VOX

MEDICAL

SPANISH
and
ENGLISH
Dictionary

VOX

MEDICAL

SPANISH
and
ENGLISH
Dictionary

New York Chicago San Francisco Lisbon London Madrid Mexico City
Milan New Delhi San Juan Seoul Singapore Sydney Toronto

The **McGraw·Hill** Companies

1 2 3 4 5 6 7 8 9 10 11 12 13 14 15   QDB/QDB   1 9 8 7 6 5 4 3 2 1 0

ISBN   978-0-07-174918-3
MHID   0-07-174918-7

Library of Congress Cataloging-in-Publication Data

Vox medical Spanish and English dictionary.
       p. ; cm. — (Vox dictionaries)
    Medical Spanish and English dictionary.
    ISBN-13: 978-0-07-174918-3 (alk. paper)
    ISBN-10: 0-07-174918-7 (alk. paper)
    1. Medicine—Dictionaries.   2. English language—Dictionaries—
Spanish.   I. Title: Medical Spanish and English dictionary.   II. Series: Vox
dictionaries.   [DNLM: 1. Medicine—Dictionary—English.   2. Medicine—
Dictionary—Spanish.   W 13]

R121.V69   2010
      610.3—dc22   2010044511

Vox (y su logotipo) es marca registrada de Larousse Editorial.
www.vox.es

Dirección editorial: Jordi Induráin Pons
Coordinación editorial: María José Simón Aragón
Informática editorial: Marc Escarmís Arasa
Realización: Marc Escarmís Arasa y Tremesú, S.L.

De la parte English-Spanish:
   Responsable: Emilio Ortega Arjonilla
   Redacción: Ana Belén Martínez López y Félix Martínez López
   Revisión: Andrew Hastings

De la parte Español-Inglés:
   Responsable: Andrew Hastings

Foreword

In the world of today, health and the prevention of disease have become the principal objective of medical interventions: from medical attention based on diagnosis and treatment, emphasis has shifted to the prevention of risk factors for disease and the need to lead a healthy life. In this context, the need to encourage and bolster the potential for communication between the English- and Spanish-speaking communities as well as the enormous scientific and terminological importance of the two languages more than justify the existence of a work of reference such as this *Vox Medical Spanish and English Dictionary*.

The *Vox Medical Spanish and English Dictionary* is primarily aimed at professionals in the field of healthcare who in the course of their work come into contact with speakers of Spanish, but it will also prove enormously useful to those users who, having Spanish as their native tongue, need to obtain an accurate English translation for terms from the fields of medicine and health in general.

This Dictionary, which consists of an extensive and detailed English-Spanish / Spanish-English bilingual glossary, aims to fill a long-felt gap in Spanish-language medical lexicography: an area where mere approximation or similarity is insufficient, where scientific and terminological precision are de rigueur. The Dictionary was compiled by a wide-ranging team of medical professionals so that not only all specialist fields might be adequately covered but also covered are nursing, diagnosis, and therapeutics.

To cover the whole range of medical topics, healthcare, well-being and nutrition, diseases, symptomatology, posology, pharmacology, diagnosis, clinical analysis, exploration, treatment, and hospitalization, and so on, an extensive headword list is required. In the first section of the dictionary, the English-Spanish glossary, there are 37,901 headwords and 34,120 sub-headwords, while in the second part, the Spanish-English glossary, there are 39,429 headwords and 35,599 sub-headwords. All of which adds up to a total of 147,049 references and makes this Dictionary a powerful tool for the use of professionals.

Prólogo

En la actualidad la salud y la prevención de las enfermedades han pasado a ser el objetivo principal de las actuaciones médicas. De la atención médica o sanitaria fundamentada en el diagnóstico y el tratamiento se ha pasado a la atención basada en la prevención de los factores de riesgo de las enfermedades y el mantenimiento de una vida sana. En este contexto, la necesidad de fortalecer y potenciar la capacidad de comunicación entre las comunidades lingüísticas anglosajona e hispana y el enorme peso científico y terminológico que poseen ambas lenguas, hacen muy adecuada la existencia de un producto de referencia como este *Vox Medical Spanish and English Dictionary*.

Es por ello que el *Vox Medical Spanish and English Dictionary* está destinado a profesionales del ámbito de la salud que por su trabajo tienen relación con personas de origen y habla hispana. Del mismo modo, su contenido puede ser de gran utilidad para todos aquellos usuarios que poseyendo el español como lengua materna, tienen la necesidad de obtener una traducción precisa y rigurosa al inglés de los términos del entorno médico y de la salud.

Es pues este Diccionario un extenso y detallado glosario bilingüe inglés-español / español-inglés que pretende cubrir una importante laguna en el ámbito léxico-médico en lengua española, un área donde no cabe una aproximación por similitud o semejanza, sino que requiere del máximo rigor científico y terminológico. En la elaboración del contenido que aquí se presenta ha trabajado un extenso equipo de profesionales en activo de la medicina para poder abarcar todas las diferentes especialidades, además de la terminología propia del ámbito de la enfermería, auxiliaría de clínica, diagnosis y terapéutica.

Los temas médicos, de salud, de bienestar y nutrición, sobre enfermedades, sintomatología, posología, farmacología, diagnosis y análisis clínico, exploración, tratamientos, ingreso hospitalario, etc., requieren de un amplio registro de entradas y subentradas: en la primera parte del diccionario, inglés-español, se presentan 37.901 entradas principales y 34.120 subentradas; mientras que en la segunda parte, español-inglés, hay 39.429 entradas y 35.599 subentradas. Todo ello suma un to-

In both the sub-headwords and in the translations in both languages, we have chosen neither to abbreviate the headword nor substitute it with any special symbol. We have done this in the interests of clarity and to help the user to find the answer to his or her queries as rapidly as possible. To distinguish them from main headwords, sub-headwords appear in italics and in a smaller typeface; this will help the user to be orientated more easily. In this way, the often extensive blocks of sub-headwords may be readily identified.

The areas of modern medicine and healthcare covered by the dictionary are of necessity very wide-ranging and inter-related. Here is an alphabetical list of some of them:

Allergology	Gynecology	Pathological anatomy
Anatomy	Hematology	Pathology
Angiology	Hepatology	Pediatrics
Biochemistry	Histology	Pharmacy
Biology	Immunology	Physiology
Cardiology	Instrumentation	Pneumology
Chemistry	Medicine	Poisoning
Cytology	Microbiology	Psychiatry
Dentistry	Nephrology	Rheumatology
Dermatology	Nutrition	Sexology
Embryology	Obstetrics	Surgery
Endocrinology	Oncology	Symptomatology
Gastrology	Ophthalmology	Therapy
Genetics	Otorhinolaryngology	Traumatology
Geriatrics	Parasitology	Urology

This *Vox Medical Spanish and English Dictionary* also contains a **summary of spanish grammar**; a complete **conjugation** of Spanish verbs (with three models for the regular conjugations and 92 models for irregular verbs); and a **Medical Spanish Phrasebook** that will prove invaluable for the production of both written and spoken messages in Spanish.

THE PUBLISHERS

tal de 147.049 registros, lo que hace de este diccionario una potente herramienta de consulta profesional. En la correlación alfabética de las voces que conforman el diccionario se ha optado por la presentación *por extenso* de las entradas, evitando en ambos idiomas el uso de elementos de abreviación o sustitución, todo ello con la idea de facilitar al máximo la consulta del diccionario y la rápida localización de las dudas del usuario. Para marcar las subentradas se ha empleado la tipografía cursiva, además de un cuerpo de letra menor, lo que facilita saber si estamos ante una voz principal o ante su conjunto, a veces extenso, de subentradas o acepciones.

Las materias que aborda el diccionario son las propias del espectro médico-sanitario, en la actualidad muy numerosas y lógicamente muy interrelacionadas. Estas son, por orden alfabético, algunas de ellas:

Alergología	Genética	Odontología
Anatomía	Geriatría	Oftalmología
Anatomía patológica	Ginecología	Oncología
Angiología	Hematología	Otorrinolaringología
Biología	Hepatología	Patología
Bioquímica	Histología	Parasitología
Cardiología	Inmunología	Pediatría
Cirugía	Instrumentación	Psiquiatría
Citología	Intoxicación	Química
Dermatología	Medicina	Reumatología
Embriología	Microbiología	Sexología
Endocrinología	Nefrología	Sintomatología
Farmacia	Neumología	Terapia
Fisiología	Nutrición	Traumatología
Gastrología	Obstetricia	Urología

El *Vox Medical Spanish and English Dictionary* se completa con un **resumen de gramática del español**, la **conjugación** completa de los tres modelos de **conjugación regular**, los **92 verbos irregulares** de más uso del español y una completa **Fraseología médica española** muy útil para elaborar mensajes hablados o escritos en español.

LOS EDITORES

Contents

Índice

Abbreviations Used in This Dictionary

Abreviaturas usadas en este diccionario

adjective	*adj.*	adjetivo
adverb	*adv.*	adverbio
feminine noun	*f.*	nombre femenino
masculine noun	*m.*	nombre masculino
noun	*n.*	nombre
verb	*v.*	verbo

English-Spanish

Inglés-Español

A*a*

abacterial *adj.* abacteriano, -na.
abalienation *n.* enajenación.
  mental abalienation enajenación mental.
abandonment *n.* abandono.
abapical *adj.* abapical.
abaptiston *n.* abaptista, abaptiston.
abarognosis *n.* abarognosia, abarognosis.
abarthrosis *n.* abartrosis.
abarticular *adj.* abarticular.
abarticulation *n.* abarticulación.
abasia *n.* abasia.
  abasia astasia abasia astasia.
  abasia trepidans abasia trepidans.
  atactic abasia abasia atáctica, abasia atáxica.
  ataxic abasia abasia atáctica, abasia atáxica.
  choreic abasia abasia coreica.
  paralytic abasia abasia paralítica.
  paroxysmal trepidant abasia abasia paroxística trepidante.
  spastic abasia abasia espástica.
abasic *adj.* abásico, -ca, abático, -ca.
abatic *adj.* abásico, -ca, abático, -ca.
abaxial *adj.* abaxial, abaxil.
abaxile *adj.* abaxial, abaxil.
abbau *n.* descomposición[1].
abdomen *n.* abdomen.
  abdomen obstipum abdomen obstipum.
  accordion abdomen abdomen en acordeón.
  acute abdomen abdomen agudo.
  boat-shaped abdomen abdomen en batea, abdomen en bote.
  carinate abdomen abdomen aquillado, abdomen carinado.
  navicular abdomen abdomen navicular.
  pendulous abdomen abdomen péndulo.
  protuberant abdomen abdomen protuberante.
  scaphoid abdomen abdomen escafoide, abdomen escafoideo.
  surgical abdomen abdomen quirúrgico.
abdominal *adj.* abdominal.
  abdominal retractor laparostato.
abdominalgia *n.* abdominalgia.
abdominocentesis *n.* abdominocentesis.
abdominocyesis *n.* abdominociesis.
abdominocystic *adj.* abdominocístico, -ca.
abdominogenital *adj.* abdominogenital.
abdominohysterotomy *n.* abdominohisterotomía.
abdominoperineal *adj.* abdominoperineal.
abdominoplasty *n.* abdominoplastia.
abdominoscopy *n.* abdominoscopia.
abdominoscrotal *adj.* abdominoescrotal, abdominoscrotal.
abdominothoracic *adj.* abdominotorácico, -ca.
abdominovaginal *adj.* abdominovaginal.
abdominovesical *adj.* abdominovesical.
abduce *v.* abducir.
abducens *adj.* abducens, abducente.

abducent *adj.* abducente.
abduct *v.* abducir.
abduction *n.* abducción.
abductor *adj.* abductor.
abembryonic *adj.* abembrionario, -ria.
abepithemia *n.* abepitimia.
abepithymia *n.* abepitimia.
aberrant *adj.* aberrante.
aberratio *n.* aberración, aberratio.
  aberratio lactis aberratio lactis.
  aberratio mensium aberratio mensium.
  aberratio testis aberratio testis.
aberration *n.* aberración.
  chromatic aberration aberración cromática, aberración del color.
  chromosomal aberration aberración cromosómica.
  chromosome aberration aberración cromosómica.
  curvature aberration aberración de curvatura.
  dioptric aberration aberración dióptrica.
  distantial aberration aberración distancial.
  lateral aberration aberración lateral.
  longitudinal aberration aberración longitudinal.
  mental aberration aberración mental.
  meridional aberration aberración meridional.
  monochromatic aberration aberración monocromática.
  Newtonian aberration aberración newtoniana.
  spherical aberration aberración de esfericidad, aberración esférica.
  ventricular aberration aberración ventricular.
aberrometer *n.* aberrómetro.
abetalipoproteinemia *n.* abetalipoproteinemia.
ability *n.* habilidad.
abiogenesis *n.* abiogenesia, abiogénesis, abiogenia.
abiogenetic *adj.* abiogenético, -ca.
abiogenous *adj.* abiógeno, -na.
abiologic *adj.* abiológico, -ca.
abiological *adj.* abiológico, -ca.
abiology *n.* abiología.
abionergy *n.* abionergia.
abiophysiology *n.* abiofisiología.
abiosis *n.* abiosis.
abiotic *adj.* abiótico, -ca.
abiotrophia *n.* abiotrofia.
  retinal abiotrophia abiotrofia retinal, abiotrofia retiniana.
abiotrophic *adj.* abiotrófico, -ca.
abiotrophy *n.* abiotrofia.
abiuretic *adj.* abiurético, -ca.
ablactation *n.* ablactación.
ablate *v.* extirpar.
ablatio *n.* ablación, ablatio.

ablatio placentae ablación placentaria, ablatio placentae.
ablatio retinae ablación retiniana, ablatio retinae.
ablepharous *adj.* abléfaro, -ra.
ablephary *n.* ablefaria.
ablepsia *n.* ablepsia.
ablepsy *n.* ablepsia.
abluent *adj.* abluente.
abluminal *adj.* abluminal.
ablution *n.* ablución.
ablutomania *n.* ablutomanía.
abneural *adj.* aneural.
abnormal *adj.* anormal.
abnormality *n.* anormalidad.
abocclusion *n.* aboclusión.
aboral *adj.* aboral.
abort *v.* abortar.
abortient *adj.* abortante.
abortifacient *adj.* abortifaciente.
abortigenic *adj.* abortante, abortifaciente.
abortion *n.* aborto.
  abortion in progress aborto en curso.
  accidental abortion aborto accidental.
  afebrile abortion aborto afebril.
  ampullar abortion aborto ampollar, aborto ampular.
  artificial abortion aborto artificial.
  cervical abortion aborto cervical.
  elective abortion aborto electivo.
  habitual abortion aborto habitual.
  idiopathic abortion aborto idiopático.
  illegal abortion aborto ilegal.
  imminent abortion aborto inminente.
  incomplete abortion aborto incompleto.
  induced abortion aborto provocado.
  inevitable abortion aborto inevitable.
  infected abortion aborto infectado.
  justifiable abortion aborto justificable.
  missed abortion aborto diferido, aborto retenido.
  recurrent abortion aborto recurrente.
  septic abortion aborto febril, aborto séptico.
  spontaneous abortion aborto espontáneo.
  therapeutic abortion aborto terapéutico.
  tubal abortion aborto tubárico.
abortionist *n.* abortista.
abortive *adj.* abortivo, -va.
abortus *n.* aborto, abortus.
abouchement *n.* abocamiento.
abrachia *n.* abraquia.
abrachiatism *n.* abraquia.
abrachiocephalia *n.* abraquiocefalia.
abrachiocephalus *n.* abraquiocéfalo.
abrachiocephaly *n.* abraquiocefalia.
abrachius *n.* abraquio.
abradant *adj.* abrasivo, -va.
abrasio *n.* abrasio, abrasión.
  abrasio corneae abrasio corneae, corneal abrasion.

abrasio dentium abrasio dentium, abrasion of the teeth, tooth abrasion.
abrasion *n.* abrasio, abrasión.
abrasion of the teeth abrasio dentium, abrasión dental, abrasión dentaria.
corneal abrasion abrasio corneae, abrasión corneal.
tooth abrasion abrasio dentium, abrasión dental, abrasión dentaria.
abrasive *adj.* abrasivo, -va.
abrasiveness *n.* abrasividad.
abrasor *n.* abrasor.
abreact *v.* abreaccionar.
abreaction *n.* abreacción.
motor abreaction abreacción motriz.
abrism *n.* abrismo.
abrosia *n.* abrosia.
abruptio *n.* abrupción, abruptio.
abruptio placentae abrupción placentaria, abruptio placentae.
abruption *n.* abrupción, abruptio.
abscess *n.* absceso.
abdominal abscess absceso abdominal.
abscess of the liver absceso hepático.
acute abscess absceso agudo.
alveolar abscess absceso alveolar.
amebic abscess absceso amebiano.
anorectal abscess absceso anorrectal.
apical abscess absceso apical.
appendiceal abscess absceso apendicular.
appendicular abscess absceso apendicular.
arthrifluent abscess absceso artrifluente.
atheromatous abscess absceso ateromatoso.
axillary abscess absceso axilar.
Bartholinian abscess absceso de Bartholin, absceso de Bartolino.
Bezold's abscess absceso de Bezold.
bicameral abscess absceso bicameral.
bile duct abscess absceso de conductos biliares.
bilharziasis abscess absceso bilharziásico, absceso bilharziótico.
biliary abscess absceso biliar.
bone abscess absceso óseo.
brain abscess absceso cerebral.
broad ligament abscess absceso del ligamento ancho.
Brodie's abscess absceso de Brodie.
bursal abscess absceso bursal.
canalicular abscess absceso canalicular.
carniform abscess absceso carniforme.
caseous abscess absceso caseoso.
cerebellar abscess absceso cerebeloso.
cerebral abscess absceso cerebral.
cheese abscess absceso caseoso.
cholangitic abscess absceso colangítico.
chronic abscess absceso crónico.
circumscribed abscess absceso circunscrito.
circumtonsillar abscess absceso peritonsilar.
cold abscess absceso frío.
collar-button abscess absceso en botón de cuello.
crypt abscess absceso críptico.
deep abscess absceso profundo.
deep-seated abscess absceso profundo.
Delpech's abscess absceso de Delpech.
dental abscess absceso dental, absceso dentoalveolar.
dentoalveolar abscess absceso dental, absceso dentoalveolar.
diffuse abscess absceso difundido, absceso difuso.
Douglas' abscess absceso de Douglas.
dry abscess absceso seco.
Dubois' abscess absceso de Dubois.
embolic abscess absceso embólico.

emphysematous abscess absceso enfisematoso.
encysted abscess absceso enquistado.
epidural abscess absceso epidural.
epiploic abscess absceso epiploico.
extradural abscess absceso extradural.
fecal abscess absceso fecal.
filarial abscess absceso filariásico.
fixation abscess absceso de fijación.
Fochier's abscess absceso de Fochier.
follicular abscess absceso folicular.
follicular collar-stud abscess absceso folicular.
frontal abscess absceso frontal.
fungal abscess absceso micótico.
gangrenous abscess absceso gangrenoso.
gas abscess absceso gaseoso.
gastric abscess absceso gástrico.
gingival abscess absceso gingival.
glandular abscess absceso ganglionar.
gravitation abscess absceso de gravitación, absceso por gravedad.
gravity abscess absceso de gravitación, absceso por gravedad.
gumboil abscess absceso gingival.
gummatous abscess absceso gomatoso.
helminthic abscess absceso helmíntico.
hemorrhagic abscess absceso hemorrágico.
hepatic abscess absceso hepático.
hot abscess absceso caliente.
hypostatic abscess absceso hipostático.
idiopathic abscess absceso idiopático.
iliac abscess absceso ilíaco.
intradural abscess absceso intradural.
intramammary abscess absceso intramamario.
intramastoid abscess absceso intramastoideo.
intratonsillar abscess absceso intraamigdalino.
ischiorectal abscess absceso isquiorrectal.
lacrimal abscess absceso lagrimal.
lacunar abscess absceso lacunar, absceso lagunar.
lateral abscess absceso lateral, absceso lateral alveolar.
lateral alveolar abscess absceso lateral, absceso lateral alveolar.
lumbar abscess absceso lumbar.
lymphatic abscess absceso linfático.
mammary abscess absceso mamario.
marginal abscess absceso marginal.
mastoid abscess absceso mastoideo.
mediastinal abscess absceso mediastínico.
medullary abscess absceso intramedular.
metastatic abscess absceso metastásico.
metastatic tuberculous abscess absceso tuberculoso metastático.
migrating abscess absceso emigrante, absceso migratorio.
miliary abscess absceso miliar.
milk abscess absceso de leche, absceso lácteo.
mother abscess absceso madre.
multiple abscess absceso múltiple.
Munro's abscess absceso de Munro.
mural abscess absceso mural.
nocardial abscess absceso nocardiásico.
orbital abscess absceso orbitario.
ossifluent abscess absceso osifluente.
Paget's abscess absceso de Paget.
palatal abscess absceso palatino.
pancreatic abscess absceso pancreático.
parafrenal abscess absceso parafrenular.
parametrial abscess absceso parametrial, absceso paramétrico.
parametric abscess absceso parametrial, absceso paramétrico.
paranephric abscess absceso paranéfrico.

parapancreatic abscess absceso parapancreático.
parapharyngeal abscess absceso parafaríngeo.
paravertebral abscess absceso paravertebral.
parietal abscess absceso parietal.
parotid abscess absceso parotídeo.
Pautrier's abscess absceso de Pautrier.
pelvic abscess absceso pélvico.
pelvirectal abscess absceso pelvirrectal.
perianal abscess absceso perianal.
periapical abscess absceso periapical.
pericemental abscess absceso pericemental.
pericoronal abscess absceso pericoronal, absceso pericoronario.
peridental abscess absceso periodóntico, absceso peridental, absceso periodontal.
perinephric abscess absceso perinéfrico, absceso perinefrítico.
periodontal abscess absceso periodóntico, absceso peridental, absceso periodontal.
peripleuritic abscess absceso peripleural, absceso peripleurítico.
perirectal abscess absceso perirrectal.
peritoneal abscess absceso peritoneal.
peritonsillar abscess absceso periamigdalino, absceso peritonsilar.
periureteral abscess absceso periureteral.
periurethral abscess absceso periuretral.
perivesical abscess absceso perivesical.
phoenix abscess absceso fénix.
postcecal abscess absceso poscecal.
Pott's abscess absceso de Pott.
premammary abscess absceso premamario.
psoas abscess absceso de psoas, absceso del psoas.
pulmonary abscess absceso pulmonar.
pulp abscess absceso pulpar.
pulpar abscess absceso pulpar.
renal abscess absceso renal.
residual abscess absceso residual.
retrocecal abscess absceso retrocecal.
retromammary abscess absceso retromamario.
retroperitoneal abscess absceso retroperitoneal.
retropharyngeal abscess absceso retrofaríngeo.
retrotonsillar abscess absceso retroamigdalino.
ring abscess absceso anular.
root abscess absceso radicular.
sacrococcygeal abscess absceso sacrococcígeo.
satellite abscess absceso satélite.
scrofulous abscess absceso escrofuloso.
secondary abscess absceso secundario.
septal abscess absceso septal.
septicemic abscess absceso septicémico.
shirt-stud abscess absceso en botón de camisa.
spermatic abscess absceso espermático.
spirillar abscess absceso espirilar.
splenic abscess absceso esplénico.
stellate abscess absceso estrellado.
stercoraceous abscess absceso estercoráceo.
stercoral abscess absceso estercoráceo.
sterile abscess absceso estéril.
stitch abscess absceso de sutura.
streptococcal abscess absceso estreptocócico.
strumous abscess absceso estrumoso.
subaponeurotic abscess absceso subaponeurótico.
subareolar abscess absceso subareolar.
subdiaphragmatic abscess absceso subdiafragmático.
subdural abscess absceso subdural.

subfascial abscess absceso subaponeurótico.
subgaleal abscess absceso subgaleal.
subhepatic abscess absceso subhepático.
submammary abscess absceso submamario.
submastoid abscess absceso constitucional.
subpectoral abscess absceso subpectoral.
subperiosteal abscess absceso subperióstico.
subperitoneal abscess absceso subperitoneal.
subphrenic abscess absceso subfrénico.
subscapular abscess absceso subescapular.
sudoriparous abscess absceso sudoríparo.
superficial abscess absceso superficial.
suprahepatic abscess absceso suprahepático.
sympathetic abscess absceso simpático.
syphilitic abscess absceso sifilítico.
thecal abscess absceso tecal.
Thornwaldt abscess absceso de Thornwaldt.
thymic abscess absceso tímico.
thymus abscess absceso tímico.
tonsillar abscess absceso amigdalino.
traumatic abscess absceso traumático.
tropical abscess absceso tropical.
tuberculous abscess absceso tuberculoso.
tuboovarian abscess absceso tuboovárico.
tympanitic abscess absceso timpánico, absceso timpanítico.
tympanocervical abscess absceso timpanocervical.
tympanomastoid abscess absceso timpanomastoideo.
urethral abscess absceso uretral.
urinary abscess absceso urinario.
urinous abscess absceso urinoso.
verminous abscess absceso verminoso.
vitreous abscess absceso vítreo.
wandering abscess absceso errante.
web-space abscess absceso interdigital.
Welch's abscess absceso de Welch.
abscessography *n.* abscesografía.
abscise *v.* abscindir.
abscission *n.* abscisión.
corneal abscission abscisión corneal.
absconsio *n.* absconsio.
absence *n.* ausencia.
atonic absence ausencia atónica.
atypical absence ausencia atípica.
complex absence ausencia compleja.
enuretic absence ausencia enurética.
epileptic absence ausencia epiléptica.
hypertonic absence ausencia hipertónica.
myoclonic absence ausencia mioclónica.
pure absence ausencia pura.
retrocursive absence ausencia retrocursiva.
simple absence ausencia simple.
sternutatory absence ausencia estornutatoria.
subclinical absence ausencia subclínica.
tussive absence ausencia tusígena.
typical absence ausencia típica.
vasomotor absence ausencia vasomotora.
Absidia *n.* Absidia.
absolute *adj.* absoluto, -ta.
absolute zero cero absoluto.
absorb *v.* absorber.
absorbance *n.* absorbancia.
absorbefacient *adj.* absorbefaciente.
absorbent *adj.* absorbente.
absorptiometer *n.* absorciómetro.
absorptiometry *n.* absorciometría.
absorption *n.* absorción.
absorption excrementitia absorción excrementicia.
absorption neta absorción neta.
agglutinin absorption absorción de aglutinina.

cutaneous absorption absorción cutánea.
disjunctive absorption absorción disyuntiva.
drug absorption absorción de fármaco.
external absorption absorción externa.
internal absorption absorción interna.
interstitial absorption absorción intersticial.
intestinal absorption absorción intestinal.
parenteral absorption absorción parenteral.
pathologic absorption absorción patológica.
pathological absorption absorción patológica.
percutaneous absorption absorción percutánea.
absorptive *adj.* absortivo, -va.
absortivity *n.* absortividad.
molar absortivity absortividad molar.
specific absortivity absortividad específica.
abstention *n.* abstención.
abstergent *adj.* abstergente.
abstinence *n.* abstinencia.
alimentary abstinence abstinencia alimentaria.
substance abstinence abstinencia de sustancias.
abstract *n.* abstracto.
abstraction *n.* abstracción.
abterminal *adj.* abterminal, aterminal.
abtorsion *n.* abtorsión.
abtropfung *n.* abtropfung.
abulia *n.* abulia.
abulic *adj.* abúlico, -ca.
abuse *n.* abuso, malos tratos.
abuse of the elderly abuso de ancianos, malos tratos al anciano.
child abuse abuso del niño, malos tratos a menores.
drug abuse abuso de medicamentos.
elder abuse abuso de ancianos, malos tratos al anciano.
emotional abuse malos tratos emocionales.
physical abuse malos tratos físicos.
psychoactive substance abuse abuso de sustancias, abuso de sustancias psicoactivas.
sexual abuse malos tratos sexuales.
sexual abuse of an adult abuso sexual del adulto.
sexual child abuse abuso sexual del niño.
substance abuse abuso de sustancias, abuso de sustancias psicoactivas.
abutment *n.* contrafuerte, lindero.
implant abutment contrafuerte del implante.
primary abutment contrafuerte primario.
acalcerosis *n.* acalcerosis.
acalcicosis *n.* acalcicosis.
acalculia *n.* acalculia.
acampsia *n.* acampsia.
acantha *n.* acanto.
acanthamebiasis *n.* acantamebiasis.
Acanthamoeba *n.* Acanthamoeba.
acanthesthesia *n.* acantestesia.
acanthion *n.* acantión.
acanthocephaliasis *n.* acantocefaliasis, acantocefalosis.
acanthocephalus *n.* acanthocephalus, acantocéfalos.
acanthocheilonemiasis *n.* acantoqueilonemiasis.
acanthocyte *n.* acantocito.
acanthocytosis *n.* acantocitosis.
acanthoid *adj.* acantoide.
acanthokeratoderma *n.* acantoqueratoderma.
acantholysis *n.* acantólisis.
acantholysis bullosa acantólisis ampollar, acantólisis bullosa.

acantholytic *adj.* acantolítico, -ca.
acanthoma *n.* acantoma.
acanthoma adenoides cysticum acantoma adenoideo, acantoma adenoquístico.
clear cell acanthoma acantoma de células claras.
Degos' acanthoma acantoma de células claras.
acanthopelvis *n.* acantopélix, acantopelvis.
acanthorrhexis *n.* acantorrexis.
acanthosis *n.* acantosis.
acanthosis nigricans acantosis nigricans.
acanthosis seborrhoeica acantosis seborreica.
acanthosis verrucosa acantosis verrugosa.
acapnia *n.* acapnia.
acapnial *adj.* acápnico, -ca.
acapnic *adj.* acápnico, -ca.
acarbia *n.* acarbia.
acardia *n.* acardia.
acardiac *adj.* acardíaco, -ca.
acardiacus *n.* acardiacus.
acardiotrophia *n.* acardiotrofia.
acardius *n.* acardio.
acarian *adj.* acariano, -na.
acariasis *n.* acariasis.
demodectic acariasis acariasis demodéctica.
psoroptic acariasis acariasis soróptica.
sarcoptic acariasis acariasis sarcóptica.
acaricide *n.* acaricida.
Acaridae *n.* Acaridae, acarídeos, acárides, acáridos.
acaridiasis *n.* acaridiasis.
Acarina *n.* Acarina.
acarine *adj.* acarino, -na.
acarinosis *n.* acarinosis, acariosis.
acarodermatitis *n.* acarodermatitis.
acarodermatitis urticaroides acarodermatitis urticaroide.
acaroid *adj.* acaroide, acaroideo, -a.
acarology *n.* acarología.
acarotoxic *adj.* acarotóxico, -ca.
Acarus *n.* Acarus.
acatalasemia *n.* acatalasemia.
acatalasia *n.* acatalasia.
acatamathesia *n.* acatamatesia.
acataphasia *n.* acatafasia.
acataposis *n.* acataposis.
acatastasia *n.* acatastasia.
acatastatic *adj.* acatastático, -ca.
acathexia *n.* acatexia.
acathexis *n.* acatexia.
acathisia *n.* acatisia.
acaudal *adj.* acaudal.
acaudate *adj.* acaudado, -da, acáudeo, -a.
accelerator *n.* acelerador.
linear accelerator acelerador lineal.
accelerometer *n.* acelerómetro.
acceptance *n.* aceptación.
acceptor *n.* aceptor.
access *n.* acceso[1].
accession *n.* accesión.
accessorius *n.* accesorio.
accessory *adj.* accesorio, -ria.
accident *n.* accidente.
cerebrovascular accident (CVA) accidente cerebrovascular (ACV).
highway accident accidente de tráfico.
industrial accident accidente de trabajo.
occupational accident accidente laboral.
professional accident accidente laboral.
traffic accident accidente de tráfico.
accidental *adj.* accidental.
accidentalism *n.* accidentalismo.
accipiter *n.* accípiter.

acclimatation *n.* aclimatación.
acclimation *n.* aclimatación.
acclimatization *n.* aclimatación.
accommodation *n.* acomodación.
  absolute accommodation acomodación absoluta.
  accommodation of the eye acomodación del ojo.
  binocular accommodation acomodación binocular.
  excessive accommodation acomodación excesiva.
  histologic accommodation acomodación histológica.
  negative accommodation acomodación negativa.
  nerve accommodation acomodación del nervio, acomodación nerviosa.
  positive accommodation acomodación positiva.
  relative accommodation acomodación relativa.
  subnormal accommodation acomodación subnormal.
  visual accommodation acomodación visual.
accommodometer *n.* acomodómetro.
accomodative *adj.* acomodativo, -va.
accomplice *n.* accomplice.
accouchement *n.* alumbramiento.
accrementition *n.* acrementación.
accretio *n.* accretio.
accretion *n.* acreción.
acculturation *n.* aculturación.
accummulation *n.* acumulación.
accumulated *adj.* acumulado, -da.
accumulator *n.* acumulador.
accuracy *n.* exactitud, precisión.
acedia *n.* acedía.
acellular *adj.* acelular.
acelomate *adj.* acelomado, -da.
acelomatous *adj.* acelomatoso, -sa.
acenesthesia *n.* acenestesia.
acentric *adj.* acéntrico, -ca.
acephalia *n.* acefalia.
acephalism *n.* acefalismo.
acephalobrachia *n.* acefalobraquia.
acephalocardia *n.* acefalocardia.
acephalochiria *n.* acefaloquiria.
acephalochirus *n.* acefaloquiro.
acephalocyst *n.* acefalocisto.
acephalogaster *n.* acefalogastro.
acephalogasteria *n.* acefalogasteria.
acephalogastria *n.* acefalogastria.
acephalopodia *n.* acefalopodia.
acephalopodius *n.* acefalópodo.
acephalorachia *n.* acefalorraquia.
acephalostomia *n.* acefalostomía.
acephalostomus *n.* acefalóstomo.
acephalothoracia *n.* acefalotoracia.
acephalous *adj.* acéfalo, -la.
acephalus *n.* acéfalo, acephalus.
  acephalus dibrachius acéfalo dibraquio, acephalus dibrachius.
  acephalus dipus acéfalo dípodo, acephalus dipus.
  acephalus monobrachius acéfalo monobraquio, acephalus monobrachius.
  acephalus monopus acéfalo monópodo, acephalus monopus.
  acephalus paracephalus acéfalo paracéfalo, acephalus paracephalus.
  acephalus simpus acéfalo simpódico, acephalus simpus.
acephaly *n.* acefalia.
aceratosis *n.* aceratosis.

acervulus *n.* acérvulo.
acescence *n.* acescencia.
acescent *adj.* acescente.
acesodyne *adj.* acesodino, -na.
acestoma *n.* acestoma.
acetabular *adj.* acetabular.
acetabulectomy *n.* acetabulectomía.
acetabuloplasty *n.* acetabuloplastia.
acetabulum *n.* acetábulo, acetabulum.
acetic *adj.* acético, -ca.
acetimeter *n.* acetímetro.
acetolysis *n.* acetólisis.
acetometer *n.* acetímetro, acetómetro.
acetone *n.* acetona.
acetonemia *n.* acetonemia.
acetonemic *adj.* acetonémico, -ca.
acetonglycosuria *n.* acetonglucosuria.
acetonumerator *n.* acetonumerador.
acetonuria *n.* acetonuria.
acetosoluble *adj.* acetosoluble.
achalasia *n.* acalasia.
  achalasia of the cardia acalasia del cardias.
  esophageal achalasia acalasia esofágica.
  pelvirectal achalasia acalasia pelvirrectal.
  sphincteral achalasia acalasia esfinteriana.
ache *n.* dolencia, dolorimiento.
  bone ache dolencia ósea.
  stomach ache dolencia gástrica.
acheilia *n.* aqueilia.
acheilous *adj.* aqueilo, -la.
acheiria *n.* aqueiria.
acheiropody *n.* aqueiropodia.
acheirous *adj.* aquiro, -ra[1].
acheirus *n.* aquiro, -ra[2].
achillobursitis *n.* aquilobursitis.
achillodynia *n.* aquilodinia.
achillorrhaphy *n.* aquilorrafia.
achillotenotomy *n.* aquilotenotomía.
  plastic achillotenotomy aquilotenotomía plástica.
achillotomy *n.* aquilotomía.
achilous *adj.* aqueilo, -la.
achiral *adj.* aquiral.
achiria *n.* aqueiria, aquiria.
achiropody *n.* aqueiropodia, aquiropodia.
achirous *adj.* aquiro, -ra[1].
achlorhydria *n.* aclorhidria.
achlorhydric *adj.* aclorhídrico, -ca.
achloroblepsia *n.* acloroblepsia.
achlorophyllous *adj.* aclorófilo, -la.
achloropsia *n.* acloropsia.
acholia *n.* acolia.
acholic *adj.* acólico, -ca.
acholuria *n.* acoluria.
acholuric *adj.* acolúrico, -ca.
achondrogenesis *n.* acondrogénesis.
achondroplasia *n.* acondroplasia.
achondroplastic *adj.* acondroplásico, -ca, acondroplástico, -ca.
achondroplasty *n.* acondroplasia.
achor *n.* acor.
achoresis *n.* acoresis.
achrencephalon *n.* acrencéfalo.
achroma *n.* acroma, acromia.
achromachia *n.* acromaquia.
achromasia *n.* acromasia.
achromate *n.* acromata.
achromatic *adj.* acromático, -ca.
achromatism *n.* acromatismo.
achromatize *v.* acromatizar.
achromatophil *adj.* acromatófilo, -la.
achromatophilia *n.* acromatofilia.
achromatopia *n.* acromatopia, acromatopsia.
achromatopic *adj.* acromatópico, -ca.
achromatopsia *n.* acromatopsia.

  atypical achromatopsia acromatopsia atípica.
  complete achromatopsia acromatopsia completa.
  incomplete achromatopsia acromatopsia incompleta.
  typical achromatopsia acromatopsia típica.
  X-linked achromatopsia acromatopsia ligada al cromosoma X.
achromatopsy *n.* acromatopsia.
achromatosis *n.* acromatosis.
achromatous *adj.* acromatoso, -sa.
achromaturia *n.* acromaturia.
achromia *n.* acromia.
  achromia parasitica acromia parasitaria.
  cortical achromia acromia cortical.
achromic *adj.* acrómico, -ca.
achromophilic *adj.* acromofílico, -ca.
achromophilous *adj.* acromófilo, -la.
achromotrichia *n.* acromotriquia.
achromycosis *n.* acromicosis.
achylia *n.* aquilia.
  achylia gastrica haemorrhagica aquilia gástrica hemorrágica.
  achylia pancreatica aquilia pancreática.
achylous *adj.* aquílico, -ca, aquiloso, -sa.
achymia *n.* aquimia.
achymosis *n.* aquimia.
acicular *adj.* acicular.
acid *n.* ácido.
  chenodeoxycholic acid (ácido) quenodesoxicólico.
  imino acid iminoácido.
  oxaloacetic acid (ácido) oxaloacético.
  oxaluric acid (ácido) oxalúrico.
  oxybutyric acid (ácido) oxibutírico.
acidalbumin *n.* acidalbúmina.
acidaminuria *n.* acidaminuria.
acidemia *n.* acidemia.
acid-fast *adj.* acidorresistente.
acidic *adj.* acídico, -ca.
acidifiable *adj.* acidificable.
acidification *n.* acidificación.
acidifier *n.* acidificador.
acidify *v.* acidificar.
acidimeter *n.* acidímetro.
acidimetry *n.* acidimetría.
acidism *n.* acidismo, acidismus.
acidismus *n.* acidismo, acidismus.
acidity *n.* acidez.
  acidity of the stomach acidez del estómago.
acidogenic *adj.* acidógeno, -na.
acidophilia *n.* acidofilia.
acidophilic *adj.* acidofílico, -ca.
acidophilism *n.* acidofilismo.
acidoresistance *n.* acidorresistencia.
acidosic *adj.* acidósico, -ca.
acidosis *n.* acidosis.
  acidosis dialysis acidosis por diálisis.
  carbon dioxide acidosis acidosis por anhídrido carbónico.
  compensated acidosis acidosis compensada.
  compensated metabolic acidosis acidosis metabólica compensada.
  compensated respiratory acidosis acidosis respiratoria compensada.
  diabetic acidosis acidosis diabética.
  distal renal tubular acidosis acidosis renal tubular distal.
  hypercapnic acidosis acidosis hipercápnica.
  hyperchloremic acidosis acidosis hiperclorémica.
  lactic acidosis acidosis láctica.
  metabolic acidosis acidosis metabólica.
  non-respiratory acidosis acidosis no respiratoria.

proximal renal tubular acidosis acidosis renal tubular proximal.
renal acidosis acidosis renal.
renal hyperchloremic acidosis acidosis renal hiperclorémica.
renal tubular acidosis acidosis renal tubular.
respiratory acidosis acidosis respiratoria.
starvation acidosis acidosis por inanición.
uncompensated acidosis acidosis descompensada.
uremic acidosis acidosis urémica.
acidosteophyte *n.* acidosteofito.
acidotic *adj.* acidótico, -ca.
acidulate *v.* acidular.
acidulated *adj.* acidulado, -da.
acidulous *adj.* acídulo, -la.
acidum *n.* ácido, acidum.
aciduria *n.* aciduria.
  acetoacetic aciduria aciduria acetoacética.
  argininosuccinic aciduria aciduria argininosuccínica.
  beta-aminoisobutyric aciduria aciduria beta-aminoisobutírica.
  beta-hydroxyisovaleric aciduria aciduria beta-hidroxiisovalérica.
  glutaric aciduria aciduria glutárica.
  methylmalonic aciduria aciduria metilmalónica.
  orotic aciduria aciduria orótica, oroticoaciduria.
aciduric *adj.* acidúrico, -ca.
acinar *adj.* acinar.
Acinetobacter *n.* Acinetobacter.
acinic *adj.* acínico, -ca.
aciniform *adj.* aciniforme.
acinitis *n.* acinitis.
acinose *adj.* acinoso, -sa.
acinotubular *adj.* acinotubular.
acinous *adj.* acinoso, -sa.
acinus *n.* ácino, acinus.
acladiosis *n.* acladiosis.
aclasis *n.* aclasia.
  diaphyseal aclasis aclasia diafisiaria.
  tarsoepiphyseal aclasis aclasia tarsoepifisaria.
aclastic *adj.* aclástico, -ca.
acleistocardia *n.* acleistocardia.
aclinic *adj.* aclínico, -ca.
acmastic *adj.* acmástico, -ca.
acme *n.* acmé.
acmesthesia *n.* acmestesia.
acne *n.* acne, acné.
  acne adoslescentium acné adolescentium.
  acne artificialis acné artificial.
  acne atrophica acné atrófica.
  acne cachecticorum acné caquéctica, acné de los caquécticos.
  acne ciliaris acné ciliar.
  acne conglobata acné conglobata.
  acne decalvans acné decalvans.
  acne disseminata acné disseminada.
  acne erythematosa acné eritematosa.
  acne estivalis acné estival.
  acne excoriée des jeunes filles acné excoriada, acné excoriada de las jovencitas.
  acne frontalis acné frontal, acné frontalis.
  acne fulminans acné fulminante.
  acne generalis acné general.
  acne hordeolaris acné hordeolaris.
  acne hypertrophica acné hipertrófica.
  acne indurata acné indurada.
  acne keratosa acné queratosa.
  acne lupoides acné luposa.
  acne mechanica acné mecánica.
  acne medicamentosa acné medicamentoso.

  acne necrotica miliaris acné necrótica miliar.
  acne neonatorum acné neonatal.
  acne papulosa acné papulosa.
  acne picealis acné picealis.
  acne punctata acné punctata.
  acne rodens acné rodens.
  acne rosacea acné rosácea.
  acne scorbutica acné escorbútica.
  acne sebacea acné sebácea.
  acne simplex acné simple.
  acne syphilitica acné sifilítica.
  acne tarsi acné tarsi.
  acne telangiectodes acné telangiectásico, acné telangiectodes.
  acne tropicalis acné tropical, acné tropicalis.
  acne urticata acné urticata.
  acne varioliformis acné varioliforme.
  acne venenata acné venenata.
  acne vulgaris acné vulgar.
  asbestos acne acné por asbestos.
  bromide acne acné brómica.
  chlorine acne acné clórica.
  common acne acné común.
  conglobate acne acné conglobata.
  contact acne acné por contacto.
  cosmetic acne acné cosmética.
  cystic acne acné quística.
  detergicans acne acné detergicans.
  epidemic acne acné epidémica.
  excoriated acne acné excoriada, acné excoriada de las jovencitas.
  halogen acne acné halógena.
  infantile acne acné infantil.
  iodide acne acné por yoduro, acné por yodo, acné yódica.
  keloid acne acné queloide.
  Mallorca acne acné Mallorca.
  mechanical acne acné mecánica.
  neonatal acne acné neonatal.
  occupational acne acné ocupacional.
  petroleum acne acné por petróleo.
  picker's acne acné del recolector.
  pomade acne acné pomada, acné por pomadas.
  premenstrual acne acné premenstrual.
  pustulosa acne acné pustulosa.
  simple acne acné simple.
  steroid acne acné esteroidea.
  tar acne acné por alquitrán.
  tropical acne acné tropical, acné tropicalis.
acneform *adj.* acneiforme.
acnegenic *adj.* acnegénico, -ca.
acneiform *adj.* acneiforme.
acnemia *n.* acnemia.
acnitis *n.* acnitis.
acoasma *n.* acoasma.
acognosy *n.* acognosia.
acomia *n.* acomia.
aconative *adj.* aconativo, -va.
acoprosis *n.* acoprosis.
acoprous *adj.* acoproso, -sa.
acor *n.* acor, agrura.
acorea *n.* acorea.
acormus *n.* acormo.
acosmia *n.* acosmia.
acoumeter *n.* acúmetro.
acoumetry *n.* acumetría.
acousma *n.* acoasma, acousma, acusma.
acousmatamnesia *n.* acusmatamnesia.
acoustic *adj.* acústico, -ca.
acousticophobia *n.* acusticofobia.
acoustics *n.* acústica.
acoustogram *n.* acustografía.
acoutometer *n.* acutómetro.
acquired *adj.* adquirido, -da.
acral *adj.* acral.

acrania *n.* acrania.
acranial *adj.* acraneal.
acrasia *n.* acrasia.
acrasia *n.* acrasia.
acraturesis *n.* acraturesis.
acremoniosis *n.* acremoniosis.
acribometer *n.* acribómetro.
acrid *adj.* acre.
acrimonia *n.* acrimonia.
acrimony *n.* acrimonia, acritud.
acrinia *n.* acrinia.
acrisia *n.* acrisia, acrisis.
acritical *adj.* acrítico, -ca.
acritochromacy *n.* acritocromacia.
acroagnosis *n.* acroagnosia, acroagnosis.
acroanesthesia *n.* acroanestesia.
acroarthritis *n.* acroartritis.
acroasphyxia *n.* acroasfixia.
  chronic acroasphyxia acroasfixia crónica.
acroblast *n.* acroblasto.
acrobrachycephaly *n.* acrobraquicefalia.
acrobystiolith *n.* acrobistiolito.
acrobystitis *n.* acrobistitis.
acrocentric *adj.* acrocéntrico, -ca.
acrocephalic *adj.* acrocefálico, -ca.
acrocephalopolysyndactyly *n.* acrocefalopolisindactilia (ACPS).
  acrocephalopolysyndactyly type I acrocefalopolisindactilia (ACPS) tipo I.
  acrocephalopolysyndactyly type II acrocefalopolisindactilia (ACPS) tipo II.
  acrocephalopolysyndactyly type III acrocefalopolisindactilia (ACPS) tipo III.
  acrocephalopolysyndactyly type IV acrocefalopolisindactilia (ACPS) tipo IV.
acrocephalosyndactyly *n.* acrocefalosindactilia.
  acrocephalosyndactyly type I acrocefalosindactilia tipo I.
  acrocephalosyndactyly type II acrocefalosindactilia tipo II.
  acrocephalosyndactyly type III acrocefalosindactilia tipo III.
  acrocephalosyndactyly type V acrocefalosindactilia tipo V.
acrocephalous *adj.* acrocéfalo, -la.
acrocephaly *n.* acrocefalia.
  acrocephaly syndactyly acrocefalia sindactilia.
acrochordon *n.* acrocordón.
acrocontracture *n.* acrocontractura.
acrocyanosis *n.* acrocianosis.
  peripheral acrocyanosis of the newborn acrocianosis periférica del recién nacido.
acrocyanotic *adj.* acrocianótico, -ca.
acrodermatitis *n.* acrodermatitis.
  acrodermatitis chronica atrophicans acrodermatitis crónica atrofiante, acrodermatitis crónica atrófica, acrodermatitis crónica de las extremidades.
  acrodermatitis continua acrodermatitis continua.
  acrodermatitis enteropathica acrodermatitis enteropática, acrodermatitis enteropática de Danbolt y Closs.
  acrodermatitis hiemalis acrodermatitis invernal.
  acrodermatitis papulosa infantum acrodermatitis papular de la niñez, acrodermatitis papulosa infantum.
  acrodermatitis perstans acrodermatitis perstans.
  continuous acrodermatitis acrodermatitis continua.
  infantil papular acrodermatitis acrodermatitis papular de la niñez, acrodermatitis papulosa infantum.

infantile acrodermatitis acrodermatitis infantil.

papular acrodermatitis of childhood acrodermatitis papular de la niñez, acrodermatitis papulosa infantum.

acrodermatosis *n.* acrodermatosis.

acrodolichomelia *n.* acrodolicomelia.

acrodont *n.* acrodonte, acrodonto.

acrodynia *n.* acrodinia.

acrodysesthesia *n.* acrodisestesia.

acrodysostosis *n.* acrodisostosis.

acroedema *n.* acroedema.

acrogeria *n.* acrogeria.

acrohyperhidrosis *n.* acrohiperhidrosis.

acrohypothermy *n.* acrohipotermia.

acrokeratoelastoidosis *n.* acroqueratoelastoidosis.

acrokeratosis *n.* acroqueratosis.

acrokeratosis verruciformis acroqueratosis verruciforme.

paraneoplastic acrokeratosis acroqueratosis paraneoplásica.

acrolein *n.* acroleína.

acroleukopathy *n.* acroleucopatía.

acromacria *n.* acromacria.

acromania *n.* acromanía.

acromastitis *n.* acromastitis.

acromegalia *n.* acromegalia.

acromegalic *adj.* acromegálico, -ca.

acromegalogigantism *n.* acromegalogigantismo.

acromegaloidism *n.* acromegaloidismo.

acromegaly *n.* acromegalia.

acromelalgia *n.* acromelalgia.

acromelia *n.* acromelia.

acromelic *adj.* acromélico, -ca.

acrometagenesis *n.* acrometagénesis.

acromial *adj.* acromial.

acromicria *n.* acromicria.

acromioclavicular *adj.* acromioclavicular.

acromiocoracoid *adj.* acromiocoracoide, acromiocoracoideo, -a.

acromiohumeral *adj.* acromiohumeral.

acromion *n.* acromion.

acromionectomy *n.* acromionectomía.

acromioscapular *adj.* acromioescapular.

acromiothoracic *adj.* acromiotorácico, -ca.

acromphalus *n.* acrónfalo.

acromyotonia *n.* acromiotonía.

acromyotonus *n.* acromiotonía, acromiotono.

acronarcotic *adj.* acronarcótico, -ca.

acroneurosis *n.* acroneurosis.

acronyx *n.* acronix.

acro-osteolysis *n.* acroosteólisis.

acropachy *n.* acropaquia.

acropachyderma *n.* acropaquidermia.

acroparalysis *n.* acroparálisis.

acroparesthesia *n.* acroparestesia.

acropathology *n.* acropatología.

acropathy *n.* acropatía.

acropetal *adj.* acrópeto, -ta.

acrophobia *n.* acrofobia.

acropigmentation *n.* acropigmentación.

acroposthitis *n.* acropostitis.

acropurpura *n.* acropúrpura.

acropustulosis *n.* acropustulosis.

infantile acropustulosis acropustulosis infantil.

acroscleroderma *n.* acroesclerodermia, acroesclerosis, acrosclerodermia.

acrosclerosis *n.* acrosclerosis.

acrosome *n.* acrosoma.

acrosphacelus *n.* acrosfacelo.

acrosphenosyndactylia *n.* acrosfenosindactilia.

acrospiroma *n.* acroespiroma, acrospiroma.

eccrine acrospiroma acrospiroma ecrino.

acrostealgia *n.* acrostealgia.

acrosyndactyly *n.* acrosindactilia.

acroteric *adj.* acrotérico, -ca.

acrotic *adj.* acrótico, -ca.

acrotism *n.* acrotismo.

acrotrophodynia *n.* acrotrofodinia.

acrotrophoneurosis *n.* acrotrofoneurosis.

acrylaldehyde *n.* acrilaldehído.

acrylic *adj.* acrílico, -ca.

act *n.* acto.

compulsive act acto compulsivo.

experiential act acto experiencial.

faulty act acto fallido.

imperious act acto imperativo.

impulsive act acto impulsivo.

indifferent act acto indiferente.

instinctive act acto instintivo.

intelligent act acto inteligente.

neutral act acto neutro.

reflex act acto reflejo.

role reversal act acto de inversión de roles.

voluntary act acto voluntario.

actin *n.* actina.

acting out *n.* acting out.

actinic *adj.* actínico, -ca.

actinicity *n.* actinicidad, actinidad.

actinine *n.* actinina.

actinism *n.* actinismo.

actinobacillosis *n.* actinobacilosis.

Actinobacillus *n.* Actinobacillus.

actinochemistry *n.* actinoquímica.

actinodermatosis *n.* actinodermatosis.

actinogenesis *n.* actinogénesis.

actinogenic *adj.* actinogénico, -na.

actinology *n.* actinología.

Actinomadura *n.* Actinomadura.

actinometer *n.* actinómetro.

actinometry *n.* actinometría.

actinomycelial *adj.* actinomicelial, actinomicético, -ca.

Actinomyces *n.* Actinomyces.

actinomycete *n.* actinomiceto.

actinomycetoma *n.* actinomicetoma.

actinomycoma *n.* actinomicoma.

actinomycosis *n.* actinomicosis.

actinomycotic *adj.* actinomicótico, -ca.

actinoneuritis *n.* actinoneuritis.

actinophage *n.* actinófago.

actinophytosis *n.* actinofitosis.

actinotherapy *n.* actinoterapia.

actinotoxemia *n.* actinotoxemia.

action *n.* acción.

ball-valve action acción de válvula esférica, acción valvular.

brachiation action acción braquial.

buffer action acción amortiguadora.

buffering action acción amortiguadora.

calorigenic action acción calorígena.

capillary action acción capilar.

cumulative action acción acumulativa.

deferred action retroactividad.

disordered action of the heart acción descontrolada del corazón (DAH).

drug action acción farmacológica.

lateral pinch action acción de pinza lateral.

reflex action acción refleja.

specific action acción específica.

specific dynamic action acción dinamicoespecífica, acción dinámica específica, acción dinamicoespecífica.

tampon action acción tampón.

thermogenic action acción termogénica.

trigger action acción desencadenante.

trophic action acción trófica.

activate *v.* activar.

activation *n.* activación.

amino acid activation activación del aminoácido.

complement activation activación del complemento.

lymphocyte activation activación de linfocitos.

monoclonal activation activación monoclonal.

ovular activation activación del óvulo, activación ovular.

ovum activation activación del óvulo, activación ovular.

plasma activation activación del plasma, activación plasmática.

polyclonal activation activación policlonal.

sperm activation activación del espermatozoide.

activator *n.* activador.

functional activator activador funcional.

monoblock activator activador monobloque.

polyclonal activator activador policlonal.

tissue plasminogen activator activador del plasminógeno tisular.

active *adj.* activo, -va.

optically active activo ópticamente.

activity *n.* actividad.

activity of daily living actividad de la vida diaria.

activity-passivity actividad-pasividad.

biological activity actividad biológica.

blocking activity actividad de bloqueo.

cholinergic activity actividad colinérgica.

enzyme activity actividad enzimática.

focussed activity actividad enfocada.

insulin-like activity actividad parecida a la insulina, actividad seudoinsulínica.

intrinsic sympathomimetic activity (ISA) actividad simpaticomimética intrínseca.

leukemia associated inhibitory activity actividad inhibitoria relacionada con la leucemia.

non-suppressible activity actividad no suprimible.

optical activity actividad óptica.

plasma renin activity actividad de renina plasmática.

purposeful activity actividad intencional.

specific activity actividad específica.

sympathoadrenal activity actividad simpaticoadrenal.

triggered activity actividad desencadenada.

actometer *n.* actómetro.

actomyosin *n.* actomiosina.

Actonia *n.* Actonia.

acufilopressure *n.* acufilopresión.

acuiparous *adj.* acuíparo, -ra.

acuity *n.* acuidad, agudeza.

resolution acuity agudeza de resolución.

Vernier acuity agudeza de Vernier.

visual acuity agudeza visual.

aculeate *adj.* aculado, -da, aculeado, -da.

acuminate *adj.* acuminado, -da.

acuophonia *n.* acufonía, acuofonía.

acupoint *n.* acupunto.

acupressure *n.* acupresión.

acupuncture *n.* acupuntura.

acupuncturist *n.* acupuntor, -ra.

acusection *n.* acusección.

acusector *n.* acusector.

acusis *n.* acusia.

acute *adj.* agudo, -da.

acutorsion *n.* acutorsión.

acyanoblepsia *n.* acianoblepsia, acianopsia.
acyanotic *adj.* acianótico, -ca.
acyclia *n.* aciclia.
acyesis *n.* aciesis.
acystia *n.* acistia.
acystinervia *n.* acistinervia, acistineuria.
ad integrum *adv.* ad integrum.
ad libitum *adv.* ad libitum.
ad nauseam *adv.* ad nauseam.
adacrya *n.* adacria.
adactylia *n.* adactilia.
adactylism *n.* adactilismo.
adactylous *adj.* adáctilo, -la.
adactyly *n.* adactilia.
adamantine *adj.* adamantino, -na.
adamantinocarcinoma *n.* adamantinocarcinoma.
adamantinoma *n.* adamantinoma, ameloblastoma.
  pigmented adamantinoma ameloblastoma pigmentado.
  pituitary adamantinoma adamantinoma pituitario, ameloblastoma hipofisario.
adamantoblast *n.* adamantoblasto.
adamantoblastoma *n.* adamantoblastoma.
adamantoma *n.* adamantoma.
adaptation *n.* adaptación.
  auditory adaptation adaptación auditiva.
  cellular adaptation adaptación celular.
  color adaptation adaptación cromática.
  dark adaptation adaptación a la oscuridad.
  enzymatic adaptation adaptación enzimática.
  light adaptation adaptación a la luz.
  phenotypic adaptation adaptación fenotípica.
  photopic adaptation adaptación fotópica.
  reality adaptation adaptación a la realidad.
  retinal adaptation adaptación retiniana.
  scotopic adaptation adaptación escotópica.
  social adaptation adaptación social.
adapter *n.* adaptador.
  band adapter adaptador de bandas.
adaptive *adj.* adaptable.
adaptometer *n.* adaptómetro.
  color adaptometer adaptómetro cromático.
adaptometry *n.* adaptometría.
adaptor *n.* adaptador.
adaxial *adj.* adaxial.
addict *n.* adicto, -ta.
  drug addict drogadicto, -ta.
  heroin addict heroinómano, -na.
addiction *n.* adicción.
  heroin addiction heroinomanía.
Addisonian *adj.* addisoniano, -na, adisoniano, -na.
Addisonism *n.* addisonismo, adisonismo.
additive *adj.* aditivo, -va.
  food additive aditivo alimentario.
  intentional additive aditivo intencional.
additivity *n.* aditividad.
adducent *adj.* aducente.
adduct *v.* aducir.
adduct *v.* adducir.
adduction *n.* adducción, aducción.
adductor *adj.* adductor, -ra, aductor, -ra.
adelomorphic *adj.* adelomórfico, -ca.
adelomorphous *adj.* adelomorfo, -fa.
adelphia *n.* adelfia.
adenalgia *n.* adenalgia.
adenase *n.* adenasa.
adenasthenia *n.* adenastenia.
  adenasthenia gastrica adenastenia gástrica.
adendric *adj.* adendrítico, -ca.
adendritic *adj.* adendrítico, -ca.

adenectomy *n.* adenectomía.
adenectopia *n.* adenectopía.
adenemphraxis *n.* adenenfraxis.
adenia *n.* adenia.
adenic *adj.* adénico, -ca.
adeniform *adj.* adeniforme.
adenine *n.* adenina.
adenitis *n.* adenitis.
  acute epidemic infectious adenitis adenitis aguda infecciosa epidémica.
  acute salivary adenitis adenitis salival aguda.
  cervical adenitis adenitis cervical.
  phlegmonous adenitis adenitis flemonosa.
  vulvovaginal adenitis adenitis vulvovaginal.
adenization *n.* adenización.
adenoacanthoma *n.* adenoacantoma.
adenoameloblastoma *n.* adenoameloblastoma.
adenocancroid *n.* adenocancroide.
adenocarcinoma *n.* adenocarcinoma.
  acinar adenocarcinoma adenocarcinoma acinar, adenocarcinoma acinoso.
  acinic cell adenocarcinoma adenocarcinoma de células acinosas.
  acinous adenocarcinoma adenocarcinoma acinar, adenocarcinoma acinoso.
  adenocarcinoma in situ adenocarcinoma in situ.
  adenocarcinoma of the kidney adenocarcinoma renal, nefrocarcinoma.
  alveolar adenocarcinoma adenocarcinoma alveolar.
  bronchiolar adenocarcinoma adenocarcinoma bronquiolar.
  follicular adenocarcinoma adenocarcinoma folicular.
  hypophyseal adenocarcinoma adenocarcinoma hipofisario.
  mucinous adenocarcinoma adenocarcinoma mucinoso.
  papillary adenocarcinoma adenocarcinoma papilar.
  polypoid adenocarcinoma adenocarcinoma polipoide.
  renal adenocarcinoma adenocarcinoma renal, nefrocarcinoma.
adenocele *n.* adenocele.
adenocellulitis *n.* adenocelulitis.
adenochondroma *n.* adenocondroma.
adenochondrosarcoma *n.* adenocondrosarcoma.
adenocyst *n.* adenoquiste.
adenocystoma *n.* adenocistoma.
  papillary adenocystoma lymphomatosum adenocistoma papilar linfomatoso.
adenodiastasis *n.* adenodiastasis.
adenodynia *n.* adenodinia.
adenoepithelioma *n.* adenoepitelioma.
adenofibroma *n.* adenofibroma.
  adenofibroma edematodes adenofibroma edematodes, adenofibroma edematoso.
adenofibromyoma *n.* adenofibromioma.
adenofibrosis *n.* adenofibrosis.
adenogenesis *n.* adenogénesis.
adenogenous *adj.* adenógeno, -na.
adenographic *adj.* adenográfico, -ca.
adenography *n.* adenografía.
adenohypersthenia *n.* adenohiperestenia.
adenohypophysis *n.* adenohipófisis.
adenohypophysitis *n.* adenohipofisitis.
adenoid *adj.* adenoide.
adenoidectomy *n.* adenoidectomía.
adenoidism *n.* adenoidismo.
adenoiditis *n.* adenoiditis.
adenoids *n.* adenoides.

adenoleiomyofibroma *n.* adenoleiomiofibroma.
adenolipoma *n.* adenolipoma.
adenolipomatosis *n.* adenolipomatosis.
  symmetric adenolipomatosis adenolipomatosis simétrica.
adenologaditis *n.* adenologaditis.
adenology *n.* adenología.
adenolymphitis *n.* adenolinfitis.
adenolymphocele *n.* adenolinfocele.
adenolymphoma *n.* adenolinfoma.
adenolysis *n.* adenólisis.
adenoma *n.* adenoma.
  acidophilic adenoma adenoma acidófilo.
  adamantine adenoma adenoma adamantino.
  adenoma alveolare adenoma alveolar.
  adenoma fibrosum adenoma fibroso.
  adenoma gelatinosum adenoma gelatinoso.
  adenoma of the kidney adenoma renal.
  adenoma tubulare testiculare ovarii adenoma tubular testicular del ovario.
  adnexal adenoma adenoma anexial.
  adrenal adenoma adenoma adrenal.
  adrenocortical adenoma adenoma adrenocortical.
  apocrine adenoma adenoma apocrino.
  apocrine sweat gland adenoma adenoma sudoríparo.
  basal cell adenoma adenoma de células basales.
  basophil adenoma adenoma basófilo.
  basophilic adenoma adenoma basófilo.
  bronchial adenoma adenoma bronquial.
  chief cell adenoma adenoma de células principales.
  chromophil adenoma adenoma cromófilo.
  chromophobe adenoma adenoma cromófobo.
  colloid adenoma adenoma coloide.
  cortical adenoma adenoma cortical.
  embryonal adenoma adenoma embrionario.
  eosinophilic adenoma adenoma eosinofílico.
  fetal adenoma adenoma fetal.
  fibroid adenoma adenoma fibroso.
  follicular adenoma adenoma folicular.
  hepatic adenoma adenoma hepático.
  hipophyseal adenoma adenoma hipofisario.
  Hürthle cell adenoma adenoma de células de Hürthle.
  islet adenoma adenoma insular.
  lactating adenoma adenoma de la lactación.
  Langerhansian adenoma adenoma de Langerhans, adenoma langerhansiano.
  macrofollicular adenoma adenoma macrofolicular.
  malignant adenoma adenoma maligno.
  microfollicular adenoma adenoma microfolicular.
  monomorphic adenoma adenoma monomórfico.
  mucinous adenoma adenoma mucinoso.
  nephrogenic adenoma adenoma nefrogénico.
  null cell adenoma adenoma de células nulas.
  ovarian tubular adenoma adenoma tubular ovárico.
  oxyphil adenoma adenoma oxífilo.
  oxyphilic granular cell adenoma adenoma de células oxífilas granulosas.
  papillary adenoma adenoma papilar.
  papillary cystic adenoma adenoma quístico papilar.
  Pick's tubular adenoma adenoma tubular de Pick.
  pituitary adenoma adenoma hipofisario.

pleomorphic adenoma adenoma pleomorfo.
polypoid adenoma adenoma polipoide.
prostatic adenoma adenoma prostático.
sebaceous adenoma adenoma sebáceo.
testicular tubular adenoma adenoma tubular testicular.
toxic adenoma adenoma tóxico.
tubular adenoma adenoma tubular.
umbilical adenoma adenoma diverticular.
villous adenoma adenoma velloso.
adenomalacia *n.* adenomalacia.
adenomatoid *adj.* adenomatoide, adenomatoideo, -a.
adenomatosis *n.* adenomatosis.
adenomatosis oris adenomatosis bucal.
erosive adenomatosis of the nipple adenomatosis erosiva del pezón.
fibrosing adenomatosis adenomatosis fibrosante.
multiple endocrine adenomatosis adenomatosis múltiple endocrina.
pluriglandular adenomatosis adenomatosis pluriglandular.
polyendocrine adenomatosis adenomatosis poliendocrina.
pulmonary adenomatosis adenomatosis pulmonar.
adenomatous *adj.* adenomatoso, -sa.
adenomectomy *n.* adenomectomía.
adenomegaly *n.* adenomegalia.
adenomere *n.* adenómero.
adenomyoepithelioma *n.* adenomioepitelioma.
adenomyoepithelioma of the stomach adenomioepitelioma del estómago.
adenomyofibroma *n.* adenomiofibroma.
adenomyoma *n.* adenomioma.
adenomyomatosis *n.* adenomiomatosis.
adenomyomatous *adj.* adenomiomatoso, -sa.
adenomyometritis *n.* adenomiometritis.
adenomyosarcoma *n.* adenomiosarcoma.
embryonal adenomyosarcoma adenomiosarcoma embrionario.
adenomyosis *n.* adenomiosis.
adenomyosis externa adenomiosis externa.
adenomyosis of the uterus adenomiosis uterina.
adenomyosis tubae adenomiosis tubaria.
adenomyosis uteri adenomiosis uterina.
external adenomyosis adenomiosis externa.
stromal adenomyosis adenomiosis del estroma.
adenomyositis *n.* adenomiositis.
adenomyxoma *n.* adenomixoma.
adenomyxosarcoma *n.* adenomixosarcoma.
adenoncus *n.* adenoncosis.
adenoneural *adj.* adenoneural.
adenopathy *n.* adenopatía.
adenopharingitis *n.* adenofaringitis.
adenophlegmon *n.* adenoflemón.
adenophthalmia *n.* adenoftalmía.
adenophyma *n.* adenofima.
adenopituicyte *n.* adenopituicito.
adenosalpingitis *n.* adenosalpingitis.
adenosarcoma *n.* adenosarcoma.
adenosarcorhabdomyoma *n.* adenosarcorrabdomioma.
adenosclerosis *n.* adenosclerosis.
adenose *adj.* adenoso, -sa.
adenosine *n.* adenosina.
adenosis *n.* adenosis.
adenosis vaginae adenosis vaginal.
blunt duct adenosis adenosis de conductos romos u obstruidos.
fibrosing adenosis adenosis fibrosante.

microglandular adenosis adenosis microglandular.
sclerosing adenosis adenosis esclerosante.
adenotome *n.* adenótomo.
adenotomy *n.* adenotomía.
adenotonsillectomy *n.* adenoamigdalectomía.
adenotyphus *n.* adenotifus.
adenous *adj.* adenoso, -sa.
adenoviral *adj.* adenoviral, adenovírico, -ca.
Adenoviridae *n.* Adenoviridae.
adenovirus *n.* adenovirus.
adenylic *adj.* adenílico, -ca.
adequacy *n.* adecuación.
velopharyngeal adequacy adecuación velofaríngea.
adermia *n.* adermia.
adermogenesis *n.* adermogénesis.
adhere *v.* adherir.
adherence *n.* adherencia.
inmune adherence adherencia inmunitaria.
primary adherence adherencia primaria.
secondary adherence adherencia secundaria.
serological adherence adherencia serológica.
sublabial adherence adherencia sublabial.
adherent *adj.* adherente.
adhesio *n.* adhesio, adhesión.
adhesion *n.* adherencia, adhesio, adhesión.
abdominal adhesion adherencia abdominal, adhesión abdominal.
amniotic adhesion adherencia amniótica, adhesión amniótica.
fibrinous adhesion adhesión fibrinosa.
fibrous adhesion adhesión fibrosa.
interthalamic adhesion adhesión intertalámica.
pericardial adhesion adherencia pericárdica, adhesión pericárdica.
platelet adhesion adhesión de las plaquetas.
primary adhesion adhesión primaria.
secondary adhesion adhesión secundaria.
traumatic uterine adhesion adherencia traumática uterina.
adhesiotomy *n.* adherenciotomía, adhesiotomía.
adhesive *adj.* adhesivo, -va.
adhesiveness *n.* adhesividad.
platelet adhesiveness adhesividad plaquetaria.
adiabatic *adj.* adiabático, -ca.
adiactinic *adj.* adiactínico, -ca.
adiadochocinesia *n.* adiadococinesia.
adiadochocinesis *n.* adiadococinesia.
adiadochokinesia *n.* adiadococinesia.
adiadochokinesis *n.* adiadococinesia.
adiadokokinesis *n.* adiadococinesia.
adiaphoresis *n.* adiaforesis.
adiaphoretic *adj.* adiaforético, -ca.
adiaphoria *n.* adiaforia.
adiapneustia *n.* adiapneustia.
adiaspiromycosis *n.* adiaspiromicosis.
adiastole *n.* adiastolia.
adiastolia *n.* adiastolia.
adiathermance *n.* adiatermancia, adiatermia.
adiathermancy *n.* adiatermancia, adiatermia.
adiathermic *adj.* adiatérmico, -ca.
adiathetic *adj.* adiatésico, -ca.
adiemorrhysis *n.* adiemorrisis.
adient *adj.* adiente.
adipectomy *n.* adipectomía.
adipocele *n.* adipocele.
adipocellular *adj.* adipocelular.
adipoceratous *adj.* adipoceratoso, -sa.
adipocere *n.* adipocera, adipocira.
adipocyte *n.* adipocito.

adipofibroma *n.* adipofibroma.
adipogenesis *n.* adipogénesis, adipogenia.
adipogenic *adj.* adipogénico, -ca.
adipogenous *adj.* adipógeno, -na.
adipoid *n.* adipoide.
adipokinesis *n.* adipocinesia, adipocinesis.
adipokinetic *adj.* adipocinético, -ca.
adipolysis *n.* adipólisis.
adipolytic *adj.* adipolítico, -ca.
adipoma *n.* adipoma.
adipomastia *n.* adipomastia.
adipometer *n.* adipómetro.
adiponecrosis *n.* adiponecrosis.
adiponecrosis subcutanea neonatorum adiponecrosis subcutánea de los recién nacidos, adiponecrosis subcutánea neonatal.
adipopectic *adj.* adipopéctico, -ca.
adipopexia *n.* adipopexia, adipopexis.
adipopexic *adj.* adipopéctico, -ca.
adipopexis *n.* adipopexia, adipopexis.
adiposalgia *n.* adiposalgia.
adipose *adj.* adiposo, -sa.
adiposis *n.* adiposis.
adiposis cerebralis adiposis cerebral.
adiposis dolorosa adiposis dolorosa.
adiposis hepatica adiposis hepática.
adiposis orchica adiposis orchalis, adiposis órquica.
adiposis tuberosa simplex adiposis tuberosa simple.
adiposis universalis adiposis universal.
adipositas *n.* adiposidad, adipositas.
adipositas abdominis adipositas abdominis.
adipositas cerebralis adiposidad cerebral, adipositas cerebralis.
adipositas cordis adipositas cordis.
adipositas ex vacuo adipositas ex vacuo.
adiposity *n.* adiposidad.
cerebral adiposity adiposidad cerebral.
pituitary adiposity adiposidad hipofisaria.
adiposuria *n.* adiposuria.
adipsia *n.* adipsia.
adipsy *n.* adipsia.
adiaspore *n.* adiaspora.
aditus *n.* aditus.
adjacent *adj.* adyacente.
adjustment *n.* ajuste.
phalangeal adjustment ajuste falángico.
adjuvant *n.* adyuvante, coadyuvante.
Freund's complete adjuvant adyuvante completo de Freund.
Freund's incomplete adjuvant adyuvante incompleto de Freund.
adjuvanticity *n.* adyuvanticidad.
Adlerian *adj.* adleriano, -na.
admaxillary *adj.* admaxilar.
admedial *adj.* admedial.
admedian *adj.* admediano, -na.
administration *n.* administración.
administration of parenteral fluids administración de líquidos parenterales.
buccal administration of medication administración bucal de la medicación.
drug administration administración de fármacos.
inhalation administration of medication administración de medicación mediante inhalación.
ophthalmic administration of medication administración oftálmica de medicamentos.
admittance *n.* admitancia.
adnerval *adj.* adnerval.
adneural *adj.* adneural.
adnexa *n.* adnexa, anejos, anexos.
adnexectomy *n.* anexectomía.

adnexitis *n.* anexitis.
adnexogenesis *n.* anexogénesis.
adnexopexy *n.* anexopexia.
adolescence *n.* adolescencia.
adolescent *n.* adolescente.
adoral *adj.* adoral.
adrenal *adj.* adrenal, suprarrenal.
adrenalectomy *n.* adrenalectomía.
adrenaline *n.* adrenalina.
adrenalinemia *n.* adrenalinemia.
adrenalinogenesis *n.* adrenalinogénesis.
adrenalinuria *n.* adrenalinuria.
adrenalism *n.* adrenalismo.
adrenalitis *n.* adrenalitis.
adrenalopathy *n.* adrenalopatía.
adrenalotropic *adj.* adrenalotrópico, -ca.
adrenarche *n.* adrenarca, adrenarquia.
adrenergic *adj.* adrenérgico, -ca.
adrenitis *n.* adrenitis.
adrenoceptive *adj.* adrenoceptivo, -va.
adrenochrome *n.* adrenocromo.
adrenocortical *adj.* adrenocortical, corticosuprarrenal.
adrenocorticomimetic *adj.* adrenocorticomimético, -ca.
adrenocorticotrophic *adj.* adrenocorticotrófico, -ca, adrenocorticotrópico, -ca, adrenocorticotropo, -pa.
adrenocorticotropic *adj.* adrenocorticotrófico, -ca, adrenocorticotrópico, -ca, adrenocorticotropo, -pa.
adrenodontia *n.* adrenodoncia.
adrenodoxin *n.* adrenodoxina.
adrenogenic *adj.* adrenogénico, -ca.
adrenogenous *adj.* adrenógeno, -na.
adrenoglomerulotropin *n.* adrenoglomerulotropina.
adrenokinetic *adj.* adrenocinético, -ca.
adrenoleukodystrophy *n.* adrenoleucodistrofia.
adrenolutin *n.* adrenolutina.
adrenolytic *adj.* adrenolítico, -ca.
adrenomedullotropic *adj.* adrenomedulotrópico, -ca.
adrenomegaly *n.* adrenomegalia.
adrenomimetic *adj.* adrenomimético, -ca.
adrenopathy *n.* adrenopatía.
adrenopausia *n.* adrenopausia.
adrenoprival *adj.* adrenoprivo, -va.
adrenoreactive *adj.* adrenorreactivo, -va.
adrenostatic *adj.* adrenostático, -ca.
adrenosterone *n.* adrenosterona.
adrenotoxin *n.* adrenotoxina.
adrenotrophic *adj.* adrenotrófico, -ca, adrenotrópico, -ca.
adrenotropic *adj.* adrenotrófico, -ca, adrenotrópico, -ca.
adrenotropin *n.* adrenotropina.
adrenotropisme *n.* adrenotropismo.
adromia *n.* adromia.
adsorb *v.* adsorber.
adsorbed *adj.* adsorbido, -da.
adsorbent *adj.* adsorbente.
adsorption *n.* adsorción.
immune adsorption adsorción inmunitaria.
adsternal *adj.* adesternal, adsternal.
adterminal *adj.* adterminal.
adult *adj., n.* adulto, -ta.
adulteration *n.* adulteración.
adulthood *n.* adultez, edad adulta.
adventitia *n.* adventicia.
adventitious *adj.* adventicio, -cia.
adynamia *n.* adinamia.
adynamia episódica hereditaria adinamia
episódica hereditaria.

adynamic *adj.* adinámico, -ca.
Aedes *n.* Aedes.
aedoeocephalus *n.* aedocéfalo.
aeluropsis *n.* aeluropsis.
aerate *v.* airear.
aeration *n.* aereación.
aerendocardia *n.* aerendocardia.
aerenterectasia *n.* aerenterectasia.
aerial *adj.* aéreo, -a.
aeriferous *adj.* aerífero, -ra.
aeriform *adj.* aeriforme.
aerobe *adj.* aerobio, -bia.
facultative aerobe aerobio facultativo.
obligate aerobe aerobio obligado.
strict aerobe aerobio estricto.
aerobic *adj.* aeróbico, -ca.
aerobiology *n.* aerobiología.
extramural aerobiology aerobiología extramural.
intramural aerobiology aerobiología intramural.
aerobioscope *n.* aerobioscopio.
aerobiosis *n.* aerobiosis, anaerobiosis.
aerobiotic *adj.* aerobiótico, -ca.
aerobullosis *n.* aerobullosis.
aerocele *n.* aerocele.
aerocolia *n.* aerocolia.
aerocolpos *n.* aerocolpos.
aerocoly *n.* aerocolia.
aerocystoscope *n.* aerocistoscopio.
aerocystoscopy *n.* aerocistoscopia.
aerodermectasia *n.* aerodermectasia.
aerodontalgia *n.* aerodontalgia.
aerodontia *n.* aerodoncia, aerodóntica.
aerodromophobia *n.* aerodromofobia.
aerodynamics *n.* aerodinámica.
aeroembolism *n.* aeroembolia, aeroembolismo.
aeroemphysema *n.* aeroenfisema.
aerogastria *n.* aerogastria.
blocked aerogastria aerogastria por bloqueo.
aerogenesis *n.* aerogénesis.
aerogenic *adj.* aerogénico, -ca.
aerogenous *adj.* aerógeno, -na.
aerohydrotherapy *n.* aerohidroterapia.
aeroionotherapy *n.* aeroionoterapia.
aeromedicine *n.* aeromedicina.
aerometer *n.* aerómetro.
Aeromonas *n.* Aeromonas.
aero-odontalgia *n.* aerodontalgia.
aero-odontodynia *n.* aerodontodinia.
aero-otitis media *n.* aerootitis media.
aeropathy *n.* aeropatía.
aeroperitoneum *n.* aeroperitoneo.
aeroperitonia *n.* aeroperitoneo.
aerophagia *n.* aerofagia.
aerophagy *n.* aerofagia.
aerophil *adj.* aerófilo, -la.
aerophile *adj.* aerófilo, -la.
aerophilic *adj.* aerofílico, -ca.
aerophilous *adj.* aerofílico, -ca.
aerophore *adj.* aeróforo, -ra.
aeropiesism *n.* aeropiecismo.
aeropiesotherapy *n.* aeropiesoterapia.
aeroplankton *n.* aeroplancton.
aeroplethysmograph *n.* aeropletismógrafo.
aeroporotomy *n.* aeroporotomía.
aerorethroscope *n.* aerouretroscopio.
aerosialophagy *n.* aerosialofagia.
aerosinusitis *n.* aerosinusitis.
aerosis *n.* aerosis.
aerosol *n.* aerosol.
aerotaxis *n.* aerotaxis.
aerotherapeutics *n.* aeroterapia.
aerotherapy *n.* aeroterapia.

aerotitis media *n.* aerotitis media.
aerotolerant *adj.* aerotolerante.
aerotonometer *n.* aerotonómetro.
aerotonometry *n.* aerotonometría.
aerotropism *n.* aerotropismo.
negative aerotropism aerotropismo negativo.
positive aerotropism aerotropismo positivo.
aerourethroscopy *n.* aerouretroscopia.
afebrile *adj.* afebril.
afetal *adj.* afetal.
affect *n.* afecto.
blunted affect afecto embotado.
constricted affect afecto constreñido.
flat affect afecto aplanado, afecto plano.
inappropiate affect afecto inapropiado.
negative affect afecto negativo.
positive affect afecto positivo.
restricted affect afecto restringido.
affected *adj.* afectado, -da, afecto, -ta.
affection *n.* afección.
affectivity *n.* afectividad.
affectomotor *adj.* afectomotor, -ra.
afferent *adj.* aferente.
affiliation *n.* afiliación.
affinity *n.* afinidad.
chemical affinity afinidad química.
elective affinity afinidad electiva.
genetic affinity afinidad genética.
residual affinity afinidad residual.
selective affinity afinidad electiva.
affinous *adj.* afín.
affirmation *n.* afirmación.
capacity affirmation afirmación de la capacidad.
afflux *n.* aflujo.
affusion *n.* afusión.
afibrillar *adj.* afibrilar.
afibrinogenemia *n.* afibrinogenemia.
afterbirth *n.* secundinas.
afterpains *n.* entuertos.
agalactia *n.* agalactia, agalaxia.
agalactorrhea *n.* agalactorrea.
agalactosis *n.* agalactosis.
agalactosuria *n.* agalactosuria.
agalactous *adj.* agaláctico, -ca, agalacto, -ta.
agalorrhea *n.* agalorrea.
agamete *n.* agameto.
agametic *adj.* agamético, -ca.
agamic *adj.* agámico, -ca.
agammaglobulinemia *n.* agammaglobulinemia.
acquired agammaglobulinemia agammaglobulinemia adquirida.
Bruton's agammaglobulinemia agammaglobulinemia de Bruton.
congenital agammaglobulinemia agammaglobulinemia congénita.
lymphopenic agammaglobulinemia agammaglobulinemia con linfocitopenia, agammaglobulinemia linfopénica.
Swiss type agammaglobulinemia agammaglobulinemia tipo Suiza.
X-linked agammaglobulinemia agammaglobulinemia congénita ligada al sexo.
agamobium *n.* agamobio.
agamogenesis *n.* agamia, agamogénesis.
agamogenetic *adj.* agamogenético, -ca.
agamogony *n.* agamogonia.
agamont *n.* agamonte.
aganglionosis *n.* aganglionosis.
agar *n.* agar, agar-agar.
agar-agar *n.* agar, agar-agar.
agarose *n.* agarosa.
agastric *adj.* agástrico, -ca.

agastroneuria *n.* agastroneuria.
age *n.* edad.
  achievement age edad de realización, edad de rendimiento.
  acquisition of language age edad de adquisición del lenguaje.
  anatomical age edad anatómica.
  Binet age edad de Binet.
  bone age edad ósea.
  childbearing age edad fértil.
  chronological age edad cronológica.
  development age edad de desarrollo.
  fertilization age edad de fertilización.
  fetal age edad fetal.
  functional age edad funcional.
  gestational age edad gestacional.
  menarcheal age edad de la menarquia.
  menarchial age edad de la menarquia.
  menstrual age edad menstrual.
  mental age edad mental.
  obstinacy age edad de la obstinación.
  physical age edad física.
  physiologic age edad fisiológica.
  physiological age edad fisiológica.
  postovulatory age edad posovulatoria.
  skeletal age edad esquelética.
  statural age edad estatural.
agenesia *n.* agenesia.
  agenesia corticalis agenesia cortical.
  agenesia of the corpus callosum agenesia del cuerpo calloso.
  callosal agenesia agenesia callosa.
  gonadal agenesia agenesia gonadal.
  nuclear agenesia agenesia nuclear.
  ovarian agenesia agenesia ovárica.
  renal agenesia agenesia renal.
  septum pellucidum agenesia agenesia del septum pellucidum.
  thymic agenesia agenesia tímica.
  vaginal agenesia agenesia vaginal.
agenesic *adj.* agenésico, -ca.
agenesis *n.* agenesia, agénesis.
ageniocephaly *n.* ageniocefalia.
agenitalism *n.* agenitalismo.
agenosomia *n.* agenosomía.
agenosomus *n.* agenosoma.
agent *n.* agente.
  activating agent agente activador.
  adrenergic blocking agent agente de bloqueo adrenérgico.
  adrenergic neuron blocking agent agente de bloqueo de neuronas adrenérgicas, agente de bloqueo neural adrenérgico.
  adrenergic neuronal blocking agent agente de bloqueo de neuronas adrenérgicas, agente de bloqueo neural adrenérgico.
  agent orange agente naranja.
  alkylating agent agente alquilante.
  alpha-adrenergic blocking agent agente de bloqueo adrenérgico alfa.
  antianxiety agent agente ansiolítico, agente antiansiedad.
  antineoplastic agent agente antineoplásico.
  antipsychotic agent agente antipsicótico.
  beta-adrenergic receptor blocking agent agente bloqueador de los receptores beta-adrenérgicos.
  beta-adrenergic blocking agent agente de bloqueo adrenérgico beta.
  bleaching agent decolorante, descolorante.
  blocking agent agente bloqueador, agente bloqueante.
  calcium channel blocking agent agente bloqueador de los canales del calcio.
  caudalizing agent agente caudalizante.

  ceruminolytic agent agente ceruminolítico.
  change agent agente de cambio.
  chelating agent agente quelante, quelante.
  chemical agent agente químico.
  chemotherapeutic agent agente quimioterápico.
  chimpanzee coryza agent agente de coriza de chimpancé.
  cholinergic blocking agent agente de bloqueo colinérgico.
  clearing agent aclarador, agente de aclaramiento.
  decalcifying agent descalcificante[2].
  depolarizing neuromuscular blocking agent agente bloqueador neuromuscular despolarizante.
  diluting agent agente diluyente.
  dispersing agent agente dispersante.
  dorsalizing agent agente dorsalizante.
  embolization agent agente embolizador.
  fixing agent agente fijadores.
  ganglionic blocking agent agente de bloqueo ganglionar.
  hypoglycemic agent hipoglucemiante.
  levigating agent agente de levigación.
  masking agent agente enmascarador.
  mesodermalizing agent agente mesodermalizador.
  mydriatic and cyclopegic agent agente midriático y ciclopéjico.
  neuroleptic agent agente neuroléptico.
  neuromuscular blocking agent agente bloqueador neuromuscular.
  non-depolarizing neuromuscular blocking agent agente bloqueador neuromuscular no despolarizante.
  oxidizing agent agente oxidante.
  pharmacological agent agente farmacológico.
  progestational agent agente progestacional.
  reducing agent agente reductor.
  slow channel blocking agent agente bloqueador de los canales lentos.
  sulfiting agent agente sulfatante.
  surfactant agent agente tensioactivo.
  synergistic agent agente sinérgico.
  teratogenic agent agente teratógeno.
  transforming agent agente transformador, agente transformante.
agerasia *n.* agerasia.
agglomerate *v.* aglomerado, -da.
agglomerated *adj.* aglomerado, -da.
agglomeration *n.* aglomeración.
agglutinable *adj.* aglutinable.
agglutinant *adj.* aglutinante.
agglutinating *adj.* aglutinador, -ra.
agglutination *n.* aglutinación.
  acid agglutination aglutinación ácida.
  bacteriogenic agglutination aglutinación bacteriógena.
  cold agglutination aglutinación de frío, aglutinación fría.
  cross agglutination aglutinación cruzada.
  group agglutination aglutinación de grupo.
  H agglutination aglutinación H.
  immune agglutination aglutinación inmune.
  non-immune agglutination aglutinación no inmune.
  O agglutination aglutinación O.
  perceptive agglutination aglutinación perceptiva.
  platelet agglutination aglutinación plaquetaria.
  salt agglutination aglutinación salina.
  somatic agglutination aglutinación somática.
agglutinative *adj.* aglutinativo, -va.

agglutinin *n.* aglutinina.
  anti-RH agglutinin aglutinina anti-RH.
  chief agglutinin aglutinina principal.
  cold agglutinin aglutinina fría.
  complete agglutinin aglutinina completa.
  cross-reacting agglutinin aglutinina de reacción cruzada.
  flagellar agglutinin aglutinina flagelar.
  group agglutinin aglutinina de grupo.
  immune agglutinin aglutinina inmune.
  incomplete agglutinin aglutinina incompleta.
  Leptospira agglutinin aglutinina de Leptospira.
  leukocyte agglutinin aglutinina leucocitaria.
  major agglutinin aglutinina específica, aglutinina mayor.
  MG agglutinin aglutinina MG.
  minor agglutinin aglutinina menor.
  normal agglutinin aglutinina normal.
  partial agglutinin aglutinina parcial.
  saline agglutinin aglutinina salina.
  somatic agglutinin aglutinina somática.
  T agglutinin aglutinina T.
  unexpected agglutinin aglutinina inesperada.
  warm agglutinin aglutinina caliente.
agglutinogen *n.* aglutinógeno.
agglutinogenic *adj.* aglutinogénico, -ca, aglutogénico, -ca.
agglutinoscope *n.* aglutinoscopio.
aggravate *v.* agravar.
aggravating *adj.* agravante.
aggregate *v.* agregar.
aggregated *adj.* agregado, -da.
aggregation *n.* agregación.
  aggregation of platelets agregación plaquetaria.
  familial aggregation agregación familiar.
  platelet aggregation agregación plaquetaria.
  red cell aggregation agregación de hematíes.
aggregometer *n.* agregómetro.
aggregometry *n.* agregometría.
aggression *n.* agresión.
  constructive aggression agresión constructiva.
  destructive aggression agresión destructiva.
  instrumental aggression agresión instrumental.
  inward aggression agresión autodestructiva, agresión interna.
  passive aggression agresión pasiva.
aggressive *adj.* agresivo, -va.
aggressiveness *n.* agresividad.
aggressivity *n.* agresividad.
aging *n.* envejecimiento.
agitated *adj.* agitado, -da.
agitation *n.* agitación.
  pyschomotor agitation agitación psicomotriz.
aglangionic *adj.* aganglionar.
aglaucopsia *n.* aglaucopsia.
aglaukopsia *n.* aglaucopsia.
aglobulia *n.* aglobulia.
aglobulism *n.* aglobulismo.
aglossia *n.* aglosia.
aglossostomia *n.* aglosostomía.
aglycemia *n.* aglucemia.
aglycosuria *n.* aglicosuria.
aglycosuric *adj.* aglicosúrico, -ca.
agmantine *n.* agmantina.
agminated *adj.* agminado, -da.
agnathia *n.* agnacia, agnatia.
agnathous *adj.* agnato, -ta.
agnogenic *adj.* agnogénico, -ca.
agnosia *n.* agnosia.

acoustic agnosia agnosia auditiva.
agnosia for faces agnosia de fisionomías.
auditory agnosia agnosia auditiva.
body-image agnosia agnosia de la imagen corporal.
cross-reacting agnosia agnosia de reacción cruzada.
finger agnosia agnosia digital.
ideational agnosia agnosia de ideación.
optic agnosia agnosia óptica.
tactile agnosia agnosia táctil.
time agnosia agnosia cronológica, agnosia temporal.
visual agnosia agnosia visual.
visual-spatial agnosia agnosia visuoespacial.
visuospatial agnosia agnosia visuoespacial.
agomphiasis *n.* agonfiasis.
agomphious *adj.* agonfo, -fa.
agomphosis *n.* agonfosis.
agonad *n.* agónada.
agonadal *adj.* agonadal.
agonadism *n.* agonadismo.
agonal *adj.* agónico, -ca.
agonist *adj.* agonista.
agony *n.* agonía.
agoraphilia *n.* agorafilia.
agoraphobia *n.* agorafobia.
agoraphobic *adj.* agorafóbico, -ca.
agouti *n.* agutí.
agrammatica *n.* agramática.
agrammatism *n.* agramatismo.
agranulocyte *n.* agranulocito.
agranulocytosis *n.* agranulocitosis.
infantile genetic agranulocytosis agranulocitosis infantil genética.
agranuloplastic *adj.* agranuloplásico, -ca, agranuloplástico, -ca.
agranulosis *n.* agranulosis.
agraphesthesia *n.* agrafoestesia.
agraphia *n.* agrafia.
absolute agraphia agrafia absoluta.
acoustic agraphia agrafia auditiva.
agraphia amnemonica agrafia amnemónica.
agraphia atactica agrafia atáctica, agrafia atáxica.
cerebral agraphia agrafia cerebral.
developmental agraphia agrafia de desarrollo.
jargon agraphia agrafia jergal.
literal agraphia agrafia literal.
mental agraphia agrafia mental.
motor agraphia agrafia motora.
musical agraphia agrafia musical.
verbal agraphia agrafia verbal.
agraphic *adj.* agráfico, -ca.
agremia *n.* agremia.
agressology *n.* agresología.
agrypnia *n.* agripnia.
ague *n.* ague.
brass foundry worker ague ague de los fundidores de latón.
brass-founder's ague ague de los fundidores de latón.
quartan ague ague cuartano.
quintan ague ague quintano.
quotidian ague ague cotidiano.
shaking ague ague agitante.
tertian ague ague terciano.
agyria *n.* agiria.
agyric *adj.* agírico, -ca.
ahaptoglobinemia *n.* ahaptoglobinemia.
ahistidasia *n.* ahistidasia.
aichmophobia *n.* ecmofobia.
ailment *n.* achaque.
ainhum *n.* ainhum.

air *n.* aire.
air swallowing aerofagia.
alveolar air aire alveolar.
compressed air aire comprimido.
factitious air aire facticio.
liquid air aire líquido.
reserve air aire de reserva.
stale air aire confinado.
stationary air aire estacionario.
airborne *adj.* aerotransportado, -da.
akanthion *n.* acantión, akantion.
akaryocyte *n.* acariocito.
akaryota *n.* acariota.
akaryote *n.* acarionte.
akatama *n.* acatama, akatama.
akatamathesia *n.* acatamatesia, akatamatesia.
akathisia *n.* acatisia, akatisia.
akeratosis *n.* aqueratosis.
akinesia *n.* acinesia, acinesis, aquinesia.
akinesia algera acinesia álgera.
akinesia amnestica acinesia amnéstica.
O'Brien akinesia acinesia de O'Brien.
reflex akinesia acinesia refleja.
akinesic *adj.* aquinésico, -ca.
akinesis *n.* aquinesia, aquinesis.
akinesthesia *n.* acinestesia.
akinetic *adj.* acinético, -ca.
akrencephalon *n.* acrencéfalo.
ala *n.* ala.
alacrima *n.* alacrima.
alactasia *n.* alactasia, alactasis.
alalia *n.* alalia.
alalia cophica alalia cófica.
alalia organica alalia orgánica.
alalia physiologica alalia fisiológica.
alalia prolongata alalia prolongada.
alalic *adj.* alálico, -ca.
alanine *n.* alanina.
alar *adj.* alar.
alarm *n.* alarma.
alastrim *n.* alastrim.
alastrimic *adj.* alastrimico, -ca.
alba *adj.* alba.
albedo *n.* albedo.
albedo retinae albedo retinae.
albidus *adj.* álbido, -da, albidus.
albinism *n.* albinismo.
autosomal recessive ocular albinism (AROA) albinismo ocular autosómico recesivo (AROA).
ocular albinism albinismo ocular.
ocular-type Forsius-Erikson albinism albinismo ocular tipo Forsius-Erikson.
oculocutaneous albinism albinismo oculocutáneo.
partial albinism albinismo parcial.
punctate oculocutaneous albinism albinismo punctata oculocutáneo.
total albinism albinismo total, albinismo universal.
tyrosinase-negative oculocutaneous albinism albinismo oculocutáneo tirosinasa negativa (ty-neg).
tyrosinase-positive oculocutaneous albinism albinismo oculocutáneo tirosinasa positivo (ty-pos).
albino *adj.* albino, -na.
albinoidism *n.* albinoidismo.
albinotic *adj.* albinótico, -ca.
albocinereous *adj.* albocinéreo, -a.
albopapuloide *adj.* albopapuloide.
albuginea *n.* albugínea.
albuginea penis albugínea penis.
albugineotomy *n.* albugineotomía.
albugineous *adj.* albugíneo, -a.

albuginitis *n.* albuginitis.
albugo *n.* albugo.
albumen *n.* albumen.
albumimeter *n.* albumímetro.
albumin *n.* albúmina.
acetosoluble albumin albúmina acetosoluble.
acid albumin albúmina ácida.
albumin A albúmina A.
alkali albumin albúmina alcalina.
Bence Jones albumin albúmina de Bence Jones.
blood albumin albúmina sanguínea.
circulating albumin albúmina circulante.
derived albumin albúmina derivada.
egg albumin albúmina de huevo.
hematin albumin albúmina hematina.
human albumin albúmina humana.
iodinated 125 I serum albumin albúmina sérica yodada con 125 I.
iodinated 131 I human serum albumin albúmina sérica humana yodada 131 I.
muscle albumin albúmina muscular.
native albumin albúmina nativa.
normal human serum albumin albúmina normal del suero humano, albúmina sérica humana normal.
organ albumin albúmina orgánica.
Patein's albumin albúmina de Patein.
radioiodinated serum albumin (RISA) albúmina sérica radioyodada.
serum albumin albúmina sérica.
vegetable albumin albúmina vegetal.
albuminate *n.* albuminato.
albuminaturia *n.* albuminaturia.
albuminemia *n.* albuminemia.
albuminiferous *adj.* albuminífero, -ra.
albuminimeter *n.* albuminímetro.
albuminimetry *n.* albuminimetría.
albuminiparous *adj.* albuminíparo, -ra.
albuminocholia *n.* albuminocolia.
albuminocytological *adj.* albuminocitológico, -ca.
albuminogenous *adj.* albuminógeno, -na.
albuminoid *n.* albuminoide.
albuminolysin *n.* albuminolisina.
albuminolysis *n.* albuminólisis.
albuminometer *n.* albuminómetro.
albuminone *n.* albuminona.
albuminoptysis *n.* albuminoptisis.
albuminoreaction *n.* albuminorreacción.
albuminorrhea *n.* albuminorrea.
albuminose *n.* albuminosa.
albuminosis *n.* albuminosis.
albuminous *adj.* albuminoso, -sa.
albuminuretic *adj.* albuminurético, -ca.
albuminuria *n.* albuminuria.
accidental albuminuria albuminuria accidental.
adolescent albuminuria albuminuria de la adolescencia, albuminuria de los adolescentes.
adventitious albuminuria albuminuria adventicia, albuminuria espontánea, albuminuria espuria.
albuminuria of athletes albuminuria de los atletas.
Bamberger's albuminuria albuminuria hematógena de Bamberger's.
Bamberger's hematogenic albuminuria albuminuria hematógena de Bamberger's.
benign albuminuria albuminuria benigna.
cardiac albuminuria albuminuria cardíaca.
colliquative albuminuria albuminuria colicuativa.
cyclic albuminuria albuminuria cíclica.

dietetic albuminuria albuminuria alimentaria, albuminuria dietética.

digestive albuminuria albuminuria digestiva.

essential albuminuria albuminuria esencial.

false albuminuria albuminuria falsa.

febrile albuminuria albuminuria febril.

functional albuminuria albuminuria funcional.

hematogenous albuminuria albuminuria hematógena.

hemic albuminuria albuminuria hémica.

hypostatic albuminuria albuminuria clinostática, albuminuria hipostática.

intermittent albuminuria albuminuria intermitente.

intrinsic albuminuria albuminuria intrínseca.

lordotic albuminuria albuminuria lordótica.

neuropathic albuminuria albuminuria neuropática.

orthostatic albuminuria albuminuria ortostática, albuminuria ortótica.

palpatory albuminuria albuminuria palpatoria.

paroxysmal albuminuria albuminuria paroxismal.

physiologic albuminuria albuminuria fisiológica.

physiological albuminuria albuminuria fisiológica.

postrenal albuminuria albuminuria posrenal.

postural albuminuria albuminuria postural.

prerenal albuminuria albuminuria prerrenal.

recurrent albuminuria albuminuria recurrente.

residual albuminuria albuminuria residual.

serous albuminuria albuminuria sérica.

toxic albuminuria albuminuria tóxica.

transient albuminuria albuminuria transitoria.

true albuminuria albuminuria verdadera.

albuminurophobia *n.* albuminurofobia.

albumoscope *n.* albuminoscopio, albumoscopio.

albumose *n.* albumosa.

Bence Jones albumose albumosa de Bence Jones.

albumosemia *n.* albumosemia.

albumosuria *n.* albumosuria.

Bence Jones albumosuria albumosuria de Bence Jones.

Bradshaw's albumosuria albumosuria de Bradshaw.

Alcaligenes *n.* Alcaligenes.

alcapton *n.* alcaptona.

alcohol *n.* alcohol.

alcoholemia *n.* alcoholemia.

alcohol-fast *adj.* alcoholresistente.

alcoholic *adj.* alcohólico, -ca.

alcoholism *n.* alcoholismo.

acute alcoholism alcoholismo agudo.

alpha alcoholism alcoholismo alfa.

beta alcoholism alcoholismo beta.

chronic alcoholism alcoholismo crónico.

delta alcoholism alcoholismo delta.

gamma alcoholism alcoholismo gamma.

alcoholization *n.* alcoholización.

alcoholize *v.* alcoholizar.

alcoholology *n.* alcohología.

alcoholometer *n.* alcoholómetro.

alcoholuria *n.* alcoholuria.

alcoholysis *n.* alcohólisis.

aldehyde *n.* aldehído.

aldosterone *n.* aldosterona.

aldosteronemia *n.* aldosteronemia.

aldosteronism *n.* aldosteronismo.

primary aldosteronism aldosteronismo primario.

pseudoprimary aldosteronism aldosteronismo seudoprimario.

secondary aldosteronism aldosteronismo secundario.

aldosteronogenesis *n.* aldosteronogénesis.

aldosteronoma *n.* aldosteronoma.

aldosteronopenia *n.* aldosteronopenia.

aldosteronuria *n.* aldosteronuria.

alemmal *adj.* alemal.

alethia *n.* alecia, aletia.

aletocyte *n.* aletocito.

aleucemia *n.* aleucemia.

aleucemia hemorrhagica aleucemia hemorrágica.

alimentary toxic aleucemia aleucemia alimentaria tóxica.

aleukemia *n.* aleucemia.

aleukemic *adj.* aleucémico, -ca.

aleukia *n.* aleucia.

aleukocytic *adj.* aleucocítico, -ca.

aleukocytosis *n.* aleucocitosis.

aleuronoid *adj.* aleuronoide.

alexeteric *adj.* alexetérico, -ca.

alexia *n.* alexia.

cortical alexia alexia cortical.

incomplete alexia alexia incompleta.

motor alexia alexia motora.

musical alexia alexia musical.

subcortical alexia alexia subcortical.

alexic *adj.* aléxico, -ca.

alexinic *adj.* alexínico, -ca.

alexipharmic¹ *adj.* alexifármaco, -ca.

alexipharmic² *n.* alexifármaco.

alexipyretic *adj.* alexipirético, -ca.

alexithymia *n.* alexitimia.

aleydigism *n.* aleydigismo.

alganesthesia *n.* alganestesia.

algefacient *adj.* algefaciente.

algeoscopy *n.* algeoscopia.

algesia *n.* algesia.

algesic *adj.* algésico, -ca, algético, -ca.

algesichronometer *n.* algesicronómetro.

algesidystrophy *n.* algesidistrofia.

algesimeter *n.* algesímetro.

algesimetry *n.* algesimetría.

algesiogenic *adj.* algesiogénico, -ca, algesiógeno, -na.

algesthesia *n.* algestesia.

algesthesis *n.* algestesia, algestesis.

algestone acetophenide *n.* algestona acetofenida.

algetic *adj.* algésico, -ca, algético, -ca.

algid *adj.* álgido, -da.

algidity *n.* algidez.

algin *n.* algina.

algioglandular *adj.* algioglandular.

algiometabolic *adj.* algiometabólico, -ca.

algiomotor *adj.* algiomotor, -ra.

algiomuscular *adj.* algiomuscular.

algiovascular *adj.* algiovascular.

algodistrophy *n.* algodistrofia.

algogenesia *n.* algogenesia, algogénesis, algogenia.

algogenesis *n.* algogenesia, algogénesis.

algogenic *adj.* algogénico, -ca.

algolagnia *n.* algolagnia.

active algolagnia algolagnia activa.

passive algolagnia algolagnia pasiva.

algologist *n.* algólogo, -ga.

algology *n.* algología.

algomenorrhea *n.* algomenorrea.

algometer *n.* algómetro.

algometry *n.* algometría.

algopareunia *n.* algopareunia.

algophobia *n.* algofobia.

algopsychalia *n.* algopsicalia.

algor *n.* algor.

algoscopy *n.* algoscopia.

algosis *n.* algosis.

algospasm *n.* algospasmo.

algovascular *adj.* algovascular.

alible *adj.* alible.

alices *n.* alices.

alicyclic *adj.* alicíclico, -ca.

alienation *n.* alienación.

alienia *n.* alienia.

alienism *n.* alienismo.

alienist *n.* alienista.

aliform *adj.* aliforme.

alignment *n.* alineación, alineamiento.

beam alignment alineación del haz.

tooth alignment alineamiento dental.

alimentary *adj.* alimentario, -ria.

alimentation *n.* alimentación.

artificial alimentation alimentación artificial.

forced alimentation alimentación forzada.

parenteral alimentation alimentación parenteral.

rectal alimentation alimentación rectal.

total parenteral alimentation alimentación parenteral total.

alimentology *n.* alimentología.

alimentotherapy *n.* alimentoterapia.

alinasal *adj.* alinasal.

aliphatic *adj.* alifático, -ca.

alipogenetic *adj.* alipogenético, -ca.

alipogenic *adj.* alipogenético, -ca.

alipotropic *adj.* alipotrópico, -ca.

aliquorrhea *n.* alicuorrea.

alisphenoid *adj.* alisfenoide.

alive *adj.* vivo, -va.

alkalemia *n.* alcalemia.

alkalescence *n.* alcalescencia.

alkalescent *adj.* alcalescente.

alkali *n.* álcali.

alkalify *v.* alcalinizar.

alkaligenous *adj.* alcalígeno, -na.

alkalimeter *n.* alcalímetro.

alkalimetry *n.* alcalimetría.

alkaline *adj.* alcalino, -na.

alkalinity *n.* alcalinidad.

alkalinization *n.* alcalinización.

alkalinize *v.* alcalinizar.

alkalinizing *n.* alcalinizador.

alkalinuria *n.* alcalinuria.

alkalipenia *n.* alcalipenia.

alkalitherapy *n.* alcaliterapia, alcaloterapia.

alkalization *n.* alcalización.

alkalize *v.* alcalinizar.

alkalizer *n.* alcalinizador, alcalizador.

alkalogenic *adj.* alcalógeno, -na.

alkaloid *n.* alcaloide.

alkalometry *n.* alcalometría.

alkalosis *n.* alcalosis.

altitude alkalosis alcalosis por la altura.

compensated alkalosis alcalosis compensada.

decompensated alkalosis alcalosis descompensada.

hypochloremic alkalosis alcalosis hipoclorémica.

hypokalemic alkalosis alcalosis hipocaliémica, alcalosis hipokaliémica, alcalosis hipopotasémica.

metabolic alkalosis alcalosis metabólica.

respiratory alkalosis alcalosis por acapnia, alcalosis respiratoria.
alkalotic *adj.* alcalótico, -ca.
alkaluria *n.* alcaluria.
alkanet *n.* orcaneta.
alkanin *n.* alcanina.
alkapton *n.* alcaptona.
alkaptonuria *n.* alcaptonuria.
alkaptonuric *adj.* alcaptonúrico, -ca.
allachesthesia *n.* alacestesia.
allantiasis *n.* alantiasis.
allantochorion *n.* alantocorion.
allantogenesis *n.* alantogénesis.
allantoic *adj.* alantoico, -ca.
allantoid *adj.* alantoide.
allantoidean *adj.* alantoideo, -a.
allantoidoangiopagus *n.* alantoidoangió-pago.
allantoin *n.* alantoína.
allantoinuria *n.* alantoinuria.
allantois *n.* alantoides.
allantotoxicon *n.* alantotoxina.
allassotherapy *n.* alasoterapia.
allaxis *n.* alaxis.
allele *n.* alelo.
  codominant allele alelo codominante, alelo isomorfo.
  dominant allele alelo dominante.
  multiple allele alelo múltiple.
  recessive allele alelo recesivo.
  silent allele alelo amorfo, alelo silencioso.
allelic *adj.* alélico, -ca.
allelism *n.* alelismo.
allelocatalysis *n.* alelocatálisis.
allelochemics *n.* aleloquímica.
allelognathia *n.* alelognatia.
allelomorph *n.* alelomorfo.
allelomorphic *adj.* alelomórfico, -ca.
allelomosphism *n.* alelomorfismo.
allelotaxy *n.* alclotaxia, alelotaxis.
allenthesis *n.* alentesis.
allergen *n.* alergeno.
  pollen allergen alergeno del polen.
allergenic *adj.* alergénico, -ca.
allergic *adj.* alérgico, -ca.
  allergic salute saludo alérgico.
allergid *n.* alérgide.
allergist *n.* alergista.
allergization *n.* alergización.
allergize *v.* alergizar.
allergized *adj.* alergizado, -da.
allergodermia *n.* alergodermia.
allergoid *n.* alergoide.
allergological *adj.* alergológico, -ca.
allergologist *n.* alergólogo, -ga.
allergology *n.* alergología.
allergometry *n.* alergometría.
allergosis *n.* alergosis.
allergy *n.* alergia.
  atopic allergy alergia atópica.
  bacterial allergy alergia bacteriana.
  bronchial allergy alergia bronquial.
  cold allergy alergia al frío.
  contact allergy alergia de contacto, alergia por contacto.
  delayed allergy alergia retardada, alergia tardía.
  drug allergy alergia a fármacos, alergia medicamentosa.
  food allergy alergia alimentaria.
  hereditary allergy alergia hereditaria.
  immediate allergy alergia inmediata.
  induced allergy alergia fisiológica, alergia normal, alergia provocada.
  insulin allergy alergia a la insulina.

latent allergy alergia latente.
multiple allergy alergia polivalente.
physical allergy alergia física.
pollen allergy alergia al polen.
polyvalent allergy alergia polivalente.
spontaneous allergy alergia espontánea.
allesthesia *n.* alestesia.
alliaceous *adj.* aliáceo, -a.
alliance *n.* alianza.
  therapeutic alliance alianza terapéutica.
  working alliance alianza de trabajo.
alloalbumin *n.* aloalbúmina.
alloalbuminemia *n.* aloalbuminemia.
alloantibody *n.* aloanticuerpo.
alloantigen *n.* aloantígeno.
allobiosis *n.* alobiosis.
allocentric *adj.* alocéntrico, -ca.
allochetia *n.* aloquecia.
allochezia *n.* aloquecia.
allochroism *n.* alocroísmo.
allochromasia *n.* alocromasia.
allocinesia *n.* alocinesia.
allocollold *n.* alocoloide.
allocortex *n.* alocorteza.
allocytophilic *adj.* alocitófilo, -la.
allodiploid *adj.* alodiploide.
allodiploidy *n.* alodiploidía.
allodromy *n.* alodromia.
allodynia *n.* alodinia.
alloeroticism *n.* aloeroticismo.
alloerotism *n.* aloerotismo.
alloesthesia *n.* alestesia, aloestesia.
allogamia *n.* alogamia.
allogeneic *adj.* alogénico, -ca.
allogenic *adj.* alogénico, -ca.
allogotrophia *n.* alogotrofia.
allograft *n.* aloinjerto.
allogroup *n.* alogrupo.
alloimmune *adj.* aloinmune.
alloimmunization *n.* aloinmunización.
allokeratoplasty *n.* aloqueratoplastia.
allokinesia *n.* alocinesia.
allokinetic *adj.* alocinético, -ca.
allomerism *n.* alomería, alomerismo.
allometric *adj.* alométrico, -ca.
allometry *n.* alometría.
allomorphism *n.* alomorfismo.
allonomous *adj.* alónomo, -ma.
allopath *n.* alópata.
allopathic *adj.* alopático, -ca.
allopathist *n.* alópata.
allopathy *n.* alopatía.
allopentaploid *adj.* alopentaploide.
allophanamide *n.* alofanamida.
allophore *adj.* alóforo, -ra.
allophtalmia *n.* aloftalmía.
alloplasia *n.* aloplasia.
alloplast *n.* aloplasto.
alloplastic *adj.* aloplástico, -ca.
alloplasty *n.* aloplastia.
alloploid *adj.* aloploide.
allopolyploid *adj.* alopoliploide.
allopolyploidy *n.* alopoliploidía.
allopsychic *adj.* alopsíquico, -ca.
allorhythmic *adj.* alorrítmico, -ca.
allosensitization *n.* alosensibilización.
allosome *n.* alosoma.
allosteric *adj.* alostérico, -ca.
allosterism *n.* alosterismo.
allostery *n.* alosteria.
allotetraploid *adj.* alotetraploide.
allothriolith *n.* alotriolito.
allotopia *n.* alotopia.
allotopic *adj.* alotópico, -ca.
allotoxin *n.* alotoxina.

allotransplantation *n.* alotrasplante.
allotriodontia *n.* alotriodoncia, alotriodontia.
allotriploid *adj.* alotriploide.
allotriuria *n.* alotriuria.
allotrophic *adj.* alotrófico, -ca.
allotropism *n.* alotropismo.
allotropy *n.* alotropía.
allotrylic *adj.* alotrílico, -ca.
allotype *n.* alotipo.
  Am allotype alotipo Am.
  Gm allotype alotipo Gm.
  Inv allotype alotipo Inv.
  Km allotype alotipo Km.
  Oz allotype alotipo Oz.
allotypic *adj.* alotípico, -ca.
allotypy *n.* alotipia.
alloxin *n.* aloxina.
alloxuremia *n.* aloxuremia.
alloxuria *n.* aloxuria.
alloxuric *adj.* aloxúrico, -ca.
all-trans-retinal *n.* todo-trans-retinal.
alochia *n.* aloquia.
alopecia *n.* alopecia.
  alopecia adnata alopecia adnata.
  alopecia androgenetica alopecia androgénica.
  alopecia areata alopecia areata.
  alopecia capitis totalis alopecia capitis totalis.
  alopecia celsi alopecia celsi.
  alopecia circumscripta alopecia circunscrita.
  alopecia congenitalis alopecia congénita.
  alopecia generalisata alopecia generalizada.
  alopecia hereditaria alopecia hereditaria.
  alopecia liminaris alopecia liminar.
  alopecia liminaris frontalis alopecia liminaris frontalis.
  alopecia marginalis alopecia marginal, alopecia marginalis.
  alopecia medicamentosa alopecia medicamentosa.
  alopecia mucinosa alopecia mucinosa.
  alopecia orbicularis alopecia orbicular.
  alopecia pityrodes alopecia pitiroides, alopecia pityrodes.
  alopecia pityroides alopecia pitiroides, alopecia pityroides.
  alopecia prematura alopecia prematura.
  alopecia seborrheica alopecia seborreica.
  alopecia senilis alopecia senil.
  alopecia symptomatica alopecia sintomática.
  alopecia syphilitica alopecia sifilítica.
  alopecia totalis alopecia total.
  alopecia toxica alopecia tóxica.
  alopecia universalis alopecia universal.
  androgenetic alopecia alopecia androgénica.
  androgenic alopecia alopecia androgénica.
  cicatricial alopecia alopecia cicatricial, alopecia cicatrisata.
  congenital alopecia alopecia congénita.
  drug alopecia alopecia farmacológica.
  Jonston's alopecia alopecia de Jonston.
  male pattern alopecia alopecia de distribución masculina, alopecia de patrón masculino, alopecia de tipo masculino.
  marginal traumatic alopecia alopecia marginal traumática.
  moth-eaten alopecia alopecia apolillada, alopecia comida por polilla.
  physiologic alopecia alopecia fisiológica.
  postpartum alopecia alopecia posparto.
  premature alopecia alopecia prematura.
  pressure alopecia alopecia por compresión, alopecia por presión.
  psychogenic alopecia alopecia psicógena.

radiation alopecia alopecia por radiación.
senile alopecia alopecia senil.
stress alopecia alopecia de estrés.
symptomatic alopecia alopecia sintomática.
syphilitic alopecia alopecia sifilítica.
traumatic alopecia alopecia traumática.
traumatic marginal alopecia alopecia traumática marginal.
X-ray alopecia alopecia por rayos X.
alopecic *adj.* alopécico, -ca.
alpha1-antitrypsin *n.* alfa1-antitripsina.
alpha2-macroblogulin *n.* alfa2-macroglobulina.
alpha-beta-blocker *n.* alfa-beta-bloqueante.
alpha-blocker *n.* alfabloqueador.
alpha-fetoprotein (AFP) *n.* alfa-fetoproteína (AFP).
alpha-globulin *n.* alfa-globulina.
alpha-hypophamine *n.* alfahipofamina.
alpha-lipoprotein *n.* alfa-lipoproteína.
alphalytic *adj.* alfalítico, -ca.
alpha-methyl dopa *n.* alfa-metildopa.
alphamimetic *adj.* alfamimético, -ca.
alphonsin *n.* alfonsino.
alphos *n.* alfos.
alteration *n.* alteración.
modal alteration alteración modal.
qualitative alteration alteración cualitativa.
quantitative alteration alteración cuantitativa.
alteregoism *n.* alteregoísmo.
alternans *n.* alternancia.
auditory alternans alternancia auditiva.
auscultatory alternans alternancia auscultatoria.
electrical alternans alternancia eléctrica.
pulsus alternans alternancia del pulso.
alternating *adj.* alternante.
alternation *n.* alternación.
cardiac alternation alternación cardíaca.
concordant alternation alternación concordante.
discordant alternation alternación discordante.
mechanical alternation alternación mecánica.
altruism *n.* altruismo.
alum *n.* alumbre.
alum-hematoxylin *n.* alumbre-hematoxilina.
aluminosis *n.* aluminosis.
alumoid *n.* albumoide.
alveobronchiolitis *n.* alveobronquiolitis.
alveobronchitis *n.* bronquioalveolitis.
alveolectomy *n.* alveolectomía.
alveolitis *n.* alveolitis.
acute pulmonary alveolitis alveolitis pulmonar aguda.
allergic alveolitis alveolitis alérgica, alveolitis alérgica extrínseca.
alveolitis sicca dolorosa alveolitis seca dolorosa.
extrinsic allergic alveolitis alveolitis alérgica, alveolitis alérgica extrínseca.
alveolobronchiolitis *n.* alveolobronquiolitis.
alveoloclasia *n.* alveoloclasia.
alveolodental *adj.* alveolodental.
alveololabial *adj.* alveololabial.
alveololingual *adj.* alveololingual.
alveolomerotomy *n.* alveolomerotomía.
alveolonasal *adj.* alveolonasal.
alveolopalatal *adj.* alveolopalatino, -na.
alveolotomy *n.* alveolotomía.
alveolus *n.* alveolo, alvéolo.
alveolysis *n.* alveólisis.
alvine *adj.* alvino, -na.
alvinolith *n.* alvinolito.
alymphia *n.* alinfia.

alymphocytosis *n.* alinfocitosis.
alymphoplasia *n.* alinfoplasia.
Nezelof type of thymic alymphoplasia alinfoplasia tímica de tipo Nezelof.
thymic alymphoplasia alinfoplasia tímica.
alymphopotent *adj.* alinfopotente.
amakrine *adj.* amacrina.
amalgam *n.* amalgama.
amalgam carrier portaamalgama.
amalgam carver tallador de amalgama.
dental amalgam amalgama dental, amalgama dentaria.
marginal integrity of amalgam integridad marginal de la amalgama.
amalgamate *v.* amalgamar.
amalgamation *n.* amalgamación.
Amanita *n.* Amanita.
amarilic *adj.* amarílico, -ca.
amarthritis *n.* amartritis.
amasesis *n.* amasesis.
amasthenic *adj.* amasténico, -ca.
amastia *n.* amastia.
amastigote *n.* amastigote.
amaurosis *n.* amaurosis.
amaurosis centralis amaurosis central.
amaurosis congenita amaurosis congénita.
amaurosis fugax amaurosis fugaz.
amaurosis partialis fugax amaurosis parcial fugaz.
cat's eye amaurosis amaurosis de ojo de gato.
central amaurosis amaurosis central.
cerebral amaurosis amaurosis central.
congenital amaurosis amaurosis congénita.
diabetic amaurosis amaurosis diabética.
hysteric amaurosis amaurosis histérica.
intoxication amaurosis amaurosis tóxica.
Leber's congenital amaurosis amaurosis congénita de Leber.
pressure amaurosis amaurosis por compresión.
reflex amaurosis amaurosis refleja.
saburral amaurosis amaurosis saburral.
toxic amaurosis amaurosis tóxica.
amaurotic *adj.* amaurótico, -ca.
amazia *n.* amacia.
ambageusia *n.* ambageusia.
ambidexter *adj.* ambidextro, -tra.
ambidexterity *n.* ambidestreza.
ambidextrality *n.* ambidextrismo.
ambidextrism *n.* ambidextrismo.
ambilateral *adj.* ambilateral.
ambilevosity *n.* ambilevosidad.
ambilevous *adj.* ambilevo, -va.
ambiopia *n.* ambiopía.
ambisexual *adj.* ambisexual.
ambivalence *n.* ambivalencia.
amblychromasia *n.* amblicromasia.
Amblyomma *n.* Amblyomma.
amblyopia *n.* ambliopía.
alcoholic amblyopia ambliopía alcohólica.
amblyopia cruciata ambliopía cruzada.
anisometropic amblyopia ambliopía anisométrica.
arsenic amblyopia ambliopía arsenical.
axial amblyopia ambliopía axil.
color amblyopia ambliopía cromática, ambliopía de color.
crossed amblyopia ambliopía cruzada.
deficiency amblyopia ambliopía nutricional.
deprivation amblyopia ambliopía por privación.
eclipse amblyopia ambliopía por eclipse.
functional amblyopia ambliopía funcional.
hysterical amblyopia ambliopía histérica.
index amblyopia ambliopía índice.

nocturnal amblyopia ambliopía nocturna.
nutritional amblyopia ambliopía nutricional.
quinine amblyopia ambliopía por la quinina, ambliopía quínica.
reflex amblyopia ambliopía refleja.
refractive amblyopia ambliopía refractiva.
relative amblyopia ambliopía relativa.
reversible amblyopia ambliopía reversible.
sensory amblyopia ambliopía sensorial.
strabismic amblyopia ambliopía estrabísmica.
tobacco amblyopia ambliopía tabáquica.
toxic amblyopia ambliopía tóxica.
traumatic amblyopia ambliopía traumática.
uremic amblyopia ambliopía urémica.
amblyopiatrics *n.* ambliopiatría.
amblyopic *n.* ambiópico, -ca.
amblyoscope *n.* ambliocospio.
ambo *n.* ambo, ambón.
ambomalleal *adj.* ambomaleal.
ambulance *n.* ambulancia.
ambulant *adj.* ambulatorio, -a.
ambulatory *adj.* ambulatorio, -a.
ambustion *n.* ambustión.
ameba *n.* ameba, amiba.
amebiasis *n.* amebiasis.
amebiasis cutis amebiasis cutis.
hepatic amebiasis amebiasis hepática.
intestinal amebiasis amebiasis intestinal.
pulmonary amebiasis amebiasis pulmonar.
amebic *adj.* amébico, -ca.
amebicidal *adj.* amebicida.
amebismo *n.* amebismo.
amebocyte *n.* amifocito.
ameboid *adj.* ameboide.
ameboidismo *n.* ameboidismo.
ameboma *n.* ameboma.
ameburia *n.* ameburia.
amelanosis *n.* amelanosis.
amelanotic *adj.* amelanótico, -ca.
amelia *n.* amelia.
amelification *n.* amelificación.
amelioration *n.* mejoría.
ameloblast *n.* ameloblasto.
amelogenesis *n.* amelogénesis.
amelogenesis imperfecta amelogénesis imperfecta.
amelus *n.* amelo.
amenia *n.* amenia.
amenorrhea *n.* amenorrea.
amenorrhea postpartum amenorrea posparto.
dietary amenorrhea amenorrea alimentaria, amenorrea dietaria.
dysponderal amenorrhea amenorrea disponderal.
emotional amenorrhea amenorrea emocional.
hyperprolactinemic amenorrhea amenorrea hiperprolactinémica.
hypophyseal amenorrhea amenorrea hipofisaria.
hypothalamic amenorrhea amenorrea hipotalámica.
jogger's amenorrhea amenorrea de las trotadoras.
lactation amenorrhea amenorrea de la lactación.
nutritional amenorrhea amenorrea nutricional.
ovarian amenorrhea amenorrea ovárica.
pathologic amenorrhea amenorrea patológica.
physiologic amenorrhea amenorrea fisiológica.
postpill amenorrhea amenorrea pospíldora.

premenopausal amenorrhea amenorrea premenopáusica.
primary amenorrhea amenorrea primaria.
relative amenorrhea amenorrea relativa.
secondary amenorrhea amenorrea secundaria.
stress amenorrhea amenorrea por estrés.
traumatic amenorrhea amenorrea traumática.
amenorrheal *adj.* amenorreico, -ca.
amenorrheic *adj.* amenorreico, -ca.
amensalismo *n.* amensalismo.
amerism *n.* amerismo.
ameristic *adj.* amerístico, -ca.
ametabolon *adj.* ametábolo, -la.
ametabolous *adj.* ametábolo, -la.
ametachromophil *adj.* ametacromófilo, -la.
ametaneutrophil *adj.* ametaneutrófilo, -la.
ametria *n.* ametria.
ametrometer *n.* ametrómetro.
ametropia *n.* ametropía, ecmetropía.
axial ametropia ametropía axil.
curvature ametropia ametropía de curvatura.
position ametropia ametropía de posición.
refractive ametropia ametropía de refracción.
ametropic *adj.* ametrópico, -ca.
amicrobic *adj.* amicrobiano, -na, amicróbico, -ca.
amiculum *n.* amículo.
amimie *n.* amimia.
amnesic amimie amimia amnésica, amimia receptiva.
aminoacid *n.* aminoácido.
essential aminoacid aminoácido esencial.
non-essential aminoacid aminoácido no esencial.
aminoacidemia *n.* aminoacidemia.
aminoacidopathy *n.* aminoacidopatía.
aminoaciduria *n.* aminoaciduria.
aminogram *n.* aminograma.
aminolipid *n.* aminolípido.
aminolipin *n.* aminolipina.
aminolysis *n.* aminólisis.
aminosis *n.* aminosis.
aminosuria *n.* aminosuria.
aminuria *n.* aminuria.
amitosis *n.* amitosis.
amitotic *adj.* amitótico, -ca.
ammoaciduria *n.* amoaciduria.
ammonia *n.* amoniaco, amoníaco.
ammoniate *adj.* amoniatado, -da, amoniatar.
ammoniemia *n.* amoniemia.
ammoniuria *n.* amoniuria.
ammotherapy *n.* amoterapia.
amnemonic *adj.* amnemónico, -ca.
amnesia *n.* amnesia.
anterograde amnesia amnesia anterógrada.
auditory amnesia amnesia auditiva.
circumscribed amnesia amnesia circunscrita.
continuous amnesia amnesia continua.
dissociative amnesia amnesia disociativa.
emotional amnesia amnesia emocional.
episodic amnesia amnesia episódica.
generalized amnesia amnesia generalizada.
infantile amnesia amnesia infantil.
lacunar amnesia amnesia lacunar, amnesia lagunar.
localized amnesia amnesia localizada.
organic amnesia amnesia orgánica.
postcontussional amnesia amnesia poscontusional.
posthypnotic amnesia amnesia posthipnótica.
posttraumatic amnesia amnesia postraumática.
retroanterograde amnesia amnesia retroanterógrada.
retrograde amnesia amnesia retrógada.

selective amnesia amnesia selectiva.
tactile amnesia amnesia táctil.
transient amnesia amnesia global transitoria.
traumatic amnesia amnesia traumática.
verbal amnesia amnesia verbal.
visual amnesia amnesia visual.
amnesic *adj.* amnésico, -ca.
amniocentesis *n.* amniocentesis.
amniochorial *adj.* amniocorial, amniocoriónico, -ca.
amniogenesis *n.* amniogénesis.
amnioma *n.* amnioma.
amnion *n.* amnios.
amnionitis *n.* amnionitis.
amniorrhea *n.* amniorrea.
amniorrhexis *n.* amniorrexis.
amnioscope *n.* amnioscopio.
amnioscopia *n.* amnioscopia.
amniotic *adj.* amniótico, -ca.
amniotitis *n.* amnionitis.
amniotome *n.* amniótomo.
amniotomy *n.* amniotomía.
Amoeba *n.* Amoeba.
amok *n.* amok.
amorpha *n.* amorfa.
amorphia *n.* amorfia.
amorphism *n.* amorfismo.
amorphous *adj.* amorfo, -fa.
amorphus *n.* amorfo.
amperage *n.* amperaje.
amperemeter *n.* amperímetro.
amphamphoterodiplopia *n.* anfanfoterodiplopía.
ampheclexis *n.* anfeclexis.
amphemerous *adj.* anfémero, -ra.
amphiarthrodial *adj.* anfiartrodial.
amphiarthrosis *n.* anfiartrosis.
amphiaster *n.* anfiáster.
amphiblastic *adj.* anfiblástico, -ca.
amphiblastula *n.* anfiblástula.
amphiblestritis *n.* anfiblestritis.
amphibolia *n.* anfibolia.
amphibolic *adj.* anfibólico, -ca.
amphicarcinogenic *adj.* anficarcinogénico, -ca.
amphicelous *adj.* anficelo, -la.
amphicentric *adj.* anficéntrico, -ca.
amphichromatic *adj.* anficromático, -ca.
amphicroic *adj.* anficroico, -ca.
amphicyte *n.* anficito.
amphidiarthrosis *n.* anfidiartrosis.
amphigastrula *n.* anfigástrula.
amphigenetic *adj.* anfigenético, -ca.
amphigony *n.* anfigonia.
amphileukemic *adj.* anfileucémico, -ca.
amphimicrobian *adj.* anfimicrobiano, -na.
amphimixis *n.* anfimixis.
amphimorula *n.* anfimórula.
amphinucleus *n.* anfinúcleo.
amphipathic *adj.* anfipático, -ca.
amphipyrenin *n.* anfipirenina.
Amphistoma *n.* Amphistoma.
Amphistoma hominis Amphistoma hominis.
amphistomiasis *n.* anfistomiasis.
amphitene *n.* anfiteno, -na.
amphitrichous *adj.* anfítrico, -ca.
amphitypy *n.* anfitipia.
amphochromatophil *adj.* anfocromatófilo, -la.
amphochromophil *adj.* anfocromófilo, -la.
amphocite *n.* anfocito.
amphodiplopy *n.* anfodiplopía.
amphogenic *adj.* anfogénico, -ca.
amphophil *adj.* anfófilo, -la.
amphophilic *adj.* anfófilo, -ca.
amphophilic basofil anfofílico basófilo.
amphophilic oxyphil anfofílico oxífilo.

amphoric *adj.* anfórico, -ca.
amphoriloquy *n.* anforiloquia.
amphorophony *n.* anforofonía.
amphoteric *adj.* anfotérico, -ca, anfótero, -ra.
amphotericity *n.* anfotericidad.
amphoterism *n.* anfoterismo.
amphoterodiplopia *n.* anfoterodiplopía.
amphotony *n.* anfotonía.
amplexation *n.* ampleción, amplexación.
amplification *n.* amplificación.
amplitude *n.* amplitud.
amplitude of accommodation amplitud de acomodación.
amplitude of convergence amplitud de convergencia.
ampoule *n.* ampolla[1], ámpula.
ampular *adj.* ampollar.
ampule *n.* ampolla[1], ámpula.
ampulla *n.* ampolla[2].
ampullary *adj.* ampollar.
ampullitis *n.* ampullitis.
ampullula *n.* ampúlula.
amputation *n.* amputación.
abdominoperineal resection amputation amputación abdominoperineal del recto.
above-knee (A-K) amputation amputación por encima de la rodilla (A-K).
Abrashanow's amputation amputación de Abrashanow.
Alanson's amputation amputación de Alanson.
Alouette's amputation amputación de Alouette.
amniotic amputation amputación amniótica.
amputation in contiguity amputación en (la) contiguidad.
amputation in continuity amputación en (la) continuidad.
aperiosteal amputation amputación aperióstica.
Beclard's amputation amputación de Béclard.
below-knee (B-K) amputation amputación por debajo de la rodilla (B-K).
Bier's amputation amputación de Bier.
birth amputation amputación natural.
bloodless amputation amputación incruenta.
Bunge's amputation amputación de Bunge.
Callander's amputation amputación de Callander.
Carden's amputation amputación de Carden.
central amputation amputación central.
cervical amputation amputación cervical.
Chopart's amputation amputación de Chopart.
cinematic amputation amputación cinemática.
cineplastic amputation amputación cineplástica.
circus amputation amputación circular.
cirular amputation amputación circular.
closed amputation amputación cerrada.
coat-sleeve amputation amputación en manga de camisa.
complete amputation amputación completa.
congenital amputation amputación congénita.
Dieffenbach's amputation amputación de Dieffenbach.
double flap amputation amputación de doble colgajo.
dry amputation amputación seca.
Dupuytren's amputation amputación de Dupuytren.

eccentric amputation amputación excéntrica.

elliptic amputation amputación elíptica.

elliptical amputation amputación elíptica.

Farabeuf's amputation amputación de Farabeuf.

flap amputation amputación con colgajos, amputación de colgajo.

flapless amputation amputación sin colgajos, amputación sin colgajos.

Forbes' amputation amputación de Forbes.

galvanocaustic amputation amputación galvanocáustica.

Gritti's amputation amputación de Gritti.

Gritti-Stokes amputation amputación de Gritti-Stokes.

guillotine amputation amputación en guillotina.

Guyon's amputation amputación de Guyon.

Hancock's amputation amputación de Hancock.

Hey's amputation amputación de Hey.

immediate amputation amputación inmediata.

interilioabdominal amputation amputación interilioabdominal.

interinnominoabdominal amputation amputación interilioabdominal.

intermediary amputation amputación intermedia, amputación intrapirética.

intermediate amputation amputación intermedia, amputación intrapirética.

interpelviabdominal amputation amputación interabdominopelviana.

intrapyretic amputation amputación intrapirética.

intrauterine amputation amputación intrauterina.

Jaboulay's amputation amputación de Jaboulay.

kineplastic amputation amputación cineplástica.

Kirk's amputation amputación de Kirk.

Langenbeck's amputation amputación de Langenbeck.

Larrey's amputation amputación de Larrey.

Le Fort's amputation amputación de Le Fort.

linear amputation amputación lineal.

Lisfranc's amputation amputación de Lisfranc.

Mackenzie's amputation amputación de Mackenzie.

Maisonneuve's amputation amputación de Maisonneuve.

major amputation amputación mayor.

Malgaigne's amputation amputación de Malgaigne.

mediate amputation amputación mediata.

mediotarsal amputation amputación mediotarsiana.

minor amputation amputación menor.

musculocutaneous amputation amputación musculocutánea.

natural amputation amputación natural.

oblique amputation amputación oblicua.

open amputation amputación abierta.

operative amputation amputación operatoria.

osteoplastic amputation amputación osteoplástica.

oval amputation amputación oval.

partial amputation amputación parcial.

pathologic amputation amputación patológica.

phalangophalangeal amputation amputación falangofalángica.

Pirogoff's amputation amputación de Pirogoff.

primary amputation amputación primaria.

pulp amputation amputación pulpar.

quadruple amputation amputación cuádruple.

racket amputation amputación en raqueta.

rectangular amputation amputación rectangular.

Ricard's amputation amputación de Ricard.

root amputation amputación de la raíz, amputación radicular.

secondary amputation amputación secundaria.

spontaneous amputation amputación espontánea.

Stokes amputation amputación de Stokes.

subastragalar amputation amputación subastragalina.

subperiosteal amputation amputación subperióstica.

Syme's amputation amputación de Syme.

synchronous amputation amputación sincrónica.

Teale's amputation amputación de Teale.

tertiary amputation amputación terciaria.

traumatic amputation amputación traumática.

Tripier's amputation amputación de Tripier.

Vladimiroff-Mikulicz amputation amputación de Vladimiroff-Mikulicz.

amputee *n.* amputado, -da.

amusia *n.* amusia, asonia.

instrumental amusia amusia instrumental.

sensory amusia amusia sensorial.

vocal motor amusia amusia motriz vocal.

amyasthenia *n.* amiastenia.

amyasthenic *n.* amiasténico, -ca.

amyctic *adj.* amíctico, -ca.

amyelencephalia *n.* amielencefalia.

amyelia *n.* amielia.

amyelinic *adj.* amielínico, -ca.

amyelotrophia *n.* amielotrofia.

amyelus *n.* amielo.

amygdala *n.* amígdala.

amygdalectomy *n.* amigdalectomía.

amygdaline *adj.* amigdalino, -na.

amygdaloid *adj.* amigdaloide.

amygdalolith *n.* amigdalolito.

amygdalopathy *n.* amigdalopatía.

amylaceous *adj.* amiláceo, -a.

amylemia *n.* amilemia.

amylism *n.* amilismo.

amyloclastic *adj.* amiloclástico, -ca.

amylodyspepsia *n.* amilodispepsia.

amylogenesis *n.* amilogénesis, amilogenia.

amylohydrolysis *n.* amilohidrólisis.

amyloid *n.* amiloide.

amyloidemia *n.* amiloidemia.

amyloidosis *n.* amiloidosis.

AA amyloidosis amiloidosis AA.

AL amyloidosis amiloidosis AL.

amyloidosis cutis amiloidosis cutánea, amiloidosis cutis.

amyloidosis of aging amiloidosis de la edad, amiloidosis de la vejez.

amyloidosis of multiple myeloma amiloidosis del mieloma múltiple.

cutaneous amyloidosis amiloidosis cutánea, amiloidosis cutis.

familial amyloidosis amiloidosis familiar.

focal amyloidosis amiloidosis focal.

hereditary amyloidosis amiloidosis hereditaria, amiloidosis heredofamiliar.

hereditary neuropathic amyloidosis amiloidosis neuropática hereditaria.

heredofamilial amyloidosis amiloidosis hereditaria, amiloidosis heredofamiliar.

idiopathic amyloidosis amiloidosis idiopática.

immuno-cyte-derived amyloidosis amiloidosis inmunoderivada.

inmunocytic amyloidosis amiloidosis inmunocítica.

lichen amyloidosis amiloidosis en liquen.

light chain-related amyloidosis amiloidosis relacionada con cadenas ligeras.

macular amyloidosis amiloidosis macular.

nodular amyloidosis amiloidosis nodular.

pericollagen amyloidosis amiloidosis pericolágena.

primary amyloidosis amiloidosis primaria.

reactive systemic amyloidosis amiloidosis sistémica reactiva.

renal amyloidosis amiloidosis renal.

secondary amyloidosis amiloidosis secundaria.

senile amyloidosis amiloidosis senil.

amylolysis *n.* amilólisis.

amylolytic *adj.* amilolítico, -ca.

amylopeptinosis *n.* amilopeptinosis.

amylophagia *n.* amilofagia.

amyloplastic *adj.* amiloplástico, -ca.

amylorrhea *n.* amilorrea.

amylosinthesis *n.* amilosíntesis.

amylosis *n.* amilosis.

amylosuria *n.* amilosuria.

amyluria *n.* amiluria.

amyocardia *n.* amiocardia.

amyoesthesis *n.* amioestesia.

amyoplasia *n.* amioplasia.

amyoplasia congenita amioplasia congénita.

amyostasia *n.* amiostasia.

amyosthenia *n.* amiostenia.

amyosthenic *adj.* amiosténico, -ca.

amyotonia *n.* amiotonía.

amyotonia congenita amiotonía congénita.

amyotrophic *adj.* amiotrófico, -ca.

amyotrophy *n.* amiotrofia.

amyotrophy neuralgica amiotrofia neurálgica.

amyotrophy spinalis progressiva amiotrofia espinal progresiva.

diabetic amyotrophy amiotrofia diabética.

hemiplegic amyotrophy amiotrofia hemipléjica.

neuralgic amyotrophy amiotrofia neurálgica.

amyous *adj.* amioso, -sa.

amyxorrhea *n.* amixorrea.

amyxorrhea gastrica amixorrea gástrica.

anabiosis *n.* anabiosis.

anabiotic *adj.* anabiótico, -ca.

anabolin *n.* anabolina.

anabolism *n.* anabolismo.

anabolite *n.* anabolito.

anabrosis *n.* anabrosis.

anabrotic *adj.* anabrótico, -ca.

anacamptometer *n.* anacamptómetro.

anacatadidymus *n.* anacatadídimo.

anacatesthesia *n.* anacatestesia.

anachoresis *n.* anacoresis.

anachoretic *adj.* anacorético, -ca.

anacidity *n.* anacidez.

gastric anacidity anacidez gástrica.

anaclasimeter *n.* anaclasímetro.

anaclasis *n.* anaclasis.

anaclisis *n.* anaclisis.

anaclitic *adj.* anaclítico, -ca.

anacmesis *n.* anacmesis.

anacrotic *adj.* anacrótico, -ca.

anacrotism *n.* anacrotismo.

anaculture *n.* anacultivo.

anadenia *n.* anadenia.
  anadenia ventriculi anadenia ventricular.
anadicrotic *adj.* anadicrótico, -ca.
anadicrotism *n.* anadicrotismo.
anadidymus *n.* anadídimo.
anadipsia *n.* anadipsia.
anadrenalism *n.* anadrenalismo.
anadrenia *n.* anadrenia.
anaerobe *adj.* anaerobio, -a.
anaerobiotic *adj.* anaerobiótico, -ca.
anaerogenic *adj.* anaerógeno, -na.
anaeroplasty *n.* anaeroplastia.
anagen *n.* anagen, anágeno.
anagenesis *n.* anagénesis.
anahormone *n.* anahormona.
anakatadidymus *n.* anacatadídimo.
anakmesis *n.* anacmesis.
anakusis *n.* anacusia, anacusis.
anal *adj.* anal.
analbuminemia *n.* analbuminemia.
analeptic *adj.* analéptico, -ca.
analgesia *n.* analgesia.
  analgesia algera analgesia álgera, analgesia álgica.
  analgesia dolorosa analgesia dolorosa.
  audio analgesia analgesia auditiva.
  continuous caudal analgesia analgesia caudal continua.
  infiltration analgesia analgesia por infiltración.
  inhalation analgesia analgesia por inhalación.
  narcolocal analgesia analgesia narcolocal.
  paretic analgesia analgesia parética.
  permeation analgesia analgesia por penetración.
  surface analgesia analgesia superficial.
analgesic *adj.* analgésico, -ca.
analgia *n.* analgia.
anallergic *adj.* analérgico, -ca.
analog *adj.* análogo, -ga.
analogy *n.* analogía.
analphalipoproteinemia *n.* analfalipoproteinemia.
analysis *n.* análisis, valoración3.
  activation analysis análisis de activación.
  analysis of variance análisis de la varianza (ANOVA).
  antigenic analysis análisis antigénico.
  biochromatic analysis análisis biocromático.
  bioelectrical impedance analysis (BIA) análisis de impedancia bioeléctrica (AIB).
  blood gas analysis análisis de gases sanguíneos.
  bradykinetic analysis análisis bradicinético.
  cephalometric analysis análisis cefalométrico.
  character analysis análisis de carácter.
  chromatographic analysis análisis cromatográfico.
  cluster analysis análisis de conjunto.
  colorimetric analysis análisis colorimétrico.
  content analysis análisis de contenido.
  data analysis análisis de datos.
  delta optical density analysis análisis de densidad óptica delta.
  densimetric analysis análisis densimétrico.
  distributive analysis análisis distributivo.
  Downs' analysis análisis de Downs.
  ego analysis análisis del yo.
  end-group analysis análisis de grupo terminal.
  gasometric analysis análisis gasométrico.
  gastric analysis análisis gástrico.
  gravimetric analysis análisis gravimétrico.

  imaging analysis análisis de imagen.
  kinetic analysis análisis cinético.
  qualitative analysis análisis cualitativo.
  qualitive analysis análisis cualitativo.
  quantitative analysis análisis cuantitativo.
  quantive analysis análisis cuantitativo.
  radiochemical analysis análisis radioquímico.
  sequential analysis análisis secuencial.
  sequential multiple analysis (SMA) análisis secuencial múltiple (ASM).
  spectroscopic analysis análisis espectroscópico.
  spectrum analysis análisis espectroscópico.
  stratographic analysis análisis estratográfico.
  tetrad analysis análisis de tétrada.
  ultimate analysis análisis último.
  vector analysis análisis vectorial.
  volumetric analysis análisis volumétrico.
analyst *n.* analista.
analytic *adj.* analítico, -ca.
analyzer *n.* analizador.
  breath analyzer analizador de aliento.
anamnesis *n.* anamnesis.
anamnestic *adj.* anamnésico, -ca.
anamniotic *adj.* anamniótico, -ca.
anamorphosis *n.* anamorfosis.
ananastasia *n.* ananastasia.
anancastia *n.* anancastia.
anaphalantiasis *n.* anafalantiasis.
anaphase *n.* anafase.
anaphia *n.* anafia, anhafia.
anaphilactin *n.* anafilactina.
anaphoresis *n.* anaforesis.
anaphoria *n.* anaforia.
anaphrodisia *n.* anafrodisia.
anaphrodisiac *adj.* anafrodisíaco, -ca.
anaphylactic *adj.* anafiláctico, -ca.
anaphylactogen *n.* anafilactógeno.
anaphylactogenesis *n.* anafilactogénesis.
anaphylatoxin *n.* anafilotoxina.
anaphylaxis *n.* anafilaxia, anafilaxis.
  acquired anaphylaxis anafilaxia adquirida.
  active anaphylaxis anafilaxia activa.
  active cutaneous anaphylaxis anafilaxia cutánea activa.
  aggregate anaphylaxis anafilaxia agregada, anafilaxia de agregación.
  antiserum anaphylaxis anafilaxia de antisuero.
  cytotoxic anaphylaxis anafilaxia citotóxica.
  generalized anaphylaxis anafilaxia generalizada.
  heterologous anaphylaxis anafilaxia heteróloga.
  homologous anaphylaxis anafilaxia homóloga.
  indirect anaphylaxis anafilaxia indirecta.
  inverse anaphylaxis anafilaxia inversa.
  local anaphylaxis anafilaxia local.
  passive anaphylaxis anafilaxia pasiva.
  passive cutaneous anaphylaxis (PCA) anafilaxia cutánea pasiva (ACP).
  reversed anaphylaxis anafilaxia invertida.
  systemic anaphylaxis anafilaxia sistémica.
anaphylodiagnosis *n.* anafilodiagnóstico.
anaphylotoxin *n.* anafilotoxina.
anaplasia *n.* anaplasia.
anaplastic *adj.* anaplásico, -ca.
anaplerosis *n.* anaplerosis.
anapnograph *n.* anapnógrafo.
anapnotherapy *n.* anapnoterapia.
anapophysis *n.* anapófisis.
anaraxia *n.* anaraxia.
anaric *adj.* anárico, -ca.

anarithmia *n.* anarritmia.
anarrhexis *n.* anarrexis.
anarthria *n.* anartria.
anasarca *n.* anasarca.
anastalsis *n.* anastalsis.
anastigmatic *adj.* anastigmático, -ca.
anastomose *v.* anastomosar.
anastomosis *n.* anastomosis.
  anastomosis arteriolovenularis glomeriformis anastomosis arteriolovenularis glomeriformis, anastomosis arteriovenosa glomeriforme, anastomosis arteriovenular glomeriforme.
  anastomosis arteriolovenularis simplex anastomosis arteriolovenular simple.
  arteriovenous anastomosis anastomosis arteriovenosa.
  Billroth I and II anastomosis anastomosis de Billroth I y II.
  Braun anastomosis anastomosis de Braun.
  heterocladic anastomosis anastomosis herocládica.
  homocladic anastomosis anastomosis homocládica.
  illorectal anastomosis anastomosis iliorrectal.
  isoperistaltic anastomosis anastomosis isoperistáltica.
  microvascular anastomosis anastomosis microvascular.
  Potts' anastomosis anastomosis de Potts.
  pyeloileocutaneous anastomosis anastomosis pieloileocutánea.
  Schmidel's anastomosis anastomosis Schmidel.
  termino-terminal anastomosis anastomosis terminoterminal.
  transureteroureteral anastomosis anastomosis transureteroureteral.
  ureteroileocutaneous anastomosis anastomosis ureteroileocutánea.
  ureteroureteral anastomosis anastomosis ureteroureteral.
anastomotic *adj.* anastomótico, -ca.
anastral *adj.* anastral.
anatomic *adj.* anatómico, -ca.
anatomical *adj.* anatómico, -ca.
anatomicopathological *adj.* anatomopatológico, -ca.
anatomist *n.* anatomista.
anatomy *n.* anatomía.
  applied anatomy anatomía aplicada.
  artificial anatomy anatomía artificial.
  artistic anatomy anatomía artística.
  clastic anatomy anatomía clástica.
  clinical anatomy anatomía clínica.
  comparative anatomy anatomía comparada.
  corrosion anatomy anatomía por corrosión.
  dental anatomy anatomía dental.
  descriptive anatomy anatomía descriptiva.
  developmental anatomy anatomía de desarrollo.
  functional anatomy anatomía funcional.
  general anatomy anatomía general.
  gross anatomy anatomía macroscópica.
  histological anatomy anatomía histológica.
  homological anatomy anatomía homológica.
  living anatomy anatomía in vivo.
  macroscopic anatomy anatomía macroscópica.
  medical anatomy anatomía médica.
  microscopic anatomy anatomía microscópica.
  minute anatomy anatomía microscópica.
  pathological anatomy anatomía patológica.
  physiognomic anatomy anatomía fisionómica.
  physiological anatomy anatomía fisiológica.

plastic anatomy anatomía plástica.
practical anatomy anatomía práctica.
radiological anatomy anatomía radiológica.
regional anatomy anatomía regional.
special anatomy anatomía especial.
surface anatomy anatomía de superficie.
surgical anatomy anatomía quirúrgica.
systematic anatomy anatomía sistemática.
topographic anatomy anatomía topográfica.
anatoxin *n.* anatoxina.
anatricrotic *adj.* anatricrótico, -ca.
anatropia *n.* anatropia.
anaxone *n.* anaxón.
anazoturia *n.* anazoúria.
anchillorrhaphy *n.* anquilorrafia.
anchorage *n.* anclaje.
  cervical anchorage anclaje cervical.
  compound anchorage anclaje compuesto.
  extramaxillary anchorage anclaje extramaxilar.
  extraoral anchorage anclaje extraoral.
  intramaxillary anchorage anclaje intramaxilar.
  intraoral anchorage anclaje intraoral.
  multiple anchorage anclaje múltiple.
  occipital anchorage anclaje occipital.
  reciprocal anchorage anclaje recíproco.
  reinforced anchorage anclaje reforzado.
  simple anchorage anclaje simple.
  stationary anchorage anclaje estacionario.
anconagra *n.* anconagra.
anconal *adj.* ancóneo, -a.
anconeal *adj.* ancóneo, -a.
anconitis *n.* anconitis.
Ancylostoma *n.* Ancylostoma.
ancylostomatic *adj.* anquilostomático, -ca.
ancylostome *n.* anquilostoma.
ancylostomiasis *n.* anquilostomiasis.
  ancylostomiasis cutis anquilostomiasis cutánea, anquilostomiasis cutis.
  cutaneous ancylostomiasis anquilostomiasis cutánea, anquilostomiasis cutis.
andreioma *n.* andreioma.
andreoblastoma *n.* andreoblastoma, androblastoma.
androblastoma *n.* androblastoma.
androgalactozemia *n.* androgalactocemia.
androgen *n.* andrógeno.
androgenesis *n.* androgénesis.
androgenization *n.* androgenización.
androgyneity *n.* androgineidad.
androgyny *n.* androginia.
android *adj.* androide.
andrology *n.* andrología.
androma *n.* androma.
andromorphous *adj.* andromorfo, -fa.
androphathy *n.* andropatía.
androphobia *n.* androfobia.
androstane *n.* androstano.
androstanedione *n.* androstanodiona.
androstenediol *n.* androstendiol.
androstenedione *n.* androstendiona.
androsterone *n.* androsterona.
anelectrotonus *n.* anelectrotono.
anemia *n.* anemia.
  achlorhydric anemia anemia aclorhídrica.
  achrestic anemia anemia acréstica.
  acute anemia anemia aguda.
  acute hemolytic anemia anemia hemolítica aguda.
  Addisonian anemia anemia addisoniana, anemia de Addison, anemia de Addison-Biermer.
  anemia hypochromica sidroachrestica hereditaria anemia hipocrómica sideroacréstica hereditaria.

anemia infantum pseudoleukemiaca anemia infantil seudoleucémica.
anemia lymphatica anemia linfática.
anemia neonatorum anemia neonatal.
anemia splenica anemia esplénica.
anhematopoietic anemia anemia anhematopoyética, anemia anhemopoyética.
anhemopoietic anemia anemia anhematopoyética, anemia anhemopoyética.
aplastic anemia anemia aplásica.
aregenerative anemia anemia arregenerativa.
asiderotic anemia anemia asiderótica.
autoimmune hemolytic anemia (AIHS) anemia hemolítica autoinmune.
Bartonella anemia anemia por Bartonella.
Biermer's anemia anemia de Biermer, anemia de Biermer-Ehrlich.
Blackfan-Diamond anemia anemia de Blackfan-Diamond.
cameloid anemia anemia cameloide.
chlorotic anemia anemia clorótica.
chronic congenital aregenerative anemia anemia arregenerativa crónica congénita.
congenital anemia of the newborn anemia congénita del neonato.
congenital hemolytic anemia anemia hemolítica congénita.
congenital hypoplastic anemia anemia hipoplásica congénita.
congenital non-spherocytic hemolytic anemia anemia hemolítica congénita no esferocítica.
Cooley's anemia anemia de Cooley.
cow's milk anemia anemia por leche de vaca.
deficiency anemia anemia carencial, anemia deficitaria.
dilution anemia anemia por dilución.
dimorphic anemia anemia dimórfica.
drug-induced immune hemolytic anemia anemia hemolítica inmune inducida por fármacos.
Ehrlich anemia anemia de Ehrlich.
elliptocitary anemia anemia eliptocitaria, anemia eliptocítica.
elliptocytotic anemia anemia eliptocitaria, anemia eliptocítica.
erythroblastic anemia of childhood anemia eritroblástica de la infancia.
familial erythroblastic anemia anemia eritroblástica familiar.
familial hypoplastic anemia anemia hipoplásica familiar.
familial megaloblastic anemia anemia megaloblástica familiar.
Fanconi's anemia anemia de Fanconi.
folic acid deficiency anemia anemia por deficiencia de ácido fólico.
globe cell anemia anemia de células globosas.
glucose-6-phosphate-dehydrogenase deficiency anemia anemia por deficiencia de glucosa-6-fosfato-deshidrogenasa.
goat's milk anemia anemia por leche de cabra.
Heinz body anemia anemia de cuerpos de Heinz.
hemolytic anemia anemia hemolítica.
hemorrhagic anemia anemia hemorrágica.
hipoplastic anemia anemia hipoplásica.
hyperchromatic anemia anemia hipercromática, anemia hipercroma, anemia hipercrómica.
hyperchromic anemia anemia hipercromática, anemia hipercroma, anemia hipercrómica.
hypochromic anemia anemia hipocroma, anemia hipocrómica.
hypochromic microcytic anemia anemia hipocrómica microcítica.

hypoferric anemia anemia hipoférrica.
icterohemolytic anemia anemia icterohemolítica.
immune hemolytic anemia anemia hemolítica inmune.
immunohemolytic anemia anemia hemolítica inmune.
infectious hemolytic anemia anemia hemolítica infecciosa.
intertropical anemia anemia intertropical.
iron deficiency anemia anemia ferropénica, anemia por deficiencia de hierro.
isochromic anemia anemia isocrómica.
juvenile pernicious anemia anemia perniciosa juvenil.
lead anemia anemia saturnina.
Lederer's anemia anemia de Lederer.
Leishman's anemia anemia de Leishman.
leukoerythroblastic anemia anemia leucoeritroblástica.
local anemia anemia local.
macrocytic anemia anemia macrocítica.
macrocytic anemia of pregnancy anemia macrocítica del embarazo.
malignant anemia anemia maligna.
Marchiafava-Micheli anemia anemia de Marchiafava-Micheli.
megaloblastic anemia anemia megaloblástica.
megalocytic anemia anemia megalocítica.
metaplastic anemia anemia metaplásica.
microangiopathic anemia anemia microangiopática.
microangiopathic hemolytic anemia anemia hemolítica microangiopática.
microcytic anemia anemia microcítica.
miners' anemia anemia de los mineros.
mountain anemia anemia de las montañas.
myelopathic anemia anemia mielopática.
myelophthisic anemia anemia mieloptísica.
normochromic anemia anemia normocrómica.
normocytic anemia anemia normocítica.
nutritional anemia anemia nutricional.
nutritional macrocytic anemia anemia macrocítica nutricional.
osteosclerotic anemia anemia osteoesclerótica.
ovalocytic anemia anemia ovalocítica.
pernicious anemia anemia perniciosa.
phenylhydrazine anemia anemia por fenilhidracina.
physiologic anemia anemia fisiológica.
polar anemia anemia polar.
posthemorrhagic anemia anemia poshemorrágica.
posthemorrhagic anemia of the newborn anemia poshemorrágica neonatal.
primaquine sensitive anemia anemia susceptible a la primaquina.
pure red cell anemia anemia de glóbulos rojos puros, anemia eritrocítica pura.
refractory anemia anemia rebelde, anemia refractaria.
scorbutic anemia anemia escorbútica.
sickle cell anemia anemia de células falciformes, anemia drepanocítica.
sideroachrestic anemia anemia sideroacréstica.
sideroblastic anemia anemia sideroblástica.
sideropenic anemia anemia sideropénica.
slaty anemia anemia pizarrosa.
spherocytic anemia anemia esferocítica.
splenic anemia anemia esplénica.
spur cell anemia anemia de células en espolón.

target cell anemia anemia de células diana.
toxic hemolytic anemia anemia hemolítica tóxica.
traumatic anemia anemia traumática.
tropical anemia anemia tropical.
anemic *adj.* anémico, -ca.
anemometer *n.* anemómetro.
anemonism *n.* anemonismo.
anemotrophy *n.* anemotrofia.
anemotropism *n.* anemotropismo.
anencephalia *n.* anencefalia.
  partial anencephalia anencefalia parcial.
anencephalic *adj.* anencefálico, -ca.
anencephalous *adj.* anencefálico, -ca.
anencephalus *n.* anencéfalo.
anenterous *adj.* anentero, -ra.
anenzimia *n.* anenzimia.
  anenzimia catalasia anenzimia catalasia.
anephric *adj.* anéfrico, -ca.
anephrogenesis *n.* anefrogénesis.
anepiploic *adj.* anepiploico, -ca.
anergasia *n.* anergasia.
anergastic *adj.* anergástico, -ca.
anergic *adj.* anérgico, -ca.
anergy *n.* anergia.
  cachectic anergy anergia caquéctica.
  negative anergy anergia negativa.
  non-specific anergy anergia inespecífica.
  positive anergy anergia positiva.
  specific anergy anergia específica.
aneroid *adj.* aneroide.
anerythroblepsia *n.* aneritroblepsia.
anerythroplasia *n.* aneritroplasia.
anerythroplastic *adj.* aneritroplásico, -ca.
anerythropoiesis *n.* aneritropoyesis.
anerythropsia *n.* aneritropsia.
anerythroregenerative *adj.* aneritrorregenerativo, -va.
anesthecinesia *n.* anestecinesia, anestequinesia.
anesthekinesia *n.* anestecinesia, anestequinesia.
anesthesia *n.* anestesia.
  adjuncts to anesthesia complementos de la anestesia.
  anesthesia dolorosa anestesia dolorosa.
  angiospastic anesthesia anestesia angioespástica.
  balanced anesthesia anestesia balanceada.
  basal anesthesia anestesia basal.
  block anesthesia anestesia bloqueante, anestesia bloqueo.
  bulbar anesthesia anestesia bulbar.
  caudal anesthesia anestesia caudal.
  central anesthesia anestesia central.
  closed anesthesia anestesia cerrada.
  colonic anesthesia anestesia cólica.
  compression anesthesia anestesia por compresión.
  conduction anesthesia anestesia por conducción.
  crossed anesthesia anestesia cruzada.
  dissociated anesthesia anestesia disociada.
  doll's head anesthesia anestesia en cabeza de muñeca.
  electric anesthesia anestesia eléctrica.
  epidural anesthesia anestesia epidural.
  facial anesthesia anestesia facial.
  frost anesthesia anestesia por congelación.
  gauntlet anesthesia anestesia en guantelete.
  general anesthesia anestesia general.
  girdle anesthesia anestesia en cinturón.
  glove anesthesia anestesia en guante.
  gustatory anesthesia anestesia gustatoria.
  Gwathmey oil-ether anesthesia anestesia de aceite etéreo de Gwathmey.

  hypotensive anesthesia anestesia con hipotensión, anestesia hipotensora.
  hypnosis anesthesia anestesia hipnótica.
  hypothermic anesthesia anestesia hipotérmica.
  hysterical anesthesia anestesia histérica.
  infiltration anesthesia anestesia por infiltración.
  inhalation anesthesia anestesia por inhalación.
  insufflation anesthesia anestesia por insuflación.
  intercostal anesthesia anestesia intercostal.
  intranasal anesthesia anestesia intranasal.
  intraoral anesthesia anestesia intrabucal.
  intraosseous anesthesia anestesia intraósea.
  intrapulpal anesthesia anestesia intrapulpar.
  intraspinal anesthesia anestesia intraspinal.
  intravenous anesthesia anestesia intravenosa.
  local anesthesia anestesia local.
  lumbar epidural anesthesia anestesia epidural lumbar.
  mixed anesthesia anestesia mixta.
  muscular anesthesia anestesia muscular.
  nausea anesthesia anestesia de la náusea.
  olfactory anesthesia anestesia olfatoria.
  open anesthesia anestesia abierta.
  paraneural anesthesia anestesia paraneural.
  paravertebral anesthesia anestesia paravertebral.
  peridural anesthesia anestesia peridural.
  perineural anesthesia anestesia perineural.
  peripheral anesthesia anestesia periférica.
  pharyngeal anesthesia anestesia faríngea.
  pressure anesthesia anestesia por presión.
  rectal anesthesia anestesia rectal.
  refrigeration anesthesia anestesia por refrigeración.
  regional anesthesia anestesia regional.
  sacral anesthesia anestesia sacra.
  saddle block anesthesia anestesia en silla de montar.
  segmental anesthesia anestesia segmentaria.
  spinal anesthesia anestesia espinal, anestesia raquídea, raquianestesia.
  splanchnic anesthesia anestesia esplácnica.
  subarachnoid anesthesia anestesia subaracnoidea.
  surface anesthesia anestesia de superficie.
  surgical anesthesia anestesia quirúrgica.
  tactile anesthesia anestesia táctil.
  thalamic hyperesthetic anesthesia anestesia hiperestética talámica.
  thermal anesthesia anestesia térmica.
  thermic anesthesia anestesia térmica.
  topical anesthesia anestesia tópica.
  total anesthesia anestesia completa.
  transsacral anesthesia anestesia transacra.
  traumatic anesthesia anestesia traumática.
  twilight anesthesia anestesia crepuscular.
  unilateral anesthesia anestesia unilateral.
  visceral anesthesia anestesia visceral.
anesthesimeter *n.* anestesímetro.
anesthesiologist *n.* anestesiólogo, -ga.
anesthesiology *n.* anestesiología.
anesthesiophore *n.* anestesióforo.
anesthetic *n.* anestésico, -ca.
  general anesthetic anestésico general.
  intravenous anesthetic anestésico endovenoso.
  local anesthetic anestésico local.
  spinal anesthetic anestésico raquídeo.
  topical anesthetic anestésico tópico.
anesthetist *n.* anestesista.
anesthetize *v.* anestesiar.

anestrus *n.* anestro.
anetoderma *n.* anetodermia.
  Jadassohn-Pellizari anetoderma anetodermia de Jadassohn, anetodermia de Jadassohn-Pellizari.
  Jadassohn's anetoderma anetodermia de Jadassohn, anetodermia de Jadassohn-Pellizari.
  perifollicular anetoderma anetodermia perifolicular.
  postinflammatory anetoderma anetodermia posinflamatoria.
  Schweninger-Buzzi anetoderma anetodermia de Schweninger-Buzzi.
anetodermia *n.* anetodermia.
aneugamy *n.* aneugamia.
aneuploid *adj.* aneuploide.
aneuploidy *n.* aneuploidía.
aneurogenic *adj.* aneurógeno, -na.
aneurolemmic *adj.* aneurolémico, -ca.
aneurysm *n.* aneurisma.
  abdominal aneurysm aneurisma abdominal.
  ampullary aneurysm aneurisma ampular.
  aneurysm by anastomosis aneurisma anastomático, aneurisma por anastomosis.
  aortic aneurysm aneurisma aórtico.
  aortic sinusal aneurysm aneurisma aórtico sinusal.
  arteriovenous aneurysm aneurisma arteriovenoso.
  arteriovenous pulmonary aneurysm aneurisma arteriovenoso pulmonar.
  atherosclerotic aneurysm aneurisma arterioesclerótico.
  axial aneurysm aneurisma axial.
  axillary aneurysm aneurisma axilar.
  bacterial aneurysm aneurisma bacteriano.
  benign bone aneurysm aneurisma óseo benigno.
  berry aneurysm aneurisma cerebral saculado.
  cardiac aneurysm aneurisma cardíaco.
  cerebral aneurysm aneurisma cerebral.
  Charcot-Bouchard aneurysm aneurisma de Charcot-Bouchard.
  cirsoid aneurysm aneurisma cirsoideo.
  compound aneurysm aneurisma compuesto.
  congenital cerebral aneurysm aneurisma cerebral congénito.
  cylindroid aneurysm aneurisma cilíndrico, aneurisma cilindroideo.
  cystogenic aneurysm aneurisma cistógeno.
  dissecting aneurysm aneurisma discante.
  ectatic aneurysm aneurisma ectático.
  embolic aneurysm aneurisma embólico.
  embolomycotic aneurysm aneurisma embolomicótico.
  false aneurysm aneurisma falso.
  fusiform aneurysm aneurisma fusiforme.
  hernial aneurysm aneurisma herniario.
  infected aneurysm aneurisma infectado.
  innominate aneurysm aneurisma braquiocefálico.
  intracranial aneurysm aneurisma intracraneal.
  lateral aneurysm aneurisma lateral.
  miliary aneurysm aneurisma miliar.
  mycotic aneurysm aneurisma micótico.
  orbital aneurysm aneurisma orbitario.
  Park's aneurysm aneurisma de Park.
  pelvic aneurysm aneurisma pélvico.
  phantom aneurysm aneurisma fantasma.
  Pott's aneurysm aneurisma de Pott.
  racemous aneurysm aneurisma racemoso.
  Rasmussen's aneurysm aneurisma de Rasmussen.
  renal aneurysm aneurisma renal.

Richet's aneurysm aneurisma de Richet.
Rodrigues' aneurysm aneurisma de Rodrigues.
saccular aneurysm aneurisma saculado, aneurisma sacular.
sacculated aneurysm aneurisma saculado, aneurisma sacular.
serpentine aneurysm aneurisma serpentino.
spurious aneurysm aneurisma espúreo, aneurisma espurio.
suprasellar aneurysm aneurisma suprasillar.
syphilitic aneurysm aneurisma sifilítico.
thoracic aneurysm aneurisma torácico.
traction aneurysm aneurisma por tracción.
traumatic aneurysm aneurisma traumático.
true aneurysm aneurisma verdadero.
tubular aneurysm aneurisma tubular.
varicose aneurysm aneurisma varicoso.
ventricular aneurysm aneurisma ventricular.
aneurysmal *adj.* aneurismático, -ca.
aneurysmectomy *n.* aneurismectomía.
aneurysmoplasty *n.* aneurismoplastia.
aneurysmorrhaphy *n.* aneurismorrafia.
aneurysmotomy *n.* aneurismotomía.
anfractuosity *n.* anfractuosidad.
anger *n.* ira.
anghropography *n.* antropografía.
angialgia *n.* angialgia.
angiasthenia *n.* angiastenia.
angiectasia *n.* angiectasia, angiectasis.
angiectasis *n.* angiectasia, angiectasis.
  congenital dysplastic angiectasis angiectasis displásica congénita.
angiectomy *n.* angiectomía.
angiectopia *n.* angiectopía.
angiemphraxis *n.* angienfraxis.
angiitis *n.* angeítis, angiítis.
  allergic cutaneous angiitis angiítis alérgica cutánea.
  allergic granulomatous angiitis angiítis granulomatosa alérgica.
  consecutive angiitis angiítis consecutiva.
  leukocytoclastic angiitis angiítis leucocitoclástica.
  necrotizing angiitis angiítis necrosante.
  nodular cutaneous angiitis angiítis nodular cutánea.
angina *n.* angina.
  abdominal angina angina abdominal.
  agranulocytic angina angina agranulocítica.
  angina abdominalis angina abdominal.
  angina abdominis angina abdominal.
  angina acuta angina aguda.
  angina catarrhalis angina catarral.
  angina cordis angina cordis.
  angina cruris angina crural.
  angina decubitus angina de decúbito.
  angina diphtheritica angina diftérica.
  angina dyspeptica angina dispéptica.
  angina epiglottidea angina epiglótica, angina epiglotídea.
  angina follicularia angina folicular.
  angina gangrenosa angina gangrenosa.
  angina inversa angina inversa.
  angina laryngea angina laríngea.
  angina membranacea angina membranosa.
  angina pectoris angina de pecho.
  angina pectoris vasomotora angina de pecho vasomotora.
  angina rheumatica angina reumática.
  angina sine dolore angina sine dolore.
  angina spuria angina espuria.
  angina trachealis angina traqueal.
  angina vasomotora angina vasomotora, angina vasomotriz.

Bretonneau's angina angina de Bretonneau.
exudative angina angina exudativa.
false angina angina falsa.
hippocratic angina angina hipocrática.
hysteric angina angina histérica.
intestinal angina angina intestinal.
lacunar angina angina lacunar.
Ludwig's angina angina de Ludwig.
malignant angina angina maligna.
monocytic angina angina monocítica.
neutropenic angina angina neutropénica.
Plaut's angina angina seudomembranosa de Plaut.
Prinzmetal's angina angina de Prinzmetal.
pseudomembranous angina angina seudomembranosa de Plaut.
pseudomembranous Plaut's angina angina seudomembranosa de Plaut.
Schultz's angina angina de Schultz.
vasomotor angina angina vasomotora, angina vasomotriz.
Vincent's angina angina de Vincent.
anginiform *adj.* anginiforme.
anginosis *n.* anginosis.
angioaccess *n.* angioacceso.
angioasthenia *n.* angioastenia.
angioataxia *n.* angioataxia.
angioblast *n.* angioblasto.
angioblastic *adj.* angioblástico, -ca.
angioblastoma *n.* angioblastoma.
angiocardiogram *n.* angiocardiograma.
angiocardiography *n.* angiocardiografía.
  radioisotope angiocardiography gamma-angiocardiografía.
angiocardiokinetic *adj.* angiocardiocinético, -ca.
angiocardiopathy *n.* angiocardiopatía.
angiocarditis *n.* angiocarditis.
angiocavernous *adj.* angiocavernoso, -sa.
angiocheiloscope *n.* angioqueiloscopio.
angiocholecistitis *n.* angiocolecistitis.
angiocholitis *n.* angiocolitis.
angiochondroma *n.* angiocondroma.
angioclast *n.* angioclasto.
angiocrine *adj.* angiocrino, -na.
angiocrinosis *n.* angiocrinosis.
angiocyst *n.* angioquiste.
angiodermatitis *n.* angiodermatitis.
angiodiascopy *n.* angiodiascopia.
angiodynia *n.* angiodinia.
angiodysplasia *n.* angiodisplasia.
angiodystrophia *n.* angiodistrofia.
  angiodystrophia ovarii angiodistrofia ovárica.
angiodystrophy *n.* angiodistrofia.
angioedema *n.* angioedema.
  hereditary angioedema angioedema hereditario.
  vibratory angioedema angioedema vibratorio.
angioedematous *adj.* angioedematoso, -sa.
angioelephantiasis *n.* angioelefantiasis.
angioendothelioma *n.* angioendotelioma.
angiofibroma *n.* angiofibroma.
  angiofibroma contagiosum tropicum angiofibroma contagioso de los trópicos.
  angiofibroma juvenile angiofibroma juvenil.
  nasopharyngeal angiofibroma angiofibroma nasofaríngeo.
angiofibrosis *n.* angiofibrosis.
angiogenesis *n.* angiogénesis.
angiogenic *adj.* angiogénico, -ca.
angioglioma *n.* angioglioma.
angiogliomatosis *n.* angiogliomatosis.
angiography *n.* angiografía.
  cerebral angiography angiografía cerebral.
  coronary angiography angiografía coronaria.

  radioisotope angiography gamma-angiografía.
  radioisotope cerebral angiography gamma-angioencefalografía.
  spinal angiography angiografía espinal.
angiohemophilia *n.* angiohemofilia.
angiohyalinosis *n.* angiohialinosis.
angiohypertonia *n.* angiohipertonía.
angiohypotonia *n.* angiohipotonía.
angioid *adj.* angioide.
angiokeratoma *n.* angioceratoma, angioqueratoma.
  angiokeratoma circumscriptum angioqueratoma circunscrito.
  angiokeratoma corporis diffusum angioqueratoma corporal difuso, angioqueratoma corporis diffusum.
  angiokeratoma of the scrotum angioqueratoma del escroto.
  diffuse angiokeratoma angioqueratoma difuso.
  Fordyce's angiokeratoma angioqueratoma de Fordyce.
  Mibelli's angiokeratoma angioqueratoma del Mibelli.
  solitary angiokeratoma angioqueratoma solitario.
angiokeratosis *n.* angioqueratosis.
angiokinesis *n.* angiocinesis.
angiokinetic *adj.* angiocinético, -ca.
angioleiomyoma *n.* angioleiomioma.
angioleucitis *n.* angioleucitis.
angioleukitis *n.* angioleucitis.
angiolipoma *n.* angiolipoma.
angiolith *n.* angiolito.
angiologia *n.* angiología.
angiology *n.* angiología.
angiolupoid *n.* angiolupoide.
angiolymphangioma *n.* angiolinfangioma.
angiolysis *n.* angiólisis.
angioma *n.* angioma.
  angioma arteriale racemosum angioma arterial racemoso.
  angioma cavernosum angioma cavernoso.
  angioma cutis angioma del cutis.
  angioma lymphaticum angioma linfático.
  angioma pigmentosum atrophicum angioma pigmentoso atrófico.
  angioma senile angioma senil.
  angioma serpiginosum angioma serpiginoso.
  angioma venosum racemosum angioma venoso racemoso.
  arteriovenous angioma of the brain angioma arteriovenoso del cerebro.
  capillary angioma angioma capilar.
  cavernous angioma angioma cavernoso.
  cherry angioma angioma en cereza.
  fissural angioma angioma fisural.
  hypertrophic angioma angioma hipertrófico.
  spider angioma angioma arácneo, angioma aracnoideo.
  strawberry angioma angioma en fresa.
  telangiectatic angioma angioma telangiectásico.
  venous angioma venoma.
angiomatosis *n.* angiomatosis.
  angiomatosis of the retina angiomatosis retiniana.
  cerebroretinal angiomatosis angiomatosis cerebrorretiniana.
  encephalofacial angiomatosis angiomatosis encefalofacial, angiomatosis encefalotrigeminal.
  encephalotrigeminal angiomatosis angio-

matosis encefalofacial, angiomatosis encefalo-trigeminal.

hepatic angiomatosis angiomatosis hepática.

retinocerebral angiomatosis angiomatosis retinocerebral.

angiomatous *adj.* angiomatoso, -sa.

angiomegaly *n.* angiomegalia.

angiometer *n.* angiómetro.

angiomyocardiac *adj.* angiomiocardíaco, -ca.

angiomyofibroma *n.* angiomiofibroma.

angiomyolipoma *n.* angiomiolipoma.

angiomyoma *n.* angiomioma.

angiomyoma cutis angiomioma cutáneo.

angiomyoneuroma *n.* angiomioneuroma.

angiomyopathy *n.* angiomiopatía.

angiomyosarcoma *n.* angiomiosarcoma.

angiomyxoma *n.* angiomixoma.

angionecrosis *n.* angionecrosis.

angioneoplasm *n.* angioneoplasia.

angioneuralgia *n.* angioneuralgia.

angioneurectomy *n.* angioneurectomía.

angioneuroedema *n.* angioneuroedema.

angioneuroma *n.* angioneuroma.

angioneuromyoma *n.* angioneuromioma.

angioneuropathic *adj.* angioneuropático, -ca.

angioneuropathy *n.* angioneuropatía.

angioneurosis *n.* angioneurosis.

angioneurotic *adj.* angioneurótico, -ca.

angioneurotomy *n.* angioneurotomía.

angionoma *n.* angionoma.

angiopancreatitis *n.* angiopancreatitis.

angioparalysis *n.* angioparálisis.

angioparesis *n.* angioparesia, angioparesis.

angiopathic *adj.* angiopático, -ca.

angiopathology *n.* angiopatología.

angiopathy *n.* angiopatía.

cerebral amyloid angiopathy angiopatía amiloide cerebral.

congophilic angiopathy angiopatía congofílica.

angiophacomatosis *n.* angiofacomatosis.

angiophakomatosis *n.* angiofacomatosis.

angioplany *n.* angioplania.

angioplasty *n.* angioplastia.

percutaneous transluminal angioplasty angioplastia transluminal percutánea.

percutaneous transluminal coronary angioplasty (PTCA) angioplastia coronaria transluminal percutánea (ACTP).

angiopoietic *adj.* angiopoyético, -ca.

angiopoioesis *n.* angiopoyesis.

angiopressure *n.* angiopresión.

angioreticuloendothelioma *n.* angiorreticuloendotelioma.

angioreticuloma *n.* angiorreticuloma.

angiorrhaphy *n.* angiorrafia.

arteriovenous angiorrhaphy angiorrafia arteriovenosa.

angiorrhexis *n.* angiorrexis.

angiosarcoma *n.* angiosarcoma.

angiosclerosis *n.* angiosclerosis.

angiosclerotic *adj.* angiosclerótico, -ca.

angioscope *n.* angioscopio.

angioscopy *n.* angioscopia.

angioscotoma *n.* angioescotoma, angioscotoma.

angioscotometry *n.* angioscotometría.

angiosialitis *n.* angiosialitis.

angiosis *n.* angiosis.

angiospasm *n.* angioespasmo, angiospasmo.

angiospastic *adj.* angioespástico, -ca, angiospástico, -ca.

angiostenosis *n.* angiostenosis.

angiosteosis *n.* angiosteosis.

angiosthenia *n.* angiostenia.

angiostomy *n.* angiostomía.

angiostrongyliasis *n.* angiostrongiliasis.

angiostrongylosis *n.* angiostrongilosis.

Angiostrongylus *n.* Angiostrongylus.

angiostrophy *n.* angiostrofia.

angiotelectasia *n.* angiotelectasia, angiotelectasis.

angiotelectasis *n.* angiotelectasia, angiotelectasis.

angiotensin *n.* angiotensina.

angiotensinogen *n.* angiotensinógeno.

angiotome *n.* angiótomo.

angiotomy *n.* angiotomía.

angiotonic *adj.* angiotónico, -ca.

angiotonin *n.* angiotonina.

angiotony *n.* angiotonía.

angiotribe *n.* angiotribo.

angiotripsy *n.* angiotripsia.

angiotrophic *adj.* angiotrófico, -ca.

angiotrophoneurosis *n.* angiotrofoneurosis.

angitis *n.* angiítis, angitis.

angle *n.* ángulo.

alpha angle ángulo alfa.

angle board tablero de ángulo.

angle of aberration ángulo de aberración.

angle of anomaly ángulo de anomalía.

angle of aperture ángulo de abertura, ángulo de abertura, ángulo de apertura.

angle of convergence ángulo de convergencia.

angle of deviation ángulo de desviación.

angle of direction ángulo de dirección.

angle of eccentricity ángulo de excentricidad.

angle of incidence ángulo de incidencia.

angle of reflection ángulo de reflexión.

angle of refraction ángulo de refracción.

axial angle ángulo axial.

carrying angle ángulo de alcance.

cephalometric angle ángulo cefalométrico, ángulo craneométrico.

critical angle ángulo crítico.

disparity angle ángulo de disparidad.

exposure angle ángulo de exposición.

horizontal angle ángulo horizontal.

impedance angle ángulo de impedancia.

meter angle ángulo métrico, ángulo metro.

minimum separable angle ángulo mínimo separable.

minimum visible angle ángulo mínimo visible.

minimum visual angle ángulo mínimo visible.

refracting angle of a prism ángulo de refracción de un prisma.

somatosplanchnic angle ángulo somatosplánicnico.

Treitz angle ángulo de Treitz.

angor *n.* angor.

angor animis angor animis.

angor pectoris angor pectoris.

angular *adj.* angular.

angulation *n.* angulación.

angulus *n.* ángulo.

anhaphia *n.* anafia, anhafia.

anhedonia *n.* anedonia, anhedonia.

anhematopoiesis *n.* anhematopoyesis.

anhidrosis *n.* anhidrosis.

thermogenic anhidrosis anhidrosis termógena.

anhidrotic *adj.* anhidrótico, -ca.

anhydration *n.* anhidratación.

anhydremia *n.* anhidremia.

anhydride *n.* anhídrido.

anhydrous *adj.* anhidro, -dra.

aniacinamidosis *n.* aniacinamidosis.

aniacinosis *n.* aniacinosis.

anianthinopsy *n.* aniantinopsia, aniaquintinopsia.

anicteric *adj.* anictérico, -ca.

anidean *adj.* anideano, -na.

anideus *n.* anídeo.

embryonic anideus anídeo embrionario, anídeo embriónico.

anidrosis *n.* anidrosis.

anidrotic *adj.* anidrótico, -ca.

anilingus *n.* anilingus.

anilinism *n.* anilinismo, anilismo.

anilinophil *adj.* anilinófilo, -la.

anilism *n.* anilinismo, anilismo.

anima *n.* ánima.

animal *n.* animal.

control animal animal de control.

decerebrate animal animal descerebrado.

experimental animal animal experimental.

Houssay animal animal de Houssay.

hyperphagic animal animal hiperfágico.

Long-Lukens animal animal de Long-Lukens.

normal animal animal normal.

spinal animal animal espinal.

thalamic animal animal talámico.

warm-blooded animal animal de sangre caliente.

animality *n.* animalidad.

animation *n.* animación.

suspended animation animación suspendida.

animism *n.* animismo.

anincretinosis *n.* anincretinosis.

anion *n.* anión.

anionic *adj.* aniónico, -ca.

aniridia *n.* aniridia.

anisakiasis *n.* anisakiasis, anisaquiasis.

Anisakis *n.* Anisakis.

Anisakis marina Anisakis marina.

aniseikonia *n.* aniseiconía.

aniseikonic *adj.* aniseicónico, -ca.

anisoaccommodation *n.* anisoacomodación.

anisochromasia *n.* anisocromasia.

anisochromatic *adj.* anisocromático, -ca.

anisochromia *n.* anisocromía.

anisocoria *n.* anisocoria.

anisocytosis *n.* anisocitosis.

anisodactylous *adj.* anisodáctilo, -la.

anisodactyly *n.* anisodactilia.

anisodiametric *adj.* anisodiamétrico, -ca.

anisodont *n.* anisodonto, -ta.

anisogamete *n.* anisogameto.

anisogametic *adj.* anisogamético, -ca.

anisogamy *n.* anisogamia.

anisognathous *adj.* anisognato, -ta.

anisoiconia *n.* aniseiconía, anisoiconía.

anisokaryosis *n.* anisocariosis.

anisomastia *n.* anisomastia.

anisomelia *n.* anisomelia.

anisomeric *adj.* anisómero, -ra.

anisometrope *adj.* anisométrope.

anisometropia *n.* anisometropía, asimetropía.

anisometropic *adj.* anisometrópico, -ca.

anisomyopia *n.* anisomiopía.

anisophoria *n.* anisoforia.

anisopia *n.* anisopía, anisopsia.

anisopiesis *n.* anisopiesis.

anisopoikilocytosis *n.* anisopoiquilocitosis.

anisorrhythmia *n.* anisorritmia.

anisosmotic *adj.* anisoosmótico, -ca.

anisosphygmia *n.* anisosfigmia.

anisosthenic *adj.* anisosténico, -ca.

anisotonic *adj.* anisotónico, -ca.

anisotropic *adj.* anisotrópico, -ca, anisótropo, -pa.

anisotropy *n.* anisotropía.
anisuria *n.* anisuria.
anitrogenous *adj.* anitrogenado, -da.
ankle *n.* tobillo.
 deck ankle tobillo de cubierta.
 tailor's ankle tobillo de sastre.
ankyloblepharon *n.* anquilobléfaron.
 ankyloblepharon filiforme adnatum anquilobléfaron filiforme congénito.
ankylocheilia *n.* anquiloquilia.
ankylocolpos *n.* anquilocolpos.
ankylodactylia *n.* anquilodactilia.
ankylodactyly *n.* anquilodactilia.
ankyloglossia *n.* anquiloglosia.
 complete ankyloglossia anquiloglosia completa.
 partial ankyloglossia anquiloglosia parcial.
ankylomele *n.* anquilómelo.
ankylophobia *n.* anquilofobia.
ankylopoietic *adj.* anquilopoyético, -ca.
ankylorrhinia *n.* anquilorrinia.
ankylosed *adj.* anquilosado, -da.
ankylosis *n.* anquilosis.
 artificial ankylosis anquilosis artificial.
 bony ankylosis anquilosis ósea.
 cricoarytenoid joint ankylosis anquilosis de la articulación cricoaritenoidea.
 dental ankylosis anquilosis dental.
 extracapsular ankylosis anquilosis extracapsular.
 false ankylosis anquilosis falsa.
 fibrous ankylosis anquilosis fibrosa.
 intracapsular ankylosis anquilosis intracapsular.
 spurious ankylosis anquilosis espuria.
 stapedial ankylosis anquilosis del estribo.
 true ankylosis anquilosis verdadera.
ankylotic *adj.* anquilótico, -ca.
ankylotomy *n.* anquilotomía.
ankylurethria *n.* anquilouretria, anquiluretria.
anlage *n.* anlaje, esbozo embrionario.
anmiotitis *n.* amniotitis.
anneal *v.* templar.
annihilation *n.* aniquilación.
annular *adj.* anular².
annuloplasty *n.* anuloplastia.
annulorrhaphy *n.* anulorrafia.
annulus *n.* anillo, annulus.
 annulus tympanicus anillo timpánico.
 annulus umbilicalis anillo umbilical.
anochromasia *n.* anocromasia.
anococcygeal *adj.* anococcígeo, -a, anocoxígeo, -a.
anodal *adj.* anodal.
anode *n.* ánodo.
 hooded anode ánodo con capucha.
 rotating anode ánodo rotatorio.
anoderm *n.* anodermo.
anodic *adj.* anódico, -ca.
anodontia *n.* anodoncia, anodontia.
 false anodontia anodoncia falsa.
 partial anodontia anodoncia parcial.
 total anodontia anodoncia total.
 true anodontia anodoncia verdadera.
anodontism *n.* anodontismo.
anodyne *adj.* anodino, -na.
anodynia *n.* anodinia.
anoetic *adj.* anoético, -ca.
anogenital *adj.* anogenital.
anomalopia *n.* anomalopía, anomalopsia.
anomaloscope *n.* anomaloscopio.
anomalotrophy *n.* anomalotrofia.
anomaly *n.* anomalía.
 Alder-Reilly anomaly anomalía de Alder, anomalía de Alder-Reilly.

Alder's anomaly anomalía de Alder, anomalía de Alder-Reilly.
Alder's constitutional granulation anomaly anomalía constitucional de la granulación de Alder.
Axenfeld's anomaly anomalía de Axenfeld.
Chédiak-Steinbrinck-Higashi anomaly anomalía de Chédiak-Steinbrinck-Higashi.
chromosomal anomaly anomalía cromosómica.
chromosome anomaly anomalía cromosómica.
congenital anomaly anomalía congénita.
congenital cardiac anomaly anomalía cardíaca congénita.
developmental anomaly anomalía de desarrollo.
Ebstein's anomaly anomalía de Ebstein.
eugnathic anomaly anomalía eugnásica.
Freund's anomaly anomalía de Freund.
gestant anomaly anomalía gestante.
Hegglin's anomaly anomalía de Hegglin.
May-Hegglin's anomaly anomalía de May-Hegglin.
morning glory anomaly anomalía en campanilla.
Pelger-Hüet anomaly anomalía Pelger-Hüet.
Peters' anomaly anomalía de Peters.
Poland's anomaly anomalía de Poland.
Rieger's anomaly anomalía de Rieger.
Shone's anomaly anomalía de Shone.
Uhl's anomaly anomalía de Uhl.
Undritz anomaly anomalía de Undritz.
anomia *n.* anomia.
anomie *n.* anomia.
anonychia *n.* anonicosis, anoniquia.
anonychosis *n.* anonicosis, anoniquia.
anoopsia *n.* anoopsia, anopsia.
anoperineal *adj.* anoperineal.
Anopheles *n.* Anopheles.
anophelicide *adj.* anofelicida.
anophelifuge *adj.* anofelífugo, -ga.
anophelism *n.* anofelismo.
anophoria *n.* anoforia.
anophthalmia *n.* anoftalmía.
 consecutive anophthalmia anoftalmía consecutiva.
 primary anophthalmia anoftalmía primaria.
 secondary anophthalmia anoftalmía secundaria.
anophthalmus *n.* anoftalmo, -ma.
anopia *n.* anopia.
anoplasty *n.* anoplastia.
anopsia *n.* anoopsia, anopsia.
anorchia *n.* anorquia, anorquidia.
anorchid *adj.* anórquido, -da.
anorchidic *adj.* anórquidico, -ca.
anorchidism *n.* anorquia, anorquidia.
anorchism *n.* anorquismo.
anorectal *adj.* anorrectal.
anorectitis *n.* anorrectitis.
anorectocolonic *adj.* anorrectocólico, -ca.
anorectum *n.* anorrecto.
anoretic *adj.* anoréxico, -ca.
anorexia *n.* anorexia.
 anorexia nervosa anorexia nerviosa.
 false anorexia anorexia falsa.
anorexiant *n.* anorexígeno.
anorexic *adj.* anoréxico, -ca.
anorexigenic *adj.* anorexígeno, -na.
anorganic *adj.* anorgánico, -ca.
anorganology *n.* anorganología.
anorgasmia *n.* anorgasmia.
anorgasmy *n.* anorgasmia.
anorthography *n.* anortografía.
anorthopia *n.* anortopia.

anorthosis *n.* anortosis.
anoscope *n.* anoscopio.
anoscopy *n.* anoscopia.
anosigmoidoscopic *adj.* anosigmoidoscópico, -ca.
anosigmoidoscopy *n.* anosigmoidoscopia.
anosmatic *adj.* anosmático, -ca.
anosmia *n.* anosmia.
 anosmia gustatoria anosmia gustatoria.
 anosmia respiratoria anosmia respiratoria.
 preferential anosmia anosmia preferencial.
anosmic *adj.* anósmico, -ca.
anosognosia *n.* anosognosia.
anosognosic *adj.* anosognósico, -ca.
anospinal *adj.* anoespinal, anospinal.
anosteoplasia *n.* anosteoplasia.
anostosis *n.* anostosis.
anotia *n.* anotia.
anotropia *n.* anotropía.
anotus *n.* anoto.
anovaginal *adj.* anovaginal.
anovaria *n.* anovaria.
anovarianism *n.* anovarianismo.
anovarism *n.* anovarismo.
anovesical *adj.* anovesical.
anovular *adj.* anovular.
anovulation *n.* anovulación.
anovulatory *adj.* anovulatorio, -a.
anovulomenorrhea *n.* anovulomenorrea.
anoxemia *n.* anoxemia, anoxihemia.
anoxemic *adj.* anoxémico, -ca.
anoxia *n.* anoxia.
 altitude anoxia anoxia de altitud, anoxia de altura.
 anemic anoxia anoxia anémica.
 anoxia neonatorum anoxia del neonato.
 anoxic anoxia anoxia anóxica.
 diffusion anoxia anoxia por difusión.
 histotoxic anoxia anoxia histotóxica.
 oxygen affinity anoxia anoxia por afinidad con el oxígeno.
 stagnant anoxia anoxia estasis, anoxia por estancamiento.
anoxic *adj.* anóxico, -ca.
ansa *n.* ansa, asa.
ansate *adj.* ansado, -da.
ansiform *adj.* ansiforme.
ansotomy *n.* ansotomía.
antacid *n.* antiácido, -da.
antagonism *n.* antagonismo.
 bacterial antagonism antagonismo bacteriano.
antagonist *adj.* antagonista, antistático, -ca.
 aldosterone antagonist antagonista aldosterona.
 associated antagonist antagonista asociado.
 calcium antagonist antagonista del calcio.
 competitive antagonist antagonista competitivo.
 direct antagonist antagonista directo.
 enzyme antagonist antagonista enzimático.
 folic acid antagonist antagonista del ácido fólico.
 narcotic antagonist antagonista de los narcóticos, antagonista narcótico.
antalgesia *n.* antialgesia.
antalgesic *adj.* antálgico, -ca, antiálgico, -ca.
antalgic *adj.* antálgico, -ca, antiálgico, -ca.
antalkaline *adj.* antialcalino, -na.
antapoplectic *adj.* antiapoplético, -ca.
antarthritic *adj.* antiartrítico, -ca.
antasthenic *adj.* antiasténico, -ca.
antasthmatic *adj.* antiasmático, -ca.
antatrophic *adj.* antiatrófico, -ca.
ante cibum *adj., adv.* ante cibum.
ante mortem *adj., adv.* ante mortem.

ante partum *adj., adv.* ante partum, anteparto.
antebrachial *adj.* antebraquial.
antebrachium *n.* antebrachium, antebrazo.
antecardium *n.* antecardio.
antecedent *n.* antecedente.
antecubital *adj.* antecubital.
antecurvature *n.* antecurvatura.
antefebrile *adj.* antefebril.
anteflex *adj.* anteflexo, -xa.
anteflexio *n.* anteflexio, anteflexión.
anteflexion *n.* anteflexio, anteflexión.
  anteflexion of the iris anteflexión del iris.
  uterine anteflexion anteflexio uteri, anteflexión uterina.
antehypophysis *n.* antehipófisis.
antelocation *n.* antelocación.
antenatal *adj.* antenatal.
anteposition *n.* anteposición.
anteprostate *n.* antepróstata.
anteprostatitis *n.* anteprostatitis.
antepyretic *adj.* antepirético, -ca.
antergia *n.* antergia.
antergic *adj.* antérgico, -ca.
anterior *adj.* anterior.
anteroclusion *n.* anteroclusión.
anteroexternal *adj.* anteroexterno, -na.
anterograde *adj.* anterógrado, -ra.
anteroinferior *adj.* anteroinferior.
anterointernal *adj.* anterointerno, -na.
anterolateral *adj.* anterolateral.
anteromedial *adj.* anteromedio, -dia.
anteromedian *adj.* anteromediano, -na.
anteroposterior *adj.* anteroposterior.
anteroseptal *adj.* anteroseptal.
anterosuperior *adj.* anterosuperior.
anterotic *adj.* antierótico, -ca.
anteroventral *adj.* anteroventral.
antesystole *n.* antesístole.
anteversion *n.* anteversión.
anteverted *adj.* antevertido, -da.
anthelix *n.* antehélix, anthélix, antihélix.
anthelminthic *adj.* antihelmíntico, -ca.
anthelmintic *adj.* antihelmíntico, -ca, antiscólico, -ca.
anthelone *n.* antelona.
anthelotic *adj.* antelótico, -ca, antihelótico, -ca.
anthema *n.* antema.
anthemorrhagic *adj.* antihemorrágico, -ca.
antherpetic *adj.* antiherpético, -ca.
anthocyanidin *n.* antocianidina.
anthocyaninemia *n.* antocianinemia.
anthocyanins *n.* antocianinas.
anthocyaninuria *n.* antocianinuria.
anthophobia *n.* antofobia.
anthorisma *n.* antorisma.
anthracemia *n.* antracemia.
anthracia *n.* antracia.
anthracic *adj.* antrácico, -ca.
anthracidal *adj.* antrácico, - ca.
anthracoid *adj.* antracoide.
anthracometer *n.* antracómetro.
anthraconecrosis *n.* antraconecrosis, antranecrosis.
anthracosilicosis *n.* antracosilicosis.
anthracosis *n.* antracosis.
  anthracosis linguae antracosis lingual.
anthracotic *adj.* antracótico, -ca.
anthrapurpurin *n.* antrapurpurina.
anthrax *n.* carbunco.
  cerebral anthrax carbunco cerebral.
  cutaneous anthrax carbunco cutáneo.
  gastrointestinal anthrax carbunco gastrointestinal.
  inhalational anthrax carbunco por inhalación.

  intestinal anthrax carbunco intestinal.
  meningeal anthrax carbunco meníngeo.
  pulmonary anthrax carbunco pulmonar.
anthropobiology *n.* antropobiología.
anthropocentric *adj.* antropocéntrico, -ca.
anthropocracy *n.* antropocracia.
anthropogenetic *adj.* antropogénico, -ca.
anthropogenic *adj.* antropogénico, -ca.
anthropogeny *n.* antropogenia.
anthropoid *adj.* antropoide.
anthropokinetics *n.* antropocinética.
anthropology *n.* antropología.
  applied anthropology antropología aplicada.
  criminal anthropology antropología criminal.
  cultural anthropology antropología cultural.
  physical anthropology antropología física.
anthropometer *n.* antropómetro.
anthropometric *adj.* antropométrico, -ca.
anthropometrist *n.* antropometrista.
anthropometry *n.* antropometría.
anthropomorphic *adj.* antropomórfico, -ca, antropomorfo, -fa.
anthropomorphism *n.* antropomorfismo.
anthroponomy *n.* antroponomía.
anthropopathy *n.* antropopatía.
anthropophilic *adj.* antropofílico, -ca, antropófilo, -la.
anthropophobia *n.* antropofobia.
anthroposcopy *n.* antroposcopia.
anthroposomatology *n.* antroposomatología.
anthroposophy *n.* antroposofía.
anthropozoonosis *n.* antropozoonosis.
anthropozoophilic *adj.* antropozoófilo, -la.
antiabortifacient *n.* antiabortivo.
antiacid *n.* antiácido, -da.
antiadrenergic *n.* antiadrenérgico, -ca.
antiagglutinating *adj.* antiaglutinante.
antialexic *adj.* antialéxico, -ca.
antiallergic *adj.* antialérgico, -ca.
antiamylase *n.* antiamilasa.
antianabolic *adj.* antianabólico, -ca.
antianaphylaxis *n.* antianafilaxia, antianafilaxis.
antiandrogen *n.* antiandrógeno.
antiandrogenic *adj.* antiandrógeno, -na.
antianemic *adj.* antianémico, -ca.
antianopheline *n.* antianofelina.
antiantibody *n.* antianticuerpo.
antiantidote *n.* antiantídoto.
antiantitoxin *n.* antiantitoxina.
antiapoplectic *adj.* antiapoplético, -ca.
antiarachnolysin *n.* antiaracnolisina.
antiarin *n.* antiarina.
antiarrhythmic *adj.* antiarrítmico, -ca.
antiarsenin *n.* antiarsenina.
antiarthritic *adj.* antiartrítico, -ca.
antiasthmatic *adj.* antiasmático, -ca.
antiatherogenic *adj.* antiaterógeno, -na.
antiautolysin *n.* antiautolisina.
antibacterial *adj.* antibacteriano, -na, antibactérico, -ca.
antibacteriolytic *adj.* antibacteriolítico, -ca.
antibechic *adj.* antibéquico, -ca.
antibiogram *n.* antibiograma, antibioticograma.
antibiotic *adj.* antibiótico, -ca.
antibiotic-resistant *adj.* antibioticorresistente.
antibiotin *n.* antibiotina.
antiblastic *adj.* antiblástico, -ca.
antiblennorrhagic *adj.* antiblenorrágico, -ca.
antibody *n.* anticuerpo.
  agglutinating antibody anticuerpo aglutinante.
  allocytophilic antibody anticuerpo alocitófilo.

  anaphylactic antibody anticuerpo anafiláctico.
  antiacetylcholine receptor antibody anticuerpo antirreceptor de acetilcolina.
  anti-basement membrane antibody anticuerpo antimembrana basal.
  anti-D antibody anticuerpo anti-D.
  anti-DNA antibody anticuerpo anti-ADN.
  anti-glomerular basement membrane antibody anticuerpo antimembrana basal glomerular (anti-MBG).
  antiglyadin antibody anticuerpo antigliadina.
  anti-idiotype antibody anticuerpo antiidiotipo.
  antimicrosomal antibody anticuerpo antimicrosomal.
  antimitochondrial antibody anticuerpo antimitocondrial, anticuerpo antimitocóndrico.
  antinuclear antibody (ANA) anticuerpo antinuclear (ANA).
  antireceptor antibody anticuerpo antirreceptor.
  antithyroglobulin antibody anticuerpo antitiroglobulina.
  antithyroid antibody anticuerpo antitiroideo.
  antologous antibody anticuerpo autólogo.
  auto-anti-idiotypic antibody anticuerpo autoantiidiotípico.
  bispecific antibody anticuerpo biespecífico.
  bivalent antibody anticuerpo bivalente.
  blocking antibody anticuerpo bloqueante.
  cell-bound antibody anticuerpo fijo a célula, anticuerpo ligado a la célula.
  cell-fixed antibody anticuerpo fijo a célula, anticuerpo ligado a la célula.
  cold antibody anticuerpo frío, anticuerpo frío-reactivo.
  cold-reactive antibody anticuerpo frío, anticuerpo frío-reactivo.
  complement-fixing antibody anticuerpo fijador del complemento.
  complete antibody anticuerpo completo.
  cross-reacting antibody anticuerpo de reacción cruzada.
  cytophilic antibody anticuerpo citófilo.
  cytotoxic antibody anticuerpo citotóxico.
  cytotropic antibody anticuerpo citotrópico.
  despeciated antibody anticuerpo desespeciado.
  detectable circulating antibody anticuerpo circulante.
  fluorescent antibody anticuerpo fluorescente.
  Forsmann antibody anticuerpo de Forssman.
  heteroclitic antibody anticuerpo heteroclítico.
  heterocytotropic antibody anticuerpo heterocitotrópico.
  heterogenetic antibody anticuerpo heterogenético.
  heterophil antibody anticuerpo heterófilo.
  heterophile antibody anticuerpo heterófilo.
  homocytotropic antibody anticuerpo homocitotrópico.
  horse-type antibody anticuerpo de tipo equino.
  hybrid antibody anticuerpo híbrido.
  idiotype antibody anticuerpo idiotipo.
  immune antibody anticuerpo inmunitario.
  incomplete antibody anticuerpo incompleto.
  inhibiting antibody anticuerpo inhibidor.
  isophil antibody anticuerpo isófilo.
  lymphocytotoxic antibody anticuerpo linfocitotóxico.
  mitochondrial antibody anticuerpo mitocondrial.
  monoclonal antibody anticuerpo monoclonal.

natural antibody anticuerpo natural.
neutralizing antibody anticuerpo neutralizante.
normal antibody anticuerpo normal.
polyclonal antibody anticuerpo policlonal.
Prausnitz-Küstner antibody anticuerpo de Prausnitz-Küstner.
protective antibody anticuerpo protector.
reaginic antibody anticuerpo reagínico.
Rh antibody anticuerpo Rh.
saline antibody anticuerpo salino.
sensitizing antibody anticuerpo sensibilizante.
treponema-immobilizing antibody anticuerpo antitreponema.
treponemal antibody anticuerpo treponémico.
TSH-displacing antibody (TDA) anticuerpo inhibidor de la TSH (TDA).
univalent antibody anticuerpo univalente.
warm antibody anticuerpo caliente, anticuerpo caliente-reactivo.
warm-reactive antibody anticuerpo caliente, anticuerpo caliente-reactivo.
Wassermann antibody anticuerpo Wassermann.
antibromic *adj.* antibrómico, -ca.
antibubonic *adj.* antibubónico, -ca.
anticachectic *adj.* anticaquéctico, -ca.
anticalculous *adj.* anticalculoso, -sa.
anticancer *adj.* anticanceroso, -sa.
anticarcinogen *adj.* anticarcinógeno, -na.
anticarcinogenic *adj.* anticarcinogénico, -ca.
anticariogenic *adj.* anticariogénico, -ca.
anticarious *adj.* anticarioso, -sa.
anticatalyzer *adj.* anticatalizador, -ra.
anticataphylactic *adj.* anticatafiláctico, -ca.
anticatarrhal *adj.* anticatarral.
anticathexis *n.* contracatexis.
anticathode *n.* anticátodo.
anticaustic *adj.* anticáustico, -ca.
anticephalalgic *adj.* anticefalálgico, -ca.
anticherotonus *n.* antiqueirotonía.
antichlorotic *adj.* anticlorótico, -ca.
anticholagogue *adj.* anticolagogo, -ga.
anticholinergic *adj.* anticolinérgico, -ca.
anticholinesterase *n.* anticolinesterasa.
antichymosin *n.* antiquimosina.
anticipation *n.* anticipación.
anticipatory *adj.* anticipado, -da.
anticnemion *n.* anticnemion.
anticoagulant *adj.* anticoagulante.
circulating anticoagulant anticoagulante circulante.
anticoagulation *n.* anticoagulación.
anticoagulin *n.* anticoagulina.
anticodon *n.* anticodón.
anticollagenase *n.* anticolagenasa.
anticolloidoclastic *adj.* anticoloidoclástico, -ca.
anticomplement *n.* anticomplemento.
anticomplementary *adj.* anticomplementario, -ria.
anticontagious *adj.* anticontagioso, -sa.
anticonvulsive *adj.* anticonvulsivo, -va.
anticritical *adj.* anticrítico, -ca.
anticurare *n.* anticurare.
anticytolysin *n.* anticitolisina.
anticytotoxin *n.* anticitotoxina.
antidepressant *adj.* antidepresivo, -va.
antidiabetic *adj.* antidiabético, -ca.
antidiarrheal *adj.* antidiarreico, -ca.
antidiarrheic *adj.* antidiarreico, -ca.
antidiastase *n.* antidiastasa.
antidiuresis *n.* antidiuresis.

antidiuretic *adj.* antidiurético, -ca.
antidiuretin *n.* antidiuretina.
antidotal *adj.* antidotal.
antidote *n.* antídoto.
chemical antidote antídoto químico.
mechanical antidote antídoto mecánico.
physiologic antidote antídoto fisiológico.
universal antidote antídoto universal.
antidromic *adj.* antidrómico, -ca.
antidysenteric *adj.* antidisentérico, -ca.
antidysrhythmic *adj.* antidisrítmico, -ca.
antidysuric *adj.* antidisúrico, -ca.
antieczematic *adj.* antieccemático, -ca.
antieczematous *adj.* antieccematoso, -sa.
antiedematous *adj.* antiedematoso, -sa.
antiedemic *adj.* antiedematoso, -sa.
antiembolism hose *n.* medias antiembolia.
antiemetic *adj.* antemético, -ca, antiemético, -ca.
antiemulsin *n.* antiemulsina.
antiendotoxic *adj.* antiendotóxico, -ca.
antiendotoxin *n.* antiendotoxina.
antienergic *adj.* antienérgico, -ca.
antienzyme *n.* antienzima.
antiepileptic *adj.* antiepiléptico, -ca.
antiepithelial *adj.* antiepitelial.
antiesterase *n.* antiesterasa.
antiestreptokinase *n.* antiestreptoquinasa.
antiestrogen *n.* antiestrógeno.
antifebrile *adj.* antifebril.
antiferment *n.* antifermento.
antifibrillatory *adj.* antifibrilatorio, -ria.
antifibrinolysin *n.* antifibrinolisina.
antifibrinolytic *adj.* antifibrinolítico, -ca.
antiflatulent *adj.* antiflatulento, -ta.
antifol *n.* antifol.
antifolate *n.* antifolato.
antifolic *adj.* antifólico, -ca.
antifungal *adj.* antifúngico, -ca.
antigalactagogue *adj.* antigalactagogo, -ga.
antigalactic *adj.* antigaláctico, -ca.
antigametocytic *adj.* antigametocítico, -ca.
antigelatinase *n.* antigelatinasa.
antigen *n.* antígeno.
allogenic antigen antígeno alogénico.
Australia antigen antígeno Australia.
beef heart antigen antígeno corazón de vacuno.
blood group antigen antígeno de grupo sanguíneo.
Boivin's antigen antígeno Boivin.
C carbohydrate antigen antígeno carbohidrato C.
capsular antigen antígeno capsular.
carbohydrate antigen antígeno hidrocarbonado.
carcinoembryonic antigen antígeno carcinoembrionario (CEA).
cholesterinized antigen antígeno colesterinizado.
class I antigen antígeno clase I.
class II antigen antígeno clase II.
class III antigen antígeno clase III.
common acute lymphoblastic leukemia antigen (calla) antígeno de la leucemia linfoblástica aguda común (calla).
common antigen antígeno común.
common leukocyte antigen antígeno leucocitario común.
complete antigen antígeno completo.
conjugated antigen antígeno conjugado.
cross-reacting antigen antígeno de reacción cruzada.
delta antigen antígeno delta.
envelope antigen antígeno de cubierta.
extractable nuclear antigen (ena) antígeno

nuclear extraíble (ena).
F antigen antígeno F.
febrile antigen antígeno febril.
flagellar antigen antígeno flagelar.
Forssman antigen antígeno Forssman.
Gm antigen antígeno Gm.
group antigen antígeno de grupo.
H antigen antígeno H.
heat-aggregated protein antigen antígeno de proteína agregada por calor.
hepatitis antigen antígeno de hepatitis.
hepatitis associated antigen (HAA) antígeno asociado a hepatitis.
hepatitis B core antigen antígeno central de la hepatitis B, antígeno core del virus de la hepatitis B.
hepatitis b surface antigen (hbsag) antígeno de superficie del virus de la hepatitis b.
heterogenetic antigen antígeno heterogénico, antígeno heterógeno.
heterologous antigen antígeno heterólogo.
heterophil antigen antígeno heterófilo.
histocompatibility antigen antígeno de histocompatibilidad.
histocompatibility major antigen antígeno de histocompatibilidad mayor.
histocompatibility minor antigen antígeno de histocompatibilidad menor.
homologous antigen antígeno homólogo.
human leukemia-associated antigen antígeno asociado a las leucemias humanas.
human lymphocyte antigen (HLA) antígeno de los linfocitos humanos (hla), antígeno leucocitario humano.
H-Y antigen antígeno H-Y.
Ia antigen antígeno Ia.
isogenic antigen antígeno isogénico.
isophile antigen antígeno isófilo.
K antigen antígeno K.
Km antigen antígeno Km.
Kveim antigen antígeno Kveim.
LD antigen antígeno LD.
Ly antigen antígeno Ly, antígeno Lyt.
Lyb antigen antígeno Lyb.
lymphocyte-defined (ld) antigen antígeno linfocito-definido (ld).
Lyt antigen antígeno Ly, antígeno Lyt.
mumps skin test antigen antígeno para la prueba cutánea de la parotiditis.
nuclear antigen antígeno nuclear.
o antigen antígeno o.
oncofetal antigen antígeno oncofetal.
organ-specific antigen antígeno específico de órgano.
Oz antigen antígeno Oz.
pancreatic oncofetal antigen (poa) antígeno oncofetal pancreático (ofp).
partial antigen antígeno parcial.
pollen antigen antígeno del polen.
private antigen antígeno privado.
prostate specific antigen antígeno prostático específico (psa).
public antigen antígeno público.
R antigen antígeno r.
recall antigen antígeno de recuerdo.
Rhus toxicodendron antigen antígeno Rhus toxicodendron.
Rhus venenata antigen antígeno Rhus venenata.
S antigen antígeno s.
self-antigen antígeno propio.
sensitized antigen antígeno sensibilizado.
sequestered antigen antígeno secuestrado.
sero-defined antigen antígeno serodefinido (sd).

serologically defined antigen antígeno serodefinido (sd).
serum-hepatitis (SH) antigen antígeno de hepatitis sérica.
shock antigen antígeno de shock.
Sm antigen antígeno Sm.
soluble antigen antígeno soluble.
somatic antigen antígeno somático.
species-specific antigen antígeno específico de especie.
specific antigen antígeno específico.
SS-a antigen antígeno SS-a.
SS-b antigen antígeno SS-b.
streptococcus m antigen antígeno m estreptocócico.
t antigen antígeno t.
Tac antigen antígeno Tac.
T-dependent antigen antígeno T-dependiente.
theta antigen antígeno theta, antígeno Thy.
Thy antigen antígeno theta, antígeno Thy.
t-independent antigen antígeno t-independiente.
tissue-specific antigen antígeno específico de tejido.
tl antigen antígeno tl.
transplantation antigen antígeno de trasplante.
tumor antigen antígeno tumoral.
tumor associated antigen antígeno asociado a tumor.
tumor-specific antigen (TSA) antígeno específico de tumor.
tumor-specific transplantation antigen (ttet) antígeno de trasplante específico del tumor.
Vi antigen antígeno Vi.
xenogeneic antigen antígeno xenógeno.
antigenemia n. antigenemia.
antigenemic adj. antigenémico, -ca.
antigenic adj. antigénico, -ca.
antigenicity n. antigenicidad.
antigenophil adj. antigenófilo, -la.
antigenotherapy n. antigenoterapia.
antigentophil adj. antigenófilo, -la.
antigentotherapy n. antigenoterapia.
antiglobulin n. antiglobulina.
antigoitrogenic adj. antibociógeno, -na.
antigonadotrophic adj. antigonadotrópico, -ca.
antigonorrheic adj. antigonorreico, -ca.
antigrowth adj. anticrecimiento.
anti-hbc n. anti-hbc.
anti-hbs n. anti-hbs.
antihelix n. antehélix.
antihelminthic adj. antihelmíntico, -ca, antivermicular, antiverminoso, -sa.
· **antihemagglutinin** n. antihemaglutinina.
antihemolysin n. antihemolisina.
antihemolytic adj. antihemolítico, -ca.
antihemorrhagic adj. antihemorrágico, -ca.
antiherpetic adj. antiherpético, -ca.
antiheterolysin n. antiheterolisina.
antihistamine n. antihistamina.
antihistaminic adj. antihistamínico, -ca.
antihormone n. antihormona.
antihydrophobic adj. antihidrofóbico, -ca.
antihydropic adj. antihidrópico, -ca.
antihydrotic adj. antihidrótico, -ca.
antihypercholesteronemic adj. antihipercolesterolémico, -ca.
antihyperglycemic adj. antihiperglucémico, -ca.
antihyperlipoproteinemic adj. antihiperlipoproteico, -ca.

antihypertensive adj. antihipertensivo, -va.
antihypnotic adj. antihipnótico, -ca.
antihypotensive adj. antihipotensor, -ra.
anti-icteric adj. antictérico, -ca, antiictérico, -ca.
anti-idiotype n. antiidiotipo.
anti-immune adj. antiinmune.
anti-infectious adj. antiinfeccioso, -sa.
anti-infective n. antiinfeccioso.
anti-inflammatory adj. antiinflamatorio, -ria.
antiinitiator n. antiiniciador.
anti-insulin n. antiinsulina.
anti-isolysin n. antiisolisina.
antikataphylactic adj. anticatafiláctico, -ca.
antikenotoxin n. antiquenotoxina.
antiketogenesis n. anticetogénesis.
antiketogenetic adj. anticetogénico, -ca.
antiketogenic adj. anticetógeno, -na, antiquetógeno, -na.
antikinase n. anticinasa.
antilactoserum n. antilactosuero.
antileishmanial adj. antileishmaniásico, -ca.
antilemic adj. antilémico, -ca.
antileprotic adj. antileproso, -sa.
antileukocidin n. antileucocidina.
antileukocytic n. antileucocito.
antileukotoxin n. antileucotoxina.
antilifarial adj. antifilárico, -ca.
antilipase n. antilipasa.
antilipemic adj. antilipémico, -ca.
antilipoid n. antilipoide.
antilipotropic adj. antilipotrópico, -ca.
antilipotropism n. antilipotropismo.
antilithic adj. antilítico, -ca[2].
antilobium n. antilobium.
antiluetic adj. antiluético, -ca.
antiluteogenic adj. antiluteogénico, -ca.
antilysic adj. antilísico, -ca.
antilysin n. antilisina.
antilysis n. antilisis.
antilytic adj. antilítico, -ca[1].
antimalarial adj. antimalárico, -ca.
antimaniacal adj. antimaníaco, -ca.
antimephitic adj. antimefítico, -ca.
antimer n. antímero.
antimere n. antímero.
antimesenteric adj. antimesentérico, -ca.
antimetabolite n. antimetabolito.
antimethemoglobinemic adj. antimetahemoglobinémico, -ca.
antimetropia n. antimetropía.
antimiasmatic adj. antimiasmático, -ca.
antimicrobial adj. antimicrobiano, -na.
antimicrobic adj. antimicrobiano, -na.
antimineralocorticoid n. antimineralocorticoide.
antimitotic adj. antimitótico, -ca.
antimongolism n. antimongolismo.
antimorph n. antimorfo.
antimorphic adj. antimórfico, -ca.
antimuscarinic adj. antimuscarínico, -ca.
antimutagen n. antimutágeno.
antimutagenic adj. antimutagénico, -ca.
antimyasthenic adj. antimiasténico, -ca.
antimycotic adj. antimicótico, -ca.
antimydriatic adj. antimidriásico, -ca.
antinarcotic adj. antinarcótico, -ca.
antinatriferic adj. antinatriférico, -ca.
antinatriuresis n. antinatriuresis.
antinauseant adj. antinauseante, antinauseoso, -sa.
antineoplastic adj. antineoplásico, -ca.
antineoplaston n. antineoplaston.
antinephritic adj. antinefrítico, -ca.
antineuralgic adj. antineurálgico, -ca.

antineuritic adj. antineurítico, -ca.
antineurotoxin n. antineurotoxina.
antiniad n. antiníade.
antinial adj. antinial.
antinion n. antiinión, antinión.
antinomy n. antinomia.
antinuclear adj. antinuclear.
antiodontalgic adj. antiodontálgico, -ca.
antioncogene n. antioncogen.
antioncotic adj. antioncótico, -ca.
antiorgastic adj. antiorgástico, -ca.
antiovaluatory adj. antiovulatorio, -ria.
antioxidant n. antioxidante.
antioxidase n. antioxidasa.
antioxidation n. antioxidación.
antipaludial adj. antipalúdico, -ca.
antiparallel adj. antiparalelo, -la.
antiparalytic adj. antiparalítico, -ca.
antiparasitic adj. antiparasitario, -ria.
antiparastata n. antiparastata.
antiparastitis n. antiparastitis.
antiparasympathomimetic adj. antiparasimpaticomimético, -ca.
antiparkinsonian adj. antiparkinsoniano, -na.
antipedicular adj. antipedicular, antipediculoso, -sa.
antipediculotic adj. antiftiríaco, -ca, antipediculótico, -ca.
antiperiodic adj. antiperiódico, -ca, antitíptico, -ca.
antiperistalsis n. antiperistalsis, antiperistaltismo.
antiperistaltic adj. antiperistáltico, -ca.
antiperspirant adj. antiperspirante, antisudoríparo, -ra.
antiphagin n. antifagina.
antiphagocytic adj. antifagocítico, -ca.
antiphlogistic adj. antiflogístico, -ca.
antiphobic adj. antifóbico, -ca.
antiphrynolysin n. antifrinolisina.
antiphthiriac adj. antiptírico, -ca.
antiphthisic adj. antitísico, -ca.
antiplague adj. antipestoso, -sa.
antiplasmin n. antiplasmina.
antiplasmodial adj. antiplasmódico, -ca.
antiplastic adj. antiplásico, -ca, antiplástico, -ca.
antiplatelet adj. antiplaquetario, -ria.
antipneumococcal adj. antineumocócico, -ca, antipneumocócico, -ca.
antipneumococcic adj. antineumocócico, -ca, antipneumocócico, -ca.
antipodagric adj. antipodágrico, -ca.
antipodal adj. antipodal.
antipode n. antípoda.
optical antipode antípoda óptica.
antipolycythemic adj. antipolicitémico, -ca.
antiport n. antiporte.
antiporter adj. antiportador, -ra.
antiprecipitin n. antiprecipitina.
antiprogestin n. antiprogestágeno.
antiprostate n. antipróstata.
antiprostatitis n. antiprostatitis.
antiprothrombin n. antiprotrombina.
antiprotozoal adj. antiprotozoario, -ria.
antipruritical adj. antipruriginoso, -sa, antiprurítico, -ca, antipruritoso, -sa.
antipsonin n. antiopsonina.
antipsoriatic adj. antipsoriásico, -ca.
antipsoric adj. antipsórico, -ca.
antipsychotic adj. antipsicótico, -ca.
antiputrefactive adj. antipútrido, -da.
antipyogenic adj. antipiogénico, -ca, antipiógeno, -na.
antipyresis n. antipiresis.
antipyretic adj. antipirético, -ca.

antipyrotic *adj.* antipirótico, -ca.
antirabic *adj.* antirrábico, -ca.
antirachitic *adj.* antirraquítico, -ca.
antirheumatic *adj.* antirreumático, -ca.
antirickettsial *adj.* antirrickettsiásico, -ca.
antiruminant *n.* antirrumiante.
antisaluresis *n.* antisaluresis.
antiscabietic *adj.* antiescabiético, -ca, antiescabioso, -sa.
antiscarlatinal *adj.* antiescarlatinoso, -sa.
antischistosomal *adj.* antiesquistosómico, -ca.
antiscorbutic *adj.* antiescorbútico, -ca.
antiseborrheic *adj.* antiseborreico, -ca.
antisecretory *adj.* antisecretor, -ra, antisecretorio, -ria.
antisense *n.* antisentido.
antisepsis *n.* antisepsia, antisepsis.
antlseptic *adj.* antiséptico, -ca.
antisepticism *n.* antisepticismo.
antiserotonin *n.* antiserotonina.
antiserum *n.* antisuero.
  blood group antiserum antisuero de grupos sanguíneos.
  Erysipelothrix rhusiopathiae antiserum antisuero Erysipelothrix rhusiopathiae.
  heterologous antiserum antisuero heterólogo.
  homologous antiserum antisuero homólogo.
  monovalent antiserum antisuero monovalente.
  nerve growth factor antiserum antisuero contra el factor de crecimiento nervioso.
  polyvalent antiserum antisuero polivalente.
  Rh antiserum antisuero Rh.
  specific antiserum antisuero específico.
antisialagogue *adj.* antisialagogo, -ga.
antisialic *adj.* antisiálico, -ca.
antisideric *adj.* antisidérico, -ca.
antisocial *adj.* antisocial.
antisocialism *n.* antisocialismo.
antispasmodic[1] *adj.* antiespasmódico, -ca, antispasmódico, -ca.
antispasmodic[2] *n.* antiespasmódico, antispasmódico.
  billiary antispasmodic antiespasmódico biliar.
  bronchial antispasmodic antiespasmódico bronquial.
antispastic *adj.* antiespástico, -ca.
antispermotoxin *n.* antiespermotoxina.
antispirochetic *adj.* antiespiroquético, -ca.
antistaphylococcic *adj.* antiestafilocócico, -ca.
antistaphylohemolysin *n.* antiestafilohemolisina.
antistaphylolysin *n.* antiestafilolisina.
antisteapsin *n.* antiesteapsina, antiesteapsina.
antistreptococcic *adj.* antiestreptocócico, -ca.
antistreptokinase *n.* antiestreptocinasa.
antistreptolysin *n.* antiestreptolisina.
antisudoral *adj.* antisudoral.
antisudorific *adj.* antisudorífico, -ca.
antisympathetic *adj.* antisimpático, -ca.
antisyphilitic *adj.* antisifilítico, -ca.
antitetanic *adj.* antitetánico, -ca.
antithenar *adj.* antitenar.
antithermic *adj.* antitérmico, -ca.
antithrombin *n.* antitrombina.
  normal antithrombin antitrombina normal.
antithromboplastin *n.* antitromboplastina.
antithrombotic *adj.* antitrombótico, -ca.
antithyroid *adj.* antitiroideo, -a.
antithyrotoxic *adj.* antitirotóxico, -ca.
antithyrotropic *adj.* antitirotrópico, -ca.
antitonic *adj.* antitónico, -ca.
antitoxic *adj.* antitóxico, -ca.
antitoxigen *n.* antitoxígeno.
antitoxin *n.* antitoxina.

bivalent gas gangrene antitoxin antitoxina bivalente de la gangrena gaseosa.
bothropic antitoxin antitoxina botrófica.
bothrops antitoxin antitoxina botrófica.
botulinum antitoxin antitoxina botulínica.
botulism antitoxin antitoxina botulínica.
bovine antitoxin antitoxina bovina.
crotalus antitoxin antitoxina crotalus.
despeciated antitoxin antitoxina despeciada.
diphtheria antitoxin antitoxina diftérica.
dysentery antitoxin antitoxina disentérica.
gas gangrene antitoxin antitoxina de la gangrena gaseosa.
normal antitoxin antitoxina normal.
pentavalent gas gangrene antitoxin antitoxina pentavalente de la gangrena gaseosa.
plant antitoxin antitoxina vegetal.
scarlet fever antitoxin antitoxina de la escarlatina.
staphylococcus antitoxin antitoxina del estafilococo.
tetanus and gas gangrene antitoxin antitoxina tetánica y de la gangrena gaseosa.
tetanus antitoxin antitoxina tetánica.
tetanus-perfringens antitoxin antitoxina tetánica perfringens.
antitoxinogen *n.* antitoxinógeno.
antitragus *n.* antitrago, antitragus.
antitreponemal *adj.* antitreponémico, -ca.
antitrichomonal *adj.* antitricomoniásico, -ca.
antitrismus *n.* antitrismo.
antitrope *n.* antítrope, antítropo.
antitropic *adj.* antitrópico, -ca.
antitropin *n.* antitropina.
antitrypanosomal *adj.* antitripanosomásico, -ca.
antitrypsic *adj.* antitrípsico, -ca antitríptico, -ca.
antitrypsin *n.* antitripsina.
antitryptic *adj.* antitríptico, -ca.
antitubercular *adj.* antituberculoso, -sa.
antituberculin *n.* antituberculina.
antituberculous *adj.* antituberculoso, -sa.
antitubulin *n.* antitubulina.
antitumorigenesis *n.* antitumorigénesis.
antitumorigenic *adj.* antitumorígeno, -na.
antitussive *adj.* antitusígeno, -na, antitusivo, -va.
antityphoid *adj.* antitífico, -ca, antitifoideo, -a, antitifoídico, -ca.
antiulcerative *adj.* antiulceroso, -sa.
antiuratic *adj.* antiurático, -ca.
antiurease *n.* antiureasa.
antiurokinase *n.* antiurocinasa.
antivenene *n.* antiveneno.
antivenereal *adj.* antivenéreo, -ca.
antivenin *n.* antiponzoñoso, -sa, antitoxina, antiveneno.
  black widow spider antivenin antitoxina contra la araña viuda negra, antiveneno de araña viuda negra.
antivenom *adj.* antiofídico, -ca.
antivenomous *adj.* antivenenoso, -sa.
antiviral *adj.* antiviral, antivírico, - ca.
antivirotic *adj.* antivirósico, -ca.
antivirulin *n.* antivirulina.
antivirus *n.* antivirus.
antivitamin *n.* antivitamina.
antivivisection *n.* antivivisección.
antixerophthalmic *adj.* antixeroftálmico, -ca.
antixerotic *adj.* antixerótico, -ca.
antizymohexase *n.* anticimohexasa.
antizymotic *adj.* anticimótico, -ca.
antophthalmic *adj.* antioftálmico, -ca.
antral *adj.* antral, ántrico, -ca.

antrectomy *n.* antrectomía.
antritis *n.* antritis.
antroatticotomy *n.* antroaticotomía.
antrobuccal *adj.* antrobucal.
antrocele *n.* antracele, antrocele.
antroduodenectomy *n.* antroduodenectomía.
antrodynia *n.* antrodinia.
antronalgia *n.* antronalgia.
antronasal *adj.* antronasal.
antroneurolysis *n.* antroneurólisis.
antrophore *n.* antróforo.
antrophose *n.* antrofosia.
antropogeny *n.* antropogénesis.
antropyloric *adj.* antropilórico, -ca.
antroscope *n.* antroscopio.
antroscopy *n.* antroscopia.
antrostomy *n.* antrostomía.
antrotome *n.* antrótomo.
antrotomy *n.* antrotomía.
antrotonia *n.* antrotonía.
antrotympanic *adj.* antrotimpánico, -ca.
antrotympanitis *n.* antrotimpanitis.
antrum *n.* antro, antrum.
anuclear *adj.* anuclear.
anuresis *n.* anuresis.
anuretic *adj.* anurético, -ca.
anuria *n.* anuria.
  angioneurotic anuria anuria angioneurótica.
  calculus anuria anuria calculosa.
  obstructive anuria anuria obstructiva.
  postrenal anuria anuria posrenal.
  prerenal anuria anuria prerrenal.
  renal anuria anuria renal.
  suppressive anuria anuria por supresión.
anuric *adj.* anúrico, -ca.
anurous *adj.* anuro, -ra.
anus *n.* ano, anus.
  anus tibiarum ano tibiarum.
  anus vesicalis ano vesical.
  artificial anus ano artificial, ano contra natura.
  ectopic anus ano ectópico.
  imperforate anus ano imperforado.
  vestibular anus ano vestibular, ano vulvovaginal.
  vulvovaginal anus ano vestibular, ano vulvovaginal.
anusitis *n.* anusitis.
anvil *n.* yunque.
anxietas tibiarum *n.* anxietas tibiarum.
anxiety *n.* angustia, ansiedad.
  anticipatory anxiety ansiedad anticipatoria, ansiedad de señal.
  automatic anxiety angustia automática.
  basic anxiety ansiedad básica.
  castration anxiety ansiedad de castración.
  free-floating anxiety ansiedad flotante.
  noetic anxiety ansiedad noética.
  reality anxiety angustia real.
  separation anxiety ansiedad de separación.
  situation anxiety ansiedad de situación.
  situational anxiety ansiedad circunstancial.
  stranger anxiety ansiedad ante los extraños.
  traumatic anxiety ansiedad traumática.
anxiolytic *adj.* ansiolítico, -ca.
aorta *n.* aorta.
aortactia *n.* aortactia.
aortal *adj.* aortal.
aortalgia *n.* aortalgia.
aortectasis *n.* aortectasia, aortectasis.
aortectomy *n.* aortectomía.
aortic *adj.* aórtico, -ca.
aorticorenal *adj.* aorticorrenal.
aortismus *n.* aortismo, aortismus.

aortismus abdominalis aortismo abdominal, aortismus abdominalis.
aortitis *n.* aortitis.
 giant cell aortitis aortitis gigantocelular.
 luetic aortitis aortitis luética.
 rheumatic aortitis aortitis reumática.
 syphilitic aortitis aortitis sifilítica.
aortocoronary *adj.* aortocoronario, -ria.
aortogram *n.* aortograma.
aortography *n.* aortografía.
 abdominal aortography aortografía abdominal.
 retrograde aortography aortografía retrógrada.
 translumbar aortography aortografía translumbar.
aortopathy *n.* aortopatía.
aortoplasty *n.* aortoplastia.
aortoptosia *n.* aortoptosis.
aortorrhaphy *n.* aortorrafia.
aortosclerosis *n.* aortoesclerosis, aortosclerosis.
aortostenosis *n.* aortoestenosis, aortostenosis.
aortotomy *n.* aortotomía.
aosmia *n.* aosmia.
apallic *adj.* apálico, -ca.
apancrea *n.* apancria.
apancreatic *adj.* apancreático, -ca.
apanthropia *n.* apantropía.
apanthropy *n.* apantropía.
aparalytic *adj.* aparalítico, -ca.
aparathyreosis *n.* aparatireosis.
aparathyroidism *n.* aparatiroidismo.
aparathyrosis *n.* aparatirosis.
apareunia *n.* apareunia.
aparthrosis *n.* apartrosis.
apathetic *adj.* apático, -ca.
apathic *adj.* apático, -ca.
apathism *n.* apatismo.
apathy *n.* apatía.
apatite *n.* apatita.
apeidosis *n.* apeidosis.
apellous *adj.* apelo, -la, apeloso, -sa.
apenteric *adj.* apentérico, -ca.
apepsia *n.* apepsia.
apepsinia *n.* apepsinia.
aperiodic *adj.* aperiódico, -ca.
aperistalsis *n.* aperistalsis, aperistaltismo.
apertognathia *n.* apertognatia.
apertometer *n.* apertómetro.
apertura *n.* abertura.
aperture *n.* abertura, apertura.
 angular aperture abertura angular.
Apex *n.* ápice.
apex *n.* apex, ápex.
apexcardiogram *n.* apexcardiograma, apexicardiograma.
apexcardiography *n.* apexicardiografía.
apexification *n.* apexificación.
apexigraph *n.* apexígrafo, apexógrafo.
aphagia *n.* afagia.
 aphagia algera afagia álgera, afagia dolorosa.
aphagopraxia *n.* afagopraxia.
aphakia *n.* afaquia.
aphakial *adj.* afaquial.
aphakic *adj.* afaco, -ca, afáquico, -ca.
aphalangia *n.* afalangia, afalangiasis.
aphasia *n.* afasia.
 acoustic aphasia afasia acústica.
 acquired epileptic aphasia afasia epiléptica adquirida.
 amnesic aphasia afasia amnésica.
 amnestic aphasia afasia amnésica.
 anomic aphasia afasia anómica.
 anosmic aphasia afasia anósmica.

aphasia lethica afasia amnemónica, afasia lética.
 associative aphasia afasia asociativa.
 ataxic aphasia afasia atáxica.
 auditory aphasia afasia auditiva.
 Broca's aphasia afasia de Broca.
 central aphasia afasia central.
 childhood aphasia afasia infantil.
 combined aphasia afasia combinada.
 commisural aphasia afasia comisural.
 complete aphasia afasia completa.
 conduction aphasia afasia de conducción.
 dysnomic aphasia afasia amnésica.
 expressive aphasia afasia expresiva.
 fluent aphasia afasia fluente, afasia fluida.
 functional aphasia afasia funcional.
 global aphasia afasia global.
 graphic aphasia afasia gráfica, afasia grafomotora.
 graphomotor aphasia afasia gráfica, afasia grafomotora.
 impressive aphasia afasia impresiva.
 jargon aphasia afasia en jeringonza, afasia jergal.
 Kussmaul's aphasia afasia de Kussmaul.
 mixed aphasia afasia mixta.
 motor aphasia afasia motora.
 nominal aphasia afasia nominal.
 optic aphasia afasia óptica.
 pathematic aphasia afasia patemática.
 pictorial aphasia afasia pictórica.
 psychosensory aphasia afasia psicosensitiva, afasia psicosensorial.
 receptive aphasia afasia receptiva.
 semantic aphasia afasia semántica.
 sensory aphasia afasia sensitiva, afasia sensorial.
 subcortical aphasia afasia subcortical.
 syntactical aphasia afasia sintáctica.
 temporoparietal aphasia afasia temporoparietal.
 transcortical aphasia afasia transcortical.
 verbal aphasia afasia verbal.
 visual aphasia afasia visual.
 Wernicke's aphasia afasia de Wernicke.
aphasiac *n.* afásico, -ca[1].
aphasic *adj.* afásico, -ca[2].
aphasiologist *n.* afasiólogo, -ga.
aphasiology *n.* afasiología.
aphemia *n.* afemia.
aphephobia *n.* afefobia.
apheresis *n.* aféresis.
Aphiochaeta *n.* Aphiochaeta.
 Aphiochaeta ferruginea Aphiochaeta ferruginea.
apholyte *n.* anfólito.
aphonia *n.* afonía.
 aphonia clericorum afonía de los clérigos.
 aphonia paralytica afonía paralítica.
 hysterical aphonia afonía histérica.
 spastic aphonia afonía espástica.
aphonic *adj.* afónico, -ca.
aphonogelia *n.* afonogelia.
aphonous *adj.* áfono, -na.
aphoresis *n.* aforesis.
aphose *n.* afosia.
aphosphagenic *adj.* afosfágeno, -na.
aphosphorosis *n.* afosforosis.
aphotesthesia *n.* afotestesia.
aphotic *adj.* afótico, -ca.
aphrasia *n.* afrasia.
aphrodisia *n.* afrodisia.
aphrodisiac *adj.* afrodisíaco, -ca.
aphrodisiomania *n.* afrodisiomanía.
aphtha *n.* afta.
aphthoid *adj.* aftoide.

aphthongia *n.* aftongía.
aphthosis *n.* aftosis.
aphthous *adj.* aftoso, -sa.
Aphthovirus *n.* Aphtovirus.
aphylactic *adj.* afiláctico, -ca.
aphylaxis *n.* afilaxia.
apical *adj.* apexiano, -na, apical.
apicectomy *n.* apectomía, apicectomía.
apiceotomy *n.* apiceotomía.
apicitis *n.* apicitis.
apicoectomy *n.* apicectomía, apicoectomía.
apicolocator *n.* apicolocalizador.
apicolysis *n.* apicólisis.
apicostome *n.* apicóstomo.
apicostomy *n.* apicostomía.
apicotomy *n.* apicotomía.
apiculate *adj.* apiculado, -da.
apicurettage *n.* apicuretaje.
apinealism *n.* apinealismo.
apinoid *adj.* apinoide.
apiotherapy *n.* apiterapia.
apisination *n.* apisinación.
apitoxin *n.* apitoxina.
apituitarism *n.* apituitarismo.
aplacental *adj.* aplacentario, -ria.
aplanatic *adj.* aplanático, -ca.
aplanatism *n.* aplanatismo.
aplasia *n.* aplasia.
 aplasia axialis extracorticalis congenita aplasia congénita extracortical axial.
 aplasia cutis congenita aplasia congénita del cutis, aplasia cutis congénita.
 aplasia of the ovary aplasia ovárica.
 aplasia pilorum propia aplasia pilorum propia.
 congenital aplasia of the thymus aplasia congénita del timo.
 germinal aplasia aplasia germinal, aplasia germinativa.
 gonadal aplasia aplasia gonadal.
 nuclear aplasia aplasia nuclear.
 ovarian aplasia aplasia ovárica.
 pure red cell aplasia aplasia eritrocitaria pura, aplasia eritrocítica pura.
 thymic aplasia aplasia tímica.
aplasmic *adj.* aplásmico, -ca.
aplastic *adj.* aplásico, -ca.
apleuria *n.* apleuria.
apnea *n.* apnea, apneustia.
 apnea neonatorum apnea neonatal.
 apnea vera apnea vera, apnea verdadera.
 cardiac apnea apnea cardíaca.
 central apnea apnea central.
 central sleep apnea apnea central del sueño.
 deglutition apnea apnea de deglución.
 induced apnea apnea inducida.
 late apnea apnea tardía.
 mixed sleep apnea apnea del sueño mixta.
 obstructive apnea apnea obstructiva.
 obstructive sleep apnea apnea obstructiva del sueño (SAOS).
 periodic apnea of the newborn apnea periódica del recién nacido.
 peripheral apnea apnea periférica.
 primary apnea apnea primaria.
 reflex apnea apnea refleja.
 secondary apnea apnea secundaria.
 sleep apnea apnea del sueño.
 sleep-induced apnea apnea inducida por el sueño.
 true apnea apnea vera, apnea verdadera.
apneic *adj.* apneico, -ca.
apneumatic *adj.* apneumático, -ca.
apneumatosis *n.* apneumatosis.
apneumia *n.* aneumia, apneumia.

apneusis *n.* apneusia, apneusis.
apneustic *adj.* apneústico, -ca.
apobiosis *n.* apobiosis.
apocamnosis *n.* apocamnosis.
apocenosis *n.* apocenosis.
apochromatic *adj.* apocromático, -ca.
apocope *n.* apócope.
apocoptic *adj.* apocóptico, -ca.
apocrine *adj.* apocrino, -na.
apocrinitis *n.* apocrinitis.
apodal *adj.* apodal, ápodo, -da.
apodia *n.* apodia.
apodous *adj.* ápodo, -da.
apody *n.* apodia.
apoenzyme *n.* apoenzima.
apoferritin *n.* apoferritina.
apogee *n.* apogeo.
apokamnosis *n.* apocamnosis.
apolar *adj.* apolar.
apolegamic *adj.* apolegámico, -ca.
apolegamy *n.* apolegamia.
apolepsis *n.* apolepsia, apolepsis.
apolipoprotein *n.* apolipoproteína.
apomixia *n.* apomixia.
apomixis *n.* apomixia, apomixis.
aponeurectomy *n.* aponeurectomía.
aponeurology *n.* aponeurología.
aponeurorrhaphy *n.* aponeurorrafia.
aponeurosis *n.* aponeurosis.
aponeurositis *n.* aponeurositis.
aponeurotic *adj.* aponeurótico, -ca.
aponeurotome *n.* aponeurótomo.
aponeurotomy *n.* aponeurotomía.
aponia *n.* aponia.
aponic *adj.* apónico, -ca.
apophlegmatic *adj.* apoflemático, -ca.
apophylactic *adj.* apofiláctico, -ca.
apophylaxis *n.* apofilaxis.
apophysary *adj.* apofisario, -ria.
apophyseal *adj.* apofisial.
apophyseopathy *n.* apofisopatía.
apophysial *adj.* apofisial.
apophysis *n.* apófisis.
apophysitis *n.* apofisitis.
  apophysitis tibialis adolescentium apofisitis tibial de los adolescentes.
apoplasmia *n.* apoplasmia.
apoplectic *adj.* apopléctico, -ca, apoplético, -ca.
apoplectiform *adj.* apoplectiforme.
apoplectoid *adj.* apoplectoide.
apoplexia *n.* apoplejía.
  apoplexia uterina apoplejía uterina.
apoplexy *n.* apoplejía.
  abdominal apoplexy apoplejía abdominal.
  adrenal apoplexy apoplejía suprarrenal.
  Broadbent's apoplexy apoplejía de Broadbent.
  bulbar apoplexy apoplejía bulbar.
  cerebellar apoplexy apoplejía cerebelar, apoplejía cerebelosa.
  cutaneous apoplexy apoplejía cutánea.
  delayed apoplexy apoplejía tardía.
  embolic apoplexy apoplejía embólica.
  functional apoplexy apoplejía funcional.
  heat apoplexy apoplejía por calor.
  ingravescent apoplexy apoplejía ingravescente.
  intestinal apoplexy apoplejía intestinal.
  neonatal apoplexy apoplejía neonatorum.
  pancreatic apoplexy apoplejía pancreática.
  pituitary apoplexy apoplejía hipofisaria, apoplejía pituitaria.
  placental apoplexy apoplejía placentaria.
  pontil apoplexy apoplejía pontina.
  pontile apoplexy apoplejía pontina.

  Raymond's apoplexy apoplejía tipo Raymond.
  renal apoplexy apoplejía renal.
  serous apoplexy apoplejía serosa.
  spasmodic apoplexy apoplejía espasmódica.
  spinal apoplexy apoplejía medular.
  thrombotic apoplexy apoplejía trombótica.
  uteroplacental apoplexy apoplejía uteroplacentaria.
apoprotein *n.* apoproteína.
apoptosis *n.* apoptosis.
aporepressor *n.* aporrepresor.
aposia *n.* aposia.
apostasis *n.* apostasis.
apostaxis *n.* apostaxia.
aposthia *n.* apostia.
apothanasia *n.* apotanasia.
apotoxin *n.* apotoxina.
apotripsis *n.* apotripsis.
apoxemena *n.* apoxemena.
apoxesis *n.* apoxesis.
apparatus *n.* aparato[1].
  Abbé-Zeiss apparatus aparato de Abbé-Zeiss.
  apparatus digestorius aparato digestivo.
  attachment apparatus aparato de fijación.
  Barcroft's apparatus aparato de Barcroft, aparato de Barcroft-Warburg.
  Barcroft-Warburg apparatus aparato de Barcroft, aparato de Barcroft-Warburg.
  Beckmann's apparatus aparato de Beckmann.
  digestive apparatus aparato digestivo.
  Fell-O'Dwyer apparatus aparato de Fell-O'Dwyer.
  Heyns' abdominal decompression apparatus aparato de descompresión abdominal de Heyns.
  Kirschner's apparatus aparato de Kirschner.
  masticatory apparatus aparato masticatorio.
  mucus trap suction apparatus aparato de aspiración de moco con válvula.
  respiratory apparatus aparato respiratorio.
  Sayre's apparatus aparato de Sayre.
  Soxhlet's apparatus aparato de Soxhlet.
  Taylor's apparatus aparato de Taylor.
  Tiselius apparatus aparato de Tiselius.
  Tobold's apparatus aparato de Tobold.
  urinary apparatus aparato urinario.
  Wangenstgeen's apparatus aparato de Wangestgeen.
  Warburg's apparatus aparato de Warburg.
appearance *n.* apariencia.
appendage *n.* apéndice.
appendalgia *n.* apendalgia, apendicalgia.
appendectomy *n.* apendectomía.
appendical *adj.* apendicular.
appendiceal *adj.* apendicular.
appendicectasis *n.* apendicectasia.
appendicectomy *n.* apendicectomía, apendicotomía.
appendicism *n.* apendicismo.
appendicitis *n.* apendicitis.
  actinomycotic appendicitis apendicitis actinomicótica.
  acute appendicitis apendicitis aguda.
  appendicitis by contiguity apendicitis por contigüedad.
  bilharzial appendicitis apendicitis bilharzial.
  chronic appendicitis apendicitis crónica.
  focal appendicitis apendicitis focal.
  foreign-body appendicitis apendicitis por cuerpo extraño.
  fulminating appendicitis apendicitis fulminante.

  gangrenous appendicitis apendicitis gangrenosa.
  left-sided appendicitis apendicitis izquierda.
  lumbar appendicitis apendicitis lumbar.
  obstructive appendicitis apendicitis obstructiva.
  perforating appendicitis apendicitis destructiva, apendicitis perforante, apendicitis perforativa.
  purulent appendicitis apendicitis purulenta.
  recurrent appendicitis apendicitis recurrente.
  segmental appendicitis apendicitis segmentaria.
  stercoral appendicitis apendicitis estercorácea.
  stercoreal appendicitis apendicitis estercorácea.
  subperitoneal appendicitis apendicitis subperitoneal.
  suppurative appendicitis apendicitis supurada, apendicitis supurativa.
  traumatic appendicitis apendicitis traumática.
  verminous appendicitis apendicitis verminosa.
appendiclausis *n.* apendiclausia, apendiclausis.
appendicocecostomy *n.* apendicocecostomía.
appendicocele *n.* apendicocele.
appendicoenterostomy *n.* apendicoenterostomía.
appendicolith *n.* apendicolito.
appendicolithiasis *n.* apendicolitiasis.
appendicolysis *n.* apendicólisis.
appendicopathia *n.* apendicopatía.
appendicopathy *n.* apendicopatía, apendicosis.
appendicostomy *n.* apendicostomía.
appendicular *adj.* apendicular.
appendix *n.* apéndice.
appendolithiasis *n.* apendicolitiasis.
apperception *n.* apercepción.
apperceptive *adj.* aperceptivo, -va.
appestat *n.* apestato.
appetite *n.* apetito.
  perverted appetite apetito pervertido.
appetition *n.* apetencia.
appetitive *adj.* apetitivo, -va.
applanation *n.* aplanación.
appliance *n.* aparato[2], dispositivo[1].
  Andresen appliance dispositivo de Andresen.
  Begg appliance dispositivo Begg.
  Bimler appliance dispositivo de Bimler.
  craniofacial appliance aparato craneofacial.
  Crozat appliance dispositivo de Crozat.
  Denholz appliance dispositivo de Denholz.
  edgewise appliance aparato de canto, dispositivo de borde.
  expansion plate appliance dispositivo de placa expansiva.
  extraoral appliance dispositivo extrabucal.
  extraoral fracture appliance aparato de fractura extraoral.
  extraoral orthodontic appliance dispositivo ortodóncico extraoral.
  fixed appliance dispositivo fijo.
  fixed orthodontic appliance dispositivo ortodóncico fijo.
  habit-braking appliance dispositivo rompe hábito.
  intraloral fracture appliance aparato de fractura intraoral.
  intraoral orthodontic appliance dispositivo ortodóncico intraoral.
  Jackson appliance dispositivo de Jackson.
  Johnson twin wire appliance dispositivo de alambre gemelo, dispositivo de alambre gemelo de Johnson.

jumping-the-bite appliance dispositivo de saltamordida.

Kesling appliance dispositivo de Kesling.

Kingsley appliance dispositivo de Kingsley.

Kloehn cervical extraoral orthodontic appliance aparato ortodóncico extraoral cervical de Kloehn.

labiolingual appliance aparato labiolingual, dispositivo labiolingual.

labiolingual fixed orthodontic appliance aparato ortodóncico labiolingual fijo.

light wire appliance aparato de alambre liviano.

monoblock appliance dispositivo monobloque.

obturator appliance aparato obturador.

orthodontic appliance aparato ortodóncico, dispositivo ortodóncico.

permanent appliance dispositivo permanente.

pin and tube fixed orthodontic appliance aparato ortodóncico fijo con clavijas y tubos.

removable orthodontic appliance aparato extraíble de ortodoncia.

retaining orthodontic appliance aparato ortodóncico de retención.

ribbon arch appliance aparato de arco de goma, dispositivo de arco de cinta.

Roger Anderson pin fixation appliance aparato de fijación con pernos de Roger Anderson.

Schwarz appliance dispositivo de Schwarz.

split plate appliance dispositivo de placa dividida.

straight wire fixed orthodontic appliance aparato ortodóncico fijo con alambre recto.

twin wire appliance dispositivo de alambre gemelo, dispositivo de alambre gemelo de Johnson.

twin-wire fixed orthodontic appliance aparato ortodóncico fijo con alambres gemelos.

universal appliance dispositivo universal.

Walker appliance dispositivo de Walker.

applicator *n.* aplicador.

apposition *n.* aposición.

apprehension *n.* aprehensión.

approach *n.* abordaje.

approximation *n.* aproximación.

apractagnosia *n.* apractagnosia.

apractic *adj.* apráctico, -ca.

apragmatism *n.* apragmatismo.

apraxia *n.* apraxia.

akinetic apraxia apraxia acinética.

amnestic apraxia apraxia amnésica.

apraxia for dressing apraxia del vestido.

Bruns' apraxia of gait apraxia de Bruns de la marcha.

constructional apraxia apraxia constructiva, apraxia de construcción.

cortical apraxia apraxia cortical.

developmental apraxia apraxia del desarrollo.

gait apraxia apraxia de la marcha.

ideational apraxia apraxia ideomotriz, apraxia de ideación, apraxia ideatoria.

ideokinetic apraxia apraxia clásica.

ideomotor apraxia apraxia ideomotora.

idiokinetic apraxia apraxia ideocinética.

innervation apraxia apraxia de inervación, apraxia inervatoria.

kinetic apraxia apraxia cinética.

limb-kinetic apraxia apraxia cinética de las extremidades, apraxia limbocinética.

motor apraxia apraxia motora, apraxia motriz.

ocular motor apraxia apraxia oculomotora (de Cogan).

sensory apraxia apraxia sensitiva.

transcortical apraxia apraxia transcortical.

apraxic *adj.* apráxico, -ca.

aproctia *n.* aprocia, aproctia.

aprosexia *n.* aprosexia.

aprosody *n.* aprosodia.

aprosopia *n.* aprosopia.

aprosopus *n.* aprósopo.

aprotinin *n.* aprotinina.

apselaphesia *n.* apselafesia.

apsithyria *n.* apsitiria.

aptitude *n.* aptitud.

aptness *n.* aptitud.

aptyalia *n.* aptialia.

aptyalism *n.* aptialismo.

apudoma *n.* apudoma.

apulmonism *n.* apulmonismo.

apyogenous *adj.* apiógeno, -na.

apyretic *adj.* apirético, -ca.

apyrexia *n.* apirexia.

apyrexial *adj.* apirético, -ca.

apyrogenic *adj.* apirógeno, -na.

aquagenic *adj.* acuagénico, -ca.

aquapuncture *n.* acuapuntura.

aquatic *adj.* acuático, -ca.

aqueduct *n.* acueducto, aqueductus.

aqueductus *n.* acueducto, aqueductus.

aqueous *adj.* acuoso, -sa.

aquocapsulitis *n.* acuocapsulitis.

aquosity *n.* acuosidad.

arabinosis *n.* arabinosis.

arabinosuria *n.* arabinosuria.

arachnidism *n.* aracnidismo.

arachnids *n.* arácnidos.

arachnitis *n.* aracnitis.

arachnodactyly *n.* aracnodactilia.

arachnoid *adj.* aracnoide.

arachnoidal *adj.* aracnoidal.

arachnoidea *n.* aracnoides.

arachnoidism *n.* aracnidismo, aracnoidismo.

arachnoiditis *n.* aracnoiditis.

chronic adhesive arachnoiditis aracnoiditis crónica adhesiva.

arachnolysin *n.* aracnolisina.

arachnopia *n.* aracnopía.

arachnorhinitis *n.* aracnorrinitis.

araneism *n.* araneísmo.

arbitrary inference *n.* inferencia arbitraria.

arbor *n.* árbol, árbor.

arboreal *adj.* arbóreo, -a.

arborescent *adj.* arborescente.

arborization *n.* arborización.

arboviral *adj.* arboviral.

Arbovirus *n.* Arbovirus.

arcade *n.* arcada.

dental arcade arcada Alveolar, arcada dentaria.

arch *n.* arco.

pharyngeal arch arco faríngeo.

reflex arch arco reflejo.

archaic *adj.* arcaico, -ca.

archecentric *adj.* arquecéntrico, -ca.

archencephalon *n.* arquencéfalo.

archenteron *n.* arquenterón.

archeocerebellum *n.* arquicerebelo.

archeocinetic *adj.* arqueocinético, -ca.

archeocortex *n.* arquicórtex, arquicorteza.

archeocyte *n.* arqueocito.

archeokinetic *adj.* arqueocinético, -ca.

archepyon *n.* arquepion.

archetype *n.* arquetipo.

archiblast *n.* arquiblasto.

archiblastic *adj.* arquiblástico, -ca.

archicerebellum *n.* arquicerebelo.

archicortex *n.* arquicórtex, arquicorteza.

archigaster *n.* arquigastro.

archinephros *n.* arquinefros.

archipallium *n.* arquipalio.

archiplasm *n.* arquiplasma.

archistoma *n.* arquistoma.

archistome *n.* arquistoma.

architis *n.* arquitis.

archocele *n.* arcocele.

archocystosyrinx *n.* arcocistosirinx.

archoptoma *n.* arcoptoma.

archoptosis *n.* arcoptosis.

archorrhagia *n.* arcorragia.

archorrhea *n.* arcorrea.

archostenosis *n.* arcostenosis.

archosyrinx *n.* arcosirinx.

arciform *adj.* arciforme.

arctation *n.* arctación, artación.

arcual *adj.* arcual.

arcuate *adj.* arcuato, -ta, arqueado, -da.

arcus *n.* arco, arcus.

arcus senilis arco senil.

ardanesthesia *n.* ardanestesia.

ardent *adj.* ardiente.

ardor *n.* ardor, escozor.

heartburn ardor ardor epigástrico.

area *n.* área, zona.

area germinativa área germinal, área germinativa.

area opaca área opaca.

area pellucida área pelúcida.

area vasculosa área vascular.

Broca's (motor speech) area área motora del habla de Broca.

Cohnheim's area área de Cohnheim.

denture foundation area área de sostén de dentadura.

denture-bearing area área de sostén de dentadura.

denture-supporting area área de sostén de dentadura.

embryonal area área embrionaria.

embryonic area área embrionaria.

general sensory area área somatosensitiva.

germinal area área germinal, área germinativa.

motor speech area of Broca área motora del habla de Broca.

paraolfactory area of Broca área paraolfatoria de Broca, área parolfatoria.

parolfactory area área paraolfatoria de Broca, área parolfatoria.

pressure area zona de presión.

relief area área de alivio, zona de descarga.

rest area área de descanso, zona de apoyo.

silent area of the brain área silenciosa.

somatic sensory area área somatosensitiva.

somatosensory area área somatosensitiva.

stress-bearing area área de soporte de tensión.

supporting area área de soporte.

areata *adj.* areata.

areflexia *n.* arreflexia.

aregenerative *adj.* arregenerativo, -va.

arenation *n.* arenación.

Arenaviridae *n.* Arenaviridae.

Arenavirus *n.* Arenavirus.

areola *n.* areola, aréola.

areola mammae areola de la mama, areola del pezón.

areola of mammary gland areola de la mama, areola del pezón.

areola of the nipple areola de la mama, areola del pezón.

areola papillaris areola papilar.

areola umbilicus areola umbilical.

Chaussier's areola areola de Chaussier.

second areola areola secundaria.

umbilical areola areola umbilical.
vaccinal areola areola vacunal.
areolar *adj.* areolar.
areolitis *n.* areolitis.
areometer *n.* areómetro.
areometric *adj.* areométrico, -ca.
areometry *n.* areometría.
argamblyopia *n.* argambliopía.
Argas *n.* Argas.
argasid *n.* argasino.
argema *n.* argema.
argentaffinoma *n.* argentafinoma.
  argentaffinoma of the bronchus argentafinoma bronquial.
argentation *n.* argentación.
argentoproteinum *n.* angentoproteína.
arginuria *n.* arginuria.
argiocardiography *n.* angiocardiografía.
argipresssin *n.* argipresina.
argyremia *n.* argiremia.
argyria *n.* argiria.
  argyria nasalis argiria nasal.
argyriasis *n.* argiriasis.
argyric *adj.* argírico, -ca.
argyrism *n.* argirismo.
argyrosis *n.* argirosis.
ariboflavinosis *n.* arriboflavinosis.
aristegenics *n.* aristogenia, aristogénica.
aristogenesis *n.* aristogénesis.
aristolochic *adj.* aristolóquico, -ca.
arithmomania *n.* aritmomanía.
arm *n.* brazo[1], brazo[2].
  arm swing braceo.
  bar clasp arm brazo en barra, brazo sujetador de barra.
  brawny arm brazo musculoso.
  chromosome arm brazo cromosoma.
  circumferential clasp arm brazo en broche circunferencial, brazo sujetador circunferencial.
  clasp arm brazo en broche.
  dynein arm brazo de dineína.
  glass arm brazo de vidrio.
  golf arm brazo de golfista.
  Krukenberg's arm brazo de Krukenberg.
  lawn tennis arm brazo de tenista.
  reciprocal arm brazo recíproco.
  retention arm brazo de retención.
  retentive arm brazo retentivo.
  retentive circumferential clasp arm brazo en broche circunferencial retentivo.
  stabilizing arm brazo estabilizador.
  stabilizing circumferential clasp arm brazo en broche circunferencial estabilizante.
armature *n.* armadura.
Armigeres *n.* Armigeres.
Armillifer *n.* Armillifer.
armless *adj.* manco, -ca.
armpit *n.* axila.
aroma *n.* aroma.
aromatic *adj.* aromático, -ca.
aromaticus *adj.* aromático, -ca.
aromatization *n.* aromatización.
arousal *n.* despertar[1].
arrachement *n.* arrancamiento.
arrangement *n.* disposición.
  tooth arrangement disposición de dientes.
arrector *adj.* arrector, -ra.
arrhaphia *n.* arrafia.
arrhenoblastoma *n.* arrenoblastoma.
arrhenogenic *adj.* arrenogénico, -ca.
arrhenoma *n.* arrenoma.
arrhinencephalia *n.* arrinencefalia.
arrhinencephaly *n.* arrinencefalia.
arrhinia *n.* arrinia.

arrhythmia *n.* arritmia.
  cardiac arrhythmia arritmia cardíaca.
  continuous arrhythmia arritmia continua.
  juvenile arrhythmia arritmia juvenil.
  perpetual arrhythmia arritmia perpetua.
  phasic arrhythmia arritmia fásica.
  respiratory arrhythmia arritmia respiratoria.
  sinus arrhythmia arritmia de seno, arritmia sinusal.
arrhythmic *adj.* arrítmico, -ca.
arrhythmogenic *adj.* arritmogénico, -ca.
arrhythmokinesis *n.* arritmocinesis.
arseniasis *n.* arseniasis.
arsenicalism *n.* arsenicalismo, arseniciasis, arsenicismo.
arsenic-fast *adj.* arsenicorresistente.
arsenicophagy *n.* arsenicofagia.
arsenism *n.* arsenismo.
arsenization *n.* arsenización.
arsenoactivation *n.* arsenoactivación.
arsenoatohemotherapy *n.* arsenoautohemoterapia.
arsenoautohemotherapy *n.* arsenoautohematoterapia.
arsenophagy *n.* arsenofagia.
arsenorelapsing *n.* arsenorrecidiva.
arsenoresistant *adj.* arsenorresistente.
arsenotherapy *n.* arsenoterapia.
arsonvalization *n.* arsonvalismo, arsonvalización.
artefact *n.* artefacto.
arteralgia *n.* arteralgia.
arterectomy *n.* arterectomía, arteriectomía.
arteria *n.* arteria.
arteriactia *n.* arteriactia.
arterial *adj.* arterial.
arterialization *n.* arterialización, arterización.
arteriectasia *n.* arteriectasia, arteriectasis.
arteriectasis *n.* arteriectasis.
arteriectomy *n.* arterectomía, arteriectomía.
arteriectopia *n.* arteriectopía.
arterioatony *n.* arterioatonía.
arteriocapillary *adj.* arteriocapilar.
arteriodilating *n.* arteriodilatación.
arteriogenesis *n.* arteriogénesis.
arteriogram *n.* arteriograma.
arteriographic *adj.* arteriográfico, -ca.
arteriography *n.* arteriografía.
  catheter arteriography arteriografía por sonda.
  cerebral arteriography arteriografía cerebral.
  selective coronary arteriography arteriografía selectiva coronaria.
  spinal arteriography arteriografía espinal.
arteriola *n.* arteriola.
arteriolar *adj.* arteriolar.
arteriole *n.* arteriola.
arteriolith *n.* arteriolito.
arteriolitis *n.* arteriolitis.
  necrotizing arteriolitis arteriolitis necrosante.
arteriology *n.* arteriología.
arteriolonecrosis *n.* arteriolonecrosis.
arteriolonephrosclerosis *n.* arteriolonefroesclerosis.
arteriolosclerosis *n.* arteriolosclerosis.
arteriolosclerotic *adj.* arteriolosclerótico, -ca.
arteriolovenous *adj.* arteriolovenoso, -sa.
arteriolovenular *adj.* arteriolovenular.
arteriomalacia *n.* arteriomalacia.
arteriometer *n.* arteriómetro.
arteriomotor *adj.* arteriomotor, -ra.
arteriomyomatosis *n.* arteriomiomatosis.
arterionecrosis *n.* arterionecrosis.
arterionephrosclerosis *n.* arterionefroesclerosis.

arteriopalmus *n.* arteriopalmus.
arteriopathy *n.* arteriopatía.
  hypertensive arteriopathy arteriopatía hipertensiva.
  plexogenic pulmonary arteriopathy arteriopatía pulmonar plexogénica.
arterioperissia *n.* arterioperisia.
arterioplania *n.* arterioplania.
arterioplasty *n.* arterioplastia.
arteriopressor *adj.* arteriopresor, -ra.
arteriorenal *adj.* arteriorrenal.
arteriorrhagia *n.* arteriorragia.
arteriorrhaphy *n.* arteriorrafia.
arteriorrhexis *n.* arteriorrexis.
arteriosclerosis *n.* arterioesclerosis, arteriosclerosis.
  arteriosclerosis obliterans arterioesclerosis obliterante.
  cerebral arteriosclerosis arterioesclerosis cerebral.
  coronary arteriosclerosis arterioesclerosis coronaria.
  diffuse arteriosclerosis arterioesclerosis difusa.
  hyaline arteriosclerosis arterioesclerosis hialina.
  hypertensive arteriosclerosis arterioesclerosis hipertensiva.
  infantile arteriosclerosis arterioesclerosis infantil.
  medial arteriosclerosis arterioesclerosis de la túnica media, arterioesclerosis medial.
  Mönckeberg's arteriosclerosis arterioesclerosis de Mönckeberg.
  nodular arteriosclerosis arterioesclerosis nodular, arterioesclerosis nudosa.
  peripheral arteriosclerosis arterioesclerosis periférica.
  presenile arteriosclerosis arterioesclerosis presenil.
  senile arteriosclerosis arterioesclerosis senil.
arteriosclerotic *adj.* arterioesclerótico, arteriosclerótico, -ca.
arteriospasm *n.* arterioespasmo, arteriospasmo.
arteriospastic *adj.* arterioespástico, -ca, arteriospástico, -ca.
arteriostenosis *n.* arterioestenosis, arteriostenosis.
arteriosteogenesis *n.* arteriosteogénesis.
arteriosteose *n.* arteriosteosis, arteriostosis.
arteriostosis *n.* arteriosteosis, arteriostosis.
arteriostrepsis *n.* arteriostrepsia, arteriostripsia, arteriotrepsia.
arteriosympathectomy *n.* arteriosimpatectomía.
arteriotome *n.* arteriótomo.
arteriotomy *n.* arteriotomía.
arteriotony *n.* arteriotonía.
arteriotrepsis *n.* arteriostrepsia, arteriostripsia, arteriotrepsia.
arterious *adj.* arterioso, -sa.
arteriovenosus *adj.* arteriovenoso, -sa.
arteriovenous *adj.* arteriovenoso, -sa.
arteritis *n.* arteritis.
  arteritis deformans arteritis deformante.
  arteritis hyperplastica arteritis hiperplásica.
  arteritis obliterans arteritis obliterante.
  arteritis umbilicalis arteritis umbilical.
  arteritis verrucosa arteritis verrugosa.
  coronary arteritis arteritis coronaria.
  cranial arteritis arteritis craneal.
  giant cell arteritis arteritis de células gigantes, arteritis gigantocelular.
  granulomatous arteritis arteritis granulomatosa.

Horton's arteritis arteritis de Horton.
infantile arteritis arteritis infantil.
localized visceral arteritis arteritis visceral localizada.
obliterating arteritis arteritis obliterante.
rheumatic arteritis arteritis reumática.
rheumatoid arteritis arteritis reumatoidea.
syphilitic arteritis arteritis sifilítica.
temporal arteritis arteritis temporal.
tuberculous arteritis arteritis tuberculosa.
arterocapillary *adj.* arteriocapilar.
artery *n.* arteria.
arthragra *n.* artragra.
arthral *adj.* artral.
arthralgia *n.* artralgia, artronalgia.
  arthralgia saturnina artralgia saturnina.
  intermittent arthralgia artralgia intermitente.
  periodic arthralgia artralgia periódica.
arthralgic *adj.* artrálgico, -ca.
arthrectomy *n.* artrectomía.
arthrempyesis *n.* artrempiesis.
arthresthesia *n.* artrestesia.
arthrifuge *n.* artrífugo, -ga.
arthritic *adj.* artrítico, -ca.
arthritide *n.* artrítide.
arthritis *n.* artritis.
  acute arthritis artritis aguda.
  acute gouty arthritis artritis gotosa aguda.
  acute rheumatic arthritis artritis reumática aguda.
  acute suppurative arthritis artritis aguda supurativa.
  arthritis deformans artritis deformante.
  arthritis fungosa artritis fúngica, artritis fungosa.
  arthritis hiemalis artritis hiemal, artritis hiemalis.
  arthritis mutilans artritis mutilante.
  arthritis nodosa artritis nudosa.
  arthritis sicca artritis seca.
  arthritis uratica artritis urática.
  arthritis urethritica artritis uretrítica.
  atrophic arthritis artritis atrófica.
  bacterial arthritis artritis bacteriana.
  Bechterew's arthritis artritis de Bechterew.
  chlamydial arthritis artritis clamidial.
  chronic inflammatory arthritis artritis inflamatoria crónica.
  chronic villous arthritis artritis vellosa crónica.
  climactic arthritis artritis climatérica.
  cricoarytenoid joint arthritis artritis cricoaritenoidea.
  degenerative arthritis artritis degenerativa.
  dysenteric arthritis artritis disentérica.
  exudative arthritis artritis exudativa.
  filarial arthritis artritis filarial.
  fungal arthritis artritis fúngica, artritis fungosa.
  gonoccocal arthritis artritis blenorrágica, artritis gonocócica, artritis gonorreica.
  gouty arthritis artritis gotosa.
  infectious arthritis artritis infecciosa.
  juvenile arthritis artritis juvenil, artritis juvenil crónica.
  juvenile chronic arthritis artritis juvenil, artritis juvenil crónica.
  juvenile rheumatoid arthritis artritis reumatoide juvenil.
  lyme arthritis artritis de lyme.
  menopausal arthritis artritis menopáusica.
  mycotic arthritis artritis micótica.
  neuropathic arthritis artritis neuropática.
  ochronotic arthritis artritis ocronótica.
  proliferative arthritis artritis proliferante.
  psoriatic arthritis artritis psoriásica.

  rheumatoid arthritis artritis reumatoide.
  rheumatoid arthritis of the spine artritis reumatoide del raquis.
  septic arthritis artritis séptica.
  suppurative arthritis artritis supurada.
  syphilitic arthritis artritis sifilítica.
  tuberculous arthritis artritis tuberculosa.
  uratic arthritis artritis urática.
  urethral arthritis artritis uretral.
  venereal arthritis artritis venérea.
  vertebral arthritis artritis vertebral.
  viral arthritis artritis vírica.
arthritism *n.* artritismo.
Arthrobacter *n.* Artrobacteria.
arthrocace *n.* artrocace.
arthrocele *n.* artrocele.
arthrocentesis *n.* artrocentesis.
arthrochalasis *n.* artrocalasia.
  arthrochalasis multiplex congenita artrocalasia múltiple congénita.
arthrochondritis *n.* artrocondritis.
arthroclasia *n.* artroclasia.
arthroclisis *n.* artrocleisis, artroclisis.
arthrodesis *n.* artrodesis.
  triple arthrodesis artrodesis triple.
arthrodia *n.* artrodia.
arthrodial *adj.* artrodial.
arthrodynia *n.* artrodinia.
arthrodynic *adj.* artrodínico, -ca.
arthrodysplasia *n.* artrodisplasia.
arthroempyesis *n.* artroempiesis.
arthroendoscopy *n.* artroendoscopia.
arthroereisis *n.* artroereisis.
arthrogenous *adj.* artrógeno, -na.
arthrogram *n.* artrograma.
arthrography *n.* artrografía.
arthrogriposis *n.* artrogriposis.
  arthrogriposis multiplex congenita artrogriposis congénita múltiple.
  congenital multiple arthrogriposis artrogriposis congénita múltiple.
arthrokatadysis *n.* artrocatadisis.
arthrokleisis *n.* artrocleisis, artroclisis.
arthrolith *n.* artrolito.
arthrologia *n.* artrología.
arthrology *n.* artrología.
arthrolysis *n.* artrólisis.
arthrometer *n.* artrómetro.
arthrometry *n.* artrometría.
arthroneuralgia *n.* artroneuralgia.
arthro-onychodysplasia *n.* artroonicodisplasia.
arthropathia *n.* artropatía.
  arthropathia ovariopriva artropatía ovariopriva.
  arthropathia psoriasica artropatía psoriásica.
arthropathic *adj.* artropático, -ca.
arthropathology *n.* artropatología.
arthropathy *n.* artropatía.
  Charcot's arthropathy artropatía de Charcot.
  chondrocalcific arthropathy artropatía condrocalcificada.
  diabetic arthropathy artropatía diabética.
  inflammatory arthropathy artropatía inflamatoria.
  neurogenic arthropathy artropatía neurógena.
  neuropathic arthropathy artropatía neuropática.
  osteopulmonary arthropathy artropatía osteopulmonar.
  static arthropathy artropatía estática.
  syphilitic arthropathy artropatía sifilítica.
  tabetic arthropathy artropatía tabética.
arthrophlysis *n.* artroflisis.
arthrophyma *n.* artrofima.

arthrophyte *n.* artrofito.
arthroplastic *adj.* artroplástico, -ca.
arthroplasty *n.* artroplastia.
arthropneumography *n.* artroneumografía.
arthropneumoroentgenography *n.* artroneumorradiografía.
arthropod *n.* artrópodo.
arthropodan *adj.* artropódico, -ca.
arthropodiasis *n.* artropodiasis.
arthropodic *adj.* artropódico, -ca.
arthropodous *adj.* artropódico, -ca.
arthropyosis *n.* artropiosis.
arthrorheumatism *n.* artrorreumatismo.
arthrorrhaphy *n.* artrorrafia.
arthroscintigram *n.* artrocentelleograma.
arthroscintigraphy *n.* artrocentelleografía.
arthrosclerosis *n.* artrosclerosis.
arthroscope *n.* artroscopio.
arthroscopy *n.* artroscopia.
arthrosis *n.* artrosis.
  arthrosis deformans artrosis deformans, artrosis deformante.
  temporomandibular arthrosis artrosis temporomandibular.
arthrospore *n.* artrospora.
arthrosteitis *n.* artrosteítis.
arthrostomy *n.* artrostomía.
arthrosynovitis *n.* artrosinovitis.
arthrotome *n.* artrótomo.
arthrotomy *n.* artrotomía.
arthrotropic *adj.* artrotrópico, -ca.
arthrotropy *n.* artrotropía.
articulare *n.* articulare.
articulate *adj.* articular.
articulated *adj.* articulado, -da.
articulatio *n.* articulación, articulatio.
articulation *n.* articulación.
articulator *n.* articulador.
  adjustable articulator articulador ajustable.
  dental articulator articulador dental.
  hinge articulator articulador en bisagra.
  line articulator articulador en plano.
  plain articulator articulador en plano.
  semiadjustable articulator articulador semiajustable.
articulatory *adj.* articulatorio, -ria.
articulostat *n.* articulóstato.
articulus *n.* artículo, articulus.
artifact *n.* artificio.
artificial *adj.* artificial.
artiodactylous *adj.* artiodáctilo, -la.
artrobacterium *n.* artrobacterium.
aryepiglottic *adj.* ariepiglótico, -ca.
aryepiglottidean *adj.* ariepiglótico, -ca.
arytenoepiglottic *adj.* aritenoepiglótico, -ca.
arytenoid *adj.* aritenoides.
arytenoidectomy *n.* aritenectomía, aritenoidectomía.
arytenoiditis *n.* aritenoiditis.
arytenoidopexia *n.* aritenoidopexia.
arytenoidopexy *n.* aritenoidopexia.
asacria *n.* asacria.
asaphia *n.* asafia.
asbestosis *n.* asbestosis.
ascariasis *n.* ascariasis.
  sarcoptic ascariasis ascariasis sarcóptica.
ascaricidal *adj.* ascaricida[2].
ascaricide *n.* ascaricida[1].
ascarid *n.* ascáride.
ascaridiasis *n.* ascaridiasis, ascaridosis.
ascaridole *n.* ascaridol.
ascaridosis *n.* ascaridiasis, ascaridosis.
Ascaris *n.* Ascaris.
ascertainment *n.* comprobación, determinación[1], indagación.

complete ascertainment comprobación completa, determinación completa, indagación completa.

incomplete ascertainment comprobación incompleta, determinación incompleta.

multiple ascertainment comprobación múltiple.

single ascertainment comprobación única, determinación aislada, indagación única.

truncate ascertainment comprobación truncada, determinación trunca, indagación truncada.

ascetospora *n.* ascetospora.

aschelminth *n.* asquelminto.

ascia *n.* ascia.

ascites *n.* ascitis.

ascites adiposus ascitis adiposa.

ascites chylosus ascitis quilosa.

ascites praecox ascitis precoz.

bloody ascites ascitis sanguinolenta.

chyliform ascites ascitis quiliforme.

chylous ascites ascitis quilosa.

exudative ascites ascitis exudativa.

fatty ascites ascitis grasa.

hemorrhagic ascites ascitis hemorrágica.

hydremic ascites ascitis hidrémica.

milky ascites ascitis lechosa.

preagonal ascites ascitis preagónica.

pseudochylous ascites ascitis seudoquilosa.

transudative ascites ascitis transudativa.

ascitic *adj.* ascítico, -ca.

ascitogenous *adj.* ascitógeno, -na.

Ascobolus *n.* Ascobolus.

ascorbemia *n.* ascorbemia, ascorbicemia.

ascorburia *n.* ascorburia.

asecretory *adj.* asecretorio, -ria.

asemasia *n.* asemasia.

asemia *n.* asemia.

asemia graphica asemia gráfica.

asemia mimica asemia mímica.

asemia verbalis asemia verbal.

asepsis *n.* asepsia, asepsis.

born out of asepsis nacido, -da sin asepsia.

integral asepsis asepsia integral.

aseptic *adj.* aséptico, -ca.

asepticism *n.* asepticismo.

asequence *n.* asecuencia.

asexual *adj.* asexual.

asexuality *n.* asexualidad.

asexualization *n.* asexualización.

asialia *n.* asialia.

asiaticoside *n.* asiaticósido.

asiderosis *n.* asiderosis.

asitia *n.* asitia.

asjike *n.* asjike.

asocial *adj.* asocial.

asoma *n.* asoma.

aspalosoma *n.* aspalosoma.

aspartylglycosaminuria *n.* aspartilglucosaminuria.

aspect *n.* aspecto.

dorsal aspect aspecto dorsal.

aspergillar *adj.* aspergilar.

aspergilloma *n.* aspergiloma.

aspergillomycosis *n.* aspergilomicosis.

aspergillosis *n.* aspergilosis.

aural aspergillosis aspergilosis aural, aspergilosis auricular.

bronchopneumonic aspergillosis aspergilosis bronconeumónica.

bronchopulmonary aspergillosis aspergilosis broncopulmonar.

disseminated aspergillosis aspergilosis diseminada.

invasive aspergillosis aspergilosis invasiva.

pulmonary aspergillosis aspergilosis pulmonar.

aspergillus *n.* Aspergillus.

aspergillustoxicosis *n.* aspergilotoxicosis.

aspermatism *n.* aspermia.

aspermia *n.* aspermia.

aspersion *n.* aspersión.

asphygmia *n.* asfigmia.

asphyxia *n.* asfixia.

asphyxia carbonica asfixia carbónica.

asphyxia livida asfixia lívida.

asphyxia neonatorum asfixia neonatal, asfixia neonatorum.

asphyxia pallida asfixia pálida.

asphyxia reticularis asfixia reticular.

blue asphyxia asfixia azul.

cyanotic asphyxia asfixia cianótica.

fetal asphyxia asfixia fetal.

local asphyxia asfixia local.

secondary asphyxia asfixia secundaria.

traumatic asphyxia asfixia traumática.

white asphyxia asfixia blanca.

asphyxial *adj.* asfíctico, -ca.

asphyxiant *adj.* asfixiante.

asphyxiate *v.* asfixiar.

aspirate *adj.* aspirado, -da, aspirar.

aspiration *n.* aspiración.

bronchoscopic aspiration aspiración broncoscópica.

meconium aspiration aspiración de meconio, aspiración meconial.

post-tussive aspiration aspiración postusiva.

vacuum aspiration aspiración al vacío.

aspirator *n.* aspirador.

vacuum aspirator aspirador de vacío.

asplenia *n.* asplenia.

asplenic *adj.* asplénico, -ca.

asporogenic *adj.* asporogénico, -ca.

asporogenous *adj.* asporógeno, -na.

asporous *adj.* asporoso, -sa.

asporulate *adj.* asporulado, -da.

assay *n.* ensayo, valoración[1].

aleatory assay ensayo aleatorio.

blastogenesis assay ensayo de blastogénesis.

CH50 assay ensayo CH50.

clonogenic assay ensayo clonogénico.

competitive binding assay ensayo de unión por competencia.

complement binding assay ensayo por unión del complemento.

double blind clinical assay ensayo clínico doble ciego.

clinical drug assay ensayo clínico de medicamentos.

EAC rosette assay ensayo de roseta EAC.

enzyme-linked immunosorbent assay ensayo de inmunoadsorción ligado a enzimas, ensayo enzimoinmunoensayo.

fourpoint assay valoración de cuatro puntos.

Grunstein-Hogness assay ensayo de Grunstein-Hogness.

hemolytic plaque assay ensayo de placa hemolítica.

immune assay valoración inmunitaria.

immunochemical assay ensayo inmunoquímico.

immunoradiometric assay ensayo inmunorradiométrico.

indirect assay ensayo indirecto.

Jerne plaque assay ensayo de la placa de Jerne.

lymphocyte proliferation assay ensayo de proliferación linfocitaria.

microbiological assay valoración microbiológica.

microhemagglutination assay for Treponema pallidum (MHA-TP) ensayo de microhemaglutinación-Treponema pallidum (MHA-TO).

microtoxicity assay ensayo de microtoxicidad.

radioligand assay ensayo de radioligando.

radioreceptor assay ensayo de radiorreceptores.

Raji cell assay ensayo de célula Raji.

rosette assay ensayo de roseta.

stem cell assay valoración de células madre.

Treponema pallidum hemagglutination assay (TPHA) ensayo de hemaglutinación por Treponema pallidum (EHTP).

assessment *n.* valoración[2].

assessment of the aging patient valoración del paciente anciano.

auditory system assessment valoración del sistema auditivo.

Brazelton assessment valoración de Brazelton.

Dubowitz assessment valoración de Dubowitz.

female reproductive system assessment valoración del aparato reproductor femenino.

gastrointestinal system assessment valoración del sistema gastrointestinal.

Gessel developmental assessment valoración del desarrollo de Gesell.

gestational assessment valoración gestacional.

home assessment valoración del domicilio.

integumentary system assessment valoración del sistema tegumentario.

lift assessment valoración del traslado.

musculoskeletal system assessment valoración del sistema musculoesquelético.

neurologic assessment valoración neurológica.

optic system assessment valoración del sistema óptico.

pain assessment valoración del dolor.

physical assessment valoración física.

respiratory assessment valoración respiratoria.

urinary system assessment valoración del aparato urinario.

assimilable *adj.* asimilable.

assimilation *n.* asimilación.

cultural assimilation asimilación cultural.

social assimilation asimilación social.

assistant *n.* soporte.

auxiliary assistant soporte auxiliar.

foil assistant soporte de oro laminar.

intermediate assistant soporte intermedio.

multiple assistant soporte múltiple.

primary assistant soporte primario.

secondary assistant soporte secundario.

terminal assistant soporte terminal.

associated *adj.* asociado, -da.

association *n.* asociación.

association of ideas asociación de ideas.

controlled association asociación controlada, asociación dirigida.

dream association asociación de sueño, asociación onírica.

free association asociación libre.

genetic association asociación genética.

assonance *n.* asonancia.

assortment *n.* agrupación.

astasia *n.* astasia.

astasia-abasia astasia abasia.

astatic *adj.* astático, -ca.

asteatosis *n.* asteatosis.

asteatosis cutis asteatosis del cutis.
aster *n.* áster.
sperm aster áster espermático.
astereognosis *n.* astereognosia, astereognosis.
astereognosy *n.* astereognosia, astereognosis.
asterion *n.* asterión.
asterixis *n.* asterixis.
asternal *adj.* asternal.
asternia *n.* asternia.
asteroid *n.* asteroide.
asthenia *n.* astenia, languidez.
asthenia gravis hypophyseogenea astenia grave hipofisiógena.
myalgic asthenia astenia miálgica.
neurocirculatory asthenia astenia neurocirculatoria.
tropical anhidrotic asthenia astenia anhidrótica tropical.
asthenic *adj.* asténico, -ca.
asthenobiosis *n.* astenobiosis.
asthenocoria *n.* astenocoria.
asthenometer *n.* astenómetro.
asthenope *n.* asténope.
asthenophobia *n.* astenofobia.
asthenopia *n.* astenopía.
accommodative asthenopia astenopía acomodativa.
muscular asthenopia astenopía muscular.
nervous asthenopia astenopía nerviosa, astenopía retinal.
neurasthenic asthenopia astenopía neurasténica.
asthenopic *adj.* astenópico, -ca.
asthenospermia *n.* astenospermia.
asthenoxia *n.* astenoxia.
asthma *n.* asma.
abdominal asthma asma abdominal.
allergic asthma asma alérgica.
alveolar asthma asma alveolar.
asthma convulsivum asma convulsiva.
atopic asthma asma atópica.
bacterial asthma asma bacteriana.
bronchial asthma asma bronquial.
bronchitic asthma asma bronquítica.
cardiac asthma asma cardíaca.
cat asthma asma de los gatos.
catarrhal asthma asma catarral.
cotton dust asthma asma por polvo de algodón.
diisocyanate asthma asma por diisocianato.
dust asthma asma por polvo.
essential asthma asma esencial.
extrinsic asthma asma extrínseca.
food asthma asma alimentaria.
hay asthma asma del heno.
Heberden's asthma asma de Heberden, asma enfisematosa.
horse asthma asma caballar, asma equina.
humid asthma asma húmeda.
infective asthma asma infecciosa.
intrinsic asthma asma intrínseca.
isocyanate asthma asma por isocianato.
Kopp's asthma asma de Kopp.
Millar's asthma asma de Millar.
miner's asthma asma de los mineros.
nervous asthma asma nerviosa.
pollen asthma asma por polen.
potter's asthma asma de los alfareros.
reflex asthma asma refleja.
renal asthma asma renal.
sexual asthma asma sexual.
spasmodic asthma asma espasmódica.
summer asthma asma de verano.
thymic asthma asma tímica.
true asthma asma verdadera.

Wichmann's asthma asma de Wichmann.
asthmatic *adj.* asmático, -ca.
asthmatogenic *adj.* asmógeno, -na.
asthmogenic *adj.* asmógeno, -na.
astigmagraph *n.* astigmágrafo.
astigmatic *adj.* astigmático, -ca.
astigmatism *n.* astigmatismo.
acquired astigmatism astigmatismo adquirido.
astigmatism against the rule astigmatismo anormal.
astigmatism with the rule astigmatismo de regla, astigmatismo de regla, astigmatismo normal.
compound astigmatism astigmatismo compuesto.
compound myopic astigmatism astigmatismo miópico compuesto.
congenital astigmatism astigmatismo congénito.
corneal astigmatism astigmatismo corneal.
direct astigmatism astigmatismo directo.
hypermetropic astigmatism astigmatismo hipermetrópico, astigmatismo hiperópico.
hyperopic astigmatism astigmatismo hipermetrópico, astigmatismo hiperópico.
inverse astigmatism astigmatismo inverso.
irregular astigmatism astigmatismo irregular.
lenticular astigmatism astigmatismo lenticular.
mixed astigmatism astigmatismo mixto.
myopic astigmatism astigmatismo miópico.
oblique astigmatism astigmatismo oblicuo.
physiological astigmatism astigmatismo fisiológico.
regular astigmatism astigmatismo regular.
reversed astigmatism astigmatismo revertido.
simple myopic astigmatism astigmatismo miópico simple.
astigmatometer *n.* astigmatómetro.
astigmatometry *n.* astigmatometría.
astigmatoscope *n.* astigmatoscopio.
astigmatoscopy *n.* astigmatoscopia.
astigmometer *n.* astigmómetro.
astigmometry *n.* astigmometría.
astigmoscope *n.* astigmoscopio.
astigmoscopy *n.* astigmoscopia.
astomatida *n.* astomatida.
astomatous *adj.* astomatoso, -sa.
astomia *n.* astomia.
astomous *adj.* ástomo, -ma.
astragalar *adj.* astragalino, -na.
astragalectomy *n.* astragalectomía.
astragalocalcanean *adj.* astragalocalcáneo, -a.
astragalocrural *adj.* astragalocrural.
astragalofibular *adj.* astragaloperoneo, -a.
astragaloscaphoid *adj.* astragaloescafoide.
astragalotibial *adj.* astragalotibial.
astragalus *n.* astrágalo.
astral *adj.* astral.
astriction *n.* astricción, astringencia.
astringent *n.* astringente.
astroblast *n.* astroblasto.
astroblastoma *n.* astroblastoma.
astrocinetic *adj.* astrocinético, -ca.
astrocyte *n.* astrocito.
astrocyte protoplasmaticum astrocito protoplasmático.
fibrous astrocyte astrocito fibroso.
protoplasmic astrocyte astrocito protoplásmico.
reactive astrocyte astrocito reactivo.
astrocytin *n.* astrocitina.
astrocytoma *n.* astrocitoma.

anaplastic astrocytoma astrocitoma anaplásico.
astrocytoma fibrillare astrocitoma fibrilar.
astrocytoma protoplasmaticum astrocitoma protoplasmático.
grade I astrocytoma astrocitoma de grado I.
grade II astrocytoma astrocitoma de grado II.
grade III astrocytoma astrocitoma de grado III.
grade IV astrocytoma astrocitoma de grado IV.
pilocytic astrocytoma astrocitoma pilocítico.
piloid astrocytoma astrocitoma piloide.
astrocytosis *n.* astrocitosis.
astroependymoma *n.* astroependimoma.
astroglia *n.* astroglia.
astroid *adj.* astroide.
astrokinetic *adj.* astrocinético, -ca.
astroma *n.* astroma.
astrosphere *n.* astrosfera.
astrostatic *adj.* astrostático, -ca.
asulfurosis *n.* asulfurosis.
asylum *n.* asilo.
asymbolia *n.* asimbolia.
pain asymbolia asimbolia dolorosa.
asymmetric *adj.* asimétrico, -ca.
asymmetrical *adj.* asimétrico, -ca.
asymmetry *n.* asimetría.
chromatic asymmetry asimetría cromática.
asymphytous *adj.* asínfitos.
asymptomatic *adj.* asintomático, -ca.
asynapsis *n.* asinapsis.
asynchronism *n.* asincronismo.
asynchrony *n.* asincronía.
asynclitism *n.* asinclitismo.
anterior asynclitism asinclitismo anterior.
posterior asynclitism asinclitismo posterior.
asyndesis *n.* asindesis.
asynechia *n.* asinequia.
asynergia *n.* asinergia.
asynergic *adj.* asinérgico, -ca.
asynergy *n.* asinergia.
asynertic *adj.* asinérgico, -ca.
asynesia *n.* asinesia.
asynesis *n.* asinesia.
asynovia *n.* asinovia.
asystematic *adj.* asistemático, -ca.
asystole *n.* asistolia.
asystolia *n.* asistolia.
asystolic *adj.* asistólico, -ca.
atactic *adj.* atáctico, -ca.
atactiform *adj.* atactiforme.
ataractic *adj.* ataráctico, -ca.
ataralgesia *n.* ataragelsia.
ataraxia *n.* ataraxia.
ataraxic *adj.* ataráxico, -ca.
atavic *adj.* atávico, -ca.
atavism *n.* atavismo.
atavistic *adj.* atávico, -ca.
ataxaphasia *n.* ataxafasia.
ataxia *n.* ataxia.
acute ataxia ataxia aguda.
acute cerebellar ataxia ataxia cerebelosa aguda.
alcoholic ataxia ataxia alcohólica.
ataxia cordis ataxia cardíaca, ataxia cordis.
ataxia telangiectasia ataxia telangiectasia.
autonomic ataxia ataxia autónoma.
Briquet's ataxia ataxia de Briquet.
Broca's ataxia ataxia de Broca.
central ataxia ataxia central.
cerebellar ataxia ataxia cerebelosa.
cerebral ataxia ataxia cerebral.
Ferguson and Critchley's ataxia ataxia de Ferguson y Critchley.

Friedreich's ataxia ataxia de Friedreich, ataxia familiar de Friedreich.
frontal ataxia ataxia frontal.
hereditary ataxia ataxia hereditaria.
hereditary cerebellar ataxia ataxia cerebelosa hereditaria.
hereditary spinal ataxia ataxia espinal hereditaria.
hysterical ataxia ataxia histérica.
intrapsychic ataxia ataxia intrapsíquica.
kinetic ataxia ataxia cinética, ataxia dinámica.
labyrinthic ataxia ataxia laberíntica.
Leyden's ataxia ataxia de Leyden.
locomotor ataxia ataxia locomotora, ataxia locomotriz.
Marie's ataxia ataxia de Marie.
motor ataxia ataxia motora, ataxia motriz.
ocular ataxia ataxia ocular.
optic ataxia ataxia óptica.
Sanger Brown ataxia ataxia de sanger brown.
sensory ataxia ataxia sensitiva.
spinal ataxia ataxia espinal.
spinocerebellar ataxia ataxia espinocerebelosa.
static ataxia ataxia estática.
thermal ataxia ataxia térmica.
truncal ataxia ataxia troncal.
vasomotor ataxia ataxia vasomotora.
vestibular ataxia ataxia vestibular.
vestibulocerebellar ataxia ataxia vestibulocerebelosa.
ataxiadynamia *n.* ataxiadinamia.
ataxiaphasia *n.* ataxafasia.
ataxic *adj.* atáxico, -ca.
ataxiophemia *n.* ataxiofemia, ataxofemia.
ataxiophobia *n.* ataxiofobia.
ataxoadynamia *n.* ataxiadinamia, ataxoadinamia.
ataxophobia *n.* ataxiofobia, ataxofobia.
atelectasis *n.* atelectasia.
acquired absorption atelectasis atelectasia por absorción adquirida.
acquired atelectasis atelectasia adquirida.
compression atelectasis atelectasia compresiva.
congenital atelectasis atelectasia congénita.
initial atelectasis atelectasia inicial.
lobular atelectasis atelectasia lobular.
obstructive atelectasis atelectasia obstructiva.
patchy atelectasis atelectasia irregular.
primary atelectasis atelectasia primaria.
relaxation atelectasis atelectasia por relajación.
resorption atelectasis atelectasia por resorción.
secondary atelectasis atelectasia secundaria.
segmental atelectasis atelectasia segmentaria.
atelectatic *adj.* atelectásico, -ca.
atelencephalia *n.* atelencefalia.
atelia *n.* atelia[1].
atelocardia *n.* atelocardia.
atelocephalous *adj.* atelocéfalo, -la.
atelocephaly *n.* atelocefalia.
atelocheilia *n.* ateloqueilia.
atelocheiria *n.* ateloquiria.
ateloencephalia *n.* ateloencefalia.
ateloglossia *n.* ateloglosia.
atelognathia *n.* atelognatia.
atelomyelia *n.* atelomielia.
atelopodia *n.* atelopodia.
ateloprosopia *n.* ateloprosopia.
atelorachidia *n.* atelorraquidia.
atelostomia *n.* atelostomía.
athelia *n.* atelia[2].

athermal *adj.* atermal.
athermancy *n.* atermancia.
athermanous *adj.* atérmano, -na.
athermic *adj.* atérmico, -ca.
athermosystaltic *adj.* atermosistáltico, -ca.
atheroembolism *n.* ateroembolia, ateroembolismo.
atheroembolus *n.* ateroémbolo.
atherogenesis *n.* aterogénesis.
atherogenic *adj.* aterogenético, -ca, aterogénico, -ca.
atheroma *n.* ateroma.
atheromatosis *n.* ateromatosis.
atheromatous *adj.* ateromatoso, -sa.
atheronecrosis *n.* ateronecrosis.
atherosclerosis *n.* aterosclerosis.
atherosclerotic *adj.* aterosclerótico, -ca.
atherosis *n.* aterosis.
atherothrombosis *n.* aterotrombosis.
atherothrombotic *adj.* aterotrombótico, -ca.
athetoid *adj.* atetoide.
athetosic *adj.* atetósico, -ca, atetótico, -ca.
athetosis *n.* atesia, atetosis.
double congenital athetosis atetosis congénita doble.
posthemiplegic athetosis atetosis poshemipléjica.
pupillary athetosis atetosis pupilar.
athetotic *adj.* atetósico, -ca, atetótico, -ca.
athiaminosis *n.* atiaminosis.
athletic *adj.* atlético, -ca.
athrepsia *n.* atrepsia.
athrocytosis *n.* atrocitosis.
athrombia *n.* atrombasis, atrombia.
athrophagocytosis *n.* atrofagocitosis.
athrophedema *n.* atrofedema.
athymia *n.* atimia.
athymism *n.* atimismo.
athyrea *n.* atirea.
athyreosis *n.* atireosis, atirosis.
athyreotic *adj.* atireótico, -ca, atirótico, -ca.
athyria *n.* atiria.
athyroidemia *n.* atiroidemia.
athyroidism *n.* atiroidismo, atiroismo.
athyroidosis *n.* atiroidia, atiroidosis.
athyrosis *n.* atireosis, atirosis.
athyrotic *adj.* atireótico, -ca, atirótico, -ca.
atlantal *adj.* atlantal.
atlantoaxial *adj.* atlantoaxil.
atlantoaxoid *adj.* atloidoaxoideo, -a.
atlantodidymus *n.* atlantodídimo.
atlantoepistrophic *adj.* atloidoepistrófico, -ca.
atlantomastoid *adj.* atlantomastoideo, -a.
atlanto-occipital *adj.* atlantooccipital.
atlanto-odontoid *adj.* atlantoodontoideo, -a.
atlas *n.* atlas.
atloaxoid *adj.* atloaxoide.
atlodidymus *n.* atlódimo.
atloid *adj.* atloideo, -a.
atloido-occipital *n.* atloidooccipital.
atmiatrics *n.* atmiatría, atmidiatría.
atmiatry *n.* atmiatría, atmidiatría.
atmocausis *n.* atmocausis.
atmocautery *n.* atmocauterio.
atmograph *n.* atmógrafo.
atmolysis *n.* atmólisis.
atmometer *n.* atmómetro.
atmotherapy *n.* atmoterapia.
atocia *n.* atocia, atoquia.
atom *n.* átomo.
excited atom átomo excitado.
ionized atom átomo ionizado.
radioactive atom átomo radiactivo.
atomization *n.* atomización.
atomizer *n.* atomizador.

atonic *adj.* atónico, -ca.
atonicity *n.* atonicidad.
atony *n.* atonía.
atopen *n.* atopeno.
atopia *n.* atopia.
atopic *adj.* atópico, -ca.
atopognosia *n.* atopognosia.
atoxic *adj.* atóxico, -ca.
atransferrinemia *n.* atransferrinemia.
atraumatic *adj.* atraumático, -ca.
atremia *n.* atremia.
atresia *n.* atresia.
anal atresia atresia del ano.
aortic atresia atresia aórtica.
atresia iridis atresia del iris, atresia irídica.
aural atresia atresia aural.
biliary atresia atresia biliar.
choanal atresia atresia de las coanas.
duodenal atresia atresia duodenal.
esophageal atresia atresia esofágica.
follicular atresia atresia folicular.
intestinal atresia atresia intestinal.
mitral atresia atresia mitral.
prepyloric atresia atresia prepilórica.
pulmonary atresia atresia pulmonar.
tricuspid atresia atresia tricúspide, atresia tricuspídea.
vaginal atresia atresia vaginal.
atresic *adj.* atrésico, -ca, atrético, -ca.
atretoblepharia *n.* atretoblefaria.
atretocephalus *n.* atretocéfalo.
atretocormus *n.* atretocormo.
atretocystia *n.* atretocistia.
atretogastria *n.* atretogastria.
atretolemia *n.* atretolemia.
atretometria *n.* atretometría.
atretopsia *n.* atretopsia.
atretorrhinia *n.* atretorrinia.
atretostomia *n.* atretostomía.
atreturethria *n.* atreturetria.
atrial *adj.* atrial.
atrichia *n.* atriquia, atriquiasis.
universal congenital atrichia atriquia universal congénita.
atrichosis *n.* atricosis.
atrichous *adj.* atricoso, -sa.
atriocommissuropexy *n.* atriocomisuropexia.
atriomegaly *n.* atriomegalia.
atriopeptigen *n.* atriopeptinógeno.
atriopeptin *n.* atriopeptina.
atrioseptopexy *n.* atrioseptopexia.
atrioseptoplasty *n.* atrioseptoplastia.
atrioseptostomy *n.* atrioseptostomía.
atriotome *n.* atriótomo.
atriotomy *n.* atriotomía.
atrioventricular *adj.* atrioventricular.
atrioventricularis comunis *n.* atrioventricularis comunis.
atriplicism *n.* atriplicismo.
atrium *n.* atrio, atrium, aurícula.
atrophia *n.* atrofia.
atrophic *adj.* atrófico, -ca.
atrophied *adj.* atrofiado, -da.
atrophoderma *n.* atrofoderma, atrofodermia.
atrophoderma albidum atrofodermia álbida.
atrophoderma biotripticum atrofoderma biotripticum, atrofodermia biotríptica.
atrophoderma diffussum atrofodermia difusa.
atrophoderma neuriticum atrofoderma neuriticum, atrofodermia neurítica.
atrophoderma pigmentosum atrofodermia pigmentoso.
atrophoderma reticulatum symmetricum faciei atrofoderma reticulatum simetricum

faciei, atrofodermia reticular simétrica facial.

atrophoderma senile atrofodermia senil.

atrophoderma vermiculare atrofodermia vermicular.

senile atrophoderma atrofodermia senil.

atrophodermatosis *n.* atrofodermatosis.

atrophy *n.* aridura, atrofia.

acute yellow atrophy of the liver atrofia amarilla aguda del hígado.

Aran-Duchenne muscular atrophy atrofia muscular de Aran-Duchenne, atrofia muscular de Duchenne-Aran.

arthritic atrophy atrofia artrítica.

atrophy bulbi atrofia del globo ocular.

atrophy choroideae et retinae atrofia coroidea retiniana.

atrophy corticostriatospinal atrofia corticostriatospinal.

atrophy cutis atrofia cutis.

atrophy cutis idiopathica atrofia dérmica idiopática.

atrophy maculosa cutis atrofia maculosa cutánea.

atrophy maculosa varioliformis cutis atrofia maculosa varioliformis cutis.

atrophy mesenterica atrofia mesentérica.

atrophy muscularum lipomatosa atrofia muscular lipomatosa.

atrophy of disuse atrofia por desuso, atrofia por inacción.

atrophy striata et maculosa atrofia estriada y maculosa.

atrophy unguium atrofia ungueal.

blue atrophy atrofia azul.

bone atrophy atrofia ósea.

brown atrophy atrofia parda.

Buchwald's atrophy atrofia de Buchwald.

cerebellar atrophy atrofia cerebelosa.

Charcot-Marie-Tooth type peroneal muscular atrophy atrofia de Charcot-Marie-Tooth.

circumscribed cerebral atrophy atrofia cerebral circunscrita.

compensatory atrophy atrofia compensadora, atrofia compensatoria.

compression atrophy atrofia por compresión.

concentric atrophy atrofia concéntrica.

correlated atrophy atrofia correlativa.

Cruveilhier's atrophy atrofia de Cruveilhier.

cyanotic atrophy atrofia cianótica.

cyanotic atrophy of the liver atrofia cianótica hepática.

degenerative atrophy atrofia degenerativa.

Déjerine-Sottas type atrophy atrofia de Déjerine-Sottas.

Déjerine-Thomas atrophy atrofia de Déjerine-Thomas.

denervated muscle atrophy atrofia muscular por denervación.

Duchenne-Aran muscular atrophy atrofia muscular de Aran-Duchenne, atrofia muscular de Duchenne-Aran.

eccentric atrophy atrofia excéntrica.

Eichhort's atrophy atrofia de Eichhort.

endocrine atrophy atrofia endocrina.

endometrial atrophy atrofia endometrial.

essential atrophy of the iris atrofia esencial del iris.

exhaustion atrophy atrofia por agotamiento.

facioscapulohumeral atrophy atrofia fascioescapulohumeral.

familial spinal muscular atrophy atrofia muscular espinal familiar.

fatty atrophy atrofia adiposa, atrofia grasa.

Fazio-Londe atrophy atrofia de Fazio-Londe.

Fuchs' atrophy atrofia de Fuchs.

gastric atrophy atrofia gástrica, gastratrofia.

gingival atrophy atrofia gingival.

granular atrophy of the kidney atrofia granular del riñón, atrofia granulosa del riñón.

gray atrophy atrofia gris.

gyrate atrophy of choroid and retina atrofia anular de la coroides y la retina, atrofia girada de la coroides y la retina.

healed yellow atrophy atrofia amarilla cicatrizada.

hemifacial atrophy atrofia hemifacial.

hemilingual atrophy atrofia hemilingual.

Hoffmann's muscular atrophy atrofia de Hoffmann.

Hunt's atrophy atrofia de Hunt.

idiopathic muscular atrophy atrofia muscular idiopática.

infantile atrophy atrofia infantil.

inflammatory atrophy atrofia inflamatoria.

interstitial atrophy atrofia intersticial.

ischemic muscular atrophy atrofia muscular isquémica.

Jadassohn's macular atrophy atrofia maculosa de Jadassohn.

juvenile muscular atrophy atrofia muscular juvenil.

Kienböck's atrophy atrofia de Kienböck.

lactation atrophy atrofia de la lactación.

leaping atrophy atrofia saltatoria.

Leber's hereditary optic atrophy atrofia óptica de Leber.

linear atrophy atrofia lineal.

lobar atrophy atrofia lobular.

marantic atrophy atrofia marántica.

muscular atrophy atrofia muscular.

myelopathic muscular atrophy atrofia muscular mielopática.

myopathic muscular atrophy atrofia miopática.

neuritic atrophy atrofia neurítica.

neuritic muscular atrophy atrofia muscular neurítica.

neurogenic atrophy atrofia neurogénica.

neuropathic atrophy atrofia neuropática.

neurotic atrophy atrofia neurótica.

neurotrophic atrophy atrofia neurotrófica.

numeric atrophy atrofia numérica.

olivopontocerebellar atrophy atrofia olivopontocerebelosa.

optic atrophy atrofia óptica.

pallidal atrophy atrofia pálida.

Parrot atrophy of the newborn atrofia de Parrot de los recién nacidos, atrofia de Parrot del neonato.

pathologic atrophy atrofia patológica.

periodontal atrophy atrofia periodontal.

physiologic atrophy atrofia fisiológica.

Pick's convolutional atrophy atrofia de Pick de las circunvoluciones.

pigmentary atrophy atrofia pigmentaria.

post-traumatic atrophy of bone atrofia postraumática de los huesos.

pressure atrophy atrofia por compresión.

primary optic atrophy atrofia óptica primaria.

progressive choroidal atrophy atrofia coroidea progresiva.

progressive muscular atrophy atrofia muscular progresiva.

progressive neuropathic peroneal muscular atrophy atrofia muscular peronea neuropática progresiva.

progressive unilateral facial atrophy atrofia facial unilateral progresiva.

pulp atrophy atrofia de la pulpa, atrofia pulpar.

receptoric atrophy atrofia receptora.

red atrophy atrofia roja.

rheumatic atrophy atrofia reumática.

scapulohumeral atrophy atrofia escapulohumeral.

Schweninger-Buzzi macular atrophy atrofia maculosa de Schweninger-Buzzi.

secondary optic atrophy atrofia óptica secundaria.

senile atrophy atrofia senil.

senile atrophy of the skin atrofia senil cutánea, atrofia senil de la piel.

serous atrophy atrofia serosa.

simple atrophy atrofia simple.

spinal atrophy atrofia espinal.

spinal muscular atrophy atrofia muscular espinal.

subacute yellow atrophy of the liver atrofia amarilla subaguda del hígado.

Sudeck's atrophy atrofia de Sudeck, atrofia ósea de Sudeck.

toxic atrophy atrofia tóxica.

traction atrophy atrofia por tracción.

transneuronal atrophy atrofia transneuronal.

trophoneurotic atrophy atrofia trofoneurótica.

vascular atrophy atrofia vascular.

von Leber's atrophy atrofia de von Leber.

Vulpian's atrophy atrofia de Vulpian.

Werdnig-Hoffmann atrophy atrofia de Werdnig-Hoffmann.

Werdnig-Hoffmann spinal muscular atrophy atrofia muscular espinal de Werdnig-Hoffmann.

white atrophy atrofia blanca.

Zimmerlin's atrophy atrofia de Zimmerlin.

atropinism *n.* atropinismo, atropismo.

atropinization *n.* atropinización.

attachment *n.* inserción, unión[1].

edgewise attachment unión por el borde.

epithelial attachment (of Gottlieb) inserción epitelial (de Gottlieb), unión epitelial (de Gottlieb).

extracoronal attachment unión extracoronal.

friction attachment unión de fricción, unión friccional.

frictional attachment unión de fricción, unión friccional.

internal attachment unión interna.

internal friction attachment inserción de fricción interna, inserción de fricción paralela.

intracoronal attachment unión intracoronal.

key attachment unión en llave, unión llave y paso de llave.

key-and-keyway attachment unión en llave, unión llave y paso de llave.

orthodontic attachment unión ortodóntica.

parallel attachment unión paralela.

parallel friction attachment inserción de fricción interna, inserción de fricción paralela.

pericemental attachment unión pericemental.

precision attachment inserción de precisión, unión de precisión.

slotted attachment unión intracoronal.

attack *n.* acceso[2], ataque.

heart attack ataque cardíaco.

panic attack ataque de pánico.

salaam attack ataque salutatorio.

sleep attack ataque de sueño.

transient ischemic attack ataque isquémico transitorio.

vagal attack ataque vagal.

vasovagal attack ataque vasovagal.

attention *n.* atención.

attenuant *adj.* atenuador, -ra, atenuante.
attenuate *v.* atenuar.
attenuation *n.* atenuación.
attenuator *n.* atenuador.
attic *n.* ático.
atticitis *n.* aticitis.
atticoantrotomy *n.* aticoantrotomía.
atticomastoid *adj.* aticomastoideo, -a.
atticotomy *n.* aticotomía.
attitude *n.* actitud.
  antalgic attitude actitud antálgica.
  attitude of combat actitud de combate.
  cruxifixion attitude actitud de crucifijo, actitud de crucifixión.
  deflexion attitude actitud de deflexión.
  Devergie's attitude actitud de Devergie.
  discobolus attitude actitud de discóbolo.
  emotional attitude actitud emocional.
  fetal attitude actitud fetal.
  forced attitude actitud forzada.
  frozen attitude actitud glacial.
  illogical attitude actitud ilógica.
  passional attitude actitud pasional.
  passionate attitude actitud apasionada.
  pugilistic attitude actitud de boxeador.
  stereotyped attitude actitud estereotipada.
  Wernicke-Mann's attitude actitud de Wernicke-Mann.
attraction *n.* atracción.
  capillary attraction atracción capilar.
  chemical attraction atracción química.
  electric attraction atracción eléctrica.
  magnetic attraction atracción magnética.
attrition *n.* atrición.
atypia *n.* atipia.
atypical *adj.* atípico, -ca.
atypism *n.* atipismo.
au-antigenemia *n.* au-antigenemia.
audible *adj.* audible.
audimutitas *n.* audimutismo.
audioanalgesia *n.* audioanalgesia.
audiogenic *adj.* audiogénico, -ca.
audiogram *n.* audiograma.
audiologist *n.* audiólogo, -ga.
audiology *n.* audiología.
audiometer *n.* audiómetro.
  automatic audiometer audiómetro automático.
  Békésy audiometer audiómetro de Békésy.
  evoked response audiometer audiómetro de respuesta evocada.
  group audiometer audiómetro de grupo.
  limited range audiometer audiómetro de rango limitado.
  pure tone audiometer audiómetro de tonos puros.
  speech audiometer audiómetro de lenguaje.
  wide range audiometer audiómetro de rango amplio.
audiometric *adj.* audiométrico, -ca.
audiometrician *n.* audiometrista.
audiometrist *n.* audiometrista.
audiometry *n.* audiometría.
  Békésy audiometry audiometría de Békésy.
  brainstem evoked response (BSER) audiometry audiometría de respuesta evocada del tronco encefálico.
  cortical audiometry audiometría cortical.
  diagnostic audiometry audiometría diagnóstica.
  electrocochleographic audiometry audiometría electrococleográfica.
  electrodermal audiometry audiometría electrodérmica.
  group audiometry audiometría de grupo.

  localization audiometry audiometría de localización.
  pure tone audiometry audiometría de tonos puros.
  speech audiometry audiometría del habla, audiometría del lenguaje.
audition *n.* audición.
  chromatic audition audición coloreada, audición cromática.
  gustatory audition audición gustativa, audición gustatoria.
auditive *adj.* auditivo, -va.
auditognosis *n.* auditognosis.
auditory *adj.* auditivo, -va.
augmentor *adj.* aumentador, -ra.
augnathus *n.* augnato.
auliplexus *n.* auliplexo.
aura *n.* aura.
  auditory aura aura auditiva.
  aura asthmatica aura asmática.
  aura hysterica aura histérica.
  electric aura aura eléctrica.
  epigastric aura aura epigástrica.
  epileptic aura aura epiléptica.
  intellectual aura aura intelectual.
  kinesthetic aura aura cinestésica.
  reminescent aura aura reminiscente.
  vertiginous aura aura vertiginosa.
aural *adj.* aural.
auramine *n.* auramina.
aurantiasis *n.* aurantiasis.
auriasis *n.* auriasis.
auric *adj.* aúrico, -ca.
auricle *n.* orejuela.
auricula *n.* orejuela.
auricular *adj.* auricular.
  auricular finger auricular, meñique.
auriculocranial *adj.* auriculocraneal.
auriculotemporal *adj.* auriculotemporal.
auriculotherapy *n.* auriculoterapia.
auriculoventricular *adj.* auriculoventricular.
auriform *adj.* auriforme.
aurinasal *adj.* aurinasal.
auripuncture *n.* auripuntura.
auris *n.* oído.
  auris externa auris externa, oído externo.
  auris interna auris interna, oído interno.
  auris media auris media, oído medio.
auriscalpium *n.* auriscalpo.
auriscope *n.* auriscopio.
aurist *n.* otólogo, -ga.
aurochromoderma *n.* aurocromodermia.
aurometer *n.* aurómetro.
aurotherapy *n.* auroterapia.
auscult *v.* auscultar.
auscultate *v.* auscultar.
auscultation *n.* auscultación.
  direct auscultation auscultación directa.
  immediate auscultation auscultación inmediata.
  Korányi's auscultation auscultación de Korányi.
  mediate auscultation auscultación mediata.
  obstetric auscultation auscultación obstétrica.
auscultatory *adj.* auscultatorio, -ria.
auscultoscope *n.* auscultoscopio.
austral *n.* haustral.
autacoid *n.* autacoide.
autarcesiology *n.* autarcesiología.
autarcesis *n.* autarcesis.
autarcetic *adj.* autarcético, -ca.
autecic *adj.* autécico, -ca.
autemesia *n.* autemesia.
autism *n.* autismo.
autistic *adj.* autista.
autoactivation *n.* autoactivación.

autoagglutination *n.* autoaglutinación.
autoagglutinin *n.* autoaglutinina.
  cold autoagglutinin crioautoaglutinina.
autoallergic *adj.* autoalérgico, -ca.
autoallergization *n.* autoalergización.
autoallergy *n.* autoalergia.
autoamputation *n.* autoamputación.
autoanalysis *n.* autoanálisis.
autoanalyzer *n.* autoanalizador.
autoanamnesis *n.* autoanamnesis.
autoanaphylaxis *n.* autoanafilaxia, autoanafilaxis.
autoantibody *n.* autoanticuerpo.
  cold autoantibody autoanticuerpo frío.
  warm autoantibody autoanticuerpo caliente.
autoanticomplement *n.* autoanticomplemento.
autoantigen *n.* autoantígeno.
autoantisepsis *n.* autoantisepsia.
autoantitoxin *n.* autoantitoxina.
autoassay *n.* autoensayo.
autoaudible *adj.* autoaudible.
autobacteriophage *n.* autobacteriófago.
autocatalysis *n.* autocatálisis.
autocatalytic *adj.* autocatalítico, -ca.
autocatharsis *n.* autocatarsis.
autocatheterism *n.* autocateterismo.
autocholecystectomy *n.* autocolecistectomía.
autocinesis *n.* autocinesis.
autoclasia *n.* autoclasia, autoclasis.
autoclasis *n.* autoclasis.
autoclave *n.* autoclave.
autoconduction *n.* autoconducción.
autocystoplasty *n.* autocistoplastia.
autocytolysin *n.* autocitolisina.
autocytolysis *n.* autocitólisis.
autocytolytic *adj.* autocitolítico, -ca.
autocytotoxin *n.* autocitotoxina.
autodermic *adj.* autodérmico, -ca.
autodigestion *n.* autodigestión.
autodrainage *n.* autodrenaje.
autoecholalia *n.* autoecolalia.
autoerotic *adj.* autoerótico, -ca.
autoeroticism *n.* autoeroticismo, autoerotismo.
autoerotism *n.* autoeroticismo, autoerotismo.
autoerythrophagocytosis *n.* autoeritrofagocitosis.
autofundoscope *n.* autofundoscopio.
autofundoscopy *n.* autofundoscopia.
autogenesis *n.* autogénesis.
autogenetic *adj.* autogenético, -ca.
autogenic *adj.* autogénico, -ca.
autogenous *adj.* autógeno, -na.
autognosia *n.* autognosia, autognosis.
autognosis *n.* autognosia, autognosis.
autognostic *adj.* autognóstico, -ca.
autograft *n.* autoinjerto.
autographism *n.* autografismo.
autohemoagglutination *n.* autohemoaglutinación.
autohemolysis *n.* autohemólisis.
autohemolytic *adj.* autohemolítico, -ca.
autohemotherapy *n.* autohemoterapia.
autohemotransfusion *n.* autohemotransfusión.
autoimmune *adj.* autoinmune, autoinmunitario, -ria.
autoimmunity *n.* autoinmunidad.
autoimmunization *n.* autoinmunización.
autoimmunocytopenia *n.* autoinmunocitopenia.
autoinfection *n.* autoinfección.
autoinoculable *adj.* autoinoculable.
autoinoculation *n.* autoinoculación.

autointoxicant *adj.* autointoxicante.
autointoxication *n.* autointoxicación.
autokeratoplasty *n.* autoqueratoplastia.
autokinesis *n.* autocinesis.
autokinetic *adj.* autocinético, -ca.
autolaryngoscopy *n.* autolaringoscopia.
autolesion *n.* autolesión, automutilación.
autoleukocytotherapy *n.* autoleucocitoterapia.
autologous *adj.* autólogo, -ga.
autolysate *n.* autolisado.
autolysin *n.* autolisina.
autolysis *n.* autólisis.
automatism *n.* automatismo.
  ambulatory automatism automatismo ambulatorio, automatismo deambulante.
  command automatism automatismo de orden.
  immediate posttraumatic automatism automatismo postraumático inmediato.
automatograph *n.* automatógrafo.
autonephrectomy *n.* autonefrectomía.
autonomic *adj.* autonómico, -ca.
autonomotropic *adj.* autonomotrópico, -ca.
autonomous *adj.* autónomo, -ma.
autonomy *n.* autonomía.
autopathography *n.* autopatografía.
autopepsia *n.* autopepsia.
autophagia *n.* autofagia.
autophagic *adj.* autofágico, -ca.
autophagolysosome *n.* autofagolisosoma.
autophagosome *n.* autofagosoma.
autophil *adj.* autófilo, -la.
autophilia *n.* autofilia.
autophonia *n.* autofonía.
autophonometry *n.* autofonometría.
autophthalmoscope *n.* autooftalmoscopio.
autoplasmotherapy *n.* autoplasmoterapia.
autoplast *n.* autoplasto.
autoplastic *adj.* autoplástico, -ca.
autoplasty *n.* autoplastia.
autoploid *n.* autoploide.
autopolyploid *adj.* autopoliploide.
autopolyploidy *n.* autopoliploidia.
autoprotection *n.* autoprotección.
autoproteolysis *n.* autoproteólisis.
autopsia *n.* autopsia.
autopsy *n.* autopsia.
  psychological autopsy autopsia psicológica.
autoreactive *adj.* autorreactivo, -va.
autoregulation *n.* autorregulación.
  heterometric autoregulation autorregulación heterométrica.

  homeometric autoregulation autorregulación homeométrica.
autoreinfection *n.* autorreinfección.
autoreinfusion *n.* autorreinfusión.
autorrhaphy *n.* autorrafia.
autoscopy *n.* autoscopia.
autosensitization *n.* autosensibilización.
autosepticemia *n.* autosepticemia.
autoserotherapy *n.* autoseroterapia, autosueroterapia.
autoserum *n.* autosuero.
autosite *n.* autósito.
autositic *adj.* autosítico, -ca.
autosmia *n.* autosmia.
autosomal *adj.* autosómico, -ca.
autosomatognosis *n.* autosomatognosis.
autosomatognostic *adj.* autosomatognóstico, -ca.
autosome *n.* autosoma.
autosplenectomy *n.* autoesplenectomía.
autosterilization *n.* autoesterilización.
autostimulation *n.* autoestimulación.
autotherapy *n.* autoterapia.
autotomia *n.* autotomía.
autotomy *n.* autotomía.
autotopagnosia *n.* autotopagnosia.
autotoxic *adj.* autotóxico, -ca.
autotransfusion *n.* autotransfusión.
autotransplantation *n.* autotrasplante.
autovaccine *n.* autovacuna.
auxanology *n.* auxanología.
auxesis *n.* auxesia.
auxetic *adj.* auxético, -ca.
auxocardia *n.* auxocardia.
auxohormone *n.* auxohormona.
auxology *n.* auxología.
auxometry *n.* auxometría.
auxoneurotropic *adj.* auxoneurotrópico, -ca.
avalvular *adj.* avalvular.
avariosis *n.* avariosis.
avascular *adj.* avascular.
avascularization *n.* avascularización.
average *n.* medio, medium.
avidin *n.* avidina.
avirulent *adj.* avirulento, -ta.
avitaminosis *n.* avitaminosis.
avivement *n.* avivamiento.
avoidance *n.* evitación.
avulsion *n.* avulsión.
axanthopsia *n.* axantopsia.
axenic *adj.* axénico, -ca.
axifugal *adj.* axófugo, -ga.

axilla *n.* axila.
axillary *adj.* axilar.
axioversion *n.* axioversión.
axis *n.* axis, eje.
  axis cylinder cilindroeje.
  cardiac electrical axis eje eléctrico del corazón.
  electrical axis of the heart eje eléctrico del corazón.
  embryonic axis eje embrionario.
  instantaneous electrical axis eje eléctrico instantáneo.
  normal axis eje normal.
  optic axis eje óptico.
  principal axis eje principal.
  sagittal axis of the eye eje sagital del ojo.
  secondary axis eje secundario.
axofugal *adj.* axófugo, -ga.
axoid *adj.* axoide, axoideo, -a.
axoidean *adj.* axoide, axoideo, -a.
axolysis *n.* axólisis.
axon *n.* axón.
axonal *adj.* axonal, axónico, -ca.
axonapraxia *adj.* axonapraxia.
axonography *n.* axonografía.
axonotmesis *n.* axonotmesis.
axopetal *adj.* axópeto, -ta.
axoplasm *n.* axoplasma.
axoplasmic *adj.* axoplásmico, -ca.
axosomatic *adj.* axosomático, -ca.
axotomy *n.* axotomía.
azimia *n.* azimia.
azoospermatism *n.* azoospermia.
azoospermia *n.* azoospermia.
azotemia *n.* azoemia, hiperazoemia.
  chloropenic azotemia hiperazoemia cloropénica.
  extrarenal azotemia hiperazoemia extrarrenal.
  hypochloremic azotemia hiperazoemia hipoclorémica.
  prerenal azotemia hiperazoemia prerrenal.
azotemic *adj.* azoémico, -ca.
azothermia *n.* azotermia.
azotorrhea *n.* azorrea.
azoturia *n.* azoturia, azouria.
azoturic *adj.* azotúrico, -ca, azoúrico, -ca.
azurophilia *n.* azurofilia.
azurophilic *adj.* azurófilo, -la.
azygogram *n.* acigograma.
azygography *n.* acigografía.
azygos *adj.* ácigos.

B b

babbling *n.* balbuceo[1].
Babesia *n.* Babesia.
babesiasis *n.* babesiasis.
Babesiidae *n.* Babesiidae.
babesiosis *n.* babesiasis, babesiosis.
baby *n.* bebé, neonato.
  battered baby bebé maltratado.
  blue baby bebé azul, neonato azul.
  blueberry muffin baby neonato en "bollito de arándanos".
  collodion baby bebé de colodión, neonato de colodión.
  giant baby neonato gigante.
  immature baby bebé inmaduro.
  test-tube baby bebé probeta.
babyhood *n.* infancia.
baccate *adj.* bacciforme.
bacciform *adj.* bacciforme.
Bacillaceae *n.* Bacillaceae.
bacillar *adj.* bacilar.
bacillary *adj.* bacilar.
bacilleferous *adj.* bacilífero, -ra.
bacillemia *n.* bacilemia.
bacilliculture *n.* bacilicultivo, bacilicultura.
bacilliform *adj.* baciliforme.
bacilligenic *adj.* baciligénico, -ca.
bacilliparous *adj.* baciliparo, -ra.
bacillogenic *adj.* baciligénico, -ca.
bacillogenous *adj.* bacilógeno, -na.
bacilloscopy *n.* baciloscopia.
bacillosis *n.* bacilosis.
bacillotherapy *n.* baciloterapia.
bacilluria *n.* baciluria.
Bacillus *n.* Bacillus.
bacillus *n.* bacilo.
back *n.* dorso, espalda.
  adolescent round back espalda curvada juvenil.
  flat back espalda plana.
  functional back espalda funcional.
  hollow back espalda hueca.
  hump back espalda jorobada.
  hunch back espalda jorobada.
  poker back espalda de jugador de póquer.
  saddle back espalda en silla de montar.
backache *n.* dorsalgia.
backbone *n.* espinazo.
background *n.* antecedentes.
backscatter *n.* backscatter.
bacteremia *n.* bacteremia.
bacterial *adj.* bacteriano, -na.
bactericholia *n.* bactericolia.
bactericidal *adj.* bactericida[2].
bactericide *n.* bactericida[1].
  specific bactericide bactericida específico.
bactericidin *n.* bactericidina.
bacterid *n.* bactéride.
  pustular bacterid bactéride pustulosa.
bacteriemia *n.* bacteriemia.
bacteriform *adj.* bacteriforme.

bacterin *n.* bacterina.
bacterinia *n.* bacterinia.
bacterioagglutinin *n.* bacterioaglutinina.
bacteriochlorophyll *n.* bacterioclorofila.
bacteriocidal *adj.* bactericida[2].
bacteriocide *n.* bactericida[1].
bacteriocidin *n.* bacteriocidina.
bacteriocin *n.* bacteriocina.
bacteriocinogen *n.* bacteriocinógeno.
bacteriocinogenic *adj.* bacteriocinogénico, -ca.
bacterioclasis *n.* bacterioclasis.
bacteriofluorescin *n.* bacteriofluoresceína.
bacteriogenic *adj.* bacteriogénico, -ca.
bacteriogenous *adj.* bacteriogeno, -na.
bacteriohemolysin *n.* bacteriohemolisina.
bacterioid *n.* bacterioide.
bacteriologic *adj.* bacteriológico, -ca.
bacteriological *adj.* bacteriológico, -ca.
bacteriologist *n.* bacteriólogo, -ga.
bacteriology *n.* bacteriología.
  clinical diagnostic bacteriology bacteriología clínica.
  medical bacteriology bacteriología médica.
  public health bacteriology bacteriología higiénica.
  sanitary bacteriology bacteriología sanitaria.
  systematic bacteriology bacteriología sistemática.
bacteriolysant *n.* bacteriolisante.
bacteriolysin *n.* bacteriolisina.
bacteriolysis *n.* bacteriólisis.
bacteriolytic *adj.* bacteriolítico, -ca.
Bacterionema *n.* Bacterionema.
  Bacterionema matruchotii Bacterionema matruchotii.
bacterio-opsonin *n.* bacterioopsonina.
bacteriopexia *n.* bacteriopexia.
bacteriopexy *n.* bacteriopexia.
bacteriophage *n.* bacteriófago, microbívoro.
  defective bacteriophage bacteriófago defectuoso.
  filamentous bacteriophage bacteriófago filamentoso.
  mature bacteriophage bacteriófago maduro.
  temperate bacteriophage bacteriófago atemperado, bacteriófago de plantilla.
  typhoid bacteriophage bacteriófago tifoideo.
  vegetative bacteriophage bacteriófago vegetativo.
  virulent bacteriophage bacteriófago virulento.
bacteriophagia *n.* bacteriofagia.
bacteriophagic *adj.* bacteriofágico, -ca.
bacteriophagology *n.* bacteriofagología.
bacteriopheophytin *n.* bacteriofeofitina.
bacteriophobia *n.* bacteriofobia.
bacteriophytoma *n.* bacteriofitoma.
bacterioplasmin *n.* bacterioplasmina.
bacterioprecipitin *n.* bacterioprecipitina.

bacterioprotein *n.* bacterioproteína.
bacteriopsonic *adj.* bacteriopsónico, -ca.
bacteriopsonin *n.* bacteriopsonina.
bacteriorhodopsin *n.* bacteriorrodopsina.
bacterioscopic *adj.* bacterioscópico, -ca.
bacterioscopy *n.* bacterioscopia.
bacteriosis *n.* bacteriosis.
bacteriospermia *n.* bacteriospermia.
bacteriostasis *n.* bacteriostasis.
bacteriostatic *adj.* bacteriostático, -ca.
bacteriotherapy *n.* bacterioterapia.
bacteriotoxemia *n.* bacteriotoxemia.
bacteriotoxic *adj.* bacteriotóxico, -ca.
bacteriotoxin *n.* bacteriotoxina.
bacteriotropic *adj.* bacteriotrópico, -ca.
bacteriotropin *n.* bacteriotropina.
bacteritic *adj.* bacterítico, -ca.
bacterium *n.* bacteria.
bacteriuria *n.* bacteriuria.
  asymptomatic bacteriuria bacteriuria asintomática.
  pregnancy bacteriuria bacteriuria gravídica.
  significant bacteriuria bacteriuria significativa.
bacteriuric *adj.* bacteriúrico, -ca.
bacteroid *n.* bacteroide.
Bacteroidaceae *n.* Bacteroidaceae.
Bacteroides *n.* Bacteroides.
bacteroides *n.* bacteroides.
bacteroidosis *n.* bacteroidosis.
bacteruria *n.* bacteriuria.
baculiform *adj.* baculiforme.
bag *n.* bolsa[1].
  Ambu bag bolsa Ambu.
  bag of waters bolsa de aguas.
  Barnes' bag bolsa de Barnes.
  breathing bag bolsa de respiración.
  Bunyan bag bolsa de Bunyan.
  Champetier de Ribes bag bolsa de Champetier de Ribes.
  colostomy bag bolsa de colostomía.
  Douglas bag bolsa de Douglas.
  forewaters bag bolsa de aguas.
  Hagner bag bolsa de Hagner.
  ice bag bolsa de hielo.
  ileostomy bag bolsa de ileostomía.
  micturition bag bolsa para micción.
  nuclear bag bolsa nuclear.
  Perry bag bolsa de Perry.
  Petersen's bag bolsa de Petersen.
  Pilcher bag bolsa de Pilcher.
  Plummer's bag bolsa de Plummer.
  Politzer's bag bolsa Politzer.
  rebreathing bag bolsa de reinspiración.
  reservoir bag bolsa de reserva, bolsa de reservorio.
  testicular bag bolsa testicular.
  Voorhees' bag bolsa de Voorhees.
bagasscosis *n.* bagazosis.
bagassosis *n.* bagazosis.

bagging *n.* bolseo.
balance *n.* balance, balanza, equilibrio.
  acid-base balance balance acidobásico, equilibrio ácido-base, equilibrio acidobásico.
  calcium balance balance cálcico.
  electrolyte balance balance electrolítico, equilibrio electrolítico.
  energy balance balance calórico, balance energético.
  enzyme balance balance enzimático.
  fluid balance balance líquido.
  genic balance balance genético.
  glomerulotubular balance balance glomérulo-tubular.
  inhibition-action balance balance de inhibición y acción.
  metabolic balance equilibrio metabólico.
  nitrogen balance balance de nitrógeno, balance nitrogenado, equilibrio nitrogenado, equilibrio nitrógeno.
  occlusal balance balance oclusal, equilibrio oclusal.
  torsion balance balanza de torsión.
  water balance balance hídrico.
  Wilhelmy balance balanza de Wilhelmy.
  zero fluid balance equilibrio líquido cero.
balanic *adj.* balánico, -ca.
balanitis *n.* balanitis.
  balanitis circinata balanitis circinada, balanitis circinata.
  balanitis circumscripta plasmacellularis balanitis circunscripta plasmacelular, balanitis circunscrita plasmocelular.
  balanitis diabetica balanitis diabética.
  balanitis gangrenosa balanitis gangrenosa.
  balanitis of Zoon balanitis de Zoon.
  balanitis plasmocellulare balanitis de plasmocitos, balanitis plasmocelular, balanitis plasmocitaria.
  balanitis plasmocellularis balanitis de plasmocitos, balanitis plasmocelular, balanitis plasmocitaria.
  balanitis xerotica obliterans balanitis xerotica obliterans, balanitis xerótica obliterante.
  candidal balanitis balanitis candidiásica.
  erosive balanitis balanitis erosiva.
  Follmann's balanitis balanitis de Follmann.
  gangrenous balanitis balanitis gangrenosa.
  phagadenic balanitis balanitis fagedénica.
  plasma cell balanitis balanitis de células plasmáticas.
balanoblennorrhea *n.* balanoblenorrea.
balanocele *n.* balanocele.
balanochlamyditis *n.* balanoclamiditis.
balanoplasty *n.* balanoplastia.
balanoposthitis *n.* balanopostitis.
  balanoposthitis chronica circumscripta plasmocellularis balanopostitis crónica circunscrita plasmocelular, balanopostitis plasmocítica circunscrita crónica.
  chronic circumscribed plasmocytic balanoposthitis balanopostitis crónica circunscrita plasmocelular, balanopostitis plasmocítica circunscrita crónica.
  specific gangrenous and ulcerative balanoposthitis balanopostitis gangrenosa y ulcerativa específica.
balanoposthomycosis *n.* balanopostomicosis.
balanopreputial *adj.* balanoprepucial.
balantidiasis *n.* balantidiasis, balantidiosis.
Balantidium *n.* Balantidium.
  Balantidium coli Balantidium coli.
balantidosis *n.* balantidiasis, balantidiosis.
balanus *n.* balanus.
balata *n.* balata.

bald *adj.* calvo, -va.
baldness *n.* calvicie.
  common male baldness calvicie masculina común.
  congenital baldness calvicie congénita.
  male pattern baldness calvicie de distribución masculina.
  pubic baldness calvicie del pubis.
ball *n.* bola, pelota.
  chondrin ball bola de condrina, pelota de condrina.
  fatty ball of Bichat bola adiposa de Bichat, bola grasa de Bichat.
  food ball bola alimentaria, bola de alimento, pelota de comida.
  fungus ball bola fúngica, bola micótica.
  Marchi ball bola de Marchi.
  pleural fibril ball bola pleural de fibrina.
ballism *n.* balismo.
ballismus *n.* balismo.
ballistic *adj.* balístico, -ca.
ballistics *n.* balística.
  forensic ballistics balística médico-legal.
  wound ballistics balística de las heridas.
ballistocardiogram *n.* balistocardiograma.
ballistocardiograph *n.* balistocardiógrafo.
ballistocardiography *n.* balistocardiografía.
ballistophobia *n.* balistofobia.
balloon *n.* balón[1], balonizar.
  balloon angioplasty angioplastia con balón.
  balloon bezoar balón bezoar.
  Shea-Anthony antral balloon balón antral de Shea-Anthony.
  sinus balloon balón sinusal.
ballottable *adj.* balotable.
ballottement *n.* ballottement, balotamiento, peloteo.
  abdominal ballottement peloteo abdominal.
  indirect ballottement peloteo indirecto.
  renal ballottement ballottement renal.
balm *n.* bálsamo[1].
balneology *n.* balneología.
balneotherapeutics *n.* balneoterapia.
balneotherapy *n.* balneoterapia.
balopticon *n.* balopticón.
balsam *n.* bálsamo[2].
balsamic *adj.* balsámico, -ca.
bancroftiasis *n.* bancroftiasis, bancroftosis.
bancroftosis *n.* bancroftiasis, bancroftosis.
band *n.* banda, bandaleta, bandeleta, cintilla.
  absorption band banda de absorción.
  adjustable orthodontic band banda ortodóncica ajustable.
  amniotic band banda amniótica.
  anchor band banda de anclaje.
  annular band banda anular.
  anogenital band banda anogenital.
  band of Gennari banda de Gennari.
  band of Kaes-Bechterew banda de Kaes-Bechterew.
  band pusher colocador de bandas.
  Bechterew's band banda de Bechterew.
  belly band banda abdominal.
  Büngner's band banda de Büngner.
  C band banda C.
  chromosome band banda cromosómica.
  Clado's band banda de Clado.
  clamp band banda abrazadera, banda clamp.
  contoured band banda contorneada.
  contraction band banda de contracción.
  elastic band banda elástica.
  Essick's cell bands bandas celulares de Essick.
  furrowed band banda estriada.
  G band banda G.
  Harris' band banda de Harris.

  Henle's band banda de Henle.
  horny band banda córnea.
  Lane's bands bandas de Lane.
  limbic bands bandas límbicas.
  M band banda M.
  Mach's band banda de Mach.
  Matas' band banda de Matas.
  matrix band banda matriz.
  molar band banda molar.
  N band banda N.
  orthodontic band banda ortodóncica, banda ortodóntica.
  Parham band banda de Parham.
  pecten band banda del pecten.
  Q band banda Q.
  R band banda R.
  Soret band banda de Soret.
  Streeter's band banda de Streeter.
  T band banda T.
  Vicq d'Azyr band banda de Vicq d'Azyr.
bandage[1] *n.* venda, vendaje.
  abdominal bandage vendaje abdominal.
  adhesive bandage vendaje adhesivo.
  Barton's bandage vendaje de Barton.
  Baynton's bandage vendaje de Baynton.
  capeline bandage vendaje capelar, vendaje en capelina.
  circular bandage vendaje circular.
  compression bandage vendaje compresivo.
  crucial bandage vendaje crucial, vendaje en cruz.
  demigauntlet bandage vendaje en semiguantelete.
  Desault's bandage vendaje de Desault.
  elastic bandage venda elástica, vendaje elástico.
  Esmarch's bandage vendaje de Esmarch.
  figure-of-eight bandage vendaje en figura de ocho, vendaje en ocho.
  four-tailed bandage vendaje de cuatro cabos, vendaje de cuatro colas.
  Galen's bandage vendaje de Galeno.
  gauntlet bandage vendaje en guante, vendaje en guantelete.
  gauze bandage vendaje de gasa.
  Gibney's fixation bandage vendaje en fijación de Gibney.
  Gibson's bandage vendaje de Gibson.
  hammock bandage vendaje en hamaca.
  Heliodorus' bandage vendaje de Heliodoro.
  immobilizing bandage vendaje de inmovilización.
  immovable bandage vendaje inamovible, vendaje inmóvil.
  many-tailed bandage vendaje de cabos múltiples, vendaje de múltiples colas, vendaje de múltiples extremos.
  Martin's bandage venda de Martin, vendaje de Martin.
  plate bandage vendaje enyesado.
  pressure bandage vendaje compresivo.
  protective bandage vendaje protectivo, vendaje protector.
  recurrent bandage vendaje recurrente.
  reversed bandage vendaje inverso.
  roller bandage vendaje en rollo, vendaje enrollado.
  scarf bandage vendaje en chalina.
  Scultetus' bandage vendaje de Scultetus.
  spica bandage vendaje en espica, vendaje en espiga.
  spiral bandage vendaje espiral.
  spiral reverse bandage vendaje espiral inverso.
  starch bandage vendaje almidonado, venda-

je dextrinado, vendaje gelatinado, vendaje silicado.

suspensory bandage vendaje suspensor, vendaje suspensorio.

T-bandage vendaje en T.

triangular bandage vendaje triangular.

Velpeau's bandage vendaje de Velpeau.

bandage² *v.* vendar.

bandaletta *n.* bandaleta, bandeleta.

bandelette *n.* bandaleta, bandeleta.

bandicoot *n.* bandicoot.

banding *n.* bandaje, bandeo, banding.

BrDU banding bandeo BrDU.

C banding bandeo C, bandeo centromérico (de la heterocromatina céntrica).

centromeric banding bandeo C, bandeo centromérico (de la heterocromatina céntrica).

chromosome banding bandeo cromosómico, bandeo de cromosomas.

G banding bandeo de Giemsa, bandeo G.

Giemsa banding bandeo de Giemsa, bandeo G.

high resolution banding bandeo de alta resolución.

NOR banding bandeo NOR.

prometaphase banding bandeo de prometafase.

prophase banding bandeo de profase.

pulmonary artery banding bandeo de la arteria pulmonar, banding pulmonar.

Q banding bandeo Q.

quinacrine banding bandeo de cinacrina.

R banding bandeo R.

reverse banding bandeo inverso.

tooth banding bandeo dental.

bane *n.* tósigo.

bank *n.* banco.

blood bank banco de sangre.

embryo bank banco de embriones.

eye bank banco de ojos.

gene bank banco de genes.

semen bank banco de semen.

serum bank banco de suero.

sperm bank banco de esperma.

bar *n.* barra.

arch bar barra de arco, barra de la arcada, barra en arco.

buccal bar barra bucal.

chromatoid bar barra cromatoide.

connector bar barra conectora.

Erich arch bar barra de Erich.

hyoid bar barra hioidea.

Kazanjian T bar barra en T de Kazanjian.

Kennedy bar barra de Kennedy.

labial bar barra labial.

lingual bar barra lingual.

median bar barra media.

occlusal rest bar barra de resto oclusal.

palatal bar barra palatina.

Passavant's bar barra de Passavant.

prism bar barra prismática.

spreader bar barra tensora.

sternal bar barra esternal.

terminal bar barra terminal.

baragnosis *n.* baragnosis.

barba *n.* barba.

barbaralalia *n.* barbaralalia.

barbeiro *n.* barbeiro.

barbitalism *n.* barbitalismo.

barbituism *n.* barbiturismo.

barbiturate *n.* barbitúrico.

barbiturism *n.* barbiturismo.

barbotage *n.* barbotaje, bombeo.

barbula hirci *n.* barbula hirci.

baresthesia *n.* barestesia.

baresthesiometer *n.* barestesiómetro.

bariatric *adj.* bariátrico, -ca.

bariatrics *n.* bariatría.

baric *adj.* bárico, -ca.

baricity *n.* baricidad.

baritosis *n.* baritosis.

barium *n.* bario.

barium sulfate sulfato de bario.

baroagnosis *n.* baroagnosis.

baroceptor *n.* baroceptor.

barodontalgia *n.* barodontalgia.

baroelectroesthesiometer *n.* baroelectroestesiómetro.

barognosis *n.* barognosis.

barograph *n.* barógrafo.

baromacrometer *n.* baromacrómetro.

barometer *n.* barómetro.

barometric *adj.* barométrico, -ca.

barometrograph *n.* barometrógrafo.

barootitis *n.* barootitis.

barophilic *adj.* barofílico, -ca, barófilo, -la.

baroreceptor *n.* barorreceptor.

baroreflex *n.* barorreflejo.

baroscope *n.* baroscopio, manoscopio.

barosinusitis *n.* barosinusitis.

barospirator *n.* barospirador.

barostat *n.* baróstato.

barotaxis *n.* barotaxis.

barotitis *n.* barotitis.

barotitis media barotitis media.

barotrauma *n.* barotrauma, barotraumatismo.

otic barotrauma barotraumatismo ótico, barotraumatismo otítico.

otitic barotrauma barotraumatismo ótico, barotraumatismo otítico.

sinus barotrauma barotraumatismo sinusal.

barotropism *n.* barotropismo.

barrier *n.* barrera.

architectural barrier barrera arquitectónica.

blood-air barrier barrera hematoaérea.

blood-aqueous barrier barrera hematoacuosa.

blood-brain barrier (BBB) barrera hematocerebral, barrera hematoencefálica (BHE).

blood-cerebral barrier barrera hematocerebral, barrera hematoencefálica (BHE).

blood-cerebrospinal fluid barrier barrera hematocerebroespinal.

blood-CSF barrier barrera hemato-LCR.

blood-gas barrier barrera hematogaseosa.

blood-testis barrier barrera hematotesticular.

blood-thymus barrier barrera hematotímica.

filtration barrier barrera de filtración.

gastric mucosal barrier barrera de la mucosa gástrica, barrera mucosa.

histohematic connective tissue barrier barrera histohemática de tejido conectivo.

incest barrier barrera incestuosa.

placental barrier barrera placentaria.

primary protective barrier barrera protectora primaria.

protective barrier barrera protectora.

radiation barrier barrera de radiación.

secondary protective barrier barrera protectora secundaria.

skin barrier barrera cutánea.

synovial barrier barrera sinovial.

bartholinitis *n.* bartholinitis, bartolinitis.

Bartonella *n.* Bartonella.

Bartonella bacilliformis Bartonella bacilliformis.

Bartonellaceae *n.* Bartonellaceae.

bartonelliasis *n.* bartoneliasis.

bartonellosis *n.* bartonellosis, bartonelosis.

baryesthesia *n.* bariestesia.

baryglossia *n.* bariglosia.

barylalia *n.* barilalia.

barymazia *n.* barimastia, barimazia.

barytosis *n.* baritosis.

basal *adj.* basal.

basalioma *n.* basalioma.

basaloid *adj.* basaloide.

basaloma *n.* basalioma, basaloma.

base *n.* base.

acidifiable base base acidificable.

acrylic resin base base de resina acrílica.

alloxuris base base aloxúrica.

apical base base apical.

Brønsted base base de Brønsted.

Brønsted-Lowry base base de Brønsted-Lowry.

cavity preparation base base de preparación cavitaria.

cement base base de cemento.

cheoplastic base base queoplástica.

conjugate base base conjugada.

denture base base de dentadura, base de la dentadura artificial, base dental.

film base base de película.

hexone base base de hexona.

histone base base de histona.

Lewis base base de Lewis.

metal base base metálica.

nitrogenous base base nitrogenada.

nucleic acid base base de ácidos nucleicos.

ointment base base de pomada.

plastic base base plástica.

pressor base base presora.

purine base base púrica, base purínica.

pyrimidine base base pirimidínica.

Schiff's base base de Schiff.

shellac base base de goma laca.

tinted denture base base de dentadura teñida, base dental coloreada, base dental teñida.

tooth-borne base base de apoyo dental.

vegetable base base vegetal.

basedoid *adj.* basedoide.

basedowian *adj.* basedowiano, -na.

basedowiform *adj.* basedowiforme.

basedowoïde *adj.* basedovoide.

Basel Nomina Anatomica *n.* Basilea Nomina Anatomica.

basial *adj.* basial.

basialis *adj.* basial.

basialveolar *adj.* basialveolar.

basiarachnitis *n.* basiaracnitis.

basiarachnoiditis *n.* basiaracnoiditis.

basic *adj.* básico, -ca.

basicity *n.* basicidad.

basicranial *adj.* basicraneal.

Basidiobolus *n.* Basidiobolus.

Basidiobolus haptosporus Basidiobolus haptosporus.

Basidiobolus meristoporus Basidiobolus meristoporus.

basidiocarp *n.* basidiocarpo.

Basidiomycetes *n.* Basidiomycetes.

basidiomycetous *n.* basidiomiceto.

basidiospore *n.* basidiospora.

basidium *n.* basidio, basidium.

basifacial *adj.* basifacial.

basihyal *n.* basihial.

basihyoid *n.* basihioide, basihioides.

basilar *adj.* basilar.

basilaris *adj.* basilar, basilaris.

basilaris cranii basilaris cranii.

basilateral *adj.* basilateral.

basilemma *n.* basilema.

basilic *adj.* basílico, -ca.

basilicus *n.* basílico.

basiloma *n.* basalioma, basiloma.

basin *n*. bacía.
  emesis basin bacía para vómitos.
  kidney basin bacía renal.
  pus basin bacía de pus.
basinasal *adj*. basinasal.
basioccipital *adj*. basioccipital.
basioglossus *n*. basiogloso.
basion *n*. basión.
basiotribe *n*. basiotribo.
basiotripsy *n*. basiotripsia.
basipetal *adj*. basípeto, -ta.
basiphobia *n*. basifobia, basofobia.
basirhinal *adj*. basirrino, -na.
basis *n*. base², basis.
basisphenoid *n*. basiesfenoides, basisfenoides.
basitemporal *adj*. basitemporal.
basivertebral *adj*. basivertebral.
basocyte *n*. basocito.
basocytopenia *n*. basocitopenia.
basocytosis *n*. basocitosis.
basoerythrocyte *n*. basoeritrocito.
basoerythrocytosis *n*. basoeritrocitosis.
basograph *n*. basógrafo.
basolateral *adj*. basolateral.
basometachromophil *adj*. basometacromófilo, -la.
basometachromophile *adj*. basometacromófilo, -la.
basopenia *n*. basopenia.
basophil *n*. basófilo, -la.
  beta basophil basófilo beta.
  Crooke-Russell basophil basófilo de Crooke-Russell.
  delta basophil basófilo delta.
  tissue basophil basófilo hístico.
basophile *adj*. basofílico, -ca.
basophilia *n*. basofilia.
  Grawitz's basophilia basofilia de Grawitz.
  punctate basophilia basofilia punteada.
basophilic *adj*. basofílico, -ca.
basophilism *n*. basofilismo.
  Cushing's basophilism basofilismo de Cushing.
  pituitary basophilism basofilismo hipofisario, basofilismo pituitario.
basophilocyte *n*. basofilocito.
basophobia *n*. basifobia, basofobia.
basoplasm *n*. basoplasma.
bath *n*. baño.
  acid bath baño ácido.
  air bath baño de aire.
  alcohol bath baño de alcohol.
  alkaline bath baño alcalino.
  alum bath baño de alumbre.
  antipyretic bath baño antipirético.
  antiseptic bath baño antiséptico.
  aromatic bath baño aromático.
  astringent bath baño astringente.
  blanket bath baño con manta.
  borax bath baño boratado, baño de bórax.
  bran bath baño de salvado.
  Brand's bath baño de Brand.
  bubble bath baño de burbujas.
  cabinet bath baño de gabinete, baño en cabina.
  camphor bath baño alcanforado, baño de alcanfor.
  carbon dioxide bath baño de dióxido de carbono.
  cold bath baño frío.
  colloid bath baño coloidal, baño coloide, baño de coloide.
  complete bed bath baño completo en la cama.
  continuous bath baño continuo, baño continuo en bañera.
  continuous tub bath baño continuo, baño continuo en bañera.

  contrast bath baño de contraste.
  cool bath baño frío.
  creosote bath baño de creosota.
  douche bath baño de ducha.
  Dowsing bath baño de inmersión lumínica, baño Dowsing.
  earth bath baño de tierra.
  electric bath baño eléctrico.
  electrotherapeutic bath baño electroterapéutico.
  emollient bath baño emoliente.
  Finnish bath baño finlandés.
  Finsen bath baño de Finsen.
  foam bath baño de espuma, baño de Sandor, baño espumoso.
  full bath baño completo.
  gelatin bath baño de gelatina.
  glycerin bath baño de glicerina.
  grease bath baño de grasa, baño oleoso.
  Greville bath baño de Greville.
  hafussi bath baño hafussi.
  herb bath baño de hierbas.
  hip bath baño de asiento.
  hot bath baño caliente.
  hot-air bath baño de aire caliente.
  hydroelectric bath baño hidroeléctrico.
  hyperthermal bath baño hipertérmico.
  immersion bath baño de inmersión.
  iron bath baño de hierro, baño ferruginoso.
  light bath baño de luz.
  linseed bath baño de linaza.
  lukewarm bath baño templado.
  medicamented bath baño medicamentoso.
  medicated tub bath baño medicado en bañera.
  milk bath baño de leche.
  mood bath baño de barro, baño de fango, baño de limo, baño de lodo.
  mud bath baño de barro.
  Naunheim bath baño de Nauheim.
  needle bath baño de agujas.
  oil bath baño de aceite.
  pack bath baño de envoltura.
  paraffin bath baño de parafina.
  peat bath baño de turba.
  Russian bath baño ruso.
  sand bath baño de arena.
  sauna bath baño de sauna.
  sea bath baño de mar.
  seawater bath baño de agua de mar.
  sedative bath baño sedante.
  sheet bath baño de sábana.
  sitz bath baño de asiento.
  sponge bath baño con esponja, baño de esponja.
  stimulant bath baño estimulante.
  sun bath baño de sol.
  sweat bath baño de sudor.
  tepid bath baño tibio.
  vapor bath baño de vapor.
  water bath baño de agua, baño de María.
  wax bath baño de cera.
  whirlpool bath baño de remolino, baño de torbellino.
bathmotropic *adj*. batmotrópico, -ca.
  negatively bathmotropic batmotrópico negativamente, batmotrópico negativo.
  positively bathmotropic batmotrópico positivamente, batmotrópico positivo.
bathmotropism *n*. batmotropismo.
bathochrome *n*. batocromo.
bathochromy *n*. batocromía.
bathocromic *adj*. batocrómico, -ca.
bathoflore *n*. batoflora.
bathomorphic *adj*. batomórfico, -ca.
bathophobia *n*. batofobia.

bathrocephaly *n*. batrocefalia.
bathyanesthesia *n*. batianestesia.
bathycardia *n*. baticardia.
bathyesthesia *n*. batiestesia.
bathygastry *n*. batigastria.
bathyhyperesthesia *n*. batihiperestesia.
bathyhypesthesia *n*. batihipoestesia.
bathypnea *n*. batipnea.
batrachoplasty *n*. batracoplastia.
batrachotoxin *n*. batracotoxina.
battarism *n*. batarismo.
battarismus *n*. batarismo.
battery *n*. batería.
  battery of tests batería de pruebas.
  Halstead-Reitan battery batería de Halstead-Reitan.
  Kaufman battery batería de Kaufman.
  Luria-Nebraska neuropsychological battery batería neuropsicológica de Luria-Nebraska.
  Reitan-Indiana battery batería de Reitan-Indiana.
  standardized aphasia battery batería estandarizada de tests de afasia.
  Woodcock-Johnson battery batería de Woodcock-Johnson.
batteyin *n*. bateína.
bay *n*. bahía.
  celomic bay bahía celómica.
bayonet *n*. bayoneta.
Bdella *n*. Bdella.
  Bdella cardinalis Bdella cardinalis.
Bdellovibrio *n*. Bdellovibrio.
bdellovibrio *n*. bdellovibrión.
beam *n*. balancín¹, haz², traviesa.
  beam restrictor limitador del haz.
  primary beam haz útil.
  useful beam haz útil.
  X-ray beam haz de rayos X.
beard *n*. barba.
beat *n*. latido, latir.
  apex beat latido apexiano, latido de la punta.
  atrial fusion beat latido de fusión auricular.
  automatic beat latido automático.
  capture beat latido de captura.
  ciliary beat latido ciliar.
  combination beat latido de combinación.
  complex ectopic beat latido ectópico complejo.
  coupled beat latido acoplado.
  dependent beat latido dependiente.
  Dressler beat latido de Dressler.
  dropped beat latido fallido, latido omitido.
  echo beat latido eco.
  ectopic beat latido ectópico.
  escape beat latido de escape.
  escaped beat latido de escape.
  extra beat latido extra.
  forced beat latido forzado.
  fusion beat latido de fusión.
  heart beat latido cardíaco.
  interference beat latido de interferencia.
  mixed beat latido mixto.
  paired beat latido apareado.
  parasystolic beat latido parasistólico.
  premature beat latido prematuro.
  reciprocal beat latido recíproco.
  retrograde beat latido retrógrado.
  summation beat latido por agregado.
  ventricular fusion beat latido de fusión ventricular.
bechic *adj*. béquico, -ca.
bed *n*. lecho.
  capillary bed lecho capilar.
  nail bed lecho ungueal.

Bedsonia *n.* Bedsonia.
beeturia *n.* betacianinuria.
behavior *n.* comportamiento, conducta.
  sexual behavior comportamiento sexual.
behaviorism *n.* behaviorismo, conductismo.
behaviorist *adj.* conductista.
bejel *n.* bejel.
Belascaris *n.* Belascaris.
belch *n.* eructar, eructo.
belemnoid *adj.* belemnoide.
bell *n.* campana.
belly *n.* vientre.
  drum belly vientre de tambor.
  wooden belly vientre de madera, vientre en tabla.
belonephobia *n.* belonefobia.
belonoid *adj.* belonoide.
belonoskiascopy *n.* belonosquiascopia.
bends *n.* bends.
benign *adj.* benigno, -na.
bentiromide *n.* bentiromida.
benzapyrene *n.* benzopireno.
benzene *n.* benceno.
benzenoid *adj.* bencenoide.
benzolism *n.* benzolismo.
benzopurpurin 4B *n.* benzopurpurina 4-B.
benzopyrene *n.* benzopireno.
benzotherapy *n.* benzoterapia.
bereavement *n.* aflicción, duelo.
  normal bereavement duelo normal.
  pathological bereavement duelo patológico.
beriberi *n.* beriberi.
  atrophic beriberi beriberi atrófico.
  cerebral beriberi beriberi cerebral.
  dry beriberi beriberi seco.
  infantile beriberi beriberi infantil.
  paralytic beriberi beriberi paralítico.
  ship beriberi beriberi de los barcos, beriberi de los navíos.
  wet beriberi beriberi húmedo.
beriberic *adj.* beribérico, -ca.
Bertiella *n.* Bertiella.
  Bertiella satyri Bertiella satyri, Bertiella studeri.
  Bertiella studeri Bertiella satyri, Bertiella studeri.
bertielliasis *n.* bertieliasis, bertielosis.
bertiellosis *n.* bertieliasis, bertielosis.
berylliosis *n.* beriliosis.
besiclometer *n.* besiclómetro.
bestiality *n.* bestialidad, bestialismo.
beta *n.* beta.
  beta fetoprotein beta fetoproteína.
  beta globulin betaglobulina.
  beta oxidation beta oxidación.
  pregnancy-specific beta globulin betaglobulina específica de embarazo.
beta-alaninemia *n.* betaalaninemia.
beta-blocker *n.* betabloqueante.
beta-carotene *n.* betacaroteno.
betacism *n.* betacismo.
betacyaninuria *n.* betacianinuria.
beta-lipoprotein *n.* beta-lipoproteína.
beta-lysine *n.* betalisina.
beta-oxibutyria *n.* betaoxibutiria.
betapropiolactone *n.* betapropiolactona.
betathromboglobulin *n.* betatromboglobulina.
betatron *n.* betatrón.
bête rouge *n.* bête rouge.
bevel *n.* bisel[1], biselar.
  cavosurface bevel bisel cavosuperficial, bisel de cavosuperficie.
  reverse bevel bisel inverso.
bezoar *n.* bezoar.

bhang *n.* bhang.
biamniotic *adj.* biamniótico.
biangular *adj.* biangular.
biarticular *adj.* biarticular.
biarticulate *adj.* biarticulado, -da.
bias *n.* desviación[1], sesgo.
  detection bias sesgo de detección.
biasteric *adj.* biastérico, -ca.
biasterionic *adj.* biasteriónico, -ca.
biauricular *adj.* biauricular[1], diótico, -ca.
biaxillary *adj.* biaxilar.
bibasic *adj.* bibásico, -ca.
bibliokleptomania *n.* bibliocleptomanía.
bibliomania *n.* bibliomanía.
bibliophobia *n.* bibliofobia.
bibliotherapy *n.* biblioterapia.
bibulous *adj.* bíbulo, -la.
bicameral *adj.* bicamaral, bicameral.
bicapsular *adj.* bicapsular.
bicarbonate *n.* bicarbonato.
  bicarbonate of sosa bicarbonato de sosa.
  blood bicarbonate bicarbonato sanguíneo.
  plasma bicarbonate bicarbonato del plasma.
  sodium bicarbonate bicarbonato de sodio, bicarbonato sódico.
  standard bicarbonate bicarbonato estándar.
bicarbonatemia *n.* bicarbonatemia.
bicaudal *adj.* bicaudal.
bicaudate *adj.* bicaudado, -da.
bicellular *adj.* bicelular.
bicephalus *n.* bicéfalo.
biceps *n.* bíceps.
bicho *n.* bicho.
biciliate *adj.* biciliado, -da.
bicipital *adj.* bicipital.
biclonal *adj.* biclonal.
biclonality *n.* biclonalidad.
biconcave *adj.* bicóncavo, -va.
biconvex *adj.* biconvexo, -xa.
bicornate *adj.* bicorne.
bicornous *adj.* bicorne.
bicornuate *adj.* bicorne.
bicoronal *adj.* bicoronal.
bicorporate *adj.* bicorporal.
bicuspid *n.* bicúspide.
bicuspidization *n.* bicuspidización.
bicuspoid *adj.* bicuspoide.
bidactyly *n.* bidactilia.
bidelt *n.* bidelto.
bidentate *adj.* bidentado, -da.
bidermoma *n.* bidermoma.
bidet *n.* bidé, bidet.
bidimensional *adj.* bidimensional.
bidiscoidal *adj.* bidiscoide.
biduotertian *n.* biduoterciana.
biduous *adj.* bidial.
bifascicular *adj.* bifascicular.
bifid *adj.* bífido, -da.
Bifidobacterium *n.* Bifidobacterium.
bifidobacterium *n.* bifidobacteria.
bifidus *adj.* bífido, -da.
bifocal *adj.* bifocal.
biforate *adj.* biforado, -da.
bifurcate *adj.* bifurcado, -da.
bifurcated *adj.* bifurcado, -da.
bifurcatio *n.* bifurcación, bifurcatio.
  bifurcatio aortae bifurcatio aortae.
  bifurcatio aortica bifurcatio aortae.
  bifurcatio carotidis bifurcatio carotidis.
  bifurcatio trunci pulmonalis bifurcatio trunci pulmonalis.
bifurcation *n.* bifurcación, bifurcatio.
  bifurcation of the aorta bifurcación aórtica, bifurcación de la aorta, bifurcatio aortae.
  bifurcation of the pulmonary trunk bifur-

cación del tronco pulmonar, bifurcatio trunci pulmonalis.
  bifurcation of the trachea bifurcación de la tráquea.
  carotid bifurcation bifurcación de la carótida, bifurcatio carotidis.
bigemina *n.* bigemina.
bigeminal *adj.* bigeminado, -da, bigeminal.
bigeminy *n.* bigeminia, bigeminidad, bigeminismo.
  atrial bigeminy bigeminismo auricular.
  atrioventricular nodal bigeminy bigeminismo nodal, bigeminismo nodal auriculoventricular.
  escape-capture bigeminy bigeminismo de escape-captura.
  nodal bigeminy bigeminismo nodal, bigeminismo nodal auriculoventricular.
  reciprocal bigeminy bigeminismo recíproco.
  ventricular bigeminy bigeminismo ventricular.
bigerminal *adj.* bigerminal.
bigonial *adj.* bigonial.
bilabe *n.* bilabio, bilabo.
bilaminar *adj.* bilaminar.
bilateral *adj.* bilateral.
bilateralism *n.* bilateralismo.
bile *n.* bilis.
  A bile bilis A.
  B bile bilis B.
  C bile bilis C.
  cystic bile bilis cística.
  gall-bladder bile bilis de la vesícula biliar.
  limy bile bilis caliza.
  Platner's crystalized bile bilis cristalizada de Platner.
  white bile bilis blanca.
Bilharzia *n.* Bilharzia.
bilharzial *adj.* bilharzial.
bilharziasis *n.* bilharziasis.
bilharzioma *n.* bilharzioma.
bilharziosis *n.* bilharziasis, bilharziosis.
biliary *adj.* biliar.
bilicyanin *n.* bilicianina.
bilidigestive *adj.* bilidigestivo, -va.
bilifaction *n.* bilifacción.
biliferous *adj.* bilífero, -ra.
bilification *n.* bilificación.
biliflavin *n.* biliflavina.
bilifuscin *n.* bilifuscina.
biligenesis *n.* biligénesis, biligenia.
biligenetic *adj.* biligenético, -ca.
biligenic *adj.* biligénico, -ca.
biligulate *adj.* biligulado, -da.
bilihumin *n.* bilihumina.
bilin *n.* bilina.
biline *n.* bilina.
bilious *adj.* bilioso, -sa.
biliousness *n.* biliosidad.
biliprasin *n.* biliprasina.
biliptysis *n.* biliptisis.
bilirachia *n.* bilirraquia.
bilirubin *n.* bilirrubina.
  conjugated bilirubin bilirrubina conjugada.
  direct bilirubin bilirrubina directa.
  direct reacting bilirubin bilirrubina de reacción directa.
  free bilirubin bilirrubina libre.
  indirect bilirubin bilirrubina indirecta.
  indirect reacting bilirubin bilirrubina de reacción indirecta.
  total bilirubin bilirrubina total.
  unconjugated bilirubin bilirrubina no conjugada.
bilirubinemia *n.* bilirrubinemia.
bilirubinglobulin *n.* bilirrubinglobulina.

bilirubinic *adj.* bilirrubínico, -ca.
bilirubinoids *n.* bilirrubinoides.
bilirubinuria *n.* bilirrubinuria.
biliuria *n.* biliuria.
biliverdin *n.* biliverdina.
biliverdine *n.* biliverdina.
biliverdinglobin *n.* biliverdinglobina.
bilobate *adj.* bilobulado, -da.
bilobed *adj.* bilobulado, -da, bilobular.
bilobular *adj.* bilobulillado, -da.
bilobulate *adj.* bilobulillado, -da.
bilocular *adj.* bilocular.
biloculate *adj.* biloculado, -da.
biloma *n.* biloma.
bilophodont *adj.* bilofodonte.
bimanual *adj.* bimanual.
bimastoid *adj.* bimastoideo, -a.
bimaxillary *adj.* bimaxilar.
bimeter *n.* bímetro.
bimodal *adj.* bimodal.
bimolecular *adj.* bimolecular.
binangle *n.* biangular.
binary *adj.* binario, -ria.
binaural *adj.* biauricular[2].
binauricular *adj.* binauricular.
bind *v.* unir, vendar.
binder *n.* faja[1].
   abdominal binder faja abdominal.
binegative *n.* binegativo.
binocular *n.* binocular.
binoculus *n.* binóculo.
binomial *adj.* binomial.
binophthalmoscope *n.* binoftalmoscopio.
binoscope *n.* binoscopio.
binotic *adj.* binótico, -ca.
binovular *adj.* biovular.
binuclear *adj.* binuclear.
binucleate *adj.* binucleado, -da.
binucleation *n.* binucleación.
binucleolate *adj.* binucleolado, -da.
bioacoustics *n.* bioacústica.
bioactive *adj.* bioactivo, -va.
bioactivity *n.* bioactividad.
bioaeration *n.* bioaereación.
bioaminergic *adj.* bioaminérgico, -ca.
bioassay *n.* bioanálisis, bioensayo.
bioastronautics *n.* bioastronáutica.
bioavailability *n.* biodisponibilidad.
bioblast *n.* bioblasto.
biocatalyst *n.* biocatalizador.
biocenosis *n.* biocenosis.
biocenotic *adj.* biocenótico, -ca.
biochemical *adj.* bioquímico, -ca.
biochemistry *n.* bioquímica.
biochemorphic *adj.* bioquemórfico, -ca, bio-quimórfico, -ca.
biochemorphology *n.* bioquemorfología, bioquimorfología.
biocidal *adj.* biocida[2].
biocide *n.* biocida[1].
bioclimatologist *n.* bioclimatólogo, -ga.
bioclimatology *n.* bioclimatología.
biocolloid *n.* biocoloide.
biocompatibility *n.* biocompatibilidad.
biocompatible *adj.* biocompatible.
biocybernetics *n.* biocibernética.
biocycle *n.* biociclo.
biocytin *n.* biocitina.
biodegradability *n.* biodegradabilidad.
biodegradable *adj.* biodegradable.
biodegradation *n.* biodegradación.
biodetritus *n.* biodetritus.
biodynamic *adj.* biodinámico, -ca.
biodynamics *n.* biodinámica.
bioecology *n.* bioecología.

bioelectricity *n.* bioelectricidad.
bioelement *n.* bioelemento.
bioeletronics *n.* bioelectrónica.
bioenergetics *n.* bioenergética.
bioenergy *n.* bioenergía.
bioengineering *n.* bioingeniería.
bioequivalence *n.* bioequivalencia.
bioequivalent *adj.* bioequivalente.
bioethics *n.* bioética.
biofeedback *n.* biorretroalimentación.
   alpha biofeedback biorretroalimentación alfa.
bioflavonoid *n.* bioflavonoide.
biogenesis *n.* biogénesis.
biogenetic *adj.* biogenético, -ca.
biogenic *adj.* biogénico, -ca.
biogenous *adj.* biógeno, -na.
biogeny *n.* biogenia.
biogeochemistry *n.* biogeoquímica.
biogeography *n.* biogeografía.
biograph *n.* biógrafo.
biogravics *n.* biogravedad.
biohazard *n.* biorriesgo, peligro biológico.
biohydraulic *adj.* biohidráulico, -ca.
bioimplant *n.* bioimplante.
bioincompatibility *n.* bioincompatibilidad.
bioinstrument *n.* bioinstrumento.
biokinetics *n.* biocinética.
biologic *adj.* biológico, -ca.
biological *adj.* biológico, -ca.
   biological plausibility verosimilitud biológica.
biologist *n.* biólogo, -ga.
biology *n.* biología.
   cellular biology biología celular.
   molecular biology biología molecular.
   oral biology biología bucal.
   radiation biology biología de la radiación, biología de radiación.
bioluminiscence *n.* bioluminiscencia.
biolysis *n.* biólisis.
biolytic *adj.* biolítico, -ca.
biomarker *n.* biomarcador.
biomass *n.* biomasa.
biomaterial *n.* biomaterial.
biomathematics *n.* biomatemáticas.
biome *n.* bioma, biomo.
biomechanics *n.* biomecánica.
   dental biomechanics biomecánica dental.
biomedical *adj.* biomédico, -ca.
biomedicine *n.* biomedicina.
biomembrane *n.* biomembrana.
biomembranous *adj.* biomembranoso, -sa.
biometeorologist *n.* biometeorólogo, -ga.
biometeorology *n.* biometeorología.
biometer *n.* biómetro.
biometrician *n.* biómetra.
biometrics *n.* biometría.
biometry *n.* biometría.
biomicroscope *n.* biomicroscopio.
   slit-lamp biomicroscope biomicroscopio de lámpara de hendidura.
biomicroscopy *n.* biomicroscopía.
biomolecule *n.* biomolécula.
biomotor *n.* biomotor.
Biomphalaria *n.* Biomphalaria.
bion *n.* bion.
bionecrosis *n.* bionecrosis.
bionic *adj.* biónico, -ca.
bionics *n.* biónica.
bionomics *n.* bionómica.
bionomy *n.* bionomía.
bionosis *n.* bionosis.
bionucleonics *n.* bionucleónica.
bio-osmotic *adj.* bioosmótico, -ca.
biophage *n.* biófago, -ga[1].
biophagism *n.* biofagismo.

biophagous *adj.* biófago, -ga[2].
biophagy *n.* biofagia.
biopharmaceutics *n.* biofarmacéutica.
biopharmacy *n.* biofarmacia.
biophase *n.* biofase.
biophilia *n.* biofilia.
biophotometer *n.* biofotómetro.
biophylactic *adj.* biofiláctico, -ca.
biophylaxis *n.* biofilaxis.
biophysical *adj.* biofísico, -ca.
biophysics *n.* biofísica.
   dental biophysics biofísica dental.
biophysiography *n.* biofisiografía.
biophysiology *n.* biofisiología.
bioplasia *n.* bioplasia.
biopoiesis *n.* biopoyesis.
biopolymer *n.* biopolímero.
bioprosthesis *n.* bioprótesis.
biopsy *n.* biopsia.
   aspiration biopsy biopsia por aspiración.
   bite biopsy biopsia fraccionaria.
   bone biopsy biopsia ósea.
   brush biopsy biopsia por cepillado, biopsia por cepillo.
   cerebral biopsy biopsia cerebral.
   cervix uterinic biopsy biopsia del cuello uterino.
   chorionic biopsy biopsia coriónica.
   chorionic villus biopsy (CVB) biopsia de vellosidad coriónica (BVC).
   cone biopsy biopsia cónica, biopsia de cono.
   cytological biopsy biopsia citológica.
   endometrium biopsy biopsia del endometrio.
   endoscopic biopsy biopsia endoscópica.
   excision biopsy biopsia escisional, biopsia por escisión.
   exploratory biopsy biopsia de exploración.
   fine-needle aspiration biopsy biopsia por punción-aspiración con aguja fina.
   gastric biopsy gastrobiopsia.
   incision biopsy biopsia incisional.
   liver biopsy biopsia hepática.
   muscular biopsy biopsia muscular.
   needle biopsy biopsia por aguja, biopsia por punción.
   negative biopsy biopsia negativa.
   open biopsy biopsia a cielo abierto.
   percutaneous biopsy biopsia percutánea.
   percutaneous renal biopsy biopsia renal percutánea.
   positive biopsy biopsia positiva.
   punch biopsy biopsia con sacabocados, biopsia de sacabocado.
   renal biopsy biopsia renal.
   sponge biopsy biopsia con esponja.
   sternal biopsy biopsia esternal.
   surface biopsy biopsia de superficie, biopsia exfoliativa, biopsia superficial.
   surgical biopsy biopsia quirúrgica.
   transvenous renal biopsy biopsia renal transvenosa.
   trephine biopsy biopsia por trepanación.
   wedge biopsy biopsia en cuña.
biopsychic *adj.* biopsíquico, -ca.
biopsychology *n.* biopsicología.
biopsychosocial *adj.* biopsicosocial.
biopterin *n.* biopterina.
biopyoculture *n.* biopiocultivo.
biorational *adj.* biorracional.
biorbital *adj.* biorbital, biorbitario, -ria.
bioreversible *adj.* biorreversible.
biorgan *n.* biórgano.
biorheology *n.* biorreología.
biorhythm *n.* biorritmo.

bios *n.* bios.
bioscience *n.* biociencia.
bioscopy *n.* bioscopia.
biosis *n.* biosis.
biosmosis *n.* biósmosis.
biosocial *adj.* biosocial.
biospectrometry *n.* bioespectrometría.
biospectroscopy *n.* bioespectroscopia.
biospeleology *n.* bioespeleología.
biosphere *n.* biosfera.
biostatics *n.* bioestática, biostática.
biostatistician *n.* bioestadístico, -ca.
biostatistics *n.* bioestadística.
biostereometrics *n.* bioestereométrica.
biosynthesls *n.* biosíntesis.
biosynthetic *adj.* biosintético, -ca.
biosystem *n.* biosistema.
biota *n.* biota.
biotaxis *n.* biotaxis.
biotaxy *n.* biotaxia.
biotechnology *n.* biotecnología.
　improvement biotechnology biotecnología mejorativa.
　medical biotechnology biotecnología médica.
biotelemetry *n.* biotelemetría.
biotherapy *n.* bioterapia.
biothesiometer *n.* biotesiómetro.
biotic *adj.* biótico, -ca.
biotics *n.* biótica.
biotin *n.* biotina.
biotinides *n.* biotínidos.
biotinyllysine *n.* biotinilisina.
biotome *n.* biotomo.
biotomy *n.* biotomía.
biotope *n.* biotopo.
biotoxication *n.* biotoxicación.
biotoxicology *n.* biotoxicología.
biotoxin *n.* biotoxina.
biotransformation *n.* biotransfomación.
biotropism *n.* biotropismo.
biotype *n.* biotipo.
biotypology *n.* biotipología.
biovar *n.* biovar.
biovular *adj.* biovular.
bipalatinoid *adj.* bipalatinoide.
biparasitic *adj.* biparásito, -ta.
biparasitism *n.* biparasitismo.
biparental *adj.* biparental.
biparietal *adj.* biparietal.
biparous *adj.* bíparo, -a.
bipartite *adj.* bipartido, -da.
biped *n.* bípedo, -da.
bipedal *adj.* bipedal, bipédico, -ca.
bipennate *adj.* bipenato, -ta.
bipenniform *adj.* bipenniforme, bipenniforme.
biperforate *adj.* biperforado, -da.
biphasic *adj.* bifásico, -ca.
biphenotypic *adj.* bifenotípico, -ca.
biphenotypy *n.* bifenotipia.
bipolar *adj.* bipolar.
bipositive *adj.* bipositivo, -va.
bipotential *adj.* bipotencial.
bipotentiality *n.* bipotencialidad.
　bipotentiality of the gonad bipotencialidad de la gónada.
biramous *adj.* birramoso, -sa.
birefringence *n.* birrefringencia.
　crystalline birefringence birrefringencia cristalina.
　flow birefringence birrefringencia de flujo.
　form birefringence birrefringencia de forma.
　intrinsic birefringence birrefringencia intrínseca.
　strain birefringence birrefringencia de tensión.

　streaming birefringence birrefringencia de corriente.
birefringent *adj.* birrefringente.
birotation *n.* birrotación.
birth *n.* nacimiento.
　complete birth nacimiento completo.
　cross birth nacimiento transversal.
　dead birth nacimiento con producto muerto.
　head birth nacimiento de vértice.
　multiple birth nacimiento múltiple.
　post-term birth nacimiento tardío.
　preterm birth nacimiento prematuro, nacimiento pretérmino.
birthmark *n.* antojo[2].
bisacromial *adj.* biacromial, bisacromial.
bisalbuminemia *n.* bisalbuminemia.
biscuit *n.* bizcocho.
　hard biscuit bizcocho duro.
　medium biscuit bizcocho medio.
　soft biscuit bizcocho blando.
bisection *n.* bisección.
bisegmentectomy *n.* bisegmentectomía.
biseptate *adj.* biseptado, -da.
bisexual *adj.* bisexual.
bisexuality *n.* ambisexualidad, bisexualidad.
bisferient *adj.* bífero, -ra, bisferiens.
bisferious *adj.* bífero, -ra, bisferiens.
bisiliac *adj.* bisilíaco, -ca.
bismuthia *n.* bismutia.
bismuthosis *n.* bismutosis.
bisque *n.* bisque.
　high bisque bisque alto.
　low bisque bisque bajo.
　medium bisque bisque medio.
bistephanic *adj.* biestefánico, -ca.
bisteroid *n.* bisteroide.
Biston betularia *n.* Biston betularia.
bistoury *n.* bisturí[1].
bistratal *adj.* biestratificado, -da.
bite *n.* bocado, dentellada, mordedura, mordida, mordisco.
　balanced bite mordida balanceada.
　check bite mordida para registro.
　closed bite mordida cerrada.
　cross bite mordida cruzada.
　edge-to-edge bite mordida borde a borde.
　normal bite mordida normal.
　open bite mordida abierta.
　scissor bite mordida en tijera.
　underhung bite mordida sobresaliente.
　wax bite mordida sobre cera.
bitemporal *adj.* bitemporal.
biterminal *adj.* biterminal.
Bithynia *n.* Bithynia.
bitrochanteric *adj.* bitrocantéreo, -a, bitrocántrico, -ca.
bitropic *adj.* bitrópico, -ca.
bitter *adj.* amargo, -ga.
bituminosis *n.* bituminosis.
biuret *n.* biuret.
bivalence *n.* bivalencia.
bivalency *n.* bivalencia.
bivalent *adj.* bivalente.
bivalve *adj.* bivalvo, -va.
biventer *n.* biventer.
biventral *adj.* bivenrral.
biventricular *adj.* biventricular.
bivitelline *adj.* bivitelino, -na.
bizarre *adj.* bizarro, -rra.
bizygomatic *adj.* bicigomático, -ca.
black *adj.* negro, -gra.
blackout *n.* desmayo.
　visual blackout desmayo visual.
bladder *n.* vejiga.
　atonic bladder vejiga atónica.

　atonic neurogenic bladder vejiga atónica neurógena.
　automatic bladder vejiga automática.
　autonomic bladder vejiga autónoma, vejiga autonómica.
　autonomic neurogenic bladder vejiga neurogénica autonóma.
　chard bladder vejiga medular.
　cord bladder vejiga en cuerda.
　fasciculate bladder vejiga de la hiel, vejiga fasciculada.
　flaccid bladder vejiga fláccida.
　hypertonic bladder vejiga espasmódica, vejiga hipertónica.
　ileal bladder vejiga ileal.
　irritable bladder vejiga irritable, vejiga nerviosa.
　low-compliance bladder vejiga de baja elasticidad.
　neurogenic bladder vejiga neurógena, vejiga neurogénica.
　neuropathic bladder vejiga neuropática.
　non-reflex bladder vejiga no refleja.
　pseudoneurogenic bladder vejiga seudoneurogénica.
　reflex bladder vejiga refleja.
　reflex neurogenic bladder vejiga neurogénica refleja.
　spastic bladder vejiga espástica.
　uninhibited neurogenic bladder vejiga neurogénica desinhibida.
　urinary bladder vejiga de la orina, vejiga urinaria, vesica urinalis, vesica urinaria.
bland *adj.* blando, -da.
blank *adj.* blanco, -ca[3].
blanket *n.* manta.
　bath blanket manta de baño.
　hypothermia blanket manta de hipotermia.
blast *n.* blast, blasto.
blastation *n.* blastación.
blastema *n.* blastema.
　nephric blastema blastema néfrico.
blastemic *adj.* blastémico, -ca.
blastic *adj.* blástico, -ca.
blastid *n.* blástida, blástide.
blastide *n.* blástida, blástide.
blastin *n.* blastina.
blastocele *n.* blastocele.
blastocelic *adj.* blastocélico, -ca.
blastochyle *n.* blastoquilo.
blastocoele *n.* blastocele.
blastocoelic *adj.* blastocélico, -ca.
blastocyst *n.* blastocisto.
Blastocystis hominis *n.* Blastocystis hominis.
blastocyte *n.* blastocito.
blastocytoma *n.* blastocitoma.
blastoderm *n.* blastodermo.
　bilaminar blastoderm blastodermo bilaminar.
　embryonic blastoderm blastodermo embrionario.
　extraembryonic blastoderm blastodermo extraembrionario.
　trilaminar blastoderm blastodermo trilaminar.
blastoderma *n.* blastodermo.
blastodermal *adj.* blastodermal.
blastodermic *adj.* blastodérmico, -ca.
blastodisc *n.* blastodisco.
blastodisk *n.* blastodisco.
blastogenesis *n.* blastogénesis.
blastogenetic *adj.* blastogenético, -ca.
blastogenic *adj.* blastogénico, -ca.
blastogeny *n.* blastogenia.
blastokinin *n.* blastocinina.

blastolysis *n.* blastólisis.
blastolytic *adj.* blastolítico, -ca.
blastoma *n.* blastoma.
　autochthonous blastoma blastoma autóctono.
　heterochthonous blastoma blastoma heteróctono, blastoma teratógeno.
　pluricentric blastoma blastoma pluricéntrico, blastoma pluricentro.
　unicentric blastoma blastoma unicéntrico.
blastomatoid *adj.* blastomatoide.
blastomatosis *n.* blastomatosis.
blastomatous *adj.* blastomatoso, -sa.
blastomere *n.* blastómera, blastómero.
blastomerotomy *n.* blastomerotomía.
blastomogenic *adj.* blastomogénico, -ca.
blastomogenous *adj.* blastomógeno, -na.
blastomyces *n.* blastomices.
Blastomyces *n.* Blastomyces.
blastomycete *n.* blastomiceto.
blastomycosis *n.* blastomicosis.
　Brazilian blastomycosis blastomicosis brasileña.
　cutaneous blastomycosis blastomicosis cutánea.
　European blastomycosis blastomicosis europea.
　keloidal blastomycosis blastomicosis queloide.
　North American blastomycosis blastomicosis norteamericana.
　South American blastomycosis blastomicosis sudamericana.
　systemic blastomycosis blastomicosis generalizada.
blastoneuropore *n.* blastoneuroporo.
blastophore *n.* blastóforo.
blastophthoria *n.* blastoftoria.
blastophthoric *adj.* blastoftórico, -ca.
blastophyllum *n.* blastófilo.
blastopore *n.* blastoporo.
blastosphere *n.* blastosfera.
blastostroma *n.* blastostroma.
blastotomy *n.* blastotomía.
blastozooid *n.* blastozoide.
blastula *n.* blástula.
blastular *adj.* blastular.
blastulation *n.* blastulación.
bleaching *adj.* blanqueamiento, decolorante, descolorante.
　coronal bleaching blanqueamiento coronal.
bleb *n.* ampolla3.
bleed *v.* sangrar.
bleeder *n.* sangrador.
bleeding[1] *adj.* sangrador, -ra.
bleeding[2] *n.* desangramiento, hemorragia, sangrado, sangramiento.
　arterial bleeding hemorragia arterial.
　breakthrough bleeding hemorragia de disrupción.
　dysfunctional uterine bleeding sangrado uterino disfuncional.
　gastrointestinal bleeding hemorragia gastrointestinal.
　implantation bleeding hemorragia por implantación.
　occult bleeding hemorragia oculta.
　summer bleeding hemorragia estival.
　withdrawal bleeding hemorragia por privación.
blennadenitis *n.* blenadenitis.
blennemesis *n.* blenemesis.
blennogenic *adj.* blenogénico, -ca.
blennogenous *adj.* blenógeno, -na.
blennoid *adj.* blenoide.

blennophthalmia *n.* blenoftalmia, blenoftalmía.
blennorrhagia *n.* blenorragia.
blennorrhagic *adj.* blenorrágico, -ca.
blennorrhea *n.* blenorrea.
　blennorrhea conjunctivalis blenorrea conjuntival.
　blennorrhea neonatorum blenorrea de los recién nacidos, blenorrea del neonato, blenorrea neonatorum.
　inclusion blennorrhea blenorrea de inclusión.
　Stoerk's blennorrhea blenorrea de Stoerk.
blennostasis *n.* blenostasis.
blennostatic *adj.* blenostático, -ca.
blennothorax *n.* blenotórax.
blennuria *n.* blenuria.
blenorrheal *adj.* blenorreico, -ca.
blepharadenitis *n.* blefaradenitis.
blepharal *adj.* blefárico, -ca.
blepharectomy *n.* blefarectomía.
blepharedema *n.* blefaredema.
blepharelosis *n.* blefarelosis.
blepharism *n.* blefarismo.
blepharitis *n.* blefaritis.
　blepharitis acarica blefaritis acárica.
　blepharitis angularis blefaritis angular.
　blepharitis ciliaris blefaritis ciliar.
　blepharitis follicularis blefaritis folicular.
　blepharitis marginalis blefaritis marginal.
　blepharitis oleosa blefaritis oleosa.
　blepharitis parasitica blefaritis parasitaria.
　blepharitis phthiriatica blefaritis ftiriásica.
　blepharitis rosacea blefaritis rosácea.
　blepharitis sicca blefaritis seca.
　blepharitis squamosa blefaritis escamosa.
　blepharitis ulcerosa blefaritis ulcerosa.
　ciliary blepharitis blefaritis ciliar.
　demodectic blepharitis blefaritis demodéctica.
　marginal blepharitis blefaritis marginal.
　Meibomian blepharitis blefaritis meibomiana.
　non-ulcerative blepharitis blefaritis no ulcerativa, blefaritis no ulcerosa.
　pediculous blepharitis blefaritis pediculosa.
　pustular blepharitis blefaritis pustular.
　seborrheic blepharitis blefaritis seborreica.
　squamous seborrheic blepharitis blefaritis seborreica escamosa.
　staphylococcic blepharitis blefaritis estafilocócica.
　ulcerative blepharitis blefaritis ulcerosa.
blepharoadenitis *n.* blefaradenitis, blefaroadenitis.
blepharoadenoma *n.* blefaroadenoma.
blepharoatheroma *n.* blefaroateroma.
blepharochalasis *n.* blefarocalasia.
blepharochromidrosis *n.* blefarocromidrosis.
blepharoclonus *n.* blefaroclono.
blepharocoloboma *n.* blefarocoloboma.
blepharoconjunctivitis *n.* blefaroconjuntivitis.
blepharodermatitis *n.* blefarodermatitis.
blepharodiastasis *n.* blefarodiastasis.
blepharoedema *n.* blefaroedema.
blepharokeratoconjunctivitis *n.* blefaroqueratoconjuntivitis.
blepharomelasma *n.* blefaromelasma.
blepharon *n.* blefaron.
blepharoncus *n.* blefaroncosis.
blepharopachynsis *n.* blefaropaquinsis.
blepharophimosis *n.* blefarofimosis.
blepharophyma *n.* blefarofima.
blepharoplast *n.* blefaroplasto.
blepharoplastic *adj.* blefaroplástico, -ca.
blepharoplasty *n.* blefaroplastia.

blepharoplegia *n.* blefaroplejía.
blepharoptosia *n.* blefaroptosis.
　blepharoptosia adiposa blefaroptosis adiposa.
　false blepharoptosia blefaroptosis falsa.
blepharoptosis *n.* blefaroptosis.
blepharopyorrhea *n.* blefaropiorrea.
blepharorrhaphy *n.* blefarorrafia.
blepharospasm *n.* blefaroespasmo, blefaroespasmo.
　essential blepharospasm blefaroespasmo esencial.
　reflex blepharospasm blefaroespasmo reflejo.
　sympathetic blepharospasm blefaroespasmo simpático.
　symptomatic blepharospasm blefaroespasmo sintomático.
blepharospasmus *n.* blefaroespasmo.
blepharosphincterectomy *n.* blefarosfinterectomía.
blepharostat *n.* blefaróstato.
blepharostenosis *n.* blefarostenosis.
blepharosynechia *n.* blefarosinequia.
blepharotomy *n.* blefarotomía.
blind *adj.* ciego, -ga.
blindness *n.* ceguera.
　Bright's blindness ceguera de Bright.
　color blindness ceguera para los colores.
　cortical blindness ceguera cortical.
　eclipse blindness ceguera por eclipse.
　flight blindness ceguera de vuelo.
　green blindness ceguera verde.
　hysterical blindness ceguera histérica.
　letter blindness ceguera literal.
　mind blindness ceguera mental.
　music blindness ceguera musical.
　night blindness ceguera nocturna.
　object blindness ceguera objetiva.
　psychic blindness ceguera psíquica.
　river blindness ceguera de los ríos.
　sign blindness ceguera para los signos.
　smell blindness ceguera para el olfato.
　snow blindness ceguera de la nieve.
　taste blindness ceguera para el gusto.
　text blindness ceguera verbal.
　word blindness ceguera verbal.
blinking *n.* parpadeo.
blister *n.* ampolla3, blíster, vesícula.
　blood blister blíster hemorrágico, vesícula hemorrágica.
　fever blister vesícula febril.
　water blister vesícula acuosa.
bloat *n.* timpanitis.
block *n.* bloque, bloquear, bloqueo1.
　air block bloqueo de aire.
　alveolar-capillary block bloqueo alveolar-capilar, bloqueo alvéolocapilar.
　anesthetic block bloqueo anestésico.
　anterograde block bloqueo anterógrado.
　arborization block bloqueo de arborización.
　atrioventricular block bloqueo auriculoventricular bloqueo A-V).
　atrioventricular heart block bloqueo cardíaco auriculoventricular.
　A-V block bloqueo auriculoventricular bloqueo A-V).
　Bier's block bloqueo de Bier.
　bite-block bloque de mordida.
　block out bloqueo5.
　bone block bloqueo de huesos.
　bundle branch block bloqueo cardíaco de rama.
　bundle-branch block (BBB) bloqueo de rama (BR).
　Bunnel block bloque de Bunnel.
　caudal block bloqueo caudal.

complete atrioventricular block bloqueo auriculoventricular completo, bloqueo auriculoventricular de tercer grado.

complete heart block (CHB) bloqueo cardíaco completo (BCC).

congenital complete heart block bloqueo cardíaco congénito.

congenital heart block bloqueo cardíaco congénito.

cryogenic block bloqueo criogénico, bloqueo criógeno.

depolarization block bloqueo de despolarización.

depolarizing block bloqueo de despolarización.

dynamic block bloqueo dinámico.

ear block bloqueo auditivo.

entrance block bloqueo de entrada.

epidural block bloqueo epidural.

exit block bloqueo de salida.

fascicular block bloqueo fascicular.

field block bloqueo de campo.

first degree atrioventricular block bloqueo auriculoventricular de primer grado.

first degree heart block bloqueo auriculoventricular de primer grado.

heart block bloqueo cardíaco, bloqueo del corazón.

incomplete heart block bloqueo cardíaco incompleto.

infranodal block bloqueo infranodal.

intercostal block bloqueo intercostal.

intercostal nerve block bloqueo de los nervios intercostales.

interventricular block bloqueo de rama (BR).

intra-atrial block bloqueo intraauricular.

intranasal block bloqueo intranasal.

intraspinal block bloqueo intraespinal.

intravenous block bloqueo de Bier.

intraventricular block bloqueo intraventricular.

metabolic block bloqueo metabólico.

Mobitz block bloqueo tipo Mobitz.

Mobitz type I heart block bloqueo cardíaco de tipo Mobitz I, bloqueo tipo Mobitz I.

Mobitz type II heart block bloqueo cardíaco de tipo Mobitz II, bloqueo tipo Mobitz II.

nerve block bloqueo nervioso.

neuromuscular block bloqueo neuromuscular.

non-depolarizing block bloqueo no despolarizante.

paracervical block bloqueo paracervical.

paraneural block bloqueo paraneural.

parasacral block bloqueo parasacro.

paravertebral block bloqueo paravertebral.

partial heart block bloqueo cardíaco parcial.

peri-infarction block bloqueo periinfarto.

perineural block bloqueo perineural.

phase I block bloqueo de fase I.

phase II block bloqueo de fase II.

phenol block bloqueo fenólico.

presacral block bloqueo presacro.

protective block bloqueo protector.

pudendal block bloqueo pudendo.

retrograde block bloqueo retrógrado.

right bundle branch block (RBBB) bloqueo de rama derecha.

sacral block bloqueo sacro.

saddle block bloqueo en silla de montar.

second degree atrioventricular block bloqueo auriculoventricular de segundo grado.

second degree heart block bloqueo auriculoventricular de segundo grado.

sinoatrial block bloqueo cardíaco sinoauricular (SA).

sinoatrial exit block bloqueo cardíaco sinoauricular (SA).

sinoauricular block bloqueo sinoauricular.

sinotrial block bloqueo sinoatrial.

sinus block bloqueo sinusal.

sinus exit block bloqueo cardíaco sinoauricular (SA).

spinal block bloqueo espinal.

spinal-subarachnoid block bloqueo espinal subaracnoideo.

splanchnic block bloqueo esplácnico.

stellate block bloqueo estrellado.

subarachnoid block bloqueo subaracnoideo.

suprahisian block bloqueo suprahisiano.

sympathetic block bloqueo simpático.

third degree heart block bloqueo auriculoventricular completo, bloqueo auriculoventricular de tercer grado.

trans-sacral block bloqueo trans-sacro.

tubal block bloqueo tubárico.

unidirectional block bloqueo unidireccional.

uterosacral block bloqueo uterosacro.

ventricular block bloqueo ventricular.

Wenckebach block bloqueo de Wenckebach.

Wenckebach heart block bloqueo cardíaco de Wenckebach.

Wilson block bloqueo de Wilson.

Wolff-Chaikoff block bloqueo de Wolff-Chaikoff.

blockade *n.* bloqueo².

"beta-adrenergic blockade; beta-blockade" bloqueo adrenérgico beta.

adrenergic blockade bloqueo adrenérgico.

adrenergic neuron blockade bloqueo de neurona adrenérgica.

alpha-adrenergic blockade bloqueo adrenérgico alfa.

alpha-blockade bloqueo adrenérgico alfa.

cholinergic blockade bloqueo colinérgico.

ganglionic blockade bloqueo ganglionar.

methadone blockade bloqueo por metadona.

myoneural blockade bloqueo mioneural.

narcotic blockade bloqueo narcótico.

neuromuscular blockade bloqueo neuromuscular.

renal blockade bloqueo renal.

sympathetic blockade bloqueo simpático.

vagal blockade bloqueo vagal.

vagus nerve blockade bloqueo vagal.

virus blockade bloqueo viral.

blockage *n.* blocaje, bloqueo³.

tendon blockage bloqueo de tendón.

blocker *n.* bloqueador, -ra, bloqueante.

alpha-blocker bloqueante alfa-adrenérgico.

beta-blocker bloqueante beta-adrenérgico.

calcium channel blocker bloqueante de la vía del calcio, bloqueante de los canales de calcio.

blocking¹ *adj.* bloqueador, -ra.

blocking² *n.* bloqueo⁴.

affective blocking bloqueo afectivo, bloqueo emocional.

mental blocking bloqueo mental.

thought blocking bloqueo del pensamiento.

block-out *n.* blockout, bloqueo⁵.

blood *n.* sangre.

anticoaglated blood sangre anticoagulable.

arterial blood sangre arterial.

blood iron sideremia.

blood volume volemia.

central blood sangre central.

cord blood sangre del cordón.

defibrinated blood sangre desfibrinada.

laked blood sangre lacada.

laky blood sangre lacada.

mixed venous blood sangre venosa mixta.

occult blood sangre oculta.

peripheral blood sangre periférica.

sludged blood sangre estancada, sangre lodosa.

splanchnic blood sangre esplácnica.

strawberry cream blood sangre en crema de fresa.

venous blood sangre venosa.

whole blood sangre entera, sangre total.

bloodless *adj.* incruento, -ta.

bloodletter *n.* sangrador.

bloodletting *n.* sangradura, sangría.

general bloodletting sangría general.

local bloodletting sangría local.

bloom *n.* florescencia.

blowpipe *n.* soplete.

blurring *n.* borrosidad.

focus blurring borrosidad de foco, borrosidad geométrica.

kinetic blurring borrosidad cinética.

photographic blurring borrosidad fotográfica.

Bodo *n.* Bodo.

body *n.* cuerpo.

alcoholic hyaline body cuerpo hialino alcohólico.

Alder body cuerpo de Alder.

alkapton body cuerpo alcaptónico.

amylaceous body amyloid body cuerpo amiláceo, cuerpo amiloide.

amyloid body of the prostate cuerpo amiloide de la próstata.

apoptotic body cuerpo apoptótico.

Arnold's body cuerpo de Arnold.

asbestos body cuerpo de amianto, cuerpo de asbestosis.

asbestosis body cuerpo de asbestosis.

Aschoff body cuerpo de Aschoff.

asteroid body cuerpo asteroide.

atretic luteum body cuerpo amarillo atrésico.

Auer body cuerpo de Auer.

Babès-Ernst body cuerpo de Babès-Ernst.

Balbiani's body cuerpo de Balbiani.

bamboo body cuerpo de bambú.

Barr body cuerpo de Barr.

Barr chromatin body cuerpo de cromatina de Barr.

basal body cuerpo basal, cuerpo basal del cilio.

basal body of the cilia cuerpo basal, cuerpo basal del cilio.

Behla's body cuerpo de Behla.

bigeminal body cuerpo bigémino.

Bracht-Wächter body cuerpo de Bracht-Wächter.

brassy body cuerpo bronceado.

Cabot's ring body cuerpo anular de Cabot.

Call-Exner body cuerpo de Call-Exner.

cancer body cuerpo de cáncer.

carotid body cuerpo carotídeo.

cell body cuerpo celular.

chromaffin body cuerpo cromafín, cuerpo cromafínico.

chromatin body cuerpo cromatínico, cuerpo de cromatina.

chromatinic body cuerpo cromatínico, cuerpo de cromatina.

chromatoid body cuerpo cromatoide.

chromophilous body cuerpo cromófilo.

Civatte body cuerpo de Civatte.

coccoid X body cuerpo cocoide X.

colloid body cuerpo coloide.

colostrum body cuerpo del calostro.

conchoidal body cuerpo concoidal.

corneal foreign body cuerpo extraño corneal.

Councilman body cuerpo de Councilman.

Cowdry's type A inclusion body cuerpo de inclusión tipo A de Cowdry.
Cowdry's type B inclusion body cuerpo de inclusión tipo B de Cowdry.
creola body cuerpo de criollo.
cystoplasmic inclusion body cuerpo citoplasmático de inclusión.
cytoid body cuerpo citoide.
Deetjen's body cuerpo de Deetjen.
dense body cuerpo denso.
Döhle body cuerpo de Döhle.
Donné's body cuerpo de Donné.
Dutcher body cuerpo de Dutcher.
Ehrlich's inner body cuerpo internos de Ehrlich.
elementary body cuerpo elemental.
Elschnig body cuerpo de Elschnig.
end body cuerpo final.
ferruginous body cuerpo ferruginoso.
foreign body cuerpo extraño.
foreign body in the ear cuerpo extraño auditivo.
foreign body in the esophagus cuerpo extraño esofágico.
foreign body in the eye cuerpo extraño ocular.
foreign body in the larynx cuerpo extraño laríngeo.
foreign body in the throat cuerpo en la garganta.
fuchsin body cuerpo de fucsina.
gamma-Favre body cuerpo gamma de Favre.
Gamma-Gandy body cuerpo de Gamma-Gandy, cuerpo de Gandy-Gamma.
Gandy-Gamma body cuerpo de Gamma-Gandy, cuerpo de Gandy-Gamma.
glomus body cuerpo de glomus, cuerpo glómico.
Gordon's elementary body cuerpo elemental de Gordon.
Guarnieri body cuerpo de Guarnieri.
habenular body cuerpo habenular.
Halberstaedter-Prowazek body cuerpo de Halberstaedter-Prowazek.
Harting body cuerpo Harting.
Hassall-Henle body cuerpo de Hassall-Henle.
Hassall's body cuerpo de Hassall.
Heinz body cuerpo de Heinz.
Heinz-Ehrlich body cuerpo de Heinz-Ehrlich.
hematoxylin body cuerpo hematoxifílico, cuerpo hematoxilínico.
hematoxyphil body cuerpo hematoxifílico, cuerpo hematoxilínico.
Hensen's body cuerpo de Hensen.
Herring body cuerpo de Herring.
Howell-Jolly body cuerpo de Howell, cuerpo de Howell-Jolly.
Howell's body cuerpo de Howell, cuerpo de Howell-Jolly.
hyaline body cuerpo hialino.
hyaline body of the pituitary cuerpo hialino de la hipófisis.
hyaloid body cuerpo hialoideo.
immune body cuerpo inmune.
inclusion body cuerpo de inclusión, cuerpo de inclusión nuclear.
inner body cuerpo interno.
intraocular foreign body cuerpo extraño intraocular.
Jaworski's body cuerpo de Jaworski.
Joest body cuerpo de Joest.
Jolly's body cuerpo de Jolly.
ketone body cuerpo cetónico.

Koch's blue body cuerpo azul de Koch.
Lafora body cuerpo de Lafora.
Landolt's body cuerpo de Landolt.
LCL body cuerpo de Levinthal-Coles-Lillie, cuerpo LCL.
LD body cuerpo de Leishman-Donovan, cuerpo LD.
LE body cuerpo LE.
Leishman-Donovan body cuerpo de Leishman-Donovan, cuerpo LD.
Levinthal-Coles-Lillie body cuerpo de Levinthal-Coles-Lillie, cuerpo LCL.
Lewy body cuerpo de Lewy.
Lindner's body cuerpo de Lindner.
Lindner's initial body cuerpo inicial de Lindner.
Lispchütz body cuerpo de Lipschütz.
loose body cuerpo suelto.
Lostorfer's body cuerpo de Lostorfer.
Luschka's body cuerpo de Luschka.
Luse body cuerpo de Luse.
Mallory's body cuerpo de Mallory.
Malpighian body cuerpo de Malpighi.
Marchal body cuerpo de Marchal.
Masson body cuerpo de Masson.
melon-seed body cuerpo de semilla de melón.
Michaelis-Gutman body cuerpo de Michaelis-Gutman.
Miyagawa body cuerpo de Miyagawa.
Mooser body cuerpo de Mooser.
Mott body cuerpo de Mott.
multilamellar body cuerpo multilaminar.
myelin body cuerpo de mielina.
Negri body cuerpo de Negri.
Neill-Mooser body cuerpo de Neill-Mooser.
nerve cell body cuerpo neuronal.
neuroepithelial body cuerpo neuroepitelial.
Nissl body cuerpo de Nissl.
nodular body cuerpo nodular.
Nothnagel's body cuerpo de Nothnagel.
nuclear inclusion body cuerpo de inclusión, cuerpo de inclusión nuclear.
Odland body cuerpo de Odland.
Pacchionian body cuerpo de Pacchioni.
Pappenheimer body cuerpo de Pappenheimer.
paraaortic body cuerpo paraaórtico.
paranephric body cuerpo paranéfrico.
paraphyseal body cuerpo parafisiario.
Paschen body cuerpo de Paschen.
pheochrome body cuerpo feocromo.
Pick's body cuerpo de Pick.
Plimmer's body cuerpo de Plimmer.
presegmenting body cuerpo presegmentae.
Prowazek body cuerpo de Prowazek, cuerpo de Prowazek-Greef.
Prowazek-Greef body cuerpo de Prowazek, cuerpo de Prowazek-Greef.
psammoma body cuerpo de psamoma.
psittacosis inclusion body cuerpo de inclusión de la psitacosis.
pyknotic body cuerpo picnótico.
Reilly body cuerpo de Reilly.
Renaut body cuerpo de Renaut.
residual body cuerpo residual.
residual body of Regaud cuerpo residual de Regaud.
restiform body cuerpo restiforme.
rice body cuerpo de arroz, cuerpo riciforme.
Ross's body cuerpo de Ross.
Russell body cuerpo de Russell.
sand body cuerpo arenáceo, cuerpo de arena.
Schaumann body cuerpo de Schaumann.
Schmorl body cuerpo de Schmorl.

sclerotic body cuerpo esclerótico.
segmenting body cuerpo segmentante.
spherical body cuerpo esférico.
subtarsal foreign body cuerpo extraño subtarsal.
tigroid body cuerpo tigroide.
Torres-Texeira body cuerpo de Torres-Texeira.
trachoma body cuerpo de tracoma.
tuffstone body cuerpo tobáceo.
ultimobranchial body cuerpo ultimobranquial.
vermiform body cuerpo vermiforme.
Verocay body cuerpo de Verocay.
Virchow-Hassall body cuerpo de Virchow-Hassall.
vitelline body cuerpo vitelino.
vitreous body cuerpo vítreo, cuerpo vítreo.
Weibel-Palade body cuerpo de Weibel-Palade.
Winkler's body cuerpo de Winkler.
Wolffian body cuerpo de Wolff.
Wolff-Orton body cuerpo de Wolff-Orton.
yellow body cuerpo amarillo.
yellow body of the ovary cuerpo amarillo del ovario.
yuxtaglomerular body cuerpo yuxtaglomerular.
zebra body cuerpo de cebra.
boil *n.* botón[1], divieso, furúnculo.
Aleppo boil botón de Aleppo.
Baghdad boil botón de Bagdad.
Biskra boil botón de Biskra.
blind boil furúnculo ciego.
Delhi boil furúnculo de Delhi.
Jericho boil furúnculo de Jericó.
Oriental boil botón de Oriente, botón oriental.
tropical boil furúnculo tropical.
Boletus satanas *n.* Boletus satanas.
bolometer *n.* bolómetro.
boloscope *n.* boloscopio.
bolus *n.* bolo.
alimentary bolus bolo alimentario, bolo alimenticio.
chondrin bolus bolo de condrina.
fecal bolus bolo fecal.
fungus bolus bolo fúngico.
intravenous bolus bolo endovenoso, bolo intravenoso.
bombard *v.* bombardear.
bombesin *n.* bombesina.
bond *n.* enlace.
bonding *n.* vinculación, vinculación afectiva.
maternal-infant bonding vinculación maternoinfantil.
bone *n.* hueso.
bone architecture arquitectura ósea.
bonelet *n.* huesecillo.
bony *adj.* óseo, -a.
boot *n.* bota.
abduction boot bota abductora.
Gibney's boot bota de Gibney.
Junod's boot bota de Junod.
Unna's boot bota de Unna.
Unna's paste boot bota de pasta de Unna.
borated *adj.* boratado, -da.
borborygmus *n.* borborigmo.
border *n.* borde[1].
brush border borde en cepillo.
denture border borde de dentadura, borde dentado, borde dental.
striated border borde estriado.
vermilion border borde bermellón.
borderline *adj.* borderline, limítrofe.

Bordetella *n.* Bordetella.
  Bordetella parapertussis Bordetella parapertussis.
  Bordetella pertussis Bordetella pertussis.
borism *n.* borismo.
boron *n.* boro.
Borrelia *n.* Borrelia.
borreliosis *n.* borreliosis.
boss *n.* giba.
  parietal boss giba parietal.
bosselated *adj.* boselado, -da, giboso, -sa.
botanic *adj.* botánico, -ca.
botany *n.* botánica.
  medical botany botánica médica.
botfly *n.* moscardón.
bothriocephaliasis *n.* botriocefaliasis.
bothriocephalus *n.* botriocéfalo.
bothrium *n.* botrio.
botryoid *adj.* botrioide.
Botryomyces *n.* Botryomyces.
botryomycoma *n.* botriomicoma.
botryomycosis *n.* micodesmoide, micofibroma.
botryomycosis *n.* botriomicosis.
botryomycotic *adj.* botriomicótico, -ca.
botrytimycosis *n.* botritimicosis.
bottle *n.* botella, frasco.
  blow bottle botella de espiración.
  Castaneda bottle botella de Castaneda.
  Mariotte bottle botella de Mariotte, frasco de Mariotte.
  nursing bottle biberón.
  Spritz bottle botella de Spritz.
  volumetric bottle frasco volumétrico.
  wash bottle botella para lavado, frasco lavador.
  Woulfe's bottle botella de Woulfe.
botuliform *adj.* botuliforme.
botulin *n.* botulina.
botulinal *adj.* botulínico, -ca.
botulinogenic *adj.* botulinogénico, botulinógeno, -na, botulogénico, -ca.
botulism *n.* botulismo.
  infant botulism botulismo del lactante, botulismo infantil.
  wound botulism botulismo en heridas, botulismo por herida.
botulismotoxin *n.* botulismotoxina.
botulogenic *adj.* botulogénico, -ca.
bouba *n.* bouba.
bouche de tapir *n.* bouche de tapir.
bougie *n.* bujía[1].
  caustic bougie bujía cáustica.
  conic bougie bujía cónica.
  cylindrical bougie bujía cilíndrica.
  dilating bougie bujía dilatable.
  ear bougie bujía auditiva.
  elastic bougie bujía elástica.
  elbowed bougie bujía acodada.
  filiform bougie bujía filiforme.
  following bougie bujía agregada.
  fusiform bougie bujía fusiforme.
  Hurst's bougie bujía de Hurst.
  Maloney's bougie bujía de Maloney.
  olive-tipped bougie bujía con punta de oliva.
  tapered bougie bujía ahusada.
  wax bougie bujía de cera.
  wax-tipped bougie bujía con extremo cubierto de cera, bujía con punta de cera.
  whip bougie bujía en látigo, bujía móvil.
bougienage *n.* bougienage.
bouillon *n.* caldo.
bound *adj.* fijado, -da.
bouquet *n.* bouquet, ramillete.
  bouquet de Riolan bouquet de Riolan.

bourdonnement *n.* zumbido.
bout *n.* brote[1].
bouton *n.* botón[2], bouton.
  axonal terminal bouton botón terminal axónico.
  Baghdad bouton botón de Bagdad.
  Biskra bouton botón de Biskra.
  bouton d'Orient botón de Oriente, botón oriental.
  bouton en chemise botón de camisa.
  bouton terminale botón terminal, bouton terminale.
  synaptic bouton botón sináptico.
  terminal bouton botón terminal, bouton terminale.
boutonnière *n.* boutonnière.
bovovaccination *n.* bovovacunación.
bovovaccine *n.* bovovacuna.
bowenoid *adj.* bowenoide.
bowl *n.* cubeta.
box *n.* caja.
  CAAT box caja de CAAT.
  CENP-B box caja de CENP-B.
  Skinner box caja de Skinner.
  tata box caja tata.
  viewing box negatoscopio.
boxel *n.* boxel.
brace *n.* abrazadera, braguero[1], corsé.
  derotation brace abrazadera de desrotación.
  Griswald brace abrazadera de Griswald.
  Milwaukee brace corsé de Milwaukee.
  Taylor brace corsé de Taylor.
  Taylor's back brace abrazadera de Taylor, braguero dorsal de Taylor.
bracelet *n.* brazalete.
  Nageotte's bracelet brazalete de Nageotte.
  Nussbaum's bracelet brazalete de Nussbaum.
brachial *adj.* braquial.
brachialgia *n.* braquialgia.
  brachialgia statica paresthestica braquialgia estática parestésica.
brachiametacarpia *n.* braquiametacarpia, braquimetacarpia.
brachiametatarsia *n.* braquiametatarsia, braquimetatarsia.
brachicephalous *adj.* braquicéfalo, -la.
brachiocephalic *adj.* braquiocefálico, -ca.
brachiocrural *adj.* braquiocrural.
brachiocubital *adj.* braquiocubital.
brachiocyllosis *n.* braquiocilosis.
brachiocyrtosis *n.* braquiocirtosis.
brachiofaciolingual *adj.* braquiofaciolingual.
brachiogram *n.* braquiograma.
brachioplasty *n.* braquioplastia.
brachium *n.* brachium, brazo[2].
brachybasia *n.* braquibasia.
brachybasocamptodactyly *n.* braquibasocamptodactilia.
brachybasophalangia *n.* braquibasofalangia.
brachycardia *n.* braquicardia.
brachycephalia *n.* braquicefalia.
brachycephalic *adj.* braquicefálico, -ca.
brachycephalism *n.* braquicefalismo.
brachycephaly *n.* braquicefalia.
brachycheilia *n.* braquiqueilia, braquiquilia.
brachychilia *n.* braquiqueilia, braquiquilia.
brachychronic *adj.* braquicrónico, -ca.
brachycnemic *adj.* braquicnémico, -ca.
brachycranial *adj.* braquicranio, -nia.
brachycranic *adj.* braquicránico, -ca.
brachydactylia *n.* braquidactilia.
brachydactylic *adj.* braquidactílico, -ca.
brachydactyly *n.* braquidactilia.
brachyesophagus *n.* braquiesófago.
brachyfacial *adj.* braquifacial.

brachyglossal *n.* braquigloso, -sa.
brachygnathia *n.* braquignatia.
brachygnathous *adj.* braquignato, -ta.
brachykerkic *adj.* braquicérquico, -ca, braquiquérquico, -ca.
brachyknemic *adj.* braquicnémico, -ca.
brachymelia *n.* braquimelia.
brachymesophalangia *n.* braquimesofalangia.
brachymetacarpalia *n.* braquimetacarpia.
brachymetacarpalism *n.* braquimetacarpia.
brachymetacarpia *n.* braquimetacarpia.
brachymetapody *n.* braquimetapodia.
brachymetatarsia *n.* braquimetatarsia.
brachymetropia *n.* braquimetropía.
brachymetropic *adj.* braquimétrope, braquimotrópico, -ca.
brachymorphic *adj.* braquimórfico, -ca, braquimorfo, -fa.
brachyodont *adj.* braquiodonte.
brachypellic *adj.* braquipélvico, -ca.
brachypelvic *adj.* braquipélvico, -ca.
brachyphalangia *n.* braquifalangia.
brachypodous *adj.* braquípodo, -da.
brachyprosopic *adj.* braquiprosópico, -ca.
brachyrhinia *n.* braquirrinia.
brachyrhynchus *n.* braquirrinco.
brachyskelic *adj.* braquisquélico, -ca.
brachyskelous *adj.* braquisquelo, -la.
brachystaphyline *adj.* braquistafilino, -na.
brachystasis *n.* braquistasis.
brachysyndactyly *n.* braquisindactilia.
brachytelephalangia *n.* braquitelefalangia.
brachytherapy *n.* braquiterapia.
brachytype *n.* braquitipo.
brachytypical *adj.* braquitípico, -ca.
brachyuranic *adj.* braquiuránico, -ca.
bracket *n.* bracket.
braditrophia *n.* braditrofia.
bradyacusia *n.* bradiacusia.
bradyarrhythmia *n.* bradiarritmia.
bradyarthria *n.* bradiartria.
bradyauxesis *n.* bradiauxesis.
bradycardia *n.* bradicardia.
  Branham's bradycardia bradicardia de Branham.
  cardiomuscular bradycardia bradicardia cardiomuscular.
  central bradycardia bradicardia central.
  essential bradycardia bradicardia esencial.
  fetal bradycardia bradicardia fetal.
  idiopathic bradycardia bradicardia idiopática.
  nodal bradycardia bradicardia nodal.
  postinfectious bradycardia bradicardia posinfecciosa, bradicardia postinfecciosa.
  postinfective bradycardia bradicardia posinfecciosa, bradicardia postinfecciosa.
  sinoatrial bradycardia bradicardia sinoauricular.
  sinus bradycardia bradicardia sinusal.
  vagal bradycardia bradicardia vagal.
  ventricular bradycardia bradicardia ventricular.
bradycardiac *adj.* bradicárdico.
bradycardic *adj.* bradicárdico.
bradycinesia *n.* bradicinesia.
bradycrotic *adj.* bradicrótico, -ca.
bradydiastalsis *n.* bradidiastalsis.
bradydiastole *n.* bradidiástole.
bradyecoia *n.* bradiecoia.
bradyesthesia *n.* bradiestesia.
bradygenesis *n.* bradigénesis.
bradyglossia *n.* bradiglosia.
bradykinesia *n.* bradicinesia, bradiquinesia.
bradykinetic *adj.* bradicinético, -ca.

bradylalia *n.* bradilalia.
bradylexia *n.* bradilexia.
bradylogia *n.* bradilogía.
bradypepsia *n.* bradipepsia.
bradyphagia *n.* bradifagia.
bradyphasia *n.* bradifasia.
bradyphemia *n.* bradifemia.
bradyphrasia *n.* bradifrasia.
bradyphrenia *n.* bradifrenia.
bradypnea *n.* bradipnea.
bradypragia *n.* bradipragia, bradipraxia.
bradypsychia *n.* bradipsiquia.
bradyrhythmia *n.* bradirritmia.
bradyspermatism *n.* bradiespermatismo, bradispermatismo.
bradysphygmia *n.* bradisfigmia.
bradystalsis *n.* bradistalsia, bradistalsis.
bradytachycardia *n.* braditaquicardia.
bradyteleocinesia *n.* bradi*teleocinesia, braditeleocinesis, braditeleoquinesia.
bradyteleokinesis *n.* braditeleocinesia, braditeleocinesis, braditeleoquinesia.
bradytocia *n.* braditocia.
bradytrophic *adj.* braditrófico, -ca.
bradyuria *n.* bradiuria.
bradyzoite *n.* bradizoíto.
braidism *n.* braidismo.
braille *n.* braille.
brain *n.* cerebro, encéfalo.
  brain stem neuroeje.
  isotopic brain scintigraphy gammaencefalografía.
branch *n.* rama, ramo.
branchia *n.* branquia.
branchial *adj.* branquial.
branching *adj.* ramificado, -da.
branchiogenic *adj.* branquiogénico, -ca.
branchiogenous *adj.* branquiógeno, -na.
branchioma *n.* branquioma.
branchiomere *n.* branquiómero.
branchiomeric *adj.* branquiomérico, -ca.
branchiomerism *n.* branquiomerismo.
branchiomotor *adj.* branquiomotor, -ra.
Branhamella *n.* Branhamella.
brash *n.* acedías.
  water brash acedías acuosas.
  weaning brash acedías del destete.
brazilein *n.* brasileína.
brazilin *n.* brasilina.
break *n.* ruptura.
breast *n.* mama.
breast-feeding *n.* lactancia materna.
  effective breast-feeding lactancia materna eficaz.
  ineffective breast-feeding lactancia materna ineficaz.
  interrumpted breast-feeding lactancia materna interrumpida.
breath *n.* aliento.
  bad breath aliento fétido, mal aliento.
  lead breath aliento plúmbico.
  liver breath aliento hepático.
  uremic breath aliento urémico.
breathing *n.* respiración.
  continuous positive pressure breathing respiración con presión positiva continua.
  glossopharyngeal breathing respiración glosofaríngea.
  intermittent positive pressure breathing respiración con presión positiva intermitente.
  mouth breathing respiración oral.
  positive-negative pressure breathing respiración con presión positiva negativa.
  shallow breathing respiración superficial.
bregma *n.* bregma.

bregmatic *adj.* bregmático, -ca.
bregmatodymia *n.* bregmatodimia.
brei *n.* brei.
bremsstrahlung *n.* bremsstrahlung.
brephic *adj.* bréfico, -ca.
brephoplastic *adj.* brefoplástico, -ca.
brephotropic *adj.* brefotrópico, -ca.
Brevibacteriaceae *n.* Brevibacteriaceae.
Brevibacterium *n.* Brevibacterium.
brevicollis *adj.* brevicollis.
brevilineal *adj.* brevilíneo, -a.
breviradiate *adj.* brevirradiado, -da.
bridge *n.* puente².
bridle *n.* brida.
brightic *adj.* brígtico, -ca.
brim *n.* borde².
brinolase *n.* brinolasa.
brisement forcé *n.* brisement forcé.
broach *n.* broca, escariador.
  barbed broach broca barbada, escariador barbado.
  pathfinder broach escariador de exploración.
  root canal broach escariador del conducto radicular.
  smooth broach broca lisa, escariador liso.
brochospirochetosis *n.* broncospiroquetosis.
bromated *adj.* bromado, -da.
bromatherapy *n.* bromatoterapia.
bromatologist *n.* bromatólogo, -ga.
bromatology *n.* bromatología.
bromatotherapy *n.* bromatoterapia.
bromatotoxin *n.* bromatotoxina.
bromatotoxismus *n.* bromatotoxismo.
bromatoxism *n.* bromatoxismo.
bromhidrosiphobia *n.* bromhidrosifobia, bromidrosifobia.
bromhidrosis *n.* bromhidrosis.
bromic *adj.* brómico, -ca.
bromide *n.* brómide.
bromidrosiphobia *n.* bromhidrosifobia, bromidrosifobia.
bromidrosis *n.* bromidrosis.
brominated *adj.* bromado, -da.
brominism *n.* brominismo.
brominized *adj.* bromado, -da.
bromism *n.* bromismo.
bromization *n.* bromuración.
bromized *adj.* bromado, -da.
bromoderma *n.* bromoderma, bromodermia.
bromohyperhidrosis *n.* bromohiperhidrosis.
bromoiodism *n.* bromoyodismo.
bromomania *n.* bromomanía.
bromopnea *n.* bromopnea.
bromphenol *n.* bromofenol.
bronchadenitis *n.* broncoadenitis.
bronchial *adj.* bronquial.
bronchiarctia *n.* bronquiarctia.
  capillary bronchiectasia bronquiectasia capilar.
  cylindrical bronchiectasia bronquiectasia cilíndrica.
  cystic bronchiectasia bronquiectasia quística.
  dry bronchiectasia bronquiectasia seca, bronquiectasia sicca.
  follicular bronchiectasia bronquiectasia folicular.
  saccular bronchiectasia bronquiectasia sacular.
bronchiectasia *n.* bronquiectasis.
bronchiectasic *adj.* bronquiectásico, -ca.
bronchiectasis *n.* bronquiectasis.
bronchiectatic *adj.* bronquiectático, -ca.
bronchiloquy *n.* bronquiloquia.
bronchiocele *n.* bronquiocele.
bronchiogenic *adj.* bronquiogénico, -ca.
bronchiole *n.* bronquiolo, bronquíolo.

  alveolar bronchiole bronquiolo respiratorio.
  lobular bronchiole bronquiolo lobulillar.
  respiratory bronchiole bronquiolo respiratorio.
  terminal bronchiole bronquiolo terminal.
bronchiolectasia *n.* bronquiolectasia, bronquiolectasis.
bronchiolectasis *n.* bronquiolectasia, bronquiolectasis.
bronchiolitis *n.* bronquiolitis.
  acute obliterating bronchiolitis bronquiolitis aguda obliterante.
  bronchiolitis exudativa bronquiolitis exudativa.
  bronchiolitis fibrosa obliterans bronquiolitis fibrosa obliterante.
  bronchiolitis obliterans bronquiolitis obliterante.
  exudative bronchiolitis bronquiolitis exudativa.
  proliferative bronchiolitis bronquiolitis proliferativa.
  vesicular bronchiolitis bronquiolitis vesicular.
bronchiolopulmonary *adj.* bronquiolopulmonar.
bronchiolus *n.* bronquiolo, bronquíolo.
bronchiospasm *n.* bronquiospasmo.
bronchiostenosis *n.* broncostenosis, bronquioestenosis.
bronchismus *n.* broncoespasmo.
  paradoxical bronchismus broncoespasmo paradójico.
bronchitic *adj.* bronquítico, -ca.
bronchitis *n.* bronquitis.
  acute bronchitis bronquitis aguda.
  acute laryngotracheal bronchitis bronquitis laringotraqueal aguda.
  asthmatic bronchitis bronquitis asmatiforme.
  bronchitis obliterans bronquitis obliterante.
  capillary bronchitis bronquitis capilar.
  Castellani's bronchitis bronquitis de Castellani.
  catarrhal bronchitis bronquitis catarral.
  cheesy bronchitis bronquitis caseosa.
  chronic bronchitis bronquitis crónica.
  croupous bronchitis bronquitis crupal.
  dry bronchitis bronquitis seca.
  epidemic bronchitis bronquitis epidémica.
  epidemic capillary bronchitis bronquitis capilar epidémica, bronquitis epidémica capilar.
  ether bronchitis bronquitis por éter.
  exudative bronchitis bronquitis exudativa.
  fibrinous bronchitis bronquitis fibrinosa.
  hemorrhagic bronchitis bronquitis hemorrágica.
  infectious asthmatic bronchitis bronquitis asmática infecciosa.
  mechanic bronchitis bronquitis mecánica.
  membranous bronchitis bronquitis membranosa.
  obliterative bronchitis bronquitis obliterante.
  phthinoid bronchitis bronquitis ftinoide.
  plastic bronchitis bronquitis plástica.
  polypoid bronchitis bronquitis polipoide.
  productive bronchitis bronquitis productiva.
  pseudomembranous bronchitis bronquitis seudomembranosa.
  putrid bronchitis bronquitis fétida, bronquitis pútrida.
  secondary bronchitis bronquitis secundaria.
  staphylococcus bronchitis bronquitis estafilocócica.
  streptococcal bronchitis bronquitis estreptocócica.
  suffocative bronchitis bronquitis sofocante.
  verminous bronchitis bronquitis verminosa.

vesicular bronchitis bronquitis vesicular.
bronchoadenitis *n.* broncoadenitis.
bronchoalveolar *n.* broncoalveolar.
bronchoalveolitis *n.* broncoalveolitis.
bronchoaspergillosis *n.* broncoaspergilosis.
bronchoaspiration *n.* broncoaspiración.
bronchoblastomycosis *n.* broncoblastomicosis.
bronchoblennorrhea *n.* broncoblenorrea.
bronchocandidiasis *n.* broncocandidiasis.
bronchocavernous *adj.* broncocavernoso, -sa.
bronchocele *n.* broncocele.
bronchocephalitis *n.* broncocefalitis.
bronchoconstriction *n.* broncoconstricción.
bronchoconstrictor *n.* broncoconstrictor.
bronchodilatation *n.* broncodilatación.
bronchodilation *n.* broncodilación.
bronchodilator *n.* broncodilatador.
  adrenergic bronchodilator broncodilatador adrenérgico.
  autonomic-active bronc hodilator broncodilatador activo sobre el sistema autónomo.
  sympathomimetic bronchodilator broncodilatador simpaticomimético.
bronchoedema *n.* broncoedema.
bronchoegophony *n.* broncoegofonía.
bronchoesophageal *adj.* broncoesofágico, -ca.
bronchoesophagology *n.* broncoesofagología.
bronchoesophagoscopy *n.* broncoesofagoscopia.
bronchofiberscope *n.* broncofibroscopio.
bronchofiberscopy *n.* broncofibroscopia.
bronchofibroscope *n.* broncofibroscopio.
bronchofibroscopy *n.* broncofibroscopia.
bronchogenic *adj.* broncogénico, -ca, broncógeno, -na.
bronchogram *n.* broncograma.
  air bronchogram broncograma aéreo.
bronchographic *adj.* broncográfico, -ca.
bronchography *n.* broncografía.
broncholith *n.* broncolito.
broncholithiasis *n.* broncolitiasis.
bronchologic *adj.* broncológico, -ca.
bronchology *n.* broncología.
bronchomalacia *n.* broncomalacia.
bronchomoniliasis *n.* broncomoniliasis.
bronchomotor *n.* broncomotor.
bronchomucotropic *adj.* broncomucotrópico, -ca.
bronchomycosis *n.* broncomicosis.
bronchonocardiosis *n.* bronconocardiosis.
broncho-oidosis *n.* broncooidosis.
bronchopancreatic *adj.* broncopancreático, -ca.
bronchopathy *n.* broncopatía.
bronchophony *n.* broncofonía.
  pectoriloquous bronchophony broncofonía con pectoriloquia.
  sniffling bronchophony broncofonía ruidosa.
  whispered bronchophony broncofonía de murmullo, broncofonía de susurro, broncofonía en susurro.
bronchoplasty *n.* broncoplastia.
bronchoplegia *n.* broncoplejía.
bronchopleural *adj.* broncopleural.
bronchopleuropneumonia *n.* broncopleuroneumonía.
bronchopneumonia *n.* bronconeumonía.
  postoperative bronchopneumonia bronconeumonía postoperatoria.
  subacute bronchopneumonia bronconeumonía subaguda.
  tuberculous bronchopneumonia bronconeumonía tuberculosa.
  virus bronchopneumonia bronconeumonía por virus.

bronchopneumonic *adj.* bronconeumónico, -ca.
bronchopneumonitis *n.* bronconeumonitis.
bronchopneumopathy *n.* bronconeumopatía.
bronchopulmonary *adj.* broncopulmonar.
bronchorrhagia *n.* broncorragia.
bronchorrhaphy *n.* broncorrafia.
bronchorrhea *n.* broncorrea.
bronchoscope *n.* broncoscopio.
  fiberoptic bronchoscope broncoscopio fibroóptico.
bronchoscopic *adj.* broncoscópico, -ca.
bronchoscopy *n.* broncoscopia.
  fiberoptic bronchoscopy broncoscopia de fibra óptica, broncoscopia fibroóptica.
  laser bronchoscopy broncoscopia láser.
bronchosinusitis *n.* broncosinusitis.
bronchospasm *n.* broncoespasmo, broncospasmo.
bronchospirochetosis *n.* broncoespiroquetosis.
bronchospirography *n.* broncoespirografía, broncospirografía.
bronchospirometer *n.* broncoespirómetro, broncospirómetro.
bronchospirometry *n.* broncoespirometría, broncospirometría.
bronchostaxis *n.* broncostaxis.
bronchostenosis *n.* broncoestenosis, broncostenosis.
bronchostomy *n.* broncostomía.
bronchotome *n.* broncótomo.
bronchotomogram *n.* broncotomograma.
bronchotomy *n.* broncotomía.
bronchotracheal *adj.* broncotraqueal.
bronchotyphus *n.* broncotifus.
bronchovesicular *adj.* broncovesicular.
bronchus *n.* bronchus, bronquio.
  stem bronchus bronquio de sostén, bronquio fuente.
  tracheal bronchus bronquio traqueal.
brontophobia *n.* brontofobia.
broth *n.* caldo.
brucella *n.* brucella.
Brucella *n.* Brucella.
Brucellaceae *n.* Brucellaceae.
brucellar *adj.* brucelar.
brucellergin *n.* brucelergina.
brucellin *n.* brucelina.
brucellosis *n.* brucelosis.
Brugia *n.* Brugia.
  Brugia malayi Brugia malayi.
  Brugia pahangi Brugia pahangi.
bruise *n.* magulladura.
bruissement *n.* bruissement.
bruit *n.* ruido.
  aneurysmal bruit ruido aneurismático.
  bruit de canon ruido de cañón.
  bruit de clapotement ruido de chapoteo.
  bruit de claquement ruido de chasquido.
  bruit de drapeau ruido de bandera.
  bruit de galop ruido de galope.
  bruit de grelot ruido de cascabel.
  bruit de Leudet ruido de Leudet.
  bruit de lime ruido de lima.
  bruit de moulin ruido de molino.
  bruit de parchemin ruido de pergamino.
  bruit de rape ruido de sierra.
  bruit de rappel ruido de redoble.
  bruit de Roger ruido de Roger.
  bruit de scie ruido de sierra.
  bruit de soufflet ruido de fuelle.
  bruit de tambour ruido de tambor.
  bruit de triolet ruido de trío.
  bruit du diable ruido del diablo.

  thyroid bruit ruido tiroideo.
  Verstraeten's bruit ruido de Verstraeten.
brunneroma *n.* brunneroma.
brunnerosis *n.* brunnerosis.
brush *n.* cepillo.
  Ayre brush cepillo de Ayre.
  bronchoscopic brush cepillo broncoscópico.
  denture brush cepillo dental.
  Kruse's brush cepillo de Kruse.
  polishing brush cepillo de pulimento.
bruxism *n.* bruxismo.
  centric bruxism bruxismo céntrico.
bruxomania *n.* bruxomanía.
brychomania *n.* bricomanía.
Bryobia *n.* Bryobia.
  Bryobia praetiosa Bryobia praetiosa.
buaki *n.* buaki.
buba *n.* buba, bubas.
  buba madre buba madre.
bubas *n.* buba, bubas.
bubo *n.* bubón.
  bubo d'emblée bubón d'emblée.
  bullet bubo bubón en bala, bubón en forma de bala.
  chancroid bubo bubón chancroidal, bubón chancroide.
  chancroidal bubo bubón chancroidal, bubón chancroide.
  climatic bubo bubón climático.
  gonorrheal bubo bubón gonorreico.
  indolent bubo bubón indolente.
  malignant bubo bubón maligno.
  parotid bubo bubón parotídeo.
  pestilential bubo bubón pestilencial.
  primary bubo bubón primario, bubón primitivo, bubón protopático.
  sympathetic bubo bubón simpático, bubón simple.
  syphilitic bubo bubón sifilítico.
  tropical bubo bubón tropical.
  venereal bubo bubón venéreo.
  virulent bubo bubón virulento.
bubonalgia *n.* bubonalgia.
bubonic *adj.* bubónico, -ca.
bubonocele *n.* bubonocele.
bubonulus *n.* bubónulo.
bucca cavi oris *n.* bucca cavi oris.
buccal *adj.* bucal.
buccoaxial *adj.* bucoaxial, bucoaxil.
buccoaxiocervical *adj.* bucoaxiocervical.
buccoaxiogingival *adj.* bucoaxiogingival.
buccocervical *adj.* bucocervical.
buccoclination *n.* bucoclinación.
buccoclusal *adj.* bucoclusal.
buccoclusion *n.* bucoclusión.
buccodistal *adj.* bucodistal.
buccogingival *adj.* bucogingival.
buccoglossopharyngitis *n.* bucoglosofaringitis.
  buccoglossopharyngitis sicca bucoglosofaringitis seca.
buccolabial *adj.* bucolabial.
buccolingual *adj.* bucolingual.
buccomaxillary *adj.* bucomaxilar.
buccomesial *adj.* bucomesial.
bucco-oclusal *adj.* bucooclusal.
bucco-oclusion *n.* bucooclusión.
buccopharyngeal *adj.* bucofaríngeo, -a.
buccoplacement *n.* bucorregresión.
buccopulpal *adj.* bucopulpar.
buccoversion *n.* bucoversión.
bucky *n.* bucky.
buckytherapy *n.* buckyterapia.
bucnemia *n.* bucnemia.
bud *n.* brote[2], yema.

bronchial bud brote bronquial, yema bronquial.
end bud brote terminal.
limb bud brote de la extremidad, brote de los miembros, yema de la extremidad.
liver bud brote hepático, yema hepática.
lung bud brote pulmonar, yema pulmonar.
metanephric bud brote metanéfrico, yema metanéfrica.
periosteal bud brote perióstico, yema perióstica.
tail bud brote caudal.
tooth bud brote dental, yema dental.
ureteric bud brote ureteral, yema ureteral.
vascular bud brote vascular, yema vascular.
budding *n.* gemación.
buffer *n.* amortiguador, buffer, tampón[1].
bicarbonate buffer tampón de bicarbonato.
blood buffer tampón sanguíneo.
cacodylate buffer tampón de cacodilato.
phosphate buffer tampón de fosfato.
protein buffer tampón de proteínas.
TRIS buffer tampón TRIS.
veronal buffer tampón de veronal.
buffering *n.* amortiguamiento[1].
bufotherapy *n.* bufoterapia.
bufotoxin *n.* bufotoxina.
bulb *n.* bulbo, bulbus.
bulbar *adj.* bulbar.
bulbiform *adj.* bulbiforme.
bulbitis *n.* bulbitis.
bulboatrial *adj.* bulboauricular.
bulbogastrone *n.* bulbogastrona.
bulboid *adj.* bulboide, bulboideo, -a.
bulbonuclear *adj.* bulbonuclear.
bulbopontine *adj.* bulbopontino, -na.
bulbosacral *adj.* bulbosacro.
bulbospinal *adj.* bulboespinal, bulbospinal.
bulbourethral *adj.* bulbouretral.
bulbous *adj.* bulboso, -sa.
bulbus *n.* bulbo, bulbus.
bulbus venae jugularis superior golfo de la vena yugular interna.
bulesis *n.* bulesis.
bulimia *n.* bulimia.
bulimia nervosa bulimia nerviosa.
bulimic *adj.* bulímico, -ca.
bulkage *n.* formador de masa.
bulla *n.* bulla.
bulla ethmoidalis bulla etmoidal.
bulla ossea bulla ossea.
emphysematous bulla bulla enfisematosa.
ethmoid bulla bulla etmoidal.
ethmoidal bulla bulla etmoidal.
pulmonary bulla bulla pulmonar.
bullosis *n.* bullosis.
diabetic bullosis bullosis diabética.
bullous *adj.* bulloso, -sa.
bundle *n.* banda, fascículo.
aberrant bundle banda aberrante.
Vicq d'Azyr bundle banda de Vicq d'Azyr.
bungarotoxin *n.* bungarotoxina.
buninoid *adj.* buninoide.
bunioectomy *n.* buniectomia.
bunion *n.* bunio, juanete.
tailor's bunion bunio de sastre.
bunionectomy *n.* bunionectomía.
Keller bunionectomy bunionectomía de Keller.
Mayo bunionectomy bunionectomía de Mayo.
bunionette *n.* bunionete.
bunodont *adj.* bunodonte.
bunoselenodont *adj.* bunoselenodonte.
Bunyaviridae *n.* Bunyaviridae.
buphthalmia *n.* buftalmía.

buphthalmos *n.* buftalmos.
buphthalmus *n.* buftalmía.
bur *n.* fresa.
cross-cut bur fresa de corte transversal.
end-cutting bur fresa con borde cortante.
finishing bur fresa de terminación.
fissure bur fresa para fisuras.
inverted cone bur fresa en cono invertido.
round bur fresa redonda.
burden *n.* carga.
body burden carga corporal.
tumor burden carga tumoral.
buret *n.* buret, bureta, burette.
burette *n.* buret, bureta, burette.
burn *n.* quemadura.
acid burn quemadura ácida.
alkali burn quemadura por álcalis.
brush burn quemadura por fricción.
cement burn quemadura por cemento.
chemical burn quemadura química.
concrete burn quemadura por cemento.
conjunctival burn quemadura conjuntival.
contact burn quemadura por contacto.
electric burn quemadura eléctrica.
electrical burn quemadura eléctrica.
first degree burn quemadura de primer grado.
flash burn quemadura por fulguración, quemadura por relámpago.
friction burn quemadura por fricción.
full-thickness burn quemadura de espesor total.
matt burn quemadura por fricción.
napalm burn quemadura por napalm.
partial-thickness burn quemadura de espesor parcial.
radiation burn quemadura por radiación.
respiratory burn quemadura respiratoria.
rope burn quemadura por cuerda, quemadura por soga.
second degree burn quemadura de segundo grado.
solar burn quemadura solar.
sun burn quemadura solar.
superficial burn quemadura superficial.
thermal burn quemadura por agentes térmicos, quemadura térmica.
third degree burn quemadura de tercer grado.
X-ray burn quemadura por rayos X.
burning *n.* quemazón.
burnisher *n.* bruñidor.
burnishing *n.* bruñido.
burquism *n.* burquismo.
bursa *n.* bolsa[2], bursa.
bursal *adj.* bursal.
bursalogy *n.* bursalogía.
bursectomy *n.* bursectomía.
bursitis *n.* bursitis.
Achilles bursitis bursitis aquilea, bursitis aquiliana.
adhesive bursitis bursitis adhesiva.
anserine bursitis bursitis anserina.
anterior Achilles bursitis bursitis aquilea anterior.
calcaneal bursitis bursitis calcaneana.
calcific bursitis bursitis calcificada.
ischiogluteal bursitis bursitis isquioglútea.
olecranal bursitis bursitis del olécranon, bursitis oleocraniana.
omental bursitis bursitis epiploica, bursitis omental.
pharyngeal bursitis bursitis faríngea.
popliteal bursitis bursitis poplítea.
posterior Achilles bursitis bursitis aquilea posterior.
prepatellar bursitis bursitis prerrotuliana.

radiohumeral bursitis bursitis radiohumeral.
retrocalcaneal bursitis bursitis retrocalcánea.
scapulohumeral bursitis bursitis escapulohumeral.
subacromial bursitis bursitis subacromial.
subdeltoid bursitis bursitis subdeltoidea.
Thornwaldt's bursitis bursitis de Thornwaldt, bursitis de Tornwaldt.
Tornwaldt's bursitis bursitis de Thornwaldt, bursitis de Tornwaldt.
bursogram *n.* bursograma.
bursographic *adj.* bursográfico, -ca.
bursography *n.* bursografía.
bursolith *n.* bursolito.
bursopathy *n.* bursopatía.
bursotomography *n.* bursotomografía.
bursotomy *n.* bursotomía.
burst *n.* explosión[2].
metabolic burst explosión metabólica.
respiratory burst explosión respiratoria.
spider burst explosión en araña.
burst-supression *n.* burst-supression.
bursula *n.* bursula.
bursula testium bursula testium.
buserelin *n.* buserelina.
BUT *n.* BUT.
butt *v.* topar.
butterfly *n.* mariposa.
Buttiauxella *n.* Buttiauxella.
button *n.* botón[3].
Amboyna button botón de Amboina.
Biskra button botón de Biskra.
bromide button botón de bromuro.
dermal button botón dérmico, botón intradérmico.
iodide button botón de yoduro.
Jaboulay button botón de Jaboulay.
mammary button botón mamario.
mescal button botón de mescal, botón de mezcal.
Murphy's button botón de Murphy.
Oriental button botón de Oriente, botón oriental.
peritoneal button botón peritoneal.
skin button botón cutáneo.
taste button botón gustativo.
buttonhole *n.* ojal.
mitral buttonhole ojal mitral.
buttonhook *n.* broche.
butyraceous *adj.* butiráceo, -a.
Butyribacterium *n.* Butyribacterium.
butyroid *adj.* butiroide.
butyrometer *n.* butirómetro.
butyroscope *n.* butiroscopio.
butyrous *adj.* butiroso, -sa.
by pass *n.* derivación[1].
aortocoronary by pass derivación aortocoronaria.
aortofemoral by pass derivación aortofemoral.
aortoiliac by pass derivación aortoilíaca.
aortorenal by pass derivación aortorrenal.
biliary by pass derivación biliar.
bowel by pass derivación intestinal.
cardiopulmonary by pass derivación cardiopulmonar.
coronary artery by pass derivación aortocoronaria.
coronary by pass derivación coronaria.
extracranial-intracranial by pass derivación extracraneal-intracraneal.
femoropopliteal by pass derivación femoropoplítea.
gastric by pass derivación gástrica.
ileal by pass derivación ileal.
internal mammary artery by pass deriva-

ción de arteria mamaria interna.

intestinal by pass derivación intestinal.

jejunoileal by pass derivación yeyunoileal.

left heart by pass derivación cardíaca izquierda.

partial by pass derivación parcial.

partial ileal by pass derivación ileal parcial.

right heart by pass derivación cardíaca derecha.

by-pass *n.* by-pass.

byproduct *n.* subproducto.

byssinosis *n.* bisinosis.

byssinotic *adj.* bisinótico, -ca.

byssocausis *n.* bisocausis.

C*c*

cabinet *n.* gabinete.
  pneumatic cabinet gabinete neumático.
  Sauerbruch's cabinet gabinete de Sauerbruch.
cacaerometer *n.* cacaerómetro.
cachectic *adj.* caquéctico, -ca.
cachet *n.* cachet, sello[1].
cachexia *n.* caquexia.
  cachexia aphthosa caquexia aftosa.
  cachexia aquosa caquexia acuosa.
  cachexia exophthalmica caquexia exoftálmica.
  cachexia hypophyseopriva caquexia hipofisopriva.
  cachexia mercurialis caquexia mercurial.
  cachexia strumipriva caquexia estrumipriva.
  cachexia suprarrenalis caquexia suprarrenal.
  cachexia thyroidea caquexia tiroidea.
  cachexia thyropriva caquexia tiropriva.
  cancerous cachexia caquexia cancerosa.
  fluoric cachexia caquexia fluórica.
  malarial cachexia caquexia palúdica.
  pituitary cachexia caquexia hipofisaria, caquexia pituitaria.
  verminous cachexia caquexia verminosa.
cacoethic *adj.* cacoético, -ca.
cacogenesis *n.* cacogénesis.
cacogenic *adj.* cacogénico, -ca.
cacogeusia *n.* cacogeusia.
cacomelia *n.* cacomelia.
cacomorphosis *n.* cacomorfosis.
cacoplastic *adj.* cacoplásico, -ca.
cacorhythmic *adj.* cacorrítmico, -ca.
cacosmia *n.* cacosmia.
cacostomia *n.* cacostomía.
cacotrophy *n.* cacotrofia.
cacumen *n.* cacumen.
cacuminal *adj.* cacuminal.
cadaver *n.* cadáver.
cadaveric *adj.* cadavérico, -ca.
cadaverous *adj.* cadavérico, -ca.
cadherins *n.* cadherinas.
cadmiosis *n.* cadmiosis.
caduca *n.* caduca.
caduceus *n.* caduceo.
caecum *n.* caecum, ciego.
caecus *n.* caecus.
caffeinism *n.* cafeinismo, cafeísmo.
cage *n.* jaula.
  Faraday's cage jaula de Faraday.
  population cage jaula de población.
  thoracic cage jaula torácica.
calamus *n.* cálamo.
calcaneal *adj.* calcáneo, -a.
calcanean *adj.* calcáneo, -a.
calcaneitis *n.* calcaneítis.
calcaneoapophysitis *n.* calcaneoapofisitis.
calcaneoastragaloid *adj.* calcaneoastragalino, -na, calcaneoastragaloide, calcaneoastragaloideo, -a.
calcaneocavus *n.* calcaneocavo.

calcaneocuboid *adj.* calcaneocuboide, calcaneocuboideo, -a.
calcaneodynia *n.* calcaneodinia.
calcaneofibular *adj.* calcaneoperoneo, -a.
calcaneonavicular *adj.* calcaneonavicular.
calcaneoplantar *adj.* calcaneoplantar.
calcaneoscaphoid *adj.* calcaneoescafoideo, -a, calcaneoscafoideo, -a.
calcaneotibial *adj.* calcaneotibial.
calcaneus *n.* calcáneo.
calcanodynia *n.* calcaneodinia, calcanodinia.
calcar *n.* calcar.
calcareous *adj.* calcáreo, -a.
calcarine *adj.* calcarino, -na.
calcariuria *n.* calcariuria.
calcaroid *adj.* calcaroide.
calcemia *n.* calcemia.
calcergy *n.* calcergia.
calcibilia *n.* calcibilia.
calcic *adj.* cálcico, -ca.
calcicosilicosis *n.* calcicosilicosis.
calcicosis *n.* calcicosis.
calcifames *n.* calcifames.
calciferous *adj.* calcífero, -ra.
calcification *n.* calcificación.
  dystrophic calcification calcificación distrófica.
  eggshell calcification calcificación en cáscara de huevo.
  metastatic calcification calcificación metastásica.
  Mönckeberg's calcification calcificación de Mönckeberg.
  Mönckeberg's medial calcification calcificación medial de Mönckeberg.
  pathologic calcification calcificación patológica.
  pulp calcification calcificación de la pulpa.
calcify *v.* calcificar.
calcigerous *adj.* calcígero, -ra.
calcimeter *n.* calcímetro.
calcination *n.* calcinación.
calcinosis *n.* calcinosis.
  calcinosis circumscripta calcinosis circunscrita.
  calcinosis cutis calcinosis cutánea.
  calcinosis interstitialis calcinosis intersticial.
  calcinosis intervertebralis calcinosis intervertebral.
  calcinosis universalis calcinosis universal.
  dystrophic calcinosis calcinosis distrófica.
  reversible calcinosis calcinosis reversible.
  tumoral calcinosis calcinosis tumoral.
calcioglobule *n.* calcioglóbulo.
calciokinesis *n.* calciocinesis.
calciokinetic *adj.* calciocinético, -ca.
calciorrhachia *n.* calciorraquia.
calciotropism *n.* calciotropismo.
calcipectic *adj.* calcipéctico, -ca.
calcipenia *n.* calcipenia.

calcipenic *adj.* calcipénico, -ca.
calcipexia *n.* calcipexia.
calcipexic *adj.* calcipéxico, -ca.
calcipexis *n.* calcipexia, calcipexis.
calcipexy *n.* calcipexia, calcipexis.
calciphilia *n.* calcifilia.
calciphylactic *adj.* calcifiláctico, -ca.
calciphylaxis *n.* calcifilaxia.
  systemic calciphylaxis calcifilaxia general, calcifilaxia sistémica.
  topical calciphylaxis calcifilaxia tópica.
calciprivia *n.* calciprivia.
calciprivic *adj.* calciprivo, -va.
calcitherapy *n.* calciterapia.
calcium *n.* calcio.
calciuria *n.* calciuria.
calcodynia *n.* calcodinia.
calcoglobulin *n.* calcoglobulina.
calcophorous *adj.* calcóforo, -ra.
calcospherite *n.* calcosferito.
calculary *adj.* calcular.
calculosis *n.* calculosis.
calculous *adj.* calculoso, -sa.
calculus *n.* cálculo, calculus.
  alternating calculus cálculo alternante.
  alvine calculus cálculo alvino.
  apatite calculus cálculo de apatita.
  arthritic calculus cálculo artrítico.
  articular calculus cálculo articular.
  biliary calculus cálculo biliar.
  bladder calculus cálculo de la vejiga.
  blood calculus cálculo sanguíneo.
  branched calculus cálculo ramificado.
  bronchial calculus cálculo bronquial.
  cardiac calculus cálculo cardíaco.
  cerebral calculus cálculo cerebral.
  cholesterol calculus cálculo de colesterol.
  combination calculus cálculo combinado, cálculo compuesto.
  coral calculus cálculo coraliforme, cálculo coralino.
  cystine calculus cálculo de cistina.
  decubitus calculus cálculo por decúbito.
  dendritic calculus cálculo dendrítico.
  dental calculus cálculo dental, cálculo dentario.
  encysted calculus cálculo enquistado.
  fibrin calculus cálculo de fibrina.
  gastric calculus cálculo gástrico.
  gonecystic calculus cálculo gonequístico, cálculo gonoquístico.
  hematogenic calculus cálculo hematógeno, cálculo hémico.
  hemic calculus cálculo hematógeno, cálculo hémico.
  hepatic calculus cálculo hepático.
  indigo calculus cálculo de índigo.
  infection calculus cálculo de infección, cálculo infeccioso.
  intestinal calculus cálculo intestinal.

lacteal calculus cálculo lácteo.
lung calculus cálculo pulmonar.
mammary calculus cálculo mamario.
matrix calculus cálculo de matriz.
metabolic calculus cálculo metabólico.
mulberry calculus cálculo en mora, cálculo moriforme.
nasal calculus cálculo nasal.
oxalate calculus cálculo de oxalato.
pancreatic calculus cálculo pancreático.
pharyngeal calculus cálculo faríngeo.
phosphate calculus cálculo de fosfato, cálculo fosfático.
phosphatic calculus cálculo de fosfato, cálculo fosfático.
pleural calculus cálculo pleural.
pocketed calculus cálculo embolsado.
preputial calculus cálculo prepucial.
primary renal calculus cálculo renal primario.
prostatic calculus cálculo prostático.
pulp calculus cálculo de la pulpa.
renal calculus cálculo renal.
salivary calculus cálculo salival.
secondary renal calculus cálculo renal secundario.
serumal calculus cálculo serumal, cálculo seruminal.
spermatic calculus cálculo espermático.
staghorn calculus cálculo en asta de ciervo.
stomachic calculus cálculo gástrico.
struvite calculus cálculo de estruvita.
subgingival calculus cálculo subgingival.
submorphous calculus cálculo submorfo.
supragingival calculus cálculo supragingival.
tonsillar calculus cálculo amigdalino, cálculo tonsilar.
urate calculus cálculo de urato.
urethral calculus cálculo de la uretra, cálculo uretral.
uric acid calculus cálculo de ácido úrico.
urinary calculus cálculo urinario.
uterine calculus cálculo uterino.
vesical calculus cálculo vesical.
vesicoprostatic calculus cálculo vesicoprostático.
Weddellite calculus cálculo de wedelita.
Whewellite calculus cálculo de whewelita.
xanthic calculus cálculo xantínico.
calefacient *adj.* calefaciente.
calentura *n.* calentura.
calenture *n.* calentura.
calf *n.* pantorrilla.
calibration *n.* calibración.
calicectasis *n.* calicectasia, calicectasis.
calicectomy *n.* calicectomía.
caliciform *adj.* caliciforme.
Caliciviridae *n.* Caliciviridae.
Calicivirus *n.* Calicivirus.
calicotomy *n.* calicotomía.
caliculus *n.* calículo, caliculus.
caliectasis *n.* calicectasia, calicectasis, caliectasia, caliectasis.
caliectomy *n.* calicectomía, caliectomía.
caligation *n.* caligación.
caligo *n.* caligo.
calioplasty *n.* calicoplastia, calioplastia.
caliorrhaphy *n.* caliorrafia.
caliotomy *n.* calicotomía, caliotomía.
calipers *n.* compás.
skinfold calipers compás de espesor dérmico, compás de pliegue cutáneo.
Callimastix *n.* Callimastix.
Calliphora *n.* Calliphora.
Calliphoridae *n.* Calliphoridae.
callosal *adj.* calloso², -sa.

callositas *n.* callosidad.
callosity *n.* callosidad.
callosomarginal *adj.* callosomarginal.
callous *adj.* calloso, -sa¹.
callus *n.* callo.
asbestos callus callo de amianto.
bony callus callo óseo.
central callus callo central.
definitive callus callo definitivo.
ensheathing callus callo envainante, callo invaginante.
external callus callo externo.
exuberant callus callo exuberante.
hard callus callo duro.
inner callus callo interno.
intermediate callus callo intermedio.
internal callus callo interno.
medullary callus callo medular.
myelogenous callus callo mielógeno.
permanent callus callo permanente.
provisional callus callo provisional.
seed callus callo de semilla.
soft callus callo blando.
temporary callus callo temporal.
calmative *n.* calmante.
calmodulin *n.* calmodulina.
calor *n.* calor.
calor febrilis calor febril.
calor fervens calor fervens.
calor innatus calor innato.
calor internus calor interno.
calor mordax calor mordente.
calor mordicans calor mordente.
calorescence *n.* calorescencia.
caloric *adj.* calórico, -ca.
caloricity *n.* calorificación.
calorie *n.* caloría.
calorifacient *adj.* calorifaciente.
calorific *adj.* calorífico, -ca.
calorigenetic *adj.* calorígeno, -na.
calorigenic *adj.* calorígeno, -na.
calorimeter *n.* calorímetro.
bomb calorimeter calorímetro a bomba, calorímetro de bomba.
compensating calorimeter calorímetro compensado.
respiration calorimeter calorímetro respiratorio.
calorimetric *adj.* calorimétrico, -ca.
calorimetry *n.* calorimetría.
direct calorimetry calorimetría directa.
indirect calorimetry calorimetría indirecta.
caloripuncture *n.* caloripuntura.
caloriscope *n.* caloriscopio.
caloritropic *adj.* caloritrópico, -ca.
calotte *n.* calota.
calsequestrin *n.* calsecuestrina.
calvaria *n.* calvaria, calvario.
calvarial *adj.* calvárico, -ca.
Calvatia *n.* Calvatia.
calvities *n.* calvicie.
calycectomy *n.* calicectomía.
calyciform *adj.* caliciforme.
calycle *n.* calículo, caliculus.
calycoplasty *n.* calicoplastia.
calycotomy *n.* calicotomía.
calyectasis *n.* calicectasia, calicectasis, caliectasia, caliectasis.
Calymmatobacterium *n.* Calymmatobacteria.
Calymmatobacterium granulomatis Calymmatobacteria granulomatis.
calyoplasty *n.* calicoplastia, calioplastia.
calyx *n.* cáliz, calyx.
cambium *n.* cambium.

camera *n.* cámara.
Abbé-Zeiss counting camera cámara contadora de Abbé-Zeiss, cámara cuentaglóbulos de Abbé-Zeiss.
acoustic camera cámara acústica.
air-equivalent ionization camera cámara aérea de ionización equivalente.
altitude camera cámara de altitud, cámara de altura.
Anger camera cámara de Anger.
bubble camera cámara de burbujas.
camera lucida cámara clara, cámara lúcida.
cloud camera cámara de nube.
counting camera cámara cuentaglóbulos.
detonating camera cámara detonante.
diffusion camera cámara de difusión.
free-air ionization camera cámara de ionización de aire libre.
gamma camera cámara gamma.
Haldane camera cámara de Haldane.
hyperbaric camera cámara hiperbárica.
ionization camera cámara de ionización.
lethal camera cámara letal.
Petroff-Hauser counting camera cámara de Petroff-Hauser.
pulp camera cámara pulpar.
scintillation camera cámara de centelleos.
standard ionization camera cámara estándar de ionización.
Storm Van Leeuwen camera cámara de Storm Van Leeuwen.
thimble camera cámara dedal.
tomographic gamma camera tomocámara.
camphor *n.* alcanfor.
camphoraceous *adj.* alcanforáceo, -a.
camphorated *adj.* alcanforado, -da.
camphorism *n.* alcanforismo, canforismo.
campimeter *n.* campímetro.
campimetry *n.* campimetría.
campospasm *n.* campoespasmo.
camptocormia *n.* camptocormia.
camptocormy *n.* camptocormia.
camptodactylia *n.* camptodactilia.
camptodactylism *n.* camptodactilia.
camptodactyly *n.* camptodactilia.
camptomelia *n.* camptomelia.
camptomelic *adj.* camptomélico, -ca.
camptospasm *n.* camptoespasmo, camptospasmo.
Campylobacter *n.* Campylobacter.
campylobacteriosis *n.* campilobacteriosis, campylobacteriosis.
campylodactyly *n.* campilodactilia.
campylognathia *n.* campilognatia.
canal *n.* canal.
irruption canal canal de irrupción.
persistent atrioventricular canal canal auriculoventricular persistente.
canalicular *adj.* canalicular.
canaliculitis *n.* canaliculitis.
canaliculization *n.* canaliculización.
canaliculodacryocystostomy *n.* canaliculodacriocistostomía.
canaliculorhinostomy *n.* canaliculorrinostomía.
canaliculus *n.* canalículo, canaliculus.
bile canaliculus canalículo biliar.
biliary canaliculus canalículo biliar.
canalis *n.* canal.
canalization *n.* canalización.
cancellated *adj.* canceloso, -sa.
cancellous *adj.* canceloso, -sa.
cancer *n.* cáncer.
acinar cancer cáncer acinoso.

acinous cancer cáncer acinoso.

aniline cancer cáncer de los trabajadores de anilina, cáncer por anilina.

apinoid cancer cáncer apinoide.

atrophicans cancer cáncer atrófico.

betel cancer cáncer de betel, cáncer por betel.

black cancer cáncer negro.

bone cancer cáncer óseo.

boring cancer cáncer terebrante.

breast cancer cáncer de mama.

buyo cheek cancer cáncer del buyo del carrillo.

cancer à deux cáncer de a dos.

cancer en cuirasse cáncer en coraza, cáncer en escudo.

cancer in situ cáncer in situ.

cerebriform cancer cáncer cerebriforme.

chimney-sweep's cancer cáncer de deshollinador.

claypipe cancer cáncer por pipa de arcilla.

colloid cancer cáncer coloidal, cáncer coloide.

colloidal cancer cáncer coloidal, cáncer coloide.

conjugal cancer cáncer conyugal.

contact cancer cáncer por contacto.

corset cancer cáncer en corsé.

cystic cancer cáncer quístico.

dendritic cancer cáncer dendrítico.

duct cancer cáncer canalicular.

dye worker's cancer cáncer de los trabajadores de anilina.

endothelial cancer cáncer endotelial.

epidermoid cancer cáncer epidérmico, cáncer epidermoide.

epithelial cancer cáncer adenoideo, cáncer epitelial.

familial cancer cáncer familiar.

fungous cancer cáncer fungoso.

hard cancer cáncer duro.

jacket cancer cáncer en chaleco.

kang cancer cáncer kang, cáncer kangri.

kangri cancer cáncer kang, cáncer kangri.

latent cancer cáncer latente.

liver cancer cáncer de hígado.

lung cancer cáncer de pulmón.

medullary cancer cáncer medular.

melanotic cancer cáncer melanótico.

mucinous cancer cáncer mucinoso.

mule-spinner's cancer cáncer de los tejedores.

occult cancer cáncer oculto.

paraffin cancer cáncer de parafina, cáncer por parafina.

pipe-smoker's cancer cáncer de los fumadores de pipa.

pitch-worker's cancer cáncer por alquitrán, cáncer por brea.

roetgenologist's cancer cáncer de los radiólogos.

scar cancer cáncer cicatricial.

scar cancer of the lungs cáncer cicatricial de los pulmones.

scirrhous cancer cáncer escirroso.

soft cancer cáncer blando.

spindle cell cancer cáncer de células fusiformes.

stump cancer cáncer del muñón.

tar cancer cáncer por alquitrán, cáncer por brea.

telangiectatic cancer cáncer telangiectásico.

tubular cancer cáncer tubular.

water cancer cáncer acuático, cáncer de agua.

canceration *n.* cancerización.

canceremia *n.* canceremia.

cancericidal *adj.* cancericida.

cancerigenic *adj.* cancerígeno, -na.

cancerism *n.* cancerismo.

cancerization *n.* cancerización.

cancerocidal *adj.* cancericida, cancerocida.

cancerogenic *adj.* cancerígeno, -na.

cancerology *n.* cancerología, carcinología.

cancerous *adj.* canceroso, -sa, carcinoso, -sa.

cancerphobia *n.* cancerofobia.

cancriform *adj.* cancriforme.

cancroid *n.* cancroide.

cancrum *n.* cancrum.

  cancrum nasi cancrum nasi.

  cancrum oris cancrum oris.

candela *n.* bujía², candela.

candicans *adj.* candicans.

Candida *n.* Candida.

candidemia *n.* candidemia.

candidiasis *n.* candidiasis, candidiosis.

  cutaneous candidiasis candidiasis cutánea.

  endocardial candidiasis candidiasis endocárdica.

candidid *n.* candídide.

candidosis *n.* candidosis.

candiduria *n.* candiduria.

candle *n.* bujía², candela.

cane *n.* bastón.

  adjustable cane bastón ajustable.

  English cane bastón inglés.

  quadripod cane bastón cuadrípode.

  tripod cane bastón trípode.

canescent *adj.* canescente.

canine *n.* canino.

caniniform *adj.* caniniforme.

canister *n.* canasta.

canities *n.* canicie.

  canities canities canicie canities.

  canities circumscripta canicie circunscrita.

  canities unguium canicie ungular.

  rapid canities canicie rápida.

cannabis *n.* cannabis.

cannabism *n.* canabismo, cannabismo.

cannula *n.* cánula.

  granulation cannula cánula de granulación.

  Karman cannula cánula de Karman.

  Kuhn's cannula cánula de Kuhn.

  Lindemann's cannula cánula de Lindemann.

  perfusion cannula cánula de doble corriente, cánula de perfusión.

  tracheostomy cannula cánula de traqueostomía.

  washout cannula cánula para lavado de arrastre.

cannulation *n.* canulación.

cannulization *n.* canulización.

canon *n.* canon.

canthariasis *n.* cantariasis.

cantharidin *n.* cantaridina.

cantharidism *n.* cantaridismo.

cantharis *n.* cantárida.

canthectomy *n.* cantectomía.

canthitis *n.* cantitis.

cantholisis *n.* cantólisis.

canthoplasty *n.* cantoplastia.

canthorrhaphy *n.* cantorrafia.

canthotomy *n.* cantotomía.

canthus *n.* canto.

cantus galli *n.* cantus galli.

cap *n.* capuchón.

  Phrygian cap gorro frigio.

capacitance *n.* capacitancia.

capacitation *n.* capacitación.

capacity *n.* capacidad.

  buffer capacity capacidad buffer.

  contractual capacity capacidad contractual.

  diffusion capacity capacidad de difusión.

  forced vital capacity (FVC) capacidad vital (CV), capacidad vital forzada (CVF).

  functional residual capacity (FRC) capacidad residual funcional (CRF).

  heat capacity capacidad térmica.

  hypnotic capacity capacidad hipnótica.

  inspiratory capacity capacidad inspiratoria.

  iron-binding capacity (IBC) capacidad de fijación de hierro (CFH).

  oxygen capacity capacidad de oxígeno.

  residual capacity capacidad residual.

  respiratory capacity capacidad respiratoria.

  thermal capacity capacidad térmica.

  total lung capacity (TLC) capacidad pulmonar total (CPT).

  vital capacity (VC) capacidad vital (CV), capacidad vital forzada (CVF).

capeline *n.* capelina.

caphalomelus *n.* cefalómelo.

capillaopathy *n.* capilaropatía.

capillarectasia *n.* capilarectasia.

Capillaria philippinensis *n.* Capillaria philippinensis.

capillariasis *n.* capilariasis.

  intestinal capillariasis capilariasis intestinal.

capillarioscopy *n.* capilarioscopia, capilaroscopia.

capillaritis *n.* capilaritis.

capillarity *n.* capilaridad.

capillaroscopy *n.* capilarioscopia, capilaroscopia.

capillary *n.* capilar.

capillus *n.* cabello, capillus.

capistration *n.* capistración.

capital *adj.* capital.

capitate *adj.* capitado, -da.

capitellum *n.* capitellum.

capitonnage *n.* capitonaje.

capitopedal *adj.* capitopedal.

capitular *adj.* capitular.

capitulum *n.* capitulum.

Capnocytophaga *n.* Capnocytophaga.

capnogram *n.* capnograma.

capnograph *n.* capnógrafo.

capnophilic *adj.* capnófilo, -la.

capotement *n.* bazuqueo.

capping *v.* cubrir.

capriloquism *n.* capriloquia, capriloquismo.

caprizant *adj.* caprizante.

capsid *n.* cápsida, cápside.

capsitis *n.* capsitis.

capsomer *n.* capsómero.

capsomere *n.* capsómero.

capsula *n.* capsula, cápsula.

  capsula vasculosa lentis cápsula lenticular vascular, capsula vasculosa lentis.

capsular *adj.* capsular.

capsulation *n.* capsulación.

capsule *n.* capsula, cápsula.

  adherent capsule cápsula adherente.

  auditory capsule cápsula auditiva.

  bacterial capsule cápsula bacteriana.

  Bowman's capsule cápsula de Bowman.

  Crosby capsule cápsula de Crosby.

  nasal capsule cápsula nasal.

  optic capsule cápsula óptica.

  otic capsule cápsula ótica.

  radiotelemetering capsule cápsula radiotelemétrica.

capsulectomy *n.* capsulectomía.

capsulitis *n.* capsulitis.

  adhesive capsulitis capsulitis adhesiva.

  hepatic capsulitis capsulitis hepática.

capsulolenticular *adj.* capsulolenticular.

capsuloplasty *n.* capsuloplastia.

capsulorraphy *n.* capsulorrafia.
capsulotome *n.* capsulótomo.
capsulotomy *n.* capsulotomía.
   renal capsulotomy capsulotomía renal.
captation *n.* captación.
capture *n.* captura.
   atrial capture captura auricular.
   electron capture captura de electrones.
   k capture captura k.
   ventricular capture captura ventricular.
caput *n.* cabeza, caput.
   caput medusae cabeza de medusa, caput medusae.
   caput natiforme naticefalia.
   caput quadratum cabeza cuadrada, caput quadratum.
carate *n.* carata, carateas.
carbhemoglobin *n.* carbohemoglobina.
carbohemia *n.* carbohemia, carbonemia.
carbohemoglobin *n.* carbohemoglobina.
carbohydraturia *n.* carbohidraturia.
carbolism *n.* carbolismo.
carboluria *n.* carboluria.
carbometer *n.* carbómetro.
carbometry *n.* carbometría.
carbon *n.* carbono.
carbonometer *n.* carbonómetro.
carbonometry *n.* carbonometría.
carbonuria *n.* carbonuria.
carboxyhemoglobin *n.* carboxihemoglobina.
carboxyhemoglobinemia *n.* carboxihemoglobinemia.
carboxylation *n.* carboxilación.
carbuncle *n.* ántrax.
   renal carbuncle ántrax renal.
carcinelcosis *n.* carcinelcosis.
carcinemia *n.* carcinemia.
carcinoembryonic *adj.* carcinoembrionario, -ria.
carcinogen *n.* carcinógeno.
   complet carcinogen carcinógeno completo.
carcinogenesis *n.* carcinogénesis, carcinogenia.
carcinogenic *adj.* carcinogénico, -ca.
carcinoid *n.* carcinoide.
carcinolysis *n.* carcinólisis.
carcinolytic *adj.* carcinolítico, -ca.
carcinoma *n.* carcinoma.
   acinar carcinoma carcinoma acinar, carcinoma acinoso.
   acinic cell carcinoma carcinoma acinocelular.
   acinous carcinoma carcinoma acinar, carcinoma acinoso.
   adenoid cystic carcinoma carcinoma adenoide quístico.
   adenoid squamous cell carcinoma carcinoma adenoide escamocelular.
   adnexal carcinoma carcinoma anexal.
   adrenal cortical carcinoma carcinoma corticosuprarrenal.
   alveolar cell carcinoma carcinoma alveolar.
   anaplastic carcinoma carcinoma anaplásico.
   apocrine carcinoma carcinoma apocrino.
   basal cell carcinoma carcinoma basocelular.
   basal squamous cell carcinoma carcinoma basoescamocelular.
   basaloid carcinoma carcinoma basaloide.
   basosquamous carcinoma carcinoma basiescamoso.
   bronchioalveolar carcinoma carcinoma broncoalveolar.
   bronchiolar carcinoma carcinoma bronquiolar.
   bronchogenic carcinoma carcinoma broncogénico.
   carcinoma ex pleomorphic adenoma carcinoma ex adenoma pleomórfico.

carcinoma in situ carcinoma in situ.
carcinoma mucocellulare carcinoma mucocelular.
clear cell carcinoma of the kidney carcinoma de células claras del riñón.
colloid carcinoma carcinoma coloide.
cylindromatous carcinoma carcinoma cilindromatoso.
cystic carcinoma carcinoma quístico.
duct carcinoma carcinoma ductal.
ductal carcinoma carcinoma ductal.
embryonal carcinoma carcinoma embrionario.
endometrioid carcinoma carcinoma endometrioide.
epidermoid carcinoma carcinoma epidermoide.
exophytic carcinoma carcinoma exofítico.
fibrolamellar liver cell carcinoma carcinoma de células hepáticas fibrolaminillares.
follicular carcinoma carcinoma folicular.
giant cell carcinoma carcinoma de células gigantes.
giant cell carcinoma of the thyroid gland carcinoma gigantocelular del tiroides.
hepatocellular carcinoma carcinoma hepatocelular.
Hürthle cell carcinoma carcinoma de células de Hürthle.
inflammatory carcinoma carcinoma inflamatorio.
intraductal carcinoma carcinoma intraductal.
intraepidermal carcinoma carcinoma intraepidérmico.
intraepithelial carcinoma carcinoma intraepitelial.
invasive carcinoma carcinoma invasor.
juvenile carcinoma carcinoma juvenil.
kangri burn carcinoma carcinoma de quemadura kangri.
large cell carcinoma carcinoma de células grandes.
latent carcinoma carcinoma latente.
lateral aberrant thyroid carcinoma carcinoma tiroideo aberrante lateral.
leptomeningeal carcinoma carcinoma leptomeníngeo.
liver cell carcinoma carcinoma de células hepáticas.
lobular carcinoma carcinoma lobular.
lobular carcinoma in situ carcinoma lobular in situ.
medullary carcinoma carcinoma medular.
meningeal carcinoma carcinoma meníngeo.
mesometanephric carcinoma carcinoma mesometanéfrico.
metaplastic carcinoma carcinoma metaplásico.
metastatic carcinoma carcinoma metastásico.
microinvasive carcinoma carcinoma microinvasor.
mucinous carcinoma carcinoma mucinoso, carcinoma mucoso.
mucoepidermoid carcinoma carcinoma mucoepidermoide.
noninfiltrating lobular carcinoma carcinoma lobular no infiltrativo.
oat cell carcinoma carcinoma de células en grano de arena, carcinoma de células pequeñas.
occult carcinoma carcinoma oculto.
papillary carcinoma carcinoma papilar.
preinvasive carcinoma carcinoma preinvasivo.
primary carcinoma carcinoma primario.
primary neuroendocrine carcinoma of the

skin carcinoma primario neuroendocrino de la piel.
renal cell carcinoma carcinoma de células renales, nefrocarcinoma.
sarcomatoid carcinoma carcinoma sarcomatoide.
scar carcinoma carcinoma cicatricial.
scirrhous carcinoma carcinoma escirroso.
secondary carcinoma carcinoma secundario.
secretory carcinoma carcinoma secretor.
signet-ring cell carcinoma carcinoma de células de anillo de sello.
small cell carcinoma carcinoma de células en grano de arena, carcinoma de células pequeñas.
spindle cell carcinoma carcinoma fusocelular.
squamous cell carcinoma carcinoma escamocelular, carcinoma escamoso.
sweat gland carcinoma carcinoma de glándulas sudoríparas.
trabecular carcinoma carcinoma trabecular.
transitional cell carcinoma carcinoma de células de transición.
tubular carcinoma carcinoma tubular.
verrucous carcinoma carcinoma verrugoso.
villous carcinoma carcinoma velloso.
Wolffian duct carcinoma carcinoma del conducto de Wolff.
carcinomatosis *n.* carcinomatosis.
   leptomeningeal carcinomatosis carcinomatosis leptomeníngea.
   meningeal carcinomatosis carcinomatosis meníngea.
carcinomatous *adj.* carcinomatoso, -sa.
carcinophilia *n.* carcinofilia.
carcinophobia *n.* carcinofobia.
carcinosarcoma *n.* carcinosarcoma.
   embryonal carcinosarcoma carcinosarcoma embrionario.
carcinosis *n.* carcinosis.
carcinostatic *adj.* carcinostático, -ca.
cardia *n.* cardias.
cardiac *adj.* cardíaco, -ca.
   cardiac ballet ballet cardíaco.
cardialgia *n.* cardialgia.
cardiasthenia *n.* cardiastenia.
cardiasthma *n.* cardiasma.
cardiataxia *n.* cardiataxia.
cardiatelia *n.* cardiatelia.
cardiectasia *n.* cardiectasia.
cardiectomized *n.* cardiectomizado.
cardiectomy *n.* cardiectomía.
cardiectopia *n.* cardiectopia.
cardinal *adj.* cardinal.
cardioaccelerator *adj.* cardioacelerador, -ra.
cardioactive *adj.* cardioactivo, -va.
cardioangiography *n.* cardioangiografía.
cardioangiology *n.* cardioangiología.
cardioaortic *adj.* cardioaórtico, -ca.
cardioarterial *adj.* cardioarterial.
cardiobacterium *n.* Cardiobacterium.
   cardiobacterium hominis cardiobacterium hominis.
cardiocairograph *n.* cardiocairógrafo.
cardiocele *n.* cardiocele.
cardiocentesis *n.* cardiocentesis.
cardiochalasia *n.* cardiocalasia.
cardiocirrhosis *n.* cardiocirrosis.
cardioclasia *n.* cardioclasia.
cardiodilator *n.* cardiodilatador.
cardiodiosis *n.* cardiodiosis.
cardiodynamics *n.* cardiodinámica.
cardiodynia *n.* cardiodinia.
cardioesophageal *adj.* cardioesofágico, -ca.
cardiogenesis *n.* cardiogénesis.

cardiogenic *adj.* cardiogénico, -ca.
cardiogram *n.* cardiograma.
  apex cardiogram apexcardiograma, apexicardiograma.
  esophageal cardiogram cardiograma esofágico.
cardiograph *n.* cardiógrafo.
cardiography *n.* cardiografía.
cardiohemothrombus *n.* cardiohemotrombo.
cardiohepathic *adj.* cardiohepático, -ca.
cardiohepatomegaly *n.* cardiohepatomegalia.
cardioid *adj.* cardioide.
cardioinhibitory *adj.* cardioinhibitorio, -ria.
cardiokinetic *adj.* cardiocinético, -ca.
cardiokymogram *n.* cardioquimograma.
cardiokymograph *n.* cardioquimógrafo.
cardiokymography *n.* cardioquimografía.
cardiolith *n.* cardiolito.
cardiologist *n.* cardiólogo, -ga.
cardlology *n.* cardiología.
cardiolysis *n.* cardiólisis.
cardiomalacla *n.* cardiomalacia.
cardiomegaly *n.* cardiomegalia.
  glycogen cardiomegaly cardiomegalia glucógena, cardiomegalia glucogénica.
  glycogenic cardiomegaly cardiomegalia glucógena, cardiomegalia glucogénica.
cardiomentopexy *n.* cardiomentopexia.
cardiometry *n.* cardiometría.
cardiomotility *n.* cardiomotilidad.
cardiomuscular *adj.* cardiomuscular.
cardiomyoliposis *n.* cardiomioliposis.
cardiomyopathy *n.* cardiomiopatía.
  alcoholic cardiomyopathy cardiomiopatía alcohólica.
  congestive cardiomyopathy cardiomiopatía congestiva.
  dilated cardiomyopathy cardiomiopatía de dilatación.
  familial hypertrophic cardiomyopathy cardiomiopatía familiar hereditaria hipertrófica.
  hypertrophic cardiomyopathy cardiomiopatía hipertrófica.
  Idiopathic cardiomyopathy cardiomiopatía idiopática.
  postpartum cardiomyopathy cardiomiopatía posparto, cardiomiopatía postpartum.
  primary cardiomyopathy cardiomiopatía primaria.
  restrictive cardiomyopathy cardiomiopatía restrictiva.
  secondary cardiomyopathy cardiomiopatía secundaria.
cardiomyopexy *n.* cardiomiopexia.
cardiomyoplasty *n.* cardiomioplastia.
cardiomyotomy *n.* cardiomiotomía.
cardionecrosis *n.* cardionecrosis.
cardionector *n.* cardionector.
cardionephric *adj.* cardionéfrico, -ca.
cardioneural *adj.* cardioneural.
cardiopaludism *n.* cardiopaludismo.
cardiopath *n.* cardiópata.
cardiopathia *n.* cardiopatía.
  cardiopathia nigra cardiopatía negra.
cardiopathy *n.* cardiopatía.
cardiopericardiopexy *n.* cardiopericardiopexia.
cardiopericarditis *n.* cardiopericarditis.
cardiophobia *n.* cardiofobia.
cardiophone *n.* cardiófono.
cardioplasty *n.* cardioplastia.
cardioplegia *n.* cardioplejía.
cardioplegic *adj.* cardiopléjico, -ca.
cardiopneumatic *adj.* cardioneumático, -ca.

cardioptosis *n.* cardioptosis.
cardiopulmonary *adj.* cardiopulmonar.
cardiopyloric *adj.* cardiopilórico, -ca.
cardiorenal *adj.* cardiorrenal.
cardiorrhaphy *n.* cardiorrafia.
cardiorrhexis *n.* cardiorrexis.
cardioschisis *n.* cardiosquisis.
cardiosclerosis *n.* cardiosclerosis.
cardioscope *n.* cardioscopio.
cardioselective *adj.* cardioselectivo, -va.
cardioselectivity *n.* cardioselectividad.
cardiospasm *n.* cardioespasmo, cardiospasmo.
cardiosphygmograph *n.* cardiosfigmógrafo.
cardiosymphysis *n.* cardiosínfisis.
cardiotachometer *n.* cardiotacómetro, cardiotaquímetro.
cardiotherapy *n.* cardioterapia.
cardiothrombus *n.* cardiotrombo.
cardiothyrotoxicosis *n.* cardiotireosis, cardiotirotoxicosis.
cardiotomy *n.* cardiotomía.
cardiotonic *adj.* cardiotónico, -ca.
cardiotopometry *n.* cardiotopometría.
cardiotoxic *adj.* cardiotóxico, -ca.
cardiovalvulitis *n.* cardiovalvulitis.
cardiovalvulotome *n.* cardiovalvulótomo.
cardiovalvulotomy *n.* cardiovalvulotomía.
cardiovascular *adj.* cardiovascular.
cardiovasculorenal *adj.* cardiovasculorrenal.
cardioversion *n.* cardioversión.
cardioverter *n.* cardioversor.
carditis *n.* carditis.
  rheumatic carditis carditis reumática.
care *n.* cuidado.
  comprehensive medical care cuidado médico total.
  critical care cuidado crítico.
  intensive care cuidado intensivo.
  medical care cuidado médico.
  palliative care cuidado paliativo.
  postoperative care cuidado posoperatorio.
  postpartal care cuidado posparto.
  preoperative care cuidado preoperatorio.
  primary medical care cuidado médico primario.
  secondary medical care cuidado médico secundario.
  terminal care cuidado terminal.
  tertiary medical care cuidado médico terciario.
carebaria *n.* carebaria.
caribi *n.* caribi.
caries *n.* caries.
  active caries caries activa.
  arrested dental caries caries dental detenida.
  buccal caries caries bucal.
  caries sicca caries seca.
  cemental caries caries cementaria.
  central caries caries central.
  compound caries caries compuesta.
  dental caries caries dentaria.
  distal caries caries distal.
  dry caries caries seca.
  fissure caries caries de fisura.
  incipient caries caries incipiente.
  interdental caries caries interdentaria.
  mesial caries caries mesial.
  necrotic caries caries necrótica.
  occlusal caries caries oclusal.
  pit and fissure caries caries de fosa y fisura.
  pit caries caries de fosa.
  primary caries caries primaria.
  proximal caries caries proximal.
  radiation caries caries por radiación.
  recurrent caries caries recurrente.

  root caries caries radicular.
  secondary caries caries secundaria.
  senile dental caries caries senil.
  smooth surface caries caries lisa.
  spinal caries caries vertebral.
carina *n.* carina.
carinate *adj.* carinado, -da.
cariogenesis *adj.* cariogénesis[2].
cariogenicity *n.* cariogenicidad.
cariostatic *adj.* cariostático, -ca.
carious *adj.* carioso, -sa.
carmalum *n.* carmalum.
carneous *adj.* carnoso, -sa.
carnification *n.* carnificación.
carnivorous *adj.* carnívoro, -ra.
carnoslnemia *n.* carnosinemia.
carnosity *n.* carnosidad.
carotene *n.* caroteno.
carotenemia *n.* carotenemia, carotinemia.
carotenosis *n.* carotenosis.
carotic *adj.* carótico, -ca.
caroticotympanlc *adj.* caroticotimpánico, -ca.
carotid *n.* carótida, carotídeo, -a.
carotidynia *n.* carotidinia.
carotin *n.* carotina.
carotinemia *n.* carotinemia.
carotinosis cutis *n.* carotenosis, carotinosis.
carpal *adj.* carpiano, -na.
carpectomy *n.* carpectomía.
carphology *n.* carfología.
carpocarpal *adj.* carpocarpiano, -na.
carpometacarpal *adj.* carpometacarpiano, -na.
carpopedal *adj.* carpopedal.
carpophalangeal *adj.* carpofalángico, -ca.
carpoptosia *n.* carpoptosia.
carpoptosis *n.* carpoptosia, carpoptosis.
carpus *n.* carpo.
  carpus curvus carpo curvo, carpocifosis.
carrier *n.* portador, - ra.
  amalgam carrier portador de amalgama.
  gametocyte carrier portador de gametocitos.
  hemophilia carrier portador de hemofilia.
cartilage *n.* cartílago.
  branchial cartilage cartílago branquial.
  calcified cartilage cartílago calcificado.
  metaphyseal cartilage cartílago de crecimiento, cartílago metafisario.
  ossifying cartilage cartílago de osificación.
  precursory cartilage cartílago precursor.
  primordial cartilage cartílago primordial.
  Reichert's cartilage cartílago de Reichert.
  temporary cartilage cartílago temporal.
cartilaginification *n.* cartilaginificación.
cartilaginiform *adj.* cartilaginiforme.
cartilaginoid *adj.* cartilaginoideo, -a.
cartilaginous *n.* cartilaginoso.
cartilago *n.* cartílago.
caruncle *n.* carúncula.
  hymenal caruncle carúncula himenal.
  urethral caruncle carúncula uretral.
caruncula *n.* carúncula.
carver *n.* modelador.
caryogenic *adj.* cariogénico, -ca[2].
caryotheca *n.* carioteca.
case *n.* caso.
  borderline case caso dudoso.
  index case caso índice.
  trial case caso de ensayo.
caseation *n.* caseificación.
caseinogen *n.* caseinógeno.
caseous *adj.* caseoso, -sa.
cassette *n.* bastidor.
cast *n.* cilindro, enyesado, escayola, modelo, molde, moldear, yeso[1].
  bacterial cast cilindro bacteriano.

bilateral long-leg spica cast yeso bilateral en espiga de pierna completa.
bivalve cast yeso bivalvo.
blood cast cilindro hemático.
coma cast cilindro del coma.
decidual cast cilindro decidual, molde decidual.
dental cast cilindro modelo dental, modelo dental, yeso dental.
diagnostic cast cilindro modelo diagnóstico, modelo de diagnóstico, molde diagnóstico.
epithelial cast cilindro epitelial.
false cast cilindro falso.
fatty cast cilindro graso.
fibrinous cast cilindro fibrinoso, molde fibrinoso.
four-poster cast escayola de cuatro apoyos.
gnathostatic cast modelo gnatostático, molde gnatostático.
granular cast cilindro granular, molde granular.
hair cast cilindro capilar, molde del pelo.
halo cast cilindro ensayado en halo, enyesado en halo, yeso halo.
hanging cast enyesado colgante.
hyaline cast cilindro hialino.
investment cast cilindro modelo de revestimiento, modelo de revestimiento.
leg cylinder cast yeso cilíndrico de pierna.
long-arm cast yeso de brazo completo.
long-leg cast yeso de pierna completa.
long-leg cast with walker yeso largo de pierna con tacón.
master cast cilindro modelo patrón, modelo patrón, molde maestro.
mucous cast cilindro mucoso.
plaster cast escayola de yeso.
preoperative cast modelo preoperatorio.
Quengle cast yeso de Quengle.
red blood cell cast cilindro de células rojas, cilindro de células rojas de la sangre.
red cell cast cilindro de células rojas, cilindro de células rojas de la sangre.
refractory cast cilindro modelo refractario, modelo refractario, molde refractario.
renal cast cilindro renal.
Risser cast yeso de Risser.
short-arm cast yeso de antebrazo.
short-leg cast yeso de pierna.
short-leg cast with walker yeso de pierna con andador.
shoulder spica cast yeso en espiga para el hombro.
spica cast yeso en espiga.
spurious cast cilindro espurio.
study cast modelo de estudio.
tube cast cilindro en tubo.
urinary cast cilindro urinario.
walking cast yeso de marcha.
waxy cast cilindro céreo.
white blood cell cast cilindro de células blancas de la sangre.
casting *n.* colado, escayolar, moldeado, vaciado.
gold casting colado funda de oro.
vacuum casting moldeado en vacío, vaciado al vacío.
castrate *v.* castrar¹.
castration *n.* castración.
functional castration castración funcional.
casuistics *n.* casuística.
catabasial *adj.* catabasial.
catabasis *n.* catabasis.
catabiosis *n.* catabiosis.
catabiotic *adj.* catabiótico, -ca.
catabolic *adj.* catabólico, -ca.

catabolism *n.* catabolismo.
catabolite *n.* catabolito.
catachronobiology *n.* catacronobiología.
catacrotic *adj.* catacrótico, -ca.
catacrotism *n.* catacrotismo.
catadicrotic *adj.* catadicrótico, -ca.
catadicrotism *n.* catadicrotismo.
catadidymus *n.* catadídimo.
catadioptric *adj.* catadióptrico, -ca.
catagen *n.* catágeno.
catagenesis *n.* catagénesis.
catalepsy *n.* catalepsia.
cataleptic *adj.* cataléptico, -ca.
cataleptiform *adj.* cataleptiforme.
cataleptoid *adj.* cataleptoide.
catalysis *n.* catálisis.
contact catalysis catálisis por contacto.
surface catalysis catálisis de superficie.
catalyst *n.* catalizador.
inorganic catalyst catalizador inorgánico.
negative catalyst catalizador negativo.
organic catalyst catalizador orgánico.
positive catalyst catalizador positivo.
catalyzer *n.* catalizador.
catamenia *n.* catamenia.
catamenial *adj.* catamenial.
catamenogenic *adj.* catamenógeno, -na.
catamnesis *n.* catamnesis.
catamnestic *adj.* catamnésico, -ca.
catapasm *n.* catapasma.
cataphoresis *n.* cataforesis.
cataphoretic *adj.* cataforético, -ca.
cataphoria *n.* cataforia.
cataphylaxis *n.* catafilaxis.
cataplasia *n.* cataplasia.
cataplasis *n.* cataplasia.
cataplasm *n.* cataplasma.
cataplectic *adj.* catapléctico, -ca.
cataplexy *n.* cataplejía, cataplexia.
cataract *n.* catarata.
annular cataract catarata anular.
arborescent cataract catarata arborescente.
atopic cataract catarata atópica.
axial cataract catarata axial.
axillary cataract catarata axilar.
black cataract catarata negra.
blue cataract catarata azul.
calcareous cataract catarata calcárea.
capsular cataract catarata capsular.
capsulolenticular cataract catarata capsulolenticular.
cataract ossea catarata ósea.
central cataract catarata central.
cerulean cataract catarata cerúlea.
complete cataract catarata completa, catarata general.
complicated cataract catarata complicada.
concussion cataract catarata por concusión.
congenital cataract catarata congénita.
copper cataract catarata por cobre.
coralliform cataract catarata coraliforme.
coronary cataract catarata coronaria.
cortical cataract catarata cortical.
crystalline cataract catarata cristalina.
cuneiform cataract catarata cuneiforme.
cupuliform cataract catarata cupuliforme.
dendritic cataract catarata dendrítica.
diabetic cataract catarata diabética.
disk-shaped cataract catarata en forma de disco.
electric cataract catarata eléctrica.
embryonic cataract catarata embrionaria.
embryopathic cataract catarata embriopática.
fibrinous cataract catarata fibroide, catarata fibrosa.

fibroid cataract catarata fibroide, catarata fibrosa.
floriform cataract catarata floriforme.
furnacemen's cataract catarata de los fogoneros.
fusiform cataract catarata fusiforme.
galactose cataract catarata por galactosa.
glassworker's cataract catarata de los vidrieros.
glaucomatous cataract catarata glaucomatosa.
gray cataract catarata gris.
hard cataract catarata dura.
hook-shaped cataract catarata en forma de gancho.
hypermature cataract catarata hipermadura.
hypocalcemic cataract catarata hipocalcémica.
immature cataract catarata inmadura.
incipient cataract catarata incipiente.
infantile cataract catarata infantil.
infrared cataract catarata infrarroja.
intumescent cataract catarata intumescente.
juvenile cataract catarata juvenil.
lamellar cataract catarata lamelar, catarata laminar.
life-belt cataract catarata en salvavidas.
mature cataract catarata madura.
membranous cataract catarata membranosa.
Morgagni's cataract catarata de Morgagni.
myotonic cataract catarata miotónica.
nuclear cataract catarata nuclear.
overripe cataract catarata supermadura.
perinuclear cataract catarata perinuclear.
peripheral cataract catarata periférica.
pisciform cataract catarata pisciforme.
polar cataract catarata polar.
posterior subcapsular cataract catarata subcapsular posterior.
progresssive cataract catarata progresiva.
punctate cataract catarata punteada.
pyramidal cataract catarata piramidal.
radiation cataract catarata por radiación.
reduplicated cataract catarata reduplicada.
ripe cataract catarata madura.
rubella cataract catarata por rubéola.
saucer-shaped cataract catarata en forma de platillo.
secondary cataract catarata secundaria.
sedimentary cataract catarata sedimentaria.
senile cataract catarata senil.
siderotic cataract catarata siderótica.
siliculose cataract catarata aridosiliuada, catarata aridosiliculosa, catarata siliculosa, catarata silicuosa.
siliquose cataract catarata aridosiliuada, catarata aridosiliculosa, catarata siliculosa, catarata silicuosa.
soft cataract catarata blanda.
spindle cataract catarata en huso.
stationary cataract catarata estacionaria.
stellate cataract catarata estrellada.
subcapsular cataract catarata subcapsular.
sugar cataract catarata por azúcar.
sutural cataract catarata sutural.
syndermatotic cataract catarata sindermatótica.
tetany cataract catarata tetánica.
total cataract catarata total.
toxic cataract catarata tóxica.
traumatic cataract catarata traumática.
umbilicated cataract catarata umbilicada.
vascular cataract catarata vascular.
zonular cataract catarata zonular.
cataracta *n.* catarata.
cataracta adiposa catarata adiposa.
cataracta brunescens catarata brunescens.

cataracta dermatogenes catarata dermatógena.
cataracta fibrosa catarata fibroide, catarata fibrosa.
cataracta membranacea accreta catarata membranácea accreta.
cataracta neurodermica catarata neurodérmica.
cataracta nodiformis catarata nodular.
cataractogenesis *n.* cataratogénesis.
cataractogenic *adj.* cataratogénico, -ca.
catarrh *n.* catarro.
  atrophic catarrh catarro atrófico.
  Bostock's catarrh catarro de Bostock.
  hypertrophic catarrh catarro hipertrófico.
  Laennec's catarrh catarro pituitoso de Laennec.
  suffocative catarrh catarro sofocante.
catarrhal *adj.* catarral.
catastalsis *n.* catastalsis.
catastaltic *adj.* catastáltico, -ca.
catastasis *n.* catástasis.
catatonia *n.* catatonía.
  excited catatonia catatonía excitada.
  stuporous catatonia catatonía estuporosa.
catatonic *adj.* catatónico, -ca.
catatrichy *n.* catatriquia.
catatricrotic *adj.* catatricrótico, -ca.
catatricrotism *n.* catatricrotismo.
cataxia *n.* cataxia.
catechin *n.* catequina.
catecholamine *n.* catecolaminas.
catenating *adj.* catenario, -ria, encadenante.
catenoid *adj.* catenoide.
catgut *n.* catgut.
  chromic catgut catgut cromado, catgut crómico.
  iki catgut catgut iki.
  silvered catgut catgut plateado.
catharsis *n.* catarsis.
cathartic *adj.* catárrico, -ca.
cathemoglobin *n.* cathemoglobina.
catheresis *n.* catéresis.
catheretic *adj.* caterético, -ca.
catheter *n.* catéter.
  acorn-tipped catheter catéter de punta en bellota.
  balloon catheter catéter de balón.
  balloon-tip catheter catéter de punta en balón.
  bicoudate catheter catéter biacodado.
  Braasch catheter catéter de Braasch.
  brush catheter catéter en cepillo.
  cardiac catheter catéter cardíaco.
  catheter bicoudé catéter biacodado.
  catheter coudé catéter acodado.
  central venous catheter catéter venoso central.
  conical catheter catéter cónico.
  double-channel catheter catéter de doble canal.
  Drew- Smythe catheter catéter de Drew-Smythe.
  elbowed catheter catéter acodado.
  eustachian catheter catéter de eustaquio.
  female catheter catéter hembra.
  Fogarty's catheter catéterde Fogarty.
  Foley's catheter catéter de Foley.
  Gouley's catheter catéter de Gouley.
  indwelling catheter catéter permanente.
  intracardiac catheter catéter intracardíaco.
  Malecot catheter catéter de Malecot.
  Nélaton's catheter catéter de Nélaton.
  olive-tip catheter catéter de punta en oliva.
  pacing catheter catéter marcapaso.

  Pezzer catheter catéter de Pezzer.
  Phillips' catheter catéter de Philips.
  prostatic catheter catéter prostático.
  Robinson catheter catéter de Robinson.
  self-retaining catheter catéter autorretentivo.
  spiral-tip catheter catéter de punta en espiral.
  Swan-Ganz catheter catéter de Swan-Ganz.
  two-way catheter catéter de dos vías.
  vertebrated catheter catéter vertebrado.
  whistle-tip catheter catéter de punta en silbato.
  winged catheter catéter alado.
catheterization *n.* cateterismo, cateterización.
  cardiac catheterization cateterismo cardiovascular.
  female catheterization sondaje femenino.
  male catheterization sondaje masculino.
  retrourethral catheterization cateterismo retrouretral.
catheterostat *n.* cateteróstato.
cathexis *n.* catexis.
cathodal *adj.* catódico, -ca.
cathode *n.* cátodo.
cathodic *adj.* catódico, -ca.
catholysis *n.* católisis.
cation *n.* catión.
catoptric *adj.* catóptrico, -ca.
cauda *n.* cauda.
caudal *adj.* caudal.
caudate *adj.* caudado, -da.
caudatolenticular *adj.* caudatolenticular.
caudocephalad *n.* caudocefalad.
caudolenticular *adj.* caudolenticular.
caul *n.* cofia.
caumesthesia *n.* caumestesia.
causalgia *n.* causalgia.
cause *n.* causa.
  constitutional cause causa constitucional.
  exciting cause causa excitante.
  immediate cause causa inmediata.
  local cause causa local.
  necessary cause causa necesaria.
  precipitating cause causa causante.
  predisposing cause causa predisponente.
  primary cause causa primaria.
  proximate cause causa próxima.
  remote cause causa remota.
  secondary cause causa secundaria.
  specific cause causa específica.
  sufficient cause causa suficiente.
  ultimate cause causa última.
caustic *adj.* cáustico, -ca.
cauterant *adj.* cauterizante.
cauterization *n.* cauterización.
cauterize *v.* cauterizar.
cautery *n.* cauterio.
cavagram *n.* cavagrama.
caval *adj.* caval.
cavascope *n.* cavascopio.
cave *n.* cueva.
caveola *n.* cavéola.
caveolin *n.* caveolina.
cavern *n.* caverna.
caverniloquy *n.* caverniloquia.
cavernitis *n.* cavernitis.
  fibrous cavernitis cavernitis fibrosa.
cavernoscope *n.* cavernoscopio.
cavernoscopy *n.* cavernoscopia.
cavernostomy *n.* cavernostomía.
cavernous *adj.* cavernoso, -sa.
cavitary *adj.* cavitario, -ria.
cavitas *n.* cavidad.
cavitation *n.* cavitación.
cavitis *n.* cavitis.

cavity *n.* cavidad.
  amniotic cavity cavidad amniótica.
  celomic cavity cavidad celómica.
  perivisceral cavity cavidad perivisceral.
  primitive perivisceral cavity cavidad perivisceral primitiva.
  splanchnic cavity cavidad esplácnica.
  tension cavity cavidad de tensión.
  tooth-decay cavity cavidad cariosa, cavidad de caries.
cavogram *n.* cavograma.
cavography *n.* cavografía.
cavum *n.* cavum.
cebocephalia *n.* cebocefalia.
cecal *adj.* cecal.
cecectomy *n.* cecectomía.
cecitis *n.* cecitis.
cecocele *n.* cecocele.
cecocolon *n.* cecocolon.
cecocolostomy *n.* cecocolostomía.
cecoileostomy *n.* cecoileostomía.
cecopexy *n.* cecopexia.
cecoplication *n.* cecoplicación.
cecorrhaphy *n.* cecorrafia.
cecosigmoidostomy *n.* cecosigmoidostomía.
cecostomy *n.* cecostomía.
cecotomy *n.* cecotomía.
Cecum *n.* cecum.
cecum *n.* caecum.
celarium *n.* celario.
celiac *adj.* celíaco, -ca.
  celiac disease celiaquía.
celiagra *n.* celiagra.
celialgia *n.* celialgia.
celiectomy *n.* celiectomía.
celiocentesis *n.* celiocentesis.
celiocolpotomy *n.* celiocolpotomía.
celioenterotomy *n.* celioenterotomía.
celiogastrostomy *n.* celiogastrostomía.
celiohysterectomy *n.* celiohisterectomía.
celiohysterotomy *n.* celiohisterotomía.
celioma *n.* celioma.
celiomyalgia *n.* celiomialgia.
celiomyomectomy *n.* celiomiomectomía.
celioparacentesis *n.* celioparacentesis.
celiorrhaphy *n.* celiorrafia.
celiosalpingectomy *n.* celiosalpingectomía.
celiosalpingotomy *n.* celiosalpingotomía.
celioscope *n.* celioscopio.
celioscopy *n.* celioscopia.
celiotomy *n.* celiotomía.
  vaginal celiotomy celiotomía vaginal.
cell *n.* célula.
  A cell célula A.
  absorptive cell of the intestine célula absorbente del intestino.
  acidophil cell célula acidófila.
  acidophil cell of anterior lobe of the hypophysis célula acidófila del lóbulo anterior de la hipófisis.
  acinar cell célula acinar, célula acinosa, célula del ácino.
  acinous cell célula acinar, célula acinosa, célula del ácino.
  adipose cell célula adiposa.
  adventitial cell célula adventicia.
  alpha cell célula alfa.
  alpha cell of anterior lobe of the hypophysis célula alfa del lóbulo anterior de la hipófisis.
  alpha cell of the pancreas célula alfa del páncreas.
  alveolar cell célula alveolare.
  Alzheimer's cell célula de Alzheimer.
  amacrine cell célula amacrina.
  ameboid cell célula ameboide.

amnion cell célula del epitelio del amnios.
anabiotic cell célula anabiótica.
anaplastic cell célula anaplásica.
angioblastic cell célula angioblástica.
Anitschkow cell célula de Anitschkow.
anterior horn cell célula del asta anterior de la médula espinal.
antigen-presenting cell célula presentadora del antígeno.
antigen-sensitive cell célula antigenosensible.
apoptotic cell célula apoptósica.
APUD cell célula APUD, célula del sistema APUD.
argentaffin cell célula argentafin.
argyrophilic cell célula argirófila.
Armanni-Ebstein cell célula de Armanni-Ebstein.
Aschoff cell célula de Aschoff.
Askanazy cell célula de Askanazy.
astroglia cell célula de astroglia.
atrophyc cell célula atrófica.
auditory receptor cell célula receptora auditiva.
balloon cell célula de balón, célula en balón, célula globosa.
band cell célula en banda.
basal cell célula basal, célula basilar.
basket cell célula en cesto.
basophil cell célula basófila.
basophil cell of anterior lobe of the hypophysis célula basófila de la hipófisis anterior.
B-cell célula B.
Beale's cell célula de Beale.
Berger cell célula de Berger.
Bergmann cell célula de Bergmann.
beta cell célula beta.
beta cell of the anterior lobe of the hypophysis célula beta del lóbulo anterior de la hipófisis.
beta cell of the pancreas célula beta del páncreas.
Betz cell célula de Betz.
bipolar cell célula bipolar.
bipolar retinal cell célula bipolar de la retina.
bitufted cell célula bipenachada.
blast cell célula blástica.
blood cell célula sanguínea.
B-memory cell célula de memoria.
Boettcher cell célula de Boettcher.
Boll's cell célula de Boll.
bone cell célula ósea.
Bowen's cell célula de Bowen.
bronchic cell célula bronquial.
bronchiolar exocrine cell célula bronquiolar exocrina.
brood cell célula madre.
C cell célula C.
Cajal-Retzius's cell célula de Cajal-Retzius.
Cajal's cell célula horizontal de Cajal.
caliciform cell célula caliciforme, célula en cáliz.
cardiac muscle cell célula muscular estriada cardíaca.
cardiac muscle cell of the myocardium célula miocárdica.
carrier cell célula transportadora.
cartilage cell célula cartilaginosa.
castrate cell célula de castración.
castration cell célula de castración.
cell of somatic senses célula sensitiva.
cell of the corneal epithelium célula córnea, célula corneal.
cell of the impulse-conducting system célula cardionectora, célula cardiovectora.

cell reticularis célula reticularis.
cell with flagellum célula flagelada.
chalice cell célula caliciforme, célula en cáliz.
chief cell of the corpus pineale célula principal del cuerpo pineal.
chief cell of the parathyroid gland célula principal oscura de la paratiroides.
chief cell of the stomach célula principal del estómago.
choroid plexus epithelial cell célula de los plexos coroideos.
chromaffin cell célula cromafin.
chromophobe cell célula cromófoba.
ciliated cell célula ciliada.
Clara cell célula de Clara.
Clarke cell célula de Clarke.
Claudius' cell célula de Claudius.
clear cell célula clara.
cleavage cell célula de segmentación.
cleaved cell célula hendida.
column cell célula fascicular.
columnar cell célula cilíndrica.
commissural cell célula comisural.
cone cell of the retina célula en cono de la retina.
connective cell célula conjuntiva.
connective tissue cell célula del tejido conjuntivo.
continuously renewing cell célula en división continua, célula lábil.
contractile cell célula contráctil.
contrasuppressor cell célula contrasupresora.
Corti's cell célula de Corti.
craneospinal ganglion neuron cell célula ganglionar de los ganglios craneoespinales.
crescent cell célula en media luna, célula semilunar.
cuboidal cell célula cúbica, célula cuboidea.
Custer cell célula de Custer.
cyomegalic cell célula citomegálica.
cytotoxic cell célula citotóxica.
cytotrophoblastic cell célula citotrofoblástica.
D cell célula D.
dark cell célula oscura.
daughter cell célula hija.
decidual cell célula decidual.
decoy cell célula señuelo.
Deiters' cell célula de Deiters.
delta cell of the anterior lobe of the hypophysis célula delta del lóbulo anterior de la hipófisis.
delta cell of the pancreas célula delta del páncreas.
dendritic cell célula dendrítica.
Dogiel's cell célula de Dogiel.
Downey cell célula de Downey.
Drysdale cell célula de Drysdale.
dust cell célula del polvo.
EC cell célula EC.
ECL cell célula ECL.
effector cell célula efectora.
egg cell célula cigoto, célula huevo.
Ehrlich cell célula de Ehrlich.
embryonic cell célula embrionaria.
enamel cell célula del esmalte.
endodermal cell célula endodérmica, célula entodérmica.
endothelial cell célula endotelial.
endothelioid cell célula endotelioide.
enterochromaffin cell célula enterocromafina.
enteroendocrine cell célula enteroendocrinas.

entodermal cell célula endodérmica, célula entodérmica.
ependymal cell célula ependimaria.
epidermic cell célula epidérmica.
epithelial cell célula epitelial.
epithelial reticular cell célula nodriza del timo, célula reticular epitelial del timo.
epithelioid cell célula epitelioide.
erythroid cell célula eritroide.
Fañanás cell célula de Fañanás.
fasciculata cell célula fasciculada.
fat cell célula grasa.
fat-storing cell célula almacenadora de grasa del hígado.
Ferrata's cell célula de Ferrata.
foam cell célula espumosa.
follicular cell célula folicular.
follicular epithelial cell célula epitelial folicular.
follicular ovarian cell célula ovárica folicular.
foreign body giant cell célula gigante de cuerpo extraño.
foveolar cell of the stomach célula foveolar del estómago.
fuchsinophil cell célula fucsinófila.
fusiform cell of the cerebral cortex célula fusiforme de la corteza cerebral.
G cell célula G.
gametoid cell célula gametoide.
ganglion cell célula ganglionar.
ganglion cell of the retina célula ganglionar de la retina.
Gaucher cell célula de Gaucher.
germinal cell célula germinal.
ghost cell célula fantasma.
giant cell célula gigante.
Gierke cell célula de Gierke.
gitter cell célula gitter.
glia cell célula glial.
globet cell célula caliciforme, célula en cáliz.
globoid cell célula globoide.
glomerulous cell célula glomerular.
glomus cell célula glómica.
Golgi epithelial cell célula epitelial de Golgi.
Golgi's cell célula de Golgi.
granule cell célula de los granos.
granulosa lutein cell célula luteínica de la granulosa.
great alveolar cell célula alveolar grande.
gustatory cell célula gustativa.
hair cell célula ciliada de tipo 1 y de tipo 2.
hair vestibular cell célula receptora del sentido del equilibrio.
hairy cell célula vellosa.
heart failure cell célula de la insuficiencia cardíaca congestiva.
hecatomeral cell célula hecatómera.
HeLa cell célula HeLa.
helper cell célula colaboradora.
HEMPAS cell célula HEMPAS.
Hensen's cell célula de Hensen.
heteromeric cell célula heterómera, célula heteromérica.
hilus cell célula hiliar.
Höfbauer cell célula de Höfbauer.
homomeric cell célula homómera, célula homomérica.
horizontal cell of Cajal célula horizontal de Cajal.
horizontal cell of the retina célula horizontal de la retina.
Hürthle cell célula de Hürthle.
hyperchromatic cell célula hipercromática.
hypertrophic cell célula hipertrófica.
inducer cell célula inductora.

inner hair cell célula ciliada interna.
inner phalangeal cell célula falángica interna.
inner pillar cell célula de los pilares internos.
intercalary cell célula intercalar.
intercapillary cell célula intercapilar.
interplexiform cell célula interplexiforme.
interstitial cell of the kidney célula intersticial del riñón.
interstitial testicular cell célula intersticial del testículo.
islet cell célula de los islotes.
Ito cell célula de Ito.
juvenile cell célula juvenil.
juxtaglomerular cell célula yuxtaglomerulare.
keratinized cell célula queratinizada.
killer cell célula asesina.
Kulchitsky cell célula de Kulchitsky.
Kupffer cell célula de Kupffer.
Lacis cell célula de Lacis.
lactotroph cell célula lactotropa.
lacunar cell célula lacunar.
Langerhans' cell célula de Langerhans.
Langhans' cell célula de Langhans.
LE cell célula LE.
Leishman's chrome cell célula de Leishman.
lepra cell célula de la lepra.
Leydig's cell célula de Leydig.
light cell of the thyroid célula clara del tiroides.
lining cell célula de revestimiento.
Lipschütz cell célula de Lipschütz.
lupus erythematosus cell célula de lupus eritematoso.
luteal cell célula luteínica.
lutein cell célula luteínica.
lymphoid cell célula linfoide.
macroglia cell célula de macroglia.
Malpighian cell célula de Malpighi.
mamotroph cell célula mamotropa.
Marchand's wandering cell célula de Marchand.
Martinotti's cell célula de Martinotti.
mast cell célula cebada.
Max-Clara cell célula de Max-Clara.
mesangial cell célula mesangial.
mesenchymal cell célula mesenquimal, célula mesenquimática.
mesothelial cell célula mesotelial.
metaplasic cell célula metaplásica.
Meynert's cell célula de Meynert.
microglia cell célula de microglia.
microglial cell célula de microglia.
migrant cell célula emigrante.
migratory cell célula migrante, célula migratoria.
Milkulicz's cell célula de Mikulicz.
mirror image cell célula en imagen de espejo.
mitral cell célula mitral.
mother cell célula madre.
mucous cell célula mucosa.
mucous neck cell célula mucosa del cuello, célula mucosas cervical.
Müller cell célula de Müller.
Müller's radial cell célula radial de Müller.
multipolar cell célula multipolar.
mural cell célula mural.
myeloid cell célula mieloidea.
myoepithelial cell célula mioepitelial.
myoid cell célula mioide.
natural killer cell célula citotóxica natural.
necrotic cell célula necrótica.
nerve cell célula nerviosa.
neuroendocrine transducer cell célula transductora neuroendocrina.
neuroepithelial cell célula neuroepitelial.

neuroglia cell célula de neuroglia.
neurogliform cell célula neurogliforme.
neurosecretory cell célula neurosecretora.
nevus cell célula de nevo.
Niemann-Pick cell célula de Niemann-Pick.
NK cell célula NK.
noble cell célula noble.
nodal cell célula nodal.
nonclonogenic cell célula no clonógena.
nucleated cell célula nucleada.
nurse cell célula nodriza.
oat cell célula en avena.
olfactory cell célula olfatoria.
olfactory receptor cell célula receptora olfatoria.
oligodendroglia cell célula de oligodendroglia.
osseous cell célula ósea.
osteogenic cell célula osteógena.
osteoprogenitor cell célula osteoprogenitora.
outer hair cell célula ciliada externa.
outer phalangeal cell célula falángica externa.
outer pillar cell célula de los pilares externos.
ovarian interstitial cell célula intersticial del ovario.
oxyntic cell célula oxíntica.
oxyphil cell célula oxífila.
packed human blood cell célula sanguínea humana centrifugada.
Pagetoid cell célula pagetoide.
Paget's cell célula de Paget.
Paneth cell célula de Paneth.
parafollicular cell célula parafolicular.
paraluteal cell célula paraluteínica.
parenchymal cell célula parenquimatosa.
parenchymatous cell of the corpus pineale célula parenquimatosa del cuerpo pineal.
parietal cell célula parietal.
peptic cell célula péptica.
pericapillary cell célula pericapilar.
permissive cell célula permisiva.
pessary cell célula en pesario.
phagocytic cell célula fagocitaria, célula fagocítica.
phalangeal cell célula falángica.
pheochrome cell célula feocroma.
photoreceptor cell célula fotorreceptora.
physaliphorous cell célula fisalífera.
Pick cell célula de Pick.
pigment cell célula pigmentaria.
pigment cell of the iris célula pigmentaria del iris.
pigment cell of the retina célula pigmentaria de la retina.
pigment cell of the skin célula pigmentaria de la piel.
pigmented cell célula pigmentada.
pillar cell célula de los pilares.
pineal cell célula pineal.
plasma cell célula plasmática.
pluripotent cell célula pluripotencial.
polychromatophil cell célula policromatófila.
PP cell célula PP.
pregnancy cell célula del embarazo.
pregranulosa cell célula pregranulosa.
prickle cell célula espinosa.
primordial cell célula primordial.
prolactin cell célula prolactínica.
protective cell célula protectora.
pseudo-Gaucher cell célula seudo-Gaucher.
pseudounipolar cell célula seudomonopolar, célula seudounipolar.
pseudoxanthoma cell célula de seudoxantoma.

Purkinje's cell célula de Purkinje.
pus cell célula de pus.
pyramidal cell célula piramidal.
pyrrhol cell célula de pirrol.
pyrrol cell célula de pirrol.
quiescent cell célula en reposo.
Raji cell célula de Raji.
red blood cell célula roja de la sangre.
Reed cell célula de Reed.
Reed-Sternberg cell célula de Reed-Sternberg.
Renshaw cell célula de Renshaw.
reticular cell célula reticular.
reticuloendothelial cell célula reticuloendotelial.
retinal pigment epithelium cell célula del epitelio pigmentario de la retina.
retinal rod cell célula en cono de la retina.
Rieder cell célula de Rieder.
Rindfleisch's cell célula de Rindfleisch.
rod cell célula en bastón.
rod cell or retina célula en bastón de la retina.
Rolando's cell célula de Rolando.
rosette forming cell célula formadora de rosetas.
Rouget cell célula de Rouget.
satellite cell célula satélite.
satellite cell of skeletal muscle célula satélite del músculo esquelético.
scavenger cell célula recolectora.
Schilling's band cell célula en banda de Schilling.
Schultze's cell célula de Schultze.
Schwann cell célula de Schwann.
segmented cell célula segmentada.
sensitized cell célula sensibilizada.
sensory cell célula sensorial.
septal cell célula septal.
Sertoli's cell célula de Sertoli.
Sézary-Lutzner cell célula de Sézary-Lutzner.
sickle cell célula en hoz, célula falciforme.
siderophil cell célula siderófila.
signet ring cell célula en anillo de sello.
silver cell célula de plata.
skeletal muscle cell célula muscular estriada esquelética.
small cleaved cell célula hendida pequeña.
smooth muscle cell célula muscular lisa.
somatic cell célula somática.
somatotroph cell célula somatotropa.
sperm cell célula espermática.
spherical cell célula redonda.
spindle cell célula fusiforme.
spine cell célula espinosa.
splenic cell célula esplénica.
splenic endothelial cell célula en duela.
squamous cell célula escamosa, célula pavimentosa, célula plana.
stab cell célula en cayado.
staff cell célula en cayado.
stellate cell of the cerebral cortex célula estrelladas de la corteza cerebral.
stem cell célula germinativa.
Sternberg cell célula de Sternberg.
Sternberg-Reed cell célula de Sternberg-Reed.
strap cell célula en correa, célula faja.
striated muscle cell célula muscular estriada.
supporting cell célula de sostén.
suppressor cell célula supresora.
surface mucous cell of the stomach célula de la superficie mucosa del estómago.
sustentacular cell célula sustentacular.
sustentacular cell of the taste buds célula oscura de los botones gustativos.

sympathochromaffin cell célula simpatico-cromafin.
synovial cell célula sinovial.
T cell célula T.
T cytotoxic cell célula T citotóxica, célula TC.
tactile cell célula táctil.
target cell célula diana, célula en diana.
tart cell célula en tarta.
taste cell célula gustativa.
TC cell célula T citotóxica, célula TC.
TH cell célula T colaboradora, célula TH.
theca lutein cell célula luteínica de la teca.
thecal cell célula de la teca.
T-helper cell célula T colaboradora, célula TH.
thyroid follicular cell célula del folículo tiroideo.
thyrotroph cell célula tirotropa.
totipotent cell célula totipotencial, célula totipotente.
Touton giant cell célula gigante de Touton.
transducer cell célula transductora.
transformed cell célula transformada por virus.
transformed virus cell célula transformada por virus.
transitional cell célula de transición.
triangular-shape cell célula triangular.
trophoblast cell célula trofoblástica.
TS cell célula T supresora, célula TS.
T-suppressor cell célula T supresora, célula TS.
tufted cell célula en penacho.
tunnel cell célula del túnel de Corti.
Türck cell célula de Türck.
type I cell célula tipo I.
type II cell célula tipo II.
Tzanck cell célula de Tzanck.
undifferentiated cell célula indiferenciada.
unipolar cell célula unipolar.
veil cell célula velada.
veiled cell célula velada.
vestibular hair cell célula pilosa vestibular.
Virchow's cell célula de Virchow.
visual receptor cell célula receptora visual.
vitreous cell célula vítrea.
wandering cell célula errante, célula migrante, célula migratoria.
Warthin-Finkeldey cell célula de Warthin-Finkeldey.
wasserhelle cell célula principal clara de la paratiroides.
water clear cell of the parathyroid gland célula principal clara de la paratiroides.
wic. 38 cell célula wic. 38.
zymogenic cell célula cimógena.
cella *n.* celda, celdilla.
celloidin *n.* celoidina.
cellophane *n.* celofán.
cellular *adj.* celular.
cellularity *n.* celularidad.
cellulicidal *adj.* celulicida.
cellulifugal *adj.* celulífugo, -ga.
cellulite *n.* celulito.
cellulitis *n.* celulitis.
acute scalp cellulitis celulitis aguda del cuero cabelludo.
anaerobic cellulitis celulitis anaeróbica.
dissecting cellulitis celulitis disecante.
gangrenous cellulitis celulitis gangrenosa.
necrotizing cellulitis celulitis necrotizante.
orbital cellulitis celulitis orbitaria.
pelvic cellulitis celulitis pélvica.
phlegmonous cellulitis celulitis flemosa.
cellulitoxic *adj.* celulotóxico, -ca.

celluloid *n.* celuloide.
celluloneuritis *n.* celuloneuritis.
celom *n.* celoma.
celomic *adj.* celómico, -ca.
celonychia *n.* celoniquia.
celosomia *n.* celosomía.
celosomus *n.* celosomo.
celotomy *n.* celotomía.
celozoic *adj.* celozoico, -ca.
celulipetal *adj.* celulípeto, -ta.
cement *n.* cemento.
afibrillar cement cemento afibrilar.
composite dental cement cemento dental compuesto.
copper phosphate cement cemento de fosfato de cobre.
dental cement cemento dental.
eugenol cement cemento de óxido de cinc, cemento eugenol modificado.
inorganic dental cement cemento dental inorgánico.
modified zinc oxide cement cemento de óxido de cinc, cemento eugenol modificado.
polycarboxylate cement cemento de policarboxilato.
resin cement cemento de resina.
silicate cement cemento de silicato.
tooth cement cemento dental.
zinc phosphate cement cemento de fosfato de cinc.
cementation *n.* cementación.
cementicle *n.* cementículo.
cementification *n.* cementificación.
cementitis *n.* cementitis.
cementoblast *n.* cementoblasto.
cementoblastoma *n.* cementoblastoma.
benign cementoblastoma cementoblastoma benigno.
cementoclasia *n.* cementoclasia.
cementoclast *n.* cementoclasto.
cementocyte *n.* cementocito.
cemento-exostosis *n.* cementoexostosis.
cementome *n.* cementoma.
gigantiform cementome cementoma gigantiforme.
true cementome cementoma verdadero.
cementosis *n.* cementosis.
cementum *n.* cemento, cementum.
cenadelphus *n.* cenadelfo.
cenencephalocele *n.* cenencefalocele.
cenesthesia *n.* cenestesia.
cenesthesic *adj.* cenestésico, -ca.
cenesthesiopathy *n.* cenestesiopatía.
cenesthetic *adj.* cenestésico, -ca.
cenesthopathy *n.* cenestopatía.
cenocyte *n.* cenocito, coenocito.
cenocytic *adj.* cenocítico, -ca.
cenogenesis *n.* cenogénesis.
cenosite *n.* cenosito, coenosito.
cenotoxin *n.* cenotoxina.
censorship *n.* censura.
center *n.* centro.
active center centro activo.
anospinal center centro anospinal.
Broca's center centro de Broca.
catalytic center centro catalítico.
cell center centro celular.
center of ossification centro de osificación.
center of ridge centro del reborde.
center of rotation centro de rotación.
chondrification center centro de condrificación.
ciliospinal center centro ciliospinal.
dentary center centro dentario.
diaphysial center centro diafisario.

epiotic center centro epiótico.
expiratory center centro espiratorio.
feeding center centro de la alimentación.
germinal center of Flemming centro germinal de Flemming.
inspiratory center centro inspiratorio.
Kerckring's center centro de kerckring.
medullary center centro medular.
motor speech center centro motor del habla.
ossific center centro de osificación.
reaction center centro de reacción.
respiratory center centro respiratorio.
rotation center centro de rotación.
satiety center centro de la saciedad.
secondary center of ossification centro secundario de osificación.
semioval center centro semioval.
sensory speech center centro sensitivo del habla.
speech center centro del lenguaje.
sphenotic center centro esfenótico.
vasomotor center centro vasomotor.
vital center centro vitales.
Wernicke's center centro de wernicke.
centesis *n.* centesis.
centrage *n.* centraje.
central *adj.* central.
centrecephalic *adj.* centrecefálico, -ca.
centric *adj.* céntrico, -ca.
centrifugal *adj.* centrífugo, -ga.
centrifugalization *n.* centrifugacion.
centrifugation *n.* centrifugacion.
band centrifugation centrifugacion por bandas.
density gradient centrifugation centrifugacion por gradiente de densidad.
zone centrifugation centrifugacion por zonas.
centrifuge *n.* centrífuga, centrifugador.
centrilobular *adj.* centrilobular.
centriole *n.* centriolo, centríolo.
distal centriole centríolo distal.
proximal centriole centríolo proximal.
centripetal *adj.* centrípeto, -ta.
centroblast *n.* centroblasto.
Centrocestus *n.* Centrocesto.
centrocyte *n.* centrocito.
centrokinesia *n.* centrocinesia.
centrokinetic *adj.* centrocinético, -ca.
centrolecithal *adj.* centrolecítico, -ca.
centromere *n.* centrómero.
centroplasm *n.* centroplasma.
centrosome *n.* centrosoma.
centrosphere *n.* centrosfera.
centrostaltic *adj.* centrostáltico, -ca.
centrum *n.* centro, centrum.
centrum ovale centro oval.
centrum semiovale centro semioval.
primary centrum of ossification centro primario de osificación.
Vicq d'Azyr centrum semiovale centro semioval de Vicq d'Azyr.
Vieussens' centrum centro oval de Vieussens.
cenuriasis *n.* cenuriasis, cenurosis.
cenuris *n.* cenuro.
cenurosis *n.* cenurosis.
ceofixation *n.* cecofijación.
cepahlonia *n.* cefalonía.
cephalalgia *n.* cefalalgia.
Horton's cephalalgia cefalalgia de Horton.
cephalemia *n.* cefalemia.
cephalhematocele *n.* cefalohematocele.
cephalhematoma *n.* cefalohematoma.
cephalic *adj.* cefálico, -ca.
cephalin *n.* cefalina.

cephalitis *n.* cefalitis.
cephalization *n.* cefalización.
cephalocathartic *adj.* cefalocatártico, -ca.
cephalocaudal *adj.* cefalocaudal.
cephalocele *n.* cefalocele.
cephalocentesis *n.* cefalocentesis.
cephalochord *n.* cefalocordio.
cephalocyst *n.* cefaloquiste.
cephalodidymus *n.* cefalodídimo.
cephalodiprosopus *n.* cefalodiprosopo.
cephalogenesis *n.* cefalogénesis.
cephalogyric *adj.* cefalógiro, -ra.
cephalohematocele *n.* cefalohematocele.
  Stromeyer's cephalohematocele cefalohematocele de Stromeyer.
cephalohematoma *n.* cefalohematoma.
cephalohemometer *n.* cefalohemómetro.
cephalohydrocele *n.* cefalohidrocele.
cephalomegaly *n.* cefalomegalia.
cephalomelvimetry *n.* cefalopelvimetría.
cephalomenia *n.* cefalomenia.
cephalomeningitis *n.* cefalomeningitis.
cephalometer *n.* cefalómetro.
cephalometry *n.* cefalometría.
  ultrasonic cephalometry cefalometría ultrasónica.
cephalomotor *adj.* cefalomotor, -ra.
cephalopagus *n.* cefalópago.
cephalopathy *n.* cefalopatía.
cephalopelvic *adj.* cefalopélvico, -ca.
cephaloplegia *n.* cefaloplejía.
cephalorrhachidian *adj.* cefalorraquídeo, -a.
cephalostat *n.* cefalóstato.
cephalostyle *n.* cefalostilo.
cephalothoracic *adj.* cefalotorácico, -ca.
cephalothoracopagus *n.* cefalotoracópago.
  cephalothoracopagus asymmetros cefalotoracópago asimétrico.
  cephalothoracopagus disymmetros cefalotoracópago disimétrico.
  cephalothoracopagus monosymmetros cefalotoracópago monosimétrico.
cephalotome *n.* cefalótomo.
cephalotomy *n.* cefalotomía.
ceptor *n.* ceptor.
  chemical ceptor ceptor químico.
  contact ceptor ceptor de contacto.
  distance ceptor ceptor a distancia.
ceramide *n.* ceramida.
cerasin *n.* cerasina.
ceratin *n.* queratina.
ceratocricoid *adj.* ceratocricoides.
ceratohyal *adj.* ceratohial, queratohial.
cercaria *n.* cercaria.
cerclage *n.* cerclaje.
Cercocystis *n.* cercocisto, Cercocystis.
cercomer *n.* cercómero.
cercomonad *n.* cercomónada.
cercomonas *n.* cercomonas.
cerebellar *adj.* cerebelar, cerebeloso -sa.
cerebellifugal *adj.* cerebelífugo, -ga.
cerebellin *n.* cerebelina.
cerebellipetal *adj.* cerebelípeto, -ta.
cerebellitis *n.* cerebelitis.
cerebellolental *adj.* cerebelolenticular.
cerebellomedullary *adj.* cerebelobulbar.
cerebello-olivary *adj.* cerebeloolivar.
cerebellopontine *adj.* cerebelopontino, -na.
cerebellorubral *adj.* cerebelorrúbrico, -ca.
cerebellospinal *adj.* cerebeloespinal.
cerebellum *n.* cerebelo.
cerebral *adj.* cerebral.
cerebralgia *n.* cerebralgia.
cerebrasthenia *n.* cerebrastenia.
cerebration *n.* cerebración.

cerebriform *adj.* cerebriforme.
cerebrifugal *adj.* cerebrífugo, -ga.
cerebripetal *adj.* cerebrípeto, -ta.
cerebritis *n.* cerebritis.
  suppurative cerebritis cerebritis supurativa.
cerebrocardiac *adj.* cerebrocardíaco, -ca.
cerebrogalactoside *n.* cerebrogalactósido.
cerebroid *adj.* cerebroide.
cerebroma *n.* cerebroma.
cerebromalacia *n.* cerebromalacia.
cerebromeningeal *adj.* cerebromeníngeo, -a.
cerebromeningitis *n.* cerebromeningitis.
cerebropathia *n.* cerebropatía.
cerebropathy *n.* cerebropatía.
cerebrosclerosis *n.* cerebroesclerosis, cerebrosclerosis.
cerebroside *n.* cerebrósido.
cerebrosidosis *n.* cerebrosidosis.
cerebrosis *n.* cerebrosis.
cerebrospinal *adj.* cerebroespinal, cerebromedular, cerebrorraquídeo, -a, cerebrospinal.
cerebrosterol *n.* cerebrosterol.
cerebrostomy *n.* cerebrostomía.
cerebrotomy *n.* cerebrotomía.
cerebrotonia *n.* cerebrotonía.
cerebrovascular *adj.* cerebrovascular.
cerebrum *n.* cerebro, cerebrum.
cerecloth *n.* encerado.
ceroid *n.* ceroide.
ceroma *n.* ceroma.
ceroplasty *n.* ceroplastia.
certification *n.* certificación.
cerulein *n.* ceruleína.
ceruloplasmin *n.* ceruloplasmina.
cerumen *n.* cerumen.
  cerumen inspissatum cerumen espesado.
  inspissated cerumen cerumen espesado.
ceruminal *adj.* ceruminal.
ceruminolytic *adj.* ceruminolítico, -ca.
ceruminoma *n.* ceruminoma.
ceruminosis *n.* ceruminosis.
ceruminous *adj.* ceruminoso, -sa.
cervical *adj.* cervical.
cervicectomy *n.* cervicectomía.
cervicitis *n.* cervicitis.
cervicoaxillary *adj.* cervicoaxilar.
cervicobrachial *adj.* cervicobraquial.
cervicobuccal *adj.* cervicobucal.
cervicodorsal *adj.* cervicodorsal.
cervicodynia *n.* cervicodinia.
cervicofacial *adj.* cervicofacial.
cervicography *n.* cervicografía.
cervicolabial *adj.* cervicolabial.
cervicolingual *adj.* cervicolingual.
cervicolinguoaxial *adj.* cervicolinguoaxial.
cervico-occipital *adj.* cervicooccipital.
cervicoplasty *n.* cervicoplastia.
cervicoscapular *adj.* cervicoescapular, cervicoscapular.
cervicothoracic *adj.* cervicotorácico, -ca.
cervicovesical *adj.* cervicovesical.
cervix *n.* cérvix, cuello.
  incompetent cervix cuello incompetente.
cesarean *n.* cesárea.
  cesarean operation tomotocia.
cestode *n.* cestodos.
cestodiasis *n.* cestodiasis.
cestoid *adj.* cestoideo, -a.
chagoma *n.* chagoma.
chain *n.* cadena.
chaining *n.* encadenamiento.
chair *n.* silla.
  birthing chair silla de parto.
chalasia *n.* calasia.
chalasis *n.* calasia, calasis.

chalastodermia *n.* calastodermia.
chalazion *n.* calacio, chalazión.
  acute chalazion chalazión agudo.
  collar-stud chalazion chalazión en botón de camisa.
chalcosis *n.* calcosis.
  chalcosis lentis calcosis del cristalino.
chalicosis *n.* calicosis.
chalinoplasty *n.* calinoplastia.
chalkitis *n.* calquitis.
chalybeate *adj.* calibeado, -da.
chamaecephalic *adj.* quemocéfalo, -la.
chamaecephaly *n.* quemocefalia.
chamber *n.* cámara.
  Abbé-Zeiss counting chamber cámara contadora de Abbé-Zeiss, cámara cuentaglóbulos de Abbé-Zeiss.
  acoustic chamber cámara acústica.
  air-equivalent ionization chamber cámara aérea de ionización equivalente.
  altitude chamber cámara de altitud, cámara de altura.
  anechoic chamber cámara anecoica.
  Boyden chamber cámara de Boyden.
  decompression chamber cámara de descompresión.
  diffusion chamber cámara de difusión.
  free-air ionization chamber cámara de ionización de aire libre.
  Haldane chamber cámara de Haldane.
  high altitude chamber cámara de gran altitud.
  hyperbaric chamber cámara hiperbárica.
  ionization chamber cámara de ionización.
  pulp chamber cámara pulpar.
  sinuatrial chamber cámara sinoauricular.
  Storm Van Leeuwen chamber cámara de Storm Van Leeuwen.
  Thoma's counting chamber cámara contadora de Thoma-Zeiss, cámara cuentaglóbulos de Thoma-Zeiss.
  Thoma-Zeiss counting chamber cámara contadora de Thoma-Zeiss, cámara cuentaglóbulos de Thoma-Zeiss.
  Zappert counting chamber cámara contadora de Zappert.
  Zappert's chamber cámara de Zappert.
chamecephalic *adj.* camecefálico, -ca.
chamecephalous *adj.* camecéfalo, -la.
chamecephaly *n.* camecefalia.
chameprosopic *adj.* cameprosópico, -ca, cameprósopo, -pa.
chameprosopy *n.* cameprosopia.
chamfer *n.* bisel[2].
chancre *n.* chancro.
  chancre redux reinduración.
  hard chancre chancro duro, chancro sifilítico.
  mixed chancre chancro mixto.
  monorecidive chancre chancro monorrecidivante.
  redux chancre chancro redux.
  soft chancre chancro blando.
  sporotrichositic chancre chancro esporotricótico.
chancroid *n.* chancroide.
chancroidal *adj.* chancroideo, -a.
chancrous *adj.* chancroso, -sa.
change *n.* cambio.
  Armanni-Ebstein change cambio de Armanni-Ebstein.
  Baggenstoss change cambio de Baggenstoss.
  Crooke-Russel change cambio de Crooke, cambio de Crooke-Russel.
  Crooke's change cambio de Crooke, cambio de Crooke-Russel.

Crooke's hyaline change cambio hialino de Crooke.

fatty change cambio graso.

harlequin color change cambio en color de arlequín.

trophic change cambio trófico.

chappa *n.* chapa.

character *n.* carácter.

compound character carácter compuesto.

dominant character carácter dominante.

inherited character carácter hereditario.

Mendelian character carácter mendeliano.

primary sex character carácter sexual primario.

recessive character carácter recesivo.

secondary sex character carácter sexual secundario.

sex-linked character carácter ligado al sexo.

characteristic[1] *adj.* característico, -ca.

characteristic[2] *n.* característica.

receiver operating characteristic (ROC) característica operativa receptora (ROC).

characterization *n.* caracterización.

denture characterization caracterización protésica.

chart *n.* cuadro, gráfica, gráfico[2].

Amsler's chart gráfica de Amsler.

Guibor's chart gráfica de Guibor.

quality control chart gráfica de control de calidad.

reading chart gráfica de lectura.

Reuss color chart gráfica de colores de Reuss.

Walker's chart gráfica de Walker.

charting *n.* graficación.

chasma *n.* grieta.

cheek *n.* carrillo, mejilla.

cheilalgia *n.* queilalgia.

cheilangioscopy *n.* queiloangioscopia.

cheilectomy *n.* queilectomía.

cheilectropion *n.* queilectropión.

cheilion *n.* queilión.

cheilitis *n.* queilitis.

actinic cheilitis queilitis actínica.

angular cheilitis queilitis angular.

apostematous cheilitis queilitis apostematosa.

cheilitis exfoliativa queilitis exfoliativa.

cheilitis glandularis queilitis glandular.

cheilitis glandularis apostematosa queilitis glandular apostematosa.

cheilitis granulomatosa queilitis granulomatosa.

cheilitis venenata queilitis venenata, queilitis venenosa.

commisural cheilitis queilitis comisural.

contact cheilitis queilitis de contacto, queilitis por contacto.

impetiginous cheilitis queilitis impetiginosa.

migrating cheilitis queilitis migratoria.

solar cheilitis queilitis solar.

Volkmann's cheilitis queilitis de Volkmann.

cheiloalveoloschisis *n.* queiloalveolosquisis.

cheiloangioscopy *n.* queiloangioscopia.

cheilocarcinoma *n.* queilocarcinoma.

cheilognathoglossoschisis *n.* queilognatoglososquisis.

cheilognathopalatoschisis *n.* queilognatopalatosquisis.

cheilognathoprosoposchisis *n.* queilognatoprosoposquisis.

cheilognathoschisis *n.* queilognatosquisis.

cheilognathouranoschisis *n.* queilognatouranosquisis.

cheiloncus *n.* queilonco.

cheilophagia *n.* queilofagia.

cheiloplasty *n.* queiloplastia.

cheilorrhaphy *n.* queilorrafia.

cheiloschisis *n.* queilosquisis.

cheiloscopy *n.* queiloscopia.

cheilosis *n.* queilosis.

angular cheilosis queilosis angular.

cheilostomatoplasty *n.* queilostomatoplastia.

cheilotomy *n.* queilotomía.

cheiragra *n.* queiragra.

cheiralgia *n.* queiralgia.

cheiralgia paresthetica queiralgia parestésica.

cheirarthritis *n.* queirartritis, quirartritis.

cheirobrachialgia *n.* queirobraquialgia.

cheirocinesthesia *n.* queirocinestesia.

cheirognomy *n.* queirognomía, quirognomía.

cheirognostic *adj.* queirognóstico, -ca.

cheirokinesthesia *n.* queirocinestesia.

cheirokinesthesic *adj.* queirocinestésico, -ca.

cheirology *n.* queirología.

cheiromegaly *n.* queiromegalia.

cheiroplasty *n.* queiroplastia.

cheiropompholyx *n.* queiroponfólix.

cheiroscope *n.* queiroscopio.

cheirospasm *n.* queiroespasmo, queirospasmo.

chelate[1] *adj.* quelado, -da.

chelate[2] *n.* quelato.

chelate[3] *v.* quelato.

chelation *n.* quelación.

cheloid *n.* queloide, queloides.

cheloidosis *n.* queloidosis.

cheloma *n.* queloma, quelos.

chemabrasion *n.* quimioabrasión.

chemexfoliation *n.* quimioexfoliación.

chemical *adj.* químico, -ca[2].

chemical protector radioprotector.

chemicobiological *adj.* quimicobiológico, -ca.

chemicocautery *n.* quimicocauterio.

chemicophysical *adj.* quimicofísico, -ca.

chemicophysiologic *adj.* quimicofisiológico, -ca, quimiofisiológico, -ca.

chemiluminiscence *n.* quimioluminiscencia.

cheminosis *n.* quiminosis.

chemism *n.* quimismo.

chemisorption *n.* quemisorción.

chemist *n.* químico, -ca[1].

chemistry *n.* química.

analytic chemistry química analítica.

analytical chemistry química analítica.

applied chemistry química aplicada.

biological chemistry química biológica.

clinical chemistry química clínica.

colloid chemistry química coloidal, química coloide.

dental chemistry química dental.

electroanalytic chemistry química electroanalítica.

forensic chemistry química forense.

industrial chemistry química industrial.

inorganic chemistry química inorgánica.

medical chemistry química médica, química patológica.

medicinal chemistry química medicinal.

metabolic chemistry química metabólica.

mineral chemistry química mineral.

nuclear chemistry química nuclear.

organic chemistry química orgánica.

pharmaceutical chemistry química farmacéutica.

physiologic chemistry química fisiológica.

physiological chemistry química fisiológica.

radiation chemistry química de las radiaciones, radioquímica.

structural chemistry química estructural.

surface chemistry química de superficie.

synthetic chemistry química de síntesis.

chemoattractant *adj.* quimioatractivo, -va.

chemoautotroph *n.* quimioautótrofo[2].

chemoautotrophic *adj.* quimioautotrófico, -ca, quimioautótrofo, -fa[1].

chemobiodynamics *n.* quimiobiodinamia.

chemocauterize *v.* quimiocauterizar.

chemocautery *n.* quimiocauterio, quimiocauterización.

chemocephalia *n.* quemocefalia.

chemocephalic *adj.* quemocéfalo, -la.

chemocephaly *n.* quemocefalia.

chemoceptor *n.* quimioceptor$$ra.

chemocoagulation *n.* quimiocoagulación.

chemodectoma *n.* quemodectoma, quimiodectoma.

chemodectomatosis *n.* quimiodectomatosis.

chemodifferentiation *n.* quimiodiferenciación.

chemoheterotroph *n.* quimioheterótrofo.

chemoheterotrophic *adj.* quimioheterotrófico, -ca.

chemohormonal *adj.* quimiohormonal.

chemoimmunology *n.* quimioinmunología.

chemokinesis *n.* quimiocinesis.

chemokinetic *adj.* quimiocinético, -ca.

chemolithotroph *n.* quimiolitótrofo.

chemolithotrophic *adj.* quimiolitotrófico, -ca.

chemoluminiscence *n.* quimioluminiscencia.

chemolysis *n.* quimiólisis.

chemomorphosis *n.* quimiomorfosis.

chemonucleolysis *n.* nucleólisis, quimionucleólisis.

chemo-organotroph *n.* quimioorganotrofo.

chemo-organotrophic *adj.* quimioorganotrófico, -ca.

chemopallidectomy *n.* quimiopalidectomía.

chemopallidothalamectomy *n.* quimiopalidotalamectomía.

chemopallidotomy *n.* quimiopalidotomía.

chemopharmacodynamic *adj.* quimiofarmacodinámico, -ca.

chemophysiology *n.* quimiofisiología.

chemoprevention *n.* quimioprevención.

chemoprophylaxis *n.* quimioprofilaxis.

primary chemoprophylaxis quimioprofilaxis primaria.

secondary chemoprophylaxis quimioprofilaxis secundaria.

chemopsychiatry *n.* quimiopsiquiatría.

chemoreception *n.* quimiorrecepción.

chemoreceptor *n.* quimiorreceptor.

central chemoreceptor quimiorreceptor central.

medullary chemoreceptor quimiorreceptor bulbar.

peripheral chemoreceptor quimiorreceptor periférico.

chemoreflex *n.* quimiorreflejo.

chemoresistance *n.* quimiorresistencia.

chemosensitive *adj.* quimiosensible.

chemosensory *adj.* quimiosensorial.

chemoserotherapy *n.* quimioseroterapia.

chemosis *n.* quemosis.

conjunctival chemosis quemosis conjuntival.

chemosmosis *n.* quimioósmosis, quimiósmosis.

chemosmotic *adj.* quimiosmótico, -ca.

chemosorption *n.* quimiosorción.

chemostat *n.* quimiostato.

chemosterilant *adj.* quimioesterilizante.

chemosurgery *n.* quimiocirugía.

chemosynthesis *n.* quimiosíntesis.

chemosynthetic *adj.* quimiosintético, -ca.
chemotactic *adj.* quimiotáctico, -ca.
chemotaxin *n.* quimiotaxina.
chemotaxis *n.* quimiotactismo, quimiotaxis.
  leukocyte chemotaxis quimiotaxis leucocitaria.
  negative chemotaxis quimiotaxis negativa.
  positive chemotaxis quimiotaxis positiva.
chemothalamectomy *n.* quimiotalamectomía.
chemothalamotomy *n.* quimiotalamotomía.
chemotherapeutic *adj.* quimioterapéutico, -ca, quimioterápico, -ca.
chemotherapy *n.* quimioterapia.
  adjuvant chemotherapy quimioterapia adyuvante.
  chemotherapy (unsealed radioactive) quimioterapia radioactiva.
  combination chemotherapy quimioterapia combinada.
  consolidation chemotherapy quimioterapia de consolidación.
  induction chemotherapy quimioterapia de inducción.
  intensification chemotherapy quimioterapia de intensificación.
  intraarterial chemotherapy quimioterapia I.A., quimioterapia intraarterial.
  salvage chemotherapy quimioterapia de salvataje.
chemotic *adj.* quemótico, -ca.
chemotroph *n.* quimiótrofo.
chemotrophic *adj.* quimiotrófico, -ca.
chemotropic *adj.* quimiotrópico, -ca.
chemotropism *n.* quimiotropismo.
chenodeoxycholylglycine *n.* quenodesoxicolilglicina.
chenodeoxycholyltaurine *n.* quenodesoxicoliltaurina.
chenotherapy *n.* quenoterapia.
cheromania *n.* queromanía.
cherophobia *n.* querofobia.
cherubism *n.* querubismo.
chest *n.* pecho, tórax.
  alar chest tórax alar.
  barrel chest tórax en tonel, tórax globoso.
  barrel-shaped chest tórax en tonel.
  blast chest tórax de estallido.
  cobbler's chest tórax de zapatero.
  emphysematous chest tórax enfisematoso.
  flail chest tórax batiente, tórax inestable.
  flat chest tórax plano.
  funnel chest tórax infundibuliforme.
  keeled chest tórax asténico, tórax en quilla, tórax raquítico.
  paralytic chest tórax de Traube, tórax paralítico.
  pigeon chest tórax de paloma, tórax de pichón.
  pterygoid chest tórax pterigoideo.
  tetrahedron chest tórax tetraédrico.
chiasm *n.* quiasma.
  Camper's chiasm quiasma de Camper.
  chiasm of the digits of the hand quiasma de los dedos de la mano, quiasma tendinoso, quiasma tendinoso del músculo flexor superficial de los dedos, quiasma tendinum digitorum manus.
  optic chiasm quiasma óptico.
  tendinous chiasm of the digital tendons quiasma de los dedos de la mano, quiasma tendinoso, quiasma tendinoso del músculo flexor superficial de los dedos, quiasma tendinum digitorum manus.
  tendinous chiasm of the flexor digitorum

sublimis muscle quiasma de los dedos de la mano, quiasma tendinoso, quiasma tendinoso del músculo flexor superficial de los dedos, quiasma tendinum digitorum manus.
chiasma *n.* quiasma.
  chiasma opticum quiasma óptico.
  chiasma tendinum digitorum manus quiasma de los dedos de la mano, quiasma tendinoso, quiasma tendinoso del músculo flexor superficial de los dedos, quiasma tendinum digitorum manus.
chiasmapexy *n.* quiasmapexia.
chiasmatic *adj.* quiasmático, -ca.
chiasmometer *n.* quiasmómetro.
chiastometer *n.* quiastómetro.
chickenpox *n.* varicela.
chilalgia *n.* quilalgia.
chilblain *n.* sabañón.
  necrotized chilblain sabañón necrosado.
child *n.* niño, -ña.
childhood *n.* infancia, niñez.
chilectomy *n.* quilectomía.
chilectropion *n.* quilectropión.
chilitis *n.* quilitis.
chill *n.* escalofrío.
  brass chill escalofrío de los fundidores.
  brazier chill escalofrío de los fundidores.
  congestive chill escalofrío congestivo.
  creeping chill escalofrío reptante.
  nervous chill escalofrío nervioso.
  urethral chill escalofrío uretral.
  zinc chill escalofrío de cinc.
chiloalveoloschisis *n.* quiloalveolosquisis.
chilognathoglossoschisis *n.* quilognatoglososquisis.
chilognathopalatoschisis *n.* quilognatopalatosquisis.
chilognathoprosoposchisis *n.* quilognatoprosoposquisis.
chilognathoschisis *n.* quilognatosquisis.
chilognathouranoschisis *n.* quilognatouranosquisis.
chilomastigiasis *n.* quilomastigiasis, quilomastixiasis.
Chilomastix *n.* Chilomastix.
chilomastixiasis *n.* quilomastigiasis, quilomastixiasis.
chilomastosis *n.* quilomastosis.
chilophagia *n.* quilofagia.
chiloplasty *n.* quiloplastia.
chilopodiasis *n.* quilopodiasis.
chilorrhaphy *n.* quilorrafia.
chiloschisis *n.* quilosquisis.
chilosis *n.* quilosis[1].
chilostomatoplasty *n.* quilostomatoplastia.
chilotomy *n.* quilotomía.
chimaera *n.* quimera.
chimera *n.* quimera.
  DNA chimera quimera de ADN.
  heterologous chimera quimera heteróloga.
  homologous chimera quimera homóloga.
  isologous chimera quimera isóloga.
  radiation chimera quimera por radiación.
chimeric *adj.* quimérico, -ca.
chimerism *n.* quimerismo.
chin *n.* barbilla, mentón.
  chin cap mentonera.
chiomera *n.* quimera.
chionablepsia *n.* quionablepsia.
chip *n.* esquirla.
chiragra *n.* quiragra.
chiral *adj.* quiral.
chiralgia *n.* quiralgia.
chirality *n.* quiralidad.
chirobrachialgia *n.* quirobraquialgia.

chirognostic *adj.* quirognóstico, -ca.
chirokinesthesia *n.* quirocinestesia.
chirokinesthetic *adj.* quirocinestésico, -ca.
chirology *n.* quirología.
chiromegaly *n.* quiromegalia.
chiroplasty *n.* quiroplastia.
chiropodalgia *n.* queiropodalgia, quiropodalgia.
chiropompholyx *n.* quiroponfólix.
chiropractics *n.* quiropráctica, quiropraxia.
chiropractor *n.* quiropráctico$$ca, quiropractor$$ra.
chiroscope *n.* quiroscopio.
chirospasm *n.* quiroespasmo, quirospasmo.
chirurgenic *adj.* quirurgénico, -ca.
chirurgic *adj.* quirúrgico, -ca.
chisel *n.* escoplo.
  binangle chisel escoplo biangulado.
chitin *n.* quitina.
chitinase *n.* quitinasa.
chitinous *adj.* quitinoso, -sa.
chitoneure *n.* quitoneuro.
chiufa *n.* chiufa.
Chlamydia *n.* Chlamydia, clamidia.
Chlamydiaceae *n.* Chlamydiaceae.
chlamydial *adj.* clamidial.
chlamydiosis *n.* clamidiasis.
chloasma *n.* cloasma.
  chloasma bronzinum cloasma broncíneo.
chlorable *n.* clorolabe.
chloracne *n.* cloracné.
chloranemia *n.* cloranemia.
chloremia *n.* cloremia.
chlorhydria *n.* clorhidria.
chloridemia *n.* cloridemia.
chloridimeter *n.* cloridímetro, clorurómetro.
chloridimetry *n.* cloridimetría, clorurometría.
chloriduria *n.* cloriduria.
chlorinated *adj.* clorado, -da, clorinado, -da.
chloroform *n.* cloroformo.
chloroformism *n.* cloroformismo.
chloroformization *n.* cloroformización.
chloroiodized *adj.* cloroyodado, -da.
chloroleukemia *n.* cloroleucemia.
chloroma *n.* cloroleucosarcomatosis, clorolinfosarcoma, cloroma.
chlorometry *n.* clorometría.
chloromyeloma *n.* cloromieloma, cloromielosarcomatosis.
chloronaftalene *n.* cloronaftaleno.
chloropenia *n.* cloropenia.
chloropexia *n.* cloropexia.
chlorophane *n.* clorófano.
chloroplast *n.* cloroplasto.
chloroprivic *adj.* cloroprivo, -va.
chloropsia *n.* cloropía, cloropsia.
chlorosarcolymphadeny *n.* clorosarcolinfadenia.
chlorosis *n.* clorosis.
chlorotic *adj.* clorótico, -ca.
chlorous *adj.* cloroso, -sa.
chloruremic *adj.* clorurémico, -ca.
chloruresis *n.* cloruresis.
chloruretic *adj.* clorurético, -ca.
chloruria *n.* cloruria.
chlostridial *adj.* clostridial.
chlourectic *adj.* clourético, -ca.
chlouresis *n.* cloruresis, clouresis.
chlouretic *adj.* clourético, -ca.
choana *n.* coana.
  primary choana coana primaria, coana primitiva.
  primitive choana coana primaria, coana primitiva.
  secondary choana coana secundaria.

choanal *adj.* coanal.
choanate *adj.* coanado, -da.
choanoid *adj.* coanoide.
choice *n.* elección.
   free choice of doctor libre elección de médico.
   object choice elección de objeto.
choke *n.* ahogo.
cholalic *adj.* colálico, -ca.
cholaligenic *adj.* colaligénico, -ca.
cholaneresis *n.* colaneresis.
cholangeitis *n.* colangeítis, colangitis.
cholangia *n.* colangia.
cholangiectasis *n.* colangiectasia.
cholangiocarcinoma *n.* colangiocarcinoma.
cholangiocholecystocholedochectomy *n.* colangiocolecistocoledocectomía.
cholangiocholecystography *n.* colangiocolecistografía.
   CT cholangiocholecystography colangiocolecistografía TC.
   intravenous cholangiocholecystography colangiocolecistografía intravenosa.
   retrogressive cholangiocholecystography colangiocolecistografía retrógada.
cholangioenterostomy *n.* colangioenterostomía.
cholangiofibrosis *n.* colangiofibrosis.
cholangiogastrostomy *n.* colangiogastrostomía.
cholangiogram *n.* colangiograma.
cholangiography *n.* colangiografía.
   cystic duct cholangiography colangiografía del conducto cístico.
   endoscopic retrograde cholangiography colangiografía endoscópica retrógrada, colangiografía retrógrada endoscópica (CPRE).
   intravenous cholangiography colangiografía intravenosa.
   percutaneous cholangiography colangiografía percutánea.
   percutaneous transhepatic cholangiography colangiografía transhepática percutánea.
   T tubule cholangiography colangiografía tubular en T.
   transhepatic cholangiography colangiografía transhepática.
   transjugular cholangiography colangiografía transyugular.
   transparietohepatic cholangiography colangiografía transparietohepática.
cholangiohepatitis *n.* colangiohepatitis.
cholangiohepatoma *n.* colangiohepatoma.
cholangiojejunostomy *n.* colangioyeyunostomía.
cholangiolar *adj.* colangiolar.
cholangiole *n.* colangiolo.
cholangiolitis *n.* colangiolitis.
cholangioma *n.* colangioma.
cholangiopancreatography *n.* colangiopancreatografía.
   endoscopic retrograde cholangiopancreatography (ERCP) colangiopancreatografía endoscópica retrógrada, colangiopancreatografía retrógrada endoscópica (CPRE).
cholangioscopy *n.* colangioscopia.
cholangiostomy *n.* colangiostomía.
cholangiotomy *n.* colangiotomía.
cholangitis *n.* colangitis.
   acute cholangitis colangitis aguda.
   cholangitis lenta colangitis lenta.
   chronic nonsuppurative destructive cholangitis colangitis destructiva crónica no supurada.
   primary sclerosing cholangitis colangitis esclerosante primaria.
   progressive nonsuppurative cholangitis colangitis progresiva no supurada.
   sclerosing cholangitis colangitis esclerosante.
cholanopoiesis *n.* colanopoyesis.
cholanopoietic *adj.* colanopoyético, -ca.
cholascos *n.* colascos.
cholebilirubin *n.* colebilirrubina.
cholechromopoiesis *n.* colecromopoyesis.
cholecyanin *n.* colocianina.
cholecyst *n.* colecisto.
cholecystagogic *adj.* colecistagógico, -ca.
cholecystagogue *adj.* colecistagogo, -ga.
cholecystalgia *n.* colecistalgia.
cholecystanony *n.* colecistatonía.
cholecystectasia *n.* colecistectasia.
cholecystectomy *n.* colecistectomía.
   laparoscopic cholecystectomy colecistectomía laparoscópica.
cholecystendysis *n.* colecistendisis.
cholecystenteric *adj.* colecistentérico, -ca, colecistoentérico, -ca.
cholecystenteroanastomosis *n.* colecistenteroanastomosis, colecistoenteroanastomosis.
cholecystenterorrhaphy *n.* colecistenterorrafia, colecistoenterorrafia.
cholecystenterostomy *n.* colecistenterostomía, colecistoenterostomía.
cholecystic *adj.* colecístico, -ca.
cholecystitis *n.* colecistitis.
   acute cholecystitis colecistitis aguda.
   cholecystitis glandularis proliferans colecistitis glandular proliferativa.
   chronic cholecystitis colecistitis crónica.
   emphysematous cholecystitis colecistitis enfisematosa.
   follicular cholecystitis colecistitis folicular.
   gaseous cholecystitis colecistitis gaseosa.
   xanthogranulomatous cholecystitis colecistitis xantogranulomatosa.
cholecystocholangiogram *n.* colecistocolangiograma.
cholecystocolonic *adj.* colecistocólico, -ca.
cholecystocolostomy *n.* colecistocolostomía.
cholecystocolotomy *n.* colecistocolotomía.
cholecystoduodenostomy *n.* colecistoduodenostomía.
cholecystogastric *adj.* colecistogástrico, -ca.
cholecystogastrostomy *n.* colecistogastrostomía.
cholecystogogic *adj.* colecistogógico, -ca.
cholecystogram *n.* colecistograma.
cholecystoileostomy *n.* colecistoileostomía.
cholecystointestinal *adj.* colecistointestinal.
cholecystojejunostomy *n.* colecistoyeyunostomía.
cholecystokinetic *adj.* colecistocinético, -ca.
cholecystokinin *n.* colecistocinina, colecistoquinina.
cholecystolithiasis *n.* colecistoliatiasis.
cholecystolithotripsy *n.* colecistolitotripsia.
cholecystonephrostomy *n.* colecistonefrostomía.
cholecystopathy *n.* colecistopatía.
cholecystopexy *n.* colecistopexia.
cholecystoplasty *n.* colecistoplastia.
cholecystoptosis *n.* colecistoptosis.
cholecystopyelostomy *n.* colecistopielostomía.
cholecystorrhaphy *n.* colecistorrafia.
cholecystosis *n.* colecistosis.
cholecystosonography *n.* colecistosonografía.
cholecystostomy *n.* colecistostomía.
cholecystotomy *n.* colecistotomía.
cholecystotyphoid *adj.* colecistotifoidea.
cholecystrography *n.* colecistografía.
choledocal *adj.* coledocal.
choledoch *n.* colédoco.
choledochal *adj.* coledociano, -na, coledocócico, -ca.
choledochectomy *n.* coledocectomía, coledoquectomía.
choledochendysis *n.* coledocendisis, coledoquendisis.
choledochiartia *n.* coledociartia.
choledochitis *n.* coledocitis.
choledochocele *n.* coledocele.
choledochocholedochostomy *n.* coledococoledocostomía.
choledochoduodenostomy *n.* coledocoduodenostomía.
choledochoenterostomy *n.* coledocoenterostomía.
choledochogastrostomy *n.* coledocogastrostomía.
choledochogram *n.* coledocograma.
choledochography *n.* coledocografía.
choledochohepatostomy *n.* coledocohepatostomía.
choledochoileostomy *n.* coledocoileostomía.
choledochojejunostomy *n.* coledocoyeyunostomía.
choledocholith *n.* coledocolito.
choledocholithiasis *n.* coledocolitiasis.
choledocholithotomy *n.* coledocolitotomía.
choledocholithotripsy *n.* coledocolitotricia, coledocolitotripsia.
choledochoplasty *n.* coledocoplastia.
choledochorrhaphy *n.* coledocorrafia.
choledochostomy *n.* coledocostomía.
choledochotomy *n.* coledocotomía.
choledochous *adj.* coledocoso, -sa.
choledoscope *n.* coledoscopio.
choleglobin *n.* coleglobina.
cholehematin *n.* colohematina.
cholehemia *n.* colehemia, colemia.
choleic *adj.* coleico, -ca.
cholelith *n.* colelito.
cholelithiasis *n.* colelitiasis, cololitiasis.
cholelithic *adj.* colelítico, -ca, cololítico, -ca.
cholelithotomy *n.* colelitomía.
cholelithotripsy *n.* colelitotricia, colelitotripsia.
cholemesis *n.* colemesis.
cholemia *n.* colemia.
cholemic *adj.* colémico, -ca.
cholemimetry *n.* colemimetría.
cholepathia *n.* colepatía.
   cholepathia spastica colepatía espástica.
choleperitoneum *n.* coleperitoneo.
choleperitonitis *n.* coleperitonitis.
cholepoiesis *n.* colepoyesis.
cholepoietic *adj.* colepoyético, -ca.
choleprasin *n.* coleprasina.
cholera *n.* cólera.
   Asiatic cholera cólera asiático.
   cholera infantum cólera infantil.
   cholera morbus cólera morbo.
   cholera sicca cólera fulminante, cólera seco.
   dry cholera cólera fulminante, cólera seco.
   typhoid cholera cólera tífico, cólera tifoídico.
choleraic *adj.* coleraico, -ca.
cholerangen *n.* colerágeno.
choleraphage *n.* coleráfago.
cholereic *adj.* colereico, -ca.
choleresis *n.* coleresis.
choleretic *adj.* colerético, -ca.
choleriform *adj.* coleriforme.
cholerigenous *adj.* colerígeno, -na.

cholerine *n.* colerina.
cholerization *n.* colerización.
cholerogenic *adj.* colerigénico, -ca.
choleroid *adj.* coleroide.
cholerrhagia *n.* colerragia.
cholerrhagic *adj.* colerrágico, -ca.
cholescintigram *n.* colescintigrama.
cholescintigraphy *n.* colescintigrafía.
cholestanol *n.* colestanol.
cholestasia *n.* colestasia.
cholestasis *n.* colestasia, colestasis.
cholestatic *adj.* colestático -ca.
cholesteatoma *n.* colesteatoma.
  cholesteatoma tympani colesteatoma timpánico.
cholesteatomatous *adj.* colesteatomatoso, -sa.
cholesteatosis *n.* colesteatosis.
cholesterase *n.* colesterasa.
cholesteremia *n.* colesteremia.
cholesterinemia *n.* colesterinemia.
cholesterinosis *n.* colesterinosis.
  cerebrotendinous cholesterinosis colesterinosis cerebrotendinosa.
cholesterinuria *n.* colesterinuria.
cholesteroderma *n.* colesterodermia.
cholesterogenesis *n.* colesterogénesis.
cholesterohistechia *n.* colesterohistequia.
cholesterohydrothorax *n.* colesterohidrotórax.
cholesterol *n.* colesterol.
cholesterolemia *n.* colesterolemia.
cholesteroleresis *n.* colesteroléresis.
cholesterologenesis *n.* colesterologénesis.
cholesterolosis *n.* colesterolosis.
  extracellular cholesterolosis colesterolosis extracelular.
cholesteroluria *n.* colesteroluria.
cholesteropoiesis *n.* colesteropoyesis.
cholesterosis *n.* colesterosis.
  cholesterosis cutis colesterosis cutánea, colesterosis cutis.
  extracellular cholesterosis colesterosis extracelular.
choletherapy *n.* coleterapia.
choleuria *n.* coleuria.
cholicele *n.* colicele.
choline *n.* colina.
cholinephritis *n.* colinefritis.
cholinergic *adj.* colinérgico, -ca.
cholinoceptive *adj.* colinoceptivo, -va.
cholinoceptor *n.* colinoceptor.
cholinomimetic *adj.* colinomimético, -ca.
cholinoreactive *adj.* colinorreactivo, -va.
cholinoreceptor *n.* colinoceptor, colinorreceptor.
cholocholecystostomy *n.* colocolecistostomía.
cholochrome *n.* colocromo.
cholocyanin *n.* colocianina.
chologenetic *adj.* cologénico, -ca.
cholohematin *n.* colohematina.
cholohemothorax *n.* colohemotórax.
chololith *n.* colelito, cololito.
chololithiasis *n.* cololitiasis.
chololithic *adj.* cololítico, -ca.
choloplania *n.* coloplania.
cholopoiesis *n.* colepoyesis, colopoyesis.
choloscopy *n.* coloscopia.
cholothorax *n.* colotórax.
choluria *n.* coleuria, coluria.
choluric *adj.* colúrico, -ca.
chondral *adj.* condral.
chondralgia *n.* condralgia.
chondralloplasia *n.* condraloplasia.
chondrectomy *n.* condrectomía.

chondric *adj.* cóndrico, -ca.
chondrification *n.* condrificación.
chondrin *n.* condrina.
chondriocont *n.* condrioconto.
chondriosome *n.* condriosoma.
chondritis *n.* condritis.
  chondritis intervertebralis calcarea condritis invertebral calcárea.
  costal chondritis condritis costal.
chondroadenoma *n.* condroadenoma.
chondroangioma *n.* condroangioma.
chondroblast *n.* condroblasto.
chondroblastoma *n.* condroblastoma.
chondrocalcinosis *n.* condrocalcinosis.
chondrocarcinoma *n.* condrocarcinoma.
chondroclast *n.* condroclasto.
chondrocostal *adj.* condrocostal.
chondrocranium *n.* condrocráneo.
chondrocyte *n.* condrocito.
  isogenous chondrocyte condrocito isógeno.
chondrodermatitis *n.* condrodermatitis.
  chondrodermatitis nodularis chronica helicis condrodermatitis nodular crónica helical.
chondrodistrophy *n.* condrodistrofia.
chondrodynia *n.* condrodinia.
chondrodysplasia *n.* condrodisplasia.
  chondrodysplasia punctata condrodisplasia punctata, condrodisplasia punteada, condrodisplasia puntiforme.
  hereditary deforming chondrodysplasia condrodisplasia deformante hereditaria.
chondrodystrophia *n.* condrodistrofia.
  asphyxiating thoracic chondrodystrophia condrodistrofia torácica asfixiante.
  chondrodystrophia calcificans congenita condrodistrofia calcificante congénita, condrodistrofia congénita puntiforme, condrodistrofia fetal calcificada.
  chondrodystrophia congenita punctata condrodistrofia punteada congénita.
  chondrodystrophia malacia condrodistrofia malácica.
  familial chondrodystrophia condrodistrofia familiar.
  hyperplastic chondrodystrophia condrodistrofia hiperplásica.
  hypoplastic chondrodystrophia condrodistrofia hipoplásica.
  hypoplastic fetal chondrodystrophia condrodistrofia fetal hipoplásica.
chondroectodermal *adj.* condroectodérmico, -ca.
chondroendothelioma *n.* condroendotelioma.
chondroepiphyseal *adj.* condroepifisario, -ria.
chondroepiphysitis *n.* condroepifisitis.
chondrofibroma *n.* condrofibroma.
chondrogen *n.* condrígeno.
chondrogenesis *n.* condrogénesis.
chondrogenic *adj.* condrógeno, -na.
chondroglossous *adj.* condrogloso, -sa.
chondrography *n.* condrografía.
chondrohypoplasia *n.* condrohipoplasia.
chondroid *adj.* condroide.
chondroitic *adj.* condroítico.
chondroitinuria *n.* condroitinuria.
chondrolipoma *n.* condrolipoma.
chondrology *n.* condrología.
chondrolysis *n.* condrólisis.
chondroma *n.* condrocele, condroma.
  chondroma sarcomatosum condroma sarcomatoso.
  extraskeletal chondroma condroma extraesquelético.
  joint chondroma condroma articular.
  synovial chondroma condroma sinovial.

  true chondroma condroma verdadero.
chondromalacia *n.* condromalacia.
  chondromalacia fetalis condromalacia fetal.
  chondromalacia of the larynx condromalacia de la laringe.
  chondromalacia patellae condromalacia patelar, condromalacia rotuliana.
  generalized chondromalacia condromalacia generalizada.
  systemic chondromalacia condromalacia sistémica.
chondromatosise *n.* condromatosis.
  multiple chondromatosise condromatosis múltiple.
  synovial chondromatosise condromatosis sinovial.
chondromatous *adj.* condromatoso, -sa.
chondromere *n.* condrómera.
chondrometaplasia *n.* condrometaplasia.
  synovial chondrometaplasia condrometaplasia sinovial.
  tenosynovial chondrometaplasia condrometaplasia tenosinovial.
chondromucin *n.* condromucina.
chondromucoprotein *n.* condromucoproteína.
chondromyoma *n.* condromioma.
chondromyxofibroma *n.* condromixofibroma.
chondromyxoid *adj.* condromixoide.
chondromyxoma *n.* condromixoma.
chondromyxosarcoma *n.* condromixosarcoma.
chondronecrosis *n.* condronecrosis.
chondro-osseous *adj.* condroóseo, -a.
chondro-osteodystrophy *n.* condroosteodistrofia.
chondropathia *n.* condropatía.
  chondropathia tuberosa condropatía tuberosa.
chondropathology *n.* condropatología.
chondrophyte *n.* condrofima, condrófito.
chondroplasia *n.* condroplasia.
  chondroplasia punctata condroplasia puntiforme.
chondroplast *n.* condroblasto, condroplasto.
chondroplastic *adj.* condroplástico, -ca.
chondroplasty *n.* condroplastia.
chondroporosis *n.* condroporosis.
chondroprotein *n.* condroproteína.
chondrosarcoma *n.* condrosarcoma.
  central chondrosarcoma condrosarcoma central.
  mesenchymal chondrosarcoma condrosarcoma mesenquimatoso.
chondrosarcomatosis *n.* condrosarcomatosis.
chondrosarcomatous *adj.* condrosarcomatoso, -sa.
chondroseptum *n.* condroseptum.
chondrosis *n.* condrosis.
chondroskeleton *n.* condroesqueleto, condrosqueleto.
chondrosteoma *n.* condrosteoma.
chondrosternal *adj.* condroesternal, condrosternal.
chondrosternoplasty *n.* condroesternoplastia, condrosternoplastia.
chondrotome *n.* condrótomo.
chondrotomy *n.* condrotomía.
chondrotrophic *adj.* condrotrófico, -ca.
chondroxiphoid *adj.* condroxifoide, condroxifoideo, -a.
chonechondrosternon *n.* conecondrosternón.
chorda *n.* cuerda.

chordal *adj.* cordal.
chorda-mesoderm *n.* cordamesodermo.
chordee *n.* encordamiento.
chordencephalon *n.* cordencéfalo.
chorditis *n.* corditis.
  chorditis cantorum corditis de los cantantes.
  chorditis fibrinosa corditis fibrinosa.
  chorditis nodosa corditis nudosa.
  chorditis tuberosa corditis tuberosa.
  chorditis vocalis corditis vocal.
  chorditis vocalis inferior corditis vocal inferior.
chordoblastoma *n.* cordoblastoma.
chordocarcinoma *n.* cordocarcinoma.
chordoepithelioma *n.* cordoepitelioma.
chordoid *adj.* cordoide.
chordoma *n.* cordoma.
chordosarcoma *n.* cordosarcoma.
chordoskeleton *n.* cordoesqueleto.
chorea *n.* corea.
  acute chorea corea aguda.
  automatic chorea corea automática.
  button maker's chorea corea de fabricantes de botones.
  chorea cordis corea cardíaca.
  chorea dimidiata corea dimidiata.
  chorea festinans corea festinante.
  chorea gravidarum corea gravidarum, corea gravídica.
  chorea major corea major, corea mayor.
  chorea minor corea menor, corea minor.
  chorea nutans corea nutans.
  chronic chorea corea crónica.
  chronic progressive chorea corea crónica progresiva, corea crónica progresiva hereditaria.
  chronic progressive hereditary chorea corea crónica progresiva, corea crónica progresiva hereditaria.
  chronic progressive non-hereditary chorea corea crónica progresiva no hereditaria.
  dancing chorea corea danzante.
  degenerative chorea corea degenerativa.
  diaphragmatic chorea corea diafragmática.
  electric chorea corea eléctrica.
  epidemic chorea corea epidémica.
  fibrillary chorea corea fibrilar.
  habit chorea corea habitual.
  hemilateral chorea corea hemilateral.
  Henoch's chorea corea de Henoch.
  hereditary chorea corea hereditaria.
  Huntington's chorea corea de Huntington.
  hyoscine chorea corea por hioscina.
  hysteric chorea corea histérica.
  hysterical chorea corea histérica.
  juvenile chorea corea juvenil.
  laryngeal chorea corea laríngea.
  limp chorea corea fláccida.
  methodic chorea corea metódica.
  mimetic chorea corea mimética.
  Morvan's chorea corea de Morvan.
  onesided chorea corea unilateral.
  paralytic chorea corea paralítica.
  posthemiplegic chorea corea poshemipléjica.
  prehemiplegic chorea corea prehemipléjica.
  procursive chorea corea procursiva.
  rheumatic chorea corea reumática.
  rhythmic chorea corea rítmica.
  rotary chorea corea rotatoria.
  saltatory chorea corea saltatoria.
  senile chorea corea senil.
  Sydenham's chorea corea de Sydenham.
  tetanoid chorea corea tetanoide.
chorea-acanthocytosis *n.* corea-acantocitosis.

choreal *adj.* coreal.
choreic *adj.* coreico, -ca.
choreiform *adj.* coreiforme.
choreoathetoid *adj.* coreoatetoide.
choreoathetosis *n.* coreoatetosis.
choreoid *adj.* coreoide.
choreophrasia *n.* coreofrasia.
chorial *adj.* corial.
chorioadenoma *n.* corioadenoma.
  chorioadenoma destruens corioadenoma destructivo, corioadenoma destruens.
chorioallantoic *adj.* corioalantoico, -ca, corioalantoideo, -a.
chorioallantois *n.* corioalantoides.
chorioamnionic *adj.* corioamniótico, -ca.
chorioamnionitis *n.* corioamnionitis.
chorioangiofibroma *n.* corioangiofibroma.
chorioangioma *n.* corioangioma.
chorioangiomatosis *n.* corioangiomatosis.
chorioangiosis *n.* corioangiosis.
chorioblastoma *n.* corioblastoma.
chorioblastosis *n.* corioblastosis.
choriocarcinoma *n.* coriocarcinoma.
choriocele *n.* coriocele.
chorioepithelioma *n.* corioepitelioma.
choriogenesis *n.* coriogénesis.
choriogonadotropin *n.* coriogonadotropina.
chorioid *adj.* corioideo, - a.
chorioma *n.* corioma.
choriomeningitis *n.* coriomeningitis.
  lymphocytic choriomeningitis coriomeningitis linfocítica.
chorion *n.* corion.
  gingival chorion corion gingival.
  previllous chorion corion prevelloso.
  primitive chorion corion primitivo.
  shaggy chorion corion hirsuto, corion velloso.
  smooth chorion corion liso.
chorionic *adj.* coriónico, -ca.
chorioplacental *adj.* corioplacentario, -ria.
chorioretinal *adj.* coriorretiniano, -na.
chorioretinitis *n.* coriorretinitis.
  chorioretinitis sclopetaria coriorretinitis esclopetaria.
chorioretinopathy *n.* coriorretinopatía.
  central serous chorioretinopathy coriorretinopatía serosa central.
chorista *n.* coristo.
choristoblastoma *n.* coristoblastoma.
choristoma *n.* coristoma.
choroidal *adj.* coroidal, coroideo, -a.
choroidea *n.* coroides.
choroidectomy *n.* coroidectomía.
choroideremia *n.* coroideremia.
choroiditis *n.* coroiditis.
  anterior choroiditis coroiditis anterior.
  areolar choroiditis coroiditis areolar.
  diffuse choroiditis coroiditis difusa, coroiditis diseminada.
  disseminated choroiditis coroiditis difusa, coroiditis diseminada.
  exudative choroiditis coroiditis exudativa.
  juxtapupillary choroiditis coroiditis yuxtapupilar.
  metastatic choroiditis coroiditis metastásica.
  multifocal choroiditis coroiditis multifocal.
  posterior choroiditis coroiditis posterior.
  proliferative choroiditis coroiditis proliferante.
  senile macular exudative choroiditis coroiditis senil macular maculosa exudativa.
  serous choroiditis coroiditis serosa.
  serpiginous choroiditis coroiditis serpiginosa.

  suppurative choroiditis coroiditis supurada, coroiditis supurativa.
choroidocyclitis *n.* coroidociclitis.
choroidoiritis *n.* coroidoiritis.
choroidopathy *n.* coroidopatía.
  areolar choroidopathy coroidopatía areolar.
  central serous choroidopathy coroidopatía serosa central.
  Doyne's honeycomb choroidopathy coroidopatía de Doyne en panal.
  geographic choroidopathy coroidopatía geográfica.
  guttate choroidopathy coroidopatía guttata.
  helicoid choroidopathy coroidopatía helicoidal.
  myopic choroidopathy coroidopatía miópica.
  senile guttate choroidopathy coroidopatía guttata senil.
  serpiginous choroidopathy coroidopatía serpiginosa.
choroidoretinitis *n.* coroidorretinitis.
choroidosis *n.* coroidosis.
  myopic choroidosis coroidosis miópica.
chorology *n.* corología.
chromadocryorrhea *n.* cromodacriorrea.
chromaffin *adj.* cromafin, cromafínico, -ca.
chromaffinity *n.* cromafinidad.
chromaffinoma *n.* cromafinoma.
chromaffinopathy *n.* cromafinopatía.
chromaphil *adj.* cromafílico, -ca, cromáfilo, -la.
chromargentaffin *n.* cromargentafin.
chromatelopsia *n.* cromatelopsia.
chromatic *adj.* cromático, -ca.
chromatid *n.* cromátida, cromátide.
chromatin *n.* cromatina.
  heteropyknotic chromatin cromatina heteropicnótica.
  nucleolar chromatin cromatina nuclear.
  nucleolar-associated chromatin cromatina asociada al núcleo.
  nucleous chromatin cromatina nuclear.
  nucleus-associated chromatin cromatina asociada al núcleo.
  oxyphil chromatin cromatina oxifílica.
  sex chromatin cromatina sexual.
chromatinic *adj.* cromatínico, -ca.
chromatin-negative *adj.* cromatín-negativo.
chromatinolysis *n.* cromatinólisis.
chromatinorrhexis *n.* cromatinorrexis.
chromatin-positive *adj.* cromatín-positivo.
chromatism *n.* cromatismo.
chromatodysopia *n.* cromatodisopía.
chromatogenous *adj.* cromatógeno, -na.
chromatogram *n.* cromatograma.
chromatograph *n.* cromatógrafo.
chromatographic *adj.* cromatográfico, -ca.
chromatography *n.* cromatografía.
  adsorption chromatography cromatografía por adsorción.
  affinity chromatography cromatografía de afinidad.
  column chromatography cromatografía en columna.
  exclusion chromatography cromatografía por exclusión.
  gas chromatography cromatografía de gases.
  gas-liquid chromatography cromatografía de gas y líquido, cromatografía líquido-gaseosa.
  gas-solid chromatography cromatografía de gas y sólido.
  gel filtration chromatography cromatografía de filtración en gel.
  gel permeation chromatography cromatografía de filtración en gel.

high pressure liquid chromatography cromatografía de líquido de alta presión.
ion exchange chromatography cromatografía de intercambio iónico.
liquid-liquid chromatography cromatografía de líquido y líquido, cromatografía líquido-líquida.
molecular sieve chromatography cromatografía de tamiz molecular.
paper chromatography cromatografía sobre papel.
partition chromatography cromatografía de partición.
thin layer chromatography cromatografía en capa fina.
two-dimensional chromatography cromatografía bidimensional.
chromatoid *adj.* cromatoide.
chromatokinesis *n.* cromatocinesis.
chromatology *n.* cromatología.
chromatolysis *n.* cromatólisis.
central chromatolysis cromatólisis central.
retrograde chromatolysis cromatólisis retrógrada.
chromatolytic *adj.* cromatolítico, -ca.
chromatometer *n.* cromatómetro.
chromatopathy *n.* cromatopatía.
chromatopectic *adj.* cromatopéctico, -ca.
chromatopexis *n.* cromatopexia.
chromatophil *adj.* cromatófilo, -la.
chromatophile *adj.* cromatófilo, -la.
chromatophilia *n.* cromatofilia.
chromatophilic *adj.* cromatofílico ca.
chromatophobia *n.* cromatofobia.
chromatophoroma *n.* cromatoforoma.
chromatoplasm *n.* cromatoplasma.
chromatopseudopsis *n.* cromatoseudopsis.
chromatopsia *n.* cromatopsia.
chromatoptometer *n.* cromatoptómetro.
chromatoptometry *n.* cromatoptometría.
chromatoscope *n.* cromatoscopio.
chromatoscopy *n.* cromatoscopia.
gastric chromatoscopy cromatoscopia gástrica.
chromatosis *n.* cromatosis.
chromatoskiameter *n.* cromatosquiámetro.
chromatotoxic *adj.* cromotóxico, -ca.
chromatotropism *n.* cromatotropismo.
chromaturia *n.* cromaturia.
chromesthesia *n.* cromestesia.
chromhidrosis *n.* cromhidrosis, cromidrosis, cromohidrosis.
apocrine chromhidrosis cromhidrosis apocrina.
chromidial *adj.* cromidial.
chromidiation *n.* cromidiación.
chromidiosis *n.* cromhidrosis, cromidrosis, cromohidrosis.
chromobacteriosis *n.* cromobacteriosis.
chromoblast *n.* cromoblasto.
chromoblastomycosis *n.* cromoblastomicosis.
chromocenter *n.* cromocentro.
chromocholoscopy *n.* cromocoloscopia.
chromocrinia *n.* cromocrinia.
chromocystoscopy *n.* cromocistoscopia.
chromodiagnosis *n.* cromodiagnosis, cromodiagnóstico.
chromogen *n.* cromógeno.
Porter-Silber chromogen cromógeno de Porter-Silber.
chromogenesis *n.* cromogénesis.
chromogenic *adj.* cromogénico, -ca.
chromoisomerism *n.* cromoisomería.
chromolipoid *n.* cromolipoide.
chromolysis *n.* cromólisis.

chromomere *n.* cromómero.
chromometer *n.* cromómetro.
chromomycosis *n.* cromomicosis.
chromonema *n.* cromonema.
chromonemal *adj.* cromonémico, -ca.
chromonychia *n.* cromoniquia.
chromoparic *adj.* cromopárico, -ca.
chromopathy *n.* cromopatía.
chromopectic *adj.* cromopéctico.
chromoperturbation *n.* cromoperturbación.
chromopexic *adj.* cromopéctico, cromopéxico, -ca.
chromopexy *n.* cromopexia.
chromophage *adj.* cromatófago, -ga, cromófago.
chromophane *n.* cromófano.
chromophilic *adj.* cromofílico, -ca.
chromophilous *adj.* cromofílico, -ca.
chromophobe *n.* cromófobo.
chromophobia *n.* cromofobia.
chromophobic *adj.* cromofóbico, -ca.
chromophore *n.* cromóforo.
chromophoric *adj.* cromofórico, -ca.
chromophose *n.* cromofosia.
chromophototherapy *n.* cromofototerapia.
chromoprotein *n.* cromoproteína.
chromopsia *n.* cromopsia.
chromoptometer *n.* cromoptómetro.
chromoradiometer *n.* cromorradiómetro.
chromoretinography *n.* cromorretinografía.
chromorhinorrhea *n.* cromorrinorrea.
chromosantonin *n.* cromosantonina.
chromoscope *n.* cromoscopio.
chromoscopy *n.* cromoscopia.
gastric chromoscopy cromoscopia gástrica.
chromosomal *adj.* cromosómico, -ca.
chromosome *n.* cromosoma.
accessory chromosome cromosoma accesorio.
acentric chromosome cromosoma acéntrico.
acrocentric chromosome cromosoma acrocéntrico.
bivalent chromosome cromosoma bivalente.
Christchurch chromosome cromosoma de Christchurch.
daughter chromosome cromosoma hijo.
derivative chromosome cromosoma derivativo.
dicentric chromosome cromosoma dicéntrico.
fragile X chromosome cromosoma X frágil.
gametic chromosome cromosoma gamético.
giant chromosome cromosoma gigante.
heterologous chromosome cromosoma heterólogo.
heterotypical chromosome cromosoma heterotípico.
homologous chromosome cromosoma homólogo.
late replicative chromosome cromosoma replicativo tardío.
M chromosome cromosoma M.
metacentric chromosome cromosoma metacéntrico.
nonhomologous chromosome cromosoma no homólogo.
nucleolar chromosome cromosoma nucleolar.
Ph1 chromosome cromosoma Ph[1].
Philadelphia chromosome cromosoma de Filadelfia.
recombinant chromosome cromosoma recombinante.
ring chromosome cromosoma anular, cromosoma en anillo.
sex chromosome cromosoma sexual.

somatic chromosome cromosoma somático.
submetacentric chromosome cromosoma submetacéntrico.
supernumerary chromosome cromosoma supernumerario.
telocentric chromosome cromosoma telocéntrico.
translocation chromosome cromosoma de translocación.
unpaired chromosome cromosoma no apareado.
X chromosome cromosoma X.
X-linked chromosome cromosoma ligado a X.
Y chromosome cromosoma Y.
yeast artificial chromosome cromosoma artificial de levaduras.
Y-linked chromosome cromosoma ligado a Y.
chromosomic complement *n.* dotación cromosómica.
chromospermism *n.* cromospermia.
chromotherapy *n.* cromoterapia.
chromotrichia *n.* cromotriquia.
chromotrichial *adj.* cromotriquial.
chromotrope *n.* cromótropo.
chromotrope 2R cromótropo 2R.
chromotropic *adj.* cromotrópico, -ca.
chromoureteroscopy *n.* cromoureteroscopia.
chromourinography *n.* cromourinografía.
chronaxia *n.* cronaxia.
chronaxie *n.* cronaxia.
chronaximeter *n.* cronaxímetro.
chronaximetric *adj.* cronaximétrico, -ca.
chronaximetry *n.* cronaximetría.
chronaxis *n.* cronaxia.
chronaxy *n.* cronaxia.
chronic *adj.* crónico, -ca.
chronicity *n.* cronicidad.
chroniosepsis *n.* croniosepsis, croniosepticemia.
chronobiologic *adj.* cronobiológico, -ca.
chronobiological *adj.* cronobiológico, -ca.
chronobiologist *n.* cronobiólogo, -ga.
chronobiology *n.* cronobiología.
chronognosis *n.* cronognosis.
chronograph *n.* cronógrafo.
chronologic *adj.* cronológico, -ca.
chronometry *n.* cronometría.
mental chronometry cronometría mental, cronometría psíquica.
chronomyometer *n.* cronomiómetro.
chrono-oncology *n.* cronooncología.
chronopharmacology *n.* cronofarmacología.
chronophobia *n.* cronofobia.
chronophotograph *n.* cronofotografía.
chronopsychophysiology *n.* cronopsicofisiología.
chronoscope *n.* cronoscopio.
chronosphygmograph *n.* cronoesfigmógrafo.
chronotaraxis *n.* cronotaraxia, cronotaraxis.
chronothanatodiagnosis *n.* cronotanatodiagnóstico.
chronotropic *adj.* cronotrópico, -ca.
chronotropism *n.* cronotropismo.
negative chronotropism cronotropismo negativo.
positive chronotropism cronotropismo positivo.
chrysiasis *n.* crisiasis.
chrysocianosis *n.* crisocianosis.
chrysoderma *n.* crisodermia.
chrysoidin *n.* crisoidina.
Chrysomya *n.* Chrysomya.
chrysophoresis *n.* crisoforesis.
Chrysops *n.* Chrysops.

chrysosis *n.* crisiasis, crisosis.
Chrysosporium parvum *n.* Chrysosporium parvum.
chrysotheraphy *n.* crisoterapia.
chylangioma *n.* quilangioma.
chylaqueous *adj.* quilacuoso, -sa, quiloacuoso, -sa.
chyle *n.* quilo.
chylectasia *n.* quilectasia.
chylemia *n.* quilemia.
chylidrosis *n.* quilhidrosis, quilidrosis.
chylifacient *adj.* quilifaciente.
chylifaction *n.* quilifacción.
chylifactive *adj.* quilifactivo, -va.
chyliferous *adj.* quilífero, -ra.
chylification *n.* quilificación.
chyliform *adj.* quiliforme.
chylocele *n.* quilocele.
chyloderma *n.* quilodermia.
chyloid *adj.* quiloide.
chylology *n.* quilología.
chylomediastinum *n.* quilomediastino.
chylomicrograph *n.* quilomicrografía.
chylomicron *n.* quilomicrón.
chylomicronemia *n.* quilomicronemia.
chylopericarditis *n.* quilopericarditis.
chylopericardium *n.* quilopericardio.
chyloperitoneum *n.* quiloperitoneo.
chylophoric *adj.* quilóforo, -ra.
chylopleura *n.* quilopleura.
chylopneumothorax *n.* quiloneumotórax.
chylopoiesis *n.* quilopoyesis.
chylopoietic *adj.* quilopoyético, -ca.
chylorrhea *n.* quilorrea.
chylosis *n.* quilosis[2].
chylothorax *n.* quilotórax.
chylous *adj.* quiloso, -sa.
chyluria *n.* quiluria.
chymase *n.* quimasa.
chyme *n.* quimo.
chymification *n.* quimificación.
chymodenin *n.* quimodenina.
chymopapain *n.* quimopapaína.
chymopoiesis *n.* quimopoyesis.
chymorrhea *n.* quimorrea.
chymosin *n.* quimosina.
chymotrypsin *n.* quimotripsina.
chymotrypsinogen *n.* quimiotripsinógeno.
chymous *adj.* quimoso, -sa.
cibophobia *n.* cibofobia.
cicatrectomy *n.* cicatrectomía.
cicatricial *adj.* cicatrizal.
cicatricotomy *n.* cicatricotomía.
cicatrisotomy *n.* cicatricotomía, cicatrisotomía.
cicatrix *n.* cicatriz.
  brain cicatrix cicatriz cerebral.
  filtering cicatrix cicatriz filtrante.
  meningocerebral cicatrix cicatriz meningocerebral.
  vicious cicatrix cicatriz viciosa.
cicatrizal *adj.* cicatricial.
cicatrizant *adj.* cicatrizante.
cicatrization *n.* cicatrización, ulesis.
ciguatera *n.* ciguatera.
ciguatoxin *n.* ciguatoxina.
ciliaroscope *n.* ciliaroscopio.
ciliarotomy *n.* ciliarotomía.
ciliary *adj.* ciliar.
ciliastatic *adj.* ciliastático, -ca.
ciliate *adj.* ciliado, ciliado, -da.
ciliectomy *n.* ciliectomía.
ciliogenesis *n.* ciliogénesis.
cilioretinal *adj.* ciliorretiniano, -na.
cilioscleral *adj.* cilioescleral.

ciliospinal *adj.* cilioespinal, ciliospinal.
ciliotomy *n.* ciliotomía.
ciliotoxicity *n.* ciliotoxicidad.
cilium *n.* cilio, cilium.
cillosis *n.* cilosis.
cimex *n.* cimex.
cimicid *n.* cimicida.
cinanesthesia *n.* cinanestesia.
cinchonism *n.* cinconismo.
cinclisis *n.* cinclisis.
cineangiocardiography *n.* cineangiocardiografía.
  radioisotope cineangiocardiography gammacámara.
cineangiography *n.* cineangiografía.
cinedensigraphy *n.* cinedensigrafía.
cinefluorography *n.* cinefluorografía.
cinefluoroscopy *n.* cinefluoroscopia.
cinegastroscopy *n.* cinegastroscopia.
cinematics *n.* cinemática.
cinematization *n.* cinematización.
cinematography *n.* cinematografía.
cinematoradiography *n.* cinematorradiografía.
cinephotomicrography *n.* cinemicrofotografía.
cineplastics *n.* cineplastia.
cineplasty *n.* cineplastia.
cineradiography *n.* cinerradiografía.
cinerea *n.* cinérea.
cinereal *adj.* cinéreo, -a.
cineritious *adj.* cinéreo, -a.
cineroentgenography *n.* cinerroentgenografía.
cinesalgia *n.* cinesalgia, cinesialgia.
cinesismography *n.* cinesismografía.
cineurography *n.* cineurografía.
cingulate *adj.* cingulado, -da, cingular.
cingulectomy *n.* cingulectomía.
cingulotomy *n.* cingulotomía.
cingulum *n.* cíngulo.
cinoxate *n.* cinoxato.
cionitis *n.* cionitis.
cionoptosis *n.* cionoptosis.
cionorrhaphy *n.* cionorrafia.
cionotomy *n.* cionotomía.
circadian *adj.* circadiano, -na.
circellus *n.* circellus.
circinate *adj.* circinado, -ca.
circle *n.* círculo.
  Berry's circle círculo de Berry.
  closed circle círculo cerrado.
  defensive circle círculo defensivo.
  least diffusion circle círculo de menor difusión.
  Pagenstecher's circle círculo de Pagenstecher.
  semi-closed circle círculo semicerrado.
  vicious circle círculo vicioso.
circuit *n.* circuito.
  anesthetic circuit circuito anestésico.
  gamma circuit circuito gamma.
  Granit's circuit circuito de Granit.
  memory circuit circuito de memoria.
  Papez circuit circuito de Papez.
  reflex circuit circuito reflejo.
  reverberating circuit circuito reverberante.
  vector circuit circuito vector.
circular *adj.* circular.
circulation *n.* circulación.
  allantoic circulation circulación alantoidea.
  assisted circulation circulación asistida.
  capillary circulation circulación capilar.
  collateral circulation circulación colateral.
  compensatory circulation circulación compensadora, circulación compensatoria.

coronary circulation circulación coronaria.
cross circulation circulación cruzada.
derivative circulation circulación derivativa.
embryonic circulation circulación embrionaria.
enterohepatic circulation circulación enterohepática.
extracorporeal circulation circulación extracorpórea.
fetal circulation circulación fetal.
greater circulation circulación mayor.
hypothalamohypophyseal portal circulation circulación portal hipotalamohipofisaria.
lesser circulation circulación menor.
lymph circulation circulación linfática.
omphalomesenteric circulation circulación onfalomesentérica.
placental circulation circulación placentaria.
portal circulation circulación de la vena porta, circulación portal.
pulmonary circulation circulación pulmonar.
sinusoidal circulation circulación sinusoidal.
systemic circulation circulación general, circulación sistémica.
vitelline circulation circulación vitelina.
circulatory *adj.* circulatorio, -ria.
circulus *n.* círculo.
circumanal *adj.* circumanal, circunanal.
circumarticular *adj.* circunarticular.
circumaxillary *adj.* circumaxilar.
circumbulbar *adj.* circumbulbar.
circumcise *v.* circuncidar.
circumcision *n.* circuncisión.
  pharaonic circumcision circuncisión faraónica.
circumcorneal *adj.* circuncorneal.
circumduction *n.* circunducción.
circumference *n.* circunferencia.
circumflex *adj.* circunflejo, -ja.
circumgemmal *adj.* circungemal.
circumintestinal *adj.* circunintestinal.
circummandibular *adj.* circunmandibular.
circumnuclear *adj.* circunnuclear.
circumocular *adj.* circunocular.
circumoral *adj.* circumoral, circunoral.
circumorbital *adj.* circunorbitario, -ria.
circumpolarization *n.* circumpolarización.
circumrenal *adj.* circunrenal.
circumscribed *adj.* circunscrito, -ta.
circumscriptus *adj.* circunscripto, -ta, circunscrito, -ta.
circumstantiality *n.* circunstancialidad.
circumvascular *adj.* circunvascular.
circumventricular *adj.* circunventricular.
circumvolute *adj.* circunvolutivo.
circunvallate *adj.* circunvalado, -da.
cirrhogenic *adj.* cirrogénico, -ca.
cirrhogenous *adj.* cirrógeno, -na.
cirrhonosus *n.* cirronosis.
cirrhosis *n.* cirrosis.
  alcoholic cirrhosis cirrosis alcohólica.
  atrophic cirrhosis cirrosis atrófica.
  biliary cirrhosis cirrosis biliar.
  biliary cirrhosis of children cirrosis biliar de los niños.
  Budd's cirrhosis cirrosis de Budd.
  capsular cirrhosis cirrosis capsular, cirrosis capsular del hígado.
  capsular cirrhosis of the liver cirrosis capsular, cirrosis capsular del hígado.
  cardiac cirrhosis cirrosis cardíaca.
  cholangiolitic cirrhosis cirrosis colangiolítica.
  congestive cirrhosis cirrosis congestiva.
  cryptogenic cirrhosis cirrosis criptogénica.
  fatty cirrhosis cirrosis grasa.

Glisson's cirrhosis cirrosis de Glisson.
Hanot's cirrhosis cirrosis de Hanot.
hypertrophic cirrhosis cirrosis hipertrófica.
juvenile cirrhosis cirrosis juvenil.
Laennec cirrhosis cirrosis de Laennec.
necrotic cirrhosis cirrosis necrótica.
nutritional cirrhosis cirrosis nutricional.
periportal cirrhosis cirrosis periportal.
pigment cirrhosis cirrosis de pigmento, cirrosis pigmentaria.
pigmentary cirrhosis cirrosis de pigmento, cirrosis pigmentaria.
portal cirrhosis cirrosis portal.
posthepatitic cirrhosis cirrosis poshepática.
postnecrotic cirrhosis cirrosis posnecrótica.
primary biliary cirrhosis cirrosis biliar primaria.
pulmonary cirrhosis cirrosis pulmonar.
stasis cirrhosis cirrosis por estasis.
syphilitic cirrhosis cirrosis sifilítica.
Todd's cirrhosis cirrosis de Todd.
toxic cirrhosis cirrosis tóxica.
unilobular cirrhosis cirrosis unilobulillar.
cirrhotic *adj.* cirrótico, -ra.
cirrose *adj.* cirroso, -sa.
cirrous *adj.* cirroso, -sa.
cirrus *n.* cirro.
cirsectomy *n.* cirsectomía.
cirsenchysis *n.* cirsenquisis.
cirsocele *n.* cirsocele.
cirsodesis *n.* cirsodesia, cirsodesis.
cirsoid *adj.* cirsoide, cirsoideo, -a.
cirsomphalos *n.* cirsónfalo.
cirsophthalmia *n.* cirsoftalmía.
cirsotome *n.* cirsótomo.
cirsotomy *n.* cirsotomía.
cistern *n.* cisterna.
cisterna *n.* cisterna.
cisternal *adj.* cisternal.
cisternography *n.* cisternografía.
cerebellopontine cisternography cisternografía cerebelopontina.
radionuclide cisternography cisternografía con radionúclidos.
cistostaxis *n.* cististaxis.
cistron *n.* cistrón.
Citrobacter *n.* Citrobacter.
citrullinemia *n.* citrulinemia.
citrullinuria *n.* citrulinuria.
cladiosis *n.* cladiosis.
cladosporiosis *n.* cladosporiosis.
cerebral cladosporiosis cladosporiosis cerebral.
cutaneous cladosporiosis cladosporiosis cutánea.
Cladosporium *n.* Cladosporium.
clairvoyance *n.* clarividencia.
clamp *n.* clamp.
Cope's clamp clamp de Cope.
Crawford clamp clamp de Crawford.
Crile's clamp clamp de Crile.
Doyen's clamp clamp de Doyen.
Fogarty clamp clamp de Fogarty.
Gant's clamp clamp de Gant.
Gaskell's clamp clamp de Gaskell.
gingival clamp clamp gingival.
Goldblatt's clamp clamp de Goldblatt.
Gussenbauer's clamp clamp de Gussenbauer.
Joseph's clamp clamp de Joseph.
Kelly clamp clamp de Kelly.
Kocher clamp clamp de Kocher.
Mikulicz clamp clamp de Mikulicz.
Mogen clamp clamp Mogen.
mosquito clamp clamp mosquito.
Ochsner clamp clamp de Ochsner.
Payr's clamp clamp de Payr.

pedicle clamp clamp para pedículos.
Potts clamp clamp de Potts.
Rankin's clamp clamp de Rankin.
rubber dam clamp clamp para dique de goma.
Willet's clamp clamp de Willet.
Yellen clamp clamp de Yellen.
clapotage *n.* clapoteo.
clapotement *n.* chapoteo, clapoteo.
clarificant *adj.* clarificador, -ra.
clarification *n.* clarificación.
clarifier *n.* aclarador.
clasmatosis *n.* clasmatosis.
clasp *n.* gancho[1].
Adams' clasp gancho de Adams.
bar clasp gancho de barra, gancho en barra.
circumferential clasp gancho circunferencial.
continuous clasp gancho continuo.
continuous lingual clasp gancho continuo.
extended clasp gancho extendido.
Roach's clasp gancho de Roach.
class *n.* clase.
classification *n.* clasificación.
clastic *adj.* clástico, -ca.
clastogen *n.* clastógeno.
clastogenic *adj.* clastogénico, -ca.
clastothrix *n.* clastotrix.
claudication *n.* claudicación.
cerebral claudication claudicación cerebral.
intermittent claudication claudicación intermitente.
triceps surae claudication claudicación del tríceps sural.
venous claudication claudicación venosa.
claudicatory *adj.* claudicante, claudicatorio, -ria.
claustral *adj.* claustral.
claustrophilia *n.* claustrofilia.
claustrophobia *n.* claustrofobia.
claustrophobic *adj.* claustrofóbico, -ca.
claustrum *n.* antemuro, claustro, claustrum.
clava *n.* clava.
claval *adj.* claval.
clavate *adj.* claviforme.
clavicle *n.* clavícula.
clavicotomy *n.* clavicotomía.
clavicula *n.* clavícula.
clavicular *adj.* clavicular.
claviculus *n.* clavículo.
clavipectoral *adj.* clavipectoral.
clavus *n.* clavo[1].
claw *n.* garra.
claw hand garra cubital.
cleaning *n.* higienización, limpieza.
ultrasonic cleaning limpieza ultrasónica.
clearance *n.* aclaramiento, limpieza.
creatinine clearance aclaramiento de creatinina.
drug clearance aclaramiento de fármaco.
free water clearance aclaramiento de agua libre.
ineffective airway clearance limpieza ineficaz de la vía aérea.
inulin clearance aclaramiento de inulina.
osmolarity clearance aclaramiento osmolar.
urea clearance aclaramiento de urea.
clearer *n.* aclarador.
clear-sightedness *n.* clarividencia.
cleavage *n.* escisión[1], segmentación.
abnormal cleavage of the cardiac valve segmentación anormal de las válvulas cardíacas.
accessory cleavage segmentación accesoria.
adequal cleavage segmentación casi igual.
determinate cleavage segmentación determinada.
discoidal cleavage segmentación discoidal, segmentación discoide.

enamel cleavage segmentación del esmalte.
equal cleavage segmentación igual.
equatorial cleavage segmentación ecuatorial.
holoblastic cleavage segmentación holoblástica.
hydrolytic cleavage segmentación hidrolítica.
indeterminate cleavage segmentación indeterminada.
meridional cleavage escisión meridional, segmentación meridional.
meroblastic cleavage segmentación incompleta parcial, segmentación meroblástica.
mosaic cleavage segmentación en mosaico.
partial cleavage segmentación parcial.
phosphoroclastic cleavage segmentación fosforoclástica.
superficial cleavage segmentación superficial.
thioclastic cleavage segmentación tioclástica, segmentación tioclástica.
total cleavage segmentación completa, segmentación total.
unequal cleavage segmentación desigual.
yolk cleavage segmentación de la yema.
cleft *adj.* hendido, -da, ranura.
cleidagra *n.* cleidagra.
cleidal *adj.* cleidal.
cleidarthritis *n.* cleidartritis.
cleidocostal *adj.* cleidocostal.
cleidocranial *adj.* cleidocraneal.
cleidomastoid *adj.* cleidomastoideo, -a.
cleidorrhexis *n.* cleidorrexis.
cleidotomy *n.* cleidotomía.
cleidotripsy *n.* cleidotripsia.
cleoid *n.* cleoide.
clidagra *n.* cleidagra, clidagra.
clidal *adj.* cleidal, clidal.
clidocostal *adj.* clidocostal.
clidocranial *adj.* clidocraneal.
climacophobia *n.* climacofobia.
climacterium *n.* climaterio.
climate *n.* clima.
climatic *adj.* climático, -ca.
climatology *n.* climatología.
climatotherapy *n.* climatoterapia.
climax *n.* clímax.
climograph *n.* climógrafo.
cline *n.* clino.
clinic *n.* clínica.
clinical *adj.* clínico, -ca[1].
clinician *n.* clínico, -ca[2].
clinicopathologic *adj.* clinicopatológico, -ca.
clinocephalic *adj.* clinocéfalo, -la.
clinocephalous *adj.* clinocéfalo, -la.
clinocephaly *n.* clinocefalia, clinocefalismo.
clinodactyly *n.* clinodactilia.
clinography *n.* clinografía.
clinoid *adj.* clinoide.
clinology *n.* clinología.
clinomania *n.* clinomanía.
clinometer *n.* clinómetro.
clinoscope *n.* clinoscopio.
clinostatic *adj.* clinostático, -ca.
clinostatism *n.* clinostatismo.
clinotherapy *n.* clinoterapia.
clip *n.* grapa.
clithrophobia *n.* clitrofobia.
clition *n.* clitión.
clitoral *adj.* clitorídeo, -a.
clitorectomy *n.* clitorectomía.
clitoridean *adj.* clitorídeo, -a.
clitoridectomy *n.* clitoridectomía.
clitoriditis *n.* clitoriditis.

clitoridotomy *n.* clitoridotomía.
clitoris *n.* clítoris.
clitorism *n.* clitorismo.
clitoritis *n.* clitoritis.
clitoromegaly *n.* clitoromegalia.
clitorotomy *n.* clitorotomía.
clivus *n.* clivus.
cloaca *n.* cloaca.
cloacal *adj.* cloacal.
clonal *adj.* clonal.
clone *n.* clon, clonar, clono.
clonic *adj.* clónico, -ca.
clonicity *n.* clonicidad.
clonicotonic *adj.* clonicotónico, -ca.
cloning *n.* clonación.
clonism *n.* clonismo.
clonogenic *adj.* clonogénico, -ca, clonógeno, -na.
clonograph *n.* clonógrafo.
clonorchiasis *n.* clonorquiasis, clonorquiosis.
clonorchiosis *n.* clonorquiasis, clonorquiosis.
Clonorchis sinensis *n.* Clonorchis sinensis.
clonospasm *n.* clonoespasmo, clonospasmo.
clonus *n.* clonus.
   ankle clonus clonus del tobillo.
   cathodal opening clonus clonus de apertura catódica.
   patellar clonus clonus rotuliano.
   toe clonus clonus de los dedos del pie.
   wrist clonus clonus de la muñeca.
clostridium *n.* clostridio.
Clostridium *n.* Clostridium.
closure *n.* cierre.
   flask closure cierre de la mufla.
   velopharyngeal closure cierre velofaríngeo.
clot *n.* coágulo, grumo.
   agonal clot coágulo agónico, coágulo de la agonía.
   agony clot coágulo agónico, coágulo de la agonía.
   antemortem clot coágulo ante mortem.
   blood clot coágulo sanguíneo.
   chicken fat clot coágulo en grasa de pollo.
   chromatin clot grumo de cromatina.
   closing clot coágulo de cierre.
   currant jelly clot coágulo en gelatina de grosella, coágulo en jalea de grosella.
   distal clot coágulo distal.
   external clot coágulo externo.
   heart clot coágulo cardíaco.
   internal clot coágulo interno.
   laminated clot coágulo laminado.
   marantic clot coágulo marántico.
   Nissl clot grumo de Nissl.
   passive clot coágulo pasivo.
   plastic clot coágulo plástico.
   post mortem clot coágulo post mortem.
   proximal clot coágulo proximal.
   Schede's clot coágulo de Schede.
   spider web clot coágulo en telaraña.
   stratified clot coágulo estratificado.
   washed clot coágulo lavado.
   white clot coágulo blanco.
cloth *n.* tela.
clownism *n.* clounismo, clownismo.
clubbing *n.* clubbing.
clubhand *n.* clubhand.
clump *v.* agrumar.
clyster *n.* clíster.
cnemial *adj.* cnemial, cnémico, -ca.
cnemis *n.* cnemis.
cnemitis *n.* cnemitis.
cnemoscoliosis *n.* cnemoscoliosis.
cnidosis *n.* cnidosis.
coadaptation *n.* coadaptación.
coadunation *n.* coadunación.

coadunition *n.* coadunación.
coagglutination *n.* coaglutinación.
coaglutinin *n.* coaglutinina.
coagulability *n.* coagulabilidad.
coagulable *adj.* coagulable.
coagulant *adj.* coagulante.
coagulation *n.* coagulación.
   closing coagulation coagulación cerrada.
   diffuse intravascular coagulation coagulación intravascular difusa.
   disseminated intravascular coagulation (DIC) coagulación intravascular diseminada (CID).
   massive coagulation coagulación masiva.
   plasmatic coagulation coagulación plasmática.
coagulative *adj.* coagulativo, -va.
coagulator *n.* coagulador.
coagulogram *n.* coagulograma.
coagulopathy *n.* coagulopatía.
   consumption coagulopathy coagulopatía por consumo de factores.
coagulum *n.* coágulo.
coalescence *n.* coalescencia.
coalescent *adj.* coalescente.
coaptation *n.* coaptación.
coarctate *adj.* coartado, -da.
coarctation *n.* coartación.
   adult type coarctation of the aorta coartación aórtica de tipo adulto.
   coarctation of the aorta coartación aórtica, coartación de la aorta.
   infantile type coarctation of the aorta coartación aórtica de tipo infantil.
   reversed coarctation coartación invertida.
coarctotomy *n.* coartotomía.
coarticulation *n.* coarticulación.
coat *n.* capa[1].
cobalt bomb *n.* bomba de cobalto.
cobaltosis *n.* cobaltosis.
cobaltous *adj.* cobaltoso, -sa.
cobraism *n.* cobraísmo.
cocain *n.* cocaína.
cocaine *n.* cocaína.
cocainism *n.* cocainismo, cocainomanía.
cocainist *n.* cocainómano, -na.
cocainization *n.* cocainización.
cocarcinogen *n.* cocarcinógeno.
cocarcinogenesis *n.* cocarcinogénesis.
cocardiform *adj.* cocardiforme.
coccal *adj.* cócico, -ca.
Coccidia *n.* Coccidia.
coccidial *adj.* coccidial.
coccidian *adj.* coccidiano, -na.
coccidioidal *adj.* coccidioide.
Coccidioides *n.* Coccidioides.
coccidioidial *adj.* coccidioideo, -a.
coccidioidina *n.* coccidioidina.
coccidioidoma *n.* coccidioidoma.
coccidioidomycosis *n.* coccidioidomicosis.
   asymptomatic coccidioidomycosis coccidioidomicosis asintomática.
   disseminate coccidioidomycosis coccidioidomicosis diseminada.
   latent coccidioidomycosis coccidioidomicosis latente.
   primary coccidioidomycosis coccidioidomicosis primaria.
   primary extrapulmonary coccidioidomycosis coccidioidomicosis extrapulmonar primaria.
   secondary coccidioidomycosis coccidioidomicosis secundaria.
coccidioidosis *n.* coccidioidosis.
coccidiosis *n.* coccidiosis.
coccidiostatic *adj.* coccidiostático, -ca.
coccidium *n.* coccidio.
Coccidium *n.* Coccidium.

coccigenic *adj.* coccigénico, -ca, coccígeno, -na.
coccobacillary *adj.* cocobacilar.
coccobacillus *n.* cocobacilo.
Coccobacillus *n.* Coccobacillus.
coccobacteria *n.* cocobacteria.
coccogenic *adj.* cocógeno, -na.
coccogenous *adj.* cocógeno, -na.
coccoid *adj.* cocoideo, -a.
coccus *n.* coco.
coccyalgia *n.* coccialgia.
coccycephaly *n.* coccicefalia.
coccydinia *n.* coccidinia.
coccygalgia *n.* coccialgia, coccigalgia.
coccygeal *adj.* coccígeo, -a.
coccygectomy *n.* coccigectomía.
coccygodynia *n.* coccigodinia.
coccygotomy *n.* coccigotomía.
coccyodinia *n.* cocciodinia.
coccyodynia *n.* coccigodinia.
coccyx *n.* cóccix, cóxis.
cochlea *n.* caracol, cóclea.
cochlear *adj.* coclear.
cochleariform *adj.* cocleariforme.
cochleitis *n.* cocleítis.
cochleosacculotomy *n.* cocleosaculotomía.
cochleotopic *adj.* cocleotópico, -ca.
cochleovestibular *adj.* cocleovestibular.
Cochliomyia *n.* Cochliomyia.
cochlitis *n.* coclitis.
cocktail *n.* cocktail, cóctel.
coconscious *adj.* coconsciente.
coconsciousness *n.* coconsciencia.
cocontraction *n.* cocontracción.
coctoantigen *n.* coctoantígeno.
coctoimmunogen *n.* coctoinmunógeno.
coctolabile *adj.* coctolábil.
coctoprecipitin *n.* coctoprecipitina.
coctoprotein *n.* coctoproteína.
coctostabile *adj.* coctoestable, coctostable.
coctostable *adj.* coctoestable, coctostable.
cocultivation *n.* cocultivo.
code *n.* código.
   analogical code código analógico.
   digital code código digital.
   genetic code código genético.
coding *n.* codificación.
codocyte *n.* codocito.
codominance *n.* codominancia.
codominant *adj.* codominante.
codon *n.* codón.
   initiating codon codón de iniciación.
   initiation codon codón de iniciación.
   termination codon codón de terminación.
coefficient *n.* coeficiente.
coelom *n.* celoma.
   extraembryonic coelom celoma extraembrionario.
   intraembryonic coelom celoma intraembrionario.
Coenerus *n.* Coenerus.
coenurasis *n.* cenuriasis, cenurosis.
coenzyme *n.* coenzima.
coenzymometer *n.* coenzimómetro.
coetaneous *adj.* coetáneo, -a.
coexcitation *n.* coexcitación.
cofactor *n.* cofactor.
cognition *n.* cognición.
cognitive *adj.* cognitivo, -va.
   cognitive structuring estructuración cognitiva.
coherence *n.* coherencia.
cohesion *n.* cohesión.
cohesive *adj.* cohesivo, -va.
cohesiveness *n.* cohesividad.
cohort *n.* cohorte.
coil *adj.* bobina, espirador, -ra.

coilonychia *n.* celoniquia.
coin-counting *n.* cuentamonedas.
coinnervation *n.* coinervación.
coinosite *n.* coinosito.
coisogenic *adj.* coisogénico, -ca.
coital *adj.* coital.
coitalgia *n.* coitalgia.
coitophobia *n.* coitofobia.
coitus *n.* coito.
col *n.* col.
colation *n.* coladura.
colature *n.* colaturo.
cold *n.* enfriamiento, frío, resfriado.
  cold in the head resfriado de la cabeza.
  head cold resfriado de la cabeza.
colectasia *n.* colectasia.
colectomy *n.* colectomía.
  subtotal colectomy colectomía subtotal.
  total colectomy colectomía total.
  transverse colectomy colectomía transversa.
coleocele *n.* coleocele, colpocele.
coleoptosis *n.* coleoptosis.
coleotomy *n.* coleotomía.
coles *n.* coles.
colibacillemia *n.* colibacilemia.
colibacillosis *n.* colibacilosis.
  colibacillosis gravidarum colibacilosis graví-dica.
colibacilluria *n.* colibaciluria.
colibacillus *n.* colibacilo.
colic[1] *adj.* cólico, -ca.
colic[2] *n.* cólico.
  appendicular colic cólico apendicular.
  biliary colic cólico biliar, cólico bilioso.
  copper colic cólico cúprico.
  Devonshire colic cólico de Devonshire.
  endemic colic cólico endémico.
  flatulent colic cólico flatulento, cólico gaseo-so, cólico ventoso.
  gallstone colic cólico colelitiásico, cólico por cálculo biliar.
  gastric colic cólico gástrico.
  hepatic colic cólico hepático.
  infantile colic cólico del lactante.
  intestinal colic cólico intestinal.
  lead colic cólico de plomo, cólico plúmbico.
  meconial colic cólico meconial.
  menstrual colic cólico menstrual.
  nephritic colic cólico nefrítico.
  ovarian colic cólico ovárico.
  painter's colic cólico de los pintores.
  pancreatic colic cólico pancreático.
  renal colic cólico renal.
  salivary colic cólico salival.
  saturnine colic cólico saturnino.
  stercoral colic cólico estercoráceo.
  tubal colic cólico tubárico, cólico tubario.
  ureteral colic cólico ureteral.
  uterine colic cólico uterino.
  vermicular colic cólico vermicular.
  verminous colic cólico verminoso.
  zinc colic cólico cíncico, cólico por cinc.
colicinogen *n.* colicinógeno.
colicinogenic *adj.* colicinogénico, -ca.
colicinogeny *n.* colicinogenia.
colicoplegia *n.* colicoplejía.
colicystitis *n.* colicistitis.
colicystopyelitis *n.* colicistopielitis.
colifixation *n.* colifijación.
coliform *adj.* coliforme.
colinearity *n.* colinealidad.
colipase *n.* colipasa.
coliplication *n.* coliplicación.
colipuncture *n.* colipuntura.
colisepsis *n.* colisepsis.

colitis *n.* colicolitis, colitis.
  amebic colitis colitis amebiana.
  balantidial colitis colitis balantidiásica.
  colitis cystica profunda colitis quística pro-funda.
  colitis cystica superficialis colitis quística su-perficial.
  colitis gravis colitis grave.
  colitis polyposa colitis poliposa.
  colitis ulcerativa colitis ulcerosa.
  collagenous colitis colitis colagenosa.
  granulomatous colitis colitis granulomatosa.
  hemorrhagic colitis colitis hemorrágica.
  ischemic colitis colitis isquémica.
  mucous colitis colitis mucosa, micoangio-neurosis.
  myxomembranous colitis colitis mixomem-branosa.
  pseudomembranous colitis colitis seudo-membranosa.
  regional colitis colitis regional.
  segmental colitis colitis segmentaria.
  transmural colitis colitis transmural.
  ulcerative colitis colitis ulcerosa.
  uremic colitis colitis urémica.
colitoxemia *n.* colitoxemia.
colitoxicosis *n.* colitoxicosis.
colitoxin *n.* colitoxina.
coliuria *n.* coliuria.
collagen *n.* colágena, colágeno.
  type I collagen colágeno tipo I.
  type II collagen colágeno tipo II.
  type III collagen colágeno tipo III.
  type IV collagen colágeno tipo IV.
collagenation *n.* colagenación, colageniza-ción.
collagenic *adj.* colagénico, -ca.
collagenitis *n.* colagenitis.
collagenogenic *adj.* colagenogénico, -ca.
collagenolysis *n.* colagenólisis.
collagenolytic *adj.* colagenolítico, -ca.
collagenosis *n.* colagenosis.
  reactive perforating collagenosis colageno-sis perforante activa.
collagenous *adj.* colágeno, -na.
collapse *n.* colapso.
  absorption collapse colapso por absorción.
  bronchiolar collapse colapso bronquiolar.
  circulatory collapse colapso circulatorio.
  collapse of the dental arch colapso del arco dentario.
  collapse of the lung colapso pulmonar.
  hypostatic lung collapse colapso pulmonar hipostático.
  massive collapse colapso masivo.
  passive lung collapse colapso pulmonar pa-sivo.
  pressure collapse colapso por presión.
  pulmonary collapse colapso pulmonar.
collapsotherapy *n.* colapsoterapia.
collar *n.* collar.
  Casal's collar collar de Casal.
  cervical collar collar ortopédico, collarín cer-vical.
  collar of pearls collar de perlas.
  collar of Stokes collar de Stokes.
  collar of Venus collar de Venus, collar venéreo.
  periosteal bone collar collar de hueso periós-tico.
  Spanish collar collar español.
  venereal collar collar de Venus, collar vené-reo.
collarette *n.* collarete.
collastin *n.* colastina.
collateral *adj.* colateral.

collateralization *n.* colateralización.
  coronary collateralization colateralización coronaria.
collection *n.* toma.
  timed collection toma programada.
collector *n.* colector.
colliculectomy *n.* coliculectomía.
colliculitis *n.* coliculitis.
colliculus *n.* colículo, colliculus.
colligation *n.* coligación.
colligative *adj.* coligativo, -va.
collimation *n.* colimación.
  beam collimation colimación del haz.
collimator *n.* colimador.
collinearity *n.* colinealidad.
colliotomy *n.* coliotomía.
colliquation *n.* colicuación.
  ballooning colliquation colicuación balón, colicuación en globo.
  reticulating colliquation colicuación reticu-lar.
colliquative *adj.* colicuativo, -va.
collision *n.* colisión.
collochemistry *n.* coloidoquímica.
collodiaphyseal *adj.* colodiafisario, -ria.
collodion *n.* collodium, colodión.
  blistering collodion colodión ampollante.
  cantharidal collodion colodión cantarídeo.
  collodion elastique colodión elástico.
  flexible collodion colodión flexible.
  hemostatic collodion colodión hemostático.
  iodized collodion colodión yodado.
  salicylic acid collodion colodión de ácido sa-licílico.
  styptic collodion colodión estíptico.
collodium *n.* collodium, colodión.
  collodium vesicans colodión vesicante.
colloid *n.* coloide.
colloidal *adj.* coloidal, coloideo, -a.
colloidin *n.* coloidina.
colloidoclasia *n.* coloidoclasia.
colloidoclasis *n.* coloidoclasia, coloidoclasis.
colloidoclastic *adj.* coloidoclástico, -ca.
colloidogen *n.* coloidógeno.
colloidopexy *n.* coloidopexia.
colloidophagia *n.* coloidofagia.
colloidophagy *n.* coloidofagia.
colloma *n.* coloma.
collum *n.* collum, cuello.
  collum distortum collum distortum, cuello torcido.
collunarium *n.* colunario.
collutorium *n.* colutorio.
collutory *n.* colutorio.
  Miller's collutory colutorio de Miller.
coloboma *n.* coloboma.
  atypical coloboma coloboma atípico.
  bridge coloboma coloboma en puente.
  choroidal coloboma coloboma de la coroides.
  coloboma at optic nerve entrance colobo-ma en la entrada del nervio óptico.
  coloboma iridis coloboma del iris.
  coloboma lentis coloboma del cristalino.
  coloboma lobuli coloboma lobular.
  coloboma of the choroid coloboma de la co-roides.
  coloboma of the ciliary body coloboma del cuerpo ciliar.
  coloboma of the fundus coloboma del fun-dus.
  coloboma of the iris coloboma del iris.
  coloboma of the lens coloboma del cristali-no.
  coloboma of the optic disc coloboma del dis-co óptico, coloboma del nervio óptico.

coloboma of the optic nerve coloboma del disco óptico, coloboma del nervio óptico.

coloboma of the retina coloboma de la retina, coloboma retiniano.

coloboma of the vitreous humor coloboma del humor vítreo, coloboma vítreo.

coloboma palpebrale coloboma palpebral.

coloboma retinae coloboma de la retina, coloboma retiniano.

complete coloboma coloboma completo.

Fuch's coloboma coloboma de Fuch.

macular coloboma coloboma macular.

palpebral coloboma coloboma palpebral.

peripapillary coloboma coloboma peripapilar.

retinochoroidal coloboma coloboma retinocoroidal.

typical coloboma coloboma típico.

colocecostomy *n.* colocecostomía.

colocentesis *n.* colocentesis.

coloclysis *n.* coloclisis.

coloclyster *n.* coloclister.

colocolic *adj.* colocólico, -ca.

colocolostomy *n.* colocolostomía.

colocutaneous *adj.* colocutáneo, -a.

colocynthidism *n.* coloquintidismo.

colodyspepsia *n.* colodispepsia.

coloenteritis *n.* coloenteritis.

colofixation *n.* colofijación.

colohepatopexy *n.* colohepatopexia.

coloileal *n.* coloileal.

cololysis *n.* colólisis.

colometrometer *n.* colometrómetro.

colon *n.* colon.

colon pelvinum colon pelviano.

giant colon colon gigante.

inactive colon colon inactivo.

irritable colon colon irritable.

lazy colon colon perezoso.

lead-pipe colon colon en caño de plomo.

pelvic colon colon pelviano.

colonalgia *n.* colicodinia, colonalgia.

colonic *adj.* colónico, -ca.

colonitis *n.* colonitis.

colonization *n.* colonización.

genetic colonization colonización genética.

colonogram *n.* colonograma.

colonometer *n.* colonómetro.

colonopathy *n.* colonopatía.

colonorrhagia *n.* colonorragia.

colonorrhea *n.* colonorrea.

colonoscope *n.* colonoscopio, coloscopio.

colonoscopy *n.* colonoscopia.

colony *n.* colonia.

colopathy *n.* colopatía.

colopexostomy *n.* colopexostomía.

colopexotomy *n.* colopexotomía.

colopexy *n.* colopexia.

coloplication *n.* coliplicación, coloplicación, coloplicatura.

coloproctectomy *n.* coloproctectomía.

coloproctia *n.* coloproctia.

coloproctitis *n.* coloproctitis.

coloproctostomy *n.* coloproctostomía.

coloptosia *n.* coloptosia.

coloptosis *n.* coloptosis.

colopuncture *n.* colopunción, colopuntura.

color *n.* color.

complementary color color complementario.

confusion color color de confusión.

contrast color color de contraste.

extrinsic color color extrínseco.

gingival color color gingival.

harlequin color color de arlequín.

incidental color color incidental.

intrinsic color color intrínseco.

metameric color color metamérico.

Munsell's color color de Munsell.

opponent color color oponente.

primary color color primario.

pseudoisochromatic color color seudoisocromático.

pure color color puro.

reflected color color reflejado.

saturated color color de saturación, color saturado.

saturation color color de saturación, color saturado.

simple color color simple.

solid color color sólido.

tone color color del tono.

colorectal *adj.* colorrectal.

colorectitis *n.* colorrectitis.

colorectostomy *n.* colorrectostomía.

colorimeter *adj.* colorimétrico, -ca, colorímetro.

Duboscq's colorimeter colorímetro de Duboscq.

titration colorimeter colorímetro de titulación.

colorimetry *n.* colorimetría.

colorrhagia *n.* colorragia.

colorrhaphy *n.* colorrafia.

colorrhea *n.* colorrea.

colosigmoidostomy *n.* colosigmoidostomía.

colosigmoiodoscopy *n.* colosigmoidoscopia.

colostomate *adj.* colostomizado, -da.

colostomy *n.* colostomía.

dry colostomy colostomía seca.

ileotransverse colostomy colostomía ileotransversa.

lateral colostomy colostomía lateral.

loop colostomy colostomía en asa.

terminal colostomy colostomía terminal.

wet colostomy colostomía húmeda.

colostration *n.* calostración.

colostric *adj.* calóstrico, -ca.

colostrorrhea *n.* calostrorrea.

colostrous *adj.* calostroso, -sa.

colostrum *n.* calostro.

colostrum gravidum calostro gravídico.

colostrum puerperarum calostro puerperal.

colotomy *n.* colotomía.

colotyphoid *adj.* colotifoidea.

colovaginal *adj.* colovaginal.

colovesical *adj.* colovesical.

colpalgia *n.* colpalgia.

colpatresia *n.* colpatresia.

colpectasia *n.* colpectasia.

colpectomy *n.* colpectomía.

colpeurisis *n.* colpeurisis.

colpeurynter *n.* colpeurinter.

colpexia *n.* colpexia.

colpismus *n.* colpismo.

colpitic *adj.* colpítico, -ca.

colpitis *n.* colpitis.

colpitis emphysematosa colpitis enfisematosa.

colpitis mycotica colpitis micótica.

colpitis senile colpitis senil, colpitis vetularum.

emphysematous colpitis colpitis enfisematosa.

colpocele *n.* colpocele, elitrocele.

colpoceliocentesis *n.* colpoceliocentesis.

colpocleisis *n.* colpocleisis.

colpocystitis *n.* colpocistitis.

colpocystocele *n.* colpocistocele.

colpocystoplasty *n.* colpocistoplastia.

colpocystotomy *n.* colpocistotomía.

colpocystoureterotomy *n.* colpocistoureterotomía.

colpocytogram *n.* colpocitograma.

colpocytology *n.* colpocitología.

colpodynia *n.* colpodinia.

colpoepisiorrhaphy *n.* colpoepisiorrafia.

colpography *n.* colpografia.

colpohyperplasia *n.* colpohiperplasia.

colpohyperplasia cystica colpohiperplasia quística.

colpohyperplasia emphysematosa colpohiperplasia enfisematosa.

colpohysterectomy *n.* colpohisterectomía.

colpohysteropexy *n.* colpohisteropexia.

colpohysterorrhaphy *n.* colpohisterorrafia.

colpohysterotomy *n.* colpohisterotomía.

colpomicroscope *n.* colpomicroscopio.

colpomicroscopic *adj.* colpomicroscópico, -ca.

colpomicroscopy *n.* colpomicroscopia.

colpomycosis *n.* colpomicosis.

colpomyomectomy *n.* colpomiomectomía, colpomiotomía.

colpopathy *n.* colpopatía.

colpoperineoplasty *n.* colpoperineoplastia.

colpoperineorrhaphy *n.* colpoperineorrafia.

colpopexy *n.* colpopexia.

colpoplasty *n.* colpoplastia.

colpoptosis *n.* colpoptosis.

colporectopexy *n.* colporrectopexia.

colporrhagia *n.* colporragia.

colporrhaphy *n.* colporrafia.

colporrhexis *n.* colporrexis.

colposcope *n.* colposcopio.

colposcopic *adj.* colposcópico, -ca.

colposcopy *n.* colposcopia.

colpospasm *n.* colpospasmo.

colpospat *n.* colpóstato.

colpostenotomy *n.* colpostenotomía.

colposteonosis *n.* colpostenosis.

colposuspension *n.* colposuspensión.

colpotherm *n.* colpotermo.

colpotomy *n.* colpotomía.

posterior colpotomy colpotomía posterior.

colpoureterocystotomy *n.* colpoureterocistotomía.

colpoureterotomy *n.* colpoureterotomía.

colpoxerosis *n.* colpoxerosis.

columella *n.* columella.

column *n.* columna.

affinity column columna de afinidad.

Bertin's column columna de Bertin.

branchial efferent column columna branquial eferente.

general somatic afferent column columna aferente somática general.

general visceral splanchnic afferent column columna aferente visceral, esplácnica general.

special somatic afferent column columna aferente somática especial.

vertebral column columna vertebral.

columna *n.* columna.

columnella *n.* columnela.

columnization *n.* columnización.

colypeptic *adj.* colipéptico, -ca.

coma *n.* coma.

agrypnodal coma coma agripnótico.

alcoholic coma coma alcohólico.

alpha coma coma alfa.

apoplectic coma coma apopléctico.

barbiturate coma coma por barbitúricos.

carcinomatous coma coma carcinomatoso.

coma hepaticum coma hepático.

coma hypochloraemicum coma hipoclorémico.

coma vigil coma vigil.
diabetic coma coma diabético.
hepatic coma coma hepático.
hyperosmolar coma coma hiperosmolar.
hyperosmolar hyperglycemic non-ketonic coma coma hiperosmolar hiperglucémico no cetónico.
hyperosmolar nonketotic coma coma hiperosmolar no cetósico.
hypoglycemic coma coma hipoglucémico.
irreversible coma coma irreversible.
Kussmaul's coma coma de Kussmaul.
metabolic coma coma metabólico.
thyrotoxic coma coma tirotóxico.
trance coma coma de trance.
uremic coma coma urémico.
comasculation n. comasculación.
comatose adj. comatoso, -sa.
combination n. combinación.
binary combination combinación binaria.
new combination combinación nueva.
combustible adj. combustible.
combustion n. combustión.
spontaneous combustion combustión espontánea.
comedo n. comedón.
closed comedo comedón cerrado.
open comedo comedón abierto.
whitehead comedo comedón blanco.
comedocarcinoma n. comedocarcinoma.
comedogenecity n. comedogeneidad.
comedogenic adj. comedogénico, -ca, comedógeno, -na.
comedomastitis adj. comedomastitis.
comes n. comes.
comissurotomy n. comisurotomía.
mitral comissurotomy comisurotomía mitral.
commensal n. comensal.
commensalism n. comensalismo.
comminuted adj. conminuto, -ta.
comminution n. conminución.
commissura n. comisura.
commissurorrhaphy n. comisurorrafia.
commissurotomy n. comisurotomía.
commisural adj. comisural.
commisure n. comisura.
commitment n. internamiento.
commotio n. conmoción.
commotio cerebri conmoción cerebral.
commotio of the labyrinth conmoción del laberinto.
commotio retinae conmoción de la retina.
commotio spinalis conmoción espinal.
medullar commotio conmoción medular.
communicable adj. comunicable.
communicans adj. comunicante.
communication n. comunicación.
congruent communication comunicación congruente.
dyadic interpersonal communication comunicación interpersonal diádica.
dysfunctional communication comunicación disfuncional.
impaired verbal communication comunicación verbal alterada.
incongruent communication comunicación incongruente.
community n. comunidad.
biotic community comunidad biótica.
climax community comunidad clímax.
therapeutic community comunidad terapéutica.
comorbidity n. comorbilidad.
compact adj. compacto, -ta.

compacta n. compacta.
compaction n. compacción.
compages n. ensambladura.
companion adj. acompañante.
comparascope n. comparascopio.
comparator n. comparador.
compartment n. compartimento.
compartmentalization n. compartimentación.
compatibility n. compatibilidad.
compatible adj. compatible.
compensation n. compensación.
depth compensation compensación en profundidad.
dosage compensation compensación de dosis.
compensatory adj. compensador, -ra.
competence n. competencia, suficiencia.
cardiac competence competencia cardíaca.
embryonic competence competencia embrionaria, suficiencia embrionaria.
immunological competence competencia inmunológica, suficiencia inmunológica.
competition n. competición.
complement n. complemento.
chromosome complement complemento cromosómico.
dominant complement complemento dominante.
complementarity n. complementariedad.
complementary adj. complementario, - ria.
complementation n. complementación.
interallelic complementation complementación interalélica.
intergenic complementation complementación intergénica.
complemented adj. complementado, -da.
complementoid n. complementoide.
complementophil adj. complementófilo, -la.
complex n. complejo, -ja.
aberrant complex complejo aberrante.
AIDS dementia complex (ADC) complejo demencia SIDA (CDS).
AIDS related complex (ARC) complejo relacionado con el SIDA (CRS).
amyotrophic-lateral-sclerosis-parkinsonism-demential complex complejo de parkinsonismo, demencia y esclerosis lateral amiotrófica.
anomalous complex complejo anómalo.
antigen-antibody complex complejo antígeno-anticuerpo.
antigenic complex complejo antigénico.
apical complex complejo apical.
atrial complex complejo auricular.
auricular complex complejo auricular.
brother complex complejo fraternal.
Cain complex complejo de Caín.
castration complex complejo de castración.
caudal pharyngeal complex complejo faríngeo caudal.
charge transfer complex complejo transferencia de carga.
Diana complex complejo de Diana.
diphasic complex complejo bifásico.
EAHF complex complejo EAFH.
Eisenmenger's complex complejo de Eisenmenger.
Electra complex complejo de Electra.
electrocardiographic complex complejo electrocardiográfico.
equiphasic complex complejo equifásico.
factor IX complex complejo de factor IX.
femininity complex complejo de femineidad.
Gohn's complex complejo de Gohn.

Golgi complex complejo de Golgi.
hapten-carrier complex complejo hapteno-portador.
hemoglobin-haptoglobin complex complejo hemoglobina-haptoglobina.
HLA complex complejo HLA.
immune complex complejo inmune, complejo inmunológico.
inclusion complex complejo de inclusión.
inferiority complex complejo de inferioridad.
iron-dextran complex complejo hierro-dextrán.
isodiphasic complex complejo isobifásico.
J-G complex complejo Y-G, complejo yuxtaglomerular.
Jocasta complex complejo de Yocasta.
junctional complex complejo de unión.
juxtaglomerular complex complejo Y-G, complejo yuxtaglomerular.
K complex complejo K.
Lear complex complejo de Lear.
major histocompatibility complex (MHC) complejo mayor de histocompatibilidad (CMH), complejo principal de histocompatibilidad.
membrane attack complex complejo de ataque de membrana.
Meyemburg's complex complejo de Meyemburg.
monophasic complex complejo monofásico.
mother complex complejo materno.
mother superior complex complejo de madre superiora.
Oedipus complex complejo de Edipo.
perhypoglossal complex complejo perihipogloso, perihipogloso nuclear.
perihypoglossal nuclear complex complejo perihipogloso, perihipogloso nuclear.
pore complex complejo del poro.
primary inoculation complex complejo primario de inoculación.
primary tuberculous complex complejo tuberculoso primario.
QRS complex complejo QRS.
QRST complex complejo QRST.
ribosome-lamella complex complejo ribosoma-laminilla.
sex complex complejo sexual.
sicca complex complejo sicca.
spike and wave complex complejo de espiga y onda.
Steidele's complex complejo de Steidele.
superiority complex complejo de superioridad.
synaptonemal complex complejo sinaptonémico.
Tacaribe complex of viruses complejo Tacaribe de virus.
ternary complex complejo ternario.
triple symptom complex complejo triple de síntomas.
ureterotrigonal complex complejo ureterotrigonal.
VATER complex complejo VATER.
ventricular complex complejo ventricular.
vitamin B complex complejo vitamínico B.
complexion n. complexión.
compliance n. adaptabilidad, compliance, compliancia, complianza.
brain compliance compliancia cerebral.
compliance of the heart compliancia del corazón.
dynamic compliance of the lung compliancia dinámica del pulmón.
effective compliance compliancia eficaz.

lung compliance compliancia pulmonar.
specific compliance compliancia específica.
static compliance compliancia estática.
thoracic compliance compliancia torácica.
ventilatory compliance compliancia ventilatoria.
complicated *adj.* complicado, -da.
complication *n.* complicación.
medical complication complicación médica.
surgical complication complicación quirúrgica.
vascular complication complicación vascular.
composition *n.* composición.
base composition composición de bases.
modeling composition composición para modelar.
compound *adj.* componer, compuesto, -ta.
comprehension *n.* comprensión.
compress *n.* compresa.
cold compress compresa fría.
graduated compress compresa graduada.
gynecologic compress compresa ginegológica.
hot compress compresa caliente.
perinal compress compresa perineal.
wet compress compresa húmeda.
compressibility *n.* compresibilidad.
compression *n.* compresión.
cardiac compression compresión cardíaca.
cerebral compression compresión cerebral, compresión del cerebro.
compression of the brain compresión cerebral, compresión del cerebro.
digital compression compresión digital.
instrumental compression compresión instrumental.
medullar compression compresión medular.
nerve compression compresión nerviosa.
spinal compression compresión espinal, compresión raquídea.
spinal cord compression compresión de la médula espinal.
compressor *n.* compresor.
air compressor compresor de aire.
Deschamps' compressor compresor de Deschamps.
shot compressor compresor de perdigón.
compulsion *n.* compulsión.
repetition compulsion compulsión a la repetición.
compulsive *adj.* compulsivo.
computer *n.* ordenador.
conarium *n.* conario.
conation *n.* conación.
conative *adj.* conativo, -va.
conatus *n.* conato.
concameration *n.* concameración.
concatenate *adj.* concatenado, -da.
concatenation *n.* concatenación.
concave *adj.* cóncavo, -va.
concavity *n.* concavidad.
concavoconcave *adj.* concavocóncavo, -va.
concavoconvex *adj.* concavoconvexo, -xa.
conceive *v.* concebir.
concentrate *v.* concentrado, concentrar.
frozen red blood concentrate concentrado de hematíes congelados.
liver concentrate concentrado de hígado.
packed cell concentrate concentrado celular.
plant protease concentrate concentrado de proteasa vegetal.
platelet concentrate concentrado de plaquetas.
prothrombin concentrate concentrado complejo protrombínico.

red blood cell concentrate concentrado de hematíes.
red blood concentrate leucocytes removed concentrado de hematíes pobre en leucocitos.
vitamin concentrate concentrado vitamínico.
washed red blood concentrate concentrado de hematíes lavados.
concentrated *adj.* concentrado, -da.
concentration *n.* concentración.
hemodialysate concentration concentración de hemodiálisis.
hydrogen ion concentration concentración de hidrogeniones.
ionic concentration concentración iónica.
limiting isorrheic concentration (LIC) concentración isorreica limitante (CIL).
M concentration concentración M.
mass concentration concentración de masa.
maximal urine concentration máxima capacidad de concentración urinaria.
maximum cell concentration (MC) concentración celular máxima (CM).
maximum urinary concentration (MUC) concentración urinaria máxima (CUM).
mean cell hemoglobin concentration concentración de hemoglobina celular media.
minimal alveolar concentration (anesthetic) concentración alveolar mínima (anestésica).
minimal bactericidal concentration concentración bactericida mínima.
minimal lethal concentration (MLC) concentración letal mínima (MCL).
minimum inhibitory concentration concentración inhibitoria mínima.
molar concentration concentración molar.
normal concentration concentración normal.
oxygen concentration in blood concentración sérica de oxigeno.
peak concentration concentración máxima.
concentric *adj.* concéntrico, -ca.
concept *n.* concepto.
no-threshold concept concepto de no umbral.
conception *n.* concepción.
imperative conception concepción imperativa.
conceptive *adj.* conceptivo, -va.
conceptual *adj.* conceptual.
conceptus *n.* conceptus.
concha *n.* concha, cornete.
conchiform *adj.* conchiforme.
conchiolinosteomyelitis *n.* conquiolinosteomielitis.
conchitis *n.* conchitis, conquitis.
conchoidal *adj.* concoideo, -a.
conchoscope *n.* concoscopio.
conchotome *n.* concótomo.
conchotomy *n.* concotomía.
conclination *n.* conclinación.
concoction *n.* concocción.
concomitance *n.* concomitancia.
concomitant *adj.* concomitante.
conconscious *n.* conconsciente.
concordance *n.* concordancia.
concordant *adj.* concordante.
concrescence *n.* concrescencia.
concretio *n.* concreción, concretio.
concretio cordis concreción cardíaca.
concretion *n.* concreción.
alvine concretion concreción alvina.
calculous concretion concreción calculosa.
prostatic concretion concreción prostástica.

tophic concretion concreción tofácea, concreción tófica.
concretization *n.* concretización.
concussion *n.* concusión.
abdominal concussion concusión abdominal.
concussion of the brain concusión cerebral, concusión del cerebro.
concussion of the labyrinth concusión del laberinto.
concussion of the retina concusión de la retina.
concussion of the spinal cord concusión de la médula espinal.
hydraulic concussion concusión hidráulica.
pulmonary concussion concusión pulmonar.
spinal concussion concusión espinal.
concussor *n.* concusor.
condensation *n.* condensación.
condenser *n.* condensador.
Abbé's condenser condensador de Abbé.
amalgam condenser condensador amalgama.
automatic condenser condensador automático.
automatic mallet condenser condensador de martillo automático.
back-action condenser condensador de acción retorno.
bayonet condenser condensador en bayoneta.
cardioid condenser condensador cardioide.
darkfield condenser condensador de campo oscuro.
electromallet condenser condensador de martillo eléctrico.
foot condenser condensador de pie.
gold condenser condensador de oro.
hand condenser condensador de mano.
Hollenback condenser condensador Hollenback.
mechanical condenser condensador mecánico.
paraboloid condenser condensador parabólico.
parallelogram condenser condensador paralelogramo.
pneumatic condenser condensador neumático.
condition *n.* acondicionar, condición.
basal condition condición basal.
conditioning *n.* condicionamiento.
assertive conditioning condicionamiento asertivo.
aversive conditioning condicionamiento aversivo.
avoidance conditioning condicionamiento de evitación.
classic conditioning condicionamiento clásico.
classical conditioning condicionamiento clásico.
escape conditioning condicionamiento de escape.
high order conditioning condicionamiento de orden superior.
instrumental conditioning condicionamiento instrumental.
operant conditioning condicionamiento operante, condicionamiento operativo.
Pavlovian conditioning condicionamiento de Pavlov, condicionamiento pavloviano.
respondent conditioning condicionamiento de respuesta.
second-order conditioning condicionamiento de segundo orden.

Skinnerian conditioning condicionamiento de Skinner.

trace conditioning condicionamiento de traza.

condom *n.* condón, preservativo.

conduction *n.* conducción.

aberrant ventricular conduction conducción ventricular aberrante.

accelerated conduction conducción acelerada.

aerial conduction conducción aérea.

aerotympanal conduction conducción aerotimpánica.

air conduction conducción aérea.

anomalous conduction conducción anómala.

anterograde conduction conducción anterógrada.

antidromic conduction conducción antidrómica.

atrioventricular conduction (A-V) conducción auriculoventricular (A-V).

avalanche conduction conducción en alud, conducción en avalancha.

bone conduction conducción ósea.

concealed conduction conducción oculta.

conduction of the nervous impulse conducción del impulso nervioso.

cranial conduction conducción craneal.

decremental conduction conducción decreciente.

delayed conduction conducción demorada, conducción retardada.

forward conduction conducción anterior.

intraventricular conduction conducción intraventricular.

nerve conduction conducción nerviosa.

orthodromic conduction conducción ortodrómica.

osteotympanic conduction conducción osteotimpánica.

Purkinje's conduction conducción de Purkinje.

retrograde conduction conducción retrógrada.

saltatory conduction conducción saltatoria.

supranormal conduction conducción supranormal.

synaptic conduction conducción sináptica.

ventricular conduction conducción ventricular.

ventriculoatrial conduction (V-A) conducción ventriculoauricular (V-A).

conductive *adj.* conductor, -ra.

conductor *n.* conductor.

conduplicate *adj.* conduplicado, -da.

conduplicato-corpore *n.* conduplicato corpore.

condylar *adj.* condilar, condíleo, -a.

condylarthrosis *n.* condiloartrosis.

condyle *n.* cóndilo.

condylectomy *n.* condilectomía.

condylion *n.* condilión.

condyloid *adj.* condiloide, condiloideo, -a.

condyloma *n.* condiloma.

condyloma acuminatum condiloma acuminado, condiloma acuminatum.

condyloma latum condiloma lato.

flat condyloma condiloma plano.

giant condyloma condiloma gigante.

pointed condyloma condiloma puntiagudo.

condylomatoid *adj.* condilomatoide.

condylomatosis *n.* condilomatosis.

condylomatous *adj.* condilomatoso, -sa.

condylotomy *n.* condilotomía.

cone *n.* cono.

achrosomal cone cono acrosómico.

antipodal cone cono antípoda, cono antipódico.

arterial cone cono arterial, cono arterioso.

axonic cone cono axónico.

bifurcation cone cono de bifurcación.

cerebellar pressure cone cono de presión, cono de presión cerebelosa.

cone of light cono luminoso, cono luminoso de Politzer.

congenital cone cono congénito.

distraction cone cono de distracción.

ether cone cono de éter, para éter.

fertilization cone cono de fecundación, cono de fertilización.

growth cone cono de crecimiento.

gutta-percha cone cono gutapercha.

implantation cone cono de implantación.

keratosic cone cono queratósico, cono queratótico.

l-cone cono l.

long cone cono largo.

m-cone cono m.

myopic cone cono miópico.

Politzer's cone cono de Politzer.

Politzer's luminous cone cono luminoso, cono luminoso de Politzer.

pressure cone cono de presión, cono de presión cerebelosa.

primitive cone cono primitivo.

pulmonary cone cono pulmonar.

retinal cone cono de la retina, cono retinal.

s-cone cono-s.

short cone cono corto.

silver cone cono plata.

supertraction cone cono de supertracción.

theca interna cone cono de la teca interna.

Tyndall cone cono de Tyndall.

cones *n.* conos.

conespecific *adj.* conespecífico, -ca.

confabulation *n.* confabulación.

confertus *n.* conferto, confertus.

confidence *n.* confianza.

basic confidence confianza básica, confianza fundamental.

fundamental confidence confianza básica, confianza fundamental.

confidentiality *n.* confidencialidad.

configuration *n.* configuración.

conflict *n.* conflicto.

approach-approach conflict conflicto de acercamiento-acercamiento, conflicto de enfoque-enfoque.

approach-avoidance conflict conflicto de acercamiento-evitación, conflicto enfoque-evitación.

avoidance-avoidance conflict conflicto de evitación-evitación.

double approach conflict conflicto de doble acercamiento.

double conflict conflicto doble.

double-avoidance conflict conflicto de doble evitación.

extrapsychic conflict conflicto extrapsíquico.

intrapsychic conflict conflicto intrapersonal, conflicto intrapsíquico.

motivational conflict conflicto motivación.

paternal role conflict conflicto de función paterna.

role conflict conflicto de rol.

confluent *adj.* confluente.

conformation *n.* conformación.

conformer *adj.* conformador, -ra.

confrication *n.* confricación.

confrontation *n.* confrontación.

congelation *n.* congelación[1].

congener *n.* congénere.

congeneric *adj.* congenérico, -ca.

congenital *adj.* congénito, -ta.

congested *adj.* congestionado, -da.

congestion *n.* congestión.

active congestion congestión activa.

brain congestion congestión cerebral.

bronchial congestion congestión bronquial.

functional congestion congestión funcional.

hypostatic congestion congestión hipostática.

neurotonic congestion congestión neurotónica.

passive congestion congestión pasiva.

physiologic congestion congestión fisiológica.

pulmonary congestion congestión pulmonar.

rebound congestion congestión de rebote.

venous congestion congestión venosa.

congestive *adj.* congestivo, -va.

conglobate *adj.* conglobado, -da.

conglobation *n.* conglobación.

conglomerate *n.* conglomerado, -da.

conglutinatio *n.* conglutinación, conglutinatio.

conglutination *n.* conglutinación, conglutinatio.

congophilic *adj.* congófilo, -la.

congruent *adj.* congruente.

conic *adj.* cónico, -ca.

conical *adj.* cónico, -ca.

Conidiobolus *n.* Conidiobolus.

conidiogenous *adj.* conidiógeno, -na.

conidiophore *n.* conidióforo.

Phialophore-type conidiophore conidióforo tipo Phialophora.

coniology *n.* coniología.

coniolymphestasis *n.* coniolinfestasia.

coniometer *n.* conímetro, coniómetro.

coniosis *n.* coniosis.

coniosporosis *n.* coniosporosis.

coniotomia *n.* coniotomía.

coniotomy *n.* coniotomía.

coniotoxicosis *n.* coniotoxicosis.

conization *n.* conización.

cautery conization conización por cauterio.

cervical conization conización cervical.

cold conization conización en frío.

conjugate[1] *adj.* conjugado, -da.

conjugate[2] *n.* conjugado.

conjugation *n.* conjugación.

conjugon *n.* conjugón.

conjunctiva *n.* conjuntiva.

bulbar conjunctiva conjuntiva bulbar.

palpebral conjunctiva conjuntiva palpebral.

conjunctival *adj.* conjuntival.

conjunctive *adj.* conjuntivo, -va.

conjunctiviplasty *n.* conjuntiviplastia.

conjunctivitis *n.* conjuntivitis.

actinic conjunctivitis conjuntivitis actínica, conjuntivitis arco luminoso.

acute conjunctivitis conjuntivitis aguda.

acute catarrhal conjunctivitis conjuntivitis catarral, conjuntivitis catarral aguda.

acute contagious conjunctivitis conjuntivitis contagiosa aguda.

acute epidemic conjunctivitis conjuntivitis epidémica aguda.

acute follicular conjunctivitis conjuntivitis folicular aguda.

acute hemorrhagic conjunctivitis conjuntivitis hemorrágica aguda.

allergic conjunctivitis conjuntivitis alérgica, conjuntivitis anafiláctica.

angular conjunctivitis conjuntivitis angular.

arc-flash conjunctivitis conjuntivitis por destello de arco.

atopic conjunctivitis conjuntivitis atópica.

atropine conjunctivitis conjuntivitis atropínica.

bacterial conjunctivitis conjuntivitis bacteriana.

Béal's conjunctivitis conjuntivitis de Béal.

blenorrheal conjunctivitis conjuntivitis blenorrágica.

calcareous conjunctivitis conjuntivitis calcárea.

catarrhal conjunctivitis conjuntivitis catarral, conjuntivitis catarral aguda.

chemical conjunctivitis conjuntivitis química.

chronic follicular conjunctivitis conjuntivitis folicular crónic.

cicatricial conjunctivitis conjuntivitis cicatricial, conjuntivitis cicatrizal.

conjunctivitis arida conjuntivitis árida.

conjunctivitis medicamentosa conjuntivitis medicamentosa.

conjunctivitis of the newborn conjuntivitis de los recién nacidos, conjuntivitis del recién nacido.

conjunctivitis petrificans conjuntivitis petrificante.

conjunctivitis tularensis conjuntivitis tularémica, conjuntivitis tularensis.

contagious granular conjunctivitis conjuntivitis granular contagiosa.

croupous conjunctivitis conjuntivitis crupal.

diphtheritic conjunctivitis conjuntivitis diftérica.

diplobacillary conjunctivitis conjuntivitis diplobacilar.

eczematous conjunctivitis conjuntivitis eccematosa.

Egyptian conjunctivitis conjuntivitis egipcia.

epidemic conjunctivitis conjuntivitis aguda contagiosa, conjuntivitis epidémica.

epidemic hemorrhagic conjunctivitis conjuntivitis hemorrágica epidémica.

follicular conjunctivitis conjuntivitis folicular.

gonococcal conjunctivitis conjuntivitis gonocócica.

gonorrheal conjunctivitis conjuntivitis gonorreica.

granular conjunctivitis conjuntivitis granular, conjuntivitis granulosa.

inclusion conjunctivitis conjuntivitis de inclusión.

infantile purulent conjunctivitis conjuntivitis infantil purulenta, conjuntivitis purulenta infantil.

Koch-Weeks conjunctivitis conjuntivitis de Koch-Weeks.

lacrimal conjunctivitis conjuntivitis lagrimal.

larval conjunctivitis conjuntivitis larval.

ligneous conjunctivitis conjuntivitis leñosa.

lithiasis conjunctivitis conjuntivitis litiásica.

Meibomian conjunctivitis conjuntivitis de Meibomio.

membranous conjunctivitis conjuntivitis membranosa.

meningococcus conjunctivitis conjuntivitis meningocócica.

molluscum conjunctivitis conjuntivitis del molusco, conjuntivitis por molusco.

Morax-Axenfeld conjunctivitis conjuntivitis de Morax-Axenfeld.

mucopurulent conjunctivitis conjuntivitis mucopurulenta.

necrotic infectious conjunctivitis conjuntivitis infecciosa necrótica, conjuntivitis necrótica infecciosa.

neonatal conjunctivitis conjuntivitis neonatal.

Parinaud's conjunctivitis conjuntivitis de Parinaud.

Pascheff's conjunctivitis conjuntivitis de Pascheff.

phlyctenular conjunctivitis conjuntivitis escrofulosa, conjuntivitis flictenular.

prairie conjunctivitis conjuntivitis de las praderas.

pseudomembranous conjunctivitis conjuntivitis seudomembranosa.

purulent conjunctivitis conjuntivitis purulenta.

shipyard conjunctivitis conjuntivitis de los astilleros.

simple conjunctivitis conjuntivitis simple.

snow conjunctivitis conjuntivitis de la nieve.

spring conjunctivitis conjuntivitis primaveral.

squirrel plague conjunctivitis conjuntivitis de la peste de las ardillas.

swimming pool conjunctivitis conjuntivitis de las piscinas.

toxicogenic conjunctivitis conjuntivitis toxicogénica.

trachomatous conjunctivitis conjuntivitis tracomatosa.

tularemic conjunctivitis conjuntivitis tularémica, conjuntivitis tularensis.

uratic conjunctivitis conjuntivitis urática.

vaccinial conjunctivitis conjuntivitis vacunal.

vernal conjunctivitis conjuntivitis vernal.

viral conjunctivitis conjuntivitis vírica.

welder's conjunctivitis conjuntivitis de soldador.

Widmark's conjunctivitis conjuntivitis de Widmark.

conjunctivodacryocystorhinostomy *n.* conjuntivodacriocistorrinostomía.

conjunctivodacryocystostomy *n.* conjuntivodacriocistostomía.

conjunctivoma *n.* conjuntivoma.

conjunctivoplasty *n.* conjuntiviplastia, conjuntivoplastia.

conjunctivorhinostomy *n.* conjuntivorrinostomía.

connatal *adj.* connatal.

connectins *n.* conectinas.

connection *n.* conexión.

  clamp connection conexión de pinza.

connective *adj.* conectivo, -va.

  connective tissue disease conectivopatía.

connector *n.* conector.

  major connector conector mayor.

  minor connector conector menor, conector secundario.

connexon *n.* conexón.

connexus *n.* conexión.

conoid *adj.* conoide, conoideo, -a.

conophthalmus *n.* conoftalmía.

consanguineous *adj.* consanguíneo, -a.

consanguinity *n.* consanguinidad.

conscience *n.* consciencia.

conscious *adj.* consciente.

consciousness *n.* conciencia.

  clouding consciousness conciencia nublada.

  double consciousness conciencia doble.

  dual consciousness conciencia doble.

  moral consciousness conciencia moral.

consecutive *adj.* consecutivo, -va.

consensual *adj.* consensual.

conservation *n.* conservación.

conservation of energy conservación de la energía.

conservation of matter conservación de la materia.

conservative *adj.* conservador, -ra.

consistence *n.* consistencia.

  gingival consistence consistencia gingival.

consolidant *adj.* consolidante.

consolidate *adj.* consolidado, -da.

consolidation *n.* consolidación.

consonance *n.* consonancia.

consonation *n.* consonación.

conspicuous *adj.* conspicuo, -cua.

constancy *n.* constancia.

  cell constancy constancia celular.

  object constancy constancia de los objetos, constancia del objeto.

  perceptive constancy constancia perceptiva, constancia perceptual.

  perceptual constancy constancia perceptiva, constancia perceptual.

constant *n.* constante.

  absorption rate constant constante de tasa de absorción.

  association constant constante de asociación.

  Avogadro's constant constante de Avogadro.

  binding constant constante de conjugación.

  constant of gravitation constante de gravitación, constante gravitacional.

  desintegration constant constante de desactivación, constante de desintegración.

  dielectric constant constante dieléctrica.

  diffusion constant constante de difusión.

  dissociation constant constante de disociación.

  equilibrium constant constante de equilibrio.

  Faraday's constant constante de Faraday.

  gas constant constante de los gases.

  gravitational constant constante de gravitación, constante gravitacional.

  ionization constant constante de ionización.

  Lapicque's constant constante de Lapicque.

  Michaelis constant constante de Michaelis.

  Newtonian constant of gravitation constante newtoniana de gravitación.

  Planck's constant constante cuántica, constante de Planck.

  radioactive constant constante de radiactividad, constante radiactiva.

  Rohrer constant constante de Rohrer.

  sedimentation constant constante de sedimentación.

  velocity constant constante de velocidad.

constellation *n.* constelación.

constipated *adj.* estreñido, -da.

constipation *n.* estreñimiento.

  atonia constipation estreñimiento atónico, estreñimiento por atonía.

  colonic constipation estreñimiento colónico.

  gastrojejunal constipation estreñimiento gastroyeyunal.

  obstructive constipation estreñimiento obstructivo.

  perceived constipation estreñimiento subjetivo.

  rectal constipation estreñimiento rectal.

  spastic constipation estreñimiento espástico.

constituent *n.* componente.

  anterior constituent componente anterior, componente anterior de fuerza.

  anterior constituent of force componente anterior, componente anterior de fuerza.

  constituent of complement componente del complemento.

constituent of force componente de fuerza.

constituent of mastication componente de la masticación.

constituent of occlusion componente de la oclusión.

group specific constituent componente específico del grupo.

M constituent componente M.

metabolic constituent componente metabólico.

respiratory constituent componente respiratorio.

secretory constituent componente secretor.

somatic motor constituent componente somático motor.

somatic sensory constituent componente somático sensitivo.

splanchnic motor constituent componente esplácnico motor, componente visceral motor.

splanchnic sensory constituent componente esplácnico sensitivo, componente visceral sensitivo.

constitution *n.* constitución.

lymphatic constitution constitución linfática.

constitutional *adj.* constitucional.

constriction *n.* constricción.

duodenopyloric constriction constricción duodenopilórica.

primary constriction constricción primaria.

secondary constriction constricción secundaria.

constrictive *adj.* constrictivo, -va.

constrictor *n.* constrictor.

constructive *adj.* constructivo, -va.

consumption *n.* consumo, consunción.

damaging consumption consumo perjudicial.

oxygen consumption consumo de oxígeno.

passive smoking consumption consumo pasivo de tabaco.

systemic oxygen consumption consumo sistémico de oxígeno.

consumptive *adj.* consuntivo, -va.

contact *n.* contacto.

balancing contact contacto balanceado, contacto de balance.

centric contact contacto céntrico.

complete contact contacto completo.

contact with reality contacto con la realidad.

deflective contact contacto deflectivo.

deflective occlusal contact contacto oclusal deflectivo.

direct contact contacto directo.

immediate contact contacto inmediato.

initial contact contacto inicial.

initial occlusal contact contacto oclusal inicial.

interceptive occlusal contact contacto oclusal interceptiva.

mediate contact contacto indirecto.

occlusal contact contacto oclusal.

premature contact contacto prematuro.

proximal contact contacto proximal, contacto próximo.

proximate contact contacto proximal, contacto próximo.

weak contact contacto débil.

working contact contacto de trabajo.

contactant *adj.* contactante.

contagion *n.* contagio.

immediate contagion contagio directo, contagio inmediato.

mediate contagion contagio indirecto.

psychic contagion contagio mental, contagio psíquico.

contagiosity *n.* contagiosidad.

contagious *adj.* contagioso, -sa.

contaminant *adj.* contaminante.

contamination *n.* contaminación.

content *n.* contenido.

carbon dioxide content contenido de anhídrido carbónico.

latent content contenido latente del sueño.

manifest content contenido manifiesto del sueño.

polymorphism information content contenido de información del polimorfismo (PIC).

context *n.* contexto.

contiguous *adj.* contiguo, -a.

continence *n.* continencia.

fecal continence continencia fecal.

urinary continence continencia urinaria.

continent *adj.* continente.

contortion *n.* contorsión.

contour *n.* contorno.

buccal contour contorno bucal.

flange contour contorno de la aleta.

gingival contour contorno gingival.

gum contour contorno de la encía.

restoration contour contorno de restauración.

contoured *adj.* contorneado, -da.

contourning *n.* contorneo.

contra-angle *n.* contraángulo.

contra-aperture *n.* contraabertura, contraapertura.

contrabevel *n.* contrabisel.

contraception *n.* anticoncepción, contracepción.

hormonal contraception contracepción hormonal.

intrauterine contraception contracepción intrauterina.

contraceptive *adj.* anticonceptivo, -va, contraceptivo.

barrier contraceptive anticonceptivo de barrera.

combination oral contraceptive anticonceptivo oral combinado.

oral contraceptive anticonceptivo oral.

sequential oral contraceptive anticonceptivo oral secuencial.

contractile *adj.* contráctil.

contractility *n.* contractilidad.

cardiac contractility contractilidad cardíaca.

galvanic contractility contractilidad galvánica.

idiomuscular contractility contractilidad idiomuscular.

contraction *n.* contracción.

anodal closure contraction contracción de cierre anódico.

anodal contraction contracción anodal.

anodal opening contraction contracción de abertura anódica, contracción de apertura anódica.

automatic contraction contracción automática.

automatic ventricular contraction contracción ventricular automática.

Braxton-Hicks contraction contracción Braxton Hicks.

carpopedal contraction contracción carpopedal, contracción carpopedia.

cathodal closure contraction contracción de cierre catódico.

cathodal opening contraction contracción de abertura catódica, contracción de apertura catódica.

closing contraction contracción de cierre.

concentric contraction contracción concéntrica.

Dupuytren's contraction contracción de Dupuytren.

eccentric contraction contracción excéntrica.

escaped contraction escaped ventricular contraction contracción de escape, contracción de escape ventricular.

escaped ventricular contraction contracción ventricular de escape.

false Dupuytren's contraction contracción de dupuytren falsa.

fibrillary contraction contracción fibrilar.

front-tap contraction contracción de golpe delantero.

Gowers' contraction contracción de Gowers.

hourglass contraction contracción en reloj de arena.

hunger contraction contracción de hambre.

idiomuscular contraction contracción idiomuscular.

isometric contraction contracción isométrica.

isotonic contraction contracción isotónica.

isovolumetric contraction contracción isovolumétrica.

myotatic contraction contracción miotática.

opening contraction contracción de abertura, contracción de abertura anódica, contracción de apertura anódica, contracción de apertura anódica.

paradoxical contraction contracción paradójica.

postural contraction contracción postural.

premature atrial contraction contracción auricular prematura.

premature contraction contracción prematura.

premature ventricular contraction (PVC) contracción ventricular prematura (CVP).

tetanic contraction contracción tetánica.

tonic contraction contracción tónica.

Trousseau's contraction contracción espasmódica de Trousseau.

twich contraction contracción de sacudida.

twiching contraction contracción espasmódica.

uterine contraction contracción uterina.

contracture *n.* contractura.

defense contracture contractura de defensa.

Dupuytren's contracture contractura de Dupuytren.

functional contracture contractura funcional.

hypertonic contracture contractura hipertónica.

hysterical contracture contractura histérica.

ischemic contracture contractura isquémica.

ischemic contracture of the left ventricle contractura isquémica del ventrículo izquierdo.

painful contracture contractura dolorosa.

physiologic contracture contractura fisiológica.

postpoliomyelitic contracture contractura pospoliomielítica.

veratrin contracture contractura por veratrina.

Volkmann's contracture contractura de Volkmann.

contrafissure *n.* contrafisura.

contraincision *n.* contraincisión.

contraindicate *v.* contraindicar.

contraindicated *adj.* contraindicado, -da.

contraindication *n.* contraindicación.

contrainsular *adj.* contrainsular.

contralateral *adj.* contralateral.
contraparetic *adj.* contraparético, -ca.
contrast *n.* contraste.
  baric contrast contraste baritado.
  double contrast contraste doble.
  ferromagnetic contrast contraste ferromagnético.
  film contrast contraste de la película.
  hydrosoluble contrast contraste hidrosoluble.
  hyperosmolar contrast contraste hiperosmolar.
  iodate contrast contraste iodado, contraste yodado.
  ionic contrast contraste iónico.
  iso-osmolar contrast contraste isoosmolar.
  liposoluble contrast contraste liposoluble.
  negative contrast contraste negativo.
  non-ionic contrast contraste no iónico.
  normo-osmolar contrast contraste norosmolar.
  objective contrast contraste objetivo.
  paramagnetic contrast contraste paramagnético.
  positive contrast contraste positivo.
  radiographic contrast contraste radiográfico.
  subjective contrast contraste subjetivo.
contrastimulant *adj.* contraestimulante.
contrastimulism *n.* contraestimulismo.
contrastimulus *n.* contraestímulo.
contravolitional *adj.* contravolitivo, -va.
contrecoup *n.* contragolpe.
control *n.* control.
  automatic control control automático.
  aversive control control aversivo.
  biological control control biológico.
  birth control control de la natalidad, control natal.
  control of hemorrhage control de la hemorragia.
  control with placebo in investigation control con placebo en investigación.
  feedback control control por retroalimentación.
  idiodynamic control control idiodinámico.
  local control control local.
  nudge control control por presión.
  own control control propio.
  quality control control de calidad.
  reflex control control reflejo.
  regional control control regional.
  respiratory control control respiratorio.
  sex control control del sexo.
  social control control social.
  stimulus control control de estímulos, control del estímulo.
  synergic control control sinérgico.
  time-varied gain control control de ganancia tiempo-variada.
  tonic control control tónico.
  vestibulo-equilibratory control control vestibuloequilibratorio.
  volitional control control volitivo, control voluntario.
  voluntary control control volitivo, control voluntario.
controversy *n.* controversia.
contusion *n.* contusión.
  brain contusion contusión cerebral.
  contusion of the spinal cord contusión de la médula espinal.
  countercoup contusion contusión por contragolpe.
  medullar contusion contusión medular.
  renal contusion contusión renal.

  scalp contusion contusión del cuero cabelludo.
  stone contusion contusión por piedra.
  temporal lobe contusion contusión del lóbulo temporal.
  wind contusion contusión aérea.
conular *adj.* conular.
conus *n.* cono, conus.
convalescence *n.* convalecencia.
convalescent *adj.* convaleciente.
conventional *adj.* convencional.
convergence *n.* convergencia.
  accommodative convergence convergencia acomodativa, convergencia de acomodación.
  fusional convergence convergencia de fusión.
  negative convergence convergencia negativa.
  positive convergence convergencia positiva.
convergiometer *n.* convergiómetro.
conversion *n.* conversión.
  freebasing conversion conversión en base libre.
converter *n.* conversor.
  analog-digital converter conversor analógico-digital.
  D-A converter conversor D-A.
  digital-to-analog converter conversor digital-analógico.
convex *adj.* convexo, -xa.
convexity *n.* convexidad.
  cortical convexity convexidad cortical.
convexobaxia *n.* convexobasia.
convexoconcave *adj.* convexocóncavo, -va.
convexoconvex *adj.* convexoconvexo, -xa.
convolute *adj.* convoluto, -ta.
convoluted *adj.* convoluto, -ta.
convolution *n.* circunvolución.
convulsant *adj.* convulsionante.
convulsion *n.* convulsión.
  clonic convulsion convulsión clónica.
  complex partial convulsion convulsión parcial compleja.
  coordinate convulsion convulsión coordinada.
  ether convulsion convulsión por éter.
  febrile convulsion convulsión febril.
  generalized tonic-clonic convulsion convulsión tónico-clónica generalizada.
  hysterical convulsion convulsión histérica, convulsión histeroide.
  hysteroid convulsion convulsión histérica, convulsión histeroide.
  immediate posttraumatic convulsion convulsión postraumática inmediata.
  infantile convulsion convulsión infantil.
  mimetic convulsion convulsión mímica.
  mimic convulsion convulsión mímica.
  partial convulsion convulsión parcial.
  puerperal convulsion convulsión puerperal.
  salaam convulsion convulsión en "salaam".
  static convulsion convulsión estática.
  tetanic convulsion convulsión tetánica.
  tonic convulsion convulsión tónica.
convulsivant *adj.* convulsivante.
convulsive *adj.* convulsivo, -va.
convulsotherapy *n.* convulsoterapia.
coordenate *n.* coordenada.
coordination *n.* coordinación.
  motor coordination coordinación motora.
  visual-motor coordination coordinación visualmotora.
co-ossification *n.* coosificación.
copepod *n.* copépodo.
coping *n.* afrontamiento.

  compromised coping afrontamiento comprometido.
  defensive coping afrontamiento defensivo.
  ineffective family coping afrontamiento familiar ineficaz.
copiopia *n.* copiopía, copiopsia.
copolymer *n.* copolímero.
copracrasia *n.* copracrasia.
coprecipitation *n.* coprecipitación.
coprecipitin *n.* coprecipitina.
copremesis *n.* copremesis.
copremia *n.* copremia.
coproantibody *n.* coproanticuerpo.
coproculture *n.* coprocultivo.
coprofagous *adj.* coprófago, -ga.
coprolagnia *n.* coprolagnia.
coprolalia *n.* coprolalia.
coprolith *n.* coprolito.
coprology *n.* coprología.
coproma *n.* coproma.
copromimia *n.* copromimia.
coprophagy *n.* coprofagia.
coprophemie *n.* coprofemia.
coprophil *adj.* coprofílico, -ca, coprófilo, -la.
coprophilia *n.* coprofilia.
coprophilic *adj.* coprofílico, -ca, coprófilo, -la.
coprophrasia *n.* coprofrasia.
coproplanesia *n.* coproplanesia.
coproporphyria *n.* coproporfiria.
coproporphyrin *n.* coproporfirina.
coproporphyrinuria *n.* coproporfirinuria.
coprostanol *n.* coprostanol.
coprostasis *n.* coprostasia, coprostasis.
coprostasophobia *n.* coprostasofobia.
coprostenol *n.* coprostenol.
coprosterin *n.* coprosterina.
coprozoa *n.* coprozoarios.
coprozoic *adj.* coprozoico, -ca.
coptosis *n.* coptosis.
coptosystole *n.* coptosístole.
copula *n.* cópula.
copulation *n.* copulación.
cor *n.* cor, corazón.
  cor adiposum cor adiposum, corazón adiposo.
  cor mobile cor mobile, corazón móvil.
  cor pulmonale cor pulmonale, corazón pulmonar.
  cor triloculare cor triloculare, corazón de tres cavidades.
coracoacromial *adj.* coracoacromial.
coracoid *adj.* coracoideo, -a.
coracoiditis *n.* coracoiditis.
coralliform *adj.* coraliforme.
coralloid *adj.* coraloide.
corasthma *n.* corasma.
cord *n.* cordón, cuerda.
  dental cord cordón dental.
  enamel cord cordón de esmalte.
  genital cord cordón genital.
  germinal cord cordón germinal.
  gonadal cord cordón gonadal.
  medullary cord cordón medular.
  nephrogenic cord cordón nefrogénico, cordón nefrógeno.
  nuchal cord cordón nucal.
  ovigerous cord cordón ovígero.
  rete cord cordón de la rete.
  sex cord cordón sexual.
  sexual cord cordón sexual.
  umbilical cord cordón umbilical.
  vitelline cord cordón vitelino.
  vocal cord cuerda vocal.
cordabrasion *n.* cordabrasión.
cordectomy *n.* cordectomía.

cordial *n.* cordial.
cordiale *adj.* cordial.
cordiform *adj.* cordiforme.
corditis *n.* corditis.
cordopexy *n.* cordopexia.
cordotomy *n.* cordotomía.
 anterolateral cordotomy cordotomía anterolateral.
 open cordotomy cordotomía abierta.
 posterior column cordotomy cordotomía del haz posterior.
 spinothalamic cordotomy cordotomía espinotalámica.
 stereotactic cordotomy cordotomía estereotáctica.
cordylobiasis *n.* cordilobiasis.
coreclisis *n.* coreclisis.
corectasis *n.* corectasia, corectasis.
corectomedialysis *n.* corectomediálisis.
corectomy *n.* corectomía.
corectopia *n.* corectopia.
corediastasis *n.* corediastasis.
corelysis *n.* corélisis.
coremorphosis *n.* coremorfosis.
corenclisis *n.* coreclisis, corenclisis.
coreometer *n.* coreómetro.
coreometry *n.* coreometría.
coreoplasty *n.* coreoplastia.
corepexy *n.* corepexia.
corepraxy *n.* corepraxia.
corestenoma *n.* corestenoma.
 corestenoma congenitum corestenoma congénito.
coretomedialysis *n.* corectomediálisis, coretomediálisis.
coretomy *n.* coretomía.
coriaceous *adj.* coriáceo, -a.
corification *n.* corificación.
coriodiastasis *n.* corodiastasis.
corium *n.* corion, corium.
 corium frondosum corion frondoso.
 corium laeve corion leve, corion leve, corium laeve.
cornea *n.* córnea.
 conical cornea córnea cónica.
 cornea farinata córnea farinácea.
 cornea plana congenita familiaris córnea plana congénita familiar.
 cornea urica córnea úrica.
 cornea verticillata córnea verticilada, córnea verticillata.
 guttate cornea córnea guttata.
corneal *adj.* corneal, corneano, -na.
corneitis *n.* corneítis.
corneoblepharon *n.* corneobléfaron.
corneocyte *n.* corneocito.
corneoiritis *n.* corneoiritis.
corneosclera *n.* corneoesclerótica.
corneoscleral *adj.* corneoescleral.
corneous *adj.* córneo, -a.
corniculate *adj.* corniculado, -da.
corniculum *n.* cornículo.
cornification *n.* cornificación.
cornified *adj.* cornificado, -da.
cornu *n.* cuerno.
cornucommissural *adj.* cornucomisural.
cornucopia *n.* cornucopia.
corodiastasis *n.* corediastasis.
corometer *n.* coreómetro, corómetro.
corona *n.* corona.
 corona radiata corona radiada, corona radiante.
 corona seborrheica corona seborreica.
 corona veneris corona de Venus, corona venérea, corona veneris.

coronal *adj.* coronal.
coronale *adj.* coronal, coronale.
coronariography *n.* coronariografía.
coronarism *n.* coronarismo.
coronaritis *n.* coronaritis.
coronary *adj.* coronario, -ria.
Coronavirus *n.* Coronavirus.
coronion *n.* coronión.
coronoid *adj.* coronoide, coronoideo, -a.
coronoidectomy *n.* coronoidectomía.
coroparelcysis *n.* coroparelcisis, coroparelquisis.
coroplasty *n.* coreoplastia, coroplastia.
coroscopy *n.* coroscopia.
corotomy *n.* corotomía.
corporeal *adj.* corporal, corpóreo, -a.
corporectomy *n.* corporectomía.
corpus *n.* corpus.
 corpus albicans cuerpo albicans.
 corpus fibrosum cuerpo fibroso.
 corpus hemorrhagicum cuerpo hemorrágico.
 corpus luteum cuerpo lúteo.
corpuscle *n.* corpúsculo.
 amylaceous corpuscle corpúsculo amiláceo, corpúsculo amiloide.
 amyloid corpuscle corpúsculo amiláceo, corpúsculo amiloide.
 Barr's corpuscle corpúsculo de Barr.
 basal corpuscle corpúsculo basal.
 Bennet's small corpuscle corpúsculo pequeño de Bennet.
 Bizzozero's corpuscle corpúsculo de Bizzozero.
 blood corpuscle corpúsculo sanguíneo.
 bone corpuscle corpúsculo óseo.
 bridge corpuscle corpúsculo en puente.
 bulboid corpuscle corpúsculo bulboide, corpúsculo bulboideo.
 cement corpuscle corpúsculo de cemento.
 chorea corpuscle corpúsculo de corea, corpúsculo de la corea.
 chromophil corpuscle corpúsculo cromófilo.
 chyle corpuscle corpúsculo del quilo.
 colostrum corpuscle corpúsculo del calostro.
 concentrated human red blood corpuscle corpúsculo sanguíneo rojo humano concentrado.
 concentric corpuscle corpúsculo concéntrico, corpúsculo concéntrico de Hassall.
 corneal corpuscle corpúsculo corneal.
 Dogiel's corpuscle corpúsculo de Dogiel.
 Donne's corpuscle corpúsculo de Donné.
 Drysdale's corpuscle corpúsculo de Drysdale.
 Eichhorst's corpuscle corpúsculo de Eichhorst.
 exudation corpuscle corpúsculo de exudación.
 genital corpuscle corpúsculo genital.
 Gierke's corpuscle corpúsculo de Gierke.
 Gluge's corpuscle corpúsculo de Gluge.
 Golgi-Mazzoni corpuscle corpúsculo de Golgi-Mazzoni.
 Golgi's corpuscle corpúsculo de Golgi.
 Grandy's corpuscle corpúsculo de Grandy, corpúsculo de Grandy-Merkel.
 Guarnieri's corpuscle corpúsculo de Guarnieri.
 gustatory corpuscle corpúsculo del gusto, corpúsculo gustativo.
 Hassall's concentric corpuscle corpúsculo concéntrico, corpúsculo concéntrico de Hassall.
 Hassall's corpuscle corpúsculo de Hassall.
 inflammatory corpuscle corpúsculo inflamatorio.

 Jaworski's corpuscle corpúsculo Jaworski.
 Krause's corpuscle corpúsculo de Krause.
 Leber's corpuscle corpúsculo de Leber.
 Lostorfer's corpuscle corpúsculo de Lostorfer.
 lymph corpuscle corpúsculo de la linfa, corpúsculo linfático, corpúsculo linfoide.
 lymphatic corpuscle corpúsculo de la linfa, corpúsculo linfático, corpúsculo linfoide.
 lymphoid corpuscle corpúsculo de la linfa, corpúsculo linfático, corpúsculo linfoide.
 Malpighian corpuscle corpúsculo de Malpighi.
 Mazzoni's corpuscle corpúsculo de Mazzoni.
 meconium corpuscle corpúsculo del meconio, corpúsculo meconales.
 Meissner's corpuscle corpúsculo de Meissner.
 Merkel corpuscle corpúsculo de Merkel.
 Mexican hat corpuscle corpúsculo en sombrero mexicano.
 milk corpuscle corpúsculo de la leche.
 mucous corpuscle corpúsculo mucoso.
 Negri's corpuscle corpúsculo de Negri.
 Nissl corpuscle corpúsculo de Nissl.
 Norris' corpuscle corpúsculo de Norris.
 oval corpuscle corpúsculo oval.
 Pacchionian corpuscle corpúsculo de Pacchioni.
 Pacini's corpuscle corpúsculo de Pacini.
 Paschen's corpuscle corpúsculo de Paschen.
 pessary corpuscle corpúsculo en pesario.
 phantom corpuscle corpúsculo fantasma.
 plastic corpuscle corpúsculo plástico.
 Purkinje's corpuscle corpúsculo de Purkinje.
 pus corpuscle corpúsculo de pus.
 red corpuscle corpúsculo rojo de la sangre.
 renal corpuscle corpúsculo renal.
 reticulated corpuscle corpúsculo reticulado.
 Ruffini's corpuscle corpúsculo de Ruffini.
 salivary corpuscle corpúsculo salival.
 Schwalbe's corpuscle corpúsculo de Schwalbe.
 tactile corpuscle of Meissner corpúsculo táctil, corpúsculo táctil de Meissner.
 taste corpuscle corpúsculo del gusto, corpúsculo gustativo.
 tendon corpuscle corpúsculo tendinoso.
 third corpuscle corpúsculo tercero.
 thymic corpuscle corpúsculo del timo, corpúsculo tímico.
 thymus corpuscle corpúsculo del timo, corpúsculo tímico.
 Timofeew's corpuscle corpúsculo de Timofeew.
 touch corpuscle corpúsculo del tacto.
 Toynbee's corpuscle corpúsculo de Toynbee.
 Traube's corpuscle corpúsculo de Traube.
 Tröltsch's corpuscle corpúsculo Tröltsch.
 typhic corpuscle corpúsculo tífico.
 Valentin's corpuscle corpúsculo de Valentin.
 Vater-Pacini corpuscle corpúsculo de Vater, corpúsculo de Vater-Pacini.
 Vater's corpuscle corpúsculo de Vater, corpúsculo de Vater-Pacini.
 Virchow's corpuscle corpúsculo de Virchow.
 white corpuscle corpúsculo blanco.
 Zimmermann's corpuscle corpúsculo de Zimmermann.
corpuscular *adj.* corpuscular.
corpusculum *n.* corpúsculo.
correction *n.* corrección.
 Allen correction corrección de Allen.
 occlusal correction corrección oclusal.
 spontaneous correction of the placenta

previa corrección espontánea de la placenta previa.
corrective *adj.* corrector, -ra.
corrector *n.* corrector.
function corrector corrector de función.
correlation *n.* correlación.
correspondence *n.* correspondencia.
anomalous correspondence correspondencia anómala.
anomalous retinal correspondence correspondencia retiniana anómala.
anormal retinal correspondence correspondencia retiniana anormal.
dysharmonious correspondence correspondencia inarmónica.
harmonious correspondence correspondencia armoniosa.
normal retinal correspondence correspondencia retiniana normal.
retinal correspondence correspondencia retiniana.
corrosion *n.* corrosión.
corrosive *adj.* corrosivo, -va.
corrugator *n.* corrugador.
corruption *n.* corrupción.
corset *n.* corsé.
Minerva's corset corsé de Minerva.
cortex *n.* corteza.
fetal cortex corteza fetal.
provisional cortex corteza provisional.
cortical *adj.* cortical.
corticalization *n.* corticalización.
corticalosteotomy *n.* corticalosteotomía.
corticate *adj.* corticado, -da.
corticectomy *n.* corticectomía.
corticifugal *adj.* corticífugo, -ga, corticófugo, -ga.
corticipetal *adj.* corticípeto, -ta, corticópeto, -ta.
corticoadrenal *adj.* corticosuprarrenal.
corticoafferent *adj.* corticoaferente.
corticoautonomic *adj.* corticoautónomo, -ma.
corticobulbar *adj.* corticobulbar.
corticocerebellum *n.* corticocerebelo.
corticocerebral *adj.* corticocerebral.
corticodiencephalic *adj.* corticodiencefálico, -ca.
corticoefferent *adj.* corticoeferente.
corticofugal *adj.* corticófugo, -ga.
corticoid *n.* corticoide.
corticomedial *adj.* corticomedial.
corticomesencephalic *adj.* corticomesencefálico, -ca.
corticopeduncular *adj.* corticopeduncular.
corticopetal *adj.* corticópeto, -ta.
corticopleuritis *n.* corticopleuritis.
corticopontine *adj.* corticopontino, -na.
corticospinal *adj.* corticoespinal, corticomedular, corticospinal.
corticosteroid *n.* corticoesteroide, corticosteroide.
corticosterone *n.* corticosterona.
corticosuprarrenaloma *n.* corticosuprarrenaloma.
corticosuprarrenoma *n.* corticosuprarrenoma.
corticothalamic *adj.* corticotalámico, -ca.
corticotrope *n.* corticotropa.
corticotroph *n.* corticotrofo.
corticotroph-lipotroph *n.* corticotrofo-lipotrofo.
corticotropic *adj.* corticotrópico, -ca.
corticotropinoma *n.* corticotropinoma.
cortilymph *n.* cortilinfa.
cortisol *n.* cortisol.
cortisolemia *n.* cortisolemia.

cortisoluria *n.* cortisoluria.
coruscation *n.* coruscación.
corybantism *n.* coribantismo.
corymbiform *adj.* corimbiforme.
corynebacterium *n.* corinebacteria.
coryneform *adj.* corineforme.
coryza *n.* coriza.
allergic coryza coriza alérgica.
coryza spasmodica coriza espasmódica.
pollen coryza coriza del polen.
costa *n.* costa, costilla.
costa cervicalis costilla cervical.
costal *adj.* costal.
costalgia *n.* costalgia.
costectomy *n.* costectomía.
costicartilage *n.* costicartílago.
costicervical *adj.* costicervical, costocervical.
costiferous *adj.* costífero, -ra.
costiform *adj.* costiforme.
costive *adj.* estreñido, -da.
costiveness *n.* estreñimiento.
costoabdominal *adj.* costoabdominal.
costocentral *adj.* costocentral.
costochondral *adj.* costocondral.
costochondritis *n.* costocondrítis.
costoclavicular *adj.* costoclavicular.
costocoracoid *adj.* costocoracoideo, -a.
costogenic *adj.* costogénico, -ca.
costoinferior *adj.* costoinferior.
costophrenic *adj.* costofrénico, -ca.
costopleural *adj.* costopleural.
costopneumopexy *n.* costoneumopexia.
costopubic *adj.* costopúbico, -ca.
costoscapular *adj.* costoescapular, costoscapular.
costospinal *n.* costoespinal, costospinal.
costosternal *adj.* costoesternal, costosternal.
costosternoplasty *n.* costoesternoplastia.
costosuperior *adj.* costosuperior.
costotome *n.* costótomo.
costotomy *n.* costotomía.
costotransverse *adj.* costotransverso, -sa.
costotransversectomy *n.* costotransversectomía.
costovertebral *adj.* costovertebral.
costoxiphoid *adj.* costoxifoideo, -a.
costrous *adj.* costroso, -sa.
cothromboplastin *n.* cotromboplastina.
cotransport *n.* cotransporte.
cotton *n.* algodón.
cottonoids *n.* lentinas.
cotyle *n.* cótilo.
cotyledon *n.* cotiledón.
cotyloid *adj.* cotiloide, cotiloideo, -a.
cotylopubic *adj.* cotilopúbico, -ca.
cotylosacral *adj.* cotilosacro, -cra.
cough *n.* tos.
asthmatic cough tos asmática.
Balme's cough tos de Balme.
bitonal cough tos bitonal.
brassy cough tos metálica.
compression cough tos por compresión.
dry cough tos seca.
ear cough tos auditiva, tos auricular.
extrapulmonary cough tos extrapulmonar.
hacking cough tos perruna, tos seca.
hebetic cough tos hebética.
mechanical cough tos mecánica.
Morton's cough tos de Morton.
non-productive cough tos no productiva.
paroxysmal cough tos espasmódica, tos paroxística.
productive cough tos productiva, tos simpática.
reflex cough tos refleja.

stomach cough tos gástrica.
Sydenham's cough tos de Sydenham.
tea taster's cough tos de catadores de té.
tooth cough tos dentaria.
trigeminal cough tos trigémina, tos trigeminal.
weaver's cough tos del tejedor.
wet cough tos blanda, tos húmeda.
whooping cough tos convulsa, tos coqueluchoide, tos ferina, tos quintosa, tosferina.
winter cough tos invernal.
count *n.* numeración, recuento.
Addis count recuento de Addis.
Arneth count recuento de Arneth.
blood count numeración globular, recuento de sangre, recuento sanguíneo.
complete blood count recuento sanguíneo completo.
differential count recuento diferencial.
differential white blood count recuento sanguíneo diferencial de glóbulos blancos.
direct platelet count recuento directo de plaquetas.
egg count numeración de los huevos.
epidermal ridge count recuento de la cresta epidérmica.
filament-non-filament count recuento de filamentos y no filamentos.
indirect platelet count recuento indirecto de plaquetas.
lymph node differential cell count adenograma.
parasite count recuento de parásitos.
Schilling's blood count recuento de Schilling.
counter *n.* contador.
automated differential leukocyte counter contador automático diferencial de leucocitos.
colony counter contador de colonias.
compensated flow meter counter contador de flujo compensado.
Coulter counter contador de Coulter.
electronic cell counter contador electrónico celular.
gamma counter contador gamma.
Geiger counter contador de Geiger, contador Geiger-Müller.
Geiger-Müller counter contador de Geiger, contador Geiger-Müller.
proportional counter contador proporcional.
scintillation counter contador de centelleo.
whole-body counter contador para todo el cuerpo.
counteraction *n.* contratracción.
counterbalancing *n.* contrabalanceo.
counterconditioning *n.* contracondicionamiento.
countercurrent *n.* contracorriente.
counterdepressant *adj.* contradepresor.
counterextension *n.* contraextensión.
counterimmunoelectrophoresis *n.* contrainmunoelectroforesis.
counterincision *n.* contraincisión.
counterinjunction *n.* contraorden.
counterirritant *adj.* contrairritante.
counterirritation *n.* contrairritación.
counteropening *n.* contraabertura, contraapertura.
counterphobia *n.* contrafobia.
counterphobic *adj.* contrafóbico, -ca.
counterpoison *n.* contraveneno.
counterpulsation *n.* contrapulsación.
external counterpulsation contrapulsación externa.
counterpunture *n.* contrapunción.
counterregulation *n.* contrarregulación.

countershock *n.* contrachoque.
counterstain *n.* contracolorante.
countersuggestion *n.* contrasugestión.
countertransference *n.* contratransferencia.
countertransport *n.* contratransporte.
counting *n.* detección.
  coincidence counting detección por coincidencia.
couperose *n.* cuperosis.
coupling *n.* acoplamiento, emparejamiento.
  fixed coupling acoplamiento fijo.
course *n.* decurso.
couvercle *n.* couvercle.
coverglass *n.* cubreobjeto.
cover-slip *n.* cubreobjeto.
cow *n.* vaca.
cowdriosis *adj.* cowdriosis.
Cowperian *adj.* cowperiano, -na.
cowperitis *n.* cowperitis.
cowpox *n.* cowpox.
coxa *n.* cadera, coxa.
  coxa adducta coxa adducta.
  coxa flexa coxa flexa.
  coxa magna coxa magna.
  coxa plana coxa plana.
  coxa valga coxa valga.
  coxa valga subluxans coxa valga subluxans.
  coxa vara coxa vara.
  coxa vara luxans coxa vara luxans, coxa vara luxante.
  false coxa vara coxa vara falsa.
coxalgia *n.* coxalgia.
  coxalgia fugax coxalgia fugaz.
coxarthria *n.* coxartria.
coxarthritis *n.* coxartritis.
coxarthrocace *n.* coxartrocace.
coxarthropathy *n.* coxartropatía.
coxarthrosis *n.* coxartrosis.
Coxiella *n.* Coxiella.
  Coxiella burnetii Coxiella burnetii.
coxitis *n.* coxitis.
  coxitis fugax coxitis fugaz.
  coxitis senile coxitis senil.
  fugitive coxitis coxitis fugaz.
  tuberculous coxitis coxitis tuberculosa.
coxodynia *n.* coxodinia.
coxofemoral *adj.* coxofemoral.
coxotomy *n.* coxotomía.
coxotuberculosis *n.* coxotuberculosis.
Coxsackie *n.* Coxsackie.
Coxsackievirus *n.* Coxsackievirus.
crab *n.* ladilla.
crablouse *n.* ladilla.
crackle *n.* crujido.
cradle *n.* cuna.
cramp *n.* calambre.
  accessory cramp calambre accesorio.
  heat cramp calambre por calor.
  intermittent cramp calambre intermitente.
  miner's cramp calambre de minero.
  musician's cramp calambre de músico.
  pianist's cramp calambre de pianista.
  recumbency cramp calambre por decúbito.
  seamstress' cramp calambre de las costureras.
  stoker's cramp calambre de fogonero.
  stomach cramp retortijón.
  tailor's cramp calambre de los sastres.
  violinist's cramp calambre de violinista.
  waiter's cramp calambre de camarero.
  watchmaker's cramp calambre de relojero.
  writers' cramp calambre de los escritores.
craneomalacia *n.* craneomalacia.
  circumscribed craneomalacia craneomalacia circunscrita.
craniad *adv.* craniad.

cranial *adj.* craneal, craneano, -na.
craniamphitomy *n.* cranianfitomía.
craniectomy *n.* craniectomía.
  linear craniectomy craniectomía lineal.
cranioacromial *adj.* craneoacromial.
cranioamphitomy *n.* craneoanfitomía.
cranioaural *adj.* craneoaural.
craniobucal *adj.* craneobucal.
craniocaudal *adj.* craneocaudal.
craniocele *n.* craneocele.
craniocerebral *adj.* craneocerebral.
craniocervical *adj.* craneocervical.
craniocleidodysostosis *n.* craneocleidodisostosis.
craniodidymus *n.* craneodídimo.
craniofacial *adj.* craneofacial.
craniofenestria *n.* craneofenestria.
craniognomy *n.* craneognomía.
craniograph *n.* craneógrafo.
craniography *n.* craneografía.
craniolacunia *n.* craneolacunia.
craniology *n.* craneología.
craniomeningocele *n.* craneomeningocele.
craniometer *n.* craneómetro.
craniometric *adj.* craneométrico, -ca.
craniometry *n.* craneometría.
craniopagus *n.* craneópago.
  craniopagus occipitalis craneópago occipital.
  craniopagus parasiticus craneópago parásito.
  craniopagus parietalis craneópago parietal.
craniopathy *n.* craneopatía.
  metabolic craniopathy craneopatía metabólica.
craniopharyngeal *adj.* craneofaríngeo, -a.
craniopharyngioma *n.* craneofaringioma.
  cystic papillomatous craniopharyngioma craneofaringioma papilomatoso quístico.
craniophore *n.* craneóforo.
cranioplasty *n.* craneoplastia.
craniopuncture *n.* craneopuntura.
craniorachischisis *n.* craneorraquisquisis.
craniorrhachidian *adj.* craneorraquídeo, -a.
craniosacral *adj.* craneosacral, craneosacro, -cra.
cranioschisis *n.* craneosquisis.
craniosclerosis *n.* craneoesclerosis, craneosclerosis.
cranioscopy *n.* craneoscopia.
craniospinal *adj.* craneoespinal, craneospinal.
craniostenosis *n.* craneoestenosis, craneostenosis.
craniostosis *n.* craneostosis.
craniosynostosis *n.* craneosinostosis.
craniotabes *n.* craneotabes.
craniotome *n.* craneótomo.
craniotomy *n.* craneotomía.
  attached craniotomy craneotomía unida.
  detached craniotomy craneotomía separada.
  osteoplastic craniotomy craneotomía osteoplástica.
craniotonoscopy *n.* craneotonoscopia.
craniotopography *n.* craneotopografía.
craniotrypesis *n.* craneotripesis.
craniotympanic *adj.* craneotimpánico, -ca.
cranitis *n.* craneítis.
cranium *n.* cráneo, cranium.
  cranium bifidum cráneo bífido, cranium bifidum.
  cranium bifidum occultum cráneo bífido oculto.
crapulent *adj.* crapulento, -ta.
crapulous *adj.* crapuloso, -sa.
crasis *n.* crasis.
crater *n.* cráter.
  gingival crater cráter gingival.
  interdental crater cráter interdental.

craterlform *adj.* crateriforme.
craterization *n.* craterización.
cratomania *n.* cratomanía.
craunology *n.* craunología, crenología.
craunotherapy *n.* craunoterapia, crenoterapia.
craw-craw *n.* craw-craw.
cream *n.* crema.
creatine *n.* creatina.
creatinemia *n.* creatinemia.
creatinin *n.* creatinina.
creatinine *n.* creatinina.
  creatinine height index creatinina de 24 horas.
creatinuria *n.* creatinuria.
creatorrhea *n.* creatorrea.
creatotoxism *n.* creatotoxismo.
creep *n.* resbalamiento.
cremasteric *adj.* cremastérico, -ca.
cremation *n.* cremación.
crematorium *n.* crematorio.
cremnophobia *n.* cremnofobia.
crenate *adj.* crenado, -da.
crenated *adj.* crenado, -da.
crenation *n.* crenación.
crenocyte *n.* crenocito.
crenocytosis *n.* crenocitosis.
crenology *n.* crenología.
crenotherapy *n.* crenoterapia.
crenulation *n.* crenulación.
creophagism *n.* creofagia.
creophagy *n.* creofagia.
creotoxin *n.* creotoxina.
creotoxism *n.* creotoxismo.
crepitant *adj.* crepitante.
crepitation *n.* crepitación.
crepitus *n.* crepitación, crépito, crepitus.
  articular crepitus crepitación articular, crépito articular.
  bony crepitus crepitación ósea, crépito óseo.
  crepitus indux crepitus indux.
  crepitus redux crepitación de retorno, crepitus redux.
  false crepitus crepitación falsa.
  joint crepitus crepitación articular, crépito articular.
  painful tendon crepitus crepitación dolorosa de los tendones.
  silken crepitus crepitación de seda.
crepuscular *adj.* crepuscular.
crescent *adj.* creciente, medialuna, semiluna.
  crescent of Giannuzzi semiluna de Giannuzzi.
  epithelial crescent semiluna epitelial.
  Giannuzzi's crescent semiluna de Giannuzzi.
  glomerular crescent semiluna glomerular.
  malarial crescent semiluna palúdica.
  myopic crescent semiluna miópica.
  sublingual crescent semiluna sublingual.
crescograph *n.* crescógrafo.
cresomania *n.* cresomanía.
crest *n.* cresta, crista.
  acousticofacial crest cresta acusticofacial.
cretin *n.* cretino, -na[1].
cretinism *n.* cretinismo.
  athyreotic cretinism cretinismo atireótico.
  familial cretinism cretinismo familiar.
  goitrous cretinism cretinismo bocioso.
  spontaneous cretinism cretinismo espontáneo, cretinismo esporádico.
  sporadic cretinism cretinismo espontáneo, cretinismo esporádico.
  sporadic goitrous cretinism cretinismo esporádico bocioso.
cretinoid *adj.* cretinoide.

cretinous *adj.* cretino, -na[2].
crevice *n.* grieta.
 gingival crevice grieta gingival.
crib *n.* criba.
 Jackson crib criba de Jackson.
 tongue crib criba lingual.
cribrate *adj.* cribado, -da.
cribration *n.* cribado.
cribriform *adj.* cribiforme.
cribrum *n.* cribrum.
cricoarytenoid *adj.* cricoaritenoideo, -a.
cricoid *adj.* cricoide, cricoideo, -a.
cricoidectomy *n.* cricoidectomía.
cricoidynia *n.* cricoidinia.
cricopharyngeal *adj.* cricofaríngeo, -a.
cricothyreotomy *n.* cricotireotomía.
cricothyroid *adj.* cricotiroideo, -a.
cricothyroidotomy *n.* cricotiroidotomía.
cricothyrotomy *n.* cricotirotomía.
cricotomy *n.* cricotomía.
cricotracheotomy *n.* cricotraqueotomía.
criminology *n.* criminología.
crinogenic *adj.* crinogénico, -ca, crinógeno, -na.
crinology *n.* crinología.
crinophagy *n.* crinofagia.
criptotia *n.* criptotia.
crisis *n.* acceso[2], crisis[2].
 Addison crisis crisis addisoniana, crisis de Addison.
 Addisonian crisis crisis addisoniana, crisis de Addison.
 adolescent crisis crisis de adolescencia.
 adrenal crisis crisis adrenal, crisis suprarrenal.
 adventitious crisis crisis adventicia.
 anaphylactoid crisis crisis anafilactoide.
 aplastic crisis crisis aplásica.
 blast crisis crisis blástica, crisis de blastos.
 blood crisis crisis sanguínea.
 bronchial crisis crisis bronquial.
 cardiac crisis crisis cardíaca.
 catathymic crisis crisis de catatimia.
 celiac crisis crisis celíaca.
 clitoris crisis crisis clitorídea.
 colinergic crisis crisis colinérgica.
 desglobulinization crisis crisis de desglobulinización.
 developmental crisis crisis del desarrollo.
 Dietl's crisis crisis de Dietl.
 false crisis crisis falsa.
 febrile crisis crisis febril.
 gastric crisis crisis gástrica.
 genital crisis of the newborn crisis genital del neonato.
 glaucomatocyclitic crisis crisis glaucomatociclítica.
 hepatic crisis crisis hepática.
 hypertensive crisis crisis hipertensiva.
 identity crisis crisis de identidad.
 intestinal crisis crisis intestinal.
 laryngeal crisis crisis laríngea.
 maturational crisis crisis de maduración.
 midlife crisis crisis de la mediana edad.
 myasthenic crisis crisis de miastenia, crisis miasténica.
 myelocytic crisis crisis mielocítica.
 nefast crisis crisis nefasta.
 nephralgic crisis crisis nefrálgica.
 ocular crisis crisis ocular.
 oculogiric crisis crisis oculógira.
 pharyngeal crisis crisis faríngea.
 puberal crisis crisis puberal.
 rejection crisis crisis de rechazo.
 renal crisis crisis renal.
 salt depletion crisis crisis con agotamiento salino.

 salt-losing crisis crisis con pérdida salina.
 sickle cell crisis crisis drepanocítica.
 situational crisis crisis de situación.
 tabetic crisis crisis tabética.
 therapeutic crisis crisis terapéutica.
 thoracic crisis crisis torácica.
 thyroid crisis crisis tiroidea, crisis tirotóxica.
 thyrotoxic crisis crisis tiroidea, crisis tirotóxica.
 visceral crisis crisis visceral.
crispation *n.* crispación.
crista *n.* cresta, crista.
criterion *n.* criterio.
 abnormality criterion criterio de anormalidad.
 frequency normality criterion criterio de normalidad de frecuencia.
 functional normality criterion criterio de normalidad funcional.
 ideal normality criterion criterio de normalidad ideal.
 Jones' criterion criterio de Jones.
 normality criterion criterio de normalidad.
 social normality criterion criterio de normalidad social.
 Spiegelberg's criterion criterio de Spiegelberg.
 subjective normality criterion criterio de normalidad subjetivo.
critical *adj.* crítico, -ca.
crocein *n.* croceína.
crocidismus *n.* crocidismo.
cromophilus *n.* cromófilo.
cross *n.* cruce, cruz.
 back cross cruce reversivo.
 clavicular cross cruz clavicular.
 cross of the heart cruz del corazón.
 dihybrid cross cruce dihíbrido.
 double back cross cruce reversivo doble.
 hair cross cruz del pelo.
 monohybrid cross cruce monohíbrido.
 phage cross cruce de fago.
 polyhybrid cross cruce polihíbrido.
 Ranvier's cross cruz de Ranvier.
 silver cross cruz argéntica.
 trihybrid cross cruce trihíbrido.
 two-factor cross cruce de dos factores.
crossbreed *adj.* cruzado, -da[2].
crossed *adj.* cruzado, -da[1].
cross-eye *n.* estrabismo.
cross-eyed *adj.* bizco, -ca.
crossing over *n.* cruzamiento.
crossing-over *n.* crossing-over, entrecruzamiento.
 genetic crossing-over entrecruzamiento de genes, entrecruzamiento genético.
 somatic crossing-over entrecruzamiento somático.
 unequal crossing-over entrecruzamiento desigual.
 uneven crossing-over entrecruzamiento desigual.
cross-match *n.* cross-match.
crossover *n.* cruzamiento.
crotaphion *n.* crotafión.
croup *n.* croup, crup.
 catarrhal croup crup catarral.
 diphtheritic croup crup diftérico.
 membranous croup crup fibrinoso, crup membranoso.
 pseudomembranous croup crup seudomembranoso.
 spasmodic croup crup espasmódico, crup espástico.
croupous *adj.* crupal, cruposo, -sa.
croupy *adj.* crupal, cruposo, -sa.
crowding *n.* apiñamiento.

crown *n.* corona.
 artificial crown corona artificial.
 bell-shaped crown corona acampanada.
 jacket crown corona funda.
 partial crown corona parcial.
 radiate crown corona radiada, corona radiante.
 static crown corona estática.
crowning *n.* coronamiento.
crucial *adj.* crucial.
crucible *n.* crisol, crucíbulo.
cruciform *adj.* cruciforme.
cruentation *n.* cruentación.
cruomania *n.* cruomanía.
cruor *n.* crúor.
crural *adj.* crural.
cruris *adj.* cruris.
cruropelvimeter *n.* cruropelvímetro.
crush *n.* aplastamiento, aplastar.
crusotomy *n.* crusotomía.
crust *n.* costra.
 milk crust costra de leche, costra láctea.
crusta *n.* costra, crusta.
 crusta inflammatoria costra inflamatoria.
 crusta lactea costra de leche, costra láctea, crusta lactea.
 crusta phlogistica costra flogística.
crustal *adj.* costroso, -sa.
crutch *n.* muleta.
cry *n.* grito.
 arthritic cry grito articular, grito artrítico.
 articular cry grito articular, grito artrítico.
 cephalic cry grito cefálico.
 epileptic cry grito epiléptico.
 joint cry grito articular, grito artrítico.
 night cry grito nocturno.
cryalgesia *n.* crialgesia.
cryanalgesia *n.* crianalgesia.
cryanesthesia *n.* crianestesia.
cryesthesia *n.* criestesia.
crymoanesthesia *n.* crimoanestesia.
crymodinia *n.* crimodinia.
crymophilic *adj.* crimófilo, -la.
crymotherapy *n.* crimoterapia, crioterapia.
cryoaglutinine *n.* crioaglutinina.
cryoanalgesia *n.* crioanalgesia.
cryoanesthesia *n.* crioanestesia.
cryobank *n.* criobanco.
cryobiology *n.* criobiología.
cryocardioplegia *n.* criocardioplejía.
cryocautery *n.* criocauterio, criocauterización.
cryoconization *n.* crioconización.
cryoextraction *n.* crioextracción.
cryoextractor *n.* crioextractor.
cryofibrinogen *n.* criofibrinógeno.
cryofibrinogenemia *n.* criofibrinogenemia.
cryogammaglobulin *n.* criogammaglobulina.
cryogen *n.* criógeno.
cryogenic *adj.* criogénico, -ca.
cryoglobulin *n.* crioglobulina.
cryoglobulinemia *n.* crioglobulinemia.
 crystal cryoglobulinemia crioglobulinemia cristalina.
cryohypophysectomy *n.* criohipofisectomía.
cryolysis *n.* criólisis.
cryometer *n.* criómetro.
cryopallidectomy *n.* criopalidectomía.
cryopathy *n.* criopatía.
cryopexy *n.* criopexia.
cryophile *adj.* criófilo, -la.
cryophylactic *adj.* criofiláctico, -ca.
cryoprecipitability *n.* crioprecipitabilidad.
cryoprecipitate *n.* crioprecipitado.
cryoprecipitation *n.* crioprecipitación.
cryopreservation *n.* crioconservación, criopreservación.

cryoprobe *n.* criosonda.
cryoprostatectomy *n.* crioprostatectomía.
cryoprotective *n.* crioprotector.
cryoprotein *n.* crioproteína.
cryopulvinectomy *n.* criopulvinectomía.
cryorit *n.* criórito.
cryoscope *n.* crioscopio.
cryoscopical *adj.* crioscópico, -ca.
cryoscopy *n.* crioscopia.
cryospasm *n.* crioespasmo.
cryospray *n.* crioaspersión.
cryostat *n.* crióstato.
cryostylet *n.* crioestilete.
cryostylette *n.* crioestilete.
cryosurgery *n.* criocirugía.
cryothalamectomy *n.* criotalamectomía.
cryotherapy *n.* crioterapia.
cryotolerant *adj.* criotolerante.
cryounit *n.* criounidad.
crypt *n.* cripta.
cryptanamnesia *n.* criptanamnesia.
cryptectomy *n.* criptectomía.
cryptesthesia *n.* criptestesia.
cryptic *adj.* críptico, -ca.
cryptitis *n.* criptitis.
cryptocephalus *n.* criptocéfalo.
cryptococcoma *n.* criptococoma.
cryptococcosis *n.* criptococosis.
Cryptococcus *n.* Cryptococcus.
cryptocrystalline *adj.* criptocristalino, -na.
cryptodeterminant *adj.* criptodeterminante.
cryptodidymus *n.* criptodídimo.
cryptoempyema *n.* criptoempiema.
cryptogenetic *adj.* criptogénico, -ca.
cryptogenic *adj.* criptogénico, -ca, criptógeno, -na.
cryptoglioma *n.* criptoglioma.
cryptolith *n.* criptolito.
cryptomenorrhea *n.* criptomenorrea.
cryptomere *n.* criptómero.
cryptomerorachischisis *n.* criptomerorraquisquisis.
cryptomnesia *n.* criptomnesia.
cryptomnesic *adj.* criptomnésico, -ca.
cryptophthalmia *n.* criptoftalmía.
cryptopiosis *n.* criptopiosis.
cryptoplasmic *adj.* criptoplásmico, -ca.
cryptopodia *n.* criptopodia.
cryptopsychic *adj.* criptopsíquico, -ca.
cryptopsychism *n.* criptopsiquismo.
cryptoradiometer *n.* criptorradiómetro.
cryptorchid *adj.* criptorquídico, -ca.
cryptorchidectomy *n.* criptorquidectomía.
cryptorchidism *n.* criptorquidismo.
cryptorchidopexy *n.* criptorquidopexia.
cryptorchidy *n.* criptorquidia.
cryptorchism *n.* criptorquismo.
cryptorrhea *n.* criptorrea.
cryptorrheic *adj.* criptorreico, -ca.
cryptoscope *n.* criptoscopio.
cryptoscopy *n.* criptoscopia.
cryptosporidiosis *n.* criptosporidiosis, cryptosporidiosis.
Cryptosporidium *n.* Cryptosporidium.
cryptotoxic *adj.* criptotóxico, -ca.
cryptozoite *n.* criptozoíto.
cryptozygous *adj.* criptocigo, -ga.
crystal *n.* cristal².
  asthma crystal cristal de asma.
  blood crystal cristal hemático.
  Böttcher's crystal cristal de Böttcher.
  Charcot-Leyden crystal cristal de Charcot-Leyden.
  Charcot-Neumann crystal cristal de Charcot-Neumann.

Charcot-Robin crystal cristal de Charcot-Robin.
  chiral crystal cristal quiral.
  coffin lid crystal cristal en tapa de ataúd.
  crystal of Reinke cristal de Reinke.
  dumbell crystal cristal del halterio.
  ear crystal cristal del oído.
  Florence crystal cristal de Florence.
  hedgehog crystal cristal en erizo.
  hematoidin crystal cristal de hematoidina.
  hydrate crystal cristal de hidrato.
  knife-rest crystal cristal en mango de cuchillo.
  leukocytic crystal cristal leucocítico.
  Leyden's crystal cristal de Leyden.
  liquid crystal cristal líquido.
  Lubarsch's crystal cristal de Lubarsch.
  rock crystal cristal de roca.
  sperm crystal cristal de esperma.
  spermin crystal cristal de espermina.
  Teichmann's crystal cristal de Teichmann.
  thorn apple crystal cristal de estramonio.
  twin crystal cristal gemelo.
  Virchow's crystal cristal de Virchow.
  whetstone crystal cristal en piedra de afilar.
  Wood's glass crystal cristal de Wood.
crystalbumin *n.* cristalbúmina.
crystallin *n.* cristalina.
  gamma crystallin cristalina gamma.
crystalline *adj.* cristalino, -na.
crystallization *n.* cristalización.
  fern-leaf crystallization cristalización en hojas de helecho.
crystallogram *n.* cristalograma.
crystallography *n.* cristalografía.
crystalloid *n.* cristaloide.
  Charcot-Böttcher crystalloid cristaloide de Charcot-Böttcher.
  crystalloid of Reinke cristaloide de Reinke.
crystallophobia *n.* cristalofobia.
crystalluria *n.* cristaluria.
crytophthalmus *n.* criptoftalmos.
Ctenocephalides *n.* Ctenocephalides.
Ctenus *n.* Ctenus.
cubital *adj.* cubital.
cubitocarpal *adj.* cubitocarpal, cubitocarpiano, -na.
cubitopalmar *adj.* cubitopalmar.
cubitorradial *adj.* cubitorradial.
cubitus *n.* cúbito, cubitus.
  cubitus valgus cúbito valgo, cubitus valgus.
  cubitus varus cúbito varus, cubitus varus.
cuboid *adj.* cuboide, cuboideo, -a, cuboides.
cuboidal *adj.* cuboide, cuboideo, -a.
cudbear *n.* orchilla.
cue *n.* señal.
  vocal cue señal vocal.
cuff *n.* brazal, manguito.
  Dacron cuff manguito de Dacron.
  musculotendinous cuff manguito musculotendinoso.
  pressure cuff manguito de presión.
  rotator cuff manguito rotador del hombro.
cul-de-sac *n.* cul-de-sac.
culdocentesis *n.* culdocentesis.
culdoplasty *n.* culdoplastia.
culdoscope *n.* culdoscopio.
culdoscopy *n.* culdoscopia.
culdotomy *n.* culdotomía.
Culex *n.* Culex.
culicifuge *adj.* culicífugo, -ga.
Culicoides *n.* Culicoides.
culicosis *n.* culicosis.
culmen *n.* culmen.
culture *n.* cultivo.
cumulative *adj.* acumulativo, -va.

cumulus *n.* cúmulo, cumulus.
  cumulus oophorus cúmulo prolígero.
cuneiform *n.* cuneiforme.
cuneocuboid *adj.* cuneocuboide.
cuneonavicular *adj.* cuneonavicular.
cuneoscaphoid *adj.* cuneoescafoide, cuneoscafoide.
cuneus *n.* cuña, cuneus.
cuniculus *n.* cunículo, cuniculus.
cup *n.* copa, taza, ventosa.
  Diogenes cup copa de Diógenes.
  dry cup ventosa seca.
  eye cup copa ocular.
  glaucomatous cup copa glaucomatosa, ventosa glaucomatosa.
  heel cup taza de talón.
  optic cup ventosa óptica.
  physiologic cup copa fisiológica, ventosa fisiológica.
  suction cup ventosa de succión.
  wet cup ventosa escarificada, ventosa húmeda.
cupola *n.* cúpula.
cupped *adj.* acopado, -da.
cupping glass *n.* ventosa.
cupremia *n.* cupremia.
cupric *adj.* cúprico, -ca.
cupriuresis *n.* cupriuresis.
cupriuria *n.* cupriuria.
cuprous *adj.* cuproso, -sa.
cupruresis *n.* cupriuresis, cupruresis.
cupruretic *adj.* cuprurético, -ca.
cupula *n.* cúpula.
cupular *adj.* cupular.
cupuliform *adj.* cupuliforme.
cupulogram *n.* cupulograma.
cupulolithiasis *n.* cupulolitiasis.
cupulometry *n.* cupulometría.
curative *adj.* curativo, -va.
cure *n.* cura.
curet *n.* cureta, legra, legrar.
  Hartmann's curet cureta de Hartmann, legra de Hartmann.
curettage *n.* curetaje, legrado, legrado uterino, raspado.
  apical curettage raspado apical.
  root curettage raspado radicular.
  subgingival curettage raspado subgingival.
  suction curettage raspado por aspiración.
  vacuum curettage raspado por vacío.
curiass *n.* coraza.
  analgesic curiass coraza analgésica.
  tabetic curiass coraza tabética.
curiegram *n.* curiegrama.
curietherapy *n.* curieterapia.
current *n.* corriente.
curvated *adj.* curvado, -da.
curvature *n.* curvatura.
  angular curvature curvatura angular.
  angular spinal curvature curvatura vertebral angular.
  anterior curvature curvatura anterior.
  backward curvature curvatura posterior.
  compensating curvature curvatura de compensación.
  Ellis-Daimoseau's curvature curvatura de Ellis-Daimoseau.
  lateral curvature curvatura lateral.
  lateral spinal curvature curvatura vertebral lateral.
  pontine curvature curvatura protuberancial.
  Pott's curvature curvatura de Pott.
  spinal curvature curvatura espinal, curvatura vertebral.
curve *n.* curva.
  aligment curve curva de alineación.

anti-Monson curve curva anti-Monson.

attenuation curve curva atenuación.

audibility curve curva de audibilidad.

Barnes curve curva de Barnes.

Bragg curve curva de Bragg.

buccal curve curva bucal.

camel curve curva de camello.

carbon dioxide titration curve curva de titulación del dióxido de carbono.

characteristic curve curva característica.

clearance curve curva de aclaramiento.

compensating curve curva de compensación.

curve dose-response curve curva de dosis-efecto, curva de dosis-reacción, curva de dosis-respuesta.

curve of occlusion curva de oclusión.

curve of Spee curva de Spee.

Damoiseau curve curva de Damoiseau.

dental curve curva dental.

distribution curve curva de distribución.

dye-dilution curve curva de dilución de colorante.

epidemic curve curva epidémica.

flow-volume curve curva de flujo-volumen.

Frank-Starling curve curva de Frank-Starling.

frequency curve curva de frecuencia.

Friedman curve curva de Friedman.

Gaussian curve curva de Gauss, curva gaussiana.

glow curve curva de luminiscencia.

growth curve curva de crecimiento.

indicator-dilution curve curva de dilución de indicador.

intracardiac pressure curve curva de presión intracardíaca.

intrauterine growth curve curva de crecimiento intrauterino.

isodose curve curva de isodosis.

isovolume pressure-flow curve curva isovolumétrica de presión-flujo.

Kaplan-Meier survival curve curva de supervivencia de Kaplan-Meier.

labial curve curva labial.

logistic curve curva logística.

milled-in curve curva contorneada.

Monson curve curva de Monson.

muscle curve curva muscular.

nitrogen washout curve curva de lavado del nitrógeno.

normal curve of distribution curva de distribución normal, curva normal de distribución.

oxygen dissociation curve curva de disociación de oxihemoglobina, curva de disociación del oxígeno, curva de disociación oxígeno-hemoglobina.

oxyhemoglobin dissociation curve curva de disociación de oxihemoglobina, curva de disociación del oxígeno, curva de disociación oxígeno-hemoglobina.

pleasure curve curva de pleasure.

Price-Jones curve curva de Price-Jones.

probability curve curva de probabilidad.

pulse curve curva de pulso, curva de pulso.

reverse curve curva inversa, curva invertida.

Starling's curve curva de Starling.

strength-duration curve curva de fuerza-duración.

stress-strain curve curva de tensión-esfuerzo.

survival curve curva de supervivencia.

temperature curve curva de temperatura, curva térmica.

tension curve curva de tensión.

Traube-Hering curve curva de Traube, curva de Traube-Hering.

visibility curve curva de visibilidad.

volume-pressure curve curva de presión-volumen.

von Spee's curve curva de von Spee.

whole-body titration curve curva de titulación de todo el cuerpo.

curvilinear *adj.* curvilíneo, -a.

Cushingoid *adj.* cushingoide.

cusp *n.* cúspide.

cuspad *adv.* cuspad.

cuspid *adj.* cuspídeo, -a.

cuspidate *adj.* cuspidado, -da.

cuspis *n.* cúspide, cuspis, valva[1].

cut *n.* corte.

cone cut corte cónico.

coronal cut corte coronal.

frozen cut corte congelado, corte por congelación.

paraffin cut corte de parafina, corte en parafina.

saggital cut corte sagital.

transversal cut corte transversal.

cutaneomucosal *adj.* cutaneomucoso, -sa.

cutaneous *n.* cutáneo, -a.

cutdown *n.* venostomía.

venous cutdown venostomía.

Cuterebra *n.* Cuterebra.

cuticle *n.* cutícula.

cuticle of the hair cutícula del pelo, cutícula pilosa.

cuticle of the root sheath cutícula de la vaina de la raíz, cutícula de la vaina del folículo piloso.

dental cuticle cutícula dentaria.

enamel cuticle cutícula del esmalte.

keratose cuticle cutícula queratosa.

Nasmyth's cuticle cutícula de Nasmyth.

cuticula *n.* cutícula.

cuticula dentis cutícula dentaria.

cuticula pili cutícula del pelo, cutícula pilosa.

cuticularization *n.* cuticularización.

cutinization *n.* cutinización.

cutireaction *n.* cutirreacción.

cutis *n.* cutis.

cutis anserina cutis anserina, fricasmo.

cutis hyperelastica cutis hiperelástico.

cutis laxa cutis laxa.

cutis marmorata cutis marmorata, cutis marmóreo.

cutis rhomboidalis nuchae cutis romboidal de la nuca.

cutis unctuosa cutis testácea, cutis untuosa.

cutis vera cutis vera, cutis verdadero.

cutis verticis gyrata cutis verticis gyrata.

cutisector *n.* cutisector.

cutization *n.* cutinización, cutización.

cyanephidrosis *n.* cianefridrosis.

Cyanobacteria *n.* cianobacterias.

cyanogenic *adj.* cianogénico, -ca.

cyanophil *n.* cianófilo.

cyanophile *n.* cianófilo.

cyanophilous *adj.* cianófilo, -la.

cyanopia *n.* cianopía.

cyanopsia *n.* cianopía, cianopsia.

cyanosed *adj.* cianosado, -da.

cyanosis *n.* cianosis.

compression cyanosis cianosis por compresión.

cyanosis retinae cianosis de la retina.

enterogenous cyanosis cianosis enterógena.

false cyanosis cianosis falsa.

hereditary methemoglobinemic cyanosis cianosis hereditaria metahemoglobinúrica.

late cyanosis cianosis tardía.

shunt cyanosis cianosis por movimiento.

tardive cyanosis cianosis tardía.

toxic cyanosis cianosis tóxica.

cyanotic *adj.* cianótico, -ca.

cyanuria *n.* cianuria.

cyanurin *n.* cianurina.

cybernetics *n.* cibernética.

cybrid *n.* cíbrido.

cyclarthrodial *adj.* ciclartrodial.

cyclarthrosis *n.* ciclartrosis.

cycle *n.* ciclo.

anovulatory cycle ciclo anovulatorio.

brain wave cycle ciclo de las ondas cerebrales.

carbon cycle ciclo del anhídrico carbónico, ciclo del carbono.

carbon dioxide cycle ciclo del anhídrico carbónico, ciclo del carbono.

cardiac cycle ciclo cardíaco.

cell cycle ciclo celular.

chewing cycle ciclo masticatorio.

citric acid cycle ciclo del ácido cítrico.

cori cycle ciclo de cori.

cycle per second ciclo por segundo.

dicarboxylic acid cycle ciclo del ácido dicarboxílico.

endogenous cycle ciclo endógeno.

estrous cycle ciclo estrual.

exoerythrocytic cycle ciclo exoeritrocítico.

exogenous cycle ciclo exógeno.

fatty acid oxidation cycle ciclo de oxidación de ácidos grasos.

force cycle ciclo forzado.

genesial cycle ciclo genésico.

hair cycle ciclo del pelo.

Krebs cycle ciclo de Krebs.

Krebs-Henseleit cycle ciclo de Krebs-Henseleit.

life cycle ciclo vital.

menstrual cycle ciclo menstrual.

nitrogen cycle ciclo del nitrógeno.

ornithine cycle ciclo de la ornitina.

ovarian cycle ciclo oogenético, ciclo ovárico.

pentose phosphate cycle ciclo de las pentosa fosfato.

reproductive cycle ciclo reproductivo.

restored cycle ciclo restaurado.

returning cycle ciclo de retorno.

Ross cycle ciclo de Ross.

succinic acid cycle ciclo del ácido succínico.

tricarboxilic acid cycle ciclo del ácido tricarboxílico.

urea cycle ciclo de la urea.

visual cycle ciclo visual.

cyclectomy *n.* ciclectomía.

cyclencephalia *n.* ciclencefalia.

cyclencephaly *n.* ciclencefalia.

cyclic *adj.* cíclico, -ca.

cyclicotomy *n.* ciclicotomía.

cyclitis *n.* ciclitis.

heterochromic cyclitis ciclitis heterocrómica.

plastic cyclitis ciclitis plástica.

purulent cyclitis ciclitis purulenta.

cyclocephalia *n.* ciclocefalia.

cyclocephaly *n.* ciclocefalia.

cyclochoroiditis *n.* ciclocoroiditis.

cyclocryotherapy *n.* ciclocrioterapia.

cyclodialysis *n.* ciclodiálisis.

cyclodiathermy *n.* ciclodiatermia.

cycloduction *n.* cicl
ducción.

cycloelectrolysis *n.* cicloelectrólisis.

cyclogeny *n.* ciclogenia.

cyclogram *n.* ciclograma.

cycloid *n.* cicloide.

cyclokeratitis *n.* cicloqueratitis.

cyclomastopathy *n.* ciclomastopatía.

cyclopea *n.* ciclopea, ciclopía.

cyclopean *adj.* ciclópeo, -a.

cyclopentenophenanthrene *n.* ciclopenta-nofenantreno.

cyclophoria *n.* cicloforia.

cyclophorometer *n.* cicloforómetro.

cyclophotocoagulation *n.* ciclofotocoagu-lación.

cyclophrenia *n.* ciclofrenia.

cyclopia *n.* ciclopía.

cyclopian *adj.* ciclopiano, -na.

cycloplegia *n.* cicloplejía.

cycloplegic *adj.* cicloplejico, -ca.

cyclops *adj.* ciclope, cíclope.

cyclosis *n.* ciclosis.

cyclospasm *n.* cicloespasmo, ciclospasmo.

cyclostat *n.* cicloóstato.

cyclothymia *n.* ciclotimia.

cyclothymiac *adj.* ciclotímico, -ca.

cyclotome *n.* ciclótomo.

cyclotomy *n.* ciclotomía.

cyclotorsion *n.* clotorsión.

cyclotron *n.* ciclotrón.

cyclotropia *n.* ciclotropía.

cyclotymic *adj.* ciclotímico, ca.

cyesis *n.* ciesis.

cylinder *n.* cilindro.

  Bence Jones cylinder cilindro de Bence Jones.

  crossed cylinder cilindro cruzado.

  Külz's cylinder cilindro de Külz.

cylindrarthrosis *n.* cilindrartrosis.

cylindraxis *n.* cilindroeje.

cylindrical *adj.* cilíndrico, -ca.

cylindriform *adj.* cilindriforme.

cylindroadenoma *n.* cilindroadenoma.

cylindrocellular *adj.* cilindrocelular.

cylindroid *n.* cilindroide.

cylindroma *n.* cilindroma.

cylindruria *n.* cilindruria.

cyllosoma *n.* cilosoma.

cyllosomus *n.* cilósomo.

cymba conchae *n.* cimba.

cymbocephalia *n.* cimbocefalia.

cymbocephalic *adj.* cimbocefálico, -ca.

cymbocephalous *adj.* cimbocefálico, -ca.

cynanche *n.* cinanquia.

cynanthropy *n.* cinantropía.

cynocephalus *n.* cinocéfalo.

cynocephaly *n.* cinocefalia.

cynodont *n.* cinodonto.

Cynomya *n.* Cynomya.

cynophobia *n.* cinofobia.

cynorexia *n.* cinorexia.

cypridophobia *n.* cipridofobia, ciprifobia.

cyrtograph *n.* cirtógrafo.

cyrtometer *n.* cirtómetro.

cyrtosis *n.* cirtosis.

cyst *n.* quiste.

  Acrel's cyst quiste de Acrel.

  allantoic cyst quiste alantoico.

  alveolar cyst quiste alveolar.

  alveolar hydatid cyst quiste hidatídico alveolar.

  amnionic cyst quiste amniótico.

  aneurysmal bone cyst quiste óseo aneurismático.

  angioblastic cyst quiste angioblástico.

  apical cyst quiste apical.

  apical periodontal cyst quiste apical periodontal, quiste periodontal apical.

  arachnoid cyst quiste aracnoideo.

  atheromatous cyst quiste ateromatoso.

  Baker's cyst quiste de Baker.

  Bartholin's cyst quiste de Bartholin, quiste de Bartolino.

  benign multilocular cyst quiste renal multilocular.

  Blessig's cyst quiste de Blessig.

  blood cyst quiste hemático, quiste hemorrágico, quiste sanguíneo.

  blue dome cyst quiste abovedado azul, quiste en cúpula azul.

  bone cyst quiste óseo.

  Boyer's cyst quiste de Boyer.

  branchial cleft cyst quiste de la hendidura branquial.

  branchial cyst quiste branquial, quiste branquiógeno.

  branchiogenetic cyst quiste branquial, quiste branquiógeno.

  branchiogenous cyst quiste branquial, quiste branquiógeno.

  bronchial cyst quiste broncogénico, quiste broncógeno, quiste broncopulmonar, quiste bronquial.

  bronchogenic cyst quiste broncogénico, quiste broncógeno, quiste broncopulmonar, quiste bronquial.

  bronchopulmonary cyst quiste broncogénico, quiste broncógeno, quiste broncopulmonar, quiste bronquial.

  bursal cyst quiste bursal.

  butter cyst quiste en mantequilla.

  calcifying and keratinizing odontogenic cyst quiste odontogénico y queratinizante.

  calcifying odontogenic cyst quiste odontogénico calcificante.

  cerebellar cyst quiste cerebeloso.

  cervical cyst quiste cervical.

  chocolate cyst quiste achocolatado, quiste de chocolate.

  choledochal cyst quiste del colédoco.

  choledochus cyst quiste del colédoco.

  chyle cyst quiste de quilo.

  colloid cyst quiste coloidal, quiste coloide, quiste coloideo.

  colloidal cyst quiste coloidal, quiste coloide, quiste coloideo.

  compound cyst quiste compuesto.

  congenital cyst quiste congénito.

  congenital preauricular cyst quiste preauricular congénito.

  corpora lutea cyst quiste del cuerpo amarillo.

  corpus luteum cyst quiste del cuerpo amarillo.

  Cowper's cyst quiste de Cowper.

  craniobuccal cyst quiste craneobucal.

  craniopharyngeal duct cyst quiste del conducto craneofaríngeo.

  cutaneous cyst quiste cutáneo, quiste cuticular.

  cuticular cyst quiste cutáneo, quiste cuticular.

  cyst of the liver quiste hepático.

  Dandy-Walker cyst quiste de Dandy-Walker.

  daughter cyst quiste hijo.

  dental cyst quiste dental.

  dental lamina cyst quiste de la lámina dental.

  dentigerous cyst quiste dentígero.

  dentoalveolar cyst quiste dentoalveolar.

  dermoid cyst quiste dermoide, quiste dermoideo.

  dermoid cyst of the ovary quiste dermoide del ovario.

  dilatation cyst quiste por dilatación.

  distention cyst quiste por distensión.

  duplication cyst quiste por duplicación.

  echinococcus cyst quiste de equinococos, quiste equinocócico.

  endometrial cyst quiste endometrial.

  endothelial cyst quiste endotelial.

  enteric cyst quiste entérico, quiste enterógeno.

  enterogenous cyst quiste entérico, quiste enterógeno.

  ependymal cyst quiste ependimario.

  epidermal cyst quiste epidérmico.

  epidermal inclusion cyst quiste epidérmico de inclusión.

  epidermoid cyst quiste epidermoide, quiste epidermoideo.

  epididymal cyst quiste de epidídimo.

  epithelial cyst quiste epitelial.

  eruption cyst quiste de erupción.

  extravasation cyst quiste por extravasación.

  exudation cyst quiste de exudación, quiste por exudación.

  fissural cyst quiste fisural.

  follicular cyst quiste folicular.

  gallbladder cyst quiste bursal.

  ganglionic cyst quiste ganglionar.

  Gartnerian cyst quiste de Gartner, quiste gartneriano.

  Gartner's cyst quiste de Gartner, quiste gartneriano.

  Gartner's duct cyst quiste de Gartner, quiste gartneriano.

  gas cyst quiste gaseoso.

  gingival cyst quiste gingival.

  globulomaxillary cyst quiste globulomaxilar.

  Gorlin cyst quiste de Gorlin.

  granddaughter cyst quiste nieto.

  hemorrhagic cyst quiste hemático, quiste hemorrágico.

  hepatic cyst quiste hepático.

  hydatid cyst quiste hidatídico.

  implantation cyst quiste de implantación, quiste por implantación, quiste por inclusión.

  implantation dermoid cyst quiste dermoide de implantación.

  inclusion cyst quiste de implantación, quiste por implantación, quiste por inclusión.

  inclusion dermoid cyst quiste dermoide de inclusión.

  intracordal cyst quiste vocal.

  intraepithelial cyst quiste intraepitelial.

  intraluminal cyst quiste intraluminal.

  intrapituitary cyst quiste intrapituitario.

  involution cyst quiste de involución, quiste por involución.

  Iwanoff's cyst quiste de Iwanoff.

  junctional cyst quiste de unión.

  keratinous cyst quiste queratinizante, quiste queratinoso.

  lacteal cyst quiste láctico.

  lateral periodontal cyst quiste lateral periodontal, quiste periodontal lateral.

  leptomeningeal cyst quiste leptomeníngeo.

  luteal cyst quiste luteínico, quiste lúteo.

  lutein cyst quiste luteínico, quiste lúteo.

  median anterior maxillary cyst quiste maxilar anterior mediano.

  median mandibular cyst quiste mandibular mediano.

  median palatal cyst quiste del paladar mediano, quiste palatino mediano.

  Meibomian cyst quiste de Meibomio, quiste meibomiano.

  mesenteric cyst quiste mesentérico.

  mesonephroid cyst quiste mesonéfrico, quiste mesonefroide.

  milk cyst quiste de la leche, quiste de leche.

  mother cyst quiste madre.

  mucoid cyst quiste mucoide.

  mucous cyst quiste mucoso.

  multilocular cyst quiste multilocular, quiste renal multilocular.

  multilocular hydatid cyst quiste hidatídico multiloculado, quiste hidatídico multilocular.

  multiloculate hydatid cyst quiste hidatídico multiloculado, quiste hidatídico multilocular.

myxoid cyst quiste mixoide.
nasoalveolar cyst quiste nasoalveolar, quiste nasolabial.
nasolabial cyst quiste nasoalveolar, quiste nasolabial.
nasopalatine duct cyst quiste del conducto nasopalatino.
necrotic cyst quiste necrótico.
neural cyst quiste neural.
neurenteric cyst quiste neurentérico.
nevoid cyst quiste nevoide.
odontogenic cyst quiste odontogénico, quiste odontógeno.
oil cyst quiste oleoso.
omental cyst quiste epiploico.
oophoritic cyst quiste ooforético.
osseous hydatid cyst quiste hidatídico óseo, quiste óseo hidatídico.
ovarian cyst quiste del ovario, quiste ovárico.
pancreatic cyst quiste pancreático.
paranephric cyst quiste paranéfrico, quiste pararrenal.
paraovarian cyst quiste paraovárico, quiste parovárico, quiste parovárico.
parasitic cyst quiste parasitario, quiste parásito.
parvilocular cyst quiste parvilocular.
pearl cyst quiste en perla, quiste perlado.
periapical cyst quiste periapical.
pericardial cyst quiste pericárdico.
periodontal cyst quiste periodontal.
phaeomycotic cyst quiste feomicótico.
pilar cyst quiste pilar, quiste pilífero, quiste piloso.
piliferous cyst quiste pilar, quiste pilífero, quiste piloso.
pilonidal cyst quiste pilonidal.
placental cyst quiste placentario.
porencephalic cyst quiste porencefálico.
primordial cyst quiste primordial.
proliferating tricholemmal cyst quiste proliferante del tricolema.
proliferation cyst quiste proliferante, quiste proliferativo.
proliferative cyst quiste proliferante, quiste proliferativo.
proligerous cyst quiste prolígero.
protozoan cyst quiste de protozoarios.
pseudomucinous cyst quiste pseudomucinoso, quiste seudomucinoso, quiste seudomucinoso.
radiculodental cyst quiste de la raíz, quiste radicular, quiste radiculodental.
Rathke's cyst quiste de Rathke.
Rathke's pouch cyst quiste de la bolsa de Rathke.
renal cyst quiste renal.
residual cyst quiste residual.
rete cyst of ovary quiste de la red ovárica.
retention cyst quiste por retención.
root cyst quiste de la raíz, quiste radicular, quiste radiculodental.
Sampson's cyst quiste de Sampson.
sanguineous cyst quiste sanguíneo.
sebaceous cyst quiste sebáceo.
secondary cyst quiste secundario.
secretory cyst quiste secretorio.
seminal cyst quiste seminal.
sequestration cyst quiste por secuestración.
serous cyst quiste seroso.
simple bone cyst quiste óseo solitario.
simple cyst quiste simple.
simple renal cyst quiste renal simple.
soap cyst quiste de jabón.
solitary bone cyst quiste óseo solitario.
Stafne bone cyst quiste óseo de Stafne.

sterile cyst quiste estéril.
subchondral cyst quiste subcondral.
sublingual cyst quiste sublingual.
subsynovial cyst quiste subsinovial.
suprasellar cyst quiste supraselar.
synovial cyst quiste sinovial.
Tarlov's cyst quiste de Tarlov.
tarry cyst quiste alquitranado.
tarsal cyst quiste tarsal, quiste tarsiano.
teratomatous cyst quiste teratomatoso.
thecal cyst quiste tecal.
theca-lutein cyst quiste tecaluteínico.
thymic cyst quiste tímico.
thyroglossal cyst quiste tirogloso, quiste tirolingual.
thyroglossal duct cyst quiste del conducto tirogloso.
thyroid dermoid cyst quiste dermoide tiroideo.
thyrolingual cyst quiste tirogloso, quiste tirolingual.
Tornwaldt's cyst quiste de Tornwaldt.
traumatic bone cyst quiste óseo solitario.
trichilemmal cyst quiste tricolémico, quiste triquilemal.
true cyst quiste verdadero.
tubal dermoid cyst quiste dermoide tubárico.
tubo-ovarian cyst quiste tuboovárico.
tubular cyst quiste tubular.
umbilical cyst quiste umbilical.
unicameral bone cyst quiste unicameral, quiste unilocular.
unicameral cyst quiste unicameral, quiste unilocular.
unilocular cyst quiste unicameral, quiste unilocular.
unilocular hydatid cyst quiste hidatídico unilocular.
urachal cyst quiste del uraco, quiste uracal.
urinary cyst quiste urinario.
vaginal cyst quiste vaginal.
vitellointestinal cyst quiste vitelointestinal.
Wolffian cyst quiste de Wolff, quiste wolffiano.
cystadenocarcinoma *n.* cistadenocarcinoma.
cystadenoma *n.* cistadenoma.
mucinous cystadenoma cistadenoma mucinoso.
papillary cystadenoma cistadenoma papilar.
papillary cystadenoma lymphomatosum cistadenoma papilar linfomatoso.
pseudomucinous cystadenoma cistadenoma seudomucinoso.
serous cystadenoma cistadenoma seroso.
cystalgia *n.* cistalgia.
cystathioninuria *n.* cistationinuria.
cystatrophia *n.* cistatrofia.
cystauchenitis *n.* cistauquenitis.
cystauchenotomy *n.* cistauquenotomía.
cystduodenostomy *n.* quistoduodenostomía.
cystectasia *n.* cistectasia.
cystectasy *n.* cistectasia.
cystectomy *n.* cistectomía, quistectomía.
Bartholin's cystectomy cistectomía de Bartholin.
partial cystectomy cistectomía parcial.
radical cystectomy cistectomía radical.
total cystectomy cistectomía total.
cystelcosis *n.* cistelcosis.
cystendesis *n.* cistendesis.
cystgastrostomy *n.* quistogastrostomía.
cystic *adj.* cístico, -ca, quístico, -ca[1].
cysticercoid *n.* cisticercoide.
cysticercosis *n.* cisticercosis.
Cysticercus *n.* cisticerco, Cysticercus.
cysticolithectomy *n.* cisticolitectomía.

cysticolithotripsy *n.* cisticolitotripsia.
cysticotomy *n.* cisticotomía.
cysticotrachelotomy *n.* cisticotraquelotomía.
cystifelleotomy *n.* cistifeleotomía, cistifelotomía.
cystiform *adj.* cistiforme.
cystigerous *adj.* cistífero, -ra, cistígero, -ra.
cystinemia *n.* cistinemia.
cystinosis *n.* cistinosis.
cystinuria *n.* cistinuria.
familial cystinuria cistinuria familiar.
cystiphorous *adj.* cistíforo, -ra.
cystirrhagia *n.* cistirragia, cistorragia.
cystistaxis *n.* cististaxis.
cystitis *n.* cistitis.
acute catarrhal cystitis cistitis aguda.
allergic cystitis cistitis alérgica.
bacterial cystitis cistitis bacteriana.
croupous cystitis cistitis crupal.
cystitis colli cistitis cervical, cistitis del cuello.
cystitis cystica cistitis quística.
cystitis glandularis cistitis glandular.
cystitis papillomatosa cistitis papilomatosa.
cystitis senilis cistitis senil.
diphtheritic cystitis cistitis diftérica.
emphysematous cystitis cistitis enfisematosa.
eosinophilic cystitis cistitis eosinófila.
exfoliative cystitis cistitis exfoliativa.
follicular cystitis cistitis folicular.
hemorrhagic cystitis cistitis hemorrágica.
incrusted cystitis cistitis incrustada.
interstitial cystitis cistitis intersticial crónica.
viral cystitis cistitis vírica.
cystitome *n.* cistítomo.
cystitomy *n.* cistitomía.
cystoadenoma *n.* cistadenoma, cistoadenoma.
cystoblast *n.* cistoblasto.
cystocarcinoma *n.* cistocarcinoma.
cystocele *n.* cistocele.
cystochromoscopy *n.* cistocromoscopia.
cystocolostomy *n.* cistocolostomía.
cystocopy *n.* cistoscopia.
cystodiverticulum *n.* cistodivertículo.
cystoduodenostomy *n.* cistoduodenostomía.
cystodynia *n.* cistodinia.
cystoelytroplasty *n.* cistoelitroplastia.
cystoenterocele *n.* cistoenterocele.
cystoenterostomy *n.* cistoenterostomía.
cystoepiplocele *n.* cistoepiplocele.
cystoepithelioma *n.* cistoepitelioma.
cystofibroma *n.* cistofibroma.
cystogastrostomy *n.* cistogastrostomía.
cystogram *n.* cistograma.
voiding cystogram cistograma de evacuación.
cystography *n.* cistografía, quistografía.
cystoid *n.* cistoide.
cystojejunostomy *n.* quistoyeyunostomía.
cystolith *n.* cistolito.
cystolithectomy *n.* cistolitectomía.
cystolithiasis *n.* cistolitiasis.
cystolithic *adj.* cistolítico, -ca.
cystolithotomy *n.* cistolitotomía.
cystoma *n.* cistoma.
cystoma serosum simplex cistoma seroso simple.
cystometer *n.* cistómetro.
cystometrogram *n.* cistometrograma.
cystometrography *n.* cistometrografía.
cystometry *n.* cistometría.
cystomorphous *adj.* cistomorfo, -fa.
cystomyoma *n.* cistomioma.
cystomyxoadenoma *n.* cistomixoadenoma.
cystomyxoma *n.* cistomixoma.
cystonephrosis *n.* cistonefrosis.

cystoneuralgia *n.* cistoneuralgia.
cystopanendoscopy *n.* cistopanendoscopia.
cystoparalysis *n.* cistoparálisis.
cystopericystectomy *n.* quistoperiquistectomía.
   subtotal cystopericystectomy quistoperiquistectomía subtotal.
   total cystopericystectomy quistoperiquistectomía total.
cystopexy *n.* cistopexia.
cystopherous *adj.* cistífero, -ra, cistófero, -ra.
cystophorous *adj.* cistífero, -ra, cistóforo, -ra.
cystophotography *n.* cistofotografía.
cystopielography *n.* cistopielografía.
cystoplasty *n.* cistoplastia.
cystoplegia *n.* cistoplejía.
cystoproctostomy *n.* cistoproctostomía.
cystoptosis *n.* cistoptosis.
cystopyelitis *n.* cistopielitis.
cystopyelonephritis *n.* cistopielonefritis.
cystoradiography *n.* cistorradiografía.
cystorectostomy *n.* cistorrectostomía.
cystorraphy *n.* cistorrafia.
cystorrhagia *n.* cistorragia.
cystorrhea *n.* cistorrea.
cystosarcoma *n.* cistosarcoma.
   cystosarcoma phylloides cistosarcoma filoides.
   cystosarcoma phylloides of the breast cistosarcoma filoides.
cystoschisis *n.* cistosquisis.
cystosclerosis *n.* cistoesclerosis, cistosclerosis.
cystoscope *n.* cistoscopio.
cystoscopic *adj.* cistoscópico, -ca.
cystose *adj.* quístico, -ca².
cystospasm *n.* cistoespasmo, cistospasmo.
cystostaxis *n.* cistostaxis.
cystostomy *n.* cistostomía.
cystotome *n.* cistótomo.
cystotomy *n.* cistotomía.
   suprapubic cystotomy cistotomía hipogástrica, cistotomíasuprapúbica.
cystotrachelotomy *n.* cistotraquelotomía.
cystoureteritis *n.* cistoureteritis.
cystoureterogram *n.* cistoureterograma.
cystoureteropyelitis *n.* cistoureteropielitis.
cystourethritis *n.* cistouretritis.
cystourethrocele *n.* cistouretrocele.
cystourethrogram *n.* cistouretrograma.
cystourethrography *n.* cistouretrografía.
cystourethroscope *n.* cistouretroscopio.
cystous *adj.* cístico, -ca, quístico, -ca².

cystoyreterography *n.* cistoureterografía.
cystron *n.* cistrón.
cystygerous *adj.* cistífero, -ra.
cytapheresis *n.* citaféresis.
cytemia *n.* citemia.
cythemolysis *n.* citemólisis.
cytoarchitectonic *adj.* citoarquitectónico, -ca.
cytoarchitectonics *n.* citoarquitectura.
cytoarchitectural *adj.* citoarquitectónico, -ca.
cytoarchitecture *n.* citoarquitectura.
cytobiology *n.* citobiología.
cytobiotaxis *n.* citobiotaxis.
cytocentrum *n.* citocentro.
cytochalasins *n.* citocalasinas.
cytochemistry *n.* citoquímica.
cytocidal *adj.* citocida².
cytocide *n.* citocida¹.
cytocinesis *n.* citocinesis.
cytoclasis *n.* citoclasia, citoclasis.
cytoclastic *adj.* citoclástico, -ca.
cytodiagnosis *n.* citodiagnóstico.
cytodieresis *n.* citodiéresis.
cytogenesis *n.* citogénesis, citogenia.
cytogeneticist *n.* citogenetista.
cytogenetics *n.* citogenética.
cytogenic *adj.* citogénico, -ca.
cytogenous *adj.* citógeno, -na.
cytoglycopenia *n.* citoglucopenia.
cytoid *adj.* citoide.
cytokine *n.* citocina.
cytologic *adj.* citológico, -ca.
cytologist *n.* citólogo, -ga.
cytology *n.* citología.
   aspiration biopsy cytology citología biópsica por aspiración.
   cervicovaginal cytology citología cervicovaginal.
   exfoliative cytology citología exfoliativa.
cytolysin *n.* citolisina.
cytolysis *n.* citólisis.
cytolysosome *n.* citolisosoma.
cytolytic *adj.* citolítico, -ca.
cytomegalic *adj.* citomegálico, -ca.
cytomegaloviruria *n.* citomegaloviruria.
cytomegalovirus *n.* citomegalovirus.
cytomembrane *n.* citomembrana.
cytomere *n.* citómera, citómero.
cytometaplasia *n.* citometaplasia.
cytometer *n.* citómetro.
cytometry *n.* citometría.
   flow cytometry citometría de flujo.

cytomorphology *n.* citomorfología.
cytomorphosis *n.* citomorfosis.
cytomycosis *n.* citomicosis.
cytopathic *adj.* citopático, -ca.
cytopathogenic *adj.* citopatógénico, -ca.
cytopathologic *adj.* citopatológico, -ca.
cytopathological *adj.* citopatológico, -ca.
cytopathologist *n.* citopatólogo, -ga.
cytopathology *n.* citopatología.
cytopathy *n.* citopatía.
cytopempsis *n.* citopempsis.
cytopenia *n.* citopenia.
cytophagous *adj.* citófago, -ga.
cytophagy *n.* citofagia.
cytophil *adj.* citófilo, -la.
cytophilaxis *n.* citofilaxis.
cytophiletic *adj.* citofilético, -ca.
cytophilic *adj.* citofílico, -ca.
cytophotometry *n.* citofotometría.
cytophylactic *adj.* citofiláctico, -ca.
cytopipette *n.* citopipeta.
cytoplasm *n.* citoplasma.
cytoplasmic *adj.* citoplasmático, -ca.
cytopoiesis *n.* citopoyesis.
cytopreparation *n.* citopreparación.
cytoscopy *n.* citoscopia.
cytosis *n.* citosis.
cytoskeleton *n.* citoesqueleto.
cytosmear *n.* citofrotis.
cytosome *n.* citosoma.
cytostasis *n.* citostasis.
cytotactic *adj.* citotáctico, -ca.
cytotaxia *n.* citotaxia.
cytotaxis *n.* citotaxia, citotaxis.
cytotherapy *n.* citoterapia.
cythesis *n.* citotesis.
cytotoxic *adj.* citotóxico, -ca.
cytotoxicity *n.* citotoxicidad.
   antibody dependent cell-mediated cytotoxicity citotoxicidad celular anticuerpo-dependiente, citotoxicidad celular dependiente de anticuerpo.
   lymphocyte-mediated cytotoxicity citotoxicidad mediada por linfocitos.
cytotoxin *n.* citotoxina.
cytotrophoblast *n.* citotrofoblasto.
cytotropism *n.* citotropismo.
cytozoic *adj.* citozoico, -ca.
cytozoon *n.* citozoario, citozoo.
cytozyme *n.* citocima, citozima.
cyturia *n.* cituria.

D d

dacryadenalgia *n.* dacriadenalgia, dacrioadenalgia.

dacryadenitis *n.* dacriadenitis.

dacryagogatresia *n.* dacriagogatresia.

dacryagogic *adj.* dacriagógico, -ca, dacriogógico, -ca.

dacrycystoptosia *n.* dacriocistoptosia, dacriocistoptosis.

dacryelcosis *n.* dacrielcosis, dacrihelcosis, dacriohelcosis, dacrionoma.

dacryoadenectomy *n.* dacriadenectomía.

dacryoadenitis *n.* dacriadenitis, dacrioadenitis.

dacryoblennorrhea *n.* dacrioblenorrea.

dacryocanaliculitis *n.* dacriocanaliculitis.

dacryocele *n.* dacriocele.

dacryocistitome *n.* dacriocistítomo, dacriocistótomo.

dacryocyst *n.* dacriocisto.

dacryocystalgia *n.* dacriocistalgia.

dacryocystectasia *n.* dacriocistectasia.

dacryocystectomy *n.* dacriocistestomía.

dacryocystis *n.* dacriocisto.

dacryocystitis *n.* dacriocistitis.

dacryocystoblennorrhea *n.* dacriocistoblennorrea.

dacryocystocele *n.* dacriocistocele.

dacryocystoethmoidostomy *n.* dacriocistoetmoidostomía.

dacryocystogram *n.* dacriocistograma.

dacryocystograph *n.* dacriocistografía.

dacryocystoptosis *n.* dacriocistoptosia, dacriocistoptosis, dacrioooptosis.

dacryocystorhinostenosis *n.* dacriocistorrinoestenosis.

dacryocystorhinostomy *n.* dacriocistorrinotomía.

dacryocystorhinotomy *n.* dacriocistorrinotomía.

dacryocystostenosis *n.* dacriocistostenosis.

dacryocystostomy *n.* dacriocistostomía.

dacryocystosyringotomy *n.* dacriocistosiringotomía.

dacryocystotome *n.* dacriocistítomo, dacriocistótomo.

dacryodenalgia *n.* dacriadenalgia, dacrioadenalgia.

dacryogenic *adj.* dacriógeno, -na.

dacryohelcosis *n.* dacrielcosis, dacrihelcosis, dacriohelcosis.

dacryohemorrhea *n.* dacriohemorragia, dacriohemorrea.

dacryolith *n.* dacriolito.

Desmarres' dacryolith dacriolito de Desmarres.

dacryolithiasis *n.* dacriolitiasis.

dacryoma *n.* dacrioma.

dacryon *n.* dacrión.

dacryops *n.* dacriops.

dacryopyorrhea *n.* dacriopiorrea.

dacryopyosis *n.* dacriopiosis.

dacryorhinocystotomy *n.* dacriorrinocistotomía.

dacryorrhea *n.* dacriorrea, dacriorrisis.

dacryoscintigraphy *n.* dacriocentellografía.

dacryosinusitis *n.* dacriosinusitis.

dacryosolenitis *n.* dacriosolenitis.

dacryostenosis *n.* dacrioestenosis, dacriostenosis.

dacryosyrinx *n.* dacriosirinx.

dactilar *adj.* dactilar.

dactiliform *adj.* dactiliforme.

dactyl *n.* dáctilo.

dactylagra *n.* dactilagra.

dactylalgia *n.* dactilalgia.

dactyledema *n.* dactiledema.

dactylia *n.* dactilia.

dactylion *n.* dactilio, dactilión.

dactylitis *n.* dactilitis.

sickle cell dactylitis dactilitis drepanocítica.

strumous dactylitis dactilitis estrumosa.

syphilitic dactylitis dactilitis sifilítica.

tuberculous dactylitis dactilitis tuberculosa.

dactylium *n.* dactilio, dactilión, dactylium.

dactylocampsiasis *n.* dactilocampsia, dactilocampsis.

dactylocampsis *n.* dactilocampsia, dactilocampsis.

dactylocampsodynia *n.* dactilocampsodinia.

dactylodinia *n.* dactilodinia.

dactylogram *n.* dactilograma.

dactylography *n.* dactilografía.

dactylogryposis *n.* dactilogriposis.

dactylology *n.* dactilolalia, dactilología.

dactylolysis *n.* dactilólisis.

dactylolysis spontanea dactilólisis espontánea.

dactylomegaly *n.* dactilomegalia.

Dactylomyia *n.* Dactylomyia.

dactylophasia *n.* dactilofasia.

dactyloscopy *n.* dactiloscopia.

dactylospasm *n.* dactiloespasmo, dactilospasmo.

daisy *n.* margarita.

daltonian *adj.* daltónico, -ca.

daltonism *n.* daltonismo.

dam *n.* dique.

post dam dique posterior.

rubber dam dique de goma, dique de hule.

damping *n.* amortiguación, amortiguamiento².

dance *n.* danza.

brachial dance danza humeral.

hilar dance danza hiliar.

hilus dance danza del hilio.

Saint Anthony's dance danza de san Antonio.

Saint John's dance danza de san Juan.

Saint Vitus dance baile de san Vito, danza de san Vito.

spatial dance danza espacial.

dandruff *n.* caspa.

dark *adj.* oscuro, -ra.

dartoic *adj.* dartoico, -ca.

dartoid *adj.* dartoideo, -a.

dartos *n.* dartos.

dartos mullebris dartos femenino.

dartre *n.* dartros.

dartrous *adj.* dartroso, -sa.

Darwinian *adj.* darwiniano, -na.

Darwinism *n.* darwinismo.

database *n.* base de datos.

daturism *n.* daturismo.

deacidification *n.* desacidificación.

dead *adj.* muerto, -ta.

deadly *adj.* mortífero, -ra.

deaf *adj.* sordo, -da.

deafferentation *n.* desaferenciación, desaferentación.

deaf-mute *adj., n.* sordomudo, -da.

deaf-mutism *n.* sordomudez.

endemic deaf-mutism sordomudez endémica.

deafness *n.* cofosis, sordera.

acoustic trauma deafness sordera por traumatismo acústico, sordera traumática acústica.

Alexander's deafness sordera de Alexander.

boilermaker's deafness sordera del calderero.

central deafness sordera central.

cerebral deafness sordera cerebral, sordera cortical.

conductive deafness sordera de conducción.

cortical deafness sordera cerebral, sordera cortical.

functional deafness sordera funcional.

high frequency deafness sordera de alta frecuencia.

industrial deafness sordera industrial.

labyrinthine deafness sordera laberíntica.

low tone deafness sordera de tonos bajos.

malarial deafness sordera palúdica.

midbrain deafness sordera mesencefálica.

Mondini deafness sordera de Mondini.

music deafness sordera musical.

nerve deafness sordera nerviosa, sordera neural, sordera neurosensorial.

neural deafness sordera nerviosa, sordera neural, sordera neurosensorial.

occupational deafness sordera ocupacional.

organic deafness sordera orgánica.

perceptive deafness sordera perceptiva.

postlingual deafness sordera poslingual.

prelingual deafness sordera prelingual.

psychogenic deafness sordera psicogénica.

retrocochlear deafness sordera retrococlear.

Scheibe's deafness sordera de Scheibe.

sensorioneural deafness sordera sensitivo-nerviosa, sordera sensorioneural.

tone deafness sordera de tonos, sordera para los tonos.

word deafness sordera de las palabras, sordera verbal.
dealbation *n.* dealbación.
dealcoholization *n.* desalcoholización.
deallergization *n.* desalergización.
deallergize *v.* desalergizar.
deamidation *n.* desamidación.
deamidization *n.* desamidización.
deamidize *v.* desamidizar.
deamination *n.* desaminación.
deaminization *n.* desaminización.
deaminize *v.* desaminizar.
deaquation *n.* deacuación.
dearterialization *n.* desarterialización.
death *n.* deceso, muerte.
  accidental death muerte accidental.
  apparent death mors putativa, muerte aparente.
  assisted death muerte asistida.
  black death muerte negra.
  brain death muerte encefálica.
  cell death muerte celular.
  cerebral death muerte cerebral.
  cot death muerte en la cuna.
  early fetal death muerte fetal temprana.
  fetal death muerte fetal.
  functional death muerte funcional.
  genetic death muerte genética.
  infant death muerte infantil.
  intermediate fetal death muerte fetal intermedia.
  late fetal death muerte fetal tardía.
  liver death muerte hepática.
  local death muerte local.
  maternal death muerte materna.
  molecular death muerte molecular.
  natural death muerte natural.
  neocortical death muerte neocortical.
  neonatal death muerte neonatal.
  perinatal death muerte perinatal.
  somatic death muerte somática.
  sudden cardiac death muerte cardíaca súbita.
  sudden death mors subitanea, muerte súbita.
  systemic death muerte sistémica.
  true death muerte real.
  unexpected death mors subitanea, muerte súbita.
  violent death muerte a mano airada, muerte violenta, occisión.
debanding *v.* desatar, desbandamiento.
debilitant *n.* debilitante.
debilitation *n.* debilitación.
debility *n.* debilidad.
  mental debility debilidad mental.
débouchement *n.* desembocadura[1].
débride *v.* desbridar.
débridement *n.* desbridamiento.
  enzymatic débridement desbridamiento enzimático.
  epithelial débridement desbridamiento epitelial.
  surgical débridement desbridamiento quirúrgico.
débris *n.* desecho[1], detritos.
debt *n.* deuda.
  alactic oxygen debt deuda de oxígeno aláctico.
  lactacid oxygen debt deuda de oxígeno lactácido.
  oxygen debt deuda de oxígeno.
decalcification *n.* decalcificación, descalcificación.
decalcifier *n.* descalcificante[2].
decalcify *v.* descalcificar.
decalcifying *adj.* decalcificante, descalcificante[1].

decalvans *adj.* decalvante.
decalvant *adj.* decalvante.
decannulation *n.* descanulación.
decant *v.* decantar.
decantation *n.* decantación, decupelación.
decapacitation *n.* descapacitación.
decapitate *adj.* decapitado, -da, decapitar.
decapitation *n.* decapitación.
decapsulation *n.* decapsulación, descapsulación.
  decapsulation of the kidney descapsulación renal.
decarbonization *n.* descarbonización.
decarboxylation *n.* descarboxilación.
decay *n.* decaimiento, descomposición[2], desintegración[2].
decease *n.* deceso, óbito.
deceleration *n.* desaceleración.
  early deceleration desaceleración inicial.
  late deceleration desaceleración tardía.
  variable deceleration desaceleración variable.
decenter *v.* descentrar.
decentration *n.* decentración, descentración.
deceration *n.* desceración.
decerebellation *n.* descerebelación.
decerebrate *adj.* descerebrado, -da.
decerebration *n.* decerebración, descerebración.
  bloodless decerebration descerebracion exangüe, descerebracion incruenta.
dechloridation *n.* decloruración, decoluración, descloruración.
dechlorination *n.* decloruración, descloruración.
dechlorurant *n.* desclorurante.
dechloruration *n.* decloruración, descloruración.
decholesterinization *n.* descolesterinización.
decholesterolization *n.* descolesterolización.
decidua *n.* decidua.
  basal decidua decidua basal.
  capsular decidua decidua capsular.
  decidua basalis decidua basal.
  decidua capsularis decidua capsular.
  decidua mentrualis decidua menstrual.
  decidua parietalis decidua parietal.
  decidua polyposa decidua poliposa.
  decidua reflexa decidua refleja.
  decidua serotina decidua serotina.
  decidua spongiosa decidua esponjosa.
  decidua vera decidua vera, decidua verdadera.
  ectopic decidua decidua ectópica.
  parietal decidua decidua parietal.
  true decidua decidua vera, decidua verdadera.
decidual *adj.* decidual.
deciduate *adj.* deciduado, -da.
deciduation *n.* deciduación.
deciduitis *n.* deciduitis.
deciduo *adj.* deciduo, -a.
deciduoma *n.* deciduoma.
  Loeb's deciduoma deciduoma de Loeb.
deciduomatosis *n.* deciduomatosis.
deciduosarcoma *n.* deciduosarcoma.
deciduosis *n.* deciduosis.
deciduous *adj.* deciduo, -a.
declination *n.* declinación.
decline *n.* decaimiento.
decoagulant *n.* descoagulante.
decoction *n.* decocción.
decollation *n.* decolación.
décollement *n.* despegamiento.
decoloration *n.* decoloración, descoloración.
decolorize *v.* decolorar, descolorar.
decompensation *n.* descompensación.

corneal decompensation descompensación corneal.
decomplementize *v.* descomplementar.
decomposition *n.* descomposición[3].
  anaerobic decomposition descomposición anaerobia.
  decomposition of movement descomposición del movimiento.
  movement decomposition descomposición del movimiento.
decompression *n.* descompresión.
  abdominal decompression descompresión abdominal.
  cardiac decompression descompresión cardíaca.
  cerebral decompression descompresión cerebral.
  decompression of the heart descompresión del corazón.
  decompression of the pericardium descompresión pericárdica.
  decompression of the spinal cord descompresión de la médula espinal.
  explosive decompression descompresión explosiva.
  internal decompression descompresión interna.
  nerve decompression descompresión nerviosa.
  orbital decompression descompresión orbitaria.
  pericardial decompression descompresión pericárdica.
  rapid decompression descompresión rápida.
  spinal decompression descompresión espinal.
  suboccipital decompression descompresión suboccipital.
  subtemporal decompression descompresión subtemporal.
  trigeminal decompression descompresión trigeminal.
deconditioning *n.* desacondicionamiento.
decongestant *n.* descongestionante, descongestivo, descongestivo, -va.
  nasal decongestant descongestivo nasal.
decongestive *adj.* descongestivo, -va.
decontamination *n.* descontaminación.
decortication *n.* decorticación.
  brain decortication decorticación cerebral.
  decortication of the lung decorticación pulmonar.
  renal decortication decorticación renal.
  reversible decortication decorticación reversible.
decortization *n.* decorticación, decortización.
decrease *n.* disminución.
decrement *n.* decremento.
decrementum *n.* decremento.
decrepitate *v.* decrepitar.
decrepitation *n.* decrepitación.
decrudescence *n.* decrudescencia.
decrustation *n.* descostramiento.
decubation *n.* decubación.
decubitus *n.* decúbito.
  acute decubitus decúbito agudo.
  Andral's decubitus decúbito de Andral.
  dorsal decubitus decúbito dorsal.
  lateral decubitus decúbito lateral.
  supine decubitus position decúbito supino.
decurrent *adj.* decurrente.
decussate *adj.* decusado, -da.
decussatio *n.* decusación.
decussation *n.* decusación.
decussorium *n.* decusorio.

dedentition *n.* dedentición.
dedifferentation *n.* desdiferenciación[1].
dedolate *v.* dedolar.
dedolation *n.* dedolación.
de-efferentation *n.* deseferentación.
deemanate *n.* desemanación.
deep *adj.* profundo, -da.
de-epicardialization *n.* desepicardialización.
defatigation *n.* desfatigación.
defatted *adj.* desgrasado, -da.
defecation *n.* defecación.
defecography *n.* defecografía.
defect *n.* defecto.
 acquired defect defecto adquirido.
 acyanotic congenital defect defecto congénito acianótico.
 aortic septal defect defecto septal aórtico.
 aorticopulmonary septal defect defecto septal aorticopulmonar.
 birth defect defecto congénito, defecto de nacimiento.
 cardiac conduction defect defecto de conducción cardíaca.
 congenital ectodermal defect defecto ectodérmico congénito.
 diffusion defect defecto de difusión.
 Embden-Meyerhof defect defecto de Embden-Meyerhof.
 endocardial cushion defect defecto de las almohadillas endocárdicas, defecto de relieve endocárdico.
 fibrous cortical defect defecto cortical fibroso.
 filling defect defecto de llenado, defecto de relleno.
 genetic defect defecto genético.
 intraventricular conduction defect (ICD) defecto de conducción intraventricular (DCI).
 luteal phase defect defecto de la fase luteínica.
 metaphysial fibrous cortical defect defecto cortical fibroso metafisario.
 neural-tube defect defecto del tubo neural.
 ostium primum defect defecto de ostium primum.
 ostium secundum defect defecto de ostium secundum.
 perceptual defect defecto de percepción, defecto perceptual.
 polytropic field defect defecto de campo politrópico.
 retention defect defecto de retención.
 septal defect defecto del tabique, defecto septal.
 ventilation-perfusion defect defecto de ventilación-perfusión.
 ventricular septal defect defecto septal ventricular.
 visual field defect defecto del campo visual.
defective *adj.* defectuoso, -sa.
defemination *n.* desfeminación.
defeminization *n.* defeminación, defeminización, desfeminización.
defense *n.* defensa.
 muscular defense defensa muscular.
deferent *adj.* deferente.
deferentectomy *n.* deferentectomía.
deferential *n.* deferencial.
deferentitis *n.* deferentitis.
defervescence *n.* defervescencia.
deffeedaction *n.* retroactividad.
defibrillation *n.* desfibración, desfibrilación.
defibrillator *n.* desfibrilador.
 automatic implantable cardioverter defi-

brillator desfibrilador automático implantable.
 external defibrillator desfibrilador externo.
defibrinated *adj.* desfibrinado, -da.
defibrination *n.* desfibrinación.
deficiency *n.* carencia, deficiencia.
 17-hydroxylase deficiency deficiencia de 17-hidroxilasa.
 adult lactase deficiency deficiencia de lactasa en el adulto.
 antitrypsin deficiency deficiencia de antitripsina.
 congenital sucrase-isomaltase deficiency deficiencia congénita de sucrasa isomaltasa.
 debrancher deficiency deficiencia desramificante.
 deficiency of sweating hiposudoración.
 familial high-density lipoprotein deficiency deficiencia familiar de lipoproteínas de alta densidad (HDL).
 familial lipoprotein deficiency deficiencia familiar de lipoproteínas.
 galactokinase deficiency deficiencia de galactoquinasa.
 glucosephosphate isomerase deficiency deficiencia de glucosafosfato isomerasa.
 HDL deficiency deficiencia familiar de lipoproteínas de alta densidad (HDL).
 inmune deficiency deficiencia de inmunidad, deficiencia inmune, deficiencia inmunitaria, deficiencia inmunológica.
 intestinal lactase deficiency deficiencia de lactasa intestinal.
 isolated IgA deficiency deficiencia de IgA aislada.
 lactase deficiency deficiencia de lactasa.
 LCAT deficiency deficiencia de LCAT.
 leukocyte G6PD deficiency deficiencia de G6PD leucocitaria.
 luteal phase deficiency deficiencia de la fase luteínica.
 oxygen deficiency deficiencia de oxígeno.
 phosphohexose isomerase deficiency deficiencia de fosfohexosa isomerasa.
 placental sulfatase deficiency deficiencia de sulfatasa placentaria.
 proximal femoral focal deficiency (PFFD) deficiencia focal femoral proximal.
 pseudocholinesterase deficiency deficiencia de seudocolinesterasa.
 pyruvate kinase deficiency deficiencia de piruvato quinasa.
 riboflavin deficiency deficiencia de riboflavina.
 secondary antibody deficiency deficiencia de anticuerpo secundario.
 selective IgA deficiency deficiencia de IgA selectiva.
 thymus-dependent deficiency deficiencia dependiente del timo.
deficit *n.* déficit.
 base deficit déficit de base.
 oxygen deficit déficit de oxígeno.
 pulse deficit déficit del pulso.
 pyruvate kinase deficit déficit de piruvatocinasa.
 saturation deficit déficit de saturación.
 sensory deficit déficit sensitivo.
 vitamin deficit déficit vitamínico.
definition *n.* definición.
definitive *adj.* definitivo, -va.
deflection *n.* deflexión, desflexión.
 H deflection deflexión H.
 V deflection (HBE) deflexión V (EFH).
defloration *n.* desfloración.

defluoridation *n.* desfluoridación.
defluvium *n.* defluvium.
 defluvium capillorum defluvium capillorum.
defluxion *n.* deflujo, defluxión.
deformation *n.* deformación.
deformed *adj.* viciado, -da.
deforming *adj.* deformante.
deformity *n.* deformidad.
 Akerlund deformity deformidad de Akerlund.
 Arnold-Chiari deformity deformidad de Arnold-Chiari.
 boutonnière deformity deformidad en ojal.
 cloverleaf skull deformity deformidad craneal en trébol.
 contracture deformity deformidad por contractura.
 Erlenmeyer flask deformity deformidad en frasco de Erlenmeyer.
 gunstock deformity deformidad en caja de escopeta, deformidad en caja de fusil.
 Haglund's deformity deformidad de Haglund.
 Ilfeld-Holder deformity deformidad de Ilfeld-Holder.
 J-sella deformity deformidad selar en J.
 keyhole deformity deformidad en ojo de cerradura.
 lobster-claw deformity deformidad en pinza de langosta.
 Madelung's deformity deformidad de Madelung.
 mermaid deformity deformidad de sirena.
 pseudolobster-claw deformity deformidad en pseudopinza de langosta.
 reduction deformity deformidad por reducción.
 rotational deformity decalaje.
 seal-fin deformity deformidad en aleta de foca.
 silver-fork deformity deformidad en dorso de tenedor.
 Sprengel's deformity deformidad de Sprengel.
 swan-neck deformity deformidad en cuello de cisne.
 Velpeau's deformity deformidad de Velpeau.
 Volkmann's deformity deformidad de Volkmann.
 whistling deformity deformidad en silbato, deformidad en silbido.
 Whitehead deformity deformidad de Whitehead.
defurfuration *n.* defurfuración, desfurfuración.
deganglionate *v.* desganglionar.
degassing *n.* desgasificación.
degenerate[1] *adj.* degenerado, -da,.
degenerate[2] *v.* degenerar.
degeneratio *n.* degeneración, degeneratio.
 degeneratio hyaloidea granuliformis degeneración hialoidea granuliforme.
degeneration *n.* degeneración.
 Abercombie's degeneration degeneración de Abercrombie.
 adipose degeneration degeneración adiposa.
 adiposogenital degeneration degeneración adiposogenital.
 amyloid degeneration degeneración amiloidea.
 angiolithic degeneration degeneración angiolítica.
 Armanni-Ebstein's degeneration degeneración de Armanni-Ebstein.

ascending degeneration degeneración ascendente.

atheromatous degeneration degeneración ateromatosa.

ballooning degeneration degeneración en balón.

Biber-Haab-Dimmer degeneration degeneración de Haab-Biber-Dimmer.

blastophthoric degeneration degeneración blastoftórica.

calcareous degeneration degeneración calcárea.

carneous degeneration degeneración cárnea.

caseous degeneration degeneración caseosa.

cellulose degeneration degeneración celulosa.

cerebromacular degeneration (CMD) degeneración cerebromacular (CMD).

cerebroretinal degeneration degeneración cerebrorretiniana.

chitinous degeneration degeneración quitinosa.

combined degeneration degeneración combinada.

cone degeneration degeneración de conos.

congenital macular degeneration degeneración macular congénita.

Crooke's hyaline degeneration degeneración hialina de Crooke.

cystic degeneration degeneración quística.

cystoid macular degeneration degeneración macular cistoidea.

descending degeneration degeneración descendente.

disciform macular degeneration degeneración macular disciforme.

ectatic marginal degeneration of the cornea degeneración ectásica marginal de la córnea.

elastoid degeneration degeneración elastoidea.

elastotic degeneration degeneración elastósica.

familial pseudoinflamatory macular degeneration degeneración macular seudoinflamatoria familiar.

fascicular degeneration degeneración fascicular.

fatty degeneration degeneración grasa.

fibrinoid degeneration degeneración fibrinoide.

fibroid degeneration degeneración fibrinoide.

fibrous degeneration degeneración fibroide, degeneración fibrosa.

glycogenic degeneration degeneración glucógena.

granulovacuolar degeneration degeneración granulovacuolar.

gray degeneration degeneración gris.

hematohyaloid degeneration degeneración hematohialoidea.

hepatolenticular degeneration degeneración hepatolenticular, degeneración hepatolenticular de Kinnear Wilson.

heredomacular degeneration degeneración heredomacular.

Holmes degeneration degeneración de Holmes.

Horn degeneration degeneración de Horn.

hyaline degeneration degeneración hialina.

hyaloideoretinal degeneration degeneración hialoideorretiniana.

hydropic degeneration degeneración hidrópica.

infantile neuronal degeneration degeneración neuronal infantil.

keratoid degeneration degeneración queratoidea.

Kuhnt-Junius degeneration degeneración de Kuhnt-Junius.

lardaceous degeneration degeneración lardácea.

lenticular progressive degeneration degeneración lenticular progresiva.

lipoidal degeneration degeneración lipoidea.

liquefaction degeneration degeneración por licuefacción.

macular degeneration degeneración macular.

macular disciform degeneration degeneración disciforme macular.

Maragliano degeneration degeneración de Maragliano.

marginal corneal degeneration degeneración corneal marginal.

Mönkeberg's degeneration degeneración de Mönkeberg.

mucinoid degeneration degeneración mucinosa.

mucoid medial degeneration degeneración mucoide medial.

myelin mucoid degeneration degeneración mucoidea mielínica.

myelinic degeneration degeneración mielínica.

myxoid degeneration degeneración mixoide, degeneración mixomatosa.

myxomatous degeneration degeneración mixoide, degeneración mixomatosa.

neurofibrillary degeneration degeneración neurofibrilar.

Nissl degeneration degeneración de Nissl.

olivopontocerebellar degeneration degeneración olivopontocerebelosa.

orthograde degeneration degeneración ortógrada.

Paschutin's degeneration degeneración de Paschutin.

pigmentary degeneration degeneración pigmentaria.

polypid degeneration degeneración polipoide.

primary neuronal degeneration degeneración neuronal primaria.

primary pigmentary degeneration of the retina degeneración pigmentaria primaria de la retina.

primary progressive cerebelar degeneration degeneración cerebelosa primaria progresiva.

pseudotubular degeneration degeneración seudotubular.

Quain's degeneration degeneración de Quain.

red degeneration degeneración roja.

reticular degeneration degeneración reticular.

retrograde degeneration degeneración retrógrada.

Rosenthal's degeneration degeneración de Rosenthal.

sclerotic degeneration degeneración esclerótica.

secondary degeneration degeneración secundaria.

senile degeneration degeneración senil.

senile exudative macular degeneration degeneración macular exudativa senil.

serous degeneration degeneración serosa.

Sorsby's macular degeneration degeneración macular de Sorsby.

spongy degeneration degeneración esponjosa.

subacute combined degeneration of the spinal cord degeneración combinada subaguda de la médula espinal.

tapetoretinal degeneration degeneración tapetorretiniana.

Terrien's marginal degeneration degeneración marginal de Terrien.

trabecular degeneration degeneración trabecular.

traumatic degeneration degeneración traumática.

Türck's degeneration degeneración de Türck.

uratic degeneration degeneración urática, degeneración úrica.

vacuolar degeneration degeneración vacuolar.

Virchow's degeneration degeneración de Virchow.

viteliform degeneration degeneración viteliforme.

vitelliruptive degeneration degeneración vitelirruptiva.

vitreous degeneration degeneración vítrea.

Wallerian degeneration degeneración de Waller, degeneración walleriana.

waxy degeneration degeneración cérea.

xerotic degeneration degeneración xerótica.

Zenker's degeneration degeneración de Zenker.

degenerative *adj.* degenerativo, -va.

degenitalize *v.* desgenitalizar.

degerm *v.* desgerminar.

degloving *n.* desenguantamiento.

deglutition *n.* deglución.

deglutitive *adj.* deglutivo, -va.

degradation *n.* degradación.

degranulation *n.* desgranulación.

degree *n.* grado[1].

degree of freedom grado de libertad.

validity degree grado de validez.

degrowth *n.* decrecimiento.

degustation *n.* degustación.

dehematize *v.* deshematizar.

dehemoglobinize *v.* deshemoglobinizar.

dehiscence *n.* dehiscencia.

dehiscence of the uterus dehiscencia del útero.

iris dehiscence dehiscencia del iris.

root dehiscence dehiscencia radicular.

wound dehiscence dehiscencia de una herida.

Zuckerkandl's dehiscence dehiscencia de Zuckerkandl.

dehumanization *n.* deshumanización.

dehumidifier *n.* deshumectante.

dehydrant *adj.* deshidratante.

dehydrate *v.* deshidratar.

dehydration *n.* dehidración, deshidratación.

absolute dehydration deshidratación absoluta.

dehydration of gingivae deshidratación de las encías.

hypernatremic dehydration deshidratación hipernatrémica.

interstitial dehydration deshidratación intersticial.

intracellular dehydration deshidratación intracelular.

intravascular dehydration deshidratación intravascular.

relative dehydration deshidratación relativa.
voluntary dehydration deshidratación voluntaria.
dehydrogenase *n.* deshidrogenasa.
dehydrogenate *v.* deshidrogenar.
dehydrogenation *n.* deshidrogenación.
dehypnotize *v.* deshipnotizar.
deiodination *n.* desyodación.
deionization *n.* desionización.
déjà entendu *n.* déjà entendu.
déjà pensé *n.* déjà pensé.
déjà vécu *n.* déjà vécu.
déjà vu *n.* déjà vu.
dejection *n.* deyección.
delacrimation *n.* deslagrimación, lagrimeo.
delactation *n.* delactación, deslactación.
de-lead *v.* desplomar.
deleterious *adj.* delétereo, -a.
deletion *n.* deleción, pérdida.
chromosomal deletion deleción cromosómica.
gene deletion deleción parcial.
interstitial deletion deleción intersticial.
terminal deletion deleción terminal.
delimitation *n.* delimitación.
deliquescence *n.* delicuescencia.
deliquescent *adj.* delicuescente.
deliriant *adj.* delirante.
delirium *n.* delirium.
delirium tremens delirium tremens.
delitescence *n.* delitescencia.
delivery *n.* extracción, parto.
abdominal delivery extracción abdominal, parto abdominal.
breech delivery extracción de nalgas.
forceps delivery extracción con fórceps.
postmortem delivery extracción post morten.
premature delivery parto prematuro.
spontaneous delivery extracción expontánea, parto espontáneo, parto eutócico, parto eutócico.
vaginal delivery parto vaginal.
dellen *n.* hoyuelo.
delomorphous *adj.* delomórfico, -ca, delomorfo, -fa.
delousing *n.* despiojamiento.
delta *n.* delta.
delta mesoscapulae delta mesoscapular.
Galton's delta delta de Galton.
deltoid *adj.* deltoide, deltoideo, -a.
deltoide *adj.* deltoide, deltoideo, -a.
deltoiditis *n.* deltoiditis.
delusion *n.* delirio.
acute delusion delirio agudo.
chronic delusion delirio crónico.
delusion of control delirio de control.
delusion of grandeur delirio de grandeza.
delusion of infidelity delirio de infidelidad.
delusion of jealousy delirio de celos.
delusion of negation delirio de negación.
delusion of persecution delirio de persecución.
delusion of reference delirio de referencia.
delusion of self-accusation delirio de autoacusación.
delusion of transformation delirio de transformación.
febrile delusion delirio febril.
furious delusion delirio furioso.
low delusion delirio bajo.
mood-congruent delusion delirio congruente con el estado de ánimo.
mood-incongruent delusion delirio incongruente con el estado de ánimo.

mystic delusion delirio místico.
nihilistic delusion delirio nihilista.
oneiric delusion delirio onírico.
paranoiac delusion delirio paranoico, delirio paranoide.
polymorphic delusion delirio polimorfo.
postraumatic delusion delirio postraumático.
senile delusion delirio senil.
somatic delusion delirio somático.
symptomatic delusion delirio sintomático.
systematized delusion delirio sistematizado.
traumatic delusion delirio traumático.
demarcation *n.* demarcación.
demasculinization *n.* desmasculinización.
demented *adj.* demente.
dementia *n.* demencia.
Alzheimer's dementia demencia de Alzheimer.
Binswanger's dementia demencia de Binswanger.
catatonic dementia demencia catatónica.
dementia myoclonica demencia mioclónica.
dementia paralytica demencia paralítica.
dyalisis dementia demencia por diálisis.
epileptic dementia demencia epiléptica.
hebephrenic dementia demencia hebefrénica.
multi-infarct dementia demencia multiinfarto.
myoclonic dementia demencia mioclónica.
paralytic dementia demencia paralítica.
paretic dementia demencia parética.
posttraumatic dementia demencia postraumática.
presenile dementia demencia presenil.
primary dementia demencia primaria.
secondary dementia demencia secundaria.
senile dementia demencia senil.
toxic dementia demencia tóxica.
vascular dementia demencia vascular.
demifacet *n.* hemicarilla.
demilune *n.* semiluna.
serous demilune semiluna serosas.
demineralization *n.* desmineralización.
demography *n.* demografía.
demonomania *n.* demonomanía.
demorphinization *n.* desmorfinización.
demucosation *n.* desmucosación.
demulcent *adj.* demulcente.
demutization *n.* desmutización.
demyelinate *v.* desmielinizar.
demyelination *n.* desmielinación.
segmentary demyelination desmielinación segmentaria.
demyelinization *n.* desmielinización.
denarcotize *v.* desnarcotizar.
denatality *n.* desnatalidad.
denaturant *n.* desnaturalizante.
denaturation *n.* desnaturalización.
protein denaturation desnaturalización de proteínas.
denatured *adj.* desnaturalizado, -da.
dendriform *adj.* dendriforme.
dendrite *n.* dendrita.
dendrodendritic *adj.* dendrodendrítico, -ca.
dendroid *adj.* dendroide.
dendron *n.* dendrón.
dendrophagocytosis *n.* dendrofagocitosis.
denervation *n.* desnervación.
dengue *n.* dengue.
hemorrhagic dengue dengue hemorrágico.
denial *n.* denegación, negación.
denicotinized *adj.* desnicotinizado, -da.
denidation *n.* denidación, desnidación.

denitration *n.* desnitratación.
denitrification *n.* desnitrificación.
denitrifier *adj.* desnitrificante.
denitrify *v.* desnitrificar.
denitrogenation *n.* desnitrogenación.
dens *n.* dens, diente.
dens caninus colmillo.
dens lacteus diente de leche.
dens serotinus diente serotino.
densimeter *n.* densímetro.
densitometer *n.* densitómetro.
densitometry *n.* densitometría.
bone densitometry densitometría ósea.
density *n.* densidad.
count density densidad de recuento.
flux density densidad de flujo.
optical density densidad óptica.
photon density densidad de fotones.
proton density densidad de protones.
dental *adj.* dental, dentario, -ria.
dental engine torno dental.
dental germectomy germectomía.
dentalgia *n.* dentalgia.
dentatum *adj.* dentado, -da.
dentibucal *adj.* dentibucal.
denticle *n.* dentículo.
denticulate *adj.* denticulado, -da.
denticulated *adj.* denticulado, -da.
dentification *n.* dentificación.
dentiform *adj.* dentiforme.
dentifrice *n.* dentífrico.
dentigerous *adj.* dentígero, -ra.
dentilabial *adj.* dentilabial.
dentilingual *adj.* dentilingual.
dentimeter *n.* dentímetro.
dentin *n.* dentina.
adventitious dentin dentina adventicia.
hypersensitive dentin dentina hipersensible.
primary dentin dentina primaria.
secondary dentin dentina secundaria.
sensitive dentin dentina sensible.
tertiary dentin dentina terciaria.
transparent dentin dentina transparente.
dentinal *adj.* dentinal, dentinario, -ria.
dentinification *n.* dentinificación.
dentinoid *adj.* dentinoide.
dentiparous *adj.* dentíparo, -ra.
dentist *n.* dentista.
dentistry *n.* odontología.
community dentistry odontología comunitaria.
cosmetic dentistry odontología cosmética.
esthetic dentistry odontología estética.
forensic dentistry odontología forense.
geriatric dentistry odontología geriátrica.
legal dentistry odontología legal.
operative dentistry odontología operatoria.
pediatric dentistry odontología pediátrica.
preventive dentistry odontología preventiva.
psychosomatic dentistry odontología psicosomática.
public health dentistry odontología de salud pública.
restorative dentistry odontología de restauración, odontología restauradora.
dentition *n.* dentición.
first dentition dentición primaria, primera dentición.
mixed dentition dentición mixta.
primary dentition dentición primaria, primera dentición.
secondary dentition dentición secundaria, segunda dentición.
dentoalvelolitis *n.* dentoalveolitis.
dentofacial *adj.* dentofacial.
dentography *n.* dentografía.

dentoid *adj.* dentoide.
dentoliva *n.* dentoliva.
dentoma *n.* dentoma.
dentonomy *n.* dentonomía.
denture *n.* dentadura.
  artificial denture dentadura artificial.
  feline denture dentadura felina.
denturism *n.* ortodoncia.
denturist *adj.* ortodoncista.
denucleated *adj.* desnucleado, -da.
denudation *n.* denudación.
denutrition *n.* desnutrición.
deobstruent *adj.* desobstruyente.
deodorant *n.* desodorante.
deodorize *v.* desodorizar.
deodorizer *n.* desodorizante.
deontology *n.* dentología, deontología.
deoppilation *n.* desopilación.
deoppilative *adj.* desopilativo, -va.
deorsum *adv.* deorsum.
deorsumduction *n.* deorsumducción.
deorsumversion *n.* deorsumversión.
deossification *n.* desosificación.
deoxidation *n.* desoxidación[1].
deoxidize *v.* desoxidar.
deoxycholaneresis *n.* desoxicolaneresis.
deoxygenation *n.* desoxigenación.
deoxyribonucleic *n.* desosirribonucleico, -ca.
  deoxyribonucleic acid (DNA) ácido desosirribonucleico (ADN).
deoxyribonucleoside *n.* desoxirribonucleósido.
deoxyribonucleotide *n.* desoxirribonucleótido.
deoxyvirus *n.* desoxivirus.
deozonize *v.* desozonizar.
depancratize *v.* despancreatizar.
department *n.* servicio.
  emergency department servicio de urgencias.
dependence *n.* dependencia.
depersonalization *n.* despersonalización.
depigmentation *n.* depigmentación, despigmentación.
depilation *n.* depilación.
  electric depilation depilación electrica.
depilatory *n.* depilatorio, -ria.
deplasmolysis *n.* desplasmólisis.
deplete *v.* agotar.
depletion *n.* depleción.
  plasma depletion depleción de plasma.
depolarization *n.* despolarización.
  dendritic depolarization despolarización dendrítica.
  slow diastolic depolarization despolarización diastólica lenta.
depolarize *v.* despolarizar.
depolarizer *n.* despolarizador.
depolymerization *n.* despolimerización.
depolymerize *v.* despolimerizar.
depopulation *n.* despoblación.
deposit *n.* depósito.
  brickdust deposit depósito de polvo de ladrillo.
depravation *n.* depravación.
depravity *n.* depravación.
depressant *n.* depresor, -ra.
  Sims' depressant depresor de Sims.
  tongue depressant depresor de la lengua.
depressed *adj.* deprimido, -da.
depression *n.* abatimiento, depresión.
  anaclitic depression depresión anaclítica.
  atypical depression depresión atípica.
  auricular depression depresión auricular.
  cataract depression depresión de la catarata.
  late depression depresión involutiva.

mental depression depresión mental.
neurotic depression depresión neurótica.
postnatal depression depresión posparto.
reactive depression depresión reactiva.
secondary depression depresión secundaria.
symptomatic depression depresión sintomática.
depressomotor *adj.* depresomotor, -ra.
deprimens oculi *n.* deprimens oculi.
deprivation *n.* deshabituación, privación.
deproteinization *n.* desproteinización.
depth *n.* profundidad.
  anesthetic depth profundidad anestésica.
depurant *adj.* depurador, -ra, depurante.
depuration *n.* depuración.
deradelphus *n.* deradelfo.
derailment *n.* descarrilamiento.
deranencephaly *n.* deranencefalia.
derangement *n.* desarreglo.
  Hey's internal derangement desarreglo interno de Hey.
derealization *n.* desrealización.
dereflection *n.* desreflexión.
dereism *n.* dereísmo.
dereistic *adj.* dereístico, -ca, irreal.
  dereistic thinking dereísmo.
derencephalia *n.* derencefalia.
derencephalocele *n.* derencefalocele.
derencephalus *n.* derencéfalo.
derencephaly *n.* derencefalia.
derepression *n.* desrepresión.
derism *n.* derismo.
derivation *n.* derivación[2].
derivative *adj.* derivativo, -va.
derma *n.* derma.
dermabrader *n.* dermoabrador.
dermabrasion *n.* dermabrasión, dermoabrasión.
Dermacentor *n.* Dermacentor.
dermad *adv.* dermad.
dermahemia *n.* dermahemia.
dermal *adj.* dermal.
dermalaxia *n.* dermalaxia.
dermalgia *n.* dermalgia.
dermametropathism *n.* dermametropatismo.
dermanaplasty *n.* dermanaplastia.
dermatalgia *n.* dermatalgia.
dermatergosis *n.* dermatergosis.
dermatic *adj.* dermático, -ca.
dermatitis *n.* dermatitis.
  actinic dermatitis dermatitis actínica.
  allergic contact dermatitis dermatitis por contacto alérgica.
  allergic dermatitis dermatitis alérgica.
  ammonia dermatitis dermatitis amoniacal, dermatitis por amoniaco.
  ancylostoma dermatitis dermatitis anquilostomiásica, dermatitis por anquilostomiasis.
  atopic dermatitis dermatitis atópica.
  berlock dermatitis dermatitis de berloque.
  berloque dermatitis dermatitis de berloque.
  blastomycetic dermatitis dermatitis blastomicética, dermatitis blastomicótica.
  brown-tail moth dermatitis dermatitis por polilla de cola parda.
  brucella dermatitis dermatitis brucelósica.
  bubble gum dermatitis dermatitis por goma de mascar.
  caterpillar dermatitis dermatitis por orugas.
  cercarial dermatitis dermatitis cercarial.
  chemical dermatitis dermatitis química.
  contact dermatitis dermatitis de contacto, dermatitis por contacto.
  contagious pustular dermatitis dermatitis pustulosa contagiosa.

  cosmetic dermatitis dermatitis cosmética, dermatitis por cosméticos.
  cutting oil dermatitis dermatitis por aceite de corte.
  dermatitis aestivalis dermatitis estival.
  dermatitis ambustionis dermatitis ambustionis, dermatitis por ambustión.
  dermatitis artefacta dermatitis artefacta, dermatitis artificial.
  dermatitis atrophicans dermatitis atrófica.
  dermatitis autophytica dermatitis autofítica.
  dermatitis blastomycotica dermatitis blastomicética, dermatitis blastomicótica.
  dermatitis bullosa striata pratensis dermatitis bullosa striata pratensis.
  dermatitis calorica dermatitis calórica.
  dermatitis combustionis dermatitis por combustión.
  dermatitis congelationis dermatitis por congelación.
  dermatitis exfoliativa dermatitis exfoliativa.
  dermatitis exfoliativa infantum dermatitis exfoliativa de los niños, dermatitis exfoliativa del neonato, dermatitis exfoliativa del recién nacido, dermatitis exfoliativa infantil, dermatitis exfoliativa neonatal.
  dermatitis exfoliativa neonatorum dermatitis exfoliativa de los niños, dermatitis exfoliativa del neonato, dermatitis exfoliativa del recién nacido, dermatitis exfoliativa infantil, dermatitis exfoliativa neonatal.
  dermatitis gangrenosa infantum dermatitis gangrenosa infantil, dermatitis gangrenosa infantum.
  dermatitis gestationis dermatitis gravídica.
  dermatitis herpetiformis dermatitis herpetiforme.
  dermatitis hiemalis dermatitis hiemal, dermatitis hiemalis, dermatitis invernal.
  dermatitis lichenoides chronica atrophicans dermatitis liquenoide crónica atrófica.
  dermatitis medicamentosa dermatitis medicamentosa.
  dermatitis micropapulosa dermatitis micropapulosa, eritematosa e hiperhidrótica de la nariz.
  dermatitis moluscum contagiosum dermatitis por molusco.
  dermatitis multiformis dermatitis multiforme.
  dermatitis nodosa dermatitis nudosa.
  dermatitis nodularis necrotica dermatitis nodular necrótica.
  dermatitis papillaris capillitii dermatitis papilar capilar, dermatitis papillaris capillitii.
  dermatitis pediculoides ventricosus dermatitis pediculoides ventricosus.
  dermatitis repens dermatitis repens.
  dermatitis seborrheica dermatitis seborreica.
  dermatitis simplex dermatitis simple.
  dermatitis striata pratensis bullosa dermatitis estriada pratense ampollosa.
  dermatitis vegetans dermatitis vegetante.
  dermatitis venenata dermatitis venenata, dermatitis venenosa.
  dermatitis verrucosa dermatitis verrugosa.
  dhobie mark dermatitis dermatitis del lavandero, dermatitis del tintorero, dermatitis dhobie, dermatitis por tinta de marcar.
  diaper dermatitis dermatitis del pañal.
  eczematous dermatitis dermatitis eccematosa.
  exfoliative dermatitis dermatitis exfoliativa.
  exudative discoid and lichenoid dermatitis dermatitis exudativa discoide y liquenoide.

factitial dermatitis dermatitis facticia, dermatitis ficticia.

grass dermatitis dermatitis por césped.

industrial dermatitis dermatitis industrial.

infectious eczematoid dermatitis dermatitis eccematoide infecciosa, dermatitis eccematoidea infecciosa, dermatitis eccematosa infecciosa.

infectious eczematous dermatitis dermatitis eccematoide infecciosa, dermatitis eccematoidea infecciosa, dermatitis eccematosa infecciosa, dermatitis infecciosa eccematoide, dermatitis infecciosa eccematoidea, dermatitis infecciosa eccematosa.

insect dermatitis dermatitis por insectos.

io-moth dermatitis dermatitis por polilla io.

irritant dermatitis dermatitis por irritante, dermatitis por irritante primario.

Jacquet's dermatitis dermatitis de Jacquet.

livedoid dermatitis dermatitis livedoide.

mango dermatitis dermatitis del mango.

marine dermatitis dermatitis marina.

meadow dermatitis dermatitis de los prados.

meadow-grass dermatitis dermatitis de la hierba de las praderas.

moth dermatitis dermatitis por polilla.

napkin dermatitis dermatitis del área del pañal.

nickel dermatitis dermatitis por níquel.

nummular dermatitis dermatitis numular.

nummular eczematous dermatitis dermatitis eccematosa numular.

occupational dermatitis dermatitis ocupacional.

onion mite dermatitis dermatitis por ácaro de la cebolla.

Oppenheim's dermatitis dermatitis de Oppenheim.

papular dermatitis of pregnancy dermatitis papulosa del embarazo.

perfume dermatitis dermatitis por perfume, dermatitis por perfumes.

perioral dermatitis dermatitis peribucal, dermatitis perioral.

photoallergic contact dermatitis dermatitis fotoalérgica de contacto, dermatitis por contacto fotoalérgico.

photocontact dermatitis dermatitis por fotocontacto.

phototoxic contact dermatitis dermatitis fototóxica, dermatitis fototóxica de contacto.

phototoxic dermatitis dermatitis fototóxica, dermatitis fototóxica de contacto.

phytophototoxicity dermatitis dermatitis fitofototóxica.

pigmented purpuric lichenoid dermatitis dermatitis liquenoide purpúrica pigmentada, dermatitis pigmentada purpúrica liquenoide, dermatitis purpúrica pigmentada liquenoide.

plant dermatitis dermatitis vegetal.

poison ivy dermatitis dermatitis por zumaque venenoso.

precancerous dermatitis dermatitis precancerosa.

primary dermatitis dermatitis primaria.

primary irritant dermatitis dermatitis por irritante, dermatitis por irritante primario, dermatitis primaria irritante.

professional dermatitis dermatitis profesional.

radiation dermatitis dermatitis por radiación.

rat-mite dermatitis dermatitis del ácaro de la rata, dermatitis por ácaros de la rata.

rhus dermatitis dermatitis por hiedra venenosa, dermatitis por plantas del género Rhus, dermatitis por rhus.

Roentgen ray dermatitis dermatitis por rayos X.

sandal strap dermatitis dermatitis por correas de sandalias.

Schamberg's dermatitis dermatitis de Schamberg.

schistosomal dermatitis dermatitis esquistosomiásica, dermatitis esquistosómica.

schistosome dermatitis dermatitis esquistosomiásica, dermatitis esquistosómica.

seborrheic dermatitis dermatitis seborreica.

shoe dye dermatitis dermatitis por betún para calzado.

solar dermatitis dermatitis solar.

stasis dermatitis dermatitis por estasis.

subcorneal pustular dermatitis dermatitis pustulosa subcorneal.

swimmer's dermatitis dermatitis de los nadadores.

traumatic dermatitis dermatitis traumática.

uncinarial dermatitis dermatitis uncinariásica.

vanilla dermatitis dermatitis por vainilla.

verrucous dermatitis dermatitis verrugosa.

weeping dermatitis dermatitis húmeda.

dermatoarthritis *n.* dermatoartritis.

lipid dermatoarthritis dermatoartritis lípida, dermatoartritis lipoide.

lipoid dermatoarthritis dermatoartritis lípida, dermatoartritis lipoide.

dermatoautoplasty *n.* dermatoautoplastia.

Dermatobia *n.* Dermatobia.

dermatobiasis *n.* dermatobiasis.

dermatocandidiasis *n.* dermatocandidiasis.

dermatocele *n.* dermatocele.

dermatocellulitis *n.* dermatocelulitis.

dermatochalasia *n.* dermatocalasia, dermatocalasis.

dermatochalasis *n.* dermatocalasia, dermatocalasis.

dermatochalazia *n.* dermatocalasia, dermatocalasis.

dermatoconiosis *n.* dermatoconiosis.

dermatoconjunctivitis *n.* dermatoconjuntivitis.

dermatocyst *n.* dermatocisto, dermatoquiste.

dermatodynia *n.* dermatodinia.

dermatodysplasia *n.* dermatodisplasia.

dermatofibroma *n.* dermatofibroma.

dermatofibroma protuberans dermatofibroma protuberans.

dermatofibrosarcoma *n.* dermatofibrosarcoma.

dermatofibrosarcoma protuberans dermatofibrosarcoma protuberans, dermatofibrosarcoma protuberante.

pigmented dermatofibrosarcoma protuberans dermatofibrosarcoma protuberante pigmentado.

dermatofibrosis *n.* dermatofibrosis.

dermatofibrosis lenticularis disseminata dermatofibrosis lenticular diseminada, dermatofibrosis lenticularis disseminata.

dermatoglyphics *n.* dermatoglifia.

dermatograph *n.* dermatógrafo.

dermatographia *n.* dermatografía.

dermatographic *adj.* dermatográfico, -ca.

dermatographism *n.* dermatografismo.

black dermatographism dermatografismo negro.

white dermatographism dermatografismo blanco.

dermatography *n.* dermatografía.

dermatoheteroplasty *n.* dermatoheteroplastia.

dermatohistopathology *n.* dermatohistopatología.

dermatoid *adj.* dermatoide.

dermatokelidoisis *n.* dermatoquelidosis.

dermatologic *adj.* dermatológico, -ca.

dermatologist *n.* dermatólogo, -ga.

dermatology *n.* dermatología.

dermatolysis *n.* dermatólisis.

dermatolysis palpebrarum dermatólisis de los párpados, dermatólisis palpebral.

dermatoma *n.* dermatoma[1].

dermatome *n.* dermatoma[2], dermátomo.

Brown dermatome dermátomo de Brown.

Castroviejo dermatome dermátomo de Castroviejo.

electric dermatome dermátomo eléctrico.

Padgett dermatome dermátomo de Padgett.

Reese dermatome dermátomo de Reese.

dermatomegaly *n.* dermatomegalia.

dermatomere *n.* dermatómera.

dermatomic *adj.* dermatómico, -ca.

dermatomyces *n.* dermatomices.

dermatomycin *n.* dermatomicina.

dermatomycosis *n.* dermatomicosis.

dermatomycosis pedis dermatomicosis del pie.

dermatomyoma *n.* dermatomioma.

dermatomyositis *n.* dermatomiositis.

dermatoneurology *n.* dermatoneurología.

dermatoneurosis *n.* dermatoneurosis.

dermatonosology *n.* dermatonosología.

dermato-ophthalmitis *n.* dermatooftalmitis.

dermatopathia *n.* dermatopatía.

dermatopathic *adj.* dermatopático, -ca.

dermatopatholgy *n.* dermatopatología.

dermatopathy *n.* dermatopatía.

dermatopharmacology *n.* dermatofarmacología.

dermatophiliasis *n.* dermatofiliasis.

dermatophilosis *n.* dermatofilosis.

dermatophobia *n.* dermatofobia.

dermatophone *n.* dermatófono.

dermatophyte *n.* demafito, dermatofito.

dermatophytid *n.* dermatofitide.

dermatophytosis *n.* dermatofitosis.

dermatoplastic *adj.* dermatoplástico, -ca.

dermatopolyneuritis *n.* dermatopolineuritis.

dermatorrhea *n.* dermatorrea.

dermatorrhexis *n.* dermatorrexis.

dermatosclerosis *n.* dermatoesclerosis, dermatosclerosis.

dermatoscopy *n.* dermatoscopia.

dermatosis *n.* dermatosis.

acarine dermatosis dermatosis acarina.

acute febrile neutrophilic dermatosis dermatosis neutrófila aguda, dermatosis neutrófila febril aguda.

acute neutrophilic dermatosis dermatosis neutrófila aguda, dermatosis neutrófila febril aguda.

Auspitz's dermatosis dermatosis de Auspitz.

benign chronic bullous dermatosis of childhood dermatosis ampollar crónica benigna de la niñez.

dermatolytic bullous dermatosis dermatosis ampollosa dermatolítica.

dermatosis cenicienta dermatosis cenicienta, dermatosis cenicienta de Ramírez.

dermatosis industrialis dermatosis industrial.

dermatosis medicamentosa dermatosis medicamentosa.

dermatosis papulosa nigra dermatosis papulosa negra, dermatosis papulosa nigra.

dermolytic bullous dermatosis dermatosis dermolítica ampollar.

industrial dermatosis dermatosis industrial.

lichenoid dermatosis dermatosis liquenoide.
pigmented purpuric lichenoid dermatosis dermatosis liquenoide purpúrica pigmentada.
professional dermatosis dermatosis profesional.
progressive pigmentary dermatosis dermatosis pigmentada progresiva, dermatosis pigmentaria progresiva.
radiation dermatosis dermatosis por radiación.
Schamberg's dermatosis dermatosis de Schamberg, dermatosis purpúrica pigmentada progresiva de Schamberg.
Schamberg's progressive pigmented purpuric dermatosis dermatosis de Schamberg, dermatosis purpúrica pigmentada progresiva de Schamberg.
seborrheic dermatosis dermatosis seborreica.
subcorneal pustular dermatosis dermatosis pustular subcorneal, dermatosis pustulosa subcorneal.
transient acantholytic dermatosis (TAD) dermatosis acantolítica pasajera, dermatosis acantolítica transitoria.
ulcerative dermatosis dermatosis ulcerosa.
dermatoskeleton *n.* dermatoesqueleto.
dermatosparaxis *n.* dermatosparaxis.
dermatotherapy *n.* dermatoterapia.
dermatotome *n.* dermatótomo.
dermatotropic *adj.* dermatotrópico, -ca.
dermatoxenoplasty *n.* dermatoxenoplastia.
dermatoxerasia *n.* dermatoxerasia.
dermatozoiasis *n.* dermatozoiasis.
dermatozoon *n.* dermatozoario, dermatozoo.
dermatozoonosis *n.* dermatozoonosis.
dermatrophia *n.* dermatrofia.
dermatrophy *n.* dermatrofia.
dermenchysis *n.* dermenquisis.
dermic *adj.* dérmico, -ca.
dermis *n.* dermis.
dermoanergy *n.* dermoanergia.
dermoblast *n.* dermoblasto.
dermocyma *n.* dermócimo.
dermocymus *n.* dermócimo.
dermodeictomy *n.* dermoidectomía.
dermoepidermal *adj.* dermoepidérmico, -ca.
dermograph *n.* dermógrafo.
dermographia *n.* dermografía.
dermographic *adj.* dermográfico, -ca.
dermographism *n.* dermografismo.
dermography *n.* dermografía.
dermohygrometer *n.* dermohigrómetro.
dermoid *n.* dermoide.
implantation dermoid dermoide de implantación.
inclusion dermoid dermoide de inclusión.
sequestration dermoid dermoide de secuestro.
dermolipectomy *n.* dermolipectomía.
dermolipoma *n.* dermolipoma.
dermolysin *n.* dermolisina.
dermolysis *n.* dermólisis.
dermometer *n.* dermómetro.
dermometry *n.* dermometría.
dermomycosis *n.* dermomicosis.
dermomyotome *n.* dermomiotoma.
dermonecrotic *adj.* dermonecrótico, -ca.
dermoneurosis *n.* dermoneurosis.
dermoneurotropic *adj.* dermoneurotrópico, -ca.
dermonosology *n.* dermonosología.
dermopathic *adj.* dermopático, -ca.
dermopathy *n.* dermopatía.
diabetic dermopathy dermopatía diabética.
dermophlebitis *n.* dermoflebitis.
dermophyte *n.* dermófito.

dermoplasty *n.* dermatoplastia, dermoplastia.
dermoskeleton *n.* dermoesqueleto, dermosqueleto.
dermostenosis *n.* dermoestenosis, dermostenosis.
dermosynovitis *n.* dermosinovitis.
dermosyphilopathy *n.* dermosifilopatía.
dermotactile *adj.* dermotáctil.
dermotoxin *n.* dermotoxina.
dermotropic *adj.* dermotrópico, -ca, dermótropo, -pa.
dermovaccine *n.* dermovacuna.
dermovascular *adj.* dermovascular.
dermovirus *n.* dermovirus.
derodidymus *n.* derodídimo, derodimo.
derotation *n.* desrotación.
desalination *n.* desalinación.
desalivation *n.* desalivación.
desamidize *v.* desamidizar.
desaturate *v.* desaturar.
desaturation *n.* desaturación.
descemetitis *n.* descemetitis.
descemetocele *n.* descemetocele.
descendens *adj.* descendens.
descending *adj.* descendente.
descensus *n.* descenso, descensus.
descensus funiculi umbilicalis descensus funiculi umbilicalis.
descensus paradoxus testis descenso paradójico del testículo.
descensus testis descenso del testículo, descenso testicular.
descensus uteri descenso del útero, descenso uterino.
descensus ventriculi descenso del vientre, descenso ventricular, descenso ventriculi.
descensus aberrans testis descenso aberrante del testículo.
descent *n.* descenso.
descent of the testis descenso del testículo, descenso testicular.
vaginal descent descenso vaginal.
vapor pressure lowering descent descenso de la presión de vapor.
desensitization *n.* desensibilización.
heterologous desensitization desensibilización heteróloga.
homologous desensitization desensibilización homóloga.
phobic desensitization desensibilización fóbica.
systematic desensitization desensibilización sistemática.
systemic desensitization desensibilización general.
desensitize *v.* desensibilizar.
desexualize *v.* desexualizar.
deshydremia *n.* deshidremia.
desiccant *adj.* desecante[1], desecante[2].
desiccate *v.* desecar.
desiccation *n.* desecación[1].
electric desiccation desecación eléctrica.
desiccative *adj.* desecativo, -va.
desiccator *n.* desecador, desecante[2].
vacuum desiccator desecador al vacío.
design *n.* diseño.
barrier-free design diseño sin barreras.
experimental design diseño experimental.
desmalgia *n.* desmalgia.
desmectasia *n.* desmectasia.
desmectasis *n.* desmectasis.
desmepithelium *n.* desmepitelio.
desmin *n.* desmina.
desmiognathus *n.* desmiognato.
desmitis *n.* desmitis.

desmocranium *n.* desmocráneo.
desmocytoma *n.* desmocitoma.
desmodontium *n.* desmodontio.
Desmodus *n.* Desmodus.
desmodynia *n.* desmodinia.
desmogenous *adj.* desmógeno, -na.
desmography *n.* desmografía.
desmohemoblast *n.* desmohemoblasto.
desmoid *n.* desmoide.
extra-abdominal desmoid desmoide extra-abdominal.
desmolase *n.* desmolasa.
desmology *n.* desmología.
desmolysis *n.* desmólisis.
desmoma *n.* desmoma.
desmoneoplasm *n.* desmoneoplasia.
desmopathy *n.* desmopatía.
desmopexia *n.* desmopexia.
desmoplakin *n.* desmoplaquina.
desmoplasia *n.* desmoplasia, desmoplastia.
desmoplastic *adj.* desmoplásico, -ca, desmoplástico, -ca.
desmopressin *n.* desmopresina.
desmopyknosis *n.* desmopicnosis.
desmorrhexis *n.* desmorrexia, desmorrexis.
desmosis *n.* desmosis.
desmosome *n.* desmosoma.
desmosterol *n.* desmosterol.
desmotomy *n.* desmotomía.
desmotropism *n.* desmotropía.
desorb *v.* desorber.
desorption *n.* desorción.
despeciate *v.* despeciar.
despeciation *n.* despeciación.
despecification *n.* despecificación.
desquamate *v.* descamar.
desquamation *n.* descamación.
branny desquamation descamación en salvado.
furfuraceous desquamation descamación furfurácea.
desquamative *adj.* descamativo, -va.
dessicant *adj.* secante.
desternalization *n.* desternalización.
destructive *adj.* destructivo, -va.
destrudo *n.* destrudo.
Desulfomonas *n.* Desulfomonas.
detachment *n.* desprendimiento.
choroidal detachment desprendimiento de coroides.
detachment of members desprendimiento de los miembros.
detachment of the placenta desprendimiento de la placenta, desprendimiento placentario.
detachment of the retina desprendimiento de la retina, desprendimiento de retina, desprendimiento retiniano.
epiphytical detachment desprendimiento epifisario.
exudative retinal detachment desprendimiento de retina exudativo, desprendimiento exudativo de la retina.
placental detachment desprendimiento de la placenta, desprendimiento placentario.
posterior vitreous detachment desprendimiento posterior del vítreo.
retinal detachment desprendimiento de la retina, desprendimiento de retina, desprendimiento retiniano.
retinal pigment epithelium detachment desprendimiento del epitelio pigmentario.
rhegmatogenous retinal detachment desprendimiento regmatógeno de la retina.
vitreous detachment desprendimiento vítreo.

detect *v.* detectar.
detection *n.* detección.
  heterozygote detection detección de heterocigotos.
detector *n.* detector.
  air detector detector de aire.
  automatic infiltration detector detector automático de infiltración.
  ceramic detector detector cerámico.
  lie detector detector de mentiras.
  proportional gas detector detector proporcional de gas.
  radiation detector detector de radiación.
  scintillation detector detector de centelleo.
detergent *adj., n.* detergente.
deterioration *n.* deterioro.
  alcoholic deterioration deterioro alcohólico.
  senile deterioration deterioro senil.
determinant *n.* determinante.
  allotypic determinant determinante alotípico.
  anterior determinant of cusp determinante anterior de la cúspide.
  antigenic determinant determinante antigénico.
  determinant of occlusion determinante de oclusión.
  disease determinant determinante de enfermedad.
  gait determinant determinante de la marcha.
  genetic determinant determinante genético.
  hidden determinant determinante oculto.
  idiotypic antigenic determinant determinante antigénico idiotípico.
  immunogenic determinant determinante inmunogénico.
  isoallotypic determinant determinante isoalotípico.
  psychic determinant determinante psíquico.
  sequential determinant determinante secuencial.
determination *n.* determinación².
  blood gas determination determinación de gases en sangre.
  embryonic determination determinación embrionaria.
  serial determination determinación en serie.
  sex determination determinación del sexo, determinación sexual.
determinism *n.* determinismo.
  psychic determinism determinismo psíquico.
detersive *n.* detersivo.
dethyroidism *n.* detiroidismo.
dethyroidize *v.* detiroidizar.
detonation *n.* detonación.
detorsion *n.* destorsión, detorsión.
detoxicate *v.* desintoxicar, destoxicar.
detoxication *n.* desintoxicación, destoxicación.
detoxification *n.* desintoxicación, destoxificación.
detoxify *v.* desintoxicar, destoxificar, detoxificar.
detrition *n.* desgaste, detrición.
detritus *n.* desecho², detrito, detritus.
detrusor *adj.* detrusor.
detubation *n.* destubación.
detumescence *n.* detumescencia.
deturgescence *n.* deturgescencia.
deutan *adj., n.* deutan.
deutencephalon *n.* deutencéfalo.
deuteranomal *n.* deuteranómalo, -la².
deuteranomalopia *n.* deuteranomalopía.
deuteranomalous *adj.* deuteranómalo, -la¹.
deuteranomaly *n.* deuteranomalía.

deuteranope *n.* deuteranope.
deuteranopia *n.* deuteranopía.
deuteranopic *adj.* deuteranópico, -ca.
deuteranopsia *n.* deuteranopsia.
deuterofat *n.* deuterograsa.
deuterohemin *n.* deuterohemina.
deuterohemophilia *n.* deuterohemofilia.
deuteromerite *n.* deuteromerito.
deuteromycete *n.* deuteromiceto.
Deuteromycetes *n.* Deuteromyces, Deuteromycetae, Deuteromycetes.
deuteronomalopsia *n.* deuteronomalopsia.
deuteropathic *adj.* deuteropático, -ca.
deuteropathy *n.* deuteropatía.
deuteroplasm *n.* deuteroplasma.
deuterosome *n.* deuterosoma.
deuterotoky *n.* deuterotocia, deuterotoquia.
deutogenic *adj.* deutogénico, -ca.
deutomerite *n.* deutomerito.
deutoplasm *n.* deutoplasma.
deutoplasmic *adj.* deutoplasmático, -ca.
deutoplasmigenon *adj.* deutoplasmígeno, -na.
deutoplasmolysis *n.* deutoplasmólisis.
devascularization *n.* desvascularización.
development *n.* desarrollo.
  arrested development desarrollo detenido.
  child development desarrollo infantil.
  cognitive development desarrollo cognitivo.
  embryologic development desarrollo embrionario.
  libidinal development desarrollo libidinal.
  life-span development desarrollo de por vida.
  mosaic development desarrollo en mosaico.
  postnatal development desarrollo posnatal.
  prenatal development desarrollo prenatal.
  psychomotor and physical development of infants desarrollo físico y psicomotor de los lactantes.
  psychomotor development desarrollo psicomotor.
  psychosexual development desarrollo psicosexual.
  psychosocial development desarrollo psicosocial.
  regulative development desarrollo regulador.
deviance *n.* desviación².
deviant *adj.* desviado, -da.
  sexual deviant desviado sexual.
deviation *n.* desviación², desviación³.
  animal deviation desviación animal.
  axis deviation desviación del eje, desviación del eje eléctrico.
  complement deviation desviación del complemento.
  conjugate deviation desviación conjugada, desviación conjugada de los ojos.
  conjugate deviation of the eyes desviación conjugada, desviación conjugada de los ojos.
  deviation from normal desviación de la norma.
  deviation of the teeth desviación de los dientes.
  deviation of the tongue desviación de la lengua.
  deviation to the left desviación a la izquierda, desviación hacia la izquierda.
  deviation to the right desviación a la derecha, desviación hacia la derecha.
  dissociated vertical deviation desviación vertical disociada.
  eye deviation desviación del ojo.
  Hering-Hellebrand deviation desviación de Hering-Hellebrand.

  immune deviation desviación inmunitaria, desviación inmunológica.
  latent deviation desviación latente.
  left axis deviation (LAD) desviación izquierda del eje.
  manifest deviation desviación manifiesta.
  minimal deviation desviación mínima.
  minimum deviation desviación mínima.
  organic deviation desviación orgánica.
  primary deviation desviación primaria.
  right axis deviation (RAD) desviación derecha del eje.
  sample standard deviation desviación estándar de una muestra.
  secondary deviation desviación secundaria.
  sexual deviation desviación sexual.
  skew deviation desviación oblicua, desviación sesgada.
  social deviation desviación social.
  spinal column deviation desviación de la columna vertebral.
  squint deviation desviación estrábica.
  standard deviation (SD) desviación estándar (DE).
  strabismal deviation desviación estrábica.
  strabismic deviation desviación estrábica.
  uterine deviation desviación uterina.
device *n.* dispositivo².
  adaptive device dispositivo de adaptación.
  central-bearing device dispositivo de apoyo central, dispositivo de soporte central.
  central-bearing tracing device dispositivo de soporte central trazador, dispositivo trazador de apoyo central.
  contraceptive device dispositivo anticonceptivo, dispositivo contraceptivo.
  flotation device dispositivo de flotación.
  fluoroscopic compression device dispositivo de compresión fluoroscópica.
  input device dispositivo de entrada.
  intra-aortic balloon device dispositivo intraaórtico en balón.
  intrauterine device (IUD) dispositivo intrauterino (DIU), dispositivo intrauterino anticonceptivo (DIUA).
  intrauterine contraceptive device dispositivo intrauterino (DIU), dispositivo intrauterino anticonceptivo (DIUA).
  left-ventricular assist device (LVAD) dispositivo de asistencia ventricular izquierda (DAVI).
  output device dispositivo de salida.
  pulsatile assist device (PAD) dispositivo de ayuda pulsátil (DAP).
  vascular access device (DAV) dispositivo de acceso vascular (DAV).
  venous access device dispositivo de acceso venoso.
deviometer *n.* desviómetro.
devisceration *n.* desvisceración.
devitalization *n.* desvitalización.
  pulp devitalization desvitalización pulpar.
devitalize *v.* desvitalizar.
devitalized *adj.* desvitalizado, -da.
devolution *n.* devolución.
devolutive *adj.* devolutivo, -va.
dewar *n.* dewar.
dexiocardia *n.* dexiocardia.
dexiotropic *adj.* dexiotrópico, -ca.
dextogram *n.* dextrograma.
dextrad *adj.* dextrad.
dextrality *n.* dextralidad.
dextraural *adj.* dextraural.
dextrinosis *n.* dextrinosis.
  debranching deficiency limit dextrinosis

dextrinosis límite, dextrinosis límite por deficiencia de desramificación.

dextrinuria *n.* dextrinuria.

dextrocardia *n.* dextrocardia.

  corrected dextrocardia dextrocardia corregida.

  dextrocardia with situs inversus dextrocardia con situs inversus.

  false dextrocardia dextrocardia falsa.

  isolated dextrocardia dextrocardia aislada.

  mirror-image dextrocardia dextrocardia en imagen en espejo.

  secondary dextrocardia dextrocardia secundaria.

  type 1 dextrocardia dextrocardia tipo 1.

  type 2 dextrocardia dextrocardia tipo 2.

  type 3 dextrocardia dextrocardia tipo 3.

  type 4 dextrocardia dextrocardia tipo 4.

dextrocardiogram *n.* dextrocardiograma.

dextrocerebral *adj.* dextrocerebral.

dextroclination *n.* dextroclinación.

dextrocular *adj.* dextrocular, dextroocular.

dextrocularity *n.* dextrocularidad.

dextrocycloduction *n.* dextrocicloducción.

dextroduction *n.* dextroducción.

dextrogastria *n.* dextrogastria.

dextrogyral *adj.* dextrógiro, -ra.

dextrogyration *n.* dextrogiración.

dextromanual *adj.* dextromano, -na, dextromanual, diestro, -tra.

dextropedal *adj.* dextropedal.

dextroposition *n.* dextroposición.

  dextroposition of the heart dextroposición del corazón.

dextrorotary *adj.* dextrorrotatorio, -ria.

dextrorotation *n.* dextrorrotación.

dextrorotatory *adj.* dextrorrotatorio, -ria.

dextrosinistral *adj.* dextrosinistro, -tra.

dextrosuria *n.* dextrosuria.

dextrotorsion *n.* dextrotorsión.

dextrotropic *adj.* dextrotrópico, -ca.

dextroversion *n.* dextroversión.

  dextroversion of the heart dextroversión del corazón.

dextroverted *adj.* dextrovertido, -da.

diabetes *n.* diabetes.

  adult-onset diabetes diabetes de comienzo en la edad adulta.

  alimentary diabetes diabetes alimentaria.

  alloxan diabetes diabetes aloxánica, diabetes por aloxano.

  artificial diabetes diabetes artificial.

  brittle diabetes diabetes frágil, diabetes inestable.

  bronze diabetes diabetes bronceada.

  calcinuric diabetes diabetes calcinúrica.

  cerebrospinal diabetes diabetes cerebroespinal.

  chemical diabetes diabetes química.

  clinical diabetes diabetes clínica.

  diabetes albuminurinicus diabetes albuminúrica.

  diabetes innocens diabetes inocente.

  diabetes inositus diabetes inositus.

  diabetes insipidus diabetes insípida.

  diabetes intermittens diabetes intermitente.

  diabetes mellitus (DM) diabetes azucarada, diabetes glucémica, diabetes mellitus (DM), diabetes sacarina.

  endocrine diabetes mellitus diabetes mellitus endocrina.

  experimental diabetes diabetes experimental.

  gestational diabetes mellitus (GDM) diabetes mellitus gestacional (DMG).

  growth-onset diabetes diabetes de comienzo en el crecimiento.

  iatrogenic diabetes diabetes iatrogénica.

  idiopathic diabetes diabetes idiopática.

  insulin-deficient diabetes diabetes con deficiencia de insulina.

  insulin-dependent diabetes diabetes insulinodependiente.

  insulin-dependent diabetes mellitus (IDDM) diabetes mellitus insulinodependiente (DMID).

  juvenile diabetes diabetes juvenil.

  juvenile onset diabetes diabetes de comienzo en la juventud.

  ketosis-prone diabetes diabetes con tendencia a la cetosis.

  ketosis-resistant diabetes diabetes resistente a la cetosis.

  latent diabetes diabetes latente.

  lipoatrophic diabetes diabetes lipoatrófica.

  lipogenous diabetes diabetes lipógena.

  lipoplethoric diabetes diabetes lipopletórica.

  lipuric diabetes diabetes lipúrica.

  masked diabetes diabetes disimulada.

  maturity-onset diabetes diabetes de comienzo en la madurez.

  maturity-onset diabetes of youth (MODY) diabetes de comienzo en la madurez de la juventud.

  Mosler's diabetes diabetes de Mosler.

  nephrogenic diabetes diabetes nefrogénica.

  nephrogenic diabetes insipidus diabetes insípida nefrogénica.

  neurogenous diabetes diabetes nerviosa, diabetes neurógena.

  non-insulin dependent diabetes diabetes no insulinodependiente.

  non-insulin dependent diabetes (NIDD) diabetes no insulinodependiente (DNID).

  non-insulin-dependent diabetes mellitus (NIDDM) diabetes mellitus no insulinodependiente (DMNID).

  overflow diabetes diabetes por derramamiento.

  overt diabetes diabetes manifiesta.

  pancreatic diabetes diabetes de Lancereaux, diabetes pancreática.

  phlorhizin diabetes diabetes floricínica.

  phosphate diabetes diabetes fosfatúrica.

  potencial diabetes diabetes potencial.

  preclinic diabetes diabetes preclínica.

  pregnancy diabetes diabetes del embarazo.

  puncture diabetes diabetes por punción.

  renal diabetes diabetes renal.

  simple diabetes diabetes simple.

  skin diabetes diabetes cutánea.

  starvation diabetes diabetes por inanición.

  steroid diabetes diabetes esteroide, diabetes esteroidea.

  subclinical diabetes diabetes frustrada, diabetes subclínica.

  temporary diabetes diabetes pasajera, diabetes temporal.

  thiazide diabetes diabetes por tiazida.

  toxic diabetes diabetes tóxica.

  true diabetes diabetes verdadera.

  type I diabetes diabetes tipo I.

  type II diabetes diabetes del adulto, diabetes tipo II.

diabetic *adj.* diabético, -ca.

diabetid *n.* diabétide.

diabetogenic *adj.* diabetogénico, -ca.

diabetogenous *adj.* diabetógeno, -na.

diabetograph *n.* diabetógrafo.

diabetology *n.* diabetología.

diabetometer *n.* diabetómetro.

diabolepsy *n.* diabolepsia.

diabrosis *n.* diabrosis.

diabrotic *adj.* diabrótico, -ca.

diacetemia *n.* diacetemia.

diaceticaciduria *n.* diaceticaciduria.

diacetonuria *n.* diacetonuria.

diaceturia *n.* diaceturia.

diachronic *adj.* diacrónico, -ca.

diacid *n.* diácido.

diaclasia *n.* diaclasia, diaclasis.

diaclasis *n.* diaclasia, diaclasis.

diaclast *n.* diaclasto.

diacrinous *adj.* diacrino, -na.

diacrisis *n.* diacrisis.

diacritic *adj.* diacrítico, -ca.

diacritical *adj.* diacrítico, -ca.

diactinic *adj.* diactínico, -ca.

diactinism *n.* diactinismo.

diaderm *n.* diadermo.

diadermic *adj.* diadérmico, -ca.

diadochokinesia *n.* diadococinesia.

diadochokinesis *adj.* diadococinético, -ca.

diagnose *v.* diagnosticar.

diagnosis *n.* diagnóstico.

  antenatal diagnosis diagnóstico antenatal.

  biological diagnosis diagnóstico biológico.

  clinical diagnosis diagnóstico clínico.

  cytohistologic diagnosis diagnóstico citohistológico, diagnóstico citológico.

  diagnosis by exclusion diagnóstico por exclusión.

  diagnosis ex-juvantibus diagnóstico ex juvantibus.

  differential diagnosis diagnóstico diferencial.

  direct diagnosis diagnóstico directo.

  Ficker diagnosis diagnóstico de Ficker.

  laboratory diagnosis diagnóstico de laboratorio.

  neonatal diagnosis diagnóstico neonatal.

  niveau diagnosis diagnóstico de nivel.

  pathologic diagnosis diagnóstico patológico.

  physical diagnosis diagnóstico físico.

  prenatal diagnosis diagnóstico prenatal.

  provocative diagnosis diagnóstico provocado.

  serum diagnosis diagnóstico serológico.

  topographic diagnosis diagnóstico topográfico.

diagnostician *n.* diagnosticador, -ra.

diagnosticum *n.* diagnosticum.

diagram *n.* diagrama.

  Werner diagram diagrama de Werner.

diagrammatic *adj.* diagramático, -ca.

diagraph *n.* diágrafo.

diakinesis *n.* diacinesis.

dial *n.* dial.

dialysance *n.* dialisancia, dialización.

dialysate *n.* dializador, -ra.

dialysis *n.* diálisis.

  continuous ambulatory peritoneal dialysis (CAPD) diálisis peritoneal ambulatoria continua (DPAC).

  cross dialysis diálisis cruzada.

  dialysis retinae diálisis de la retina, diálisis retiniana.

  equilibrium dialysis diálisis por equilibrio.

  extracorporeal dialysis diálisis extracorpórea.

  lymph dialysis diálisis de linfa.

  peritoneal dialysis diálisis peritoneal.

  renal dialysis diálisis renal.

  single-needle dialysis unipunción, unipuntura.

dialyzable *adj.* dializable.

dialyze *v.* dializar.
dialyzer *n.* dializadorr.
diamagnetic *adj.* diamagnético, -ca.
diamagnetism *n.* diamagnetismo.
diameter *n.* diámetro.
diaminuria *n.* diaminuria.
diamnotic *adj.* diamnótico, -ca.
diamorphosis *n.* diamorfosis.
diancephalic *adj.* diencefálico, -ca.
diandria *n.* diandria.
diandry *n.* diandria.
dianoetic *adj.* dianoético, -ca.
Diantamoeba *n.* Diantamoeba.
diantebrachia *n.* diantebraquia.
diapason *n.* diapasón.
diapause *n.* diapausa.
embryonic diapause diapausa embrionaria.
diapedesis *n.* diapédesis.
diaphane *adj.* diáfano, -na.
diaphaneity *n.* diafanidad.
diaphanometer *n.* diafanómetro.
diaphanometry *n.* diafanometría.
diaphanoscope *n.* diafanoscopio.
diaphanoscopy *n.* diafanoscopia.
diaphemetric *adj.* diafemétrico, -ca.
diaphoresis *n.* diaforesis.
diaphoretic *adj.* diaforético, -ca.
diaphragm *n.* diafragma¹, diafragma².
Akerlund diaphragm diafragma de Akerlund.
arcing spring contraceptive diaphragm diafragma anticonceptivo de espiral.
Bucky diaphragm diafragma de Bucky, diafragma de Bucky-Potter.
Bucky-Potter diaphragm diafragma de Bucky, diafragma de Bucky-Potter.
coil-spring contraceptive diaphragm diafragma anticonceptivo de muelle espiral.
contraceptive diaphragm diafragma anticonceptivo.
flat spring contraceptive diaphragm diafragma anticonceptivo de resorte plano.
Potter-Bucky diaphragm diafragma de Potter-Bucky.
vaginal diaphragm diafragma vaginal.
diaphragma *n.* diaphragma.
diaphragmalgia *n.* diafragmalgia.
diaphragmatic *adj.* diafragmático, -ca.
diaphragmatocele *n.* diafragmatocele.
diaphragmitis *n.* diafragmatitis.
diaphragmodynia *n.* diafragmodinia.
diaphyseal *adj.* diafisario, -ria.
diaphysectomy *n.* diafisectomía.
diaphysis *n.* diáfisis.
diaphysitis *n.* diafisistis.
diapiresis *n.* diapiresis.
diaplacenta *adj.* diaplacentario, -ria.
diaplasis *n.* diaplasis.
diaplastic *adj.* diaplástico, -ca.
diaplexus *n.* diaplex, diaplexo.
diapnoic *adj.* diapnoico, -ca.
diapnotic *adj.* diapnótico, -ca.
diapophysis *n.* diapófisis.
diapyesis *n.* diapiesis.
diapyetic *adj.* diapiético, -ca.
diarrhea *n.* diarrea.
acute diarrhea diarrea aguda.
chewing gum diarrhea diarrea por chicle.
choleraic diarrhea diarrea coleraica, diarrea coleriforme.
colliquative diarrhea diarrea colicuativa.
congenital chloride diarrhea diarrea congénita con cloruro.
critical diarrhea diarrea crítica.
diarrhea ablactatorum diarrea del destete.

diarrhea ablactorum diarrea ablactorum.
diarrhea alba diarrea alba.
diarrhea chylosa diarrea quilosa.
diarrhea tubular diarrea tubular.
dietetic food diarrhea diarrea por alimentación dietética.
dysentric diarrhea diarrea disentérica.
enteral diarrhea diarrea entérica, diarrea intestinal.
epidemic diarrhea of the newborn diarrea epidémica del neonato, diarrea epidémica del recién nacido.
familial chloride diarrhea diarrea familiar con cloruro.
fatty diarrhea diarrea grasa.
fermental diarrhea diarrea fermentativa.
fermentative diarrhea diarrea fermentativa.
flagellate diarrhea diarrea por flagelados.
gastrogenous diarrhea diarrea gastrógena.
hill diarrhea diarrea de las alturas, diarrea de las colinas.
infantile diarrhea diarrea infantil.
irritative diarrhea diarrea irritativa.
lienteric diarrhea diarrea lientérica.
mecanical diarrhea diarrea mecánica.
membranous diarrhea diarrea membranosa.
morning diarrhea diarrea matinal.
mucous diarrhea diarrea mucosa.
neonatal diarrhea diarrea neonatal.
nocturnal diarrhea diarrea nocturna.
osmotic diarrhea diarrea osmótica.
pancreatogenous diarrhea diarrea pancreatógena.
paradoxical diarrhea diarrea paradójica.
parenteral diarrhea diarrea parenteral.
promontory diarrhea diarrea promontoria.
purulent diarrhea diarrea purulenta.
putrefactive diarrhea diarrea putrefactiva.
serous diarrhea diarrea serosa.
simple diarrhea diarrea simple.
stercoral diarrhea diarrea estercorácea.
summer diarrhea diarrea estival.
traveler's diarrhea diarrea del viajero.
trench diarrhea diarrea de las trincheras.
tropical diarrhea diarrea tropical.
uremic diarrhea diarrea urémica.
virus diarrhea diarrea por virus, diarrea viral, diarrea virósica.
watery diarrhea diarrea acuosa.
white diarrhea diarrea blanca.
diarrheal *adj.* diarreico, -ca.
diarrheic *adj.* diarreico, -ca.
diarrheogenic *adj.* diarreógeno, -na.
diarthric *adj.* diártrico, -ca.
diarthrodial *adj.* diartrodial.
diarthrosis *n.* diartrosis.
rotatory diarthrosis diartrosis rotatoria.
diarticular *v.* diarticular.
diaschisis *n.* diasquisis.
diascope *n.* diascopio.
diascopy *n.* diascopia.
diaspironecrosis *n.* diaspironecrosis.
diastalsis *n.* diastalsis.
diastaltic *adj.* diastáltico, -ca.
diastasic *adj.* diastásico, -ca.
diastasimetry *n.* diastasimetría.
diastasis *n.* diastasis.
diastasis cordis diastasis cardíaca, diastasis cordis.
diastasis recti abdominis diastasis recti abdominis.
iris diastasis diastasis del iris.
diastasuria *n.* diastasuria.
diastatic *adj.* diastásico, -ca, diastático, -ca.
diastema *n.* diastema.

diastematocrania *n.* diastematocrania.
diastematomyelia *n.* diastematomielia.
diastematopyelia *n.* diastematopielia.
diaster *n.* diáster.
diastole *n.* diástole.
cardiac diastole diástole cardíaca.
diastolic *adj.* diastólico, -ca.
diastrophism *n.* diastrofia, diastrofismo.
diataxia *n.* diataxia.
cerebral diataxia diataxia cerebral.
diatela *n.* diatela.
diathermal *adj.* diatérmico, -ca.
diathermancy *n.* diatermancia.
diathermocoagualtion *n.* diatermocoagulación.
diathermy *n.* diatermia.
short wave diathermy diatermia de onda corta.
surgical diathermy diatermia quirúrgica.
ultrashort wave diathermy diatermia por ondas ultracortas.
diathesis *n.* diátesis.
aneurysmal diathesis diátesis aneurismática.
arthritic diathesis diátesis artrítica.
asthenic diathesis diátesis asténica.
bilious diathesis diátesis biliosa.
catharral diathesis diátesis catarral.
contractural diathesis diátesis de contractura.
cystic diathesis diátesis quística.
Czerny's diathesis diátesis de Czerny, diátesis exudativa linfática.
exudative diathesis diátesis exudativa.
fibroplastic diathesis diátesis fibroplástica.
gouty diathesis diátesis diastrófica, diátesis gotosa.
hemorrhagic diathesis diátesis hemorrágica.
hemorrhagic diathesis of the newborn diátesis hemorrágica del neonato.
inopectic diathesis diátesis inopéctica.
lupus diathesis diátesis lupoide.
neuropathic diathesis diátesis neuropática.
ossifying diathesis diátesis osificante.
oxalic diathesis diátesis oxálica.
psychopathic diathesis diátesis psicopática.
rheumatic diathesis diátesis reumática.
spasmodic diathesis diátesis espasmódica, diátesis espasmofílica.
spasmophilic diathesis diátesis espasmódica, diátesis espasmofílica.
tuberculous diathesis diátesis tuberculosa.
urica diathesis diátesis úrica.
diathetic *adj.* diatésico, -ca.
diatomic *adj.* diatómico, -ca.
diatoric *n.* diatórico.
diauchenos *n.* diauqueno.
diazonal *adj.* diazonal.
diazone *n.* diazona.
dibasic *adj.* dibásico, -ca.
dibrachia *n.* dibraquia.
dibrachius *n.* dibraquio.
dicelous *adj.* díceleo, -a, dicelo, -la.
dicentric *adj.* dicéntrico, -ca.
dicephalus *n.* dicéfalo, -la.
dicephalus diauchenos dicéfalo diauqueno.
dicephalus dipus dibrachius dicéfalo dipus dibrachius.
dicephalus dipus tetrabrachius dicéfalo dipus tetrabrachius.
dicephalus dipygus dicéfalo dipygus.
dicephalus monauchenos dicéfalo monauqueno.
dicephalus parasiticus dicéfalo parásito.
dicephaly *n.* dicefalia.
dicheilia *n.* diqueilia.

dicheiria *n.* diquiria.
dicheirus *n.* diquiro, -ra.
dichilia *n.* diqueilia.
dichiria *n.* diquiria.
dichogeny *n.* dicogenia.
dichorial *adj.* dicorial.
dichorionic *adj.* dicoriónico, -ca.
dichotomization *n.* dicotomización.
dichotomy *n.* dicotomía.
dichroic *adj.* dicroico, -ca.
dichroism *n.* dicroísmo.
dichromasy *n.* dicromasia.
dichromat *adj.* dicrómata.
dichromatic *adj.* dicromático, -ca.
dichromatism *n.* dicromatismo.
dichromatopsia *n.* dicromatopsia.
dichromic *adj.* dicrómico, -ca.
dichromophil *adj.* dicromófilo, -la.
dichromophile *adj.* dicromófilo, -la.
dichromophilism *n.* dicromofilia.
dichuchwa *n.* dichuchwa.
dicliditis *n.* dicliditis.
diclodostosis *n.* diclidistosis, diclidostosis.
diclodotomy *n.* diclidotomía.
dicoria *n.* dicoria.
dicrotic *adj.* dicrótico, -ca.
dicrotism *n.* dicrotismo.
dictyokinesis *n.* dictiocinesis.
dictyosome *n.* dictiosoma.
dictyotene *n.* dictiotene, dictioteno.
didactylism *n.* didactilismo.
didactylous *adj.* didactilo, -la.
didelphia *n.* didelfia.
didelphic *adj.* didélfico, -ca.
didymalgia *n.* didimalgia.
didymitis *n.* didimitis.
didymodinia *n.* didimodinia.
didymus *n.* dídimo.
die *v.* morir.
diechoscope *n.* diecoscopio.
dielectric *adj.* dieléctrico, -ca.
dielectrolysis *n.* dielectrolisis.
diembryony *n.* diembrionía.
diencephalohypophyseal *adj.* diencefalohipofisiario, -ria.
diencephalon *n.* diencéfalo.
Dientamoeba *n.* Dientamoeba.
dieresis *n.* diéresis.
　spontaneous dieresis diéresis espontánea.
dieretic *adj.* dierético, -ca.
diesophagus *n.* diesófago.
diet *n.* dieta, régimen.
　absolute diet dieta absoluta.
　acid-ash diet dieta ácida, dieta de cenizas ácidas.
　adequate diet dieta adecuada.
　alkali-ash diet dieta alcalina, dieta de cenizas alcalinas.
　balanced diet dieta equilibrada.
　basal diet dieta basal.
　basic diet dieta básica.
　Cantani's diet dieta de Cantani.
　challenge diet dieta de provocación.
　clear liquid diet dieta hídrica, dieta líquida clara.
　diabetic diet dieta diabética, dieta para diabéticos, régimen diabético.
　Duke diet dieta de Duke.
　elemental diet dieta elemental.
　elimination diet dieta de eliminación, régimen de eliminación.
　Feingold diet dieta de Feingold.
　fiber diet dieta fibrosa.
　full diet dieta completa.
　full liquid diet dieta líquida completa.

　Giordano-Giovannetti diet dieta de Giordano-Giovanneti.
　gluten-free diet dieta libre de gluten, dieta sin gluten.
　gouty diet dieta para gotosos.
　high calorie diet dieta rica en calorías.
　high fat diet dieta rica en grasas.
　high fiber diet dieta rica en fibra.
　high protein diet dieta rica en proteínas.
　high-potassium diet dieta rica en potasio.
　high-vitamin diet dieta rica en vitaminas.
　Keith's low ionic diet dieta de Keith.
　Kempner's diet dieta de Kempner.
　ketogenic diet dieta cetógenica.
　light diet dieta libre de purinas ligera, dieta ligera.
　liquid diet dieta líquida.
　low calorie diet dieta baja en calorías, dieta pobre en calorías.
　low fat diet dieta pobre en grasas.
　low oxalate diet dieta pobre en oxalato.
　low purine diet dieta pobre en purina.
　low residue diet dieta pobre en residuos.
　low salt diet dieta hiposódica.
　low-calcium diet dieta pobre en calcio.
　low-caloric diet dieta hipocalórica.
　low-cholesterol diet dieta pobre en colesterol.
　low-saturated-fat diet dieta pobre en grasas saturadas.
　macrobiotic diet dieta macrobiótica.
　milk diet dieta láctea.
　mixed diet dieta mixta.
　Moro-Heisler diet dieta de Moro-Heisler.
　optimal diet dieta óptima.
　protein sparing diet dieta de conservación de proteínas.
　provocative diet dieta desencadenante.
　purine restricted diet dieta con restricción de purina.
　purine-low diet dieta baja en purinas.
　rachitic diet dieta raquítica.
　reducing diet dieta reductora.
　reduction diet dieta de adelgazamiento.
　regular diet dieta regular.
　rice diet dieta de arroz.
　salt-free diet dieta sin sal.
　Schemm diet dieta de Schemm.
　Schmidt diet dieta de Schmidt, dieta Schmidt-Strassburger.
　Schmidt-Strassburger diet dieta de Schmidt, dieta Schmidt-Strassburger.
　Sippy diet dieta de Sippy.
　smooth diet dieta suave.
　soft diet dieta blanda.
　subsistence diet dieta de subsistencia.
　Taylor's diet dieta de Taylor.
dietary allowance *n.* aporte dietético.
dietetic *adj.* dietético, -ca.
dietetics *n.* dietética.
dietitian *n.* dietetista, dietista.
dietogenetics *n.* dietogenética.
dietotherapy *n.* dietoterapia.
dietotoxicity *n.* dietotoxicidad.
difference *n.* diferencia.
　alveolar-arterial oxygen difference diferencia de oxígeno alveolar-arterial.
　arteriovenous carbon dioxide difference diferencia arteriovenosa de dióxido de carbono.
　arteriovenous oxygen difference diferencia arteriovenosa de oxígeno.
　individual difference diferencia individual.
　light difference diferencia luminosa.
differential *adj.* diferencial.

differentiate *v.* diferenciar.
differentiated *adj.* diferenciado, -da.
differentiation *n.* diferenciación.
　correlative differentiation diferenciación correlativa.
　dependent differentiation diferenciación dependiente.
　functional differentiation diferenciación funcional.
　invisible differentiation diferenciación invisible.
　regional differentiation diferenciación regional.
　self differentiation diferenciación propia.
diffraction *n.* difracción.
　X-ray diffraction difracción de rayos X.
diffuse *adj.* difundido, -ca, difundir, difuso, -sa.
diffusible *adj.* difusible.
diffusiometer *n.* difusiómetro.
diffusion *n.* difusión.
　double diffusion difusión doble.
　double diffusion in one dimension difusión doble unidimensional.
　double diffusion in two dimensions difusión doble bidimensional.
　exchange diffusion difusión de recambio.
　facilitated diffusion difusión facilitada.
　free diffusion difusión libre.
　gel diffusion difusión de geles, difusión en gel.
　impeded diffusion difusión impedida.
　single diffusion difusión simple.
　single radial diffusion difusión simple radial.
digametic *adj.* digamético, -ca.
digastric *adj.* digástrico, -ca.
digenea *n.* digenea.
digenesis *n.* digenesia.
digest *v.* digerir.
digestant *adj.* digestivo, -va.
digestion *n.* digestión.
　artificial digestion digestión artificial.
　bile digestion digestión biliar.
　difficult digestion digestión laboriosa.
　gastric digestion digestión gástrica.
　gastrointestinal digestion digestión gastrointestinal.
　intercellular digestion digestión intercelular.
　intestinal digestion digestión intestinal.
　intracellular digestion digestión intracelular.
　lipolytic digestion digestión lipolítica.
　pancreatic digestion digestión pancreática.
　parenteral digestion digestión parenteral.
　peptic digestion digestión péptica.
　primary digestion digestión primaria.
　secondary digestion digestión secundaria.
　sludge digestion digestión del cieno.
digit *n.* dígito.
　clubbed digit dígito claviforme.
digital *adj.* digital.
　digital tomosynthesis tomosíntesis digital.
digitalgia paresthetica *n.* digitalalgia parestésica.
digitalis *n.* digitial.
digitalism *n.* digitalismo.
digitalization *n.* digitalización.
digitate *adj.* digitado, -da.
digitatio *n.* digitatio.
digitation *n.* digitación.
digitiform *adj.* digitiforme.
digitoplantar *adj.* digitoplantar.
digitoxicity *n.* digitoxicidad.
digitus *n.* dígito, digitus.
　digitus valgus digitus valgus.
　digitus varus digitus varus.
diglossia *n.* diglosia.

dignathus *n.* dignato.
digynia *n.* diginia.
digyny *n.* diginia.
diheterozygote *n.* diheterocigoto.
dihybrid *n.* dihíbrido.
dihydrated *adj.* dihidratado, -da.
dihydric *adj.* dihídrico, -ca.
dihysteria *n.* dihisteria, dihisterismo.
diktyoma *n.* dictioma.
dilaceration *n.* dilaceración, dislaceración.
  radicular dilaceration dilaceración radicular.
  root dilaceration dilaceración radicular.
dilatancy *n.* dilatancia.
dilatation *n.* dilatación.
  ab ingestis dilatation dilatación ab ingestis.
  cardiac dilatation dilatación cardíaca.
  cervical dilatation dilatación cervical.
  digital dilatation dilatación digital.
  dilatation and curettage (D & C) dilatación y legrado.
  dilatation of the stomach dilatación del estómago.
  fractional dilatation and curettage dilatación y legrado fraccionados.
  gastric dilatation dilatación gástrica.
  idiopathic dilatation dilatación idiopática.
  post-stenotic dilatation dilatación postestenótica.
  prognathic dilatation dilatación del prognatión, dilatación prognática.
  toxic dilatation of the colon dilatación tóxica del colon.
  urethral dilatation dilatación de la uretra, dilatación uretral.
dilation *n.* dilatación.
  ab ingestis dilation dilatación ab ingestis.
  cardiac dilation dilatación cardíaca.
  cervical dilation dilatación cervical.
  digital dilation dilatación digital.
  dilation and curettage (D & C) dilatación y legrado.
  dilation of the stomach dilatación del estómago.
  fractional dilation and curettage dilatación y legrado fraccionados.
  gastric dilation dilatación gástrica.
  idiopathic dilation dilatación idiopática.
  post-stenotic dilation dilatación postestenótica.
  prognathic dilation dilatación del prognatión, dilatación prognática.
  toxic dilation of the colon dilatación tóxica del colon.
  urethral dilation dilatación de la uretra, dilatación uretral.
dilator *n.* dilatador.
  anal dilator dilatador anal.
  Arnott's dilator dilatador de Arnott.
  Einhorn's dilator dilatador de Einhorn.
  Goodell's dilator dilatador de Goodell.
  Hanks' dilator dilatador de Hanks.
  Hegar's dilator dilatador de Hegar.
  hydrostatic dilator dilatador hidrostático.
  Kollmann's dilator dilatador de Kollmann.
  laryngeal dilator dilatador laríngeo.
  Plummer's dilator dilatador de Plummer.
  Seigneux's dilator dilatador de Seigneux.
  Starck's dilator dilatador de Starck.
  Tubbs' dilator dilatador de Tubbs.
  Walther's dilator dilatador de Walther.
dildo *n.* dildo.
dilecanus *n.* dilecanus.
diluent *adj.* diluente, diluyente.
dilute[1] *adj.* diluido, -da.
dilute[2] *v.* diluir.

diluted *adj.* diluido, -da.
dilution *n.* dilución.
  doubling dilution dilución de duplicación.
  nitrogen dilution dilución de nitrógeno.
  serial dilution dilución seriada.
dimelia *n.* dimelia.
dimelus *n.* dimelo.
dimension *n.* dimensión.
  buccolingual dimension dimensión bucolingual.
  occlusal vertical dimension dimensión vertical oclusal.
  postural dimension dimensión de postura.
  rest vertical dimension dimensión vertical en reposo.
  vertical dimension dimensión vertical.
dimensionless *adj.* adimensional.
dimetria *n.* dimetria.
dimidiate *v.* dimidiar.
dimorphobiotic *adj.* dimorfobiótico, -ca.
dimple *n.* hoyuelo.
dineric *adj.* dinérico, -ca.
dineuric *adj.* dinéurico, -ca.
dinical *adj.* dínico, -ca.
dinitroresorcinol *n.* dinitrorresorcinol.
dinophobia *n.* dinofobia.
diocoele *n.* diocele.
diopsimeter *n.* diopsímetro.
diopter *n.* dioptría.
  prism diopter dioptría prismática.
dioptometer *n.* dioptómetro, dioptrómetro.
dioptometry *n.* dioptometría, dioptrometría.
dioptric *adj.* dióptrico, -ca.
dioptrics *n.* dióptrica.
dioptroscopy *n.* dioptroscopia.
diorthosis *n.* diortosis.
diovular *adj.* diovular.
diovulatory *adj.* diovulatorio, -a.
dioxide *n.* dióxido.
dip *n.* dip.
dipetalonemiasis *n.* dipetalonemiasis.
diphalia *n.* difalia.
diphallus *n.* difalia.
diphasic *adj.* difásico, -ca.
diphonia *n.* difonía.
diphterial *adj.* difterial.
diphtheria *n.* difteria.
  avian diphtheria difteria aviaria.
  Bretonneau diphtheria difteria de Bretonneau.
  circumscribed diphtheria difteria circunscrita.
  cutaneous diphtheria difteria cutánea, difteria dérmica.
  diphtheria gravis difteria grave.
  false diphtheria difteria falsa.
  faucial diphtheria difteria faucial.
  gangrenous diphtheria difteria gangrenosa.
  laryngeal diphtheria difteria laríngea, garrotillo.
  malignant diphtheria difteria maligna.
  nasal diphtheria difteria nasal.
  nasopharyngeal diphtheria difteria nasofaríngea.
  pharyngeal diphtheria difteria faríngea.
  septic diphtheria difteria séptica.
  surgical diphtheria difteria quirúrgica.
  umbilical diphtheria difteria umbilical.
  wound diphtheria difteria de las heridas.
diphtheritic *adj.* diftérico, -ca.
diphtheritis *n.* difteritis.
diphtheroid *adj.* difteroide.
diphthongia *n.* diftongia.
Diphyllobothriidae *n.* Diphyllobothriidae.
diplacusis *n.* diplacusia.

diplacusis binauralis diplacusia biaural.
diplacusis binauralis dysharmonica diplacusia diaural disarmónica.
diplacusis dysharmonica diplacusia disarmónica.
diplacusis echoica diplacusia ecoica.
diplacusis monauralis diplacusia monoaural.
diplegia *n.* diplejía.
  atonic diplegia diplejía atónica.
  cerebral infantile diplegia diplejía cerebral infantil.
  congenital facial diplegia diplejía facial congénita.
  facial diplegia diplejía facial.
  masticatory diplegia diplejía masticatoria.
  spastic diplegia diplejía espástica.
diplegic *adj.* dipléjico, -ca.
diploalbuminuria *n.* diploalbuminuria.
diplobacillus *n.* diplobacilo.
  Morax- Axenfeld diplobacillus diplobacilo de Morax- Axenfeld.
diplobacteria *n.* diplobacteria.
diploblastic *adj.* diploblástico, -ca.
diplocardia *n.* diplocardia.
diplocephalus *n.* diplocéfalo.
diplocephaly *n.* diplocefalia.
diplocheiria *n.* diploqueiria, diploquiria.
diplochiria *n.* diploquciria, diploquiria.
diplococcemia *n.* diplococemia.
diplococcoid *adj.* diplocócico, -ca, diplococoide.
diplococcus *n.* diplococo.
diplocoria *n.* diplocoria.
diplodiatoxicosis *n.* diplodiatoxicosis.
diploë *n.* diploe.
diploetic *adj.* diploético, -ca.
diplogenesis *n.* diplogénesis.
diplogram *n.* diplograma.
diploic *adj.* diploico, -ca.
diploid *adj.* diploide.
diploidy *n.* diploidía.
diplomelituria *n.* diplomelituria.
diplomyelia *n.* diplomielia.
diploneural *adj.* diploneural.
diplont *n.* diplonte.
diplopagus *adj.* diplópago, -ga.
diplophase *n.* diplofase.
diplophonia *n.* diplofonia.
diplopia *n.* diplopía, diploscopía.
  binocular diplopia diplopía binocular.
  crossed diplopia diplopía cruzada.
  direct diplopia diplopía directa, diplopía simple.
  heteronymous diplopia diplopía heterónima.
  homonymous diplopia diplopía homónima.
  horizontal diplopia diplopía horizontal.
  monocular diplopia diplopía monocular, diplopía unicular.
  paradoxical diplopia diplopía paradójica.
  physiological diplopia diplopía fisiológica.
  stereoscopic diplopia diplopía estereoscópica.
  torsional diplopia diplopía de torsión.
  vertical diplopia diplopía vertical.
diplopiometer *n.* diplopiomietro.
diplopodia *n.* diplopodia.
diploscope *n.* diploscopio.
diplosomatia *n.* diplosomancia.
diplosome *n.* diplosoma.
diplosomia *n.* diplosomía.
diplotene *n.* diplotene, diploteno.
dipodia *n.* dipodia.
diprosopus *n.* diprósopo.
  diprosopus tetrophthalmus diprósopo tetroftalmo.

diprotrizoate *n.* diprotrizoato.
dipsesis *n.* dipsesis.
dipsetic *adj.* dipséptico, -ca.
dipsogen *n.* dipsógeno.
dipsogenic *adj.* dipsogénico, -ca.
dipsomania *n.* dipsomanía.
dipsosis *n.* dipsosis.
dipsotherapy *n.* dipsoterapia.
dipus *n.* dipo.
dipygus *n.* dipigo, dipygus.
direct *adj.* directo, -ta.
directive *n.* instrucción.
  advance directive instrucción previa.
director *n.* director, -ra.
  grooved director director acanalado.
  medical director director médico.
directoscope *n.* directoscopio.
dirhinic *adj.* dirrínico, -ca.
dirigation *n.* dirigación.
dirigomotor *adj.* dirigomotor, -ra.
disability *n.* discapacidad, incapacidad.
  developmental disability incapacidad del desarrollo.
  developmental disability (DD) discapacidad de desarrollo (DD).
  disability to sustain spontaneous ventilation incapacidad para mantener la ventilación espontánea.
  learning disability discapacidad para el aprendizaje.
  mental disability incapacidad mental.
  occupational disability discapacidad profesional.
disacchariduria *n.* disacariduria.
disacidify *v.* desacidificar.
disaggregation *n.* desagregación, disgregación.
disarticulation *n.* desarticulación.
  Chopart's disarticulation desarticulación de Chopart.
  Larrey's disarticulation desarticulación de Larrey.
  Mackenzie's disarticulation desarticulación de Mackenzie.
  Malgaigne's disarticulation desarticulación de Malgaigne.
  Syme's disarticulation desarticulación de Syme.
  Tripier's disarticulation desarticulación de Tripier.
disassociation *n.* disasociación.
disavowal *n.* renegación.
disc *n.* disco.
  abrasive disc disco abrasivo.
  Bardeen's primitive disc disco primitivo de Bardeen.
  Bardeen's disc disco de Bardeen.
  Blake's disc disco de Blake.
  blastodermic disc disco blastodérmico.
  blood disc disco sanguíneo.
  Burlew disc disco de Burlew.
  carborundum disc disco de carborundo.
  choked disc disco obstruido.
  cloth disc disco de tela.
  conic disc disco cónico.
  cupped disc disco en forma de copa.
  cutting disc disco cortante.
  cuttlefish disc disco de sepia.
  dental disc disco dental.
  diamond disc disco de diamante.
  ectodermal disc disco ectodérmico.
  embryonic disc disco embrionario.
  emery disc disco de esmeril.
  gelatin disc disco de gelatina.
  germ disc disco germinal, disco germinativo.

  germinal disc disco germinal, disco germinativo.
  herniated disc disco herniado.
  intercalated disc disco intercalado.
  interpubic disc disco interpúbico.
  intra-articular disc disco intraarticular.
  Merkel's disc disco de Merkel.
  micrometer disc disco micrométrico.
  Newton's disc disco de Newton.
  Plácido's disc disco de Plácido.
  polishing disc disco pulidor.
  proligerous disc disco prolígero.
  protruded disc disco protruido.
  Rekoss disc disco de Rekoss.
  rod disc disco de las células de los bastones.
  ruptured disc disco roto, disco rupturado.
  sacrococcygeal disc disco sacrococcígeo.
  sandpaper disc disco de papel de lija.
  Schiefferdecker's disc disco de Schiefferdecker.
  stenopaic disc disco estenopaico, disco estenopeico.
  stenopeic disc disco estenopaico, disco estenopeico.
  stroboscopic disc disco estroboscópico.
discectomy *n.* discectomía.
  percutaneous discectomy discectomía percutánea.
discharge *n.* alta, descarga[1].
  absolute discharge alta definitiva.
  brush discharge descarga de cepillo.
  disruptive discharge descarga de desorganización.
  electric discharge descarga electrica.
  epileptic discharge descarga epiléptica.
  involuntary discharge alta involuntaria.
  nervous discharge descarga nerviosa.
  systolic discharge descarga sistólica.
dischronation *n.* discronación.
disciform *adj.* disciforme.
discission *n.* discisión.
  cataract discission discisión de la catarata.
  discission of the cervix uteri discisión del cuello uterino.
  discission of the pleura discisión de la pleura.
  posterior discission discisión posterior.
discitis *n.* discitis.
disclination *n.* disclinación.
discoblastic *adj.* discoblástico, -ca.
discoblastula *n.* discoblástula.
discocyte *n.* discocito.
discogastrula *n.* discogástrula.
discogenetic *adj.* discogenético, -ca.
discogenic *adj.* discogénico, -ca.
discogram *n.* discograma.
discography *n.* discografía.
discoid *n.* discoide.
discoidectomy *n.* discoidectomía.
discontinuous *adj.* discontinuo, -a.
discopathy *n.* discopatía.
  traumatic cervical discopathy discopatía cervical traumática.
discophorous *adj.* discóforo, -ra.
discoplasm *n.* discoplasma.
discordance *n.* discordancia.
discordant *adj.* discordante.
discoria *n.* discoria[1].
discrepancy *n.* discrepancia.
  tooth size discrepancy discrepancia de las dimensiones dentales.
discrete *adj.* discreto, -ta.
discrimination *n.* discriminación.
  tactile discrimination discriminación táctil.
discriminator *n.* discriminador.
  lower level discriminator (LLD) discriminador de bajo nivel (DBN).

  upper level discriminator (ULD) discriminador de alto nivel (DAN).
discus *n.* disco, discus.
  discus proligerus disco prolígero.
discussive *n.* disolvente[2].
discutient *n.* disolvente[2].
disdiaclast *n.* disdiaclasto.
disease *n.* enfermedad.
  aaa disease enfermedad aaa.
  accumulation disease enfermedad por acumulación.
  Acosta's disease enfermedad de Acosta.
  Adams-Stokes disease enfermedad de Adams-Stokes.
  Addison-Biermer disease enfermedad de Addison-Biermer.
  Addison's disease enfermedad de Addison.
  adenoid disease enfermedad adenoidea.
  akamushi disease enfermedad akamushi.
  Albers-Schönberg disease enfermedad de Albers-Schönberg.
  Albert's disease enfermedad de Albert.
  Albright's disease enfermedad de Albright.
  Alexander's disease enfermedad de Alexander.
  Alpers disease enfermedad de Alpers.
  Alzheimer's disease enfermedad de Alzheimer.
  anarthritic rheumatoid disease enfermedad anartrítica reumatoidea.
  Anders' disease enfermedad de Anders.
  antibody deficiency disease enfermedad por deficiencia de anticuerpos.
  aortoiliac occlusive disease enfermedad aortoilíaca oclusiva.
  Aran-Duchenne disease enfermedad de Aran-Duchenne.
  Armstrong's disease enfermedad de Armstrong.
  Aujeszky's disease enfermedad de Aujeszky.
  Australian X disease enfermedad X australiana.
  autoimmune disease enfermedad autoinmune.
  aviator's disease enfermedad de los aviadores.
  Ayerza's disease enfermedad de Arrillaga-Ayerza, enfermedad de Ayerza.
  Baelz's disease enfermedad de Baelz.
  Ballet's disease enfermedad de Ballet.
  Baló's disease enfermedad de Baló.
  Bamberger-Marie disease enfermedad de Bamberger-Marie.
  Bamberger's disease enfermedad de Bamberger.
  Bannister's disease enfermedad de Bannister.
  Barclay-Baron disease enfermedad de Barclay-Baron.
  Barlow's disease enfermedad de Barlow.
  Barraquer's disease enfermedad de Barraquer, enfermedad de Barraquer-Simons.
  Basedow's disease enfermedad de Basedow.
  Batten-Mayou disease enfermedad de Batten-Mayou.
  bauxite worker's disease enfermedad de los trabajadores de bauxita.
  Bazin's disease enfermedad de Bazin.
  Beauvais' disease enfermedad de Beauvais.
  Bechterew's disease enfermedad de Bechterew.
  Begbie's disease enfermedad de Begbie.
  Béguez César disease enfermedad de Béguez César.
  Behçet's disease enfermedad de Behçet.
  Behr's disease enfermedad de Behr.
  Benson's disease enfermedad de Benson.

Bernhardt's disease enfermedad de Bernhardt, enfermedad de Bernhardt-Roth.

Besnier-Boeck-Schaumann disease enfermedad de Besnier-Boeck-Schaumann.

Best's disease enfermedad de Best.

Bielschowsky's disease enfermedad de Bielschowsky.

Binswanger's disease enfermedad de Binswanger.

blinding disease enfermedad cegadora.

Bloch-Sulzberger disease enfermedad de Bloch-Sulzberger.

Blocq's disease enfermedad de Blocq.

Blount-Barber disease enfermedad de Blount, enfermedad de Blount-Barber.

Blount's disease enfermedad de Blount, enfermedad de Blount-Barber.

blue disease enfermedad azul.

Bornholm disease enfermedad de Bornholm.

Bouchard's disease enfermedad de Bouchard.

Bouillaud's disease enfermedad de Bouillaud.

Bourneville-Pringle disease enfermedad de Bourneville-Pringle.

Bourneville's disease enfermedad de Bourneville.

Bowen's disease enfermedad de Bowen.

Brailsford-Morquio disease enfermedad Brailsford-Morquio.

Breda's disease enfermedad de Breda.

Bright's disease enfermedad de Bright.

Brill's disease enfermedad de Brill, enfermedad de Brill-Zinsser.

Brill-Symmers disease enfermedad de Brill-Symmers.

Brill-Zinsser disease enfermedad de Brill, enfermedad de Brill-Zinsser.

Brocq's disease enfermedad de Brocq.

Brodie's disease enfermedad de Brodie.

bronzed disease enfermedad bronceada.

Brooke's disease enfermedad de Brooke.

Bruck's disease enfermedad de Bruck.

Brushfield-Wyatt disease enfermedad de Brushfield-Wyatt.

Bruton's disease enfermedad de Bruton.

Buerger's disease enfermedad de Buerger.

Bürger-Grütz disease enfermedad de Bürger-Grütz.

Bury's disease enfermedad de Bury.

Buschke's disease enfermedad de Buschke.

Busquet's disease enfermedad de Busquet.

Busse-Buschke disease enfermedad de Busse-Buschke.

Byler's disease enfermedad de Byler.

Caffey's disease enfermedad de Caffey.

caisson disease enfermedad de los cajones.

Calvé-Perthes disease enfermedad de Calvé-Perthes, enfermedad de Legg, enfermedad de Legg-Calvé-Perthes, enfermedad de Legg-Perthes.

Canavan's disease enfermedad de Canavan.

Caroli's disease enfermedad de Caroli.

Carrión's disease enfermedad de Carrión.

cat-bite disease enfermedad por mordedura de gato.

cat-scratch disease enfermedad por arañazo de gato.

celiac disease celiaquía, enfermedad celíaca.

central core disease enfermedad del núcleo central.

cerebrovascular disease enfermedad cerebrovascular.

Chagas' disease enfermedad de Chagas, enfermedad de Chagas-Cruz.

Chagas-Cruz disease enfermedad de Chagas, enfermedad de Chagas-Cruz.

Charcot-Marie-Tooth disease enfermedad de Charcot-Marie-Tooth.

Charcot's disease enfermedad de Charcot.

Charlouis' disease enfermedad de Charlouis.

Cheadle's disease enfermedad de Cheadle.

Chiari's disease enfermedad de Chiari.

Chicago disease enfermedad de Chicago.

cholesterol ester storage disease enfermedad por almacenamiento de ésteres de colesterol.

Christian's disease enfermedad de Christian.

Christmas disease enfermedad de Christmas.

chronic active liver disease enfermedad hepática crónica activa.

chronic hypertensive disease enfermedad hipertensiva crónica.

chronic mountain disease enfermedad crónica de la montaña.

chronic obstructive pulmonary disease (COPD) enfermedad pulmonar obstructiva crónica (EPOC).

cytomegalic inclusion disease enfermedad de inclusiones citomegálicas.

circling disease enfermedad de los círculos.

Coats' disease enfermedad de Coats.

Cockayne's disease enfermedad de Cockayne.

collagen-vascular disease enfermedad colágena, enfermedad colagenovascular.

combined system disease enfermedad de sistemas combinados.

communicable disease enfermedad comunicable.

Conradi's disease enfermedad de Conradi.

constitutional disease enfermedad constitucional.

contagious disease enfermedad contagiosa.

Cori's disease enfermedad de Cori.

coronary artery disease coronariopatía.

Corrigan's disease enfermedad de Corrigan.

Cotunnius disease enfermedad de Cotugnof, enfermedad de Cotunnius.

Cowden's disease enfermedad de Cowden.

Creutzfeldt-Jakob disease enfermedad de Creutzfeldt-Jakob.

Crigler-Najjar disease enfermedad de Crigler-Najjar.

Crocq's disease enfermedad de Crocq.

Crohn's disease enfermedad de Crohn.

Crouzon's disease enfermedad de Crouzon.

Cruveilhier-Baumgarten disease enfermedad de Cruveilhier-Baumgarten.

Cruveilhier's disease enfermedad de Cruveilhier.

Csillag's disease enfermedad de Csillag.

Curschmann's disease enfermedad de Curschmann.

Cushing's disease enfermedad de Cushing.

cystic disease of renal medulla enfermedad quística de la médula renal.

cystic disease of the breast enfermedad quística de la mama.

cystine storage disease enfermedad por almacenamiento de cistina.

Czerny's disease enfermedad de Czerny.

dancing disease enfermedad danzante.

Darier's disease enfermedad de Darier.

Darling's disease enfermedad de Darling.

Davies' disease enfermedad de Davies.

De Quervain's disease enfermedad de De Quervain.

decompression disease enfermedad por descompresión.

deficiency disease enfermedad por deficiencia.

degenerative joint disease enfermedad articular degenerativa.

Degos' disease enfermedad de Degos.

Déjerine's disease enfermedad Déjerine, enfermedad Déjerine-Sottas.

Déjerine-Sottas disease enfermedad Déjerine, enfermedad Déjerine-Sottas.

dense-deposit disease enfermedad con depósitos densos.

Dercum's disease enfermedad de Dercum.

Deutschländer's disease enfermedad de Deutschländer.

Devic's disease enfermedad de Devic.

Di Guglielmo's disease enfermedad de Di Guglielmo.

disappearing bone disease enfermedad de hueso desaparecido.

Döhle disease enfermedad de Döhle.

Donohue's disease enfermedad de Donohue.

drug-induced disease enfermedad inducida por fármacos.

Dubini's disease enfermedad de Dubini.

Dubois' disease enfermedad de Dubois.

Duchenne's disease enfermedad de Duchenne.

Duhring 's disease enfermedad de Duhring.

Dukes' disease enfermedad de Dukes, enfermedad de Dukes-Filatov.

Duncan's disease enfermedad de Duncan.

Duplay's disease enfermedad de Duplay.

Dupuytren's disease of the foot enfermedad del pie de Dupuytren.

Durand-Nicolas-Favre disease enfermedad de Durand-Nicolas-Favre.

Duroziez's disease enfermedad de Duroziez.

Eales' disease enfermedad de Eales.

Ebstein's disease enfermedad de Ebstein.

Eisenmenger's disease enfermedad de Eisenmenger.

emotional disease enfermedad emocional.

Engelmann's disease enfermedad de Engelmann.

Epstein's disease enfermedad de Epstein.

Erb-Charcot disease enfermedad de Erb-Charcot.

Erb-Goldflam disease enfermedad de Erb-Goldflam.

Erb's disease enfermedad de Erb.

Erdheim disease enfermedad de Erdheim.

Eulenburg's disease enfermedad de Eulenburg.

exanthematous disease enfermedad exantemática.

extramammary Paget's disease enfermedad de Paget extramamaria.

extrapyramidal disease enfermedad extrapiramidal.

Fabry's disease enfermedad de Fabry.

Fahr's disease enfermedad de Fahr.

Fahr-Volhard disease enfermedad de Fahr-Volhard.

Farber's disease enfermedad de Farber.

fat-deficiency disease enfermedad por deficiencia de grasas.

Favre-Durand-Nicolas disease enfermedad de Favre-Durand-Nicolas.

Feer's disease enfermedad de Feer.

femoropopliteal occlusive disease enfermedad femoropoplítea oclusiva.

Fenwick's disease enfermedad de Fenwick.

fibrocystic disease of the breast enfermedad fibroquística de la mama.

fibrocystic disease of the pancreas enfermedad fibroquística del páncreas.

Fiedler's disease enfermedad de Fiedler.
fifth disease enfermedad quinta.
Filatov's disease enfermedad de Filatov, enfermedad de Filatow.
Flajani disease enfermedad de Flajani.
Flatau-Schilder disease enfermedad de Flatau-Schilder.
Flegel's disease enfermedad de Flegel.
Fleischner's disease enfermedad de Fleischner.
flint disease enfermedad de pedernal.
Folling's disease enfermedad de Folling.
Forbes' disease enfermedad de Forbes.
Fordyce's disease enfermedad de Fordyce.
Forrestier's disease enfermedad de Forrestier.
Fothergill's disease enfermedad de Fothergill.
Fournier's disease enfermedad de Fournier.
Fox-Fordyce disease enfermedad de Fox-Fordyce.
Francis' disease enfermedad de Francis.
Frei disease enfermedad de Frei.
Freiberg's disease enfermedad de Freiberg.
Friedländer disease enfermedad de Friedländer.
Friedmann's disease enfermedad de Friedmann.
Friedreich's disease enfermedad de Friedreich.
Frommel's disease enfermedad de Frommel.
Fuerstner's disease enfermedad de Fuerstner.
fusospirochetal disease enfermedad fusoespiroquetal.
Gaisböck's disease enfermedad de Gaisböck.
Gamma's disease enfermedad de Gamma.
Gamstorp's disease enfermedad de Gamstorp.
Gandy-Nanta disease enfermedad de Gandy-Nanta.
garapata disease enfermedad de las garrapatas.
Garré's disease enfermedad de Garré.
Gaucher's disease enfermedad de Gaucher.
Gee-Herter disease enfermedad de Gee, enfermedad de Gee-Herter, enfermedad de Gee-Herter-Heubner, enfermedad de Gee-Thaysen.
Gee-Herter-Heubner disease enfermedad de Gee, enfermedad de Gee-Herter, enfermedad de Gee-Herter-Heubner, enfermedad de Gee-Thaysen.
Gee's disease enfermedad de Gee, enfermedad de Gee-Herter, enfermedad de Gee-Herter-Heubner, enfermedad de Gee-Thaysen.
Gee-Thaysen disease enfermedad de Gee, enfermedad de Gee-Herter, enfermedad de Gee-Herter-Heubner, enfermedad de Gee-Thaysen.
Gerhardt's disease enfermedad de Gerhardt.
Gerlier's disease enfermedad de Gerlier.
Gibney's disease enfermedad de Gibney.
Gierke's disease enfermedad de Gierke.
Gilbert's disease enfermedad de Gilbert.
Gilchrist's disease enfermedad de Gilchrist.
Gilles de la Tourette's disease enfermedad de Gilles de la Tourette.
Glanzmann's disease enfermedad de Glanzmann.
glycogen-storage disease enfermedad por almacenamiento de glucógeno.
Goldflam disease enfermedad de Goldflam.
Gorham's disease enfermedad de Gorham.
Gougerot and Blum disease enfermedad de Gougerot y Blum.

Gougerot-Ruiter disease enfermedad de Gougerot-Ruiter.
Gougerot-Sjögren disease enfermedad de Gougerot-Sjögren.
Gowers disease enfermedad de Gowers.
Graefe's disease enfermedad de Graefe.
graft versus host disease enfermedad de injerto versus huésped.
Graves' disease enfermedad de Graves.
Gross disease enfermedad de Gross.
Grover's disease enfermedad de Grover.
Guinon's disease enfermedad de Guinon.
GVH disease enfermedad IVH.
H disease enfermedad H.
Haff disease enfermedad de Haff.
Haglund's disease enfermedad de Haglund.
Hailley and Hailley disease enfermedad de Hailley y Hailley.
Hallervorden-Spatz disease enfermedad de Hallervorden-Spatz.
Hand-Schüller-Christian disease enfermedad de Hand-Schüller-Christian.
Hansen's disease enfermedad de Hansen.
Harada's disease enfermedad de Harada.
Hartnup disease enfermedad de Hartnup.
Hashimoto's disease enfermedad de Hashimoto.
Heberden's disease enfermedad de Heberden.
Hebra's disease enfermedad de Hebra.
Heck's disease enfermedad de Heck.
Heine-Medin disease enfermedad de Heine-Medin.
hemorrhagic disease of the newborn enfermedad hemorrágica del neonato, enfermedad hemorrágica del recién nacido.
hepatolenticular disease enfermedad hepatolenticular.
hereditary disease enfermedad hereditaria.
Herlitz's disease enfermedad de Herlitz.
herring-worm disease enfermedad del gusano del arenque.
Hers' disease enfermedad de Hers.
Heubner's disease enfermedad de Heubner.
hidebound disease enfermedad de la piel endurecida.
hip-joint disease coxartropatía.
Hippel-Lindau disease enfermedad de Hippel, enfermedad de Hippel-Lindau.
Hippel's disease enfermedad de Hippel, enfermedad de Hippel-Lindau.
Hirschsprung's disease enfermedad de Hirschsprung.
His disease enfermedad de His-Werner.
His-Werner disease enfermedad de His-Werner.
Hodgkin's disease enfermedad de Hodgkin.
Hodgson's disease enfermedad de Hodgson.
Hoffa's disease enfermedad de Hoffa.
hookworm disease enfermedad de uncinarias.
Hoppe-Goldflam disease enfermedad de Hoppe-Goldflam.
Horton's disease enfermedad de Horton.
Huchard's disease enfermedad de Huchard.
Huntington's disease enfermedad de Huntington.
Hunt's disease enfermedad de Hunt.
Hutchinson-Gilford disease enfermedad de Hutchinson-Gilford.
Hutinel's disease enfermedad de Hutinel.
hyaline membrane disease enfermedad de la membrana hialina.
hydatic disease enfermedad hidatídica.
Hyde's disease enfermedad de Hyde.

Iceland disease enfermedad de Islandia.
I-cell disease enfermedad de células I.
idiopathic Bamberger-Marie disease enfermedad idiopática de Bamberger-Marie.
immune complex disease enfermedad de inmunocomplejos.
immunodeficiency disease enfermedad de inmunodeficiencia.
immunoproliferative small intestinal disease enfermedad inmunoproliferativa del intestino delgado.
inclusion body disease enfermedad de cuerpos de inclusión.
industrial disease enfermedad industrial.
infectious disease enfermedad infecciosa.
infective disease enfermedad infecciosa.
interstitial disease enfermedad intersticial.
iron-storage disease enfermedad por almacenamiento de hierro.
island disease enfermedad de las islas.
Jaffe-Lichtenstein disease enfermedad de Jaffe-Lichtenstein.
Jakob-Creuzfeldt disease enfermedad de Jakob, enfermedad de Jakob-Creutzfeldt.
Jansky-Bielschowsky disease enfermedad de Jansky-Bielschowsky.
Jensen's disease enfermedad de Jensen.
Johnson-Stevens disease enfermedad de Johnson-Stevens.
Jüngling's disease enfermedad de Jüngling.
kakke disease kakke, kakké.
Katayama disease enfermedad de Katayama.
Kawasaki disease enfermedad de Kawasaki.
Kiembock's disease enfermedad de Kiemböck, enfermedad del martillo neumático.
Kimmelstiel-Wilson disease enfermedad de Kimmelstiel-Wilson.
Kimura's disease enfermedad de Kimura.
kinky-hair disease enfermedad de cabello ensortijado.
Kinnier-Wilson disease enfermedad de Kinnier-Wilson.
Kirkland's disease enfermedad de Kirkland.
Köhler's disease enfermedad de Köhler.
Köhlmeier-Degos disease enfermedad de Köhlmeier-Degos.
Krabbe's disease enfermedad de Krabbe.
Krishaber's disease enfermedad de Krishaber.
Kufs disease enfermedad de Kufs.
Kugelberg-Welander disease enfermedad de Kugelberg-Welander.
Kuhnt-Junius disease enfermedad de Kuhnt-Junius.
Kümmel's disease enfermedad de Kümmel.
Kyrle's disease enfermedad de Kyrle.
La Peyronie's disease enfermedad de La Peyronie.
Laënnec's disease enfermedad de Laënnec.
Lafora body disease enfermedad de cuerpos de Lafora.
Lafora's disease enfermedad de Lafora.
Landouzy's disease enfermedad de Landouzy.
laughing disease enfermedad de la risa.
L-chain disease enfermedad de cadena L.
Legg disease enfermedad de Legg, enfermedad de Legg-Calvé-Perthes, enfermedad de Legg-Perthes.
Legg-Perthes disease enfermedad de Legg, enfermedad de Legg-Calvé-Perthes, enfermedad de Legg-Perthes.
legionnaires' disease enfermedad de los legionarios.
linear IgA bullous disease in children enfermedad ampollar de IgA lineal en niños.

Little's disease enfermedad de Little.
Lyme disease enfermedad de Lyme.
lysosomal disease enfermedad lisosomal.
Madelung's disease enfermedad de Madelung.
Malassez's disease enfermedad de Malassez.
Malherbe's disease enfermedad de Malherbe.
maple syrup urine disease enfermedad de la orina en jarabe de arce.
marble bone disease enfermedad de hueso de mármol.
Marburg virus disease enfermedad por virus de Marburg.
Marchiafava-Micheli disease enfermedad de Marchiafava-Micheli.
Marie-Strümpell disease enfermedad de Marie-Strümpell.
Marsh's disease enfermedad de Marsh.
McArdle's disease enfermedad de McArdle.
Mediterranean-hemoglobin E disease enfermedad mediterránea-hemoglobina.
Meige's disease enfermedad de Meige.
Ménétrier's disease enfermedad de Ménétrier.
Ménière's disease enfermedad de Ménière.
mental disease enfermedad mental.
Meyer's disease enfermedad de Meyer.
miasmatic disease enfermedad miasmática.
microcystic disease of the renal medulla enfermedad microquística de la médula renal.
micrometastatic disease enfermedad micrometastásica.
Miller's disease enfermedad de Miller.
Milroy's disease enfermedad de Milroy.
Milton's disease enfermedad de Milton.
Minamata disease enfermedad de Minamata.
miner's disease enfermedad de los mineros.
minimal-change disease enfermedad de cambios mínimos.
mixed connective-tissue disease enfermedad mixta del tejido conjuntivo.
molecular disease enfermedad molecular.
Monge's disease enfermedad de Monge.
Morgagni's disease enfermedad de Morgagni.
Morquio's disease condrosteodistrofia, enfermedad de Morquio.
Morton's disease enfermedad de Morton.
Morvan's disease enfermedad de Morvan.
motor neuron disease enfermedad de las neuronas motoras.
multicore disease enfermedad multifocal.
Nicolas-Favre disease enfermedad de Nicolas-Favre.
Niemann-Pick disease enfermedad de Niemann-Pick.
nil disease enfermedad nil, enfermedad nula.
Nonne-Milroy disease enfermedad de Nonne-Milroy.
notifiable disease enfermedad notificable.
occupational disease enfermedad ocupacional.
Ollier's disease enfermedad de Ollier.
Oppenheim disease enfermedad de Oppenheim.
organic disease enfermedad orgánica.
Ormond's disease enfermedad de Ormond.
Osler's disease enfermedad de Osler.
Paget's disease enfermedad de Paget.
paper mill worker's disease enfermedad de los trabajadores de fábricas de papel.
parasitic disease enfermedad parasitaria.
Parkinson's disease enfermedad de Parkinson.
Parrot's disease enfermedad de Parrot.
Parry's disease enfermedad de Parry.

Pauzat's disease enfermedad de Pauzat.
Pavy's disease enfermedad de Pavy.
Paxton's disease enfermedad de Paxton.
Payr's disease enfermedad de Payr.
pearl-worker's disease enfermedad de los que trabajan con perlas.
Pel-Ebstein disease enfermedad de Pel-Ebstein.
Pelizaeus-Merzbacher disease enfermedad de Pelizaeus-Merzbacher.
Pellegrini's disease enfermedad de Pellegrini, enfermedad de Pellegrini-Stieda.
Pellegrini-Stieda disease enfermedad de Pellegrini, enfermedad de Pellegrini-Stieda.
pelvic inflammatory disease enfermedad inflamatoria de la pelvis.
periodic disease enfermedad periódica.
perna disease enfermedad perna.
Perthes disease enfermedad de Perthes.
Peyronie's disease enfermedad de Peyronie.
Pfeiffer's disease enfermedad de Pfeiffer.
Pick's disease enfermedad de Pick.
pink disease enfermedad rosada.
Plummer's disease enfermedad de Plummer.
polycystic disease of the kidneys enfermedad poliquística de los riñones.
polycystic liver disease enfermedad poliquística del hígado.
Pompe's disease enfermedad de Pompe.
Posada-Wernicke disease enfermedad de Posada-Wernicke.
Potter's disease enfermedad de Potter.
Pott's disease enfermedad de Pott.
Preiser's disease enfermedad de Preiser.
primary disease enfermedad primaria.
Pringle's disease enfermedad de Pringle.
Profichet's disease enfermedad de Profichet.
pulpy kidney disease enfermedad del riñón pulposo.
Purtscher's disease enfermedad de Purtscher.
Pyle's disease enfermedad de Pyle.
quiet hip disease enfermedad de cadera quieta.
Quincke's disease enfermedad de Quincke.
Quinquaud's disease enfermedad de Quinquaud.
radiation disease enfermedad por radiaciones.
ragpicker's disease enfermedad de los traperos.
ragsorter's disease enfermedad de los traperos.
Raynaud's disease enfermedad de Raynaud.
Recklinghausen's disease enfermedad de Recklinghausen.
Recklinghausen's disease of the bone enfermedad ósea de Recklinghausen.
Reed-Hodgkin disease enfermedad de Reed-Hodgkin.
Refsum's disease enfermedad de Refsum.
Reiter's disease enfermedad de Reiter.
Rendu-Osler-Weber disease enfermedad de Rendu-Osler-Weber.
rheumatic disease enfermedad reumática.
rheumatic heart disease enfermedad cardíaca reumática.
rheumatoid disease enfermedad reumatoidea.
Riedel's disease enfermedad de Riedel.
Riga-Fede disease enfermedad de Riga-Fede.
Ritter's disease enfermedad de Ritter.
Robinson's disease enfermedad de Robinson.
Robles' disease enfermedad de Robles.
Rokitansky's disease enfermedad de Rokitansky.

Romberg's disease enfermedad de Romberg.
Rose disease enfermedad de Rose.
Rosenbach's disease enfermedad de Rosenbach.
Rossbach's disease enfermedad de Rossbach.
Roth-Bernhardt disease enfermedad de Roth, enfermedad de Roth-Bernhardt.
Roth's disease enfermedad de Roth, enfermedad de Roth-Bernhardt.
Rougnon-Heberden disease enfermedad de Rougnon-Heberden.
Roussy-Lévy disease enfermedad de Roussy-Lévy.
Sandhoff's disease enfermedad de Sandhoff.
sandworm disease enfermedad del gusano de arena.
Saunders disease enfermedad de Saunders.
Schamberg's disease enfermedad de Schamberg.
Schaumann's disease enfermedad de Schaumann.
Schaumberg's disease enfermedad de Schaumberg.
Schenck's disease enfermedad de Schenck.
Scheuermann's disease enfermedad de Scheuermann.
Schilder's disease enfermedad de Schilder.
Schimmelbusch's disease enfermedad de Schimmelbusch.
Schlatter-Osgood disease enfermedad de Schlatter, enfermedad de Schlatter-Osgood.
Schlatter's disease enfermedad de Schlatter, enfermedad de Schlatter-Osgood.
Schönlein's disease enfermedad de Schönlein.
Schottmüller's disease enfermedad de Schottmüller.
Schroeder's disease enfermedad de Schroeder.
Schultz's disease enfermedad de Schultz.
Schwediauer's disease enfermedad de Schwediauer.
sclerocystic disease of the ovary enfermedad escleroquística del ovario.
sea-blue histiocyte disease enfermedad de histiocitos de color azul marino.
secondary disease enfermedad secundaria.
Selter's disease enfermedad de Selter.
Senear-Usher disease enfermedad de Senear-Usher.
sexually transmitted disease (STD) enfermedad de transmisión sexual (ETS).
Shaver's disease enfermedad de Shaver.
shimamushi disease enfermedad de Shimamushi.
sickle cell disease enfermedad drepanocítica.
sickle cell-thalassemia disease enfermedad de talasemia drepanocítica.
Siemerling-Creutzfeldt disease enfermedad Siemerling-Creutzfeldt.
silo-filler's disease enfermedad de los silos.
Simmonds' disease enfermedad de Simmonds.
Simon's disease enfermedad de Simon.
sixth disease enfermedad sexta.
sixth venereal disease enfermedad sexta venérea.
Sjögren's disease enfermedad de Sjögren.
skinbound disease enfermedad de la piel endurecida.
Sneddon-Wilkinson disease enfermedad de Sneddon-Wilkinson.
specific disease enfermedad específica.
Spencer's disease enfermedad de Spencer.
Spielmeyer-Sjögren disease enfermedad de Spielmeyer-Sjögren.

Spielmeyer-Stock disease enfermedad Spielmeyer-Stock.

Spielmeyer-Vogt disease enfermedad de Spielmeyer-Vogt.

Stargardt's disease enfermedad de Stargardt.

Steele-Richardson-Olszewski disease enfermedad de Steele-Richardson-Olszewski.

Steinert's disease enfermedad de Steinert.

Sternberg's disease enfermedad de Sternberg.

Sticker's disease enfermedad de Sticker.

Stieda's disease enfermedad de Stieda.

Still's disease enfermedad de Still.

Stokes-Adams disease enfermedad de Stokes-Adams.

stone-masons' disease enfermedad de los albañiles.

storage disease enfermedad por almacenamiento.

Strümpell-Marie disease enfermedad de Strümpell-Marie.

Sturge's disease enfermedad de Sturge.

Stuttgart disease enfermedad de Stuttgart.

Sudeck's disease enfermedad de Sudeck.

Sulzberger-Garbe disease enfermedad de Sulzberger-Garbe.

Sutton's disease enfermedad de Sutton.

Swediauer's disease enfermedad de Swediauer.

Sweet's disease enfermedad de Sweet.

Swift-Feer disease enfermedad de Swift, enfermedad de Swift-Feer.

Swift's disease enfermedad de Swift, enfermedad de Swift-Feer.

swineherd's disease enfermedad de los porquerizos.

Sydenham's disease enfermedad de Sydenham.

Sylvest's disease enfermedad de Sylvest.

systemic autoimmune disease enfermedad autoinmune sistémica.

systemic-febrile disease enfermedad febril sistémica.

Takahara's disease enfermedad de Takahara.

Takayasu's disease enfermedad de Takayasu.

Talma's disease enfermedad de Talma.

Tangier disease enfermedad de Tánger.

Taussig-Bing disease enfermedad de Taussig-Bing.

Taylor's disease enfermedad de Taylor.

Tay-Sachs disease enfermedad de Tay-Sachs.

Thiemann's disease enfermedad de Thiemann.

third disease enfermedad tercera.

Thomsen's disease enfermedad de Thomsen.

Thygeson's disease enfermedad de Thygeson.

thyrocardiac disease enfermedad tirocardíaca.

Tietze's disease enfermedad de Tietze.

Tillaux's disease enfermedad de Tillaux.

Tommaselli's disease enfermedad de Tommaselli.

Tornwaldt's disease enfermedad de Tornwaldt.

Tourette's disease enfermedad de Tourette.

tsutsugamushi disease enfermedad de tsutsugamushi.

Underwood's disease enfermedad de Underwood.

Unna's disease enfermedad de Unna.

Unverricht's disease enfermedad de Unverricht.

Urbach-Wiethe disease enfermedad de Urbach-Wiethe.

vagabond's disease enfermedad del vagabundo.

valvular heart disease valvulopatía cardíaca.

van Buren's disease enfermedad de van Buren.

Vaquez-Osler disease enfermedad de Vaquez, enfermedad de Vaquez-Osler.

Vaquez's disease enfermedad de Vaquez, enfermedad de Vaquez-Osler.

venereal disease enfermedad venérea.

veno-occlusive disease of the liver enfermedad venooclusiva del hígado.

Vidal's disease enfermedad de Vidal.

Vincent's disease enfermedad de Vincent.

Virchow's disease enfermedad de Virchow.

Vogt-Spielmeyer disease enfermedad de Vogt-Spielmeyer.

von Gierke's disease enfermedad de von Gierke.

von Hippel-Lindau disease enfermedad de von Hippel-Lindau.

von Meyenburg's disease enfermedad de von Meyenburg.

von Recklinghausen's disease enfermedad de von Recklinghausen.

von Willebrand's disease enfermedad de von Willebrand.

Voorhoeve's disease enfermedad de Voorhoeve.

Vrolik's disease enfermedad de Vrolik.

Wagner's disease enfermedad de Wagner.

Wardrop's disease enfermedad de Wardrop.

Wartenberg disease enfermedad de Wartenberg.

Weber-Christian disease enfermedad de Weber-Christian.

Weber's disease enfermedad de Weber.

Wegner's disease enfermedad de Wegner.

Weil's disease enfermedad de Weil.

Weir-Mitchell's disease enfermedad de Weir-Mitchell.

Werdnig-Hoffmann disease enfermedad de Werdnig-Hoffmann.

Werlhof's disease enfermedad de Werlhoff.

Werner-His disease enfermedad de Werner-His.

Werner-Schultz disease enfermedad de Werner-Schultz.

Wernicke's disease enfermedad de Wernicke.

Werther's disease enfermedad de Werther.

Wesphal's disease enfermedad de Westphal.

Whitmore's disease enfermedad de Whitmore.

Whytt's disease enfermedad de Whytt.

Wilkie's disease enfermedad de Wilkie.

Wilson's disease enfermedad de Wilson.

Winckel's disease enfermedad de Winckel.

Winiwarter-Buerger disease enfermedad de Winiwarter-Buerger.

Winkelman's disease enfermedad de Winkelman.

Winkler's disease enfermedad de Winkler.

Whipple's disease enfermedad de Whipple.

Wolman's disease enfermedad de Wolman.

Woringer-Kolopp disease enfermedad de Woringer-Kolopp.

X disease enfermedad X.

yellow disease enfermedad amarilla.

Ziehen-Oppenheim disease enfermedad de Ziehen-Oppenheim.

disequilibrium *n.* desequilibrio[1], desequilibrio[2].

genetic disequilibrium desequilibrio genético.

linkage disequilibrium desequilibrio de enlace, desequilibrio de ligamiento, desequilibrio por ligadura.

disharmony *n.* disarmonía.

occlusal disharmony disarmonía oclusal.

disimmune *adj.* desinmune.

disimmunity *n.* desinmunidad.

disimmunize *v.* desinmunizar.

disimpaction *n.* desimpactación.

disinfect *v.* desinfectar.

disinfectant *n.* desinfectante.

complete disinfectant desinfectante completo.

incomplete disinfectant desinfectante incompleto.

disinfection *n.* desinfección.

concomitant disinfection desinfección concomitante, desinfección concurrente.

concurrent disinfection desinfección concomitante, desinfección concurrente.

terminal disinfection desinfección terminal.

thermometer disinfection desinfección del termómetro.

disinfestation *n.* desinfestación.

disinhibition *n.* desinhibición.

disinsected *adj.* desinsectado, -da.

disinsection *n.* desinsectación.

disinsectization *n.* desinsectización.

disinsertion *n.* desinserción.

disintegrant *n.* desintegrante.

disintegration *n.* desintegración[1].

alpha disintegration desintegración alfa.

beta disintegration desintegración beta.

radioactive disintegration desintegración radiactiva.

disinvagination *n.* desinvaginación.

radiologic disinvagination desinvaginación radiológica.

disjoint *v.* desarticular.

disjunction *n.* disyunción.

coodination disjunction disyunción de la coordinación.

craniofacial disjunction disyunción craneofacial.

disk *n.* disco.

diskectomy *n.* discectomía.

diskeratosis *n.* disqueratosis.

benign diskeratosis disqueratosis benigna.

congenital diskeratosis disqueratosis congénita.

diskeratosis congenita disqueratosis congénita.

hereditary benign intraepithelial diskeratosis disqueratosis intraepitelial hereditaria benigna.

intraepithelial diskeratosis disqueratosis intraepitelial.

isolated diskeratosis follicularis disqueratosis folicular aislada.

malignant diskeratosis disqueratosis maligna.

diskeratotic *adj.* disqueratósico, -ca.

diskitis *n.* discitis, disquitis.

diskogram *n.* discograma.

diskography *n.* discografía.

dislocatio *n.* dislocación.

dislocatio erecta dislocación erecta.

dislocation *n.* descoyuntamiento, dislocación, lluxatio, luxación.

Bell-Dally dislocation luxación de Bell-Dally.

closed dislocation luxación cerrada.

complete dislocation luxación completa.

compound dislocation luxación compuesta.

congenital dislocation luxación congénita.

congenital dislocation of the hip luxación congénita de cadera.

consecutive dislocation luxación consecutiva.

dislocation of the clavicle luxación de la clavícula.

dislocation of the finger luxación del dedo.

dislocation of the hip luxación de cadera.

dislocation of the knee luxación de la rodilla.

dislocation of the lens luxación del cristalino.

dislocation of the shoulder luxación del hombro.

divergent dislocation luxación divergente.

fractura dislocation luxación y fractura.

habitual dislocation luxación habitual, luxación iterativa, luxación recidivante.

incomplete dislocation luxación incompleta.

intrauterine dislocation luxación intrauterina.

Kienböck's dislocation luxación de Kienböck.

Lisfranc dislocation luxación de Lisfranc.

Malgaigne's dislocation luxación de Malgaigne.

metacarpophalangeal joint dislocation luxación de la articulación metacarpofalángica.

Monteggia dislocation luxación de Monteggia.

Nélaton's dislocation luxación de Nélaton.

obturator dislocation luxación del obturador.

old dislocation luxación antigua, luxación inveterada.

open dislocation luxación abierta.

partial dislocation luxación parcial.

pathologic dislocation luxación patológica.

perineal dislocation luxación perineal.

primitive dislocation luxación primitiva.

recent dislocation luxación reciente.

sciatic dislocation luxación ciática.

simple dislocation luxación simple.

Smith dislocation luxación de Smith.

subastragalar dislocation luxación subastragalina.

subpubic dislocation luxación subpúbica.

subspinous dislocation luxación subespinosa.

traumatic dislocation luxación traumática.

dismemberment *n.* desmembramiento.

disocclude *v.* disocluir.

disome *n.* disoma.

disomic *adj.* disómico, -ca.

disomus *n.* disomo.

disomy *n.* disomía.

uniparental disomy disomía uniparental.

disorder *n.* desorden, trastorno.

academic skill disorder trastorno específicos del desarrollo del aprendizaje escolar.

acute stress disorder trastorno por estrés agudo.

adjustment disorder trastorno adaptativo.

affective disorder trastorno afectivo.

amnestic disorder trastorno amnésicos.

antisocial personality disorder trastorno antisocial de la personalidad.

anxiety disorder trastorno de ansiedad.

Asperger's disorder trastorno de Asperger.

attention-deficit hyperactive disorder trastorno por déficit de atención con hiperactividad.

autistic disorder trastorno autista, trastorno autístico.

behavior disorder trastorno del comportamiento.

behavior disorder of childhood and adolescence trastorno del comportamiento en la niñez y en la adolescencia.

bipolar disorder trastorno bipolar.

bipolar I disorder trastorno bipolar I.

bipolar II disorder trastorno bipolar II.

body dysmorphic disorder trastorno dismórfico corporal.

central auditory processing disorder trastorno de procesamiento auditivo central.

collagen disorder trastorno de la colágena.

conversion disorder trastorno de conversión.

cyclotimic disorder trastorno ciclotímico.

delusional disorder trastorno delirante.

dependent personality disorder trastorno de la personalidad por dependencia.

despersonalization disorder trastorno de despersonalización.

developmental disorder trastorno del desarrollo.

disorder related to substances trastorno relacionado con sustancias.

dissociative disorder trastorno disociativo.

dissociative identity disorder trastorno de identidad disociativo.

dysthymic disorder trastorno distímico.

eating disorder trastorno de la conducta alimentaria.

factitious disorder trastorno facticio.

functional disorder trastorno funcional.

gait disorder trastorno de la marcha.

generalized anxiety disorder trastorno de ansiedad generalizada.

histrionic personality disorder trastorno histriónico de la personalidad.

hypochondriac disorder trastorno hipocondríaco.

immunodeficiency disorder trastorno por inmunodeficiencia.

impulse control disorder trastorno del control de impulsos.

inherited disorder trastorno hereditario.

intermittent explosive disorder trastorno explosivo intermitente.

LDL-receptor disorder trastorno de receptor LDL.

learning disorder trastorno del aprendizaje.

major depressive disorder trastorno depresivo mayor.

maniac-depressive disorder trastorno maniacodepresivo.

Mendelian disorder trastorno mendeliano.

mental disorder trastorno mental.

metabolic disorder trastorno metabólico.

monogenic disorder trastorno monogénico.

mood disorder trastorno del estado del ánimo.

multifactorial disorder trastorno multifactorial.

multiple personality disorder trastorno de personalidad múltiple.

narcissistic personality disorder trastorno narcisista de la personalidad.

neurotic disorder trastorno neurótico.

obsessive-compulsive personality disorder trastorno obsesivo-compulsivo de la personalidad.

organic mental disorder trastorno mental orgánico.

pain disorder trastorno por dolor.

panic disorder trastorno de pánico.

paranoid personality disorder trastorno paranoide de la personalidad.

pervasive development disorder trastorno general del desarrollo, trastorno generalizado del desarrollo.

post-traumatic stress disorder trastorno por estrés postraumático.

psychological development disorder trastorno del desarrollo psicológico.

Rett disorder trastorno de Rett.

schizoaffective disorder trastorno esquizoafectivo.

schizoid personality disorder trastorno esquizoide de la personalidad.

schizophreniform disorder trastorno esquizofreniforme.

schizotypal personality disorder trastorno esquizotípico de la personalidad.

seasonal affective disorder (SAD) trastorno afectivo estacional (TAE).

separative anxiety disorder trastorno de ansiedad por separación.

sexual disorder trastorno sexual.

sexual identity disorder trastorno de la identidad sexual.

shared psychotic disorder trastorno psicótico compartido.

simple-gen disorder trastorno por gen simple.

sleep disorder trastorno del sueño.

somatization disorder trastorno de somatización.

somatoform disorder trastorno somatomorfo.

spinocerebellar disorder trastorno espinocerebeloso.

substance abuse disorder trastorno por abuso de sustancias.

substance-induced anxiety disorder trastorno de ansiedad inducido por sustancias.

substance-induced psychotic disorder trastorno psicótico inducido por sustancias.

tic disorder trastorno de tics.

disorganization *n.* desorganización.

disorientation *n.* desorientación.

spatial disorientation desorientación espacial.

dispar *adj.* dispar.

dispareunia *n.* dispareunia.

organic dispareunia dispareunia orgánica.

disparity *n.* disparidad.

conjugate disparity disparidad conjugada.

fixation disparity disparidad de fijación.

retinal disparity disparidad retinal.

dispermia *n.* dispermia[1].

dispermy *n.* dispermia[1].

dispersion *n.* dispersión[1].

chromatic dispersion dispersión cromática.

optical rotatory dispersion (ORD) dispersión óptica rotatoria (DOR).

temporal dispersion dispersión temporal.

dispersoid *n.* dispersoide.

dispira *n.* dispira.

dispireme *n.* dispirema.

displaceability *n.* desplazabilidad.

tissue displaceability desplazabilidad de tejidos.

displacement *n.* decalaje, desplazamiento[1].

affect displacement desplazamiento del afecto.

character displacement desplazamiento de carácter.

competitive displacement desplazamiento competitivo.

condylar displacement desplazamiento condíleo.

fetal displacement desplazamiento fetal.

fish-hook displacement desplazamiento en anzuelo.

gallbladder displacement desplazamiento vesicular.

lateral pelvic displacement desplazamiento pélvico lateral.

tissue displacement desplazamiento hístico, desplazamiento tisular.
disposition *n.* disposición.
disproportion *n.* desproporción.
 cephalopelvic disproportion (CPD) desproporción cefalopélvica (DCP).
disruption *n.* disrupción.
disruptive *adj.* disruptivo, -va.
dissect *v.* disecar.
dissecting *adj.* disector, -ra.
dissection *n.* disección.
 aortic dissection disección aórtica.
 blunt dissection disección roma.
 functional neck dissection disección cervical funcional.
 neck dissection disección cervical.
 radical dissection disección radical.
 radical neck dissection disección cervical radical, disección radical de cuello.
 retroperitoneal lymph node dissection disección de los ganglios linfáticos retroperitoneales.
 sharp dissection disección cortante.
dissector *n.* disector.
disseminated *adj.* diseminado, -da.
dissemination *n.* diseminación.
dissepiment *n.* disepimiento.
dissimilate *v.* desasimilar.
dissimilation *n.* desasimilación, disimilación.
dissimulation *n.* disimulo.
dissociable *adj.* disociable.
dissociated *adj.* disociado, -da.
dissociation *n.* disociación.
 albuminocytologic dissociation disociación albuminocelular, disociación albuminocitológica.
 atrial dissociation disociación auricular.
 atrioventricular dissociation disociación auriculoventricular (AV).
 bacterial dissociation disociación bacteriana.
 complete atrioventricular dissociation disociación auriculoventricular completa.
 complete AV dissociation disociación auriculoventricular completa.
 dissociation by interference disociación de interferencia.
 electromechanical dissociation disociación electromecánica.
 incomplete atrioventricular dissociation disociación auriculoventricular incompleta.
 incomplete AV dissociation disociación auriculoventricular incompleta.
 interference dissociation disociación de interferencia.
 ionic dissociation disociación iónica.
 isorhythmic dissociation disociación isorrítmica.
 longitudinal dissociation disociación longitudinal.
 microbic dissociation disociación microbiana.
 peripheral dissociation disociación periférica.
 sleep dissociation disociación del sueño.
 syringomyelic dissociation disociación siringomiélica.
 tabetic dissociation disociación tabética.
 thermoalgesic dissociation disociación termoalgésica.
dissolution *n.* disolución.
 salting dissolution disolución salina.
dissolvent *n.* disolvente[1].
dissonance *n.* disonancia.
 cognitive dissonance disonancia cognitiva.
distal *adj.* distal, distalis.

distalis *adj.* distal, distalis.
distance *n.* distancia.
 angular distance distancia angular.
 cone-surface distance distancia cono-superficie.
 focal distance distancia focal.
 infinite distance distancia infinita.
 interarch distance distancia interarcos.
 interocclusal distance distancia interoclusal.
 interocular distance distancia interocular.
 interpediculate distance distancia interpedicular.
 interpupillary distance distancia interpupilar.
 interridge distance distancia interrebordes.
 large interarch distance distancia grande interarcos.
 map distance distancia de mapa, distancia de mapeo.
 object-film distance distancia objeto-película.
 pupillary distance distancia pupilar.
 reduced interarch distance distancia interarcos reducida.
 small interarch distance distancia pequeña interarcos.
 sociometric distance distancia sociométrica.
 source-cone distance distancia fuente-cono.
 target-skin distance distancia blanco-piel.
 working distance distancia de trabajo.
distend *v.* distender[1].
distensibility *n.* distensibilidad.
distension *n.* distensión[1].
 gas distension distensión gaseosa.
distention *n.* distensión[1].
distichia *n.* distiquia.
 acquired distichia distiquia adquirida.
distichiasis *n.* distiquiasis.
distichous *adj.* dístico, -ca.
distill *v.* destilar.
distillate *n.* destilado.
distillation *n.* destilación.
 destructive distillation destilación destructiva.
 dry distillation destilación seca.
 fractional distillation destilación fraccionada, destilación fraccional.
 molecular distillation destilación molecular.
 vacuum distillation destilación al vacío, destilación en el vacío.
distoaxiogingival *adj.* distoaxiogingival.
distoaxioincisal *adj.* distoaxioincisal.
distoaxio-occlusal *adj.* distoaxiooclusal.
distobuccal *adj.* distobucal.
distobucco-occlusal *adj.* distobucooclusal.
distobuccopulpal *adj.* distobucopulpar.
distocervical *adj.* distocervical.
distoclination *n.* distoclinación.
distoclusal *adj.* distooclusal.
distoclusion *n.* distoclusión, distooclusión.
distogingival *adj.* distogingival.
distoincisal *adj.* distoincisal.
distolabial *adj.* distolabial.
distolabioincisal *adj.* distolabioincisal.
distolabiopulpal *adj.* distolabiopulpar.
distolingual *adj.* distolingual.
distolinguoincisal *adj.* distolinguoincisal.
distolinguo-occlusal *adj.* distolinguoocclusal.
distolinguopulpal *adj.* distolinguopulpar.
Distoma *n.* Distoma.
distomatosis *n.* distomatosis.
distomia *n.* distomia.
distomiasis *n.* distomiasis.
 hemic distomiasis distomiasis hémica, distomiasis sanguínea.

 hepatic distomiasis distomiasis hepática.
 pulmonary distomiasis distomiasis pulmonar.
distomolar *n.* distomolar.
distomus *n.* dístomo.
disto-occlusal *adj.* distooclusal.
disto-occlusion *n.* distooclusión.
distoplacement *n.* distocolocación.
distopulpal *adj.* distopulpar.
distopulpolabial *adj.* distopulpolabial.
distopulpolingual *adj.* distopulpolingual.
distorted *adj.* viciado, -da.
distortion *n.* distorsión.
 cognitive distortion distorsión cognitiva.
 distortion oris distorsión oris.
 parataxic distortion distorsión parataxica.
 perceptive distortion distorsión perceptiva.
distoversion *n.* distoversión.
distractibility *n.* distractibilidad, distraibilidad.
distraction *n.* distracción.
 bone distraction distracción ósea.
distractor *n.* distractor.
distress *n.* distrés, sufrimiento.
 adult respiratory distress distrés respiratorio del adulto.
 fetal distress sufrimiento fetal.
 idiopathic respiratory distress of the newborn (type I) distrés respiratorio del recién nacido tipo I.
distribution *n.* distribución.
 Bernouilli distribution distribución de Bernouilli.
 bimodal distribution distribución bimodal.
 binomial distribution distribución binomial.
 chi-square distribution distribución chi-cuadrado.
 chi-squared distribution distribución chi-cuadrado.
 countercurrent distribution distribución por contracorriente.
 dose distribution distribución de dosis.
 drug distribution distribución del fármaco.
 exponential distribution distribución exponencial.
 F distribution distribución F.
 frequency distribution distribución de frecuencia.
 Gaussian distribution distribución de Gauss, distribución gausiana.
 normal distribution distribución normal.
 Poisson distribution distribución de Poisson.
 probability distribution distribución de probabilidad.
 standard normal distribution distribución normal estándar.
districhiasis *n.* distriquia, distriquiasis.
distrix *n.* distrix.
diurea *n.* diurea.
diuresis *n.* diuresis.
 alcohol diuresis diuresis alcohólica.
 osmotic diuresis diuresis osmótica, diuresis tubular.
 water diuresis diuresis acuosa.
diuretic *n.* diurético, -ca.
 cardiac diuretic diurético cardíaco.
 direct diuretic diurético directo.
 high-ceiling diuretic diurético del asa, diurético del asa ascendente.
 indirect diuretic diurético indirecto.
 loop diuretic diurético del asa, diurético del asa ascendente.
 mercurial diuretic diurético de mercurio, diurético mercurial.
 osmotic diuretic diurético osmótico.

potassium-sparing diuretic diurético ahorrador de potasio, diurético de recambio de potasio.
thiazide diuretic diurético tiacídico.
diuria *n.* diuria.
diurnule *n.* diúrnula.
divagation *n.* divagación.
divalence *n.* divalencia.
divalency *n.* divalencia.
divalent *adj.* divalente.
divarication *n.* divaricación.
divergence *n.* divergencia.
 negative vertical divergence divergencia vertical negativa.
 positive vertical divergence divergencia vertical positiva.
divergent *adj.* divergente.
diverticular *adj.* diverticular.
diverticulectomy *n.* diverticulectomía.
diverticulitis *n.* diverticulitis.
diverticulization *n.* diverticulización.
diverticulogram *n.* diverticulograma.
diverticuloma *n.* diverticuloma.
diverticulopexy *n.* diverticulopexia.
diverticulosis *n.* diverticulosis.
diverticulum *n.* divertículo, diverticulum.
 acquired diverticulum divertículo adquirido.
 cervical diverticulum divertículo cervical.
 diverticulum ilei verum divertículo ilei verum.
 functional diverticulum divertículo funcional.
 ganglion diverticulum divertículo de ganglión.
 Ganser's diverticulum divertículo de Ganser.
 Graser's diverticulum divertículo de Graser.
 hepatic diverticulum divertículo hepático.
 Meckel's diverticulum divertículo de Meckel.
 Pertik's diverticulum divertículo de Pertik.
 pressure diverticulum divertículo de presión, divertículo por presión, divertículo por pulsión.
 pulsion diverticulum divertículo de pulsión, divertículo por pulsión.
 Rokitansky's diverticulum divertículo Rokitansky.
 synovial diverticulum divertículo sinovial.
 thyroglossal diverticulum divertículo tirogloso, divertículo tiroideo.
 thyroid diverticulum divertículo tirogloso, divertículo tiroideo.
 traction diverticulum divertículo por tracción.
 true diverticulum divertículo verdadero.
 urethral diverticulum divertículo uretral.
 ventricular diverticulum divertículo ventricular.
 vesical diverticulum divertículo vesical.
divisio *n.* división.
division *n.* división.
 cell division división celular.
 cleavage division división por segmentación.
 conjugate division división conjugada.
 craniosacral division división craneosacra.
 direct cell division división celular directa.
 direct nuclear division división nuclear directa.
 equation division división por ecuación.
 equational division división ecuacional.
 indirect cell division división celular indirecta.
 indirect nuclear division división nuclear indirecta.
 maturation division división de maduración.
 meiotic division división meiótica.

 mitotic division división mitótica.
 multiplicative division división multiplicativa.
 reduction division división de reducción, división por reducción, división reduccional.
 Remak's nuclear division división nuclear de Remak.
divulsion *n.* divulsión.
divulsor *n.* divulsor.
dizygotic *adj.* dicigótico, -ca, dicigoto, -ta.
dizygous *adj.* dicigótico, -ca, dicigoto, -ta.
dizziness *n.* aturdimiento, desvanecimiento, mareo.
docimasia *n.* docimasia.
 agony docimasia docimasia de la agonía.
 bacteriological docimasia docimasia bacteriológica.
 diaphragmatic docimasia docimasia diafragmática.
 gastrointestinal docimasia docimasia gastrointestinal.
 hepatic docimasia docimasia hepática.
 hydrostatic docimasia docimasia hidrostática.
 nutritional docimasia docimasia alimenticia.
 otic docimasia docimasia ótica.
 pulmonary docimasia docimasia pulmonar.
 radiologic docimasia docimasia radiológica.
 sialic docimasia docimasia siálica.
 suprarenal docimasia docimasia suprarrenal.
docimastic *adj.* docimásico, -ca.
doctor *n.* doctor, -ra.
doctrine *n.* doctrina.
 humoral doctrine doctrina humoral.
 Monro-Kellie doctrine doctrina de Monro, doctrina de Monro-Kellie.
 Monro's doctrine doctrina de Monro, doctrina de Monro-Kellie.
 neuron doctrine doctrina neuronal.
doigt mort *n.* doigt mort.
dolabrate *adj.* dolabrado, -da.
dolabriform *adj.* dolabriforme.
dolichocephalic *adj.* dolicocefálico, -ca.
dolichocephalism *n.* dolicocefalismo.
dolichocephalous *adj.* dolicocéfalo, -la.
dolichocephaly *n.* dolicocefalia.
dolichocolon *n.* dolicocolon.
dolichocranial *adj.* dolicocraneal.
dolichoderus *n.* dolicodero.
dolichofacial *adj.* dolicofacial.
dolichogastry *n.* dolicogastria.
dolichohieric *adj.* dolicohiérico, -ca.
dolichokerkic *adj.* dolicocérquico, -ca.
dolichoknemic *adj.* dolicocnémico, -ca.
dolichomorphic *adj.* dolicomorfo, -fa.
dolichopellic *adj.* dolicopélico, -ca.
dolichopelvic *adj.* dolicopélvico, -ca.
dolichoprosopic *adj.* dolicoprosópico, -ca.
dolichoprosopous *adj.* dolicoprosopo, -pa.
dolichostenomelia *n.* dolicoestenomelia, dolicostenomelia.
dolichouranic *adj.* dolicouránico, -ca, dolicuránico, -ca.
dolichuranic *adj.* dolicouránico, -ca, dolicuránico, -ca.
dolor *n.* dolor.
 dolor capitis dolor capitis, dolor de cabeza.
 dolor coxae dolor de coxis.
 dolor praesagiente dolor presagiente.
 dolor vagus dolor vagus.
dolorific *adj.* dolorífico, -ca, doloroso, -sa.
dolorimeter *n.* dolorímetro.
dolorimetry *n.* dolorimetría.
dolorogenic *adj.* dolorógeno, -na.
dolorology *n.* dolorología.

domain *n.* dominio.
domaria *n.* domaria.
domiciliary *adj.* domiciliario, -ria.
dominance *n.* dominancia.
 cerebral dominance dominancia cerebral.
 eye dominance dominancia ocular.
 false dominance dominancia falsa.
 genetic dominance dominancia genética.
 incomplete dominance dominancia incompleta.
 lateral dominance dominancia lateral.
 ocular dominance dominancia ocular.
 one-sided dominance dominancia unilateral.
 partial dominance dominancia parcial.
dominant *adj.* dominante.
donor *n.* dador, donador, -ra, donante.
 blood donor donante de sangre.
 cadaveric donor donante de cadáver.
 F donor donante F.
 general donor donante general.
 hydrogen donor donante de hidrógeno.
 living donor donante vivo.
 universal donor donante universal.
 xenogenic donor donante xenogénico.
Donovania granulomatis *n.* Donovania granulomatis.
donovanosis *n.* donovanosis.
dope *v.* dopar.
Doppler *n.* Doppler.
 color Doppler Doppler color.
 continuous Doppler Doppler continuo.
 duplex Doppler Doppler dúplex.
 pulsed Doppler Doppler pulsado.
 transcranial Doppler Doppler transcraneal.
dormancy *n.* dormancia.
dormifacient *adj.* dormifaciente.
dorsabdominal *adj.* dorsoabdominal.
dorsal *adj.* dorsal, dorsalis.
dorsalgia *n.* dorsalgia.
 benign dorsalgia dorsalgia benigna.
dorsalis *adj.* dorsal, dorsalis.
dorsalization *n.* dorsalización.
dorsiacromial *adj.* dorsoacromial.
dorsicervical *adj.* dorsocervical.
dorsiduct *adj.* dorsiductor, -ra.
dorsiflect *v.* dorsiflexionar.
dorsiflexion *n.* dorsiflexión.
dorsimesial *adj.* dorsimesial.
dorsimetric *adj.* dorsimétrico, -ca.
dorsiscapular *adj.* dorsiescapular.
dorsispinal *adj.* dorsiespinal.
dorsoanterior *adj.* dorsoanterior.
dorsocephalad *adj.* dorsocefálico, -ca.
dorsodynia *n.* dorsodinia.
dorsointercostal *adj.* dorsointercostal.
dorsolateral *adj.* dorsolateral.
dorsolumbar *adj.* dorsolumbar.
dorsomedian *adj.* dorsomedial.
dorsomesial *adj.* dorsomesial.
dorsonasal *adj.* dorsonasal.
dorsonuchal *adj.* dorsonucal.
dorsoposterior *adj.* dorsoposterior.
dorsoradial *adj.* dorsorradial.
dorsoscapular *adj.* dorsoescapular.
dorsoventrad *adv.* dorsoventrad.
dorsoventral *adj.* dorsoventral.
dorsum *n.* dorso, dorsum.
dosage *n.* dosificación.
 pediatric dosage dosificación pediátrica.
dose *n.* dosis.
 absorbance dose dosis absorbida, dosis absorbida de radiación.
 absorbed dose dosis absorbida, dosis absorbida de radiación.

accumulated dose equivalent dosis equivalente acumulada.

average dose dosis promedio.

booster dose dosis de refuerzo.

cumulative dose dosis acumulada, dosis acumulativa.

cumulative radiation dose dosis de radiación acumulativa.

curative dose dosis curativa.

daily dose dosis diaria.

depth dose dosis de profundidad, dosis profunda.

divided dose dosis dividida.

dose ratemeter medidor de ritmo de dosis.

dose to skin dosis en piel.

doubling dose dosis de duplicación.

effective dose (ED) dosis efectiva, dosis efficax (DE), dosis eficaz.

emergency dose dosis de urgencia.

epilation dose dosis de depilación.

equianalgesic dose dosis equianalgésica.

equivalent dose dosis equivalente.

erythema dose dosis eritema.

exit dose dosis de salida.

fetal dose dosis fetal.

fractional dose dosis fraccionada.

genetically significant dose (GSD) dosis genéticamente significativa (DGS).

gonadal dose dosis gonadal.

infective dose dosis infectante.

initial dose dosis inicial.

integral absorbed dose dosis integral, dosis integral absorbida.

integral dose dosis integral, dosis integral absorbida.

intoxicating dose dosis intoxicante.

L dose dosis L.

L+d dose dosis L+d.

lethal dose (LD) dosis mortal, dosis letal (DL).

Lf dose dosis Lf.

limes nul dose dosis L D, dosis limes cero, dosis limes nul.

limes zero dose dosis L D, dosis limes cero, dosis limes nul.

Lo dose dosis Lo.

loading dose dosis de ataque.

Lr dose dosis Lr.

maintenance dose dosis de mantenimiento.

maximal dose dosis máxima.

maximal permissible dose dosis máxima permisible, dosis máxima permitida (DMP).

maximum permissible dose (MPD) dosis máxima permisible, dosis máxima permitida (DMP).

median curative dose dosis curativa mediana.

median effective dose (ED50) dosis eficaz media, dosis eficaz mediana (DE50).

median infective dose dosis infectante mediana.

median lethal dose dosis mortal media, dosis mortal mediana.

median lethal dose (LD50) dosis letal media (DL50).

median tissue culture infective dose dosis infectante media en cultivo de tejidos.

median toxic dose (TD50) dosis tóxica media (DT50).

minimal dose dosis mínima.

minimal infecting dose (MID) dosis mínima infecciosa (DMI).

minimal lethal dose dosis mortal mínima.

minimal lethal dose (MLD) dosis letal mínima (DLM).

minimal reacting dose (MRD) dosis mínima reactiva (DMR).

minimum dose dosis mínima.

minimum lethal dose dosis mortal mínima.

optimal dose dosis óptima.

optimum dose dosis óptima.

organ tolerance dose dosis de tolerancia de órganos.

permissible dose dosis permisible.

personal dose dosis personal.

preventive dose dosis preventiva.

priming dose dosis de cebamiento.

protracted dose dosis prolongada.

radiation absorbed dose dosis absorbida, dosis absorbida de radiación.

reacting dose dosis reactiva.

sensitizing dose dosis sensibilizante.

shocking dose dosis de shock.

skin dose dosis cutánea, dosis dérmica.

sublethal dose dosis subletal.

superficial dose dosis superficial.

therapeutic dose dosis terapéutica.

threshold dose dosis umbral.

threshold erythema dose dosis umbral de eritema.

tissue dose dosis tisular.

tolerance dose dosis de tolerancia, dosis tolerada.

toxic dose (TD) dosis tóxica (DT).

unit dose dosis unitaria.

volume dose dosis de volumen.

dosimeter *n.* dosímetro.

area dosimeter dosímetro de área.

duplex dosimeter dosímetro dúplex.

film dosimeter dosímetro de película.

Fricke dosimeter dosímetro de Fricke.

individual dosimeter dosímetro individual.

integrating dosimeter dosímetro integrador.

dosimetrist *n.* dosimetrista.

dosimetry *n.* dosimetría.

hydrostatic dosimetry dosimetría hidrostática.

photographic dosimetry dosimetría fotográfica.

thermoluminiscence dosimetry dosimetría de termoluminiscencia, dosimetría por termoluminiscencia.

X-ray dosimetry dosimetría de rayos X.

dosis *n.* dosis.

dosis curativa dosis curativa.

dosis efficax dosis efectiva, dosis efficax (DE), dosis eficaz.

dosis refracta dosis refracta.

dosis tolerata dosis tolerata.

dossier *n.* expediente.

dot *n.* mancha.

Gunn's dot mancha de Gunn.

Marcus Gunn's dot mancha de Marcus Gunn.

Maurer's dot mancha de Maurer.

Mittendorf's dot mancha de Mittendorf.

Schüffner's dot mancha de Schüffner.

Trantas' dot mancha de Trantas.

double *adj.* doble.

doublet *n.* doblete.

Wollaston's doublet doblete de Wollaston.

douche *n.* ducha.

air douche ducha de aire.

fan douche ducha en abanico.

Scotch douche ducha escocesa.

transition douche ducha alternante.

douglascele *n.* douglascele.

douglasitis *n.* douglasitis.

dracontiasis *n.* dracontiasis.

dracuncular *adj.* dracuncular.

dracunculiasis *n.* dracunculiasis.

Dracunculoidea *n.* Dracunculoidea.

dracunculosis *n.* dracunculosis.

Dracunculus *n.* Dracunculus.

Dracunculus medinensis Dracunculus medinensis.

drag *n.* arrastre.

dragée *n.* gragea.

drain[1] *n.* dren, drenaje[1].

cigarette drain dren en cigarrillo.

controlled drain dren controlado.

Mikulicz's drain dren de Mikulicz.

Penrose's drain dren de Penrose.

quarantine drain dren de cuarentena.

stab drain dren transfixión.

stab wound drain dren por contraabertura.

drain[2] *v.* drenar.

drainage *n.* drenaje[2].

Barraya's drainage drenaje de Barraya.

basal drainage drenaje basal.

bronchial drainage drenaje bronquial.

Bülau's drainage drenaje de Bülau.

button drainage drenaje con botón, drenaje en botón.

capillary drainage drenaje capilar.

closed drainage drenaje cerrado.

closed pleural drainage drenaje pleural cerrado.

closed-wound suction drainage drenaje de una herida cerrada.

continuous suction drainage drenaje continuo por aspiración.

definitive drainage drenaje definitivo.

gravity drainage drenaje por gravedad.

infusion-aspiration drainage drenaje por infusión-aspiración.

Mikulicz's drainage drenaje de Mikulicz.

Monaldi's drainage drenaje de Monaldi.

open drainage drenaje abierto.

Penrose's drainage drenaje de Penrose.

postural drainage drenaje postural.

Redon's drainage drenaje de Redon.

stab drainage drenaje por contraabertura.

suction drainage drenaje aspirativo, drenaje por aspiración, drenaje por succión.

through drainage drenaje total.

through-and-through drainage drenaje por irrigación.

tidal drainage drenaje periódico.

underwater seal drainage drenaje hermético bajo agua.

Wagensteen's drainage drenaje de Wagensteen.

dramatism *n.* dramatismo.

dramatization *n.* dramatización.

drastic *n.* drástico, -ca.

draw-sheet *n.* zalea.

dream *n.* ensueño, sueño[1].

anxiety dream sueño ansioso, sueño de ansiedad.

clairvoyant dream ensueño clarividente.

day dream ensueño diurno, sueño diurno.

punishment dream sueño de castigo.

drepanocyte *n.* drepanocito.

drepanocytemia *n.* drepanocitemia[1].

drepanocytic *adj.* drepanocítico, -ca.

drepanocytosis *n.* drepanocitosis[1].

dressing *n.* apósito, vendaje.

drift *n.* deriva, desplazamiento[2], desviación[4].

antigenic drift deriva antigénica, desplazamiento antigénico, desviación antigénica.

genetic drift deriva genética, desplazamiento genético, desviación genética.

random genetic drift deriva genética.

ulnar drift desviación cubital.

drifting *n.* desplazamiento[3].

drill[1] *n.* trépano.
  cannulated drill trépano canulado.
drill[2] *v.* perforar.
drip *n.* goteo.
  alkaline milk drip goteo de leche alcalina, goteo de leche alcalinizada de Winkelstein.
  alkalinized milk drip of Winkelstein goteo de leche alcalina, goteo de leche alcalinizada de Winkelstein.
  intravenous drip goteo intravenoso.
  Murphy drip goteo de Murphy.
  postnasal drip goteo posnasal.
drive *n.* impulso[1], pulsión[1].
  acquired drive impulso adquirido.
  aggressive drive impulso agresivo, pulsión agresiva, pulsión destructiva.
  exploratory drive impulso exploratorio.
  learned drive impulso aprendido.
  meiotic drive impulso meiótico.
  physiological drive impulso fisiológico.
  primary drive impulso primario.
  secondary drive impulso secundario.
  sexual drive impulso sexual, pulsión sexual.
driving *n.* impulsión[1].
  photic driving impulsión fótica.
dromic *adj.* drómico, -ca.
dromograph *n.* dromógrafo.
dromotropic *adj.* dromotrópico, -ca.
dromotropism *n.* dromotropismo.
  negative dromotropism dromotropismo negativo.
  positive dromotropism dromotropismo positivo.
drop *n.* gota[1].
  drop attack drop attack.
  ear drop gota para el oído.
  enamel drop gota de esmalte.
  eye drop gota ocular, gota para los ojos.
  hanging drop gota colgante.
  knock-out drop gota knock-out.
  nose drop gota nasal.
  stomach drop gota estomacal.
dropacism *n.* dropacismo.
droplet *n.* gotita.
dropper *n.* cuentagotas, gotero.
dropsical *adj.* hidrópico, -ca.
dropsy *n.* hidropepsía, hidropesia.
  abdominal dropsy hidropesia abdominal.
  acute anemic dropsy hidropesia anémica aguda.
  articular dropsy hidropesia articular.
  cardiac dropsy hidropesia cardíaca.
  cutaneous dropsy hidropesia cutánea.
  dropsy of the amnion hidropesia del amnios.
  dropsy of the chest hidropesia del tórax.
  dropsy of the head hidropesia de la cabeza.
  dropsy of the pericardium hidropesia del pericardio.
  epidemic dropsy hidropesia epidémica.
  famine dropsy hidropesia del hambre.
  hepatic dropsy hidropesia hepática.
  peritoneal dropsy hidropesia peritoneal.
  renal dropsy hidropesia renal.
  war dropsy hidropesia de guerra.
  wet dropsy hidropesia húmeda.
Drosophila melanogaster *n.* Drosophila melanogaster.
drowning *n.* ahogamiento.
  near drowning ahogamiento incompleto.
  secondary drowning ahogamiento secundario.
drowsiness *n.* modorra, sopor.
drug *n.* droga, drogar, fármaco, medicamento.
  antagonistic drug droga antagonista.
  crude drug droga bruta, droga cruda.

designer drug droga de diseño.
drug dependence drogodependencia.
  habit-forming drug droga que produce hábito.
  nephrotoxic drug droga nefrotóxica.
  sulfa drug sulfamida.
drug-fast *n.* drogarresistente.
drunkenness *n.* embriaguez.
drusen *n.* drusa, drüsen.
  drusen of the optic disk drusa de la papila óptica.
  giant drusen drusa gigantes.
  optic nerve drusen drusa del nervio óptico.
dry *adj.* seco, -ca.
dualism *n.* dualismo.
duality of CNS control *n.* dualidad de control del SNC.
duct *n.* conducto.
  aberrant duct conducto aberrante.
  Cuvier's duct conducto de Cuvier.
  hypophyseal duct conducto hipofisario.
  pronephric duct conducto pronéfrico.
  thyroglossal duct conducto tirogloso.
  thyrolingual duct conducto tirolingual.
ductal *adj.* ductal.
ductile *adj.* dúctil.
duction *n.* ducción.
  forced duction ducción forzada.
  passive duction ducción pasiva.
ductulus *n.* dúctulo, ductulus.
ductus *n.* conducto, ductus.
dullness *n.* embotamiento, matidez.
  emotional dullness embotamiento afectivo.
  postcardial dullness matidez poscordial.
  precardial dullness matidez precordial.
  shifting dullness matidez móvil.
  tympanitic dullness matidez timpanítica.
dumb *adj.* mudo, -da.
dumbbell *n.* halterio.
dumbness *n.* mudez.
duocrinin *n.* duocrinina.
duodenal *adj.* duodenal.
duodenectomy *n.* duodenectomía.
duodenitis *n.* duodenitis.
duodenocholangeitis *n.* duodenocolangeítis, duodenocolangitis.
duodenocholecystostomy *n.* duodenocolecistostomía.
duodenocholedochotomy *n.* duodenocoledocotomía.
duodenocolic *adj.* duodenocólico, -ca.
duodenocystostomy *n.* duodenocistostomía.
duodenoduodenostomy *n.* duodenoduodenostomía.
duodenoenterostomy *n.* duodenoenterostomía.
duodenogram *n.* duodenograma.
duodenography *n.* duodenografía.
duodenohepatic *adj.* duodenohepático, -ca.
duodenoileostomy *n.* duodenoileostomía.
duodenojejunostomy *n.* duodenoyeyunostomía.
duodenolysis *n.* duodenólisis.
duodenorrhaphy *n.* duodenorrafia.
duodenoscope *n.* duodenoscopio.
duodenoscopy *n.* duodenoscopia.
duodenostomy *n.* duodenostomía.
duodenotomy *n.* duodenotomía.
duodenum *n.* duodeno.
duoparental *adj.* duoparental.
duovirus *n.* duovirus.
duplication *n.* duplicación.
  conservative duplication duplicación conservadora.
  dispersive duplication duplicación dispersora.

  duplication of chromosomes duplicación cromosómica.
  semiconservative duplication duplicación semiconservadora.
duplicitas *n.* duplicidad.
  duplicitas anterior duplicidad anterior.
  duplicitas asymmetros duplicidad asimétrica.
  duplicitas completa duplicidad completa.
  duplicitas cruciata duplicidad cruzada.
  duplicitas incompleta duplicidad incompleta.
  duplicitas inferior duplicidad inferior.
  duplicitas media duplicidad media.
  duplicitas parallela duplicidad paralela.
  duplicitas posterior duplicidad posterior.
  duplicitas superior duplicidad superior.
  duplicitas symmetros duplicidad simétrica.
dupp *n.* dupp.
dura *n.* dura.
  dura mater duramadre, duramater.
dural *adj.* dural.
duralumin *n.* duraluminio.
duramatral *adj.* dural.
duraplasty *n.* duraplastia.
duration *n.* duración.
  half amplitude pulse duration duración de semiamplitud del pulso.
  pulse duration duración del pulso.
duroarachnitis *n.* duroaracnitis.
dust-borne *adj.* transmitido, -da por polvo.
dwarf *n.* enano, -na.
  achondroplasic dwarf enano acondroplásico.
  asexual dwarf enano asexual.
  ateliotic dwarf enano ateliótico.
  bird-headed dwarf of Seckel enano con cabeza de pájaro, enano con cabeza de pájaro de Seckel.
  bird-headed dwarf enano con cabeza de pájaro, enano con cabeza de pájaro de Seckel.
  Brissaud's dwarf enano de Brissaud.
  cretin dwarf enano cretino.
  diastrophic dwarf enano diastrófico.
  Fröhlich's dwarf enano de Fröhlich.
  geleophysic dwarf enano geleofísico.
  hypophyseal dwarf enano hipofisario.
  hypothyroid dwarf enano hipotiroideo.
  idiopathic dwarf enano idiopático.
  infantile dwarf enano infantil.
  micromelic dwarf enano micromélico.
  normal dwarf enano normal.
  Paltauf's dwarf enano de Paltauf.
  phocomelic dwarf enano focomélico.
  physiologic dwarf enano fisiológico.
  pituitary dwarf enano pituitario.
  primordial dwarf enano primordial.
  pure dwarf enano puro.
  rachitic dwarf enano raquítico.
  renal dwarf enano renal.
  rhizomelic dwarf enano rizomélico.
  Russell dwarf enano de Russell.
  Seckel dwarf enano de Seckel.
  sexual dwarf enano sexual.
  thanatophoric dwarf enano tanatofórico.
  true dwarf enano verdadero.
dwarfism *n.* enanismo.
  achondroplastic dwarfism enanismo acondroplásico.
  acromelic dwarfism enanismo acromélico.
  aortic dwarfism enanismo aórtico.
  Brissaud's dwarfism enanismo de Brissaud.
  camptomelic dwarfism enanismo camptomélico.
  chondrodystrophic dwarfism enanismo condrodistrófico.

deprivation dwarfism enanismo carencial.
diastrophic dwarfism enanismo diastrófico.
hypophyseal dwarfism enanismo hipofisario.
hypothyroid dwarfism enanismo hipotiroideo.
infantile dwarfism enanismo infantil.
Laron type dwarfism enanismo de Laron, enanismo tipo Laron.
lethal dwarfism enanismo mortal.
Lorain-Lévi dwarfism enanismo de Lorain-Lévi.
mesomelic dwarfism enanismo mesomélico.
metatropic dwarfism enanismo metatrófico.
micromelic dwarfism enanismo micromélico.
mulibrey dwarfism enanismo mulibrey.
phocomelic dwarfism enanismo focomélico.
physiologic dwarfism enanismo fisiológico.
pituitary dwarfism enanismo pituitario.
primordial dwarfism enanismo primordial.
senile dwarfism enanismo senil.
Silver-Russell dwarfism enanismo de Silver-Russell.
snub-nose dwarfism enanismo de nariz respingada.
thanatophoric dwarfism enanismo tanatofórico.
true dwarfism enanismo verdadero.
Walt Disney dwarfism enanismo de Walt Disney.
dyad *n.* díada.
dye *n.* colorante.
dyeing *adj.* colorante.
dying *adj.* moribundo, -da.
dynamic *adj.* dinámico, -ca.
dynamics *n.* dinámica.
  group dynamics dinámica de grupo.
dynamism *n.* dinamismo.
dynamization *n.* dinamización.
dynamogenesis *n.* dinamogénesis.
dynamogenic *adj.* dinamogénico, -ca, dinamógeno, -na.
dynamogeny *n.* dinamogenia.
dynamograph *n.* dinamógrafo.
dynamometer *n.* dinamómetro.
dynamopathic *adj.* dinamopático, -ca.
dynamoscope *n.* dinamoscopio.
dynamoscopy *n.* dinamoscopia.
dynein *n.* dineína.
dyonisiac *adj.* dionisíaco, -ca.
dyonism *n.* dionismo.
dysacousia *n.* disacusia, disacusis, disacusma.
dysacusia *n.* disacusia, disacusis, disacusma.
dysacusis *n.* disacusia, disacusis, disacusma.
dysadaptation *n.* desadaptación.
dysadrenalism *n.* disadrenalismo.
dysadrenia *n.* disadrenia.
dysallilognathia *n.* disalelognatia.
dysanagnosia *n.* disanagnosia.
dysantigraphia *n.* disantigrafía.
dysaphia *n.* disafia.
dysaphic *adj.* disáfico, -ca.
dysaptation *n.* desadaptación, disaptación.
dysarteriotony *n.* disarteriotonía.
dysarthria *n.* disartria.
  dysarthria literalis disartria literal.
  dysarthria syllabaris spasmodica disartria silábica espasmódica.
  rigid dysarthria disartria espástica.
  spastic dysarthria disartria espástica.
dysarthric *adj.* disártrico, -ca.
dysarthrosis *n.* disartrosis.
dysautonomia *n.* disautonomía.
  familial dysautonomia disautonomía familiar.

dysbarism *n.* disbarismo.
dysbasia *n.* disbasia.
  dysbasia angiosclerotica angiosclerótica intermitente, disbasia angioesclerótica, disbasia angiosclerótica.
  dysbasia angiospastica disbasia angioespástica.
  dysbasia intermittens angiosclerotica angiosclerótica intermitente, disbasia angioesclerótica, disbasia angiosclerótica.
  dysbasia lordotica progressiva disbasia lordótica progresiva.
  dysbasia neurasthenica intermittens disbasia neurasténica intermitente.
dysbetalipoproteinemia *n.* disbetalipoproteinemia.
dysbolism *n.* disbolismo.
dysboulia *n.* disbulia.
dysboulic *adj.* disbúlico, -ca.
dysbulia *n.* disbulia.
dysbulic *adj.* disbúlico, -ca.
dyscalculia *n.* discalculia.
dyscephalia *n.* discefalia.
  dyscephalia mandibulo-oculofacialis discefalia mandibulooculofacial.
dyscephaly *n.* discefalia.
  mandibulo-oculofacial dyscephaly discefalia mandibulooculofacial.
dyscheiral *adj.* disquirial.
dyscheiria *n.* disquiria.
dyschesia *n.* disquecia, disquesia.
dyschezia *n.* disquecia, disquezia.
dyschilia *n.* disquilia.
dyschiral *adj.* disquirial.
dyschiria *n.* disquiria.
dyscholia *n.* discolia.
dyschondrogenesis *n.* discondrogénesis.
dyschondroplasia *n.* discondroplasia.
  dyschondroplasia with hemangiomas discondroplasia con hemangiomas.
  Ollier's dyschondroplasia discondroplasia de Ollier.
dyschondrosteosis *n.* discondrosteosis.
dyschroa *n.* discroa, discroia.
dyschroia *n.* discroa, discroia.
dyschromasia *n.* discromasia.
dyschromatopsia *n.* discromatopsia.
  chromatic dyschromatopsia discromatopsia cromática.
  dyschromatic dyschromatopsia discromatopsia discromática.
dyschromatosis *n.* discromatosis.
dyschromia *n.* dicromodermia, discromía, paracromía.
dyschronism *n.* discronismo.
dyschronometry *n.* discronometría.
dyschylia *n.* disquilia.
dyscinesia *n.* discinesia, disquinesia.
dyscontrol *n.* descontrol.
dyscoria *n.* discoria².
dyscorticism *n.* discorticismo.
dyscrasia *n.* discrasia.
  blood dyscrasia discrasia sanguínea.
  plasma cell dyscrasia discrasia de las células plasmáticas.
dyscrasic *adj.* discrásico, -ca.
dyscratic *adj.* discrásico, -ca.
dysdiadochokinesia *n.* disdiadococinesia.
dysdiadochokinetic *adj.* disdiadococinético, -ca.
dysdipsia *n.* disdipsia.
dysecoia *n.* disecoia.
dysembryoma *n.* disembrioma.
dysembryoplasia *n.* disembrioplasia.
dysemia *n.* disemia, dissemia.

dysencephalia splanchnocystica *n.* disencefalia esplacnoquística.
dysendography *n.* disendografía.
dyseneia *n.* diseneia.
dysenteric *adj.* disentérico, -ca.
dysenteriform *adj.* disenteriforme.
dysentery *n.* disentería.
  amebic dysentery disentería amebiana, disentería amibiana.
  asylum dysentery disentería de los asilos.
  bacillary dysentery disentería bacilar.
  balantidial dysentery disentería balantidiana, disentería balantidiásica.
  bilharzial dysentery disentería bilharziana.
  catharral dysentery disentería catarral.
  chronic dysentery disentería crónica.
  ciliary dysentery disentería ciliar, disentería por ciliados.
  ciliate dysentery disentería ciliar, disentería por ciliados.
  epidemic dysentery disentería epidémica.
  flagellate dysentery disentería por flagelados.
  Flexner's dysentery disentería de Flexner.
  fulminating dysentery disentería fulminante.
  giardiasis dysentery disentería giardiásica.
  helminthic dysentery disentería helmíntica.
  institutional dysentery disentería de las instituciones.
  Japanese dysentery disentería japonesa.
  malarial dysentery disentería palúdica.
  malignant dysentery disentería maligna.
  protozoal dysentery disentería por protozoarios.
  schistosoma dysentery disentería esquistosomiásica.
  scorbutic dysentery disentería escorbútica.
  Sonne dysentery disentería de Sonne.
  spirillar dysentery disentería espirilar.
  sporadic dysentery disentería esporádica.
  viral dysentery disentería viral, disentería virósica.
dysequilibrium *n.* desequilibrio².
dyserethesia *n.* diseretesia.
dyserethism *n.* diseretismo.
dysergia *n.* disergia.
dysesthesia *n.* disestesia.
  auditory dysesthesia disacusia, disacusis, disestesia auditiva.
dysesthetic *adj.* disestésico, -ca, disestético, -ca.
dysfibrinogenemia *n.* disfibrinogenemia.
dysfunction *n.* disfunción.
  constitutional hepatic dysfunction disfunción constitucional del hígado, disfunción hepática constitucional.
  dental dysfunction disfunción dentaria.
  erectile dysfunction disfunción eréctil.
  esophageal dysfunction disfunción esofágica.
  female sexual dysfunction disfunción sexual femenina.
  male sexual dysfunction disfunción sexual masculina.
  minimal brain dysfunction disfunción cerebral mínima.
  myofascial pain dysfunction disfunción por dolor miofascial.
  non-organic sexual dysfunction disfunción sexual no orgánica.
  orgasmic dysfunction disfunción orgásmica.
  papillary muscle dysfunction disfunción muscular papilar.
  placental dysfunction disfunción placentaria.

sensory integrative dysfunction disfunción de la integración sensitiva.

sexual dysfunction disfunción sexual.

speech dysfunction disfunción del lenguaje.

temporomandibular dysfunction disfunción temporomandibular.

temporomandibular joint dysfunction (TMD) disfunción de la articulación temporomandibular.

ventricular dysfunction disfunción ventricular.

dysfunctional *adj.* disfuncional.

dysgalactia *n.* disgalactia.

dysgammaglobulinemia *n.* disgammaglobulinemia.

dysgenesia *n.* disgenesia[1].

dysgenesis *n.* disgenesia[2].

brain dysgenesis disgenesia cerebral.

epiphyseal dysgenesis disgenesia epifisaria.

gonadal dysgenesis disgenesia gonadal.

iridocorneal mesodermal dysgenesis disgenesia mesodérmica iridocorneal.

mixed gonadal dysgenesis disgenesia gonadal mixta.

pure gonadal dysgenesis disgenesia gonadal pura.

reticular dysgenesis disgenesia reticular.

seminiferous tubule dysgenesis disgenesia de los túbulos seminíferos.

dysgenitalism *n.* disgenitalismo.

dysgerminoma *n.* disgerminoma.

dysgeusia *n.* disgeusia.

dysglandular *adj.* disglandular.

dysglobulinemia *n.* disglobulinemia.

dysglycemia *n.* disglucemia.

dysgnathia *n.* disgnatia.

dysgnathic *adj.* disgnático, -ca.

dysgnosia *n.* disgnosia.

dysgonic *adj.* disgónico, -ca.

dysgrammatism *n.* disgramatismo.

dysgraphia *n.* disgrafia.

dyshematopoiesis *n.* dishematopoyesis.

dyshematopoietic *adj.* dishematopoyético, -ca.

dyshemopoiesis *n.* dishemopoyesis.

dyshemopoietic *adj.* dishemopoyético, -ca.

dyshepatia *n.* dishepatía.

lipogenic dyshepatia dishepatía lipogénica.

dyshesion *n.* dishesión.

dyshidria *n.* disidria, dishidria.

dyshidrosis *n.* disidrosis, dishidrosis.

dyshormonal *adj.* dishormonal.

dyshormonic *adj.* dishormónico, -ca.

dyshormonism *n.* dishormonismo.

dyshormonogenesis *n.* dishormonogénesis.

dysimmunity *n.* disinmunidad.

dyskaliemia *n.* discaliemia.

dyskaryosis *n.* discariosis.

dyskaryotic *adj.* discariótico, -ca.

dyskeratoma *n.* disqueratoma.

warty dyskeratoma disqueratoma verrugoso.

dyskinesia *n.* disquinesia.

biliary dyskinesia disquinesia biliar.

ciliar dyskinesia disquinesia ciliar.

dyskinesia algera disquinesia álgera.

dyskinesia intermittens disquinesia intermitente.

extrapiramidal dyskinesia disquinesia extrapiramidales.

orofacial dyskinesia disquinesia bucofacial.

tardive dyskinesia disquinesia tardía.

tardive oral dyskinesia disquinesia oral tardía.

tracheobronchial dyskinesia disquinesia traqueobronquial.

dyskinetic *adj.* discinético, -ca.

dyslalia *n.* dislalia.

dyslexia *n.* dislexia.

dyslexic *adj.* disléxico, -ca.

dyslipidemia *n.* dislipidemia.

dyslipidosis *n.* dislipidosis.

dyslipoidosis *n.* dislipidosis.

dyslipoproteinemia *n.* dislipoproteinemia.

dysmasesis *n.* dismasesis.

dysmature *adj.* dismaduro, -ra.

dysmaturity *n.* dismadurez.

pulmonary dysmaturity dismadurez pulmonar.

dysmegalopsia *n.* dismegalopsia.

dysmelia *n.* dismelia.

dysmenorrhea *n.* dismenorrea.

acquired dysmenorrhea dismenorrea adquirida.

congestive dysmenorrhea dismenorrea congestiva.

dysmenorrhea intermenstrualis dismenorrea intermenstrual.

essential dysmenorrhea dismenorrea esencial.

functional dysmenorrhea dismenorrea funcional.

inflammatory dysmenorrhea dismenorrea inflamatoria.

intrinsic dysmenorrhea dismenorrea intrínseca.

mechanical dysmenorrhea dismenorrea mecánica.

membranous dysmenorrhea dismenorrea membranosa.

nervous dysmenorrhea dismenorrea nerviosa.

obstructive dysmenorrhea dismenorrea obstructiva.

ovarian dysmenorrhea dismenorrea ovárica.

primary dysmenorrhea dismenorrea primaria.

psychogenic dysmenorrhea dismenorrea psicógena.

secondary dysmenorrhea dismenorrea secundaria.

spasmodic dysmenorrhea dismenorrea espasmódica.

tubal dysmenorrhea dismenorrea tubaria, dismenorrea tubárica.

ureteric dysmenorrhea dismenorrea uretérica.

uterine dysmenorrhea dismenorrea uterina.

vaginal dysmenorrhea dismenorrea vaginal.

dysmetabolism *n.* dismetabolismo.

dysmetria *n.* dismetría.

ocular dysmetria dismetría ocular.

dysmetropsia *n.* dismetropsia.

dysmimia *n.* dismimia.

dysmnesia *n.* dismnesia.

dysmnesic *adj.* dismnésico, -ca.

dysmorphia *n.* dismorfia.

craniofacial dysmorphia dismorfia craneofacial.

mandibulo-oculofacial dysmorphia dismorfia mandibulo-oculofacial.

dysmorphic *adj.* dismórfico, -ca.

dysmorphism *n.* dismorfismo.

dysmorphogenesis *n.* dismorfogénesis.

dysmorphologist *n.* dismorfologista.

dysmorphology *n.* dismorfología.

dysmorphophobia *n.* dismorfofobia.

dysmorphosis *n.* dismorfosis.

dysmyelination *n.* dismielinación.

dysmyotonia *n.* dismiotonía.

dysnomia *n.* disnomia.

color dysnomia disnomia para los colores.

dysnystaxis *n.* disnistaxis.

dysodontiasis *n.* disodontiasis.

dysoemia *n.* disoemia.

dysonthology *n.* disontología.

dysontogenesis *n.* disontogénesis, disontogenia.

dysontogenetic *adj.* disontogenético, -ca, disontogénico, -ca.

dysopia *n.* disopía.

dysopia algera disopía álgera.

dysopsia *n.* disopsia.

dysorexia *n.* disorexia.

dysorganoplasia *n.* disorganoplasia.

dysoria *n.* disoria.

dysoric *adj.* disórico, -ca.

dysosmia *n.* disosmia.

dysosteogenesis *n.* disosteogénesis.

dysostosis *n.* disostosis.

acrofacial dysostosis disostosis acrofacial, disostosis acrofacial de Nager.

cleidocranial dysostosis disostosis cleidocraneal, disostosis cleidocraneal congénita.

clidocranial dysostosis disostosis cleidocraneal, disostosis cleidocraneal congénita.

craniofacial dysostosis disostosis craneofacial, disostosis craneofacial hereditaria.

craniofacial hereditary dysostosis disostosis craneofacial, disostosis craneofacial hereditaria.

craniometaphyseal dysostosis disostosis craneometafisaria.

dysostosis cleidocranialis congenita disostosis cleidocraneal, disostosis cleidocraneal congénita.

dysostosis enchondralis epiphysaria disostosis encondral epifisaria.

dysostosis multiplex disostosis múltiple.

mandibuloacral dysostosis disostosis mandibuloacral.

mandibulofacial dysostosis disostosis mandibulofacial, disostosis maxilofacial.

mandibulofacial dysostosis with epibulbar dermoids disostosis mandibulofacial con dermoides epibulbares.

metaphyseal dysostosis disostosis metafisaria.

metaphysial dysostosis disostosis metafisaria.

Nager's acrofacial dysostosis disostosis acrofacial, disostosis acrofacial de Nager.

orodigitofacial dysostosis disostosis orodigitofacial.

otomandibular dysostosis disostosis otomandibular.

peripheral dysostosis disostosis periférica.

dysoxidative *adj.* disoxidativo, -va.

dyspallia *n.* dispalia.

dyspancreatism *n.* dispancreatismo.

dysparathyroidism *n.* disparatiroidismo.

dyspepsia *n.* dispepsia.

acid dyspepsia dispepsia ácida.

adhesion dyspepsia dispepsia por adherencia.

appendicular dyspepsia dispepsia apendicular.

appendix dyspepsia dispepsia apendicular.

atonic dyspepsia dispepsia atónica.

biliary dyspepsia biliar dispepsia.

catarrhal dyspepsia dispepsia catarral.

cholelithic dyspepsia dispepsia colelitiásica, dispepsia colelítica.

colon dyspepsia dispepsia cólica.

fermentative dyspepsia dispepsia fermentativa.

flatulent dyspepsia dispepsia flatulenta.

functional dyspepsia dispepsia funcional.

gastric dyspepsia dispepsia gástrica.
idiopathic dyspepsia dispepsia idiopática.
intestinal dyspepsia dispepsia intestinal.
nervous dyspepsia dispepsia nerviosa.
ovarian dyspepsia dispepsia ovárica.
reflex dyspepsia dispepsia refleja.
salivary dyspepsia dispepsia salival.
sulphuretted dyspepsia dispepsia sulfhídrica.
dyspeptic *adj.* dispéptico, -ca.
dysperistalsis *n.* disperistalsis.
dysphagia *n.* disfagia.
dysphagia inflammatoria disfagia inflamatoria.
dysphagia lusoria disfagia lusoria.
dysphagia nervosa disfagia nerviosa.
dysphagia paralytica disfagia paralítica.
dysphagia spastica disfagia espástica.
dysphagia valsalviana disfagia de Valsalva.
dysphagocytosis *n.* disfagocitosis.
congenital dysphagocytosis disfagocitosis congénita.
dysphagy *n.* disfagia.
Bayford-Autenrieth's dysphagy disfagia de Bayford-Autenrieth.
contractile ring dysphagy disfagia por anillo contráctil.
nervous dysphagy disfagia nerviosa.
sideropenic dysphagy disfagia sideropénica.
vallecular dysphagy disfagia valecular.
Valsalva's dysphagy disfagia de Valsalva.
dysphasia *n.* disfasia.
dysphemia *n.* disfemia.
dysphonia *n.* disfonía.
dysphonia clericorum disfonía de los clérigos.
dysphonia plicae ventricularis disfonía de las cuerdas vocales falsas.
dysphonia puberum disfonía de los púberes, disfonía puberal.
dysphonia spastica disfonía espasmódica, disfonía espástica.
dysplastic dysphonia disfonía displástica.
functional dysphonia disfonía funcional.
spasmodic dysphonia disfonía espasmódica, disfonía espástica.
spastic dysphonia disfonía espasmódica, disfonía espástica.
dysphonic *adj.* disfónico, -ca.
dysphoretic *adj.* disforético, -ca.
dysphoria *n.* disforia.
postcoitus dysphoria disforia postcoital.
dysphoriant *adj.* disforiante.
dysphoric *adj.* disfórico, -ca.
dyspigmentation *n.* dispigmentación.
dyspituitarism *n.* dispituitarismo.
dysplasia *n.* displasia.
anhidrotic ectodermal dysplasia displasia ectodérmica anhidrótica.
anterofacial dysplasia displasia anterofacial, displasia anteroposterior, displasia anteroposterior facial.
anteroposterior dysplasia displasia anterofacial, displasia anteroposterior, displasia anteroposterior facial.
anteroposterior facial dysplasia displasia anterofacial, displasia anteroposterior, displasia anteroposterior facial, displasia facial anteroposterior.
asphyxiating thoracic dysplasia displasia torácica asfixiante.
atriodigital dysplasia displasia auriculodigital.
bronchopulmonary dysplasia displasia broncopulmonar.
cerebral dysplasia displasia cerebral.
cervical dysplasia displasia cervical.
chondroectodermal dysplasia displasia condroectodérmica.

cleidocranial dysplasia displasia cleidocraneal, displasia clidocraneal.
clidocranial dysplasia displasia cleidocraneal, displasia clidocraneal.
congenital ectodermal dysplasia displasia ectodérmica congénita.
craniocarpotarsal dysplasia displasia craneocarpotarsiana.
craniodiaphyseal dysplasia displasia craneodiafisaria.
craniodiaphysial dysplasia displasia craneodiafisaria.
craniometaphyseal dysplasia displasia craneometafisaria.
craniometaphysial dysplasia displasia craneometafisaria.
cretinoid dysplasia displasia cretinoide.
dental dysplasia displasia dental.
dentin dysplasia displasia de la dentina, displasia dentinaria.
dentinal dysplasia displasia de la dentina, displasia dentinaria.
dentoalveolar dysplasia displasia dentoalveolar.
diaphyseal dysplasia displasia diafisaria, displasia diafisaria progresiva.
diaphysial dysplasia displasia diafisaria, displasia diafisaria progresiva.
dysplasia epiphysealis hemimelica displasia epifisaria hemimelia, displasia epifisaria hemimélica.
dysplasia epiphysealis punctata displasia epifisaria punteada.
dysplasia epiphysialis hemimelia displasia epifisaria hemimelia, displasia epifisaria hemimélica.
dysplasia epiphysialis multiplex displasia epifisaria múltiple.
dysplasia epiphysialis punctata displasia epifisaria punteada.
dysplasia linguofacialis displasia linguofacial.
dysplasia of the cervix displasia del cuello uterino.
ectodermal dysplasia displasia ectodérmica.
enamel dysplasia displasia del esmalte.
encephalo-ophthalmic dysplasia displasia encefalooftálmica.
epiphyseal dysplasia displasia epifisaria.
epithelial dysplasia displasia epitelial.
faciodigitogenital dysplasia displasia faciodigitogenital.
faciogenital dysplasia displasia faciogenital.
familial fibrous dysplasia of the jaws displasia fibrosa familiar de los maxilares, displasia fibrosa mandibular.
familial white folded mucosal dysplasia displasia familiar de pliegues blancos.
fibromuscular dysplasia displasia fibromuscular.
fibrous dysplasia displasia fibrosa.
fibrous dysplasia of bone displasia fibrosa de los huesos, displasia fibrosa ósea.
hereditary bone dysplasia displasia hereditaria de los huesos, displasia ósea hereditaria.
hereditary renal-retinal dysplasia displasia renal-retiniana hereditaria.
hidrotic ectodermal dysplasia displasia ectodérmica hidrótica.
hypohidrotic ectodermal dysplasia displasia ectodérmica hipohidrótica.
lymphopenic thymic dysplasia displasia tímica linfopénica.
mammary dysplasia displasia mamaria.
mandibulofacial dysplasia displasia maxilofacial.

metaphyseal dysplasia displasia metafisaria.
metaphysial dysplasia displasia metafisaria.
Mondini dysplasia displasia de Mondini.
monostotic fibrous dysplasia displasia fibrosa monostótica.
mucoepithelial dysplasia displasia mucoepitelial.
multiple epiphysial dysplasia displasia epifisaria múltiple.
Namaqualand hip dysplasia displasia de cadera de Namaqualand.
oculoauricular dysplasia displasia oculoauricular, displasia oculoauriculovertebral (OAV).
oculoauriculovertebral (OAV) dysplasia displasia oculoauricular, displasia oculoauriculovertebral (OAV).
oculodentodigital dysplasla (ODD) displasia oculodentodigital (ODD), displasia oculodentoóseo (ODOD).
oculodento-osseous dysplasia (ODOD) displasia oculodentodigital (ODD), displasia oculodentoóseo (ODOD).
oculovertebral dysplasia displasia oculovertebral.
odontogenic dysplasia displasia odontogénica.
ophthalmomandibulomelic dysplasia displasia oftalmomandibulomélica (OMM).
periapical cemental dysplasia displasia cemental periapical.
polyostotic dysplasia displasia fibrosa poliostótica.
progressive diaphyseal dysplasia displasia diafisaria, displasia diafisaria progresiva.
pseudoachondroplastic spondyloepiphysial dysplasia displasia espondiloepifisaria seudoacondroplásica.
renal dysplasia displasia renal.
retinal dysplasia displasia retiniana.
septo-optic dysplasia displasia septoóptica.
skeletal dysplasia displasia del esqueleto.
skeletodental dysplasia displasia esqueletodental.
spondyloepiphyseal dysplasia displasia espondiloepifisaria.
spondyloepiphysial dysplasia displasia espondiloepifisaria.
Streeter's dysplasia displasia de Streeter.
thymic dysplasia displasia tímica.
ureteral neuromuscular dysplasia displasia ureteral neuromuscular.
ventriculoradial dysplasia displasia ventriculorradial.
dysplastic *adj.* displásico, -ca.
dyspnea *n.* disnea.
cardiac dyspnea disnea cardíaca.
dyspnea at rest disnea de reposo.
exertional dyspnea disnea de ejercicio, disnea de esfuerzo.
expiratory dyspnea disnea espiratoria.
functional dyspnea disnea funcional.
inspiratory dyspnea disnea inspiratoria.
nocturnal dyspnea disnea nocturna.
non-expansional dyspnea disnea no expansiva.
orthostatic dyspnea disnea ortostática.
paroxysmal nocturnal dyspnea (PND) disnea nocturna paroxística, disnea paroxística nocturna (DPN).
renal dyspnea disnea renal.
sighing dyspnea disnea suspirosa.
dyspneic *adj.* disneico, -ca.
dyspoiesis *n.* dispoyesis.
dysponderal *adj.* disponderal.
dyspragia *n.* dispragia.

dyspragia intermittens angiosclerotica intestinalis dispragia intermitente angiosclerótica intestinal.
dyspraxia *n.* dispraxia.
developmental dyspraxia dispraxia del desarrollo.
dysprosody *n.* disprosodia.
Monrod-Krohn's dysprosody disprosodia de Monrod-Krohn.
dysproteinemia *n.* disproteinemia.
dysproteinemic *adj.* disproteinémico, -ca.
dysraphia *n.* disrafia.
occult spinal dysraphia disrafia vertebral oculta.
spinal dysraphia disrafia raquídea.
dysraphism *n.* disrafismo.
dysreflexia *n.* disreflexia.
autonomic dysreflexia disreflexia autonómica.
dysrhaphia *n.* disrafia.
dysrhaphism *n.* disrafismo.
dysrhythmia *n.* disritmia.
cardiac dysrhythmia disritmia cardíaca.
cerebral dysrhythmia disritmia cerebral.
circadian dysrhythmia disritmia circadiana.
electroencephalographic dysrhythmia disritmia electroencefalográfica.
esophageal dysrhythmia disritmia esofágica.
paroxysmal cerebral dysrhythmia disritmia cerebral paroxística.
dyssomnia *n.* disomnia.
dysspermia *n.* dispermia[2].
dysspondylism *n.* disespondilismo.
dysstasia *n.* disestasia.
dysstatic *adj.* disestático, -ca, distásico, -ca.
dyssymbolia *n.* disimbolia.
dyssymboly *n.* disimbolia.
dyssymmetry *n.* disimetría.
dyssynergia *n.* disinergia.
biliary dyssynergia disinergia biliar.
detrusor sphincter dyssynergia disinergia detrusor-esfínter.
dyssynergia cerebellaris myoclonica disinergia cerebelosa mioclónica, disinergia mioclónica cerebelosa.
dyssynergia cerebellaris progressiva disinergia cerebelosa progresiva.
dyssystole *n.* disistolia.
dystasia *n.* disestasia, distasia, distasis.
hereditary areflexic dystasia distasia arrefléxica hereditaria.
hereditary ataxic dystasia distasia atáxica hereditaria, distasia de Roussy-Lévy.
Roussy-Lévy hereditary ataxic dystasia distasia atáxica hereditaria, distasia de Roussy-Lévy.
dystassia *n.* distasia, distasis.
dystaxia *n.* distaxia.
dystectia *n.* distectia.
dysteleology *n.* disteleología.
dystelephalangy *n.* distelefalangia.
dysthymia *n.* distimia.
dysthymic *adj.* distímico, -ca.
dysthymism *n.* distimismo.
dysthyreosis *n.* distireosis.
dysthyroid *adj.* distiroideo, -a.
dysthyroidal *adj.* distiroideo, -a.
dysthyroidism *n.* distiroidismo.
dystithia *n.* distitia.
dystocia *n.* distocia.
cervical dystocia distocia cervical.
constriction ring dystocia distocia por anillo de constricción.
contraction ring dystocia distocia por anillo de constricción.
fetal dystocia distocia fetal.

maternal dystocia distocia materna.
placental dystocia distocia placentaria.
dystonia *n.* distonía.
dystonia deformans progressiva distonía deformante muscular, distonía deformante progresiva.
dystonia lenticularis distonía lenticular.
dystonia musculorum deformans distonía deformante muscular, distonía deformante progresiva, distonía muscular deformante.
kinesigenic dystonia distonía kinesigénica.
paroxysmal dystonia distonía paroxística.
tardive dystonia distonía tardía.
torsion dystonia distonía de torsión, distonía por torsión.
dystonic *adj.* distónico, -ca.
dystopia *n.* distopia.
dystopia canthorum distopia de los cantos.
dystopia testis distopia testis.
dystopic *adj.* distópico, -ca.
dystrophia *n.* distrofia.
dystrophia adiposa corneae distrofia adiposa de la córnea.
dystrophia adiposogenitalis distrofia adiposogenital.
dystrophia brevicollis distrofia brevicollis.
dystrophia diffusa distrofia difusa.
dystrophia endothelialis corneae distrofia endotelial de la córnea.
dystrophia epithelialis corneae distrofia epitelial de la córnea.
dystrophia hypophysopriva chronica distrofia hipofiseopriva crónica, distrofia hipofisopriva crónica.
dystrophia mediana canaliformis distrofia canaliforme mediana.
dystrophia mesodermalis congenita hyperplastica distrofia mesodérmica congénita hiperplástica.
dystrophia myotonica distrofia miotónica.
dystrophia periostalis hyperplastica familiar distrofia perióstica hiperplástica familiar.
dystrophia unguis mediana canaliformis distrofia canaliforme mediana de la uña, distrofia ungueal mediana canaliforme.
dystrophia unguium distrofia ungueal, distrofia ungular.
dystrophic *adj.* distrófico, -ca.
dystrophin *n.* distrofina.
dystrophinopathy *n.* distrofinopatía.
dystrophoneurosis *n.* distrofoneurosis.
dystrophy *n.* distrofia.
adiposogenital dystrophy distrofia adiposogenital.
adult pseudohypertrophic muscular dystrophy distrofia muscular seudohipertrófica adulta.
Albright's dystrophy distrofia de Albright.
asphyxiating thoracic dystrophy (ATD) distrofia asfíctica torácica.
Barnes' dystrophy distrofia de Barnes.
Becker type muscular dystrophy distrofia muscular de Becker.
Becker type tardive muscular dystrophy distrofia muscular tardía tipo Becker.
Becker's dystrophy distrofia de Becker.
Becker's muscular dystrophy distrofia muscular de Becker.
benign pseudohypertrophic muscular dystrophy distrofia muscular benigna seudohipertrófica.
Biber-Haab-Dimmer dystrophy distrofia de Biber-Haab-Dimmer.
childhood muscular dystrophy distrofia muscular infantil.

cleidocranial dystrophy distrofia cleidocraneal.
Cogan's microcystic dystrophy distrofia microquística de Cogan.
cones dystrophy distrofia de los conos.
corneal dystrophy distrofia corneal.
craniocarpotarsal dystrophy distrofia craneocarpotarsiana.
Déjerine-Landouzy dystrophy distrofia de Déjerine-Landouzy.
distal muscular dystrophy distrofia muscular distal.
Duchenne-Landouzy dystrophy distrofia de Duchenne-Landouzy.
Duchenne's dystrophy distrofia de Duchenne.
Duchenne's muscular dystrophy distrofia muscular de Duchenne.
endothelial dystrophy of the cornea distrofia endotelial de la córnea.
epithelial dystrophy distrofia epitelial.
Erb's dystrophy distrofia de Erb.
Erb's muscular dystrophy distrofia muscular de Erb.
facioscapulohumeral muscular dystrophy distrofia muscular facioescapulohumeral, distrofia muscular fascioscapulohumeral.
familial osseous dystrophy distrofia ósea familiar.
Favre's dystrophy distrofia de Favre.
fingerprint dystrophy distrofia como impresiones digitales, distrofia en huellas dactilares.
fleck dystrophy of the cornea distrofia manchada de la córnea.
Fuchs' dystrophy distrofia de Fuchs.
Fuchs' epithelial dystrophy distrofia epitelial de Fuchs.
Gowers muscular dystrophy distrofia muscular de Gowers.
granular corneal dystrophy (Groenouw's type I) distrofia corneal granular (de Groenouw tipo I).
granular stromal dystrophy distrofia granular de la estroma.
gutter dystrophy of the cornea distrofia en gotera de la córnea.
hereditary vitelliform dystrophy distrofia viteliforme hereditaria.
hypophyseal dystrophy distrofia hipofisaria.
juvenile epithelial dystrophy distrofia epitelial juvenil.
Landouzy-Déjerine type dystrophy distrofia de Landouzy-Déjerine.
lattice corneal dystrophy distrofia en enrejado de la córnea.
lattice dystrophy(of cornea) distrofia en encaje (de la córnea).
Leyden-Möbius muscular dystrophy distrofia de Leyden-Möbius, distrofia muscular de Leyden Möbius, distrofia muscular de Leyden-Möbius.
limb-girdle muscular dystrophy distrofia muscular de las cinturas de las extremidades, distrofia muscular de las cinturas escapulohumeral o pélvica.
macular corneal dystrophy (Groenouw's type II) distrofia corneal macular (de Groenouw tipo II).
macular stromal dystrophy distrofia macular de la estroma.
map-dot-fingerprint dystrophy distrofia mapa-puntos-impresiones digitales.
Meesman dystrophy distrofia de Meesman.
microcystic epithelial dystrophy distrofia epitelial microquística.

muscular dystrophy distrofia muscular.
myotonic dystrophy distrofia miotónica.
myotonic muscular dystrophy distrofia muscular miotónica.
oculocerebrorenal dystrophy distrofia oculocerebrorrenal.
oculopharyngeal muscular dystrophy distrofia muscular oculofaríngea.
papillary and pigmentary dystrophy distrofia papilar y pigmentaria.
pelvofemoral muscular dystrophy distrofia muscular pelvifemoral.
posterior polymorphous dystrophy distrofia polimorfa posterior.
progressive muscular dystrophy distrofia muscular progresiva.
progressive tapetochoroidal dystrophy distrofia taperocoroidea progresiva, distrofia tapetocoroidea.
pseudohypertrophic muscular dystrophy distrofia muscular seudohipertrófica.

Reis-Bucklers' dystrophy distrofia de Reis-Bucklers.
reticular dystrophy of the cornea distrofia reticular de la córnea.
ring-like corneal dystrophy distrofia anular de la córnea.
Salzmann's dystrophy distrofia de Salzmann.
Salzmann's nodular corneal dystrophy distrofia corneal nodular de Salzmann.
scapulohumeral muscular dystrophy distrofia muscular escapulohumeral.
Simmerlin's dystrophy distrofia de Simmerlin.
Steinert's muscular dystrophy distrofia muscular de Steinert.
sympathetic reflex dystrophy distrofia refleja simpática, distrofia simpática refleja.
tapetochoroidal dystrophy distrofia taperocoroidea progresiva, distrofia tapetocoroidea.
thoracic-pelvic-phalangeal dystrophy distrofia torácica-pélvica-falángica.
thyroneural dystrophy distrofia tironerviosa, distrofia tironeural.
twenty-nail dystrophy distrofia de las veinte uñas.
vitelliform dystrophy distrofia viteliforme.
vitreo-tapetoretinal dystrophy distrofia vítreotapetorretiniana.
Welander's muscular dystrophy distrofia muscular tipo Welander.
wound dystrophy distrofia de heridas.

dystrypsia *n.* distripsia.
dysuresia *n.* disuresia.
dysuria *n.* alginuresis, disuria.
psychic dysuria disuria psíquica.
spasmodic dysuria disuria espasmódica, disuria espástica.
spastic dysuria disuria espasmódica, disuria espástica.
dysuriac *adj.* disúrico, -ca.
dysuric *adj.* disúrico, -ca.
dysury *n.* disuria.
dysvitaminosis *n.* disvitaminosis.
dyszoospermia *n.* diszoospermia.

E e

ear *n.* oído, oreja.
  aviator's ear oído de aviador.
  Aztec ear oreja azteca.
  bat ear oreja de murciélago.
  beach ear oído de playa.
  Blainville ear oreja de blainville.
  boxer's ear oreja de boxeador.
  Cagot ear oreja de Cagot.
  cat's ear oreja de gato.
  cauliflower ear oreja de coliflor, oreja en coliflor.
  cup ear oreja en taza.
  Darwin's ear oreja de darwin.
  external ear auris externa, oído externo.
  hairy ear oreja pilosa.
  Hong Kong ear oído de Hong Kong.
  hot weather ear oído de tiempo caliente.
  inner ear auris interna, oído interno.
  internal ear auris interna, oído interno.
  loop ear oreja en asa.
  lop ear oreja caída.
  middle ear auris media, oído medio.
  Morel's ear oreja de macaco, oreja de Morel.
  Mozart ear oreja de Mozart.
  outer ear auris externa, oído externo.
  prizefighter ear oreja de boxeador.
  scroll ear oreja de sátiro, oreja en pergamino, oreja en punta, oreja en punta de sátiro, oreja en rollo de papel.
  Singapore ear oído de Singapur.
  Stahl ear oreja de Stahl nº 1, oreja de Stahl nº 2.
  swimmer's ear oído de nadador.
  tank ear oído de tanque.
  tropical ear oído tropical.
  Wildermuth's ear oreja de Wildermuth.
eardrum *n.* tambor², tímpano.
ebonation *n.* ebonación.
ébranlement *n.* ébranlement.
ebriety *n.* ebriedad.
ebrious *adj.* ebrio, -a.
ebullism *n.* ebullismo.
ebullition *n.* ebullición.
ebur *n.* ebur.
  ebur dentis ebur dentis.
eburnation *n.* eburnación.
  eburnation of dentin eburnación de la dentina.
eburneous *adj.* ebúrneo, -a.
eburnitis *n.* eburnitis.
écarteur *n.* écarteur.
ecaudate *adj.* ecaudado, -a.
ecbolic *adj.* ecbólico, -ca.
ecbovirus (Enteric Cytopathic Bovine Orphan) *n.* ecbovirus.
eccentric *adj.* excéntrico, -ca.
eccentricity *n.* excentricidad.
eccentrochondroplasia *n.* eccentrochondroplasia, excentrocondroplasia.
eccentroosteochondrodysplasia *n.* eccentroosteocondrodisplasia.

eccentropiesis *n.* excentropiesis.
eccephalosis *n.* excefalosis.
ecchondroma *n.* econdroma, excondroma.
  ecchondroma physaliphora econdroma fisaliforme.
ecchondrosis *n.* excondrosis.
  ecchondrosis physaliformis excondrosis fisalifora, excondrosis fisaliforme.
  ecchondrosis physaliphora excondrosis fisalifora, excondrosis fisaliforme.
ecchondrotome *n.* econdrótomo, excondrótomo.
ecchymoma *n.* equimoma.
ecchymosed *adj.* equimosado, -da.
ecchymosis *n.* equimosis.
  cadaveric ecchymosis equimosis cadavérica.
  palpebral ecchymosis equimosis palpebral.
  Tardieu's ecchymosis equimosis de Tardieu.
ecchymotic *adj.* equimótico, -ca.
eccrine *adj.* ecrino, -na.
eccrinology *n.* ecrinología.
eccrisiology *n.* ecrisiología.
eccrisis *n.* ecrisis.
eccritic *adj.* ecrítico, -ca.
eccyesis *n.* ecciesis, exciesis.
ecdemic *adj.* ecdémico, -ca.
echinate *adj.* equinado, -da.
echinenone *n.* equinenona.
echinocacciasis *n.* equinococosis.
  renal echinococciasis equinococosis renal.
  retrovesical echinococciasis equinococosis retrovesical.
echinococcosis *n.* equinococosis.
echinococcotomy *n.* equinococotomía.
Echinococcus *n.* Echinococcus.
echinococcus *n.* equinococo.
echinocyte *n.* equinocito.
echinophthalmia *n.* equinoftalmía.
echinosis *n.* equinosis.
echinostomiasis *n.* equinostomiasis.
echinulate *adj.* equinulado, -da.
echo *n.* eco.
  amphoric echo eco anfórico.
  atrial echo eco auricular.
  beat echo eco del latido.
  echo nodus sinuatrialis eco del nódulo sinoauricular.
  metallic echo eco metálico.
  thought hearing echo eco del pensamiento.
ECHO virus *n.* echovirus.
echoacousia *n.* ecoacusia.
echoaortography *n.* ecoaortografía.
echocardiogram *n.* ecocardiograma.
echocardiography *n.* ecocardiografía.
  B-mode two dimensional echocardiography ecocardiografía bidimensional.
  cross-sectional echocardiography ecocardiografía de sección transversal.
  Doppler echocardiography ecocardiografía Doppler.

  transesophageal echocardiography ecocardiografía transesofágica.
echoencephalogram *n.* ecoencefalograma.
echoencephalograph *n.* ecoencefalógrafo.
echoencephalography *n.* ecoencefalografía.
echogenic *adj.* ecogénico, -ca, ecógeno, -na.
echogenicity *n.* ecogenicidad.
echogram *n.* ecograma.
echographer *n.* ecógrafo.
echographia *n.* ecografía.
echographic *adj.* ecográfico, -ca.
echographist *n.* ecografista.
echography *n.* ecografía.
  A mode echography ecografía en modo A.
  B mode echography ecografía en modo B.
  Doppler echography ecografía Doppler.
  M mode echography ecografía en modo M.
  real time echography ecografía en tiempo real.
  static echography ecografía estática.
echokinesia *n.* ecocinesia, ecocinesis, ecoquinesis.
echokinesis *n.* ecocinesia, ecocinesis, ecoquinesis.
echolalia *n.* ecolalia.
  delayed echolalia ecolalia tardía.
echolucent *adj.* ecolúcido, -da.
echomatism *n.* ecomatismo, ecomotismo.
echomimia *n.* ecomimia.
echomotism *n.* ecomatismo, ecomotismo.
echopathy *n.* ecopatía.
echophonia *n.* ecofonía.
echophonocardiography *n.* ecofonocardiografía.
echophony *n.* ecofonía.
echophotony *n.* ecofotonía.
echophrasia *n.* ecofrasia.
echopraxia *n.* ecopraxia.
echopraxis *n.* ecopraxia.
echoscope *n.* ecoscopio.
echostructure *n.* ecoestructura.
echovirus *n.* ecovirus.
echovirus (Enteric Cytopathic Human Orphan) *n.* ECHOvirus.
eclabium *n.* eclabio.
eclampsia *n.* eclampsia.
  puerperal eclampsia eclampsia puerperal.
  uremic eclampsia eclampsia urémica.
eclampsism *n.* eclampsismo, eclamptismo.
eclamptic *adj.* eclámpsico, -ca, eclámptico, -ca.
eclamptism *n.* eclampsismo, eclamptismo.
eclamptogenic *adj.* eclamptogénico, -ca.
eclamptogenous *adj.* eclamptógeno, -na.
eclipse *n.* eclipse.
eclysis *n.* eclisis.
ecmnesia *n.* ecmnesia.
ecochleation *n.* ecocleación.
ecogenetic *adj.* ecogenético, -ca.
ecogenetics *n.* ecogenética.
ecologist *n.* ecólogo, -ga.

ecology *n.* ecología.
  human ecology ecología humana.
economic *adj.* económico, -ca.
economy *n.* economía.
  animal economy economía animal.
  token economy economía simbólica.
ecosite *n.* ecoparásito, ecósito.
ecosystem *n.* ecosistema.
ecotaxis *n.* ecotaxis.
ecotone *n.* ecotono.
ecphyadectomy *n.* ecfiadectomía.
ecphyaditis *n.* ecfiaditis.
ecphylactic *adj.* ecfiláctico, -ca.
ecphylaxis *n.* ecfilaxis.
ecphyma *n.* ecfima.
ecsomatics *n.* ecsomática.
ecstasy *n.* éxtasis.
ecstatic *adj.* extático, -ca.
ecstrophe *n.* extrofia.
ecstrophy *n.* extrofia.
ectacolia *n.* ectacolia.
ectal *adj.* ectal.
ectasia *n.* ectasia,, ectasis.
  alveolar ectasia ectasia alveolar.
  annuloaortic ectasia ectasia anuloaórtica.
  corneal ectasia ectasia corneal.
  diffuse arterial ectasia ectasia arterial difusa.
  ectasia cordis ectasia cardíaca.
  ectasia ventriculi paradoxa ectasia paradójica del vientre.
  hypostatic ectasia ectasia hipostática.
  mammary duct ectasia ectasia de conductos mamarios.
  papillary ectasia ectasia papilar.
  scleral ectasia ectasia de la esclerótica, ectasia escleral.
  senile ectasia ectasia senil.
  tubular ectasia ectasia tubular.
  ureteral ectasia ectasia ureteral.
ectasis *n.* ectasia,, ectasis.
ectatic *adj.* ectásico, -ca, ectático, -ca.
ectental *adj.* ectental, ectoental.
ecterograph *n.* ecterógrafo.
ectethmoid *n.* ectetmoides.
ecthyma *n.* ectima, ectimosis.
  contagious ecthyma ectima contagioso.
  ecthyma gangrenosum ectima gangrenoso.
  ecthyma shyphiliticum ectima sifilítico.
ecthymatiform *adj.* ectimatiforme.
ecthymiform *adj.* ectimiforme.
ecthyreosis *n.* ectireosis.
ectiris *n.* ectiris.
ectobiology *n.* ectobiología.
ectoblast *n.* ectoblasto.
ectocardia *n.* ectocardia.
ectocardiac *adj.* ectocardíaco, -ca.
ectocardial *adj.* ectocardíaco, -ca.
ectocervical *adj.* ectocervical.
ectocervix *n.* ectocérvix.
ectochoroidea *n.* ectocoroides.
ectocinerea *n.* ectocinérea.
ectocolon *n.* ectocolon.
ectocondyle *n.* ectocóndilo.
ectocornea *n.* ectocórnea.
ectocyst *n.* ectoquiste.
ectocytic *adj.* ectocítico, -ca.
ectoderm *n.* ectodermo.
  amniotic ectoderm ectodermo amniótico.
  basal ectoderm ectodermo basal.
  chorionic ectoderm ectodermo coriónico.
  epithelial ectoderm ectodermo epitelial.
  extraembryonic ectoderm ectodermo extraembrionario.
  neural ectoderm ectodermo neural.
  superficial ectoderm ectodermo superficial.

ectodermatosis *n.* ectodermatosis.
ectodermic *adj.* ectodérmico, -ca.
ectodermosis *n.* ectodermosis.
  ectodermosis erosiva pluriorificialis ectodermosis erosiva pluriorificial.
ectoental *adj.* ectental, ectoental.
ectogenic *adj.* ectógeno, -na.
ectogenous *adj.* ectógeno, -na.
ectoglia *n.* ectoglia.
ectoglobular *adj.* ectoglobular.
ectogony *n.* ectogonia.
ectolecithal *adj.* ectolecito, -ta.
ectolysis *n.* ectólisis.
ectomeninx *n.* ectomeninge.
ectomere *n.* ectómera, ectómero.
ectomerogony *n.* ectomerogonia.
ectomesoblast *n.* ectomesoblasto.
ectonuclear *adj.* ectonuclear.
ectopagus *n.* ectópago.
ectoparasite *n.* ectoparásito.
ectoparasiticide *n.* ectoparasiticida.
ectoparasitism *n.* ectoparasitismo.
ectoperitoneal *adj.* ectoperitoneal.
ectoperitonitis *n.* ectoperitonitis.
ectopia *n.* ectopia.
  ectopia cloacae ectopia de la cloaca.
  ectopia cordis ectopia cardiaca, ectopia cordis.
  ectopia cordis abdominalis ectopia cordis abdominalis.
  ectopia iridis ectopia del iris.
  ectopia lentis ectopia del cristalino, ectopia lentis.
  ectopia maculae ectopia macular.
  ectopia pupillae ectopia pupilar.
  ectopia pupillae congenita ectopia congénita de la pupila.
  ectopia renis ectopia renal.
  ectopia testis ectopia testicular.
  ectopia vesicae ectopia de la vejiga, ectopia vesical.
  pectoral ectopia cordis ectopia cordis pectoral.
ectopic *adj.* ectópico, -ca.
ectoplacenta *n.* ectoplacenta.
ectoplacental *adj.* ectoplacentario, -ria.
ectoplasm *n.* ectoplasma.
ectoplasmatic *adj.* ectoplasmático, -ca.
ectoplast *n.* ectoplasto.
ectoplastic *adj.* ectoplástico, -ca.
ectopotomy *n.* ectopotomía.
ectopy *n.* ectopia.
  cervical ectopy ectopia cervical.
  crossed renal ectopy ectopia renal cruzada.
  pupillary ectopy ectopia pupilar.
  renal ectopy ectopia renal.
ectoretina *n.* ectorretina.
ectoscopy *n.* ectoscopia.
ectosite *n.* ectósito.
ectoskeleton *n.* ectoesqueleto, ectosqueleto.
ectosteal *adj.* ectósteo, -a, ectóstico, -ca.
ectostosis *n.* ectostosis.
ectosuggestion *n.* ectosugestión.
ectothrix *n.* ectotrix.
ectozoon *adj.* ectozoario, ectozoo, -a.
ectrocheiry *n.* ectroqueiria, ectroquiria.
ectrochiry *n.* ectroqueiria, ectroquiria.
ectrodactilia *n.* ectrodactilia.
ectrodactylism *n.* ectrodactilismo.
ectrodactyly *n.* ectrodactilia.
ectrofalangia *n.* ectrofalangia.
ectrogenic *adj.* ectrogénico, -ca.
ectrogeny *n.* ectrogenia.
ectromelia *n.* ectromelia.
ectromelic *adj.* ectromélico, -ca.

ectromelus *n.* ectromelo.
ectrometacarpia *n.* ectrometacarpia.
ectrometatarsia *n.* ectrometatarsia.
ectropion *n.* ectropía, ectropión.
  atonic ectropion ectropión atónico.
  cervical ectropion ectropión cervical.
  cicatricial ectropion ectropión cicatrizal.
  ectropion luxurians ectropión lujuriante.
  ectropion of pigment layer ectropión de la capa pigmentaria.
  ectropion sarcomatosum ectropión sarcomatoso.
  ectropion uveae ectropión uveal.
  flaccid ectropion ectropión fláccido.
  paralytic ectropion ectropión paralítico.
  senile ectropion ectropión senil.
  spastic ectropion ectropión espástico.
  uveal ectropion ectropión uveal.
ectropionize *v.* ectropionizar.
ectropody *n.* ectropodia.
ectrosis *n.* ectrosis.
ectrosyndactylia *n.* ectrosindactilia.
ectrosyndactyly *n.* ectrosindactilia.
ectrotic *adj.* ectrótico, -ca.
ectypia *n.* ectipia.
eczema *n.* eccema, ezcema.
  acute eczema eccema agudo.
  allergic eczema eccema alérgico.
  asteatotic eczema eccema asteatótico.
  atopic eczema eccema atópico, eccema constitucional.
  baker's eczema eccema de los panaderos.
  chronic eczema eccema crónico.
  contact eczema eccema de contacto.
  dry seborrheic eczema eccema seborreico seco.
  eczema capitis eccema capitis.
  eczema craquelé eccema agrietado.
  eczema diabeticorum eccema diabético.
  eczema epilans eccema depilatorio, eccema epilante.
  eczema erythematosum eccema eritematoso.
  eczema herpeticum eccema herpético.
  eczema hypertrophicum eccema hipertrófico.
  eczema madidans eccema madidans.
  eczema marginatum eccema marginado, eccema marginatum.
  eczema nummulare eccema numular.
  eczema papulosum eccema papuloso.
  eczema parasiticum eccema parasitario.
  eczema pustulosum eccema pustuloso.
  eczema rubrum eccema rojo.
  eczema squamosum eccema escamoso.
  eczema tyloticum eccema tilótico.
  eczema vaccinatum eccema vacunal.
  eczema verrucosum eccema verrugoso.
  eczema vesiculosum eccema simple, eccema vesiculoso.
  erythematous eczema eccema eritematoso.
  flexural eczema eccema de los pliegues de flexión, eccema flexural.
  follicular eczema eccema folicular.
  hand eczema eccema de las manos.
  housewives' eczema eccema de las amas de casa.
  impetiginous eczema eccema impetiginizado, eccema impetiginoso.
  infantile eczema eccema de la niñez, eccema infantil.
  lichenoid eczema eccema liquenoide.
  microbic eczema eccema microbiano.
  moist eczema eccema húmedo.
  nummular eczema eccema numular.

orbicular eczema eccema orbicular.
seborrheic eczema eccema seborreico.
solar eczema eccema solar.
stasis eczema eccema por estasis.
tropical eczema eccema tropical.
varicose eczema eccema varicoso.
weeping eczema eccema exudativo, eccema rezumante.
winter eczema eccema invernal.
xerotic eczema eccema xerótico.
eczematid *n.* eccemátide.
eczematization *n.* eccematización.
eczematogenic *adj.* eccematogénico, -ca, eccematógeno, -na, eccemógeno, -na.
eczematold *adj.* eccematolde.
eczematosis *n.* eccematosis.
eczematous *adj.* eccematoso, -sa.
edema *n.* edema.
acute circumscribed edema edema agudo circunscrito.
acute essential edema edema agudo esencial.
acute paroxysmal edema edema agudo paroxístico.
alimentary edema edema alimentario.
alveolar edema edema alveolar.
angioneurotic edema edema angioneurótico.
Berlin's edema edema de Berlín.
blue edema edema azul.
brain edema edema cerebral, edema del cerebro.
brown edema edema pardo.
bullous edema edema ampollar.
bullous vesicae edema edema ampollar de la vejiga, edema ampolloso vesical.
cachectic edema edema caquéctico.
Calabar edema edema de Calabar.
cardiac edema edema cardíaco.
cerebral edema edema cerebral, edema del cerebro.
circumscribed edema edema circunscrito.
conjunctival edema edema conjuntival, edema de la conjuntiva.
corneal edema edema corneal.
cyclic idiopathic edema edema cíclico idiopático.
cystoid macular edema edema macular quístico.
dependent edema edema por declive, edema postural.
edema bullosum vesicae edema ampollar de la vejiga, edema ampolloso vesical.
edema calidum edema cálido.
edema frigidum edema frígido.
edema fugax edema fugaz.
edema neonatorum edema neonatal, edema neonatorum.
edema of the glottis edema de la glotis.
edema of the lung edema de pulmón, edema pulmonar.
edema of the optic disk edema del disco óptico.
famine edema edema de hambre.
gaseous edema edema gaseoso.
gestational edema edema gestacional.
heat edema edema por calor.
hepatic edema edema hepático.
hereditary angioneurotic edema edema angioneurótico hereditario.
high-altitude edema edema de altitud.
high-altitude pulmonary edema edema pulmonar de las grandes alturas.
hunger edema edema de hambre.
hysterical edema edema histérico.
inflammatory edema edema inflamatorio.

insulin edema edema por insulina.
local intracutaneous edema edema intradérmico local.
lymphatic edema edema linfático.
macular diabetic edema edema macular diabético.
malignant edema edema de Pirogoff, edema maligno.
marantic edema edema marántico.
menstrual edema edema menstrual.
migratory edema edema migratorio.
Milton's edema edema de Milton.
mucous edema edema mucoso.
neuropathic edema edema neuropático.
non-inflammatory edema edema no inflamatorio.
nutritional edema edema nutricional.
palpebral edema edema palpebral.
papilar edema edema de papila.
paroxysmal pulmonary edema edema pulmonar paroxístico.
passive edema edema pasivo.
periodic edema edema periódico.
periorbital edema edema periorbitario.
periretinal edema edema perirretiniano.
pitting edema edema compresible, edema depresible.
placental edema edema placentario.
prehepatic edema edema prehepático.
premenstrual edema edema premenstrual.
pressure edema edema por presión.
pulmonary edema edema de pulmón, edema pulmonar.
purulent edema edema purulento.
Quincke's edema edema de Quincke.
Reinke's edema edema de Reinke.
renal edema edema renal.
rheumatic edema edema reumático.
salt edema edema salino.
scrotal edema edema del escroto.
solid edema edema sólido.
solid edema of the lungs edema sólido de los pulmones.
terminal edema edema terminal.
toxic edema edema tóxico.
traumatic edema of the retina edema traumático de la retina.
vasogenic edema edema vasógeno.
venous edema edema venoso.
vernal edema of the lung edema vernal del pulmón.
wandering edema edema errante.
war edema edema de guerra.
Yangtze edema edema Yangtze.
edemagen *n.* edemágeno.
edematigenous *adj.* edematígeno, -na, edematógeno, -na, edemígeno, -na.
edematization *n.* edematización.
edematogenic *adj.* edemarígeno, -na, edematógeno, -na.
edematous *adj.* edematoso, -sa.
edentia *n.* edencia.
edeocephalus *n.* edeocéfalo.
edge *n.* borde3.
cutting edge borde cortante.
denture edge borde de dentadura, borde dentado, borde dental.
edge-strength resistencia del borde.
incisal edge borde incisal, borde incisivo.
leading edge borde conductor.
eduction *n.* educción.
effacement *n.* borradura, borramiento.
effect *n.* efecto.
abscopal effect efecto abscopal.
additive effect efecto aditivo.

adverse drug effect efecto farmacológico adverso.
anachoretic effect efecto anacorético.
anodic effect efecto anódico.
Anrep effect efecto de Anrep.
Arias Stella effect efecto de Arias-Stella.
autocrine effect efecto autocrino.
autokinetic effect efecto autocinético.
Bernoulli effect efecto de Bernoulli.
biologic effect efecto biológico.
Bohr effect efecto de Bohr.
Compton effect efecto de Compton.
contrary effect efecto contrario.
Cotton effect efecto de Cotton.
Crabtree effect efecto de Crabtree.
cumulative effect efecto acumulativo.
curtain effect efecto velo.
Cushing effect efecto de Cushing.
cytopathic effect efecto citopático.
Danysz effect efecto de Danysz.
dead space effect efecto de espacio muerto.
Deelman effect efecto de Deelman.
Doppler effect efecto Doppler.
effect of sleep deprivation efecto de la privación del sueño.
electrophonic effect efecto electrofónico.
Emerson effect efecto de Emerson.
experimenter's effect efecto del experimentador.
Fahraeus-Lindqvist effect efecto de Fahraeus-Lindqvist.
Fenn effect efecto de Fenn.
founder effect efecto fundador.
gene dosage effect efecto de dosificación genética.
gonadal effect of radiation efecto gonadal de la radioterapia.
Haldane effect efecto Haldane.
Hallwachs effect efecto de Hallwachs.
Hawthorne effect efecto Hawthorne.
heel effect efecto de talón.
hematologic effect efecto hematológico.
ionization effect efecto de ionización.
isomorphic effect efecto isomórfico.
Mierzejewski effect efecto de Mierzejewski.
Nagler effect efecto de Nagler.
Orbeli effect efecto de Orbeli.
oxygen effect efecto oxígeno.
pair formation effect efecto de formación de pares.
Pasteur effect efecto de Pasteur.
photechic effect efecto fotéquico, efecto fotéxico.
photographic effect efecto fotográfico.
piezoelectric effect efecto piezoeléctrico.
placebo effect efecto placebo.
position effect efecto de posición.
pressure effect efecto de presión.
psychological effect of abortion efecto psicológico del aborto.
Purkinje effect efecto de Purkinje.
radioactive effect efecto radiactivo.
Rivero-Carvallo effect efecto Rivero-Carvallo.
Russell effect efecto de Russell.
second gas effect efecto del segundo gas.
secundary effect efecto secundario.
side effect efecto colateral.
sigma effect efecto sigma.
Somogyi effect efecto de Somogyi.
Soret effect efecto de Soret.
specific dynamic effect efecto dinámico específico.
Staub-Traugott effect efecto de Staub-Traugott.

Stiles-Crawford effect efecto de Stiles-Crawford.
training effect efecto del entrenamiento.
Tyndall effect efecto de Tyndall.
Venturi effect efecto de Venturi.
Vulpian's effect efecto de Vulpian.
Wedensky effect efecto de Wedensky.
wind chill effect efecto enfriador del viento.
Wolff-Chaikoff effect efecto de Wolff-Chaikoff.
Zeeman effect efecto de Zeeman.
effectiveness *n.* efectividad, eficacia.
biologic effectiveness eficacia biológica.
contraceptive effectiveness eficacia anticonceptiva.
cost effectiveness eficacia de costes.
effectiveness of a program efectividad de un programa.
relative biological effectiveness eficacia biológica relativa.
theoretic effectiveness eficacia teórica.
use effectiveness eficacia de uso.
effector *n.* efector.
efferent *adj.* eferente.
effervescence *n.* efervescencia.
effervescent *adj.* efervescente.
efficiency *n.* eficiencia.
visual efficiency eficiencia visual.
efflorescence *n.* eflorescencia.
effluve *n.* efluvio.
anagen effluve efluvio anágeno.
telogen effluve efluvio telógeno.
effluvium *n.* efluvio.
effort *n.* esfuerzo².
distributed effort esfuerzo distribuido.
effraction *n.* efracción.
effumability *n.* efumabilidad.
effuse *adj.* esparcido, -da.
effusion *n.* derrame, efusión.
abdominal effusion derrame abdominal.
articular effusion derrame articular.
cerebral effusion derrame cerebral.
hemorrhagic effusion derrame hemorrágico.
joint effusion derrame articular, derrame sinovial.
pericardial effusion derrame pericárdico.
pericardium effusion derrame pericárdico.
peritoneum effusion derrame peritoneal.
pleural effusion derrame pleural, derrame pleurítico.
purulent effusion derrame purulento.
sanguineous effusion derrame sanguíneo.
serous effusion derrame seroso.
egagropilus *n.* egagrópilo.
egesta *n.* excremento.
egilops *n.* egílope, egilops.
eglandulous *adj.* eglanduloso, -sa.
ego *n.* ego, yo.
ego ideal yo ideal.
undifferentiated family ego mass yo familiar indiferenciado.
egobronchophony *n.* egobroncofonía.
egocentric *adj.* egocéntrico, -ca.
egocentricity *n.* egocentrismo.
egocentrism *n.* egocentrismo.
ego-dystonic *adj.* egodistónico, -ca.
egoism *n.* egoísmo.
egomania *n.* egomanía.
egophonic *adj.* egofónico, -ca.
egophony *n.* egofonía.
ego-syntonic *adj.* egosintónico, -ca.
egotism *n.* egoísmo.
Ehrlichia *n.* Ehrlichia.
Ehrlichieae *n.* Ehrlichieae.
ehrlichiosis *n.* ehrliquiosis.

eiconometer *n.* eiconómetro.
eidetic *adj.* eidético, -ca.
eidogen *n.* eidógeno.
eidopometry *n.* eidopometría, eidoptometría.
eidoptometry *n.* eidopometría, eidoptometría.
Eikenella *n.* Eikenella.
eikonometer *n.* eiconómetro.
eiloid *adj.* eiloide.
eisanthema *n.* eisantema.
eisodic *adj.* eisódico, -ca.
ejaculate *adj.* eyaculado, -da.
ejaculatio *n.* eyaculación.
ejaculatio deficiens eyaculación deficiente.
ejaculatio praecox eyaculación precoz.
ejaculatio retardata eyaculación retardada.
ejaculation *n.* eyaculación.
premature ejaculation eyaculación prematura.
retarded ejaculation eyaculación retardada.
retrograde ejaculation eyaculación retrógrada.
ejaculator *adj.* eyaculador, -ra.
ejaculatory *adj.* eyaculatorio, -ria.
ejecta *n.* eyecta.
ejection *n.* eyección.
milk ejection eyección de la leche.
ventricular ejection eyección ventricular.
ejector *n.* eyector.
saliva ejector eyector de saliva.
ektoplasmic *adj.* ectoplásmico, -ca.
ektoplastic *adj.* ectoplástico, -ca.
elaboration *n.* elaboración.
secondary elaboration elaboración secundaria.
elaiometer *n.* elaiómetro, eleómetro, oleómetro.
elaiopathy *n.* elaiopatía, eleopatía.
elaioplast *n.* elaioplasto, eleoplasto.
elastance *n.* elastancia.
cerebral elastance elastancia cerebral.
elastic *n.* elástico, -ca.
elasticin *n.* elasticina.
elasticity *n.* elasticidad.
physical elasticity of muscle elasticidad física del músculo.
physiologic elasticity of muscle elasticidad fisiológica del músculo.
total elasticity of muscle elasticidad total del músculo.
elastin *n.* elastina.
elastofibroma *n.* elastofibroma.
elastofibroma dorsi elastofibroma dorsal.
elastogenesis *n.* elastogénesis.
elastoidosis *n.* elastoidosis.
nodular elastoidosis elastoidosis nodular.
elastolysis *n.* elastólisis.
generalized elastolysis elastólisis generalizada.
elastolytic *adj.* elastolítico, -ca.
elastoma *n.* elastoma.
juvenile elastoma elastoma juvenil.
Miescher's elastoma elastoma de Miescher.
elastometer *n.* elastómetro.
elastometry *n.* elastometría.
elastopathy *n.* elastopatía.
elastorrhexis *n.* elastorrexis.
elastosis *n.* elastosis.
actinic elastosis elastosis actínica.
elastosis colloidalis conglomerata elastosis coloidal conglomerada.
elastosis dystrophica elastosis distrófica.
elastosis perforans serpiginosa elastosis reactiva perforante, elastosis serpiginosa perforante.

nodular elastosis of Favre and Racouchot elastosis nodular de Favre-Racouchot.
perforating elastosis elastosis reactiva perforante, elastosis serpiginosa perforante.
perifollicular elastosis elastosis perifolicular.
postinflammatory elastosis elastosis posinflamatoria.
senile elastosis elastosis senil.
solar elastosis elastosis solar.
elbow *n.* codo.
baseball pitcher's elbow codo de lanzador.
dropped elbow codo péndulo.
golfer's elbow codo de golfista.
Little Leaguer's elbow codo de Little Leaguer.
miner's elbow codo de los mineros.
nursemaid's elbow codo de las niñeras.
pulled elbow codo dislocado.
student elbow codo del estudiante.
tennis elbow codo de tenista.
elbowed *adj.* acodado, -da.
elctrogustometry *n.* electrogustometría.
elective *adj.* electivo, -va.
electricity *n.* electricidad.
electrization *n.* electrización.
electroacupucnture *n.* electroacupuntura.
electroanalgesia *n.* electroanalgesia.
electroanalysis *n.* electroánalisis.
electroanesthesia *n.* electroanestesia.
electroappendectomy *n.* electroapendicectomía.
electroaxonography *n.* electroaxonografía.
electrobasograph *n.* electrobasógrafo.
electrobasography *n.* electrobasografía.
electrobiology *n.* electrobiología.
electrobioscopy *n.* electrobioscopia.
electrocardiogram (ECG) *n.* electrocardiograma (ECG).
scalar electrocardiogram electrocardiograma escalar.
stress electrocardiogram electrocardiograma de esfuerzo.
unipolar electrocardiogram electrocardiograma unipolar.
electrocardiograph *n.* electrocardiógrafo.
electrocardiography *n.* electrocardiografía.
fetal electrocardiography electrocardiografía fetal.
intracardiac electrocardiography electrocardiografía intracardíaca.
precordial electrocardiography electrocardiografía precordial.
electrocardiophonogram *n.* electrocardiofonograma.
electrocardiophonograph *n.* electrocardiofonógrafo.
electrocardiophonography *n.* electrocardiofonografía.
electrocardioscopy *n.* electrocardioscopia.
electrocatalysis *n.* electrocatálisis.
electrocauterization *n.* electrocauterización.
electrocautery *n.* electrocauterio.
electrochemical *adj.* electroquímico, -ca.
electrochemistry *n.* electroquímica.
electrocholecystectomy *n.* electrocolecistectomía.
electrocholecystocausis *n.* electrocolecistocausis.
electrochromatography *n.* electrocromatografía.
electrocoagulation *n.* electrocoagulación.
electrocochleogram *n.* electrococleograma.
electrocochleographic *adj.* electrococleográfico, -ca.
electrocochleography *n.* electrococleografía.

electrocontractility *n.* electrocontractilidad.
electroconvulsive *adj.* electroconvulsivo, -va.
electrocorticogram *n.* electrocorticograma.
electrocorticography *n.* electrocorticografía.
electrocryptectomy *n.* electrocriptectomía.
electrocution *n.* electrocución.
electrocystography *n.* electrocistografía.
electrode *n.* electrodo.
electrodermal *adj.* electrodérmico, -ca.
electrodermatome *n.* electrodermátomo.
electrodesiccation *n.* electrodesecación.
electrodiagnosis *n.* electrodiagnóstico.
electrodialysis *n.* electrodiálisis.
electrodialyzer *n.* electrodializador.
electrodynamic *adj.* electrodinámico, -ca.
electrodynograph *n.* electrodinógrafo.
electroencephalogram *n.* electroencefalograma.
   flat isoelectric electroencephalogram electroencefalograma isoeléctrico plano.
electroencephalograph *n.* electroencefalógrafo.
   electroencephalograph technologist electroencefalografista.
electroencephalographer *n.* electroencefalografista.
electroencephalography *n.* electroencefalografía.
electroencephaloscope *n.* electroencefaloscopio.
electroendosmosis *n.* electroendósmosis.
electroespectrogram *n.* electroespectrograma.
electrogastrogram *n.* electrogastrograma.
electrogastrograph *n.* electrogastrógrafo.
electrogastrography *n.* electrogastrografía.
electrogram *n.* electrograma.
   His bundle electrogram electrograma del haz de His.
   His electrogram hisiograma.
electrography *n.* electrografía.
   His bundle electrography electrografía del haz de His.
electrohemodynamics *n.* electrohemodinámica.
electrohemostasis *n.* electrohemostasia, electrohemostasis.
electrohysterogram *n.* electrohisterograma.
electrohysterograph *n.* electrohisterógrafo.
electrohysterography *n.* electrohisterografía.
electroimmunodiffusion *n.* electroinmunodifusión.
electrokinetic *adj.* electrocinético, -ca.
electrolithotrity *n.* electrolitotricia.
electrolysis *n.* electrólisis.
electrolyte *n.* electrolito.
   amphoteric electrolyte electrolito anfótero.
   colloidal electrolyte electrolito coloidal.
electrolytic *adj.* electrolítico, -ca.
electrolyzer *n.* electrolizador.
electromagnet *n.* electroimán.
electromagnetic *adj.* electromagnético, -ca.
electromagnetism *n.* electromagnetismo.
electromanometer *n.* electromanómetro.
electromassage *n.* electromasaje.
electrometer *n.* electrómetro.
electrometrogram *n.* electrometrograma.
electrometrography *n.* electrometrografía.
electromicturation *n.* electromicción.
electromigratory *adj.* electromigratorio, -ria.
electromorph *adj.* electromorfo, -fa.
electromyogram *n.* electromiograma.
electromyograph *n.* electromiógrafo.
electromyographer *n.* electromiografista.
electromyography *n.* electromiografía.

kinesiologic electromyography electromiografía cinesiológica.
ureteral electromyography electromiografía ureteral.
electron *n.* electrón.
   Auger electron electrón de Auger.
   emission electron electrón de emisión.
   internal conversion electron electrón de conversión, electrón de conversión interna.
   positive electron electrón positivo.
   valence electron electrón de valencia.
electronarcosis *n.* electronarcosis.
electronegative *adj.* electronegativo, -va.
electronegativity *n.* electronegatividad.
electroneurography *n.* electroneurografía.
electroneurolysis *n.* electroneurólisis.
electroneuromyography *n.* electroneuromiografía.
electronic *adj.* electrónico, -ca.
electronics *n.* electrónica.
electronograph *n.* electronógrafo.
electronystagmogram *n.* electronistagmograma.
electronystagmograph *n.* electronistagmógrafo.
electronystagmography (ENG) *n.* electronistagmografía (ENG).
electro-oculogram *n.* electrooculograma.
electro-oculography *n.* electrooculografía.
electro-olfactogram *n.* electroolfatograma.
electro-osmosis *n.* electrosmosis.
electropacing *n.* electrosistolia.
electroparacentesis *n.* electroparacentesis.
electropathology *n.* electropatología.
electropherogram *n.* electroferograma, electroforegrama.
electrophil *adj.* electrófilo, -la.
electrophile *adj.* electrófilo, -la.
electrophilic *adj.* electrofílico, -ca.
electrophoregram *n.* electroferograma, electroforegrama.
electrophoresis *n.* electroforesis.
   capillary electrophoresis electroforesis capilar.
   disc electrophoresis electroforesis de disco.
   gel electrophoresis electroforesis en gel.
   hemoglobin electrophoresis electroforesis de hemoglobina.
   isoenzyme electrophoresis electroforesis de isoenzimas.
   lipoprotein electrophoresis electroforesis de lipoproteínas.
   moving boundary electrophoresis electroforesis de fronteras móviles.
   paper electrophoresis electroforesis en papel.
   protein electrophoresis electroforesis de proteína.
   pulsed field gradient electrophoresis electroforesis de gradiente en un campo de pulsos.
   thin-layer electrophoresis (TLE) electroforesis en capas delgadas.
   zone electrophoresis electroforesis de zona.
electrophoretic *adj.* electroforético, -ca.
electrophoretogram *n.* electroforetograma.
electrophorus *n.* electróforo.
electrophotometer *n.* electrofotómetro.
electrophototherapy *n.* electrofototerapia.
electrophrenic *adj.* electrofrénico, -ca.
electrophysiologic *adj.* electrofisiológico, -ca.
electrophysiological *adj.* electrofisiológico, -ca.
electrophysiology *n.* electrofisiología.
electropneumograph *n.* electroneumógrafo.
electroporation *n.* electroporación.

electropositive *adj.* electropositivo, -va.
electropuncture *n.* electropuntura, galvanopuntura.
electroradiology *n.* electrorradiología.
electroradiometer *n.* electrorradiómetro.
electroradioscopy *n.* electrorradioscopia.
electroresection *n.* electrorresección.
electroretinogram *n.* electrorretinograma.
electroretinograph *n.* electrorretinógrafo.
electroretinography *n.* electrorretinografía.
electrosalivograma *n.* electrosialograma.
electroscission *n.* electroescisión.
electroscope *n.* electroscopio.
electrosection *n.* electrosección.
electroshock *n.* electrochoque, electroshock.
electrosleep *n.* electrosueño.
electrospectrography *n.* electroespectrografía.
electrospinogram *n.* electroespinograma, electrospinograma.
electrospinography *n.* electroespinografía.
electrostatic *adj.* electrostático, -ca.
electrostenolysis *n.* electroestenólisis, electrostenólisis.
electrostethograph *n.* electroestetógrafo.
electrostimulation *n.* electroestimulación.
electrostriatogram *n.* electrostriatograma.
electrostriction *n.* electrostricción.
electrosurgery *n.* electrocirugía.
electrosynthesis *n.* electrosíntesis.
electrotaxis *n.* electrotaxis.
   negative electrotaxis electrotaxis negativa.
   positive electrotaxis electrotaxis positiva.
electrothanasia *n.* electrotanasia.
electrotherapeutics *n.* electroterapia.
   cerebral electrotherapeutics electroterapia cerebral.
electrotherapy *n.* electroterapia.
electrotherm *n.* electrotermo.
electrotome *n.* electrótomo.
electrotomy *n.* electrotomía.
electrotonic *adj.* electrotónico, -ca.
electrotonus *n.* electrotono.
electrotrephine *n.* electrotrépano.
electrotropism *n.* electrotropismo.
   negative electrotropism electrotropismo negativo.
   positive electrotropism electrotropismo positivo.
electroultrafiltration *n.* electroultrafiltración.
electroureterogram *n.* electroureterograma.
electroureterography *n.* electroureterografía.
electrovagogram *n.* electrovagograma.
electrovalence *n.* electrovalencia.
electrovalent *adj.* electrovalente.
electroversion *n.* electroversión.
eleidin *n.* eleidina.
element *n.* elemento.
   trace element oligoelemento.
elementary *adj.* elemental.
elementum *n.* elemento.
eleometer *n.* eleómetro, oleómetro.
eleopathy *n.* eleopatía.
eleoplast *n.* eleoplasto.
eleotherapy *n.* eleoterapia, oleoterapia.
elephantiasic *adj.* elefantiásico, -ca.
elephantiasis *n.* elefantiasis.
   congenital elephantiasis elefantiasis congénita.
   elephantiasis chirurgica elefantiasis quirúrgica.
   elephantiasis congenita angiomatosa elefantiasis angiomatosa congénita.

elephantiasis filariensis elefantiasis filariásica.
elephantiasis gingivae elefantiasis gingival.
elephantiasis graecorum elefantiasis de los griegos, elefantiasis griega.
elephantiasis neuromatosa elefantiasis neuromatosa, elefantiasis tubárica.
elephantiasis nostras elefantiasis nostras.
elephantiasis oculi elefantiasis ocular.
elephantiasis scroti elefantiasis del escroto, elefantiasis escrotal.
elephantiasis vulvae elefantiasis vulvar.
gingival elephantiasis elefantiasis gingival.
lymphangiectatic elephantiasis elefantiasis linfangiectásica, elefantiasis linfangiectodes.
nevoid elephantiasis elefantiasis nevoide.
telangiectodes elephantiasis elefantiasis telangiectoide.
elephantoid *adj.* elefantoide, elefantoideo, -a.
elevator *n.* elevador.
angular elevator elevador angular.
apical elevator elevador apical.
cross bar elevator elevador de barra cruzada.
Cryer elevator elevador de Cryer.
elevator periosteum elevador perióstico.
periosteal elevator elevador perióstico.
root elevator elevador de raíz.
screw elevator elevador a tornillo.
straight elevator elevador recto.
T-bar elevator elevador de barra en T.
wedge elevator elevador dental, elevador en cuña.
eliminant *adj.* eliminador, -ra, eliminante.
elimination *n.* eliminación.
carbon dioxide elimination eliminación de dióxido de carbono.
immune elimination eliminación inmunitaria.
elinguation *n.* elinguación.
elinin *n.* elinina.
ELISA *n.* ELISA.
elixir *n.* elixir.
ellipsis *n.* elipse, clipsis.
ellipsoid *adj.* elipsoide.
ellipsoidal *adj.* elipsoide.
elliptocytary *adj.* eliptocitario, -ria.
elliptocyte *n.* eliptocito.
elliptocytosis *n.* eliptocitosis.
elliptocytotic *adj.* eliptocitótico, -ca.
elongation *n.* elongación.
elute *v.* eluir.
elution *n.* elución.
elutriate *v.* elutriar.
elutriation *n.* elutriación.
centrifugal elutriation elutriación por centrifugación.
elypocytic *adj.* elipocítico, -ca.
emaciation *n.* demacración, emaciación.
emaculation *n.* emaculación.
emanation *n.* emanación.
emanator *n.* emanador.
emanatorium *n.* emanatorio.
emancipation *n.* emancipación.
emanotherapy *n.* emanoterapia.
emarginate *adj.* emarginado, -da.
emargination *n.* emarginación.
emasculation *n.* emasculación.
Embadomonas *n.* Embadomonas.
embalm *v.* embalsamar.
embalming *n.* embalsamamiento.
emboitement *n.* encaje.
headgear emboitement encaje cefálico.
embole *n.* embolia[1].
embolectomy *n.* embolectomía.
embolemia *n.* embolemia.
embolic *adj.* embólico, -ca.

emboliform *adj.* emboliforme.
embolism *n.* embolia[2].
air embolism embolia aérea.
amniotic fluid embolism embolia amniótica.
arterial embolism embolia arterial.
atheroma embolism embolia por ateroma.
bacillary embolism embolia bacilar.
bone marrow embolism embolia de médula ósea.
capillary embolism embolia capilar.
cellular embolism embolia celular.
cerebral embolism embolia cerebral.
cholesterol embolism embolia por colesterol.
coronary embolism embolia coronaria.
cotton-fiber embolism embolia por fibras de algodón.
crossed embolism embolia cruzada.
direct embolism embolia directa.
embolism cutis medicamentosa embolia cutis medicamentosa.
fat embolism embolia adiposa, embolia grasa.
gas embolism embolia gaseosa.
hematogenous embolism embolia hematógena.
infective embolism embolia infecciosa.
lymph embolism embolia linfática, embolia linfógena.
lymphogenous embolism embolia linfática, embolia linfógena.
miliary embolism embolia miliar, embolia múltiple.
multiple embolism embolia miliar, embolia múltiple.
obturating embolism embolia obturante.
oil embolism embolia oleosa.
pantaloon embolism embolia en pantalón.
paradoxical embolism embolia paradójica.
plasmodium embolism embolia por plasmodios.
pulmonary embolism embolia pulmonar.
pyemic embolism embolia piémica.
retinal embolism embolia de la retina.
retrograde embolism embolia retrógrada.
riding embolism embolia cabalgante.
saddle embolism embolia en silla de montar.
septic embolism embolia séptica.
septical embolism embolia séptica.
spinal embolism embolia espinal.
straddling embolism embolia a horcajadas.
trichinous embolism embolia triquinosa.
tumor embolism embolia tumoral.
venous embolism embolia venosa.
embolization *n.* embolización.
percutaneous embolization embolización percutánea.
embolomycotic *adj.* embolomicótico, -ca.
embolotherapy *n.* emboloterapia.
embolus *n.* émbolo.
air embolus émbolo gaseoso.
cancer embolus émbolo canceroso.
catheter embolus émbolo de catéter.
cell embolus émbolo celular.
fat embolus émbolo adiposo.
foam embolus émbolo espumoso.
obturating embolus émbolo obturador.
riding embolus émbolo cabalgante.
saddle embolus émbolo en silla de montar.
emboly *n.* embolia[1].
embouchement *n.* desembocadura[2].
embriopathy *n.* embriopatía.
embryo *n.* embrión.
heterogametic embryo embrión heterogamético.
homogametic embryo embrión homogamético.

Janösik's embryo embrión de Janösik.
presomite embryo embrión presomita.
previllous embryo embrión prevelloso.
somite embryo embrión somita.
Spee's embryo embrión de Spee.
embryoblast *n.* embrioblasto.
embryocardia *n.* embriocardia.
jugular embryocardia embriocardia yugular.
embryocardial *adj.* embriocárdico, -ca.
embryogenesis *n.* embriogénesis.
embryogenetic *adj.* embriogenético, -ca.
embryogenic *adj.* embriogénico, -ca.
embryogeny *n.* embriogenia.
embryoid *adj.* embrioide.
embryoism *n.* embrionismo.
embryologist *n.* embriólogo, -ga.
embryology *n.* embriología.
causal embryology embriología causal.
comparative embryology embriología comparada.
descriptive embryology embriología descriptiva.
experimental embryology embriología experimental.
embryoma *n.* embrioma.
embryoma of the kidney embrioma del riñón.
embryomorphous *adj.* embriomorfo, -fa.
embryonal *adj.* embrionario, -ria.
embryonate *adj.* embrionado, -da.
embryonic *adj.* embrionario, -ria.
embryoniform *adj.* embrioniforme.
embryonism *n.* embrionismo.
embryonization *n.* embrionización.
embryonoid *adj.* embrionoide.
embryony *n.* embrionia.
embryopathia *n.* embriopatía.
rubella embryopathia embriopatía rubeolar, embriopatía rubeólica.
embryopathology *n.* embriopatología.
embryoplastic *adj.* embrioplásico, -ca.
embryotome *n.* embriótomo.
embryotomy *n.* embriotomía.
embryotoxic *adj.* embriotóxico, -ca.
embryotoxicity *n.* embriotoxicidad.
embryotoxon *n.* embriotoxon.
posterior embryotoxon embriotoxon posterior.
embryotroph *n.* embriotrofo.
embryotrophic *adj.* embriotrófico, -ca.
embryotrophy *n.* embriotrofia.
emedullate *v.* desmedular[1], emedular.
emeiocytosis *n.* emeiocitosis.
emergence *n.* despertar[2].
emergency *n.* emergencia, urgencia[1].
emergent *adj.* emergente.
emesia *n.* emesia, emesis.
gastric emesia emesia gástrica.
nervous emesia emesia nerviosa.
emesis *n.* emesia, emesis.
emesis gravidarum emesia gravidarum, emesia gravídica.
emetatrophia *n.* emetatrofia.
emetic *adj.* emético, -ca, emetizante.
central emetic emético central.
direct emetic emético directo.
indirect emetic emético indirecto.
mechanical emetic emético mecánico.
systemic emetic emético sistémico.
emeticology *n.* emeticología.
emetocathartic *adj.* emetocatártico, -ca.
emetology *n.* emetología.
emetophobia *n.* emetofobia.
emigration *n.* emigración.
eminence *n.* eminencia, eminentia.

eminentia *n.* eminencia, eminentia.
emiocytosis *n.* emiocitosis.
emissarium *n.* emisaria, emissarium.
emissary *adj.* emisario, -ria.
emmenagogic *adj.* emenagógico, -ca.
emmenagogue *n.* emenagogo.
  direct emmenagogue emenagogo directo.
  indirect emmenagogue emenagogo indirecto.
emmenia *n.* emenia.
emmenic *adj.* eménico, -ca.
emmeniopathy *n.* emeniopatía, emenopatía.
emmenology *n.* emenología.
emmetrope *adj.* emétrope.
emmetropia *n.* emetropía.
emmetropic *adj.* emetrópico, -ca.
emmetropization *n.* emetropización.
emollient *adj.* emoliente.
emotional *adj.* emocional.
emotivity *n.* emotividad.
empacho *n.* empacho.
empathic *adj.* empático, -ca.
empathize *v.* empatizar.
empathy *n.* empatía.
  generative empathy empatía generativa.
emperipolesis *n.* emperiopolesis, emperipolesis.
emphlysis *n.* enflisis.
emphractic *adj.* enfráctico, -ca.
emphraxis *n.* enfraxis.
emphysema *n.* enfisema.
  alveolar emphysema enfisema alveolar.
  atrophic emphysema enfisema atrófico.
  centriacinar emphysema enfisema centriacinar, enfisema centriacinoso.
  centrilobular emphysema enfisema centrilobulillar.
  compensating emphysema enfisema compensador, enfisema compensatorio, enfisema suplementario, enfisema vicariante.
  compensatory emphysema enfisema compensador, enfisema compensatorio, enfisema suplementario, enfisema vicariante.
  cutaneous emphysema enfisema cutáneo.
  diffuse emphysema enfisema difuso.
  ectatic emphysema enfisema ectásico.
  false emphysema enfisema falso.
  familial emphysema enfisema familiar.
  gangrenous emphysema enfisema gangrenoso.
  generalized emphysema enfisema generalizado.
  interlobular emphysema enfisema interlobulillar.
  interstitial emphysema enfisema intersticial.
  mediastinal emphysema enfisema mediastínico.
  panacinar emphysema enfisema panacinar, enfisema panacinoso.
  panlobular emphysema enfisema panlobulillar.
  paraseptal emphysema enfisema paraseptal.
  pulmonary emphysema enfisema pulmonar.
  senile emphysema enfisema senil.
  subcutaneous emphysema enfisema subcutáneo.
  subgaleal emphysema enfisema subgaleal.
  surgical emphysema enfisema quirúrgico.
  traumatic emphysema enfisema traumático.
  vesicular emphysema enfisema vesicular.
emphysematous *adj.* enfisematoso, -sa.
empiric *adj.* empírico, -ca.
empirical *adj.* empírico, -ca.
emprosthotonos *n.* emprostótonos.
emprosthotonus *n.* emprostótonos.

emptysis *n.* emptisis.
empyema *n.* empiema.
  empyema benignum empiema benigno.
  empyema necessitatis empiema de necesidad, empiema necessitatis.
  empyema of the chest empiema torácico.
  empyema of the gallblader empiema vesicular.
  empyema of the pericardium empiema del pericardio, empiema pericárdico.
  epidural empyema empiema epidural.
  gallbladder empyema empiema vesicular.
  interlobar empyema empiema interlobular.
  latent empyema empiema latente.
  loculated empyema empiema loculado.
  mastoid empyema empiema mastoideo.
  metapneumonic empyema empiema metapneumónico.
  pneumococcal empyema empiema neumocócico.
  pulsating empyema empiema pulsátil.
  putrid empyema empiema pútrido.
  streptococcal empyema empiema estreptocócico.
  subdural empyema empiema subdural.
  sypneumonic empyema empiema sinneumónico.
  thoracic empyema empiema torácico.
  tuberculous empyema empiema tuberculoso.
empyesis *n.* empiesis.
empyemic *adj.* empiémico, -ca.
empyocele *n.* empiocele.
empyreuma *n.* empireuma.
empyreumatic *adj.* empireumático, -ca.
emulgent *n.* emulgente.
emulsifier *n.* emulsionante.
emulsify *v.* emulsionar.
emulsion *n.* emulsión.
emulsive *adj.* emulsivo, -va.
emulsoid *n.* emulsoide.
emunctory *adj.* emuntorio, -ria.
enamel *n.* esmalte.
  curled enamel esmalte rizado.
  dental enamel esmalte dental.
  dwarfed enamel esmalte enano, esmalte enanoide.
  gnarled enamel esmalte nudoso.
  hereditary brown enamel esmalte marrón hereditario, esmalte pardo hereditario.
  hypoplastic enamel esmalte hipoplásico.
  mottled enamel esmalte moteado.
  nanoid enamel esmalte enano, esmalte enanoide, esmalte nanoide.
  straight enamel esmalte recto.
  whorled enamel esmalte con remolinos.
enameloblast *n.* esmaltoblasto.
enameloblastoma *n.* esmaltoblastoma.
enamelogenesis *n.* enamelogénesis.
  enamelogenesis imperfecta enamelogénesis imperfecta.
enameloma *n.* enameloma, esmaltoma.
enanthem *n.* enantema.
enanthema *n.* enantema.
enanthematous *adj.* enantematoso, -sa.
enanthesis *n.* enantesis.
enanthrope *adj.* enantrópico, -ca.
enantiobiosis *n.* enantiobiosis.
enarthritis *n.* enartritis.
enarthrodial *adj.* enartrodial.
enarthrosis *n.* enartrodia, enartrosis.
encapsulated *adj.* encapsulado, -da.
encapsulation *n.* encapsulación.
encapsuled *adj.* encapsulado, -da.
encarditis *n.* encarditis.

encatarrhaphy *n.* encatarrafia.
encelialgia *n.* encelialgia.
enceliitis *n.* encelitis.
encelitis *n.* encelitis.
encepahlauxe *n.* encefalauxa, encefalauxia.
encephalalgia *n.* encefalalgia.
encephalatrophic *adj.* encefalatrófico, -ca.
encephalatrophy *n.* encefalatrofia.
encephalemia *n.* encefalemia.
encephalic *adj.* encefálico, -ca.
encephalitic *adj.* encefalítico, -ca.
encephalitis *n.* encefalitis.
  acute diseminated encephalitis encefalitis aguda diseminada.
  acute hemorrhagic encephalitis encefalitis hemorrágica, encefalitis hemorrágica aguda.
  acute necrotizing encephalitis encefalitis aguda necrosante, encefalitis necrosante aguda.
  Australian X encephalitis encefalitis australiana X.
  B encephalitis encefalitis B.
  benign myalgic encephalitis encefalitis miálgica benigna.
  Binswanger's encephalitis encefalitis de Binswanger.
  Bunyavirus encephalitis encefalitis por Bunyavirus.
  California encephalitis encefalitis de California.
  Central European encephalitis encefalitis de Europa Central.
  chikungunya encephalitis encefalitis chikungunya.
  cortical encephalitis encefalitis cortical.
  Coxsackie encephalitis encefalitis por Coxsackie.
  Dawson's encephalitis encefalitis de Dawson.
  encephalitis C encefalitis C.
  encephalitis corticalis encefalitis cortical.
  encephalitis epidemica encefalitis epidémica.
  encephalitis hemorrhagica superior encefalitis hemorrágica superior.
  encephalitis hyperplastica encefalitis hiperplásica.
  encephalitis japonica encefalitis japonesa, encefalitis japonica.
  encephalitis neonatorum encefalitis neonatal.
  encephalitis periaxialis encefalitis periaxial, encefalitis periaxil concéntrica.
  encephalitis periaxialis concentrica encefalitis periaxial, encefalitis periaxil concéntrica.
  encephalitis periaxialis diffusa encefalitis periaxial difusa.
  epidemic encephalitis encefalitis epidémica.
  experimental allergic encephalitis encefalitis alérgica experimental.
  forest-spring encephalitis encefalitis primaveral de los bosques.
  hemorrhagic arsphenamine encephalitis encefalitis hemorrágica por arsfenamina.
  hemorrhagic encephalitis encefalitis hemorrágica, encefalitis hemorrágica aguda.
  herpes simplex encephalitis encefalitis herpética.
  herpetic encephalitis encefalitis herpética.
  hyperergic encephalitis encefalitis hiperérgica.
  Ilheus encephalitis encefalitis de Ilheus, encefalitis Ilhéus.
  inclusion body encephalitis encefalitis por cuerpos de inclusión.

influenzal encephalitis encefalitis por influenza.

Japanese B encephalitis encefalitis japonesa B.

Japanese encephalitis encefalitis japonesa, encefalitis japonica.

lead encephalitis encefalitis por plomo.

lethargic encephalitis encefalitis letárgica.

Mengo encephalitis encefalitis Mengo.

Murray-Valley encephalitis encefalitis de Murray-Valley.

necrotizing encephalitis encefalitis necrosante.

postinfectious encephalitis encefalitis posinfecciosa.

postvaccinal encephalitis encefalitis posvacunal.

Powassan encephalitis encefaliris de Powassan.

purulent encephalitis encefalitis purulenta.

pyogenic encephalitis encefalitis piógena, encefalitis piogénica.

Russian autumn encephalitis encefalitis rusa otoñal.

Russian endemic encephalitis encefalitis rusa endémica.

Russian forest-spring encephalitis encefalitis rusa de primavera y verano, encefalitis rusa primaveral de los bosques.

Russian spring-summer encephalitis encefalitis rusa de primavera y verano, encefalitis rusa primaveral de los bosques.

Russian spring-summer encephalitis (Eastern subtype) encefalitis rusa vernoestival (subtipo oriental).

Russian tick-borne encephalitis encefalitis rusa transmitida por garrapatas.

secondary encephalitis encefalitis secundaria.

Semliki forest encephalitis encefalitis del bosque Semliki.

St Louis encephalitis encefalitis de San Luis.

subacute inclusion body encephalitis encefalitis subaguda por cuerpos de inclusión.

summer encephalitis encefalitis estival.

suppurative encephalitis encefalitis supurada, encefalitis supurativa.

tick-borne encephalitis (Eastern subtype) encefalitis transmitida por garrapatas (subtipo oriental).

toxoplasmic encephalitis encefalitis toxoplásmica.

vaccinal encephalitis encefalitis vacunal.

van Bogaert's encephalitis encefalitis de van Bogaert.

varicella encephalitis encefalitis de la varicela.

vernal encephalitis encefalitis vernal.

vernoestival encephalitis encefalitis vernoestival.

Vienna encephalitis encefalitis de Viena.

von Economo's encephalitis encefalitis de von Economo.

woodcutter's encephalitis encefalitis del leñador.

encephalitogen *n.* encefalitógeno.

encephalitogenic *adj.* encefalitogénico, -ca.

encephalization *n.* encefalización.

encephalo-arteriography *n.* encefaloarteriografía.

encephalocele *n.* encefalocele.

encephaloclastic *adj.* encefaloclástico, -ca.

encephalocystocele *n.* encefalocistocele.

encephalodyalisis *n.* encefalodiálisis.

encephalodynia *n.* encefalodinia.

encephalodysplasia *n.* encefalodisplasia.

encephalogram *n.* encefalograma.

encephalography *n.* encefalografía.

gamma encephalography encefalografía gamma.

encephaloid *adj.* encefaloide.

encephalolith *n.* encefalolito.

encephalology *n.* encefalología.

encephaloma *n.* encefaloma.

encephalomalacia *n.* encefalomalacia.

encephalomeningitis *n.* encefalomeningitis.

encephalomeningocele *n.* encefalomeningocele.

encephalomeningopathy *n.* encefalomeningopatía.

encephalomere *n.* encefalómero.

encephalometer *n.* encefalómetro.

encephalometric *adj.* encefalométrico, -ca.

encephalomyelitis *n.* encefalomielitis.

acute disseminated encephalomyelitis encefalomielitis aguda diseminada, encefalomielitis diseminada aguda.

Eastern equine encephalomyelitis encefalomielitis equina del Este.

equine encephalomyelitis encefalomielitis equina.

experimental allergic encephalomyelitis encefalomielitis alérgica experimental.

granulomatous encephalomyelitis encefalomielitis granulomatosa.

postinfectious encephalomyelitis encefalomielitis posinfecciosa.

postvaccinal encephalomyelitis encefalomielitis posvacunal.

toxoplasmic encephalomyelitis encefalomielitis toxoplásmica.

Venezuelan equine encephalomyelitis encefalomielitis equina venezolana.

viral encephalomyelitis encefalomielitis por virus, encefalomielitis viral, encefalomielitis virósica.

virus encephalomyelitis encefalomielitis por virus, encefalomielitis viral, encefalomielitis virósica.

Western equine encephalomyelitis encefalomielitis equina del Oeste.

zoster encephalomyelitis encefalomielitis zoster.

encephalomyelocele *n.* encefalomielocele.

encephalomyeloneuropathy *n.* encefalomieloneuropatía.

non-specific encephalomyeloneuropathy encefalomieloneuropatía inespecífica.

encephalomyelopathy *n.* encefalomielopatía.

carcinomatous encephalomyelopathy encefalomielopatía carcinomatosa.

epidemic myalgic encephalomyelopathy encefalomielopatía miálgica epidémica.

mitochondrial encephalomyelopathy encefalomielopatía mitocondrial.

paracarcinomatous encephalomyelopathy encefalomielopatía paracarcinomatosa.

postinfection encephalomyelopathy encefalomielopatía posinfecciosa.

postvaccinial encephalomyelopathy encefalomielopatía posvacunal.

subacute necrotizing encephalomyelopathy encefalomielopatía necrosante, encefalomielopatía necrosante subaguda.

encephalomyeloradiculitis *n.* encefalomielorradiculitis.

encephalomyeloradiculoneuritis *n.* encefalomielorradiculoneuritis.

encephalomyeloradiculopathy *n.* encefalomielorradiculopatía.

encephalomyocarditis *n.* encefalomiocarditis.

encephalon *n.* encéfalo.

encephalopathia *n.* encefalopatía.

encephalopathic *adj.* encefalopático, -ca.

encephalopathy *n.* encefalopatía.

acute necrotizing hemorrhagic encephalopathy encefalopatía necrosante hemorrágica aguda.

Addisonian encephalopathy encefalopatía de Addison.

biliary encephalopathy encefalopatía biliar.

bilirubin encephalopathy encefalopatía bilirrubínica, encefalopatía por bilirrubina.

Binswanger's encephalopathy encefalopatía de Binswanger.

bovine spongiform encephalopathy encefalopatía espongiforme bovina.

demyelinating encephalopathy encefalopatía desmielinizante.

dialysis encephalopathy encefalopatía de diálisis, encefalopatía por diálisis.

familial encephalopathy encefalopatía familiar.

hepatic encephalopathy encefalopatía hepática.

hypernatremic encephalopathy encefalopatía hipernatrémica.

hypertensive encephalopathy encefalopatía hipertensiva.

hypoglycemic encephalopathy encefalopatía hipoglucémica.

lead encephalopathy encefalopatía por plomo.

metabolic encephalopathy encefalopatía metabólica.

myoclonic encephalopathy of childhood encefalopatía mioclónica infantil.

palindromic encephalopathy encefalopatía palindrómica.

pancreatic encephalopathy encefalopatía pancreática.

portal-systemic encephalopathy encefalopatía portal sistemática, encefalopatía portosistemática.

postanoxic encephalopathy encefalopatía posanóxica.

progressive subcortical encephalopathy encefalopatía subcortical progresiva.

punch-drunk encephalopathy encefalopatía de los boxeadores.

recurrent encephalopathy encefalopatía recurrente.

saturnine encephalopathy encefalopatía saturnina.

spongiform encephalopathy encefalopatía espongiforme.

subacute necrotizing encephalopathy encefalopatía necrosante subaguda.

subacute spongiform encephalopathy encefalopatía espongiforme subaguda.

subcortical arteriosclerotic encephalopathy encefalopatía arteriosclerótica subcortical.

thyrotoxic encephalopathy encefalopatía tirotóxica.

transmissible encephalopathy of mink encefalopatía transmisible del visón.

transmissible spongiform encephalopathy encefalopatía espongiforme transmisible.

transmissible spongiform virus encephalopathy encefalopatía transmisible por virus espongiforme.

traumatic progressive encephalopathy encefalopatía traumática progresiva.

uremic encephalopathy encefalopatía urémica.

encephalophyma *n.* encefalofima.
encephalopsy *n.* encefalopsia.
encephalopuncture *n.* encefalopuntura.
encephalopyosis *n.* encefalopiosis.
encephalorachidian *adj.* encefalorraquídeo, -a.
encephaloradiculitis *n.* encefalorradiculitis.
encephalorrhagia *n.* encefalorragia.
encephaloschisis *n.* encefalosquisis.
encephalosclerosis *n.* encefaloesclerosis, encefalosclerosis.
encephaloscope *n.* encefaloscopio.
encephaloscopy *n.* encefaloscopia.
encephalosepsis *n.* encefalosepsis.
encephalosis *n.* encefalosis.
encephalospinal *adj.* encefaloespinal, encefalospinal.
encephalothlipsis *n.* encefalotlipsis.
encephalotome *n.* encefalótomo.
encephalotomy *n.* encefalotomía.
encheiresis *n.* enquiresis.
enchima *n.* enquima.
enchondral *adj.* encondral.
enchondroma *n.* encondroma.
 multiple congenital enchondroma encondroma congénito múltiple.
enchondromatosis *n.* encondromatosis.
 multiple enchondromatosis encondromatosis múltiple.
 skeletal enchondromatosis encondromatosis esquelética.
enchondromatous *adj.* encondromatoso, -sa.
enchondrosarcoma *n.* encondrosarcoma.
enchondrosis *n.* encondrosis.
enclave *n.* enclave.
encoding *n.* codificación.
encolpitis *n.* encolpitis.
encopresis *n.* encopresis.
 non-organic encopresis encopresis no orgánica.
encranial *adj.* encraneal.
encranius *n.* encráneo.
encyesis *n.* enciesis.
encyopyelitis *n.* enciopielitis.
encysted *adj.* enquistado, -da.
encystment *n.* enquistamiento.
end *n.* extremo.
 cohesive end extremo cohesivo.
 sticky end extremo cohesivo.
endadelphos *n.* endadelfo.
Endamoeba *n.* Endamoeba.
endamoebiasis *n.* endamebiasis, endamoebiasis.
endangeitis *n.* endangeítis, endangiítis, endangitis.
 endangeitis obliterans endangeítis obliterante.
endangiitis *n.* endangeítis, endangiítis, endangitis.
endangitis *n.* endangeítis, endangiítis, endangitis.
endangium *n.* endangio.
endaortic *adj.* endoaórtico, -a.
endaortitis *n.* endoaortitis.
 bacterial endaortitis endoaortitis bacteriana.
endarterectomy *n.* endoarteriectomía.
 carotid endarterectomy endoarteriectomía carotídea.
 coronary endarterectomy endoarteriectomía coronaria.
 gas endarterectomy endoarteriectomía por gas.
endarterial *adj.* endoarterial.
endarteritis *n.* endoarteritis.
 bacterial endarteritis endoarteritis bacteriana.

endarteritis deformans endoarteritis deformante.
endarteritis obliterans endoarteritis obliterante.
endarteritis proliferans endoarteritis proliferante.
Heubner's specific endarteritis endoarteritis específica de Heubner.
endarterium *n.* endoarteria.
endarteropathy *n.* endoarteriopatía.
 digital endarteropathy endoarteriopatía digital.
endeictic *adj.* endeíctico, -ca.
endemia *n.* endemia.
endemic *adj.* endémico, -ca.
endemoepidemic *adj.* endemoepidémico, -ca.
endemy *n.* endemia.
endermatic *adj.* endermático, -ca.
endermic *adj.* endérmico, -ca.
endermism *n.* endermismo.
endermosis *n.* endermosis.
enderon *n.* enderón.
enderonic *adj.* enderónico, -ca.
ending *n.* terminación.
 nerve ending terminación nerviosa.
endoabdominal *adj.* endoabdominal.
endoaneurysmoplasty *n.* endoaneurismoplastia.
endoangiitis *n.* endangeítis, endangiítis, endangitis.
endoangitis *n.* endangeítis, endangiítis, endangitis.
endoantitoxin *n.* endoantitoxina.
endoaortic *adj.* endoaórtico, -ca.
endoaortitis *n.* endoaortitis.
endoappendicitis *n.* endoapendicitis.
endoarteritis *n.* endoarteritis.
endoauscultation *n.* endoauscultación.
endobacillary *adj.* endobacilar.
endobasion *n.* endobasión.
endobiotic *adj.* endobiótico, -ca.
endoblast *n.* endoblasto, entoblasto.
endoblastic *adj.* endoblástico, -ca.
endobronchial *adj.* endobronquial.
endobronchitis *n.* endobronquitis.
endocardiac *adj.* endocardíaco, -ca.
endocardial *adj.* endocárdico, -ca.
endocardiography *n.* endocardiografía.
endocarditic *adj.* endocardítico, -ca.
endocarditis *n.* endocarditis.
 abacterial thrombotic endocarditis endocarditis abacteriana trombótica.
 acute bacterial endocarditis endocarditis bacteriana aguda.
 atypical verrucous endocarditis endocarditis verrugosa atípica, endocarditis verrugosa no bacteriana.
 bacterial endocarditis endocarditis bacteriana.
 cachectic endocarditis endocarditis caquéctica.
 chronic endocarditis endocarditis crónica.
 constrictive endocarditis endocarditis constrictiva.
 endocarditis chordalis endocarditis cordal.
 endocarditis lenta endocarditis lenta.
 fungal endocarditis endocarditis por hongos.
 infectious endocarditis endocarditis infecciosa.
 infective endocarditis endocarditis infecciosa.
 isolated parietal endocarditis endocarditis parietal aislada.
 Libman-Sacks endocarditis endocarditis de Libman-Sacks.

 Löffler's endocarditis endocarditis de Löffler.
 Löffler's parietal fibroplastic endocarditis endocarditis fibroplásica parietal de Löffler.
 lupus endocarditis endocarditis lúpica.
 malignant endocarditis endocarditis maligna.
 marantic endocarditis endocarditis marántica.
 mural endocarditis endocarditis mural.
 mycotic endocarditis endocarditis micótica.
 non-bacterial thrombotic endocarditis endocarditis trombótica no bacteriana.
 non-bacterial verrucous endocarditis endocarditis verrugosa atípica, endocarditis verrugosa no bacteriana.
 Osler's endocarditis endocarditis de Osler.
 parietal endocarditis endocarditis parietal.
 polypous endocarditis endocarditis poliposa.
 prosthetic valve endocarditis endocarditis por válvula de prótesis.
 pulmonic endocarditis endocarditis pulmonar.
 pustulous endocarditis endocarditis pustulosa.
 rheumatic endocarditis endocarditis reumática.
 rickettsial endocarditis endocarditis rickettsiana.
 right-sided endocarditis endocarditis derecha.
 septic endocarditis endocarditis séptica.
 subacute bacterial endocarditis endocarditis bacteriana subaguda.
 syphilitic endocarditis endocarditis sifilítica.
 terminal endocarditis endocarditis terminal.
 tuberculous endocarditis endocarditis tuberculosa.
 ulcerative endocarditis endocarditis ulcerada, endocarditis ulcerativa.
 valvular endocarditis endocarditis valvular.
 vegetative endocarditis endocarditis vegetante, endocarditis vegetativa.
 verrucous endocarditis endocarditis verrucosa, endocarditis verrugosa.
endocardium *n.* endocardio.
endoceliac *adj.* endocelíaco, -ca.
endocellular *adj.* endocelular.
endocervical *adj.* endocervical.
endocervicitis *n.* endocervicitis.
endocervix *n.* endocérvix.
endochondral *adj.* endocondral.
endochorion *n.* endocorion.
endochrome *n.* endocromo.
endocolitis *n.* endocolitis.
endocolpitis *n.* endocolpitis.
endocommensal *n.* endocomensal.
endoconidiotoxicosis *n.* endoconidiotoxicosis.
endocorpuscular *adj.* endocorpuscular.
endocranial *adj.* endocraneal, entocraneal.
endocraniosis *n.* endocraneosis.
endocranitis *n.* endocranitis.
endocranium *n.* endocráneo, entocráneo.
endocrine *adj.* endocrino, -na.
endocrinism *n.* endocrinismo.
endocrinologist *n.* endocrinólogo, -a.
endocrinology *n.* endocrinología.
 reproductive endocrinology endocrinología reproductora.
endocrinoma *n.* endocrinoma.
 multiple endocrinoma endocrinoma múltiple.
endocrinopath *n.* endocrinópata.
endocrinopathic *adj.* endocrinopático, -ca.

endocrinopathy *n.* endocrinopatía.
multiple endocrinopathy endocrinopatía múltiple.
endocrinosis *n.* endocrinosis.
endocrinotherapy *n.* endocrinoterapia.
endocrinous *adj.* endocrino, -na.
endocyclic *adj.* endocíclico, -ca.
endocyst *n.* endoquiste.
endocystitis *n.* endocistitis.
endocyte *n.* endocito.
endocytosis *n.* endocitosis.
receptor-mediated endocytosis endocitosis mediada por receptor.
endoderm *n.* endodermo, entodermo.
yolk-sac endoderm endodermo del saco vitelino.
endodermal *adj.* endodérmico, -ca, entodérmico, -da.
endodermoreaction *n.* endodermorreacción.
endodiascope *n.* endodiascopio.
endodiascopy *n.* endodiascopia.
endodontia *n.* endodoncia.
endodontics *n.* endodoncia.
endodontist *n.* endodoncista, endodontista.
endodontium *n.* endodontitis.
endodontum *n.* endodonto.
endodontologist *n.* endodontólogo, -ga.
endodontology *n.* endodontología.
endoenteritis *n.* endoenteritis.
endoenzyme *n.* endoenzima.
endoepidermal *adj.* endoepidérmico, -ca.
endoepithelial *adj.* endoepitelial.
endoesophagitis *n.* endoesofagitis.
endoexoteric *adj.* endoexotérico, -ca.
endofaradism *n.* endofaradismo.
endogalvanism *n.* endogalvanismo.
endogamous *adj.* endógamo, -ma.
endogamy *n.* endogamia.
endogastric *adj.* endogástrico, -ca.
endogastritis *n.* endogastritis.
endogenetic *adj.* endogenético, -ca.
endogenic *adj.* endogénico, -ca.
endogenote *n.* endogenota, endogenoto.
endogenous *adj.* endógeno, -na.
endoglobar *adj.* endoglobular.
endoglobular *adj.* endoglobular.
endognathion *n.* endognatio, endognation.
endoherniorrhaphy *n.* endoherniorrafia.
endointoxication *n.* endointoxicación.
endolabyrinthitis *n.* Endolaberintitis.
endolaryngeal *adj.* endolaríngeo, -a.
endolarynx *n.* endolaringe.
endolith *n.* endolito.
endolymph *n.* endolinfa.
endolympha *n.* endolinfa.
endolymphatic *adj.* endolinfático, -ca.
endolymphic *adj.* endolínfico, -ca.
endolysin *n.* endolisina.
leukocytic endolysin endolisina leucocitaria, endolisina leucocítica.
endolysis *n.* endólisis.
endolysosome *n.* endolisosoma.
endomastoiditis *n.* endomastoiditis.
endomeninx *n.* endomeninge.
endomesoderm *n.* endomesodermo.
endometrectomy *n.* endometrectomía.
endometrial *adj.* endometrial.
endometrioid *adj.* endometrioide.
endometrioma *n.* endometrioma.
endometriosis *n.* endometriosis.
direct endometriosis endometriosis directa.
endometriosis externa endometriosis externa.
endometriosis interna endometriosis interna.

endometriosis ovarii endometriosis ovárica.
endometriosis uterina endometriosis uterina.
endometriosis vesicae endometriosis vesical.
implantation endometriosis endometriosis de implantación.
metastatic endometriosis endometriosis metastásica.
ovarian endometriosis endometriosis ovárica.
peritoneal endometriosis endometriosis peritoneal.
primary endometriosis endometriosis primaria.
stromal endometriosis endometriosis del estroma.
transplantation endometriosis endometriosis transplantada.
tuberculous endometriosis endometriosis tuberculosa.
endometritis *n.* endometritis.
bacteriotoxic endometritis endometritis bacteriotóxica.
cervical endometritis endometritis cervical.
decidual endometritis endometritis decidual.
endometritis dissecans endometritis disecante, endometritis exfoliativa.
endometritis tuberosa papulosa endometritis tuberosa papulosa.
glandular endometritis endometritis glandular.
hyperplastic endometritis endometritis hiperplásica.
membranous endometritis endometritis membranosa.
puerperal endometritis endometritis puerperal.
syncytial endometritis endometritis sincicial.
tuberculous endometritis endometritis tuberculosa.
endometrium *n.* endometrio.
Swiss cheese endometrium endometrio en queso suizo, endometrio gruyère.
endometropic *adj.* endometrópico, -ca.
endometry *n.* endometría.
endomitosis *n.* endomitosis.
endomitotic *adj.* endomitótico, -ca.
endomixis *n.* endomixis.
endomorph *n.* endomorfo, -fa.
endomorphic *adj.* endomórfico, -ca.
endomorphy *n.* endomorfia.
endomotorsonde *n.* endomotorsonda.
endomyocardial *adj.* endomiocárdico, -ca.
endomyocarditis *n.* endomiocarditis.
endomyometritis *n.* endomiometritis.
endomysium *n.* endomisio.
endonasal *adj.* endonasal.
endonephritis *n.* endonefritis.
endoneural *adj.* endoneural, endonéurico, -ca.
endoneuritis *n.* endoneuritis.
endoneurium *n.* endoneurio, endoneuro.
endoneurolysis *n.* endoneurólisis.
endonuclear *adj.* endonuclear.
endonucleolus *n.* endonucléolo.
endoparasite *n.* endoparásito.
endoparasitism *n.* endoparasitismo.
endopelvic *adj.* endopélvico, -ca.
endoperiarteritis *n.* endoperiarteritis.
endopericardiac *adj.* endopericardíaco, -ca.
endopericardial *adj.* endopericárdico, -ca.
endopericarditis *n.* endopericarditis.
endoperimyocarditis *n.* endoperimiocarditis.
endoperineuritis *n.* endoperineuritis.

endoperitoneal *adj.* endoperitoneal.
endoperitonitis *n.* endoperitonitis.
endophlebitis *n.* endoflebitis.
endophoria *n.* endoforia.
endophthalmitis *n.* endoftalmía, endoftalmitis.
bacterial endophthalmitis endoftalmitis bacteriana.
endophthalmitis ophthalmia nodosa endoftalmitis nudosa.
endophthalmitis phacoanaphylactica endoftalmitis facoanafiláctica.
granulomatous endophthalmitis endoftalmitis granulomatosa.
phacoallergic endophthalmitis endoftalmitis facoalérgica.
phacoanaphylactic endophthalmitis endoftalmitis facoanafiláctica.
retarded endophthalmitis endoftalmitis por gérmenes lentos.
sterile endophthalmitis endoftalmitis estéril.
endophylaxination *n.* endofilaxis.
endoplasm *n.* endoplasma.
endoplasmatic *adj.* endoplasmático, -ca.
endoplasmic *adj.* endoplásmico, -ca.
endoplyploidy *n.* endopliploidía.
endopolygeny *n.* endopoligenia.
endopolyploid *adj.* endopoliploide.
endoprothesis *n.* endoprótesis.
endoradiosonde *n.* endorradiosonda.
endoreduplication *n.* endorreduplicación.
endorhinitis *n.* endorrinitis.
endorphin *n.* endorfina.
endorphinergic *adj.* endorfinérgico, -ca.
endorrhachis *n.* endorraquis.
endosalpingiosis *n.* endosalpingiosis, endosalpingiosis.
endosalpingitis *n.* endosalpingitis.
endosalpingosis *n.* endosalpingiosis, endosalpingiosis.
endosalpinx *n.* endosálpinx.
endosarc *n.* endosarco.
endoscope *n.* endoscopio.
endoscopic *adj.* endoscópico, -ca.
endoscopist *n.* endoscopista.
endoscopy *n.* endoscopia.
peroral endoscopy endoscopia perbucal.
transcolonic endoscopy endoscopia transcólica.
endosecretory *adj.* endosecretorio, -ria.
endosepsis *n.* endosepsis.
endosite *n.* endósito.
endoskeleton *n.* endoesqueleto, endosqueleto.
endosmometer *n.* endosmómetro.
endosmosis *n.* endósmosis, enósmosis.
endosmotic *adj.* endosmótico, -ca.
endosome *n.* endosoma.
endosonoscopy *n.* endosonoscopia.
endosteal *adj.* endóstico, -ca.
endosteitis *n.* endostitis.
endosteoma *n.* endosteoma.
endostethoscope *n.* endoestetoscopio, endostetoscopio.
endosteum *n.* endostio.
endostitis *n.* endostitis.
endostoma *n.* endosteoma, endostoma.
endostosis *n.* endostosis.
endosymbiosis *n.* endosimbiosis.
endotendineum *n.* endotendón.
endotenon *n.* endotendón.
endothelial *adj.* endotelial.
endothelioblastoma *n.* endotelioblastoma.
endotheliochorial *adj.* endoteliocorial.
endotheliocyte *n.* endoteliocito.

endotheliocytosis *n.* endoteliocitosis.
endothelioid *adj.* endotelioide.
endotheliolysin *n.* endoteliolisina.
endotheliolytic *adj.* endoteliolítico, -ca.
endothelioma *n.* endotelioma.
 diffuse endothelioma endotelioma difuso.
 dural endothelioma endotelioma dural.
 endothelioma angiomatosum endotelioma angiomatoso.
 endothelioma capitis endotelioma capitis.
 endothelioma cutis endotelioma cutis.
endotheliomatosis *n.* endoteliomatosis.
endotheliosarcoma *n.* endoteliosarcoma.
endotheliosis *n.* endoteliosis.
endotheliotoxin *n.* endoteliotoxina.
endothelitis *n.* endotelitis.
endothelium *n.* endotelio.
endothelization *n.* endotelización.
endotherm *n.* endotermo.
endothermic *adj.* endotérmico, -ca.
endothermy *n.* endotermia.
endothrix *n.* endotrix.
endothyropexy *n.* endotiroidopexia, endotiropexia.
endotoscope *n.* endotoscopio.
endotoxemia *n.* endotoxinemia.
endotoxic *adj.* endotóxico, -ca.
endotoxicosis *n.* endotoxicosis.
endotoxin *n.* Endotoxina.
endotracheal *adj.* endotraqueal.
endovasculitis *n.* endovasculitis.
 hemorrhagic endovasculitis endovasculitis hemorrágica.
endovenitis *n.* endovenitis.
endovenous *adj.* endovenoso, -sa.
endyma *n.* endima.
enema *n.* enema, lavativa.
 analeptic enema enema analéptico.
 barium enema enema baritado, enema de bario.
 blind enema enema ciego.
 contrast enema enema de contraste, enema opaco.
 double contrast enema enema de doble contraste.
 flatus enema enema para flato.
 high enema enema alto.
 nutrient enema enema nutriente.
 nutritive enema enema nutriente.
 turpentine enema enema de trementina.
energometer *n.* energómetro.
energy *n.* energía.
enervation *n.* enervación.
engagement *n.* encajamiento.
engastrius *n.* engastrio.
engine *n.* machina, máquina.
 dental engine máquina dental.
 high-speed engine máquina de alta velocidad.
 surgical engine máquina quirúrgica.
 ultraspeed engine máquina ultrarrápida.
engineering *n.* ingeniería.
 biomedical engineering ingeniería biomédica.
 dental engineering ingeniería dental.
 genetic engineering ingeniería genética.
 medical engineering ingeniería médica.
englobement *n.* englobamiento.
engorged *adj.* ingurgitado, -da.
engorgement *n.* ingurgitación, inigurgitación.
engram *n.* engrama.
engraphia *n.* engrafia.
enhancement *n.* acrecentamiento, intensificación.

 shadow casting enhancement intensificación de sombras.
enhematospore *n.* enhematospora.
enhemospore *n.* enhemospora.
enkatarrhaphy *n.* encatarrafia.
enkephalin *n.* encefalina.
enkephalinergic *adj.* encefalinérgico, -ca.
enlargement *n.* agrandamiento.
 cervical enlargement agrandamiento cervical.
 gingival enlargement agrandamiento gingival.
enophthalmos *n.* enoftalmos.
enophthalmus *n.* enoftalmía.
enorchia *n.* enorquia.
enostosis *n.* enostasis, enostosis, entostosis.
enrichment *n.* enriquecimiento.
ensisternum *n.* ensisternón, ensisternum.
ensomphalus *n.* ensónfalo.
enstrophe *n.* enstrofia.
entamebiasis *n.* entamebiasis.
Entamoeba *n.* Entamoeba.
entaredinitis *n.* enteradenitis.
entasia *n.* entasia.
entasis *n.* entasia, éntasis.
entatic *adj.* entático, -ca.
entepicondyle *n.* entepicóndilo.
enteraden *n.* enteradeno.
enteral *adj.* enteral.
enteralgia *n.* enteralgia.
enterangiemphraxis *n.* enterangienfraxis.
enterauxe *n.* enterauxa.
enterectasis *n.* enterectasia, enterectasis.
enterectomy *n.* enterectomía.
enterelcosis *n.* enterelcosis.
enteric *adj.* entérico, -ca.
entericold *adj.* entericoide.
enteritis *n.* enteritis.
 anaphylactic enteritis enteritis alérgica, enteritis anafiláctica.
 choleriform enteritis enteritis coleriforme.
 chronic cicatrizing enteritis enteritis cicatricial, enteritis cicatrizante crónica.
 diphtheritic enteritis enteritis diftérica.
 enteritis cystica chronica enteritis quística crónica.
 enteritis necroticans enteritis necrosante, enteritis necrótica, enteritis necrotizante.
 enteritis nodularis enteritis nodular.
 enteritis polyposa enteritis poliposa.
 feline enteritis enteritis felina, enteritis felina específica, enteritis felina infecciosa.
 feline infectious enteritis enteritis felina, enteritis felina específica, enteritis felina infecciosa.
 granulomatous enteritis enteritis granulomatosa.
 mucomembranous enteritis enteritis membranosa, enteritis mucomembranosa.
 mucous enteritis enteritis mucosa.
 necrotizing enteritis enteritis necrosante, enteritis necrótica, enteritis necrotizante.
 phlegmonous enteritis enteritis flemonosa.
 protozoan enteritis enteritis por protozoarios, enteritis protozoaria.
 pseudomembranous enteritis enteritis seudomembranosa.
 regional enteritis enteritis regional.
 segmental enteritis enteritis segmentaria.
 specific feline enteritis enteritis felina, enteritis felina específica, enteritis felina infecciosa.
 terminal enteritis enteritis terminal.
 tuberculous enteritis enteritis tuberculosa.
enteroanastomosis *n.* enteroanastomosis.
enteroantigen *n.* enteroantígeno.

enteroapocleisis *n.* enteroapocleisis.
Enterobacter *n.* Enterobacter.
Enterobacteriaceae *n.* Enterobacteriaceae.
enterobacterial *adj.* enterobacteriano, -na.
enterobiasis *n.* enterobiasis.
enterobiliary *adj.* enterobiliar.
Enterobius *n.* Enterobius.
enterobrosia *n.* enterobrosia, enterobrosis.
enterobrosis *n.* enterobrosia, enterobrosis.
enterocele *n.* enterocele, enterocelo.
enterocentesis *n.* enterocentesis.
enterocholecystostomy *n.* enterocolecistostomía.
enterochromaffin *adj.* enterocromafin.
enterocinesia *n.* enterocinesis, enteroquinesia, enteroquinesis.
enterocinesis *n.* enterocinesis, enteroquinesia, enteroquinesis.
enterocinetic *adj.* enterocinético, -ca.
enterocleisis *n.* enterocleisis.
 omental enterocleisis enterocleisis del epiplón, enterocleisis epiploica.
enteroclysis *n.* diaclismosis, enteroclisis, enteroclisma.
enterococcemia *n.* enterococemia.
Enterococcus *n.* Enterococcus, enterococo.
enterocoele *n.* enterocele, enterocelo.
enterocolectomy *n.* enterocolectomía.
enterocolitis *n.* enterocolitis.
 antibiotic enterocolitis enterocolitis antibiótica.
 antibiotic-associated enterocolitis enterocolitis relacionada con antibióticos.
 hemorrhagic enterocolitis enterocolitis hemorrágica.
 necrotizing enterocolitis enterocolitis necrosante.
 pseudomembranous enterocolitis enterocolitis seudomembranosa.
 regional enterocolitis enterocolitis regional.
enterocolostomy *n.* enterocolostomía.
enterocutaneous *adj.* enterocutáneo, -a.
enterocyst *n.* enteroquiste.
enterocystocele *n.* enterocistocele.
enterocystoma *n.* enteroquistoma.
enterocyte *n.* enterocito.
enterodynia *n.* enterodinia.
enteroenterostomy *n.* enteroenterostomía.
enteroepiplocele *n.* enteroepiplocele.
enterogastric *adj.* enterogástrico, -ca.
enterogastritis *n.* enterogastritis.
enterogenous *adj.* enterógeno, -na.
enterogram *n.* enterograma.
enterograph *n.* enterógrafo.
enterography *n.* enterografía.
enterohepatitis *n.* enterohepatitis.
 infectious enterohepatitis enterohepatitis infecciosa.
enterohepatocele *n.* enterohepatocele.
enterohydrocele *n.* enterohidrocele.
enteroidea *adj.* enteroide, enteroidea.
enterointestinal *adj.* enterointestinal.
enterokinesia *n.* enterocinesis, enteroquinesia, enteroquinesis.
enterokinesis *n.* enterocinesis, enteroquinesia, enteroquinesis.
enterokinetic *adj.* enterocinético, -ca, enteroquinético, -ca.
enterokinin *n.* enterocinina.
enterolith *n.* enterolito.
enterolithiasis *n.* enterolitiasis.
enterology *n.* enterología.
enterolysis *n.* enterólisis.
enteromegalia *n.* enteromegalia.
enteromegaly *n.* enteromegalia.

enteromenia *n.* enteromenia.
enteromere *n.* enterómera.
enteromerocele *n.* enteromerocele.
enterometer *n.* enterómetro.
Enteromonas *n.* Enteromonas.
 Enteromonas hominis Enteromonas hominis.
enteromycodermitis *n.* enteromicodermitis.
enteromycosis *n.* enteromicosis.
 enteromycosis bacteriacea enteromicosis bacteriana.
enteromyiasis *n.* enteromiiasis.
enteron *n.* enteron.
enteroneuritis *n.* enteroneuritis.
enteronitis *n.* enteronitis.
entero-oxyntin *n.* enteroxintina.
enteroparesis *n.* enteroparálisis, enteroparesia.
enteropathogen *n.* enteropatógeno.
enteropathogenesis *n.* enteropatogenia.
enteropathogenic *adj.* enteropatogénico, -ca.
enteropathy *n.* enteropatía.
 eosinophilic enteropathy enteropatía eosinofílica.
 exudative enteropathy enteropatía exudativa.
 gluten enteropathy enteropatía por gluten.
 protein-losing enteropathy enteropatía con pérdida de proteínas, enteropatía con pérdida proteínica.
enteropexy *n.* enteropexia.
enteroplasty *n.* enteroplastia.
enteroplegia *n.* enteroplejía.
enteroplex *n.* enteroplex.
enteroplexy *n.* enteropexia, enteroplexia.
enteroproctia *n.* enteroproccia, enteroproctia.
enteroptosia *n.* enteroptosis.
enteroptosis *n.* enteroptosis.
enteroptotic *adj.* enteroptósico, -ca.
enteroptychia *n.* enteroptiquia.
enteroptychy *n.* enteroptiquia.
enterorenal *adj.* enterorrenal.
enterorrhagia *n.* enterorragia.
enterorrhaphy *n.* enterorrafia.
 circular enterorrhaphy enterorrafia circular, enterorrafia terminoterminal.
enterorrhea *n.* enterorrea.
enterorrhexis *n.* enterorrexia, enterorrexis.
enteroscope *n.* enteroscopio.
enterosepsis *n.* enterosepsis.
enterosite *n.* enterósito.
enterosorption *n.* enterosorción.
enterospasm *n.* enteroespasmo, enterospasmo.
enterostasis *n.* enterostasis.
enterostaxis *n.* enterostaxis.
enterostenosis *n.* enteroestenosis, enterostenosis.
enterostomal *adj.* enterostómico, -ca.
enterostomy *n.* enterostomía.
 double enterostomy enterostomía doble.
 gun-barrel enterostomy enterostomía en cañón de escopeta.
enterotome *n.* enterótomo.
 Dupuytren's enterotome enterótomo de Dupuytren.
enterotomy *n.* enterotomía.
enterotoxemia *n.* enterotoxemia.
enterotoxication *n.* enterotoxicación.
enterotoxigenic *adj.* enterotoxigénico, -ca, enterotoxígeno, -na.
enterotoxin *n.* enterotoxina.
 cholera enterotoxin enterotoxina del cólera.
 cytotonic enterotoxin enterotoxina citotónica.

Escherichia coli enterotoxin enterotoxina de Escherichia coli.
 staphylococcal enterotoxin enterotoxina estafilocócica.
enterotoxism *n.* enterotoxismo.
enterotropic *adj.* enterotrópico, -ca.
enterotyphus *n.* enterotifus.
enterovaginal *adj.* enterovaginal.
enterovenous *adj.* enterovenoso, -sa.
enterovesical *adj.* enterovesical.
enteroviral *adj.* enterovirósico, -ca.
enterovirus *n.* enterovirus.
enterozoic *adj.* enterozoico, -ca.
enterozoon *n.* enterozoo.
enteruria *n.* enteruria.
enthalpy *n.* entalpía.
enthesis *n.* entesis.
enthesitis *n.* entesitis.
enthesopathic *adj.* entesopático, -ca.
enthesopathy *n.* entesopatía.
enthetic *adj.* entésico, -ca, entético, -ca.
enthetobiosis *n.* entetobiosis.
enthlasis *n.* entlasis.
entire *n.* entero.
entiris *n.* entiris.
entity *n.* entidad.
entoblast *n.* endoblasto, entoblasto.
entocele *n.* entocele.
entochondrostosis *n.* entocondrostosis.
entochoroidea *n.* entocoroides.
entocnemial *adj.* entocnémico, -ca.
entocondyle *n.* entocóndilo.
entocone *n.* entocono.
entoconid *n.* entoconida, entoconidio.
entocornea *n.* entocórnea.
entocranial *adj.* endocraneal, entocraneal.
entocranium *n.* endocráneo, entocráneo.
entocyte *n.* entocito.
entoderm *n.* endodermo, entodermo.
entodermal *adj.* endodérmico, -ca, entodérmico, -da.
entodermic *adj.* endodérmico, -ca, entodérmico, -da.
entome *n.* entomo.
entomere *n.* entómera.
entomesoderm *n.* endomesodermo, entomesodermo.
entomion *n.* entomión.
entomologist *n.* entomólogo, -a.
entomology *n.* entomología.
 cadaveric entomology entomología cadavérica.
entomophobia *n.* entomofobia.
Entomophthoraceae *n.* Entomophthoraceae.
entomophthoramycosis *n.* entomoftoramicosis.
 entomophthoramycosis basidiobolae entomoftoramicosis basidiobolae.
 entomophthoramycosis conidiobolae entomoftoramicosis conidiobolae.
entophtalmia *n.* endoftalmía, entoftalmía.
entophyte *n.* entófito.
entopic *adj.* entópico, -ca.
entoplasm *n.* endoplasma, entoplasma.
entoplastic *adj.* entoplásico, -ca.
entoptic *adj.* entóptico, -ca.
entoptoscope *n.* entoptoscopio.
entoptoscopy *n.* entoptoscopia.
entoretina *n.* entorretina.
entostosis *n.* enostosis, enostosis, entostosis.
entotic *adj.* entótico, -ca.
entotympanic *adj.* entotimpánico, -ca.
entozoon *n.* entozoario, entozoo.
entropion *n.* entropión.
 atonic entropion entropión atónico.

cicatricial entropion entropión cicatricial, entropión cicatrizal.
 congenital entropion entropión congénito.
 involutive entropion entropión involutivo.
 senile entropion entropión senil.
 spasmodic entropion entropión espasmódico.
 spastic entropion entropión espástico.
 uvea entropion entropión uveal.
entropionize *v.* entropionizar.
entropy *n.* entropía.
entypy *n.* entipia.
enucleated *adj.* enucleado, -da.
enucleation *n.* enucleación.
 enucleation of the eyeball enucleación ocular.
enucleator *n.* cnucleador.
enula *n.* enula.
enuresis *n.* enuresis.
 diurnal enuresis enuresis diurna.
 nocturnal enuresis enuresis nocturna.
enuretic *adj.* enurético, -ca.
envelope *n.* cubierta, envoltura[1].
 nuclear envelope envoltura nuclear.
 viral envelope envoltura virósica.
environment *n.* ambiente.
envy *n.* envidia.
 penis envy envidia del pene.
enzygotic *adj.* encigótico, -ca.
enzymatic *adj.* enzimático, -ca.
enzyme *n.* enzima.
enzyme-immunoassay *n.* enzimoinmunoensayo.
enzymohistochemistry *n.* enzimohístoquímica.
enzymologist *n.* enzimólogo, -a.
enzymology *n.* enzimología.
enzymolysis *n.* enzimólisis, enzimosis.
enzymopathy *n.* enzimopatía.
enzymuria *n.* enzimuria.
eosinocyte *n.* eosinocito.
eosinopenia *n.* eosinopenia.
eosinophil *n.* eosinófilo.
eosinophile *n.* eosinófilo.
eosinophilia *n.* eosinofilia.
 asthmatic eosinophilia eosinofilia asmática.
 Löffler's eosinophilia eosinofilia de Löffler, eosinofilia pulmonar simple.
 pulmonary infiltration eosinophilia eosinofilia con infiltración pulmonar.
 simple pulmonary eosinophilia eosinofilia de Löffler, eosinofilia pulmonar simple.
 tropical eosinophilia eosinofilia tropical, eosinofilia tropical pulmonar.
 tropical pulmonary eosinophilia eosinofilia tropical, eosinofilia tropical pulmonar.
eosinophilic *adj.* eosinofílico, -ca.
eosinophilosis *n.* eosinofilosis.
eosinophilotactic *adj.* eosinofilotáctico, -ca.
eosinophiluria *n.* eosinofiluria.
eosinophylopoietin *n.* eosinofilopoyetina.
eosinotactic *adj.* eosinotáctico, -ca.
eosinotaxis *n.* eosinotaxis.
epacmastic *adj.* epacmástico, -ca.
epacme *n.* epacmo.
epallobiosis *n.* epalobiosis.
epamniotic *adj.* epamniótico, -ca.
eparsalgia *n.* eparsalgia, epersalgia.
eparterial *adj.* eparterial.
epaxial *adj.* epaxial, epaxil.
epencephalic *adj.* epencefálico, -ca.
epencephalon *n.* epencéfalo.
ependimocytoma *n.* ependimocitoma.
ependopathy *n.* ependopatía.

ependyma *n.* epéndimo.
ependymal *adj.* ependimario, -ria.
ependymitis *n.* ependimitis.
ependymoblast *n.* ependimoblasto.
ependymoblastoma *n.* ependimoblastoma.
ependymocyte *n.* ependimocito.
ependymoma *n.* ependimoma.
  intramedullary ependymoma ependimoma intramedular.
  myxopapillary ependymoma ependimoma mixopapilar.
ependymopathy *n.* ependimopatía.
epersalgia *n.* eparsalgia, epersalgia.
eperythrozoonosis *n.* eperitrozoonosis.
ephapse *n.* efapsis.
ephaptic *adj.* efáptico, -ca.
ephebic *adj.* efébico, -ca.
ephelides *n.* efélide.
ephemeral *adj.* efímero, -ra.
Ephemerida *n.* Ephemerida.
ephidrosis *n.* efidrosis.
epiblast *n.* epiblasto.
epiblastic *adj.* epiblástico, -ca.
epiblepharon *n.* epibléfaron.
epibole *n.* epibolia.
epiboly *n.* epibolia.
epibulbar *adj.* epibulbar.
epicanthal *adj.* epicántico, -ca.
epicanthic *adj.* epicántico, -ca.
epicanthus *n.* epicanto.
  epicanthus inversus epicanto invertido.
epicardia *n.* epicardias.
epicardial *adj.* epicardial, epicárdico, -ca.
epicardiectomy *n.* epicardiectomía.
epicardiolysis *n.* epicardiólisis.
epicarditis *n.* epicarditis.
epicardium *n.* epicardio.
epicauma *n.* epicauma.
epicentral *adj.* epicentral.
epichorion *n.* epicorion.
epicoeloma *n.* epiceloma.
epicomus *n.* epicomo.
epicondylalgia *n.* epicondialgia, epicondilalgia.
  externa epicondylalgia epicondialgia externa.
epicondyle *n.* epicóndilo.
epicondylian *adj.* epicondilar, epicondíleo, -a.
epicondylic *adj.* epicondilar, epicondíleo, -a.
epicondylitis *n.* epicondilitis.
  lateral humeral epicondylitis epicondilitis humeral externa, epicondilitis humeral lateral.
epicondylus *n.* epicóndilo.
epicoracoid *adj.* epicoracoideo, -a.
epicorneoscleritis *n.* epicorneoescleritis.
epicostal *adj.* epicostal.
epicranium *n.* epicráneo.
epicranius *n.* epicráneo.
epicrisis *n.* epicrisis.
epicritic *adj.* epicrítico, -ca.
epicystitis *n.* epicistitis.
epicystotomy *n.* epicistotomía.
epicyte *n.* epicito.
epidemic *n.* epidemia, epidémico, -ca.
  point epidemic epidemia puntual.
epidemicity *n.* epidemicidad.
epidemiography *n.* epidemiografía.
epidemiologist *n.* epidemiólogo, -a.
epidemiology *n.* epidemiología.
  analytic epidemiology epidemiología analítica.
  descriptive epidemiology epidemiología descriptiva, epidemiología observacional.
  experimental epidemiology epidemiología experimental.

  substantive epidemiology epidemiología sustantiva.
epiderm *n.* epidermis, epidermo.
epidermalization *n.* epidermalización.
epidermatic *adj.* epidermático, -ca.
epidermatitis *n.* epidermatitis.
epidermatoplasty *n.* epidermatoplastia.
epidermic *adj.* epidérmico, -ca.
epidermicula *n.* epidermícula.
epidermidalization *n.* epidermización.
epidermidosis *n.* epidermidosis.
epidermis *n.* epidermis, epidermo.
epidermitis *n.* epidermitis.
epidermization *n.* epidermización.
epidermodysplasia *n.* epidermodisplasia.
  epidermodysplasia verruciformis epidermodisplasia verruciforme.
epidermoid *adj.* epidermoide.
epidermolysis *n.* epidermólisis.
  acquired epidermolysis bullosa epidermólisis ampollar adquirida.
  albopapuloid epidermolysis bullosa dystrophica epidermólisis ampollar distrófica albopapuloide.
  bullous epidermolysis of Weber-Cockayne epidermólisis ampollar de Weber-Cockayne.
  dominant epidermolysis bullosa dystrophica epidermólisis ampollar distrófica dominante.
  dysplastic epidermolysis bullosa dystrophica epidermólisis ampollar distrófica displásica.
  epidermolysis acquisita epidermólisis adquirida.
  epidermolysis bullosa epidermólisis ampollar.
  epidermolysis bullosa acquisita epidermólisis ampollar adquirida.
  epidermolysis bullosa dystrophica epidermólisis ampollar distrófica.
  epidermolysis bullosa hereditaria epidermólisis ampollar hereditaria.
  epidermolysis bullosa lethalis epidermólisis ampollar letal, epidermólisis ampollar mortal.
  epidermolysis bullosa simplex epidermólisis ampollar simple, epidermólisis ampollar simple generalizada.
  generalized epidermolysis bullosa simplex epidermólisis ampollar simple, epidermólisis ampollar simple generalizada.
  hyperplastic epidermolysis bullosa epidermólisis ampollar hiperplásica.
  hyperplastic epidermolysis bullosa dystrophica epidermólisis ampollar distrófica hiperplásica.
  junctional epidermolysis bullosa epidermólisis ampollar de las articulaciones.
  polydysplastic epidermolysis bullosa epidermólisis ampollar polidisplásica.
  polydysplastic epidermolysis bullosa dystrophica epidermólisis ampollar distrófica polidisplásica.
  recessive epidermolysis bullosa dystrophica epidermólisis ampollar distrófica recesiva.
  toxic bullous epidermolysis epidermólisis ampollar tóxica.
epidermolytic *adj.* epidermolítico, -ca.
epidermoma *n.* epidermoma.
epidermomycosis *n.* epidermomicosis.
epidermophytid *n.* epidermofítide.
Epidermophyton *n.* Epidermophyton.
epidermophytosis *n.* epidermofitosis.
  epidermophytosis cruris epidermofitosis cruris.
  epidermophytosis interdigitale epidermofitosis interdigital.

epidermosis *n.* epidermosis.
epidermotropic *adj.* epidermotrófico, -ca, epidermotrópico, -ca.
epidermotropism *n.* epidermotropismo.
epidialysis *n.* epidiálisis.
epidiascope *n.* epidiascopio.
epididymal *adj.* epididimal, epididimario, -ria.
epididymectomy *n.* epididimectomía.
epididymis *n.* epidídimo.
epididymisoplasty *n.* epididimisoplastia.
epididymitis *n.* epididimitis.
  acute epididymitis epididimitis inespecífica.
  tuberculous epididymitis epididimitis tuberculosa.
epididymodeferentectomy *n.* epididimodeferentectomía.
epididymodeferential *adj.* epididimodeferencial.
epididymo-orchitis *n.* epididimoorquitis.
epididymoplasty *n.* epididimoplastia.
epididymotomy *n.* epididimotomía.
epididymovasectomy *n.* epididimovasectomía.
epididymovasostomy *n.* epididimovasostomía.
epididymovesiculography *n.* epididimovesiculografía.
epidural *adj.* epidural.
epidurography *n.* epidurografía.
epifascial *adj.* epifascial.
epigamic *adj.* epigámico, -ca.
epigaster *n.* epigáster.
epigastralgia *n.* epigastralgia.
epigastric *adj.* epigástrico, -ca.
epigastrium *n.* epigastrio.
epigastrius *n.* epigastrios, epigastrius.
epigastrocele *n.* epigastrocele.
epigastrorrhaphy *n.* epigastrorrafia.
epigenesis *n.* epigénesis.
epigenetic *adj.* epigenético, -ca.
epigenetics *n.* epigenética.
epigenic *adj.* epigenético, -ca.
epigeny *n.* epigénesis.
epiglottectomy *n.* epiglectomía, epiglotectomía.
epiglottic *adj.* epiglótico, -ca.
epiglottidean *adj.* epiglotídeo, -a.
epiglottidectomy *n.* epiglotidectomía.
epiglottis *n.* epiglotis.
epiglottitis *n.* epiglotitis.
  acute epiglottitis epiglotitis aguda.
epignathus *n.* epignato.
epihyal *adj.* epihial.
epihyoid *adj.* epihioideo, -a.
epikeratophakia *n.* epiqueratofaquia.
epikeratoprosthesis *n.* epiqueratoprótesis.
epilamellar *adj.* epilamelar, epilaminillar.
epilemma *n.* epilema.
epilemmal *adj.* epilémico, -ca.
epilepidoma *n.* epilepidoma.
epilepsia *n.* epilepsia.
  epilepsia nutans epilepsia nutatoria.
  epilepsia partialis continua epilepsia parcial continua.
epilepsy *n.* epilepsia.
  abdominal epilepsy epilepsia abdominal.
  acquired epilepsy epilepsia adquirida.
  activated epilepsy epilepsia activada.
  akinetic epilepsy epilepsia acinética.
  anosognosic epilepsy epilepsia anosognósica.
  atonic epilepsy epilepsia atónica.
  audiogenic epilepsy epilepsia audiogénica.
  automatic epilepsy epilepsia automática.
  autonomic epilepsy epilepsia autónoma.

benign childhood epilepsy epilepsia benigna del niño, epilepsia benigna infantil.
benign childhood epilepsy with occipital paroxysms epilepsia infantil con paroxismos occipitales.
centrencephalic epilepsy epilepsia centroencefálica.
chronic focal epilepsy epilepsia focal crónica.
complex precipitated epilepsy epilepsia precipitada compleja.
continuous spike-and wave epilepsy during sleep epilepsia con punta-onda continuada del sueño.
cortical epilepsy epilepsia cortical.
cryptogenic epilepsy epilepsia criptogenética, epilepsia criptogénica.
diencephalic epilepsy epilepsia diencefálica.
diurnal epilepsy epilepsia diurna.
early posttraumatic epilepsy epilepsia postraumática precoz.
eating epilepsy epilepsia por comida.
essential epilepsy epilepsia esencial.
familial epilepsy epilepsia familiar.
focal epilepsy epilepsia focal.
generalized epilepsy epilepsia generalizada.
generalized flexion epilepsy epilepsia generalizada en flexión.
generalized tonic-clonic epilepsy epilepsia tonico-clónica generalizada.
grand mal epilepsy epilepsia de gran mal, epilepsia de grand mal.
hysterical epilepsy epilepsia histérica.
idiopathic epilepsy epilepsia idiopática.
Jacksonian epilepsy epilepsia de Bravais-Jackson, epilepsia jacksoniana.
juvenile myoclonic epilepsy epilepsia mioclónica juvenil.
Kojewnikoff's epilepsy epilepsia de Kojewnikoff.
larval epilepsy epilepsia larvada.
laryngeal epilepsy epilepsia laríngea.
late epilepsy epilepsia demorada, epilepsia tardía.
latent epilepsy epilepsia latente.
local epilepsy epilepsia local, epilepsia localizada.
localized epilepsy epilepsia local, epilepsia localizada.
major epilepsy epilepsia major, epilepsia mayor.
masked epilepsy epilepsia enmascarada.
matutinal epilepsy epilepsia del despertar, epilepsia matutina.
minor epilepsy epilepsia menor, epilepsia minor.
minor focal epilepsy epilepsia focal menor.
musicogenic epilepsy epilepsia musicógena, epilepsia musicogénica.
myoclonic astatic epilepsy epilepsia astática mioclónica.
myoclonic epilepsy epilepsia mioclónica.
nocturnal epilepsy epilepsia nocturna.
organic epilepsy epilepsia orgánica.
partial epilepsy epilepsia parcial.
pattern sensitive epilepsy epilepsia sensible a un patrón.
petit mal epilepsy epilepsia de pequeño mal, epilepsia de petit mal.
photic epilepsy epilepsia fótica.
photogenic epilepsy epilepsia fotógena, epilepsia fotogénica.
photosensitive epilepsy epilepsia fotosensible.
physiologic epilepsy epilepsia fisiológica.
posttraumatic epilepsy epilepsia postraumática.

primary generalized epilepsy epilepsia generalizada primaria, epilepsia primaria generalizada.
procursive epilepsy epilepsia procursiva.
progressive familial myoclonic epilepsy epilepsia mioclónica progresiva, epilepsia mioclónica progresiva familiar.
progressive myoclonic epilepsy epilepsia mioclónica progresiva, epilepsia mioclónica progresiva familiar.
psychomotor epilepsy epilepsia psicomotora.
reading epilepsy epilepsia primaria de la lectura.
reflex epilepsy epilepsia refleja.
rolandic epilepsy epilepsia rolándica.
secondary generalized epilepsy epilepsia generalizada secundaria, epilepsia secundaria generalizada.
sensory epilepsy epilepsia sensitiva, epilepsia sensorial.
sensory precipitated epilepsy epilepsia precipitada sensorial.
serial epilepsy epilepsia seriada.
sleep epilepsy epilepsia del sueño.
somnambulic epilepsy epilepsia del sonámbulo.
spinal epilepsy epilepsia espinal.
startle epilepsy epilepsia por sobresalto, epilepsia sobresalto.
temporal lobe epilepsy epilepsia del lóbulo temporal.
tonic epilepsy epilepsia tónica.
tornado epilepsy epilepsia en tornado.
traumatic epilepsy epilepsia traumática.
uncinate epilepsy epilepsia uncinada.
vasomotor epilepsy epilepsia vasomotora.
vasovagal epilepsy epilepsia vasovagal.
visceral epilepsy epilepsia visceral.
epileptic *adj.* epiléptico, -ca.
epileptiform *adj.* epileptiforme.
epileptogenic *adj.* epileptogénico, -ca.
epileptogenous *adj.* epileptógeno, -na.
epileptoid *adj.* epileptoide.
epileptologist *n.* epileptólogo, -ga.
epileptology *n.* epileptología.
epileptosis *n.* epileptosis.
epilesional *adj.* epilesional.
epiloia *n.* epiloia.
epimandibular *adj.* epimandibular.
epimastical *adj.* epimastical.
epimastigote *n.* epimastigote, epimastigoto.
epimenorrhagia *n.* epimenorragia.
epimenorrhea *n.* epimenorrea.
epimer *n.* epímero.
epimerization *n.* epimerización.
epimicroscope *n.* epimicroscopio.
epimorphic *adj.* epimórfico, -ca.
epimorphosis *n.* epimorfosis.
epimysiotomy *n.* epimisiotomía.
epimysium *n.* epimisio.
epinephrine *n.* epinefrina.
epinephrinemia *n.* epinefrinemia.
epinephritis *n.* epinefritis.
epinephros *n.* epinefros.
epineural *adj.* epineural[1].
epineurial *adj.* epineural[2].
epineurium *n.* epineurio, epineuro.
epinosic *adj.* epinósico, -ca.
epinosis *n.* epinosis.
epiotic *adj.* epiótico, -ca.
epiparonychia *n.* epiparoniquia.
epipastic *adj.* epipástico, -ca.
epipericardial *adj.* epipericárdico, -ca.
epipharingitis *n.* epifaringitis.
epiphenomenon *n.* epifenómeno.

epiphora *n.* epífora.
atonic epiphora epífora atónica.
epiphylaxis *n.* epifilaxis.
epiphyseal *adj.* epifisario, -ria.
epiphyseodesis *n.* epifisiodesis.
epiphysial *adj.* epifisario, -ria.
epiphysiodesis *n.* epifisiodesis.
epiphysioid *adj.* epifisioide.
epiphysiolysis *n.* epifisiólisis.
epiphysiometer *n.* epifisiómetro.
epiphysiopathy *n.* epifisiopatía.
epiphysis *n.* epífisis.
femoral epiphysis epífisis femoral.
pressure epiphysis epífisis por presión.
slipped epiphysis epífisis desprendida.
stippled epiphysis epífisis punteada.
traction epiphysis epífisis por tracción.
epiphysitis *n.* epifisitis.
vertebral epiphysitis epifisitis vertebral.
epipial *adj.* epipial.
epiplocele *n.* epiplocele.
epiploectomy *n.* epiplectomía, epiploectomía.
epiploenterocele *n.* epiplenterocele, epiploenterocele.
epiploic *adj.* epiploico, -ca.
epiploitis *n.* epiploítis.
epiplomerocele *n.* epiplomerocele.
epiplomphalocele *n.* epiplonfalocele.
epiploon *n.* epiplón.
epiplopexy *n.* epiplopexia.
epiploplasty *n.* epiploplastia.
epiplorrhaphy *n.* epiplorrafia.
epiplosarcomphalocele *n.* epiplosarconfalocele.
epiploscheocele *n.* epiplosqueocele.
epipteric *adj.* epiptérico, -ca.
epipygus *n.* epípigo.
epipyramis *n.* epipiramidal.
epirotulian *adj.* epirrotuliano, -na.
episclera *n.* epiesclerótica, episclera, episclerótica.
episcleral *adj.* epiescleral, epiesclerótico, -ca, episcleral, episclerótico, -ca.
episcleritis *n.* epiescleritis, epiesclerotitis, episcleritis.
episcleritis multinodularis epiescleritis multinodular.
episcleritis nodular epiescleritis nodular.
episcleritis periodica fugax epiescleritis periódica fugaz.
episclerotitis *n.* episclerotitis.
episiotomy *n.* episiotomía.
episode *n.* episodio.
acute schizophrenic episode episodio esquizofrénico agudo.
affective episode episodio afectvo.
depressive episode episodio depresivo.
hypomaniac episode episodio hipomaníaco.
major depressive episode episodio depresivo grave.
major depressive episode with psychotic symptoms episodio depresivo grave con síntomas psicóticos.
major depressive episode without psychotic symptoms episodio depresivo grave sin síntomas psicóticos.
manic episode episodio maníaco.
mixed episode episodio mixto.
psycholeptic episode episodio psicoléptico.
episome *n.* episoma.
resistance-transferring episome episoma que transfiere resistencia.
epispadia *n.* epispadias.
balanic epispadia epispadias balánico, epispadias glandular.

balanitic epispadia epispadias balánico.
clitoric epispadia epispadias clitorídeo.
complete epispadia epispadias completo.
penile epispadia epispadias peniano.
penopubic epispadia epispadias penopubiano.
subsymphyseal epispadia epispadias subsinfisario.
epispadiac *adj.* epispádico, -ca.
epispadias *n.* epispadias.
epispastic *adj.* epispástico, -ca.
epispinal *adj.* epiespinal, epispinal.
episplenitis *n.* epiesplenitis, episplenitis.
epistasis *n.* epistasia, epistasis.
epistasy *n.* epistasia, epistasis.
epistatic *adj.* epistático, -ca.
epistaxis *n.* epistaxis.
renal epistaxis epistaxis renal.
epistemology *n.* epistemología.
evolutive epistemology epistemología evolutiva.
genetic epistemology epistemología genética.
episternal *adj.* epiesternal.
episternum *n.* epiesternón, episternón.
episthotonos *n.* epistótonos.
epistropheus *n.* epistrofeo.
epitaxy *n.* epitaxia, epitaxis.
epitela *n.* epitela.
epitendineum *n.* epitendineo, epitendineum.
epitenon *n.* epitenón.
epithalamic *adj.* epitalámico, -ca.
epithalamus *n.* epitálamo.
epithalaxia *n.* epitalaxia, epitalaxis.
epithelial *adj.* epitelial.
epithelialization *n.* epitelización.
epithelloblastoma *n.* epitelloblastoma.
epithelioceptor *n.* epitelioceptor.
epitheliochorial *adj.* epiteliocorial.
epitheliocyte *n.* epiteliocito.
epitheliofibril *n.* epiteliofibrilla.
epitheliogenic *adj.* epiteliogenético, -ca.
epithelioglandular *adj.* epitelioglandular.
epithelioid *adj.* epitelioide.
epitheliolysis *n.* epiteliólisis.
epitheliolytic *adj.* epiteliolítico, -ca.
epithelioma *n.* epitelioma.
basal cell epithelioma epitelioma basocelular, epitelioma de células basales.
Borst-Jadassohn type intraepidermal epithelioma epitelioma intraepidérmico tipo Borst-Jadassohn.
chorionic epithelioma epitelioma coriónico.
columnar epithelioma epitelioma cilíndrico.
cylindrical epithelioma epitelioma cilíndrico.
epithelioma adamantinum epitelioma adamantino.
epithelioma adenoides cysticum epitelioma adenoide quístico, epitelioma adenoideo quístico.
epithelioma cuniculatum epitelioma cuniculado.
Malherbe's calcifying epithelioma epitelioma calcificante de Malherbe.
malignant ciliary epithelioma epitelioma ciliar maligno.
multiple benign cystic epithelioma epitelioma quístico benigno múltiple.
multiple self-healing squamous epithelioma epitelioma escamoso de involución espontánea, epitelioma escamoso múltiple autocicatrizante, epitelioma escamoso múltiple autocurable, epitelioma escamoso múltiple de involución espontánea.
prickle cell epithelioma epitelioma espinocelular.

sebaceous epithelioma epitelioma sebáceo.
epitheliomatosis *n.* epiteliomatosis.
epitheliomatous *adj.* epiteliomatoso, -sa.
epitheliomuscular *adj.* epiteliomuscular.
epitheliopathy *n.* epiteliopatía.
pigment epitheliopathy epiteliopatía pigmentaria.
epitheliosis *n.* epiteliosis.
epitheliosis desquamativa conjunctivae epiteliosis descamativa de la conjuntiva, epiteliosis exfoliativa conjuntival.
epitheliotoxin *n.* epiteliotoxina.
epithelite *n.* epitelito.
epithelitis *n.* epitelitis.
epithelium *n.* epitelio, epithelium.
anterior epithelium of the cornea epitelio anterior de la córnea.
anterius epithelium corneae epitelio anterior de la córnea.
capsular epithelium epitelio capsular.
ciliated epithelium epitelio ciliado.
columnar epithelium epitelio columnar.
corneal epithelium epitelio corneal, epitelio de la cornea.
cubical epithelium epitelio cúbico simple.
cuboidal epithelium epitelio cúbico simple.
cylindrical epithelium epitelio cilíndrico.
enamel epithelium epitelio del esmalte.
epithelium corneae epitelio corneal, epitelio de la cornea.
epithelium lentis epitelio del cristalino.
epithelium mucosae epitelio de las mucosas, epitelio de superficies húmedas, epitelio no queratinizado.
epithelium of the lens epitelio del cristalino.
epithelium pigmentosum iridis epitelio pigmentado del iris.
external dental epithelium epitelio externo del esmalte, epitelio externo dental.
external enamel epithelium epitelio externo del esmalte, epitelio externo dental.
glandular epithelium epitelio glandular.
laminated epithelium epitelio laminado.
muscle epithelium epitelio muscular.
olfactory epithelium epitelio olfatorio.
pigmented epithelium of the iris epitelio pigmentado del iris.
pseudostrafied epithelium epitelio seudoestratificado.
respiratory epithelium epitelio respiratorio.
retinal pigmentary epithelium epitelio pigmentario de la retina.
seminiferous epithelium epitelio germinal masculino, epitelio seminífero.
sense epithelium epitelio sensorial.
sensory epithelium epitelio sensorial.
simple epithelium epitelio simple.
squamous epithelium epitelio escamoso.
stratified epithelium epitelio estratificado, epitelio multiestratificado, epitelio poliestratificado.
subcapsular epithelium epitelio subcapsular.
transitional epithelium epitelio de transición, epitelio transicional.
epithelization *n.* epitelización.
epithem *n.* epítema.
epithesis *n.* epítesis.
epitonic *adj.* epitónico, -ca.
epitope *n.* epitopo.
epitrichial *adj.* epitriquial.
epitrichium *n.* epitriquio.
epitrochlea *n.* epitróclea.
epitrochlear *adj.* epitrocleano, -na, epitroclear.
epitrochleytis *n.* epitrocleítis.

epituberculosis *n.* epituberculosis.
epitympanic *adj.* epitimpánico, -ca.
epitympanum *n.* epitímpano.
epityphlitis *n.* epitiflitis.
epizoic *adj.* epizoico, -ca.
epizoicide *adj.* epizoicida.
epizoo *n.* epizoario, epizoo.
epizoon *n.* epizoario, epizoo.
epizoonosis *n.* epizoonosis.
eponychia *n.* eponiquia.
eponychium *n.* eponiquio.
eponym *n.* epónimo.
eponymic *adj.* eponímico, -ca.
eponymous *adj.* epónimo, -ma.
epoophorectomy *n.* epooforectomía.
epulis *n.* épulis.
congenital epulis épulis congénito, épulis congénito del recién nacido.
congenital epulis of the newborn épulis congénito, épulis congénito del recién nacido.
epulis fibromatosa épulis fibromatoso.
epulis fissurata épulis fisurado.
epulis granulomatosa épulis granulomatoso.
epulis gravidarum épulis del embarazo.
epulis of the newborn épulis del neonato.
giant cell epulis épulis de células gigantes, épulis gigantocelular.
pigmented epulis épulis pigmentado.
telangiectatic epulis épulis telangiectásico.
epulofibroma *n.* epulofibroma.
epuloid *adj.* epuloide, epuloideo, -a.
epulosis *n.* epulosis.
epulotic *adj.* epulótico, -ca.
equalization *n.* ecualización.
equate *v.* igualar.
equation *n.* ecuación.
equator *n.* ecuador.
equator of the cell ecuador de la célula.
equatorial *adj.* ecuatorial.
equiaxial *adj.* equiaxial, equiaxil.
equicaloric *adj.* equicalórico, -ca.
equilibration *n.* equilibración.
mandibular equilibration equilibración mandibular.
occlusal equilibration equilibración oclusal.
equilibrator *n.* equilibrador.
equilibrium *n.* equilibrio.
acid-base equilibrium equilibrio ácido-base, equilibrio acidobásico.
body equilibrium equilibrio corporal.
carbon equilibrium equilibrio del carbono.
colloid equilibrium equilibrio coloide.
Donnan equilibrium equilibrio de Donnan.
dynamic equilibrium equilibrio dinámico.
fluid equilibrium equilibrio hídrico.
genetic equilibrium equilibrio genético.
Gibbs-Donnan equilibrium equilibrio de Gibbs-Donnan.
Hardy-Weinberg equilibrium equilibrio de Hardy-Weinberg.
homeostatic equilibrium equilibrio homeostático.
linkage equilibrium equilibrio de enlace.
membrane equilibrium equilibrio de membrana.
nitrogen equilibrium equilibrio nitrogenado, equilibrio nitrógeno.
nitrogenous equilibrium equilibrio nitrogenado, equilibrio nitrógeno.
nutritive equilibrium equilibrio nutritivo.
physiologic equilibrium equilibrio fisiológico.
protein equilibrium equilibrio proteínico.
radioactive equilibrium equilibrio radiactivo.
random mating equilibrium equilibrio de acople arbitrario.

stable equilibrium equilibrio estable.
static equilibrium equilibrio estático.
unstable equilibrium equilibrio inestable.
equimolar *adj.* equimolar.
equimolecular *adj.* equimolecular.
equination *n.* equinación.
equinia *n.* equinia.
equinovalgus *adj.* equinovalgo, -ga, equinovalgus.
equinovarus *adj.* equinovaro, -ra, equinovarus.
equipment *n.* equipo[1].
equipotential *adj.* equipotencial.
equitoxic *adj.* equitóxico, -ca.
equivalence *n.* equivalencia.
equivalency *n.* equivalencia.
equivalent *n.* equivalente.
Eratyrus *n.* Eratyrus.
erectile *adj.* eréctil.
erection *n.* erección.
 penile erection erección peneana.
erector *adj.* erector.
eremacausis *n.* eremacausia.
erethism *n.* eretismo.
Erethmapodites *n.* Erethmapodites.
ergastoplasm *n.* ergastoplasma.
ergodynamograph *n.* ergodinamógrafo.
ergoesthesiograph *n.* ergoestesiógrafo.
ergogenic *adj.* ergogénico, -ca.
ergogram *n.* ergograma.
ergograph *n.* ergógrafo.
 Mosso's ergograph ergógrafo de Mosso.
ergographic *adj.* ergográfico, -ca.
ergometer *n.* ergómetro.
 bicycle ergometer ergómetro de bicicleta.
ergonomics *n.* ergonomía.
ergoplasm *n.* ergoplasma.
ergosome *n.* ergosoma.
ergostat *n.* ergóstato.
ergotherapy *n.* ergoterapia.
ergothioneine *n.* ergotioneína.
ergotism *n.* ergotismo.
ergotized *adj.* ergotizado, -da.
ergotoxicosis *n.* ergotoxicosis.
ergotropic *adj.* ergotrópico, -ca.
ergotropy *n.* ergotropía.
eriometry *n.* eriometría.
erisiphake *n.* erisífaco.
erisophake *n.* erisífaco, erisófaco.
erode *v.* erosionar.
erogastrocolia *n.* aerogastrocolia.
erogeneity *n.* erogeneidad.
erogenous *adj.* erógeno, -na.
eros *n.* eros.
erosion *n.* erosión.
 cervical erosion erosión cervical.
 dental erosion erosión dental, erosión dentaria.
 Dieulafoy's erosion erosión de Dieulafoy.
 recurrent corneal erosion erosión corneal recurrente.
erosive *adj.* erosivo, -va.
erotic *adj.* erótico, -ca.
eroticism *n.* eroticismo.
erotism *n.* erotismo.
 anal erotism erotismo anal.
 muscle erotism erotismo muscular.
 oral erotism erotismo oral.
 urethral erotism erotismo uretral.
erotization *n.* erotización.
erotize *v.* erotizar.
erotogenesis *n.* erotogénesis.
erotogenic *adj.* erotogénico, -ca, erotógeno, -na.
erotomania *n.* erotomanía.

erotomaniac *adj.* erotomaníaco, -ca, erotómano, -na.
erotophobia *n.* erotofobia.
erratic *adj.* errático, -ca.
error *n.* error.
 allowable error error permisible.
 laboratory error error de laboratorio.
 medical error error médico.
 medication error error de medicacion.
 random error error aleatorio.
 refractive error error de refracción.
 standard error error estándar.
 systematic error error sistemático.
 systemic error error sistemático.
 type I error error de tipo I.
 type II error error de tipo II.
erubescence *n.* erubescencia, rubefacción.
erubescent *adj.* erubescente.
eructation *n.* eructación.
eruption *n.* erupción.
 accelerated eruption erupción acelerada.
 acneiform drug eruption erupción farmacológica acneiforme.
 active eruption erupción activa.
 bullous eruption erupción ampollosa.
 clinical eruption erupción clínica.
 continuous eruption erupción continua.
 creeping eruption erupción reptante, erupción serpiginosa.
 delayed eruption erupción demorada, erupción retardada.
 drug eruption erupción farmacológica, erupción por drogas.
 eruption of the teeth erupción del diente, erupción dentaria.
 erythematous eruption erupción eritematosa.
 feigned eruption erupción fingida.
 fixed drug eruption erupción fija medicamentosa, erupción medicamentosa fija.
 fixed eruption erupción fija.
 iodine eruption erupción por yodo.
 Kaposi's varicelliform eruption erupción variceliforme de Kaposi.
 macular eruption erupción macular, erupción maculosa.
 maculopapular eruption erupción maculopapulosa.
 medicinal eruption erupción medicamentosa, erupción medicinal.
 passive eruption erupción pasiva.
 petechial eruption erupción petequial.
 polymorphic light eruption erupción luminosa polimorfa.
 polymorphous eruption erupción polimorfa.
 polymorphous light eruption erupción polimorfa lumínica.
 pustular eruption erupción pustulosa.
 seabather's eruption erupción de los bañistas.
 serum eruption erupción por suero, erupción sérica.
 surgical eruption erupción quirúrgica.
 tooth eruption erupción del diente, erupción dentaria.
 vesicobullous eruption erupción vesiculosa.
eruptive *adj.* eruptivo, -va.
erysipelas *n.* erisipela.
 ambulant erysipelas erisipela ambulante.
 coast erysipelas erisipela de la costa.
 erysipelas grave internum erisipela grave interna.
 erysipelas internum erisipela interna.
 erysipelas migrans erisipela migratoria.

 erysipelas perstans erisipela perstans, erisipela perstans facial.
 erysipelas perstans faciei erisipela perstans, erisipela perstans facial.
 erysipelas pustulosum erisipela pustulosa.
 erysipelas verrucosum erisipela verrugosa.
 erysipeloid erysipelas erisipela crónica.
 facial erysipelas erisipela facial.
 gangrenous erysipelas erisipela gangrenosa.
 malignant erysipelas erisipela maligna.
 necrotizing erysipelas erisipela necrosante.
 phlegmonous erysipelas erisipela flemonosa.
 recurrent erysipelas erisipela recurrente.
 surgical erysipelas erisipela quirúrgica.
 wandering erysipelas erisipela errante.
 white erysipelas erisipela blanca, erisipela linfática.
 zoonotic erysipelas erisipela zoonótica.
erysipelatous *adj.* erisipelatoso, -sa.
erysipeloid *n.* erisipeloide.
erythema *n.* eritema.
 acrodynic erythema eritema acrodínico.
 Bazin's indurative erythema eritema indurado de Bazin.
 cold erythema eritema del frío.
 diaper erythema eritema amoniacal.
 epidemic arthritic erythema eritema epidémico artrítico.
 epidemic erythema eritema epidémico.
 erythema ab igne eritema ab igne.
 erythema annulare eritema anular.
 erythema annulare centrifugum eritema anular centrífugo.
 erythema annulare rheumaticum eritema anular reumático.
 erythema bullosum eritema ampollar.
 erythema caloricum eritema calórico.
 erythema chromicum melanodermicum eritema chromicum melanodermicum.
 erythema chronicum migrans eritema crónico migratorio, eritema migratorio crónico.
 erythema circinatum eritema circinado.
 erythema dyschromicum perstans eritema discrómico persistente, eritema dyschromicum perstans.
 erythema ecarlatinoides eritema escarlatiniforme, eritema escarlatinoide.
 erythema elevatum diutinum eritema elevado, eritema elevatum, eritema elevatum diutinum.
 erythema exfoliativa eritema exfoliativo.
 erythema figuratum eritema figuratum.
 erythema figuratum perstans eritema figurado perstans, eritema figuratum perstans.
 erythema fugax eritema fugaz.
 erythema induratum eritema indurado.
 erythema infectiosum eritema infeccioso.
 erythema intertrigo eritema intertrigo.
 erythema iris eritema en iris, eritema iris.
 erythema keratodes eritema queratoide.
 erythema marginatum eritema marginado reumático.
 erythema marginatum rheumaticum eritema marginado reumático.
 erythema migrans eritema migratorio.
 erythema migrans linguae eritema migratorio de la lengua.
 erythema multiforme eritema multiforme.
 erythema multiforme bullosum eritema multiforme ampollar.
 erythema multiforme exudativum eritema multiforme exudativo.
 erythema multiforme major eritema multiforme mayor.

erythema multiforme minor eritema multiforme menor.

erythema necroticans eritema necroticans.

erythema neonatorum eritema del recién nacido, eritema neonatal.

erythema neonatorum toxicum eritema neonatal tóxico.

erythema nodosum eritema nodoso, eritema nudoso.

erythema nodosum leprosum eritema leproso nudoso, eritema nudoso leproso.

erythema nodosum migrans eritema nudoso migratorio.

erythema nodosum syphiliticum eritema nudoso sifilítico.

erythema palmare eritema palmar.

erythema palmare hereditarium eritema palmar hereditario.

erythema papulatum eritema papuloso.

erythema papulosum eritema papuloso.

erythema paratrimma eritema paratrimma.

erythema pernio eritema pernio.

erythema perstans eritema persistente.

erythema simplex eritema simple, eritema simplex.

erythema solare eritema solar.

erythema streptogenes eritema estreptógeno.

erythema toxicum eritema tóxico, eritema venenatum.

erythema toxicum neonatorum eritema tóxico del neonato, eritema tóxico del recién nacido.

erythema toxicum of the newborn eritema tóxico del neonato, eritema tóxico del recién nacido.

erythema traumaticum eritema traumático.

erythema tuberculatum eritema tuberculatum.

figurate erythema eritema figuratum.

generalized erythema eritema generalizado.

gluteal erythema eritema glúteo.

gyrate erythema eritema gyratum, eritema gyratum perstans.

hemorrhagic exudative erythema eritema exudativo hemorrágico.

Jacquet's erythema eritema de Jacquet.

macular erythema eritema macular.

Milian's erythema eritema de Milian.

napkin erythema eritema por pañal.

necrolytic migratory erythema eritema migratorio necrolítico, eritema necrolítico migratorio.

palmar erythema eritema palmar.

polymorphe erythema eritema polimorfo.

scalatiniform erythema eritema escarlatiniforme, eritema escarlatinoide.

symptomatic erythema eritema sintomático.

toxic erythema eritema tóxico, eritema venenatum.

erythematogenic *adj.* eritematogénico, -ca.

erythematopultaceous *adj.* eritematopultáceo, -a.

erythematous *adj.* eritematoso, -sa.

erythematovesicular *adj.* eritematovesicular.

erythemogenic *adj.* eritemógeno, -na.

erythophose *n.* eritrofosia.

erythralgia *n.* eritralgia.

erythrasma *n.* eritrasma.

erythredema *n.* eritredema, eritroedema.

erythrederma *n.* eritredermia.

erythremia *n.* eritremia.

altitude erythremia eritremia de altura.

erythremomelalgia *n.* eritremomelalgia.

erythrism *n.* eritrismo.

erythristic *adj.* eritrístico, -ca.

erythroblast *n.* eritroblasto, hemonormoblasto.

acidophilic erythroblast eritroblasto acidófilo.

basophilic erythroblast eritroblasto basófilo.

definitive erythroblast eritroblasto definitivo.

early erythroblast eritroblasto temprano.

eosinophilic erythroblast eritroblasto eosinófilo.

intermediate erythroblast eritroblasto intermedio.

late erythroblast eritroblasto tardío.

orthochromatic erythroblast eritroblasto ortocromático.

oxyphilic erythroblast eritroblasto oxífilo.

polychromatic erythroblast eritroblasto policromático.

primitive erythroblast eritroblasto primitivo.

erythroblastemia *n.* eritroblastemia.

erythroblastic *adj.* eritroblástico, -ca.

erythroblastoma *n.* eritroblastoma.

erythroblastomatosis *n.* eristroblastomatosis.

erythroblastopenia *n.* eritroblastopenia.

erythroblastosis *n.* eritroblastosis.

erythroblastosis fetalis eritroblastosis fetal.

erythroblastosis neonatorum eritroblastosis neonatal.

erythrocatalysis *n.* eritrocatálisis.

erythrochromia *n.* eritrocromía.

erythroclasis *n.* eritroclasia, eritroclasis.

erythroclast *n.* eritroclasto.

erythroclastic *adj.* eritroclástico, -ca.

erythrocyanosis *n.* eritrocianosis.

erythrocytapheresis *n.* eritrocitaféresis.

erythrocyte *n.* eritrocito.

achromic erythrocyte eritrocito acrómico.

basophilic erythrocyte eritrocito básófilo.

crenated erythrocyte eritrocito crenado.

hypochromic erythrocyte eritrocito hipocrómico.

immature erythrocyte eritrocito inmaduro.

Mexican hat erythrocyte eritrocito en sombrero mexicano.

normochromic erythrocyte eritrocito normocrómico.

nucleated erythrocyte eritrocito nucleado.

orthochromatic erythrocyte eritrocito ortocromático.

polychromatic erythrocyte eritrocito policromático, eritrocito policromatofílico, eritrocito policromatófilo.

polychromatophilic erythrocyte eritrocito policromático, eritrocito policromatofílico, eritrocito policromatófilo.

sickled erythrocyte eritrocito falciforme.

stippled erythrocyte critocito básófilo.

target erythrocyte eritrocito en diana.

erythrocythemia *n.* eritrocitemia.

erythrocytic *adj.* eritrocitario, -ria, eritrocítico, -ca.

erythrocytoblast *n.* eritrocitoblasto.

erythrocytolisis *n.* eritrocitólisis.

erythrocytolysin *n.* eritrocitolisina.

erythrocytometer *n.* eritrocitómetro.

erythrocytopenia *n.* eritrocitopenia.

erythrocytophagous *adj.* eritrocitófago, -ga.

erythrocytophagy *n.* eritrocitofagia.

erythrocytopoiesis *n.* eritrocitopoyesis.

erythrocytorrhexis *n.* eritrocitorrexia, eritrocitorrexis.

erythrocytoschisis *n.* eritrocitosquisis.

erythrocytosis *n.* eritrocitosis.

leukemic erythrocytosis eritrocitosis leucémica.

erythrocyturia *n.* eritrocituria.

erythrodegenerative *adj.* eritrodegenerativo, -va.

erythroderma *n.* eritrodermia.

bullous congenital ichthyosiform erythroderma eritrodermia ictiosiforme congénito bulloso.

congenital ichthyosiform erythroderma eritrodermia ictiosiforme, eritrodermia ictiosiforme congénito.

erythroderma desquamativum eritrodermia descamativa.

erythroderma psoriaticum eritrodermia psoriásica.

exfoliative erythroderma eritrodermia exfoliativa.

ichthyosiform erythroderma eritrodermia ictiosiforme, eritrodermia ictiosiforme congénito.

lymphomatous erythroderma eritrodermia linfomatoso.

non-bullous congenital ichthyosiform erythroderma eritrodermia ictiosiforme congénito no bulloso.

Sézary erythroderma eritrodermia de Sézary.

erythrodermatitis *n.* eritrodermatitis, eritrodermitis.

erythrodontia *n.* eritrodoncia.

erythrogenesis *n.* eritrogénesis, eritrogenia.

erythrogenesis imperfecta eritrogénesis imperfecta.

erythrogenic *adj.* eritrogénico, -ca, eritrógeno, -na.

erythrogonium *n.* eritrogonio.

erythroid *adj.* eritroide.

erythrokeratoderma *n.* eritroqueratodermia.

erythrokeratoderma variabilis eritroqueratodermia variable.

erythrokinetics *n.* eritrocinética.

erythrolabe *n.* eritrolabo.

erythroleukemia *n.* eritroleucemia.

erythroleukoblastosis *n.* eritroleucoblastosis.

erythroleukosis *n.* eritroleucosis.

erythroleukothrombocythemia *n.* eritroleucotrombocitemia.

erythrolysis *n.* eritrólisis.

erythromelalgia *n.* eritromelalgia.

erythromelalgia of the head eritromelalgia de la cabeza.

erythromelia *n.* eritromelia.

erythrometer *n.* eritrómetro.

erythron *n.* eritrón.

erythroneocytosis *n.* eritroneocitosis.

erythronoclastic *adj.* eritronoclástico, -ca.

erythroparasite *n.* eritroparásito.

erythropenia *n.* eritropenia.

erythrophage *n.* eritrófago.

erythrophagia *n.* eritrofagia.

erythrophagocyte *n.* eritrofagocito.

erythrophagocytosis *n.* eritrofagocitosis.

erythropheresis *n.* eritroféresis.

erythrophil *n.* eritrófilo.

erythrophilic *adj.* eritrofílico, -ca.

erythrophilous *adj.* eritrófilo, -la.

erythrophobic *adj.* eritrófobo, -ba.

erythrophore *n.* eritróforo.

erythrophyll *n.* eritrófilo3.

erythropia *n.* eritropía.

erythroplakia *n.* eritroplaquia.

speckled erythroplakia eritroplaquia moteada.

erythroplasia *n.* eritroplasia.
erythroplasia of Queyrat eritroplasia de Queyrat.
Zoon's erythroplasia eritroplasia de Zoon.
erythroplastid *n.* eritroplástide.
erythropoiesis *n.* eritropoyesis.
erythropoietic *adj.* eritropoyético, -ca.
erythroprosopalgia *n.* eritroprosopalgia.
erythropsia *n.* eritropía, eritropsia.
erythropyknosis *n.* eritropicnosis.
erythrorrhexis *n.* eritrorrexia, eritrorrexis.
érythrose *n.* eritrosa, eritrosis.
érythrose peribuccale pigmentaire eritrosis peribucal pigmentaria.
érythrose péribuccale pigmentaire of Brocq eritrosa peribucal pigmentaria de Brocq.
erythrosedimentation *n.* eritrosedimentación.
erythrosis *n.* eritrosa, eritrosis.
erythrosis pigmentata faciei eritrosis peribucal pigmentaria, eritrosis pigmentaria facial.
erythrostasis *n.* eritrostasis.
erythrothioneine *n.* eritrotioneína.
erythruria *n.* eritruria.
erytroblastotic *adj.* eritroblastósico, -ca.
escape *n.* escape.
aldosterone escape escape de aldosterona.
nodal escape escape nodal.
vagal escape escape vagal.
ventricular escape escape ventricular.
eschar *n.* escara[1].
escharotic *adj.* escarótico, -ca.
escharotomy *n.* escarotomía.
Escherichia *n.* Escherichia.
eschrolalia *n.* escrolalia.
escopophilia *n.* escoptofilia.
escutcheon *n.* blasón.
eseptate *adj.* eseptado, -da.
esocataphoria *n.* esocataforia.
esodeviaton *n.* esodesviación.
esodic *adj.* esódico, -ca.
esoethmoiditis *n.* esoetmoiditis.
esophagalgia *n.* esofagalgia.
esophageal *adj.* esofágico, -ca.
esophagectasia *n.* esofagectasia, esofagectasis, esofagoectasia.
esophagectasis *n.* esofagectasia, esofagectasis, esofagoectasia.
esophagectomy *n.* esofagectomía, esofagoectomía.
subtotal esophagectomy esofagectomía subtotal.
total esophagectomy esofagectomía total.
esophagism *n.* esofagismo.
esophagitis *n.* esofagitis.
caustic esophagitis esofagitis cáustica.
chronic peptic esophagitis esofagitis péptica crónica.
esophagitis dissecans superficialis esofagitis disecante superficial.
reflux esophagitis esofagitis de reflujo, esofagitis por reflujo.
esophagocardioplasty *n.* esofagocardioplastia.
esophagocele *n.* esofagocele.
esophagocologastrostomy *n.* esofagocologastrostomía.
esophagocoloplasty *n.* esofagocoloplastia.
esophagoduodenostomy *n.* esofagoduodenostomía.
esophagodynia *n.* esofagodinia.
esophagoenterostomy *n.* esofagoenterostomía.
esophagofiberscope *n.* esofagofibroscopio.
esophagogastrectomy *n.* esofagogastrectomía.

esophagogastric *adj.* esofagogástrico, -ca.
esophagogastroanastomosis *n.* esofagogastroanastomosis.
esophagogastrojejunostomy *n.* esofagogastroyeyunostomía.
esophagogastromyotomy *n.* esofagogastromiotomía.
esophagogastroplasty *n.* esofagogastroplastia.
esophagogastroscopy *n.* esofagogastroscopia.
esophagogastrostomy *n.* esofagogastrostomía.
esophagogram *n.* esofagograma.
esophagography *n.* esofagografía.
esophagojejunogastrostomosis *n.* esofagoyeyunogastrostomosis.
esophagojejunogastrostomy *n.* esofagoyeyunogastrostomía.
esophagojejunoplasty *n.* esofagoyeyunoplastia.
esophagojejunostomy *n.* esofagoyeyunostomía.
esophagolaryngectomy *n.* esofagolaringectomia.
esophagology *n.* esofagología.
esophagomalacia *n.* esofagomalacia.
esophagomycosis *n.* esofagomicosis.
esophagomyotomy *n.* esofagomiotomía.
esophagopharynx *n.* esofagofaringe.
esophagoplasty *n.* esofagoplastia.
esophagoplication *n.* esofagoplicación, esofagoplicatura.
esophagoptosis *n.* esofagoptosis.
esophagoscope *n.* esofagoscopio.
esophagoscopy *n.* esofagoscopia.
esophagospasm *n.* esofagoespasmo, esofagospasmo.
esophagostenosis *n.* esofagoestenosis, esofagostenosis.
esophagostoma *n.* esofagostoma.
esophagostomiasis *n.* esofagostomiasis.
esophagostomy *n.* esofagostomía.
esophagotome *n.* esofagótomo.
esophagotomy *n.* esofagotomía.
esophagotracheal *adj.* esofagotraqueal.
esophagram *n.* esofagograma.
esophagus *n.* esófago.
corkscrew esophagus esófago en sacacorchos.
nutcracker esophagus esófago cascanueces, esófago en cascanueces.
esophoria *n.* esoforia.
basic esophoria esoforia básica.
consecutive esophoria esoforia consecutiva.
mixed esophoria esoforia mixta.
non-accommodative esophoria esoforia no acomodativa.
non-refractive accommodative esophoria esoforia acomodativa no refractiva.
refractive accommodative esophoria esoforia acomodativa refractiva.
esophoric *adj.* esofórico, -ca.
esotropia *n.* esotropía.
esotropic *adj.* esotrópico, -ca.
esquillectomy *n.* esquilectomía.
esquinancea *n.* esquinancia, esquinencia.
essence *n.* esencia.
essential *adj.* esencial.
ester *n.* éster.
esthesia *n.* estesia.
esthesic *adj.* estésico, -ca.
esthesiodic *adj.* estesiódico, -ca.
esthesiogenesis *n.* estesiogénesis.
esthesiogenic *adj.* estesiogénico, -ca, estesiógeno, -na.

esthesiography *n.* estesiografía.
esthesiometer *n.* estesiómetro.
esthesiometry *n.* estesiometría, hafemetría.
esthesioneuroblastoma *n.* estesioneuroblastoma.
olfactory esthesioneuroblastoma estesioneuroblastoma olfatorio.
esthesioneurocytoma *n.* estesioneurocitoma.
esthesiophysiology *n.* estesiofisiología.
esthesioscopy *n.* estesioscopia.
esthesodic *adj.* estesiódico, -ca, estesódico, -ca.
estimate *n.* estimación.
biased estimate estimación sesgada.
consistent estimate estimación consistente.
interval estimate estimación en un intervalo.
point estimate estimación puntual.
product-limit estimate estimación del límite del producto.
unbiased estimate estimación no sesgada.
estivation *n.* estivación.
estrin *n.* estrina.
estriol *n.* estriol.
estrogen *n.* estrógeno.
estrogenic *adj.* estrogénico, -ca.
estrophilin *n.* estrofilina.
estruation *n.* estruación.
estrus *n.* oestro.
ethanol *n.* etanol.
ethanolism *n.* etanolismo.
ether *n.* éter.
ethereal *adj.* etéreo, -a.
etherification *n.* eterificación.
etherism *n.* eterismo.
etherization *n.* eterización.
etheromania *n.* eteromanía.
etherometer *n.* eterómetro.
ethics *n.* ética.
agreement ethics ética de consenso.
biomedical ethics ética biomédica.
descriptive ethics ética descriptiva.
empiric ethics ética empírica.
medical ethics ética médica.
ethmocarditis *n.* etmocarditis.
ethmocephalia *n.* etmocefalia.
ethmocephalus *n.* etmocéfalo.
ethmocranial *adj.* etmocraneal.
ethmofrontal *adj.* etmofrontal.
ethmoid *adj.* etmoide, etmoideo, -a.
ethmoid bone etmoides.
ethmoidal *adj.* etmoidal.
ethmoidale *adj.* etmoidal.
ethmoidectomy *n.* etmoidectomía.
ethmoiditis *n.* etmoiditis.
ethmoidotomy *n.* etmoidotomía.
ethmolacrimal *adj.* etmolagrimal.
ethmomaxillary *adj.* etmomaxilar.
ethmonasal *adj.* etmonasal.
ethmopalatal *adj.* etmopalatino, -na.
ethmosphenoid *adj.* etmoesfenoidal, etmoesfenoideo, -a.
ethmoturbinal *adj.* etmoturbinal.
ethmovomerine *adj.* etmovomeriano, -na, etmovomerino, -na.
ethnobiology *n.* etnobiología.
ethnology *n.* etnología.
ethological *adj.* etológico, -ca.
ethologist *n.* etólogo, -ga.
ethology *n.* etología.
ethopharmacology *n.* etofarmacología.
ethylation *n.* etilación.
ethylism *n.* etilismo.
etiolated *adj.* etiolado, -da.
etiolation *n.* etiolación.
etiologic *adj.* etiológico, -ca.
etiological *adj.* etiológico, -ca.

etiology *n.* etiología.
  etiology and pathogenesis etiopatogenia.
etiopathic *adj.* etiopático, -ca.
etiopathogenesis *n.* etiopatogenia.
etiotropic *adj.* etiotrópico, -ca.
etnography *n.* etnografía.
euadrenocorticism *n.* euadrenocorticismo.
eubacterium *n.* eubacteria.
Eubacterium *n.* Eubacterium.
eubiotics *n.* eubiótica.
eucapnia *n.* eucapnia.
eucarion *n.* eucarion, eucarión.
eucaryosis *n.* eucariosis.
eucaryote *n.* eucariota.
eucaryotic *adj.* eucariótico, -ca.
euchlorhydria *n.* euclorhidria.
eucholia *n.* eucolia.
euchromatic *adj.* eucromático, -ca.
euchromatin *n.* eucromatina.
euchromatopsy *n.* eucromatopsia.
euchylia *n.* euquilia.
eucorticalism *n.* eucorticalismo.
eudiaphoresis *n.* eudiaforesis.
eudiemorrhysis *n.* eudiemorrisis.
eudiometer *n.* eudiómetro.
eudipsia *n.* eudipsia.
euergasis *n.* euergasia.
euesthesia *n.* Euestesia.
eugamy *n.* eugamia.
eugenetics *n.* eugenesia, eugenética.
eugenics *n.* eugenesia, eugénesis, eugenia.
  negative eugenics eugenesia negativa.
  positive eugenics eugenesia positiva.
euglycemia *n.* euglucemia.
euglycemic *adj.* euglucémico, -ca.
eugnathia *n.* eugnatia.
eugnathic *adj.* eugnático, -ca.
eugnosia *n.* eugnosia.
eugnostic *adj.* eugnóstico, -ca.
eugonic *adj.* eugónico, -ca.
euhydratation *n.* euhidratación.
eukarion *n.* eucarion, eucarión.
eukaryocyte *adj.* eucariocito, -ta.
eukaryosis *n.* eucariosis.
eukaryote *n.* eucariota.
eukaryotic *adj.* eucariótico, -ca.
eukinesia *n.* eucinesia.
eukinetic *adj.* eucinético, -ca.
eumastia *n.* eumastia.
eumelanosome *n.* eumelanosoma.
eumenorrhea *n.* eumenorrea.
eumetria *n.* eumetría.
eumorphics *n.* eumorfia.
eumorphism *n.* eumorfismo.
eumycetoma *n.* eumicetoma.
eunuch *n.* eunuco.
eunuchism *n.* eunuquismo.
  pituitary eunuchism eunuquismo hipofisario.
eunuchoid *n.* eunucoide.
eunuchoidism *n.* eunucoidismo.
  female eunuchoidism eunucoidismo femenino.
  hypergonadotropic eunuchoidism eunucoidismo hipergonadotrópico.
  hypogonadotropic eunuchoidism eunucoidismo hipogonadotrópico.
euosmia *n.* euosmia.
eupancreatism *n.* eupancreatismo.
eupepsia *n.* eupepsia.
eupepsy *n.* eupepsia.
eupeptic *adj.* eupéptico, -ca.
euperistalsis *n.* euperistalsis.
euphenic *adj.* eufénico, -ca.
euphenics *n.* eufenia.

euphoretic *adj.* euforético, -ca.
euphoria *n.* euforia.
euphoriant *adj.* euforizante.
euphoric *adj.* eufórico, -ca.
euphorigenic *adj.* euforígeno, -na.
eupirexia *n.* eupirexia.
euplasia *n.* euplasia.
euplastic *adj.* euplásico, -ca.
euploid *adj.* euploide.
euploidy *n.* euploidía.
eupnea *n.* eupnea.
eupneic *adj.* eupneico, -ca.
eupractic *adj.* eupráctico, -ca, eupráxico, -ca.
eupraxia *n.* eupraxia.
eupraxic *adj.* eupráctico, -ca, eupráxico, -ca.
eupyrene *n.* eupireno.
eurhythmia *n.* eurritmia.
eurycranial *adj.* euricraneal.
eurygnathic *adj.* eurignático, -ca.
eurygnathism *n.* eurignatismo.
eurygnathous *adj.* eurignato, -ta.
euryon *n.* eurion.
euryopia *n.* euriopía.
euryphotic *adj.* eurifótico, -ca.
eurysomatic *adj.* eurisomático, -ca.
eurythermal *adj.* euritermo, -ma.
eurythermic *adj.* euritérmico, -ca.
eusitia *n.* eusitia.
eusplanchnia *n.* eusplacnia.
eustachitis *n.* eustaquitis.
eusthenia *n.* eustenia.
eusthenuria *n.* eustenuria.
eustress *n.* euestrés.
eusystole *n.* eusístole, eusistolia.
eusystolic *adj.* eusistólico, ca.
eutectic *adj.* eutéctico, -ca.
eutelegenesis *n.* eutelegenesia, eutelegénesis.
eutenothenics *n.* eugenotenia.
euthanasia *n.* eutanasia.
  active euthanasia eutanasia activa.
  involuntary euthanasia eutanasia involuntaria.
  legal euthanasia eutanasia legal.
  neonatal euthanasia eutanasia neonatal.
  passive euthanasia eutanasia pasiva.
  voluntary euthanasia eutanasia voluntaria.
eutherapeutic *adj.* euterapéutico, -ca.
euthermic *adj.* eutérmico, -ca.
euthymia *n.* eutimia.
euthymic *adj.* eutímico, -ca.
euthymism *n.* eutimismo.
euthyphoria *n.* eutiforia.
euthyroid *adj.* eutiroideo, -a.
euthyroidism *n.* eutireosis, eutiroidismo.
eutocia *n.* eutocia.
eutonic *adj.* eutónico, -ca.
eutopic *adj.* eutópico, -ca.
eutrichosis *n.* eutricosis.
eutrophia *n.* eutrofia.
eutrophic *adj.* eutrófico, -ca.
eutrophication *n.* eutroficación.
euvolia *n.* euvolia.
evacuate *v.* evacuar.
evacuation *n.* evacuación.
evacuator *n.* evacuador.
  Ellik evacuator evacuador de Ellik.
evagination *n.* evaginación.
evaluation *n.* evaluación.
  cognitive evaluation evaluación cognitiva.
  neuropsychological evaluation evaluación neuropsicológica.
  prevocational evaluation evaluación prelaboral.
evanescent *adj.* evanescente.
evaporation *n.* evaporación.
evasion *n.* evasión.

eventration *n.* eventración.
  eventration of the diaphragm eventración, eventración del diafragma.
  umbilical eventration eventración umbilical.
eversion *n.* eversión.
eviration *n.* eviración.
evisceration *n.* evisceración.
  anterior pelvic evisceration evisceración pélvica anterior.
  orbital evisceration evisceración orbitaria.
  pelvic evisceration evisceración pélvica.
  posterior pelvic evisceration evisceración pélvica posterior.
  total pelvic evisceration evisceración pélvica total.
evitative *adj.* evitativo, -va.
evocation *n.* evocación.
evocator *n.* evocador.
evolution *n.* evolución.
  bathmic evolution evolución bátmica.
  biological evolution evolución biológica.
  convergent evolution evolución convergente.
  Denman's spontaneous evolution evolución espontánea de Denman.
  determinant evolution evolución determinante.
  emergent evolution evolución emergente.
  evolution of infarction evolución del infarto.
  organic evolution evolución orgánica.
  orthogenic evolution evolución ortogénica.
  parallel evolution evolución paralela.
  saltatory evolution evolución saltatoria.
  spontaneous evolution evolución espontánea.
evolutive *adj.* evolutivo, -va.
evulsio *n.* evulsión.
evulsion *n.* evulsión.
exacerbation *n.* exacerbación.
exairesis *n.* exairesis, exéresis.
exaltation *n.* exaltación.
examination *n.* examen.
  bacteriologic sputum examination examen bacteriológico de esputo.
  breast examination examen de mama.
  cytologic examination examen citológico.
  cytologic sputum examination examen citológico del esputo.
  double contrast examination examen con doble contraste.
  fresh examination examen directo.
  mental examination examen mental.
  mental status examination examen del estado mental.
  mini mental state examination mini examen del estado mental.
  neurologic examination examen neurológico.
  Papanicolaou examination examen de Papanicolaou.
  physical examination examen físico.
  postmortem examination examen post mortem.
exangia *n.* exangia.
exania *n.* exania.
exanimation *n.* exanimación.
exanthema *n.* exantema.
  exanthema arthrosia exantema arthrosia.
  exanthema subitum exantema súbito.
exanthematous *adj.* exantemático, -ca, exantematoso, -sa.
exanthesis *n.* exantesis.
exanthrope *adj.* exántropo, -pa.
exanthropic *adj.* exantrópico, -ca.
exarteritis *n.* exarteritis.

exarticulation *n.* exarticulación.
excalation *n.* excalación.
excarnation *n.* excarnación.
excavatio *n.* excavación.
excavation *n.* excavación.
 atrophic excavation excavación atrófica.
 dental excavation excavación dental.
 glaucomatous excavation excavación glaucomatosa.
excavator *n.* excavador.
 dental excavator excavador dental.
 hoe excavator excavador en azada.
 spoon excavator excavador en cucharilla.
excementosis *n.* excementosis.
excentric *adj.* excéntrico, -ca.
excerebration *n.* excerebración.
excernent *adj.* excernente.
excess *n.* exceso.
 antibody excess exceso de anticuerpos.
 antigen excess exceso de antígeno.
 base excess exceso de base.
 convergence excess exceso de convergencia.
 negative base excess exceso de base negativo.
exchange *n.* intercambio.
 gaseous exchange intercambio gaseoso.
 impaired gas exchange intercambio gaseoso alterado.
 sister chromatid exchange intercambio de cromátides hermanas.
exchanger *n.* cambiador.
 heat exchanger cambiador de calor.
 ionic exchanger intercambiador iónico.
excipient *n.* excipiente.
excise *v.* escindir, excindir, extirpar.
excision *n.* escisión², excisión, rescisión.
 wound excision desbridamiento.
excitability *n.* excitabilidad.
 nerve excitability excitabilidad nerviosa.
 supernormal excitability excitabilidad supranormal.
 supranormal excitability excitabilidad supranormal.
excitable *adj.* excitable.
excitant *adj.* excitante.
excitation *n.* excitación¹.
 anomalous atrioventricular excitation excitación auriculoventricular anómala.
 direct excitation excitación directa.
 indirect excitation excitación indirecta.
 proton excitation excitación protónica.
excitatory *adj.* excitativo, -va.
excitement *n.* excitación².
 catatonic excitement excitación catatónica.
 maniac excitement excitación maníaca.
excitoanabolic *adj.* excitoanabólico, -ca.
excitocatabolic *adj.* excitocatabólico, -ca.
excitoglandular *adj.* excitoglandular.
excitometabolic *adj.* excitometabólico, -ca.
excitomotor *adj.* excitomotor, -ra.
excitomotory *adj.* excitomotor, -ra.
excitomuscular *adj.* excitomuscular.
excitonutrient *adj.* excitonutritivo, -va.
excitosecretory *adj.* excitosecretor, -ra, excitosecretorio, -ria.
excitovascular *adj.* excitovascular.
exclusion *n.* exclusión.
 allelic exclusion exclusión alélica.
 competitive exclusion exclusión competitiva.
 Devine exclusion exclusión de Devine.
 exclusion of the pupil exclusión de la pupila.
excochleation *n.* excocleación.
excoriation *n.* excoriación.
 neurotic excoriation excoriación neurótica.
excrement *n.* excremento.

excrementitious *adj.* excrementicio, -cia.
excrescence *n.* excrecencia.
 cauliflower excrescence excrecencia en coliflor.
 fungating excrescence excrecencia fungosa.
 fungous excrescence excrecencia fungosa.
 skin tag excrescence excrecencia cutánea.
excreta *n.* excremento.
excretion *n.* excreción.
 pseudouridine excretion excreción de seudouridina.
 radioactive iodine excretion excreción de yodo radiactivo.
excretory *adj.* excretor, -ra.
excursion *n.* excursión.
 lateral excursion excursión lateral.
 protrusive excursion excursión protrusiva.
 retrusive excursion excursión retrusiva.
excycloduction *n.* excicloducción.
excyclophoria *n.* excicloforia.
excyclotropia *n.* exciclotropía.
excyclovergence *n.* exciclovergencia.
excystation *n.* exquistación, exquistamiento.
exemia *n.* exemia.
exencephalia *n.* exencefalia.
exencephalic *adj.* exencefálico, -ca.
exencephalocele *n.* exencefalocele.
exencephalus *n.* exencéfalo.
exencephaly *n.* exencefalia.
exenteration *n.* evisceración, exenteración.
exenteritis *n.* exenteritis.
exercise *n.* ejercicio.
 active assisted exercise ejercicio activo asistido.
 active exercise ejercicio activo.
 active resistance exercise ejercicio de resistencia activa.
 active resistive exercise ejercicio activo contra resistencia.
 aerobic exercise ejercicio aeróbico.
 anaerobic exercise ejercicio anaeróbico.
 Buerger postural exercise ejercicio postural de Buerger.
 chopping exercise ejercicio de leñador.
 Codman's exercise ejercicio de Codman.
 corrective exercise ejercicio correctivo.
 daily adjusted progressive resistance exercise ejercicio de resistencia progresiva de ajuste diario.
 deep breathing and coughing exercise ejercicio de respiración profunda y de tos.
 free exercise ejercicio libre.
 Frenkel exercise ejercicio de Frenkel.
 graduated resistance exercise ejercicio de resistencia graduada.
 isokinetic exercise ejercicio isocinético.
 isometric exercise ejercicio isométrico.
 isotonic exercise ejercicio isotónico.
 Kegel's exercise ejercicio de Kegel.
 muscle-setting exercise ejercicio de preparación muscular, ejercicio estático.
 passive exercise ejercicio pasivo.
 physical exercise ejercicio físico.
 postmastectomy exercise ejercicio posmastectomía.
 progressive assistive exercise ejercicio asistido progresivo.
 progressive resistance exercise ejercicio con resistencia progresiva.
 pubococcygeous exercise ejercicio pubococcígeo.
 range of motion exercise ejercicio de arco de movilidad.
 therapeutic exercise ejercicio terapéutico.
 underwater exercise ejercicio bajo el agua.

exeresis *n.* exairesis, exéresis.
exergic *adj.* exérgico, -ca.
exergonic *adj.* exergónico, -ca.
exesion *n.* exesión.
exfoliation *n.* exfoliación.
 exfoliation areata linguae exfoliación areata de la lengua.
 exfoliation of the lens exfoliación del cristalino.
 lamellar exfoliation of the newborn exfoliación laminar del neonato, exfoliación laminar del recién nacido.
exfoliative *adj.* exfoliativo, -va.
exhalation *n.* exhalación.
exhausted *adj.* exhausto, -ta.
exhaustion *n.* agotamiento, extenuación.
 anhidrotic heat exhaustion agotamiento por calor anhidrótico, agotamiento por calor del tipo II.
 combat exhaustion agotamiento de combate.
 heat exhaustion agotamiento por calor.
 heat exhaustion type II agotamiento por calor anhidrótico, agotamiento por calor del tipo II.
 nervous exhaustion agotamiento nervioso.
exhibitionism *n.* exhibicionismo.
exhibitionist *n.* exhibicionista.
exocardia *n.* exocardia.
exocardial *adj.* exocardíaco, -ca.
exocataphoria *n.* exocataforia.
exocele *n.* exocele.
exocellular *adj.* exocelular.
exocervix *n.* exocérvix.
exochorion *n.* exocorion.
exocoelom *n.* exoceloma.
exocoeloma *n.* exoceloma.
exocolitis *n.* exocolitis.
exocrin *adj.* exocrino, -na.
exocrine *adj.* exocrino, -na.
exocrinology *n.* exocrinología.
exocytosis *n.* exocitosis.
exodontia *n.* exodoncia².
exodontics *n.* exodoncia¹.
exodontist *n.* exodontista.
exoergic *adj.* exérgico, -ca.
exoerythrocytic *adj.* exoeritrocítico, -ca.
exogamy *n.* exogamia.
exogastric *adj.* exogástrico, -ca.
exogastritis *n.* exogastritis.
exogenic *adj.* exógeno, -na.
exogenous *adj.* exógeno, -na.
exognathia *n.* exognatia.
exognathion *n.* exognatio, exognation.
exohemophylaxis *n.* exohemofilaxia.
exolever *n.* exopalanca.
exometer *n.* exómetro.
exomphalos *n.* exónfalo, exonfalocele.
exon *n.* exón.
exopathic *adj.* exopático, -ca.
exopathy *n.* exopatía.
exophoria *n.* exoforia.
exophoric *adj.* exofórico, -ca.
exophtalmus *n.* exoftalmos.
exophthalmia *n.* exoftalmía.
 endocrine exophthalmia exoftalmía endocrina.
 malignant exophthalmia exoftalmía maligna.
 pulsating exophthalmia exoftalmía pulsátil.
exophthalmic *adj.* exoftálmico, -ca.
exophthalmogenic *adj.* exoftalmógeno, -na.
exophthalmometer *n.* exoftalmómetro, proptómetro.
exophthalmometric *adj.* exoftalmométrico, -ca.

exophthalmometry *n.* exoftalmometría.
exophthalmos *n.* exoftalmos.
　thyrotoxic exophthalmos exoftalmos tiro-
　tóxico.
　thyrotropic exophthalmos exoftalmos tiro-
　trópico.
exophylaxis *n.* exofilaxis.
exophytic *adj.* exofítico, -ca.
exoplasm *n.* exoplasma.
exorbitism *n.* exorbitis, exorbitismo.
exormia *n.* exormía.
exoserosis *n.* exoserosis.
exoskeleton *n.* exoesqueleto, exosqueleto.
exosmosis *n.* exosmosis, exósmosis.
exosplenopexy *n.* exosplenopexia.
exostectomy *n.* exostectomía.
exostosectomy *n.* exostosectomía.
exostosis *n.* exostosis.
　dental exostosis exostosis dental, exostosis
　dentaria.
　exostosis bursata exostosis bursata.
　exostosis cartilaginea exostosis cartilagino-
　sa.
　hereditary multiple exostosis exostosis
　múltiple, exostosis múltiple hereditaria.
　ivory exostosis exostosis ebúrnea.
　multiple exostosis exostosis múltiple, exos-
　tosis múltiple hereditaria.
　osteocartilaginous exostosis exostosis os-
　teocartilaginosa, exostosis osteocartilaginosa
　solitaria.
　solitary osteocartilaginous exostosis exos-
　tosis osteocartilaginosa, exostosis osteocarti-
　laginosa solitaria.
exostotic *adj.* exostóxico, -ca.
exoteric *adj.* exotérico, -ca.
exothelioma *n.* exotelioma.
exothermal *adj.* exotérmico, -ca.
exothermic *adj.* exotérmico, -ca.
exothermy *n.* exotermia.
exothymopexy *n.* exotimopexia.
exothyropexy *n.* exotiropexia.
exotic *adj.* exótico, -ca.
exotropia *n.* exotropía.
　basic exotropia exotropía básica.
　divergence excess exotropia exotropía por
　exceso de divergencia.
　divergence insufficiency exotropia exotro-
　pía por insuficiencia de divergencia.
exotropic *adj.* exotrópico, -ca.
expander *n.* expansor.
　plasma expander expansor del plasma.
　tissue expander expansor tisular.
expansion *n.* expansión.
　clonal expansion expansión clonal.
　cubical expansion expansión cúbica.
　expansion of the arch expansión del arco.
　extracellular volume expansion expansión
　del volumen extracelular.
　hygroscopic expansion expansión higroscó-
　pica.
　maxillary expansion expansión del maxilar.
　perceptual expansion expansión perceptual.
　setting expansion expansión de fraguado.
　thermal expansion expansión térmica.
　wax expansion expansión de cera.
expansiveness *n.* expansividad.
expectorant *n.* expectorante.
　liquefying expectorant expectorante coli-
　cuativo.
　stimulant expectorant expectorante estimu-
　lante.
expectoration *n.* expectoración.
experience *n.* experiencia.
　internal experience vivencia.

experiment *n.* experimento.
experimental *adj.* experimental.
experimentation *n.* experimentación.
　clinical experimentation experimentación
　clínica.
expiration *n.* espiración, expiración.
　active expiration espiración activa.
　passive expiration espiración pasiva.
expiratory *adj.* espiratorio, -ria.
expire *v.* expirar.
exploration *n.* exploración.
　gynecological exploration exploración gi-
　necológica.
　physical exploration exploración física.
　psychologic exploration exploración psico-
　lógica.
exploratory *adj.* explorador, -ra.
explorer *n.* explorador[1].
explosion *n.* explosión[1].
explosive *adj.* explosivo, -va.
exponent *n.* exponente.
exponential *adj.* exponencial.
exposure *n.* exposición.
　acute exposure exposición aguda, exposi-
　ción aguda a la radiación.
　acute radiation exposure exposición aguda,
　exposición aguda a la radiación.
　automatic exposure exposición automática.
　chronic exposure exposición crónica, exposi-
　ción crónica a la radiación.
　chronic radiation exposure exposición cró-
　nica, exposición crónica a la radiación.
　entrance exposure exposición de entrada.
　radiation exposure exposición a la radiación.
expression *n.* expresión.
　early expression expresión temprana.
expressivity *n.* expresividad.
expulsion *n.* expulsión.
expulsive *adj.* expulsivo, -va.
exsanguinate *adj.* exanguinado, -da.
exsanguination *n.* exanguinación.
exsanguine *adj.* exangüe.
exsanguinotransfusion *n.* exanguinotrans-
　fusión.
exsiccant *n.* desecador, desecante[2].
exsiccate *v.* desecar.
exsiccation *n.* desecación[1], desecación[2].
exsiccosis *n.* exicosis.
exsomatize *v.* exsomatizar.
exstrophy *n.* extrofia.
　cloacal exstrophy extrofia de la cloaca.
　exstrophy of the bladder extrofia de la vejiga,
　extrofia vesical.
　exstrophy of the cloaca extrofia de la cloaca.
exsufflation *n.* exsuflación.
exsufflator *n.* exsuflador.
extension *n.* extensión.
　Buck's extension extensión de Buck.
　Codivilla's extension extensión de Codivilla.
　extension per contiguitatem extensión por
　contigüidad.
　extension per continuitatem extensión con-
　tinua.
　extension per saltam extensión saltatoria.
　infarct extension extensión del infarto.
　life extension extensión de la vida.
　nail extension extensión del clavo.
　parasellar extension extensión paraselar.
　ridge extension extensión de rebordes, ex-
　tensión del reborde alveolar, extensión margi-
　nal.
　skeletal extension extensión esquelética.
　suprasellar extension extensión supraselar.
extensometer *n.* extensómetro.
extensor *adj.* extensor, -ra.

exterior *n.* exterior.
external *adj.* externo, -na.
externality *n.* externalidad.
externalization *n.* externalización.
externalize *v.* externalizar.
exteroceptive *adj.* exteroceptivo, -va.
exteroceptor *n.* exteroceptor.
exterofection *n.* exterofección.
exterofective *adj.* exterofectivo, -va.
extinction *n.* extinción.
　sensory extinction extinción sensitiva.
　specific extinction extinción específica.
extirpation *n.* extirpación.
extorsion *n.* extorsión.
extra-adrenal *adj.* extrasuprarrenal.
extra-anthropic *adj.* extraantrópico, -ca.
extra-articular *adj.* extraarticular.
extrabronchial *adj.* extrabronquial.
extrabuccal *adj.* extrabucal.
extrabulbar *adj.* extrabulbar.
extracaliceal *adj.* extracaliceal.
extracapsular *adj.* extracapsular.
extracardiac *adj.* extracardíaco, -ca.
extracardial *adj.* extracardíaco, -ca.
extracarpal *adj.* extracarpiano, -na.
extracellular *adj.* extracelular.
extracerebral *adj.* extracerebral.
extrachromosomal *adj.* extracromosómi-
co, -ca.
extracorporal *adj.* extracorporal.
extracorporeal *adj.* extracorporal, extracorpóreo, -a.
extracorpored *adj.* extracorporal, extracorpóreo, -a.
extracorticospinal *adj.* extracorticoespinal.
extracranial *adj.* extracraneal, extracraneano, -na.
extract *n.* extracto, extraer.
extraction *n.* extracción.
　breech extraction extracción de nalgas.
　cataract extraction extracción de una catara-
　ta.
　extracapsular cataract extraction extrac-
　ción extracapsular de una catarata.
　extracapsular extraction of the lens extrac-
　ción extracapsular del cristalino.
　fetal extraction extracción fetal.
　intracapsular cataract extraction extrac-
　ción intracapsular de una catarata.
　intracapsular extraction of the lens extrac-
　ción intracapsular del cristalino.
　podalic extraction extracción podálica.
　progressive extraction extracción en serie,
　extracción seriada.
　selected extraction extracción en serie, ex-
　tracción seriada.
　serial extraction extracción en serie, extrac-
　ción seriada.
　tooth extraction extracción dental.
extractive *adj.* extractivo, -va.
extractor *n.* extractor.
extracystic *adj.* extracístico, -ca.
extradural *adj.* extradural.
extraembryonic *adj.* extraembrionario, -ria.
extraepiphyseal *adj.* extraepifisario, -ria.
extraepiphysial *adj.* extraepifisario, -ria.
extragenic *adj.* extragénico, -ca.
extragenital *adj.* extragenital.
extrahepatic *adj.* extrahepático, -ca.
extrajection *n.* extrayección.
extraligamentous *adj.* extraligamentoso, -sa.
extramarginal *adj.* extramarginal.
extramastoiditis *n.* extramastoiditis.
extramedullary *adj.* extramedular.
extrameningeal *adj.* extrameníngeo, -a.

extramural *adj.* extramural.
extraneous *adj.* extraño, ña[1].
extranuclear *adj.* extranuclear.
extraocular *adj.* extraocular.
extraoculogram *n.* extraoculograma.
extraoral *adj.* extraoral.
extraosseous *adj.* extraóseo, -a.
extraovular *adj.* extraovular.
extrapapillary *adj.* extrapapilar.
extraparenchymal *adj.* extraparenquimático, -ca, extraparenquimatoso, -sa.
extrapelvic *adj.* extrapélvico, -ca.
extrapericardial *adj.* extrapericárdico, -ca.
extraperineal *adj.* extraperineal.
extraperiosteal *adj.* extraperióstico, -ca.
extraperitoneal *adj.* extraperitoneal.
extraplacental *adj.* extraplacentario, -ria.
extraplantar *adj.* extraplantar.
extrapleural *adj.* extrapleural.
extrapolation *n.* extrapolación.
extraprostatic *adj.* extraprostático, -ca.
extraprostatitis *n.* extraprostatitis.
extrapsychic *adj.* extrapsíquico, -ca.
extrapulmonary *adj.* extrapulmonar.
extrapyramidal *adj.* extrapiramidal.
extrasensory *adj.* extrasensorial.
extraserous *adj.* extraseroso, -sa.
extrasomatic *adj.* extrasomático, -ca.
extrasystole *n.* extrasístole, extrasistolia.
 atrial extrasystole extrasístole auricular.
 atrioventricular extrasystole extrasístole auriculoventricular.
 atrioventricular nodal extrasystole extrasístole nodular auriculoventricular.
 auricular extrasystole extrasístole auricular.
 auriculoventricular extrasystole extrasístole auriculoventricular.
 concealed junctional extrasystole extrasístole de la unión oculta.
 extrasystole atrioventriculare extrasístole auriculoventricular.
 infranodal extrasystole extrasístole infranodular.
 interpolated extrasystole extrasístole interpolada.
 junctional extrasystole extrasístole de la unión.
 lower nodal extrasystole extrasístole nodular inferior.
 midnodal extrasystole extrasístole mesonodular.
 nodal extrasystole extrasístole nodular.
 retrograde extrasystole extrasístole retrógada.
 return extrasystole extrasístole de retorno.
 supraventricular extrasystole extrasístole supraventricular.
 upper nodal extrasystole extrasístole nodular superior.

 ventricular extrasystole extrasístole ventricular.
extratarsal *adj.* extratarsal.
extratensive *adj.* extratensivo, -va.
extrathoracic *adj.* extratorácico, -ca.
extratracheal *adj.* extratraqueal.
extratubal *adj.* extratubárico, -ca, extratubario, -ria.
extratympanic *adj.* extratimpánico, -ca.
extrauterine *adj.* extrauterino, -na.
extravaginal *adj.* extravaginal.
extravasate *n.* extravasado.
extravasation *n.* extravasación.
 extravasation punctiforme extravasación puntiforme.
extravascular *adj.* extravascular.
extraventricular *adj.* extraventricular.
extraversion *n.* extraversión, extroversión.
extravisual *adj.* extravisual.
extraxial *adj.* extraaxial.
extreme *n.* extremo.
 amino extreme extremo amino.
extremity *n.* extremidad.
extrinsic *adj.* extrínseco, -ca.
extrogastrulation *n.* extrogastrulación.
extrophia *n.* extrofia.
extrospection *n.* extrospección.
extroversion *n.* extroversión.
extrude *v.* extrudir.
extrudoclusion *n.* extrudoclusión.
extrusion *n.* extrusión.
 extrusion of a tooth extrusión dentaria.
extubate *v.* extubar.
extubation *n.* extubación.
exuberant *adj.* exuberante.
exudate *n.* exudado.
 cotton-wool exudate exudado algodonoso.
exudation *n.* exudación.
exudative *adj.* exudativo, -va.
exulcerans *adj.* exulcerante.
exulceratio *n.* exulceración.
 exulceratio simplex exulceración simple.
exumbilication *n.* exumbilicación.
exutory *n.* exutorio.
exuviation *n.* exuviación.
eye *n.* ojo.
 amaurotic cat's eye ojo de gato amaurótico.
 aphakic eye ojo afáquico.
 artificial eye ojo artificial.
 bank eye banco de ojo.
 black eye ojo negro.
 bleary eye ojo blefarítico, ojo legañoso.
 cinema eye ojo de cinematógrafo.
 cyclopean eye ojo de cíclope.
 cyclopian eye ojo de cíclope.
 cystic eye ojo quístico.
 dark-adapted eye ojo adaptado a la oscuridad.

 deviating eye ojo desviado.
 dominant eye ojo dominante.
 exciting eye ojo de excitación, ojo excitante.
 fixating eye ojo de fijación, ojo fijador.
 fixing eye ojo de fijación, ojo fijador.
 following eye ojo errante.
 hare's eye ojo de liebre.
 heavy eye ojo pesado.
 hot eye ojo caliente.
 Klieg eye ojo de Klieg.
 light-adapted eye ojo adaptado a la luz.
 Listing's reduced eye ojo reducido de Listing.
 master eye ojo maestro, ojo maestro dominante.
 master-dominant eye ojo maestro, ojo maestro dominante.
 median eye ojo mediano de Nairobi.
 monochromatic eye ojo monocromático.
 phakic eye ojo fáquico.
 photopic eye ojo fotópico.
 pink eye ojo rosado, ojo sonrosado.
 primary eye ojo primario.
 pseudophakic eye ojo seudofáquico.
 raccoon eye ojo de mapache.
 reduced eye ojo reducido.
 schematic eye ojo esquemático.
 scotopic eye ojo escotópico.
 secondary eye ojo secundario.
 shipyard eye ojo de los astilleros.
 Snellen's reform eye ojo de Snellen.
 squinting eye ojo bizco, ojo estrábico.
 sympathizing eye ojo simpatizante.
 web eye ojo membranoso.
eyebrow *n.* ceja.
eyecup *n.* lavaojos.
eyelash *n.* pestaña.
 ectopic eyelash pestaña ectópica.
 piebald eyelash pestaña partialbina.
eyelet *n.* ojete.
eyelid *n.* párpado.
eyepiece *n.* ocular[2].
 comparison eyepiece ocular de comparación.
 compensating eyepiece ocular compensador, ocular compensatorio, ocular de compensación.
 demonstration eyepiece ocular de demostración.
 high-eyepoint eyepiece ocular con el punto de mira elevado.
 Huygens' eyepiece ocular de Huygens.
 Huyguenian eyepiece ocular de Huygens.
 negative eyepiece ocular negativo.
 positive eyepiece ocular positivo.
 Ramsden's eyepiece ocular de Ramsden.
 wide field eyepiece ocular de amplio campo, ocular de campo amplio.

F f

fabella *n.* fabela.
fabulation *n.* fabulación.
face *n.* cara, facies, faz.
  acromegalic face facies acromegálica.
  adenoid face facies adenoide, facies adenoidea.
  aortic face facies aórtica.
  bird face braquignatia, cara de pájaro.
  cherubic face facies angélica, facies querúbica.
  Corvisart's face facies de Corvisart.
  cow face cara de vaca, facies bovina, facies de vaca.
  dish face cara de plato.
  elfin face facies de duende.
  frog face cara de sapo.
  hippocratic face cara hipocrática, facies agónica, facies descompósita, facies hipocrática.
  hound-dog face facies de sabueso.
  Hutchinson's face facies de Hutchinson.
  leonine face facies leonina.
  Marshall Hall's face facies de Marshall Hall.
  masklike face facies de máscara, cara de máscara.
  mitral face facies mitral.
  moon face cara de luna llena, facies de luna, facies lunar.
  myasthenic face facies miasténica.
  myopathic face facies miopática.
  Parkinsonian face facies de Parkinson, facies marmórea, facies parkinsoniana.
  Parkinson's face facies de Parkinson, facies marmórea, facies parkinsoniana.
  Potter's face facies de Potter.
facet *n.* faceta.
  articular facet faceta articular.
  clavicular facet faceta clavicular.
  corneal facet faceta corneal.
  locked facet faceta trabada.
facetectomy *n.* facetectomía.
facette *n.* faceta.
facial *adj.* facialis.
facialis *adj.* facialis.
facies *n.* facies.
  facies abdominalis facies abdominal.
  facies bovina facies de vaca.
  facies dolorosa facies dolorosa.
  facies hepatica facies hepática.
  facies hippocratica facies agónica, facies descompósita, facies hipocrática.
  facies leonina facies leonina.
  facies scaphoidea facies escafoidea.
  facies uterina facies uterina.
facilitation *n.* facilitación.
facilitative *adj.* facilitatorio, -ria.
facing *n.* carilla.
faciobrachial *adj.* faciobraquial.
faciocephalalgia *n.* faciocefalalgia.
faciocervical *adj.* faciocervical.
faciolingual *adj.* faciolingual.
facioplasty *n.* facioplastia.

facioplegia *n.* facioplejía.
facioscapulohumeral *adj.* facioescapulohumeral.
faciostenosis *n.* facioestenosis, faciostenosis.
factitial *adj.* facticio, -cia.
factitious *adj.* facticio, -cia.
factor *n.* factor.
factorial *n.* factorial.
facultative *adj.* facultativo, -va.
faculty *n.* facultad.
  fusion faculty facultad de fusión.
  rational faculty razón[1].
failure *n.* fallo, insuficiencia.
  acute circulatory failure insuficiencia circulatoria aguda.
  acute renal failure insuficiencia renal aguda.
  acute respiratory failure (ARF) insuficiencia respiratoria aguda (IRA).
  chronic renal failure insuficiencia renal crónica.
  circulatory failure insuficiencia circulatoria.
  compensated heart failure insuficiencia cardíaca compensada.
  congestive heart failure (CHF) insuficiencia cardíaca congestiva (ICC).
  end-stage renal failure insuficiencia renal crónica terminal.
  heart failure insuficiencia cardíaca.
  left ventricular failure insuficiencia cardíaca izquierda, insuficiencia cardíaca ventricular izquierda.
  left-heart failure insuficiencia cardíaca izquierda, insuficiencia cardíaca ventricular izquierda.
  liver failure insuficiencia hepática.
  mitral failure insuficiencia mitral.
  polyuric acute renal failure insuficiencia renal aguda poliúrica.
  postrenal acute renal failure insuficiencia renal aguda posrenal.
  prerenal failure insuficiencia prerrenal.
  renal failure insuficiencia renal.
  respiratory failure insuficiencia respiratoria.
  right ventricular failure insuficiencia cardíaca derecha, insuficiencia cardíaca ventricular derecha.
  right-heart failure insuficiencia cardíaca derecha, insuficiencia cardíaca ventricular derecha.
faint *n.* desfallecimiento, desmayo.
falcate *adj.* falcado, -da.
falcial *adj.* falcial.
falciform *adj.* falcicular, falciforme.
falcine *adj.* falcino, -na.
falcula *n.* fálcula.
falcular *adj.* falcular.
false *adj.* falso, -sa.
  false negative falsonegativo.
  false positive falsopositivo.
falsetto *n.* falsete.

falsification *n.* falsificación.
  retrospective falsification falsificación retrospectiva.
falx *n.* falx, hoz.
familial *adj.* familiar.
family *n.* familia.
  cancer family familia de cáncer.
  nuclear family familia nuclear.
fang *n.* colmillo.
fantascope *n.* fantascopio.
fantasy *n.* ensoñación, fantasía.
faradaic *adj.* farádico, -ca.
faradic *adj.* farádico, -ca.
faradimeter *n.* faradímetro.
faradism *n.* faradismo.
faradization *n.* faradización.
faradocontractility *n.* faradocontractilidad.
faradomuscular *adj.* faradomuscular.
faradopalpation *n.* faradopalpación.
faradotherapy *n.* faradoterapia.
farcy *n.* farcinosis, muermo.
fardel *n.* fardo.
fascia *n.* fascia.
fasciagraphy *n.* fasciagrafía.
fascial *adj.* fascial.
fascicle *n.* fascículo.
fascicular *adj.* fascicular.
fasciculate *adj.* fasciculado, -da.
fasciculated *adj.* fasciculado, -da.
fasciculation *n.* fasciculación.
fasciculus *n.* fascículo.
fasciitis *n.* fascitis.
  eosinophilic fasciitis fascitis eosinofílica.
  exudative calcifying fasciitis fascitis exudativa calcificante.
  necrotizing fasciitis fascitis necrosante.
  nodular fasciitis fascitis nodular.
  parosteal fasciitis fascitis paróstica.
  perirenal fasciitis fascitis perirrenal.
  proliferative fasciitis fascitis proliferativa.
  pseudosarcomatous fasciitis fascitis seudosarcomatosa.
fasciodesis *n.* fasciodesis.
Fasciola *n.* Fasciola.
fasciollasls *n.* fascioliasis.
fasciolid *n.* fasciólido.
fasciolopsiasis *n.* fasciolopsiasis.
fascioplasty *n.* fascioplastia.
fasciorrhaphy *n.* fasciorrafia.
fasciotomy *n.* fasciotomía.
fastigium *n.* fastigio, fastigium.
fat *n.* grasa.
  bound fat grasa conjugada.
  brown fat grasa parda.
  chyle fat grasa del quilo.
  corpse fat grasa cadavérica, grasa de cadáver.
  fetal fat grasa fetal.
  grave fat grasa grave.
  grave-wax fat grasa cadavérica, grasa de cadáver.

masked fat grasa disimulada.
milk fat grasa de la leche.
moruloid fat grasa moruloide.
mulberry fat grasa moruloide.
multilocular fat grasa multilocular.
neutral fat grasa neutra.
polyunsaturated fat grasa poliinsaturada.
saturated fat grasa saturada.
split fat grasa desdoblada.
unilocular fat grasa unilocular.
unsaturated fat grasa insaturada.
white fat grasa blanca.
fatal *adj.* fatal.
fatality *n.* fatalidad.
fate *n.* destino.
prospective fate destino prospectivo.
fatherhood *n.* paternidad.
fatigability *n.* fatigabilidad.
fatigable *adj.* fatigable.
fatigue *n.* fatiga.
auditory fatigue fatiga auditiva.
battle fatigue fatiga de batalla, fatiga de las batallas.
combat fatigue fatiga de combate.
pseudocombat fatigue fatiga de seudocombate.
stimulation fatigue fatiga de estimulación.
fatty *adj.* graso, -sa.
fauces *n.* fauces.
faucial *adj.* faucial.
faucitis *n.* faucitis.
faveolate *adj.* faveolado, -da, faveolar.
favid *n.* fávide.
favus *n.* favo, favus.
fear *n.* miedo, temor.
febricant *adj.* febricante.
febricide *n.* febricida.
febricity *n.* febricidad.
febricula *n.* febrícula.
febrifacient *adj.* febrifaciente.
febriferous *adj.* febrífero, -a.
febrific *adj.* ca, febrífico.
febrifugal *adj.* febrífugo, -ga.
febrifuge *n.* febrífugo.
febrile *adj.* febril.
febris *adj.* febris.
fecal *adj.* fecal.
fecalith *n.* fecalito.
fecaloid *adj.* fecaloide.
fecaloma *n.* fecaloma.
fecaluria *n.* fecaluria.
feces *n.* heces.
feculent *adj.* feculento, -ta.
fecund *adj.* fecundo, -da.
fecundate *v.* fecundar.
fecundatio *n.* fecundación.
fecundatio ab extra fecundación ab extra.
fecundation *n.* fecundación.
artificial fecundation fecundación artificial.
external fecundation fecundación externa.
in vitro fecundation fecundación in vitro.
internal fecundation fecundación interna.
fecundity *n.* fecundidad.
feedback *n.* feedback, retroacción, retroalimentación.
negative feedback retroalimentación negativa.
positive feedback retroalimentación positiva.
feeding *n.* alimentación.
artificial feeding alimentación artificial.
bottle feeding alimentación con biberón.
breast feeding alimentación al pecho.
complementary feeding alimentación complementaria.
extrabuccal feeding alimentación extrabucal.
fictitious feeding alimentación ficticia.

Finkelstein's feeding alimentación de Finkelstein.
forced feeding alimentación forzada.
forcible feeding alimentación forzada.
gastric feeding alimentación gástrica.
gastrostomy feeding alimentación mediante gastrostomía.
infant feeding alimentación del lactante.
intravenous feeding alimentación intravenosa.
nasogastric feeding alimentación nasogástrica.
sham feeding alimentación simulada.
tube feeding alimentación por sonda.
feeling *n.* sentimiento.
feeling of guilt sentimiento de culpabilidad.
feeling of inferiority sentimiento de inferioridad.
female *n.* hembra.
femenine *adj.* femenino, -na.
feminism *n.* feminismo.
feminization *n.* feminización.
testicular feminization feminización testicular.
femoral *adj.* femoral.
femorocele *n.* femorocele.
femoroiliac *adj.* femoroilíaco, -ca.
femorotibial *adj.* femorotibial.
femur *n.* fémur.
fenestra *n.* fenestra, ventana.
fenestra cochleae fenestra cochleae, ventana coclear, ventana de la cóclea.
fenestra novovalis fenestra novovalis, ventana novovalis.
fenestra of the cochlea fenestra cochleae, ventana coclear, ventana de la cóclea.
fenestra of the vestibule fenestra vestibuli, ventana del vestíbulo, ventana vestibular.
fenestra ovalis fenestra ovalis, ventana oval.
fenestra vestibuli fenestra vestibuli, ventana del vestíbulo, ventana vestibular.
fenestrate *v.* fenestrar.
fenestrated *adj.* fenestrado, -da.
fenestration *n.* fenestración.
alveolar plate fenestration fenestración de la placa alveolar.
apical fenestration fenestración apical.
tracheal fenestration fenestración traqueal.
feral *adj.* feral.
ferment *n.* fermento.
fermentable *adj.* fermentable.
fermentation *n.* fermentación.
acetic fermentation fermentación acética, fermentación acetosa.
acetous fermentation fermentación acética, fermentación acetosa.
alcoholic fermentation fermentación alcohólica.
ammoniacal fermentation fermentación amoniacal.
amylic fermentation fermentación amílica.
butyric fermentation fermentación butírica.
caseous fermentation fermentación caseosa.
diastatic fermentation fermentación diastásica.
lactic acid fermentation fermentación láctica.
storing fermentation fermentación de almacenamiento.
viscous fermentation fermentación viscosa.
fermentative *adj.* fermentativo, -va.
fermentoid *n.* fermentoide.
fermentum *n.* fermento, fermentum.
ferrialbuminic *adj.* ferrialbumínico, -ca.
ferricytochrome *n.* ferricitocromo.
ferrihemoglobin *n.* ferrihemoglobina.

ferritin *n.* ferritina.
ferrocytochrome *n.* ferrocitocromo.
ferrohemochrome *n.* ferrohemocromo.
ferrokinetic *adj.* ferrocinético, -ca.
ferrokinetics *n.* ferrocinética.
ferropexy *n.* ferropexia.
ferroporphyrin *n.* ferroporfirina.
ferroproteins *n.* ferroproteínas.
ferroprotoporphyrin *n.* ferroprotoporfirina.
ferrotherapy *n.* ferroterapia.
ferrugination *n.* ferruginación.
ferruginous *adj.* ferruginoso, -sa.
ferrule *n.* casquillo, gatillo[1].
ferrum *n.* ferrum, hierro.
fertile *adj.* fértil.
fertility *n.* fertilidad.
fertilization *n.* fertilización.
fertilizin *n.* fertilicina, fertilisina.
fervescence *n.* fervescencia.
festinant *adj.* festinante.
festination *n.* festinación.
festoon *n.* festón.
gingival festoon festón gingival.
McCall festoon festón de mcCall.
festooning *adj.* festoneado, -da.
fetal *adj.* fetal.
fetalism *n.* fetalismo.
fetalization *n.* fetalización.
feticide *n.* feticidio.
fetid *adj.* fétido, -da.
fetish *n.* fetiche.
fetishism *n.* fetichismo.
transvestic fetishism fetichismo travestido.
fetoglobulin *n.* fetoglobulina.
fetology *n.* fetología.
fetometry *n.* fetometría.
fetopathy *n.* fetopatía.
diabetic fetopathy fetopatía diabética.
fetoplacental *adj.* fetoplacentario, -ria.
fetoprotein *n.* fetoproteína.
fetor *n.* fetor.
fetor exoris fetor exoris.
fetor hepaticus fetor hepaticus.
fetor oris fetor oris.
fetoscope *n.* fetoscopio.
fetoscopy *n.* fetoscopia.
fetotoxic *adj.* fetotóxico, -ca.
fetotoxicity *n.* fetotoxicidad.
fetus *n.* feto.
calcified fetus feto calcificado.
fetus acardius feto acardíaco, feto acardio.
fetus amorphus feto amorfo.
fetus compressus feto compressus.
fetus in fetu feto in fetu.
fetus sanguinolentus feto sanguinolento.
harlequin fetus feto arlequín.
impacted fetus feto retenido.
mummified fetus feto momificado.
papyraceous fetus feto papiráceo.
parasitic fetus feto parásito.
viable fetus feto viable.
fever *n.* fiebre.
absorption fever fiebre de absorción, fiebre por absorción.
acclimating fever fiebre de aclimatación.
Aden fever fiebre de Adén.
adynamic fever fiebre adinámica.
African tick fever fiebre africana por garrapatas.
algid pernicious fever fiebre álgida perniciosa.
aphthous fever fiebre aftosa.
Argentine hemorrhagic fever fiebre argentina hemorrágica.
Argentinian hemorrhagic fever fiebre argentina hemorrágica.

artificial fever fiebre artificial.
aseptic fever fiebre aséptica.
Assam fever fiebre de assam.
asthenic fever fiebre asténica.
Australian Q fever fiebre australiana Q.
autumn fever fiebre otoñal.
black fever fiebre negra.
blackwater fever fiebre de aguas negras.
blue fever fiebre azul.
boutonneuse fever fiebre botonosa.
brass founders' fever fiebre de los fundido-res.
Brazilian purpuric fever fiebre purpúrea de Brasil.
Brazilian spotted fever fiebre exantemática brasileña.
Bullis fever fiebre de Bullis.
Bwamba fever fiebre Bwamba.
cachectic fever fiebre caquéctica.
cachexial fever fiebre caquéctica.
camp fever fiebre castrense, fiebre de los campamentos.
cane-field fever fiebre de los campos de azúcar.
canicola fever fiebre canícola.
cat-bite fever fiebre por mordedura de gato.
cat-scratch fever fiebre por arañazo de gato.
central fever fiebre central.
cerebrospinal fever fiebre cerebral, fiebre cerebroespinal.
cesspool fever fiebre de las letrinas.
Chagres fever fiebre de Chagres, fiebre de Panamá.
Charcot's fever fiebre de Charcot.
Colombian tick fever fiebre colombiana por garrapata.
Congolian red fever fiebre roja del Congo.
continued fever fiebre continuada.
continuous fever fiebre continua.
Cyprus fever fiebre de Chipre.
dandy fever fiebre dandy.
dehydration fever fiebre por deshidratación.
dengue fever fiebre dengue, fiebre rompehuesos, fiebre solar.
dengue hemorrhagic fever fiebre hemorrágica dengue.
desert fever fiebre del desierto.
digestive fever fiebre digestiva.
double quartan fever fiebre cuartana doble.
drug fever fiebre medicamentosa.
Dumdum fever fiebre Dumdum.
Dutton's relapsing fever fiebre recurrente de Dutton.
elephantoid fever fiebre elefantoidea.
enteric fever fiebre entérica, fiebre entericoide.
entericoid fever fiebre entérica, fiebre entericoide.
ephemeral fever fiebre de un día, fiebre efímera.
epidemic hemorrhagic fever fiebre hemorrágica epidémica.
eruptive fever fiebre eruptiva.
exanthematous fever fiebre exantemática.
familial Mediterranean fever fiebre mediterránea familiar.
famine fever fiebre por hambre.
fatigue fever fiebre de fatiga, fiebre por fatiga.
fever of unknown origin (FUO) fiebre de origen desconocido (FOD).
field fever fiebre de los campos.
five-day fever fiebre de los cinco días.
Fort Bragg fever fiebre de Fuerte Bragg.
Gibraltar fever fiebre de Gibraltar.
Hankow fever fiebre de Hankow.
Hasami fever fiebre de Hasami.
hay fever fiebre del heno.

hectic fever fiebre cacoquímica, fiebre colicuativa, fiebre consecutiva, fiebre héctica, fiebre lenta.
hemoglobinuric fever fiebre biliosa hematúrica, fiebre hemoglobinúrica.
hemorrhagic fever fiebre hemorrágica, fiebre hemorrágica aguda epidémica.
herpetic fever fiebre herpética.
hospital fever fiebre de los hospitales.
inanition fever fiebre de inanición.
influenza fever fiebre catarral epidémica.
intermenstrual fever fiebre intermenstrual.
intermittent fever fiebre crónica, fiebre intermitente.
intermittent hepatic fever fiebre hepática intermitente.
inundation fever fiebre de inundación, fiebre de las inundaciones.
Jaccoud's dissociated fever fiebre disociada de Jaccoud.
Japanese flood fever fiebre fluvial japonesa.
Japanese river fever fiebre fluvial japonesa.
jungle fever fiebre de las selvas.
jungle yellow fever fiebre amarilla de la jungla, fiebre amarilla de las selvas.
Junin fever fiebre de Junín.
Katayama fever fiebre de Katayama.
Korin fever fiebre de Korin.
Lassa fever fiebre de Lassa.
malarial fever fiebre malárica, fiebre perniciosa.
Malta fever fiebre de Malta, fiebre napolitana.
Manchurian fever fiebre de Manchuria.
Marseille fever fiebre de Marsella.
Mediterranean fever fiebre del Mediterráneo, fiebre exantemática del mediterráneo.
metal fume fever fiebre de los humos de metales, fiebre de los humos metálicos.
milk fever fiebre láctea, fiebre láctica.
Mossman fever fiebre de Mossman.
mud fever fiebre del lodo.
Murchinson-Pel-Ebstein fever fiebre de Murchinson-Pel-Ebstein.
nanukayami fever fiebre japonesa de los siete días, fiebre nanukayami.
ninemile fever fiebre de las nueve millas.
o'nyong-nyong fever fiebre de o'nyong-nyong.
Oroya fever fiebre de Oroya.
paludal fever fiebre palúdica.
pappataci fever fiebre de chitral, fiebre pappataci.
paratyphoid fever fiebre paratifoidea.
parenteric fever fiebre parenteral.
parturient fever fiebre de las parturientas.
Pel-Ebstein fever fiebre de Pel-Ebstein.
periodic fever fiebre periódica.
petechial fever fiebre petequial.
Pfeiffer's glandular fever fiebre de Pfeiffer.
pharyngoconjunctival fever fiebre faringoconjuntival.
phlebotomus fever fiebre flebotoma, fiebre por flebotomos.
pinta fever fiebre de pinta.
polyleptic fever fiebre poliléptica.
Pomona fever fiebre de Pomona.
pretibial fever fiebre pretibial.
prison fever fiebre de las cárceles, fiebre de las prisiones.
protein fever fiebre de proteínas, fiebre por proteínas.
puerperal fever fiebre puerperal.
pulmonary fever fiebre pulmonar.
Q fever fiebre cuadrilátera, fiebre de Queensland, fiebre Q.

quartan fever fiebre cuartana.
quintan fever fiebre quintana.
quotidian fever fiebre cotidiana.
rabbit fever fiebre de los conejos.
rat-bite fever fiebre por mordedura de rata.
recurrent fever fiebre recurrente.
relapsing fever fiebre recidivante.
remittent fever fiebre remitente.
rice-field fever fiebre de los arrozales, fiebre de los campos de arroz.
Rocky Mountain spotted fever fiebre de las montañas rocosas, fiebre exantemática de las montañas rocosas.
rose fever fiebre de rose.
salt fever fiebre por sal.
San Joaquin fever fiebre de San Joaquín.
Schottmüller fever fiebre de Schottmüller.
septic fever fiebre séptica.
seven-day fever fiebre de los siete días.
ship fever fiebre contagiosa de los barcos.
Sindbis fever fiebre Sindbis.
slime fever fiebre del cieno.
Songo fever fiebre de Songo.
South African tickbite fever fiebre sudafricana por garrapatas.
spirillum fever fiebre por espirilos.
splenic fever fiebre esplénica.
suppurative fever fiebre supurativa.
swamp fever fiebre de los pantanos.
syphilitic fever fiebre sifilítica.
tertian fever fiebre terciana.
thermic fever fiebre térmica.
three-day fever fiebre de los tres días, fiebre estival de tres días.
tick fever fiebre de las garrapatas, fiebre por garrapatas.
Tobia fever fiebre de Tobia.
traumatic fever fiebre de fractura, fiebre traumática.
trench fever fiebre de las trincheras, fiebre de schee, fiebre tibiálgica.
tsutsugamushi fever fiebre tsutsugamushi.
typhoid fever fiebre pitogénica, fiebre tifoidea.
undulant fever fiebre ondulante, fiebre oscilante.
urethral fever fiebre uretral.
urinary fever fiebre urinaria, fiebre urinosa.
uveoparotid fever fiebre uveoparotídea.
viral hemorrhagic fever fiebre hemorrágica vírica.
yellow fever fiebre amarilla, fiebre biliosa perniciosa, fiebre flava, fiebre gástrica.
zinc fever fiebre del cinc.
fiber *n.* fibra.
   Sharpey's fiber fibra de Sharpey.
fibercolonoscope *n.* fibrocolonoscopio.
fibergastroscope *n.* fibrogastroscopio.
fiberoptic *adj.* fibroóptico, -ca, fibróptico, -ca.
fiberoptics *n.* fibroóptica, fibróptica.
fiberscope *n.* fibroscopio.
fibremia *n.* fibremia.
fibril *n.* fibrilla.
fibrillar *adj.* fibrilar².
fibrillary *adj.* fibrilar².
fibrillate *v.* fibrilar¹.
fibrillated *adj.* fibrilado, -da.
fibrillation *n.* fibrilación.
   atrial fibrillation fibrilación auricular.
   auricular fibrillation fibrilación auricular.
   ventricular fibrillation fibrilación ventricular.
fibrilloblast *n.* fibrilloblasto.
fibrilloflutter *n.* fibriloflúter.
fibrillogenesis *n.* fibrilogénesis.
fibrillolysis *n.* fibrilólisis.

fibrillolytic *adj.* fibrilolítico, -ca.
fibrin *n.* fibrina.
 stroma fibrin fibrina del estroma.
fibrinemia *n.* fibrinemia.
fibrinocellular *adj.* fibrinocelular.
fibrinogen *n.* fibrinógeno.
 human fibrinogen fibrinógeno humano.
fibrinogenemia *n.* fibrinogenemia.
fibrinogenesis *n.* fibrinogénesis.
fibrinogenic *adj.* fibrinogénico, -ca.
fibrinogenolysis *n.* fibrinogenólisis.
fibrinogenolytic *adj.* fibrinogenolítico, -ca.
fibrinogenopenia *n.* fibrinogenopenia.
fibrinogenopenic *adj.* fibrinogenopénico, -ca.
fibrinogenous *adj.* fibrinógeno, -na.
fibrinoid *n.* fibrinoide.
fibrinolysis *n.* fibrinólisis.
fibrinolytic *adj.* fibrinolítico, -ca.
fibrinopenia *n.* fibrinopenia.
fibrinopeptide *n.* fibrinopéptido.
fibrinoplastic *adj.* fibrinoplásico, -ca.
fibrinoplastin *n.* fibrinoplastina, fibrinoplasto.
fibrinopurulent *adj.* fibrinopurulento, -ta.
fibrinorrhea *n.* fibrinorrea.
fibrinoscopy *n.* fibrinoscopia.
fibrinous *adj.* fibrinoso, -sa.
fibrinuria *n.* fibrinuria.
fibroadenia *n.* fibroadenia.
fibroadenoma *n.* fibroadenoma.
 giant fibroadenoma fibroadenoma gigante.
 giant fibroadenoma of the breast fibroadenoma gigante de las mamas.
 intracanalicular fibroadenoma fibroadenoma intracanalicular.
 pericanalicular fibroadenoma fibroadenoma pericanalicular.
fibroadenosis *n.* fibroadenosis.
fibroadipose *adj.* fibroadiposo, -sa.
fibroangioma *n.* fibroangioma.
 nasopharyngeal fibroangioma fibroangioma nasofaríngeo.
fibroareolar *adj.* fibroareolar.
fibroatrophy *n.* fibroatrofia.
fibroblast *n.* fibroblasto.
fibroblastic *adj.* fibroblástico, -ca.
fibroblastoma *n.* fibroblastoma.
 perineural fibroblastoma fibroblastoma perineural.
fibrobronchitis *n.* fibrobronquitis.
fibrocalcific *adj.* fibrocalcificado, -da.
fibrocarcinoma *n.* fibrocarcinoma.
fibrocartalaginous *adj.* fibrocartilaginoso, -sa.
fibrocartilage *n.* fibrocartílago.
fibrocaseous *adj.* fibrocaseoso, -sa.
fibrocellular *adj.* fibrocelular.
fibrochondritis *n.* fibrocondritis.
fibrocollagenous *adj.* fibrocolágeno, -na.
fibrocongestive *adj.* fibrocongestivo, -va.
fibrocyst *n.* fibroquiste.
fibrocystic *adj.* fibroquístico, -ca.
fibrocystoma *n.* fibrocistoma.
fibrocyte *n.* fibrocito.
fibrocytogenesis *n.* fibrocitogénesis.
fibrodysplasia *n.* fibrodisplasia.
fibroelastic *adj.* fibroelástico, -ca.
fibroelastosis *n.* fibroelastosis.
 endocardial fibroelastosis fibroelastosis endocárdica.
 endomyocardial fibroelastosis fibroelastosis endomiocárdica.
fibroenchondroma *n.* fibroenchondroma.
fibroepithelioma *n.* fibroepitelioma.
fibrofatty *adj.* fibrograso, -sa.
fibrofolliculoma *n.* fibrofoliculoma.
fibrogenesis *n.* fibrogénesis.

fibrogenic *adj.* fibrogénico, -ca.
fibroglia *n.* fibroglia.
fibroglioma *n.* fibroglioma.
fibrogliosis *n.* fibrogliosis.
fibrohemorrhagic *adj.* fibrohemorrágico, -ca.
fibrohistiocytic *adj.* fibrohistiocítico, -ca.
fibroid *adj.* fibriforme, fibroide.
fibroidectomy *n.* fibroidectomía.
fibrokeratoma *n.* fibroqueratoma.
fibroleiomyoma *n.* fibroleiomioma.
fibrolipoma *n.* fibrolipoma.
fibrolipomatous *adj.* fibrolipomatoso, -sa.
fibroma *n.* fibroma.
 ameloblastic fibroma fibroma ameloblástico.
 aponeurotic fibroma fibroma aponeurótico.
 central cementifying fibroma fibroma cimentante.
 chondromyxoid fibroma fibroma condromixoide.
 concentric fibroma fibroma concéntrico.
 cystic fibroma fibroma quístico.
 desmoplastic fibroma fibroma desmoplásico.
 fibroma cavernosum fibroma cavernoso.
 fibroma molle fibroma blando, fibroma molle.
 fibroma molle gravidarum fibroma blando del embarazo.
 fibroma myxomatodes fibroma mixomatodes, fibroma mixomatoide, fibroma mixomatoso.
 fibroma pendulum fibroma péndulo, fibroma pendulum.
 fibroma thecocellulare xanthomatodes fibroma tecocelular xantomatodes.
 intracanalicular fibroma fibroma intracanalicular.
 juvenile nasopharyngeal fibroma fibroma nasofaríngeo juvenil.
 non-osteogenic fibroma fibroma no osteogénico.
 odontogenic fibroma fibroma odontogénico, fibroma odontógeno.
 ossifying fibroma fibroma osificante.
 peripheral ossifying fibroma fibroma osificante periférico.
 periungual fibroma fibroma periungueal.
 recurring digital fibroma of childhood fibroma digital recurrente de la infancia.
fibromatogenic *adj.* fibromatogénico, -ca.
fibromatoid *adj.* fibromatoide.
fibromatosis *n.* fibromatosis.
 abdominal fibromatosis fibromatosis abdominal.
 congenital generalized fibromatosis fibromatosis congénita generalizada.
 fibromatosis colli fibromatosis cervical.
 fibromatosis gingivae fibromatosis gingival.
 fibromatosis ventriculi fibromatosis ventricular.
 gingival fibromatosis fibromatosis gingival.
 infantile digital fibromatosis fibromatosis digital, fibromatosis digital infantil, fibromatosis infantil digital.
 palmar fibromatosis fibromatosis palmar.
 penile fibromatosis fibromatosis peniana.
 plantar fibromatosis fibromatosis plantar.
 subcutaneous pseudosarcomatous fibromatosis fibromatosis subcutánea seudosarcomatosa.
fibromatous *adj.* fibromatoso, -sa.
fibromectomy *n.* fibromectomía.
fibromembranous *adj.* fibromembranoso, -sa.
fibromuscular *adj.* fibromuscular.
fibromyectomy *n.* fibromiectomía.
fibromyitis *n.* fibromiítis.
fibromyoma *n.* fibromioma.

fibromyomectomy *n.* fibromiomectomía.
fibromyositis *n.* fibromiositis.
 nodular fibromyositis fibromiositis nodular.
fibromyotomy *n.* fibromiotomía.
fibromyxoma *n.* fibromixoma.
fibromyxosarcoma *n.* fibromixosarcoma.
fibronectin *n.* fibronectina.
 plasma fibronectin fibronectina plasmática.
fibroneuroma *n.* fibroneuroma.
fibronuclear *adj.* fibronuclear.
fibro-osteoma *n.* fibroosteoma.
fibropapilloma *n.* fibropapiloma.
fibroplasia *n.* fibroplasia.
 retrolental fibroplasia (RLF) fibroplasia retrolenticular.
 retrolenticular fibroplasia fibroplasia retrolenticular.
fibroplastic *adj.* fibroplástico, -ca.
fibroplastin *n.* fibroplastina.
fibropolypus *n.* fibropólipo.
fibropsamoma *n.* fibropsamoma.
fibropurulent *adj.* fibropurulento, -ta.
fibroreticulate *adj.* fibrorreticulado, -da.
fibrosarcoma *n.* fibrosarcoma.
fibroserous *adj.* fibroseroso, -sa.
fibrosis *n.* fibrosis.
 African endomyocardial fibrosis fibrosis endomiocárdica, fibrosis endomiocárdica africana.
 congenital hepatic fibrosis fibrosis hepática congénita.
 cystic fibrosis fibrosis quística, fibrosis quística del páncreas.
 cystic fibrosis of the pancreas fibrosis quística, fibrosis quística del páncreas.
 endomyocardial fibrosis fibrosis endomiocárdica, fibrosis endomiocárdica africana.
 idiopathic pulmonary fibrosis fibrosis pulmonar idiopática.
 idiopathic retroperitoneal fibrosis fibrosis retroperitoneal, fibrosis retroperitoneal idiopática.
 mediastinal fibrosis fibrosis del mediastino.
 nodular subepidermal fibrosis fibrosis nodular subepidérmica.
 panmural fibrosis of the bladder fibrosis panmural de la vejiga.
 pericentral fibrosis fibrosis pericentral.
 perimuscular fibrosis fibrosis perimuscular.
 periureteric fibrosis fibrosis periureteral.
 postfibrinous fibrosis fibrosis posfibrinosa.
 proliferative fibrosis fibrosis neoplásica, fibrosis proliferativa.
 replacement fibrosis fibrosis de sustitución.
 retroperitoneal fibrosis fibrosis retroperitoneal, fibrosis retroperitoneal idiopática.
 subadventitial fibrosis fibrosis subadventicia.
fibrositis *n.* fibrofascitis, fibrositis.
fibrosteoma *n.* fibroosteoma.
fibrothorax *n.* fibrotórax.
fibrotic *adj.* fibrótico, -ca.
fibrous *adj.* fibroso, -sa.
 fibrous release codivilla.
fibrovascular *adj.* fibrovascular.
fibroxanthoma *n.* fibroxantoma.
fibula *n.* fíbula, peroné.
fibular *adj.* fibular.
fibulocalcaneal *adj.* fibulocalcáneo, -a.
ficosis *n.* ficosis.
field *n.* campo.
 auditory field campo auditivo.
 Broca's field campo de Broca.
 Brodmann's field campo citoarquitectónico de Brodmann, campo cortical de Brodmann.

Cohnheim's field campo de Cohnheim.
cribriform field of vision campo de visión cribiforme.
field of fixation campo de fijación.
Flechsig's field campo de Flechsig.
gamma field campo gamma.
high-power field campo de gran aumento.
individuation field campo de individualización.
low-power field campo de poco aumento.
magnetic field campo magnético.
microscopic field campo de un microscopio, campo microscópico.
morphogenetic field campo morfogenético.
myelinogenetic field campo mielogenético.
nerve field campo nervioso.
primary nail field campo ungueal primario.
visual field campo de visión, campo visual.
figolabile *adj.* frigolábil.
figure *n.* figura.
flame figure figura en llama.
fortification figure figura de fortificación.
mitotic figure figura mitótica.
Purkinje's figure figura de Purkinje.
Stifel's figure figura de Stifel.
Zöllner's figure figura de zöllner.
filaceous *adj.* filáceo, -a.
filaggrin *n.* filagrina.
filamen *n.* filamen.
filament *n.* filamento, filamentum.
Billroth's filament filamento de Billroth.
cytokeratin filament filamento de citoqueratina.
intermediate filament filamento intermedio.
keratin filament filamento de queratina.
lateral enamel filament filamento lateral del esmalte.
lymphatic anchoring filament filamento linfático de anclaje.
myosin filament filamento de miosina.
polar injecting filament filamento polar.
spermatic filament filamento espermático.
Z filament filamento Z.
filamentous *adj.* filamentoso, -sa.
filamentum *n.* filamento, filamentum.
filar *adj.* filar.
Filaria *n.* Filaria.
filarial *adj.* filarial.
filariasis *n.* filariasis, filariosis.
Bancroftian filariasis filariasis bancroftiana, filariasis brancrofti, filariasis de Bancroft.
Brugian filariasis filariasis de Brug.
Brug's filariasis filariasis de Brug.
filariasis bancrofti filariasis bancroftiana, filariasis brancrofti, filariasis de Bancroft.
filariasis malayi filariasis malaya.
Malayan filariasis filariasis malaya.
occult filariasis filariasis oculta.
Ozzard's filariasis filariasis de Ozzard.
filaricidal *adj.* filaricida[2].
filaricide *n.* filaricida[1].
filariform *adj.* filariforme.
Filarioidea *n.* Filarioidea.
file *n.* lima[1].
bone file lima para hueso.
endodontic file lima endodóntica.
gold file lima de oro.
Hirschfeld-Dunlop file lima de Hirschfeld-Dunlop.
periodontal file lima periodontal.
root canal file lima del conducto radicular.
filial *adj.* filial.
filiation *n.* filiación.
filiform *adj.* filiforme.
filipuncture *n.* filipunción.

fillet *n.* filete.
filling *n.* obturación[1].
retrograde filling obturación retrógrada.
root canal filling obturación del conducto radicular.
temporary filling obturación temporal.
film *n.* película[2].
cine film película de cine.
dental film película dental.
direct-exposure film película de exposición directa.
double-emulsion film película de emulsión doble.
duplicating film película duplicadora.
fixed blood film película de sangre fijada.
localization film película de localización.
panoramic X-ray film película radiográfica panorámica.
sulfa film película de sulfa.
filopressure *n.* filopresión.
filovaricosis *n.* filovaricosis.
filter *n.* filtrar, filtro.
filterable *adj.* filtrable.
filtrable *adj.* filtrable.
filtrate *n.* filtrado.
filtration *n.* filtración.
gel filtration filtración en gel, gelcromatografía.
filum *n.* filum.
fimbria *n.* fimbria, franja.
fimbriate *adj.* fimbriado, -da.
fimbriated *adj.* fimbriado, -da.
fimbriation *n.* fimbriación.
fimbriectomy *n.* fimbriectomía.
fimbriocele *n.* fimbriocele.
fimbrioplasty *n.* fimbroplastia.
finger *n.* dedo[1].
baseball finger dedo de jugador de béisbol.
bolster finger dedo acolchado.
drumstick finger dedo en palillo de tambor.
hammer finger dedo en llave, dedo en martillo, dedo trabado.
Madonna's finger dedo de Madonna.
mallet finger dedo en maza.
ring finger anular[1].
sausage finger dedo en salchicha.
spade finger dedo en pala.
spider finger dedo arácnido, dedo de araña.
spring finger dedo en resorte.
trigger finger dedo en gatillo.
waxy finger dedo céreo, dedo de cera.
fingernail *n.* uña.
fingerprint *n.* huella digital.
first-aid kit *n.* botiquín.
fission *n.* fisión.
binary fission fisión binaria.
cellular fission fisión celular.
multiple fission fisión múltiple.
nuclear fission fisión atómica, fisión nuclear.
fissura *n.* fisura, hendidura.
fissural *adj.* fisural.
fissuration *n.* fisuración.
fissure *n.* cisura, fisura, hendidura.
Ammon's fissure fisura de ammon.
anal fissure fisura anal, fisura del ano, fisura in ano.
fistula *n.* fístula.
abdominal fistula fístula abdominal.
anal fistula fístula anal, fístula del ano.
arteriovenous fistula fístula arteriovenosa.
biliary fistula fístula biliar.
blind fistula fístula ciega.
branchial fistula fístula branquial, fístula congénita cervical.
bronchoesophageal fistula fístula broncoesofágica.

bronchopleural fistula fístula broncopleural.
carotid-cavernous fistula fístula carotídea cavernosa.
cervical fistula fístula cervical.
cholecystoduodenal fistula fístula colecistoduodenal.
coccygeal fistula fístula coccígea.
coloileal fistula fístula coloileal.
colonic fistula fístula cólica, fístula colónica.
colovaginal fistula fístula colovaginal.
colovesical fistula fístula colovesical.
complete fistula fístula completa.
congenital preauricular fistula fístula preauricular congénita.
congenital pulmonary arteriovenous fistula fístula arteriovenosa pulmonar congénita.
coronary arteriovenous fistula fístula arteriovenosa coronaria.
coronary artery fistula fístula arterial coronaria.
craniosinus fistula fístula craniosinus.
dental fistula fístula alveolar, fístula dental, fístula dentaria.
Eck's fistula fístula de Eck.
Eck's fistula in reverse fístula de Eck invertida.
enterocutaneous fistula fístula enterocutánea.
enterovaginal fistula fístula enterovaginal.
enterovesical fistula fístula enterovesical.
external fistula fístula externa.
fecal fistula fístula fecal.
fistula bimucosa fístula bimucosa.
fistula cervicovaginalis laqueatica fístula cervicovaginal, fístula cervicovaginal laqueática.
fistula corneae fístula corneal.
fistula in ano fístula anal, fístula del ano.
fistula lymphatica fístula linfática.
gastric fistula fístula gástrica.
gastrocolic fistula fístula gastrocólica, fístula gastrocolónica.
gastroduodenal fistula fístula gastroduodenal.
gastrointestinal fistula fístula gastrointestinal.
genitourinary fistula fístula genitourinaria.
gingival fistula fístula gingival.
hepatic fistula fístula hepática.
horseshoe fistula fístula en herradura.
incomplete fistula fístula incompleta.
internal fistula fístula interna.
intestinal fistula fístula intestinal.
lacrimal fistula fístula lacrimal, fístula lagrimal.
lacteal fistula fístula láctea.
lymphatic fistula fístula linfática.
Mann-Bollman fistula fístula de Mann-Bollman.
metroperitoneal fistula fístula histeroperitoneal.
oroantral fistula fístula oroantral.
orofacial fistula fístula orofacial.
oronasal fistula fístula oronasal.
parietal fistula fístula parietal.
perineovaginal fistula fístula perineovaginal.
pharyngeal fistula fístula faríngea.
pilonidal fistula fístula pilonidal, fístula sacrococcígea.
pulmonary fistula fístula pulmonar.
rectolabial fistula fístula rectolabial.
rectourethral fistula fístula rectouretral.
rectovaginal fistula fístula rectovaginal.
rectovesical fistula fístula rectovesical.
rectovestibular fistula fístula rectovestibular.

rectovulvar fistula fístula rectovulvar.
salivary fistula fístula salival.
spermatic fistula fístula espermática.
stercoral fistula fístula estercorácea.
submental fistula fístula submentoniana.
Thiry's fistula fístula de Thiry.
Thiry-Vella fistula fístula de Thiry-Vella.
thoracic fistula fístula torácica.
tracheal fistula fístula traqueal.
tracheoesophageal fistula fístula traqueoesofágica.
umbilical fistula fístula onfaloentérica, fístula umbilical.
urachal fistula fístula del uraco, fístula umbilicourinaria, fístula uracal.
ureterocutaneous fistula fístula ureterocutánea.
ureterovaginal fistula fístula ureterovaginal.
urinary fistula fístula urinaria.
urogenital fistula fístula urogenital.
uteroperitoneal fistula fístula uteroperitoneal.
vesical fistula fístula vesical.
vesicocolic fistula fístula vesicocólica, fístula vesicolónica.
vesicocutaneous fistula fístula vesicocutánea.
vesicointestinal fistula fístula vesicointestinal.
vesicouterine fistula fístula vesicouterina.
vesicovaginal fistula fístula vesicovaginal.
vitelline fistula fístula vitelina.
fistulatome *n.* fistulátomo, fistulótomo.
fistulectomy *n.* fistulectomía.
fistulization *n.* fistulización.
fistuloenterostomy *n.* fistuloenterostomía.
fistulotomy *n.* fistulotomía.
fistulous *adj.* fistuloso, -sa.
fixation *n.* contención, fijación.
autotrophic fixation fijación autotrófica.
bifoveal fixation fijación bifoveal.
binocular fixation fijación binocular.
carbon dioxide fixation fijación del dióxido de carbono.
circumalveolar fixation fijación circunalveolar.
circummandibular fixation fijación circunmandibular.
complement fixation fijación de alexina, fijación del complemento.
craneofacial fixation fijación craneofacial.
crossed fixation fijación cruzada.
elastic band fixation fijación por banda elástica.
external fixation fijación externa.
external pin fixation fijación externa por clavos.
intermaxillary fixation fijación intermaxilar.
internal fixation fijación interna.
intraosseous fixation fijación intraósea.
mandibulomaxillary fixation fijación mandibulomaxilar.
maxilomandibular fixation fijación maxilomandibular.
nitrogen fixation fijación de nitrógeno.
skeletal fixation fijación esquelética.
tooth fixation fijación del diente.
fixative *adj.* fijador, fijador, -ra.
flabellum *n.* flabelo.
flaccid *adj.* fláccido, -da, flácido, -da.
flagellar *adj.* flagelar.
flagellate *adj.* flagelado, -da.
flagellated *adj.* flagelado, -da.
flagellation *n.* flagelación.
flagelliform *adj.* flageliforme.
flagellosis *n.* flagelosis.

flagellum *n.* flagelo.
flame *v.* flamear.
flange *n.* aleta.
buccal flange aleta bucal.
labial flange aleta labial.
lingual flange aleta lingual.
flank *n.* flanco.
flap *n.* colgajo.
Abbe's flap colgajo de Abbe.
advacement flap colgajo de avance.
arterial flap colgajo arterial.
axial flap colgajo axial.
axial pattern flap colgajo con configuración axial.
bilobed flap colgajo bilobulado.
bipedicle flap colgajo bipediculado.
bladder flap colgajo vesical.
bone flap colgajo óseo.
buried flap colgajo sepultado.
caterpillar flap colgajo en oruga.
cellulocutaneous flap colgajo celulocutáneo.
composite flap colgajo compuesto.
compound flap colgajo compuesto.
cross flap colgajo cruzado.
delayed flap colgajo diferido.
delayed transfer flap colgajo de transferencia tardía.
deltopectoral flap colgajo deltopectoral.
direct flap colgajo directo.
direct transfer flap colgajo de transferencia directa, colgajo de transferencia inmediata.
distant flap colgajo a distancia, colgajo distante.
double pedicle flap colgajo de doble cabo, colgajo de pedículo doble.
Eloesser flap colgajo de Eloesser.
envelope flap colgajo de cobertura, colgajo de envoltura.
Estlander flap colgajo de Estlander.
fascial flap colgajo fascial.
Filatov flap colgajo de Filatov, colgajo de Filatov-Gillies.
Filatov-Gillies flap colgajo de Filatov, colgajo de Filatov-Gillies.
flag flap colgajo en bandera.
flat flap colgajo plano.
free bone flap colgajo óseo libre.
free flap colgajo libre, colgajo libre vascularizado.
French flap colgajo francés.
full thickness flap colgajo de espesor completo.
gauntlet flap colgajo de guantelete.
Gillies' flap colgajo de Gillies.
gingival flap colgajo gingival.
groin flap colgajo inguinal.
hinged flap colgajo en bisagra.
immediate flap colgajo inmediato.
immediate transfer flap colgajo de transferencia directa, colgajo de transferencia inmediata.
Indian flap colgajo indio.
interpolated flap colgajo interpolado.
island flap colgajo en isla, colgajo insular.
Italian flap colgajo italiano.
jump flap colgajo en salto.
Langebeck pedicle mucoperiosteal flap colgajo mucoperióstico bipendiculado de Langebeck.
Limberg's flap colgajo de Limberg.
lined flap colgajo tapizado.
lingual tongue flap colgajo linguopalatino.
local flap colgajo local.
michrochirurgic free flap colgajo libre microquirúrgico.

modified Widman flap colgajo modificado de Widman.
mucoperichondral flap colgajo mucoperichondral.
mucoperiosteal flap colgajo mucoperióstico.
muscular flap colgajo muscular.
musculocutaneous flap colgajo musculocutáneo.
myocutaneous flap colgajo miocutáneo.
neurovascular flap colgajo neurovascular.
open flap colgajo abierto.
osteomiocutaneous flap colgajo osteomiocutáneo.
parabiotic flap colgajo parabiótico.
partial thickness flap colgajo de espesor parcial.
pectoralis muscle flap colgajo de pectoral.
pedicle flap colgajo pediculado.
pericoronal flap colgajo pericoronal.
permanent pedicle flap colgajo pediculado permanente.
radial forearm flap colgajo radial.
random pattern flap colgajo de distribución al azar, colgajo randomizado.
rectus abdominis muscle flap colgajo de músculo recto abdominal.
rope flap colgajo de cuerda, colgajo en cordel.
rotation flap colgajo de rotación, colgajo por rotación.
sickle flap colgajo falciforme.
skin flap colgajo cutáneo, colgajo de piel.
sliding flap colgajo deslizante, colgajo por deslizamiento.
split thickness flap colgajo de espesor parcial.
subcutaneous flap colgajo subcutáneo.
tongue flap colgajo lingual.
TRAM flap colgajo TRAM.
translation flap colgajo de traslación.
tubed flap colgajo de tubo, colgajo pediculado tubular, colgajo tubular.
tunnel flap colgajo de túnel.
turnover flap colgajo doblado.
VRAM flap colgajo VRAM.
V-Y flap colgajo en V-Y.
Z flap colgajo en Z.
flare *n.* enrojecimiento.
flask *n.* balón^2, mufla.
casting flask balón de moldeo.
crown flask balón coronal.
denture flask balón dental.
Dewar flask balón de Dewar.
Erlenmeyer flask balón de Erlenmeyer.
Fernbach flask balón de Fernbach.
Florence flask balón de Florence.
injection flask balón de inyección.
refractory flask balón refractario.
vacuum flask balón de vacío.
volumetric flask balón volumétrico.
flatulence *n.* flatulencia.
flatulent *adj.* flatulento, -ta.
flatus *n.* flato.
flatus vaginalis garrulitas vulvae.
flavectomy *n.* flavectomía.
flavedo *n.* flavedo.
flavescent *adj.* flavescente.
flavism *n.* flavismo.
Flavivirus *n.* Flavivirus.
Flavobacterium *n.* Flavobacterium.
flavoprotein *n.* flavoproteína.
flavor *n.* sabor.
flebectasia *n.* flebectasia.
fletcherism *n.* fletcherismo.
flex *v.* flexionar.
flexibility *n.* flexibilidad.
flexible *adj.* flexible.

fleximeter *n.* flexímetro.
flexion *n.* flexión[1].
flexoplasty *n.* flexoplastia.
flexor *adj.* flexor, -ra.
flexura *n.* flexión[2], flexura.
flexural *adj.* flexural.
flexure *n.* flexión[2].
  cephalic flexure flexión cefálica.
  cerebral flexure flexión cerebral.
  cranial flexure flexión craneal.
  mesencephalic flexure flexión mesencefálica.
flicker *n.* destello.
floaters *n.* moscas volantes.
floc *n.* floc.
floccose *adj.* flocoso, -sa.
flocculable *adj.* floculable.
flocculate *v.* flocular[1].
flocculation *n.* floculación.
flocculence *n.* floculencia.
flocculent *adj.* floculento, -ta.
flocculoreaction *n.* floculorreacción.
flocculus *n.* flocculus, flóculo.
  accessory flocculus flóculo accesorio, flóculo secundario.
flocular *adj.* flocular[2].
flooding *n.* inundación.
floor *n.* suelo.
flora *n.* flora.
  intestinal flora flora intestinal.
florid *adj.* florido, -da.
flotation *n.* flotación.
flow *n.* flujo[1].
  axoplasmic flow flujo axoplasmático.
  forced expiratory flow (FEF) flujo espiratorio forzado.
  gene flow flujo genético.
  local cerebral blood flow (LCBF) flujo sanguíneo cerebral local (FSCL).
  peak expiratory flow flujo espiratorio máximo.
  renal plasma flow (RPF) flujo plasmático renal (RPF).
  retrograde flow flujo retrógrado.
  total renal blood flow (TRBF) flujo sanguíneo renal total (FSRT).
flowmeter *n.* flujómetro, medidor de flujo.
flu *n.* gripe.
  avian flu gripe aviar.
  bird flu gripe aviar.
  swine flu gripe A, gripe porcina.
flucrylate *n.* flucrilato.
fluctuant *adj.* fluctuante.
fluctuation *n.* fluctuación.
fluent *adj.* fluente.
fluid *n.* fluido, líquido[1].
  allantoic fluid líquido alantoico, líquido alantoideo.
  amniotic fluid líquido amniótico.
  ascitic fluid líquido ascítico.
  body fluid líquido corporal.
  cerebrospinal fluid líquido cefalorraquídeo.
  Condy's fluid líquido de Condy.
  crevicular fluid líquido crevicular.
  Dakin's fluid líquido de Dakin.
  decalcifying fluid líquido descalcificante.
  Delafield's fluid líquido de Delafield.
  dialysis fluid líquido de diálisis, líquido dializador.
  Ecker's fluid líquido de Ecker.
  extravascular fluid líquido extravascular.
  Flemming's fixing fluid líquido fijador de Flemming.
  follicular fluid líquido folicular, liquor folliculi.
  gingival fluid líquido gingival.

  interstitial fluid líquido intersticial.
  intracellular fluid líquido intracelular.
  intraocular fluid líquido intraocular.
  Kaiserling's fluid líquido de Kaiserling.
  labyrinthine fluid líquido laberíntico.
  Lang's fluid líquido de Lang.
  Locke's fluid líquido de Locke.
  Müller's fluid líquido de Müller.
  pericardial fluid líquido pericárdico.
  peritoneal fluid líquido peritoneal.
  Piazza's fluid líquido de Piazza.
  pleural fluid líquido pleural.
  prostatic fluid líquido prostático.
  Rees and Ecker diluting fluid líquido de dilución de Rees y Ecker.
  Rees-Ecker fluid líquido de Rees-Ecker.
  Scarpa's fluid líquido de Scarpa.
  seminal fluid líquido seminal.
  serous fluid líquido seroso.
  spinal fluid líquido espinal.
  sulcular fluid líquido sulcular.
  synovial fluid líquido sinovial.
  Thoma's fluid líquido de Thoma.
  tissue fluid líquido hístico, líquido tisular.
  transcellular fluid líquido transcelular.
  uterine fluid líquido uterino.
  ventricular fluid líquido ventricular.
  Waldeyer's fluid líquido de Waldeyer.
  Wickersheimer's fluid líquido de Wickersheimer.
  Zenker's fluid líquido de Zenker.
fluidity *n.* fluidez.
fluke *n.* duela.
  blood fluke duela sanguínea.
  human liver fluke duela hepática, duela hepática humana.
  intestinal fluke duela intestinal.
  liver fluke duela hepática, duela hepática humana.
  lung fluke duela pulmonar.
flumina pilorum *n.* flumina pilorum.
fluorescein *n.* fluoresceína.
fluoresceinuria *n.* fluoresceinuria.
fluorescence *n.* fluorescencia.
fluorescent *adj.* fluorescente.
fluoridation *n.* fluoración.
fluoridization *n.* fluoridización.
fluorimetry *n.* fluorimetría.
fluorochrome *n.* fluorocromo.
fluorochroming *n.* fluorocromación.
fluorocyte *n.* fluorocito.
fluorography *n.* fluorografía.
fluoroimmunoassay *n.* fluoroinmunoensayo.
fluorometer *n.* fluorómetro.
fluorometry *n.* fluorofotometría, fluorometría.
fluoronephelometer *n.* fluoronefelómetro.
fluororoentgenography *n.* fluorroentgenografía.
fluororoentgeonography *n.* fluororradiografía.
fluoroscope *n.* fluoroscopio.
  biplane fluoroscope fluoroscopio biplano.
fluoroscopic *adj.* fluoroscópico, -ca.
fluoroscopy *n.* fluoroscopia.
fluorosis *n.* fluorosis.
  chronic endemic fluorosis fluorosis endémica crónica.
  dental fluorosis fluorosis dental.
flush *n.* rubor, sofoco.
  hectic flush rubor héctico.
  malar flush rubor malar.
flutter *n.* aleteo, flúter.
  atrial flutter aleteo atrial, flúter auricular.
  auricular flutter aleteo auricular.

  diaphragmatic flutter aleteo diafragmático, flúter diafragmático.
  impure flutter aleteo impuro, flúter impuro.
  mediastinal flutter flúter mediastínico.
  ocular flutter aleteo ocular.
  pure flutter flúter puro.
  ventricular flutter aleteo ventricular.
  ventricular flutter (VFI) flúter ventricular.
flutter-fibrillation *n.* aleteo-fibrilación.
flux *n.* flujo[2].
  celiac flux flujo celíaco.
  ionic flux flujo iónico.
  luminous flux flujo luminoso.
  menstrual flux flujo menstrual.
  Newtonian flux flujo newtoniano.
fluxion *n.* fluxión.
fly *n.* mosca.
foam *n.* espuma.
focal *adj.* focal.
focimeter *n.* focómetro.
focus *n.* foco.
  aplanatic focus foco aplanático.
  Assmann focus foco de Assmann.
  conjugate focus foco conjugado.
  epileptogenic focus foco epileptógeno.
  Gohn's focus foco de Gohn.
  natural focus of infection foco natural de infección.
  principal focus foco principal.
  real focus foco real.
  Simon focus foco de Simon.
  virtual focus foco virtual.
fogging *n.* veladura.
fold *n.* pliegue.
  genital fold pliegue genital.
  Jonnesco's fold pliegue de Jonnesco.
  Juvara's fold pliegue de Juvara.
  Rathke's fold pliegue de Rathke.
  Schultze's fold pliegue de Schultze.
follicle *n.* folículo.
follicular *adj.* folicular.
folliculitis *n.* foliculitis.
  agminate folliculitis foliculitis agminada.
  eosinophilic pustular folliculitis foliculitis pustulosa eosinofílica.
  folliculitis abscedens et suffodiens foliculitis abscedens et suffodiens.
  folliculitis barbae foliculitis de la barba.
  folliculitis decalvans foliculitis decalvante.
  folliculitis externa foliculitis externa.
  folliculitis gonorrheica foliculitis blenorrágica, foliculitis gonorreica.
  folliculitis interna foliculitis interna.
  folliculitis keloidalis foliculitis queloide.
  folliculitis nares perforans foliculitis perforante de la nariz.
  folliculitis ulerythematosa reticulata foliculitis uleritematosa reticulada.
  folliculitis varioliformis foliculitis varioliformis.
  gram-negative folliculitis foliculitis gram-negativa.
  keloidal folliculitis foliculitis queloide.
  perforating folliculitis foliculitis perforante.
folliculoma *n.* foliculoma.
  lipidic folliculoma foliculoma lipoídico.
follitropin *n.* folitropina.
fomentation *n.* fomentación.
fomite *n.* fomite.
fontanel *n.* fontanela.
fonticulus *n.* fontículo.
food *n.* alimento, comida.
  base-forming food alimento formador de bases.
  dietetic food alimento dietético.

food exchange list alimento equivalentes.
organic food alimento orgánico.
foot *n.* pie.
athlete's foot pie de atleta.
Charcot's foot pie de Charcot.
claw foot pie en garra.
cleft foot pie hendido.
club foot pie zambo.
drop foot pie caído.
flat foot pes planus, pie plano.
forced foot pie forzado.
Friedreich's foot pie de Friedreich.
fungous foot pie micótico.
Hong-Kong foot pie de Hong-Kong.
immersion foot pie de inmersión.
madura foot pie de madura.
march foot pie de marcha.
Morand's foot pie de Morand.
Morton's foot pie de Morton.
mossy foot pie musgoso.
perivascular foot pie chupador, pie perivas
cular.
sandal foot pie en sandalia.
spastic flat foot pie plano espástico.
spatula foot pie en espátula.
trench foot pie de trinchera.
forage *n.* forage.
foramen *n.* agujero, foramen.
foraminiferal *adj.* foraminífero, -ra.
foraminiferous *adj.* foraminífero, -ra.
foraminotomy *n.* foraminotomía.
foration *n.* foración.
force *n.* fuerza[1].
animal force fuerza animal.
bite force fuerza de mordida.
catabolic force fuerza catabólica.
centrifugal force fuerza centrífuga.
centripetal force fuerza centrípeta.
coercitive force fuerza coercitiva de los músculos.
electromotive force (EMF) fuerza electromotriz (FEM).
extraoral force fuerza extrabucal.
force of mastication fuerza de masticación,
fuerza de masticación.
frictional force fuerza de fricción.
London force fuerza de Londres.
nerve force fuerza nerviosa.
nervous force fuerza nerviosa.
occlusal force fuerza oclusal.
relative centrifugal force (RCF) fuerza centrífuga relativa (FCR).
reserve force fuerza de reserva, fuerza radical.
rest force fuerza de reposo.
van der Waals' force fuerza de van der Waals.
vital force fuerza vital.
forceps *n.* fórceps, pinzas.
Adson forceps pinzas de Adson.
alligator forceps fórceps aligátor, pinzas alligator.
Allis forceps fórceps de Allis.
Arruga's forceps pinzas de Arruga.
arterial forceps pinzas arterial.
Asch forceps fórceps de Asch.
axis-traction forceps fórceps de tracción
axial.
Bailey-Williamson forceps fórceps de Bailey-
Williamson.
Barton forceps fórceps de Barton.
bone forceps pinzas para huesos.
Brown-Adson forceps pinzas de Brown-Adson.
bulldog forceps pinzas bulldog.
bullet forceps pinzas para proyectiles.
capsule forceps pinzas para cápsula.
cup biopsy forceps pinzas para biopsias.

cutting forceps pinzas para cortar.
DeLee forceps fórceps de DeLee.
dental forceps fórceps dental, pinzas dental.
dressing forceps pinzas para vendajes.
Elliot forceps fórceps de Elliot.
Evans forceps pinzas de Evans.
extracting forceps pinzas de extracción.
Garrison's forceps fórceps de Garrison.
Graefe forceps pinzas de Graefe.
Hawks-Dennen forceps fórceps de Hawks-
Dennen.
hemostatic forceps pinzas hemostática.
high forceps fórceps alto.
jeweler's forceps pinzas de joyero.
Kielland's forceps fórceps de Kielland.
Kjelland's forceps fórceps de Kjelland.
Kocher forceps fórceps de Kocher.
Koeberlé forceps fórceps de Koeberlé.
Lahey forceps pinzas Lahey.
Laplace's forceps pinzas de Laplace.
Levret's forceps fórceps de Levret.
low forceps fórceps bajo.
Löwenberg's forceps pinzas de Löwenberg.
Luikart forceps fórceps de Luikart.
mouse-tooth forceps pinzas diente de ratón.
needle forceps pinzas para agujas.
obstetrical forceps fórceps obstétrico.
O'Hara forceps pinzas O'Hara.
outlet forceps fórceps de salida.
Piper forceps fórceps de Piper.
Randall stone forceps de Randall, pinzas
para cálculos.
Simpson's forceps fórceps de Simpson.
speculum forceps pinzas especular.
Tarnier's forceps fórceps de Tarnier.
tubular forceps pinzas tubular.
Tucker-McLean forceps fórceps de Tucker-
McLean.
vulsellum forceps pinzas vulsellum.
Walsham's forceps fórceps de Walsham.
Willett forceps fórceps de Willett, pinzas de
Willett.
forcipressure *n.* forcipresión.
forearm *n.* antebrachium, antebrazo.
forefoot *n.* antepié.
forehead *n.* frente.
Olympian forehead frente olímpica.
foreign *adj.* extraño, -ña[1], extraño, -ña[2].
forensic *adj.* forense.
forensic scientist forense[1].
forgetting *n.* olvido.
form *n.* forma.
accollé form forma accolée.
appliqué form forma appliquée.
arch form forma arqueada, forma de arco.
boat form forma de bote.
cavity preparation form forma de preparación cavitaria.
chair form forma de silla.
extension form forma de extensión.
face form forma facial.
half-chair form forma en media silla.
involution form forma de involución.
juvenile form forma joven, forma juvenil.
L form forma L.
occlusal form forma oclusal.
outline form forma de contorno.
posterior tooth form forma de diente posterior.
replicative form forma replicativa.
resistance form forma de resistencia.
retencion form forma de retención.
ring form forma de anillo.
skew form forma sesgada.
tooth form forma dental.

twist form forma retorcida.
wave form forma de onda.
wax form forma cérea.
young form forma joven, forma juvenil.
formalinize *v.* formalinizar.
formation *n.* formación.
compromise formation formación de compromiso.
palisade formation formación en empalizada.
formication *n.* formicación, hormigueo.
formiciasis *n.* formiciasis.
formula *n.* fórmula.
formulate *v.* formular.
fornix *n.* fórnix.
foruncle *n.* forúnculo.
fosso *n.* fosa.
fossula *n.* foseta, fosita.
foundation *n.* fundación.
denture foundation fundación dental.
founder *n.* fundador, -ra.
fovea *n.* fóvea.
foveate *adj.* foveado, -da.
foveated *adj.* foveado, -da.
foveation *n.* foveación.
foveola *n.* foveola.
foveolar *adj.* foveolar.
foveolate *adj.* foveolado, -da.
fraction *n.* fracción.
amorphous fraction of adrenal cortex fracción amorfa de la corteza suprarrenal.
blood plasma fraction fracción del plasma.
dried human plasma protein fraction fracción proteica del plasma humano desecado.
ejection fraction (EF) fracción de eyección
(FE), fracción de eyección sistólica.
filtration fraction (FF) fracción de filtración
(FF).
human plasma protein fraction fracción
proteica del plasma humano.
mole fraction fracción molar.
recombination fraction fracción de recombinación.
regurgitant fraction fracción de regurgitación.
systolic ejection fraction fracción de eyección (FE), fracción de eyección sistólica.
fractional *adj.* fraccionario, -ria.
fractionation *n.* fraccionamiento.
fracture *n.* fractura.
depressed cranial fracture hundimiento craneal.
fragiform *adj.* fragiforme.
fragilitas *n.* fragilidad, fragilitas.
fragility *n.* fragilidad.
capillary fragility fragilidad capilar, fragilitas
crinium.
erythrocyte fragility fragilidad de la sangre.
fragility of bone fragilidad de los huesos, fragilitas ossium.
fragility of the blood fragilidad de la sangre.
fragilocyte *n.* fragilocito.
fragilocytosis *n.* fragilocitosis.
fragment *n.* fragmento.
acentric fragment fragmento acéntrico.
butterfly fragment fragmento en mariposa.
Fab fragment fragmento Fab.
Fc. fragment fragmento Fc.
one-carbon fragment fragmento de un carbono.
Spengler's fragment fragmento de Spengler.
two-carbon fragment fragmento de dos carbonos.
fragmentation *n.* fragmentación.
fraise *n.* fresa.
frambesiform *adj.* frambesiforme.

frambesioma *n.* frambesioma.
frame *n.* armazón, marco.
  electric frame armazón de calentamiento.
  heat frame armazón de calentamiento.
  ice frame armazón de hielo.
  reading frame marco de lectura.
  trial frame armazón de ensayo.
framework *n.* esqueleto.
  appendicular framework esqueleto apendicular.
  articulated framework esqueleto articulado.
  axial framework esqueleto axial, esqueleto axil.
  cardiac framework esqueleto cardíaco, esqueleto del corazón.
  jaw framework esqueleto maxilar.
  sclera framework esqueleto de la esclerótica.
  visceral framework esqueleto visceral.
Francisella *n.* Francisella.
frank *adj.* franco, -ca.
franklinic *adj.* franclínico, -ca.
franklinization *n.* franklinización.
freckle *n.* peca.
  Hutchinson's freckle peca de Hutchinson.
  iris freckle peca del iris.
  melanotic freckle peca melanótica.
freeze-drying *n.* congelación-desecación, criodesecación.
freeze-etching *n.* criosombreado.
freeze-fracturing *n.* criofractura.
freeze-substitution *n.* congelación-sustitución.
freezing *n.* congelación[1].
  gastric freezing congelación gástrica.
fremitus *n.* frémito.
  bronchial fremitus frémito bronquial.
  friction fremitus frémito por fricción.
  pericardial fremitus frémito pericárdico.
  pleural fremitus frémito pleural.
  rhonchal fremitus frémito rónquico.
  subjective fremitus frémito subjetivo.
  tactile fremitus frémito táctil.
  tussive fremitus frémito tusígeno.
  vocal fremitus frémito vocal.
frenotomy *n.* frenotomía.
frenulum *n.* frenillo.
frenum *n.* freno.
frenzy *n.* frenesí.
frequency *n.* frecuencia.
  breathing respiration frequency frecuencia de la respiración.
  critical flicker fusion frequency frecuencia de fusión crítica de destellos.
  frequency of micturition frecuencia de micción.
  fundamental frequency frecuencia fundamental.
  gene frequency frecuencia genética.
fretting *n.* desgaste.
Freudian *adj.* freudiano, -na.
friability *n.* friabilidad.
friable *adj.* friable.
fricative *adj.* fricativo, -va.
friction *n.* fricción, friega.
  dynamic friction fricción dinámica.
  starting friction fricción de iniciación.
  static friction fricción estática.
fright *n.* susto.
frigid *adj.* frígido, -da.
frigidity *n.* frigidez.
frigostable *adj.* frigoestable.
frigotherapy *n.* frigoterapia.
fringe *n.* franja.
  cervical fringe franja cervical.

  costal fringe franja costal.
frit *n.* frito.
frontal *adj.* frontal.
frontipetal *adj.* frontípeto, -ta.
frontofocometer *n.* frontofocómetro.
frontomalar *adj.* frontomalar.
frontomaxillary *adj.* frontomaxilar.
frontonasal *adj.* frontonasal.
fronto-occipital *adj.* frontooccipital.
frontotemporal *adj.* frontotemporal.
frontozygomatic *adj.* frontocigomático, -ca.
frostbite *n.* congelación[2].
  deep frostbite congelación profunda.
  superficial frostbite congelación superficial.
frotoparietal *adj.* frontoparietal.
frottement *n.* frotamiento.
fructosemia *n.* fructosemia.
fructosuria *n.* fructosuria.
  essential fructosuria fructosuria esencial.
frustration *n.* frustración.
fuchsin *n.* fucsina.
fuchsinophil *adj.* fucsinófilo, fucsinófilo, -la.
fuchsinophilia *n.* fucsinofilia.
fuchsinophilic *adj.* fucsinofílico, -ca.
fucosidosis *n.* fucosidosis.
fugacity *n.* fugacidad.
fugitive *adj.* fugaz.
fugue *n.* fuga.
  epileptic fugue fuga epiléptica.
  psychogenic fugue fuga de ideas.
fuguism *n.* fuguismo.
fulcrum *n.* fulcro.
fulgurant *adj.* fulgurante.
fulguration *n.* fulguración.
fulliculosis *n.* foliculosis.
fulminant *adj.* fulminante.
fumigate *v.* fumigar.
fumigation *n.* fumigación.
funcigide *n.* fungicida.
functio laesa *n.* functio laesa.
function *n.* función.
  allomeric function función alomérica.
  arousal function función de despertar.
  atrial transport function función de transporte auricular.
  cumulative distribution function función de distribución acumulable.
  discriminant function función discriminante.
  distribution function función de distribución.
  isomeric function función isomérica.
  mapping function función de mapeo.
  modulation transfer function función de transferencia de modulación.
  probability density function función de densidad de probabilidad.
functional *adj.* funcional.
fundament *n.* fundamento.
fundamental *adj.* fundamental.
fundectomy *n.* fundectomía, fundosectomía, fundusectomía.
fundic *adj.* fúndico, -ca.
fundiform *adj.* fundiforme.
fundoplication *n.* fundoplicación.
fundus *n.* fondo, fundus.
  albinotic fundus fondo albinótico.
  fundus albipunctatus fondo albipunctatus.
  fundus diabeticus fondo diabético.
  fundus flavimaculatus fondo flavimaculatus.
  fundus gastricus fondo de estómago.
  fundus meatus acustici interni fondo del meato auditivo interno.
  fundus oculi fondo de ojo.

  fundus of internal acoustic meatus fondo del conducto auditivo interno.
  fundus of stomach fondo de estómago.
  fundus of the urinary bladder fondo de la vejiga urinaria, fondo vesical.
  fundus of the uterus fondo del útero, fondo uterino.
  fundus of the vagina fondo de la vagina.
  fundus tigre fondo tigroide.
  fundus tympani fondo timpánico.
  fundus uteri fondo del útero, fondo uterino.
  fundus vaginae fondo de la vagina.
  fundus vesicae urinariae fondo de la vejiga urinaria, fondo vesical.
  leopard fundus fondo en leopardo.
  tesellated fundus fondo en mosaico, fondo teselado.
  tigroid fundus fondo tigroide.
funduscope *n.* fundoscopio.
funduscopy *n.* fundoscopia.
fundusectomy *n.* fundisectomía.
fungal *adj.* fungal.
fungemia *n.* fungemia.
fungiforme *adj.* fungiforme.
fungiliform *adj.* fungiliforme.
fungistasis *n.* fungistasis.
fungistatic *adj.* fungistático, -ca.
fungitoxic *adj.* fungifitóxico, -ca, fungitóxico, -ca.
fungitoxicity *n.* fungitoxicidad.
fungoid *adj.* fungoide.
fungosity *n.* fungosidad.
fungous *adj.* fungoso, -sa.
fungus *n.* fungus, hongo.
funic *adj.* fúnico, -ca.
funicle *n.* funículo, funiculus.
funiculalgia *n.* funiculalgia.
funicular *adj.* funicular.
funiculitis *n.* funiculitis.
  endemic funiculitis funiculitis endémica.
  filarial funiculitis funiculitis filariásica.
funiculopexy *n.* funiculopexia.
funiculus *n.* cordón, funículo, funiculus.
  funiculus umbilicalis cordón umbilical.
funiform *adj.* funiforme.
funis *n.* funis.
furcation *n.* furcación.
furfur *n.* fúrfura.
furfuraceous *adj.* furfuráceo, -a.
furrow *n.* surco.
furuncle *n.* forúnculo.
furuncular *adj.* furuncular.
furunculoid *adj.* furunculoide.
furunculosis *n.* furunculosis.
  furunculosis blastomycetica furunculosis blastomicética.
  furunculosis cryptococcica furunculosis criptocócica.
  furunculosis orientalis furunculosis oriental.
furunculous *adj.* furunculoso.
Fusarium *n.* Fusarium.
fuscin *n.* fuscina.
fuse *v.* fundir.
fusiform *adj.* fusiforme.
fusimotor *adj.* fusimotor, -ra.
fusion *n.* fusión.
  cell fusion fusión celular.
  centric fusion fusión céntrica.
  nuclear fusion fusión nuclear.
Fusobacterium *n.* Fusobacterium.
fusocellular *adj.* fusocelular.
fusospirillosis *n.* fusoespirilosis.
fusospirochetosis *n.* fusoespiroquetosis.
fututrix *n.* fututrix.

G g

GABA *n.* GABA.
GABAergic *adj.* gabaminérgico, -ca.
gadfly *n.* tábano.
gag *n.* abrebocas, mordaza.
Davis-Crowe mouth gag mordaza bucal de Davis-Crowe.
gain *n.* beneficio, ganancia.
antigen gain ganancia de antígeno.
brightness gain ganancia en brillo.
primary gain beneficio primario de la enfermedad, ganancia primaria.
secondary gain beneficio secundario de la enfermedad, ganancia secundaria.
therapeutic gain ganancia terapéutica.
time compensation gain (TCG) ganancia de compensación de tiempo.
time-compensated gain ganancia de compensación de tiempo.
time-varied gain (TVG)]) ganancia tiempo-variada.
gait *n.* marcha.
antalgic gait marcha antálgica.
ataxic gait marcha atáxica.
calcaneous gait marcha calcánea.
cautious gait marcha cautelosa.
cerebellar gait marcha cerebelosa, marcha oscilante.
compensated gluteal gait marcha glútea compensada.
crutch gait marcha con muletas.
dorsiflexor gait marcha de dorsiflexión.
double step gait marcha de paso doble.
drag-to gait marcha arrastrada, marcha de arrastre.
drop foot gait marcha de pie caído.
dystrophic gait marcha distrófica, marcha miopática.
equine gait marcha equina.
festinating gait marcha festinante.
four-point gait marcha de cuatro puntos.
gastrocnemius gait marcha gemelar.
gluteal gait marcha glútea.
heel-toe gait marcha de talón y dedos, marcha taloneante.
helicopod gait marcha helicópoda.
hemiplegic gait marcha de segador, marcha hemipléjica.
high steppage gait marcha en estepaje, marcha en estepaje alto.
Parkinsonian gait marcha parkinsoniana.
Petren's gait marcha de Petren.
pigeon gait marcha de paloma.
quadriceps gait marcha del cuádriceps.
scissors gait marcha en tijeras.
spastic gait marcha espasmódica, marcha espástica.
stamping gait marcha de talón y dedos, marcha taloneante.
stepping gait marcha a pequeños pasos.
tabetic gait marcha tabética.

three-point gait marcha de tres puntos, marcha en tres apoyos.
Trendelenburg gait marcha de Trendelenburg.
two point gait marcha de dos apoyos, marcha de dos puntos.
uncompensated gluteal gait marcha glútea descompensada.
waddling gait marcha de ánade.
galactacrasia *n.* galactacrasia.
galactagogue *n.* galactagogo.
galactemia *n.* galactemia.
galactic *adj.* galáctico, -ca.
galactidrosis *n.* galacthidrosis, galactidrosis, galactohidrosis.
galactischia *n.* galactisquia.
galactoblast *n.* galactoblasto.
galactobolic *adj.* galactobólico, -ca.
galactocele *n.* galactocele.
galactocrasia *n.* galactocrasia.
galactogen *n.* galactógeno.
galactogenous *adj.* galactógeno, -na.
galactogogue *n.* galactogogo, -ga.
galactography *n.* galactografía.
galactokinase *n.* galactocinasa, galactoquinasa.
galactolipid *n.* galactolípido.
galactolipin *n.* galactolipina.
galactoma *n.* galactoma.
galactometastasis *n.* galactometástasis.
galactometer *n.* galactómetro.
galactopexy *n.* galactopexia.
galactophagous *adj.* galactófago, -ga.
galactophlebitis *n.* galactoflebitis.
galactophlysis *n.* galactóflisis.
galactophore *n.* galactóforo.
galactophoritis *n.* galactoforitis.
galactophorous *adj.* galactóforo, -ra.
galactophygous *adj.* galactófigo, -ga.
galactoplania *n.* galactoplania.
galactopoiesis *n.* galactopoyesis.
galactopoietic *adj.* galactopoyético, -ca.
galactopyra *n.* galactópira.
galactorrhea *n.* galactia, galactorrea.
galactoschesis *n.* galactosquesis.
galactoscope *n.* galactoscopio.
galactose *n.* galactosa.
galactosemia *n.* galactosemia.
classic galactosemia galactosemia congénita.
congenital galactosemia galactosemia congénita.
galactokinase deficiency galactosemia galactosemia por déficit de galactocinasa.
galactoside *n.* galactósido.
galactosis *n.* galactosis.
galactostasis *n.* galactostasia, galactostasis.
galactosuria *n.* galactosuria.
galactosylceramidase *n.* galactosilceramidasa.
galactotherapy *n.* galactoterapia.

galactotoxin *n.* galactotoxina.
galactotoxism *n.* galactotoxismo.
galactotrophy *n.* galactotrofia.
galactoxism *n.* galactoxismo.
galacturia *n.* galacturia.
galea *n.* galea.
galea aponeurotica galea aponeurótica.
galea capitis galea capitis.
galeatomy *n.* galeatomía.
galeatus *adj.* galeado, -da.
galenica *n.* galenicales, galénicos.
galenicals *n.* galenicales, galénicos.
galenics *n.* galenicales, galénicos.
galeropia *n.* galeropía.
galeropsia *n.* galeropsia.
gall *n.* rozadura.
gallein *n.* galeína.
gallop *n.* galope.
atrial gallop galope auricular.
presystolic gallop galope presistólico.
protodiastolic gallop galope protodiastólico.
summation gallop galope de sumación.
systolic gallop galope sistólico.
gallstone *n.* cálculo.
opacifying gallstone cálculo biliar opacificador.
silent gallstone cálculo biliar silencioso.
galvanic *adj.* galvánico, -ca.
galvanism *n.* galvanismo.
dental galvanism galvanismo dental.
galvanization *n.* galvanización.
galvanocaustia *n.* galvanocaustia.
chemical galvanocaustia galvanocaustia química.
thermal galvanocaustia galvanocaustia térmica.
galvanocautery *n.* galvanocauterio.
galvanochemical *adj.* galvanoquímico, -ca.
galvanocontractility *n.* galvanocontractilidad.
galvanofaradization *n.* galvanofaradización.
galvanogustometer *n.* galvanogustómetro.
galvanoionization *n.* galvanoionización.
galvanolysis *n.* galvanólisis.
galvanometer *n.* galvanómetro.
d'Arsonval galvanometer galvanómetro de bovina móvil, galvanómetro de cuadro móvil, galvanómetro de d'Arsonval.
Einthoven's galvanometer galvanómetro de Einthoven, galvanómetro de filamento, galvanómetro de hilo.
Einthoven's string galvanometer galvanómetro de Einthoven, galvanómetro de filamento, galvanómetro de hilo.
galvanomuscular *adj.* galvanomuscular.
galvanonarcosis *n.* galvanonarcosis.
galvanonervous *adj.* galvanonervioso, -sa.
galvanopalpation *n.* galvanopalpación.
galvanoscope *n.* galvanoscopio.
galvanosurgery *n.* galvanocirugía.

galvanotaxis *n.* galvanotaxia, galvanotaxis.
galvanotherapeutics *n.* galvanoterapia.
galvanotherapy *n.* galvanoterapia.
galvanotonus *n.* galvanotonía, galvanotono.
galvanotropism *n.* galvanotropismo.
gambling *n.* ludopatía.
game *n.* juego.
  compulsive game juego compulsivo.
  controlled game juego controlado.
  model game juego modelo.
  pathologic game juego patológico.
gamete *n.* gameto.
gametic *adj.* gamético, -ca.
gametocide *n.* gametocida[1].
gametocydal *adj.* gametocida[2].
gametocyst *n.* gametoquiste.
gametocyte *n.* gametocito.
gametocytemia *n.* gametocitemia.
gametogenesis *n.* gametogénesis, gametogenia.
gametogenic *adj.* gametogénico, -ca.
gametogonia *n.* gametogonia.
gametogony *n.* gametogonia.
gametoid *adj.* gametoide.
gametokinetic *adj.* gametocinético, -ca.
gametologist *n.* gametólogo, -ga.
gametology *n.* gametología.
gametopathy *n.* gametopatía.
gametophagia *n.* gametofagia.
gametotropic *adj.* gametotrópico, -ca.
gamic *adj.* gámico, -ca.
gammacardiogram *n.* gammacardiograma.
gammacardiography *n.* gammacardiografía.
gammacism *n.* gamacismo, gammacismo.
gammaencephalogram *n.* gammaencefalograma.
gammaglobulin *n.* gammaglobulina.
gammaglobulinopathy *n.* gammaglobulinopatía.
gammaglutamyltranspeptidase *n.* gammaglutamiltransferasa, gammaglutamiltranspeptidasa.
gammagram *n.* gammagrama.
gammagraphic *adj.* gammagráfico, -ca.
gammagraphy *n.* gammagrafía.
  gammagraphy of the brain gammaencefalografía.
gamma-orbitography *n.* gammaorbitografía.
gammatherapy *n.* gammaterapia.
gammatomography *n.* gammatomografía.
gammavenography *n.* gammaflebografía.
gammopathy *n.* gammapatía.
  benign monoclonal gammopathy gammapatía monoclonal benigna, gammapatía monoclónica benigna.
  monoclonal gammopathy gammapatía monoclonal, gammapatía monoclónica.
  polyclonal gammopathy gammapatía policlonal, gammapatía policlónica.
gamobium *n.* gamobio.
gamogenesis *n.* gamogénesis.
gamogony *n.* gamogonia.
gamont *n.* gamonte, gamonto.
gamophagia *n.* gamofagia.
gamophobia *n.* gamofobia.
gampsodactyly *n.* gampsodactilia.
gangliasthenia *n.* gangliastenia.
gangliate *adj.* gangliado, -da.
gangliated *adj.* gangliado, -da.
gangliectomy *n.* gangliectomía.
gangliitis *n.* gangliítis, ganglitis.
ganglioblast *n.* ganglioblasto.
gangliocyte *n.* gangliocito.
gangliocytoma *n.* gangliocitoma.
ganglioform *adj.* ganglioforme.

ganglioglioma *n.* ganglioglioma.
ganglioglioneuroma *n.* ganglioglioneuroma.
gangliolysis *n.* gangliólisis.
  percutaneous radiofrequency gangliolysis gangliólisis percutánea por radiofrecuencia.
gangliolytic *adj.* gangliolítico, -ca.
ganglioma *n.* ganglioma.
  sympathetic embryonic ganglioma ganglioma embrionario simpático.
ganglion *n.* ganglio, ganglión.
  Acrel's ganglion ganglión de Acrel.
  compound ganglion ganglión compuesto.
  diffuse ganglion ganglión difuso.
  primary ganglion ganglión primario.
  simple ganglion ganglión simple.
  synovial ganglion ganglión sinovial.
ganglionated *adj.* ganglionado, -da.
ganglionectomy *n.* ganglionectomía.
ganglioneuroblastoma *n.* ganglioneuroblastoma.
ganglioneurofibroma *n.* ganglioneurofibroma.
ganglioneuroma *n.* ganglioneuroma.
  central ganglioneuroma ganglioneuroma central.
  dumbbell ganglioneuroma ganglioneuroma en pesa de gimnasia.
ganglioneuromatosis *n.* ganglioneuromatosis.
ganglionic *adj.* ganglionar.
ganglionitis *n.* ganglionitis.
  acute posterior ganglionitis ganglionitis posterior aguda.
  Gasserian ganglionitis ganglionitis de Gasser.
ganglionostomy *n.* ganglionostomía.
ganglioplegic *adj.* gangliopléjico, -ca.
gangliosialidosis *n.* gangliosidosis.
ganglioside *n.* gangliósido.
  ganglioside GM1 gangliósido GM1.
  ganglioside GM2 gangliósido GM2.
gangliosidosis *n.* gangliosidosis.
  adult GM1 gangliosidosis gangliosidosis GM1 del adulto, gangliosidosis GM1 tipo 3.
  adult GM2 gangliosidosis gangliosidosis GM2 del adulto.
  generalized gangliosidosis gangliosidosis generalizada.
  GM1 gangliosidosis gangliosidosis GM1.
  GM2 gangliosidosis gangliosidosis GM2.
  infantile GM1 gangliosidosis gangliosidosis GM1 infantil, gangliosidosis GM1 tipo 1.
  infantile GM2 gangliosidosis gangliosidosis GM2 infantil, gangliosidosis GM2 tipo 1.
  juvenile GM1 gangliosidosis gangliosidosis GM1 juvenil, gangliosidosis GM1 tipo 2.
  juvenile GM2 gangliosidosis gangliosidosis GM2 juvenil, gangliosidosis GM2 tipo 3.
  type 1 GM1 gangliosidosis gangliosidosis GM1 infantil, gangliosidosis GM1 tipo 1.
  type 1 GM2 gangliosidosis gangliosidosis GM2 infantil, gangliosidosis GM2 tipo 1.
  type 2 GM1 gangliosidosis gangliosidosis GM1 juvenil, gangliosidosis GM1 tipo 2.
  type 2 GM2 gangliosidosis gangliosidosis GM2 tipo 2, gangliosidosis GM2 variante 0.
  type 3 GM1 gangliosidosis gangliosidosis GM1 del adulto, gangliosidosis GM1 tipo 3.
  type 3 GM2 gangliosidosis gangliosidosis GM2 juvenil, gangliosidosis GM2 tipo 3.
  variant 0 GM2 gangliosidosis gangliosidosis GM2 tipo 2, gangliosidosis GM2 variante 0.
gangliosympathectomy *n.* gangliosimpatectomía.
gangosa *n.* gangosa.
gangrene *n.* gangrena.
  anemic gangrene gangrena anémica.

  angiosclerotic gangrene gangrena angioesclerótica.
  arteriosclerotic gangrene gangrena arterioesclerótica.
  carbolic gangrene gangrena carbólica.
  circumscribed gangrene gangrena circunscrita.
  cold gangrene gangrena fría.
  cutaneous gangrene gangrena cutánea.
  decubital gangrene gangrena por decúbito.
  diabetic gangrene gangrena diabética.
  diphtheritic gangrene gangrena diftérica.
  disseminated cutaneous gangrene gangrena cutánea diseminada.
  dry gangrene gangrena seca.
  embolic gangrene gangrena embólica.
  emphysematous gangrene gangrena enfisematosa.
  epidemic gangrene gangrena epidémica.
  eyelid benign gangrene gangrena benigna de los párpados.
  Fournier's gangrene gangrena de Fournier.
  fulminant gangrene gangrena fulminante.
  fulminant gangrene in the genital member gangrena fulminante de los órganos genitales.
  gas gangrene gangrena gaseosa.
  gaseous gangrene gangrena gaseosa.
  glycemic gangrene gangrena glucémica.
  hemorrhagic gangrene gangrena hemorrágica.
  hot gangrene gangrena caliente.
  humid gangrene gangrena húmeda.
  inflammatory gangrene gangrena inflamatoria.
  Lasègue's gangrene gangrena de Lasègue.
  Meleney's gangrene gangrena de Meleney.
  Meleney's synergistic gangrene gangrena sinérgica, gangrena sinérgica de Meleney, gangrena sinergística de Meleney.
  mephitic gangrene gangrena mefítica.
  mixed gangrene gangrena mixta.
  moist gangrene gangrena húmeda.
  molecular gangrene gangrena molecular.
  multiple gangrene gangrena múltiple.
  neurotic gangrene gangrena neurótica.
  oral gangrene gangrena oral.
  Pott's gangrene gangrena de Pott.
  presenile gangrene gangrena presenil.
  presenile spontaneous gangrene gangrena presenil espontánea.
  pressure gangrene gangrena por presión.
  primary gangrene gangrena primaria.
  progressive bacterial synergistic gangrene gangrena sinérgica bacteriana progresiva, gangrena sinergística progresiva.
  progressive gangrene gangrena progresiva.
  progressive synergistic gangrene gangrena sinérgica bacteriana progresiva, gangrena sinergística progresiva.
  pulmonary gangrene gangrena pulmonar.
  Raynaud's gangrene gangrena de Raynaud.
  secondary gangrene gangrena secundaria.
  senile gangrene gangrena senil.
  spontaneous gangrene of the newborn gangrena espontánea del recién nacido.
  static gangrene gangrena estática, gangrena por estasis.
  symmetrical gangrene gangrena simétrica.
  symmetrical gangrene on both sides gangrena simétrica de las extremidades.
  sympathetic gangrene gangrena simpática.
  thrombotic gangrene gangrena trombótica.
  traumatic gangrene gangrena traumática.
  trophic gangrene gangrena trófica.

venous gangrene gangrena venosa.
wet gangrene gangrena húmeda.
white gangrene gangrena blanca.
gangrenosis *n.* gangrenosis.
gangrenous *adj.* gangrenoso, -sa.
ganoblaste *n.* ganoblasto.
gap *n.* brecha, intervalo.
air-bone gap brecha aire-hueso.
anion gap intervalo aniónico.
auscultatory gap brecha auscultatoria.
chromosomal gap brecha cromosómica.
DNA gap brecha de ADN, brecha de DNA.
osmolal gap intervalo osmolal.
silent gap brecha silenciosa.
Gardnerella *n.* Gardnerella.
gargalanesthesia *n.* gargalanestesia.
gargalesthesia *n.* gargalestesia.
gargalesthetic *adj.* gargalestésico, -ca.
gargarism *n.* gargarismo.
gargle¹ *n.* gárgara.
gargle² *v.* gargarizar.
gargoylysm *n.* gargoilismo, gargolismo.
gas *n.* gas.
alveolar gas gas alveolar.
ammoniac gas gas amoníaco.
blood gas gas sanguíneo.
Clayton's gas gas de Clayton.
coal gas gas del alumbrado.
deleterious gas gas deletéreo.
expired gas gas espirado.
gas in the stomach gas del estómago.
hemolytic gas gas hemolítico.
inert gas gas inerte.
inspired gas gas aspirado.
intestinal gas gas intestinal.
laughing gas gas hilarante.
liver gas gas hepático.
marine acid gas gas ácido marino.
marsh gas gas de los pantanos.
mustard gas gas mostaza.
nitrous gas gas nitroso.
noble gas gas noble.
olefiant gas gas olefiante, gas oleificante.
sewer gas gas de albañal, gas de las alcantarillas.
sneezing gas gas estornutatorio.
sternutatory gas gas estornutatorio.
suffocating gas gas asfixiante, gas sofocante.
tear gas gas lacrimógeno.
vesicating gas gas vesicante.
vomiting gas gas vomitivo.
war gas gas de guerra.
wild gas gas silvestre.
gaseous *adj.* gaseoso, -sa.
gasiform *adj.* gaseiforme, gasiforme.
gasogenic *adj.* gasógeno, -na.
gasometer *n.* gasómetro.
gasometric *adj.* gasométrico, -ca.
gasometry *n.* gasometría.
gasserectomy *n.* gasserectomía.
Gasserian *adj.* gasseriano, -na.
Gasterophilus hemorrhoidalis *n.* Gasterophilus hemorrhoidalis.
gastradenitis *n.* gastroadenitis.
gastralgia *n.* gastralgia.
appendicular gastralgia gastralgia apendicular.
gastralgokenosis *n.* gastralgocenocis, gastralgoquenosis.
gastramorphus *n.* gastroamorfo.
gastrectasia *n.* gastrectasia.
acute gastrectasia gastrectasia aguda.
gastrectasis *n.* gastrectasis.
gastrectomy *n.* gastrectomía.
partial gastrectomy gastrectomía parcial, gastrectomía subtotal.

Pólya gastrectomy gastrectomía de Pólya.
subtotal gastrectomy gastrectomía parcial, gastrectomía subtotal.
total gastrectomy gastrectomía total.
gastric *adj.* gástrico, -ca.
gastrinaemia *n.* gastrinemia.
gastrine *n.* gastrina.
gastrinoma *n.* gastrinoma.
gastrinosis *n.* gastrinosis.
gastritic *adj.* gastrítico, -ca.
gastritis *n.* gastritis.
antral gastritis gastritis antral, gastritis del antro.
antrum gastritis gastritis antral, gastritis del antro.
atrophic gastritis gastritis atrófica.
atrophic hyperplastic gastritis gastritis atrófica hiperplásica.
catarrhal gastritis gastritis catarral.
chemical gastritis gastritis química.
chronic cystic gastritis gastritis quística crónica.
chronic follicular gastritis gastritis folicular crónica.
cirrhotic gastritis gastritis cirrótica.
corrosive gastritis gastritis corrosiva.
eosinophilic gastritis gastritis eosinófila.
erosive gastritis gastritis erosiva.
exfoliative gastritis gastritis exfoliativa.
follicular gastritis gastritis folicular.
gastritis cystica poliposa gastritis poliposa quística.
gastritis fibroplastica gastritis fibroplástica.
giant hypertrophic gastritis gastritis hipertróhica gigante.
hemorrhagic gastritis gastritis hemorrágica.
hyperpeptic gastritis gastritis hiperpéptica.
hypertrophic gastritis gastritis hipertrófica.
interstitial gastritis gastritis intersticial.
mycosis gastritis gastritis micótica.
phlegmonous gastritis gastritis flemonosa.
polypous gastritis gastritis poliposa.
pseudomembranous gastritis gastritis seudomembranosa.
radiation gastritis gastritis por radiación.
sclerotic gastritis gastritis esclerótica.
toxic gastritis gastritis tóxica.
gastroacephalus *n.* gastroacéfalo.
gastroadynamic *adj.* gastroadinámico, -ca.
gastroalbumorrhea *n.* gastroalbumorrea.
gastroanastomosis *n.* gastroanastomosis.
gastroatrophy *n.* gastroatrofia.
gastroblennorrhea *n.* gastroblenorrea.
gastrocamera *n.* gastrocámara.
gastrocardiac *adj.* gastrocardíaco, -ca.
gastrocele *n.* gastrocele.
gastrocnemius *n.* gastrocnemio.
gastrocoele *n.* gastrocelo.
gastrocolic *adj.* gastrocólico, -ca.
gastrocolitis *n.* gastrocolitis.
gastrocolostomy *n.* gastrocolostomía.
gastrocolotomy *n.* gastrocolotomía.
gastrocutaneous *adj.* gastrocutáneo, -a.
gastrodialysis *n.* gastrodiálisis.
gastrodiaphany *n.* gastrodiafanía, gastrodiafanoscopia.
gastrodidymus *n.* gastrodídimo.
gastrodisciasis *n.* gastrodisciasis.
Gastrodiscoides hominis *n.* Gastrodiscoides hominis.
gastroduodenal *adj.* gastroduodenal.
gastroduodenectomy *n.* gastroduodenectomía.
gastroduodenitis *n.* gastroduodenitis.
gastroduodenoenterostomy *n.* gastroduodenoenterostomía.

gastroduodenoscopy *n.* gastroduodenoscopia.
gastroduodenostomy *n.* gastroduodenostomía.
gastrodynia *n.* gastrodinia.
gastroenteralgia *n.* gastroenteralgia.
gastroenteric *adj.* gastroentérico, -ca.
gastroenteritis *n.* gastroenteritis.
acute infectious gastroenteritis gastroenteritis infecciosa aguda.
acute infectious non-bacterial gastroenteritis gastroenteritis infecciosa no bacteriana aguda.
endemic infectious non-bacterial infantile gastroenteritis gastroenteritis infantil, gastroenteritis infantil no bacteriana endémica.
eosinophilic gastroenteritis gastroenteritis eosinófila.
epidemic non-bacterial gastroenteritis gastroenteritis no bacteriana epidémica.
infantile gastroenteritis gastroenteritis infantil, gastroenteritis infantil no bacteriana endémica.
Norwalk gastroenteritis gastroenteritis de Norwalk.
Salmonella paratyphi B gastroenteritis gastroenteritis paratifosa B, gastroenteritis paratifosa tipo B.
Salmonella typhosa gastroenteritis gastroenteritis tifosa.
viral gastroenteritis gastroenteritis viral.
gastroenteroanastomosis *n.* gastroenteroanastomosis.
gastroenterocolitis *n.* gastroenterocolitis.
gastroenterocolostomy *n.* gastroenterocolostomía.
gastroenterologist *n.* gastroenterólogo, -ga.
gastroenterology *n.* gastroenterología.
gastroenteropathy *n.* gastroenteropatía.
gastroenteroplasty *n.* gastroenteroplastia.
gastroenteroptosis *n.* gastroenteroptosis.
gastroenterostomy *n.* gastroenterostomía.
gastroenterotomy *n.* gastroenterotomía.
gastroepiploic *adj.* gastroepiploico, -ca.
gastroesophageal *adj.* gastroesofágico, -ca.
gastroesophagectomy *n.* gastroesofagectomía.
gastroesophagitis *n.* gastroesofagitis.
gastroesophagostomy *n.* gastroesofagostomía.
gastrofiberscope *n.* gastrofibroscopio.
gastrofiberscopy *n.* gastrofibroscopia.
gastrogastrostomy *n.* gastrogastrostomía.
gastrogavage *n.* gastrogavaje.
gastrogenic *adj.* gastrogénico, -ca.
gastrograph *n.* gastrógrafo.
gastrohepatic *adj.* gastrohepático, -ca.
gastrohepatitis *n.* gastrohepatitis.
gastrohypertonic *adj.* gastrohipertónico, -ca.
gastrohypertony *n.* gastrohipertonía.
gastroileac *adj.* gastroilíaco, -ca.
gastroileitis *n.* gastroileítis.
gastroileostomy *n.* gastroileostomía.
gastrointestinal *adj.* gastrointestinal.
gastrojejunocolic *adj.* gastroyeyunocólico, -ca.
gastrojejuno-esophogostomy *n.* gastroyeyunoesofagostomía.
gastrojejunostomy *n.* gastroyeyunostomía.
gastrokinesograph *n.* gastrocinesiógrafo.
gastrolavage *n.* gastrolavado.
gastrolienal *adj.* gastrolienal.
gastrolith *n.* gastrolito.
gastrolithiasis *n.* gastrolitiasis.
gastrologist *n.* gastrólogo, -ga.
gastrology *n.* gastrología.
gastrolysis *n.* gastrólisis.
gastromalacia *n.* gastromalacia, malacogastria.

gastromegaly *n.* gastromegalia.
gastromelus *n.* gastromelo.
gastromycosis *n.* gastromicosis.
gastromyotomy *n.* gastromiotomía.
gastromyxorrhea *n.* gastromixorrea.
gastrone *n.* gastrona.
gastronesteostomy *n.* gastronesteostomía.
gastropancreatitis *n.* gastropancreatitis.
gastroparalysis *n.* gastroparálisis.
 gastroparalysis diabeticorum gastroparálisis diabética.
gastroparasitus *n.* gastroparásito.
gastroparesis *n.* gastroparesia, gastroparesis.
gastroparietal *adj.* gastroparietal.
gastropathic *adj.* gastropático, -ca.
gastropathy *n.* gastropatía.
 hypertrophic hypersecretory gastropathy
 gastropatía hipertrófica hipersecretoria.
gastroperiodynia *n.* gastroperiodinia.
gastroperitonitis *n.* gastroperitonitis.
gastropexy *n.* gastropexia.
 Hill posterior gastropexy gastropexia posterior de Hill.
Gastrophilus hemorrhoidalis *n.* Gastrophilus
 hemorrhoidalis.
gastrophotography *n.* gastrofotografía.
gastrophrenic *adj.* gastrofrénico, -ca.
gastrophthisis *n.* gastrotisis.
gastroplasty *n.* gastroplastia.
 Collis gastroplasty gastroplastia de Collis.
 vertical banded gastroplasty gastroplastia
 en banda vertical.
gastroplegia *n.* gastroplejía.
gastroplegy *n.* gastroplejía.
gastroplication *n.* gastroplicación.
gastroplicature *n.* gastroplicación.
gastropneumonic *adj.* gastroneumónico, -ca.
gastroptosia *n.* gastroptosi.
gastroptosis *n.* gastroptosi, gastroptosis.
gastroptyxis *n.* gastroptixis.
gastropulmonary *adj.* gastropulmonar.
gastropylorectomy *n.* gastropilorectomía.
gastropyloric *adj.* gastropilórico, -ca.
gastroradiculitis *n.* gastrorradiculitis.
gastrorrhagia *n.* gastrorragia.
gastrorrhaphy *n.* gastrorrafia.
gastrorrhea *n.* gastrorrea.
gastrorrhexis *n.* gastrorrexis.
gastroschisis *n.* gastrosquisis.
gastroscope *n.* gastroscopio.
 fiberoptic gastroscope gastroscopio fibróptico.
gastroscopic *adj.* gastroscópico, -ca.
gastroscopy *n.* gastroscopia.
gastroselective *adj.* gastroselectivo, -va.
gastrosia *n.* gastrosia.
 gastrosia fungosa gastrosia micótica.
gastrosis *n.* gastrosia, gastrosis.
gastrospasm *n.* gastroespasm, gastrospasmo.
gastrospiry *n.* gastrospiria.
gastrosplenic *adj.* gastroesplénico, -ca, gastrosplénico, -ca.
gastrostaxis *n.* gastrostaxis.
gastrostenosis *n.* gastroestenosis, gastrostenosis.
gastrostogavage *n.* gastrostogavaje.
gastrostolavage *n.* gastrostolavado.
gastrostoma *n.* gastrostoma.
gastrostomy *n.* gastrostomía, gastrostomosis.
 Beck's gastrostomy gastrostomía de Beck.
 Glassman's gastrostomy gastrostomía de
 Glassman.
 Stamm's gastrostomy gastrostomía de Stamm.
 Witzel's gastrostomy gastrostomía de Witzel.
gastrosuccorrhea *n.* gastrosucorrea.

 digestive gastrosuccorrhea gastrosucorrea
 digestiva.
gastrothoracopagus *n.* gastrotoracópago.
gastrotome *n.* gastrótomo.
gastrotomy *n.* gastrotomía.
gastrotonometer *n.* gastrotonómetro.
gastrotonometry *n.* gastrotonometría.
gastrotoxic *adj.* gastrotóxico, -ca.
gastrotoxin *n.* gastrotoxina.
gastrotrachelotomy *n.* gastrotraquelotomía.
gastrotropic *adj.* gastrotrópico, -ca.
gastrotympanites *n.* gastrotimpanitis.
gastroxia *n.* gastroxia.
gastroxynsis *n.* gastroxinsis.
gastrula *n.* gástrula.
gastrulation *n.* gastrulación.
gating *n.* compartimentación.
gatism *n.* gatismo.
gauge *n.* calibrador.
 bite gauge calibrador de mordida.
 Boley gauge calibrador de Boley.
 catheter gauge calibrador de catéteres.
 strain gauge calibrador de tensiones.
 undercut gauge calibrador de zonas retentivas.
gauntlet *n.* guantelete.
Gaussian *adj.* gaussiano, -na.
gauze *n.* gasa.
 absorbable gauze gasa absorbible.
 absorbent gauze gasa absorbente.
 hydrophile gauze gasa hidrófila.
 petrolatum gauze gasa vaselinada.
 sterile absorbent gauze gasa absorbente estéril.
 zinc gelatin impregnated gauze gasa impregnada en gelatina de cinc.
gavage *n.* gavaje.
gay *n.* gay.
Gedoelstia *n.* Gedoelstia.
gedoelstiosis *n.* gedoelstiosis.
gegenhalten *n.* gegenhalten.
gel *n.* gel.
 colloidal gel gel coloidal.
 pharmacopeial gel gel farmacopeico.
gelase *n.* gelasa.
gelasmus *n.* gelasma, gelasmo.
gelastic *adj.* gelástico, -ca.
gelate *v.* gelar, gelificar.
gelatification *n.* gelatificación, gelatinización.
gelatigenous *adj.* gelatígeno, -na.
gelatin *n.* gelatina.
 gelatin of Wharton gelatina de Wharton.
 glycerinated gelatin gelatina de glicerina, gelatina glicerinada.
 Irish moss gelatin gelatina de musgo de Irlanda.
 medicated gelatin gelatina medicada.
 Piorkowski's gelatin gelatina de Piorkowski.
 vegetable gelatin gelatina vegetal.
 zinc gelatin gelatina de cinc.
gelatiniferous *adj.* gelatinífero, -ra.
gelatinize *v.* gelatinizar.
gelatinoid *adj.* gelatinoide.
gelatinolytic *adj.* gelatinolítico, -ca.
gelatinous *adj.* gelatiniforme, gelatinoso, -sa.
gelation *n.* gelación, gelatión.
gelification *n.* gelificación.
gelometer *n.* gelómetro.
gelosis *n.* gelosis.
gelotherapy *n.* geloterapia.
gelotherapy *n.* geloterapia.
gelotripsy *n.* gelotripsia.
gelsolin *n.* gelsolina.
Gemella haemolysans *n.* Gemella haemolysans.
gemellary *adj.* gemelar.

gemellipara *n.* gemelípara.
gemellology *n.* gemelología.
geminate *adj.* geminado, -da.
gemination *n.* geminación.
geminous *adj.* geminoso, -sa.
geminus *n.* gemelo, -la, gémino, -na.
gemistocyte *n.* gemistocito.
gemistocytic *adj.* gemistocítico, -ca.
gemistocytoma *n.* gemistocitoma.
gemma *n.* gema.
gemmangioma *n.* gemangioma.
gemmation *n.* gemación.
gemmule *n.* gémula.
gena *n.* gena.
genal *adj.* genal.
gender *n.* género^2.
gene *n.* gen.
 allelic gene gen alélico.
 autosomal gene gen autosómico.
 cell interaction gene gen de interacción celular.
 CI gene gen CI.
 codominant gene gen codominante.
 complementary gene gen complementario.
 control gene gen de control.
 derepressed gene gen desreprimido.
 dominant gene gen dominante.
 gene library biblioteca genética, genoteca.
 H gene gen de histocompatibilidad, gen H.
 histocompatibility gene gen de histocompatibilidad, gen H.
 holandric gene gen holándrico.
 immune response gene gen de inmunorrespuesta, gen de reacción inmunitaria.
 immune suppressor gene gen supresor inmunitario.
 inmunoglobulin gene gen de inmunoglobulinas.
 Ir gene gen Ir.
 Is gene gen Is.
 leaky gene gen de fuga.
 lethal gene gen letal.
 major gene gen mayor.
 mimic gene gen mímico.
 mitochondrial gene gen mitocondrial.
 mutant gene gen mutante.
 operator gene gen operador.
 penetrant gene gen penetrante.
 pleiotropic gene gen pleiotrópico, gen pleyotrópico.
 recessive gene gen recesivo.
 reciprocal gene gen recíproco.
 regulator gene gen regulador.
 regulatory gene gen regulador.
 repressed gene gen reprimido.
 repressor gene gen represor.
 sex-conditioned gene gen condicionado por
 el sexo.
 sex-influenced gene gen influido por el sexo.
 sex-limited gene gen limitado por el sexo.
 sex-linked gene gen ligado al sexo.
 silent gene gen silencioso.
 split gene gen dividido.
 structural gene gen estructural.
 sublethal gene gen subletal.
 syntenic gene gen sinténicos.
 transfer gene gen de transferencia.
 wild-type gene gen de tipo salvaje.
 X-linked gene gen ligado a X.
 Y-linked gene gen ligado a Y.
genealogy *n.* genealogía.
general *adj.* general.
 general practitioner generalista.
generalization *n.* generalización.
generalized *adj.* generalizado, -da.
generation *n.* generación.

alternate generation generación alternada, generación alternante.

asexual generation generación asexual.

direct generation generación directa.

F1 generation generación filial primera.

F2 generation generación filial segunda.

first filial generation generación filial primera.

non-sexual generation generación no sexual.

parental generation generación parental, generación paterna.

second filial generation generación filial segunda.

sexual generation generación sexual.

skipped generation generación saltada.

spontaneous generation generación espontánea.

virgin generation generación virgen.

viviparous generation generación vivípara.

generative *adj.* generativo, -va.

generator *n.* generador.

aerosol generator generador de aerosoles.

asynchronous pulse generator generador de pulso asincrónico.

atrial synchronous pulse generator generador de pulso sincrónico auricular.

atrial triggered pulse generator generador de pulso desencadenado auricular.

demand pulse generator generador de pulso de demanda.

fixed rate pulse generator generador de pulso de frecuencia fija.

pulse generator generador de pulso.

radionuclide generator generador de radionúclido.

standby pulse generator generador de pulso standby.

ventricular inhibited pulse generator generador de pulso inhibido ventricular.

ventricular synchronous pulse generator generador de pulso sincrónico ventricular.

generic *adj.* genérico, -ca.

genesial *adj.* genesíaco, -ca.

genesic *adj.* genésico, -ca.

genesiology *n.* genesiología.

genesis *n.* génesis.

genesistasis *n.* genesistasia, genesistasis.

genestatic *adj.* genestático, -ca.

genetic *adj.* genético, -ca.

genetic load lastre genético.

geneticist *n.* genetista.

genetics *n.* genética.

bacterial genetics genética bacteriana.

behavior genetics genética de la conducta.

clinical genetics genética clínica.

Galtonian genetics genética galtoniana.

human genetics genética humana.

mathematical genetics genética matemática.

medical genetics genética médica.

Mendelian genetics genética mendeliana.

microbial genetics genética microbiana.

molecular genetics genética molecular.

population genetics genética de población, genética poblacional.

quantitative genetics genética cuantitativa.

reverse genetics genética inversa.

statistical genetics genética estadística.

transplantation genetics genética de trasplantes.

genetotrophic *adj.* genetotrófico, -ca.

genial *adj.* geniano, -na.

genian *adj.* geniano, -na.

genic *adj.* génico, -ca.

genicular *adj.* genicular.

geniculate *adj.* geniculado, -da.

geniculated *adj.* geniculado, -da.

geniculum *n.* genículo, geniculum.

geniocheiloplasty *n.* geniqueiloplastia, geniquiloplastia.

geniohyoid *adj.* geniohioideo, -a[2].

genion *n.* genión.

genioplasty *n.* genioplastia.

genital *adj.* genital.

genitalia *n.* genitales, genitalia.

ambiguous external genitalia genitales externos ambiguos.

external genitalia genitales externos.

indifferent genitalia genitales indiferentes.

internal genitalia genitales internos.

genitaloid *adj.* genitaloide, genitaloideo, -a.

genitals *n.* genitales, genitalia.

genitocrural *adj.* genitocrural.

genitofemoral *adj.* genitofemoral.

genitoinfectious *adj.* genitoinfeccioso, -sa.

genitoplasty *n.* genitoplastia.

genitourinary *adj.* genitourinario, ria.

genoblast *n.* genoblasto.

genodermatology *n.* genodermatología.

genodermatosis *n.* genodermatosis.

genome *n.* genoma.

human genome genoma humano.

genomic *adj.* genómico, -ca.

genoneurodermatosis *n.* genoneurodermatosis.

genophobia *n.* genofobia.

genospecies *n.* genoespecie.

genote *n.* genoto.

genotoxic *adj.* genotóxico, -ca.

genotoxicity *n.* genotoxicidad.

genotype *n.* genotipo.

genotypic *adj.* genotípico, -ca.

genotypical *adj.* genotípico, -ca.

gentianin *n.* gencianina.

gentianophil *n.* gencianófilo, -la[1].

gentianophilic *adj.* gencianofílico, -ca, gencianófilo, -la[2].

gentianophilous *adj.* gencianofílico, -ca, gencianófilo, -la[2].

gentianophobic *adj.* gencianófobo, -ca.

gentianophobous *adj.* gencianófobo, -ca.

genu *n.* genu, rodilla.

genu extrorsum genu varo, genu varum.

genu introrsum genu valgo, genu valgum.

genu recurvatum genu recurvatum.

genu valgum genu valgo, genu valgum.

genu varum genu varo, genu varum.

genual *adj.* genual.

genucubital *adj.* genucubital.

genufacial *adj.* genufacial.

genuine *adj.* genuina.

genupectoral *adj.* genupectoral.

genus *n.* género[1], genus.

genyantralgia *n.* geniantralgia.

genyantritis *n.* geniantritis.

genyantrum *n.* geniantro.

genycheiloplasty *n.* geniqueiloplastia, geniquiloplastia.

genyplasty *n.* geniplastia, genoplastia.

geocarcinology *n.* geocancerología, geocarcinología.

geochemistry *n.* geoquímica.

geode *n.* geoda.

geomedicine *n.* geomedicina.

geopathology *n.* geopatología.

geophagia *n.* geofagia.

geophagism *n.* geofagismo.

geophagist *n.* geofagista, geófago, -ga.

geophagy *n.* geofagia.

geophilic *adj.* geofílico, -ca.

Geophilus *n.* Geophilus.

geotactic *adj.* geotáctico, -ca.

geotaxis *n.* geotactismo, geotaxia, geotaxis.

geotragia *n.* geotragia.

geotrichosis *n.* geotricosis.

Geotrichum candidum *n.* Geotrichum candidum.

geotropic *adj.* geotrópico, -ca.

geotropism *n.* geotropismo.

negative geotropism geotropismo negativo.

positive geotropism geotropismo positivo.

gephyrophobia *n.* gefirofobia.

geratic *adj.* gerático, -ca.

geratology *n.* geratología.

gerbil *n.* gerbo.

gereology *n.* gereología.

geriatric *adj.* geriátrico, -ca.

geriatrician *n.* geriatra.

geriatrics *n.* geriatría.

dental geriatrics geriatría dental.

geriodontics *n.* geriodóntica.

geriodontist *n.* geriodontista.

germ *n.* germen.

dental germ germen del diente, germen dental, germen dental de reserva, germen dentario.

enamel germ germen del esmalte.

germ cell gameto.

hair germ germen del pelo.

reserve tooth germ germen del diente, germen dental, germen dental de reserva, germen dentario.

tooth germ germen del diente, germen dental, germen dental de reserva, germen dentario.

germicidal *adj.* germicida[2].

germicide *n.* germicida[1].

germinal *adj.* germinal.

germination *n.* germinación.

germinative *adj.* germinativo, -va.

germinoma *n.* germinoma.

germogen *n.* germógeno.

gerocomia *n.* gerocomía.

gerocomy *n.* gerocomía.

gerodermia *n.* gerodermia.

gerodontic *adj.* gerodóntico, -ca.

gerodontics *n.* gerodoncia.

gerodontist *n.* gerodontista.

gerodontology *n.* gerodontología.

gerokomy *n.* gerocomía.

geromarasmus *n.* geromarasmo.

geromosphism *n.* geromorfismo.

cutaneous geromosphism geromorfismo cutáneo.

gerontal *adj.* geriátrico, -ca, geróntico, -ca.

gerontologist *n.* gerontólogo, -ga.

gerontology *n.* gerontología.

gerontophile *n.* gerontófilo.

gerontophilia *n.* gerontofilia.

gerontophobia *n.* gerontofobia.

gerontopia *n.* gerontopía, gerontopsia.

gerontotherapeutics *n.* gerontoterapéutica.

gerontotherapy *n.* gerontoterapia.

gerontotoxon *n.* gerontotoxón.

gerontoxon *n.* gerontoxón.

geropsychiatry *n.* gerontopsiquiatría.

geruestmark *n.* geruestmark.

gestagen *n.* gestágeno[1].

gestagenic *adj.* gestágeno, -na[2].

gestaltism *n.* gestaltismo.

gestation *n.* gestación.

gestational *adj.* gestacional.

gestosis *n.* gestosis.

giant *n.* gigante.

Giardia *n.* Giardia.

Giardia intestinalis Giardia intestinalis.

Giardia lamblia Giardia lamblia.

giardiasis *n.* giardiasis.

gibbosity *n.* gibosidad.
gibbous *adj.* giboso, -sa.
gibbus *n.* giba.
giddiness *n.* mareo, vahído.
gigantism *n.* gigantismo.
  acromegalic gigantism gigantismo acromegálico.
  cerebral gigantism gigantismo cerebral.
  eunuchoid gigantism gigantismo eunucoide, gigantismo eunucoideo.
  fetal gigantism gigantismo fetal.
  hyperpituitary gigantism gigantismo hiperhipofisario.
  normal gigantism gigantismo normal, gigantismo primordial.
  pituitary gigantism gigantismo hipofisario.
  primordial gigantism gigantismo normal, gigantismo primordial.
gigantoblast *n.* gigantoblasto.
gigantochromoblast *n.* gigantoblasto.
gigantocyte *n.* gigantocito.
gigantomastia *n.* gigantomastia.
gigantosoma *n.* gigantosoma.
gikiyami *n.* gikiyami.
ginger *adj.* pelirrojo, -ja, taheño, -ña, tajeño, -ña.
gingiva *n.* encía, gingiva.
  alveolar gingiva encía alveolar.
  areolar gingiva encía areolar.
  attached gingiva encía adherida.
  buccal gingiva encía bucal.
  cemental gingiva encía cemental.
  free gingiva encía libre, encía no adherida.
  interdental gingiva encía interdental, encía interdentaria.
  interproximal gingiva encía interproximal.
  labial gingiva encía labial.
  lingual gingiva encía lingual.
  papillary gingiva encía papilar.
  septal gingiva encía septal.
gingival *adj.* gingival.
  gingival blanching blanqueo gingival.
gingivalgia *n.* gingivalgia.
gingivectomy *n.* gingivectomía.
gingivitis *n.* gingivitis.
  acute necrotizing gingivitis gingivitis necrosante aguda.
  acute necrotizing ulcerative gingivitis (ANUG) gingivitis ulcerosa necrosante aguda.
  acute ulcerative gingivitis gingivitis ulceromembranosa, gingivitis ulceromembranosa aguda, gingivitis ulcerosa aguda, gingivitis ulcerosa necrosante.
  acute ulceromembranous gingivitis gingivitis ulceromembranosa, gingivitis ulceromembranosa aguda, gingivitis ulcerosa aguda, gingivitis ulcerosa necrosante.
  atrophic senile gingivitis gingivitis atrófica senil.
  bismuth gingivitis gingivitis por bismuto.
  chronic desquamative gingivitis gingivitis descamativa crónica.
  cotton-roll gingivitis gingivitis por rollos de algodón.
  desquamative gingivitis gingivitis descamativa.
  Dilantin gingivitis gingivitis por Dilantin.
  diphenylhydantoin gingivitis gingivitis por difenilhidantoína.
  eruptive gingivitis gingivitis eruptiva.
  fusospirillary gingivitis gingivitis fusoespirilar, gingivitis fusospiroquetósica.
  fusospirochetal gingivitis gingivitis fusoespirilar, gingivitis fusospiroquetósica.
  generalized marginal gingivitis gingivitis marginal generalizada.

  gingivitis gravidarum gingivitis de la gravidez.
  hemorrhagic gingivitis gingivitis hemorrágica.
  herpetic gingivitis gingivitis herpética.
  hormonal gingivitis gingivitis hormonal.
  hyperplastic gingivitis gingivitis hiperplásica.
  hyperplastic leukemic gingivitis gingivitis leucémica hiperplásica.
  marginal gingivitis gingivitis marginal.
  necrotizing ulcerative gingivitis gingivitis ulceromembranosa, gingivitis ulceromembranosa aguda, gingivitis ulcerosa aguda, gingivitis ulcerosa necrosante.
  phagedenic gingivitis gingivitis fagedénica.
  pregnancy gingivitis gingivitis del embarazo.
  proliferative gingivitis gingivitis proliferativa.
  simple marginal gingivitis gingivitis marginal simple.
  streptococcal gingivitis gingivitis estreptocócica.
  suppurating gingivitis gingivitis supurante.
  suppurative marginal gingivitis gingivitis marginal supurativa.
  tuberculous gingivitis gingivitis tuberculosa.
  ulceromembranous gingivitis gingivitis ulceromembranosa, gingivitis ulceromembranosa aguda, gingivitis ulcerosa aguda, gingivitis ulcerosa necrosante.
  Vincent's gingivitis gingivitis de Vincent.
gingivoaxial *adj.* gingivoaxial, gingivoaxil.
gingivobuccoaxial *adj.* gingivobucoaxil.
gingivoglossitis *n.* gingivoglositis.
gingivolabial *adj.* gingivolabial.
gingivolinguoaxial *adj.* gingivolinguoaxial.
gingivo-osseous *adj.* gingivoóseo, -a.
gingivoperiodontis *n.* gingivoperiodontis.
  necrotizing ulcerative gingivoperiodontis gingivoperiodontis ulcerosa necrosante.
gingivoplasty *n.* gingivoplastia.
gingivorrhagia *n.* gingivorragia.
gingivosis *n.* gingivosis.
gingivostomatitis *n.* gingivoestomatitis.
  herpetic gingivostomatitis gingivoestomatitis herpética.
  necrotizing ulcerative gingivostomatitis gingivoestomatitis ulcerosa necrosante.
ginglyform *adj.* gingliforme.
ginglymoarthrodial *adj.* ginglimoartrodial.
ginglymoid *adj.* ginglimoide, ginglimoideo, -a.
ginglymus *n.* gínglimo.
gingovolinguoaxial *adj.* gingivolinguoaxil.
girdle *n.* cintura.
  Hitzig's girdle cintura de Hitzig.
  Neptune's girdle cintura de Neptuno.
  shoulder girdle cintura escapular.
  thoracic girdle cintura torácica.
githagism *n.* gitagismo.
glabella *n.* glabela.
glabellum *n.* glabela.
glabrous *adj.* glabro, -bra.
glacial *adj.* glacial.
  glacial acetic acid glacial ácido acético.
gladiate *adj.* gladiado, -da.
gladiomanubrial *adj.* gladiomanubrial.
glairin *n.* glairidina, glairina.
gland *n.* glándula.
  absorbent gland glándula absorbente.
  accessory adrenal gland glándula adrenal accesoria.
  accessory gland glándula accesoria.
  accessory parotid gland glándula parótida accesoria.

  accessory suprarenal gland glándula suprarrenal accesoria.
  acid gland glándula ácida.
  acinar gland glándula acinar, glándula acinosa.
  acinotubular gland glándula acinotubular.
  acinous gland glándula acinar, glándula acinosa.
  admaxillary gland glándula admaxilar.
  adrenal gland glándula adrenal, glándula adrenalis.
  aggregate gland glándula agregada.
  Albarran's gland glándula de Albarrán.
  albuminous gland glándula albuminosa.
  alveolar gland glándula alveolar.
  anal gland glándula anal.
  anteprostatic gland glándula anteprostática.
  anterior lingual gland (of Blandin and Nuhn) glándula lingual anterior.
  apical gland glándula apical, glándula apical de la lengua.
  apical gland of the tongue glándula apical, glándula apical de la lengua.
  apocrine gland glándula apocrina.
  aporic gland glándula apórica.
  areolar gland glándula areolar.
  arterial gland glándula arterial.
  arytenoid gland glándula aritenoide, glándula aritenoidea.
  Aselli's gland glándula de Aselli.
  Bartholin's gland glándula de Bartholin.
  Bauhin's gland glándula de Bauhin.
  Baumgarten's gland glándula de Baumgarten.
  Blandin and Nuhn's gland glándula de Blandin, glándula de Blandin y Nuhn.
  Blandin's gland glándula de Blandin, glándula de Blandin y Nuhn.
  Boerhaave's gland glándula de Boerhaave.
  Bowman's gland glándula de Bowman.
  bronchial gland glándula bronquial.
  Bruch's gland glándula de Bruch.
  Brunner's gland glándula de Brunner.
  buccal gland glándula bucale.
  bulbocavernous gland glándula bulbocavernosa.
  bulbourethral gland glándula bulbouretral.
  cardiac gland glándula cardial, glándula del cardias.
  cardiac gland of the esophagus glándula cardial del esófago.
  carotid gland glándula carotídea.
  celiac gland glándula celiaca.
  ceruminous gland glándula ceruminosa.
  cervical gland glándula cervical, glándula cervical del útero.
  cervical gland of the uterus glándula cervical, glándula cervical del útero.
  Ciaccio's gland glándula de Ciaccio.
  ciliary gland glándula ciliar, glándula ciliar de la conjuntiva.
  ciliary gland of the conjunctiva glándula ciliar, glándula ciliar de la conjuntiva.
  circumanal gland glándula circumanal.
  closed gland glándula cerrada, glándula clausa.
  Cobelli's gland glándula de Cobelli.
  coil gland glándula enroscada.
  compound gland glándula compuesta, glándula conglomerada.
  conglobate gland glándula conglobada.
  conjunctival gland glándula conjuntival.
  convoluted gland glándula contorneada.
  Cowper's gland glándula de Cowper.
  cutaneous gland glándula cutáne.

duodenal gland glándula duodenal.
Duverney's gland glándula de Duverney.
Ebner's gland glándula de Ebner.
eccrine gland glándula ecrina.
endocrine gland glándula anómala, glándula endocrina.
esophageal gland glándula esofágica.
excretory gland glándula excretoria.
exocrine gland glándula abierta, glándula anacrina, glándula de secreción externa, glándula exocrina.
fundic gland of the stomach glándula fúndica.
fundus gland glándula fúndica.
Galeati's gland glándula de Galeati (duodenal).
gastric gland glándula gástrica.
Gay's gland glándula de Gay.
genal gland glándula genal, glándula geniana.
genital gland glándula genital.
gingival gland glándula gingival.
gland of internal secretion glándula de secreción interna.
gland of larynx glándula laríngea.
gland of Lieberkühn glándula de Lieberkühn.
gland of the biliary mucosa glándula de la mucosa biliar.
gland of the mouth glándula de la boca, glándula oral.
gland of the pharynx glándula faríngea.
gland of Tyson glándula de Tyson.
gland of Wolfring glándula de Wolfring.
gland of Zeis glándula de Zeis.
Gley's gland glándula de Gley.
greater vestibular gland glándula vestibular mayor.
gustatory gland glándula gustatoria.
Havers' gland glándula de Havers.
Haversian gland glándula de Havers.
hemal gland glándula hemática.
hemal lymph gland glándula hemolinfática.
hematopoietic gland glándula hematopoyética.
hemolymph gland glándula hemolinfática.
Henle's gland glándula de Henle.
heterocrine gland glándula heterocrina.
holocrine gland glándula holocrina.
intercarotid gland glándula intercarotídea.
interstitial gland glándula intersticial.
intestinal gland glándula intestinal.
Krause's gland glándula de Krause.
labial gland glándula labiales de la boca.
labial gland of the mouth glándula labiales de la boca.
lacrimal gland glándula lagrimal.
lactiferous gland glándula mamaria.
laryngeal gland glándula laríngea.
Lieberkühn's gland glándula de Lieberkühn.
Littre's gland glándula de Littre.
Luschka's cystic gland glándula cística de Luschka.
Luschka's gland glándula de Luschka.
lymph gland glándula linfática.
lymphatic gland glándula linfática.
major salivary gland glándula salival mayor.
mammary gland glándula mamaria.
maxillary gland glándula submaxilar.
Meibomian gland glándula de Meibomio.
merocrine gland glándula merocrina.
milk gland glándula mamaria.
minor salivary gland glándula salival menor.
mixed gland glándula mixta.
molar gland glándula molar.
Moll's gland glándula de Moll.
monoptychic gland glándula monoptíquica.
Montgomery's gland glándula de Montgomery.
Morgagni's gland glándula de Morgagni.

muciparous gland glándula mucípara, glándula mucosa.
mucous gland glándula mucípara, glándula mucosa.
Nuhn's gland glándula de Nuhn.
odoriferous gland glándula odorífica.
odoriferous gland of the prepuce glándula prepucial.
oil gland glándula sebácea.
olfactory gland glándula olfatoria.
oxyntic gland glándula oxíntica.
Pacchionian gland glándula de Pacchioni.
palatine gland glándula palatina.
palpebral gland glándula palpebral.
parathyroid gland glándula paratiroide.
paraurethral gland glándula parauretral.
parotid gland glándula parótida.
peptic gland glándula péptica.
perspiratory gland glándula perspiratoria.
pharyngeal gland glándula faríngea.
pileous gland glándula pilosa.
pituitary gland glándula pituitaria.
polyptychic gland glándula poliptíquica.
prehyoid gland glándula prehioide.
preputial gland glándula prepucial.
proper gastric gland glándula fúndica.
prostate gland glándula prostática.
pyloric gland glándula pilórica.
racemose gland glándula racemosa.
retromolar gland glándula molar.
Rivinus' gland glándula de Rivinus.
Rosenmüller's gland glándula de Rosenmüller.
saccular gland glándula sacular.
salivary gland glándula salival.
Sandström's gland glándula de Sandström.
Schüller's gland glándula de Schüller.
sebaceous gland glándula sebácea.
sentinel gland glándula centinela.
seromucous gland glándula seromucosa.
serous gland glándula serosa.
Serres' gland glándula de Serres.
sexual gland glándula sexual.
Sigmund's gland glándula de Sigmund.
simple gland glándula simple.
Skene's gland glándula de Skene.
staphyline gland glándula estafilina.
sublingual gland glándula sublingual.
submandibular gland glándula submandibular.
submaxillary gland glándula submaxilar.
sudoriferous gland glándula sudorípara.
sudoriparous gland glándula sudorípara.
suprarenal gland glándula suprarrenal.
Suzanne's gland glándula de Suzanne.
sweat gland glándula sudorípara.
synovial gland glándula sinovial.
target gland glándula blanco.
tarsal gland glándula tarsal.
tarsoconjunctival gland glándula tarsal.
Theile's gland glándula de Theile.
thymus gland glándula timo.
thyroid gland glándula tiroides.
Tiedemann's gland glándula de Tiedemann.
tubular gland glándula tubular, glándula tubulosa.
tubuloacinar gland glándula tubuloacinar.
Tyson's gland glándula de Tyson.
unicellular gland glándula unicelular.
urethral gland glándula uretral.
uterine gland glándula uterina.
vascular gland glándula vascular.
vestibular gland glándula vestibular.
vulvovaginal gland glándula vulvovaginal.
Wasmann's gland glándula de Wasmann.
Weber's gland glándula de Weber.

Woelfler's gland glándula de Woelfler.
Zuckerkandl's gland glándula de Zuckerkandl.
glanders *n.* muermo.
glandilemma *n.* glandilema.
glandula *n.* glándula.
glandula adrenalis glándula adrenal, glándula adrenalis.
glandula atrabiliaris glándula atrabiliar, glándula atrabiliaria.
glandula basilaris glándula basilar.
glandula bronchiale glándula bronquial.
glandula buccale glándula bucale.
glandula bulbo-urethralis glándula bulbouretral.
glandula bulbourethralis (Cowperii) glándula bulbouretral.
glandula ceruminosa glándula ceruminosa.
glandula gastrica propria glándula fúndica.
glandula lacrimalis glándula lagrimal.
glandula mammaria glándula mamaria.
glandula mucosa glándula mucípara, glándula mucosa.
glandula parotidea glándula parótida.
glandula parotidea accesoria glándula parótida accesoria.
glandula parotis glándula parótida.
glandula pituitaria glándula pituitaria.
glandula prostatica glándula prostática.
glandula seromucosa glándula seromucosa.
glandula serosa glándula serosa.
glandula sublingualis glándula sublingual.
glandula submandibularis glándula submandibular.
glandula submaxillaris glándula submaxilar.
glandula suprarenales accessoriae glándula suprarrenal accesoria.
glandula suprarenalis glándula suprarrenal.
glandula thyroidea glándula tiroides.
glandula vestibularis major glándula de Bartholin, glándula vestibular mayor.
glandular *adj.* glandular.
glandule *n.* glandulilla.
glandulous *adj.* glanduloso, -sa.
glans *n.* glande, glans.
glans clitoridis glande del clítoris, glans clitoridis.
glans penis glande del pene, glans penis.
glare *n.* deslumbramiento[1].
blinding glare deslumbramiento cegador.
dazzling glare deslumbramiento ofuscador.
direct glare deslumbramiento directo.
indirect glare deslumbramiento indirecto.
peripheral glare deslumbramiento periférico.
specular glare deslumbramiento especular.
veiling glare deslumbramiento velador.
glarometer *n.* glarómetro.
Glaserian *adj.* glaseriano, -na.
glass *n.* cristal[1], vidrio.
glasses *n.* gafas.
bifocal glasses gafas bifocales.
Franklin glasses gafas bifocales.
safety glasses gafas de seguridad.
glaucoma *n.* glaucoma.
absolute glaucoma glaucoma absoluto.
acute angle-closure glaucoma glaucoma de ángulo cerrado agudo.
acute congestive glaucoma glaucoma congestivo agudo.
acute glaucoma glaucoma agudo.
air-block glaucoma glaucoma por bloqueo de aire.
angle-closure glaucoma glaucoma de ángulo cerrado.
angle-recession glaucoma glaucoma de recesión del ángulo.

aphakic glaucoma glaucoma afáquico.
apoplectic glaucoma glaucoma apopléctico.
auricular glaucoma glaucoma auricular.
capsular glaucoma glaucoma capsular.
chronic angle-closure glaucoma glaucoma de ángulo cerrado crónico.
chronic glaucoma glaucoma crónico.
chronic narrow-angle glaucoma glaucoma crónico de ángulo estrecho.
chronic simple glaucoma glaucoma crónico simple.
chymotrypsin-induced glaucoma glaucoma inducido por quimotripsina, glaucoma por quimotripsina.
closed-angle glaucoma glaucoma de cierre de ángulo, glaucoma por cierre del ángulo.
combined glaucoma glaucoma combinado.
compensated glaucoma glaucoma compensado.
congenital glaucoma glaucoma congénito.
congestive glaucoma glaucoma congestivo.
contusion glaucoma glaucoma por contusión.
corticosteroid glaucoma glaucoma inducido por corticosteroides, glaucoma por esteroides.
Donders' glaucoma glaucoma de Donders.
enzyme glaucoma glaucoma enzimático.
ghost cell glaucoma glaucoma por células fantasmas.
glaucoma consummatum glaucoma consumado.
glaucoma fulminans glaucoma fulminante.
glaucoma without hypertension glaucoma de baja tensión.
hemorrhagic glaucoma glaucoma hemorrágico.
hypersecretion glaucoma glaucoma por hipersecreción.
infantile glaucoma glaucoma infantil.
inflammatory glaucoma glaucoma inflamatorio.
intermittent angle-closure glaucoma glaucoma de ángulo cerrado intermitente.
juvenile glaucoma glaucoma juvenil.
latent angle-closure glaucoma glaucoma de ángulo cerrado latente.
lenticular glaucoma glaucoma lenticular.
low-tension glaucoma glaucoma de baja tensión, glaucoma de tensión baja.
malignant glaucoma glaucoma maligno.
melanomalytic glaucoma glaucoma melanomalítico.
narrow-angle glaucoma glaucoma de ángulo estrecho.
neovascular glaucoma glaucoma neovascular.
non-congestive glaucoma glaucoma no congestivo.
obstructive glaucoma glaucoma obstructivo.
open-angle glaucoma glaucoma de ángulo abierto.
phacogenic glaucoma glaucoma facógeno, glaucoma facolítico, glaucoma facomórfico.
phacolytic glaucoma glaucoma facógeno, glaucoma facolítico, glaucoma facomórfico.
phacomorphic glaucoma glaucoma facógeno, glaucoma facolítico, glaucoma facomórfico.
pigmentary glaucoma glaucoma pigmentario.
primary glaucoma glaucoma primario.
prodromal glaucoma glaucoma prodrómico.
pseudoexfoliative capsular glaucoma glaucoma capsular seudoexfoliativo.
pupillary block glaucoma glaucoma por bloqueo pupilar.
secondary glaucoma glaucoma secundario.
simple glaucoma glaucoma simple, glaucoma simplex.

steroid glaucoma glaucoma por esteroides.
traumatic glaucoma glaucoma traumático.
vitreous block glaucoma glaucoma por bloqueo de humor vítreo.
wide-angle glaucoma glaucoma de ángulo amplio.
glaucomatocyclitic *adj.* glaucomatociclítico, -ca.
glaucomatous *adj.* glaucomatoso, -sa.
glaucosis *n.* glaucosis.
glaucosuria *n.* glaucosuria.
glaze *n.* vidriado.
glenohumeral *adj.* glenohumeral.
glenoid *adj.* glenoide, glenoideo, -a.
glia *n.* glía.
ameboid glia glía ameboide.
cytoplasmic glia glía citoplásmica.
fibrillary glia glía fibrilar.
glia of Fañanás glía de Fañanás.
gliacyte *n.* gliacito.
glial *adj.* glial.
glide *n.* deslizamiento.
mandibular glide deslizamiento del maxilar inferior, deslizamiento mandibular.
occlusal glide deslizamiento oclusal.
slipped femoral epiphysis glide deslizamiento de la epifisis femoral.
gliobacteria *n.* gliobacteria.
glioblast *n.* glioblasto.
glioblastoma multiforme *n.* glioblastoma multiforme.
glioblastosis cerebri *n.* glioblastosis cerebral.
gliococcus *n.* gliococo.
gliocyte *n.* gliocito.
gliocytoma *n.* gliocitoma.
gliofibrillary *adj.* gliofibrilar.
gliogenous *adj.* gliógeno, -na.
glioma *n.* glioma.
astrocytic glioma glioma astrocítico.
ependymal glioma glioma ependimario.
ganglionic glioma glioma ganglionar.
gigantocellular glioma glioma gigantocelular.
glioma endophytum glioma endofitico, glioma endófito.
glioma exophytum glioma exofítico, glioma exófito.
glioma of optic chiasm glioma del quiasma óptico.
glioma of the spinal cord glioma de la médula espinal.
glioma retinae glioma de la retina, glioma retiniano.
glioma telangiectodes glioma telangiectásico, glioma telangiectodes.
mixed glioma glioma mixto.
nasal glioma glioma nasal.
optic glioma glioma óptico.
optic nerve glioma glioma óptico.
peripheral glioma glioma periférico.
telangiectatic glioma glioma telangiectásico, glioma telangiectodes.
gliomatosis *n.* gliomatosis.
gliomatous *adj.* gliomatoso, -sa.
gliomyoma *n.* gliomioma.
gliomyxoma *n.* gliomixoma.
glioneurona *n.* glioneuroma.
gliophagia *n.* gliofagia.
gliosarcoma *n.* gliosarcoma.
gliosis *n.* gliosis.
diffuse gliosis gliosis difusa.
hemispheric gliosis gliosis hemisférica.
hypertrophic nodular gliosis gliosis nodular hipertrófica.
isomorphic gliosis gliosis isomorfa, gliosis isomórfica.

isomosphous gliosis gliosis isomorfa, gliosis isomórfica.
perivascular gliosis gliosis perivascular.
piloid gliosis gliosis piloide.
spinal gliosis gliosis espinal, gliosis raquídea.
unilateral gliosis gliosis unilateral.
gliosome *n.* gliosoma.
glischrin *n.* gliscrina.
glischruria *n.* gliscruria.
glissade *n.* glissade.
glissonitis *n.* glisonitis, glissonitis.
globi *n.* globos.
globin *n.* globina.
globinometer *n.* globinómetro.
globoid *adj.* globoide.
globose *adj.* globoso, -sa.
globoside *adj.* globósido, -da.
globular *adj.* globular.
globule *n.* glóbulo.
dentin globule glóbulo de dentina.
Dobie's globule glóbulo de Dobie.
Marchi's globule glóbulo de Marchi.
milk globule glóbulo de leche.
Morgagni's globule glóbulo de Morgagni.
myelin globule glóbulo de mielina.
globuliferous *adj.* globulífero, -ra.
globulimeter *n.* globulímetro.
globulin *n.* globulina.
alpha globulin globulina alfa.
antidiphtheritic globulin globulina antidiftérica.
anti-human globulin globulina antihumana.
anti-human serum globulin globulina antihumana sérica.
antilymphocyte globulin (ALG) globulina antilinfocito (ALG).
antithymocyte globulin (ATG) globulina antitimocito (ATG).
antitoxic globulin globulina antitóxica.
beta globulin globulina beta.
chickenpox immune (human) globulin globulina inmune de la varicela humana, globulina inmunitaria de la varicela humana.
gamma globulin globulina gamma.
hepatitis B immune globulin globulina inmune de hepatitis B, globulina inmunitaria de hepatitis B.
immune globulin globulina inmune, globulina inmunitaria.
immune human serum globulin globulina sérica humana inmune, globulina sérica humana inmunitaria.
measles immune globulin globulina inmune de sarampión, globulina inmunitaria de sarampión.
pertussis immune globulin globulina inmune contra (de) la tos ferina, globulina inmunitaria contra (de) la tos ferina.
pertussis immune human globulin globulina inmune de la tos, globulina Inmunitaria de la tos ferina.
poliomyelitis immune globulin globulina Inmune de poliomielitis, globulina inmunitaria de poliomielitis.
rabies immune globulin globulina inmune contra (de), globulina inmunitaria contra (de) la rabia.
RH0 (D) immune globulin globulina inmune de RH0 (D), globulina inmunitaria de RH0 (D).
serum accelerator globulin globulina aceleradora del suero.
serum globulin globulina séricas.
specific immune serum globulin globulina inmune específica, globulina inmune sérica específica, globulina inmunitaria específica, globulina inmunitaria sérica específica.

testosterone-estradiol-binding globulin (TEBG) globulina conjugadora de testosterona-estradiol.

tetanus immune human globulin globulina inmune tetánica humana, globulina inmunitaria tetánica humana.

thyroxine-binding globulin (TBG) globulina conjugadora (fijadora) de tiroxina, globulina que conjuga tiroxina.

vaccinia immune human globulin globulina inmune humana vacunal, globulina inmunitaria humana vacunal.

varicella-zoster immune globulin (VZIG) globulina inmune contra la varicela zóster, globulina inmunitaria contra la varicela zóster.

zoster immune globulin globulina inmune al zóster, globulina inmune antizóster, globulina inmunitaria al zóster, globulina inmunitaria antizóster.

globulinemia *n.* globulinemia.

globulinuria *n.* globulinuria.

globulolysis *n.* globulólisis.

globulolytic *adj.* globulolítico, -ca.

globulose *n.* globulosa.

globulysis *n.* globulisis.

globus *n.* globo, globus.

  globus hystericus globo histérico.

  globus of the eye globo del ojo, globo ocular.

  globus pallidus globo pálido, globus pallidus.

  globus pallidus lateralis globo pálido lateral.

  globus pallidus medialis globo pálido medial.

glomal *adj.* glómico, -ca.

glomangioma *n.* glomangioma.

glomangiosis *n.* glomangiosis.

  pulmonary glomangiosis glomangiosis pulmonar.

glomectomy *n.* glomectomía.

glomerate *adj.* glomerado, -da.

glomerular *adj.* glomerular.

  glomerular hyperfiltration hiperfiltración glomerular.

glomerule *n.* glomérulo.

glomerulitis *n.* glomerulitis.

glomerulonephritis *n.* glomerulonefritis.

  acute crescentic glomerulonephritis glomerulonefritis semilunar aguda.

  acute glomerulonephritis glomerulonefritis aguda (GNA).

  acute hemorrhagic glomerulonephritis glomerulonefritis hemorrágica aguda.

  acute poststreptococcal glomerulonephritis glomerulonefritis posestreptocócica aguda.

  antibasement membrane glomerulonephritis glomerulonefritis antimembrana basal.

  Berger's focal glomerulonephritis glomerulonefritis focal de Berger.

  chronic glomerulonephritis glomerulonefritis crónica.

  chronic hypocomplementemic glomerulonephritis glomerulonefritis hipocomplementémica crónica.

  diffuse glomerulonephritis glomerulonefritis difusa.

  exudative glomerulonephritis glomerulonefritis exudativa.

  focal embolic glomerulonephritis glomerulonefritis embólica focal.

  focal glomerulonephritis glomerulonefritis focal.

  hypocomplementemic glomerulonephritis glomerulonefritis hipocomplementémica.

  IgA glomerulonephritis glomerulonefritis por IgA.

  lobular glomerulonephritis glomerulonefritis lobular.

  local glomerulonephritis glomerulonefritis local.

  malignant glomerulonephritis glomerulonefritis maligna.

  membranoproliferative glomerulonephritis glomerulonefritis membranoproliferativa.

  membranous glomerulonephritis glomerulonefritis membranosa.

  mesangial proliferative glomerulonephritis glomerulonefritis proliferativa, glomerulonefritis proliferativa mesangial.

  mesangiocapillary glomerulonephritis glomerulonefritis mesangiocapilar.

  nodular glomerulonephritis glomerulonefritis nodular.

  proliferative glomerulonephritis glomerulonefritis proliferativa, glomerulonefritis proliferativa mesangial.

  rapidly progressive glomerulonephritis glomerulonefritis de progresión rápida, glomerulonefritis rápidamente progresiva.

  segmental glomerulonephritis glomerulonefritis segmentaria.

  subacute glomerulonephritis glomerulonefritis subaguda.

glomerulonephropathy *n.* glomerulonefropatía.

glomerulopathy *n.* glomerulopatía.

  diabetic glomerulopathy glomerulopatía diabética.

  focal sclerosing glomerulopathy glomerulopatía esclerosante focal.

glomerulosclerosis *n.* glomeruloesclerosis, glomerulosclerosis.

  diabetic glomerulosclerosis glomeruloesclerosis diabética.

  focal segmentary glomerulosclerosis glomeruloesclerosis segmentada focal, glomeruloesclerosis segmentaria focal.

  intercapillary glomerulosclerosis glomeruloesclerosis intercapilar.

glomerulose *adj.* glomeruloso, -sa.

glomerulotropin *n.* glomerulotropina.

glomerulus *n.* glomérulo.

  caudal glomerulus glomérulo caudal.

  coccygeal arterial glomerulus glomérulo arterial coccígeo.

  glomerulus arteriosi cochleae glomérulo arterioso coclear.

  glomerulus of the kidney glomérulo de Ruysch, glomérulo renal, glomérulo del riñón.

  glomerulus of mesonephros glomérulo del mesonefros.

  Malpighian glomerulus glomérulo de Malpighi, glomérulo de Malpigio.

  non-encapsulated nerve glomerulus glomérulo nervioso no encapsulado.

  olfactory glomerulus glomérulo olfatorio.

  renal glomerulus glomerulus renis glomérulo de Ruysch, glomérulo renal, glomérulo del riñón.

  Ruysch's glomerulus glomérulo de Ruysch, glomérulo renal, glomérulo del riñón.

glomic *adj.* glómico, -ca.

glomoid *adj.* glomoide.

glomus *n.* glomo, glomus.

  body glomus glomo carotídeo, glomus caroticum, glomus carotídeo.

  carotid glomus glomo carotídeo, glomus caroticum, glomus carotídeo.

  choroid glomus glomo coroideo, glomus choroideum.

  coccygeal glomus glomo coccígeo, glomus coccygeum.

  cutaneous glomus glomo cutáneo.

  digital glomus glomo digital.

  glomus caroticum glomo carotídeo, glomus caroticum, glomus carotídeo.

  intravagal glomus glomo intravagal.

  neuromyoarterial glomus glomo neuromioarterial.

  pulmonary glomus glomo pulmonar.

glosomantia *n.* glosomantia.

glossagra *n.* glosagra.

glossal *adj.* glosal.

glossalgia *n.* glosalgia.

glossectomy *n.* glosectomía.

Glossina *n.* Glossina.

  Glossina morsitans Glossina morsitans.

  Glossina pallidipes Glossina pallidipes.

  Glossina palpalis Glossina palpalis.

glossitis *n.* glositis.

  atrophic glossitis glositis atrófica.

  benign migratory glossitis glositis migratoria benigna.

  glossitis areata exfoliativa glositis areata exfoliativa, glositis areata marginada, glositis exfoliativa.

  glossitis desiccans glositis desecante.

  glossitis migrans glositis migratoria.

  Hunter's glossitis glositis de Hunter.

  idiopathic glossitis glositis idiopática.

  median rhomboid glossitis glositis rómbica media, glositis romboidal media, glositis romboidal mediana, glositis romboidea media.

  Möller's glossitis glositis de Möller.

  phlegmonous glossitis glositis flemonosa.

glossocele *n.* glosocele.

glossocinesthesic *adj.* glosocinestésico, -ca.

glossocoma *n.* glosocoma.

glossodontotropism *n.* glosodontotropismo.

glossodynamometer *n.* glosodinamómetro.

glossodynia *n.* glosodinia.

  glossodynia exfoliativa glosodinia exfoliativa.

glossodyniotropism *n.* glosodiniotropismo.

glossoepiglottic *adj.* glosoepiglótico, -ca.

glossoepiglottidean *adj.* glosoepiglótico, -ca.

glossograph *n.* glosógrafo.

glossohyal *adj.* glosohial, glosohioideo, -a.

glossokinesthetic *adj.* glosocinestésico, -ca.

glossolabial *adj.* glosolabial.

glossolalia *n.* glosolalia.

glossology *n.* glosología.

glossolysis *n.* glosólisis.

glossomania *n.* glosomanía.

glossoncus *n.* glosonco.

glossopalatine *adj.* glosopalatino, -na.

glossopalatinus *n.* glosopalatino.

glossopathy *n.* glosopatía.

glossopexy *n.* glosopexia.

glossopharyngeal *adj.* glosofaríngeo, -a.

glossopharyngeus *n.* glosofaríngeo.

glossophobia *n.* glosofobia.

glossophytia *n.* glosofitia.

glossoplasty *n.* glosoplastia.

glossoplegia *n.* glosoplejía.

glossoptosis *n.* glosoptosia, glosoptosis.

glossopyrosis *n.* glosopirosis.

glossorrhaphy *n.* glosorrafia.

glossoscopy *n.* glososcopia.

glossospasm *n.* glosoespasmo, glosospasmo.

glossosteresis *n.* glosoestéresis, glosostéresis.

glossotilt *n.* glosotractor.

glossotomy *n.* glosotomía.

glossotrichia *n.* glosotriquia.

glossy-skin *n.* glossy-skin.

glottal *adj.* glotal.

glottic *adj.* glótico, -ca.

glottidospasm *n.* glotidoespasmo.

glottis *n.* glotis.
  glottis vocalis glotis vocal.
  intercartilaginous glottis glotis intercartilaginosa.
  respiratory glottis glotis respiratoria.
glottitis *n.* glotitis.
glottogram *n.* glosograma.
glottography *n.* glosografía.
glottology *n.* glosología, glotología.
glucagon *n.* glucagón.
glucagonoma *n.* glucagonoma.
glucase *n.* glucasa.
glucatonia *n.* glucatonía.
glucide *n.* glúcido.
gluciphore *n.* glucíforo.
glucocerebrosidase *n.* glucocerebrosidasa.
glucocerebroside *n.* glucocerebrósido.
glucocorticoid *n.* glucocorticoide.
glucocorticotrophic *adj.* glucocorticotrófico, -ca.
glucogen *n.* glucógeno.
glucogenesis *n.* glucogénesis.
glucogenetic *adj.* glucogenético, -ca.
glucogenic *adj.* glucogénico, -ca.
glucohemia *n.* glucohemia.
glucokinase *n.* glucocinasa.
glucokinetic *adj.* glucocinético, -ca.
glucolysis *n.* glucólisis.
glucolytic *adj.* glucolítico, -ca.
gluconeogenesis *n.* gluconeogénesis.
gluconeogenetic *adj.* gluconeogénico, -ca.
glucopenia *n.* glucopenia.
glucophore *n.* glucóforo.
glucoproteinase *n.* glucoproteinasa.
glucoptyalism *n.* glucoptialismo, glucotialismo.
glucose *n.* glucosa.
glucosin *n.* glucosina.
glucosuria *n.* glucosuria.
glucuronic acid conjugation *n.* glucuronidoconjugación.
glucuronide *n.* glucurónido.
glucuronuria *n.* glucuronuria.
glutamyl *n.* glutamil, glutamilo.
  glutamyl transferase glutamil transferasa, glutamil transpeptidasa.
  glutamyl transpeptidase glutamil transferasa, glutamil transpeptidasa.
glutathionaemia *n.* glutationemia.
glutathione *n.* glutatión.
glutathionemia *n.* glutationemia.
glutathionuria *n.* glutationuria.
gluteal *adj.* glúteo, -a.
gluten *n.* gluten.
gluteofemoral *adj.* gluteofemoral.
gluteoinguinal *adj.* gluteoinguinal.
glutinous *adj.* glutinoso, -sa.
glutitis *n.* glutitis.
glutolin *n.* glutolina.
glutoscope *n.* glutoscopio.
glycase *n.* glucasa.
glycation *n.* glucación.
glycemia *n.* glicemia, glucemia.
glycemin *n.* glicemina.
glycerate *n.* glicerado, glicerato.
glyceridaemia *n.* gliceridemia.
glycerin *n.* glicerina.
glycerinated *adj.* glicerinado, -na.
glycerinum *n.* glicerina, glicerinum.
glycerogel *n.* glicerogel.
glycerogelatin *n.* glicerogelatina.
glycerol *n.* glicerol.
glycerolize *v.* glicerolizar.
glycerophilic *adj.* glicerófilo, -la.
glycine *n.* glicina.
glycinemia *n.* glicinemia.

glycinuria *n.* glicinuria.
  familial glycinuria glicinuria familiar.
glycocalyx *n.* glucocálix, glucocáliz.
glycocoll *n.* glicocola.
glycocorticoid *n.* glicocorticoide.
glycocyaminase *n.* glucociaminasa.
glycogen *n.* glicógeno.
glycogenase *n.* glucogenasa.
glycogenesis *n.* glicogénesis, glucogenogénesis.
glycogenetic *adj.* glicogenético, -ca.
glycogenic *adj.* glicogénico, -ca.
glycogenolysis *n.* glucogenólisis.
glycogenolytic *adj.* glucogenolítico, -ca.
glycogenopexy *n.* glucogenopexia.
glycogenosis *n.* glucogenosis.
  brancher deficiency glycogenosis glucogenosis por deficiencia de enzima ramificante.
  generalized glycogenosis glucogenosis generalizada.
  glucose 6-phosphatase hepatorenal glycogenosis glucogenosis hepatorrenal de glucosa 6-fosfatasa.
  hepatophosphorylase deficiency glycogenosis glucogenosis por deficiencia de fosforilasa hepática.
  myophosphorylase deficiency glycogenosis glucogenosis por deficiencia de miofosforilasa.
  type I glycogenosis glucogenosis tipo I.
  type II glycogenosis glucogenosis tipo II.
  type III glycogenosis glucogenosis tipo III.
  type IV glycogenosis glucogenosis tipo IV.
  type V glycogenosis glucogenosis tipo V.
  type VI glycogenosis glucogenosis tipo VI.
glycogenous *adj.* glucogenoso, -sa.
glycogeusia *n.* glucogeusia.
glycoglycinuria *n.* glucoglicinuria.
glycohemia *n.* glucohemia.
glycohemoglobin *n.* glucohemoglobina.
glycohistechia *n.* glucohistequia.
glycolysis *n.* glicólisis.
glycolytic *adj.* glucolítico, -ca.
glycometabolic *adj.* glucometabólico, -ca.
glycometabolism *n.* glucometabolismo.
glyconeogenesis *n.* gluconeogénesis.
glycopenia *n.* glucopenia.
glycopexic *adj.* glucopéxico, -ca.
glycopexis *n.* glucopexia.
Glycophagus *n.* Glycophagus.
glycophilia *n.* glucofilia.
glycophorin *n.* glucoforina.
glycopolyuria *n.* glucopoliuria.
glycoprival *n.* glucoprivo.
glycoprotein *n.* glicoproteína, glucoproteína.
glycoptyalism *n.* glucoptiolismo.
glycoregulation *n.* glucorregulación.
glycoregulatory *adj.* glucorregulatorio, -ria.
glycorrhachia *n.* glucorraquia.
glycorrhea *n.* glucorrea.
glycosecretory *adj.* glucosecretorio, -ria.
glycosemia *n.* glicosemia, glucosemia.
glycosialia *n.* glucosialia.
glycosialorrhea *n.* glucosialorrea.
glycosometer *n.* glucosómetro.
glycosphingolipidosis *n.* glucosfingolipidosis.
glycostatic *adj.* glucostático, -ca.
glycosuria *n.* glucosuria.
  alimentary glycosuria glucosuria alimentaria.
  benign glycosuria glucosuria benigna.
  digestive glycosuria glucosuria digestiva.
  emotional glycosuria glucosuria emocional.
  epinephrine glycosuria glucosuria por adrenalina.
  hyperglycemic glycosuria glucosuria hiperglucémica.

  magnesium glycosuria glucosuria por magnesio.
  nervous glycosuria glucosuria nerviosa.
  non-diabetic glycosuria glucosuria no diabética.
  non-hyperglycemic glycosuria glucosuria no hiperglucémica.
  normoglycemic glycosuria glucosuria normoglucémica.
  orthoglycemic glycosuria glucosuria ortoglucémica.
  pathologic glycosuria glucosuria patológica.
  phlorhizin glycosuria glucosuria floricínica, glucosuria por floridzina.
  phloridzin glycosuria glucosuria floricínica, glucosuria por floridzina.
  renal glycosuria glucosuria renal.
  toxic glycosuria glucosuria tóxica.
glycosylation *n.* glucosilación.
glycotaxis *n.* glucotaxis.
glycotrophic *adj.* glucotrófico, ca.
glycotropic *adj.* glucotrópico, -ca.
glycuresis *n.* glucuresis.
glycuronic *adj.* glucurónico, -ca.
  glycuronic acid conjugation glucuronidoconjugación.
  glycuronic conjugation glucuroconjugación.
glycuronide *adj.* glicurónido, -da.
glycuronuria *n.* glucuronuria.
glykemia *n.* glicemia, glucemia.
glyoxalase *n.* glioxalasa.
gnashing *n.* rechinamiento.
gnat *n.* jején.
gnathalgia *n.* gnatalgia.
gnathic *adj.* gnático, -ca.
gnathion *n.* gnatión.
gnathitis *n.* gnatitis.
gnathocephalus *n.* gnatocéfalo.
gnathodynamics *n.* gnatodinámica.
gnathodynamometer *n.* gnatodinamómetro.
gnathodynia *n.* gnatodinia.
gnathography *n.* gnatografía.
gnathologic *adj.* gnatológico, -ca.
gnathological *adj.* gnatológico, -ca.
gnathology *n.* gnatología.
gnathopalatoschisis *n.* gnatopalatosquisis.
gnathoplasty *n.* gnatoplastia.
gnathoschisis *n.* gnatosquisis.
gnathostat *n.* gnatostato.
gnathostatics *n.* gnatostática.
Gnathostoma spinigerum *n.* Gnathostoma spinigerum.
gnathostomiasis *n.* gnatostomiasis.
gnosia *n.* gnosia.
gnotobiology *n.* gnotobiología.
gnotobiota *n.* gnotobiota.
gnotobiote *n.* gnotobiote, gnotobioto.
gnotobiotic *adj.* gnotobiótico, -ca.
gnotobiotics *n.* gnotobiótica.
gnotophoresis *n.* gnotoforesis.
gnotophoric *adj.* gnotofórico, -ca.
goal *n.* meta.
goggles *n.* anteojeras.
goiter *n.* bocio.
  aberrant goiter bocio aberrante.
  acute goiter bocio agudo.
  adenomatous goiter bocio adenomatoso.
  Basedow's goiter bocio de Basedow.
  colloid goiter bocio coloidal, bocio coloide.
  congenital goiter bocio congénito.
  cystic goiter bocio quístico.
  diffuse goiter bocio difuso.
  diving goiter bocio buceador, bocio buzo, bocio móvil.
  ectopic goiter bocio ectópico.

endemic goiter bocio endémico.
exophthalmic goiter bocio exoftálmico.
familial goiter bocio familiar.
fibrous goiter bocio fibroso.
follicular goiter bocio folicular.
intrathoracic goiter bocio intratorácico.
iodide goiter bocio por yoduro.
lingual goiter bocio lingual.
lymphadenoid goiter bocio linfadenoide.
microfollicular goiter bocio microfolicular.
multinodular goiter bocio multinodular.
nodular goiter bocio nodular.
non-toxic goiter bocio no tóxico.
parenchymatous goiter bocio parenquimatoso.
perivascular goiter bocio perivascular.
plunging goiter bocio zambullidor.
retrovascular goiter bocio retrovascular.
simple goiter bocio simple.
sternal goiter bocio esternal.
substernal goiter bocio retrosternal, bocio subesternal.
suffocative goiter bocio sofocante.
thoracic goiter bocio torácico.
toxic goiter bocio tóxico.
toxic multinodular goiter bocio multinodular tóxico.
toxic nodular goiter bocio nodular tóxico.
vascular goiter bocio vascular.
wandering goiter bocio errante.
goitrogen *n.* bociógeno.
goitrogenic *adj.* bociogénico, -ca.
goitrogenicity *n.* bociogenicidad.
goitrogenous *adj.* bociogénico, -ca.
goitrous *adj.* bocioso, -sa.
gold *n.* oro.
cohesive gold oro cohesivo.
colloidal gold oro coloidal.
colloidal radioactive gold oro coloidal radiactivo.
direct gold oro directo.
fibrous gold oro fibroso.
gold foil oro laminado.
matt gold oro mate.
non-cohesive gold oro no cohesivo.
non-cohesive gold foil oro laminado no cohesivo.
platinized gold foil oro laminado platinado.
powdered gold oro en polvo.
radioactive gold oro radiactivo.
white gold oro blanco.
golgiokinesis *n.* golgiocinesis.
golgiosome *n.* golgiosoma.
gomitoli *n.* gomitoli.
gomphiasis *n.* gonfiasis.
gomphosis *n.* gonfosis.
gonacratia *n.* gonacracia.
gonad *n.* gónada.
indifferent gonad gónada indiferente.
streak gonad gónada en tiras.
third gonad gónada tercera.
gonadal *adj.* gonadal.
gonadectomy *n.* gonadectomía.
gonadial *adj.* gonádico, -da.
gonadoblastoma *n.* gonadoblastoma.
gonadocrin *n.* gonadocrina.
gonadogenesis *n.* gonadogénesis.
gonadoinhibitory *adj.* gonadoinhibidor, gonadoinhibitorio, -ria.
gonadokinetic *adj.* gonadocinético, -ca.
gonadopathy *n.* gonadopatía.
gonadopause *n.* gonadopausia.
gonadostimuline *n.* gonadostimulina.
gonadotherapy *n.* gonadoterapia.
gonadotrope *n.* gonadotropa.
gonadotroph *n.* gonadotrofa, gonadotrofo.

gonadotrophic *adj.* gonadotrófico, -ca.
gonadotrophin *n.* gonadotrofina.
anterior pituitary gonadotrophin gonadotrofina anterohipofisaria, gonadotrofina pituitaria anterior.
chorionic gonadotrophin (CG) gonadotrofina coriónica (CG).
human chorionic gonadotrophin gonadotrofina coriónica humana (HCG).
human menopausal gonadotrophin gonadotrofina menopáusica humana (HMG).
pregnant mare serum gonadotrophin gonadotrofina equina, gonadotrofina sérica de yegua preñada (PMSG).
gonadotropic *adj.* gonadotrópico, -ca.
gonadotropin *n.* gonadotropina.
gonaduct *n.* gonaducto.
gonagra *n.* gonagra.
gonalgia *n.* gonalgia.
gonane *n.* gonano.
gonangiectomy *n.* gonangiectomía.
gonarthritis *n.* gonartritis.
gonarthrocace *n.* gonartrocace.
gonarthromeningitis *n.* gonartromeningitis.
gonarthrosis *n.* gonartrosis.
gonarthrotomy *n.* gonartrotomía.
gonatagra *n.* gonatagra.
gonatocele *n.* gonatocele.
gonecyst *n.* gonecisto.
gonecystis *n.* gonecisto.
gonecystitis *n.* gonecistitis.
gonecystolith *n.* gonecistolito.
gonecystopyosis *n.* gonecistopiosis.
Gongylonema *n.* Gongylonema.
Gongylonema pulchrum Gongylonema pulchrum, Gongylonema scutatum.
Gongylonema scutatum Gongylonema pulchrum, Gongylonema scutatum.
gongylonemiasis *n.* gongilonemiasis.
gonia *n.* gonia.
gonial *adj.* gonial.
goniocraniometry *n.* goniocraneometría, goniocraniometría.
goniodysgenesis *n.* goniodisgenesia.
gonioma *n.* gonioma.
goniometer *n.* goniómetro.
finger goniometer goniómetro digital.
gonion *n.* gonión.
goniophotography *n.* goniofotografía.
goniopuncture *n.* goniopunción.
gonioscope *n.* gonioscopio.
gonioscopic *adj.* gonioscópico, -ca.
gonioscopy *n.* gonioscopia, goniscopia.
goniospasis *n.* goniospasis.
goniosynechia *n.* goniosinequia.
goniotomy *n.* goniotomía.
gonitis *n.* goneítis, gonitis.
gonoblennorrhea *n.* gonoblenorrea.
gonocampsis *n.* gonocampsis.
gonocele *n.* gonocele.
gonochorism *n.* gonocorismo.
gonochorismus *n.* gonocorismo.
gonocide *n.* gonocida.
gonococcal *adj.* gonocócico, -ca.
gonococcemia *n.* gonococemia.
gonococcia *n.* gonococia.
gonococcic *adj.* gonocócico, -ca.
gonococcidal *adj.* gonococida.
gonococcoidal *adj.* gonococicida.
gonococcus *n.* gonococo.
gonocyte *n.* gonocito.
gonocytoma *n.* gonocitoma.
gonohemia *n.* gonohemia.
gonophage *n.* gonófago.
gonophore *n.* gonóforo.

gonophorus *n.* gonóforo.
gonoreaction *n.* gonorreacción.
gonorrhea *n.* gonorrea.
gonorrheal *adj.* gonorreico, -ca.
gonotome *n.* gonótomo.
gonotoxemia *n.* gonotoxemia.
gonotoxin *n.* gonotoxina.
Gonyaulax catanella *n.* Gonyaulax catanella.
gonycampsis *n.* goniacampsia, gonicampsis.
gonycrotesis *n.* gonicrótesis.
gonyectyposis *n.* goniectíposis.
gonyocele *n.* goniocele.
gonyoncus *n.* gonioncо.
Gordius *n.* Gordius.
Gordius aquaticus Gordius aquaticus.
gorget *n.* gola, gorjerete.
probe gorget sonda gorjerete.
gorondou *n.* gorondou, gorondú.
gouge *n.* gubia.
Kelley gouge gubia de Kelley.
goundou *n.* goundou, gundo, gundú.
gout *n.* gota[2].
abarticular gout gota abarticular.
acute gout gota aguda.
articular gout gota articular.
calcium gout gota cálcica, gota por calcio.
chalky gout gota cretácea.
idiopathic gout gota idiopática.
irregular gout gota irregular.
latent gout gota latente.
lead gout gota por plomo.
masked gout gota enmascarada.
oxalic gout gota oxálica.
polyarticular gout gota poliarticular.
primary gout gota primaria.
regular gout gota regular.
retrocedent gout gota retrocedente, gota retropulsa.
rheumatic gout gota reumática.
saturnine gout gota saturnina.
secondary gout gota secundaria.
tophaceous gout gota tofácea.
gouty *adj.* gotoso, -sa.
Graafian *adj.* graafiano, -na.
gracile *adj.* grácil.
gracilis *adj.* gracilis.
grade *n.* grado[2].
Gleason's tumor grade grado tumoral de Gleason.
gradient *n.* gradiente.
atrioventricular gradient gradiente auriculoventricular.
density gradient gradiente de densidad.
electrochemical gradient gradiente electroquímico.
mitral gradient gradiente mitral.
systolic gradient gradiente sistólico.
ventricular gradient gradiente ventricular.
graduated *adj.* graduado, -da.
graft *n.* injertar, injerto.
accordion graft injerto en acordeón.
activated graft injerto activado.
adipodermal graft injerto adipodérmico.
allogeneic graft injerto alogénico, injerto alógeno.
anastomosed graft injerto anastomosado.
animal graft injerto animal.
aponeurotic graft injerto aponeurótico.
arterial graft injerto arterial.
augmentation graft injerto de aumento.
autochthonous graft injerto autóctono.
autodermic graft injerto autodérmico.
autoepidermic graft injerto autoepidérmico.
autogenous graft injerto autógeno.
autologous graft injerto autólogo.

autologous venous graft injerto de vena autóloga.

autoplastic graft injerto autoplástico.

avascular graft injerto avascular.

Blair-Brown graft injerto de Blair-Brown.

bone graft injerto de hueso.

brephoplastic graft injerto brefoplástico.

cable graft injerto en cable.

cadaver graft injerto de cadáver.

cartilage graft injerto de cartílago.

chessboard graft injerto en tablero de ajedrez.

chip graft injerto en trocitos.

chorioallantoic graft injerto corioalantoico, injerto corioalantoideo.

columellar graft injerto de columela.

composite graft injerto compuesto.

compound graft injerto compuesto.

corneal graft injerto corneal.

cutis graft injerto de cutis.

Davis graft injerto de Davis.

Delagenière's osteoperiostic graft injerto osteoperióstico de Delagenière.

delayed graft injerto diferido, injerto retrasado.

dermal graft injerto dérmico.

dermal-fat graft injerto dermoadiposo, injerto dermograso.

dermic graft injerto dérmico.

diced cartilage graft injerto en cubitos de cartílago.

Douglas graft injerto de Douglas.

epidermic graft injerto epidérmico.

Esser graft injerto de Esser.

fascia graft injerto de fascia.

fascicular graft injerto fascicular.

fat graft injerto adiposo, injerto de grasa.

fibula graft injerto de peroné.

filler graft injerto de relleno.

free graft injerto libre.

full-thickness graft injerto de espesor completo, injerto de espesor total.

funicular graft injerto funicular.

H graft injerto H.

hair graft injerto de pelo.

heterodermic graft injerto heterodérmico.

heterologous graft injerto heterólogo.

heteroplastic graft injerto heteroplástico.

heterospecific graft injerto heteroespecífico.

homologous graft injerto homólogo.

homoplastic graft injerto homoplástico.

hyperplastic graft injerto hiperplásico, injerto hiperplástico.

implantation graft injerto de implantación.

infusion graft injerto de infusión.

inlay graft injerto de incrustación.

interspecific graft injerto interespecífico.

isogeneic graft injerto isogeneico, injerto isogénico.

isologous graft injerto isólogo.

isoplastic graft injerto isoplástico.

jump graft injerto saltón.

Krause graft injerto de Krause, injerto de Krause-Wolfe.

Krause-Wolfe graft injerto de Krause, injerto de Krause-Wolfe.

lamellar graft injerto laminar.

mesh graft injerto en malla, injerto en red.

mucosal graft injerto mucoso.

nerve graft injerto de nervio, injerto nervioso, injerto neural.

omental graft injerto epiploico, injerto epiplónico.

onlay bone graft injerto óseo sobrepuesto.

onlay graft injerto de revestimiento, injerto directo.

orthotopic graft injerto ortotópico.

osseous graft injerto óseo.

osteoarticular graft injerto osteoarticular.

osteochondral graft injerto osteocondral.

osteoperiosteal graft injerto osteoperiostal, injerto osteoperióstico.

outlay graft "injerto "outlay".

partial-thickness graft injerto de espesor parcial.

patch graft injerto en parche.

pedicle graft injerto pediculado.

penetrating graft injerto penetrante.

periosteal graft injerto perióstico.

Phemister graft injerto de Phemister.

pinch graft injerto de pellizco.

porcine graft injerto porcino.

postage stamp graft injerto en sello de correos.

primary skin graft injerto cutáneo primario.

punch graft injerto de sacabocados.

Reverdin graft injerto de Reverdin.

rib graft injerto costal.

scalp graft injerto de pelo.

sieve graft injerto en criba.

skin graft injerto cutáneo, injerto de piel.

sleeve graft injerto en manga, injerto en manguito.

split-skin graft injerto cutáneo parcial, injerto de piel dividida.

split-thickness graft injerto de espesor dividido.

spongeous graft injerto de esponjosa.

spreader graft injerto expansivo.

Stent graft injerto de Stent.

syngeneic graft injerto singeneico, injerto singénico.

tendinous graft injerto tendinoso.

tendon graft injerto tendinoso.

thick-split graft injerto parcial grueso.

Thiersch graft injerto de Thiersch.

tube graft injerto en tubo.

tunnel graft injerto en túnel.

vascularized graft injerto vascularizado.

venous graft injerto venoso.

white graft injerto blanco.

Wolfe-Krause graft injerto de Wolfe-Krause.

Wolfe's graft injerto de Wolfe.

xenogeneic graft injerto xenogénico.

zooplastic graft injerto zooplástico.

grain *n.* grano.

gram-negative *adj.* gramnegativo, -va.

gram-positive *adj.* grampositivo, -va.

grancement *n.* rechinamiento.

grandiose *adj.* grandioso, -sa.

grandiosity *n.* grandiosidad.

granoplasm *n.* granoplasma.

granular *adj.* granular.

granular-fatty *adj.* granulograsoso, -sa.

granulated *n.* granulado.

granulatio *n.* granulación.

granulation *n.* granulación.

arachnoidal granulation granulación aracnoide, granulación aracnoidea.

Bayle's granulation granulación de Bayle.

Bright's granulation granulación de Bright.

cell granulation granulación celular.

cerebral granulation granulación cerebral.

exuberant granulation granulación exuberante.

Pacchionian granulation granulación de Pacchioni.

pyroninophilic granulation granulación pironinófila.

Reilly granulation granulación de Reilly.

Virchow's granulation granulación de Virchow.

granule *n.* gránulo.

acidophil granule gránulo acidófilo.

acrosomal granule gránulo acrosómico.

albuminous granule gránulo albuminoso.

aleuronoid granule gránulo aleuronoides.

alpha granule gránulo alfa.

Altmann's granule gránulo de Altmann.

amphophil granule gránulo anfófilo.

argentaffin granule gránulo argentafin.

atrial granule gránulo atrial.

azure granule gránulo azur, gránulo azurófilo.

azurophil granule gránulo azur, gránulo azurófilo.

azurophilic granule gránulo azur, gránulo azurófilo.

Babès-Ernst granule gránulo de Babès-Ernst.

basal granule gránulo basal.

basophil granule gránulo basófilo.

Bensley's specific granule gránulo específico de Bensley.

beta granule gránulo beta.

Birbeck granule gránulo de Birbeck.

Bollinger granule gránulo de Bollinger.

Bütschli's granule gránulo de Bütschli.

chromatic granule gránulo cromático, gránulo cromófilo.

chromophil granule gránulo cromático, gránulo cromófilo.

chromophilic granule gránulo cromático, gránulo cromófilo.

chromophobe granule gránulo cromófobo.

Crooke's granule gránulo de Crooke.

cytoplasmic granule gránulo citoplásmico.

delta granule gránulo delta.

Ehrlich-Heinz granule gránulo de Ehrlich, gránulo de Ehrlich-Heinz.

eosinophil granule gránulo eosinófilo.

Fordyce's granule gránulo de Fordyce.

fuchsinophil granule gránulo fucsinófilo.

gamma granule gránulo gamma.

Grawitz's granule gránulo de Grawitz.

Heinz granule gránulo de Heinz.

iodophil granule gránulo yodófilo.

Isaacs' granule gránulo de Isaacs.

juxtaglomerular granule gránulo yuxtaglomerulares.

kappa granule gránulo kappa.

keratohyalin granule gránulo de queratohialina, gránulo queratohialino.

Kölliker's interstitial granule gránulo intersticial de Kölliker.

Kretz's granule gránulo de Kretz.

Langerhans' granule gránulo de Langerhans.

Langley's granule gránulo de Langley.

melon seed body granule gránulo riciforme.

membrane-coating granule gránulo con membrana recubierta.

meningeal granule gránulo meníngeo.

metachromatic granule gránulo metacromático.

Much's granule gránulo de Much.

mucinogen granule gránulo de mucinógeno.

Neusser's granule gránulo de Neusser.

neutrophil granule gránulo neutrófilo.

Nissl granule gránulo de Nissl.

oxyphil granule gránulo oxífilo.

Palade granule gránulo de Palade.

Paschen granule gránulo de Paschen.

pigment granule gránulo de pigmento.

Plehn's granule gránulo de Plehn.

proacrosomal granule gránulo proacrosómicos.

prosecretion granule gránulo de prosecreción.

protein granule gránulo proteínico.

Schrön-Much granule gránulo de Schrön-Much.

Schüffner's granule gránulo de Schüffner.
secretion granule gránulo de secreción.
secretory granule gránulo de secreción.
seminal granule gránulo seminal.
specific atrial granule gránulo auricular específico.
sphere granule gránulo esférico.
sulfur granule gránulo de azufre.
toxic granule gránulo tóxico.
vermiform granule gránulo vermiforme.
volutin granule gránulo de volutina.
Zimmermann's granule gránulo de Zimmermann.
zymogen granule gránulo de cimógeno.
granuliform *adj.* granuliforme.
granulitis *n.* granulia.
granuloadipose *adj.* granuloadiposo, -sa.
granulocorpuscle *n.* granulocorpúsculo.
granulocyte *n.* granulocito.
  band form granulocyte granulocito en banda.
  immature granulocyte granulocito inmaduro.
  segmented granulocyte granulocito segmentado.
granulocytic *adj.* granulocitario, -ria, granulocítico, -ca.
granulocytopathy *n.* granulocitopatía.
granulocytopenia *n.* granulocitopenia.
granulocytopoiesis *n.* granulocitopoyesis.
granulocytopoietic *adj.* granulocitopoyético, -ca.
granulocytosis *n.* granulocitosis.
granuloma *n.* granuloma.
  amebic granuloma granuloma amebiano, granuloma amibiano.
  apical granuloma granuloma apical.
  beryllium granuloma granuloma por berilio.
  bilharzial granuloma granuloma bilharzial.
  candida granuloma granuloma candidiásico, granuloma por candida.
  candidal granuloma granuloma candidiásico, granuloma por candida.
  giant cell reparative granuloma granuloma de reparación de células gigantes.
  giant cell reparative granuloma, central granuloma de reparación de células gigantes, central.
  giant cell reparative granuloma, peripheral granuloma de reparación de células gigantes, periférico.
  cholesterol granuloma granuloma por colesterol.
  coccidioidal granuloma granuloma coccidioide, granuloma coccidioideo.
  dental granuloma granuloma dental, granuloma dentario.
  eosinophilic granuloma granuloma eosinofílico de los huesos, granuloma eosinófilo.
  eosinophilic granuloma of the bone granuloma eosinofílico de los huesos, granuloma eosinófilo.
  foreign body granuloma granuloma de cuerpo extraño.
  giant cell granuloma granuloma de células gigantes.
  giant cell reparative granuloma granuloma de reparación de células gigantes, granuloma reparador de células gigantes.
  giant cell reparative granuloma, central granuloma de reparación de células gigantes, central.
  giant cell reparative granuloma, peripheral granuloma de reparación de células gigantes, periférico.
  granuloma annulare granuloma anular.

  granuloma endemicum granuloma endémico.
  granuloma epidemicum granuloma endémico.
  granuloma faciale granuloma facial, granuloma facial eosinofílico.
  granuloma fissuratum granuloma fisurado.
  granuloma fungoides granuloma fungoide.
  granuloma gangraenescens granuloma gangrenoso.
  granuloma gluteale infantum granuloma glúteo infantil.
  granuloma gravidarum granuloma del embarazo.
  granuloma inguinale granuloma inguinal.
  granuloma inguinale tropicum granuloma inguinal tropical.
  granuloma iridis granuloma del iris.
  granuloma multiforme granuloma multiforme.
  granuloma pudendi granuloma pudendo.
  granuloma pudens tropicum granuloma pudendo tropical.
  granuloma telangiectaticum granuloma telangiectásico.
  granuloma tropicum granuloma tropical.
  Hodgkin's granuloma granuloma de Hodgkin.
  infectious granuloma granuloma infeccioso.
  laryngeal granuloma granuloma laríngeo.
  lethal midline granuloma granuloma mortal de la línea media.
  lipoid granuloma granuloma lipoide, granuloma lipoideo.
  lipophagic granuloma granuloma lipofágico.
  lycopodium granuloma granuloma por licopodio.
  Majocchi granuloma granuloma de Majocchi.
  malarial granuloma granuloma palúdico.
  malignant granuloma granuloma maligno.
  midline granuloma granuloma de la línea media.
  Mignon's eosinophilic granuloma granuloma eosinófilo de Mignon.
  monilial granuloma granuloma moniliásico.
  oily granuloma granuloma oleoso.
  parasitic granuloma granuloma parasitario.
  periapical granuloma granuloma periapical.
  plasma cell granuloma granuloma de células plasmáticas.
  pseudopyogenic granuloma granuloma seudopiogénico.
  pyogenic granuloma granuloma piogénico, granuloma piógeno.
  reparative giant cell granuloma granuloma de células gigantes reparador.
  reticulohistiocytic granuloma granuloma reticulohistiocítico.
  rheumatic granuloma granuloma reumático.
  root end granuloma granuloma radicular.
  sarcoidal granuloma granuloma sarcoide.
  schistosome granuloma granuloma esquistosómico.
  sea urchin granuloma granuloma de erizo de mar.
  swimming pool granuloma granuloma de las albercas, granuloma de las piscinas, granuloma de los balnearios.
  trichophytic granuloma granuloma tricofítico.
  ulcerating granuloma of the pudenda granuloma ulcerativo de los genitales, granuloma ulceroso de las regiones pudendas.
  umbilical granuloma granuloma umbilical.
  venereal granuloma granuloma venéreo.
  xanthomatous granuloma granuloma xantomatoso.

  zirconium granuloma granuloma por circonio.
granulomatosis *n.* granulomatosis.
  allergic granulomatosis granulomatosis alérgica.
  bronchocentric granulomatosis granulomatosis broncocéntrica.
  granulomatosis disciformis progressiva et chronica granulomatosis disciforme crónica y progresiva.
  granulomatosis siderotica granulomatosis siderótica.
  Langerhans cell granulomatosis granulomatosis de células de Langerhans.
  lipid granulomatosis granulomatosis lipídica, granulomatosis lipoide.
  lipoid granulomatosis granulomatosis lipídica, granulomatosis lipoide.
  lipophagic intestinal granulomatosis granulomatosis intestinal lipofágica.
  lymphomatoid granulomatosis granulomatosis linfomatoide, granulomatosis linfomatoidea.
  malignant granulomatosis granulomatosis maligna.
  Miescher granulomatosis granulomatosis de Miescher.
  necrotizing respiratory granulomatosis granulomatosis respiratoria necrosante.
  Wegener's granulomatosis granulomatosis de Wegener.
granulomatous *adj.* granulomatoso, -sa.
granulomere *n.* granulómero.
granulopenia *n.* granulopenia.
granulopexis *n.* granulopexia.
granulopexy *n.* granulopexia.
granuloplasm *n.* granuloplasma.
granuloplastic *adj.* granuloplástico, -ca.
granulopoiesis *n.* granulopoyesis.
granulopoietic *adj.* granulopoyético, -ca.
granulopoietin *n.* granulopoyetina.
granulopotent *adj.* granulopotente.
granulose *adj.* granulosa, granuloso, -sa.
granulosis *n.* granulosis.
  granulosis rubra nasi granulosis nasal roja, granulosis rubra nasi.
granulosity *n.* granulosidad.
granulovacuolar *adj.* granulovacuolar.
granum *n.* grano, granum.
graph *n.* gráfica, gráfico.
graphanesthesia *n.* grafanestesia.
graphesthesia *n.* grafestesia.
graphic *adj.* gráfico, -ca.
graphite *n.* grafito.
graphitosis *n.* grafitosis.
graphoanalysis *n.* grafoanálisis.
graphocatharsis *n.* grafocatarsis.
graphokinesthetic *adj.* grafocinestésico, -ca.
graphology *n.* grafología.
graphomania *n.* grafomanía.
graphomotor *adj.* grafomotor, -ra.
graphopathology *n.* grafopatología.
graphophobia *n.* grafofobia.
graphorrhea *n.* graforrea.
graphoscope *n.* grafoscopio.
graphospasm *n.* grafoespasmo, grafospasmo.
grass *n.* gramínea.
gratification *n.* gratificación.
grattage *n.* grattage.
grave *adj.* grave.
gravedo *n.* gravedo.
gravel *n.* gravela, gravilla.
gravid *n.* grávida.
gravida *n.* grávida.
gravidic *adj.* gravídico, -ca.

gravidism *n.* gravidismo.
graviditas *n.* gravidez, graviditas.
  graviditas examnialis gravidez examinal, graviditas examnialis.
  graviditas exochorialis gravidez excorial, graviditas exochorialis.
gravidity *n.* gravidez.
gravidocardiac *adj.* gravidocardiaco, -ca.
gravidopuerperal *adj.* gravidopuerperal.
gravimeter *n.* gravímetro.
gravimetric *adj.* gravimétrico, -ca.
gravireceptors *n.* gravirreceptores.
gravis *adj.* grave.
gravistatic *adj.* gravistático, -ca.
gravitation *n.* gravitación.
gravitometer *n.* gravitómetro.
gravity *n.* gravedad.
  standard gravity gravedad estándar.
gray *adj.* gris.
  perihypoglossal gray gris perihipogloso.
  silver gray gris de plata.
  steel gray gris de acero.
green *adj.* verde.
greffotome *n.* grefótomo.
gregaloid *adj.* gregaloide.
gregariousness *n.* gregarismo.
gression *n.* gresión.
grid *n.* grilla.
  Wetzel grid grilla de Wetzel.
grief *n.* aflicción, duelo, pena.
griffin claw *n.* gafedad.
grinding *n.* abrasio, abrasión, desgaste, lijado, trituración[1].
  selective grinding abrasión selectiva, desgaste selectivo, lijado selectivo.
  spot grinding abrasión puntual, lijado de punto.
grip *n.* asimiento, gripe.
  endemic grip gripe endémica.
  hook grip asimiento en gancho.
  power grip asimiento de fuerza.
  precision grip asimiento de precisión.
gripe *n.* retortijón.
grippal *adj.* gripal.
grippe *n.* gripe.
  grippe aurique gripe áurica.
groin *n.* ingle.
groove *n.* corredera, surco.
gross *adj.* grueso, -sa.
ground *n.* terreno.
group *n.* grupo.
  blood group grupo sanguíneo.
  CMN group grupo CMN.
  colon-typhoid-dysentery group grupo colon-tifóidico-disentérico, grupo de colon, tifoidea y disentería.
  control group grupo de control.
  cytophil group grupo citófilo.
  determinant group grupo determinante.
  diagnosis-related group (DRG) grupo de diagnósticos relacionados (GDR), grupos relacionados por diagnóstico.
  E group grupo E.
  encounter group grupo de encuentro.
  experimental group grupo experimental.
  glucophore group grupo glucóforo.
  group agglutination grupo aglutinación.
  hemorrhagic-septicemia group grupo de septicemia hemorrágica.
  Lancefield group of streptococci grupo de Lancefield.
  linkage group grupo de ligamiento.
  matched group grupo emparejado.
  paratyphoid-enteriditis group grupo de paratifoidea y enteritis, grupo paratifoidenteritis Salmonella.

  sensitivity group grupo de sensibilidad.
  sensitivity training group grupo de entrenamiento de la sensibilidad.
  specific group grupo específico.
  T group grupo T.
  task oriented group grupo de tareas.
  therapeutic group grupo terapéutico.
  training group grupo de capacitación, grupo de entrenamiento.
grouping *n.* agrupamiento.
  blood grouping agrupamiento sanguíneo.
growth *n.* crecimiento.
  absolute growth crecimiento absoluto.
  accretionary growth crecimiento acrecionario, crecimiento por acreción.
  allometric growth crecimiento alométrico.
  appositional growth crecimiento por aposición.
  auxetic growth crecimiento auxético.
  catch-up growth crecimiento compensador.
  condylar growth crecimiento condíleo.
  differential growth crecimiento diferencial.
  heterogonous growth crecimiento heterógono.
  histiotypic growth crecimiento histiotípico.
  interstitial growth crecimiento intersticial.
  intrauterine retarded growth crecimiento intrauterino retardado.
  isometric growth crecimiento isométrico.
  multiplicative growth crecimiento de multiplicación.
  new growth crecimiento nuevo.
  organotypic growth crecimiento organotípico.
  relative growth crecimiento relativo.
grumose *adj.* grumoso, -sa.
grumous *adj.* grumoso, -sa.
grunting *n.* quejido.
gryochrome *n.* griocromo.
gryphosis *n.* grifosis.
gryposis *n.* griposis.
  gryposis penis griposis del pene.
  gryposis ungulum griposis ungueal, griposis ungulum.
guaiac *n.* guayacán, guayaco.
guanidine *n.* guanidina.
guanidinemia *n.* guanidinemia.
guanophore *n.* guanóforo.
guard *n.* guarda.
  bite guard guarda de mordida.
  mouth guard guarda bucal, guardaboca.
  night guard guarda nocturna.
  occlusal guard guarda oclusal.
gubernacular *adj.* gubernacular.
gubernaculum *n.* gubernáculo.
  chorda gubernaculum gubernáculo del cordón.
  gubernaculum dentis gubernáculo dental, gubernáculo dentis.
  gubernaculum testis gubernáculo de Hunter, gubernáculo testicular, gubernáculo testis.
  Hunter's gubernaculum gubernáculo de Hunter, gubernáculo testicular, gubernáculo testis.
guiac *n.* guayacán, guayaco.
guidance *n.* guía.
  catheter guidance guía de catéter.
  condylar guidance guía condílea.
  incisal guidance guía incisal.
guide *n.* guía.
  adjustable anterior guide guía ajustable anterior.
  anterior guide guía anterior.
  condylar guide guía condílea.
  incisal guide guía incisal.
guideline *n.* guía.
guillotine *n.* guillotina.

guinea pig *n.* cobaya, cobayo.
gullet *n.* gaznate.
gum *n.* encía, goma[1].
gumma *n.* goma[2].
  tuberculous gumma goma tuberculosa.
gummatous *adj.* gomatoso, -sa[1], gomoso, -sa.
gummy *adj.* gomatoso, -sa[2], gomoso, -sa.
gurgling *n.* gorgoteo.
gurgulio *n.* gurgulio.
gurney *n.* gurney.
gustation *n.* gustación.
  colored gustation gustación coloreada.
gustatism *n.* gustatismo.
gustatory *adj.* gustativo, -va.
gustin *n.* gustina.
gustometer *n.* gustómetro.
gustometry *n.* gustometría.
gut *n.* intestino, intestinum.
  blind gut intestino ciego.
  postanal gut intestino posanal.
  primitive gut intestino primitivo.
  tail gut intestino de la cola.
gutta *n.* gota[2], gutta.
  gutta rosacea gutta rosácea.
  gutta serena gota serena, gutta serena.
gutta-percha *n.* gutapercha.
guttate *n.* gutada, guttata.
gutter *n.* gotiera.
guttering *n.* acanaladura.
guttural *adj.* gutural.
gutturophony *n.* guturofonía.
gutturotetany *n.* guturotetania.
gymnastics *n.* gimnasia.
  ocular gymnastics gimnasia ocular.
  Swedish gymnastics gimnasia sueca.
Gymnoascus *n.* Gymnoascus.
gymnobacterium *n.* gimnobacteria.
gymnocyte *n.* gimnocito.
gymnophobia *n.* gimnofobia.
gymnoplast *n.* gimnoplasto.
gymnoscopic *adj.* gimnoscópico, -ca.
gymnosophy *n.* gimnosofía.
gynander *n.* ginandro.
gynandria *n.* ginandria.
gynandrism *n.* ginandrismo.
gynandroblastoma *n.* ginandroblastoma.
gynandroid *n.* ginandroide.
gynandromorph *n.* ginandromorfo.
gynandromorphism *n.* ginandromorfismo.
gynandromorphous *adj.* ginandromorfo, -fa.
gynandry *n.* ginandria.
gynanthropia *n.* ginantropía.
gynanthropism *n.* ginantropismo.
gynatresia *n.* ginatresia.
gynecogen *n.* ginecógeno.
gynecogenic *adj.* ginecogénico, -ca.
gynecoid *adj.* ginecoide, ginecoideo, -a.
gynecologic *adj.* ginecológico, -ca.
gynecological *adj.* ginecológico, -ca.
gynecologist *n.* ginecólogo, -ga.
gynecology *n.* ginecología.
gynecomania *n.* ginecomanía.
gynecomastia *n.* ginecomastia.
  nutritional gynecomastia ginecomastia nutricional.
  refeeding gynecomastia ginecomastia de realimentación.
  rehabilitation gynecomastia ginecomastia de rehabilitación.
gynecomastism *n.* ginecomatismo.
gynecopathy *n.* ginecopatía.
gynecotocology *n.* ginecotocología.
gyneduct *n.* gineducto.
gynephilia *n.* ginefilia.
gynephobia *n.* ginefobia.

gyneplasty *n.* gineplastia.
gyniatrics *n.* giniatría.
gyniatry *n.* giniatría.
gynogenesis *n.* ginogénesis.
gynoid *adj.* ginecoide.
gynomerogon *n.* ginomerogono.
gynomerogony *n.* ginomerogonia.
gynopathic *adj.* ginopático, -ca.

gynopathy *n.* ginopatía.
gynophobia *n.* ginofobia.
gynoplastics *n.* ginoplastia.
gynoplasty *n.* ginoplastia.
gypsum *n.* yeso^2.
gyrate *v.* girar.
gyrectomy *n.* girectomía.
   frontal gyrectomy girectomía frontal.

gyrencephalic *adj.* girencefálico, girencéfalo.
gyromagnetic *adj.* giromagnético, -ca.
gyrometer *n.* girómetro.
gyrosa *n.* girosa, girosis.
gyrospasm *n.* giroespasmo, girospasmo.
gyrotrope *n.* girotropo.
gyrus *n.* giro, gyrus.
gysgenopathy *n.* disgenopatía.

H h

habeas corpus *n.* habeas corpus.
habena *n.* habena.
habenal *adj.* habenal, habenar.
habenar *adj.* habenal, habenar.
habenula *n.* habénula.
habenular *adj.* habenular.
habit *n.* hábito, rutina[1].
habitat *n.* hábitat.
habitual *adj.* habitual.
habituation *n.* habituación.
habitus *n.* hábito.
Haemagogus *n.* Haemagogus.
Haemamoeba *n.* haemamoeba.
Haemaphysalis *n.* Haemaphysalis.
Haementeria *n.* Haementeria.
Haemodipsus *n.* Haemodipsus.
Haemophylus *n.* Haemophilus.
haemorrhagia *n.* hemorragia.
Haemosporidium *n.* Haemosporidium.
haemosporidium *n.* hemosporidio.
Hafnia *n.* Hafnia.
hair *n.* cabello, capillus, pelo, vello.
  auditory hair pelo auditivo.
  bamboo hair pelo de bambú.
  burrowing hair pelo horadante.
  cast hair cilindro de pelo.
  club hair pelo claviforme.
  exclamation point hair pelo en signo de admiración.
  Frey's irritation hair pelo irritantes de Frey.
  ingrown hair pelo encarnado, pelo invaginado.
  kinky hair pelo ensortijado.
  lanugo hair pelo lanugo.
  nettling hair pelo urticante.
  pubic hair vello pubiano, vello púbico.
  ringed hair pelo anular.
  Schridde's cancer hair pelo canceroso de Schridde.
  stellate hair pelo estrellado.
  taste hair pelo gustativo.
  woolly hair pelo lanudo.
hairy *adj.* peludo, -da.
halation *n.* deslumbramiento[2].
half-caste *adj.* mestizo, -za.
half-life *n.* semidesintegración, semivida.
  biologic half-life semivida biológica.
haliphagia *n.* halifagia.
halisteresis *n.* halistéresis.
  halisteresis cerea halistéresis cérea.
halisteretic *adj.* halisterético, -ca.
halitosis *n.* halitosis.
halituous *adj.* halitoso, -sa.
halitus *n.* hálito.
hallucination *n.* alucinación.
  alcoholic hallucination alucinación alcohólica.
  auditory hallucination alucinación auditiva.
  formed visual hallucination alucinación visual formada.

gustatory hallucination alucinación gustativa.
haptic hallucination alucinación háptica.
hypnagogic hallucination alucinaciónhipnagógica.
hypnopompic hallucination alucinación hipnopómpica.
kinesthetic hallucination alucinación cenestésica.
Lilliputian hallucination alucinación liliputiense.
olfactory hallucination alucinación olfatoria.
somatic hallucination alucinación somática.
stump hallucination alucinación del muñón.
tactile hallucination alucinación táctil.
unformed visual hallucination alucinación visual no formada.
visual hallucination alucinación visual.
hallucinogen *n.* alucinógeno.
hallucinosis *n.* alucinosis.
  acute hallucinosis alucinosis aguda.
  organic hallucinosis alucinosis orgánica.
hallucinotic *adj.* alucinante.
hallux *n.* hallux.
  hallux dolorosus hallux dolorosus.
  hallux extensus hallux extensus.
  hallux flexus hallux flexus.
  hallux malleus hallux malleus.
  hallux rigidus hallux rigidus.
  hallux valgus hallux valgus.
  hallux varus hallux varus.
halmatogenesis *n.* halmatogénesis.
halo *n.* halo.
  anemic halo halo anémico.
  Fick's halo halo Fick.
  glaucomatous halo halo glaucomatoso.
  halo glaucomatosus halo glaucomatoso.
  halo nevus halo nevus.
  senile halo halo senil.
Halobacteriaceae *n.* Halobacteriaceae.
Halobacterium *n.* Halobacterium.
Halococcus *n.* Halococcus.
halodermia *n.* halodermia.
halogen *n.* halógeno.
halogenation *n.* halogenación.
haluid *adj.* haloide, haloideo, -a.
halometer *n.* halómetro.
halometry *n.* halometría.
halophil *n.* halófilo, -la.
halophile *n.* halófilo, -la.
halophilic *adj.* halofílico, -ca.
halosteresis *n.* halostéresis.
hamarthritis *n.* hamartritis.
hamartia *n.* hamartia.
hamartial *adj.* hamarcial, hamartial.
hamartoblastoma *n.* hamartoblastoma.
hamartochondromatosis *n.* hamartocondromatosis.
hamartoma *n.* hamartoma.
  fibrous hamartoma of infancy hamartoma fibroso del lactante.

neuronal hamartoma hamartoma neuronal.
neuronal hypothalamic hamartoma hamartoma neuronal hipotalámico.
pulmonary hamartoma hamartoma pulmonar.
renal hamartoma hamartoma renal.
retinal pigment epithelium hamartoma hamartoma epitelial fragmentario de la retina.
hamartomatosis *n.* hamartomatosis.
hamartomatous *adj.* hamartomatoso, -sa.
hamartoplasia *n.* hamartoplasia.
hamate *adj.* ganchoso, -sa.
  hamate bone hamatum.
hamatum *n.* hamatum.
hammer *n.* martillo.
  reflex hammer martillo de reflejos.
hamular *adj.* hamelar, hamular.
hamulus *n.* gancho[2], hamulus.
hand *n.* mano.
  accoucheur's hand mano de comadrón, mano de partero.
  alien hand mano ajena.
  benediction hand mano apostólica, mano de predicador.
  claw hand mano en garra.
  cleft hand mano en horquilla, mano fisurada, mano hendida.
  club hand mano zamba.
  crab hand mano de cangrejo.
  dead hand mano muerta.
  drop hand mano caída, mano péndula.
  frozen hand mano congelada.
  ghoul hand mano de vampiro.
  lobster-claw hand mano en pinzas de langosta.
  Marinesco's succulent hand mano suculenta de Marinesco.
  mirror hand mano en espejo.
  mitten hand mano en guantelete.
  monkey hand mano de mono, mano de simio, mano simiesca.
  obstetrical hand mano obstétrica.
  opera-glass hand mano en anteojo, mano en gemelo, mano en gemelos de teatro.
  phantom hand mano fantasma.
  skeleton hand mano de esqueleto, mano esquelética.
  spade hand mano en pala.
  split hand mano dividida.
  trench hand mano de trinchera.
  trident hand mano en tridente.
  writing hand mano de escritor.
handedness *n.* manualidad.
handicap *n.* impedimento.
  mental handicap minusvalía mental.
handicapped *adj.* inválido, -da, minusválido, -da.
handle *n.* mango.
hangnail *n.* padrastro.
hapalonychia *n.* hapaloniquia.

haphalgesia *n.* hafalgesia.
haplodermatitis *n.* haplodermatitis, haplodermitis.
haplodont *adj.* haplodonto, -ta.
haploid *adj.* haploide.
haploidentical *adj.* haploidéntico, -ca.
haploidentity *n.* haploidentidad.
haploidy *n.* haploidía.
haplology *n.* haplología.
haplomycosis *n.* haplomicosis.
haplont *n.* haplonto.
haplopathy *n.* haplopatía.
haplophase *n.* haplofase.
haplopia *n.* haplopía.
haploscope *n.* haploscopio.
   mirror haploscope haploscopio en espejo.
haploscopic *adj.* haploscópico, -ca.
haplotype *n.* haplotipo.
hapten *n.* hapteno.
   bacterial hapten hapteno bacterial.
   group A hapten hapteno grupo A.
haptene *n.* hapteno.
haptenic *adj.* hapténico, -ca.
haptic *adj.* háptico, -ca.
haptics *n.* háptica, haptología.
haptometer *n.* haptómetro.
haptophil *adj.* haptófilo, -la.
haptophile *adj.* haptófilo, -la.
haptophore *n.* haptóforo.
haptophoric *adj.* haptofórico, -ca.
haptophorous *adj.* haptofórico, -ca.
harara *n.* harara.
hard *adj.* duro, -ra.
hardening *n.* endurecimiento.
hardness *n.* dureza.
   diamond pyramid hardness dureza de la pirámide del diamante.
   hardness of X-rays dureza de los rayos X.
   indentation hardness dureza de indentación.
   permanent hardness dureza permanente.
   temporary hardness dureza temporal.
harmonia *n.* harmonia.
harpoon *n.* arpón.
Hartmanella *n.* Hartmanella.
hartmannelliasis *n.* hartmanneliasis.
harvest *v.* cultivar.
hashish *n.* hachís.
hatchet *n.* hacha.
   enamel hatchet hacha esmalte.
Hauch *n.* hauch.
haustration *n.* haustración.
haustrum *n.* haustrum.
Haverhillia multiformis *n.* Haverhillia multiformis.
hawkinsinuria *n.* hawkinsinuria.
head *n.* cabeza.
   bulldog head cabeza de bulldog.
   head injury descalabradura.
   head wound descalabradura.
   hourglass head cabeza en reloj de arena.
   medusa head cabeza de medusa.
   saddle head cabeza en silla de montar.
   square head cabeza cuadrada.
headache *n.* cefalea.
   cluster headache cefalea acuminada, cefalea en grupo, cefalea en racimo.
   histaminic headache cefalea histamínica.
   Horton's headache cefalea de Horton.
   migraine headache cefalea migrañosa.
   sinusal vacuum headache cefalea por efecto del vacío.
   spinal headache cefalea espinal.
   tension headache cefalea tensional.
   tension-type headache cefalea tensional.
headgear *n.* casco cefálico.

head-nodding *n.* cabeceo.
healing *n.* curación.
   healing by first intention curación por primera intención.
   healing by second intention curación por segunda intención.
   healing by third intention curación por tercera intención.
health *n.* salud, sanitas.
   community mental health salud mental comunitaria.
   environmental health salud medioambiental.
   family health salud familiar.
   industrial health salud laboral.
   mental health salud mental.
   mental health consultation interconsulta de salud mental.
   occupational health salud profesional.
   sexual health salud sexual.
healthy *adj.* sano, -na.
hear *v.* oír.
hearing aid *n.* audífono.
heart *n.* cor, corazón.
   armor heart corazón en armadura.
   armored heart corazón blindado.
   artificial heart corazón artificial.
   athlete's heart corazón atlético, corazón de atleta.
   athletic heart corazón atlético, corazón de atleta.
   beer heart corazón de bebedor de cerveza, corazón de cerveza.
   boat-shaped heart corazón navicular.
   bony heart corazón óseo.
   drop heart corazón caído.
   fat heart corazón adiposo, corazón graso.
   fatty heart corazón adiposo, corazón graso.
   flask-shaped heart corazón en matriz.
   frosted heart corazón congelado, corazón recubierto.
   hairy heart corazón piloso.
   hanging heart corazón colgante.
   horizontal heart corazón horizontal.
   hypoplastic heart corazón hipoplásico.
   icing heart corazón de hielo.
   intermediate heart corazón intermedio.
   irritable heart corazón irritable.
   left heart corazón izquierdo.
   movable heart corazón móvil.
   myxedema heart corazón mixedematoso.
   parchment heart corazón de pergamino.
   pear-shaped heart corazón piriforme.
   pneumatic heart driver impulsor cardíaco neumático.
   pulmonary heart corazón pulmonar.
   Quain's fatty heart corazón graso de Quain.
   right heart corazón derecho.
   round heart corazón redondeado.
   sabot heart corazón en zueco.
   semihorizontal heart corazón semihorizontal.
   semivertical heart corazón semivertical.
   skin heart corazón cutáneo.
   soldier's heart corazón de soldado, corazón militar.
   stone heart corazón de piedra.
   suspended heart corazón suspendido.
   systemic heart corazón sistémico.
   tabby cat heart corazón en pecho de tordo.
   teardrop heart corazón en forma de lágrima.
   three-chambered heart cor triloculare, corazón de tres cavidades.
   tiger heart corazón de tigre, corazón tigroide.
   tobacco heart corazón tabáquico.

   venous heart corazón venoso.
   vertical heart corazón vertical.
   wandering heart corazón errante.
heat *n.* calor.
   conductive heat calor conductivo, calor de conducción.
   convective heat calor convectivo, calor de convección.
   conversive heat calor de conversión.
   delayed heat calor de relajación.
   dry heat calor seco.
   heat of combustion calor de combustión.
   heat of compression calor de compresión.
   heat of crystallization calor de cristalización.
   heat of dissociation calor de disociación.
   heat of evaporation calor de evaporación.
   heat of formation calor de formación.
   heat of fusion calor de fusión.
   heat of sublimation calor de sublimación.
   heat of vaporization calor de vaporización.
   initial heat calor inicial.
   innate heat calor innato.
   latent heat calor latente.
   latent heat of fusion calor latente de fusión.
   latent heat of sublimation calor latente de sublimación.
   latent heat of vaporization calor latente de vaporización.
   molecular heat calor molecular.
   radiant heat calor radiante.
   recovery heat calor de recuperación.
   sensible heat calor sensible.
   specific heat calor específico.
hebephrenia *n.* hebefrenia.
hebetic *adj.* hebético, -ca.
hebetomy *n.* hebetomía.
hebotomy *n.* hebetomía, hebotomía.
hecatomeral *adj.* hecatomérico, -ca, hecatómero, -ra.
hecatomeric *adj.* hecatomérico, -ca.
hectic *adj.* héctico, -ca.
hedatresia *n.* hedatresia.
hedonia *n.* hedonismo.
hedonic *adj.* hedónico, -ca.
hedonism *n.* hedonismo.
hedratresia *n.* hedatresia, hedratresia.
hedrocele *n.* hedrocele.
heel *n.* talón, tacón.
   anterior heel talón anterior.
   basketball heel talón de jugador de baloncesto.
   black heel talón negro.
   gonorrheal heel talón gonocócico.
   jogger's heel talón de footing.
   painful heel talón doloroso.
   policeman's heel talón de policía.
   prominent heel talón prominente.
   Thomas heel talón de Thomas.
   walking heel tacón.
height *n.* altura, estatura, talla.
   anterior facial height altura facial anterior.
   apex height altura apical.
   cusp height altura cuspídea.
   facial height altura facial.
   fundal height altura del fondo del útero.
   height of contour altura del contorno.
   lower facial height altura facial inferior.
   nasal height altura nasal.
   orbital height altura orbitaria.
   posterior facial height altura facial posterior.
   surveyed height of contour altura límite del contorno.
   upper facial height altura facial superior.
helcoid *adj.* helcoide.
helcology *n.* helcología.

helcoma *n.* helcoma.
helcomenia *n.* helcomenia.
helcoplasty *n.* helcoplastia.
helcosis *n.* helcosis.
Heleidae *n.* Heleidae.
helical *adj.* helicoidal, helicoide.
Helicobacter *n.* Helicobacter.
helicoid *adj.* helicoidal, helicoide.
helicoidal *adj.* helicoidal, helicoide.
helicopod *adj.* helicópodo, -da.
helicopodia *n.* helicopodia.
helicotrema *n.* helicotrema.
heliencephalitis *n.* heliencefalitis, helioencefalitis.
helioaerotherapy *n.* helioaeroterapia.
heliophobia *n.* heliofobia.
heliosis *n.* heliosis.
heliotherapy *n.* helioterapia.
helix *n.* hélice, hélix.
helminth *n.* helminto.
helminthagogue *adj.* helmintagogo, -ga.
helminthiasis *n.* helmintiasis, helmintogénesis.
helminthic *adj.* helmíntico, -ca.
helminthism *n.* helmintismo.
helminthoid *adj.* helmintoide.
helminthoma *n.* helmintoma.
helminthous *adj.* helmíntico, -ca.
heloma *n.* heloma.
   heloma durum heloma duro, heloma durum.
   heloma molle heloma blando, heloma molle.
Helophilus *n.* Helophilus.
helosis *n.* helosis.
helotomy *n.* helotomía.
hem *n.* hem.
hemabarometer *n.* hemabarómetro.
hemachromatosis *n.* hemacromatosis, hemocromatosis.
hemachromatotic *adj.* hemacromatósico, -ca, hemocromatósico, -ca.
hemachrome *n.* hemacromo.
hemachrosis *n.* hemacrosis.
hemacyte *n.* hemacito.
hemacytometer *n.* hemacitómetro.
hemacytometry *n.* hemacitometría.
hemacytopoiesis *n.* hemacitopoyesis.
hemacytozoon *n.* hemacitozoo.
hemaden *n.* hemadeno.
hemadenology *n.* hemadenología.
hemadostenosis *n.* hemadostenosis.
hemadsorbent *adj.* hemadsorbente.
hemadsorption *n.* hemadsorción.
hemadynamometer *n.* hemadinamómetro.
hemadynamometry *n.* hemadinamometría.
hemafacient *adj.* hemafaciente.
hemafecia *n.* hemafecia.
hemagglutination *n.* hemaglutinación.
   indirect hemagglutination hemaglutinación indirecta.
   passive hemagglutination hemaglutinación pasiva.
   viral hemagglutination hemaglutinación viral, hemaglutinación virósica.
hemagglutinative *adj.* hemaglutinante.
hemagiectasa *n.* hemangiectasia, hemangiectasis.
hemaglutinin *n.* hemaglutinina.
   bacterial hemagglutinin bacteriohemaglutinina.
hemagogic *adj.* hemagógico, -ca.
hemagogue *n.* hemagogo.
hemagonium *n.* hemagonio.
hemal *adj.* hemal.
hemalum *n.* hemalum, hemalumbre.
hemamebiasis *n.* hemamebiasis.

hemanalysis *n.* hemanálisis.
hemangiectasis *n.* hemangiectasia, hemangiectasis.
hemangioameloblastoma *n.* hemangioameloblastoma.
hemangioblast *n.* hemoangioblasto.
hemangioblasto *n.* hemangioblasto.
hemangioblastoma *n.* hemangioblastoma.
hemangioendothelioblastoma *n.* hemangioendotelioblastoma.
hemangioendothelioma *n.* hemangioendotelioma.
   benign hemangioendothelioma hemangioendotelioma benigno.
   hemangioendothelioma tuberosum multiplex hemangioendotelioma tuberoso múltiple.
   malignant hemangioendothelioma hemangioendotelioma maligno.
hemangiofibroma *n.* hemangiofibroma, hemoangiofibroma.
   juvenile hemangiofibroma hemangiofibroma juvenil.
hemangioma *n.* hemangioma.
   ameloblastic hemangioma hemangioma ameloblástico.
   arterial hemangioma hemangioma arterial.
   capillary hemangioma hemangioma capilar.
   cavernous hemangioma hemangioma cavernoso.
   choroidal hemangioma hemangioma coroideo.
   congenital hemangioma hemangioma congénito.
   hemangioma planum extensum hemangioma plano extenso.
   hemangioma simplex hemangioma simple.
   racemose hemangioma hemangioma racemoso.
   sclerosing hemangioma hemangioma esclerosante.
   senile hemangioma hemangioma senil.
   strawberry hemangioma hemangioma en fresa.
   superficial fading infantile hemangioma hemangioma infantil superficial evanescente.
   venous hemangioma hemangioma venoso.
   verrucous hemangioma hemangioma verrugoso.
   vertebral hemangioma hemangioma vertebral.
hemangiomatosis *n.* hemangiomatosis.
hemangiomatous *adj.* hemangiomatoso, -sa.
hemangiopericyte *n.* hemangiopericito.
hemangiosarcoma *n.* hemangiosarcoma.
hemapheic *adj.* hemafeico, -ca.
hemaphein *n.* hemafeína.
hemapheism *n.* hemafeísmo.
hemapheresis *n.* hemaféresis.
hemaphotograph *n.* hemafotografía.
hemapoiesis *n.* hemapoyesis.
hemapoietic *adj.* hemapoyético, -ca.
hemapophysis *n.* hemapófisis.
hemarthros *n.* hemartros.
hemarthrosis *n.* hemartrosis.
hemartoma *n.* hemartoma.
hemastrontium *n.* hemastroncio.
hemataerometer *n.* hemataerómetro.
hematapostema *n.* hematapostema.
hematein *n.* hemateína.
   Baker's acid hematein hemateína ácida de Baker.
hematemesis *n.* hematemesis.
   Goldstein's hematemesis hematemesis Goldstein.

hematencephalon *n.* hematencéfalo.
hematherapy *n.* hematerapia, hemoterapia.
hemathermal *adj.* hematérmico, -ca, hematermo, -ma.
hemathermous *adj.* hematérmico, -ca, hematermo, -ma.
hemathidrosis *n.* hemathidrosis, hematidrosis.
hemathorax *n.* hematórax.
hematic *adj.* hemático, -ca.
hematidrosis *n.* hemathidrosis, hematidrosis.
hematimetry *n.* hematimetría.
hematin *n.* hematina, hemocroína.
hematinemia *n.* hematinemia.
hematinic *adj.* hematínico, -ca.
hematinogen *n.* hematinógeno.
hematinometer *n.* hematinómetro.
hematinuria *n.* hematinuria.
hematischesis *n.* hematisquesis.
hematobilia *n.* hematobilia.
hematobium *n.* hematobio.
hematoblast *n.* hematoblasto.
hematocele *n.* hematocele.
   parametric hematocele hematocele paramétrico, hematocele periuterino, hematocele retrouterino.
   pudendal hematocele hematocele pudendo.
   retrouterine hematocele hematocele paramétrico, hematocele periuterino, hematocele retrouterino.
   scrotal hematocele hematocele del escroto, hematocele escrotal.
   vaginal hematocele hematocele vaginal.
hematocelia *n.* hematocelia.
hematocephalus *n.* hematocéfalo.
hematocephaly *n.* hematocefalia.
hematochezia *n.* hematoquecia, hematoquezia.
hematochlorin *n.* hematoclorina.
hematochromatosis *n.* hematocromatosis.
hematochyluria *n.* hematoquiluria.
hematocoelia *n.* hematocelia.
hematocolpometra *n.* hematocolpómetra.
hematocolpos *n.* hematocolpos.
hematocornea *n.* hematocórnea.
hematocrit *n.* hematocrito.
   large vessel hematocrit hematocrito de gran vaso.
   total body hematocrit hematocrito corporal total, hematocrito de cuerpo entero.
   whole body hematocrit hematocrito corporal total, hematocrito de cuerpo entero.
   Wintrobe hematocrit hematocrito de Wintrobe.
hematocyst *n.* hematocisto, hematoquiste.
hematocyte *n.* hematocito.
hematocytoblast *n.* hematocitoblasto.
hematocytolysis *n.* hematocitólisis.
hematocytometer *n.* hematocitómetro.
hematocytopenia *n.* hematocitopenia.
hematocyturia *n.* hematocituria, hematocituria.
hematodialysis *n.* hematodiálisis.
hematodyscrasia *n.* hematodiscrasia.
hematodystrophy *n.* hematodistrofia.
hematoencephalic *adj.* hematoencefálico, -ca.
hematogenesis *n.* hematogénesis.
hematogenic *adj.* hematogénico, -ca.
hematogenous *adj.* hematógeno, -na.
hematoglobin *n.* hematoglobina.
hematoglobinuria *n.* hematoglobinuria.
hematoglobulin *n.* hematoglobulina.
hematogone *n.* hematogonia,, hematógono.
hematohidrosis *n.* hematohidrosis.
hematohyaloid *n.* hematohialoide.
hematoid *adj.* hematoide.

hematoidin *n.* hematoidina.
hematokolpos *n.* hematocolpos.
hematokrit *n.* hematocrito.
hematolin *n.* hematolina.
hematolith *n.* hematolito.
hematologist *n.* hematólogo, -ga.
hematology *n.* hematología.
hematolymphangioma *n.* hematolinfagioma.
hematolysis *n.* hematólisis.
hematolytic *adj.* hematolítico, -ca.
hematoma *n.* hematoma.
aneurysmal hematoma hematoma aneurismático.
cerebellum hematoma hematoma de cerebelo.
corpus luteum hematoma hematoma del cuerpo amarillo.
hematoma auris hematoma auricular, hematoma auris.
intracranial hematoma hematoma intracraneal.
intraparenchymatous hematoma hematoma intraparenquimatoso.
pelvic hematoma hematoma pélvico.
perianal hematoma hematoma perianal.
periorbital hematoma hematoma en antifaz.
posttraumatic perirenal hematoma hematoma perirrenal espontáneo, hematoma perirrenal traumático.
posttraumatic spontaneous hematoma hematoma perirrenal espontáneo, hematoma perirrenal traumático.
retroplacental hematoma hematoma retroplacentario.
retrouterine hematoma hematoma retrouterino.
spontaneous cerebral hematoma hematoma intracerebral espontáneo.
subchorionic tuberous hematoma hematoma tuberoso subcoriónico.
subdural hematoma hematoma subdural.
subgaleal hematoma hematoma subgaleal.
subperiostial hematoma hematoma subperióstico.
subungual hematoma hematoma subungueal.
hematometra *n.* hematómetra.
hematomole *n.* hematomola.
hematomphalocele *n.* hematonfalocele.
hematomphalus *n.* hematónfalo.
hematomycosis *n.* hematomicosis.
hematomyelia *n.* hematomielia.
hematomyelitis *n.* hematomielitis.
hematomyelopore *n.* hematomieloporosis.
hematoncometry *n.* hematoncometría.
hematonephrosis *n.* hematonefrosis.
hematonic *adj.* hematónico, -ca.
hematonosis *n.* hematonosis.
hematopahgocyte *n.* hematofagocito.
hematopathology *n.* hematopatología.
hematopathy *n.* hematopatía.
hematopedesis *n.* hematopedesis.
hematopenia *n.* hematopenia.
hematopericardium *n.* hematopericardio.
hematoperitoneum *n.* hematoperitoneo.
hematopexis *n.* hematopexis, hemopexis.
hematophage *n.* hematófago.
hematophagia *n.* hematofagia.
hematophagous *adj.* hematófago, -ga.
hematophagy *n.* hematofagia.
hematophilia *n.* hematofilia.
hematophobia *n.* hematofobia.
hematophyte *n.* hematofito.
hematophytic *adj.* hematofítico, -ca.
hematopiesis *n.* hematopiesis.

hematoplania *n.* hematoplanía.
hematoplastic *adj.* hematoplásico, -ca.
hematopneic *adj.* hematopneico, -ca.
hematopoiesis *n.* hematopoyesis.
hematopoietic *adj.* hematopoyético, -ca.
hematoporphyria *n.* hematoporfiria.
hematoporphyrin *n.* hematoporfirina.
hematoporphyrinemia *n.* hematoporfirinemia.
hematoporphyrinism *n.* hematoporfirinismo.
hematoporphyrinuria *n.* hematoporfirinuria.
hematopsia *n.* hematopsia.
hematorrhachis *n.* hematorraquis.
hematorrhea *n.* hematorrea.
hematosalphinx *n.* hematosalpinge, hematosálpinx.
hematoscheocele *n.* hematosqueocele, hemosqueocele.
hematoscope *n.* hematoscopio.
hematoscopy *n.* hematoscopia.
hematosepsis *n.* hematosepsis.
hematoside *n.* hematósido.
hematosin *n.* hematosina.
hematosis *n.* hematosis.
hematospectrophotometer *n.* hematoespectrofotómetro, hematospectrofotómetro.
hematospectroscope *n.* hematoespectroscopio.
hematospectroscopy *n.* hematoespectroscopia.
hematospermatocele *n.* hematoespermatocele, hematospermatocele.
hematospermia *n.* hematoespermia, hematospermia.
hematospherinemia *n.* hematoesferinemia.
hematosporida *n.* hematosporidios.
hematosteon *n.* hematósteon.
hematotherapy *n.* hematoterapia.
hematothermal *adj.* hematotérmico, -ca.
hematothorax *n.* hematotórax.
hematotoxic *adj.* hematotóxico, -ca.
hematotoxicosis *n.* hematotoxicosis.
hematotoxin *n.* hematotoxina.
hematotrachelos *n.* hematotraquelo.
hematotropic *n.* hematotrópico.
hematotympanum *n.* hematotímpano.
hematoxic *adj.* hematóxico, -ca.
hematoxin *n.* hematoxina.
hematoxylin *n.* hematoxilina.
hematozoic *adj.* hematozoico, -ca.
hematozoon *n.* hematozoo.
hematrometry *n.* hematometría.
hematuresis *n.* hematuresis.
hematuria *n.* hematuria.
benign familial hematuria hematuria familiar benigna.
benign recurrent hematuria hematuria recurrente familiar.
Egyptian hematuria hematuria egipcia.
endemic hematuria hematuria endémica.
essential hematuria hematuria esencial.
false hematuria hematuria falsa.
initial hematuria hematuria inicial.
macroscopic hematuria hematuria macroscópica.
microscopic hematuria hematuria microscópica.
nephrological hematuria hematuria nefrológica.
painful hematuria hematuria dolorosa.
painless hematuria hematuria indolora.
primary hematuria hematuria primaria.
renal hematuria hematuria renal.
terminal hematuria hematuria terminal.
urethral hematuria hematuria uretral.
vesical hematuria hematuria vesical.

hemelytrometra lateralis *n.* hemelitrómetra lateralis.
hemeralope *adj.* hemerálope.
hemeralopia *n.* hemeralopía, hemeropía.
hemiablepsia *n.* hemiablepsia.
hemiacardius *n.* hemiacardio.
hemiacephalus *n.* hemiacéfalo.
hemiachromatopsia *n.* hemiacromatopsia.
hemiacrosomia *n.* hemiacrosomía.
hemiageusia *n.* hemiageusia, hemiageustia.
hemiageustia *n.* hemiageusia, hemiageustia.
hemialbumin *n.* hemialbúmina.
hemialbumose *n.* hemialbumosa.
hemialbumosuria *n.* hemialbumosuria.
hemialgia *n.* hemialgia.
hemiamaurosis *n.* hemiamaurosis.
hemiamblyopia *n.* hemiambliopía.
hemiamyosthenia *n.* hemiamiostenia.
hemianacusia *n.* hemianacusia.
hemianalgesia *n.* hemianalgesia.
hemianencephaly *n.* hemianencefalia.
hemianesthesia *n.* hemianestesia.
alternate hemianesthesia hemianestesia alternada, hemianestesia alternante.
cerebral hemianesthesia hemianestesia cerebral.
crossed hemianesthesia hemianestesia cruzada.
hemianesthesia cruciata hemianestesia cruzada.
mesocephalic hemianesthesia hemianestesia mesocefálica.
pontile hemianesthesia hemianestesia mesocefálica.
spinal hemianesthesia hemianestesia espinal.
hemianopia *n.* hemianopía, hemianopsia.
hemianopic *adj.* hemianóptico, -ca.
hemianopsia *n.* hemianopía, hemianopsia, hemianopsis.
absolute hemianopsia hemianopsia absoluta.
altitudinal hemianopsia hemianopsia altitudinal.
bilateral hemianopsia hemianopsia bilateral.
binasal hemianopsia hemianopsia binasal.
binocular hemianopsia hemianopsia binocular.
bitemporal hemianopsia hemianopsia bitemporal.
complete hemianopsia hemianopsia completa, hemianopsia total.
congruous hemianopsia hemianopsia congruente.
crossed hemianopsia hemianopsia cruzada.
equilateral hemianopsia hemianopsia equilateral.
heteronymous hemianopsia hemianopsia heterónima, hemianopsia vertical.
homonymous hemianopsia hemianopsia homónima.
horizontal hemianopsia hemianopsia horizontal.
incomplete hemianopsia hemianopsia incompleta, hemianopsia parcial.
incongruous hemianopsia hemianopsia incongruente.
lateral hemianopsia hemianopsia lateral.
nasal hemianopsia hemianopsia nasal.
quadrant hemianopsia hemianopsia cuadrántica, hemianopsia de cuadrantes.
quadrantic hemianopsia hemianopsia cuadrántica, hemianopsia de cuadrantes.
relative hemianopsia hemianopsia relativa.
temporal hemianopsia hemianopsia temporal.

true hemianopsia hemianopsia verdadera.

unilateral hemianopsia hemianopsia unilateral.

uniocular hemianopsia hemianopsia uniocular.

hemianoptic *adj.* hemianóptico, -ca.

hemianosmia *n.* hemianosmia.

hemiapraxia *n.* hemiapraxia.

hemiarthroplasty *n.* hemiartroplastia.

hemiarthrosis *n.* hemiartrosis.

hemiasynergia *n.* hemiasinergia.

hemiataxia *n.* hemiataxia.

hemiataxy *n.* hemiataxia.

hemiathetosis *n.* hemiatetosis.

hemiatrophy *n.* hemiatrofia.

facial hemiatrophy hemiatrofia facial.

progressive lingual hemiatrophy hemiatrofia lingual progresiva.

hemiautotroph *n.* hemiautótrofo.

hemiautotrophic *adj.* hemiautotrófico, -ca.

hemiballism *n.* hemibalismo.

hemiballismus *n.* hemibalismo.

hemibladder *n.* hemivejiga.

hemiblock *n.* hemibloqueo.

ventricular hemiblock hemibloqueo ventricular.

hemic *adj.* hémico, -ca.

hemicanities *n.* hemicanicie.

hemicardia *n.* hemicardia.

hemicardia dextra hemicardia derecha, hemicardia dextra.

hemicardia sinistra hemicardia izquierda, hemicardia sinistra.

hemicardius *n.* hemicardio.

hemicentrum *n.* hemicentro.

hemicephalia *n.* hemicefalia, hemiencefalia.

hemicephalus *n.* hemicéfalo.

hemicerebrum *n.* hemicerebro.

hemichorea *n.* hemicorea.

hemichromatopsia *n.* hemicromatopsia.

hemichromosome *n.* hemicromosoma.

hemicolectomy *n.* hemicolectomía.

left hemicolectomy hemicolectomía izquierda.

right hemicolectomy hemicolectomía derecha.

hemicorporectomy *n.* hemicorporectomía.

hemicorticectomy *n.* hemicorticectomía.

hemicrania *n.* hemicránea, hemicrania.

hemicranial *adj.* hemicraneal.

hemicraniectomy *n.* hemicraniectomía.

hemicraniosis *n.* hemicraniosis.

hemidecortication *n.* hemidecorticación.

hemidesmosome *n.* hemidesmosoma.

hemidiaphoresis *n.* hemidiaforesis.

hemidiaphragm *n.* hemidiafragma.

hemidrosis *n.* hemidrosis.

hemidysergia *n.* hemidisergia.

hemidysesthesia *n.* hemidisestesia.

hemidystrophy *n.* hemidistrofia.

hemiectromelia *n.* hemiectromelia.

hemiencephalus *n.* hemiencéfalo.

hemiepilepsy *n.* hemiepilepsia.

hemifacial *adj.* hemifacial.

hemigastrectomy *n.* hemigastrectomía.

hemigigantism *n.* hemigigantismo.

hemiglobin *n.* hemiglobina, hemoglobina.

hemiglossal *adj.* hemiglósico, -ca.

hemiglossectomy *n.* hemiglosectomía.

hemiglossitis *n.* hemiglositis.

hemignatia *n.* hemignatia.

hemihepatectomy *n.* hemihepatectomía.

hemihidrosis *n.* hemidrosis, hemihidrosis.

hemihypalgesia *n.* hemihipalgesia.

hemihyperesthesia *n.* hemihiperestesia.

hemihyperhidrosis *n.* hemihiperhidrosis.

hemihyperidrosis *n.* hemihiperhidrosis.

hemihypermetria *n.* hemihipermetría.

hemihyperplasia *n.* hemihiperplasia.

hemihypertonia *n.* hemihipertonía.

hemihypertrophy *n.* hemihipertrofia.

facial hemihypertrophy hemihipertrofia facial.

hemihypesthesia *n.* hemihipoestesia.

hemihypoesthesia *n.* hemihipoestesia.

hemihypometria *n.* hemihipometría.

hemihypophysectomy *n.* hemihipofisectomía.

hemihypoplasia *n.* hemihipoplasia.

hemihypotonia *n.* hemihipotonía.

hemikaryon *n.* hemicarion.

hemilaminectomy *n.* hemilaminectomía.

hemilaryngectomy *n.* hemilaringectomía.

hemilateral *adj.* dimidiado, -da, hemilateral.

hemilesion *n.* hemilesión.

hemilingual *adj.* hemilingual.

hemimacroglossia *n.* hemimacroglosia.

hemimandibulectomy *n.* hemimandibulectomía.

hemimaxillectomy *n.* hemimaxilectomía.

hemimegalencephaly *n.* hemimegaloencefalia.

hemimelia *n.* hemimelia.

cubital hemimelia hemimelia cubital.

fibular hemimelia hemimelia peronea, peroneal.

peroneal hemimelia hemimelia peronea, peroneal.

radial hemimelia hemimelia radial.

tibial hemimelia hemimelia tibial.

ulnar hemimelia hemimelia cubital.

hemimelus *n.* hemimelo.

hemimembrane *n.* hemimembrana.

hemimyelomeningocele *n.* hemimielomeningocele.

heminephrectomy *n.* heminefrectomía.

heminephrourectomy *n.* heminefrourectomía.

hemineurasthenia *n.* hemineurastenia.

hemiobesity *n.* hemiobesidad.

hemiopalgia *n.* hemiopalgia.

hemiopia *n.* hemiopía.

hemiopic *adj.* hemiópico, -ca.

hemipagus *n.* hemípago, hemipagos.

hemiparalysis *n.* hemiparálisis.

hemiparaplegia *n.* hemiparaplejía.

hemiparesis *n.* hemiparesia.

hemiparesthesia *n.* hemiparestesia.

hemiparetic *adj.* hemiparético, -ca.

hemiparkinsonism *n.* hemiparkinsonismo.

hemipelvectomy *n.* hemipelvectomía.

hemipeptone *n.* hemipeptona.

hemiphalangectomy *n.* hemifalangectomía.

hemiplacenta *n.* hemiplacenta.

hemiplegia *n.* hemiplejía.

alternate hemiplegia hemiplejía alterna, hemiplejía alternada.

alternating hemiplegia hemiplejía alterna, hemiplejía alternada.

alternating oculomotor hemiplegia hemiplejía alterna oculomotriz.

ascending hemiplegia hemiplejía ascendente.

capsular hemiplegia hemiplejía capsular.

cerebral hemiplegia hemiplejía cerebral.

contralateral hemiplegia hemiplejía contralateral.

crossed hemiplegia hemiplejía cruzada.

facial hemiplegia hemiplejía facial.

faciobraquial hemiplegia hemiplejía faciobraquial.

faciolingual hemiplegia hemiplejía faciolingual.

flaccid hemiplegia hemiplejía fláccida.

hemiplegia alternans hypoglossica hemiplejía alternans hypoglossica.

hemiplegia cruciata hemiplejía cruzada.

infantile hemiplegia hemiplejía infantil.

puerperal hemiplegia hemiplejía puerperal.

spastic hemiplegia hemiplejía espasmódica, hemiplejía espástica.

spinal hemiplegia hemiplejía espinal.

hemiplegic *adj.* hemipléjico, -ca.

hemiprostatectomy *n.* hemiprostatectomía.

Hemiptera *n.* Hemiptera.

hemipterous *adj.* hemíptero, -ra.

hemipylorectomy *n.* hemipilorectomía.

hemipyonephrosis *n.* hemipionefrosis.

hemirachischisis *n.* hemirraquisquisis.

hemisacralization *n.* hemisacralización.

hemiscotoma *n.* hemiscotoma.

hemiscotosis *n.* hemiscotosis.

hemisection *n.* hemisección.

hemisectomy *n.* hemisectomía.

hemisensory *adj.* hemisensorial.

hemisoantibody *n.* hemisoanticuerpo.

hemisomnambulism *n.* hemisonambulismo.

hemisomus *n.* hemisoma.

hemisotonic *adj.* hemisotónico, -ca.

hemispasm *n.* hemiespasmo.

hemispherectomy *n.* hemisferectomía, hemisfinterectomía.

hemispherium *n.* hemisferio.

hemisphygmia *n.* hemisfigmia.

Hemispora stellata *n.* Hemispora stellata.

hemispore *n.* hemisporosis.

hemistrumectomy *n.* hemistrumectomía.

hemisyndrome *n.* hemisíndrome.

hemisystole *n.* hemisístole, hemisistolia.

hemiteras *n.* hemiteria.

hemiteratic *adj.* hemitérico, -ca.

hemitetany *n.* hemitetania.

hemithermoanesthesia *n.* hemitermoanestesia.

hemithorax *n.* hemitórax.

hemithyroidectomy *n.* hemitiroidectomía.

hemitonia *n.* hemitonía.

hemitoxin *n.* hemitoxina.

hemitremor *n.* hemitemblor.

hemivagotony *n.* hemivagotonía.

hemivertebra *n.* hemivértebra.

hemizygosity *n.* hemicigosidad, hemicigotia.

hemizygote *n.* hemicigoto.

hemizygotic *adj.* hemicigótico, -ca.

hemizygous *adj.* hemicigótico, -ca.

hemoaccess *n.* hemoacceso.

hemoagglutination *n.* hemoaglutinación.

hemoagglutinin *n.* hemoaglutinina.

hemoalkalimeter *n.* hemoalcalímetro.

hemoanalysis *n.* hemoanálisis.

hemoantitoxin *n.* hemoantitoxina.

hemobilia *n.* hemobilia.

hemobilinuria *n.* hemobilinuria.

hemoblast *n.* hemoblasto.

hemoblastosis *n.* hemoblastosis.

hemocatharsis *n.* hematocatarsis, hemocatarsis.

hemocatheresis *n.* hemocatéresis.

hemocatheretic *adj.* hemocaterético, -ca.

hemocele *n.* hemocele.

hemocelom *n.* hemoceloma.

hemocholecystitis *n.* hemocolecistitis.

hemochorial *adj.* hemocorial.

hemochromatosis *n.* hemocromatosis.

exogenous hemochromatosis hemocromatosis exógena.

hereditary hemochromatosis hemocromatosis hereditaria.

idiopathic hemochromatosis hemocromatosis idiopática.

primary hemochromatosis hemocromatosis primaria.

secondary hemochromatosis hemocromatosis secundaria.

hemochromatotic *adj.* hemocromatósico, -ca.

hemochromogen *n.* hemocromógeno.

hemochromometer *n.* hemocromómetro.

hemochromometry *n.* hemocromometría.

hemoclasia *n.* hemoclasia, hemoclasis.

hemoclasis *n.* hemoclasia, hemoclasis.

hemoclastic *adj.* hemoclástico, -ca.

hemoclip *n.* hemoclip.

hemocoagulin *n.* hemocoagulina.

hemocoelom *n.* hemoceloma.

hemocoeloma *n.* hemoceloma.

hemoconcentration *n.* hemoconcentración.

hemoconiosis *n.* hemoconiosis.

hemocrine *adj.* hemocrino, -na.

hemocrinia *n.* hemocrinia.

hemocrinotherapy *n.* hemocrinoterapia.

hemocryoscopy *n.* hemocrioscopia.

hemoculture *n.* hemocultivo.

hemocyte *n.* hemocito.

hemocytoblast *n.* hemocitoblasto.

hemocytoblastoma *n.* hemocitoblastoma.

hemocytocatheresis *n.* hemocitocatéresis.

hemocytology *n.* hemocitología.

hemocytolysis *n.* hemocitólisis.

hemocytoma *n.* hemocitoma.

hemocytometer *n.* hemocitómetro.

hemocytometry *n.* hemocitometría.

hemocytophagia *n.* hemocitofagia.

hemocytophagic *adj.* hemocitofágico, -ca.

hemocytophagy *n.* hemocitofagia.

hemocytopoiesis *n.* hemocitopoyesis.

hemocytotripsis *n.* hemocitotripsia.

hemocytozoon *n.* hemocitozoo.

hemodia *n.* hemodia.

hemodiagnosis *n.* hemodiagnóstico.

hemodialysis *n.* hemodiálisis.

home hemodialysis hemodiálisis domiciliaria.

hospital hemodialysis hemodiálisis hospitalaria.

hemodialyzer *n.* hemodializador.

hemodiapedesis *n.* hemodiapédesis.

hemodilution *n.* hemodilución.

hemodynamic *adj.* hemodinámico, -ca.

hemodynamics *n.* hemodinámica.

intrarenal hemodynamics hemodinámica intrarrenal.

hemodynamometer *n.* hemodinamómetro.

hemodynamometry *n.* hemodinamometría.

hemodyscrasia *n.* hemodiscrasia.

hemodystrophy *n.* hemodistrofia.

hemoendothelial *adj.* hemoendotelial.

hemoendothelioma *n.* hemoendotelioma.

hemofilter *n.* hemofiltro.

hemofiltration *n.* hemofiltración.

hemoflagellate *adj.* hemoflagelado, -da.

hemogenesis *n.* hemogenesia, hemogénesis.

hemoglobin *n.* hemoglobina.

hemoglobinated *adj.* hemoglobinado, -da.

hemoglobinemia *n.* hemoglobinemia.

puerperal hemoglobinemia hemoglobinemia puerperal.

hemoglobiniferous *adj.* hemoglobinífero, -ra.

hemoglobinocholia *n.* hemoglobinobilia, hemoglobinocolia.

hemoglobinolysis *n.* hemoglobinólisis.

hemoglobinometer *n.* hemoglobinómetro.

hemoglobinopathy *n.* hemoglobinopatía.

hemoglobinopepsia *n.* hemoglobinopepsia.

hemoglobinophilia *n.* hemoglobinofilia.

hemoglobinophilic *adj.* hemoglobinofilico, -ca.

hemoglobinorrhea *n.* hemoglobinorrea.

hemoglobinous *adj.* hemoglobinoso, -sa.

hemoglobinuria *n.* hemoglobinuria.

bacillary hemoglobinuria hemoglobinuria bacilar.

cold hemoglobinuria hemoglobinuria al frío, hemoglobinuria por frío.

epidemic hemoglobinuria hemoglobinuria epidémica.

malarial hemoglobinuria hemoglobinuria malárica, hemoglobinuria palúdica.

march hemoglobinuria hemoglobinuria de la marcha.

paroxysmal hemoglobinuria hemoglobinuria paroxística "a frigore", hemoglobinuria intermitente".

paroxysmal nocturnal hemoglobinuria (PNH) hemoglobinuria paroxística nocturna (HPN).

toxic hemoglobinuria hemoglobinuria tóxica.

hemoglobinuric *adj.* hemoglobinúrico, -ca.

hemogram *n.* hemograma.

hemoid *adj.* hemoide.

hemokinesis *n.* hemocinesis.

hemokinetic *adj.* hemocinético, -ca.

hemolamella *n.* hemolaminilla.

hemoleukocyte *n.* hemoleucocito.

hemoleukocytic *adj.* hemoleucocitario, -ria, hemoleucocítico, -ca.

hemolisoid *n.* hemolisoide.

hemolith *n.* hemolito.

hemolization *n.* hemolización.

hemology *n.* hemología.

hemolymph *n.* hemolinfa.

hemolymphangioma *n.* hemolinfangioma.

hemolysate *n.* hemolisado.

hemolysin *n.* hemolisina.

hemolysin immune inmunohemolisina.

hemolysis *n.* hemólisis.

alpha hemolysis hemólisis alfa.

beta hemolysis hemólisis beta.

biologic hemolysis hemólisis biológica.

conditioned hemolysis hemólisis condicionada.

contact hemolysis hemólisis por contacto.

gamma hemolysis hemólisis gamma.

immune hemolysis hemólisis inmune, hemólisis inmunitaria.

passive hemolysis hemólisis pasiva.

venom hemolysis hemólisis por veneno, hemólisis venenosa.

viridans hemolysis hemólisis viridans.

hemolysophilic *adj.* hemolisofílico, -ca.

hemolytic *adj.* hemolítico, -ca.

hemolyzable *adj.* hemolizable.

hemolyze *v.* hemolizar.

hemomediastium *n.* hemomediastino.

hemometer *n.* hemómetro.

hemometra *n.* hemómetra.

hemometry *n.* hemometría.

hemomyelosis *n.* hemomielosis.

hemonephrosis *n.* hemonefrosis.

hemopathology *n.* hemopatología.

hemopathy *n.* hemopatía.

hemoperfusion *n.* hemoperfusión.

hemopericardium *n.* hemopericardio.

hemoperitoneum *n.* hemoperitoneo.

hemopexin *n.* hemopexina.

hemophage *n.* hemófago.

hemophagia *n.* hemofagia.

hemophagocyte *n.* hemofagocito.

hemophagocytosis *n.* hemofagocitosis.

hemophil *adj.* hemófilo, -la.

hemophile *adj.* hemófilo, -la.

hemophilia *n.* hemofilia.

classical hemophilia hemofilia clásica.

hemophilia A hemofilia A.

hemophilia B hemofilia B.

hemophilia C hemofilia C.

hemophilia neonatorum hemofilia neonatal.

Leyden hemophilia hemofilia de Leyden.

vascular hemophilia hemofilia vascular.

hemophiliac *n.* hemofílico.

hemophilic *adj.* hemofílico, -ca.

hemophilioid *adj.* hemofilioide.

Hemophilus *n.* Haemophilus, Hemophilus.

hemophobia *n.* hemafobia, hemofobia.

hemophoresis *n.* hemoforesis.

hemophoric *adj.* hemofórico, -ca.

hemophotograph *n.* hemofotografía.

hemophotometer *n.* hemofotómetro.

hemophtalmos *n.* hemoftalmia, hemoftalmos.

hemophthalmus *n.* hemoftalmia, hemoftalmos.

hemophthisis *n.* hemotisis.

hemopiezometer *n.* hemopiesímetro, hemopiesómetro, hemopiezómetro.

hemoplastic *adj.* hemoplásico, -ca.

hemopleura *n.* hemopleura.

hemopneumopericardium *n.* hemoneumopericardio.

hemopneumothorax *n.* hemoneumotórax.

hemopoiesic *adj.* hemopoyésico, -ca.

hemopoiesis *n.* hemopoyesis.

hemopoietic *adj.* hemopoyético, -ca.

hemoporphyrin *n.* hemoporfirina.

hemoprecipitin *n.* hemoprecipitina.

hemoproctia *n.* hemoproccia, hemoproctia.

hemoprotein *n.* hemoproteína.

hemoptic *adj.* hemóptico, -ca.

hemoptysic *adj.* hemoptísico, -ca.

hemoptysis *n.* hemoptisis.

cardiac hemoptysis hemoptisis cardiaca.

cardiovascular hemoptysis hemoptisis cardiaca.

endemic hemoptysis hemoptisis endémica.

Goldstein's hemoptysis hemoptisis de Goldstein.

oriental hemoptysis hemoptisis de Manson.

parasitic hemoptysis hemoptisis parasitaria.

hemopyelectasis *n.* hemopielectasia.

hemorepellant *adj.* hemorrepelente.

hemorheology *n.* hemorreología.

hemorrhachis *n.* hemorraquis.

hemorrhage *n.* hemorragia.

alveolar hemorrhage hemorragia alveolar.

antepartum hemorrhage hemorragia anteparto.

basal ganglia hemorrhage hemorragia en ganglios basales.

brain hemorrhage hemorragia cerebral.

brainstem hemorrhage hemorragia del tronco encefálico.

capillary hemorrhage hemorragia capilar.

capsuloganglionic hemorrhage hemorragia capsuloganglionar.

cerebellar hemorrhage hemorragia cerebelosa.

cerebral hemorrhage hemorragia cerebral.

delayed postpartum hemorrhage hemorragia posparto retardada.

digestive hemorrhage hemorragia digestiva.

dysfunctional uterine hemorrhage (DUB) hemorragia uterina disfuncional (HUD).

essential hemorrhage hemorragia esencial.

expulsive hemorrhage hemorragia expulsiva.
external hemorrhage hemorragia externa.
extradural hemorrhage hemorragia extradural.
fetomaternal hemorrhage hemorragia fetomaterna.
flame-shaped hemorrhage hemorragia en llamas.
gastric hemorrhage hemorragia gástrica.
gastroesophageal hemorrhage hemorragia gastroesofágica.
hemispheric hemorrhage hemorragia hemisférica.
intermediate hemorrhage hemorragia intermedia.
internal hemorrhage hemorragia interna.
intestinal hemorrhage hemorragia intestinal.
intracerebral hemorrhage hemorragia intracerebral.
intracranial hemorrhage hemorragia intracraneal.
intramedullary hemorrhage hemorragia de la médula espinal, hemorragia intramedular.
intraparenchymatous hemorrhage hemorragia intraparenquimatosa.
intrapartum hemorrhage hemorragia intraparto.
intraventricular hemorrhage hemorragia intraventricular.
lobar hemorrhage hemorragia lobular.
lower digestive hemorrhage hemorragia digestiva baja.
massive hemorrhage hemorragia masiva.
nasal hemorrhage hemorragia nasal.
oozing hemorrhage hemorragia en sábana.
parenchymatous hemorrhage hemorragia parenquimatosa.
petechial hemorrhage hemorragia petequial.
plasma hemorrhage hemorragia plasmática.
pontine hemorrhage hemorragia pontina.
postpartum hemorrhage hemorragia posparto.
primary hemorrhage hemorragia primaria, hemorragia primitiva, hemorragia traumática.
puerperal hemorrhage hemorragia puerperal.
pulmonary hemorrhage hemorragia pulmonar.
punctate hemorrhage hemorragia puntiforme.
recurring hemorrhage hemorragia recidivante, hemorragia recurrente.
renal hemorrhage hemorragia renal.
secondary hemorrhage hemorragia secundaria.
splinter hemorrhage hemorragia en astilla.
spontaneous cerebral hemorrhage hemorragia cerebral espontánea.
spontaneous hemorrhage hemorragia espontánea.
subarachnoid hemorrhage hemorragia subaracnoidea HSA.
subdural hemorrhage hemorragia subdural.
subgaleal hemorrhage hemorragia subgaleal.
syringomyelic hemorrhage hemorragia siringomiélica.
unavoidable hemorrhage hemorragia inevitable.
upper digestive hemorrhage hemorragia digestiva alta.
uterine hemorrhage hemorragia uterina.
vaginal hemorrhage hemorragia vaginal.

vitreous hemorrhage hemorragia vítrea.
hemorrhagenic *adj.* hemorragénico, -ca, hemorrágeno, -na.
hemorrhagic *adj.* hemorrágico, -ca.
hemorrhagiparous *adj.* hemorragíparo, -ra.
hemorrhea *n.* hemorrea.
hemorrheology *n.* hemorreología.
hemorrhoidal *adj.* hemorroidal.
hemorrhoidectomy *n.* hemorroidectomía.
hemorrhoidolysis *n.* hemorroidólisis.
hemorrhoids *n.* hemorroides.
　combined hemorrhoids hemorroides combinadas.
　cutaneous hemorrhoids hemorroides cutáneas.
　external hemorrhoids hemorroides externas.
　internal hemorrhoids hemorroides internas.
　mixed hemorrhoids hemorroides mixtas.
　mucocutaneous hemorrhoids hemorroides mucocutáneas.
　prolapsed hemorrhoids hemorroides prolapsadas.
　sentinel hemorrhoids hemorroides centinelas.
　strangulated hemorrhoids hemorroides estranguladas.
　thrombosed hemorrhoids hemorroides trombosadas.
hemosalpinx *n.* hemosálpinx.
hemoscope *n.* hemoscopio.
hemosialemesis *n.* hemosialemesis.
hemosiderinuria *n.* hemosiderinuria, hemosideruria.
hemosiderosis *n.* hemosiderosis.
　hepatic hemosiderosis hemosiderosis hepática.
　idiopathic pulmonary hemosiderosis hemosiderosis pulmonar idiopática.
　nutritional hemosiderosis hemosiderosis nutricional.
　pulmonary hemosiderosis hemosiderosis pulmonar.
hemosite *n.* hemósito.
hemospasia *n.* hemospasia.
hemospermia *n.* hemospermia.
　hemospermia espuria hemospermia espúrea.
　hemospermia vera hemospermia verdadera.
hemosporidium *n.* hemosporidio.
hemostasia *n.* hemostasia, hemostasis.
　surgical hemostasia hemostasis quirúrgica.
hemostasis *n.* hemostasis.
hemostat *n.* hemóstato.
hemostatic *adj.* hematostático, -ca, hemostático, -ca.
hemostyptic *adj.* hemostíptico, -ca.
hemotasis *n.* hematostaxis.
hemotherapeutics *n.* hemoterapia.
hemotherapy *n.* hemoterapia.
hemothorax *n.* hemotórax.
hemotoxic *adj.* hemotóxico, -ca.
hemotoxin *n.* hemotoxina.
hemotroph *n.* hemotrofo.
hemotrophe *n.* hemotrofo.
hemotrophic *adj.* hemotrófico, -ca.
hemotropic *adj.* hemotrópico, -ca.
hemotympanum *n.* hemotímpano.
hemovitreous *adj.* hemovítreo, -a.
hemoxometer *n.* hemoxímetro, hemoxómetro.
hemozoon *n.* hemozoo.
hemuresis *n.* hemuresis.
henogenesis *n.* henogenesia, henogenesis.
henoma *n.* henoma.
henosis *n.* henosis.
hepaptosis *n.* hepaptosis.

hepar *n.* hígado.
heparin *n.* heparina.
　heparin calcium heparina cálcica.
　heparin sodium heparina sódica.
heparinemia *n.* heparinemia.
heparinization *n.* heparinización.
heparinize *v.* heparinizar.
hepatalgia *n.* hepatalgia.
hepatargia *n.* hepatargia.
hepatargy *n.* hepatargia.
hepatectomize *v.* hepatectomizar.
hepatectomy *n.* hepatectomía.
　left lobar hepatectomy hepatectomía izquierda.
　right lobar hepatectomy hepatectomía derecha.
　total hepatectomy hepatectomía total.
hepatic *adj.* hepático, -ca.
hepatichodochotomy *n.* hepaticocoledostomía, hepaticodocotomía.
hepaticocholangiojejunostomy *n.* hepaticocolangioyeyunostomía.
hepaticoduodenostomy *n.* hepaticoduodenostomía.
hepaticoenterostomy *n.* hepaticoenterostomía.
hepaticogastronomy *n.* hepaticogastronomía.
hepaticojejunostomy *n.* hepaticoyeyunostomía.
hepaticoliasis *n.* hepaticoliasis.
hepaticolithotomy *n.* hepaticolitotomía.
hepaticolithotripsy *n.* hepaticolitotripsia, hepatolitotripsia.
hepaticopulmonary *adj.* hepaticopulmonar.
hepaticostomy *n.* hepaticostomía.
hepaticotomy *n.* hepaticotomía.
hepatism *n.* hepatismo.
hepatitic *adj.* hepatítico, -ca.
hepatitis *n.* hepatitis.
　acute anicteric hepatitis hepatitis anictérica aguda.
　alcoholic hepatitis hepatitis alcohólica.
　anicteric hepatitis hepatitis anictérica.
　cholangiolitic hepatitis hepatitis colangiolítica.
　cholangitic hepatitis hepatitis colangiolítica.
　cholestatic hepatitis hepatitis colestásica.
　chronic hepatitis hepatitis crónica.
　chronic active hepatitis hepatitis crónica activa.
　chronic agressive hepatitis hepatitis crónica agresiva.
　chronic interstitial hepatitis hepatitis crónica intersticial.
　chronic persisting hepatitis hepatitis crónica persistente.
　delta agent hepatitis hepatitis por agente delta, hepatitis viral D, hepatitis viral de tipo D.
　delta hepatitis hepatitis delta.
　drug-induced hepatitis hepatitis inducida por tóxicos o fármacos.
　epidemic hepatitis hepatitis epidémica.
　familial hepatitis hepatitis familiar.
　fulminant hepatitis hepatitis fulminante.
　fulminating hepatitis hepatitis fulminante.
　giant cell hepatitis hepatitis de células gigantes.
　halothane hepatitis hepatitis por halotano.
　hepatitis A hepatitis A.
　hepatitis B hepatitis B.
　hepatitis C hepatitis C.
　hepatitis D hepatitis D.
　hepatitis E hepatitis E.
　hepatitis externa hepatitis externa.

homologous serum hepatitis hepatitis por suero homólogo.

infectious hepatitis hepatitis infecciosa.

inoculation hepatitis hepatitis por inoculación.

long-incubation hepatitis hepatitis de incubación prolongada.

lupoid hepatitis hepatitis lupoide.

MS-1 hepatitis hepatitis MS-1.

MS-2 hepatitis hepatitis MS-2.

NANB hepatitis hepatitis no-A, NANB, no-B.

neonatal hepatitis hepatitis neonatal.

neonatal giant cell hepatitis hepatitis neonatal de células gigantes.

persistent chronic hepatitis hepatitis crónica persistente.

plasma cell hepatitis hepatitis de células plasmáticas.

post-transfusion hepatitis hepatitis postransfusional.

recrudescent hepatitis hepatitis recrudescente.

serum hepatitis hepatitis por suero, hepatitis sérica.

short-incubation hepatitis hepatitis de incubación breve.

subacute hepatitis hepatitis subaguda.

suppurative hepatitis hepatitis supurada.

toxic hepatitis hepatitis tóxica.

transfusion hepatitis hepatitis tranfusional, por transfusión.

viral hepatitis hepatitis por virus, hepatitis viral, hepatitis vírica.

viral hepatitis type A hepatitis viral A, hepatitis viral de tipo A.

viral hepatitis type B hepatitis viral B, hepatitis viral de tipo B.

viral hepatitis type C hepatitis viral C, hepatitis viral de tipo C.

viral hepatitis type E hepatitis viral de tipo E, hepatitis viral E.

virus hepatitis hepatitis por virus, hepatitis viral, hepatitis vírica.

hepatization *n.* hepatización.

gray hepatization hepatización gris.

red hepatization hepatización roja.

yellow hepatization hepatización amarilla.

hepatized *adj.* hepatizado, -da.

hepatobiliary *adj.* hepatobiliar.

hepatoblastoma *n.* hepatoblastoma.

hepatobronchial *adj.* hepatobronquial.

hepatocarcinogenesis *n.* hepatocarcinogénesis.

hepatocarcinogenetic *adj.* hepatocarcinogenético, -ca.

hepatocarcinoma *n.* hepatocarcinoma.

hepatocele *n.* hepatocele.

hepatocellular *adj.* hepatocelular.

hepatocholangiocystoduodenostomy *n.* hepatocolangiocistoduodenostomía.

hepatocholangioenterostomy *n.* hepatocolangioenterostomía.

hepatocholangiostomy *n.* hepatocolangiostomía.

hepatocholangitis *n.* hepatocolangitis.

hepatocirrhosis *n.* hepatocirrosis.

hepatocolic *adj.* hepatocólico, -ca.

hepatocystic *adj.* hepatocístico, -ca.

hepatocyte *n.* hepatocito.

hepatodynia *n.* hepatodinia.

hepatodystrophy *n.* hepatodistrofia.

hepatoenteric *adj.* hepatoentérico, -ca.

hepatofugal *adj.* hepatófugo, -ga.

hepatogenic *adj.* hepatogénico, -ca.

hepatogenous *adj.* hepatógeno, -na.

hepatography *n.* hepatografía.

hepatoid *adj.* hepatoide.

hepatojugular *adj.* hepatoyugular.

hepatolenticular *adj.* hepatolenticular.

hepatolienal *adj.* hepatoesplénico, -ca, hepatolienal.

hepatolith *n.* hepatolito.

hepatolithectomy *n.* hepatolitectomía.

hepatolithiasis *n.* hepatolitiasis.

hepatolysin *n.* hepatolisina.

hepatolysis *n.* hepatólisis.

hepatoma *n.* hepatoma, hepatonco.

hepatomalacia *n.* hepatomalacia.

hepatomegalia *n.* hepatomegalia.

hepatomegaly *n.* hepatomegalia.

hepatomelanosis *n.* hepatomelanosis.

hepatomphalocele *n.* hepatonfalocele.

hepatomphalos *n.* hepatónfalo.

hepatonephromegaly *n.* hepatonefromegalia.

hepatopathy *n.* hepatopatía.

hepatopetal *adj.* hepatópeto, -ta.

hepatopexy *n.* hepatopexia.

hepatophage *n.* hepatófago.

hepatophlebitis *n.* hepatoflebitis.

hepatoptosis *n.* hepatoptosis.

hepatorenal *adj.* hepatorrenal.

hepatorrhagia *n.* hepatorragia.

hepatorrhaphy *n.* hepaticorrafia, hepatorrafia.

hepatorrhea *n.* hepatorrea.

hepatorrhexis *n.* hepatorrexis.

hepatoscopy *n.* hepatoscopia.

hepatosis *n.* hepatosis.

hepatosplenitis *n.* hepatoesplenitis.

hepatosplenography *n.* hepatoesplenografía.

hepatosplenomegaly *n.* hepatoesplenomegalia, hepatosplenomegalia.

hepatostomy *n.* hepatostomía.

hepatotherapy *n.* hepatoterapia.

hepatotomy *n.* hepatotomía.

transthoracic hepatotomy hepatotomía transtorácica.

hepatotoxemia *n.* hepatotoxemia.

hepatotoxic *adj.* hepatotóxico, -ca.

hepatotoxicity *n.* hepatotoxicidad.

hepatotoxin *n.* hepatotoxina.

hepatotrophia *n.* hepatotrofia.

hepatotrophy *n.* hepatotrofia.

hepatotropic *adj.* hepatotrópico, -ca.

heptachromic *adj.* heptacrómico, -ca.

heptose *n.* heptosa.

heptosuria *n.* heptosuria.

hereditability *n.* heredabilidad.

hereditary *adj.* hereditario, -ria.

heredity *n.* herencia[2].

autosomal heredity herencia autosómica.

collateral heredity herencia colateral.

extrachromosomal heredity herencia extracromosómica.

extranuclear heredity herencia extranuclear.

Galtonian heredity herencia galtoniana.

Mendelian heredity herencia mendeliana.

mosaic heredity herencia en mosaico, herencia mosaica.

recessive heredity herencia recesiva.

sex-influenced heredity herencia influida por el sexo.

sex-limited heredity herencia limitada por el sexo.

sex-linked heredity herencia ligada al sexo.

X-linked heredity herencia ligada al cromosoma X.

Y-linked heredity herencia ligada al cromosoma Y.

heredoataxia *n.* heredoataxia.

heredodegeneration *n.* heredodegeneración.

heredofamilial *adj.* heredofamiliar.

heredoimmunity *n.* heredoinmunidad.

heredoinfection *n.* heredoinfección.

heredolues *n.* heredolúes.

heredoluetic *adj.* heredoluético, -ca.

heredopathia *n.* heredopatía.

heredopathia atactica polyneuritiformis heredopatía atáxica polineuritiforme.

heredoretinopathia congenita *n.* heredorretinopatía congénita.

heredosyphilis *n.* heredosífilis.

heredosyphilitic *adj.* heredosifilítico, -ca.

heredosyphilology *n.* heredosifilología.

heredotaxia *n.* heredoataxia.

heritability *n.* heredabilidad, herencia[1].

hermaphrodism *n.* hermafrodismo.

hermaphrodite *n.* hermafrodita.

true hermaphrodite hermafrodita verdadero.

hermaphroditism *n.* hermafroditismo.

adrenal hermaphroditism hermafroditismo suprarrenal.

bilateral hermaphroditism hermafroditismo bilateral.

dimidiate hermaphroditism hermafroditismo dimidiado, hermafroditismo partido.

false hermaphroditism hermafroditismo falso.

female hermaphroditism hermafroditismo femenino.

lateral hermaphroditism hermafroditismo alterno, hermafroditismo externo, hermafroditismo lateral.

male hermaphroditism hermafroditismo masculino.

spurious hermaphroditism hermafroditismo espurio.

transverse hermaphroditism hermafroditismo transverso.

true hermaphroditism hermafroditismo completo, hermafroditismo verdadero.

unilateral hermaphroditism hermafroditismo unilateral.

Hermetia illucens *n.* Hermetia illucens.

hermetic *adj.* hermético, -ca.

hermoplasmodium *n.* hemoplasmodio.

hernia *n.* hernia.

abdominal hernia hernia abdominal.

acquired hernia hernia adquirida.

antevesical hernia hernia prevesical.

axial hiatal hernia hernia hiatal axial.

Barth's hernia hernia de Barth.

Béclard's hernia hernia de Béclard.

bilocular femoral hernia hernia bilocular femoral, hernia femoral bilocular.

Birkett's hernia hernia de Birkett.

Bochdaleck's hernia hernia de Bochdaleck.

cecal hernia hernia cecal.

cerebral hernia hernia cerebral.

Cloquet's hernia hernia de Cloquet.

complete hernia hernia completa.

concealed hernia hernia oculta.

congenital diaphragmatic hernia hernia diafragmática congénita.

congenital hernia hernia congénita.

Cooper's hernia hernia de Cooper.

crural hernia hernia crural.

cystic hernia hernia cística.

diaphragmatic hernia hernia diafragmática.

direct hernia hernia directa.

direct inguinal hernia hernia inguinal directa, hernia inguinal interna.

diverticular hernia hernia diverticular.

double loop hernia hernia de asa doble.

dry hernia hernia seca.

duodenojejunal hernia hernia duodenoyeyunal.
encysted hernia hernia enquistada.
epigastric hernia hernia epigástrica.
external hernia hernia externa.
extrasacular hernia hernia extrasacular.
fascial hernia hernia fascial.
fatty hernia hernia grasa.
femoral hernia hernia femoral.
foraminal hernia hernia foraminal.
funicular hernia hernia funicular.
gastroesophageal hernia hernia gastroesofágica.
gluteal hernia hernia glútea.
Gruber's hernia hernia de Gruber.
Grynfelt hernia hernia de Grynfelt.
hernia adiposa hernia adiposa.
hernia cerebri hernia cerebral.
hernia en bissac hernia en doble saco.
hernia of the broad ligament of the uterus hernia del ligamento ancho uterino.
hernia of the iris hernia del iris.
Hesselbach's hernia hernia de Hesselbach.
Hey's hernia hernia de Hey.
hiatal hernia hernia de hiato, hernia de hiato esofágico, hernia hiatal.
hiatus hernia hernia de hiato, hernia hiatal.
Holthouse's hernia hernia de Holthouse.
iliacosubfascial hernia hernia iliacosubfascial.
incarcerated hernia hernia encarcelada, hernia incarcerada.
incisional hernia hernia incisional.
incomplete hernia hernia incompleta.
indirect hernia hernia indirecta.
indirect inguinal hernia hernia inguinal externa, hernia inguinal indirecta.
infantile hernia hernia infantil.
inguinal hernia hernia inguinal.
inguinocrural hernia hernia inguinocrural.
inguinoescrotal hernia hernia inguinoescrotal.
inguinofemoral hernia hernia inguinofemoral.
inguinolabial hernia hernia inguinolabial.
inguinosuperficial hernia hernia inguinosuperficial.
intermuscular hernia hernia intermuscular.
internal hernia hernia interna.
interparietal hernia hernia interparietal.
intersigmoid hernia hernia intersigmoidea.
interstitial hernia hernia intersticial.
intrapelvic hernia hernia intrapelviana.
irreducible hernia hernia irreductible.
ischiatic hernia hernia isquiática.
ischiorectal hernia hernia isquiorrectal.
Krönlein's hernia hernia de Krönlein.
Küster's hernia hernia de Küster.
labial hernia hernia labial.
lateral ventral hernia hernia anteroexterna.
Laugier's hernia hernia de Laugier.
levator hernia hernia del elevador.
Littré's hernia hernia de Littré.
lumbar hernia hernia lumbar.
Malgaigne's hernia hernia de Malgaigne.
meningeal hernia hernia meníngea.
mesenteric hernia hernia mesentérica.
mesocolic hernia hernia mesocólica.
Morgagni's hernia hernia de Morgagni.
mucosal hernia hernia mucosa.
muscular hernia hernia muscular.
oblique hernia hernia oblicua.
obturator hernia hernia del obturador, hernia obturatriz.
omental hernia hernia epiploica, hernia omental.
orbital hernia hernia orbitaria.

ovarian hernia hernia ovárica.
pannicular hernia hernia panicular.
paraesophageal hernia hernia paraesofágica.
parahiatal hernia hernia parahiatal.
paraperitoneal hernia hernia paraperitoneal.
parasaccular hernia hernia parasacular.
parietal hernia hernia parietal.
pectineal hernia hernia pectínea.
perineal hernia hernia perineal.
Petit's hernia hernia de Petit.
posterior labial hernia hernia labial posterior.
posterior vaginal hernia hernia vaginal posterior.
prevascular hernia hernia prevascular.
properitoneal hernia hernia properitoneal.
properitoneal inguinal hernia hernia inguinal properitoneal, hernia inguinoproperitoneal.
pudendal hernia hernia pudenda.
pulsion hernia hernia por pulsión.
rectovaginal hernia hernia rectovaginal.
reducible hernia hernia coercible, hernia reducible, hernia reductible.
retrocecal hernia hernia retrocecal.
retrograde hernia hernia retrógrada.
retroperitoneal hernia hernia retroperitoneal.
retropubic hernia hernia retropubiana.
retrosternal hernia hernia retrosternal.
retrovascular hernia hernia retrovascular.
Richter's hernia hernia de Richter.
Rieux' hernia hernia de Rieux.
Rokitansky's hernia hernia de Rokitansky.
rolling hernia hernia por rodamiento.
sciatic hernia hernia ciática.
scrotal hernia hernia escrotal.
Serafini's hernia hernia de Serafini.
sliding esophageal hiatal hernia hernia hiatal esofágica deslizante.
sliding hernia hernia deslizada, hernia deslizante, hernia por deslizamiento.
sliding hiatal hernia hernia hiatal deslizante, hernia hiatal por deslizamiento.
slipped hernia hernia deslizada, hernia deslizante, hernia por deslizamiento.
Spiegelian hernia hernia de Spiegel.
stomal hernia hernia paraestomal.
strangulated hernia hernia estrangulada.
subpubic hernia hernia subpúbica.
synovial hernia hernia sinovial.
Treitz's hernia hernia de Treitz.
umbilical hernia hernia umbilical.
uterine hernia hernia uterina.
vaginal hernia hernia vaginal.
vaginolabial hernia hernia vaginolabial.
Velpeau's hernia hernia de Velpeau.
ventral hernia hernia ventral.
vesical hernia hernia de la vejiga, hernia vesical.
vesicle hernia hernia vesiculosa.
vitreous hernia hernia del vítreo.
von Bergmann's hernia hernia de von Bergmann.
W hernia hernia en W.
herniary *adj.* herniario, -ria.
herniated *adj.* herniado, -da.
herniation *n.* herniación.
caudal transtentorial herniation herniación transtentorial caudal.
central herniation herniación central.
cerebral herniation herniación cerebral.
cingulate herniation herniación del cíngulo.
foraminal herniation herniación foraminal.

herniation of the intervertebral disk herniación de disco intervertebral.
herniation of the nucleus pulposus herniación del núcleo pulposo.
rostral transtentorial herniation herniación transtentorial rostral.
sphenoidal herniation herniación esfenoidal.
subfacial herniation herniación subfacial.
tentorial herniation herniación tentorial.
tonsillar herniation herniación amigdalina, herniación tonsilar.
transtentorial herniation herniación transtentorial.
uncal herniation herniación del uncus, herniación uncal.
hernioappendectomy *n.* hernioapendicectomía.
hernioenterotomy *n.* hernioenterotomía.
herniography *n.* herniografía.
hernioid *adj.* hernioide.
herniolaparotomy *n.* herniolaparotomía.
herniology *n.* herniología.
hernioplasty *n.* hernioplastia.
herniopuncture *n.* herniopunción, herniopuntura.
herniorrhaphy *n.* herniorrafia.
inguinal herniorrhaphy herniorrafia inguinal.
herniotome *n.* herniótomo.
Cooper's herniotome herniótomo de Cooper.
herniotomy *n.* herniotomía.
Petit's herniotomy herniotomía de Petit.
herpangina *n.* herpangina.
herpes *n.* herpes.
genital herpes herpes genital.
herpes catarrhalis herpes catarral.
herpes circinatus bullosus herpes circinado ampolloso.
herpes corneae herpes corneal.
herpes desquamans herpes descamativo.
herpes digitalis herpes digital.
herpes facialis herpes facial.
herpes febrilis herpes febril.
herpes generalisatus herpes generalizado.
herpes genitalis herpes genital.
herpes gestationis herpes gestacional, herpes gravídico.
herpes gladiatorum herpes de los gladiadores.
herpes labialis herpes labial.
herpes menstrualis herpes menstrual.
herpes progenitalis herpes progenital.
herpes recurrens herpes recurrente.
herpes simplex herpes simple.
herpes simplex encephalitis herpesencefalitis.
herpes zoster herpes zoster.
herpes zoster auricularis herpes auricular posterior.
herpes zoster ophthalmicus herpes zoster oftálmico.
herpes zoster oticus herpes zoster ótico.
herpes zoster varicellosus herpes zoster varicelloso.
iris herpes herpes del iris, herpes iris.
neonatal herpes herpes neonatal.
oral herpes herpes oral.
recurrent herpes herpes recurrente.
relapsing herpes herpes recidivante.
traumatic herpes herpes traumático.
wrestler's herpes herpes de los luchadores.
Herpesviridae *n.* Herpesviridae.
herpesvirus *n.* herpesvirus.

herpesvirus hominis herpesvirus hominis.
herpesvirus suis herpesvirus suis.
herpetic adj. herpético, -ca.
herpetiform adj. herpetiforme.
herpetoide adj. herpetoide.
Herpetoviridae n. Herpetoviridae.
herpetovirus n. herpetovirus.
hersage n. hersaje.
herzstoss n. herzstoss.
hesperanopia n. hesperanopía, hesperanopsia.
heteradelphia n. heteradelfia.
heteradelphus n. heteradelfo.
heteradenia n. heteradenia.
heteradenic adj. heteradénico, -ca.
heteralius n. heteralio, heteralo.
heterauxesis n. heterauxesis, heterauxesis, heterauxia.
heteraxial adj. heteraxial, heteraxil.
heterecious adj. heterecio, -cia.
hetereoimmunity n. heteroinmunidad.
heterergic adj. heterérgico, -ca.
heteresthesia n. heterestesia.
hetericism n. heterecismo.
heteroagglutination n. heteroaglutinación.
heteroagglutinin n. heteroaglutinina.
heteroalbuminosuria n. heteroalbuminosuria.
heteroalbumose n. heteroalbumosa.
heteroallele n. heteroalelo.
heteroantibody n. heteroanticuerpo.
heteroantigen n. heteroantígeno.
heteroantiserum n. heteroantisuero.
heteroatom n. heteroátomo.
Heterobilharzia n. Heterobilharzia.
heteroblastic adj. heteroblásico, -ca.
heterocellular adj. heterocelular.
heterocentric adj. heterocéntrico, -ca.
heterocephalus n. heterocéfalo.
heterocheiral adj. heteróquiro, -ra.
heterochiral adj. heteróquiro, -ra.
heterochromatic adj. heterocromático, -ca.
heterochromatin n. heterocromatina.
  constitutive heterochromatin heterocromatina constitutiva.
  facultative heterochromatin heterocromatina facultativa.
  satellite-rich heterochromatin heterocromatina rica en satélite.
heterochromatinization n. heterocromatinización.
heterochromatization n. heterocromatización.
heterochromatosis n. heterocromatosis.
heterochromia n. heterocromía.
  atrophic heterochromia heterocromía atrófica.
  binocular heterochromia heterocromía binocular.
  iris heterochromia heterocromía del iris.
  simple heterochromia heterocromía simple.
  sympathetic heterochromia heterocromía simpática.
heterochromosome n. heterocromosoma.
heterochromous adj. heterocrómico, -ca, heterocromo, -ma.
heterochron adj. heterócrono, -na.
heterochronia n. heterocronía.
heterochronic adj. heterocrónico, -ca.
heterochronous adj. heterocrónico, -ca.
heterochylia n. heteroquilia.
heterocladic adj. heterocládico, -ca.
heterocomplement n. heterocomplemento.
heterocrine adj. heterocrino, -na.
heterocrinia n. heterocrinia.

heterocyclic adj. heterocíclico, -ca.
heterocytolysin n. heterocitolisina.
heterocytotoxin n. heterocitotoxina.
heterocytotropic adj. heterocitotrópico, -ca.
Heterodera radicicola n. Heterodera radicicola.
heterodermic adj. heterodérmico, -ca.
heterodesmotic adj. heterodesmótico, -ca.
heterodidymus n. heterodídimo.
heterodimer n. heterodímero.
heterodisperse adj. heterodisperso, -sa.
heterodont adj. heterodonto, -ta.
heterodromous adj. heteródromo, -ma.
heteroduplex n. heterodúplex.
heteroecious adj. heteroecio, -cia.
heteroerotic adj. heteroerótico, -ca.
heteroeroticism n. heteroerotismo.
heteroerotism n. heteroerotismo.
heterofermentation n. heterofermentación.
heterofermenter n. heterofermentador.
heterogamete n. heterogameto.
heterogametic adj. heterogamético, -ca.
heterogamety n. heterogametismo.
heterogamous adj. heterogámico, -ca, heterógamo, -ma.
heterogamy n. heterogamia.
heteroganglionic adj. heteroganglionar.
heterogeneic adj. heterogénico, -ca.
heterogeneity n. heterogeneidad, heterogenicidad.
  genetic heterogeneity heterogeneidad genética.
  allelic genetic heterogeneity heterogeneidad genética alélica.
  locus genetic heterogeneity heterogeneidad genética de locus.
heterogeneous adj. heterogéneo, -a.
heterogenesis n. heterogénesis.
heterogenetic adj. heterogenético, -ca.
heterogenic adj. heterogénico, -ca.
heterogenote n. heterogenoto.
heterogenous adj. heterogéneo, -a, heterogénico, -ca, heterógeno, -na.
heterogeny n. heterogenia.
heteroglobulose n. heteroglobulosa.
heterogony n. heterogonia.
heterograft n. heteroinjerto.
heterography n. heterografía.
heterohemagglutination n. heterohemaglutinación.
heterohemagglutinin n. heterohemaglutinina.
heterohypnosis n. heterohipnosis.
heteroimmune adj. heteroinmune.
heteroinfection n. heteroinfección.
heteroinoculation n. heteroinoculación.
heterokaryon n. heterocarion.
heterokaryosis n. heterocariosis.
heterokaryotic adj. heterocariótico, -ca.
heterokeratoplasty n. heteroqueratoplastia.
heterokinesia n. heterocinesia.
heterokinesis n. heterocinesis.
heterolateral adj. heterolateral.
heterolipids n. heterolípidos.
heterolith n. heterolito.
heterologous adj. heterólogo, -ga.
heterology n. heterología.
heterolysin n. heterolisina.
heterolysis n. heterólisis.
heterolytic adj. heterolítico, -ca.
heteromastigote adj. heteromastigoto, -ta.
heteromeric adj. heteromérico, -ca.
heteromerous adj. heterómero, -ra.
heterometaplasia n. heterometaplasia.
heterometropia n. heterometropía.
heteromorphism n. heteromorfismo.

heteromorphosis n. heteromorfosis.
heteromorphous adj. heteromorfo, -fa.
heteronomous adj. heterónomo, -ma.
heteronomy n. heteronomía.
heteronymous adj. heterónimo, -ma.
hetero-osteoplasty n. heteroosteoplastia.
heteropagus n. heterópago.
heteropancreatism n. heteropancreatismo.
heterophagy n. heterofagia.
heterophil n. heterófilo.
heterophile n. heterófilo.
heterophilic adj. heterofílico, -ca.
heterophonia n. heterofonía.
heterophoria n. heteroforia.
heterophoric adj. heterofórico, -ca.
heterophthalmia n. heteroftalmía.
heterophthalmos n. heteroftalmos.
heterophtongia n. heteroftongia.
heterophyasis n. heterofiasis.
heterophyd n. heterófido.
heterophydiasis n. heterofidiasis.
Heterophyes n. Heterophyes.
Heterophyidae n. Heterophyidae.
heteroplasia n. heteroplasia.
heteroplasm n. heteroplasma.
heteroplastic adj. heteroplástico, -ca.
heteroplastid n. heteroplástido.
heteroplasty n. heteroplastia.
heteroploid adj. heteroploide.
heteroploidy n. heteroploidía.
heteropodal adj. heterópodo, -da.
heteropolymer adj. heteropolímero, -ra.
heteropolymeric adj. heteropolimérico, -ca.
heteroprosopus n. heteroprosopus.
heteropsia n. heteropía, heteropsia.
heteropyknosis n. heteropicnosis.
  negative heteropyknosis heteropicnosis negativa.
  positive heteropyknosis heteropicnosis positiva.
heterosaccharide n. heterosacárido.
heteroscope n. heteroscopio.
heteroscopy n. heteroscopia.
heteroserotherapy n. heterosueroterapia.
heterosexism n. heterosexismo.
heterosexual adj. heterosexual.
heterosexuality n. heterosexualidad.
heterosis n. heterosis.
heterosmia n. heterosmia.
heterosome n. heterosoma.
heterospecific adj. heteroespecífico, -ca.
heterosuggestion n. heterosugestión.
heterotaxia n. heterotaxia, heterotaxis.
  cardiac heterotaxia heterotaxia cardíaca.
heterotaxic adj. heterotáxico, -ca.
heterotaxis n. heterotaxia, heterotaxis.
heterotaxy n. heterotaxia, heterotaxis.
heterotherapy n. heteroterapia.
heterotherm adj. heterotermo, -ma.
heterothermic adj. heterotérmico, -ca.
heterothermy n. heterotermia.
heterotic adj. heterótico, -ca.
heterotonia n. heterotonía.
heterotonic adj. heterotónico, -ca.
heterotopia n. heterotopia.
  heterotopia maculae heterotopia macular.
  neuronal heterotopia heterotopia neuronal.
heterotopic adj. heterotópico, -ca.
heterotopy n. heterotopia.
heterotoxin n. heterotoxina.
heterotransplant n. heterotrasplante[1].
heterotransplantation n. heterotrasplante[2].
heterotrichosis n. heterotricosis.
  heterotrichosis superciliorum heterotricosis superciliar.

heterotrichous *adj.* heterótrico, -ca.
heterotroph *n.* heterótrofo.
heterotrophia *n.* heterotrofia.
heterotrophic *adj.* heterotrófico, -ca.
heterotrophy *n.* heterotrofia.
heterotropia *n.* heterotropía.
heterotropy *n.* heterotropía.
heterotypic *adj.* heterotípico, -ca.
heterovaccine *n.* heterovacuna.
heteroxenous *adj.* heteroxénico, -ca, heteroxeno, -na.
heteroxeny *n.* heteroxenia.
heterozoic *adj.* heterozoico, -ca.
heterozygosis *n.* heterocigosis.
heterozygosity *n.* heterocigosidad, heterocigotia.
heterozygote *n.* heterocigoto, heterozigoto.
  compound heterozygote heterocigoto compuesto.
  double heterozygote heterocigoto doble.
  manifesting heterozygote heterocigoto manifiesto.
  obligate heterozygote heterocigoto obligado.
heterozygous *adj.* heterocigótico, -ca.
hetroinoculable *adj.* heteroinoculable.
heuristic *adj.* heurístico, -ca.
hexabasic *adj.* hexabásico, -ca.
hexacanth *n.* hexacanto.
hexachromic *adj.* hexacrómico, -ca.
hexad *n.* héxada.
hexadactylia *n.* hexadactilia.
hexadactylism *n.* hexadactilismo.
hexadactyly *n.* hexadactilia.
Hexagenia bilineata *n.* Hexagenia bilineata.
hexamer *n.* hexámero.
hexaploid *adj.* hexaploide.
hexaploidy *n.* hexaploidía.
hexatomic *adj.* hexatómico, -ca.
hexavaccine *n.* hexavacuna.
hexenmilch *n.* hexenmilch.
hexiology *n.* hexiología.
hiatal *adj.* hiatal.
hiatus *n.* hiato.
hibernation *n.* hibernación.
  artificial hibernation hibernación artificial.
hibernoma *n.* hibernoma.
hiccough *n.* hipo.
hiccup *n.* hipo.
hidradenitis *n.* hidradenitis.
  hidradenitis axillaris hidradenitis axilar.
  hidradenitis axillaris of Verneuil hidradenitis axilar de Verneuil.
  hidradenitis suppurativa hidradenitis supurada, hidradenitis supurativa.
hidradenoid *adj.* hidradenoide.
hidradenoma *n.* hidradenoma.
  clear cell hidradenoma hidradenoma de células claras.
  hidradenoma eruptivum hidradenoma eruptivo.
  hidradenoma papilliferum hidradenoma papilar.
  nodular hidradenoma hidradenoma nodular.
  papillary hidradenoma hidradenoma papilar.
hidroadenoma *n.* hidroadenoma.
hidropoiesis *n.* hidropoyesis.
hidrosadenitis *n.* hidrosadenitis.
hidrosis *n.* hidrosis.
hidrotic *adj.* hidrótico, -ca.
hiemal *adj.* hiemal.
hieralgia *n.* hieralgia.
hierarchy *n.* jerarquía.
  Maslow's hierarchy jerarquía de Maslow, jerarquía de necesidades de Maslow.

  Maslow's hierarchy of need jerarquía de Maslow, jerarquía de necesidades de Maslow.
  response hierarchy jerarquía de respuesta.
hierolisthesis *n.* hierolistesis.
hilar *adj.* hiliar.
hilitis *n.* hilitis.
hilum *n.* hilio.
himantosis *n.* himantosis.
hip *n.* cadera.
  snapping hip cadera de resorte.
hippocampal *adj.* hipocámpico, -ca.
hippocampus *n.* hipocampo, hippocampus.
hippocratic *adj.* hipocrático, -ca.
hippocratism *n.* hipocratismo.
hippuria *n.* hipuria.
hippus *n.* hippus.
  pupillar hippus hippus pupilar.
  respiratory hippus hippus respiratorio.
hircismus *n.* hircismo.
hirsute *adj.* hirsuto, -ta.
hirsutism *n.* hirsutismo.
  Apert's hirsutism hirsutismo de Apert.
  constitutional hirsutism hirsutismo constitucional.
  idiopathic hirsutism hirsutismo idiopático.
hirudicidal *adj.* hirudicida[2].
hirudicide *n.* hirudicida[1].
hirudiniasis *n.* hirudiniasis.
hirudinization *n.* hirudinización.
hirudinize *v.* hirudinizar.
histamine *n.* histamina.
histaminemia *n.* histaminemia.
histaminergic *adj.* histaminérgico, -ca.
histaminuria *n.* histaminuria.
histanoxia *n.* histanoxia.
histic *adj.* hístico, -ca.
histidinemia *n.* histidinemia.
histidinuria *n.* histidinuria.
histioblast *n.* histioblasto.
histiocyte *n.* histiocito.
  sea-blue histiocyte histiocito azul marino.
histiocytic *adj.* histiocítico, -ca.
histiocytoma *n.* histiocitoma, histiocitoma.
  fibrous histiocytoma histiocitoma fibroso.
  generalized eruptive histiocytoma histiocitoma eruptivo generalizado.
  lipoid histiocytoma histiocitoma lipoide.
  malignant fibrous histiocytoma histiocitoma fibroso maligno.
histiocytosis *n.* histiocitosis.
  accumulative histiocytosis histiocitosis acumulativa.
  Langerhans cell histiocytosis histiocitosis de células de Langerhans.
  lipid histiocytosis histiocitosis lipídica, histiocitosis lipoídica.
  malignant histiocytosis histiocitosis maligna.
  nodular non-X histiocytosis histiocitosis nodular no X.
  regressing atypical histiocytosis histiocitosis atípica con regresión.
  sinus histiocytosis histiocitosis sinusal.
  X histiocytosis histiocitosis X.
  Y histiocytosis histiocitosis Y.
histioid *adj.* histioide, histioideo, -a.
histioincompatibility *n.* histioincompatibilidad.
histio-irritative *adj.* histioirritante.
histioma *n.* histioma.
histionic *adj.* histiónico, -ca.
histoangic *adj.* histoángico, -ca.
histoblast *n.* histoblasto.
histochemical *adj.* histoquímico, -ca.
histochemistry *n.* histoquímica.

histochromatosis *n.* histocromatosis.
histoclastic *adj.* histoclástico, -ca.
histoclinical *adj.* histoclínico, -ca.
histocompatibility *n.* histocompatibilidad.
histocompatible *adj.* histocompatible.
histocyte *n.* histocito.
histocytoma *n.* histiocitoma.
histocytosis *n.* histiocitosis, histocitosis.
histodiagnosis *n.* histodiagnosis.
histodialysis *n.* histodiálisis.
histodifferentiation *n.* histodiferenciación.
histofluorescence *n.* histofluorescencia.
histogenesis *n.* histogénesis.
histogenetic *adj.* histogenético, -ca.
histogenous *adj.* histógeno, -na.
histogeny *n.* histogenia.
histogram *n.* histograma.
histography *n.* histografía.
histohematogenous *adj.* histohematógeno, -na.
histohydria *n.* histohidria.
histohypoxia *n.* histohipoxia.
histoid *adj.* histioide, histoide, histoideo, -a.
histoincompatible *adj.* histoincompatible.
histokinesis *n.* histocinesis.
histologic *adj.* histológico, -ca.
histological *adj.* histológico, -ca.
histologist *n.* histólogo, -ga.
histology *n.* histología.
  normal histology histología normal.
  pathologic histology histología patológica.
histolysate *n.* histolisado.
histolytic *adj.* histolítico, -ca.
histoma *n.* histioma, histoma.
histometaplastic *adj.* histometaplásico, -ca.
histomorphology *n.* histomorfología.
histomorphometry *n.* histomorfometría.
histone *n.* histona.
  histone nucleinate histona nucleinato de.
histonectomy *n.* histonectomía.
histoneurology *n.* histoneurología.
histonomy *n.* histonomía.
histonuria *n.* histonuria.
histopathogenesis *n.* histopatogenia.
histopathology *n.* histopatología.
histophagus *n.* histófago.
histophysiology *n.* histofisiología.
Histoplasma *n.* Histoplasma.
histoplasmona *n.* histoplasmona.
histoplasmosis *n.* histoplasmosis.
  African histoplasmosis histoplasmosis africana.
  ocular histoplasmosis histoplasmosis ocular.
  presumed ocular histoplasmosis histoplasmosis ocular presunta.
historadiography *n.* historradiografía.
historetention *n.* historretención.
historrhexis *n.* historrexis.
history *n.* antecedentes, historia.
  case history historia personal y familiar.
  clinical history historia clínica.
  complete health history historia clínica completa.
  family history historia familiar.
  health history historia clínica.
  history of present illness historia actual, historia de la enfermedad actual.
  occupational history historia laboral.
  personal and social history antecedentes personales y sociales.
  psychiatric history historia psiquiátrica.
  sexual history historia sexual.
histoteliosis *n.* histoteliosis.
histothanatology *n.* histotanatología.
histotherapy *n.* histoterapia.

histothrombin *n.* histotrombina.
histotome *n.* histótomo.
histotomy *n.* histotomía.
histotoxic *adj.* histotóxico, -ca.
histotroph *n.* histotrofo.
histotrophe *n.* histotrofo.
histotrophic *adj.* histotrófico, -ca.
histotropic *adj.* histotrópico, -ca.
histozoic *adj.* histozoico, -ca.
histrionic *adj.* histriónico, -ca.
histrionism *n.* histrionismo.
histyocytomatosis *n.* histiocitomatosis.
hive *n.* habón.
hoarse *adj.* ronco, -ca.
hoarseness *n.* ronquera.
hodoneuromere *n.* hodoneurómera.
holandric *adj.* holándrico, -ca.
holarthritic *adj.* holoartrítico, -ca.
holarthritis *n.* holartritis.
holder *n.* soporte.
 foil holder soporte de oro laminar.
 weight holder soporte del peso.
hollow *n.* hoyo², hueco.
holoacardius *n.* holoacardio.
 holoacardius acephalus holoacardio acéfalo.
 holoacardius acormus holoacardio acórmico.
 holoacardius amorphus holoacardio amorfo.
holoacrania *n.* holoacrania.
holoanencephaly *n.* holoanencefalia.
holoantigen *n.* holoantígeno.
holoarthritis *n.* holoartritis.
holoblastic *adj.* holoblástico, -ca.
holocephalic *adj.* holocefálico, -ca, holocéfalo, -la.
holocord *n.* holocordón.
holocrine *adj.* holocrino, -na.
holoendemic *adj.* holoendémico, -ca.
hologamy *n.* hologamia.
hologastroschisis *n.* hologastrosquisis.
hologenesis *n.* hologénesis.
hologram *n.* holograma.
holography *n.* holografía.
 acoustical holography holografía acústica.
hologynic *adj.* hologínico, -ca.
holomastigote *adj.* holomastigoto, -ta.
holomorphosis *n.* holomorfosis.
holomyarial *adj.* holomiarial.
holophytic *adj.* holofítico, -ca.
holoprosencephaly *n.* holoprosencefalia.
 familial alobar holoprosencephaly holoprosencefalia familiar alobular.
holorachischisis *n.* holorraquisquisis.
holoschisis *n.* holosquisis.
holosystolic *adj.* holosistólico, -ca.
holotelencephaly *n.* holotelencefalia.
Holothyrus *n.* Holothyrus.
holotonia *n.* holotonía.
holotonic *adj.* holotónico, -ca.
holotopy *n.* holotopia.
holotrichous *adj.* holotrico, -ca.
holotype *n.* holotipo.
holoxenic *adj.* holoxénico, -ca.
holozoic *adj.* holozoico, -ca.
holter monitoring *n.* holter.
homalocephalous *adj.* homalocéfalo, -la.
homalography *n.* homalografía.
Homalomyia *n.* Homalomyia.
homaluria *n.* homaluria.
homaxial *adj.* homaxil.
homeochrome *adj.* homeocromo, -ma.
homeodynamics *n.* homeodinámica.
homeokinesis *n.* homeocinesia, homeocinesis.
homeometric *adj.* homeométrico, -ca.
homeomorphous *adj.* homeomorfo, -fa.

homeo-osteoplasty *n.* homeosteoplastia.
homeopath *n.* homeópata.
homeopathic *adj.* homeopático, -ca.
homeopathist *n.* homeópata.
homeopathy *n.* homeopatía.
homeoplasia *n.* homeoplasia.
homeoplastic *adj.* homeoplásico, -ca.
homeorrhexis *n.* homeorrexis.
homeosis *n.* homeosis.
homeostasis *n.* homeostasia, homeostasis.
 Bernard-Cannon homeostasis homeostasis Bernard-Cannon.
 genetic homeostasis homeostasis genética.
 Lerner homeostasis homeostasis de Lerner.
 ontogenic homeostasis homeostasis ontogénica.
 physiological homeostasis homeostasis fisiológica.
 Waddingtonian homeostasis homeostasis waddingtoniana.
homeostatic *adj.* homeostático, -ca.
homeotherapeutic *adj.* homeoterapéutico, -ca.
homeotherapeutics *n.* homeoterapia.
homeotherapy *n.* homeoterapia.
homeotherm *adj.* homeotermo, -ma.
homeothermic *adj.* homeotérmico, -ca.
homeothermism *n.* homeotermismo.
homeothermy *n.* homeotermia.
homeotic *adj.* homeótico, -ca.
homeotransplant *n.* homeotransplante, homeotrasplante.
homeotransplantation *n.* homeotransplante, homeotrasplante.
homeotypic *adj.* homeotípico, -ca.
homeotypical *adj.* homeotípico, -ca.
homicide *n.* homicidio.
 simple homicide homicidio simple.
homing *n.* nostocitosis.
 lymphocytic homing tráfico linfocitario.
hominid *adj.* homínido, -da.
Hominidae *n.* Hominidae.
hominoid *adj.* hominoide.
Hominoidea *n.* Hominoidea.
Homo *n.* Homo.
 Homo sapiens Homo sapiens.
homoblastic *adj.* homoblástico, -ca.
homobody *n.* homocuerpo.
homocarnosinosis *n.* homocarnosinosis.
homocentric *adj.* homocéntrico, -ca.
homochronous *adj.* homócrono, -na.
homocladic *adj.* homocládico, -ca.
homocyclic *adj.* homocíclico, -ca.
homocystinemia *n.* homocistinemia.
homocystinuria *n.* homocistinuria.
homocytotropic *adj.* homocitotrópico, -ca.
homodesmotic *adj.* homodesmótico, -ca.
homodimer *n.* homodímero.
homodont *n.* homodonto, -ta.
homodromous *adj.* homódromo, -ma.
homoeosis *n.* homeosis, homoeosis.
homoerotic *adj.* homoerótico, -ca.
homoeroticism *n.* homoerotismo.
homoerotism *n.* homoerotismo.
homofermentation *n.* homofermentación.
homofermenter *n.* homofermentador.
homogamete *n.* homogameto.
homogametic *adj.* homogamético, -ca.
homogamous *adj.* homógamo, -ma.
homogamy *n.* homogamia.
homogenate *n.* homogenado.
homogeneity *n.* homogeneidad.
homogeneization *n.* homogeneización.
homogeneous *adj.* homogéneo, -a.
homogenesis *n.* homogenesia, homogénesis.

homogenetic *adj.* homogenético, -ca.
homogenic *adj.* homogénico, -ca.
homogenicity *n.* homogenicidad.
homogenize *v.* homogeneizar.
homogenized *adj.* homogeneizado, -da.
homogenote *n.* homogenoto.
homogentisuria *n.* homogentisinuria, homogentisuria.
homogeny *n.* homogenia.
homoglandular *adj.* homoglandular.
homograft *n.* homoinjerto.
homoiopodal *adj.* homoyopódico, -ca.
homoiostasis *n.* homoiostasis.
homokaryon *n.* homocarion.
homokaryotic *adj.* homocariótico, -ca.
homokeratoplasty *n.* homoqueratoplastia.
homolactic *adj.* homoláctico, -ca.
homolateral *adj.* homolateral.
homolipids *n.* homolípidos.
homolog *adj.* homólogo, -ga.
homologous *adj.* homólogo, -ga.
homolysin *n.* homolisina.
homolysis *n.* homólisis.
homomorphic *adj.* homomórfico, -ca.
homomorphosis *n.* homomorfosis.
homonomous *adj.* homónomo, -ma.
homonuclear *adj.* homonuclear.
homonymous *adj.* homónimo, -ma.
homophil *n.* homófilo.
homophilic *adj.* homofílico, -ca.
homophobia *n.* homofobia.
homoplastic *adj.* homoplástico, -ca.
homoplasty *n.* homoplastia.
homorganic *adj.* homoorgánico, -ca, homorgánico, -ca.
homosexual *adj.* homosexual.
homosexuality *n.* homosexualidad.
 ego-dystonia homosexuality homosexualidad egodistónica.
 female homosexuality homosexualidad femenina.
 latent homosexuality homosexualidad latente.
 overt homosexuality homosexualidad manifiesta.
 unconscious homosexuality homosexualidad inconsciente.
homostimulant *adj.* homoestimulante.
homostimulation *n.* homoestimulación.
homothallic *adj.* homotálico, -ca.
homothallism *n.* homotalismo.
homotherm *adj.* homeotermo, -ma, homotermo.
homothermal *adj.* homotérmico, -ca.
homothermal *adj.* homeotérmico, -ca.
homothermic *adj.* homeotérmico, -ca, homotérmico, -ca.
homotonic *adj.* homotónico, -ca.
homotopic *adj.* homotópico, -ca.
homotransplant *n.* homotrasplante.
homotransplantation *n.* homotrasplante.
homotropism *n.* homotropismo.
homotype *n.* homotipo.
homotypic *adj.* homotípico, -ca.
homotypical *adj.* homotípico, -ca.
homoxenous *adj.* homoxénico, -ca.
homozoic *adj.* homozoico, -ca.
homozygosis *n.* homocigosis.
homozygosity *n.* homocigosidad.
homozygote *adj.* homocigoto, -ta, homozigoto.
 homozygote by descent homocigoto por descendencia.
homozygous *adj.* homocigótico, -ca.
homunculus *n.* homúnculo.
honey *n.* miel.

hook *n.* gancho[2].
  blunt hook gancho de llave, gancho romo.
  Bose's hook gancho de Bose.
  Braun's hook gancho de Braun.
  calvarial hook gancho calvárico.
  dissecting hook erina.
  Dujarier's hook gancho de Dujarier.
  hook of the hamate bone gancho del hueso ganchoso.
  lacrimal hook gancho del unguis, gancho lagrimal.
  Loughnane's hook gancho de Loughnane.
  Malpaigne's hook gancho de Malpaigne.
  muscle hook gancho muscular.
  obtuse hook gancho obtuso.
  Pajot's hook gancho de Pajot.
  palate hook gancho del paladar, gancho palatino.
  pancreas hook gancho del páncreas.
  pterygoid hook gancho de la apófisis pterigoides, gancho de la pterigoides.
  Ramsbotham's hook gancho de Ramsbotham.
  sliding hook gancho deslizable.
  squint hook gancho de estrabismo.
  tracheotomy hook gancho para traqueotomía.
  Tyrrell's hook gancho de Tyrrell.
hookworm *n.* uncinaria.
  New World hookworm uncinaria americana, uncinaria del Nuevo Mundo.
  Old World hookworm uncinaria del Viejo Mundo, uncinaria europea.
hopelessness *n.* desesperanza.
hordeolum *n.* orzuelo.
  hordeolum externum orzuelo externo.
  hordeolum internum orzuelo interno.
  hordeolum meibomianum orzuelo de Meibomio, orzuelo meibomiano.
horizon *n.* horizonte.
  clinical horizon horizonte clínico.
  developmental horizon horizonte del desarrollo.
horizontal pursuit *n.* seguimiento horizontal.
hormesis *n.* hormesis.
hormion *n.* hormión.
hormonagogue *adj.* hormonagogo, -ga.
hormonal *adj.* hormonal.
hormone *n.* hormona.
hormonic *adj.* hormónico, -ca.
hormonogenesis *n.* hormonogénesis.
hormonogenic *adj.* hormonogenia, hormonogénico, -ca.
hormonology *n.* hormonología.
hormonopexic *adj.* hormonopéxico, -ca.
hormonopoiesis *n.* hormonopoyesis, hormonopoyesis.
hormonopoietic *adj.* hormonopoyético, -ca.
hormonoprivia *n.* hormonoprivia.
hormonosis *n.* hormonosis.
hormonotherapy *n.* hormonoterapia.
horn *n.* cuerno.
  cicatricial horn cuerno cicatricial, cuerno cicatrizal.
  cutaneous horn cuerno cutáneo.
  nail horn cuerno ungular.
  pulp horn cuerno de la pulpa, cuerno pulpar.
  sebaceous horn cuerno sebáceo.
horny *adj.* córneo, -a.
horripilation *n.* horripilación.
horror *n.* horror.
horsefly *n.* tábano.
hospital *n.* hospital.
  general hospital hospital general.
  geriatric day care hospital hospital geriátrico de día.

maternity hospital hospital de maternidad, hospital materno.
  mental hospital manicomio.
  psychiatric hospital hospital psiquiátrico.
hospitalization *n.* hospitalización.
  partial hospitalization hospitalización parcial.
host *n.* hospedador, huésped.
hostility *n.* hostilidad.
hue *n.* matiz.
hum *n.* zumbido.
  venous hum zumbido venoso.
humectant *adj.* humectante.
humectation *n.* humectación.
humeral *adj.* humeral.
humerorradial *adj.* humerorradial.
humeroscapular *adj.* humeroescapular, humeroscapular.
humeroulnar *adj.* humerocubital.
humerus *n.* húmero.
humidification *n.* humidificación.
humidifier *n.* humidificador.
  bubble diffusion humidifier humidificador de difusión de burbujas.
  cascade humidifier humidificador en cascada.
  hygroscopic humidifier humidificador higroscópico.
  jet humidifier humidificador de chorro.
  wick humidifier humidificador de mecha.
humidity *n.* humedad.
  absolute humidity humedad absoluta.
  relative humidity humedad relativa.
humor *n.* humor.
  crystalline humor humor cristalino.
  humor aquosus humor acuoso.
  humor cristallinus humor cristalino.
  humor vitreus humor vítreo.
  ocular humor humor ocular.
  plasmoid humor humor plasmoide.
  vitreous humor humor vítreo.
humoral *adj.* humoral.
hump *n.* giba, joroba.
  buffalo hump joroba de búfalo.
  Hampton's hump giba de Hampton.
humpback *n.* corcova, gibosidad, joroba.
hunchback *n.* gibosidad.
hunger *n.* hambre.
hyalin *n.* hialina.
  alcoholic hyalin hialina alcohólica.
  Crooke's hyalin hialina de Crooke.
  hematogenous hyalin hialina hematógena.
hyaline *adj.* hialino, -na.
hyalinization *n.* hialinización.
hyalinosis *n.* hialinosis.
  hyalinosis cutis et mucosae hialinosis cutis et mucosae.
hyalinuria *n.* hialinuria.
hyalitis *n.* hialitis.
  hyalitis punctata hialitis punctata.
  hyalitis suppurativa hialitis supurativa.
  punctate hyalitis hialitis punctata.
  suppurative hyalitis hialitis supurativa.
hyalocyte *n.* hialocito.
hyalogen *n.* hialógeno, -na.
hyalohyphomycosis *n.* hialohifomicosis.
hyaloid *adj.* hialoide, hialoideo, -a.
hyaloiditis *n.* hialoiditis.
hyalomere *n.* hialómera, hialómero.
hyalomitome *n.* hialomitoma.
Hyalomma *n.* Hyalomma.
hyalomucoid *adj.* hialomucoide.
hyalonyxis *n.* hialonixis.
hyalophagia *n.* hialofagia.
hyalophagy *n.* hialofagia.
hyaloplasm *n.* hialoplasma, paramiotoma.

nuclear hyaloplasm hialoplasma nuclear.
hyaloplasma *n.* hialoplasma.
hyaloserositis *n.* hialoserositis.
  progressive multiple hyaloserositis hialoserositis múltiple progresiva.
hyalosis *n.* hialosis.
  asteroid hyalosis hialosis asteroide.
  punctate hyalosis hialosis punteada.
hyalosome *n.* hialosoma.
hybaroxia *n.* hibaroxia.
hybrid *n.* híbrido, -da.
  false hybrid híbrido falso.
  SV40-adenovirus hybrid híbrido SV40-adenovirus.
hybridism *n.* hibridismo.
hybridity *n.* hibridez.
hybridization *n.* hibridación.
  cell hybridization hibridación celular.
  DNA hybridization hibridación de ADN.
  fluorescence in situ hybridization hibridación in situ fluorescente.
  nucleic acid hybridization hibridación de ácidos nucleicos.
  somatic cell hybridization hibridación de células somáticas.
hybridoma *n.* hibridoma.
hydatid *n.* hidátide.
hydatidiform *adj.* hidatidiforme.
hydatidocele *n.* hidatidocele.
hydatidosis *n.* hidatidosis.
hydatidostomy *n.* hidatidostomía.
hydatiduria *n.* hidatiduria.
hydatiform *adj.* hidatiforme.
Hydatigena *n.* Hydatigena.
hydatism *n.* hidatismo.
hydatodoma *n.* hidatidoma.
hydatoid *n.* hidatoide, hidatoides.
hydraeroperitoneum *n.* hidroaeroperitoneo.
hydragog *adj.* hidragogo, -ga.
hydramnion *n.* hidramnios.
hydramnios *n.* hidramnios.
hydranencephaly *n.* hidranencefalia, hidrencefalia.
hydrangiography *n.* hidrangiografía.
hydrangiology *n.* hidrangiología.
hydrangiotomy *n.* hidrangiotomía.
hydrargirosis *n.* hidrargirosis.
hydrargyria *n.* hidrargiria.
hydrargyrism *n.* hidrargirismo.
hydrargyromania *n.* hidrargiromanía.
hydrarthrodial *adj.* hidrartródico, -ca, hidrartrósico, -ca.
hydrarthrosis *n.* hidrartrosis.
  intermittent hydrarthrosis hidrartrosis intermitente, hidrartrosis periódica.
hydrate *n.* hidrato.
hydrated *adj.* hidratado, -da.
hydration *n.* hidratación.
hydraulics *n.* hidráulica.
hydremia *n.* hidremia.
hydrencephalocele *n.* hidrencefalocele.
hydrencephalomeningocele *n.* hidrencefalomeningocele, hidroencefalomeningocele.
hydrencephalus *n.* hidrencéfalo.
hydrepigastrium *n.* hidrepigastrio.
hydriatic *adj.* hidriático, -ca.
hydriatics *n.* hidriatría.
hydriatric *adj.* hidriático, -ca, hidriátrico, -ca.
hydric *adj.* hídrico, -ca.
hydroa *n.* hidroa.
hydroanencephalia *n.* hidroanencefalia.
hydroappendix *n.* hidroapéndice.
hydroblepharon *n.* hidrobléfaron.
hydrocalicosis *n.* hidrocalicosis.
hydrocalyx *n.* hidrocáliz.

hydrocarbon *n.* hidrocarburo.
hydrocarburism *n.* hidrocarburismo.
hydrocardia *n.* hidrocardia.
hydrocele *n.* hidrocele.
  acute hydrocele hidrocele agudo.
  cervical hydrocele del cuello, hidrocele cervical.
  chylous hydrocele hidrocele quiloso.
  communicating hydrocele hidrocele comunicante.
  congenital hydrocele hidrocele congénito.
  diffused hydrocele hidrocele difuso.
  Dupuytren's hydrocele hidrocele de Dupuytren.
  encysted hydrocele hidrocele enquistado.
  filarial hydrocele hidrocele filiriásico.
  funicular hydrocele hidrocele funicular.
  hernial hydrocele hidrocele herniario.
  hydrocele feminae hidrocele femenino, hidrocele muliebris.
  hydrocele of the neck del cuello, hidrocele cervical.
  hydrocele renalis hidrocele renal.
  infantile hydrocele hidrocele del lactante.
  Maunoir's hydrocele hidrocele de Maunoir.
  Nuck's hydrocele hidrocele de Nuck.
  scrotal hydrocele hidrocele escrotal externo.
  spinal hydrocele hidrocele espinal.
hydrocelectomy *n.* hidrocelectomía.
hydrocenosis *n.* hidrocenosis.
hydrocephalia *n.* hidrocefalia.
  communicating hydrocephalia hidrocefalia comunicante.
  congenital hydrocephalia hidrocefalia congénita.
  double compartment hydrocephalia hidrocefalia de compartimento doble.
  ex vacuo hydrocephalia hidrocefalia ex vacuo.
  external hydrocephalia hidrocefalia externa.
  hyperproductive hydrocephalia hidrocefalia hiperproductiva.
  hyporeabsortive hydrocephalia hidrocefalia hiporreabsortiva.
  internal hydrocephalia hidrocefalia interna.
  non-communicating hydrocephalia hidrocefalia no comunicante.
  normal pressure hydrocephalia hidrocefalia a presión normal.
  normal pressure occult hydrocephalia hidrocefalia oculta, hidrocefalia oculta a presión normal.
  normal-pressure hydrocephalia hidrocefalia normotensa.
  obstructive hydrocephalia hidrocefalia obstructiva.
  occult hydrocephalia hidrocefalia oculta, hidrocefalia oculta a presión normal.
  otitic hydrocephalia hidrocefalia otítica.
  postmeningitic hydrocephalia hidrocefalia posmeningítica.
  posttraumatic hydrocephalia hidrocefalia postraumática.
  primary hydrocephalia hidrocefalia primaria.
  secondary hydrocephalia hidrocefalia secundaria.
  thrombotic hydrocephalia hidrocefalia trombótica.
  toxic hydrocephalia hidrocefalia tóxica.
hydrocephalic *adj.* hidrocefálico, -ca.
hydrocephalocele *n.* hidrocefalocele.
hydrocephaloid *adj.* hidrocefaloide.
hydrocephalus *n.* hidrocéfalo, -la.
hydrocholecystis *n.* hidrocolecisto.
hydrocholeresis *n.* hidrocoleresis.

hydrocholeretic *adj.* hidrocolerético, -ca.
hydrocholesterol *n.* hidrocolesterol.
hydrocirsocele *n.* hidrocirsocele.
hydrocolloid *n.* hidrocoloide.
  irreversible hydrocolloid hidrocoloide irreversible.
  reversible hydrocolloid hidrocoloide reversible.
hydrocolpocele *n.* hidrocolpocele.
hydrocolpos *n.* hidrocolpos.
hydroconion *n.* hidroconión.
hydrocortisone *n.* hidrocortisona.
hydrocyanism *n.* hidrocianismo.
hydrocyst *n.* hidroquiste.
hydrocystadenoma *n.* hidrocistadenoma.
hydrocystoma *n.* hidrocistoma.
hydrodictiotomy *n.* hidrodictiotomía.
hydrodiffusion *n.* hidrodifusión.
hydrodiuresis *n.* hidrodiuresis.
hydroelectric *adj.* hidroeléctrico, -ca.
hydroencephalocele *n.* hidroencefalocele.
hydroencephalomeningocele *n.* hidroence falomeningocele.
hydrogen *n.* hidrógeno.
hydrogenate *v.* hidrogenar.
hydrogenation *n.* hidrogenación.
hydrogenoid *n.* hidrogenoide.
hydrohematonephrosis *n.* hidrohematonefrosis.
hydrohepatosis *n.* hidrohepatosis.
hydrohymenitis *n.* hidrohimenitis.
hydrokinesitherapy *n.* hidrocinesiterapia.
hydrokinetic *adj.* hidrocinético, -ca.
hydrokinetics *n.* hidrocinética.
hydrolabile *adj.* hidrolábil.
hydrolability *n.* hidrolabilidad.
hydrolabyrinth *n.* hidrolaberinto.
hydrolite *n.* hidrólito.
hydrolysate *n.* hidrolizado, -da.
hydrolysis *n.* hidrólisis.
hydrolytic *adj.* hidrolítico, -ca.
hydrolyze *v.* hidrolizar.
hydroma *n.* hidroma, higroma.
hydromassage *n.* hidromasaje.
hydromeningitis *n.* hidromeningitis.
hydromeningocele *n.* hidromeningocele.
hydrometer *n.* hidrómetro.
hydrometra *n.* hidrómetra.
hydrometric *adj.* hidrométrico, -ca.
hydrometrocolpos *n.* hidrometrocolpos.
hydrometry *n.* hidrometría.
hydromicrocephaly *n.* hidromicrocefalia.
hydromphalus *n.* hidrónfalo.
hydromyelia *n.* hidromielia.
hydromyelocele *n.* hidromielocele.
hydromyelomeningocele *n.* hidromielomeningocele.
hydromyoma *n.* hidromioma.
hydronephrosis *n.* hidronefrosis.
  closed hydronephrosis hidronefrosis cerrada.
  open hydronephrosis hidronefrosis abierta.
hydronephrotic *adj.* hidronefrótico, -ca.
hydroparasalpinx *n.* hidroparasálpinx.
hydroparotitis *n.* hidroparotitis.
hydropenia *n.* hidropenia.
hydropenic *adj.* hidropénico, -ca.
hydropericarditis *n.* hidropericarditis.
hydropericardium *n.* hidropericardio.
hydroperinephrosis *n.* hidroperinefrosis.
hydroperion *n.* hidroperion.
hydroperitoneum *n.* hidroperitoneo.
hydropexia *n.* hidropexia.
hydropexic *adj.* hidropéxico, -ca.
hydropexis *n.* hidropexia, hidropexis.
hydrophagocytosis *n.* hidrofagocitosis.

hydrophil *adj.* hidrófilo, -la.
hydrophile *adj.* hidrófilo, -la.
hydrophilia *n.* hidrofilia.
hydrophilic *adj.* hidrofílico, -ca.
hydrophilism *n.* hidrofilismo.
hydrophobia *n.* fobodipsia, hidrofobia.
hydrophobic *adj.* hidrofóbico, -ca.
hydrophobophobia *n.* hidrofobofobia.
hydrophorograph *n.* hidroforógrafo.
hydrophthalmia *n.* hidroftalmía.
hydrophthalmus *n.* hidroftalmos.
  hydrophthalmus anterior hidroftalmos anterior.
  hydrophthalmus posterior hidroftalmos posterior.
  hydrophthalmus totalis hidroftalmos total.
hydrophysometra *n.* hidrofisómetra.
hydropic *adj.* hidrópico, -ca.
hydropigenous *adj.* hidropígeno, -na.
hydroplasma *n.* hidroplasma.
hydropneumatosis *n.* hidroneumatosis.
hydropneumogony *n.* hidroneumogonia.
hydropneumopericardium *n.* hidroneumopericardio.
hydropneumoperitoneum *n.* hidroneumoperitoneo.
hydropneumothorax *n.* hidroneumotórax.
hydropoietic *adj.* hidropoyético, -ca.
hydropotherapy *n.* hidropoterapia.
hydrops *n.* hidropepsía, hidropesia.
  endolymphatic hydrops hidropesia endolinfática.
  fetal hydrops hidropesia fetal.
  hydrops ad matulam hidropesia ad matulam.
  hydrops articuli hidropesia articular.
  hydrops fetalis hidropesia fetal.
  hydrops folliculi hidropesia folicular.
  hydrops gravidarum hidropesia gravídica.
  hydrops ovarii hidropesia ovárica.
  hydrops tubae hidropesia tubárica.
  hydrops tubae profluens hidropesia tubae profluens, hidropesia tubárica intermitente.
  immune fetal hydrops hidropesia fetal inmune.
  labyrinthine hydrops hidropesia del laberinto, hidropesia laberíntica.
  meningeal hydrops hidropesia meníngea.
  non-immune fetal hydrops hidropesia fetal no inmune.
hydropyonephrosis *n.* hidropionefrosis.
hydrorachis *n.* hidrorraquis.
hydrorachitis *n.* hidrorraquitis.
hydrorrhea *n.* hidrorrea.
  hydrorrhea gravidarum hidrorrea gravídica.
  nasal hydrorrhea hidrorrea nasal.
hydrosalpinx *n.* hidrosálpinx.
  hydrosalpinx follicularis hidrosálpinx follicular.
  hydrosalpinx simplex hidrosálpinx simple.
  intermittent hydrosalpinx hidrosálpinx intermitente.
hydrosarcocele *n.* hidrosarcocele.
hydroscheocele *n.* hidroosqueocele.
hydroschesis *n.* hidrosquesis.
hydroscope *n.* hidroscopio.
hydrosolubility *n.* hidrosolubilidad.
hydrosoluble *adj.* hidrosoluble.
hydrosphygmograph *n.* hidroesfigmógrafo, hidrosfigmógrafo.
hydrospirometer *n.* hidroespirómetro, hidrospirómetro.
hydrostable *n.* hidroestable.
hydrostat *n.* hidróstato.
hydrostatic *adj.* hidrostático, -ca.
hydrostatics *n.* hidrostática.

hydrosynthesis *n.* hidrosíntesis.
hydrosyringomyelia *n.* hidrosiringomielia.
hydrotaxis *n.* hidrotaxia, hidrotaxis.
hydrotherapeutic *adj.* hidroterapéutico, -ca, hidroterápico, -ca.
hydrotherapeutics *n.* hidroterapia.
hydrotherapy *n.* hidroterapia.
hydrothermal *adj.* hidrotérmico, -ca.
hydrothionammonemia *n.* hidrotionamonemia.
hydrothionemia *n.* hidrotionemia.
hydrothionuria *n.* hidrotionuria.
hydrothorax *n.* hidrotórax.
  chylous hydrothorax hidrotórax quiloso.
hydrotomy *n.* hidrotomía.
hydrotropism *n.* hidrotropismo.
hydrotubation *n.* hidrotubación.
hydroureter *n.* hidrouréter, hidroureterosis.
hydroureteronephrosis *n.* hidroureteronefrosis.
hydrouria *n.* hidrouria, hidruria.
hydrous *adj.* hidratado, -da, hidroso, -sa.
hydrovarium *n.* hidroovario, hidrovario.
hydroxykynereninuria *n.* hidroxiquinurreninuria.
hydroxyphenyluria *n.* hidroxifeniluria.
hydroxyprolinemia *n.* hidroxiprolinemia.
hydruria *n.* hidruria.
hydruric *adj.* hidrúrico, -ca.
hygiene *n.* higiene.
  bronchial hygiene higiene bronquial.
  bronchopulmonary hygiene higiene broncopulmonar.
  dental hygiene higiene dental.
  mental hygiene higiene mental.
  mouth hygiene higiene bucal.
  oral hygiene higiene oral.
hygienic *adj.* higiénico, -ca.
hygienist *n.* higienista.
hygric *adj.* hígrico, -ca.
hygroblepharic *adj.* higroblefárico, -ca.
hygroma *n.* higroma.
  cystic hygroma higroma quístico.
  hygroma axillare higroma axilar.
  hygroma colli cystum higroma cervical.
  hygroma cysticum higroma quístico.
  hygroma praepatellare higroma prepatelar, higroma prerrotuliano.
  mesothelial hygroma higroma mesotelial.
  subdural hygroma higroma subdural.
hygromatous *adj.* higromatoso, -sa.
hygrometer *n.* higrómetro.
hygrometric *adj.* higrométrico, -ca.
hygrometry *n.* higrometría.
hygroscopic *adj.* higroscópico, -ca.
hyla *n.* hila.
hylergography *n.* hilergografía.
hylogeny *n.* hilogénesis, hilogenia.
hylology *n.* hilología.
hyloma *n.* hiloma.
  mesenchymal hyloma hiloma mesenquimático.
  mesothelial hyloma hiloma mesotelial.
hylotropic *adj.* hilotrópico, -ca.
hylotropy *n.* hilotropía.
hymen *n.* himen.
  annular hymen himen anular.
  circular hymen himen circular.
  cribriform hymen himen cribriforme.
  denticular hymen himen denticulado, himen denticular, himen franjeado.
  denticulate hymen himen denticulado, himen denticular.
  falciform hymen himen falciforme.
  fenestrated hymen himen fenestrado.

  hymen bifenestratus himen bifenestrado.
  hymen biforis himen bifenestrado.
  hymen sculptatus himen esculpido.
  hymen septate himen tabicado.
  hymen septus himen septado.
  hymen subseptus himen subseptus, himen subtabicado.
  imperforated hymen himen imperforado.
  infundibuliform hymen himen infundibuliforme.
  septate hymen himen septado.
  vertical hymen himen vertical.
hymenal *adj.* himenal.
hymenectomy *n.* himenectomía.
hymenitis *n.* himenitis.
hymenolepiasis *n.* himenolepiasis.
hymenolepidid *adj.* himenolépido, -da.
hymenopterism *n.* himenopterismo.
hymenorrhaphy *n.* himenorrafia.
hymenotomy *n.* himenotomía.
hyoepiglottic *adj.* hioepiglótico, -ca.
hyoepiglottidean *adj.* hioepiglótico, -ca.
hyoglossal *adj.* hiogloso, -sa.
hyoid *adj.* hioide, hioideo, -a, hioides.
hyopharyngeal *adj.* hiofaríngeo, -a.
hyothyroid *adj.* hiotiroide, hiotiroideo, -a.
hypacidemia *n.* hipacidemia, hipoacidemia.
hypacusia *n.* hipacusia, hipoacusia, hipoacusis.
hypacusis *n.* hipacusis, hipoacusia, hipoacusis.
hypalbuminemia *n.* hipalbuminemia, hipoalbuminemia.
hypalbuminosis *n.* hipoalbuminosis,.
hypalgesia *n.* hipalgesia, hipoalgesia.
hypalgesic *adj.* hipalgésico, -ca, hipoalgésico, -ca.
hypalgetic *adj.* hipalgésico, -ca, hipoalgésico, -ca.
hypalgia *n.* hipoalgia.
hypamnesia *n.* hipoamnesia.
hypamnion *n.* hipoamnios.
hypamnios *n.* hipamnios, hipoamnios.
hyparterial *adj.* hiparterial, hipoarterial.
hypaxial *adj.* hipaxial, hipaxil, hipoaxial.
hypencephalon *n.* hipencéfalo.
hypenchime *n.* hipénquima.
hyperabsorption *n.* hiperabsorción.
hyperacanthosis *n.* hiperacantosis.
hyperacid *adj.* hiperácido, -da.
hyperacidaminuria *n.* hiperacidaminuria.
hyperacidity *n.* hiperacidez.
  gastric hyperacidity hiperacidez gástrica.
hyperactive *adj.* hiperactivo, -va.
hyperactivity *n.* hiperactividad.
hyperacuity *n.* hiperacusia.
hyperacusia *n.* hiperacusia.
hyperacusis *n.* hiperacusis.
hyperacute *adj.* hiperagudo, -da.
hyperadenosis *n.* hiperadenosis.
hyperadiposis *n.* hiperadiposis.
hyperadiposity *n.* hiperadiposidad.
hyperadrenalcorticalism *n.* hiperadrenocorticalismo.
hyperadrenalinemia *n.* hiperadrenalinemia.
hyperadrenalism *n.* hiperadrenalismo, hiperadrenia.
hyperadrenocorticalism *n.* hiperadrenocorticalismo.
hyperadrenocorticism *n.* hiperadrenocorticismo.
hyperalbuminemia *n.* hiperalbuminemia.
hyperalbuminosis *n.* hiperalbuminosis.
hyperaldosteronemia *n.* hiperaldosteronemia.
hyperaldosteronism *n.* hiperaldosteronismo.
hyperalgesia *n.* hiperalgesia.

  auditory hyperalgesia hiperalgesia auditiva.
  muscular hyperalgesia hiperalgesia muscular.
hyperalgesic *adj.* hiperalgésico, -ca.
hyperalgetic *adj.* hiperalgético, -ca.
hyperalgia *n.* hiperalgia.
hyperalimentation *n.* hiperalimentación.
  parenteral hyperalimentation hiperalimentación parenteral.
hyperalimentosis *n.* hiperalimentosis.
hyperkalescence *n.* hiperalcalescencia.
hyperalkalinity *n.* hiperalcalinidad.
hyperallantoinuria *n.* hiperalantoinuria.
hyperalonemia *n.* hiperalonemia.
hyperalphalipoproteinemia *n.* hiperalfalipoproteinemia.
hyperaminoacidemia *n.* hiperaminoacidemia.
hyperaminoaciduria *n.* hiperaminoaciduria.
hyperammonemia *n.* hiperamonemia, hiperamoniemia.
  cerebroatrophic hyperammonemia hiperamonemia cerebroatrófica.
  type I congenital hyperammonemia hiperamonemia congénita tipo I.
  type II congenital hyperammonemia hiperamonemia congénita tipo II.
hyperammonuria *n.* hiperamonuria.
hyperamylasemia *n.* hiperamilasemia.
hyperandrogenemia *n.* hiperandrogenemia.
hyperandrogenism *n.* hiperandrogenismo.
hyperaphia *n.* hiperafia.
hyperaphic *adj.* hiperáfico, -ca.
hyperargininemia *n.* hiperargininemia.
hyperazotemia *n.* hiperazoemia.
hyperazoturia *n.* hiperazoturia.
hyperbaric *adj.* hiperbárico, -ca.
hyperbarism *n.* hiperbarismo.
hyperbasophilic *adj.* hiperbasofílico, -ca.
hyperbetalipoproteinemia *n.* hiperbetalipoproteinemia.
  familial hyperbetalipoproteinemia hiperbetalipoproteinemia familiar.
  familial hyperbetalipoproteinemia and hyperprebetalipoproteinemia hiperbetalipoproteinemia familiar e hiperprebetalipoproteinemia.
hyperbicarbonatemia *n.* hiperbicarbonatemia.
hyperbilirubinemia *n.* hiperbilirrubinemia.
  congenital hyperbilirubinemia hiperbilirrubinemia congénita.
  conjugated hyperbilirubinemia hiperbilirrubinemia conjugada.
  hyperbilirubinemia of the newborn hiperbilirrubinemia del recién nacido.
  neonatal hyperbilirubinemia hiperbilirrubinemia neonatal.
  unconjugated hyperbilirubinemia hiperbilirrubinemia no conjugada.
hyperblastosis *n.* hiperblastosis.
hyperbrachycephalic *adj.* hiperbraquicefálico, -ca.
hyperbrachycephaly *n.* hiperbraquicefalia.
hyperbradykinemia *n.* hiperbradicinemia.
hyperbradykininism *n.* hiperbradicininismo.
hypercalcemia *n.* hipercalcemia.
  familial hypocalciuric hypercalcemia hipercalcemia hipocalciúrica familiar.
  idiopathic hypercalcemia hipercalcemia idiopática, hipercalcemia idiopática del lactante.
  idiopathic hypercalcemia of infants hipercalcemia idiopática, hipercalcemia idiopática del lactante.

hypercalcinemia *n.* hipercalcinemia.
hypercalcinuria *n.* hipercalcinuria.
hypercalcipexy *n.* hipercalcipexia.
hypercalcitoninemia *n.* hipercalcitoninemia.
hypercalciuria *n.* hipercalciuria.
  absortive hypercalciuria hipercalciuria absortiva.
  idiopathic hypercalciuria hipercalciuria idiopática.
  renal hypercalciuria hipercalciuria renal.
hypercalcuria *n.* hipercalcuria.
hypercapnia *n.* hipercapnia.
hypercapnic *adj.* hipercápnico, -ca.
hypercarbia *n.* hipercarbia.
hypercardia *n.* hipercardia.
hypercarotenemia *n.* hipercarotinemia.
hypercarotinemia *n.* hipercarotinemia.
hypercatharsis *n.* hipercatarsis.
hypercathartic *adj.* hipercatártico, -ca.
hypercellular *adj.* hipercelular.
hypercellularity *n.* hipercelularidad.
hypercementosis *n.* hipercementosis.
hypercetonuria *n.* hipercetonuria, hiperquetonuria.
hyperchloremia *n.* hipercloremia.
hyperchloremic *adj.* hiperclorémico, -ca.
hyperchlorhydria *n.* hiperclorhidria.
hyperchloruration *n.* hipercloruración.
hyperchloruria *n.* hipercloruria.
hypercholesteremia *n.* hipercolesteremia.
hypercholesteremic *adj.* hipercolesterémico, -ca.
hypercholesterinemia *n.* hipercolesterinemia.
hypercholesterolemia *n.* hipercolesterolemia.
  familial hypercholesterolemia hipercolesterolemia familiar.
  familial hypercholesterolemia with hyperlipemia hipercolesterolemia familiar con hiperlipemia.
hypercholesterolemic *adj.* hipercolesterolémico, -ca.
hypercholesterolia *n.* hipercolesterolia.
hypercholia *n.* hipercolia.
hyperchondroplasia *n.* hipercondroplasia.
hyperchromaffinism *n.* hipercromafinismo.
hyperchromasia *n.* hipercromasia.
hyperchromatic *adj.* hipercromático, -ca.
hyperchromatism *n.* hipercromatismo, hipercromatosis.
hyperchromatopsia *n.* hipercromatopsia.
hyperchromemia *n.* hipercromemia.
hyperchromia *n.* hipercromía.
hyperchromic *adj.* hipercrómico, -ca.
hyperchylia *n.* hiperquilia.
hyperchylomicronemia *n.* hiperquilomicronemia.
  familial hyperchylomicronemia hiperquilomicronemia familiar.
  familial hyperchylomicronemia with hyperprebetalipoproteinemia hiperquilomicronemia familiar con hiperprebetalipoproteinemia.
hypercoagulability *n.* hipercoagulabilidad.
hypercoagulable *adj.* hipercoagulable.
hypercoria *n.* hipercoria.
hypercorticalism *n.* hipercorticalismo.
hypercorticism *n.* hipercorticismo.
hypercorticoidism *n.* hipercorticoidismo.
hypercortisolemia *n.* hipercortisolemia.
hypercortisolism *n.* hipercortisolismo.
hypercreatinemia *n.* hipercreatinemia.
hypercrine *adj.* hipercrino, -na.
hypercrinia *n.* hipercrinia, hipercrinismo.
hypercrisia *n.* hipercrisia.
hypercrupremia *n.* hipercupremia.

hypercryalgesia *n.* hipercrialgesia.
hypercryesthesia *n.* hipercriestesia.
hypercupriuria *n.* hipercupriuria.
hypercyanotic *adj.* hipercianótico, -ca.
hypercyesis *n.* hiperciesis.
hypercythemia *n.* hipercitemia.
hypercytochromia *n.* hipercitocromía.
hypercytosis *n.* hipercitosis.
hyperdactylism *n.* hiperdactilismo.
hyperdactyly *n.* hiperdactilia.
hyperdens *adj.* hiperdenso, -sa.
hyperdensity *n.* hiperdensidad.
hyperdiastole *n.* hiperdiástole.
hyperdicrotic *adj.* hiperdicrótico, -ca.
hyperdicrotism *n.* hiperdicrotismo.
hyperdiploid *adj.* hiperdiploide.
hyperdipsia *n.* hiperdipsia.
hyperdistension *n.* hiperdistensión.
hyperdiuresis *n.* hiperdiuresis.
hyperdontia *n.* hiperdontia.
hyperdynamia *n.* hiperdinamia.
  hyperdynamia uteri hiperdinamia uterina.
hyperdynamic *adj.* hiperdinámico, -ca.
hypereccrisia *n.* hiperecrisia.
hypereccrisis *n.* hiperecrisis.
hypereccritic *adj.* hiperecrítico, -ca.
hyperechema *n.* hiperequema.
hyperechogenic *adj.* hiperecogénico, -ca.
hyperechogenicity *n.* hiperecogenicidad.
hyperechoic *adj.* hiperecoico, -ca.
hyperelectrolytemia *n.* hiperelectrolitemia.
hyperemesis *n.* hiperemesis.
  hyperemesis gravidarum hiperemesis del embarazo, hiperemesis gravídica.
  hyperemesis lactentium hiperemesis de la lactancia, hiperemesis lactentium.
hyperemetic *adj.* hiperemético, -ca.
hyperemia *n.* hiperemia.
  active hyperemia hiperemia activa, hiperemia arterial.
  arterial hyperemia hiperemia activa, hiperemia arterial.
  Bier's hyperemia hiperemia de Bier.
  collateral hyperemia hiperemia colateral.
  constriction hyperemia hiperemia por constricción.
  fluxionary hyperemia hiperemia congestiva, hiperemia fluxionaria.
  leptomeningeal hyperemia hiperemia leptomeníngea.
  passive hyperemia hiperemia pasiva.
  peristatic hyperemia hiperemia peristática.
  reactive hyperemia hiperemia reactiva.
  venous hyperemia hiperemia venosa.
hyperemic *adj.* hiperémico, -ca.
hyperemization *n.* hiperemización.
hyperencephalus *n.* hiperencéfalo.
hyperencephaly *n.* hiperencefalia.
hyperendemic *adj.* hiperendémico, -ca.
hyperendocrinism *n.* hiperendocrinismo.
hypereosinophilia *n.* hipereosinofilia.
  filarial hypereosinophilia hipereosinofilia filarial.
hyperephidrosis *n.* hiperefidrosis.
hyperepinephrinemia *n.* hiperepinefrinemia.
hyperepithymia *n.* hiperepitemia, hiperepitimia.
hyperequilibrium *n.* hiperequilibrio.
hypererethism *n.* hipereretismo.
hyperergasia *n.* hiperergasia.
hyperergia *n.* hiperergia.
hyperergic *adj.* hiperérgico, -ca.
hyperergy *n.* hiperergia.
hypererytrocythemia *n.* hipereritrocitemia.
hyperesophoria *n.* hiperesoforia.

hyperesthesia *n.* hiperestesia.
  auditory hyperesthesia hiperestesia acústica, hiperestesia auditiva.
  cerebral hyperesthesia hiperestesia cerebral.
  cervical hyperesthesia hiperestesia cervical.
  gustatory hyperesthesia hiperestesia gustatoria.
  hyperesthesia optica hiperestesia óptica.
  muscular hyperesthesia hiperestesia muscular.
  oneiric hyperesthesia hiperestesia onírica.
  tactile hyperesthesia hiperestesia táctil.
hyperesthetic *adj.* hiperestésico, -ca.
hyperestrinemia *n.* hiperestrinemia.
hyperestrinism *n.* hiperestrinismo.
hyperestrogenemia *n.* hiperestrogenemia.
hyperestrogenism *n.* hiperestrogenismo.
hypereuryopia *n.* hipereuriopía, hipereuropía.
hyperevolutism *n.* hiperevolutismo.
hyperexcretory *adj.* hiperexcretorio, -ria.
hyperexophoria *n.* hiperexoforia.
hyperexplesia *n.* hiperexplexia.
hyperextension *n.* hiperextensión.
hyperferremia *n.* hiperferremia.
hyperferremic *adj.* hiperferrémico, -ca.
hyperferricemia *n.* hiperferricemia.
hyperfibrinogenemia *n.* hiperfibrinogenemia.
hyperfibrinolysis *n.* hiperfibrinólisis.
hyperflexion *n.* hiperflexión.
hyperfolliculinemia *n.* hiperfoliculinemia.
hyperfolliculinism *n.* hiperfoliculismo.
hyperfolliculinuria *n.* hiperfoliculinuria.
hyperfolliculoidism *n.* hiperfoliculoidismo.
hyperfunction *n.* hiperfunción.
  adrenal hyperfunction hiperfunción suprarrenal.
hyperfunctioning *n.* hiperfuncionamiento.
hypergalactia *n.* hipergalactia.
hypergalactosis *n.* hipergalactosis.
hypergammaglobulinemia *n.* hipergammaglobulinemia.
  monoclonal hypergammaglobulinemia hipergammaglobulinemia monoclonal.
hypergastrinemia *n.* hipergastrinemia.
hypergenesis *n.* hipergénesis.
hypergenetic *adj.* hipergenético, -ca.
hypergenitalism *n.* hipergenitalismo.
hypergeusesthesia *n.* hipergeusestesia.
hypergeusia *n.* hipergeusia.
hypergia *n.* hipoergia.
hyperglandular *adj.* hiperglandular.
hyperglobulinemia *n.* hiperglobulinemia.
hyperglucagonemia *n.* hiperglucagonemia.
hyperglucogenolysis *n.* hiperglucogenólisis.
hyperglycemia *n.* hiperglicemia, hiperglucemia.
  non-ketotic hyperglycemia hiperglucemia no cetósica.
  posthypoglycemic hyperglycemia hiperglucemia poshipoglucémica.
hyperglyceridemia *n.* hipergliceridemia.
  endogenous hyperglyceridemia hipergliceridemia endógena.
  exogenous hyperglyceridemia hipergliceridemia exógena.
hyperglyceridemic *adj.* hipergliceridémico, -ca.
hyperglycinemia *n.* hiperglicinemia.
hyperglycinuria *n.* hiperglicinuria.
  hyperglycinuria with hyperglycinemia hiperglicinuria con hiperglicinemia.
hyperglycistia *n.* hiperglicistia.
hyperglycorrhachia *n.* hiperglucorraquia.
hyperglycosemia *n.* hiperglucosemia.
hyperglycosuria *n.* hiperglucosuria.
hyperglyoxylemia *n.* hiperglioxilemia.

hypergonadism *n.* hipergonadismo.
hypergonadotropic *adj.* hipergonadotrópico, -ca.
hypergranulosis *n.* hipergranulosis.
hyperguanidinemia *n.* hiperguanidinemia.
hypergynecosmia *n.* hiperginecosmia.
hyperhemoglobinemia *n.* hiperhemoglobinemia.
hyperheparinemia *n.* hiperheparinemia.
hyperhepathia *n.* hiperhepatía.
hyperhidrosis *n.* hiperhidrosis, hiperidrosis.
 gustatory hyperhidrosis hiperhidrosis gustatoria.
 hyperhidrosis oleosa hiperhidrosis oleosa.
 hyperhidrosis unilateralis hiperhidrosis lateral.
hyperhidrotic *adj.* hiperhidrótico, -ca.
hyperhormonism *n.* hiperhormonismo.
hyperhydrochloria *n.* hiperhidrocloria.
hyperhydropexis *n.* hiperhidropexia.
hyperhydropexy *n.* hiperhidropexia.
hyperhydroxyprolinemia *n.* hiperhidroxiprolinemia.
hyperhypophysism *n.* hiperhipofisismo.
hyperimidodipeptiuria *n.* hiperimidodipeptiuria.
hyperimmune *adj.* hiperinmune.
hyperimmunity *n.* hiperinmunidad.
hyperimmunization *n.* hiperinmunización.
hyperimmunoglobulinemia *n.* hiperinmunoglobulinemia.
 hyperimmunoglobulinemia E hiperinmunoglobulinemia E.
hyperindicanemia *n.* hiperindicanemia.
hyperinfection *n.* hiperinfección.
hyperingesta *n.* sobreingesta.
hyperingestion *n.* hiperingestión, sobreingestión.
hyperinosemia *n.* hiperinosemia.
hyperinosis *n.* hiperinosis.
hyperinsuflation *n.* hiperinsuflación.
 periodic hyperinsuflation hiperinsuflación periódica.
hyperinsular *adj.* hiperinsular.
hyperinsulinemia *n.* hiperinsulinemia.
hyperinsulinism *n.* hiperinsulinismo.
 alimentary hyperinsulinism hiperinsulinismo alimentario.
hyperintense *adj.* hiperintenso, -sa.
hyperintensity *n.* hiperintensidad.
hyperiodemia *n.* hiperyodemia.
hyperirritability *n.* hiperirritabilidad.
hyperisotonia *n.* hiperisotonía.
hyperisotonic *adj.* hiperisotónico, -ca.
hyperkalemia *n.* hipercaliemia.
hyperkaliemia *n.* hipercaliemia.
hyperkaluresis *n.* hipercaliuresis.
hyperkeratinization *n.* hiperqueratinización.
hyperkeratomycosis *n.* hiperqueratomicosis.
hyperkeratosis *n.* hiperqueratosis.
 eccentric hyperkeratosis hiperqueratosis excéntrica.
 epidermolytic hyperkeratosis hiperqueratosis epidermolítica.
 follicular hyperkeratosis hiperqueratosis folicular.
 hyperkeratosis congenita hiperqueratosis congénita.
 hyperkeratosis figurata centrifuga atrophica hiperqueratosis figurada centrífuga atrófica.
 hyperkeratosis follicularis hiperqueratosis folicular.
 hyperkeratosis follicularis et parafollicularis hiperqueratosis folicular y parafolicular.
 hyperkeratosis follicularis et parafollicula-

ris in cutem penetrans hiperqueratosis follicularis et parafollicularis in cutem penetrans, hiperqueratosis follicularis in cutem penetrans.
 hyperkeratosis follicularis in cutem penetrans hiperqueratosis follicularis et parafollicularis in cutem penetrans, hiperqueratosis follicularis in cutem penetrans.
 hyperkeratosis lacunaris hiperqueratosis lacunar, hiperqueratosis lagunar.
 hyperkeratosis lenticularis perstans hiperqueratosis lenticularis perstans.
 hyperkeratosis of palms and soles hiperqueratosis congénita palmar y plantar, hiperqueratosis palmar y plantar.
 hyperkeratosis penetrans hiperqueratosis penetrans, hiperqueratosis penetrante.
 hyperkeratosis subungualis hiperqueratosis subungueal.
 progressive dystrophic hyperkeratosis hiperqueratosis distrófica progresiva.
hyperketonemia *n.* hipercetonemia.
hyperketonuria *n.* hipercetonuria, hiperquetonuria.
hyperketosis *n.* hipercetosis, hiperquetosis.
hyperkinemia *n.* hipercinemia.
hyperkinemic *adj.* hipercinémico, -ca.
hyperkinesia *n.* hipercinesia, hiperquinesia.
hyperkinesis *n.* hipercinesia, hipercinesis.
hyperkinetic *adj.* hipercinético, -ca.
hyperkoria *n.* hipercoria.
hyperlactacidemia *n.* hiperlactacidemia.
hyperlactation *n.* hiperlactación.
hyperlaxicity *n.* hiperlaxitud.
hyperlecithinemia *n.* hiperlecitinemia.
hyperleukocytosis *n.* hiperleucocitosis.
hyperlexia *n.* hiperlexia.
hyperleydigism *n.* hiperleydigismo.
hyperlipemia *n.* hiperlipemia.
 carbohydrate-induced hyperlipemia hiperlipemia inducida por carbohidratos, hiperlipemia provocada por carbohidratos.
 combined fat-and carbohydrate-induced hyperlipemia hiperlipemia combinada inducida por grasas y carbohidratos.
 essential familial hyperlipemia hiperlipemia familiar esencial.
 fat-induced hyperlipemia hiperlipemia inducida por grasas, hiperlipemia provocada por grasas.
 idiopathic hyperlipemia hiperlipemia idiopática.
 mixed hyperlipemia hiperlipemia mixta.
hyperlipidemia *n.* hiperlipidemia.
hyperlipoidemia *n.* hiperlipidemia, hiperlipoidemia.
hyperlipoproteinemia *n.* hiperlipoproteinemia.
 acquired hyperlipoproteinemia hiperlipoproteinemia adquirida.
 combined hyperlipoproteinemia hiperlipoproteinemia combinada familiar.
 familial hyperlipoproteinemia hiperlipoproteinemia familiar.
 mixed hyperlipoproteinemia hiperlipoproteinemia mixta.
 type I familial hyperlipoproteinemia hiperlipoproteinemia familiar de tipo I.
 type II familial hyperlipoproteinemia hiperlipoproteinemia familiar de tipo II.
 type IIa familial hyperlipoproteinemia hiperlipoproteinemia familiar de tipo IIa.
 type IIb familial hyperlipoproteinemia hiperlipoproteinemia familiar de tipo IIb.
 type III familial hyperlipoproteinemia hiperlipoproteinemia familiar de tipo III.

 type IV familial hyperlipoproteinemia hiperlipoproteinemia familiar de tipo IV.
 type V familial hyperlipoproteinemia hiperlipoproteinemia familiar de tipo V.
hyperliposis *n.* hiperliposis.
hyperlithemia *n.* hiperlitemia.
hyperlithic *adj.* hiperlítico, -ca.
hyperlithuria *n.* hiperlituria.
hyperlordosis *n.* hiperlordosis.
hyperlucency *n.* hiperlucencia.
hyperlucent *adj.* hiperlucente.
hyperluteinization *n.* hiperluteinización.
hyperlysinemia *n.* hiperlisinemia.
hyperlysinuria *n.* hiperlisinuria.
hypermagnesemia *n.* hipermagnesemia.
hypermastia *n.* hipermastia.
hypermastigote *n.* hipermastigoto.
hypermature *adj.* hipermaduro, -ra.
hypermelanotic *adj.* hipermelanótico, -ca.
hypermenorrhea *n.* hipermenorrea.
hypermetabolic *adj.* hipermetabólico, -ca.
hypermetabolism *n.* hipermetabolismo.
 extrathyroidal hypermetabolism hipermetabolismo extratiroideo.
hypermetaplasia *n.* hipermetaplasia.
hypermetria *n.* hipermetría.
hypermetrope *n.* hipermétrope.
hypermetropia *n.* hipermetropía.
 absolute hypermetropia hipermetropía absoluta.
 axial hypermetropia hipermetropía axial, hipermetropía axil.
 curvature hypermetropia hipermetropía de curvatura.
 facultative hypermetropia hipermetropía facultativa.
 latent hypermetropia hipermetropía latente.
 manifest hypermetropia hipermetropía manifiesta.
 relative hypermetropia hipermetropía relativa.
 total hypermetropia hipermetropía total.
hypermetropy *n.* hipermetropía.
hypermimia *n.* hipermimia.
hypermineralization *n.* hipermineralización.
hypermnesia *n.* hipermnesia.
hypermnesic *adj.* hipermnésico, -ca.
hypermobility *n.* hipermovilidad.
hypermodal *adj.* hipermodal.
hypermorph *n.* hipermorfo, -fa.
hypermotility *n.* hipermotilidad.
hypermyesthesia *n.* hipermiestesia.
hypermyotonia *n.* hipermiotonía.
hypermyotrophy *n.* hipermiotrofia.
hypernasality *n.* hipernasalidad.
hypernatremia *n.* hipernatremia.
 hypodipsic hypernatremia hipernatremia hipodípsica.
hypernatremic *adj.* hipernatrémico, -ca.
hypernatronemia *n.* hipernatronemia.
hyperneocytosis *n.* hiperneocitosis.
hypernephroid *adj.* hipernefroide.
hypernephroma *n.* hipernefroma, nefroepitelioma.
hypernitremia *n.* hipernitremia.
hypernutrition *n.* hipernutrición.
hyperoncotic *adj.* hiperoncótico, -ca.
hyperonychosis *n.* hiperonicosis, hiperoniquia.
hyperope *n.* hipérope.
hyperopia *n.* hiperopía.
hyperopic *adj.* hiperópico, -ca.
hyperorchidism *n.* hiperorquidismo.
hyperorexia *n.* hiperorexia.
hyperornithinemia *n.* hiperornitinemia.
hyperorthocytosis *n.* hiperortocitosis.

hyperosmolality *n.* hiperosmolalidad.
hyperosmolarity *n.* hiperosmolaridad.
hyperosmotic *adj.* hiperosmótico, -ca.
hyperosteogeny *n.* hiperosteogenia.
hyperosteoidosis *n.* hiperosteoidosis.
hyperostosis *n.* hiperostosis.
 ankylosing age-related vertebral hyperostosis hiperostosis vertebral senil anquilosante.
 ankylosing hyperostosis hiperostosis anquilosante.
 child cortical hyperostosis hiperostosis cortical infantil.
 diffuse idiopathic skeletal hyperostosis hiperostosis esquelética idiopática difusa.
 flowing hyperostosis hiperostosis confluente, hiperostosis de flujo.
 frontal internal hyperostosis hiperostosis de Morgagni, hiperostosis frontal interna.
 generalized cortical hyperostosis hiperostosis cortical generalizada.
 hyperostosis corticalis deformans hiperostosis cortical deformante.
 hyperostosis corticalis deformans juvenilis hiperostosis cortical juvenil deformante.
 hyperostosis cranii hiperostosis craneal.
 hyperostosis frontalis interna hiperostosis de Morgagni, hiperostosis frontal interna.
 infantile cortical hyperostosis hiperostosis cortical del lactante.
 senile ankylosing hyperostosis of the spine hiperostosis anquilosante senil del raquis.
 streak hyperostosis hiperostosis veteada.
hyperostotic *adj.* hiperostósico, -ca, hiperostótico, -ca.
hyperovarianism *n.* hiperovarismo.
hyperovarism *n.* hiperovarismo.
hyperoxaluria *n.* hiperoxaluria.
 enteric hyperoxaluria hiperoxaluria entérica.
 primary hyperoxaluria hiperoxaluria primaria.
 primary hyperoxaluria and oxalosis hiperoxaluria primaria y oxalosis.
 type I primary hyperoxaluria hiperoxaluria primaria tipo I.
 type II primary hyperoxaluria hiperoxaluria primaria tipo II.
hyperoxemia *n.* hiperoxemia.
hyperoxia *n.* hiperoxia.
hyperoxic *adj.* hiperóxico, -ca.
hyperoxidation *n.* hiperoxidación.
hyperoxygenation *n.* hiperoxigenación.
hyperpallesthesia *n.* hiperpalestesia.
hyperpancreatism *n.* hiperpancreatismo.
hyperpancreorrhea *n.* hiperpancreorrea.
hyperparasite *n.* hiperparásito.
 second degree hyperparasite hiperparásito de segundo grado.
hyperparasitism *n.* hiperparasitismo.
hyperparathyroidism *n.* hiperparatiroidismo.
 primary hyperparathyroidism hiperparatiroidismo primario.
 secondary hyperparathyroidism hiperparatiroidismo secundario.
 tertiary hyperparathyroidism hiperparatiroidismo terciario.
hyperparotidism *n.* hiperparotidismo.
hyperpathia *n.* hiperpatía.
hyperpepsia *n.* hiperpepsia.
hyperpepsinemia *n.* hiperpepsinemia.
hyperpepsinia *n.* hiperpepsinia.
hyperpepsinuria *n.* hiperpepsinuria.
hyperperistalis *n.* hiperperistalsis.
hyperperistalsis *n.* hiperperistaltismo.
hyperpermeability *n.* hiperpermeabilidad.

hyperpexia *n.* hiperpexia.
hyperpexy *n.* hiperpexia.
hyperphagia *n.* hiperfagia.
hyperphalangia *n.* hiperfalangia.
hyperphalangism *n.* hiperfalangismo.
hyperphasia *n.* hiperfasia.
hyperphenylalaninemia *n.* hiperfenilalaninemia.
hyperphonesis *n.* hiperfonesis.
hyperphonia *n.* hiperfonía.
hyperphoria *n.* hiperforia.
hyperphosphatasemia *n.* hiperfosfatasemia.
 chronic congenital idiopathic hyperphosphatasemia hiperfosfatasemia idiopática congénita crónica.
 hyperphosphatasemia tarda hiperfosfatasemia tardía.
hyperphosphatasia *n.* hiperfosfatasia.
hyperphosphatemia *n.* hiperfosfatemia.
hyperphosphaturia *n.* hiperfosfaturia.
hyperphosphoremia *n.* hiperfosforemia.
hyperpiesia *n.* hiperpiesia, hiperpiesis.
hyperpietic *adj.* hiperpiético, -ca.
hyperpigmentation *n.* hiperpigmentación.
hyperpinealism *n.* hiperpinealismo.
hyperpipecolatemia *n.* hiperpipecolatemia.
hyperpituitarism *n.* hiperpituitarismo.
hyperplasia *n.* hiperplasia.
 adenoid hyperplasia hiperplasia adenoidea.
 adrenal medullary hyperplasia hiperplasia medular suprarrenal.
 adrenocortical hyperplasia hiperplasia corticosuprarrenal.
 angiofollicular lymph node hyperplasia hiperplasia ganglionar mediastínica angiofolicular.
 angiolymphoid hyperplasia hiperplasia angiolinfoide, hiperplasia angiolinfoide con eosinofilia.
 angiolymphoid hyperplasia with eosinophilia hiperplasia angiolinfoide, hiperplasia angiolinfoide con eosinofilia.
 atypical melanocytic hyperplasia hiperplasia melanocítica atípica.
 basal cell hyperplasia hiperplasia basocelular.
 benign mediastinal lymph node hyperplasia hiperplasia ganglionar mediastínica benigna.
 benign prostatic hyperplasia hiperplasia prostática benigna (HBP).
 chronic perforating pulp hyperplasia hiperplasia perforante crónica de la pulpa.
 congenital adrenal hyperplasia hiperplasia adrenal congénita, hiperplasia suprarrenal congénita.
 corticotroph hyperplasia hiperplasia corticotropa.
 cutaneous lymphoid hyperplasia hiperplasia linfoide cutánea.
 cystic hyperplasia hiperplasia quística.
 cystic hyperplasia of the breast hiperplasia quística de la mama.
 denture hyperplasia hiperplasia de la dentadura.
 Dilantin hyperplasia hiperplasia por Dilantín.
 ductal hyperplasia hiperplasia canalicular.
 endometrial hyperplasia hiperplasia del endometrio, hiperplasia endometrial.
 fibromuscular hyperplasia hiperplasia fibromuscular.
 fibrous inflammatory hyperplasia hiperplasia inflamatoria, hiperplasia inflamatoria fibrosa.

 focal epithelial hyperplasia hiperplasia epitelial focal.
 giant follicular hyperplasia hiperplasia folicular gigante.
 gingival hyperplasia hiperplasia gingival.
 hyperplasia cementum hiperplasia del cemento.
 inflammatory fibrous hyperplasia hiperplasia fibrosa inflamatoria.
 inflammatory hyperplasia hiperplasia inflamatoria, hiperplasia inflamatoria fibrosa.
 inflammatory papillary hyperplasia hiperplasia papilar inflamatoria.
 intravascular papillary endothelial hyperplasia hiperplasia endotelial papilar intravascular.
 juxtaglomerular cell hyperplasia hiperplasia de células yuxtaglomerulares.
 lactotroph hyperplasia hiperplasia lactótropa.
 lipoid hyperplasia hiperplasia lipoide.
 neoplastic hyperplasia hiperplasia neoplásica.
 nodular hyperplasia of the prostate hiperplasia nodular de próstata.
 nodular lymphoid hyperplasia hiperplasia linfoide nodular.
 nodular regenerative hyperplasia hiperplasia regenerativa nodular.
 ovarian stromal hyperplasia hiperplasia ovárica del estroma.
 parathyroid hyperplasia hiperplasia paratiroidea.
 pituitary hyperplasia hiperplasia hipofisaria.
 polar hyperplasia hiperplasia polar.
 pseudocarcinomatous hyperplasia hiperplasia seudocarcinomatosa.
 pseudoepitheliomatous hyperplasia hiperplasia seudoepiteliomatosa.
 thyrotroph hyperplasia hiperplasia tireotropa.
 verrucous hyperplasia hiperplasia verrugosa.
hyperplasmia *n.* hiperplasmia.
hyperplastic *adj.* hiperplásico, -ca.
hyperploid *adj.* hiperploide.
hyperploidy *n.* hiperploidía.
hyperpnea *n.* hiperpnea.
hyperpneic *adj.* hiperpneico, -ca.
hyperpolarization *n.* hiperpolarización.
hyperpolypeptidemia *n.* hiperpolipeptidemia.
hyperponesis *n.* hiperponesis.
hyperponetic *adj.* hiperponético, -ca.
hyperposia *n.* hiperposia.
hyperpotassemia *n.* hipercalemia, hiperpotasemia.
hyperpragia *n.* hiperpragia.
hyperprebetalipoproteinemia *n.* hiperprebetalipoproteinemia.
 familial hyperprebetalipoproteinemia hiperprebetalipoproteinemia familiar.
hyperpresbyopia *n.* hiperpresbiopía.
hyperproinsulinemia *n.* hiperproinsulinemia.
hyperprolactinemia *n.* hiperprolactinemia.
hyperprolactinemic *adj.* hiperprolactinémico, -ca.
hyperprolinemia *n.* hiperprolinemia.
hyperprosexia *n.* hiperprosexia.
hyperproteinemia *n.* hiperproteinemia.
hyperproteosis *n.* hiperproteosis.
hyperpselaphesia *n.* hiperpselafesia.
hyperptyalism *n.* hiperptialismo.
hyperpyremia *n.* hiperpiremia.
hyperpyretic *adj.* hiperpirético, -ca.

hyperpyrexia *n.* hiperpirexia.
  fulminant hyperpyrexia hiperpirexia fulminante.
  heat hyperpyrexia hiperpirexia por calor.
  malignant hyperpyrexia hiperpirexia maligna.
hyperpyrexial *adj.* hiperpirático, -ca, hiperpiréxico, -ca.
hyperreactive *adj.* hiperreactivo, -va.
hyperreactivity *n.* hiperreactividad.
  bronchial hyperreactivity hiperreactividad bronquial.
hyperreflexia *n.* hiperreflexia.
  autonomic hyperreflexia hiperreflexia autónoma.
hyperreninemia *n.* hiperreninemia.
hyperreninemic *adj.* hiperreninémico, -ca.
hypersalemia *n.* hipersalemia.
hypersaline *adj.* hipersalino, -na.
hypersalivation *n.* hipersalivación.
hypersarcosinemia *n.* hipersarcosinemia.
hypersecretion *n.* hipersecreción.
  gastric hypersecretion hipersecreción gástrica.
hypersegmentation *n.* hipersegmentación.
hypersensitivity *n.* hipersensibilidad.
  anaphylactic hypersensitivity hipersensibilidad anafiláctica.
  contact hypersensitivity hipersensibilidad por contacto.
  cutaneous basophil hypersensitivity hipersensibilidad basófila cutánea.
  cytotoxic hypersensitivity hipersensibilidad citotóxica.
  delayed hypersensitivity (DH) de tipo retardado (HTR), hipersensibilidad retardada (HR).
  delayed-type hypersensitivity (DTH) de tipo retardado (HTR), hipersensibilidad retardada (HR).
  immediate hypersensitivity hipersensibilidad inmediata.
  immune complex hypersensitivity hipersensibilidad por inmunocomplejos.
  pencil hypersensitivity hipersensibilidad de lápiz.
  rebound hypersensitivity hipersensibilidad de rebote.
  tuberculin-type hypersensitivity hipersensibilidad tipo tuberculina.
  type I hypersensitivity hipersensibilidad de tipo I.
  type II hypersensitivity hipersensibilidad de tipo II.
  type III hypersensitivity hipersensibilidad de tipo III.
hypersensitization *n.* hipersensibilización.
hyperserotonemia *n.* hiperserotonemia.
hypersexuality *n.* hipersexualidad.
hyperskeocytosis *n.* hiperesqueocitosis.
hypersomatotropism *n.* hipersomatotropismo.
hypersomia *n.* hipersomía.
hypersomnia *n.* hipersomnia.
hypersomnolence *n.* hipersomnolencia.
  primary hypersomnolence hipersomnolencia primaria.
hyperspadias *n.* hiperespadias.
hypersphyxia *n.* hiperesfixia.
hypersplenia *n.* hiperesplenia.
hypersplenism *n.* hiperesplenismo.
hypersteatosis *n.* hiperesteatosis.
hyperstereoroentgenography *n.* hiperestereorroentgenografía.
hypersthenia *n.* hiperestenia.

hypersthenic *adj.* hiperesténico, -ca.
hypersthenuria *n.* hiperestenuria.
hypersuprarenalism *n.* hipersuprarrenalismo.
hypersusceptibility *n.* hipersusceptibilidad.
hypersympathicotonus *n.* hipersimpaticotonía.
hypersystole *n.* hipersístole, hipersistolia.
hypersystolic *adj.* hipersistólico, -ca.
hypertarachia *n.* hipertaraquia.
hypertaurodontism *n.* hipertaurodontismo.
hypertelorism *n.* hipertelorismo.
  canthal hypertelorism hipertelorismo cántico.
  ocular hypertelorism hipertelorismo ocular.
  orbital hypertelorism hipertelorismo orbitario.
hypertension *n.* hipertensión.
  accelerated hypertension hipertensión acelerada.
  adrenal hypertension hipertensión suprarrenal.
  arterial hypertension hipertensión arterial.
  benign hypertension hipertensión benigna, hipertensión roja.
  benign arterial hypertension hipertensión arterial benigna.
  benign intracranial hypertension hipertensión intracraneal benigna.
  border-line arterial hypertension hipertensión arterial limítrofe.
  essential hypertension hipertensión esencial.
  essential arterial hypertension hipertensión arterial esencial.
  Goldblatt's hypertension hipertensión de Goldblatt.
  hyperreninemic arterial hypertension hipertensión arterial hiperreninémica.
  hypertensive crisis hypertension hipertensión arterial paroxística.
  idiopathic hypertension hipertensión idiopática.
  intracranial hypertension hipertensión intracraneal.
  labile hypertension hipertensión en los límites, hipertensión lábil.
  labile arterial hypertension hipertensión arterial lábil.
  low-renin hypertension hipertensión con renina baja.
  malignant hypertension hipertensión maligna.
  malignant arterial hypertension hipertensión arterial maligna.
  mild pregnancy-induced arterial hypertension hipertensión arterial transitoria del embarazo.
  ocular hypertension hipertensión ocular.
  pale hypertension hipertensión pálida.
  portal hypertension hipertensión portal.
  postpartum hypertension hipertensión posparto.
  primary hypertension hipertensión primaria.
  pulmonary hypertension hipertensión pulmonar.
  pulmonary arterial hypertension hipertensión arterial pulmonar.
  renal hypertension hipertensión renal.
  renal parenchymal arterial hypertension hipertensión arterial nefrógena.
  renovascular hypertension hipertensión renovascular.
  renovascular arterial hypertension hiper-

tensión arterial vasculorrenal, hipertensión vasculorrenal.
  secondary hypertension hipertensión secundaria.
  secondary arterial hypertension hipertensión arterial secundaria.
  splenoportal hypertension hipertensión esplenoportal.
  symptomatic hypertension hipertensión sintomática.
  systemic arterial hypertension hipertensión arterial sistémica.
  systemic venous hypertension hipertensión venosa sistémica.
  vascular hypertension hipertensión vascular.
  white coat arterial hypertension hipertensión arterial de bata blanca.
hypertensive *adj.* hipertensivo, -va, hipertenso, -sa.
hypertensor *adj.* hipertensor, -ra.
hypertermesthesia *n.* hipertermestesia, hipertermoestesia.
hypertestoidism *n.* hipertestoidismo.
hypertetraploid *adj.* hipertetraploide.
hyperthecosis *n.* hipertecosis.
  ovarian hyperthecosis hipertecosis ovárico.
  stromal hyperthecosis hipertecosis estromal.
  testoid hyperthecosis hipertecosis testoide.
hyperthelia *n.* hipertelia.
hyperthermalgesia *n.* hipertermalgesia.
hyperthermesthesia *n.* hipertermestesia.
hyperthermia *n.* hipertermia.
  habitual hyperthermia hipertermia habitual.
  hyperthermia of anesthesia hipertermia de la anestesia.
  intraoperative hyperthermia hipertermia intraoperatoria.
  limb hyperthermia hipertermia de las extremidades.
  malignant hyperthermia (MH) hipertermia maligna (HM).
  regional hyperthermia hipertermia regional.
  therapeutic hyperthermia hipertermia terapéutica.
hyperthermoesthesia *n.* hipertermestesia, hipertermoestesia.
hyperthrombinemia *n.* hipertrombinemia.
hyperthymia *n.* hipertimia.
hyperthymic *adj.* hipertímico, -ca.
hyperthymism *n.* hipertimismo.
hyperthyreosis *n.* hipertireosis.
hyperthyroid *adj.* hipertiroide, hipertiroideo, -a.
hyperthyroidism *n.* hipertiroidismo.
  apathetic hyperthyroidism hipertiroidismo apático.
  iodine-induced hyperthyroidism hipertiroidismo inducido por yodo.
  masked hyperthyroidism hipertiroidismo enmascarado.
  ophthalmic hyperthyroidism hipertiroidismo oftálmico.
  primary hyperthyroidism hipertiroidismo primario.
  secondary hyperthyroidism hipertiroidismo secundario.
hyperthyroidosis *n.* hipertiroidosis.
hyperthyroxinemia *n.* hipertiroxinemia.
  familial dysalbuminemic hyperthyroxinemia hipertiroxinemia disalbuminémica familiar.
hypertonia *n.* hipertonía.
  hypertonia polycythemica hipertonía policitémica.
  sympathetic hypertonia hipertonía simpática.

hypertonic *adj.* hipertónico, -ca.
hypertonicity *n.* hipertonicidad.
hypertoxic *adj.* hipertóxico, -ca.
hypertoxicity *n.* hipertoxicidad.
hypertrichiasis *n.* hipertriquiasis.
hypertrichophrydia *n.* hipertricofridia.
hypertrichosis *n.* hipertricosis.
  hypertrichosis lanuginosa hipertricosis lanuginosa.
  hypertrichosis lanuginosa acquisita hipertricosis lanuginosa adquirida.
  hypertrichosis partialis hipertricosis parcial.
  hypertrichosis pinae auris hipertricosis del pabellón auricular.
  hypertrichosis universalis hipertricosis universal.
  nevoid hypertrichosis hipertricosis nevoide.
hypertriploid *adj.* hipertriploide.
hypertroph *n.* hipertrofo.
hypertrophic *adj.* hipertrófico, -ca.
hypertrophy *n.* hipertrofia.
  adaptative hypertrophy hipertrofia adaptativa, hipertrofia de adaptación.
  adenoid hypertrophy hipertrofia adenoide.
  asimmetrical septal hypertrophy hipertrofia septal asimétrica.
  benign prostatic hypertrophy hipertrofia prostática benigna.
  Billroth hypertrophy hipertrofia de Billroth.
  cardiac hypertrophy hipertrofia cardíaca.
  compensatory hypertrophy hipertrofia compensadora.
  compensatory hypertrophy of the heart hipertrofia compensadora del corazón.
  compensatory renal hypertrophy hipertrofia renal, hipertrofia renal compensadora.
  complementary hypertrophy hipertrofia complementaria.
  concentric hypertrophy hipertrofia concéntrica.
  eccentric hypertrophy hipertrofia excéntrica.
  false hypertrophy hipertrofia falsa.
  functional hypertrophy hipertrofia funcional.
  giant hypertrophy of the gastric mucosa hipertrofia gigante de la mucosa gástrica.
  hemangiectatic hypertrophy hipertrofia hemangiectásica.
  hemifacial hypertrophy hipertrofia hemifacial.
  hypertrophy of the heart hipertrofia del corazón.
  lipomatous hypertrophy hipertrofia lipomatosa.
  mammary hypertrophy hipertrofia mamaria.
  Marie's hypertrophy hipertrofia de Marie.
  numerical hypertrophy hipertrofia numérica.
  physiologic hypertrophy hipertrofia fisiológica.
  prostatic hypertrophy hipertrofia prostática.
  pseudomuscular hypertrophy hipertrofia seudomuscular.
  quantitative hypertrophy hipertrofia cuantitativa.
  renal hypertrophy hipertrofia renal, hipertrofia renal compensadora.
  simple hypertrophy hipertrofia simple.
  true hypertrophy hipertrofia verdadera.
  unilateral hypertrophy hipertrofia unilateral.
  ventricular hypertrophy hipertrofia ventricular.
  vicarious hypertrophy hipertrofia vicaria, hipertrofia vicariante.

hypertropia *n.* hipertropía.
hypertryglyceridemia *n.* hipertrigliceridemia.
  carbohydrate-induced hypertryglyceridemia hipertrigliceridemia inducida por carbohidratos.
  familial hypertryglyceridemia hipertrigliceridemia familiar.
hyperuresis *n.* hiperuresis.
hyperuricemia *n.* hiperuricemia.
  hereditary hyperuricemia hiperuricemia hereditaria.
hyperuricemic *adj.* hiperuricémico, -ca.
hyperuricosuria *n.* hiperuricosuria.
hyperuricuria *n.* hiperuricuria.
hypervalinemia *n.* hipervalinemia.
hyperventilation *n.* hiperventilación.
  neurogenic central hyperventilation hiperventilación neurógena central.
hypervigilance *n.* hipervigilancia.
hyperviscosity *n.* hiperviscosidad.
hypervitaminosis *n.* hipervitaminosis.
  hypervitaminosis A hipervitaminosis A.
  hypervitaminosis D hipervitaminosis D.
hypervitaminotic *adj.* hipervitaminósico, -ca.
hypervolemia *n.* hipervolemia.
hypervolemic *adj.* hipervolémico, -ca.
hypervolia *n.* hipervolia.
hypesthesia *n.* hipestesia, hipoestesia.
hypesuprarenalemia *n.* hipersuprarrenalemia.
hypha *n.* hifa.
hyphema *n.* hipema.
hyphemia *n.* hipohemia.
  intertropical hyphemia hipohemia intertropical.
  tropical hyphemia hipohemia tropical.
hyphidrosis *n.* hipidrosis.
hyphomycetes *n.* hifomiceto.
hyphomycosis *n.* hifomicosis.
hypnagogic *adj.* hipnagógico, -ca.
hypnagogue *n.* hipnagogo.
hypnalgia *n.* hipnalgia.
hypnapagogic *adj.* hipnapagógico, -ca.
hypnic *adj.* hípnico, -ca.
hypnoanalysis *n.* hipnoanálisis.
hypnoanalytic *adj.* hipnoanalítico, -ca.
hypnocatharsis *n.* hipnocatarsis.
hypnocinematogrph *n.* hipnocinematógrafo.
hypnodontics *n.* hipnodóntica.
hypnogenic *adj.* hipnogénico, -ca.
hypnogenous *adj.* hipnógeno, -na.
hypnoid *adj.* hipnoideo, -a.
hypnoidization *n.* hipnoidización.
hypnologist *n.* hipnólogo, -ga.
hypnology *n.* hipnología.
hypnonarcoanalysis *n.* hipnonarcoanálisis.
hypnonarcosis *n.* hipnonarcosis.
hypnopompic *adj.* hipnopómpico, -ca.
hypnosia *n.* hipnosia.
hypnosis *n.* hipnosis.
  lethargic hypnosis hipnosis letárgica.
  major hypnosis hipnosis mayor.
  minor hypnosis hipnosis menor.
hypnosophy *n.* hipnosofia.
hypnotherapy *n.* hipnoterapia.
hypnotic *adj.* hipnótico, -ca.
hypnotism *n.* hipnotismo.
hypnotist *n.* hipnotizador, -ra.
hypnotization *n.* hipnotización.
hypnotize *v.* hipnotizar.
hypoacidity *n.* hipoacidez.
hypoactive *adj.* hipoactivo, -va.
hypoactivity *n.* hipoactividad.
hypoacusia *n.* hipoacusia, hipoacusis.

  conductive hypoacusia hipoacusia conductiva.
  mixed hypoacusia hipoacusia mixta.
  sensorineural hypoacusia hipoacusia neurosensorial.
  sudden hypoacusia hipoacusia súbita.
hypoacusis *n.* hipoacusia, hipoacusis.
hypoadenia *n.* hipoadenia.
hypoadrenalism *n.* hipoadrenalismo.
hypoadrenia *n.* hipoadrenia.
hypoadrenocorticism *n.* hipoadrenocorticismo.
hypoalbuminemia *n.* hipoalbuminemia.
hypoalbuminosis *n.* hipalbuminosis, hipoalbuminosis,.
hypoaldosteronemia *n.* hipoaldosteronemia.
hypoaldosteronism *n.* hipoaldosteronismo.
  hyporeninemic hypoaldosteronism hipoaldosteronismo hiporreninémico.
  isolated hypoaldosteronism hipoaldosteronismo aislado.
  selective hypoaldosteronism hipoaldosteronismo selectivo.
hypoaldosteronuria *n.* hipoaldosteronuria.
hypoalimentation *n.* hipoalimentación.
hypoalkaline *adj.* hipoalcalino, -na.
hypoalkalinity *n.* hipoalcalinidad.
hypoallergenic *adj.* hipoalérgenico, -ca.
hypoalonemia *n.* hipoalonemia.
hypoaminoacidemia *n.* hipoaminoacidemia.
hypoanakinesia *n.* hipoanacinesia.
hypoanakinesis *n.* hipoanacinesis.
hypoandrogenism *n.* hipoandrogenismo.
hypoanesthesia *n.* hipnoanestesia.
hypoazoturia *n.* hipazouria, hipoazoturia.
hypobaria *n.* hipobaria.
hypobaric *adj.* hipobárico, -ca.
hypobarism *n.* hipobarismo.
hypobaropathy *n.* hipobaropatía.
hypobasemia *n.* hipobasemia.
hypobetalipoproteinemia *n.* hipobetalipoproteinemia.
  familial hypobetalipoproteinemia hipobetalipoproteinemia familiar.
hypobilirubinemia *n.* hipobilirrubinemia.
hypoblast *n.* hipoblasto.
hypoblastic *adj.* hipoblástico, -ca.
hypobranchial *adj.* hipobranquial.
hypocalcemia *n.* hipocalcemia.
hypocalcia *n.* hipocalcia.
hypocalcification *n.* hipocalcificación.
  enamel hypocalcification hipocalcificación del esmalte.
hypocalcipectic *adj.* hipocalcipéctico, -ca.
hypocalcipexy *n.* hipocalcipexia.
hypocalciuria *n.* hipocalciuria.
hypocapnia *n.* hipocapnia.
hypocapnic *adj.* hipocápnico, -ca.
hypocarbia *n.* hipocarbia.
hypocellular *adj.* hipocelular.
hypocellurarity *n.* hipocelularidad.
hypocelom *n.* hipoceloma.
hypochloremia *n.* hipocloremia.
hypochloremic *adj.* hipoclorémico, -ca.
hypochlorhydria *n.* hipoclorhidria.
hypochloridation *n.* hipocloridación.
hypochloridemia *n.* hipocloridemia.
hypochlorization *n.* hipoclorización, hipocloruración.
hypochloruria *n.* hipocloruria.
hypocholesteremic *adj.* hipocolesterémico, -ca.
hypocholesterinemia *n.* hipocolesterinemia.
hypocholesterolemia *n.* hipocolesterolemia.
hypocholesterolemic *adj.* hipocolesterolémico, -ca.

hypocholia *n.* hipocolia.
hypocholuria *n.* hipocoluria.
hypochondria *n.* hipocondría.
hypochondriac *n.* hipocondríaco, -ca[1].
hypochondriacal *adj.* hipocondríaco, -ca[2].
hypochondriasis *n.* hipocondriasis.
hypochondroplasia *n.* hipocondroplasia.
hypochordal *adj.* hipocordal.
hypochromasia *n.* hipocromasia.
hypochromatic *adj.* hipocromático, -ca.
hypochromatism *n.* hipocromatismo.
hypochromatosis *n.* hipocromatosis.
hypochromemia *n.* hipocromatemia, hipocromemia.
hypochromia *n.* hipocromía.
hypochromic *adj.* hipocrómico, -ca.
hypochrosis *n.* hipocrosis.
hypochylia *n.* hipoquilia.
hypocitraturia *n.* hipocitraturia.
hypocitremia *n.* hipocitremia.
hypocitruria *n.* hipocitruria.
hypocoagulability *n.* hipocoagulabilidad.
hypocoagulable *adj.* hipocoagulable.
hypocoelom *n.* hipoceloma.
hypocomplementemia *n.* hipocomplementemia.
hypocomplementemic *adj.* hipocomplementémico, -ca.
hypocondylar *adj.* hipocondíleo, -a.
hypocone *n.* hipocono.
hypoconid *n.* hipocónido.
hypoconule *n.* hipocónulo.
hypoconulid *n.* hipoconúlido.
hypocorticalism *n.* hipocorticalismo.
hypocorticoidism *n.* hipocorticismo.
hypocupremia *n.* hipocupremia.
hypocyclosis *n.* hipociclosis.
hypocystotomy *n.* hipocistotomía.
hypocythemia *n.* hipocitemia.
 progressive hypocythemia hipocitemia progresiva.
hypocytosis *n.* hipocitosis.
hypodactylia *n.* hipodactilia.
hypodactylism *n.* hipodactilismo.
hypodactyly *n.* hipodactilia.
hypodense *adj.* hipodenso, -sa.
hypodensity *n.* hipodensidad.
hypoderm *n.* hipodermis.
hypodermatoclysis *n.* hipodermatoclisis.
hypodermatomy *n.* hipodermatomía.
hypodermatosis *n.* hipodermatosis.
hypodermic *adj.* hipodérmico, -ca.
hypodermis *n.* hipodermis.
hypodermoclysis *n.* hipodermoclisis.
hypodermolithiasis *n.* hipodermolitiasis.
hypodiaphragmatic *adj.* hipodiafragmático, -ca.
hypodinamia *n.* hipodinamia.
 hypodinamia cordis hipodinamia cordis.
 primary uterine hypodinamia hipodinamia uterina primaria.
 secondary uterine hypodinamia hipodinamia uterina secundaria.
 uterine hypodinamia hipodinamia uterina.
hypodiploid *adj.* hipodiploide.
hypodipsia *n.* hipodipsia.
hypodipsic *adj.* hipodípsico, -ca.
hypodontia *n.* hipodontia.
hypodynamic *adj.* hipodinámico, -ca.
hypoeccrisia *n.* hipoecrisia.
hypoeccrisis *n.* hipoecrisia, hipoecrisis.
hypoeccritic *adj.* hipoecrítico, -ca.
hypoechogenic *adj.* hipoecogénico, -ca.
hypoechogenicity *n.* hipoecogenicidad.
hypoechois *adj.* hipoecoico, -ca.

hypoelectrolytemia *n.* hipoelectrolitemia.
hypoendocrinia *n.* hipoendocrinia.
hypoendocrinial *n.* hipoendocrinismo.
hypoeosinophilia *n.* hipoeosinofilia.
hypoergasia *n.* hipoergasia.
hypoergia *n.* hipoergia.
hypoergic *adj.* hipoérgico, -ca.
hypoergy *n.* hipoergia.
hypoesophoria *n.* hipoesoforia.
hypoesthesia *n.* hipoestesia.
hypoestrinemia *n.* hipoestrinemia.
hypoestrogenemia *n.* hipoestrogenemia.
hypoestrogenism *n.* hipoestrogenismo.
hypoevolutism *n.* hipoevolutismo.
hypoexophoria *n.* hipoexoforia.
hypoexposition *n.* hipoexposición.
hypoferremia *n.* hipoferremia.
hypoferrism *n.* hipoferrismo.
hypofertile *adj.* hipofértil.
hypofertility *n.* hipofertilidad.
hypofibrinogenemia *n.* hipofibrinogenemia.
hypofunction *n.* hipofunción, hipofuncionamiento.
hypogalactia *n.* hipogalactia.
hypogalactous *adj.* hipogalactoso, -sa.
hypogammaglobinemia *n.* hipogammaglobinemia.
hypogammaglobulinemia *n.* hipogammaglobulinemia.
 acquired hypogammaglobulinemia hipogammaglobulinemia adquirida.
 congenital hypogammaglobulinemia hipogammaglobulinemia congénita.
 physiologic hypogammaglobulinemia hipogammaglobulinemia fisiológica.
 primary hypogammaglobulinemia hipogammaglobulinemia primaria.
 secondary hypogammaglobulinemia hipogammaglobulinemia secundaria.
 transient hypogammaglobulinemia hipogammaglobulinemia pasajera.
 transient hypogammaglobulinemia of infancy hipogammaglobulinemia transitoria de la infancia.
 X-linked hypogammaglobulinemia hipogammaglobulinemia infantil ligada a X, hipogammaglobulinemia ligada a X.
 X-linked infantile hypogammaglobulinemia hipogammaglobulinemia infantil ligada a X, hipogammaglobulinemia ligada a X.
hypoganglionosis *n.* hipoganglionosis.
hypogastric *adj.* hipogástrico, -ca.
hypogastrium *n.* hipogastrio.
hypogastrocele *n.* hipogastrocele.
hypogastropagus *n.* hipogastrodídimo, hipogastrópago.
hypogastroschisis *n.* hipogastrosquisis.
hypogenesis *n.* hipogénesis, hipogenia.
 polar hypogenesis hipogénesis polar.
hypogenetic *adj.* hipogenético, -ca.
hypogenitalism *n.* hipogenitalismo.
hypogeusesthesia *n.* hipogeusestesia.
hypogeusia *n.* hipogeusia.
hypoglandular *adj.* hipoglandular.
hypoglossal *adj.* hipogloso, -sa.
hypoglossus *adj.* hipogloso, -sa.
hypoglottis *n.* hipoglotis.
hypoglucagonemia *n.* hipoglucagonemia.
hypoglycemia *n.* hipoglucemia.
 factitial hypoglycemia hipoglucemia facticia.
 fasting hypoglycemia hipoglucemia en ayunas.
 ketotic hypoglycemia hipoglucemia cetósica.
 leucine-induced hypoglycemia hipoglucemia inducida por leucina.
 mixed hypoglycemia hipoglucemia mixta.

 neonatal hypoglycemia hipoglucemia neonatal.
 reactive hypoglycemia hipoglucemia reactiva.
hypoglycemic *adj.* hipoglucémico, -ca.
hypoglycogenolysis *n.* hipoglucogenólisis.
hypoglycorrhachia *n.* hipoglucorraquia.
hypognathous *adj.* hipognato, -ta.
hypogonadia *n.* hipogonadía.
hypogonadism *n.* hipogonadismo.
 eugonadotropic hypogonadism hipogonadismo eugonadotrópico.
 familial hypogonadotropic hypogonadism hipogonadismo hipogonadotrópico familiar.
 hypergonadotropic hypogonadism hipogonadismo hipergonadotrópico.
 hypogonadism with anosmia hipogonadismo con anosmia.
 hypogonadotropic hypogonadism hipogonadismo hipogonadotrópico.
 male hypogonadism hipogonadismo masculino.
 primary hypogonadism hipogonadismo primario.
 secondary hypogonadism hipogonadismo secundario.
hypogonadotropic *adj.* hipogonadotrópico, -ca.
hypogranulocytosis *n.* hipogranulocitosis.
hypohepathia *n.* hipohepatía.
hypohidrosis *n.* hipohidrosis.
hypohidrotic *adj.* hipohidrótico, -ca.
hypohormonal *adj.* hipohormonal.
hypohormonic *adj.* hipohormónico, -ca.
hypohydremia *n.* hipohidremia.
hypohydrochloria *n.* hipohidrocloria.
hypohyloma *n.* hipohiloma.
hypohypnotic *adj.* hipohipnótico, -ca.
hypohypophisism *n.* hipohipofisismo.
hypoimmunity *n.* hipoinmunidad.
hypoinsulinemia *n.* hipoinsulinemia.
hypoinsulinism *n.* hipoinsulinismo.
hypointense *adj.* hipointenso, -sa.
hypointensity *n.* hipointensidad.
hypoisotonic *adj.* hipoisotónico, -ca.
hypokalemia *n.* hipocalemia, hipocaliemia.
hypokalemic *adj.* hipocaliémico, -ca.
hypokaliemia *n.* hipocaliemia.
hypokinemia *n.* hipocinemia.
hypokinesia *n.* hipocinesia, hipoquinesia.
hypokinesis *n.* hipocinesia, hipocinesis.
hypokolasia *n.* hipocolasia.
hypolactasia *n.* hipolactasia.
hypolarynx *n.* hipolaringe.
hypolemmal *adj.* hipolemal.
hypolepidoma *n.* hipolepidoma.
hypolethal *adj.* hipoletal.
hypoleukemia *n.* hipoleucemia.
hypoleydigism *n.* hipoleydigismo.
hypolipemia *n.* hipolipemia, hipolipidemia.
hypolipidemic *adj.* hipolipémico, -ca.
hypolipoproteinemia *n.* hipolipoproteinemia.
hypoliposis *n.* hipoliposis.
hypoliquorrhea *n.* hipolicuorrea.
hypolucency *n.* hipolucencia.
hypolucent *adj.* hipolucente.
hypolymphemia *n.* hipolinfemia.
hypomagnesemia *n.* hipomagnesemia.
hypomagnesuria *n.* hipomagnesuria.
hypomania *n.* hipomanía.
hypomaniac *n.* hipomaníaco, -ca.
hypomastia *n.* hipomastia.
hypomazia *n.* hipomacia.
hypomelanosis *n.* hipomelanismo, hipomelanosis.

idiopathic guttate hypomelanosis hipomelanosis idiopática guttata.
Ito's hypomelanosis hipomelanosis de Ito.
hypomelia *n.* hipomelia.
hypomenorrhea *n.* hipomenorrea.
hypomere *n.* hipómera.
hypometabolic *adj.* hipometabólico, -ca.
hypometabolism *n.* hipometabolismo.
euthyroid hypometabolism hipometabolismo eutiroideo.
hypometria *n.* hipometría.
hypomicrosoma *n.* hipomicrosomía.
hypomimia *n.* hipomimia.
hypomineralization *n.* hipomineralización.
hypomobility *n.* hipomovilidad.
hypomodal *adj.* hipomodal.
hypomorph *n.* hipomorfo, -fa.
hypomotility *n.* hipomotilidad.
hypomyelination *n.* hipomielinización.
hypomyelinogenesis *n.* hipomielinogénesis.
hypomyotonia *n.* hipomiotonía.
hypomyxia *n.* hipomixia, hipomixis.
hyponanosoma *n.* hiponanosomía.
hyponasality *n.* hiponasalidad.
hyponatremia *n.* hiponatremia.
depletional hyponatremia hiponatremia por depleción.
dilutional hyponatremia hiponatremia por dilución.
hyperlipemic hyponatremia hiponatremia hiperlipémica.
hyponatruria *n.* hiponatruria.
hyponeocytosis *n.* hiponeocitosis.
hyponitremia *n.* hiponitremia.
hyponychial *adj.* hiponiquial.
hyponychium *n.* hiponiquio.
hyponychon *n.* hiponicón.
hypooncotic *adj.* hipooncótico, -ca.
hypo-orchidia *n.* hipoorquidia.
hypoorchidism *n.* hipoorquidismo.
hypoorthocytosis *n.* hipoortocitosis.
hypoosmolality *n.* hipoosmolalidad.
hypoosmolar *adj.* hipoosmolar.
hypoosmolarity *n.* hipoosmolaridad.
hypoovarinism *n.* hipoovarismo.
hypopancreatism *n.* hipopancreatismo.
hypopancreorrhea *n.* hipopancreorrea.
hypoparathyreosis *n.* hipoparatireosis.
hypoparathyroidism *n.* hipoparatiroidia, hipoparatiroidismo.
familial hypoparathyroidism hipoparatiroidismo familiar.
hypopepsia *n.* hipopepsia.
hypopepsinia *n.* hipopepsinia.
hypoperfusion *n.* hipoperfusión.
renal hypoperfusion hipoperfusión renal.
hypoperistalsis *n.* hipoperistalsis, hipoperistaltismo.
hypopexia *n.* hipopexia.
hypopexy *n.* hipopexia.
hypophalangism *n.* hipofalangismo.
hypopharyngeal *adj.* hipofaríngeo, -a.
hypopharyngoscope *n.* hipofaringoscopio.
hypopharyngoscopy *n.* hipofaringoscopia.
hypopharynx *n.* hipofaringe.
hypophonesis *n.* hipofonesis.
hypophonia *n.* hipofonía.
hypophoria *n.* hipoforia.
hypophosphatasemia *n.* hipofosfatasemia.
hypophosphatasia *n.* hipofosfatasia.
hypophosphatemia *n.* hipofosfatemia.
familial hypophosphatemia hipofosfatemia familiar.
hypophosphatemic *adj.* hipofosfatémico, -ca.
hypophosphaturia *n.* hipofosfaturia.

hypophosphoremia *n.* hipofosforemia.
hypophrenium *n.* hipofrenio.
hypophyseal *adj.* hipofisario, -ria.
hypophysectomize *v.* hipofisectomizar.
hypophysectomy *n.* hipofisectomía.
hypophyseoportal *adj.* hipofisoportal.
hypophyseoprivic *adj.* hipofisioprivo, -va, hipofisoprivo, -va.
hypophyseotropic *adj.* hipofisiotrópico, -ca, hipofisotrópico, -ca.
hypophysial *adj.* hipofisario, -ria.
hypophysioportal *adj.* hipofisioportal.
hypophysioprivic *adj.* hipofisioprivo, -va.
hypophysiotropic *adj.* hipofisiotrópico, -ca, hipofisotrópico, -ca.
hypophysis *n.* hipófisis.
hypophysitis *n.* hipofisitis.
lymphocytic hypophysitis hipofisitis linfoide.
hypophysoma *n.* hipofisoma.
hypopiesis *n.* hipopiesis.
orthostatic hypopiesis hipopiesis ortostática.
hypopietic *adj.* hipopiético, -ca.
hypopigmentation *n.* hipopigmentación.
hypopinealism *n.* hipopinealismo.
hypopituitarism *n.* hipopituitarismo.
hypoplasia *n.* hipoplasia.
cartilage-hair hypoplasia hipoplasia de cartílago y pelo.
enamel hypoplasia hipoplasia del esmalte.
focal dermal hypoplasia hipoplasia dérmica-focal.
hereditary enamel hypoplasia hipoplasia hereditaria del esmalte.
hypoplasia of the mesenchyme hipoplasia del mesénquima.
oligomeganephronic renal hypoplasia hipoplasia renal oligomeganefrónica.
optic nerve hypoplasia hipoplasia del nervio óptico.
renal hypoplasia hipoplasia renal.
right ventricular hypoplasia hipoplasia del ventrículo derecho.
segmental renal hypoplasia hipoplasia renal segmentaria.
thymic hypoplasia hipoplasia tímica.
true hypoplasia hipoplasia renal simple.
Turner's hypoplasia hipoplasia de Turner.
hypoplastic *adj.* hipoplásico, -ca.
hypoplasty *n.* hipoplasia.
hypoploid *n.* hipoploide.
hypoploidy *n.* hipoploidía.
hypopnea *n.* hipopnea.
hypopneic *adj.* hipopneico, -ca.
hypoponesis *n.* hipoponesis.
hypoporosis *n.* hipoporosis.
hypoposia *n.* hipoposia.
hypopotassemia *n.* hipopotasemia.
hypopotassemic *adj.* hipopotasémico, -ca.
hypopotentia *n.* hipopotencia.
hypopraxia *n.* hipopraxia, hipopraxis.
hypoproaccelerinemia *n.* hipoproacelerinemia.
hypoproconvertinemia *n.* hipoproconvertinemia.
hypoprolactinemia *n.* hipoprolactinemia.
hypoprolanemia *n.* hipoprolanemia.
hypoprosexia *n.* hipoprosexia.
hypoprosody *n.* hipoprosodia.
hypoproteinemia *n.* hipoproteinemia.
prehepatic hypoproteinemia hipoproteinemia prehepática.
hypoproteinia *n.* hipoproteinia.
hypoproteinic *adj.* hipoproteínico, -ca.
hypoproteinosis *n.* hipoproteinosis.

hypoprothrombinemia *n.* hipoprotrombinemia.
hypopselaphesia *n.* hipopselafesia.
hypoptyalism *n.* hipoptialismo.
hypopyon *n.* hipopión.
recurrent hypopyon hipopión recurrente.
hyporeactive *adj.* hiporreactivo, -va.
hyporeflexia *n.* hiporreflexia.
hyporeninemia *n.* hiporreninemia.
hyporeninemic *adj.* hiporreninémico, -ca.
hyporiboflavinosis *n.* hiporriboflavinosis.
hyporreninism *n.* hiporreninismo.
hyporrhea *n.* hiporrea.
hyposalemia *n.* hiposalemia.
hyposalivation *n.* hiposalivación.
hyposcheotomy *n.* hiposqueotomía.
hyposcleral *adj.* hipoescleral, hipoesclerótico, -ca.
hyposecretion *n.* hiposecreción.
hyposensitive *adj.* hiposensitivo, -va.
hyposensitivity *n.* hiposensibilidad.
hyposensitization *n.* hiposensibilización.
hyposexuality *n.* hiposexualidad.
hyposialadenitis *n.* hiposialadenitis.
hyposialosis *n.* hiposialosis.
hyposkeocytosis *n.* hipoesqueocitosis.
hyposmia *n.* hiposmia.
hyposmosis *n.* hipoósmosis.
hyposmotic *adj.* hipoosmótico, -ca.
hyposomatotropism *n.* hiposomatotropismo.
hyposomia *n.* hiposomía.
hyposomnia *n.* hiposomnia.
hypospadiac *n.* hipospádico.
hypospadias *n.* hipospadia, hipospadias.
anterior hypospadias hipospadia balánico, hipospadia balanítico.
balanic hypospadias hipospadia balánico, hipospadia balanítico.
balanopreputial hypospadias hipospadia balanoprepucial.
female hypospadias hipospadia femenino.
glandular hypospadias hipospadia glandular.
penile hypospadias hipospadia peneano.
penoscrotal hypospadias hipospadia peneano-escrotal.
perineal hypospadias hipospadia perineal.
posterior hypospadias hipospadia perineal.
pseudovaginal hypospadias hipospadia seudovaginal.
hyposphresia *n.* hiposfresia.
hyposphyxia *n.* hipoesfixia.
hyposplenism *n.* hipoesplenismo, hiposplenismo.
hypostasis *n.* hipostasis.
post morten hypostasis hipostasis post morten.
pulmonary hypostasis hipostasis pulmonar.
hypostatic *adj.* hipostático, -ca.
hyposteatolysis *n.* hiposteatólisis.
hyposteatosis *n.* hipoesteatosis.
hyposthenia *n.* hipoestenia.
**hypos
theniant** *adj.* hipoestenizante.
hyposthenic *adj.* hipoesténico, -ca.
hyposthenuria *n.* hipoestenuria.
tubular hyposthenuria hipoestenuria tubular.
hypostome *n.* hipostoma.
hypostomia *n.* hipostomía.
hypostomial *adj.* hipostomial.
hypostosis *n.* hipostosis.
hyposuprarenalism *n.* hiposuprarrenalemia, hiposuprarrenalismo.
hyposympathicotonous *n.* hiposimpaticotonía.

hyposynergia *n.* hiposinergia.
hyposystole *n.* hiposístole, hiposistolia.
hypotaxia *n.* hipotaxia.
hypotelorism *n.* hipotelorismo.
  ocular hypotelorism hipotelorismo ocular.
  orbital hypotelorism hipotelorismo orbitario.
hypotension *n.* hipotensión.
  arterial hypotension hipotensión arterial.
  chronic idiopathic orthostatic hypotension hipotensión ortostática crónica, hipotensión ortostática idiopática crónica.
  chronic orthostatic hypotension hipotensión ortostática crónica, hipotensión ortostática idiopática crónica.
  controlled hypotension hipotensión controlada, hipotensión deliberada.
  induced hypotension hipotensión inducida.
  intracranial hypotension hipotensión intracraneal.
  orthostatic hypotension hipotensión ortostática.
  postural hypotension hipotensión postural.
  supine hypotension hipotensión en supino.
  symtomatic hypotension hipotensión sintomática.
  vascular hypotension hipotensión vascular.
hypotensive *adj.* hipotensivo, -va, hipotenso, -sa.
hypotensor *adj.* hipotensor, -ra.
hypotetraploid *adj.* hipotetraploide.
hypothalamia *n.* hipotalamia.
hypothalamic *adj.* hipotalámico, -ca.
hypothalamohypophyseal *adj.* hipotalamohipofisario, -ria.
hypothalamotomy *n.* hipotalamotomía.
hypothalamus *n.* hipotálamo.
hypothenar *n.* hipotenar.
hypothermal *adj.* hipotérmico, -ca.
hypothermia *n.* hipotermia.
  accidental hypothermia hipotermia accidental.
  endogenous hypothermia hipotermia endógena.
  local hypothermia hipotermia local.
  moderate hypothermia hipotermia moderada.
  profound hypothermia hipotermia profunda.
  regional hypothermia hipotermia regional.
  total body hypothermia hipotermia corporal total.
hypothesis *n.* hipótesis.
  alternative hypothesis hipótesis alternativa.
  autocrine hypothesis hipótesis autocrina.
  Avogadro's hypothesis hipótesis de Avogadro.
  biogenic amine hypothesis hipótesis de las aminas biógenas.
  chemiosmotic hypothesis hipótesis quimiosmótica.
  Dreyer and Bennet hypothesis hipótesis de Dreyer y Bennet.
  drift hypothesis hipótesis de la deriva.
  Gad's hypothesis hipótesis de Gad.
  gate-control hypothesis hipótesis del control de compuerta.
  Gompertz's hypothesis hipótesis de Gompertz.
  insular hypothesis hipótesis insular.
  jelly roll hypothesis hipótesis de rollo de jalea.
  Lyon's hypothesis hipótesis de Lyon.
  Makeham's hypothesis hipótesis de Makeham.

  Michaelis-Menten hypothesis hipótesis de Michaelis-Menten.
  null hypothesis hipótesis nula.
  one gene-one enzyme hypothesis hipótesis un gen-una enzima.
  one gen-one polypeptide chain hypothesis hipótesis un gen-una cadena polipeptídica.
  permissive hypothesis hipótesis permisiva.
  predictive hypothesis hipótesis predictiva.
  scientific hypothesis hipótesis científica.
  segregation hypothesis hipótesis de la segregación.
  sliding filament hypothesis hipótesis de filamentos deslizantes.
  social cause hypothesis hipótesis de la causa social.
  Starling's hypothesis hipótesis de Starling.
  unitarian hypothesis hipótesis unitaria.
  wobble hypothesis hipótesis de la inestabilidad, hipótesis del balanceo.
  zwitter hypothesis hipótesis zwitter.
hypothrepsia *n.* hipotrepsia.
hypothrombinemia *n.* hipotrombinemia.
hypothromboplastinemia *n.* hipotromboplastinemia.
hypothymia *n.* hipotimia.
hypothymic *adj.* hipotímico, -ca.
hypothymism *n.* hipotimismo.
hypothyreosis *n.* hipotireosis.
hypothyroid *adj.* hipotiroideo, -a.
hypothyroidation *n.* hipotiroidación.
hypothyroidism *n.* hipotiroidía, hipotiroidismo.
  infantile hypothyroidism hipotiroidismo del lactante.
  secondary hypothyroidism hipotiroidismo secundario.
hypothyroxinemia *n.* hipotiroxinemia.
hypotonic *adj.* hipotónico, -ca.
hypotonicity *n.* hipotonicidad.
hypotonus *n.* hipotono.
hypotony *n.* hipotonía.
  benign congenital hypotony hipotonía congénita benigna.
  hypotony oculi hipotonía ocular.
hypotoxicity *n.* hipotoxicidad.
hypotrichiasis *n.* hipotriquiasis.
hypotrichosis *n.* hipotricosis.
hypotrichous *adj.* hipotricoso, -sa.
hypotriploid *adj.* hipotriploide.
hypotrophy *n.* hipotrofia.
hypotropia *n.* hipotropía.
hypotympanotomy *n.* hipotimpanotomía.
hypotympanum *n.* hipotímpano.
hypouremia *n.* hipouremia.
hypouresis *n.* hipouresis.
hypouricemia *n.* hipouricemia.
hypouricuria *n.* hipouricosuria, hipouricuria.
hypourocrinia *n.* hipourocrinia.
hypovarism *n.* hipoovarismo, hipovarismo.
hypovenosity *n.* hipovenosidad.
hypoventilation *n.* hipoventilación.
hypovigilance *n.* hipovigilancia.
hypovitaminosis *n.* hipovitaminosis.
hypovolemia *n.* hipovolemia.
hypovolemic *adj.* hipovolémico, -ca.
hypovolia *n.* hipovolia.
hypoxemia *n.* hipoxemia.
hypoxia *n.* hipoxia.
  acute hypoxia hipoxia aguda.
  anemic hypoxia hipoxia anémica.
  chronic hypoxia hipoxia crónica.
  diffusion hypoxia hipoxia por difusión.
  histotoxic hypoxia hipoxia histotóxica.
  hypoxic hypoxia hipoxia hipóxica.

  ischemic hypoxia hipoxia isquémica.
  oxygen affinity hypoxia hipoxia por afinidad con el oxígeno.
  stagnant hypoxia hipoxia estancada, hipoxia por estasis.
hypoxic *adj.* hipóxico, -ca.
hypoxidosis *n.* hipoxidosis.
hypsarrhythmia *n.* hipsarritmia.
hypsibrachycephalic *adj.* hipsobraquicefálico, -ca.
hypsibrachycephaly *n.* hipsobraquicefalia.
hypsicephalic *adj.* hipsicefálico, -ca, hipsocefálico, -ca.
hypsicephaly *n.* hipsicefalia, hipsocefalia.
hypsiloid *adj.* hipsiloide.
hypsistaphylia *n.* hipsistafilia.
hypsitenocephalic *adj.* hipsitenocefálico, -ca.
hypsochromic *adj.* hipsocrómico, -ca.
hypsochromy *n.* hipsocromía.
hypsodont *n.* hipsodonto.
hypsokinesis *n.* hipsocinesia, hipsocinesis.
hypsotherapy *n.* hipsoterapia.
hypurgia *n.* hipurgia.
hysteralgia *n.* histeralgia.
hysteratresia *n.* histeratresia.
hysterectomy *n.* histerectomía, metrostéresis.
  abdominal hysterectomy histerectomía abdominal.
  abdominovaginal hysterectomy histerectomía abdominovaginal.
  cesarean hysterectomy histerectomía cesárea.
  complete hysterectomy histerectomía completa.
  modified radical hysterectomy histerectomía radical modificada.
  paravaginal hysterectomy histerectomía paravaginal.
  partial hysterectomy histerectomía parcial.
  Porro hysterectomy histerectomía de Porro.
  radical hysterectomy histerectomía radical.
  subtotal hysterectomy histerectomía subtotal.
  supracervical hysterectomy histerectomía supracervical.
  supravaginal hysterectomy histerectomía supravaginal.
  total hysterectomy histerectomía total.
  vaginal hysterectomy histerectomía vaginal.
hysteresis *n.* histéresis.
  protoplasmic hysteresis histéresis protoplásmica.
  static hysteresis histéresis estática.
hystereurysis *n.* histereurisis.
hysteria *n.* histeria.
  anxiety hysteria histeria de angustia.
  conversion hysteria histeria de conversión.
  hypnoid hysteria histeria hipnoide.
  traumatic hysteria histeria traumática.
hysteric *adj.* histérico, -ca.
hysterical *adj.* histérico, -ca.
hysteriform *adj.* histeriforme.
hysteritis *n.* histeritis.
hysterobubonocele *n.* histerobubonocele.
hysterocele *n.* histerocele.
hysterocleisis *n.* histerocleisis.
hysterocolposcope *n.* histerocolposcopio.
hysterocystic *adj.* histerocístico, -ca.
hysterocystocleisis *n.* histerocistocleisis.
hysterocystopexy *n.* histerocistopexia.
hysterodynia *n.* histerodinia.
hysteroepilepsy *n.* histeroepilepsia.
hysterogram *n.* histerograma.
hysterograph *n.* histerógrafo.
hysterography *n.* histerografía.

hysteroid *adj.* histeroide.
hysterolaparotomy *n.* histerolaparotomía.
hysterolith *n.* histerolito.
hysterology *n.* histerología.
hysterolysis *n.* histerólisis.
hysterometer *n.* histerómetro.
hysterometry *n.* histerometría.
hysteromyoma *n.* histeromioma.
hysteromyomectomy *n.* histeromiomectomía.
hysteromyotomy *n.* histeromiotomía.
hysteronarcolepsy *n.* histeronarcolepsia.
hysteroneurasthenia *n.* histeroneurastenia.
hystero-oophorectomy *n.* histerooforectomía.
hysteropathy *n.* histeropatía.
hysteropexy *n.* histeropexia, metropexia.
  abdominal hysteropexy histeropexia abdominal.
  vaginal hysteropexy histeropexia vaginal.
hysterophore *n.* histeróforo.

hysteropia *n.* histeropía.
hysteroplasty *n.* histeroplastia.
hysteroptosis *n.* histeroptosia, histeroptosis.
hysterorrhaphy *n.* histerorrafia.
hysterorrhea *n.* histerorrea.
hysterorrhexis *n.* histerorrexis.
hysterosalpingectomy *n.* histerosalpingectomía, histerosalpinguectomía.
hysterosalpingogram *n.* histerosalpingograma.
hysterosalpingography *n.* histerosalpingografía.
hysterosalpingo-oophorectomy *n.* histerosalpingooforectomía.
hysterosalpingostomy *n.* histerosalpingostomía.
hysteroscope *n.* histeroscopio.
hysteroscopy *n.* histeroscopia.
hysterostat *n.* histeróstato.
hysterostomatocleisis *n.* histerostomatocleisis.
hysterosystole *n.* histerosístole.

hysterotabetism *n.* histerotabetismo.
hysterothermometry *n.* histerotermometría.
hysterotome *n.* histerótomo.
hysterotomy *n.* histerotomía, metratomía.
  abdominal hysterotomy histerotomía abdominal.
  vaginal hysterotomy histerotomía vaginal.
hysterotrachelectasia *n.* histerotraquelectasia.
hysterotrachelectomy *n.* histerotraquelectomía.
hysterotracheloplasty *n.* histerotraqueloplastia.
hysterotrachelorrhaphy *n.* histerotraquelorrafia.
hysterotrachelotomy *n.* histerotraquelotomía.
hysterotubography *n.* histerotubografía.
hysterovaginoenterocele *n.* histerovaginoenterocele.
hystiogenic *adj.* histiogénico, -ca.
hystolisis *n.* histólisis.
hystriciasis *n.* histriquiasis.

I i

ianthinopsia *n.* yantinopsia.
iathergy *n.* iatergia.
iatraliptic *adj.* iatraléptico, -ca, iatralíptico, -ca, yatraléptico, -ca, yatralíptico, -ca.
iatraliptics *n.* iatraléptica, iatralíptica, yatraléptica, yatralíptica.
iatreusiology *n.* iatreusiología, yatreusiología.
iatreusis *n.* iatreusis, yatreusis.
iatric *adj.* iátrico, -ca, yátrico, -ca.
iatrogenesis *n.* yatrogénesis.
iatrogenia *n.* iatrogenia.
iatrogenic *adj.* iatrogénico, -ca, iatrógeno, -na, yatrogénico, -ca, yatrógeno, -na.
iatrogeny *n.* yatrogenia.
iatrology *n.* iatrología,, yatrología.
iatrophysics *n.* iatrofísica, yatrofísica.
iatrotechnics *n.* iatrotécnica.
iatrotechnique *n.* iatrotécnica.
ichnogram *n.* icnograma.
ichor *n.* icor.
ichoremia *n.* icoremia.
ichoroid *adj.* icoroide.
ichorous *adj.* icoroso, -sa.
ichorrea *n.* icorrea.
ichorrhemia *n.* icorremia.
ichthyhemotoxism *n.* ictiohemotoxismo.
ichthyism *n.* ictismo.
ichthyoacanthotoxin *n.* ictioacantotoxina.
ichthyoacanthotoxism *n.* ictioacantotoxismo.
ichthyocolla *n.* ictiocola.
ichthyohemotoxin *n.* ictiohemotoxina.
ichthyoid *adj.* ictioide.
ichthyology *n.* ictiología.
ichthyootoxin *n.* ictiootoxina.
ichthyootoxism *n.* ictiootoxismo.
ichthyophagia *n.* ictiofagia.
ichthyophagous *adj.* ictiófago, -ga.
ichthyophobia *n.* ictiofobia.
ichthyosarcotoxin *n.* ictiosarcotoxina.
ichthyosarcotoxism *n.* ictiosarcotoxismo.
ichthyosiform *adj.* ictiosiforme.
ichthyosis *n.* ictiosis.
  acquired ichthyosis ictiosis adquirida.
  congenital ichthyosis ictiosis congénita.
  ichthyosis congenita ictiosis congénita.
  ichthyosis congenita neonatorum ictiosis congénita neonatal.
  ichthyosis corneae ictiosis córnea.
  ichthyosis fetalis ictiosis fetal.
  ichthyosis follicularis ictiosis folicular.
  ichthyosis hystrix ictiosis hystrix.
  ichthyosis intrauterina ictiosis intrauterina.
  ichthyosis linearis circumflexa ictiosis lineal circunfleja.
  ichthyosis linearis circumscripta ictiosis lineal circunscripta.
  ichthyosis palmaris et plantaris ictiosis palmar y plantar.
  ichthyosis sauroderma ictiosis sauroderma, ictiosis saurodérmica.

  ichthyosis scutulata ictiosis escutiforme.
  ichthyosis sebacea ictiosis sebácea.
  ichthyosis sebacea cornea ictiosis sebácea córnea.
  ichthyosis simplex ictiosis simple.
  ichthyosis spinosa ictiosis espinosa.
  ichthyosis vulgaris ictiosis vulgar.
  lamellar ichthyosis ictiosis lamelar, ictiosis laminar, ictiosis laminillar.
  nacreous ichthyosis ictiosis nacarada, ictiosis nácrea.
  sex-linked ichthyosis ictiosis ligada al sexo.
  X-linked ichthyosis ictiosis ligada al cromosoma X.
ichthyosismus *n.* ictiosismo.
  ichthyosismus exanthematicus ictiosismo exantemático.
ichthyotic *adj.* ictiósico, -ca, ictiótico, -ca.
ichthyotoxic *adj.* ictiotóxico, -ca.
ichthyotoxicology *n.* ictiotoxicología.
ichthyotoxicon *n.* ictiotoxicon.
ichthyotoxin *n.* ictiotoxina.
ichthyotoxism *n.* ictiotoxismo.
iconomania *n.* iconomanía.
icosahedral *adj.* icosaédrico, -ca.
ictal *adj.* ictal.
icteric *adj.* ictérico, -ca.
icteroanemia *n.* icteroanemia.
  hemolytic icteroanemia icteroanemia hemolítica.
icterogenic *adj.* icterogénico, -ca.
icterogenicity *n.* icterogenicidad.
icterohematuria *n.* icterohematuria.
icterohematuric *adj.* icterohematúrico, -ca.
icterohemoglobinuria *n.* icterohemoglobinuria.
icterohepatitis *n.* icterepatitis, icterohepatitis.
icteroid *adj.* icteroide.
icterus *n.* ictericia, icterus.
  acquired hemolytic icterus icterus hemolítico adquirido.
  benign familial icterus icterus familiar benigno.
  chronic familial icterus ictericia familiar crónica, icterus familiar crónico.
  congenital familial icterus ictericia familiar congénita.
  congenital hemolytic icterus ictericia hemolítica congénita, icterus hemolítico congénito.
  cythemolytic icterus icterus citohemolítico.
  epidemic catarrhal icterus ictericia catarral epidémica.
  icterus gravis ictericia grave, icterus gravis.
  icterus gravis neonatorum ictericia grave del recién nacido, ictericia neonatal grave.
  icterus melas icterus melas.
  icterus neonatorum ictericia del neonato, ictericia neonatal, icterus neonatal.
  icterus praecox ictericia precoz, icterus praecox.

  infectious icterus ictericia infecciosa, icterus infeccioso.
  nuclear icterus ictericia nuclear.
  physiologic icterus ictericia fisiológica, icterus fisiológico.
ictometer *n.* ictómetro.
ictus *n.* ictus.
  ictus cordis ictus cordis.
  ictus epilepticus ictus epiléptico.
  ictus paralyticus ictus paralyticus.
  ictus sanguinis ictus hemorrágico.
  ictus solis ictus solis.
id id, ide.
idea *n.* idea.
  autochthonous idea idea autóctona.
  compulsive idea idea compulsiva.
  delirious idea idea delirante.
  deliroid idea idea deliroide.
  fixed idea idea fija.
  idea of persecution idea de persecución.
  idea of reference idea de referencia, idea referencial.
  imperative idea idea imperativa, idea imperiosa.
  obsessional idea idea obsesiva.
  overvalued idea idea sobrevalorada.
  primary delirious idea idea delirante primaria.
  referential idea idea de referencia, idea referencial.
  secondary delirious idea idea delirante secundaria.
ideal *n.* ideal.
  ego ideal ideal del ego, ideal del yo.
idealization *n.* idealización.
  primitive idealization idealización primitiva.
ideation *n.* ideación.
  paranoid ideation ideación paranoide.
  suicidal ideation ideación suicida.
ideational *adj.* ideacional.
ideatum ideatum.
identification *n.* identificación.
  aggressor identification identificación con el agresor.
  competitive identification identificación competitiva.
  cosmic identification identificación cósmica.
  dental identification identificación dental.
  positive identification identificación positiva.
  projective identification identificación proyectiva.
identity *n.* identidad.
  basic group identity identidad básica de grupo.
  core gender identity identidad de género.
  ego identity identidad del ego, identidad del yo.
  gender identity identidad de género.
  negative identity identidad negativa.

personal identity identidad personal.
sexual identity identidad sexual.
ideodynamism *n.* ideodinamismo.
ideogenetic *adj.* ideógeno, -na.
ideoglandular *adj.* ideoglandular.
ideology *n.* ideología.
ideometabolic *adj.* ideometabólico, -ca.
ideometabolism *n.* ideometabolismo.
ideomotion *n.* ideomoción.
ideomotor *adj.* ideomotor, -ra.
ideomuscular *adj.* ideomuscular.
ideophobia *n.* ideofobia.
ideophrenia *n.* ideofrenia.
ideophrenic *adj.* ideofrénico, -ca.
ideoplastia *n.* ideoplastia.
ideovascular *adj.* ideovascular.
idioagglutinin *n.* idioaglutinina.
idioblapsis *n.* idioblapsis.
idioblaptic *adj.* idiobláptico, -ca.
idioblast *n.* idioblasto.
idiochromatin *n.* idiocromatina.
idiochromidia *n.* idiocromidio.
idiochromosome *n.* idiocromosoma.
idiocrasy *n.* idiocrasia.
idiocratic *adj.* idiocrático, -ca.
idiocy *n.* idiocia, idiotez.
amaurotic familial idiocy idiocia amaurotica familiar, idiocia familiar amaurótica.
amaurotic idiocy idiocia amaurotica familiar.
Aztec idiocy idiocia azteca.
cretinoid idiocy idiocia cretinoide.
erethistic idiocy idiocia eretística.
Kalmuk idiocy idiocia de Kalmuk.
microcephalic idiocy idiocia microcefálica.
Mongolian idiocy idiocia mongólica.
moral idiocy idiocia moral.
idiodynamic *adj.* idiodinámico, -ca.
idiogenesis *n.* idiogénesis.
idioglossia *n.* idioglosia.
idioglottic *adj.* idioglótico, -ca.
idiogram *n.* idiograma.
idiographic *adj.* idiográfico, -ca.
idioheteroagglutinin *n.* idioheteroaglutinina.
idioheterolysin *n.* idioheterolisina.
idiohypnotism *n.* idiohipnotismo.
idioisoagglutinin *n.* idioisoaglutinina.
idioisolysin *n.* idioisolisina.
idiokinetic *adj.* ideocinético, -ca.
idiolalia *n.* idiolalia.
idiolog *n.* idiólogo.
idiologism *n.* idiologismo.
idiolysin *n.* idiolisina.
idiomere *n.* idiómero.
idiomuscular *adj.* idiomuscular.
idionodal *adj.* idionodal.
idiopathetic *adj.* idiopatético, -ca.
idiopathic *adj.* idiopático, -ca.
idiopathy *n.* idiopatía.
idiophore *n.* idióforo.
idiopsychologic *adj.* idiopsicológico, -ca.
idioreflex *n.* idiorreflejo.
idioretinal *adj.* idiorretinal.
idiosoma *n.* idiosoma.
idiosome *n.* idiosoma.
idiospasm *n.* idioespasmo, idiospasmo.
idiosyncrasy *n.* idiosincrasia.
idiosyncrasy to a drug idiosincrasia a un fármaco.
idiosyncratic *adj.* idiosincrático, -ca.
idiot *n.* idiota.
idiot savant idiota sabio, idiota sapiente, idiota-sabio.
idiotope *n.* idiótopo.
idiotopy *n.* idiotopía.
idiotoxin *n.* idiotoxina.

idiotrophic *adj.* idiotrófico, -ca.
idiotropic *adj.* idiotrópico, -ca.
idiotype *n.* idiotipo.
idiotypic *adj.* idiotípico, -ca.
idiovariation *n.* idiovariación.
idioventricular *adj.* idioventricular.
iduronate-2-sulfatase *n.* iduronato-2-sulfatasa.
igniextirpation *n.* igniextirpación.
ignioperation *n.* ignioperación.
ignipedites *n.* ignipedites.
ignipuncture *n.* ignipuntura.
ignis infernalis ignis infernalis.
ignization *n.* ignización.
ikota *n.* ikota.
ileac *adj.* iléaco, -ca.
ileadelphus *n.* ileadelfo.
ileal *adj.* ileal.
ileectomy *n.* ileectomía.
ileitis *n.* ileítis.
backwash ileitis ileítis retrógrada.
distal ileitis ileítis distal.
regional ileitis ileítis regional.
terminal ileitis ileítis terminal.
ileocecal *adj.* ileocecal.
ileocecostomy *n.* ileocecostomía.
ileocecum *n.* ileociego.
ileocolic *adj.* ileocólico, -ca.
ileocolitis *n.* ileocolitis.
ileocolitis ulcerosa chronica ileocolitis ulcerosa crónica.
tuberculous ileocolitis ileocolitis tuberculosa.
ileocolonic *adj.* ileocolónico, -ca.
ileocolostomy *n.* ileocolostomía.
ileocolotomy *n.* ileocolotomía.
ileocystoplasty *n.* ileocistoplastia.
ileocystostomy *n.* ileocistostomía.
ileoenterectropy *n.* ileoentectropia.
ileography *n.* ileografía.
ileoileostomy *n.* ileoileostomía.
ileojejunitis *n.* ileoyeyunitis.
ileopexy *n.* ileopexia.
ileoproctostomy *n.* ileoproctostomía.
ileorectal *adj.* ileorrectal.
ileorectostomy *n.* ileorrectostomía.
ileorrhaphy *n.* ileorrafia.
ileosigmoid *adj.* ileosigmoide.
ileosigmoidostomy *n.* ileosigmoidostomía.
ileostomate *adj.* ileostomizado, -da.
ileostomy *n.* ileostomía.
Brooke ileostomy ileostomía de Brooke.
continent ileostomy ileostomía de continencia.
Kock ileostomy ileostomía de Kock.
urinary ileostomy ileostomía urinaria.
ileotomy *n.* ileotomía.
ileotransversostomy *n.* ileotransversostomía.
ileum *n.* íleon.
duplex ileum íleon doble.
ileus *n.* íleo, íleus.
adynamic ileus íleo adinámico.
biliary ileus íleo biliar.
dynamic ileus íleo dinámico.
gallstone ileus íleo por cálculos biliares.
hyperdynamic ileus íleo hiperdinámico.
ileus paralyticus íleo paralítico.
mechanical ileus íleo mecánico.
meconial ileus íleo meconial.
meconium ileus íleo meconial.
occlusive ileus íleo oclusivo.
paralytic ileus íleo paralítico.
postoperative ileus íleo postoperatorio.
spastic ileus íleo espástico.
terminal ileus íleo terminal.

verminous ileus íleo verminoso.
iliac *adj.* ilíaco[2], -ca.
iliacus *n.* ilíaco[1].
iliadelphus *n.* iliadelfo.
iliocapsular *adj.* iliocapsular.
iliococcygeal *adj.* iliococcígeo, -a.
iliocolotomy *n.* iliocolotomía.
iliocostal *adj.* iliocostal.
iliofemoral *adj.* iliofemoral.
iliofemoroplasty *n.* iliofemoroplastia.
iliohypogastric *adj.* iliohipogástrico, -ca.
ilioinguinal *adj.* ilioinguinal.
iliolumbar *adj.* iliolumbar.
iliolumbocostoabdominal *adj.* iliolumbocostoabdominal.
iliometer *n.* iliómetro.
iliopagus *n.* iliópago.
iliopectineal *adj.* iliopectíneo, -a.
iliopelvic *adj.* iliopélvico, -ca.
iliopubic *adj.* iliopubiano, -na.
iliosacral *adj.* iliosacro, -cra.
iliosciatic *adj.* iliociático, -ca, ilioisquiático, -ca.
iliospinal *adj.* ilioespinal, iliospinal.
iliothoracopagus *n.* iliotoracópago.
iliotibial *adj.* iliotibial.
iliotrocanteric *adj.* iliotrocantéreo, -a.
ilioxiphopagus *n.* ilioxifópago.
ilium *n.* ilion, ilium.
ill *adj.* enfermo, -ma.
illaqueation *n.* ilaqueación.
illinition *n.* ilinación, ilinición.
illness *n.* enfermedad.
functional illness enfermedad funcional.
mental illness enfermedad mental.
ill-treatment *n.* sevicia.
illumination *n.* iluminación.
axial illumination iluminación axial, iluminación axil.
central illumination iluminación central.
contact illumination iluminación de contacto, iluminación por contacto.
critical illumination iluminación crítica.
dark-field illumination iluminación de campo oscuro, iluminación en campo oscuro.
dark-ground illumination iluminación en fondo oscuro.
direct illumination iluminación directa.
erect illumination iluminación erecta.
focal illumination iluminación focal.
Köhler illumination iluminación de Köhler.
lateral illumination iluminación lateral.
oblique illumination iluminación oblicua.
through illumination iluminación de lado a lado.
vertical illumination iluminación vertical.
illuminator *n.* iluminador.
Abbe's illuminator iluminador de Abbe.
illusion *n.* ilusión.
catatimic illusion ilusión catatímica.
illusion for inattention ilusión por inatención.
illusion of doubles ilusión de dobles.
illusion of movement ilusión de movimiento.
oculogravic illusion ilusión oculográvica.
oculogyral illusion ilusión oculógira.
optical illusion ilusión óptica.
paraeidolic illusion ilusión pareidólica.
illusional *adj.* ilusional, ilusivo, -va.
illutation *n.* ilutación.
ima ima.
image *n.* imagen.
accidental image imagen accidental.
amorphous image imagen amorfa.

analogic image imagen analógica.

aseptic body image imagen aséptica del cuerpo.

body image imagen corporal.

bull's-eye image imagen en ojo de buey.

catatropic image imagen catatrópica.

compromise body image imagen corporal de compromiso.

consecutive image imagen consecutiva.

decompression image imagen de descompresión.

digital image imagen digital.

direct image imagen directa.

doughnut image imagen en donuts.

dual-energy image imagen de energía dual.

dynamic image imagen dinámica.

eidetic image imagen eidética.

electrostatic image imagen electrostática.

erect image imagen erecta, imagen erguida.

false image imagen falsa.

Fourier transform image imagen de transformación de Fourier.

functional image imagen funcional.

further image imagen de adición.

guided image imagen guiada.

hallucinoid image imagen alucinoide.

heteronymous image imagen heterónima.

homonymous image imagen homónima.

hypnagogic image imagen hipnagógica.

hypnopompic image imagen hipnopómpica.

idealized image imagen idealizada.

image intensifier intensificador de imagen.

image matrix imagen matriz.

incidental image imagen incidental.

inverted image imagen invertida.

latent image imagen latente.

localizer image imagen localizadora.

magnetic resonance image (MRI) imagen por resonancia magnética (IRM).

memory image imagen de memoria.

mental image imagen mental.

mirror image imagen de espejo.

mnemic image imagen mnémica.

motor image imagen motora.

optical image imagen óptica.

parent image imagen paterna.

phantom image imagen fantasma.

primordial image imagen primordial.

Purkinje image imagen de Purkinje.

Purkinje-Sanson image imagen de Purkinje-Sanson.

Purkinje-Sanson mirror image imagen en espejo de Purkinje-Sanson.

radioisotope image imagen de radioisótopo.

real image imagen real.

real-time image imagen en tiempo real.

retinal image imagen retinal, imagen retiniana.

Sanson's image imagen de Sanson.

sensory image imagen sensitiva, imagen sensorial.

snowfall image imagen en nevada.

specular image imagen especular.

subtraction image imagen de sustracción.

tactile image imagen táctil.

unequal retinal image imagen retiniana desigual.

virtual image imagen virtual.

visual image imagen visual.

imagery *n.* imaginería[1].

eidetic imagery eideísmo.

imaginal *adj.* imaginal.

imagination *n.* imaginación.

creative imagination imaginación creadora.

productive imagination imaginación productiva.

reproductive imagination imaginación reproductiva.

imaging *n.* imaginería[2].

imago imago.

imagocide *adj.* imagocida.

imbalance *n.* desequilibrio[1], imbalance.

autonomic imbalance desequilibrio autónomo.

binocular imbalance desequilibrio binocular.

occlusal imbalance desequilibrio oclusivo.

sex chromosome imbalance desequilibrio de cromosomas sexuales.

vasomotor imbalance desequilibrio vasomotor.

imbalanced *adj.* desequilibrado, -da.

imbecile *n.* imbécil.

imbecility *n.* imbecilidad.

moral imbecility imbecilidad moral.

imbibition *n.* imbibición.

hemoglobin imbibition imbibición de hemoglobina.

imbricate *adj.* imbricado, -da, imbricar.

imbricated *adj.* imbricado, -da.

imbrication *n.* imbricación.

horizontal imbrication imbricación horizontal.

iminoglycinuria *n.* iminoglicinuria.

iminohydrolase *n.* iminohidrolasa.

iminourea *n.* iminourea.

immature *adj.* inmaduro, -ra.

immaturity *n.* inmadurez.

affective immaturity inmadurez afectiva.

psychomotor immaturity inmadurez psicomotriz.

immediate *adj.* inmediato, -ta.

immersion *n.* inmersión.

homogeneous immersion inmersión homogénea.

oil immersion inmersión en aceite.

water immersion inmersión en agua.

immiscible *adj.* inmiscible.

immitance *n.* inmitancia.

immobility *n.* inmovilidad.

immobilization *n.* inmovilización.

immobilize *v.* inmovilizar.

immortalization *n.* inmortalización.

immune *adj.* inmune.

immunisin *n.* inmunisina.

immunity *n.* inmunidad.

acquired immunity inmunidad adquirida.

active immunity inmunidad activa.

adoptive immunity inmunidad adoptiva.

antibacterial immunity inmunidad antibacteriana, inmunidad bacteriolítica.

antitoxic immunity inmunidad antitóxica.

antiviral immunity inmunidad antiviral, inmunidad antivírica, inmunidad antivirósica.

artificial active immunity inmunidad activa artificial.

artificial passive immunity inmunidad pasiva artificial.

bacteriophage immunity inmunidad a bacteriófagos.

cell-mediated immunity (CMI) inmunidad de mediación celular, inmunidad mediada por células (IMC), inmunidad mediada por células T (IMCT).

cellular immunity inmunidad celular.

community immunity inmunidad de comunidad.

concomitant immunity inmunidad concomitante.

congenital immunity inmunidad congénita.

cross immunity inmunidad cruzada.

familial immunity inmunidad familiar.

general immunity inmunidad general.

genetic immunity inmunidad genética.

group immunity inmunidad de grupo.

herd immunity inmunidad colectiva, inmunidad de rebaño.

humoral immunity inmunidad humoral.

individual immunity inmunidad individual.

infection immunity inmunidad a la infección.

inherent immunity inmunidad inherente.

inherited immunity inmunidad hereditaria.

innate immunity inmunidad innata.

intrauterine immunity inmunidad intrauterina.

local immunity inmunidad local.

maternal immunity inmunidad materna.

native immunity inmunidad nativa.

natural non-specific immunity inmunidad inespecífica natural.

non-specific immunity inmunidad inespecífica.

passive immunity inmunidad pasiva.

racial immunity inmunidad racial.

relative immunity inmunidad relativa.

species immunity inmunidad de especie.

specific active immunity inmunidad activa específica.

specific immunity inmunidad específica.

specific passive immunity inmunidad pasiva específica.

stress immunity inmunidad al estrés.

T cell-mediated immunity (TCMI) inmunidad de mediación celular, inmunidad mediada por células (IMC), inmunidad mediada por células T (IMCT).

tissue immunity inmunidad tisular.

immunization *n.* inmunización.

active immunization inmunización activa.

passive immunization inmunización pasiva.

immunizator *adj.* inmunizador, -ra, inmunizante.

immunize *v.* inmunizar.

immunoadjuvant *adj.* inmunoadyuvante.

immunoadsorbent *n.* inmunoadsorbente.

immunoadsorption *n.* inmunoadsorción.

immunoagglutination *n.* inmunoaglutinación.

immunoassay *n.* inmunoanálisis, inmunoensayo, inmunovaloración.

enzyme immunoassay inmunoensayo enzimático.

enzyme-multiplied immunoassay (EMIT) inmunoensayo multiplicado por enzimas.

solid phase immunoassay inmunoensayo en fase sólida.

thin-layer immunoassay inmunoensayo en capa delgada.

immunobiology *n.* inmunobiología.

immunoblast *n.* inmunoblasto.

immunoblastic *adj.* inmunoblástico, -ca.

immunocatalysis *n.* inmunocatálisis.

immunochemical *adj.* inmunoquímico, -ca.

immunochemistry *n.* inmunoquímica.

immunochemotherapy *n.* inmunoquimioterapia.

immunocoadjuvant *n.* inmunocoadyuvante.

immunocompetence *n.* inmunocompetencia, inmunosuficiencia.

immunocompetent *adj.* inmunocompetente, inmunosuficiente.

immunocomplex *n.* inmunocomplejo.

immunocompromised *adj.* inmunocomprometido, -da.

immunoconglutinin *n.* inmunoconglutinina.

immunocyte *n.* inmunocito.

immunocytoadherence *n.* inmunocitoadherencia.

immunocytochemistry *n.* inmunocitoquímica.
immunodeficiency *n.* inmunodeficiencia.
cellular immunodeficiency with abnormal immunoglobulin synthesis inmunodeficiencia celular con síntesis anormal de inmunoglobulinas.
combined immunodeficiency inmunodeficiencia combinada.
common variable immunodeficiency inmunodeficiencia común variable, inmunodeficiencia variable común.
common variable unclassifiable immunodeficiency inmunodeficiencia variable común inclasificable.
hyper IgM syndrome immunodeficiency inmunodeficiencia con hiperproducción de IgM.
immunodeficiency with elevated IgM inmunodeficiencia con aumento de IgM.
immunodeficiency with hyper-IgM inmunodeficiencia con hiper IgM.
immunodeficiency with hypoparathyroidism inmunodeficiencia con hipoparatiroidismo.
immunodeficiency with short-limbed dwarfism inmunodeficiencia con enanismo de miembros cortos.
immunodeficiency with thymoma inmunodeficiencia asociada a timoma.
primary immunodeficiency inmunodeficiencia primaria.
secondary immunodeficiency inmunodeficiencia secundaria.
severe combined immunodeficiency (SCID) inmunodeficiencia combinada grave, inmunodeficiencia combinada severa (IDCG).
immunodeficient *adj.* inmunodeficiente.
immunodepression *n.* inmunodepresión.
immunodepressive *adj.* inmunodepresor, -ra.
immunodermatology *n.* inmunodermatología.
immunodiagnosis *n.* inmunodiagnosis, inmunodiagnóstico.
immunodiffusion *n.* inmunodifusión.
double immunodiffusion inmunodifusión doble.
radial immunodiffusion inmunodifusión radial (IDR).
single immunodiffusion inmunodifusión simple.
immunodominance *n.* inmunodominancia.
immunodominant *adj.* inmunodominante.
immunoelectrodiffusion *n.* inmunoelectrodifusión.
immunoelectrophoresis *n.* inmunoelectroforesis.
counter immunoelectrophoresis inmunoelectroforesis contra corriente.
countercurrent immunoelectrophoresis inmunoelectroforesis contra corriente.
crossed immunoelectrophoresis inmunoelectroforesis cruzada.
rocket immunoelectrophoresis inmunoelectroforesis en cohete.
two-dimensional immunoelectrophoresis inmunoelectroforesis bidimensional.
immunoenhancement *n.* inmunofomento.
immunoenhancer *n.* inmunoestimulador.
immunoferritin *n.* inmunoferritina.
immunofiltration *n.* inmunofiltración.
immunofluorescence *n.* inmunofluorescencia.
direct immunofluorescence inmunofluorescencia directa.
indirect immunofluorescence inmunofluorescencia indirecta.

immunogen *n.* inmunógeno.
behavioral immunogen inmunógeno por conducta.
immunogenetic *adj.* inmunogenético, -ca.
immunogenetics *n.* inmunogenética.
immunogenic *adj.* inmunogénico, -ca.
immunogenicity *n.* inmunogenicidad.
immunoglobulin *n.* inmunoglobulina.
anti-D immunoglobulin inmunoglobulina anti-D.
chickenpox immunoglobulin inmunoglobulina de la varicela.
hepatitis B immunoglobulin (HBIG) inmunoglobulina contra la hepatitis B (IgHB).
human normal immunoglobulin inmunoglobulina humana normal.
immunoglobulin A (IgA) inmunoglobulina A (IgA).
immunoglobulin A deficiency inmunoglobulina A deficitaria.
immunoglobulin D (IgD) inmunoglobulina D (IgD).
immunoglobulin E (IgE) inmunoglobulina E (IgE).
immunoglobulin G (IgG) inmunoglobulina G (IgG).
immunoglobulin M (IgM) inmunoglobulina M (IgM).
immunoglobulin M deficiency inmunoglobulina M deficitaria.
measles immunoglobulin inmunoglobulina del sarampión.
monoclonal immunoglobulin inmunoglobulina monoclonal.
pertussis immunoglobulin inmunoglobulina contra la tos ferina, inmunoglobulina del pertussis.
poliomyelitis immunoglobulin inmunoglobulina de la poliomielitis.
rabies immunoglobulin inmunoglobulina antirrábica, inmunoglobulina de la rabia.
Rh0 immunoglobulin (DD) inmunoglobulina Rh0 (D).
secretory immunoglobulin A inmunoglobulina A secretoria.
specific immunoglobulin inmunoglobulina específica.
tetanus immunoglobulin (TIG) inmunoglobulina del tétanos (IGT), inmunoglobulina tetánica.
thyroid growth stimulating immunoglobulin inmunoglobulina estimulantes del crecimiento del tiroides.
thyroid-binding inhibitory immunoglobulin (TBII) inmunoglobulina inhibitoria de fijación del tiroides.
thyroid-stimulating immunoglobulin inmunoglobulina estimulantes del tiroides (TSI).
TSH-binding inhibitory immunoglobulin (TBII) inmunoglobulina inhibitoria de la fijación de la TSH (TBII).
varicellazoster immunoglobulin (VZIG) inmunoglobulina de la varicela zoster (IGVZ).
zoster immunoglobulin (ZIG) inmunoglobulina zoster (ZIG).
immunoglobulinopathy *n.* inmunoglobulinopatía.
immunohematology *n.* inmunohematología.
immunoheterogeneity *n.* inmunoheterogeneidad.
immunoheterogeneous *adj.* inmunoheterogéneo, -a.
immunohistochemical *adj.* inmunohistoquímico, -ca.

immunohistochemistry *n.* inmunohistoquímica.
immunohistofluorescence *n.* inmunohistofluorescencia.
immunoincompetent *adj.* inmunoinsuficiente.
immunologic *adj.* inmunológico, -ca.
immunological *adj.* inmunológico, -ca.
immunologist *n.* inmunólogo, -ga.
immunology *n.* inmunología.
immunomodulation *n.* inmunomodulación.
immunomodulator *n.* inmunomodulador.
immunoparasitology *n.* inmunoparasitología.
immunoparesis *n.* inmunoparálisis.
immunopathogenesis *n.* inmunopatogenia.
immunopathologic *adj.* inmunopatológico, -ca.
immunopathology *n.* inmunopatología.
immunoperoxidase *n.* inmunoperoxidasa.
immunophysiology *n.* inmunofisiología.
immunopotency *n.* inmunopotencia.
immunopotentiation *n.* inmunopotenciación.
immunopotentiator *n.* inmunopotenciador.
immunoprecipitation *n.* inmunoprecipitación.
immunoproliferative *adj.* inmunoproliferativo, -va.
immunoprophylaxis *n.* inmunoprofilaxis.
immunoprotein *n.* inmunoproteína.
immunoradiometric *adj.* inmunorradiométrico, -ca.
immunoradiometry *n.* inmunorradiometría.
immunoreactant *adj.* inmunorreactivo, -va.
glucagon immunoreactant inmunorreactivo de glucagón.
immunoreaction *n.* inmunorreacción.
immunoreactive *adj.* inmunorreactivo, -va.
immunoregulation *n.* inmunorregulación.
immunoselection *n.* inmunoselección.
immunosenescence *n.* inmunosenectud.
immunosorbent *adj.* inmunosorbente.
immunostaining *n.* inmunomarcaje.
immunostimulant *adj.* inmunoestimulante.
immunostimulation *n.* inmunoestimulación.
immunosuppresant *n.* inmunosupresor.
immunosuppresive *adj.* inmunosupresivo, -va.
immunosuppression *n.* inmunosupresión.
immunosurgery *n.* inmunocirugía.
immunosurveillance *n.* inmunovigilancia.
immunotherapy *n.* inmunoterapia.
active specific immunotherapy inmunoterapia específica activa.
adoptive immunotherapy inmunoterapia adoptiva.
venom immunotherapy inmunoterapia con veneno.
immunotolerance *n.* inmunotolerancia.
immunotoxin (IT) *n.* inmunotoxina (IT).
immunotransfusion *n.* inmunotransfusión.
immunotropic *adj.* inmunotrópico, -ca.
impact *n.* impacto.
impaction *n.* impacción[1].
ceruminal impaction impacción de cerumen.
dental impaction impacción dental, impacción dentaria.
fecal impaction impacción fecal.
food impaction impacción de alimentos.
inertial impaction impacción por inercia.
mucus impaction impacción mucosa.
impairment *n.* deterioro.
mental impairment deterioro mental.
impalpable *adj.* impalpable.

impaludation *n.* impaludación, impaludismo.
impar *adj.* impar.
impardigitate *adj.* impardigitado, -da.
impatency *n.* impatencia.
impatent *adj.* impatente.
impedance *n.* impedancia.
　acoustic impedance impedancia acústica.
imperative *adj.* imperativo, -va.
imperception *n.* impercepción.
imperforate *adj.* imperforado, -da.
imperforation *n.* imperforación.
imperious *adj.* imperioso, -sa.
impermeability *n.* impermeabilidad.
impermeable *adj.* impermeable.
impermeant *adj.* impermeante.
impersistence *n.* impersistencia.
　motor impersistence impersistencia motora.
impervious *adj.* impenetrable, impervio, -via.
impetiginization *n.* impetiginización.
impetiginous *adj.* impetiginoso, -sa.
impetigo *n.* impétigo.
　Bockhart's impetigo impétigo de Bockhart.
　bullous impetigo of the newborn impétigo ampollar del recién nacido.
　follicular impetigo impétigo folicular.
　impetigo bullosa impétigo ampollar, impétigo bulloso.
　impetigo circinata impétigo circinado.
　impetigo contagiosa impétigo contagioso.
　impetigo contagiosa bullosa impétigo contagioso bulloso.
　impetigo eczematodes impétigo eccematodes, impétigo eccematoide.
　impetigo herpetiformis impétigo herpetiforme.
　impetigo neonatorum impétigo neonatal.
　impetigo vulgaris impétigo vulgar.
　staphylococcal impetigo impétigo estafilocócico.
　streptococcal impetigo impétigo estreptocócico.
impetus *n.* ímpetu.
implant¹ *n.* implante.
　bag-gel implant implante de bolsa-gel.
　carcinomatous implant implante carcinomatoso.
　cell implant implante de células.
　cochlear implant implante coclear.
　dental implant implante dental.
　endodontic implant implante de endodoncia.
　endometrial implant implante endometrial.
　endo-osseous implant implante endoóseo.
　endosseous implant implante endoóseo, implante intraóseo.
　endosteal implant implante endóstico.
　hypodermic implant implante hipodérmico.
　inflatable implant implante inflable.
　intramucosal implant implante intramucoso.
　intraocular implant implante intraocular.
　intraperiosteal implant implante intraperióstico.
　lens implant implante de cristalino.
　magnetic implant implante magnético.
　orbital implant implante orbitario.
　osseointegrated implant implante osteointegrado.
　penile implant implante peniano.
　pin implant implante a perno.
　post implant implante en poste.
　submucosal implant implante submucoso.
　subperiosteal implant implante subperióstico.
　supraperiosteal implant implante supraperióstico.

　tissue implant implante de tejidos.
implant² *v.* implantar.
implantation *n.* implantación.
　central implantation implantación central.
　circumferential implantation implantación circunferencial.
　cortical implantation implantación cortical.
　eccentric implantation implantación excéntrica.
　hypodermic implantation implantación hipodérmica.
　interstitial implantation implantación intersticial.
　nerve implantation implantación de nervio, implantación nerviosa.
　pellet implantation implantación de pellet.
　periosteal implantation implantación perióstica.
　subcutaneous implantation implantación subcutánea.
　subperiosteal implantation implantación subperióstica.
　superficial implantation implantación superficial.
implantodontics *n.* implantodoncia.
implantodontist *n.* implantodoncista.
implantodontology *n.* implantodontología.
implantologist *n.* implantólogo, -ga.
implantology *n.* implantología.
　dental implantology implantología dental, implantología oral.
　oral implantology implantología dental, implantología oral.
implementing *n.* ejecución.
implosion *n.* implosión.
impotence *n.* impotencia, impotentia.
　atonic impotence impotencia atónica.
　functional impotence impotencia funcional.
　hormonal impotence impotencia hormonal.
　learned impotence impotencia aprendida.
　medicamentous impotence impotencia medicamentosa.
　neurogenic impotence impotencia atónica, impotencia neurológica.
　psychogenic impotence impotencia psicógena.
　vasculogenic impotence impotencia vasculogénica.
　venous impotence impotencia venosa.
impotency *n.* impotencia, impotentia.
impotentia *n.* impotencia, impotentia.
impregnate *v.* impregnar.
impregnation *n.* impregnación.
impressio *n.* impresión.
　impressio cardiaca hepatis impresión cardíaca del hígado.
　impressio cardiaca pulmonis impresión cardíaca del pulmón.
　impressio colica impresión cólica, impresión cólica del hígado.
　impressio colica hepatis impresión cólica, impresión cólica del hígado.
　impressio duodenalis impresión duodenal, impresión duodenal del hígado.
　impressio duodenalis hepatis impresión duodenal, impresión duodenal del hígado.
　impressio esophagea impresión esofágica del hígado.
　impressio esophagea hepatis impresión esofágica, impresión esofágica del hígado.
　impressio gastrica impresión gástrica.
　impressio gastrica hepatis impresión gástrica del hígado.
　impressio gastrica renis impresión gástrica del riñón.

　impressio hepatica renis impresión hepática, impresión hepática del riñón.
　impressio ligamenti costoclavicularis impresión del ligamento costoclavicular.
　impressio muscularis renis impresión muscular renal.
　impressio petrosa pallii impresión petrosa, impresión petrosa del palio.
　impressio renalis impresión renal, impresión renal del hígado.
　impressio renalis hepatis impresión renal, impresión renal del hígado.
　impressio suprarenalis impresión suprarrenal, impresión suprarrenal del hígado.
　impressio suprarenalis hepatis impresión suprarrenal, impresión suprarrenal del hígado.
　impressio trigeminalis impresión trigémina, impresión trigémina del hueso temporal.
　impressio trigeminalis ossis temporalis impresión trigémina, impresión trigémina del hueso temporal.
　impressio trigemini ossis temporalis impresión trigémina, impresión trigémina del hueso temporal.
　impressiones gyrorum impresiones gyrorum.
impression *n.* impresión.
　anatomic impression impresión anatómica.
　basilar impression impresión basilar.
　bridge impression impresión de puente.
　cardiac impression impresión cardíaca.
　cardiac impression of the liver impresión cardíaca del hígado.
　cardiac impression of the lung impresión cardíaca del pulmón.
　cleft palate impression impresión de fisura paladar, impresión de paladar hendido.
　colic impression impresión cólica, impresión cólica del hígado.
　colic impression of the liver impresión cólica, impresión cólica del hígado.
　complete denture impression impresión de dentadura completa o total, impresión para prótesis completa o total.
　deltoid impression impresión deltoidea, impresión deltoidea del húmero.
　deltoid impression of the humerus impresión deltoidea, impresión deltoidea del húmero.
　dental impression impresión dental.
　digastric impression impresión digástrica.
　digital impression impresión digitada, impresión digital.
　digitate impression impresión digitada, impresión digital.
　direct bone impression impresión ósea directa.
　duodenal impression impresión duodenal, impresión duodenal del hígado.
　duodenal impression of the liver impresión duodenal, impresión duodenal del hígado.
　esophageal impression impresión esofágica, impresión esofágica del hígado.
　esophageal impression of the liver impresión esofágica, impresión esofágica del hígado.
　final impression impresión definitiva, impresión final.
　gastric impression impresión gástrica.
　gastric impression of the liver impresión gástrica del hígado.
　gyrate impression impresiones gyrorum.
　hydrocolloid impression impresión hidrocoloide.
　impression for costoclavicular ligament impresión del ligamento costoclavicular.

lower impression impresión inferior.
mandibular impression impresión del maxilar inferior.
maxillary impression impresión maxilar superior.
mental impression impresión mental.
partial denture impression impresión de dentadura parcial, impresión para prótesis parcial.
petrosal impression of the pallium impresión petrosa, impresión petrosa del palio.
preliminary impression impresión preliminar.
primary impression impresión primaria.
renal impression impresión renal, impresión renal del hígado.
renal impression of the liver impresión hepática, impresión hepática del riñón, impresión renal, impresión renal del hígado.
rhomboid impression impresión romboidea, impresión romboidea de la clavícula.
rhomboid impression of the clavicle impresión romboidea, impresión romboidea de la clavícula.
secondary impression impresión secundaria.
sectional impression impresión seccional.
suprarenal impression impresión suprarrenal, impresión suprarrenal del hígado.
suprarenal impression of the liver impresión suprarrenal, impresión suprarrenal del hígado.
trigeminal impression impresión trigémina, impresión trigémina del hueso temporal.
trigeminal impression of the temporal bone impresión angular para el ganglio de Gasser, impresión trigémina, impresión trigémina del hueso temporal.
upper impression impresión superior.
imprint *n.* impronta².
imprinting *n.* imprimación, impronta¹, troquelado.
impuberal *n.* impúber.
impulse *n.* impulso².
apex impulse impulso apical.
apical impulse impulso apical.
cardiac impulse impulso cardíaco.
ectopic impulse impulso ectópico.
episternal impulse impulso episternal.
escape impulse impulso de escape.
irresistible impulse impulso irresistible.
kinetic impulse impulso cinético.
left parasternal impulse impulso paraesternal izquierdo.
morbid impulse impulso morboso.
nerve impulse impulso nervioso.
neural impulse impulso neural.
premature impulse impulso prematuro.
right parasternal impulse impulso paraesternal derecho.
impulsion *n.* impulsión².
impulsive *adj.* impulsivo, -va.
impulsiveness *n.* impulsividad.
impulsivity *n.* impulsividad.
imu *n.* imu.
in articulo mortis in articulo mortis.
in extremis in extremis.
in loco parentis in loco parentis.
in situ in situ.
in utero in utero.
in vacuo in vacuo.
in vitro in vitro.
in vivo in vivo.
inacidity *n.* inacidez.
inaction *n.* inacción.
inactivate *v.* inactivar.

inactivation *n.* inactivación.
complement inactivation inactivación del complemento, inactivación del suero.
heat inactivation inactivación por calor.
inactivation of complement inactivación del complemento, inactivación del suero.
X inactivation inactivación X.
inactivator *n.* inactivador.
inagglutinable *adj.* inaglutinable.
inanimate *adj.* inanimado, -da.
inanition *n.* inanición¹.
inapparent *adj.* inaparente.
inappetence *n.* inapetencia.
inarticulate *adj.* inarticulado, -da.
inassimilable *adj.* inasimilable.
inattention *n.* inatención.
selective inattention inatención selectiva.
sensory inattention inatención sensitiva.
visual inattention inatención visual.
inaxon *n.* inaxón.
inborn *adj.* ingénito, -ta.
inbred *adj.* endocriado, -da.
inbreeding *n.* endocría, endogamia.
incandescence *n.* incandescencia.
incandescency *n.* incandescencia.
incandescent *adj.* incasdescente.
incarcerated *adj.* encarcelado, -da, incarcerado, -da.
incarceration *n.* incarceración.
incarnant *adj.* encarnante.
incarnatio *n.* encarnamiento.
incarnation *n.* encarnadura, encarnamiento.
incarnative *adj.* incarnativo, -va.
incendiarism *n.* incendiarismo.
incentive *n.* incentivo.
incertae sedis incertae sedis.
incest *n.* incesto.
incestuous *adj.* incestuoso, -sa.
inchacao *n.* inchacao.
incidence *n.* incidencia.
incident *adj.* incidente.
incineration *n.* incineración.
incipient *adj.* incipiente.
incisal *adj.* incisal.
incise *v.* incidir.
incision *n.* incisión.
Agnew-Verhoeff incision incisión de Agnew-Verhoeff.
Battle-Jalaguier-Kammerer incision incisión de Battle-Jalaguier-Kammerer.
Battle's incision incisión de Battle.
Bevan's incision incisión de Bevan.
bucket-handle incision incisión en asa de cubo.
celiotomy incision incisión de celiotomía.
Cherney incision incisión de Cherney.
chevron incision incisión en cabrio.
Deaver's incision incisión de Deaver.
Dührssen's incision incisión de Dührssen.
endaural incision incisión endaural.
Fergusson's incision incisión de Fergusson.
flank incision incisión del flanco.
Kammerer-Battle incision incisión de Kammerer-Battle.
Kocher's incision incisión de Kocher.
Maylard incision incisión de Maylard.
McBurney's incision incisión de McBurney.
Munro-Kerr incision incisión de Munro-Kerr.
Nagamatsu incision incisión de Nagamatsu.
paramedian incision incisión paramedia, incisión paramediana.
paravaginal incision incisión paravaginal.
Pfannenstiel's incision incisión de Pfannenstiel.
relief incision incisión de alivio.

Rockey-Davis incision incisión de Rockey-Davis.
Schuchardt's incision incisión de Schuchardt.
transverse abdominal incision incisión abdominal transversa.
Warren's incision incisión de Warren.
incisive *adj.* incisivo², -va.
incisolabial *adj.* incisolabial.
incisolingual *adj.* incisolingual.
incisoproximal *adj.* incisoproximal.
incisor *adj.* incisivo¹, incisor.
central incisor incisivo central.
first incisor incisivo primero.
Hutchinson's incisor incisivo de Hutchinson.
lateral incisor incisivo lateral.
medial incisor incisivo medial.
second incisor incisivo segundo.
shovel-shaped incisor incisivo en forma de ala.
winged incisor incisivo en ala.
incisura *n.* incisura.
incisure *n.* incisura.
incitant *adj.* incitante.
incitogram *n.* incitograma.
inclinatio *n.* inclinación.
inclinatio pelvis inclinación de la pelvis, inclinación pélvica.
inclination *n.* inclinación.
condylar guidance inclination inclinación de guía condílea.
condylar guide inclination inclinación de guía condílea.
dental inclination inclinación dental.
enamel rod inclination inclinación de los prismas del esmalte.
inclination of the pelvis inclinación de la pelvis, inclinación pélvica.
lateral condylar inclination inclinación condílea lateral.
lingual inclination inclinación lingual.
pelvic inclination inclinación de la pelvis, inclinación pélvica.
incline *n.* inclinación.
incline of the pelvis inclinación de la pelvis, inclinación pélvica.
pelvic incline inclinación de la pelvis, inclinación pélvica.
inclinometer *n.* inclinómetro.
inclusion *n.* inclusión.
cell inclusion inclusión celular.
dental inclusion inclusión dental.
Döhle inclusion inclusión de Döhle.
fetal inclusion inclusión fetal.
Guarnieri's inclusion inclusión de Guarnieri.
intranuclear inclusion inclusión intranuclear.
leukocyte inclusion inclusión leucocitaria, inclusión leucocítica.
nuclear inclusion inclusión nuclear.
Walthard's inclusion inclusión de Walthard.
incoagulability *n.* incoagulabilidad.
incoagulable *adj.* incoagulable.
incoercible *adj.* incoercible.
incoherence *n.* incoherencia.
incoherent *adj.* incoherente.
incompatibility *n.* incompatibilidad.
chemical incompatibility incompatibilidad química.
physiologic incompatibility incompatibilidad fisiológica.
Rh incompatibility incompatibilidad Rh.
therapeutic incompatibility incompatibilidad terapéutica.
incompatible *adj.* incompatible.
incompetence *n.* incompetencia.

aortic incompetence incompetencia aórtica.

cardiac incompetence incompetencia cardíaca.

mitral incompetence incompetencia mitral.

muscular incompetence incompetencia muscular.

pulmonary incompetence incompetencia pulmonar.

pulmonic incompetence incompetencia pulmonar.

pyloric incompetence incompetencia pilórica.

tricuspid incompetence incompetencia tricuspídea.

valvular incompetence incompetencia valvular.

incompetency *n.* incompetencia.

incompetent *adj.* incompetente.

inconstant *adj.* inconstante.

incontinence *n.* incontinencia.

active incontinence incontinencia activa.

affective incontinence incontinencia afectiva.

anal incontinence incontinencia anal.

continuous incontinence incontinencia continua.

fecal incontinence incontinencia fecal.

incontinence of pigment incontinencia de pigmento, incontinencia pigmentaria, incontinentia pigmenti.

incontinence of the feces incontinencia de excremento.

incontinence of urine incontinencia urinaria.

overflow incontinence incontinencia de orina por rebosamiento, incontinencia rebosamiento.

paradoxical incontinence incontinencia paradójica.

paralytic incontinence incontinencia paralítica.

rectal incontinence incontinencia rectal.

stress incontinence incontinencia de esfuerzo, incontinencia por tensión.

stress urinary incontinence incontinencia de orina de esfuerzo genuina.

urge incontinence incontinencia con urgencia miccional.

urgency incontinence incontinencia con urgencia miccional.

urinary exertional incontinence incontinencia urinaria por esfuerzo.

urinary incontinence incontinencia urinaria.

urinary stress incontinence incontinencia urinaria por estrés.

incontinent *adj.* incontinente.

incontinentia *n.* incontinencia, incontinentia.

Bloch-Sulzberger incontinentia pigmenti incontinencia pigmentaria de Bloch-Sulzberger.

incontinentia alvi incontinencia alva.

incontinentia pigmenti incontinencia de pigmento, incontinencia pigmentaria, incontinentia pigmenti.

incontinentia pigmenti achromians incontinencia pigmentaria acrómica.

incontinentia urinae incontinencia urinaria.

Naegeli's incontinentia pigmenti incontinencia pigmentaria de Naegeli.

incoordination *n.* incoordinación.

cricopharyngeal incoordination incoordinación cricofaríngea.

incorporation *n.* incorporación.

incostapedial *adj.* incoestapedio, -dia.

increment *n.* incremento.

incretodiagnosis *n.* incretodiagnóstico.

incretogenous *adj.* incretógeno, -na.

incretology *n.* incretología.

incretopathy *n.* incretopatía.

incretotherapy *n.* incretoterapia.

incrustation *n.* encostración, encostradura, incostración, incrustación[1].

incubate *n.* incubado.

incubation *n.* incubación.

incubator *n.* incubadora.

isolation incubator incubadora de aislamiento.

incubus *n.* íncubo, incubus.

incudal *adj.* incudal, incúdeo, -a.

incudectomy *n.* incudectomía.

incudiform *adj.* incudiforme.

incudomalleal *adj.* incudomaleolar.

incudostapedial *adj.* Incudoestapedio, -dia, incudostapedio, -dia.

incurable *adj.* incurable.

incus *n.* incus, yunque.

incycloduction *n.* inciclinoducción.

incyclophoria *n.* inciclforia.

incyclotropia *n.* inciclotropía.

indenization *n.* indenización.

indentation *n.* indentación.

scleral indentation indentación escleral.

independence *n.* independencia.

professional independence independencia profesional.

index *n.* índice.

absorbancy index índice de absorbancia.

ACH index índice ACH.

altitudinal index índice de altura.

alveolar index índice alveolar.

anesthetic index índice anestésico.

antitryptic index índice antitríptico.

Apgar index índice de Apgar.

Arneth index índice de Arneth.

auricular index índice auricular.

auriculoparietal index índice auriculoparietal.

auriculovertical index índice auriculovertical.

baric index índice bárico.

Barthel index (BI) índice de Barthel (IB).

baseline fetal heart index índice cardíaco fetal basal.

basilar index índice basilar.

Becker-Lennhoff index índice de Becker-Lennhoff.

Bödecker index índice de Bödecker.

body mass index índice de masa corporal.

Bouchard's index índice de Bouchard.

braquial index índice braquial.

Brugsch's index índice de Brugsch.

buffer index índice buffer.

calcium index de calcio, índice cálcico.

Calculus Surface index índice de superficie de cálculos.

cardiac index índice cardíaco.

cardiothoracic index índice cardiotorácico.

centromeric index índice centromérico.

cephalic index index cefálico, índice cefálico.

cephalo-orbital index índice cefaloorbitario.

cephalorachidian index índice cefalorraquídeo.

cephalospinal index índice cefaloespinal.

cerebral index índice cerebral.

cerebrospinal index índice cerebrospinal.

chemotherapeutic index índice quimioterapéutico.

color index (CI) índice colorimétrico, índice del color (IC).

corofrontal index índice coronofrontal.

cranial index índice craneal.

Dean's fluorosis index índice de fluorosis de Dean.

def caries index índice DEF, índice def de caries, índice DEF de caries.

degenerative index índice degenerativo.

dental index index dental, índice dental, índice dentario.

DF caries index índice DF, índice df de caries, índice DF de caries.

DMF caries index índice DMF, índice dmf de caries, índice DMF de caries.

DMFS caries index índice DMFS de caries, índice dmfs de caries, índice DMS.

effective temperature index índice de temperatura efectiva, índice efectivo de temperatura.

empathic index índice de empatía, índice empático.

empathy index índice de comprensión de los sentimientos, índice de empatía, índice empático.

endemic index índice endémico.

erythrocyte index índice eritrocitario, índice eritrocítico.

facial index índice facial.

femorohumeral index índice femorohumeral.

Flower's dental index índice dental de Flower.

Flower's index índice de Flower.

forearm-hand index índice de antebrazo y mano.

Fourmentin's thoracic index índice torácico de Fourmentin.

free thyroxine index índice de tiroxina libre.

gingival index índice gingival.

gingival-periodontal index índice gingivoperiodontal.

gnathic index índice gnático.

habitus index índice de hábito.

hair index índice de pelo.

hand index índice de la mano.

height index índice de altura.

height-length index índice de altura-largo.

hematopneic index índice hematopneico.

hemorenal index índice hemorrenal.

hemorenal salt index índice hemorrenal de sal.

icteric index índice de icterus, índice ictérico.

icterus index índice de icterus, índice ictérico.

jaundice index índice de icterus, índice ictérico.

juxtaglomerular index índice yuxtaglomerular.

karyopyknotic index índice cariopicnótico.

Kaup index índice de Kaup.

length-breadth index índice entre longitud y anchura, índice largo-ancho.

length-height index índice de longitud y altura, índice largo altura.

Lennhoff's index índice de Lennhoff.

leukopenic index índice leucopénico.

lower leg-foot index índice inferior de pierna y pie.

maturation index índice de maduración.

maxilloalveolar index índice maxiloalveolar.

metacarpal index índice metacarpiano.

mitotic index índice mitótico.

molar absorbancy index índice de absorbancia molar.

nasal index índice nasal.

nucleocytoplasmic index índice nucleocitoplásmico.

nucleoplasmic index índice nucleoplásmico.

obesity index índice de obesidad.

opsonic index índice opsónico.

oral hygiene index índice de higiene oral.

orbital index (of Broca) índice orbitario (de Broca).

orbitonasal index índice orbitonasal.

palatal index índice palatino.

palatine index índice palatino.

palatomaxillary index índice palatomaxilar.

parasite index índice parasitario.

pelvic index índice pélvico.

periodontal index índice periodontal.

phagocytic index í fagocítico, índice fagocitario.

physiognomonic upper face index índice fisiognomónico de la parte superior de la cara.

Pirquet's index índice de Pirquet.

plaque index índice de placa.

PMA index índice PMA.

ponderal index índice ponderal.

pressure-volume index índice de presión-volumen.

pulse index índice de pulso.

quality of life index índice de calidad de vida.

Quetelet's index índice de Quetelet.

radiohumeral index índice radiohumeral.

red cell index índice de hematíes, índice eritrocitario, índice eritrocítico.

refraction index índice de refracción.

refractive index índice de refracción.

Reid index índice de Reid.

repetition index índice de repetición.

respiration index índice respiratorio.

Robinson index índice de Robinson.

Röhrer's index índice de Röhrer.

root caries index índice de caries en raíces.

sacral index índice del sacro.

saturation index índice de saturación.

saturation index of hemoglobin índice de saturación de la hemoglobina.

Schilling's index índice de Schilling.

sedimentation index índice de sedimentación.

shock index índice de shock.

short increment sensitivity index (SISI) índice de incremento corto de la sensibilidad.

simplified oral hygiene index índice de higiene oral simplificado.

slew index índice de torsión.

spleen index índice esplénico.

splenic index índice esplénico.

splenometric index índice esplenométrico.

staphylo-opsonic index índice estafiloopsónico.

steroid production index índice de producción de esteroides.

steroid secretory index índice secretorio de esteroides.

stroke volume index índice de volumen sistólico.

stroke work index índice de trabajo sistólico.

therapeutic index índice terapéutico.

thoracic index index torácico, índice torácico.

tibiofemoral index índice tibiofemoral.

tibioradial index índice tibiorradial.

Tiffeneau's index índice de Tiffeneau.

transversovertical index índice transversovertical.

trunk index índice del tronco.

tuberculo-opsonic index índice tuberculoopsónico.

uricolytic index índice uricolítico.

vertical index índice vertical.

vital index índice vital.

voiding flow index índice de flujo de micción.

volume index índice de volumen.

wind chill index índice de frío del aire.

zygomaticoauricular index índice cigomaticoauricular.

indican *n.* indicán, indicano.

metabolic indican indicán metabólico.

indicanemia *n.* indicanemia.

indicanidrosis *n.* indicanhidrosis, indicanidrosis.

indicanmeter *n.* indicánmetro.

indicanorachia *n.* indicanorraquia.

indicant *n.* indicante.

indicanuria *n.* indicanuria.

indicatio *n.* indicación.

indicatio causalis indicación causal.

indicatio curativa indicación curativa.

indicatio morbi indicación mórbida, indicación morbosa.

indicatio symptomatica indicación sintomática.

indication *n.* indicación.

indication for surgery indicación operatoria, indicación quirúrgica.

indicator *n.* indicador, -ra.

alizarin indicator indicador de alizarina.

anaerobic indicator indicador anaerobio.

Andrade's indicator indicador de Andrade.

chemical indicator indicador químico.

dew point indicator indicador de temperatura de condensación.

oxidation-reduction indicator indicador de oxidación-reducción.

radioactive indicator indicador radiactivo.

redox indicator indicador redox.

Schneider's indicator indicador de Schneider.

indicophose *n.* indicofosia.

indifference *n.* indiferencia.

attentional indifference indiferencia atencional.

belle indifference indiferencia bella.

indifferentiation *n.* indiferenciación.

indigence *n.* indigencia.

medical indigence indigencia médica.

indigenous *n.* indígena.

indigestible *adj.* indigerible.

indigestion *n.* indigestión.

acid indigestion indigestión ácida.

fat indigestion indigestión grasa.

gastric indigestion indigestión gástrica.

intestinal indigestion indigestión intestinal.

nervous indigestion indigestión nerviosa.

sugar indigestion indigestión de azúcares.

indigitation *n.* indigitación.

indigo *n.* índigo.

indigogen *n.* indigógeno.

indigopurpurine *n.* indigopurpurina.

indigotin *n.* indigotina.

indigouria *n.* indigouria.

indiguria *n.* indiguria.

indirect *adj.* indirecto, -ta.

indirubin *n.* indirrubina.

indirubinuria *n.* indirrubinuria.

indiscriminate *adj.* indiscriminado, -da.

indisposition *n.* indisposición.

indiversion *n.* indiversión.

individualism *n.* individualismo.

individuality *n.* individualidad.

individuation *n.* individuación, individualización.

indolaceturia *n.* indolaceturia.

indole *n.* indol.

indolent *adj.* indolente, indoloro, -ra.

indologenous *adj.* indológeno, -na.

indoluria *n.* indoluria.

indoxyl *n.* indoxilo.

indoxylemia *n.* indoxilemia.

indoxyl-sulfate *n.* indoxilsulfato.

indoxyluria *n.* indoxiluria.

induce *v.* inducir.

induced *adj.* inducido, -da.

inducer *n.* inductora.

inductance *n.* inductancia.

induction *n.* inducción.

autonomous induction inducción autónoma.

complementary induction inducción complementaria.

elective induction of labor inducción electiva del parto.

electromagnetic induction inducción electromagnética.

enzyme induction inducción enzimática.

induction of anesthesia inducción de la anestesia.

induction of labor inducción del parto.

lysogenic induction inducción lisogénica.

medical induction of labor inducción médica del parto.

Spemann's induction inducción de Spemann.

spinal induction inducción espinal, inducción raquídea.

inductor *n.* inductor[1], -ra.

inductorium *n.* inductor[2].

inductotherm *n.* inductotermo.

inductothermy *n.* inductotermia.

indulin *n.* indulina.

indulinophil *n.* indulinófilo[1].

indulinophile *n.* indulinófilo[1].

indulinophilic *adj.* indulinófilo[2], -la.

indurated *adj.* indurado, -da.

induration *n.* induración.

black induration induración negra.

brawny induration induración carnosa.

brown induration induración parda.

brown induration of the lung induración marrón del pulmón.

cyanotic induration induración cianótica.

fibrous induration induración fibroide.

Froriep's induration induración de Froriep.

granular induration induración granular, induración granulosa.

gray induration induración gris.

laminate induration induración laminada, induración laminar.

parchment induration induración en parche.

penile induration induración del pene.

pigment induration of the lung induración pigmentaria del pulmón.

plastic induration induración plástica, induración plástica del pene.

red induration induración roja.

indurative *adj.* indurativo, -va.

inebriant *adj.* inebriante, inebriativo, -va.

inebriation *n.* embriaguez, inebriación.

light inebriation embriaguez ligera.

serious inebriation embriaguez grave.

subclinical inebriation embriaguez subclínica.

inedia *n.* inedia.

inelastic *adj.* inelástico, -ca.

inemia *n.* inemia.

Inermicapsifer Inermicapsifer.

inert *adj.* inerte.

inertia *n.* inercia.

colonic inertia inercia del colon.

immunological inertia inercia inmunológica.

magnetic inertia inercia magnética.

psychic inertia inercia psíquica.

INF *n.* INF), interferón (IFN.

infancy *n.* infancia, lactancia².
infant *n.* lactante.
  infant of a diabetic mother hijo de madre diabética.
  infant of an addicted mother hijo de madre adicta.
  nursing infant lactante.
infanticide *n.* infanticida, infanticidio.
infantile *adj.* infantil.
infantilism *n.* infantilismo.
  Brissaud's infantilism infantilismo de Brissaud.
  cachectic infantilism infantilismo caquéctico.
  celiac infantilism infantilismo celíaco.
  dysthyroidal infantilism infantilismo distiroideo, infantilismo distiróidico.
  hepatic infantilism infantilismo hepático.
  Herter's infantilism infantilismo de Herter.
  hypophyseal infantilism infantilismo hipofisario.
  hypothyroid infantilism infantilismo hipotiroideo.
  idiopathic infantilism infantilismo idiopático.
  intestinal infantilism infantilismo intestinal.
  Lévi-Lorain infantilism infantilismo de Lévi-Lorain.
  Lorain-Lévi infantilism infantilismo de Lorain-Lévi.
  Lorain's infantilism infantilismo de Lorain.
  lymphatic infantilism infantilismo linfático.
  myxedematous infantilism infantilismo mixedematoso.
  pancreatic infantilism infantilismo pancreático.
  partial infantilism infantilismo parcial.
  pituitary infantilism infantilismo hipofisario, infantilismo pituitario.
  proportionate infantilism infantilismo proporcionado.
  regressive infantilism infantilismo regresivo, infantilismo reversivo, infantilismo tardío.
  renal infantilism infantilismo renal.
  sexual infantilism infantilismo del sexo, infantilismo sexual.
  static infantilism infantilismo estático.
  symptomatic infantilism infantilismo sintomático.
  universal infantilism infantilismo universal.
infarct *n.* infarto.
  anemic infarct infarto anémico.
  bilirubin infarct infarto de bilirrubina.
  bland infarct infarto blando.
  bone infarct infarto óseo.
  Brewer's infarct infarto de Brewer.
  calcareous infarct infarto calcáreo.
  cystic infarct infarto quístico.
  embolic infarct infarto embólico.
  hemorrhagic infarct infarto hemorrágico.
  pale infarct infarto pálido.
  red infarct infarto rojo.
  scalp infarct infarto del cuero cabelludo.
  septic infarct infarto séptico.
  thrombotic infarct infarto trombótico.
  uric acid infarct infarto de ácido úrico.
  white infarct infarto blanco.
  Zahn's infarct infarto de Zahn.
infarctectomy *n.* infarctectomía.
infarction *n.* infarto.
  acute myocardial infarction (AMI) infarto agudo de miocardio (IAM).
  anterior myocardial infarction infarto anterior del miocardio.
  anterior pituitary lobe infarction infarto del lóbulo anterior de la hipófisis.

  anteroinferior myocardial infarction infarto anteroinferior del miocardio.
  anterolateral myocardial infarction infarto anterolateral del miocardio.
  anteroseptal myocardial infarction infarto anteroseptal del miocardio.
  atrial infarction infarto auricular.
  cardiac infarction infarto cardíaco.
  cerebral infarction infarto cerebral.
  diaphragmatic myocardial infarction infarto diafragmático del miocardio.
  hepatic infarction infarto hepático.
  inferior myocardial infarction infarto inferior del miocardio.
  inferolateral myocardial infarction infarto inferolateral del miocardio.
  intestinal infarction infarto intestinal.
  lacunar infarction infarto lacunar.
  lateral myocardial infarction infarto lateral del miocardio.
  liver infarction infarto hepático.
  mesenteric infarction infarto mesentérico.
  myocardial infarction (MI) infarto del miocardio (IM).
  myocardial infarction in H-form infarto del miocardio en forma de H.
  non-transmural myocardial infarction infarto no transmural del miocardio.
  posterior myocardial infarction infarto posterior del miocardio.
  pulmonary infarction (PI) infarto pulmonar (IP).
  renal infarction infarto renal.
  septal myocardial infarction infarto septal del miocardio.
  silent myocardial infarction infarto silencioso del miocardio.
  subendocardial infarction infarto subendocárdico, infarto subendocárdico del miocardio.
  subendocardial myocardial infarction infarto subendocárdico, infarto subendocárdico del miocardio.
  through-and-through myocardial infarction infarto a través del miocardio.
  transmural infarction infarto transmural, infarto transmural del miocardio.
  transmural myocardial infarction infarto transmural, infarto transmural del miocardio.
  watershed infarction infarto en vertiente.
infaust *adj.* infausto, -ta.
infect *v.* infectar.
infectible *adj.* infectable.
infection *n.* infección.
  aerogenous infection infección aerógena.
  agonal infection infección agonal, infección agónica.
  airborne infection infección aérea, infección transmitida por el aire.
  anaerobic infection infección por anacrobios.
  apical infection infección apical.
  colonization infection infección colonizadora.
  community-acquired infection infección extrahospitalaria.
  complicated urinary infection infección urinaria complicada.
  concurrent infection infección concurrente.
  cross infection infección cruzada.
  cryptogenic infection infección criptogenética, infección criptogena, infección criptogénica.
  droplet infection infección por gotillas, infección transmitida por gotitas.
  dust-borne infection infección transportada por polvo.

  ectogenous infection infección ectógena.
  endogenous infection infección endógena.
  enteric infection infección intestinal.
  epidural infection infección epidural.
  exogenous infection infección exógena.
  extracranial infection infección extracraneal.
  extradural infection infección extradural.
  focal infection infección focal.
  fungal infection infección fúngica.
  gastrointestinal infection infección gastrointestinal.
  germinal infection infección germinal.
  hospital-acquired infection infección adquirida en el hospital.
  iatrogenic infection infección iatrogénica, infección yatrogénica.
  infection following splenectomy infección secundaria a esplenectomía.
  intraventicular infection infección intraventricular.
  latent infection infección latente.
  LCR shunts infection infección de las derivaciones de LCR.
  local infection infección local.
  low-grade infection infección leve.
  mass infection infección masiva.
  mixed infection infección mixta.
  nosocomial infection infección nosocomial.
  opportunistic infection infección oportunista.
  periapical infection infección periapical.
  pin track infection infección del trayecto del clavo.
  polymicrobic infection infección polimicrobiana.
  protozoal infection infección protozoaria.
  psychic infection infección psíquica.
  pyogenic infection infección piógena.
  respiratory tract infection infección del tracto respiratorio.
  retrograde infection infección retrógrada.
  secondary infection infección secundaria.
  spinal infection infección raquimedular.
  staphylococcal infection infección estafilocócica.
  streptococcal infection infección estreptocócica.
  subacute infection infección subaguda.
  subclinical infection infección subclínica.
  subdural infection infección subdural.
  systemic infection infección sistémica.
  terminal infection infección terminal.
  trypanosomal infection infección tripanosómica.
  uncomplicated infection infección urinaria no complicada.
  upper respiratory infection infección de las vías respiratorias superiores.
  urinary infection infección urinaria.
  urinary tract infection (UTI) infección del tracto urinario (ITU).
  vector-borne infection infección transmitida por un vector.
  Vincent's infection infección de Vincent.
  viral infection infección vírica, viriasis.
  water-borne infection infección transmitida por agua.
  zoonotic infection infección zoonótica.
infection-immunity *n.* infección-inmunidad.
infectiosity *n.* infecciosidad.
infectious *adj.* infeccioso, -sa.
infectiousness *n.* infecciosidad.
infective *adj.* infectivo, -va.
infectivity *n.* infectividad.
inferent *adj.* inferente.

inferior *adj.* inferior.

inferiority *n.* inferioridad.

inferolateral *adj.* inferoexterno, -na, inferolateral.

inferomedial *adj.* inferointerno, -na.

inferomedian *adj.* inferomedial, inferomediano, -na.

inferonasal *adj.* inferonasal.

inferoposterior *adj.* inferoposterior.

inferotemporal *adj.* inferotemporal.

infertility *n.* infertilidad.

  primary infertility infertilidad primaria.

  secondary infertility infertilidad secundaria.

infest *v.* infestar.

infestation *n.* infestación.

infibulation *n.* infibulación.

infiltrate[1] *n.* infiltrado.

  Assmann's tuberculous infiltrate infiltrado de Assmann, infiltrado tuberculoso de Assmann.

  infraclavicular infiltrate infiltrado infraclavicular.

infiltrate[2] *v.* infiltrar.

infiltration *n.* infiltración.

  adipose infiltration infiltración adiposa.

  calcareous infiltration infiltración calcárea.

  calcium infiltration infiltración cálcica.

  cellular infiltration infiltración celular.

  epituberculous infiltration infiltración epituberculosa.

  fatty infiltration infiltración grasa.

  fatty infiltration of the heart infiltración grasa del corazón.

  gelatinous infiltration infiltración gelatinosa.

  glycogen infiltration infiltración de glucógeno, infiltración glucogénica.

  gray infiltration infiltración gris.

  inflammatory infiltration infiltración inflamatoria.

  lipomatous infiltration infiltración lipomatosa.

  lymphocytic infiltration of the skin infiltración linfocítica de la piel.

  paraneural infiltration infiltración paraneural.

  perineural infiltration infiltración perineural.

  sanguineous infiltration infiltración sanguínea.

  serous infiltration infiltración serosa.

  tissular infiltration infiltración de los tejidos.

  tuberculous infiltration infiltración tuberculosa.

  urinous infiltration infiltración de orina, infiltración urinaria, infiltración urinosa.

infinity *n.* infinito.

infirm *adj.* enfermizo, -za, infirme.

infirmity *n.* achaque, dolencia.

inflammagen *n.* inflamágeno.

inflammation *n.* inflamación.

  acute inflammation inflamación aguda.

  adhesive inflammation inflamación adherente, inflamación adhesiva.

  allergic inflammation inflamación alérgica.

  alterative inflammation inflamación alterante.

  atrophic inflammation inflamación atrófica.

  bacterial inflammation inflamación bacteriana.

  catarrhal inflammation inflamación catarral.

  chronic inflammation inflamación crónica.

  cirrhotic inflammation inflamación cirrótica.

  croupous inflammation inflamación crupal, inflamación cruposa.

  degenerative inflammation inflamación degenerativa.

  diffuse inflammation inflamación difusa.

  disseminated inflammation inflamación diseminada.

  exudative inflammation inflamación exudativa.

  fibrinopurulent inflammation inflamación fibrinopurulenta.

  fibrinous inflammation inflamación fibrinosa.

  fibroid inflammation inflamación fibroide.

  fibrosing inflammation inflamación fibroide.

  focal inflammation inflamación focal.

  granulomatous inflammation inflamación granulomatosa.

  hyperplastic inflammation inflamación hiperplásica, inflamación hiperplástica.

  hypertrophic inflammation inflamación hipertrófica.

  immune inflammation inflamación inmune.

  inflammation of the liver inflamación del hígado.

  interstitial inflammation inflamación intersticial.

  metastatic inflammation inflamación metastásica, inflamación metastática.

  necrotic inflammation inflamación necrótica.

  necrotizing inflammation inflamación necrosante.

  obliterative inflammation inflamación obliterante, inflamación obliterativa.

  parenchymatous inflammation inflamación parenquimatosa.

  plastic inflammation inflamación plástica, inflamación plástica.

  productive inflammation inflamación productiva.

  proliferative inflammation inflamación proliferativa.

  proliferous inflammation inflamación proliferante.

  pseudomembranous inflammation inflamación seudomembranosa.

  purulent inflammation inflamación purulenta.

  reactive inflammation inflamación reactiva.

  sclerosing inflammation inflamación esclerosante.

  serofibrinous inflammation inflamación serofibrinosa.

  seroplastic inflammation inflamación seroplástica, inflamación seroplástica.

  serous inflammation inflamación serosa, inflamación serótica.

  simple inflammation inflamación simple.

  specific inflammation inflamación específica.

  subacute inflammation inflamación subaguda.

  suppurative inflammation inflamación supurativa.

  toxic inflammation inflamación tóxica.

  traumatic inflammation inflamación traumática.

  ulcerative inflammation inflamación ulcerativa, inflamación ulcerosa.

inflammatory *adj.* inflamatorio, -ria.

inflation *n.* inflación.

inflator *n.* inflador.

inflection *n.* inflexión.

inflexibility *n.* inflexibilidad.

inflexion *n.* inflexión.

influenza *n.* influenza.

  Asian influenza influenza asiática.

  endemic influenza influenza endémica.

  Hong Kong influenza influenza de Hong Kong.

  influenza A influenza a.

  influenza B influenza B.

  influenza C influenza C.

  influenza nostras influenza nostras.

  Russian influenza influenza rusa.

  Spanish influenza influenza española.

influenzal *adj.* influenzal.

Influenzavirus Influenzavirus.

information processing *n.* procesamiento de la información.

informativeness *n.* informatividad.

informed consent *adj.* consentimiento informado.

informosome *n.* informosoma.

infra-axillary *adj.* infraaxilar.

infrabulge *n.* subecuador.

infracardiac *adj.* infracardíaco, -ca.

infracerebral *adj.* infracerebral.

infraciliature *n.* infraciliatura.

infraclass *n.* infraclase.

infraclavicular *adj.* infraclavicular.

infraclusion *n.* infraclusión.

infraconstrictor *adj.* infraconstrictor, -ra.

infracortical *adj.* infracortical.

infracostal *adj.* infracostal.

infracotyloid *adj.* infracotiloideo, -a.

infracristal *adj.* infracrestal.

infraction *n.* infracción.

  Freiberg's infraction infracción de Freiberg.

infracture *n.* infractura.

infradentale *n.* infradental.

infradian *adj.* infradiano, -na.

infradiaphragmatic *adj.* infradiafragmático, -ca.

infraduction *n.* infraducción.

infraglenoid *adj.* infraglenoideo, -a.

infraglottic *adj.* infraglótico, -ca.

infrahepatic *adj.* infrahepático, -ca.

infrahyoid *adj.* infrahioideo, -a.

infrainguinal *adj.* infrainguinal.

inframamillary *adj.* inframamilar.

inframammary *adj.* inframamario, -ria.

inframandibular *adj.* inframandibular.

inframarginal *adj.* inframarginal.

inframaxillary *adj.* inframaxilar.

infranuclear *adj.* infranuclear.

infraocclusion *n.* infraoclusión.

infraorbital *adj.* infraorbital, infraorbitario, -ria.

infrapatellar *adj.* infrapatelar, infrarrotuliano, -na.

infrapsychic *adj.* infrapsíquico, -ca.

infrared *adj.* infrarrojo, -ja.

  far infrared infrarrojo distante.

  long-wave infrared infrarrojo de onda larga.

  near infrared infrarrojo cercano.

  short-wave infrared infrarrojo de onda corta.

infrascapular *adj.* infraescapular, infrascapular.

infrasonic *adj.* infrasónico, -ca.

infrasound *n.* infrasonido.

infraspinous *adj.* infraespinoso, -sa, infraspinoso, -sa.

infrasplenic *adj.* infraesplénico, -ca, infrasplénico, -ca.

infrasternal *adj.* infraesternal, infrasternal.

infrastructure *n.* infraestructura.

infrasubspecific *adj.* infrasubespecífico, -ca.

infratemporal *adj.* infratemporal.

infratentorial *adj.* infratentorial.

infrathoracic *adj.* infratorácico, -ca.

infratonsillar *adj.* infraamigdalino, -na, infratonsilar.

infratracheal *adj.* infratraqueal.

infratrochlear *adj.* infratroclear.

infratubal *adj.* infratubárico, -ca.

infraturbinal *adj.* infraturbinal.

infraumbilical *adj.* infraumbilical.

infravergence *n.* infravergencia.

infraversion *n.* infraversión.

infriction *n.* infricción.

infundibular *adj.* infundibular.

infundibulectomy *n.* infundibulectomía.

  Brock's infundibulectomy infundibulectomía de Brock.

infundibuliform *adj.* infundibuliforme.

infundibulin *n.* infundibulina.

infundibulofolliculitis *n.* infundibulofoliculitis.

  disseminated recurrent infundibulofolliculitis infundibulofoliculitis diseminada recurrente.

infundibuloma *n.* infundibuloma.

infundibulopelvic *adj.* infundibulopélvico, -ca.

infundibulum infundíbulo, infundibulum.

infusate *adj.* infundido, -da.

infusible *adj.* infusible.

infusion *n.* infusión.

  cold infusion infusión fría.

  interstitial infusion infusión intersticial.

  intraosseous infusion infusión intraósea.

  intravenous infusion infusión endovenosa, infusión intravenosa.

  meat infusion infusión de carne.

  saline infusion infusión salina.

  subcutaneous infusion infusión subcutánea.

infusodecoction *n.* infusodecocción.

ingesta *n.* ingesta.

ingestant *n.* ingestante.

ingestion *n.* ingestión.

ingestive *adj.* ingestivo, -va.

ingravescent *adj.* ingravescente.

ingredient *n.* ingrediente.

ingrowing toenail *n.* uñero.

ingrown toenail *n.* uñero.

ingrowth *n.* increscencia.

  epithelial ingrowth increscencia epitelial.

inguen *n.* ingle.

inguinal *adj.* inguinal.

inguinoabdominal *adj.* inguinoabdominal.

inguinocrural *adj.* inguinocrural.

inguinodynia *n.* inguinodinia.

inguinolabial *adj.* inguinolabial.

inguinoperitoneal *adj.* inguinoperitoneal.

inguinoscrotal *adj.* inguinoescrotal, inguinoscrotal.

inhalant *n.* inhalante.

  antifoaming inhalant inhalante antiespumante.

inhalation *n.* inhalación.

  isoproterenol sulfate inhalation inhalación de sulfato de isoproterenol.

  smoke inhalation inhalación de humo.

  solvent inhalation inhalación de solventes.

inhale *v.* inhalar.

inhaler *n.* inhalador.

  ether inhaler inhalador de éter.

  H.H. inhaler inhalador H.H.

  metered dose inhaler inhalador de dosis fija.

inherent *adj.* inherente.

inheritance *n.* herencia[2].

  alternative inheritance herencia alternativa.

  amphigenous inheritance herencia anfígona.

  autosomal dominant inheritance herencia autosómica dominante.

  autosomal inheritance herencia autosómica.

  autosomal recessive inheritance herencia autosómica recesiva.

biparental inheritance herencia biparenteral.

blending inheritance herencia mezclada.

complemental inheritance herencia complementaria.

crisscross inheritance herencia cruzada.

cytoplasmic inheritance herencia citoplasmática, herencia citoplásmica.

duplex inheritance herencia doble.

holandric inheritance herencia holándrica.

hologynic inheritance herencia hologínica.

homochronous inheritance herencia homócrona.

homotropic inheritance herencia homotrópica.

intermediate inheritance herencia intermedia.

maternal inheritance herencia materna.

mitochondrial inheritance herencia mitocondrial.

monofactorial inheritance herencia monofactorial.

multifactorial inheritance herencia multifactorial.

polygenic inheritance herencia poligénica.

quantitative inheritance herencia cuantitativa.

quasidominant inheritance herencia cuasidominante.

supplemental inheritance herencia suplementaria.

X-linked dominant inheritance herencia dominante ligada al cromosoma X.

X-linked inheritance herencia ligada al cromosoma X.

X-linked recessive inheritance herencia recesiva ligada al cromosoma X.

inhibin *n.* inhibina.

inhibit *v.* inhibir.

inhibition *n.* inhibición.

  allogeneic inhibition inhibición alogénica.

  allogenic inhibition inhibición alogénica.

  allosteric inhibition inhibición alostérica.

  central inhibition inhibición central.

  competitive inhibition inhibición competitiva.

  contact inhibition inhibición de contacto.

  endproduct inhibition inhibición de producto terminal.

  feedback inhibition inhibición de retroalimentación, inhibición por retroalimentación.

  hapten inhibition of precipitation inhibición de precipitación por hapteno.

  hemagglutination inhibition IHA), inhibición de hemaglutinación (IH.

  inhibition of enzymes inhibición enzimática.

  inhibition of the reflexes inhibición de reflejos, inhibición refleja.

  latent inhibition inhibición latente.

  non-competitive inhibition inhibición no competitiva.

  potassium inhibition inhibición por potasio.

  proactive inhibition inhibición proactiva.

  reciprocal inhibition inhibición recíproca.

  reflex inhibition inhibición de reflejos, inhibición refleja.

  residual inhibition inhibición residual.

  retroactive inhibition inhibición retroactiva.

  selective inhibition inhibición selectiva.

  social inhibition inhibición social.

  suicide inhibition inhibición suicida.

  Wedensky inhibition inhibición de Wedensky.

inhibitive *adj.* inhibidor[2], -ra.

inhibitor *n.* inhibidor[1].

alpha1-trypsin inhibitor inhibidor de alpha1-tripsina.

angiotensin converting enzyme inhibitor (ACE) inhibidor de la enzima convertidora de angiotensina, inhibidor de la enzima de conversión, inhibidor de la enzima de conversión de la angiotensina (ECA).

appetite inhibitor inhibidor del apetito.

C1 esterase inhibitor inhibidor de C1 (C1 INH), inhibidor de C1 esterasa.

C1 inhibitor (C1 INH) inhibidor de C1 (C1 INH), inhibidor de C1 esterasa.

carbonate dehydratase inhibitor inhibidor de carbonato deshidratasa.

carbonic anhydrase inhibitor inhibidor de la anhidrasa carbónica.

cholesterol inhibitor inhibidor del colesterol.

cholinesterase inhibitor inhibidor de la colinesterasa.

competitive inhibitor inhibidor competitivo.

human alpha1 proteinase inhibitor inhibidor de alfa1 proteinasa humana.

mitotic inhibitor inhibidor mitótico.

monoamine oxidase inhibitor (MAOI) inhibidor de la monoaminaoxidasa, inhibidor de la monoaminooxidasa (IMAO).

non-reversible inhibitor inhibidor no reversible.

plasminogen activator inhibitor (PAI-1) inhibidor del activador del plasminógeno-1 (PAI-1).

residual inhibitor inhibidor residual.

trypsin inhibitor inhibidor de tripsina.

uncompetitive inhibitor inhibidor no competitivo.

inhibitory *adj.* inhibidor[2], -ra, inhibitorio, -ria.

inhibitrope *adj.* inhibítropo, -pa.

inhomogeneity *n.* inhomogeneidad.

inhomogeneous *adj.* inhomogéneo, -a.

iniac *adj.* iniaco, -ca.

iniad iniad.

inial *adj.* inial.

iniencephalus *n.* iniencéfalo.

iniencephaly *n.* iniencefalia.

iniodymus *n.* iniodimo.

inion *n.* inión.

iniopagus *n.* iniópago.

iniops *n.* iniope, iniops.

initial *adj.* inicial.

initiation *n.* iniciación.

initiator *n.* iniciador.

initis *n.* initis.

inject *v.* inyectar.

injectable *adj.* inyectable.

injected *adj.* inyectado, -da.

injection *n.* inyección.

  anatomical injection inyección anatómica.

  booster injection inyección de recuerdo.

  circumcorneal injection inyección circuncorneal.

  coarse injection inyección burda.

  depot injection inyección depot, inyección por depósito.

  dextrose and sodium chloride injection inyección de cloruro de sodio y dextrosa, inyección de cloruro sódico y dextrosa.

  endermic injection inyección endodérmica.

  epifascial injection inyección epifascial.

  fine injection inyección fina.

  fructose injection inyección de fructosa.

  gaseous injection inyección gaseosa.

  gelatin injection inyección gelatinosa.

  hypodermic injection inyección hipodérmica.

insulin injection inyección de insulina.
intraarticular injection inyección intraarticular.
intracutaneous injection inyección intracutánea.
intradermal injection inyección intradermal, inyección intradérmica.
intradermic injection inyección intradermal, inyección intradérmica.
intramuscular injection inyección intramuscular.
intrathecal injection inyección intratecal.
intravascular injection inyección intravascular.
intravenous injection inyección intravenosa.
intraventricular injection inyección intraventricular.
iodinated I125 albumin injection inyección de albúmina marcada con^{125} I.
iodinated I131 albumin injection inyección de albúmina marcada con^{131} I.
iron dextran injection inyección de hierro dextrán.
iron sorbitex injection inyección de hierro sorbitex.
jet injection inyección a chorro, inyección de chorro.
lactated Ringer's injection inyección de lactato de Ringer, inyección lactada de Ringer.
opacifying injection inyección opacificante.
paraperiosteal injection inyección paraperióstica.
parenchymatous injection inyección parenquimatosa.
posterior pituitary injection inyección de hipófisis posterior.
preservative injection inyección preservativa.
protamine sulfate injection inyección de sulfato de protamina.
protein hydrolysate injection inyección de hidrolizado proteico.
regular insulin injection inyección regular de insulina.
Ringer's injection inyección de Ringer.
sclerosing injection inyección esclerosante.
sensitizing injection inyección sensibilizadora, inyección sensibilizante.
sodium chloride injection inyección de cloruro de sodio.
sodium lactate injection inyección de lactato sódico.
sodium pertenechtate Tc99m injection inyección de pertenectato de sodio marcado con Tc99m.
sodium radiochromate injection inyección de radiocromato de sodio.
subcutaneous injection inyección subcutánea.
vasopressin injection inyección de vasopresina.
Z-tract injection inyección en Z.
injector *n.* inyector.
jet injector inyector a chorro.
injunction *n.* interdicto.
injure *v.* lesionar.
injury *n.* injuria, lesión.
birth injury lesión de parto.
blast injury lesión por explosión.
cold injury lesión por frío.
contrecoup injury lesión por contragolpe.
contrecoup injury of the brain lesión en contragolpe del cerebro.
coup injury of the brain lesión en golpe del cerebro.

deceleration injury lesión por desaceleración.
egg-white injury lesión de clara de huevo.
Goyrand's injury lesión de Goyrand.
head injury lesión de la cabeza.
hyperextension-hyperflexion injury lesión de hiperextensión-hiperflexión.
injury of the intervertebral disk lesión del disco intervertebral.
internal injury lesión interna.
ionizing radiation injury lesión por radiación ionizante.
roindage injury lesión por explosión.
spinal cord injury lesión de la médula espinal.
vital injury lesión vital.
inlay *n.* incrustación², inlay.
epithelial inlay incrustación epitelial.
gold inlay incrustación de oro.
porcelain inlay incrustación de porcelana.
wax inlay incrustación de cera.
inlet *n.* entrada.
innate *adj.* innato, ta.
innervation *n.* inervación.
double innervation inervación doble.
reciprocal innervation inervación recíproca.
innidation *n.* anidación, innidación.
innidiation *n.* inidiación.
innocent *adj.* inocente.
innocuous *adj.* innocuo, -cua, inocuo, -cua.
innominatal *adj.* innominático, -ca.
innominate *adj.* innominado, -da.
innoxious *adj.* innocuo, -cua.
inochondritis *n.* inocondritis.
inoculability *n.* inoculabilidad.
inoculable *adj.* inoculable.
inoculate *v.* inocular.
inoculation *n.* inoculación.
protective inoculation inoculación protectora.
stress inoculation inoculación de estrés, inoculación para estrés.
inoculum *n.* inóculo.
inogenesis *n.* inogénesis.
inoglia *n.* inoglia.
inohymenitis *n.* inohimenitis.
inolith *n.* inolito.
inomyositis *n.* inomiositis.
inoperable *adj.* inoperable.
inophragma *n.* inofragma.
inorganic *adj.* inorgánico, -ca.
inosclerosis *n.* inoesclerosis, inosclerosis.
inoscopy *n.* inoscopia.
inosculate *v.* inoscular.
inosculation *n.* inosculación.
inose *n.* inosa, inose.
inosemia *n.* inosemia.
inosite *n.* inosita.
inositis *n.* inositis.
inositol *n.* inositol.
inositol-1-4-5-triphosphate inositol -1-4-5-trisfosfato (IP3).
inositoluria *n.* inositoluria.
inosituria *n.* inosituria.
inostosis *n.* inostosis.
inosuria *n.* inosuria.
inotagma *n.* inotagma.
inotropic *adj.* inotrópico, -ca, inótropo, -pa.
negatively inotropic inotrópico negativo.
positively inotropic inotrópico positivo.
inotropism *n.* inotropismo.
inpatient *adj.* hospitalizado, -da.
inquiline *n.* inquilino.
inruction *n.* inructación.
insalivate *v.* insalivar.
insalivation *n.* insalivación.
insalubrious *adj.* insalubre.

insane *adj.* insano, -na, loco, -ca.
insanitary *adj.* antihigiénico, -ca, insanitario, -ria.
insanity *n.* alienación mental, insania, locura.
Basedowian insanity insania de Basedow.
insatiable *adj.* insaciable.
inscriptio *n.* inscripción.
inscriptio tendinea inscripción tendinosa.
inscription *n.* inscripción.
tendinous inscription inscripción tendinosa.
tendinous inscription of the rectus abdominis muscle inscripción tendinosa del músculo rectoabdominal.
insect *n.* insecto.
Insecta Insecta.
insectarium *n.* insectario, insectarium.
insecticide *n.* insecticida.
insectifuge *n.* insectífugo, -ga.
insemination *n.* inseminación.
artificial insemination inseminación artificial.
artificial insemination-donor (AID) inseminación artificial de donante (IAD).
artificial insemination-husband (AIH) inseminación artificial del cónyuge (IAC).
donor insemination inseminación de donador.
heterologous insemination inseminación heteróloga.
homologous insemination inseminación homóloga.
insenescence *n.* insenescencia.
insensibility *n.* insensibilidad.
insensible *adj.* insensible.
insert *n.* inserción, insertar.
intramucosal insert inserción intramucosa.
mucosal insert inserción intramucosa.
insertio *n.* inserción.
insertio velamentosa inserción velamentosa.
insertion *n.* inserción.
radium insertion inserción de radio.
thinking insertion inserción del pensamiento.
thought insertion inserción del pensamiento.
velamentous insertion inserción velamentosa.
insheathed *adj.* envainado, -da.
insidious *adj.* insidioso, -sa.
insight *n.* insight, introspección.
insilinism *n.* insulinismo.
insolation *n.* insolación.
asphyxial insolation insolación asfíctica.
hyperpyrexial insolation insolación hiperpiréxica.
insoluble *adj.* insoluble.
insomnia *n.* insomnio.
familial fatal insomnia insomnio familiar fatal.
insomniac *adj.* insomne.
insomnic *adj.* insomne.
insorption *n.* insorción.
inspection *n.* inspección.
inspectionism *n.* inspeccionismo.
inspersion *n.* inspersión.
inspirate *v.* inspirar.
inspiration *n.* inspiración.
crowing inspiration inspiración en forma de silbido áspero.
forced inspiration inspiración forzada.
forcible inspiration inspiración forzada.
inspiration hold inspiración mantenida.
periodic deep inspiration inspiración profunda periódica.
inspiratory *adj.* inspiratorio, -ria.
inspirometer *n.* aspirómetro, inspirómetro.
inspissated *adj.* espesado, -da.

inspissation *n.* inspisación.
inspissator *n.* espesador.
instability *n.* inestabilidad.
  attentional instability inestabilidad atencional.
  genetic instability inestabilidad genética.
  joint instability inestabilidad articular.
  tumor instability inestabilidad tumoral.
  vertebral cervical instability inestabilidad vertebral cervical.
instep *n.* empeine.
instillation *n.* instilación.
  BCG instillation in bladder cancer instilación vesical con BCG.
  eardrop instillation instilación de gotas óticas.
  nasal instillation of medication instilación nasal de medicamentos.
  rectal instillation of medication instilación rectal de medicamentos.
  thiotepa instillation in bladder cancer instilación vesical con tiotepa.
  vaginal instillation of medication instilación vaginal de fármacos.
instillator *n.* instilador.
instinct *n.* instinto, pulsión[1].
  aggressive instinct instinto agresivo, pulsión agresiva, pulsión destructiva.
  death instinct instinto de muerte, instinto mortal, pulsión de muerte.
  ego instinct instinto del ego, instinto del yo, pulsión del yo.
  herd instinct instinto de grupo, instinto de rebaño.
  instinct of self-preservation pulsión de autoconservación.
  instinct to master pulsión de dominio.
  life instinct instinto de vida, instinto vital, pulsión de vida.
  mother instinct instinto materno.
  sexual instinct instinto sexual, pulsión sexual.
  social instinct instinto social.
instinctive *adj.* instintivo, -va.
instinctual *adj.* instintivo, -va.
institutionalize *v.* hospitalizar.
instrument *n.* instrumento.
  diamond cutting instrument instrumento cortante de diamantes.
  Krueger instrument stop instrumento tope de Krueger.
  plugging instrument instrumento para obturar.
  purse-string instrument instrumento para sutura en tabaquera.
  research instrument instrumento de investigación.
  stereotactic instrument instrumento estereotáxico.
  stereotaxic instrument instrumento estereotáxico.
  test handle instrument instrumento de mango de prueba.
instrumental *adj.* instrumental[1].
instrumentarium *n.* instrumental[2], instrumentario.
instrumentation *n.* instrumentación.
  Dwyer instrumentation instrumentación de Dwyer.
  Harrington instrumentation instrumentación de Harrington.
insucation *n.* insucación.
insudation *n.* insudación.
insufficiency *n.* insuficiencia.
  accommodative insufficiency insuficiencia acomodativa.

active insufficiency insuficiencia activa.
  acute adrenocortical insufficiency insuficiencia corticosuprarrenal aguda.
  adrenal insufficiency insuficiencia capsular, insuficiencia suprarrenal.
  adrenocortical insufficiency insuficiencia corticosuprarrenal.
  aortic insufficiency insuficiencia aórtica.
  arterial insufficiency insuficiencia arterial.
  arterial insufficiency of the lower extremities insuficiencia arterial de las extremidades inferiores.
  backward heart insufficiency insuficiencia cardíaca retrógrada.
  basilar insufficiency insuficiencia vertebrobasilar.
  cardiac insufficiency insuficiencia cardíaca.
  chronic adrenocortical insufficiency insuficiencia corticosuprarrenal crónica.
  circulatory insufficiency insuficiencia circulatoria.
  convergence insufficiency insuficiencia por convergencia.
  coronary insufficiency insuficiencia coronaria.
  divergence insufficiency insuficiencia por divergencia.
  electric insufficiency insuficiencia eléctrica.
  forward heart insufficiency insuficiencia cardíaca anterógrada.
  gastric insufficiency insuficiencia gástrica.
  gastromotor insufficiency insuficiencia gastromotora.
  gonadal insufficiency insuficiencia gonadal.
  hepatic insufficiency insuficiencia hepática.
  ileocecal insufficiency insuficiencia ileocecal.
  insufficiency of the externi insuficiencia de los músculos externos.
  insufficiency of the eyelids insuficiencia de los párpados, insuficiencia palpebral.
  insufficiency of the interni insuficiencia de los músculos internos.
  insufficiency of the valves insuficiencia valvular.
  latent adrenocortical insufficiency insuficiencia corticosuprarrenal latente.
  mitral insufficiency insuficiencia mitral.
  muscular insufficiency insuficiencia muscular.
  myocardial insufficiency insuficiencia del miocardio.
  pancreatic insufficiency insuficiencia pancreática.
  parathyroid insufficiency insuficiencia paratiroidea.
  partial adrenocortical insufficiency insuficiencia corticosuprarrenal parcial.
  pituitary insufficiency insuficiencia hipofisaria.
  placental insufficiency insuficiencia placentaria.
  primary adrenocortical insufficiency insuficiencia corticosuprarrenal primaria.
  pulmonary insufficiency insuficiencia pulmonar.
  pyloric insufficiency insuficiencia pilórica.
  renal insufficiency insuficiencia renal.
  respiratory insufficiency insuficiencia respiratoria.
  secondary adrenocortical insufficiency insuficiencia corticosuprarrenal secundaria.
  thyroid insufficiency insuficiencia tiroidea.
  tricuspid insufficiency insuficiencia tricuspídea.
  uterine insufficiency insuficiencia uterina.

valvular insufficiency insuficiencia valvular.
  vascular insufficiency insuficiencia vascular.
  velopharyngeal insufficiency insuficiencia velofaríngea.
  venous insufficiency insuficiencia venosa.
  vertebrobasilar insufficiency insuficiencia vertebrobasilar.
insufflate *v.* insuflar.
insufflation *n.* insuflación.
  cranial insufflation insuflación craneal.
  endotracheal insufflation insuflación endotraqueal, insuflación intratraqueal.
  insufflation of the lungs de los pulmones, insuflación pulmonar.
  perirenal insufflation insuflación perirrenal.
  presacral insufflation insuflación presacra.
  tubal insufflation insuflación tubaria, insuflación tubárica.
insufflator *n.* insuflador.
insula *n.* ínsula.
insular *adj.* insular.
insular-pancreatotropic *adj.* insularpancreatotrópico, -ca.
insulation *n.* aislamiento[1].
insulator *n.* aislante.
insulin *n.* insulina.
  atypical insulin insulina atípica.
  biphasic insulin insulina bifásica.
  globin insulin insulina globina.
  globin zinc insulin insulina cíncica globina, insulina con cinc y globina.
  human insulin insulina humana.
  immunoreactive insulin insulina inmunorreactiva.
  intermediate-acting insulin insulina de acción intermedia.
  isophane insulin insulina isofánica.
  lente insulin insulina lenta.
  long-acting insulin insulina de acción prolongada.
  lyspro insulin insulina lispro.
  NPH (Neutral Protamine Hagedorn) insulin insulina NPH (Neutral Protamine Hagedorn).
  protamine zinc insulin insulina protamina cinc, insulina protamina cíncica.
  rapid-acting insulin insulina de acción rápida.
  regular insulin insulina regular.
  semilente insulin insulina semilenta.
  short-acting insulin insulina de acción corta.
  single component insulin insulina de componente único.
  slow-acting insulin insulina de acción lenta.
  synthetic insulin insulina sintética.
  three-to-one insulin insulina de tres a uno.
insulinase *n.* insulinasa.
insulinemia *n.* insulinemia.
insulinogenesis *n.* insulinogénesis.
insulinogenic *adj.* insulinogénico, -ca.
insulinoid *adj.* insulinoide.
insulinolipodystrophy *n.* insulinolipodistrofia.
insulinoma *n.* insulinoma.
insulinopenic *adj.* insulinopénico, -ca.
insulitis *n.* insulitis.
insulogenic *adj.* insulogénico, -ca.
insuloma *n.* insuloma.
insulopathic *adj.* insulopático, -ca.
insult *n.* insulto.
insusceptibility *n.* insusceptibilidad.
intake *n.* ingesta, ingreso.
  acceptable daily intake (ADI) ingesta diaria permisible (IDP).
  caloric intake ingesta calórica.

fluid intake ingesta de líquidos.
salt dietary intake ingesta de sal.
integrase *n.* integrasa.
integration *n.* integración.
  biological integration integración biológica.
  personality integration integración de la personalidad.
  sensory integration integración sensitiva.
  structural integration integración estructural.
integrator *n.* integrador.
integrin *n.* integrina.
integument *n.* integumento, integumentum, tegumento.
integumentum *n.* integumento, integumentum, tegumento.
  integumentum commune integumento común, integumentum commune.
intellect *n.* intelecto.
intellection *n.* intelección.
intellectualization *n.* intelectualización.
intelligence *n.* inteligencia.
  abstract intelligence inteligencia abstracta.
  artificial intelligence (AI) inteligencia artificial (IA).
  crystallized intelligence inteligencia cristalizada.
  fluid intelligence inteligencia fluida.
  measured intelligence inteligencia medida.
  mechanical intelligence inteligencia mecánica.
  social intelligence inteligencia social.
intemperance *n.* intemperancia.
intensimeter *n.* intensímetro.
intensionometer *n.* intensionómetro.
intensity *n.* intensidad.
  electric intensity intensidad del campo eléctrico.
  intensity of sound intensidad del sonido.
  intensity of x-rays intensidad de los rayos roentgen.
  luminous intensity intensidad luminosa.
  signal intensity intensidad de señal.
intensive *adj.* intensivo, -va.
intention *n.* intención.
  paradoxical intention intención paradójica.
interaccessory *adj.* interaccesorio, -ria.
interacinar *adj.* interacinar.
interacinous *adj.* interacinoso, -sa.
interaction *n.* interacción.
  drug-drug interaction interacción medicamentosa.
  drug-food interaction interacción fármaco-alimentos, interacciones entre alimentos y fármacos.
  food and drug interaction interacción entre alimentos y fármacos.
  knee-ankle interaction interacción rodilla-tobillo.
  nurse-client interaction interacción enfermero-paciente.
interagglutination *n.* interaglutinación.
interalveolar *adj.* interalveolar.
interangular *adj.* interangular.
interannular *adj.* interanular.
interarch *n.* interarcos.
interarticular *adj.* interarticular.
interarytenoid *adj.* interaritenoideo, -a.
interasteric *adj.* interastérico, -ca.
interatrial *adj.* interatrial.
interauricular *adj.* interauricular.
interbody *adj.* intercuerpos.
interbrain *n.* intercerebro.
intercadence *n.* intercadencia.
intercadent *adj.* intercadente.

intercalary *adj.* intercalado, -da.
intercalate *v.* intercalar.
intercalation *n.* intercalación.
intercanalicular *adj.* intercanalicular.
intercapillary *adj.* intercapilar.
intercarotic *adj.* intercarotídeo, -a.
intercarotid *adj.* intercarotídeo, -a.
intercarpal *adj.* intercarpal, intercarpiano, -na.
intercartilaginous *adj.* intercartilaginoso, -sa.
intercavernous *adj.* intercavernoso, -sa.
intercellular *adj.* intercelular.
intercentral *adj.* intercentral.
interception *n.* intercepción.
intercerebral *adj.* intercerebral.
interchange *n.* intercambio.
  Hamburger interchange intercambio de Hamburger.
interchondral *adj.* intercondral.
intercilium *n.* intercilium.
interclavicular *adj.* interclavicular.
interclinoid *adj.* interclinoide.
intercoccygeal *adj.* intercoccígeo, -a.
intercolumnar *adj.* intercolumnar, intercolumnario, -ria.
intercondylar *adj.* intercondilar.
intercondyloid *adj.* intercondiloideo, -a.
intercondylous *adj.* intercondíleo, -a.
intercostal *adj.* intercostal.
intercostohumeral *adj.* intercostohumeral.
intercourse *n.* intercambio.
  sexual intercourse intercambio sexual.
intercricothyrotomy *n.* intercricotirotomía.
intercristal *adj.* intercrestal, intercristal.
intercritical *adj.* intercrítico, -ca.
intercross *n.* entrecruzamiento.
intercrural *adj.* intercrural.
intercurrent *adj.* intercurrente.
intercuspation *n.* intercuspación.
intercusping *n.* intercuspidación.
intercutaneomucous *adj.* intercutaneomucoso, -sa.
interdeferential *adj.* interdeferencial.
interdental *adj.* interdental, interdentario, -ria.
interdental spillway *n.* aliviadero interdentario.
interdentium *n.* interdentium.
interdigit *n.* interdígito.
interdigital *adj.* interdigital.
interdigitate *v.* interdigitar.
interdigitation *n.* interdigitación.
interdisciplinary *adj.* interdisciplinario, -ria.
interface *n.* interfase.
  crystalline interface interfase cristalina.
  dermoepidermal interface interfase dermoepidérmica.
  metal interface interfase metálica.
  structural interface interfase estructural.
interfacial *adj.* interfacial.
interfascicular *adj.* interfascicular.
interfeminium *n.* interfeminium.
interfemoral *adj.* interfemoral.
interference *n.* interferencia.
  bacterial interference interferencia bacteriana.
  constructive interference interferencia constructiva.
  cuspal interference interferencia de las cúspides.
  destructive interference interferencia destructiva.
  occlusal interference interferencia oclusal.
  proactive interference interferencia proactiva.
  retroactive interference interferencia retroactiva.
interferometer *n.* interferómetro.

  electron interferometer interferómetro electrónico.
interferometry *n.* interferometría.
  electron interferometry interferometría electrónica.
interferon (IFN) *n.* INF), interferón (IFN).
interfibrillar *adj.* interfibrilar.
interfibrous *adj.* interfibroso, -sa.
interfilamentous *adj.* interfilamentoso, -sa.
interfilar *adj.* interfilar.
interfrontal *adj.* interfrontal.
interfurca *n.* interhorquilla.
interganglionic *adj.* interganglionar.
intergemmal *adj.* intergemal.
intergenic *adj.* intergénico, -ca.
interglobular *adj.* interglobular.
intergluteal *adj.* interglúteo, -a.
intergonial *adj.* intergonial.
intergradation *n.* intergradación.
intergrade *n.* intergrado.
intergranular *adj.* intergranular, intergranuloso, -sa.
intergyral *adj.* intergiral.
interhemicerebral *adj.* interhemicerebral.
interhemispheric *adj.* interhemisférico, -ca.
interictal *adj.* interictal.
interior *adj.* interior.
interischiadic *adj.* interisquiático, -ca.
interkinesis *n.* intercinesia, intercinesis.
interlabial *adj.* interlabial.
interlamellar *adj.* interlamelar, interlaminillar.
interleukin (IL) *n.* interleucina (IL), interleuquina (IL).
interligamentary *adj.* interligamentario, -ria.
interligamentous *adj.* interligamentoso, -sa.
interlobar *adj.* interlobar, interlobular.
interlobitis *n.* interlobitis, interlobulitis.
interlobular *adj.* interlobulillar.
interlocking *n.* trabamiento.
intermalleolar *adj.* intermaleolar.
intermamillary *adj.* intermamilar.
intermammary *adj.* intermamario, -ria.
intermarriage *n.* intermatrimonio.
intermaxilla *n.* intermaxila.
intermaxillary *adj.* intermaxilar.
intermediary *adj.* intermediario, -ria, intermedio¹, -dia.
intermediate *adj.* intermediario, -ria, intermedio¹, -dia, intermedio².
intermediolateral *adj.* intermediolateral.
intermembranous *adj.* intermembranoso, -sa.
intermeningeal *adj.* intermeníngeo, -a.
intermenstrual *adj.* intermenstrual.
intermenstruum *n.* intermenstruo.
intermetacarpal *adj.* intermetacarpiano, -na.
intermetameric *adj.* intermetamérico, -ca.
intermetatarsal *adj.* intermetatarsiano, -na.
intermission *n.* interludio, intermisión.
intermit *v.* intermitir.
intermitotic *adj.* intermitótico, -ca.
intermittence *n.* intermitencia.
intermittency *n.* intermitencia.
intermittent *adj.* intermitente.
intermolecular *adj.* intermolecular.
intermural *adj.* intermural.
intermuscular *adj.* intermuscular.
intern *n.* interno², -na.
internal *adj.* interno¹, -na.
internalization *n.* interiorización, internalización.
internarial *adj.* internarinal.
internasal *adj.* internasal.
internation *n.* internación.
interne *n.* interno², -na.

interneuromeric *adj.* interneuromérico, -ca.
interneuron *n.* interneurona.
internist *n.* internista.
internodal *adj.* internodal.
internode *n.* internodo, internudo.
 internode of Ranvier internudo de Ranvier.
internodular *adj.* internodular.
internship *n.* internado.
internuclear *adj.* internuclear.
internuncial *adj.* internuncial.
interocclusal *adj.* interoclusal.
interoceptive *adj.* interoceptivo, -va.
interoceptor *n.* interoceptor.
interofection *n.* interofección.
interofective *adj.* interofectivo, -va.
interoinferior *adj.* interoinferior.
interolivary *adj.* interolivar.
interorbital *adj.* interorbitario, -ria.
interosseal *adj.* interóseo, -a.
interosseous *adj.* interóseo, -a.
interpalpebral *adj.* interpalpebral.
interparietal *adj.* interparietal.
interparoxysmal *adj.* interparoxismal, interparoxísmico, -ca, interparoxístico, -ca.
interpediculate *adj.* interpediculado, -da, interpedicular.
interpeduncular *adj.* interpeduncular.
interpersonal *adj.* interpersonal.
interphalangeal *adj.* interfalángico, -ca.
interphase *n.* interfase.
interphyletic *adj.* interfilético, -ca.
interpial *adj.* interpial.
interplant *n.* interplante.
interplanting *n.* interplantación.
Interpleural *adj.* interpleural.
interpolar *adj.* interpolar[1].
interpolate *v.* Interpolar[2].
interpolation *n.* interpolación.
interposition *n.* interposición.
interpretation *n.* interpretación.
 doomwatcher interpretation interpretación catastrofista.
 interpretation of dreams interpretación de los sueños.
interprotometamere *adj.* interprotometámera, interprotometamérico, -ca.
interproximal *adj.* interproximal.
interpubic *adj.* interpúbico, -ca.
interpupillary *adj.* interpupilar.
interradial *adj.* interradial.
interrenal *adj.* interrenal.
interrupted *adj.* interrumpido, -da.
interscapular *adj.* interescapular.
interscapulum interscapulum.
intersciatic *adj.* interciático, -ca.
intersectio *n.* intersección.
 intersectiones tendineae musculi recti abdominis intersecciones tendinosas del músculo rectoabdominal.
intersection *n.* intersección.
 tendinous intersection intersección tendinosa.
intersegment *n.* intersegmento.
intersegmental *adj.* intersegmentario, -ria.
interseptal *adj.* interseptal.
interseptovalvular *adj.* interseptovalvular.
interseptum interseptum.
intersex *n.* intersexual[1].
 female intersex intersexual femenino.
 male intersex intersexual masculino.
 true intersex intersexual verdadero.
intersexual *adj.* intersexual[2].
intersexuality *n.* intersexualidad.
interspace *n.* interespacio.
 dineric interspace interespacio dinérico.

interspinal *adj.* interespinal.
interspinous *adj.* interespinoso, -sa.
intersternal *adj.* interesternal.
interstice *n.* intersticio.
 interstice of the kidney intersticio renal.
interstitial *adj.* intersticial.
interstitium *n.* intersticio.
intersystole *n.* intersístole.
intertarsal *adj.* intertarsal, intertarsiano, -na.
interthalamic *adj.* intertalámico, -ca.
intertransverse *adj.* intertransverso, -sa.
intertriginous *adj.* intertriginoso, -sa.
intertrigo *n.* intertrigo.
 intertrigo labialis intertrigo labial.
intertrochanteric *adj.* intertrocantéreo, -a.
intertubercular *adj.* intertubercular, intertuberculoso, -sa.
intertubular *adj.* intertubular.
interureteral *adj.* interureteral.
interureteric *adj.* interuretérico, -ca.
intervaginal *adj.* intervaginal.
interval *n.* intervalo.
 1 interval (G 1) intervalo 1 (G 1).
 2 interval (G 2) intervalo 2 (G 2).
 A-H interval intervalo A-H.
 A-N interval intervalo A-N.
 atriocarotid interval (a-c) intervalo auriculocarotídeo (a-c).
 auriculoventricular interval intervalo auriculoventricular.
 A-V interval intervalo A-V.
 BH interval intervalo BH.
 cardioarterial interval (c-a) intervalo cardioarterial (c-a).
 cardioarterious interval intervalo cardioarterial (c-a).
 coupling interval intervalo de acoplamiento, intervalo de acople.
 escape interval intervalo de escape.
 fixed interval (FI) of reinforcement intervalo fijo (IF) de refuerzo.
 focal interval intervalo focal, intervalo focal de Sturm.
 H-V interval intervalo H-V.
 interectopic interval intervalo ectópico.
 isometric interval intervalo isométrico.
 lucid interval intervalo lúcido.
 P-A interval intervalo P-A.
 passive interval intervalo pasivo.
 postsphygmic interval intervalo posesfígmico, intervalo postesfígmico.
 P-P interval intervalo P-P.
 P-Q interval intervalo P-Q.
 P-R interval intervalo P-R.
 presphygmic interval intervalo preesfígmico, intervalo presfígmico.
 Q-R interval intervalo Q-R.
 Q-RB interval intervalo Q-RB.
 Q-RS interval intervalo Q-RS.
 Q-RST interval intervalo Q-RST.
 Q-S interval intervalo Q-S.
 Q-T interval intervalo Q-T.
 reference interval intervalo de referencia.
 R-R interval intervalo R-R.
 sphygmic interval intervalo esfígmico.
 S-T interval intervalo S-T.
 Sturm's interval intervalo de Sturm.
 systolic time interval intervalo de tiempo sistólico.
 tolerance interval intervalo de tolerancia.
intervalvular *adj.* intervalvular.
intervascular *adj.* intervascular.
intervention *n.* intervención.
 crisis intervention intervención de crisis, intervención en crisis.

 dependent intervention intervención dependiente.
 directive intervention intervención directiva.
 neuroreflexotherapy intervention (NRT) intervención neurorreflejoterápica (NRT).
 no directive intervention intervención no directiva.
 nursing intervention intervención de enfermería.
 psychological intervention intervención psicológica.
 Senning intervention intervención de Senning.
interventricular *adj.* interventricular.
intervertebral *adj.* intervertebral.
interview *n.* entrevista.
 clinical interview entrevista clínica.
 descriptive interview entrevista descriptiva.
 direct interview entrevista directa.
 directive interview entrevista directiva.
 direct-question interview entrevista de preguntas directas.
 emergency interview entrevista en urgencias.
 enclosed interview entrevista cerrada.
 indirect interview entrevista indirecta.
 non-directive interview entrevista no directiva.
 open interview entrevista abierta.
 psychiatric interview entrevista psiquiátrica.
 standardized interview entrevista estandarizada.
 structured interview entrevista estructurada.
 therapeutic interview entrevista terapéutica.
 unstructured interview entrevista no estructurada.
intervillous *adj.* intervelloso, -sa.
intestinal *adj.* intestinal.
intestine *n.* intestino, intestinum.
 blind intestine intestino ciego.
 empty intestine intestino vacío.
 foregut intestine intestino anterior.
 iced intestine intestino congelado.
 ileum intestine intestino íleon.
 jejunoileal intestine intestino delgado mesenterial, intestino delgado mesentérico.
 jejunum intestine intestino yeyuno.
 large intestine intestino grueso.
 mesenterial intestine intestino mesenterial.
 rectum intestine intestino recto.
 small intestine intestino delgado.
 straight intestine intestino recto.
intestinotoxin *n.* intestinotoxina.
intestinum *n.* intestino, intestinum.
 intestinum caecum intestino ciego.
 intestinum cecum intestino ciego.
 intestinum crassum intestino grueso.
 intestinum ileum intestino íleon.
 intestinum jejunum intestino yeyuno.
 intestinum rectum intestino recto.
 intestinum tenue intestino delgado.
 intestinum tenue mesenteriale intestino delgado mesenterial, intestino delgado mesentérico.
intima *adj.* íntima.
intimacy *n.* intimidad.
 affective intimacy intimidad afectiva.
intimitis *n.* intimitis.
 proliferative intimitis intimitis proliferativa.
intolerance *n.* intolerancia.
 acetate intolerance intolerancia al acetato.
 activity intolerance intolerancia a la actividad.
 congenital lactose intolerance intolerancia congénita a la lactosa.

congenital lysine intolerance intolerancia congénita a la lisina.

congenital sucrose intolerance intolerancia congénita a la sacarosa.

disaccharide intolerance intolerancia a los disacáridos.

drug intolerance intolerancia a fármacos.

fructose intolerance intolerancia a la fructosa.

glucose intolerance (IGT) intolerancia a la glucosa (IGT).

gluten intolerance intolerancia al gluten.

hereditary fructose intolerance intolerancia hereditaria a la fructosa.

lactose intolerance intolerancia a la lactosa.

lysine intolerance intolerancia a la lisina.

lysinuric protein intolerance intolerancia proteínica con lisinuria.

intorsion *n.* intorsión.

intorter *n.* intorsor.

intoxation *n.* intoxación.

intoxicant *adj.* intoxicante, toxicante.

intoxication *n.* intoxicación.

acid intoxication intoxicación ácida, intoxicación por ácidos.

acute alcohol intoxication intoxicación aguda debida al consumo de alcohol.

alcohol idiosyncratic intoxication intoxicación alcohólica idiosincrática.

aluminum intoxication intoxicación por aluminio.

anaphylactic intoxication intoxicación anafiláctica.

bongkrek intoxication intoxicación por bongkrek.

citrate intoxication intoxicación con citrato.

intestinal intoxication intoxicación intestinal.

pathological intoxication intoxicación patológica.

saturnine intoxication intoxicación saturnina.

septic intoxication intoxicación séptica.

water intoxication intoxicación acuosa, intoxicación hídrica, intoxicación por agua.

intra-abdominal *adj.* intraabdominal.

intra-acinous *adj.* intraacinoso, -sa.

intra-adenoidal *adj.* intraadenoideo, -a.

intra-apendicular *adj.* intraapendicular.

intra-arachnoid *adj.* intraaracnoideo, -a.

intra-arterial *adj.* intraarterial.

intra-articular *adj.* intraarticular.

intra-atomic *adj.* intraatómico, -ca.

intra-atrial *adj.* intraauricular.

intra-aural *adj.* intraaural, intraótico, -ca, intraural.

intrabronchial *adj.* intrabronquial.

intrabuccal *adj.* intrabucal.

intracanalicular *adj.* intracanalicular.

intracapsular *adj.* intracapsular.

intracardiac *adj.* intracardíaco, -ca.

intracarpal *adj.* intracarpal, intracarpiano, -na.

intracartilaginous *adj.* intracartilaginoso, -sa.

intracatheter *n.* intracatéter.

intracavitary *adj.* intracavitario, -ria.

intracelial *adj.* intracelíaco, -ca, intracelial.

intracellular *adj.* intracelular.

intracephalic *adj.* intracefálico, -ca.

intracerebellar *adj.* intracerebelar, intracerebeloso, -sa.

intracerebral *adj.* intracerebral.

intracervical *adj.* intracervical.

intrachondral *adj.* intracondral.

intrachondrial *adj.* intracondrial.

intrachordal *adj.* intracordal.

intracisternal *adj.* intracisternal.

intracistronic *adj.* intracistrónico, -ca.

intracolic *adj.* intracólico, -ca.

intracordal *adj.* intracordial.

intracoronal *adj.* intracoronal.

intracorporal *adj.* intracorporal.

intracorporeal *adj.* intracorpóreo, -a.

intracorpuscular *adj.* intracorpuscular.

intracostal *adj.* intracostal.

intracranial *adj.* intracraneal.

intractable *adj.* intratable.

intracutaneous *adj.* intracutáneo, -a.

intracystic *adj.* intracístico, -ca, intraquístico, -ca.

intracytoplasmic *adj.* intracitoplasmático, -ca.

intrad intrad.

intradermal *adj.* intradérmico, -ca.

intradermoreaction *n.* intradermorreacción.

intraduct *n.* intraconducto.

intraductal *adj.* intraductal.

intraduodenal *adj.* intraduodenal.

intradural *adj.* intradural.

intraembryonic *adj.* intraembrionario, -ria.

intraepidermal *adj.* intraepidérmico, -ca.

intraepiphyseal *adj.* intraepifisario, -ria.

intraepithelial *adj.* intraepitelial.

intraerythrocytic *adj.* intraeritrocítico, -ca.

intraesternal *adj.* intraesternal.

intrafaradization *n.* intrafaradización.

intrafascicular *adj.* intrafascicular.

intrafat *adj.* intragraso, -sa.

intrafebrile *adj.* intrafebril.

intrafetation *n.* intrafetación.

intrafilar *adj.* intrafilar.

intrafissural *adj.* intrafisural.

intrafistular *adj.* intrafistular, intrafistuloso, -sa.

intrafollicular *adj.* intrafolicular.

intrafusal *adj.* intrafusal.

intragalvanization *n.* intragalvanización.

intragastric *adj.* intragástrico, -ca.

intragemmal *adj.* intragemal, intragemario, -ria.

intragenic *adj.* intragénico, -ca.

intraglandular *adj.* intraglandular.

intraglobular *adj.* intraglobular.

intragyral *adj.* intragiral, intragírico, -ca.

intrahepatic *adj.* intrahepático, -ca.

intrahyoid *adj.* intrahioideo, -a.

intraictal *adj.* intraictal.

intraintestinal *adj.* intraintestinal.

intrajugular *adj.* intrayugular.

intralamellar *adj.* intralaminar.

intralaryngeal *adj.* intralaríngeo, -a.

intralesional *adj.* intralesional.

intraleukocytic *adj.* intraleucocitario, -ria, intraleucocítico, -ca.

intraligamentous *adj.* intraligamentario, -ria, intraligamentoso, -sa.

intralingual *adj.* intralingual.

intralobar *adj.* intralobar, intralobular.

intralobular *adj.* intralobulillar.

intralocular *adj.* intralocular.

intraluminal *adj.* intraluminal.

intramammary *adj.* intramamario, -ria.

intramarginal *adj.* intramarginal.

intramastoiditis *n.* intramastoiditis.

intramedullary *adj.* intrabulbar, intramedular.

intramembranous *adj.* intramembranoso, -sa.

intrameningeal *adj.* intrameníngeo, -a.

intramolecular *adj.* intramolecular.

intramural *adj.* intramural.

intramuscular *adj.* intramuscular.

intramyocardial *adj.* intramiocárdico, -ca.

intramyometrial *adj.* intramiometrial.

intranasal *adj.* intranasal.

intranatal *adj.* intranatal.

intraneural *adj.* intraneural.

intranuclear *adj.* intranuclear.

intraocular *adj.* intraocular.

intraoperative *adj.* intraoperatorio, -ria.

intraoral *adj.* intraoral.

intraorbital *adj.* intraorbital, intraorbitario, -ria.

intraosseous *adj.* intraóseo, -a.

intraosteal *adj.* intraosteal.

intraovarian *adj.* intraovárico, -ca.

intraovular *adj.* intraovular.

intraparenchymatous *adj.* intraparenquimatoso, -sa.

intraparietal *adj.* intraparietal.

intrapartum intraparto.

intrapelvic *adj.* intrapélvico, -ca.

intrapericardiac *adj.* intrapericárdico, -ca.

intrapericardial *adj.* intrapericárdico, -ca.

intraperineal *adj.* intraperineal.

intraperitoneal *adj.* intraperitoneal.

intrapersonal *adj.* intrapersonal.

intrapial *adj.* intrapial.

intraplacental *adj.* intraplacentario, -ria.

intrapleural *adj.* intrapleural.

intrapontine *adj.* intrapontino, -na.

intraprostatic *adj.* intraprostático, -ca.

intraprotoplasmic *adj.* intraprotoplasmático, -ca, intraprotoplásmico, -ca.

intrapsychic *adj.* intrapsíquico, -ca.

intrapsychical *adj.* intrapsíquico, -ca.

intrapulmonary *adj.* intrapulmonar.

intrapyretic *adj.* intrapirético, -ca.

intrarachidian *adj.* intrarraquídeo, -a.

intrarectal *adj.* intrarrectal.

intrarenal *adj.* intrarrenal.

intraretinal *adj.* intrarretiniano, -na.

intrascleral *adj.* intraescleral, intraesclerótico, -ca, intrascleral, intrasclerótico, -ca.

intrascrotal *adj.* intraescrotal, intrascrotal.

intrasellar *adj.* intraselar, intrasillar.

intraserous *adj.* intraseroso, -sa.

intraspinal *adj.* intraespinal, intraspinal.

intrasplenic *adj.* intraesplénico, -ca, intrasplénico, -ca.

intrastitial *adj.* intrasticial.

intrastromal *adj.* intraestromático, -ca, intraestrómico, -ca.

intrastromatic *adj.* intrastromático, -ca.

intrastromic *adj.* intrastrómico, -ca.

intrasynovial *adj.* intrasinovial.

intratarsal *adj.* intratarsal, intratarsiano, -na.

intratesticular *adj.* intratesticular.

intrathecal *adj.* intratecal.

intrathenar *adj.* intratenar.

intrathoracic *adj.* intratorácico, -ca.

intratonsillar *adj.* intraamigdalino, -na, intratonsilar.

intratrabecular *adj.* intratrabecular.

intratracheal *adj.* intratraqueal.

intratubal *adj.* intratubárico, -ca, intratubario, -ria.

intratubular *adj.* intratubular.

intratympanic *adj.* intratimpánico, -ca.

intraureteral *adj.* intraureteral.

intraurethral *adj.* intrauretral.

intrauterine *adj.* intrauterino, -na.

intravaginal *adj.* intravaginal.

intravasation *n.* intravasación.

intravascular *adj.* intravascular.

intravenation *n.* intravenación.

intravenous *adj.* intravenoso, -sa.

intravenous controller controlador intravenoso.

intraventicular *adj.* intraventricular.
intravertebral *adj.* intravertebral.
intravesical *adj.* intravesical.
intravillous *adj.* intravelloso, -sa.
intravital *adj.* intravital.
intravitelline *adj.* intravitelino, -na.
intravitreous *adj.* intravítreo, -a.
intrinsic *adj.* intrínseco, -ca.
introducer *n.* introductor.
introflexion *n.* introflexión.
introgastric *adj.* introgástrico, -ca.
introgression *n.* introgresión.
introitus *n.* introito.
  introitus vaginae introito vaginal.
introjection *n.* introyección.
intromission *n.* intromisión.
intromittent *adj.* intromitente.
intron *n.* intrón.
introspection *n.* introspección.
introspective *adj.* introspectivo, -va.
introsusception *n.* introsuscepción.
introversion *n.* introversión.
introvert *adj.* introvertido, -da, introvertir.
intrusion *n.* intrusión.
intubador *n.* intubador.
intubate *v.* intubar.
intubation *n.* intubación.
  altercursive intubation intubación altercursiva.
  aqueductal intubation intubación acueductal.
  blind nasotracheal intubation intubación nasotraqueal ciega.
  endotracheal intubation intubación endotraqueal.
  gastric intubation sondaje gástrico.
  intratracheal intubation intubación intratraqueal.
  nasal intubation intubación nasal.
  nasogastric intubation intubación nasogástrica.
  nasotracheal intubation intubación nasotraqueal.
  oral intubation intubación bucal, intubación oral.
  orotracheal intubation intubación bucotraqueal, intubación orotraqueal.
intubationist *n.* intubacionista.
intuition *n.* intuición.
  delirious intuition intuición delirante.
intumesce *v.* intumecer, intumescer.
intumescence *n.* intumescencia, intumescentia.
  cervical intumescence intumescencia cervical.
  lumbar intumescence intumescencia lumbar.
intumescent *adj.* intumescente.
intumescentia *n.* intumescencia, intumescentia.
  intumescentia cervicalis intumescencia cervical.
  intumescentia lumbalis intumescencia lumbar.
  intumescentia lumbosacralis intumescencia lumbosacra.
intussusception *n.* intususcepción.
  agonic intussusception intususcepción agónica.
  colic intussusception intususcepción cólica.
  double intussusception intususcepción doble.
  ileal intussusception intususcepción ileal.
  ileocecal intussusception intususcepción iliocecal.
  intestinal intussusception intususcepción intestinal.

  jejunogastric intussusception intususcepción yeyunogástrica.
  postmortem intussusception intususcepción postmortem.
  retrograde intussusception intususcepción retrógrada.
intussusceptive *adj.* intususceptivo, -va.
intussusceptum intussusceptum, intususceptum.
intussuscipiens intussuscipiens, intususcipiens.
inulase *n.* inulasa.
inulin *n.* inulina.
inulinase *n.* inulinasa.
inunction *n.* inunción.
invaccination *n.* invacunación.
invaginate *v.* invaginar.
invagination *n.* invaginación.
  basilar invagination invaginación basilar.
invaginator *n.* invaginador.
invalid *n.* inválido, -da.
invalidism *n.* invalidez.
invasion *n.* invasión.
invasive *adj.* invasivo, -va, invasor, -ra.
invasiveness *n.* invasibilidad, invasividad.
inventory *n.* inventario.
  Beck's diagnostic inventory (BDI) inventario diagnóstico de Beck (IDB).
  Millon clinical multiaxial inventory (MCMI) inventario clínico multiaxial de Millón (MCMI).
  Minnesota multiphasic personality inventory (MMPI) inventario multifásico de la personalidad de Minnesota.
  personality inventory inventario de personalidad.
invermination *n.* inverminación.
inversion *n.* inversión.
  adrenaline inversion inversión de adrenalina.
  carbohydrate inversion inversión de carbohidratos.
  chromosome inversion inversión cromosómica.
  epinephrine inversion inversión de adrenalina.
  inversion of the uterus inversión del útero, inversión uterina.
  narcotic inversion inversión narcótica.
  paracentric inversion inversión paracéntrica.
  pericentric inversion inversión pericéntrica.
  pressure inversion inversión por presión.
  sexual inversion inversión sexual.
  thermic inversion inversión térmica.
  uterine inversion inversión del útero, inversión uterina.
  visceral inversion inversión visceral.
invert *n.* invertido, -da.
invertase *n.* invertasa.
invertebrate *n.* invertebrado, -da.
invertin *n.* invertina.
invertor *n.* inversor.
investigation *n.* investigación.
  clinical investigation investigación clínica.
  clinical investigation in the third world investigación clínica en el tercer mundo.
  investigation in animals investigación científica en animales.
  non-therapeutic investigation investigación no terapéutica.
  scientific investigation investigación científica.
  therapeutic investigation investigación terapéutica.
inveterate *adj.* inveterado, -da.

inviscation *n.* inviscación.
involucre *n.* involucro.
involucrin *n.* involucrina.
involucrum *n.* involucro.
involuntary *adj.* involuntario, -ria.
involuntomotory *adj.* involuntomotor, -ra.
involution *n.* involución.
  involution of the uterus involución del útero, involución uterina.
  senile involution involución senil.
  uterine involution involución del útero, involución uterina.
involutional *adj.* involucional, involutivo, -va.
iodate *adj.* iodado, -da.
iodbasedow *n.* yodobasedow.
iodemia *n.* iodemia, yodemia.
ioderma *n.* iodermia.
iodic *adj.* yódico, -ca.
iodide *n.* yoduro.
iodinate *v.* yodar.
iodinated *adj.* yodado, -da.
iodination *n.* yodación.
iodine *n.* iodo, yodo.
  butanol-extractable iodine (BEI) yodo extraído con butanol, yodo soluble en butanol.
  Gram's iodine yodo de Gram.
  protein-bound iodine (PBI) yodo ligado a proteínas, yodo unido a proteínas.
  radioactive iodine radioiodo, yodo radiactivo.
iodine-fast *adj.* yodorresistente.
iodinophil *adj.* yodófilo, yodófilo, -la.
iodinophile *adj.* yodófilo, yodófilo, -la.
iodinophilous *adj.* yodófilo, -la.
iodipamide *n.* yodipamida.
iodism *n.* yodismo.
iodize *v.* yodar, yodizar.
iodized *adj.* yodado, -da.
iodoacetamide *n.* yodoacetamida.
iodocholesterol *n.* iodocolesterol, yodocolesterol.
iododerma *n.* yódide, yododermia.
iodoformism *n.* yodoformismo.
iodogenic *adj.* yodogénico, -ca.
iodoglobulin *n.* yodoglobulina.
iodometric *adj.* yodométrico, -ca.
iodometry *n.* yodimetría, yodometría.
iodophil *n.* yodófilo.
iodophilia *n.* yodofilia.
  extracellular iodophilia yodofilia extracelular.
  intracellular iodophilia yodofilia intracelular.
iodophthalein *n.* yodoftaleína.
iodoproteins *n.* yodoproteínas.
iodopsin *n.* yodopsina.
iodopyracet *n.* yodopiracet.
iodotherapy *n.* yodoterapia.
iodothyronine *n.* yodotironinas.
iodothyronines *n.* iodotironinas.
iodotyrosine *n.* yodotirosinas.
iodotyrosines *n.* iodotirosinas.
iodoventriculography *n.* yodoventriculografía.
iodovolatilization *n.* yodovolatilización.
ioduria *n.* yoduria.
iohexol *n.* iohexol.
iometer *n.* ionómero.
ion *n.* ión.
  dipolar ion ión bipolar, ión dipolar.
  hydride ion ión hidruro.
  hydrogen ion ión de hidrógeno.
  hydronium ion ión de hidronio, ión hidronio.
  ion ammonium ión amonio.
  oxonium ion ión oxonio.

spectator ion ión espectador.
sulfonium ion ión sulfonio.
ionic *adj.* iónico, -ca.
ionization *n.* dialectolisis, ionización.
  avalanche ionization ionización en avalancha.
  Townsend ionization ionización de Townsend.
ionize *v.* ionizar.
ionocolorimeter *n.* ionocolorímetro.
ionogenic *adj.* ionógeno, -na.
ionogram *n.* ionograma.
ionometer *n.* ionómetro.
ionopherogram *n.* ionoferograma.
ionophore *n.* ionóforo.
ionophoresis *n.* ionoforesis.
ionophoretic *adj.* ionoforético, -ca.
ionophose *n.* ionofosia, yonofosia.
ionoscope *n.* ionoscopio.
ionosphere *n.* ionósfera.
ionotherapy *n.* ionoterapia.
ion-protein *n.* ión-proteína.
iontophoresis *n.* iontoforesis.
iontophoretic *adj.* iontoforético, -ca.
iontoquantimeter *n.* iontocuantímetro.
iontoradiometer *n.* iontorradiómetro.
iontotherapy *n.* iontoterapia.
iopamidol *n.* iopamidol.
iophobia *n.* iofobia.
iotacism *n.* iotacismo.
iotacisme *n.* yotacismo.
iothalamate *n.* iotalamato.
  iothalamate meglumine iotalamato meglumina.
  iothalamate sodium iotalamato sódico.
ioxaglate *n.* ioxaglato.
ipsation *n.* ipsación.
ipsilateral *adj.* ipsilateral, ipsolateral.
ipsism *n.* ipsismo.
iradiocobalt *n.* radiocobalto.
irascibility *n.* irascibilidad.
iridal *adj.* iridal.
iridalgia *n.* iridalgia.
iridauxesis *n.* iridauxesis.
iridectasis *n.* iridectasia.
iridectome *n.* iridéctomo.
iridectomesodialysis *n.* iridectomesodiálisis.
iridectomize *v.* iridectomizar.
iridectomy *n.* iridectomía.
  basal iridectomy iridectomía basal.
  buttonhole iridectomy iridectomía en ojal.
  complete iridectomy iridectomía completa.
  optic iridectomy iridectomía óptica.
  optical iridectomy iridectomía óptica.
  peripheral iridectomy iridectomía periférica.
  preliminary iridectomy iridectomía preliminar.
  preparatory iridectomy iridectomía preparatoria.
  sector iridectomy iridectomía en sector, iridectomía sectorial.
  stenopeic iridectomy iridectomía estenopeica.
  therapeutic iridectomy iridectomía terapéutica.
iridectopia *n.* iridectopia.
iridectropium *n.* iridectropión.
iridemia *n.* iridemia.
iridencleisis *n.* iridencleisis, iridenclisis.
iridentropium *n.* iridentropión.
irideremia *n.* irideremia.
iridescence *n.* iridescencia, iridiscencia.
iridescent *adj.* iridescente, iridiscente.
iridesis *n.* iridesis.
iridiagnosis *n.* iridiagnosis.

iridial *adj.* iridial.
iridian *adj.* iridiano, -na.
iridic *adj.* irídico, -ca.
iridization *n.* iridización.
iridoavulsion *n.* iridoavulsión.
iridocapsulitis *n.* iridocapsulitis.
iridocele *n.* iridocele.
iridochoroiditis *n.* iridocoroiditis.
iridocoloboma *n.* iridocoloboma.
iridoconstrictor *n.* iridoconstrictor, -ra.
iridocorneal *adj.* iridocorneal.
iridocorneosclerectomy *n.* iridocorneosclerectomía.
iridocyclectomy *n.* iridociclectomía.
iridocyclitis *n.* iridociclitis.
  Fuchs' heterochromic iridocyclitis iridociclitis Heterocrómica, iridociclitis Heterocrómica de Fuchs.
  heterochromic iridocyclitis iridociclitis Heterocrómica, iridociclitis Heterocrómica de Fuchs.
  hypertensive iridocyclitis iridociclitis hipertensiva.
  iridocyclitis septica iridociclitis séptica.
iridocyclochoroiditis *n.* iridociclocoroiditis.
iridocystectomy *n.* iridocistectomía.
iridodesis *n.* iridodesis.
iridodiagnosis *n.* iridodiagnosis, iridodiagnóstico.
iridodialyisis *n.* iridodiálisis.
iridodiastasis *n.* iridodiastasis.
iridodilator *n.* iridodilatador, -ra.
iridodonesis *n.* iridodonesis.
iridokeratitis *n.* iridoqueratitis.
iridokinesia *n.* iridocinesia.
iridokinesis *n.* iridocinesia, iridocinesis.
iridokinetic *adj.* iridocinético, -ca.
iridoleptynsis *n.* iridoleptinsis.
iridology *n.* iridología.
iridolysis *n.* iridólisis.
iridomalacia *n.* iridomalacia.
iridomesodialysis *n.* iridomesodiálisis.
iridomotor *adj.* iridomotor, -ra.
iridoncosis *n.* iridoncosis.
iridoncus *n.* iridonco.
iridoparalysis *n.* iridoparálisis.
iridopathy *n.* iridopatía.
iridoperiphakitis *n.* iridoperifacitis, iridoperifaquitis.
iridoplegia *n.* iridoplejía.
  accommodation iridoplegia iridoplejía de acomodación.
  complete iridoplegia iridoplejía completa.
  reflex iridoplegia iridoplejía refleja.
  sympathetic iridoplegia iridoplejía simpática.
iridoptosis *n.* iridoptosis.
iridopupillary *adj.* iridopupilar.
iridorhexis *n.* iridorrexis.
iridoschisis *n.* iridosquisis.
iridoschisma *n.* iridosquisma.
iridosclerotomy *n.* iridoesclerotomía, iridosclerotomía.
iridosteresis *n.* iridostéresis.
iridotasis *n.* iridotasis.
iridotomy *n.* iridotomía.
iris *n.* iris.
  detached iris iris separado.
  iris bombé iris abombado, iris bombé.
  plateau iris iris en meseta.
  tremulous iris iris tremulans, iris trémulo.
  umbrella iris iris en sombrilla.
irisopsia *n.* irisopsia.
iritectomy *n.* iritoectomía.
iritic *adj.* irítico, -ca.

iritis *n.* iritis.
  diabetic iritis iritis diabética.
  Doyne's guttate iritis iritis guttata de Doyne.
  fibrinous iritis iritis fibrinosa.
  follicular iritis iritis folicular.
  gouty iritis iritis gotosa.
  hemorrhagic iritis iritis hemorrágica.
  iritis blennorrhagique à rechutes iritis blenorrágica con recaídas.
  iritis catamenialis iritis catamenial.
  iritis glaucomatosa iritis glaucomatosa.
  iritis obturans iritis obturante.
  iritis papulosa iritis papulosa.
  iritis recidivans staphylococcoallergica iritis estafilococoalérgica recidivante.
  nodular iritis iritis nodular.
  plastic iritis iritis plásica, iritis plástica.
  primary iritis iritis primaria.
  purulent iritis iritis purulenta.
  quiet iritis iritis silenciosa, iritis tranquila.
  secondary iritis iritis secundaria.
  serous iritis iritis serosa.
  spongy iritis iritis esponjosa.
  sympathetic iritis iritis simpática.
  uratic iritis iritis urática.
iritomy *n.* iritomía, irotomía.
iron *n.* hierro.
irradiate *adj.* irradiado, -da, irradiar[1].
irradiation *n.* irradiación.
  local graft irradiation irradiación local del injerto.
  total body irradiation irradiación corporal total.
  total lymphoid irradiation (TLI) irradiación linfoide total (ILT).
irreducible *adj.* irreducible.
irregular *adj.* irregular.
irregularity *n.* irregularidad.
  irregularity of the pulse irregularidad del pulso.
irreinoculability *n.* irreinoculabilidad.
irrespirable *adj.* irrespirable.
irresponsibility *n.* irresponsabilidad.
  criminal irresponsibility irresponsabilidad criminal.
irresucitable *adj.* irresucitable.
irreversible *adj.* irreversible.
irrigate *v.* irrigar.
irrigation *n.* irrigación.
  acetic acid irrigation irrigación de ácido acético.
  aminoacetic acid irrigation irrigación de ácido aminoacético.
  bladder irrigation irrigación vesical.
  cold caloric irrigation irrigación fría.
  colonic irrigation irrigación colónica.
  colostomy irrigation irrigación de la colostomía.
  continuous irrigation irrigación continua.
  drip-suck irrigation irrigación goteo-aspiración.
  gingival blood irrigation irrigación gingival.
  mediate irrigation irrigación mediata.
  ostomy irrigation irrigación de la ostomía.
  Ringer's irrigation irrigación de Ringer.
  saline irrigation irrigación salina.
  sodium chloride irrigation irrigación de cloruro sódico.
  vaginal irrigation irrigación vaginal.
  wound irrigation irrigación de una herida.
irrigator *n.* irrigador.
irrigoradioscopy *n.* irrigorradioscopia.
irrigoscopy *n.* irrigoscopia.
irritability *n.* irritabilidad.
  chemical irritability irritabilidad química.

electric irritability irritabilidad eléctrica.
irritability of the bladder irritabilidad vesical.
irritability of the stomach irritabilidad del estómago.
mechanical irritability irritabilidad mecánica.
muscular irritability irritabilidad muscular.
myotatic irritability irritabilidad miotática.
nervous irritability irritabilidad nerviosa.
tactile irritability irritabilidad táctil.
irritable *adj.* irritable.
irritant *n.* irritante.
primary irritant irritante primario.
irritation *n.* irritación.
direct irritation irritación directa.
functional irritation irritación funcional.
sympathetic irritation irritación simpática.
irritative *adj.* irritativo, -va.
isauxesis *n.* isauxesis.
ischemia *n.* isquemia.
cerebral ischemia isquemia cerebral.
chronic intestinal ischemia isquemia intestinal crónica.
ischemia retinae isquemia retiniana.
myocardial ischemia isquemia del miocardio, isquemia miocárdica.
postural ischemia isquemia postural.
renal ischemia isquemia renal.
silent ischemia isquemia silenciosa, isquemia subclínica.
uterine ischemia isquemia uterina.
ischemic *adj.* isquémico, -ca.
ischesis *n.* isquesis.
ischiac *adj.* isquiaco, -ca.
Ischladelphus *n.* isquadelfo.
ischiadic *adj.* isquiádico, -ca.
ischiadicus *adj.* isquiádico, -ca.
ischial *adj.* isquiádico, -ca, isquial.
ischialgia *n.* isquialgia.
ischias *n.* isquias.
ischiatic *adj.* isquiádico, -ca, isquiático, -ca.
ischidrosis *n.* isquidrosis.
ischiectomy *n.* isquiectomía.
ischioanal *adj.* isquioanal.
ischiobulbar *adj.* isquiobulbar.
ischiocapsular *adj.* isquiocapsular.
ischiocavernous *adj.* isquiocavernoso, -sa.
ischiocele *n.* isquiocele.
ischiochimia *n.* isquioquimia.
ischiococcygeal *adj.* isquiococcígeo, -a.
ischiodidymus *n.* isquiodídimo.
ischiodymia *n.* isquiodimia.
ischiodynia *n.* isquiodinia.
ischiofemoral *adj.* isquiofemoral.
ischiofibular *adj.* isquioperoneo, -a.
ischiohebotomy *n.* isquiohebotomía.
ischiomelus *n.* isquiómelo.
ischioneuralgia *n.* isquioneuralgia.
ischionitis *n.* isquionitis.
ischiopagia *n.* isquiopagia.
ischiopagus *n.* isquiópago.
ischiopagy *n.* isquiopagia.
ischioperineal *adj.* isquioperineal.
ischiopubic *adj.* isquiopúbico, -ca.
ischiorectal *adj.* isquiorrectal.
ischiosacral *adj.* isquiosacral, isquiosacro, -cra.
ischiothoracopagus *n.* isquiotoracópago.
ischiotibial *adj.* isquiotibial.
ischiovaginal *adj.* isquiovaginal.
ischiovertebral *adj.* isquiovertebral.
ischium ischium, isquion.
ischiuretic *n.* isquiurético, -ca.
ischiuria *n.* isquiuria.
ischiuria spastica isquiuria espástica.
ischogyria *n.* iscogiria.

ischuretic *adj.* iscúrico, -ca.
ischuria *n.* iscuria.
ischuria paradoxa iscuria paradójica.
ischuria spastica iscuria espasmódica, iscuria espástica.
isciatic *adj.* ciático, -ca.
iseiconia *n.* iseiconía.
iseiconic *adj.* iseicónico, -ca.
island *n.* isla.
blood island isla sanguínea.
bone island isla ósea.
island of Calleja isla de Calleja.
island of Langerhans isla de Langerhans.
island of the pancreas isla del páncreas, isla pancreática.
olfactory island isla olfatoria.
pancreatic island isla del páncreas, isla pancreática.
Pander's island isla de Pander.
islet *n.* islote.
blood islet islote sanguíneo.
islet of Calleja islote de Calleja.
islet of Langerhans islote de Langerhans.
pancreatic islet islote pancreático.
Walthard's islet islote de Walthard.
isoadrenocorticism *n.* isoadrenocorticismo.
isoagglutination *n.* isoaglutinación.
isoagglutinin *n.* isoaglutinina.
isoagglutinogen *n.* isoaglutinógeno, -na.
isoallele *n.* isoalelo.
isoallelism *n.* isoalelismo.
isoamylase *n.* isoamilasa.
isoanaphylaxis *n.* isoanafilaxia, isoanafilaxis.
isoantibody *n.* isoanticuerpo.
isoantigen *n.* isoantígeno.
isobar *n.* isóbaro.
isobaric *adj.* isobárico, -ca.
isobody *n.* isocuerpo.
isobolism *n.* isobolismo.
isocaloric *adj.* isocalórico, -ca.
isocapnia *n.* isocapnia.
isocapnic *adj.* isocápnico, -ca.
isocellular *adj.* isocelular.
isocenter *n.* isocentro.
isocentric *adj.* isocéntrico, -ca.
isochoria *n.* isocoria.
isochoric *adj.* isocórico, -ca.
isochromatic *adj.* isocromático, -ca.
isochromatophil *adj.* isocromatófilo, -la.
isochromatophile *adj.* isocromatófilo, -la.
isochromosome *n.* isocromosoma.
isochron *adj.* isócrono, -na.
isochronal *adj.* isocronal.
isochronia *n.* isocronía.
isochronic *adj.* isocrónico, -ca.
isochronism *n.* isocronismo.
isochronous *adj.* isócrono, -na.
isochroous *adj.* isocroo, -a.
isocline *n.* isoclina.
isocoagulase *n.* isocoagulasa.
isocomplement *n.* isocomplemento.
isocomplementophilic *adj.* isocomplementófilo, -la.
isocortex *n.* isocórtex, isocorteza.
isocyclic *adj.* isocíclico, -ca.
isocytolysin *n.* isocitolisina.
isocytosis *n.* isocitosis.
isocytotoxin *n.* isocitotoxina.
isodactylism *n.* isodactilia, isodactilismo.
isodense *adj.* isodenso, -sa.
isodiametric *adj.* isodiamétrico, -ca.
isodontic *adj.* isodonto, -ta.
isodose *n.* isodosis.
isodynamic *adj.* isodinámico, -ca.
isodynamogenic *adj.* isodinamógeno, -na.

isoechogenic *adj.* isoecogénico, -ca.
isoeffect *n.* isoefecto.
isoelectric *adj.* isoeléctrico, -ca.
isoenergetic *adj.* isoenergético, -ca.
isoenzyme *n.* isoenzima.
fraction isoenzyme CPK isoenzima CPK.
Regan isoenzyme isoenzima de Regan.
isoerythrolysis *n.* isoeritrólisis.
neonatal isoerythrolysis isoeritrólisis neonatal.
isoflows *n.* isoflujo.
isogamete *n.* isogameto.
isogametic *adj.* isogamético, -ca.
isogamety *n.* isogametía.
isogamus *n.* isógamo.
isogamy *n.* isogamia.
isogeneic *adj.* isogeneico, -ca.
isogeneric *adj.* isogenérico, -ca.
isogenesis *n.* isogénesis, isogenia.
isogenic *adj.* isogénico, -ca.
isogenous *adj.* isógeno, -na.
isognathous *adj.* isognato, -ta.
isograft *n.* isoinjerto.
isohemagglutination *n.* isohemaglutinación.
isohemagglutinin *n.* isohemaglutinina.
isohemolysin *n.* isohemolisina.
isohemolysis *n.* isohemólisis.
isohemolytic *adj.* isohemolítico, -ca.
isohydric *adj.* isohídrico, -ca.
isohydruria *n.* isohidruria.
isohypercytosis *n.* isohipercitosis.
isohypocytosis *n.* isohipocitosis.
isoiconia *n.* isoiconía.
isoiconic *adj.* isoicónico, -ca.
isoimmunization *n.* isoinmunización.
Rh isoimmunization isoinmunización Rh.
isointense *adj.* isointenso, -sa.
isokinetic *adj.* isocinético, -ca.
isolated *adj.* aislado, -da.
isolation *n.* aislamiento².
attitudinal isolation aislamiento de actitud.
behavioral isolation aislamiento conductal.
infectious isolation aislamiento infeccioso.
protective isolation aislamiento protector.
reversed isolation aislamiento inverso.
social isolation aislamiento social.
isolator *n.* aislante.
surgical isolator aislante quirúrgico.
isolecithal *adj.* isolecítico, -ca, isolecito, -ta.
isoleucine *n.* isoleucina.
isoleukoagglutinin *n.* isoleucoaglutinina.
isologous *n.* isólogo, -ga.
isolysin *n.* isolisina.
isolysis *n.* isólisis.
isolytic *adj.* isolítico, -ca.
isomastigote *adj.* isomastigoto, -ta.
isomer *adj.* isómero, -ra.
isomerase *n.* isomerasa.
isomeric *adj.* isomérico, -ca.
isomerism *n.* isomerismo.
isomerization *n.* isomerización.
isometric *adj.* isométrico, -ca.
isometropia *n.* isometropía.
isometry *n.* isometría.
isomicrogamete *n.* isomicrogameto.
isomorphic *adj.* isomórfico, -ca.
isomorphism *n.* isomorfismo.
isomorphous *adj.* isomorfo, -fa.
isoncotic *adj.* isoncótico, -ca.
iso-oncotic *adj.* isooncótico, -ca.
iso-osmotic *adj.* isoosmótico, -ca.
isopathy *n.* isopatía.
isophagy *n.* isofagia.
isophenolization *n.* isofenolización.
isophoria *n.* isoforia.

isophotometer *n.* isofotómetro.
isopia *n.* isopía.
isoplassonts *n.* isoplasontes.
isoplastic *adj.* isoplástico, -ca.
isoplasty *n.* isoplastia.
isopleth *n.* isopleta.
isopotential *n.* isopotencial.
isoprecipitin *n.* isoprecipitina.
isopter *n.* isóptero.
isopyknic *adj.* isopícnico, -ca.
isopyknosis *n.* isopicnosis.
isopyknotic *adj.* isopicnótico, -ca.
isorrhea *n.* isorrea.
isorrheic *adj.* isorreico, -ca.
isorrhopic *adj.* isorrópico, -ca.
isoscope *n.* isoscopio.
isosensitization *n.* isosensibilización.
isoserotherapy *n.* isosueroterapia.
isoserum *n.* isosuero.
isosexual *adj.* isosexual.
isosmotic *adj.* isosmótico, -ca.
isosmoticity *n.* isosmoticidad.
isospermotoxin *n.* isospermotoxina.
Isospora Isospora.
  Isospora belli Isospora belli.
  Isospora hominis Isospora hominis.
isosporiasis *n.* isosporiasis.
isostere *n.* isóstero.
isosthenuria *n.* isostenuria.
isostimulation *n.* isoestimulación.
isotherapy *n.* isoterapia.
isothermic *adj.* isotérmico, -ca.
isotone *n.* isotono.
isotonia *n.* isotonía.
isotonic *adj.* isotónico, -ca.
isotonicity *n.* isotonicidad.
isotope *n.* isótopo.
  radiactive isotope isótopo radiactivo.

isotopic *adj.* isotópico, -ca.
isotopology *n.* isotopología.
isotoxic *adj.* isotóxico, -ca.
isotoxin *n.* isotoxina.
isotransplantation *n.* isotrasplantación, isotrasplante.
isotrimorphism *n.* isotrimorfismo.
isotrimorphous *adj.* isotrimorfo, -fa.
isotron *n.* isotrón.
isotropic *adj.* isotrópico, -ca.
isotropous *adj.* isótropo, -pa.
isotropy *n.* isotropía.
isotype *n.* isotipo.
isotypical *adj.* isotípico, -ca.
isovolume *n.* isovolumen.
isovolumetric *adj.* isovolumétrico, -ca.
isovolumic *adj.* isovolúmico, -ca.
isozyme *n.* isozima.
issue *n.* exutorio.
isthmectomy *n.* istmectomía.
isthmian *adj.* ístmico, -ca.
isthmic *adj.* ístmico, -ca.
isthmitis *n.* istmitis.
isthmoparalysis *n.* istmoparálisis.
isthmoplegia *n.* istmoplejía.
isthmospasm *n.* istmoespasmo.
isthmus *n.* istmo.
isuria *n.* isuria.
it *n.* ello.
itch *n.* comezón, prurito.
  baker's itch prurito del panadero.
  bath itch prurito del baño.
  coolie itch prurito del coolie.
  Cuban itch prurito cubano.
  frost itch prurito de escarcha.
  grain itch prurito por cereales.
  ground itch prurito del suelo.
  lumberman's itch prurito del leñador.

  Norway itch prurito de noruega.
  poultryman's itch prurito de avicultor.
  Saint Ignatius' itch prurito de san Ignacio.
  senile itch prurito senil.
  swamp itch prurito de los pantanos.
  swimmer's itch prurito del nadador.
  symptomatic itch prurito sintomático.
  toe itch prurito de los dedos de los pies.
  winter itch prurito de invierno.
itching *n.* picazón.
iter iter.
  iter ad infundibulum iter ad infundibulum.
  iter chordae anterius iter chordae anterius.
  iter chordae posterius iter chordae posterius.
  iter dentium iter dentis, iter dentium.
  iter of Sylvius iter de Silvio.
Iteral *adj.* iteral.
iteration *n.* iteración.
iteroparity *n.* iteroparidad.
iteroparous *adj.* iteróparo, -ra.
ivory *n.* marfil.
Ixodes Ixodes.
  Ixodes bicornis Ixodes bicornis.
  Ixodes cavipalpus Ixodes cavipalpus.
  Ixodes dammini Ixodes dammini.
  Ixodes frequens Ixodes frequens.
  Ixodes pacificus Ixodes pacificus.
  Ixodes persulcatus Ixodes persulcatus.
  Ixodes ricinus Ixodes ricinus.
  Ixodes scapularis Ixodes scapularis.
ixodiasis *n.* ixodiasis.
ixodic *adj.* ixódico, -ca.
ixodid *n.* ixódido.
Ixodidae Ixodidae.
Ixodides Ixodides.
ixodism *n.* ixodismo.
Ixodoidea Ixodoidea.
ixomyelitis *n.* ixomielitis.

J j

jabbering *n.* farfulla.
jacket *n.* chaleco, corsé, funda.
  diaper restraint jacket corsé en forma de pañal.
  flexion jacket corsé de flexión.
  Minerva jacket chaleco Minerva.
  restraint jacket corsé de restricción.
  Riser jacket corsé de Riser.
  Sayre's jacket chaleco de Sayre, corsé de Sayre.
jackscrew *n.* gato.
jactatio *n.* jactación.
  jactatio capitis nocturna jactación cefálica nocturna.
jactitation *n.* jactitación.
jaculiferous *adj.* jaculífero, -ra.
janiceps *n.* janicéfalo, janiceps.
  janiceps assymmetrus janicéfalo asimétrico.
  janiceps parasiticus janicéfalo parásito.
jar *n.* jarra.
  bell jar jarra en campana.
  Leyden jar jarra de Leyden.
jargon *n.* jerga.
jargon aphasia *n.* jargonafasia.
jargonaphasia *n.* jargonafasia.
jaundice *n.* ictericia.
  acholuric familial jaundice ictericia acolúrica familiar.
  acholuric jaundice ictericia acolúrica.
  anhepatic jaundice ictericia anhepática, ictericia anhepatógena.
  anhepatogenous jaundice ictericia anhepática, ictericia anhepatógena.
  black jaundice ictericia negra.
  breast milk jaundice ictericia por leche materna.
  Budd's jaundice ictericia de Budd.
  catarrhal jaundice ictericia catarral.
  choleric jaundice ictericia colérica.
  cholestatic jaundice ictericia colestática.
  chronic acholuric jaundice ictericia acolúrica crónica.
  chronic familial jaundice ictericia familiar crónica, ictericia familiar crónico.
  chronic idiopathic jaundice ictericia idiopática crónica.
  congenital familial jaundice ictericia familiar congénita.
  congenital familial non-hemolytic jaundice ictericia no hemolítica congénita, ictericia No hemolítica congénito familiar.
  congenital hemolytic jaundice ictericia hemolítica congénita, icterus hemolítico congénito.
  congenital jaundice ictericia congénita.
  congenital nonhemolytic jaundice ictericia no hemolítica congénita, ictericia No hemolítica congénito familiar.
  Crigler-Najjar jaundice ictericia de Crigler-Najjar.
  epidemic jaundice ictericia epidémica.
  familial acholuric jaundice ictericia acolúrica familiar.
  familial non-hemolytic jaundice ictericia no hemolítica familiar.
  febrile jaundice ictericia febril.
  gravidic jaundice ictericia gravídica.
  hematogenous jaundice ictericia hematógena.
  hemolytic jaundice ictericia hemolítica.
  hemorrhagic jaundice ictericia hemorrágica.
  hepatocellular jaundice ictericia hepatocelular.
  hepatogenic jaundice ictericia hepatógena.
  hepatogenous jaundice ictericia hepatógena.
  homologous serum jaundice ictericia por suero homólogo, por suero humano.
  human serum jaundice ictericia por suero homólogo, por suero humano.
  Infectious Jaundice ictericia infecciosa, icterus infeccioso.
  infective jaundice ictericia infecciosa, icterus infeccioso.
  jaundice of the newborn ictericia del recién nacido.
  latent jaundice ictericia latente.
  leptospiral jaundice ictericia por leptospiras.
  malignant jaundice ictericia maligna.
  mechanical jaundice ictericia mecánica.
  neonatal jaundice ictericia neonatal, icterus neonatal.
  non-hemolytic jaundice ictericia no hemolítica.
  non-obstructive jaundice ictericia no obstructiva.
  nuclear jaundice ictericia nuclear.
  obstructive jaundice ictericia obstructiva.
  painless jaundice ictericia indolora.
  physiologic jaundice ictericia fisiológica, icterus fisiológico.
  picric acid jaundice ictericia por ácido pícrico.
  post-arsphenamine jaundice ictericia de la arsfenamina.
  posthepatic jaundice ictericia posthepática.
  regurgitation jaundice ictericia de regurgitación.
  retention jaundice ictericia de retención.
  Schmorl's jaundice ictericia de Schmorl.
  spherocytic jaundice ictericia esferocítica.
  spirochetal jaundice ictericia espiroquetósica.
  Sumatra jaundice ictericia de Sumatra.
  toxemic jaundice ictericia toxémica.
  toxic jaundice ictericia tóxica.
jaw *n.* maxilar[1], quijada.
  bird beak jaw quijada en pico de pájaro.
  cleft jaw quijada hendida.
  crackling jaw quijada crujiente.
  Habsburg jaw quijada de Habsburgo.
  parrot jaw quijada de cotorra.
  pipe jaw quijada de pipa.
jecorize *v.* jecorizar.

jejunal *adj.* yeyunal.
jejunectomy *n.* yeyunectomía.
jejunitis *n.* yeyunitis.
jejunocecostomy *n.* yeyunocecostomía.
jejunocolostomy *n.* yeyunocolostomía.
jejunography *n.* yeyunografía.
jejunoileal *adj.* yeyunoileal.
jejunoileitis *n.* yeyunoileítis.
jejunoileostomy *n.* yeyunoileostomía.
jejunojejunostomy *n.* yeyunoyeyunostomía.
jejunoplasty *n.* yeyunoplastia.
jejunorrhaphy *n.* yeyunorrafia.
jejunostomy *n.* yeyunostomía.
jejunotomy *n.* yeyunotomía.
jejunum *n.* yeyuno.
jelly *n.* gelatina, jalea.
  cardiac jelly gelatina cardíaca, jalea cardíaca.
  contraceptive jelly jalea anticonceptiva, jalea contraceptiva.
  Elsner's jelly gelatina de Elsner.
  enamel jelly gelatina de esmalte.
  glycerin jelly gelatina de glicerina, gelatina glicerinada, jalea de glicerina.
  lidocaine hydrochloride jelly jalea de clorhidrato de lidocaína.
  mineral jelly gelatina mineral.
  nutrient jelly gelatina nutriente.
  pramoxine hydrochloride jelly jalea de clorhidrato de pramoxina.
  Stilling's jelly gelatina de Stilling.
  vaginal jelly jalea vaginal.
  vegetable jelly gelatina vegetal.
  Wharton's jelly gelatina de Wharton, jalea de Wharton.
Jennerian *adj.* jeneriano, -na.
jennerization *n.* jenerización, jennerización.
jerk *n.* sacudida.
  Achiles jerk sacudida de Aquiles.
  ankle jerk sacudida del tobillo.
  biceps jerk sacudida del bíceps.
  chin jerk sacudida del mentón.
  crossed adductor jerk sacudida aductora cruzada.
  crossed jerk sacudida cruzada.
  crossed knee jerk sacudida cruzada de la rodilla.
  elbow jerk sacudida del codo.
  jaw jerk sacudida del maxilar.
  knee jerk sacudida de la rodilla.
  quadriceps jerk sacudida del cuádriceps.
  supinator jerk sacudida del supinador.
  tendon jerk sacudida tendinosa.
  triceps surae jerk sacudida del tríceps crural.
jet lag *n.* jet lag.
jitter *n.* jitter.
jodbasedow *n.* yodobasedow.
juccuya *n.* juccuya, jucuya.
judgement call *n.* apelación al buen juicio.
judgment *n.* juicio.
jugal *adj.* yugal.

jugomaxillary *adj.* yugomaxilar.
jugular *adj.* yugular.
jugulation *n.* yugulación.
jugulum jugulum.
jugum jugum, yugo.
  jugum cerebralia ossium cranii yugo cerebral de los huesos del cráneo.
  jugum penis yugo para el pene.
  jugum sphenoidale yugo esfenoidal.
juice *n.* jugo.
  appetite juice jugo del apetito.
  cancer juice jugo canceroso, jugo de cáncer.
  cherry juice jugo de cereza.
  gastric juice jugo gástrico.
  intestinal juice jugo intestinal.
  pancreatic juice jugo pancreático.
  press juice jugo de exprimido.
  prostatic juice jugo prostático.
  raspberry juice jugo de frambuesa.
Jukes *n.* Jukes.
jumentous *adj.* jumentoso, -sa.
junction *n.* unión².
  adherent junction unión adherente.
  amelodental junction unión amelodentinaria, unión amelodentínica.
  amelodentinal junction unión amelodentinaria, unión amelodentínica.
  amnioembryonic junction unión amnioembrionaria.
  bony junction unión ósea.
  cardioesophageal junction unión cardioesofágica.
  cementodentinal junction unión cemento-dentinaria, unión de cemento y dentina.
  cementoenamel junction unión cemento-esmalte, unión de cemento y esmalte.
  choledochoduodenal junction unión coledocoduodenal.
  communicating junction unión de intersticio.
  corticomedullary junction unión corticomedular.
  dentinocemental junction unión de dentina y cemento, unión dentinocementaria.
  dentinoenamel junction unión de dentina y esmalte, unión dentina-esmalte.
  dentogingival junction unión dentogingival.
  dermoepidermal junction unión dermoepidérmica.
  electrotonic junction unión electrotónica.
  esophagogastric junction unión esofagogástrica.
  fibromuscular junction unión fibromuscular.
  gap junction unión de brecha, unión de hendidura, unión de nexo, unión nexo.
  gastroesophageal junction unión gastroesofágica.
  ileocecal junction unión ileocecal.
  intercellular junction unión intercelular.
  junction of the lips unión de los labios.
  mucocutaneous junction unión mucocutánea.
  muscle-tendon junction unión musculotendinosa.
  myoneural junction unión mioneural.
  neuroectodermal junction unión neuroectodérmica.
  neuromuscular junction unión neuromuscular.
  neurosomatic junction unión neurosomática.
  occluding junction unión ocluyente.
  osseous junction unión ósea.
  squamocolumnar junction unión escamocolumnar.
  ST junction unión ST.
  synaptic junction unión sináptica.
  thight junction unión ocluyente.
  tight junction unión estrecha.
  tympanostapedial junction unión timpanoestapedia.
  ureteropelvic junction unión ureteropélvica.
  ureterovesical junction unión ureterovesical.
junctional *adj.* yuncional.
Jungian *adj.* jungiano, -na.
jurisprudence *n.* jurisprudencia.
  dental jurisprudence jurisprudencia dental.
  medical jurisprudence jurisprudencia médica.
justo justo.
  justo major justo major.
  justo minor justo minor.
juvenile *adj.* juvenil.
juxta-articular *adj.* yuxtaarticular.
juxtaepiphyseal *adj.* yuxtaepifisario, -ria.
juxtaepiphysial *adj.* yuxtaepifisario, -ria.
juxtaglomerular *adj.* yuxtaglomerular.
juxtamedullary *adj.* yuxtamedular.
juxtangina *n.* yuxtaangina, yuxtangina.
juxtaposition *n.* yuxtaposición.
juxtapyloric *adj.* yuxtapilórico, -ca.
juxtaspinal *adj.* yuxtaespinal, yuxtaspinal.
juxtavesical *adj.* yuxtavesical.

K k

kabure *n.* kabure.
kafindo *n.* kafindo.
kaif *n.* kaif.
kakidrosis *n.* caquidrosis.
kakke *n.* kakke, kakké.
kala-azar *n.* kala-azar.
kaliemia *n.* caliemia.
kaligenous *adj.* calígeno, na.
kalimeter *n.* kalímetro.
kaliopenia *n.* caliopenia, kaliopenia.
kaliopenic *adj.* caliopénico, -ca, kaliopénico, -ca.
kalium kalium.
kaliuresis *n.* caliuresis, kaliuresis.
kaliuretic *adj.* caliurético, -ca, kaliurético, -ca.
kallak *n.* kallak.
Kallikak *n.* Kallikak.
kallikrein *n.* kalicreína.
kallikreinogen *n.* calicreinógeno.
kaluresis *n.* kaliuresis.
kaluretic *adj.* kaliurético, -ca.
kaniemba *n.* kaniemba, kanyemba.
kansasiin *n.* kansasina.
kanyemba *n.* kaniemba, kanyemba.
kaodzera *n.* kaodzera.
kaolinosis *n.* caolinosis.
kappacism *n.* kappacismo.
karnofsky *n.* karnofsky.
karyapsis *n.* cariapsis.
karyochromatophil *adj.* cariocromatófilo, -la, cariocromófilo, -la.
karyogamy *n.* cariogamia.
karyogenesis *n.* cariogénesis[1].
karyogenic *adj.* cariogénico[1], -ca.
karyokinesis *n.* cariocinesis.
    asymmetrical karyokinesis cariocinesis asimétrica.
karyoklasis *n.* carioclasis.
karyolitic *adj.* cariolítico, -ca.
karyology *n.* cariología.
karyolymph *n.* cariolinfa.
karyolysis *n.* cariólisis.
karyomere *n.* cariómera.
karyomitosis *n.* cariomitosis.
karyomitotic *adj.* cariomItótico, -ca.
karyomorphism *n.* cariomorfismo.
karyoplasm *n.* carioplasma.
karyopyknosis *n.* cariopicnosis.
karyorrhexis *n.* cariorrexis.
karyosome *n.* cariosoma.
karyostasis *n.* cariostasis.
karyotheca *n.* carioteca.
karyotype *n.* cariotipo.
kasai *n.* kasai.
katal *n.* katal.
katathermometer *n.* catatermómetro.
keloid *n.* queloide, queloides.
    acne keloid queloide de acné.
    Addison's keloid queloide de Addison.
    Alibert's keloid queloide de Alibert.

cicatricial keloid queloide cicatricial.
    false keloid queloide falso.
    Hawkins' keloid queloide de Hawkins.
    keloid of the gums queloide de las encías.
keloidosis *n.* queloidosis.
keloplasty *n.* queloplastia.
kelotomy *n.* quelotomía.
kenotoxin *n.* quenotoxina.
keratalgia *n.* queratalgia.
keratan sulfate *n.* queratán-sulfato.
keratansulfaturia *n.* queratansulfaturia.
keratectasia *n.* queratectasia.
keratectomy *n.* keratectomía, queratectomía.
    photo-refractive keratectomy queratectomía fotorrefractiva, queratectomía fotorrefringente.
keratein *n.* querateína.
keratiasis *n.* queratiasis.
keratic *adj.* querático, -ca.
keratin *n.* queratina.
keratinase *n.* queratinasa.
keratinization *n.* queratinización.
keratinize *v.* queratinizar.
keratinized *adj.* queratinizado, -da.
keratinocyte *n.* queratinocito.
keratinoid *adj.* queratinoide.
keratinosome *n.* queratinosoma.
keratinous *adj.* queratinoso, -sa.
keratitis *n.* queratitis.
    acne rosacea keratitis queratitis de acné rosácea.
    actinic keratitis queratitis actínica.
    aerosol keratitis queratitis de los aerosoles.
    alphabet keratitis queratitis alfabética, queratitis en alfabeto.
    alphabetical keratitis queratitis alfabética, queratitis en alfabeto.
    anaphylactic keratitis queratitis anafiláctica.
    annular keratitis queratitis anular.
    artificial silk keratitis queratitis de la seda artificial.
    aspergillus keratitis queratitis por aspergillus.
    band keratitis queratitis en banda.
    band-shaped keratitis queratitis en banda.
    deep keratitis queratitis profunda.
    dendriform keratitis queratitis dendriforme, queratitis dendrítica.
    dendritic keratitis queratitis dendriforme, queratitis dendrítica.
    desiccation keratitis queratitis de desecación.
    Dimmer's keratitis queratitis de Dimmer.
    disciform keratitis queratitis disciforme, queratitis discoide.
    epithelial diffuse keratitis queratitis epitelial difusa.
    exfoliative keratitis queratitis exfoliativa.
    exposure keratitis queratitis por exposición.
    fascicular keratitis queratitis fascicular.
    filamentary keratitis queratitis filamentosa.

furrow keratitis queratitis arrugada.
    geographic keratitis queratitis geográfica.
    herpetic keratitis queratitis herpética.
    hypopyon keratitis queratitis con hipopión, queratitis de hipopión.
    interstitial keratitis queratitis intersticial.
    keratitis arborescens queratitis arborescente.
    keratitis bandelette qucratitis cn banda.
    keratitis bullosa queratitis ampollosa.
    keratitis filamentosa queratitis filamentosa.
    keratitis linearis migrans queratitis lineal migratoria.
    keratitis nummularis queratitis numular.
    keratitis periodica fugax queratitis fugaz periódica.
    keratitis petrificans queratitis petrificans.
    keratitis profunda queratitis profunda.
    keratitis punctata queratitis punctata, queratitis punteada.
    keratitis punctata profunda queratitis punteada profunda.
    keratitis pustuliformis profunda q pustuliforme profunda, queratitis pustulosa profunda.
    keratitis ramificata superficialis queratitis ramificada superficial.
    keratitis sicca queratitis seca.
    lagophthalmic keratitis queratitis lagoftálmica.
    lattice keratitis queratitis entretejida.
    marginal keratitis queratitis marginal.
    metaherpetic keratitis queratitis metaherpética.
    mycotic keratitis queratitis micótica.
    necrogranulomatous keratitis queratitis necrogranulomatosa.
    neuroparalytic keratitis queratitis neuroparalítica.
    neurotrophlc keratltis queratitis neurotrófica.
    nummular keratitis queratitis numular.
    parenchymatous keratitis queratitis parenquimatosa.
    phlyctenular keratitis queratitis flictenular.
    polymorphic superficial keratitis queratitis superficial polimorfa.
    punctate keratitis queratitis punctata, queratitis punteada.
    purulent keratitis queratitis purulenta.
    reaper's keratitis queratitis de los segadores.
    reticular keratitis queratitis reticular.
    ribbon-like keratitis queratitis en banda.
    rosacea keratitis queratitis rosácea.
    sclerosing keratitis queratitis esclerosante.
    scrofulous keratitis queratitis escrofulosa.
    secondary keratitis queratitis secundaria.
    serpiginous keratitis queratitis serpiginosa.
    striate keratitis queratitis estríada.
    superficial linear keratitis queratitis lineal superficial.

superficial punctate keratitis queratitis punteada superficial.
suppurative keratitis queratitis supurativa.
Thygeson superficial punctate keratitis queratitis puntiforme superficial de Thygeson.
trachomatous keratitis queratitis tracomatosa.
trophic keratitis queratitis trófica.
vascular keratitis queratitis vascular.
vasculonebulous keratitis queratitis vasculonebulosa.
vesicular keratitis queratitis vesicular.
xerotic keratitis queratitis xerótica.
zonular keratitis queratitis zonular.
keratoacanthoma *n.* queratoacantoma.
keratoangioma *n.* queratoangioma.
keratoatrophoderma *n.* queratoatrofodermia.
keratocele *n.* queratocele.
keratocentesis *n.* queratocentesis.
keratoconjunctivitis *n.* queratoconjuntivitis.
atopic keratoconjunctivitis queratoconjuntivitis atópica.
epidemic keratoconjunctivitis queratoconjuntivitis epidémica.
flash keratoconjunctivitis queratoconjuntivitis en flash, queratoconjuntivitis por destello.
herpetic keratoconjunctivitis queratoconjuntivitis herpética.
keratoconjunctivitis sicca queratoconjuntivitis seca.
phlyctenular keratoconjunctivitis queratoconjuntivitis flictenular.
shipyard keratoconjunctivitis queratoconjuntivitis de los astilleros.
superior limbic keratoconjunctivitis queratoconjuntivitis límbica superior.
ultraviolet keratoconjunctivitis queratoconjuntivitis ultravioleta.
vernal keratoconjunctivitis queratoconjuntivitis primaveral, queratoconjuntivitis vernal.
viral keratoconjunctivitis queratoconjuntivitis viral, queratoconjuntivitis virósica.
virus keratoconjunctivitis queratoconjuntivitis viral, queratoconjuntivitis virósica.
keratoconus *n.* queratocono.
keratocyte *n.* queratocito.
keratoderma *n.* queratodermia.
diffuse palmoplantar keratoderma queratodermia palmoplantar difusa.
endocrine keratoderma queratodermia endocrina.
keratoderma blennorrhagicum queratodermia blenorrágica, queratodermia plantar fisurada.
keratoderma climactericum queratodermia climatérica.
keratoderma eccentrica queratodermia excéntrica.
keratoderma palmare et plantare queratodermia palmar y plantar, queratodermia palmoplantar.
keratoderma palmaris et plantaris queratodermia palmar y plantar, queratodermia palmoplantar.
keratoderma plantare sulcatum queratodermia plantar surcada.
keratoderma symmetrica queratodermia simétrica.
lymphedematous keratoderma queratodermia linfedematosa.
mutilating keratoderma queratodermia mutilante.
palmoplantar keratoderma queratodermia palmar y plantar, queratodermia palmoplantar.

punctate keratoderma queratodermia punteada.
senile keratoderma queratodermia senil.
symmetric keratoderma queratodermia simétrica.
Vohwinkel's keratoderma queratodermia de Vohwinkel.
Vorner's keratoderma queratodermia de Vorner.
keratodermatitis *n.* queratodermatitis.
keratodermatocele *n.* queratodermatocele.
keratoectasia *n.* queratoectasia.
keratogenesis *n.* queratogénesis.
keratogenetic *adj.* queratogénico, -ca.
keratogenous *adj.* queratógeno, -na.
keratoglobus *n.* queratoglobo.
keratohelcosis *n.* queratohelcosis.
keratohemia *n.* queratohemia.
keratohyal *adj.* queratohial.
keratohyalin *n.* queratohialina.
keratoid *adj.* queratoide, queratoideo, -a.
keratoiditis *n.* queratoiditis.
keratoiridocyclitis *n.* queratoiridociclitis.
keratoiridoscope *n.* queratoiridoscopio.
keratoiritis *n.* queratoiritis.
hypopyon keratoiritis queratoiritis de hipopión.
keratoleptynsis *n.* queratoleptinsis.
keratoleukoma *n.* queratoleucoma.
keratolysis *n.* queratólisis.
keratolysis exfoliativa queratólisis exfoliativa.
keratolysis neonatorum queratólisis del recién nacido, queratólisis neonatal.
keratolysis plantare sulcatum queratólisis plantar surcada.
pitted keratolysis queratólisis excavada.
keratolytic *adj.* queratolítico, -ca.
keratoma *n.* queratoma.
keratoma hereditarium mutilans queratoma hereditario mutilante.
keratoma palmare et plantare queratoma palmar y plantar.
keratoma senile queratoma senil.
keratomalacia *n.* queratomalacia.
keratome *n.* querátomo.
keratometer *n.* queratómetro.
keratometric *adj.* queratométrico, -va.
keratometry *n.* queratometría.
keratomileusis *n.* queratomileusis.
keratomycosis *n.* queratomicosis.
keratomycosis linguae queratomicosis de la lengua, queratomicosis lingual.
lingual keratomycosis queratomicosis de la lengua, queratomicosis lingual.
keratonosus *n.* queratonosis.
keratopathy *n.* queratopatía.
band keratopathy queratopatía en banda.
band-shaped keratopathy queratopatía en banda.
bullous keratopathy queratopatía ampollar, queratopatía bullosa.
climatic keratopathy queratopatía climática.
filamentary keratopathy queratopatía filamentosa.
Labrador keratopathy queratopatía del Labrador.
lipid keratopathy queratopatía lipídica.
striate keratopathy queratopatía estríada.
vesicular keratopathy queratopatía vesicular.
keratophakia *n.* queratofaquia.
keratoplasia *n.* queratoplasia.
keratoplasty *n.* queratoplastia.
allopathic keratoplasty queratoplastia alopática.

autogenous keratoplasty queratoplastia autógena.
lamellar keratoplasty queratoplastia lamelar.
non-penetrating keratoplasty queratoplastia no penetrante.
optic keratoplasty queratoplastia óptica.
penetrating keratoplasty queratoplastia penetrante.
refractive keratoplasty queratoplastia de refracción.
tectonic keratoplasty queratoplastia tectónica.
keratoprosthesis *n.* queratoprótesis.
keratoprotein *n.* queratoproteína.
keratorhexis *n.* queratorrexis.
keratoscleritis *n.* queratoescleritis, queratoscleritis.
keratoscope *n.* queratoscopio.
keratoscopy *n.* queratoscopia.
keratosis *n.* queratosis.
actinic keratosis queratosis actínica.
arsenic keratosis queratosis arsenical, queratosis por arsénico.
arsenical keratosis queratosis arsenical, queratosis por arsénico.
gonorrheal keratosis queratosis gonorreica.
keratosis blennorrhagica queratosis blenorrágica.
keratosis follicularis queratosis folicular.
keratosis follicularis contagiosa queratosis folicular contagiosa.
keratosis linguae queratosis lingual.
keratosis nigricans queratosis nigricans.
keratosis obturans queratosis obturadora, queratosis obturante, queratosis obturatriz.
keratosis palmaris et plantaris queratosis palmar y plantar.
keratosis pharyngea queratosis faríngea.
keratosis pilaris queratosis pilar, queratosis pilaris, queratosis pilosa.
keratosis punctata queratosis punteada.
keratosis rubra figurata queratosis rubra figurata.
keratosis seborrheica queratosis seborreica.
keratosis senilis queratosis senil.
radiation keratosis queratosis por radiación.
roentgen keratosis queratosis por rayos roentgen.
seborrheic keratosis queratosis seborreica.
senile keratosis queratosis senil.
solar keratosis queratosis solar.
stucco keratosis queratosis del estuco.
tar keratosis queratosis por alquitrán.
keratosulfate *n.* queratosulfato.
keratotic *adj.* queratósico, -ca.
keratotome *n.* queratótomo.
keratotomy *n.* queratotomía.
delimiting keratotomy queratotomía delimitante.
laser excimer keratotomy queratotomía con láser excímer.
radial keratotomy queratotomía radial.
refractive keratotomy queratotomía refractiva.
keratotorus *n.* queratótoro.
kerectasis *n.* querectasia, querectasis.
kerectomy *n.* querectomía.
kerion *n.* kerión, querión.
Celsus kerion querión de Celso.
kerion celsi querión de Celso.
kerion of Celso querión de Celso.
kermes *n.* kermes.
kernel *n.* kernel.
kernicterus *n.* kerníctero, kernicterus, querníctero.

keroid *adj.* queroideo, -a.
kerotherapy *n.* queroterapia.
kerotohyaline *adj.* queratohialino, -na.
ketoacidosis *n.* acidocetosis, cetoacidosis.
ketoaciduria *n.* cetoaciduria.
 branched chain ketoaciduria cetoaciduria de cadena ramificada.
ketogenesis *n.* cetogénesis.
ketogenetic *adj.* cetogenético, -ca.
ketogenic *adj.* cetogénico, -ca.
ketolysis *n.* cetólisis.
ketolytic *adj.* cetolítico, -ca.
ketone *n.* cetona.
ketonemia *n.* cetonemia.
ketonic *adj.* cetónico, -ca.
ketonization *n.* cetonización.
ketonuria *n.* cetonuria.
 branched chain ketonuria cetonuria de cadena ramificada.
ketosis *n.* cetosis.
ketosteroid *n.* cetosteroide.
kibisotome *n.* quibisítomo.
kidney *n.* riñón.
 amyloid kidney riñón adiposo, riñón amiloide, riñón amiloideo, riñón lardáceo.
 Armanni-Ebstein kidney riñón de Armanni-Ebstein.
 arteriolosclerotic kidney riñón arterioloesclerótico.
 arteriosclerotic kidney riñón arterioesclerótico.
 artificial kidney riñón artificial.
 Askr-Upmark kidney riñón de Askr-Upmark.
 atrophic kidney riñón atrófico.
 cake kidney riñón en torta.
 cicatricial kidney riñón cicatricial.
 contracted kidney riñón contraído.
 cow kidney riñón de vaca.
 crush kidney riñón aplastado.
 cystic kidney riñón quístico.
 disk kidney riñón discoide.
 duplex kidney riñón doble.
 fatty kidney riñón graso.
 flea-bitten kidney riñón picado por pulgas.
 floating kidney riñón ectópico, riñón flotante.
 Formad's kidney riñón de Formad.
 fused kidney riñón fusionado.
 Goldblatt kidney riñón de Goldblatt.
 granular kidney riñón granular.
 head kidney riñón cefálico, riñón delantero.
 hind kidney riñón trasero.
 horseshoe kidney riñón en herradura.
 medullary sponge kidney riñón meduloesponjoso.
 mortar kidney riñón de argamasa.
 movable kidney riñón movible.
 mural kidney riñón mural, riñón parietal.
 pancake kidney riñón en panqueque.
 pelvic kidney riñón pélvico.
 polycystic kidney riñón poliquístico.
 primordial kidney riñón primordial.
 putty kidney riñón de masilla.
 pyelonephritic kidney riñón pielonefrítico.
 Roser-Bradford kidney riñón de Roser-Bradford.
 sclerotic kidney riñón esclerótico.
 supernumerary kidney riñón supernumerario.
 wandering kidney riñón errante.
 waxy kidney riñón céreo.
kimputu *n.* kimputu.
kinanesthesia *n.* cinanestesia.
kinase *n.* quinasa.
 insulin kinase insulinocinasa.

kinematics *n.* cinemática.
kinemometer *n.* cinemómetro.
kineplastics *n.* cineplastia.
kinesalgia *n.* cinesalgia, kinesialgia.
kinescopy *n.* cinescopio.
kinesia *n.* cinesia, cinesis.
kinesialgia *n.* kinesialgia.
kinesiatrics *n.* kinesiatría.
kinesics *n.* kinésica.
kinesiestesiometer *n.* cinesiestesiómetro.
kinesimeter *n.* cinesímetro, kinesímetro, kinesiómetro.
kinesiologist *n.* kinesiólogo, -ga.
kinesiology *n.* cinesiología, kinesiología.
kinesiometer *n.* cinesímetro, cinesiómetro.
kinesioneurosis *n.* cinesioneurosis.
kinesiotherapy *n.* cinesioterapia, cinesiterapia.
kinesipathist *n.* kinesiópata, kinesioterapeuta, kinesiterapeuta.
kinesipathy *n.* kinesiopatía.
kinesis *n.* cinesia, cinesis, kinesis.
kinesitherapy *n.* cinesiatría, cinesioterapia, cinesiterapia, kinesioterapia, kinesiterapia.
kinesodic *adj.* cinesódico, -ca.
kinesophobia *n.* cinesofobia, kinesofobia.
kinesthesia *n.* cinestesia, kinestesia.
kinesthesiometer *n.* cinestesiómetro, kinestesiómetro.
kinesthetic *adj.* cinestésico, -ca, kinestésico, -ca.
kinetic *adj.* cinético, -ca.
kinetics *n.* cinética.
 chemical kinetics cinética química.
kinetism *n.* cinetismo.
kinetocardiogram *n.* cinetocardiograma.
kinetocardiograph *n.* cinetocardiógrafo.
kinetochore *n.* cinetocoro.
kinetogenic *adj.* cinetogénico -ca, cinetógeno, -na.
kinetonucleus *n.* cinetonúcleo.
kinetoplasm *n.* kinetoplasma.
kinetoplast *n.* cinetoplasto.
kinetoscope *n.* cinetoscopio.
kinetoscopy *n.* cinetoscopia.
kinetosis *n.* cinetosis.
kinetosome *n.* cinetosoma.
kinetotherapy *n.* cinesioterapia, cinesiterapia, cinetoterapia.
Kingella Kingella.
kininogen *n.* cininógeno.
kink *n.* acodadura, acodamiento.
 ileal kink acodadura de Lane.
 Lane's kink acodadura de Lane.
kinohapt *n.* cinohapto.
kinomometer *n.* cinomómetro, kinomómetro.
kinotoxin *n.* kinotoxina.
kiotome *n.* quiótomo.
kiotomy *n.* quiotomía.
Klebsiella Klebsiella.
Klebsielleae Klebsielleae.
kleptolagnia *n.* cleptolagnia.
kleptomania *n.* cleptomanía.
kleptomaniac *n.* cleptomaníaco, cleptómano.
kleptophobia *n.* cleptofobia.
klexography *n.* klexografía.
Kluyvera Kluyvera.
kneading *n.* amasamiento.
knee *n.* rodilla.
 Brodie's knee rodilla de Brodie.
 capped knee rodilla distendida.
 housemaid's knee rodilla de mucama.
 locked knee rodilla bloqueada.
 rugby knee rodilla de rugby.

kneeguard *n.* rodillera.
kneippism *n.* kneippismo.
knife *n.* bisturí[2], cuchilla, cuchillo.
 amputation knife cuchillo de amputación.
 Beer's knife cuchillo de Beer.
 buck knife bisturí de banco, cuchillo de banco.
 button knife cuchillo de botón.
 cartilage knife cuchillo para cartílago.
 cataract knife cuchillo de catarata.
 cautery knife bisturí eléctrico, cuchillo de cauterización.
 chemical knife cuchillo químico.
 electric knife bisturí eléctrico, cuchillo eléctrico.
 electrocautery knife bisturí eléctrico.
 electrode knife cuchillo electrodo.
 endotermic knife cuchillo endotérmico.
 Fox knife cuchilla de Fox.
 free-hand knife bisturí a pulso.
 gold knife cuchilla de oro.
 Goldman-Fox knife bisturí de Goldman-Fox, cuchilla de Goldman-Fox, cuchillo de Goldman-Fox.
 Graefe's knife cuchillo de Graefe.
 hernia knife cuchillo de hernia.
 Hymby knife cuchillo de Hymby.
 Joseph knife bisturí de Joseph.
 Kirkland knife bisturí de Kirkland, cuchillo de Kirkland.
 lenticular knife cuchillo lenticular.
 Liston's knife bisturí de Liston, cuchillo de Liston.
 Merrifield's knife bisturí de Merrifield, cuchillo de Merrifield.
 Ramsbotham's sickle knife cuchillo falciforme de Ramsbotham.
 ring knife bisturí en anillo.
 rocker knife cuchillo balancín.
 spoke-shave knife bisturí en anillo.
knismogenic *adj.* cnismogénico, -ca, quenismógeno, -na.
knismolagnia *n.* cnismolagnia.
knitting *n.* entretejido.
knock-kneed *n.* patizambo, -ba, zambo, -ba.
knot *n.* nudo.
 clove-hitch knot nudo de ballestrinque.
 double knot nudo doble.
 enamel knot nudo del esmalte.
 false knot of the umbilical cord nudo falso del cordón umbilical.
 friction knot nudo de fricción.
 granny knot nudo de rizo mal cruzado.
 reef knot nudo cruzado.
 ret knot nudo de redecilla.
 sailor's knot nudo de marinero.
 square knot nudo cuadrado.
 stay knot nudo de retén.
 surgeon's knot nudo de cirujano.
 surgical knot nudo quirúrgico.
 true knot of the umbilical cord nudo verdadero del cordón umbilical.
knot-carrier *n.* portanudos.
knuckle *n.* nudillo.
 aortic knuckle nudillo aórtico.
 cervical aortic knuckle nudillo cervical aórtico.
kocherization *n.* kocherización.
koilocyte *n.* coilocito.
koilocytosis *n.* coilocitosis.
koilonychia *n.* celoniquia, coiloniquia.
koilosternia *n.* coilosternia.
koinonia *n.* coinonía.
koinotropy *n.* coinotropía.
kolypeptic *adj.* colipéptico, -ca.

kolytic *adj.* colítico, -ca.
konimeter *n.* conímetro, coniómetro.
koniocortex *n.* coniocorteza.
konometer *n.* conímetro, coniómetro, conómetro.
kophemia *n.* cofemia.
kopophobia *n.* copofobia.
koro *n.* koro.
kra-kra *n.* kra-kra.
kratometer *n.* cratómetro.
krauomania *n.* crauomanía.
kraurosis *n.* craurosis.
 kraurosis penis craurosis del pene.
 kraurosis vulvae craurosis vulvar.

kreotoxin *n.* creotoxina.
kreotoxism *n.* creotoxismo.
kresofuchsin *n.* cresofucsina.
kubisagari *n.* kubisagari, kubisagaru, kubisgari.
kubisagaru *n.* kubisagari, kubisagaru, kubisgari.
kubisgari *n.* kubisagari, kubisagaru, kubisgari.
Kurthia Kurthia.
kurtosis *n.* curtosis.
kuru *n.* kuru.
kwashiorkor *n.* kwashiorkor.
kwaski *n.* kwaski.
kyllosis *n.* quilosis[3].

kymocyclograph *n.* quimociclógrafo.
kymogram *n.* quimograma.
kymograph *n.* cimógrafo, quimógrafo.
kymography *n.* cimografía, quimografía.
 roentgen kymography quimografía roentgen.
kymoscope *n.* cimoscopio[1].
kynophobia *n.* cinofobia.
kyogenic *adj.* quiógeno, -na.
kyphoscoliosis *n.* cifoescoliosis, cifoscoliosis.
kyphosis *n.* cifosis.
 Scheuermann's kyphosis cifosis de Scheuermann.
kyrtorrhachic *adj.* quirtorráquico, -ca.

L l

label *n.* marcaje.
  radioactive label marcaje radiactivo.
labeling *adj.* etiquetado, -da.
labial *adj.* labial.
labialism *n.* labialismo.
labially *adv.* labialmente.
labile *adj.* lábil.
  heat labile termolábil.
lability *n.* labilidad.
labioalveolar *adj.* labioalveolar.
labioaxiogingival *adj.* labioaxiogingival.
labiocervical *adj.* labiocervical.
labiochorea *n.* labiocorea.
labioclination *n.* labioinclinación.
labiodental *adj.* labiodental.
labiogingival *adj.* labiogingival.
labioglossolaryngeal *adj.* labioglosolaríngeo, -a.
labioglossopharyngeal *adj.* labioglosofaríngeo, -a.
labiograph *n.* labiógrafo.
labioincisal *adj.* labioincisal.
labiolingual *adj.* labiolingual.
labiologic *adj.* labiológico, -ca.
labiology *n.* labiología.
labiomental *adj.* labiomentoniano, -na.
labiomycosis *n.* labiomicosis.
labionasal *adj.* labionasal.
labiopalatine *adj.* labiopalatino, -na.
labioplacement *n.* labiocolocación, labioposición.
labioplasty *n.* labioplastia.
labiotenaculum *n.* labiotenáculo.
labioversion *n.* labioversión.
labitome *n.* labítomo.
labium *n.* labio.
labor *n.* parto.
  artificial labor parto artificial.
  atonic labor parto atónico.
  complicated labor parto complicado.
  false labor parto falso.
  induced labor parto inducido, parto provocado.
  instrumental labor parto instrumental.
  labor coach instructor, -ra del parto.
  multiple labor parto múltiple.
  precipitate labor parto precipitado.
  prolonged labor parto prolongado.
laboratory *n.* laboratorio.
  clinical laboratory laboratorio clínico.
labrale labrale.
labrum labrum.
labyrinth *n.* laberinto.
labyrinthectomy *n.* laberintectomía.
labyrinthine *adj.* laberíntico, -ca.
labyrinthitis *n.* laberintitis.
labyrinthotomy *n.* laberintotomía.
labyrinthus *n.* laberinto.
lacerable *adj.* lacerable.
lacerated *adj.* lacerado, -da, rasgado, -da.

laceration *n.* laceración.
  brain laceration laceración cerebral.
  scalp laceration laceración del cuero cabelludo.
  vaginal laceration laceración vaginal.
lacertus lacertus.
lachrymal *adj.* lacrimal, lagrimal[1], lagrimal[2].
lachrymation *n.* lacrimación, lagrimación.
lacocystorhinostomy *n.* lacocistorrinostomía.
lacrimal *n.* lacrimal, lagrimal[1], lagrimal[2].
  lacrimal bone unguis.
lacrimalin *n.* lacrimalina.
lacrimation *n.* lacrimación, lagrimación, lagrimeo.
lacrimator *adj.* lacrimógeno, -na.
lacrimatory *adj.* lacrimatorio, -a.
lacrimonasal *adj.* lacrimonasal.
lacrimotome *n.* lacrimótomo.
lacrimotomy *n.* lacrimotomía.
lactacidemia *n.* lactacidemia.
lactacidosis *n.* lactacidosis.
lactaciduria *n.* lactaciduria.
lactagogue *adj.* lactagogo, -ga.
lactate *v.* lactar.
lactation *n.* lactación, lactancia[1].
lactational *adj.* lactacional.
lacteal *adj.* lácteo, -a.
lactescence *n.* lactescencia.
lactescent *adj.* lactescente.
lactic *adj.* láctico, -ca.
lacticacidemia *n.* lacticacidemia.
lacticemia *n.* lacticemia.
lactiferous *adj.* lactífero, -ra.
lactifugal *adj.* lactífugo, -ga.
lactifuge *adj.* lactífugo, -ga.
lactigenous *adj.* lactígeno, -na.
lactigerous *adj.* lactígero, -ra.
lactin *n.* lactina.
lactivorous *adj.* lactívoro, -ra.
Lactobacillaceae Lactobacillaceae.
Lactobacilleae Lactobacilleae.
lactobacillin *n.* lactobacilina.
Lactobacillus Lactobacillus.
  Lactobacillus acidophilus Lactobacillus acidophilus.
  Lactobacillus bifidus Lactobacillus bifidus.
  Lactobacillus bulgaricus Lactobacillus bulgaricus.
lactobacillus *n.* lactobacilo.
lactobutyrometer *n.* lactobutirómetro.
lactocele *n.* lactocele.
lactocrit *n.* lactocrito.
lactodensimeter *n.* lactodensímetro.
lactofarinaceous *adj.* lactofarináceo, -a.
lactoferrin *n.* lactoferrina.
lactogen *n.* lactógeno[1].
  human placental lactogen (HPL) lactógeno placentario humano (HPL).
lactogenesis *n.* lactogénesis.

lactogenic *adj.* lactogénico, -ca, lactógeno[2], -na.
lactoglobulin *n.* lactoglobulina.
lactometer *n.* lactómetro.
lacto-ovovegetarian *adj.* lactoovovegetariano, -na.
lactoprecipitin *n.* lactoprecipitina.
lactoprotein *n.* lactoproteína.
lactorrhea *n.* lactorrea.
lactoscope *n.* lactoscopio.
lactose *n.* lactosa.
lactoside *n.* lactósido.
lactosidosis *n.* lactosidosis.
  ceramide lactosidosis lactosidosis de ceramida.
lactosuria *n.* lactosuria.
lactosyl *n.* lactosil.
  lactosyl ceramidase lactosil-ceramidasa.
  lactosyl ceramide lactosil-ceramida.
  lactosyl ceramidosis lactosilceramidosis.
lactotherapy *n.* lactoterapia.
lactotoxin *n.* lactotoxina.
lactotrope *n.* lactótropa.
lactotropin *n.* lactotropina.
lactovegetarian *adj.* lactovegetariano, -na.
lacuna *n.* laguna.
  Blessig's lacunae laguna de Blessig.
  cerebral lacuna laguna cerebral.
  Howship's lacuna laguna de Howship.
  resorption lacuna laguna de absorción, laguna de reabsorción.
lacunar *adj.* lacunar, lagunar.
lacunule *n.* lagunilla, lagúnula.
lacus lacus, lago.
laeve *adj.* leve[1].
lag *n.* tardanza.
  nitrogen lag tardanza del nitrógeno.
lagena *n.* lagena.
lageniform *adj.* lageniforme.
lagnesis *n.* lagneomanía, lagnesis.
lagnosis *n.* lagnosis.
lagophthalmos *n.* lagoftalmía, lagoftalmos.
lagophthalmus *n.* lagoftalmía.
laiose *n.* layosa.
lake[1] *n.* lacado, lago.
lake[2] *v.* lacar.
laliatry *n.* laliatría.
lallation *n.* lalación.
lalochezia *n.* laloquecia.
lalognosis *n.* lalognosis.
laloneurosis *n.* laloneurosis.
lalopathology *n.* lalopatología.
lalopathy *n.* lalopatía.
lalophobia *n.* lalofobia.
laloplegia *n.* laloplejía.
lalorrhea *n.* lalorrea.
lambartry *n.* lumbartria.
lambda *n.* lambda.
lambdacism *n.* lambdacismo.
lambdacismus *n.* lambdacismo.
lambliasis *n.* lambliasis.

lambliosis *n.* lambliasis.
lamboloid *adj.* lambdoideo, -a.
lame *adj.* cojo -ja.
lamella *n.* lamella, laminilla[1].
  annulate lamella laminilla anular.
  bone lamella laminilla ósea.
  enamel lamella laminilla del esmalte.
  glandulopreputial lamella laminilla glandoprepucial.
lamellar *adj.* lamelar, laminal, laminillar.
lamelliform *adj.* lameliforme.
lamellipodia *n.* lamelipodio.
lameness *n.* cojera.
lamina *n.* lámina.
laminagram *n.* laminagrama.
laminagraph *n.* laminágrafo.
laminagraphy *n.* laminagrafía.
laminar *adj.* laminar.
laminated *adj.* laminado, -da, laminoso, -sa.
lamination *n.* laminación.
  fascial membrane lamination laminación de la membrana fascial.
laminectomy *n.* laminectomía.
laminin *n.* laminina.
laminitis *n.* laminitis.
laminogram *n.* laminograma.
laminograph *n.* laminógrafo.
laminography *n.* laminografía.
laminotomy *n.* laminotomía.
lamp *n.* lámpara.
  annealing lamp lámpara de recocción.
  arc lamp lámpara de arco.
  carbon arc lamp lámpara de arco carbónico.
  diagnostic lamp lámpara de diagnóstico.
  Eldridge-Green lamp lámpara de Eldridge-Green.
  Finsen lamp lámpara de Finsen.
  Gullstrand's slit lamp lámpara de Gullstrand.
  heat lamp lámpara de calor.
  hollow cathode lamp lámpara catódica hueca.
  mercury vapor lamp lámpara de vapor de mercurio.
  mignon lamp lámpara mignon.
  quartz lamp lámpara de cuarzo.
  slit lamp lámpara de hendidura.
  spirit lamp lámpara de alcohol.
  tungsten arc lamp lámpara de arco de tungsteno.
  ultraviolet lamp lámpara ultravioleta.
  Wood's lamp lámpara de Wood.
lamprophonia *n.* lamprofonía.
lamprophonic *adj.* lamprofónico, -ca.
lanceolate *adj.* lanceolado, -da.
lancet *n.* lanceta, sangradera.
  abscess lancet lanceta de absceso.
  acne lancet lanceta de acné.
  gum lancet lanceta gingival.
  laryngeal lancet lanceta laríngea.
  spring lancet lanceta con resorte, lanceta de muelle.
  thumb lancet lanceta en pulgar.
lancinating *adj.* lancinante.
landfill *n.* vertedero.
  sanitary landfill vertedero sanitario.
language *n.* lenguaje[1].
  body language lenguaje corporal.
  sensory-based language lenguaje sensitivo.
  sign language lenguaje de signos.
  verbal language lenguaje verbal.
laniary *adj.* laniario, -ria.
lantalgy *n.* lantalgia.
lanthanic *adj.* lantánico, -ca.
lanuginous *adj.* lanuginoso, -sa.
lanugo *n.* lanugo.
lapactic *adj.* lapáctico, -ca.

laparectomy *n.* laparectomía.
laparocele *n.* laparocele.
laparocholecystotomy *n.* laparocolecistotomía.
laparocolectomy *n.* laparocolectomía.
laparocolostomy *n.* laparocolostomía.
laparocolotomy *n.* laparocolotomía.
laparocystectomy *n.* laparocistectomía.
laparocystostomy *n.* laparocistotomía.
laparoenterostomy *n.* laparoenterostomía.
laparoenterotomy *n.* laparoenterotomía.
laparogastroscopy *n.* laparogastroscopia.
laparogastrostomy *n.* laparogastrostomía.
laparogastrotomy *n.* laparogastrotomía.
laparohepatotomy *n.* laparohepatotomía.
laparohysterectomy *n.* laparohisterectomía.
laparohystero-oophorectomy *n.* laparohisterooforectomía.
laparohysteropexy *n.* laparohisteropexia.
laparohysterosalpingo-oophorectomy *n.* laparohisterosalpingooforectomía.
laparohysterotomy *n.* laparohisterotomía.
laparoileotomy *n.* laparoileotomía.
laparomonodidymus *n.* laparomonodídimo.
laparomyitis *n.* laparomiitis.
laparomyomectomy *n.* laparomiomectomía.
laparomyositis *n.* laparomiositis.
laparonephrectomy *n.* laparonefrectomía.
laparorrhaphy *n.* laparorrafia.
laparosalpingectomy *n.* laparosalpingectomía.
laparosalpingo-oophorectomy *n.* laparosalpingooforectomía.
laparosalpingotomy *n.* laparosalpingotomía.
laparoscope *n.* laparoscopio.
laparoscopy *n.* laparoscopia.
laparosplenectomy *n.* laparoesplenectomía, laparosplenectomía.
laparosplenotomy *n.* laparoesplenotomía, laparosplenotomía.
laparotomaphilia *n.* laparotomafilia.
laparotome *n.* laparótomo.
laparotomy *n.* laparotomía.
  exploration laparotomy laparotomía exploradora.
  midline laparotomy laparotomía media.
  pararectal laparotomy laparotomía pararrectal.
  Pfannestiel's laparotomy laparotomía de Pfannestiel.
  staging laparotomy laparotomía de estadiaje.
  subcostal laparotomy laparotomía subcostal.
  transverse laparotomy laparotomía transversa.
laparotyphlotomy *n.* laparotiflotomía.
lapsus *n.* lapsus.
  lapsus calami lapsus calami.
  lapsus linguae lapsus linguae.
  lapsus memoriae lapsus memoriae.
lardacein *n.* lardaceína.
larva *n.* larva.
larvaceous *adj.* larváceo, -a.
larvacide *adj.* larvicida.
larval *adj.* larval.
larvate *adj.* larvado, -da.
larviposition *n.* larviposición.
laryngalgia *n.* laringalgia, laringodinia.
laryngeal *adj.* laríngeo, -a.
laryngectomee *n.* laringuectomizado, -da.
laryngectomized *adj.* laringuectomizado, -da.
laryngectomy *n.* laringuectomía.
  supraglottic laryngectomy laringuectomía supraglótica.

  total laryngectomy laringuectomía total.
laryngemphraxis *n.* laringenfraxis.
laryngendoscope *n.* laringoendoscopio.
laryngismal *adj.* laringísmico, -ca.
laryngitis *n.* laringitis.
  acute catarrhal laryngitis laringitis aguda, laringitis catarral aguda.
  atrophic laryngitis laringitis atrófica.
  chronic catarrhal laryngitis laringitis catarral crónica.
  chronic subglottic laryngitis laringitis subglótica, laringitis subglótica crónica.
  croupous laryngitis laringitis crupal, laringitis cruposa.
  diphtheritic laryngitis laringitis diftérica.
  laryngitis sicca laringitis seca.
  laryngitis stridulosa laringitis estridulosa.
  membranous laryngitis laringitis membranosa.
  phlegmonous laryngitis laringitis flemonosa.
  spasmodic laryngitis laringitis espasmódica.
  subglottic laryngitis laringitis subglótica, laringitis subglótica crónica.
  syphilitic laryngitis laringitis sifilítica.
  tuberculous laryngitis laringitis tuberculosa.
  vestibular laryngitis laringitis vestibular.
laryngocele *n.* laringocele.
  laryngocele ventricularis laringocele ventricular.
  ventricular laryngocele laringocele ventricular.
laryngocentesis *n.* laringocentesis.
laryngofission *n.* laringofisión.
laryngofissure *n.* laringofisura.
laryngogram *n.* laringograma.
laryngograph *n.* laringógrafo.
laryngography *n.* laringografía.
laryngohypopharynx *n.* laringohipofaringe.
laryngology *n.* laringología.
laryngomalacia *n.* laringomalacia.
laryngometry *n.* laringometría.
laryngoparalysis *n.* laringoparálisis.
laryngopathy *n.* laringopatía.
laryngophantom *n.* laringofantoma.
laryngopharyngeal *adj.* laringofaríngeo, -a.
laryngopharyngectomy *n.* laringuefaringectomía.
laryngopharyngitis *n.* laringofaringitis.
laryngopharynx *n.* laringofaringe.
laryngophone *n.* laringófono.
laryngophony *n.* laringofonía.
laryngophthisis *n.* laringotisis.
laryngoplasty *n.* laringoplastia.
laryngoplegia *n.* laringoplejía.
laryngoptosis *n.* laringoptosis.
laryngopyocele *n.* laringopiocele.
laryngorhinology *n.* laringorrinología.
laryngorrhagia *n.* laringorragia.
laryngorrhaphy *n.* laringorrafia.
laryngorrhea *n.* laringorrea.
laryngoscleroma *n.* laringoescleroma, laringoscleroma.
laryngoscope *n.* laringoscopio.
  Bullard's laryngoscope laringoscopio de Bullard.
  Miller's laryngoscope laringoscopio de Miller.
laryngoscopic *adj.* laringoscópico, -ca.
laryngoscopist *n.* laringoscopista.
laryngoscopy *n.* laringoscopia.
  direct laryngoscopy laringoscopia directa.
  indirect laryngoscopy laringoscopia de espejo, laringoscopia indirecta.
  suspension laryngoscopy laringoscopia por suspensión.

laryngospasm *n.* laringoespasmo, laringospasmo.

laryngostasis *n.* laringoestasis, laringostasis.

laryngostat *n.* laringóstato.

laryngostenosis *n.* laringoestenosis, laringostenosis.

laryngostomy *n.* laringostomía.

laryngostroboscope *n.* laringoestroboscopio, laringostroboscopio.

laryngotome *n.* laringótomo.

  dilating laryngotome laringótomo de dilatación.

laryngotomy *n.* laringotomía.

  complete laryngotomy laringotomía total.

  inferior laryngotomy laringotomía inferior.

  median laryngotomy laringotomía mediana.

  subhyoid laryngotomy laringotomía subhioidea.

  superior laryngotomy laringotomía superior.

  thyrohyoid laryngotomy laringotomía tirohioidea.

laryngotracheal *adj.* laringotraqueal.

laryngotracheitis *n.* laringotraqueítis.

laryngotracheobronchitis *n.* laringotraqueobronquitis.

  acute laryngotracheobronchitis laringotraqueobronquitis aguda.

laryngotracheobronchoscopy *n.* laringotraqueobroncoscopia.

laryngotracheoscopy *n.* laringotraqueoscopia.

laryngotracheotomy *n.* laringotraqueotomía.

laryngoxerosis *n.* laringoxerosis.

laryngytic *adj.* laringítico, -ca.

larynx *n.* laringe.

  artificial larynx laringe artificial.

lasanum *n.* lasánum.

lascivia *n.* lascivia.

laser *n.* láser.

  argon laser láser de argón.

  carbon-dioxide laser láser de dióxido de carbono.

  CO2 laser láser de CO2.

  dye laser láser de colorante.

  excimer laser láser de excímero.

  galium-arsenide laser láser de arseniuro de galio.

  helium-neon laser láser de helio y neón.

  high power laser láser de alta potencia.

  ion laser láser iónico.

  krypton laser láser de criptón.

  neodymium: yttrium-aluminium-garnet (Nd: YAG) laser láser de neodimio: itrio-aluminio-granate (Nd: YAG).

  surgical laser láser quirúrgico.

Lasiohelea Lasiohelea.

lassitude *n.* lasitud.

late *adj.* tardío, -a.

latenciation *n.* latenciación.

latency *n.* latencia.

  distal latency latencia distal.

latent *adj.* latente[1].

lateraabdominal *adj.* lateroabdominal.

lateral *adj.* lateral.

lateral decentering *n.* descentramiento lateral.

laterality *n.* lateralidad.

  crossed laterality lateralidad cruzada.

  dominant laterality lateralidad dominante.

lateralization *n.* lateralización.

laterodeviation *n.* laterodesviación.

lateroduction *n.* lateroducción.

lateroflexion *n.* lateroflexión.

lateroposition *n.* lateroposición.

lateropulsion *n.* lateropulsión.

laterotorsion *n.* laterotorsión.

laterotrusion *n.* laterotrusión.

lateroversion *n.* lateroversión.

lathyrism *n.* latirismo.

lathyritic *adj.* latírico, -ca.

lathyrogen *adj.* latirógeno, -na.

latitude *n.* latitud.

latrodectism *n.* latrodectismo.

Latrodectus Latrodectus.

laudabilis *adj.* laudable.

laugh *n.* risa.

lavage *n.* lavado.

  blood lavage lavado de la sangre, lavado general, lavado sanguíneo.

  bronchial lavage lavado bronquial.

  bronchopulmonary lavage lavado broncopulmonar, lavado gástrico.

  gastric lavage lavado del estómago.

  peritoneal lavage lavado peritoneal.

  pleural lavage lavado pleural.

  vesical lavage lavado vesical.

laveur *n.* lavador.

law *n.* ley.

  Allen's paradoxic law ley paradójica de Allen.

  all-or-none law ley del todo o nada.

  Ambard's law ley de Ambard.

  Angström's law ley de Angström.

  Aran's law ley de Aran.

  Arndt-Schutz's law ley de Arndt-Schulz.

  Avogadro's law ley de Avogadro.

  Baer's law ley de Baer.

  Barfurth's law ley de Barfurth.

  Bartian-Bruns law ley de Bastian, ley de Bastian-Bruns.

  Baruch's law ley de Baruch.

  Bastian's law ley de Bastian, ley de Bastian-Bruns.

  Beer's law ley de Beer.

  Behring's law ley de Behring.

  Bell's law ley de Bell, ley de Bell-Magendie.

  Bergonié-Tribondeau law ley de Bergonié-Tribondeau.

  biogenetic law ley biogenética.

  Bowditch's law ley de Bowditch.

  Boyle's law ley de Boyle.

  Bunsen-Roscoe law ley de Bunsen-Roscoe.

  Camerer's law ley de Camerer.

  Charles' law ley de Charles.

  Cope's law ley de Cope.

  Coulomb's law ley de Coulomb.

  Courvoisier's law ley de Courvoisier.

  Coutard's law ley de Coutard.

  Dalton-Henry law ley de Dalton-Henry.

  Dalton's law ley de Dalton.

  Descartes' law ley de Descartes.

  Desmarres' law ley de Desmarres.

  Dollo's law ley de Dollo.

  Donders' law ley de Donders.

  Draper's law ley de Draper.

  Du Bois-Reymond's law ley de Du Bois-Reymond.

  Dulong-Petit's law ley de Dulong-Petit.

  Einstein-Starck law ley de Einstein-Starck.

  Einthoven's law ley de Einthoven.

  Elliot's law ley de Elliot.

  Ewald's law ley de Ewald.

  Fajans' law ley de Fajans.

  Faraday's law ley de Faraday.

  Farr's law ley de Farr.

  Fechner-Weber law ley de Fechner-Weber.

  Ferry-Porter law ley de Ferry-Porter.

  Flatau's law ley de Flatau.

  Flint's law ley de Flint.

  Flourens' law ley de Flourens.

  Froriep's law ley de Froriep.

  Gay-Lussac law ley de Gay-Lussac.

  Giraud-Teulon law ley de Giraud-Teulon.

  Godelier's law ley de Godelier.

  Golgi's law ley de Golgi.

  Gompertz's law ley de Gompertz.

  Graham's law ley de Graham.

  Grasset's law ley de Grasset.

  Grotthus' law ley de Grotthus.

  Grotthus-Draper's law ley de Grotthus-Draper.

  Gudden's law ley de Gudden.

  Guldberg-Waage law ley de Guldberg-Waage.

  Gullstrand's law ley de Gullstrand.

  Gull-Toynbee law ley de Gull-Toynbee.

  Haeckel's law ley de Haeckel.

  Hanau's law of articulation ley de Hanau de la articulación.

  Hardy-Weinberg law ley de Hardy-Weinberg.

  Heidenhain's law ley de Heidenhain.

  Hellin's law de Hellin-Zeleny, ley de Hellin.

  Henry's law ley de Henry.

  Hering's law ley de Hering.

  Hilton's law ley de Hilton.

  Houghton's fatigue law ley de la fatiga de Houghton.

  ideal gas law ley de los gases perfectos.

  inverse square law ley del cuadrado inverso de la distancia.

  isodynamic law ley de la isodinamia.

  Jackson's law ley de Jackson.

  Kahler's law ley de Kahler.

  Knapp's law ley de Knapp.

  Koch's law ley de Koch.

  Küstner's law ley de Küstner.

  Lambert's cosine law ley del coseno de Lambert.

  Landouzy-Grasset law ley de Landouzy-Grasset.

  Lapicque's law ley de Lapicque.

  Laplace's law ley de Laplace.

  law of articulation ley de articulación.

  law of association ley de asociación.

  law of average localization ley de la localización promedio.

  law of conservation of energy ley de conservación de la energía.

  law of conservation of matter ley de conservación de la materia.

  law of constant numbers in ovulation ley del número constante de ovulación.

  law of contrary innervation ley de la inervación contraria.

  law of denervation ley de denervación.

  law of excitation ley de la excitación.

  law of independent assortment ley de la combinación independiente.

  law of initial value ley del valor inicial.

  law of isochronism ley del isocronismo.

  law of isolated conduction ley de la conducción aislada.

  law of mass action ley de la acción de masas.

  law of multiple proportions ley de las proporciones múltiples.

  law of multiple variants ley de las variantes múltiples.

  law of partial pressures ley de las presiones parciales.

  law of recapitulation ley de la recapitulación.

  law of reciprocal proportions ley de las proporciones recíprocas.

  law of referred pain ley del dolor referido.

law of refraction ley de la refracción.
law of segregation ley de la segregación.
law of sines ley de los senos.
law of the heart ley del corazón.
law of the intestine ley del intestino.
law of the minimum ley del mínimo.
law of universal gravitation ley de la gravitación universal.
Listing's law ley de Listing.
Louis' law ley de Louis.
Madgendie's law ley de Madgendie.
Malthusian law ley de Malthus.
Marey's law ley de Marey.
Marfan's law ley de Marfan.
Mariotte's law ley de Mariotte.
mass law ley de las masas.
Maxwell-Boltzmann distibrution law ley de distribución de Maxwell-Boltzmann.
Meltzer's law ley de Meltzer.
Mendeleiev's law ley de Mendeleiev.
Mendel's law ley de Mendel.
Meyer's law ley de Meyer.
Müller-Haeckel law ley de Müller-Haeckel.
Nerst's law ley de Nernst.
Newland's law ley de Newland.
Newton's law ley de Newton.
Nysten's law ley de Nysten.
Ochoa's law ley de Ochoa.
Ohm's law ley de Ohm.
Ollier's law ley de Ollier.
Pajot's law ley de Pajot.
Pascal's law ley de Pascal.
periodic law ley periódica.
Petit's law ley de Petit.
Pflueger's law ley de Pflueger.
Prévost's law ley de Prévost.
Profeta's law ley de Profeta.
Raoult's law ley de Raoult.
reciprocity law ley de la reciprocidad.
Ritter's law ley de Ritter.
Rosenbach's law ley de Rosenbach.
Rubner's law of growth ley de Rubner del crecimiento.
Schoeder van der Kolk's law ley de Schoeder van der Kolk.
Schütz's law de Schütz-Borissov, ley de Schütz.
Semon-Rosenbach law de Semon-Rosenbach, ley de Semon.
Semon's law de Semon-Rosenbach, ley de Semon.
Sherrington's law ley de Sherrington.
Snell's law ley de Snell.
Spallanzani's law ley de Spallanzani.
Starling's law of the heart ley de Starling del corazón.
Stokes' law ley de Stokes.
Teevan's law ley de Teevan.
Toynbee's law ley de Toynbee.
van der Kolk's law ley de van der Kolk.
Van't Hoff's law ley de Van't Hoff.
Virchow's law ley de Virchow.
Waller's law ley de Waller.
Walton's law ley de Walton.
Weber-Fechner law ley de Weber-Fechner.
Weber's law ley de Weber.
Weigert's law ley de Weigert.
Wilder's law of initial value ley de Wilder del valor inicial.
Williston's law ley de Williston.
Wolff's law ley de Wolff.
Wund-Lamansky law ley de Wund-Lamansky.
lax *adj.* laxo, -xa.
laxation *n.* laxación.

laxative *n.* laxante.
laxator *adj.* laxador, -ra.
laxity *n.* laxitud.
layer *n.* capa².
lead *n.* derivación³.
  ABC lead derivación ABC.
  aVf lead derivación aVF.
  aVl lead derivación aVL.
  aVr lead derivación aVR.
  bipolar lead derivación bipolar.
  CB lead derivación CB.
  CF lead derivación CF.
  chest lead derivación torácica.
  CL lead derivación CL.
  CR lead derivación CR.
  direct lead derivación directa.
  electrocardiograph lead derivación electrocardiográfica.
  esophageal lead derivación esofágica.
  indirect lead derivación indirecta.
  Intracardiac lead derivación intracardíaca.
  limb lead derivación de las extremidades, derivación de los miembros, derivación del miembro.
  precordial lead derivación precordial.
  semidirect lead derivación semidirecta.
  standard lead derivación estándar.
  unipolar lead derivación unipolar.
  V lead derivación V.
  Wilson's lead derivación de Wilson.
leaflet *n.* hojuela.
leanness *n.* delgadez.
learned helplessness *n.* indefensión aprendida.
learning *n.* aprendizaje.
  affective learning aprendizaje afectivo.
  latent learning aprendizaje latente.
  learning and humor aprendizaje y humor.
  learning and stress aprendizaje y estrés.
  psychomotor learning aprendizaje psicomotor.
  sexual learning in children aprendizaje sexual en los niños.
  state-dependent learning aprendizaje dependiente del estado.
leash *n.* gavilla.
lecanopagus *n.* lecanópago.
lechopyra *n.* lecopira.
lectotype *n.* lectotipo.
leech *n.* sanguisucción.
leeching *n.* hirudinización.
left-eyed *adj.* sinistrocular.
left-footed *adj.* sinistropedal.
left-handed *n.* zurdo, -da.
left-handed *adj.* sinistrómano, -na.
leg *n.* pierna.
  Barbados leg pierna de Barbados.
  bow leg pierna en arco.
  elephant leg pierna de elefante.
  milk leg pierna de leche.
  restless leg pierna inquietas.
  rider's leg pierna del jinete.
  tennis leg pierna de tenista.
  white leg pierna blanca.
Legionella Legionella.
Legionellaceae Legionellaceae.
legionellosis *n.* legionelosis.
leguminivorous *adj.* leguminívoro, -ra.
leiasthenia *n.* leiastenia, liastenia.
leiodermia *n.* leiodermia.
leiodystonia *n.* leiodistonía.
leiomyoblastoma *n.* leiomioblastoma.
leiomyofibroma *n.* leiomiofibroma, liomiofibroma.
leiomyoma *n.* leiomioma, liomioma.

  cutis leiomyoma liomioma cutáneo, liomioma cutis.
  epithelioid leiomyoma leiomioma epitelioide.
  leiomyoma cutis leiomioma cutáneo, leiomioma cutis.
  leiomyoma uteri leiomioma uterino.
  parasitic leiomyoma leiomioma parasitario.
  vascular leiomyoma leiomioma vascular.
leiomyomatosis *n.* leiomiomatosis.
leiomyosarcoma *n.* leiomiosarcoma.
leiotrichous *adj.* leiótrico, -ca.
Leishmania Leishmania.
leishmaniasis *n.* leishmaniasis, leishmaniosis.
leishmanicidal *adj.* leishmanicida.
leishmanid *n.* leishmánide.
leishmanin leishmanina.
leishmaniosis *n.* leishmaniosis.
  acute cutaneous leishmaniosis leishmaniosis cutánea aguda.
  American leishmaniosis leishmaniosis americana.
  anergic leishmaniosis anérgica cutánea, leishmaniosis anérgica.
  anthroponotic cutaneous leishmaniosis leishmaniosis cutánea antroponótica.
  canine leishmaniosis leishmaniosis canina.
  chronic cutaneous leishmaniosis leishmaniosis cutánea crónica.
  cutaneous anergic leishmaniosis anérgica cutánea, leishmaniosis anérgica.
  cutaneous leishmaniosis leishmaniosis cutánea, leishmaniosis dérmica.
  diffuse cutaneous leishmaniosis leishmaniosis cutánea difusa.
  disseminated cutaneous leishmaniosis leishmaniosis cutánea diseminada.
  dry cutaneous leishmaniosis leishmaniosis cutánea seca.
  infantile leishmaniosis leishmaniosis infantil.
  leishmaniosis americana leishmaniosis americana.
  leishmaniosis recidivans leishmaniosis recidivante.
  leishmaniosis tegumentaria diffusa leishmaniosis tegumentaria difusa.
  lupoid leishmaniosis leishmaniosis lupoide.
  mucocutaneous leishmaniosis leishmaniosis cutaneomucosa, leishmaniosis mucocutánea.
  nasopharyngeal leishmaniosis leishmaniosis nasobucal, leishmaniosis nasofaríngea, leishmaniosis nasooral.
  New Word leishmaniosis leishmaniosis del Nuevo Mundo.
  Old Word leishmaniosis leishmaniosis del Viejo Mundo.
  post-kala-azar dermal leishmaniosis leishmaniosis dérmica ulterior a kala-azar.
  pseudolepromatous leishmaniosis leishmaniosis seudolepromatosa.
  rural cutaneous leishmaniosis leishmaniosis cutánea rural.
  urban cutaneous leishmaniosis leishmaniosis cutánea urbana.
  urban leishmaniosis leishmaniosis urbana.
  visceral leishmaniosis leishmaniosis visceral.
  wet cutaneous leishmaniosis leishmaniosis cutánea húmeda.
  zoonotic cutaneous leishmaniosis leishmaniosis cutánea zoonótica.
leishmanoid *n.* leishmanoide.
  dermal leishmanoid leishmanoide dérmica, leishmanoide dérmica post-kala-azar.
  post-kala-azar dermal leishmanoid leish-

manoide dérmica, leishmanoide dérmica post-kala-azar.

lema *n.* lema.

lemic *adj.* lémico, -ca.

lemniscus *n.* lemnisco.

lemography *n.* lemografía.

lemology *n.* lemología.

lemoparalysis *n.* lemoparálisis.

lemostenosis *n.* lemoestenosis.

length *n.* longitud.
  arch length longitud de arco, longitud de la arcada.
  available arch length longitud de arcada disponible, longitud de arco disponible.
  basialveolar length longitud basialveolar.
  basinasal length longitud basinasal.
  crown-heel length longitud vértex a talón, longitud vértice-talón.
  crown-rump length (CRL) longitud vértex a rabadilla, longitud vértice-nalgas.
  effective wave length longitud efectiva de onda.
  equivalent wave length longitud efectiva de onda.
  focal length longitud focal.
  stem length longitud truncal.

lenitive *adj.* lenitivo, -va.

lens *n.* cristalino, lente.
  achromatic lens lente acromática.
  acrylic lens lente de acrílico.
  adherent lens lente adherente.
  anastigmatic lens lente anastigmática.
  aniseikonic lens lente aniseicónica.
  aplanatic lens lente aplanática, lente aplanética.
  apochromatic lens lente apocromática.
  aspheric lens lente asférica.
  astigmatic lens lente astigmática.
  biconcave lens lente bicóncava.
  biconvex lens lente biconvexa.
  bicylindrical lens lente bicilíndrica.
  bifocal lens lente bifocal.
  bispherical lens lente biesférica.
  Brücke lens lente de Brücke.
  cataract lens lente de catarata.
  compound lens lente compuesta.
  concave lens lente cóncava.
  concavoconcave lens lente concavocóncava.
  concavoconvex lens lente concavoconvexa.
  condensing lens lente condensadora.
  contact lens lente de contacto, lentilla.
  convergent lens lente convergente.
  converging meniscus lens lente en menisco convergente.
  convex lens lente convexa.
  convexoconcave lens lente convexocóncava.
  convexoconvex lens lente convexoconvexa.
  coquille lens lente de Coquille.
  corneal contact lens lente de contacto corneal.
  corneal lens lente corneal.
  Crookes' lens lente de Crookes.
  crossed lens lente cruzada.
  crystalline lens lente cristalina.
  cylindrical lens lente cilíndrica.
  decentered lens lente descentrada.
  diverging lens lente divergente.
  diverging meniscus lens lente en menisco divergente.
  double concave lens lente doble cóncava.
  double convex lens lente doble convexa.
  flat lens lente plana.
  Franklin's lens lente de Franklin.
  gas permeable contact lens lente de contacto permeable al gas.

  hard contact lens lente de contacto dura.
  honeybee lens lente ojo de abeja.
  immersion lens lente de inmersión.
  iseikonic lens lente iseicónica.
  lens crystallina lente cristalina.
  meniscus lens lente de menisco.
  meter lens lente metro.
  minus lens lente minus.
  multifocal lens lente multifocal.
  negative meniscus lens lente en menisco negativa.
  ocular lens lente ocular.
  omnifocal lens lente omnifocal.
  orthoscopic lens lente ortoscópica.
  periscopic concave lens lente periscópica cóncava.
  periscopic convex lens lente periscópica convexa.
  periscopic lens lente periscópica.
  photosensitive lens lente fotosensible.
  plane lens lente nivelada.
  plano lens lente nivelada.
  planoconcave lens lente planocóncava.
  planoconvex lens lente planoconvexa.
  plus lens lente plus.
  positive meniscus lens lente en menisco positiva.
  punktal lens lente puntal.
  safety lens lente de seguridad.
  scleral contact lens lente de contacto escleral.
  size lens lente de tamaño.
  slab-off lens lente dividida.
  soft contact lens lente de contacto blanda.
  spherical lens lente esférica.
  spherocylindrical lens lente esferocilíndrica.
  stigmatic lens lente estigmática.
  toric lens lente tórica.
  trial lens lente de prueba.
  trifocal lens lente trifocal.

lensectomy *n.* lensectomía.

lensometer *n.* lentómetro.

lentectomize *v.* lentectomizar.

lentectomy *n.* lentectomía.

lenticonus *n.* lenticono.

lenticula *n.* lentícula.

lenticular *adj.* lenticular.

lenticulo-optic *adj.* lenticuloóptico, -ca.

lenticulopapular *adj.* lenticulopapular.

lenticulostriate *adj.* lenticuloestríado, -da.

lenticulothalamic *adj.* lenticulotalámico, -ca.

lenticulus lentículo.

lentiform *adj.* lentiforme.

lentiginosis *n.* lentiginosis.
  centrofacial lentiginosis lentiginosis centrofacial.
  generalized lentiginosis lentiginosis generalizada.
  periorificial lentiginosis lentiginosis periorificial.
  progressive cardiomyopathic lentiginosis lentiginosis cardiomiopática progresiva.

lentiginous *adj.* lentiginoso, -sa.

lentiglobus *n.* lentiglobo.

lentigo *n.* léntigo.
  juvenile lentigo léntigo juvenil.
  lentigo maligna léntigo maligno.
  lentigo simplex léntigo simplex.
  malignant lentigo léntigo maligno.
  nevoid lentigo léntigo nevoide.
  senile lentigo léntigo senil.
  solar lentigo léntigo solar.

lentigomelanosis *n.* lentigomelanosis.

lentitis *n.* lentitis.

lentivirus *n.* lentivirus.

lentoptosis *n.* lentoptosis.

lentula *n.* léntula.

leontiasis *n.* leontiasis.
  leontiasis ossea leontiasis ósea.

leotropic *adj.* leotrópico, -ca.

leper *adj.* leproso, -sa.

lepidic *adj.* lepídico, -ca.

lepidosis *n.* lepidosis.

lepothrix *n.* lepotrix.

lepra *n.* lepra.

leprechaunism *n.* leprechaunismo.

leprid *n.* lépride.

leprologist *n.* leprólogo, -ga.

leprology *n.* leprología.

leproma *n.* leproma.

lepromatous *adj.* lepromatoso, -sa.

lepromin *n.* lepromina.

leprosarium *n.* leprosario.

leprosary *n.* leprosería.

leprose *adj.* leproso, -sa.

leprostatic *adj.* leprostático, -ca.

leprosy *n.* lepra.
  borderline lepromatous leprosy lepra limítrofe lepromatosa.
  borderline leprosy lepra fronteriza, lepra limítrofe.
  borderline tuberculous leprosy lepra limítrofe tuberculoide.
  cutaneous leprosy lepra cutánea.
  diffuse leprosy of Lucio lepra difusa de Lucio.
  dimorphous leprosy lepra dimorfa.
  histoid leprosy lepra histoide.
  indeterminate leprosy lepra indeterminada.
  intermediate leprosy lepra intermedia.
  Lazarine leprosy lepra lazarina.
  lepromatous leprosy lepra lepromatosa.
  leprosy nodule leproma.
  Lucio's leprosy lepra de Lucio.
  macular leprosy lepra macular, maculoanestésica.
  Malabar leprosy lepra de Malabar.
  neural leprosy lepra neural.
  nodular leprosy lepra nodular.
  reactional leprosy lepra reaccional.
  smooth leprosy lepra lisa.
  tuberculoid leprosy lepra tuberculoide.
  uncharacteristic leprosy lepra no característica.

leprotic *adj.* leprótico, -ca.

leprous *adj.* leproso, -sa.

leptocephalic *adj.* leptocefálico, -ca.

leptocephalous *adj.* leptocefálico, -ca.

leptocephalus *adj.* leptocéfalo, -la.

leptocephaly *n.* leptocefalia.

leptochromatic *adj.* leptocromático, -ca.

Leptoconops Leptoconops.

leptocyte *n.* leptocito.

leptocytosis *n.* leptocitosis.

leptodactylous *adj.* leptodáctilo, -la.

leptodactyly *n.* leptodactilia.

leptodermia *n.* leptodermia.

leptodermic *adj.* leptodérmico, -ca.

leptodontus *adj.* leptodonto, -ta.

leptomeningeal *adj.* leptomeníngeo, -a.

leptomeninges *n.* leptomeninges.

leptomeningioma *n.* leptomeningioma.

leptomeningitis *n.* leptomeningitis.
  basilar leptomeningitis leptomeningitis basilar.
  sarcomatous leptomeningitis leptomeningitis sarcomatosa.

leptomeningopathy *n.* leptomeningopatía.

leptopellic *adj.* leptopélvico, -ca, leptopiélico, -ca.

leptophonia *n.* leptofonía.

leptophonic *adj.* leptofónico, -ca.

leptopodia *n.* leptopodia.
leptoprosope *adj.* leptoprosopo, -pa.
leptoprosopia *n.* leptoprosopia.
leptoprosopic *adj.* leptoprosópico, -ca.
leptorrhine *adj.* leptorrino, -na.
leptoscope *n.* leptoscopio.
leptosomatic *adj.* leptosomático, -ca.
Leptospira Leptospira.
Leptospiraceae Leptospiraceae.
leptospiral *adj.* leptospirósico, -ca.
leptospire *n.* leptospira.
leptospirosis *n.* leptospirosis.
　anicteric leptospirosis leptospirosis anictérica.
　benign leptospirosis leptospirosis benigna.
　equine leptospirosis leptospirosis equina.
　leptospirosis icterohaemorraghica leptospirosis icterohemorrágica.
leptospiruria *n.* leptospiuria.
leptostaphyline *adj.* leptoestafilino, -na.
Leptosylla Leptosylla.
leptotene *n.* leptotene, leptoteno.
leptothrix leptotrix.
Leptotrichia Leptotrichia.
　Leptotrichia buccalis Leptotrichia buccalis.
leptotrichosis *n.* leptotricosis.
　leptotrichosis conjunctivae leptotricosis de la conjuntiva.
leresis *n.* leresis.
lesbian *adj.* lesbiana.
lesbianism *n.* lesbianismo.
lesion *n.* lesión.
　Armanni-Ebstein lesion lesión de Armanni-Ebstein.
　Baehr-Löhlein lesion lesión de Baehr-Löhlein.
　Bankart's lesion lesión de Bankart.
　benign lymphoepithelial lesion lesión linfoepitelial benigna.
　birds' nest lesion lesión en nido de pájaro.
　birth lesion lesión de nacimiento.
　Blumenthal lesion lesión de Blumenthal.
　Bracht-Wächter lesion lesión de Bracht-Wächter.
　caviar lesion lesión en caviar.
　central lesion lesión central.
　closed head lesion lesión cefálica cerrada.
　coin lesion of the lungs lesión numular de los pulmones.
　Councilman's lesion lesión de Councilman.
　counter-coup lesion lesión por contragolpe.
　degenerative lesion lesión degenerativa.
　destructive lesion lesión destructiva.
　diffuse axonal lesion lesión axonal difusa.
　diffuse lesion lesión difusa, lesión diseminada.
　diffuse lesion and coma lesión difusa y coma.
　discharging lesion lesión de descarga.
　Duret's lesion lesión de Duret.
　Ebstein's lesion lesión de Ebstein.
　focal lesion lesión focal.
　Ghon's primary lesion lesión primaria de Ghon.
　glomerular lesion lesión glomerular.
　gross lesion lesión macroscópica, lesión manifiesta.
　Hill-Sachs lesion lesión de Hill-Sachs.
　histologic lesion lesión histológica.
　impaction lesion lesión por impacción.
　irritative lesion lesión irritativa.
　Janeway lesion lesión de Janeway.
　Lennert's lesion lesión de Lennert.
　local lesion lesión local.
　Mallory-Weiss lesion lesión de Mallory-Weiss.

　medullar lesion lesión medular.
　molecular lesion lesión molecular.
　onion scale lesion lesión en cáscara de cebolla.
　onionskin lesion lesión en cáscara de cebolla.
　open head lesion lesión cefálica abierta.
　organic lesion lesión orgánica.
　partial lesion lesión parcial.
　peripheral lesion lesión periférica.
　pneumatic lesion lesión por un neumático.
　point lesion lesión puntual.
　precancerous lesion lesión precancerosa.
　primary lesion lesión primaria.
　radial sclerosing lesion lesión esclerosante radial.
　ring-wall lesion lesión anular de pared, lesión en anillo de pared.
　solitary coin lesion lesión numular solitaria.
　structural lesion lesión estructural.
　supranuclear lesion lesión supranuclear.
　systemic lesion lesión sistémica.
　total lesion lesión total.
　traumatic lesion lesión traumática.
　trophic lesion lesión trófica.
　upper motor neuron lesion lesión de la neurona motora superior.
　whiplash lesion lesión en látigo.
　wire-loop lesion lesión en asa, lesión en asa de alambre.
let-down *n.* subida de leche.
lethal *adj.* letal.
lethality *n.* letalidad.
lethargy *n.* letargia, letargo.
　African lethargy letargo africano.
　hysteric lethargy letargia histérica, letargo histérico.
　induced lethargy letargo inducido.
　lucid lethargy letargo lúcido.
lethologica *n.* letología.
leucapheresis *n.* leucaféresis.
leucine *n.* leucina, leukina.
leucinosis *n.* leucinosis.
leucinuria *n.* leucinuria.
leucismus *n.* leucismo.
leucitis *n.* leucitis.
leucocoria *n.* leucocoria.
leucocytic *adj.* leucocítico, -ca.
leucosin *n.* leucosina.
Leucothrix Leukothrix.
leucyl *n.* leucilo.
leukapheresis *n.* leucaféresis, leucoféresis.
leukemia *n.* leucemia.
　acute childhood leukemia leucemia aguda infantil.
　acute leukemia leucemia aguda.
　acute lymphoblastic leukemia leucemia linfoblástica aguda.
　acute lymphocytic leukemia leucemia linfocítica aguda.
　acute megakaryoblastic leukemia leucemia megacarioblástica aguda.
　acute monoblastic leukemia leucemia monoblástica aguda (M5).
　acute monocytic leukemia leucemia monocítica aguda.
　acute myelocytic leukemia (AML) leucemia mielocítica aguda (LMA).
　acute myeloid leukemia leucemia mieloide aguda.
　acute myelomonocytic leukemia leucemia mielomonocítica aguda (M4).
　acute non-lymphoblastic leukemia leucemia no linfoblástica aguda.
　acute non-lymphocytic leukemia leucemia aguda no linfocítica.

　acute promyelocytic leukemia leucemia promielocítica, leucemia promielocítica aguda.
　adult T-cell leukemia leucemia de células T en adultos.
　aleukemic leukemia leucemia aleucémica, leucemia aleucocitémica.
　aleukocythemic leukemia leucemia aleucémica, leucemia aleucocitémica.
　basophilic leukemia leucemia basófila, leucemia basofílica.
　basophilocytic leukemia leucemia basófila, leucemia basofílica.
　B-prolymphocytic leukemia leucemia prolinfocítica de origen B.
　chronic granulocytic leukemia leucemia granulocítica crónica.
　chronic lymphocytic leukemia (LLC) leucemia linfocítica crónica (LLC).
　chronic myelocytic leukemia leucemia mielocítica crónica, leucemia mieloide crónica (LMC).
　chronic myelomonocytic leukemia leucemia mielomonocítica crónica.
　differentiated acute myeloid leukemia leucemia mieloide aguda diferenciada.
　embryonal leukemia leucemia embrionaria.
　eosinophilic leukemia leucemia eosinofílica.
　erythromyeloblastic leukemia leucemia eritromieloblástica.
　granulocytic leukemia leucemia granulocítica.
　Gross' leukemia leucemia de Gross.
　hairy-cell leukemia leucemia de células peludas, leucemia de células pilosas, leucemia de células vellosas.
　hemoblastic leukemia leucemia hemoblástica, leucemia hemocitoblástica.
　hemocytoblastic leukemia leucemia hemoblástica, leucemia hemocitoblástica.
　histiocytic leukemia leucemia histiocítica.
　large granular lymphocytes leukemia leucemia de linfocitos grandes granulares (LLG).
　leukemia cutis leucemia cutánea.
　leukemic leukemia leucemia leucémica.
　leukopenic leukemia leucemia leucopénica.
　lymphatic leukemia leucemia linfática.
　lymphoblastic leukemia leucemia linfoblástica.
　lymphocytic leukemia leucemia linfocítica.
　lymphogenous leukemia leucemia linfógena.
　lymphoid leukemia leucemia linfoide.
　lymphoidocytic leukemia leucemia linfoidocítica.
　lymphosarcoma cell leukemia leucemia de células de linfosarcoma.
　mast cell leukemia leucemia de células cebadas, leucemia de mastocitos, leucemia mastocítica.
　mature cell leukemia leucemia de células maduras.
　megakarycytic leukemia leucemia megacariocítica.
　meningeal leukemia leucemia meníngea.
　micromyeloblastic leukemia leucemia micromieloblástica.
　mixed cell leukemia leucemia de células mixtas.
　mixed leukemia leucemia mixta.
　monoblastic leukemia leucemia monoblástica.
　monocytic leukemia leucemia monocítica.
　myeloblastic acute leukemia leucemia aguda mieloblástica.

myeloblastic leukemia leucemia mieloblástica.
myelocytic leukemia leucemia mielocítica.
myelogenous leukemia leucemia mielógena.
myeloid granulocytic leukemia leucemia granulocítica mieloide.
myelomonocytic leukemia leucemia mielomonocítica.
Naegeli's leukemia leucemia de Naegeli.
neutrophilic leukemia leucemia neutrófila.
plasma cell leukemia leucemia de células plasmáticas.
plasmacytic leukemia leucemia plasmática.
polymorphocytic leukemia leucemia polimorfocítica.
promyelocytic leukemia leucemia promielocítica, leucemia promielocítica aguda.
Rieder's cell leukemia leucemia de células de Rieder.
Schilling's leukemia leucemia de Schilling.
splenic leukemia leucemia esplénica.
stem cell leukemia leucemia de células blásticas, leucemia de células madre.
subleukemic leukemia leucemia subleucémica.
T-prolymphocytic leukemia leucemia prolinfocítica de origen T.
undifferentiated acute myeloid leukemia leucemia mieloide aguda indiferenciada (M1).
undifferentiated cell leukemia leucemia aguda indiferenciada, leucemia de células indiferenciadas.
leukemic *adj.* leucémico, -ca.
leukemid *n.* leucémide.
leukemogen *adj.* leucemógeno, -na.
leukemogenesis *n.* leucemogénesis.
leukemogenic *adj.* leucemogénico, -ca.
leukemoid *adj.* leucemoide.
leukencephalitis *n.* leucencefalitis, leucoencefalitis.
  acute epidemic leukencephalitis leucoencefalitis epidémica aguda.
  acute hemmorrhagic leukencephalitis leucoencefalitis hemorrágica aguda.
  leukencephalitis periaxialis concentrica leucoencefalitis periaxil concéntrica.
  subacute sclerosing leukencephalitis leucoencefalitis esclerosante subaguda.
  van Bogaert's sclerosing leukencephalitis leucoencefalitis esclerosante de Van Bogaert.
leukin *n.* leuquina.
leukina *n.* leucina, leukina.
leukoagglutinin *n.* leucoaglutinina.
leukoaraiosis *n.* leucoaraiosis.
leukoblast *n.* leucoblasto.
  granular leukoblast leucoblasto granuloso.
leukoblastosis *n.* leucoblastosis.
leukochloroma *n.* leucocloroma.
leukocidin *n.* leucocidina.
  Panton-Valentine (P-V) leukocidin leucocidina de Panton-Valentine (P-V).
leukocrit *n.* leucócrito.
leukocytal *adj.* leucocitario, -a, leucocítico, -ca.
leukocytaxia *n.* leucocitaxia.
leukocytaxis *n.* leucocitaxia, leucocitaxis.
leukocyte *n.* leucocito.
  acidophilic leukocyte leucocito acidófilo.
  agranular leukocyte leucocito agranuloso.
  basophilic leukocyte leucocito basófilo.
  cystonotic leukocyte leucocito cistonótico.
  eosinophilic leukocyte leucocito eosinófilo.
  filament polymorphonuclear leukocyte leucocito polimorfonuclear filamentoso.
  granular leukocyte leucocito granuloso.
  heterophilic leukocyte leucocito heterófilo.

labeled leukocyte leucocito marcados.
lymphoid leukocyte leucocito linfoide.
mast leukocyte leucocito cebado.
motile leukocyte leucocito móvil.
multinuclear leukocyte leucocito multinuclear.
neutrophilic leukocyte leucocito neutrófilo.
non-filament polymorphonuclear leukocyte leucocito polimorfonuclear no filamentoso.
non-granular leukocyte leucocito no granulosos.
non-motile leukocyte leucocito inmóvil, leucocito no mótil.
oxyphilic leukocyte leucocito oxífilo.
polymorphonuclear leukocyte leucocito polimorfonuclear.
polynuclear leukocyte leucocito polinuclear.
polynuclear neutrophilic leukocyte leucocito neutrófilo polinuclear.
segmented leukocyte leucocito segmentado.
leukocythemia *n.* leucocitemia.
leukocytic *adj.* leucocitario, -a, leucocítico, -ca.
leukocytoblast *n.* leucocitoblasto.
leukocytoclasis *n.* leucocitoclasia.
leukocytogenesis *n.* leucocitogénesis.
leukocytoid *adj.* leucocitoide, leucocitoideo, -a.
leukocytolisin *n.* leucocitolisina.
leukocytolysis *n.* leucocitólisis.
  venom leukocytolysis leucocitólisis venenosa.
leukocytolytic *adj.* leucocitolítico, -ca.
leukocytoma *n.* leucocitoma.
leukocytometer *n.* leucocitómetro.
leukocytopenia *n.* leucocitopenia.
leukocytophagy *n.* leucocitofagia.
leukocytoplania *n.* leucocitoplania.
leukocytopoiesis *n.* leucocitopoyesis.
leukocytosis *n.* leucocitosis.
  absolute leukocytosis leucocitosis absoluta.
  agonal leukocytosis leucocitosis agonal, leucocitosis agónica.
  basophilic leukocytosis leucocitosis basófila.
  digestive leukocytosis leucocitosis digestiva, leucocitosis gravídica.
  distribution leukocytosis leucocitosis de distribución.
  emotional leukocytosis leucocitosis emocional.
  eosiniphilic leukocytosis leucocitosis eosinófila.
  leukocytosis of the newborn leucocitosis del neonato.
  lymphocytic leukocytosis leucocitosis linfocítica.
  monocytic leukocytosis leucocitosis monocítica.
  mononuclear leukocytosis leucocitosis mononuclear.
  neutrophilic leukocytosis leucocitosis neutrófila.
  pathologic leukocytosis leucocitosis patológica.
  physiologic leukocytosis leucocitosis fisiológica.
  pure leukocytosis leucocitosis pura.
  relative leukocytosis leucocitosis relativa.
  terminal leukocytosis leucocitosis terminal.
  toxic leukocytosis leucocitosis tóxica.
leukocytotactic *adj.* leucocitotáctico, -ca.
leukocytotaxis *n.* leucocitotaxia, leucocitotaxis.
leukocytotherapy *n.* leucocitoterapia.
leukocytotoxin *n.* leucocitotoxina.
leukocytotropic *adj.* leucocitotrópico, -ca.

leukocyturia *n.* leucocituria.
leukoderma *n.* leucodermia.
  acquired leukoderma leucodermia adquirida.
  congenital leukoderma leucodermia congénita.
  leukoderma acquisitum centrifugum leucodermia centrífuga adquirida.
  leukoderma colli leucodermia cervical, leucodermia del cuello.
  occupational leukoderma leucodermia profesional.
  postinflammatory leukoderma leucodermia postinflamatoria.
  syphilitic leukoderma leucodermia sifilítica.
leukodermatous *adj.* leucodermatoso, -sa.
leukodermia *n.* leucodermia.
leukodontia *n.* leucodontia.
leukodystrophy *n.* leucodistrofia.
  globoid cell leukodystrophy leucodistrofia de células globoides, leucodistrofia globoide.
  globoid leukodystrophy leucodistrofia de células globoides, leucodistrofia globoide.
  hereditary cerebral leukodystrophy leucodistrofia cerebral hereditaria.
  Krabbe's leukodystrophy leucodistrofia de Krabbe.
  leukodystrophy cerebri progressiva leucodistrofia cerebral progresiva.
  metachromatic leukodystrophy leucodistrofia metacromática.
  spongiform leukodystrophy leucodistrofia espongiforme.
  sudanophilic leukodystrophy leucodistrofia sudanófila.
leukoencephalopathy *n.* leucoencefalopatía.
  metachromatic leukoencephalopathy leucoencefalopatía metacromática.
  progressive multifocal leukoencephalopathy leucoencefalopatía multifocal progresiva.
  subacute sclerosing leukoencephalopathy leucoencefalopatía esclerosante subaguda.
leukoencephaly *n.* leucoencefalia.
  metachromatic leukoencephaly leucoencefalia metacromática.
leukoenkephalin *n.* leucoencefalina.
leukoerythroblastosis *n.* leucoeritroblastosis.
leukogram *n.* leucograma.
leukokeratosis *n.* leucoqueratosis.
leukokinesis *n.* leucocinesia.
leukokinetic *adj.* leucocinético, -ca.
leukokinetics *n.* leucocinética.
leukokinin *n.* leucocinina.
leukokraurosis *n.* leucocraurosis.
leukolymphosarcoma *n.* leucolinfosarcoma.
leukolysin *n.* leucolisina.
leukolysis *n.* leucólisis.
leukolytic *adj.* leucolítico, -ca.
leukoma *n.* leucoma.
  adherent leukoma leucoma adherente.
leukomaine *n.* leucomaína.
leukomainemia *n.* leucomainemia.
leukomainic *adj.* leucomaínico, -ca.
leukomalacia *n.* leucomalacia.
leukomatous *adj.* leucomatoso, -sa.
leukomyelitis *n.* leucomielitis.
leukomyelopathy *n.* leucomielopatía.
leukomyoma *n.* leucomioma.
leukonecrosis *n.* leuconecrosis.
leukonychia *n.* leuconiquia.
leukopathia *n.* leucopatía.
  acquired leukopathia leucopatía adquirida.
  congenital leukopathia leucopatía congénita.

leukopathia punctata reticularis symmetrica leucopatía punteada reticular simétrica.
leukopathia unguis leucopatía de las uñas, leucopatía ungueal.
leukopedesis *n.* leucopédesis.
leukopenia *n.* leucopenia.
basophilic leukopenia leucopenia basófila.
congenital leukopenia leucopenia congénita.
eosinophilic leukopenia leucopenia eosinófila.
malignant leukopenia leucopenia maligna.
monocytic leukopenia leucopenia monocítica.
neutrophilic leukopenia leucopenia neutrófila.
pernicious leukopenia leucopenia perniciosa.
leukopenic *adj.* leucopénico, -ca.
leukophagocytosis *n.* leucofagocitosis.
leukophlegmasia *n.* leucoflegmasía.
leukophlegmasia dolens leucoflegmasía dolens.
leukophoresis *n.* leucoforesis.
leukoplakia *n.* leucoplaquia.
leukoplasia *n.* leucoplasia.
cervical leukoplasia leucoplasia de cuello.
hairy leukoplasia leucoplasia peluda, leucoplasia pilosa.
laryngeal leukoplasia leucoplasia vocal.
leukoplasia buccalis leucoplasia bucal.
leukoplasia lingualis leucoplasia lingual.
leukoplasia vulvae leucoplasia de vulva.
oral leukoplasia leucoplasia oral.
speckled leukoplasia leucoplasia moteada.
vulval leukoplasia leucoplasia de vulva.
leukopoiesis *n.* leucopoyesis.
leukopoietic *adj.* leucopoyético, -ca.
leukopoietin *n.* leucopoyetina.
leukoprecipitin *n.* leucoprecipitina.
leukoprophylaxis *n.* leucoprofilaxis.
leukoprotease *n.* leucoproteasa.
leukopsin *n.* leucopsina.
leukorrhea fluor albus, leucorrea, uterorrea.
menstrual leukorrhea leucorrea menstrual, leucorrea periódica.
leukorrheal *adj.* leucorreico, -ca.
leukosarcoma *n.* leucosarcoma.
leukoscope *n.* leucoscopio.
leukosis *n.* leucosis.
acute leukosis leucosis aguda.
lymphoid leukosis leucosis linfoide.
myeloblastic leukosis leucosis mieloblástica.
myelocytic leukosis leucosis mielocítica.
skin leukosis leucosis cutánea.
leukotactic *adj.* leucotáctico, -ca.
leukotaxia *n.* leucotaxia.
leukotaxine *n.* leucotaxina.
leukotaxis *n.* leucotaxis.
leukotherapy *n.* leucoterapia.
preventive leukotherapy leucoterapia preventiva.
Leukothrix Leukothrix.
leukothrombin *n.* leucotrombina.
leukotic *adj.* leucótico, -ca.
leukotome *n.* leucótomo.
leukotomy *n.* leucotomía.
transorbital leukotomy leucotomía transorbitaria.
leukotoxic *adj.* leucotóxico, -ca.
leukotoxin *n.* leucotoxina.
leukotrichia *n.* leucotriquia.
leukotrichia annularis leucotriquia anular.
leukotrichous *adj.* leucotrico, -ca.
leukourobilin *n.* leucourobilina.

levator *n.* elevador, levator.
level *n.* nivel.
acoustic reference level nivel de referencia acústica.
blood level nivel sanguíneo.
blood level of glucose nivel sanguíneo de glucosa.
Clark's level nivel de Clark.
hearing level nivel auditivo.
isoelectric level nivel isoeléctrico.
level of consciousness nivel de consciencia.
operant level nivel operativo.
peak level nivel máximo.
phenobarbitalphenytoin serum level nivel plasmático de fenobarbitalfenitoína.
serum creatinine level nivel de creatinina en suero.
significance level nivel de significación.
sound pressure level nivel de presión del sonido.
window level nivel de ventana.
lever *n.* palanca.
dental lever palanca dental.
levigation *n.* levigación.
levitation *n.* levitación.
levocardia *n.* levocardia.
isolated levocardia levocardia aislada.
mixed levocardia levocardia mixta.
levocardiogram *n.* levocardiograma.
levoclination *n.* levoclinación.
levocycloduction *n.* levocicloducción.
levoduction *n.* levoducción.
levoform *n.* levoforma.
levogiration *n.* levogiración.
levogram *n.* levograma.
levogyral *adj.* levógiro, -ra.
levogyrate *adj.* levógiro, -ra.
levogyrous *adj.* levógiro, -ra.
levophobia *n.* levofobia.
levorotation *n.* levorrotación.
levorotatory *adj.* levorrotatorio, -a.
levotorsion *n.* levotorsión.
levoversion *n.* levoversión.
levulosemia *n.* levulosemia.
levulosuria *n.* levulosuria.
levuride *n.* levadúrido, levúrido.
leydigarche *n.* leydigarquia.
liberation *n.* liberación.
liberator *n.* liberador.
histamine liberator liberador de histamina.
liberomotor *adj.* liberomotor, -ra.
libidinal *adj.* libidinal.
libidinization *n.* libidinización.
libidinous *adj.* libinidoso, -sa.
libido *n.* líbido.
bisexual libido líbido bisexual.
lichen *n.* liquen.
lichen acuminatus liquen acuminado.
lichen agrius liquen agrio.
lichen albus liquen albo.
lichen amyloidosus liquen amiloideo, liquen amiloidoso.
lichen annularis liquen anular.
lichen corneus hypertrophicus liquen córneo hipertrófico.
lichen fibromucinoidosus liquen fibromucinoidoso.
lichen hemorrhagicus liquen hemorrágico.
lichen infantum liquen infantil.
lichen iris liquen iris.
lichen myxedematosus liquen mixedematoso.
lichen nitidus liquen nítido.
lichen nuchae liquen de la nuca.
lichen obtusus liquen obtuso.

lichen obtusus corneus liquen obtuso córneo.
lichen pilaris liquen pilar.
lichen planopilaris liquen planopilar, liquen planopiloso.
lichen planus liquen plano.
lichen planus annularis liquen plano anular.
lichen planus atrophicus liquen plano atrófico.
lichen planus bullous liquen plano bulloso.
lichen planus erythematosus liquen plano eritematoso.
lichen planus et acuminatus atrophicans liquen planus et acuminatus atrophicans.
lichen planus follicularis liquen plano folicular.
lichen planus hypertrophicus liquen plano hipertrófico.
lichen planus verrucosus liquen plano verrugoso.
lichen planus vesiculobullous liquen plano bulloso-vesicular.
lichen ruber moniliformis liquen rojo moniliforme.
lichen ruber planus liquen rojo plano.
lichen ruber verrucosus liquen rojo verrugoso.
lichen sclerosus liquen escleroso.
lichen sclerosus et atrophicus liquen escleroatrófico.
lichen scrofulosus liquen escrofuloso.
lichen simplex chronicus liquen crónico simple, liquen simple crónico.
lichen spinulosus liquen espinuloso.
lichen striatus liquen estriado.
lichen strophulosus liquen estrofuloso.
lichen syphiliticus liquen sifilítico.
lichen tropicus liquen trópico.
lichen urticatus liquen urticado.
lichen variegatus liquen variegatus.
oral erosive lichen liquen plano bucal erosivo.
oral non-erosive lichen liquen plano bucal no erosivo.
tropical lichen liquen tropical.
Wilson's lichen liquen de Wilson.
lichenification *n.* liquenificación.
lichenoid *adj.* liquenoide.
lien *n.* bazo, lien.
lien mobilis bazo movible, bazo móvil.
lienal *adj.* lienal.
lienculus *n.* liénculo.
lienectomy *n.* lienectomía.
lienitis *n.* lienitis.
lienography *n.* lienografía.
lienomalacia *n.* lienomalacia.
lienomedullary *adj.* lienomedular.
lienomyelogenous *adj.* lienomielógeno, -na.
lienomyelomalacia *n.* lienomielomalacia.
lienopancreatic *adj.* lienopancreático, -ca.
lienopathy *n.* lienopatía.
lienorenal *adj.* lienorrenal.
lienotoxin *n.* lienotoxina.
lienteric *adj.* lientérico, -ca.
lientery *n.* lientería.
lienunculus *n.* lienúnculo.
life *n.* vida.
artificial life vida artificial.
average life vida media.
biological half life vida media biológica.
effective half life (EHL) vida media efectiva, vida media eficaz (VME).
latent life vida latente.
physical half life vida media física.
plasma half life vida media plasmática.
postnatal life vida posnatal.

potential life vida potencial.
prenatal life vida antenatal, vida intrauterina, vida prenatal, vida uterina.
radionuclide half life vida media de un radionúclido.
sexual life vida sexual.
vegetative life vida vegetativa.
life island *n.* burbuja.
lifting *n.* lifting.
  brow lifting lifting de las cejas.
  facial lifting lifting facial.
ligament *n.* ligamento.
  periodontal ligament ligamento periodontal.
ligamentopexis *n.* ligamentopexia.
ligamentous *adj.* ligamentoso, -sa.
ligamentum *n.* ligamento, ligamentum.
ligand *n.* ligando.
ligate *v.* ligar.
ligation *n.* ligación, ligadura¹.
  banding ligation ligadura con banda elástica.
  Barron ligation ligadura de Barron.
  rubber-band ligation ligadura con banda elástica.
  teeth ligation ligadura dental.
  tubal ligation ligadura tubaria, tubárica.
ligature *n.* ligadura².
  chain ligature ligadura catenaria, ligadura en cadena.
  elastic ligature ligadura elástica.
  grass-line ligature ligadura con fibra vegetal.
  interlacing ligature ligadura entrelazada.
  interlocking ligature ligadura entrelazada.
  intravascular ligature ligadura intravascular.
  Larrey's ligature ligadura de Larrey.
  lateral ligature ligadura lateral.
  occluding ligature ligadura oclusiva.
  pole ligature ligadura polar.
  provisional ligature ligadura provisional.
  soluble ligature ligadura soluble.
  suboccluding ligature ligadura suboclusiva.
  surgical ligature ligadura quirúrgica.
  terminal ligature ligadura terminal.
  thread-elastic ligature ligadura de hilo elástico.
  vascular ligature ligadura vascular.
light *n.* lux, luz.
  actinic light luz actínica.
  black light luz negra.
  coherent light luz coherente.
  cold light luz fría.
  diffused light luz difusa.
  idioretinal light luz idiorretiniana.
  infrared light luz infrarroja.
  intrinsic light luz intrínseca.
  light minimum luz mínima.
  monochromatic light luz monocromática.
  oblique light luz oblicua.
  polarized light luz polarizada.
  reflected light luz reflejada.
  refracted light luz refractada.
  stray light luz difusa.
  transmitted light luz transmitida.
  Tyndall light luz de Tyndall.
  ultraviolet light luz ultravioleta.
  vein light luz venosa.
  visible light luz visible.
  white light luz blanca.
  Wood's light luz de Wood.
lightening *n.* aligeramiento, liviandad.
ligneous *adj.* leñoso, -sa.
limb *n.* extremidad, miembro.
  anacrotic limb miembro anacrótico.
  catacrotic limb miembro catacrótico.
  inferior limb miembro inferior.

lower limb miembro inferior.
superior limb miembro superior.
thoracic limb miembro torácico.
upper limb miembro superior.
limbal *adj.* limbal.
limbic *adj.* límbico, -ca.
limbus *n.* limbo.
lime *n.* lima².
limen *n.* limen.
liminal *adj.* liminal, liminar.
liminometer *n.* liminómetro.
limit *n.* límite.
  assimilation limit límite de asimilación.
  audibility limit límite auditivo, límite de la audibilidad.
  elastic limit límite elástico.
  Hayflick's limit límite de Hayflick.
  limit of flocculation límite de floculación.
  limit of perception límite de percepción.
  limit of the confidentiality límite de la confidencialidad.
  proportional limit límite proporcional.
  saturation limit límite de saturación.
  short-term exposure limit (STEL) límite para exposición corta.
limitans *adj.* limitante.
limitation *n.* limitación.
  eccentric limitation limitación excéntrica.
  hip limitation limitación de la cadera.
  limitation of motion limitación del movimiento.
limitrophic *adj.* limitrófico, -ca.
limnemia *n.* limnemia.
limnemic *adj.* limnémico, -ca.
limnology *n.* limnología.
limophthisis *n.* limitisis, limoptisis, limotisis.
limosis *n.* limosis.
limotherapy *n.* limoterapia.
limp *n.* cojera.
line *n.* línea.
  absorption line línea de absorción.
  accretion line línea de acreción.
  Aldrich-Mees line línea de Aldrich-Mees.
  arterial line línea arterial.
  base-apex line línea entre base y vértice.
  Beau's line línea de Beau.
  Bechterew's line línea de Bechterew.
  bismuth line línea de bismuto.
  Bismuth's line línea de Bismutia.
  black line línea negra.
  blood line línea de sangre.
  blue line línea azul.
  Borsieri's line línea de Borsieri.
  Bruton's line línea de Burton.
  calcification line of Retzius línea de calcificación de Retzius.
  cell line línea celular.
  cementing line línea del cemento.
  cleavage line línea de tensión.
  copper line línea de cobre.
  demarcation line of the retina línea de demarcación de la retina.
  Dennie's line línea de Dennie.
  developmental line línea de desarrollo, línea surco del desarrollo.
  digastric line línea digástrica.
  dynamic line línea dinámica.
  ectental line línea ectental.
  Ehrlich-Türk line línea de Ehrlich-Türk.
  Ellis' line línea de Ellis, línea de Ellis-Garland.
  Ellis-Garland line línea de Ellis, línea de Ellis-Garland.
  embryonic line línea embrionaria.
  epiphysial line línea epifisaria.
  established line línea celular establecida.

Fleishner line línea de Fleischner.
fulcrum line línea de palanca, línea del fulcro.
fulcrum retentive line línea de palanca de retención.
Galton's line línea de Galton.
germ line línea germinal.
Hampton line línea de Hampton.
Harris' line línea de Harris.
Head's line línea de Head.
Hensen's line línea de Hensen.
high lip line línea de altura labial.
Hunter-Schreger line línea de Hunter-Schreger.
imbrication line of cementum línea de imbricación del cemento.
imbrication line of von Ebner línea de imbricación de von Ebner.
incremental line línea de incremento.
incremental line of cementum línea de incremento del cemento.
incremental line of von Ebner línea de incremento de Ebner.
intraperiod line línea intraperiódica.
isoeffect line línea de isoefecto.
isoelectric line línea isoeléctrica.
Jadelot's line línea de Jadelot.
Kerley-B line línea B de Kerley-B.
labial line línea labial.
lead line línea de plomo.
line nigra línea nigra.
line of demarcation línea de demarcación.
line of Ebner línea de Ebner.
line of expression línea de expresión.
line of fixation línea de fijación.
line of gravity línea de gravedad.
line of minimal tension línea de tensión mínima.
line of occlusion línea de oclusión.
line of vision línea de la visión.
line of Zahn línea de Zahn.
low lip line línea bala del labio.
magnetic line of force línea de fuerza magnética, línea magnética de fuerza.
major period line línea periódica mayor.
McGregor's line línea de McGregor.
Mees' line línea de Mees.
mercurial line línea mercurial.
Morgan's line línea de Morgan.
Muehrcke's line línea Muehrcke.
nasal line línea nasal.
neonatal line línea neonatal.
Obersteiner-Redlich line línea de Obersteiner-Redlich.
oblique line línea oblicua.
oculozygomatic line línea oculocigomática.
Ogsten line línea de Ogsten.
Ohngren's line línea de Ohngren.
orbitolmeatal line línea orbitomeatal.
orthostatic line línea ortostática.
Owen's line línea de Owen.
Paris line línea de París.
Pastia's line línea de Pastia.
period line línea periódica.
pleuroesophageal line línea pleuroesofágica.
recessional line línea de recesión.
Reid's base line línea base de Reid.
relaxed skin tension line línea de tensión de la piel relajada.
sagittal line línea sagital.
Salter's incremental line línea incremental de Salter.
Salter's line línea de Salter.
Schreger's line línea de Schreger.
Sergent's white adrenal line línea suprarrenal blanca de Sergent.

silver line línea argentina.
stabilizing fulcrum line línea de palanca estabilizante, línea estabilizadora del fulcro.
survey line línea guía.
thyroid red line línea roja tiroidea.
Trümmerfeld line línea de Trümmerfeld.
venous line línea venosa.
vibrating line línea vibratoria.
Zöllner's line línea de Zöllner.
linea *n.* línea.
linea albicantes línea albicante.
lineage *n.* descendencia, linaje.
cell lineage linaje celular.
linear *adj.* lineal.
lingua *n.* lengua, lingua.
lingua fissurata lengua fisurada, lingua fissurata.
lingua geographica lengua geográfica, lingua geographica.
lingual *adj.* lingual.
linguale *n.* linguale.
lingualis *adj.* lingual.
Linguatula Linguatula.
linguatuliasis *n.* linguatuliasis.
linguatulosis *n.* linguatuliasis, linguatulosis.
linguiform *adj.* lingüiforme.
lingula *n.* língula.
lingular *adj.* lingular.
lingulectomy *n.* lingulectomía.
linguoaxial *adj.* linguoaxil.
linguoaxiogingival *adj.* linguoaxiogingival.
linguocervical *adj.* linguocervical.
linguoclination *n.* linguoclinación.
linguoclusion *n.* linguoclusión.
linguodental *adj.* linguodental.
linguodistal *adj.* linguodistal.
linguogingival *adj.* linguogingival.
linguoincisal *adj.* linguoincisal.
linguomesial *adj.* linguomesial.
linguo-occlusal *adj.* linguoocclusal.
linguopapilitis *n.* linguopapilitis.
linguoplacement *n.* linguoubicación.
linguopulpal *adj.* linguopulpal.
linguoversion *n.* linguoversión.
liniment *n.* linimento.
linimentum *n.* linimento.
lining *n.* revestimiento.
linitis *n.* linitis.
linitis plastica linitis plástica.
linkage *n.* ligamiento, linkage.
genetic linkage ligamiento genético.
medical record linkage ligamiento de registros clínicos.
sex linkage ligamiento sexual.
linked *adj.* ligado, -da.
linker *n.* ligador.
lip *n.* labio.
cleft lip labio fisurado, labio hendido.
lipacidemia *n.* lipacidemia.
lipaciduria *n.* lipaciduria.
liparodypnea *n.* liparodisnea.
liparoid *adj.* liparoide, liparoideo, -a.
liparomphalus *n.* liparónfalo.
lipase *n.* lipasa.
lipasic *adj.* lipásico, -ca.
lipasuria *n.* lipasuria.
lipectomy *n.* lipectomía.
suction lipectomy lipectomía por succión.
lipedema *n.* lipedema.
lipemia *n.* lipemia.
alimentary lipemia lipemia alimentaria.
diabetic lipemia lipemia diabética.
lipemia retinalis lipemia retiniana.
postprandial lipemia lipemia posprandial.
lipid *n.* lípido.

compound lipid lípido compuesto.
lipid bilayer bicapa lipídica.
lipid reducer hipolipidemiante.
simple lipid lípido simple.
lipidase *n.* lipidasa.
lipidemia *n.* lipidemia.
lipidic *adj.* lipídico, -ca.
lipidolysis *n.* lipidólisis.
lipidolytic *adj.* lipidolítico, -ca.
lipidosis *n.* lipidosis.
cerebral lipidosis lipidosis cerebral.
cerebroside lipidosis lipidosis por cerebrósidos.
galactosylceramide lipidosis lipidosis de galactósido de ceramida, lipidosis galactosilceramida.
ganglioside lipidosis lipidosis por gangliósidos.
glucosyl cerebroside lipidosis lipidosis de cerebrósidos glucosílicos.
glucosylceramide lipidosis lipidosis de glucósido de ceramida.
glycolipid lipidosis lipidosis por glucolípidos.
sphingomyelin lipidosis lipidosis por esfingomielina.
sulfatide lipidosis lipidosis por sulfátidos.
lipiduria *n.* lipiduria.
lipin *n.* lipina.
liplike *adj.* labiado, -da.
lipoadenoma *n.* lipoadenoma.
lipoarthritis *n.* lipartritis, lipoartritis.
lipoatrophia *n.* lipoatrofia.
insulin lipoatrophia lipoatrofia por insulina.
lipoatrophia circumscripta lipoatrofia circunscrita.
partial lipoatrophia lipoatrofia parcial.
lipoblast *n.* lipoblasto.
lipoblastoma *n.* lipoblastoma.
lipoblastomatosis *n.* lipoblastomatosis.
lipocaic *n.* lipocaico.
lipocardiac *adj.* lipocardíaco, -ca.
lipocatabolic *adj.* lipocatabólico, -ca.
lipocele *n.* lipocele.
lipoceratous *adj.* lipoceratoso, -sa.
lipocere *n.* lipocera.
lipochondrodystrophy *n.* lipocondrodistrofia.
lipochondroma *n.* lipocondroma.
lipochrome *n.* lipocromo.
lipoclasis *n.* lipoclasis.
lipoclastic *adj.* lipoclástico, -ca.
lipocrit *n.* lipócrito.
lipocyte *n.* lipocito.
lipodermoid *n.* lipodermoide.
lipodieretic *adj.* lipodierético, -ca.
lipodystrophia *n.* lipodistrofia.
lipodystrophia intestinalis lipodistrofia intestinal.
lipodystrophia progressiva lipodistrofia progressiva.
lipodystrophia progressiva superior lipodistrofia progresiva superior.
lipodystrophy *n.* lipodistrofia.
bitrochanteric lipodystrophy lipodistrofia bitrocantérea.
congenital generalized lipodystrophy lipodistrofia congénita generalizada.
congenital progressive lipodystrophy lipodistrofia congénita progresiva.
generalized lipodystrophy lipodistrofia generalizada.
insulin lipodystrophy lipodistrofia insulínica, lipodistrofia por insulina.
intestinal lipodystrophy lipodistrofia intestinal.

partial lipodystrophy lipodistrofia parcial.
progressive congenital lipodystrophy lipodistrofia progresiva congénita.
progressive partial lipodystrophy lipodistrofia parcial.
total lipodystrophy lipodistrofia total.
lipoedema *n.* lipoedema.
lipoferous *adj.* lipófero, -ra, lipoferoso, -sa.
lipofibroma *n.* lipofibroma.
lipogenesis *n.* lipogénesis, lipogenia.
lipogenetic *adj.* lipogenético, -ca.
lipogenic *adj.* lipogénico, -ca, lipógeno, -na.
lipogranuloma *n.* lipogranuloma.
lipogranulomatosis *n.* lipogranulomatosis.
disseminated lipogranulomatosis lipogranulomatosis diseminada.
Farber's lipogranulomatosis lipogranulomatosis de Farber.
lipohemarthrosis *n.* lipohemartrosis.
lipohistiodieresis *n.* lipohistiodiéresis.
lipohyalin *n.* lipohialina.
lipohyperprophy *n.* lipohipertrofia.
lipoid *adj.* lipoidal, lipoide.
lipoidemia *n.* lipoidemia.
lipoidic *adj.* lipoídico, -ca.
lipoidosis *n.* lipoidosis.
arterial lipoidosis lipoidosis arterial.
lipoidosis corneae lipoidosis corneal.
lipoidosis cutis et mucosae lipoidosis cutis et mucosae.
renal lipoidosis lipoidosis renal.
lipoidproteinosis *n.* lipoidoproteinosis.
lipoidsiderosis *n.* lipoidosiderosis.
lipoiduria *n.* lipiduria, lipoiduria.
lipolipoidosis *n.* lipolipoidosis.
lipolysis *n.* lipólisis.
lipolytic *adj.* lipolítico, -ca.
lipoma *n.* lipoma.
atypical lipoma lipoma atípico.
diffuse lipoma lipoma difuso.
fat cell lipoma lipoma de células grasas, lipoma de células grasas fetales.
fetal lipoma lipoma fetal.
infiltrating lipoma lipoma infiltrativo.
intradural lipoma lipoma intradural.
lipoblastic lipoma lipoma lipoblástico.
lipoma annulare colli lipoma anular del cuello.
lipoma arborescens lipoma arborescente.
lipoma capsulare lipoma capsular.
lipoma cavernosum lipoma cavernoso.
lipoma diffusu renis lipoma difuso renal.
lipoma dolorosa lipoma doloroso.
lipoma fibrosum lipoma fibroso.
lipoma myxomatodes lipoma mixomatoso.
lipoma ossificans lipoma osificante.
lipoma sarcomatodes lipoma sarcomatoso.
lipoma sarcomatosum lipoma sarcomatoso.
lipoma telangiectodes lipoma telangiectásico.
pleomorphic lipoma lipoma pleomórfico.
spindle cell lipoma lipoma de células fusiformes.
telangiectatic lipoma lipoma telangiectásico.
lipomatoid *adj.* lipomatoide, lipomatoideo, -a.
lipomatosis *n.* lipomatosis.
congenital lipomatosis of the pancreas lipomatosis congénita del páncreas.
diffuse lipomatosis lipomatosis difusa.
lipomatosis atrophicans lipomatosis atrófica.
lipomatosis dolorosa lipomatosis dolorosa.
lipomatosis gigantea lipomatosis gigante.
lipomatosis neurotica lipomatosis neurótica.

lipomatosis renis lipomatosis de restitución del riñón, lipomatosis renal, lipomatosis renis.
  multiple lipomatosis lipomatosis múltiple.
  multiple symmetric lipomatosis lipomatosis simétrica múltiple.
  nodular circumscribed lipomatosis lipomatosis nodular circunscrita.
  renal lipomatosis lipomatosis de restitución del riñón, lipomatosis renal, lipomatosis renis.
  symmetric lipomatosis lipomatosis simétrica.
  symmetrical lipomatosis lipomatosis simétrica.
lipomatous *adj.* lipomatoso, -sa.
lipomeningocele lipomeningocele.
lipomerla *n.* lipomería.
lipometabolic *adj.* lipometabólico, -ca.
lipometabolism *n.* lipometabolismo.
lipomicron *n.* lipomicrón.
lipomucopolysaccharidosis *n.* lipomucopolisacaridosis.
lipomyohemangioma *n.* lipomiohemangioma.
lipomyoma *n.* lipomioma.
lipomyxoma *n.* lipomixoma.
liponephrosis *n.* liponefrosis.
lipopathy *n.* lipopatía.
lipopectic *adj.* lipopéctico, -ca.
lipopenia *n.* lipopenia.
lipopenic *adj.* lipopénico, -ca.
lipopexia *n.* lipopexia.
lipopexic *adj.* lipopéxico, -ca.
lipophage *n.* lipófago, -ga.
lipophagia *n.* lipofagia.
lipophagic *adj.* lipofágico, -ca.
lipophagy *n.* lipofagia.
  granulomatous lipophagy lipofagia granulomatosa.
lipophanerosis *n.* lipofanerosis.
lipophil *adj.* lipófilo, -la.
lipophilia *n.* lipofilia.
lipophilic *adj.* lipófilo, -la.
lipopolysaccharide *n.* lipopolisacárido.
lipoprotein *n.* lipoproteína.
lipoproteinemia *n.* lipoproteinemia.
lipoproteinosis *n.* lipoproteinosis.
liposarcoma *n.* liposarcoma.
liposis *n.* liposis.
liposolubility *n.* liposolubilidad.
liposoluble *adj.* liposoluble.
liposome *n.* liposoma.
lipostomy *n.* lipostomía.
liposuction *n.* lipoaspiración.
liposuction *n.* liposucción.
lipothymia *n.* lipotimia.
lipotrophic *adj.* lipotrófico, -ca.
lipotrophy *n.* lipotrofia.
lipotropic *adj.* lipotrópico, -ca.
lipotropism *n.* lipotropismo.
lipotropy *n.* lipotropía.
lipovaccine *n.* lipovacuna.
lipovitellin *n.* lipovitelina.
lipoxeny *n.* lipoxenia.
lipoxidase *n.* lipoxidasa.
lipoxygenase *n.* lipoxigenasa.
lipoxysm *n.* lipoxismo.
lipping *n.* labiación.
lippitude *n.* lipitud.
lippitudo *n.* lipitud.
lipsotrichia *n.* lipsotriquia.
lipuria *n.* lipuria.
lipuric *adj.* lipúrico, -ca.
liquefacient *adj.* licuefaciente.
liquefaction *n.* licuación, licuefacción.
  gas liquefaction licuación de un gas.

liquefactive *adj.* licuefactivo, -va.
liquenoid *adj.* liquinoideo, -a.
liquescent *adj.* licuescente.
liquid *adj.* líquido, -da², líquido¹.
  Müller's liquid líquido de Müller.
liquiform *adj.* liquiforme.
liquogel *n.* licuogel.
liquor *n.* licor, líquido¹, liquor.
  liquor cerebrospinalis líquido cefalorraquídeo, líquido cerebrospinal, liquor cerebrospinalis.
  liquor chorii liquor chorii.
  liquor cotunnii liquor cotunnii.
  liquor folliculi líquido folicular, liquor folliculi.
  liquor gastricus liquor gastricus.
  liquor of Scarpa liquor de Scarpa.
  liquor pancreaticus liquor pancreaticus.
  liquor prostaticus liquor prostaticus.
  liquor puris liquor puris.
  liquor sanguinis liquor sanguinis.
  liquor scarpae liquor de Scarpa.
  liquor seminis liquor seminis.
  mother liquor liquor madre.
liquoral *adj.* licuoral.
liquorrhea *n.* licuorrea.
lisping *n.* ceceo.
lissencephalia *n.* lisencefalia.
lissencephalic *adj.* lisencefálico, -ca.
lissencephaly *n.* lisencefalia.
lissive *adj.* miorrelajante.
lissosphincter *n.* lisoesfínter.
lissotrichic *adj.* lisótrico, -ca.
lissotrichous *adj.* lisótrico, -ca.
Listerela Listerella.
listerellosis *n.* listerelosis.
Listeria Listeria.
  Listeria monocytogenes Listeria monocytogenes.
Listerial *adj.* listerial.
listeriosis *n.* listeriosis.
listerism *n.* listerismo.
lithagogectasia *n.* litagogectasia.
lithagogue *adj.* litagogo, -ga.
lithangiuria *n.* litangiuria.
lithecbole *n.* litecbolia.
lithectasy *n.* litectasia.
lithectomy *n.* litectomía.
lithemia *n.* litemia.
lithemic *adj.* litémico, -ca.
lithiasic *adj.* litiásico, -ca.
lithiasis *n.* litiasis.
  appendicular lithiasis litiasis apendicular.
  lithiasis conjunctivae litiasis conjuntival.
  pancreatic lithiasis litiasis pancreática.
  urinary lithiasis litiasis urinaria.
lithic *adj.* lítico, -ca².
lithium *n.* litio.
lithocenosis *n.* litocenosis.
lithoclast *n.* litoclasto.
lithoclysmia *n.* litoclisma.
lithocystotomy *n.* litocistotomía.
lithodialysis *n.* litodiálisis.
lithogenesis *n.* litogénesis.
lithogenic *adj.* litógeno, -na.
lithogenous *adj.* litógeno, -na.
lithogeny *n.* litogenia.
lithoid *adj.* litoide.
lithokelyphopedion *n.* litocelifopedio, litoquelifopedion.
lithokelyphopedium *n.* litocelifopedio, litocelifopedion.
lithokelyphos *n.* litocelifo, litoquelifos.
lithokonion *n.* litoconion.
litholabe *n.* litolabo.

litholapaxy *n.* litolapaxia.
lithology *n.* litología.
litholysis *n.* litólisis.
litholyte *n.* litolito.
litholytic *adj.* litolítico, -ca.
lithometer *n.* litómetro.
lithomil *n.* litómilo.
lithonephria *n.* litonefria, litonefrosis.
lithonephritis *n.* litonefritis.
lithonephrotomy *n.* litonefrotomía.
lithontriptic *adj.* litontríptico, -ca.
lithopedion *n.* litopedion.
lithopedium *n.* litopedion.
lithophone *n.* litófono.
lithoscope *n.* litoscopio.
lithotome *n.* litótomo.
lithotomist *n.* litotomista.
lithotomy *n.* litotomía.
  high lithotomy litotomía alta.
  lateral lithotomy litotomía lateral.
  marian lithotomy litotomía mariana.
  median lithotomy litotomía mediana.
  mediolateral lithotomy litotomía mediolateral.
  perineal lithotomy litotomía perineal.
  prerectal lithotomy litotomía prerrectal.
  rectal lithotomy litotomía rectal, litotomía rectovesical.
  rectovesical lithotomy litotomía rectal, litotomía rectovesical.
  suprapubic lithotomy litotomía suprapúbica.
  vaginal lithotomy litotomía vaginal, litotomía vesicovaginal.
  vesical lithotomy litotomía vesical.
  vesicovaginal lithotomy litotomía vaginal, litotomía vesicovaginal.
lithotony *n.* litotonía.
lithotresis *n.* litotresis.
  ultrasonic lithotresis litotresis ultrasónica.
lithotripsy *n.* litotripsia.
lithotripter *n.* litotriptor.
lithotriptic *adj.* litontríptico, -ca, litotríptico, -ca.
lithotriptoscope *n.* litotriptoscopio.
lithotriptoscopy *n.* litotriptoscopia.
lithotrite *n.* litotritor.
lithotrity *n.* litotricia.
lithous *adj.* litoso, -sa.
lithoxiduria *n.* litoxiduria.
lithuresis *n.* lituresis.
lithureteria *n.* lituretería.
lithuria *n.* lituria.
litmus *n.* tornasol.
litter *n.* camilla.
littritis *n.* litritis, littritis.
liveborn *adj.* nacido, -da vivo, -va.
livedo *n.* livedo.
  idiopathic livedo reticularis livedo reticular idiopática.
  livedo postmortem livedo post mortem.
  livedo racemosa livedo anular, livedo racemosa.
  livedo reticularis livedo reticular, livedo reticularis.
  livedo telangiectatica livedo telangiectásica.
  symptomatic livedo reticularis livedo reticular sintomática.
livedoid *adj.* livedoide, livedoideo, -a.
liver *n.* hígado.
  albuminoid liver hígado albuminoide.
  amyloid liver hígado amiloide.
  biliary cirrhotic liver hígado cirrótico biliar.
  bronze liver hígado de bronce.
  cardiac liver hígado cardíaco.

cirrhotic liver hígado cirrótico.
degraded liver hígado degradado.
fatty liver hígado adiposo, hígado graso.
foamy liver hígado espumoso.
hobnail liver hígado claveteado.
infantile liver hígado infantil.
lardaceous liver hígado lardáceo.
nutmeg liver hígado de nuez moscada.
pigmented liver hígado pigmentado.
polycystic liver hígado poliquístico.
stasis liver hígado de estasis.
wandering liver hígado errante, hígado flotante.
waxy liver hígado céreo.
livid *adj.* lívido, -da, plomizo, -za.
lividity *n.* lividez.
postmortem lividity lividez postmortem.
living will *n.* testamento vital.
livor *n.* livor.
livor mortis livor mortis.
lixiviation *n.* lixiviación.
lixivium lixivio, lixivium.
lobar *adj.* lobar.
lobate *adj.* lobado, -da.
lobation *n.* lobulación.
lobe *n.* lóbulo, lobus.
lobectomy *n.* lobectomía.
lobitis *n.* lobitis.
Loboa loboi Loboa loboi.
lobopod *n.* lobopodio, lobópodo.
lobopodium *n.* lobopodio.
lobotomy *n.* lobotomía.
frontal lobotomy lobotomía frontal.
prefrontal lobotomy lobotomía prefrontal.
transorbital lobotomy lobotomía transorbitaria.
lobular *adj.* lobular.
lobulated *adj.* lobulado, -da.
lobulation *n.* lobulación.
portal lobulation lobulación portal.
renal lobulation lobulación renal.
lobule *n.* lobulillo, lobulus.
lobulose *adj.* lobuloso, -sa.
lobulous *adj.* lobuloso, -sa.
lobulus *n.* lobulillo, lobulus.
lobus *n.* lóbulo, lobus.
local *adj.* local.
localization *n.* localización.
auditory localization localización auditiva.
cerebral localization localización cerebral.
germinal localization localización germinal.
spatial localization localización espacial.
stereotaxic localization localización estereotáxica.
tactile localization localización táctil.
localized *adj.* localizado, -da.
localizer *n.* localizador.
abutment localizer localizador de confín.
Berman-Moorhead localizer localizador de Berman-Moorhead.
electroacoustic localizer localizador electroacústico.
Moorhead foreign body localizer localizador de Berman-Moorhead.
locator *n.* localizador.
lochia *n.* lochia, loquios.
lochia alba loquios blancos.
lochia cruenta lochia cruenta, loquios cruentos.
lochia purulenta loquios purulentos.
lochia rubra loquios rojos.
lochia sanguinolenta loquios sanguinolentos.
lochia serosa loquios serosos.
lochial *adj.* loquial.

lochiocolpos *n.* loquiocolpos.
lochiometra *n.* loquiómetra.
lochiorrhea *n.* loquiorrea.
lochioschesis *n.* loquioesquesis, loquiosquesis.
lochiostasis *n.* loquiostasis.
loci loci.
locomotion *n.* locomoción.
braquial locomotion locomoción braquial.
locomotive *adj.* locomotor, -a.
locomotor *adj.* locomotor, -a.
locomotory *adj.* locomotor, -a.
locular *adj.* locular.
loculate *adj.* loculado, -da.
loculation *n.* loculación.
loculus *n.* lóculo.
locus *n.* locus, lugar.
locus of infection lugar de infección.
loemology *n.* loemología.
loempe *n.* loempe.
logadectomy *n.* logadectomía.
logaditis *n.* logaditis.
logagnosia *n.* logoagnosia.
logagraphia *n.* logoagrafia.
logamnesia *n.* logamnesia, logoamnesia.
logaphasia *n.* logafasia, logoafasia.
logasthenia *n.* logoastenia.
logoclonia *n.* logoclonía.
logoklony *n.* logoclonía.
logokophasis *n.* logocofasis, logocofosia.
logomania *n.* logomanía.
logoneurosis *n.* logoneurosis.
logopathy *n.* logopatía.
logopedia *n.* logopedia.
logopedics *n.* logopedia.
logoplegia *n.* logoplejía.
logorrhea *n.* logorrea.
logospasm *n.* logoespasmo, logospasmo.
logotherapy *n.* logoterapia.
loiasis *n.* loyasis.
loimic *adj.* loímico, -ca.
loimographia *n.* loimografía.
loimology *n.* loimología.
loin *n.* lomo.
loliism *n.* lolismo.
longevity *n.* longevidad.
longilineal *adj.* longilíneo, -a.
longimanous *adj.* longímano, -na.
longipedate *adj.* longípedo, -da.
longiradiate *adj.* longirradiado, -da.
longitudinal *adj.* longitudinal.
longitudinalis *adj.* longitudinal.
longitypical *adj.* longitípico, -ca.
loop *n.* asa, bucle.
flow-volume loop bucle de flujo-volumen.
r-loop bucle-r.
lophodont *adj.* lofodonto, -ta.
lophotrichous *adj.* lofotrico, -ca.
lordoscoliosis *n.* lordoescoliosis.
lordosis *n.* lordosis.
lordotic *adj.* lordótico, -ca.
loss *n.* deterioro.
hearing loss deterioro auditivo.
lotio *n.* loción.
lotion *n.* loción.
loupe *n.* lupa.
corneal loupe lupa corneal.
louse *n.* piojo.
loxarthrosis *n.* loxartrosis.
Loxoceles Loxoceles.
loxophthalmus *n.* loxoftalmía.
Loxoscelidae Loxoscelidae.
loxoscelism *n.* loxoscelismo.
viscerocutaneous loxoscelism loxoscelismo viscerocutáneo.

loxotomy *n.* loxotomía.
lucid *adj.* lúcido, -da.
lucidification *n.* lucidificación.
lucidity *n.* lucidez.
lucifugal *adj.* lucífugo, -ga.
lucipetal *adj.* lucípeto, -ta.
lues *n.* lúe, lúes.
lues venerea lúe venérea.
luetic *adj.* luético, -ca.
lumbago *n.* lumbago.
ischemic lumbago lumbago isquémico.
lumbar *adj.* lumbar.
lumbarization *n.* lumbalización, lumbarización.
lumboabdominal *adj.* lumboabdominal.
lumbocolostomy *n.* lumbocolostomía.
lumbocolotomy *n.* lumbocolotomía.
lumbocostal *adj.* lumbocostal.
lumbocrural *adj.* lumbocrural.
lumbodorsal *adj.* lumbodorsal.
lumbodynia *n.* lumbodinia.
lumboiliac *adj.* lumboilíaco, -ca.
lumboinguinal *adj.* lumboinguinal.
lumbo-ovarian *adj.* lumboovárico, -ca.
lumbosacral *adj.* lumbosacro, -cra.
lumbricide *adj.* lumbricida.
lumbricoid *adj.* lumbricoide, lumbricoideo, -a.
lumbricosis *n.* lumbricosis.
lumbricus *n.* lombriz.
lumen *n.* lumen.
residual lumen lumen residual.
luminal *adj.* luminal.
luminescence *n.* luminiscencia.
luminiferous *adj.* luminífero, -ra.
luminiscency *n.* luminiscencia.
luminophore *adj.* luminóforo, -ra.
luminous *adj.* luminoso, -sa.
lumpectomy *n.* cachectomía.
lunatomalacia *n.* lunatomalacia.
lung *n.* pulmón.
air-conditioner lung pulmón por acondicionador de aire.
bird-breeder's lung pulmón de criador de aves.
bird-fancier's lung pulmón de criador de aves.
cardiac lung pulmón cardíaco.
cheese worker's lung pulmón de trabajadores del queso.
coalminer's lung pulmón de los mineros del carbón.
drowned lung pulmón ahogado.
farmer's lung pulmón de granjero.
fibroid lung pulmón fibroide.
honeycomb lung pulmón en panal, pulmón en panal de abeja.
iron lung pulmón de acero.
mason's lung pulmón de albañil.
mushroom-worker's lung pulmón de los trabajadores con hongos.
postperfusion lung pulmón posperfusión.
quiet lung pulmón quieto.
thresher's lung pulmón de trillador.
uremic lung pulmón urémico.
welder's lung pulmón de soldador.
wet lung pulmón húmedo.
white lung pulmón blanco.
lunula *n.* lúnula.
lupiform *adj.* lupiforme.
lupinosis *n.* lupinosis.
lupoid *adj.* lúpico, -ca, lupoide.
lupous *adj.* luposo, -sa.
lupus *n.* lupus.
chilblain lupus lupus eritematoso en sabañones.

chilblain lupus erythematosus lupus eritematoso en sabañones.

chronic discoid lupus erythematosus lupus eritematoso discoide crónico.

cutaneous lupus erythematosus lupus eritematoso cutáneo.

discoid lupus erythematosus lupus eritematoso discoide, lupus eritematoso discoideo.

disseminated lupus erythematosus lupus eritematoso diseminado.

drug-induced lupus lupus inducido por fármacos.

hypertrophic lupus erythematosus lupus eritematoso hipertrófico.

lupus erythematosus (LE) lupus eritematoso.

lupus erythematosus profundus lupus eritematoso profundo.

lupus erythematosus tumidus lupus eritematoso túmido.

lupus hypertrophicus lupus hipertrófico.

lupus livido lupus lívido.

lupus miliaris disseminatus faciei lupus miliar diseminado de la cara, lupus miliar diseminado facial.

lupus nephritis lupus nefrítico.

lupus papillomatosus lupus papilomatoso.

lupus pernio lupus pernio.

lupus psoriasis lupus psoriásico.

lupus sebaceus lupus sebáceo.

lupus serpiginosus lupus serpiginoso.

lupus superficialis lupus superficial.

lupus tumidus lupus túmido, lupus tumidus.

lupus verrucosus lupus verrucoso, lupus verrugoso.

lupus vulgaris lupus vulgar.

lupus vulgaris erythematoides lupus eritematoso vulgar.

neonatal lupus lupus neonatal.

systemic lupus erythematosus (SLE) lupus eritematoso sistémico (LES).

transient neonatal systemic lupus erythematosus lupus eritematoso sistémico neonatal transitorio.

lura lura.

lusus naturae *n.* lusus naturae.

luteal *adj.* lúteo, -a.

luteectomy *n.* lutectomía.

lutein *n.* luteína.

luteinization *n.* luteinización.

luteogenic *adj.* luteogénico, -ca.

luteohormone *n.* luteohormona.

luteoid *adj.* luteoide, luteoideo, -a.

luteol *n.* luteol.

luteole *n.* luteol.

luteolysis *n.* luteólisis.

luteoma *n.* luteoma.

pregnancy luteoma luteoma del embarazo.

luteotrope *n.* luteotropa.

luteotroph *n.* luteotrofa.

luteotrophic *adj.* luteotrófico, -ca.

luteotrophin *n.* luteotrofina.

luteotropic *adj.* luteotrópico, -ca.

luteotropin *n.* luteotropina.

lutropin *n.* lutropina.

Lutzomyia Lutzomyia.

lux *n.* lux, luz.

luxatio *n.* luxatio, luxación.

luxatio erecta luxación erecta.

luxatio imperfecta luxación imperfecta.

luxation *n.* lluxatio, luxación.

complicated luxation luxación complicada.

dental luxation luxación dentaria.

luxuriant *adj.* lujuriante.

luxus *n.* lujo, luxus.

lycanthropy *n.* licantropía.

lycomania *n.* licomanía.

lycoperdonosis *n.* licoperdonosis.

lycorexia *n.* licorexia.

lygophilia *n.* ligofilia.

lymph *n.* linfa.

aplastic lymph linfa aplástica.

blood lymph linfa sanguínea.

corpuscular lymph linfa corpuscular.

croupous lymph linfa cruposa.

euplastic lymph linfa euplástica.

fibrinous lymph linfa fibrinosa.

inflammatory lymph linfa inflamatoria.

intercellular lymph linfa intercelular.

intravascular lymph linfa intravascular.

plastic lymph linfa plástica.

tissue lymph linfa hística, linfa tisular.

vaccine lymph linfa de vaccinia, linfa de vacuna.

vaccinia lymph linfa de vaccinia, linfa de vacuna.

lymphadenectasis *n.* linfadenectasia.

lymphadenectomy *n.* linfadenectomía.

lymphadenhypertrophy *n.* linfadenehipertrofia.

lymphadenia *n.* linfadenia.

lymphadenitis *n.* linfadenitis.

caseous lymphadenitis linfadenitis caseosa.

dermatopathic lymphadenitis linfadenitis dermatopática.

mesenteric lymphadenitis linfadenitis mesentérica.

paratuberculous lymphadenitis linfadenitis paratuberculosa.

regional granulomatous lymphadenitis linfadenitis granulomatosa regional.

regional lymphadenitis linfadenitis regional.

tuberculoid lymphadenitis linfadenitis tuberculoide.

tuberculous lymphadenitis linfadenitis tuberculosa.

lymphadenocele *n.* linfadenocele.

lymphadenocyst *n.* linfadenoquiste.

lymphadenogram *n.* linfadenograma.

lymphadenography *n.* linfadenografía.

lymphadenoma *n.* linfadenoma.

lymphadenomatosis *n.* linfadenomatosis.

lymphadenopathy *n.* linfadenopatía.

angioimmunoblastic lymphadenopathy with dysproteinemia (AILD) linfadenopatía angioinmunoblástica con disproteinemia (LAID).

dermatopathic lymphadenopathy linfadenopatía dermatopática.

immunoblastic lymphadenopathy linfadenopatía inmunoblástica.

tuberculous lymphadenopathy linfadenopatía tuberculosa.

lymphadenosis *n.* linfadenosis.

benign lymphadenosis linfadenosis benigna.

lymphadenosis cutis benigna linfadenosis cutánea benigna.

lymphadenotomy *n.* linfadenotomía.

lymphadenovarix *n.* linfadenovárice.

lymphagogue *n.* linfagogo.

lymphangeitis *n.* linfangeítis.

lymphangial *adj.* linfangial.

lymphangiectasia *n.* linfangiectasia.

cavernous lymphangiectasia linfangiectasia cavernosa.

cystic lymphangiectasia linfangiectasia quística.

intestinal lymphangiectasia linfangiectasia intestinal.

simple lymphangiectasia linfangiectasia simple.

lymphangiectatic *adj.* linfangiectásico, -ca.

lymphangiectodes *n.* linfangiectodes.

lymphangiectomy *n.* linfangiectomía, linfangioectomía.

lymphangiitis *n.* linfangiítis.

lymphangioadenogram *n.* linfangioadenograma.

lymphangioadenography *n.* linfangioadenografía.

lymphangioendothelioblastoma *n.* linfangioendotelioblastoma.

lymphangioendothelioma *n.* linfangioendotelioma.

lymphangiogram *n.* linfangiograma.

lymphangiography *n.* linfangiografía.

lymphangioleiomyomatosis *n.* linfangioleiomiomatosis.

lymphangiology *n.* linfangiología.

lymphangioma *n.* linfangioma.

capillary lymphangioma linfangioma capilar.

cavernous lymphangioma linfangioma cavernoso.

cystic lymphangioma linfangioma quístico.

lymphangioma capillare varicosum linfangioma capilar varicoso.

lymphangioma cavernosum linfangioma cavernoso.

lymphangioma circumscriptum linfangioma circunscrito.

lymphangioma simplex linfangioma simple.

lymphangioma superficium simplex linfangioma superficial simple.

simple lymphangioma linfangioma simple.

lymphangiomatous *adj.* linfangiomatoso, -sa.

lymphangiomyomatosis *n.* linfangiomiomatosis.

lymphangion *n.* linfangion.

lymphangiophlebitis *n.* linfangioflebitis.

lymphangioplasty *n.* linfangioplastia.

lymphangiosarcoma *n.* linfangiosarcoma.

lymphangiotomy *n.* linfangiotomía.

lymphangitis *n.* linfangitis.

gummatous lymphangitis linfangitis gomatosa.

lymphangitis carcinomatosa linfangitis carcinomatosa.

lymphapheresis *n.* linfaféresis.

lymphatic *adj.* linfático, -ca.

lymphaticostomy *n.* linfaticostomía.

lymphatism *n.* linfatismo.

lymphatitis *n.* linfatitis.

lymphatogenous *adj.* linfatógeno, -na.

lymphatology *n.* linfatología.

lymphatolysis *n.* linfatólisis.

lymphatolytic *adj.* linfatolítico, -ca.

lymphatome *n.* linfatomo.

lymphectasia *n.* linfectasia.

lymphedema *n.* linfedema.

congenital lymphedema linfedema congénito.

hereditary lymphedema linfedema hereditario.

lymphedema praecox linfedema precoz.

primary lymphedema linfedema primario.

lymphemia *n.* linfemia.

lymphendotelioma *n.* linfendotelioma.

lymphenteritis *n.* linfenteritis.

lymphepithelioma *n.* linfepitelioma.

lymphization *n.* linfización.

lymphoadenoma *n.* linfoadenoma.

lymphoblast *n.* linfoblasto.

lymphoblastic *adj.* linfoblástico, -ca.

lymphoblastoma *n.* linfoblastoma.

giant follicular lymphoblastoma linfoblastoma folicular gigante.

lymphoblastomatosis *n.* linfoblastomatosis.
lymphoblastomatous *adj.* linfoblastomatoso, -sa.
lymphoblastomid *n.* linfoblastómide.
lymphoblastosis *n.* linfoblastosis.
lymphocinesia *n.* linfocinesia.
lymphocitapheresis *n.* linfocitaféresis.
lymphocitosis *n.* linfocitosis.
acute infectious lymphocitosis linfocitosis infecciosa aguda.
lymphocoele *n.* linfocele.
lymphocyst *n.* linfocisto.
lymphocyte *n.* linfocito.
amplifier T lymphocyte linfocito T amplificador.
B lymphocyte linfocito B.
cytotoxic T lymphocyte linfocito T citotóxicos.
helper T lymphocyte linfocito T ayudador.
killer lymphocyte linfocito asesino.
large granular lymphocyte linfocito granular grande.
Rieder's lymphocyte linfocito de Rieder.
T lymphocyte linfocito T.
thymus independent lymphocyte linfocito independiente del timo.
thymus-dependent lymphocyte linfocito dependiente del timo.
transformed lymphocyte linfocito transformado.
lymphocythemia *n.* linfocitemia.
lymphocytic *adj.* linfocítico, -ca.
lymphocytoblast *n.* linfocitoblasto.
lymphocytoma *n.* linfocitoma.
benign lymphocytoma cutis linfocitoma benigno de la piel.
lymphocytoma cutis linfocitoma cutáneo, linfocitoma cutis.
lymphocytomatosis *n.* linfocitomatosis.
lymphocytopenia *n.* linfocitopenia.
lymphocytopheresis *n.* linfocitoféresis.
lymphocytopoiesis *n.* linfocitopoyesis.
lymphocytopoietic *adj.* linfocitopoyético, -ca.
lymphocytorrhexis *n.* linfocitorrexis.
lymphocytotic *adj.* linfocitósico, -ca.
lymphocytotoxicity *n.* linfocitotoxicidad.
lymphocytotoxin *n.* linfocitotóxina.
lymphodermia *n.* linfodermia.
lymphoduct *n.* linfoducto.
lymphoepithelioma *n.* linfoepitelioma.
lymphoganglin *n.* linfoganglina.
lymphogenesis *n.* linfogénesis, linfogenia.
lymphogenic *adj.* linfogénico, -ca.
lymphogenous *adj.* linfógeno, -na.
lymphogram *n.* linfograma.
lymphogranuloma *n.* linfogranuloma.
lymphogranuloma benignum linfogranuloma benigno.
lymphogranuloma inguinale linfogranuloma inguinal.
lymphogranuloma venereum linfogranuloma venéreo.
venereal lymphogranuloma linfogranuloma venéreo.
lymphogranulomatosis *n.* linfogranulomatosis.
benign lymphogranulomatosis linfogranulomatosis benigna.
lymphogranulomatosis cutis linfogranulomatosis maligna de la piel.
lymphogranulomatosis inguinalis linfogranulomatosis inguinal.
lymphography *n.* linfografía.
lymphohistiocytosis *n.* linfohistiocitosis.
lymphohistioplasmacytic *adj.* linfohistioplasmático, -ca.

lymphoid *adj.* linfoide, linfoideo, -a.
lymphoidectomy *n.* linfoidectomía.
lymphoidotoxemia *n.* linfoidotoxemia.
lymphokine *n.* linfocina.
lymphokinesis *n.* linfocinesia, linfocinesis, linfoquinesia.
lymphology *n.* linfología.
lympholysis *n.* linfólisis.
lympholytic *adj.* linfolítico, -ca.
lymphoma *n.* linfoma.
adult T cell lymphoma linfoma de células T del adulto.
African lymphoma linfoma africano.
benign lymphoma of the rectum linfoma benigno del recto.
Burkitt's lymphoma linfoma de Burkitt.
convoluted T-cell lymphoma linfoma de células T contorsionado.
cutaneous T-cell lymphoma linfoma de células T cutáneo.
diffuse lymphoma linfoma difuso.
follicular center cell lymphoma linfoma de células del centro folicular.
follicular lymphoma linfoma folicular.
giant follicle lymphoma linfoma folicular gigante.
granulomatous lymphoma linfoma granulomatoso.
histiocytic lymphoma linfoma histiocítico.
Hodgkin's lymphoma linfoma de Hodgkin.
inmunoblastic lymphoma linfoma inmunoblástico.
intestinal T-cell lymphoma linfoma intestinal T.
large cell lymphoma linfoma de células grandes.
Lennert's lymphoma linfoma de Lennert.
lymphoblastic lymphoma linfoma linfoblástico.
lymphocytic lymphoma linfoma linfocítico.
lymphoepithelioid cell lymphoma linfoma linfoepitelioide.
lymphoma cutis linfoma cutis.
lymphoplasmocytic lymphoma linfoma linfoplasmocítico.
malignant lymphoma linfoma maligno.
MALT lymphoma linfoma MALT.
Mediterranean lymphoma linfoma del Mediterráneo, linfoma mediterráneo.
mixed lymphocytic-histiocytic lymphoma linfoma mixto linfocítico e histiocítico.
monocytoid lymphoma linfoma monocitoide.
nodular histiocytic lymphoma linfoma nodular histiocítico.
nodular lymphoma linfoma nodular.
non-Hodgkin's lymphoma linfoma no de Hodgkin.
peripheral T-cell lymphoma linfoma T periférico.
plasmacytoid lymphocytic lymphoma linfoma linfocítico plasmacitoide.
pleomorphic lymphoma linfoma pleomorfo.
poorly differentiated lymphocytic lymphoma linfoma linfocítico mal diferenciado.
poorly differentiated lymphocytic malignant lymphoma linfoma linfocítico maligno mal diferenciado.
real histiocytic lymphoma linfoma histiocítico verdadero.
small B-cell lymphoma linfoma de células B pequeñas.
small lymphocytic lymphoma linfoma linfocítico pequeño.
small lymphocytic T-cell lymphoma linfoma de células T de pequeños linfocitos.

stem cell lymphoma linfoma de células madre.
T-cell lymphoma linfoma de células T.
thyroid lymphoma linfoma tiroideo.
U-cell (undefined) lymphoma linfoma de células U (indefinido).
undifferentiated lymphoma linfoma indiferenciado.
undifferentiated malignant lymphoma linfoma maligno indiferenciado.
well-differentiated lymphocytic lymphoma linfoma linfocítico bien diferenciado.
well-differentiated lymphocytic malignant lymphoma linfoma linfocítico maligno bien diferenciado.
lymphomatoid *adj.* linfomatoide, linfomatoideo, -a.
lymphomatosis *n.* linfomatosis.
neural lymphomatosis linfomatosis neural.
ocular lymphomatosis linfomatosis ocular.
lymphomatous *adj.* linfomatoso, -sa.
lymphomyeloma *n.* linfomieloma.
lymphomyxoma *n.* linfomixoma.
lymphonoditis *n.* linfonoditis.
lymphonodulus *n.* linfonódulo.
lymphopathia *n.* linfopatía.
lymphopathy *n.* linfopatía.
ataxic lymphopathy linfopatía atáxica.
lymphopathy venereum linfopatía venérea.
lymphopenia *n.* linfopenia.
lymphoplasia *n.* linfoplasia.
cutaneous lymphoplasia linfoplasia cutánea.
lymphoplasm *n.* linfoplasma.
lymphoplasmapheresis *n.* linfoplasmaféresis.
lymphoplasty *n.* linfoplastia.
lymphopoiesis *n.* linfopoyesis.
lymphopoietic *adj.* linfopoyético, -ca.
lymphoproliferative *adj.* linfoproliferativo, -va.
lymphoreticular *adj.* linforreticular.
lymphoreticulosis *n.* linforreticulosis.
benign (inoculation) lymphoreticulosis linforreticulosis benigna (de inoculación).
lymphorrhagia *n.* linforragia.
lymphorrhea *n.* linforrea.
lymphorrhoid *n.* linforroide.
lymphosarcoma *n.* linfosarcoma.
lymphosarcomatosis *n.* linfosarcomatosis.
lymphostasis *n.* linfostasia.
lymphotasis *n.* linfostasis.
lymphotaxis *n.* linfotaxis.
lymphotism *n.* linfotismo.
lymphotome *n.* linfatomo, linfotomo.
lymphotoxemia *n.* linfotoxemia.
lymphotoxin *n.* linfotoxina.
lymphotrophy *n.* linfotrofia.
lymphotropic *adj.* linfotrópico, -ca.
lymphous *adj.* linfoso, -sa.
lymphuria *n.* linfuria.
lymph-vascular *adj.* linfovascular.
lyonization *n.* lionización.
lyonized *adj.* lionizado, -da.
lyophile *adj.* liófilo, -la.
lyophilic *adj.* liofílico, -ca.
lyophilization *n.* liofilización.
lyophilize *v.* liofilizar.
lyophilizer *n.* liofilizador.
lyophobe *adj.* liófobo, -ba.
lyophobic *adj.* liofóbico, -ca, liófobo, -ba.
lyosorption *n.* lioadsorción, liosorción.
lyotropic *adj.* liotrópico, -ca.
Lyponyssus Lyponyssus.
lypressin *n.* lipresina.
lyra *n.* lira.
lysate *n.* lisado, lisado, -da.

lyse[1] *n.* lisa.
lyse[2] *v.* lisar.
lysemia *n.* lisemia.
lysimeter *n.* lisímetro.
lysin *n.* lisina.
lysine *n.* lisina.
lysinemia *n.* lisinemia.
lysinogen *adj.* lisinógeno, -na.
lysinogenesis *n.* lisinogénesis.
lysinosis *n.* lisinosis.
lysinuria *n.* lisinuria.
lysis *n.* lisis.

lysobacteria *n.* lisobacteria.
lysocythin *n.* lisocitina.
lysogen *adj.* lisógeno, -na.
lysogenesis *n.* lisiogenia, lisogénesis.
lysogenic *adj.* lisogénico, -ca.
lysogenicity *n.* lisogenicidad.
lysogenization *n.* lisogenización.
lysogeny *n.* lisogenia.
lysokinase *n.* lisocinasa.
lysosomal *adj.* lisosómico, -ca.
lysosome *n.* lisosoma.
   definitive lysosome lisosoma definitivo.

   primary lysosome lisosoma primario.
   secondary lysosome lisosoma secundario.
lysotripping *n.* lisorremoción.
lysotype *n.* lisotipo.
lysozyme *n.* lisozima.
lysozymuria *n.* lisozimuria.
lyssa *n.* lisa.
lyssic *adj.* lísico, -ca.
lyssodexis *n.* lisodexia.
lyssoid *adj.* lisoide.
lyssophobia *n.* lisofobia.
lytic *adj.* lítico, -ca[1].

M m

macerate[1] *n.* macerado.

macerate[2] *v.* macerar.

maceration *n.* maceración.

macerative *adj.* macerativo, -va.

machine *n.* machina, máquina.

 anesthesia machine máquina de anestesia.

 heart-lung machine máquina cardiopulmonar, máquina corazón-púlmón.

 kidney machine máquina renal.

 panoramic rotating machine máquina rotativa panorámica.

machismo *n.* machismo.

macies macies.

macradenous *adj.* macroadenoso, -sa.

macrencephalia *n.* macrencefalia, macroencefalia.

macrencephaly *n.* macroencefalia.

macroaggregate *n.* macroagregado.

macroamylase *n.* macroamilasa.

macroamylasemia *n.* macroamilasemia.

macroamylasemic *adj.* macroamilasémico, -ca.

macroanalysis *n.* macroanálisis.

macroaneurysm *n.* macroaneurisma.

macroangiopathy *n.* macroangiopatía.

macrobacterium *n.* macrobacteria.

macrobiosis *n.* macrobiosis.

macrobiote *n.* macrobiota.

macrobiotic *adj.* macrobiótico, -ca.

macrobiotics *n.* macrobiótica.

macroblast *n.* macroblasto.

macroblepharia *n.* macroblefaria.

macrobrachia *n.* macrobraquia.

macrocardia *n.* macrocardia.

macrocardius *n.* macrocardio.

macrocephalia *n.* macrocefalia.

macrocephalic *adj.* macrocefálico, -ca.

macrocephalus *n.* macrocéfalo, megalocéfalo, -la.

macrocephaly *n.* macrocefalia.

macrocheilia *n.* macroqueilia.

macrocheiria *n.* macroqueiria.

macrochemical *adj.* macroquímico, -ca.

macrochemistry *n.* macroquímica.

macrochilia *n.* macroqueilia, macroquilia.

macrochiria *n.* macroqueiria, macroquiria.

macrochylomicron *n.* macroquilomicrón.

macroclitoris *n.* macroclítoris.

macrocnemia *n.* macrocnemia.

macrococcus *n.* macrococo.

macrocolon *n.* macrocolia, macrocolon.

macrocornea *n.* macrocórnea.

macrocrania *n.* macrocrania.

macrocranium *n.* macrocráneo.

macrocryoglobulin *n.* macrocrioglobulina.

macrocryoglobulinemia *n.* macrocrioglobulinemia.

macrocyst *n.* macrocisto, macroquiste.

macrocyte *n.* macrocito.

macrocythemia *n.* macrocitemia.

macrocytic *adj.* macrocítico, -ca.

macrocytosis *n.* macrocitosis.

macrodactylia *n.* macrodactilia.

macrodactylism *n.* macrodactilismo.

macrodactyly *n.* macrodactilia.

macrodont *n.* macrodonte, macrodonto.

macrodontia *n.* macrodoncia, macrodontia.

macrodontic *adj.* macrodóntico, -ca.

macrodontism *n.* macrodontismo.

macrodrip *n.* macrogotero.

macrodystrophia *n.* macrodistrofia.

 macrodystrophia lipomatosa progressiva macrodistrofia lipomatosa progresiva.

macroelement *n.* macroelemento.

macroencephalon *n.* macroencéfalo.

macroencephaly *n.* macroencefalia.

macroerythroblast *n.* macroeritroblasto.

macroerythrocyte *n.* macroeritrocito.

macroesthesia *n.* macroestesia, macrostesia.

macrofauna *n.* macrofauna.

macroflora *n.* macroflora.

macrogamete *n.* macrogameto.

macrogametocyte *n.* macrogametocito.

macrogamont *n.* macrogamonte, macrogamonto.

macrogastria *n.* macrogastria.

macrogenesy *n.* macrogenesia, macrogénesis.

macrogenia *n.* macrogenia.

macrogenitosomia *n.* macrogenitosomía.

 macrogenitosomia precox macrogenitosomía precoz.

macrogeny *n.* macrogenia.

macrogingivae *n.* macroencías.

macroglia *n.* macroglia.

macroglobulin *n.* macroglobulina.

 total macroglobulins macroglobulinas totales.

macroglobulinemia *n.* macroglobulinemia.

 Waldenström's macroglobulinemia macroglobulinemia de Waldenström.

macroglossia *n.* macroglosia.

macrognathia *n.* macrognatia, macrognatismo.

macrographia *n.* macrografía.

macrogyria *n.* macrogiria.

macrolabia *n.* macrolabia.

macrolecithal *adj.* macrolecito, -ta.

macroleukoblast *n.* macroleucoblasto.

macrolide *n.* macrólido.

macrolymphocyte *n.* macrolinfocito.

macrolymphocytosis *n.* macrolinfocitosis.

macromania *n.* macromanía.

macromastia *n.* macromastia.

macromazia *n.* macromastia.

macromelanosome *n.* macromelanosoma.

macromelia *n.* macromelia.

macromerozoite *n.* macromerozoíto.

macromerus *n.* macrómera, macrómero.

macromethod *n.* macrométodo.

macromolecular *adj.* macromolecular.

macromolecule *n.* macromolécula.

macromonocyte *n.* macromonocito.

macromyeloblast *n.* macromieloblasto.

macronodular *adj.* macronodular.

macronormoblast *n.* macronormoblasto.

macronormochromoblast *n.* macronormocromoblasto.

macronucleus *n.* macronúcleo.

macronutrient *n.* macronutriente.

macronychia *n.* macroniquia.

macroorchidism *n.* macroorquidia, macroorquidismo, macrorquidismo.

macroparasite *n.* macroparásito.

macropathology *n.* macropatología.

macropenis *n.* macropene, macropenisomía.

macrophage *n.* macrófago.

 alveolar macrophage macrófago alveolar.

 fixed macrophage macrófago fijo.

 free macrophage macrófago libre.

 Hansemann macrophage macrófago de Hansemann.

 tissue macrophage macrófago tisular.

macrophagocyte *n.* macrofagocito.

macrophallus *n.* macrofalia, macrofalo.

macrophthalmia *n.* macroftalmía.

macrophthalmous *adj.* macroftálmico, -ca.

macropia *n.* macropía.

macroplasia *n.* macroplasia.

macroplastia *n.* macroplasia, macroplastia.

macropodia *n.* macropodia.

macropolycyte *n.* macropolicito, macropolocito.

macroprolactinoma *n.* macroprolactinoma.

macropromyelocyte *n.* macropromielocito.

macroprosopia *n.* macroprosopia.

macroprosopous *adj.* macroprosópico, -ca.

macropsia *n.* macropsia.

macroradiography *n.* macrorradiografía.

macroreentry *n.* macrorreentrada.

macrorhinia *n.* macrorrinia.

macroscelia *n.* macroscelia.

macroscopic *adj.* macroscópico, -ca.

macroscopical *adj.* macroscópico, -ca.

macroscopy *n.* macroscopia.

macrosigmoid *n.* macrosigmoide.

macrosis *n.* macrosis.

macrosmatic *adj.* macrosmático, -ca.

macrosomatia *n.* macrosomatia.

macrosomia *n.* macrosomía.

macrosplanchnic *adj.* macroesplácnico, -ca, macrosplácnico, -ca.

macrostereognosia *n.* macroestereognosia.

macrostereognosis *n.* macroestereognosia, macrostereognosia, macrostereognosis.

macrostomia *n.* macrostomía.

macrostructural *adj.* macroestructural.

macrotia *n.* macrotia.

macrotome *n.* macrótomo.

macrotooth *n.* macrodiente.

macula *n.* macula, mácula.

false macula mácula falsa.
macula acustica sacculi mácula acústica del sáculo.
macula acustica utriculi mácula acústica del utrículo.
macula adherens mácula adherente.
macula albida mácula álbida, mácula blanca.
macula atrophica mácula atrófica, macula atrophica.
macula cerulea macula cerulea, mácula cerúlea.
macula communis mácula común.
macula corneae mácula corneal.
macula cribosa mácula cribosa.
macula cribosa inferior mácula cribosa inferior.
macula cribosa media mácula cribosa media.
macula cribosa superior mácula cribosa superior.
macula flava mácula flava.
macula folliculi mácula folicular.
macula germinativa mácula germinativa.
macula gonorrhoica mácula gonorreica, macula gonorrhoica.
macula lactea mácula láctea.
macula lutea mácula lútea.
macula pellucida macula pellucida.
macula retinae mácula blanca de la retina, mácula de la retina, mácula lútea de la retina.
macula sacculi mácula del sáculo.
macula tendinea mácula tendínea.
macula utriculi mácula utriculi.
mongolian macula mácula mongólica.
Saenger's macula mácula de Saenger.
macular *adj.* macular.
maculate *adj.* maculado, -da.
maculation *n.* maculación.
maculocerebral *adj.* maculocerebral.
maculoerythematous *adj.* maculoeritematoso, -sa.
maculopapular *adj.* maculopapular.
maculopapule *n.* maculopápula.
maculopathy *n.* maculopatía.
diabetic maculopathy maculopatía diabética.
maculovesicular *adj.* maculovesicular.
mad *adj.* loco, -ca.
madarosis *n.* madarosis, madesis.
madescent *adj.* madescente.
madidans *adj.* madidans.
madness *n.* locura.
Madurella Madurella.
maduromycosis *n.* maduromicosis.
mageiric *adj.* mageírico, -ca.
magenstrasse *n.* magenstrasse.
magistral *adj.* magistral.
magma *n.* magma.
magnesemia *n.* magnesemia.
magnesite *n.* magnesita.
magnesium *n.* magnesio, magnesium.
magnet *n.* imán.
denture magnet imán de dentadura.
Grüning's magnet imán de Grüning, imán de Haab, imán de Hirschberg.
Haab's magnet imán de Grüning, imán de Haab, imán de Hirschberg.
Hirschberg's magnet imán de Grüning, imán de Haab, imán de Hirschberg.
permanent magnet imán permanente.
resistive magnet imán resistivo.
superconducting magnet imán superconductivo.
temporary magnet imán temporal.
magnetic *adj.* magnético, -ca.
magnetism *n.* magnetismo.
magnetization *n.* magnetización.

magnetocardiograph *n.* magnetocardiógrafo.
magnetocardiography *n.* magnetocardiografía.
magnetoconstriction *n.* magnetoconstricción.
magnetoelectricity *n.* magnetoelectricidad.
magnetoencephalogram (MEG) *n.* magnetoencefalograma (MEG).
magnetoencephalograph *n.* magnetoencefalógrafo.
magnetoencephalography *n.* magnetoencefalografía.
magnetology *n.* magnetología.
magnetometer *n.* magnetómetro.
magneton *n.* magnetón.
magnetotherapy *n.* magnetoterapia.
magnetron *n.* magnetrón.
magnetropism *n.* magnetropismo.
magnicellular *adj.* magnicelular.
magnification *n.* magnificación.
radiographic magnification magnificación radiográfica.
magnify *v.* magnificar.
magnitude *n.* magnitud.
mahamari *n.* mahamari.
MAID MAID.
maidism *n.* maidismo.
maim *v.* mutilar.
main *n.* mano.
main d'accoucheur mano de comadrón, mano de partero.
main en squelette mano de esqueleto, mano esquelética.
main succulente mano suculenta.
maintainer *n.* mantenedor.
space maintainer mantenedor de espacio.
maintenance *n.* mantenimiento.
mal *n.* mal.
mal de Cayenne mal de Cayenne.
mal de Meleda mal de Meleda.
mal de mer mal de mar, mal marino.
mal del pinto mal de los pintos, mal de Pinto.
mal morado mal morado.
mal rouge mal rojo.
petit mal mal pequeño, pequeño mal.
malabsorption *n.* malabsorción.
congenital lactose malabsorption malabsorción congénita de lactosa.
congenital sucrose-isomaltose malabsorption malabsorción congénita de sucrosa-isomaltosa.
glucose-galactose malabsorption malabsorción familiar de glucosa-galactosa.
malacia *n.* malacia.
malacia traumatica malacia traumática.
metaplastic malacia malacia metaplástica.
parotic malacia malacia parótica.
malacic *adj.* malácico, -ca.
malacoma *n.* malacoma.
malacoplakia *n.* malacoplaquia, malacoplasia.
malacoplakia vesicae malacoplaquia vesical.
malacosarcosis *n.* malacosarcosis.
malacosis *n.* malacosis.
malacosteon *n.* malacosteon.
malacotic *adj.* malacótico, -ca.
malacotomy *n.* malacotomía.
malactic *adj.* maláctico, -ca.
maladjusted *adj.* maladaptado, -da.
maladjustment *n.* inadaptación, maladaptación.
social maladjustment inadaptación social.
malagma *n.* malagma.
malaise *n.* malestar.
malalignment *n.* malalineación.

malar *adj.* malar.
malaria *n.* helópira, malaria, paludismo.
algid malaria paludismo álgido.
autochthonous malaria paludismo autóctono.
benign tertian malaria paludismo terciano, paludismo terciano benigno.
bilious remittent malaria paludismo bilioso remitente.
cerebral malaria paludismo cerebral.
hemolytic malaria paludismo hemolítico.
induced malaria paludismo inducido, paludismo terapéutico.
intermittent malaria paludismo intermitente.
malaria comatosa paludismo comatoso.
malaria falciparum paludismo falciparum.
malaria vivax paludismo vivax.
malignant tertian malaria paludismo terciano maligno.
nonan malaria paludismo nono.
ovale malaria paludismo oval, paludismo oval terciano.
ovale tertian malaria paludismo oval, paludismo oval terciano.
pernicious malaria paludismo pernicioso.
quartan malaria paludismo cuartano.
quotidian malaria paludismo cotidiano.
remittent malaria paludismo remitente.
tertian malaria paludismo terciano, paludismo terciano benigno.
malariacidal *adj.* malaricida.
malariatherapy *n.* malariaterapia.
malariologist *n.* malariólogo, -ga.
malariology *n.* malariología.
malariometry *n.* malariometría.
malariotherapy *n.* malarioterapia.
malarious *adj.* malárico, -ca.
malassimilation *n.* malasimilación.
malaxate *n.* malaxación.
malaxation *n.* malaxación.
maldevelopment *n.* maldesarrollo.
maldigestion *n.* maladigestión, maldigestión.
male *n.* macho, varón.
malemission *n.* malaemisión, malemisión.
maleruption *n.* malaerupción, malerupción.
malformation *n.* malformación.
Arnold Chiari malformation malformación de Arnold Chiari.
malfunction *n.* malfunción.
maliasmus *n.* maliasmo.
malignancy *n.* malignidad.
malignant *adj.* maligno, -na.
malignin *n.* malignina.
malignogram *n.* malignograma.
mali-mali *n.* mali-mali.
malinterdigitation *n.* malainterdigitación, malinterdigitación.
malleability *n.* maleabilidad.
malleable *adj.* maleable.
malleal *adj.* maleal.
mallear *adj.* malear.
malleation *n.* maleación.
malleinization *n.* malleinización.
malleoidosis *n.* malleoidosis.
malleoincudal *adj.* maleoincúdeo, -a.
malleolar *adj.* maleolar.
malleolus *n.* maléolo.
malleotomy *n.* maleotomía.
mallochorion *n.* malocorion.
malnutrition *n.* desnutrición, malnutrición.
energy-protein malnutrition malnutrición proteicocalórica.
malignant malnutrition desnutrición maligna, malnutrición maligna.

protein malnutrition malnutrición de proteínas.

malocclusion *n.* maloclusión.

close-bite malocclusion maloclusión de mordida cerrada.

open-bite malocclusion maloclusión de mordida abierta.

telescoping malocclusion maloclusión en telescopio.

Malpighian *adj.* malpighiano, -na.

malposed *adj.* malpuesto, -ta.

malposition *n.* malposición.

malpractice *n.* mala práctica.

malpraxis *n.* malpraxis.

malpresentation *n.* malapresentación.

malrotation *n.* malarrotación.

maltoside *n.* maltósido.

maltosuria *n.* maltosuria.

maltreatment *n.* maltrato.

malturned *adj.* malrotado, -da.

malunion *n.* malaunión, malunión.

mamalgia *n.* mamalgia.

mamatroph *adj.* mamatrófico, -ca.

mamelon *n.* mamelón.

mamelonated *adj.* mamelonado, -da.

mamelonation *n.* mamelonación.

mamilla *n.* mamila.

mamillary *adj.* mamilar.

mamillate *adj.* mamilado, -da.

mamillated *adj.* mamilado, -da.

mamillation *n.* mamilación.

mamilliform *adj.* mamiliforme.

mamilliplasty *n.* mamiloplastia.

mamillitis *n.* mamilitis.

mamiloplasty *n.* mamiloplastia.

mammaplasty *n.* mamaplastia.

mammectomy *n.* mamectomía.

mammiform *adj.* mamiforme.

mammilliform *adj.* mamiliforme.

mammillitis *n.* mamilitis.

mammitis *n.* mamitis.

mammogen *n.* mamógeno.

mammogenesis *n.* mamogénesis.

mammogram *n.* mamograma.

mammograph *n.* mamógrafo.

mammographic *adj.* mamográfico, -ca.

mammography *n.* mamografía.

film screen mammography mamografía de barrido.

mammoplasty *n.* mamoplasia, mamoplastia.

Aries-Pitanguy mammoplasty mamoplastia de Aries-Pitanguy.

augmentation mammoplasty mamoplastia de aumento, mamoplastia de incremento.

Biesenberger mammoplasty mamoplastia de Biesenberger.

Conway mammoplasty mamoplastia de Conway.

reconstructive mammoplasty mamoplastia reconstructiva.

reduction mammoplasty mamoplastia de reducción.

Strömbeck mammoplasty mamoplastia de Strömbeck.

mammosomatotroph *n.* mamosomatotrofo.

mammothermography *n.* mamotermografía.

mammotomy *n.* mamotomía.

mammotroph *n.* mamótrofa.

mammotrophic *adj.* mamotrófico, -ca.

mammotropic *adj.* mamotrófico, -ca, mamotrópico, -ca.

mammotropin *n.* mamotropina.

manchette *n.* manchette.

mandama mandama.

mandible *n.* mandíbula.

crackling mandible mandíbula crujiente.

lower mandible mandíbula inferior.

lumpy mandible mandíbula abultada.

parrot mandible mandíbula de loro.

upper mandible mandíbula superior.

mandibular *adj.* mandibular.

mandibulectomy *n.* mandibulectomía.

mandibulofacial *adj.* mandibulofacial.

mandibulo-oculofacial *adj.* mandibulooculofacial.

mandibulopharyngeal *adj.* mandibulofaríngeo, -a.

mandrel *n.* mandril, mandrina.

mandril *n.* mandril, mandrina.

maneuver *n.* maniobra.

accordion maneuver maniobra de acordeón.

Allen's maneuver maniobra de Allen.

alloplastic maneuver maniobra aloplástica.

aspirant maneuver maniobra de aspiración.

autoplastic maneuver maniobra autoplástica.

Bill's maneuver maniobra de Bill.

Bracht's maneuver maniobra de Bracht.

Brandt-Andrews maneuver maniobra de Brandt-Andrews.

Buzzard's maneuver maniobra de Buzzard.

Credé's maneuver maniobra de Credé.

DeLee's maneuver maniobra de DeLee.

Ejrup maneuver maniobra de Ejrup.

Fowler maneuver maniobra de Fowler.

Gowers' maneuver maniobra de Gowers.

Halstead's maneuver maniobra de Halstead.

Hampton maneuver maniobra de Hampton.

Heimlich's maneuver maniobra de Heimlich.

Hoguet's maneuver maniobra de Hoguet.

Hueter's maneuver maniobra de Hueter.

Jendrassik's maneuver maniobra de Jendrassik.

key-in-lock maneuver maniobra de la llave en el cerrojo.

Kocher maneuver maniobra de Kocher.

Lasegue's maneuver maniobra de Lasegue.

Leopold's maneuver maniobra de Leopold.

Mauriceau's maneuver maniobra de Mauriceau.

Mauriceau-Smellie-Vett maneuver maniobra de Mauriceau-Smellie-Vett.

McDonald's maneuver maniobra de Mc Donald.

Müller's maneuver maniobra de Müller.

Munro Kerr maneuver maniobra de Munro Kerr.

Nägeli's maneuver maniobra de Nägeli.

Pajot's maneuver maniobra de Pajot, maniobra de Saxtorph.

Phalen's maneuver maniobra de Phalen.

Pinard's maneuver maniobra de Pinard.

Prague maneuver maniobra de Praga.

Pringle's maneuver maniobra de Pringle.

Ritgen's maneuver maniobra de Ritgen.

Scanzoni's maneuver maniobra de Scanzoni.

Schatz's maneuver maniobra de Schatz.

Schreiber's maneuver maniobra de Schreiber.

Sellick maneuver maniobra de Sellick.

Toynbee maneuver maniobra de Toynbee.

Valsalva's maneuver maniobra de Valsalva.

manganism *n.* manganesismo, manganismo.

mange *n.* mange.

demodectic mange mange demodéctico, mange folicular.

follicular mange mange demodéctico, mange folicular.

psoroptic mange mange psoróptico.

sarcoptic mange mange sarcóptico.

mania *n.* manía.

mania à potu manía a potu.

maniac *adj.* maníaco, -ca.

maniac-depressive *adj.* maniacodepresivo, -va.

manicy *n.* manicia.

manifestation *n.* manifestación.

manikin *n.* maniquí.

maniloquism *n.* manilocuismo.

maniphalanx *n.* manifalange.

manipulation *n.* manipulación.

conjoined manipulation manipulación conjunta.

genetic manipulation manipulación genética.

spinal manipulation manipulación vertebral.

mannerism *n.* manerismo, manierismo.

mannosidosis *n.* manosidosis.

manometer *n.* manómetro.

aneroid manometer manómetro aneroide.

dial manometer manómetro de dial.

differential manometer manómetro diferencial.

mercurial manometer manómetro de mercurio, manómetro mercurial.

manometric *adj.* manométrico, -ca.

manometry *n.* manometría.

manoptoscope *n.* manoptoscopio.

manoscopy *n.* manoscopia.

Mansonella Mansonella.

mansonelliasis *n.* mansoneliasis.

mansonellosis *n.* mansonelosis.

Mansonia Mansonia.

mantle *n.* manto.

manual *adj.* manual.

Bergey's manual manual de Bergey.

manubrium *n.* manubrio.

manudynamometer *n.* manodinamómetro, manudinamómetro.

manus mano, manus.

manus extensa mano extendida.

manus flexa mano en flexión.

manus plana mano plana.

manus superextensa mano superextendida.

manus valga mano valga.

manus vara mano vara.

map *n.* mapa.

bone map mapa óseo.

brain electric activity map (BEAM) mapa de actividad eléctrica cerebral (MAEC).

chromosomal map mapa cromosómico.

cognitive map mapa cognitivo.

cytologic map mapa citológico.

linkage map mapa de ligadura, mapa de ligamiento.

physical map mapa físico.

mapping *n.* mapeo.

marantic *adj.* marántico, -ca.

marasmatic *adj.* marasmático, -ca.

marasmic *adj.* marásmico, -ca.

marasmoid *adj.* marasmoide.

marasmus *n.* marasmo.

marble *adj.* marmóreo, -a.

marc *n.* bagazo.

marfanoid *adj.* marfanoide.

margin *n.* borde[4], margen.

anterior margin margen anterior.

ciliary margin margen ciliar.

inferior margin margen inferior.

margin of safety margen de seguridad.

pupillary margin of the iris margen pupilar del iris.

social margin margen social.

superior margin margen superior.

marginal *adj.* marginal, marginalis.

margination *n.* marginación.
marginoplasty *n.* marginoplastia.
margo *n.* borde[4], margen, margo.
marinotherapy *n.* marinoterapia.
mariposia *n.* mariposia.
mariscal *adj.* mariscal.
maritonucleus *n.* maritonúcleo.
mark *n.* marca.
  beauty mark marca de belleza.
  birth mark marca de nacimiento.
  Pohl's mark marca de Pohl.
  scoring mark marca lineal.
  strawberry mark marca de fresa, marca en frambuesa.
marker *n.* marcador.
  biochemical marker marcador bioquímico.
  cell-surface marker marcador celular de superficie.
  genetic marker marcador genético.
  tumor marker marcador tumoral.
marking *n.* marcación.
marmoreal *adj.* marmóreo, -a.
marmot *n.* marmota.
marmotte *n.* marmota.
marrow *n.* médula.
  depressed marrow médula deprimida.
  gelatinous marrow médula gelatinosa.
  red bone marrow médula ósea roja.
  red marrow médula roja.
  yellow bone marrow médula ósea amarilla.
marsupialization *n.* marsupialización.
maschaladenitis *n.* mascaladenitis.
maschalephidrosis *n.* mascalefidrosis.
maschalhyperhidrosis *n.* mascalhiperhidrosis.
maschaloncus mascaloma, mascalonco, mascaloncus.
masculinity *n.* masculinidad.
masculinization *n.* masculinización.
masculinize *v.* masculinizar.
masculinovoblastoma *n.* masculinovoblastoma.
MASER *n.* MASER.
  optic MASER MASER óptico.
mask *n.* máscara, mascarilla.
  BLB mask mascarilla BLB, mascarilla de Boothby-Lovelace-Bulbulia.
  Boothby-Lovelace-Bulbulian mask mascarilla BLB, mascarilla de Boothby-Lovelace-Bulbulia.
  ecchymotic mask máscara equimótica.
  full face mask mascarilla total de la cara.
  Hutchinson's mask mascarilla de Hutchinson.
  laringeal mask mascarilla laríngea.
  luetic mask máscara luética.
  mask of pregnancy máscara del embarazo.
  non-rebreathing mask máscara de sentido único, máscara respiratoria única.
  oxygen mask mascarilla de oxígeno.
  Parkinson's mask máscara de Parkinson.
  tabetic mask mascarilla tabética.
  tropical mask máscara tropical.
  Venturi's mask mascarilla de Venturi.
masked *adj.* enmascarado, -da.
masking *n.* enmascaramiento.
masochism *n.* masoquismo.
masochist *n.* masoquista.
masochistic *adj.* masoquístico, -ca.
mass *n.* masa, massa.
  achromatic mass masa acromática.
  appendiceal mass masa apendicular.
  appendix mass masa apendicular.
  atomic mass masa atómica.
  body cell mass masa de las células corporales.

cell mass masa celular.
  injection mass masa de inyección.
  inner cell mass masa celular interna.
  intermediate cell mass masa intermedia.
  lateral mass of atlas masa lateral de atlas.
  lean body mass masa magra, masa magra corporal.
  mass lateralis vertebrae masa vertebral lateral.
  pill mass masa de píldoras, masa pilular.
  pilular mass masa de píldoras, masa pilular.
  sclerotic cemental mass masa cementaria esclerótica.
  tigroid mass masa tigroide.
  tubular excretory mass masa excretoria tubular.
  ventrolateral mass masa ventrolateral.
massa *n.* masa, massa.
  massa innominata masa innominada.
  massa lateralis atlantis masa lateral de atlas.
massage *n.* masaje.
  cardiac massage masaje cardíaco.
  closed chest massage masaje a tórax cerrado.
  electrovibratory massage masaje electrovibratorio.
  external cardiac massage masaje cardíaco externo.
  gingival massage masaje gingival.
  heart massage masaje cardíaco.
  open chest massage masaje a tórax abierto.
  prostatic massage masaje prostático.
  Sweddish massage masaje sueco.
  vapor massage masaje de vapor.
  vibratory massage masaje vibratorio, vibroterapéutica.
masseteric *adj.* maseterino, -na.
masseur *n.* masajista.
massotherapy *n.* masoterapia.
mastadenitis *n.* mastadenitis.
mastadenoma *n.* mastadenoma.
Mastadenovirus Mastadenovirus.
mastalgia *n.* mastalgia.
mastatrophia *n.* mastatrofia.
mastatrophy *n.* mastatrofia.
mastauxe *n.* mastauxa.
mast-cell *n.* mastocito.
mastectomy *n.* mastectomía.
  extended radical mastectomy mastectomía radical ampliada.
  Halsted's mastectomy mastectomía de Halsted.
  mastectomy lumpectomy mastectomía lumpectomía.
  Meyer's mastectomy mastectomía de Meyer.
  modified radical mastectomy mastectomía radical modificada.
  radical mastectomy mastectomía radical.
  simple mastectomy mastectomía simple.
  subcutaneous mastectomy mastectomía subcutánea.
  total mastectomy mastectomía total.
masthelcosis *n.* mastelcosis.
mastication *n.* masticación.
masticatory *adj.* masticatorio, -ria.
mastigote *n.* mastigoto.
mastitis *n.* mastitis.
  acute mastitis mastitis aguda.
  chronic cystic mastitis mastitis quística crónica.
  chronic tuberculous mastitis mastitis tuberculosa crónica.
  cystic mastitis mastitis quística.
  gargantuan mastitis mastitis de Gargantúa, mastitis gigante.
  glandular mastitis mastitis glandular.

granulomatous mastitis mastitis granulomatosa.
  interstitial mastitis mastitis intersticial.
  mastitis neonatorum mastitis del recién nacido, mastitis neonatal.
  parenchymatous mastitis mastitis parenquimática, mastitis parenquimatosa.
  periductal mastitis mastitis periductal, mastitis retroareolar.
  phlegmonous mastitis mastitis flemonosa.
  plasma cell mastitis mastitis de células plasmáticas, mastitis plasmocitaria, mastitis plasmocítica.
  retromammary mastitis mastitis retromamaria.
  stagnation mastitis mastitis de estancamiento, mastitis estancada.
  submammary mastitis mastitis submamaria.
  suppurative mastitis mastitis supurativa.
mastocarcinoma *n.* mastocarcinoma.
mastochondroma *n.* mastocondroma, mastocondrosis.
mastocyte *n.* mastocito.
mastocytogenesis *n.* mastocitogénesis.
mastocytoma *n.* mastocitoma.
mastocytosis *n.* mastocitosis.
  diffuse cutaneous mastocytosis mastocitosis cutánea difusa.
  diffuse mastocytosis mastocitosis difusa.
  systemic mastocytosis mastocitosis sistémica.
mastodynia *n.* mastodinia.
mastogram *n.* mastograma.
mastography *n.* mastografía.
mastoid *adj.* mastoideo, -a.
mastoidalgia *n.* mastoidalgia.
mastoidectomy *n.* mastoidectomía.
  modified radical mastoidectomy mastoidectomía radical modificada.
  radical mastoidectomy mastoidectomía radical.
mastoideocentesis *n.* mastoideocentesis, mastoidocentesis.
mastoiditis *n.* mastoiditis.
  Bezold's mastoiditis mastoiditis de Bezold.
  sclerosing mastoiditis mastoiditis esclerosante.
  silent mastoiditis mastoiditis silenciosa.
mastoidotomy *n.* mastoidotomía.
mastoidotympanectomy *n.* mastoidotimpanectomía.
mastoncus mastonco, mastoncus.
mastooccipital *adj.* mastoccipital, mastooccipital.
mastoparietal *adj.* mastoparietal.
mastopathy *n.* mastopatía.
mastopexy *n.* mastopexia.
mastoplastia *n.* mastoplastia.
mastoplasty *n.* mastoplastia.
mastopsis *n.* mastoptosis.
mastoptosis *n.* mastoptosis.
mastorrhagia *n.* mastorragia.
mastoscirrhus *n.* mastocirrus, mastoscirro.
mastosis *n.* mastosis.
mastosquamous *adj.* mastoescamoso, -sa, mastoscamoso, -sa.
mastosyrinx *n.* mastosyrinx.
mastotic *adj.* mastótico, -ca.
mastotomy *n.* mastotomía.
masturbation *n.* masturbación.
materia *n.* materia.
  materia alba materia blanca.
material *n.* material.
  alloplastic material material aloplástico.
  base material material de base.
  baseplate material material de placa base.

crossreacting material (CRM) material de reacción cruzada.
dental material material dental.
genetic material material genético.
impression material material de impresión.
sharp material material punzante.
suture material material de sutura.
tissue equivalent material material equivalente de tejido.
maternal *adj.* maternal, materno, -na.
maternity *n.* maternidad.
mating *n.* apareamiento.
assortative mating apareamiento concordante, apareamiento selectivo.
assorted mating apareamiento concordante, apareamiento selectivo.
assortive mating apareamiento concordante, apareamiento selectivo.
matiniose *n.* matiniosa.
matlazahuatl *n.* matlazáhuatl.
matrass *n.* matraz.
matrical *adj.* matrical, matricial.
matricial *adj.* matricial.
matriclinous *adj.* matriclinoso, -sa.
matrilineal *adj.* matrilineal.
matrix *n.* matriz[1], matriz[2].
amalgam matrix matriz de amalgama.
bone matrix matriz ósea.
capsular matrix matriz capsular.
cartilage matrix matriz de cartílago.
cell matrix matriz celular.
cytoplasmic matrix matriz citoplasmática.
extracellular matrix matriz extracelular.
falling of the matrix matriz caída.
functional matrix matriz funcional.
hair matrix matriz de pelo.
interstitial matrix matriz intersticial.
interterritorial matrix matriz interterritorial.
matrix unguis matriz de la uña, matriz ungueal, matriz ungular.
mitochondrial matrix matriz mitocondrial.
nail matrix matriz de la uña, matriz ungueal, matriz ungular.
sarcoplasmic matrix matriz sarcoplásmica.
territorial matrix matriz territorial.
matroclinous *adj.* matróclino, -na.
matrocliny *n.* matroclinia.
matter *n.* materia.
maturant *n.* madurante.
maturation *n.* maduración.
affinity maturation maduración de afinidad.
bone maturation maduración ósea.
cervical maturation maduración cervical.
mature *adj.* madurar, maduro, -ra.
maxilla *n.* maxilar[1].
maxillary *adj.* maxilar[2].
maxillectomy *n.* maxilectomía.
maxillitis *n.* maxilitis.
maxillodental *adj.* maxilodental, maxilodentario, -ria.
maxilloethmoidectomy *n.* maxiloetmoidectomía.
maxillofacial *adj.* maxilofacial.
maxillojugal *adj.* maxiloyugal.
maxillolabial *adj.* maxilolabial.
maxillomandibular *adj.* maxilomandibular.
maxillopalatine *adj.* maxilopalatino, -na.
maxillopharyngeal *adj.* maxilofaríngeo, -a.
maxillotomy *n.* maxilotomía.
maximum *n.* máximo.
transport maximum (Tm) máximo transporte (Tm).
tubular maximum (Tm) máximo tubular (Tm).
mayidism *n.* mayidismo.
mazic *adj.* mácico, -ca.

mazolysis *n.* mazolisis.
mazopathy *n.* mazopatía.
mazoplasia *n.* mazoplasia.
meal *n.* comida.
mean *n.* media.
arithmetic mean media aritmética.
geometric mean media geométrica.
population mean media de la población.
sample mean media muestral.
standard error of the mean error estándar de la media.
measles *n.* sarampión.
atypical measles sarampión atípico.
black measles sarampión negro.
German measles sarampión alemán.
hemorrhagic measles sarampión hemorrágico.
three-day measles sarampión de los tres días.
tropical measles sarampión tropical.
measure *n.* medida.
measurement *n.* determinación[2], medición, valoración[2].
direct measurement of blood pressure determinación directa de la tensión arterial.
research measurement valoración de la investigación.
meatal *adj.* meatal.
meatomastoidectomy *n.* meatomastoidectomía.
meatome *n.* meátomo.
meatometer *n.* meatómetro.
meatoplasty *n.* meatoplastia.
meatorrhaphy *n.* meatorrafia.
meatoscope *n.* meatoscopio.
meatoscopy *n.* meatoscopia.
meatotome *n.* meatótomo.
meatotomy *n.* meatotomía.
meatus *n.* meato, meatus.
mecanotherapy *n.* mecanoterapia.
mechanical *adj.* mecánico, -ca.
mechanicoreceptor *n.* mecanicorreceptor.
mechanicotherapeutics *n.* mecanicoterapeútica.
mechanicotherapy *n.* mecanicoterapeútica.
mechanics *n.* mecánica.
animal mechanics mecánica animal.
body mechanics mecánica corporal.
developmental mechanics mecánica del desarrollo.
quantum mechanics mecánica cuántica.
mechanism *n.* mecanismo.
countercurrent mechanism mecanismo a contra corriente.
defense mechanism mecanismo de defensa.
double displacement mechanism mecanismo de doble desplazamiento.
Douglas mechanism mecanismo de Douglas.
Duncan's mechanism mecanismo de Duncan.
escape mechanism mecanismo de escape.
Frank-Starling mechanism mecanismo de Frank-Starling.
gating mechanism mecanismo de compuerta.
host defense mechanism mecanismo de defensa del huésped.
immunological mechanism mecanismo inmunológico.
mechanism of labor mecanismo del parto.
mechanism of urine concentration mecanismo de concentración urinaria.
mental mechanism mecanismo mental.
oculogyric mechanism mecanismo oculógiro.
pain mechanism mecanismo del dolor.
ping-pong reaction mechanism mecanismo de reacción de ping-pong.

ping-pong mechanism mecanismo de ping-pong.
proprioceptive mechanism mecanismo propioceptivo.
reentrant mechanism mecanismo reentrante.
Schultze's mechanism mecanismo de Schultze.
mechanocardiography *n.* mecanocardiografía.
mechanocyte *n.* mecanocito.
mechanogymnastics *n.* mecanogimnasia.
mechanophobia *n.* mecanofobia.
mechanoreceptor *n.* mecanorreceptor.
mechanoreflex *n.* mecanorreflejo.
mechanotherapy *n.* mecanoterapia.
mechanothermy *n.* mecanotermia.
mecism *n.* mecismo.
mecistocephalic *adj.* mecistocéfalo, la.
mecistocephalous *adj.* mecistocéfalo, -la.
meckelectomy *n.* meckelectomía.
mecocephalic *adj.* mecocéfalo, -la.
mecocephaly *n.* mecocefalia.
mecometer *n.* mecómetro.
meconiorrhea *n.* meconiorrea.
meconism *n.* meconismo.
meconium *n.* meconio.
mecystasis *n.* mecistasia.
mediad *adj.* mediad.
medial *adj.* medial.
medialecithal *adj.* medialecital.
medialecithe *n.* medialecito.
medialis *adj.* medial.
mediameter *n.* mediámetro.
median *adj.* mediana, mediano, -na.
mediastinal *adj.* mediastínico, -ca.
mediastinitis *n.* mediastinitis.
fibrous mediastinitis mediastinitis fibrosa.
idiopathic fibrous mediastinitis mediastinitis fibrosa idiopática.
indurative mediastinitis mediastinitis indurativa.
mediastinogram *n.* mediastinograma.
mediastinography *n.* mediastinografía.
mediastinopericarditis *n.* mediastinopericarditis.
mediastinoscope *n.* mediastinoscopio.
mediastinoscopic *adj.* mediastinoscópico, -ca.
mediastinoscopy *n.* mediastinoscopia.
mediastinotomy *n.* mediastinotomía.
mediastinum *n.* mediastino.
mediate *v.* mediar.
mediation *n.* mediación.
mediator *n.* mediador.
medicable *adj.* medicable.
medical *adj.* médico, -ca.
medical consultation interconsulta médica.
medical illustrator ilustrador médico.
medicamentous *adj.* medicamentoso, -sa.
medicated *adj.* medicado, -da.
medication *n.* medicación.
arrhenic medication medicación arrénica.
conservative medication medicación conservadora.
hypodermic medication medicación hipodérmica.
intravenous medication medicación intravenosa.
ionic medication medicación iónica.
preanesthetic medication medicación preanestésica.
sublingual medication medicación sublingual.
substitutive medication medicación derivativa, medicación sustitutiva.
transduodenal medication medicación transduodenal.

medicator *n.* medicador.
medicinal *adj.* medicinal.
medicine *n.* medicamento, medicina.
  aerospace medicine medicina aeroespacial, medicina aeronáutica.
  allopathic medicine medicina alopática.
  alternative medicine medicina alternativa.
  aviation medicine medicina de aviación, medicina de la aviación.
  behavioral medicine medicina de la conducta, medicina del comportamiento.
  clinical medicine medicina clínica.
  comparative medicine medicina comparada.
  compound medicine medicamento compuesto.
  defensive medicine medicina defensiva.
  dosimetric medicine medicina dosimétrica.
  emergency medicine medicina de urgencia.
  environmental medicine medicina ambiental.
  evidence based medicine medicina basada en la evidencia.
  experimental medicine medicina experimental.
  family medicine medicina de familia, medicina familiar.
  fetal medicine medicina fetal.
  forensic medicine medicina forense.
  geriatric medicine medicina geriátrica.
  holistic medicine medicina holística.
  hyperbaric medicine medicina hiperbárica.
  internal medicine medicina interna.
  ionic medicine medicina iónica.
  legal medicine medicina legal.
  medicine community medicina comunitaria.
  military medicine medicina militar.
  neonatal medicine medicina neonatal.
  nuclear medicine medicina nuclear.
  occupational medicine medicina del trabajo.
  osteopathic medicine medicina osteopática.
  patent medicine medicamento sin receta.
  pediatric medicine medicina pediátrica.
  perinatal medicine medicina perinatal.
  physical medicine medicina física.
  preclinical medicine medicina preclínica.
  preventive medicine medicina preventiva.
  proprietary medicine medicamento patentado.
  prospective medicine medicina prospectiva.
  psychosomatic medicine medicina psicosomática.
  rational medicine medicina racional.
  scientific medicine medicina ciéntifica.
  social medicine medicina social.
  socialized medicine medicina socializada.
  space medicine medicina espacial.
  sports medicine medicina del deporte, medicina deportiva.
  state medicine medicina estatal.
  tropical medicine medicina tropical.
medicobiologic *adj.* medicobiológico, -ca.
medicobiological *adj.* medicobiológico, -ca.
medicochirurgical *adj.* medicoquirúrgico, -ca.
medicodental *adj.* medicodental.
medicolegal *adj.* medicolegal.
medicomechanical *adj.* medicomecánico, -ca.
medicosocial *adj.* medicosocial.
medicotopographical *adj.* medicotopográfico, -ca.
medicozoological *adj.* medicozoológico, -ca.
medifrontal *adj.* mediofrontal.
mediocarpal *adj.* mediocarpiano, -na.
mediodens *n.* mediodens.
mediolateral *adj.* mediolateral.

medionecrosis *n.* medionecrosis.
medio-occipital *adj.* mediooccipital.
mediotarsal *adj.* mediotarsiano, -na.
mediotrusion *n.* mediotrusión.
mediotype *n.* mediotipo.
medisect *n.* medisección, mediseccionar.
medium *n.* medio, medium.
  active medium medio activo.
  clearing medium medio aclarador, medio aclarante.
  complete medium medio completo.
  contrast medium medio de contraste.
  culture medium medio de cultivo.
  disperse medium medio de dispersión.
  dispersion medium medio de dispersión.
  dispersive medium medio de dispersión.
  external medium medio externo.
  motility test medium medio para prueba de motilidad.
  mounting medium medio de montaje, medio montador.
  passive medium medio pasivo.
  radioactive contrast medium medio de contraste radiactivo.
  radiolucent medium medio radiolúcido.
  radiopaque medium medio radioopaco.
  selective medium medio selectivo.
  separating medium medio de separación, medio separador.
  support medium medio de soporte.
  transport medium medio de transporte.
  Wickersheimer medium medio de Wickersheimer.
medulla *n.* médula.
medullary *adj.* medular.
medullated *adj.* medulado, -da.
medullation *n.* medulación.
medullectomy *n.* medulectomía.
medulliadrenal *adj.* meduloadrenal.
medullitis *n.* medulitis.
medullization *n.* medulización.
medulloadrenal *adj.* meduloadrenal.
medulloarthritis *n.* meduloartritis.
medulloblast *n.* meduloblasto.
medulloblastoma *n.* meduloblastoma.
medullocell *n.* medulocélula.
medulloencephalic *adj.* meduloencefálico, -ca.
medulloepithelioma *n.* meduloepitelioma.
medulloid *adj.* meduloide.
medullomyoblastoma *n.* medulomioblastoma.
medullosuprarenoma *n.* medulosuprarrenoma.
medullotherapy *n.* meduloterapia.
megabacterium *n.* megabacteria.
megabladder *n.* megavejiga.
megacalycosis *n.* megacalicosis, megacaliosis.
megacardia *n.* megacardia.
megacecum *n.* megaciego.
megacephalic *adj.* megacefálico, -ca.
megacephalous *adj.* megacéfalo, -la.
megacephaly *n.* megacefalia.
megacholedochus *n.* megacolédoco.
megaclitoris *n.* megaclítoris.
megacoccus *n.* megacoco.
megacolon *n.* megacolon, megalocolia.
  acquired functional megacolon megacolon adquirido funcional.
  acquired megacolon megacolon adquirido.
  acute megacolon megacolon agudo.
  aganglionic megacolon megacolon aganglionar, megacolon agangliónico.
  congenital megacolon megacolon congénito.

  idiopathic megacolon megacolon idiopático.
  megacolon congenitum megacolon congénito.
  toxic megacolon megacolon tóxico.
megacystis *n.* megacistis.
megadactylia *n.* megadactilia.
megadactylism *n.* megadactilia.
megadactyly *n.* megadactilia.
megadolichocolon *n.* megadolicocolon.
megadont *n.* megadonte, megadonto.
megadontia *n.* megadoncia.
megadontic *adj.* megadóntico, -ca.
megadontism *n.* megadontismo.
megadose *n.* megadosis.
megaduodenum *n.* megaduodeno.
megaesophagus *n.* megaesófago.
megagamete *n.* megagameto.
megagnathia *n.* megagnatia.
megakaryoblast *n.* megacarioblasto.
megakaryocite *n.* megacariocito.
megakaryocyte *n.* megalocariocito.
megakaryocytopoiesis *n.* megacariocitopoyesis.
megakaryocytosis *n.* megacariocitosis.
megalakria *n.* megalacria.
megalecithal *adj.* megalecítico, -ca, megalecito, -ta.
megalencephaly *n.* megaloencefalia.
megalgia *n.* megalgia.
megaloblast *n.* megaloblasto.
megaloblastoid *adj.* megaloblastoide.
megalocardia *n.* megalocardia.
megalocephalic *adj.* megalocefálico, -ca.
megalocephaly *n.* megalocefalia.
megalocheiria *n.* megaloqueiria, megaloquiria.
megalochiria *n.* megaloqueiria, megaloquiria.
megaloclitoris *n.* megaloclítoris.
megalocornea *n.* megalocórnea.
megalocystis *n.* megalocisto.
megalocyte *n.* megalocito.
megalocythemia *n.* megalocitemia.
megalocytosis *n.* megalocitosis.
megalodactylia *n.* megalodactilia.
megalodactylism *n.* megalodactilismo.
megalodactyly *n.* megalodactilia.
megalodontia *n.* megalodoncia.
megaloencephalic *adj.* megaloencefálico, -ca.
megaloencephalon *n.* megaloencéfalo.
megaloenteron *n.* megaloenterón.
megaloesophagus *n.* megaloesófago.
megalogastria *n.* megalogastria.
megaloglossia *n.* megaloglosia.
megalographia *n.* megalografía.
megalography *n.* megalografía.
megalomania *n.* megalomanía.
megalomaniac *adj.* megalomaníaco, -ca, megalómano, -na.
megalomelia *n.* megalomelia.
megalonychia *n.* megaloniquia.
megalonychosis *n.* megalonicosis.
megalopenis *n.* megalopene.
megalophallus *n.* megalofalo.
megalophtalmus *n.* megaloftalmo.
megalophthalmos *n.* megaloftalmía.
  anterior megalophthalmos megaloftalmía anterior.
megalopia *n.* megalopía.
megalopodia *n.* megalopodia.
megalopsia *n.* megalopsia.
Megalopyge Megalopyge.
  Megalopyge opercularis Megalopyge opercularis.
megaloscope *n.* megaloscopio.
megalosplanchnic *adj.* megaloesplácnico, megalosplácnico, -ca.

megalosplenia *n.* megaloesplenia, megalosplenia.
megalosyndactyly *n.* megalosindactilia.
megaloureter *n.* megalouréter.
megalourethra *n.* megalouretra.
megamerozoite *n.* megamerozoíto.
meganucleus *n.* meganúcleo.
megaophthalmos *n.* megaoftalmía.
megaprosopia *n.* megaprosopia.
megaprosopous *adj.* megaprosópico, -ca, megaprosopo, -pa.
megarectum *n.* megarrecto.
Megaselia Megaselia.
megaseme *n.* megasema, megasemo.
megasigmoid *n.* megasigmoide.
megasoma *n.* megasoma.
megasomia *n.* megasomía.
megathrombocyte *n.* megatrombocito.
megaureter *n.* megauréter.
megaurethra *n.* megauretra.
megavitamin *n.* megavitamina.
megavoltage *n.* megavoltaje.
megoxicyte *n.* megoxicito.
megoxyphil *n.* megoxífilo.
mehlnährschaden *n.* mehlnährschaden.
meibomianitis *n.* mebiomianitis.
meibomitis *n.* meibomitis.
meicephalalgia *n.* hemicefalalgia.
meiocyte *n.* meiocito.
meiogenic *adj.* meiogénico, -ca, meiógeno, -na.
meiosis *n.* meiosis.
meiotic *adj.* meiótico, -ca.
melagra *n.* melagra.
melalgia *n.* melalgia.
melanedema *n.* melanoedema, -ma.
melanemesis *n.* melanemesis.
melanemia *n.* melanemia.
melanidrosis *n.* melanidrosis.
melaniferous *adj.* melanífero, -ra.
melanin *n.* melanina.
artificial melanin melanina artificial, melanina ficticia.
factitious melanin melanina artificial, melanina ficticia.
melanism *n.* melanismo.
melanistic *adj.* melanístico, -ca.
melano *n.* melano.
melanoacanthoma *n.* melanoacantoma.
melanoameloblastoma *n.* melanoameloblastoma.
melanoblast *n.* melanoblasto.
melanoblastoma *n.* melanoblastoma.
melanoblastosis *n.* melanoblastosis.
melanocarcinoma *n.* melanocarcinoma.
melanocomous *adj.* melanocomo, -ca.
melanocyte *n.* melanocito.
dendritic melanocyte melanocito dendrítico.
melanocytic *adj.* melanocítico, -ca.
melanocytoma *n.* melanocitoma.
compound melanocytoma melanocitoma compuesto.
dermal melanocytoma melanocitoma dérmico.
melanocytoma of the optic disk melanocitoma del disco óptico.
melanocytosis *n.* melanocitosis.
melanocytosis toxica lichenoides melanocitosis tóxica liquenoide.
oculodermal melanocytosis melanocitosis oculodérmica.
melanodendrocyte *n.* melanodendrocito.
melanoderm *n.* melanodermo.
melanoderma *n.* melanodermia.
melanoderma cachecticorum melanodermia caquéctica.

parasitic melanoderma melanodermia parasitaria.
racial melanoderma melanodermia racial.
senile melanoderma melanodermia senil.
melanodermatitis *n.* melanodermatitis.
melanodermatitis toxica lichenoides melanodermatitis tóxica liquenoide.
melanodermic *adj.* melanodérmico, -ca.
melanoepithelioma *n.* melanoepitelioma.
melanogen *n.* melanógeno.
melanogenemia *n.* melanogenemia.
melanogenesis *n.* melanogénesis.
melanogenic *adj.* melanogénico, -ca.
melanoglossia *n.* melanoglosia.
melanohidrosis *n.* melanohidrosis.
melanoid *n.* melanoide.
melanokeratosis *n.* melanoqueratosis.
Melanolestes Melanolestes.
Melanolestes picipes Melanolestes picipes.
melanoleukoderma *n.* melanoleucodermia.
melanoleukoderma colli melanoleucodermia cervical, melanoleucodermia colli.
melanoma *n.* melanoma.
acral lentiginous melanoma melanoma acral lentiginoso, melanoma lentiginoso acral.
amelanic melanoma melanoma amelánico, melanoma amelanótico.
amelanotic melanoma melanoma amelánico, melanoma amelanótico.
benign juvenile melanoma melanoma juvenil, melanoma juvenil benigno.
choroidal malignant melanoma melanoma coroideo maligno.
choroidal melanoma melanoma de úvea.
Cloudman melanoma melanoma de Cloudman.
Cloudman's S 91 melanoma melanoma S91 de Cloudman.
halo melanoma melanoma de aureola, melanoma de halo.
Harding-Passey melanoma melanoma de Harding-Passey.
in situ malignant melanoma melanoma maligno in situ.
in-situ melanoma melanoma in situ.
juvenile melanoma melanoma juvenil, melanoma juvenil benigno.
lentigo maligna melanoma melanoma de léntigo maligno.
malignant melanoma melanoma maligno, melanoscirro.
minimal deviation melanoma melanoma con desviación mínima.
nodular melanoma melanoma nodular.
primary cutaneous melanoma melanoma cutáneo primario.
subungual melanoma melanoma subungueal, melanoma subungular.
superficial spreading melanoma melanoma de extensión superficial.
melanomatosis *n.* melanomatosis.
melanomatous *adj.* melanomatoso, -sa.
melanonichya *n.* melanoniquia.
melanopathy *n.* melanopatía.
melanophage *n.* melanófago.
melanophore *n.* melanóforo.
melanophorin *n.* melanoforina.
melanoplakia *n.* melanoplaquia, melanoplasia.
melanoprecipitation *n.* melanoprecipitación.
melanoptysis *n.* melanoptisis.
melanorrhagia *n.* melanorragia.
melanorrhea *n.* melanorrea.
melanosarcoma *n.* melanosarcoma.
melanosarcomatosis *n.* melanosarcomatosis.

melanoscirrhus *n.* melanoescirro.
melanosis *n.* melanosis.
circumscribed precancerous melanosis of Dubreuilh melanosis precancerosa circunscrita de Dubreuilh.
conjunctival melanosis melanosis conjuntival.
melanosis circumscripta precancerosa melanosis circunscrita precancerosa.
melanosis coli melanosis coli, melanosis de colon.
melanosis corii degenerativa melanosis corii degenerativa.
melanosis iridis melanosis del iris, melanosis iridiana.
melanosis lenticularis progressiva melanosis progresiva lenticular.
melanosis of the iris melanosis del iris, melanosis iridiana.
melanosis recti nigrosis rectal.
neonatal pustular melanosis melanosis pustulosa neonatal.
neurocutaneous melanosis melanosis neurocutánea.
oculocutaneous melanosis melanosis oculocutánea, melanosis oculodérmica.
oculodermal melanosis melanosis oculocutánea, melanosis oculodérmica.
precancerous melanosis of Dubreuilh melanosis precancerosa de Dubreuilh.
Riehl's melanosis melanosis de Riehl.
tar melanosis melanosis por alquitrán.
melanosity *n.* melanosidad.
melanosome *n.* melanosoma.
giant melanosome melanosoma de células gigantes.
melanotic *adj.* melanótico, -ca.
melanotonin *n.* melanotonina.
melanotrichia *n.* melanotriquia.
melanotrichous *adj.* melanotrico, -ca.
melanotroph *n.* melanotrofo.
melanotropic *adj.* melanotrópico, -ca.
melanotropin *n.* melanotrofina, melanotropina.
melanuresis *n.* melanuresis.
melanuric *adj.* melanúrico, -ca.
melanurie *n.* melanuria.
melanurin *n.* melanurina.
melasma *n.* melasma.
melasma addisonnii melasma addisoniano, melasma de Addison.
melasma gravidarum melasma gravídico, melasma uterino.
melasma suprarenale melasma suprarrenal.
melasma universale melasma universal.
melatonin *n.* melatonina.
melena *n.* melena.
melena neonatorum melena del recién nacido, melena neonatal.
melena spuria melena espuria, melena falsa.
melena vera melena verdadera.
melenemesis *n.* melenémesis.
melenic *adj.* melénico, -ca.
melicera *n.* melicera.
meliceris *n.* melicera, meliceris.
melioidosis *n.* melioidosis.
acuta melioidosis melioidosis aguda.
chronic melioidosis melioidosis crónica.
melissophobia *n.* melisofobia.
melissotherapy *n.* melisoterapia.
melitis *n.* melitis.
melitoptyalism *n.* melitoptialismo.
melitoptyalon *n.* melitoptialón.
melocervicoplasty *n.* melocervicoplastia.
melodidymus *n.* melodídimo.

melomelia *n.* melomelia.
melomelus *n.* melómelo.
meloncus *n.* melonco.
meloplasty *n.* meloplastia.
melorheostosis *n.* melorreostosis.
melosalgia *n.* melosalgia.
meloschisis *n.* melosquisis.
melotia *n.* melotia.
member *n.* miembro.
 phantom member miembro fantasma.
 siren member miembro sirena.
 virile member miembro viril.
membrana *n.* membrana.
 membrana perforata membrana perforada.
 membrana preformativa membrana preformativa.
 membrana pupilaris membrana pupilar.
 membranae deciduae decidua.
membranaceous *adj.* membranáceo, -a.
membranate *adj.* membranado, -da.
membrane *n.* membrana.
 alveolocapillary membrane membrana alveolocapilar.
 animal membrane membrana animal.
 aponeurotic membrane membrana aponeurótica.
 arachnoid membrane membrana aracnoidea.
 basement membrane membrana fundamental.
 biocompatible membrane of dialysis membrana de diálisis biocompatible.
 birth membrane membrana del nacimiento.
 cell membrane membrana celular.
 closing membrane membrana de cierre.
 croupous membrane membrana cruposa.
 cyclitic membrane membrana ciclítica.
 dentinoenamel membrane membrana de dentina y esmalte.
 diphtheritic membrane membrana diftérica.
 dysmenorrheal membrane membrana dismenorreica.
 egg membrane membrana del huevo.
 embryonic membrane membrana embrionaria.
 endoneural membrane membrana endoneural.
 epipapillary membrane membrana epipapilar.
 epiretinal membrane membrana epirretinal.
 external limiting membrane membrana limitante externa.
 extraembryonic membrane membrana extraembrionaria, membrana fetal.
 fetal membrane membrana extraembrionaria, membrana fetal.
 fusca membrane membrana fusca.
 germinal membrane membrana germinal, membrana germinativa.
 gradocol membrane membrana de gradocol.
 Haller's membrane membrana de Haller.
 Heuser's membrane membrana de Heuser.
 hyaline membrane membrana hialina.
 internal limiting membrane membrana limitante interna.
 Jackson's membrane membrana de Jackson.
 keratogenous membrane membrana queratógena.
 limiting membrane of the neural tube membrana limitante del tubo neural.
 Nitabuch's membrane membrana de Nitabuch.
 nuclear membrane membrana nuclear.
 outer limiting membrane membrana limitante externa.

 placental membrane membrana placentaria.
 plasma membrane membrana plasmática.
 pleuropericardial membrane membrana pleuropericárdica.
 pleuroperitoneal membrane membrana pleuroperitoneal.
 presynaptic membrane membrana presináptica.
 pyogenic membrane membrana piógena.
 pyophylactic membrane membrana piofiláctica.
 semipermeable membrane of dialysis membrana de diálisis semipermeable.
 urogenital membrane membrana genitourinaria, membrana urogenital.
 urorectal membrane membrana urorrectal.
 viteline membrane membrana vitelina.
 Volkmann's membrane membrana de Volkmann.
membranectomy *n.* membranectomía.
membranella *n.* membranela.
membraniform *adj.* membraniforme.
membranin *n.* membranina.
membranocartilaginous *adj.* membranocartilaginoso, -sa.
membranoid *adj.* membranoide.
membranolysis *n.* membranólisis.
membranous *adj.* membranoso, -sa.
membrum *n.* miembro.
 membrum inferius miembro inferior.
 membrum muliebre miembro de la mujer.
 membrum superius miembro superior.
 membrum virile miembro viril.
memory *n.* memoria.
 affect memory memoria afectiva.
 anterograde memory memoria anterógrada.
 direct-access memory memoria de acceso directo.
 echoic memory memoria ecoica.
 eye memory memoria ocular.
 inmunologic memory memoria inmunológica.
 kinesthetic memory memoria cinestésica.
 long term memory (LTM) memoria a largo plazo (MLP).
 random-access memory (RAM) memoria de acceso aleatorio (RAM).
 read-only memory (ROM) memoria sólo de lectura (ROM).
 remote memory memoria remota.
 retrograde memory memoria retrógrada.
 screen memory memoria de pantalla, memoria protectora.
 selective memory memoria selectiva.
 senile memory memoria senil.
 short-term memory (STM) memoria a corto plazo (MCP).
 subconscious memory memoria subconsciente.
 visual memory memoria visual.
menacme *n.* menacma.
menalgia *n.* menalgia.
menaquinone (MK) *n.* menaquinona (MK).
menarchal *adj.* menarcal.
menarche *n.* menarca, menarquia, menarquía.
menarcheal *adj.* menárquico, -ca.
menarchial *adj.* menárquico, -ca.
Mendelian *adj.* mendeliano, -na.
Mendelism *n.* mendelismo.
mendelizing *adj.* mendelizante.
menhidrosis *n.* menhidrosis.
meningeal *adj.* meníngeo, -a.
meningematoma *n.* meningohematoma.
meningeocortical *adj.* meningeocortical.
meningeoma *n.* meningeoma, meningioma.

meningeorrhaphy *n.* meningeorrafia.
meninginitis *n.* meninginitis.
meningioma *n.* meningioma.
 angioblastic meningioma meningioma angioblástico.
 cutaneous meningioma meningioma cutáneo.
 optic nerve meningioma meningioma del nervio óptico.
 orbit meningioma meningioma orbitario.
 psammomatous meningioma meningioma psamomatoso.
 spinal meningioma meningioma intrarraquídeo, meningioma raquídeo.
 ventricular meningioma meningioma intraventricular.
meningiomatosis *n.* meningiomatosis.
meningism *n.* meningismo.
meningitic *adj.* meningítico, -ca.
meningitis *n.* meningitis.
 acute aseptic meningitis meningitis aséptica, meningitis aséptica aguda.
 aseptic meningitis meningitis aséptica, meningitis aséptica aguda.
 bacterial meningitis meningitis bacteriana.
 basilar meningitis meningitis basal, meningitis basilar.
 carcinomatous meningitis meningitis carcinomatosa.
 cerebral meningitis meningitis cerebral.
 cerebrospinal meningitis meningitis cefalorraquídea, meningitis cerebroespinal.
 eosinophilic meningitis meningitis eosinófila.
 epidemic cerebrospinal meningitis meningitis cefalorraquídea epidémica, meningitis cerebroespinal epidémica.
 gummatous meningitis meningitis gomatosa.
 listeria meningitis meningitis listeria.
 lymphocytic meningitis meningitis linfocítica, meningitis linfocítica benigna.
 meningitis ossificans meningitis osificante.
 meningitis serosa circumscripta meningitis serosa circunscrita, meningitis serosa circunscrita quística.
 meningitis sympathica meningitis simpática.
 meningococcal meningitis meningitis meningocócica.
 Mollaret's meningitis meningitis de Mollaret.
 neoplastic meningitis meningitis neoplásica.
 occlusive meningitis meningitis oclusiva.
 otitic meningitis meningitis otítica.
 plague meningitis meningitis por peste.
 pneumococcal meningitis meningitis neumocócica.
 purulent meningitis meningitis purulenta.
 Quincke's meningitis meningitis de Quincke.
 serous meningitis meningitis serosa.
 spinal meningitis meningitis espinal.
 sterile meningitis meningitis estéril.
 traumatic meningitis meningitis traumática.
 tubercular meningitis meningitis tuberculosa.
 tuberculous meningitis meningitis tuberculosa.
 viral meningitis meningitis viral, meningitis virásica.
meningoarteritis *n.* meningoarteritis.
meningoblastoma *n.* meningoblastoma.
meningocele *n.* meningocele.
 cranial meningocele meningocele craneal.
 spinal meningocele meningocele raquídeo.
 spurious meningocele meningocele espurio.

traumatic meningocele meningocele traumático.
meningocerebritis *n.* meningocerebritis.
meningococcemia *n.* meningococemia, meningococia.
acute fulminating meningococcemia meningococemia fulminante aguda.
meningococci *n.* meningococo.
meningococcosis *n.* meningococosis.
meningocortical *adj.* meningocortical.
meningocystocele *n.* meningocistocele.
meningocyte *n.* meningocito.
meningoencephalitis *n.* meningoencefalitis.
acute primary hemorrhagic meningoencephalitis meningoencefalitis hemorrágica primaria aguda.
biundulant meningoencephalitis meningoencefalitis biondulante.
herpetic meningoencephalitis meningoencefalitis herpética.
mumps meningoencephalitis meningoencefalitis de las paperas, meningoencefalitis por parotiditis.
primary amebic meningoencephalitis meningoencefalitis amebiana primaria.
syphilitic meningoencephalitis meningoencefalitis sifilítica.
meningoencephalocele *n.* meningoencefalocele.
meningoencephalomyelitis *n.* meningoencefalomielitis.
meningoencephalomyelopathy *n.* meningoencefalomielopatía.
meningoencephalopathy *n.* meningoencefalopatía.
meningofibroblastoma *n.* meningofibroblastoma.
meningogenic *adj.* meningógeno, -na.
meningoma *n.* meningioma, meningoma.
meningomalacia *n.* meningomalacia.
meningomyelitis *n.* meningomielitis.
meningomyelocele *n.* meningomielocele.
meningomyeloencephalitis *n.* meningomieloencefalitis.
meningomyeloradiculitis *n.* meningomielorradiculitis.
meningo-osteophlebitis *n.* meningoosteoflebitis, meningosteoflebitis.
meningopathy *n.* meningopatía.
meningorachidian *adj.* meningorraquídeo, -a.
meningoradicular *adj.* meningorradicular.
meningoradiculitis *n.* meningorradiculitis.
meningorrhagia *n.* meningorragia.
meningorrhaphy *n.* meningorrafia.
meningosis *n.* meningosis.
meningothelioma *n.* meningotelioma.
meningovascular *adj.* meningovascular.
meninguria *n.* meninguria.
meninx *n.* meninge.
meninx primitiva meninge primitiva.
meniscal *adj.* meniscal.
meniscectomy *n.* meniscectomía.
menischesis *n.* menisquesis.
meniscitis *n.* meniscitis.
meniscocyte *n.* meniscocito.
meniscocytosis *n.* meniscocitosis.
meniscorrhaphy *n.* meniscorrafia.
meniscosynovial *adj.* meniscosinovial.
meniscotome *n.* meniscótomo.
meniscus *n.* menisco.
menocelis *n.* menocelis.
menometrorrhagia *n.* menometrorragia.
menopausal *adj.* menopáusico, -ca.
menopause *n.* menopausia, menopausis.

artificial menopause menopausia artificial.
male menopause menopausia masculina.
menopause praecox menopausia precoz, menopausia prematura.
surgical menopause menopausia quirúrgica.
menophania *n.* menofanía.
menoplania *n.* menometástasis, menoplanía.
menorralgia *n.* menorralgia.
menorrhagia *n.* menorragia.
menorrhea *n.* menorrea.
menorrheal *adj.* menorreico, -ca.
menoschesis *n.* menosquesia, menosquesis.
menostasia *n.* menostasia.
menostasis *n.* menostasia, menostasis.
menostaxis *n.* menostaxis.
menotropin *n.* menotropina.
menouria *n.* menouria.
menoxenia *n.* menoxenia.
menstrual *adj.* menstrual, menstrualis.
menstruant *adj.* menstruante.
menstruate *v.* menstruar.
menstruation *n.* menstruación.
anovular menstruation menstruación anovular, menstruación anovulatoria.
anovulatory menstruation menstruación anovular, menstruación anovulatoria.
delayed menstruation menstruación retrasada.
difficult menstruation menstruación difícil.
non-ovulational menstruation menstruación no ovulatoria, menstruación sin ovulación.
regurgitant menstruation menstruación regurgitante, menstruación retrógrada.
retrograde menstruation menstruación regurgitante, menstruación retrógrada.
supplementary menstruation menstruación complementaria, menstruación suplementaria.
suppressed menstruation menstruación suprimida.
vicarious menstruation menstruación sustitutiva, menstruación vicariante.
menstruous *adj.* menstruoso, -sa.
menstruum *n.* menstruo.
mental *adj.* mental, mentoniano, -na.
mentalis *adj.* mentoniano, -na.
mentality *n.* mentalidad.
mentation *n.* mentación.
menticide *n.* menticida.
mentimeter *n.* mentímetro.
mentolabial *adj.* mentolabial.
menton *n.* mentón.
mentoplasty *n.* mentoplastia.
mentotransverse *adj.* mentotransversa.
mentula *n.* méntula.
mentulagra *n.* mentulagra.
mentulate *n.* mentulado.
mentum *n.* mentón.
mephitis *n.* fetidez.
meralgia *n.* meralgia.
meralgia paresthetica meralgia parestésica.
mercurialism *n.* mercurialismo.
mercurialization *n.* mercurialización.
mercurialized *adj.* mercurializado, -da.
mercuric *adj.* mercúrico, -ca.
mercurous *adj.* mercurioso, -sa.
mercury *n.* mercurio.
merergasia *n.* merergasia.
merergastic *adj.* merergástico, -ca.
merisis *n.* merisis.
merism *n.* merismo.
meristic *adj.* merístico, -ca.
meroacrania *n.* meroacrania.
meroanencephaly *n.* meroanencefalia.

meroblastic *adj.* meroblástico, -ca.
merocele *n.* merocele.
merocoxalgia *n.* merocoxalgia.
merocrine *adj.* merocrino, -na.
merocyst *n.* merocisto.
merocyte *n.* merocito.
merodiastolic *adj.* merodiastólico, -ca.
meroergasia *n.* meroergasia.
merogamy *n.* merogamia.
merogastrula *n.* merogástrula.
merogenesis *n.* merogénesis.
merogenetic *adj.* merogenético, -ca.
merogenic *adj.* merogénico, -ca.
merogonic *adj.* merogónico, -ca.
merogony *n.* merogonia.
diploid merogony merogonia diploide.
parthenogenetic merogony merogonia partenogenética.
merology *n.* merología.
meromelia *n.* meromelia.
meromicrosomia *n.* meromicrosomía.
meromorphosis *n.* meromorfosis.
meromyosin *n.* meromiosina.
meronecrobiosis *n.* meronecrobiosis.
meronecrosis *n.* meronecrosis.
meropia *n.* meropía, meropsia.
merorachischisis *n.* merorraquisquisis.
meroscope *n.* meroscopio.
meroscopy *n.* meroscopia.
merosmia *n.* meroosmia, merosmia.
merostotic *adj.* merosteósico, -ca.
merosystolic *adj.* merosistólico, -ca.
merotomy *n.* merotomía.
merozoite *n.* merozoíto.
Merulius lacrymans merulius lacrymans.
merycism *n.* mericismo.
mesad mesad.
mesal *adj.* mesal.
mesangial *adj.* mesangial.
mesangiocapillary *adj.* mesangiocapilar.
mesangium *n.* mesangio.
extraglomerular mesangium mesangio extraglomerular.
mesaortitis *n.* mesaortitis.
mesaraic *adj.* mesaraico, -ca, mesareico, -ca.
mesarteritis *n.* mesarteritis.
mesaticephalic *adj.* mesaticefálico, -ca.
mesatipellic *adj.* mesatipélico, -ca.
mesatipelvic *adj.* mesatipélvico, -ca.
mesaxon *n.* mesaxón.
mesectic *adj.* meséctico, -ca.
mesectoblast *n.* mesectoblasto.
mesectoderm *n.* mesectodermo.
mesencephalic *adj.* mesencefálico, -ca.
mesencephalitis *n.* mesencefalitis.
mesencephalohypophyseal *adj.* mesencefalohipofisiario, -ria.
mesencephalon *n.* mesencéfalo, mesoencéfalo.
mesencephalotomy *n.* mesencefalotomía.
mesenchyma *n.* mesénquima.
mesenchymal *adj.* mesenquimático, -ca, mesenquimatoso, -sa.
mesenchymoma *n.* mesenquimoma.
benign mesenchymoma mesenquimoma benigno.
malignant mesenchymoma mesenquimoma maligno.
mesenterectomy *n.* mesenterectomía.
mesenteric *adj.* mesentérico, -ca.
mesenteriolum *n.* mesenteriolo.
mesenteriopexy *n.* mesenteriopexia.
mesenteriorrhaphy *n.* mesenteriorrafia.
mesenteriplication *n.* mesenterioplicación.
mesenteritis *n.* mesenteritis.

mesenterium mesenterio, mesenterium.
mesenterium commune mesenterio común, mesenterio dorsal común.
mesenterium dorsale commune mesenterio común, mesenterio dorsal común.
mesenteron *n.* mesenteroblasto, mesénteron.
mesentery *n.* mesenterio.
primitive mesentery mesenterio primitivo.
ventral mesentery mesenterio ventral.
mesentomere *n.* mesentómero.
mesentorrhaphy *n.* mesentorrafia.
mesh *n.* malla.
mesiad mesad, mesiad.
mesial *adj.* mesial.
mesially *adj.* mesial.
mesien *adj.* mesino, -na.
mesiobuccal *adj.* mesiobucal.
mesiobucco-occlusal *adj.* mesiobucooclusal.
mesiobuccopulpal *adj.* mesiobucopulpal, mesiobucopulpar.
mesiocclusion *n.* mesioclusión, mesiooclusión.
mesiocervical *adj.* mesiocervical.
mesioclination *n.* mesioclinación.
mesiodens *n.* mesiodens, mesiodiente.
mesiodistal *adj.* mesiodistal.
mesiodistocclusal (MOD) *adj.* mesiodistooclusal (MOD).
mesiogingival *adj.* mesiogingival.
mesiognathic *adj.* mesiognático, -ca.
mesioincisal *adj.* mesioincisal.
mesioincisodistal *adj.* mesioincisodistal.
mesiolabial *adj.* mesiolabial.
mesiolabioincisal *adj.* mesiolabioincisal.
mesiolingual *adj.* mesiolingual.
mesiolinguoincisal *adj.* mesiolinguoincisal.
mesiolinguo-occlusal *adj.* mesiolinguooclusal.
mesiolinguopulpal *adj.* mesiolinguopulpar.
mesion *n.* mesión.
mesio-occlusal *adj.* mesiooclusal.
mesio-occlusion *n.* mesiooclusión.
mesio-occlusodistal *adj.* mesiooclusodistal.
mesiopulpal *adj.* mesiopulpal, mesiopulpar.
mesiopulpolabial *adj.* mesiopulpolabial.
mesiopulpolingual *adj.* mesiopulpolingual.
mesioversion *n.* mesioversión.
mesiplacement *n.* mesiocolocación.
mesiris *n.* mesoiris.
mesoaortitis *n.* mesoaortitis.
mesoaortitis syphilitica mesoaortitis sifilítica.
mesoappendicitis *n.* mesoapendicitis.
mesoappendix *n.* mesoapéndice.
mesoarial *adj.* mesoarial.
mesoarium *n.* mesoario, mesoarium.
mesoblast *n.* mesoblasto.
mesoblastema *n.* mesoblastema.
mesoblastemic *adj.* mesoblastémico, -ca.
mesoblastic *adj.* mesoblástico, -ca.
mesobronchitis *n.* mesobronquitis.
mesocardia *n.* mesocardia.
mesocardium *n.* mesocardio.
arterial mesocardium mesocardio arterial.
dorsal mesocardium mesocardio dorsal.
lateral mesocardium mesocardio lateral.
venous mesocardium mesocardio venoso.
ventral mesocardium mesocardio ventral.
mesocarpal *adj.* mesocarpiano, -na, mesocárpico, -ca.
mesocecal *adj.* mesocecal.
mesocecum *n.* mesociego.
mesocephalic *adj.* mesocefálico, -ca, mesocéfalo, -la.
mesocephalon *n.* mesocéfalo.

mesochondrium *n.* mesocondrio.
mesochoroidea *n.* mesocoroides.
mesococcus *n.* mesococo.
mesocolic *adj.* mesocólico, -ca.
mesocolon *n.* mesocolon.
mesocolopexy *n.* mesocolopexia.
mesocoloplication *n.* mesocoloplegadura, mesocoloplicación.
mesocord *n.* mesocordio, mesocordón.
mesocornea *n.* mesocórnea.
mesocranic *adj.* mesocráneo, -a.
mesocuneiform *adj.* mesocuneiforme.
mesocyst *n.* mesocisto.
mesocytoma *n.* mesocitoma.
mesoderm *n.* mesodermo.
branchial mesoderm mesodermo branquial.
extraembryonic mesoderm mesodermo extraembrionario.
gastral mesoderm mesodermo gastral.
intermediate mesoderm mesodermo intermedio.
intraembryonic mesoderm mesodermo intraembrionario.
lateral mesoderm mesodermo lateral.
paraxial mesoderm mesodermo paraxial.
secondary mesoderm mesodermo secundario.
somatic mesoderm mesodermo somático.
splanchnic mesoderm mesodermo esplácnico.
visceral mesoderm mesodermo visceral.
mesodermic *adj.* mesodérmico, -ca.
mesodiastolic *adj.* mesodiastólico, -ca.
mesodont *n.* mesodonte, mesodonto.
mesodontic *adj.* mesodóntico, -ca.
mesodontism *n.* mesodontismo.
mesoduodenal *adj.* mesoduodenal.
mesoduodenum *n.* mesoduodeno.
mesoenteriolum *n.* mesoenteriolo.
mesoepididymis *n.* mesoepidídimo.
mesoepithelium *n.* mesoepitelio.
mesoesophagus *n.* mesoesófago.
mesogaster *n.* mesogaster.
mesogastric *adj.* mesogástrico, -ca.
mesogastrium *n.* mesogastrio.
mesogenital *adj.* mesogenital.
mesoglia *n.* mesoglia.
mesoglioma *n.* mesoglioma.
mesogluteal *adj.* mesoglúteo, -a.
mesognathic *adj.* mesognático, -ca.
mesognathion *n.* mesognation.
mesognathous *adj.* mesognático, -ca.
Mesogonimus Mesogonimus.
mesohyloma *n.* mesohiloma.
mesoileum *n.* mesoíleon.
mesojejunum *n.* mesoyeyuno.
mesolepidoma *n.* mesolepidoma.
mesolobotomy *n.* mesolobotomía.
mesology *n.* mesología.
mesolymphocyte *n.* mesolinfocito.
mesomelia *n.* mesomelia.
mesomelic *adj.* mesomélico, -ca.
mesomere *n.* mesómera, mesómero.
mesomeric *adj.* mesomérico, -ca.
mesomerism *n.* mesomerismo.
mesometritis *n.* mesometritis.
mesometrium *n.* mesometrio.
mesomorph *n.* mesomorfo.
mesomorphic *adj.* mesomórfico, -ca.
mesomorphy *n.* mesomorfia.
mesomula *n.* mesómula.
meson *n.* mesón.
mesonasal *adj.* mesonasal.
mesonephric *adj.* mesonéfrico, -ca.
mesonephroma *n.* mesonefroma.

mesonephron *n.* mesonefros.
mesonephros *n.* mesonefros.
mesoneuritis *n.* mesoneuritis.
meso-omentum *n.* mesoomento.
meso-ontomorph *n.* mesontomorfo.
mesopallium *n.* mesopalio.
mesopexy *n.* mesopexia.
mesophil *n.* mesófilo.
mesophile *n.* mesófilo.
mesophilic *adj.* mesofílico, -ca.
mesophlebitis *n.* mesoflebitis.
mesophragma *n.* mesofragma.
mesophryon *n.* mesofrión.
mesopia *n.* mesopía.
mesopic *adj.* mesópico, -ca.
mesopneumon *n.* mesoneumo.
mesoprosopic *adj.* mesoprosópico, -ca.
mesopsychic *adj.* mesopsíquico, -ca.
mesopulmonum *n.* mesopulmón.
mesorchial *adj.* mesorquial.
mesorchium *n.* mesorquio.
mesorectum *n.* mesorrecto.
mesoretine *n.* mesorretina.
mesoropter *n.* mesoróptero.
mesorrhaphy *n.* mesorrafia.
mesorrhine *adj.* mesorrino, -na.
mesosalpinx *n.* mesosálpinx.
mesoscope *n.* mesoscopio.
mesoseme *adj.* mesosemo, -ma.
mesosigmoid *n.* mesosigmoide, mesosigmoides.
mesosigmoiditis *n.* mesosigmoiditis.
mesosigmoidopexy *n.* mesosigmoidopexia.
mesoskelic *adj.* mesosquélico, -ca.
mesosomatous *adj.* mesosomatoso, -sa, mesosomo, -ma.
mesosome *n.* mesosoma.
mesosomia *n.* mesosomía.
mesostenium *n.* mesostenio.
mesosternum *n.* mesoesternón, mesosternón.
mesostroma *n.* mesoestroma.
mesosyphilis *n.* mesosífilis.
mesosystolic *adj.* mesosistólico, -ca.
mesotarsal *adj.* mesotarsiano, -na.
mesotaurodontism *n.* mesotaurodontismo.
mesotendon *n.* mesotendón.
mesotenon *n.* mesotenon.
mesothelial *adj.* mesotelial.
mesothelioma *n.* mesotelioma.
benign mesothelioma of the genital tract mesotelioma benigno del tracto genital.
mesothelium *n.* mesotelio.
mesotropic *adj.* mesotrópico, -ca.
mesotympanum *n.* mesotímpano.
mesouranic *adj.* mesouránico, -ca.
mesovarium *n.* mesoovario, mesovario.
messenger *n.* mensajero.
second messenger segundo mensajero.
mesuranic *adj.* mesouránico, -ca, mesuránico, -ca.
meta-arthritic *adj.* metaartrítico, -ca.
metabasis *n.* metábasis.
metabiosis *n.* metabiosis.
metabolic *adj.* metabólico, -ca.
metabolimeter *n.* metabolímetro.
metabolimetry *n.* metabolimetría.
metabolin *n.* metabolina.
metabolism *n.* metabolismo.
acid-base metabolism metabolismo acido-básico.
ammonotelic metabolism metabolismo amonotélico.
anaerobic metabolism metabolismo anaeróbico.
basal metabolism metabolismo basal.

carbohydrate metabolism metabolismo de carbohidratos, metabolismo de los hidratos de carbono.

cholesterol metabolism metabolismo del colesterol.

drug metabolism metabolismo farmacológico.

electrolyte metabolism metabolismo de los electrólitos.

endogenous metabolism metabolismo endógeno.

energy metabolism metabolismo energético.

exogenous metabolism metabolismo exógeno.

fat metabolism metabolismo de las grasas, metabolismo graso.

intermediary metabolism metabolismo intermediario.

iron metabolism metabolismo del hierro.

protein metabolism metabolismo de las proteínas, metabolismo proteico.

renal metabolism metabolismo renal.

respiratory metabolism metabolismo respiratorio.

ureotelic metabolism metabolismo ureotélico.

uricotelic metabolism metabolismo uricotélico.

metabolite *n.* metabolito.

metabolizable *adj.* metabolizable.

metabolize *v.* metabolizar.

metacarpal *adj.* metacarpiano, -na.

metacarpectomy *n.* metacarpectomía.

metacarpophalangeal *adj.* metacarpofalángico, -ca.

metacarpus *n.* metacarpo.

metacele *n.* metacelio, metacelo.

metacentric *adj.* metacéntrico, -ca.

metachromasia *n.* metacromasia, metacromatismo.

metachromatic *adj.* metacromático, -ca.

metachromatin *n.* metacromatina.

metachromia *n.* metacromía.

metachromic *adj.* metacrómico, -ca.

metachromophil *adj.* metacromatófilo, -la, metacromófilo, -la.

metachromophile *adj.* metacromatófilo, -la.

metachromosome *n.* metacromosoma.

metachronous *adj.* metacrónico, -ca, metacrono, -na.

metachysis *n.* metaquisis.

metacoele *n.* metacelio.

metacoeloma *n.* metaceloma.

metacone *n.* metacono.

metaconid *n.* metacónido, -da.

metacontrast *n.* metacontraste.

metaconule *adj.* metacónulo, -la.

metacromophile *adj.* metacromófilo, -la.

metacryptozoite *n.* metacriptozoíto.

metacyesis *n.* metaciesis.

metaduodenum *n.* metaduodeno.

metadysentery *n.* metadisentería.

metagaster *n.* metagastrio.

metagastrula *n.* metagástrula.

metagenesis *n.* metagenesia, metagénesis.

metagglutinin *n.* metaaglutinina.

metaglobulin *n.* metaglobulina.

metagonimiasis *n.* metagonimiasis.

Metagonimus Metagonimus.

Metagonimus yokogawai Metagonimus yokogawai.

metagrippal *adj.* metagripal.

metaherpes *n.* metaherpes.

metaicteric *adj.* metaictérico, -ca.

metainfective *adj.* metainfeccioso, -sa.

metakinesis *n.* metacinesia, metacinesis.

metal *n.* metal.

metalbumin *n.* metaalbúmina.

metallaxis *n.* metalaxia.

metallergy *n.* metaalergia, metalergia.

metallesthesia *n.* metalestesia.

metallic *adj.* metálico, -ca.

metallization *n.* metalización.

metallized *adj.* metalizado, -da.

metallizing *adj.* metalizante.

metalloflavoprotein *n.* metaloflavoproteína.

metalloid *n.* metaloide.

metallophilia *n.* metalofilia.

metallophilic *adj.* metalófilo, -la.

metalloscopy *n.* metaloscopia.

metallotherapy *n.* metaloterapia.

metallothionein *n.* metalotioneína.

metaluetic *adj.* metaluético, -ca.

metamer *n.* metámera, metámero.

metamere *n.* metámera.

metameric *adj.* metamérico, -ca.

metamerism *n.* metamería, metamerismo.

metamorphopsia *n.* metamorfopsia.

metamorphosis *n.* metamorfosis.

fatty metamorphosis metamorfosis adiposa, metamorfosis grasa.

platelet metamorphosis metamorfosis plaquetaria.

retrograde metamorphosis metamorfosis retrógrada, metamorfosis retrogresiva.

retrogressive metamorphosis metamorfosis retrógrada, metamorfosis retrogresiva.

revisionary metamorphosis metamorfosis de revisión.

viscous metamorphosis metamorfosis estructural, metamorfosis viscosa.

metamorphotic *adj.* metamórfico, -ca, metamorfósico, -ca, metamorfótico, -ca.

metamyelocite *n.* metamielocito.

metanephric *adj.* metanéfrico, -ca.

metanephrine *n.* metanefrina.

metanephro *n.* metanefrón.

metanephrogenic *adj.* metanefrogénico, -ca, metanefrógeno, -na.

metanephron *n.* metanefrón.

metanephros *n.* metanefrón, metanefros.

metaneutrophil *adj.* metaneutrófilo, -la.

metaneutrophile *adj.* metaneutrófilo, -la.

metanucleus *n.* metanúcleo.

metapeptone *n.* metapeptona.

metaphase *n.* metafase.

metaphrenia *n.* metafrenia.

metaphyseal *adj.* metafisario, -ria.

metaphysial *adj.* metafisario, -ria.

metaphysis *n.* metáfisis.

metaphysitis *n.* metafisitis.

metaplasia *n.* metaplasia.

agnogenic myeloid metaplasia metaplasia mieloide agnógena, metaplasia mieloide agnogénica.

apocrine metaplasia metaplasia apocrina.

intestinal metaplasia metaplasia intestinal.

myeloid metaplasia metaplasia mieloide.

postpolycythemic myeloid metaplasia metaplasia mieloide pospolicitémica.

primary myeloid metaplasia metaplasia mieloide primaria.

pseudopyloric metaplasia metaplasia seudopilórica.

secondary myeloid metaplasia metaplasia mieloide secundaria.

squamous metaplasia metaplasia escamosa.

symptomatic myeloid metaplasia metaplasia mieloide sintomática.

metaplasis *n.* metaplasis.

metaplasm *n.* metaplasma.

metaplastic *adj.* metaplásico, -ca.

metaplexus *n.* metaplexo.

metapneumonic *adj.* metaneumónico, -ca.

metapodalia *n.* metapodalia.

metapophysis *n.* metaapófisis, metapófisis.

metapore *n.* metaporo.

metaprotein *n.* metaproteína.

metapsychics *n.* metapsíquica.

metapsychology *n.* metapsicología.

metapyretic *adj.* metapirético, -ca.

metarteriole *n.* metarteriola, metarteriola.

metarubricyte *n.* metarrubricito.

metastable *adj.* metaestable, metastable.

metastasectomy *n.* metastasectomía.

metastasis *n.* metaptosis, metástasis.

biochemical metastasis metástasis bioquímica.

calcareous metastasis metástasis calcárea.

contact metastasis metástasis de contacto.

crossed metastasis metástasis cruzada.

direct metastasis metástasis directa.

paradoxical metastasis metástasis paradójica.

pulsating metastasis metástasis pulsátil.

retrograde metastasis metástasis retrógrada.

satellite metastasis metástasis satélite.

metastatic *adj.* metastásico, -ca, metastático, -ca.

metasternum *n.* metaesternón, metasternón.

metasynapsis *n.* metasinapsis.

metasyncrisis *n.* metasincrisis.

metasyndesis *n.* metasindesis.

metasyphilis *n.* metalúes, metasífilis.

metasyphilitic *adj.* metasifilítico, -ca.

metatarsal *adj.* metatarsiano, -na.

metatarsalgia *n.* metatarsalgia.

metatarsectomy *n.* metatarsectomía.

metatarsophalangeal *adj.* metatarsofalángico, -ca.

metatarsus *n.* metatarso, metatarsus.

metatarsus adductocavus metatarso aducto cavo.

metatarsus adductovarus metatarso aducto varo.

metatarsus adductus metatarso aducido, metatarso aducto.

metatarsus atavicus metatarso atávico.

metatarsus brevis metatarso breve.

metatarsus latus metatarso ancho, metatarsus latus.

metatarsus primus varus metatarso primo varo.

metatarsus valgus metatarso valgo.

metatarsus varus metatarso varo.

metathalamus *n.* metatálamo.

metathesis *n.* metátesis.

metathetic *adj.* metatésico, -ca.

metathrombin *n.* metatrombina.

metatroph *n.* metatrófo.

metatrophic *adj.* metatrófico, -ca.

metatrophy *n.* metatrofia.

metatropic *adj.* metatrópico, -ca.

metatypic *adj.* metatípico, -ca.

metatypical *adj.* metatípico, -ca.

metazonal *adj.* metazonal.

metazoonosis *n.* metazoonosis.

metecious *n.* metecio.

metencephalic *adj.* metaencefálico, -ca, metencefálico, -ca.

metencephalon *n.* metaencéfalo, metencéfalo.

metencephalospinal *adj.* metencefaloespinal.

metenkephalin *n.* metencefalina.

meteorism *n.* meteorismo.

meteoropathology *n.* meteoropatología.

meteoropathy *n.* meteoropatía.
meteororesistant *adj.* meteororresistente.
meteorosensitive *adj.* meteorolábil, meteorosensitivo, -va.
meteorotropic *adj.* meteorotrópico, -ca.
meteorotropism *n.* meteorotropismo.
metepencephalon *n.* metepencéfalo.
meter *n.* metro.
 dosage meter metro de posología.
 light meter metro de luz.
 peak flow meter metro de flujo máximo.
metergasia *n.* metergasia, metergasis.
metergasis *n.* metergasia, metergasis.
metestrum *n.* metaestro.
metestrus *n.* metaestro.
methadone *n.* metadona.
methanogen *n.* metanógeno.
methanogenic *adj.* metanógeno, -na.
methanolysis *n.* metanólisis.
methectic *adj.* metéctico, -ca.
methemalbumin *n.* metahemalbúmina.
methemalbuminemia *n.* metahemalbuminemia.
metheme *n.* metahem.
methemoglobin *n.* metahemoglobina.
 methemoglobin reductase (NADPH) metahemoglobina reductasa (NADPH).
methemoglobinemia *n.* metahemoglobinemia.
 acquired methemoglobinemia metahemoglobinemia adquirida.
 congenital methemoglobinemia metahemoglobinemia congénita.
 enterogenous methemoglobinemia metahemoglobinemia enterógena.
 hereditary methemoglobinemia metahemoglobinemia hereditaria.
 primary methemoglobinemia metahemoglobinemia primaria.
 secondary methemoglobinemia metahemoglobinemia secundaria.
methemoglobinemic *adj.* metahemoglobinémico, -ca.
methemoglobinuria *n.* metahemoglobinuria.
methilepsia *n.* metilepsia.
method *n.* método.
 Abbott's method método de Abbott.
 ABC method método ABC.
 abortive method método abortivo.
 absorption method método de absorción.
 acid hematin method método de la hematina ácida, método para la hemoglobina.
 Altmann-Gersh method método de Altmann-Gersh.
 Bloor, Pelkan and Allen's method método de Bloor, Pelkan y Allen.
 Aristotelian method método aristotélico.
 Ashby's method método de Ashby.
 Askenstedt's method método de Askenstedt.
 Autenrieth and Barth's method método para el ácido oxálico.
 autoclave method método de autoclave.
 auxanographic method método auxanográfico.
 Barger's method método de Barger.
 Barraquer's method método de barraquer.
 barrier method método de barrera.
 basal body temperature method of family planning método de planificación familiar mediante la temperatura basal.
 basal temperature method método de temperatura basal.
 Baudelocque's method método de Baudelocque.
 Beck's method método de Beck.

 Benassi method método de Benassi.
 Bertel's method método de Bertel.
 Billings method método de Billings.
 Blackett-Healy method método Blackett-Healy.
 Bock and Benedict's method método de Bock y Benedict.
 Born method of wax plate reconstruction método de Born de reconstrucción con placas de cera.
 Bradley's method método de Bradley.
 Brasdor's method método de Brasdor.
 Brehmer's method método de Brehmer.
 calendar method of family planning método del calendario de planificación familiar.
 caliper method método del calibre.
 Callahan's method método de Callahan.
 Carrel-Dakin method método de Carrel-Dakin.
 Carrel's method método de Carrel.
 Castañeda's method método de Castañeda.
 cervical mucus method of family planning método de planificación familiar del moco cervical.
 charcoal method método ABC.
 Charters' method método de Charters.
 Chayes' method método de Chayes.
 Chick-Martin method método de Chick-Martin.
 chloropercha method método de la cloropercha.
 Ciaccio's method método de Ciaccio.
 Clark-Collip method método de Clark-Collip.
 closed circuit method método de circuito cerrado.
 closed system helium dilution method método de dilución de helio en sistema cerrado.
 confrontation method método de confrontación.
 contourned adducted trochanteric controlled alignment method método de alineación controlada del contorno trocantérico en aducción.
 contraceptive method método contraceptivo.
 Converse method método de Converse.
 copper sulfate method método del sulfato de cobre.
 Corley and Denis' method método de Corley y Denis.
 correlational method método correlativo.
 Couette method método de Couette.
 Coutard's method método de Coutard.
 Credé's method método de Credé.
 Cronin method método de Cronin.
 cross-sectional method método de cortes transversales.
 Cuignet's method método de Cuignet.
 culture media method método microbiológicos.
 Denis and Leche's method método de Denis y Leche.
 Denman's method método de Denman.
 Dickinson method método de Dickinson.
 Dick-Read method método de Dick-Read.
 Dieffenbach's method método de Dieffenbach.
 diffusion method método de difusión.
 direct method método directo.
 direct method for making inlays método directo para hacer incrustaciones.
 disk diffusion method método de difusión en disco.
 disk sensitivity method método de sensibilidad por discos.

 double antibody method método de doble anticuerpo.
 Duke's method método de Duke.
 Eicken's method método de Eicken.
 Ellinger's method método de Ellinger.
 Epstein's method método de Epstein.
 experimental method método experimental.
 Fahraeus method método de Fahraeus.
 Faust's method método de Faust.
 Feulgen stainning method método de tinción de Feulgen.
 Fick method método de Fick.
 Fiske and Subbarow's method método de Fiske y Subbarow.
 Fiske's method método de Fiske.
 fixed base method método para las bases fijas, método para las bases fijas totales.
 flash method método del flash.
 flotation method método de flotación.
 Folin and Wu's method método de Folin y Wu.
 Folin's method método de Folin.
 Fone's method método de Fone.
 frozen section method método de sección congelada.
 Fülleborn's method método de Fülleborn.
 Gärtner's method método de Gärtner.
 Gerota's method método de Gerota.
 Givens' method método de Givens.
 glucose oxidase method método de glucosa oxidasa.
 gold number method método del número de oro.
 Greulich-Pyle method método Greulich-Pyle.
 Gruber's method método de Gruber.
 Gunson method método Gunson.
 Haas method método de Haas.
 Hamilton's method método de Hamilton.
 Hammerschlag's method método de Hammerschlag.
 Heintz's method método de Heintz.
 hemoglobin method método de la hematina ácida, método para la hemoglobina.
 Henschen method método de Henschen.
 Herter and Foster method método para el indol, método de Herter y Foster.
 Heublein's method método de Heublein.
 hexokinase method método de hexocinasa.
 Hirschberg's method método de Hirschberg.
 Hirschfeld's method método de Hirschfeld.
 Holmgren method método de Holmgren.
 Home's silver precipitation method método de la precipitación de plata de Home.
 Howell's method método de Howell.
 Hung's method método de Hung.
 immunofluorescence method método de inmunofluorescencia.
 indirect method for making inlays método indirecto para hacer incrustaciones.
 indophenol method método de indofenol.
 introspective method método introspectivo.
 Ivy's method método de Ivy.
 Jaboulay's method método de Jaboulay.
 Johnson's method método de Johnson.
 Judd method método de Judd.
 Karr's method método de Karr.
 Kasabach method método de Kasabach.
 Kendall's method método de Kendall, método para el yodo.
 Kety-Schmidt method método de Kety-Schmidt.
 Kirstein's method método de Kirstein.
 Kite method método de Kite.
 Kjedahl's method método de Kjeldahl.
 Klapp's method método de Klapp.

Klüver-Barrera method método de Klüver-Barrera.

Knaus-Ogino's method método de Knaus-Ogino.

Kuchendorf method método Kuchendorf.

Laborde's method método de Laborde.

Lamaze method método de Lamaze.

Lane method método de Lane.

lateral condensation method método de condensación lateral.

Lauenstein method método de Lauenstein.

Law method método de Law.

Leboyer method método de Leboyer.

Leboyer method of delivery método de expulsión de Leboyer.

Lee-White method método de Lee-White.

limited fluctuation method of dosing método de dosificación de fluctuación limitada.

Ling's method método de Ling.

longitudinal method método longitudinal.

Lysholm method método de Lysholm.

macro-Kjeldahl method método macro-Kjeldahl.

Marchi's method método de Marchi.

Marshall's method método de Marshall.

McCrudden method método de McCrudden.

Meltzer's method método de Meltzer.

method for acid soluble phosphorus método para el fósforo acidosoluble.

method for aminoacid nitrogen método para el nitrógeno de aminoácidos.

method for amoniac nitrogen método para el nitrógeno de amoniaco.

method for calcium método para el calcio.

method for chlorides método para los cloruros.

method for cholesterol método para el colesterol.

method for creatine método para la creatina.

method for dextrose método para la dextrosa.

method for fatty acids método para los ácidos grasos.

method for glucose método para la glucosa.

method for guanidine método para la guanidina.

method for indican método para el indicán.

method for inorganic phosphates método para los fosfatos inorgánicos.

method for iron método para el hierro.

method for peptic activity método para la actividad péptica.

method for protein-free blood filtrate método para el filtrado de sangre libre de proteínas.

method for purine bodies método para los cuerpos púricos.

method for sugar método para los azúcares.

method for total fixed base método para las bases fijas, método para las bases fijas totales.

Meyer's method método de Meyer.

micro-Kjeldahl method método micro-Kjeldahl.

Mohr's method método de Mohr.

Moore's method método de Moore.

multiple cone method método del cono múltiple.

Murphy method método de Murphy.

Myers and Wardell's method método de Myers y Wardell.

natural family planning method método de planificación familiar natural.

natural method método natural.

Needles' split cast method método de Needles del modelo dividido.

Nikiforoff's method método de Nikiforoff.

Ogata's method método de Ogata.

Ogino-Knaus method método de Ogino-Knaus.

open circuit method método de circuito abierto.

optical density method método de la densidad óptica.

Orr method método de Orr.

Orsi-Grocco method método de Orsi-Grocco.

Osborne and Folin's method método de Osborne y Folin.

ova concentration method método para la concentración de huevecillos.

ovulation method of family planning método de la ovulación para planificación familiar.

Paracelsian method método de Paracelso.

paraffin method método de la parafina.

parallax method método parallax.

Parker's method método de Parker.

Pavlov method método de Pavlov.

peak method of dosing método de dosificación máxima.

Porges method método de Porges.

Price-Jones method método de Price-Jones.

Purman's method método de Purman.

Read method método de Read.

Rehfuss method método de Rehfuss.

Reverding's method método de Reverding.

rhythm method método del ritmo.

Ritchie's formol ether method método del formol y éter de Ritchie.

Ritgen's method método de Ritgen.

Roux's method método de Roux.

Sahli's method método de Sahli.

Saling's method método de Saling.

Salkowski, Autenrieth and Barth's method método de Salkowski, Autenrieth y Barth.

Satterthwaite method método de Satterthwaite.

Scarpa's method método de Scarpa.

Schaffer method método de Schaffer.

Scherer's method método de Scherer.

Schick's method método de Schick.

Schmidt-Thannhauser method método de Schmidt-Thannhauser.

Schüller's method método de Schüller.

scientific method método científico.

sectional method método de segmentación, método seccional.

segmentation method método de segmentación, método seccional.

Shohl and Pedley's method método de Shohl y Pedley.

Siffert's method método de Siffert.

silver cone method método del cono de plata.

silver point method método del punto de plata.

single cone method método de cono único.

Sluder's method método de Sluder.

Smellie's method método de Smellie.

split cast method método del modelo dividido, método del molde dividido.

Stas-Otto method método de Stas-Otto.

Stehle's method método de Stehle.

Stroganoff's method método de Stroganoff.

Sumner's method método de Sumner.

suspension method método de suspensión.

Sweet localization method método de localización de Sweet.

symptothermal method of family planning método sintotérmico de planificación familiar.

Thane's method método de Thane.

Theden's method método de Theden.

Thiersch's method método de Thiersch.

thiochrome method método de tiocromo.

total method for sulfur método para el azufre total.

tourniquet infusion method método de infusión con torniquete.

tracer depot method método del trazador depot.

trial and error method método empírico.

ultropaque method método ultraopaco.

van Gehuchten's method método de van Gehuchten.

van Slyke and Cullen method método para el dióxido de carbono, método para la reserva alcalina.

Van Slyke and Cullen's method método de van Slyke y Cullen.

van Slyke and Fitz method método para la reserva alcalina.

van Slyke and Fitz's method método de van Slyke y Fitz.

van Slyke and Meyer method método de van Slyke y Meyer.

van Slyke and Palmer method método de van Slyke y Palmer.

van Slyke's method método de van Slyke.

vertical condensation method método de condensación vertical.

Walker's method método de Walker.

Waring's method método de Waring.

Weber's method método de Weber.

Welcker's method método de Welcker.

Welker's method método de Welker.

Westergren's method método de Westergren.

Wheeler's method método de Wheeler.

Whipple's method método de Whipple.

Wiechowski and Handorsky's method método Wiechowski y Handorsky.

Wilson's method método de Wilson.

Wintrobe and Landsberg's method método de Wintrobe y Landsberg.

Wintrobe method método de Wintrobe.

withdrawal method método de la retirada.

Wolfe's method método de Wolfe.

Wolter's method método de Wolter.

Wynn's method método de Wynn.

methodology *n.* metodología.

methomania *n.* metomanía.

methylate *v.* metilar.

methylated *adj.* metilado, -da.

methylation *n.* metilación.

DNA methylation metilación de ADN.

methylcellulose *n.* metilcelulosa.

methylic *adj.* metílico, -ca.

metmyoglobin *n.* metamioglobina, metomioglobina.

metonymy *n.* metonimia.

metopagus *n.* metópago.

metopic *adj.* metópico, -ca.

metopion *n.* metopión.

metopism *n.* metopismo.

metoplasty *n.* metoplastia.

metopodynia *n.* metopodinia.

metopon *n.* metopón.

metopopagus *n.* metópago.

metopoplasty *n.* metopoplastia.

metoposcopy *n.* metoposcopia.

metralgia *n.* metralgia.

metratonia *n.* metratonía.

metratrophia *n.* metraatrofia, metratrofia.

metratrophy *n.* metraatrofia.

metrechoscopy *n.* metrecoscopia.

metrectasia *n.* metrectasia.
metrectomy *n.* metrectomía.
metrectopia *n.* metrectopia.
metreurynter *n.* metreurínter.
metreurysis *n.* metreurisis.
metria *n.* metria.
metriocephalic *adj.* metriocefálico, -ca.
metritis *n.* metritis.
  dissecting metritis metritis disecante.
  metritis dissecans metritis disecante.
  puerperal metritis metritis puerperal.
metrocarcinoma *n.* metrocarcinoma.
metrocele *n.* metrocele.
metrocolpocele *n.* metrocolpocele.
metrocystosis *n.* metrocistosis.
metrodynia *n.* metrodinia.
metroendometritis *n.* metroendometritis.
metrofibroma *n.* metrofibroma.
metrogenous *adj.* metrógeno, -na.
metrography *n.* metrografía.
metroleukorrhea *n.* metroleucorrea.
metrology *n.* metrología.
metrolymphangitis *n.* metrolinfangitis.
metromalacia *n.* metromalacia.
metromalacoma *n.* metromalacoma.
metromalacosis *n.* metromalacosis.
metromenorrhagia *n.* metromenorragia.
metronoscope *n.* metronoscopio.
metroparalysis *n.* metroparálisis.
metropathic *adj.* metropático, -ca.
metropathy *n.* metropatía.
  metropathy hemorrhagica metropatía hemorrágica.
metroperitoneal *adj.* metroperitoneal.
metroperitonitis *n.* metroperitonitis.
metrophlebitis *n.* metroflebitis.
metroplasty *n.* metroplastia.
metroptosis *n.* metroptosia, metroptosis.
metrorrhagia *n.* metrorragia, uterorragia.
metrorrhea *n.* metrorrea.
metrorrhexis *n.* metrorrexia, metrorrexis.
metrosalpingitis *n.* metrosalpingitis.
metrosalpingography *n.* metrosalpingografía.
metroscope *n.* metroscopio.
metrostaxis *n.* metrostaxis.
metrostenosis *n.* metroestenosis, metrostenosis.
metrotomy *n.* metrotomía.
metrotoxin *n.* metrotoxina.
metrotubography *n.* metrotubografía.
miana *n.* miana.
miasma *n.* miasma.
miasmatic *adj.* miasmático, -ca.
micaceous *adj.* micáceo, -a.
mication *n.* micación.
micatosis *n.* micatosis.
micciometry *n.* micciometría.
micella *n.* micela.
micellar *adj.* micelar.
micelle *n.* micela.
micoplasma *n.* micoplasma.
  T-strain micoplasma micoplasma de cepa T.
micorradiographic *adj.* microrradiográfico, -ca.
micracoustic *adj.* micracústico, -ca.
micranatomy *n.* microanatomía.
micrangium *n.* micrangio.
micrencephalon *n.* microencéfalo.
micrencephalous *adj.* microencefálico, -ca.
micrencephaly *n.* microencefalia.
micrergy *n.* micrergia.
microabscess *n.* microabsceso.
  Munro microabscess microabsceso de Munro.

Pautrier's microabscess microabsceso de Pautrier.
microacoustic *adj.* microacústico, -ca.
microadenoma *n.* microadenoma.
microadenopathy *n.* microadenopatía.
microaerobion *n.* microaerobio.
microaerophilic *adj.* microaerófilo, -la.
microaerosol *n.* microaerosol.
microaerotonometer *n.* microaerotonómetro.
microaggregate *n.* microagregado.
microalbuminuria *n.* microalbuminuria.
microanalysis *n.* microanálisis.
microanastomosis *n.* microanastomosis.
microanatomist *n.* microanatomista.
microanatomy *n.* micranatomía.
microaneurysm *n.* microaneurisma.
microangiography *n.* microangiografía.
microangiopathic *adj.* microangiopático, -ca.
microangiopathy *n.* micrangiopatía, microangiopatía.
  thrombotic microangiopathy microangiopatía trombótica.
microangioscopy *n.* microangioscopia.
microarteriographic *adj.* microarteriográfico, -ca.
microarteriography *n.* microarteriografía.
microbacterium *n.* microbacteria.
Microbacterium Microbacterium.
microbalance *n.* microbalanza.
microbe *n.* microbio.
microbial *adj.* microbiano, -na.
microbian *adj.* microbiano, -na.
microbic *adj.* microbiano, -na.
microbicidal *adj.* microbicida[1].
microbicide *n.* microbicida[1].
microbid *n.* micróbide.
microbiemia *n.* microbiemia, microbihemia, microbiohemia.
microbioassay *n.* microbioensayo, microbioinvestigación.
microbiological *adj.* microbiológico, -ca.
microbiologist *n.* microbiólogo, -ga.
microbiology *n.* microbiología.
microbiophotometer *n.* microbiofotómetro.
microbiota *n.* microbiota.
microbiotic *adj.* microbiótico, -ca.
microbism *n.* microbiosis, microbismo.
microblast *n.* microblasto.
microblepharia *n.* microblefaria.
microblepharism *n.* microblefarismo.
microblepharon *n.* microbléfaron.
microbrachia *n.* microbraquia.
microbrachius *n.* microbraquio.
microbrenner *n.* microbrenner, microfulgurador.
microburet *n.* microbureta.
microcalcification *n.* microcalcificación.
microcalix *n.* microcáliz.
microcalorie *n.* microcaloría.
microcalyx *n.* microcáliz.
microcardia *n.* microcardia.
microcaulia *n.* microcaulia.
microcentrum *n.* microcentro.
microcephalia *n.* microcefalia.
microcephalic *adj.* microcefálico, -ca.
microcephalism *n.* microcefalismo.
microcephalous *adj.* microcefálico, -ca.
microcephalus *n.* microcéfalo.
microcephaly *n.* microcefalia.
microcheilia *n.* microqueilia.
microcheiria *n.* microqueiria.
microchemical *adj.* microquímico, -ca.
microchemistry *n.* microquímica.
microchilia *n.* microqueilia, microquilia.

microchiria *n.* microqueiria, microquiria.
microcinematography *n.* microcinematografía.
microcirculation *n.* microcirculación.
microcircunvolution *n.* microcircunvolución.
microcnemia *n.* microcnemia.
Micrococaceae micrococaceae, Micrococáceas.
Micrococcus Micrococcus.
micrococcus *n.* micrococo.
microcolitis *n.* microcolitis.
microcolon *n.* microcolon.
microcolony *n.* microcolonia.
microconcentration *n.* microconcentración.
microconidium *n.* microconidio.
microcoria *n.* microcoria.
microcornea *n.* microcórnea.
microcrania *n.* microcrania.
microcrystal *n.* microcristal.
microcrystalline *adj.* microcristalino, -na.
microcyst *n.* microquiste.
microcystometer *n.* microcistómetro.
microcyte *n.* microcito.
microcythemia *n.* microcitemia.
microcytic *adj.* microcítico, -ca.
microcytosis *n.* microcitosis.
microcytotoxicity *n.* microcitotoxicidad.
microdactilia *n.* microdactilia.
microdactylous *adj.* microdáctilo, -la.
microdactyly *n.* microdactilia.
microdeletion *n.* microdeleción.
microdensitometer *n.* microdensitómetro.
microdentism *n.* microdentismo.
microdermatome *n.* microdermatomo.
microdetermination *n.* microdeterminación.
microdisection *n.* microdisección.
microdont *n.* microdonto.
microdontia *n.* microdoncia, microdontia.
microdontic *adj.* microdóntico, -ca.
microdontism *n.* microdontismo.
microdosage *n.* microdosificación.
microdose *n.* microdosis.
microdrepanocytic *adj.* microdrepanocitico, -ca.
microdrepanocytosis *n.* microdrepanocitosis.
microdrip *n.* microgotero.
microecology *n.* microecología.
microelectrode *n.* microelectrodo.
microelectrophoresis *n.* microelectroforesis.
microelectrophoretic *adj.* microelectroforético, -ca.
microelement *n.* microelemento.
microembolus *n.* microémbolo.
microencapsulation *n.* microcapsulación.
microenvironment *n.* microambiente.
microerythrocyte *n.* microeritrocito.
microestimation *n.* microestimación.
microfauna *n.* microfauna.
microfibril *n.* microfibrilla.
microfilament *n.* microfilamento.
microfilaremia *n.* microfilaremia.
microfilaria *n.* microfilaria.
microflora *n.* microflora.
microfluorometry *n.* microfluorometría.
microgamete *n.* microgameto.
microgametocyte *n.* microgametocito.
microgamont *n.* microgamonte, microgamonto.
microgamy *n.* microgamia.
microgastria *n.* microgastria.
microgenesis *n.* microgénesis.
microgenia *n.* microgenia.
microgenitalism *n.* microgenitalia, microgenitalismo.
microglia *n.* microglia.

microgliacyte *n.* microgliacito, microgliocito.
microglial *adj.* microglial.
microgliocyte *n.* microgliocito.
microglioma *n.* microglioma.
microgliomatosis *n.* microgliomatosis.
microgliosis *n.* microgliosis.
microglobulin *n.* microglobulina.
microglossia *n.* microglosia.
micrognathia *n.* micrognacia, micrognatia.
 micrognathia with peromelia micrognacia con peromelia.
microgonioscope *n.* microgonioscopio.
micrograft *n.* microinjerto.
micrograph *n.* micrógrafo.
micrography *n.* micrografía.
microgyria *n.* microgiria.
 sclerotic microgyria microgiria esclerótica.
microgyrus *n.* microgiro.
microhematocrit *n.* microhematocrito.
microhepatia *n.* microhepatía.
microhistology *n.* microhistología.
microincineration *n.* microincineración.
microincision *n.* microincisión.
microinfarct *n.* microinfarto.
microinjector *n.* microinyector.
microinvasion *n.* microinvasión.
microinvasive *adj.* microinvasor, -ra.
microkinematography *n.* microcinematografía.
microlaryngoscopy *n.* microlaringoscopia.
microlecithal *adj.* microlecito, -ta.
microlentia *n.* microlentia.
microlesion *n.* microlesión.
microleukoblast *n.* microleucoblasto.
microlith *n.* microlito.
microlithiasis *n.* microlitiasis.
 alveolar microlithiasis microlitiasis alveolar, microlitiasis alveolar pulmonar.
 pulmonary alveolar microlithiasis microlitiasis alveolar, microlitiasis alveolar pulmonar.
microlymphoidocyte *n.* microlinfoidocito.
micromania *n.* micromanía.
micromanipulation *n.* micromanipulación.
micromanipulator *n.* micromanipulador.
micromanometer *n.* micromanómetro.
micromanometric *adj.* micromanométrico, -ca.
micromastia *n.* micromastia.
micromaxilla *n.* micromaxilia.
micromazia *n.* micromazia.
micromegalopsia *n.* micromegalopsia.
micromelia *n.* micromelia.
micromere *n.* micrómera, micrómero.
micromerozoite *n.* micromerozoíto.
micrometabolism *n.* micrometabolismo.
micrometastasic *adj.* micrometastático, -ca.
micrometastasis *n.* micrometástasis.
micrometer *n.* micrómetro.
 caliper micrometer micrómetro a compás.
 slide micrometer micrómetro para portaobjetos.
micromethod *n.* micrométodo.
micrometry *n.* micrometría.
micromolar *adj.* micromolar.
micromolecular *adj.* micromolecular.
Micromonospora Micromonospora.
Micromonosporaceae Micromonosporaceae.
micromotoscope *n.* micromotoscopio.
micromyelia *n.* micromielia.
micromyeloblast *n.* micromieloblasto.
micromyelolymphocyte *n.* micromielolinfocito.
micron *n.* micron.
microneedle *n.* microaguja.
microneme *n.* micronema.

microneurosurgery *n.* microneurocirugía.
micronic *adj.* micrónico, -ca.
micronize *v.* micronizar.
micronodular *adj.* micronodular.
micronormoblast *n.* micronormoblasto.
micronucleus *n.* micronúcleo.
micronutrient *n.* micronutriente.
micronychia *n.* microniquia.
micronychosis *n.* micronicosis.
micro-orchidism *n.* microorquidismo.
microorganic *adj.* microorgánico, -ca.
microorganism *n.* microorganismo.
microparasite *n.* microparásito.
micropathology *n.* micropatología.
micropenis *n.* micropene.
microperfusion *n.* microperfusión.
microphage *n.* micrófago, -ga.
microphagocyte *n.* microfagocito.
microphakia *n.* microfaquia, microfasia.
microphallus *n.* microfalia.
microphone *n.* micrófono.
microphonia *n.* microfonía.
microphonic *adj.* microfónico, -ca.
microphony *n.* microfonía.
microphotograph *n.* microfotografía.
microphthalmos *n.* microftalmía, microftalmos.
microphthalmoscope *n.* microftalmoscopio.
microphthalmus *n.* microftalmía, microftalmos.
microphysics *n.* microfísica.
microphyte *n.* microfito.
micropia *n.* micropía.
micropinocytosis *n.* micropinocitosis.
micropipet *n.* micropipeta.
microplasia *n.* microplasia.
microplethysmography *n.* micropletismografía.
micropodia *n.* micropodia.
micropolariscope *n.* micropolariscopio.
micropolygyria *n.* micropoligiria.
microprecipitation *n.* microprecipitación.
microprobe *n.* microsonda.
microprojection *n.* microproyección.
microprojector *n.* microproyector.
microprolactinoma *n.* microprolactinoma.
microprosopia *n.* microprosopia.
microprosopus *n.* microprosopo.
micropsia *n.* micropsia.
microptic *adj.* micróptico, -ca.
micropuncture *n.* micropunción, micropuntura.
micropus *n.* micrópodo.
microradiogram *n.* microrradiograma.
microradiography *n.* microrradiografía.
microrchidia *n.* microorquia, microorquidia.
microreentry *n.* microrreentrada.
microrefractometer *n.* microrrefractómetro.
microrespirometer *n.* microrrespirómetro.
microrhinia *n.* microrrinia.
microsaccades *n.* microsacudidas.
microscelia *n.* microscelia.
microscintigraphy *n.* microescintigrafía.
microscope *n.* microscopio.
 acoustic microscope microscopio acústico, microscopio ultrasónico.
 beta ray microscope microscopio de rayos beta.
 capillary microscope microscopio capilar.
 centrifuge microscope microscopio centrífugo.
 color-contrast microscope microscopio de contraste de color.
 comparator microscope microscopio comparativo, microscopio de comparación.

 compound microscope microscopio compuesto.
 dark-field microscope microscopio de campo oscuro.
 electron microscope microscopio electrónico.
 fluorescence microscope microscopio de fluorescencia, microscopio fluorescente.
 Greenough microscope microscopio de Greenough.
 hypodermic microscope microscopio hipodérmico.
 infrared microscope microscopio infrarrojo.
 integrating microscope microscopio de integración.
 interference microscope microscopio de interferencia.
 ion microscope microscopio iónico.
 laser microscope microscopio láser.
 light microscope microscopio de luz.
 opaque microscope microscopio opaco.
 operating microscope microscopio de operaciones, microscopio operatorio, microscopio quirúrgico.
 polarization microscope microscopio de polarización, microscopio polarizante.
 polarizing microscope microscopio de luz polarizada.
 projection X ray microscope microscopio de proyección de rayos X.
 reflecting microscope microscopio reflejante.
 Rheinberg microscope microscopio de Rheinberg.
 scanning electron microscope microscopio eléctronico de centelleo.
 scanning electron microscope (SEM) microscopio electrónico de barrido (MEG).
 scanning microscope microscopio de barrido.
 slit lamp microscope microscopio de lámpara de hendidura.
 stereoscopic microscope microscopio estereoscópico.
 stroboscopic microscope microscopio estroboscópico.
 transmission scanning electron microscope microscopio electrónico de barrido de transmisión.
 trinocular microscope microscopio trinocular.
 ultraviolet microscope microscopio ultravioleta.
 X-ray microscope microscopio de rayos X.
microscopic *adj.* microscópico, -ca.
microscopical *adj.* microscópico, -ca.
microscopist *n.* microscopista.
microscopy *n.* microscopía.
 clinical microscopy microscopía clínica.
 electron microscopy microscopía electrónica.
 fluorescence microscopy microscopía de fluorescencia, microscopía fluorescente.
 fundus microscopy microscopía de fondo, microscopía fúndica.
 immersion microscopy microscopía de inmersión.
 immune electron microscopy microscopía inmunoelectrónica.
 immunofluorescence microscopy microscopía de inmunofluorescencia, microscopía inmunofluorescente.
 scanning electron microscopy microscopía electrónica de barrido.
 transmission scanning electron microscopy (TSEM) microscopía electrónica de barrido de transmisión (MEBT).

ultraviolet microscopy microscopía ultravioleta.
microsection *n.* microsección.
microseme microsemo, -ma.
microsmatic *adj.* microosmático, -ca.
microsoma *n.* microsoma.
microsomal *adj.* microsomático, -ca.
microspectrophotometer *n.* microespectrofotómetro.
microspectrophotometry *n.* microespectrofotometría.
microspectroscope *n.* microespectroscopio, microspectroscopio.
microspherocyte *n.* microesferocito.
microspherocytosis *n.* microesferocitosis.
microspherolith *n.* microsferolito.
microsphygmia *n.* microsfigmia.
microsphygmy *n.* microsfigmia.
microsphyxia *n.* microsfixia.
microsplanchnic *adj.* microesplácnico, -ca, microsplácnico, -ca.
microsplenia *n.* microesplenia, microsplenia.
microsplenic *adj.* microesplénico, -ca.
Microspora Microspora.
Microsporasida Microsporasida.
microspore *n.* microspora.
microsporid *n.* microspóride.
Microsporida Microsporida.
microsporosis *n.* microsporosis.
Microsporum Microsporum.
microstat *n.* microstato.
microstethoscope *n.* microestetófono, microestetoscopio.
microsthenic *adj.* microsténico, -ca.
microstomy *n.* microstomía.
microstrabismus *n.* microestrabismo.
microsurgery *n.* microcirugía.
microsuture *n.* microsutura.
microsyringe *n.* microjeringa.
microthelia *n.* microtelia.
microthermy *n.* microtermia.
microthrombosis *n.* microtrombosis.
microthrombus *n.* microtrombo.
microtia *n.* microtia.
microtiter *n.* microtítulo.
microtome *n.* microtomo.
microtomy *n.* microtomía.
microtonometer *n.* microtonómetro.
microtransfusion *n.* microtransfusión.
microtrauma *n.* microtrauma.
Microtrombidium Microtrombidium.
microtropia *n.* microtropía.
microtubule *n.* microtúbulo.
microtus *n.* microto.
microunit *n.* microunidad.
microvascular *adj.* microvascular.
microvasculature *n.* microvasculatura.
mlcrovesicle *n.* microvesícula.
microvillus *n.* microvellosidad.
microviscosimeter *n.* microviscosímetro.
microvivisection *n.* microvivisección.
microvoltimeter *n.* microvoltímetro.
microwelding *n.* microsoldadura.
microxycyte *n.* microxicito.
microxyphil *n.* microxifilo.
microzoaria *n.* microzoario.
microzoon *n.* microzoo.
micrurgic *adj.* micrúrgico, -ca.
micrurgy *n.* micrurgia.
Micrurus micruroides, Micrurus.
miction *n.* micción.
micturition *n.* micturición.
midbody *n.* mediocuerpo, mesocuerpo.
midcarpal *adj.* mediocarpiano, -na.
midfrontal *adj.* mediofrontal.

midge *n.* jején.
midget *n.* enano, -na.
midgracile *adj.* mesográcil.
midmenstrual *adj.* mediomestrual, mesomestrual.
midoccipital *adj.* mediooccipital, mesooccipital.
midpain *n.* mesodolor.
midsternum *n.* mesoesternón, mesosternón.
midtarsal *adj.* mediotarsal.
midwife *n.* comadrona, matrona.
miectomy *n.* miectomía.
mielasthenia *n.* mielastenia.
Miescheria Miescheria.
migraine *n.* jaqueca, migraña.
  abdominal migraine jaqueca abdominal, migraña abdominal.
  accompanied migraine migraña acompañada.
  acute confusional migraine jaqueca confusional aguda, migraña confusional aguda.
  basilar-artery migraine migraña basilar.
  classic migraine migraña clásica.
  common migraine migraña común.
  fulgurating migraine jaqueca fulgurante, migraña fulgurante.
  Harris migraine migraña de Harris.
  hemiplegic migraine jaqueca hemipléjica, migraña hemipléjica.
  migraine with aura migraña con aura.
  migraine without aura migraña sin aura.
  ophthalmic migraine jaqueca oftálmica, migraña oftálmica.
  ophthalmoplegic migraine jaqueca oftalmopléjica, migraña oftalmopléjica.
migrainous *adj.* migrañoso, -sa.
migranoid *adj.* jaquecoso, -sa.
migranous *adj.* jaquecoso, -sa.
migration *n.* migración.
  anodic migration migración anódica.
  cathodic migration migración catódica.
  cellular migration migración celular.
  external migration migración externa.
  internal migration migración interna.
  migration of the ovum migración del óvulo.
  pathologic tooth migration migración dental patológica.
  physiological tooth migration migración dental fisiológica.
  retrograde migration migración retrógrada.
  transperitoneal migration migración transperitoneal.
milammeter *n.* milámetro.
mild *adj.* leve^2.
miliampere *n.* miliamperio.
miliaria *n.* miliaria.
  miliaria alba miliaria alba cristalina.
  miliaria rubra miliaria roja, miliaria rubra.
miliary *adj.* miliar.
  miliary nevofibroma nevofibroma miliar.
milk *n.* leche.
milking *n.* ordeño.
milk-leg *n.* leucoflegmasía.
millia neonatorum *n.* miliosis neonatal.
milliammeter *n.* miliámetro.
milliamperemeter *n.* miliamperímetro.
milliequivalent *n.* miliequivalente.
milling-in milling-in.
millium milio, millium.
  colloid millium milio coloidal.
milphosis *n.* milfosis.
Mima Mima.
mimesis *n.* mimesis.
mimetic *adj.* mimético, -ca.
mimic *adj.* mímica, mímico, -ca.

mimicry *n.* mimetismo.
mimmation *n.* mimación, mimmación.
mimosis *n.* mimosis.
mind *n.* mente.
  wandering mind mente errante.
mineral *n.* mineral.
mineralcorticoid *n.* mineralcorticoide, mineralocorticoide.
mineralization *n.* mineralización.
mineralized *adj.* mineralizado, -da.
miniabdominoplasty *n.* miniabdominoplastia.
minify *v.* minificar.
minilaparatomy *n.* minilaparatomía.
  pelvic minilaparatomy minilaparatomía pélvica.
minim *n.* mínima.
minimization *n.* minimización.
minimum *n.* mínimo.
  light minimum mínimo de luz.
  minimum audibile mínimo audible.
  minimum cognoscibile mínimo cognoscible.
  minimum legibile mínimo legible.
  minimum separabile mínimo separable.
  visibile minimum mínimo visible.
minuthesis *n.* minutesis.
miofibrosis *n.* miofibrosis.
  miofibrosis cordis miofibrosis cardíaca.
mioplasty *n.* mioplastia.
miopragia *n.* meyopragia, miopragía.
miosis *n.* miosis.
  irritative miosis miosis irritativa.
  paralytic miosis miosis paralítica.
  spastic miosis miosis espasmódica, miosis espástica.
miracidium *n.* miracidio.
mirage *n.* espejismo.
mire *n.* mira.
mirror *n.* espejo.
  concave mirror espejo cóncavo.
  convex mirror espejo convexo.
  dental mirror espejo dental.
  frontal mirror espejo de frente, espejo frontal.
  Glatzel's mirror espejo de Glatzel.
  head mirror espejo de frente, espejo frontal.
  laryngeal mirror espejo laríngeo.
  mouth mirror espejo bucal.
  nasographic mirror espejo nasográfico.
  plane mirror espejo plano.
misanthropia *n.* misantropía.
misanthropy *n.* misandria, misantropía.
miscarriage *n.* malogro.
miscegenation *n.* miscegenación.
miscible *adj.* miscible.
miserotia *n.* miserotia.
misogamy *n.* misogamia.
misogyny *n.* misoginia.
misologia *n.* misología.
misoneism *n.* misoneísmo.
misopedia *v.* misopedia.
misopedy *n.* misopedia.
missexual *adj.* malsexual.
mitapsis *n.* mitapsis.
mite *n.* ácaro.
mitella *n.* mitela.
mitere *n.* mitor.
mithridatism *n.* mitridatismo.
miticidal *adj.* miticida.
miticide *n.* acaricida.
mitigate *v.* mitigar.
mitochondria *n.* mitocondria.
mitochondrial *adj.* mitocondrial.
mitogen *n.* mitógeno.
mitogenesis *n.* mitogénesis, mitogenia.
mitogenetic *adj.* mitogenético, -ca.

mitokinetic *adj.* mitocinético, -ca.
mitome *n.* mitoma.
mitoplasm *n.* mitoplasma.
mitoschisis *n.* mitosquisis.
mitosis *n.* mitosis.
  akinetic mitosis mitosis acinética.
  anastral mitosis mitosis anastral.
  astral mitosis mitosis astral.
  heterotype mitosis mitosis heterotípica.
  homeotypic mitosis mitosis homeotípica.
  multicentric mitosis mitosis multicéntrica.
  pathologic mitosis mitosis patológica.
  pluripolar mitosis mitosis pluripolar.
  somatic mitosis mitosis somática.
mitosome *n.* mitosoma.
mitotic *adj.* mitótico, -ca.
mitral *adj.* mitral.
mitralization *n.* mitralizacion.
mittelschmerz *n.* mittelschmerz.
mittor *n.* mitor.
mixed *adj.* mixto, -ta.
mixing *n.* mezclado.
mixochondroma *n.* mixocondroma.
mixoscopia *n.* mixoscopia.
mixotroph *n.* mixótrofo.
mixotrophic *adj.* mixotrófico, -ca.
mixture *n.* mezcla, mixtura.
  extemporaneous mixture mezcla extemporánea.
mneme *n.* mneme.
mnemic *adj.* mnémico, -ca, mnemónico, -ca, mnésico, -ca, mnéstico, -ca.
mnemism *n.* mnemismo.
mnemonics *n.* mnemónica.
mnemotechnics *n.* mnemotecnia.
mobility *n.* movilidad.
  electrophoretic mobility movilidad electroforética.
mobilization *n.* movilización.
mobilize *v.* movilizar.
mobilometer *n.* movilómetro.
mock up *n.* maqueta.
modality *n.* modalidad.
model¹ *n.* modelar.
  medical model modelo médico.
model² *v.* modelar.
modeling *n.* modelado.
  urea kinetic modeling modelo cinético de la urea.
modification *n.* modificación.
  behavior modification modificación de conducta.
modioliform *adj.* modioliforme.
modiolus *n.* modiolo.
modulation *n.* modulación.
  antigenic modulation modulación antigénica.
modulator *n.* modulador.
mogiarthria *n.* mogiartria.
mogigraphia *n.* mogigrafía.
mogilalia *n.* mogilalia.
mogiphonia *n.* mogifonía.
moist *adj.* húmedo, -da.
molal *adj.* molal.
molality *n.* molalidad.
molar *adj.* molar, muela.
  first molar primer molar.
  Moon's molar molar de Moon.
  mulberry molar molar en mora, molar moriforme.
  second molar segundo molar.
  sixth-year molar molar de los seis años, molar del sexto años.
  third molar tercer molar.
  twelfth-year molar molar de los doce años.

molariform *adj.* molariforme.
molarity *n.* molaridad.
mold¹ *n.* moho, molde.
mold² *v.* moldear.
molding *n.* moldeado.
mole *n.* mola.
  blood mole mola sanguínea.
  Breus' mole mola de Breus.
  cystic mole mola quística.
  false mole mola falsa.
  fleshy mole mola carnosa.
  hydatid mole mola hidatídica, mole hidatiforme.
  hydatidiform mole mola hidatídica, mole hidatiforme.
  invasive mole mola invasiva, mola invasora.
  malignant mole mola maligna, mola metastatizante.
  spider mole mola aracnoidea.
  stone mole mola pétrea.
  true mole mola verdadera.
  tubal mole mola tubaria.
  vesicular mole mola vesicular.
molecular *adj.* molecular.
molecule *n.* molécula.
  adhesion molecule molécula de adhesión.
  coestimulatory molecule molécula coestimuladora.
  complement protein molecule molécula proteica del complemento.
  middle molecule molécula media.
  signal molecule molécula señal.
molilalia *n.* molilalia.
molimen *n.* molimen.
molismophobia *n.* molismofobia.
mollin *n.* jabonadura.
mollities mollities.
  mollities ossium mollities ossium.
molluscacidal *adj.* moluscocida.
molluscacide *n.* moluscocida.
molluscum *n.* molusco.
  molluscum contagiosum molusco contagioso.
  molluscum fibrosum molusco fibroso.
  molluscum verrucosum molusco verrugoso.
molybdenic *adj.* molibdénico, -ca.
molybdenosis *n.* molibdenosis.
molybdenous *adj.* molibdenoso, -sa.
molybdenum *n.* molibdeno.
molybdoprotein *n.* molibdoproteína.
molybdous *adj.* molibdoso, -sa.
monamine oxidase *n.* monoaminooxidasa.
monangle *adj.* monoangular, monoángulo.
monarthritis *n.* monartritis, monoartritis.
  monarthritis deformans monartritis deformante.
monaster *n.* monáster.
monatomic *adj.* monoatómico, -ca.
monauchenos *n.* monauqueno.
monavitaminosis *n.* monoavitaminosis.
monaxonic *adj.* monoaxónico, -ca.
moner *n.* mónera.
monerula *n.* monérula.
monesthetic *adj.* monestésico, -ca.
mongolism *n.* mongolismo.
  translocation mongolism mongolismo por traslocación.
mongoloid *adj.* mongoloide.
monhydric *adj.* monohídrico, -ca.
monilated *adj.* monilado, -da.
monilethrix *n.* monilétrix.
Monilia Monilia.
monilial *adj.* monilial.
moniliasis *n.* moniliasis.
monilid *n.* monílide.

moniliform *adj.* moniliforme.
moniliosis *n.* moniliosis.
monism *n.* monismo.
monitor *n.* monitor, monitorizar.
  blood pressure monitor monitor de presión arterial.
  cardiac monitor monitor cardíaco.
  central venous pressure monitor monitor de presión venosa central.
  CVP monitor monitor de PVC.
  electronic fetal monitor monitor fetal electrónico.
  Holter monitor monitor Holter.
monoamelia *n.* monoamelia.
monoamide *n.* monoamida.
monoamine *n.* monoamina.
monoaminergic *adj.* monoaminérgico, -ca.
monoaminuria *n.* monoaminuria.
monoamniotic *adj.* monoamniótico, -ca.
monoanesthesia *n.* monoanestesia.
monoarticular *adj.* monoarticular.
monoassociated *adj.* monoasociado, -da.
monoathetosis *n.* monoatetosis.
monoaural *adj.* monoaural.
monobasic *adj.* monobásico, -ca.
monoblast *n.* monoblasto.
monoblastoma *n.* monoblastoma.
monobrachia *n.* monobraquia.
monobrachius *n.* monobraquio.
monobromated *adj.* monobromado, -da.
monocalcic *adj.* monocálcico, -ca.
monocardian *adj.* monocardio, -a.
monocelled *adj.* monocelular.
monocellular *adj.* monocelular.
monocephalus *n.* monocéfalo.
  monocephalus tetrapus dibrachius monocéfalo tetrápodo dibraquio.
  monocephalus tripus dibrachius monocéfalo trípodo dibraquio.
monochord *n.* monocordio.
monochorea *n.* monocorea.
monochorial *adj.* monocorial, monocorionico, -ca.
monochroic *adj.* monocroico, -ca.
monochromasia *n.* monocromasia.
monochromat *n.* monocrómata.
monochromatic *adj.* monocromático, -ca.
monochromatism *n.* monocromatismo.
monochromatophil *n.* monocromatófilo.
monochromic *adj.* monocrómico, -ca.
monochromophil *adj.* monocromófilo, -la.
monochromophile *adj.* monocromófilo, -la.
monoclonal *adj.* monoclonal, monoclónico, -ca.
monocontaminated *adj.* monocontaminado, -da.
monocontamination *n.* monocontaminación.
monocorditis *n.* monocorditis.
monocrotic *adj.* monocrótico, -ca.
monocrotism *n.* monocrotismo.
monocular *adj.* monocular.
monoculus *n.* monóculo.
monocyclic *adj.* monocíclico, -ca.
monocyesis *n.* monociesis.
monocyte *n.* monocito.
monocytic *adj.* monocítico, -ca.
monocytoid *adj.* monocitoide.
monocytopenia *n.* monocitopenia.
monocytopoiesis *n.* monocitopoiesis.
monocytosis *n.* monocitosis.
monodactylia *n.* monodactilia.
monodactylism *n.* monodactilismo.
monodactyly *n.* monodactilia.
monodelt *n.* monodelto.

monodermoma *n.* monodermoma.
monodiplopia *n.* monodiplopía.
monodisperse *adj.* monodisperso, -sa.
monoesthetic *adj.* monoestético, -ca.
monoestrous *adj.* monoestro, -ra, monoestrual.
monofilament *n.* monofilamento.
monogametic *adj.* monogamético, -ca.
monoganglial *adj.* monoganglionar.
monogastric *adj.* monogástrico, -ca.
monogenesis *n.* monogénesis, monogenia.
monogenetic *adj.* monogenético, -ca.
monogenic *adj.* monogénico, -ca.
monogerminal *adj.* monogerminal.
monohybrid *adj.* monohíbrido, -da.
monohydrated *adj.* monohidratado, -da.
monoideism *n.* monoideísmo.
monoinfection *n.* monoinfección.
monoiodotyrosine *n.* monoyodotirosina.
monokaryote *n.* monocariota.
monokaryotic *adj.* monocariótico, -ca.
monokine *n.* monocina.
monolayer *n.* monocapa.
monolepsis *n.* monolepsis.
monolocular *adj.* monolocular.
monomania *n.* monomanía.
monomaniac *n.* monomaníaco.
monomastigote *n.* monomastigoto.
monomaxillary *adj.* monomaxilar.
monomelic *adj.* monomélico, -ca.
monomer *n.* monómero.
monomeric *adj.* monomérico, -ca.
monometallic *adj.* monometálico, -ca.
monomicrobic *adj.* monomicrobiano, -na.
monomioplegia *n.* monomioplejía.
monomolecular *adj.* monomolecular.
monomorphic *adj.* monomórfico, -ca.
monomorphism *n.* monomorfismo.
monomorphous *adj.* monomorfo, -fa.
monomphalus *n.* monónfalo.
monomyositis *n.* monomiositis.
mononeural *adj.* mononeural.
mononeuralgia *n.* mononeuralgia.
mononeuric *adj.* mononeúrico, -ca.
mononeuritis *n.* mononeuritis.
  diabetic mononeuritis mononeuritis diabética.
  mononeuritis multiplex mononeuritis múltiple.
mononeuropathy *n.* mononeuropatía.
mononoea *n.* mononoea.
monont *n.* mononte.
mononuclear *adj.* mononuclear.
mononucleate *adj.* mononucleado, -da.
mononucleosis *n.* mononucleosis.
  cytomegalovirus mononucleosis mononucleosis por citomegalovirus.
  Infectious mononucleosis mononucleosis infecciosa.
  post-transfusion mononucleosis mononucleosis postransfusional.
mononucleotide *n.* mononucleótido.
mono-osteitic *adj.* monoosteítico, -ca.
mono-ovular *adj.* monoovular.
monooxygenase *n.* monooxigenasa.
monoparesis *n.* monoparesia.
monoparesthesia *n.* monoparestesia.
monopathic *adj.* monopático, -ca.
monopathy *n.* monopatía.
monopenia *n.* monopenia.
monophagia *n.* monofagia.
monophagism *n.* monofagismo.
monophasia *n.* monofasia.
monophasic *adj.* monofásico, -ca.
monophobia *n.* monofobia.

monophthalmos *n.* monoftalmo.
monophyletic *adj.* monofilético, -ca.
monophyletism *n.* monofiletismo.
monophyletist *n.* monofiletista.
monophyodont *adj.* monofiodonto, -ta.
monoplasmatic *adj.* monoplasmático, -ca.
monoplastic *adj.* monoplástico, -ca.
monoplegia *n.* monoplejía.
monoplegic *adj.* monopléjico, -ca.
monopodia *n.* monopodia.
monopodial *adj.* monopodial.
monopoiesis *n.* monopoyesis.
monoptychial *adj.* monoptiquial.
monopus *n.* monopo.
monorchia *n.* monorquia.
monorchidic *adj.* monorquídico, -ca.
monorchidism *n.* monorquidismo.
monorchism *adj.* monorquidia, monorquismo.
monorhinic *adj.* monorrinico, -ca.
monosaccharide *n.* monosacárido.
monosaccharose *n.* monosacarosa.
monoscelous *adj.* monoscelo, -la.
monoscenism *n.* monoescenismo.
monosemia *n.* monosomía.
monosome *n.* monosoma.
monosomic *adj.* monosómico, -ca.
monosomous *adj.* monosomo.
monospasm *n.* monospasmo, monoespasmo.
monospecific *adj.* monoespecífico, -ca.
monospermy *n.* monoespermia, monospermia.
monostotic *adj.* monostótico, -ca.
monostratal *adj.* monoestratal.
monostratified *adj.* monoestratificado, -da.
monosyfilide *n.* monosifílide.
monosymptom *n.* monosíntoma.
monosymptomatic *adj.* monosintomático, -ca.
monosynaptic *adj.* monosináptico, -ca.
monoterminal *adj.* monoterminal.
monothermia *n.* monotermia.
monotic *adj.* monótico, -ca.
monotocous *adj.* monotoco, -ca, monotocoso, -sa.
monotricate *adj.* monotricado, -da.
monotrichous *adj.* monotrico, -ca.
monovalent *adj.* monovalente.
monovular *adj.* monoovular, monovular.
monovulatory *adj.* monoovulatorio, -a.
monoxenic *adj.* monoxénico, -ca.
monoxenous *adj.* monoxénico, -ca.
monoxide *n.* monóxido.
monoxygenase *n.* monoxigenasa.
monozoic *adj.* monozoico, -ca.
monozygosity *n.* monocigosidad.
monozygotic *adj.* monocigótico, -ca.
monozygous *adj.* monocigoto, -ta.
mons mons, monte.
  mons veneris monte de venus.
monster *n.* monstruo.
monstricide *n.* monstruicidio.
monstrosity *n.* monstruosidad.
monstrum monstrum, monstruo.
monticulus *n.* montículo.
morbid *adj.* mórbido, -da, morboso, -sa.
morbidity *n.* morbidad, morbosidad.
morbidostatic *adj.* morbidostático, -ca.
morbific *adj.* morbífico, -ca.
morbility *n.* morbilidad.
  puerperal morbility morbilidad puerperal.
morbilli morbilia.
morbilliform *adj.* morbiliforme.
morbillous *adj.* morbilloso, -sa.
morbus morbus.
  morbus Addisonii morbus Addisonii.

morbus coxae senilis morbus coxae senilis.
morbus moniliformis morbus moniliformis.
morcel *v.* morcelar.
morcellation *n.* morcelación.
morcellement *n.* morcelamiento.
mordant *n.* mordente, mordiente.
morfogen *n.* morfógeno.
Morganella Morganella.
morgibenous *adj.* morbígeno, -na.
morgue *n.* morgue.
moria *n.* moria.
moribund *adj.* moribundo, -da.
moron *n.* morón.
moronism *n.* moronismo.
moronity *n.* moronismo.
morosis *n.* morosis.
morphallactic *adj.* morfaláctico, -ca.
morphallaxis *n.* morfalaxia.
morphea *n.* morfea.
  generalized morphea morfea generalizada.
  guttate morphea morfea gutada, morfea guttata.
  linear morphea morfea lineal.
  morphea acroterica morfea acrotérica.
  morphea alba morfea alba.
  morphea guttata morfea gutada, morfea guttata.
  morphea herpetiformis morfea herpetiformis.
  morphea linearis morfea lineal.
  morphea pigmentosa morfea nigra, morfea pigmentosa.
morphine *n.* morfina.
morphinic *adj.* morfinico, -ca.
morphinism *n.* morfinismo.
morphinist *adj.* morfinómano, -na.
morphinistic *adj.* morfinístico, -ca.
morphinization *n.* morfinización.
morphinomania *n.* morfinomanía.
morphiomania *n.* morfinomanía.
morphodifferentiation *n.* morfodiferenciación.
morphogenesis *n.* morfogénesis.
morphogenetic *adj.* morfogenético, -ca.
morphogeny *n.* morfogenia.
morphography *n.* morfografía.
morphological *adj.* morfológico, -ca.
morphology *n.* morfología.
morpholysis *n.* morfólisis.
morphometric *adj.* morfométrico, -ca.
morphometry *n.* morfometría.
morphon *n.* morfón.
morphophyly *n.* morfofilia.
morphophysics *n.* morfofísica.
morphoplasm *n.* morfoplasma.
morphosis *n.* morfosis.
morphotic *adj.* morfótico, -ca.
morrhuin *n.* morruina.
morsal *adj.* morsal.
mortal *adj.* mortal.
mortality *n.* mortalidad.
  fetal mortality mortalidad fetal.
  infant mortality mortalidad infantil.
  maternal mortality mortalidad maternal.
  neonatal mortality mortalidad neonatal.
  perinatal mortality mortalidad perinatal.
  prenatal mortality mortalidad prenatal.
mortalogram *n.* mortalograma.
mortar *n.* mortero.
mort-aux-rats *n.* raticida.
Mortierella Mortierella.
mortification *n.* mortificación.
mortified *adj.* mortificado, -da.
mortinatalidad *n.* mortinatalidad.
mortuary[1] *adj.* mortuorio, -ia.

mortuary[2] *n.* mortuorio, necrocomio.
morula *n.* mórula.
morular *adj.* morular.
morulation *n.* morulación.
moruloid *adj.* moruloide.
mosaic *n.* mosaico.
  colposcopic mosaic mosaico cervical.
  sex chromosomic mosaic mosaico de cromosomas sexuales.
  sex mosaic mosaico sexual.
mosaicism *n.* mosaicismo, mosaiquismo.
  cellular mosaicism mosaicismo celular.
  chromosome mosaicism mosaicismo cromosómico.
  erythrocyte mosaicism mosaicismo eritrocítico.
  gene mosaicism mosaicismo de genes.
  germ line mosaicism mosaicismo de línea germinal.
  germinal mosaicism mosaicismo germinal.
  gonadal mosaicism mosaicismo gonadal.
mosquito *n.* mosquito.
mosquitocide *n.* mosquitocida.
mote *n.* mota.
mother *n.* madre.
  birth mother madre de nacimiento.
  mother of vinegar madre del vinagre.
  surrogate mother madre de alquiler, madre sustituta.
motherhood *n.* maternidad.
  genetic motherhood maternidad genética.
  gestational motherhood maternidad gestacional.
  legal motherhood maternidad legal.
  surrogate motherhood maternidad de alquiler, maternidad subrogada.
motile *adj.* mótil, movible, móvil.
motilin *n.* motilina.
motility *n.* motilidad.
motion *n.* moción.
motivation *n.* motivación.
  achievement motivation motivación de logro.
  extrinsic motivation motivación extrínseca.
  intrinsic motivation motivación intrínseca.
  organic motivation motivación orgánica.
  personal motivation motivación personal.
  physiological motivation motivación fisiológica.
  social motivation motivación social.
motive *adj.* motivo.
  achievement motive motivo de éxito, motivo de logro.
  mastery motive motivo de dominio.
motoceptor *n.* motoceptor.
motofacient *adj.* motofaciente.
motoneuron *n.* motoneurona.
  alfa motoneuron motoneurona alfa.
  gamma motoneuron motoneurona gamma.
  heteronymous motoneuron motoneurona heterónima.
  homonymous motoneuron motoneurona homónima.
  lower motoneuron motoneurona inferior.
  peripheral motoneuron motoneurona periférica.
  upper motoneuron motoneurona central, motoneurona superior.
motor *n.* motor.
motorial *adj.* motórico, -ca.
motoricity *n.* motricidad.
motorium *n.* motorium.
motormeter *n.* motormetro.
motorogerminative *adj.* motorogerminativo, -va.
motorpathy *n.* motorpatía.

mottled *adj.* moteado, -da.
mottling *n.* moteado.
moulting *n.* muda.
mount[1] *n.* monte.
  mount of venus monte de venus.
mount[2] *v.* montar.
mountant *n.* montante.
mounting *n.* montaje.
mourning *n.* duelo.
mouse *n.* ratón.
  cancer-free white (CFW) mouse ratón CFW.
  joint mouse ratón articular.
  New Zealand Black (NAB) mouse ratón de Nueva Zelanda (ratón NAB).
  nu/nu mouse ratón nu/nu.
  nude mouse ratón desnudo.
mouth *n.* boca.
  carp mouth boca de carpa.
  Ceylon sore mouth boca ulcerada de Ceylán.
  denture sore mouth boca lastimada por prótesis, boca ulcerada por dentadura.
  dry mouth boca seca.
  glass-blowers' mouth boca de los sopladores de vidrio.
  saburral mouth boca saburral.
  sore mouth boca ulcerada.
  tapir mouth boca de tapir.
  trench mouth boca de trinchera.
  white mouth boca blanca.
mouthwash *n.* colutorio, gargarismo.
movement *n.* movimiento.
  accessory movement movimiento accesorio.
  active movement movimiento activo.
  adversive movement movimiento adversivo.
  ameboid movement movimiento ameboide.
  angular movement movimiento angular.
  assistive movement movimiento asistivo, movimiento auxiliar.
  associated movement movimiento asociado.
  automatic movement movimiento automático.
  ballistic movement movimiento balístico.
  Bennett movement movimiento de Bennett.
  body movement movimiento corporal.
  border movement movimiento de bordes, movimiento de límites.
  border tissue movement movimiento hístico de bordes, movimiento hístico de límites.
  Brownian movement movimiento browniano, movimiento brunoniano.
  Brown-Zsigmondy movement movimiento de Brown-Zsigmondy.
  cardinal movement of labor movimiento cardinal del parto.
  cardinal ocular movement movimiento ocular cardinal.
  choreic movement movimiento coreico, movimiento coreiforme.
  ciliary movement movimiento ciliar.
  circus movement movimiento circular, movimiento de circo.
  cogwheel ocular movementmovement movimiento ocular de piñón.
  conjugate movement of the eyes movimiento conjugado de los ojos.
  continuous passive movement movimiento pasivo continuo.
  contralateral associated movement movimiento contralateral asociado.
  decortical movement movimiento de decorticación.
  decorticated posturing movement movimiento de decorticación.
  disconjugate movement of the eyes movimiento no conjugado de los ojos.

  dystonic movement movimiento distónico.
  euglenoid movement movimiento euglenoide.
  excursive movement movimiento de excursión.
  fetal movement movimiento fetal.
  fixational ocular movement movimiento ocular de fijación.
  forced movement movimiento forzado.
  free mandibular movement movimiento libre del maxilar inferior, movimiento mandibular libre.
  Frenkel's movement movimiento de Frenkel.
  functional mandibular movement movimiento funcional del maxilar, movimiento mandibular funcional.
  fusional movement movimiento fusional.
  gliding movement movimiento deslizante.
  hinge movement movimiento en bisagra.
  intermediary movement movimiento intermediario, movimiento intermedio.
  intermediate movement movimiento intermediario, movimiento intermedio.
  inverse ocular movement movimiento ocular inverso.
  jaw movement movimiento del maxilar inferior, movimiento mandibular.
  lateral movement movimiento lateral.
  Magnan's movement movimiento de Magnan.
  Magnan's trombone movement movimiento de trombón de Magnan.
  mandibular movement movimiento del maxilar inferior, movimiento mandibular.
  mass movement movimiento de masa.
  masticatory movement movimiento masticatorio.
  molecular movement movimiento molecular.
  morphogenetic movement movimiento morfogenético.
  muscular movement movimiento muscular.
  neurobiotactic movement movimiento neurobiotáctico.
  non-rapid eye movement movimiento ocular no rápido.
  nucleopetal movement movimiento nucleópeto.
  opening movement movimiento apertura, movimiento de abertura.
  paradoxical movement of the eyelids movimiento paradójico de los párpados.
  passive movement movimiento pasivo.
  pendular movement movimiento pendular.
  perverted ocular movement movimiento ocular pervertido.
  precordial movement movimiento precordial.
  protoplasmatic movement movimiento protoplasmático.
  rapid eye movement (REM) movimiento ocular rápido.
  reflex movement movimiento reflejo.
  resistive movement movimiento de resistencia, movimiento resistido.
  saccadic movement movimiento a tirones, movimiento sacádico, movimiento sacudido.
  scissor movement movimiento en tijeras.
  segmentation movement movimiento de segmentación.
  smooth pursuit eye movement movimiento ocular de búsqueda uniforme.
  spontaneous movement movimiento espontáneo.
  streaming movement movimiento de corriente, movimiento de flujo.

Swedish movement movimiento sueco.
synkinetic movement movimiento sincinético.
translatory movement movimiento de traslación, movimiento traslatorio.
vermicular movement movimiento vermicular.
moxa *n.* moxa.
moxibustion *n.* moxibustión.
moyamoya *n.* moyamoya.
mucicarmine *n.* mucicarmin.
mucid *adj.* múcido, -da.
muciferous *adj.* mucífero, -ra.
mucification *n.* mucificación.
muciform *adj.* muciforme.
mucigenous *adj.* mucígeno, -na.
mucilage *n.* mucílago.
mucilagenous *adj.* mucilaginoso, sa.
mucin *n.* mucina.
mucinase *n.* mucinasa.
mucinemia *n.* mucinemia.
mucinoblast *n.* mucinoblasto.
mucinogen *n.* mucinógeno.
mucinolytic *adj.* mucinolítico, -ca.
mucinosis *n.* mucinosis.
  follicular mucinosis mucinosis folicular.
  papular mucinosis mucinosis papular.
mucinous *adj.* mucinoso, -sa.
mucinuria *n.* mucinuria.
mucionoid *adj.* mucinoide.
muciparous *adj.* mucíparo, -ra.
mucitis *n.* mucitis.
mucoanguineous *adj.* mucosanguíneo, -a.
mucoantibody *n.* mucoanticuerpo.
mucocartilage *n.* mucocartílago.
mucocele *n.* mucocele.
mucoclasis *n.* mucoclasia.
mucocolpos *n.* mucocolpos.
mucocutaneous *adj.* mucocutáneo, -a.
mucocyst *n.* mucoquiste.
mucocyte *n.* mucocito.
mucoderm *n.* mucoderma.
mucodermal *adj.* mucodérmico, -ca.
mucoepidermoid *adj.* mucoepidermoide.
mucofibrous *adj.* mucofibroso, -sa.
mucoflocculent *adj.* mucofloculento, -ta.
mucoglobulin *n.* mucoglobulina.
mucoid *adj.* mucoide.
  urine mucoid mucoide urinario.
mucolipidosis *n.* mucolipidosis.
mucolysis *n.* mucolisis.
mucolytic *adj.* mucolítico, -ca.
mucomembranous *adj.* mucomembranoso, -sa.
mucopeptide *n.* mucopéptido.
mucoperichondrial *adj.* mucopericondrial.
mucoperichondrium *n.* mucopericondrio.
mucoperiosteal *adj.* mucoperióstico, -ca.
mucoperiosteum *n.* mucoperiostio.
mucopolysaccharidosis *n.* mucopolisacaridosis.
mucopolysaccharidase *n.* mucopolisacaridasa.
mucopolysaccharide *n.* mucopolisacárido.
mucopolysacchariduria *n.* mucopolisacariduria.
  Tamm-Horsfall mucopolysacchariduria mucopolisacariduria de Tamm-Horsfall.
mucoprotein *n.* mucoproteína.
mucopurulent *adj.* mucopurulento, -ta.
mucopus *n.* mocopús, mucopús.
mucormycosis *n.* mucormicosis.
mucosa *n.* mucosa.
mucosectomy *n.* mucosectomía.
mucosedative *adj.* mucosedante.

mucoserous *adj.* mucoseroso, -sa.
mucosin *n.* mucosina.
mucositis *n.* mucositis.
mucosocutaneous *adj.* mucosocutáneo, -a.
mucostatic *adj.* mucostático, -ca.
mucosulfatidosis *n.* mucosulfatidosis.
mucotome *n.* mucótomo.
mucous *adj.* mucoso, -sa.
mucoviscidosis *n.* mucoviscidosis.
mucro *n.* mucro.
  mucro cordis mucro cardíaco.
  mucro sternis mucro esternal.
mucronate *adj.* mucronato, -ta.
mucroniform *adj.* mucroniforme.
mucus *n.* moco, mucosidad, mucus.
muffle *n.* mufla.
mular *adj.* mular.
mulatto *adj., n.* mulato, -ta.
muliebria *n.* muliebria.
muliebrity *n.* muliebridad.
muller *n.* moleta.
müllerianoma *n.* müllerianoma.
multiallelic *adj.* multialélico, -ca.
multiangular *adj.* multiangular.
multiarticular *adj.* multiarticular.
multiaxial *adj.* multiaxial.
multibaccilary *adj.* multibacilar.
multicapsular *adj.* multicapsular.
multicell *n.* multicélula.
multicellular *adj.* multicelular.
multicellularity *n.* multicelularidad.
multicentric *adj.* multicéntrico, -ca.
multicontaminated *adj.* multicontaminado, -da.
multicuspid *adj.* multicúspide.
multicuspidate *adj.* multicúspide, multicuspídeo, -a.
multicystic *adj.* multiquístico, -ca.
multidentate *adj.* multidentado, -da.
multidimensional *adj.* multidimensional.
multifactorial *adj.* multifactorial.
multifamilial *adj.* multifamiliar.
multifetation *n.* multifetación.
multifidus *adj.* multífido, -da.
multifocal *adj.* multifocal.
multiform *adj.* multiforme.
multiganglionic *adj.* multiganglionar.
multigesta *adj.* multigesta.
multiglandular *adj.* multiglandular.
multigravida *adj.* multigrávida.
multihallucalism *n.* multihalucalismo.
multihallucism *n.* multihalucismo.
multi-infection *n.* multiinfección.
multilobar *adj.* multilobular.
multilobular *adj.* multilobulillar.
multilocal *adj.* multilocal.
multilocular *adj.* multilocular.
multimammae *n.* multimamia.
multinodal *adj.* multinodal.
multinodular *adj.* multinodular.
multinuclear *adj.* multinuclear.
multipara *adj.* multípara.
multiparity *n.* multiparidad.
multiparous *adj.* multíparo, -ra.
multipartial *adj.* multiparcial.
multiplanar *adj.* multiplanar.
multiple *adj.* múltiple.
multiplication *n.* multiplicación.
multiplicitas *n.* multiplicidad.
  multiplicitas cordis multiplicidad cardíaca.
multipolar *adj.* multipolar.
multipollicalism *n.* multipolicalismo.
multirooted *adj.* multirradicular.
multirotation *n.* multirrotación.
multiscan *n.* multicorte.

multisensitivity *n.* multisensibilidad.
multiterminal *adj.* multiterminal.
multituberculate *adj.* multituberculado, -da.
multivalent *adj.* multivalente.
mumbling *n.* mascullamiento.
mummification *n.* momificación.
mummy *n.* momia.
mumps *n.* paperas.
munity *n.* munidad.
mural *adj.* mural.
muramidase *n.* muramidasa.
murein *n.* mureína.
muriform *adj.* muriforme.
murmur *n.* murmullo, soplo.
  accidental murmur soplo accidental.
  anemic murmur soplo anémico.
  aortic murmur soplo aórtico.
  aortic regurgitant murmur soplo de regurgitación aórtica.
  apex murmur soplo de la punta.
  arterial murmur soplo arterial.
  atriosystolic murmur soplo auriculosistólico.
  Austin Flint murmur soplo de Austin Flint.
  bellows murmur soplo de fuelle.
  brain murmur soplo cerebral.
  Cabot-Locke murmur soplo de Cabot-Locke.
  cardiopulmonary murmur soplo cardiopulmonar, soplo cardiorrespiratorio.
  cardiorespiratory murmur soplo cardiopulmonar, soplo cardiorrespiratorio.
  Carey-Coombs' murmur soplo de Carey-Coombs.
  Cole-Cecil murmur soplo de Cole-Cecil.
  continuous murmur soplo continuo.
  Coombs murmur soplo de Coombs.
  crescendo murmur soplo creciente, soplo in crescendo.
  Cruveilhier-Baumgarten murmur soplo de Cruveilhier-Baumgarten.
  diamond-shaped murmur soplo en forma de rombo.
  diastolic murmur soplo diastólico.
  Duroziez's murmur soplo de Duroziez.
  dynamic murmur soplo dinámico.
  early diastolic murmur soplo diastólico inicial.
  ejection murmur soplo de eyección.
  endocardial murmur soplo endocárdico.
  exocardial murmur soplo exocardíaco, soplo extracardíaco.
  extracardiac murmur soplo exocardíaco, soplo extracardíaco.
  Flint's murmur soplo de Flint.
  Fräntzel's murmur soplo de Fräntzel.
  functional murmur soplo funcional.
  Gibson's murmur soplo de Gibson.
  Graham-Steell's murmur soplo de Graham-Steell.
  heart murmur soplo cardíaco.
  hemic murmur soplo hemático.
  Hodgkin-Key murmur soplo de Hodgkin-Key.
  holosystolic murmur soplo holosistólico.
  hourglass murmur soplo en reloj de arena.
  innocent murmur soplo inocente.
  inorganic murmur soplo inorgánico.
  late apical systolic murmur soplo sistólico apical tardío.
  late diastolic murmur soplo diastólico tardío.
  late systolic murmur soplo telesistólico.
  machinery murmur soplo de maquinaria.
  mid-diastolic murmur soplo mesodiastólico.
  mill wheel murmur soplo en rueda de molino.
  mitral murmur soplo mitral.
  muscular murmur soplo muscular.

musical murmur soplo musical.
nun's murmur soplo de monja.
organic murmur soplo orgánico.
pansystolic murmur soplo pansistólico.
pericardial murmur soplo pericárdico.
physiological murmur soplo fisiológico.
pleuropericardial murmur soplo pleuroperi-cárdico.
prediastolic murmur soplo prediastólico.
presystolic murmur soplo presistólico.
pulmonary murmur soplo pulmonar.
regurgitant murmur soplo de regurgitación, soplo regurgitante.
respiratory murmur soplo respiratorio.
Roger's murmur soplo de Roger.
sea gull murmur soplo de gaviota.
seesaw murmur soplo en sube y baja.
Steell's murmur soplo de Steell.
stenosal murmur soplo de estenosis, soplo es-tenótico.
Still's murmur soplo de Still.
systolic murmur soplo sistólico.
to-and-fro murmur soplo de vaivén, soplo en vaivén.
tricuspid murmur soplo tricuspídeo.
vascular murmur soplo vascular.
venous murmur soplo venoso.
vesicular murmur soplo vesicular.
water wheel murmur soplo en rueda hidráu-lica.
musca *n.* mosca.
Musca Musca.
muscacide *n.* muscacida.
muscarinic *adj.* muscarínico, -ca.
muscarinique *n.* muscarina.
muscarinism *n.* muscarinismo.
muscicide *n.* muscicida.
muscle *n.* músculo.
agonistic muscle músculo agonista.
antigravity muscle músculo antigravitatorio.
antogonistic muscle músculo antagonista.
articular muscle músculo articular.
extrinsic muscle músculo extrínseco.
intrafusal muscle músculo intrafusal.
intrinsic muscle músculo intrínseco.
involuntary muscle músculo involuntario.
isometric muscle músculo isométrico.
myotomic muscle músculo miotómico.
nonstriated muscle músculo liso.
prime muscle músculo principal.
smooth muscle músculo de fibra lisa, múscu-lo liso.
striated muscle músculo de fibra estriada, músculo estriado.
synergitic muscle músculo sinérgico.
voluntary muscle músculo voluntario.
muscular *adj.* muscular.
muscularity *n.* muscularidad.
musculature *n.* musculatura.
musculoaponeurotic *adj.* musculoaponeuró-tico, -ca.
musculocutaneous *adj.* musculocutáneo, -a.
musculodermic *adj.* musculodérmico, -ca.
musculoelastic *adj.* musculoelástico, -ca.
musculointestinal *adj.* musculointestinal.
musculomembranous *adj.* musculomembra-noso, -sa.
musculophrenic *adj.* musculofrénico, -ca.
musculoskeletal *adj.* musculoesquelético, -ca.
musculotendinous *adj.* musculotendino-so, -sa.
musculotonic *adj.* musculotónico, -ca.
musculus *n.* músculo.
musicogenic *adj.* musicogénico, -ca.
musicotherapy *n.* musicoterapia.

mussitation *n.* musitación.
mutacism *n.* mutacismo.
mutagen *n.* mutágeno.
mutagenesis *n.* mutagénesis.
insertional mutagenesis mutagénesis inser-cional.
mutagenic *adj.* mutagénico, -ca.
mutagenicity *n.* mutagenicidad.
mutant *n.* mutante.
mutarotation *n.* mutarrotación.
mutation *n.* mutación.
addition-deletion mutation mutación por inserción-deleción.
allelic mutation mutación alélica.
auxotrophic mutation mutación auxotrófica.
back mutation mutación retrógrada.
biochemical mutation mutación bioquímica.
chromosomal mutation mutación cromosó-mica.
clear plaque mutation mutación en placa cla-ra.
cold-sensitive mutation mutación sensible al frío.
conditional lethal mutation mutación con-dicional mortal.
conditional mutation mutación condicional.
constitutive mutation mutación constitutiva.
forward mutation mutación hacia delante.
frameshift mutation mutación de desvia-ción de la estructura.
genomic mutation mutación genómica.
germinal mutation mutación germinal.
homeotic mutation mutación homeótica.
induced mutation mutación inducida.
lethal mutation mutación letal, mutación mortal.
missense mutation mutación de sentido erróneo.
natural mutation mutación natural.
neutral mutation mutación neutra.
nutritional mutation mutación nutricional.
opal mutation mutación opalina.
point mutation mutación de punto, muta-ción puntiforme.
reading-frame-shift mutation mutación de desviación de la estructura de la lectura, muta-ción por cambio de encuadre.
reverse mutation mutación corregida, muta-ción inversa.
silent mutation mutación silente.
somatic mutation mutación somática.
spontaneous mutation mutación espontá-nea.
supressor mutation mutación supresora.
temperature-sensitive mutation mutación sensible a la temperatura.
visible mutation mutación visible.
mutational *adj.* mutacional.
mute *adj.* mudo, -da.
mutein *n.* muteína.
mutilation *n.* mutilación.
mutism *n.* mutismo.
akinetic mutism mutismo acinético.
deaf mutism mutismo sordo.
elective mutism mutismo electivo.
muton *n.* mutón.
mutualism *n.* mutualismo.
mutualist *adj.* mutualista.
myalgia *n.* mialgia.
epidemic myalgia mialgia epidémica.
lumbar myalgia mialgia lumbar.
myalgia abdominis mialgia abdominal.
myalgia capitis mialgia cefálica, mialgia cra-neal.
myalgia cervicalis mialgia cervical.

myalgia thermica mialgia térmica.
myasis *n.* miasis.
African furuncular myasis miasis foruncular africana.
creeping myasis miasis reptante.
human botfly myasis miasis por moscardón humano.
intestinal myasis miasis intestinal.
nasal myasis miasis nasal.
ocular myasis miasis ocular.
subcutaneous myasis miasis subcutánea.
traumatic myasis miasis traumática.
tumbu myasis miasis dérmica tumbu.
wound myasis miasis de heridas.
myasteniform *adj.* miasteniforme.
myasthenia *n.* miastenia
myasthenia gastrica miastenia gástrica.
myasthenia gravis miastenia grave, miaste-nia grave seudoparalítica.
myasthenia gravis pseudoparalytica mias-tenia grave, miastenia grave seudoparalítica.
myasthenia laryngis miastenia laríngea.
neonatal myasthenia miastenia neonatal.
myasthenic *adj.* miasténico, -ca.
myatonia *n.* miatonía.
myatonia congenita miatonía congénita.
myatony *n.* miatonía.
myatrophy *n.* miatrofia.
mycelial *adj.* micélico, -ca.
mycelian *adj.* miceliano, -na.
mycelioid *adj.* micelioide.
mycelium *n.* micelio.
aerial mycelium micelio aéreo.
non-septate mycelium micelio no septado.
septate mycelium micelio septado, micelio tabicado.
mycete *n.* miceto.
mycethemia *n.* micetemia.
mycetismus *n.* micetismo.
mycetismus cerebris micetismo cerebral.
mycetismus choleriformis micetismo coleri-forme.
mycetismus gastrointestinalis micetismo gastrointestinal.
mycetismus nervosus micetismo nervioso.
mycetismus sanguinarius micetismo san-guinario.
mycetogenetic *adj.* micetogénico, -ca.
mycetogenic *adj.* micetógeno, -na.
mycetogenous *adj.* micetógeno, -na.
mycetoma *n.* micetoma.
actimomycotic mycetoma micetoma actino-micótico.
Bouffardi's black mycetoma micetoma ne-gro de Bouffardi.
Bouffardi's white mycetoma micetoma blanco de Bouffardi.
Brumpt's white mycetoma micetoma blan-co de Brumpt.
Carter's black mycetoma micetoma negro de Carter.
eumycotic mycetoma micetoma eumicótico.
Nicolle's white mycetoma micetoma blanco de Nicolle.
Vincent's white mycetoma micetoma blan-co de Vincent.
mycid *adj.* mícide.
mycoagglutinin *n.* micoaglutinina.
mycobacteria *n.* micobacteria.
anonymous mycobacteria micobacteria anónima, micobacteria atípica.
atypical mycobacteria micobacteria anóni-ma, micobacteria atípica.
Mycobacteriaceae Mycobacteriaceae.
mycobacteriosis *n.* micobacteriosis.

Mycobacterium Mycobacterium.
mycobactin *n.* micobactina.
mycocide *n.* micocida.
mycoderma *n.* micoderma.
mycodermatitis *n.* micodermatitis.
mycodermomycosis *n.* micodermomicosis.
mycogastritis *n.* micogastritis.
mycohemia *n.* micohemia.
mycologist *n.* micólogo, -ga.
mycology *n.* micetología, micología.
 medical mycology micología médica.
mycomyringitis *n.* micomiringitis.
mycopathology *n.* micopatología.
mycophage *n.* micófago.
mycophagy *n.* micofagia.
Mycoplasma Mycoplasma.
mycoplasmal *adj.* micoplasmático, -ca.
Mycoplasmataceae Mycoplasmataceae.
mycoprecipitin *n.* micoprecipitina.
mycoproteination *n.* micoproteinación.
mycopus *n.* micopús.
mycosis *n.* micetosis, micosis.
 mycosis chronica micosis crónica.
 mycosis framboesioides micosis framboesioides.
 mycosis fungoides micosis fungoides.
 mycosis intestinalis micosis intestinal, micosis intestinalis.
 mycosis leptotrica micosis leptótrica.
 Posadas mycosis micosis de Posadas.
mycostasis *n.* micostasis.
mycostatic *adj.* micostático, -ca.
mycosterols *n.* micoesteroles.
mycotic *adj.* micótico, -ca.
mycotoxicosis *n.* micotoxicosis.
mycotoxin *n.* micotoxina.
mycotoxinization *n.* micotoxinización.
mycovirus *n.* micovirus.
mycronystagmus *n.* micronistagmo.
mycteric *adj.* mictérico, -ca.
mycteroxerosis *n.* micteroxerosis.
mydaleine *n.* midaleína.
mydatoxine *n.* midatoxina.
mydriasis *n.* midriasis, platicoria.
 alternating mydriasis midriasis alternante.
 amaurotic mydriasis midriasis amaurótica.
 paralytic mydriasis midriasis paralítica.
 pharmacologic mydriasis midriasis artificial, midriasis farmacológica.
 spasmodic mydriasis midriasis espasmódica.
 spastic mydriasis midriasis espástica.
 spinal mydriasis midriasis espinal.
mydriatic *adj.* midriático, -ca.
myectopia *n.* miectopia.
myectopy *n.* miectopia.
myelacephalus *n.* mielacéfalo.
myelalgia *n.* mielalgia.
myelanalosis *n.* mielanalosis.
myelapoplexy *n.* mielapoplejía.
myelatelia *n.* mielatelia.
myelatrophy *n.* mielatrofia.
myelauxe *n.* mielauxa.
myelemia *n.* mielemia.
myelencephalitis *n.* mielencefalitis.
myelencephalon *n.* mielencéfalo.
myelencephalospinal *adj.* mielencefaloespinal.
myeleterosis *n.* mieleterosis.
myelic *adj.* miélico, -ca.
myelin *n.* mielina.
myelinated *adj.* mielinado, -da, mielinizado, -da.
myelinic *adj.* mielínico, -ca.
myelinization *n.* mielinización.
myelinoclasis *n.* mielinoclasia, mielinoclasis.

myelinolysin *n.* mielinolisina.
myelinolysis *n.* mielinólisis.
 central pontine myelinolysis mielinólisis central pontina.
myelinopathy *n.* mielinopatía.
myelinosis *n.* mielinosis.
myelitic *adj.* mielítico, -ca.
myelitis *n.* mielitis.
 acute ascending myelitis mielitis ascendente, mielitis ascendente aguda.
 acute myelitis mielitis aguda.
 acute transverse myelitis mielitis transversa aguda, mielitis transversal aguda.
 ascending myelitis mielitis ascendente, mielitis ascendente aguda.
 bulbar myelitis mielitis bulbar.
 central myelitis mielitis central.
 chronic myelitis mielitis crónica.
 compression myelitis mielitis por compresión.
 concussion myelitis mielitis por concusión, mielitis por conmoción.
 cornual myelitis mielitis cornual.
 descending myelitis mielitis descendente.
 diffuse myelitis mielitis difusa.
 disseminated myelitis mielitis diseminada.
 Foix-Alajouaine myelitis mielitis de Foix-Alajouaine.
 funicular myelitis mielitis funicular.
 hemorrhagic myelitis mielitis hemorrágica.
 myelitis vaccinia mielitis por vacuna.
 neuro-optic myelitis mielitis neuroóptica.
 periependymal myelitis mielitis periependimaria.
 postvaccinal myelitis mielitis por vacuna.
 subacute necrotizing myelitis mielitis necrosante subaguda.
 transverse myelitis mielitis transversa, mielitis transversal.
 traumatic myelitis mielitis traumática.
myeloarchitecture *n.* mieloarquitectura.
myeloblast *n.* mieloblasto.
myeloblastemia *n.* mieloblastemia.
myeloblastoma *n.* mieloblastoma.
myeloblastosis *n.* mieloblastosis.
myelocele *n.* mielocele.
myelocentric *adj.* mielocéntrico, -ca.
myelocephalus *n.* mielocéfalo.
myelocist *n.* mielocisto.
myelocitomatosis *n.* mielocitomatosis.
myeloclast *n.* mieloclasto.
myelocoele *n.* mielocelo.
myelocone *n.* mielocono.
myelocyst *n.* mieloquiste.
myelocystele *n.* mielocistocele.
myelocystic *adj.* mielocístico, -ca, mieloquístico, -ca.
myelocystomenyngocele *n.* mielocistomeningocele.
myelocyte *n.* mielocito.
myelocythemia *n.* mielocitemia.
myelocytic *adj.* mielocítico, -ca.
myelocytoma *n.* mielocitoma.
myelocytosis *n.* mielocitosis.
myelodiastasia *n.* mielodiastasis.
myelodiastasis *n.* mielodiastasia.
myelodysplasia *n.* mielodisplasia.
myeloencephalic *adj.* mieloencefálico, -ca.
myeloencephalitis *n.* mieloencefalitis.
 eosinophilic myeloencephalitis mieloencefalitis eosinofílica.
myelofibrosis *n.* mielofibrosis.
 osteosclerosis myelofibrosis mielofibrosis osteoesclerótica.
myelofugal *adj.* mielófugo, -ga.

myelogenesis *n.* mielinogénesis, mielogénesis.
myelogenetic *adj.* mielinogenético, -ca, mielogenético, -ca.
myelogenic *adj.* mielogénico, -ca.
myelogenous *adj.* mielógeno, -na.
myelogeny *n.* mielinogenia, mielogenia.
myelogone *n.* mielogonia.
myelogonic *adj.* mielogónico, -ca.
myelogram *n.* mielograma.
myelography *n.* mielografía.
myeloic *adj.* mieloico, -ca.
myeloid *adj.* mieloide, mieloideo, -a.
myeloidin *n.* mieloidina.
myeloidosis *n.* mieloidosis.
myeloleukemia *n.* mieloleucemia.
myelolipoma *n.* mielolipoma.
myelolymphangioma *n.* mielolinfangioma.
myelolymphocyte *n.* mielolinfocito.
myelolysis *n.* mielólisis.
myelolytic *adj.* mielolítico, -ca.
myeloma *n.* mieloma.
 Bence-Jones myeloma mieloma de Bence-Jones.
 endothelial myeloma mieloma endotelial.
 extramedullary myeloma mieloma extramedular.
 indolent myeloma mieloma indolente.
 L-chain myeloma mieloma de cadena L.
 localized myeloma mieloma localizado.
 multiple myeloma mieloma múltiple.
 non-secretory myeloma mieloma no secretorio.
 peripheral plasma cell myeloma mieloma de células plasmáticas periféricas.
 plasma cell myeloma mieloma de células plasmáticas.
 solitary myeloma mieloma solitario.
myelomalacia *n.* mielomalacia.
myelomatoid *adj.* mielomatoide.
myelomatosis *n.* mielomatosis.
myelomenia *n.* mielomenia.
myelomeningitis *n.* mielomeningitis.
myelomeningocele *n.* mielomeningocele.
myelomere *n.* mielómera, mielómero.
myelomonocyte *n.* mielomonocito.
myelomyces *n.* mielomices.
myeloneuritis *n.* mieloneuritis.
myelonic *adj.* mielónico, -ca.
myelonotoxicity *n.* mielinotoxicidad.
myelo-opticoneuropathy *n.* mieloopticoneuropatía.
myeloparalysis *n.* mieloparálisis.
myelopathic *adj.* mielopático, -ca.
myelopathy *n.* mielopatía.
 ascending myelopathy mielopatía ascendente.
 carcinomatous myelopathy mielopatía carcinomatosa.
 cervical myelopathy mielopatía cervical.
 cervical spondylotic myelopathy mielopatía cervical espondilótica.
 compressive myelopathy mielopatía compresiva, mielopatía por compresión.
 concussion myelopathy mielopatía por concusión, mielopatía por conmoción.
 descending myelopathy mielopatía descendente.
 diabetic myelopathy mielopatía diabética.
 funicular myelopathy mielopatía funicular.
 hemorrhagic myelopathy mielopatía hemorrágica.
 paracarcinomatous myelopathy mielopatía paracarcinomatosa.
 radiation myelopathy mielopatía por radiaciones.

spondylotic cervical myelopathy mielopatía cervical espondilótica.
transverse myelopathy mielopatía transversa.
traumatic myelopathy mielopatía traumática.
myeloperoxidase *n.* mieloperoxidasa.
myelopetal *adj.* mielópeto, -ta.
myelophage *n.* mielófago.
myelophthisic *adj.* mielotísico, -ca.
myelophthisis *n.* mielotisis.
myeloplaque *n.* mieloplaca.
myeloplast *n.* mieloplasto.
myeloplax *n.* mieloplaxa.
myeloplegia *n.* mieloplejía.
myelopoiesis *n.* mielopoyesis.
  ectopic myelopoiesis mielopoyesis ectópica.
  extramedullary myelopoiesis mielopoyesis extramedular.
myelopoietic *adj.* mielopoyético, -ca.
myelopore *n.* mieloporo.
myeloproliferative *adj.* mieloproliferativo, -va.
myeloradiculitis *n.* mielorradiculitis.
myeloradiculodysplasia *n.* mielorradiculodisplasia.
myeloradiculopathy *n.* mielorradiculopatía.
myeloradiculopolyneuronitis *n.* mielorradiculopolineuronitis.
myelorrhagia *n.* mielorragia.
myelorrhaphy *n.* mielorrafia.
myelosarcoma *n.* mielosarcoma.
myelosarcomatosis *n.* mielosarcomatosis.
myeloschisis *n.* mielosquisis.
myeloscintogram *n.* mielocintigrama, mieloescintigrama.
myelosclerosis *n.* mieloesclerosis, mielosclerosis.
myelosis *n.* mielosis.
  aleukemic myelosis mielosis aleucémica.
  chronic non-leukemic myelosis mielosis crónica no leucémica, mielosis no leucémica crónica.
  erythremic myelosis mielosis eritrémica.
  funicular myelosis mielosis funicular.
  leukemic myelosis mielosis leucémica.
  leukopenic myelosis mielosis leucopénica.
  non-leukemic myelosis mielosis no leucémica.
  subleukemic myelosis mielosis subleucémica.
myelospasm *n.* mieloespasmo.
myelospongium *n.* mielospongio.
myelosuppression *n.* mielosupresión.
myelosuppressive *adj.* mielosupresor, -ra.
myelosyphilis *n.* mielosífilis.
myelosyringosis *n.* mielosiringosis.
myelotherapy *n.* mieloterapia.
myelotome *n.* mielótomo.
myelotomography *n.* mielotomografia.
myelotomy *n.* mielotomía.
  Bischof's myelotomy mielotomía de Bischof.
  commissural myelotomy mielotomía comisural.
  midline myelotomy mielotomía de la línea media.
  T myelotomy mielotomía en T.
myelotoxic *adj.* mielotóxico, -ca.
myelotoxicity *n.* mielotoxicidad.
myelotoxin *n.* mielotoxina.
myenteric *adj.* mientérico, -ca.
myenteron *n.* mienteron.
myesthesia *n.* miestesia.
myiasis *n.* miasis, miiasis.
myitis *n.* miitis.
mylohyoid *adj.* milohioideo, -a.

myoadenylate deaminase *n.* mioadenilato desaminasa.
myoalbumin *n.* mioalbúmina.
myoarchitectonic *adj.* mioarquitectónico, -ca.
myoasthenia *n.* mioastenia.
myoatrophy *n.* miatrofia, mioatrofia.
myoautonomy *n.* mioautonomía.
myoblast *n.* mioblasto.
myoblastic *adj.* mioblástico, -ca.
myoblastoma *n.* mioblastoma.
myoblastomyoma *n.* mioblastomioma.
myobradia *n.* miobradia.
myocardia *n.* miocardia.
myocardiac *adj.* miocárdico, -ca.
myocardial *adj.* miocárdico, -ca.
myocardiogram *n.* miocardiograma.
myocardiograph *n.* miocardiógrafo.
myocardiolysis *n.* miocardiólisis.
myocardiopathy *n.* miocardiopatía.
  alcoholic myocardiopathy miocardiopatía alcohólica.
  beer-drinker myocardiopathy miocardiopatía del bebedor de cerveza.
  chagasic myocardiopathy miocardiopatía chagásica.
  congestive myocardiopathy miocardiopatía congestiva.
  constrictive myocardiopathy miocardiopatía constrictiva.
  diabetic myocardiopathy miocardiopatía diabética.
  dilated myocardiopathy miocardiopatía dilatada.
  hypertrophic myocardiopathy miocardiopatía hipertrófica.
  hypertrophic obstructive myocardiopathy miocardiopatía hipertrófica obstructiva.
  idiopathic myocardiopathy miocardiopatía idiopática.
  infiltrative myocardiopathy miocardiopatía infiltrante.
  peripartum myocardiopathy miocardiopatía periparto.
  post partum myocardiopathy miocardiopatía posparto.
  primary myocardiopathy miocardiopatía primaria.
  restrictive myocardiopathy miocardiopatía restrictiva.
  secondary myocardiopathy miocardiopatía secundaria.
myocardiorrhaphy *n.* miocardiorrafia.
myocardiosis *n.* miocardiosis.
myocarditic *adj.* miocardítico, -ca.
myocarditis *n.* miocarditis.
  acute bacterial myocarditis miocarditis bacteriana aguda.
  acute isolated myocarditis miocarditis aguda aislada, miocarditis aislada aguda.
  acute primary myocarditis miocarditis aguda primaria.
  acute secondary myocarditis miocarditis aguda secundaria.
  acute septic myocarditis miocarditis séptica aguda.
  chronic myocarditis miocarditis crónica.
  diphtheritic myocarditis miocarditis diftérica.
  fibrous myocarditis miocarditis fibrosa.
  Fieldler's myocarditis miocarditis de Fieldler.
  fragmentation myocarditis miocarditis de fragmentación.
  giant cell myocarditis miocarditis de células gigantes.
  idiopathic myocarditis miocarditis idiopática.

  indurative myocarditis miocarditis indurativa.
  interstitial myocarditis miocarditis intersticial.
  parenchymatous myocarditis miocarditis parenquimosa.
  rheumatic myocarditis miocarditis reumática.
  toxic myocarditis miocarditis tóxica.
  tuberculous myocarditis miocarditis tuberculosa.
myocardium *n.* miocardio.
  stunned myocardium miocardio aturdido.
myocardosis *n.* miocardiosis, miocardosis.
myocele *n.* miocele.
myocelialgia *n.* miocelialgía.
myocelitis *n.* miocelitis.
myocellulitis *n.* miocelulitis.
myocephalon *n.* miocéfalo.
myoceptor *n.* mioceptor.
myocerosis *n.* miocerosis.
myochorditis *n.* miocorditis.
myochrome *n.* miocromo.
myochronoscope *n.* miocronoscopio.
myoclonia *n.* mioclonía.
  cortical myoclonia mioclonía cortical.
  disseminated myoclonia mioclonía generalizada.
  fibrillary myoclonia mioclonía fibrilar.
  focal myoclonia mioclonía focal.
  multiplex myoclonia mioclonía múltiple.
  myoclonia epileptica mioclonía epiléptica.
  myoclonia fibrillaris multiplex mioclonía fibrilar múltiple.
  palatal myoclonia mioclonía palatina, mioclonía velopalatina.
  pseudoglottic myoclonia mioclonía seudoglótica.
  reticular myoclonia mioclonía reticular.
  segmental myoclonia mioclonía parcelar.
  spinal myoclonia mioclonía espinal.
  stimulus sensitive myoclonia mioclonía sensible a los estímulos.
myoclonic *adj.* mioclónico, -ca.
myoclonus *n.* mioclono.
  nocturnal myoclonus mioclono nocturno.
myocoele *n.* miocelo.
myocolpitis *n.* miocolpitis.
myocrismus *n.* miocrismo.
myoctonine *n.* mioctonina.
myoculator *n.* mioculador.
myocutaneous *adj.* miocutáneo, -a.
myocyte *n.* miocito.
myocytolisis *n.* miocitólisis.
myocytoma *n.* miocitoma.
myodegeneration *n.* miodegeneración.
myodemia *n.* miodemia.
myodermal miodérmico.
myodesopsia *n.* miodesopsia, miiodesopsia, miiodopsia.
myodiastasis *n.* miodiastasis.
myodidymus *n.* miodídimo.
myodiopter *n.* miodioptría.
myodynamia *n.* miodinamia.
myodynamic *adj.* miodinámico, -ca.
myodynamics *n.* miodinámica.
myodynamometer *n.* miodinamómetro.
myodynia *n.* miodinia.
myodystonia *n.* miodistonía.
myodystony *n.* miodistonía.
myodystrophia *n.* miodistrofia.
  myodystrophia fetalis miodistrofia fetal.
myodystrophy *n.* miodistrofia.
myoedema *n.* mioedema.
myoelastic *adj.* mioelástico, -ca.
myoelectric *adj.* mioeléctrico, -ca.
myoelectrical *adj.* mioeléctrico, -ca.

myoendocarditis *n.* mioendocarditis.
myoephitelial *adj.* mioepitelial.
myoepithelioma *n.* mioepitelioma.
myoepithelium *n.* mioepitelio.
myoesthesia *n.* mioestesia.
myofascial *adj.* miofascial.
myofascitis *n.* miofascitis.
myofibril *n.* miofibrilla.
myofibrillar *adj.* miofibrilar.
myofibroblast *n.* miofibroblasto.
myofibroma *n.* miofibroma.
myofibrositis *n.* miofibrositis.
myofunctional *adj.* miofuncional.
myogelosis *n.* miogelosis.
myogen *n.* miógeno.
myogenesis *n.* miogénesis.
myogenetic *adj.* miogenético, -ca.
myogenic *adj.* miogénico, -ca.
myogenous *adj.* miógeno, -na.
myoglia *n.* mioglia.
myoglobin *n.* mioglobina.
myoglobinuria *n.* mioglobinuria.
myoglobulin *n.* mioglobulina.
myoglobulinuria *n.* mioglobulinuria.
myognathus *n.* miognato.
myogram *n.* miograma.
myograph *n.* miógrafo.
myographic *adj.* miográfico, -ca.
myography *n.* miografía.
myohematin *n.* miohematina.
myohemoglobin *n.* miohemoglobina.
myohypertrophia *n.* miohipertrofia.
myoid *adj.* mioide, mioideo, -a.
myoidema *n.* mioidema.
myoidism *n.* mioidismo.
myoinositol *n.* mioinositol.
myoischemia *n.* mioisquemia.
myokimia *n.* miocimia.
myokinase *n.* mioquinasa.
myokinesemeter *n.* mioquinesímetro.
myokinesimeter *n.* miocinesímetro.
myokinesis *n.* mioquinesia, mioquinesis.
myokinetic *adj.* mioquinético, -ca.
myokinin *n.* mioquinina.
myolecithal *adj.* miolecito, -ta.
myolemma *n.* miolema.
myolipoma *n.* miolipoma.
myologia *n.* miología.
myology *n.* miología.
myolysis *n.* miólisis.
  cardiotoxic myolysis miólisis cardiotóxica, miólisis cordis tóxica.
  myolysis cardiotoxica miólisis cardiotóxica, miólisis cordis tóxica.
myoma *n.* mioma.
  myoma previum mioma previo.
  myoma sarcomatodes mioma sarcomatodes.
  myoma striocellulare mioma estriocelular.
myomagenesis *n.* miomagénesis.
myomalacia *n.* miomalacia.
myomatectomy *n.* miomatectomía.
myomatosis *n.* miomatosis.
myomatous *adj.* miomatoso, -sa.
myomectomy *n.* miomectomía.
myomelanosis *n.* miomelanosis.
myomere *n.* miómera.
myometer *n.* miómetro.
myometrial *adj.* miometrial.
myometritis *n.* miometritis.
myometrium *n.* miometrio.
myomitochondrion *n.* miomitocondria.
myomohysterectomy *n.* miomohisterectomía.
myomotomy *n.* miomotomía.
myon *n.* mion.
myonecrosis *n.* mionecrosis.

clostridial myonecrosis mionecrosis clostridial, mionecrosis por clostridios.
myoneme *n.* mionema.
myonephropexy *n.* mionefropexia.
myoneural *adj.* mioneural.
myoneurasthenia *n.* mioneurastenia.
myoneure *n.* mioneura, mioneuro.
myoneuroma *n.* mioneuroma.
myonosus *n.* mionosis.
myonymy *n.* mionimia.
myopachynsis *n.* miopaquinsis.
myopalmus *n.* miopalmo.
myoparalysis *n.* mioparálisis.
myoparesis *n.* mioparesis.
myopathic *adj.* miopático, -ca.
myopathy *n.* miopatía.
  acromegalic myopathy miopatía en la acromegalia.
  alcoholic myopathy miopatía alcohólica.
  carcinomatous myopathy miopatía carcinomatosa.
  central core myopathy miopatía central core.
  centronuclear myopathy miopatía centronuclear.
  distal myopathy miopatía distal.
  mitochondrial myopathy miopatía mitocondrial.
  myopathy cordis miopatía cardíaca.
  myopathy with fiber type disproportion miopatía con desproporción congénita de los tipos de fibras.
  myotonic myopathy miopatía miotónica.
  myotubular myopathy miopatía miotubular.
  nemaline myopathy miopatía nemalínica.
  ocular myopathy miopatía ocular.
  rod myopathy miopatía de bastoncillos.
  steroid myopathy miopatía esteroidea.
  thyrotoxic myopathy miopatía tirotóxica.
myope *adj.* miope.
myopericarditis *n.* miopericarditis.
myophage *n.* miófago.
myophagism *n.* miofagia, miofagismo.
myophone *n.* miófono.
myopia *n.* miopía.
  axial myopia miopía axil.
  chromatic myopia miopía cromática.
  curvature myopia miopía de curvatura.
  degenerative myopia miopía degenerativa.
  index myopia miopía de índice.
  malignant myopia miopía maligna, miopía perniciosa.
  myopia magna miopía magna.
  night myopia miopía nocturna.
  pathologic myopia miopía patológica.
  premature myopia miopía prematura.
  primary myopia miopía primaria.
  prodromal myopia miopía prodrómica.
  progressive myopia miopía progresiva.
  simple myopia miopía simple.
  space myopia miopía espacial.
  transient myopia miopía transitoria.
myopic *adj.* miópico, -ca.
myoplasm *n.* mioplasma.
myoplastic *adj.* mioplástico, -ca.
myopolar *adj.* miopolar.
myoprotein *n.* mioproteína.
myopsis *n.* miopsia.
myopsychic *adj.* miopsíquico, -ca.
myopsychopathy *n.* miopsicopatía.
myopsychosis *n.* miopsicosis.
myopus *n.* miopo, miopus.
myorraphy *n.* miorrafia.
myorreceptor *n.* miorreceptor.
myorrhexis *n.* miorrexis.
myosalgia *n.* miosalgia.

myosalpingitis *n.* miosalpingitis.
myosalpinx *n.* miosálpinx.
myosan *n.* miosán.
myosarcoma *n.* miosarcoma.
myosclerosis *n.* mioesclerosis, miosclerosis.
myoscope *n.* mioscopio.
myoseism *n.* mioseísmo, miosismia.
myoseptum *n.* miotabique.
myoserum *n.* miosuero.
myosin *n.* miosina.
myosinogen *n.* miosinógeno.
myosinose *n.* miosinosa.
myosinuria *n.* miosinuria.
myosis *n.* miosis.
myositic *adj.* miosítico, -ca.
myositis *n.* miositis.
  acute disseminated myositis miositis aguda diseminada.
  acute progressive myositis miositis aguda progresiva.
  anaerobic myositis miositis anaeróbica.
  cervical myositis miositis cervical.
  infectious myositis miositis infecciosa.
  interstitial myositis miositis intersticial.
  multiple myositis miositis múltiple.
  myositis a frigore miositis a frigore.
  myositis fibrosa miositis fibrosa.
  myositis ossificans miositis osificante.
  myositis ossificans circumscripta miositis osificante circunscrita.
  myositis ossificans progressiva miositis osificante progresiva.
  myositis ossificans traumatica miositis osificante traumática.
  myositis purulenta miositis purulenta, miositis supurativa.
  myositis purulenta tropica miositis tropical purulenta.
  myositis serosa miositis serosa.
  myositis trichinosa miositis triquinosa.
  orbital myositis miositis orbitaria.
  parenchymatous myositis miositis parenquimatosa.
  primary multiple myositis miositis primaria múltiple.
  proliferative myositis miositis proliferativa, myositis proliferante.
  rheumatoid myositis miositis reumatoidea.
  spontaneous bacterial myositis miositis bacteriana espontánea.
  traumatic myositis miositis traumática.
  tropical myositis miositis tropical.
myospasia *n.* miospasia.
myospasm *n.* mioespasmo, miospasmo.
myospasmia *n.* mioespasmia, miospasmia.
myospherulosis *n.* mioesferulosis.
myosphygmia *n.* miosfigmia.
myostasis *n.* miostasia.
myostatic *adj.* miostático, -ca.
myostenometer *n.* miostenómetro.
myosteoma *n.* miosteoma.
myosthenic *adj.* miosténico, -ca.
myosthenometer *n.* mioestenómetro.
myostroma *n.* mioestroma, miostroma.
myostromin *n.* mioestromina.
myosuria *n.* miosuria.
myosuture *n.* miosutura.
myosynizesis *n.* miosinézesis, miosinicesis.
myotactic *adj.* miotáctico, -ca.
myotamponade *n.* miotaponamiento.
myotasis *n.* miotasis.
myotatic *adj.* miotático, -ca.
myotenoplasty *n.* miotenoplastia.
myotenositis *n.* miotenositis.
myotenotomy *n.* miotenotomía.

myothermic *adj.* miotérmico, -ca.
myotic *adj.* miótico, -ca.
myotility *n.* miotilidad.
myotome *n.* miotoma, miótomo.
myotomy *n.* miotomía.
myotone *n.* miotono.
myotonia *n.* miotonía.
  myotonia acquisita miotonía adquirida.
  myotonia atrophica miotonía atrófica.
  myotonia dystrophica miotonía distrófica.
  myotonia neonatorum miotonía neonatal.
myotonic *adj.* miotónico, -ca.
myotonoid *adj.* miotonoide.
myotonometer *n.* miotonómetro.
myotonus *n.* miotono.
myotrophic *adj.* miotrófico, -ca.
myotrophy *n.* miotrofia.
myotropic *adj.* miotrópico, -ca.
myringa *n.* miringe.
myringitis *n.* miringitis.
  bullous myringitis miringitis ampollar, miringitis vesicular.
  infectious myringitis miringitis infecciosa.
  myringitis bullosa miringitis ampollar, miringitis vesicular.
myringodectomy *n.* miringectomía, miringodectomía.
myringodermatitis *n.* miringodermatitis.
myringomycosis *n.* miringomicosis.
  myringomycosis aspergillina miringomicosis aspergilina.
myringoplasty *n.* miringoplastia.
myringostapediopexy *n.* miringoestapediopexia.
myringotome *n.* miringótomo.
myringotomy *n.* miringotomía.
myrinx *n.* miringe.
myristicin *n.* miristicina.
myrmecia *n.* mirmecia.
myrtiform *adj.* mirtiforme.

mysophilia *n.* misofilia.
mysophobia *n.* misofobia.
mysophobiac *n.* misófobo, -ba.
mysophobic *adj.* misofóbico, -ca.
mysosarcomatous *adj.* mixosarcomatoso, -sa.
mytacism *n.* metacismo, mitacismo, mutacismo.
mythomania *n.* mitomanía.
mythophobia *n.* mitofobia.
mytilotoxine *n.* mitilotoxina.
mytilotoxism *n.* mitilotoxismo.
myxadenitis *n.* mixadenitis.
myxadenoma *n.* mixadenoma.
myxangitis *n.* mixangitis.
myxangoitis *n.* mixoangoítis.
myxasthenia *n.* mixastenia.
myxedema *n.* mixedema.
  childhood myxedema mixedema infantil.
  circumscribed myxedema mixedema circunscrito.
  congenital myxedema mixedema congénito.
  infantile myxedema mixedema infantil.
  nodular myxedema mixedema nodular.
  operative myxedema mixedema operatorio.
  papular myxedema mixedema papular.
  pituitary myxedema mixedema hipofisario.
  pretibial myxedema mixedema pretibial.
  secondary myxedema mixedema secundario.
myxedematoid *adj.* mixedematoide, mixedematoideo, -a.
myxedematous *adj.* mixedematoso, -sa.
myxemia *n.* mixemia.
myxidiocy *n.* mixidiocia.
myxoadenitis *n.* mixoadenitis.
myxoadenoma *n.* mixoadenoma.
myxoblastome *n.* mixoblastoma.
myxochandrofibrosarcoma *n.* mixocondrofibrosarcoma.
myxochondroma *n.* mixocondroma.
myxochondrosarcoma *n.* mixocondrosarcoma.
myxocystitis *n.* mixocistitis.

myxocystoma *n.* mixocistoma.
myxocyte *n.* mixocito.
myxoenchondroma *n.* mixoencondroma.
myxoendothelioma *n.* mixoendotelioma.
myxofibroma *n.* mixofibroma.
myxofibrosarcoma *n.* mixofibrosarcoma.
myxogliomia *n.* mixoglioma.
myxoglobulosis *n.* mixoglobulosis.
myxoid *adj.* mixoide.
myxoinoma *n.* mixoinoma.
myxolipoma *n.* mixolipoma.
myxoma *n.* mixoma.
  atrial myxoma mixoma auricular.
  cystic myxoma mixoma quístico.
  enchondromatous myxoma mixoma encondromatoso.
  erectile myxoma mixoma eréctil.
  lipomatous myxoma mixoma lipomatoso.
  myxoma enchondromatosum mixoma encondromatoso.
  myxoma fibrosum mixoma fibroso.
  myxoma lipomatosum mixoma lipomatoso.
  myxoma sarcomatosum mixoma sarcomatoso.
  ondontogenic myxoma mixoma odontogénico, mixoma odontógeno.
  vascular myxoma mixoma vascular.
myxomatosis *n.* mixomatosis.
myxomatous *adj.* mixomatoso, -sa.
myxomiome *n.* mixomioma.
myxoneuroma *n.* mixoneuroma.
myxoneurosis *n.* mixoneurosis.
myxopapilloma *n.* mixopapiloma.
myxopoiesis *n.* mixopoyesis.
myxorrhea *n.* mixorrea.
  myxorrhea gastrica mixorrea gástrica.
  myxorrhea intestinalis mixorrea intestinal.
myxosarcoma *n.* mixosarcoma.
myzesis *n.* micesis.
Myzorhynchus Myzorhynchus.

nacelle *n.* nacela.
nacreous *adj.* nacarado, -da.
nadir *n.* nadir.
Naegleria Naegleria.
naegleriasis *n.* naegleriasis.
naevocancer *n.* nevocáncer.
naevoxanthoendothelioma *n.* nevoxantoendotelioma.
naevus *n.* naevus, nevo.
  naevus anemicus nevo anémico.
  naevus angiectodes nevo angiectodeo.
  naevus angiomatodes nevo angiomatodieo.
  naevus arachnoideus nevo arácneo, nevo aracnoideo.
  naevus araneosus nevo arácneo, nevo aracnoideo.
  naevus araneus nevo arácneo, nevo aracnoideo.
  naevus cavernosus nevo cavernoso.
  naevus comedonicus nevo comedónico.
  naevus despigmentosus nevo despigmentado.
  naevus elasticus nevo elástico.
  naevus elasticus of Lewandowsky nevo elástico de Lewandowsky.
  naevus flammeus nevo flámeo, nevo flamígero.
  naevus follicularis nevo folicular.
  naevus follicularis keratosis nevo folicular queratoso.
  naevus fuscoceruleus acromiodeltoideus nevo fuscocerúleo acromiodeltoideo.
  naevus lipomatoides nevo lipomatoso.
  naevus lipomatosus cutaneus superficialis nevo lipomatoso cutáneo superficial.
  naevus of Ito nevo de Ito.
  naevus of Ota nevo de Ota.
  naevus papillomatosus nevo papilomatoso.
  naevus pigmentosus nevo pigmentado, nevo pigmentario, nevo pigmentoso.
  naevus pilosus nevo piloso.
  naevus sanguineus nevo sanguíneo.
  naevus sebaceus nevo sebáceo, nevo sebáceo de Jadassohn.
  naevus sebaceus of Jadassohn nevo sebáceo, nevo sebáceo de Jadassohn.
  naevus spilus nevo plano.
  naevus sanguineus nevo sanguíneo.
  naevus spilus tardus nevo plano tardío.
  naevus syringocystadenomatosus papilliferus nevo siringoquístico adenomatoso papilífero.
  naevus syringocystadenosus papilliferus nevo siringocistadenoso papilífero.
  naevus unius lateris naevus unius lateris, nevo unilateral, naevus unius lateris.
  naevus vascularis nevo vascular.
  naevus vasculosus nevo vascular.
  naevus venosus nevo venoso.
  naevus verrucosus nevo verrucoide, nevo verrucoso, nevo verrugoso.

nail[1] *n.* clavo[2], uña.
  double-edge nail uña de doble borde.
  eggshell nail uña en cáscara de huevo.
  half and half nail uña mitad y mitad.
  hippocratic nail uña hipocrática.
  ingrown nail uña encarnada, uña incardinada.
  parrot beak nail uña en pico de loro.
  pincer nail uña en pinza.
  pitted nail uña con hoyuelos.
  racket nail uña en raqueta.
  reedy nail uña acanalada, uña en caña.
  shell nail uña en vaina.
  spoon nail uña en cuchara.
  Terry's nail uña de Terrry.
  turtle-back nail uña en dorso de tortuga.
  watch-crystal nail uña en vidrio de reloj.
  yellow nail uña amarilla.
nail[2] *n.* clavar.
nailing *n.* enclavamiento.
  intramedullary nailing enclavamiento intramedular.
  medullary nailing enclavamiento medular.
name *n.* nombre.
  generic name nombre genérico.
  non-proprietary name nombre no patentado, nombre no registrado.
  proprietary name nombre patentado, nombre registrado.
  systematic name nombre sistemático.
  trivial name nombre trivial, nombre vulgar.
nanism *n.* nanismo.
nanocephalia *n.* nanocefalia.
nanocephalic *adj.* nanocefálico, -ca.
nanocephalous *adj.* nanocéfalo, -la.
nanocephaly *n.* nanocefalia.
nanocormia *n.* nanocormia.
nanoid *adj.* nanoide.
nanomelia *n.* nanomelia.
nanomelus *n.* nanomelo.
nanophthalmia *n.* nanoftalmia.
nanophthalmos *n.* nanoftalmos.
nanosomia *n.* nanosomía.
nanosomus *n.* nanósomo, -ma.
nanukayami *n.* nanukayami.
nape *n.* nuca.
naphthylpararosaniline *n.* naftilpararrosanilina.
naphtolism *n.* naftolismo.
napiform *adj.* napiforme.
naprapath *n.* naprápata.
naprapathy *n.* naprapatía.
narcism *n.* narcismo.
narcissism *n.* narcisismo.
narcissistic *adj.* narcisista.
narcoanalysis *n.* narcoanálisis.
narcoanesthesia *n.* narcoanestesia.
narcocatharsis *n.* narcocatarsis.
narcodiagnosis *n.* narcodiagnóstico.
narcohypnia *n.* narcohipnia.
narcohypnosis *n.* narcohipnosis.

narcolepsia *n.* narcolepsia.
narcolepsy *n.* narcolepsia.
narcoleptic *adj.* narcoléptico, -ca.
narcoma *n.* narcoma.
narcomania *n.* narcomanía.
narcose *adj.* narcoso, -sa.
narcosis *n.* narcosis.
  basal narcosis narcosis basal.
  intravenous narcosis narcosis intravenosa.
  medullary narcosis narcosis bulbar, narcosis medular.
  narcosis basis narcosis basal.
  nitrogen narcosis narcosis por nitrógeno.
  Nussbaum's narcosis narcosis de Nussbaum.
narcostimulant *adj.* narcoestimulante, narcostimulante.
narcosynthesis *n.* narcosíntesis.
narcotherapy *n.* narcoterapia.
narcotic *adj.* narcótico, -ca.
  narcotic anodyne narcótico anodino.
  narcotic hypnoytic narcótico hipnótico.
  narcotic sedative narcótico sedante.
narcotico-acrid *adj.* narcoácrido, -da.
narcotico-irritant *adj.* narcoirritante.
narcotize *v.* narcotizar.
narcous *adj.* narcoso, -sa.
naris narina, naris.
nasal *adj.* nasal.
nasalis *adj.* nasal.
nascent *adj.* naciente.
nasioiniac *adj.* nasioiníaco, -ca, nasioníaco, -ca.
nasion *n.* nasión.
nasitis *n.* nasitis.
nasoantral *adj.* nasoantral.
nasoantrostomy *n.* nasoantrostomía.
nasobronchial *adj.* nasobronquial.
nasociliary *adj.* nasociliar.
nasofrontal *adj.* nasofrontal.
nasogastric *adj.* nasogástrico, -ca.
nasograph *n.* nasógrafo.
nasolabial *adj.* nasolabial.
nasolacrimal *adj.* nasolacrimal, nasolagrimal.
nasomanometer *n.* nasomanómetro.
nasonnement *n.* nasalidad.
naso-oral *adj.* nasobucal, nasooral.
nasopalatine *adj.* nasopalatino, -na.
nasopalpebral *adj.* nasopalpebral.
nasopharyngeal *adj.* nasofaríngeo, -a.
nasopharyngitis *n.* nasofaringitis.
nasopharyngography *n.* nasofaringografía.
nasopharyngolaryngoscope *n.* nasofaringolaringoscopio.
nasopharyngoscope *n.* nasofaringoscopio.
nasopharyngoscopy *n.* nasofaringoscopia.
nasopharynx *n.* nasofaringe.
nasorostral *adj.* nasorrostral.
nasoscope *n.* nasoscopio.
nasoseptal *adj.* nasoseptal.
nasoseptitis *n.* nasoseptitis.
nasosinusitis *n.* nasosinusitis.

nasoturbinal *adj.* nasoturbinal.
nasus nariz, nasus.
natal *adj.* natal.
natality *n.* natalidad.
nates nates.
natimortality *n.* natimortalidad.
native *adj.* nativo, -va.
natremia *n.* natremia.
natriemia *n.* natremia.
natriferic *adj.* natriférico, -ca.
natrium natrium.
natriuresis *n.* natriuresis, natruresis.
natriuretic *adj.* natriurético, -ca.
natriuria *n.* natriuria.
natruresis *n.* natruresis.
natruretic *adj.* natriurético, -ca.
natural *adj.* natural.
naturalism *n.* naturalismo.
naturalization *n.* naturalización.
nature *n.* naturaleza.
naturopath *n.* naturópata.
naturopathic *adj.* naturopático, -ca.
naturopathy *n.* naturopatía.
naupathia *n.* naupatía.
nausea *n.* náusea.
  nausea epidemica náusea epidémica.
  nausea gravidarum náusea gravídica.
  nausea marina náusea marítima, náusea naval.
nauseant *adj.* nauseabundo, -da, nauseante.
nauseous *adj.* nauseoso, -sa.
navel *n.* ombligo.
  blue navel ombligo azul.
  enamel navel ombligo del esmalte.
navicula *n.* navícula.
navicular *adj.* navicular.
navicularthritis *n.* navicularitis.
nealogy *n.* nealogía.
nearthrosis *n.* neartrosis.
nebula *n.* nébula.
nebulization *n.* nebulización.
nebulize *v.* nebulizar.
nebulizer *n.* nebulizador.
  jet nebulizer nebulizador a chorro.
  spinning disk nebulizer nebulizador de disco giratorio.
  ultrasonic nebulizer nebulizador ultrasónico.
necatoriasis *n.* necatoriasis.
necessity *n.* necesidad.
  basic human necessity necesidad básica.
  dependency necessity necesidad de dependencia.
neck *n.* cuello.
  bull neck cuello de toro.
  Madelung's neck cuello de Madelung.
  neck of a tooth cuello dentario.
  webbed neck cuello membranoso.
  wry neck cuello rígido.
necklace *n.* corbata.
  Casal's necklace corbata de Casal.
necrectomy *n.* necrectomía.
necrobiosis *n.* necrobiosis.
  necrobiosis lipoidica necrobiosis lipídica, necrobiosis lipoídica.
  necrobiosis lipoidica diabeticorum necrobiosis lipídica diabética, necrobiosis lipoidea de los diabéticos, necrobiosis lipoídica diabética.
necrobiotic *adj.* necrobiótico, -ca.
necrocytosis *n.* necrocitosis.
necrocytotoxin *n.* necrocitotoxina.
necrogenic *adj.* necrogénico, -ca.
necrogenous *adj.* necrógeno, -na.
necrogranulomatous *adj.* necrogranulomatoso, -sa.
necrologic *adj.* necrológico, -ca.

necrologist *n.* necrólogo, -ga.
necrology *n.* necrología.
necrolysis *n.* necrólisis.
  toxic epidermal necrolysis (TEN) necrólisis epidérmica tóxica (NET).
necromania *n.* necromanía.
necrometer *n.* necrómetro.
necromimesis *n.* necromimesis.
necronectomy *n.* necronectomía.
necroparasite *n.* necroparásito.
necropathy *n.* necropatía.
necrophagia *n.* necrofagia.
necrophagous *adj.* necrófago, -ga.
necrophile *n.* necrófilo.
necrophilia *n.* necrofilia.
necrophilic *adj.* necrofílico, -ca.
necrophilism *n.* necrofilismo.
necrophilous *adj.* necrófilo, -la.
necrophily *n.* necrofilia.
necrophobia *n.* necrofobia.
necropneumonia *n.* necroneumonía.
necropsy *n.* necropsia.
  medicolegal necropsy necropsia médico-legal.
necrosadism *n.* necrosadismo.
necroscopy *n.* necroscopia.
necrosis *n.* necrosis.
  acute tubular necrosis (ATN) necrosis tubular aguda (NTA).
  arteriolar necrosis necrosis arteriolar.
  aseptic bone necrosis necrosis ósea aséptica.
  aseptic necrosis necrosis aséptica.
  avascular necrosis necrosis avascular.
  Balser's fatty necrosis necrosis grasa de Balser.
  bridging necrosis necrosis confluente, necrosis hepática en puente.
  caseation necrosis necrosis caseosa.
  caseous necrosis necrosis caseosa.
  central necrosis necrosis central.
  cheesy necrosis necrosis caseosa.
  coagulation necrosis necrosis coagulativa, necrosis por coagulación.
  colliquative necrosis necrosis colicuativa.
  cystic medial necrosis necrosis medial quística, necrosis medial quística de Erdheim.
  dry necrosis necrosis seca.
  embolic necrosis necrosis embólica.
  epiphyseal ischemic necrosis necrosis isquémica epifisaria.
  Erdheim's cystic medial necrosis necrosis medial quística, necrosis medial quística de Erdheim.
  exanthematous necrosis necrosis exantematosa.
  fat necrosis necrosis adiposa, necrosis grasa.
  fibrinoid necrosis necrosis fibrinoide.
  focal necrosis necrosis focal.
  gangrenous necrosis necrosis gangrenosa.
  hyaline necrosis necrosis hialina.
  ischemic necrosis necrosis isquémica.
  liquefaction necrosis necrosis licuefactiva, necrosis por licuefacción.
  liquefactive necrosis necrosis licuefactiva, necrosis por licuefacción.
  massive hepatic necrosis necrosis hepática masiva.
  medial necrosis necrosis medial.
  mercurial necrosis necrosis mercurial.
  moist necrosis necrosis húmeda.
  mummification necrosis necrosis por momificación.
  necrosis of renal papillae necrosis de las papilas renales, necrosis papilar renal.
  Paget's quiet necrosis necrosis silenciosa de Paget.

  peripheral necrosis necrosis periférica.
  phosphorus necrosis necrosis por fósforo.
  piecemeal necrosis necrosis fragmentaria.
  pressure necrosis necrosis por presión.
  progressive emphysematous necrosis necrosis enfisematosa progresiva, necrosis progresiva enfisematosa.
  radiation necrosis necrosis por radiación.
  radium necrosis necrosis por radio.
  renal papillary necrosis necrosis de las papilas renales, necrosis papilar renal.
  septic necrosis necrosis séptica.
  subcutaneous fat necrosis of the newborn necrosis adiposa subcutánea del recién nacido.
  superficial necrosis necrosis superficial.
  suppurative necrosis necrosis supurativa.
  syphilitic necrosis necrosis sifilítica.
  total necrosis necrosis total.
  tubular necrosis necrosis tubular.
  Zenker's necrosis necrosis de Zenker.
  zonal necrosis necrosis zonal.
necrospermia *n.* necrospermia.
necrotactism *n.* necrotactismo.
necrotic *adj.* necrótico, -ca.
necrotizing *adj.* necrosante, necrotizante.
necrotomy *n.* necrotomía.
  osteoplastic necrotomy necrotomía osteoplástica.
necrozoospermia *n.* necrozoospermia.
need *n.* necesidad.
  compulsion need necesidad compulsiva.
needle *n.* aguja.
  Abram's needle aguja de Abraham.
  aneurysm needle aguja de aneurisma.
  aspirating needle a. de aspiración, aguja aspiradora, aguja aspirante.
  aspiration needle a. de aspiración, aguja aspiradora, aguja aspirante.
  atraumatic needle aguja atraumática.
  Babcock's needle aguja de Babcock.
  biopsy needle aguja de corte, aguja gruesa, aguja para biopsia.
  Brockenbrough's needle aguja de Brockenbrough.
  cataract needle aguja de catarata.
  Chiba's needle aguja de Chiba.
  Colapinto's needle aguja de Colapinto.
  Cope's needle aguja de Cope.
  Deschamps needle aguja de Deschamps.
  double entry needle aguja de doble acceso.
  Emmet's needle aguja de Emmet.
  exploring needle aguja exploradora.
  fine needle aguja fina.
  Francke's needle aguja de Francke.
  Frazier's needle aguja de Frazier.
  Gillmore needle aguja de Gillmore.
  Hagedorn needle aguja de Hagedorn.
  hypodermic needle aguja hipodérmica.
  intramuscular needle aguja intramuscular.
  intravenous needle aguja endovenosa, aguja intravenosa.
  knife needle aguja de bisturí, aguja-cuchilla.
  Kopan's needle aguja de Kopan.
  ligature needle aguja de ligadura.
  lumbar puncture needle aguja para punción lumbar.
  Menghini needle aguja de Menghini.
  radium needle aguja de radio.
  Reverdin's needle aguja de Reverdin.
  round needle aguja cilíndrica, aguja redonda.
  Salah's sternal puncture needle aguja de Salah para punción esternal.
  scalp vein needle aguja para vena del cuero cabelludo.
  skinny needle aguja cutánea.

spatula needle aguja en espátula.
stop needle aguja con tope, aguja de stop.
straight needle aguja recta.
triangular needle aguja triangular.
Tuohy's needle aguja de Tuohy.
Vim-Silverman needle aguja de Vim-Silverman.
needle-carrier *n.* portaagujas.
needle-driver *n.* portaagujas.
needle-holder *n.* portaagujas.
neencephalon *n.* neencéfalo.
nefluorophotometer *n.* nefluorofotómetro.
nefroureterolithiasis *n.* nefroureterolitiasis.
negation *n.* negación.
negative *adj.* negativo, -va.
negativism *n.* negativismo.
negativity *n.* negatividad.
negatoscope *n.* negatoscopio.
neglect *n.* descuido.
unilateral neglect descuido unilateral.
negligence *n.* negligencia.
Neisseria Neisseria.
Neisseriaceae Neisseriaceae.
neisserial *adj.* neissérico, -ca.
nelavan *n.* nelauna, nelavan, neláván.
nelavane *n.* nelauna, nelavan, neláván.
nemathelminth *n.* nematelminto.
nemathelminthiasis *n.* nematelmintiasis.
nematicide *adj.* nematicida.
nematization *n.* nematización.
nematoblast *n.* nematoblasto.
nematocidal *adj.* nematicida, nematocida[2].
nematocide *n.* nematocida[1].
Nematoda Nematoda.
nematode *n.* nematodo.
nematodiasis *n.* nematodiasis.
nematoid *adj.* nematoide, nematoideo, -a.
nematosis *n.* nematosis.
nematospermia *n.* nematospermia.
nemic *adj.* némico, -ca.
neoantigen *n.* neoantígeno.
neoarthrosis *n.* neoartrosis.
neobehaviorism *n.* neoconductismo.
neobiogenesis *n.* neobiogénesis.
neoblastic *adj.* neoblástico, -ca.
neocerebellum *n.* neocerebelo.
neocinetic *adj.* neocinético, -ca.
neocortex *n.* neocórtex, neocorteza.
neocystostomy *n.* neocistostomía.
neocyte *n.* neocito.
neocytopheresis *n.* neocitoféresis.
neocytosis *n.* neocitosis.
neo-Darwinism *n.* neodarvinismo, neodarwinismo.
neodiathermy *n.* neodiatermia.
neoencephalon *n.* neoencéfalo.
neofetal *adj.* neofetal.
neofetus *n.* neofeto.
neoformation *n.* neoformación.
neoformative *adj.* neoformativo, -va.
neogala *n.* neogala.
neogenesis *n.* neogénesis.
neogenetic *adj.* neogenético, -ca.
neoglottic *adj.* neoglótico, -ca.
neoglottis *n.* neoglotis.
neoglycogenesis *n.* neoglicogénesis, neoglucogénesis.
neohymen *n.* neohimen.
neokinetic *adj.* neocinético, -ca.
neokinetics *n.* neocinética.
neolalia *n.* neolalia.
neolalism *n.* neolalismo.
neolipogenesis *n.* neolipogénesis.
neologism *n.* neologismo.
neomembrane *n.* neomembrana.

neomorph *adj.* neomorfo, -fa.
neomorphism *n.* neomorfismo.
neonatal *adj.* neonatal.
neonate *n.* neonato.
malformed neonate neonato malformado.
mentally handicapped neonate neonato deficiente.
neonatologist *n.* neonatólogo, -ga.
neonatology *n.* neonatología.
neonatometer *n.* neonatómetro.
neopallium neopalio, neopallium.
neopathy *n.* neopatía.
neophilia *n.* neofilia.
neoplasia *n.* neoplasia.
benign neoplasia neoplasia benigna.
histoid neoplasia neoplasia histoide.
malignant neoplasia neoplasia maligna.
mixed neoplasia neoplasia mixta.
multiple endocrine neoplasia neoplasia endocrina múltiple.
organoid neoplasia neoplasia organoide.
type I neoplasia neoplasia endocrina múltiple, tipo I.
type II neoplasia neoplasia endocrina múltiple, tipo II.
type III neoplasia neoplasia endocrina múltiple, tipo III.
neoplasm *n.* neoplasma.
benign neoplasm neoplasma benigno.
histoid neoplasm neoplasma histoide.
malignant neoplasm neoplasma maligno.
neoplastic *adj.* neoplásico, -ca, neoplástico, -ca.
neoplastigenic *adj.* neoplastigénico, -ca.
neoplasty *n.* neoplastia.
neorickettsious *n.* neorickettsiosa.
neostomy *n.* neostomía.
neostriatal *adj.* neostriatal.
neostriatum neoestriado, -da, neostriado, -da, neostriatum.
neostrophingic *adj.* neostrófico, -ca.
neothalamus *n.* neotálamo.
neovascularization *n.* neovascularización.
retinal neovascularization neovascularización retiniana.
nepenthic *adj.* nepéntico, -ca.
nepheloid *adj.* nefeloide.
nephelometer *n.* nefelómetro.
nephelometric *adj.* nefelométrico, -ca.
nephelometry *n.* nefelometría.
nephelopia *n.* nefelopía, nefelopsia.
nephradenoma *n.* nefradenoma, nefroadenoma.
nephralgia *n.* nefralgia, nefrodinia.
nephralgic *adj.* nefrálgico, -ca.
nephrapostasis *n.* nefrapostasis.
nephrasthenia *n.* nefrastenia.
nephratonia *n.* nefratonía.
nephratony *n.* nefratonía.
nephrauxa *n.* nefrauxa.
nephrauxe *n.* nefrauxa.
nephrectasia *n.* nefrectasia.
nephrectasis *n.* nefrectasia, nefrectasis.
nephrectasy *n.* nefrectasia.
nephrectomize *v.* nefrectomizar.
nephrectomy *n.* nefrectomía.
abdominal nephrectomy nefrectomía abdominal.
anterior nephrectomy nefrectomía anterior.
lumbar nephrectomy nefrectomía lumbar.
paraperitoneal nephrectomy nefrectomía paraperitoneal.
partial nephrectomy nefrectomía parcial.
posterior nephrectomy nefrectomía posterior.
radical nephrectomy nefrectomía radical.

subcapsular nephrectomy nefrectomía subcapsular.
nephredema *n.* nefredema, nefroedema.
nephrelcosis *n.* nefrelcosis, sefrohelcosis.
nephremia *n.* nefremia.
nephremphraxis *n.* nefrenfraxis.
nephrhydrotic *adj.* nefrohidrótico, -ca.
nephria *n.* nefria.
nephric *adj.* néfrico, -ca.
nephridium *n.* nefridio.
nephrism *n.* nefrismo.
nephritic *adj.* nefrítico, -ca.
nephritides *n.* nefrítides.
nephritis *n.* nefritis, renitis.
acute interstitial nephritis nefritis intersticial aguda.
acute nephritis nefritis aguda.
acute supurative nephritis nefritis supurativa aguda.
acute tubulointerstitial nephritis nefritis tubulointersticial aguda.
analgesic nephritis nefritis por analgésicos.
anti-basement membrane nephritis nefritis antimembrana basal.
arteriosclerotic nephritis nefritis arteriosclerótica.
azotemic nephritis nefritis hiperazoémica.
bacterial nephritis nefritis bacteriana.
Balkan nephritis nefritis de los Balcanes.
Balkan tubulointerstitial nephritis nefritis tubulointersticial de los Balcanes.
capsular nephritis nefritis capsular.
caseous nephritis nefritis caseosa.
cheesy nephritis nefritis caseosa.
chronic nephritis nefritis crónica.
chronic parenchymatous nephritis nefritis parenquimatosa crónica.
chronic suppurative nephritis nefritis supurativa crónica.
congenital nephritis nefritis congénita.
crupous nephritis nefritis cruposa.
dropsical nephritis nefritis hidrópica.
Ellis type 2 nephritis nefritis de Ellis, tipo 2.
exudative nephritis nefritis exudativa.
fibrolipomatous nephritis nefritis fibrolipomatosa.
focal nephritis nefritis focal.
glomerular nephritis nefritis glomerular.
glomerulocapsular nephritis nefritis glomerulocapsular.
hemorrhagic nephritis nefritis hemorrágica.
hereditary nephritis nefritis hereditaria.
immune complex nephritis nefritis por inmunocomplejos.
indurative nephritis nefritis indurativa.
infective tubulointerstitial nephritis nefritis tubulointersticial infecciosa.
interstitial nephritis nefritis intersticial.
Lancereaux's nephritis nefritis de Lancereaux.
lipomatous nephritis nefritis lipomatosa.
lupus nephritis nefritis del lupus, nefritis lúpica.
Masugi-type nephritis nefritis de Masugi.
mesangial nephritis nefritis mesangial.
nephritis caseosa nefritis caseosa.
nephritis dolorosa nefritis dolorosa.
nephritis gravidarum nefritis de la gravidez, nefritis gravídica.
nephritis of pregnancy nefritis del embarazo.
nephritis repens nefritis repentina.
neumococcus nephritis nefritis neumocócica.
parenchymatous nephritis nefritis parenquimatosa.
potassium-losing nephritis nefritis crónica por pérdida de potasio.

productive nephritis nefritis productiva.
salt-losing nephritis nefritis con pérdida de sal.
saturnine nephritis nefritis saturnina.
scarlatinal nephritis nefritis escarlatínica, nefritis por escarlatina.
subacute nephritis nefritis subaguda.
suppurative nephritis nefritis supurativa.
syphilitic nephritis nefritis sifilítica.
tartrate nephritis nefritis por tartrato.
transfusion nephritis nefritis por transfusión.
trench nephritis nefritis de las trincheras.
tubal nephritis nefritis tubular.
tuberculous nephritis nefritis tuberculosa.
tubular nephritis nefritis tubular.
tubulointerstitial nephritis nefritis tubulo-intersticial.
uranium nephritis nefritis por uranio.
war nephritis nefritis de guerra.
nephritogenic *adj.* nefritogénico, -ca, nefritógeno, -na.
nephroabdominal *adj.* nefroabdominal.
nephroangiosclerosis *n.* nefroangioesclerosis, nefroangiosclerosis.
nephrobiopsy *n.* nefrobiopsia.
nephroblastema *n.* nefroblastema.
nephroblastoma *n.* nefroblastoma.
nephroblastomatosis *n.* nefroblastomatosis.
nephrocalcinosis *n.* nefrocalcinosis.
nephrocapsectomy *n.* nefrocapsectomía.
nephrocardiac *adj.* nefrocardíaco, -ca.
nephrocele *n.* nefrocele.
nephrocelom *n.* nefroceloma.
nephrocolic *n.* nefrocólico[1].
nephrocolopexy *n.* nefrocolopexia.
nephrocoloptosis *n.* nefrocoloptosis.
nephrocystanastomosis *n.* nefrocistanastomosis.
nephrocystitis *n.* nefrocistitis.
nephrocystoanastomosis *n.* nefrocistoanastomosis.
nephrocystosis *n.* nefrocistosis.
nephroerysipelas *n.* nefroerisipela.
nephrogastric *adj.* nefrogástrico, -ca.
nephrogenetic *adj.* nefrogenético, -ca, nefrogénico, -ca, nefrógeno, -na.
nephrogram *n.* nefrograma.
nephrography *n.* nefrografía.
nephrography with splenography nefroesplenografía.
nephrohemia *n.* nefrohemia.
nephrohydrosis *n.* nefrohidrosis.
nephrohypertrophy *n.* nefrohipertrofia.
nephroid *n.* nefroide, nefroideo, -a.
nephrolith *n.* nefrolito.
nephrolithiasis *n.* nefrolitiasis.
nephrolithotomy *n.* nefrolitotomía.
percutaneous nephrolithotomy nefrolitotomía percutánea.
nephrologist *n.* nefrólogo, -ga.
nephrology *n.* nefrología.
nephrolysine *n.* nefrolisina.
nephrolysis *n.* nefrólisis.
nephrolytic *adj.* nefrolítico, -ca.
nephroma *n.* nefroma.
embryonal nephroma nefroma embrionario.
mesoblastic nephroma nefroma mesoblástico.
nephromalacia *n.* nefromalacia.
nephromegaly *n.* nefromegalia.
nephromere *n.* nefrómera.
nephron *n.* nefrón, nefrona.
nephronophthisis *n.* nefronoptisis.
familial juvenile nephronophthisis nefro-

noptisis familiar juvenil, nefronoptisis hereditaria del niño.
nephro-omentopexy *n.* nefroomentopexia.
nephroparalysis *n.* nefroparálisis.
nephropathia *n.* nefropatía.
nephropathia epidemica nefropatía epidémica.
nephropathic *adj.* nefropático, -ca.
nephropathy *n.* nefropatía.
analgesic nephropathy nefropatía por analgésicos.
Balkan nephropathy nefropatía balcánica, nefropatía de los Balcanes.
chronic nephropathy nefropatía crónica.
chronic tubular nephropathy nefropatía tubular crónica.
dropsical nephropathy nefropatía hidrópésica.
endemic Balkan nephropathy nefropatía endémica balcánica.
epidemic nephropathy nefropatía epidémica.
gouty nephropathy nefropatía gotosa.
hepatitis B virus related nephropathy nefropatía por virus de la hepatitis B.
hepatitis C virus related nephropathy nefropatía por virus de la hepatitis C.
hereditary nephropathy nefropatía hematúrica familiar con sordera.
hypazoturic nephropathy nefropatía hipoazoúrica.
hypercalcemic nephropathy nefropatía hipercalcémica.
hypochloruric nephropathy nefropatía hipoclorúrica.
hypokalemic nephropathy nefropatía hipopotasémica.
IgA nephropathy nefropatía por IgA.
IgM nephropathy nefropatía por IgM.
osmotic nephropathy nefropatía osmótica.
potassium-losing nephropathy nefropatía con pérdida de potasio.
reflux nephropathy nefropatía de reflujo, nefropatía por reflujo.
salt-losing nephropathy nefropatía con pérdida de sal.
transfusion nephropathy nefropatía postransfusional.
nephropexy *n.* nefropexia.
nephrophagiasis *n.* nefrofagiasis.
nephrophthisis *n.* nefroptisis.
nephropoietic *adj.* nefropoyético, -ca.
nephropoietin *n.* nefropoyetina.
nephroptosia *n.* nefroptisis, nefroptosia.
nephroptosis *n.* nefroptisis, nefroptosis.
nephropyelitis *n.* nefropielitis.
nephropyelography *n.* nefropielografía.
nephropyelolithotomy *n.* nefropielolitotomía.
nephropyeloplasty *n.* nefropieloplastia.
nephropyosis *n.* nefropiosis.
nephrorrhagia *n.* nefrorragia.
nephrorrhaphy *n.* nefrorrafia.
nephroscleria *n.* nefroesclerosis.
nephrosclerosis *n.* nefroesclerosis, nefrosclerosis.
arterial nephrosclerosis nefroesclerosis arterial.
arteriolar nephrosclerosis nefroesclerosis arteriolar.
benign nephrosclerosis nefroesclerosis benigna.
hyaline arteriolar nephrosclerosis nefroesclerosis arteriolar hialina.
hyperplastic arteriolar nephrosclerosis nefroesclerosis arteriolar hiperplásica.

intercapillary nephrosclerosis nefroesclerosis intercapilar.
malignant nephrosclerosis nefroesclerosis maligna.
senile nephrosclerosis nefroesclerosis senil.
nephrosclerotic *adj.* nefroesclerótico, -ca.
nephroscope *n.* nefroscopio.
percutaneous nephroscope nefroscopio percutáneo.
nephroscopy *n.* nefroscopia.
nephrosialidosis *n.* nefrosialidosis.
nephrosis *n.* nefrosis.
acute nephrosis nefrosis aguda.
amyloid nephrosis nefrosis amiloidea.
cholemic nephrosis nefrosis colémica.
chronic nephrosis nefrosis crónica.
Epstein's nephrosis nefrosis de Epstein.
familial nephrosis nefrosis familiar.
glycogen nephrosis nefrosis de glucógeno.
hemoglobinuric nephrosis nefrosis hemoglobinúrica.
hydropic nephrosis nefrosis hidrópica.
hypokalemic nephrosis nefrosis hipopotasémica.
hypoxic nephrosis nefrosis hipóxica.
larval nephrosis nefrosis larvada.
lipoid nephrosis nefrosis lípida, nefrosis lipoide, nefrosis lipoidea.
lower nephron nephrosis nefrosis de la nefrona inferior.
necrotizing nephrosis nefrosis necrosante.
osmotic nephrosis nefrosis osmótica.
toxic nephrosis nefrosis tóxica.
vacuolar nephrosis nefrosis vacuolar.
nephrosonography *n.* nefrosonografía.
nephrosplenopexy *n.* nefroesplenopexia.
nephrostogram *n.* nefrostograma.
nephrostolithotomy *n.* nefrostolitotomía.
nephrostoma *n.* nefrostoma.
nephrostome *n.* nefrostoma.
nephrostomy *n.* nefrostomía.
anatrophic nephrostomy nefrostomía anatrófica.
nephrothisis *n.* nefrotisis.
nephrotic *adj.* nefrótico, -ca.
nephrotome *n.* nefrotoma, nefrótomo.
nephrotomic *adj.* nefrotómico, -ca.
nephrotomogram *n.* nefrotomograma.
nephrotomography *n.* nefrotomografía.
nephrotomy *n.* nefrotomía.
abdominal nephrotomy nefrotomía abdominal.
lumbar nephrotomy nefrotomía lumbar.
nephrotoxic *adj.* nefrotóxico, -ca.
nephrotoxicity *n.* nefrotoxicidad.
nephrotoxin *n.* nefrotoxina.
nephrotresis *n.* nefrotresis, nefrotriesis.
nephrotrophic *adj.* nefrotrófico, -ca.
nephrotropic *adj.* nefrotrópico, -ca.
nephrotuberculosis *n.* nefrotuberculosis.
nephrotyphoid *adj.* nefrotifoidea.
nephrotyphus nefrotifo, nefrotifus.
nephroureterectomy *n.* nefroureterectomía.
nephroureterocystectomy *n.* nefroureterocistectomía.
nephrydrosis *n.* nefridrosis.
nephrydrotic *adj.* nefrohidrótico, -ca.
nepiology *n.* nepiología.
neropathy *n.* neropatía.
nerve *n.* nervio.
seventh cranial nerve séptimo par craneal.
sixth cranial nerve sexto par craneal.
tenth cranial nerve décimo par craneal.
twelfth cranial nerve duodécimo par craneal.
nerves *n.* nervios.

nervimotility *n.* nervimotilidad, nervimovilidad.
nervimotion *n.* nervimoción.
nervimuscular *adj.* nervimuscular.
nervine *adj.* nervino, -na.
nervomuscular *adj.* nervimuscular.
nervone *n.* nervona.
nervosism *n.* nerviosismo.
nervosity *n.* nerviosidad.
nervotabes *n.* nervotabes.
nervous *adj.* nervioso, -sa.
nervousness *n.* nerviosismo.
nervus nervio, nervus.
nesidiectomy *n.* nesidiectomía.
nesidioblast *n.* nesidioblasto.
nesidioblastoma *n.* nesidioblastoma.
nesidioblastosis *n.* nesidioblastosis.
Nesslerization *n.* nesslerización.
nest *n.* nido.
  Brunn's epithelial nest nido epitelial de Brunn.
  epithelial nest nido epitelial.
  swallow nest nido de golondrina.
  Waltard cell nest nido de Waltard.
nesteostomy *n.* nesteostomía.
nestiatria *n.* nestiatría.
nestitherapy *n.* nestiterapia.
nestotherapy *n.* nestoterapia.
net *n.* red.
nettle *n.* ortiga.
neumofasciography *n.* neumofasciografía.
neuradynamia *n.* neuradinamia.
neuragmia *n.* neuragmia.
neural *adj.* neural.
neuralgia *n.* neuralgia.
  cardiac neuralgia neuralgia cardíaca.
  cervicobrachial neuralgia neuralgia cervicobraquial.
  cervico-occipital neuralgia neuralgia cervicooccipital.
  cranial neuralgia neuralgia craneal.
  degenerative neuralgia neuralgia degenerativa.
  Fothergill's neuralgia neuralgia de Fothergill.
  geniculate neuralgia neuralgia geniculada.
  glossopharyngeal neuralgia neuralgia glosofaríngea.
  hallucinatory neuralgia neuralgia alucinatoria.
  Harris' migrainous neuralgia neuralgia jaquecosa, neuralgia jaquecosa de Harris.
  herpetic neuralgia neuralgia herpética.
  Hunt's neuralgia neuralgia de Hunt.
  idiopathic neuralgia neuralgia idiopática.
  intercostal neuralgia neuralgia intercostal.
  mammary neuralgia neuralgia mamaria.
  mandibular joint neuralgia neuralgia de la articulación temporomaxilar.
  migrainous cranial neuralgia neuralgia craneal migrañosa.
  migrainous neuralgia neuralgia jaquecosa, neuralgia jaquecosa de Harris.
  Morton's plantar neuralgia neuralgia plantar de Morton.
  nasociliary neuralgia neuralgia nasociliar.
  neuralgia facialis vera neuralgia facial verdadera.
  otic neuralgia neuralgia ótica.
  peripheral neuralgia neuralgia periférica.
  red neuralgia neuralgia roja.
  reminiscent neuralgia neuralgia reminiscente.
  sciatic neuralgia neuralgia ciática.
  Sluder's neuralgia neuralgia de Sluder.
  sphenopalatine neuralgia neuralgia esfenopalatina.
  stump neuralgia neuralgia del muñón.
  supraorbital neuralgia neuralgia supraorbitaria.
  symptomatic neuralgia neuralgia sintomática.
  trifacial neuralgia neuralgia trifacial.
  trifocal neuralgia neuralgia trifacial.
  trigeminal neuralgia neuralgia del trigémino.
  vidian neuralgia neuralgia vidiana.
  visceral neuralgia neuralgia visceral.
neuralgic *adj.* neurálgico, -ca.
neuralgiform *adj.* neuralgiforme.
neuranagenesis *n.* neuranagénesis.
neurangiosis *n.* neurangiosis, neuroangiosis.
neurapophysis *n.* neurapófisis, neuroapófisis.
neurapraxia *n.* neurapraxia, neuroapraxia.
neurarchy *n.* neurarquia.
neurarthropathy *n.* neurartropatía.
neurasthenia *n.* neurastenia.
neurasthenic *adj.* neurasténico, -ca.
neurataxia *n.* neurataxia.
neurataxy *n.* neurataxia.
neuratria *n.* neuriatría.
neuratrophia *n.* neuratrofia, neuroatrofia.
neuratrophy *n.* neuratrofia, neuroatrofia.
neuraxial *adj.* neuroaxial.
neuraxis *n.* neuraxis, neuroaxis.
neuraxon *n.* neuraxón, neuroaxón.
neuraxone *n.* neuraxón.
neure *n.* neura.
neurectasia *n.* neurectasia.
neurectasis *n.* neurectasia, neurectasis.
neurectasy *n.* neurectasia.
neurectomy *n.* neurectomía.
  gastric neurectomy neurectomía gástrica.
neurectopia *n.* neurectopia.
neurectopy *n.* neurectopia.
neurenteric *adj.* neurentérico, -ca.
neurergic *adj.* neurérgico, -ca.
neurexeresis *n.* neurexéresis.
neuriatry *n.* neuriatría.
neurilemma *n.* neurilema.
neurilemmal *adj.* neurilémico, -ca.
neurilemmitis *n.* neurilemitis.
neurilemmoma *n.* neurilemoma, neurolemoma.
  acoustic neurilemoma neurilemoma acústico.
neurility *n.* neurilidad.
neurimotility *n.* neurimotilidad.
neurinoma *n.* neurinoma.
  acoustic neurinoma neurinoma acústico.
  benign neurinoma neurinoma benigno.
  trigeminal neurinoma neurinoma del trigémino.
neurinomatosis *n.* neurinomatosis.
neurit *n.* neurita.
neurite *n.* neurita.
neuritic *adj.* neurítico, -ca.
neuritis *n.* neuritis.
  adventitial neuritis neuritis adventicia.
  alcoholic neuritis neuritis alcohólica.
  axial neuritis neuritis axial, neuritis axonal.
  brachial neuritis neuritis braquial.
  central neuritis neuritis central.
  descending neuritis neuritis descendente.
  dietetic neuritis neuritis dietética.
  disseminated neuritis neuritis diseminada.
  endemica neuritis neuritis endémica, neuritis endémica múltiple.
  facial neuritis neuritis facial.
  Fallopian neuritis neuritis de Falopio.
  Gombault's neuritis neuritis de Gombault.
  hypertrophic interstitial neuritis neuritis intersticial hipertrófica.
  interstitial neuritis neuritis intersticial.
  intraocular neuritis neuritis intraocular.
  latent neuritis neuritis latente.
  leprous neuritis neuritis leprosa.
  malarial multiple neuritis neuritis palúdica múltiple.
  malarial neuritis neuritis palúdica.
  migrating neuritis neuritis migratoria.
  multiple neuritis neuritis múltiple.
  neuritis migrans neuritis migratoria.
  neuritis multiplex endemica neuritis endémica, neuritis endémica múltiple.
  neuritis nodosa neuritis nodosa.
  neuritis puerperalis traumatica neuritis puerperal traumática.
  neuritis saturnina neuritis saturnina.
  optic neuritis neuritis óptica.
  orbital optic neuritis neuritis óptica orbitaria.
  parenchymatous neuritis neuritis parenquimatosa.
  periaxial neuritis neuritis periaxial.
  peripheral neuritis neuritis periférica.
  porphyric neuritis neuritis porfírica.
  postfebrile neuritis neuritis posfebril.
  postocular neuritis neuritis postocular.
  pressure neuritis neuritis por presión.
  radiation neuritis neuritis por radiación.
  radicular neuritis neuritis radicular.
  retrobulbar neuritis neuritis retrobulbar.
  rheumatic neuritis neuritis reumática.
  segmental neuritis neuritis segmentaria.
  senile neuritis neuritis senil.
  serum neuritis neuritis sérica.
  shoulder-girdle neuritis neuritis de la cintura escapular.
  syphilitic neuritis neuritis sifilítica.
  tabetic neuritis neuritis tabética.
  toxic neuritis neuritis tóxica.
  traumatic neuritis neuritis traumática.
neuroallergy *n.* neuroalergia.
neuroamebiasis *n.* neuroamibiasis.
neuroanastomosis *n.* neuroanastomosis.
neuroanatomy *n.* neuroanatomía.
neuroarthropathy *n.* neuroartropatía.
neuroastrocytoma *n.* neuroastrocitoma.
neuroaugmentation *n.* neuroamplificación.
neuroaxone *n.* neuroaxón.
neurobehavioral *adj.* neuroconductual.
neurobiologist *n.* neurobiólogo, -ga.
neurobiology *n.* neurobiología.
neurobiotaxis *n.* neurobiotaxis.
neuroblast *n.* neuroblasto.
neuroblastoma *n.* neuroblastoma.
neuroborreliosis *n.* neuroborreliosis.
neurocardiac *adj.* neurocardíaco, -ca.
neurocele *n.* neurocele, neurocelo.
neurocentral *adj.* neurocentral.
neurocentrum *n.* neurocentro.
neuroceptor *n.* neuroceptor.
neurocheck *n.* mini examen nervioso.
neurochemistry *n.* neuroquímica.
neurochondrite *n.* neurocondrita.
neurochorioretinitis *n.* neurocoriorretinitis.
neurochoroiditis *n.* neurocoroiditis.
neurocladism *n.* neurocladismo.
neuroclonic *adj.* neuroclónico, -ca.
neurocranial *adj.* neurocraneal.
neurocranium *n.* neurocráneo.
  cartilaginous neurocranium neurocráneo cartilaginoso.
  membranous neurocranium neurocráneo membranoso.
neurocrine *adj.* neurocrino, -na.
neurocrinia *n.* neurocrinia.
neurocristopathy *n.* neurocristopatía.

neurocutaneous *adj.* neurocutáneo, -a.
neurocyte *n.* neurocito.
neurocytology *n.* neurocitología.
neurocytolysis *n.* neurocitólisis.
neurocytoma *n.* neurocitoma.
neurodealgia *n.* neurodealgia.
neurodeatrophia *n.* neurodeatrofia.
neurodegenerative *adj.* neurodegenerativo, -va.
neurodendrite *n.* neurodendrita.
neurodendron *n.* neurodendrón.
neuroderm *n.* neurodermo.
neurodermatitis *n.* neurodermatitis.
  circumscribed neurodermatitis neurodermatitis crónica circunscrita.
  disseminated neurodermatitis neurodermatitis diseminada.
  exudative neurodermatitis neurodermatitis exudativa.
  neurodermatitis disseminata neurodermatitis diseminada.
  nummular neurodermatitis neurodermatitis numular.
neurodermitis *n.* neurodermitis.
neurodiagnosis *n.* neurodiagnóstico.
neurodocitis *n.* neurodocitis.
neurodynamic *adj.* neurodinámico, -ca.
neurodynia *n.* neurodinia.
neuroectoderm *n.* neuroectodermo.
neuroectodermal *adj.* neuroectodérmico, -ca.
neuroectomy *n.* neurectomía, neuroectomía.
neuroeffector *adj.* neuroefector, -ra.
neuroelectricity *n.* neuroelectricidad.
neuroelectrotherapeutics *n.* neuroelectroterapia.
neuroelectrotherapy *n.* neuroelectroterapia.
neuroencephalomyelopathy *n.* neuroencefalomielopatía.
  optic neuroencephalomyelopathy neuroencefalomielopatía óptica.
neuroendarteriectomy *n.* neuroendarteriectomía.
neuroendocrine *adj.* neuroendocrino, -na.
neuroendocrinology *n.* neuroendocrinología.
neuroepidermal *adj.* neuroepidérmico, -ca.
neuroepithelial *adj.* neuroepitelial.
neuroepithelioma *n.* neuroepitelioma.
neuroepithelium *n.* neuroepitelio.
neurofiber *n.* neurofibra.
neurofibra *n.* neurofibra.
neurofibril *n.* neurofibrilla.
neurofibrillar *adj.* neurofibrilar.
neurofibroma *n.* neurofibroma.
  plexiform neurofibroma neurofibroma plexiforme.
  storiform neurofibroma neurofibroma estoriforme.
neurofibromatosis *n.* neurofibromatosis.
  abortive neurofibromatosis neurofibromatosis abortiva.
  incomplete neurofibromatosis neurofibromatosis incompleta.
neurofibrosarcomatosis *n.* neurofibrosarcomatosa.
neurofilament *n.* neurofilamento.
neurofixation *n.* neurofijación.
neuroganglitis *n.* neuroganglitis.
neurogastric *adj.* neurogástrico, -ca.
neurogenesis *n.* neurogénesis.
neurogenetic *adj.* neurogenético, -ca.
neurogenic *adj.* neurogénico, -ca.
neurogenous *adj.* neurógeno, -na.
neuroglia *n.* neuroglía.
  interfascicular neuroglia neuroglía interfascicular.

  peripheral neuroglia neuroglía periférica.
neuroglial *adj.* neuroglial.
neurogliar *adj.* neuroglial, neurogliar.
neurogliocyte *n.* neurogliocito.
neurogliocytoma *n.* neurogliocitoma.
neuroglioma *n.* neuroglioma.
  neuroglioma ganglionare neuroglioma ganglionar.
neuroglycopenia *n.* neuroglucopenia.
neurography *n.* neurografía.
neurohemal *adj.* neurohemal.
neurohistology *n.* neurohistología.
neurohormonal *adj.* neurohormonal.
neurohormone *n.* neurohormona.
neurohumor *n.* neurohumor.
neurohumoral *adj.* neurohumoral.
neurohypnology *n.* neurohipnología.
neurohypophyseal *adj.* neurohipofisario, -a.
neurohypophysectomy *n.* neurohipofisectomía.
neurohypophysis *n.* neurohipófisis.
neuroid *adj.* neuroide, neuroideo, -a.
neuroimmunologic *adj.* neuroinmunológico, -ca.
neuroimmunology *n.* neuroinmunología.
neuroinidia *n.* neuroinidia.
neurokinet *n.* neuroquineto.
neurokyme *n.* neuroquimo.
neurolabyrinthitis *n.* neurolaberintitis.
neurolathyrism *n.* neurolatirismo.
neurolema *n.* neurilema, neurolema.
neurolemma *n.* neurilema, neurolema.
neurolemmitis *n.* neurilemitis, neurolemitis.
neurolemmoma *n.* neurilemoma, neurolemoma.
neuroleptanalgesic *adj.* neuroleptoanalgésico, -ca.
neuroleptanesthesia *n.* neuroleptoanestesia.
neuroleptanesthetic *adj.* neuroleptoanestésico, -ca.
neuroleptic *adj.* neuroléptico, -ca.
neuroleptoanalgesia *n.* neuroleptoanalgesia.
neurolinguistics *n.* neurolingüística.
neurolipomatosis dolorosa *n.* neurolipomatosis dolorosa.
neurologic *adj.* neurológico, -ca.
neurologist *n.* neurólogo, -ga.
neurology *n.* neurología.
  clinical neurology neurología clínica.
neurolophoma *n.* neurolofoma.
neurolues *n.* neurolúes.
neurolymph *n.* neurolinfa.
neurolymphomatosis *n.* neurolinfomatosis.
  peripheral neurolymphomatosis neurolinfomatosis periférica.
neurolysin *n.* neurolisina.
neurolysis *n.* neurólisis.
neurolytic *adj.* neurolítico, -ca.
neuroma *n.* neuroma.
  acoustic neuroma neuroma acústico.
  amputation neuroma neuroma de amputación.
  amyelinic neuroma neuroma amielínico.
  false neuroma neuroma falso.
  fascicular neuroma neuroma fascicular.
  fibrillary neuroma neuroma fibrilar.
  ganglionar neuroma neuroma ganglionado, neuroma ganglionar, neuroma ganglónico.
  ganglionated neuroma neuroma ganglionado, neuroma ganglionar, neuroma ganglónico.
  ganglionic neuroma neuroma ganglionado, neuroma ganglionar, neuroma ganglónico.
  malignant neuroma neuroma maligno.
  multiple neuroma neuroma múltiple.

  myelinic neuroma neuroma mielínico.
  neuroma cutis neuroma cutáneo.
  neuroma telangiectodes neuroma telangiectásico, neuroma telangiectodes.
  nevoid neuroma neuroma nevoide.
  plexiform neuroma neuroma plexiforme.
  stump neuroma neuroma del muñón.
  traumatic neuroma neuroma traumático.
  true neuroma neuroma verdadero.
  Verneuil's neuroma neuroma de Verneuil.
neuromalacia *n.* neuromalacia.
neuromalakia *n.* neuromalacia.
neuromatosis *n.* neuromatosis.
neuromatous *adj.* neuromatoso, -sa.
neuromechanism *n.* neuromecanismo.
neuromelitococcosis *n.* neuromelitococia.
neuromeningeal *adj.* neuromeníngeo, -a.
neuromere *n.* neurómero.
neuromery *n.* neuromería.
neuromimetic *adj.* neuromimético, -ca.
neuromittor *n.* neuroemisor, neuromisor, neuromitor.
neuromodulation *n.* neuromodulación.
neuromodulator *n.* neuromodulador.
neuromotor *adj.* neuromotor, -ra.
neuromuscular *adj.* neuromuscular.
neuromyal *adj.* neuromial.
neuromyasthenia *n.* neuromiastenia.
  epidemic neuromyasthenia neuromiastenia epidémica.
neuromyelitis *n.* neuromielitis.
  neuromyelitis optica neuromielitis óptica.
neuromyic *adj.* neurómico, -ca.
neuromyopathic *adj.* neuromiopático, -ca.
neuromyopathy *n.* neuromiopatía.
  carcinomatous neuromyopathy neuromiopatía carcinomatosa.
neuromyositis *n.* neuromiositis.
neuromyotonia *n.* neuromiotonía.
neuron *n.* neurona.
  afferent neuron neurona aferente.
  bipolar neuron neurona bipolar.
  central neuron neurona central.
  connector neuron neurona de conexión.
  correlation neuron neurona de correlación.
  efferent neuron neurona eferente.
  Golgi type I neuron neurona de Golgi del tipo I.
  Golgi type II neuron neurona de Golgi del tipo II.
  intercalary neuron neurona de asociación, neurona intercalar.
  intercalated neuron neurona de asociación, neurona intercalar.
  internuncial neuron neurona internuncial.
  long neuron neurona larga.
  motor neuron neurona motora.
  multiform neuron neurona multiforme.
  multipolar neuron neurona multipolar.
  peripheral motor neuron neurona motora periférica.
  peripheral sensory neuron neurona sensitiva periférica, neurona sensorial periférica.
  polymorphic neuron neurona polimórfica.
  postganglionic neuron neurona posganglionar.
  preganglionic neuron neurona preganglionar.
  premotor neuron neurona premotora.
  projection neuron neurona de proyección.
  pseudounipolar neuron neurona seudounipolar.
  sensory neuron neurona sensitiva, neurona sensorial.
  short neuron neurona corta.

unipolar neuron neurona unipolar.
neuronagenesis *n.* neuronagénesis.
neuronal *adj.* neuronal.
neuroncology *n.* neuroncología.
neurone *n.* neurona.
neuronephric *adj.* neuronéfrico, -ca.
neuronevus *n.* neuronevo.
neuronic *adj.* neurónico, -ca.
neuronin *n.* neuronina.
neuronitis *n.* neuronitis.
neuronixis *n.* neuronixis.
neuronoatrophy *n.* neuronoatrofia.
neuronopathy *n.* neuronopatía.
  sensory neuronopathy neuronopatía sensorial.
neuronophage *n.* neuronófago.
neuronophagia *n.* neurofagia, neuronofagia.
neuronophagy *n.* neuronofagia.
neuronosis *n.* neuronosis.
neuronotropic *adj.* neuronotrópico, -ca.
neuronymy *n.* neuronimia.
neuro-ophthalmology *n.* neuroftalmología, neurooftalmología.
neuro-otology *n.* neurootología, neurotología.
neuropacemaker *n.* neuromarcapasos.
neuropapillitis *n.* neuropapilitis.
neuroparalysis *n.* neuroparálisis.
neuroparalytic *adj.* neuroparalítico, -ca.
neuropath *n.* neurópata.
neuropathic *adj.* neuropático, -ca.
neuropathogenesis *n.* neuropatogénesis, neuropatogenia.
neuropathogenicity *n.* neuropatogenicidad.
neuropathologist *n.* neuropatólogo, -ga.
neuropathology *n.* neuropatología.
neuropathy *n.* neuropatía.
  acute anterior ischemic optic neuropathy neuropatía anterior isquémica aguda.
  alcoholic neuropathy neuropatía alcohólica.
  ascending neuropathy neuropatía ascendente.
  asymmetric motor neuropathy neuropatía motora asimétrica.
  brachial plexus neuropathy neuropatía del plexo braquial.
  descending neuropathy neuropatía descendente.
  diabetic neuropathy neuropatía diabética.
  diphtheritic neuropathy neuropatía diftérica.
  entrapment neuropathy neuropatía de atrapamiento.
  familiar amyloid neuropathy neuropatía amiloidea familiar.
  glial axonal neuropathy neuropatía axonal glial.
  hereditary optic neuropathy neuropatía óptica hereditaria de Lieber.
  hereditary sensory radicular neuropathy neuropatía radicular sensitiva hereditaria.
  ischemic optic neuropathy neuropatía óptica isquémica.
  isoniazid neuropathy neuropatía por isoniazida.
  lead neuropathy neuropatía por plomo.
  leprous neuropathy neuropatía leprosa.
  Lieber's hereditary optic neuropathy neuropatía óptica hereditaria de Lieber.
  Lieber's optic neuropathy neuropatía óptica hereditaria de Lieber.
  metabollic neuropathy neuropatía metabólica.
  motor dapsone neuropathy neuropatía motora por dapsona.

  paraneoplastic neuropathy neuropatía paraneoplásica.
  periaxial neuropathy neuropatía periaxial.
  peripheral neuropathy neuropatía periférica.
  progressive hypertrophic interstitial neuropathy neuropatía intersticial hipertrófica progresiva.
  progressive hypertrophic neuropathy neuropatía hipertrófica progresiva.
  segmental neuropathy neuropatía segmentaria.
  serum neuropathy neuropatía sérica.
  serum sickness neuropathy neuropatía sérica.
  symmetric distal neuropathy neuropatía distal simétrica.
  tomaculous neuropathy neuropatía tomacular.
neuropeptide *n.* neuropéptido.
neurophage *n.* neurófago.
neuropharmacological *adj.* neurofarmacológico, -ca.
neuropharmacology *n.* neurofarmacología.
neurophilic *adj.* neurofílico, -ca, neurófilo, -la.
neurophthalmology *n.* neuroftalmología.
neurophthisis *n.* neuroptisis.
neurophylaxy *n.* neurofilaxia.
neurophysiologist *n.* neurofisiólogo, -ga.
neurophysiology *n.* neurofisiología.
neuropil *n.* neurópilo.
neuropile *n.* neurópilo.
neuropilem *n.* neuropilema.
neuroplasm *n.* neuroplasma.
neuroplasmic *adj.* neuroplásmico, -ca.
neuroplasty *n.* neuroplastia.
neuroplegia *n.* neuroplejia, neuroplejía.
neuroplegic *adj.* neuropléjico, -ca.
neuroplexus *n.* neuroplexo.
neuropodion *n.* neuropodio, neurópodo.
neuropore *n.* neuroporo.
  anterior neuropore neuroporo anterior.
  caudal neuropore neuroporo caudal.
  posterior neuropore neuroporo posterior.
  rostral neuropore neuroporo rostral.
neuropotential *n.* neuropotencial.
neuropraxia *n.* neuropraxia.
neuroprobasia *n.* neuroprobasia, neuroprobasis.
neuropsychiatric *adj.* neuropsiquiátrico, -ca.
neuropsychiatry *n.* neuropsiquiatría.
neuropsychic *adj.* neuropsíquico, -ca.
neuropsychochemistry *n.* neuropsicoquímica.
neuropsychofarmacology *n.* neuropsicofarmacología.
neuropsychologic *adj.* neuropsicológico, -ca.
neuropsychological *adj.* neuropsicológico, -ca.
neuropsychology *n.* neuropsicología.
neuropsychosis *n.* neuropsicosis.
neuroradiologist *n.* neurorradiólogo, -ga.
neuroradiology *n.* neurorradiología.
  interventional neuroradiology neurorradiología intervencional.
neuroreceptor *n.* neurorreceptor.
neurorecidive *n.* neurorrecidiva.
neurorecurrence *n.* neurorrecurrencia.
neurorelapse *n.* neurorrecaída, neurorrelapso.
neuroretinitis *n.* neurorretinitis.
neuroretinopathy *n.* neurorretinopatía.
  hypertensive neuroretinopathy neurorretinopatía hipertensiva.
neuroroentgenography *n.* neurorroentgenografía.

neurorrhaphy *n.* neurorrafia.
neurorrhexis *n.* neurorrexis.
Neurorrhyctes hydrophobiae Neurorrhyctes hydrophobiae.
neurosarcocleisis *n.* neurosarcocleisis.
neurosarcoidosis *n.* neurosarcoidosis.
neurosarcoma *n.* neurosarcoma.
neurosciences *n.* neurociencias.
neuroscientist *n.* neurocientífico, -ca.
neurosclerosis *n.* neuroesclerosis, neurosclerosis.
neurosecretion *n.* neurosecreción.
neurosecretory *adj.* neurosecretor, -ra, neurosecretorio, -ria.
neurosegmental *adj.* neurosegmentario, -ria.
neurosensory *adj.* neurosensitivo, -va, neurosensorial.
neurosis *n.* neurosis.
  actual neurosis neurosis actual.
  anxiety neurosis neurosis de angustia, neurosis de ansiedad.
  cardiac neurosis neurosis cardíaca.
  character neurosis neurosis de carácter.
  combat neurosis neurosis de combate, neurosis del corazón del soldado.
  compulsion neurosis neurosis compulsiva, neurosis de compulsión.
  conversion neurosis neurosis de conversión.
  depressive neurosis neurosis depresiva.
  experimental neurosis neurosis experimental.
  failure neurosis neurosis de fracaso.
  family neurosis neurosis familiar.
  fatigue neurosis neurosis de fatiga.
  gastric neurosis neurosis gástrica.
  hypochondriacal neurosis neurosis hipocondríaca.
  hypochondrial neurosis neurosis hipocondríaca.
  hysterical neurosis neurosis histérica.
  mixed neurosis neurosis mixta.
  narcissistic neurosis neurosis narcisista.
  neurasthenic neurosis neurosis neurasténica.
  neurosis of abandonment neurosis de abandono.
  obsessional neurosis neurosis obsesiva, neurosis obsesivo-compulsiva.
  phobic neurosis neurosis fóbica.
  transference neurosis neurosis de transferencia.
  traumatic neurosis neurosis traumática.
  vegetative neurosis neurosis vegetativa.
  war neurosis neurosis de guerra.
neurosism *n.* neurosismo.
neuroskeletal *adj.* neuroesquelético, -ca, neurosquelético, -ca.
neuroskeleton *n.* neuroesqueleto, neurosqueleto.
neurosome *n.* neurosoma.
neurospasm *n.* neuroespasmo, neurospasmo.
neurosplanchnic *adj.* neuroesplácnico, -ca, neurosplácnico, -ca.
neurospongioma *n.* neuroespongioma, neurospongioma.
neurospongium *n.* neuroespongio, neurospongio.
neurosschwannoma *n.* neuroschwannoma.
neurostatus *n.* neuroestado, neuroestatus.
neurosthenia *n.* neurostenia.
neurosthenic *adj.* neurosténico, -ca.
neurostimulation *n.* neuroestimulación.
neurostimulator *n.* neuroestimulador.
neurosurgeon *n.* neurocirujano.
neurosurgery *n.* neurocirugía.
  functional neurosurgery neurocirugía funcional.

neurosuture *n.* neurosutura.
neurosyphilis *n.* neurosífilis.
asymptomatic neurosyphilis neurosífilis asintomática.
meningovascular neurosyphilis neurosífilis meningovascular.
parenchymatous neurosyphilis neurosífilis parenquimatosa.
paretic neurosyphilis neurosífilis parética.
neurotabes *n.* neurotabes.
neurotagma *n.* neurotagma.
neurotendinous *adj.* neurotendinoso, -sa.
neurotension *n.* neurotensión.
neuroterminal *adj.* neuroterminal.
neurothekeoma *n.* neurotequeoma.
neurotherapeutics *n.* neuroterapia.
neurotherapy *n.* neuroterapia.
neurothlipsia *n.* neurotlipsia.
neurothlipsis *n.* neurotlipsia, neurotlipsis.
neurotic *adj.* neurótico, -ca.
neuroticism *n.* neuroticismo, neurotismo.
neurotization *n.* neurotización.
neurotize *v.* neurotizar.
neurotmesis *n.* neurotmesis.
neurotology *n.* neurotología.
neurotome *n.* neurotoma, neurótomo.
neurotomography *n.* neurotomografía.
neurotomy *n.* neurotomía.
opticociliary neurotomy neurotomía opticociliar.
radiofrequency neurotomy neurotomía por radiofrecuencia.
retro-Gasserian neurotomy neurotomía retrogasseriana.
neurotonia *n.* neurotonía.
neurotonic *adj.* neurotónico, -ca.
neurotonometer *n.* neurotonómetro.
neurotony *n.* neurotonía.
neurotoxia *n.* neurotoxia.
neurotoxic *adj.* neurotóxico, -ca.
neurotoxicity *n.* neurotoxicidad.
neurotransducer *n.* neurotransductor.
neurotransmission *n.* neurotransmisión.
neurotransmitter *n.* neurotransmisor.
false neurotransmitter neurotransmisor falso.
neurotrauma *n.* neurotrauma.
neurotripsy *n.* neurotripsia.
neurotrophasthenia *n.* neurotrofastenia, neurotrofoastenia.
neurotrophic *adj.* neurotrófico, -ca.
neurotrophy *n.* neurotrofia.
neurotropic *adj.* neurotrópico, -ca.
neurotropism *n.* neurotropismo.
neurotropy *n.* neurotropía.
neurotrosis *n.* neurotrosis.
neurotubule *n.* neurotúbulo.
neurovaccine *n.* neurovacuna.
neurovaricosis *n.* neurovaricosis.
neurovaricosity *n.* neurovaricosidad.
neurovariola *n.* neurovariola.
neurovascular *adj.* neurovascular.
neurovegetative *adj.* neurovegetativo, -va.
neurovirulence *n.* neurovirulencia.
neurovirulent *adj.* neurovirulento, -ta.
neurovirus *n.* neurovirus.
neurovisceral *adj.* neurovisceral.
neurula *n.* néurula.
neurulation *n.* neurulación.
neururgic *adj.* neurúrgico, -ca.
neutral *adj.* neutral, neutro, -tra.
neutralism *n.* neutralismo.
neutrality *n.* neutralidad.
neutralization *n.* neutralización.
viral neutralization neutralización viral.

neutralize *v.* neutralizar.
neutretto *n.* neutreto.
neutrino *n.* neutrino.
neutroclusion *n.* neutroclusión.
neutrocyte *n.* neutrocito.
neutrocytopenia *n.* neutrocitopenia.
neutrocytophilia *n.* neutrocitofilia.
neutrocytosis *n.* neutrocitosis.
neutrography *n.* neutrografía.
neutron *n.* neutrón.
neutropenia *n.* neutropenia.
chronic benign neutropenia of childhood neutropenia crónica benigna de la infancia.
chronic hypoplastic neutropenia neutropenia hipoplásica crónica.
congenital neutropenia neutropenia congénita.
cyclic neutropenia neutropenia cíclica.
familial benign chronic neutropenia neutropenia familiar crónica benigna.
hypersplenic neutropenia neutropenia hiperesplénica.
idiopathic neutropenia neutropenia idiopática.
Kostmann neutropenia neutropenia de Kostmann.
malignant neutropenia neutropenia maligna.
neonatal neutropenia neutropenia neonatal.
periodic neutropenia neutropenia periódica.
peripheral neutropenia neutropenia periférica.
primary splenic neutropenia neutropenia esplénica primaria.
transitory neonatal neutropenia neutropenia neonatal transitoria.
neutrophil *n.* neutrófilo.
band neutrophil neutrófilo en banda.
filamented neutrophil neutrófilo filamentado.
giant neutrophil neutrófilo gigante.
hypersegmented neutrophil neutrófilo hipersegmentado.
immature neutrophil neutrófilo inmaduro.
juvenile neutrophil neutrófilo juvenil.
mature neutrophil neutrófilo maduro.
rod neutrophil neutrófilo en bastoncillo.
segmented neutrophil neutrófilo segmentado.
stab neutrophil neutrófilo en banca.
neutrophilia *n.* neutrofilia.
neutrophilic *adj.* neutrofílico, -ca.
neutrophilopenia *n.* neutrofilopenia.
neutrophilous *adj.* neutrófilo, -la.
neutropism *n.* neutropismo.
neutrotaxis *n.* neutrotaxis.
nevoblast *n.* nevoblasto.
nevocarcinoma *n.* nevocarcinoma.
nevocyte *n.* nevocito.
nevocytic *adj.* nevocítico, -ca.
nevoid *adj.* nevoide, nevoideo, -a.
nevolipoma *n.* nevolipoma.
nevoxanthoendothelioma *n.* nevoxantoendotelioma.
nevus *n.* naevus, nevo.
achromic nevus nevo acrómico.
acquired nevus nevo adquirido.
amelanotic nevus nevo amelanótico.
balloon cell nevus nevo celular baloniforme, nevo celular en balón.
basal cell nevus nevo de células basales.
bathing trunk nevus nevo en traje de baño.
Becker's nevus nevo de Becker.
blue nevus nevo ampolla de forma azul, nevo azul.

blue rubber bleb nevus nevo azul con flictenas de goma, nevo azul en pezón, nevo azul en tetina de goma.
capillary nevus nevo capilar.
cellular blue nevus nevo azul celular, nevo celular azul.
cellular nevus nevo celular.
chromatophore nevus of Naegeli nevo cromatóforo de Naegeli.
compound nevus nevo compuesto.
congenital nevus nevo congénito.
connective tissue nevus nevo de tejido conjuntivo.
dermal nevus nevo dérmico.
dysplastic nevus nevo displásico.
epidermal nevus nevo epidérmico.
epidermic-dermic nevus nevo dermoepidérmico.
epithelial nevus nevo epitelial.
epithelioid cell nevus nevo de células epitelioides.
fatty nevus nevo graso.
faun tail nevus nevo cola de fauno.
flame nevus nevo en llama.
giant congenital pigmented nevus nevo gigante congénito pigmentado.
giant hairy nevus nevo gigante velloso.
giant pigmented nevus nevo gigante pigmentado, nevo pigmentado gigante.
hair follicle nevus nevo de los folículos pilosos.
hairy nevus nevo piloso, nevo velloso.
halo nevus nevo en halo.
hepatic nevus nevo hepático.
intradermal nevus nevo intradérmico.
Ito's nevus nevo de Ito.
Jadassohn's nevus nevo de Jadassohn.
Jadassohn-Tièche nevus nevo azul de Jadassohn-Tièche.
junction nevus nevo de transición, nevo de unión, nevo intermedio.
junctional nevus nevo de unión.
linear nevus nevo lineal.
melanocytic nevus nevo melanocítico.
nape nevus nevo de la nuca.
neural nevus nevo neural.
neuroid nevus nevo neural.
nevocellular nevus nevo nevocelular.
nevocytic nevus nevo nevocítico.
nevus-cell nevus nevo de células névicas.
nodular connective tissue nevus nevo nodular de tejido conjuntivo.
non-pigmented nevus nevo no pigmentado.
nuchal nevus nevo de la nuca.
oral epithelial nevus nevo epitelial oral.
organoid nevus nevo organoide.
Ota's nevus nevo de Ota.
pigmented hairy epidermal nevus nevo epidérmico piloso pigmentado, nevo epidérmico velloso pigmentado.
pigmented nevus nevo pigmentado, nevo pigmentario, nevo pigmentoso.
pilose nevus nevo piloso.
spider nevus nevo en araña.
spindle and epithelioid cell nevus nevo de células fusiformes y epitelioides.
spindle cell nevus nevo de células fusiformes.
Spitz nevus nevo de Spitz.
stellar nevus nevo estelar.
strawberry nevus nevo en frambuesa, nevo en fresa.
Sutton's nevus nevo de Sutton.
systemized nevus nevo sistemizado.
telangiectatic nevus nevo telangiectásico.
Unna's nevus nevo de Unna.

vascular nevus nevo vascular.
verrucoid nevus nevo verrucoide, nevo verrucoso, nevo verrugoso.
verrucous nevus nevo verrucoide, nevo verrucoso, nevo verrugoso.
white sponge nevus nevo esponjoso blanco.
newborn *n.* recién nacido.
nexus nexo, nexus.
niacinamide *n.* niacinamida.
niche *n.* nicho.
  Barclay's niche nicho de Barclay.
  ecologic niche nicho ecológico.
  ecological niche nicho ecológico.
  enamel niche nicho del esmalte.
  Haudek's niche nicho de Haudek.
  niche of round window nicho de la ventana redonda.
nick *n.* muesca.
nicking *n.* escotamiento.
  AV nicking huella AV.
nicotinamide *n.* nicotinamida.
nicotinamidemia *n.* nicotinamidemia.
nicotine *n.* nicotina.
nicotinism *n.* nicotinismo.
nicotinolytic *adj.* nicotinolítico, -ca.
nicotinomimetic *adj.* nicotinomimético, -ca.
nictation *n.* nictación.
nictemeral *adj.* nictémero, -ra.
nictitating *adj.* nictitante.
nictitation *n.* nictificación, nictitación.
nictophonia *n.* nictofonía.
nicturia *n.* nicturia.
nidal *adj.* nidal.
nidation *n.* nidación.
nidus *n.* nido.
  cancer nidus nido de cáncer.
  nidus avis nido de ave.
  nidus hirundinis nido de golondrina.
nightmare *n.* pesadilla.
nigral *adj.* nigral.
nigrities nigrities.
  nigrities linguae nigrities linguae.
nigrosin *n.* nigrosina.
nigrosine *n.* nigrosina.
nigrostriatal *adj.* nigroestriado, -da.
nihilism *n.* nihilismo.
  therapeutic nihilism nihilismo terapéutico.
niphablepsia *n.* nifablepsia.
niphotyphlosis *n.* nifotiflosis.
nipple *n.* pezón.
nit *n.* liendre.
nitremia *n.* nitremia.
nitrification *n.* nitrificación.
nitrituria *n.* nitrituria.
nitrogen *n.* nitrógeno.
nitrogen-fixing *n.* nitrogenación.
nitrogenization *n.* nitrogenización.
nitrogenous *adj.* nitrogenado, -da.
nitrometer *n.* nitrómetro.
nitron *n.* nitrón.
njovera *n.* njovera.
Nocardia Nocardia.
Nocardiaceae Nocardiaceae.
nocardial *adj.* nocardial.
nocardiasis *n.* nocardiasis.
nocardioform *adj.* nocardioforme.
Nocardiopsis Nocardiopsis.
nocardiosis *n.* nocardiosis.
  granulomatous nocardiosis nocardiosis granulomatosa.
nocebo *n.* nocebo.
nociassociation *n.* nociasociación.
nociception *n.* nocicepción.
nociceptive *adj.* nociceptivo, -va.
nociceptor *n.* nociceptor.

  polymodal nociceptor nociceptor polimodal.
nocifensor *adj.* nocifensor, -ra.
noci-influence *n.* nociinfluencia.
nociperception *n.* nocipercepción.
noctalbuminuria *n.* noctalbuminuria.
noctambulation *n.* noctambulación.
noctambulic *adj.* noctámbulo, -la.
noctambulism *n.* noctambulismo.
noctiphobia *n.* nictofobia, noctifobia.
nocturia *n.* nicturia, nocturia.
nocturnal *adj.* nocturno, -na.
nocuity *n.* nocuidad.
nodal *adj.* nodal.
node *n.* nódulo^2, nudo.
  Aschoff-Tawara's node nódulo de Aschoff-Tawara.
  atrioventricular node nódulo auriculoventricular.
  Bouchard's node nódulo de Bouchard.
  Féréol's node nódulo de Féréol.
  Haygarth's node nódulo de Haygarth.
  Heberden's node nódulo de Heberden.
  Meynet's node nódulo de Meynet.
  Osler's node nódulo de Osler.
  Schmidt's node nudo de Schmidt.
  Schmorl's node nudo de Schmorl.
  singer's node nódulo de cantante.
  sinoatrial node nódulo sinoauricular, nódulo sinusal.
  sinoauricular node nódulo sinoauricular, nódulo sinusal.
  syncytial node nudo sincitial.
  syphilitic node nódulo sifilítica.
  Tawara's node nódulo de Tawara.
  teacher's node nódulo de profesor.
nodose *adj.* nudoso, -sa.
nodositas *n.* nudosidad.
nodosity *n.* nudosidad.
nodous *adj.* nudoso, -sa.
nodular *adj.* nodular.
nodulate *adj.* nodulado, -da.
nodulated *adj.* nodulado, -da.
nodulation *n.* nodulación.
nodule *n.* nódulo^1.
nodulectomy *n.* nodulectomía.
nodulitis *n.* nodulitis.
  rheumatoid nodulitis nodulitis reumatoide.
nodulosis *n.* nodulosis.
  rheumatoid nodulosis nodulosis reumatoide.
nodulous *adj.* noduloso, -sa.
nodulus nódulo^1, nodulus.
nodus nodus, nudo.
noematic *adj.* noemático, -ca.
noematochometer *n.* noematocómetro.
noesis *n.* noesis.
noetic *adj.* noético, -ca.
noise *n.* ruido.
  ambient noise ruido ambiental.
noma *n.* noma.
  noma pudendi noma de la vulva, noma pudendi.
  noma vulvae noma de la vulva, noma pudendi.
nomadic *adj.* nómada.
nomatophobia *n.* nomatofobia.
nomenclature *n.* nomenclatura.
  binary nomenclature nomenclatura binaria, nomenclatura binomial.
  binomial nomenclature nomenclatura binaria, nomenclatura binomial.
  chromosomal nomenclature nomenclatura cromosómica.
Nomina Anatomica (NA) *n.* Nomina Anatomica (NA).

nomogenesis *n.* nomogénesis.
nomogram *n.* nomograma.
  blood volume nomogram nomograma del volumen sanguíneo.
  breathing nomogram nomograma respiratorio.
  Cartesian nomogram nomograma cartesiano.
  Radford nomogram nomograma de Radford.
  Siggard-Andersen nomogram nomograma de Siggard-Andersen.
  West nomogram nomograma de West.
nomography *n.* nomografía.
nomothetic *adj.* nomotético, -ca.
nomotopic *adj.* nomotópico, -ca.
non compos mentis *adj.* non compos mentis.
nona *n.* nona.
non-adherent *adj.* no adherente.
nonan *adj.* nonana.
non-antigenic *adj.* no antigénico, -ca.
non-cariogenic *adj.* no cariogénico, -ca.
non-cellular *adj.* no celular.
non-compliance *n.* incumplimiento.
non-conductor *adj.* no conductor, -ra.
non-depolarizer *adj.* no despolarizador, -ra.
non-disease *n.* no enfermedad.
non-disjunction *n.* no disyunción.
non-electrolyte *n.* no electrolito.
non-heme *adj.* no hem.
non-immune *adj.* no inmune.
non-immunity *n.* no inmunidad.
non-infectious *adj.* no infeccioso, -sa.
non-invasive *adj.* no invasivo, -va.
non-involution *n.* no involución.
non-ionic *adj.* no iónico, -ca.
non-medullated *adj.* no mielínico, -ca.
non-myelinic *adj.* no mielínico, -ca.
non-neoplastic *adj.* no neoplásico, -ca.
non-nucleated *adj.* no nucleado, -da.
non-occlusion *n.* no oclusión.
non-oliguric *adj.* no oligúrico, -ca.
non-oncogenic *adj.* no oncógeno, -na.
non-opaque *adj.* no opaco, -ca.
non-penetrance *n.* no penetrancia.
non-photochromogen *n.* no fotocromógeno.
non-polar *adj.* no polar.
non-radiable *adj.* no radiable.
non-rotation *n.* no rotación.
non-secretor *n.* no secretor, -ra.
non-septate *adj.* no septado, -da.
non-specific *adj.* inespecífico, -ca.
non-taster *adj.* no gustador, -ra.
non-toxic *adj.* no tóxico, -ca.
non-union *n.* no unión.
non-valent *adj.* no valente.
non-vascular *adj.* no vascular.
non-verbal *adj.* no verbal.
non-viable *adj.* inviable, no viable.
nooanaleptic *adj.* nooanaléptico, -ca.
nookleptia *n.* noocleptia.
norma *n.* norma^2.
normal *adj.* normal.
normality *n.* normalidad.
normalization *n.* normalización.
normalize *v.* normalizar.
normergic *adj.* normérgico, -ca, normoérgico, -ca.
normoblast *n.* normoblasto.
  acidophilic normoblast normoblasto acidófilo.
  basophilic normoblast normoblasto basófilo.
  early normoblast normoblasto temprano.
  eosinophilic normoblast normoblasto eosinófilo.
  intermediate normoblast normoblasto intermedio.

late **normoblast** normoblasto tardío.
orthochromatic normoblast normoblasto ortocromático.
oxyphilic **normoblast** normoblasto oxífilo.
polychromatic **normoblast** normoblasto policromático.
normoblastic *adj.* normoblástico, -ca.
normoblastosis *n.* normoblastosis.
normocalcemia *n.* normocalcemia.
normocalcemic *adj.* normocalcémico, -ca.
normocapnia *n.* normocapnia.
normocholesterolemia *n.* normocolesterolemia.
normocholesterolemic *adj.* normocolesterolémico, -ca.
normochromia *n.* normocromía.
normochromic *adj.* normocrómico, -ca.
normochromocyte *n.* normocromocito.
normocyte *n.* normocito.
normocytic *adj.* normocítico, -ca.
normocytosis *n.* normocitosis.
normodromous *adj.* normodrómico, -ca.
normoerythrocyte *n.* normoeritrocito.
normogenesis *n.* normogénesis.
normoglycemia *n.* normoglucemia.
normoglycemic *adj.* normoglucémico, -ca.
normokalemia *n.* normopotasemia.
normokaliemia *n.* normopotasemia.
normolineal *adj.* normolineal.
normolipidemia *n.* normolipedemia, normolipemia.
normonormocytosis *n.* normonormocitosis.
normo-orthocytosis *n.* normoortocitosis.
normoplasia *n.* normoplasia.
normosexuality *n.* normosexualidad.
normospermia *n.* normoespermia.
normosqueocitosis *n.* normosqueocitosis.
normosthenuria *n.* normostenuria.
normotensive *adj.* normotenso, -sa.
normothermia *n.* normotermia.
normotonia *n.* normotonía.
normotonic *adj.* normotónico, -ca.
normotopic *n.* normotopo.
normovolemia *n.* normovolemia.
normoxia *n.* normoxemia, normoxia.
nose *n.* nariz.
  brandy **nose** nariz de brandy.
  cleft **nose** nariz hendida.
  copper **nose** nariz de cobre.
  dog **nose** nariz de perro.
  hammer **nose** nariz en martillo.
  potato **nose** nariz en patata.
  rum **nose** nariz de ron.
  saddle **nose** nariz en silla de montar.
  saddle-back **nose** nariz en dorso de silla de montar.
  swayback **nose** nariz en lomo equino.
  toper's **nose** nariz de bebedor.
  upturned **nose** nariz respingona.
nosebleed *n.* epistaxis.
nosegay *n.* ramillete.
  Riolan's **nosegay** ramillete de Riolano.
nosencephalus *n.* nosencéfalo.
nosetiology *n.* nosetiología.
nosochthonography *n.* nosoctonografía.
nosocomial *adj.* nosocomial.
nosocomium *n.* nosocomio.
nosogenesis *n.* nosogénesis.
nosogeny *n.* nosogenia.
nosogeography *n.* nosogeografía.
nosographic *adj.* nosográfico, -ca.
nosographist *n.* nosógrafo, -fa.
nosography *n.* nosografía.
nosohemia *n.* nosemia, nosohemia.
nosointoxication *n.* nosointoxicación.

nosologic *adj.* nosológico, -ca.
nosology *n.* nosología.
  psychiatric **nosology** nosología psiquiátrica.
nosomania *n.* nosomanía.
nosometry *n.* nosometría.
nosomycosis *n.* nosomicosis.
nosonomy *n.* nosonomía.
nosoparasite *n.* nosoparásito.
nosophilia *n.* nosofilia.
nosophobe *adj.* nosófobo, -ba.
nosophobia *n.* nosofobia.
nosophyte *n.* nosófito.
nosopoietic *adj.* nosopoyético, -ca.
nosotaxy *n.* nosotaxia.
nosotherapy *n.* nosoterapia.
nosotoxic *adj.* nosotóxico, -ca.
nosotoxicosis *n.* nosotoxicosis.
nosotoxin *n.* nosotoxina.
nosotrophy *n.* nosotrofia.
nosotropic *adj.* nosotrópico, -ca.
nostalgia *n.* nostalgia.
nostology *n.* nostología.
nostomania *n.* nostomanía.
nostophobia *n.* nostofobia.
nostrum *n.* nostrum.
notal *adj.* notal.
notancephalia *n.* notancefalia.
notanencephalia *n.* notanencefalia.
notch *n.* escotadura, muesca.
notched *adj.* escotado, -da.
notencephalocele *n.* notencefalia, notencefalocele.
notochord *n.* notocorda, notocordio.
notochordal *adj.* notocordal.
notochordoma *n.* notocordoma.
notogenesis *n.* notogénesis.
notomelia *n.* notomelia.
notomelus *n.* notomelo.
notomyelitis *n.* notomielitis.
noumenon *n.* noúmeno.
noxa *n.* noxa.
noxious *adj.* nocivo, -va.
nucha *n.* nuca.
nuchal *adj.* nucal.
nuclear *adj.* nuclear.
nucleated *adj.* nucleado, -da.
nucleation *n.* nucleación.
nucleide *n.* nucleido.
nucleiform *adj.* nucleiforme.
nuclein *n.* nucleína.
nucleoalbumium *n.* nucleoalbúmina.
nucleocapsid *n.* nucleocápsida, nucleocápside.
nucleochylema *n.* nucleoquilema.
nucleochyme *n.* nucleoquima.
nucleofugal *adj.* nucleofugal, nucleófugo, -ga.
nucleohistone *n.* nucleohistona.
nucleohyaloplasm *n.* nucleohialoplasma.
nucleoid *adj.* nucleoide.
nucleolar *adj.* nucleolar.
nucleoliform *adj.* nucleoliforme.
nucleolin *n.* nucleolina.
nucleolinus *n.* nucleolino.
nucleoloid *adj.* nucleoloide.
nucleololus *n.* nucleólolo.
nucleolonema *n.* nucleolonema.
nucleoloneme *n.* nucleolonema.
nucleolus *n.* nucleólo.
  chromatin **nucleolus** nucléolo de cromatina.
  false **nucleolus** nucléolo falso.
  nucleinic **nucleolus** nucléolo nucleínico.
  secondary **nucleolus** nucléolo secundario.
nucleomicrosome *n.* nucleomicrosoma.
nucleon *n.* nucleón.
nucleonic *adj.* nucleónico, -ca.

nucleopetal *adj.* nucleópeto, -ta.
nucleophagocytosis *n.* nucleofagocitosis.
nucleophil *adj.* nucleófilo, -la.
nucleophile *adj.* nucleófilo, -la.
nucleoplasm *n.* nucleoplasma.
nucleoproteid *n.* nucleoproteido.
nucleoprotein *n.* nucleoproteína.
nucleorrhexis *n.* nucleorrexis.
nucleorthesis *n.* nucleortesis.
nucleosidase *n.* nucleosidasa.
nucleoside *n.* nucleósido.
nucleosome *n.* nucleosoma.
nucleospindle *n.* nucleohuso.
nucleotherapy *n.* nucleoterapia.
nucleotide *n.* nucleótido.
nucleotoxin *n.* nucleotoxina.
nuclephilic *adj.* nucleofílico, -ca.
nucleus núcleo, nucleus.
  Béclard's **nucleus** núcleo de Béclard.
  Klein-Gumprecht shadow **nucleus** núcleo de Klein-Gumprecht.
  segmentation **nucleus** núcleo de segmentación.
  yolk **nucleus** núcleo vitelino.
nuclide *n.* núclido.
nudomania *n.* nudomanía.
nudophobia *n.* nudofobia.
nulligravida *n.* nuligrávida.
nullipara *n.* nulípara.
nulliparity *n.* nuliparidad.
number *n.* número.
  acetyl **number** número acetilo.
  acid **number** número ácido.
  atomic **number (z)** número atómico (z).
  Avogadro's **number** número de Avogado.
  Brinell hardness **number** número de dureza de Brinell.
  chromosome **number** número cromosómico.
  dibucaine **number** número de dibucaína.
  electronic **number** número electrónico.
  hardness **number** número de dureza.
  Hehner **number** número de Hehner.
  Hittorf **number** número de Hittorf.
  Hübl **number** número de Hübl, número de Huebl.
  Huebl **number** número de Hübl, número de Huebl.
  hydrogen **number** número de hidrógeno.
  iodine **number** número de yodo.
  isotopic **number** número isotópico.
  Knoop hardness **number** número de dureza de Knoop.
  Looschmidt's **number** número de Looschmidt.
  mass **number** número de masa, número másico.
  oxidation **number** número de oxidación.
  polar **number** número polar.
  Polenske **number** número de Polenske.
  Reichert-Meissl **number** número de Reichert-Meissl.
  Rockwell hardness **number** número de dureza de Rockwell.
  saponification **number** número de saponificación.
  transport **number** número de transporte.
  turnorver **number** número de recambio.
numbness *n.* adormecimiento, entumecimiento.
  waking **numbness** entumecimiento al despertar.
numerical *adj.* numérico, -ca.
nummiform *adj.* numiforme.
nummular *adj.* numular.
nummulation *n.* numulación.
nunnation *n.* nunación.

nuptiality *n.* nupcialidad.
nurse *n.* enfermero, -ra.
  male nurse enfermero.
  wet nurse nodriza.
nursing *n.* enfermería.
nutation *n.* nutación.
nutatory *adj.* nutatorio, -ria.
nutrient *n.* nutriente.
nutriment *n.* nutrimento.
nutriology *n.* nutriología.
nutripump *n.* nutripompa.
nutrition *n.* nutrición.
  adequate nutrition nutrición adecuada.
  parenteral nutrition nutrición parenteral.
  total parenteral nutrition (tpn) nutrición parenteral total (npt).
nutritional *adj.* nutricional.
nutritionist *n.* nutrista.
nutritious *adj.* nutricio, -cia.
nutritive *adj.* alimenticio, -cia, nutritivo, -va.
nyctalgia *n.* nictalgia.
nyctalope *adj.* nictálope.
nyctalopia *n.* nictalopía.
  nyctalopia with congenital myopia nictalopía con miopía congénita.
nyctanopia *n.* nictanopía.
nyctaphonia *n.* nictafonía.
nycterine *adj.* nicterino, -na.
nycterohemeral *adj.* nicterohemeral.
nyctohemeral *adj.* nictohemeral.
nyctophilia *n.* nictofilia.
nyctophobia *n.* nictofobia.
Nyctotherus Nyctotherus.
nyctotyphlosis *n.* nictotiflosis, nictotiplosis.
nycturia *n.* nicturia.
nymph *n.* ninfa.
  nymph of Krause ninfa de Krause.
nympha *n.* ninfa.
nymphal *adj.* ninfal.
nymphectomy *n.* ninfectomía.
nymphitis *n.* ninfitis.
nymphocaruncular *adj.* ninfocaruncular.
nymphohymeneal *adj.* ninfohimenal, ninfohimeneal.

nympholabial *adj.* ninfolabial.
nympholepsy *n.* ninfolepsia.
nymphomania *n.* ninfomanía.
nymphomaniac *n.* ninfómana.
nymphomaniacal *adj.* ninfomaníaco, -ca.
nymphoncus *n.* ninfonco.
nymphotomy *n.* ninfotomía.
Nyssorhynchus Nyssorhynchus.
nystagmic *adj.* nistágmico, -ca.
nystagmiform *adj.* nistagmiforme.
nystagmogram *n.* nistagmograma.
nystagmograph *n.* nistagmógrafo.
nystagmography *n.* nistagmografía.
nystagmoid *adj.* nistagmoide.
nystagmometry *n.* nistagmometría.
nystagmus nistagmo, nistagmus.
  amaurotic nystagmus nistagmo amaurótico.
  amblyopic nystagmus nistagmo ambliópico.
  ataxic nystagmus nistagmo atáxico.
  aural nystagmus nistagmo aural.
  caloric nystagmus nistagmo calórico.
  central nystagmus nistagmo central.
  Cheyne's nystagmus nistagmo de Cheyne, nistagmo de Cheyne-Stokes.
  congenital hereditary nystagmus nistagmo congénito.
  congenital nystagmus nistagmo congénito.
  conjugate nystagmus nistagmo conjugado.
  convergence nystagmus nistagmo convergente.
  deviational nystagmus nistagmo desviacional.
  dissociated nystagmus nistagmo disociado.
  downbeat nystagmus nistagmo vertical hacia abajo.
  dysjunctive nystagmus nistagmo disyuntivo.
  electrical nystagmus nistagmo eléctrico.
  end-position nystagmus nistagmo de posición final, nistagmo de posición terminal.
  fatigue nystagmus nistagmo de fatiga.
  fixation nystagmus nistagmo de fijación.
  galvanic nystagmus nistagmo galvánico.
  gaze nystagmus nistagmo de la mirada.
  jerk nystagmus nistagmo en sacudidas.

  jerky nystagmus nistagmo en sacudidas.
  labyrinthine nystagmus nistagmo laberíntico.
  latent nystagmus nistagmo latente.
  lateral nystagmus nistagmo lateral.
  miner's nystagmus nistagmo de los mineros.
  nystagmus in caloric tests nistagmo calórico.
  nystagmus myoclonus nistagmo mioclónico.
  nystagmus retractorius nistagmo de retracción.
  ocular nystagmus nistagmo ocular.
  ondulatory nystagmus nistagmo ondulatorio, nistagmo oscilante, nistagmo oscilatorio.
  opticokinetic nystagmus nistagmo opticocinético, nistagmo optocinético, nistagmo optoquinético.
  optokinetic nystagmus nistagmo opticocinético, nistagmo optocinético, nistagmo optoquinético.
  palatal nystagmus nistagmo palatino.
  paretic nystagmus nistagmo parético.
  pendular nystagmus nistagmo pendular.
  positional nystagmus nistagmo posicional.
  railroad nystagmus nistagmo de ferrocarril.
  resilient nystagmus nistagmo adaptable.
  retraction nystagmus nistagmo de retracción.
  rhythmical nystagmus nistagmo rítmico.
  rotatory nystagmus nistagmo rotatorio.
  secondary nystagmus nistagmo secundario.
  see-saw nystagmus nistagmo en sierra.
  spontaneous nystagmus nistagmo espontáneo.
  unilateral nystagmus nistagmo unilateral.
  upbeat nystagmus nistagmo vertical hacia arriba.
  vertical nystagmus nistagmo vertical.
  vestibular nystagmus nistagmo vestibular.
  vibratory nystagmus nistagmo vibratorio.
  visual nystagmus nistagmo visual.
  voluntary nystagmus nistagmo voluntario.
nystaxis *n.* nistaxis.
nyxis *n.* nixis.

O o

oasis *n.* oasis.
oath *n.* juramento.
  hippocratic oath juramento de Hipócrates, juramento hipocrático.
  Nightingale oath juramento de Nightingale.
  oath of Hippocrates juramento de Hipócrates, juramento hipocrático.
obdormition *n.* obdormición.
obducent *adj.* obducente.
obduction *n.* obducción.
obeliac *adj.* obelíaco, -ca.
obeliad obeliad.
obelion *n.* obelión.
obese *adj.* obeso, -sa.
obesity *n.* obesidad.
  adult-onset obesity obesidad de iniciación en la edad adulta.
  alimentary obesity obesidad alimentaria.
  cushingoid obesity obesidad cushingoide.
  endogenous obesity obesidad endógena.
  exogenous obesity obesidad exógena.
  generalized obesity obesidad armónica.
  hyperadrenal obesity obesidad hipersuprarrenal.
  hyperinsulinar obesity obesidad hiperinsulínica.
  hyperplasmic obesity obesidad hiperplásmica.
  hyperplastic-hypertrophic obesity obesidad hiperplásica e hipertrófica.
  hypertrophic obesity obesidad hipertrófica.
  hypogonad obesity obesidad hipogonádica.
  hypoplasmic obesity obesidad hipoplásmica.
  hypothalamic obesity obesidad hipotalámica.
  hypothyroid obesity obesidad hipotiroidea.
  lifelong obesity obesidad de toda la vida.
  morbid obesity obesidad mórbida.
  simple obesity obesidad simple.
  truncal obesity obesidad troncular.
obesogenous *adj.* obesógeno, -na.
Obesumbacterium Obesumbacterium.
obex *n.* óbex.
obfuscation *n.* obfuscación, ofuscación, ofuscamiento.
object *n.* objeto.
  choice object objeto de elección.
  object permanence permanencia del objeto.
  sex object objeto sexual.
  test object objeto de prueba.
  transitional object objeto transicional.
objective *n.* objetivo.
  achromatic objective objetivo acromático.
  apochromatic objective objetivo apocromático.
  dry objective objetivo seco.
  flat field objective objetivo de campo plano.
  fluorite objective objetivo de fluorita.
  immersion objective objetivo de inmersión.
  semiapochromatic objective objetivo semiapocromático.

obligate *adj.* obligado, -da.
oblique *adj.* oblicuo, -cua.
obliquity *n.* oblicuidad.
  Litzmann's obliquity oblicuidad de Litzmann.
  Nägele's obliquity oblicuidad de Nägele.
  obliquity of the pelvis oblicuidad de la pelvis.
obliquus *adj.* oblicuo, -cua.
obliterans *adj.* obliterans.
obliteration *n.* obliteración.
  cortical obliteration obliteración cortical.
oblongata *adj.* oblongada.
obnubilation *n.* obnubilación de la conciencia.
observer *n.* observador.
  non-participant observer observador no participante.
  participant observer observador participante.
observoscope *n.* observoscopio.
obsession *n.* obsesión.
  impulsive obsession obsesión impulsiva.
  inhibitory obsession obsesión inhibitoria.
obsessive *adj.* obsesivo, -va.
obsessive-compulsive *adj.* obsesivo-compulsivo, -va.
obsolescence *n.* obsolescencia.
obstetric *adj.* obstétrico, -ca.
obstetrical *adj.* obstétrico, -ca.
obstetrician *n.* obstetra, tocólogo, -ga.
obstetrics *n.* obstetricia.
  medico-legal obstetrics obstetricia médico-legal.
obstinate *adj.* obstinado, -da.
obstipation *n.* obstipación.
obstruction *n.* obstrucción.
  airway obstruction obstrucción de la vía aérea.
  biliary obstruction obstrucción biliar.
  chronic airway obstruction obstrucción crónica de las vías respiratorias.
  closed-loop obstruction obstrucción de bucle cerrado, obstrucción en ansa cerrada.
  false colonic obstruction obstrucción falsa del colon.
  foreign body obstruction obstrucción por cuerpo extraño.
  intestinal obstruction obstrucción intestinal.
  mechanical intestinal obstruction obstrucción intestinal mecánica.
  nasal obstruction obstrucción nasal.
  pyloric obstruction and dilatation obstrucción y dilatación pilóricas.
  retinal central arterial obstruction obstrucción de la arteria central de la retina.
  retinal central venous obstruction obstrucción de la vena central de la retina.
  strangulating intestinal obstruction obstrucción intestinal estrangulante.
  upper airway obstruction (UAO) obstruc-

ción de las vías respiratorias superiores (OVRS).
  ureteropelvic obstruction obstrucción ureteropelviana.
  ureterovesical obstruction obstrucción ureterovesical.
  ventricular obstruction obstrucción ventricular.
obstructive *adj.* obstructivo, -va.
obstruent *n.* obstruyente.
obtund *v.* obtundir.
obtundation *n.* obtunción.
obtundent *n.* obtundente.
obturation *n.* obturación².
  canal obturation obturación de un canal, obturación de un conducto.
obturator *n.* obturador¹.
  Cripp's obturator obturador de Cripp.
obtuse *adj.* obtuso, -sa.
obtusion *n.* obtusión.
occipital *adj.* occipital.
occipitalis *adj.* occipital, occipitalis.
occipitalization *n.* occipitalización.
occipitoanterior *adj.* occipitoanterior.
occipitoatloid *adj.* occipitoatloideo, -a.
occipitoaxial *adj.* occipitoaxial.
occipitoaxoid *adj.* occipitoaxoideo, -a.
occipitobasilar *adj.* occipitobasilar.
occipitobregmatic *adj.* occipitobregmático, -ca.
occipitocalcarine *adj.* occipitocalcarino, -na.
occipitocervical *adj.* occipitocervical.
occipitofacial *adj.* occipitofacial.
occipitofrontal *adj.* occipitofrontal.
occipitomastoid *adj.* occipitomastoideo, -a.
occipitomental *adj.* occipitomentoniano, -na.
occipitoparietal *adj.* occipitoparietal.
occipitoposterior *adj.* occipitoposterior.
occipitotemporal *adj.* occipitotemporal.
occipitothalamic *adj.* occipitotalámico, -ca.
occiput *n.* occipucio.
occlude *v.* ocluir.
occluded *adj.* ocluido, -da.
occluder *n.* oclusor.
occlusal *adj.* oclusal, oclusional.
occlusion *n.* oclusión.
  abnormal occlusion oclusión anormal.
  acentric occlusion oclusión acéntrica.
  afunctional occlusion oclusión afuncional.
  anatomic occlusion oclusión anatómica.
  anterior occlusion oclusión anterior.
  balanced occlusion oclusión balanceada, oclusión equilibrada.
  basilar artery occlusion oclusión de la arteria basilar.
  bimaxillary protrusive occlusion oclusión protrusiva bimaxilar.
  buccal occlusion oclusión bucal.
  centric occlusion oclusión central, oclusión céntrica.

coronary occlusion oclusión coronaria.
dental occlusion oclusión dental.
distal occlusion oclusión distal.
eccentric occlusion oclusión excéntrica.
edge-to-edge occlusion oclusión a borde, oclusión borde con borde, oclusión de borde, oclusión de borde a borde.
end-to-end occlusion oclusión extremo con extremo, oclusión terminoterminal.
enteromesenteric occlusion oclusión enteromesentérica.
functional occlusion oclusión funcional.
habitual occlusion oclusión habitual.
hyperfunctional occlusion oclusión hiperfuncional.
ideal occlusion oclusión ideal.
intestinal occlusion oclusión intestinal.
labial occlusion oclusión labial.
lateral occlusion oclusión lateral.
lingual occlusion oclusión lingual.
mechanically balanced occlusion oclusión mecánicamente balanceada.
mesenteric artery occlusion oclusión de la arteria mesentérica.
mesial occlusion oclusión mesial.
neutral occlusion oclusión neutra.
normal occlusion oclusión normal.
occlusion of the pupil oclusión de la pupila.
pathogenic occlusion oclusión patógena, oclusión patogénica.
physiologic occlusion oclusión fisiológica.
physiological occlusion oclusión fisiológica.
physiologically balanced occlusion oclusión fisiológicamente balanceada.
posterior occlusion oclusión posterior.
postnormal occlusion oclusión posnormal.
prenormal occlusion oclusión prenormal.
protrusive occlusion oclusión protrusiva.
retrusive occlusion oclusión retrusiva.
spherical form of occlusion forma esférica de oclusión, oclusión en forma esférica.
terminal occlusion oclusión terminal.
torsive occlusion oclusión torsiva.
traumatic occlusion oclusión traumática.
traumatogenic occlusion oclusión traumatógena, oclusión traumatogénica.
working occlusion oclusión de trabajo.
occlusive *adj.* oclusivo, -va.
occlusocervical *adj.* oclusocervical.
occlusometer *n.* oclusómetro.
occult *adj.* oculto, -ta.
occupancy *n.* ocupación.
ocellus *n.* ocelo.
ochlesis *n.* oclesis.
ochlophobia *n.* oclofobia.
ochrodermia *n.* ocrodermia.
ochrometer *n.* ocrómetro.
ochronosis *n.* ocronosis.
  exogenous ochronosis ocronosis exógena.
ochronosus *n.* ocronosis.
ochronotic *adj.* ocronoso, -sa, ocronótico, -ca.
ocrylate *n.* ocrilato.
octan *n.* octana.
octapeptide *n.* octapéptido.
octaploid *adj.* octaploide.
octaploidic *adj.* octaploídico, -ca.
octaploidy *n.* octaploidía.
octarius *n.* octario.
octavalent *adj.* octavalente.
octet *n.* octeto.
octigravida *n.* octigrávida, octográvida.
octipara *n.* octípara.
Octomitidae Octomitidae.
Octomyces Octomyces.
  Octomyces etiennei Octomyces etiennei.

octopamine *n.* octopamina.
octose *n.* octosa.
ocufilcon *n.* ocufilcón.
ocular *adj.* ocular¹, ocular².
  compensating ocular ocular compensador, ocular compensatorio, ocular de compensación.
  Huygens' ocular ocular de Huygens.
  ocular bobbing bobbing ocular.
  ocular motor oculomotor, -ra.
  Ramsden's ocular ocular de Ramsden.
  wide field ocular ocular de amplio campo, ocular de campo amplio.
ocularist *n.* ocularista.
oculist *n.* oculista.
oculistics *n.* oculística.
oculoauriculovertebral *adj.* oculoauriculovertebral.
oculocardiac *adj.* oculocardíaco, -ca.
oculocephalogyric *adj.* oculocefalógiro, -ra.
oculocerebrorenal *adj.* oculocefalorrenal.
oculocutaneous *adj.* oculocutáneo, -a.
oculodentodigital *adj.* oculodentodigital.
oculodermal *adj.* oculodérmico, -ca.
oculodynia *n.* oculodinia.
oculofacial *adj.* oculofacial.
oculography *n.* oculografía.
  photosensor oculography oculografía fotosensora.
oculogyration *n.* oculogiración.
oculogyria *n.* oculogiria.
oculogyric *adj.* oculogírico, -ca, oculógiro, -ra.
oculomandibulodyscephaly *n.* oculomandibulodiscefalia.
oculometroscope *n.* oculometroscopio.
oculomotor *adj.* oculomotor, -ra.
oculomycosis *n.* oculomicosis.
oculonasal *adj.* oculonasal.
oculopalpebral *adj.* oculopalpebral.
oculopathy *n.* oculopatía.
oculoplastic *adj.* oculoplástico, -ca.
oculoplethysmography *n.* oculopletismografía.
oculopneumoplethysmography *n.* oculoneumopletismografía.
oculopupillary *adj.* oculopupilar.
oculospinal *adj.* oculoespinal, oculospinal.
oculosympathetic *adj.* oculosimpático, -ca.
oculovertebral *adj.* oculovertebral.
oculozygomatic *adj.* oculocigomático, -ca.
oculus oculus, ojo.
ocytocin *n.* ocitocina.
odaxesmus *n.* odaxesmo.
odaxetic *n.* odaxético, -ca.
odditis *n.* odditis, oditis.
odogenesis *n.* odogénesis.
odondectomy *n.* odondectomía.
odon-eki *n.* odon-eki.
odontagra *n.* odontagra.
odontalgia *n.* odontalgia.
  odontalgia dentalis odontalgia dental.
odontalgic *adj.* odontálgico, -ca.
odontectomy *n.* odontectomía.
odonterism *n.* odonterismo.
odontexesis *n.* odontexesis.
odontiasis *n.* odontiasis.
odontiatria *n.* odontiatría.
odontiatrogenic *adj.* odontiatrogénico, -ca, odontoyatrógeno, -na.
odontic *adj.* odóntico, -ca.
odontinoid *n.* odontinoide.
odontitis *n.* odontitis.
odontoameloblastoma *n.* odontoameloblastoma.
odontoblast *n.* odontoblasto.

odontoblastoma *n.* odontoblastoma.
odontobothritis *n.* odontobotritis.
odontocia *n.* odontocia.
odontoclamis *n.* odontoclamis.
odontoclast *n.* odontoclasto.
odontodynia *n.* odontodinia.
odontodysplasia *n.* odontodisplasia.
odontogen *n.* odontogén.
odontogenesis *n.* odontogénesis.
  odontogenesis imperfecta odontogénesis imperfecta.
odontogenetic *adj.* odontogenético, -ca.
odontogenic *adj.* odontogénico, -ca, odontógeno, -na.
odontogenous *adj.* odontogénico, -ca.
odontogeny *n.* odontogenia.
odontogram *n.* odontograma.
odontograph *n.* odontógrafo.
odontography *n.* odontografía.
odontoid *adj.* odontoide, odontoides.
odontolith *n.* odontolito.
odontolithiasis *n.* odontolitiasis.
odontologist *n.* odontólogo, -ga.
odontology *n.* odontología.
  forensic odontology odontología forense.
  four-handed odontology odontología a cuatro.
odontoloxia *n.* odontoloxia.
odontoloxy *n.* odontoloxia.
odontolysis *n.* odontólisis.
odontoma *n.* odontoma.
  ameloblastic odontoma odontoma ameloblástico.
  complex odontoma odontoma complejo.
  composite odontoma odontoma compuesto.
  compound odontoma odontoma compuesto.
  coronal odontoma odontoma coronal, odontoma coronario.
  coronary odontoma odontoma coronal, odontoma coronario.
  embryoplastic odontoma odontoma embrioplásico.
  fibrous odontoma odontoma fibroso.
  mixed odontoma odontoma mixto.
  odontoma adamantinum odontoma adamantino.
  radicular odontoma odontoma radicular.
odontonecrosis *n.* odontonecrosis.
odontoneuralgia *n.* odontoneuralgía.
odontonomy *n.* odontonimia, odontonomía.
odontonosology *n.* odontonosología.
odontopathic *adj.* odontopático, -ca.
odontopathy *n.* odontopatía.
odontoperiosteum *n.* odontoperiostio.
odontophobia *n.* odontofobia.
odontoplast *n.* odontoplasto.
odontoplasty *n.* odontoplastia.
odontoplerosis *n.* odontoplerosis.
odontoprisis *n.* odontoprisis.
odontoptosis *n.* odontoptosis.
odontoradiograph *n.* odontorradiografía.
odontorrhagia *n.* odontorragia.
odontorthosis *n.* odontortosis.
odontoschism *n.* odontocisma, odontosquisis.
odontoscope *n.* odontoscopio.
odontoscopy *n.* odontoscopia.
odontoseisis *n.* odontoseisis.
odontosis *n.* odontosis.
odontotechny *n.* odontotecnia.
odontotheca *n.* odontoteca.
odontotherapy *n.* odontoterapia.
odontotomy *n.* odontotomía.
  prophylactic odontotomy odontotomía profiláctica.

odontotripsis *n.* odontotripsia, odontotripsis.
odor odor, olor.
  body odor olor corporal.
  butcher's shop odor olor a carnicería.
  minimal identifiable odor olor mínimo identificable.
odorant *adj.* odorante.
odoriferous *adj.* odorífero, -ra.
odorimeter *n.* odorímetro.
odorimetry *n.* odorimetría.
odoriphore *n.* odoríforo.
odorivection *n.* odorivección.
odorivector *adj.* odorivector, -ra.
odorography *n.* odorografía.
odorous *adj.* oloroso, -sa.
odynacusis *n.* odinacusia, odinacusis, odinoacusia.
odynolysis *n.* odinólisis.
odynometer *n.* odinómetro.
odynophagia *n.* odinofagia.
odynophobia *n.* odinofobia.
odynophonia *n.* odinofonía.
odynphagia *n.* odinofagia.
Oeciacus hirudinis Oeciacus hirudinis.
oesophagostomiasis *n.* esofagostomiasis,oesofagostomiasis.
Oesophagostomum Oesophagostomum.
  Oesophagostomum apiostomum Oesophagostomum apiostomum.
  Oesophagostomum bifurcum Oesophagostomum bifurcum.
  Oesophagostomum brumpti Oesophagostomum brumpti.
oesophagus *n.* oesófago.
oestriasis *n.* oestriasis.
Oestridae Oestridae.
oestrosis *n.* oestrosis.
oestrum *n.* oestro.
oestrus *n.* oestro.
Oestrus Oestrus.
  Oestrus hominis Oestrus hominis.
  Oestrus ovis Oestrus ovis.
official *adj.* oficial.
ogive *n.* ojiva.
ogo *n.* ogo.
ohmammeter *n.* ohmámetro.
ohmmeter *n.* óhmetro.
ohne Hauch *n.* ohne Hauch.
oidiomycin *n.* oidiomicina.
oidiomycosis *n.* oidiomicosis.
oidiomycotic *adj.* oidiomicótico, -ca.
oikosite *n.* oicosito.
oil *n.* aceite.
oily *adj.* oleoso, -sa.
oinomania *n.* oinomanía.
ointment *n.* pomada, ungüento, unguentum.
  eye ointment ungüento ocular, ungüento oftálmico.
  ophthalmic ointment ungüento ocular, ungüento oftálmico.
old age *n.* vejez.
oleaginous *adj.* oleaginoso, -sa.
oleandrin *n.* oleandrina.
oleandrism *n.* oleandrismo.
olecranal *adj.* olecraneal.
olecranarthritis *n.* olecranartritis.
olecranarthrocace *n.* olecranartrocace.
olecranarthropaty *n.* olecranartropatía.
olecranoid *adj.* olecranoide.
olecranon *n.* olécrano, olécranon.
oleinfusion *n.* oleoinfusión.
oleinitis *n.* oleinitis.
oleoarthrosis *n.* oleoartrosis.
oleochrysotherapy *n.* oleocrisoterapia.
oleogranuloma *n.* oleogranuloma.

oleoma *n.* oleoma.
oleometer *n.* oleómetro.
oleonucleoprotein *n.* oleonucleoproteína.
oleoperitoneography *n.* oleoperitoneografía.
oleosus *adj.* oleoso, -sa.
oleotherapy *n.* oleoterapia.
oleothorax *n.* oleotórax.
oleovitamin *n.* oleovitamina.
olfact *n.* olfato.
olfactie *n.* olfatía.
olfaction *n.* olfacción.
olfactism *n.* olfatismo.
olfactology *n.* olfatología.
olfactometer *n.* olfatómetro.
olfactometry *n.* olfatometría.
olfactophobia *n.* olfatofobia.
olfactory *adj.* olfatorio, -ria.
olfactus *n.* olfato.
olfacty *n.* olfatía.
oligakisuria *n.* oligaquisuria.
oligemia *n.* oligemia.
olighidria *n.* olighidria.
oligidria *n.* oligidria.
oligoamnios *n.* oligoamnios.
oligoblast *n.* oligoblasto.
oligocardia *n.* oligocardia.
oligocholia *n.* oligocolia.
oligochromasia *n.* oligocromasia.
oligochromemia *n.* oligocromemia.
oligochylia *n.* oligoquilia.
oligochymia *n.* oligoquimia.
oligocystic *adj.* oligocístico, -ca, oligoquístico, -ca.
oligocythemia *n.* oligocitemia.
oligocythemic *adj.* oligocitémico, -ca.
oligocytosis *n.* oligocitosis.
oligodactylia *n.* oligodactilia.
oligodactyly *n.* oligodactilia.
oligodendria *n.* oligodendria.
oligodendroblast *n.* oligodendroblasto.
oligodendroblastoma *n.* oligodendroblastoma.
oligodendrocyte *n.* oligodendrocito.
oligodendroglia *n.* oligodendroglia, oligodendroglía.
oligodendroglioma *n.* oligodendroglioma.
oligodipsia *n.* oligodipsia.
oligodontia *n.* oligodoncia, oligodontia.
oligodynamic *adj.* oligodinámico, -ca.
oligoencephalon *n.* oligoencéfalo.
oligogalactia *n.* oligogalactia, oligogalia.
oligogenic *adj.* oligogénico, -ca.
oligogenics *n.* oligogénesis, oligogenia.
oligoglia *n.* oligoglía.
oligoglobulia *n.* oligoglobulia.
oligohemia *n.* oligohemia.
oligohemic *adj.* oligohémico, -ca.
oligohidria *n.* oligohidria.
oligohydramnios *n.* oligohidramnios.
oligohydruria *n.* oligohidruria.
oligohypermenorrhea *n.* oligohipermenorrea.
oligohypomenorrhea *n.* oligohipomenorrea.
oligolecithal *adj.* oligolecito, -ta.
oligoleukocythemia *n.* oligoleucocitemia.
oligoleukocytosis *n.* oligoleucocitosis.
oligomeganephronia *n.* oligomeganefronia.
oligomeganephronic *adj.* oligomeganefrónico, -ca.
oligomenorrhea *n.* oligomenorrea.
oligomer *n.* oligómero.
oligometallic *adj.* oligometálico, -ca.
oligomorphic *adj.* oligomorfo, -fa, oligomúrfico, -ca.
oligonatality *n.* oligonatalidad.

oligonecrospermia *n.* oligonecrospermia.
oligonephronic *adj.* oligonefrónico, -ca.
oligonitrophilic *adj.* oligonitrófilo, -la.
oligonucleotide *n.* oligonucleótido.
oligo-ovulation *n.* oligoovulación.
oligopepsia *n.* oligopepsia.
oligopeptide *n.* oligopéptido.
oligophosphaturia *n.* oligofosfaturia.
oligophrenia *n.* oligofrenia.
  phenylpyruvate oligophrenia oligofrenia fenilpirúvica.
  phenylpyruvic oligophrenia oligofrenia fenilpirúvica.
oligophrenic *adj.* oligofrénico, -ca.
oligoplasmia *n.* oligoplasmia.
oligoplastic *adj.* oligoplástico, -ca.
oligopnea *n.* oligopnea.
oligoposia *n.* oligoposia.
oligopsychia *n.* oligopsiquia.
oligoptyalism *n.* oligoptialismo, oligotialismo.
oligopyrene *adj.* oligopirénico, -ca.
oligopyrous *adj.* oligopiroso, -sa.
oligoria *n.* oligoria.
oligosaccharide *n.* oligosacárido.
oligosialia *n.* oligosialia.
oligosideremia *n.* oligosideremia.
oligospermatism *n.* oligospermatismo.
oligospermia *n.* oligospermia.
oligosymptomatic *adj.* oligosintomático, -ca.
oligosynaptic *adj.* oligosináptico, -ca.
oligothymia *n.* oligotimia.
oligotrichia *n.* oligotriquia.
oligotrichosis *n.* oligotricosis.
oligotrophia *n.* oligotrofia.
oligotrophic *adj.* oligotrófico, -ca.
oligotrophy *n.* oligotrofia.
oligozoospermatism *n.* oligozoospermia.
oligozoospermia *n.* oligozoospermia.
oliguresia *n.* oliguresia.
oliguresis *n.* oliguresis.
oliguria *n.* oliguria.
oliguric *adj.* oligúrico, -ca.
olisthy *n.* olistía.
oliva *n.* oliva.
  oliva inferior oliva inferior.
olivary *adj.* olivar.
olive *n.* oliva.
  inferior olive oliva inferior.
olivifugal *adj.* olivífugo, -ga.
olivipetal *adj.* olivípeto, -ta.
olivocochlear *adj.* olivococlear.
olivopontocerebellar *adj.* olivopontocerebeloso, -sa.
olophonia *n.* olofonía.
omacephalus *n.* omacéfalo.
omagra *n.* omagra.
omalgia *n.* omalgia.
omarthritis *n.* omartritis.
ombrophobia *n.* ombrofobia.
ombrophore *n.* ombróforo.
omega *n.* omega.
  omega melancholicum omega melancólica.
omental *adj.* omental.
omentectomy *n.* omentectomía.
omentitis *n.* omentitis.
omentofixation *n.* omentofijación.
omentopexy *n.* omentopexia.
omentoplasty *n.* omentoplastia.
omentoportography *n.* omentoportografía.
omentorrhaphy *n.* omentorrafia.
omentosplenopexy *n.* omentoesplenopexia, omentosplenopexia.
omentotomy *n.* omentotomía.
omentovolvulus *n.* omentovólvulo.

omentum *n.* epiplón, omento.
omentumectomy *n.* omentumectomía.
omission *n.* omisión.
omitis *n.* omitis.
ommochrome *n.* omocromo.
omnipotence *n.* omnipotencia.
omnivorous *adj.* omnívoro, -ra.
omocephalus *n.* omocéfalo.
omoclavicular *adj.* omoclavicular.
omodynia *n.* omodinia.
omohyoid *adj.* omohioideo, -a.
omophagia *n.* omofagia.
omoplata *n.* omoplato, omóplato.
omosternum *n.* omoesternón.
omothyroid *n.* omotiroides.
omotocia *n.* omotocia.
omphalectomy *n.* onfalectomía.
omphalelcosis *n.* onfalelcosis.
omphalic *adj.* onfálico, -ca.
omphalitis *n.* onfalitis.
omphaloangiopagus *n.* onfaloangiópago.
omphalocele *n.* onfalocele.
omphalochorion *n.* onfalocorion.
omphalodidymus *n.* onfalodídimo, onfalomonodídimo.
omphaloenteric *adj.* onfaloentérico, -ca.
omphalogenesis *n.* onfalogenesia, onfalogénesis.
omphaloma *n.* onfaloma.
omphalomesaraic *adj.* onfalomesaraico, -ca.
omphalomesenteric *adj.* onfalomesentérico, -ca.
omphaloncus *n.* onfalonco.
omphalopagus *n.* onfalópago.
omphalophlebitis *n.* onfaloflebitis.
omphaloproptosis *n.* onfaloproptosis, onfaloptosis.
omphalorrhagia *n.* onfalorragia.
omphalorrhea *n.* onfalorrea.
omphalorrhexis *n.* onfalorrexis.
omphalosite *n.* onfalósito.
omphalospinous *adj.* onfaloespinoso, -sa.
omphalotomy *n.* onfalotomía.
omphalotribe *n.* onfalotribo.
omphalotripsy *n.* onfalotricia, onfalotripsia.
omphalovesical *adj.* onfalovesical.
omphalus *n.* ónfalo.
omunono *n.* omunono.
onanism *n.* onanismo.
onaye *n.* onaya.
Onchocerca Onchocerca.
   Onchocerca caecutiens Onchocerca caecutiens.
   Onchocerca volvulus Onchocerca volvulus.
onchocerciasis *n.* oncocerciasis.
onchocercoma *n.* oncocercoma.
onchocercosis *n.* oncocercosis.
Oncocerca Onchocerca, Oncocerca.
oncocyte *n.* oncocito.
oncocytic *adj.* oncocítico, -ca.
oncodnavirus *n.* oncodnavirus.
oncogene *n.* oncogén, oncogene.
oncogenesis *n.* oncogenesia, oncogénesis, oncogenia.
oncogenetic *adj.* oncogenético, -ca.
oncogenic *adj.* oncogénico, -ca.
oncogenicity *n.* oncogenicidad.
oncogenous *adj.* oncógeno, -na.
oncograph *n.* oncógrafo.
oncography *n.* oncografía.
oncoides *n.* oncoide, oncoides.
oncologic *adj.* oncológico, -ca.
oncologist *n.* oncólogo, -ga.
   radiation oncologist oncólogo radioterapeuta.
oncology *n.* oncología.

radiation oncology oncología radioterápica.
oncolysate *n.* oncolizado.
oncolysis *n.* oncólisis.
oncolytic *adj.* oncolítico, -ca.
oncoma *n.* oncoma.
Oncomelania Oncomelania.
oncometer *n.* oncómetro.
oncometric *adj.* oncométrico, -ca.
oncometry *n.* oncometría.
Oncornavirus Oncornavirus.
oncosis *n.* oncosis.
oncosphere *n.* oncosfera.
oncotherapy *n.* oncoterapia.
oncothlipsis *n.* oncotlipsis.
oncotic *adj.* oncótico, -ca.
oncotomy *n.* oncotomía.
oncotropic *adj.* oncotrópico, -ca.
oncovirus *n.* oncovirus.
ondometer *n.* ondómetro.
one-armed *adj.* manco, -ca.
one-eyed *adj.* tuerto, -ta.
oneiric *adj.* onírico, -ca.
oneirism *n.* oneirismo, onirismo.
oneiroanalysis *n.* oneiroanálisis.
oneirocritical *adj.* onirocrítico, -ca.
oneirodynia *n.* oneirodinia, onirodinia.
   oneirodynia activa onirodinia activa.
   oneirodynia gravis onirodinia grave.
oneirogenic *adj.* oneirógeno, -na, onirógeno, -na.
oneirogmus *n.* oneirogmo, onirogma.
oneiroid *adj.* oneiroide, oniroide.
oneirology *n.* onirología.
oneirophonia *n.* onirofonía.
oneirophrenia *n.* oneirofrenia, onirofrenia.
oneiroscopy *n.* oniroscopia.
oniomania *n.* oniomanía.
onkinocele *n.* onquinocele.
onlay *n.* onlay.
onomatomania *n.* onomatomanía.
onomatophobia *n.* onomatofobia.
onomatopoiesis *n.* onomatopoyesis.
onset of action *n.* inicio de la acción.
ontogenesis *n.* ontogenesia, ontogénesis.
ontogenetic *adj.* ontogenético, -ca.
ontogenic *adj.* ontogénico, -ca.
ontogeny *n.* ontogenia.
onyalai onialai, onyalai.
onychalgia *n.* onicalgia.
onychatrophia *n.* onicatrofia, onicoatrofia.
onychatrophy *n.* onicatrofia, onicoatrofia.
onychauxis *n.* onicauxis.
onychectomy *n.* onicectomía, oniquectomía.
onychia *n.* oniquia.
   onychia lateralis oniquia lateral.
   onychia maligna oniquia maligna.
   onychia periungualis oniquia periungueal.
   onychia sicca oniquia seca.
onychitis *n.* oniquitis.
onychoclasis *n.* onicoclasis.
onychocryptosis *n.* onicocriptosis.
onychodynia *n.* onicodinia.
onychodystrophy *n.* onicodistrofia.
onychogenic *adj.* onicogénico, -ca.
onychogram *n.* onicograma.
onychograph *n.* onicógrafo.
onychogryphosis *n.* onicogrifosis, onicogriposis.
onychogryposis *n.* onicogriposis.
onychoheterotopia *n.* onicoheterotopia.
onychoid *adj.* onicoide.
onychology *n.* onicología.
onycholysis *n.* onicólisis.
onychoma *n.* onicoma.
onychomadesis *n.* onicomadesis.

onychomalacia *n.* onicomalacia.
onychomycosis *n.* onicomicosis.
   dermatophytic onychomycosis onicomicosis dermatofítica.
onychonosis *n.* oniconosis.
onycho-osteodysplasia *n.* onicoosteodisplasia.
onychopathic *adj.* onicopático, -ca.
onychopathology *n.* onicopatología.
onychopathy *n.* onicopatía.
onychophagia *n.* onicofagia.
onychophagist *n.* onicófag, -ga.
onychophagy *n.* onicofagia.
onychophosis *n.* onicofosis.
onychophyma *n.* onicofima.
onychoplasty *n.* onicoplastia.
onychoptosis *n.* onicoptosis.
onychorrhexis *n.* onicorrexis.
onychoschizia *n.* onicosquisis.
onychosis *n.* onicosis.
onychostroma *n.* onicoestroma.
onychotillomania *n.* onicotilomanía.
onychotomy *n.* onicotomía.
onychotrophy *n.* onicotrofia.
O'nyong-nyong O'nyong-nyong.
onyx ónix, onyx.
onyxis *n.* onixis.
onyxitis *n.* onixitis.
oocephalous *adj.* oocéfalo[2], -la.
oocephalus *n.* oocéfalo[1], -la.
oocinesia *n.* oocinesis.
oocinete *n.* oocineto.
oocyan *adj.* ociano, -na.
oocyanin *n.* oocianina.
oocyesis *n.* oociesis.
oocyst *n.* oocisto, ooquiste.
oocytase *n.* oocitasa.
oocyte *n.* oocito.
   primary oocyte oocito de primer orden, oocito primario.
   secondary oocyte oocito de segundo orden,
oocito secundario.
oodeocele *n.* oodeocele.
oogamous *adj.* oogamo, -ma.
oogamy *n.* oogamia.
oogenesis *n.* oogenesia, oogénesis, oogenia.
oogenetic *adj.* oogenético, -ca.
oogenic *adj.* oogénico, -ca, oógeno, -na.
oogonium *n.* oogonia.
ookinesia *n.* oocinesis.
ookinesis *n.* oocinesis.
oolemma *n.* oolema.
oophagia *n.* oofagia.
oophagy *n.* oofagia.
oophoralgia *n.* ooforalgia.
oophorectomize *v.* ooforectomizar.
oophorectomy *n.* ooforectomía.
oophoritis *n.* ooforitis.
   auntoinmune oophoritis ooforitis autoinmune.
   oophoritis parotidea ooforitis parotídea.
oophorocystectomy *n.* ooforocistectomía.
oophorocystosis *n.* ooforocistosis.
oophorogenous *adj.* ooforógeno, -na.
oophorohysterectomy *n.* ooforohisterectomía.
oophoroma *n.* ooforoma.
   oophoroma folliculare ooforoma folicular.
oophoron *n.* oóforo.
oophoropathy *n.* ooforopatía.
oophoropexy *n.* ooforopexia.
oophoroplasty *n.* ooforoplastia.
oophororrhaphy *n.* oofororrafia.
oophorosalpingectomy *n.* ooforosalpingectomía.

oophorosalpingitis *n.* ooforosalpingitis.
oophorostomy *n.* ooforostomía.
oophorotomy *n.* ooforotomía.
oophorrhagia *n.* oofororragia.
ooplasm *n.* ooplasma.
ooporphyrin *n.* ooporfirina.
oorhodein *n.* oorrodeína.
oosperm *n.* oospermo.
oospore *n.* oospora.
ootheca *n.* ooteca.
ootherapy *n.* ooterapia.
ootid *n.* oótide.
ootype *n.* ootipo.
ooxanthine *n.* ooxantina.
oozooid *n.* oozoide.
opacification *n.* opacamiento, opacificación.
  posterior capsule opacification opacificación de la cápsula posterior.
opacified *adj.* opacificado, -da.
opacity *n.* opacidad.
  Caspar's ring opacity opacidad anular de Caspar.
opalescent *adj.* opalescente.
opalescin *n.* opalescina.
opaline *n.* opalgia.
opaline *adj.* opalino, -na.
opalisin *n.* opalisina.
opaque *adj.* opaco, -ca.
opeidoscope *n.* opeidoscopio.
opening *n.* abertura.
operability *n.* operabilidad.
operable *adj.* operable.
operant *adj.* operante.
operate *v.* operar.
operating room *n.* quirófano.
operation *n.* operación.
  Abbé-Estlander operation operación de Abbé-Estlander.
  Abbe's operation operación de Abbe.
  Adam's operation for ectropion operación de Adams.
  Akin operation operación de Akin.
  Albee-Delbet operation operación de Albee-Delbet.
  Albee's operation operación de Albee.
  Albert's operation operación de Albert.
  Alexander-Adams operation operación de Alexander-Adams.
  Alexander's operation operación de Alexander.
  Alouette operation operación de Alouette.
  Ammon's operation operación de Ammon.
  Amussat's operation operación de Amussat.
  Anagnostakis' operation operación de Anagnostakis.
  Aries-Pitanguy operation operación de Aries-Pitanguy.
  Arlt's operation operación de Arlt.
  Asch operation operación de Asch.
  Babcock's operation operación de Babcock.
  Baldy's operation operación de Baldy.
  Baldy-Webster operation operación de Baldy-Webster.
  Ball's operation operación de Ball.
  Barkan's operation operación de Barkan.
  Barker operation operación de Barker.
  Barraquer's operation operación de Barraquer.
  Barsky's operation operación de Barsky.
  Barton's operation operación de Barton.
  Basset's operation operación de Basset.
  Bassini's operation operación de Bassini.
  Battle's operation operación de Battle.
  Baudelocque's operation operación de Baudelocque.

  Beer's operation operación de Beer.
  Belsey Mark IV operation operación de Belsey Mark IV.
  Belsey operation operación de Belsey.
  Berger's operation operación de Berger.
  Berke operation operación de Berke.
  Bevan's operation operación de Bevan.
  Bier's operation operación de Bier.
  Biesenberger's operation operación de Biesenberger.
  Billroth's operation I operación de Billroth I.
  Billroth's operation II operación de Billroth II.
  Blair-Brown operation operación de Blair-Brown.
  Blalock-Hanlon operation operación de Blalock-Hanlon.
  Blalock-Taussig operation operación de Blalock-Taussig.
  Blaskovics' operation operación de Blaskovics.
  bloodless operation operación exangüe.
  Bonnet's operation operación de Bonnet.
  Bowman's operation operación de Bowman.
  Bozeman's operation operación de Bozeman.
  Bricker's operation operación de Bricker.
  Brock operation operación de Brock.
  Brophy's operation operación de Brophy.
  Browne operation operación de Browne.
  Brunschwig's operation operación de Brunschwig.
  Buck's operation operación de Buck.
  Burow's operation operación de Burow.
  Caldwell-Luc operation operación de Caldwell-Luc.
  Carmody-Batson operation operación de Carmody-Batson.
  Carpue's operation operación de Carpue.
  Cecil's operation operación de Cecil.
  Celsian operation operación de Celso.
  cesarean operation operación cesárea.
  Chopart's operation operación de Chopart.
  Colonna's operation operación de Colonna.
  Commando's operation operación de Commando.
  Conway operation operación de Conway.
  cosmetic operation operación plástica.
  Cotte's operation operación de Cotte.
  Cotting's operation operación de Cotting.
  Dana's operation operación de Dana.
  Dandy's operation operación de Dandy.
  Daviel's operation operación de Daviel.
  de Vincentiis operation operación de Vincentiis.
  debulking operation operación de reducción.
  Denonvilliers' operation operación de Denonvilliers.
  Dieffenbach's operation operación de Dieffenbach.
  Doyle's operation operación de Doyle.
  Duhamel operation operación de Duhamel.
  Duplay's operation operación de Duplay.
  Dupuy-Dutemps operation operación de Dupuy-Dutemps.
  Dupuytren's operation operación de Dupuytren.
  Elliot's operation operación de Elliot.
  Emmet's operation operación de Emmet.
  equilibrating operation operación equilibrante.
  Esser's operation operación de Esser.
  Estes' operation operación de Estes.
  Eversbusch's operation operación de Eversbusch.

  exploratory operation operación exploradora, operación exploratoria.
  fenestration operation operación de fenestración, operación de fenestración de Lempert.
  Fergusson's operation operación de Fergusson.
  Filatov's operation operación de Filatov.
  filtering operation operación filtrante.
  Finney's operation operación de Finney.
  flap operation operación de colgajo.
  Foley operation operación de Foley.
  Fontan operation operación de Fontan.
  Fothergill's operation operación de Fothergill.
  Franco's operation operación de Franco.
  Frank's operation operación de Frank.
  Frazier-Spiller operation operación de Frazier-Spiller.
  Fredet-Ramstedt operation operación de Fredet-Ramstedt.
  Freund's operation operación de Freund.
  Freyer's operation operación de Freyer.
  Frost-Lang's operation operación de Frost-Lang.
  Fukala's operation operación de Fukala.
  Fuller's operation operación de Fuller.
  Gifford's operation operación de Gifford.
  Gigli's operation operación de Gigli.
  Gilliam's operation operación de Gilliam.
  Gillies' operation operación de Gillies.
  Gil-Vernet operation operación de Gil-Vernet.
  Girdlestone operation operación de Girdlestone.
  Glenn's operation operación de Glenn.
  Graefe's operation operación de Graefe.
  Gritti's operation operación de Gritti.
  Grondahl-Finney operation operación de Grondahl-Finney.
  Guyon's operation operación de Guyon.
  Halsted's operation operación de Halsted.
  Hancock's operation operación de Hancock.
  Hartmann's operation operación de Hartmann.
  Haultain's operation operación de Haultain.
  Heaney's operation operación de Heaney.
  Heath's operation operación de Heath.
  Heineke-Mikulicz operation operación de Heinecke-Mikulicz.
  Heine's operation operación de Heine.
  Heller's operation operación de Heller.
  Herbert's operation operación de Herbert.
  Hey's operation operación de Hey.
  Hibbs' operation operación de Hibbs.
  Hill operation operación de Hill.
  Hoffa-Lorenz operation operación de Hoffa, operación de Hoffa-Lorenz.
  Hoffa's operation operación de Hoffa, operación de Hoffa-Lorenz.
  Hofmeister's operation operación de Hofmeister.
  Holth's operation operación de Holth.
  Horsley's operation operación de Horsley.
  Hotz-Anagnostakis operation operación de Hotz-Anagnostakis.
  Huggins' operation operación de Huggins.
  Hummelsheim's operation operación de Hummelsheim.
  Huntington's operation operación de Huntington.
  Indian operation operación hindú.
  interposition operation operación de interposición.
  interval operation operación de intervalo.
  Irving's sterilization operation operación de esterilización de Irving.

Italian operation operación italiana.
Jaboulay's operation operación de Jaboulay.
Jacobaeus operation operación de Jacobaeus.
Jansen's operation operación de Jansen.
Juvara's operation operación de Juvara.
Kader's operation operación de Kader.
Kasai operation operación de Kasai.
Kazanjian's operation operación de Kazanjian.
Keen's operation operación de Keen.
Keller operation operación de Keller.
Kelly's operation operación de Kelly.
Killian-Freer operation operación de Killian-Freer.
Killian's operation operación de Killian.
King's operation operación de King.
Knapp's operation operación de Knapp.
Kocher's operation operación de Kocher.
Köerte-Ballance operation operación de Köerte-Ballance.
Kondoleon operation operación de Kondoleon.
Kraske's operation operación de Kraske.
Krimer's operation operación de Krimer.
Krogius' operation operación de Krogius.
Krönlein operation operación de Krönlein.
Kuhnt's operation operación de Kuhnt.
Küstner operation operación de Küstner.
Ladd's operation operación de Ladd.
Lagrange's operation operación de Lagrange.
Lambrinudi operation operación de Lambrinudi.
Landolt's operation operación de Landolt.
Lane's operation operación de Lane.
Lapidus operation operación de Lapidus.
Laroyenne's operation operación de Laroyenne.
Larrey's operation operación de Larrey.
Lash's operation operación de Lash.
Le Fort-Neugebauer operation operación de le fort, operación de Le Fort-Neugebauer.
Le Fort's operation operación de le fort, operación de Le Fort-Neugebauer.
Lempert's fenestration operation operación de fenestración, operación de fenestración de Lempert.
Leriche's operation operación de Leriche.
Lindner's operation operación de Lindner.
Lisfranc's operation operación de Lisfranc.
Liston's operation operación de Liston.
Lizars' operation operación de Lizars.
Longmire's operation operación de Longmire.
Lorenz's operation operación de Lorenz.
Luc's operation operación de Luc.
Macewen's operation operación de Macewen.
Madlener operation operación de Madlener.
major operation operación mayor.
Manchester operation operación de Manchester.
Marshall-Marchetti-Krantz operation operación de Marshall-Marchetti-Krantz.
Mason's operation operación de Mason.
mastoid operation operación mastoides.
Matas' operation operación de Matas.
Mayo's operation operación de Mayo.
McBride operation operación de McBride.
McBurney's operation operación de McBurney.
McReynolds' operation operación de McReynolds.
McVay's operation operación de McVay.

Meller's operation operación de Meller.
Mikulicz's operation operación de Mikulicz.
Miles' operation operación de Miles.
minor operation operación menor.
morcellation operation operación de morcelación.
Moschcowitz's operation operación de Moschcowitz.
Motais' operation operación de Motais.
Mules' operation operación de Mules.
mustard operation operación de mustard.
Naffziger operation operación de Naffziger.
Nissen's operation operación de Nissen.
Norton's operation operación de Norton.
Ober's operation operación de Ober.
Ogston-Luc operation operación de Ogston-Luc.
Olshausen's operation operación de Olshausen.
open operation operación abierta.
Patey's operation operación de Patey.
Payne operation operación de Payne.
Phelps' operation operación de Phelps.
Phemister operation operación de Phemister.
plastic operation operación plástica.
Pólya's operation operación de Pólya.
Pomeroy's operation operación de Pomeroy.
Porro operation operación de Porro.
Potts operation operación de Potts.
Puttio-Platt operation operación de Puttio-Platt.
radical operation operación radical.
Ramstedt operation operación de Ramstedt.
Rastelli operation operación de Rastelli.
Récamier's operation operación de Récamier.
Regnoli's operation operación de Regnoli.
Ridell operation operación de Ridell.
Roux operation operación de Roux, operación de Roux en Y.
Roux-en-Y operation operación de Roux, operación de Roux en Y.
Saemisch's operation operación de Saemisch.
Saenger's operation operación de Saenger.
Scanzoni's operation operación de Scanzoni.
Schauta vaginal operation operación vaginal de Schauta.
Schauta's operation operación de Schauta.
Schede's operation operación de Schede.
Scheie's operation operación de Scheie.
Schönbein's operation operación de Schönbein.
Schröder's operation operación de Schröder.
Schuchardt's operation operación de Schuchardt.
second-look operation operación de reexploración.
Sédillot's operation operación de Sédillot.
Senning operation operación de Senning.
Serre's operation operación de Serre.
seton operation operación con seton.
Sever's operation operación de Sever.
Shirodkar's operation operación de Shirodkar.
Silver operation operación de Silver.
Sistrunk's operation operación de Sistrunk.
Smith-Boyce's operation operación de Smith-Boyce.
Smith-Indian operation operación india de Smith.
Smith-Robinson's operation operación de Smith-Robinson.
Smith's operation operación de Smith.

Soave operation operación de Soave.
Sorrin's operation operación de Sorrin.
Spinelli's operation operación de Spinelli.
Ssabanejew-Frank operation operación de Ssabanejew-Frank.
stapes mobilization operation operación de movilización del estribo.
State operation operación de State.
Stein operation operación de Stein.
Steindler operation operación de Steindler.
Stoffel's operation operación de Stoffel.
Stokes' operation operación de Stokes.
Stookey-Scarff operation operación de Stookey-Scarff.
Strassmann's operation operación de Strassmann.
Strömbeck operation operación de Strömbeck.
Sturmdorf's operation operación de Sturmdorf.
subcutaneous operation operación subcutánea.
Swenson's operation operación de Swenson.
Syme's operation operación de Syme.
Tagliacotian operation operación de Tagliacozzi, operación tagliacotiana.
Tanner's operation operación de Tanner.
Teale's operation operación de Teale.
TeLinde operation operación de TeLinde.
Thiersch's operation operación de Thiersch.
Torek operation operación de Torek.
Torkildsen's operation operación de Torkildsen.
Toti's operation operación de Toti.
Trendelenburg's operation operación de Trendelenburg.
van Hook's operation operación de van Hook.
Vineberg operation operación de Vineberg.
Vladimiroff operation operación de Vladimiroff.
Waterston operation operación de Waterston.
Watkins' operation operación de Watkins.
Webster's operation operación de Webster.
Wertheim's operation operación de Wertheim, operación de Wertheim-Meigs.
Wheelhouse's operation operación de Wheelhouse.
Whitehead's operation operación de Whitehead.
White's operation operación de White.
Whitman's operation operación de Whitman.
Young's operation operación de Young.
Ziegler's operation operación de Ziegler.
operationalization of behavior *n.* operacionalización de la conducta.
operative *adj.* operativo, -va.
operator *n.* operador, -ra.
opercular *adj.* opercular.
operculectomy *n.* operculectomía.
operculitis *n.* operculitis.
operculum *n.* opérculo.
 dental operculum opérculo dental.
 operculum dentale opérculo dental.
 trophoblastic operculum opérculo trofoblástico.
operon *n.* operón.
ophiasis *n.* ofiasis.
ophidiasis *n.* ofidiasis.
ophidic *adj.* ofídico, -ca.
ophidiophobia *n.* ofidiofobia.
ophidism *n.* ofidismo.
ophiotoxemia *n.* ofiotoxemia.

ophitoxemia *n.* ofitoxemia.
ophryitis *n.* ofriítis.
ophryogenes *n.* ofriogenes.
ophryon *n.* ofrio, ofrión.
ophryosis *n.* ofriosis.
ophrytis *n.* ofritis.
ophthalmagra *n.* oftalmagra.
ophthalmalgia *n.* oftalmalgia.
ophthalmatrophia *n.* oftalmatrofia.
ophthalmectomy *n.* oftalmectomía.
ophthalmencephalon *n.* oftalmencéfalo.
ophthalmia *n.* oftalmía.
　actinic ray ophthalmia oftalmía por rayos actínicos.
　Brazilian ophthalmia oftalmía brasileña.
　catarrhal ophthalmia oftalmía catarral.
　caterpillar ophthalmia oftalmía de pelo de oruga.
　caterpillar-hair ophthalmia oftalmía de pelo de oruga.
　Egyptian ophthalmia o de Egipto, oftalmía egipcia.
　electric ophthalmia oftalmía eléctrica.
　flash ophthalmia oftalmía de destello.
　gonorrheal ophthalmia oftalmía gonorreica.
　granular ophthalmia oftalmía granular, oftalmía granulosa.
　hepatic ophthalmia oftalmía hepática.
　metastatic ophthalmia oftalmía metastásica.
　migratory ophthalmia oftalmía migratoria.
　mucous ophthalmia oftalmía mucosa.
　neuroparalytic ophthalmia oftalmía neuroparalítica.
　ophthalmia eczematosa oftalmía eccematosa.
　ophthalmia hepatica oftalmía hepática.
　ophthalmia lenta oftalmía lenta.
　ophthalmia neonatorum oftalmía del recién nacido, oftalmía neonatal.
　ophthalmia nivalis oftalmía de la nieve, oftalmía nivalis.
　ophthalmia nodosa oftalmía nodosa, oftalmía nudosa.
　phlyctenular ophthalmia oftalmía flictenular.
　pseudotuberculous ophthalmia oftalmía seudotuberculosa.
　purulent ophthalmia oftalmía purulenta.
　reaper's ophthalmia oftalmía del cosechador.
　scrofulous ophthalmia oftalmía escrofulosa.
　spring ophthalmia oftalmía primaveral.
　strumous ophthalmia oftalmía estrumosa.
　sympathetic ophthalmia oftalmía simpática.
　transferred ophthalmia oftalmía transferida.
　ultraviolet ray ophthalmia oftalmía por rayos ultravioleta.
　varicose ophthalmia oftalmía varicosa.
　vegetable ophthalmia oftalmía vegetal.
ophthalmiac *adj.* oftalmíaco, -ca.
ophthalmiatrics *n.* oftalmíatría.
ophthalmic *adj.* oftálmico, -ca.
ophthalmitic *adj.* oftalmítico, -ca.
ophthalmitis *n.* oftalmitis.
ophthalmoblennorrhea *n.* oftalmoblenorrea.
ophthalmocele *n.* oftalmocele.
ophthalmocopia *n.* oftalmocopia.
ophthalmodesmitis *n.* oftalmodesmitis.
ophthalmodiaphanoscope *n.* oftalmodiafanoscopio.
ophthalmodiastimeter *n.* oftalmodiastímetro.
ophthalmodonesis *n.* oftalmodonesis.
ophthalmodynamometer *n.* oftalmodinamómetro.
　Bailliart's ophthalmodynamometer oftalmodinamómetro de Bailliart.
　suction ophthalmodynamometer oftalmodinamómetro de succión.

ophthalmodynamometry *n.* oftalmodinamometría.
ophthalmodynia *n.* oftalmodinia.
ophthalmoeikonometer *n.* oftalmoeiconómetro.
ophthalmoencephalon *n.* oftalmoencéfalo.
ophthalmofundoscope *n.* oftalmofundoscopio.
ophthalmogram *n.* oftalmograma.
ophthalmograph *n.* oftalmógrafo.
ophthalmography *n.* oftalmografía.
ophthalmogyric *adj.* oftalmogírico, -ca, oftalmógiro, -ra.
ophthalmoleukoscope *n.* oftalmoleucoscopio.
ophthalmolith *n.* oftalmolito.
ophthalmologic *adj.* oftalmológico, -ca.
ophthalmological *adj.* oftalmológico, -ca.
ophthalmologist *n.* oftalmólogo, -ga.
ophthalmology *n.* oftalmología.
ophthalmomalacia *n.* oftalmomalacia.
ophthalmomelanosis *n.* oftalmomelanosis.
ophthalmometer *n.* oftalmómetro.
ophthalmometroscope *n.* oftalmometroscopio.
ophthalmometry *n.* oftalmometría.
ophthalmomycosis *n.* oftalmomicosis.
ophthalmomyiasis *n.* oftalmomiasis, oftalmomiiasis.
ophthalmomyitis *n.* oftalmomiitis, oftalmomitis.
ophthalmomyositis *n.* oftalmomiositis.
ophthalmomyotomy *n.* oftalmomiotomía.
ophthalmoneuritis *n.* oftalmoneuritis.
ophthalmoneuromyelitis *n.* oftalmoneuromielitis.
ophthalmopathy *n.* oftalmopatía.
　endocrine ophthalmopathy oftalmopatía endocrina.
　external ophthalmopathy oftalmopatía externa.
　Graves' ophthalmopathy oftalmopatía de Graves-Basedow.
　Graves-Basedow's ophthalmopathy oftalmopatía de Graves-Basedow.
　internal ophthalmopathy oftalmopatía interna.
　thyroid ophthalmopathy oftalmopatía tiroidea.
ophthalmophacometer *n.* oftalmofacómetro.
ophthalmophantom *n.* oftalmofantasma, oftalmofantoma.
ophthalmophlebotomy *n.* oftalmoflebotomía.
ophthalmophthisis *n.* oftalmoftisis.
ophthalmoplasty *n.* oftalmoplastia.
ophthalmoplegia *n.* oftalmoplejía.
　basal ophthalmoplegia oftalmoplejía basal, oftalmoplejía basilar.
　exophthalmic ophthalmoplegia oftalmoplejía exoftálmica.
　external ophthalmoplegia oftalmoplejía externa.
　fascicular ophthalmoplegia oftalmoplejía fascicular.
　internal ophthalmoplegia oftalmoplejía interna.
　internuclear ophthalmoplegia oftalmoplejía internuclear.
　nuclear ophthalmoplegia oftalmoplejía nuclear.
　orbital ophthalmoplegia oftalmoplejía orbitaria.
　Parinaud's ophthalmoplegia oftalmoplejía de Parinaud.
　partial ophthalmoplegia oftalmoplejía parcial.

　progressive external ophthalmoplegia oftalmoplejía progresiva externa.
　progressive ophthalmoplegia oftalmoplejía progresiva.
　Tolosa-Hunt's ophthalmoplegia oftalmoplejía dolorosa de Tolosa-Hunt.
　total ophthalmoplegia oftalmoplejía total.
ophthalmoplegic *adj.* oftalmopléjico, -ca.
ophthalmorrhagia *n.* oftalmorragia.
ophthalmorrhea *n.* oftalmorrea.
ophthalmorrhexis *n.* oftalmorrexis.
ophthalmoscope *n.* oftalmoscopio.
　binocular ophthalmoscope oftalmoscopio binocular.
　demonstration ophthalmoscope oftalmoscopio de demostración.
　direct ophthalmoscope oftalmoscopio directo.
　indirect ophthalmoscope oftalmoscopio indirecto.
ophthalmoscopic *adj.* oftalmoscópico, -ca.
ophthalmoscopy *n.* oftalmoscopia.
　direct ophthalmoscopy oftalmoscopia directa.
　indirect ophthalmoscopy oftalmoscopia indirecta.
　medical ophthalmoscopy oftalmoscopia médica.
　metric ophthalmoscopy oftalmoscopia métrica.
　ophthalmoscopy with reflected light oftalmoscopia con luz reflejada.
ophthalmospasm *n.* oftalmospasmo.
ophthalmospectroscope *n.* oftalmoespectroscopio.
ophthalmospectroscopy *n.* oftalmoespectroscopia.
ophthalmostasis *n.* oftalmostasis.
ophthalmostat *n.* oftalmostato.
ophthalmostatometer *n.* oftalmostatómetro.
ophthalmosteresis *n.* oftalmostéresis.
ophthalmosynchysis *n.* oftalmosinquisis.
ophthalmothermometer *n.* oftalmotermómetro.
ophthalmotomy *n.* oftalmotomía.
ophthalmotonometer *n.* oftalmotonómetro.
ophthalmotonometry *n.* oftalmotonometría.
ophthalmotoxin *n.* oftalmotoxina.
ophthalmotrope *n.* oftalmótropo.
ophthalmotropometer *n.* oftalmotropómetro.
ophthalmotropometry *n.* oftalmotropometría.
ophthalmovascular *adj.* oftalmovascular.
ophthalmoxyster *n.* oftalmoxistro.
opiate *adj.* opiáceo, -a, opiado, -da.
opilação *n.* opilación.
opioid *n.* opioide.
opiomania *n.* opiomanía.
opiomaniac *adj.* opiomaníaco, -ca, opiómano, -na.
opiomelanocortin *n.* opiomelanocortina.
opiophagism *n.* opiofagismo.
opiophagy *n.* opiofagia.
opisthenar *n.* opistenar.
opisthencephalon *n.* opistencéfalo.
opisthiobasial *adj.* opistiobasial.
opisthion *n.* opistión.
opisthionasial *adj.* opistionasial.
opisthocheilia *n.* opistoqueilia.
opisthochilia *n.* opistoquilia, opistoquilia.
opisthocranion *n.* opistocráneo.
opisthogenia *n.* opistogenia.
opisthoporeia *n.* opistoporeia.
opisthorchiasis *n.* opistorquiasis.

opisthorchid *n.* opistórquido.
Opisthorchiidae Opisthorchiidae.
Opisthorchis Opisthorchis.
opisthorchosis *n.* opistorcosis.
opisthotic *adj.* opistótico, -ca.
opisthotonic *adj.* opistotónico, -ca.
opisthotonoid *adj.* opistotonoide.
opisthotonos *n.* opistótonos.
opisthotonus *n.* opistótonos.
  opisthotonus fetalis opistótonos fetal.
opistognathism *n.* opistognatismo.
opium opio, opium.
  Boston opium opio de Boston.
  crude opium opio bruto.
  denarcotized opium opio desnarcotizado.
  deodorized opium opio desodorizado.
  granulated opium opio granulado.
  lettuce opium opio de lechuga.
  opium deodoratum opio desodorizado.
  opium granulatum opio granulado.
  opium pulveratum opio en polvo.
  powdered opium opio en polvo.
  pudding opium opio de budín.
opocephalous *adj.* opocéfalo, -la.
opocephalus *n.* opocéfalo.
opodidymus *n.* opodídimo.
opodymus *n.* opódimo.
opossum *n.* zarigüeya.
opotherapy *n.* opoterapia.
oppilation *n.* opilación.
oppilative *adj.* opilativo, -va.
opponens *adj.* oponente.
opportunistic *adj.* oportunista.
opposing *adj.* oponente.
oppositipolar *adj.* opositipolar.
opsialgia *n.* opsialgia.
opsigenes *adj.* opsígeno, -na.
opsin *n.* opsina.
opsinogen *n.* opsinógeno.
opsiometer *n.* opsiómetro.
opsiuria *n.* opsiuria.
opsoclonia *n.* opsoclonía.
opsoclonus opsoclono, opsoclonus.
opsogen *n.* opsógeno.
opsomania *n.* opsomanía.
opsone *n.* opsona.
opsonic *adj.* opsónico, -ca.
opsoniferous *adj.* opsonífero, -ra.
opsonification *n.* opsonificación.
opsonify *v.* opsonificar.
opsonin *n.* opsonina.
  common opsonin opsonina común.
  immune opsonin opsonina inmune.
  normal opsonin opsonina normal.
  specific opsonin opsonina específica.
  thermolabile opsonin opsonina termolábil.
  thermostable opsonin opsonina termoestable.
opsoninopathy *n.* opsoninopatía.
  consumptive opsoninopathy opsoninopatía por utilización.
opsonization *n.* opsonización.
opsonize *v.* opsonizar.
opsonocytophagic *adj.* opsonocitofágico, -ca.
opsonogen *n.* opsonógeno.
opsonology *n.* opsonología.
opsonometry *n.* opsonometría.
opsonophilia *n.* opsonofilia.
opsonophilic *adj.* opsonófilo, -la.
opsonophoric *adj.* opsonóforo, -ra.
opsonotherapy *n.* opsonoterapia.
optesthesia *n.* optestesia.
opththalmoxerosis *n.* oftalmoxerosis.
optic *adj.* óptico[1], -ca.
optical *adj.* óptico[1], -ca.

optician *n.* óptico[2], -ca.
opticist *n.* óptico[2], -ca.
opticochiasmatic *adj.* opticoquiasmático, -ca.
opticociliary *adj.* opticociliar.
opticocinerea *n.* opticocinérea.
opticokinetic *adj.* opticocinético, -ca.
opticonasion *n.* opticonasión.
opticopupillary *adj.* opticopupilar.
optics *n.* óptica.
  fiber optics óptica de fibras.
  Nomarski optics óptica de Nomarski.
optimal *adj.* óptimo, -ma.
optimeter *n.* optímetro.
optimism *n.* optimismo.
  therapeutic optimism optimismo terapéutico.
optimum óptimo, optimum.
optist *n.* óptico[2], -ca.
optoblast *n.* optoblasto.
optochiasmic *adj.* optoquiasmático, -ca.
optogram *n.* optograma.
optokinetic *adj.* optocinético, -ca.
optomeninx *n.* optomeninge.
optometer *n.* optómetro.
  objective optometer optómetro objetivo.
optometrist *n.* optometrista.
optometry *n.* optometría.
optomyometer *n.* optomiómetro.
optophone *n.* optófono.
optostriate *adj.* optostriado, -da.
optotype *n.* optotipo.
ora serrata *n.* ora serrata, ora serrata retinae.
  ora serrata retinae ora serrata, ora serrata retinae.
orad orad.
oral *adj.* oral[1].
orale *n.* oral[2].
orality *n.* oralidad.
orange *n.* naranja.
orangeophil *adj.* naranjófilo, -la.
orbicular *adj.* orbicular[1].
orbiculare *n.* orbiculare.
orbicularis orbicular[2], orbicularis.
orbiculus *n.* orbículo.
orbit *n.* órbita.
orbita *n.* órbita.
orbital *adj.* orbital[2].
orbitale *n.* orbital[1].
orbitalis *adj.* orbitario, -ria.
orbitectomy *n.* orbitectomía.
orbitography *n.* orbitografía.
orbitonasal *adj.* orbitonasal.
orbitonometer *n.* orbitonómetro.
orbitonometry *n.* orbitonometría.
orbitopagus *n.* orbitópago.
orbitosphenoid *adj.* orbitoesfenoidal.
orbitostat *n.* orbitóstato.
orbitotemporal *adj.* orbitotemporal.
orbitotomy *n.* orbitotomía.
orbivirus *n.* orbivirus.
orcein *n.* orceína.
orchectomy *n.* orquectomía.
orchella *n.* orcela, orchella.
orchialgia *n.* orquialgia.
orchiatrophy *n.* orquiatrofia.
orchic *adj.* órquico, -ca.
orchicatabasis *n.* orquicatabasis.
orchichorea *n.* orquicorea.
orchidalgia *n.* orquidalgia.
orchidectomy *n.* orquidectomía.
orchidic *adj.* orquídico, -ca.
orchiditis *n.* orquiditis.
orchidoepididymectomy *n.* orquidoepididimectomía.
orchidometer *n.* orquidómetro.

orchidoncus *n.* orquidonco.
orchidopathy *n.* orquidopatía.
orchidopexy *n.* orquidopexia.
orchidoplasty *n.* orquidoplastia.
orchidoptosis *n.* orquidoptosis, orquioptosis.
orchidorrhaphy *n.* orquidorrafia.
orchidotherapy *n.* orquidoterapia.
orchidotomy *n.* orquidotomía.
orchiectomy *n.* orquectomía, orquiectomía.
  orchiectomy in prostate adenocarcinoma orquiectomía subalbugínea.
  orchiectomy in testicular carcinoma orquiectomía por cáncer de testículo.
orchiepididymitis *n.* orquidoepididimitis, orquiepididimitis, orquioepididimitis.
orchilytic *adj.* orquiolítico, -ca.
orchiocatabasis *n.* orquiocatabasis.
orchiocele *n.* orquiocele.
orchiodynia *n.* orquiodinia.
orchiofuniculisis *n.* orquidofuniculisis.
orchioncus *n.* orquionco.
orchioneuralgia *n.* orquioneuralgia.
orchiopathy *n.* orquiopatía.
orchiopexy *n.* orquiopexia.
orchioplasty *n.* orquioplastia.
orchiorrhaphy *n.* orquiorrafia.
orchioscheocele *n.* orquiosqueocele.
orchioscirrhus *n.* orquioescirro, orquioscirro.
orchiotherapy *n.* orquioterapia.
orchiotomy *n.* orquidotomía, orquiotomía.
orchis orchis, orquis.
orchitic *adj.* orquítico, -ca.
orchitis *n.* orquitis.
  metastatic orchitis orquitis metastática.
  orchitis parotidea orquitis parótida, orquitis parotídea, orquitis parotídica.
  orchitis variolosa orquitis variolosa.
  spermatogenic granulomatous orchitis orquitis granulomatosa espermatógena.
  traumatic orchitis orquitis traumática.
orchitolytic *adj.* orquitolítico, -ca.
orchotomy *n.* orcotomía.
orcin *n.* orcina.
orcinol *n.* orcinol.
order *n.* orden[1], orden[2].
  DNR order orden de no reanimación, orden de no resucitar.
  do-not-resuscitate-without-consent order orden de no reanimación sin consentimiento.
  do-not-resuscitate order orden de no reanimación, orden de no resucitar.
  medication order orden de tratamiento.
  nursing order orden de enfermería.
  order of procedure orden de procedimiento.
  pecking order orden forzado.
ordinate *n.* ordenada.
orectic *adj.* oréctico, -ca.
orexia *n.* orexia.
orexigenic *adj.* orexigénico, -ca, orexígeno, -na.
oreximania *n.* oreximanía.
orexis *n.* orexia.
orf *n.* orf.
organ *n.* órgano.
  accessory organ órgano accesorio.
  accessory organ of the eye órgano accesorio del ojo.
  acoustic organ órgano acústico.
  anulospiral organ órgano anuloespiral.
  cell organ órgano celular.
  cement organ órgano del cemento.
  Chievitz's organ órgano de Chievitz.
  circumventricular organ órgano circunventricular.

Corti's organ órgano de Corti.
critical organ órgano crítico.
digestive organ órgano digestivo.
effector organ órgano efector.
enamel organ órgano del esmalte, órgano esmalte.
end organ órgano final, órgano terminal.
external genital organ órgano genital externo.
extraperitoneal organ órgano extraperitoneal.
female genital organ órgano genital femenino.
female reproductive organ órgano reproductor femenino.
floating organ órgano flotante.
flower-spray organ of Ruffini órgano en ramillete de Ruffini.
Golgi's tendon organ órgano tendinoso de Golgi.
gustatory organ órgano del gusto, órgano gustativo, órgano gustatorio.
homologous organ órgano homólogo.
internal genital organ órgano genital interno.
intromittent organ órgano introductor, órgano intromitente.
Jacobson's organ órgano de Jacobson.
lymphatic organ órgano linfático.
lymphoid organ órgano linfoide.
male genital organ órgano genital masculino.
male reproductive organ órgano reproductor del varón.
Meyer's organ órgano de Meyer.
neurotendinous organ órgano neurotendinoso.
olfactory organ órgano del olfato, órgano olfatorio.
organ of Corti órgano de Corti.
organ of Giraldès órgano de Giraldès.
organ of Golgi órgano de Golgi.
organ of hearing órgano de la audición.
organ of Rosenmüller órgano de Rosenmüller.
organ of Ruffini órgano de Ruffini.
organ of shock órgano de choque.
organ of smell órgano del olfato, órgano olfatorio.
organ of taste órgano del gusto, órgano gustativo, órgano gustatorio.
organ of touch órgano del tacto.
organ of vision órgano de la visión, órgano visual.
primary lymphoid organ órgano linfoide primario.
primitive fat organ órgano primitivo de grasa.
ptotic organ órgano ptótico.
reproductive organ órgano reproductor.
retroperitoneal organ órgano retroperitoneal.
Rosenmüller's organ órgano de Rosenmüller.
rudimentary organ órgano rudimentario.
Ruffini's organ órgano de Ruffini.
secondary lymphoid organ órgano linfoide secundario.
segmental organ órgano segmentario.
sense organ órgano de los sentidos, órgano de un sentido, órgano sensorial.
sensory end organ órgano sensitivo terminal.
sensory organ órgano de los sentidos, órgano sensorial.
spiral organ órgano espiral.
subcommissural organ órgano subcomisural.

subfornical organ órgano subfornical.
supernumerary organ órgano supernumerario.
target organ órgano blanco, órgano diana.
taste organ órgano del gusto, órgano gustativo, órgano gustatorio.
terminal organ órgano terminal.
touch receptor organ órgano del tacto.
urinary organ órgano urinario.
vestibular organ órgano vestibular.
vestibulocochlear organ órgano vestibulococlear.
vestigial organ órgano vestigial.
visual organ órgano de la visión, órgano visual.
vomeronasal organ órgano vomeronasal.
wandering organ órgano errante.
Weber's organ órgano de Weber.
organacidia *n.* organacidia.
organella *n.* organela, organelo.
organelle *n.* organela, organelo.
holdfast organelle organela cristal de reloj, organela Lieberkühn.
organic *adj.* orgánico, -ca.
organicism *n.* organicismo.
organicist *n.* organicista.
organism *n.* organismo.
calculated mean organism (CMO) organismo medio calculado.
consumer organism organismo consumidor.
fastidious organism organismo exigente.
hypothetical mean organism (HMO) organismo medio hipotético.
nitrifying organism organismo nitrificante.
nitrosifying organism organismo nitrosificante.
pleuropneumonia-like organism (PPLO) organismo tipo pleuroneumonía.
organization *n.* organización.
preferred provider organization (PPO) organización de prestadores seleccionados (OPS).
pregenital organization organización pregenital.
professional organization organización profesional.
organizer *n.* organizador, -ra.
nucleolar organizer organizador del nucléolo, organizador nucleolar.
nucleolus organizer organizador del nucléolo, organizador nucleolar.
primary organizer organizador primario, organizador principal.
procentriole organizer organizador de los procentríolos, organizador procentríolo.
secondary organizer organizador secundario.
tertiary organizer organizador terciario.
organochlorine *n.* organocloro.
organofaction *n.* organofacción.
organoferric *adj.* organoférrico, -ca.
organogel *n.* organogel.
organogen *n.* organógeno.
organogenesis *n.* organogenesia, organogénesis.
organogenetic *adj.* organogenético, -ca.
organogenic *adj.* organogénico, -ca.
organogeny *n.* organogenia.
organography *n.* organografía.
organoid *n.* organoide.
organoleptic *adj.* organoléptico, -ca.
organology *n.* organología.
organoma *n.* organoma.
organomegaly *n.* organomegalia.
organomercurial *adj.* organomercurial.

organometallic *adj.* organometálico, -ca.
organon *n.* órgano.
organon gustus órgano del gusto, órgano gustativo, órgano gustatorio.
organon olfactus órgano del olfato, órgano olfatorio.
organonomy *n.* organonomía.
organonymy *n.* organonimia.
organopathy *n.* organopatía.
organopexia *n.* organopexia.
organopexy *n.* organopexia.
organophilic *adj.* organofílico, -ca, organófilo, -la.
organophosphate *n.* organofosfato.
organophosphorated *adj.* organofosforado, -da.
organophosphorus *n.* organofósforo.
organoscopy *n.* organoscopia.
organosol *n.* organosol.
organotaxis *n.* organotaxis.
organotherapy *n.* organoterapia.
heterologous organotherapy organoterapia heteróloga.
homologous organotherapy organoterapia homóloga.
organotrope *n.* organótropo.
organotrophic *adj.* organotrófico, -ca.
organotropic *adj.* organotrópico, -ca.
organotropism *n.* organotropismo.
organotropy *n.* organotropía.
organ-specific *adj.* organoespecífico, -ca.
organule *n.* orgánulo.
organum *n.* órgano.
organum auditus órgano auditivo.
organum extraperitoneale órgano extraperitoneal.
organum gustatorium órgano del gusto, órgano gustativo, órgano gustatorio.
organum gustus órgano del gusto, órgano gustativo, órgano gustatorio.
organum olfactorium órgano del olfato, órgano olfatorio.
organum olfactus órgano del olfato, órgano olfatorio.
organum retroperitoneale órgano retroperitoneal.
organum spirale órgano espiral.
organum subcommissurale órgano subcomisural.
organum subfornicale órgano subfornical.
organum tactus órgano del tacto.
organum vestibulocochleare órgano vestibulococlear.
organum visuale órgano de la visión, órgano visual.
organum visus órgano de la visión, órgano visual.
organum vomeronasale órgano vomeronasal.
orgasm *n.* orgasmo.
orgasmic *adj.* orgásmico, -ca, orgástico, -ca.
orgasmic maturity madurez orgásmica.
orient *v.* orientar.
orientation *n.* orientación.
personal orientation orientación personal.
reality orientation orientación de la realidad.
sexual orientation orientación sexual.
orifice *n.* orificio.
orificial *adj.* orificial.
orificialist *n.* orificialista.
orificium *n.* orificio.
origin *n.* origen.
orinotherapy *n.* orinoterapia.
ornate *n.* ornado.
ornithine *n.* ornitina.

ornithine carbamoyltransferase ornitina carbamiltransferasa, ornitina carbamoiltransferasa.

ornithine decarboxylase ornitina descarboxilasa.

ornithine transcarbamoylase ornitina transcarbamoilasa.

ornithinemia *n.* ornitinemia.

ornithinuria *n.* ornitinuria.

Ornithodoros Ornithodoros.

Ornithonyssu bacoti Ornithonyssu bacoti.

ornithosis *n.* ornitosis.

orodiagnosis *n.* orodiagnóstico.

orodigitofacial *adj.* orodigitofacial.

orofacial *adj.* orofacial.

orogranulocyte *n.* orogranulocito.

orogranulocytic *adj.* orogranulocítico, -ca.

oroimmunity *n.* oroinmunidad.

orokinase *n.* oroquinasa.

orolingual *adj.* orolingual.

oromaxillary *adj.* oromaxilar.

oromeningitis *n.* oromeningitis.

oronasal *adj.* oronasal.

oropharyngeal *adj.* orofaríngeo, -a.

oropharyngolaryngitis *n.* orofaringolaringitis.

oropharynx *n.* mesofaringe, orofaringe.

Oropsylla Oropsylla.

Oropsylla idahoensis Oropsylla idahoensis.

Oropsylla silantiewi Oropsylla silantiewi.

orosomucoid *n.* orosomucoide.

orotate *n.* orotato.

orotherapy *n.* oroterapia.

oroticaciduria *n.* orotic aciduria, oroticaciduria.

orotidine *n.* orotidina.

orotidylato *n.* orotidilato.

orrhodiagnosis *n.* orrodiagnosis, orrodiagnóstico.

orrhoimmunity *n.* orroinmunidad.

orrhology *n.* orrología.

orrhomeningitis *n.* orromeningitis.

orrhoreaction *n.* orrorreacción.

orrhorrhea *n.* orrorrea.

orrhotherapeutic *adj.* orroterapéutico, -ca.

orrhotherapy *n.* orroterapia.

orseillin BB *n.* orseilina BB.

orthergasia *n.* ortergasia.

orthesis *n.* ortesis.

  ankle-foot orthesis (AFO) ortesis tobillo-pie (OTP).

  electric spinal orthesis ortesis raquídea eléctrica.

  Engen extension orthesis Engen extensión ortesis.

  free-form foot orthesis ortesis de pie de formato libre.

  Newington orthesis ortesis de Newington.

orthetic *adj.* ortésico, -ca.

orthetics *n.* ortésica, ortética.

orthetist *n.* ortetista.

orthoacid *n.* ortoácido.

orthoarteriotony *n.* ortoarteriotonía.

ortho-arteriotony *n.* ortoarteriotonía.

orthobiosis *n.* ortobiosis.

orthocephalic *adj.* ortocefálico, -ca.

orthocephalous *adj.* ortocéfalo, -la.

orthochorea *n.* ortocorea.

orthochromatic *adj.* ortocromático, -ca.

orthochromia *n.* ortocromía.

orthochromophil *adj.* ortocromófilo, -la.

orthochromophile *adj.* ortocromófilo, -la.

orthocresol *n.* ortocresol.

orthocytosis *n.* ortocitosis.

orthodactylous *adj.* ortodáctilo, -la.

orthodentin *n.* ortodentina.

orthodeoxia *n.* ortodesoxia.

orthodiagram *n.* ortodiagrama.

orthodiagraph *n.* ortodiágrafo.

orthodiagraphy *n.* ortodiagrafía.

orthodiametry *n.* ortodiametría.

orthodiascope *n.* ortodiascopio.

orthodiascopy *n.* ortodiascopia.

orthodigita *n.* ortodígita.

orthodontia *n.* ortodoncia.

orthodontic *adj.* ortodóntico, -ca.

orthodontics *n.* ortodoncia.

  corrective orthodontics ortodoncia correctiva.

  interperceptive orthodontics ortodoncia interperceptiva.

  preventive orthodontics ortodoncia preventiva.

  prophylactic orthodontics ortodoncia preventiva.

  surgical orthodontics ortodoncia quirúrgica.

orthodontist *adj.* ortodentista, ortodoncista, ortodontista.

orthodontology *n.* ortodontología.

orthodromic *adj.* ortodrómico, -ca.

orthogenesis *n.* ortogénesis, ortogenia.

orthogenic *adj.* ortogénico, -ca.

orthogenics *n.* ortogénica.

orthoglycemic *adj.* ortoglucémico, -ca.

orthognathia *n.* ortognatia.

orthognathic *adj.* ortognático, -ca.

orthognathics *n.* ortognática.

orthognathism *n.* ortognatismo.

orthognathous *adj.* ortognato, -ta.

orthograde *adj.* ortógrado, -da.

orthokeratology *n.* ortoqueratología.

orthokeratosis *n.* ortoqueratosis.

orthokinetics *n.* ortocinética.

orthomechanical *adj.* ortomecánico, -ca.

orthomechanotherapy *n.* ortomecanoterapia.

orthomelic *adj.* ortomélico, -ca.

orthometer *n.* ortómetro.

orthomolecular *adj.* ortomolecular.

orthomorphia *n.* ortomorfia.

Orthomyxoviridae Orthomyxoviridae.

orthomyxovus *n.* ortomixovirus.

orthoneutrophil *adj.* ortoneutrófilo, -la.

orthopantograph *n.* ortopantografía.

orthopantomograph *n.* ortopantomógrafo.

orthopantomography *n.* ortopantomografía.

orthopedic *adj.* ortopédico, -ca.

orthopedics *n.* ortopedia.

  dental orthopedics ortopedia dental.

  functional jaw orthopedics ortopedia funcional de los maxilares.

orthopedist *n.* ortopedista.

orthopercussion *n.* ortopercusión.

orthophony *n.* ortofonía.

orthophoria *n.* ortoforia.

orthophoric *adj.* ortofórico, -ca.

orthophosphate *n.* ortofosfato.

  inorganic orthophosphate (pi) ortofosfato inorgánico (pi).

orthophrenia *n.* ortofrenia.

orthopia *n.* ortopía, ortopsia.

orthoplastocyte *n.* ortoplastocito.

orthoplessimeter *n.* ortoplexímetro.

orthopnea *n.* ortopnea.

  two-pillow orthopnea ortopnea de dos almohadas.

orthopneic *adj.* ortopneico, -ca.

orthopod *n.* ortopeda.

Orthopoxvirus Orthopoxvirus, Ortopoxvirus.

orthoprosthesis *n.* ortoprótesis.

orthopsychiatry *n.* ortopsiquiatría.

orthoptic *adj.* ortóptico, -ca.

orthoptics *n.* ortóptica.

orthoptist *n.* ortoptista.

orthoptoscope *n.* ortoptoscopio.

orthorhombic *adj.* ortorrómbico, -ca.

orthorrhachic *adj.* ortorráquico, -ca.

orthoscope *n.* ortoscopio.

orthoscopic *adj.* ortoscópico, -ca.

orthoscopy *n.* ortoscopia.

orthosis *n.* ortosis.

orthoskiagraph *n.* ortosquiágrafo.

orthoskiagraphy *n.* ortosquiagrafía.

orthostatic *adj.* ortostático, -ca.

orthostatism *n.* bipedestación, ortostatismo.

orthostereoscope *n.* ortoestereoscopio.

orthostereoscope *n.* ortostereoscopio.

orthosympathetic *n.* ortosimpático, -ca.

orthotast *n.* ortotasto.

orthoterion *n.* ortoterion.

orthothanasia *n.* ortotanasia.

orthotherapy *n.* ortoterapia.

orthotic *adj.* ortótico, -ca.

orthotics *n.* ortótica.

orthotist *n.* ortotista.

orthotolidine *n.* ortotolidina.

orthotonos *n.* ortótonos.

orthotonus *n.* ortótonos.

orthotopic *adj.* ortotópico, -ca.

orthotrophy *n.* ortotrofia.

orthotropic *adj.* ortotrópico, -ca.

orthotyphoid *n.* ortotifoidea.

orthovoltage *n.* ortovoltaje.

orthropsia *n.* ortropsia.

orthuria *n.* orturia.

oryzenin *n.* oricenina.

os *n.* boca, hueso, os.

  os lacrimale unguis.

osamine *n.* osamina.

osazone *n.* osazona.

oscedo *n.* oscedo.

oscheal *adj.* osqueal.

oscheitis *n.* osqueítis.

oschelephantiasis *n.* osqueoelefantiasis.

oscheocele *n.* osqueocele.

oscheohydrocele *n.* osqueohidrocele.

oscheolith *n.* osqueolito.

oscheoma *n.* osqueoma.

oscheoncus *n.* osqueonco.

oscheoplasty *n.* osqueoplastia.

oschitis *n.* osquitis.

oscillation *n.* oscilación.

  bradykinetic oscillation oscilación bradicinética.

oscillator *n.* oscilador.

oscillatory *adj.* oscilatorio, -ria.

oscillogram *n.* oscilograma.

oscillograph *n.* oscilógrafo.

oscillography *n.* oscilografía.

oscillometer *n.* oscilómetro.

oscillometric *adj.* oscilométrico, -ca.

oscillometry *n.* oscilometría.

oscillopsia *n.* oscilopsia.

oscilloscope *n.* osciloscopio.

  cathode ray oscilloscope osciloscopio de rayos catódicos.

  storage oscilloscope osciloscopio de almacenamiento.

oscitate *v.* oscitar.

oscitation *n.* oscitación.

osculum *n.* ósculo, osculum.

ose *n.* ose.

osmate *n.* osmato.

osmatic *adj.* osmático, -ca.

osmesis *n.* osmesis.

osmesthesia *n.* osmestesia.

osmicate *v.* osmicar.

osmication *n.* osmificación.
osmics *n.* ósmica.
osmidrosis *n.* osmidrosis.
osmification *n.* osmificación.
osmiophilic *adj.* osmiófilo, -la.
osmiophobic *adj.* osmiófobo, -ba.
osmoceptor *n.* osmoceptor.
osmodysphoria *n.* osmodisforia.
osmogram *n.* osmograma.
osmol *n.* osmol.
osmolagnia *n.* osmolagnia.
osmolality *n.* osmolalidad.
  calculated serum osmolality osmolalidad calculada del suero.
osmolar *adj.* osmolar.
osmolarity *n.* osmolaridad.
  blood osmolarity osmolaridad sanguínea.
  serum osmolarity osmolaridad del suero, osmolaridad sérica.
  urine osmolarity osmolaridad de la orina, osmolaridad urinaria.
osmole *n.* osmol.
osmology *n.* osmología.
osmolute *n.* osmoluto.
osmometer *n.* osmómetro.
  freezing point osmometer osmómetro de punto de congelación.
  Hepp osmometer osmómetro de Hepp.
  membrane osmometer osmómetro de membrana.
osmometry *n.* osmometría.
osmonosology *n.* osmonosología.
osmophilic *adj.* osmofílico, -ca, osmófilo, -la.
osmophobia *n.* osmofobia.
osmophore *n.* osmóforo.
osmoreceptor *n.* osmorreceptor.
osmoregulation *n.* osmorregulación.
osmoregulatory *adj.* osmorregulador, -ra.
osmoscope *n.* osmoscopio.
osmose *v.* osmosar.
osmosis *n.* osmosis, ósmosis.
  reverse osmosis osmosis inversa.
osmosity *n.* osmosidad.
osmosology *n.* osmosología.
osmostat *n.* osmostato.
osmotaxis *n.* osmotaxis.
osmotherapy *n.* osmoterapia.
osmotic *adj.* osmótico, -ca.
osphresiolagnia *n.* osfresiolagnia.
osphresiologic *adj.* osfresiológico, -ca.
osphresiology *n.* osfresiología.
osphresiometer *n.* osfresiómetro.
osphresiophilia *n.* osfresiofilia.
osphresiophobia *n.* osfresiofobia.
osphresis *n.* osfresis.
osphretic *adj.* osfrético, -ca.
osphyalgia *n.* osfialgia.
osphyarthrosis *n.* osfiartrosis.
osphyomyelitis *n.* osfiomielitis.
osphyotomy *n.* osfiotomía.
ossature *n.* osamenta.
ossein *n.* oseína.
osseoalbumoid *n.* osteoalbumoide.
osseoaponeurotic *adj.* osteoaponeurótico, -ca.
osseocartilaginous *adj.* oseocartilaginoso, -sa.
osseofibrous *adj.* osteofibroso, -sa.
osseomucin *n.* oseomucina.
osseomucoid *n.* oseomucoide.
osseosonometer *n.* oseosonómetro.
osseosonometry *n.* oseosonometría.
osseous *adj.* óseo, -a.
ossicle *n.* huesecillo, osículo.
  sphenoturbinal ossicle esfenoturbinal.
ossicular *adj.* osicular.
ossiculectomy *n.* osiculectomía.

ossiculotomy *n.* osiculotomía.
ossiculum osículo, ossiculum.
ossidesmosis *n.* osidesmosis.
ossiferous *adj.* osífero, -ra.
ossific *adj.* osífico, -ca.
ossification *n.* osificación.
  cartilaginous ossification osificación cartilaginosa.
  ectopic ossification osificación ectópica.
  endochondral ossification osificación encondral, osificación endocondral.
  heterotopic ossification osificación heterotópica.
  intramembranous ossification osificación intramembranosa.
  membranous ossification osificación membranosa.
  metaplastic ossification osificación accidental, osificación metaplásica.
  perichondral ossification osificación pericondral.
  periosteal ossification osificación perióstica.
ossiform *adj.* osiforme.
ossify *v.* osificar.
ossifying *adj.* osificante.
ossiphone *n.* osífono.
ostalgia *n.* ostalgia.
ostarthritis *n.* ostartritis.
osteal *adj.* osteal, osteico, -ca.
ostealbumoid *n.* osteoalbumoide.
ostealgia *n.* ostealgia.
ostealgic *adj.* osteálgico, -ca.
osteameba *n.* ostameba, osteameba, osteamiba.
osteanagenesis *n.* osteanagenesia, osteanagénesis.
osteanaphysis *n.* ostcanáfisis.
ostearthritis *n.* osteartritis.
ostectomy *n.* ostectomía.
ostectopy *n.* ostectopía.
osteectomy *n.* osteectomía.
osteectopia *n.* osteectopía.
ostein *n.* osteína.
osteine *n.* osteína.
osteite *n.* osteíto.
osteitic *adj.* osteítico, -ca.
osteitis *n.* osteítis.
  acute osteitis osteítis aguda.
  alveolar osteitis osteítis alveolar, osteítis alveolar localizada.
  carious osteitis osteítis cariosa.
  central osteitis osteítis central.
  Garré's chronic non-suppurative osteitis osteítis crónica no supurativa de Garré.
  chronic non-suppurative osteitis osteítis no supurativa crónica.
  chronic osteitis osteítis crónica.
  condensing osteitis osteítis condensante.
  cortical osteitis osteítis cortical.
  formative osteitis osteítis formativa.
  gommatous osteitis osteítis gomatosa.
  hematogenous osteitis osteítis hematógena.
  localized alveolar osteitis osteítis alveolar, osteítis alveolar localizada.
  localized osteitis fibrosa osteítis fibrosa localizada.
  multifocal osteitis fibrosa osteítis fibrosa multifocal.
  necrotic osteitis osteítis necrótica.
  osteitis albuminosa osteítis albuminosa.
  osteitis carnosa osteítis carnosa.
  osteitis condensans generalisata osteítis condensante generalizada.
  osteitis condensans ilii osteítis condensante ilíaca.

  osteitis deformans osteítis deformante.
  osteitis fibrosa circumscripta osteítis fibroquística circunscripta.
  osteitis fibrosa cystica osteítis fibrosa quística, osteítis fibrosaquística, osteítis quística.
  osteitis fibrosa cystica generalisata osteítis fibrosa quística generalizada.
  osteitis fibrosa disseminata osteítis fibrosa diseminada.
  osteitis fibrosa localisata osteítis fibrosa localizada.
  osteitis fibrosa osteoplastica osteítis fibrosa osteoplástica.
  osteitis fragilitans osteítis fragilizante.
  osteitis fungosa osteítis fungosa.
  osteitis granulosa osteítis granulosa.
  osteitis of the glenoid cavity glenoiditis.
  osteitis ossificans osteítis osificante.
  osteitis pubis osteítis púbica.
  osteitis tuberculosa multiplex cystica osteítis tuberculosa quística múltiple.
  parathyroid osteitis osteítis paratiroidea.
  productive osteitis osteítis productiva.
  rarefying osteitis osteítis rarefaciente, osteítis rareficante.
  renal osteitis fibrosa osteítis fibrosa renal.
  sclerosing osteitis osteítis esclerosante.
  secondary hyperplastic osteitis osteítis hiperplásica secundaria.
  vascular osteitis osteítis vascular.
ostemia *n.* ostemia.
ostempyesis *n.* ostempiesis.
osteoacusis *n.* osteacusia, osteoacusis.
osteoanagenesis *n.* osteoanagénesis.
osteoanesthesia *n.* osteoanestesia.
osteoaneurysm *n.* osteoaneurisma.
osteoarthritis *n.* osteoartritis.
  chronic osteoarthritis osteoartritis crónica.
  endemic osteoarthritis osteoartritis endémica.
  erosive osteoarthritis osteoartritis erosiva.
  hyperplastic osteoarthritis osteoartritis hiperplásica, osteoartritis hiperplástica.
  interphalangeal osteoarthritis osteoartritis interfalángica.
  osteoarthritis deformans osteoartritis deformante.
osteoarthropathy *n.* osteoartropatía.
  hypertrophic pneumic osteoarthropathy osteoartropatía hipertrófica neumónica, osteoartropatía neumónica hipertrófica.
  hypertrophic pulmonary osteoarthropathy osteoartropatía hipertrófica pulmonar, osteoartropatía pulmonar, osteoartropatía pulmonar hipertrófica.
  idiopathic hypertrophic osteoarthropathy osteoartropatía hipertrófica idiopática.
  pneumogenic osteoarthropathy osteoartropatía neumogénica.
  primary hypertrophic osteoarthropathy osteoartropatía hipertrófica primaria.
  pulmonary osteoarthropathy osteoartropatía pulmonar, osteoartropatía pulmonar hipertrófica.
  secondary hypertrophic osteoarthropathy osteoartropatía hipertrófica secundaria.
osteoarthrosis *n.* osteoartrosis.
osteoarthrotomy *n.* osteoartrotomía.
osteoarticular *adj.* osteoarticular.
osteoblast *n.* osteoblasto.
osteoblastic *adj.* osteoblástico, -ca.
osteoblastoma *n.* osteoblastoma.
osteocachectic *adj.* osteocaquéctico, -ca.
osteocachexia *n.* osteocaquexia.
osteocalcin *n.* osteocalcina.

osteocampsia *n.* osteocampsia.
osteocampsis *n.* osteocampsis.
osteocarcinoma *n.* osteocarcinoma.
osteocartilaginous *adj.* osteocartilaginoso, -sa.
osteocele *n.* osteocele.
osteocementum *n.* osteocemento.
osteochodropathy *n.* osteocondropatía.
  polyglucose (dextran) sulfate-induced osteochodropathy osteocondropatía inducida por sulfato de poliglucosa (dextrán).
osteochondral *adj.* osteocondral.
osteochondritis *n.* osteocondritis.
  calcaneal osteochondritis osteocondritis calcánea.
  juvenile deforming metatarsophalangeal osteochondritis osteocondritis deformante metatarsofalángica juvenil.
  osteochondritis deformans juvenilis osteocondritis deformante juvenil, osteocondritis juvenil deformante, osteocondritis juvenil deformante.
  osteochondritis deformans juvenilis dorsi osteocondritis deformante juvenil dorsal.
  osteochondritis dissecans osteocondritis disecante.
  osteochondritis ischiopubica osteocondritis isquiopúbica.
  osteochondritis necroticans osteocondritis necrosante.
  osteochondritis ossis metacarpi et metatarsi osteocondritis de los huesos metatarsianos y metacarpianos.
  syphilitic osteochondritis osteocondritis sifilítica.
osteochondrodysplasia *n.* osteocondrodisplasia.
osteochondrodystrophia *n.* osteocondrodistrofia.
  osteochondrodystrophia deformans osteocondrodistrofia deformante.
osteochondrodystrophy *n.* osteocondrodistrofia.
  familial osteochondrodystrophy osteocondrodistrofia familiar.
osteochondrofibroma *n.* osteocondrofibroma.
osteochondrolysis *n.* osteocondrólisis.
osteochondroma *n.* osteocondroma.
  fibrosing osteochondroma osteocondroma fibrosante.
osteochondromatosis *n.* osteocondromatosis.
  synovial osteochondromatosis osteocondromatosis sinovial.
osteochondromyxoma *n.* osteocondromixoma.
osteochondropathia *n.* osteocondropatía.
  osteochondropathia cretinoidea osteocondropatía cretinoide.
osteochondrophyte *n.* osteocondrófito.
osteochondrosarcoma *n.* osteocondrosarcoma.
osteochondrosis *n.* osteocondrosis.
  navicular osteochondrosis osteocondrosis del escafoides, osteocondrosis del navicular.
  osteochondrosis deformans tibiae osteocondrosis tibial deformante.
  tibial tubercle osteochondrosis osteocondrosis de la tuberosidad de la tibia.
  vertebral osteochondrosis osteocondrosis vertebral.
osteochondrous *adj.* osteocondrósico, -ca, osteocondroso, -sa, osteocondrótico, -ca.
osteoclasia *n.* osteoclasia.
osteoclasis *n.* osteoclasis.
osteoclast *n.* osteoclasto.
osteoclastic *adj.* osteoclástico, -ca.

osteoclastoma *n.* osteoclastoma.
osteoclasty *n.* osteoclastia.
osteocomma *n.* osteocoma.
osteocondensans *adj.* osteocondensante.
osteocope *n.* osteócopo.
osteocopic *adj.* osteocópico, -ca.
osteocranium *n.* osteocráneo, osteocranium.
osteocystoma *n.* osteocistoma.
osteocyte *n.* osteocito.
osteodensitometer *n.* osteodensitómetro.
osteodentin *n.* osteodentina.
osteodentinoma *n.* osteodentinoma.
osteodermatopoikilosis *n.* osteodermatopoikilosis.
osteodermatous *adj.* osteodermatoso, -sa.
osteodermia *n.* osteodermia.
osteodiastasis *n.* osteodiastasis.
osteodynia *n.* osteodinia.
osteodysplasty *n.* osteodisplasia.
osteodystrophia *n.* osteodistrofia.
osteodystrophy *n.* osteodistrofia.
  Albright's hereditary osteodystrophy osteodistrofia hereditaria de Albright.
  renal osteodystrophy osteodistrofia renal.
osteoectasia *n.* osteoectasia.
  familial osteoectasia osteoectasia familiar.
osteoectomy *n.* osteoectomía.
osteoenchondroma *n.* osteoencondroma.
osteoepiphysis *n.* osteoepífisis.
osteofibrochondrosarcoma *n.* osteofibrocondrosarcoma.
osteofibroma *n.* osteofibroma.
osteofibromatosis *n.* osteofibromatosis.
  cystic osteofibromatosis osteofibromatosis quística.
osteofibrosis *n.* osteofibrosis.
  periapical osteofibrosis osteofibrosis periapical.
osteofibrous *adj.* osteofibroso, -sa.
osteofluorosis *n.* osteofluorosis.
osteogen *n.* osteógeno.
osteogenesis *n.* osteogenesia, osteogénesis.
  defective osteogenesis osteogenesia imperfecta.
  electrically stimulated osteogenesis osteogenesia estimulada eléctricamente.
  osteogenesis imperfecta osteogenesia imperfecta.
osteogenetic *adj.* osteogenético, -ca.
osteogenic *adj.* osteogénico, -ca.
osteogenous *adj.* osteógeno, -na.
osteogeny *n.* osteogenia.
osteogram *n.* osteograma.
osteography *n.* osteografía.
osteohalisteresis *n.* osteohalistéresis.
osteohydatidosis *n.* osteohidatidosis.
osteohypertrophy *n.* osteohipertrofia.
osteoid *adj.* osteoide.
osteoinduction *n.* osteoinducción.
osteolipochondroma *n.* osteolipocondroma.
osteolipoma *n.* osteolipoma.
osteologia *n.* osteología.
osteologist *n.* osteólogo, -ga.
osteology *n.* osteología.
osteolysis *n.* osteólisis.
osteolytic *adj.* osteolítico, -ca.
osteoma *n.* osteoma.
  cavalryman's osteoma osteoma de soldado de caballería.
  compact osteoma osteoma compacto.
  dental osteoma osteoma dental.
  giant osteoid osteoma osteoma osteoide gigante.
  ivory osteoma osteoma ebúrneo.
  osteoid osteoma osteoma osteoide.

  osteoma cutis osteoma cutáneo.
  osteoma durum osteoma duro.
  osteoma medullare osteoma medular.
  osteoma sarcomatosum osteoma sarcomatoso.
  spongy osteoma osteoma esponjoso.
osteomalacia *n.* osteomalacia.
  hepatic osteomalacia osteomalacia hepática.
  infantile osteomalacia osteomalacia infantil.
  juvenile osteomalacia osteomalacia juvenil.
  puerperal osteomalacia osteomalacia puerperal.
  renal tubular osteomalacia osteomalacia tubular renal.
  senile osteomalacia osteomalacia senil.
  X-linked hypophosphatemic osteomalacia ostcomalacia hipofosfatémica ligada al cromosoma X.
osteomalacic *adj.* osteomalácico, -ca.
osteomalacosis *n.* osteomalacosis.
osteomatoid *adj.* osteomatoide, osteomatoideo, -a.
osteomatosis *n.* osteomatosis.
osteomere *n.* osteómera, osteómero.
osteomesopyknosis *n.* osteomesopicnosis.
osteometry *n.* osteometría.
osteomiositis *n.* osteomiositis.
osteomucin *n.* osteomucina.
osteomyelitic *adj.* osteomielítico, -ca.
osteomyelitis *n.* osteomielitis.
  conchiolin osteomyelitis osteomielitis por conciolina.
  cranial osteomyelitis osteomielitis craneal.
  Garré's osteomyelitis osteomielitis de Garré.
  malignant osteomyelitis osteomielitis maligna.
  osteomyelitis variolosa osteomielitis variolosa.
  salmonella osteomyelitis osteomielitis salmonella.
  sclerosing non-suppurative osteomyelitis osteomielitis esclerosante no supurada.
  typhoid osteomyelitis osteomielitis tifoidea.
  vertebral osteomyelitis osteomielitis vertebral.
osteomyelodysplasia *n.* osteomielodisplasia.
osteomyelography *n.* osteomielografía.
osteomyxochondroma *n.* osteomixocondroma.
osteon *n.* osteón.
osteoncus *n.* osteonco.
osteone *n.* osteona.
osteonecrosis *n.* osteonecrosis.
osteoneuralgia *n.* osteoneuralgia.
osteonosus *n.* osteonosis.
osteo-odontoma *n.* osteoodontoma.
osteo-onychodysplasia *n.* osteoonicodisplasia.
osteopath *n.* osteópata.
osteopathia *n.* osteopatía.
  osteopathia condensans generalisata osteopatía condensante generalizada.
  osteopathia hyperostotica congenita osteopatía hiperostótica congénita.
  osteopathia hyperostotica multiplex infantilis osteopatía hiperostótica múltiple infantil.
osteopathic *adj.* osteopático, -ca.
osteopathology *n.* osteopatología.
osteopathy *n.* osteopatía.
  alimentary osteopathy osteopatía alimentaria.
  condensing osteopathy osteopatía condensante.
  disseminated condensing osteopathy osteopatía condensante diseminada.

hunger osteopathy osteopatía de hambre, osteopatía por hambre.

myelogenic osteopathy osteopatía mielógena, osteopatía mielogénica.

pubis osteopathy osteopatía de pubis.

striated osteopathy osteopatía estriada.

osteopecilia *n.* osteopecilia.

osteopedion *n.* osteopedion.

osteopenia *n.* osteopenia.

osteopenic *adj.* osteopénico, -ca.

osteoperiosteal *adj.* osteoperióstico, -ca.

osteoperiostitis *n.* osteoperiostitis.

osteopetrosis *n.* osteopetrosis.

osteopetrotic *adj.* osteopetrósico, -ca, osteopetrótico, -ca.

osteophage *n.* osteófago.

osteophagia *n.* osteofagia.

osteophlebitis *n.* osteoflebitis.

osteophone *n.* osteófono.

osteophony *n.* osteofonía.

osteophyma *n.* osteofima.

osteophyte *n.* osteófito.

osteophytosis *n.* ostcofitosis.

osteoplaque *n.* osteoplaca.

osteoplasia *n.* osteoplasia.

osteoplast *n.* osteoplasto.

osteoplastic *adj.* osteoplástico, -ca.

osteoplasty *n.* osteoplastia.

osteopoikilosis *n.* osteopoiquilosis.

osteopoikilotic *adj.* osteopoiquilótico, -ca.

osteoporomalacia *n.* osteoporomalacia.

osteoporosis *n.* osteoporosis.

 juvenile osteoporosis osteoporosis juvenil.

 osteoporosis circumscripta cranii osteoporosis craneal circunscrita.

 osteoporosis of disuse osteoporosis por desuso, osteoporosis por reposo excesivo.

 postmenopausal osteoporosis osteoporosis posmenopáusica.

 post-traumatic osteoporosis osteoporosis postraumática.

 senile osteoporosis osteoporosis senil.

osteoporotic *adj.* osteoporótico, -ca.

osteopsathyrosis *n.* osteopsatirosis.

osteoradiodensitometry *n.* osteodensitometría.

osteoradionecrosis *n.* osteorradionecrosis.

osteorrhagia *n.* osteorragia.

osteorrhaphy *n.* osteorrafia.

osteosarcoma *n.* osteosarcoma.

 chondroblastic osteosarcoma osteosarcoma condroblástico.

 extraskeletal osteosarcoma osteosarcoma extraesquelético.

 fibroblastic osteosarcoma osteosarcoma fibroblástico.

 juxtacortical osteosarcoma osteosarcoma yuxtacortical.

 multifocal osteosarcoma osteosarcoma multifocal.

 osteoblastic osteosarcoma osteosarcoma osteoblástico.

 periostic osteosarcoma osteosarcoma perióstico.

 small cell osteosarcoma osteosarcoma de células pequeñas.

 telangiectatic osteosarcoma osteosarcoma telangiectásico.

osteosarcomatous *adj.* osteosarcomatoso, -sa.

osteosclerosis *n.* osteoesclerosis.

 disseminated osteosclerosis osteoesclerosis diseminada.

 Faneras' osteosclerosis osteoesclerosis endóstica pneumica de Faneras.

 fluor osteosclerosis osteoesclerosis del flúor.

osteopetrosis osteosclerosis osteoesclerosis osteopetrosis.

osteosclerosis congenita osteoesclerosis congénita.

osteosclerosis fragilis osteoesclerosis frágil.

osteosclerosis fragilis generalisata osteoesclerosis frágil generalizada.

osteosclerosis myelofibrosis osteoesclerosis mielofibromatosa.

osteosclerotic *adj.* osteoesclerótico, -ca.

osteoscope *n.* osteoscopio.

osteoseptum *n.* osteosepto, osteoseptum.

osteosis *n.* osteosis.

 osteosis cutis osteosis cutánea.

 osteosis eburnisans monomelica osteosis eburnizante monomélica.

 parathyroid osteosis osteosis paratiroidea.

 renal fibrocystic osteosis osteosis fibroquística renal.

osteospongioma *n.* osteoespongioma, osteospongioma.

osteosteatoma *n.* osteoesteatoma.

osteostixis *n.* osteostixis.

osteosuture *n.* osteosutura.

osteosynovitis *n.* osteosinovitis.

osteosynthesis *n.* osteosíntesis.

osteotabes *n.* osteotabes.

osteotelangiectasia *n.* osteotelangiectasia.

osteothrombophlebitis *n.* osteotromboflebitis.

osteothrombosis *n.* osteotrombosis.

osteotome *n.* osteótomo.

osteotomoclasia *n.* osteotomoclasia.

osteotomoclasis *n.* osteotomoclasia, osteotomoclasis.

osteotomy *n.* osteotomía.

 abduction osteotomy osteotomía de abducción.

 adduction osteotomy osteotomía de adducción.

 angulation osteotomy osteotomía de angulación.

 block osteotomy osteotomía en bloque.

 C sliding osteotomy osteotomía deslizante en.

 Chiari's osteotomy osteotomía de Chiari.

 cuneiform osteotomy osteotomía cuneiforme.

 cup-and-ball osteotomy osteotomía esférica.

 displacement osteotomy osteotomía de desplazamiento.

 hinge osteotomy osteotomía en bisagra.

 horizontal osteotomy osteotomía horizontal.

 iliac osteotomy osteotomía ilíaca.

 innominate osteotomy osteotomía ilíaca.

 linear osteotomy osteotomía lineal.

 Lorenz's osteotomy osteotomía de Lorenz.

 opening abductory wedge osteotomy (OAWO) osteotomía abductora en cuña de apertura (OACA).

 opening wedge osteotomy osteotomía en cuña de apertura.

 pelvic osteotomy osteotomía pélvica, osteotomía púbica.

 sagittal split mandibular osteotomy osteotomía mandibular dividida sagital.

 segmental alveolar osteotomy osteotomía alveolar segmentaria.

 sliding oblique osteotomy osteotomía deslizante oblicua.

 valgus osteotomy osteotomía valguizante, osteotomía varizante.

 varus osteotomy osteotomía valguizante, osteotomía varizante.

 vertical osteotomy osteotomía vertical.

osteotribe *n.* osteotribo.

osteotrite *n.* osteotrito.

osteotrophy *n.* osteotrofia.

osteotylus *n.* osteotilo.

osthexia *n.* ostexia.

osthexy *n.* ostexia.

ostial *adj.* ostial.

ostiary *adj.* ostiario, -ria.

ostitic *adj.* ostítico, -ca.

ostitis *n.* ostitis.

ostium *n.* abertura, ostium.

 ostium primum defect ostium primum.

 ostium secundum defect ostium secundum.

ostomate *adj.* ostomado, -da, ostomizado, -da.

ostomy *n.* ostomía.

ostosis *n.* ostosis.

ostraceous *adj.* ostráceo, -a.

ostracosis *n.* ostracosis.

ostreotoxism *n.* ostreotoxismo.

otagra *n.* otagra.

otalgia *n.* otalgia.

 geniculate otalgia otalgia geniculada.

 otalgia dentalis otalgia dental.

 otalgia intermittens otalgia intermitente.

 reflex otalgia otalgia refleja.

 secondary tabetic otalgia otalgia tabética secundaria.

otalgic *adj.* otálgico, -ca.

otaphone *n.* otáfono.

othematoma *n.* otohematoma.

othemorrhagia *n.* otohemorragia.

otiatria *n.* otiatría.

otiatrics *n.* otiatría.

otic *adj.* ótico, -ca.

otitic *adj.* otítico, -ca.

otitis *n.* otitis.

 adhesive otitis otitis adhesiva.

 adhesive otitis media otitis media adhesiva.

 aviation otitis o del aviador, otitis de aviación, otitis de los aviadores.

 barotraumatic otitis media otitis media barotraumática.

 external otitis otitis externa.

 fibroadhesive otitis media otitis media fibroadhesiva.

 furuncular otitis o furunculosa, otitis foruncular.

 malignant otitis externa otitis externa maligna.

 mucosus otitis otitis mucosa.

 otitis crouposa otitis crupal, otitis cruposa.

 otitis desquamativa otitis descamativa.

 otitis diphtheritica otitis diftérica.

 otitis externa otitis externa.

 otitis externa circumscripta otitis externa circunscrita.

 otitis externa diffusa otitis externa difusa.

 otitis externa furunculosa otitis externa forunculosa.

 otitis furunculosa o furunculosa, otitis foruncular.

 otitis interna otitis interna.

 otitis intima otitis íntima.

 otitis labyrinthica otitis laberíntica.

 otitis mastoidea otitis mastoidea.

 otitis media otitis media.

 otitis media adhesiva otitis media adhesiva.

 otitis media catarrhalis acuta otitis media catarral aguda.

 otitis media catarrhalis chronica otitis media catarral crónica.

 otitis media purulenta otitis media purulenta.

 otitis media purulenta acuta otitis media purulenta aguda.

 otitis media purulenta chronica otitis media purulenta crónica.

otitis media sclerotica otitis media esclerótica.
otitis media serosa otitis media serosa.
otitis media suppurativa otitis media supurada, otitis media supurativa.
otitis media vasomotorica otitis vasomotora.
otitis mycotica otitis micótica.
otitis sclerotica otitis esclerótica.
reflux otitis media otitis media de reflujo.
secretory otitis media otitis media secretoria.
serous otitis otitis serosa.
serous otitis media otitis media serosa.
otoantritis *n.* otoantritis.
otoblennorrhea *n.* otoblenorrea.
otocephalus *n.* otocéfalo.
otocephaly *n.* otocefalia.
otocerebritis *n.* otocerebritis.
otocleisis *n.* otocleisis.
otoconia *n.* otoconias.
otocranial *adj.* otocraneal.
otocranium *n.* otocráneo.
otocyst *n.* otocisto.
otodynia *n.* otodinia.
otoencephalitis *n.* otoencefalitis.
otoganglion *n.* otoganglio.
otogenic *adj.* otogénico, -ca.
otogenous *adj.* otógeno, -na.
otography *n.* otografía.
otohemineurasthenia *n.* otohemineurastenia.
otolaryngologist *n.* otolaringólogo, -ga.
otolaryngology *n.* otolaringología.
otolite *n.* otolito.
otolith *n.* otolito.
otolithiasis *n.* otolitiasis.
otologic *adj.* otológico, -ca.
otologist *n.* otólogo, -ga.
otology *n.* otología.
otomastoiditis *n.* otomastoiditis.
otomucormycosis *n.* otomucormicosis.
otomyasthenia *n.* otomiastenia.
Otomyces Otomyces.
otomycosis *n.* otomicosis.
otomyiasis *n.* otomiasis.
otoneuralgia *n.* otoneuralgia.
otoneurasthenia *n.* otoneurastenia.
otoneurologic *adj.* otoneurológico, -ca.
otoneurology *n.* otoneurología.
otopalatodigital *adj.* otopalatodigital.
otopathy *n.* otopatía.
otopharyngeal *adj.* otofaríngeo, -a.
otophone *n.* otófono.
otoplasty *n.* otoplastia.
otopolypus *n.* otopólipo.
otopyorrhea *n.* otopiorrea.
otopyosis *n.* otopiosis.
otor *adj.* ótico, -ca.
otorhinolaryngologist *n.* otorrinolaringólogo, -ga.
otorhinolaryngology *n.* otorrinolaringología.
otorhinology *n.* otorrinología.
otorrhagia *n.* otorragia.
otorrhea *n.* otorrea.
  cerebrospinal fluid otorrhea otorrea de líquido cefalorraquídeo.
otosalpinx *n.* otosalpinge, otosalpinx.
otosclerosis *n.* otoesclerosis, otosclerosis.
otosclerotic *adj.* otoesclerótico, -ca, otosclerótico, -ca.
otoscope *n.* otoscopio.
  Brunton's otoscope otoscopio de Brunton.
  Siegle's otoscope otoscopio de Siegle.
  Tonybee's otoscope otoscopio de Toynbee.
otoscopy *n.* otoscopia.

otosis *n.* otosis.
otospongiosis *n.* otoespongiosis, otospongiosis.
ototomy *n.* ototomía.
ototoxic *adj.* ototóxico, -ca.
ototoxicity *n.* ototoxicidad.
oulectomy *n.* oulectomía, ulectomía.
oulitis *n.* oulitis, ulitis.
oulonitis *n.* oulonitis.
oulorragia *n.* ulorragia.
oulorrhagia *n.* oulorragia.
outlet *n.* salida.
outlier *n.* dato aberrante.
output *n.* gasto, salidas.
  cardiac output gasto cardíaco.
  energy output gasto de energía.
  stroke output gasto por contracción.
  urinary output gasto urinario.
oval *adj.* oval, ovalado, -da.
ovalbumin *n.* ovalbúmina.
ovalocytary *adj.* ovalocitario, -ria.
ovalocyte *n.* ovalocito.
ovalocytosis *n.* ovalocitosis.
ovarialgia *n.* ovarialgia.
ovarian *adj.* ovárico, -ca.
ovariectomy *n.* ovariectomía.
ovariocele *n.* ovariocele.
ovariocentesis *n.* ovariocentesis.
ovariocyesis *n.* ovariociesis.
ovariodysneuria *n.* ovariodisneuria.
ovariogenic *adj.* ovariogénico, -ca, ovariógeno, -na.
ovariohysterectomy *n.* ovariohisterectomía.
ovariolytic *adj.* ovariolítico, -ca.
ovarioncus *n.* ovarionco.
ovariopathy *n.* ovariopatía.
ovariopexy *n.* ovariopexia.
ovariorrhexis *n.* ovariorrexis.
ovariosalpingectomy *n.* ovariosalpingectomía.
ovariosalpingitis *n.* ovariosalpingitis.
ovariosteresis *n.* ovariostéresis.
ovariostomy *n.* ovariostomía.
ovariotestis *n.* ovariotestis.
ovariotherapy *n.* ovarioterapia.
ovariotomy *n.* ovariotomía.
  abdominal ovariotomy ovariotomía abdominal.
  vaginal ovariotomy ovariotomía vaginal.
ovariotubal *adj.* ovariotubárico, -ca.
ovaritis *n.* ovaritis.
ovarium ovario, ovarium.
  ovarium bipartitum ovario bipartito.
  ovarium gyratum ovarium gyratum.
  ovarium lobatum ovario lobulado.
  ovarium masculinum ovario masculino.
ovarotherapy *n.* ovaroterapia.
ovary *n.* ovario.
  adenocystic ovary ovario adenoquístico.
  oyster ovary ovario de ostra.
  polycystic ovary ovario poliquístico.
overbite *n.* sobremordida.
overcorrection *n.* sobrecorrección.
overdetermination *n.* sobredeterminación.
overdosage *n.* sobredosificación.
overdose *n.* sobredosis.
overextension *n.* sobreextensión.
overfeeding *n.* sobrealimentación.
overhydration *n.* hiperhidratación.
overinclusiveness *n.* hiperinclusividad.
overjet *n.* resalto.
overjut *n.* resalto.
overlap *n.* superposición.
  horizontal overlap superposición horizontal.
  vertical overlap superposición vertical.

overlay *n.* añadido.
  functional overlay cobertura funcional.
overloading *n.* sobrecarga.
overriding *n.* cabalgamiento.
oversampling *n.* superposición.
overstrain *n.* sobrefatiga.
overwintering *n.* invernación.
ovicidal *adj.* ovicida[2].
ovicide *n.* ovicida[1].
oviducal *adj.* oviductal.
oviduct *n.* oviducto.
oviductal *adj.* oviductal.
oviferous *adj.* ovífero, -ra.
oviform *adj.* oviforme.
ovigenesis *n.* ovigénesis.
ovigenetic *adj.* ovigenético, -ca.
ovigenic *adj.* ovigénico, -ca.
ovigenous *adj.* ovígeno, -na.
ovigerm *n.* ovigermen.
ovigerous *adj.* ovígero, -ra.
oviparity *n.* oviparidad.
oviposition *n.* oviposición, ovipostura.
ovisac *n.* ovísaco.
ovocyte *n.* ovocito.
ovogenesis *n.* ovogenesia, ovogénesis.
ovoglobulin *n.* ovoglobulina.
ovoid *n.* ovoide.
  fetal ovoid ovoide fetal.
  Manchester ovoid ovoide de Manchester.
ovolysin *n.* ovolisina.
ovolytic *adj.* ovolítico, -ca.
ovomucin *n.* ovomucina.
ovomucoid *n.* ovomucoide.
ovoplasm *n.* ovoplasma.
ovoprecipitin *n.* ovoprecipitina.
ovoprotogen *n.* ovoprotógeno.
ovotestis *n.* ovotestículo, ovotestis.
ovotherapy *n.* ovoterapia.
ovotransferrin *n.* ovotransferrina.
ovovitelin *n.* ovovitelina.
ovovitellin *n.* ovovitelina.
ovular *adj.* ovular.
ovulase *n.* ovulasa.
ovulation *n.* ovulación.
  amenstrual ovulation ovulación amenstrual.
  paracyclic ovulation ovulación paracíclica.
  supplementary ovulation ovulación complementaria.
ovulatory *adj.* ovulativo, -va, ovulatorio, -ria.
ovule *n.* óvulo,.
  Graafian ovule óvulo de Graaf.
  Naboth's ovule óvulo de Naboth.
  Peter's ovule óvulo de Peters.
  primitive ovule óvulo primitivo.
  primordial ovule óvulo primordial.
ovulocyclic *adj.* ovulocíclico, -ca.
ovulogenous *adj.* ovulógeno, -na.
ovum *n.* huevo, óvulo,, ovum.
  fertilized ovum óvulo fecundado, óvulo fertilizado.
  Peter's ovum óvulo de Peters.
  primitive ovum óvulo primitivo.
  primordial ovum óvulo primordial.
  vaginal ovum óvulo vaginal.
oxalate *n.* oxalato.
oxalated *adj.* oxalatado, -da.
oxalation *n.* oxalación.
oxalemia *n.* oxalemia.
oxalism *n.* oxalismo.
oxaloacetate *n.* oxalacetato, oxaloacetato.
oxalosis *n.* oxalosis.
oxaluria *n.* oxaluria.
oxamide *n.* oxamida.
oxamniquine *n.* oxamniquina.
oxandrolone *n.* oxandrolona.

oxidant *adj.* oxidante.
oxidasis *n.* oxidasis.
oxidation *n.* oxidación.
 beta oxidation oxidación beta.
 biological oxidation oxidación biológica.
 coupled oxidation oxidación acoplada.
 fatty acid oxidation oxidación de ácidos grasos.
 omega oxidation omega oxidación.
oxidation-reduction *n.* oxidación-reducción, oxidorreducción.
oxidative *adj.* oxidativo, -va.
oxide *n.* óxido.
 ethyl oxide óxido de etilo.
 ethylene oxide óxido de etileno.
 indifferent oxide óxido indiferente.
 neutral oxide óxido neutro.
 nitric oxide óxido nítrico.
 nitrous oxide óxido nitroso.
 red mercuric oxide óxido mercúrico rojo.
 yellow mercuric oxide óxido mercúrico amarillo.
oxidization *n.* oxidización.
oxidize *v.* oxidar.
oxidized *adj.* oxidado, -da.
oxidoreductase *n.* oxidorreductasa.
oxidosis *n.* oxidosis.
oxigeusia *n.* oxigeusia.
oximeter *n.* oxímetro.
 cuvette oximeter oxímetro de cubeta.
 ear oximeter oxímetro auditivo.
 intracardiac oximeter oxímetro intracardíaco.
oximetry *n.* oximetría.
oximinotransferase *n.* oximinotransferasa.
oxiphil *adj.* oxífilo, -la.
oxiphonia *n.* oxifonía.
oxonemia *n.* oxonemia.
oxonuria *n.* oxonuria.
oxoprolinuria (5-oxoprolinuria) *n.* 5-oxoprolinuria.
oxozone *n.* oxozono.
oxyacoia *n.* oxiacoia.
oxyakoia *n.* oxiacoia.
oxyaphia *n.* oxiafia.
oxybarbiturate *n.* oxibarbitúrico.
oxyblepsia *n.* oxiblepsia, oxiblepsis.
oxybutyria *n.* oxibutiria, oxibutiruria.
oxybutyricacidemia *n.* oxibutiricacidemia.
oxycalorimeter *n.* oxicalorímetro.
oxycephalia *n.* oxicefalia.
oxycephalic *adj.* oxicefálico, -ca.
oxycephalous *adj.* oxicéfalo, -la.

oxycephaly *n.* oxicefalia.
oxycholine *n.* oxicolina.
oxychromatic *adj.* oxicromático, -ca.
oxychromatin *n.* oxicromatina.
oxycinesia *n.* oxicinesia.
oxydoreductase *n.* oxidorreductasa.
oxyecoia *n.* oxiecoia.
oxyesthesia *n.* oxiestesia.
oxygen *n.* oxígeno.
 excess oxygen oxígeno en exceso.
 heavy oxygen oxígeno pesado.
 high pressure oxygen oxígeno de presión elevada, oxígeno hiperbárico.
 hyperbaric oxygen oxígeno de presión elevada, oxígeno hiperbárico.
 molecular oxygen oxígeno molecular.
 nascent oxygen oxígeno naciente.
 singlet oxygen oxígeno singulete, oxígeno singlete.
 transtracheal oxygen oxígeno transtraqueal.
oxygenase *n.* oxigenasa.
oxygenate *v.* oxigenar.
oxygenated *adj.* oxigenado, -da.
oxygenation *n.* oxigenación.
 apneic oxygenation oxigenación apneica.
 extracorporeal oxygenation oxigenación extracorpórea.
 hyperbaric oxygenation oxigenación hiperbárica.
oxygenator *n.* oxigenador.
 disk oxygenator oxigenador de disco, oxigenador de disco giratorio.
 film oxygenator oxigenador de película.
 membrane oxygenator oxigenador de membrana.
 rotating disk oxygenator oxigenador de disco, oxigenador de disco giratorio.
 screen oxygenator oxigenador de pantalla.
oxygenic *adj.* oxigénico, -ca.
oxygenize *v.* oxigenizar.
oxygentherapy *n.* oxigenoterapia.
oxyheme *n.* oxihem.
oxyhemochromogen *n.* oxihemocromógeno.
oxyhemocyanine *n.* oxihemocianina.
oxyhemoglobin *n.* oxihemoglobina.
oxyhemoglobinometer *n.* oxihemoglobinómetro.
oxyhemogram *n.* oxihemograma.
oxyhemograph *n.* oxihemógrafo.
oxyhydrocephalus *n.* oxihidrocéfalo.
oxyiodide *n.* oxiyoduro.
oxylalia *n.* oxilalia.

Oxymonadida Oxymonadida.
oxymyoglobin *n.* oximioglobina.
oxynervon *n.* oxinervona.
oxynervone *n.* oxinervona.
oxyntic *adj.* oxíntico, -ca.
oxyopia *n.* oxiopía, oxiopsia.
oxyopter *n.* oxioptría.
oxyosis *n.* oxidosis, oxiosis.
oxyosmia *n.* oxiosmia.
oxyosphresia *n.* oxiosfresia.
oxyparaplastin *n.* oxiparaplastina.
oxypathia *n.* oxipatía.
oxyperitoneum *n.* oxiperitoneo.
oxyphilic *adj.* oxifílico, -ca.
oxyphilous *adj.* oxifílico, -ca.
oxyphonia *n.* oxifonía.
oxyphorase *n.* oxiforasa.
oxyplasm *n.* oxiplasma.
oxypurinase *n.* oxipurinasa.
oxypurine *n.* oxipurina.
oxyrhine *adj.* oxirrino, -na.
Oxyspirura Oxyspirura.
oxytalan *n.* oxitalán.
oxytalanolysis *n.* oxitalanólisis.
oxytocia *n.* oxitocia.
oxytocic *adj.* oxitócico, -ca.
oxytocin (OXT) *n.* oxitocina (OXT).
oxytoxin *n.* oxitoxina.
oxytropism *n.* oxitropismo.
oxytuberculin *n.* oxituberculina.
oxyuria *n.* oxiuria.
oxyuriasis *n.* oxiuriasis.
oxyuricide *n.* oxiuricida.
oxyurid *n.* oxiúrido.
oxyurifuge *adj.* oxiurífugo, -ga.
oxyuriosis *n.* oxiuriosis.
oxyuris *n.* oxiuro.
oxyuroid *n.* oxiuroide.
Oxyuroidea Oxyuroidea.
ozena *n.* ocena, ozena.
 ozena laryngis ozena laríngea.
ozenous *adj.* ocenoso, -sa.
ozonator *n.* ozonador.
ozone *n.* ozono.
ozonide *n.* ozónido.
ozonize *v.* ozonizar.
ozonizer *n.* ozonizador.
ozonolysis *n.* ozonólisis.
ozonometer *n.* ozonómetro.
ozonophore *n.* ozonóforo.
ozonoscope *n.* ozonoscopio.
ozostomia *n.* ozostomía.

P*p*

pabular *adj.* pabular.
pabulum *n.* pábulo.
pacemaker *n.* marcapaso, marcapasos.
  artificial cardiac pacemaker marcapaso cardíaco artificial.
  artificial pacemaker marcapaso artificial.
  asynchronous pacemaker marcapaso asincrónico.
  cilium pacemaker marcapaso ciliar.
  demand pacemaker marcapaso de demanda, marcapaso por demanda.
  ectopic pacemaker marcapaso ectópico.
  electric cardiac pacemaker marcapaso cardíaco eléctrico.
  external pacemaker marcapaso externo.
  fixed-rate pacemaker marcapaso de frecuencia fija, marcapaso de ritmo fijo.
  gastric pacemaker marcapaso gástrico.
  implanted internal pacemaker marcapaso implantado interno.
  natural pacemaker marcapaso natural.
  pacemaker of the heart marcapaso del corazón.
  permanent pacemaker marcapaso permanente.
  pervenous pacemaker marcapaso pervenoso.
  programmable pacemaker marcapaso programable.
  radiofrequency pacemaker marcapaso de radiofrecuencia.
  shifting pacemaker marcapaso deslizable.
  sinus pacemaker marcapaso sinusal.
  subsidiary atrial pacemaker marcapaso auricular subsidiario.
  synchronous pacemaker marcapaso sincrónico.
  temporary pacemaker marcapaso transitorio.
  transthoracic pacemaker marcapaso transtorácico.
  transvenous catheter pacemaker catéter marcapaso transvenoso.
  wandering atrial pacemaker marcapaso auricular errante.
  wandering pacemaker marcapaso errante, marcapaso migratorio.
pachometer *n.* pacómetro, paquímetro.
pachyacria *n.* paquiacria.
pachyblepharon *n.* paquibléfaron.
pachycephaly *n.* paquicefalia.
pachycheilia *n.* paquiqueilia.
pachychilia *n.* paquiquilia.
pachycholia *n.* paquicolia.
pachychromatic *adj.* paquicromático, -ca.
pachycolpismus *n.* paquicolpismo.
pachydactylia *n.* paquidactilia.
pachydermatocele *n.* paquidermatocele.
pachydermatosis *n.* paquidermatosis.
pachydermia *n.* paquidermia.
  pachydermia laryngis paquidermia laríngea.

pachydermia lymphangiectatica paquidermia linfangiectásica.
pachyemia *n.* paquiemia.
pachyglossia *n.* paquiglosia.
pachygnatous *adj.* paquignato, -ta.
pachyhemia *n.* paquihemia.
pachylosis *n.* paculosis, paquilosis.
pachymenia *n.* paquimenia.
pachymeningitis *n.* paquimeningitis.
  hemorrhagic internal pachymeningitis paquimeningitis hemorrágica interna.
  hypertrophic cervical pachymeningitis paquimeningitis cervical hipertrófica.
  pachymeningitis intralamellaris paquimeningitis intralaminar.
  purulent pachymeningitis paquimeningitis purulenta.
  serous internal pachymeningitis paquimeningitis serosa interna.
pachymeninx *n.* paquimeninge.
pachymeter *n.* paquímetro.
pachynema *n.* paquinema.
pachynsis *n.* paquinsis.
pachyonychia *n.* paquioniquia.
pachyotia *n.* paquiotia.
pachypelviperitonitis *n.* paquipelviperitonitis.
pachyperiosteoderma *n.* paquiperiosteoderma.
pachyperiostitis *n.* paquiperiostitis.
pachyperitonitis *n.* paquiperitonitis.
pachypleuritis *n.* paquipleuritis.
pachysalpingitis *n.* paquisalpingitis.
pachysalpingo-ovaritis *n.* paquisalpingoovaritis.
pachyvaginalitis *n.* paquivaginalitis.
pachyvaginitis *n.* paquivaginitis.
  pachyvaginitis cystica paquivaginitis quística.
pack *n.* envoltura², taponamiento.
  Mikulicz pack taponamiento de Mikulicz.
  periodontal pack taponamiento periodontal.
  throat pack taponamiento faríngeo.
packer *n.* empacador, taponador².
packing *n.* empacamiento, taponamiento.
  denture packing empacamiento protésico.
  nasal packing taponamiento nasal.
pad *n.* almohadilla.
  abdominal pad almohadilla abdominal.
  Bichat's fat pad almohadilla adiposa de Bichat.
  buccal fat pad almohadilla grasa bucal.
  corn pad almohadilla para callo.
  dinner pad almohadilla de alimentación.
  donut pad almohadilla en donut.
  fat pad almohadilla adiposa, almohadilla grasa.
  girdle pad almohadilla pélvica.
  infrapatellar fat pad almohadilla grasa infrarrotuliana.
  Kelly's pad almohadilla de Kelly.

  kidney pad almohadilla renal.
  knuckle pad almohadilla de los nudillos.
  laparotomy pad almohadilla de laparotomía.
  navicular pad almohadilla navicular.
  Passavant's pad almohadilla de Passavant.
  periarterial pad almohadilla periarterial.
  retromolar pad almohadilla retromolar.
  sucking pad almohadilla de succión.
  suctorial pad almohadilla de succión.
pagetoid *adj.* pagetoide.
pain *n.* algia, dolor.
  abdominal pain dolor abdominal.
  acute pain dolor agudo.
  appendicitis pain dolor de apendicitis.
  atypical facial pain algia facial atípica.
  bearing-down pain dolor "para abajo", dolor de pujos".
  boring pain dolor terebrante.
  burning pain dolor urente.
  cardiac pain dolor cardíaco.
  central pain dolor central.
  chest pain dolor torácico.
  chronic intractable pain dolor crónico resistente al tratamiento.
  chronic pain dolor crónico.
  dilating pain dolor de dilatación.
  dream pain dolor en sueños.
  dull pain dolor sordo.
  epigastric pain dolor epigástrico.
  expulsive pain dolor de expulsión, dolor expulsivo.
  fulgurant pain dolor fulgurante.
  gas pain dolor de gas.
  girdle pain dolor en cinturón.
  growing pain dolor de crecimiento, dolor del crecimiento.
  heterotopic pain dolor heterotópico.
  homotopic pain dolor homotópico.
  hunger pain dolor de hambre.
  ideogenous pain dolor ideógeno.
  imperative pain dolor imperativo.
  intermenstrual pain dolor intermenstrual.
  intractable pain dolor intratable, dolor resistente al tratamiento.
  ischemic pain dolor isquémico.
  jumping pain dolor saltante.
  labor pain dolor de parto.
  lightning pain dolor lancinante.
  low back pain dolor de la región inferior de la espalda, lumbalgia.
  mind pain dolor de la mente, dolor mental.
  nerve pain dolor nervioso.
  night pain dolor nocturno.
  organic pain dolor orgánico.
  osteocopic pain dolor osteocópico.
  parietal pain dolor parietal.
  pelvic pain dolor pélvico.
  phantom limb pain dolor de la extremidad fantasma.
  postprandial pain dolor posprandial.

precordial pain dolor precordial.
premonitory pain dolor premonitorio.
psychic pain dolor psíquico.
psychogenic pain dolor psicogénico.
psychosomatic pain dolor psicosomático.
referred pain dolor referido.
rest pain dolor de reposo, dolor en reposo.
root pain dolor de raíz.
spot pains dolor en manchas.
starting pain dolor sobresaltante.
tracheal pain dolor traqueal.
visceral pain dolor visceral.
wandering pain dolor errante, dolor errático.
paint *n.* pincelación.
pairing *n.* apareamiento.
base pairing apareamiento de bases.
chromosome pairing apareamiento de los cromosomas.
random pairing apareamiento al azar.
palatal *adj.* palatal.
palate *n.* paladar.
artificial palate paladar artificial.
cleft palate paladar fisurado, paladar hendido.
falling palate paladar caído.
smoker's palate paladar del fumador.
palatiform *adj.* palatiforme.
palatine *adj.* palatino, -na.
palatitis *n.* palatitis.
palatoglossal *adj.* palatogloso, -sa.
palatognathous *adj.* palatognato, -ta.
palatography *n.* palatografía.
palatomaxillary *adj.* palatomaxilar.
palatomyography *n.* palatomiografía.
palatonasal *adj.* palatonasal.
palatopagus *n.* palatópago.
palatopharyngeal *adj.* palatofaríngeo, -a.
palatoplasty *n.* palatoplastia.
palatoplegia *n.* palatoplejía.
palatorrhaphy *n.* palatorrafia.
palatosalpingeus *n.* palatosalpíngeo, -a.
palatoschisis *n.* palatosquisis.
palatum paladar, palatum.
paleocinetic *adj.* paleocinético, -ca.
paleocortex *n.* paleocórtex, paleopalio.
paleogenesis *n.* paleogénesis.
paleokinetic *adj.* paleocinético, -ca.
paleostriatum paleoestriado, paleostriatum.
paleothalamus *n.* paleotálamo.
palilalia *n.* palilalia.
palinesthesia *n.* palinestesia.
palingenesis *n.* palingénesis.
palinopsia *n.* palinopsia.
paliphrasia *n.* palifrasia.
palisade *n.* empalizada.
pallanesthesia *n.* palanestesia.
pallescense *n.* palescencia.
pallesthesia *n.* palestesia, vibrosensibilidad.
pallial *adj.* palial.
palliate *v.* paliar.
palliative *adj.* paliativo, -va.
pallidal *adj.* palidal.
pallium palio, pallium.
pallor *n.* palidez.
palm *n.* palma.
hand ball palm palma de deportista.
liver palm palma hepática.
palmanesthesia *n.* palanestesia, palmanestesia.
palmar *adj.* palmar.
palmature *n.* palmatura.
palmesthesia *n.* palestesia, palmestesia.
palmic *adj.* pálmico, -ca.
palmoscopy *n.* palmoscopia.
palmprint *n.* huella palmar.
palmus *n.* palmo, palmus.

palpable *adj.* palpable.
palpation *n.* palpación.
bimanual palpation palpación bimanual.
palpatometry *n.* palpatometría.
palpatopercussion *n.* palpatopercusión.
palpebra *n.* párpado.
palpebral *adj.* palpebral.
palpebration *n.* palpebración.
palpebritis *n.* palpebritis.
palpitation *n.* palpitación.
paludal *adj.* palúdico, -ca.
paludide *n.* palúdide.
paludism *n.* paludosis.
pamphobia *n.* panfobia.
panangiitis *n.* panangeítis.
panarteritis *n.* panarteritis.
panarthritis *n.* panartritis.
panasthesia *n.* panastesia.
pancarditis *n.* pancarditis.
pancreas *n.* páncreas.
accessory pancreas páncreas accesorio.
annular pancreas páncreas anular.
Asselli's pancreas páncreas de Aselli.
pancreas accessorium páncreas accesorio.
pancreas minus páncreas menor.
small pancreas páncreas menor.
Willis' pancreas páncreas de Willis.
Winslow's pancreas páncreas de Winslow.
pancreatalgia *n.* pancreatalgia.
pancreatectomy *n.* pancreatectomía.
pancreatemphraxis *n.* pancreatenfraxis.
pancreaticocholecistostomy *n.* Pancreaticocolecistostomía.
pancreaticoduodenal *adj.* pancreaticoduodenal.
pancreaticoduodenostomy *n.* pancreaticoduodenostomía.
pancreaticoenterestomy *n.* pancreaticoenterostomía.
pancreaticojejunostomy *n.* pancreaticoyeyunostomía.
pancreaticosplenic *adj.* pancreaticoesplénico, -ca.
pancreatism *n.* pancreatismo.
pancreatitis *n.* pancreatitis.
acute pancreatitis pancreatitis aguda.
calcareous pancreatitis pancreatitis calcárea.
centrilobar pancreatitis pancreatitis centrilobular.
chronic pancreatitis pancreatitis crónica.
chronic relapsing pancreatitis pancreatitis recidivante crónica.
interstitial pancreatitis pancreatitis intersticial.
purulent pancreatitis pancreatitis purulenta.
pancreatoduodenectomy *n.* pancreatoduodenectomía.
pancreatogenic *adj.* pancreatógeno, -na.
pancreatogenous *adj.* pancreatógeno, -na.
pancreatography *n.* pancreatografía.
pancreatolith *n.* pancreatolito.
pancreatolithectomy *n.* pancreatolitectomía.
pancreatolithotomy *n.* pancreatolitotomía, pancreolitotomía.
pancreatolysis *n.* pancreatólisis.
pancreatomy *n.* pancreaticotomía.
pancreatoncus *n.* pancreatonco.
pancreatopathy *n.* pancreatopatía, pancreopatía.
pancreatotomy *n.* pancreatotomía.
pancreatotropic *adj.* pancreatotrópico, -ca.
pancreatropic *adj.* pancreatrópico, -ca.
pancreectomy *n.* pancreectomía.
pancreolysis *n.* pancreólisis.

pancreoprivic *adj.* pancreoprivo, -va.
pancreotherapy *n.* pancreoterapia.
pancreozymin *n.* pancreocimina.
pancretomy *n.* pancreatomía.
pancystitis *n.* pancistitis.
pancytopenia *n.* pancitopenia.
congenital pancytopenia pancitopenia congénita.
Falconi's pancytopenia pancitopenia de Fanconi.
pandemia *n.* pandemia.
pandemic *adj.* pandémico, -ca.
pandiculation *n.* pandiculación.
panelectroscope *n.* panelectroscopio.
panencephalitis *n.* panencefalitis.
subacute sclerosing panencephalitis panencefalitis esclerosante subaguda.
panesthesia *n.* panestesia.
pangenesis *n.* pangénesis, pangenia.
panglossia *n.* panglosia.
panhematopenia *n.* panhematopenia.
panhidrosis *n.* panhidrosis, panidrosis.
panhyperemia *n.* panhiperemia.
panhystero-oophorectomy *n.* panhisterosalpingooforectomía.
panic *n.* pánico.
panimmunity *n.* paninmunidad.
panmixia *n.* panmixia.
panmyelopathy *n.* panmielopatía.
constitutional infantile panmyelopathy panmielopatía constitucional infantil.
panmyelophthisis *n.* panmieloptisis, panmielotisis.
panneuritis *n.* panneuritis.
panniculalgia *n.* paniculalgia.
panniculitis *n.* paniculitis.
relapsing febrile nodular non-suppurative panniculitis paniculitis nodular no supurativa, paniculitis nodular no supurativa recurrente febril.
subacute nodular migratory panniculitis paniculitis migratoria nodular subaguda.
Weber-Christian panniculitis paniculitis de Weber-Christian.
panniculus paníiculo, panniculus.
pannus pannus, paño.
panophthalmia *n.* panoftalmía.
panophthalmitis *n.* panoftalmitis.
panoptosis *n.* panoptosis.
panosteitis *n.* panosteítis.
panotitis *n.* panotitis.
panphobia *n.* pantofobia.
panplegia *n.* panplejía.
pansclerosis *n.* panesclerosis.
pansinusitis *n.* pansinusitis.
panspermatism *n.* panespermatismo.
panspermia *n.* panespermia.
pant *v.* jadear.
pantachromatic *adj.* pantacromático, -ca.
pantamorphia *n.* pantamorfia.
pantanencephalia *n.* pantanencefalia.
pantanencephaly *n.* pantanencefalia.
pantatrophia *n.* pantatrofia.
pantatrophy *n.* pantatrofia.
panthodic *adj.* pantódico, -ca.
panting *n.* jadeo.
pantogamy *n.* pantogamia.
pantograph *n.* pantógrafo.
pantomograph *n.* pantomógrafo.
pantomography *n.* pantomografía.
pantomorphic *adj.* pantomórfico, -ca.
pantoscopic *adj.* pantoscópico, -ca.
pantropic *adj.* pantrópico, -ca.
panuveitis *n.* panuveítis.
papilla *n.* papila.

papillary *adj.* papilar.
papillate *adj.* papilar.
papillectomy *n.* papilectomía.
papilledema *n.* papiledema.
papilliferous *adj.* papilífero, -ra.
papilliform *adj.* papiliforme.
papillitis *n.* papilitis.
 necrotizing papillitis papilitis necrosante.
 necrotizing renal papillitis papilitis renal necrosante.
papilloadenocystoma *n.* papiloadenocistoma.
papillocarcinoma *n.* papilocarcinoma.
papilloma *n.* papiloma.
 Hopmann's papilloma papiloma de Hopmann.
 hornifying papilloma papiloma córneo.
 intracystic papilloma papiloma intracístico.
 intraductal papilloma papiloma intracanicular.
 papilloma acuminatum papiloma acuminado.
 papilloma diffusum papiloma difuso, papiloma múltiple.
 papilloma neuropathicum papiloma neuropático.
 papilloma venereum papiloma venéreo.
 villous papilloma papiloma velloso.
papillomatosis *n.* papilomatosis.
papilloretinitis *n.* papilorretinitis.
papillotomy *n.* papilotomía.
pappus pappus.
papulation *n.* papulación, papulización.
papule *n.* pápula.
 Celsus' papule pápula de Celso.
papuliferous *adj.* papulífero, -ra.
papuloerythematous *adj.* papuloeritematoso, -sa.
papuloid *adj.* papuloide.
papulopostular *adj.* papulopustuloso, -sa.
papulosis *n.* papulosis.
 malignant atrophic papulosis papulosis atrófica maligna.
papulosquamous *adj.* papuloescamoso, -sa.
papulovesicular *adj.* papulovesicular.
papyraceous *adj.* papiráceo, -a.
para-analgesia *n.* paraanalgesia.
para-anesthesia *n.* paraanestesia.
para-appendicitis *n.* paraapendicitis.
parabiosis *n.* parabiosis.
 dialytic parabiosis parabiosis dialítica.
 vascular parabiosis parabiosis vascular.
parablepsia *n.* parablepsia.
paracanthoma *n.* paracantoma.
paracanthosis *n.* paracantosis.
paracardiac *adj.* paracardíaco, -ca.
paracarmine *n.* paracarmín.
paracele *n.* paracelo.
paracentesis *n.* paracentesis.
 abdominal paracentesis paracentesis abdominal.
 paracentesis oculi paracentesis ocular.
 tympanic paracentesis paracentesis timpánica.
paracentral *adj.* paracentral.
paracephalus *n.* paracéfalo.
paracholera *n.* paracólera.
parachordal *adj.* paracordal.
parachroia *n.* paracroia.
parachromatism *n.* paracromatismo.
parachromatopsia *n.* paracromatopsia.
parachromatosis *n.* paracromatosis.
paracinesia *n.* paracinesia.
paracinesis *n.* paracinesia, paracinesis.
paracme *n.* paracmé.

paracnemidion *n.* paracnemidion.
paracnemis *n.* paracnemis.
paracoenesthesia *n.* paracenestesia.
paracolitis *n.* paracolitis.
paracolpitis *n.* paracolpitis.
paracolpium *n.* paracolpio.
paracone *n.* paracono.
paracoxalgia *n.* paracoxalgia.
paracusia *n.* paracusia.
 false paracusia paracusia falsa.
 paracusia acris paracusia acris.
 paracusia duplicata paracusia doble.
 Willis' paracusia paracusia de Willis, paracusia willisiana.
paracusis *n.* paracusia, paracusis.
paracystitis *n.* paracistitis.
paracystium *n.* paracistio.
paradenitis *n.* paradenitis.
paradental *adj.* paradental.
paradentitis *n.* paradentitis.
paradentosis *n.* paradentosis, paradontosis.
paradiabetes *n.* paradiabetes.
paradidymis *n.* paradídimo, paraepicele.
paradiphtheritic *adj.* paradiftérico, -ca.
paradox *n.* paradoja.
 Opie paradox paradoja de Opie.
 Weber's paradox paradoja de Weber.
paradoxical *adj.* paradójico, -ca.
paradysentery *n.* paradisentería.
paraeccrisis *n.* paraecrisis.
paraepilepsy *n.* paraepilepsia.
paraesthesia *n.* paraestesia.
paraffinoma *n.* parafinoma.
paraflagellum *n.* paraflagelo.
parafunctional *adj.* parafuncional.
paraganglioma *n.* paraganglioma.
 medullary paraganglioma paraganglioma medular.
 non-chromaffin paraganglioma paraganglioma no cromafin.
paraganglion *n.* paraganglio.
parageusia *n.* parageusia.
paragglutination *n.* paraglutinación.
paraglobulin *n.* paraglobina, paraglobulina.
paraglobulinuria *n.* paraglobulinuria.
paraglossa *n.* paraglosia, paraglosis.
paraglossitis *n.* paraglositis.
paragnatus *n.* paragnato.
paragrammatism *n.* paragramatismo.
paragraphia *n.* paragrafia.
parahemoglobin *n.* parahemoglobina.
parahepatic *adj.* parahepático, -ca.
parahepatitis *n.* parahepatitis.
parahormone *n.* parahormona.
parainfection *n.* parainfección.
parainfluenza *adj.* paragripal.
parakeratosis *n.* paraceratosis, paraqueratosis.
 parakeratosis psoriasiformis paraqueratosis psoriasiforme.
 parakeratosis scutularis paraqueratosis escutular.
paralalia *n.* paralalia.
paralambdacism *n.* paralambdacismo.
paralexia *n.* paralexia.
paralgesia *n.* paralgesia.
paralgia *n.* paralgia.
parallax *n.* paralaje, paralax.
 binocular parallax paralaje binocular.
parallergia *n.* paralergia.
parallergic *adj.* paralérgico, -ca.
paralysis *n.* parálisis.
 acoustic paralysis parálisis acústica.
 acute ascending paralysis parálisis ascendente aguda.
 acute bulbar paralysis parálisis bulbar aguda.

 alcoholic paralysis parálisis alcohólica.
 alternate paralysis parálisis alterna.
 ambiguo-accessorius paralysis parálisis ambiguoaccesoria.
 ambiguo-accessorius-hypoglossal paralysis parálisis ambiguoaccesoriohipoglosa.
 ambiguous hypoglossal paralysis parálisis ambiguohipoglosa.
 ambiguous pinothalamic paralysis parálisis ambiguoespinotalámica.
 anesthesia paralysis parálisis de la anestesia.
 arsenical paralysis parálisis arsenical.
 ascending paralysis parálisis ascendente.
 association paralysis parálisis de asociación.
 asthenic bulbar paralysis parálisis bulbar asténica.
 asthenobulbospinal paralysis parálisis astenobulboespinal.
 Bell's paralysis parálisis de Bell.
 brachial paralysis parálisis braquial.
 brachifacial paralysis parálisis braquiofacial.
 Brown-Séquard's paralysis parálisis de Brown-Séquard.
 bulbar paralysis parálisis bulbar.
 bulbospinal paralysis parálisis bulboespinal.
 central paralysis parálisis central.
 centrocortical paralysis parálisis centrocortical.
 cerebral paralysis parálisis cerebral.
 cincumflex paralysis parálisis circunfleja.
 complete paralysis parálisis completa.
 compression paralysis parálisis por compresión.
 creeping paralysis parálisis reptante.
 crossed paralysis parálisis cruzada.
 crural paralysis parálisis crural.
 decubitus paralysis parálisis por decúbito.
 diphtheritic paralysis parálisis diftérica.
 diver's paralysis parálisis de los buzos.
 Duchenne-Erb paralysis parálisis de Duchenne-Erb.
 Duchenne's paralysis parálisis de Duchenne.
 emotional paralysis parálisis emocional.
 Erb-Duchenne paralysis parálisis de Erb-Duchenne.
 false paralysis parálisis falsa.
 familial periodic paralysis parálisis periódica familiar.
 flaccid paralysis parálisis fláccida.
 glossolabial paralysis parálisis glosolabial.
 glossolabiolaryngeal paralysis parálisis labioglosolaríngea.
 glossolabiopharyngeal paralysis parálisis labioglosofaríngea.
 glossopharyngolabial paralysis parálisis glosofaringolabial.
 Gluber's paralysis parálisis de Gluber.
 Hunt's juvenile paralysis agitans parálisis agitante juvenil (de Hunt).
 hysterical paralysis parálisis histérica.
 incomplete paralysis parálisis incompleta.
 infantile paralysis parálisis infantil.
 ischemic paralysis parálisis isquémica, parálisis isquémica de Volkmann.
 Klumpke-Déjerine paralysis parálisis de Klumpke, parálisis de Klumpke-Déjerine.
 Klumpke's paralysis parálisis de Klumpke, parálisis de Klumpke-Déjerine.
 Landry's paralysis parálisis de Landry.
 Lissauer's paralysis parálisis de Lissauer.
 local paralysis parálisis local.
 medullary tegmental paralysis parálisis bulbar tegmentaria.
 Millard-Gluber paralysis parálisis de Millard-Gluber.

mimetic paralysis parálisis mimética.
myopathic paralysis parálisis miopática.
nuclear paralysis parálisis nuclear.
obstetrical paralysis parálisis obstétrica.
ocular paralysis parálisis ocular.
painful paralysis algoparálisis.
paralysis agitans parálisis agitante.
paralysis of accommodation parálisis de la acomodación.
peripheral paralysis parálisis periférica.
phonetic paralysis parálisis fonética.
postdiphtheritic paralysis parálisis posdiftérica.
progressive bulbar paralysis parálisis bulbar progresiva.
pseudobulbar paralysis parálisis seudobulbar.
pseudohypertrophic paralysis parálisis seudohipertrófica.
psychic paralysis parálisis psíquica.
Ramsay Hunt paralysis parálisis de Ramsay Hunt.
reflex paralysis parálisis refleja.
sleep paralysis parálisis del sueño.
spastic bulbar paralysis parálisis bulbar espástica.
spastic paralysis parálisis espasmódica, parálisis espástica.
spinal spastic paralysis parálisis espinal espasmódica.
supranuclear paralysis parálisis supranuclear.
Todd's paralysis parálisis de Todd.
trigeminal paralysis parálisis del trigémino.
Volkmann's ischemic paralysis parálisis isquémica, parálisis isquémica de Volkmann.
waking paralysis parálisis del despertar.
Weber's paralysis parálisis de Weber.
Werding-Hoffmann paralysis parálisis de Werding-Hoffmann.
writer's paralysis parálisis de los escritores.
paralyzant *n.* paralizador, -ra, paralizante.
paramagnetism *n.* paramagnetismo.
paramastitis *n.* paramastitis.
paramastoiditis *n.* paramastoiditis.
paramedian *adj.* paramediano, -na.
paramesial *adj.* paramesial.
parameter *n.* parámetro.
parametritis *n.* parametritis.
anterior parametritis parametritis anterior.
posterior parametritis parametritis posterior.
parametrium *n.* parametrio.
paramimia *n.* paramimia.
paramnesia *n.* paramnesia.
Paramoeba Paramoeba.
paramolar *n.* paramolar.
paramorphia *n.* paramorfia.
paramphistomiasis *n.* paranfistomiasis.
paramyoclonus *n.* paramioclonía.
paramyoclonus multiplex paramioclonía múltiple.
paramyosinogen *n.* paramiosinógeno.
paramyotonia *n.* paramiotonía.
congenital paramyotonia paramiotonía congénita.
paramyotonus *n.* paramiotono.
paranalgesia *n.* paranalgesia.
paranephritis *n.* paranefritis.
paranephroma *n.* paranefroma.
paranesthesia *n.* hemiparanestesia, paranestesia.
paraneural *adj.* paraneural, paranéurico, -ca.
paranoia *n.* paranoia.
paranoiac *adj.* paranoico, -ca.

paranoid *adj.* paranoide.
paranormal *adj.* paranormal.
paranucleus *n.* paranúcleo.
paraomphalic *adj.* paraonfálico, -ca.
paraoperative *adj.* paraoperatorio, -ria.
parapancreatic *adj.* parapancreático, -ca.
paraparesis *n.* paraparesia.
parapedesis *n.* parapedésis.
paraperitoneal *adj.* paraperitoneal.
parapestis *n.* parapeste.
paraphasia *n.* parafasia, parafemia.
literal paraphasia parafasia fonémica, parafasia literal.
verbal paraphasia parafasia verbal.
paraphia *n.* parafia.
paraphilia *n.* parafilia.
paraphimosis *n.* parafimosis.
paraphonia *n.* parafonía.
paraphonia puberum parafonía puberum.
paraphrenia *n.* parafrenia.
paraphrenitis *n.* parafrenitis.
paraphysis *n.* paráfisis.
paraplectic *adj.* parapléjico, -ca.
paraplegia *n.* paraplejía.
alcoholic paraplegia paraplejía alcohólica.
ataxic paraplegia paraplejía atáxica.
cerebral paraplegia paraplejía cerebral.
congenital spastic paraplegia paraplejía espástica congénita.
flaccid paraplegia paraplejía fláccida.
infantile spastic paraplegia paraplejía espástica infantil.
paraplegia superior paraplejía superior.
peripheral paraplegia paraplejía periférica.
Pott's paraplegia paraplejía de Pott.
spastic paraplegia paraplejía espástica.
toxic paraplegia paraplejía tóxica.
paraplegic *adj.* parapléjico, -ca.
paraplegiform *adj.* paraplejiforme.
parapleuritis *n.* parapleuritis.
paraplexus *n.* paraplexo.
parapneumonia *n.* paraneumonía.
parapophysis *n.* parapófisis.
parapraxia *n.* parapraxia.
paraproctitis *n.* paraproctitis.
paraproctium *n.* paraproctio.
paraprotein *n.* paraproteína.
paraproteinemia *n.* paraproteinemia.
parapsia *n.* parapsia, parapsis.
parapsoriasis *n.* parapsoriasis.
parapsychology *n.* parapsicología.
parareaction *n.* pararreacción.
pararectal *n.* pararrectal.
parareflexia *n.* pararreflexia.
pararenal *adj.* pararrenal.
pararhizoclasia *n.* pararrizoclasia.
pararhotacism *n.* pararrotacismo.
pararrhythmia *n.* pararritmia.
parasacral *adj.* parasacro, -cra.
parasagittal *adj.* parasagital.
parasalpingitis *n.* parasalpingitis.
parasigmatism *n.* parasigmatismo.
parasinoidal *adj.* parasinoidal, parasinusal.
parasite *n.* parásito.
accidental parasite parásito accidental.
auxiliary parasite parásito auxiliar.
commensal parasite parásito comensal.
facultative parasite parásito facultativo.
incidental parasite parásito incidental.
inquiline parasite parásito inquilino.
obligate parasite parásito obligado.
specific parasite parásito específico.
parasitemia *n.* parasitemia.
parasitic *adj.* parasitario, -ria, parasítico, -ca.
parasiticidal *adj.* parasiticida[2].

parasiticide *n.* parasiticida[1].
parasitifer *n.* parasitífero.
parasitism *n.* parasitismo.
parasitogenic *adj.* parasitogénico, -ca.
parasitoid *adj.* parasitoide.
parasitologist *n.* parasitólogo, -ga.
parasitology *n.* parasitología.
parasitophobia *n.* parasitofobia.
parasitosis *n.* parasitosis.
parasitotrope *adj.* parasitótropo, -pa.
parasitotropy *n.* parasitotropía, parasitotropismo.
parasomnia *n.* parasomnia.
paraspadia *n.* paraspadias.
paraspadias *n.* paraspadias.
paraspecific *adj.* paraespecífico, -ca.
parasplenic *adj.* parasplénico, -ca.
parasteatosis *n.* paraesteatosis.
parasternal *adj.* paraesternal.
parasthenia *n.* parastenia.
parastruma *n.* parastruma.
parasympathetic *adj.* parasimpático, -ca.
parasympathicotonia *n.* parasimpaticotonía.
parasympatholytic *adj.* parasimpaticolítico, -ca.
parasympathomimetic *adj.* parasimpaticomimético, -ca.
parasynovitis *n.* parasinovitis.
parasyphilis *n.* parasífilis.
parasyphilosis *n.* parasifilosis.
parasystole *n.* parasístole.
paratarsium *n.* paratarso.
paratenon *n.* paratendón.
paratereseomania *n.* paratereseomanía.
paraterminal *adj.* paraterminal.
parathormone *n.* parathormona, paratormona.
parathymia *n.* paratimia.
parathyrin *n.* paratirina.
parathyroid *adj.* paratiroideo, -a, paratiroides.
parathyroidectomy *n.* paratiroidectomía.
parathyroidoma *n.* paratiroidoma.
parathyroprivia *n.* paratiroprivia.
parathyrotropic *adj.* paratirotrópico, -ca.
paratonia *n.* paratonía.
paratrichosis *n.* paratricosis.
paratripsis *n.* paratripsis.
paratriptic *adj.* paratríptico, -ca.
paratrophy *n.* paratrofia.
paratuberculosis *n.* paratuberculosis.
paratyhpoid *n.* paratifoidea.
paratyphlitis *n.* paratiflitis.
paratyphoid *n.* paratifoide.
paratypical *adj.* paratípico, -ca.
paraumbilical *adj.* paraumbilical.
paraurethra *n.* parauretra.
paraurethritis *n.* parauretritis.
parauterine *adj.* parauterino, -na.
paravaccinia *n.* paravacuna.
paravaginal *adj.* paravaginal.
paravaginitis *n.* paravaginitis.
paravenous *adj.* paravenoso, -sa.
paravertebral *adj.* paravertebral.
paravesical *adj.* paravesical.
paravitaminosis *n.* paravitaminosis.
paraxial *adj.* paraxial, paraxil.
parazoon *n.* parazoo.
parectasia *n.* parectasia.
parectasis *n.* parectasia, parectasis.
parectropia *n.* parectropía.
pareidolia *n.* pareidolia.
parelectrotomy *n.* parelectrotomía.
parencephalia *n.* parencefalia.
parencephalitis *n.* parencefalitis.
parencephalocele *n.* parencefalocele.

parencephalon *n.* parencéfalo.
parenchyma *n.* parénquima.
parenchymatitis *n.* parenquimatitis.
parental *adj.* parental.
parenteral *adj.* parenteral, parentérico, -ca.
parepicele *n.* parepicele.
parepithymia *n.* parepitimia.
parergasia *n.* parergasia.
paresis *n.* paresia.
 galloping paresis paresia galopante.
 general paresis paresia general.
 painful paresis algoparesia.
 stationary paresis paresia estacionaria.
paresthesia *n.* parestesia.
 Bernhardt's paresthesia parestesia de Bernhardt.
paretic *adj.* parético, -ca.
pareunia *n.* pareunia.
paridrosis *n.* parahidrosis, paridrosis.
parietal *adj.* parietal.
parietitis *n.* parietitis.
parietofrontal *adj.* parietofrontal.
parieto-occipital *adj.* parietooccipital.
parietosphenoid *adj.* parietoesfenoidal.
parietosplanchnic *adj.* parietosplácnico, -ca.
parietosquamosal *adj.* parietoescamoso, -sa.
parietotemporal *adj.* parietotemporal.
parietovisceral *adj.* parietovisceral.
parity *n.* paridad.
parkinsonism *n.* parkinsonismo.
parodontitis *n.* parodontitis.
parodontium *n.* paradencio, parodoncio, parodontio.
parodontosis *n.* parodontosis.
parolivary *adj.* parolivar.
paromphalocele *n.* paraonfalocele.
paroneiria *n.* paroniria.
paroniria *n.* paroniria.
paronychosis *n.* paronicosis.
parophthalmia *n.* paroftalmía, paroftalmitis.
paropsia *n.* paropsia, paropsis.
paropsis *n.* paropsia.
parorchidium *n.* parorquidia.
parorexia *n.* parorexia.
parosmia *n.* parosmia.
parosphresia *n.* parosfresia.
parosteitis *n.* parosteítis.
parosteosis *n.* parosteosis.
parostitis *n.* parosteítis, parostitis.
parostosis *n.* parosteosis, parostosis.
parotic *adj.* parótico, -ca.
parotid *adj.* parótida, parotídeo, -a.
parotidectomy *n.* parotidectomía.
parotiditis *n.* parotiditis.
 epidemic parotiditis parotiditis contagiosa, parotiditis epidémica.
 parotiditis phlegmonosa parotiditis flemonosa.
 postoperative parotiditis parotiditis posoperatoria.
parotidoauricularis *adj.* parotidoauricular.
parotidosclerosis *n.* parotidoesclerosis.
parotitis *n.* parotitis.
parovariotomy *n.* parovariotomía.
parovaritis *n.* parovaritis.
paroxysm *n.* paroxismo.
paroxysmal *adj.* paroxismal, paroxísmico, -ca, paroxístico, -ca.
pars *n.* pars, parte.
 pars planitis pars planitis.
parsimony *n.* parsimonia.
part *n.* parte.
parthenogenesis *n.* partenogénesis.
parthenoplasty *n.* partenoplastia.
partialism *n.* parcialismo.

particle *n.* partícula.
 alpha particle partícula alfa.
 beta particle partícula beta.
 colloid particle partícula coloide.
 Dane particle partícula de Dane.
 F particle partícula F.
 Zimmermann's elementary particle partícula elemental de Zimmermann.
partimutism *n.* partimutismo.
partition *n.* tabique.
parturient *adj.* parturienta.
parturifacient *n.* parturifaciente.
parturiometer *n.* parturiómetro.
partus *n.* parto.
parulis *n.* párulis.
paruria *n.* paruria.
parvicellular *adj.* parvicelular.
parvule *adj.* párvulo, -la.
passage *n.* paso².
passion *n.* pasión.
passive *adj.* pasivo, -va.
past pointing *n.* señalización pasada.
paste *n.* pasta.
pasteurella *n.* pasteurella.
pasteurization *n.* pasteurización.
patch *n.* placa¹.
 Bitot's patch placa de Bitot.
 herald patch placa heráldica.
 Hutchinson's patch placa de Hutchinson.
 mucous patch placa mucosa.
 salmon patch placa asalmonada.
 smoker's patch placa de los fumadores.
 soldier's patch placa de los soldados.
patefaction *n.* patefacción.
patella *n.* patela, rótula.
 floating patella rótula flotante.
 slipping patella rótula deslizable.
patellapexy *n.* patelapexia.
patellar *adj.* patelar.
patellectomy *n.* patelectomía.
patelliform *adj.* pateliforme.
patellofemoral *adj.* patelofemoral.
paternalism *n.* paternalismo.
path *n.* trayecto, vía.
 condyle path vía condílea.
 copulation path vía de copulación.
 incisor path vía incisiva.
 placement path vía de colocación.
pathema *n.* patema.
pathematology *n.* patematología.
pathergasia *n.* patergasia.
pathergy *n.* patergia.
pathetic *adj.* patético, -ca.
pathetism *n.* patetismo.
pathoanatomy *n.* patoanatomía.
pathobiology *n.* patobiología.
pathobolism *n.* patobolismo.
pathoclisis *n.* patoclisis.
pathocrinia *n.* patocrinia.
pathodontia *n.* patodoncia.
pathogen *n.* patógeno.
pathogenic *adj.* patógeno, -na.
pathogenicity *n.* patogenicidad.
pathogeny *n.* patogénesis, patogenia.
pathognomonia *n.* patognomía.
pathognomonic *adj.* patognomónico, -ca.
pathognostic *adj.* patognóstico, -ca.
pathography *n.* patografía.
pathologic *adj.* patológico, -ca.
pathological *adj.* patológico, -ca.
pathologist *n.* patólogo, -ga.
 speech-language pathologist logopeda.
pathology *n.* patología.
 cellular pathology patología celular.
 clinical pathology patología clínica.

 comparative pathology patología comparada.
 dental pathology patología dental.
 experimental pathology patología experimental.
 external pathology patología externa.
 functional pathology patología funcional.
 general pathology patología general.
 geographical pathology patología geográfica.
 humoral pathology patología humoral.
 internal pathology patología interna.
 medical pathology patología médica.
 mental pathology patología mental.
 special pathology patología especial.
 speech pathology logopedia.
 surgical pathology patología quirúrgica.
patholysis *n.* patólisis.
pathomeiosis *n.* patomeiosis.
pathometabolism *n.* patometabolismo.
pathomimesis *n.* patomimesis.
pathomorphism *n.* patomorfismo, patomorfología.
pathomorphosis *n.* patomorfosis.
pathoneurosis *n.* patoneurosis.
pathonomia *n.* patonomía.
pathonomy *n.* patonomía.
patho-occlusion *n.* patooclusión.
pathophilia *n.* patofilia.
pathophobia *n.* patofobia.
pathophoresis *n.* patoforesis.
pathopsychology *n.* patopsicología.
pathopsychosis *n.* patopsicosis.
pathosis *n.* patosis.
pathotropism *n.* patotropismo.
pathway *n.* vía.
 accessory pathway vía accesoria.
 afferent pathway vía aferente.
 alternative complement pathway vía alternativa del complemento.
 alternative pathway vía alternativa.
 alternative pathway of complement activation vía alternativa de la activación del complemento.
 auditory pathway vía auditiva.
 biosynthetic pathway vía biosintética.
 efferent pathway vía eferente.
 Embden-Meyerhof pathway vía de Embden-Meyerhof.
 Embden-Meyerhof-Parnas pathway vía de Embden-Meyerhof-Parnas.
 final common pathway vía final común.
 internuncial pathway vía internuncial.
 metabolic pathway vía metabólica.
 motor pathway vía motora.
 pentose phosphate pathway vía del fosfato de pentosa, vía del fosfogluconato.
 reentrant pathway vía de reentrada.
 sensory pathway vía sensitiva.
 visual pathway vía visual.
patient *n.* paciente.
patrilineal *adj.* patrilineal.
patroclinous *adj.* patróclino, -na.
patrogenesis *n.* patrogénesis.
pattern *n.* patrón.
 action pattern patrón de acción.
 airflow pattern patrón de flujo aéreo.
 behavior pattern patrón de conducta.
 capsular pattern patrón capsular.
 combined pattern patrón combinado.
 fixed action pattern patrón de acción fija.
 hourglass pattern patrón de reloj de arena.
 muscle pattern patrón muscular.
 occlusal pattern patrón oclusal.
 reflex inhibiting pattern (RIP) patrón de inhibición refleja (PIR).

startle pattern patrón de sobresalto.
stimulus pattern patrón de estímulo.
wax pattern patrón de cera.
patulous *adj.* patuloso, -sa.
pauciarticular *adj.* pauciarticular.
paucibacillary *adj.* paucibacilar.
paucisynaptic *adj.* paucisináptico, -ca.
pause *n.* pausa.
apneic pause pausa apneica.
compensatory pause pausa compensatoria.
postextrasystolic pause pausa posextrasistólica.
pavementing *n.* pavimentación.
pavilion *n.* pabellón.
pavor *n.* pavor.
pavor nocturnus pavor nocturno.
P-congenitale P-congénita.
P-dextrocardiale P-dextrocardial.
pearl *n.* perla.
Elschnig pearl perla de Elschnig.
enamel pearl perla de esmalte.
epithelial pearl perla epitelial.
Epstein's pearl perla de Epstein.
gouty pearl perla gotosa.
keratin pearl perla de queratina.
squamous pearl perla escamosa.
pecant *adj.* pecante.
pechyagra *n.* pequiagra.
pecicecitis *n.* pericecitis.
pecten *n.* peine.
pectenitis *n.* pectenitis.
pectenosis *n.* pectenosis.
pectenotomy *n.* pectenotomía.
pectinate *adj.* pectinado, -da.
pectineal *adj.* pectíneo, -a.
pectiniform *adj.* pectiniforme.
pectoral *adj.* pectoral.
pectoralgia *n.* pectoralgia.
pectoriloquy *n.* pectoriloquia.
aphonic pectoriloquy pectoriloquia afónica.
whispering pectoriloquy pectoriloquia susurrante.
pectorophony *n.* pectorofonía.
pectus *n.* pecho.
pedal *adj.* pedal.
pedarthrocace *n.* pedartrocace.
pedatrophia *n.* paidoatrofia, pedatrofia.
pedatrophy *n.* paidoatrofia, pedatrofia.
pediadontia *n.* pediadoncia.
pediadontology *n.* pediadontología.
pediatric *adj.* pediátrico, -ca.
pediatrician *n.* pediatra.
pediatrics *n.* pediatría.
pedicel *n.* pedicelo.
pedicellate *adj.* pedicelado, -da.
pedicellated *adj.* pedicelado, -da.
pedicellation *n.* pedicelación.
pedicle *n.* pedículo.
optic pedicle pedículo óptico.
pedicular *adj.* pedicular.
pediculate *adj.* pediculado, -da.
pediculation *n.* pediculación.
pediculicide *n.* pediculicida.
pediculosis *n.* pediculosis.
pediculosis capitis pediculosis capitis.
pediculosis corporis pediculosis corporis.
pediculosis palpebrarum pediculosis palpebrarum.
pediculosis pubis pediculosis pubis.
pediculous *adj.* pediculoso, -sa.
Pediculus Pediculus.
pediculus *n.* pedículo, pediculus, piojo.
pedicure *n.* pedicura, pedicuría.
pediluvium *n.* pediluvio.
pediphalanx *n.* pedifalange.

pedodontics *n.* pedodoncia.
pedodynamometer *n.* pedodinamómetro.
pedogamy *n.* pedogamia.
pedogenesis *n.* pedogénesis.
pedograph *n.* pedógrafo.
pedography *n.* pedografía.
pedometer *n.* pedómetro.
pedomorphic *adj.* pedomórfico, -ca.
pedomorphism *n.* pedomorfismo.
pedopathy *n.* pedopatía.
pedophile *n.* pedófilo[1], -la.
pedophilia *n.* paidofilia, pedofilia.
pedophilic *adj.* pedofílico, -ca, pedófilo[2], -la.
pedophobia *n.* pedofobia.
pedrogram *n.* pedograma.
peduncle *n.* pedúnculo.
peduncular *adj.* peduncular.
pedunculated *adj.* pedunculado, -da.
pedunculotomy *n.* pedunculotomía.
pedunculus *n.* pedúnculo.
peg *n.* clavija.
pelagism *n.* pelagismo.
pelidnoma *n.* pelidnoma.
pelioma *n.* pelioma.
peliosis *n.* peliosis.
peliosis hepatis peliosis hepática.
pellagra *n.* pelagra.
infantile pellagra pelagra infantil.
pellagra sine pellagra pelagra sin pelagra.
secondary pellagra pelagra secundaria.
typhoid pellagra pelagra tifoidea.
pellagragenic *adj.* pelagrágeno, -na.
pellagral *adj.* pelagral.
pellagroid *adj.* pelagroide.
pellagrologist *n.* pelagrólogo, -ga.
pellagrology *n.* pelagrología.
pellagrosis *n.* pelagrosis.
pellagrous *adj.* pelagroso, -sa.
pellicle *n.* película[1].
absorbable gelatin pellicle película de gelatina absorbible.
acquired pellicle película adquirida.
brown pellicle película marrón, película parda.
tear pellicle película lagrimal.
pellicular *adj.* pelicular.
pelliculous *adj.* peliculoso, -sa.
pellucid *adj.* pelúcido, -da.
pelmatic *adj.* pelmático, -ca.
pelmatogram *n.* pelmatograma.
peltate *adj.* peltado, -da.
peltation *n.* peltación.
pelvic *adj.* pelviano, -na, pélvico, -ca.
pelvicaliceal *adj.* pelvicalicial.
pelvicalyceal *adj.* pelvicalicial.
pelvicellulitis *n.* pelvicelulitis.
pelvicephalometry *n.* pelvicefalomerría.
pelvifermoral *adj.* pelvifemoral.
pelvifixation *n.* pelvifijación.
pelvigraph *n.* pelvígrafo.
pelvilithotomy *n.* pelvilitotomía.
pelvimeter *n.* pelvímetro.
pelvimetry *n.* pelvimetría.
clinical pelvimetry pelvimetría clínica.
manual pelvimetry pelvimetría manual.
planographic pelvimetry pelvimetría planográfica.
stereoscopic pelvimetry pelvimetría estereoscópica.
X-ray pelvimetry pelvimetría con rayos X.
pelviograph *n.* pelviógrafo.
pelviography *n.* pelvigrafía, pelviografía.
pelvioileoneocystostomy *n.* pelvioileoneocistostomía.
pelviolithotomy *n.* pelviolitotomía.

pelvioneostomy *n.* pelvioneostomía.
pelvioplasty *n.* pelvioplastia.
pelvioradiography *n.* pelviorradiografía.
pelvioscopy *n.* pelvioscopia, pelviscopia.
pelviotomy *n.* pelviotomía.
pelviperitonitis *n.* pelvioperitonitis, pelviperitonitis.
pelviradiography *n.* pelvirradiografía.
pelvirectal *adj.* pelvirrectal.
pelviroentgenography *n.* pelvirroentgenografía.
pelvis *n.* pelvis.
android pelvis pelvis androide.
anthropoid pelvis pelvis antropoide.
assimilation pelvis pelvis asimilada.
beaked pelvis pelvis en pico.
brachypellic pelvis pelvis braquipélica.
caoutchouc pelvis pelvis de caucho, pelvis de goma.
contracted pelvis pelvis contraída.
cordate pelvis pelvis cordiforme.
cordiform pelvis pelvis cordiforme.
coxalgic pelvis pelvis coxálgica.
dolichopellic pelvis pelvis dolicopélica.
dwarf pelvis pelvis enana.
extrarenal pelvis pelvis extrarrenal.
flat pelvis pelvis plana.
frozen pelvis pelvis congelada.
funnel-shaped pelvis pelvis en embudo, pelvis infundibuliforme.
gynecoid pelvis pelvis ginecoide.
hardened pelvis pelvis endurecida.
heart-shaped pelvis pelvis en forma de corazón.
infantile pelvis pelvis infantil.
inverted pelvis pelvis invertida.
justo major pelvis pelvis gigante.
juvenile pelvis pelvis juvenil.
kyphoscoliotic pelvis pelvis cifoescoliótica.
kyphotic pelvis pelvis cifótica.
longitudinal oval pelvis pelvis oval longitudinal.
lordotic pelvis pelvis lordótica.
masculine pelvis pelvis masculina.
mesatipellic pelvis pelvis mesatipélica.
Nägele's pelvis pelvis de Nägele, pelvis oblicua.
osteomalacic pelvis pelvis osteomalácica.
Otto pelvis pelvis de Otto.
pelvis obtecta pelvis obtecta.
pelvis of the gallbladder pelvis de la vesícula biliar.
pelvis renalis pelvicilla renal.
pelvis spinosa pelvis espinosa.
platypellic pelvis pelvis platipélica.
Prague pelvis pelvis de Praga.
pseudo-osteomalacic pelvis pelvis seudoosteomalácica.
rachitic pelvis pelvis raquítica.
renal pelvis pelvicilla renal, pelvis renal.
reniform pelvis pelvis reniforme.
Robert's pelvis pelvis de Robert.
Rokitansky's pelvis pelvis de Rokitansky.
rostrate pelvis pelvis rostrata.
round pelvis pelvis redonda.
scoliotic pelvis pelvis escoliótica.
split pelvis pelvis hendida.
spondylolisthetic pelvis pelvis espondilolistética.
transverse oval pelvis pelvis oval transversa.
pelvisacral *adj.* pelvisacral.
pelvisacrum *n.* pelvisacro.
pelviscope *n.* pelvioscopio, pelviscopio.
pelvisection *n.* pelvisección.
pelvisternum *n.* pelviesternón.

pelvitherm *n.* pelvitermo.
pelvitomy *n.* pelviotomía, pelvitomía.
pelviureterography *n.* pelviureterografía.
pelvospondylitis ossificans *n.* pelvoespondilitis osificante.
pemphigoid *n.* penfigoide.
 benign mucosal pemphigoid penfigoide mucoso benigno.
 bulbous pemphigoid penfigoide ampollar.
 cicatricial pemphigoid penfigoide cicatricial.
 ocular pemphigoid penfigoide ocular.
pemphigus *n.* pénfigo.
 familial benign chronic pemphigus pénfigo familiar benigno crónico.
 ocular pemphigus pénfigo ocular.
 pemphigus acutus pénfigo agudo.
 pemphigus contagiosus pénfigo contagioso.
 pemphigus crouposus pénfigo crupal, pénfigo cruposo.
 pemphigus diphtheriticus pénfigo diftérico.
 pemphigus erythematosus pénfigo eritematoso.
 pemphigus foliaceus pénfigo foliáceo.
 pemphigus gangrenosus pénfigo gangrenoso.
 pemphigus leprosus pénfigo leproso.
 pemphigus neonatorum pénfigo neonatal.
 pemphigus vegetans pénfigo vegetante.
 pemphigus vulgaris pénfigo vulgar.
pendelluft pendelluft.
pendular *adj.* pendular.
penectomy *n.* penectomía.
penetrability *n.* penetrabilidad.
penetrance *n.* penetrancia.
penetrating *adj.* penetrante.
penetration *n.* penetración.
penetrology *n.* penetrología.
penetrometer *n.* penetrómetro.
penial *adj.* peneano, -na.
penicillate *adj.* peniciliado, -da.
penicilliosis *n.* peniciliosis.
penicillus *n.* penicilio.
penile *adj.* peneano, -na.
penis *n.* pene, verga.
 clubbed penis pene claviforme, pene en masa.
 concealed penis pene oculto.
 double penis pene doble.
 femineus penis pene femenino.
 penis palmatus pene palmado, verga palmeada.
 plastica penis pene plástico.
 webbed penis pene membranoso, verga palmeada.
penischisis *n.* penisquisis
penitis *n.* penitis.
penniform *adj.* penniforme.
penoscrotal *adj.* penoescrotal.
penotomy *n.* penotomía.
pentachromic *adj.* pentacrómico, -ca.
pentadactyl *adj.* pentadáctilo, -la.
pentadactyle *adj.* pentadáctilo, -la.
pentalogy *n.* pentalogía.
 pentalogy of Fallot pentalogía de Fallot.
pentamer *n.* pentámero.
pentaploid *adj.* pentaploide.
pentaploidy *n.* pentaploidía.
pentasomy *n.* pentasomía.
pentastomiasis *n.* pentastomiasis.
pentose *n.* pentosa.
pentosemia *n.* pentosemia.
pentosuria *n.* pentosuria.
 alimentary pentosuria pentosuria alimentaria.
 essential pentosuria pentosuria esencial.
 primary pentosuria pentosuria primaria.

pentosuric *adj.* pentosúrico, -ca.
peotomy *n.* peotomía.
peplomer *n.* peplómero.
peplos *n.* peplo.
pepsinuria *n.* pepsinuria.
peptic *adj.* péptico, -ca.
Peptococcaceae Peptococcaceae.
Peptococcus Peptococcus.
peptocrinine *n.* peptocrinina.
peptogenic *adj.* peptogénico, -ca.
peptogenous *adj.* peptógeno, -na.
peptolysis *n.* peptólisis.
peptolytic *adj.* peptolítico, -ca.
peptonization *n.* peptonización.
peptonize *v.* peptonizar.
peptonuria *n.* peptonuria.
 enterogenous peptonuria peptonuria enterógena.
 hepatogenous peptonuria peptonuria hepatógena.
 nephrogenic peptonuria peptonuria nefrógena.
 puerperal peptonuria peptonuria puerperal.
 pyogenic peptonuria peptonuria piógena.
Peptostreptococcus Peptostreptococcus.
per os *adj.* per os, peroral.
peracephalus *n.* peracéfalo.
peracidity *n.* peracidez.
peracute *adj.* peragudo, -da.
peraxillary *adj.* peraxilar.
percentile *n.* percentil.
percept *n.* percepto.
perception *n.* percepción.
 conscious perception percepción consciente.
 depth perception percepción de la profundidad.
 extrasensory perception (ESP) percepción extrasensorial (PES).
 facial perception percepción facial.
 simultaneous perception percepción simultánea.
perceptive *adj.* perceptivo, -va.
perceptivity *n.* perceptividad.
percipient *adj.* perceptor, -ra.
percussible *adj.* percutible.
percussion *n.* percusión.
 auscultatory percussion percusión auscultatoria.
 bimanual percussion percusión bimanual.
 clavicular percussion percusión clavicular.
 deep percussion percusión profunda.
 direct percussion percusión directa.
 finger percussion percusión digital.
 immediate percussion percusión inmediata.
 mediate percussion percusión mediata.
 palpatory percussion percusión palpatoria.
 threshold percussion percusión umbral.
percussopunctator *n.* percusopuntor.
percussor *n.* percusor.
percutaneous *adj.* percutáneo, -a.
perencephaly *n.* perencefalia.
perennial *adj.* perenne.
perfectionism *n.* perfeccionismo.
perfilometer *n.* perfilómetro.
perflation *n.* perflación.
perforans *adj.* perforante.
perforated *adj.* perforado, -da.
perforation *n.* perforación.
 Bezold's perforation perforación de Bezold.
 dental perforation perforación dental.
perforator *n.* perforador.
perfrication *n.* perfricación.
perfusate *adj.* perfundido, -da.
perfuse *v.* perfundir.
perfusion *n.* perfusión.

 regional perfusion perfusión regional.
periacinal *adj.* periacinal.
periacinous *adj.* periacinoso, -sa.
periadenitis *n.* periadenitis.
 periadenitis aphtae periadenitis aftosa.
 periadenitis mucosa necrotica recurrens periadenitis mucosa necrótica recurrente.
periadventitial *adj.* periadventicio, -a.
perialienitis *n.* perialienitis.
periampullary *adj.* periampular.
perianal *adj.* perianal.
periangiocholitis *n.* periangiocolitis.
periangioma *n.* periangioma.
periangitis *n.* periangeítis.
periaortic *adj.* periaórtico, -ca.
periaortitis *n.* periaortitis.
perlapex *n.* periápice.
periapical *adj.* periapical.
periappendicitis *n.* periapendicitis.
 periappendicitis decidualis periapendicitis decidual.
periappendicular *adj.* periapendicular.
periaqueductal *adj.* periacueductal.
periarterial *adj.* periarterial.
periarteritis *n.* periarteritis.
periarthric *adj.* periártrico, -ca.
periarthritis *n.* periartritis.
periarticular *adj.* periarticular.
periauricular *adj.* periauricular.
periaxial *adj.* periaxial.
periaxillary *adj.* periaxilar.
periaxonal *adj.* periaxónico, -ca.
periblast *n.* periblasto.
peribronchial *adj.* peribronquial.
peribronchiolar *adj.* peribronquiolar.
peribronchiolitis *n.* peribronquiolitis.
peribronchitis *n.* peribronquitis.
peribuccal *adj.* peribucal.
peribulbar *adj.* peribulbar.
peribursal *adj.* peribursal.
pericaliceal *adj.* pericaliceo, -a.
pericallosal *adj.* pericalloso, -sa.
pericanalicular *adj.* pericanalicular.
pericapsular *adj.* pericapsular.
pericardectomy *n.* pericardectomía.
pericardiac *adj.* pericardíaco, -ca, pericárdico, -ca.
pericardial *adj.* pericardíaco, -ca, pericárdico, -ca.
pericardicentesis *n.* pericardicentesis.
pericardiectomy *n.* pericardiectomía.
pericardiocentesis *n.* pericardiocentesis.
pericardiolysis *n.* pericardiólisis.
pericardiomediastinitis *n.* pericardiomediastinitis.
pericardioperitoneal *adj.* pericardioperitoneal.
pericardiophrenic *adj.* pericardiofrénico, -ca.
pericardiopleural *adj.* pericardiopleural.
pericardiorrhaphy *n.* pericardiorrafia.
pericardiostomy *n.* pericardiostomía.
pericardiotomy *n.* pericardiotomía.
pericarditic *adj.* pericardítico, -ca.
pericarditis *n.* pericarditis.
 acute benign pericarditis pericarditis benigna aguda.
 adhesive pericarditis pericarditis adherente.
 amebic pericarditis pericarditis amibiana.
 carcinomatous pericarditis pericarditis carcinomatosa.
 chronic constrictive pericarditis pericarditis constrictiva crónica.
 external pericarditis pericarditis externa.
 fibrinous pericarditis fibropericarditis, pericarditis fibrinosa.

hemorrhagic pericarditis pericarditis hemorrágica.

idiopathic pericarditis pericarditis idiopática.

internal adhesive pericarditis pericarditis adherente interna.

localized pericarditis pericarditis localizada.

pericarditis calculosa pericarditis calculosa.

pericarditis obliterans pericarditis obliterante.

pericarditis sicca pericarditis seca.

pericarditis villosa pericarditis vellosa.

pericarditis with effusion pericarditis con derrame.

purulent pericarditis pericarditis purulenta.

rheumatic pericarditis pericarditis reumática.

serofibrinous pericarditis pericarditis serofibrinosa.

suppurative pericarditis pericarditis supurativa.

tuberculous pericarditis pericarditis tuberculosa.

uremic pericarditis pericarditis urémica.

pericardium *n.* pericardio.

adherent pericardium pericardio adherente.

bread-and-butter pericardium pericardio de pan y mantequilla.

shaggy pericardium pericardio peludo.

pericardotomy *n.* pericardotomía.

pericecal *adj.* pericecal.

pericellular *adj.* pericelular.

pericemental *adj.* pericemental, pericementario, -ria.

pericementitis *n.* pericementitis.

apical pericementitis pericementitis apical.

pericementoclasia *n.* pericementoclasia.

pericementum *n.* pericemento.

pericentral *adj.* pericentral.

pericentriolar *adj.* pericentriolar.

pericephalic *adj.* pericefálico, -ca.

pericholangitis *n.* pericolangitis.

perichondral *adj.* pericondral, pericondrial.

perichondrial *adj.* pericondral, pericondrial.

perichondritis *n.* pericondritis.

peristernal perichondritis pericondritis periesternal.

relapsing perichondritis pericondritis recidivante.

perichondrium *n.* pericondrio.

perichord *n.* pericordio.

perichordal *adj.* pericordal.

perichoroidal *adj.* pericoroidal.

pericolic *adj.* pericólico, -ca.

pericolitis *n.* pericolitis.

pericolitis dextra pericolitis derecha.

pericolitis sinistra pericolitis izquierda.

pericolonitis *n.* pericolonitis.

pericolpitis *n.* pericolpitis.

pericorneal *adj.* pericorneal.

pericoronal *adj.* pericoronal.

pericoronitis *n.* pericoronitis.

pericranial *adj.* pericraneal.

pericranitis *n.* pericranitis.

pericranium *n.* pericráneo.

pericycle *n.* periciclo.

pericystic *adj.* pericístico, -ca, periquístico, -ca.

pericystitis *n.* pericistitis.

pericystium *n.* pericistio.

pericyte *n.* pericito.

pericytial *adj.* pericítico, -ca.

peridectomy *n.* peridectomía, peritectomía.

peridens *n.* peridens.

peridental *adj.* peridental.

peridentium *n.* peridencio.

periderm *n.* periderma, peridermo.

periderma *n.* periderma, peridermo.

peridermal *adj.* peridérmico, -ca.

peridermic *adj.* peridérmico, -ca.

peridesmic *adj.* peridésmico, -ca.

peridesmitis *n.* peridesmitis.

peridesmium *n.* peridesmio.

perididymis *n.* peridídimo.

perididymitis *n.* peridididimitis.

peridiverticulitis *n.* peridiverticulitis.

periduodenitis *n.* periduodenitis.

peridural *adj.* peridural.

periencephalitis *n.* periencefalitis.

perienteric *adj.* perientérico, -ca.

perienteritis *n.* perienteritis.

periependymal *adj.* periependimal.

periesophageal *adj.* periesofagico, -ca.

periesophagitis *n.* periesofagitis.

perifocal *adj.* perifocal.

perifollicular *adj.* perifolicular.

perifolliculitis *n.* perifoliculitis.

perifolliculitis capitis abscedens et suffodiens perifoliculitis capitis abscedens et suffodiens.

superficial pustular perifolliculitis perifoliculitis pustulosa superficial.

perifuse *v.* perifundir.

perifusion *n.* perifusión.

periganglionic *adj.* periganglionar.

perigastric *adj.* perigástrico, -ca.

perigastritis *n.* perigastritis.

perigemmal *adj.* perigemal.

periglandulitis *n.* periglandulitis.

periglottic *adj.* periglótico, -ca.

periglottis *n.* periglotis.

perihepatic *adj.* perihepático, -ca.

perihepatitis *n.* perihepatitis.

perihernial *adj.* perihernial.

peri-implantitis *n.* periimplantitis.

peri-implantoclasia *n.* periimplantoclasia.

perijejunitis *n.* periyeyunitis.

perikaryon *n.* pericarion.

perikeratic *adj.* periquerático, -ca.

perikyma *n.* pericima.

perilabyrinthitis *n.* perilaberintitis.

perilaryngeal *adj.* perilaríngeo, -a.

perilaryngitis *n.* perilaringitis.

perilenticular *adj.* perilenticular.

periligamentous *adj.* periligamentoso, -sa.

perilympha *n.* perilinfa.

perilymphangial *adj.* perilinfangial.

perilymphangitis *n.* perilinfangeítis.

perilymphatic *adj.* perilinfático, -ca.

perimeningitis *n.* perimeningitis.

perimeter *n.* perímetro.

arc perimeter perímetro de arco.

Goldmann perimeter perímetro de Goldmann.

projection perimeter perímetro de proyección.

Tübingen perimeter perímetro de Tubinga.

perimetric *adj.* perimetral, perimétrico, -ca.

perimetritic *adj.* perimetrítico, -ca.

perimetritis *n.* perimetritis.

perimetrium *n.* perimetrio.

perimetry *n.* perimetría.

computed perimetry perimetría computerizada.

flicker perimetry perimetría flicker.

kinetic perimetry perimetría cinética.

mesopic perimetry perimetría mesópica.

objective perimetry perimetría objetiva.

quantitative perimetry perimetría cuantitativa.

scotopic perimetry perimetría escotópica.

static perimetry perimetría estática.

perimyelis *n.* perimielo.

perimyelitis *n.* perimielitis.

perimyoendocarditis *n.* perimioendocarditis.

perimyositis *n.* perimiositis.

perimysial *adj.* perimisial.

perimysiitis *n.* perimisitis.

perimysitis *n.* perimisitis.

perimysium *n.* perimisio.

perimysium externum perimisio externo.

perimysium internum perimisio interno.

perinatal *adj.* perinatal.

perinatologist *n.* perinatólogo, -ga.

perinatology *n.* perinatología.

perineal *adj.* perineal.

perineocele *n.* perincocele.

perineometer *n.* perineómetro.

perineorrhaphy *n.* perineoplastia, perineorrafia.

perineoscrotal *adj.* perineoescrotal.

perineostomy *n.* perineostomía.

perineosynthesis *n.* perineosíntesis.

perineotomy *n.* perineotomía.

perineovaginal *adj.* perineovaginal.

perinephric *adj.* perinéfrico, -ca.

perinephritic *adj.* perinefrítico, -ca.

perinephritis *n.* perinefritis.

perinephrium *n.* perinefrio.

perineum *n.* periné, perineo.

watering-can perineum perineo en regadera.

perineural *adj.* perineúrico, -ca.

perineuritis *n.* perineuritis.

perineurium *n.* perineurio.

perinuclear *adj.* perinuclear.

periocular *adj.* periocular.

period *n.* período, regla[1].

absolute refractory period período refractario absoluto.

cap period período de capuchón, período de casquete.

cold period período de frío.

critical period período crítico.

eclipse period período de eclipse.

ejection period período de eyección.

extrinsic incubation period período de incubación extrínseca.

fertile period período fértil.

functional refractory period período refractario funcional.

incubative period período de incubación.

induction period período de inducción.

intersystolic period período intersistólico.

intrapartum period período intraparto.

isoelectric period período isoeléctrico.

isometric period período isométrico.

isometric period of cardiac cycle período isométrico del ciclo cardíaco.

latency period período de latencia, período latente.

latent period período de latencia, período latente.

masticatory silent period período silencioso masticatorio.

menstrual period período menstrual.

missed period período faltante.

mitotic period período mitótico.

oedipal period período edípico.

period of invasion período de invasión.

preejection period período de preeyección.

prodromal period período prodrómico.

puerperal period período puerperal.

refractory period período refractario.

refractory period of electronic pacemaker período refractario del marcapaso electrónico.

relative refractory period período refractario relativo.
resting period período de reposo.
silent period período silencioso.
total refractory period período refractario total.
vegetative period período vegetativo.
vulnerable (of heart) period período vulnerable (del corazón).
Wenckebach period período de Wenckebach.
periodic *adj.* periódico, -ca.
periodicity *n.* periodicidad.
  diurnal periodicity periodicidad diurna.
  filarial periodicity periodicidad filariásica.
  lunar periodicity periodicidad lunar.
  malarial periodicity periodicidad palúdica.
  norturnal periodicity periodicidad nocturna.
  subperiodic periodicity periodicidad subperiódica.
periodontal *adj.* periodontal.
periodontics *n.* periodoncia.
periodontist *n.* periodoncista.
periodontitis *n.* periodontitis.
  apical periodontitis periodontitis apical.
  complex periodontitis periodontitis compleja.
  complicated periodontitis periodontitis complicada.
  juvenile periodontitis periodontitis juvenil.
  light periodontitis periodontitis leve.
  simple periodontitis periodontitis simple.
  suppurative periodontitis periodontitis supurativa.
periodontium *n.* periodoncio, periodonto.
periodontoclasia *n.* periodontoclasia.
periodontolysis *n.* periodontólisis.
periodontosis *n.* periodontosis.
periomphalic *adj.* perionfálico, -ca.
perionychia *n.* perioniquia.
perionychium *n.* perioniquio.
perionyx *n.* periónix.
perionyxis *n.* perionixis.
perioophoritis *n.* periooforitis.
perioophorosalpingitis *n.* periooforosalpingitis.
perioperative *adj.* perioperatorio, -ria.
periophthalmic *adj.* perioftálmico, -ca.
periophthalmitis *n.* perioftalmitis.
perioral *adj.* perioral.
periorbita *n.* periórbita.
periorbital *adj.* periorbitario, -ria.
periorchitis *n.* periorquitis.
  periorchitis hemorrhagica periorquitis hemorrágica.
periosteal *adj.* perióstico, -ca.
periosteitis *n.* periosteítis.
periosteoma *n.* periosteoma.
periosteomedullitis *n.* periosteomedulitis.
periosteomyelitis *n.* periosteomielitis.
periosteopathy *n.* periosteopatía.
periosteophyte *n.* periosteofito.
periosteosis *n.* periosteosis.
periosteotome *n.* periosteótomo.
periosteotomy *n.* periosteotomía.
periosteum *n.* periostio.
  alveolar periosteum periostio alveolar.
  periosteum alveolare periostio alveolar.
  periosteum cranii periostio craneal.
periostitis *n.* periostitis.
  orbital periostitis periostitis orbitaria.
periostoma *n.* periostoma.
periostosis *n.* periostosis.
periostosteitis *n.* periostosteítis.
periostotome *n.* periostótomo.

periostotomy *n.* periostotomía.
periotic *adj.* periótico, -ca.
periovaritis *n.* periovaritis.
periovular *adj.* periovular.
peripachymeningitis *n.* peripaquimeningitis.
peripancreatitis *n.* peripancreatitis.
peripapillary *adj.* peripapilar.
peripenial *adj.* peripeniano, -na.
peripharyngeal *adj.* perifaríngeo, -a.
peripheral *adj.* periférico, -ca.
peripherocentral *adj.* periferocentral.
periphery *n.* periferia.
periphlebitic *adj.* periflebítico, -ca.
periphlebitis *n.* periflebitis.
peripolar *adj.* peripolar.
perlpolesis *n.* peripolesis.
periporitis *n.* periporitis.
periportal *adj.* periportal.
periproctitis *n.* periproctitis.
periprostatic *adj.* periprostático, -ca.
periprostatitis *n.* periprostatitis.
peripylephlebitis *n.* peripiloflebitis.
peripylic *adj.* peripílico, -ca.
peripyloric *adj.* peripilórico, -ca.
perirectal *adj.* perirrectal.
perirectitis *n.* perirrectitis.
perirenal *adj.* perirrenal.
perirhinal *adj.* perirrínico, -ca.
perirhizoclasia *n.* perirrizoclasia.
perisalpingitis *n.* perisalpingitis.
perisalpingo-ovaritis *n.* perisalpingoovaritis.
perisalpinx *n.* perisálpinx.
periscopic *adj.* periscópico, -ca.
perisigmoiditis *n.* perisigmoiditis.
perispermatitis *n.* periespermatitis.
  perispermatitis serosa periespermatitis serosa.
perisplanchnic *adj.* periesplácnico, -ca.
perisplanchnitis *n.* periesplacnitis.
perisplenic *adj.* periesplénico, -ca.
perisplenitis *n.* periesplenitis.
perispondylic *adj.* periespondílico, -ca.
perispondylitis *n.* periespondilitis.
peristalsis *n.* peristaltismo.
  mass peristalsis peristaltismo masivo.
  retrograde peristalsis peristaltismo retrógrado.
  reversed peristalsis peristaltismo invertido.
peristaltic *adj.* peristáltico, -ca.
peristaphylitis *n.* periestafilitis.
peristasis *n.* peristasis.
peristole *n.* perístole.
peristolic *adj.* peristólico, -ca.
peristomal *adj.* peristomatoso, -sa.
peristomatous *adj.* peristomatoso, -sa.
peristrumous *adj.* periestrumoso, -sa.
perisynovial *adj.* perisinovial.
peritectomy *n.* peritectomía.
peritendineum *n.* peritendíneo.
peritendinitis *n.* peritendinitis.
  peritendinitis calcarea peritendinitis calcárea.
peritenon *n.* peritenón.
peritenontitis *n.* peritenontitis.
perithelium *n.* peritelio.
  Eberth's perithelium peritelio de Eberth.
perithoracic *adj.* peritorácico, -ca.
perithyroiditis *n.* peritiroiditis.
peritomist *n.* peritomista.
peritomy *n.* peritomía.
peritoneal *adj.* peritoneal.
peritonealgia *n.* peritonealgia.
peritoneocentesis *n.* peritoneocentesis.
peritoneoclysis *n.* peritoneoclisis.
peritoneopathy *n.* peritoneopatía.

peritoneopericardial *adj.* peritoneopericárdico, -ca.
peritoneopexy *n.* peritoneopexia.
peritoneoplasty *n.* peritoneoplastia.
peritoneoscope *n.* peritoneoscopio.
peritoneoscopy *n.* peritoneoscopia.
peritoneotomy *n.* peritoneotomía.
peritoneum *n.* peritoneo.
peritonism *n.* peritonismo.
peritonitis *n.* peritonitis.
  adhesive peritonitis peritonitis adherente.
  bile peritonitis peritonitis biliar.
  chemical peritonitis peritonitis química.
  chyle peritonitis peritonitis quílica.
  circumscribed peritonitis peritonitis circunscrita.
  diaphragmatic peritonitis peritonitis diafragmática.
  diffuse peritonitis peritonitis difusa.
  fibrocaseous peritonitis peritonitis fibrocaseosa.
  gas peritonitis peritonitis gaseosa.
  general peritonitis peritonitis general.
  localized peritonitis peritonitis localizada.
  meconium peritonitis peritonitis por meconio.
  pelvic peritonitis peritonitis pélvica.
  peritonitis deformans peritonitis deformante.
  peritonitis encapsulans peritonitis encapsulante.
  productive peritonitis peritonitis productiva.
  tuberculous peritonitis peritonitis tuberculosa.
peritonsillar *adj.* periamigdalar.
peritonsillitis *n.* periamigdalitis.
peritracheal *adj.* peritraqueal.
peritrochanteric *adj.* peritrocantérico, -ca.
perityphlic *adj.* peritíflico, -ca.
periumbilical *adj.* periumbilical.
periungual *adj.* periungular.
periureteral *adj.* periureteral.
periureteric *adj.* periureteral.
periureteritis *n.* periureteritis.
  periureteritis plastica periureteritis plástica.
periurethral *adj.* periuretral.
periurethritis *n.* periuretritis.
periuterine *adj.* periuterino, -na.
periuvular *adj.* periuvular.
perivaginitis *n.* perivaginitis.
perivascular *adj.* perivascular.
perivasculitis *n.* perivasculitis.
perivenous *adj.* perivenoso, -sa.
perivertebral *adj.* perivertebral.
perivesical *adj.* perivesical.
perivisceral *adj.* perivisceral.
perivisceritis *n.* perivisceritis.
perivitelline *adj.* perivitelino, -na.
perlèche *n.* boquera, perlèche, vaharera.
permeability *n.* permeabilidad.
permeable *adj.* permeable.
permeant *adj.* permeante.
permeate *v.* permear.
permeation *n.* permeación.
pernicious *adj.* pernicioso, -sa.
perniosis *n.* perniosis.
perobrachius *n.* perobraquio.
perocephalus *n.* perocéfalo.
perodactylia *n.* perodactilia.
perodactyly *n.* perodactilia.
peromelia *n.* peromelia.
peroneal *adj.* peroneo, -a.
peroneocalcaneal *adj.* peroneocalcáneo, -a.
peroneotibial *adj.* peroneotibial.

peropus *n.* peropo.
peroral *adj.* perbucal, peroral.
perosplanchnia *n.* peroesplacnia.
petro-occipital *adj.* petrooccipital.
perosseous *adj.* peróseo, -a.
perseveration *n.* perseveración.
persistence *n.* persistencia.
persistent *adj.* persistente.
persona *n.* persona.
personality *n.* personalidad.
anal personality personalidad anal.
cyclothymic personality individuo ciclotímico.
epileptic personality personalidad epileptoide.
split personality personalidad escindida.
persuasion *n.* persuasión.
perversion *n.* perversión.
polymorphous perversion perversión polimorfa.
sexual perversion perversión sexual.
pervert *n.* perverso, -sa.
perverted *adj.* pervertido, -da.
perycaliceal *adj.* pericaliceo, -a.
pes pes, pie.
pes abductus pes abductus, pie abducto.
pes adductus pes adductus, pie aducto.
pes cavus pes cavus, pie cavo.
pes corvinus pie de cuervo.
pes equinovalgus pes equinovalgus, pie equinovalgo.
pes equinovarus pes equinovarus, pie equinovaro.
pes equinus pie equino.
pes gigas pes gigas, pie gigante.
pes planovalgus pes planovalgus, pie planovalgo.
pes planus pes planus, pie plano.
pes pronatus pes pronatus, pie en pronación.
pes supinatus pes supinatus, pie supino.
pes talus pes talus, pie talo.
pes valgus pes valgus, pie valgo.
pes varus pes varus, pie varo.
pessary *n.* pesario.
diaphragm pessary pesario de diafragma.
Gariel's pessary pesario de Gariel.
Hodge's pessary pesario de Hodge.
ring pessary pesario de anillo.
pessimism *n.* pesimismo.
therapeutic pessimism pesimismo terapéutico.
pesticemia *n.* pesticemia.
pestiferous *adj.* pestífero, -ra.
pestilence *n.* pestilencia.
pestilential *adj.* pestilente.
pestis *n.* peste.
pestis variolosa peste variolosa.
pesudocolloid *n.* seudocoloide.
petechia *n.* petequia.
Tardieu's petechia petequia de Tardieu.
petechial *adj.* petequial.
petechiasis *n.* petequiasis.
petiolate *adj.* peciolado, -da.
petiolated *adj.* peciolado, -da.
petiolus *n.* peciolo, pecíolo.
petiolus epiglottidis pecíolo epiglótico.
petroccipital *adj.* petroccipital.
petrolatum *n.* vaselina.
heavy liquid petrolatum vaselina líquida pesada.
hydrophilic petrolatum vaselina hidrófila.
light liquid petrolatum vaselina líquida ligera, vaselina líquida liviana.
liquid petrolatum vaselina líquida.
petrolatum liquidum vaselina líquida.
petrolatum liquidum leve vaselina líquida ligera, vaselina líquida liviana.

white petrolatum vaselina blanca.
petromastoid *adj.* petromastoideo, -a.
petro-occipital *adj.* petrooccipital.
petrositis *n.* petrositis.
petrosomastoid *adj.* petrosomastoideo, -a.
petrosphenoid *adj.* petroesfenoidal.
petrosquamosal *adj.* petroescamoso, -sa.
petrosquamous *adj.* petroescamoso, -sa.
petrous *adj.* pétreo, -a.
pexis *n.* pexis.
phacoanaphylaxis *n.* facoanafilaxia.
phacocele *n.* facocele.
phacocyst *n.* facocisto.
phacocystectomy *n.* facocistectomía.
phacocystitis *n.* facocistitis.
phacodonesis *n.* facodonesis.
phacoemulsification *n.* facoemulsificación, facoemulsión.
phacoerysis *n.* facoéresis, facoerisis.
phacofragmentation *n.* facofragmentación.
phacoglaucoma *n.* facoglaucoma.
phacohymenitis *n.* facohimenitis.
phacoid *adj.* facoide.
phacoidoscope *n.* facoidoscopio.
phacolysin *n.* facolisina.
phacolysis *n.* facólisis.
phacolytic *adj.* facolítico, -ca.
phacoma *n.* facoma.
phacomalacia *n.* facomalacia.
phacomatosis *n.* facomatosis.
phacometachoresis *n.* facometacoresis.
phacometecesis *n.* facometecesis.
phacopalingenesis *n.* facopalingénesis.
phacoplanesis *n.* facoplanesis.
phacosclerosis *n.* facoesclerosis, facosclerosis.
phacoscope *n.* facoscopio.
phacoscopy *n.* facoscopia.
phacoscotasmus *n.* facoscotasmo.
phacotherapy *n.* facoterapia.
phacotoxic *adj.* facotóxico, -ca.
phaeohyphomycosis *n.* feohifomicosis.
phage *n.* fago.
phagedena *n.* fagedena, fagedeno.
phagedena gangrenosa fagedena gangrenosa.
phagedena nosocomialis fagedena nosocomial.
phagedena tropica fagedena tropical.
sloughing phagedena fagedena esfacelante.
phagedenic *adj.* fagedénico, -ca.
phagocyte *n.* fagocito.
phagocytic *adj.* fagocitario, -ria, fagocítico, -ca.
phagocytin *n.* fagocitina.
phagocytize *v.* fagocitar.
phagocytolysis *n.* fagocitólisis.
phagocytolytic *adj.* fagocitolítico, -ca.
phagocytosis *n.* fagocitosis.
induced phagocytosis fagocitosis inducida.
spontaneous phagocytosis fagocitosis espontánea.
phagodynamometer *n.* fagodinamómetro.
phagokaryosis *n.* fagocariosis.
phagolysis *n.* fagólisis.
phagolysosome *n.* fagolisosoma.
phagolytic *adj.* fagolítico, -ca.
phagopyrism *n.* fagopirismo.
phagosome *n.* fagosoma.
phakitis *n.* faquitis.
phakoma *n.* facoma.
phakomatosis *n.* facomatosis.
phalacrosis *n.* falacrosis.
phalangeal *adj.* falángico, -ca.
phalangectomy *n.* falangectomia.
phalangeta *n.* falangeta.

phalangosis *n.* falangosis.
phalanx *n.* falange.
phallalgia *n.* falalgia.
phallectomy *n.* falectomía.
phallic *adj.* fálico, -ca.
phalliform *adj.* faliforme.
phallitis *n.* falitis.
phallocampsis *n.* falocampsia, falocampsis.
phallocrypsis *n.* falocripsis.
phallodynia *n.* falodinia.
phalloid *adj.* faloide.
phalloncus *n.* falonco.
phalloplasty *n.* faloplastia.
phallorrhagia *n.* falorragia.
phallorrhea *n.* falorrea.
phallotomy *n.* falotomía.
phallus *n.* falo.
phanerogenic *adj.* fanerogénico, -ca, fanerógeno, -na.
phaneroscope *n.* faneroscopio.
phanerosis *n.* fanerosis.
fatty phanerosis fanerosis grasa.
phanerozoite *n.* fanerozoíto.
phantasm *n.* fantasma.
phantasmagoria *n.* fantasmagoría.
phantasmatomoria *n.* fantasmatomoria.
phantasmoscopia *n.* fantasmoscopia.
phantasmoscopy *n.* fantasmoscopia.
phantasy *n.* fantasía.
pharmaceutic *adj.* farmacéutico[2], -ca.
pharmaceutical *adj.* farmacéutico[2], -ca.
pharmaceutics *n.* farmacia.
clinical pharmaceutics farmacia clínica.
Galenic pharmaceutics farmacia galénica.
pharmaceutist *n.* farmacéutico[1], -ca.
pharmacist *n.* farmacéutico[1], -ca.
pharmacochemistry *n.* farmacoquímica.
pharmacodiagnosis *n.* farmacodiagnóstico.
pharmacodynamic *adj.* farmacodinámico, -ca.
pharmacodynamics *n.* farmacodinamia.
pharmacoendocrinology *n.* farmacoendocrinología.
pharmacogenetics *n.* farmacogenética.
pharmacognosist *n.* farmacognosista.
pharmacognosy *n.* farmacognosia.
pharmacography *n.* farmacografía.
pharmacokinetic *adj.* farmacocinético, -ca.
pharmacokinetics *n.* farmacocinética.
pharmacologic *adj.* farmacológico, -ca.
pharmacological *adj.* farmacológico, -ca.
pharmacologist *n.* farmacólogo, -ga.
clinical pharmacologist farmacólogo clínico.
pharmacology *n.* farmacología.
clinical pharmacology farmacología clínica.
pharmacopeial *adj.* farmacopeico, -ca.
pharmacopoeia *n.* farmacopea.
pharmacotherapy *n.* farmacoterapia.
pharmacy *n.* farmacia.
pharyngalgia *n.* faringalgia.
pharyngeal *adj.* faríngeo, -a.
pharyngectasia *n.* faringectasia.
pharyngectomy *n.* faringectomía.
pharyngemphraxis *n.* faringenfraxis.
pharyngism *n.* faringismo.
pharyngismus *n.* faringismo.
pharyngitic *adj.* faringítico, -ca.
pharyngitis *n.* faringitis.
acute lymphonodular pharyngitis faringitis linfonodular aguda.
acute pharyngitis faringitis aguda.
atrophic pharyngitis faringitis atrófica.
catarrhal pharyngitis faringitis catarral.
chronic pharyngitis faringitis crónica.
croupous pharyngitis faringitis crupal, faringitis cruposa.

diphtheritic pharyngitis faringitis diftérica.
follicular pharyngitis faringitis folicular.
gangrenous pharyngitis faringitis gangrenosa.
glandular pharyngitis faringitis glandular.
granular pharyngitis faringitis granular, faringitis granulosa.
membranous pharyngitis faringitis membranosa.
pharyngitis herpetica faringitis herpética.
pharyngitis hypertrophica lateralis faringitis hipertrófica lateral.
pharyngitis keratosa faringitis queratosa.
pharyngitis sicca faringitis seca.
phlegmonous pharyngitis faringitis apostemática, faringitis flemonosa.
ulcerative pharyngitis faringitis ulcerosa.
ulceromembranous pharyngitis faringitis ulceromembranosa.
pharyngoamygdalitis *n.* faringoamigdalitis.
pharyngocele *n.* faringocele.
pharyngodynia *n.* faringodinia.
pharyngoepyglottic *adj.* faringoepiglótico, -ca.
pharyngoesophageal *adj.* faringoesofágico, -ca.
pharyngoesophagoplasty *n.* faringoesofagoplastia.
pharyngoglossal *adj.* faringogloso, -sa.
pharyngokeratosis *n.* faringoqueratosis.
pharyngolaryngeal *adj.* faringolaríngeo, -a.
pharyngolaryngitis *n.* faringolaringitis.
pharyngolith *n.* faringolito.
pharyngology *n.* faringología.
pharyngomaxillary *adj.* faringomaxilar.
pharyngomycosis *n.* faringomicosis.
pharyngonasal *adj.* faringonasal.
pharyngo-oral *adj.* faringobucal.
pharyngopalatine *adj.* faringopalatino, -na.
pharyngoparalysis *n.* faringoparálisis.
pharyngopathia *n.* faringopatía.
pharyngopathy *n.* faringopatía.
pharyngoperistole *n.* faringoperístole.
pharyngoplasty *n.* faringoplastia.
pharyngoplegia *n.* faringoplejía.
pharyngorhinitis *n.* faringorrinitis.
pharyngorrhagia *n.* faringorragia.
pharyngosalpingitis *n.* faringosalpingitis.
pharyngoscleroma *n.* faringoscleroma.
pharyngoscope *n.* faringoscopio.
pharyngoscopy *n.* faringoscopia.
pharyngospasm *n.* faringoespasmo.
pharyngostenosis *n.* faringoestenosis, faringostenosis.
pharyngotherapy *n.* faringoterapia.
pharyngotome *n.* faringótomo.
pharyngotomy *n.* faringotomía.
external pharyngotomy faringotomía externa.
internal pharyngotomy faringotomía interna.
subhyoid pharyngotomy faringotomía subhioidea.
pharyngotonsillitis *n.* faringotonsilitis.
pharyngotyphoid *n.* faringotifoidea.
pharyngoxerosis *n.* faringoxerosis.
pharyningospasm *n.* faringospasmo.
pharynx *n.* faringe.
phase *n.* fase.
acceleration phase fase de aceleración.
alpha phase fase alfa.
aqueous phase fase acuosa.
autistic phase fase autista.
be in phase estar en fase.
beta phase fase beta.
cis phase fase cis.
continuous phase fase continua.

coupling phase fase de acoplamiento.
deceleration phase fase de desaceleración.
eclipse phase fase de eclipse.
eruptive phase fase eruptiva.
expiration phase fase espiratoria.
external phase fase externa.
follicular phase fase estrogénica, fase folicular.
genital phase fase genital.
induction phase fase de inducción.
inductive phase fase de inducción.
lag phase fase demorada.
latent phase fase latente.
log phase fase de intervalo bacteriano.
logarithmic phase fase exponencial, fase logarítmica.
luteal phase fase luteínica.
meiotic phase fase meiótica.
menstrual phase fase menstrual.
motofacient phase fase motofaciente.
negative phase fase apofiláctica, fase negativa.
oedipal phase fase cdípica.
oral phase fase oral.
out of phase fuera de fase.
phallic phase fase fálica.
phase 0 fase 0.
phase 1 fase 1.
phase 2 fase 2.
phase 3 fase 3.
phase 4 fase 4.
phase of decline fase de declinación.
phase of maximum slope fase de máxima pendiente.
positive phase fase positiva.
pregenital phase fase pregenital.
premeiotic phase fase premeiótica.
preoedipical phase fase preedípica.
preoperational thought phase fase de pensamiento preoperativo.
radial growth phase fase de crecimiento radial.
reduction phase fase de reducción.
rest phase fase de descanso.
resting phase fase de reposo.
S phase fase S.
secretory phase fase secretora.
sensorimotor phase fase sensitivomotora.
stance phase of gait fase de apoyo de la marcha.
stationary phase fase estacionaria.
supernormal recovery phase fase de recuperación supernormal.
swing phase of gait fase de balanceo de la marcha.
trans phase fase trans.
vertical growth phase fase de crecimiento vertical.
vulnerable phase fase vulnerable.
phatnorrhagia *n.* fatnorragia.
phene *n.* feno.
phenetidinuria *n.* fenetidinuria.
phenobutiodil *n.* fenobutiodil.
phenocopy *n.* fenocopia.
phenodeviant *adj.* fenoanómalo, -la, fenodesviado, -da.
phenogenetics *n.* fenogenética.
phenolemia *n.* fenolemia.
phenolization *n.* fenolización.
phenologist *n.* fenologista.
phenology *n.* fenología.
phenoluria *n.* fenoluria.
phenom *n.* fenoma.
phenomenology *n.* fenomenología.
phenomenon *n.* fenómeno.
autoscopic phenomenon heautoscopia.

phenotype *n.* fenotipo.
Bombay phenotype fenotipo de bombay.
phenotypic *adj.* fenotípico, -ca.
phenozygous *adj.* fenocigo, -ga.
phenylalaninemia *n.* fenilalaninemia.
phenylketonuria (FKU) *n.* fenilcetonuria (FCU).
maternal phenylketonuria (FKU) fenilcetonuria (FCU) maternal.
pheochrome *adj.* feocromo, -ca.
pheochromoblast *n.* feocromoblasto.
pheochromocyte *n.* feocromocito.
pheochromocytoma *n.* feocromocitoma.
pheomelanin *n.* feomelanina.
pheomelanogenesis *n.* feomelanogénesis.
pheomelanosome *n.* feomelanosoma.
pheresis *n.* féresis.
pheromone *n.* feromonas.
phial *n.* fial.
phimosis *n.* fimosis.
phimotic *adj.* fimótico, -ca.
phlebalgia *n.* flebalgia.
phlebanesthesia *n.* flebanestesia, fleboanestesia.
phlebangioma *n.* flebangioma.
phlebarteriectasia *n.* flebarteriectasia.
phlebasthenia *n.* flebastenia.
phlebectasis *n.* flebectasis.
phlebectomy *n.* flebectomía.
phlebectopia *n.* flebectopia.
phlebectopy *n.* flebectopia.
phlebemphraxis *n.* flebenfraxis.
phlebepatitis *n.* flebepatitis.
phlebeurysm *n.* flebeurismo.
phlebexairesis *n.* flebexairesis.
phlebismus *n.* flebismo.
phlebitic *adj.* flebítico, -ca.
phlebitis *n.* flebitis.
adhesive phlebitis flebitis adhesiva.
anemic phlebitis flebitis anémica.
blue phlebitis flebitis azul.
chlorotic phlebitis flebitis clorótica.
gouty phlebitis flebitis gotosa.
migrating phlebitis flebitis migratoria.
obliterating phlebitis flebitis obliterante, flebitis obliterativa.
obstructive phlebitis flebitis obstructiva.
phlebitis migrans flebitis migratoria.
phlebitis nodularis necrotisans flebitis necrótica, flebitis nodular, flebitis nodular necrosante.
plastic phlebitis flebitis plástica.
productive phlebitis flebitis productiva.
proliferative phlebitis flebitis proliferativa.
puerperal phlebitis flebitis puerperal.
sclerosing phlebitis flebitis esclerosante.
septic phlebitis flebitis séptica.
sinus phlebitis flebitis sinusal.
suppurative phlebitis flebitis supurativa.
phleboclysis *n.* fleboclisis.
drip phleboclysis fleboclisis gota a gota, fleboclisis por goteo.
slow phleboclysis fleboclisis lenta.
phlebodynamics *n.* flebodinamia.
phleboestrepsis *n.* fleboestrepsis.
phlebofibrosis *n.* flebofibrosis.
phlebogenous *adj.* flebógeno, -na.
phlebogram *n.* flebograma.
phlebograph *n.* flebógrafo.
phlebography *n.* flebografía.
phleboid *adj.* fleboide.
phlebolith *n.* flebolito.
phlebolithiasis *n.* flebolitiasis.
phlebology *n.* flebología.
phlebomanometer *n.* flebomanómetro.

phlebometritis n. flebometritis.
phlebomyomatosis n. flebomiomatosis.
phlebonarcosis n. flebonarcosis.
phlebopexy n. flebopexia.
phlebophlebostomy n. fleboflebostomía.
phlebophthalmotomy n. fleboftalmotomía.
phlebopiezometry n. flebopiezometría.
phleboplasty n. fleboplastia.
phleborrhagia n. fleborragia.
phleborrhaphy n. fleborrafia.
phleborrhexis n. fleborrexis.
phlebosclerosis n. fleboesclerosis, flebosclerosis.
phlebosis n. flebosis.
phlebostasis n. flebostasia,, flebostasis.
phlebostenosis n. fleboestenosis, flebostenosis.
phlebothrombosis n. flebotrombosis.
phlebotome n. flebótomo.
phlebotomist n. flebotomista.
phlebotomize v. flebotomizar.
phlebotomy n. flebotomía.
phlegm n. flema.
phlegmasia n. flegmasía.
  cellulitic phlegmasia flegmasía celulítica.
  phlegmasia alba dolens flegmasía alba dolens.
  phlegmasia cerulea dolens flegmasía cerulea dolens.
  thrombotic phlegmasia flegmasía trombótica.
phlegmon n. flemón.
  diffuse phlegmon flemón difuso.
  emphysematous phlegmon flemón enfisematoso.
  gas phlegmon flemón gaseoso.
  pancreatic phlegmon flemón pancreático.
phlegmonosis n. flemonosis.
phlegmonous adj. flemonoso, -sa, flemoso, -sa.
phlogistic adj. flogístico, -ca.
phlogisticozymoid n. flogisticozimoide.
phlogocyte n. flogocito.
phlogocytosis n. flogocitosis.
phlogogenic adj. flogogénico, -ca.
phlogosis n. flogosis.
phlogotherapy n. flogoterapia.
phlogotic adj. flogósico, -ca.
phloxine n. floxina.
phlyctena n. flictena.
phlyctenar adj. flictenar.
phlyctenoid adj. flictenoide.
phlyctenosis n. flictenosis.
phlyctenotherapy n. flictenoterapia.
phlyctenous adj. flictenoso, -sa.
phlyctenular adj. flictenular.
phlyctenule n. flicténula.
phlyctenulosis n. flictenulosis.
phobia n. fobia.
phobic adj. fóbico, -ca.
phocomelia n. focomelia.
phocomelus n. focomelo.
phonacoscope n. fonacoscopio.
phonacoscopy n. fonacoscopia.
phonarteriogram n. fonoarteriograma.
phonarteriographic adj. fonoarteriográfico, -ca.
phonarteriography n. fonoarteriografía.
phonasthenia n. fonastenia.
phonation n. fonación.
phonatory adj. fonatorio, -ria.
phonautograph n. fonautógrafo.
phonendoscope n. fonendoscopio.
phonendoskiascope n. fonendosquiascopio.
phoniatrician n. foniatra.
phoniatrics n. foniatría.

phonic adj. fónico, -ca.
phonism n. fonismo.
phonoangiography n. fonoangiografía.
phonoauscultation n. fonoauscultación.
phonocardioagraph n. fonocardiógrafo.
phonocardiogram n. fonocardiograma.
phonocardiographic adj. fonocardiográfico, -ca.
phonocardiography n. fonocardiografía.
phonocatheter n. fonocatéter.
phonocatheterization n. fonocateterismo.
  intracardiac phonocatheterization fonocateterismo intracardiaco.
phonoelectrocardioscope n. fonoelectrocardioscopio.
phonogram n. fonograma.
phonograph n. fonógrafo.
phonomania n. fonomanía.
phonometer n. fonómetro.
phonomyoclonus n. fonomioclonía, fonomioclono.
phonomyography n. fonomiografía.
phonopathy n. fonopatía.
phonophobia n. fonofobia.
phonophore n. fonóforo.
phonophotography n. fonofotografía.
phonopsia n. fonopsia.
phonoreceptor n. fonorreceptor.
phonorenogram n. fonorrenograma.
phonoscope n. fonoscopio.
phonoscopy n. fonoscopia.
phonoselectoscope n. fonoselectoscopio.
phonostethograph n. fonoestetógrafo, fonostetógrafo.
phontactoscope n. fontactoscopio.
phoriascope n. foriascopio.
phorocytosis n. forocitosis.
phorologist n. forólogo, -ga.
phorology n. forología.
phorometer n. forómetro.
phorometry n. forometría.
phoront n. foronte.
phoro-optometer n. forooptómetro, foroptómetro.
phoroptor n. foróptero.
phoroscope n. foroscopio.
phorotone n. forótono.
phose n. fosia.
phosgenic adj. fosgénico, -ca.
phosis n. fosis.
phosphagen n. fosfágeno, fosfógeno.
phosphagenic adj. fosfagénico, -ca.
phosphastat n. fosfastat.
phosphated adj. fosfatado, -da.
phosphatemia n. fosfatemia.
phosphatidosis n. fosfatidosis.
phosphatoptosis n. fosfatoptosis.
phosphaturia n. fosfaturia.
phosphoglucomutase n. fosfoglucomutasa.
phosphoglucoprotein n. fosfoglucoproteína.
phosphoglyceride n. fosfoglicérido.
phospholipid n. fosfolípido.
phospholipidemia n. fosfolipidemia.
phosphonecrosis n. fosfonecrosis, fosforonecrosis.
phosphopenia n. fosfopenia, fosforopenia.
phosphoprotein n. fosfoproteína.
phosphorescence n. fosforescencia.
phosphorescent adj. fosforescente.
phosphorism n. fosforismo.
phosphorized adj. fosforizado, -da.
phosphorolysis n. fosforólisis.
phosphoroscope n. fosforoscopio.
phosphoruria n. fosforuria.
phosphorylation n. fosforilación.

phosphuresis n. fosfuresis.
phosphuretic adj. fosfurético, -ca.
photalgia n. fotalgia.
photallochromy n. fotalocromía.
photechy n. fotequia.
photesthesis n. fotestesia.
photic adj. fótico, -ca.
photism n. fotismo.
photoablation n. fotoablación.
photoactinic adj. fotoactínico, -ca.
photoactive adj. fotoactivo, -va.
photoallergy n. fotoalergia.
photoautotrophic adj. fotoautotrófico, -ca.
photobacteria n. fotobacteria.
photobiology n. fotobiología.
photocatalysis n. fotocatálisis.
photoceptor n. fotoceptor.
photochemical adj. fotoquímico, -ca.
photochemistry n. fotoquímica.
photochemotherapy n. fotoquimioterapia.
photochromogen n. fotocromógena.
photocoagulation n. fotocoagulación.
photocoagulator n. fotocoagulador.
  laser photocoagulator fotocoagulador de láser.
  xenon-arc photocoagulator fotocoagulador de arco de xenón.
photodermatitis n. fotodermatitis.
photodermatosis n. fotodermatosis.
photodistribution n. fotodistribución.
photodynamic adj. fotodinámico, -ca.
photodynamics n. fotodinamia.
photodynia n. fotodinia.
photoelectric adj. fotoeléctrico, -ca.
photoelectrometer n. fotoelectrómetro.
photoelectron n. fotoelectrón.
photoelement n. fotoelemento.
photoerythema n. fotoeritema.
photofluorogram n. fotofluorograma.
photofluorography n. fotofluorografía, fotorradiografía.
photofluoroscopy n. fotofluoroscopia.
photogastroscope n. fotogastroscopio.
photogen n. fotógeno.
photogenic adj. fotogénico, -ca.
photogenous adj. fotogénico, -ca.
photogram n. fotograma.
photohematachometer n. fotohematacómetro.
photoinactivation n. fotoinactivación.
photokinesis n. fotocinesia, fotocinesis.
photokinetic adj. fotocinético, -ca.
photokinetics n. fotocinética.
photokymograph n. fotoquimógrafo.
photolitic adj. fotolítico, -ca.
photology n. fotología.
photoluminescent adj. fotoluminiscente.
photoluminiscence n. fotoluminiscencia.
photolysis n. fotólisis.
photolyte n. fotolito.
photoma n. fotoma.
photomacrography n. fotomacrografía.
photomagnetism n. fotomagnetismo.
photometer n. fotómetro.
  Förster photometer fotómetro de förster.
photometry n. fotometría.
photomicrography n. fotomicrografía.
photomicroscopy n. fotomicroscopia.
photomyoclonus n. fotomioclono.
photon n. fotón.
photoncia n. fotoncia.
photonosus n. fotonosis.
photopathy n. fotopatía.
photoperceptive adj. fotoperceptivo, -va.
photoperiod n. fotoperiodicidad.

photopharmacology *n.* fotofarmacología.
photophilic *adj.* fotofílico, -ca.
photophobia *n.* fotofobia.
photophonic *adj.* fotofóbico, -ca.
photophthalmia *n.* fotoftalmía.
photopia *n.* fotopía.
photopic *adj.* fotópico, -ca.
photopsia *n.* fotopsia.
photopsin *n.* fotopsina.
photoptarmosis *n.* fotoptarmosis.
photoptometer *n.* fotoptómetro.
photoptometry *n.* fotoptometría.
photoradiation *n.* fotorradiación.
photoradiometer *n.* fotorradiómetro.
photoreaction *n.* fotorreacción.
photoreactivation *n.* fotorreactivación.
photoreceptive *adj.* fotorreceptivo, -va.
photoreceptor *n.* fotorreceptor, -ra.
photoretinitis *n.* fotorretinitis.
photoretinopathy *n.* fotorretinopatía.
photoscan *n.* fotocentelleo, fotocentelleografía.
photoscopy *n.* fotoscopia.
photosensitization *n.* fotosensibilización.
photosensor *n.* fotosensor.
photostable *adj.* fotoestable, fotostable.
photostethoscope *n.* fotoestetoscopio, fotostetoscopio.
photosthetic *adj.* fotoestético, -ca.
photostress *n.* fotoestrés.
photosynthesis *n.* fotosíntesis.
phototaxis *n.* fototactismo, fototaxia, fototaxis.
phototherapy *n.* fototerapia.
photothermal *adj.* fototérmico, -ca.
photothermy *n.* fototermia.
phototonus *n.* fototono.
phototoxic *adj.* fototóxico, -ca.
phototoxis *n.* fototoxis.
photuria *n.* foturia.
phrenalgia *n.* frenalgia.
phrenemphraxis *n.* frenenfraxis.
phrenetic *adj.* frenético, -ca.
phrenic *adj.* frénico, -ca.
phrenicectomy *n.* frenectomía, frenicectomía.
phreniclasia *n.* freniclasia, freniclasis.
phreniclasis *n.* freniclasia, freniclasis.
phrenicoexeresis *n.* frenicoexéresis.
phreniconeurectomy *n.* freniconeurectomía.
phrenicotomy *n.* frenicotomía.
phrenicotripsy *n.* frenicotripsia.
phrenitis *n.* frenitis.
phrenocolic *adj.* frenocólico, -ca.
phrenocolopexy *n.* frenocolopexia.
phrenodynia *n.* frenodinia.
phrenogastric *adj.* frenogástrico, -ca.
phrenoglottic *adj.* frenoglótico, -ca.
phrenograph *n.* frenógrafo.
phrenohepatic *adj.* frenohepático, -ca.
phrenoplasty *n.* frenoplastia.
phrenoplegia *n.* frenoparálisis, frenoplejía.
phrenoptosis *n.* frenoptosis.
phrenospasm *n.* frenoespasmo, frenospasmo.
phrenosplenic *adj.* frenoesplénico, -ca, frenosplénico, -ca.
phrictopathic *adj.* frictopático, -ca.
phrynoderma *n.* frinodermia.
phthinoid *adj.* tinoide, -a.
phthiriasis *n.* ftiriasis, ptiriasis.
  phthiriasis capitis ptiriasis de la cabeza.
  phthiriasis corporis ptiriasis del cuerpo.
  phthiriasis pubis ptiriasis del pubis.
phthisic *adj.* tísico, -ca.
phthisiogenesis *n.* tisiogénesis.

phthisiogenetic *adj.* tisiogénico, -ca, tisiógeno, -na.
phthisiology *n.* tisiología.
phthisiotherapeutical *adj.* tisioterapéutico, -ca.
phthisiotherapist *n.* tisioterapeuta.
phthisiotherapy *n.* tisioterapia.
phthisis *n.* tisis.
  abdominal phthisis tisis abdominal, tisis mesentérica.
  acute miliary phthisis tisis aguda granúlica.
  essential phthisis bulbi tisis esencial, tisis esencial del globo ocular.
  ocular phthisis tisis ocular.
  phthisis bulbi tisis del globo ocular.
  phthisis corneae tisis corneal.
phycomycetosis *n.* ficomicetosis.
phycomycetous *adj.* ficomicetoso, -sa.
phycomycosis *n.* ficomicosis.
  phycomycosis entomophthorae ficomicosis entomóftora.
  subcutaneous phycomycosis ficomicosis subcutánea.
phylacagogic *adj.* filacagogo, -ga.
phylactic *adj.* filáctico, -ca.
phylactotransfusion *n.* filactotransfusión.
phylagrypnia *n.* filagripnia.
phylaxiology *n.* filaxiología.
phylaxis *n.* filaxis.
phyletic *adj.* filético, -ca.
phyllode *adj.* filoide, filoideo, -a.
phylogenesis *n.* filogénesis.
phylogenetic *adj.* filogenético, -ca.
phylogenic *adj.* filogénico, -ca.
phylogeny *n.* filogenia.
phyma *n.* fima.
phymatology *n.* fimatología.
phymatorrhysin *n.* fimatorrisina.
phymosiectomy *n.* fimosiectomía.
physaliferous *adj.* fisalífero, -ra.
physaliform *adj.* fisaliforme.
physaliphore *adj.* fisalífero, -ra, fisalíforo, -ra.
physalis *n.* fisalis.
physalization *n.* fisalización.
physalopteriasis *n.* fisalopteriasis.
physeal *adj.* fisario, -ria, fiseal.
physiatrics *n.* fisiatría.
physiatrist *n.* fisiatra.
physical *adj.* físico, -ca.
physician *n.* médico, -ca.
  allopathic physician médico alopático.
  emergency physician médico de urgencia.
  family physician médico de familia.
  house physician médico de presencia física.
  osteopathic physician médico osteópata.
  primary care physician médico de atención primaria.
  resident physician médico residente.
physicochemical *adj.* fisicoquímico, -ca.
physicogenic *adj.* fisicogénico, -ca, fisicógeno, -na.
physics *n.* física.
physiochemical *adj.* fisioquímico, -ca.
physiochemistry *n.* fisioquímica.
physiocracy *n.* fisiocracia.
physiogenesis *n.* fisiogénesis, fisiogenia.
physiogenic *adj.* fisiogénico, -ca.
physiognomy *n.* fisionomía, fisonomía.
physiognosis *n.* fisiognomía, fisiognómica, fisiognosis.
physiologic *adj.* fisiológico, -ca.
physiological *adj.* fisiológico, -ca.
physiologicoanatomical *adj.* fisiologicoanatómico, -ca.
physiologist *n.* fisiólogo, -ga.
physiology *n.* fisiología.

  animal physiology fisiología animal.
  cellular physiology fisiología celular.
  comparative physiology fisiología comparada.
  dental physiology fisiología dental.
  developmental physiology fisiología evolutiva.
  experimental physiology fisiología experimental.
  general physiology fisiología general.
  human physiology fisiología humana.
  morbid physiology fisiología mórbida.
  pathologic physiology fisiología patológica.
  perinatal physiology fisiología perinatal.
  special physiology fisiología especial.
physiolysis *n.* fisiólisis.
physiometry *n.* fisiometría.
physiopathologic *adj.* fisiopatológico, -ca.
physiopathology *n.* fisiopatología.
physiophyly *n.* fisiofilia.
physiopyrexia *n.* fisiopirexia.
physiotherapeutic *adj.* fisioterapéutico, -ca.
physiotherapeutist *n.* fisioterapeuta.
physiotherapist *n.* fisioterapeuta.
physiotherapy *n.* fisioterapia.
physis *n.* fisis.
physocele *n.* fisocele.
physocephaly *n.* fisocefalia.
physohematometra *n.* fisohematómetra.
physohydrometra *n.* fisohidrómetra.
physometra *n.* fisómetra, metrenfisema.
physopyosalpinx *n.* fisopiosálpinx.
physostigmine *n.* fisostigmina.
physostigminism *n.* fisostigminismo.
phytobezoar *n.* fitobezoar.
phytohemagglutinin *n.* fitohemaglutinina.
phytoid *adj.* fitoide.
phytonosis *n.* fitonosis.
phytoparasite *n.* fitoparásito.
phytopathy *n.* fitopatía.
phytophlyctodermatitis *n.* fitoflictodermatitis.
phytophotodermatitis *n.* fitofodermatitis, fitofotodermatitis.
phytosis *n.* fitosis.
phytotherapy *n.* fitoterapia.
pia mater *n.* piamadre.
pia-arachnitis *n.* piaracnitis.
pial *adj.* pial.
pian *n.* pian.
piblokto *n.* piblokto.
pica *n.* pica.
pickling *n.* desoxidación^2.
picnic *adj.* pícnico, -ca.
pictograph *n.* pictógrafo.
piebaldness *n.* piebaldismo.
piece *n.* pieza.
  Fab piece pieza Fab.
  Fc piece pieza Fc.
piedra *n.* piedra.
  artificial piedra piedra artificial.
  pulp piedra piedra pulpar.
  skin piedra piedra cutánea.
  tear piedra piedra lagrimal.
  vein piedra piedra venosa.
  white piedra piedra blanca.
piesesthesia *n.* piesestesia.
piesimeter *n.* piesímetro.
  Hales' piesimeter piesímetro de Hales.
piesis *n.* piesis.
piesometer *n.* piesímetro, piesómetro.
piezochemistry *n.* piezoquímica.
piezogenic *adj.* piezogénico, -ca.
piezometer *n.* piesímetro, piezómetro.
pigment *n.* pigmento.

bile pigment pigmento biliar.

hematogenous pigment pigmento hematógeno.

hepatogenous pigment pigmento hepatógeno.

malarial pigment pigmento palúdico.

melanotic pigment pigmento melánico, pigmento melanótico.

nigrum pigment pigmento negro.

respiratory pigment pigmento respiratorio.

visual pigment pigmento visual.

wear-and-tear pigment pigmento de desgaste, pigmento residual.

pigmentary *adj.* pigmentario, -ria.

pigmentation *n.* pigmentación.

arsenic pigmentation pigmentación arsenical.

exogenous pigmentation pigmentación exógena.

pigmented *adj.* pigmentado, -da.

pigmentolysin *n.* pigmentolisina.

pila *n.* pila.

pile *n.* almorrana.

piles *n.* pilas.

pilimiction *n.* pilimicción.

pill *n.* píldora.

sugar-coated pill gragea.

pillar *n.* pilar.

pill-rolling amasado de píldoras.

pilobezoar *n.* pilobezoar.

pilocystic *adj.* piloquístico, -ca.

piloerection *n.* piloerección.

piloid *adj.* piloide.

pilojection *n.* piloyección.

pilomatrichoma *n.* pilomatricoma.

pilometer *n.* pilómetro.

pilomotor *adj.* pilomotor, -ra.

pilonidal *adj.* pilonidal.

pilose *adj.* piloso, -sa.

pilosebaceous *adj.* pilosebáceo, -a.

pilosis *n.* pilosis.

pilular *adj.* pilular.

pilus *n.* cabello, capillus.

pimeloma *n.* pimeloma.

pimelopterygium *n.* pimelopterigión.

pimelorrhea *n.* pimelorrea.

pimelorthopnea *n.* pimelortopnea.

pimelosis *n.* pimelosis.

pimeluria *n.* pimeluria.

pimple *n.* granito.

pin *n.* perno, tornillo.

self-threading pin tornillo autorroscante.

Steinmann pin perno de Steinmann.

pineal *adj.* pineal.

pinealectomy *n.* epifisectomía, pinealectomía.

pinealocyte *n.* pinealocito.

pinealoma *n.* pinealoma.

ectopic pinealoma pinealoma ectópico.

extrapineal pinealoma pinealoma extrapineal.

pinealopathy *n.* pinealopatía.

pineoblastoma *n.* pineoblastoma.

pinguecula *n.* pinguécula, pinguícula.

pinguicula *n.* pinguécula, pinguícula.

pinhole *adj.* estenopaico, -ca, estenopeico, -ca.

piniform *adj.* piniforme.

pinnal *adj.* pinal.

pinocyte *n.* pinocito.

pinocytosis *n.* pinocitosis.

pinosome *n.* pinosoma.

pinta *n.* pinta.

pintid *n.* píntide.

pintoid *adj.* pintoide.

piopithelium *n.* pioepitelio.

piorrea *n.* piorrea.

piorthopnea *n.* piortopnea.

pipet *n.* pipeta.

pipette *n.* pipeta.

piriform *adj.* piriforme.

piroplasmosis *n.* piroplasmosis.

pit *n.* hoyo[2], hueco.

pitecoid *adj.* pitecoide.

pith *v.* desmedular[2].

pithiatism *n.* pitiatismo.

pithode *n.* pitode, pitoide.

pituicyte *n.* pituicito.

pituitarigenic *adj.* hipofisógeno, -na.

pituitarism *n.* pituitarismo.

pituitarium *n.* pituitaria.

pituitary *adj.* pituitario, -ria.

pituitectomy *n.* pituitectomía.

pituitous *adj.* pituitoso, -sa.

pityriasis *n.* pitiriasis.

pityriasis alba pitiriasis alba.

pityriasis alba atrophicans pitiriasis alba atrófica.

pityriasis capitis pitiriasis capitis.

pityriasis circinata pitiriasis circinada.

pityriasis linguae pitiriasis lingual.

pityriasis maculata pitiriasis maculata, pitiriasis manchada.

pityriasis nigra pitiriasis negra.

pityriasis rosea pitiriasis rosácea, pitiriasis rosada.

pityriasis rubra pitiriasis rubra.

pityriasis rubra pilaris pitiriasis rubra pilaris.

pityriasis sicca pitiriasis seca.

pityriasis simplex pitiriasis simple.

pityriasis versicolor pitiriasis versicolor.

Pityrosporum Pityrosporum.

Pityrosporum orbiculare Pityrosporum orbiculare.

placebo *n.* placebo.

placement *n.* colocación.

lingual placement colocación lingual.

percutaneous catheter placement colocación de un catéter percutáneo.

placenta *n.* placenta.

accessory placenta placenta accesoria.

adherent placenta placenta adherente.

annular placenta placenta anular.

bilobate placenta placenta bilobulada.

bilobed placenta placenta bilobulada.

cirsoid placenta placenta cirsoide.

dimidiate placenta placenta dimidiada.

fetal placenta placenta fetal.

incarcerated placenta placenta incarcerada.

lobed placenta placenta lobulada.

maternal placenta placenta materna.

placenta bipartita placenta bipartida.

placenta circunvallata placenta circunvalada.

placenta cirsoides placenta cirsoide.

placenta diffusa placenta difusa.

placenta dimidiata placenta dimidiada.

placenta duplex placenta doble.

placenta fenestrata placenta fenestrada.

placenta fetalis placenta fetal.

placenta membranacea placenta membranácea, placenta membranosa.

placenta previa placenta previa.

placenta spuria placenta espuria.

placenta uterina placenta uterina.

retained placenta placenta retenida.

Schultze's placenta placenta de Schultze.

succenturiate placenta placenta succenturiada.

triplex placenta placenta triple.

placental *adj.* placentario, -ria.

placentation *n.* placentación.

placentitis *n.* placentitis.

placentography *n.* placentografía.

placentoid *adj.* placentoide.

placentology *n.* placentología.

placentoma *n.* placentoma.

placentotherapy *n.* placentoterapia.

placode *n.* placoda.

placoide *adj.* placoide.

pladaroma *n.* pladaroma.

pladarosis *n.* pladarosis.

plagiocephalic *adj.* plagiocefálico, -ca.

plagiocephalism *n.* plagiocefalismo.

plagiocephaly *n.* plagiocefalia.

plague *n.* peste.

ambulant plague peste ambulante, peste ambulatoria.

ambulatory plague peste ambulante, peste ambulatoria.

black plague peste negra.

bubonic plague peste bubónica.

glandular plague peste glandular.

hemorrhagic plague peste hemorrágica.

larval plague peste larval.

Pahvant Valley plague peste del valle de Pahvant.

pneumonic plague peste neumónica.

septicemic plague peste septicémica.

plane *n.* plano.

planigraphy *n.* planigrafía.

planimeter *n.* planímetro.

planing *n.* aplanamiento[2].

planocellular *adj.* planocelular.

planoconcave *adj.* planocóncavo, -va.

planoconvex *adj.* planoconvexo, -xa.

planocyte *n.* planocito.

planography *n.* planografía.

planta pedis *n.* planta del pie.

plantalgia *n.* plantalgia.

plantar *adj.* plantar.

planula *n.* plánula.

invaginate planula plánula invaginada.

planum *n.* plano, planum.

planuria *n.* planuria.

plaque *n.* placa[2].

argyrophile plaque placa argirófila.

bacterial plaque placa bacteriana.

bacteriophage plaque placa bacteriófaga.

dental plaque placa dentaria.

fibromyelinic plaque placa fibromielínica.

Hollenhorst plaque placa Hollenhorst.

senile plaque placa senil.

plasma *n.* plasma.

antihemophilic human plasma plasma humano antihemofílico.

blood plasma plasma sanguíneo.

citrated plasma plasma citratado.

muscle plasma plasma muscular.

pooled plasma plasma mezclado.

salt plasma plasma salado.

true plasma plasma verdadero.

plasmacyte *n.* plasmocito.

plasmacytoma *n.* plasmacitoma.

plasmalemma *n.* plasmalema.

plasmapheresis *n.* plasmaféresis.

plasmarrhexis *n.* plasmarrexis, plasmorrexis.

plasmatherapy *n.* plasmoterapia.

plasmatogamy *n.* plastogamia.

plasmatorrhexis *n.* plasmatorrexis.

plasmatosis *n.* plasmatosis.

plasmid *n.* plásmido.

plasmocyte *n.* plasmocito.

plasmocytoma *n.* plasmacitoma, plasmocitoma.

plasmodial *adj.* plasmodial.

plasmodiblast *n.* plasmodiblasto.

plasmodicidal *adj.* plasmodicida².
plasmodicide *n.* plasmodicida¹.
plasmodium *n.* plasmodio.
Plasmodium Plasmodium.
plasmolysis *n.* plasmólisis.
plasmoma *n.* plasmoma.
plasmoptysis *n.* plasmoptisis, plasmotisis.
plasmorrhexis *n.* plasmorrexis.
plasmoschisis *n.* plasmosquisis.
plasmotomy *n.* plasmotomía.
plasmotropic *adj.* plasmotrópico, -ca.
plasmotropism *n.* plasmotropismo.
plastein *n.* plasteína.
plaster *n.* emplasto, yeso².
  plaster of Paris yeso de París.
plastic *adj.* plástico, -ca.
plastid *n.* plástida.
plastron *n.* plastrón.
plasty *n.* plástia.
plate *n.* placa3.
  bite plate placa de mordedura.
  bone plate placa ósea.
  cardiogenic plate placa cardiógena.
  chorionic plate placa coriónica.
  cough plate placa de tos.
  counting plate placa de cuentas.
  Egger's plate placa de Egger.
  equatorial plate placa ecuatorial.
  ethmovomerine plate placa etmovomeriana.
  Kingsley plate placa de Kingsley.
  Lane's plate placa de lane.
  Moe plate placa de Moe.
  nephrotome plate placa de nefrotoma.
  neural plate placa neural.
  segmental plate placa segmentaria.
plateau *n.* meseta.
platelet *n.* plaqueta.
plateletpheresis *n.* plaquetaféresis.
platybasia *n.* platibasia, platibasis.
platycephalic *adj.* platicéfalo, -la.
platycephalous *adj.* platicéfalo, -la.
platycephaly *n.* platicefalia.
platycnemia *n.* platicnemia, platicnemismo.
platycrania *n.* platicrania.
platycyte *n.* placito.
platyhelminth *n.* platelminto.
platyhieric *adj.* platihiérico, -ca.
platymeria *n.* platimeria.
platymorphia *n.* platimorfia.
platyonychia *n.* platoniquia.
platyopia *n.* platiopía.
platypodia *n.* platipodia.
platyrrhiny *n.* platirrinia.
platyspondylia *n.* platispondilla, platispondilisis.
play *n.* juego.
  active play juego activo.
  cooperative play juego cooperativo.
  parallel play juego paralelo.
  skill play juego de habilidad.
pleasure *n.* placer.
  organ pleasure placer de órgano.
pledge *n.* juramento.
pledget *n.* tapón².
plegaphonia *n.* plegafonía.
pleiochromy *n.* pleocromía.
pleiocytosis *n.* pleiocitosis, pleocitosis.
pleiotropia *n.* pleiotropía.
pleiotropic *adj.* pleiotrópico, -ca, pleotrópico, -ca.
pleiotropy *n.* pleotropía.
pleocholia *n.* pleocolia.
pleochroism *n.* pleocroísmo.
pleochromatic *adj.* pleocroico, -ca, pleocromático, -ca.
pleochromatism *n.* pleocromatismo.

pleocytosis *n.* pleiocitosis.
pleomastia *n.* pleomastia.
pleomorphic xanthoastrocytoma *n.* xantoastrocitoma pleomórfico.
pleomorphism *n.* pleomorfia, pleomorfismo.
pleonosteosis *n.* pleonosteosis.
pleoptics *n.* pleóptica.
plerosis *n.* plerosis.
Plesiomonas Plesiomonas.
  Plesiomonas shigelloides plesiomonas shigelloides.
plesiomorphic *adj.* plesiomorfo, -fa.
plessesthesia *n.* plesestesia.
plessimeter *n.* plesímetro.
plessimetry *n.* plesimetría.
plessor *n.* plesor.
plethora *n.* plétora.
plethysmogram *n.* pletismograma.
plethysmograph *n.* pletismógrafo.
  body plethysmograph pletismógrafo corporal.
  digital plethysmograph pletismógrafo digital.
  pressure plethysmograph pletismógrafo a presión.
plethysmography *n.* pletismografía.
plethysmometry *n.* pletismometría.
pleura *n.* pleura.
pleuracentesis *n.* pleuracentesis.
pleuralgia *n.* pleuralgia.
pleurapophysis *n.* pleurapófisis.
pleurectomy *n.* pleurectomía.
pleurisy *n.* pleuresía.
  acute pleurisy pleuresía aguda.
  adhesive pleurisy pleuresía adhesiva.
  chronic pleurisy pleuresía crónica.
  chylous pleurisy pleuresía quilosa.
  costal pleurisy pleuresía costal.
  diaphragmatic pleurisy pleuresía diafragmática.
  double pleurisy pleuresía doble.
  dry pleurisy pleuresía seca.
  encysted pleurisy pleuresía enquistada.
  fibrinous pleurisy pleuresía fibrinosa.
  hemorrhagic pleurisy pleuresía hemorrágica.
  ichorous pleurisy pleuresía icorosa.
  interlobar pleurisy pleuresía interlobular.
  latent pleurisy pleuresía latente.
  mediastinal pleurisy pleuresía mediastínica.
  metapneumonic pleurisy pleuresía metaneumónica.
  pleurisy with effusion pleuresía exudativa.
  proliferating pleurisy pleuresía proliferante.
  pulmonary pleurisy pleuresía pulmonar.
  pulsating pleurisy pleuresía pulsátil.
  purulent pleurisy pleuresía purulenta.
  sacculated pleurisy pleuresía saculada.
  serofibrinous pleurisy pleuresía serofibrinosa.
  serous pleurisy pleuresía serosa.
  typhoid pleurisy pleuresía tífica.
  visceral pleurisy pleuresía visceral.
  wet pleurisy pleuresía húmeda.
pleuritis *n.* pleuritis.
pleuritogenous *adj.* pleuritógeno, -na.
pleurobronchitis *n.* pleurobronquitis.
pleurocele *n.* pleurocele.
pleurocentesis *n.* pleurocentesis.
pleurocentrum *n.* pleurocentro.
pleurocholecystitis *n.* pleurocolecistitis.
pleuroclysis *n.* pleuroclisis.
pleurocutaneous *adj.* pleurocutáneo, -a.
pleurodynia *n.* pleurodinia.
  epidemic pleurodynia pleurodinia diafragmática epidémica.
pleurogenous *adj.* pleurógeno, -na.

pleurography *n.* pleurografía.
pleurohepatitis *n.* pleurohepatitis.
pleurolith *n.* pleurolito.
pleurolysis *n.* pleurólisis.
pleuromelus *n.* pleuromelo.
pleuroneumonia *n.* pleuroperineumonía.
pleuroparietopexy *n.* pleuroparietopexia.
pleuropericarditis *n.* pleuropericarditis.
pleuroperitoneal *adj.* pleuroperitoneal.
pleuropneumonia *n.* pleuroneumonía.
pleuropneumonolysis *n.* pleuroneumólisis, pleuroneumónólisis.
pleuropulmonary *adj.* pleuropulmonar.
pleurorrhea *n.* pleurorrea.
pleuroscope *n.* pleuroscopio.
pleuroscopy *n.* pleuroscopia.
pleurosomus *n.* pleurosomo.
pleurothotonos *n.* pleurostótonos, pleurotótonos.
pleurothotonus *n.* pleurostótonos.
pleurotomy *n.* pleurotomía.
pleurotyphoid *n.* pleurotifus.
pleurovisceral *adj.* pleurovisceral.
plexiform *adj.* plexiforme.
plexigraph *n.* plesígrafo.
pleximeter *n.* plexímetro.
pleximetry *n.* pleximetría.
plexitis *n.* plexitis.
plexometer *n.* plexímetro, plexómetro.
plexor *n.* plexor.
plexus *n.* plexo.
plication *n.* plicación.
plicotomy *n.* plicotomía.
plombage *n.* plombaje.
plot¹ *n.* trazado.
plot² *v.* trazar.
plug *n.* tapón¹.
  cerumen plug tapón de cerumen.
  Dittrich's plug tapón de Dittrich.
  Ecker's plug tapón de Ecker.
  epithelial plug tapón epitelial.
  Imlach's fat plug tapón de Imlach, tapón graso de Imlach.
  mucous plug tapón mucoso, tapón mucoso cervical.
  Traube's plug tapón de Traube.
plugger *n.* atacador, obturador², taponador¹.
  amalgam plugger obturador de amalgama, taponador de amalgama.
  automatic plugger obturador automático, taponador automático.
  back-action plugger obturador de acción retrógrada, taponador de acción retrógada.
  foil plugger taponador de chapa de oro.
  foot plugger obturador en forma de pie, taponador de pie.
  gold plugger taponador de oro.
  reverse plugger taponador de reversa.
  root canal plugger obturador de conductos radiculares.
plumbism *n.* plumbismo.
plumose *adj.* plumoso, -sa.
plumula *n.* plúmula.
pluriglandular *adj.* pluriglandular.
plurigravida *n.* plurigrávida.
plurilocular *adj.* plurilocular.
plurinuclear *adj.* plurinuclear.
pluripara *n.* plurípara.
pluriparity *n.* pluriparidad.
pluripolar *adj.* pluripolar.
pluripotenciality *n.* pluripotencialidad.
pluripotent *adj.* pluripotente.
pluripotential *adj.* pluripotencial.
plutonism *n.* plutonismo.
pneogaster *n.* neogáster.

pneogram *n.* neograma.
pneograph *n.* neógrafo.
pneometer *n.* neómetro.
pneoscope *n.* neoscopio.
pneumal *adj.* neumático, -ca.
pneumarthography *n.* neumartrografía.
pneumarthrogram *n.* neumartrograma, neumoartrograma.
pneumarthrosis *n.* neumartrosis, neumoartrosis.
pneumascope *n.* neumascopio.
pneumathemia *n.* neumatemia.
pneumatics *n.* neumática.
pneumatinuria *n.* neumatinuria.
pneumatization *n.* neumatización.
pneumatized *adj.* neumatizado, -da.
pneumatocardia *n.* neumatocardia.
pneumatocele *n.* neumatocele.
  cranial pneumatocele neumatocele craneal.
  extracranial pneumatocele neumatocele extracraneal.
  intracranial pneumatocele neumatocele intracraneal.
  pneumatocele cranii neumatocele craneal.
pneumatocephalus *n.* neumatocefalia.
pneumatodyspnea *n.* neumatodisnea.
  parotid pneumatodyspnea neumatodisnea parotídeo.
pneumatogram *n.* neumatograma.
pneumatograph *n.* neumatógrafo.
pneumatohemia *n.* neumatohemia.
pneumatometer *n.* neumatómetro.
pneumatometry *n.* neumatometría.
pneumatophore *n.* neumatóforo.
pneumatorrhachis *n.* neumatorraquis.
pneumatoscope *n.* neumatoscopio.
pneumatosis *n.* neumatosis.
  intestinal pneumatosis neumatosis intestinal.
  pneumatosis cystoides intestinalis neumatosis cistoide intestinal, neumatosis cystoides intestinalis.
  pneumatosis cystoides intestinorum neumatosis cistoide intestinal, neumatosis cystoides intestinalis.
  pneumatosis intestinalis neumatosis intestinal.
  pneumatosis pulmonum neumatosis pulmonar.
pneumatotherapy *n.* neumatoterapia.
pneumatothorax *n.* neumatotórax.
pneumaturia *n.* neumaturia.
pneumatype *n.* neumatipo.
pneumectomy *n.* neumectomía.
pneumoalveolography *n.* neumoalveolografía.
pneumoamnios *n.* neumoamnios.
pneumoangiogram *n.* neumoangiograma.
pneumoangiography *n.* neumoangiografía.
pneumoarthrography *n.* neumoartrografía.
pneumobacillus *n.* neumobacilo.
  Friedlander's pneumobacillus neumobacilo de Friedlander.
pneumobulbar *adj.* neumobulbar.
pneumobulbous *adj.* neumobulboso, -sa.
pneumocardial *adj.* neumocardíaco, -ca.
pneumocardiograph *n.* neumocardiógrafo.
pneumocardiography *n.* neumocardiografía.
pneumocele *n.* neumocele.
pneumocentesis *n.* neumocentesis.
pneumocephalia *n.* neumocefalia.
pneumocholecystitis *n.* neumocolecistitis.
pneumochysis *n.* neumoquisis.
pneumococcal *adj.* neumocócico, -ca.
pneumococcemia *n.* neumococemia.

pneumococcic *adj.* neumocócico, -ca.
pneumococcidal *adj.* neumococida.
pneumococcolysis *n.* neumococólisis.
pneumococcosis *n.* neumococosis.
pneumococcosuria *n.* neumococosuria.
pneumococcus *n.* neumococo.
pneumocolon *n.* neumocolon.
pneumoconiosis *n.* neumoconiosis.
  bauxite pneumoconiosis neumoconiosis de la bauxita, neumoconiosis por bauxita.
  collagenous pneumoconiosis neumoconiosis colagenosa.
  pneumoconiosis of coal workers neumoconiosis de los mineros del carbón.
  pneumoconiosis siderotica neumoconiosis siderótica.
pneumocrania *n.* neumocránco, neumocrania.
pneumocranium *n.* neumocráneo.
pneumocystiasis *n.* neumocistiasis.
pneumocystic *adj.* neumocístico, -ca.
pneumocystography *n.* neumocistografía.
pneumocystosis *n.* neumocistosis.
pneumocystotomography *n.* neumocistotomografía.
pneumocyte *n.* neumocito.
pneumoderma *n.* neumodermia.
pneumodograph *n.* neumodógrafo.
pneumodynamics *n.* neumodinámica.
pneumoempyema *n.* neumoempiema.
pneumoencephalogram *n.* neumoencefalograma.
pneumoencephalography *n.* neumencefalografía, neumoencefalografía.
pneumoencephalomyelogram *n.* neumoencefalomielograma.
pneumoencephalomyelography *n.* neumoencefalomielografía.
pneumoencephalus *n.* neumoencéfalo.
pneumoenteritis *n.* neumoenteritis.
pneumofasciogram *n.* neumofasciograma.
pneumogalactocele *n.* neumogalactocele.
pneumogastric *adj.* neumogástrico, -ca.
pneumogastrography *n.* neumogastrografía.
pneumogastroscopy *n.* neumogastroscopia.
pneumogram *n.* neumograma.
pneumograph *n.* neumógrafo.
pneumography *n.* neumografía.
  cerebral pneumography neumografía cerebral.
  retroperitoneal pneumography neumografía retroperitoneal.
pneumogynogram *n.* neumoginograma.
pneumohemia *n.* neumohemia.
pneumohemopericardium *n.* neumohemopericardio.
pneumohemothorax *n.* neumohemotórax.
pneumohydrometra *n.* neumohidrómetra.
pneumohydropericardium *n.* neumohidropericardio.
pneumohydroperitoneum *n.* neumohidroperitoneo.
pneumohydrothorax *n.* neumohidrotórax.
pneumohypoderma *n.* neumohipodermia.
pneumokidney *n.* neumorriñón.
pneumolith *n.* neumolito.
pneumolithiasis *n.* neumolitiasis.
pneumology *n.* neumología.
pneumomalacia *n.* neumomalacia.
pneumomassage *n.* neumomasaje.
pneumomastography *n.* neumomastografía.
pneumomediastinogram *n.* neumomediastinograma.
pneumomediastinography *n.* neumomediastinografía.
pneumomediastinum *n.* neumomediastino.

pneumomelanosis *n.* neumomelanosis.
pneumometer *n.* neumómetro.
pneumomycosis *n.* neumomicosis.
pneumomyelography *n.* neumomielografía.
pneumonectasia *n.* neumoectasia, neumonectasia.
pneumonectasis *n.* neumoectasia, neumonectasis.
pneumonectomy *n.* neumonectomía.
pneumonedema *n.* neumonedema, neumonemia.
pneumonia *n.* neumonía.
  abortive pneumonia neumonía abortiva.
  acute pneumonia neumonía aguda.
  alcoholic pneumonia neumonía alcohólica.
  amebic pneumonia neumonía amibiana.
  anthrax pneumonia neumonía por carbunco.
  apex pneumonia neumonía apical.
  apical pneumonia neumonía apical.
  aspiration pneumonia neumonía por aspiración.
  atypical bronchial pneumonia neumonía bronquial atípica.
  atypical pneumonia neumonía atípica, neumonía atípica primaria.
  bacterial pneumonia neumonía bacteriana.
  bilious pneumonia neumonía biliosa.
  bronchial pneumonia neumonía bronquial.
  Buhl's desquamative pneumonia neumonía descamativa de Buhl.
  caseous pneumonia neumonía caseosa.
  central pneumonia neumonía central.
  cerebral pneumonia neumonía cerebral.
  cheesy pneumonia neumonía caseosa.
  chronic eosinophilic pneumonia neumonía crónica eosinófila.
  chronic fibrous pneumonia neumonía fibrosa crónica.
  chronic pneumonia neumonía crónica.
  cold agglutinin pneumonia neumonía por aglutininas frías.
  congenital aspiration pneumonia neumonía congénita, neumonía congénita por aspiración, neumonía por aspiración congénita.
  congenital pneumonia neumonía congénita, neumonía congénita por aspiración.
  contusion pneumonia neumonía por contusión.
  core pneumonia neumonía nuclear.
  Corrigan's pneumonia neumonía de Corrigan.
  croupous pneumonia neumonía cruposa.
  deglutition pneumonia neumonía de la deglución, neumonía por deglución.
  Desnos' pneumonia neumonía de Desnos.
  desquamative interstitial pneumonia (DIP) neumonía intersticial descamativa.
  desquamative pneumonia neumonía descamativa.
  double pneumonia neumonía doble.
  Eaton agent pneumonia neumonía por agente de Eaton.
  embolic pneumonia neumonía embólica.
  eosinophilic pneumonia neumonía eosinófila, neumonía eosinofílica.
  ephemeral pneumonia neumonía efímera.
  extrinsic allergic pneumonia neumonía alérgica extrínseca.
  fibrinous pneumonia neumonía fibrinosa.
  fibrous pneumonia neumonía fibrosa.
  Friedlander's bacillus pneumonia neumonía de Friedlander, neumonía por bacilo de Friedlander.
  Friedlander's pneumonia neumonía de Friedlander, neumonía por bacilo de Friedlander.

gangrenous pneumonia neumonía gangrenosa.

generalized pneumonia neumonía generalizada.

giant cell pneumonia neumonía de células gigantes.

Hecht's pneumonia neumonía de Hecht.

hypersensitivity pneumonia neumonía por hipersensibilidad.

hypostatic pneumonia neumonía hipostática.

indurative pneumonia neumonía indurativa.

influenza virus pneumonia neumonía por virus de la gripe.

influenzal pneumonia neumonía por virus de la gripe.

inhalation pneumonia neumonía por inhalación.

interstitial plasma cell pneumonia neumonía intersticial de células plasmáticas.

interstitial pneumonia neumonía intersticial.

intrauterine pneumonia neumonía intrauterina.

Kaufmann's pneumonia neumonía de Kaufmann.

lipoid pneumonia neumonía lípida, neumonía lipoide, neumonía lipoidea.

lobar pneumonia neumonía lobular, neumonía lobulillar.

lobular pneumonia neumonía lobular, neumonía lobulillar.

Löffler's pneumonia neumonía de Löffler.

Louisiana pneumonia neumonía de Louisiana.

lymphoid interstitial pneumonia neumonía intersticial linfoide, neumonía linfoide intersticial.

massive pneumonia neumonía masiva.

metastatic pneumonia neumonía metastásica.

migratory pneumonia neumonía migratoria.

mycoplasma pneumonia neumonía micoplasmática, neumonía por micoplasma.

mycoplasmal pneumonia neumonía micoplasmática, neumonía por micoplasma.

obstructive pneumonia neumonía obstructiva.

oil pneumonia neumonía por aceites.

parenchymatous pneumonia neumonía parenquimatosa.

Pittsburgh pneumonia neumonía de Pittsburgh.

plague pneumonia neumonía pestífera, neumonía pestosa, neumonía por peste.

plasma cell pneumonia neumonía de células plasmáticas.

pleuritic pneumonia neumonía pleurítica.

pleurogenetic pneumonia neumonía pleurógena.

pleurogenic pneumonia neumonía pleurógena.

pneumococcal pneumonia neumonía neumocócica.

Pneumocystis carinii pneumonia neumonía por Pneumocystis carinii.

pneumonia alba neumonía alba.

pneumonia dissecans neumonía disecante.

pneumonia interlobularis purulenta neumonía interlobulillar purulenta.

pneumonia malleosa neumonía maleosa.

primary atypical pneumonia neumonía atípica, neumonía atípica primaria, neumonía primaria atípica.

purulent pneumonia neumonía purulenta.

rheumatic pneumonia neumonía reumática.

Riesman's pneumonia neumonía de Riesman.

secondary pneumonia neumonía secundaria.

septic pneumonia neumonía séptica.

staphylococcal pneumonia neumonía estafilocócica.

streptococcal pneumonia neumonía estreptocócica.

superficial pneumonia neumonía superficial.

suppurative pneumonia neumonía supurativa.

terminal pneumonia neumonía terminal.

toxemic pneumonia neumonía toxémica.

transplantation pneumonia neumonía de los transplantes.

traumatic pneumonia neumonía traumática.

tuberculous pneumonia neumonía tuberculosa.

tularemic pneumonia neumonía tularémica.

typhoid pneumonia neumonía tífica, neumonía tifoidea, neumonía tifoídica.

unresolved pneumonia neumonía no resuelta.

uremic pneumonia neumonía urémica.

vagus pneumonia neumonía vagal.

varicella pneumonia neumonía por varicela.

viral pneumonia neumonía viral, neumonía vírica.

walking pneumonia neumonía errante.

wandering pneumonia neumonía errante.

white pneumonia neumonía blanca.

woolsorter's pneumonia neumonía de los cardadores de lana.

pneumonic *adj.* neumónico, -ca.

pneumonitis *n.* neumonitis.

acute interstitial pneumonitis neumonitis intersticial aguda.

aspiration pneumonitis neumonitis por aspiración.

chemical pneumonitis neumonitis química.

cholesterol pneumonitis neumonitis de colesterol.

granulomatous pneumonitis neumonitis granulomatosa.

hypersensitivity pneumonitis neumonitis por hipersensibilidad.

lymphocytic interstitial pneumonitis neumonitis intersticial linfocítica.

malarial pneumonitis neumonitis palúdica.

Pneumocystis pneumonitis neumonitis por Pneumocystis.

uremic pneumonitis neumonitis urémica.

pneumonocele *n.* neumonocele.

pneumonocentesis *n.* neumonocentesis.

pneumonocirrhosis *n.* neumonocirrosis.

pneumonococcus *n.* neumonococo.

pneumonoconiosis *n.* neumonoconiosis.

pneumonocyte *n.* neumonocito.

granular pneumonocyte neumonocito granuloso.

membranous pneumonocyte neumonocito membranoso.

pneumonoenteritis *n.* neumonoenteritis.

pneumonograph *n.* neumonografía.

pneumonography *n.* neumonografía.

pneumonokoniosis *n.* neumonoconiosis.

pneumonolipoidosis *n.* neumonolipoidosis.

pneumonology *n.* neumonología.

pneumonomelanosis *n.* neumonomelanosis.

pneumonometer *n.* neumonómetro.

pneumonomycosis *n.* neumonomicosis.

pneumonopaludism *n.* neumonopaludismo.

pneumonopathy *n.* neumonopatía.

pneumonopexy *n.* neumonopexia.

pneumonophthisis *n.* neumonotisis.

pneumonopleuritis *n.* neumonopleuritis.

pneumonorachicentesis *n.* neumonorraquicentesis.

pneumonoresection *n.* neumonorresección.

pneumonorrhagia *n.* neumonorragia.

pneumonosis *n.* neumonosis.

pneumonotherapy *n.* neumonoterapia.

pneumonotomy *n.* neumonotomía.

pneumopaludism *n.* neumopaludismo.

pneumopathy *n.* neumopatía.

pneumopericardium *n.* neumopericardio.

pneumoperitoneal *adj.* neumoperitoneal.

pneumoperitoneum *n.* neumoperitoneo.

pneumoperitonitis *n.* neumoperitonitis.

pneumopexy *n.* neumopexia.

pneumophagia *n.* neumofagia.

pneumophonia *n.* neumofonía.

pneumopleuritis *n.* neumopleuritis.

pneumopleuroparietopexy *n.* neumopleuroparietopexia.

pneumoprecordium *n.* neumoprecordio.

pneumopreperitoneum *n.* neumopreperitoneo.

pneumopyelography *n.* neumopielografía.

pneumopyopericardium *n.* neumopiopericardio.

pneumopyothorax *n.* neumopiotórax.

pneumorachis *n.* neumorraquis.

pneumoradiography *n.* neumorradiografía.

pneumoresection *n.* neumorresección.

pneumoretroperitoneum *n.* neumorretroperitoneo.

pneumoroentgenonography *n.* neumorroentgenografía.

pneumorrhagia *n.* neumorragia.

pneumorrhaphy *n.* neumonorrafia, neumorrafía.

pneumoscrotum *n.* neumoescroto.

pneumosepticemia *n.* neumosepticemia.

pneumoserosa *n.* neumoserosa.

pneumoserothorax *n.* neumoserotórax.

pneumosilicosis *n.* neumosilicosis.

pneumotachogram *n.* neumotacograma.

pneumotachograph *n.* neumotacógrafo.

Fleich pneumotachograph neumotacógrafo de Fleich.

Silverman-Lilly pneumotachograph neumotacógrafo de Silverman-Lilly.

pneumotachometer *n.* neumotacómetro.

pneumotachygraph *n.* neumotacógrafo, neumotaquígrafo.

pneumotherapy *n.* neumoterapia.

pneumothermomassage *n.* neumotermomasaje.

pneumothorax *n.* neumotórax.

catamenial pneumothorax neumotórax catamenial.

clicking pneumothorax neumotórax de chasquido.

closed pneumothorax neumotórax cerrado.

diagnostic pneumothorax neumotórax diagnóstico.

extrapleural pneumothorax neumotórax extrapleural.

open pneumothorax neumotórax abierto.

opening pneumothorax neumotórax abierto.

pressure pneumothorax neumotórax a presión.

spontaneous pneumothorax neumotórax espontáneo.

tension pneumothorax neumotórax a tensión, neumotórax hiperbárico.

valvular pneumothorax neumotórax valvular.

pneumotomography *n.* neumotomografía.

pneumotomy *n.* neumotomía.

pneumotropic *adj.* neumotrópico, -ca.
pneumotropism *n.* neumotropismo.
pneumotympanum *n.* neumotímpano.
pneumotyphus *n.* neumotifo, neumotifus.
pneumouria *n.* neumouria.
pneumoventricle *n.* neumoventrículo.
pneumoventriculography *n.* neumoventri-culografía.
Pneumovirus Pneumovirus.
pneusis *n.* neusis.
pneusometer *n.* neusímetro.
pocket *n.* bolsa³.
  gingival pocket bolsa gingival.
  infrabony pocket bolsa infraósea.
  intra-alveolar pocket bolsa intraalveolar.
  intrabony pocket bolsa intraósea.
  periodontal pocket bolsa periodontal.
  Rathke's pocket bolsa de Rathke.
  Seessel's pocket bolsa de Seessel.
  subcrestal pocket bolsa subcrestal.
pockmark *n.* hoyo¹.
poculum *n.* copa.
  poculum diogenis copa de Diógenes.
podagra *n.* podagra, podagrismo.
podalgia *n.* podalgia.
podalic *adj.* podálico, -ca.
podarthritis *n.* podartritis.
podedema *n.* podedema.
podencephalus *n.* podencéfalo.
podiatrist *adj.* podiatra.
podiatry *n.* podiatría.
pododynamometer *n.* pododinamómetro.
pododynia *n.* pododinia.
podogram *n.* podograma.
podologist *n.* podólogo, -ga.
podology *n.* podología.
pogoniasis *n.* pogoniasis.
pogonion *n.* pogonión.
poikiloblast *n.* poiquiloblasto.
poikilocyte *n.* poiquilocito.
poikilocythemia *n.* poiquilocitemia.
poikilocytosis *n.* poiquilocitosis.
poikiloderma *n.* poiquilodermia.
poikiloploid *adj.* poiquiloploide.
poikiloploidy *n.* poiquiloploidía.
poikilosmosis *n.* poiquilósmosis.
poikilosmotic *adj.* poiquilosmótico, -ca.
poikilothermic *adj.* poiquilotérmico, -ca.
poikilothermy *n.* poiquilotermia.
poikilothrombocyte *n.* poiquilotrombocito.
point *n.* punta, punto.
  absorbent point punta absorbente.
  boiling point punto de ebullición.
  cold-rigor point punto de rigor por el frío.
  end point punto terminal.
  freezing point punto de congelación.
  gutta-percha point punta de gutapercha.
  heat-rigor point punto de rigor por el calor.
  isoelectric point punto isoeléctrico.
  isoionic point punto isoiónico.
  isosbestic point punto isosbéstico.
  J point punto J.
  motor point punto motor.
  neutral point punto neutro.
  painful point punto doloroso.
  point dolorosum punto doloroso.
  point of maximal impulse punto de máximo impulso.
  point of ossification punto de osificación.
  pressure point punto de presión.
  primary point of ossification punto de osificación primario.
  secondary point of ossification punto de osificación secundario.
  silver point punta de plata.

Velleix's point punto de Velleix.
poison *n.* veneno.
  acrid poison veneno acre, veneno ácrido, veneno irritante.
  arrow poison veneno de flechas.
  fish poison veneno de los peces.
  fugu poison veneno del fugu, veneno fugu.
  narcotic poison veneno narcótico.
  puffer poison veneno de pez globo.
  whelk poison veneno de buccino.
poisoning *n.* envenenamiento, intoxicación.
  acetaminophen poisoning intoxicación por paracetamol.
  acetylsalicylic acid poisoning intoxicación por ácido acetilsalicílico.
  acute nicotine poisoning intoxicación nicotínica aguda.
  alkali poisoning intoxicación alcalina, intoxicación por álcalis.
  amphetamine poisoning intoxicación por anfetaminas.
  antimony poisoning intoxicación por antimonio.
  arsenic poisoning intoxicación por arsénico.
  aspirin poisoning intoxicación por aspirina.
  atropine sulfate poisoning intoxicación por sulfato de atropina.
  bacterial food poisoning intoxicación alimentaria bacteriana.
  benzene poisoning intoxicación por benceno.
  blood poisoning intoxicación séptica.
  cadmium poisoning intoxicación por cadmio.
  caffeine poisoning intoxicación por cafeína.
  camphor poisoning intoxicación por alcanfor.
  carbolic acid poisoning intoxicación por ácido carbólico.
  carbon dioxide poisoning intoxicación por anhídrido carbónico.
  carbon monoxide poisoning intoxicación por monóxido de carbono.
  carbon tetrachloride poisoning intoxicación por tetracloruro de carbono.
  caustic poisoning intoxicación por cáusticos.
  chlordane poisoning intoxicación por clordano.
  chlorinatedorganic insecticide poisoning intoxicación por insecticidas organoclorados.
  chronic fluoride poisoning crónica por flúor, intoxicación crónica por fluoruro.
  chronic fluorine poisoning crónica por flúor, intoxicación crónica por fluoruro.
  ciguatera poisoning intoxicación por ciguatera.
  clamp poisoning intoxicación por almejas.
  cocaine hydrochloride poisoning intoxicación por clorhidrato de cocaína.
  cyanide poisoning intoxicación por cianuro.
  DDT poisoning intoxicación por DDT.
  digitalis poisoning intoxicación por digitálicos.
  ergot poisoning intoxicación por cornezuelo del centeno.
  ethylene dichloride poisoning intoxicación por dicloruro de etileno.
  ethylene glycol poisoning intoxicación por etilenglicol.
  fish poisoning intoxicación por pescado.
  fluoride poisoning intoxicación por fluoruros.
  food poisoning intoxicación alimentaria, intoxicación alimenticia.
  gasoline poisoning intoxicación por gasolina.

  guaiacol poisoning intoxicación por guayacol.
  heavy metal poisoning intoxicación por metales pesados.
  heptachlor poisoning intoxicación por heptaclor.
  herbicide poisoning intoxicación por herbicida.
  hypochlorite poisoning intoxicación con hipoclorito.
  iodine poisoning intoxicación por yodo.
  iron poisoning intoxicación por hierro.
  iron salts poisoning intoxicación por sales de hierro.
  ivy poisoning intoxicación por zumaque venenoso.
  kerosene poisoning intoxicación por queroseno.
  lead poisoning intoxicación por plomo.
  malathion poisoning intoxicación por malatión.
  meat poisoning intoxicación por carne.
  mercury poisoning intoxicación por mercurio.
  mushroom poisoning intoxicación por setas.
  naphtalene poisoning intoxicación por naftaleno.
  naphthol poisoning intoxicación por naftol.
  narcotic poisoning intoxicación por narcóticos.
  nicotine poisoning intoxicación por nicotina.
  nitrobenzene poisoning intoxicación por nitrobenceno.
  opiate poisoning intoxicación opiácea.
  paradichlorobenzene poisoning intoxicación por paradiclorobenceno.
  paralytic shellfish poisoning intoxicación paralizante por marisco.
  paraquat poisoning intoxicación por paracuat.
  parathion poisoning intoxicación por paratión.
  pesticide poisoning intoxicación por pesticidas.
  petroleum distillate poisoning intoxicación por destilados del petróleo.
  phenol poisoning intoxicación por fenol.
  phosphorus poisoning intoxicación por fósforo.
  rodenticide poisoning intoxicación por raticida.
  salicylate poisoning intoxicación por salicilatos.
  scombroid poisoning intoxicación escombroide, intoxicación por peces escombroides.
  shellfish poisoning intoxicación por crustáceos, intoxicación por marisco.
  silver salts poisoning intoxicación por sales de plata.
  sodium arsenite poisoning intoxicación por arsenito de sodio.
  sodium fluoride poisoning intoxicación por fluoruro sódico.
  strychnine poisoning intoxicación por estricnina.
  tempeh poisoning intoxicación por bongkrek.
  thallium poisoning intoxicación por talio.
  venerupin poisoning intoxicación por venerupina.
  warfarin poisoning intoxicación por warfarina.
  zinc salt poisoning intoxicación por sal de zinc.

poisonous *adj.* venenoso, -sa.
polar *n.* polar.
polarimeter *n.* polarímetro.
polariscope *n.* polariscopio.
polaristrobometer *n.* polaristrobómetro.
polarity *n.* polaridad.
polarization *n.* polarización.
polarizer *n.* polarizador, -ra.
polarogaphy *n.* polarografía.
polarogram *n.* polarograma.
pole *n.* polo.
 animal pole polo animal.
 germinal pole polo germinativo.
 negative pole polo negativo.
 positive pole polo positivo.
 vegetative pole polo vegetativo.
policeman *n.* gendarme.
poliencephalitis *n.* poliencefalitis.
polio *n.* polio.
poliocidal *adj.* poliocida.
polioclastic *adj.* polioclástico, -ca.
poliodystrophy *n.* poliodistrofia.
polioencephalitis *n.* polioencefalitis.
polioencephalomyelitis *n.* polioencefalomielitis.
polioencephalopathy *n.* polioencefalopatía.
poliomyelencephalitis *n.* poliomielencefalitis.
poliomyelitis *n.* poliomielitis.
 acute anterior poliomyelitis poliomielitis anterior aguda.
 acute lateral poliomyelitis poliomielitis lateral aguda.
 ascending poliomyelitis poliomielitis ascendente.
 bulbar poliomyelitis poliomielitis bulbar.
 chronic anterior poliomyelitis poliomielitis anterior crónica.
 endemic poliomyelitis poliomielitis endémica.
 epidemic poliomyelitis poliomielitis epidémica.
 postinoculation poliomyelitis poliomielitis posinoculación.
 post-tonsillectomy poliomyelitis poliomielitis posamigdalectomía.
 postvaccinal poliomyelitis poliomielitis posvacunal.
 spinal paralytic poliomyelitis poliomielitis espinal paralítica.
poliomyeloencephalitis *n.* poliomieloencefalitis.
poliomyelopathy *n.* poliomielopatía.
polioneuromere *n.* polioneurómera.
poliosis *n.* poliosis, poliotriquia.
poliovirus *n.* poliovirus.
polishing *n.* pulido.
politzerization *n.* politzeración.
 negative politzerization politzeración negativa.
pollakidipsia *n.* polaquidipsia.
pollakisuria *n.* polaquisuria.
pollakiuria *n.* polaquiuria.
pollenogenic *adj.* polenogénico, -ca, polenógeno, -na.
pollenosis *n.* polenosis.
pollicization *n.* policización.
pollinosis *n.* polinosis.
pollution *n.* polución.
polocyte *n.* polocito.
polyadenitis *n.* poliadenia, poliadenitis.
polyadenoma *n.* poliadenoma.
polyadenopathy *n.* poliadenopatía.
polyadenosis *n.* poliadenosis.
polyarteritis *n.* poliarteritis.
polyarthritis *n.* poliartritis.

chronic villous polyarthritis poliartritis crónica vellosa.
polyarthritis chronica villosa poliartritis crónica vellosa.
polyarthritis destruens poliartritis deformante.
tuberculous polyarthritis poliartritis tuberculosa.
vertebral polyarthritis poliartritis vertebral.
polyarticular *adj.* poliarticular.
polyatomic *adj.* poliatómico, -ca.
polyauxotrophic *adj.* poliauxotrófico, -ca.
polyavitaminosis *n.* poliavitaminosis, polideficiencia.
polyblennia *n.* poliblenia.
polycardia *n.* policardia.
polycellular *adj.* policelular.
polycentric *adj.* policéntrico, -ca.
polycheiria *n.* poliqueiria.
polychiria *n.* poliqueiria, poliquiria.
polychloruria *n.* policloruria.
polycholia *n.* policolia.
polychondritis *n.* policondritis.
 chronic atrophic polychondritis policondritis atrófica crónica.
 polychondritis chronica atrophicans policondritis atrófica crónica.
 relapsing polychondritis policondritis recidivante.
polychondropathia *n.* policondropatía.
polychromasia *n.* policromasia.
polychromatic *adj.* policromático, -ca, policromo, -ma.
polychromatocyte *n.* policromatocito.
polychromatocytosis *n.* policromatocitosis.
polychromatophil *adj.* policromatófilo, -la.
polychromatophile *adj.* policromatófilo, -la.
polychromatophilia *n.* policromatofilia, policromofilia.
polychromatosis *n.* policromatosis.
polychromemia *n.* policromemia.
polychylia *n.* poliquilia.
polyclinic *n.* policlínica.
polyclonia *n.* policlonía.
polycoria *n.* policoria.
polycrotic *adj.* policrórico, -ca, policroto, -ta.
polycrotism *n.* policrotismo.
polycyclic *adj.* policíclico, -ca.
polycyesis *n.* policiesis.
polycystic *adj.* poliquístico, -ca.
polycythemia *n.* policitemia, poliglobulia.
 myelopathic polycythemia policitemia mielopática.
 polycythemia rubra policitemia roja, policitemia rubra.
 polycythemia vera policitemia vera, policitemia verdadera.
 relative polycythemia policitemia relativa.
 secondary polycythemia policitemia secundaria.
 splenomegalic polycythemia policitemia crónica esplenomegálica.
 spurious polycythemia policitemia espuria.
 stress polycythemia policitemia de estrés.
polydactylia *n.* polidactilia.
polydactylism *n.* polidactilismo.
polydactyly *n.* polidactilia.
polydipsia *n.* polidipsia.
polydispersoid *n.* polidispersoide.
polydysplasia *n.* polidisplasia.
 hereditary ectodermal polydysplasia polidisplasia ectodérmica hereditaria.
polyembryony *n.* poliembrionía.
polyencephalomyelitis *n.* poliencefalomielitis, polioencefalomielitis.

polyendocrine *adj.* poliendocrino, -na.
polyendocrinoma *n.* poliendocrinoma.
polyendocrinopathy *n.* poliendocrinopatía.
polyergic *adj.* poliérgico, -ca.
polyesthesia *n.* poliestesia.
polyesthetic *adj.* poliestésico, -ca.
polygalactia *n.* poligalactia, poligalia.
polyganglionic *adj.* poliganglionar.
polygene *n.* polígeno.
polygenic *adj.* poligénico, -ca.
polyglandular *n.* poliglandular.
polygnathus *n.* polignato.
polygon *n.* polígono.
polygraph *n.* polígrafo.
polygyny *n.* poliginia.
polygyria *n.* poligiria.
polyhidrosis *n.* polihidrosis.
polyhybrid *adj.* polihíbrido, -da.
polyhydramnios *n.* polihidramnios.
polyhydruria *n.* polihidruria.
polyhypermenorrhea *n.* polihipermenorrea.
polyhypomenorrhea *n.* polihipomenorrea.
polyinfection *n.* poliinfección.
polykaryocyte *n.* policariocito.
polyleptic *adj.* poliléptico, -ca.
polylogia *n.* polilogia.
polymastia *n.* polimastia.
polymazia *n.* polimazia.
polymelia *n.* polimelia.
polymer *n.* polímero.
polymeria *n.* pleomería, polimería, polimerismo.
polymerization *n.* polimerización.
polymetacarpia *n.* polimetacarpia.
polymetatarsia *n.* polimetatarsia.
polymicrobial *adj.* polimicrobiano, -na.
polymicrogyria *n.* polimicrogiria.
polymicrolipomatosis *n.* polimicrolipomatosis.
polymorphic *n.* polimórfico, -ca, polimorfo, -fa.
polymorphism *n.* polimorfismo.
polymorphocellular *adj.* polimorfocelular.
polymorphocyte *n.* polimorfocito.
polymorphonuclear *adj.* polimorfonuclear.
polymorphous *n.* polimorfo, -fa.
polymyoclonus *n.* polimioclonía.
polymyositis *n.* polimiositis.
 trichinous polymyositis polimiositis triquinosa.
polyneural *adj.* polineural, polinéurico, -ca.
polyneuralgia *n.* polineuralgia.
polyneuritis *n.* polineuritis.
 acute febrile polyneuritis polineuritis febril aguda.
 acute idiopathic polyneuritis polineuritis idiopática aguda.
 acute infective polyneuritis polineuritis infecciosa, polineuritis infecciosa aguda.
 acute postinfectious polyneuritis polineuritis posinfecciosa, polineuritis posinfecciosa aguda.
 anemic polyneuritis polineuritis anémica.
 endemic polyneuritis polineuritis endémica.
 infectious polyneuritis polineuritis infecciosa, polineuritis infecciosa aguda.
 postinfectious polyneuritis polineuritis posinfecciosa, polineuritis posinfecciosa aguda.
polyneuroradiculitis *n.* polineurorradiculitis.
polynuclear *adj.* polinuclear.
polynucleate *adj.* polinucleado, -da.
polynucleated *adj.* polinucleado, -da.
polynucleolar *adj.* polinucleolar.
polynucleosis *n.* polinucleosis.
polynucleotide *n.* polinucleótido.

polyodontia *n.* poliodoncia.
polyonychia *n.* polioniquia.
polyopia *n.* poliopía.
  polyopia monophthalmica poliopía monocular.
polyopsia *n.* poliopsia.
polyorchid *n.* poliórquido.
polyorchidism *n.* poliorquidismo.
polyorchism *n.* poliorquismo.
polyotia *n.* poliotia.
polyovular *adj.* poliovular.
polyovulatory *adj.* poliovulatorio, -ria.
polyp *n.* pólipo.
  adenomatous polyp pólipo adenomatoso.
  bleeding polyp pólipo sangrante.
  bronchial polyp pólipo bronquial.
  cardiac polyp pólipo cardíaco.
  cellular polyp pólipo celular.
  choanal polyp pólipo coanal.
  cystic polyp pólipo quístico.
  fibrinous polyp pólipo fibrinoso.
  fibrous polyp pólipo fibroso.
  fleshy polyp pólipo carnoso.
  gingival polyp pólipo gingival.
  Hopmann's polyp pólipo de Hopmann.
  hydatid polyp pólipo hidatídico.
  hyperplastic polyp pólipo hiperplásico.
  inflammatory polyp pólipo inflamatorio.
  juvenile polyp pólipo juvenil.
  laryngeal polyp pólipo laríngeo.
  lipomatous polyp pólipo lipomatoso.
  lymphoid polyp pólipo linfoide.
  metaplastic polyp pólipo metaplásico.
  mucous polyp pólipo mucoso.
  myomatous polyp pólipo miomatoso.
  nasal polyp pólipo nasal.
  osseous polyp pólipo óseo.
  placental polyp pólipo placentario.
  pulp polyp pólipo pulpar.
  retention polyp pólipo de retención.
  vascular polyp pólipo vascular.
polypapilloma *n.* polipapiloma.
polyparasitism *n.* poliparasitismo.
polypathia *n.* polipatía.
polypectomy *n.* polipectomía.
polypeptide *n.* polipéptido.
polypeptidemia *n.* polipeptidemia.
polypeptidorrhachia *n.* polipeptidorraquia.
polyphagia *n.* polifagia.
polyphalangism *n.* polifalangismo.
polypharmacy *n.* polifármacia.
polyphasic *adj.* polifásico, -ca.
polyphrasia *n.* polifrasia.
polyphyodont *adj.* polifiodonto, -ta.
polypiform *adj.* polipiforme.
polyplasmia *n.* poliplasmia.
polyplastic *adj.* poliplástico, -ca, poloplasto.
polyplegia *n.* poliplejía.
polyploid *adj.* poliploide.
polyploidy *n.* poliploidía.
polypnea *n.* polipnea.
polypodia *n.* polipodia.
polypoid *adj.* polipoide.
polyporous *adj.* poliporoso, -sa.
polyposia *n.* poliposia.
polyposis *n.* poliposis.
  gastric polyposis poliposis gástrica.
  intestinal polyposis poliposis intestinal.
polypotome *n.* polipótomo.
polypotrite *n.* polipotribo, polipotrito.
polyradiculitis *n.* polirradiculitis.
polyradiculoneuritis *n.* polirradiculoneuritis.
polyribosome *n.* polirribosoma.
polyrrhea *n.* polirrea.
polysaccharide *n.* polihósido, polisacárido.

polysarcia *n.* polisarcia.
polyscelia *n.* poliscelia, polisquelia.
polyscelus *n.* poliscelo.
polyscope *n.* poliscopio.
polyserositis *n.* poliorromeningitis, poliserositis.
polysialia *n.* polisialia.
polysome *n.* polisoma, polisomo.
polysomic *adj.* polisómico, -ca.
polysomy *n.* polisomía.
polyspermy *n.* poliespermia, polispermia.
  pathological polyspermy poliespermia patológica.
  physiological polyspermy poliespermia fisiológica.
polystichia *n.* polistiquia.
polysuspensoid *n.* polisuspensoide.
polyteny *n.* politenia.
polythelia *n.* politelia.
polythene *n.* politeno.
polytrichia *n.* politriquia.
polytrichosis *n.* politricosis.
polytrophy *n.* politrofia.
polytropic *adj.* politrópico, -ca.
polyuria *n.* poliuria.
polyvalent *adj.* polivalente.
pompholyx *n.* ponfólix.
pomphus *n.* ponfo.
ponderable *adj.* ponderable.
ponderal *adj.* ponderal.
ponograph *n.* ponógrafo.
pons *n.* puente[1].
ponticular *adj.* ponticular.
ponticulus *n.* pontículo.
pontile *adj.* pontino, -na.
pontine *adj.* pontino, -na.
pontocerebellar *adj.* pontocerebeloso, -sa.
pool *n.* pool.
poples *n.* poples.
popliteal *adj.* poplíteo, -a.
poradenitis *n.* poradenia, poradenitis.
poradenolymphitis *n.* poradenolinfitis.
pore *n.* poro.
  nuclear pore poro nuclear.
porencephalia *n.* poroencefalia.
porencephaly *n.* porencefalia.
poriomania *n.* poriomanía.
porion *n.* porión.
porocele *n.* porocele.
porocephaliasis *n.* porocefaliasis, porocefalosis.
Porocephalus Porocephalus.
porokeratosis *n.* poroqueratosis.
poroma *n.* poroma.
porosis *n.* porosis.
  cerebral porosis porosis cerebral.
porotic *adj.* porótico, -ca.
porotomy *n.* porotomía.
porous *adj.* poroso, -sa.
porphobilinogen *n.* porfobilinógeno.
porphyria *n.* porfiria.
  porphyria cutanea tarda (PCT) porfiria cutanea tarda, porfiria cutánea tardía.
  variegata porphyria porfiria variegata.
porphyrinemia *n.* porfirinemia.
porphyrinuria *n.* porfirinuria.
porphyrization *n.* porfirización.
porphyruria *n.* porfiruria.
porrigo *n.* pórrigo.
  porrigo decalvans pórrigo decalvante.
  porrigo favosa pórrigo favoso.
  porrigo larvalis pórrigo larval.
porropsia *n.* porropsia.
porta *n.* porta.
portion *n.* porción.

portligature *n.* portaligaduras.
portography *n.* portografía.
  splenic portography portografía esplénica.
position *n.* posición.
  Albert's position posición de Albert.
  anatomical position posición anatómica.
  Bonner's position posición de Bonner.
  Bozeman's position posición de Bozeman.
  Casselberry's position posición de Casselberry.
  Depage's position posición de Depage.
  depressive position posición depresiva.
  descerebrate position posición de descerebración.
  dorsal position posición dorsal.
  dorsal recumbent position posición de decúbito dorsal, posición de decúbito supino.
  dorsosacral position posición dorsosacra.
  Duncan's position posición de Duncan.
  eccentric position posición excéntrica.
  Edebohls' position posición de Edebohls.
  Elliot's position posición de Elliot.
  fetal position posición fetal.
  Fowler's position posición de Fowler.
  frontoanterior position posición frontal anterior, posición frontoanterior.
  frontoposterior position posición frontal posterior, posición frontoposterior.
  frontotransverse position posición frontal transversa, posición frontotransversa.
  functional position of the hand posición funcional de la mano.
  genucubital position posición genucubital.
  genupectoral position posición genupectoral.
  jackknife position posición en navaja de bolsillo.
  Jones' position posición de jones.
  knee-elbow position posición rodilla-codo.
  Kraske position posición de kraske.
  landmark position posición de referencia.
  lateral recumbent position posición de decúbito lateral, posición lateroabdominal.
  leapfrog position posición del salto de rana.
  lithotomy position posición de litotomía.
  mentum anterior position posición mentoanterior, posición mentoniana anterior.
  mentum posterior position posición mentoniana posterior, posición mentoposterior.
  mentum transverse position posición mentoniana transversa.
  Noble's position posición de Noble.
  obstetric position posición obstétrica.
  occipitoanterior position posición occipital anterior, posición occipitoanterior.
  occipitoposterior position posición occipital posterior, posición occipitoposterior.
  occipitotransverse position posición occipital transversa, posición occipitotransversa.
  occlusal position posición oclusal.
  orthopneic position posición ortopneica.
  paranoid-schizoid position posición esquizoparanoide.
  prone position posición de decúbito prono, posición prona.
  Rose's position posición de Rose.
  sacroanterior position posición sacra anterior, posición sacroanterior.
  sacroposterior position posición sacra posterior, posición sacroposterior.
  sacrotranverse position posición sacra transversa, posición sacrotransversa.
  scapula anterior position posición escapular anterior, posición escapuloanterior.
  scapula posterior position posición escapular posterior, posición escapuloposterior.

Simon's position posición de Simon.
Sims' position posición de Sims.
supine position posición supina.
Trendelenburg's position posición de Trendelenburg.
tripod position posición de trípode.
Valentine's position posición de Valentine.
Walcher's position posición alemana, posición de Walcher.
positive *adj.* positivo, -va.
positron *n.* positrón.
posologic *adj.* posológico, -ca.
posology *n.* posología.
post mortem *n.* post mortem.
post nares post nares.
post partum posparto, post partum.
postaxial *adj.* posaxial.
postbrachial *adj.* posbraquial.
postbuccal *adj.* posbucal, posoral.
postbulbar *adj.* posbulbar.
postcecal *adj.* poscecal.
postcentral *adj.* poscentral.
postcibal *adj.* poscibal.
postcisterna *n.* poscisterna.
postclavicular *adj.* posclavicular.
postclimacteric *adj.* posclimatérico, -ca.
postcondylar *adj.* poscondíleo, -a.
postconnubial *adj.* posconubial.
postconvulsive *adj.* posconvulsivo, -va.
postcordial *adj.* poscordial.
postcubital *adj.* poscubital.
postdiastolic *adj.* posdiastólico, -ca.
postdicrotic *adj.* posdicrótico, -ca.
postdigestive *adj.* posdigestivo, -va.
postdiphtheritic *adj.* posdiftérico, -ca.
postembryonic *adj.* posembrionario, -ria.
postencephalic *adj.* posencefálico, -ca.
postepileptic *adj.* posepiléptico, -ca.
posterior *adj.* posterior, -ra.
posteroanterior *adj.* posteroanterior.
posteroinferior *adj.* posteroinferior.
posterointernal *adj.* posterointerno, -na.
posterolateral *adj.* posterolateral.
posteromedian *adj.* posteromediano, -na.
posteroparietal *adj.* posteroparietal.
posterosuperior *adj.* posterosuperior, -ra.
posterula *n.* postérula.
postesophageal *adj.* posesofágico, -ca.
postethmoid *adj.* posetmoideo, -a.
postfebrile *adj.* posfebril.
postganglionic *adj.* posganglionar.
postglenoid *adj.* posglenoideo, -a.
posthemiplegic *adj.* poshemipléjico, -ca.
posthemorrhage *n.* poshemorragia.
posthemorrhagic *adj.* poshemorrágico, -ca.
posthepatic *adj.* poshepático, -ca.
posthetomy *n.* postetomía.
posthioplasty *n.* postioplastia.
posthitis *n.* postitis.
postholith *n.* postolito.
posthumous *adj.* póstumo, -ma.
posthyoid *adj.* poshioideo, -a.
posthypnotic *adj.* poshipnótico, -ca.
posthypoglycemic *adj.* poshipoglucémico, -ca.
posthypophysis *n.* poshipófisis.
posthypoxic *adj.* poshipóxico, -ca.
postinfluenzal *adj.* posgripal.
postmalarial *adj.* posmalárico, -ca, pospalúdico, -ca.
postmastoid *adj.* posmastoideo, -a.
postmature *adj.* posmaduro, -ra.
postmediastinal *adj.* posmediastínico, -ca.
postmeiotic *adj.* posmeiótico, -ca.
postmenopausal *adj.* posmenopáusico, -ca.
postmesenteric *adj.* posmesentérico, -ca.

postnasal *adj.* posnasal.
postnatal *adj.* posnatal.
postnecrotic *adj.* posnecrótico, -ca.
postneuritic *adj.* posneurítico, -ca.
postoperative *adj.* posoperatorio, -ria.
postorbital *adj.* posorbitario, -ria.
postpalatine *adj.* pospalatino, -na.
postparalytic *adj.* posparalítico, -ca.
postpharyngeal *adj.* posfaríngeo, -a.
postpneumonic *adj.* posneumónico, -ca.
postponent *adj.* posponente.
postprandial *adj.* posprandial.
postpubescent *adj.* pospúbero, -ra, pospubescente.
postpyknotic *adj.* pospicnótico, -ca.
postrolandic *adj.* posrolándico, -ca.
postsphenoid *n.* posesfenoides.
postsphygmic *adj.* posesfígmico, -ca.
postsplenic *adj.* posesplénico, -ca.
postsylvian *adj.* postsilviano, -na.
post-traumatic *adj.* postraumático, -ca.
post-typhoid *adj.* postifoídico, -ca.
postulate *n.* postulado.
   Koch's postulate postulado de Koch.
postural *adj.* postural.
posture *n.* postura.
postuterine *adj.* posuterino, -na.
postvaccinal *adj.* posvacunal.
potable *adj.* potable.
potassemia *n.* potasemia.
potassium *n.* potasio.
potency *n.* potencia.
potential *n.* potencial.
potential acuimeter *n.* medidor de agudeza visual potencial.
potentialization *n.* potencialización.
potentiation *n.* potenciación.
potomania *n.* potomanía.
pouch *n.* bolsa4.
   antral pouch bolsa antral.
   branchial pouch bolsa branquial.
   Broca's pouch bolsa de Broca.
   celomic pouch bolsa celómica.
   Douglas' pouch bolsa de Douglas.
   endodermal pouch bolsa endodérmica.
   Hartmann's pouch bolsa de Hartmann.
   Heidenhain pouch bolsa de Heidenhain.
   Indiana pouch bolsa de Indiana.
   J-pouch bolsa en J.
   Kock's pouch bolsa Kock.
   Mainz's pouch bolsa de Mainz.
   Mainz's pouch 2 bolsa de Mainz 2.
   paracystic pouch bolsa paracística.
   pararectal pouch bolsa pararrectal.
   paravesical pouch bolsa paravesical.
   Pavlov pouch bolsa de Pavlov.
   pharyngeal pouch bolsa faríngea.
   Physick's pouch bolsa de Physick.
   pouch of Douglas bolsa de Douglas.
   Prussak's pouch bolsa de Prussak.
   Rathke's pouch bolsa de Rathke.
   rectouterine pouch bolsa rectouterina.
   Seessel's pouch bolsa de Seessel.
   ultimobranchial pouch bolsa ultimobranquial.
power *n.* poder.
Poxviridae Poxviridae.
practice *n.* práctica.
prandial *adj.* prandial.
praxis *n.* praxis.
preagonal *adj.* preagónico, -ca.
preanal *adj.* preanal.
preanesthesia *n.* preanestesia.
preaortic *adj.* preaórtico, -ca.
preataxic *adj.* preatáxico, -ca.
preauricular *adj.* preauricular.

preaxial *adj.* preaxial, preaxil.
prebacillary *adj.* prebacilar.
prebase *n.* prebase.
precancerosis *n.* precancerosis.
precancerous *adj.* precanceroso, -sa.
precapillary *n.* precapilar.
precarcinomatous *adj.* precarcinomatoso, -sa.
precardiac *adj.* precardíaco, -ca.
precartilage *n.* precartílago.
precava *n.* precava.
precentral *adj.* precentral.
prechordal *n.* precordal.
precipitable *adj.* precipitable.
precipitant *adj.* precipitante.
precipitate *n.* precipitado.
precipitation *n.* precipitación.
precipitinogen *n.* precipitinógeno.
precirrhosis *n.* precirrosis.
preclavicular *adj.* preclavicular.
preclinical *adj.* preclínico, -ca.
precocious *adj.* precoz.
precocity *n.* precocidad.
precoma *n.* precoma.
preconscious *n.* preconsciente.
precordia *n.* precordio.
precordial *adj.* precordial.
precordialgia *n.* precordialgia.
precostal *adj.* precostal.
precritical *adj.* precrítico, -ca.
precursor *adj.* precursor, -ra.
predentin *n.* predentina.
prediabetes *n.* prediabetes.
prediastole *n.* prediástole.
predigestion *n.* predigestión.
predisposition *n.* predisposición.
prediverticular *adj.* prediverticular.
pre-eclampsia *n.* preeclampsia.
pre-epiglottic *adj.* preepiglótico, -ca.
pre-eruptive *adj.* preeruptivo, -va.
preflagellate *adj.* preflagelado, -da.
preformation *n.* preformación.
prefrontal *adj.* prefrontal.
preganglionic *adj.* preganglionar.
pregenital *adj.* pregenital.
pregnancy *n.* embarazo.
   abdominal pregnancy embarazo abdominal.
   aborted ectopic pregnancy embarazo ectópico abortado.
   ampullar pregnancy embarazo ampollar, embarazo ampular.
   ampullary tubal pregnancy embarazo tubárico ampular.
   bigeminal pregnancy embarazo bigémino.
   broad ligament pregnancy embarazo en el ligamento ancho.
   cervical pregnancy embarazo cervical.
   combined pregnancy embarazo combinado.
   cornual pregnancy embarazo cornual.
   ectopic pregnancy embarazo ectópico.
   extra-amniotic pregnancy embarazo extra-amniótico.
   extrachorial pregnancy embarazo extracorial.
   extramembranous pregnancy embarazo extramembranoso.
   extrauterine pregnancy embarazo extrauterino.
   fallopian pregnancy embarazo de Falopio, embarazo falopiano.
   false pregnancy embarazo falso.
   heterotopic pregnancy embarazo heterotópico.
   hydatid pregnancy embarazo hidatídico.
   interstitial pregnancy embarazo intersticial.
   intraligamentary pregnancy embarazo intraligamentario, embarazo intraligamentoso.

intramural pregnancy embarazo intramural.
intraperitoneal pregnancy embarazo intraperitoneal.
molar pregnancy embarazo afetal, embarazo molar.
multiple pregnancy embarazo múltiple.
mural pregnancy embarazo mural.
ovarian pregnancy embarazo ovárico.
ovarioabdominal pregnancy embarazo ovaricoabdominal, embarazo ovarioabdominal.
phantom pregnancy embarazo fantasma.
plural pregnancy embarazo plural.
postdate pregnancy embarazo posmaduro.
prolonged pregnancy embarazo prolongado.
sarcofetal pregnancy embarazo sarcofetal.
secondary abdominal pregnancy embarazo abdominal secundario.
spurious pregnancy embarazo espurio.
stump pregnancy embarazo de muñón.
tubal pregnancy embarazo tubárico.
tuboabdominal pregnancy embarazo tuboabdominal.
tubo-ovarian pregnancy embarazo tuboovárico.
tubouterine pregnancy embarazo tubouterino.
twin pregnancy embarazo gemelar.
uterine pregnancy embarazo eutópico, embarazo uterino.
uteroabdominal pregnancy embarazo uteroabdominal.
utero-ovarian pregnancy embarazo uteroovárico.
uterotubal pregnancy embarazo uterotubárico.
pregnant *adj.* embarazada.
incompetent pregnant woman mujer gestante incapaz.
pregnant woman mujer gestante.
pregonium *n.* pregonio, pregonium.
pregravidic *adj.* pregravídico, -ca.
prehallux *n.* prehallux.
prehemiplegic *adj.* prehemipléjico, -ca.
prehensile *adj.* prensil.
prehension *n.* prensión.
prehepaticus *n.* prehepático.
prehypophysis *n.* prehipófisis.
preimmunization *n.* preinmunización.
prelacrimal *adj.* prelacrimal, prelagrimal.
prelacteal *adj.* prelácteo, -a.
prelaryngeal *adj.* prelaríngeo, -a.
preleukemia *n.* preleucemia.
prelymbic *adj.* prelímbico, -ca.
premalignant *adj.* premaligno, -na.
premaniacal *adj.* premaniaco, -ca, premaníaco, -ca.
premature *n.* prematuro, -ra.
premaxillary *adj.* premaxilar.
premedication *n.* premedicación.
premenstrual *adj.* premenstrual.
premolar *n.* premolar.
premorbid *adj.* premórbido, -da.
premortal *adj.* premortal.
premunition *n.* premunición.
premunitive *adj.* premunitivo, -va.
premyeloblast *n.* premieloblasto.
premyelocyte *n.* premielocito.
prenarcosis *n.* prenarcosis.
prenasal *adj.* prenasal.
prenatal *adj.* prenatal.
preneoplastic *adj.* preneoplásico, -ca.
preoperative *adj.* preoperatorio, -ria.
preoptic *adj.* preóptico, -ca.
preoral *adj.* preoral.
prepalatal *adj.* prepalatino, -na.

preparation *n.* preparación.
radiopharmaceutical preparation radiofármaco.
prepatellar *adj.* prepatelar, prerrotuliano, -na.
preperforative *adj.* preperforativo, -va.
preperitoneal *adj.* preperitoneal.
preplacental *adj.* preplacentario, -ria.
preponderance *n.* preponderancia.
prepsychosis *n.* prepsicosis.
prepubescent *adj.* prepubescente.
prepucial *adj.* prepucial.
preputiotomy *n.* prepuciotomía.
preputium *n.* prepucio.
preputium clitoridis prepucio del clítoris.
prerectal *adj.* prerrectal.
prerenal *adj.* prerrenal.
presbyacusia *n.* presbiacusia, presbiacusis.
presbyatrics *n.* presbiatría.
presbyope *n.* presbíope.
presbyophrenia *n.* presbiofrenia.
presbyopia *n.* presbicia, presbiopía, presbitismo.
presbyopic *n.* présbita, présbite.
prescapular *adj.* preescapular.
prescription *n.* prescripción, receta.
presenile *adj.* presenil.
presenility *n.* presenilidad.
presentation *n.* presentación.
anterior presentation presentación mentoanterior.
breech complete presentation presentación de nalgas completa.
breech presentation presentación de nalgas.
brow presentation presentación de frente.
cephalic presentation presentación cefálica.
compound presentation presentación compuesta.
double breech presentation presentación doble de nalgas.
face presentation presentación de cara, presentación facial.
footing presentation presentación podálica.
funis presentation presentación funicular.
knee presentation presentación de rodillas.
oblique presentation presentación oblicua.
pelvic presentation presentación pelviana, presentación pélvica.
placental presentation presentación de la placenta.
posterior presentation presentación mentoposterior.
shoulder presentation presentación de hombros.
transverse presentation presentación transversa.
trunk presentation presentación de tronco.
vertex presentation presentación de vértice.
preservation *n.* conservación.
cold preservation conservación en frío.
preservative *n.* conservante.
presphenoid *n.* preesfenoides.
pressor *adj.* presor, -ra.
pressoreceptor *adj.* presorreceptor, -ra.
pressure *n.* presión.
alveolar distending pressure presión de apertura alveolar.
atmospheric pressure presión atmosférica.
back pressure presión de fondo, presión retrógrada.
blood pressure presión arterial.
capillary pressure presión capilar.
central venous pressure (CVP) presión venosa central (PVC).
cerebral perfusion pressure (CPP) presión de perfusión cerebral (PPC).

cerebrospinal pressure presión cefalorraquídea.
colloid osmotic pressure presión coloidosmótica.
continuous negative chest wall pressure presión torácica negativa continua.
continuous positive airway pressure (CPAP) presión positiva continua de las vías respiratorias (PPCVR).
cricoid pressure presión del cricoides.
critical pressure presión crítica.
diastolic blood pressure presión arterial diastólica.
diastolic filling pressure presión de llenado diastólico.
filling pressure presión de llenado.
high blood pressure hipertensión.
hydrostatic pressure presión hidrostática.
intra-abdominal pressure presión intraabdominal.
intracranial pressure presión intracraneal.
intraocular pressure presión intraocular.
intraventricular pressure presión intraventricular.
jugular venous pressure (JVP) presión venosa yugular (PVY).
maximum inspiratory pressure (MIP) presión inspiratoria máxima (PIM).
negative end-expiratory pressure (NEEP) presión espiratoria final negativa (PEFN).
negative pressure presión negativa.
oncotic pressure presión oncótica.
opening pressure presión de apertura.
osmotic pressure presión osmótica.
partial pressure presión parcial.
partial pressure of carbon dioxide presión parcial de anhídrido carbónico.
pleural pressure presión pleural.
positive end expiratory pressure (PEEP) presión espiratoria final positiva (PEFP).
positive pressure presión positive.
pulmonary artery wedge pressure presión de enclavamiento de la arteria pulmonar.
pulmonary pressure presión pulmonar.
pulmonary wedge pressure (PWP) presión de enclavamiento pulmonar (PEP).
pulse pressure presión del pulso.
solution pressure presión de solución.
static pressure presión estática.
systolic pressure presión sistólica.
transpulmonary pressure presión transpulmonar.
venous pressure presión venosa.
wedge pressure presión de enclavamiento.
zero-end expiratory pressure (ZEEP) presión espiratoria final cero.
presuppurative *adj.* presupurativo, -va.
presylvian *adj.* presilviano, -na.
presynaptic *n.* presináptico.
presystole *n.* presístole.
pretarsal *adj.* pretarsal, pretarsiano, -na.
prethyroid *adj.* pretiroideo, -a.
prethyroideal *adj.* pretiroideo, -a.
prethyroidean *adj.* pretiroideo, -a.
pretibial *adj.* pretibial.
pretrematic *adj.* pretremático, -ca.
pretuberculosis *n.* pretuberculosis.
pretympanic *adj.* pretimpánico, -ca.
preurethritis *n.* preuretritis.
prevalence *n.* prevalencia.
prevention *n.* prevención.
primary prevention prevención primaria.
secondary prevention prevención secundaria.
tertiary prevention prevención terciaria.

preventive *adj.* preventivo, -va.
prevertebral *adj.* prevertebral.
prevesical *adj.* prevesical.
previous *adj.* previo, -via.
previtamin *n.* previtamina.
prezygotic *adj.* precigótico, -ca.
prezymogen *n.* precimógeno.
priapism *n.* priapismo.
priapitis *n.* priapitis.
priapus *n.* priapos.
primary *adj.* primario, -ria.
primate *n.* primate.
primer *n.* imprimador.
  cavity primer imprimador de cavidad.
primigravida *n.* primigrávida.
primipara *n.* primípara.
primiparity *n.* primiparidad.
primitive *adj.* primitivo, -va.
primordial *adj.* primordial.
primordium *n.* primordio, primordium.
principle *n.* principio.
  abstinence principle principio de abstinencia.
  active principle principio activo.
  antianemia principle principio antianémico.
  closure principle principio de cierre.
  Doppler principle principio Doppler.
  epigenetic principle principio epigenético.
  Fick principle principio de Fick.
  Hardy-Weinberg equilibrium principle principio de equilibrio de Hardy-Weinberg.
  inclusiveness principle principio de inclusión.
  Le Chatelier's principle principio de Le Chatelier.
  nirvana principle principio de nirvana.
  organic principle principio orgánico.
  Pascal's principle principio de Pascal.
  pleasure principle principio de placer.
  preparedness principle principio de expectancia, principio de preparación.
  principle of constancy principio de constancia.
  prothrombin converting principle principio de conversión de protrombina.
  proximate principle principio inmediato.
  reality principle principio de realidad.
prion *n.* prión.
prism *n.* prisma.
prismoid *adj.* prismoide.
prismosphere *n.* prismoesfera, prismosfera.
prisoptometer *n.* prismoptómetro, prisoptómetro.
proacrosomal *adj.* proacrosómico, -ca.
proal *adj.* proal.
probacteriophage *n.* probacteriófago.
  defective probacteriophage probacteriófago defectuoso.
proband *n.* probando.
probe[1] *n.* sonda.
  Anel's probe sonda de Anel.
  ball probe sonda esofágica de esfera.
  blood flow probe sonda de flujo sanguíneo.
  blunt probe sonda roma.
  bristle probe sonda esofágica de cerdas.
  bullet probe sonda de proyectil, sonda para proyectiles.
  drum probe sonda de tambor.
  eyed probe sonda de ojo.
  gene probe sonda génica.
  horse hair probe sonda esofágica de cerdas.
  lacrimal probe sonda lagrimal.
  meerschaum probe sonda de magnesita.
  nucleic acid probe sonda de ácido nucleico.
  periodontal probe sonda periodontal.

  pocket probe sonda de saco.
  radioactive probe sonda radiactiva.
  scissor probe sonda de tijeras.
  sponge probe sonda esofágica de torunda.
  vertebrated probe sonda vertebrada.
  viral probe sonda viral.
  wire probe sonda de alambre.
probe[2] *v.* sondar.
probing *n.* sondeo.
probiotic *adj.* probiótico, -ca.
proboscis *n.* probóscide.
procedure *n.* intervención, procedimiento.
  Blalock-Taussing procedure procedimiento de Blalock-Taussing.
  Commando procedure procedimiento de Commando.
  Duhamel's procedure intervención de Duhamel.
  endorrectal pull-through procedure procedimiento telescópico endorrectal.
  Ewart's procedure procedimiento de Ewart.
  Fontan procedure procedimiento de Fontan.
  Friederich's procedure intervención de Friederich.
  Girdlestone procedure procedimiento de Girdlestone.
  Hartmann's procedure intervención de Hartmann.
  invasive procedure procedimiento invasivo.
  Kaplan's procedure intervención de Kaplan.
  Kasai's procedure intervención de Kasai.
  Ladd's procedure intervención de Ladd.
  mustard procedure procedimiento de mustard.
  Nicholas procedure procedimiento de Nicholas.
  Nicola procedure procedimiento de Nicola.
  Puestow's procedure intervención de Puestow, procedimiento de Puestow.
  Puttio-Platt procedure procedimiento de Puttio-Platt.
  Rashkind procedure procedimiento de Rashkind.
  shelf procedure procedimiento del estante.
  Sugiura's procedure intervención de Sugiura.
  Torkildsen's procedure procedimiento de Torkildsen.
  V-Y procedure procedimiento en V-Y.
  Warren's procedure intervención de Warren.
  Whipple's procedure intervención de Whipple.
  W-plastia procedure procedimiento W.
  Z-plastia procedure procedimiento z.
procephalic *adj.* procefálico, -ca.
process *n.* proceso.
procheilia *n.* proqueilia, proquilia.
prochilia *n.* proqueilia, proquilia.
prochirus *n.* peróquiro.
prochondral *adj.* procondral.
prochordal *adj.* procordal.
prochorion *n.* procorion.
procidentia *n.* procidencia.
  procidentia uteri procidencia del útero.
procollagen *n.* procolágeno.
procreate *n.* procrear.
procreation *n.* procreación.
proctagra *n.* proctagra.
proctalgia *n.* proctalgia.
  proctalgia fugax proctalgia fugaz.
proctatresia *n.* proctatresia.
proctectasia *n.* proctectasia.
proctectomy *n.* proctectomía.
procteurynter *n.* procteurínter.
proctitis *n.* proctitis.

  chronic ulcerative proctitis proctitis ulcerosa crónica.
  epidemic gangrenous proctitis proctitis epidémica gangrenosa, proctitis gangrenosa epidémica.
  idiopathic proctitis proctitis idiopática.
  radiation proctitis proctitis por radiación.
proctocele *n.* proctocele.
proctoclysis *n.* proctoclisis.
proctococcypexy *n.* proctococcipexia, proctocoxipexia.
proctocolectomy *n.* proctocolectomía.
proctocolitis *n.* proctocolitis.
proctocolonoscopy *n.* proctocolonoscopia.
proctocolpoplasty *n.* proctocolpoplastia.
proctocystocele *n.* proctocistocele.
proctocystoplasty *n.* proctocistoplastia.
proctocystotomy *n.* proctocistotomía.
proctodeal *adj.* proctodeico, -ca.
proctodeum *n.* proctodeo.
proctodynia *n.* proctodinia.
proctoelytroplasty *n.* proctoelitroplastia.
proctogenic *adj.* proctogénico, -ca, proctógeno, -na.
proctologic *adj.* proctológico, -ca.
proctologist *n.* proctólogo, -ga.
proctology *n.* proctología.
proctoparalysis *n.* proctoparálisis.
proctoperineoplasty *n.* proctoperineoplastia.
proctoperineorrhaphy *n.* proctoperineorrafia.
proctopexy *n.* proctopexia.
proctoplasty *n.* proctoplastia.
proctoplegia *n.* proctoplejía.
proctoptosia *n.* proctoptosia.
proctoptosis *n.* proctoptosia, proctoptosis.
proctorrhaphy *n.* proctorrafia.
proctorrhea *n.* proctorrea.
proctoscope *n.* proctoscopio.
  Tuttle's proctoscope proctoscopio de Tuttle.
proctoscopy *n.* proctoscopia.
proctosigmoidectomy *n.* proctosigmoidectomía.
proctosigmoiditis *n.* proctosigmoiditis.
proctosigmoidopexy *n.* proctosigmoidopexia.
proctosigmoidoscope *n.* proctosigmoidoscopio, rectosigmoidoscopio.
proctosigmoidoscopy *n.* proctosigmoidoscopia, rectosigmoidoscopia.
proctospasm *n.* proctoespasmo, proctospasmo.
proctostasis *n.* proctostasis.
proctostat *n.* proctóstato.
proctostenosis *n.* proctoestenosis, proctostenosis.
proctostomy *n.* proctostomía.
proctotome *n.* proctótomo.
proctotomy *n.* proctotomía.
proctotresia *n.* proctotresia.
proctovalvotomy *n.* proctovalvotomía.
procumbent *adj.* procumbente.
procursive *adj.* procursivo, -va.
procurvation *n.* procurvación.
prodomous *adj.* prodrómico, -ca.
prodrome *n.* pródromo.
prodromic *adj.* prodrómico, -ca.
product *n.* producto.
productive *adj.* productivo, -va.
proencephalon *n.* proencéfalo.
proenzyme *n.* proenzima.
proerythroblast *n.* proeritroblasto.
proestrogen *n.* proestrógeno.
proestrum *n.* proestro, proestrum.

professional intrusism *n.* intrusismo profesional.
profile *n.* perfil.
  antigenic profile perfil antigénico.
  biochemical profile perfil bioquímico.
  facial profile perfil facial.
  personality profile perfil de la personalidad.
  test profile perfil de pruebas.
  urethral pressure profile perfil de presión uretral.
progenitalis *adj.* progenital.
progenitor *n.* progenitor, -ra.
progeny *n.* progenie.
progeria *n.* progeria.
progestational *adj.* progestacional.
progesterone *n.* progesterona.
progestogen *n.* progestágeno, progestógeno.
proglossis *n.* proglosis.
proglottid *n.* proglótide.
proglottis *n.* proglotis.
prognathic *adj.* prognato, -ta.
prognathism *n.* prognatismo.
prognathometer *n.* prognatómetro.
prognosis *n.* pronóstico.
progonoma *n.* progonoma.
  progonoma of the jaw progonoma mandibular.
progravid *adj.* progravido, -da.
progress *n.* progreso.
progression *n.* progresión.
progressive *adj.* progresivo, -va.
prohormone *n.* prohormona.
proinsulin *n.* proinsulina.
proiosystole *n.* proiosístole.
proiosystolia *n.* proiosistolia.
projection *n.* proyección.
  erroneous projection proyección errónea.
  false projection proyección falsa.
  radiologic projection proyección radiológica.
  visual projection proyección visual.
prokaryote *n.* procariota.
prokaryotic *adj.* procariótico, -ca.
prolabial *adj.* prolabial.
prolabium *n.* prolabio.
prolactin *n.* prolactina.
prolapse *n.* prolapso.
  anal prolapse prolapso del ano.
  frank prolapse prolapso franco.
  mitral valve prolapse prolapso de la válvula mitral.
  prolapse of the anus prolapso del ano.
  prolapse of the cord prolapso del cordón.
  prolapse of the iris prolapso del iris.
  prolapse of the rectum prolapso del recto, prolapso rectal.
  prolapse of the umbilical cord prolapso del cordón umbilical.
  prolapse of the uterus prolapso del útero.
  rectal prolapse prolapso del recto, prolapso rectal.
prolepsis *n.* prolepsis.
proleptic *adj.* proléptico, -ca.
proliferation *n.* proliferación.
  gingival proliferation proliferación gingival.
proliferative *adj.* proliferativo, -va.
proliferous *adj.* prolífero, -ra.
prolific *adj.* prolífico, -ca.
proligerous *adj.* prolígero, -ra.
prolongation *n.* prolongación.
promegaloblast *n.* promegaloblasto.
prometaphase *n.* prometafase.
prominence *n.* prominencia.
prominent *adj.* prominente.
prominentia *n.* prominencia.

promonocyte *n.* promonocito.
promontory *n.* promontorio.
promyelocyte *n.* promielocito.
pronation *n.* pronación.
  pronation of the foot pronación del pie.
  pronation of the forearm pronación del antebrazo.
pronatis *n.* pronato.
pronator *adj.* pronador, -ra.
prone *n.* prono.
pronephros *n.* pronefros.
pronograde *adj.* pronógrado, -da.
pronometer *n.* pronómetro.
pronucleus *n.* pronúcleo.
pro-otic *adj.* proótico, -ca.
propagate *v.* propagar.
propagation *n.* propagación.
properitoneal *adj.* properitoneal.
prophase *n.* profase.
prophylactic *adj.* diafiláctico, -ca, profiláctico, -ca.
  prophylactic odontomy odontomía profiláctica.
prophylaxis *n.* profilaxis.
  active prophylaxis profilaxis activa.
  chemical prophylaxis profilaxis química.
  dental prophylaxis profilaxis dental.
  oral prophylaxis profilaxis bucal.
  passive prophylaxis profilaxis pasiva.
  serum prophylaxis profilaxis sérica.
propioception *n.* propiocepción.
propionacidemia *n.* propionacidemia.
propiospinal *adj.* propioespinal.
proplasmacyte *n.* proplasmocito.
propositus *n.* propósito.
proprioceptor *adj.* propioceptor, -ra.
proptosis *n.* proptosis.
propulsion *n.* propulsión.
prorsad prorsad.
proscolex *n.* proescólex.
prosencephalon *n.* prosencéfalo.
prosodemy *n.* prosodemia.
prosodiplegia *n.* prosopodiplejía.
prosody *n.* prosodia.
prosopagnosia *n.* prosopagnosia.
prosopagus *n.* prosópago.
prosopalgia *n.* prosopalgia, prosopodinia.
prosopalgic *adj.* prosopálgico, -ca.
prosopectasia *n.* prosopectasia.
prosoplasia *n.* prosoplasia.
prosopodysmorphia *n.* prosopodismorfia.
prosoponeuralgia *n.* prosoponeuralgia.
prosopoplegia *n.* prosopoplejía.
prosopoplegic *adj.* prosopopléjico, -ca.
prosoposchisis *n.* prosoposquisis.
prosopothoracopagus *n.* prosopotoracópago.
prospermia *n.* proespermia.
prostatalgia *n.* prostatalgia.
prostate *n.* próstata.
prostatectomy *n.* prostatectomía.
prostatic *adj.* prostático, -ca.
prostaticovesical *adj.* prostaticovesical.
prostatism *n.* prostatismo.
prostatitis *n.* prostatitis.
prostatocystitis *n.* prostatocistitis.
prostatocystotomy *n.* prostatocistotomía.
prostatodynia *n.* prostatodinia.
prostatography *n.* prostatografía.
prostatolith *n.* prostatolito.
prostatomegaly *n.* prostatomegalia.
prostatomy *n.* prostatomía.
prostatomyomectomy *n.* prostatomiomectomía.
prostatorrhea *n.* prostatorrea.
prostatotomy *n.* prostatotomía.

prostatovesiculectomy *n.* prostatovesiculectomía.
prostatovesiculitis *n.* prostatovesiculitis.
prosternation *n.* prosternación.
prosthesis *n.* prótesis.
  antireflux prosthesis prótesis antirreflujo.
  bar joint prosthesis prótesis articulada a barras.
  cardiac valve prosthesis prótesis de válvula cardíaca.
  cochlear prosthesis prótesis coclear.
  complete prosthesis prótesis completa.
  definitive prosthesis prótesis definitiva.
  dental prosthesis dentaria, prótesis dental.
  fixed partial prosthesis prótesis parcial fija.
  full prosthesis prótesis total.
  immediate insertion prosthesis prótesis de inserción inmediata.
  immediate prosthesis prótesis inmediata.
  implant prosthesis prótesis de implante.
  interim prosthesis prótesis interina.
  maxillofacial prosthesis prótesis maxilofacial.
  ocular prosthesis prótesis ocular.
  overlay prosthesis prótesis superpuesta.
  partial prosthesis prótesis parcial.
  preparatory prosthesis prótesis preparatory.
  provisional prosthesis prótesis provisional.
  removable partial prosthesis prótesis parcial removible.
  telescopic prosthesis prótesis telescópica.
  temporary prosthesis prótesis temporal.
  transitional prosthesis prótesis transitoria.
  treatment prosthesis prótesis de tratamiento.
  trial prosthesis prótesis de prueba.
prosthetic *adj.* prostético, -ca, protésico, -ca.
prostration *n.* postración.
protamine *n.* protamina.
protanomalopia *n.* protanomalopía.
protanomaly *n.* protanomalía.
protanope *adj.* protánope.
protanopia *n.* protanopía.
protean *adj.* proteico, -ca.
proteasome *n.* proteosoma.
proteid *n.* proteido.
protein *n.* proteína.
proteinaceous *adj.* proteináceo, -a.
proteinemia *n.* proteinemia.
proteinogenous *adj.* proteinógeno, -na.
proteinogram *n.* proteinograma.
proteinosis *n.* proteinosis.
  lipid proteinosis proteinosis lipídica.
  pulmonary alveolar proteinosis proteinosis alveolar pulmonar.
proteinotherapy *n.* proteinoterapia, proteoterapia.
proteinuria *n.* proteinuria, proteuria.
  accidental proteinuria proteinuria accidental.
  adventitious proteinuria proteinuria adventicia.
  athletic proteinuria proteinuria atlética.
  Bence-Jones proteinuria proteinuria de Bence-Jones.
  colliquative proteinuria proteinuria colicuativa.
  dietetic proteinuria proteinuria dietética.
  digestive proteinuria proteinuria digestiva.
  effort proteinuria proteinuria de esfuerzo.
  emulsion proteinuria proteinuria de emulsión.
  enterogenic proteinuria proteinuria enterógena.
  false proteinuria proteinuria falsa.

febrile proteinuria proteinuria febril.
functional proteinuria proteinuria funcional.
gestational proteinuria proteinuria gestacional.
globular proteinuria proteinuria globular.
gouty proteinuria proteinuria gotosa.
hematogenous proteinuria proteinuria hematógena.
hemic proteinuria proteinuria hémica.
intermittent proteinuria proteinuria intermitente.
intrinsic proteinuria proteinuria intrínseca.
isolated proteinuria proteinuria aislada.
lordotic proteinuria proteinuria lordótica.
mixed proteinuria proteinuria mixta.
orthostatic proteinuria proteinuria ortostática.
palpatory proteinuria proteinuria palpatoria.
paroxysmal proteinuria proteinuria paroxística.
physiologic proteinuria proteinuria fisiológica.
postrenal proteinuria proteinuria posrenal.
postural proteinuria proteinuria postural.
prerenal proteinuria proteinuria prerrenal.
pyogenic proteinuria proteinuria piógena.
regulatory proteinuria proteinuria regulatoria.
renal proteinuria proteinuria nefrógena, proteinuria renal.
residual proteinuria proteinuria residual.
serous proteinuria proteinuria serosa.
transient proteinuria proteinuria transitoria.
true proteinuria proteinuria verdadera.
proteoclastic *adj.* proteoclástico, -ca.
proteohormone *n.* proteohormona.
proteolipid *n.* proteolípido.
proteolysin *n.* proteolisina.
proteolysis *n.* proteólisis.
proteometabolic *adj.* proteometabólico, -ca.
proteometabolism *n.* proteometabolismo.
proteopepsis *n.* proteopepsis.
proteopexis *n.* proteopexis.
proteopexy *n.* proteopexis.
proteosuria *n.* proteosuria.
Proteus Proteus.
prothrombin *n.* protrombina.
protide *n.* prótido.
protochondrium *n.* protocondrio.
protocol *n.* protocolo.
protoconid *n.* protocónido, protocono.
protocoproporphyria *n.* protocoproporfiria.
protoderm *n.* protodermo.
protodiastolic *adj.* protodiastólico, -ca.
protoduodenum *n.* protoduodeno.
protoerythrocyte *n.* protoeritrocito.
protofilament *n.* protofilamento.
protoleukocyte *n.* protoleucocito.
proton *n.* protón.
protonephron *n.* protonefros.
protonephros *n.* protonefros.
protoneuron *n.* protoneurona.
proto-oncogene *n.* protooncogén.
protophyte *n.* protófito.
protoplasia *n.* protoplasia.
protoplasm *n.* protoplasma.
protoplasmatic *adj.* protoplasmático, -ca.
protoplasmic *adj.* protoplasmático, -ca.
protoplast *n.* protoplasto.
protoporphyria *n.* protoporfiria.
protoporphyrinuria *n.* protoporfirinuria.
protorrhagia *n.* proctorragia.
protospasm *n.* protoespasmo.
protostoma *n.* protostoma.

protosyphilis *n.* protosífilis.
protothecosis *n.* prototecosis.
prototoxin *n.* prototoxina.
prototroph *adj.* protótrofo, -fa.
prototype *n.* prototipo.
protovertebra *n.* protovértebra.
protozoacide *n.* protozoacida.
protozoal *adj.* protozoario, -ria.
protozoology *n.* protozoología.
protozoon *n.* protozoo.
protozoophage *adj.* protozoófago, -ga.
protozoosis *n.* protozoiasis, protozoosis.
protozootherapy *n.* protozooterapia.
protraction *n.* protracción.
  mandibular protraction protracción mandibular.
  maxillary protraction protracción maxilar.
protractor *n.* protractor.
protrusion *n.* protrusión.
protrypsin *n.* protripsina.
protuberance *n.* protuberancia.
proud flesh *n.* bezo.
provertebra *n.* provértebra.
provirus *n.* provirus.
provitamin *n.* provitamina.
proxemics *n.* proxémica.
proximal *adj.* proximal.
proximoataxia *n.* proximoataxia.
proximoceptor *n.* proximoceptor.
proximolabial *adj.* proximolabial.
proximolingual *adj.* proximolingual.
proximovestibular *adj.* proximovestibular.
prozone *n.* prozona.
prozygosis *n.* procigosis, prozigosis.
pruriginous *adj.* prurígeno, -na, pruriginoso, -sa.
prurigo *n.* prurigo.
  Besnier's prurigo prurigo de Besnier.
  Hebra's prurigo prurigo de Hebra.
  melanotic prurigo prurigo melanótico.
  prurigo aestivalis prurigo estival.
  prurigo agria prurigo agrio.
  prurigo chronica multiformis prurigo crónico multiforme.
  prurigo ferox prurigo ferox.
  prurigo gestationis prurigo gestacional, prurigo gestationis.
  prurigo infantilis prurigo infantil.
  prurigo nodularis prurigo nodular.
  prurigo of Besnier prurigo de Besnier.
  prurigo of Hebra prurigo de Hebra.
  prurigo simplex prurigo simple.
  summer prurigo prurigo de verano.
pruritic *adj.* prurítico, -ca.
pruritus *n.* prurito.
  essential pruritus prurito esencial, prurito generalizado, prurito idiopático.
  pruritus ani prurito anal, prurito ani.
  pruritus copra prurito por copra.
  pruritus senilis prurito senil.
  pruritus vulvae prurito vulvar.
  water pruritus prurito de agua.
psalterial *adj.* salterial, saltérico, -ca.
psalterium *n.* salterio.
psammocarcinoma *n.* psamocarcinoma.
psammoma *n.* psamoma.
psammomatous *adj.* psamomatoso, -sa.
psammous *adj.* psamoso, -sa.
pselaphesia *n.* pselafesia.
psellism *n.* pselismo.
pseudacousis *n.* seudoacusia.
pseudacousma *n.* seudacusma.
pseudacromegaly *n.* seudoacromegalia.
pseudactinomycosis *n.* seudactinomicosis.
pseudagraphia *n.* seudoagrafía.

pseudalbuminuria *n.* seudoalbuminuria.
pseudangina *n.* seudoangina.
pseudankylosis *n.* seudoanquilosis.
pseudaphia *n.* seudoafia.
pseudarrhenia *n.* seudoarrenia.
pseudarthrosis *n.* seudoartrosis.
pseudesthesia *n.* seudoestesia.
pseudinoma *n.* seudinoma.
pseudoacanthosis nigricans *n.* seudoacantosis nigricans.
pseudoacephalus *n.* seudoacéfalo.
pseudoachondroplasia *n.* seudoacondroplasia.
pseudoactinomycosis *n.* seudoactinomicosis.
pseudoagrammatism *n.* seudoagramatismo.
pseudoagraphia *n.* seudoagrafía.
pseudoalbuminuira *n.* seudoalbuminuria.
pseudoalopecia *n.* seudoalopecia atrófica.
pseudoalveolar *adj.* seudoalveolar.
pseudoanaphylactic *adj.* seudoanafiláctico, -ca.
pseudoanaphylaxis *n.* seudoanafilaxia, seudoanafilaxis.
pseudoanemia *n.* seudoanemia.
pseudoaneurysm *n.* seudoaneurisma.
pseudoangina *n.* seudoangina.
pseudoangiosarcoma *n.* seudoangiosarcoma.
  Masson's pseudoangiosarcoma seudoangiosarcoma de Masson.
pseudoankylosis *n.* seudoanquilosis.
pseudoanodontia *n.* seudoanodoncia.
pseudoanorexia *n.* seudoanorexia.
pseudoantagonist *n.* seudoantagonista.
pseudoaphia *n.* seudoafia.
pseudoapoplexy *n.* seudoapoplejía.
pseudoappendicitis *n.* seudoapendicitis.
pseudoapraxia *n.* seudoapraxia.
pseudoarthrosis *n.* seudoartrosis.
pseudoataxia *n.* seudoataxia.
pseudoathetosis *n.* seudoatetosis.
pseudoatrophoderma *n.* seudoatrofodermia.
pseudobacillus *n.* seudobacilo.
pseudobacterium *n.* seudobacteria.
pseudoblennorrhagia *n.* seudoblenorragia.
pseudobronchiectasis *n.* seudobronquiectasia.
pseudobulbar *adj.* seudobulbar.
pseudobuzzing *n.* seudozumbido.
  pseudobuzzing of the ears seudozumbido de oído.
pseudocardiac *adj.* seudocardíaco, -ca.
pseudocartilage *n.* seudocartílago.
pseudocast *n.* seudocilindro.
pseudocatilaginous *adj.* seudocartilaginoso, -sa.
pseudocele *n.* seudocele.
pseudocelom *n.* seudoceloma.
pseudocephalocele *n.* seudocefalocele.
pseudochancre *n.* seudochancro.
pseudochlorosis *n.* seudoclorosis.
pseudocholecystitis *n.* seudocolecistitis.
pseudocholesteatoma *n.* seudocolesteatoma.
pseudochorea *n.* seudocorea.
pseudochromesthesia *n.* seudocromestesia.
pseudochromhidrosis *n.* seudocromhidrosis, seudocromidrosis.
pseudochromidrosis *n.* seudocromidrosis.
pseudochromosome *n.* seudocromosoma.
pseudochylous *adj.* seudoquiloso, -sa.
pseudocirrhosis *n.* seudocirrosis.
pseudoclaudication *n.* seudoclaudicación.
pseudoclonus *n.* seudoclono.
pseudocoarctation *n.* seudocoarctación.
pseudocoelomate *adj.* seudocelomado, -da.

pseudocoloboma *n.* seudocoloboma.
pseudocolony *n.* seudocolonia.
pseudocopulation *n.* seudocopulación.
pseudocorpus luteum *n.* seudocuerpo lúteo.
pseudocowpox *n.* seudovacuna.
pseudocoxalgia *n.* seudocoxalgia.
pseudocrisis *n.* seudocrisis.
pseudocroup *n.* seudocrup.
pseudocryptorchism *n.* seudocriptorquismo.
pseudocyanin *n.* seudocianina.
pseudocyesis *n.* seudociesis.
pseudocylindroid *n.* seudocilindroide.
pseudocyst *n.* seudoquiste.
   pancreatic pseudocyst seudoquiste pancreático.
pseudodeciduosis *n.* seudodeciduosis.
pseudodementia *n.* seudodemencia.
pseudodextrocardia *n.* seudodextrocardia.
pseudodiastolic *adj.* seudodiastólico, -ca.
pseudodiphtheria *n.* seudodifteria.
pseudodiverticulum *n.* seudodivertículo.
pseudodominant *adj.* seudodominante.
pseudodysentery *n.* seudodisentería.
pseudodyspepsia *n.* seudodispepsia.
pseudoedema *n.* seudoedema.
pseudoembryonic *adj.* seudoembrionario, -ria.
pseudoemphysema *n.* seudoenfisema.
pseudoencephalus *n.* seudoencéfalo.
pseudoendometritis *n.* seudoendometritis.
pseudoeosinophil *n.* seudoeosinófilo.
pseudoepiphysis *n.* seudoepífisis.
pseudoerysipelas *n.* seudoerisipela.
pseudoesthesia *n.* seudoestesia.
pseudoexfoliation *n.* seudoexfoliación.
   pseudoexfoliation of the lens capsule seudoexfoliación de la cápsula del cristalino.
pseudoexophoria *n.* seudoexoforia.
pseudoexophthalmos *n.* seudoexoftalmia.
pseudoextrophy *n.* seudoextrofia.
pseudofluctuation *n.* seudofluctuación.
pseudofracture *n.* seudofractura.
pseudoganglion *n.* seudoganglión.
pseudogene *n.* seudogén.
pseudogeusesthesia *n.* seudogeusestesia.
pseudogeusia *n.* seudogeusia.
pseudoglioma *n.* seudoglioma.
pseudoglobulin *n.* seudoglobulina.
pseudoglomerulus *n.* seudoglomérulo.
pseudoglottic *adj.* seudoglótico, -ca.
pseudoglottis *n.* seudoglotis.
pseudogonorrhea *n.* seudogonorrea.
pseudogonorrhoea *n.* seudogonorrea.
pseudogout *n.* seudogota.
pseudographia *n.* seudografía.
pseudograze *n.* seudoerosión.
pseudogynecomastia *n.* seudoginecomastia.
pseudohallucination *n.* seudoalucinación.
pseudohaustration *n.* seudohaustración.
pseudohematuria *n.* seudohematuria.
pseudohemophilia *n.* seudohemofilia.
pseudohemophtysis *n.* seudohemoptisis.
pseudohereditary *adj.* seudohereditario, -ria.
pseudohermafroditism *n.* seudohermafroditismo.
   female pseudohermafroditism seudohermafroditismo femenino.
   male pseudohermafroditism seudohermafroditismo masculino.
pseudohermaphrodite *n.* seudohermafrodita.
   female pseudohermaphrodite seudohermafrodita femenino.
   male pseudohermaphrodite seudohermafrodita masculino.
pseudohernia *n.* seudohernia.

pseudoheterotopia *n.* seudoheterotopia.
pseudohydrarthrosis *n.* seudohidrartrosis.
   pseudohydrarthrosis of the knee seudohidrartrosis de la rodilla.
pseudohydrocephaly *n.* seudohidrocefalia.
pseudohydronephrosis *n.* seudohidronefrosis.
pseudohydrophobia *n.* seudohidrofobia.
pseudohyperparathyroidism *n.* seudohiperparatiroidismo.
pseudohypertelorism *n.* seudohipertelorismo.
pseudohypertrichosis *n.* seudohipertricosis.
pseudohypertrophic *adj.* seudohipertrófico, -ca.
pseudohypertrophy *n.* seudohipertrofia.
   muscular pseudohypertrophy seudohipertrofia muscular.
pseudohypha *n.* seudohifa.
pseudohypoaldosteronism *n.* seudohipoaldosteronismo.
pseudohyponatremia *n.* seudohiponatremia.
pseudohypoparathyroidism *n.* seudohipoparatiroidismo.
pseudohypophosphatasia *n.* seudohipofosfatasia.
pseudohypothyrodism *n.* seudohipotiroidismo.
pseudoicterous *adj.* seudoíctero, -ra.
pseudoinfarction *n.* seudoinfarto.
pseudoinfluenza *n.* seudoinfluenza.
pseudointraligamentous *adj.* seudointraligamentoso, -sa.
pseudoion *n.* seudoión.
pseudoisochromatic *adj.* seudoisocromático, -ca.
pseudoisocyanin *n.* seudoisocianina.
pseudojaundice *n.* seudoictericia.
pseudolamellar *adj.* seudolaminar.
pseudoleukemia *n.* seudoleucemia.
pseudoleukocythemia *n.* seudoleucocitemia.
pseudolipoma *n.* seudolipoma.
pseudolithiasis *n.* seudolitiasis.
pseudologia phantastica *n.* seudología fantástica.
pseudoluxation *n.* seudoluxación.
pseudolymphocyte *n.* seudolinfocito.
pseudolymphoma *n.* seudolinfoma.
pseudomalaria *n.* seudomalaria, seudopaludismo.
pseudomalignancy *n.* seudomalignidad.
pseudomamma *n.* seudomama.
pseudomegacolon *n.* seudomegacolon.
pseudomelanoma *n.* seudomelanoma.
pseudomelanosis *n.* seudomelanosis.
pseudomembrane *n.* seudomembrana.
pseudomembranous *adj.* seudomembranoso, -sa.
pseudomeningitis *n.* seudomeningitis.
pseudomenstruation *n.* seudomenstruación.
pseudometaplasia *n.* seudometaplasia.
pseudomethemoglobin *n.* seudometahemoglobina.
pseudomicrocephalus *adj.* seudomicrocéfalo, -la.
pseudomicrocephaly *n.* seudomicrocefalia.
pseudomnesia *n.* seudomnesia.
Pseudomonas Pseudomonas.
pseudomotor *adj.* seudomotor, -ra.
pseudomucin *n.* seudomucina.
pseudomucinous *adj.* seudomucinoso, -sa.
pseudomutism *n.* seudomutismo.
pseudomutuality *n.* seudomutualidad.
pseudomyasis *n.* seudomiasis.
pseudomycelium *n.* seudomicelio.

pseudomycosis *n.* seudomicosis.
pseudomyopia *n.* seudomiopía.
pseudomyxoma *n.* seudomixoma.
pseudonarcotic *adj.* seudonarcótico, -ca.
pseudonarcotism *n.* seudonarcotismo.
pseudonarrowness *n.* seudoangostura.
pseudoneoplasm *n.* seudoneoplasia.
pseudoneuralgia *n.* seudoneuralgia.
pseudoneuritis *n.* seudoneuritis.
pseudoneuroma *n.* seudoneuroma.
pseudoneuronophagia *n.* seudoneurofagia.
pseudonit *n.* seudoliendre.
pseudonystagmus *n.* seudonistagmo.
pseudo-obstruction *n.* seudoobstrucción.
pseudo-ochronosis *n.* seudoocronosis.
pseudo-optogram *n.* seudooptograma.
pseudo-osteomalacia *n.* seudoosteomalacia, seudosteomalacia.
pseudo-ovum *n.* seudoóvulo.
pseudopannus *n.* seudopaño.
pseudopapilla *n.* seudopapila.
pseudopapilledema *n.* seudopapiledema.
pseudoparalysis *n.* seudoparálisis.
   arthritic general pseudoparalysis seudoparálisis general artrítica.
   congenital atonic pseudoparalysis seudoparálisis atónica congénita.
   spastic pseudoparalysis seudoparálisis espástica.
pseudoparaphrasia *n.* seudoparafrasia, seudoparafrasis.
pseudoparaplegia *n.* seudoparaplejía.
   Basedow's pseudoparaplegia seudoparaplejía de Basedow.
pseudoparasite *n.* seudoparásito.
pseudoparasitism *n.* seudoparasitismo.
pseudoparesis *n.* seudoparesia.
pseudopeptone *n.* seudopeptona.
pseudopericardial *adj.* seudopericárdico, -ca.
pseudoperitonitis *n.* seudoperitonitis.
pseudophakia *n.* seudofaquia.
pseudophakodonesis *n.* seudofacodonesis.
pseudophlegmon *n.* seudoflemón.
pseudophotesthesia *n.* seudofotoestesia.
pseudophthisis *n.* seudotisis.
pseudoplague *n.* seudopeste.
pseudoplasm *n.* seudoplasma.
pseudoplasmodium *n.* seudoplasmodium.
pseudoplatelet *n.* seudoplaqueta.
pseudoplegia *n.* seudoplejía.
pseudopleuresy *n.* seudopleuresía.
pseudopleuritis *n.* seudopleuritis.
pseudopod *n.* seudópodo.
pseudopodium *n.* seudópodo.
pseudopoliomyelitis *n.* seudopoliomielitis.
pseudopolycythemia *n.* seudopolicitemia.
pseudopolymelia *n.* seudopolimelia.
pseudopolyp *n.* seudopólipo.
pseudopolyposis *n.* seudopoliposis.
pseudoponeumonia *n.* seudoneumonía.
pseudoporphyria *n.* seudoporfiria.
pseudopregnancy *n.* seudoembarazo.
pseudoprognathism *n.* seudoprognatismo.
pseudoproteinuria *n.* seudoproteinuria.
pseudopseudohypoparathyroidism *n.* seudoseudohipoparatiroidismo.
pseudopsia *n.* seudopsia.
pseudopterygium *n.* seudopterigión.
pseudoptosis *n.* seudoptosis.
pseudoptyalism *n.* seudoptialismo, seudotialismo.
pseudopuberty *n.* seudopubertad.
   precocious pseudopuberty seudopubertad precoz.
pseudoreaction *n.* seudorreacción.

pseudoreminiscence *n.* seudorreminiscencia.
pseudoreplica *n.* seudorréplica.
pseudoretinitis pigmentosa *n.* seudorretinitis pigmentosa.
pseudorheumatism *n.* seudorreumatismo.
pseudorickets *n.* seudorraquitismo.
pseudorosette *n.* seudorroseta.
pseudorubella *n.* seudorrubéola.
pseudosarcoma *n.* seudosarcoma.
pseudosclerema *n.* seudoesclerema, seudosclerema.
pseudosclerosis *n.* seudoesclerosis, seudosclerosis.
  Westphal's pseudosclerosis seudoesclerosis de Westphal.
  Westphal-Strümpell pseudosclerosis seudoesclerosis de Westphal-Strümpell.
pseudoscrotum *n.* seudoescroto.
pseudosmallpox *n.* seudovaricela, seudoviruela.
pseudosolution *n.* seudosolución.
pseudostoma *n.* seudoestoma, seudostoma.
pseudostrabism *n.* seudoestrabismo.
pseudostrabismus *n.* seudoestrabismo.
pseudostratification *n.* seudoestratificación.
pseudostratified *adj.* seudoestratificado, -da.
pseudotabes *n.* seudotabes.
  Friedreich's pseudotabes seudotabes de Friedreich.
pseudotetanus *n.* seudotétanos.
pseudothrill *n.* seudofrémito.
pseudotrachoma *n.* seudotracoma.
pseudotrichiniasis *n.* seudotriquinosis.
pseudotrichinosis *n.* seudotriquinosis.
pseudotrismus *n.* seudotrismo.
pseudotruncus arteriosus *n.* seudotronco arterioso.
pseudotubercle *n.* seudotubérculo.
pseudotuberculoma *n.* seudotuberculoma.
pseudotuberculosis *n.* seudotuberculosis.
  pseudotuberculosis hominis streptothrica seudotuberculosis estreptotrica humana.
pseudotumor *n.* seudotumor.
  inflammatory pseudotumor seudotumor inflamatorio.
  pseudotumor cerebri seudotumor cerebral.
pseudotyphoid *n.* seudotifoidea.
pseudotyphus *n.* seudotifus.
pseudouremia *n.* seudouremia.
pseudourticaria *n.* seudourticaria.
pseudovacuole *n.* seudovacuola.
pseudovalve *n.* seudoválvula.
pseudovariola *n.* seudovariola.
pseudoventricle *n.* seudoventrículo.
pseudovitamin *n.* seudovitamina.
pseudovoice *n.* seudovoz.
pseudovomiting *n.* seudovómito.
pseudoxanthoma *n.* seudoxantoma.
  pseudoxanthoma elasticum seudoxantoma elástico.
psilosis *n.* psilosis, silosis.
psittacosis *n.* psitacosis.
psodymus *n.* psódimo.
psoitis *n.* psoítis.
psomophagia *n.* psomofagia.
psophagy *n.* psomofagia.
psorelcosis *n.* psorelcosis.
psorenteritis *n.* psorenteritis.
psoriasiform *adj.* psoriasiforme.
psoriasis *n.* psoriasis.
  diffused psoriasis psoriasis difusa.
  exfoliative psoriasis psoriasis exfoliativa, psoriasis folicular.
  generalized pustular psoriasis of Zambusch psoriasis pustulosa generalizada de Zambusch.

  psoriasis annularis psoriasis anular.
  psoriasis annulata psoriasis anular.
  psoriasis arthropica psoriasis artropática.
  psoriasis buccalis psoriasis bucal.
  psoriasis circinata psoriasis circinada.
  psoriasis diffusa psoriasis difusa.
  psoriasis discoidea psoriasis discoidea.
  psoriasis geographica psoriasis geográfica.
  psoriasis guttata psoriasis guttata.
  psoriasis gyrata psoriasis gyrata.
  psoriasis inveterata psoriasis inveterada.
  psoriasis linguae psoriasis lingual.
  psoriasis nummularis psoriasis numular.
  psoriasis of palms and soles psoriasis palmar y plantar.
  psoriasis orbicularis psoriasis orbicular.
  psoriasis ostreacea psoriasis ostrácea.
  psoriasis punctata psoriasis punctata, psoriasis punteada.
  psoriasis rupioides psoriasis rupioides.
  psoriasis spondylitica psoriasis espondilítica.
  psoriasis universalis psoriasis universal, psoriasis universalis.
psychalgia *n.* psicalgia.
psychalia *n.* psicalia.
psychasthenia *n.* psicastenia.
psyche *n.* psique.
psychedelic *adj.* psicodélico, -ca.
psychiatrist *n.* psiquiatra.
psychiatry *n.* psiquiatría.
  biological psychiatry psiquiatría biológica.
  community psychiatry psiquiatría comunitaria.
  dynamic psychiatry psiquiatría dinámica.
  existential psychiatry psiquiatría existencial.
  forensic psychiatry psiquiatría forense.
  infantile psychiatry psiquiatría infantil.
  social psychiatry psiquiatría social.
psychic *adj.* psíquico, -ca.
psychism *n.* psiquismo.
psychoacoustics *n.* psicoacústica.
psycho-analysis *n.* psicoanálisis
psychoanalyst *n.* psicoanalista.
psychoauditory *adj.* psicoacústico, -ca, psicoauditivo, -va.
psychobiology *n.* psicobiología.
psychocatharsis *n.* psicocatarsis.
psychodiagnosis *n.* psicodiagnóstico.
psychodometry *n.* psicodometría.
psychodrama *n.* psicodrama.
psychodynamics *n.* psicodinámica.
psychoendocrinology *n.* psicoendocrinología.
psychogalvanic *adj.* psicogalvánico, -ca.
psychogenesis *n.* psicogénesis, psicogenia.
psychogeriatrics *n.* psicogeriatría.
psychologist *n.* psicólogo, -ga.
psychology *n.* psicología.
  behavioral psychology psicología conductista.
  clinical psychology psicología clínica.
  cognitive psychology psicología cognitiva.
  community psychology psicología comunitaria.
  counseling psychology psicología de la orientación.
  depth psychology psicología profunda.
  developmental psychology psicología evolutiva.
  dynamic psychology psicología dinámica.
  educational psychology psicología de la educación, psicología educacional.
  existential psychology psicología existencial.
  experimental psychology psicología experimental.

  genetic psychology psicología genética.
  Gestalt psychology psicología de la Gestalt.
  individual psychology psicología individual.
  industrial psychology psicología industrial.
  industrial-organizational psychology psicología del trabajo y de las organizaciones.
  medical psychology psicología médica.
  social psychology psicología social.
psychometry *n.* psicometría.
psychomotor *adj.* psicomotor, -ra.
psychoneurosis *n.* psiconeurosis.
psychonosology *n.* psiconosología.
psychopath *n.* psicópata.
psychopathic *adj.* psicopático, -ca.
psychopathology *n.* psicopatología.
psychopathy *n.* psicopatía.
psychopharmaceutical *n.* psicofármaco.
psychopharmacology *n.* psicofarmacología.
psychophylaxis *n.* psicofilaxis.
psychophysics *n.* psicofísica.
  clinical psychophysics psicofísica clínica.
psychophysiology *n.* psicofisiología.
psychosensory *adj.* psicosensorial.
psychosexual *adj.* psicosexual.
psychosis *n.* psicosis.
psychosocial *adj.* psicosocial.
psychosomatic *adj.* psicosomático, -ca.
psychostimulant *n.* psicoestimulante.
psychotechnics *n.* psicotecnia.
psychotherapist *n.* psicoterapeuta.
psychotherapy *n.* psicoterapia.
  analytic psychotherapy psicoterapia analítica.
  dynamic psychotherapy psicoterapia dinámica.
  existential psychotherapy psicoterapia existencial.
  Gestalt psychotherapy psicoterapia de la Gestalt.
  group psychotherapy psicoterapia de grupo, psicoterapia grupal.
  psychoanalytic psychotherapy psicoterapia psicoanalítica.
  short-term psychotherapy psicoterapia breve.
  supportive psychotherapy psicoterapia de apoyo.
  trasactional psychotherapy psicoterapia transaccional.
psychotic *adj.* psicótico, -ca.
psychotropic *adj.* psicotrópico, -ca, psicotropo, -pa.
pternalgia *n.* pternalgia.
pterygium *n.* pterigión.
pterygoid *adj.* pterigoide, pterigoideo, -a, pterigoides, terigoide, terigoideo, -a.
pterygomandibular *adj.* pterigomandibular.
pterygomaxillare *adj.* pterigomaxilar.
pterygopalatine *adj.* palatopterigoideo, -a, pterigopalatino, -na.
ptilosis *n.* ptilosis.
ptomainemia *n.* tomainemia.
ptomainotoxism *n.* tomainotoxismo.
ptomatopsia *n.* tomatopía, tomatopsia.
ptomatopsy *n.* tomatopía, tomatopsia.
ptosis *n.* ptosis.
  false ptosis ptosis falsa.
  Horner's ptosis ptosis de Horner.
  ptosis adiposa ptosis adiposa.
  ptosis lipomatosis ptosis lipomatosa.
  ptosis sympathetica ptosis simpática.
ptyalagogue *adj.* tialagogo, -ga.
ptyalectasis *n.* tialectasia.
ptyalism *n.* tialismo, tialosis.
  gravidic ptyalism tialismo gravídico.

ptyalocele *n.* tialocele.
ptyalogenic *adj.* tialogénico, -ca, tialógeno, -na.
ptyalography *n.* tialografía.
ptyalolith *n.* tialito, tialolito.
ptyalolithiasis *n.* tialolitiasis.
ptyaloreaction *n.* tialorreacción.
ptyalorrhea *n.* tialorrea.
ptyocrinous *n.* ptiocrino.
pubarche *n.* pubarquia.
puberty *n.* pubertad.
  precocious puberty pubertad precoz.
pubes pubes.
pubescence *n.* pubescencia.
pubescent *adj.* pubescente.
pubioplasty *n.* pubioplastia.
pubiotomy *n.* pubiotomía.
pubis *n.* pubis.
pubofemoral *adj.* pubiofemoral.
puboprostatic *adj.* pubioprostático, -ca.
puericulture *n.* puericultura.
puerpera *n.* puérpera.
puerperal *adj.* puerperal.
puerperium *n.* puerperio.
pull *n.* tirón.
pullulation *n.* pululación.
pulmoaortic *adj.* pulmoaórtico, -ca.
pulmolith *n.* pulmolito.
pulmometer *n.* pulmómetro.
pulmometry *n.* pulmometría.
pulmonectomy *n.* pulmonectomía.
pulmonitis *n.* pulmonía.
pulp *n.* pulpa.
  dead pulp pulpa muerta.
  dental pulp pulpa dental.
  devitalized pulp pulpa desvitalizada.
  digital pulp pulpa del dedo, pulpa digital.
  exposed pulp pulpa expuesta.
  necrotic pulp pulpa necrótica.
  non-vital pulp pulpa no vital.
  pulp of the finger pulpa del dedo, pulpa digital.
  putrescent pulp pulpa putrefacta.
  radicular pulp pulpa radicular.
  vital pulp pulpa vital.
pulpa *n.* pulpa.
  pulpa splenica pulpa esplénica.
pulpalgia *n.* pulpalgia.
pulpation *n.* pulpación.
pulpectomy *n.* pulpectomía.
pulpifaction *n.* pulpefacción.
pulpiform *adj.* pulpiforme.
pulpitis *n.* pulpitis.
  hyperplastic pulpitis pulpitis hiperplásica.
  irreversible pulpitis pulpitis irreversible.
  reversible pulpitis pulpitis reversible.
  suppurative pulpitis pulpitis supurativa.
pulpless *adj.* despulpado, -da.
pulpy *adj.* pulposo, -sa.
pulsate *v.* latir.
pulsatile *adj.* pulsátil.
pulsation *n.* pulsación.
pulsator *n.* pulsador.
pulse *n.* pulso.
  abdominal pulse pulso abdominal.
  anacrotic pulse pulso anacrótico, pulso anacroto.
  bigeminal pulse pulso bigémino.
  bisferious pulse pulso bisferiens.
  bulbar pulse pulso bulbar.
  cannon ball pulse pulso en bala de cañón.
  capillary pulse pulso capilar.
  celer pulse pulso celer.
  collapsing pulse pulso colapsante.
  cordy pulse pulso cordal.
  Corrigan's pulse pulso de Corrigan.
  coupled pulse pulso acoplado.

  dicrotic pulse pulso dicrótico, pulso dicroto.
  dorsal pedis pulse pulso pedio.
  elastic pulse pulso elástico.
  entoptic pulse pulso entóptico.
  equal pulse pulso igual.
  febrile pulse pulso febril.
  filiform pulse pulso filiforme.
  frequent pulse pulso frecuente.
  gaseous pulse pulso gaseoso.
  guttural pulse pulso gutural.
  hard pulse pulso duro.
  intermittent pulse pulso intermitente.
  irregular pulse pulso irregular.
  jugular pulse pulso yugular.
  Kussmaul's paradoxical pulse pulso paradójico, pulso paradójico de Kussmaul.
  Kussmaul's pulse pulso de Kussmaul.
  long pulse pulso largo.
  Monneret's pulse pulso de Monneret.
  monocrotic pulse pulso monocroto.
  mousetail pulse pulso en cola de ratón.
  movable pulse pulso móvil.
  nail pulse pulso ungueal, pulso ungular.
  paradoxical pulse pulso paradójico, pulso paradójico de Kussmaul.
  peripheral pulse pulso periférico.
  piston pulse pulso a pistón.
  plateau pulse pulso en meseta.
  polycrotic pulse pulso policroto.
  popliteal pulse pulso poplíteo.
  pulse cordis pulso cordis.
  pulse tremulus pulso trémulo.
  quadrigeminal pulse pulso cuadrigémino.
  Quincke's pulse pulso de Quincke.
  radial pulse pulso radial.
  rapid pulse pulso rápido.
  respiratory pulse pulso respiratorio.
  reversed paradoxical pulse pulso paradójico invertido.
  Riegel's pulse pulso de Riegel.
  slow pulse pulso lento.
  soft pulse pulso blando.
  tense pulse pulso tenso.
  tricrotic pulse pulso tricrótico, pulso tricroto.
  trigeminal pulse pulso trigeminado, pulso trigémino.
  undulating pulse pulso ondulante.
  vacuus pulse pulso vacío, pulso vacuo.
  venous pulse pulso venoso.
  vermicular pulse pulso vermicular.
  water-hammer pulse pulso en martillo de agua.
pulsion *n.* pulsión[2].
pulsus *n.* pulso.
  pulsus aequalis pulso igual.
  pulsus alternans pulso alternante.
  pulsus caprisans pulso caprizante.
  pulsus celer pulso acelerado.
  pulsus differens pulso differens.
  pulsus heterochronicus pulso heterocrónico.
  pulsus inaequalis pulso desigual.
  pulsus incongruens pulso incongruente.
  pulsus infrequens pulso infrecuente.
  pulsus irregularis perpetuus pulso irregular perpetuo.
  pulsus oppresus pulso de opresión.
  pulsus tardus pulso tardío.
  pulsus vagus pulso del vago.
pultaceous *adj.* pultáceo, -a.
pulverization *n.* pulverización.
pulverize *v.* pulverizar.
pulvinar pulvinar.
pulvinated *adj.* pulvinado, -da.
pump *n.* bomba, bombear.
  Abbott pump bomba de Abbott.
  air pump bomba de aire.

  Alvegniat's pump bomba de Alvegniat.
  amine pump bomba de aminas.
  blood pump bomba de sangre, bomba sanguínea.
  breast pump bomba mamaria, bomba para mamas, bomba sacaleches.
  calcium pump bomba de calcio.
  cardiac balloon pump bomba cardíaca de balón.
  Carrel-Lindbergh pump bomba de Carrel-Lindbergh.
  constant infusion pump bomba para infusión constante.
  dental pump bomba dental.
  Harvard pump bomba de Harvard.
  infusion pump bomba de infusión.
  infusion-withdrawal pump bomba de infusión y extracción.
  insulin infusion pump bomba de infusión de insulina.
  insulin pump bomba de insulina.
  intra-aortic balloon pump (IABP) bomba con balón intraaórtico, bomba-balón intraaórtico.
  intravenous peristaltic pump bomba peristáltica intravenosa.
  intravenous piston pump bomba intravenosa de pistón.
  intravenous syringe pump bomba de jeringa intravenosa.
  ionic pump bomba iónica.
  jet ejector pump bomba eyectora a chorro.
  Lindbergh's pump bomba de Lindbergh.
  morphine pump bomba de morfina.
  peristaltic pump bomba peristáltica.
  proton pump bomba de protones.
  saliva pump bomba para saliva.
  slip-on blood pump bomba rápida de sangre.
  sodium pump bomba de sodio.
  sodium-potassium pump bomba de Na y K, bomba de sodio-potasio.
  stomach pump bomba del estómago, bomba estomacal, bomba gástrica.
punch *n.* sacabocados.
  pin punch sacabocados de alfiler.
  plate punch sacabocados de placa.
punctiform *adj.* puntiforme.
puncture *n.* punción.
  Bernard's puncture punción de Bernard.
  cisternal puncture punción cisternal.
  cranial puncture punción craneal.
  diabetic puncture punción diabética.
  exploratory puncture punción exploratoria.
  heel puncture punción del talón.
  intracisternal puncture punción intracraneal.
  Kronecker's puncture punción de Kronecker.
  lumbar puncture (LP) punción lumbar (PL).
  Quincke's puncture punción de Quincke.
  spinal puncture punción espinal, punción raquídea.
  splenic puncture punción esplénica.
  sternal puncture punción esternal.
  suboccipital puncture punción suboccipital.
  thecal puncture punción tecal.
  ventricular puncture punción ventricular.
pupil *n.* pupila.
  Adie's pupil pupila de Adie.
  Argyll-Robertson pupil pupila de Argyll-Robertson.
  artificial pupil pupila artificial.
  Bumke's pupil pupila de Bumke.
  catatonic pupil pupila catatónica.
  cat's-eye pupil pupila en ojo de gato.
  cogwheel pupil pupila en rueda dentada.

fixed pupil pupila fija.
Gunn pupil pupila de Gunn.
Holmes-Adie pupil pupila de Holmes-Adie.
Horner's pupil pupila de Horner.
Hutchinson's pupil pupila de Hutchinson.
keyhole pupil pupila en ojo de cerradura.
Marcus-Gunn pupil pupila de Marcus-Gunn.
paradoxical pupil pupila paradójica.
pinhole pupil pupila puntiforme.
rigid pupil pupila rígida.
Robertson pupil pupila de Robertson.
Saenger pupil pupila de Saenger.
tonic pupil pupila tónica.
pupilla *n.* pupila.
pupillatonia *n.* pupilatonía.
pupillomotor *adj.* pupilomotor, -ra.
pupilloscopia *n.* pupiloscopia.
pupillostatometer *n.* pupilostatómetro.
pupilometer *n.* pupilómetro.
pupilometry *n.* pupilometría.
pupiloplegia *n.* pupiloplejía.
purgative *adj.* purgante.
 drastic purgative drástico.
puriform *adj.* puriforme.
purinemia *n.* purinemia.
puromucous *adj.* puromucoso, -sa.
purple púrpura[1].
 visual purple púrpura visual.
purpura *n.* púrpura[2].
 acute vascular purpura púrpura vascular aguda.
 allergic purpura púrpura alérgica.
 anaphylactoid purpura púrpura anafiláctica.
 angioneurotic purpura púrpura angioneurótica.
 fibrinolytic purpura púrpura fibrinolítica.
 hemorrhagic purpura púrpura hemorrágica.
 Henoch's purpura púrpura abdominal, púrpura de Henoch.
 Henoch-Schönlein purpura púrpura de Henoch-Schönlein.
 idiopathic thrombocytopenic purpura (ITP) púrpura trombocitopénica idiopática (PTI).
 immune thrombocytopenic purpura púrpura trombocitopénica inmune.
 iodic purpura púrpura yódica.
 malignant purpura púrpura maligna.
 non-thrombocytopenic purpura púrpura atrombocitopénica, púrpura no trombocitopénica.
 psychogenic purpura púrpura psicogénica.
 purpura fulminans púrpura fulminans, púrpura fulminante.
 purpura iodica púrpura yódica.
 purpura nervosa púrpura nerviosa.
 purpura rheumatica púrpura reumática.
 purpura senilis púrpura senil.
 purpura symptomatica púrpura sintomática.
 purpura urticans púrpura urticans.
 thrombocytopenic purpura púrpura trombocitopénica.
 thrombopenic purpura púrpura trombopática, púrpura trombopénica.
 thrombotic thrombocytopenic purpura (TTP) púrpura trombocitopénica trombótica (PTT).
 Waldenström's purpura púrpura de Waldenström.
purpuriferous *adj.* purpurífero, -ra.
purpurinuria *n.* purpurinuria.
purpurogenous *adj.* purpurógeno, -na.
purulence *n.* purulencia.
purulent *adj.* purulento, -ta.
puruloid *adj.* puruloide.

pus *n.* pus.
 anchovy sauce pus pus de salsa de anchoas.
 blue pus pus azul.
 cheesy pus pus caseoso, pus denso.
 curdy pus pus cuajado.
 green pus pus verde.
 lichorous pus pus licoroso.
 sanious pus pus sanioso.
pustular *adj.* pustular, pustuloso, -sa.
pustulation *n.* pustulación.
pustule *n.* pústula.
 multilocular pustule pústula multilocular.
 pock pustule pústula variólica.
 pustule postmortem pústula post mortem.
 simple pustule pústula simple.
 spongiform pustule of Kogoj pústula espongiforme de Kogoj.
 unilocular pustule pústula unilocular.
pustuliform *adj.* pustuliforme.
pustulocrustaceous *adj.* pustulocrustáceo, -a.
pustulosis *n.* pustulosis.
 pustulosis palmaris et plantaris pustulosis palmoplantar.
 pustulosis vacciniformis acuta pustulosis vacciniforme aguda.
putrefaction *n.* putrefacción, putrescencia.
putrid *adj.* pútrido, -da.
putty *n.* masilla.
pyarthrosis *n.* piartrosis.
pyelectasia *n.* pielectasia.
pyelectasis *n.* pielectasia, pielectasis.
pyelitic *adj.* pielítico, -ca.
pyelitis *n.* pielitis.
pyelocaliectasis *n.* pielocaliectasis.
pyelocalyceal *adj.* pielocaliceal.
pyelocystitis *n.* pielocistitis.
pyelofluoroscopy *n.* pielofluoroscopia.
pyelogram *n.* pielograma.
pyelography *n.* pielografía.
 antegrade pyelography pielografía antégrada.
pyelolithotomy *n.* pielolitotomía.
pyelolymphatic *adj.* pielolinfático, -ca.
pyelonephritis *n.* pielonefritis.
 acute pyelonephritis pielonefritis aguda.
 ascending pyelonephritis pielonefritis ascendente.
 chronic pyelonephritis pielonefritis crónica.
 xanthogranulomatous pyelonephritis pielonefritis xantogranulomatosa.
pyelonephrosis *n.* pielonefrosis.
pyeloplasty *n.* pieloplastia.
 Anderson-Hynes pyeloplasty pieloplastia de Anderson-Hynes.
 capsular flap pyeloplasty pieloplastia de colgajo capsular.
 Culp pyeloplasty pieloplastia de Culp.
 disjoined pyeloplasty pieloplastia desarticulada.
 dismembered pyeloplasty pieloplastia desmembrada.
 Foley Y-plasty pyeloplasty pieloplastia en Y de Foley.
 Scardino vertical flap pyeloplasty pieloplastia de colgajo vertical de Scardino.
pyeloscopy *n.* pieloscopia.
pyelostomy *n.* pielostomía.
pyelotomy *n.* pielotomía.
 extended pyelotomy pielotomía extendida.
pyeloureterectasis *n.* pieloureterectasis.
pyeloureterography *n.* pieloureterografía.
pyelovenous *adj.* pielovenoso, -sa.
pyemesis *n.* piemesis.
pyemia *n.* piemia.
 cryptogenic pyemia piemia criptogénica.
pyemic *adj.* piémico, -ca.

pyencephalus *n.* piencéfalo.
pygal *adj.* pigal.
pygmalionism *n.* pigmalionismo.
pygmy *n.* pigmeo, -a.
pygoamorphus *n.* pigoamorfo.
pygodidymus *n.* pigodídimo.
pygomelus *n.* pigomelo.
pygopagus *n.* pigópago.
pyknodysostosis *n.* picnodisostosis.
pyknophrasia *n.* picnofrasia.
pyknosis *n.* picnosis.
pyknotic *adj.* picnótico, -ca.
pylemphraxis *n.* pilenfraxis.
pylephlebectasia *n.* pileflebectasia.
pylephlebectasis *n.* pileflebectasia, pileflebectasis.
pylephlebitis *n.* pileflebitis.
pylethrombophlebitis *n.* piletromboflebitis.
pylethrombosis *n.* piletrombosis.
pylic *adj.* pílico, -ca.
pyloralgia *n.* piloralgia.
pylorectomy *n.* pilorectomía.
pyloric *adj.* pilórico, -ca.
pyloritis *n.* piloritis.
pylorodiosis *n.* pilorodiosis.
pyloroduodenitis *n.* piloroduodenitis.
pylorogastrectomy *n.* pilorogastrectomía.
pyloromyotomy *n.* piloromiotomía.
pyloroplasty *n.* piloroplastia.
 Finney pyloroplasty piloroplastia de Finney.
 Heineke-Mikulicz pyloroplasty piloroplastia de Heineke-Mikulicz.
 Jaboulay pyloroplasty piloroplastia de Jaboulay.
pyloroptosia *n.* piloroptosia.
pyloroptosis *n.* piloroptosia, piloroptosis.
pylorospasm *n.* piloroespasmo.
pylorostenosis *n.* piloroestenosis, piloroestenosis.
pylorostomy *n.* pilorostomía.
pylorotomy *n.* pilorotomía.
pylorus *n.* píloro.
pyocele *n.* piocele.
pyocelia *n.* piocelia.
pyocephalus *n.* piocefalia.
 circunscribed pyocephalus piocefalia circunscripta.
pyochezia *n.* pioquecia.
pyococcus *n.* piococo.
pyocolpocele *n.* piocolpocele.
pyocolpos *n.* piocolpos.
pyocyanic *adj.* pociánico, -ca.
pyocyanogenic *adj.* piocianógeno, -na.
pyocyanolysin *n.* piocianolisina.
pyocyst *n.* pioquiste.
pyocystitis *n.* piocistitis.
pyocyte *n.* piocito.
pyoderma *n.* piodermia.
 chancriform pyoderma piodermia chancriforme.
 primary pyoderma piodermia primario.
 pyoderma gangrenosum piodermia gangrenoso.
 pyoderma vegetans piodermia vegetante.
 secondary pyoderma piodermia secundario.
pyodermatitis *n.* piodermatitis.
pyodermatosis *n.* piodermatosis.
pyogen *n.* piógeno.
pyogenesis *n.* piogénesis.
pyogenetic *adj.* piogenético, -ca.
pyogenic *adj.* piogénico, -ca.
pyohemia *n.* piohemia.
pyohemothorax *n.* piohemotórax.
pyoid *adj.* pioide.
pyolabyrinthitis *n.* piolaberintitis.

pyometra *n.* piómetra.
pyometritis *n.* piometritis.
pyomyositis *n.* piomiositis.
  tropical pyomyositis piomiositis tropical.
pyonephritis *n.* pionefritis.
pyonephrolithiasis *n.* pionefrolitiasis.
pyonephrosis *n.* pionefrosis.
pyonephrotic *adj.* pionefrótico, -ca.
pyo-ovarium *n.* pioovario.
pyopericarditis *n.* piopericarditis.
pyopericardium *n.* piopericardio.
pyoperitoneum *n.* pioperitoneo.
pyoperitonitis *n.* pioperitonitis.
pyophthalmia *n.* pioftalmía.
pyophthalmitis *n.* pioftalmitis.
pyophysometra *n.* piofisómetra.
pyopneumocholecystitis *n.* pioneumocolecistitis.
pyopneumocyst *n.* pioneumocisto.
pyopneumohepatitis *n.* pioneumohepatitis.
pyopneumopericardium *n.* pioneumopericardio.
pyopneumoperitoneum *n.* pioneumoperitoneo.
pyopneumoperitonitis *n.* pioneumoperitonitis.
pyopneumothorax *n.* pioneumotórax.
  subdiaphragmatic pyopneumothorax pioneumotórax subdiafragmático, pioneumotórax subfrénico.

subphrenic pyopneumothorax pioneumotórax subdiafragmático, pioneumotórax subfrénico.
pyopoiesis *n.* piopoyesis.
pyopoietic *adj.* piopoyético, -ca.
pyoptysis *n.* pioptisis.
pyopyelectasis *n.* piopielectasis.
pyosalpingitis *n.* piosalpingitis.
pyosalpingo-oophoritis *n.* piosalpingooforitis.
pyosalpingo-oothecitis *n.* piosalpingootecitis.
pyosalpinx *n.* piosálpinx.
pyosemia *n.* piosemia.
pyosepticemia *n.* piosepticemia.
pyosis *n.* piosis.
  Manson's pyosis piosis de Manson.
pyospermia *n.* piospermia.
pyostatic *adj.* piostático, -ca.
pyostomatitis *n.* pioestomatitis.
  pyostomatitis vegetans pioestomatitis vegetante.
pyothorax *n.* piotórax.
pyoumbilicus *n.* pioombligo.
pyourachus *n.* piouraco.
pyoureter *n.* piouréter.
pyramid *n.* pirámide.
pyramidal *adj.* piramidal.

pyramitodomy *n.* piramidotomía.
  medullary pyramitodomy piramidotomía bulbar, piramidotomía medular.
  spinal pyramitodomy piramidotomía espinal, piramidotomía raquídea.
pyrectic *adj.* pirético, -ca.
pyrenemia *n.* pirenemia.
pyretic *adj.* pirético, -ca.
pyretogenetic *adj.* piretogenético, -ca.
pyretogenic *adj.* piretogénico, -ca.
pyrexia *n.* pirexia.
pyrexial *adj.* piréxico, -ca.
pyrogen *n.* pirógeno.
pyrogenic *adj.* pirogénico, -ca.
pyroglobulinemia *n.* piroglobulinemia.
pyrolysis *n.* pirólisis.
pyromania *n.* piromanía.
pyrometer *n.* pirómetro.
pyronine *n.* pironina.
pyroscope *n.* piroscopio.
pyrosis *n.* pirosis.
pyruvemia *n.* piruvemia.
pythogenic *adj.* pitógeno, -na.
pythogenous *adj.* pitógeno, -na.
pytogenesis *n.* pitogénesis.
pyuria *n.* piuria.
  miliary pyuria piuria miliar.

quadrangle *n.* cuadrángulo.
quadrant *n.* cuadrante.
 abdominal quadrant cuadrante abdominal.
quadrantanopia *n.* cuadrantanopia, cuadrantanopsia.
quadrantanopsia *n.* cuadrantanopia, cuadrantanopsia.
quadrat *n.* quadrat.
quadriceps *adj.* cruádriceps.
quadricepsplasty *n.* cuadricepsplastia.
quadriceptor *n.* cuadriceptor.
quadricuspid *adj.* cuadricúspide.
quadridentate *adj.* cuadridentado, -da.
quadridigitate *adj.* cuadridigitado, -da.
quadrigeminal *adj.* cuadrigémino, -na.
quadrigeminy *n.* cuadrigeminia.
quadrilateral *n.* cuadrilátero.
 Celsus' quadrilateral cuadrilátero de Celso.
quadrilocular *adj.* cuadrilocular.
quadripara *n.* cuadrípara.
quadriparesis *n.* cuadriparesia.
quadripartite *adj.* cuadripartito, -ta.

quadriplegia *n.* cuadriplejía.
quadriplegic *adj.* cuadripléjico, -ca.
quadripolar *adj.* cuadripolar.
quadrisect *v.* cuadrisectar.
quadrisection *n.* cuadrisección.
quadritubercular *adj.* cuadritubercular.
quadrivalent *adj.* cuadrivalente.
quadruplet *n.* cuatrillizo, -za.
quale *n.* quale.
qualimeter *n.* cualímetro.
qualitative *adj.* cualitativo, -va.
quality *n.* cualidad.
 beam quality cualidad del haz.
quantal *adj.* quantal.
quantimeter *n.* cuantímetro.
quantitative *adj.* cuantitativo, -va.
quantum quantum.
quarantine *n.* cuarentena.
quartan *n.* cuartana.
 double quartan cuartana doble.
 triple quartan cuartana triple.
quartile *n.* cuartil.
quartipara *n.* cuartípara.

quartisect *v.* cuartisectar.
quasidominance *n.* cuasidominancia.
quasidominant *adj.* cuasidominante.
quaternary *adj.* cuaternario, -ria.
quenching *n.* extinción.
 fluorescence quenching extinción de fluorescencia, extinción por fluorescencia.
quenuthoracoplasty *n.* quenutoracoplastia.
querulous *adj.* querulante.
querulousness *n.* querulancia.
quickening *n.* vivificación[1].
quiescent *adj.* quiescente.
quigila *n.* quijilla.
quinquecuspid *adj.* quinquecúspide.
quinquetubercular *adj.* quinquetubercular.
quintan *adj.* quintana.
quintassence *n.* quintaesencia.
quintipara *n.* quintípara.
quintisternal *adj.* quintisternal.
quintuplet *adj.* quintillizo, -za, quíntuplo, -pla.
quotidian *adj.* cotidiana.
quotient *n.* cociente.

R r

rabbeting *n.* impacción², impactación.
rabiate *adj.* rabioso, -sa.
rabic *adj.* rábico, -ca.
rabicidal *adj.* rabicida.
rabid *adj.* rabioso, -sa.
rabies *n.* rabia.
  dumb rabies rabia muda.
  false rabies rabia falsa.
  furious rabies rabia furiosa.
  paralytic rabies rabia paralítica.
rabietic *adj.* rábico, -ca.
rabific *adj.* rabífico, -ca.
rabiform *adj.* rabiforme.
rabigenic *adj.* rabígeno, -na.
race *n.* raza.
racemate *n.* racemato.
raceme *n.* raceme.
racemic *adj.* racémico, -ca.
racemization *n.* racemización.
racemose *adj.* racemoso, -sa.
rachial *adj.* raquial.
rachialbuminimeter *n.* raquialbuminómetro.
rachialbuminimetry *n.* raquialbuminometría.
rachialgia *n.* raquialgia.
rachianalgesia *n.* raquianalgesia.
rachianesthesia *n.* raquianestesia.
  hyperbaric rachianesthesia raquianestesia hiperbárica.
  hypobaric rachianesthesia raquianestesia hipobárica.
rachicentesis *n.* raquicentesis.
rachidial *adj.* raquídeo, -a.
rachidian *adj.* raquidiano, -na.
rachigraph *n.* raquígrafo.
rachilysis *n.* raquilisis.
rachiocampsis *n.* raquiocampsis.
rachiocentesis *n.* raquicentesis, raquiocentesis.
rachiochysis *n.* raquioquisis.
rachiocyphosis *n.* raquiocifosis.
rachiodynia *n.* raquiodinia.
rachiokyphosis *n.* raquiocifosis.
rachiometer *n.* raquiómetro.
rachiomyelitis *n.* raquiomielitis.
rachiopagus *n.* raquiópago, -ga.
rachiopathy *n.* raquiopatía.
rachioplegia *n.* raquioplejía.
rachioscoliosis *n.* raquioescoliosis, raquioscoliosis.
rachiotome *n.* raquiótomo.
rachiotomy *n.* raquiotomía.
rachipagus *adj.* raquiópago, -ga, raquípago, -ga.
rachipathy *n.* raquiopatía.
rachiresistance *n.* raquirresistencia.
rachiresistant *adj.* raquirresistente.
rachis *n.* raquis.
rachisagra *n.* raquisagra.
rachischisis *n.* raquisquisis.
  rachischisis posterior raquisquisis posterior.

rachischisis totalis raquisquisis total.
rachisensibility *n.* raquisensibilidad.
rachisensible *adj.* raquisensible, raquisensitivo, -va.
rachistenosis *n.* raquiestenosis.
rachitic *adj.* raquítico, -ca.
rachitis *n.* raquitis, raquitismo.
  celiac rachitis raquitismo celíaco.
  hemorrhagic rachitis raquitismo hemorrágico.
  hepatic rachitis raquitismo hepático.
  hypophosphatemic familial rachitis raquitismo hipofosfatémico familiar, raquitismo vitaminorresistente familiar hipofosfatémico de Fanconi.
  late rachitis raquitismo tardío.
  lean rachitis raquitismo magro.
  pseudodeficiency rachitis raquitismo por seudodeficiencia.
  rachitis fetalis raquitis fetal, raquitismo fetal.
  rachitis fetalis annularis raquitis fetal anular.
  rachitis fetalis micromelica raquitis fetal micromélica.
  rachitis intrauterina raquitis intrauterina.
  rachitis tarda raquitis tardía, raquitismo de los adolescentes.
  rachitis uterina raquitis uterina.
  refractory rachitis raquitismo refractario.
  renal rachitis raquitismo renal.
  resistant rachitis raquitismo vitaminorresistente.
  vitamin D-refractory rachitis raquitismo refractario a la vitamina D.
  vitamin D-resistant rachitis raquitismo resistente a la vitamina D.
  X-linked hypophosphatemic rachitis raquitismo hipofosfatémico familiar, raquitismo vitaminorresistente familiar hipofosfatémico de Fanconi.
rachitogenic *adj.* raquitógeno, -na.
rachitome *n.* raquiótomo, raquítomo.
rachitomy *n.* raquiotomía, raquitomía.
rachyochysis *n.* raquioquisis.
racial *adj.* racial.
racism *n.* racismo.
racist *adj.* racista.
radarkymography *n.* radarquimografía.
radectomy *n.* radectomía.
radiability *n.* radiabilidad.
radiable *adj.* radiable.
radiad radiad.
radial *adj.* radial.
radialis *adj.* radial.
radian *n.* radián.
radiant *n.* radiante.
radiate *v.* irradiar², radiado, -da, radiar.
radiation *n.* radiación.
  acoustic radiation radiación acústica.
  adaptive radiation radiación adaptativa.
  alpha radiation radiación alfa.

  annihilation radiation radiación de aniquilación.
  atmospheric radiation radiación atmosférica.
  auditory radiation radiación auditiva, radiación auditoria.
  background radiation radiación ambiental, radiación de fondo.
  backscatter radiation radiación de retrodispersión.
  beta radiation radiación beta.
  blemsstrahlung radiation radiación de frenado.
  breaking radiation radiación de frenado.
  characteristic radiation radiación característica.
  corpuscular radiation radiación corpuscular.
  cosmic radiation radiación cósmica.
  divergent radiation radiación divergente.
  electromagnetic radiation radiación electromagnética.
  extended field radiation radiación de campo ampliado.
  gamma radiation radiación gamma.
  geniculocalcarine radiation radiación geniculocalcarina.
  graft radiation radiación del injerto.
  Gratiolet radiation radiación de Gratiolet.
  hard radiation radiación dura.
  heterogeneous radiation radiación heterogénea.
  homogeneous radiation radiación homogénea.
  infrared radiation radiación infrarroja.
  interstitial radiation radiación intersticial.
  intrauterine radiation radiación intrauterina.
  ionizing radiation radiación ionizante.
  leakage radiation radiación por fugas.
  low-level radiation radiación de bajo grado.
  monochromatic radiation radiación monocromática.
  monoenergetic radiation radiación monoenergética.
  natural radiation radiación natural.
  non-ionizing radiation radiación no ionizante.
  nuclear radiation radiación nuclear.
  occipitothalamic radiation radiación occipitotalámica.
  off-focus radiation radiación fuera de foco.
  optic radiation radiación óptica.
  photochemical radiation radiación fotoquímica.
  primary radiation radiación primaria.
  pyramidal radiation radiación piramidal.
  radiation of Gratiolet radiación de Gratiolet.
  radiation of the thalamus radiación talámica.
  radiation protection radioprotección.

remnant radiation radiación residual.
Rollier's radiation radiación de Rollier.
scattered radiation radiación difusa, radiación dispersa.
secondary radiation radiación secundaria.
soft radiation radiación blanda.
solar radiation radiación solar.
stray radiation radiación no utilizada.
tegmental radiation radiación tegmentaria.
thalamic radiation radiación talámica.
thalamotemporal radiation radiación talamotemporal.
thermal radiation radiación térmica.
total body radiation radiación corporal total.
ultraviolet radiation radiación ultravioleta.
useful radiation radiación útil.
visible radiation radiación visible.
Wernicke radiation radiación de Wernicke.
X-radiation radiación X.
radiato *n.* radiación.
radiato corporis callosi radiación del cuerpo calloso.
radiato corporis striati radiación del cuerpo estriado.
radical *n.* radical.
acid radical ácido radical.
alcohol radical radical alcohol.
color radical radical coloreado, radical cromóforo, radical de color.
free radical radical libre.
hydroxyl radical radical hidróxilo.
oxygen derived free radical radical libre.
oxygen radical radical de oxígeno.
radiciform *adj.* radiciforme.
radicle *n.* radícula.
radicotomy *n.* radicotomía.
radicula *n.* radícula.
radiculalgia *n.* radiculalgia.
radicular *adj.* radicular.
radiculectomy *n.* radiculectomía.
radiculitis *n.* radiculitis.
acute brachial radiculitis radiculitis braquial aguda.
radiculoganglionitis *n.* radiculoganglionitis.
radiculography *n.* radiculografía.
radiculomedullary *adj.* radiculomedular.
radiculomeningomyelitis *n.* radiculomeningomielitis.
radiculomyelopathy *n.* radiculomielopatía.
radiculoneuritis *n.* radiculoneuritis.
radiculoneuropathy *n.* radiculoneuropatía.
radiculopathy *n.* radiculopatía.
radiectomy *n.* radectomía, radiectomía.
radiferous *adj.* radífero, -ra.
radioactivation *n.* radiactivación.
radioactive *adj.* radiactivo, -va, radioactivo, -va.
radioactive cow vaca radiactiva.
radioactivity *n.* radiactividad, radioactividad.
alpha radioactivity radiactividad alfa.
artificial radioactivity radiactividad artificial.
beta positive radioactivity radiactividad beta positiva.
beta radioactivity radiactividad beta.
induced radioactivity radiactividad inducida.
natural radioactivity radiactividad natural.
specific radioactivity radiactividad específica.
radioactor *n.* radiactor.
radioallergosorbent *adj.* radioalergosorbente.
radioautograph *n.* radioautógrafo.
radioautography *n.* radioautografía.
radiobicipital *adj.* radiobicipital.
radiobiologic *adj.* radiobiológico, -ca.

radiobiological *adj.* radiobiológico, -ca.
radiobiologist *n.* radiobiólogo, -ga.
radiobiology *n.* radiobiología.
radiocalcium *n.* radiocalcio.
radiocancer *n.* radiocáncer.
radiocarbon *n.* radiocarbono.
radiocarcinogenesis *n.* radiocarcinogénesis.
radiocardiogram *n.* radiocardiograma.
radiocardiography *n.* radiocardiografía.
radiocarpal *adj.* radiocarpal, radiocarpiano, -na.
radiochemical *adj.* radioquímico, -ca.
radiochemistry *n.* radioquímica.
radiochromatograpy *n.* radiocromatografía.
radiocinematograph *n.* radiocinematógrafo.
radiocinematographic *adj.* radiocinematográfico, -ca.
radiocinematography *n.* radiocinematografía.
radiocolloid *n.* radicoloide, radiocoloide.
radiocurable *adj.* radiocurable.
radiocystitis *n.* radiocistitis.
radiodense *adj.* radiodenso, -sa.
radiodensimetry *n.* radiodensimetría.
radiodensitometry *n.* radiodensitometría.
radiodensity *n.* radiodensidad.
radiodermatitis *n.* radiodermatitis.
radiodermitis *n.* radiodermitis.
radiodiagnosis *n.* radiodiagnosis, radiodiagnóstico.
radiodiagnostic *n.* radiodiagnóstico, -ca.
radiodigital *adj.* radiodigital.
radiodontics *n.* radiodoncia.
radiodontist *n.* radiodoncista.
radioecology *n.* radioecología.
radioelectrocardiogram *n.* radioelectrocardiograma.
radioelectrocardiograph *n.* radioelectrocardiógrafo.
radioelectrocardiography *n.* radioelectrocardiografía.
radioelement *n.* radielemento, radioelemento.
radioencephalogram *n.* radioencefalograma.
radioencephalography *n.* radioencefalografía.
radioepidermitis *n.* radioepidermitis.
radioepithelitis *n.* radioepitelitis.
radiofibrinogen *n.* radiofibrinógeno.
radiofrequency *n.* radiofrecuencia.
radiogallium *n.* radiogalio.
radiogen *n.* radiógeno.
radiogenesis *n.* radiogénesis.
radiogenic *adj.* radiogénico, -ca, radiógeno, -na.
radiogenics *n.* radiogenia.
radiogram *n.* radiografía², radiograma.
bite-wing radiogram radiografía con aleta.
panoramic radiogram radiografía panorámica.
radiographer *n.* radiografista.
radiographic *adj.* radiográfico, -ca.
radiography *n.* radiografía¹.
bite-wing radiography radiografía de mordida.
body-section radiography radiografía de una sección corporal, radiografía seriada por planos paralelos.
digital radiography radiografía digital.
double contrast radiography radiografía de doble contraste.
electron radiography radiografía electrónica.
magnification radiography radiografía de aumento, radiografía de magnificación, radiografía magnificada.

mass miniature radiography radiografía en miniatura en masa.
mass radiography radiografía en masa.
mucosal relief radiography radiografía del relieve de la mucosa.
occlusal radiography radiografía oclusal, radiografía oclusiva.
panoramic radiography radiografía panorámica.
periapical radiography radiografía periapical.
selective radiography radiografía selectiva.
serial radiography radiografía en serie, radiografía seriada.
slit scan radiography radiografía por barrido de hendidura.
radiohumeral *adj.* radiohumeral.
radioimmunity *n.* radioinmunidad, radioinmunización.
radioimmunoassay *n.* radioinmunoensayo.
radioimmunoassay (RIA) *n.* radioinmunoanálisis (RIA).
radioimmunodetection *n.* radioinmunodetección.
radioimmunodiffusion *n.* radioinmunodifusión.
radioimmunoelectrophoresis *n.* radioinmunoelectroforesis.
radioimmunologic *adj.* radioinmunológico, -ca.
radioimmunology *n.* radioinmunología.
radioimmunoprecipitation *n.* radioinmunoprecipitación.
radioimmunosorbent *adj.* radioinmunosorbente.
radioimmunotherapy *n.* radioinmunoterapia.
radioiodinated *adj.* radioyodado, -da.
radioiodine *n.* radioyodo.
radioiron *n.* radiohierro.
radioisotope *n.* radioisótopo.
radioisotopic *adj.* radioisotópico, -ca.
radiokymography *n.* radioquimografía.
radiolabeled *adj.* radiomarcado, -da.
radiolabeling *n.* radiomarcado, radiomarcaje.
radiolead *n.* radioplomo.
radiolesion *n.* radiolesión.
radioligand *n.* radioligando.
radiologic *adj.* radiológico, -ca.
radiological *adj.* radiológico, -ca.
radiologist *n.* radiólogo, -ga.
dental radiologist radiólogo dental.
radiology *n.* radiología.
conventional radiology radiología convencional.
dental radiology radiología dental.
diagnostic radiology radiología diagnóstica.
digital radiology radiología digital.
interventional radiology radiología intervencionista.
medical radiology radiología médica.
oral radiology radiología bucal.
pediatric radiology radiología pediátrica.
radiolucency *n.* radiolucencia, radiolucidez.
radiolucent *adj.* radiolucente, radiolúcido, -da.
radioluminiscence *n.* radioluminiscencia.
radiolysis *n.* radiólisis.
radiometer *n.* radiómetro.
film radiometer radiómetro de película.
pastille radiometer radiómetro de pastilla.
photographic radiometer radiómetro fotográfico.
radiometry *n.* radiometría.
radiomicrometer *n.* radiomicrómetro.

radiomimetic *adj.* radiomimético, -ca.
radiomuscular *adj.* radiomuscular.
radiomutation *n.* radiomutación.
radionecrosis *n.* radionecrosis.
radioneuritis *n.* radioneuritis.
radionitrogen *n.* radionitrógeno.
radionucleus *n.* radionúcleo.
radionuclide *n.* radionúclido.
radiopacity *n.* radioopacidad, radiopacidad.
radiopalmar *adj.* radiopalmar.
radiopaque *adj.* radioopaco, -ca, radiopaco, -ca.
radioparency *n.* radiotransparencia.
radiopathology *n.* radiopatología.
radiopelvigraphy *n.* radiopelvigrafía.
radiopelvimetry *n.* radiopelvimetría.
radiopharmaceutic *adj.* radiofarmacéutico, -ca[1].
radiopharmaceutical *adj.* radiofarmacéutico, -ca[1].
radiopharmacist *n.* radiofarmacéutico, -ca[2].
radiopharmacy *n.* radiofarmacia.
radiophosphorus *n.* radiofósforo.
radiophotography *n.* radiofotografía.
radiophysicist *n.* radiofísico, -ca.
radiophysics *n.* radiofísica.
radiopotassium *n.* radiopotasio.
radiopotentiation *n.* radiopotenciación.
radioreaction *n.* radiorreacción.
radioreceptor *n.* radiorreceptor.
radioresistance *n.* radiorresistencia.
  acquired radioresistance radiorresistencia adquirida.
radioresistant *adj.* radiorresistente.
radioresponsive *adj.* radiorreaccionante, radiorrespondente.
radiosclerometer *n.* radioesclerómetro, radiosclerómetro.
radioscope *n.* radioscopio.
radioscopic *adj.* radioscópico, -ca.
radioscopy *n.* radioscopia.
radiosensibility *n.* radiosensibilidad.
radiosensible *adj.* radiosensible.
radiosensitive *adj.* radiolábil, radiosensible.
radiosensitiveness *n.* radiosensibilidad.
radiosensitivity *n.* radiosensibilidad.
radiosensitizer *n.* radiosensibilizador.
radiosodium *n.* radiosodio.
radiostereoscopy *n.* radioestereoscopia, radiostereoscopia.
radiosteroscopy *n.* radioestereoscopia, radiostereoscopia.
radiostrontium *n.* radioestroncio.
radiosulfur *n.* radioazufre.
radiosurgery *n.* radiocirugía.
radiotelemetry *n.* radiotelemetría.
radiothanatology *n.* radiotanatología.
radiotherapeutic *adj.* radioterapéutico, -ca.
radiotherapeutics *n.* radioterapéutica.
radiotherapist *n.* radioterapeuta.
radiotherapy *n.* radioterapia.
  electron beam radiotherapy radioterapia con electrones.
  extended field radiotherapy radioterapia de campo ampliado.
  interstitial radiotherapy radioterapia intersticial.
  intracavitary radiotherapy radioterapia intracavitaria.
  metabolic radiotherapy radioterapia metabólica.
  negative pi meson (pion) radiotherapy radioterapia con mesones pi negativos (piones).
  whole-body radiotherapy radioterapia corporal total.

radiothermy *n.* radiotermia.
radiothyroidectomy *n.* radiotiroidectomía.
radiothyroxin *n.* radiotiroxina.
radiotomography *n.* radiotomografía.
radiotoxemia *n.* radiotoxemia.
radiotoxicity *n.* radiotoxicidad.
radiotoxicology *n.* radiotoxicología.
radiotracer *n.* radiotrazador.
radiotransparency *n.* radiotransparencia.
radiotransparent *adj.* radiotransparente.
radioulnar *adj.* radiocubital.
radisectomy *n.* radisectomía.
radium *n.* radio[1], radium.
radius radio[2], radius.
  radius curvus radio curvo.
  radius fixus radio fijo.
  radius of the lens radio del cristalino.
  van der Walls radius radio de van der Walls.
radix radix, raíz.
radon *n.* radón.
  radon 219 actinon radón 219.
  radon 220 thoron radón 220.
  radon 222 radón 222.
  radon 222 daughter products productos dependientes del radón 222.
rage *n.* ira.
  sham rage ira falsa, ira fingida.
ragocyte *n.* ragocito.
Raillietina Raillietina.
raillietiniasis *n.* raillietiniasis.
rales *n.* sibilancia.
  sibilant rales sibilancia.
  whistling rales sibilancia.
ramal *n.* ramal.
ramicotomy *n.* ramicotomía.
ramification *n.* ramificación.
  false ramification ramificación falsa.
ramified *adj.* ramificado, -da.
ramify *v.* ramificar.
ramisection *n.* ramisección.
ramisectomy *n.* ramisectomía.
ramitis *n.* ramitis.
ramose *adj.* ramoso, -sa.
ramous *adj.* ramoso, -sa.
rampart *n.* bastión.
  maxillary rampart bastión maxilar.
ramulus *n.* ramita, rámula, rámulo, ramúsculo.
ramus *n.* rama[1], ramo, ramus.
rancid *adj.* rancio, -cia.
rancidify *v.* enranciarse, ranciar.
rancidity *n.* rancidez, ranciedad.
range *n.* gama, rango.
  dynamic range rango dinámico.
  range of accommodation rango de acomodación.
  range of motion rango de movimiento.
ranine *adj.* ranino, -na.
rank *adj.* rancio, -cia.
ranula *n.* ránula.
  pancreatic ranula ránula pancreática.
ranular *adj.* ranular.
rape[1] *n.* violación.
  acquaintance rape violación por conocido.
  date rape violación por conocido.
  marital rape violación marital.
  statutory rape violación de menores.
rape[2] *v.* violar.
raphe *n.* rafe.
raphidiospore *n.* rafidiospora.
raptus *n.* rapto.
rarefaction *n.* enrarecimiento, rarefacción.
rarefy *v.* rarificarse.
rarefying *adj.* rarificante, rarificativo, -va.
rasceta *n.* rasceta.
rash *n.* exantema, rash.

ammonia rash rash amoniacal.
antitoxin rash rash antitoxina.
astacoid rash rash astacoide.
black currant rash rash en pasa negra.
Boston rash exantema de Boston.
butterfly rash exantema en alas de mariposa, exantema en mariposa, rash en mariposa.
caterpillar rash rash por orugas.
crystal rash rash cristalino.
diaper rash exantema del pañal, rash del pañal.
drug rash exantema medicamentoso, rash por drogas.
ecchymotic rash exantema equimótico.
heat rash exantema por calor, rash por calor.
hydatid rash rash hidatídico.
keratoid rash exantema queratoide.
macular rash exantema macular.
maculopapular rash exantema maculopapuloso.
medicinal rash rash por drogas.
Murray Valley rash rash del Valle del Murray.
nettle rash exantema por ortigas, rash por ortigas.
prickly heat rash rash por calor.
rose rash rash roséola.
serum rash rash sérico.
summer rash rash de verano.
syphilitic rash exantema sifilítico.
wandering rash exantema errante, rash errante.
wildfire rash rash de erisipela.
rasion *n.* rasión.
rasp *v.* raspar.
raspatory *n.* raspador.
rat *n.* rata.
rate *n.* índice, tasa, velocidad.
  abortion rate índice de abortos.
  adjusted death rate tasa de mortalidad ajustada.
  adjusted rate índice de corrección.
  attack rate índice de ataque.
  basal metabolic rate (BMR) índice metabólico basal, velocidad metabólica basal.
  birth rate índice de natalidad.
  bone formation rate tasa de formación ósea.
  case fatality rate índice de casos de mortalidad, índice de casos fatales.
  case rate índice de casos.
  circulation rate velocidad circulatoria, velocidad de circulación.
  concordance rate índice de concordancia.
  cooling rate velocidad de enfriamiento.
  critical rate índice crítico.
  crude birth rate tasa bruta de natalidad.
  crude rate índice bruto.
  death rate índice de muertes, tasa de mortalidad.
  DEF rate índice DEF, índice def de caries, índice DEF de caries.
  DMF rate índice DMF, índice dmf de caries, índice DMF de caries.
  dose rate índice de dosis.
  erythrocyte sedimentation rate (ESR) índice de eritrosedimentación, índice de sedimentación de eritrocitos, índice de sedimentación eritrocítica (ESR), velocidad de eritrosedimentación, velocidad de sedimentación de eritrocitos, velocidad de sedimentación de los glóbulos rojos, velocidad de sedimentación globular (VSG).
  expiratory exchange rate velocidad de intercambio espiratorio.
  false-negative rate tasa de falsos negativos.
  false-positive rate tasa de falsos positivos.

fatality rate índice de casos fatales.
fertility rate tasa de fertilidad.
fetal death rate índice de muertes fetales.
five-year survival rate índice de supervivencia a cinco años.
glomerular filtration rate (GFR) índice de filtración glomerular (GFR), tasa de filtración glomerular (TFG).
growth rate índice de crecimiento.
incidence rate índice de incidencia.
infant mortality rate índice de mortalidad infantil.
inherent rate velocidad inherente.
karyoplasmic rate índice carioplásmico.
lethality rate índice de letalidad.
local cerebral metabolic rate of glucose utilization (LCMRG) velocidad de metabolización cerebral local de la glucosa (VMCLG).
maternal death rate índice de muerte materna.
maternal mortality rate índice de mortalidad materna.
maximal expiratory flow rate (MEFR) velocidad máxima de flujo espiratorio (MEFR).
maximal midexpiratory flow rate velocidad máxima de flujo mesoespiratorio.
Mendelian rate índice mendeliano.
metabolic rate índice metabólico.
morbidity rate índice de morbilidad, tasa de morbididad.
mortality rate índice de mortalidad.
mutation rate índice de mutación, tasa de mutación.
neonatal mortality rate índice de mortalidad neonatal.
nutritive rate índice nutritivo.
oocyst rate índice de oocistos.
output exposure rate índice de exposición a las irradiaciones.
perfusion rate velocidad de perfusión.
perinatal mortality rate índice de mortalidad perinatal.
postnatal mortality rate índice de mortalidad perinatal.
pregnancy rate tasa de embarazos.
prevalence rate índice de prevalencia.
proportionate mortality rate (PMR) índice de mortalidad proporcionada (PMR).
puerperal mortality rate index de mortalidad puerperal, índice de mortalidad puerperal.
pulse rate velocidad de pulso.
rate of growth velocidad de crecimiento.
refined birth rate tasa de nacimientos ajustada.
respiratory exchange rate velocidad de intercambio respiratorio.
secondary attack rate índice de ataque secundario.
sedimentation rate velocidad de sedimentación.
sex rate índice sexual.
shear rate índice de corte.
sickness rate índice de enfermedad.
specific absorption rate (SAR) velocidad de absorción específica (VAE).
specific rate índice específico, tasa específica.
sporozoite rate índice de esporozoítos.
standardized death rate tasa de mortalidad estandarizada.
standarized morbidity rate (SMR) índice de morbilidad estandarizada (SMR).
standardized rate índice estandarizado.
steroid metabolic clearance rate (MCR) índice de depuración metabólica de los esteroides.
stillbirth rate índice de mortinatos.

true birth rate tasa real de nacimientos.
urea excretion rate índice de excreción de urea.
volumetric flow rate velocidad de flujo volumétrico.
zeta sedimentation rate (ZSR) índice de sedimentación zeta (ZSR).
raticide *n.* raticida.
ratio *n.* proporción, razón².
base ratio razón de bases.
ration[1] *n.* ración.
basal ration ración basal.
ration[2] *v.* racionar.
rational *adj.* racional.
rationale *n.* raciocinio.
rationality *n.* racionalidad.
ethical rationality racionalidad ética.
technical rationality racionalidad técnica.
rationalization *n.* racionalización.
rattle *n.* estertor.
amphoric rattle estertor anfórico.
atelectatic rattle estertor atelectásico.
border rattle estertor del borde.
bronchial rattle estertor bronquial.
bubbling rattle estertor burbujeante, estertor de burbujas.
cavernous rattle estertor cavernoso.
cellophane rattle estertor de celofán.
clicking rattle estertor de chasquido.
collapse rattle estertor de colapso.
consonating rattle estertor consonante.
cracking rattle estertor de crujido.
crepitant rattle estertor crepitante.
dry rattle estertor ronco, estertor seco.
gurgling rattle estertor de gorgoteo.
guttural rattle estertor extratorácico, estertor gutural.
marginal rattle estertor marginal.
metallic rattle estertor metálico.
moist rattle estertor húmedo.
mucous rattle estertor mucoso.
palpable rattle estertor palpable.
sibilant rattle estertor sibilante.
Skoda's rattle estertor de Skoda.
sonorous rattle estertor sonoro.
subcrepitant rattle estertor subcrepitante.
tracheal rattle estertor traqueal.
vesicular rattle estertor vesicular.
whistling rattle estertor de silbido.
Rattus Rattus.
rattus *n.* rata.
raucedo *n.* raucedo.
rausch rausch.
ray *n.* rayo.
actinic ray rayo actínico.
alpha ray rayo alfa.
anode ray rayo anódico.
antirachitic ray rayo antirraquítico.
astral ray rayo astral.
Becquerel ray rayo de Becquerel.
beta ray rayo beta.
border ray rayo límite, rayo limítrofe.
caloric ray rayo calórico.
cathodic ray rayo catódico, rayo negativo.
central ray rayo central.
characteristic fluorescent ray rayo fluorescentes característico.
characteristic ray rayo característico.
chemical ray rayo químico.
convergent ray rayo convergentes.
cosmic ray rayo cósmicos.
Crookes ray rayo de Crookes.
delta ray rayo delta.
digital ray rayo digital.
direct ray rayo directo.

direction ray rayo de dirección.
divergent ray rayo divergente.
dynamic ray rayo dinámico.
erythema-producing ray rayo productores de eritema.
Finsen ray rayo de Finsen.
fluorescent ray rayo fluorescente.
gamma ray rayo gamma.
glass ray rayo de vidrio.
Grenz ray rayo de Grenz.
H ray rayo H.
hard ray rayo duro.
heat ray rayo calórico.
Hertzian ray rayo hertziano.
incident ray rayo incidente.
indirect ray rayo indirecto.
infrared ray rayo infrarrojo.
infraroentgen ray rayo infrarroentgen.
intermediate ray rayo intermedio.
luminous ray rayo luminoso.
marginal ray rayo marginal.
medullary ray rayo medular.
Millikan ray rayo de Millikan.
monochromatic ray rayo monocromático.
necrobiotic ray rayo necrobiótico.
paracathodic ray rayo paracatódico.
parallel ray rayo paralelo.
paraxial ray rayo paraaxial.
positive ray rayo positivo.
primary ray rayo primario.
reflected ray rayo reflejado.
refracted ray rayo refractado.
roentgen ray rayo roentgen.
Sagnac ray rayo de Sagnac.
scattered ray rayo difuso, rayo diseminado.
secondary ray rayo secundario.
soft ray rayo blando.
supersonic ray rayo supersónico.
ultra x-ray rayo ultra X.
ultrasonic ray rayo ultrasónico.
ultraviolet ray rayo ultravioleta.
vital ray rayo vital.
W ray rayo W.
razor *n.* navaja.
reabsorb *v.* reabsorber.
reabsorbable *adj.* reabsorbible.
reabsorption *n.* reabsorción.
bone reabsorption reabsorción ósea.
external tooth reabsorption reabsorción dental externa.
gingival reabsorption reabsorción gingival.
internal reabsorption reabsorción interna.
internal tooth reabsorption reabsorción dental interna.
ridge reabsorption reabsorción de rebordes.
root reabsorption reabsorción de raíces.
tubular reabsorption reabsorción tubular.
tubular reabsorption of phosphate reabsorción tubular de fosfatos.
reachers *n.* alcanzadores.
react *v.* reaccionar.
reactance *n.* reactancia.
reactant *n.* reactante.
acute phase reactant reactante de fase aguda.
reaction *n.* reacción.
reaction-formation reacción-formación.
reactivate *v.* reactivar.
reactivation *n.* reactivación.
reactivation of serum reactivación del suero.
reactivity *n.* reactividad.
reading *n.* lectura.
lip reading lectura de labios, lectura del habla.
speech reading lectura de labios, lectura del habla.
reagent *n.* reactivo.

real *adj.* real.
reality *n.* realidad.
reamer *n.* ensanchador.
 engine reamer ensanchador a motor.
 intramedullary reamer ensanchador intramedular.
 rib spreader reamer ensanchador de costillas.
reamputation *n.* reamputación.
reattachment *n.* reinserción.
rebase *v.* rebasar.
rebound *n.* rechazo.
rebreathing *n.* reinhalación.
recalcification *n.* recalcificación.
recall *n.* recuerdo.
recanalization *n.* recanalización.
recanalize *v.* recanalizar.
 recanalize a vessel recanalizar un vaso.
recapitulation *n.* recapitulación.
receptaculum *n.* receptáculo, receptaculum.
receptoma *n.* receptoma.
receptor *n.* receptor, -ra.
 alpha-adrenergic receptor receptor alfa-adrenérgico.
 beta-adrenergic receptor receptor beta-adrenérgico.
 chemical receptor receptor químico.
 cholinergic receptor receptor colinérgico.
 contact receptor receptor de contacto.
 dopamine receptor receptor de dopamina.
 estrogen receptor receptor de estrógenos.
 Fc receptor receptor Fc.
 gustatory receptor receptor gustatorio.
 hormone receptor receptor hormonal.
 insulin receptor receptor de insulina.
 LDL receptor receptor de lipoproteínas de baja densidad (LDL).
 muscarinic receptor receptor muscarínico.
 opiate receptor receptor para opiáceo.
 pain receptor receptor de dolor.
 pressure receptor receptor de presión.
 progesterone receptor receptor de progesterona.
 sensory receptor receptor sensitivo.
 stretch receptor receptor de estiramiento.
 touch receptor receptor táctiles.
 volume receptor receptor de volumen.
recess *n.* receso.
recession *n.* recesión.
 gingival recession recesión gingival.
 recession of symptoms recesión de síntomas.
 tendon recession recesión tendinosa.
recessivity *n.* recesividad.
recessive *adj.* recesivo, -va.
recessiveness *n.* recesividad.
recessus *n.* receso, recessus.
 recessus epitympanicus epitímpano.
recidivation *n.* recidiva.
recidivism *n.* recidivismo.
recidivist *n.* recidivista.
recipe *n.* receta.
recipiomotor *adj.* recipiomotor, -ra.
reciprocation *n.* reciprocación.
recivdism *n.* recidividad.
reclination *n.* reclinación.
reclusion *n.* reclusión.
recognition *n.* reconocimiento.
 antigen recognition in cell-mediated immunity reconocimiento antigénico en la inmunidad celular.
recollection *n.* recolección.
recombinant *adj.* recombinante.
recombination *n.* recombinación.
 bacterial recombination recombinación bacteriana, recombinación genética bacteriana.

 genetic recombination recombinación genética.
recompression *n.* recompresión.
recon *n.* recón.
reconstitution *n.* reconstitución.
reconstruction *n.* reconstrucción.
 breast reconstruction reconstrucción de la mama.
 holographic reconstruction reconstrucción holográfica.
record *n.* registro.
 anesthesia record registro de anestesia.
 daily patient care record registro de cuidados diarios de pacientes.
 electrocardiographic record registro electrocardiografico.
 electroencefalographic record registro electroencefalografico.
 face-brow record registro de arco facial.
 functional chew-in record registro funcional de masticación.
 hospital record registro hospitalario.
 interocclusal record registro interoclusal.
 maxillomandibular record registro maxilomandibular.
 medical record registro médico.
 occluding centric relation record registro de la relación de oclusión céntrica.
 patient's hospital record registro hospitalario de pacientes.
 preextraction record registro preextracción.
 preoperative record registro preoperatorio.
 problem-oriented record registro orientado por problemas.
 profile record registro de perfil.
 protrusive record registro protrusivo.
 terminal jaw relation record registro de la relación intermaxilar terminal.
 three-dimensional record registro tridimensional.
 tissue record registro de tejidos.
recovery *n.* recuperación[2], restablecimiento.
 creep recovery recuperación de arrastre.
 postoperatory recovery recuperación posoperatoria.
 spontaneous recovery recuperación espontánea.
 ultrasonic egg recovery recuperación de un óvulo por ultrasonido.
recrement *n.* recremento.
recrudescence *n.* recrudecimiento, recrudescencia.
recrudescent *adj.* recrudescente.
recruitment *n.* reclutamiento.
rectal *adj.* rectal.
rectalgia *n.* rectalgia.
rectectomy *n.* rectectomía.
rectification *n.* rectificación.
rectify *v.* rectificar.
rectitis *n.* rectitis.
rectoabdominal *adj.* rectoabdominal.
rectocele *n.* rectocele.
rectoclysis *n.* rectoclisis.
rectococcipexy *n.* rectococcicopexia, rectococcipexia.
rectococcygeal *adj.* rectococcígeo, -a.
rectocolitis *n.* rectocolitis.
rectocystotomy *n.* rectocistotomía.
rectoperineal *adj.* rectoperineal.
rectoperineorrhaphy *n.* rectoperineorrafia.
rectopexy *n.* rectopexia.
rectoplasty *n.* rectoplastia.
rectorrhaphy *n.* rectorrafia.
rectoscopy *n.* rectoscopia.
rectosigmoid *n.* rectosigmoide.

rectosigmoidectomy *n.* rectosigmoidectomía.
rectostenosis *n.* rectostenosis.
rectostomy *n.* rectostomía.
rectotome *n.* rectótomo.
rectotomy *n.* rectotomía.
rectourethral *adj.* rectouretral.
rectouterine *adj.* rectouterino, -na.
rectovaginal *adj.* rectovaginal, vaginorrectal.
rectovesical *adj.* rectovesical.
rectovestibular *adj.* rectovestibular.
rectovulvar *adj.* rectovulvar.
rectum *n.* recto[1].
recumbent *adj.* recumbente.
recuperate *v.* recuperarse.
recuperation *n.* recuperación[1].
recurrence *n.* recurrencia.
recurrent *adj.* recurrente[1].
recurvation *n.* recurvación.
red *n.* rojo, rojo, -ja.
red-haired *adj.* pelirrojo, -ja, taheño, -ña, tajeño, -ña.
red-headed *adj.* pelirrojo, -ja, taheño, -ña, tajeño, -ña.
redifferentiation *n.* rediferenciación.
redintegration *n.* redintegración.
redislocation *n.* redislocación.
redness *n.* rubor.
redox *n.* redox.
redressement *n.* enderezamiento[1].
 redressement forcé enderezamiento forzado.
reduce *v.* reducir.
reducible *adj.* reducible.
reductant *n.* reductor.
reduction *n.* reducción.
 breast reduction reducción de la mama, reducción mamaria.
 closed reduction reducción cerrada.
 closed reduction of fracture reducción cerrada de fractura.
 mammaplasty reduction reducción de la mama, reducción mamaria.
 open reduction reducción abierta.
 open reduction of fracture reducción abierta de fractura.
 oxidation reduction reduccion-oxidación.
 reduction en masse reducción en masa.
 reduction of chromosomes reducción de cromosomas.
 reduction of fracture reducción de fractura.
 tuberosity reduction reducción de la tuberosidad.
 weight reduction reducción de peso.
reduplication *n.* reduplicación.
reeducation *n.* reeducación.
reefing *n.* reefing.
 stomach reefing reefing del estómago.
reentry *n.* reentrada.
refection *n.* refección.
reference *n.* referencia.
referral *n.* derivación[4].
refine *v.* refinar.
refining *n.* refinación.
reflect *v.* reflejar, reflexionar.
reflected *adj.* reflejado, -da.
reflection *n.* reflexión.
reflector *n.* reflector, -ra.
reflex *n.* reflejo, -ja.
 abdominal reflex reflejo abdominal.
 abdominocardiac reflex reflejo abdominocardíaco.
 abominal reflex reflejo cutaneoabdominal.
 Abrams' heart reflex reflejo de Abrams, reflejo cardíaco de Abrams, reflejo de Livierato.
 accommodation reflex reflejo de acomodación.

Achilles reflex reflejo aquíleo, reflejo aquiliano.

Achilles tendon reflex reflejo del tendón de Aquiles, reflejo tendinoso de Aquiles.

acousticopalpebral reflex reflejo acusticopalpebral.

acquired reflex reflejo adquirido.

acromial reflex reflejo acrominal.

adductor reflex reflejo del aductor.

allied reflex reflejo aliado.

anal reflex reflejo anal.

anal sphincter reflex reflejo del esfínter anal.

ankle reflex reflejo del tobillo.

antagonistic reflex reflejo antagónico.

aortic reflex reflejo aórtico.

aponeurotic reflex reflejo aponeurótico.

Aschner-Dagnini reflex reflejo de Aschner, reflejo de Aschner-Dagnini.

Aschner's reflex reflejo de Aschner, reflejo de Aschner-Dagnini, reflejo de Dagnini-Aschner.

attention reflex of the pupil reflejo de atención de la pupila.

attitudinal reflex reflejo de actitud.

audito-oculogyric reflex reflejo auditooculógiro.

auditory oculogyric reflex reflejo oculógiro auditivo.

auditory reflex reflejo auditivo, reflejo aural.

auriculocervical nerve reflex reflejo auriculocervical.

auriculopalpebral reflex reflejo auriculopalpebral.

auriculopressor reflex reflejo auriculopresor.

auropalpebral reflex reflejo auropalpebral.

axon reflex reflejo axónico.

Babinski reflex reflejo de Babinski.

Bainbridge reflex reflejo de Bainbridge.

Barkman's reflex reflejo de Barkman.

basal joint reflex reflejo articular basal.

Bechterew-Mendel reflex reflejo de Bechterew-Mendel.

Bechterew's reflex reflejo de Bechterew.

Benedek's reflex reflejo de Benedek.

Bezold-Jarisch reflex reflejo de Bezold-Jarisch.

biceps femoris reflex reflejo del bíceps femoral.

biceps reflex reflejo bicipital, reflejo del bíceps.

Bing's reflex reflejo de Bing.

bladder reflex reflejo urinario, reflejo vesical.

blink reflex reflejo de guiño.

bone reflex reflejo óseo.

brachioradial reflex reflejo braquiorradial.

Brain's reflex reflejo de Brain.

bregmocardiac reflex reflejo bregmocardíaco.

Brissaud's reflex reflejo de Brissaud.

Brudzinski's reflex reflejo de Brudzinski.

bulbocavernosus reflex reflejo bulbocavernoso.

bulbocavernous reflex reflejo bulbocavernoso.

bulbonimic reflex reflejo bulbonímico.

Capp's reflex reflejo de Capp.

cardiac reflex reflejo cardíaco.

carotid sinus reflex reflejo del seno carotídeo.

celiac plexus reflex reflejo del plexo celíaco.

cephalic reflex reflejo cefálico.

cephalopalpebral reflex reflejo cefalopalpebral.

cerebral cortex reflex reflejo de la corteza cerebral.

cerebropupillary reflex reflejo cerebropupilar.

Chaddock reflex reflejo de Chaddock.

chain reflex reflejo en cadena.

chin reflex reflejo mentoniano.

ciliary reflex reflejo ciliar.

ciliospinal reflex reflejo ciliospinal.

cochleo-orbicular reflex reflejo cocleoorbicular.

cochleopalpebral reflex reflejo cocleopalpebral.

cochleopupillary reflex reflejo cocleopupilar.

conditional reflex reflejo condicionado.

conditioned reflex reflejo condicionado.

conjunctival reflex reflejo conjuntival.

consensual light reflex reflejo consensual luminoso.

contralateral reflex reflejo contralateral.

coordinate reflex reflejo coordinado.

coordinated reflex reflejo compuesto, reflejo coordinado.

corneal reflex reflejo corneal.

corneomandibular reflex reflejo corneomandibular, reflejo corneomaxilar.

corneopterygoid reflex reflejo corneopterigoideo.

coronary reflex reflejo coronario.

costal arch reflex reflejo del arco costal.

cough reflex reflejo tusígeno.

cranial reflex reflejo craneal.

cremasteric reflex reflejo cremastérico.

crossed adductor reflex reflejo del aductor cruzado.

crossed reflex reflejo cruzado.

cry reflex reflejo del llanto.

cuboidodigital reflex reflejo tarsofalángico.

cutaneous pupillary reflex reflejo cutáneo pupilar, reflejo del cutáneo.

dartos reflex reflejo del dartos.

deep abdominal reflex reflejo abdominales profundo.

deep reflex reflejo profundo.

defense reflex reflejo de defensa.

digital reflex reflejo digital.

direct light reflex reflejo fotomotor, reflejo luminoso directo.

diving reflex reflejo de inmersión.

dorsal reflex reflejo dorsal.

embrace reflex reflejo del abrazo.

epigastric reflex reflejo epigástrico.

Erben's reflex reflejo de Erben.

Escherich's reflex reflejo de Escherich.

esophagosalivary reflex reflejo esofagosalival.

external oblique reflex reflejo oblícuo externo.

eye reflex reflejo ocular.

facial reflex reflejo facial.

faucial reflex reflejo faucal, reflejo faucial.

femoral reflex reflejo femoral.

femoroabdominal reflex reflejo femoroabdominal.

finger-thumb reflex reflejo índice-pulgar.

flexor reflex reflejo flexor.

forced grasping reflex reflejo de prensión, reflejo de prensión forzada.

front-tap reflex reflejo de percusión frontal.

fundus reflex reflejo del fondo de ojo.

gag reflex reflejo nauseoso.

gastrocolic reflex reflejo gastrocólico.

gastroileal reflex reflejo gastroileal, reflejo gastroilíaco.

Gault's cochleopalpebral reflex reflejo de Gault.

Geigel's reflex reflejo de Geigel.

Gifford's reflex reflejo de Gifford.

gluteal reflex reflejo glúteo.

Gordon reflex reflejo de Gordon.

grasp reflex reflejo de agarre, reflejo de prensión, reflejo de prensión forzada.

grasping reflex reflejo de prensión, reflejo de prensión forzada.

great-toe reflex reflejo del dedo gordo del pie.

Grünfelder's reflex reflejo de Grünfelder.

Guillain-Barré reflex reflejo de Guillain-Barré, reflejo plantar en hiperflexión.

gustatory-sudorific reflex reflejo gustatorio-sudorífico.

gustolacrimal reflex reflejo gustolagrimal.

Haab's reflex reflejo de Haab.

hepatojugular reflex reflejo hepatoyugular.

Hering-Breuer reflex reflejo de Hering-Breuer.

Hirschberg's reflex reflejo de Hirschberg.

Hoffmann's reflex reflejo de Hoffmann.

Hughes' reflex reflejo de Hughes.

humoral reflex reflejo humoral.

hypogastric reflex reflejo hipogástrico.

inborn reflex reflejo incondicionado.

indirect reflex reflejo indirecto.

infraspinatus reflex reflejo infraspinoso.

inguinal reflex reflejo inguinal.

interscapular reflex reflejo interescapular.

intrinsic reflex reflejo intrínseco.

inverted radial reflex reflejo radial invertido.

inverted reflex reflejo invertido.

investigatory reflex reflejo investigatorio.

ipsilateral reflex reflejo ipsilateral.

Jacobson's reflex reflejo de Jacobson.

jaw reflex reflejo del maxilar.

jaw-working reflex reflejo mandibular de guiño.

Joffroy's reflex reflejo de Joffroy.

Juster's reflex reflejo de Juster.

Kisch's reflex reflejo de Kisch.

knee reflex reflejo de la rodilla.

knee-jerk reflex reflejo de la sacudida de la rodilla, reflejo patelar.

Kocher's reflex reflejo de Kocher.

labyrinthine reflex reflejo laberíntico.

labyrinthine righting reflex reflejo laberíntico de enderezamiento.

lacrimal reflex reflejo lagrimal.

lacrimogustatory reflex reflejo lagrimogustativo.

laryngeal reflex reflejo laríngeo.

laryngospastic reflex reflejo laringoespástico.

latent reflex reflejo latente.

laughter reflex reflejo de la risa.

Lidell-Sherrington reflex reflejo de Lidell-Sherrington.

light reflex reflejo fotomotor, reflejo luminoso.

lip reflex reflejo labial.

lordosis reflex reflejo de lordosis.

Loven reflex reflejo de Loven.

lumbar reflex reflejo lumbar.

Lust's reflex reflejo de Lust.

Mac Carthy's reflex reflejo de Mac Carthy.

mass reflex reflejo en masa.

Mayer's reflex reflejo de Mayer.

McCormac's reflex reflejo de Mc Cormac.

mediopubic reflex reflejo mediopubiano.

Mendel-Bechterew reflex reflejo de Mendel-Bechterew.

metacarpohypothenar reflex reflejo metacarpohipotenar.

metacarpothenar reflex reflejo metacarpotenar.

metatarsal reflex reflejo cuboide digital, reflejo metatarsiano.

micturition reflex reflejo de micción.
milk-ejection reflex reflejo de eyección láctea.
Mondonesi's reflex reflejo de Mondonesi.
Moro reflex reflejo de Moro.
muscular reflex reflejo motor muscular, reflejo muscular.
myenteric reflex reflejo mientérico.
myopic reflex reflejo miópico.
myotatic reflex reflejo miotático.
nasal reflex reflejo nasal.
nasomental reflex reflejo nasomentoniano.
near reflex reflejo cercano.
neck reflex reflejo cervical.
nociceptive reflex reflejo nociceptivo.
nocifensor reflex reflejo nocifensor.
nose-bridge-lid reflex reflejo de nariz-puente-párpado.
nose-eye reflex reflejo de nariz-ojo.
oculocardiac reflex reflejo oculocardíaco.
oculocephalic reflex reflejo oculocefálico.
oculocephalogyric reflex reflejo oculocefalógiro.
oculopharyngeal reflex reflejo oculofaríngeo.
olecranon reflex reflejo del olécranon.
Oppenheim's reflex reflejo de Oppenheim.
opticofacial reflex reflejo opticofacial.
orbicularis oculi reflex reflejo del orbicular de los párpados.
orbicularis pupillary reflex reflejo orbicular pupilar.
orienting reflex reflejo de orientación, reflejo orientador.
palatal reflex reflejo palatino.
palatine reflex reflejo palatino.
palmar reflex reflejo palmar.
palm-chin reflex reflejo palma-mentón.
palmomental reflex reflejo palmomentoniano.
parachute reflex reflejo de paracaídas.
paradoxical extensor reflex reflejo extensor paradójico.
paradoxical flexor reflex reflejo flexor paradójico, reflejo paradójico.
paradoxical patellar reflex reflejo rotuliano paradójico.
paradoxical pupillary reflex reflejo pupilar paradójico.
paradoxical reflex reflejo paradójico.
paradoxical triceps reflex reflejo paradójico del tríceps.
patellar reflex reflejo rotuliano.
patellar tendon reflex reflejo del tendón rotuliano.
patello-adductor reflex reflejo rotuloaductor.
pathologic reflex reflejo patológico.
Pavlov's reflex reflejo de Pavlov.
pectoral reflex reflejo pectoral.
Pérez reflex reflejo de Pérez.
pericardial reflex reflejo pericárdico.
periosteal reflex reflejo perióstico.
pharyngeal reflex reflejo faríngeo.
phasic reflex reflejo fásico.
Phillipson's reflex reflejo de Phillipson.
pilomotor reflex reflejo pilomotor.
Piltz's reflex reflejo de Piltz.
plantar muscle reflex reflejo muscular plantar.
plantar reflex reflejo plantar.
pneocardiac reflex reflejo neocardíaco.
pneopneic reflex reflejo neopneico.
postural reflex reflejo postural.
pressoreceptor reflex reflejo presorreceptor.

proprioceptive reflex reflejo propioceptivo.
proprioceptive-oculocephalic reflex reflejo oculocefálico.
protective laryngeal reflex reflejo laríngeo protector.
psychocardiac reflex reflejo psicocardíaco.
psychogalvanic reflex reflejo psicogalvánico.
psychogalvanic skin reflex reflejo cutáneo psicogalvánico.
pulmonocoronary reflex reflejo pulmonocoronario.
pupillary reflex reflejo pupilar.
pupillary-skin reflex reflejo pupilar-cutáneo.
radial reflex reflejo radial.
radiobicipital reflex reflejo radiobicipital.
radioperiosteal reflex reflejo radioperióstico.
rectal reflex reflejo rectal.
rectocardiac reflex reflejo rectocardíaco.
rectolaryngeal reflex reflejo rectolaríngeo.
red reflex reflejo rojo.
Remak's reflex reflejo de Remak.
renal reflex reflejo renal.
Riddoch's mass reflex reflejo de Riddoch.
Roger's reflex reflejo de Roger.
rooting reflex reflejo de hociqueo.
Rossolimo's reflex reflejo de Rossolimo.
Ruggeri's reflex reflejo de Ruggeri.
scapulohumeral reflex reflejo escapulohumeral.
Schäffer's reflex reflejo de Schäffer.
scrotal reflex reflejo escrotal.
semimembranosus reflex reflejo semimembranoso, semitendinoso.
semitendinosus reflex reflejo semimembranoso, semitendinoso.
shot-silk reflex reflejo de la seda tornasolada.
simple reflex reflejo simple.
sinus reflex reflejo sinusal.
Snellen's reflex reflejo de Snellen.
sole reflex reflejo plantar.
sole-tap reflex reflejo de percusión plantar.
spinal reflex reflejo espinal.
Starling's reflex reflejo de Starling.
startle reflex reflejo de sobresalto.
static reflex reflejo estático, reflejo estatocinético.
statokinetic reflex reflejo estático, reflejo estatocinético.
stepping reflex reflejo de la marcha.
Stookey's reflex reflejo de Stookey.
Strümpell's reflex reflejo de Strümpell.
styloradial reflex reflejo estilorradial.
suckling reflex reflejo de succión.
superficial reflex reflejo superficial.
supination reflex reflejo de supinación.
supinator longus reflex reflejo del supinador, reflejo del supinador largo.
supinator reflex reflejo del supinador, reflejo del supinador largo.
supporting reflex reflejo de apoyo, reflejo de sostén.
supraorbital reflex reflejo supraorbital, reflejo supraorbitario.
suprapatellar reflex reflejo suprarrotuliano.
supraumbilical reflex reflejo supraumbilical.
synchronous reflex reflejo sincrónico.
tapetal light reflex reflejo luminoso tapetal.
tarsophalangeal reflex reflejo tarsofalángico.
tendon reflex reflejo tendinoso.
threat reflex reflejo de alarma, reflejo de amenaza.
thumb reflex reflejo del pulgar.
tonic reflex reflejo tónico.

trained reflex reflejo condicionado.
triceps reflex reflejo del tríceps.
triceps surae reflex reflejo del tríceps crural.
trochanter reflex reflejo del trocánter.
Trömner's reflex reflejo de Trömner.
ulnar reflex reflejo cubitopronador.
unconditioned reflex reflejo incondicionado.
upper abdominal periosteal reflex reflejo perióstico abdominal superior.
vascular reflex reflejo vascular.
vasopressor reflex reflejo vasopresor.
vasovagal reflex reflejo vasovagal.
venorespiratory reflex reflejo venorrespiratorio.
vesical reflex reflejo vesical.
vestibulospinal reflex reflejo vestibuloespinal.
virile reflex reflejo viril.
visceral reflex reflejo visceral.
visceral traction reflex reflejo de tracción visceral.
viscerocardiac reflex reflejo viscerocardíaco.
viscerogenic reflex reflejo viscerogénico.
visceromotor reflex reflejo visceromotor.
viscerosensory reflex reflejo viscerosensitivo.
viscerotrophic reflex reflejo viscerotrófico.
vomiting reflex reflejo de vómito.
Weingrow's reflex reflejo de Weingrow.
Weiss' reflex reflejo de Weiss.
Westphal pupillary reflex reflejo de Westphal, reflejo de Westphal-Piltz.
Westphal-Piltz reflex reflejo de Westphal, reflejo de Westphal-Piltz.
Westphal's pupillary reflex reflejo pupilar de Westphal.
white pupillary reflex reflejo de la pupila blanca.
wink reflex reflejo de guiño.
withdrawal reflex reflejo del retiro.
reflexogenic adj. reflexogénico, -ca.
reflexogenous adj. reflexógeno, -na.
reflexograph n. reflexógrafo.
reflexology n. reflexología.
reflexometer n. reflexómetro.
reflexophile adj. reflexófilo, -la.
reflexotherapy n. reflexoterapia.
reflux n. reflujo.
 abdominojugular reflux reflujo abdominoyugular.
 esophageal reflux reflujo esofágico.
 gastroesophageal reflux reflujo gastroesofágico.
 hepatojugular reflux reflujo hepatoyugular.
 uretrorenal reflux reflujo uretrorrenal.
 uretrovesiculo-differential reflux reflujo uretrovesiculodeferencial.
 vesicoureteral reflux reflujo vesicoureteral.
refract v. refractar.
refraction n. refracción.
 double refraction refracción doble.
 dynamic refraction refracción dinámica.
 ocular refraction refracción ocular.
 oculopharyngeal refraction refracción oculofaríngea.
 static refraction refracción estática.
refractionist adj. refraccionista.
refractionometer n. refraccionómetro.
refractive adj. refractivo, -va.
refractivity n. refractividad.
refractometer n. refractómetro.
refractometry n. refractometría.
refractory adj. refractario, -ria.
refracture n. refractura.

refrangible *adj.* refrangible.
refresh *v.* refrescar.
refrigerant *adj.* refrescante, refrigerante.
refrigeration *n.* refrigeración.
refringence *n.* refringencia.
refringent *adj.* refringente.
refusion *n.* refusión.
regainer *n.* recuperador.
regenerate *v.* regenerar.
regeneration *n.* regeneración.
  aberrant regeneration regeneración aberrante.
regimen *n.* régimen.
region *n.* región.
  abdominal region región abdominal.
regional *adj.* regional.
regression *n.* regresión.
regressive *adj.* regresivo, -va.
regular *adj.* regular.
regularity *n.* regularidad.
regulation *n.* regulación.
regulator *n.* regulador.
regulatory *adj.* regulador, -ra.
regurgitant *adj.* regurgitante.
regurgitate *v.* regurgitar.
regurgitation *n.* regurgitación.
  aortic regurgitation regurgitación aórtica.
  mitral regurgitation regurgitación mitral.
  pulmonic regurgitation regurgitación pulmonar.
  tricuspid regurgitation regurgitación tricuspídea.
  valvular regurgitation regurgitación valvular.
rehabilitation *n.* rehabilitación.
rehearsal *n.* recitado.
rehospitalize *v.* rehospitalizar.
rehydratation *n.* rehidratación.
rehydrate *v.* rehidratar.
reimplantation *n.* reimplantación.
reinfection *n.* reinfección.
reinforcement *n.* reforzamiento, refuerzo.
  contingency reinforcement refuerzo contingente.
  continuous reinforcement refuerzo continuo.
  fixed-interval reinforcement reforzamiento de intervalo fijo.
  intermittent reinforcement refuerzo intermitente.
  negative reinforcement refuerzo negativo.
  partial reinforcement refuerzo parcial.
  positive reinforcement refuerzo positivo.
  primary reinforcement refuerzo primario.
  secondary reinforcement refuerzo secundario.
  variable interval (VI) reinforcement reforzamiento de intervalo variable (IV).
  variable ratio (VR) reinforcement reforzamiento de relación variable (RV).
reinforcer *n.* reforzador.
reinnervation *n.* reinervación.
reinoculation *n.* reinoculación.
reintegration *n.* reintegración.
reintubation *n.* reintubación.
reinversion *n.* reinversión.
rejection *n.* rechazo, reyección.
  acute cellular rejection rechazo celular agudo.
  acute rejection rechazo agudo.
  humoral rejection rechazo humoral.
  organ rejection rechazo de órgano.
rejuvenescence *n.* rejuvenecimiento.
relapse *n.* recaída, recidiva.
  tumor relapse recidiva de los tumores.
relapsing *adj.* recurrente[2].

relation *n.* relación.
  absolute terminal innervation relation relación de inervación terminal absoluta.
  accommodative convergence-accommodation relation relación de acomodación-convergencia acomodativa (A/CA).
  acquired centric relation relación céntrica adquirida.
  acquired eccentric relation relación excéntrica adquirida.
  albumin-globulin (A/G) relation relación albúmina-globulina (A/G).
  ALT:AST relation relación ALT:AST.
  amylase-creatinine clearance relation relación de depuración metabólica de amilasa-creatinina.
  body-weight relation relación de peso corporal.
  buccolingual relation relación bucolingual.
  cardiothoracic relation relación cardiotorácica.
  centric jaw relation relación intermaxilar céntrica.
  dynamic relation relación dinámica.
  eccentric relation relación excéntrica.
  extraction (E) relation relación de extracción (E).
  flux relation relación de flujo.
  functional terminal innervation relation relación de inervación terminal funcional.
  hand relation relación de la mano.
  intermaxillary relation relación intermaxilar.
  IRI/G relation relación IIR/G.
  ketogenic-antiketogenic (K:A) relation relación cetogénica-anticetogénica (C:A).
  lecithin/sphingomyelin (L/S) relation relación lecitina/esfingomielina (L/E).
  M:E relation relación M:E.
  maxillomandibular relation relación maxilomandibular.
  median relation relación mediana, relación mediana retruida.
  median retruded relation relación mediana, relación mediana retruida.
  Mendelian relation relación mendeliana.
  nuclear-cytoplasmic relation relación nuclear-citoplasmática.
  nutritive relation relación nutritiva.
  occluding relation relación oclusal.
  P/O relation relación F/O.
  protrusive jaw relation relación intermaxilar protrusiva.
  protrusive relation relación protrusiva.
  relation of decayed and filled surfaces (RDFS) relación de superficies dentarias deterioradas y obturadas.
  relation of decayed and filled teeth (RDFT) relación de dientes deteriorados y obturados.
  respiratory exchange (R) relation relación de intercambio respiratorio (R).
  rest jaw relation relación intermaxilar de reposo.
  rest relation relación de reposo.
  ridge relation relación de los rebordes.
  sadomasochistic relation relación sadomasoquista.
  segregation relation relación de segregación.
  sex relation relación de sexos.
  therapeutic relation relación terapéutica.
  unstrained jaw relation relación intermaxilar sin tensión.
  ventilation/perfusion relation (Va/Q) relación ventilación/perfusión (Va/Q).
  zeta sedimentation relation (ZSR) relación de sedimentación zeta.
relationship *n.* relación.

  blood relationship relación de sangre.
  hypnotic relationship relación hipnótica.
  object relationship relación de objeto.
relative *adj.* relativo, -va.
relax *v.* relajar.
relaxant *n.* relajante.
  depolarizing relaxant relajante despolarizante.
  muscular relaxant relajante muscular.
  neuromuscular relaxant relajante neuromuscular.
  non-depolarizing relaxant relajante no despolarizante.
  smooth muscle relaxant relajante del músculo liso.
relaxation *n.* relajación, relajamiento.
  cardioesophageal relaxation relajación cardioesofágica.
  isometric relaxation relajación isométrica.
  isovolumetric relaxation relajación isovolumétrica.
  isovolumic relaxation relajación isovolúmica.
relearning *n.* reaprendizaje.
release *n.* liberación.
  prolonged release liberación prolongada.
  sustained release liberación sostenida.
  timed release liberación programada.
reliability *n.* fiabilidad.
relief *n.* alivio.
relieve *v.* aliviar.
reline *v.* recapar.
reluxation *n.* redislocación.
remanent *n.* remanente.
remediable *adj.* remediable.
remedy *n.* remedio.
  concordant remedy remedio concordante.
  inimic remedy remedio inímico.
remineralization *n.* remineralización.
reminescence *n.* reminiscencia.
remission *n.* remisión.
  spontaneous remission remisión espontánea.
remit *v.* remitir.
remittence *n.* remitencia.
remittent *adj.* remitente.
remodeling *n.* remodelación.
renal *adj.* renal.
renculus *n.* rénculo.
renicapsule *n.* renicápsula.
renicardiac *adj.* renicardíaco, -ca, renicardio, -dia.
reniculus *n.* renículo.
reniform *adj.* reniforme.
renipelvic *adj.* renipélvico, -ca.
reniportal *adj.* reniportal.
renipuncture *n.* renipuntura.
renitence *n.* renitencia.
renocutaneous *adj.* renocutáneo, -a.
renogastric *adj.* renogástrico, -ca.
renogenic *adj.* renogénico, -ca.
renogram *n.* renograma.
renography *n.* renografía.
renointestinal *adj.* renointestinal.
renomegaly *n.* renomegalia.
renopathy *n.* renopatía.
renoprival *adj.* renoprivo, -va.
renopulmonary *adj.* renopulmonar.
renotrophic *adj.* renotrófico, -ca.
renotrophin *n.* renotrofina.
renotropic *adj.* renotrópico, -ca.
renovascular *adj.* renovascular.
renunculus *n.* rénulo, renúnculo.
Reoviridae Reoviridae.
Reovirus Reovirus.
reoxidation *n.* reoxidación.

repair *n.* reparación.
reparation *n.* reparación.
  chemical reparation reparación química.
  dna reparation reparación de ADN.
  surgical reparation reparación quirúrgica.
  tissue reparation reparación tisular.
reparative *adj.* reparador, -ra, reparativo, -va.
repellent *adj.* repelente.
repercolation *n.* repercolación.
repetition-compulsion *n.* repetición-compulsión.
replacement *n.* sustitución.
  hip replacement sustitución de cadera.
  knee replacement sustitución de rodilla.
  total hip replacement sustitución total de la cadera.
  total joint replacement sustitución articular total.
replant *n.* reimplante.
replantation *n.* replantación.
repletion *n.* repleción.
replica *n.* réplica.
replicase *n.* replicasa.
replicate *v.* replicar.
replication *n.* replicación.
replicator *n.* replicador.
replicon *n.* replicón.
replisome *n.* replisoma.
repolarization *n.* repolarización.
report *n.* informe.
  BEIR-III report informe BEIR-III.
  incident report informe de incidencias.
  radiological report informe radiológico.
  Remmelink report informe Remmelink.
  Warnock's report informe Warnock.
repositioning *n.* reposición.
  gingival repositioning reposición gingival.
  jaw repositioning reposición mandibular.
  muscle repositioning reposición muscular.
repositor *n.* repositor.
representation *n.* representación.
repression *n.* represión.
reproduction *n.* reproducción.
  asexual reproduction reproducción asexual.
  cytogenic reproduction reproducción citogénica.
  sexual reproduction reproducción sexual.
  somatic reproduction reproducción somática.
reproductive *adj.* reproductivo, -va, reproductor, -ra.
repudiation *n.* repudio.
repullulation *n.* repululación.
repulsion *n.* repulsión.
request *n.* demanda.
resazurin *n.* resazurina.
research *n.* investigación.
  clinical research investigación clínica.
  nursing research investigación de enfermería.
resect *v.* resecar.
resectable *adj.* resecable.
resection *n.* resección.
  gum resection resección de las encías.
  Miles resection resección de Miles.
  muscle resection resección muscular.
  Reichel-Pólya stomach resection resección estomacal de Reichel-Pólya.
  root resection resección de raíces, resección radicular.
  scleral resection resección escleral.
  submucous resection (SMR) resección submucosa (RSM).
  transurethral resection (TUR) resección transuretral (RTU).
  wedge resection resección en cuña.

resectocopy *n.* resectoscopia.
resectoscope *n.* resectoscopio.
reserve *n.* reserva.
  alkali reserve reserva alcalina.
  breathing reserve reserva respiratoria.
  cardiac reserve reserva cardíaca.
reservoir *n.* reservorio.
  animal reservoir reservorio de virus.
  Ommaya reservoir reservorio de Ommaya.
  reservoir of infection reservorio de infección.
  reservoir of spermatozoa reservorio de espermatozoides.
residual *adj.* residual.
residue *n.* residuo, resto.
  adrenal residue resto adrenal, resto suprarrenal.
  carbon residue resto de carbono.
  day residue residuo del día, resto diurno.
  embryonic residue resto embrionario.
  epithelial residue resto epitelial.
  fetal residue resto fetal.
  Malassez's epithelial residue resto epiteliales de Malassez.
  mesonephric residue resto mesonéfrico.
  precision residue resto de precisión.
  Walthard's cell residue resto celular de Walthard.
  Wolffian residue resto de Wolff.
resilience *n.* elasticidad, resiliencia.
  psychobiologic resilience elasticidad psicobiológica.
resistance *n.* resistencia.
  acid alcohol resistance resistencia a ácidos y alcohol.
  airway resistance resistencia de las vías aéreas.
  bateriophage resistance resistencia a los bacteriófagos.
  expiratory resistance resistencia espiratoria.
  impact resistance resistencia al impacto.
  inductive resistance resistencia inductiva.
  insulin resistance resistencia a la insulina.
  mutual resistance resistencia mutua.
  peripheral resistance resistencia periférica.
  synaptic resistance resistencia sináptica.
  total peripheral resistance (TPR) resistencia periférica total (RPT).
resistor *n.* resistor.
resolution *n.* resolución.
resolve *v.* resolver.
resolvent *adj.* resolutivo, -va, resolvente.
resonance *n.* resonancia.
  amphoric resonance resonancia anfórica.
  cracked-pot resonance resonancia de olla hendida.
  electron spin resonance resonancia de espín electrónico.
  hydatic resonance resonancia hidatídica.
  magnetic resonance (mr) resonancia magnética.
  nuclear magnetic resonance (Nmr) resonancia magnética nuclear.
  skodaic resonance resonancia escódica.
  tympanitic resonance resonancia timpánica.
  vesicular resonance resonancia vesicular.
  vesiculotympanitic resonance resonancia vesiculotimpánica.
  vocal resonance (Vr) resonancia vocal.
  wooden resonance resonancia de madera.
resonant *adj.* resonante.
resonator *n.* resonador.
  Oudin resonator resonador de Oudin.
resorption *n.* resorción.
respirable *adj.* respirable.

respiration *n.* respiración.
  abdominal respiration respiración abdominal.
  aerobic respiration respiración aeróbica.
  amphoric respiration respiración anfórica.
  anaerobic respiration respiración anaeróbica.
  apneustic respiration respiración apneústica.
  artificial respiration respiración artificial.
  assisted respiration respiración asistida.
  Biot's respiration respiración de Biot.
  Bouchut's respiration respiración de Bouchut.
  bronchial respiration respiración bronquial.
  broncovesicular respiration respiración broncovesicular.
  cerebral respiration respiración cerebral.
  Cheyne-Stokes respiration respiración de Cheyne-Stokes.
  cogwheel respiration respiración en rueda dentada.
  controlled respiration respiración controlada.
  Corrigan's respiration respiración de Corrigan.
  costal respiration respiración costal.
  cutaneous respiration respiración cutánea.
  diaphragmatic respiration respiración diafragmática.
  diffusion respiration respiración por difusión.
  divided respiration respiración dividida.
  electrophrenic respiration respiración electrofrénica.
  external respiration respiración externa.
  fetal respiration respiración fetal.
  forced respiration respiración forzada.
  harsh respiration respiración ruda.
  internal respiration respiración interna.
  interrupted respiration respiración entrecortada, respiración interrumpida.
  Kussmaul respiration respiración de Kussmaul, respiración de Kussmaul-Kien.
  Kussmaul-Kien's respiration respiración de Kussmaul, respiración de Kussmaul-Kien.
  meningitic respiration respiración meningítica.
  mouth-to-mouth respiration respiración boca a boca.
  nitrate respiration respiración de nitrato.
  paradoxical respiration respiración paradójica.
  puerile respiration respiración pueril.
  rude respiration respiración ruda.
  sighing respiration respiración suspirosa.
  stertorous respiration respiración estertorosa.
  sulfate respiration respiración de sulfato.
  supplementary respiration respiración suplementaria.
  thoracic respiration respiración torácica.
  tissue respiration respiración hística.
  tubular respiration respiración tubárica, respiración tubular.
  vesicular respiration respiración vesicular.
  vesiculocavernous respiration respiración vesiculocavernosa.
respirator *n.* respirador.
  cuirass respirator respirador en coraza.
  Drinker respirator respirador de Drinker.
  pressure-controlled respirator respirador controlado por presión.
  tank respirator respirador tanque.
  volume-controlled respirator respirador controlado por volumen.

respiratory *adj.* respiratorio, -ria.
respire *v.* respirar.
respirometer *n.* respirómetro.
  Dräger respirometer respirómetro de Dräger.
  Wright respirometer respirómetro de Wright.
response *n.* respuesta.
  anamnestic response respuesta anamnéstica.
  biphasic response respuesta bifásica.
  conditioned response respuesta condicionada.
  curve response respuesta de curva.
  Cushing response respuesta de Cushing.
  depletion response respuesta de deplección.
  early-phase response respuesta de fase temprana.
  fight response respuesta de lucha.
  flight response respuesta de huida.
  galvanic skin response respuesta cutánea galvánica.
  Henry-Gauer response respuesta de Henry-Gauer.
  immune response respuesta inmune.
  isomorphic response respuesta isomórfica.
  late-phase response respuesta de fase tardía.
  no response (NR) no respuesta (NR).
  oculomotor response respuesta oculomotora.
  orienting response respuesta de orientación.
  psychogalvanic response respuesta psicogalvánica.
  psychogalvanic skin response respuesta psicogalvánica.
  recruiting response respuesta de reclutamiento.
  relaxation response respuesta de relajación.
  sonomotor response respuesta sonomotora.
  triple response respuesta triple.
  unconditioned response respuesta no condicionada.
rest *n.* apoyo[1], descanso, reposo, soporte.
  incisal rest apoyo incisal.
  occlusal rest apoyo oclusal.
  precision rest soporte de precisión.
restibrachium *n.* restibraquio.
restiform *adj.* restiforme.
restis *n.* restis.
restitutio ad integrum restitutio ad integrum.
restocythemia *n.* restocitemia.
restoration *n.* restauración.
  acid-etched restoration restauración grabada con ácido.
  combination restoration restauración combinada.
  compound restoration restauración compuesta.
  direct acrylic restoration restauración directa de acrílico.
  direct composite resin restoration restauración directa de resina, restauración directa de resina compuesta.
  direct resin restoration restauración directa de resina, restauración directa de resina compuesta.
  overhanging restoration restauración colgante.
  permanent restoration restauración permanente.
  root canal restoration restauración de conductos radiculares.
  silicate restoration restauración de silicato.
  temporary restoration restauración temporal.

restorative *adj.* reconstituyente, reparativo, va, restaurativo, -va.
restraint *n.* restricción, sujeción.
  chemical restraint sujeción química.
resublimed *adj.* resublimado, -da.
result *n.* resultado.
resuscitation *n.* reanimación, resucitación, resurrección.
  cardiopulmonary resuscitation reanimación cardiopulmonar.
  do not attempt resuscitation (DNAR) no intentar la reanimación (NIR).
  mouth-to-mouth resuscitation reanimación boca a boca.
resuscitator *n.* resucitador.
retainer *n.* retenedor.
  continuous bar retainer retenedor en barra continuo.
  direct retainer retenedor directo.
  extracoronal retainer retenedor extracoronal.
  indirect retainer retenedor indirecto.
  intracoronal retainer retenedor intracoronal.
  matrix retainer retenedor de matriz.
  space retainer retenedor de espacio.
retardate *adj.* retardado, retrasado, -da.
retardation *n.* retraso.
  mental retardation retraso mental.
  mild mental retardation retraso mental leve.
  moderate mental retardation retraso mental moderado.
  profound mental retardation retraso mental profundo.
  psychomotor retardation retraso psicomotor.
  severe mental retardation retraso mental grave.
retarder *n.* retardador.
rete *n.* red, rete.
retention *n.* retención.
  denture retention retención protésica.
  direct retention retención directa.
  indirect retention retención indirecta.
  partial denture retention retención de prótesis parciales.
  retention of the placenta retención placentaria.
  retention of placental fragments retención placentaria.
  retention of urine retención de orina.
  urine retention retención de orina.
retetestis retetestis.
rethelioma *n.* retelioma.
reticula *n.* retícula.
reticular *adj.* reticular.
reticulated *adj.* reticulado, -da.
reticulation *n.* reticulación.
reticulin *n.* reticulina.
reticulocyte *n.* reticulocito.
reticulocytopenia *n.* reticulocitopenia.
reticulocytosis *n.* reticulocitosis.
reticuloendothelial *adj.* reticuloendotelial.
reticuloendothelioma *n.* reticuloendotelioma.
reticuloendotheliosis *n.* reticuloendoteliosis.
  leukemic reticuloendotheliosis reticuloendoteliosis leucémica.
reticuloendothelium *n.* reticuloendotelio.
reticulohistiocytoma *n.* reticulohistiocitoma.
reticulohistiocytosis *n.* reticulohistiocitosis.
  multicentric reticulohistiocytosis reticulohistiocitosis multicéntrica.
reticuloid *n.* reticuloide.

actinic reticuloid reticuloide actínico.
reticuloma *n.* reticuloma.
reticulopenia *n.* reticulopenia.
reticulosarcoma *n.* reticulosarcoma.
reticulosis *n.* reticulosis, retoteliosis.
  benign inoculation reticulosis reticulosis benigna por inoculación.
  histiocytic medullary reticulosis reticulosis medular histiocítica.
  leukemic reticulosis reticulosis leucémica.
  lipomelanic reticulosis reticulosis lipomelánica.
  myeloid reticulosis reticulosis mieloide.
  pagetoid reticulosis reticulosis pagetoide.
  polymorphic reticulosis reticulosis polimórfica.
reticulospinal *adj.* reticuloespinal.
reticulothelium *n.* reticulotelio.
reticulotomy *n.* reticulotomía.
reticulum *n.* retículo.
  Ebner's reticulum retículo de Ebner.
  endoplasmic reticulum retículo endoplásmico.
  Kölliker's reticulum retículo de Kölliker.
  sarcoplasmic reticulum retículo sarcoplasmático.
  stellate reticulum retículo estrellado.
  trabecular reticulum retículo trabecular.
retiform *adj.* retiforme.
retina *n.* retina.
  coarctate retina retina comprimida.
  detached retina retina desprendida.
  fleck retina retina de kandori.
  flecked retina retina manchada, retina veteada.
  leopard retina retina de leopardo.
  shot-silk retina retina de seda tornasolada.
  tigroid retina retina tigroide.
retinaculum retináculo, retinaculum.
retinal *adj.* retinal, retiniano, -na.
retinene *n.* retineno.
retinitis *n.* dictitis, retinitis.
  actinic retinitis retinitis actínica.
  albuminuric retinitis retinitis albuminúrica.
  apoplectic retinitis retinitis apoplética.
  azotemic retinitis retinitis azoémica.
  central angiospastic retinitis retinitis angiospástica central.
  circinate retinitis retinitis circinada.
  diabetic retinitis retinitis diabética.
  exudative retinitis retinitis exudativa.
  gravidic retinitis retinitis gravídica.
  hypertensive retinitis retinitis hipertensiva.
  Jacobson's retinitis retinitis de Jacobson.
  Jensen's retinitis retinitis de Jensen.
  leukemic retinitis retinitis esplénica, retinitis leucémica.
  metastatic retinitis retinitis metastásica.
  proliferating retinitis retinitis proliferante.
  punctate retinitis retinitis punctata, retinitis punteada.
  purulent retinitis retinitis purulenta, retinitis serosa.
  recurrent central retinitis retinitis central recurrente.
  retinitis hemorrhagica retinitis hemorrágica.
  retinitis nephritica retinitis nefrítica, retinitis renal.
  retinitis pigmentosa retinitis pigmentaria, retinitis pigmentosa.
  retinitis proliferans retinitis proliferante.
  retinitis sclopetaria retinitis esclopedaria.
  retinitis syphilitica retinitis sifilítica.
  secondary retinitis retinitis secundaria.
  septic retinitis retinitis séptica.

simple retinitis retinitis simple.
solar retinitis retinitis solar.
syphilitic retinitis retinitis sifilítica.
retinoblastoma *n.* retinoblastoma.
retinochoroid *adj.* retinocoroide.
retinochoroiditis *n.* retinocoroiditis.
  bird shot retinochoroiditis retinocoroiditis en perdigón.
  retinochoroiditis juxtapapillaris retinocoroiditis yuxtapapilar.
retinocytoma *n.* retinocitoma.
retinodialysis *n.* retinodiálisis.
retinography *n.* retinografía.
retinoid *adj.* retinoide.
retinomalacia *n.* retinomalacia.
retinopapillitis *n.* retinopapilitis.
  retinopapillitis of premature infants retinopapilitis de los niños prematuros.
retinopathy *n.* retinopatía.
  angiopathic retinopathy retinopatía angiopática.
  arteriosclerotic retinopathy retinopatía arteriosclerótica.
  central angiospastic retinopathy retinopatía angioespástica central.
  central serous retinopathy retinopatía serosa central.
  circinate retinopathy retinopatía circinada.
  compression retinopathy retinopatía por compresión.
  diabetic retinopathy retinopatía diabética.
  dysoric retinopathy retinopatía disórica.
  dysproteinemic retinopathy retinopatía disproteinémica.
  eclamptic retinopathy retinopatía eclámptica.
  electric retinopathy retinopatía eléctrica.
  external exudative retinopathy retinopatía exudativa externa.
  gravidic retinopathy retinopatía gravídica.
  hypertensive retinopathy retinopatía hipertensiva.
  hypotensive retinopathy retinopatía hipotensiva.
  Leber's idiopathic stellate retinopathy retinopatía estrellada idiopática de Leber.
  leukemic retinopathy retinopatía leucémica.
  lipemic retinopathy retinopatía lipémica.
  macular retinopathy retinopatía macular.
  photo retinopathy retinopatía fótica.
  pigmentary retinopathy retinopatía pigmentaria, retinopatía pigmentosa.
  proliferative retinopathy retinopatía proliferativa.
  renal retinopathy retinopatía renal.
  retinopathy of prematurity retinopatía de los prematuros.
  retinopathy punctata albescens retinopatía punctata albescens.
  rubella retinopathy retinopatía de la rubéola.
  sickle cell retinopathy retinopatía drepanocítica.
  solar retinopathy retinopatía solar.
  stellate retinopathy retinopatía estrellada.
  tapetoretinal retinopathy retinopatía tapetorretiniana.
  toxemic retinopathy of preganancy retinopatía toxémica del embarazo.
  toxic retinopathy retinopatía tóxica.
  traumatic retinopathy retinopatía traumática.
  venous stasis retinopathy retinopatía por estasis venosa.
retinopexy *n.* retinopexia.
retinopiesis *n.* retinopiesis.

retinoschisis *n.* retinosquisis.
  juvenile retinoschisis retinosquisis juvenil.
  senile retinoschisis retinosquisis senil.
retinoscope *n.* retinoscopio.
  luminous retinoscope retinoscopio luminoso.
  reflecting retinoscope retinoscopio reflector.
retinoscopy *n.* retinoscopia.
  cylinder retinoscopy retinoscopia cilíndrica.
  fogging retinoscopy retinoscopia borrosa.
retinosis *n.* retinosis.
retisolution *n.* retisolución.
retoperithelium *n.* retoperitelio.
retort *n.* retorta.
retothelioma *n.* retotelioma.
retothelium *n.* retotelio.
retractile *adj.* retráctil.
retraction *n.* retracción.
  gingival retraction retracción gingival.
  mandibular retraction retracción mandibular.
  retraction of the chest retracción del tórax.
  uterine muscle retraction retracción del útero.
retractor *n.* retractor, separador[1].
  Moorehead's retractor retractor de Moorehead.
retrenchment *n.* cercenamiento.
retroauricular *adj.* retroauricular.
retrobronchial *adj.* retrobronquial.
retrobuccal *adj.* retrobucal.
retrobulbar *adj.* retrobulbar.
retrocalcaneobursitis *n.* retrocalcaneobursitis.
retrocardiac *adj.* retrocardíaco, -ca.
retrocatheterism *n.* retrocateterismo.
retrocecal *adj.* retrocecal.
retrocervical *adj.* retrocervical.
retrocession *n.* retrocesión, retroceso.
retroclavicular *adj.* retroclavicular.
retrocolic *adj.* retrocólico, -ca.
retrocollis *n.* retrocolis.
retrodeviation *n.* retrodesviación.
retrodisplacement *n.* retrodesplazamiento.
retroesophageal *adj.* retroesofágico, -ca.
retrofilling *n.* retroobturación.
retroflexed *adj.* retroflexionado, -da, retroflexo, -xa.
retroflexion *n.* retroflexión.
retrognathia *n.* retrognatia.
retrognathic *adj.* retrognático, -ca.
retrognathism *n.* retrognatismo.
retrograde *adj.* retrógrado, -da.
  retrograde ureteropyelography ureteropielografía retrógrada.
retrography *n.* retrografía.
retrogression *n.* retrogresión.
retroinsular *adj.* retroinsular.
retroiridian *adj.* retroiridiano, -na.
retrojection *n.* retroyección.
retrojector *n.* retroyector.
retrolabyrinthine *adj.* retrolaberíntico, -ca.
retrolental *adj.* retrolental.
retrolenticular *adj.* retrolenticular.
retrolingual *adj.* retrolingual.
retrolisthesis *n.* retrolistesis.
retromammary *adj.* retromamario, -ria.
retromandibular *adj.* retromandibular.
retromastoid *adj.* retromastoideo, -a.
retromaxillary *adj.* retromaxilar.
retromorphosis *n.* retromorfosis.
retronasal *adj.* retronasal.
retro-ocular *adj.* retroocular.
retroperitoneal *adj.* retroperitoneal.
retroperitonitis *n.* retroperitonitis.

  idiopathic fibrous retroperitonitis retroperitonitis fibrosa idiopática.
retropharyngeal *adj.* retrofaríngeo, -a.
retropharynx *n.* retrofaringe.
retroplacental *adj.* retroplacentario, -ria.
retroplasia *n.* retroplasia.
retroposed *adj.* retropuesto, -ta.
retroposition *n.* retroposición.
retroposon *n.* retroposón.
retropubic *adj.* retropúbico, -ca.
retropulsion *n.* retropulsión.
retrorectal *adj.* retrorrectal.
retrospection *n.* retrospección.
retrospective *adj.* retrospectivo, -va.
retrospondylolisthesis *n.* retroespondilolistesis, retrospondilolistesis.
retrostalsis *n.* retrostalsis.
retrosternal *adj.* retroesternal, retrosternal.
retrosymphysial *adj.* retrosinfisial.
retrotarsal *adj.* retrotarsiano, -na.
retrouterine *adj.* retrouterino, -na.
retroversioflexion *n.* retroversioflexión.
retroversion *n.* retroversión.
retroverted *adj.* retrovertido, -da.
Retroviridae Retroviridae.
retrovirus *n.* retrovirus.
retrusion *n.* retrusión.
return *n.* retorno.
  venous return retorno venoso.
revaccination *n.* revacunación.
revascularization *n.* revascularización.
reversible *adj.* reversible.
reversion *n.* reversión.
revertant *adj.* revertante.
revivification *n.* revivificación.
reviviscence *n.* reviviscencia.
revulsion *n.* derivación[2], revulsión.
revulsive *n.* revulsivo, -va.
reward *n.* recompensa.
rhabditiform *adj.* rabditiforme.
Rhabditis Rhabditis.
rhabdocyte *n.* rabdocito.
rhabdoid *adj.* rabdoide, rabdoideo, -a.
rhabdomyoblast *n.* rabdomioblasto.
rhabdomyoblastoma *n.* rabdomioblastoma.
rhabdomyochondroma *n.* rabdomiocondroma.
rhabdomyolysis *n.* rabdomiólisis.
  exertional rhabdomyolysis rabdomiólisis por esfuerzo.
  idiopathic paroxysmal rhabdomyolysis rabdomiólisis paroxística idiopática.
rhabdomyoma *n.* rabdomioma.
rhabdomyomyxoma *n.* rabdomiomixoma.
rhabdomyosarcoma *n.* rabdomiosarcoma.
  alveolar rhabdomyosarcoma rabdomiosarcoma alveolar.
  embryonal rhabdomyosarcoma rabdomiosarcoma embrionarios.
  juvenile alveolar rhabdomyosarcoma rabdomiosarcoma alveolar juvenil.
  pleomorphic rhabdomyosarcoma rabdomiosarcoma pleomórfico.
rhabdophobia *n.* rabdofobia.
rhabdosarcoma *n.* rabdosarcoma.
rhabdosphincter *n.* rabdoesfínter.
Rhabdoviridae Rhabdoviridae.
rhabdovirus *n.* rabdovirus.
rhacoma *n.* racoma.
rhadbitoid *adj.* rabditoide.
rhaebocrania *n.* raebocrania.
rhaebosis *n.* raebosis.
rhagade *n.* rágade.
rhagades *n.* rágade, ragadías.
rhagadiform *adj.* ragadiforme.

rhagiocrine *adj.* ragiocrino, -na.
rhegma *n.* regma.
rhegmetogenous *adj.* regmatógeno, -na.
rheobase *n.* reobase, reobasis.
rheobasic *adj.* reobásico, -ca.
rheocardiography *n.* reocardiografía.
rheocord *n.* reocordio.
rheoencephalogram *n.* reoencefalograma.
rheoencephalography *n.* reoencefalografía.
rheogram *n.* reograma.
rheologist *n.* reólogo, -ga.
rheology *n.* reología.
rheometer *n.* reómetro.
rheometry *n.* reometría.
rheopexy *n.* reopexia.
rheoscope *n.* reoscopio.
rheostat *n.* reóstato.
rheostosis *n.* reostosis.
rheotachygraphy *n.* reotaquigrafía.
rheotaxis *n.* reotaxis.
rheotome *n.* reótomo.
rheotrope *n.* reótropo.
rheotropism *n.* reotropismo.
rheum *n.* legaña, reuma, reúma.
rheuma *n.* reuma, reúma.
rheumatalgia *n.* reumatalgia.
rheumatic *adj.* reumático, -ca.
rheumaticosis *n.* reumaticosis.
rheumatid *n.* reumátide.
rheumatism *n.* reumatismo.
  acute articular rheumatism reumatismo articular agudo.
  cerebral rheumatism reumatismo cerebral.
  chronic articular rheumatism reumatismo articular crónico, reumatismo deformante.
  chronic rheumatism reumatismo crónico, reumatismo gotoso.
  gonorrheal rheumatism reumatismo gonorreico.
  Heberden's rheumatism reumatismo de Heberden.
  inflammatory rheumatism reumatismo inflamatorio.
  lumbar rheumatism reumatismo lumbar.
  Macleod's rheumatism reumatismo capsular de Macleod, reumatismo de Macleod.
  muscular rheumatism reumatismo muscular.
  nodose rheumatism reumatismo nudoso.
  osseous rheumatism reumatismo óseo.
  palindromic rheumatism reumatismo palindrómico.
  Poncet's rheumatism reumatismo de Poncet.
  rheumatism of the heart reumatismo cardíaco.
  subacute rheumatism reumatismo subagudo.
  tuberculous rheumatism reumatismo tuberculoso.
  visceral rheumatism reumatismo visceral.
rheumatismal *adj.* reumático, -ca.
rheumatocelis *n.* reumatocelis.
rheumatologist *n.* reumatólogo, -ga.
rheumatology *n.* reumatología.
rheumatosis *n.* reumatosis.
rhexis *n.* rotura.
rhigosis *n.* rigosis.
rhigotic *adj.* rigótico, -ca.
rhinal *adj.* rinal.
rhinalgia *n.* rinalgia.
rhinallergosis *n.* rinalergia, rinalergosis.
rhinedema *n.* rinedema, rinoedema.
rhinencephalic *adj.* rinencefálico, -ca.
rhinencephalon *n.* rinencéfalo.
rhinenchysis *n.* rinenquisis.
rhinesthesia *n.* rinestesia.

rhineurynter *n.* rineurínter.
rhinion *n.* rinión.
rhinism *n.* rinismo.
rhinitis *n.* rinitis.
  acute catarrhal rhinitis rinitis catarral aguda.
  acute rhinitis rinitis aguda.
  allergic rhinitis rinitis alérgica.
  anaphylactic rhinitis rinitis analfiláctica.
  atrophic rhinitis rinitis atrófica.
  caseous rhinitis rinitis caseosa.
  chronic rhinitis rinitis crónica.
  croupous rhinitis rinitis cruposa.
  eosinophilic non-allergic rhinitis rinitis eosinofílica no alérgica.
  fibrinous rhinitis rinitis fibrinosa.
  gangrenous rhinitis rinitis gangrenosa.
  hypertrophic rhinitis rinitis hipertrófica.
  membranous rhinitis rinitis membranosa.
  pseudomembranous rhinitis rinitis seudomembranosa.
  purulent rhinitis rinitis purulenta.
  rhinitis caseosa rinitis caseosa.
  rhinitis nervosa rinitis nerviosa.
  rhinitis purulenta rinitis purulenta.
  rhinitis sicca rinitis seca.
  scrofulous rhinitis rinitis escrofulosa.
  syphilitic rhinitis rinitis sifilítica.
  tuberculous rhinitis rinitis tuberculosa.
  vasomotor rhinitis rinitis vasomotora.
rhinnommectomy *n.* rinomectomía.
rhinoanemometer *n.* rinoanemómetro.
rhinoantritis *n.* nasoantritis.
rhinoantritis *n.* rinoantritis.
rhinobyon *n.* rinobión.
rhinocanthectomy *n.* rinocantectomía.
rhinocele *n.* rinocelo.
rhinocephalia *n.* rinencefalia, rinocefalia.
rhinocephalus *n.* rinocéfalo.
rhinocephaly *n.* rinencefalia, rinocefalia.
rhinocheiloplasty *n.* rinoqueiloplastia, rinoquiloplastia.
rhinocleisis *n.* rinocleisis.
rhinodacryolith *n.* rinodacriolito.
rhinodymia *n.* rinodimia.
rhinodynia *n.* rinodinia.
rhinogenous *adj.* rinógeno, -na.
rhinokyphectomy *n.* rinocifectomía.
rhinokyphosis *n.* rinocifosis.
rhinolalia *n.* rinolalia.
  rhinolalia aperta rinolalia abierta.
  rhinolalia clausa rinolalia cerrada.
rhinolaryngitis *n.* rinolaringitis.
rhinolaryngology *n.* rinolaringología.
rhinolith *n.* rinolito.
rhinolithiasis *n.* rinolitiasis.
rhinologic *adj.* rinológico, -ca.
rhinologist *n.* rinólogo, -ga.
rhinology *n.* riniatría, rinología.
rhinomanometry *n.* rinomanometría.
rhinometer *n.* rinómetro.
rhinomucormycosis *n.* rinomucormicosis.
rhinomycosis *n.* rinomicosis.
rhinonecrosis *n.* rinonecrosis.
rhinoneurosis *n.* rinoneurosis.
rhinopathy *n.* rinopatía.
rhinopharyngeal *adj.* rinofaríngeo, -a.
rhinopharyngitis *n.* rinofaringitis.
rhinopharyngocele *n.* rinofaringocele.
rhinopharyngolith *n.* rinofaringolito.
rhinopharynx *n.* rinofaringe.
rhinophonia *n.* rinofonía.
rhinophycomycosis *n.* rinoficomicosis.
rhinophyma *n.* rinofima.
rhinoplasty *n.* rinoplastia.
  English rhinoplasty rinoplastia inglesa.

  Indian rhinoplasty rinoplastia hindú.
  Italian rhinoplasty rinoplastia italiana.
rhinopolypus *n.* rinopólipo.
rhinoreaction *n.* rinorreacción.
rhinorrhagia *n.* rinorragia.
rhinorrhaphy *n.* rinorrafia.
rhinorrhea *n.* rinorrea.
  cerebrospinal fluid rhinorrhea rinorrea cerebroespinal, rinorrea de líquido cefalorraquídeo.
  gustatory rhinorrhea rinorrea gustativa.
rhinosalpingitis *n.* rinosalpingitis.
rhinoscleroma *n.* rinoescleroma, rinoscleroma.
rhinoscope *n.* rinoscopio.
rhinoscopy *n.* rinoscopia.
  anterior rhinoscopy rinoscopia anterior.
  median rhinoscopy rinoscopia media.
  posterior rhinoscopy rinoscopia posterior.
rhinosporidiosis *n.* rinosporidiosis.
Rhinosporidium Rhinosporidium.
rhinostenosis *n.* rinoestenosis, rinostenosis.
rhinotomy *n.* rinotomía.
rhinotracheitis *n.* rinotraqueítis.
rhinovaccination *n.* rinovacunación.
Rhinovirus Rhinovirus.
rhinovirus *n.* rinovirus.
rhizanesthesia *n.* rizanestesia.
rhizoid *adj.* rizoide.
rhizomelia *n.* rizomelia.
rhizomelic *adj.* rizomélico, -ca.
rhizomeningomyelitis *n.* rizomeningomielitis.
rhizomere *n.* rizómera.
rhizoneure *n.* rizoneura.
rhizoplast *n.* rizoplasto.
rhizopoda *n.* rizópodos.
Rhizopus Rhizopus.
rhizotomy *n.* rizotomía.
  anterior rhizotomy rizotomía anterior.
  facet rhizotomy rizotomía de facetas.
  posterior rhizotomy rizotomía posterior.
  trigeminal rhizotomy rizotomía trigeminal.
rhodamine b *n.* rodamina b.
Rhodnius prolixus Rhodnius prolixus.
rhodocyte *n.* rodocito.
rhodogenesis *n.* rodogénesis.
rhodophylactic *adj.* rodofiláctico, -ca.
rhodophylaxis *n.* rodofilaxia, rodofilaxis.
Rhodotorula Rhodotorula.
rhombencephalon *n.* rombencéfalo.
rhombic *adj.* rómbico, -ca.
rhomboatloideus *n.* romboatloideo.
rhomboid *adj.* romboide.
rhombomere *n.* rombómero.
rhopheocytosis *n.* rofeocitosis.
rhoptry *n.* roptría.
rhotacism *n.* rotacismo.
rhynomanometer *n.* rinomanómetro.
rhypophagy *n.* ripofagia.
rhythm *n.* ritmo.
  agonal rhythm ritmo agónico.
  alpha rhythm ritmo alfa.
  atrioventricular nodal rhythm ritmo nodal auriculoventricular.
  atrioventricular rhythm ritmo auriculoventricular.
  Berger rhythm ritmo de Berger.
  beta rhythm ritmo beta.
  bigeminal rhythm ritmo bigémico.
  cantering rhythm ritmo de galope.
  circadian rhythm ritmo circadiano.
  circus rhythm ritmo circular.
  coronary nodal rhythm ritmo nodal coronario.

coronary sinus rhythm ritmo sinusal coronario.
coupled rhythm ritmo acoplado.
delta rhythm ritmo delta.
ectopic rhythm ritmo ectópico.
escape rhythm ritmo de escape.
fast rhythm ritmo rápido.
fetal rhythm ritmo fetal.
idionodal rhythm ritmo idionodal.
idioventricular rhythm ritmo idioventricular.
nodal rhythm ritmo nodal.
pendulum rhythm ritmo pendular.
quadruple rhythm ritmo cuádruple.
reciprocal rhythm ritmo recíproco.
reciprocating rhythm ritmo reciprocante.
reversed reciprocal rhythm ritmo recíproco invertido.
sinus rhythm ritmo sinusal.
theta rhythm ritmo theta.
tick-tack rhythm ritmo de tic-tac.
trainwheel rhythm ritmo de ruedas de tren.
trigeminal rhythm ritmo trigeminal.
triple rhythm ritmo triple.
ultradian rhythm ritmo ultradiano.
ventricular rhythm ritmo ventricular.
rhythmical *adj.* rítmico, -ca.
rhythmophone *n.* ritmófono.
rhytidectomy *n.* ridectomía, ritidectomía.
rhytidoplasty *n.* ritidoplastia.
rhytidosis *n.* ritidosis.
rhytmeur *n.* ritmador.
rhytmotherapy *n.* ritmoterapia.
rib *n.* costa, costilla.
cervical rib costilla cervical.
slipping rib costilla deslizada, costilla deslizante.
ribavirin *n.* ribavirina.
ribbon *n.* cinta.
riboflavin *n.* riboflavina.
riboflavine *n.* riboflavina.
ribonucleoprotein *n.* ribonucleoproteína.
ribonucleoside *n.* ribonucleósido.
ribonucleotide *n.* ribonucleótido.
ribosome *n.* ribosoma.
ribosuria *n.* ribosuria.
rickets *n.* raquitismo.
acute rickets raquitismo agudo.
adult rickets raquitismo del adulto.
beryllium rickets raquitismo por berilio.
fat rickets raquitismo graso.
fetal rickets raquitismo congénito.
Glissonian rickets raquitismo de Glisson.
late rickets raquitismo de los adolescentes.
scurvy rickets raquitismo escorbútico.
Rickettsia Rickettsia.
Rickettsiaceae Rickettsiaceae.
rickettsial *adj.* rickettsial.
rickettsiosis *n.* rickettsiosis.
rickettsiostatic *adj.* rickettsiostático, -ca.
rickety *adj.* raquítico, -ca.
rictus *n.* rictus.
ridge *n.* borde5, reborde.
primitive ridge borde primitivo.
right-eyed *adj.* dextrocular.
right-footed *adj.* dextropedal.
right-handed *adj.* dextromano, -na, manidiestro, -tra.
rigidity *n.* rigidez.
anatomic rigidity rigidez anatómica.
cadaveric rigidity rigidez cadavérica.
catatonic rigidity rigidez catatónica.
cerebellar rigidity rigidez cerebelosa.
cogwheel rigidity rigidez en rueda dentada.
decerebrate rigidity rigidez de descerebración.
decorticate rigidity rigidez de decorticación.

extrapyramidal rigidity rigidez extrapiramidal.
hemiplegic rigidity rigidez hemipléjica.
lead rigidity rigidez en caño de plomo.
mydriatic rigidity rigidez midriática.
ocular rigidity rigidez ocular.
pathologic rigidity rigidez patológica.
pipe rigidity rigidez en caño de plomo.
postmortem rigidity rigidez post mortem.
scleral rigidity rigidez escleral.
rigor *n.* rigor.
acid rigor rigor ácido.
calcium rigor rigor cálcico.
heat rigor rigor térmico.
myocardiac rigor rigor mortis miocárdico.
rigor mortis rigor mortis.
rigor nervorum rigor nervorum.
rigor tremens rigor tremens.
rim *n.* borde6.
bite rim borde de mordedura.
occlusal rim borde de oclusión.
occlusion rim borde de oclusión.
record rim borde de registro.
rima *n.* rima.
rimose *adj.* rimoso, -sa.
rimula *n.* rímula.
ring *n.* anillo.
Albl's ring anillo de Albl.
Bandl's ring anillo de Bandl.
Cabot's ring anillo de Cabot.
carbocyclic ring anillo carbocíclico.
constriction ring anillo constrictor, anillo de constricción.
constrictive ring anillo constrictor, anillo de constricción.
contact ring anillo de contacto.
contractile ring anillo contráctil.
Donders' ring anillo de Donders.
Fleischer ring anillo de Fleischer, anillo de Fleischer-Strümpell.
Fleischer-Strümpell ring anillo de Fleischer, anillo de Fleischer-Strümpell.
Flieringa's ring anillo Flieringa.
germ ring anillo germinal.
glaucomatous ring anillo glaucomatoso.
Graefenberg ring anillo de Graefenberg.
heterocyclic ring anillo heterocíclico.
homocyclic ring anillo homocíclico.
isocyclic ring anillo isocíclico.
Kayser-Fleischer ring anillo corneal de Kayser-Fleischer.
Liesegang ring anillo de Liesegang.
Löwe's ring anillo de Löwe.
Lyon's ring anillo de Lyon.
Maxwell's ring anillo de Maxwell.
neck ring anillo cervical.
neonatal ring anillo neonatal.
pathologic retraction ring anillo de retracción patológica.
physiologic retraction ring anillo de retracción fisiológica.
retraction ring anillo de retracción.
ring of Soemmering anillo de Soemmering.
teething ring anillo mordedor.
tympanic ring anillo timpánico.
umbilical ring anillo umbilical.
vascular ring anillo vascular.
Vossius ring anillo lenticular de Vossius.
ringworm *n.* tiña, tinea.
black-dot ringworm tiña en mancha negra.
gray-patch ringworm tiña a parches grises.
ringworm of the face tiña de la cara.
ringworm of the feet tiña del pie, tinea pedis.
ringworm of the groin tiña de la ingle, tiña inguinal.

ringworm of the hand tiña de las manos, tinea manus.
ringworm of the nails tiña de las uñas, tiña ungueal.
ringworm of the scalp tiña del cuero cabelludo.
Tokelau ringworm tiña de Tokelau.
ripa *n.* ripa.
risk *n.* riesgo.
empiric risk riesgo empírico.
recurrence risk riesgo de recurrencia.
risus *n.* risa.
risus caninus risa canina.
risus sardonicus risa sardónica.
ritual *n.* ritual.
rivalry *n.* rivalidad.
binocular rivalry rivalidad binocular.
rivalry of the retina rivalidad de la retina.
rivus lacrimalis *n.* rivus lacrimalis.
roborant *adj.* roborante.
rod *n.* bastoncillo.
analyzing rod bastoncillo analizador.
Auer rod bastoncillo de Auer.
basal rod bastoncillo basal.
enamel rod bastoncillo del esmalte.
germinal rod bastoncillo germinal.
König's rod bastoncillo de König.
Maddox's rod bastoncillo de Maddox.
muscle rod bastoncillo muscular.
olfactory rod bastoncillo olfatorio.
Reichmann's rod bastoncillo de Reichmann.
retinal rod bastoncillo retiniano.
rod of Heidenhain bastoncillo de Heidenhain.
rods and cones conos y bastones.
rodonalgia *n.* rodonalgia.
roentgen *n.* roentgen.
roentgen equivalent-man roentgen equivalente-hombre.
roentgen equivalent-physical roentgen equivalente-físico.
roentgencinematography *n.* radiocinematografía.
roentgen-equivalent-physical rep.
roentgenism *n.* roentgenismo.
roentgenkymogram *n.* radioquimograma, roentgenoquimograma.
roentgenkymograph *n.* radioquimógrafo, roentgenoquimógrafo.
roentgenkymography *n.* radioquimografía, roentgenoquimografía.
roentgenogram *n.* roentgenograma.
roentgenography *n.* roentgenografía.
mucosal relief roentgenography roentgenografía en relieve de la mucosa.
sectional roentgenography roentgenografía seccional.
serial roentgenography roentgenografía seriada.
roentgenologist *n.* roentgenólogo, -ga.
roentgenology *n.* roentgenología.
roentgenometer *n.* roentgenómetro.
roentgenometry *n.* roentgenometría.
roentgenoscope *n.* roentgenoscopio.
roentgenoscopy *n.* roentgenoscopia.
roentgenotherapy *n.* roentgenoterapia.
role *n.* rol.
complementary role rol complementario.
gender role rol de género.
non-complementary role rol no complementario.
sexual role rol sexual.
sick role rol de enfermo.
roll *n.* rollo.
iliac roll rollo ilíaco.

scleral roll rollo escleral.
romanopexy *n.* romanopexia.
romanoscope *n.* romanoscopio.
rongeur *n.* rongeur.
roof *n.* techo.
room *n.* sala.
  delivery room paritorio, sala de partos.
  emergency room (ER) sala de urgencias (SU).
  games room sala de juegos.
  intensive therapy room sala de cuidados intensivos.
  operating room (OR) sala de operaciones (SO).
  postdelivery room sala posparto.
  predelivery room sala de dilatación.
  recovery room sala de recuperación.
  recovery room (RR) sala de reanimación.
root *n.* raíz.
rootlet *n.* raicilla.
  flagellar rootlet raicilla flagelar.
ropalocytosis *n.* ropalocitosis.
rosacea *n.* rosácea.
  hypertrophic rosacea rosácea hipertrófica.
rosanilin *n.* rosanilina.
rosary *n.* rosario.
  rachitic rosary rosario raquítico.
rose *n.* rosa.
roseola *n.* roséola.
  epidemic roseola roséola epidémica.
  idiopathic roseola roséola idiopática.
  roseola infantilis roséola infantil.
  roseola infantum roséola infantil.
  syphilitic roseola roséola sifilítica.
rosette *n.* roseta.
rostral *adj.* rostral.
rostriform *adj.* rostriforme.
rot *n.* descomposición[4].
  Barcoo rot descomposición de Barcoo.
  black rot descomposición negra.
rotameter *n.* rotámetro.
rotation *n.* rotación.
  intestinal rotation rotación intestinal.
  molecular rotation rotación molecular.

  optical rotation rotación óptica.
  specific rotation rotación específica.
rotator *adj.* rotador, rotatorio, -ria.
Rotavirus Rotavirus.
rotoscoliosis *n.* rotoescoliosis.
rototome *n.* rotótomo.
rotula *n.* rótula.
round *n.* sesión.
  teaching round sesión docente.
route *n.* vía.
  route of administration vía de administración.
rubbing *n.* roce.
  friction rubbing roce de fricción.
  pericardial friction rubbing roce de fricción pericárdica.
  pericardial rubbing roce pericárdico.
  pleuritic rubbing roce pleurítico.
rubedo *n.* rubedo.
rubefacient *adj.* rubefaciente.
rubefaction *n.* rubefacción.
rubella *n.* rubella, rubéola.
rubeola *n.* rubella, rubéola.
  rubeola scarlatiniforma rubéola escarlatinosa.
  rubeola scarlatinosa rubéola escarlatinosa.
rubeosis *n.* rubeosis.
  rubeosis iridis rubeosis iris.
  rubeosis iridis diabetica rubeosis diabética del iris.
rubescent *adj.* rubescente.
rubiginous *adj.* rubiginoso, -sa.
Rubivirus Rubivirus.
rubor *n.* rubor.
rubriblast *n.* rubriblasto.
  pernicious anemia type rubriblast rubriblasto tipo anemia perniciosa.
rubric *adj.* rúbrico, -ca.
rubricyte *n.* rubricito.
rubrospinal *adj.* rubrospinal.
ructus eructo, ructus.
rudiment *n.* rudimento.
rudimentary *adj.* rudimental, rudimentario, -ria.
rufous *adj.* rufoso, -sa.

ruga arruga, ruga.
  ruga palatina arruga palatina.
  ruga vaginale arruga vaginal.
rugine *n.* raspadera.
rugitus rugitus.
rugose *adj.* rugoso, -sa.
rugosity *n.* rugosidad.
rugous *adj.* rugoso, -sa.
rule *n.* norma[1], regla[2].
  Abegg's rule regla de Abegg.
  Cowling's rule regla de Cowling.
  Goriaew's rule regla de Goriaew.
  Haase's rule regla de Haase.
  His' rule regla de His.
  Jackson's rule regla de Jackson.
  Le Bel-van't Hoff rule regla de Le Bel-van't Hoff.
  Liebermeister's rule regla de Liebermeister.
  Nägele's rule regla de Nägele.
  Ogino-Knaus rule regla de Ogino-Knaus.
  phase rule regla de fase.
  Prentice's rule regla de Prentice.
  Quetelet's rule regla de Quetelet.
  Rolleston's rule regla de Rolleston.
  rule of bigeminy regla de bigeminia.
  rule of outlet regla del conducto de salida.
  Schütz rule regla de Schütz.
  Young's rule regla de Young.
rumination *n.* rumiación.
Ruminococcus Ruminococcus.
rump *n.* rabadilla.
rupia *n.* rupia.
  rupia escharotica rupia escarótica.
rupial *adj.* rupial.
rupioid *adj.* rupiode.
rupture *n.* rotura, ruptura.
rush *n.* oleada.
rust *n.* orín.
rutidosis *n.* rutidosis.
rutilism *n.* rutilismo.
rutin *n.* rutina[2].
rutoside *n.* rutósido.

Ss

S romanum *n* S ilíaca del colon, S romana del colon.

saburra *n.* saburra.

saburral *adj.* saburral.

sac *n.* bolsa5, saccus, saco.

  amniotic sac bolsa amniótica.

saccade *n.* sacudida.

saccadic *adj.* sacádico, -ca.

saccate *adj.* enquistado, -da.

saccharated *adj.* sacarolado, -da, sacarólico, -ca.

saccharephidrosis *n.* sacarefidrosis.

sacchariferous *adj.* sacarífero, -ra.

saccharification *n.* sacarificación.

saccharimeter *n.* sacarímetro.

saccharin *n.* sacarina.

saccharine *adj.* sacarino, -na.

saccharogalactorrhea *n.* sacarogalactorrea.

saccharolytic *adj.* sacarolítico, -ca.

saccharometabolic *adj.* saracometabólico, -ca.

saccharometabolism *n.* sacarometabolismo.

saccharometer *n.* sacarómetro.

Saccharomyces sacaromiceto, Saccharomyces.

Saccharomycetacea Saccharomycetacea.

saccharomycetic *adj.* sacaromicético, -ca.

saccharomycetolysis *n.* sacaromicetólisis.

Saccharomycopsis Saccharomycopsis.

saccharomycosis *n.* sacaromicosis.

saccharuria *n.* sacaruria.

sacciform *adj.* sacciforme, saculiforme.

saccular *adj.* sacular.

sacculated *adj.* saculado, -da.

sacculation *n.* saculación.

  sacculation of the colon saculación del colon.

saccule *n.* sáculo.

sacculocochlear *adj.* saculococlear.

sacculus *n.* sáculo.

saccus *n.* saccus, saco.

sacrad sacrad.

sacral *adj.* sacral.

sacralgia *n.* sacralgia.

sacralization *n.* sacralización.

sacrectomy *n.* sacrectomía.

sacroanterior *adj.* sacroanterior.

sacroarthogenic *adj.* sacroartrógeno, -na.

sacrococcygeal *adj.* sacrococcígeo, -a.

sacrococcyx *n.* sacrocóccix.

sacrocoxalgia *n.* sacrocoxalgia.

sacrocoxitis *n.* sacrocoxitis.

sacrodynia *n.* sacrodinia.

sacroiliac *adj.* sacroilíaco, -ca.

sacroiliitis *n.* sacroileítis, sacroilitis.

sacrolisthesis *n.* sacrolistesis.

sacrolumbar *adj.* sacrolumbar.

sacroperineal *adj.* sacroperineal.

sacroposterior *adj.* sacroposterior.

sacrosciatic *adj.* sacrociático, -ca.

sacrospinal *adj.* sacroespinal, sacroespinoso, -sa, sacrospinoso, -sa.

sacrospinalis *adj.* sacroespinoso, -sa, sacrospinoso, -sa.

sacrotomy *n.* sacrotomía.

sacrotransverse *adj.* sacrotransverso, -sa.

sacrouterine *adj.* sacrouterino, -na.

sacrovertebral *adj.* sacrovertebral.

sacrum *n.* sacro.

  tilted sacrum sacro inclinado.

sactosalpinx *n.* sactosálpinx.

sadism *n.* sadismo.

  anal sadism sadismo anal.

  oral sadism sadismo oral.

  sexual sadism sadismo sexual.

sadist *n.* sádico[1], -ca.

sadistic *adj.* sádico[2], -ca.

sadness *n.* tristeza.

sadomasochism *n.* sadomasoquismo.

sadomasochistic *adj.* sadomasoquista.

safu *n.* safu.

sagittal *adj.* sagital.

sal *n.* sal.

salicylate *v.* salicilar, salicilatar.

salicylemia *n.* salicilemia.

salicylism *n.* salicilismo.

salicyltherapy *n.* saliciloterapia, salicilterapia.

salient *n.* saliente.

salifiable *adj.* salificable.

salify *v.* salificar.

salimeter *n.* salímetro.

saline *adj.* salino, -na.

salinometer *n.* salinómetro.

saliva *n.* saliva.

  artificial saliva saliva artificial.

  chorda saliva saliva cordal, saliva de la cuerda.

  ganglionic saliva saliva ganglionar.

  lingual saliva saliva lingual.

  parotid saliva saliva parótida, saliva parotídea.

  resting saliva saliva en reposo.

  ropy saliva saliva filante.

  sublingual saliva saliva sublingual.

  submaxilar saliva saliva submaxilar.

  sympathetic saliva saliva simpática.

salivant *adj.* salivante.

salivaria *n.* salivaria.

salivarian *adj.* salivariano, -na.

salivary *adj.* salival.

salivate *v.* salivar.

salivation *n.* salivación.

salivator *adj.* salivador, -ra.

salivatory *adj.* salivatorio, -ria.

salivolithiasis *n.* salivolitiasis.

salmonella *n.* salmonela.

Salmonella Salmonella.

salmonellosis *n.* salmonelosis.

salpingectomy *n.* salpingectomía.

  abdominal salpingectomy salpingectomía abdominal.

salpingemphraxis *n.* salpingenfraxis.

salpingian *adj.* salpíngeo, -a, salpingiano, -na.

salpingioma *n.* salpingioma.

salpinglon *n.* salpinglón.

salpingitic *adj.* salpingítico, -ca.

salpingitis *n.* salpingitis.

  chronic interstitial salpingitis salpingitis intersticial crónica.

  chronic vegetating salpingitis salpingitis vegetativa crónica.

  eustachian salpingitis salpingitis de Eustaquio.

  foreign body salpingitis salpingitis por cuerpo extraño.

  gonococcal salpingitis salpingitis gonocócica.

  gonorrheal salpingitis salpingitis gonorreica.

  hemorrhagic salpingitis salpingitis hemorrágica.

  hypertrophic salpingitis salpingitis hipertrófica.

  mural salpingitis salpingitis mural.

  nodular salpingitis salpingitis nodular.

  parenchymatous salpingitis salpingitis parenquimatosa.

  pseudofollicular salpingitis salpingitis seudofolicular.

  purulent salpingitis salpingitis purulenta, salpingitis serosa.

  pyogenic salpingitis salpingitis piógena.

  salpingitis isthmica nodosa salpingitis ístmica nudosa.

  tuberculous salpingitis salpingitis tuberculosa.

salpingocatheterism *n.* salpingocateterismo.

salpingocele *n.* salpingocele.

salpingocyesis *n.* salpingociesis.

salpingography *n.* salpingografía.

salpingolithiasis *n.* salpingolitiasis.

salpingolysis *n.* salpingólisis.

salpingo-oophorectomy *n.* salpingooforectomía.

salpingo-oophoritis *n.* salpingooforitis.

salpingo-oophorocele *n.* salpingooforocele.

salpingo-ovariectomy *n.* salpingoovariectomía.

salpingoperitonitis *n.* salpingoperitonitis.

salpingopexy *n.* salpingopexia.

salpingopharyngeal *adj.* salpingofaríngeo, -a.

salpingopharyngeus *n.* salpingofaríngeo.

salpingoplasty *n.* salpingoplastia.

salpingorrhagia *n.* salpingorragia.

salpingorrhaphy *n.* salpingorrafia.

salpingoscope *n.* salpingoscopio.

salpingoscopy *n.* salpingoscopia.

salpingostaphyline *adj.* salpingoestafilino, -na.

salpingostomy *n.* salpingostomía.

salpingotomy *n.* salpingotomía.

salpinx *n.* salpinge, salpinx, sálpinx.

salt *n.* sal.

saltation *n.* saltación.

saltatorial *adj.* saltatorio, -ria.
saltatoric *adj.* saltatorio, -ria.
saltatory *adj.* saltatorio, -ria.
salubrious *adj.* salubre.
salubrity *n.* salubridad.
saluresis *n.* saluresis.
saluretic *adj.* salurético, -ca.
salutary *adj.* saludable, salutífero, -ra.
sample *n.* muestra.
　biased sample muestra sesgada.
　random sample muestra al azar.
sampling *n.* muestreo, toma.
　chorionic villi sampling toma de muestras de las vellosidades coriónicas.
　random sampling muestreo aleatorio.
sanative *adj.* sanativo, -va.
sanatorium *n.* sanatorio.
sane *n.* cuerdo, -da.
sanguicolous *adj.* sanguícola.
sanguifacient *adj.* sanguifaciente.
sanguiferous *adj.* sanguífero, -ra.
sanguification *n.* sanguificación.
sanguimotor *adj.* sanguimotor, -ra.
sanguine *adj.* sanguíneo, -a.
sanguineous *adj.* sanguíneo, -a.
sanguinolent *adj.* sanguinolento, -ta.
sanguinopoietic *adj.* sanguinopoyético, -ca.
sanguinopurulent *adj.* sanguinopurulento, -ta.
sanguinous *adj.* sanguinoso, -sa.
sanguivorous *adj.* sanguívoro, -ra.
sanies *n.* sanies.
saniopurulent *adj.* saniopurulento, -ta.
sanioserous *adj.* sanioseroso, -sa.
sanious *adj.* sanioso, -sa.
sanitary *adj.* sanitario, -ria.
sanitation *n.* saneamiento, sanidad.
sanitize *v.* sanear.
sanity *n.* cordura, sanidad.
saphena *n.* safena.
saphenectomy *n.* safenectomía.
saphenous *adj.* safeno, -na.
sapid *adj.* sápido, -da.
sapo *n.* jabón.
　sapo domesticus jabón doméstico.
　sapo mollis jabón blando.
　sapo mollis medicinalis jabón medicinal blando.
　sapo viridis jabón verde.
saponaceous *adj.* saponáceo, -a.
saponatus *adj.* jabonoso, -sa.
saponification *n.* saponificación.
sapophore *n.* sapóforo.
sapphism *n.* safismo.
sapremia *n.* sapremia.
saprobic *adj.* sapróbico, -ca.
saprodontia *n.* saprodoncia.
saprogenic *adj.* saprogénico, -ca.
saprogenous *adj.* saprógeno, - na.
sapronosis *n.* sapronosis.
saprophilous *adj.* saprófilo, -la.
saprophyte *n.* saprófilo, saprofito, saprófito.
saprophytic *adj.* saprofítico, -ca.
saprophytism *n.* saprofitismo.
saprozoic *adj.* saprozoico, -ca.
saprozoite *n.* saprozoíto.
saprozoonosis *n.* saprozoonosis.
Sarcina Sarcina.
sarcine *n.* sarcina.
sarcitis *n.* sarcitis.
sarcoadenoma *n.* sarcoadenoma.
sarcoblast *n.* sarcoblasto.
sarcocarcinoma *n.* sarcocarcinoma.
sarcocele *n.* sarcocele.
sarcocyst *n.* sarcocisto.

Sarcocystis Sarcocystis.
sarcocystosis *n.* sarcocistosis.
sarcocyte *n.* sarcocito.
Sarcodina Sarcodina.
sarcoenchondroma *n.* sarcoencondroma.
sarcogenic *adj.* sarcogénico, -ca, sarcógeno, -na.
sarcohydrocele *n.* sarcohidrocele.
sarcoid *n.* sarcoide.
　Boeck's sarcoid sarcoide de Boeck.
　Carier-Roussy sarcoid sarcoide de Carier-Roussy.
　sarcoid of Boeck sarcoide de Boeck.
　Schaumann's sarcoid sarcoide de Schaumann.
　Spiegler-Fendt sarcoid sarcoide de Spiegler-Fendt.
sarcoidosis *n.* sarcoidosis.
　hypercalcemic sarcoidosis sarcoidosis hipercalcémica.
　muscular sarcoidosis sarcoidosis muscular.
　sarcoidosis cordis sarcoidosis cardíaca, sarcoidosis cordis.
sarcolemma *n.* sarcolema.
sarcolemmic *adj.* sarcolémico, -ca.
sarcolemmous *adj.* sarcolemoso, -sa.
sarcology *n.* sarcología.
sarcolysis *n.* sarcólisis.
sarcolyte *n.* sarcólito.
sarcolytic *adj.* sarcolítico, -ca.
sarcoma *n.* sarcoma.
　Abernethy's sarcoma sarcoma de Abernethy.
　adipose sarcoma sarcoma adiposo.
　alveolar soft part sarcoma sarcoma alveolar de las partes blandas.
　ameloblastic sarcoma sarcoma ameloblástico.
　angiolithic sarcoma sarcoma angiolítico.
　botryoid sarcoma sarcoma botrioide, sarcoma botrioideo, sarcoma botrioides.
　chloromatous sarcoma sarcoma cloromatoso.
　chondroblastic sarcoma sarcoma condroblástico.
　embryonal sarcoma sarcoma embrionario.
　endometrial stromal sarcoma sarcoma del estroma endometrial, sarcoma estrómico endometrial.
　Ewing's sarcoma sarcoma de Ewing.
　fascial sarcoma sarcoma fascial.
　fascicular sarcoma sarcoma fasciculado.
　fibroblastic sarcoma sarcoma fibroblástico.
　giant cell sarcoma sarcoma de células gigantes, sarcoma gigantocelular.
　granulocytic sarcoma sarcoma granulocítico.
　Hodgkin's sarcoma sarcoma de Hodgkin.
　idiopathic multiple pigmented hemorrhagic sarcoma sarcoma hemorrágico pigmentado idiopático simple.
　immunoblastic sarcoma sarcoma inmunoblástico.
　immunoblastic sarcoma of B cells sarcoma inmunoblástico de células B.
　immunoblastic sarcoma of T cells sarcoma inmunoblástico de células T.
　juxtacortical osteogenic sarcoma sarcoma osteogénico yuxtacortical.
　Kaposi's sarcoma sarcoma de Kaposi.
　Kupffer cell sarcoma sarcoma de células de Kupffer.
　leukocytic sarcoma sarcoma leucocítico.
　lymphatic sarcoma sarcoma linfático.
　medullary sarcoma sarcoma medular.
　melanotic sarcoma sarcoma melanótico.
　mixed cell sarcoma sarcoma de células mixtas.
　multiple idiopathic hemorrhagic sarcoma sarcoma hemorrágico idiopático múltiple.
　myelogenic sarcoma sarcoma mielógeno.

　osteoblastic sarcoma sarcoma osteoblástico.
　osteogenic sarcoma sarcoma osteogénico.
　parosteal sarcoma sarcoma parósteo.
　periosteal sarcoma sarcoma perióstico.
　polymorphous sarcoma sarcoma polimorfo.
　pseudo-Kaposi sarcoma sarcoma seudo-Kaposi.
　reticulum cell sarcoma sarcoma de células reticulares.
　reticulum cell sarcoma of the brain sarcoma reticulocítico, sarcoma reticuloendotelial.
　round cell sarcoma sarcoma de células redondas.
　sarcoma botryoides sarcoma botrioide, sarcoma botrioideo, sarcoma botrioides.
　sarcoma colli uteri hydropicum papillare sarcoma hidrópico papilar del cuello uterino.
　spindle cell sarcoma sarcoma de células fusiformes, sarcoma fusocelular.
　synovial sarcoma sarcoma sinovial.
　telangiectatic sarcoma sarcoma osteogénico telangiectático, sarcoma telangiectásico.
　X-ray sarcoma radiosarcoma.
sarcomagenesis *n.* sarcomagénesis.
sarcomagenic *adj.* sarcomagénico, -ca, sarcomágeno, -na.
sarcomastosis *n.* sarcomatosis.
sarcomatoid *adj.* sarcomatoide, sarcomatoideo, -a.
sarcomatous *adj.* sarcomatoso, -sa.
sarcomelanin *n.* sarcomelanina.
sarcomere *n.* sarcómera, sarcómero.
sarconeme *n.* sarconema.
sarconphalocele *n.* sarconfalocele.
Sarcophagidae Sarcophagidae.
sarcoplasm *n.* sarcoplasma.
sarcoplasmic *adj.* sarcoplásmico, -ca.
sarcoplast *n.* sarcoplasto.
sarcopoietic *adj.* sarcopoyético, -ca.
Sarcoptes Sarcoptes.
sarcoptic *adj.* sarcóptico, -ca.
sarcoptid *n.* sarcóptido.
sarcoptidosis *n.* sarcoptidosis.
sarcosinemia *n.* sarcosinemia.
sarcosis *n.* sarcosis.
Sarcosporidia Sarcosporidia.
sarcosporidiasis *n.* sarcosporidiasis.
sarcosporidiosis *n.* sarcosporidiasis, sarcosporidiosis.
sarcosporidium *n.* sarcosporidio.
sarcostosis *n.* sarcosteosis, sarcostosis.
sarcostyle *n.* sarcostilo.
sarcotherapeutics *n.* sarcoterapia.
sarcotherapy *n.* sarcoterapia.
sarcotic *adj.* sarcótico, -ca.
sarcotripsy *n.* sarcotripsia.
sarcotubules *n.* sarcotúbulos.
sarcous *adj.* sarcoso, -sa.
sarsapogenin *n.* zarzasapogenina.
satellite *n.* satélite.
　chromosome satellite satélite cromosoma, satélite cromosómico.
　nucleolar satellite satélite nucleolar.
　perineuronal satellite satélite perineuronal.
satellitism *n.* satelitismo.
satellitosis *n.* satelitosis.
satiety *n.* saciedad.
saturated *adj.* saturado, -da.
saturation *n.* saturación.
　arterial oxygen saturation saturación arterial en oxígeno.
　central venous oxygen saturation (CVSO2) saturación venosa central de oxígeno (SVCO2).
　hemoglobin oxygen saturation saturación de oxígeno en la hemoglobina.

hemoglobin saturation saturación de hemoglobina.

iron saturation saturación de hierro.

oxygen saturation saturación de oxígeno.

oxyhemoglobin saturation saturación de oxihemoglobina.

secondary saturation saturación secundaria.

saturnine *adj.* saturnino, -na.

saturnism *n.* saturnismo.

saturnotherapy *n.* saturnoterapia.

satyriasis *n.* satiriasis.

saucerization *n.* aplanamiento[1], saucerización.

sauriasis *n.* sauriasis.

sauriderma *n.* sauridermia.

sauriosis *n.* sauriasis, sauriosis.

sauroderma *n.* sauridermia, saurodermia.

sauroid *adj.* sauroide.

saw *n.* sierra.

Adam's saw sierra de Adams.

amputating saw sierra de amputación.

bayonet saw sierra de bayoneta.

Butcher's saw sierra de Butcher.

cast saw sierra de escayola.

chain saw sierra de cadena.

crown saw sierra de corona.

Farabeuf's saw sierra de Farabeuf.

Gigli's saw sierra de Gigli.

Gigli's wire saw sierra de alambre de Gigli.

Hey's saw sierra de Hey.

hole saw sierra de perforación.

separating saw sierra de separación.

Shrady's saw sierra de Shrady, sierra subcutánea.

Stryker saw sierra de Stryker.

subcutaneous saw sierra de Shrady, sierra subcutánea.

scab *n.* escara[2].

scabetic *adj.* escabético, -ca, escabiético, -ca, escabioso, -sa.

scabicidal *adj.* escabicida.

scabicide *adj.* escabicida.

scabies *n.* escabiasis, sarna.

crusted scabies escabiasis costrosa.

Norway scabies escabiasis de Noruega, sarna de Noruega.

Norwegian scabies escabiasis de Noruega, sarna de Noruega.

scabietic *adj.* escabético, -ca, escabiético, -ca, escabioso, -sa, sarnoso, -sa.

scabieticide *n.* escabieticida.

scabrities scabrities.

scabrities unguium scabrities unguium.

scala *n.* rampa.

scalar *adj.* escalar.

scald *n.* escaldadura.

scale *n.* descamar, escala, escama[2], gama.

scalenectomy *n.* escalenectomía.

scalenotomy *n.* escalenotomía.

scaler *n.* escarificador[2], raspador.

deep scaler escarificador profundo.

double-ended scaler escarificador de doble filo.

hoe scaler escarificador de azada, raspador en azada.

sickle scaler escarificador en hoz.

sonic scaler raspador sónico.

superficial scaler escarificador superficial.

ultrasonic scaler escarificador ultrasónico.

wing scaler escarificador en ala.

scaling *n.* escarificación[2].

deep scaling escarificación profunda.

ultrasonic scaling escarificación ultrasónica.

scalp cuero cabelludo.

scalpel *n.* escalpelo.

scalpriform *adj.* escalpriforme.

scalprum *n.* escalpro.

scaly *adj.* escamoso, -sa.

scan *n.* rastreo, scan.

isotopic body scan in thyroid carcinoma rastreo isotópico en el carcinoma de tiroides.

isotopic scan rastreo isotópico.

linear scan rastreo lineal.

Meckel scan rastreo de Meckel.

ventilation-perfusion scan rastreo de ventilación-perfusión.

scanner *n.* escáner.

scanning *n.* barrido.

scanography *n.* escanografía.

scapha scapha.

scaphocephalic *adj.* escafocefálico, -ca.

scaphocephalism *n.* escafocefalismo.

scaphocephalous *adj.* escafocéfalo, -la.

scaphocephaly *n.* escafocefalia.

scaphohydrocephalus *n.* escafohidrocéfalo.

scaphohydrocephaly *n.* escafohidrocefalia.

scaphoid *adj.* escafoide, escafoideo, -a, escafoides.

scaphoiditis *n.* escafoidiris.

scapula *n.* escápula.

alar scapula escápula alada, escápula alata, scapula alata.

floating scapula escápula flotante.

Graves' scapula escápula de Graves.

scaphoid scapula escápula escafoide, escápula escafoidea.

scapula alata escápula alada, escápula alata, scapula alata.

winged scapula escápula alada, escápula alata, scapula alata.

scapulalgia *n.* escapulalgia.

scapular *adj.* escapular.

scapulary *n.* escapulario.

scapulectomy *n.* escapulectomía.

scapuloanterior *adj.* escapuloanterior.

scapuloclavicular *adj.* escapuloclavicular.

scapulodynia *n.* escapulodinia.

scapulohumeral *adj.* escapulohumeral.

scapulopexy *n.* escapulopexia.

scapuloposterior *adj.* escapuloposterior.

scar *n.* cicatriz.

cigarette-paper scar cicatriz en papel de cigarrillo.

hypertrophic scar cicatriz hipertrófica.

papyraceous scar cicatriz papirácea.

shilling scar cicatriz en chelín.

scarification *n.* escarificación[1].

scarificator *n.* escarificador[1].

scarlatina *n.* escarlatina.

anginose scarlatina escarlatina anginosa.

latent scarlatina escarlatina frustrada, escarlatina latente.

puerperal scarlatina escarlatina puerperal.

scarlatina anginosa escarlatina anginosa.

scarlatina hemorrhagica escarlatina hemorrágica.

scarlatina latens escarlatina frustrada, escarlatina latente.

scarlatina maligna escarlatina maligna.

scarlatina rheumatica escarlatina reumática.

scarlatina simplex escarlatina simple.

scarlatinal *adj.* escarlatínico, -ca.

scarlatinella *n.* escarlatinela.

scarlatiniform *adj.* escarlatiniforme.

scarlatinoid *adj.* escarlatinoide.

scatemia *n.* escatemia, escoretemia.

scatologia *n.* escatología.

scatologic *adj.* escatológico, -ca.

scatology *n.* escatología.

telephone scatology escatología telefónica.

scatoma *n.* escatoma.

scatophagy *n.* escatofagia.

scatophilia *n.* escatofilia.

scatoscopy *n.* escatoscopia.

scatter *n.* dispersión[2].

Compton scatter dispersión de Compton.

Thompson scatter dispersión de Thompson.

scattergram *n.* difusograma, dispersograma.

scattering *n.* dispersión[2].

scelalgia *n.* escelalgia.

scelotyrbe *n.* escelotirba, escelotirbe.

schema *n.* esquema.

schematic *adj.* esquemático, -ca.

schematograph *n.* esquematógrafo.

scheme *n.* esquema.

scheroma *n.* esqueroma.

schiencephaly *n.* esquiencefalia.

schindylesis *n.* esquindilesis.

schistasis *n.* esquistasis.

schistocelia *n.* esquistocelia.

schistocephalus *n.* esquistocéfalo.

schistocormia *n.* esquistocormia.

schistocormus *n.* esquistocormo.

schistocystis *n.* esquistocistis.

schistocyte *n.* esquistocito.

schistocytosis *n.* esquistocitosis.

schistoglossia *n.* esquistoglosia.

schistomelia *n.* esquistomelia.

schistomelus *n.* esquistomelo.

schistometer *n.* esquistómetro.

schistoprosopia *n.* esquistoprosopia.

schistoprosopus *n.* esquistoprosopo.

schistorhachis *n.* esquistorraquis.

schistosis *n.* esquistosis.

Schistosoma Schistosoma.

schistosomal *adj.* esquistosomiásico, -ca.

schistosome *n.* esquistosoma, tecosoma.

schistosomia *n.* esquistosomía.

schistosomiasis *n.* esquistosomiasis.

asiatic schistosomiasis esquistosomiasis asiática.

bladder schistosomiasis esquistosomiasis vesical.

cutaneous schistosomiasis esquistosomiasis cutánea.

ectopic schistosomiasis esquistosomiasis ectópica.

hepatic schistosomiasis esquistosomiasis hepática.

intestinal schistosomiasis esquistosomiasis intestinal.

Japanese schistosomiasis esquistosomiasis japonesa, esquistosomiasis japonica.

Manson's schistosomiasis esquistosomiasis de Manson, esquistosomiasis mansoni.

Oriental schistosomiasis esquistosomiasis oriental.

pulmonary schistosomiasis esquistosomiasis pulmonar.

schistosomiasis haematobium esquistosomiasis haematobia, esquistosomiasis haematobium.

schistosomiasis intercalatum esquistosomiasis intercalatum.

schistosomiasis japonica esquistosomiasis japonesa, esquistosomiasis japonica.

schistosomiasis mansoni esquistosomiasis de Manson, esquistosomiasis mansoni.

schistosomiasis mekongi esquistosomiasis del Mekong.

urinary schistosomiasis esquistosomiasis urinaria.

visceral schistosomiasis esquistosomiasis visceral.

schistosomicidal *adj.* esquistosomicida.

schistosomulum *n.* esquistosómula.

schistosomus *n.* esquistosomo.

schistosternia *n.* esquistosternia.
schistothorax *n.* esquistotórax.
schistotrachelus *n.* esquistotraquelo.
schizencephalic *adj.* esquizencefálico, -ca.
schizencephaly *n.* esquizencefalia.
schizoaffective *adj.* esquizoafectivo, -va.
Schizoblastosporium Schizoblastosporium.
schizocephalia *n.* esquizocefalia.
schizocytosis *n.* esquizocitosis.
schizoencephalia *n.* esquizoencefalia.
schizogenesis *n.* esquizogénesis.
schizogenous *adj.* esquizógeno, -na.
schizogony *n.* esquizogonia.
schizogyria *n.* esquizogiria.
schizoid *adj.* esquizoide.
schizokinesis *n.* esquizocinesia.
schizomycete *n.* esquizomiceto.
schizomycosis *n.* esquizomicosis.
schizont *n.* esquizonte.
schizonticide *n.* esquizonticida.
schizonychia *n.* esquizoniquia.
schizophasia *n.* esquizofasia.
schizophrenia *n.* esquizofrenia.
  acute schizophrenia esquizofrenia aguda.
  catatonic schizophrenia esquizofrenia catatónica.
  childhood schizophrenia esquizofrenia infantil.
  disorganized schizophrenia esquizofrenia desorganizada.
  hebephrenic schizophrenia esquizofrenia hebefrénica.
  latent schizophrenia esquizofrenia latente.
  paranoid schizophrenia esquizofrenia paranoide.
  pseudoneurotic schizophrenia esquizofrenia seudoneurótica.
  residual schizophrenia esquizofrenia residual.
  simple schizophrenia esquizofrenia simple.
  undifferentiated schizophrenia esquizofrenia indiferenciada.
schizophrenic *adj.* esquizofrénico, -ca.
schizophreniform *adj.* esquizofreniforme.
Schizopyrenida Schizopyrenida.
schizothorax *n.* esquizotórax.
schizothymia *n.* esquizotimia.
schizotrichia *n.* esquizotriquia.
schizotropic *adj.* esquizotrópico, -ca.
schizotrypanosomiasis *n.* esquizotripanosomiasis.
schizotypal *adj.* esquizotípico, -ca.
schizozoite *n.* esquizozoíto.
schlusskoagulum *n.* schlusskoagulum.
Schultze mode *n.* modo Schultze.
schwannitis *n.* schwannitis.
schwannoglioma *n.* schwannoglioma.
schwannoma *n.* schwannoma, schwanoma.
  granular cell schwannoma schwannoma de células granulosas.
schwannosis *n.* schwannosis.
scialyscope *n.* escialiscopio.
sciatica *n.* ciática.
scieropia *n.* escieropía.
scinticisternography *n.* centellocisternografía.
scintigram *n.* centellograma, escintigrama.
scintigraphic *adj.* centellográfico, -ca.
scintigraphy *n.* centellografía, escintigrafía.
scintillascope *n.* centelloscopio, escintilascopio.
scintillation *n.* centelleo, escintilación.
scintillator *n.* centelleador.
scintillometer *n.* centellómetro.
scintiphotography *n.* centellofotografía.
scintiscan *n.* centellobarrido.
sciopody *n.* esciopodia.

scirrhencanthis *n.* escirrencantis.
scirrhoid *adj.* escirroide.
scirrhoma *n.* escirroma.
scirrhopthalmia *n.* escirroftalmía.
scirrhosity *n.* escirrosidad.
scirrhous *adj.* escirroso, -sa.
scirrhus *n.* escirro.
scission *n.* escisión^2.
scissors *n.* tijeras.
  canalicular scissors tijeras canalicular.
  cannula scissors tijeras de cánula.
  craniotomy scissors tijeras de craneotomía.
  Fox scissors tijeras de Fox.
  Liston's scissors tijeras de Liston.
  Smellie's scissors tijeras de Smellie.
  Wecker's scissors tijeras de Wecker.
scissura *n.* cisura.
sclera *n.* esclera.
scleradenitis *n.* escleradenitis.
scleral *adj.* escleral.
scleratitis *n.* escleratitis, esclerotitis.
scleratogenous *adj.* escleratógeno, -na.
sclerectasia *n.* esclerectasia.
sclerectoiridectomy *n.* esclerectoiridectomía.
sclerectoiridodialysis *n.* esclerectoiridodiálisis.
sclerectome *n.* escleréctomo.
sclerectomy *n.* esclerectomía.
scleredema *n.* escleredema.
  scleredema adultorum escleredema del adulto.
sclerema *n.* esclerema.
  sclerema adiposum esclerema adiposo.
  sclerema neonatorum esclerema de los recién nacidos, esclerema neonatal.
sclerencephaly *n.* esclerencefalia.
scleriasis *n.* escleriasis.
scleriritomy *n.* escleriritomía, escleroiritomía.
scleritis *n.* escleritis.
  annular scleritis escleritis anular.
  anterior necrotizing scleritis escleritis necrosante anterior.
  anterior scleritis escleritis anterior.
  brawny scleritis escleritis marginal.
  deep scleritis escleritis profunda.
  diffuse scleritis escleritis difusa.
  gelatinous scleritis escleritis gelatinosa.
  malignant scleritis escleritis maligna.
  necrotizing scleritis escleritis necrosante, escleritis necrotizante.
  nodular scleritis escleritis nodular.
  posterior scleritis escleritis posterior.
scleroadipose *adj.* escleroadiposo, -sa.
scleroatrophy *n.* escleroatrofia.
scleroblastema *n.* escleroblastema.
scleroblastemic *adj.* escleroblastémico, -ca.
sclerocataracta *n.* esclerocatarata.
sclerochoroidal *adj.* esclerocoroideo, -a.
sclerochoroiditis *n.* esclerocoroiditis.
  anterior sclerochoroiditis esclerocoroiditis anterior.
  posterior sclerochoroiditis esclerocoroiditis posterior.
scleroconjunctival *adj.* escleroconjuntival.
scleroconjunctivitis *n.* escleroconjuntivitis.
sclerocornea *n.* esclerocórnea.
sclerocorneal *adj.* esclerocorneal.
sclerodactylia *n.* esclerodactilia.
sclerodactyly *n.* esclerodactilia.
scleroderma *n.* escirrosarca, escleremia, esclerodermia.
  circumscribed scleroderma esclerodermia circunscrita.
  diffuse scleroderma esclerodermia difusa.
  generalized scleroderma esclerodermia generalizada.

  linear scleroderma esclerodermia lineal.
  localized scleroderma esclerodermia localizada.
  systemic scleroderma esclerodermia sistémica.
sclerodermatitis *n.* esclerodermatitis, esclerodermitis.
sclerodermatous *adj.* esclerodermatoso, -sa.
sclerodermoid *adj.* esclerodermoide.
sclerodesmia *n.* esclerodesmia.
sclerogenic *adj.* esclerogénico, -ca.
sclerogenous *adj.* esclerógeno, -na.
sclerogummatous *adj.* esclerogomatoso, -sa, esclerogomoso, -sa.
scleroid *adj.* escleroide.
scleroiritis *n.* escleroiritis.
sclerokeratitis *n.* escleroqueratitis.
sclerokeratoiritis *n.* escleroqueratoiritis.
sclerokeratosis *n.* escleroqueratosis.
scleroma *n.* escleroma.
  respiratory scleroma escleroma respiratorio.
scleromalacia *n.* escleromalacia.
  scleromalacia perforans escleromalacia perforante.
scleromere *n.* esclerómero.
sclerometer *n.* esclerómetro.
scleromyxedema *n.* escleromixedema.
scleronychia *n.* escleroniquia, esclerotonixis.
scleronyxis *n.* escleronixis.
sclero-oophoritis *n.* esclero-ooforitis.
sclero-oothecitis *n.* esclerootecitis.
sclerophthalmia *n.* escleroftalmía, escleroftalmía.
scleroplasty *n.* escleroplastia.
scleroprotein *n.* escleroproteína.
sclerosal *adj.* escleroso, -sa.
sclerosant *adj.* esclerosante.
sclerosarcoma *n.* esclerosarcoma.
scleroscope *n.* escleroscopio.
sclerosed *adj.* esclerosado, -da.
sclerosing *adj.* esclerosante.
sclerosis *n.* esclerismo, escleropatía, esclerosis.
  Alzheimer's sclerosis esclerosis de Alzheimer.
  amyotrophic lateral sclerosis esclerosis lateral simétrica.
  amyotrophic lateral sclerosis (ALS) esclerosis lateral amiotrófica (ELA).
  anterolateral sclerosis esclerosis anterolateral.
  arterial sclerosis esclerosis arterial, esclerosis arteriocapilar.
  arteriocapillary sclerosis esclerosis arterial, esclerosis arteriocapilar.
  arteriolar sclerosis esclerosis arteriolar.
  bone sclerosis esclerosis ósea.
  Canavan's sclerosis esclerosis de Canavan.
  central areolar choroidal sclerosis esclerosis coroidal areolar central.
  combined sclerosis esclerosis combinada.
  dentinal sclerosis esclerosis dentinal, esclerosis dentinaria.
  diaphyseal sclerosis esclerosis diafisaria.
  diffuse infantile familial sclerosis esclerosis familiar infantil difusa.
  diffuse sclerosis esclerosis difusa.
  diffuse systemic sclerosis esclerosis sistémica difusa.
  disseminated sclerosis esclerosis diseminada.
  endocardial sclerosis esclerosis endocárdica.
  Erb's sclerosis esclerosis de Erb.
  familial centrolobar sclerosis esclerosis centrolobulillar familiar.
  focal glomerular sclerosis esclerosis glomerular focal.
  focal sclerosis esclerosis focal.

gastric sclerosis esclerosis gástrica.
glomerular sclerosis esclerosis glomerular.
hippocampal sclerosis esclerosis hipocámpica.
hyperplastic sclerosis esclerosis hiperplásica.
idiopathic hypercalcemic sclerosis of infants esclerosis hipercalcémica idiopática infantil.
insular sclerosis esclerosis insular.
intimal sclerosis esclerosis de la íntima.
laminar cortical sclerosis esclerosis cortical laminar.
lateral sclerosis esclerosis lateral.
lateral spinal sclerosis esclerosis espinal lateral.
lobar sclerosis esclerosis lobular.
mantle sclerosis esclerosis del manto.
Marie's sclerosis esclerosis de Marie.
menstrual sclerosis esclerosis menstrual.
mesial temporal sclerosis esclerosis del lóbulo temporal.
miliary sclerosis esclerosis miliar.
Mönckeberg's sclerosis esclerosis de Mönckeberg.
multiple sclerosis (MS) esclerosis múltiple (EM).
nodular sclerosis esclerosis nodular.
nuclear sclerosis esclerosis nuclear.
ovulational sclerosis esclerosis ovulatoria.
Pelizaeus-Merzbacher sclerosis esclerosis de Pelizaeus-Merzbacher.
physiologic sclerosis esclerosis fisiológica.
posterior sclerosis esclerosis posterior.
posterior spinal sclerosis esclerosis espinal posterior.
posterolateral sclerosis esclerosis posterolateral.
primary lateral sclerosis esclerosis lateral primaria.
progressive systemic sclerosis (PSS) esclerosis sistémica progresiva (ESP).
renal sclerosis esclerosis renal.
sclerosis corii esclerosis coriónica.
sclerosis cutanea esclerosis cutánea.
sclerosis of white matter esclerosis de la sustancia blanca.
subendocardial sclerosis esclerosis subendocárdica.
systemic sclerosis esclerosis sistémica.
tuberous sclerosis esclerosis tuberosa.
unicellular sclerosis esclerosis unicelular.
valvular sclerosis esclerosis valvular.
vascular sclerosis esclerosis vascular.
venous sclerosis esclerosis venosa.
ventrolateral sclerosis esclerosis ventrolateral.
scleroskeleton *n.* escleroesqueleto.
sclerostenosis *n.* escleroestenosis, esclerostenosis.
sclerostomy *n.* esclerostomía.
sclerotherapy *n.* escleroterapia.
sclerothrix *n.* esclerotrix.
sclerotic *adj.* esclerótico, -ca.
sclerotica *n.* esclerótica.
scleroticectomy *n.* escleroticectomía.
scleroticochoroiditis *n.* escleroticocoroiditis.
scleroticonyxis *n.* escleroticonixis.
scleroticopuncture *n.* escleroticopunción.
sclerotitis *n.* esclerotitis.
sclerotome *n.* esclerotoma, esclerótomo.
sclerotomy *n.* esclerotomía.
anterior sclerotomy esclerotomía anterior.
posterior sclerotomy esclerotomía posterior.
sclerotrichia *n.* esclerotriquia.
sclerotycotomy *n.* escleroticotomía.

sclerotylosis *n.* esclerotilosis.
sclerous *adj.* escleroso, -sa.
sclerozone *n.* esclerozona.
scoleciasis *n.* escoleciasis.
scoleciform *adj.* escoleciforme.
scolecoid *adj.* escolecoide.
scolex *n.* escólex.
scoliokyphosis *n.* escoliocifosis.
scoliometer *n.* escoliómetro.
scoliometry *n.* escoliometría.
scoliosis *n.* escoliosis.
antalgic scoliosis escoliosis antálgica, escoliosis antiálgica.
Brissaud's scoliosis escoliosis de Brissaud.
cicatricial scoliosis escoliosis cicatricial, escoliosis cicatrizal.
congenital scoliosis escoliosis congénita.
coxitic scoliosis escoliosis coxítica, escoliosis isquiática.
empyemic scoliosis escoliosis empiemática, escoliosis empiémica.
essential scoliosis escoliosis esencial.
habit scoliosis escoliosis habitual, escoliosis por hábito.
idiopathic scoliosis escoliosis idiopática.
inflammatory scoliosis escoliosis inflamatoria.
myopathic scoliosis escoliosis miopática.
neuropathic scoliosis escoliosis neuropática.
ocular scoliosis escoliosis ocular, escoliosis oftálmica.
ophthalmic scoliosis escoliosis ocular, escoliosis oftálmica.
osteopathic scoliosis escoliosis osteopática.
pain scoliosis escoliosis antálgica, escoliosis antiálgica.
paralytic scoliosis escoliosis paralítica.
postural scoliosis escoliosis postural.
rachitic scoliosis escoliosis raquítica.
rheumatic scoliosis escoliosis reumática.
sciatic scoliosis escoliosis ciática.
static scoliosis escoliosis estática.
structured scoliosis escoliosis estructurada.
syringomyelic scoliosis escoliosis siringomiélica.
scoliotic *adj.* escoliótico, -ca.
scoliotone *n.* escoliótono.
Scolopendra Scolopendra.
scolopsia *n.* escolopsia.
scoop *n.* cucharilla, legra.
Mulles' scoop legra de Mulles.
scopometer *n.* escopómetro.
scopometry *n.* escopometría.
scopophilia *n.* escopofilia, voyeurismo.
scopophobia *n.* escopofobia.
scoptolagnia *n.* escoptolagnia.
scoptophilia *n.* escoptofilia.
scoptophobia *n.* escopofobia, escoptofobia.
Scopulariopsis Scopulariopsis.
scorbutic *adj.* escorbútico, -ca.
scorbutigenic *adj.* escorbutigénico, -ca, escorbutígeno, -na.
scordinema *n.* escordinema.
scorpionism *n.* escorpionismo.
Scotobacteria Scotobacteria.
scotobacterium *n.* escotobacteria.
scotochromogenicity *n.* escotocromogenicidad.
scotoma *n.* escotoma.
absolute scotoma escotoma absoluto.
annular scotoma escotoma anular.
arcuate scotoma escotoma arqueado.
aural scotoma escotoma auditivo, escotoma aural, escotoma auricular.
Bjerrum's scotoma escotoma de Bjerrum.

cecocentral scotoma escotoma cecocentral.
central scotoma escotoma central.
centrocecal scotoma escotoma centrocecal.
color scotoma escotoma de color.
eclipse scotoma escotoma eclíptico.
flittering scotoma escotoma fluctuante.
glaucomatous nerve-fiber-bundle scotoma escotoma glaucomatoso de haces de fibras nerviosas.
hemianopic scotoma escotoma hemianópico.
insular scotoma escotoma insular.
negative scotoma escotoma negativo.
paracentral scotoma escotoma paracentral.
pericentral scotoma escotoma pericentral.
peripapillary scotoma escotoma peripapilar.
peripheral scotoma escotoma periférico.
positive scotoma escotoma positivo.
quadrantic scotoma escotoma cuadrántico.
relative scotoma escotoma relativo.
ring scotoma escotoma anular.
scintillating scotoma escotoma centelleante.
scotoma auris escotoma auditivo, escotoma aural, escotoma auricular.
Seidel's scotoma escotoma de Seidel.
sickle scotoma escotoma falciforme.
zonular scotoma escotoma zonular.
scotomagraph *n.* escotomatógrafo.
scotomatous *adj.* escotomatoso, -sa.
scotometer *n.* escotómetro.
scotometry *n.* escotometría.
scotomization *n.* escotomización.
scotopia *n.* escotopía, escotopsia.
scotopic *adj.* escotópico, -ca.
scototherapy *n.* escototerapia.
scratch *n.* rascadura.
screen *n.* pantalla.
Bjerrum screen pantalla de Bjerrum.
fluorescent screen pantalla fluorescente.
intensifying screen pantalla intensificadora.
tangent screen pantalla tangente.
screening *n.* detección, screening.
genetic screening detección selectiva genética.
multiphasic screening detección selectiva multifásica.
scrobiculate *adj.* escrobiculado, -da.
scrobilulus *n.* escrobículo.
scrofulide *n.* escrofúlide.
scrofuloderma *n.* escrofulodermia.
papular scrofuloderma escrofulodermia papulosa.
scrofuloderma gummosa escrofulodermia gomosa.
tuberculous scrofuloderma escrofulodermia tuberculosa.
ulcerative scrofuloderma escrofulodermia ulcerosa.
verrucous scrofuloderma escrofulodermia verrugosa.
scrofulosis *n.* escrofulosis.
scrofulotuberculosis *n.* escrofulotuberculosis.
scrotal *adj.* escrotal.
scrotectomy *n.* escrotectomía.
scrotiform *adj.* escrotiforme.
scrotitis *n.* escrotitis.
scrotocele *n.* escrotocele.
scrotoplasty *n.* escrotoplastia.
scrotum *n.* escroto.
scrupulosity *n.* escrupulosidad.
scurvy *n.* escorbuto.
Alpine scurvy escorbuto alpino, escorbuto de los Alpes.
hemorrhagic scurvy escorbuto hemorrágico.

infantile scurvy escorbuto infantil.
land scurvy escorbuto terrestre.
sea scurvy escorbuto marino, escorbuto marítimo.
scutate *adj.* escutado, -da.
scute *n.* escudo[1].
scutiform *adj.* escutiforme.
scutular *adj.* escutular.
scutulum escútula, scutulum.
scutum scutum.
scybalous *adj.* escibaloso, -sa.
scybalum *n.* escíbalo.
scyntography *n.* escintigrafía.
scyphiform *adj.* esciiforme.
scyphoid *adj.* escifoide.
scytoblastema *n.* escitoblastema.
seal[1] *n.* sellado, sello[2].
border seal sellado de bordes, sello de bordes.
double seal sello doble.
palatal seal sellado palatino, sellado palatino posterior.
peripheral seal sellado periférico.
posterior palatal seal sellado palatino, sellado palatino posterior, sello palatino posterior.
postpalatal seal sellado pospalatino.
tip seal sello terminal.
velopharyngeal seal sellado velofaríngeo, sello velofaríngeo.
seal[2] *v.* sellar, sembrar.
sealant *n.* sellador.
dental sealant sellador dental.
fissure sealant sellador de fisuras.
pit and fissure sealant sellador de huecos y fisuras.
seam *n.* costura.
pigment seam costura de pigmento.
searcher *n.* explorador[2].
searching *n.* investigación.
relation searching investigación de relación.
season *n.* estación[1].
seat *n.* asiento.
basal seat asiento basal.
sebaceous *adj.* sebáceo, -a.
sebaceus *adj.* sebáceo, -a.
sebiagogic *adj.* sebiagógico, -ca.
sebiferous *adj.* sebífero, -ra.
sebiparous *adj.* sebíparo, -ra.
sebolith *n.* sebolito.
seborrhea *n.* seborragia, seborrea.
concrete seborrhea seborrea concreta, seborrea costrosa.
eczematoid seborrhea seborrea eccematosa.
seborrhea adiposa seborrea adiposa.
seborrhea capitis seborrea capilar, seborrea capitis, seborrea de la cabeza.
seborrhea cerea seborrea cérea.
seborrhea corporis seborrea corporal.
seborrhea faciei seborrea de la cara, seborrea facial.
seborrhea nigra seborrea nigra, seborrea nigricans.
seborrhea of the face seborrea de la cara, seborrea facial.
seborrhea oleosa seborrea oleosa.
seborrhea sicca seborrea seca.
seborrhea squamosa neonatorum seborrea escamosa neonatal.
seborrheic *adj.* seborreico, -ca.
seborrhoid *n.* seborroide.
sebotropic *adj.* sebotrópico, -ca.
sebum *n.* sebo, sebum.
seclusion *n.* seclusión.
seclusion of the pupil seclusión de la pupila.
secodont *adj.* secodonto, -ta.
secondary *n.* secundario, -ria.

secreta *n.* secreta.
secretagogue *adj.* secretagogo, -ga.
secrete *v.* secretar, segregar.
secreted *adj.* secretado, -da.
secretion *n.* secreción.
apocrine secretion secreción apocrina.
autocrine secretion secreción autocrina.
bronchial secretion secreción bronquial.
external secretion secreción externa.
holocrine secretion secreción holocrina.
internal secretion secreción interna.
merocrine secretion secreción merocrina.
paracrine secretion secreción paracrina.
paralytic secretion secreción paralítica.
secretogogue *adj.* secretagogo, -ga.
secretoinhibitory *adj.* secretoinhibidor, -ra, secretoinhibitorio, -ria.
secretomotor *adj.* secretomotor, -ra.
secretor *n.* secretor.
secretory *adj.* secretor, -ra.
sectarian *adj.* sectario, -ria.
sectile *n.* séctil.
sectio *n.* sección.
sectio alta sección alta, sección hipogástrica, sección suprapúbica.
sectio lateralis sección lateral.
sectio mediana sección mediana.
section *n.* corte, sección.
abdominal section sección abdominal.
celloidin section sección de celoidina.
cervical cesarean section sección cesárea cervical.
cesarean section sección cesárea.
classical cesarean section sección cesárea clásica.
coronal section sección coronal.
C-section sección C.
detached cranial section sección craneal separada.
frontal section corte frontal, sección frontal.
frozen section corte congelado, corte por congelación, sección congelada.
Latzko's cesarean section sección cesárea de Latzko.
low cervical cesarean section sección cesárea cervical baja, sección cesárea cervical inferior.
lower segment cesarean section sección cesárea del segmento inferior.
Munro Kerr cesarean section sección cesárea de Munro Kerr.
paraffin section corte de parafina, corte en parafina.
perineal section sección perineal.
Pitres' section corte de Pitres.
pituitary stalk section sección del tallo hipofisario.
Saemisch's section sección de Saemisch.
sagittal section sección sagital.
serial section corte en serie.
thin section sección fina.
transversal section corte transversal.
ultrathin section sección ultrafina.
sector *n.* sector.
sectorial *adj.* sectorial.
secundigravida *n.* secundigrávida.
secundina uteri *n.* secundina uterina.
secundines *n.* secundinas.
secundipara *n.* secundípara.
secundiparity *n.* secundiparidad.
sedation *n.* sedación.
sedative *n.* sedante, sedativo, -va.
cardiac sedative sedante cardíaco.
cerebral sedative sedante cerebral.
gastric sedative sedante gástrico.

general sedative sedante general.
intestinal sedative sedante intestinal.
nerve trunk sedative sedante de tronco nervioso.
nervous sedative sedante nervioso.
respiratory sedative sedante respiratorio.
spinal sedative sedante raquídeo.
vascular sedative sedante vascular.
sedativus *n.* sedante, sedativo, -va.
sedentary *adj.* sedentario, -ria.
sediment *n.* sedimento.
urinary sediment sedimento urinario.
sedimentable *adj.* sedimentable.
sedimentation *n.* sedimentación.
erythrocyte sedimentation sedimentación eritrocitaria, sedimentación eritrocítica.
formalin ether sedimentation (Ritchie) sedimentación con formol y éter (Ritchie).
sedimentator *n.* sedimentador.
seduction *n.* seducción.
seed *n.* semilla.
radiogold seed (198 Au) semilla de oro radiactivo (198 Au).
seeding *n.* siembra.
segment *n.* segmento.
segmental *adj.* segmentario, -ria.
segmentation *n.* segmentación.
haustral segmentation segmentación haustral.
segmenter *n.* segmentador.
Segmentina Segmentina.
segmentum *n.* segmento.
segregation *n.* segregación.
segregator *n.* segregador.
seisesthesia *n.* seisestesia.
seismesthesia *n.* seismestesia.
seismocardiogram *n.* seismocardiograma.
seismocardiography *n.* seismocardiografía.
seismotherapy *n.* seismoterapia.
seizure *n.* acceso[2], convulsión, crisis[1].
absence seizure crisis de ausencia.
akinetic seizure convulsión acinética.
anosognosic seizure crisis anosognósica.
atonic seizure crisis atónica.
clonic seizure convulsión clónica.
convulsive seizure crisis convulsiva.
epileptic seizure crisis epiléptica.
febrile seizure convulsión febril.
focal seizure convulsión focal.
generalized seizure crisis generalizada.
generalized tonic-clonic seizure convulsión tónico-clónica generalizada.
grand mal seizure crisis de gran mal.
hysterical seizure convulsión histérica, convulsión histeroide.
Jacksonian seizure crisis jacksoniana.
motor seizure crisis motora.
myoclonic seizure crisis mioclónica.
neonatal seizure convulsión neonatal.
partial complex seizure crisis parcial compleja.
partial seizure convulsión parcial, crisis parcial.
partial simple seizure crisis parcial simple.
petit mal seizure crisis de pequeño mal.
secondarily generalized seizure crisis generalizada secundaria.
tonic seizure convulsión tónica.
tonic-clonic seizure crisis generalizada tónico-clónica.
selection *n.* selección.
artificial selection selección artificial.
cytologic selection selección citológica.
directional selection selección direccional.
disruptive selection selección disruptiva.

diversifying selection selección diversificante.
medical selection selección médica.
multiphasic selection selección multifásica.
multiple selection selección múltiple.
natural selection selección natural.
neonatal selection selección neonatal.
prenatal selection selección prenatal.
progeny selection selección de descendencia.
random selection selección aleatoria.
sexual selection selección sexual.
stabilizing selection selección estabilizante.
truncate selection selección sesgada, selección truncada.
selective *adj.* selectivo, -va.
selectivity *n.* selectividad.
selene *n.* semiluna.
selene unguium selene unguium.
Selenomonas Selenomonas.
selenosis *n.* selenosis.
self *n.* sí mismo.
self-awareness *n.* autoconciencia.
self-control *n.* autocontrol.
self-differentiation *n.* autodiferenciación.
self-digestion *n.* autodigestión.
self-discovery *n.* autodescubrimiento.
self-fertilization *n.* autofecundación.
self-knowledge *n.* autoconocimiento.
self-limited *adj.* autolimitado, -da.
self-poisoning *n.* autoenvenenamiento.
self-stimulation *n.* autoestimulación.
self-tolerance *n.* autotolerancia.
sella *n.* sella, silla.
denture base sella silla de la base de dentadura.
sella turcica sella turcica.
sellar *adj.* sillar.
semeiography *n.* semiografía.
semeiology *n.* semiología.
semeiotic *adj.* semiótico, -ca.
semeiotics *n.* semiótica.
semelincident *adj.* semelincidente.
semelparity *n.* semelparidad.
semelparous *adj.* semélparo, -ra.
semen *n.* semen.
semenology *n.* semenología, seminología.
semenuria *n.* semenuria, seminuria.
semiantigen *n.* semiantígeno.
semicanal *n.* semicanal, semiconducto.
semicanalis *n.* semiconducto.
semicartilaginous *adj.* semicartilaginoso, -sa.
semicircular *adj.* semicircular.
semicoma *n.* semicoma.
semicomatose *adj.* semicomatoso, -sa.
semiconductor *n.* semiconductor.
semiconscious *n.* semiconsciente.
semicrista *n.* semicresta.
semicuantitative *adj.* semicuantitativo, -va.
semidecussation *n.* semidecusación.
semiflexion *n.* semiflexión.
semifluctuating *adj.* semifluctuante.
semilunar *adj.* semilunar.
semilune *n.* semiluna.
semiluxation *n.* semiluxación.
semimembranous *adj.* semimembranoso, -sa.
semimonstrosity *n.* semimostruosidad.
seminal *adj.* seminal.
semination *n.* seminación.
seminiferous *adj.* seminífero, -ra.
seminologist *n.* seminólogo, -ga.
seminology *n.* seminología.
seminoma *n.* seminoma.
ovarian seminoma seminoma del ovario, seminoma ovárico.
spermacytic seminoma seminoma espermatocítico.

seminuria *n.* semenuria, seminuria.
semiography *n.* semiografía.
semiology *n.* semiología.
semiorbicular *adj.* semiorbicular.
semiotic *adj.* semiótico, -ca.
semiotics *n.* semiótica.
semiparasite *n.* semiparásito.
semipenniform *adj.* semipenniforme.
semipermeable *adj.* semipermeable.
semiplegia *n.* semiplejía.
semipronation *n.* semipronación.
semiprone *adj.* semiprono, -na.
semirecumbent *adj.* semirrecostado, -da, semirrecumbente.
semisideratio *n.* semisideración.
semisideration *n.* semisideración.
semispeculum *n.* semiespéculo.
semisulcus *n.* semisurco.
semisupination *n.* semisupinación.
semisupine *adj.* semisupino, -na.
semisynthetic *adj.* semisintético, -ca.
semitendinous *adj.* semitendinoso, -sa.
semitertian *n.* semiterciana.
sender *n.* transmisor, -ra.
senemologist *n.* semenólogo, -ga.
senescence *n.* senescencia.
dental senescence senescencia dental, senescencia dentaria.
senescent *adj.* senescente.
senile *adj.* senil.
senilism *n.* senilismo.
senility *n.* senilidad.
senium *n.* senectud.
senograph *n.* senógrafo.
senography *n.* senografía.
senopia *n.* senopía, senopsia.
sensation *n.* sensación.
cincture sensation sensación de cinto, sensación en cintura.
delayed sensation sensación diferida, sensación retardada, sensación retrasada.
dermal sensation sensación dérmica.
epigastric sensation sensación epigástrica.
general sensation sensación general.
girdle sensation sensación de cinto, sensación en cintura.
light sensation sensación luminosa.
new sensation sensación nueva.
objective sensation sensación objetiva.
primary sensation sensación primaria.
proprioceptive sensation sensación propioceptiva.
referred sensation sensación referida.
reflex sensation sensación refleja.
sensation of warmth sensación de calor.
skin sensation sensación cutánea.
special sensation sensación especial.
strain sensation sensación de esfuerzo.
subjective sensation sensación subjetiva.
superficial sensation sensación superficial.
tactile sensation sensación táctil.
transferred sensation sensación transferida.
vascular sensation sensación vascular.
sense *n.* sentido.
chemical sense sentido químico.
color sense sentido del color.
form sense sentido de la forma.
internal sense sentido interno.
joint sense sentido articular.
kinesthetic sense sentido cinestésico.
labyrinthine sense sentido laberíntico.
light sense sentido luminoso.
muscle sense sentido muscular.
muscular sense sentido muscular.
obstacle sense sentido de los obstáculos.

pain sense sentido del dolor.
position sense sentido de la posición, sentido de la postura.
posture sense sentido de la posición, sentido de la postura.
pressure sense sentido de la presión.
proprioceptive sense sentido propioceptivo.
sense of equilibrium sentido del equilibrio.
seventh sense sentido séptimo.
sixth sense sentido sexto.
space sense sentido del espacio, sentido espacial.
special sense sentido especial, sentido específico.
static sense sentido estático.
stereognostic sense sentido estereognóstico.
tactile sense sentido táctil.
temperature sense sentido de la temperatura.
thermic sense sentido térmico.
time sense sentido del tiempo.
tone sense sentido del tono.
vibratory sense sentido vibratorio.
visceral sense sentido visceral.
sensibiligen *adj.* sensibilígeno, -na.
sensibilisin *n.* sensibilisina.
sensibility *n.* sensibilidad[1].
articular sensibility sensibilidad articular.
bone sensibility sensibilidad ósea.
cortical sensibility sensibilidad cortical.
deep sensibility sensibilidad profunda.
electromuscular sensibility sensibilidad electromuscular.
epicritic sensibility sensibilidad epicrítica.
joint sensibility sensibilidad articular.
mesoblastic sensibility sensibilidad mesoblástica.
pallesthetic sensibility sensibilidad palestésica, sensibilidad palmestésica.
proprioceptive sensibility sensibilidad propioceptiva.
protopathic sensibility sensibilidad protopática.
splanchnesthetic sensibility sensibilidad esplacnestésica.
vibratory sensibility sensibilidad vibratoria.
sensiferous *adj.* sensífero, -ra.
sensigenous *adj.* sensígeno, -na.
sensimeter *n.* sensímetro.
sensitinogen *n.* sensitinógeno.
sensitive *adj.* sensible.
sensitivity *n.* sensibilidad[2].
acquired sensitivity sensibilidad adquirida.
antibiotic sensitivity sensibilidad a los antibióticos.
contrast sensitivity sensibilidad de contraste.
cross sensitivity sensibilidad cruzada.
diagnostic sensitivity sensibilidad diagnóstica.
idiosyncratic sensitivity sensibilidad idiosincrática.
pacemaker sensitivity sensibilidad marcapaso.
photoallergic sensitivity sensibilidad fotoalérgica.
phototoxic sensitivity sensibilidad fototóxica.
primaquine sensitivity sensibilidad a la primaquina.
proportional sensitivity sensibilidad proporcional.
relativa sensitivity sensibilidad relativa.
salt sensitivity sensibilidad a la sal.
sensitization *n.* sensibilización.
active sensitization sensibilización activa.
autoerythrocyte sensitization sensibilización autoeritrocítica.

covert sensitization sensibilización encubierta.
cross sensitization sensibilización cruzada.
passive sensitization sensibilización pasiva.
photodynamic sensitization sensibilización fotodinámica.
protein sensitization sensibilización proteica, sensibilización proteínica.
Rh sensitization sensibilización Rh.
sensitized *adj.* sensibilizado, -da.
sensitizer *adj.* sensibilizador, -ra, sensibilizante.
sensitogen *adj.* sensitógeno, -na.
sensitometer *n.* sensitómetro.
sensomobile *adj.* sensomóvil.
sensomobility *n.* sensomovilidad.
sensomotor *adj.* sensomotor, -triz.
sensor *n.* sensor, -ra.
sensorial *adj.* sensorial.
sensoriglandular *adj.* sensoriglandular, sensorioglandular.
sensorimotor *adj.* sensitivomotor, -ra, sensoriomotor, -triz.
sensorimuscular *adj.* sensorimuscular, sensoriomuscular.
sensorineural *adj.* sensitivoneural.
sensoriometabolism *n.* sensoriometabolismo.
sensorium *n.* sensorio.
sensorivascular *adj.* sensoriovascular.
sensorivasomotor *adj.* sensoriovasomotor, -triz.
sensory *adj.* sensitivo, -va.
sensual *adj.* sensual.
sensualism *n.* sensualidad, sensualismo.
sentiment *n.* sentimiento.
separation *n.* separación.
jaw separation separación de los maxilares.
separation of teeth separación de dientes.
separation of the retina separación de la retina.
separation-individuation separación-individuación.
separator *n.* separador².
sepodonogenesis *n.* sepedogénesis, sepedonogénesis.
sepsis *n.* sepsis.
catheter sepsis sepsis del catéter.
incarcerated sepsis sepsis incarcerada.
mouse sepsis sepsis murina.
murine sepsis sepsis murina.
puerperal sepsis sepsis puerperal.
sepsis agranulocytica sepsis agranulocítica.
sepsis intestinalis sepsis intestinal.
sepsis lenta sepsis lenta.
septal *adj.* septal.
septan *adj.* septana, septano, -na.
septate *adj.* septado, -da, tabicado, -da.
septation *n.* septación.
septatome *n.* septátomo.
septectomy *n.* septectomía.
septemia *n.* septemia.
septic *adj.* séptico, -ca.
septicemia *n.* septicemia.
acute fulminating meningococcal septicemia septicemia meningocócica fulminante aguda.
cryptogenic septicemia septicemia criptógena.
fungal septicemia septicemia fúngica.
morphine injector's septicemia septicemia de los morfinómanos.
phlebitic septicemia septicemia flebítica.
plague septicemia septicemia de la peste.
puerperal septicemia septicemia puerperal.
sputum septicemia septicemia del esputo.
typhoid septicemia septicemia tifoidea, septicemia tifoídica.

septicemic *adj.* septicémico, -ca.
septicophlebitis *n.* septicoflebitis.
septicopyemia *n.* septicopiohemia.
cryptogenic septicopyemia septicopiohemia criptógena.
metastatic septicopyemia septicopiohemia metastásica.
spontaneous septicopyemia septicopiohemia espontánea.
septicopyemic *adj.* septicopiohémico, -ca.
septicozymoid *adj.* septicocimoide, septicocimoideo, -a.
septiferous *adj.* septífero, -ra.
septigravida *n.* septigrávida.
septimetritis *n.* septimetritis.
septineuritis *n.* septineuritis.
Nicolau's septineuritis septineuritis de Nicolau.
septipara *n.* septípara.
septomarginal *adj.* septomarginal.
septonasal *adj.* septonasal.
septoplasty *n.* septoplastia.
septorhinoplasty *n.* rinoseptoplastia.
septostomy *n.* septostomía.
balloon atrial septostomy septostomía auricular por pelota, septostomía con balón.
balloon septostomy septostomía auricular por pelota, septostomía con balón.
septotome *n.* septótomo.
septotomy *n.* septotomía.
septulum *n.* séptulo.
septulum testis séptulo testis.
septum *n.* septo, septum, tabique.
septuplet *adj.* septúpleto, -ta.
sequela *n.* secuela.
sequence *n.* secuencia.
ALU sequence secuencia ALU.
coding sequence secuencia de codificación.
consensus sequence secuencia consensuada.
cross-sequence secuencia cruzada.
developmental sequence secuencia del desarrollo.
flanking sequence secuencia colindante.
insertion sequence secuencia de inserción.
intervening sequence secuencia de intervención, secuencia intercalada.
palindromic sequence secuencia palindrómica.
regulatory sequence secuencia reguladora.
termination sequence secuencia de terminación.
sequester *v.* secuestrar.
sequestral *adj.* secuestral.
sequestrant *adj.* secuestrante.
sequestration *n.* secuestro.
drug sequestration secuestro farmacológico.
pulmonary sequestration secuestro pulmonar.
subclavian sequestration secuestro subclavio.
sequestrectomy *n.* secuestrectomía.
sequestrotomy *n.* secuestrotomía.
sequestrum *n.* secuestro.
primary sequestrum secuestro primario.
secondary sequestrum secuestro secundario.
tertiary sequestrum secuestro terciario.
sequoiosis *n.* secoyosis.
seralbumin *n.* seroalbúmina.
serangitis *n.* serangitis.
serapheresis *n.* seraféresis.
sere *n.* sere.
serempion *n.* serempión.
serendipity *n.* serendipia, serendipidad.
serial *adj.* seriado, -da, serial.
serialograph *n.* serialógrafo.

sericite *n.* sericita.
series *n.* serie.
basophil series serie basófila, serie basofílica.
basophilic series serie basófila, serie basofílica.
eosinophil series serie eosinófila, serie eosinofílica.
eosinophilic series serie eosinófila, serie eosinofílica.
erythrocyte series serie de eritrocitos, serie eritrocítica.
erythrocytic series serie de eritrocitos, serie eritrocítica.
granulocyte series serie de granulocitos, serie granulocítica.
granulocytic series serie de granulocitos, serie granulocítica.
Hofmeister series serie de Hofmeister.
leukocytic series serie leucocítica.
lymphocyte series serie de linfocitos, serie linfocítica.
lymphocytic series serie de linfocitos, serie linfocítica.
lyotropic series serie liotrópica.
monocyte series serie monocítica.
monocytic series serie monocítica.
myeloid series serie mielocítica, serie mieloide.
neutrophil series serie de neutrófilos, serie neutrofílica.
neutrophilic series serie de neutrófilos, serie neutrofílica.
plasmacyte series serie de plasmocitos, serie plasmocítica.
plasmacytic series serie de plasmocitos, serie plasmocítica.
thrombocyte series serie de trombocitos, serie trombocítica.
thrombocytic series serie de trombocitos, serie trombocítica.
seriflux *n.* seriflujo.
serifuge *n.* serifuga.
seriograph *n.* seriógrafo.
seriography *n.* seriografía.
serioscopy *n.* seriescopía, serioscopía.
seriscission *n.* seriscisión.
seroalbuminous *adj.* seroalbuminoso, -sa.
seroalbuminuria *n.* seroalbuminuria.
seroanaphylaxis *n.* seroanafilaxis.
serochrome *n.* serocromo.
serocolitis *n.* serocolitis.
seroconversion *n.* seroconversión.
seroconvert *v.* seroconvertir.
seroculture *n.* serocultivo.
serocystic *adj.* seroquístico, -ca.
serodiagnosis *n.* serodiagnosis, serodiagnóstico.
seroenteritis *n.* seroenteritis.
seroepidemiologic *adj.* seroepidemiológico, -ca.
seroepidemiological *adj.* seroepidemiológico, -ca.
seroepidemiology *n.* seroepidemiología.
serofast *adj.* serorresistente.
serofibrinous *adj.* serofibrinoso, -sa.
serofibrous *adj.* serofibroso, -sa.
seroflocculation *n.* serofloculación.
serofluid *n.* serofluido.
serogastria *n.* serogastria.
serogenesis *n.* serogenesia, serogénesis.
seroglobulin *n.* seroglobulina.
seroglycoid *n.* seroglucoide.
serogroup *n.* serogrupo.
serohemorrhagic *adj.* serohemorrágico, -ca.
serohepatitis *n.* serohepatitis.
seroimmunity *n.* seroinmunidad.

seroinversion *n.* seroinversión.
serolactescent *adj.* serolactescente.
serolemma *n.* serolema.
serolipase *n.* serolipasa.
serologic *adj.* serológico, -ca.
serological *adj.* serológico, -ca.
serologist *n.* serólogo, -ga.
serology *n.* serología.
 diagnostic serology serología diagnóstica.
serolysin *n.* serolisina.
seroma *n.* seroma.
seromembranous *adj.* seromembranoso, -sa.
seromocus *n.* seromoco.
seromucoid *adj.* seromucoide, seromucoideo, -a.
seromucous *adj.* seromucoso, -sa.
seromuscular *adj.* seromuscular.
seronegative *adj.* seronegativo, -va.
seronegativity *n.* seronegatividad.
seroperitoneum *n.* seroperitoneo.
seropheresis *n.* seraféresis, seroféresis.
serophilic *adj.* serofílico, -ca.
serophysiology *n.* serofisiología.
seroplastic *adj.* seroplástico, -ca.
seropneumothorax *n.* seroneumotórax.
seropositive *adj.* seropositivo, -va.
seropositivity *n.* seropositividad.
seroprevalence *n.* seroprevalecencia.
seroprevention *n.* seroprevención.
seroprognosis *n.* seropronóstico.
seroprophylaxis *n.* seroprofilaxia, seroprofilaxis.
seropurulent *adj.* seropurulento, -ta.
seroreaction *n.* serorreacción.
serorelapse *n.* serorrecaída.
seroresistant *adj.* serorresistente.
serosa *n.* serosa.
serosal *adj.* seroso, -sa.
serosamucin *n.* serosamucina.
serosanguineous *adj.* serosanguíneo, -a.
serosanguinous *adj.* serosanguíneo, -a.
seroscopy *n.* seroscopia.
serose *n.* serosa.
seroserous *adj.* seroseroso, -sa.
serositis *n.* serositis.
 multiple serositis serositis múltiple.
serosity *n.* serosidad.
serosurvey *n.* seroencuesta, serovigilancia.
serosynovial *adj.* serosinovial.
serosynovitis *n.* serosinovitis.
serotaxis *n.* serotaxis.
serotherapist *n.* seroterapeuta.
serotherapy *n.* seroterapia.
serothorax *n.* serotórax.
serotonin *n.* serotonina.
serotoninergic *adj.* serotoninérgico, -ca.
serotype[1] *n.* serotipo.
serotype[2] *v.* serotipificar.
serous *adj.* seroso, -sa.
serovaccination *n.* serovacunación.
serovar *n.* serovariedad.
serozyme *n.* serocima.
serpiginous *adj.* serpiginoso, -sa.
serpigo *n.* serpigio.
serrated *adj.* serrado, -da, serratus.
Serratia Serratia.
serratus *adj.* serrado, -da, serrato, -ta, serratus.
serrefine *n.* serrefina.
serrulate *adj.* serrulado, -da.
serrulated *adj.* serrulado, -da.
serum *n.* serum, suero.
 anticomplementary serum suero anticomplementario.
 antilymphocyte serum (ALS) suero antilinfocitario, suero antilinfocítico (SAL).

 antipertussis serum suero contra la tos ferina.
 antiplatelet serum suero antiplaquetario.
 blood grouping serum suero de determinación de grupos sanguíneos.
 blood serum suero sanguíneo.
 convalescent serum suero de convalecencia, suero de convalecente.
 Coombs serum suero de Coombs.
 dried human serum suero humano desecado.
 foreign serum suero extraño.
 human measles immune serum suero inmune de sarampión humano.
 human pertussis immune serum suero inmune de tos ferina humana.
 human scarlet-fever immune serum suero inmune de escarlatina humana.
 human serum suero humano.
 hyperimmune serum suero hiperinmune.
 immune serum suero inmune.
 liquid human serum suero humano líquido.
 measles convalescent serum suero de convaleciente de sarampión.
 muscle serum suero muscular.
 normal human serum suero humano normal.
 normal serum suero normal.
 pooled blood serum suero combinado, suero sanguíneo combinado.
 pooled serum suero combinado, suero sanguíneo combinado.
 salted serum suero salado.
 thyrotoxic serum suero tirolítico, suero tirotóxico.
serumal *adj.* sérico, -ca.
serum-fast *adj.* serorresistente.
serumuria *n.* serumuria.
service *n.* servicio.
 basic health service servicio básico de salud.
 day health care service servicio de hospital de día.
 detoxification service servicio de toxicología.
 diagnostic service servicio diagnóstico.
 environmental service servicio interno.
 health-related service servicio relacionado con la salud.
 maternal and child (MCH) service servicio de salud maternoinfantil.
 psychiatric emergency service servicio de urgencias de psiquiatría.
 shared service servicio compartido.
sesamoid *adj.* sesamoide, sesamoideo, -a.
sesamoiditis *n.* sesamoiditis.
sessile *adj.* sésil.
set *n.* reposicionamiento.
seta *n.* seta.
setaceous *adj.* setáceo, -a.
setiferous *adj.* setífero, -ra.
setigerous *adj.* setífero, -ra, setígero, -ra.
seton *n.* sedal.
setup *n.* montaje.
sex *v.* sexar, sexo.
 chromosomal sex sexo cromosómico.
 endocrinologic sex sexo endocrinológico.
 genetic sex sexo genético.
 gonadal sex sexo gonadal.
 morphological sex sexo morfológico.
 nuclear sex sexo nuclear.
 psychological sex sexo psicológico.
 safe sex sexo seguro.
 social sex sexo social.
sex-controlled *adj.* controlado, -da por el sexo.
sexdigitate *adj.* sexdigitado, -da.
sexdigitism *n.* sexdigitismo.
sex-influenced *adj.* influido, -da por el sexo.
sexism *n.* sexismo.

sex-limited *adj.* limitado, -a por el sexo.
sexology *n.* sexología.
sexopathy *n.* sexopatía.
sextan *n.* sextana.
sextigravida *n.* sextigrávida.
sextipara *n.* sextípara.
sextuplet *adj.* sextillizo, -za, sextúpleto, -ta.
sexual *adj.* sexual.
 sexual harassment acoso sexual.
sexuality *n.* sexualidad.
 infantile sexuality sexualidad infantil.
shadow *n.* sombra.
 acoustic shadow sombra acústica.
 breast shadow sombra mamaria.
shadow-casting *n.* sombreado.
shaft *n.* diáfisis.
shakes *n.* sacudidas.
 hatter's shakes sacudidas del sombrero.
 kwaski shakes sacudidas kwaski.
shaping *n.* modelación.
shashitsu *n.* shashitsu.
sheath *n.* vaina.
 caudal sheath vaina caudal.
 fenestrated sheath vaina fenestrada.
 fibrous sheath vaina fibrosa.
 medullary sheath vaina medular.
 mitochondrial sheath vaina mitocondrial.
 myelin sheath vaina de mielina, vaina mielínica.
 resectoscope sheath vaina del resectoscopio.
 root sheath vaina radicular.
shell *n.* concha, valva[1].
shield *n.* escudo[2].
 Buller's shield escudo de Büller.
 contact shield escudo de contacto.
 embryonic shield escudo embrionario.
 eye shield escudo ocular.
 lead shield escudo de plomo.
 nipple shield escudo de pezón, escudo para el pezón.
 oral shield escudo bucal, escudo orale.
 phallic shield escudo fálico.
shielding *n.* blindaje.
shift *n.* desplazamiento[4], desviación[5].
 axis shift desplazamiento axial, desviación axial.
 chemical shift desviación química.
 chloride shift desplazamiento de cloruros, desviación de cloruros.
 Doppler shift desplazamiento de Doppler.
 luteoplacental shift desviación luteoplacentaria.
 Purkinje shift desplazamiento de Purkinje, desviación de Purkinje.
 regenerative blood shift desviación sanguínea regenerativa.
 shift to the left desplazamiento hacia la izquierda, desviación hacia la izquierda.
 shift to the right desplazamiento hacia la derecha, desviación hacia la derecha.
 threshold shift desplazamiento del umbral.
Shigella Shigella.
shigellosis *n.* shigellosis.
shimming *n.* homogeneización.
shin *n.* espinilla.
 cucumber shin espinilla en pepino.
 saber shin espinilla en sable.
 shin splints espinilla en férula.
 toasted shin espinilla tostada.
shiver *n.* estremecimiento[1].
shock *n.* choque, shock.
 anaphylactic shock choque anafiláctico.
 anaphylactoid shock choque anafilactoide.
 anesthetic shock choque anestésico, choque por anestesia.

bacteriemic shock choque bacteriémico.
break shock choque por interrupción.
cardiogenic shock choque cardiogénico.
chronic shock choque crónico.
cultural shock choque cultural, shock cultural.
declamping shock choque por descompresión.
deferred shock choque diferido.
delayed shock choque diferido.
delirious shock choque delirante.
electric shock choque eléctrico.
endotoxic shock choque endotóxico.
endotoxin shock choque por endotoxinas.
erethistic shock choque eretístico.
hematogenic shock choque hematogénico.
hemorrhagic shock choque hemorrágico.
histamine shock choque histamínico.
hypovolemic shock choque hipovolémico.
insulin shock choque insulínico.
irreversible shock choque irreversible.
neurogenic shock choque neurogénico.
nitroid shock choque nitroide.
oligemic shock choque oligohémico.
osmotic shock choque osmótico.
primary shock choque primario.
protein shock choque proteico.
reversible shock choque reversible.
secondary shock choque secundario.
septic shock choque séptico.
serum shock choque sérico.
speed shock choque por exceso de rapidez.
spinal shock choque espinal, choque medular.
surgical shock choque quirúrgico.
traumatic shock choque traumático.
vasogenic shock choque vasogénico.
war shock shock de guerra.
wet shock choque húmedo.
shoe *n.* zapato.
cast shoe zapato para escayola.
normal last shoe zapato de horma normal.
orthopedic Oxford shoe zapato ortopédico de tacón bajo.
shoulder *n.* hombro.
drop shoulder hombro caído.
frozen shoulder hombro congelado.
knocked-down shoulder hombro trabado.
loose shoulder hombro flojo.
stubbed shoulder hombro en tocón.
shower *n.* ducha, shower.
uric acid shower shower de ácido úrico.
shudder *n.* estremecimiento[2].
shunt *n.* derivación[5], shunt.
arteriovenous (A-V) shunt derivación arteriovenosa (AV).
cardiovascular shunt derivación cardiovascular.
Denver shunt derivación de Denver.
dialysis shunt derivación para diálisis.
Dickens shunt derivación de Dickens.
distal splenorenal shunt derivación esplenorrenal, derivación esplenorrenal distal.
external shunt derivación externa.
Glenn shunt derivación de Glenn.
Glenn's shunt derivación de Glenn.
hexose monophosphate shunt derivación de la hexosa monofosfato, derivación del monofosfato de hexosa.
intrapulmonary shunt derivación intrapulmonar.
left to right shunt derivación desde izquierda hacia derecha.
LeVeen peritonovenous shunt derivación peritoneovenosa, derivación periventosa de LeVeen.

LeVeen shunt derivación de LeVeen.
lumboperitoneal shunt derivación lumboperitoneal.
mesocaval shunt derivación mesocava.
pentose shunt derivación de pentosa.
peritoneovenous shunt derivación peritoneovenosa, derivación periventosa de LeVeen.
portacaval shunt derivación portocava, derivación poscava.
portocaval shunt derivación portocava, derivación poscava.
postcaval shunt derivación portocava, derivación poscava.
Rapoport-Luebering shunt derivación de Rapoport-Luebering.
renal-splenic venous shunt derivación venosa renal-esplénica.
reversed shunt derivación invertida.
right-to-left shunt derivación de derecha a izquierda.
spinofallopian tube shunt derivación espinotubárica.
splenorenal shunt derivación esplenorrenal, derivación esplenorrenal distal.
tracheoesophageal shunt derivación traqueoesofágica.
ventriculoatrial shunt derivación ventriculoauricular.
ventriculofallopian tube shunt derivación ventriculotubárica.
ventriculoperitoneal shunt derivación ventriculoperitoneal.
ventriculopleural shunt derivación ventriculopleural.
ventriculovenous shunt derivación ventriculovenosa.
Warburg-Lipmann-Dickens shunt derivación de Warburg-Lipmann-Dickens.
Warren shunt derivación de Warren.
Waterson shunt derivación de Waterson.
siagantritis *n.* siagantritis.
siagonantritis *n.* siagonantritis.
siagonatra *n.* siagonagra.
sialaden *n.* sialadeno.
sialadenectomy *n.* sialadenectomía.
sialadenitis *n.* sialadenitis.
chronic non-specific sialadenitis sialadenitis inespecífica crónica.
sialadenography *n.* sialadenografía.
sialadenoncus *n.* sialadenonco.
sialadenosis *n.* sialadenosis.
sialadenotomy *n.* sialadenotomía.
sialagogue *adj.* sialagogo, -ga, sialogogo, -ga.
sialaporia *n.* sialaporía.
sialectasia *n.* sialectasia.
sialemesis *n.* sialemesis.
sialic *adj.* siálico, -ca.
sialine *adj.* sialino, -na.
sialism *n.* sialismo.
sialismus *n.* sialismo.
sialoadenectomy *n.* sialoadenectomía.
sialoadenitis *n.* sialoadenitis.
sialoadenotomy *n.* sialoadenotomía.
sialoaerophagia *n.* sialoaerofagia.
sialoaerophagy *n.* sialoaerofagia.
sialoangiectasis *n.* sialoangiectasia, sialoangiectasis.
sialoangiitis *n.* sialoangitis.
sialoangiography *n.* sialoangiogafía.
sialoangitis *n.* sialoangitis.
sialocele *n.* sialocele.
sialodochitis *n.* sialodoquitis.
sialodochoplasty *n.* sialodocoplastia.
sialoductitis *n.* sialoductitis.
sialogastrone *n.* sialogastrona.

sialogenous *adj.* sialógeno, -na.
sialogogic *adj.* sialogógico, -ca.
sialogogue *adj.* sialagogo, -ga, sialogogo, -ga.
sialogram *n.* sialograma.
sialography *n.* sialografía.
sialolith *n.* sialolito.
sialolithiasis *n.* sialolitiasis.
sialolithotomy *n.* sialolitotomía.
sialology *n.* sialología.
sialometaplasia *n.* sialometaplasia.
necrotizing sialometaplasia sialometaplasia necrosante.
sialomucin *n.* sialomucina.
sialophagia *n.* sialofagia.
sialophagy *n.* sialofagia.
sialorrhea *n.* sialorrea.
sialoschesis *n.* sialosquesis.
sialosemeiology *n.* sialosemiología.
sialosemiology *n.* sialosemiología.
sialosis *n.* sialosis.
sialostenosis *n.* sialoestenosis, sialostenosis.
sialosyrinx *n.* sialojeringa.
sialotic *adj.* sialótico, -ca.
sibilant *adj.* sibilante.
sibling *n.* mellizo.
sibship *n.* consanguinidad.
siccant *adj.* secante.
siccative *adj.* secativo, -va, sicativo, -va.
sicchasia *n.* sicasia.
sick *adj.* enfermo, -ma, mareado, -da, nauseado, -da.
sicklemia *n.* drepanocitemia[2].
sickling *n.* drepanocitosis[2].
sickness *n.* enfermedad.
African sleeping sickness enfermedad del sueño africano.
altitude sickness enfermedad de las alturas.
car sickness enfermedad terrestre.
decompression sickness enfermedad por descompresión.
falling sickness enfermedad de la caída.
functional sickness enfermedad funcional.
green sickness enfermedad verde.
Indian sickness enfermedad india.
laughing sickness enfermedad de la risa.
morning sickness enfermedad matinal.
motion sickness enfermedad del movimiento.
mountain sickness enfermedad de la montaña.
serum sickness enfermedad del suero.
sleeping sickness enfermedad del sueño.
side *n.* lado.
sideration *n.* sideración.
siderism *n.* siderismo.
sideroblast *n.* sideroblasto.
siderocyte *n.* siderocito.
sideroderma *n.* siderodermia.
siderofibrosis *n.* siderofibrosis.
siderogenous *adj.* siderógeno, -na.
sideropenic *adj.* ferriprivo, -va.
siderophage *n.* siderófago, -ga.
siderophil *n.* siderófilo.
siderophilous *adj.* siderófilo, -la.
siderophore *n.* sideróforo.
sideroscope *n.* sideroscopio.
siderosilicosis *n.* siderosilicosis.
siderosis *n.* siderosis.
hepatic siderosis siderosis hepática.
nutritional siderosis siderosis nutricional.
pulmonary siderosis siderosis pulmonar.
siderosis bulbi siderosis bulbar.
siderosis conjunctivae siderosis conjuntival.
urinary siderosis siderosis urinaria.
siderotic *adj.* siderótico, -ca.

siderous *adj.* sideroso, -sa.
sieve *n.* tamiz.
  molecular sieve tamiz molecular.
sieving *n.* tamización.
sigh *n.* suspiro.
sight *n.* visión, vista.
  day sight visión diurna, vista diurna.
  far sight visión de lejos.
  long sight visión de lejos, vista larga, vista lejana.
  near sight visión de cerca.
  night sight vista nocturna.
  short sight visión corta, vista cercana, vista corta.
sigmasism *n.* sigmatismo.
sigmatism *n.* sigmatismo.
sigmoid *adj.* sigmoide, sigmoideo, -a, sigmoides.
sigmoidectomy *n.* sigmoidectomía.
sigmoiditis *n.* sigmoiditis.
sigmoidopexy *n.* sigmoidopexia.
sigmoidoproctostomy *n.* sigmoidoproctostomía.
sigmoidorectostomy *n.* sigmoidorrectostomía.
sigmoidoscope *n.* sigmoidoscopio.
sigmoidoscopy *n.* sigmoidoscopia.
sigmoidosigmoidostomy *n.* sigmoidosigmoidostomía.
sigmoidostomy *n.* sigmoidostomía.
sigmoidotomy *n.* sigmoidotomía.
sigmoidovesical *adj.* sigmoidovesical.
sigmoscope *n.* sigmoscopio.
sign *n.* signo.
  Aaron's sign signo de Aaron.
  Abadie's sign signo de Abadie.
  Abadie's sign of tabes dorsalis signo de Abadie de tabes dorsal.
  accessory sign signo accesorio.
  Ahlfeld's sign signo de Ahlfeld.
  Allis' sign signo de Allis.
  Amoss' sign signo de Amoss.
  André-Thomas sign signo de André-Thomas.
  Angelescu's sign signo de Angelescu.
  antecedent sign signo antecedente.
  anterior drawer sign signo del cajón anterior.
  Argyll-Robertson's sign signo de Argyll-Robertson.
  Arroyo's sign signo de Arroyo.
  Auenbrugger's sign signo de Auenbrugger.
  Aufrecht's sign signo de Aufrecht.
  Auspitz's sign signo de Auspitz.
  Babinski's sign signo de Babinski.
  Babinski's toe sign signo de Babinski del dedo gordo.
  Bacelli's sign signo de Bacelli.
  Baillarger's sign signo de Baillarger.
  Ballance's sign signo de Ballance.
  Bard's sign signo de Bard.
  Baruch's sign signo de Baruch.
  Bassler's sign signo de Bassler.
  Bastedo's sign signo de Bastedo.
  Battle's sign signo de Battle.
  Becker's sign signo de Becker.
  Béclard's sign signo de Béclard, signo de madurez de Béclard.
  Béhier-Hardy sign signo de Béhier-Hardy.
  Bell's sign signo de Bell.
  Bespaloff's sign signo de Bespalov.
  Bezold's sign signo de Bezold.
  Biederman's sign signo de Biederman.
  Bielschowsky's sign signo de Bielschowsky.
  Biermer's sign signo de Biermer.
  Biernacki's sign signo de Biernacki.
  Binda's sign signo de Binda.
  Biot's sign signo de Biot.

  Bird's sign signo de Bird.
  Bjerrum's sign signo de Bjerrum.
  Bonnet's sign signo de Bonnet.
  Bordier-Frankel sign signo de Bordier-Frankel.
  Borsieri's sign signo de Borsieri.
  Bouveret's sign signo de Bouveret.
  Bragard's sign signo de Bragard.
  Branham's sign signo de Branham.
  Braun-Fernwald sign signo de Braun-Fernwald.
  Braxton-Hicks sign signo de Braxton-Hicks.
  Brissaud sign signo de Brissaud.
  Brittain's sign signo de Brittain.
  Broadbent's sign signo de Broadbent.
  Brodie's sign signo de Brodie.
  bronchogram sign signo del broncograma aéreo.
  Brudzinski's sign signo de Brudzinski.
  Bryant's sign signo de Bryant.
  Bryson's sign signo de Bryson.
  Bychowski's sign signo de Bychowski.
  Cantelli's sign signo de Cantelli.
  Cardarelli's sign signo de Cardarelli.
  cardinal sign (of inflammation) signo cardinal (de inflamación).
  Carman's sign signo de Carman.
  Carvallo's sign signo de Carvallo.
  Cejka's sign signo de Cejka.
  Chaddock's sign signo de Chaddock.
  Chadwick's sign signo de Chadwick.
  Charcot-Marie's sign signo de Charcot-Marie.
  Charcot's sign signo de Charcot.
  Charcot-Vulpian's sign signo de Charcot-Vulpian.
  Chase's sign signo de Chase.
  Cheyne-Stokes sign signo de Cheyne-Stokes.
  clavicular sign signo clavicular.
  Cleeman's sign signo de Cleeman.
  clenched fist sign signo del puño cerrado de Pitres.
  Codman's sign signo de Codman.
  cogwheel sign signo de la rueda dentada.
  coin sign signo de la moneda.
  Cole's sign signo de Cole.
  commemorative sign signo conmemorativo.
  Comolli's sign signo de Comolli.
  complementary opposition sign signo de oposición complementaria.
  contralateral sign signo contralateral.
  Coopernail sign signo de Coopernail.
  Cope's sign signo de Cope.
  Corrigan's sign signo de Corrigan.
  Courvoisier's sign signo de Courvoisier.
  Crichton-Browne's sign signo de Crichton-Browne.
  Crowe's sign signo de Crowe.
  Cullen's sign signo de Cullen.
  Dalrymple's sign signo de Dalrympe.
  Damoisseau's sign signo de Damoisseau.
  Dance's sign signo de Dance.
  Darier's sign signo de Darier.
  Davidsohn's sign signo de Davidsohn.
  Déjerine's sign signo de Déjerine.
  Delbet's sign signo de Delbet.
  Demianoff's sign signo de Demianoff.
  Deuel's sign signo de Deuel.
  doll's eye sign signo de los ojos de la muñeca.
  Dubois' sign signo de Dubois.
  Duchenne's sign signo de Duchenne.
  duct sign signo del doble conducto.
  Duncan-Bird's sign signo de Duncan-Bird.
  Duroziez's sign signo de Duroziez.
  Erichsen's sign signo de Erichsen.

  Ewart's sign signo de Ewart.
  Faget's sign signo de Faget.
  Fajersztajn crossed sciatic sign signo ciático cruzado de Fajersztajn.
  fan sign signo del abanico.
  Forscheimer's sign signo de Forcsheimer.
  Fothergill's sign signo de Fothergill.
  Friedreich's sign signo de Friedreich.
  Froment's paper sign signo de Froment del papel.
  Froment's sign signo de Froment.
  Gaenslen's sign signo de Gaenslen.
  Galeazzi's sign signo de Galeazzi.
  Gauss' sign signo de Gauss.
  Gerhardt's sign signo de Gerhardt.
  Gianelli's sign signo de Gianelli.
  Gibson's sign signo de Gibson.
  Gifford's sign signo de Gifford.
  Glasgow's sign signo de Glasgow.
  Gordon's sign signo de Gordon.
  Gotron's sign signo de Gotron.
  Gowers' sign signo de Gowers.
  Graefe's sign signo de Graefe, signo de von Graefe.
  Grasset's sign signo de Grasset.
  Grey-Turner's sign signo de Grey-Turner.
  Griesinger's sign signo de Griesinger.
  Guedel's sign's signo de Guedel.
  Guillain's sign signo de Guillain.
  Gunn's sign signo de Gunn.
  Guntz's sign signo de Guntz.
  Guttmann's sign signo de Guttmann.
  Guye's sign signo de Guye.
  Hahn's sign signo de Hahn.
  Hamman's sign signo de Hamman.
  harlequin sign signo del arlequín.
  Heberden's sign signo de Heberden.
  Hefke-Turner sign signo de Hefke-Turner.
  Hegar's sign signo de Hegar.
  Heim-Kreysig sign signo de Heim-Kreysig.
  Heimlich sign signo de Heimlich.
  Hellat's sign signo de Hellat.
  Hennebert's sign signo de Hennebert.
  Hertwig-Magendie sign signo de Hertwig-Magendie.
  Heryng's sign signo de Heryng.
  Hick's sign signo de Hicks.
  Higoumenakis sign signo de Higoumenakis.
  hilar obliteration sign signo del hilio tapado.
  Hoffmann's sign signo de Hoffmann.
  Hoffmann-Tinel's sign signo de Hoffmann-Tinel.
  Holmes' sign signo de Holmes.
  Homans sign signo de Homans.
  Hoover's sign signo de Hoover.
  Horn's sign signo de Horn.
  Hoster's sign signo de Hoster.
  Howship-Romberg sign signo de Howship-Romberg.
  Hueter's sign signo de Hueter.
  Hutchinson's pupillary sign signo de Hutchinson.
  Hutter's sign signo de Hutter.
  indexical sign signo indexal.
  interossei sign signo interóseo.
  Jaccoud's sign signo de Jaccoud.
  Jacquemier's sign signo de Jacquemier.
  Jellinek's sign signo de Jellinek.
  Jendrassik's sign signo de Jendrassik.
  Joffroy's sign signo de Joffroy.
  Keen's sign signo de Keen.
  Kehrer's sign signo de Kehrer.
  Kehr's sign signo de Kehr.
  Kerandel's sign signo de Kerandel.
  Kernig's sign signo de Kerning.

Klein's sign signo de Klein.

Kocher's sign signo de Kocher.

Koplik's sign signo de Koplik.

Koranyi's sign signo de Koranyi.

Kreysig's sign signo de Kreysig.

Kussmaul's sign signo de Kussmaul.

Küstner's sign signo de Küstner.

Langoria's sign signo de Langoria.

Lasègue's sign signo de Lasègue.

Laugier's sign signo de Laugier.

Lebhardt's sign signo de Lebhardt.

Leri's sign signo de Leri.

Leser-Trélat sign signo de Leser-Trélat.

Lesieur's sign signo de Lesieur.

Lewinson's sign signo de Lewinson.

Lhermitte's sign signo de Lhermitte.

Lian's sign signo de Lian.

Lichtheim's sign signo de Lichtheim.

local sign signo local.

Ludloff's sign signo de Ludloff.

Lust's sign signo de Lust.

Magendie-Hertwig sign signo de Magendie, signo de Magendie-Hertwig.

Magnan's sign signo de Magnan.

Mahler's sign signo de Mahler.

Marañón's sign signo de Marañón.

Marcus Gunn pupil sign signo de la pupila de Marcus Gunn, signo pupilar de Marcus Gunn.

Marcus Gunn's pupillary sign signo de la pupila de Marcus Gunn, signo pupilar de Marcus Gunn.

Marcus Gunn's sign signo de Marcus Gunn.

Marie-Foix sign signo de Marie-Foix.

Marie's sign signo de Marie.

McBurney's sign signo de McBurney.

McEwen's sign signo de McEwen.

meningeal sign signo meníngeo.

meniscus sign signo del menisco.

Mennell's sign signo de Mennell.

Milian's sign signo de Milian, signo del máximo periférico de Milian.

Minor's sign signo de Minor.

Möbius' sign signo de Möbius.

Müller's sign signo de Müller.

Murphy's sign signo de Murphy.

Musset's sign signo de Musset.

Myerson's sign signo de Myerson.

Naffziger sign signo de Naffziger.

Naunyn's sign signo de Naunyn.

neck sign signo del cuello.

Negro's sign signo de Negro.

Neri's sign signo de Neri.

Nikolsky's sign signo de Nikolsky.

objective sign signo objetivo.

obturator sign signo del obturador.

Oliver's sign signo de Oliver-Cardarelli.

Oppenheim's sign signo de Oppenheim.

Osler's sign signo de Osler.

Parkinson's sign signo de Parkinson.

Parrot's sign signo de Parrot.

Pastia's sign signo de Pastia.

Payr's sign signo de Payr.

peak mucus sign signo del pico de moco.

physical sign signo físico.

Piskacek's sign signo de Piskacek.

Pitres' sign signo de Pitres.

placental sign signo placentario.

Pool-Schlesinger sign signo de Pool-Schlesinger.

Porter's sign signo de Porter.

positive sign of pregnancy signo positivo de embarazo.

posterior drawer sign signo del cajón posterior.

Prehn's sign signo de Prehn.

presumptive sign signo de presunción.

probable sign signo probable.

prodromic sign signo prodrómico.

psoas sign signo de psoas.

Queckenstedt's sign signo de Queckenstedt.

Quincke's sign signo de Quincke.

Radovici's sign signo de Radovici.

Raynaud's sign signo de Raynaud.

Remak's sign signo de Remak.

Revilliod's sign signo de Revilliod.

Riesman's sign signo de Riesman.

Roche's sign signo de Roche.

Romaña's sign signo de Romaña.

Romberg-Howship sign signo de Romberg-Howship.

rope sign signo de la cuerda.

Rosenbach's sign signo de Rosenbach.

Rossolimo's sign signo de Rossolimo.

Rovsing's sign signo de Rovsing.

Rumpel-Leede sign signo de Rumpel-Leede.

Sanders' sign signo de Sanders.

Saunders' sign signo de Saunders.

Schlesinger's sign signo de Schlesinger.

Schultze's sign signo de Schultze.

scimitar sign signo de la cimitarra.

Seitz's sign signo de Seitz.

setting-sun sign signo de la puesta del sol.

sign of the orbicularis signo orbicular.

silhouette sign signo de la silueta.

soft neurologic sign signo neurológico leve.

Souques' sign signo de Souques.

Spalding's sign signo de Spalding.

Stellwag's sign signo de Stellwag.

Sternberg's sign signo de Sternberg.

Stewart-Holmes sign signo de Stewart-Holmes.

Stierlin's sign signo de Stierlin.

Stiller's sign signo de Stiller.

Strümpell's sign signo de Strümpell.

Suker's sign signo de Suker.

Sumner's sign signo de Sumner.

swinging flashing sign signo de destello oscilante.

Tellais' sign signo de Tellais.

Ten-Horn's sign signo de Ten-Horn.

Thomas' sign signo de Thomas.

Thomayer's sign signo de Thomayer.

thumb sign signo del pulgar.

toe sign signo del dedo gordo.

Tournay's sign signo de Tournay.

Trendelenburg's sign signo de Trendelenburg.

Troisier's sign signo de Troisier.

Trömner's sign signo de Trömner.

Trousseau's sign signo de Trousseau.

Turner's sign signo de Turner.

Turyn's sign signo de Turyn.

Vanzetti's sign signo de Vanzetti.

vein sign signo de la vena.

Vigouroux's sign signo de Vigouroux.

visual sign signo visual.

vital sign signo vital.

Voltolini's sign signo de Voltolini.

von Graefe's sign signo de von Graefe.

Wahl's sign signo de Wahl.

Walker's sign signo de Walker.

Wartenberg's sign signo de Wartenberg.

Weber's sign signo de Weber.

Weiss' sign signo de Weiss.

Wenckebach's sign signo de Wenckebach.

Wernicke's sign signo de Wernicke.

Westermark's sign signo de Westermark.

Westphal's sign signo de Westphal.

Widowitz's sign signo de Widowitz.

Winterbottom's sign signo de Winterbottom.

Wintrich's sign signo de Wintrich.

Wood's sign signo de Wood.

Zaufal's sign signo de Zaufal.

signal *n.* señal.

signal of anxiety señal de angustia.

significance *n.* significación.

statistical significance significación estadística.

silence *n.* silencio.

electrocerebral silence (ECS) silencio electrocerebral.

silent *adj.* silencioso, -sa, silente.

silhouette *n.* silueta.

cardiac silhouette silueta cardíaca.

silicatosis *n.* silicatosis.

siliceous *adj.* silíceo, -a.

silicious *adj.* silíceo, -a.

silicoanthrocosis *n.* silicoantrocosis.

silicone *n.* silicona.

injectable silicone silicona inyectable.

silicosis *n.* silicosis.

silicotic *adj.* silicótico, -ca.

silicotuberculosis *n.* silicotuberculosis.

silicous *adj.* silicoso, -sa.

silk *n.* seda.

surgical silk seda quirúrgica.

virgin silk seda virgen.

simesthesia *n.* simestesia.

similia similibus curantur similia similibus curantur.

similimum similimum.

simillimum simillimum.

simple *adj.* simple.

simulation *n.* simulación.

simulator *adj.* simulador, simulador, -ra.

Simulium Simulium.

simultagnosia *n.* simultagnosia, simultanagnosia.

simultanagnosia *n.* simultagnosia, simultanagnosia.

simultaneous *adj.* simultáneo, -a.

sinal *adj.* sinal.

sincipital *adj.* sincipital.

sinciput *n.* sincipucio.

sinew *n.* tendón.

singultation *n.* singultación.

singultous *adj.* singultoso, -sa.

sinistral *adj.* sinistral.

sinistrality *n.* sinistralidad.

sinistraural *adj.* sinistraural.

sinistrocardia *n.* sinistrocardia.

sinistrocerebral *adj.* sinistrocerebral.

sinistrocular *adj.* sinistrocular.

sinistrocularity *n.* sinistrocularidad.

sinistromanual *adj.* sinistrómano, -na.

sinistropedal *adj.* sinistropedal.

sinistrotorsion *n.* sinistrotorsión.

sinoatrial *adj.* sinoatrial.

sinoauricular *adj.* sinoauricular.

sinobronchitis *n.* sinobronquitis.

sinopulmonary *adj.* sinopulmonar.

sinospiral *adj.* sinoespiral.

sinoventricular *adj.* sinuventricular.

sinoviorthese *n.* sinoviortesia.

sinter *n.* sínter.

sinuate *adj.* sinuoso, -sa.

sinuous *adj.* sinuoso, -sa.

sinus seno, sinus.

sinusal *adj.* sinusal.

sinusitis *n.* sinuitis, sinusitis.

chronic sinusitis sinusitis crónica.

ethmoid sinusitis sinusitis etmoidea.

frontal sinusitis sinusitis frontal.

infectious sinusitis of turkeys sinusitis infecciosa del pavo.

sinusitis abscendens sinusitis abscendante.
sinusoid *n.* sinusoide.
sinusoidal *adj.* sinusoidal.
sinusoidalization *n.* sinusoidalización.
sinusotomy *n.* sinusotomía.
sinuspiral *adj.* sinuspiral.
sinuventricular *adj.* sinuventricular.
Siphunculina Siphunculina.
sirenomelia *n.* sirenomelia.
sirenomelus *n.* sirenomelo.
siriasis *n.* siriasis.
sismotherapy *n.* seismoterapia, sismoterapia.
site lugar, sitio, situs, zona.
  active site sitio activo.
  allosteric site sitio alostérico.
  binding site lugar de unión.
  cleavage site sitio de segmentación.
  fragile site sitio frágil.
  insertion site lugar de inserción.
  privileged site sitio privilegiados.
  psychoanalytic site situs psicoanalítica.
  receptor site sitio receptor.
  restriction site sitio de restricción.
  switching site sitio de cambio.
sitiology *n.* sitiología.
sitology *n.* sitiología, sitología.
sitophobia *n.* sitiofobia, sitofobia.
sitotherapy *n.* sitioterapia, sitoterapia.
sitotoxism *n.* sitotoxismo.
sitotropism *n.* sitiotropismo, sitotropismo.
situation *n.* situación.
situs *n.* sitio, situs.
  situs inversus viscerum situs inversus viscerum.
  situs perversus situs perversus.
  situs solitus situs solitus.
  situs transversus situs transversus.
skelalgia *n.* escelalgia.
skelasthenia *n.* esquelastenia.
skeletal *adj.* esquelético, -ca.
skeletization *n.* esqueletización.
skeletogenous *adj.* esqueletógeno, -na.
skeletogeny *n.* esqueletogenia.
skeleton *n.* esqueleto.
  cartilaginous skeleton esqueleto cartilaginoso.
  fibrous skeleton of the heart esqueleto fibroso del corazón.
  skeleton appendiculare esqueleto apendicular.
  skeleton axiale esqueleto axial, esqueleto axil.
  skeleton membri inferioris liberi esqueleto libre de los miembros inferiores.
  skeleton membri superioris liberi esqueleto libre de los miembros superiores.
  skeleton of free inferior limb esqueleto de la extremidad inferior libre.
  skeleton of free superior limb esqueleto de la extremidad superior libre.
  skeleton of the thorax esqueleto torácico.
  thoracic skeleton esqueleto torácico.
skeletopia *n.* esquelotopia.
skeletopy *n.* esquelotopia.
skeneitis *n.* esquenitis.
skeneoscope *n.* esqueneoscopio, esquenoscopio.
skenitis *n.* esquenitis.
skenoscope *n.* esqueneoscopio, esquenoscopio.
skeocytosis *n.* esqueocitosis.
skeptophylaxis *n.* esceptofilaxis.
skiameter *n.* esquiámetro.
skiametry *n.* esciametría.
skiascope *n.* esquiascopio.
skiascopy *n.* esquiascopia.

skiascotometry *n.* esquiascotometría.
skill *n.* destreza, habilidad.
  gross motor skill habilidad motora.
skin *n.* piel.
  bronzed skin piel bronceada.
  crocodile skin piel de cocodrilo, piel de lagarto.
  deciduous skin piel decidua.
  elastic skin piel elástica.
  farmer's skin piel de agricultor.
  fish skin piel de pescado.
  glabrous skin piel lampiña.
  glossy skin piel brillante.
  loose skin piel laxa.
  nail skin piel de las uñas.
  parchment skin piel apergaminada.
  piebald skin piel multicolor.
  pig skin piel de cerdo.
  porcupine skin piel de puercoespín.
  sailor's skin piel de marinero.
  shagreen skin piel de zapa.
  skin of the teeth piel de los dientes.
  toad skin piel de sapo.
  writing skin escritura en la piel.
  yellow skin piel amarilla.
skull *n.* cráneo.
  bifid skull cráneo bífido, cranium bifidum.
  maplike skull cráneo en mapa.
  natiform skull cráneo natiforme.
  steeple skull cráneo en campanario.
  tower skull cráneo en torre.
slant *n.* inclinación, pendiente.
  slant of the occlusal plane inclinación del plano oclusal.
slaver *n.* baba.
sleep somnus, sueño².
  active sleep sueño activo.
  crescendo sleep sueño creciente, sueño en crescendo.
  deep sleep sueño profundo.
  desynchronized sleep sueño desincronizado.
  dreaming sleep sueño con sueños.
  electric sleep sueño eléctrico.
  electrotherapeutic sleep sueño electroterapéutico.
  fast sleep sueño rápido.
  fast wave sleep sueño de onda rápida.
  frozen sleep sueño congelado.
  hypnotic sleep sueño hipnótico.
  light sleep sueño ligero, sueño liviano.
  non-rapid eye movement sleep sueño que no es de movimientos oculares rápidos.
  NREM sleep sueño NREM.
  orthodox sleep sueño ortodoxo.
  paradoxical sleep sueño paradójico.
  paroxysmal sleep sueño paroxístico.
  pathologic sleep sueño patológico.
  prolonged sleep sueño prolongado.
  rapid eye movement sleep sueño de movimientos oculares rápidos (MOR).
  REM sleep sueño de movimientos oculares rápidos (MOR), sueño REM.
  S sleep sueño S.
  synchronized sleep sueño sincronizado.
  temple sleep sueño templo.
  twilight sleep sueño crepuscular.
  winter sleep sueño invernal.
sleeptalking *n.* somniloquia.
sleepwalker *n.* sonámbulo, -la.
sleepwalking *n.* sonambulismo.
slide *n.* laminilla², portaobjetos.
sling *n.* cabestrillo, fronda.
slit *v.* hender.
slop *n.* declive.
slope *n.* vertiente.

slough *n.* esfacelo.
sloughing *adj.* esfacelación, esfacelado, -da.
sludge *n.* barro.
sludging *n.* sedimentación.
slurry *n.* lechada.
smallpox *n.* viruela.
  black smallpox viruela negra.
  coherent smallpox viruela coherente.
  confluent smallpox viruela confluente, viruela confluyente.
  discrete smallpox viruela discreta.
  fulminating smallpox viruela fulminante.
  hemorrhagic smallpox viruela hemorrágica.
  malignant smallpox viruela maligna.
  modified smallpox viruela modificada, viruela variceloide.
  West Indian smallpox viruela antillana.
smear *n.* frotis.
  alimentary tract smear frotis del tracto alimentario.
  blood smear frotis sanguíneo.
  buccal smear frotis bucal.
  cervical smear frotis cervical.
  colonic smear frotis colónico.
  cul-de-sac smear frotis del fondo de saco.
  cytologic smear frotis citológico.
  duodenal smear frotis duodenal.
  ectocervical smear frotis ectocervical.
  endocervical smear frotis endocervical.
  endometrial smear frotis endometrial.
  esophageal smear frotis esofágico.
  fast smear frotis rápido.
  FGT cytologic smear frotis citológico FGT.
  gastric smear frotis gástrico.
  lateral vaginal wall smear frotis de la pared vaginal lateral.
  lower respiratory tract smear frotis del tracto respiratorio inferior.
  oral smear frotis oral.
  pancervical smear frotis pancervical.
  Pap smear frotis de Pap, frotis de Papanicolaou.
  sputum smear frotis de esputo.
  urinary smear frotis urinario.
  vaginal smear frotis vaginal.
smegma *n.* esmegma.
  smegma clitoridis esmegma del clítoris.
  smegma preputii esmegma del prepucio.
smegmalith *n.* esmegmalito, esmegmolito.
smegmatic *adj.* esmegmático, -ca.
smegmolith *n.* esmegmalito, esmegmolito.
smell *v.* oler.
snake *n.* serpiente.
snare *n.* snare.
  cold snare snare frío.
  galvanocaustic snare snare caliente, snare galvanocáustico.
sneeze *n.* estornudo.
snore *n.* ronquido.
snuffbox *n.* tabaquera.
  anatomic snuffbox tabaquera anatómica.
  anatomical snuffbox tabaquera anatómica.
  anatomist's snuffbox tabaquera anatómica.
snuffles *n.* romadizo.
snuffling *n.* nasalización.
soap *n.* jabón.
  animal soap jabón animal.
  carbolic soap jabón fenicado.
  Castile soap jabón de Castilla.
  curd soap jabón de cuajada.
  domestic soap jabón doméstico.
  green soap jabón verde.
  hard soap jabón duro.
  hexachlorophene liquid soap jabón líquido de hexaclorofeno.

insoluble soap jabón insoluble.
marine soap jabón marino.
medicinal soft soap jabón medicinal blando.
potash soap jabón de potasa.
salt water soap jabón de agua salada.
soft soap jabón blando.
soluble soap jabón soluble.
superfatted soap jabón supergraso.
tallow soap jabón de sebo.
zinc soap jabón de cinc.
socia parotidis socia parotidis.
sociology *n.* sociología.
socket *n.* alveolo, alvéolo.
dry socket alvéolo seco.
sodemia *n.* sodemia.
sodium *n.* sodio.
sodium ipodate ipodato sódico.
sodoku *n.* sodoku.
sodomy *n.* sodomía.
softening *n.* reblandecimiento.
sokosho *n.* sokosho.
sol *n.* sol.
solar *adj.* solar.
solarium *n.* solarium.
solenoid *n.* solenoide.
solenoma *n.* solenoma.
solenonychia *n.* solenoniquia.
solid *n.* sólido, -da.
solidification *n.* solidificación.
solipsism *n.* solipsismo.
solitary *adj.* solitario, -ria.
solubility *n.* solubilidad.
soluble *adj.* soluble.
solum solum, suelo.
solute *n.* soluto.
solutio *n.* solución, solutio.
solution solución, solutio.
solvate *n.* solvato.
solvation *n.* solvatación.
solvolysis *n.* solvólisis.
soma *n.* soma.
somatagnosia *n.* somatoagnosia.
somatalgia *n.* somatalgia.
somatesthesia *n.* somatestesia.
somatesthesic *adj.* somatestésico, -ca.
somatic *adj.* somático, -ca.
somaticosplanchnic *adj.* somaticoesplácnico, -ca.
somaticovisceral *adj.* somaticovisceral.
somatist *n.* somatista.
somatization *n.* somatización.
somatoceptor *n.* somatoceptor.
somatoderm *n.* somatoderma, somatodermo.
somatodidymus *n.* somatodídimo, -ma.
somatodymia *n.* somatodimia.
somatoform *adj.* somatoforme.
somatogenesis *n.* somatogenesis, somatogénesis, somatogenia.
somatogenetic *adj.* somatogenético, -ca.
somatogenic *adj.* somatogénico, -ca.
somatogram *n.* somatograma.
somatoliberin *n.* somatoliberina.
somatology *n.* somatología.
somatome *n.* somátomo.
somatomegaly *n.* somatomegalia.
somatometry *n.* somatometría.
somatomic *adj.* somatómico, -ca.
somatommamotropin *n.* somatomamotropina.
chorionic somatommamotropin somatomamotropina coriónica, somatomamotropina coriónica humana (HCS).
human chorionic somatommamotropin (HCS) somatomamotropina coriónica, somatomamotropina coriónica humana (HCS).

somatopagus *n.* somatópago.
somatopathic *adj.* somatopático, -ca.
somatopathy *n.* somatopatía.
somatopleura *n.* somatopleura.
somatopleural *adj.* somatopleural.
somatopleure *n.* somatopleura.
somatoprosthetics *n.* somatoprótesis.
somatopsychic *adj.* somatopsíquico, -ca.
somatoschisis *n.* somatosquisis.
somatoscopy *n.* somatoscopia.
somatosensory *adj.* somatosensorial.
somatosexual *adj.* somatosexual.
somatosplanchcnic *adj.* somatoesplácnico, -ca.
somatosplanchnopleuric *adj.* somatoesplacnopléurico, -ca.
somatostatin *n.* somatostatina.
somatostatinoma *n.* somatostatinoma.
somatotherapy *n.* somatoterapia.
somatotonia *n.* somatotonía.
somatotopagnosia *n.* somatotopoagnosia.
somatotopagnosis *n.* somatotopoagnosia.
somatotopic *adj.* somatotópico, -ca.
somatotopy *n.* somatotopia.
somatotridymus *n.* somatotrídimo.
somatotroph *n.* somatotrofo.
somatotrophic *adj.* somatotrófico, -ca.
somatotropic *adj.* somatotrópico, -ca.
somatotype *n.* somatotipo.
somatotyping *n.* somatotipificación.
somatotypology *n.* somatotipología.
somatotypy *n.* somatotipia.
somite *n.* somita, somite, somito.
occipital somite somita occipital.
somnambulance *n.* sonambulismo.
somnambulism *n.* sonambulismo.
somnambulist *n.* sonámbulo, -la.
somnifacient *adj.* somnifaciente.
somniferous *adj.* somnífero, -ra.
somnific *adj.* somnífero, -ra.
somnifugous *adj.* somnífugo, -ga.
somniloquence *n.* somnilocuencia.
somniloquism *n.* somniloquismo.
somniloquist *n.* somnílocuo, -cua.
somniloquy *n.* somniloquia.
somnipathist *n.* somnípata.
somnipathy *n.* somnipatía.
somnocinematograph *n.* somnocinematógrafo.
somnocinematography *n.* somnocinematografía.
somnolence *n.* somnolencia.
somnolency *n.* somnolencia.
somnolent *adj.* somnoliento, -ta.
somnolentia *n.* somnolencia.
somosphere *n.* somosfera, somósfera.
sonic *adj.* sónico, -ca.
sonicate[1] *adj.* sonicado, -da.
sonicate[2] *v.* sonicar.
sonication *n.* sonicación.
sonifer *n.* sonífero.
sonification *n.* sonificación.
sonifier *n.* sonificador.
sonitus ruido, sonido, sonitus.
sonochemistry *n.* sonoquímica.
sonogram *n.* sonograma.
sonograph *n.* sonógrafo.
sonographic *adj.* sonográfico, -ca.
sonography *n.* sonografía.
sonolucency *n.* sonolucidez.
sonolucent *adj.* sonolúcido, -da.
sonomotor *adj.* sonomotor, -ra.
sonorous *adj.* sonoro, -ra.
sophistication *n.* sofisticación.
sopor *n.* sopor.
soporiferous *adj.* soporífero, -ra.

soporific *n.* soporífico, -ca.
soporose *adj.* soporoso, -sa.
soporous *adj.* soporoso, -sa.
sorb *v.* sorber.
sorbefacient *adj.* sorbefaciente.
sorbent *adj.* sorbente.
sordes *n.* fuliginosidad, sordes.
sore , llaga, ulcus.
hard sore ulcus durum.
pressure sore llaga por presión.
tropical sore ulcus tropicum.
sororiation *n.* sororiación.
souffle *n.* soplo.
apical diastolic souffle soplo diastólico apical.
basal diastolic souffle soplo diastólico basal.
cardiac souffle soplo cardíaco.
ejection souffle soplo de eyección.
fetal souffle soplo fetal.
funic souffle soplo funicular.
funicular souffle soplo funicular.
mammary souffle soplo mamario.
mitral souffle soplo mitral.
physiological souffle soplo fisiológico.
placental souffle soplo placentario.
pulmonary souffle soplo pulmonar.
splenic souffle soplo esplénico.
tricuspid souffle soplo tricuspídeo.
umbilical souffle soplo umbilical.
uterine souffle soplo uterino.
sound[1] *n.* ruido, sonda sonido.
amphoric breath sound ruido respiratorio anfórico, sonido respiratorio anfórico.
amphoric voice sound ruido vocal anfórico.
anvil sound ruido de yunque.
atrial sound ruido auricular.
auscultatory sound ruido auscultatorio, sonido auscultatorio.
bandbox sound ruido de tambor.
Beatty-Bright friction sound ruido de Beatty-Bright, sonido de fricción de Beatty-Bright.
bell sound ruido de campana.
Bellocq's sound sonda de Bellocq.
bellows sound sonido de fuelle.
Béniqué's sound sonda de Béniqué.
bottle sound sonido de botella.
bowel sound ruido intestinal.
Bowman's sound sonda de Bowman.
bronchial breath sound ruido respiratorio bronquial.
bronchovesicular sound sonido broncovesicular.
Campbell sound sonda de Campbell.
cardiac sound ruido cardíaco.
cavernous voice sound ruido vocal cavernoso.
coconut sound ruido de coco.
cracked-pot sound ruido de olla hendida.
Davis interlocking sound sonda articulada de Davis.
double-shock sound ruido de doble shock.
ejection sound ruido de expulsión.
entotic sound sonido entótico.
esophageal sound sonda esofágica.
flapping sound sonido de aleteo.
friction sound ruido de fricción, sonido de fricción.
Guisez's sound sonda de Guisez.
heart sound ruido del corazón, sonido cardíaco.
hippocratic sound ruido hipocrático, sonido hipocrático.
Jewett sound sonda de Jewett.
Korotkoff sound sonido de Korotkoff, ruido de Korotkoff.
lacrimal sound sonda lagrimal.

Le Fort sound sonda de Le Fort.
McCrea sound sonda de McCrea.
Mercier's sound sonda de Mercier.
metallic sound ruido metálico, sonido metálico.
muscle sound ruido muscular, sonido muscular.
peacock sound sonido de pavo real.
percussion sound ruido de percusión, sonido de percusión.
pericardial friction sound ruido de fricción pericárdica.
physiological sound sonido fisiológico.
pistol-shot femoral sound ruido femoral de disparo de revólver.
pistol-shot sound ruido de disparo.
post-tussis suction sound ruido de succión postussis.
pulmonic sound sonido pulmonar.
respiratory sound ruido respiratorio, sonido respiratorio.
sail sound ruido de vela de barco.
Santini's booming sound ruido de Santini.
Simpson uterine sound sonda uterina de Simpson.
Sims uterine sound sonda uterina de Sims.
succussion sound ruido de bazuqueo, ruido de sucusión.
tick-tack sound ruido de tic-tac.
tracheal breath sound ruido respiratorio traqueal, sonido respiratorio traqueal.
urethral sound sonda uretral.
uterine sound sonda uterina.
Van Buren sound sonda de Van Buren.
vesicular breath sound ruido respiratorio vesicular, sonido respiratorio vesicular.
water-whistle sound ruido de silbido de agua.
white sound sonido blanco.
Winternitz's sound sonda de Winternitz.
xiphisternal crunching sound sonido de crepitación xifiesternal.
sound[2] *v.* sondar.
sounding *n.* sondeo.
sour *adj.* agrio, -a.
space *n.* espacio.
anatomical dead space espacio muerto anatómico.
Blessig's space espacio de Blessig.
cell spaces espacios celulares.
chyle space espacio del quilo.
Crookes' space espacio de Crookes.
Czermak's space espacio de Czermak.
escapement space espacio de escape.
freeway space espacio de vía libre.
Haversian space espacio de Havers.
intercristal space espacio intercrestal.
interocclusal rest space espacio interoclusal de reposo, espacio interoclusal en reposo.
interosseous space espacio interóseo.
K space espacio K.
mechanical dead air space espacio aéreo mecánico muerto.
mitochondrial membrane space espacio de la membrana mitocondrial.
perineuronal space espacio perineural.
perinuclear space espacio perinuclear.
perivascular space espacio perivascular.
physiologic dead space espacio muerto fisiológico.
Poiseuille's space espacio de Poiseuille.
presacral space espacio presacro.
thiocyanate space espacio de tiocianato.
spallation *n.* estallido.
span *n.* envergadura.

spaniomenorrhea *n.* espanomenorrea.
Spaniopsis Spaniopsis.
spanopnea *n.* espanopnea.
sparganosis *n.* esparganosis.
ocular sparganosis esparganosis ocular.
Sparganum Sparganum.
spasm *n.* espasmo.
affect spasm espasmo afectivos.
anorectal spasm espasmo anorrectal.
athetoid spasm espasmo atetoide.
Bell's spasm espasmo de Bell.
bronchial spasm espasmo bronquial.
cadaveric spasm espasmo cadavérico.
canine spasm espasmo canino.
carpopedal spasm espasmo carpopedal, espasmo carpopédico.
cerebral spasm espasmo cerebral.
cervical spasm espasmo cervical.
choreiform spasm espasmo coreiforme.
ciliary muscle spasm espasmo del músculo ciliar.
clonic spasm espasmo clónico.
coronary artery spasm espasmo arterial coronario.
cynic spasm espasmo cínico.
dancing spasm espasmo danzante, espasmo de danza.
diffuse esophageal spasm espasmo esofágico, espasmo esofágico difuso.
epidemic transient diaphragmatic spasm espasmo diafragmático transitorio epidémico.
esophageal spasm espasmo esofágico, espasmo esofágico difuso.
facial spasm espasmo facial.
fixed spasm espasmo fijo.
functional spasm espasmo de fatiga, espasmo funcional.
glottic spasm espasmo glótico.
habit spasm espasmo habitual, espasmo por hábito.
hemifacial spasm espasmo hemifacial.
infantile massive spasm espasmo infantil, espasmo infantil masivo.
infantile spasm espasmo infantil, espasmo infantil masivo.
intention spasm espasmo intencional.
lock spasm espasmo de trabamiento.
malleatory spasm espasmo maleatorio.
masticatory spasm espasmo masticatorio.
mimic spasm espasmo mímico.
mixed spasm espasmo mixto.
mobile spasm espasmo móvil.
myopathic spasm espasmo miopático.
nictitating spasm espasmo nictitante.
occupation spasm espasmo ocupacional.
occupational spasm espasmo ocupacional.
perineal spasm espasmo perineal.
phonatory spasm espasmo fonatorio.
phonic spasm espasmo fonatorio.
professional spasm espasmo profesional.
progressive torsion spasm espasmo de torsión progresiva, espasmo progresivo de torsión.
pyloric spasm espasmo pilórico.
pyloric spasm of the newborn gastropilorospasmo del recién nacido.
respiratory spasm espasmo respiratorio.
retrocollic spasm espasmo retrocervical, espasmo retrocólico, retrocolis.
Romberg's spasm espasmo de Romberg.
rotatory spasm espasmo rotatorio.
salaam spasm espasmo salaam, espasmo salutatorio.
saltatory spasm espasmo saltatorio.
sewing spasm espasmo de las costureras.

spasm of accommodation espasmo de acomodación.
synclonic spasm espasmo sinclónico.
tailors' spasm espasmo de los sastres.
tetanic spasm espasmo tetánico.
tonic spasm espasmo tónico.
tonoclonic spasm espasmo tonicoclónico.
tooth spasm espasmo dentario.
torsion spasm espasmo de torsión.
toxic spasm espasmo tóxico.
twitch spasm espasmo muscular.
vaginal spasm espasmo vaginal.
vasomotor spasm espasmo vasomotor.
winking spasm espasmo de guiños, espasmo de parpadeo.
writer's spasm espasmo de los escritores.
spasmodic *adj.* espasmódico, -ca.
spasmogen *n.* espasmógeno.
spasmogenic *adj.* espasmogénico, -ca.
spasmology *n.* espasmología.
spasmolygmus *n.* espasmoligmo.
spasmolysant *adj.* espasmolisante.
spasmolysis *n.* espasmólisis.
spasmolytic *adj.* espasmolítico, -ca.
spasmophile *adj.* espasmófilo, -a.
spasmophilia *n.* espasmofilia.
spasmophilic *adj.* espasmofílico, -ca.
spasmus espasmo, spasmus.
spasmus coordinatus espasmo coordinado.
spasmus glottidis espasmo de la glotis.
spasmus nutans espasmo nutans.
spastic *adj.* espástico, -ca.
spasticity *n.* espasticidad.
spatial *adj.* espacial.
spatium *n.* espacio.
spatula *n.* espátula.
spay *v.* castrar[2].
specialist *n.* especialista.
species *n.* especie.
type species especie tipo.
specific *adj.* específico, -ca.
specificity *n.* especificidad.
bond specificity especificidad de unión.
diagnostic specificity especificidad diagnóstica.
enzymatic specificity especificidad enzimática.
organ specificity especificidad de órgano.
relative specificity especificidad relativa.
specificity of association especificidad de asociación.
stereoisomer specificity especificidad de estereoisomérica.
specillum *n.* especilo.
specimen *n.* espécimen, muestra.
clean-catch specimen muestra no contaminada.
cytologic specimen muestra citológica.
midstream-catch urine specimen muestra de orina de mitad de micción.
random voided specimen muestra miccional aleatoria.
sputum specimen muestra de esputo.
spectacles *n.* anteojos, gafas.
Bartels' spectacles anteojos de Bartels.
bifocal spectacles anteojos bifocales.
clerical spectacles anteojos de clérigo, anteojos de predicador.
compound spectacles anteojos compuestos.
crutch spectacles anteojos de muleta.
decentered spectacles anteojos descentrados.
divers' spectacles anteojos de buzo.
divided spectacles anteojos divididos.
half-glass spectacles anteojos de media lente.

industrial spectacles anteojos industriales.
Masselon's spectacles anteojos de Masselon.
mica spectacles anteojos de mica.
orthoscopic spectacles anteojos ortoscópicos.
pantoscopic spectacles anteojos pantoscópicos.
periscopic spectacles anteojos periscópicos.
photochromic spectacles anteojos fotocrómicos.
prismatic spectacles anteojos prismáticos.
protective spectacles anteojos protectores.
pulpit spectacles anteojos de púlpito.
safety spectacles anteojos de seguridad.
stenopaic spectacles anteojos estenopeicos.
stenopeic spectacles anteojos estenopeicos.
tinted spectacles anteojos entintados.
trifocal spectacles anteojos trifocales.
wire frame spectacles anteojos de armazón de alambre.
spectral *adj.* espectral.
spectrochemistry *n.* espectroquímica.
spectrocolorimeter *n.* espectrocolorímetro.
spectrofluorometer *n.* espectrofluorómetro.
spectrogram *n.* espectrograma.
spectrograph *n.* espectrógrafo.
  mass spectrograph espectrógrafo de masa.
spectrography *n.* espectrografía.
spectrometer *n.* espectrómetro.
  mass spectrometer espectrómetro de masa.
  Mössbauer spectrometer espectrómetro de Mössbauer.
spectrometry *n.* espectrometría.
spectrophobia *n.* espectrofobia.
spectrophotofluorimetry *n.* espectrofotofluorimetría.
spectrophotofluorometer *n.* espectrofotofluorómetro.
spectrophotometer *n.* espectrofotómetro.
spectrophotometry *n.* espectrofotometría.
  atomic absorption spectrophotometry espectrofotometría por absorción atómica.
  flame emission spectrophotometry espectrofotometría por emisión de llama.
spectropolarimeter *n.* espectropolarímetro.
spectropyrheliometer *n.* espectropireliómetro.
spectroscope *n.* espectroscopio.
  direct vision spectroscope espectroscopio de visión directa.
spectroscopic *adj.* espectroscópico, -ca.
spectroscopy *n.* espectroscopia.
  infrared spectroscopy espectroscopia infrarroja.
  magnetic resonance spectroscopy espectroscopia por resonancia magnética.
spectrum *n.* espectro.
  absorption spectrum espectro de absorción.
  action spectrum espectro de acción.
  antimicrobial spectrum espectro antimicrobiano.
  broad spectrum espectro amplio.
  chemical spectrum espectro químico.
  chromatic spectrum espectro cromático.
  color spectrum espectro de color.
  continuous spectrum espectro continuo.
  continuous X-ray spectrum espectro de rayos X continuo.
  diffraction spectrum espectro de difracción.
  electromagnetic spectrum espectro electromagnético.
  fortification spectrum espectro de fortificación.
  gaseous spectrum espectro gaseoso.
  infrared spectrum espectro infrarrojo.

invisible spectrum espectro invisible.
ocular spectrum espectro ocular.
prismatic spectrum espectro prismático.
solar spectrum espectro solar.
thermal spectrum espectro calorífico, espectro térmico.
toxin spectrum espectro de toxinas.
visible spectrum espectro visible.
wide spectrum espectro amplio.
X-ray spectrum espectro de rayos X.
speculum *n.* espéculo.
  bivalve speculum espéculo bivalvo.
  Bozeman's speculum espéculo de Bozeman.
  Brinkerhoff's speculum espéculo de Brinkerhoff.
  Cooke's speculum espéculo Cooke, espéculo de Cook.
  Cook's speculum espéculo Cooke, espéculo de Cook.
  duckbill speculum espéculo de pico de pato, espéculo en pico de pato.
  duck-billed speculum espéculo de pico de pato, espéculo en pico de pato.
  ear speculum espéculo de oído.
  eye speculum espéculo ocular.
  Fergusson's speculum espéculo de Fergusson.
  Fränkel speculum espéculo de Fränkel.
  Gruber's speculum espéculo de Gruber.
  Hartmann's speculum espéculo de Hartmann.
  Kelly's rectal speculum espéculo rectal de Kelly.
  Kelly's speculum espéculo de Kelly.
  Martin and Davy speculum espéculo de Martin, espéculo de Martin y Davy.
  Martin's speculum espéculo de Martin, espéculo de Martin y Davy.
  Mathews speculum espéculo de Mathews.
  nasal speculum espéculo nasal.
  Pedersen's speculum espéculo de Pedersen.
  Politzer's speculum espéculo de Politzer.
  Sims' speculum espéculo de Sims.
  stop speculum espéculo con tope, espéculo de detención, espéculo graduado.
  wire bivalve speculum espéculo metálico bivalvo.
speech *n.* habla, lenguaje[2].
  adenoid speech habla adenoidea.
  alaryngeal speech habla alaríngea.
  aphonic speech lenguaje afónico.
  ataxic speech lenguaje atáxico.
  automatic speech lenguaje automático.
  cerebellar speech habla cerebelosa, lenguaje cerebeloso.
  clipped speech habla cercenada, lenguaje cercenado.
  echo speech ecolalia, habla ecolálica.
  esophageal speech habla esofágica, lenguaje esofágico.
  explosive speech habla explosiva, lenguaje explosivo.
  incoherent speech habla incoherente.
  jumbled speech habla confusa.
  mirror speech en espejo, habla en espejo, lenguaje especular.
  non-spontaneous speech habla no espontánea.
  plateau speech habla en meseta.
  pressured speech habla apremiante, habla apresurada.
  scamping speech lenguaje cercenado.
  scanning speech habla escándida, lenguaje escándido.
  serial speech lenguaje seriado.

slurring speech habla arrastrada.
spastic speech habla espástica.
staccato speech habla entrecortada, lenguaje en staccato.
syllabic speech habla silábica.
speed *n.* velocidad.
spelencephaly *n.* espelencefalia.
speleostomy *n.* espeleostomía.
sperm *n.* esperma.
spermacrasia *n.* espermacrasia.
spermagglutination *n.* espermaglutinación.
spermalist *n.* espermalista.
spermatemphraxis *n.* espermatenfraxis.
spermatic *adj.* espermático, -ca.
spermaticidal *adj.* espermaticida[2], espermatocida[2].
spermaticide *n.* espermaticida[1], espermatocida[1].
spermatid *n.* espermátide.
spermatitis *n.* espermatitis.
spermatocele *n.* espermatocele.
spermatocelectomy *n.* espermatocelectomía.
spermatocidal *adj.* espermaticida[2], espermatocida[2].
spermatocide *n.* espermaticida[1], espermatocida[1].
spermatocyst *n.* espermatocele, espermatocisto.
spermatocystectomy *n.* espermatocistectomía.
spermatocystitis *n.* espermatocistitis.
spermatocystotomy *n.* espermatocistotomía.
spermatocytal *adj.* espermatocítico, -ca.
spermatocyte *n.* espermatocito.
  primary spermatocyte espermatocito primario.
  secondary spermatocyte espermatocito secundario.
spermatocytogenesis *n.* espermatocitogénesis.
spermatocytoma *n.* espermatocitoma.
spermatogenesis *n.* espermatogénesis.
spermatogenetic *adj.* espermatogenético, -ca.
spermatogenic *adj.* espermatogénico, -ca.
spermatogenous *adj.* espermatógeno, -na.
spermatogeny *n.* espermatogenia.
spermatogonium *n.* espermatogonia, espermatogonio.
spermatoid *adj.* espermatoide.
spermatolysis *n.* espermatólisis.
spermatolytic *adj.* espermatolítico, -ca.
spermatopathia *n.* espermatopatía.
spermatopathy *n.* espermatopatía.
spermatophobia *n.* espermatofobia.
spermatopoietic *adj.* espermatopoyético, -ca.
spermatorrhea *n.* espermatorrea.
spermatoschesis *n.* espermatosquesis.
spermatotoxin *n.* espermatotoxina.
spermatozoal *adj.* espermatozoico, -ca.
spermatozoid *n.* espermatozoide.
spermatozoon *n.* espermatozoo.
spermaturia *n.* espermaturia.
spermectomy *n.* espermectomía.
spermiation *n.* espermiación.
spermicidal *adj.* espermicida[2].
spermicide *n.* espermicida[1].
spermiduct *n.* espermiducto.
spermiocyte *n.* espermiocito.
spermiogenesis *n.* espermiogénesis.
spermiogram *n.* espermiograma.
spermioteleosis *n.* espermioteliosis.
spermioteleotic *adj.* espermioteliótico, -ca.
spermium *n.* espermio.
spermoblast *n.* espermoblasto.
spermocytoma *n.* espermocitoma.

spermogonium *n.* espermogonio.
spermolith *n.* espermolito.
spermoloropexis *n.* espermoloropexis.
spermoloropexy *n.* espermoloropexia.
spermolysis *n.* espermólisis.
spermolytic *adj.* espermolítico, -ca.
spermoneuralgia *n.* espermoneuralgia.
spermophleboectasia *n.* espermoflebectasia.
spermospore *n.* espermoespora, espermospora.
spermotoxic *adj.* espermotóxico, -ca.
spermotoxin *n.* espermotoxina.
sphacelation *n.* esfacelación.
sphaceloderma *n.* esfacelodermia.
sphacelous *adj.* esfacelado, -da.
sphacelus *n.* esfacelo.
sphagitis *n.* esfagitis.
sphenetmoid *adj.* esfenoetmoides.
sphenion *n.* esfenión.
sphenobasilar *adj.* esfenobasilar.
sphenocephalus *n.* esfenocéfalo.
sphenocephaly *adj.* esfenocefalia.
sphenoethmoid *adj.* esfenoetmoidal, esfenoetmoides.
sphenofrontal *adj.* esfenofrontal.
sphenoid *adj.* esfenoideo, -a, esfenoides.
sphenoidal *adj.* esfenoidal.
sphenoiditis *n.* esfenoiditis.
sphenoidostomy *n.* esfenoidostomía.
sphenoidotomy *n.* esfenoidotomía.
sphenomalar *adj.* esfenomalar.
sphenomaxillary *adj.* esfenomaxilar.
sphenometer *n.* esfenómetro.
spheno-occipital *adj.* esfenooccipital.
sphenopagus *n.* esfenópago.
sphenopalatine *adj.* esfenopalatino, -na.
sphenoparietal *adj.* esfenoparietal.
sphenopetrosal *adj.* esfenopetroso, -sa.
sphenorbital *adj.* esfenoorbital, esfenoorbitario, - ria.
sphenosquamosal *adj.* esfenoescamoso, -sa, esfenoscamoso, -sa.
sphenotemporal *adj.* esfenotemporal.
sphenotic *adj.* esfenótico, -ca.
sphenotresia *n.* esfenotresia.
sphenotribe *n.* esfenotribo.
sphenotripsy *n.* esfenotripsia.
sphenoturbinal *adj.* esfenoturbinal.
sphenovomerine *adj.* esfenovomeriano, -na, esfenovomerino, -na.
sphenozygomatic *adj.* esfenocigomático, -ca.
sphere *n.* esfera.
  attraction sphere esfera de atracción.
  embryotic sphere esfera embriótica.
  Morgagni's sphere esfera de Morgagni.
  segmentation sphere esfera de segmentación.
  vitelline sphere esfera vitelina.
  yolk sphere esfera vitelina.
spherical *adj.* esférico, -ca.
spherocylinder *n.* esferocilindro.
spherocyte *n.* esferocito.
spherocytic *adj.* esferocítico, -ca.
spherocytosis *n.* esferocitosis.
  hereditary spherocytosis esferocitosis hereditaria.
spheroid *adj.* esferoide.
spheroidal *adj.* esferoidal.
spherolith *n.* esferolito.
spherometer *n.* esferómetro.
spherophakia *n.* esferofaquia.
spheroplast *n.* esferoplasto.
spheroprism *n.* esferoprisma.
spherospermia *n.* esferospermia.
spherule *n.* esférula.

spherule of Fulci esférula de Fulci.
spherulin *n.* esferulina.
sphigmobologram *n.* esfigmobolograma.
sphincter *n.* esfinter.
  AMS-800 artificial sphincter esfinter artificial AMS-800.
  artificial sphincter esfinter artificial.
  extrinsic sphincter esfinter extrínseco.
  microscopic sphincter esfinter microscópico.
  Nélaton's sphincter esfinter de Nélaton.
  Oddi's sphincter esfinter de Oddi.
  ostial sphincter esfinter ostial.
  pathologic sphincter esfinter patológico.
sphincteralgia *n.* esfinteralgia.
sphincterectomy *n.* esfinterectomía.
sphincterial *adj.* esfinteriano, -na.
sphincterismus *n.* esfinterismo.
sphincteritis *n.* esfinteritis.
sphincteroid *adj.* esfinteroide.
sphincterolysis *n.* esfinterólisis.
sphincteroplasty *n.* esfinteroplastia.
sphincteroscope *n.* esfinteroscopio.
sphincteroscopy *n.* esfinteroscopia.
sphincterotome *n.* esfinterótomo.
sphincterotomy *n.* esfinterotomía.
  endoscopic sphincterotomy esfinterotomía endoscópica.
  lateral sphincterotomy esfinterotomía lateral interna.
  transduodenal sphincterotomy esfinterotomía transduodenal.
  urethral sphincterotomy esfinterotomía uretral.
sphingogalactoside *n.* esfingogalactósido.
sphingolipid *n.* esfingolípido.
sphingolipidosis *n.* esfingolipidosis.
  cerebral sphingolipidosis esfingolipidosis cerebral.
  infantile cerebral sphingolipidosis esfingolipidosis cerebral infantil.
sphingolipodystrophy *n.* esfingolipodistrofia.
sphingomyelin *n.* esfingomielina.
sphingomyelinosis *n.* esfingomielinosis.
sphygmic *adj.* esfígmico, -ca.
sphygmobolometer *n.* esfigmobolómetro.
sphygmobolometry *n.* esfigmobolometría.
sphygmocardiogram *n.* esfigmocardiograma.
sphygmocardiograph *n.* esfigmocardiógrafo.
sphygmocardioscope *n.* esfigmocardioscopio.
sphygmochronograph *n.* esfigmocronógrafo.
sphygmodynamometer *n.* esfigmodinamómetro.
sphygmogenin *n.* esfigmogenina.
sphygmogram *n.* esfigmograma.
sphygmograph *n.* esfigmógrafo.
sphygmographic *adj.* esfigmográfico, -ca.
sphygmography *n.* esfigmografía.
sphygmoid *adj.* esfigmoide, esfigmoideo, -a.
sphygmology *n.* esfigmología.
sphygmomanometer *n.* esfigmomanómetro.
  Mosso's sphygmomanometer esfigmomanómetro de Mosso.
  Rogers' sphygmomanometer esfigmomanómetro de Rogers.
sphygmomanometry *n.* esfigmomanometría.
sphygmometer *n.* esfigmómetro.
sphygmometrograph *n.* esfigmometrógrafo.
sphygmometroscope *n.* esfigmometroscopio.
sphygmometry *n.* esfigmometría.
sphygmo-oscillometer *n.* esfigmooscilómetro.
sphygmopalpation *n.* esfigmopalpación.
sphygmophone *n.* esfigmófono.

sphygmoplethysmograph *n.* esfigmopletismógrafo.
sphygmoscope *n.* esfigmoscopio.
  Bishop's sphygmoscope esfigmoscopio de Bishop.
sphygmoscopy *n.* esfigmoscopia.
sphygmosystole *n.* esfigmosístole.
sphygmotonograph *n.* esfigmotonógrafo.
sphygmotonometer *n.* esfigmotonómetro.
sphygmoviscosimetry *n.* esfigmoviscosimetría.
spicular *adj.* espicular.
spicule *n.* espícula.
spiculum *n.* espícula.
spider *n.* araña.
  arterial spider araña arterial.
  vascular spider araña vascular.
spill *n.* derramamiento.
spillway *n.* derramadero, vertedero.
  occlusal spillway vertedero oclusivo.
spiloma *n.* espiloma.
spiloplaxia *n.* espiloplaxia.
spilus *n.* espilo.
spin *n.* spin.
  nuclear spin spin nuclear.
spina *n.* espina.
  spina bifida espina bífida.
  spina bifida anterior espina bífida anterior.
  spina bifida aperta espina bífida abierta.
  spina bifida cystica espina bífida quística.
  spina bifida manifesta espina bífida manifiesta.
  spina bifida occulta espina bífida oculta.
  spina bifida posterior espina bífida posterior.
  spina ventosa espina ventosa.
spinal *adj.* espinal.
spinalgia *n.* espinalgia.
spinate *adj.* espinado, -da.
spindle *n.* huso.
  aortic spindle huso aórtico.
  Axenfeld-Krukenberg spindle huso de Axenfeld-Krukenberg, huso de Krukenberg.
  central spindle huso central.
  cleavage spindle huso de segmentación.
  enamel spindle huso del esmalte.
  His spindle huso de His.
  Kühne's spindle huso de Kühne.
  mitotic spindle huso mitótico.
  muscle spindle huso muscular.
  muscular spindle huso muscular.
  neuromuscular spindle huso neuromuscular.
  neurotendinous spindle huso neurotendinoso.
  nuclear spindle huso nuclear.
  tigroid spindle huso tigroide.
  urine spindle huso urinaria.
spine *n.* espina.
  bamboo spine espina de bambú.
  bifid spine espina bífida.
  Civinni's spine espina de Civinni.
  cleft spine espina dividida, espina hendida.
  dendritic spine espina dendrítica.
  dorsal spine espina dorsal.
  poker spine espina dorsal rígida.
  railway spine espina de ferrocarril.
spinifugal *adj.* espinífugo, -ga.
spinipetal *adj.* espinípeto, -ta, espinópeto, -ta.
spinnbarkeit *n.* spinnbarkeit.
spinobulbar *adj.* espinobulbar.
spinocellular *adj.* espinocelular.
spinocerebellar *adj.* espinocerebeloso, -sa.
spinocollicular *adj.* espinocolicular.
spinocortical *adj.* espinocortical.
spinocostalis *n.* espinocostal.
spinogalvanization *n.* espinogalvanización.

spinoglenoid *adj.* espinoglenoideo, -a.
spinomuscular *adj.* espinomuscular.
spinoneural *adj.* espinoneural.
spino-olivar *adj.* espinoolivar.
spinopetal *adj.* espinípeto, -ta, espínopeto, -ta.
spinoreticular *adj.* espinorreticular.
spinotectal *adj.* espinotectal.
spinothalamic *adj.* espinotalámico, -ca.
spintharicon *n.* espintaricón.
spinthariscope *n.* espintariscopio, espinteroscopio.
spintherism *n.* espinterismo, espinteropía, espinteropsia.
spintherometer *n.* espinterómetro.
spiradenitis *n.* espiradenitis.
spiradenoma *n.* espiradenoma.
  cylindromatous spiradenoma espiradenoma cilindromatoso.
  eccrine spiradenoma espiradenoma ecrino.
spiral *adj., n.* espiral.
  Curschmann's spiral espiral de Curschmann.
  spiral of Tillaux espiral de Tillaux.
spirillar *adj.* espirilar.
spirillemia *n.* espirilemia.
spirillicidal *adj.* espirilicida.
spirillicidin *n.* espirilicidina.
spirillosis *n.* espirilosis.
spirillum *n.* espirilo.
spirilotropic *adj.* espirilotrópico, -ca.
spirochaeta *n.* espiroqueta.
spirochetal *adj.* espiroquetal.
spirochete *n.* espiroqueta, espirosoma.
spirochetemia *n.* espiroquetemia.
spirocheticidal *adj.* espiroqueticida.
spirochetogenous *adj.* espiroquetógeno, -ña.
spirochetolysin *n.* espiroquetolisina.
spirochetolysis *n.* espiroquetólisis.
spirochetosis *n.* espiroquetosis.
  bronchopulmonary spirochetosis espiroquetosis broncopulmonar.
  spirochetosis arthritica espiroquetosis artrítica.
spirochetotic *adj.* espiroquetósico, -ca.
spirocheturia *n.* espiroqueturia.
spirogram *n.* espirograma.
spirograph *n.* espirógrafo.
spirography *n.* espirografía.
spiroid *adj.* espiroidal, espiroideo.
spiro-index *n.* espiro-índice.
spiroma *n.* espiroma.
spirometer *n.* espirómetro.
  chain-compensated spirometer espirómetro compensado por una cadena.
  Krogh spirometer espirómetro de Krogh.
  Tissot's spirometer espirómetro de Tissot.
  wedge spirometer espirómetro en cuña.
Spirometra Spirometra.
spirometric *adj.* espirométrico, -ca.
spirometry *n.* espirometría.
  bronchoscopic spirometry espirometría broncoscópica.
  incentive spirometry espirometría incentivada.
spirophore *n.* espiróforo.
spiroscope *n.* espiroscopio.
spiroscopy *n.* espiroscopia.
spissated *adj.* espesado, -da.
spitting *n.* gargajeo.
spittoon *n.* escupidera.
splachnapophysis *n.* esplacnapófisis.
splanchnapophyseal *adj.* esplacnapofisario, -ria, esplacnoapofisario, -ria.
splanchnapophysial *adj.* esplacnapofisario, -ria, esplacnoapofisario, -ria.
splanchnapophysis *n.* esplacnoapófisis.
splanchnectopia *n.* esplacnectopia, esplacnotopia.

splanchnemphraxis *n.* esplacnenfraxis.
splanchnesthesia *n.* esplacnestesia.
splanchnesthetic *adj.* esplacnestésico, -ca.
splanchnic *adj.* esplácnico, -ca.
splanchnicectomy *n.* esplacnicectomía.
splanchnicotomy *n.* esplacnicotomía.
splanchnoblast *n.* esplacnoblasto.
splanchnocele *n.* esplacnocele.
splanchnocranium *n.* esplacnocráneo.
splanchnoderm *n.* esplacnodermo.
splanchnodiastasis *n.* esplacnodiastasis.
splanchnography *n.* esplacnografía.
splanchnolith *n.* esplacnolito.
splanchnology *n.* esplacnología.
splanchnomegalia *n.* esplacnomegalia.
splanchnomegaly *n.* esplacnomegalia.
splanchnomicria *n.* esplacnomicria.
splanchnopathy *n.* esplacnopatía.
splanchnopleura *n.* esplacnopleura.
splanchnopleural *adj.* esplacnopleural.
splanchnopleure *n.* esplacnopleura.
splanchnopleuric *adj.* esplacnopléurico, -ca.
splanchnoptosia *n.* esplacnoptosis.
splanchnoptosis *n.* esplacnoptosis.
splanchnosclerosis *n.* esplacnoesclerosis, esplacnosclerosis.
splanchnoscopy *n.* esplacnoscopia.
splanchnoskeletal *adj.* esplacnoesquelético, -ca.
splanchnoskeleton *n.* esplacnoesqueleto, esplacnosqueleto.
splanchnosomatic *adj.* esplacnosomático, -ca.
splanchnotomy *n.* esplacnotomía.
splanchnotribe *n.* esplacnotribo.
splay *n.* splay.
spleen *n.* bazo.
  accessory spleen bazo accesorio.
  bacon spleen bazo de tocino.
  cyanotic spleen bazo cianótico.
  diffuse waxy spleen bazo céreo difuso.
  enlarged spleen bazo aumentado de tamaño.
  flecked spleen of Feitis bazo moteado de Feitis.
  floating spleen bazo flotante.
  Gandy-Gamna spleen bazo Gandy-Gamna.
  hard-baked spleen bazo durococido.
  lardaceous spleen bazo lardáceo.
  movable spleen bazo movible, bazo móvil.
  porphyria spleen bazo de porfiria, bazo porfídico.
  prophyry spleen bazo de porfiria, bazo porfídico.
  sago spleen bazo jaspeado, bazo sagú.
  speckled spleen bazo moteado.
  sugar-coated spleen bazo azucarado, bazo recubierto de azúcar.
  wandering spleen bazo errante.
  waxy spleen bazo céreo.
splen *n.* bazo.
splenadenoma *n.* esplenadenoma, esplenoadenoma.
splenalgia *n.* esplenalgia.
splenatrophy *n.* esplenatrofia.
splenauxe *n.* esplenauxa.
splenceratosis *n.* esplenoceratosis.
splenculus *n.* esplénculo.
splenectasis *n.* esplenectasia, esplenoectasia.
splenectomy *n.* esplenectomía.
  partial splenectomy esplenectomía parcial.
splenectopia *n.* esplenectopia.
splenectopy *n.* esplenectopia.
splenelcosis *n.* esplenelcosis.
splenemia *n.* esplenemia, esplenohemia.
splenemphraxis *n.* esplenenfraxis.
spleneolus *n.* esplenéolo.

splenetic *adj.* esplenético, -ca.
splenial *adj.* esplenial.
splenic *adj.* esplénico, -ca.
splenicterus *n.* esplenícterus.
spleniculus *n.* esplenículo, esplenúnculo.
splenification *n.* esplenificación.
spleniform *adj.* espleniforme.
spleniserrate *adj.* espleniserrato, -ta.
splenitis *n.* esplenitis.
  spodogenous splenitis esplenitis espodógena.
splenium *n.* esplenio, splenium.
  splenium corporis callosi splenium del cuerpo calloso.
splenization *n.* esplenización.
  hypostatic splenization esplenización hipostática.
splenoblast *n.* esplenoblasto.
splenocele *n.* esplenocele.
splenoceratosis *n.* esplenoceratosis.
splenocleisis *n.* esplenocleisis.
splenocolic *adj.* esplenocólico, -ca.
splenocyte *n.* esplenocito.
splenodynia *n.* esplenodinia.
splenogenous *adj.* esplenógeno, -na.
splenogram *n.* esplenograma.
splenography *n.* esplenografía.
splenohepatomegalia *n.* esplenohepatomegalia.
splenohepatomegaly *n.* esplenohepatomegalia.
splenoid *adj.* esplenoide, esplenoideo, -a.
splenokeratosis *n.* esplenoqueratosis.
splenolaparotomy *n.* esplenolaparotomía.
splenology *n.* esplenología.
splenolymphatic *adj.* esplenolinfático, -ca.
splenolysis *n.* esplenólisis.
splenoma *n.* esplenocitoma, esplenoma.
splenomalacia *n.* esplenomalacia.
splenomedullary *adj.* esplenomedular.
splenomegaly *n.* esplenomegalia.
  congestive splenomegaly esplenomegalia congestiva.
  Egyptian splenomegaly esplenomegalia egipcia.
  febrile tropical splenomegaly esplenomegalia tropical, esplenomegalia tropical febril.
  Gaucher splenomegaly esplenomegalia de Gaucher.
  hemolytic splenomegaly esplenomegalia hemolítica.
  hyperreactive malarious splenomegaly esplenomegalia palúdica hiperreactiva.
  infectious splenomegaly esplenomegalia infecciosa.
  infective splenomegaly esplenomegalia infecciosa.
  myelopthisic splenomegaly esplenomegalia mielotísica.
  Niemann splenomegaly esplenomegalia de Niemann.
  siderotic splenomegaly esplenomegalia siderótica.
  thrombophlebitic splenomegaly esplenomegalia tromboflebítica.
  tropical splenomegaly esplenomegalia tropical, esplenomegalia tropical febril.
splenometry *n.* esplenometría.
splenomyelogenous *adj.* esplenomielógeno, -na.
splenomyelomalacia *n.* esplenomielomalacia.
splenoncus *n.* esplenonco.
splenonephric *adj.* esplenonéfrico, -ca.
splenonephroptosis *n.* esplenonefroptosis.

splenopancreatic *adj.* esplenopancreático, -ca.
splenoparectasis *n.* esplenoparectasia.
splenopathy *n.* esplenopatía.
splenopexia *n.* esplenopexia.
splenopexis *n.* esplenopexia.
splenophrenic *adj.* esplenofrénico, -ca.
splenoplexy *n.* esplenopexia.
splenopneumonia *n.* esplenoneumonía, esplenopulmonitis.
splenoportogram *n.* esplenoportograma.
splenoportography *n.* esplenoportografía.
   direct splenoportography esplenoportografía directa.
   indirect splenoportography esplenoportografía indirecta.
splenoptosia *n.* esplenoptosia, esplenoptosis.
splenoptosis *n.* esplenoptosia, esplenoptosis.
splenorenal *adj.* esplenorrenal.
splenorenopexia *n.* esplenorrenopexia.
splenorrhagia *n.* esplenorragia.
splenorrhaphy *n.* esplenorrafia.
splenosis *n.* esplenosis.
   pericardial splenosis esplenosis pericárdica.
splenotomy *n.* esplenotomía.
splenotoxin *n.* esplenotoxina.
splenule *n.* esplénulo.
splenulus *n.* esplénulo.
splenunculus *n.* esplenículo, esplenúnculo.
spliceosoma *n.* espliceosoma.
splicing *n.* empalme.
splint *n.* férula.
   abutment splint férula de lindero, férula de sostén.
   acid etch cemented splint férula cementada por grabado en ácido.
   active splint férula activa.
   Agnew's splint férula de Agnew.
   air splint férula de aire, férula neumática.
   airplane splint férula en abducción, férula en aeroplano.
   anchor splint férula de fijación, férula en ancla.
   Anderson splint férula de Anderson.
   Angle's splint férula de Angle.
   Asch splint férula de Asch.
   Ashhurst's splint férula de Ashhurst.
   backboard splint férula dorsal, férula posterior.
   banjo traction splint férula de tracción de banjo.
   Bavarian splint férula bávara.
   biteguard splint férula de protección de la mordida.
   Böhler's splint férula de Böhler.
   Bond's splint férula de Bond.
   bracketed splint férula de trabas.
   buccal splint férula bucal.
   Cabot's splint férula de Cabot.
   cap splint férula dental, férula en capuchón.
   Carter's intranasal splint férula intranasal de Carter.
   Charfield-Girdleston splint férula de Charfield-Girdleston.
   coaptation splint férula de coaptación.
   cockup splint férula de muñeca.
   contact splint férula de contacto.
   Cramer wire splint férula de alambre de Cramer.
   Cramer's splint férula de Cramer.
   Denis Browne splint férula de Denis Browne.
   dynamic splint férula dinámica.
   Essig splint férula de Essig.
   Essig-type splint férula de tipo de Essig.
   Fox's splint férula de Fox.
   fracture splint férula de fractura.

   Frejka pillow splint férula de almohada de Frejka.
   Frejka splint férula de Frejka.
   functional splint férula funcional.
   Gibson's walking splint férula de marcha de Gibson.
   Gilmer's splint férula de Gilmer.
   Gordon's splint férula de Gordon.
   Gunning splint férula de Gunning.
   Hodgen splint férula de Hodgen.
   inflatable splint férula inflable.
   inlay splint férula de incrustación.
   interdental splint férula interdental, férula interdentaria.
   Jones nasal splint férula nasal de Jones.
   Kanavel cockup splint férula de levantamiento de Kanavel.
   Keller-Blake splint férula de Keller-Blake.
   Kingsley splint férula de Kingsley.
   Kirschner wire splint férula de alambre de Kirschner.
   labial splint férula labial, férula vestibular.
   ladder splint férula en escalera, férula escalonada.
   Levis' splint férula de Levis.
   lingual splint férula lingual, férula palatina.
   Liston's splint férula de Liston.
   live splint férula viva.
   Mason's splint férula de Mason.
   Mclintire splint férula de Mclintire.
   night splint férula nocturna.
   opponens splint férula oponente.
   plaster splint férula de yeso.
   plastic splint férula de plástico.
   poroplastic splint férula poroplástica.
   Porzett splint férula de Porzett.
   reverse Kingsley splint férula invertida de Kingsley.
   Roger Anderson splint férula de Roger Anderson.
   Sayre's splint férula de Sayre.
   Simpson's splint férula de Simpson.
   Staeder splint férula de Staeder.
   Stromeyer's splint férula de stromeyer.
   surgical splint férula quirúrgica.
   T splint férula en T.
   Taylor's splint férula de Taylor.
   therapeutic splint férula terapéutica.
   Thomas knee splint férula de rodilla de Thomas.
   Thomas posterior splint férula posterior de Thomas.
   Thomas splint férula de thomas.
   Tobruk splint férula de Tobruk.
   Toronto splint férula Toronto.
   Valentine's splint férula de Valentine.
   Volkman splint férula de Volkman.
   Wertheim splint férula de Wertheim.
   wire splint férula de alambre.
splinter[1] *n.* astilla, esquirla.
   bone splinter astilla ósea.
splinter[2] *v.* astillar.
splinting *n.* entablillado, ferulización.
split *n.* escisión[3].
splitting *n.* desdiferenciación[2], desdoblamiento, escisión[3].
   sagittal splitting of the mandible desdoblamiento sagital de la mandíbula.
   splitting of heart sounds desdoblamiento de los ruidos cardíacos.
spodogenous *adj.* espodógeno, -na.
spodophorous *adj.* espodóforo, -ra.
spodylous *adj.* espondíleo, -a.
spondylalgia *n.* espondilalgia.
spondylarthritis *n.* espondilartritis, espondiloartritis.

   spondylarthritis ankylopoietica espondilartritis anquilopoyética.
spondylarthrosis *n.* espondilartrosis.
spondylitic *adj.* espondilítico, -ca.
spondylitis *n.* espondilitis.
   ankylosing spondylitis espondilitis anquilosante.
   Bechterew's spondylitis espondilitis de Bechterew.
   hypertrofic spondylitis espondilitis hipertrófica.
   Kümmell's spondylitis espondilitis de Kümmell.
   Marie-Strümpell spondylitis espondilitis de Marie-Strümpell.
   muscular spondylitis espondilitis muscular.
   postraumatic spondylitis espondilitis postraumática.
   rheumatoid spondylitis espondilitis reumatoide, espondilitis reumatoidea.
   rhizomelic spondylitis espondilitis rizomélica.
   spondylitis ankylopoietica espondilitis anquilopoyética.
   spondylitis ankylosans espondilitis anquilosante.
   spondylitis brucella espondilitis brucelósica.
   spondylitis deformans espondilitis deformante.
   spondylitis infectiosa espondilitis infecciosa.
   spondylitis rhizomelica espondilitis rizomélica.
   spondylitis tuberculosa espondilitis tuberculosa.
   spondylitis typhosa espondilitis tífica, espondilitis tifosa.
   traumatic spondylitis espondilitis traumática.
   tuberculous spondylitis espondilitis tuberculosa.
   vertebral spondylitis espondilitis vertebral.
spondylizema *n.* espondilicema, espondilocema.
spondyloarthrography *n.* espondiloartrografía.
spondyloarthropathy *n.* espondiloartropatía.
spondylocace *n.* espondilocace.
spondyloclisis *n.* espondiloclisis.
spondylodidymia *n.* espondilodidimia.
spondylodynia *n.* espondilodinia.
spondylolisthesis *n.* espondilolistesis.
   congenital spondylolisthesis espondilolistesis congénita.
   degenerative spondylolisthesis espondilolistesis degenerativa.
   dysplasic spondylolisthesis espondilolistesis displásica.
   isthmic spondylolisthesis espondilolistesis ístmica.
spondylolisthetic *adj.* espondilolistésico, -ca.
spondylolysis *n.* espondilólisis.
spondylomalacia *n.* espondilomalacia.
   spondylomalacia traumatica espondilomalacia traumatica.
spondylomyelitis *n.* espondilomielitis.
spondylopathy *n.* espondilopatía.
   traumatic spondylopathy espondilopatía traumática.
spondyloptosis *n.* espondiloptosis.
spondylopyosis *n.* espondilopiosis.
spondyloschisis *n.* espondilosquisis.
spondylosis *n.* espondilosis.
   cervical spondylosis espondilosis cervical.
   hyperostotic spondylosis espondilosis hiperostótica.

lumbar spondylosis espondilosis lumbar.

spondylosis chronica ankylopoietica espondilosis crónica anquilopoyética.

spondylosis uncovertebralis espondilosis uncovertebral.

spondylosyndesis *n.* espondilosindesis.

spondylothoracic *adj.* espondilotorácico, -ca.

spondylotic *adj.* espondilótico, -ca.

spondylotomy *n.* espondilotomía.

spondylous *adj.* espondiloso, -sa.

spondylozema *n.* espondilicema, espondilocema.

sponge *n.* esponja, tampón.

abdominal sponge esponja abdominal.

absorbable gelatin sponge esponja absorbible de gelatina, esponja de gelatina, esponja de gelatina absorbible, esponja gelatinada absorbible.

Bernays' sponge esponja de Bernays.

bronchoscopic sponge esponja broncoscópica.

compressed sponge esponja comprimida.

contraceptive sponge esponja anticonceptiva.

fibrin sponge esponja de fibrina.

gauze sponge esponja de gasa.

gelatin sponge esponja de gelatina, esponja de gelatina absorbible.

menstrual sponge tampón menstrual.

vaginal sponge esponja vaginal.

spongeitis *n.* espongeítis, espongiítis.

spongia *n.* esponja.

spongiform *adj.* espongiforme.

spongiitis *n.* espongeítis, espongiítis.

spongioblast *n.* espongioblasto.

spongioblastoma *n.* espongioblastoma.

multiform spongioblastoma espongioblastoma multiforme.

polar spongioblastoma espongioblastoma polar.

spongioblastoma polare espongioblastoma polar.

unipolar spongioblastoma espongioblastoma unipolar.

spongiocyte *n.* espongiocito.

spongiocytoma *n.* espongiocitoma.

spongioid *adj.* espongioide, espongioideo, -a.

spongioplasty *n.* espongioplastia.

spongiose *adj.* esponjoso, -sa.

spongiosis *n.* espongiosis.

spongiositis *n.* espongiositis.

spongiotic *adj.* espongiótico, -ca.

spongy *adj.* esponjoso, -sa.

spontaneous *adj.* espontáneo, -a.

spool *n.* canilla.

Carassini's spool canilla de Carassini.

spoon *n.* cuchara.

cataract spoon cuchara para cataratas.

Daviel's spoon cuchara de Daviel.

sharp spoon cuchara afilada, cuchara cortante.

Volkmann's spoon cuchara de Volkmann.

sporadic *adj.* esporádico, -ca.

sporadin *n.* esporadina, esporadino.

sporangial *adj.* esporángico, -ca.

sporangiophore *n.* esporangióforo.

sporangiospore *n.* esporangioespora.

sporangium *n.* esporangio.

spore *n.* espora.

sporicidal *adj.* esporicida.

sporiferous *adj.* esporífero, -ra.

sporiparous *adj.* esporíparo, -ra.

sporoagglutination *n.* esporoaglutinación.

sporoblast *n.* esporoblasto.

sporocyst *n.* esporocisto.

sporoduct *n.* esporoducto.

sporogenesis *n.* esporogénesis.

sporogenic *adj.* esporogénico, -ca, esporógeno, -na.

sporogeny *n.* esporogenia.

sporogony *n.* esporogonia.

sporonticide *n.* esporonticida.

sporonto *n.* esporonto.

sporophore *n.* esporóforo.

sporotrichosis *n.* esporotricosis.

sporotrichotic *adj.* esporotricótico, -ca.

Sporozoa Sporozoa.

sporozolte *n.* esporozoíto.

sporozooid *adj.* esporozoide, esporozooide.

sporozoon *n.* esporozoario, esporozoo.

sporozoosis *n.* esporozoosis.

sporulation *n.* esporación, esporulación.

spot *n.* mancha.

Bitot's spot mancha de Bitot.

blind spot mancha ciega.

blue spot mancha azul.

Brushfield's spot mancha de Brushfield.

café au lait spot mancha de café con leche.

Carleton's spot mancha de Carleton.

Cayenne pepper spot mancha de pimienta de Cayena.

cherry-red spot mancha de color rojo de cereza, mancha rojo cereza.

Christopher's spot mancha de Christopher.

chromatin spot mancha de cromatina.

cold spot mancha fría.

corneal spot mancha corneana, mancha de la córnea.

cotton-wool spot mancha algodonosa.

cribiform spot mancha cribiforme, mancha cribosa.

De Morgan's spot mancha de De Morgan.

Elschnig's spot mancha de Elschnig.

embryonic spot mancha embrionaria.

epigastric spot mancha epigástrica.

flame spot mancha en llama.

focal spot mancha focal.

Fordyce's spot mancha de Fordyce.

Forscheimer spot mancha de Forscheimer.

Fuchs' black spot mancha negra de Fuchs.

Fuchs' spot mancha de Fuchs.

Gaule's spot mancha de Gaule.

Graefe's spot mancha de Graefe.

hot spot mancha caliente.

hypnogenic spot mancha hipnógena.

Koplik's spot mancha de Koplik.

light spot mancha de luz.

liver spot mancha hepática.

Mariotte's spot mancha de Mariotte.

Maurer's spot mancha de Maurer, mancha perniciosa.

Maxwell's spot mancha de Maxwell.

Mongolian spot mancha de Baelz, mancha mongólica.

mulberry spot mancha en mora.

pelvic spot mancha pélvica.

Port wine spot mancha en vino de Oporto.

rose spot mancha de rosa, mancha rosáceas, mancha rosada.

Roth's spot mancha de Roth.

ruby spot mancha rubí.

saccular spot mancha sacular.

sacral spot mancha sacra.

shin spot mancha tibial.

Soemmering's spot mancha de Soemmering.

Sommer-Larcher's spot mancha esclerótica de Sommer-Larcher.

Tardieu's spot mancha de Tardieu.

Tay's spot mancha de Tay.

temperature spot mancha de temperatura, mancha por temperatura.

tendinous spot mancha tendinosa.

Trousseau's spot mancha de Trousseau.

typhoid spot mancha de tifoidea.

utricular spot mancha utricular.

white frontal spot mancha blanca frontal.

yellow spot mancha amarilla.

spotting *n.* manchado.

sprain *n.* esguince, torcedura.

cervical sprain esguince cervical.

lumbar sprain esguince lumbar.

rider's sprain esguince de los jinetes, esguince del jinete.

sprain of the ankle or foot esguince de tobillo o de pie.

sprain of the back esguince de espalda.

spray *n.* nebulización.

ether spray nebulización de éter.

needle spray nebulización de aguja.

Pickrell's spray nebulización de Pickrell.

Tucker's spray nebulización de Tucker.

tyrothricin spray nebulización de tirotricina.

spreader *n.* distribuidor, espaciador, untador.

gutta-percha spreader distribuidor de gutapercha.

root canal filling spreader espaciador del empaste del conducto radicular.

root canal spreader untador del conducto de la raíz.

spring *n.* resorte.

sprout *n.* brote[3].

syncytial sprout brote sincitial.

sprue *n.* bebedero de molde, esprue.

celiac sprue esprue celíaco.

non-tropical sprue esprue no tropical.

refractory sprue esprue refractario.

tropical sprue esprue tropical.

spurious *adj.* espúreo, -a, espurio, -ria.

sputum *n.* esputo.

squama *n.* escama[1].

squamate *adj.* escamado, -da, escamoso, -sa.

squamatization *n.* escamatización, escamización.

squame *n.* escama[1].

squamocellular *adj.* escamocelular.

squamofrontal *n.* escamofrontal.

squamomastoid *adj.* escamomastoideo, -a.

squamo-occipital *adj.* escamooccipital.

squamoparietal *adj.* escamoparietal.

squamopetrosal *adj.* escamopetroso, -sa.

squamosoparietal *adj.* escamosoparietal.

squamosphenoid *adj.* escamoesfenoidal, escamoesfenoideo, -a.

squamotemporal *adj.* escamotemporal.

squamous *adj.* escamoso, -sa.

squamozygomatic *adj.* escamocigomático, -ca.

squatting *n.* cuclillas.

squint *v.* bizquear, bizqueo, bizquera.

accommodative squint bizqueo de la acomodación.

comitant squint bizqueo concomitante.

concomitant squint bizqueo concomitante.

convergent squint bizqueo convergente.

divergent squint bizqueo divergente.

upward and downward squint bizqueo hacia arriba y hacia abajo.

stabile *adj.* estable.

stabilimeter *n.* estabilímetro.

stability *n.* estabilidad.

denture stability estabilidad de una prótesis dental.

dimensional stability estabilidad dimensional.

endemic stability estabilidad endémica.

enzootic stability estabilidad enzoótica.

suspension stability estabilidad de suspensión.

stabilization *n.* estabilización.

cast stabilization estabilización de la escayola.

stabilizer *n.* estabilizador.

endodontic stabilizer estabilizador endodóntico.

stabilograph *n.* estabilógrafo.

stable *adj.* estable.

stadiometer *n.* estadiómetro.

staff *n.* varilla.

grooved staff varilla ranurada.

staff of Wrisberg vástago de Wrisberg.

stage *n.* estadio, etapa, fase, platina.

algid stage fase álgida.

amphibolic stage fase anfibólica.

anal stage etapa anal, etapa anal-sádica, fase anal, fase anal-sádica.

anal-sadistic stage etapa anal, etapa anal-sádica, fase anal, fase anal-sádica.

Arneth stage estadio de Arneth.

asphyxial stage fase de asfixia.

cold stage fase fría.

concrete operations stage estadio de las operaciones concretas.

defervescent stage estadio defervescente, fase de defervescencia.

embryonic stage estadio embrionario.

end stage estadio terminal.

expulsive stage fase de expulsión.

fetal stage estadio fetal.

first stage fase primera (del trabajo de parto).

formal operation stage estadio de las operaciones formales.

fourth stage fase cuarta (del trabajo del parto).

genital stage etapa genital.

germinal stage estadio germinal.

hot stage fase caliente.

imperfect stage fase imperfecta.

incubative stage fase de incubación.

latency stage fase de latencia.

mirror stage fase del espejo.

oral stage etapa oral.

oral-sadistic stage fase oral sádica.

perfect stage fase perfecta.

phallic stage etapa fálica.

placental stage fase placentaria.

preconceptual stage fase preconceptual.

preeruptive stage fase preeruptiva.

premenstrual stage fase premenstrual.

preoperational stage estadio preoperacional.

preswing stance stage fase de bipedestación previa al balanceo.

prodromal stage fase prodrómico.

progestational stage fase progestacional.

proliferative stage etapa proliferativa, fase de estrina, fase proliferativa.

pyretogenic stage fase piretógena.

pyrogenic stage fase pirógena.

Ranke's stage fase de Ranke.

rest stage fase de reposo.

resting stage fase de descanso.

ring stage fase de anillo.

second stage fase segunda (del trabajo del parto).

sensoriomotor stage estadio sensoriomotor.

stage of anesthesia fase de la anestesia.

stage of dying fase de la agonía.

stage of fervescence fase de fervescencia.

stepladder stage fase en escalera.

sweating stage fase de sudación.

Tanner's stage estadio de Tanner, estadio madurativo de Tanner.

third stage fase tercera (del trabajo del parto).

transitional pulp stage fase de la pulpa transicional.

tumor stage estadio tumoral.

ugly duckling stage fase de patito feo.

vegetative stage fase vegetativa.

stagger *v.* tambalearse.

staging *n.* estadificación.

cancer staging estadificación del cáncer.

Jewett and Strong staging estadificación de Jewett y Strong.

lymphoma staging estadificación del linfoma.

TNM staging estadificación TNM.

stagnation *n.* estancamiento.

stain *v.* colorante, teñir.

staining *adj.* coloración, colorante.

stalagmon *n.* estalagmón.

stalk *n.* tallo.

abdominal stalk tallo abdominal.

belly stalk tallo ventral.

body stalk tallo corporal.

optic stalk tallo óptico.

yolk stalk tallo vitelino.

staltic *adj.* estáltico, -ca.

stammering *n.* balbuceo[2].

stance *n.* estática equilibrio.

standard *n.* estándar.

ambient air standard estándar de aire ambiental.

internal standard estándar interno.

NBS standard estándar NBS.

standardization *n.* estandarización.

standardization of a test estandarización de una prueba.

standardize *v.* tipificar.

stanniferous *adj.* estannífero, -ra.

stannosis *n.* estanosis.

stapedectomy *n.* estapedectomía.

stapedial *adj.* estapedial, estapédico, -ca.

stapediolysis *n.* estapediólisis.

stapedioplasty *n.* estapedioplastia.

stapediotenotomy *n.* estapediotenotomía.

stapediovestibular *adj.* estapediovestibular.

stapedius *n.* estapedio.

stapes *n.* estribo.

staphylagra *n.* estafilagra.

staphylectomy *n.* estafilectomía.

staphyledema *n.* estafiledema, estafiloedema.

staphylematoma *n.* estafilematoma, estafilhematoma.

staphyline *adj.* estafilino, -na.

staphylion *n.* estafilión.

staphylitis *n.* estafilitis.

staphyloangina *n.* estafiloangina.

staphylobacterin *n.* estafilobacterina.

staphylocide *n.* estafilocida.

staphylococcal *adj.* estafilocócico, -ca.

staphylococcemia *n.* estafilococemia.

staphylococcia *n.* estafilococia.

staphylococcic *adj.* estafilocócico, -ca.

staphylococcide *n.* estafilococida.

staphylococcolysin *n.* estafilococolisina.

staphylococcolysis *n.* estafilococólisis.

staphylococcosis *n.* estafilococosis.

staphylococcus *n.* estafilococo.

Staphylococcus Staphylococcus.

staphyloderma *n.* estafilodermia.

staphylodermatitis *n.* estafilodermatitis.

staphylodialysis *n.* estafilodiálisis.

staphyloedema *n.* estafiledema, estafiloedema.

staphylohemia *n.* estafilohemia.

staphylohemolysin *n.* estafilohemolisina.

staphyloleukocidin *n.* estafiloleucocidina.

staphylolysin *n.* estafilolisina.

staphyloma *n.* estafiloma.

annular staphyloma estafiloma anular.

anterior staphyloma estafiloma anterior.

ciliary staphyloma estafiloma ciliar.

corneal staphyloma estafiloma corneal, estafiloma de la córnea.

equatorial staphyloma estafiloma ecuatorial.

intercalary staphyloma estafiloma intercalar.

posterior staphyloma estafiloma posterior.

projecting staphyloma estafiloma proyectado, estafiloma proyectante.

retinal staphyloma estafiloma retiniano.

Scarpa's staphyloma estafiloma de Scarpa.

scleral staphyloma estafiloma de la esclerótica, estafiloma escleral.

staphyloma corneae racemosum estafiloma corneal racemoso.

uveal staphyloma estafiloma uveal.

staphylomatous *adj.* estafilomatoso, -sa.

staphyloncus *n.* estafilonco.

staphylopharyngorrhaphy *n.* estafilofaringorrafia.

staphyloplasty *n.* estafiloplastia.

staphyloptosia *n.* estafiloptosia, estafiloptosis.

staphyloptosis *n.* estafiloptosia, estafiloptosis.

staphylorrhaphy *n.* estafilorrafia.

staphyloschisis *n.* estafilosquisis.

staphylotome *n.* estafilótomo.

staphylotomy *n.* estafilotomía.

staphylotoxin *n.* estafilotoxina.

staphylotropic *adj.* estafilotrópico, -ca.

star *n.* estrella.

starch *n.* almidón.

startling *n.* sobresalto.

starvation *n.* inanición[2].

stasimorphia *n.* estasimorfia.

stasimorphy *n.* estasimorfia.

stasis *n.* estasia, estasis.

colon stasis estasia del colon.

ileal stasis estasia ileal.

intestinal stasis estasia intestinal.

papillary stasis estasia papilar.

pressure stasis estasia por presión.

urinary stasis estasia urinaria.

venous stasis estasia venosa.

state *n.* estado.

absence state estado de ausencia.

absent state estado de ausencia.

acute confusional state estado confusional agudo.

aggregation state estado de agregación.

alpha state estado alfa.

anxiety state estado de ansiedad.

anxiety tension state estado de ansiedad.

apallic state estado apálico.

borderline state estado limítrofe.

carrier state estado de portador.

catelectrotonic state estado catelectrotónico.

central excitatory state estado excitador central.

chronic vegetative state estado vegetativo crónico.

confusional state estado confusional.

convulsive state estado convulsivo.

crepuscular state estado crepuscular.

diabetogenic state estado diabetógeno.

dysphoric state estado de ánimo disfórico.

dreamy state estado de ensoñación, estado onírico.

elevated state estado de ánimo elevado.

equilibrium state estado de equilibrio.

eunuchoid state estado eunucoide.

eutimic state estado de ánimo eutímico.

excited state estado excitado.
expansive state estado de ánimo expansivo.
fatigue state estado de fatiga.
febrile state estado febril.
ground state estado basal.
hypnagogic state estado hipnagógico.
hypnoid state estado hipnoide.
hypnotic state estado hipnótico.
hypometabolic state estado hipometabólico.
iatrogenic state estado iatrógeno.
initial contact stance state estado de contacto inicial del apoyo.
intersexual state estado intersexual.
irritable state estado de ánimo irritable.
lacunar state estado lacunar, status lacunaris.
local excitatory state estado excitador local.
metastable state estado metaestable.
mood state estado de ánimo.
nervous state estado nervioso.
paranoid state estado paranoide.
persistent vegetative state estado vegetativo persistente.
phobic state estado fóbico.
pluripotent state estado pluripotente.
preschizophrenic state estado preesquizofrénico.
prototaxic mode state estado prototáxico.
refractory state estado refractario.
singlet state estado singulete.
state of the art estado del arte.
steady state estado estable.
subliminal self state estado subliminal.
triplet state estado de triplete, estado triplete.
twilight state estado crepuscular.
vegetative state estado vegetativo.
static *adj.* estático, -ca.
station *n.* estación².
stationary *adj.* estacionario, -a.
statistic *adj.* estadístico, -ca.
statistics *n.* estadística.
Bayesian statistics estadística bayesiana.
descriptive statistics estadística descriptiva.
inferential statistics estadística inferencial.
morbidity statistics estadística de la morbididad.
parametric statistics estadística paramétrica.
vital statistics estadística vital.
statoacoustic *adj.* estatoacústico, -ca.
statoconia *n.* estatoconios.
statocyst *n.* estatoquiste.
statokinetic *adj.* estatocinético, -ca.
statokinetics *n.* estatocinesis.
statolith *n.* estatolito.
statometer *n.* estatómetro.
statural *adj.* estatural.
stature *n.* estatura, talla.
short stature baja estatura, talla baja.
status *n.* estado, status.
mental status estado mental.
status anginosus estado anginoso, status anginosus.
status arthriticus estado artrítico.
status asthmaticus estado asmático, estado asthmaticus.
status choleraicus estado coleraico, estado colérico.
status choreicus estado coreico.
status convulsivus estado convulsivo.
status cribrosus estado criboso.
status criticus estado crítico.
status dysmyelinisatus estado desmielinizado, status dysmyelinisatus.
status dysraphicus estado disráfico, status dysraphicus.
status epilepticus estado de mal epiléptico, estado epiléptico, status epilepticus.

status hemicranicus estado hemicraneal.
status hypnoticus estado hipnótico.
status lymphaticus estado linfático.
status marmoratus estado marmóreo, status marmoratus.
status spongiosus estado esponjoso, status spongiosus.
status sternuens estado estornutatorio.
status thymicolymphaticus estado tímico, estado timicolinfático, estado timolinfático.
status thymicus estado tímico, estado timicolinfático, estado timolinfático.
status typhosus estado tifoso, status typhosus.
status verrucosum estado verrucoso.
status vertiginosus estado vertiginoso.
staurion *n.* estaurión.
stauroplegia *n.* estauroplejía.
staxis *n.* estaxis.
steal *n.* robo.
iliac steal robo ilíaco.
renal-splanchnic steal robo renal-esplácnico.
subclavian steal robo de la sublavia.
steariform *adj.* esteariforme.
stearrhea *n.* estearrea.
steatitis *n.* esteatitis.
steatocele *n.* esteatocele.
steatocystoma *n.* esteatocistoma.
steatocystoma multiplex esteatocistoma múltiple.
steatogenesis *n.* esteatogénesis.
steatogenous *adj.* esteatógeno, -na.
steatohepatitis *n.* esteatohepatitis.
steatolysis *n.* esteatólisis.
steatolytic *adj.* esteatolítico, -ca.
steatomatosis *n.* esteatomatosis.
steatomery *n.* esteatomería.
steatonecrosis *n.* esteatonecrosis.
steatopygia *n.* esteatopigia.
steatopygous *adj.* esteatopígico, -ca, esteatópigo, -ga.
steatorrhea *n.* esteatorrea.
biliary steatorrhea esteatorrea biliar.
idiopathic steatorrhea esteatorrea idiopática.
intestinal steatorrhea esteatorrea intestinal.
pancreatic steatorrhea esteatorrea pancreática.
steatorrhea simplex esteatorrea simple.
steatosis *n.* esteatosis.
hepatic steatosis esteatosis hepática.
steatosis cardiaca esteatosis cardíaca, esteatosis cordis.
steatosis cordis esteatosis cardíaca, esteatosis cordis.
stechiology *n.* estequiología.
stechiometric *adj.* estequiométrico, -ca.
stechiometry *n.* estequiometría.
stegnosis *n.* estegnosis.
stegnotic *adj.* estegnótico, -ca.
Stegomyia Stegomyia.
stellate *adj.* estrellado, -da.
stellectomy *n.* estelectomía.
stenion *n.* estenión.
stenobregmatic *adj.* estenobregmático, -ca, estenobregmato, -ta.
stenocardia *n.* estenocardia.
stenocephalia *n.* estenocefalia.
stenocephalic *adj.* estenocefálico, -ca.
stenocephalous *adj.* estenocéfalo, -la.
stenocephaly *n.* estenocefalia.
stenochoria *n.* estenocoria.
stenocompressor *n.* estenocompresor.
stenocoriasis *n.* estenocoriasis.
stenocrotaphia *n.* estenocrotafia.
stenocrotaphy *n.* estenocrotafia.

stenopaic *adj.* estenopaico, -ca, estenopeico, -ca.
stenopeic *adj.* estenopaico, -ca, estenopeico, -ca.
stenophotic *adj.* estenofótico, -ca.
stenosal *adj.* estenótico, -ca.
stenosed *adj.* estenosado, -da.
stenosis *n.* estenosis.
anal stenosis estenosis anal.
aortic stenosis estenosis aórtica.
aqueductal stenosis estenosis del acueducto de Silvio.
buttonhole stenosis estenosis en ojal.
calcific nodular aortic stenosis estenosis aórtica nodular calcificada.
cardiac stenosis estenosis cardíaca.
caroticovertebral stenosis estenosis caroticovertebral.
cervical stenosis estenosis cervical.
cicatricial stenosis estenosis cicatricial, estenosis cicatrizal.
congenital pyloric stenosis estenosis pilórica congénita.
coronary ostial stenosis estenosis coronaria ostial.
Dittrich's stenosis estenosis de Dittrich.
double aortic stenosis estenosis aórtica doble.
fish-mouth mitral stenosis estenosis mitral en boca de pez.
granulation stenosis estenosis por granulación.
hypertrophic pyloric stenosis estenosis pilórica hipertrófica.
idiopathic hypertrophic subaortic stenosis estenosis subaórtica hipertrófica idiopática.
infundibular stenosis estenosis infundibular.
laryngeal stenosis estenosis laríngea.
lateral recess stenosis estenosis del conducto.
lumbar stenosis estenosis del canal lumbar.
mitral stenosis estenosis mitral.
mitral valve stenosis estenosis de la válvula mitral.
muscular subaortic stenosis estenosis subaórtica muscular.
postdiphtheritic stenosis estenosis posdiftérica.
pulmonary stenosis estenosis pulmonar.
pyloric stenosis estenosis pilórica.
renal artery stenosis estenosis arterial renal.
spinal stenosis estenosis raquídea.
subaortic stenosis estenosis subaórtica.
subvalvular stenosis estenosis subvalvular.
subvalvular aortic stenosis estenosis aórtica subvalvular.
supravalvular stenosis estenosis supravalvular.
tricuspid stenosis estenosis tricuspídea.
valvular stenosis estenosis valvular.
stenostenosis *n.* estenoestenosis.
stenostomia *n.* estenostomía.
stenothermic *adj.* estenotérmico, -ca, estenotermo, -ma.
stenothorax *n.* estenotórax.
stenotic *adj.* estenótico, -ca.
stenoxenous *n.* estenoxeno.
stent *n.* endoprótesis.
step *n.* paso¹.
stephanion *n.* esteafanión, estefanión.
steppage *n.* estepaje.
stercolith *n.* estercolito.
stercoraceous *adj.* estercoráceo, -a.
stercoral *adj.* estercoral.
stercorarian *n.* estercoraria.
stercoremia *n.* estercoremia.

stercorolith *n.* estercorolito.
stercoroma *n.* estercoroma.
stercorome *n.* estercoroma.
stercorous *adj.* estercoroso, -sa.
stereoagnosis *n.* estereoagnosia.
stereoanesthesia *n.* estereoanestesia.
stereoarthrolysis *n.* estereoartrólisis.
stereocampimeter *n.* estereocampímetro.
stereocampimetry *n.* estereocampimetría.
stereocilium *n.* estereocilio.
stereocognosy *n.* estereocognosia, estereocognosis.
stereocolpogram *n.* estereocolpograma.
stereocolposcope *n.* estereocolposcopio.
stereoelectroencephalography *n.* estereoelectroencefalografía.
stereoencephalometry *n.* estereoencefalometría.
stereoencephalotome *n.* estereoencefalótomo.
stereoencephalotomy *n.* estereoencefalotomía.
stereofluoroscopy *n.* estereofluoroscopia.
stereognosis *n.* estereognosia, estereognosis.
stereognostic *adj.* estereognósico, -ca, estereognóstico, -ca.
stereogram *n.* estereograma.
stereograph *n.* estereógrafo.
stereography *n.* estereografía.
stereometer *n.* estereómetro.
stereometry *n.* estereometría.
stereo-ophthalmoscope *n.* estereoftalmoscopio.
stereo-orthopter *n.* estereoortóptero.
stereopathy *n.* estereopatía.
stereophantoscope *n.* estereopantoscopio.
stereophorometer *n.* estereoforómetro.
stereophoroscope *n.* estereoforoscopio.
stereophotography *n.* estereofotografía.
stereophotomicrograph *n.* estereofotomicrografía.
stereopsis *n.* estereopsia, estereopsis.
stereoradiography *n.* estereorradiografía.
stereoroentgenography *n.* estereorroentgenografía.
stereoscope *n.* estereoscopio.
stereoscopic *adj.* estereoscópico, -ca.
stereoscopy *n.* estereoscopia.
stereospecific *n.* estereoespecífico.
stereotactic *adj.* estereotáctico, -ca, estereotáxico, -ca.
stereotaxic *adj.* estereotáxico, -ca.
stereotaxis *n.* estereotaxia, estereotaxis.
stereotaxy *n.* estereotaxia, estereotaxis.
stereotropic *adj.* estereotrópico, -ca.
stereotropism *n.* estereotropismo.
stereotype *n.* estereotipo.
  dysfunctional stereotype estereotipo disfuncional.
stereotypy *n.* estereotipia.
  oral stereotypy estereotipia oral.
sterigm *n.* esterigma.
sterile *adj.* estéril.
sterilitas *n.* esterilidad.
sterility *n.* esterilidad.
  absolute sterility esterilidad absoluta.
  acquired sterility esterilidad adquirida.
  female sterility esterilidad femenina.
  male sterility esterilidad masculina.
  normospermatogenic sterility esterilidad normoespermatogénica.
  one-child sterility esterilidad de un hijo, esterilidad de un niño, esterilidad de un solo hijo.
  primary sterility esterilidad primaria.
  relative sterility esterilidad relativa.
sterilization *n.* esterilización, uperisación.

coercive sterilization esterilización coactiva.
concurrent sterilization esterilización concurrente.
dry heat sterilization esterilización por calor seco.
eugenic sterilization esterilización eugénica.
fractional sterilization esterilización fraccionada, esterilización fraccional.
gas sterilization esterilización gaseosa.
intermittent sterilization esterilización intermitente.
involuntary sterilization esterilización involuntaria.
laparoscopic sterilization esterilización laparoscópica.
steam sterilization esterilización por vapor.
sterilization of deficient persons esterilización de deficientes.
voluntary sterilization esterilización voluntaria.
sterilizer *n.* esterilizador.
  glass bead sterilizer esterilizador de perlas de vidrio.
  hot salt sterilizer esterilizador de sal caliente.
sternal *adj.* esternal.
sternalgia *n.* esternalgia.
sternebra *n.* esternebra.
sternoclavicular *adj.* esternoclavicular.
sternocleidal *adj.* esternocleidal, esternocleido, -da.
sternocleidomastoid *adj.* esternocleidomastoideo, -a.
sternocostal *n.* esternocostal.
sternodymia *n.* esternodimia.
sternodymus *n.* esternódimo.
sternodynia *n.* esternodinia.
sternoglossal *adj.* esternogloso, -sa.
sternogoniometer *n.* esternogoniómetro.
sternohyoid *adj.* esternohioideo, -a.
sternoid *adj.* esternoide.
sternomastoid *adj.* esternomastoideo, -a.
sternopagia *n.* esternopagia.
sternopagus *n.* esternópago.
sternopericardial *adj.* esternopericárdico, -ca.
sternoscapular *adj.* esternoescapular.
sternoschisis *n.* esternosquisis.
sternothyroid *adj.* esternotiroideo, -a.
sternotomy *n.* esternotomía.
  median sternotomy esternotomía media.
sternotracheal *adj.* esternotraqueal.
sternotrypesis *n.* esternotripesis.
sternovertebral *adj.* esternovertebral.
sternum esternón, sternum.
sternutatio *n.* estornudo.
sternutation *n.* estornudo.
steroauscultation *n.* estereoauscultación.
steroid *n.* esteroide.
  anabolic steroid esteroide anabólicos, esteroide anabolizante.
  steroid hydroxylase esteroide hidroxilasa.
  steroid monoxygenase esteroide monoxigenasa.
steroidal *adj.* esteroidal.
steroidogenesis *n.* esteroidogénesis.
steroidogenic *adj.* esteroidógeno, -na.
steroid-resistance *n.* corticorresistencia.
stertor *n.* estertor.
  hen-cluck stertor estertor en cloqueo de gallina.
  stertor de retour estertor de retorno.
  stertor redux estertor redux.
stertorous *adj.* estertoroso, -sa.
stethalgia *n.* estetalgia.
stetharteritis *n.* estetarteritis.
stethemia *n.* estetemia.

stethendoscope *n.* estetoendoscopio.
stethoacoustic *adj.* estetoacústico, -ca.
stethocyrtograph *n.* estetocirtógrafo.
stethocyrtometer *n.* estetocirtómetro.
stethogoniometer *n.* estetogoniómetro.
stethograph *n.* estetógrafo.
stethography *n.* estetografía.
stethokyrtograph *n.* estetocirtógrafo, estetoquirtógrafo.
stethometer *n.* estetómetro.
stethomimetic *adj.* estetomimético, -ca.
stethomyitis *n.* estetomiítis, estetomitis.
stethomyositis *n.* estetomiositis.
stethoparalysis *n.* estetoparálisis.
stethophone *n.* estetófono.
stethophonometer *n.* estetofonómetro.
stethopolyscope *n.* estetopoliscopio.
stethoscope *n.* estetoscopio.
  binaural stethoscope estetoscopio biauricular.
  Cammann's stethoscope estetoscopio de Cammann.
  diaphragm stethoscope estetoscopio diafragmático.
  differential stethoscope estetoscopio diferencial.
  electronic stethoscope estetoscopio electrónico.
  esophageal stethoscope estetoscopio esofágico.
stethoscopic *adj.* estetoscópico, -ca.
stethoscopy *n.* estetoscopia.
stethospasm *n.* estetoespasmo.
sthenia *n.* estenia.
sthenic *adj.* esténico, -ca.
sthenometer *n.* estenómetro.
sthenophotic *adj.* estenofótico, -ca.
stibialism *n.* estibialismo, estibismo.
stibiated *adj.* estibiado, -da.
stibiation *n.* estibiación.
stigma *n.* estigma.
  follicular stigma estigma del folículo de De Graaf, estigma folicular.
  Malpighian stigma estigma de Malpighi, estigma de Malpigio.
stigmatic *adj.* estigmático, -ca.
stigmatism *n.* estigmatismo.
stigmatization *n.* estigmatización.
stigmatometer *n.* estigmatómetro.
stigmatoscope *n.* estigmatoscopio.
stigmatoscopy *n.* estigmatoscopia.
stilet *n.* estilete.
stilette *n.* estilete.
stillborn *adj.* mortinato, -ta.
stillicidium *n.* estilicidio.
  stillicidium narium estilicidio nasal.
  stillicidium urinae estilicidio de la orina, estilicidio urinario.
stimulant *n.* estimulante.
  central nervous system stimulant estimulante del sistema nervioso central, neuroestimulante.
  central stimulant estimulante central.
  diffusible stimulant estimulante difusible, estimulante difusivo.
  general stimulant estimulante general.
  local stimulant estimulante local, estimulante tópico.
  uterine stimulant estimulante uterino.
stimulation *n.* estimulación.
  area stimulation estimulación de área.
  audio-visual-tactile stimulation estimulación audiovisual y táctil.
  cerebellar stimulation estimulación del cerebelo.

cortical magnetic stimulation estimulación magnética cortical.

dorsal column stimulation estimulación de los fascículos dorsales.

electrical stimulation for pain estimulación eléctrica en el dolor.

galvanic electric stimulation estimulación eléctrica galvánica.

Ganzfeld stimulation estimulación Ganzfeld.

infant stimulation estimulación del lactante.

pacing stimulation estimulación cardíaca con marcapasos.

perctaneous stimulation estimulación percutánea.

photic stimulation estimulación fótica.

punctual stimulation estimulación de punto.

repetitive stimulation estimulación repetitiva.

transcutaneous electric nerve stimulation (TENS) estimulación nerviosa eléctrica transcutánea (TENS).

transcutaneous nerve stimulation estimulación nerviosa transcutánea.

vagal stimulation estimulación del nervio vago.

stimulator *n.* estimulador.

Bimler stimulator estimulador de Bimler.

human thyroid adenylate cyclase stimulator estimulador de la adenilatociclasa tiroidea humana (HTACS).

long-acting thyroid stimulator estimulador tiroideo de acción prolongada.

pallidal stimulator estimulador palidal.

thalamic stimulator estimulador talámico.

stimulus *n.* estímulo.

adequate stimulus estímulo adecuado.

aversive stimulus estímulo aversivo.

conditioned stimulus estímulo condicionado.

discriminant stimulus estímulo discriminante.

discriminative stimulus estímulo discriminativo.

electric stimulus estímulo eléctrico.

heterologous stimulus estímulo heterólogo.

heterotopic stimulus estímulo heterotópico.

homologous stimulus estímulo homólogo.

hypoxic drive stimulus estímulo hipóxico.

inadequate stimulus estímulo inadecuado.

liminal stimulus estímulo liminal, estímulo mínimo.

maximal stimulus estímulo máximo.

mechanical stimulus estímulo mecánico.

nociceptive stimulus estímulo nociceptivo.

nomotopic stimulus estímulo nomotópico.

releasing stimulus estímulo liberador.

square wave stimulus estímulo de onda cuadrada.

subliminal stimulus estímulo subliminal.

subthreshold stimulus estímulo subumbral.

supraliminal stimulus estímulo supraliminal.

supramaximal stimulus estímulo supramáximo.

threshold stimulus estímulo de umbral, estímulo umbral.

unconditioned stimulus estímulo incondicionado, estímulo no condicionado.

sting *n.* picadura.

stippling *n.* punteado.

stirpicultural *adj.* estirpicultural.

stirpiculture *n.* estirpicultivo.

stitch[1] *n.* agujetas.

stitch[2] *v.* suturar.

stivation *n.* estivación.

stochastic *adj.* estocástico, -ca.

stock *n.* stock.

stoichiology *n.* estequiología.

stoichiometric *adj.* estequiométrico, -ca.

stoichiometry *n.* estequiometría.

stoke *n.* stoke.

stoma *n.* estoma.

Fuchs' stoma estoma de Fuchs.

loop stoma estoma en asa.

stomacace *n.* estomacace.

stomach *n.* estómago.

aberrant umbilical stomach estómago umbilical aberrante.

bilocular stomach estómago bilocular.

cascade stomach estómago en caída de agua, estómago en cascada.

cup and spill stomach estómago de copa y derrame.

drain-trap stomach estómago en trampa de drenaje.

dumping stomach estómago de vaciamiento rápido.

hourglass stomach estómago en reloj de arena.

leather-bottle stomach estómago en bota de vino.

sclerotic stomach estómago esclerótico.

thoracic stomach estómago torácico.

trifid stomach estómago trífido.

wallet stomach estómago en billetera.

water-trap stomach estómago en trampa de agua.

stomachal *adj.* estomacal.

stomachalgia *n.* estomacalgia.

stomachic *adj.* estomáquico, -ca.

stomachodynia *n.* estomacodinia.

stomachoscopy *n.* estomacoscopia.

stomal *adj.* estomal.

stomalgia *n.* estomalgia.

stomatal *adj.* estomatal.

stomatalgia *n.* estomatalgia.

stomatic *adj.* estomático, -ca.

stomatitis *n.* estomatitis.

allergic stomatitis estomatitis alérgica.

angular stomatitis estomatitis angular.

aphthous stomatitis estomatitis aftosa, estomatitis folicular.

arsenic stomatitis estomatitis arsenical, estomatitis por arsénico.

Atabrine stomatitis estomatitis por Atabrine.

bismuth stomatitis estomatitis por bismuto.

catarrhal stomatitis estomatitis catarral.

contact stomatitis estomatitis de contacto.

denture stomatitis estomatitis por dentadura.

erythematopultaceous stomatitis estomatitis eritematopultácea.

fusospirochetal stomatitis estomatitis fusoespiroquetósica.

gangrenous stomatitis estomatitis gangrenosa.

gonococcal stomatitis estomatitis gonocócica.

gonorrheal stomatitis estomatitis gonorreica.

herpetic stomatitis estomatitis herpética.

lead stomatitis estomatitis por plomo.

medicamentous stomatitis estomatitis medicamentosa.

membranous stomatitis estomatitis membranosa.

mercurial stomatitis estomatitis mercurial.

mycotic stomatitis estomatitis micótica.

primary herpetic stomatitis estomatitis herpética primaria.

pseudomembranous stomatitis estomatitis seudomembranosa.

recurrent aphthous stomatitis estomatitis aftosa recurrente.

recurrent herpetic stomatitis estomatitis herpética recurrente.

recurrent ulcerative stomatitis estomatitis ulcerativa, estomatitis ulcerosa, estomatitis ulcerosa recurrente.

simple stomatitis estomatitis simple.

stomatitis aphthosa estomatitis aftosa, estomatitis folicular.

stomatitis exantematica estomatitis exantemática.

stomatitis medicamentosa estomatitis medicamentosa.

stomatitis nicotina estomatitis por nicotina.

stomatitis parasitica estomatitis candidiásica.

stomatitis scarlatina estomatitis por escarlatina.

stomatitis scorbutica estomatitis escorbútica.

stomatitis venenata estomatitis venenata, estomatitis venenosa.

syphilitic stomatitis estomatitis sifilítica.

tropical stomatitis estomatitis tropical.

ulcerative stomatitis estomatitis ulcerativa, estomatitis ulcerosa, estomatitis ulcerosa recurrente.

uremic stomatitis estomatitis urémica.

vesicular stomatitis estomatitis vesicular.

Vincent's stomatitis estomatitis de Vincent.

water stomatitis estomatitis de agua.

stomatocatharsis *n.* estomatocatarsis.

stomatocyte *n.* estomatocito.

stomatocytosis *n.* estomacitosis, estomatocitosis.

stomatodeum *n.* estomatodeo.

stomatodynia *n.* estomatodinia.

stomatodysodia *n.* estomatodisodia.

stomatogastric *adj.* estomatogástrico, -ca.

stomatoglossitis *n.* estomatoglositis.

stomatognathic *adj.* estomatognático, -ca.

stomatography *n.* estomatografía.

stomatolalia *n.* estomatolalia.

stomatologic *adj.* estomatológico, -ca.

stomatological *adj.* estomatológico, -ca.

stomatologist *n.* estomatólogo, -ga.

stomatology *n.* estomatología.

stomatomalacia *n.* estomatomalacia.

stomatomy *n.* estomatomía.

stomatomycosis *n.* estomatomicosis.

stomatonecrosis *n.* estomatonecrosis.

stomatonoma *n.* estomatonoma.

stomatopathy *n.* estomatopatía.

stomatoplastic *adj.* estomatoplástico, -ca.

stomatoplasty *n.* estomatoplastia.

stomatorrhagia *n.* estomatorragia.

stomatoschisis *n.* estomatosquisis.

stomatoscope *n.* estomatoscopio.

stomatosis *n.* estomatosis.

stomatotherapist *n.* estomatoterapeuta.

stomatotherapy *n.* estomatoterapia.

stomatotomy *n.* estomatotomía.

stomatotyphus *n.* estomatotifo.

stomocephalus *n.* estomencéfalo, estomocéfalo.

stomodeal *adj.* estomodeal.

stomodeum *n.* estomodeo.

stomoschisis *n.* estomosquisis.

Stomoxys Stomoxys.

stool *n.* deposición, excremento, heces.

butter stool heces mantecosas.

fatty stool heces grasas.

lienteric stool heces lientérica.

mucous stool heces mucosas.

storiform *adj.* estoriforme.
storm *n.* tormenta.
 thyroid storm tormenta tiroidea, tormenta tirotóxica.
 thyrotoxic storm tormenta tiroidea, tormenta tirotóxica.
stove *n.* estufa.
strabismal *adj.* estrábico, -ca.
strabismic *adj.* estrabísmico, -ca.
strabismology *n.* estrabismología.
strabismometer *n.* estrabismómetro.
strabismometry *n.* estrabismometría.
strabismus *n.* estrabismo.
 absolute strabismus estrabismo absoluto.
 accommodative strabismus estrabismo acomodativo, estrabismo de acomodación.
 alternate day strabismus estrabismo en días alternados.
 alternating strabismus estrabismo alternado, estrabismo alternante.
 bilateral strabismus estrabismo bilateral, estrabismo binocular.
 comitant strabismus estrabismo concomitante.
 concomitant strabismus estrabismo concomitante, estrabismo muscular.
 constant strabismus estrabismo constante.
 convergent strabismus estrabismo convergente.
 cyclic strabismus estrabismo cíclico.
 divergent strabismus estrabismo divergente, estrabismo paralelo.
 external strabismus estrabismo externo.
 intermittent strabismus estrabismo intermitente.
 internal strabismus estrabismo interno.
 kinetic strabismus estrabismo cinético.
 latent strabismus estrabismo latente.
 manifest strabismus estrabismo manifiesto.
 mechanical strabismus estrabismo cicatricial, estrabismo mecánico.
 monocular strabismus estrabismo monocular.
 monolateral strabismus estrabismo monolateral, estrabismo unilateral, estrabismo uniocular.
 non-concomitant strabismus estrabismo no concomitante.
 paralytic strabismus estrabismo paralítico.
 spastic strabismus estrabismo espástico.
 strabismus deorsum vergens estrabismo deorsum vergens.
 strabismus sursum vergens estrabismo sursum vergens.
 vertical strabismus estrabismo vertical.
strabometer *n.* estrabómetro.
strabometry *n.* estrabometría.
strabotome *n.* estrabótomo.
strabotomy *n.* estrabotomía.
straight *adj.* recto[2], -ta.
strain[1] *n.* cepa, distensión[2], esfuerzo[1], estirpe.
 abdominal strain distensión abdominal.
 auxotrophic strain cepa auxotrófica.
 carrier strain cepa portadora.
 cell strain cepa celular.
 cellular strain estirpe celular.
 congenic strain cepa congénica.
 eye strain distensión ocular.
 high-jumper's strain distensión de los saltadores de altura.
 hypothetical mean strain (HMS) cepa media hipotética (CMH).
 isogenic strain cepa isogénica.
 lysogenic strain cepa lisógena.
 neotype strain cepa neotipo.

 prototrophic strain cepa prototrófica.
 pseudolysogenic strain cepa seudolisogénica.
 stock strain cepa de reserva.
 type strain cepa tipo.
 wild type strain cepa tipo salvaje.
strain[2] *v.* distender[2], forzar, tamizar.
straining *n.* tenesmo.
strait *n.* estrecho.
strand *n.* hebra.
 ADN antisense strand hebra antisentido de ADN.
 ADN complementary strand hebra complementaria de ADN.
 DNA coding strand hebra codificante de ADN.
 DNA minus strand hebra molde de ADN.
 DNA non-coding strand hebra no codificante de ADN.
 DNA plus strand hebra codificante de ADN, hebra sentido de ADN.
 DNA sense strand hebra codificante de ADN, hebra sentido de ADN.
 DNA template strand hebra molde de ADN.
strangalesthesia *n.* estrangalestesia.
strangle *n.* estrangulación.
strangulated *adj.* estrangulado, -da.
strangulation *n.* estrangulación.
 internal strangulation estrangulación interna.
 intestinal strangulation estrangulación intestinal.
stranguria *n.* estranguria.
strangury *n.* estranguria.
strap[1] *n.* esparadrapo, faja[2].
 T strap faja en T, faja T.
strap[2] *v.* fajar, vendar.
strapping *n.* strapping, vendaje.
strategy *n.* estrategia.
 cognitive strategy estrategia cognitiva.
 coping strategy estrategia de afrontamiento.
stratification *n.* estratificación.
stratified *adj.* estratificado, -da.
stratiform *adj.* estratiforme.
stratigraphy *n.* estratigrafía.
stratum *n.* estrato.
streak *n.* estría, raya.
 angioid streak estría angioide, raya angioide.
 fatty streak raya grasa.
 gravidic streak estría gravídica.
 meningitic streak raya meningítica.
 Moore lightning streak raya luminosa de Moore.
 pregnancy streak estría del embarazo.
streblomicrodactyly *n.* estreblomicrodactilia.
stremma *n.* estrema.
strength *n.* fuerza[2], intensidad.
 associative strength fuerza asociativa.
 electric field strength intensidad del campo eléctrico.
 ionic strength fuerza iónica.
 strength of association intensidad de asociación.
 tensile strength fuerza tensil.
strephenopodia *n.* estrefenopodia.
strephexopodia *n.* estrefexopodia.
strephopodia *n.* estrefopodia.
strephosymbolia *n.* estrefosimbolia.
strepitus *n.* estrépito.
strepticemia *n.* estrepticemia.
streptobacillus *n.* estreptobacilo.
Streptobacillus Streptobacillus.
streptobacteria *n.* estreptobacterias.
streptobacterin *n.* estreptobacterina.
streptocerciasis *n.* estreptocercosis.

Streptococcaceae Streptococcaceae.
streptococcal *adj.* estreptocócico, -ca.
streptococcemia *n.* estreptococemia.
streptococcic *adj.* estreptocócico, -ca.
streptococcide *n.* estreptococicida.
streptococcosis *n.* estreptococia, estreptococicosis, estreptococosis.
Streptococcus Streptococcus.
streptococcus *n.* estreptococito, estreptococo.
streptoderma *n.* estreptodermia.
streptodermatitis *n.* estreptodermatitis.
streptomicrodactyly *n.* estreptomicrodactilia.
Streptomyces Streptomyces.
Streptomycetaceae Streptomycetaceae.
streptomycete *n.* estreptomiceto.
streptosepticemia *n.* estreptosepticemia.
streptotrichiasis *n.* estreptotriquiasis.
streptotrichosis *n.* estreptotricosis.
stress *n.* estrés, tensión[1].
 occupational stress estrés laboral.
 post-traumatic stress estrés postraumático.
 psychosocial stress estrés psicosocial.
 stress breaker rompefuerzas.
 yield stress estrés de rendimiento.
stressor *adj.* estresante, estresor.
 psychic stressor estresor psíquico.
stretcher *n.* camilla.
stretching *n.* estiramiento.
 passive stretching estiramiento pasivo.
 stretching of contractures estiramiento de las contracturas.
stria *n.* estría, stria.
 cutaneous stria estría cutis.
 stria atrophica estría atrófica.
 stria cutis distensa estría cutánea distendida.
 stria distensa estría de distensión.
 stria gravidarum estría del embarazo.
 Wickham's striae estrías de Wickham.
striascope *n.* estriascopio.
striatal *adj.* estriatal.
striate *adj.* estriado, -da.
striated *adj.* estriado, -da.
striation *n.* estriación.
 tabby cat striation estriación gatuna.
 tigroid striation estriación tigroide.
striatonigral *adj.* estriatonígrico, -ca, estriatonigro, -gra.
stricture *n.* estrechez.
 anastomotic stricture estrechez anastomótica.
 annular stricture estrechez anular.
 bridle stricture estrechez en brida.
 cicatricial stricture estrechez cicatricial.
 contractile stricture estrechez contráctil.
 false stricture estrechez falsa.
 functional stricture estrechez funcional.
 Hunner's stricture estrechez de Hunner.
 impassable stricture estrechez impermeable.
 impermeable stricture estrechez impermeable.
 irritable stricture estrechez irritable.
 organic stricture estrechez orgánica.
 permanent stricture estrechez permanente.
 recurrent stricture estrechez recurrente.
 spasmodic stricture estrechez espasmódica, estrechez espástica.
 spastic stricture estrechez espasmódica, estrechez espástica.
 temporary stricture estrechez temporal.
stricturization *n.* estrechamiento.
stricturoplasty *n.* estricturoplastia.
stricturotome *n.* estricturótomo.
stricturotomy *n.* estricturotomía.

strident *adj.* estridente.
stridor *n.* estridor.
congenital laryngeal stridor estridor laríngeo congénito.
expiratory stridor estridor espiratorio.
inspiratory stridor estridor inspiratorio.
laryngeal stridor estridor laríngeo.
stridor dentium estridor dentario.
stridor serraticus estridor serrático.
systolic stridor estridor sistólico.
whoop stridor estridor convulsivo.
stridulous *adj.* estriduloso, -sa.
striocellular *adj.* estriocelular.
striocerebellar *adj.* estriocerebeloso, -sa.
striomotor *adj.* estriomotor, -ra.
striomuscular *adj.* estriomuscular.
strionigral *adj.* estriatonígrico, -ca, estriatonigro, -gra.
strip[1] *n.* desvenamiento, flebectomía, raspado, tira.
abrasive strip tira abrasiva.
linen strip tira de lino.
Mees' strip tira de Mees.
strip[2] *v.* desagotar, exprimir.
stripe *n.* banda.
stripe of Gennari banda de Gennari.
stripper *n.* desvenador.
strobila *n.* estróbila.
strobiloid *adj.* estrobiloide, estrobiloideo, -a.
strobilus *n.* estróbila, estróbilo.
stroboscope *n.* estroboscopio.
stroboscopic *adj.* estroboscópico, -ca.
stroboscopy *n.* estroboscopia.
stroke *n.* ataque.
heat stroke ataque de calor.
stroma *n.* estroma.
stromal *adj.* estromal.
stromatic *adj.* estromático, -ca.
stromatogenous *adj.* estromatógeno, -na.
stromatolysis *n.* estromatólisis.
stromatosis *n.* estromatosis.
stromic *adj.* estromal.
stromuhr *n.* stromuhr.
strongyliasis *n.* estrongiliasis, estrongilosis.
Strongyloidea Strongyloidea.
Strongyloides Strongyloides.
strongyloidiasis *n.* estrongiloidiasis, estrongiloidiosis, estrongiloidosis.
strongyloidosis *n.* estrongiloidiasis, estrongiloidiosis, estrongiloidosis.
strongylosis *n.* estrongiliasis, estrongilosis.
strontiuresis *n.* estronciouresis.
strontiuretic *adj.* estronciourético, -ca.
Strophantus Strophantus.
strophocephalus *adj.* estrofocéfalo, -la.
strophocephaly *n.* estrofocefalia.
strophosomia *n.* estrofosomía.
strophulus *n.* estrófulo.
strophulus candidus estrófulo cándido, estrófulo candidus.
strophulus intertinctus estrófulo intertinctus, estrófulo intertinto.
strophulus pruriginosus estrófulo pruriginoso, estrófulo pruriginosus.
structural *adj.* estructural.
structuralism *n.* estructuralismo.
structure *n.* estructura.
antigenic structure estructura antigénica.
brush heap structure estructura en cerdas de cepillo.
collaborative power structure estructura colaboradora de poder.
crystal structure estructura cristalina.
dentine-supporting structure estructura de sostén de dentadura.

denture-supporting structure estructura de soporte protésico.
DNA structure estructura de ADN.
family structure estructura familiar.
fine structure estructura fina.
gel structure estructura de gel.
mental structure estructura mental.
primary structure estructura primaria.
protein structure estructura de la proteína.
quaternary structure estructura cuaternaria.
secondary structure estructura secundaria.
tertiary structure estructura terciaria.
tuboreticular structure estructura tuborreticular.
struma *n.* estruma.
Hashimoto's struma estruma de Hashimoto.
ligneous struma estruma leñoso, estruma lígneo.
Riedel's struma estruma de molde de hierro, estruma de Riedel.
struma aberrata estruma aberrante.
struma calculosa estruma coloide quístico.
struma colloides estruma coloidal, estruma coloide, estruma gelatinoso.
struma fibrosa estruma fibroso.
struma lymphatica estruma linfático.
struma lymphomatosa estruma linfomatoso.
struma maligna estruma maligno.
struma medicamentosa estruma medicamentoso.
struma ovarii estruma ovárico.
struma parenchymatosa estruma folicular, estruma parenquimatoso.
struma vasculosa estruma vasculoso.
strumectomy *n.* estrumectomía.
median strumectomy estrumectomía mediana.
strumiform *adj.* estrumiforme.
strumiprivous *adj.* estrumiprivo, -va.
strumitis *n.* estrumitis.
strumous *adj.* estrumoso, -sa.
study *n.* estudio.
blind study estudio ciego.
case-control study estudio de control de casos.
cohort study estudio de cohortes.
cross sectional study estudio transversal.
cross-selectional study estudio transversal.
diachronic study estudio diacrónico.
Doppler scanning study estudio Doppler.
double blind study estudio doble ciego.
Duke longitudinal study estudio longitudinal de Duke.
dynamic image study estudio dinámico de imagen.
electrophysiologic testing study estudio electrofisiológico.
factor-search study estudio de búsqueda de factores.
fiberoptic study estudio de fibra óptica.
longitudinal study estudio longitudinal.
multivariate study estudio multivariados.
phase one study estudio en fase uno.
phase three study estudio en fase tres.
phase two study estudio en fase dos.
prospective study estudio prospectivo.
retrospective study estudio retrospectivo.
single-blind study estudio simple ciego.
synchronic study estudio sincrónico.
workup study estudio diagnóstico.
stump *n.* muñón.
conical stump muñón cónico.
duodenal stump muñón duodenal.
gastric stump muñón gástrico.
rectal stump muñón rectal.
tooth stump raigón.

stupefacient *adj.* estupefaciente.
stupefactive *adj.* estupefaciente.
stupidity *n.* estupidez.
stupor *n.* estupor.
benign stupor estupor benigno.
catatonic stupor estupor catatónico.
depressive stupor estupor depresivo.
dissociative stupor estupor disociativo.
stuporous *adj.* estuporoso, -sa.
stuttering *n.* tartamudez.
labiochoreic stuttering tartamudez labiocoreica.
urinary stuttering tartamudez urinaria, tartamudez vesical.
sty *n.* orzuelo.
external sty orzuelo externo.
internal sty orzuelo interno.
Meibomian sty orzuelo de Meibomio, orzuelo meibomiano.
Zeisian sty o zeisiano, orzuelo de Zeis.
stycosis *n.* esticosis.
stye *n.* orzuelo.
style *n.* estilete.
stylet *n.* estilete.
endotracheal stylet estilete endotraqueal.
stylette *n.* estilete.
styliform *adj.* estiliforme.
styliscus *n.* estilisco.
styloglossus *adj.* estilogloso, -sa.
stylohyal *adj.* estilohioideo, -a.
stylohyoid *adj.* estilohioideo, -a.
styloid *adj.* estiloide, estiloideo, -a.
styloiditis *n.* estiloiditis.
stylomandibular *adj.* estilomandibular.
stylomastoid *adj.* estilomastoideo, -a.
stylomaxillary *adj.* estilomaxilar.
stylomyloid *adj.* estilomiloideo, -a.
stylopodium *n.* estilopodio.
stylostaphyline *adj.* estiloestafilino, -na.
stylosteophyte *n.* estilosteófito.
stylostixis *n.* estilostixis.
stylus *n.* estilete.
stymatosis *n.* estimatosis.
styptic *adj.* estíptico, -ca.
subabdominal *adj.* subabdominal.
subabdominoperitoneal *adj.* subabdominoperitoneal.
subacetabular *adj.* subacetabular.
subacromial *adj.* subacromial.
subacute *adj.* subagudo, -da.
subanal *adj.* subanal.
subaortic *adj.* subaórtico, -ca.
subapical *adj.* subapical.
subaponeurotic *adj.* subaponeurótico, -ca.
subarachnoid *adj.* subaracnoideo, -a.
subarcuate *adj.* subarqueado, -da.
subareolar *adj.* subareolar.
subastragalar *adj.* subastragalino, -na.
subastringent *adj.* subastringente.
subatloidean *adj.* subatloideo, -a.
subatomic *adj.* subatómico, -ca.
subaural *adj.* subaural.
subauricular *adj.* subauricular.
subaxial *adj.* subaxial, subaxil.
subaxillary *adj.* subaxilar.
subbasal *adj.* subbasal, subbásico, -ca.
subbrachycephalic *adj.* subbraquicéfalo, -la, subraquicefálico, -ca.
subcalcareous *adj.* subcalcáreo, -a.
subcalcarine *adj.* subcalcarino, -na.
subcallosal *adj.* subcalloso, -sa.
subcapsular *adj.* subcapsular.
subcapsuloperiosteal *adj.* subcapsuloperióstico, -ca.
subcardinal *adj.* subcardinal.

subcartilaginous *adj.* subcartilaginoso, -sa.
subcecal *adj.* subcecal.
subcellular *adj.* subcelular.
subcentral *adj.* subcentral.
subception *n.* subcepción.
subchondral *adj.* subcondral.
subchordal *adj.* subcordal.
subchorionic *adj.* subcoriónico, -ca.
subchoroidal *adj.* subcoroidal, subcoroideo, -a.
subchronic *adj.* subcrónico, -ca.
subclass *n.* subclase.
subclavian *adj.* subclavio, -via.
subclinical *adj.* subclínico, -ca.
subcollateral *adj.* subcolateral.
subconjunctival *adj.* subconjuntival.
subconjunctivitis *n.* subconjuntivitis.
subconscious *adj.* subconsciente.
subconsciousness *n.* subconsciencia.
subcontinuous *adj.* subcontinuo, -nua.
subcoracoid *adj.* subcoracoideo, -a.
subcortical *adj.* subcortical.
subcostal *adj.* subcostal.
subcostalgia *n.* subcostalgia.
subcranial *adj.* subcraneal.
subcrepitant *adj.* subcrepitante.
subcrepitation *n.* subcrepitación.
subculture[1] *n.* subcultivo, subcultura.
subculture[2] *v.* subcultivar.
subcurative *adj.* subcurativo, -va.
subcutaneous *adj.* subcutáneo, -a.
subcuticular *adj.* subcuticular.
subcutis *n.* subcutis.
subdeltoid *adj.* subdeltoideo, -a.
subdental *adj.* subdental, subdentario, -ria.
subdermic *adj.* subdérmico, -ca.
subdiaphragmatic *adj.* subdiafragmático, -ca.
subdorsal *adj.* subdorsal.
subduct *v.* subducir.
subduction *n.* subducción.
subdural *adj.* subdural.
subendocardial *adj.* subendocardíaco, -ca, subendocárdico, -ca.
subendothelial *adj.* subendotelial.
subendothelium *n.* subendotelio.
subependymal *adj.* subependimario, -ria.
subependymal *adj.* subependimario, -ria.
subependymoma *n.* subependimoma.
subepidermal *adj.* subepidérmico, -ca.
subepidermic *adj.* subepidérmico, -ca.
subepiglottic *adj.* subepiglótico, -ca.
subepithelial *adj.* subepitelial.
suberosis *n.* suberosis.
subexcite *v.* subexcitar.
subextensibility *n.* subextensibilidad.
subfamily *n.* subfamilia.
subfascial *adj.* subfascial.
subfertile *adj.* subfecundo, -da.
subfertility *n.* subfecundidad, subfertilidad.
subfissure *n.* subcisura.
subflavous *adj.* subflavo, -va.
subfoliar *adj.* subfoliar.
subfolium *n.* subfolio, subfolium.
subgaleal *adj.* subgaleal.
subgemal *adj.* subgemal.
subgenus *n.* subgénero.
subgerminal *adj.* subgerminal.
subgingival *adj.* subgingival.
subglenoid *adj.* subglenoideo, -a.
subglossal *adj.* subglósico, -ca, subgloso, -sa.
subglossitis *n.* subglositis.
subglottic *adj.* subglótico, -ca.
subgranular *adj.* subgranular, subgranuloso, -sa.
subgrundation *n.* subgrundación.
subgyrus *n.* subcircunvolución.

subhepatic *adj.* subhepático, -ca.
subhumeral *adj.* subhumeral.
subhyaloid *adj.* subhialoideo, -a.
subhyoid *adj.* subhioideo, -a.
subicteric *adj.* subictérico, -ca.
subicular *adj.* subicular.
subiculum *n.* subículo, subiculum.
subiliac *adj.* subilíaco, -ca.
subilium *n.* subíleon, subilion.
subimbibitional *adj.* subimbibicional.
subinfection *n.* subinfección.
subinflammation *n.* subinflamación.
subinflammatory *adj.* subinflamatorio, -ria.
subintimal *adj.* subíntimo, -a.
subintrance *n.* subintrancia.
subintrant *adj.* subintrante.
subinvolution *n.* subinvolución.
   uterine subinvolution subinvolución del útero, subinvolución uterina.
subjacent *adj.* subyacente.
subject *v.* sujetar, sujeto.
subjective *adj.* subjetivo, -va.
subjectoscope *n.* subjetoscopio.
subjugal *adj.* subyugal.
sublatio sublación, sublatio.
sublation *n.* sublación.
sublesional *adj.* sublesional.
sublethal *adj.* subletal.
subleukemia *n.* subleucemia.
sublimate[1] *adj.* sublimado, -da.
   corrosive sublimate sublimado corrosivo.
sublimate[2] *v.* sublimar.
sublimation *n.* sublimación.
subliminal *adj.* subliminal.
sublingual *adj.* sublingual.
sublinguitis *n.* sublingüitis.
sublobar *adj.* sublobulillar.
sublobe *n.* sublóbulo.
sublumbar *adj.* sublumbar.
subluminal *adj.* subluminal.
subluxate *v.* subluxar.
subluxation *n.* subluxación.
   congenital subluxation of the hip subluxación congénita de cadera.
   shoulder subluxation subluxación del hombro.
   Volkmann's subluxation subluxación de Volkmann.
sublymphemia *n.* sublinfemia.
submammary *adj.* submamario, -ria.
submandibular *adj.* submandibular.
submarginal *adj.* submarginal.
submaxillaritis *n.* submaxilaritis.
submaxillary *adj.* submaxilar.
submeatal *adj.* submeatal.
submedial *adj.* submedial.
submedian *adj.* submediano, -na.
submembranous *adj.* submembranoso, -sa.
submental *adj.* submentoniano, -na.
submentovertex *n.* submentovértice.
submerged *n.* sumergido.
submersion *n.* submersión, sumersión.
   root submersion sumersión de la raíz.
submetacentric *adj.* submetacéntrico, -ca.
submicroscopal *adj.* submicroscópico, -ca.
submicroscopic *adj.* submicroscópico, -ca.
submorphous *adj.* submorfo, -fa.
submucosa *n.* submucosa.
submucosal *adj.* submucoso, -sa.
submucous *adj.* submucoso, -sa.
subnasal *adj.* subnasal.
subnasion *n.* subnasión.
subnatant *adj.* subnadante.
subneural *adj.* subneural.
subnotochordal *adj.* subnotocordal.

subnucleus *n.* subnúcleo.
subnutrition *n.* subnutrición.
suboccipital *adj.* suboccipital.
suboccipitobregmatic *adj.* suboccipitobregmático, -ca.
suboptimal *adj.* subóptimo, -ma.
suborbital *adj.* suborbitario, -ria.
suborder *n.* suborden.
suboxidation *n.* suboxidación.
suboxide *n.* subóxido.
subpapillary *adj.* subpapilar.
subpapular *adj.* subpapular.
subparalytic *adj.* subparalítico, -ca.
subparietal *adj.* subparietal.
subpatellar *adj.* subpatelar, subrotuliano, -na.
subpectoral *adj.* subpectoral.
subpelviperitoneal *adj.* subpelviperitoneal.
subpericardial *adj.* subpericardíaco, -ca, subpericárdico, -ca.
subperiosteal *adj.* subperióstico, -ca.
subperiosteocapsular *adj.* subperiostiocapsular.
subperitoneal *adj.* subperitoneal.
subperitoneoabdominal *adj.* subperitoneoabdominal.
subperitoneopelvic *adj.* subperitoneopélvico, -ca.
subpetrosal *adj.* subpetroso, -sa.
subpharyngeal *adj.* subfaríngeo, -a.
subphrenic *adj.* subfrénico, -ca.
subphylum subfilo, subphylum.
subpial *adj.* subpial.
subpituitarism *n.* subpituitarismo.
subpleural *adj.* subpleural.
subplexal *adj.* subpléxico, -ca.
subpreputial *adj.* subprepucial.
subpubic *adj.* subpubiano, -na, subpúbico, -ca.
subpulmonary *adj.* subpulmonar.
subpulpal *adj.* subpulpal.
subpyramidal *adj.* subpiramidal.
subrectal *adj.* subrectal.
subretinal *adj.* subretinal, subretiniano, -na.
subsartorial *adj.* subsartorial.
subscaphocephaly *n.* subescafocefalia.
subscapular *adj.* subescapular.
subscleral *adj.* subescleral.
subsclerotic *adj.* subesclerótico, -ca.
subserosa *n.* subserosa.
subserosal *adj.* subseroso, -sa.
subserous *adj.* subseroso, -sa.
subsibilant *adj.* subsibilante.
subsidence *n.* subsidencia.
subsistence *n.* subsistencia.
subsonic *adj.* subsónico, -ca.
subspeciality *n.* subespecialidad.
subspecies *n.* subespecie.
subspinale *n.* subespinal.
subspinous *adj.* subespinoso, -sa.
subsplenial *adj.* subesplenio, -nia.
substage *n.* subplatina.
substance *n.* sustancia.
substandard *adj.* subestándar.
substantia *n.* sustancia.
substernal *adj.* subesternal.
substernomastoid *adj.* subesternomastoideo, -a.
substituent *adj.* sustituyente.
substitute *n.* sustituto, -ta.
   blood substitute sustituto de sangre.
   mother substitute sustituto materno.
   plasma substitute sustituto plasmático.
   volume substitute sustituto de volumen.
substitution *n.* sustitución.
   creeping substitution of bone sustitución reptante del hueso.

stimulus substitution sustitución de estímulos.

symptom substitution sustitución de síntomas.

substitutive *n.* sustitutivo, -va.

subtraction *n.* sustracción.

energy substraction sustracción energética.

hybrid substraction sustracción híbrida.

temporal substraction sustracción temporal.

substrate *n.* sustrato.

substratum *n.* sustrato.

substructure *n.* subestructura.

implant denture substructure subestructura de implantes protésicos.

implant substructure subestructura de implante.

subsulcus *n.* subsurco.

subsultus tendinum subsultus tendinum.

subsylvian *adj.* subsilviano, -na.

subsystem *n.* subsistema.

subtalar *adj.* subtalar.

subtarsal *adj.* subtarsal, subtarsiano, -na.

subtegumental *adj.* subtegumentario, -ria.

subtemporal *adj.* subtemporal.

subtenial *adj.* subtenial.

subtentorial *adj.* subtentorial.

subterminal *adj.* subterminal.

subtetanic *adj.* subtetánico, -ca.

subthalamic *adj.* subtalámico, -ca.

subthalamus *n.* subtálamo.

subthyroideus *n.* subtiroideo.

subthyroidism *n.* subtiroidismo.

subtotal *adj.* subtotal.

subtrapezial *adj.* subtrapecial.

subtribe *n.* subtribu.

subtrochanteric *adj.* subtrocantéreo, -a, subtrocanteriano, -na, subtrocantérico, -ca.

subtrochlear *adj.* subtroclear.

subtuberal *adj.* subtuberal.

subtympanic *adj.* subtimpánico, -ca.

subumbilical *adj.* subumbilical.

subungual *adj.* subungueal, subungular.

suburethral *adj.* suburetral.

subvaginal *adj.* subvaginal.

subvalvular *adj.* subvalvular.

subvertebral *adj.* subvertebral.

subvitaminosis *n.* subvitaminosis.

subvitrinal *adj.* subvítreo, -a.

subvolution *n.* subvolución.

subzonal *adj.* subzonal.

subzygomatic *adj.* subcigomático, -ca.

succagogue *n.* sucagogo, -ga.

succedaneous *adj.* sucedáneo, -a.

succedaneum *n.* sucedáneo.

succenturiate *adj.* succenturiado, -da.

succinous *adj.* succinoso, -sa.

succorrhea *n.* sucorrea.

succus jugo, succus.

appetite succus jugo del apetito.

succus cerasi jugo de cereza.

succus entericus jugo intestinal.

succus gastricus jugo gástrico.

succus pancreaticus jugo pancreático.

succus prostaticus jugo prostático.

succussion *n.* sucusión.

hippocratic succussion sucusión hipocrática.

suck *v.* succionar.

suckle *v.* amamantar.

sucrose *n.* sacarosa.

sucrosemia *n.* sacarosemia, sucrosemia.

sucrosuria *n.* sacarosuria, sucrosuria.

suction *n.* succión.

post-tussive suction succión postusiva.

Wangesteen suction succión de Wangesteen.

suctorial *adj.* suctorial.

sucus sucus.

sudamen *n.* sudamen.

sudaminal *adj.* sudaminal.

sudan *n.* sudán.

sudanophilia *n.* sudanofilia.

sudanophilic *adj.* sudanófilo, -la.

sudanophilous *adj.* sudanófilo, -la.

sudanophobic *adj.* sudanófobo, -ba.

sudarium *n.* sudario.

sudation *n.* sudación.

sudogram *n.* sudograma.

sudomotor *adj.* sudomotor, -ra.

sudor *n.* sudor.

sudor cruentus sudor sanguíneo.

sudor sanguineus sudor sanguíneo.

sudor urinosus sudor urinoso.

sudoral *adj.* sudoral.

sudoresis *n.* sudoresis.

sudoriferous *adj.* sudorífero, -ra.

sudorific *adj.* sudorífico, -ca.

sudorikeratosis *n.* sudoqueratosis.

sudoriparous *adj.* sudoríparo, -ra.

sudorometer *n.* sudorómetro.

sudorrhea *n.* sudorrea.

suffering *n.* sufrimiento.

suffocation *n.* ahogamiento, opresión.

suffusion *n.* sufusión.

sugar *n.* azúcar.

suggestibility *n.* sugestibilidad, sugestionabilidad.

suggestible *adj.* sugestionable.

suggestion *n.* sugestión.

hypnotic suggestion sugestión hipnótica.

posthypnotic suggestion sugestión poshipnótica.

suggestive *adj.* sugestivo, -va.

suicidal *adj.* suicida[2].

suicide *n.* suicida[1], suicidio.

intention of suicide conamen.

suicidology *n.* suicidología.

suipestifer *n.* suipestifer.

sukkla pakla *n.* sukkla pakla.

sulcate *adj.* surcado, -da.

sulcation *n.* surcamiento.

sulciform *adj.* sulciforme.

sulculus sulculus.

sulcus *n.* sulcus, surco.

sulfamethemoglobin *n.* sulfametahemoglobina.

sulfanuria *n.* sulfanuria.

sulfatemia *n.* sulfatemia.

sulfatidosis *n.* sulfatidosis.

sulfhemoglobin *n.* sulfahemoglobina, sulfohemoglobina.

sulfhemoglobinemia *n.* sulfahemoglobinemia, sulfohemoglobinemia.

sulfmethemoglobin *n.* sulfometahemoglobina.

sulfolysis *n.* sulfólisis.

sulfomucin *n.* sulfomucina.

sulfonamide *n.* sulfamida.

sulfonamidemia *n.* sulfamidemia.

sulfonamidocholia *n.* sulfamidocolia.

sulfonamidotherapy *n.* sulfamidoterapia.

sulfonamiduria *n.* sulfamiduria.

sulfoxism *n.* sulfoxismo.

sumac *n.* zumaque.

poison sumac zumaque de los pantanos, zumaque venenoso.

swamp sumac zumaque de los pantanos, zumaque venenoso.

summation *n.* sumación.

summation of stimuli sumación de estímulos.

temporal summation sumación temporal.

superabduction *n.* superabducción.

superacid *adj.* superácido, -da.

superacidity *n.* superacidez.

superacromial *adj.* superacromial.

superactivity *n.* sobreactividad, superactividad.

superacute *adj.* sobreagudo, -da, superagudo, -da.

superalimentation *n.* sobrealimentación, superalimentación.

superalkalinity *n.* superalcalinidad.

superanal *adj.* superanal.

superaurale *n.* superaural.

supercentral *adj.* supercentral.

superciliary *adj.* superciliar.

supercilium supercilio, supercilium.

superclass *n.* superclase.

superdicrotic *adj.* superdicrótico, -ca.

superdistention *n.* superdistensión.

superduction *n.* superducción.

superego *n.* superyó.

superexcitation *n.* sobreexcitación, superexcitación.

superextended *adj.* superextendido, -da.

superextension *n.* superextensión.

superfamily *n.* superfamilia.

superfatted *adj.* supergraso, -sa.

superfecundation *n.* superfecundación.

superfetation *n.* superfetación.

superfibrination *n.* superfibrinación.

superficial *adj.* superficial.

superficialis *adj.* superficial.

superflexion *n.* superflexion.

superfunction *n.* superfunción.

superfusion *n.* superfusión.

supergenual *adj.* superrotuliano, -na.

superimpregnation *n.* superimpregnación.

superinduce *v.* superinducir.

superinfection *n.* superinfección.

superinvolution *n.* superinvolución.

superior *adj.* superior.

superjacent *adj.* superyacente.

superlactation *n.* superlactación.

superligamen *n.* superligamen.

supermaxilla *adj.* supermaxilar[1].

supermaxillary *adj.* supermaxilar[2].

supermedial *adj.* supermedial, supermediano, -na.

supermotility *n.* supermotilidad, supermovilidad.

supernatant *adj.* supernadante.

supernumerary *adj.* supernumerario, -ria.

supernutrition *n.* supernutrición.

superoccipital *adj.* superoccipital.

superolateral *adj.* superolateral.

superovulation *n.* superovulación.

superparasite *n.* superparásito.

superparasitism *n.* superparasitismo.

superpetrosal *adj.* superpetroso, -sa.

superpigmentation *n.* superpigmentación.

superposition *n.* superposición.

super-regeneration *n.* superregeneración.

supersaturate *v.* supersaturar.

supersecretion *n.* supersecreción.

supersensitivity *n.* supersensibilidad.

disuse supersensitivity supersensibilidad por desuso.

supersensitization *n.* supersesibilización.

supersonic *adj.* supersónico, -ca.

supersonics *n.* supersónica.

supersphenoid *adj.* superesfenoidal.

superstructure *n.* superestructura.

implant denture superstructure superestructura de implante, superestructura de prótesis implantada.

implant superstructure superestructura de

implante, superestructura de prótesis implantada.

supertension *n.* supertensión.

supervascularization *n.* supervascularización.

supervenosity *n.* supervenosidad.

supervention *n.* supervención.

superversion *n.* superversión.

supervirulent *adj.* supervirulento, -ta.

supervision *n.* supervisión.

supervitaminosis *n.* supervitaminosis.

supervoltage *n.* supervoltaje.

supinate *v.* supinar.

supination *n.* supinación.

   supination of the foot supinación del pie.

   supination of the forearm supinación del antebrazo.

supinator *n.* supinador.

supine *adj.* supino, -na.

suppedania *n.* supedania.

supplemental *adj.* suplementario, -ria.

support *n.* apoyo[2], soporte.

   advanced cardiac life support (ACLS) soporte vital cardíaco avanzado (SVCA).

   basic life support soporte vital básico.

   life support soporte vital.

   midstance support apoyo medio.

   mobile arm support soporte móvil para el brazo.

   pediatric advanced life support (PALS) soporte vital avanzado pediátrico (SVAP).

suppressant *n.* supresor, -ra.

suppression *n.* supresión.

   overdrive suppression supresión de la sobreconducción.

suppurant *n.* supurante.

suppurate *v.* supurar.

suppuration *n.* supuración.

   alveolodental suppuration supuración alveolodental.

suppurative *adj.* supurativo, -va.

supra-acromial *adj.* supraacromial.

supra-anal *adj.* supraanal.

supra-auricular *adj.* supraauricular.

supra-axillary *adj.* supraaxilar.

suprabuccal *adj.* suprabucal.

suprabulge *adj.* supraecuatorial.

supracardinal *adj.* supracardinal.

supracerebellar *adj.* supracerebeloso, -sa.

supracerebral *adj.* supracerebral.

suprachoroid *adj.* supracoroideo, -a.

suprachoroidea *n.* supracoroides.

supraciliary *adj.* supraciliar.

supraclavicular *adj.* supraclavicular.

supraclavicularis *n.* supraclavicular.

   supraclavicularis major supraclavicularis major.

supraclusion *n.* supraclusión.

supracondylar *adj.* supracondíleo, -a.

supracondyloid *adj.* supracondíleo, -a.

supracostal *adj.* supracostal.

supracotyloid *adj.* supracotiloideo, -a.

supracranial *adj.* supracraneal.

supracristal *adj.* supracrestal.

supradiaphragmatic *adj.* supradiafragmático, -ca.

supraduction *n.* supraducción.

supraepicondylar *adj.* supraepicondíleo, -a.

supraepitrochlear *adj.* supraepitroclear, supraepitrócleo, -a.

supraglenoid *adj.* supraglenoideo, -a.

supraglottic *adj.* supraglótico, -ca.

suprahepatic *adj.* suprahepático, -ca.

suprahyoid *adj.* suprahioideo, -a.

suprainguinal *adj.* suprainguinal.

supraintestinal *adj.* supraintestinal.

supraliminal *adj.* supraliminal.

supralumbar *adj.* supralumbar.

supramalleolar *adj.* supramaleolar.

supramammary *adj.* supramamario, -ria.

supramandibular *adj.* supramandibular.

supramarginal *adj.* supramarginal.

supramastoid *adj.* supramastoideo, -a.

supramaxilla *n.* supramaxilar[1].

supramaxillary *adj.* supramaxilar[2].

supramaximal *adj.* supramáximo, -ma.

suprameatal *adj.* suprameático, -ca.

supramental *adj.* supramentoniano, -na.

supramentale *n.* supramentale.

supranasal *adj.* supranasal.

supraneural *adj.* supraneural.

supranormal *adj.* supranormal.

supranuclear *adj.* supranuclear.

supraoccipital *adj.* supraoccipital.

supraocclusion *n.* supraoclusión.

supraocular *adj.* supraocular.

supraoptimal *adj.* supraóptimo, -ma.

supraorbital *adj.* supraorbitario, -ria.

suprapatellar *adj.* suprapatelar, suprarrotuliano, -na.

suprapelvic *adj.* suprapelviano, -na, suprapélvico, -ca.

suprapharmacologic *adj.* suprafarmacológico, -ca.

supraphysiologic *adj.* suprafisiológico, -ca.

supraphysiological *adj.* suprafisiológico, -ca.

suprapontine *adj.* suprapontino, -na.

suprapubic *adj.* suprapúbico, -ca.

suprarenal *adj.* suprarrenal.

suprarenalectomy *n.* suprarrenalectomía.

suprarenalemia *n.* suprarrenalemia.

suprarenalism *n.* suprarrenalismo.

suprarenalopathy *n.* suprarrenalopatía.

suprarenogenic *adj.* suprarrenogénico, -ca.

suprarenoma *n.* suprarrenoma.

suprarenopathy *n.* suprarrenopatía.

suprarenotropic *adj.* suprarrenotrópico, -ca.

suprarenotropism *n.* suprarrenotropismo.

suprascapular *adj.* supraescapular, suprascapular.

suprascleral *adj.* supraesclerótico, -ca.

suprasellar *adj.* supraselar.

supraseptal *adj.* supraseptal.

suprasonics *n.* suprasónica.

supraspinal *adj.* supraespinal, supraspinal.

supraspinous *adj.* supraespinoso, -sa, supraspinoso, -sa.

suprastapedial *adj.* supraestapedial.

suprasternal *adj.* supraesternal, suprasternal.

suprasylvian *adj.* suprasilviano, -na.

suprasymphysary *adj.* suprasinfisario, -ria.

supratemporal *adj.* supratemporal.

supratentorial *adj.* supratentorial.

suprathoracic *adj.* supratorácico, -ca.

supratonsillar *adj.* supraamigdalino, -na, supratonsilar.

supratrochlear *adj.* supratroclear.

supratympanic *adj.* supratimpánico, -ca.

supraumbilical *adj.* supraumbilical.

supravaginal *adj.* supravaginal.

supravalvular *adj.* supravalvular.

supraventricular *adj.* supraventricular.

supravergence *n.* supravergencia.

supraversion *n.* supraversión.

supravital *adj.* supravital.

supraxiphoid *adj.* supraxifoideo, -a.

sura *n.* sura.

sural *adj.* sural.

suralis *adj.* sural.

surdimute *adj.* sordomudo, -da.

surdimutitas *n.* sordomudez.

surface *n.* superficie.

surgeon *n.* cirujano, -na.

surgery *n.* cirugía.

   abdominal surgery cirugía abdominal.

   ambulatory surgery cirugía ambulatoria.

   antiseptic surgery cirugía antiséptica.

   aseptic surgery cirugía aséptica.

   aural surgery cirugía ótica, cirugía otológica.

   cardiac surgery cirugía cardíaca.

   cineplastic surgery cirugía cineplástica.

   clinical surgery cirugía clínica.

   closed surgery cirugía cerrada.

   conservative surgery cirugía conservadora.

   cosmetic surgery cirugía cosmética.

   craniofacial surgery cirugía craneofacial.

   dental surgery cirugía dental.

   dentofacial surgery cirugía dentofacial.

   esthetic surgery cirugía estética.

   featural surgery cirugía de las facciones.

   general surgery cirugía general.

   major surgery cirugía mayor.

   maxillofacial surgery cirugía maxilofacial.

   minor surgery cirugía menor.

   open heart surgery cirugía a corazón abierto.

   operative surgery cirugía operatoria.

   oral surgery cirugía bucal, cirugía oral.

   orthognathic surgery cirugía ortognática.

   orthopedic surgery cirugía ortopédica.

   plastic surgery cirugía plástica.

   radical surgery cirugía radical.

   reconstructive surgery cirugía reconstructiva, cirugía reconstructora.

   stereotactic surgery cirugía estereotáctica, cirugía estereotáxica.

   stereotaxic surgery cirugía estereotáctica, cirugía estereotáxica.

   structural surgery cirugía estructural.

   transsexual surgery cirugía transexual.

surgical *adj.* quirúrgico, -ca.

surrogate *n.* suplente.

sursanure *n.* sursanura.

sursumduction *n.* sursunducción.

sursumvergence *n.* sursunvergencia.

sursumversion *n.* sursunversión.

surveillance *n.* vigilancia[1].

   inmune surveillance vigilancia inmune, vigilancia inmunológica.

   inmunological surveillance vigilancia inmune, vigilancia inmunológica.

survey *n.* vigilancia[1].

   metastatic survey vigilancia metastática.

survival *n.* supervivencia.

susceptibility *n.* susceptibilidad.

   genetic susceptibility susceptibilidad genética.

susceptible *adj.* susceptible.

suscitate *v.* suscitar.

suspenopsia *n.* suspenopsia.

suspensiometer *n.* suspensiómetro.

suspension *n.* suspensión.

suspensoid *n.* suspensoide.

suspensory *n.* suspensorio, -ria.

sustentacular *adj.* sustentacular.

sustentaculum soporte, sustentáculo, sustentaculum.

susurrus *n.* susurro.

   susurrus aurium susurro auricular.

sutika *n.* sutika.

sutura *n.* sutura[1].

sutural *adj.* sutural.

suturation *n.* suturación.

suture *n.* sutura.

   absorbable surgical suture sutura absorbible.

   absorbable suture sutura absorbible.

Albert's suture sutura de Albert.
anatomical suture sutura anatómica.
Appolito's suture sutura de Appolito.
apposition suture sutura de aposición.
approximation suture sutura de afrontamiento, sutura de aproximación.
atraumatic suture sutura atraumática.
bastard suture sutura bastarda.
Bell's suture sutura de Bell.
blanket suture sutura de manta.
bolster suture sutura con soporte.
bridle suture sutura en brida.
Bunnell's suture sutura de Bunnell.
buried suture sutura enterrada, sutura incluida, sutura profunda, sutura sepultada.
button suture sutura de Billroth, sutura de botón, sutura de Bozeman, sutura en botón.
catgut suture sutura de catgut.
chain suture sutura de cadena, sutura en cadena.
circular suture sutura circular.
coaptation suture sutura de coaptación.
cobbler's suture sutura de zapatero.
compound suture sutura compuesta, sutura emplumada.
Connell's suture sutura de Connell.
continuous running suture sutura continua corrida.
continuous suture sutura continua.
Cushing's suture sutura de Cushing.
Czerny-Lembert suture sutura de Czerny-Lembert.
Czerny's suture sutura de Czerny.
delayed suture sutura demorada, sutura diferida.
dentate suture sutura dentada.
double-button suture sutura de doble botón.
doubly armed suture sutura de doble brazo.
Dupuytren's suture sutura de Dupuytren.
end-on matress suture sutura vertical de colchonero.
everting suture sutura de eversión.
Faden's suture sutura de Faden.
false suture sutura falsa.
far-and-near suture sutura de lejos y de cerca.
figure-of-8 suture sutura en forma de 8, sutura en ocho, sutura ensortijada.
Frost's suture sutura de Frost.
furrier's suture sutura de peletero.
Gaillard-Arlt suture sutura de Gaillard-Arlt.
Gély's suture sutura de Gély.
glover's suture sutura de guantero.
Gould's suture sutura de Gould.
Gussenbauer's suture sutura de Gussenbauer.
Halsted's suture sutura de Halsted.
harelip suture sutura de labio leporino.
harmonic suture sutura armónica.
hemostatic suture sutura hemostática.
horizontal mattress suture sutura horizontal de colchonero.
implanted suture sutura implantada.
interrupted suture sutura de puntos en asa, sutura de puntos en u, sutura de puntos separados, sutura en asa, sutura interrumpida.
intradermal mattress suture sutura intradérmica de colchonero.
intradermic suture sutura intradérmica.
inverting suture sutura de inversión.
Jobert de Lamballe's suture sutura de Jobert de Lamballe.
Le Dentu's suture sutura de Le Dentu.
Le Fort's suture sutura de Le Fort, sutura de Lejars.
Lembert suture sutura de Lembert.
lock-stitch suture sutura a punto pasado, sutura de Doyen, sutura de punto pasado, sutura en festón.
matress suture sutura de colchonero.
nerve suture sutura de nervio.
non-absorbable surgical suture sutura no absorbible, sutura quirúrgica no absorbible.
Pancoast's suture sutura de Pancoast.
Paré's suture sutura de Paré.
Parker-Kerr suture sutura de Parker-Kerr.
plane suture sutura por planos.
plastic suture sutura de lengüeta y surco, sutura plástica.
presection suture sutura preseccional, sutura previa al corte.
primary suture sutura primaria.
purse-string suture sutura en bolsa de tabaco, sutura en jareta.
quilled suture sutura compuesta, sutura emplumada.
quilted suture sutura acolchada.
relaxation suture sutura de relajación.
retention suture sutura de retención.
right-angle mattress suture sutura de colchonero en ángulo recto.
secondary suture sutura secundaria.
shotted suture sutura calada, sutura hendida.
silkworm gut suture sutura de tripa de gusano de seda.
Sims' suture sutura de Sims.
spiral suture sutura en espiral, sutura espiral.
subcuticular suture sutura subcuticular.
superficial suture sutura superficial.
surgical suture sutura quirúrgica.
suture plana sutura plana.
tension suture sutura de tensión.
transfixion suture sutura de transfixión.
uninterrumpted suture sutura ininterrumpida.
uninterrupted suture sutura no interrumpida.
wedge-and-groove suture sutura de cuña y surco.
wire suture sutura metálica.
suturectomy n. suturectomía.
swage v. estampar.
swager n. estampador.
swallow v. deglutir.
swarming n. inulación.
swayback n. caída de espaldas.
sweat[1] n. sudor.
  bloody sweat sudor sanguíneo.
  colliquative sweat sudor colicuativo.
  fetid sweat bromhidrosis.
  night sweat sudor nocturno.
  red sweat sudor rojo.
sweat[2] v. sudar.
swing n. balancín[2].
switch n. interruptor.
  exposure switch interruptor de exposición.
swoon n. vahído.
sycephalous adj. sicéfalo, -la.
sychnuria n. sicnuria.
sycholia n. sincolia.
sycliticism n. sinclitismo.
sycoma n. psicoma.
sycosis n. sicosis.
  coccogenic sycosis sicosis cocógena.
  lupoid sycosis sicosis lupoide.
  parasitic sycosis sicosis parasitaria.
  sycosis barbae sicosis de la barba.
  sycosis nuchae sicosis de la nuca.
  sycosis nuchae necrotisans sicosis necrotizante de la nuca.
  sycosis staphylogenes sicosis estafilógena.
  sycosis tarsi sicosis tarsal.
  sycosis vulgaris sicosis simple, sicosis vulgar.
syllepsiology n. silepsiología.
syllepsis n. silepsis.
sylvian adj. silviano, -na.
symballophone n. simbalófono.
symbiology n. simbiología.
symbionic adj. simbiónico, -ca.
symbiont n. simbionte.
symbiosis n. simbiosis.
  antagonistic symbiosis simbiosis antagónica, simbiosis antagonista.
  antipathetic symbiosis simbiosis antagónica, simbiosis antagonista.
  conjunctive symbiosis simbiosis conjuntiva.
  constructive symbiosis simbiosis constructiva.
  dyadic symbiosis simbiosis diádica.
  triadic symbiosis simbiosis triádica.
symbiote n. simbión, simbiota.
symbiotic adj. simbiótico, -ca.
symblepharon n. simbléfaron.
  anterior symblepharon simbléfaron anterior.
  posterior symblepharon simbléfaron posterior.
  total symblepharon simbléfaron total.
symblepharopterygium n. simblefaropterigión.
symbol n. símbolo.
  consensual validated symbol símbolo validado consensualmente.
  radiation symbol símbolo de radiación.
symbolia n. simbolia.
symbolism n. simbolismo.
symbolization n. simbolización.
symbrachydactylism n. simbraquidactilismo.
symbrachydactyly n. simbraquidactilia.
symmelia n. simelia.
  apodial symmelia simelia apodálica.
  tripodial symmelia simelia tripódica.
symmelus n. simelo.
symmetric adj. simétrico, -ca.
symmetrical adj. simétrico, -ca.
symmetry n. simetría.
  bilateral symmetry simetría bilateral.
  inverse symmetry simetría inversa.
  radial symmetry simetría radial.
sympathectomize v. simpatectomizar.
sympathectomy n. simpatectomía.
  periarterial sympathectomy simpatectomía periarterial.
sympathetic n. simpático.
sympatheticoparalytic adj. simpaticoparalítico, -ca.
sympatheticotherapy n. simpaticoterapia.
sympatheticotonia n. simpaticotonía.
sympatheticotonic adj. simpaticotónico, -ca.
sympathic n. simpático.
sympathicectomy n. simpaticectomía.
sympathicoblast n. simpaticoblasto.
sympathicoblastoma n. simpaticoblastoma.
sympathicogonioma n. simpaticogonioma.
sympathicolytic adj. simpaticolítico, -ca.
sympathicomimetic adj. simpaticomimético, -ca.
sympathiconeuritis n. simpaticoneuritis.
sympathicopathy n. simpaticopatía.
sympathicotonia n. simpaticotonía.
sympathicotonic adj. simpaticotónico, -ca.
sympathicotripsy n. simpaticotripsia.
sympathicotrope adj. simpaticotrópico, -ca, simpaticótropo, -pa.
sympathicotropic adj. simpaticotrópico, -ca.
sympathism n. simpatismo.
sympathizer adj. simpatizador, -ra, simpatizante.

sympathoadrenal *adj.* simpatosuprarrenal.
sympathoblast *n.* simpatoblasto.
sympathoblastoma *n.* simpatoblastoma.
sympathogonioma *n.* simpatogonioma.
sympatholytic *adj.* simpatolítico, -ca.
sympathoma *n.* simpatoma.
sympathomimetic *adj.* simpatomimético, -ca.
sympathy *n.* simpatía.
sympexion *n.* simpexión.
sympexis *n.* simpexis.
symphalangia *n.* sinfalangia.
symphalangism *n.* sinfalangismo.
symphalangy *n.* sinfalangia.
symphiseotome *n.* sinfisiótomo.
symphiseotomy *n.* sinfisiotomía.
symphisodactylla *n.* sinfisodactilia.
Symphoromyia Symphoromyia.
symphyocephalus *n.* sinfiocéfalo.
symphyogenetic *adj.* sinfiogenético, -ca.
symphyseal *adj.* sinfisial.
symphysic *adj.* sinfísico, -ca.
symphysiectomy *n.* sinfisectomía, sinfisiectomía.
symphysiolysis *n.* sinfisiólisis.
symphysion *n.* sinfisión.
symphysiorrhaphy *n.* sinfisiorrafia.
symphysiotome *n.* sinfisiótomo.
symphysiotomy *n.* sinfisiotomía.
symphysis *n.* sínfisis.
  cardiac symphysis sínfisis cardíaca.
symphysodactyly *n.* sinfisodactilia.
symplasm *n.* simplasma.
symplasmatic *adj.* simplasmático, -ca.
symplex symplex.
sympodia *n.* simpodia.
symport *n.* simporte.
symptom *n.* síntoma.
  abstinence symptom síntoma de abstinencia.
  accessory symptom síntoma accesorio.
  accidental symptom síntoma accidental.
  Anton's symptom síntoma de Anton.
  assident symptom síntoma asidente.
  Bárány's symptom síntoma de Bárány.
  Baumès symptom síntoma de Baumès.
  Béhier-Hardy symptom síntoma de Béhier-Hardy.
  Bechterew's symptom síntoma de Bechterew.
  Bezold's symptom síntoma de Bezold.
  Bolognini's symptom síntoma de Bolognini.
  Bonhoeffer's symptom síntoma de Bonhoeffer.
  Brauch-Romberg symptom síntoma de Brauch-Romberg
  Buerger's symptom síntoma de Buerger.
  Burghart's symptom síntoma de Burghart.
  Capgras symptom síntoma de Capgras.
  Cardarelli's symptom síntoma de Cardarelli.
  cardinal symptom síntoma cardinal.
  Castellani-Low symptom síntoma de Castellani-Low.
  characteristic symptom síntoma característico.
  Colliver's symptom síntoma de Colliver.
  concomitant symptom síntoma concomitante.
  consecutive symptom síntoma consecutivo.
  constitutional symptom síntoma constitucional, síntoma general.
  crossbar symptom of Fraenkel síntoma de barra cruzada de Fraenkel.
  deficiency symptom síntoma de deficiencia.
  delayed symptom síntoma aplazado, síntoma diferido, síntoma retrasado.
  Demarquay's symptom síntoma de Demarquay.

  direct symptom síntoma directo.
  dissociation symptom síntoma de disociación.
  Duroziez's symptom síntoma de Duroziez.
  endothelial symptom síntoma endotelial.
  Epstein's symptom síntoma de Epstein.
  equivocal symptom síntoma equívoco.
  esophagosalivary symptom síntoma esofagosalival.
  Fischer's symptom síntoma de Fischer.
  focal symptom síntoma focal.
  Frenkel's symptom síntoma de Frenkel.
  Fröschel's symptom síntoma de Fröschel.
  Ganser's symptom síntoma de Ganser.
  Goldthwait's symptom síntoma de Goldthwait.
  Gordon's symptom síntoma de Gordon.
  Griesinger's symptom síntoma de Griesinger.
  guiding symptom síntoma orientador.
  Haenel's symptom síntoma de Haenel.
  halo symptom síntoma del halo.
  Hochenegg's symptom síntoma de Hochenegg.
  Howship's symptom síntoma de Howship.
  incarceration symptom síntoma de encarcelación, síntoma de incarceración.
  indirect symptom síntoma indirecto.
  induced symptom síntoma inducido.
  Jellinek's symptom síntoma de Jellinek.
  Jonas symptom síntoma de Jonas.
  Kérandel's symptom síntoma de Kérandel.
  Kocher's symptom síntoma de Kocher.
  Kussmaul's symptom síntoma de Kussmaul.
  labyrinthine symptom síntoma laberíntico.
  Lade symptom síntoma de Lade.
  Liebreich's symptom síntoma de Liebreich.
  local symptom síntoma local.
  localizing symptom síntoma de localización.
  Magendie's symptom síntoma de Magendie.
  negative pathognomonic symptom síntoma patognomónico negativo.
  neighborhood symptom síntoma de vecindad.
  nostril symptom síntoma de la ventana nasal.
  objective symptom síntoma objetivo.
  Oehler's symptom síntoma de Oehler.
  passive symptom síntoma pasivo.
  pathognomonic symptom síntoma patognomónico.
  Pel-Ebstein symptom síntoma de Pel-Ebstein.
  Pratt's symptom síntoma de Prat.
  precursory symptom síntoma precursor, síntoma premonitor.
  premonitory symptom síntoma precursor, síntoma premonitor.
  presenting symptom síntoma de presentación.
  prodromal symptom síntoma prodrómico.
  rainbow symptom síntoma del arco iris, síntoma en arco iris.
  rational symptom síntoma racional.
  reflex symptom síntoma reflejo.
  Remak's symptom síntoma de Remak.
  Roger's symptom síntoma de Roger.
  Romberg-Howship symptom síntoma de Romberg-Howship.
  Séguin's signal symptom síntoma señal de Séguin.
  signal symptom síntoma señal.
  Simon's symptom síntoma de Simon.
  Sklowsky's symptom síntoma de Sklowsky.
  static symptom síntoma estático.
  Stellwag's symptom síntoma de Stellwag.
  Stierlin's symptom síntoma de Sterlin.
  subjective symptom síntoma subjetivo.
  sympathetic symptom síntoma simpático.

  target symptom síntoma diana.
  Tar's symptom síntoma de Tar.
  Trendelenburg's symptom síntoma de Trendelenburg.
  Trunecek's symptom síntoma de Trunecek.
  Wanner's symptom síntoma de Wanner.
  Wartenberg's symptom síntoma de Wartenberg.
  Weber's symptom síntoma de Weber.
  Wernicke's symptom síntoma de Wernicke.
  Westphal's symptom síntoma de Westphal.
  Winterbottom's symptom síntoma de Winterbottom.
  withdrawal symptom síntoma de retiro, síntoma de supresión.
symptomatic *adj.* sintomático, -ca.
symptomatology *n.* sintomatología.
symptomatolytic *adj.* sintomatolítico, -ca.
symptomolytic *adj.* sintomatolítico, -ca.
symptosis *n.* simptosis.
sympus sympus.
synadelphus *n.* sinadelfo.
synaetion *n.* sinetión.
synalbumin *n.* sinalbúmina.
synalgia *n.* sinalgia.
synalgic *adj.* sinálgico, -ca.
synanastomosis *n.* sinanastomosis.
synanthem *n.* sinantema.
synanthema *n.* sinantema.
synaphymenitis *n.* sinafimenitis.
synapse *n.* sinapsis.
  axoaxonic synapse sinapsis axoaxónica, sinapsis axoonoaxónica.
  axodendritic synapse sinapsis axodendrítica.
  axodendrosomatic synapse sinapsis axodendrosomática.
  axosomatic synapse sinapsis axosomática.
  dendrodendritic synapse sinapsis dendrodendrítica.
  electrotonic synapse sinapsis electrotónica.
  en passant synapse sinapsis de tránsito.
  loop synapse sinapsis en asa.
synapsis *n.* sinapsis.
synaptic *adj.* sináptico, -ca.
synaptology *n.* sinaptología.
synaptosome *n.* sinaptosoma.
synarthrodia *n.* sinartrodia.
synarthrodial *adj.* sinartrodial.
synarthrosis *n.* sinartrosis.
synarthrophysis *n.* sinartrofisis.
synathresis *n.* sinatresis.
synathroisis *n.* sinatroisis.
syncanthus *n.* sincanto.
syncaryon *n.* sincarion.
syncelom *n.* sinceloma.
syncephalus *n.* sincéfalo.
syncephaly *n.* sincefalia.
syncheilia *n.* sinquilia.
synchesis *n.* sinquesis, sínquisis.
synchilia *n.* sinquilia.
synchiria *n.* sinquiria.
synchondrectomy *n.* sincondrectomía.
synchondroseotomy *n.* sincondroseotomía.
synchondrosis *n.* sincondrosis.
synchondrotomy *n.* sincondrotomía.
synchorial *adj.* sincorial.
synchronism *n.* sincronismo.
synchronous *adj.* sincrónico, -ca.
synchroton *n.* sincrotón.
synchysis *n.* sínquisis.
  synchysis scintillans sínquisis centelleante.
syncinesis *n.* sincinesia, sincinesis.
  homolateral limb syncinesis sincinesia homolateral de los miembros.
  imitative syncinesis sincinesia imitativa.

mouth and hand syncinesis sincinesia de boca y mano.

synciput *n.* sincipucio.

synclitic *adj.* sinclítico, -ca.

synclitism *n.* sinclitismo.

synclonus *n.* sinclonía, sinclono.

syncopal *adj.* sincopal.

syncope *n.* síncope.

Adams-Stokes syncope síncope de Adams-Stokes.

cardiac syncope síncope cardíaco.

carotid sinus syncope síncope del seno carotídeo.

cough syncope síncope de la tos, síncope por tos.

digital syncope síncope digital.

laryngeal syncope síncope laríngeo.

local syncope síncope local.

micturition syncope síncope de micción, síncope miccional.

postural syncope síncope postural.

prostatic syncope síncope prostático.

stretching syncope síncope por estiramiento.

swallow syncope síncope deglutorio, síncope por deglución.

swallowing syncope síncope deglutorio, síncope por deglución.

syncope anginosa síncope anginoso.

tussive syncope síncope tusígeno.

vasodepressor syncope síncope vasodepresor.

vasovagal syncope síncope vasovagal.

syncopic *adj.* sincópico, -ca.

syncretio syncretio.

syncytial *adj.* sincitial.

syncytioma *n.* sincitioma.

syncytioma malignum sincitioma maligno.

syncytiotrophoblast *n.* sincitiotrofoblasto.

syncytium *n.* sincitio.

syncytoid *adj.* sincitioide, sincitioideo, -a.

syncytotoxin *n.* sincitotoxina.

syndactyl *n.* sindáctilo[1], -la.

syndactyle *n.* sindáctilo[1], -la.

syndactylia *n.* sindactilia.

syndactylism *n.* sindactilismo.

syndactylous *adj.* sindactílico, -ca, sindáctilo[2], -la.

syndactyly *n.* palmidactilia, sindactilia.

complete syndactyly sindactilia completa.

complicated syndactyly sindactilia complicada.

double syndactyly sindactilia doble.

partial syndactyly sindactilia parcial.

simple syndactyly sindactilia simple.

single syndactyly sindactilia sencilla.

triple syndactyly sindactilia triple.

syndectomy *n.* sindectomía.

syndelphus *n.* sindelfo.

syndemoplasty *n.* sindesmoplastia.

syndesis *n.* sindesis.

syndesmectomy *n.* sindesmectomía.

syndesmitis *n.* sindesmitis.

syndesmitis metatarsea sindesmitis metatarsiana.

syndesmography *n.* sindesmografía.

syndesmologia *n.* sindesmología.

syndesmology *n.* sindesmología.

syndesmoma *n.* sindesmoma.

syndesmo-odontoid *adj.* sindesmodontoides.

syndesmopexy *n.* sindesmopexia.

syndesmophyte *n.* sindesmófito.

syndesmorrhaphy *n.* sindesmorrafia.

syndesmosis *n.* sindesmosis.

radioulnar syndesmosis sindesmosis radiocubital.

syndesmosis radio-ulnaris sindesmosis radiocubital.

syndesmosis tibiofibularis sindesmosis tibioperonea.

syndesmosis tympanostapedia sindesmosis timpanoestapedia.

tibiofibular syndesmosis sindesmosis tibioperonea.

tympanostapedial syndesmosis sindesmosis timpanoestapedia.

syndesmotomy *n.* sindesmotomía.

syndrome *n.* síndrome.

17-hydroxylase deficiency syndrome síndrome de deficiencia de 17-hidroxilasa.

Aarskog syndrome síndrome de Aarskog-Scott.

Aarskog-Scott syndrome síndrome de Aarskog-Scott.

Aase syndrome síndrome de Aase.

abdominal muscle deficiency syndrome síndrome de deficiencia muscular abdominal.

Abercrombie syndrome síndrome de Abercrombie.

abstinence syndrome síndrome de abstinencia.

abused-child syndrome síndrome de abuso del niño.

Achard syndrome síndrome de Achard.

Achard-Thiers syndrome síndrome de Achard-Thiers.

Achenbach syndrome síndrome de Achenbach.

acquired immunodeficiency syndrome (AIDS) síndrome de inmunodeficiencia adquirida (SIDA).

acrofacial syndrome síndrome acrofacial.

acute radiation syndrome síndrome de irradiación aguda.

acute respiratory distress syndrome síndrome de dificultad respiratoria aguda.

Adair-Dighton syndrome síndrome de Adair-Dighton.

Adams-Stokes syndrome síndrome de Adams-Stokes.

Addisonian syndrome síndrome adisoniano, síndrome de Addison.

adherence syndrome síndrome de adherencia.

Adie's syndrome síndrome de Adie, síndrome de Adie-Reys.

adiposogenital syndrome síndrome adiposogenital.

adrenogenital syndrome síndrome adrenogenital.

adult respiratory distress syndrome (ARDS) síndrome de dificultad respiratoria del adulto (SDRA), síndrome de distrés respiratorio del adulto (SDRA), síndrome de insuficiencia respiratoria del adulto.

afferent loop syndrome síndrome del asa aferente.

aglossia-adactylia syndrome síndrome de aglosia-adactilia.

Ahumada-del Castillo syndrome síndrome de Ahumada-del Castillo.

Aicardi's syndrome síndrome de Aicardi.

Alajouanine's syndrome síndrome de Alajouanine.

Albright-McCune-Sternberg syndrome síndrome de Albright, síndrome de Albright-McCune-Sternberg.

Albright's syndrome síndrome de Albright, síndrome de Albright-McCune-Sternberg.

Albright-Turner's syndrome síndrome de Albright-Turner.

Aldrich syndrome síndrome de Aldrich.

Aldrich's syndrome síndrome de Aldrich.

Alezzandrini's syndrome síndrome de Alezzandrini.

Alice-in-Wonderland syndrome síndrome de Alicia en el país de las maravillas.

Allemann's syndrome síndrome de Allemann.

Allen-Masters' syndrome síndrome de Allen-Masters.

Alport's syndrome síndrome de Alport.

Alström syndrome síndrome de Alström.

amenorrhea-galactorrhea syndrome síndrome de amenorrea-galactorrea.

amnestic syndrome síndrome amnésico, síndrome amnésico-confabulatorio.

amnestic-confabulatory syndrome síndrome amnésico, síndrome amnésico-confabulatorio.

amniotic band syndrome síndrome de la banda amniótica.

amniotic infection syndrome of Blane síndrome de infección amniótica de Blane.

amyostatic syndrome síndrome amiostático.

Andersen's syndrome síndrome de Andersen.

androgen-insensitivity syndrome síndrome de insensibilidad a los andrógenos.

Angelman's syndrome síndrome de Angelman.

Angelucci syndrome síndrome de Angelucci.

Angelucci's syndrome síndrome de Angelucci.

anginal syndrome síndrome anginoso.

anginose syndrome síndrome anginoso.

angio-osteohypertrophy syndrome síndrome de angio-osteohipertrofia.

anorexia-cachexia syndrome síndrome de anorexia-caquexia.

anterior cord syndrome síndrome del cordón anterior.

anterior cornual syndrome síndrome del asta anterior.

anterior medullar syndrome síndrome medular anterior.

anterior tibial compartment syndrome síndrome del compartimiento tibial anterior.

antibody deficiency syndrome síndrome de deficiencia de anticuerpos, síndrome por deficiencia de anticuerpos.

anticholinergic syndrome síndrome anticolinérgico.

Anton's syndrome síndrome de Anton.

anxiety syndrome síndrome de ansiedad.

aortic arch syndrome síndrome del cayado aórtico.

apallic syndrome síndrome apálico.

Apert Cushing's syndrome síndrome de Apert-Cushing.

Apert syndrome síndrome de Apert.

Apert-Crouzon's syndrome síndrome de Apert-Crouzon.

argentaffinoma syndrome síndrome argentafin, síndrome de argentafinoma.

Argonz-del Castillo syndrome síndrome de Argonz-Ahumada del Castillo.

Arndt-Gottron syndrome síndrome de Arndt-Gottron.

Arnold-Chiari syndrome síndrome de Arnold-Chiari.

Ascher's syndrome síndrome de Ascher.

Asherman's syndrome síndrome de Asherman.

Asherson's syndrome síndrome de Asherson.

asplenia syndrome síndrome de asplenia.

ataxia-telangiectasia syndrome síndrome de ataxia y telangiectasia.

athletic heart syndrome síndrome del corazón atlético.

auriculotemporal syndrome síndrome auriculotemporal.

A-V strabismus syndrome síndrome de estrabismo A-V.

Avellis' syndrome síndrome de Avellis.

Axenfeld's syndrome síndrome de Axenfeld.

Axenfeld-Schürenberg syndrome síndrome de Axenfeld-Schürenberg.

Ayerza's syndrome síndrome de Ayerza.

Babinski-Fröhlich syndrome síndrome de Babinski-Frölich.

Babinski-Nageotte syndrome síndrome de Babinski-Nageotte.

Babinski's syndrome síndrome de Babinski.

Babinski-Vazquez syndrome síndrome de Babinski-Vazquez.

BADS syndrome síndrome BADS.

Bäfverstedt's syndrome síndrome de Bäfverstedt.

Balint's syndrome síndrome de Balint.

Baller Gerold syndrome síndrome de Baller-Gerold.

Bannwarth's syndrome síndrome de Bannwarth.

Banti's syndrome síndrome de Banti.

Bardet-Biedl syndrome síndrome de Bardet-Biedl.

Barlow's syndrome síndrome de Barlow.

Barraquer-Simon's syndrome síndrome de Barraquer-Simon.

Barré-Guillain syndrome síndrome de Barré-Guillain.

Barrett's syndrome síndrome de Barrett.

Bart's syndrome síndrome de Bart.

Bartter's syndrome síndrome de Bartter.

basal cell nevus syndrome síndrome de carcinoma nevoide de células basales.

basilar artery insufficiency syndrome síndrome de insuficiencia de la arteria basilar.

Bassen-Kornzweig syndrome síndrome de Bassen-Kornzweig.

Bazex's syndrome síndrome de Bazex.

Bearn-Kunkel syndrome síndrome de Bearn-Kunkel, síndrome de Bearn-Kunkel-Slater.

Bearn-Kunkel-Slater syndrome síndrome de Bearn-Kunkel, síndrome de Bearn-Kunkel-Slater.

Beckwith's syndrome síndrome de Beckwith, síndrome de Beckwith-Wiedemann.

Beckwith-Wiedemann syndrome síndrome de Beckwith, síndrome de Beckwith-Wiedemann.

Behçet's syndrome síndrome de Behçet.

Behr's syndrome síndrome de Behr.

Benedikt's syndrome síndrome de Benedikt.

Beradinelli's syndrome síndrome de Beradinelli.

Berheim's syndrome síndrome de Berheim.

Bernard-Horner syndrome síndrome de Bernard, síndrome de Bernard-Horner.

Bernard's syndrome síndrome de Bernard, síndrome de Bernard-Horner.

Bernard-Sergent syndrome síndrome de Bernard-Sergent.

Bernard-Soulier syndrome síndrome de Bernard-Soulier.

Bernhardt-Roth syndrome síndrome de Benhardt-Roth.

Bertolotti's syndrome síndrome de Bertolotti.

Bianchi's syndrome síndrome de Bianchi.

Biedl's syndrome síndrome de Biedl-Bardet.

Biemond syndrome type II síndrome de Biemond II.

Biemond syndrome síndrome de Biemond.

biotin deficiency syndrome síndrome de deficiencia de biotina.

Björnstad's syndrome síndrome de Björnstad.

Blatin's syndrome síndrome de Blatin.

blind loops syndrome síndrome del asa ciega.

Bloch-Sulzberger syndrome síndrome de Bloch-Sulzberger.

Bloom's syndrome síndrome de Bloom.

Blum's syndrome síndrome de Blum.

body of Luys syndrome síndrome del cuerpo de Luys.

Boerhaave's syndrome síndrome de Boerhaave.

Bogorad's syndrome síndrome de Bogorad.

Bonnevie-Ullrich syndrome síndrome de Bonnevie-Ullrich.

Bonnier's syndrome síndrome de Bonnier.

Böök's syndrome síndrome de Böök.

Börjesson-Forssman-Lehmann syndrome síndrome de Börjesson-Forssman-Lehmann.

Bouillaud's syndrome síndrome de Bouillaud.

bowel bypass syndrome síndrome de bypass intestinal.

brachial syndrome síndrome braquial.

bradycardia-tachycardia syndrome síndrome de bradicardia y taquicardia.

Brennemann's syndrome síndrome de Brennemann.

Briquet's syndrome síndrome de Briquet.

Brissaud-Sicard syndrome síndrome de Brissaud-Sicard.

Bristowe's syndrome síndrome de Bristowe.

brittle bone syndrome síndrome del hueso quebradizo.

brittle cornea syndrome síndrome de córnea quebradiza.

Brock syndrome síndrome de Brock.

Brocq-Pautrier syndrome síndrome de Brocq-Pautrier.

Brown's syndrome síndrome de Brown.

Brown-Séquard syndrome síndrome de Brown-Séquard.

Bruns' syndrome síndrome de Bruns.

Brunsting's syndrome síndrome de Brunsting.

Brushfield-Wyatt syndrome síndrome de Brushfield-Wyatt.

Budd-Chiari syndrome síndrome de Budd-Chiari.

bulbar syndrome síndrome bulbar.

Bürger-Grütz syndrome síndrome de Bürger-Grütz.

Burnett's syndrome síndrome de Burnett.

Buschke-Ollendorf syndrome síndrome de Buschke-Ollendorf.

Bywaters' syndrome síndrome de Bywaters.

Caffey's syndrome síndrome de Caffey, síndrome de Caffey-Silverman, síndrome de Caffey-Smith.

Caffey-Silverman syndrome síndrome de Caffey, síndrome de Caffey-Silverman, síndrome de Caffey-Smith.

Caffey-Smith syndrome síndrome de Caffey, síndrome de Caffey-Silverman, síndrome de Caffey-Smith.

callosal syndrome síndrome calloso.

camptomelic syndrome síndrome camptomélico.

Canada-Cronkhite syndrome síndrome de Canada-Cronkhite.

Capgras' syndrome síndrome de Capgras.

Caplan's syndrome síndrome de Caplan.

capsulo-thalamic syndrome síndrome capsulotalámico.

carcinoid syndrome síndrome carcinoide.

cardiofacial syndrome síndrome cardiofacial.

carpal tunnel syndrome síndrome del canal carpiano.

Carpenter's syndrome síndrome de Carpenter.

cartilage-hair hypoplasia syndrome síndrome de hipoplasia de cartílago y pelo.

cat-cry syndrome síndrome cri du chat, síndrome del maullido, síndrome del maullido de gato.

cauda equina syndrome síndrome de la cola de caballo.

caudal dysplasia syndrome síndrome de displasia caudal, síndrome de regresión caudal.

caudal regresion syndrome síndrome de displasia caudal, síndrome de regresión caudal.

Ceelen-Gellestadt syndrome síndrome de Ceelen, síndrome de Ceelen-Gellestadt.

celiac syndrome síndrome celíaco.

cellular immunity deficiency syndrome síndrome de inmunodeficiencia celular.

central cord syndrome síndrome del cordón central, síndrome de la médula espinal central.

centroposterior syndrome síndrome centroposterior.

cerebellar syndrome síndrome cerebeloso.

cerebellomedullary malformation syndrome síndrome de malformación cerebelobulbar.

cerebrocardiac syndrome síndrome cerebrocardíaco.

cerebrohepatorenal syndrome síndrome cerebrohepatorrenal.

cervical disc syndrome síndrome del disco cervical.

cervical fusion syndrome síndrome de fusión cervical.

cervical post-traumatic syndrome síndrome cervical postraumático.

cervical rib syndrome síndrome de la costilla cervical.

cervical syndrome síndrome cervical, síndrome cervicobraquial.

cervicobrachial syndrome síndrome cervical, síndrome cervicobraquial.

Cestan-Chenais syndrome síndrome de Cestan, síndrome de Cestan-Chenais.

Cestan-Raymond syndrome síndrome de Cestan-Raymond.

Cestan's syndrome síndrome de Cestan, síndrome de Cestan-Chenais.

chancriform syndrome síndrome chancriforme.

Chandler's syndrome síndrome de Chandler.

Charcot's syndrome síndrome de Charcot.

Charcot-Weiss-Baker syndrome síndrome de Charcot-Weiss-Baker.

Charlin's syndrome síndrome de Charlin.

Chauffard's syndrome síndrome de Chauffard, síndrome de Chauffard-Still.

Chauffard-Still syndrome síndrome de Chauffard, síndrome de Chauffard-Still.

Chédiak-Higashi syndrome síndrome de Chédiak-Higashi.

Chiari-Arnold syndrome síndrome de Chiari-Arnold.

Chiari-Frommel syndrome síndrome de Chiari-Frommel.

Chiari's syndrome síndrome de Chiari.

Chilaiditi's syndrome síndrome de Chilaiditi.

CHILD syndrome síndrome de CHILD.

Chotzen's syndrome síndrome de Chotzen.

Christian's syndrome síndrome de Christian.

Christ-Siemens-Touraine syndrome síndrome de Christ-Siemens-Touraine.

chromosomal instability syndrome síndrome de inestabilidad cromosómica.

chromosomal syndrome síndrome cromosómico.

chromosome 5p syndrome síndrome del cromosoma 5p.

chronic fatigue syndrome (CFS) síndrome de fatiga crónica (SFC).

chronic hyperventilation syndrome síndrome de hiperventilación, síndrome de hiperventilación crónica.

Churg-Strauss syndrome síndrome de Churg-Strauss.

Citelli's syndrome síndrome de Citelli.

Clarke-Hadefield syndrome síndrome de Clarke-Hadefield.

Claude Bernard-Horner syndrome síndrome de Claude Bernard-Horner.

Claude's syndrome síndrome de Claude.

Clerambault syndrome síndrome de Clérambault.

clic syndrome síndrome del chasquido.

closed head syndrome síndrome de la cabeza cerrada.

Clough and Richter's syndrome síndrome de Clough y Richter.

Clouston's syndrome síndrome de Clouston.

cloverleaf skull syndrome síndrome de cráneo en hoja de trébol.

Cobb's syndrome síndrome de Cobb.

Cockayne's syndrome síndrome de Cockayne.

Cogan-Reese's syndrome síndrome de Cogan-Reese.

Cogan's syndrome síndrome de Cogan.

Cohen's syndrome síndrome de Cohen.

cold agglutinin syndrome síndrome por aglutinina de frío.

Collet's syndrome síndrome de Collet, síndrome de Collet-Sicard.

Collet-Sicard syndrome síndrome de Collet, síndrome de Collet-Sicard.

combined immunodeficiency syndrome síndrome de inmunodeficiencia combinada.

compartmental syndrome síndrome compartimental.

compression syndrome síndrome de compresión.

concussion syndrome síndrome de conmoción cerebral.

Conn's syndrome síndrome de Conn.

Conradi-Hünermann syndrome síndrome de Conradi-Hünermann.

contiguous gene syndrome síndrome del gen contiguo.

Cornelia de Lange's syndrome síndrome de Cornelia de Lange.

corpus luteum deficiency syndrome síndrome de insuficiencia del cuerpo lúteo, síndrome de insuficiencia lútea.

Costen's syndrome síndrome de Costen.

costoclavicular syndrome síndrome costoclavicular.

Cotard's syndrome síndrome de Cotard.

Courvoisier-Terrier syndrome síndrome de Courvoisier-Terrier.

couvade syndrome síndrome de covada.

Cowden's syndrome síndrome de Cowden.

craniosynostosis-radial aplasia syndrome síndrome craneosinostosis-aplasia radial.

CREST syndrome síndrome CREST.

Creutzfeldt-Jakob syndrome síndrome de Creutzfeldt-Jakob.

cri-du-chat syndrome síndrome cri du chat, síndrome del maullido, síndrome del maullido de gato.

Crigler-Najjar syndrome síndrome de Crigler-Najjar.

Cronkhite-Canada syndrome síndrome de Cronkhite, síndrome de Cronkhite-Canada.

Cross-McKusick-Breen syndrome síndrome de Cross-McKusick-Breen.

Crouzon's syndrome síndrome de Crouzon.

CRST syndrome síndrome CRST.

crush syndrome síndrome de aplastamiento.

Cruveilhier-Baumgarten syndrome síndrome de Cruveilhier-Baumgarten.

cryptophthalmos syndrome síndrome de criptoftalmía.

culture-specific syndrome síndrome específico de cultura.

Curtius syndrome síndrome de Curtius.

Cushing's medicamentous syndrome síndrome medicamentoso de Cushing.

Cushing's syndrome síndrome de Cushing.

Cyriax's syndrome síndrome de Cyriax.

Cyryax syndrome síndrome de Cyriax.

Danbolt-Closs syndrome síndrome de Danbolt-Closs.

Dandy-Walker syndrome síndrome de Dandy-Walker.

Danlos' syndrome síndrome de Danlos.

De Lange's syndrome síndrome de De Lange.

De Sanctis-Cachione syndrome síndrome de De Sanctis-Cacchione.

dead fetus syndrome síndrome del feto muerto.

Debré-Sémélaigne syndrome síndrome de Debré-Sémélaigne.

defibrination syndrome síndrome de desfibrinación.

Degos' syndrome síndrome de Degos.

Déjérine-Klumpke syndrome síndrome de Déjérine-Klumpke.

Déjérine-Roussy syndrome síndrome de Déjérine-Roussy.

Dejerine's syndrome síndrome de Déjérine.

Déjérine-Sottas syndrome síndrome de Déjerine-Sottas.

del Castillo's syndrome síndrome de del Castillo.

deletion syndrome síndrome de deleción.

dengue hemorrhagic fever shock (DHFS) syndrome síndrome del choque hemorrágico del dengue (SHFS).

Dennie-Marfan syndrome síndrome de Dennie-Marfan.

dependency syndrome síndrome de dependencia.

depersonalization syndrome síndrome de despersonalización.

depressive syndrome síndrome depresivo.

Di George syndrome síndrome de Di George.

Di Guglielmo's syndrome síndrome de Di Guglielmo.

dialysis disequilibrium syndrome síndrome de desequilibrio de diálisis.

dialysis encephalopathy syndrome síndrome de encefalopatía por diálisis.

Diamond-Balckfan syndrome síndrome de Balckfan-Diamond.

diencephalic syndrome síndrome diencefálico.

Dighton-Adair syndrome síndrome de Dighton-Adair.

disc syndrome síndrome del disco.

disconnection syndrome síndrome de desconexión interhemisférica.

Donath-Landsteiner syndrome síndrome de Donath-Landsteiner.

Donohue's syndrome síndrome de Donohue.

Down's syndrome síndrome de Down.

Dresbach's syndrome síndrome de Dresbach.

Dressler's syndrome síndrome de Dressler.

Duane's syndrome síndrome de Duane.

Dubin-Johnson syndrome síndrome de Dubin-Johnson.

Dubin-Sprinz syndrome síndrome de Dubin-Sprinz.

Dubowitz syndrome síndrome de Dubowitz.

Dubreuil-Chambardel syndrome síndrome de Dubreuil-Chambardel.

Duchenne-Erb syndrome síndrome de Duchenne-Erb.

Duchenne's syndrome síndrome de Duchenne.

dumping syndrome síndrome de la evacuación gástrica en torrente, síndrome de la evacuación gástrica rápida, síndrome del dumping.

Duncan's syndrome síndrome de Duncan.

Duplay's syndrome síndrome de Duplay.

Dupré's syndrome síndrome de Dupré.

Dyke-Davidoff syndrome síndrome de Dyke-Davidoff.

dysglandular syndrome síndrome disglandular.

dyskinetic syndrome síndrome discinético.

dysplasia oculodentodigitalia syndrome síndrome de displasia oculodentodigital.

dysraphic syndrome síndrome disráfico.

Eaton-Lambert syndrome síndrome de Eaton-Lambert.

ectopic ACTH syndrome síndrome de ACTH ectópica.

ectopic-hypercalcemic syndrome síndrome de hipercalcemia ectópica.

ectrodactyly-ectodermal dysplasia-clefting syndrome síndrome ectrodactilia-displasia ectodérmica-fisuración.

Eddowes' syndrome síndrome de Eddowes.

Edwards' syndrome síndrome de Edwards.

EEC syndrome síndrome ectrodactilia-displasia ectodérmica-fisuración.

effort syndrome síndrome de esfuerzo.

egg-white syndrome síndrome de la clara de huevo.

Eisenmenger's syndrome síndrome de Eisenmenger.

Ekbom syndrome síndrome de Ekbom.

electrocardiographic-auscultatory syndrome síndrome electrocardiográfico-auscultatorio.

elfin facies syndrome síndrome de cara de diablillo.

Ellis-van Creveld syndrome síndrome de Ellis-van Creveld.

Emery-Dreifuss syndrome síndrome de Emery-Dreifuss.

EMG syndrome síndrome EMG.

endotelio-iridocorneal syndrome síndrome endotelial iridocorneal.

epiphyseal syndrome síndrome epifisario.

Epstein's syndrome síndrome de Epstein.

Erb's syndrome síndrome de Erb.

erythrodysesthesia syndrome síndrome de eritrodistesia.

euthyroid sick syndrome síndrome de enfermedad eutiroidea.

Evans' syndrome síndrome de Evans.

exomphalos-macroglossia-gigantism syn-

drome síndrome exónfalo-macroglosia-gigantismo.

exophthalmos-macroglossia-gigantism syndrome síndrome exoftalmos-macroglosia-gigantismo.

extrapyramidal syndrome síndrome extrapiramidal.

Faber's syndrome síndrome de Faber.

Fabry's syndrome síndrome de Fabry.

faciodigitogenital syndrome síndrome faciodigitogenital.

Fahr's syndrome síndrome de Fahr.

Fallot's syndrome síndrome de Fallot.

Fanconi's syndrome síndrome de Fanconi.

Farber syndrome síndrome de Farber, síndrome de Farber-Uzman.

Farber-Uzman syndrome síndrome de Farber, síndrome de Farber-Uzman.

Favre-Racouchot syndrome síndrome de Favre-Racouchot.

Fazio-Londe's syndrome síndrome de Fazio-Londe.

fear-tension-pain syndrome síndrome miedo-tensión-dolor.

Felty's syndrome síndrome de Felty.

fertile eunuch syndrome síndrome del eunuco fecundo, síndrome del eunuco fértil.

fetal alcohol syndrome síndrome alcohólico fetal, síndrome de alcoholismo fetal.

fetal aspiration syndrome síndrome de aspiración fetal.

fetal face syndrome síndrome de cara fetal.

fetal hydantoin syndrome (FHS) síndrome de la hidantonía fetal, síndrome hidantoínico fetal (SHF).

Fèvre-Languepin syndrome síndrome de Fèvre-Languepin.

fibrinogen-fibrin conversion syndrome síndrome de conversión de fibrinógeno en fibrina.

Fiessinger's syndrome síndrome de Fiessinger.

Figueira's syndrome síndrome de Figueira.

Fischer's syndrome síndrome de Fisher.

Fitz-Hugh-Curtis syndrome síndrome de Fitz-Hugh-Curtis.

Fitz's syndrome síndrome de Fitz.

flashing pain syndrome síndrome del dolor relámpago.

floppy infant syndrome síndrome del lactante blando, síndrome del lactante fláccido.

focal dermal hypoplasia syndrome síndrome de hipoplasia dérmica focal.

Foix-Alajouanine syndrome síndrome de Foix-Alajouanine.

Foix-Cavany-Marie syndrome síndrome de Foix-Cavany-Marie.

Forbes-Albright syndrome síndrome de Forbes-Albright.

Forssman's carotid syndrome síndrome carotídeo de Forssman.

Foster-Kennedy's syndrome síndrome de Foster-Kennedy.

four-day syndrome síndrome de los cuatro días.

Foville's syndrome síndrome de Foville.

fragile X syndrome síndrome del cromosoma X frágil.

Franceschetti-Jadassohn syndrome síndrome de Franceschetti-Jadassohn.

Franceschetti's syndrome síndrome de Franceschetti.

Freeman-Sheldon syndrome síndrome de Freeman-Sheldon.

Frey's syndrome síndrome de Frey.

Friderichsen-Waterhouse syndrome síndrome de Friderichsen-Waterhouse.

Friedmann's vasomotor syndrome síndrome de Friedmann.

Fröhlich's syndrome síndrome de Fröhlich.

Froin's syndrome síndrome de Froin.

Frommel-Chiari syndrome síndrome de Frommel-Chiari.

frontal lobe syndrome síndrome del lóbulo frontal.

Fuchs' syndrome síndrome de Fuchs.

functional bowel syndrome síndrome intestinal funcional.

G syndrome síndrome G.

Gailliard's syndrome síndrome de Gailliard.

galactorrhea-amenorrhea syndrome síndrome de galactorrea-amenorrea.

Ganser syndrome síndrome de Ganser.

Ganser's syndrome síndrome de Ganser.

Garcin's syndrome síndrome de Garcin.

Gardner-Diamond syndrome síndrome de Gardner-Diamond.

Gardner's syndrome síndrome de Gardner.

Gasser's syndrome síndrome de Gasser.

gastrocardiac syndrome síndrome gastrocardíaco.

gay bowel syndrome síndrome intestinal del homosexual.

Gee-Herter-Heubner syndrome síndrome de Gee-Herter-Heubner.

Gélineau's syndrome síndrome de Gélineau.

gender dysphoria syndrome síndrome de disforia de género.

general adaptation syndrome síndrome general de adaptación (SGA).

Gerhardt's syndrome síndrome de Gerhardt.

Gerlier's syndrome síndrome de Gerlier.

Gerstmann's syndrome síndrome de Gerstmann.

Gerstmann-Straussler syndrome síndrome de Gerstmann-Straussler.

Gianotti-Crosti syndrome síndrome de Gianotti-Crosti.

Gilbert's syndrome síndrome de Gilbert.

Gilles de la Tourette's syndrome síndrome de Gilles de la Tourette.

glioma-polyposis syndrome síndrome de glioma y poliposis.

glomangiomatous osseus malformation syndrome síndrome de malformación glomangiomatosa y ósea, síndrome de malformación ósea glomangiomatosa.

glucagonoma syndrome síndrome de glucagonoma.

Goldenhar's syndrome síndrome de Goldenhar.

Goltz syndrome síndrome de Goltz.

Goodman syndrome síndrome de Goodman.

Goodpasture's syndrome síndrome de Goodpasture.

Good's syndrome síndrome de Good.

Gopalan's syndrome síndrome de Gopalan.

Gorham syndrome síndrome de Gorham, síndrome de Gorham-Stout.

Gorlin-Chaudhry-Moss syndrome síndrome de Gorlin-Chaudhry-Moss.

Gorlin-Goltz syndrome nevomatosa basocelular.

Gorlin's syndrome síndrome de Gorlin.

Gougerot-Carteaud syndrome síndrome de Gougerot-Carteaud.

Gowers' syndrome síndrome de Gowers.

Gradenigo's syndrome síndrome de Gradenigo, síndrome de Gradenigo-Lannois.

Graham Little syndrome síndrome de Graham Little.

gray baby syndrome síndrome del lactante gris.

gray spinal syndrome síndrome gris espinal.

gray syndrome síndrome gris.

Griscelli syndrome síndrome de Griscelli.

Grönblad-Strandberg syndrome síndrome de Grönblad-Strandberg.

Gruber's syndrome síndrome de Gruber.

Gubler's syndrome síndrome de Gubler.

Guillain-Barré's syndrome síndrome de Guillain-Barré, síndrome de Guillain-Barré-Strohl.

Gunn's syndrome síndrome de Gunn.

Hadefield-Clarke syndrome síndrome de Hadefield-Clarke.

Hallervorden-Spatz syndrome síndrome de Hallevorden-Spatz.

Hamman-Rich syndrome síndrome de Hamman-Rich.

Hamman's syndrome síndrome de Hamman.

hand-and-foot syndrome síndrome de manos y pies.

hand-foot-uterus syndrome pie y útero, síndrome de mano.

Hand-Schüller-Christian syndrome síndrome de Hand-Schüller-Christian.

hand-shoulder syndrome síndrome de mano y hombro.

Hanhart's syndrome síndrome de Hanhart.

Harada's syndrome síndrome de Harada.

hard water syndrome síndrome del agua dura.

Hare's syndrome síndrome de Hare.

Harris' syndrome síndrome de Harris.

Hartnup syndrome síndrome de Hartnup.

Hayem-Widal syndrome síndrome de Hayem-Widal.

heart-hand syndrome síndrome de corazón y mano.

Heerfordt's syndrome síndrome de Heerfordt.

Heidenhain's syndrome síndrome de Heidenhain.

hemangioma-thrombocytopenia syndrome síndrome de hemangiomatosis y trombocitopenia, síndrome de hemangioma-trombocitopenia.

hematopoietic syndrome síndrome hematopoyético.

hemolytic-uremic syndrome síndrome hemolítico-urémico.

hemorrhagic fever syndrome síndrome de fiebre hemorrágica.

Henoch-Schönlein syndrome síndrome de Henoch-Schönlein.

hepatorenal syndrome síndrome hepatorrenal.

hereditary benign intraepithelial dyskeratosis syndrome síndrome de disqueratosis intraepitelial hereditaria benigna.

Hermansky-Pudlak syndrome síndrome de Hermansky-Pudlak.

Heyd syndrome síndrome de Heyd.

Hinman's syndrome síndrome de Hinman.

Hoffmann-Werdnig syndrome síndrome de Hoffmann-Werdnig.

holiday heart syndrome síndrome del corazón del día de fiesta.

Holmes-Adie syndrome síndrome de Holmes-Adie.

Holt-Oram syndrome síndrome de Holt-Oram.

Homén's syndrome síndrome de Homén.

Horner's syndrome síndrome de Horner, síndrome de Horner-Bernard.

Horton's syndrome síndrome de Horton.

Houssay syndrome síndrome de Houssay.

Howel-Evans' syndrome síndrome de Howel-Evans.

Hughlings-Jackson syndrome síndrome de Hughlings-Jackson.

Hunter syndrome síndrome de Hunter, síndrome de Hunter-Hurler.

Hunter-Hurler syndrome síndrome de Hunter, síndrome de Hunter-Hurler.

Hunt's syndrome síndrome de Hunt.

Hurler's syndrome síndrome de Hurler.

Hurler-Scheie syndrome síndrome de Hurler-Scheie.

Hutchinson syndrome síndrome de Hutchinson.

Hutchinson-Gilford syndrome síndrome de Hutchinson-Gilford.

hyaline membrane syndrome síndrome de la membrana hialina.

hydralazine lupus syndrome síndrome lúpico por hidralacina.

hydralazine syndrome síndrome de la hidralacina.

hyperabduction syndrome síndrome de hiperabducción.

hyperdynamic syndrome síndrome hiperdinámico.

hypereosinophilic syndrome síndrome hipereosinófilo.

hyperimmunoglobulin E syndrome síndrome de hiperinmunoglobulina E, síndrome de hiperinmunoglobulinemia E.

hyperimmunoglobulinemia E syndrome síndrome de hiperinmunoglobulina E, síndrome de hiperinmunoglobulinemia E.

hyperkinetic heart syndrome síndrome del corazón hipercinético.

hyperkinetic syndrome síndrome hipercinético.

hypersensitive xiphoid syndrome síndrome de hipersensibilidad xifoidea.

hypertrophied frenula syndrome síndrome de hipertrofia frenular.

hyperventilation syndrome síndrome de hiperventilación, síndrome de hiperventilación crónica.

hyperviscosity syndrome síndrome de hiperviscosidad.

hypoglossic-hypodactyly syndrome síndrome de hipoglosia-hipodactilia.

hypoparathyroidism syndrome síndrome de hipoparatiroidismo.

hypophyseal syndrome síndrome hipofisario.

hypoplastic left heart syndrome síndrome de hipoplasia del corazón izquierdo, síndrome del corazón izquierdo hipoplásico.

idiopathic respiratory distress syndrome síndrome de dificultad respiratoria idiopática.

Imerslund syndrome síndrome de Imerslund, síndrome de Imerslund-Graesbeck.

Imerslund-Graesbeck syndrome síndrome de Imerslund, síndrome de Imerslund-Graesbeck.

immotile cilia syndrome síndrome de los cilios inmóviles.

immunodeficiency syndrome síndrome de inmunodeficiencia.

indifference to pain syndrome síndrome de indiferencia al dolor.

inhibitory syndrome síndrome inhibitorio.

inspissated bile syndrome síndrome de bilis espesada.

institutionalism syndrome síndrome de hospitalización.

inversed jaw-winking syndrome síndrome del guiño maxilar invertido.

iris-nevus syndrome síndrome iris-nevo.

irritable bowel syndrome síndrome del intestino irritable.

irritable colon syndrome síndrome del colon irritable.

Irvine-Gass' syndrome síndrome de Irvine-Gass.

Isaac's syndrome síndrome de Isaac.

Ivemark's syndrome síndrome de Ivemark.

Jackson's syndrome síndrome de Jackson.

Jacod's syndrome síndrome de Jacod.

Jadassohn-Lewandowski syndrome síndrome de Jadassohn-Lewandowsky.

Jahnke's syndrome síndrome de Jahnke.

jaw-winking syndrome síndrome del guiño maxilar, síndrome del maxilar inferior y parpadeo.

Jervell and Lange-Nielsen syndrome síndrome de Jervell y Lange-Nielsen.

Jeune's syndrome síndrome de Jeune.

Job syndrome síndrome de Job.

jugular foramen syndrome síndrome del agujero rasgado posterior, síndrome del agujero yugular.

Kanner's syndrome síndrome de Kanner.

Kartagener's syndrome síndrome de Kartagener.

Kasabach-Merrit syndrome síndrome de Kasabach-Merrit.

Kast's syndrome síndrome de Kast.

Katayama syndrome síndrome de Katayama.

Kawasaki syndrome síndrome de Kawasaki.

Kearns-Sayre syndrome síndrome de Kearns-Sayre.

Kellgren's syndrome síndrome de Kellgren.

Kelly-Paterson syndrome síndrome de Kelly-Paterson.

Kennedy's syndrome síndrome de Kennedy.

Kimmelstiel-Wilson syndrome síndrome de Kimmelstiel-Wilson.

Klauder's syndrome síndrome de Klauder.

Kleeblattschadel syndrome síndrome de cráneo en hoja de trébol.

Kleine-Levin syndrome síndrome de Kleine-Levin.

Klein-Waardenburg syndrome síndrome de Klein-Waardenburg.

Klinefelter's syndrome síndrome de Klinefelter.

Klippel-Feil syndrome síndrome de Klippel-Feil.

Klippel-Trénaunay syndrome síndrome de Klippel-Trénaunay, síndrome de Klippel-Trénaunay-Weber.

Klippel-Trénaunay-Weber syndrome síndrome de Klippel Trénaunay, síndrome de Klippel-Trénaunay-Weber.

Klumpe-Déjerine syndrome síndrome de Klumpke-Déjerine.

Kocher-Debré-Sémélaigne syndrome síndrome de Kocher-Debré-Sémélaigne.

Koenig's syndrome síndrome de Koenig.

Koerber-Salus-Elschnig syndrome síndrome de Koerber-Salus-Elschnig.

Korsakoff's syndrome síndrome de Korsakoff, síndrome de Korsakov.

Kostmann's syndrome síndrome de Kostmann.

Krabbe's syndrome síndrome de Krabbe.

Krause's syndrome síndrome de Krause.

Labbé's neurocirculatory syndrome síndrome de Labbé.

Lambert-Eaton syndrome síndrome de Lambert-Eaton.

Landau-Kleffner's syndrome síndrome de Landau-Kleffner.

Landry syndrome síndrome de Landry.

Laron's syndrome síndrome de Laron.

Larsen's syndrome síndrome de Larsen.

Lasègue's syndrome síndrome de Lasègue.

Launois syndrome síndrome de Launois.

Launois-Cléret syndrome síndrome de Launois-Cléret.

Laurence-Moon syndrome síndrome de Laurence-Moon.

Laurence-Moon-Biedl syndrome síndrome de Laurence-Biedl, síndrome de Laurence-Moon-Bardet-Biedl, síndrome de Laurence-Moon-Biedl.

Läwen-Roth's syndrome síndrome de Läwen-Roth.

Lawford's syndrome síndrome de Lawford.

Lawrence-Seip syndrome síndrome de Lawrence-Seip.

lazy leucocyte syndrome síndrome de leucocitos perezosos.

Leigh syndrome síndrome de Leigh.

Lenègre's syndrome síndrome de Lenègre-de Bruix.

Lennox-Gastaut syndrome síndrome de Lennox-Gastaut.

lentigines syndrome síndrome de léntigos, síndrome de léntigos múltiples.

leopard syndrome síndrome del leopardo.

Leriche's syndrome síndrome de Leriche.

Leri-Weill syndrome síndrome de Leri-Weill.

Lermoyez's syndrome síndrome de Lermoyez.

Lesch-Nyham syndrome síndrome de Lesch-Nyham.

Letterer-Siwer syndrome síndrome de Letterer-Siwer.

levator syndrome síndrome del elevador.

Lev's syndrome síndrome de Lev.

Lhermitte and McAlpine syndrome síndrome de Lhermitte y McAlpine.

Libman-Sacks syndrome síndrome de Libman-Sacks.

Liddle's syndrome síndrome de Liddle.

Li-Fraumeni cancer syndrome síndrome de cáncer de Li-Fraumeni.

Lightwood's syndrome síndrome de Lightwood.

Lignac-Fanconi syndrome síndrome de Lignac, síndrome de Lignac-Fanconi.

liver-kidney syndrome síndrome de hígado y riñón.

Lobstein's syndrome síndrome de Lobstein.

local adaptation syndrome (LAS) síndrome de adaptación local (SAL).

locked-in syndrome síndrome de cautiverio, síndrome de encierro.

loculation syndrome síndrome de loculación.

Löffler's syndrome síndrome de Löffler.

Looser-Milkman syndrome síndrome de Looser-Debray-Milkman.

Lorain-Lévi syndrome síndrome de Lorain-Lévi.

Louis-Bar syndrome síndrome de Louis-Bar.

Lowe syndrome síndrome de Lowe, síndrome de Lowe-Terry-Mac Lachlan.

Lowe-Terry-Mac Lachlan syndrome síndrome de Lowe, síndrome de Lowe-Terry-Mac Lachlan.

Lown-Ganong-Levine syndrome síndrome de Lown-Ganong-Levine.

Lutenbacher's syndrome síndrome de Lutenbacher.

Lyell's syndrome síndrome de Lyell.

lymphadenopathy syndrome (LAS) síndrome de linfoadenopatía, síndrome de linfoadenopatía generalizada persistente (SLGP).

Mackenzie's syndrome síndrome de Mackenzie.

Macleod's syndrome síndrome de Macleod.

Mad Hatter syndrome síndrome de Mad Hatter.

Mafucci's syndrome síndrome de Mafucci.

malabsortion syndrome síndrome de mala absorción, síndrome de malabsorción.

malarial hyperreactive spleen syndrome síndrome del bazo palúdico hiperreactivo.

Mallory-Weiss syndrome síndrome de Mallory-Weiss.

mandibulofacial dysostosis syndrome síndrome de disostosis mandibulofacial.

mandibulo-oculofacial syndrome síndrome mandibulooculofacial.

Marañón's syndrome síndrome de Marañón.

Marchesani's syndrome síndrome de Marchesani.

Marchiafava-Micheli syndrome síndrome de Marchiafava-Micheli.

Marcus Gunn syndrome síndrome de Marcus Gunn.

Marfan syndrome síndrome de Marfan.

Marfan's syndrome síndrome de Marfan.

Margolis syndrome síndrome de Margolis.

Marie-Robinson syndrome síndrome de Marie-Robinson.

Marie's syndrome síndrome de Marie.

Marin Amat syndrome síndrome de Marín Amat.

Marinesco-Sjögren syndrome síndrome de Marinesco-Sjögren.

Markus-Adie syndrome síndrome de Markus.

Maroteaux-Lamy syndrome síndrome de Maroteaux-Lamy.

Martorell's syndrome síndrome de Martorell.

mast syndrome síndrome del marteleno.

Masters-Allen syndrome síndrome de Masters-Allen.

mastocytosis syndrome síndrome de mastocitosis.

maternal deprivation syndrome síndrome de deprivación materna.

Mauriac's syndrome síndrome de Mauriac.

Mayer-Rokitansky-Küster-Hauser syndrome síndrome de Mayer-Rokitansky-Küster-Hauser.

McArdle's syndrome síndrome de Mac Ardle, síndrome de Mac Ardle-Schmid-Pearson.

McCune-Albright syndrome síndrome de McCune-Albright.

Meadows' syndrome síndrome de Meadows.

Meckel syndrome síndrome de Meckel, síndrome de Meckel-Gruber.

Meckel-Gruber syndrome síndrome de Meckel, síndrome de Meckel-Gruber.

megacystic syndrome síndrome megacístico.

megacystis-megaureter syndrome síndrome de megacisto y megauréter.

Meige's syndrome síndrome de Meige.

Meigs' syndrome síndrome de Meigs.

Melkersson-Rosenthal syndrome síndrome de Melkersson, síndrome de Melkersson-Rosenthal.

Mendelson's syndrome síndrome de Mendelson.

Ménétrier's syndrome síndrome de Ménétrier.

Mengert's shock syndrome síndrome de choque de Mengert.

Ménière's syndrome síndrome de Ménière.

Menkes' syndrome síndrome de Menkes.

menopausal syndrome síndrome menopáusico.

methionine malabsorption syndrome síndrome de malabsorción de metionina.

Meyer-Schwickerath and Weyers syndrome síndrome de Meyer-Schwickerath y Weyers.

Meyers-Kowenaar syndrome síndrome de Meyers-Kowenaar.

microdeletion syndrome síndrome microdelecional.

middle lobe syndrome síndrome del lóbulo medio.

Mikulicz's syndrome síndrome de Mikulicz.

milk-alkali syndrome síndrome de leche y álcali, síndrome de leche y alcalinos.

Milkman's syndrome síndrome de Milkman, síndrome de Milkman-Looser.

Millard-Gubler syndrome síndrome de Millard-Gubler.

Miller-Fisher's syndrome síndrome de Miller-Fisher.

Milles' syndrome síndrome de Milles.

Minkowski-Chauffard syndrome síndrome de Minkowski-Chauffard.

Möbius' syndrome síndrome de Möbius.

Mohr syndrome síndrome de Mohr.

mucocutaneous lymph node syndrome síndrome de los ganglios linfáticos mucocutáneos.

mucocutaneous lymph node syndrome (MLNS) síndrome ganglionar mucocutáno (SGMC).

multiple glandular deficiency syndrome síndrome de insuficiencia glandular múltiple.

multiple hamartoma syndrome síndrome del hamartoma múltiple.

multiple lentigines syndrome síndrome de léntigos, síndrome de léntigos múltiples.

myasthenia gravis syndrome síndrome de miastenia grave.

myasthenic syndrome (MS) síndrome miasténico.

myeloproliferative syndrome síndrome mieloproliferativo.

myofacial pain-dysfunction syndrome síndrome de dolor y disfunción miofacial.

neglect syndrome negligencia motriz.

neural crest syndrome síndrome de la cresta neural.

nystagmus blockage syndrome síndrome del bloqueo del nistagmo.

OFD syndrome síndrome BFD.

organic anxiety syndrome síndrome de ansiedad orgánica.

orofaciodigital syndrome síndrome bucofaciodigital tipo II (BFD).

orofaciodigital syndrome type III (OFD) síndrome bucofaciodigital tipo III (BFD).

pain dysfunction syndrome síndrome de disfunción dolorosa.

painful arch syndrome síndrome del arco doloroso.

painful-bruising syndrome síndrome de equimosis dolorosa.

pallidal syndrome síndrome del globo pálido.

pelvic congestion syndrome síndrome de congestión pélvica.

pericolic membrane syndrome síndrome de la membrana pericólica.

phantom limb syndrome síndrome del miembro fantasma.

pharyngeal pouch syndrome síndrome de la bolsa faríngea.

pineal hyperplasia syndrome síndrome de hiperplasia pineal.

pituitary syndrome síndrome hipofisario.

placental dysfunction syndrome síndrome de disfunción placentaria, síndrome de insuficiencia placentaria.

polyendocrine deficiency syndrome síndrome de deficiencia poliendocrina, síndrome de deficiencia poliglandular.

polyglandular deficiency syndrome síndrome de deficiencia poliendocrina, síndrome de deficiencia poliglandular.

pontocerebellas angle syndrome síndrome del ángulo pontocerebeloso.

popliteal entrapment syndrome síndrome de atrapamiento poplíteo.

popliteal web syndrome síndrome de la membrana poplítea.

posterior cord syndrome síndrome del cordón posterior.

post-traumatic brain syndrome síndrome cerebral postraumático.

post-traumatic stress syndrome síndrome de estrés postraumático.

postviral fatigue syndrome síndrome de fatiga posvírica.

prepubertal castrate syndrome síndrome de castración funcional prepuberal.

prune-belly syndrome síndrome en ciruela pasa.

pulmonary acid aspiration syndrome síndrome de aspiración ácida pulmonar, síndrome de aspiración pulmonar de ácido.

pulmonary dysmaturity syndrome síndrome de inmadurez pulmonar.

punchdrunk syndrome síndrome de embriaguez.

rabbit syndrome síndrome del conejo.

radial aplasia-thrombocytopenia syndrome síndrome de aplasia radial-trombocitopenia.

relocation stress syndrome síndrome de dificultad respiratoria del recién nacido, síndrome de distrés respiratorio del recién nacido, síndrome de estrés por cambio de entorno.

respiratory distress syndrome of the newborn síndrome de dificultad respiratoria del recién nacido.

runting syndrome síndrome de injerto contra huésped.

salt-depletion syndrome síndrome de agotamiento de sal, síndrome de agotamiento de sal.

scalenus anterior syndrome síndrome del escaleno anterior.

scalenus anticus syndrome síndrome del escaleno.

scalenus syndrome síndrome del escaleno.

scapulocostal syndrome síndrome escapulocostal.

Sebright bantam syndrome síndrome de la gallina enana de Sebright.

Selye general adaptation syndrome (GAS) síndrome de adaptación general (SAG) de Selye.

Sertoli-cell-only syndrome síndrome de células de Sertoli únicamente.

serum sickness syndrome síndrome de enfermedad del suero.

short-bowel syndrome síndrome de intestino corto.

shoulder-hand syndrome síndrome de hombro y mano.

SIDA-wasting syndrome síndrome caquéctico-SIDA.

sleep apnea syndrome síndrome de apnea del sueño.

social breakdown syndrome síndrome del fracaso social.

Sotos syndrome síndrome de Fernández-Sotos.

spherophakia-brachymorphia syndrome síndrome de esferofaquia y braquimorfia.

splenic flexure syndrome síndrome del ángulo esplénico.

split notochord syndrome notocordodisrafia.

split-brain syndrome síndrome del cerebro dividido.

stiff heart syndrome síndrome de corazón rígido.

stiff-man syndrome síndrome del hombre rígido.

Stockholm syndrome síndrome de Estocolmo.

straight back syndrome síndrome de la espalda recta, síndrome del dorso recto.

stroke syndrome síndrome de accidente vascular.

sundowning syndrome síndrome del anochecer.

sunrise syndrome síndrome del amanecer.

superior caval syndrome síndrome cava superior.

superior mesenteric artery syndrome síndrome de la arteria mesentérica superior.

superior orbital fissure syndrome síndrome de la hendidura orbitaria superior.

supine hypontensive syndrome síndrome de hipotensión supina.

supravalvar aortic stenosis syndrome síndrome de estenosis aórtica supravalvular.

supravalvular aortic stenosis-infantile hypercalcemia syndrome síndrome de estenosis aórtica supravalvular-hipercalcemia infantil.

Sylvian aqueduct syndrome síndrome del acueducto de Silvio.

syndrome of Babinski-Nageotte síndrome de Babinski-Nageotte.

syndrome of Benedikt síndrome de Benedikt.

syndrome of corpus striatum síndrome del cuerpo estriado.

syndrome of crocodile tears síndrome de lágrimas de cocodrilo.

syndrome of retroparotid space síndrome del espacio retroparotídeo.

syndrome of sea-blue histiocyte síndrome de histiocitos de color azul marino.

syndrome of sensory dissociation with brachial amyotrophy síndrome de disociación sensorial con amiotrofia braquial.

tarsal tunnel syndrome síndrome del canal del tarso.

temporomandibular dysfunction syndrome síndrome de disfunción de la articulación temporomandibular, síndrome de disfunción temporomandibular.

temporomandibular joint pain dysfunction syndrome síndrome de disfunción dolorosa de la articulación temporomandibular.

temporomandibular joint pain-function syndrome síndrome de dolor-disfunción de la articulación temporomandibular.

temporomandibular joint syndrome síndrome de disfunción de la articulación temporomandibular, síndrome de disfunción temporomandibular, síndrome de la articulación temporomaxilar.

testicular feminization syndrome síndrome de feminización testicular.

tethered cord syndrome síndrome de la médula trabada.

thoracic outlet syndrome síndrome de estrecho torácico, síndrome del conducto de salida torácica.

tired housewife syndrome síndrome del ama de casa fatigada.

tooth-and-nail syndrome síndrome de dientes y uñas.

tourist class syndrome síndrome de la clase turista.

toxic allergic syndrome síndrome alérgico tóxico.

toxic shock syndrome (TSS) síndrome del choque tóxico (SST).

translocation Down syndrome síndrome de Down por traslocación.

tropical splenomegaly syndrome síndrome de esplenomegalia tropical.

tryptophan-induced eosinophilia-myalgia syndrome síndrome mialgia-eosinofilia inducida por triptófano.

tumor lysis syndrome síndrome de lisis tumoral.

vitreoretinal choroidopathy syndrome síndrome de coroidopatía vitreorretiniana.

whistling face syndrome síndrome de cara silbante, síndrome de cara silbante y mano en capa de molino de viento.

whistling face-windmill vane hand syndrome síndrome de cara silbante, síndrome de cara silbante y mano en capa de molino de viento.

withdrawal syndrome síndrome de abstinencia.

withdrawal syndrome for alcohol síndrome de abstinencia del alcohol.

withdrawal syndrome for cannabis síndrome de abstinencia de cannabioides.

withdrawal syndrome for hypnotics síndrome de abstinencia de hipnóticos.

withdrawal syndrome for opioids síndrome de abstinencia de opioides.

withdrawal syndrome for sedatives síndrome de abstinencia de sedantes.

X-linked lymphoproliferative syndrome síndrome linfoproliferativo ligado al cromosoma X.

syndromic *adj.* sindrómico, -ca.

syndromology *n.* sindromología.

synechenterotomy *n.* sinequenterotomía.

synechia *n.* sinequia.

annular synechia sinequia anular.

anterior synechia sinequia anterior.

circular synechia sinequia circular.

peripheral anterior synechia sinequia anterior periférica.

posterior synechia sinequia posterior.

synechia pericardii sinequia del pericardio, sinequia pericárdica.

synechia vulvae sinequia vulvar.

total anterior synechia sinequia anterior total.

total posterior synechia sinequia posterior total.

total synechia sinequia total.

synechology *n.* sinecología.

synechotome *n.* sinecótomo.

synechotomy *n.* sinecotomía.

synecrosis *n.* sinecrosis.

synencephalocele *n.* sinencefalocele.

synencephalus *n.* sinencéfalo.

synencephaly *n.* sinencefalia.

syneresis *n.* sinéresis.

synergetic *adj.* sinergético, -ca.

synergia *n.* sinergia.

synergic *adj.* sinérgico, -ca.

synergism *n.* sinergismo.

synergist *n.* sinergista.

pituitary synergist sinergista hipofisario.

synergistic *adj.* sinergístico, -ca.

synergy *n.* sinergia.

synesthesia *n.* sinestesia.

auditory synesthesia sinestesia auditiva.

synesthesia algica sinestesia álgica.

synesthesialgia *n.* sinestesialgia.

synezesis *n.* sinezesis.

syngamous *adj.* singamo, -ma.

syngamy *n.* singamia.

syngeneic *adj.* singeneico, -ca.

syngenesioplastic *adj.* singenesioplástico, -ca.

syngenesioplasty *n.* singenesioplastia.

syngenesiotransplantation *n.* singenesiotrasplante.

syngenesis *n.* singénesis.

syngenic *adj.* singénico, -ca.

syngnathia *n.* singnatia.

syngonic *adj.* singónico, -ca.

syngraft *n.* sininjerto.

synidrosis *n.* sinidrosis.

synizesis *n.* sinicesis.

synkainogenesis *n.* sincainogénesis.

synkaryon *n.* sincarion.

synkinesis *n.* sincinesia, sincinesis.

synkinetic *adj.* sincinético, -ca.

synneurosis *n.* sineurosis.

synocha *n.* sinoca.

synochal *adj.* sinocal.

synocytotoxin *n.* sinocitotoxina.

synonychia *n.* sinoniquia.

synonym *adj.* sinónimo, -ma.

objective synonym sinónimo objetivo.

senior synonym sinónimo senior.

subjective synonym sinónimo subjetivo.

synophridia *n.* sinofridia.

synophris *n.* sinofris.

synophthalmia *n.* sinoftalmía.

synophthalmus *n.* sinoftalmía.

synopsis *n.* sinopsia, sinopsis.

synopsy *n.* sinopsia, sinopsis.

synoptoscope *n.* sinoptoscopio.

synorchidism *n.* sinorquidia.

synorchism *n.* sinorquismo.

synoscheos *n.* sinósqueo.

synostatic *adj.* sinostósico, -ca.

synosteology *n.* sinosteología.

synosteotic *adj.* sinostósico, -ca.

synosteotomy *n.* sinosteotomía.

synostosis *n.* sinostosis.

tribasilar synostosis sinostosis tribasilar.

synotia *n.* sinotia.

synotus *n.* sinoto.

synovectomy *n.* sinovectomía.

synovia *n.* sinovia.

synovial *adj.* sinovial.

synovialoma *n.* sinovialoma.

synovin *n.* sinovina.

synovio *n.* sinovio.

synovioblast *n.* sinovioblasto.

synovioma *n.* sinovioma.

synoviorthese *n.* sinoviortesis.

synoviorthesis *n.* sinoviortesis.

synoviosarcoma *n.* sinoviosarcoma.

synoviparous *adj.* sinovíparo, -ra.

synovitis *n.* sinovitis.

bursal synovitis sinovitis bursal.

chronic hemorrhagic villous synovitis sinovitis vellosa hemorrágica crónica.

dry synovitis sinovitis seca.

filarial synovitis sinovitis filarial.

localized nodular synovitis sinovitis nodular localizada.

pigmented villonodular synovitis sinovitis vellonodular pigmentada.

purulent synovitis sinovitis purulenta.

serous synovitis sinovitis serosa.

simple synovitis sinovitis simple.

suppurative synovitis sinovitis supurada.

synovitis sicca sinovitis seca.

tendinous synovitis sinovitis tendinosa.

vaginal synovitis sinovitis vaginal.

vibration synovitis sinovitis de vibración, sinovitis por vibración.

synpneumonic *adj.* sinneumónico, -ca.

syntactic *adj.* sintáctico, -ca.

syntaxis *n.* sintaxis.

syntenic *adj.* sinténico, -ca.

syntenosis *n.* sintenosis.

synteny *n.* sintenia.

synteresis *n.* sintéresis.

synteretic *adj.* sinterético, -ca.

syntescope *n.* sintescopio.

syntexis *n.* síntexis.

synthermal *adj.* sintérmico, -ca.

synthesis *n.* síntesis.

inducible enzyme synthesis síntesis de enzima inducible.

synthesis of continuity síntesis de contigüidad.

synthetic *adj.* sintético, -ca.

synthorax *n.* sintórax.

syntone *adj.* sintono, -na.

syntonic *adj.* sintónico, -ca.

syntonin *n.* sintonina.

syntony *n.* sintonía.

syntopia *n.* sintopia.

syntripsis *n.* sintripsia, sintripsis.

syntrophism *n.* sintrofismo.

syntrophoblast *n.* sintrofoblasto.

syntropic *adj.* sintrópico, -ca.

syntropy *n.* sintropía.

inverse syntropy sintropía inversa.

synulosis *n.* sinulosis.

synulotic *adj.* sinulótico, -ca.

syphilid *n.* sifílide.

acuminate syphilid sifílide acuminata.

annular syphilid sifílide anular.

bullous syphilid sifílide ampollar.

corymbose syphilid sifílide corimbiforme.

ecthymatous syphilid sifílide ectimatosa.

erythematous syphilid sifílide eritematosa.

flat papular syphilid sifílide papulosa plana.

follicular syphilid sifílide folicular.

gummatous syphilid sifílide gomosa.

impetiginous syphilid sifílide impetiginosa.

lenticular syphilid sifílide lenticular.

macular syphilid sifílide maculosa pigmentaria.

miliary syphilid sifílide miliar.

nodular syphilid sifílide nodular.

nummular syphilid sifílide numular.

palmar syphilid sifílide palmar, sifílide plantar.

papular syphilid sifílide papulosa.

pigmentary syphilid sifílide pigmentaria.

plantar syphilid sifílide palmar, sifílide plantar.

rupial syphilid sifílide rupial.

secondary syphilid sifílide precoz, sifílide secundaria.

tertiary syphilid sifílide tardía, sifílide terciaria.

tubercular syphilid sifílide tuberculosa.

varioliform syphilid sifílide variceliforme, sifílide varioliforme.

syphilis *n.* sífilis.

cardiovascular syphilis sífilis cardiovascular.

congenital syphilis sífilis congénita.

early latent syphilis sífilis latente precoz, sífilis temprana latente.

early syphilis sífilis temprana.

endemic syphilis sífilis endémica.

gummatous syphilis sífilis gomosa.

hereditary syphilis sífilis hereditaria.

late benign syphilis sífilis benigna tardía.

late latent syphilis sífilis latente tardía, sífilis tardía latente.

late syphilis sífilis tardía.

latent syphilis sífilis latente.

meningovascular syphilis sífilis meningovascular.

non-venereal syphilis sífilis no venérea.

parenchymatous syphilis sífilis parenquimatosa.

primary syphilis sífilis primaria.

quaternary syphilis sífilis cuaternaria.

secondary syphilis sífilis secundaria.

syphilis hereditaria sífilis hereditaria.

syphilis hereditaria tarda sífilis hereditaria tardía.

tertiary syphilis sífilis terciaria.

syphilitic *adj.* sifilítico, -ca.

syphiloderm *n.* sifilodermia.

syphiloderma *n.* sifilodermia.

syphilogenous *adj.* sifilógeno, -na.

syphiloid *n.* sifiloide.

syphilology *n.* sifilología.

syphiloma *n.* sifiloma.

syphilopathy *n.* sifilopatía.

syphilophyma *n.* sifilofima.

syphilosis *n.* sifilosis.

syphilous *adj.* sifiloso, -sa.

syphitoxin *n.* sifitoxina.

syphon *n.* sifón.

syphonage *n.* sifonaje.

syrigmus *n.* sirigmo.

syringadenoma *n.* siringadenoma.

syringe *n.* jeringa, jeringuilla.

air syringe jeringa de aire.

Anel's syringe jeringa de Anel.

aspiration syringe jeringa de aspiración.

chip syringe jeringa de fragmentillos.

control syringe jeringa de control.

Davidson syringe jeringa de Davidson.

dental syringe jeringa dental.

fountain syringe jeringa de fuente, jeringa fuente.

hypodermic syringe jeringa hipodérmica.

Luer-Lok syringe jeringa de Luer, jeringa de Luer-Lok.

Luer's syringe jeringa de Luer, jeringa de Luer-Lok.

Neisser's syringe jeringa de Neisser.

Pitkin syringe jeringa de Pitkin.

probe syringe jeringa sonda.

ring syringe jeringa anular.

rubber-bulb syringe jeringa con bulbo de goma.

water syringe jeringa de agua.

syringectomy *n.* siringectomía.

syringitis *n.* siringitis.

syringobulbia *n.* siringobulbia.

syringocele *n.* siringocele.

syringocystadenoma *n.* siringocistoadenoma.

syringocystadenoma papilliferum siringocistoadenoma papilífero.

syringocystoma *n.* siringocistoma.

syringoencephalia *n.* siringoencefalia.

syringoid *adj.* siringoide.

syringoma *n.* siringoma.

chondroid syringoma siringoma condroide.

syringomyelia *n.* siringomielia.

syringomyelocele *n.* siringomielocele.

syringotome *n.* siringótomo.

syringotomy *n.* siringotomía.

syrup *n.* jarabe.

acacia syrup jarabe de goma arábiga.

aromatic eriodictyon syrup jarabe aromático de yerba santa.

cacao syrup jarabe de cacao.

cherry syrup jarabe de cereza.

citric acid syrup jarabe de ácido cítrico.

cocoa syrup jarabe de cocoa.

compound white pine syrup jarabe compuesto de pino blanco.

compound white pine syrup with codeine jarabe compuesto de pino blanco con codeína.

cyproheptadine hydrochloride syrup jarabe de clorhidrato de ciproheptadina.

dicyclomine hydrochloride syrup jarabe de clorhidrato de diciclomina.

dihydrocodeinone bitartrate syrup jarabe de bitartrato de dihidrocodeinona.

glyceryl guaiacolate syrup jarabe de guayacolato de glicerilo.

glycirrhiza syrup jarabe de orozuz.

hydriodic acid syrup jarabe de ácido yodhídrico.

hydrocodone bitartrate syrup jarabe de ditartrato de hidrocodona.

licorice syrup jarabe de regaliz.

methdilazine hydrochloride syrup jarabe de clorhidrato de metdilacina.

orange syrup jarabe de naranja.

piperazine citrate syrup jarabe de citrato de piperacina.

promethazine hydrochloride syrup jarabe de clorhidrato de prometacina.

raspberry syrup jarabe de frambuesa.

senna syrup jarabe de hoja sen.

simple syrup jarabe simple.

syrup of ipecac jarabe de ipecacuana.

syrup of tolu jarabe de tolú.

tolu balsam syrup jarabe de bálsamo de tolú.

wild cherry syrup jarabe de cereza silvestre.

syrupy *adj.* siruposo, -sa.

syssarcosis *n.* sisarcosis.

syssomus *n.* sísomo.

systaltic *adj.* sistáltico, -ca.

system *n.* sistema.

absolute system of units sistema absoluto de unidades.

absorbent system sistema absorbente.

accessory portal system of Sappey sistema portal accesorio, sistema portal accesorio de Sappey.

APUD system sistema APUD.

association system sistema de asociación.

autonomic nervous system sistema nervioso autónomo.

Bertillon system bertillonaje, sistema Bertillon.

blood group system sistema de grupos sanguíneos.

blood-vascular system sistema sanguíneo vascular.

buffer system sistema amortiguador.

cardiovascular system sistema cardiovascular.

centimeter-gram-second (CGS) system sistema cegesimal (CGS), sistema centímetro-gramo-segundo (CGS).

central nervous system sistema nervioso central.

cerebrospinal system sistema cefalorraquídeo.

chromaffin system sistema cromafin.

circulatory system sistema circulatorio.

colloid system sistema coloide.
conductor system of the heart sistema conductor del corazón, sistema de conducción del corazón.
craniosacral system sistema craneosacro.
dentinal system sistema de la dentina, sistema dentinal.
dermal system sistema dérmico, sistema dermoide.
digestive system sistema digestivo.
disperse system sistema disperso.
ecological system sistema ecológico.
endocrine system sistema endocrino.
esthesiodic system sistema estesiódico.
extrapyramidal motor system sistema extrapiramidal, sistema motor extrapiramidal.
feedback system sistema de retroalimentación.
foot-pound-second (FPS) system sistema pie-libra-segundo.
genital system sistema genital.
glandular system sistema glandular.
Haversian system sistema de Havers, sistema haversiano.
hematopoietic system sistema hematopoyético, sistema hemopoyético.
heterogeneous system sistema heterogéneo.
His-Tawara system sistema de His-Tawara.
homogeneous system sistema homogéneo.
hypoxia warning system sistema de aviso de hipoxia.
immune system sistema inmunitario, sistema inmunológico.
indicator system sistema indicador.
integumentary system sistema tegumentario.
international system of units sistema internacional de unidades (SI).
interofective system sistema interofectivo.
interrenal system sistema interrenal.
involuntary nervous system sistema nervioso involuntario.
kinetic system sistema cinético.
Linnaean system of nomenclature sistema de nomenclatura de Linneo.
locomotor system sistema locomotor.

lymphatic system sistema linfático.
masticatory system sistema masticatorio.
metameric nervous system sistema nervioso metamérico.
meter-kilogram-second system (MKS) sistema metro-kilogramo-segundo (MKS).
metric system sistema métrico.
mononuclear phagocyte system sistema mononuclear fagocítico.
mononuclear phagocyte system (MPS) sistema fagocítico mononuclear (SFM).
muscular system sistema muscular.
nervous system sistema nervioso.
neuromuscular system sistema neuromuscular.
non-specific system sistema no específico.
occlusal system sistema oclusal.
oculomotor system sistema oculomotor.
oxidation-reduction (O-R) system sistema de oxidación-reducción (O-R).
parasympathetic nervous system sistema nervioso parasimpático.
pedal system sistema pedal.
periodic system sistema periódico.
portal system sistema portal.
pressoreceptor system sistema presorreceptor.
projection system sistema de proyección.
properdin system sistema de la properdina.
Purkinje system sistema de Purkinje.
pyramidal system sistema piramidal.
redox system sistema redox.
renin-angiotensin system sistema renina-angiotensina.
reproductive system sistema reproductor.
reticular activating system (RAS) sistema activador reticular, sistema reticular activador ascendente.
reticuloendothelial system sistema reticuloendotelial.
second signaling system sistema de segundas señales.
skeletal system sistema esquelético.
somesthetic system sistema somestésico.
static system sistema estático.

stomatognathic system sistema estomatognático.
sympathetic nervous system sistema nervioso del tronco simpático, sistema nervioso simpático.
system of macrophages sistema macrófago.
system respiratorium sistema respiratorio.
T system sistema T.
thoracolumbar system sistema toracolumbar.
urinary system sistema urinario.
urogenital system sistema urogenital.
vascular system sistema vascular, sistema vascular sanguíneo.
vasomotor system sistema vasomotor.
vegetative nervous system sistema nervioso vegetativo, sistema vegetativo.
vertebral-basilar system sistema vertebral-basilar.
visceral nervous system sistema nervioso visceral.
systematic tabulation *n.* tabulación sistemática.
systematized *adj.* sistematizado, -da.
systematology *n.* sistematología.
systemic *adj.* sistémico, -ca.
systemoid *adj.* sistemoide.
systole *n.* sístole.
aborted systole sístole abortada.
arterial systole sístole arterial.
auricular systole sístole auricular.
electromechanical systole sístole electromecánica.
extra systole sístole extra.
late systole sístole tardía.
premature systole sístole prematura.
systole alternans sístole alternada.
ventricular systole sístole ventricular.
systolic honk *n.* graznido sistólico.
systolometer *n.* sistolómetro.
systremma *n.* sistrema.
syzygial *adj.* sicigial.
syzygium *n.* sicigio.
syzygy *n.* sicigia.

T t

tabacism *n.* tabaquismo.
tabacosis *n.* tabacosis.
tabagism *n.* tabaquismo.
tabanid *n.* tabánidos.
tabanka *n.* tabanka.
tabardillo *n.* tabardillo.
tabes *n.* tabefacción, tabes.
  cerebral tabes tabes cerebral.
  cervical tabes tabes cervical, tabes superior.
  Friedreich's tabes tabes de Friedreich, tabes familiar, tabes hereditaria.
  peripheral tabes tabes periférica.
  tabes diabetica tabes diabética.
  tabes dorsalis tabes dorsal, tabes raquídea.
  tabes ergotica tabes ergótica.
  tabes infantum tabes infantil.
  tabes mesaraica tabes mesaraica.
  tabes mesenterica tabes escrofulosa, tabes mesentérica.
  tabes spasmodica tabes espasmódica.
  tabes spinalis tabes espinal.
tabescence *n.* tabescencia.
tabetic *adj.* tabético, -ca.
tabic *adj.* tábico, -ca.
tabification *n.* tabificación.
tablature *n.* tablatura.
table *n.* mesa, tabla.
  Aub-Dubois table tabla de Aub-Dubois.
  cohort life table tabla de supervivencia.
  contingency table tabla de contingencia.
  demographic life table tabla de mortalidad, tabla de mortalidad demográfica.
  examining table mesa de examen.
  life table tabla de supervivencia.
  Mendeleiev table tabla de Mendéleiev.
  operating table mesa de operaciones.
  periodic table tabla periódica.
  Reuss' color table tabla de colores de Reuss.
  rotokinetic treatment table tabla de tratamiento rotocinético.
  Stilling color table tabla de colores de Stilling.
  Tanner growth table tabla de crecimiento de Tanner.
  tilt table mesa basculante, mesa inclinada.
tablet *n.* comprimido, tableta.
  buccal tablet tableta bucal.
  coated tablet comprimido recubierto.
  compressed tablet tableta comprimida.
  dispensing tablet tableta de preparación, tableta distribuidora.
  enteric coated tablet tableta con cubierta entérica.
  hypodermic tablet tableta hipodérmica.
  prolonged action tablet tableta de acción prolongada.
  repeat action tablet tableta de acción repetida.
  sublingual tablet tableta sublingual.
  sustained action tablet tableta de acción sostenida.

  triturate tablet tableta triturada.
taboo *n.* tabú.
taboparalysis *n.* taboparálisis.
taboparesis *n.* taboparesis.
tabu *n.* tabú.
tabula *n.* tabla, tabula.
  tabula rasa tabula rasa.
tabular *adj.* tabular.
tache *n.* mancha.
  tache blanche mancha blanca.
  tache bleuâtre mancha azul.
  tache cérébrale mancha cerebral, mancha meníngea.
  tache laiteuse mancha de leche, mancha láctea.
  tache motrice mancha motriz.
  tache noire mancha negra.
  tache spinale mancha espinal, mancha raquídea.
tachistesthesia *n.* taquistestesia.
tachistoscope *n.* taquistoscopio.
tachograph *n.* tacógrafo.
tachography *n.* tacografía, tacograma.
tachometer *n.* tacómetro.
tachyalimentation *n.* taquialimentación.
tachyarrhythmia *n.* taquiarritmia.
tachyauxesis *n.* taquiauxesia, taquiauxesis.
tachycardia *n.* taquicardia.
  atrial chaotic tachycardia taquicardia caótica auricular.
  atrial tachycardia taquicardia auricular.
  atrioventricular nodal tachycardia taquicardia nodal auriculoventricular.
  atrioventricular node reentrant tachycardia taquicardia intranodal.
  atrioventricular tachycardia taquicardia auriculoventricular.
  auriculoventricular tachycardia taquicardia auriculoventricular.
  bidirectional ventricular tachycardia taquicardia ventricular bidireccional.
  chaotic atrial tachycardia taquicardia caótica auricular.
  double tachycardia taquicardia doble.
  ectopic tachycardia taquicardia ectópica.
  essential tachycardia taquicardia esencial.
  fetal tachycardia taquicardia fetal.
  Gallavardin's tachycardia taquicardia de Gallavardin.
  junctional tachycardia taquicardia de la unión.
  nodal tachycardia taquicardia nodal.
  orthostatic tachycardia taquicardia ortostática.
  paroxysmal atrial tachycardia taquicardia paroxística auricular.
  paroxysmal nodal tachycardia taquicardia nodal paroxística.
  paroxysmal tachycardia taquicardia paroxística.

  paroxysmal ventricular tachycardia taquicardia paroxística ventricular.
  reflex tachycardia taquicardia refleja.
  sinus tachycardia taquicardia sinusal.
  supraventricular tachycardia (SVT) taquicardia supraventricular (TSV).
  tachycardia en salves taquicardia en salvas.
  tachycardia strumosa exophthalmica taquicardia estrumosa y exoftálmica.
  tachycardia torsades de pointes taquicardia en franja de puntas.
  ventricular tachycardia taquicardia ventricular.
tachycardiac *adj.* taquicárdico, -ca.
tachycardic *adj.* taquicárdico, -ca.
tachydysrhythmia *n.* taquidisritmia.
tachygastria *n.* taquigastria.
tachygenesis *n.* taquigénesis.
tachylalia *n.* taquilalia.
tachymeter *n.* taquímetro.
tachypacing *n.* taquimarcapasos.
tachyphagia *n.* taquifagia.
tachyphrasia *n.* taquifrasia.
tachyphrenia *n.* taquifrenia, taquipsiquia.
tachyphylasis *n.* taquisinecia.
tachyphylaxia *n.* taquifilaxia.
tachypnea *n.* taquipnea.
  nervous tachypnea taquipnea nerviosa.
  transient tachypnea taquipnea transitoria.
tachypragia *n.* taquipragia, taquiurgia.
tachypylaxis *n.* taquifilaxis.
tachyrhythmia *n.* taquirritmia.
tachysynthesis *n.* taquisíntesis.
tachysystole *n.* taquisistolia.
tachytrophism *n.* taquitropismo.
tachyzoite *n.* taquizoíto.
tactic *adj.* táctico, -ca.
tacticity *n.* tacticidad.
tactile *adj.* táctil.
tactile agnosia *n.* amorfognosia.
tactometer *n.* tactómetro.
tactual *adj.* táctil.
tactus *n.* tacto.
  tactus eruditus tacto erudito.
  tactus expertus tacto experimentado.
taedium vitae taedium vitae.
taenia *n.* taenia, tenia[1], tenia[2].
Taenia Taenia.
taenial *adj.* tenial.
taeniasis *n.* teniasis.
  somatic taeniasis teniasis somática.
taenifugal *adj.* tenífugo, -ga.
taenifuge *adj.* tenífugo, -ga.
taeniola *n.* taeniola, teniola.
Taijin kyofusho *n.* Taijin kyofusho.
tail *n.* cola.
talalgia *n.* talalgia.
talar *adj.* talar.
talcosis *n.* talcosis.
  pulmonary talcosis talcosis pulmonar.

taliped *adj.* talípedo, -da.
talipedic *adj.* talipédico, -ca.
talipes talipes.
  talipes arcuatus talipes arcuato.
  talipes calcaneovalgus talipes calcaneovalgo.
  talipes calcaneovarus talipes calcaneovaro.
  talipes calcaneus talipes calcáneo.
  talipes cavovalgus talipes cavovalgo.
  talipes cavus talipes cavo.
  talipes equinovalgus talipes equinovalgo.
  talipes equinovarus talipes equinovaro.
  talipes equinus talipes equino.
  talipes planovalgus talipes planovalgo.
  talipes plantaris talipes plantar.
  talipes planus talipes plano.
  talipes transversoplanus talipes transverso-plano.
  talipes valgus talipes valgo.
  talipes varus talipes varo.
talocalcaneal *adj.* talocalcáneo, -a.
talocalcanean *adj.* talocalcáneo, -a.
talocrural *adj.* talocrural.
talofibular *adj.* talofibular, taloperoneal, talo-peroneo, -a.
talonavicular *adj.* talonavicular.
talonid *n.* talónide.
taloscaphoid *adj.* taloescafoideo, -a.
talotibial *adj.* talotibial.
talus talón, talus.
tama *n.* tama.
tambour *n.* tambor[1].
tampon[1] *n.* tampón, tapón[2].
  Corner's tampon tampón de Corner, tapón de Corner.
tampon[2] *v.* raponar.
tamponade *n.* taponamiento.
  balloon tamponade taponamiento con globo.
  cardiac tamponade taponamiento cardíaco, taponamiento de Rose.
  chronic tamponade taponamiento cardíaco crónico, taponamiento crónico.
  esophagogastric tamponade taponamiento esofagogástrico.
  heart tamponade taponamiento del corazón.
  pericardial tamponade taponamiento pericárdico.
tangentiality *n.* tangencialidad.
tangle *n.* maraña.
  neurofibrillary tangle maraña neurofibrilares.
tangoreceptor *n.* tangorreceptor.
tanning *n.* bronceado.
tanspalatal *adj.* transpalatino, -na.
tantrum *n.* berrinche, rabieta.
tanycyte *n.* tanicito.
tanyphonia *n.* tanifonía.
taon *n.* taón.
tape *n.* cinta.
  adhesive tape cinta adhesiva, esparadrapo.
  dental tape cinta dental.
tapeinocephalic *adj.* tapeinocefálico, -ca.
tapeinocephaly *n.* tapeinocefalia.
tapetal *adj.* tapetal.
tapetochoroidal *adj.* tapetocoroideo, -a.
tapetoretinal *adj.* tapetorretiniano, -na.
tapetoretinopathy *n.* tapetorretinopatía.
tapetum tapetum.
tapeworm *n.* tenia[1].
taphophilia *n.* tafofilia.
tapinocephalic *adj.* tapeinocefálico, -ca, tapinocefálico, -ca.
tapinocephaly *n.* tapeinocefalia, tapinocefalia.
tapiroid *adj.* tapiroide.

tapotage *n.* tapotage.
tapotement *n.* tapotement.
tar *n.* brea.
  juniper tar brea de enebro.
  pine tar brea de pino.
tara *n.* tara[2].
taraxigen *n.* taraxígeno.
taraxy *n.* taraxia, taraxis.
tardive *adj.* tardío, -a.
tardy *adj.* tardío, -a.
tare *n.* tara[1].
target *n.* blanco[1].
tarsadenitis *n.* tarsadenitis.
tarsal *adj.* tarsal, tarsiano, -na.
tarsalgia *n.* tarsalgia.
tarsectomy *n.* tarsectomía.
  anterior tarsectomy tarsectomía anterior.
  cuneiform tarsectomy tarsectomía cuneiforme.
  posterior tarsectomy tarsectomía posterior.
tarsectopia *n.* tarsectopía.
tarsitis *n.* tarsitis.
tarsocheiloplasty *n.* tarsoqueiloplastia, tarsoquiloplastia.
tarsoclasia *n.* tarsoclasia.
tarsoclasis *n.* tarsoclasis.
tarsomalacia *n.* tarsomalacia.
tarsomegaly *n.* tarsomegalia.
tarsometatarsal *adj.* tarsometatarsiano, -na.
tarso-orbital *adj.* tarsoorbitario, -ria.
tarsophalangeal *adj.* tarsofalángico, -ca.
tarsophyma *n.* tarsofima.
tarsoplasia *n.* tarsoplasia, tarsoplastia.
tarsoplasty *n.* tarsoplastia.
tarsoptosis *n.* tarsoptosis.
tarsorrhaphy *n.* tarsorrafia.
tarsotarsal *adj.* tarsotarsal, tarsotarsiano, -na.
tarsotibial *adj.* tarsotibial.
tarsotomy *n.* tarsotomía.
tarsus *n.* tarso, tarsus.
tartar *n.* sarro.
taste *n.* gusto.
  color taste gusto coloreado, gusto del color.
  Franklinic taste gusto de Franklin, gusto franklínico.
  taste blindness ceguera al gusto.
  voltaic taste gusto voltaico.
tattoo *n.* taraceo, tatuaje.
  amalgam tattoo tatuaje de amalgama.
tattooing *n.* tatuaje.
  tattooing of the cornea tatuaje de la córnea.
taurocholaneresis *n.* taurocolaneresis.
taurocholanopoiesis *n.* taurocolanopoyesis.
taurocholemia *n.* taurocolemia.
taurodontism *n.* taurodontismo.
tautomer *adj.* tautómero, -ra.
tautomeric *adj.* tautomérico, -ca.
tautomerism *n.* tautomería, tautomerismo.
taxis *n.* taxis.
  bipolar taxis taxis bipolar.
  negative taxis taxis negativa.
  positive taxis taxis positiva.
taxon *n.* taxón.
taxonomic *adj.* taxonómico, -ca.
taxonomist *n.* taxonomista.
taxonomy *n.* taxonomía.
  numerical taxonomy taxonomía numérica.
taylorism *n.* taylorismo.
team *n.* equipo[2].
  code team equipo de reanimación.
tear[1] *n.* desgarramiento, desgarro.
  bucket-handle tear desgarro en asa de cubo.
  cemental tear desgarro del cemento.
  cementum tear desgarro del cemento.
  ligamental tear desgarro ligamentoso.

  Mallory-Weiss tear desgarro de Mallory-Weiss.
  tear of the perineum desgarro del perineo, desgarro perineal.
  vaginal tear desgarro vaginal.
tear[2] *n.* lágrima.
  artificial tear lágrima artificial.
  crocodile tear lágrima de cocodrilo.
tearing *n.* lagrimeo.
tease *v.* desmenuzar.
technique *n.* técnica.
  airbrasive technique técnica de abrasión con aire.
  Alexander technique técnica de Alexander.
  Asopa's technique técnica de Asopa.
  aspiration technique técnica de aspiración.
  assisted reproduction technique técnica de reproducción asistida.
  atrial-wall technique técnica de pared auricular.
  Barcroft-Warburg technique técnica de Barcroft-Warburg.
  Begg technique técnica de Begg.
  behavioral technique técnica conductual.
  Camey's neobladder technique técnica de Camey.
  coaxial technique técnica coaxial.
  cognitive technique técnica cognitiva.
  conditioned relaxation technique técnica de relajación condicionada.
  cross trigonal technique técnica de Cohen.
  Czepa's technique técnica de Czepa.
  DeLorme technique técnica de DeLorme.
  depilatory technique técnica depilatoria.
  Devine-Horton's technique técnica de Devine-Horton.
  digital image technique técnica de imagen digital.
  dilution-filtration technique técnica de dilución y filtración.
  direct technique técnica directa.
  Dotter's technique técnica de Dotter.
  Ficoll-Hypaque technique técnica de Ficoll-Hypaque.
  fluorescent antibody technique técnica de anticuerpos fluorescentes.
  flush technique técnica de rubor.
  Frazier's technique técnica de Frazier.
  Gregoir's technique técnica de Gregoir.
  Hakanson's technique técnica de Hakanson.
  Hampton technique técnica Hampton.
  hanging drop technique técnica de gota colgante.
  Hartel technique técnica de Hartel.
  Holtzman inkblot technique técnica de las manchas de tinta de Holtzman.
  imaginary relaxation technique técnica de relajación imaginaria.
  immunoperoxidase technique técnica de inmunoperoxidasa.
  indirect technique técnica indirecta.
  injection technique técnica de inyección.
  intravenous infusion technique técnica de infusión intravenosa.
  Jacobson's progressive relaxation technique técnica de relajación progresiva de E. Jacobson.
  Jerne plaque technique técnica de placa de Jerne.
  Judkins' technique técnica de Judkins.
  Kleinschmidt technique técnica de Kleinschmidt.
  Kronlein's technique técnica de Kronlein.
  Laurell technique técnica de Laurell.
  Leboyer technique técnica de Leboyer.

long cone technique técnica del cono largo.
Marshall-Marchetti-Kranz's technique técnica de corrección de incontinencia Marshall-Marchetti-Kranz.
McGoon technique técnica de McGoon.
Merendino technique técnica de Merendino.
Mohs' technique técnica de Mohs.
Oakley-Fulthorpe technique técnica de Oakley-Fulthorpe.
Orr technique técnica de Orr.
Oudin technique técnica de Oudin.
peroxidase-antiperoxidase technique técnica de la peroxidasa-antiperoxidasa.
rebreathing technique técnica de re-respiración.
Rebuck skin window technique técnica de ventana cutánea de Rebuck.
relaxation technique técnica de relajación.
Schultz's relaxation technique técnica de relajación de Schultz.
scintillation counting technique técnica de cuenta de centelleo.
Seldinger's technique técnica de Seldinger.
Smith-Robinson's technique técnica de Smith-Robinson.
Southern blot technique técnica de secado de Southern.
squash technique técnica de machacamiento.
sterile insect technique técnica para esterilizar insectos.
substraction technique técnica de sustracción.
supersonic vibration technique técnica de vibración supersónica.
Tennison-Randall's technique técnica de Tennison-Randall.
time diffusion technique técnica de difusión de tiempo.
Trueta technique técnica de Trueta.
washed field technique técnica del campo lavado.
Western blot technique técnica de manchado de Western, técnica de secado de Western.
Wolpe's relaxation technique técnica de relajación de Wolpe.
tectal *adj.* tectal.
tectiform *adj.* tectiforme.
tectocephalic *adj.* tectocefálico, -ca.
tectocephaly *n.* tectocefalia.
tectology *n.* tectología.
tectonic *adj.* tectónico, -ca.
tectorial *adj.* tectorial, tectorio, -ria.
tectorium tectorio, tectorium.
tectospinal *adj.* tectoespinal, tectospinal
tectum techo, tectum.
teething *n.* dentición.
tegmen tegmen, tegmento.
tegmental *adj.* tegmental, tegmentario, -ria.
tegmentotomy *n.* tegmentotomía.
tegmentum tegmento, tegmentum.
tegument *n.* tegumento.
teichopsia *n.* teicopsia.
teinodynia *n.* teinodinia.
tektin *n.* tectina.
tela *n.* tela.
telalgia *n.* telalgia[1].
telangiectasia *n.* telangiectasia.
  capillar telangiectasia telangiectasia capilar.
  cephalo-oculocutaneous telangiectasia telangiectasia cefalooculocutánea.
  essential telangiectasia telangiectasia esencial.
  generalized essential telangiectasia telangiectasia esencial generalizada.
  hereditary hemorrhagic telangiectasia te-

langiectasia hemorrágica hereditaria.
  idiopathic juxtafoveolar telangiectasia telangiectasia yuxtafoveolar idiopática.
  retinal telangiectasia telangiectasia retiniana.
  spider telangiectasia telangiectasia aracniforme, telangiectasia aracnoide.
  telangiectasia lymphatica telangiectasia linfática.
  telangiectasia macularis eruptiva perstans telangiectasia macular eruptiva persistente.
  telangiectasia verrucosa telangiectasia verrugosa.
telangiectasis *n.* telangiectasis.
telangiectatic *adj.* telangiectásico, -ca.
telangiectodes *adj.* telangiectoide.
telangiitis *n.* telangiitis, telangitis.
telangioma *n.* telangiectoma, telangioma.
telangion *n.* telangión.
telangiosis *n.* telangiosis.
telebinocular *n.* telebinocular.
telecanthus *n.* telecanto.
telecardiogram *n.* telecardiograma.
telecardiography *n.* telecardiografía.
telecardiophone *n.* telecardiófono.
teleceptive *adj.* teleceptivo, -va.
teleceptor *n.* teleceptor.
telecommand *n.* telemando.
telecord *n.* telecord.
telectrocardiogram *n.* telectrocardiograma.
telecurietherapy *n.* telecurieterapia.
teledendrite *n.* teledendrita.
teledendron *n.* teledendron.
telediagnosis *n.* telediagnóstico.
telediastolic *adj.* telediastólico, -ca.
teleelectrocardiograph *n.* teleelectrocardiógrafo.
telefluoroscopy *n.* telefluoroscopia.
telekinesis *n.* telecinesia, telecinesis, telequinesia.
telekinetic *adj.* telecinético, -ca.
telelectrocardiogram *n.* telelectrocardiograma.
telemeter *n.* telémetro.
telemetry *n.* telemetría.
telencephalic *adj.* telencefálico, -ca.
telencephalization *n.* telencefalización.
telencephalon *n.* telencéfalo.
teleneurite *n.* teleneurita.
teleological *adj.* teleológico, -ca.
teleologism *n.* teleologismo.
teleology *n.* teleología.
teleonomic *adj.* teleonómico, -ca.
teleonomy *n.* teleonomía.
teleopsia *n.* teleopsia.
teleorbitism *n.* teleorbitismo.
telepathist *n.* telépata.
telepathize *v.* telepatizar.
telepathy *n.* telepatía.
teleradiography *n.* telerradiografía.
teleradium *n.* telerradio.
telereceptive *adj.* telerreceptivo, -va.
telereceptor *n.* telerreceptor.
telergic *adj.* telérgico, -ca.
telergy *n.* telergia.
teleroentgenogram *n.* telerroentgenograma.
teleroentgenography *n.* telerroentgenografía.
teleroentgenotherapy *n.* telerroentgenoterapia.
telesis *n.* telesis.
telesthesia *n.* telestesia.
telesthetoscope *n.* telestetoscopio.
telesyphilis *n.* telesífilis.
telesystolic *adj.* telesistólico, -ca.

teletactor *n.* teletactor.
teletherapy *n.* telerradioterapia, teleterapia.
telethermometer *n.* teletermómetro.
tellurism *n.* telurismo.
telobiosis *n.* telobiosis.
telocentric *adj.* telocéntrico, -ca.
telocoele *n.* telocele.
telodendron *n.* telodendrión, telodendron.
telogen *n.* telógeno.
teloglia *n.* teloglia.
telognosis *n.* telognosis.
telognostic *adj.* telognóstico, -ca.
telolecithal *adj.* telolecital.
telolemma *n.* telolema.
telomerase *n.* telomerasa.
telomere *n.* telómero.
telopeptide *n.* telopéptido.
telophase *n.* telofase.
telophragma *n.* telofragma.
teloreceptor *n.* telorreceptor.
telorism *n.* telorismo.
telotism *n.* telotismo.
temperament *n.* temperamento.
  choleric temperament temperamento bilioso, temperamento colérico.
  melancholic temperament temperamento atrabiliario, temperamento atrabilioso, temperamento melancólico.
  phlegmatic temperament temperamento flemático, temperamento linfático.
  sanguine temperament temperamento sanguíneo.
temperature *n.* temperatura.
  absolute temperature temperatura absoluta.
  ambient temperature temperatura ambiental.
  axillary temperature temperatura axilar.
  basal body temperature temperatura corporal basal.
  basal temperature temperatura basal.
  body temperature temperatura corporal.
  core temperature temperatura central.
  critical temperature temperatura crítica.
  denaturation temperature of DNA temperatura de desnaturalización del ADN.
  maximum temperature temperatura máxima.
  mean temperature temperatura media.
  minimum temperature temperatura mínima.
  normal temperature temperatura normal.
  optimum temperature temperatura óptima.
  oral temperature temperatura oral.
  rectal temperature temperatura rectal.
  room temperature temperatura ambiental.
  sensible temperature temperatura sensible.
  subnormal temperature temperatura subnormal.
  temperature of infant temperatura del lactante.
  therapeutic temperature temperatura terapéutica.
  tympanic temperature temperatura timpánica.
template *n.* plantilla, templado.
  surgical template plantilla quirúrgica, templado quirúrgico.
temple *n.* sien.
tempolabile *adj.* tempolábil.
temporal *adj.* temporal[1].
temporalis *adj.* temporal[2].
temporoauricular *adj.* temporoauricular.
temporofacial *adj.* temporofacial.
temporofrontal *adj.* temporofrontal.
temporohyoid *adj.* temporohioideo, -a.

temporomalar *adj.* temporomalar.
temporomandibular *adj.* temporomandibular.
temporomaxillary *adj.* temporomaxilar.
temporooccipital *adj.* temporooccipital.
temporoparietal *adj.* temporoparietal.
temporopontile *adj.* temporopontil, temporopontino, -na.
temporosphenoid *adj.* temporoesfenoidal, temporoesfenoideo, -a.
temporozygomatic *adj.* temporocigomático, ca.
tempostabile *adj.* tempoestable, tempostábil.
tenacious *adj.* tenaz.
tenacity *n.* tenacidad.
tenalgia *n.* tenalgia.
tendinitis *n.* tendinitis.
  calcific tendinitis tendinitis cálcica, tendinitis calcificada.
  stenosing tendinitis tendinitis estenosante.
  tendinitis ossificans traumatica tendinitis osificante traumática.
  tendinitis stenosans tendinitis estenosante.
tendinography *n.* tendinografía.
tendinoplasty *n.* tendinoplastia.
tendinous *adj.* tendinoso, -sa.
tendo *n.* tendo, tendón.
  tendo Achillis tendón de Aquiles.
  tendo calcaneus tendón calcáneo.
tendomucin *n.* tendomucina.
tendomucoid *n.* tendomucoide.
tendon *n.* tendón.
  Achilles' tendon tendón de Aquiles.
  heel tendon tendón del talón.
  pulled tendon tendón desgarrado.
  rider's tendon tendón de jinete.
tendonitis *n.* tendinitis, tendonitis.
tendophony *n.* tendofonía.
tendosynovitis *n.* tendosinovitis.
  adhesive tendosynovitis tendosinovitis adhesiva.
  gonococcic tendosynovitis tendosinovitis gonocócica, tendosinovitis gonorreica.
  gonorrheal tendosynovitis tendosinovitis gonocócica, tendosinovitis gonorreica.
  localized nodular tendosynovitis tendosinovitis nodular localizada.
  nodular tendosynovitis tendosinovitis nodular.
  tendosynovitis acuta purulenta tendosinovitis purulenta, tendosinovitis purulenta aguda.
  tendosynovitis chronica tendosinovitis serosa, tendosinovitis serosa crónica.
  tendosynovitis crepitans tendosinovitis crepitante.
  tendosynovitis granulosa tendosinovitis granulosa.
  tendosynovitis stenosans tendosinovitis estenosante.
  tuberculous tendosynovitis tendosinovitis tuberculosa.
  villonodular pigmented tendosynovitis tendosinovitis vellonodular pigmentada.
  villonodular tendosynovitis tendosinovitis vellosonodular.
  villous tendosynovitis tendosinovitis vellosa.
tendovaginal *adj.* tendovaginal.
tendovaginitis *n.* tendovaginitis.
tenectomy *n.* tenectomía.
tenesmic *adj.* tenésmico, -ca.
tenesmus *n.* tenesmo.
  rectal tenesmus tenesmo rectal.
  vesical tenesmus tenesmo vesical.

tenia *n.* tenia².
teniacide *adj.* tenicida.
teniafugal *adj.* tenífugo, -ga.
teniafuge *adj.* tenífugo, -ga.
teniamyotomy *n.* teniamiotomía.
teniasis *n.* teniasis.
tenicide *adj.* tenicida.
teniform *adj.* teniforme.
tenifugal *adj.* tenífugo, -ga.
tenifuge *adj.* tenífugo, -ga.
teniola *n.* teniola.
teniotoxin *n.* teniotoxina.
tenodesis *n.* tenodesis, tenopexia.
tenodynia *n.* tenodinia.
tenofibril *n.* tenofibrilla.
tenography *n.* tenografía.
tenolysis *n.* tenólisis.
tenomyoplasty *n.* tenomioplastia.
tenomyotomy *n.* tenomiotomía.
tenonectomy *n.* tenonectomía.
tenonitis *n.* tenonitis.
tenonometer *n.* tenonómetro.
tenonostosis *n.* tenonostosis.
tenontagra *n.* tenontagra.
tenontitis *n.* tenontitis.
  tenontitis prolifera calcarea tenontitis proliferante calcárea, tenontitis prolífica calcárea.
tenontography *n.* tenontografía.
tenontolemmitis *n.* tenontolemitis, tenontolemnitis.
tenontomyoplasty *n.* tenontomioplastia.
tenontomyotomy *n.* tenontomiotomía.
tenontophyma *n.* tenontofima.
tenontoplastic *adj.* tenontoplástico, -ca.
tenontoplasty *n.* tenontoplastia.
tenophony *n.* tenofonía.
tenoplastic *adj.* tenoplástico, -ca.
tenoplasty *n.* tenoplastia.
tenoreceptor *n.* tenorreceptor.
tenorrhaphy *n.* tenorrafia.
tenosinovectomy *n.* tenosinovectomía.
tenositis *n.* tenositis.
tenostosis *n.* tenostosis.
tenosuspension *n.* tenosuspensión.
tenosuture *n.* tenosutura.
tenosynovectomy *n.* tenosinovectomía.
tenosynovitis *n.* tenosinovitis.
tenotome *n.* tenótomo.
tenotomize *v.* tenotomizar.
tenotomy *n.* tenotomía.
  curb tenotomy tenotomía con sujeción, tenotomía de contención, tenotomía de restricción.
  graduated tenotomy tenotomía graduada.
  subcutaneous tenotomy tenotomía subcutánea.
tenovaginitis *n.* tenovaginitis.
tense *adj.* tenso, -sa.
tensioactive *adj.* tensioactivo, -va.
tensiometer *n.* tensiómetro.
tension *n.* tensión².
  arterial tension tensión arterial.
  blood gas tension tensión de un gas sanguíneo.
  carbon-dioxide tension tensión de dióxido de carbono.
  electrical tension tensión eléctrica.
  fatigue tension tensión de fatiga.
  interfacial surface tension tensión superficial interfacial.
  intravenous tension tensión intravenosa.
  muscular tension tensión muscular.
  ocular tension tensión ocular.
  oxygen tension tensión de oxígeno.
  premenstrual tension tensión premenstrual.

  surface tension tensión superficial.
  tissue tension tensión hística, tensión tisular.
  ultimate tension tensión final, tensión límite.
  wall tension tensión de pared.
tensometer *n.* tensómetro.
tensor *n.* tensor, -ra.
tent *n.* tienda.
tentative *adj.* tentativo, -va.
tentorial *adj.* tentorial.
tentorium tentorium, tienda.
tentum tentum.
tephromalacia *n.* tefromalacia.
tephromyelitis *n.* tefromielitis.
tephrosis *n.* tefrosis.
tepid *adj.* tibio, -bia.
teras *n.* teras.
teratism *n.* teratismo.
  ceasmic teratism teratismo ceásmico.
  ectopic teratism teratismo ectópico.
  ectrogenic teratism teratismo ectrogénico.
  hypergenetic teratism teratismo hipergenético.
  symphysic teratism teratismo sinfísico.
teratoblastoma *n.* teratoblastoma.
teratocarcinogenesis *n.* teratocarcinogénesis.
teratocarcinoma *n.* teratocarcinoma.
  teratocarcinoma testis teratocarcinoma de testículo.
teratogen *n.* teratógeno¹.
teratogenesis *n.* teratogénesis, teratogenia.
teratogenetic *adj.* teratogenético, -ca.
teratogenic *adj.* teratogénico, -ca.
teratogenicity *n.* teratogenicidad.
teratogenous *adj.* teratógeno².
teratoid *adj.* teratoide².
teratologic *adj.* teratológico, -ca.
teratologist *n.* teratólogo, -ga.
teratology *n.* teratología.
teratoma *n.* teratoide¹, teratoma.
  adult teratoma teratoma adulto.
  benign cystic teratoma teratoma quístico, teratoma quístico benigno.
  cystic teratoma teratoma quístico, teratoma quístico benigno.
  immature teratoma teratoma inmaduro.
  malignant teratoma teratoma maligno.
  mature teratoma teratoma maduro.
  solid teratoma teratoma macizo.
teratomous *adj.* teratomatoso, -sa.
teratosis *n.* teratosis.
teratospermia *n.* teratospermia.
terebinthinism *n.* terebintinismo.
terebrans *adj.* terebrante.
terebrant *adj.* terebrante.
terebrating *adj.* terebrante.
terebration *n.* terebración.
term *n.* término.
terminal *n.* terminal.
  C terminal terminal C.
  cohesive terminal terminal cohesivo.
  dumb terminal terminal no inteligente.
  intelligent terminal terminal inteligente.
  video display terminal terminal de visualización de vídeo.
terminatio *n.* terminación.
termination *n.* terminación.
terminology *n.* terminología.
terminus *n.* término, terminus.
termogenin *n.* termogenina.
ternary *adj.* ternario, -ria.
terrace *n.* terrace.
territoriality *n.* territorialidad.
terror *n.* terror.
  night terror terror nocturno.

tertian *n.* terciano, -na.
  malignant tertian terciano maligna.
tertiarism *n.* terciarismo.
tertiary *adj.* terciario, -ria.
tertipara *n.* tercípara.
teslaization *n.* teslaización.
test *n.* prueba, test.
  achievement test test de rendimiento.
  acid-perfusion test test de perfusión ácida.
  Allen-Doisy test test de Allen-Doisy.
  Ames' test test de Ames.
  apomorphine test test de apomorfina.
  aptitude test test de aptitudes.
  Beery-Buktenika test of developmental visual motor integration (VMI) prueba del desarrollo de la integración visuomotora de Beery-Buktenika.
  Bending's test test de Bending.
  Denver's analytic test for development prueba de Denver para el análisis del desarrollo.
  edrophonium test test del edrofonio.
  efficiency test test de eficiencia.
  epicutaneous skin test test epicutáneo.
  Farnsworth's test test de Farnsworth.
  gestalt visualmotor test test gestáltico viso-motor.
  infusion test test de infusion.
  intelligence test test de inteligencia.
  intradermal skin test test intracutáneo.
  Kaufman test of educational achievement (K-TEA) prueba de Kaufman para logros educacionales.
  Kohs block design test prueba del diseño de bloques de Kohs.
  Langman's test test de Langman.
  Lepromin's test test de Lepromin.
  Machover draw-a-person (MDAP) test prueba de Machover del dibujo de la figura humana.
  male impotence test (MIT) prueba para la impotencia.
  Mitsuda's test test de Mitsuda.
  papaverin test test de papaverina.
  Pap's test test de Pap.
  personality test test de personalidad.
  pressure-volume test test de presión-volumen.
  projective test test proyectivo.
  radio-allergo-(inmuno)sorbent test RAST RAST.
  revised Peabody picture vocabulary test (PPVT-R) prueba de Peabody revisada de vocabulario con imágenes.
  revised Wechsler memory scale test prueba de memoria de Wechsler revisada.
  Rorschach's test test de Rorschach.
  sentence completion test (SCT) prueba de frases incompletas.
  Standford-Binet test prueba de Standford-Binet.
  thematic aperception test test de apercepción temática (TAT).
  test letter letra de prueba.
  test tube probeta.
  venereal disease research laboratory (VDRL) test prueba de investigación de laboratorio de enfermedades venéreas.
  Wada's test test de Wada.
  Wisconsin card sorting test prueba de elección de tarjetas de Wisconsin.
testalgia *n.* testalgia.
testectomy *n.* testectomía.
testicle *n.* testículo.
  Cooper's irritable testicle testículo irritable de Cooper.
  cryptorchid testicle testículo criptorquídico.
  displaced testicle testículo desplazado.
  ectopic testicle testículo ectópico.
  inverted testicle testículo invertido.
  movable testicle testículo móvil.
  obstructed testicle testículo obstruido.
  pulpy testicle testículo pulposo.
  relax testicle testículo de reducción, testículo redux, testis redux.
  retained testicle testículo retenido.
  retractile testicle testículo retráctil.
  undescended testicle testículo no descendido.
testicond *adj.* testicondo, -da.
testicular *adj.* testicular.
testiculoma *n.* testiculoma.
testimony *n.* testimonio.
testing *n.* valoración².
  gross sensory testing valoración de la sensibilidad general.
testis testículo, testis.
testitis *n.* testitis.
testitoxicosis *n.* testitoxicosis.
testoid *adj.* testiforme, testoide, testoideo, -a.
testopathy *n.* testopatía.
testosterone *n.* testosterona.
tetanal *adj.* tetanal.
tetanic *adj.* tetánico, -ca.
tetaniform *adj.* tetaniforme.
tetanigenous *adj.* tetanígeno, -na.
tetanism *n.* tetanismo.
tetanization *adj.* tetanización.
tetanize *v.* tetanizar.
tetanode *n.* tetánodo.
tetanoid *adj.* tetanoide, tetanoideo, -a.
tetanometer *n.* tetanómetro.
tetanomotor *n.* tetanomotor.
tetanospasmin *n.* tetanospasmina.
tetanus *n.* tétanos.
  acoustic tetanus tétanos acústico.
  anodal closure tetanus tétanos anódico de cierre, tétanos de cierre anódico.
  anodal duration tetanus tétanos durable anódico.
  anodal opening tetanus tétanos anódico de abertura, tétanos de abertura anódica.
  apyretic tetanus tétanos apirético.
  benign tetanus tétanos benigno.
  cathodal closure tetanus tétanos catódico de cierre, tétanos de cierre catódico.
  cathodal duration tetanus tétanos durable catódico.
  cathodal opening tetanus tétanos catódico de apertura, tétanos de abertura catódica.
  cephalic tetanus tétanos cefálico, tétanos de Janin, tétanos de Klemn, tétanos paralítico.
  cerebral tetanus tétanos cerebral.
  chronic tetanus tétanos crónico.
  complete tetanus tétanos completo.
  cryptogenic tetanus tétanos criptogénico, tétanos criptógeno, tétanos espontáneo, tétanos idiopático, tétanos médico, tétanos reumático.
  drug tetanus tétanos farmacológico, tétanos medicamentoso.
  extensor tetanus tétanos extensor.
  flexor tetanus tétanos flexor.
  generalized tetanus tétanos generalizado.
  head tetanus tétanos cefálico, tétanos de la cabeza.
  hydrophobic tetanus tétanos hidrofóbico, tétanos hidrófobo.
  imitative tetanus tétanos imitativo.
  incomplete tetanus tétanos incompleto.
  intermittent tetanus tétanos intermitente, tétanos remitente.
  local tetanus tétanos local.
  neonatal tetanus tétanos de los recién nacidos, tétanos del neonato, tétanos neonatal, tétanos neonatorum.
  partial tetanus tétanos parcial.
  physiological tetanus tétanos fisiológico.
  postserum tetanus tétanos postsérico.
  puerperal tetanus tétanos puerperal.
  Rose's cephalic tetanus tétanos cefálico de Rose.
  splanchnic tetanus tétanos de Binot, tétanos esplácnico.
  tetanus anticus tétanos anticus.
  tetanus completus tétanos completus.
  tetanus dorsalis tétanos dorsal.
  tetanus infantum tétanos infantil.
  tetanus neonatorum tétanos de los recién nacidos, tétanos del neonato, tétanos neonatal, tétanos neonatorum.
  tetanus posticus tétanos posterior, tétanos póstico, tétanos posticus.
  tetanus postpartum tétanos posparto.
  toxic tetanus tétanos tóxico.
  traumatic tetanus tétanos traumático.
  uterine tetanus tétanos uterino.
tetany *n.* tetania.
  duration tetany tetania duradera.
  epidemic tetany tetania epidémica.
  gastric tetany tetania gástrica.
  hyperventilation tetany tetania de hiperventilación, tetania por hiperventilación.
  hypocalcemic tetany tetania hipocalcémica.
  infantile tetany tetania infantil.
  latent tetany tetania latente.
  manifest tetany tetania manifiesta.
  neonatal tetany tetania del recién nacido, tetania neonatal.
  parathyroid tetany tetania paratiroidea.
  parathyroprival tetany tetania paratireopriva, tetania paratiropriva.
  phosphate tetany tetania por fosfato.
  rheumatic tetany tetania reumática.
  tetany gravidarum tetania gravídica.
  tetany of alkalosis tetania por alcalosis.
  tetany parathyreopriva tetania paratireopriva, tetania paratiropriva.
  uterine tetany tetania uterina.
tetartanope *n.* tetartánope.
tetartanopia *n.* tetartanopía, tetartanopsia.
tetartanopic *adj.* tetartanópico, -ca.
tetartocone *n.* tetartocono.
tetia *n.* tetia.
tetra-amelia *n.* tetraamelia.
tetrablastic *adj.* tetrablástico, -ca.
tetrabrachius *n.* tetrabraquio.
tetrabromophenolphthalein *n.* tetrabromofenolftaleína.
  tetrabromophenolphthalein sodium tetrabromofenolftaleína sódica.
tetrachirus *n.* tetráquiro.
tetrachromic *adj.* tetracrómico, -ca.
tetracrotic *adj.* tetracrótico, -ca.
tetracuspid *adj.* tetracúspide.
tetrad *n.* tétrada.
tetradactylous *adj.* tetradáctilo, -la.
tetradactyly *n.* tetradactilia.
tetragonum *n.* cuadrilátero, tetrágono.
  tetragonum lumbale cuadrilátero lumbar, tetrágono lumbar.
tetragonus tetragonus.
tetrahydric *adj.* tetrahídrico, -ca.
tetraiodophenolphthalein *n.* tetrayodofenolftaleína.
tetralogy *n.* tetralogía.
  Eisenmenger tetralogy tetralogía de Eisenmenger.

Fallot's tetralogy tetralogía de Fallot.
tetralogy of Fallot tetralogía de Fallot.
tetramastia *n.* tetramastia.
tetramastous *adj.* tetramasto, -ta.
tetramazia *n.* tetramazia.
tetramelus *n.* tetramelos.
tetrameric *adj.* tetramérico, -ca, tetrámero, -ra.
tetramerous *adj.* tetrámero, -ra.
Tetramitus Tetramitus.
tetranophthalmos *n.* tetranoftalmo.
tetranopsia *n.* tetranopsia.
tetraodontoxism *n.* tetraodontoxismo.
tetraophthalmus *n.* tetraoftalmo, tetranoftalmo.
tetraparesis *n.* tetraparesia.
tetraperomelia *n.* tetraperomelia.
tetraphocomelia *n.* tetrafocomelia.
tetraplegia *n.* tetraplejía.
tetraplegic *adj.* tetrapléjico, -ca.
tetraploid *adj.* tetraploide.
tetraploidy *n.* tetraploidía.
tetrapod *adj.* tetrápodo, -da.
tetrapodisis *n.* tetrapódisis.
tetrapus tetrápodo, -da, tetrapus.
tetrascelus *n.* tetrascelo, tetrasquelo.
tetrasomic *adj.* tetrasómico, -ca.
tetrasomy *n.* tetrasomía.
tetraster *n.* tetráster.
tetrastischiasis *n.* tetrastisquiasis.
Tetrastoma Tetrastoma.
tetratomic *adj.* tetratómico, -ca.
tetravaccine *n.* tetravacuna.
tetravalent *adj.* tetravalente.
tetrazolium *n.* tetrazolio.
  tetrazolium nitroblue nitroazul de tetrazolio.
tetrodotoxism *n.* tetraodontoxismo, tetrodotoxismo.
tetrophthalmus *n.* tetroftalmo.
tetrose *n.* tetrosa.
tetter *n.* sarpullido.
  crusted tetter sarpullido costroso.
  prickly heat tetter sarpullido por calor.
texis *n.* texis.
textural *adj.* textural.
texture *n.* textura.
textus tejido, textus.
thalamencephalic *adj.* talamencefálico, -ca, talamoencefálico, -ca.
thalamencephalon *n.* talamencéfalo, talamoencéfalo.
thalamic *adj.* talámico, -ca.
thalamocortical *adj.* talamocortical.
thalamolenticular *adj.* talamolenticular.
thalamomillary *adj.* talamomamilar.
thalamotegmental *adj.* talamotegmental.
thalamotomy *n.* talamotomía.
  anterior thalamotomy talamotomía anterior.
  dorsomedial thalamotomy talamotomía dorsomedial.
thalamus *n.* tálamo.
  dorsal thalamus thalamus dorsalis.
thalassemia *n.* talasemia.
  beta thalassemia talasemia beta.
  beta-delta thalassemia talasemia beta-delta.
  delta thalassemia talasemia delta.
  F thalassemia talasemia F.
  hemoglobin S thalassemia talasemia de hemoglobina S.
  Lepore thalassemia talasemia de Lepore.
  major thalassemia talasemia mayor.
  minor thalassemia talasemia menor.
  sickle cell thalassemia talasemia de células falciformes, talasemia drepanocítica.

thalassemia intermedia talasemia intermedia.
thalassophobia *n.* talasofobia.
thalassoposia *n.* talasoposia.
thalassotherapy *n.* talasoterapia.
thallitoxicosis *n.* taliotoxicosis, talotoxicosis.
thallotoxicosis *n.* taliotoxicosis.
thalposis *n.* talposis.
thalpotic *adj.* talpótico, -ca.
thamuria *n.* tamuria.
thanatobiologic *adj.* tanatobiológico, -ca.
thanatochemistry *n.* tanatoquimia.
thanatochronology *n.* tanatocronología.
thanatognomonic *adj.* tanatognomónico, -ca.
thanatoid *adj.* tanatoide.
thanatology *n.* tanatología.
thanatomania *n.* tanatomanía.
thanatometer *n.* tanatómetro.
thanatophidial *adj.* tanatofídico, -ca.
thanatophilia *n.* tanatofilia.
thanatophobia *n.* tanatofobia.
thanatophoric *adj.* tanatofórico, -ca.
thanatopsy *n.* tanatopsia.
thanatos *n.* tánatos.
thanatosis *n.* tanatosis.
thanotopsia *n.* tanotopsia.
thebaic *adj.* tebaico, -ca.
thebaism *n.* tebaísmo.
theca *n.* teca[1].
thecal *adj.* tecal.
thecitis *n.* tecitis.
thecodont *adj.* tecodonto, -ta.
thecoma *n.* tecoma.
thecomatosis *n.* tecomatosis.
thelalgia *n.* telalgia[2].
thelarche *n.* telarca, telarquia, telarquía.
theleplasty *n.* teleplastia, teloplastia.
thelerethism *n.* teleretismo.
thelitis *n.* telitis.
thelium *n.* telio.
theloncus *n.* telonco.
thelorrhagia *n.* telorragia.
thelothism *n.* teleretismo.
thelygenic *adj.* teligénico, -ca.
thenal *adj.* tenal.
thenar *adj.* tenar.
theophylline determination *n.* teofilinemia.
theorem *n.* teorema.
  Bayes theorem teorema de Bayes.
  central limit theorem teorema central del límite.
  Gibbs theorem teorema de Gibbs.
theoretical *adj.* teórico, -ca[2].
theorist *n.* teórico, -ca[1].
theory *n.* teoría.
  activity theory teoría de la actividad.
  adsorption theory of narcosis teoría de adsorción de narcosis.
  aging theory of atherosclerosis teoría del envejecimiento de la ateriosclerosis.
  Altmann's theory teoría de Altmann.
  antibody instructive theory teoría instructiva de los anticuerpos.
  antibody specific theory teoría del anticuerpo específico.
  apposition theory teoría de aposición.
  atomic theory teoría atómica.
  attribution theory teoría de la atribución.
  avalanche theory teoría de la avalancha, teoría del alud.
  Baeyer's theory teoría de Baeyer.
  balance theory teoría del equilibrio.
  balance theory of sex teoría de equilibrio de los sexos.
  bind theory teoría del vínculo.
  Bohr's theory teoría de Bohr.

Bowman's theory teoría de Bowman.
Brønsted theory teoría de Brønsted.
Buergi's theory teoría de Buergi.
Burn and Rand theory teoría de Burn y Rand.
Cannon theory teoría de Cannon.
Cannon-Bard theory teoría de Cannon-Bard.
cell theory teoría celular.
cellular immunity theory teoría de la inmunidad celular, teoría de la inmunidad celular de Metchnikov.
celomic metaplasia theory of endometriosis teoría de metaplasia celómica de la endometriosis.
clonal selection theory teoría de la selección clonal.
clonal-selection theory of immunity teoría de la selección clonal de la inmunidad.
closed circulation theory teoría de la circulación cerrada.
closed-open circulation theory teoría de la circulación cerrada y abierta.
cognitive dissonance theory teoría de la disonancia cognitiva.
Cohnheim's theory teoría de Cohnheim.
colloid theory of narcosis teoría coloidal de la narcosis.
communication theory teoría de la comunicación.
contractile ring theory teoría del anillo contráctil.
convergence-projection theory teoría de convergencia y proyección.
core conductor theory teoría del conductor central.
crisis theory teoría de la crisis.
Darwinian theory teoría darwiniana, teoría de Darwin, teoría evolucionista.
De Bordeau theory teoría de De Bordeau.
De Vries theory teoría de De Vries, teoría de las mutaciones.
Delecato-Doman theory teoría de Delecato-Doman.
developmental theory of aging teoría del desarrollo de la edad.
Dieulafoy theory teoría de Dieulafoy.
dimer theory teoría del dímero.
dipole theory teoría de los dipolos.
disengagement theory teoría de la desconexión.
double bind theory teoría del doble vínculo.
dualistic theory teoría dualista.
duplicity theory of vision teoría de la duplicidad de la visión.
ectopic focus theory teoría del foco ectópico.
Ehrlich's side-chain theory teoría de las cadenas laterales, teoría de las cadenas laterales de Ehrlich.
Ehrlich's theory teoría bioquímica de Ehrlich, teoría de Ehrlich.
electron theory teoría de los electrones.
emergency theory teoría de la emergencia, teoría de la urgencia.
emigration theory teoría de la emigración.
encrustation theory teoría de la incrustación.
enzyme inhibition theory of narcosis teoría de inhibición enzimática por la narcosis.
epigenetic theory teoría epigenética.
equilibrium theory teoría del equilibrio.
expanding surface theory teoría de la superficie en ampliación.
fast circulation theory teoría de la circulación rápida.
Flourens' theory teoría de Flourens.
forbidden clone theory teoría del clon prohibido.

free-radical theory of aging teoría del envejecimiento por los radicales libres.
frequency theory teoría de la frecuencia.
Frerich's theory teoría de Frerich.
Freud's theory teoría de Freud.
gametoid theory teoría gametoide.
gastrea theory teoría de la gastrea, teoría de la gastrea de Haeckel.
gate control theory teoría de control de compuertas, teoría del gate control.
gate theory teoría de la puerta.
gate theory of pain teoría de las compuertas del dolor.
germ layer theory teoría de la capa germinal.
germ theory teoría de los gérmenes, teoría germinal.
germ-plasm theory teoría germen-plasma.
Gestalt theory teoría de la Gestalt.
Getman visuomotor theory teoría visomotora de Getman.
Golgi's theory teoría de Golgi.
Goltz's theory teoría de Goltz.
Haeckel's gastrea theory teoría de la gastrea, teoría de la gastrea de Haeckel.
Helmholtz theory of accommodation teoría de Helmholtz de la acomodación.
Helmholtz theory of hearing teoría de Helmholtz de la audición.
hematogenous theory of endometriosis teoría hematógena de la endometriosis.
Hering's theory of color vision teoría de Hering de la visión del color.
hit theory teoría del impacto.
hydrate microcrystal theory of anesthesia teoría de hidratos microcristalinos de la anestesia.
immunologic theory of aging teoría inmunológica del envejecimiento.
implantation theory of the production of endometriosis teoría de la implantación en la producción de endometriosis.
incasement theory teoría de inclusión, teoría del encajonamiento.
information theory teoría de la información.
instructive theory teoría de la instrucción.
interactionist theory teoría de la interacción.
ionic theory teoría iónica.
James-Lange's theory teoría de James-Lange.
Jung's theory teoría de Jung.
kern-plasma relation theory teoría de kern, teoría de la relación núcleo-plasma.
Knoop theory teoría de Knoop.
Lacan's theory teoría lacaniana.
Ladd-Franklin theory teoría de Ladd-Franklin.
Lamarckian theory teoría de Lamarck.
lateral chain theory teoría de las cadenas laterales, teoría de las cadenas laterales de Ehrlich.
learning theory teoría del aprendizaje.
Liebig theory teoría de Liebig.
lipoid theory of narcosis teoría lipoide de la narcosis.
local circuit theory teoría del circuito local.
lymphatic dissemination theory of endometriosis teoría de la diseminación linfática de la endometriosis.
mass action theory teoría de acción en masa.
membrane expansion theory teoría de expansión de membranas.
membrane ionic theory teoría iónica de la membrana.
Mendelian theory teoría mendeliana.
Metchnikoff's theory teoría de Mechnikov, teoría de Metchnikoff, teoría de Metchnikov.
Metchnikov's cellular immunity theory teoría de la inmunidad celular, teoría de la inmunidad celular de Metchnikov.

Meyer-Overton theory of narcosis teoría de Meyer-Overton de la narcosis.
migration theory teoría de la migración.
Miller's chemicoparasitic theory teoría quimicoparasitaria, teoría quimioparasitaria de Miller.
molecular dissociation theory teoría de la disociación molecular.
monophyletic theory teoría monofilética.
Monro-Kellie's theory teoría de Monro-Kellie.
myoelastic theory teoría mioelástica.
myogenic theory teoría miógena, teoría miogénica.
natural selection theory teoría de la selección natural.
Nernst's theory teoría de Nernst.
neurochronaxic theory teoría neurocronáxica.
neurogenic theory teoría neurogénica.
neuron theory teoría de la neurona, teoría neuronal.
Ollier's theory teoría de Ollier.
omega-oxidation theory teoría de omega-oxidación.
ondulatory theory teoría de la onda, teoría ondulatoria.
open circulation theory teoría de la circulación abierta.
open-closed circulation theory teoría de la circulación abierta y cerrada.
opponent colors theory teoría de los colores opuestos.
overproduction theory teoría de superproducción.
oxygen deprivation theory of narcosis teoría de privación de oxígeno en la narcosis.
Pasteur's theory teoría de Pasteur.
pattern theory of pain teoría del patrón del dolor.
Pauling theory teoría de Pauling.
permeability theory of narcosis teoría de la permeabilidad en la narcosis.
place theory teoría de la posición, teoría del sitio.
Planck theory teoría de Planck.
point-de-repère theory teoría del punto de referencia.
polarization membrane theory teoría de la polarización de la membrana.
polyphyletic theory teoría polifilética.
POU theory teoría POU.
preformation theory teoría de la preformación, teoría preformacionista.
preformationism theory teoría de la preformación, teoría preformacionista.
prescriptive theory teoría prescriptiva.
quantum theory teoría cuántica, teoría de los quanta, teoría del quantum.
recapitulation theory teoría de la recapitulación.
receptor theory of drug action teoría de los receptores en la acción farmacológica.
recombinational germline theory teoría de recombinación de la línea germinal.
reed instrument theory teoría de instrumento de viento.
reentry theory teoría de reentrada, teoría de reingreso.
resonance theory of hearing teoría de la resonancia de la audición, teoría de la resonancia de Traube.
Ribbert's theory teoría de Ribbert.
Schön's theory teoría de Schön.
self-theory teoría del yo.
sensorimotor theory teoría sensorimotora.

sequestered antigen theory teoría de los antígenos secuestrados.
Shiefferdecker's symbiosis theory teoría de la simbiosis de Schiefferdecker, teoría de Schiefferdecker de la simbiosis.
side chain theory teoría de las cadenas laterales, teoría de las cadenas laterales de Ehrlich.
single hit theory teoría de un solo golpe.
situational theory teoría de situación.
sliding filament theory teoría de los filamentos deslizantes.
slow circulation theory teoría de la circulación lenta.
social cognitive theory teoría cognitiva social.
social learning theory teoría del aprendizaje social.
somatic mutation of cancer theory teoría de mutación somática del cáncer.
spindle elongation theory teoría del alargamiento del huso.
Spitzer's theory teoría de Spitzer.
ß-oxidation-condensation theory teoría de ß-oxidación-condensación.
stress-adaptation theory teoría de la adaptación al estrés.
stringed instrument theory teoría de instrumento de cuerda.
surface tension theory of narcosis teoría de la tensión superficial de la narcosis.
target theory teoría del blanco.
telephone theory teoría del teléfono.
template theory teoría de la plantilla.
thermodynamic theory of narcosis teoría termodinámica de la narcosis.
thermostat theory teoría del termostato.
trialistic theory teoría trialista.
two-sympathin theory teoría de las dos simpatinas.
unitarian theory teoría unitaria.
van't Hoff's theory teoría de van't Hoff.
Warburg's theory teoría de Warburg.
wear-and-tear theory teoría del desgaste.
Weismann's theory teoría de Weismann.
Woods-Fildes theory teoría de Woods-Fildes.
X-inactivation theory teoría de la inactivación del X.
Young-Helmholtz theory of color vision teoría de Young-Helmholtz.
theque *n.* teca².
therapeutic *adj.* terapéutico, -ca.
therapeutics terapia.
therapia *n.* terapia.
therapia sterilisans covergens terapia sterilisans covergens.
therapia sterilisans divergens terapia sterilisans divergens.
therapia sterilisans fractionata terapia sterilisans fractionata.
therapia sterilisans magna terapia esterilizante magna.
therapist *n.* terapeuta.
occupation therapist terapeuta ocupacional.
physical therapist terapeuta físico.
sexual therapist terapeuta sexual.
speech therapist terapeuta del lenguaje.
therapy *n.* terapia.
acid therapy terapia ácida.
adjuvant therapy terapia adyuvante.
aerosol bronchodilator therapy terapia broncodilatadora en aerosol.
anticoagulant therapy terapia anticoagulante.
art therapy terapia de oficio.

autogenic therapy terapia autogénica.

autoserum therapy terapia autosérica.

aversion therapy terapia aversiva, terapia de aversión.

bacterial therapy terapia bacteriana.

beam therapy terapia de haz.

behavior therapy terapia conductual, terapia de conducta.

biological therapy terapia biológica.

brief therapy terapia breve.

buffer therapy terapia de amortiguación.

carbonic therapy terapia carbónica.

Chaoul therapy terapia de Chaoul.

client-centered therapy terapia centrada en el cliente, terapia centrada en el paciente.

clinical humidity therapy terapia clínica de humidificación.

cognitive therapy terapia cognitiva.

collapse therapy terapia de colapso.

combined therapy terapia combinada.

corrective therapy terapia correctora.

Curie therapy terapia de Curie.

cytoreductive therapy terapia citorreductora.

deep roentgen-ray therapy terapia profunda de rayos X.

deleading therapy terapia del saturnismo.

depot therapy terapia por depósito.

diathermic therapy terapia diatérmica.

directive therapy terapia dirigida.

divorce therapy terapia del divorcio.

duplex therapy terapia doble.

electroconvulsive therapy terapia electroconvulsiva (TEC).

electrotherapeutic sleep therapy terapia con sueño electroterapéutico.

emanation therapy terapia de emanación.

endocrine therapy terapia endocrina.

environmental therapy terapia ambiental.

existential therapy terapia existencial.

expressive therapy terapia expresiva.

extended family therapy terapia familiar extendida.

family therapy terapia de la familia, terapia familiar, terapia familiar conjunta.

foreign protein therapy terapia con proteínas, terapia con proteínas extrañas, terapia proteínico.

functional orthodontic therapy terapia ortodóntica funcional.

gas therapy terapia gaseosa.

gene therapy terapia génica.

Gestalt therapy de la Gestalt, terapia gestáltica.

grid therapy terapia de rejilla.

group therapy terapia de grupo.

heterovaccine therapy terapia con heterovacunación, terapia vacunal.

high-voltage roentgen therapy terapia radiológico de alto voltaje.

humidification therapy terapia de humedecimiento.

hunger therapy terapia de hambre.

hyperbaric oxygen therapy terapia con oxígeno hiperbárico.

immunesuppresive therapy terapia inmunosupresora.

immunization therapy terapia de inmunización.

Indoklon therapy terapia de Indoklon.

induction therapy terapia de inducción.

infrared therapy terapia con infrarrojos.

inhalation therapy terapia de inhalación.

interference current therapy terapia de corriente interferida.

interpersonal therapy terapia interpersonal.

interstitial therapy terapia intersticial.

intracavitary therapy terapia intracavitaria.

intralesional therapy terapia intralesional.

intraosseus therapy terapia intraósea.

intravenous therapy terapia intravenosa.

irritation therapy terapia de irritación.

light therapy terapia de luz.

maintenance drug therapy terapia de mantenimiento.

malarial therapy terapia de paludización, terapia palúdica.

meditation therapy terapia de meditación.

megavitamin therapy terapia megavitamínica.

metatrophic therapy terapia metatrófica.

milieu therapy terapia del medio.

multiple family therapy terapia familiar múltiple.

myofunctional therapy terapia miofuncional.

narcosis therapy terapia de narcosis.

non-directive therapy terapia no directiva.

non-specific therapy terapia inespecífica.

occupational therapy terapia ocupacional.

opsonic therapy terapia opsónica.

organic therapy terapia orgánica.

orthodontic therapy terapia ortodóntica.

orthomolecular therapy terapia ortomolecular.

oxygen therapy terapia con oxígeno.

paraspecific therapy terapia paraespecífica.

parenteral therapy terapia parenteral.

phage therapy terapia fágica.

photodynamic therapy terapia fotodinámica.

photoradiation therapy terapia con fotorradiación.

physical therapy terapia física.

plasma exchange therapy terapia de intercambio plasmático.

plasma therapy terapia con plasma.

play therapy terapia de juego, terapia lúdica.

primal scream therapy terapia del grito primal.

proliferation therapy terapia proliferación.

protein shock therapy terapia de shock proteico.

psychoanalytic therapy terapia psicoanalítica.

pulp canal therapy terapia del conducto de la pulpa.

pulse therapy terapia con pulsos.

radiation therapy terapia con radiación, terapia con radio.

radium therapy terapia con radiación, terapia con radio.

rational emotive therapy terapia racional emotiva.

rational therapy terapia racional.

ray therapy terapia con rayos.

recreational therapy terapia recreativa.

recurrence therapy terapia de recurrencia.

reflex therapy terapia refleja.

relationship therapy terapia de relación.

relaxation therapy terapia de relajación.

release therapy terapia de liberación.

replacement therapy terapia de reposición.

role playing therapy terapia de representación de un rol.

root canal therapy terapia del conducto de la raíz.

rotation therapy terapia de rotación.

sclerosing therapy terapia de esclerosis.

sensory integrative therapy terapia de integración sensorial.

serum therapy terapia con suero, terapia sérica.

sexual therapy terapia sexual.

shock therapy terapia de choque, terapia de shock.

short wave therapy terapia de onda corta.

social network therapy terapia de red social.

social therapy terapia social.

solar therapy terapia solar.

somatic therapy terapia somática.

sparing therapy terapia de protección.

specific therapy terapia específica.

speech therapy terapia del lenguaje.

steroid hormone therapy terapia con hormonas esteroideas.

stimulation therapy terapia de estimulación.

subcoma insulin therapy terapia insulínica de coma, terapia insulínica de subcoma.

substitution therapy terapia de sustitución, terapia sustitutiva.

substitutive therapy terapia de sustitución, terapia sustitutiva.

suggestive therapy terapia de sugestión.

teleradium therapy terapia con telerradio.

thyroid therapy terapia tiroidea.

ultrasonic therapy terapia ultrasónica.

ultraviolet therapy terapia ultravioleta.

vaccine therapy terapia con vacunas.

work therapy terapia laboral.

therencephalous *adj.* terencéfalo, -la.

theriomorphism *n.* teriomorfismo.

therm *n.* terma.

thermacogenesis *n.* termacogénesis.

thermaerotherapy *n.* termaeroterapia.

thermal *adj.* termal, térmico, -ca.

thermalgesia *n.* termalgesia, termoalgesia.

thermalgia *n.* termalgia.

thermanalgesia *n.* termanalgesia, termoanalgesia.

thermanesthesia *n.* termanestesia, termoanestesia.

thermatology *n.* termatología.

thermelometer *n.* termelómetro.

thermesthesia *n.* termaestesia, termestesia, termoestesia,.

thermesthesiometer *n.* termestesiómetro, termoestesiómetro.

thermic *adj.* térmico, -ca.

thermion *n.* termión.

thermistor *n.* termistor.

thermoalgesia *n.* termoalgesia.

thermoanalgesia *n.* termoanalgesia.

thermoanesthesia *n.* termoanestesia.

thermocauterectomy *n.* termocauterectomía.

thermocautery *n.* termocauterio, termocauterización.

thermochemistry *n.* termoquímica.

thermochroic *adj.* termocroico, -ca.

thermochroism *n.* termocroísmo.

thermochrose *n.* termocrosia.

thermochrosis *n.* termocrosis.

thermochrosy *n.* termocrosia.

thermocoagulation *n.* termocoagulación.

   trigeminal thermocoagulation termocoagulación del trigémino.

thermocurrent *n.* termocorriente.

thermodiffusion *n.* termodifusión.

thermodilution *n.* termodilución.

thermoduric *adj.* termodúrico, -ca.

thermodynamics *n.* termodinámica.

thermoelectric *adj.* termoeléctrico, -ca.

thermoelectricity *n.* termoelectricidad, termomagnetismo.

thermoesthesiometer *n.* termoestesiómetro.

thermoexcitory *adj.* termoexcitador, -ra.
thermogenesis *n.* termogenesia, termogénesis.
  non-shivering thermogenesis termogénesis sin estremecimiento.
thermogenetic *adj.* termogenético, -ca.
thermogenic *adj.* termogénico, -ca.
thermogenics *n.* termogenia.
thermogenous *adj.* termogénico, -ca, termógeno, -na.
thermogram *n.* termograma.
thermograph *n.* termógrafo.
  continuous scan thermograph termógrafo de centelleo continuo.
thermographic *adj.* termográfico, -ca.
thermography *n.* termografía.
  infrared thermography termografía infrarroja.
  liquid crystal thermography termografía con cristal líquido.
  microwave thermography termografía por microondas.
thermogravimeter *n.* termogravímetro.
thermohyperalgesia *n.* termohiperalgesia.
thermohyperesthesia *n.* termohiperestesia.
thermohypesthesia *n.* termohipestesia, termohipoestesia, termohipostesia.
thermoinactivation *n.* termoinactivación.
thermoinhibitory *adj.* termoinhibidor, -ra, termoinhibitorio, -ria.
thermointegrator *n.* termointegrador.
thermokeratoplasty *n.* termoqueratoplastia.
thermolabile *adj.* termolábil.
thermolamp *n.* termolámpara.
thermolaryngoscope *n.* termolaringoscopio.
thermology *n.* termología.
thermolysis *n.* termólisis.
thermolytic *adj.* termolítico, -ca.
thermomassage *n.* termomasaje.
thermometer *n.* termómetro.
  air thermometer termómetro de aire.
  axilla thermometer termómetro axilar.
  Beckmann thermometer termómetro de Beckmann.
  bimetal thermometer termómetro bimetálico.
  Celsius thermometer termómetro centígrado, termómetro de Celsius.
  clinical thermometer termómetro clínico.
  depth thermometer termómetro de profundidad.
  differential thermometer termómetro diferencial.
  electronic thermometer termómetro electrónico.
  Fahrenheit thermometer termómetro de Fahrenheit.
  fever thermometer termómetro para la fiebre.
  gas thermometer termómetro de gas.
  half-minute thermometer termómetro de medio minuto.
  kata thermometer termómetro cata.
  Kelvin thermometer termómetro Kelvin.
  liquid-in-glass thermometer termómetro de líquido en vidrio.
  maximum thermometer termómetro de máxima.
  mercury thermometer termómetro de mercurio.
  metallic thermometer termómetro metálico.
  metastatic thermometer termómetro metastático.
  minimum thermometer termómetro de mínima.

  optic thermometer termómetro óptico.
  oral thermometer termómetro bucal.
  Rankine thermometer termómetro Rankine.
  Réaumur thermometer termómetro de Réaumur.
  recording thermometer termómetro de registro.
  rectal thermometer termómetro rectal.
  self-registering thermometer termómetro con autorregistro.
  spirit thermometer termómetro de alcohol.
  surface thermometer termómetro de superficie.
  thermocouple thermometer termómetro de termopar.
  tympanic membrane thermometer termómetro de la membrana timpánica.
thermometric *adj.* termométrico, -ca.
thermometry *n.* termometría.
  clinical thermometry termometría clínica.
  ear thermometry termometría del oído.
  invasive thermometry termometría invasiva.
thermonuclear *adj.* termonuclear.
thermopalpation *n.* termopalpación.
thermophile *adj.* termófilo, -la.
thermophilic *adj.* termofílico, -ca.
thermophore *n.* termóforo, -ra.
thermoplacentography *n.* termoplacentografía.
thermoplastic *adj.* termoplástico, -ca.
thermoplegia *n.* termoplejía.
thermopolypnea *n.* termopolipnea.
thermopolypneic *adj.* termopolipneico, -ca.
thermoprecipitation *n.* termoprecipitación.
thermoradiotherapy *n.* termorradioterapia.
thermoreceptor *n.* termorreceptor, -ra.
thermoregulation *n.* termorregulación.
  ineffective thermoregulation termorregulación ineficaz.
  neonatal thermoregulation termorregulación neonatal.
thermoregulator *n.* termorregulador, -ra.
thermoresistance *n.* termorresistencia.
thermoresistant *adj.* termorresistente.
thermoscope *n.* termoscopio.
thermostabile *adj.* termoestable, termostábil, termostable.
thermostability *n.* termoestabilidad, termostabilidad.
thermostable *adj.* termoestable.
thermostasis *n.* termoestasia, termostasia.
thermostat *n.* termostato, termóstato.
  hypothalamic thermostat termostato hipotalámico.
thermosteresis *n.* termoestéresis, termostéresis.
thermosthesia *n.* termoestesia,.
thermosystaltic *adj.* termosistáltico, -ca.
thermosystaltism *n.* termosistaltismo.
thermotactic *adj.* termotáctico, -ca.
thermotaxic *adj.* termotáxico, -ca.
thermotaxis *n.* termotaxia, termotaxis.
  negative thermotaxis termotaxia negativa.
  positive thermotaxis termotaxia positiva.
thermotherapy *n.* termoterapia.
thermotics *n.* termótica.
thermotolerant *adj.* termotolerante.
thermotonometer *n.* termotonómetro.
thermotracheotomy *n.* termotraqueotomía.
thermotropic *adj.* termotrópico, -ca.
thermotropism *n.* termotropismo.
theromorph *adj.* teromorfo, -fa.
theromorphism *n.* teromorfia, teromorfismo.
thesaurismosis *n.* tesaurismosis.
thesaurismotic *adj.* tesaurismótico, -ca.

thesaurosis *n.* tesaurosis.
thiadiazide *n.* tiadiacida, tiadiacina.
thiadiazine *n.* tiadiacida, tiadiacina.
thiazide *n.* tiacida, tiazida.
thiazin *n.* tiazina.
thiemia *n.* tiemia.
thigh *n.* muslo.
  cricket thigh muslo de cricket.
  driver's thigh muslo de los conductores, muslo del chófer.
  Heilbronner's thigh muslo de Heilbronner.
thigmotactic *adj.* tigmotáctico, -ca.
thigmotaxis *n.* haptotaxis, tigmotaxia, tigmotaxis.
thigmotropic *adj.* tigmotrópico, -ca.
thigmotropsm *n.* tigmotropismo.
thin *v.* fluidificar.
thinking *n.* pensamiento.
  abstract thinking pensamiento abstracto.
  animistic thinking pensamiento animista.
  autistic thinking pensamiento autista.
  concrete thinking pensamiento concreto.
  creative thinking pensamiento creativo.
  egocentric thinking pensamiento egocéntrico.
  hypothetical-deductive thinking pensamiento hipotético-deductivo.
  iconic thinking pensamiento icónico.
  illogical thinking pensamiento ilógico.
  paleologic thinking pensamiento paleológico.
thinness *n.* delgadez.
thiodotherapy *n.* tiodoterapia.
thioexic *adj.* tiopéxico, -ca.
thioflavine *n.* tioflavina.
  thioflavine S tioflavina S.
  thioflavine T tioflavina T.
thiogenic *adj.* tiogénico, -ca, tiógeno, -na.
thiolysis *n.* tiólisis.
thionic *adj.* tiónico, -ca.
thionin *n.* tionina.
thiopectic *adj.* tiopéctico, -ca.
thiopexy *adj.* tiopéctico, -ca, tiopexia.
thioredoxin *n.* tiorredoxina.
thiozine *n.* tiocina.
thirst *n.* sed.
  false thirst sed falsa.
  insensible thirst sed insensible.
  subliminal thirst sed subliminal.
  true thirst sed real, sed verdadera.
  twilight thirst sed crepuscular.
thixolabile *adj.* tixolábil.
thixotropic *adj.* tixotrópico, -ca.
thixotropy *n.* tixotropía, tixotropismo.
thoracalgia *n.* toracalgia.
thoracectomy *n.* toracectomía.
thoracentesis *n.* toracentesis.
thoracic *adj.* torácico, -ca.
thoracicoabdominal *adj.* toracicoabdominal.
thoracicoacromial *adj.* toracicoacromial.
thoracicohumeral *adj.* toracicohumeral.
thoracoabdominal *adj.* toracoabdominal.
thoracoacromial *adj.* toracoacromial.
thoracobronchotomy *n.* toracobroncotomía.
thoracoceloschisis *n.* toracocelosquisis.
thoracocentesis *n.* toracocentesis.
thoracocyllosis *n.* toracocilosis.
thoracocyrtosis *n.* toracocirtosis.
thoracodelphus *n.* toracodelfo.
thoracodidymus *n.* toracodídimo.
thoracodynia *n.* toracodinia.
thoracogastrodidymus *n.* toracogastrodídimo.
thoracogastroschisis *n.* toracogastrosquisis.
thoracograph *n.* toracógrafo.

thoracolaparotomy *n.* toracolaparotomía.
thoracolumbar *adj.* toracolumbar.
thoracolysis *n.* toracólisis.
thoracomelus *n.* toracomelo.
thoracometer *n.* toracómetro.
thoracometry *n.* toracometría.
thoracomyodynia *n.* toracomiodinia.
thoracopagus *n.* toracópago.
thoracoparacephalus *n.* toracoparacéfalo.
thoracopathy *n.* toracopatía.
thoracoplasty *n.* toracoplastia.
  conventional thoracoplasty toracoplastia convencional.
  costoversion thoracoplasty toracoplastia con costoversión, toracoplastia de costoversión.
thoracopneumograph *n.* toraconeumógrafo.
thoracopneumoplasty *n.* toraconeumoplastia.
thoracoschisis *n.* toracosquisis.
thoracoscope *n.* toracoscopio.
thoracoscopy *n.* toracoscopia.
thoracospinal *adj.* toracoespinal, toracospinal.
thoracostenosis *n.* toracoestenosis, toracostenosis.
thoracostomy *n.* toracostomía.
  tube thoracostomy toracostomía cerrada.
thoracotomy *n.* toracotomía.
  anterolateral thoracotomy toracotomía anteroexterna.
  posterolateral thoracotomy toracotomía posterolateral.
thoradelphus *n.* toradelfo.
thorax *n.* tórax.
  bony thorax tórax óseo.
  flail thorax tórax pulsátil.
  paralytic thorax tórax de Traube, tórax paralítico.
  Peyrot's thorax tórax de Peyrot.
  phthinoid thorax tórax ftinoide.
thorny headed worms *n.* acantocéfalos.
thought *n.* pensamiento.
  automatic thought pensamiento automático.
  operatory thought pensamiento operacional.
thread *n.* hilo.
thremmatology *n.* trematología.
threpsis *n.* trepsia, trepsis.
threshold *n.* umbral.
  absolute threshold umbral absoluto.
  achromatic threshold umbral acromático.
  auditory threshold umbral auditivo, umbral de audición.
  convulsant threshold umbral convulsivo, umbral de convulsión.
  differential threshold umbral diferencial.
  displacement threshold umbral de desplazamiento.
  dose threshold umbral de dosis.
  double point threshold umbral de doble punto, umbral de punto doble.
  epileptic threshold umbral epileptógeno.
  erythema threshold umbral de eritema.
  flicker fusion threshold umbral titilante de fusión.
  galvanic threshold umbral galvánico.
  minimum light threshold umbral luminoso mínimo.
  neuron threshold umbral neuronal.
  pain threshold umbral de dolor, umbral doloroso.
  relational threshold umbral de relación.
  renal threshold umbral renal.
  renal threshold for glucose umbral renal de la glucosa.
  seizure threshold umbral convulsivo, umbral de convulsión.

  sensitivity threshold umbral de sensibilidad, umbral sensitivo.
  sensory threshold umbral de sensibilidad, umbral sensitivo.
  stimulus threshold umbral de estímulo.
  swallowing threshold umbral de deglución.
  threshold of consciousness umbral de conciencia, umbral de consciencia, umbral del conocimiento.
  threshold of resolution umbral de resolución.
  threshold of visual sensation umbral de la sensación visual, umbral visual.
  visual threshold umbral de la sensación visual, umbral visual.
thrill *n.* thrill.
  aortic thrill thrill aórtico.
throat *n.* garganta.
  putrid throat garganta pútrida.
  septic sore throat garganta dolorida séptica.
  sore throat garganta dolorida.
throb *v.* latir.
throbbing *adj.* latente[2].
thrombapheresis *n.* trombaféresis.
thrombasthenia *n.* tromboastenia.
thrombectomy *n.* trombectomía.
thrombin *n.* trombina.
thromboangiitis *n.* tromboangeítis, tromboangitis.
  thromboangiitis obliterans tromboangeítis obliterante.
thromboclasis *n.* tromboclasis.
thromboclastic *adj.* tromboclástico, -ca.
thromboclastography *n.* tromboclastografía.
thrombocyst *n.* trombocisto.
thrombocytapheresis *n.* trombocitaféresis.
thrombocythemia *n.* trombocitemia.
  essential thrombocythemia trombocitemia esencial.
  hemorrhagic thrombocythemia trombocitemia hemorrágica.
  idiopathic thrombocythemia trombocitemia idiopática.
  primary thrombocythemia trombocitemia primaria.
thrombocytic *adj.* trombocítico, -ca.
thrombocytocrit *n.* trombocitócrito.
thrombocytolysis *n.* plastocitosis, trombocitólisis.
thrombocytopathic *adj.* trombocitopático, -ca.
thrombocytopathy *n.* trombocitopatía.
thrombocytopenia *n.* plastocitopenia, trombocitopenia.
  autoimmune thrombocytopenia trombocitopenia autoinmune.
  essential thrombocytopenia trombocitopenia esencial.
  immune thrombocytopenia trombocitopenia inmune.
  isoimmune thrombocytopenia trombocitopenia isoinmune.
thrombocytopoiesis *n.* trombocitopoyesis.
thrombocytopoietic *adj.* trombocitopoyético, -ca.
thrombocytosis *n.* trombocitosis.
thromboelastograh *n.* tromboelastografo.
thromboelastogram *n.* tromboelastograma.
thromboembolism *n.* tromboembolia, tromboembolismo.
thromboendarterectomy *n.* tromboendarterectomía.
thromboendarteritis *n.* tromboendarteritis.
thromboendocarditis *n.* tromboendocarditis.
thrombogenesis *n.* trombogénesis.
thrombogenic *adj.* trombógeno, -na.

thromboid *adj.* tromboide.
thrombokinase *n.* trombocinasa.
thrombokinesis *n.* trombocinesia, trombocinesis, tromboquinesis.
thrombokinetics *n.* trombocinética.
thrombolymphangitis *n.* trombolinfangitis.
thrombolysis *n.* trombólisis.
thrombolytic *adj.* trombolítico, -ca.
thrombopathia *n.* trombopatía.
thrombopathy *n.* trombopatía.
thrombopenia *n.* trombopenia.
thrombopeny *n.* trombopenia.
thrombophilia *n.* trombofilia.
thrombophlebitis *n.* tromboflebitis.
  postpartum iliofemoral thrombophlebitis tromboflebitis iliofemoral posparto.
  thrombophlebitis migrans tromboflebitis migratoria.
  thrombophlebitis purulenta tromboflebitis purulenta.
  thrombophlebitis saltans tromboflebitis saltarina.
thromboplastic *adj.* tromboplástico, -ca.
thromboplastid *n.* tromboplástida.
thromboplastin *n.* tromboplastina.
thrombopoiesis *n.* trombopoyesis.
thrombopoietic *adj.* trombopoyético, -ca.
thrombosed *adj.* trombosado, -da.
thrombosinusitis *n.* trombosinusitis.
thrombosis *n.* trombosis.
  agonal thrombosis trombosis agonal, trombosis de Ribert.
  atrophic thrombosis trombosis atrófica.
  cardiac thrombosis trombosis cardiaca.
  cavernous sinus thrombosis trombosis del seno cavernoso.
  cerebral thrombosis trombosis cerebral.
  compression thrombosis trombosis por compresión.
  coronary thrombosis trombosis coronaria.
  creeping thrombosis trombosis reptante.
  dilatation thrombosis trombosis por dilatación.
  infective thrombosis trombosis por infección.
  jumping thrombosis trombosis saltarina.
  marantic thrombosis trombosis marántica, trombosis marásmica.
  marasmic thrombosis trombosis marántica, trombosis marásmica.
  mesenteric arterial thrombosis trombosis mesentérica, trombosis mesentérica arterial.
  mesenteric thrombosis trombosis mesentérica, trombosis mesentérica arterial.
  mural thrombosis trombosis mural.
  placental thrombosis trombosis placentaria.
  plate thrombosis trombosis en lámina, trombosis plaquetaria.
  platelet thrombosis trombosis en lámina, trombosis plaquetaria.
  post-traumatic arterial thrombosis trombosis arterial postraumática.
  post-traumatic venous thrombosis trombosis venosa postraumática.
  propagating thrombosis trombosis propagante.
  puerperal thrombosis trombosis puerperal.
  sinus thrombosis trombosis sinusal.
  traumatic thrombosis trombosis traumática.
  venous thrombosis trombosis venosa.
thrombostasis *n.* trombostasis.
thrombostenin *n.* trombostenina.
thrombotest *n.* thrombotest.
thrombotic *adj.* trombótico, -ca.
thrombus *n.* trombo.

agglutinative thrombus trombo aglutinativo.

agonal thrombus trombo agonal.

agony thrombus trombo agónico.

annular thrombus trombo anular.

antemortem thrombus trombo ante mortem, trombo previo a la muerte.

ball thrombus trombo esférico.

bile thrombus trombo biliar.

calcified thrombus trombo calcificado.

currant jelly thrombus trombo de jalea de grosella.

fibrin thrombus trombo de fibrina, trombo fibrinoso.

hyaline thrombus trombo hialino.

infective thrombus trombo infectivo.

laminated thrombus trombo laminado.

lateral thrombus trombo lateral.

marantic thrombus trombo marasmático, trombo marásmico.

marasmatic thrombus trombo marasmático, trombo marásmico.

milk thrombus trombo lácteo.

mixed thrombus trombo mixto.

mural thrombus trombo mural.

obstructive thrombus trombo obliterante, trombo obstructivo.

occluding thrombus trombo oclusivo.

occlusive thrombus trombo oclusivo.

organized thrombus trombo organizado.

pale thrombus trombo pálido.

parasitic thrombus trombo parasitario, trombo parásito.

parietal thrombus trombo parietal.

plate thrombus trombo plaquetario.

platelet thrombus trombo plaquetario.

post mortem thrombus trombo post mortem, trombo subsecuente a la muerte.

primary thrombus trombo autóctono, trombo primario.

propagated thrombus trombo prolongado, trombo propagado.

red thrombus trombo rojo.

secondary thrombus trombo secundario.

stratified thrombus trombo estratificado.

traumatic thrombus trombo traumático.

valvular thrombus trombo valvular.

white thrombus trombo blanco.

thromophonia *n.* tromofonía.

through *n.* canalón.

thrush *n.* algodoncillo, muguet.

thumb *n.* pulgar.

tennis thumb pulgar del tenista.

thylacitis *n.* tilacitis.

thymectomize *v.* timectomizar.

thymectomy *n.* timectomía.

thymelcosis *n.* timelcosis.

thymiasis *n.* timiasis.

thymic *adj.* tímico, -ca.

thymicolymphatic *adj.* timicolinfático, -ca.

thymion *n.* timion, timión.

thymiosis *n.* timiasis, timiosis.

thymitis *n.* timitis.

thymocyte *n.* timocito.

thymogenic *adj.* timogénico, -ca, timógeno, -na.

thymokesis *n.* timoquesia, timoquesis.

thymokinetic *adj.* timocinético, -ca.

thymolysin *n.* timolisina.

thymolysis *n.* timólisis.

thymolytic *adj.* timolítico, -ca.

thymoma *n.* timoma.

thymopathic *adj.* timopático, -ca.

thymopathy *n.* timopatía.

thymopoietin *n.* timopoyetina.

thymoprivous *adj.* timoprivo, -va.

thymosin *n.* timosina.

thymotoxic *adj.* timotóxico, -ca.

thymotrophic *adj.* timotrófico, -ca.

thymus *n.* timo.

accessory thymus timo accesorio.

thymusectomy *n.* timusectomía.

thyroactive *adj.* tiroactivo, -va.

thyroadenitis *n.* tiroadenitis.

thyroaplasia *n.* tiroaplasia.

thyroarytenoid *adj.* tiroaritenoideo, -a.

thyrocardiac *adj.* tirocardíaco, -ca.

thyrocarditis *n.* tirocarditis.

thyrocele *n.* tirocele.

thyrocervical *adj.* tirocervical.

thyrochondrotomy *n.* tirocondrotomía.

thyrocricotomy *n.* tirocricotomía.

thyrodesmic *adj.* tirodésmico, -ca.

thyroepiglottic *adj.* tiroepiglótico, -ca.

thyroesophageus *n.* tiroesófago.

thyrofissure *n.* tirofisura.

thyrogenic *adj.* tirogénico, -ca.

thyrogenous *adj.* tirogénico, -ca, tirógeno, -na.

thyroglobulin *n.* tiroglobulina.

thyroglossal *adj.* tirogloso, -sa.

thyrohyal *adj.* tirohial.

thyrohyoid *adj.* tirohioideo, -a.

thyroid *adj.* tiroideo, -a.

thyroid *n.* tiroides.

thyroidectomize *v.* tiroidectomizado, -da, tiroidectomizar.

thyroidectomy *n.* tiroidectomía.

chemical thyroidectomy tiroidectomía química.

subtotal thyroidectomy tiroidectomía subtotal.

total thyroidectomy tiroidectomía total.

thyroidism *n.* tiroidismo.

thyroiditis *n.* tiroiditis.

acute non-suppurative thyroiditis tiroiditis no supurativa aguda.

acute thyroiditis tiroiditis aguda.

autoimmune thyroiditis tiroiditis autoinmune.

chronic atrophic thyroiditis tiroiditis atrófica crónica.

chronic fibrous thyroiditis tiroiditis fibrosa crónica.

chronic lymphadenoid thyroiditis tiroiditis linfadenoide crónica, tiroiditis linfocítica crónica.

chronic lymphocytic thyroiditis tiroiditis linfadenoide crónica, tiroiditis linfocítica crónica.

chronic thyroiditis tiroiditis crónica.

fibrous thyroiditis tiroiditis fibrosa.

focal lymphocytic thyroiditis tiroiditis linfocítica focal.

giant cell thyroiditis tiroiditis de células gigantes.

giant follicular thyroiditis tiroiditis folicular gigante.

granulomatous thyroiditis tiroiditis granulomatosa, tiroiditis granulomatosa subaguda.

Hashimoto's thyroiditis tiroiditis de Hashimoto.

ligneous thyroiditis tiroiditis invasora, tiroiditis leñosa, tiroiditis lígnea.

parasitic thyroiditis tiroiditis parasitaria.

Quervain's thyroiditis tiroiditis de Quervain.

Riedel's thyroiditis tiroiditis de Riedel.

subacute granulomatous thyroiditis tiroiditis granulomatosa, tiroiditis granulomatosa subaguda.

subacute lymphocytic thyroiditis tiroiditis linfocítica subaguda.

subacute thyroiditis tiroiditis subaguda.

thyroidization *n.* tiroidización.

thyroidology *n.* tiroidología.

thyroidopathy *n.* tiroidopatía.

thyroidotherapy *n.* tiroidoterapia.

thyroidotomy *n.* tiroidotomía.

thyrointoxication *n.* tirointoxicación.

thyroketonuria *n.* tirocetonuria.

thyrolaryngeal *adj.* tirolaríngeo, -a.

thyroliberin *n.* tiroliberina.

thyrolingual *adj.* tirolingual.

thyromegaly *n.* tiromegalia.

thyromimetic *adj.* tiromimético, -ca.

thyroncus *n.* tironco.

thyroparathyroidectomy *n.* tiroparatiroidectomía.

thyroparathyroprivic *adj.* tiroparatiroprivo, -va.

thyropathy *n.* tiropatía.

thyropharyngeal *adj.* tirofaríngeo, -a.

thyrophyma *n.* tirofima.

thyroplasty *n.* tiroplastia.

thyroprival *adj.* tiroprivo, -va.

thyroprivia *n.* tiroprivación, tiroprivia.

thyroptosis *n.* tiroptosis.

thyrotherapy *n.* tiroterapia.

thyrotome *n.* tirótomo.

thyrotomy *n.* tirotomía.

thyrotoxemia *n.* tirotoxemia.

thyrotoxia *n.* tirotoxia.

thyrotoxic *adj.* tirotóxico, -ca.

thyrotoxicosis *n.* tirotoxicosis.

apathetic thyrotoxicosis tirotoxicosis apática.

thyrotoxicosis medicamentosa tirotoxicosis medicamentosa.

thyrotoxin *n.* tirotoxina.

thyrotrope *n.* tirotropo.

thyrotroph *n.* tirotrofo.

thyrotropic *adj.* tirotrópico, -ca.

thyrotropin *n.* tirotropina.

thyrotropism *n.* tirotropismo.

thyroxinemia *n.* tiroxinemia.

thyroxinic *adj.* tiroxínico, -ca.

tiacarana *n.* tiacarana.

tibia *n.* tibia.

saber tibia tibia en sable.

saber-shaped tibia tibia en sable.

tibia valga tibia valga.

tibia vara tibia vara.

tibial *adj.* tibial, tibialis.

tibialgia *n.* tibialgia.

tibialis *adj.* tibial, tibialis.

tibiocalcanean *adj.* tibiocalcáneo, -a.

tibiofemoral *adj.* tibiofemoral.

tibiofibular *adj.* tibiofibular.

tibionavicular *adj.* tibionavicular.

tibioperoneal *adj.* tibioperoneo, -a.

tibioscaphoid *adj.* tibioescafoideo, -a.

tibiotarsal *adj.* tibiotarsiano, -na.

tic *n.* tic.

bowing tic tic salutatorio.

chronic tic tic crónico.

complex motor tic tic motor complejo.

complex vocal tic tic vocal complejo.

convulsive tic tic convulsivo.

diaphragmatic tic tic diafragmático, tic respiratorio.

glossopharyngeal tic tic glosofaríngeo.

habit tic tic habitual, tic por hábito.

jumping tic tic de Guinon.

local tic tic local.

mimic tic tic de mímica, tic mímico.

progressive choreic tic tic coreico progresivo.

rotatory tic tic rotatorio.

saltatory tic tic saltatorio.
simple motor tic tic motor simple.
simple vocal tic tic vocal simple.
spasmodic tic tic espasmódico.
tic de pensée tic de pensamiento, tic "de pensée".
tic de sommeil tic del sueño.
tic douloureux tic doloroso, tic doloroso de la cara.
tic facial tic facial.
tick *n.* garrapata.
tide *n.* marea.
acid tide marea ácida.
alkaline tide marea alcalina.
fat tide marea grasa.
red tide marea roja.
tigroid *adj.* tigroide.
tigrolysis *n.* tigrólisis.
tilmus *n.* tilmo.
timbre *n.* timbre.
time *n.* tiempo.
activated partial thromboplastin time (APTT) tiempo de trombloplastina parcial activada (TTPa).
apex time tiempo del ápice.
association time tiempo de asociación.
bleeding time tiempo de hemorragia, tiempo de sangría.
calcium time tiempo de calcio.
chromoscopy time tiempo de cromoscopia.
circulation time tiempo en la circulación.
clot retraction time tiempo de retracción del coágulo.
clotting time tiempo de coagulación, tiempo de formación del coágulo.
decimal reduction time tiempo de reducción decimal.
dextrinizing time tiempo de dextrinización.
doubling time tiempo de reduplicación.
fading time tiempo de desaparición.
forced expiratory time (FET) tiempo de espiración forzosa (FET).
generation time tiempo de generación.
inertia time tiempo de inercia.
left ventricular ejection time (LVET) tiempo de expulsión del ventrículo izquierdo.
normal circulation time tiempo de circulación normal.
partial thromboplastin time (PTT) tiempo de tromboplastina parcial (TTP).
prothrombin time tiempo de protrombina.
reaction time tiempo de reacción.
recalcification time tiempo de recalcificación.
recognition time tiempo de reconocimiento.
reconstruction time tiempo de reconstrucción.
relaxation time tiempo de relajación.
resolving time tiempo de resolución.
retention time tiempo de retención.
rise time tiempo de elevación.
secondary bleeding time tiempo de sangría secundaria.
sedimentation time tiempo de sedimentación.
sensation time tiempo de sensación.
sinoatrial recovery time (SART) tiempo de recuperación sinoauricular.
tissue thromboplastin inhibition time tiempo de inhibición de tromboplastina tisular.
thermal death time tiempo térmico de muerte.
timer *n.* cronómetro.
tinctable *adj.* teñible.
tinction *n.* tinción.

tinctorial *adj.* tintorial.
tincture *n.* tintura.
tinea *n.* tiña, tinea.
asbestos-like tinea tiña del tipo del asbesto.
tinea amiantacea tiña amiantácea.
tinea axillaris tiña axilar.
tinea barbae tiña de la barba.
tinea capitis tiña de la cabeza, tinea capitis.
tinea ciliorum tiña ciliar.
tinea circinata tiña circinada, tinea corporis.
tinea corporis tiña corporal, tiña del cuerpo.
tinea cruris tiña crural.
tinea faciale tiña facial, tinea faciei.
tinea faciei tiña facial, tinea faciei.
tinea favosa tiña fávica, tiña lupinosa, tiña maligna, tinea favosa.
tinea glabrosa tiña glabra, tiña glabrosa.
tinea imbricata tiña de Birmania, tiña imbricada, tinea imbricata.
tinea inguinalis tiña de la ingle, tiña inguinal.
tinea kerion tiña querion.
tinea manuum tiña de las manos, tinea manus.
tinea nigra tiña negra.
tinea nodosa tiña nudosa.
tinea pedis tiña podal.
tinea profunda tiña profunda.
tinea sycosis tiña sicosis.
tinea tarsi tiña tarsal.
tinea tonsurans tiña microspórica, tiña tonsurante, tiña tricofítica.
tinea tropicalis tiña tropical.
tinea unguium tiña de las uñas, tiña ungueal.
tinea vera tiña verdadera, tinea vera.
tinea versicolor tiña versicolor.
tingible *adj.* tingible.
tingling *n.* hormigueo.
tinkle *n.* retintín.
tinnitus *n.* acúfeno, tinnitus, zumbido.
clicking tinnitus tinnitus en clic, zumbido de chasquido.
Leudet's tinnitus zumbido de Leudet.
non-vibratory tinnitus zumbido no vibratorio.
objective tinnitus zumbido objetivo.
tinnitus aurium tinnitus aurium, zumbido auricular.
tinnitus cerebri tinnitus cerebral.
vibratory tinnitus zumbido vibratorio.
tint B *n.* tinte B.
tintometer *n.* tintómetro.
tintometry *n.* tintometría.
tiring *n.* tiring.
tissue *n.* tejido.
adenoid tissue tejido adenoide, tejido adenoideo, tejido citógeno.
adipose tissue tejido adiposo.
adrenogenic tissue tejido adrenógeno.
areolar tissue tejido areolar.
bone tissue tejido óseo.
brown adipose tissue tejido adiposo pardo.
cancellous tissue tejido esponjoso, tejido poroso.
cardiac striated tissue tejido muscular cardíaco.
cartilaginous tissue tejido cartilaginoso.
cavernous tissue tejido cavernoso.
cellular tissue tejido celular.
chondroid tissue tejido condroide.
chordal tissue tejido cordal, tejido cordoideo.
chromaffin tissue tejido cromafín.
cicatricial tissue tejido cicatricial.
compact tissue tejido compacto.
connective tissue tejido conectivo, tejido conjuntivo.
elastic tissue tejido elástico, tejido elástico amarillo.

embryonic tissue tejido embrionario, tejido primario.
endothelial tissue tejido endotelial.
episcleral tissue tejido episcleral, tejido esclerótico.
epithelial tissue tejido epitelial.
erectile tissue tejido eréctil.
fibroareolar tissue tejido fibroareolar.
fibroelastic tissue tejido fibroelástico.
fibrohyaline tissue tejido fibrohialino.
fibrous tissue tejido fibroso.
friable tissue tejido friable.
Gamgee tissue tejido de Gamgee.
gelatiginous tissue tejido gelatinoso.
gingival tissue tejido gingival.
glandular tissue tejido glandular.
hard tissue tejido duro.
hemopoietic tissue tejido hemopoyético.
heterologous tissue tejido heterólogo.
heterotopic tissue tejido heterotópico.
homologous tissue tejido homólogo.
hylic tissue tejido hílico.
hyperplastic tissue tejido hiperplástico.
interstitial tissue tejido intersticial.
investing tissue tejido de revestimiento.
junctional tissue tejido de unión.
lardaceous tissue tejido lardáceo.
lepidic tissue tejido lepídico.
loose connective tissue tejido conjuntivo laxo.
lymphadenoid tissue tejido linfadenoide.
lymphatic tissue tejido linfático.
lymphoid tissue tejido linfoide, tejido linfoideo.
mesenchymal tissue tejido mesenquimático, tejido mesenquimatoso.
mesonephric tissue tejido mesonéfrico.
metanephrogenic tissue tejido metanefrogénico.
mucous tissue tejido mucoso.
multilocular adipose tissue tejido adiposo multilocular.
muscular tissue tejido muscular.
myeloid tissue tejido mieloide.
nasion soft tissue tejido blando del nasión.
nephrogenic tissue tejido nefrogénico.
nervous tissue tejido nervioso.
nodal tissue tejido nodular.
osseous tissue tejido óseo.
osteogenic tissue tejido osteógeno.
osteoid tissue tejido osteoide.
parenchymatous tissue tejido parenquimatoso.
periapical tissue tejido periapical.
primitive pulp tissue tejido primitivo de la pulpa.
reticular tissue tejido reticulado, tejido reticular, tejido retiforme.
retiform tissue tejido reticulado, tejido reticular, tejido retiforme.
rubber tissue tejido de caucho.
scar tissue tejido cicatricial.
skeletal tissue tejido esquelético.
smooth muscular tissue tejido muscular liso.
splenic tissue tejido esplénico.
striated skeletal muscular tissue tejido muscular estríado esquelético.
subcutaneous tissue tejido subcutáneo.
target tissue tejido blanco.
tissue trimming recorte de tejidos.
tuberculosis granulation tissue tejido tuberculoso de granulación.
white adipose tissue tejido adiposo blanco.
tissular *adj.* tisular.
titer *n.* título.

titillation *n.* titilación.
titillomania *n.* titilomanía.
titmus *n.* titmus.
titrate *v.* titular.
titration *n.* titulación, valoración3.
  colorimetric titration titulación colorimétrica.
  complexometric titration titulación complexométrica.
  coulometric titration titulación coulométrica.
  Dean and Webb titration titulación de Dean y Webb.
  potentiometric titration titulación potenciométrica.
titubant *adj.* titubeante.
titubation *n.* titubeo.
tobacco *n.* tabaco.
tococardiography *n.* tococardiografía.
tocodynagraph *n.* tocodinagrafía, tocodinágrafo.
tocodynamometer *n.* tocodinamómetro.
tocograph *n.* tocógrafo.
tocography *n.* tocografía.
tocology *n.* tocología.
tocolysis *n.* tocólisis.
tocometer *n.* tocómetro.
tocotransducer *n.* tocotransductor.
toe *n.* dedo².
  hammer toe dedo en martillo.
  hippocratic toe dedo hipocrático.
  Hong Kong toe dedo de Hong Kong.
  Morton's toe dedo de Morton.
  painful toe dedo doloroso.
  pigeon toe dedo de paloma.
  stiff toe dedo rígido.
  tennis toe dedo del pie de tenista.
  toe drop dedo caído.
  webbed toe dedo palmado.
toenail *n.* uña.
  ingrowing toenail uña encarnada, uña incardinada.
Togaviridae Togaviridae.
togavirus *n.* togavirus.
toilet *n.* toilet, toilette.
  articular toilet toilet articular.
  cadaveric toilet toilet cadavérica.
toilette *n.* toilet, toilette.
tolerance *n.* tolerancia.
  acoustic tolerance tolerancia acústica.
  acquired tolerance tolerancia adquirida.
  activity tolerance tolerancia a la actividad.
  alkali tolerance tolerancia a los álcalis.
  crossed tolerance tolerancia cruzada.
  drug tolerance tolerancia a los fármacos, tolerancia farmacológica.
  exercise tolerance tolerancia al ejercicio.
  frustration tolerance tolerancia a la frustración.
  glucose tolerance tolerancia a la glucosa.
  high-zone tolerance tolerancia elevada de zona.
  immunologic tolerance tolerancia inmunológica.
  individual tolerance tolerancia individual.
  low-zone tolerance tolerancia baja de zona.
  oxygen tolerance tolerancia al oxígeno.
  split tolerance tolerancia dividida.
  tolerance pain tolerancia al dolor.
  work tolerance tolerancia al trabajo.
tolerant *adj.* tolerante.
tolerogen *n.* tolerógeno.
tolerogenesis *n.* tolerogénesis.
tolerogenic *adj.* tolerogénico, -ca, tolerógeno, -na.
toll *n.* mortandad.
tomentum *n.* tomento.

tomentum cerebri tomento cerebral.
tomoarthrography *n.* tomoartrografía.
tomodensitometry *n.* tomodensitometría.
tomogram *n.* tomograma.
tomograph *n.* tomógrafo.
tomography *n.* tomografía.
  computed tomography (CT) tomografía computadorizada (TC).
  computer axial tomography (CAT) tomografía axial computadorizada (TAC).
  emission computed tomography (ECT) tomografía computadorizada por emisión (TCE).
  full-lung tomography tomografía pulmonar completa.
  hypocycloidal tomography tomografía hipocicloidal, tomografía hipocicloide.
  linear tomography tomografía lineal.
  positron emission tomography (PET) tomografía por emisión de positrones (PET).
  single-photon emission computed tomography (SPECT) tomografía computadorizada por emisión de fotón único (SPECT).
  ultrasonic tomography tomografía ultrasónica.
tomolevel *n.* tomonivel.
tone *n.* tono.
  affective tone tono afectivo.
  bronchomotor tone tono broncomotor.
  chemical tone tono químico.
  emotional tone tono emocional.
  feeling tone tono sentimental.
  fetal heart tone (FHT) tono cardíaco fetal (TCF).
  heart tone tono cardíaco.
  muscular tone tono muscular.
  myogenic tone tono miógeno, tono neurógeno.
  Traube's double tone tono doble de Traube.
  vagal tone tono vagal.
tongs *n.* tenaza.
  Crutchfield tongs tenaza de Crutchfield.
  Gardner-Wells tongs tenaza de Gardner-Wells.
tongue *n.* lengua.
  adherent tongue lengua adherente.
  amyloid tongue lengua amiloide.
  antibiotic tongue lengua de antibióticos.
  baked tongue lengua horneada.
  bald tongue lengua calva.
  bifid tongue lengua bífida, lengua partida.
  black hairy tongue lengua negra, lengua negra vellosa, lengua vellosa negra.
  black tongue lengua negra, lengua negra vellosa.
  burning tongue lengua quemante.
  cerebriform tongue lengua cerebriforme.
  cleft tongue lengua hendida.
  coated tongue lengua cubierta.
  cobble-stone tongue lengua en guijarro.
  crocodile tongue lengua cuarteada, lengua de cocodrilo.
  dotted tongue lengua graneada, lengua punteada.
  double tongue lengua doble.
  fern leaf tongue lengua en hoja de helecho.
  fissured tongue lengua arrugada, lengua fisurada, lingua fissurata.
  flat tongue lengua plana.
  furred tongue lengua saburral.
  geographic tongue lengua disecada, lengua en mapa, lengua geográfica, lingua geographica.
  grooved tongue lengua plegada.
  hairy tongue lengua pilosa, lengua vellosa.
  hobnail tongue lengua claveteada.

  lobulated tongue lengua lobulada.
  magenta tongue lengua de color magenta, lengua de magenta.
  parrot tongue lengua de loro, lengua de perico.
  raspberry tongue lengua aframbuesada.
  red strawberry tongue lengua en frambuesa roja.
  scrotal tongue lengua escrotal.
  smoker's tongue lengua de los fumadores.
  stippled tongue lengua graneada, lengua punteada.
  strawberry tongue lengua en frambuesa, lengua en fresa.
  sulcated tongue lengua surcada.
  swallowing tongue lengua tragada.
  tie tongue lengua frenada, lengua ligada.
  white strawberry tongue lengua en frambuesa blanca.
  white tongue lengua blanca.
tonic *n.* tónico, -ca.
tonicity *n.* tonicidad.
tonicize *v.* tonificar.
tonicoclonic *adj.* tonicoclónico, -ca.
toning *n.* entonación.
tonoclonic *adj.* tonoclónico, -ca.
tonofibril *n.* tonofibrilla.
tonofilament *n.* tonofilamento.
tonogram *n.* tonograma.
tonograph *n.* tonógrafo.
tonography *n.* tonografía.
  carotid compression tonography tonografía de compresión carotídea.
tonometer *n.* tonómetro.
  applanation tonometer tonómetro de aplanamiento.
  electronic tonometer tonómetro electrónico.
  Gärtner's tonometer tonómetro de Gärtner.
  Goldmann's applanation tonometer tonómetro de aplanamiento de Goldmann.
  impression tonometer tonómetro de impresión.
  indentation tonometer tonómetro de indentación.
  MacKay-Marg electronic tonometer tonómetro electrónico de MacKay-Marg.
  McLean tonometer tonómetro de McLean.
  Mueller electronic tonometer tonómetro electrónico de Mueller.
  pneumatic tonometer tonómetro neumático.
  Recklinghausen tonometer tonómetro de Recklinghausen.
  Schiötz's tonometer tonómetro de Schiötz.
tonometry *n.* tonometría.
  applanation tonometry tonometría de aplanación, tonometría de aplanamiento.
  indentation tonometry tonometría de indentación.
tonophant *n.* tonofante, tonofanto.
tonophyte *n.* tonofito.
tonoplast *n.* tonoplasto.
tonoscillograph *n.* tonosciógrafo.
tonoscope *n.* tonoscopio.
tonotopic *adj.* tonotópico, -ca.
tonotopicity *n.* tonotopicidad.
tonotropic *adj.* tonotrópico, -ca.
tonsil *n.* amígdala.
tonsillar *adj.* tonsilar.
tonsillary *adj.* tonsilar.
tonsillectomy *n.* tonsilectomía.
tonsillith *n.* tonsilito.
tonsillitis *n.* amigdalitis, tonsilitis.
  acute parenchymatous tonsillitis amigdalitis parenquimatosa aguda.

acute tonsillitis amigdalitis aguda.

caseous tonsillitis amigdalitis caseosa.

diphtheritic tonsillitis amigdalitis diftérica.

follicular tonsillitis amigdalitis folicular.

herpetic tonsillitis amigdalitis herpética.

lacunar tonsillitis tonsilitis caseosoa, tonsilitis lacunar, tonsilitis lagunar.

lingual tonsillitis amigdalitis lingual.

mycotic tonsillitis amigdalitis micótica.

parenchymatous tonsillitis tonsilitis parenquimatosa.

preglottic tonsillitis amigdalitis preglótica.

streptococcal tonsillitis amigdalitis estreptocócica.

superficial tonsillitis amigdalitis superficial, tonsilitis superficial.

supurative tonsillitis amigdalitis supurativa.

tonsillitis lenta amigdalitis lenta.

Vincent tonsillitis tonsilitis de Vincent.

Vincent's tonsillitis amigdalitis de Vincent.

tonsilloadenoidectomy *n.* adenoamigdalectomía.

tonsillohemisporosis *n.* amigdalohemisporosis.

tonsillolith *n.* tonsilolito.

tonsillomoniliasis *n.* tonsilomoniliasis.

tonsillomycosis *n.* tonsilomicosis.

tonsillo-oidiosis *n.* amigdaloidiosis.

tonsillopathy *n.* tonsilopatía.

tonsilloprive *adj.* amigdaloprivo, -va.

tonsilloscopy *n.* tonsiloscopia.

tonsillotome *n.* amigdalótomo, tonsilótomo.

tonsillotomy *n.* amigdalotomía, tonsilotomía.

tonus *n.* tonicidad, tono, tonus.

tooth *n.* diente, muela.

acrylic resin tooth diente de acrílico, diente de resina acrílica.

anatomic tooth diente anatómico.

artificial tooth diente artificial.

buck tooth diente prominente, diente salido.

canine tooth colmillo.

cheoplastic tooth diente queoplástico.

crossbite tooth diente en mordida cruzada.

cross-pin tooth diente de clavillos cruzados.

dead tooth diente muerto.

deciduous tooth diente decidual.

devitalized tooth diente desvitalizado.

embedded tooth diente intruido.

extruded tooth diente extruido.

fluoridated tooth diente fluorado.

Fournier tooth diente de Fournier.

fused tooth diente fusionado.

geminated tooth diente geminado.

ghost tooth diente fantasma.

Goslee tooth diente de Goslee.

green tooth diente verde.

Horner's tooth diente de Horner.

impacted tooth diente impactado.

malacotic tooth diente malacótico.

malposed tooth diente en malposición.

metal insert tooth diente con inserción de metal.

migrating tooth diente migratorio.

milk tooth diente de leche.

mottled tooth diente manchado.

mulberry tooth diente en mora.

natal tooth diente natal.

neonatal tooth diente neonatal.

non-anatomic tooth diente no anatómico.

non-vital tooth diente no vital.

normally posed tooth diente en posición normal.

notched tooth diente con muescas.

permanent tooth diente permanente.

plastic tooth diente de plástico.

premature tooth diente prematuro.

premilk tooth diente prelácteo.

primary tooth diente primario.

protruding tooth diente protruido.

pulpless tooth diente despulpado.

rake tooth diente en rastrillo.

sclerotic tooth diente esclerótico.

screwdriver tooth diente de Hutchinson, diente en destornillador.

second tooth diente secundario.

snaggle tooth diente fuera de lugar.

spaced tooth diente espaciado.

straightpin tooth diente de espiga recta.

submerged tooth diente sumergido.

supernumerary tooth diente supernumerario.

supplemental tooth diente complementario.

syphilitic tooth diente sifilítico.

temporary tooth diente temporal.

tube tooth diente en tubo.

Turner's tooth diente de Turner.

unerupted tooth diente no erupcionado.

vital tooth diente vital.

wandering of a tooth diente errante.

wisdom tooth muela del juicio.

zero degree tooth diente de grado cero.

topagnosia *n.* topagnosia.

topagnosis *n.* topagnosia, topagnosis.

topalgia *n.* topalgia, topoalgia.

topesthesia *n.* topestesia.

tophaceus *adj.* tofáceo, -a.

topholipoma *n.* tofolipoma.

tophus *n.* tofo.

topical *adj.* tópico, -ca.

topicum *n.* tópico.

topistic *adj.* topístico, -ca.

topoanesthesia *n.* topoanestesia.

topochemistry *n.* topoquímica.

topodysesthesia *n.* topodisestesia.

topognosis *n.* topognosia, topognosis.

topogram *n.* topograma.

topographic *adj.* topográfico, -ca.

topographical *adj.* topográfico, -ca.

topography *n.* Tópica, topografía.

anatomical topography topografía anatómica.

topology *n.* topología.

toponarcosis *n.* toponarcosis.

toponym *n.* topónimo.

toponymy *n.* toponimia.

topoparesthesia *n.* topoparestesia.

topopathogenesis *n.* topopatogenia.

topophylaxis *n.* topofilaxia, topofilaxis.

toposcope *n.* toposcopio.

topothermesthesiometer *n.* topotermestesiómetro.

topovaccinotherapy *n.* topovacunación, topovacunoterapia.

torcula *n.* prensa, tórcula.

toric *adj.* tórico, -ca.

tormina *n.* tormina.

torminal *adj.* torminal.

torose *adj.* toroso, -sa.

torous *adj.* toroso, -sa.

torpent *adj.* torpente.

torpid *adj.* tórpido, -da.

torpidity *n.* torpidez.

torpor *n.* torpor.

torpor retinae torpor retinae, torpor retinal.

torque *n.* torque.

torsiometer *n.* torsiómetro.

torsion *n.* torsión.

clasp torsion torsión del gancho.

femoral torsion torsión femoral.

negative torsion torsión negativa.

positive torsion torsión positiva.

tibial torsion torsión tibial.

torsion of a tooth torsión de un diente.

torsion of the testis torsión del cordón espermático, torsión del testículo, torsión testicular.

torsionometer *n.* torsionómetro.

torsiversion *n.* torsiversión.

torso *n.* torso.

torsocclusion *n.* torsoclusión.

torso-occlusion *n.* torsoclusión.

torticollis *n.* torticolis, tortícolis.

congenital torticollis tortícolis congénita.

dermatogenic torticollis tortícolis dermatógena.

dystonic torticollis tortícolis distónica.

fixed torticollis tortícolis fija.

intermittent torticollis tortícolis intermitente.

labyrinthine torticollis tortícolis laberíntica.

myogenic torticollis tortícolis miógeno.

neurogenic torticollis tortícolis neurógeno.

ocular torticollis tortícolis ocular.

reflex torticollis tortícolis refleja.

rheumatoid torticollis tortícolis reumática, tortícolis reumatoide.

spasmodic torticollis tortícolis convulsiva, tortícolis espasmódica.

spurious torticollis tortícolis espuria, tortícolis falsa.

symptomatic torticollis tortícolis sintomática.

tortuous *adj.* tortuoso, -sa.

toruloma *n.* toruloma.

Torulopsis Torulopsis.

torulopsosis *n.* torulopsosis.

torulosis *n.* torulosis.

torulus *n.* torulo, tórulo.

torus *n.* toro, torus.

totemism *n.* totemismo.

totemistic *adj.* totemístico, -ca.

totipotent *adj.* totipotente.

totipotentia *n.* totipotencia.

totipotential *adj.* totipotencial.

totipotentiality *n.* totipotencialidad.

touch *n.* tacto.

abdominal touch tacto abdominal.

constant touch tacto mantenido.

double touch tacto doble.

rectal touch tacto rectal.

royal touch tacto real.

vaginal touch tacto vaginal.

vesical touch tacto vesical.

touching *n.* toque.

tour *n.* vuelta.

tour de maitre vuelta de maestro.

tourniquet *n.* torniquete.

automatic rotating tourniquet torniquete rotatorio automático.

Dupuytren tourniquet torniquete de Dupuytren.

Esmarch tourniquet torniquete de Esmarch.

pneumatic tourniquet torniquete neumático.

scalp tourniquet torniquete de cuero cabelludo.

toxalbumic *adj.* toxalbúmico, -ca.

toxanemia *n.* toxanemia.

toxemia *n.* toxemia.

alimentary toxemia toxemia alimentaria, toxemia alimenticia.

eclamptic toxemia toxemia eclámptica, toxemia eclamptogénica.

eclamptogenic toxemia toxemia eclámptica, toxemia eclamptogénica.

hydatid toxemia toxemia hidatídica.

toxemia of pregnancy toxemia del embarazo, toxemia gravídica.

toxemic *adj.* toxémico, -ca.

toxic *adj.* tóxico, -ca.
toxicemia *n.* toxicemia, toxicohemia.
toxicide *adj.* toxicida.
toxicity *n.* toxicidad.
  acute toxicity toxicidad aguda.
  cochlear toxicity toxicidad coclear.
  oxygen toxicity toxicidad del oxígeno.
  pulmonary oxygen toxicity toxicidad por oxígeno, toxicidad pulmonar por oxígeno.
  vestibular toxicity toxicidad vestibular.
toxicoderma *n.* toxicodermia.
toxicodermatitis *n.* toxicodermatitis.
toxicodermatosis *n.* toxicodermatosis.
toxicogenic *adj.* toxicogénico, -ca, toxicógeno, -na.
toxicohemla *n.* toxicemia, toxicohemia.
toxicoid *adj.* toxicoide.
toxicokinetics *n.* toxicocinética.
toxicolgy *n.* toxicología.
toxicologic *adj.* toxicológico, -ca.
toxicologist *n.* toxicólogo, -ga.
toxicomania *n.* toxicomanía.
toxicomaniac *n.* toxicómano, -na.
toxicopectic *adj.* toxicopéctico, -ca.
toxicopexia *n.* toxicopexia.
toxicopexy *n.* toxicopexia.
toxicosis *n.* toxicosis.
  alimentary toxicosis toxicosis alimentaria, toxicosis alimenticia.
  endogenic toxicosis toxicosis endógena.
  exogenic toxicosis toxicosis exógena.
  gestational toxicosis toxicosis gestacional.
  hemorrhagic capillary toxicosis toxicosis capilar hemorrágica.
  retention toxicosis toxicosis de retención.
  thyroid toxicosis toxicosis tiroidea.
  triiodothyronine (T3) toxicosis toxicosis por triyodotironina (T3).
toxiferous *adj.* toxífero, -ra, toxiferoso, -sa.
toxigenic *adj.* toxigénico, -ca, toxígeno, -na.
toxigenicity *n.* toxigenicidad.
toxignomic *adj.* toxignomónico, -ca.
toxin *n.* tóxico, toxina.
toxinemia *n.* toxinemia.
toxinfection *n.* toxiinfección.
toxinic *adj.* toxínico, -ca.
toxinogenic *adj.* toxinogénico, -ca, toxinógeno, -na.
toxinogenicity *n.* toxinogenicidad.
toxinology *n.* toxinología.
toxinosis *n.* toxinosis.
toxinotherapy *n.* toxinoterapia, toxiterapia.
toxipathic *adj.* toxipático, -ca.
toxipathy *n.* toxipatía.
toxipherous *adj.* toxicóforo, -ra.
toxocaral *adj.* toxocariásico, -ca.
toxocariasis *n.* toxocariasis.
toxogen *adj.* toxógeno, -na.
toxogenin *n.* toxogenina.
toxoglobulin *n.* toxoglobulina.
toxoid *n.* toxoide.
toxoid-antitoxoid *n.* toxoide-antitoxoide.
toxoneme *n.* toxonema.
toxonosis *n.* toxonosis.
toxopexic *adj.* toxopéxico, -ca.
toxophil *adj.* toxófilo, -la.
toxophilic *adj.* toxofílico, -ca.
toxophobia *n.* toxofobia.
toxophore *adj.* toxóforo, -ra.
Toxoplasma Toxoplasma.
toxoplasmosis *n.* toxoplasmosis.
  acquired toxoplasmosis in adults toxoplasmosis adquirida en adultos.
  congenital toxoplasmosis toxoplasmosis congénita.

toxoprotein *n.* toxoproteína.
toxuria *n.* toxuria.
trabecula *n.* trabécula.
trabecular *adj.* trabecular.
trabeculate *adj.* trabeculado, -da.
trabeculation *n.* trabeculación.
trabeculectomy *n.* trabeculectomía.
trabeculoplasty *n.* trabeculoplastia.
  laser trabeculoplasty trabeculoplastia láser.
trabeculotomy *n.* trabeculotomía.
tracer *n.* trazador.
  arrow-point tracer trazador de punta de flecha.
  isotopic tracer trazador isotópico.
  needle-point tracer trazador de punta de aguja.
  stylus tracer trazador de estilo.
trachea *n.* tráquea.
tracheal *adj.* traqueal.
trachealgia *n.* traquealgia.
trachectasy *n.* traquectasia.
tracheirrhagia *n.* traqueorragia.
tracheitis *n.* traqueítis.
trachelagra *n.* traquelagra.
trachelalis *n.* traquelalis.
trachelectomy *n.* traquelectomía.
trachelematoma *n.* traquelematoma.
trachelian *adj.* traqueliano, -na.
trachelism *n.* traquelismo.
trachelismus *n.* traquelismo.
trachelitis *n.* traquelitis.
trachelocele *n.* traquelocele.
trachelocyllosis *n.* traquelocilosis.
trachelocyrtosis *n.* traquelocirtosis.
trachelocystitis *n.* traquelocistitis.
trachelodorsal *adj.* dorsotraqueliano, -na.
trachelodynia *n.* traquelodinia.
trachelokyphosis *n.* traquelocifosis.
trachelologist *n.* traquelólogo, -ga.
trachelology *n.* traquelología.
trachelo-occipitalis *adj.* traquelooccipital.
trachelopanus *n.* traquelopano.
trachelopexy *n.* traquelopexia.
trachelophyma *n.* traquelofima.
tracheloplasty *n.* traqueloplastia.
trachelorrhaphy *n.* traquelorrafia.
tracheloschisis *n.* traquelosquisis.
trachelosyringorrhaphy *n.* traquelosiringorrafia.
trachelotomy *n.* traquelotomía.
tracheoaerocele *n.* traqueoaerocele.
tracheobiliary *adj.* traqueobiliar.
tracheobronchial *adj.* traqueobronquial.
tracheobronchitis *n.* traqueobronquitis.
tracheobronchomalacia *n.* traqueobroncomalacia.
tracheobronchomegaly *n.* traqueobroncomegalia.
tracheobronchoscopy *n.* traqueobroncoscopia.
tracheocele *n.* traqueocele.
tracheoesophageal *adj.* traqueoesofágico, -ca.
tracheofissure *n.* traqueofisura.
tracheofistulization *n.* traqueofistulización.
tracheogenic *adj.* traqueógeno, -a.
tracheolaryngeal *adj.* traqueolaríngeo, -a.
tracheolaryngotomy *n.* traqueolaringotomía.
tracheomalacia *n.* traqueomalacia.
tracheomegaly traqueomegalia.
tracheopathia *n.* traqueopatía.
  tracheopathia osteoplastica traqueopatía osteoplásica.
tracheopathy *n.* traqueopatía.
tracheopharyngeal *adj.* traqueofaríngeo, -a.
tracheophonesis *n.* traqueofonesis.

tracheophony *n.* traqueofonía.
tracheoplasty *n.* traqueoplastia.
tracheopyosis *n.* traqueopiosis.
tracheorrhaphy *n.* traqueorrafia.
tracheoschisis *n.* traqueosquisis.
tracheoscope *n.* traqueoscopio.
tracheoscopic *adj.* traqueoscópico, -ca.
tracheoscopy *n.* traqueoscopia.
tracheostenosis *n.* traqueoestenosis, traqueostenosis.
tracheostoma *n.* traqueostoma.
tracheostomize *v.* traqueostomizar.
tracheostomy *n.* traqueostomía.
tracheotome *n.* traqueótomo.
tracheotomize *v.* traqueotomizar.
tracheotomy *n.* traqueotomía.
  inferior tracheotomy traqueotomía inferior.
  superior tracheotomy traqueotomía superior.
trachitis *n.* traqueítis, traquitis.
trachoma *n.* tracoma.
  Arlt's trachoma tracoma de Arlt.
  granular trachoma tracoma folicular, tracoma granular.
  trachoma of the vocal bands tracoma de las cuerdas vocales.
  Türck's trachoma tracoma de Türck.
trachomatous *adj.* tracomatoso, -sa.
trachychromatic *adj.* traquicromático, -ca.
trachyphonia *n.* traquifonía.
tracing *n.* trazado, trazo.
track *n.* rastro.
  germ track rastro germinal.
tract *n.* haz[1], tracto.
  uveal tract úvea.
traction *n.* tracción.
  90-90 traction tracción 90-90.
  adhesive skin traction tracción cutánea adhesiva.
  ambulatory traction tracción ambulatoria.
  axis traction tracción axial, tracción por el eje.
  balanced traction tracción equilibrada.
  Bryant's traction tracción de Bryant.
  Buck's skin traction tracción cutánea de Buck.
  Buck's traction tracción de Buck.
  cutaneous traction tracción cutánea.
  Dunlop skeletal traction tracción esquelética de Dunlop.
  Dunlop skin traction tracción cutánea de Dunlop.
  elastic traction tracción elástica.
  external traction tracción externa.
  halo traction tracción en halo.
  halopelvic traction tracción halopélvica.
  head traction tracción cefálica.
  intermaxillary traction tracción intermaxilar.
  isometric traction tracción isométrica.
  isotonic traction tracción isotónica.
  maxillomandibular traction tracción maxilomandibular, tracción maxilomaxilar.
  Neufeld roller traction tracción rodante de Neufeld.
  non-adhesive skin traction tracción cutánea no adhesiva.
  orthopedic traction tracción ortopédica.
  Quigley traction tracción de Quigley.
  Russell traction tracción de Russell.
  Sayre's suspension traction tracción de suspensión de Sayre.
  skeletal traction tracción esquelética.
  skin traction tracción de la piel.
  tongue traction tracción lingual.
  weight traction tracción con peso.

tractor *n.* tractor.
Lowsley's tractor tractor de Lowsley.
prostatic tractor tractor prostático.
Syms tractor tractor de Syms.
urethral tractor tractor uretral.
Young prostatic tractor tractor prostático de Young.
tractotomy *n.* tractotomía.
anterolateral tractotomy tractotomía anterolateral.
intramedullary tractotomy tractotomía intramedular.
pyramidal tractotomy tractotomía piramidal.
Schwartz tractotomy tractotomía de Schwartz.
Sjöqvist tractotomy tractotomía de Sjöqvist.
spinal tractotomy tractotomía espinal.
spinothalamic tractotomy tractotomía espinotalámica.
trigeminal tractotomy tractotomía trigémina.
Walker tractotomy tractotomía de Walker.
tractus haz[1], tracto, tractus.
tragal *adj.* tragal.
tragion *n.* tragion, tragión.
tragomaschalia *n.* tragomascalia.
tragophonia *n.* tragofonía.
tragophony *n.* tragofonía.
tragopodia *n.* tragopodia.
tragus trago, tragus.
train *v.* entrenar.
trainable *adj.* adiestrable.
training *n.* adiestramiento, entrenamiento.
active resistance training (ART) entrenamiento de resistencia activa (ERA).
aerobic training entrenamiento aeróbico.
assertive training adiestramiento asertivo, entrenamiento afirmativo, entrenamiento asertivo.
aversive training entrenamiento aversivo.
expressive training adiestramiento expresivo.
hygienic habit training entrenamiento en hábitos higiénicos.
inspiratory resistance muscle training entrenamiento muscular con resistencia a la inspiración.
orthopic training entrenamiento ortópico.
social skills training adiestramiento en habilidades sociales, entrenamiento en habilidades sociales.
trait *n.* rasgo.
acquired trait rasgo adquirido.
Bombay trait rasgo de Bombay.
categorical trait rasgo categórico.
character trait rasgo caracterial, rasgo del carácter.
chromosomal trait rasgo cromosómico.
codominant trait rasgo codominante.
dependent trait rasgo dependiente.
dominant trait rasgo dominante.
hereditary trait rasgo hereditario.
intermediate trait rasgo intermedio.
marker trait rasgo marcador.
non-penetrant trait rasgo no penetrante.
personality trait rasgo de la personalidad.
qualitative trait rasgo cualitativo.
secretor trait rasgo secretor.
sex-conditioned trait rasgo condicionado por el sexo.
sex-influenced trait rasgo influido por el sexo.
sex-limited trait rasgo limitado por el sexo.
sex-linked trait rasgo ligado al sexo.

sickle cell trait rasgo de células drepanocíticas.
trajector *n.* trayector.
tramitis *n.* tramitis.
trance *n.* trance.
alcoholic trance trance alcohólico.
death trance trance mortal.
hypnotic trance trance hipnótico.
induced trance trance inducido.
somnambulistic trance trance de sonambulismo.
tranquilizer *n.* tranquilizante.
major tranquilizer tranquilizante mayor.
minor tranquilizer tranquilizante menor.
transabdominal *adj.* transabdominal.
transaction *n.* transacción.
false transaction transacción falsa.
ulterior transaction transacción ulterior.
transaminasemia *n.* transaminasemia.
transanimation *n.* transanimación.
transaortic *adj.* transaórtico, -ca.
transappendageal *adj.* transapendicular.
transatrial *adj.* transauricular.
transaudient *adj.* transaudiente.
transaxial *adj.* transaxil.
transbasal *adj.* transbasal.
transcalent *adj.* transcalente.
transcalvarial *adj.* transcalvarial.
transcapsidation *n.* transcapsidación.
transcatheter *adj.* transcatéter.
transcervical *adj.* transcervical.
transcondylar *adj.* transcondilar.
transcondyloid *adj.* transcondíleo, -a, transcondiloide.
transcortical *adj.* transcortical.
transcricothyroid *adj.* transcricotiroideo, -a.
transcript *adj.* transcripto, -ta.
transcription *n.* transcripción.
transcutaneous *adj.* transcutáneo, -a.
transcytosis *n.* transcitosis.
transdermal *adj.* transdérmico, -ca.
transduce *v.* transducir.
transductant *adj.* transductante.
transducter *n.* transductor.
flow transducter transductor de flujo.
transduction *n.* transducción.
abortive transduction transducción abortiva.
complete transduction transducción completa.
general transduction transducción general.
high frequency transduction transducción de alta frecuencia.
low frequency transduction transducción de baja frecuencia.
specialized transduction transducción especializada.
specific transduction transducción específica.
transdural *adj.* transdural.
transect *v.* transeccionar.
transection *n.* transección.
transepidermal *adj.* transepidérmico, -ca.
transepithelial *adj.* transepitelial.
transethmoidal *adj.* transetmoidal.
transfaunation *n.* transfaunación.
transfection *n.* transfección.
osmotic transfection transfección osmótica.
transfectoma *n.* transfectoma.
transfer *n.* transferencia[1], traslado.
charge transfer transferencia de carga.
embryo transfer transferencia embrionaria.
gene transfer transferencia génica.
group transfer transferencia de grupo.
pivot transfer traslado con pivotación.
sliding transfer traslado por deslizamiento.
tendon transfer transferencia de tendón.

transference *n.* transferencia[2].
extrasensory thought transference transferencia de pensamiento, transferencia por pensamiento extrasensorial.
negative transference transferencia negativa.
positive transference transferencia positiva.
thought transference transferencia de pensamiento, transferencia por pensamiento extrasensorial.
transfixion *n.* transfixión.
transformant *adj.* transformante.
transformation *n.* transformación.
asbestos transformation transformación por asbesto.
bacterial transformation transformación bacteriana.
blastic transformation transformación blástica.
cell transformation transformación celular.
Fourier's transformation (FT) transformación de Fourier (TF).
globular-fibrosus transformation (G-F transformation) transformación globular fibrosa transformación G-F).
Lineweaver-Burk transformation transformación de Lineweaver-Burk.
Lobry de Bruyn-van Ekenstein transformation transformación de Lobry de Bruyn-van Ekenstein.
logit transformation transformación logit.
lymphocyte transformation transformación de linfocitos, transformación linfocitaria, transformación linfocítica.
transformer *n.* transformador.
transfuse *v.* transfundir.
transfusion *n.* transfusión.
arterial transfusion transfusión arterial.
autologous transfusion transfusión autóloga.
blood transfusion transfusión de sangre.
buffy coat transfusion transfusión de leucocitos.
direct transfusion transfusión directa.
drip transfusion transfusión por goteo.
exchange transfusion transfusión de recambio.
exsanguination transfusion transfusión exanguino, transfusión por exanguinación.
fetomaternal transfusion transfusión fetomaterna.
granulocyte transfusion transfusión de granulocitos.
immediate transfusion transfusión inmediata.
indirect transfusion transfusión indirecta.
intraperitoneal transfusion transfusión intraperitoneal.
intrauterine transfusion transfusión intrauterina.
mediate transfusion transfusión mediata.
peritoneal transfusion transfusión peritoneal.
placental transfusion transfusión placentaria.
reciprocal transfusion transfusión recíproca.
replacement transfusion transfusión de reemplazo, transfusión de sustitución.
subcutaneous transfusion transfusión subcutánea.
total substitution transfusion transfusión de sustitución total, transfusión total.
twin-to-twin transfusion transfusión gemelo-gemelar.
transgenation *n.* transgenación.
transgenic *adj.* transgénico, -ca.
transhiatal *adj.* transhiatal.
transient *adj.* transitorio, -a.

transiliac *adj.* transilíaco, -ca.
transilient *adj.* transiliente.
transillumination *n.* transiluminación.
transinsular *adj.* transinsular.
transischiac *adj.* transisquiático, -ca.
transisthmian *adj.* transistmiano, -na, transístmico, -ca.
transit *n.* tránsito.
  intestinal transit tránsito intestinal.
transition *n.* transición.
  cervicothoracic transition transición cervicotorácica.
  isomeric transition transición isomérica.
  midlife transition transición de la vida media.
transitional *adj.* transicional.
translateral *adj.* translateral.
translation *n.* traducción.
  nick translation traducción de muesca.
translocation *n.* translocación, traslocación.
  balanced translocation translocación balanceada, translocación equilibrada.
  reciprocal translocation translocación recíproca.
  Robertsonian translocation translocación robertsoniana.
translucent *adj.* translúcido, -da.
transmembrane *n.* transmembrana.
transmigration *n.* transmigración.
  external transmigration transmigración externa.
  internal transmigration transmigración interna.
transmissible *adj.* transmisible.
transmission *n.* transmisión.
  duplex transmission transmisión doble.
  ephaptic transmission transmisión efáptica.
  horizontal transmission transmisión horizontal.
  iatrogenic transmission transmisión iatrogénica.
  neurochemical transmission transmisión neuroquímica.
  neurohumoral transmission transmisión neurohumoral.
  neuromuscular transmission transmisión neuromuscular.
  placental transmission transmisión placentaria.
  synaptic transmission transmisión sináptica.
  transovarial transmission transmisión transovárica.
  trans-stadial transmission transmisión transestadial.
  vertical transmission transmisión vertical.
transmittance *n.* transmitancia.
transmitter *n.* transmisor, -ra.
transmural *adj.* transmural.
transocular *adj.* transocular.
transonance *n.* trasonancia.
transorbital *adj.* transorbitario, -a.
transovarial *adj.* transovárico, -ca.
transparent *adj.* transparente.
transparietal *adj.* transparietal.
transpeptidation *n.* transpeptidación.
transperitoneal *adj.* transperitoneal.
transphosphorylation *n.* transfosforilación.
transpirable *adj.* transpirable.
transpiration *n.* transpiración.
  pulmonary transpiration transpiración pulmonar.
transpire *v.* transpirar.
transplacental *adj.* transplacentario, -a.
transplant *n.* trasplantar[1], trasplante.
  allogeneic transplant trasplante alogeneico, trasplante autoplástico.

bone marrow transplant trasplante de médula ósea.
  corneal transplant trasplante corneal, trasplante de córnea.
  fetal tissue transplant trasplante de tejido fetal.
  Gallie transplant trasplante de Gallie.
  heart transplant trasplante cardíaco, trasplante de corazón.
  heteroplastic transplant trasplante heteroplástico.
  heterotopic transplant trasplante heterotópico.
  HLA-identical transplant trasplante HLA idéntico.
  homoplastic transplant trasplante homoplástico.
  homotopic transplant trasplante homotópico.
  liver transplant trasplante hepático.
  orthotopic transplant trasplante ortotópico.
  pancreatic transplant trasplante pancreático.
  pancreaticoduodenal transplant trasplante pancreaticoduodenal.
  renal transplant trasplante renal.
  syngenesioplastic transplant trasplante singenesioplástico.
  tendon transplant trasplante del tendón, trasplante tendinosos.
  tooth transplant trasplante dental.
transplantation *n.* trasplante.
transpleural *adj.* transpleural.
transport *n.* transporte.
  active transport transporte activo.
  axoplasmic transport transporte axoplasmático.
  bone transport transporte óseo.
  bulk transport transporte de masa.
  ciliary mucus transport transporte ciliar del moco.
  iron transport transporte de hierro.
  oxygen transport transporte de oxígeno.
  passive transport transporte pasivo.
  vesicular transport transporte vesicular.
transposition *n.* transposición, trasposición.
  corrected transposition of great vessels trasposición corregida de grandes arterias, trasposición corregida de grandes vasos.
  partial transposition of great vessels trasposición parcial de grandes vasos.
  transposition of great vessels trasposición de grandes arterias, trasposición de grandes vasos, trasposición de los troncos arteriales.
transpubic *adj.* transpúbico, -ca.
transsegmental *adj.* transegmental, transegmentario, -a.
transseptal *adj.* transeptal.
transsexual *adj.* transexual.
transsexualism *n.* transexualismo.
transsphenoidal *adj.* transesfenoidal.
transsternal *adj.* transesternal.
transsynaptic *adj.* transináptico, -ca.
transtemporal *adj.* transtemporal.
transtentorial *adj.* transtentorial.
transthalamic *adj.* transtalámico, -ca.
transthermia *n.* transtermia.
transthoracic *adj.* transtorácico, -ca.
transthoracotomy *n.* transtoracotomía.
transtracheal *adj.* transtraqueal.
transtrochantericosteotomy *n.* transtrochantericosteotomía.
transtympanic *adj.* transtimpánico, -ca.
transubstantiation *n.* transustanciación.
transudate[1] *n.* transudado, trasudado.
transudate[2] *v.* transudar.

transudation *n.* transudación, trasudación.
transureteroureterostomy *n.* transureteroureterostomía.
transurethral *adj.* transuretral.
transvaginal *adj.* transvaginal.
transvaterian *adj.* transvateriano, -na.
transvector *n.* transvector.
transventricular *adj.* transventricular.
transversalis *adj.* transversal.
transverse *adj.* transverso, -sa.
transversectomy *n.* transversectomía.
transversion *n.* transversión.
transversocostal *adj.* transversocostal.
transversotomy *n.* tranversotomía.
transversus *adj.* transverso, -sa.
transvesical *adj.* transvesical.
transvestism *n.* travestismo.
transvestite *n.* travestido, -da.
trapeziform *adj.* trapeciforme.
trapeziometacarpal *adj.* trapeciometacarpiano, -na.
trapezium *n.* trapecio.
trapezoid *adj.* trapezoide, trapezoideo, -a.
trascendence *n.* trascendencia.
trascendent *adj.* trascendental, trascendente.
traslation *n.* traslación.
trasplantar *adj.* trasplantar[2].
trasplantectomy *n.* trasplantectomía.
trauma *n.* trauma.
  acoustic trauma trauma acústico.
  birth trauma trauma del nacimiento.
  birth trauma of the brachial plexus trauma obstrético del plexo braquial.
  cranioencephalic trauma trauma craneoencefálico.
  missile wound trauma trauma por herida de bala.
  occlusal trauma trauma oclusal.
  potential trauma trauma potencial.
  psychic trauma trauma psíquico.
  renal trauma trauma renal.
  spinal cord trauma trauma raquimedular.
  urethral trauma trauma uretral.
traumasthenia *n.* traumastenia.
traumatherapy *n.* traumaterapia.
traumatic *adj.* traumático, -ca.
traumatism *n.* traumatismo.
  abdominal traumatism traumatismo abdominal.
  blunt abdominal traumatism traumatismo abdominal cerrado.
  open abdominal traumatism traumatismo abdominal abierto.
  secondary occlusal traumatism traumatismo oclusal secundario.
traumatize *v.* traumatizar.
traumatogenic *adj.* traumatógeno, -na.
traumatologist *n.* traumatólogo, -ga.
traumatology *n.* traumatología.
traumatonesis *n.* traumatonesis.
traumatopathy *n.* traumatopatía.
traumatophilia *n.* traumatofilia.
traumatopnea *n.* traumatopnea.
traumatopyra *n.* traumatópira.
traumatosepsis *n.* traumatosepsis.
traumatosis *n.* traumatosis.
traumatotherapy *n.* traumatoterapia.
traumatropism *n.* traumatropismo.
tray *n.* bandeja.
  acrylic resin tray bandeja de resina acrílica.
  annealing tray bandeja de recocido.
  impression tray bandeja de impresión, bandeja para impresiones.
treat *v.* tratar.
treatment *n.* tratamiento.

active treatment tratamiento activo.

adjuvant treatment tratamiento adyuvante.

antigen treatment tratamiento antigénico.

anti-rejection treatment tratamiento anti-rrechazo.

autoserous treatment tratamiento autoséri-co, tratamiento con autosueros.

Bier's combined treatment tratamiento de Bier combinado.

Bier's treatment tratamiento de Bier.

Bouchardat's treatment tratamiento de Bouchardat.

Brehmer's treatment tratamiento de Brehmer.

Brown-Séquard's treatment tratamiento de Brown-Séquard.

causal treatment tratamiento causal.

coadjuvant treatment tratamiento coadyuvante.

coma insulinic treatment tratamiento de coma insulínico, tratamiento por coma insulínico.

combined modality treatment tratamiento combinado.

conservative treatment tratamiento conservador.

curative treatment tratamiento curativo.

diabetic treatment tratamiento de la diabetes.

dietetic treatment tratamiento dietético.

empiric treatment tratamiento empírico.

eventration treatment tratamiento de eventración.

expectant treatment tratamiento expectante.

Frenkel's treatment tratamiento de Frenkel.

Goeckerman treatment tratamiento dc Goeckerman.

Hartel's treatment tratamiento de Hartel.

high-frequency treatment tratamiento de alta frecuencia.

hygienic treatment tratamiento higiénico.

immunosuppressive treatment tratamiento inmunosupresor.

insulin shock treatment tratamiento de choque insulínico.

isoserum treatment tratamiento isosérico.

Kenny treatment tratamiento de Kenny.

Klapp's creeping treatment tratamiento reptante de Klapp.

Lerich's treatment tratamiento de Lerich.

light treatment tratamiento de luz, tratamiento luminoso.

malarial treatment tratamiento del paludismo.

Matas' treatment tratamiento de Matas.

medicinal treatment tratamiento medicinal.

neoadjuvant treatment tratamiento neoadyuvante.

organ treatment tratamiento orgánico.

Orr treatment tratamiento de Orr.

palliative treatment tratamiento paliativo.

poisoning treatment tratamiento de las intoxicaciones.

preventive treatment tratamiento preventivo.

prophylactic treatment tratamiento profiláctico.

radical treatment tratamiento radical.

root canal treatment tratamiento de conducto radicular.

salicyl treatment tratamiento con salicílicos.

Schlösser's treatment tratamiento de Schlösser.

slush treatment tratamiento de mascarilla.

solar treatment tratamiento solar.

specific treatment tratamiento específico.

stepped treatment tratamiento escalonado.

string method treatment tratamiento con el método del hilo.

subcoma insulin treatment tratamiento de subcoma insulínico.

substitutive treatment tratamiento sustitutivo.

supporting treatment tratamiento de sostén.

surgical treatment tratamiento quirúrgico.

symptomatic treatment tratamiento sintomático.

Tallerman treatment tratamiento de Tallermann.

tannic acid treatment taninación.

teleradium treatment tratamiento con teleradio.

three-dye treatment tratamiento de tres colorantes.

thymus treatment tratamiento con timo.

thyroid treatment tratamiento con tiroides.

Trueta treatment tratamiento de Trueta.

underwater treatment tratamiento bajo el agua.

zone treatment tratamiento zonal.

trema *n.* trema.

Trematoda Trematoda.

trematodes *n.* Trematodes, trematodos.

trematodiasis *n.* trematodiasis.

tremogram *n.* tremograma.

tremograph *n.* tremógrafo.

tremolabile *adj.* tremolábil.

tremor *n.* temblor, tremor.

action tremor temblor de acción.

alternating tremor temblor alternante.

arsenical tremor temblor arsenical, temblor por arsénico.

benign essential tremor temblor esencial, temblor esencial benigno, temblor esencial hereditario.

cerebellar tremor temblor cerebeloso.

coarse tremor temblor burdo, temblor grueso, temblor tosco.

continuous tremor temblor continuo.

essential tremor temblor esencial, temblor esencial benigno, temblor esencial hereditario.

familial tremor temblor familiar.

fibrillary tremor temblor fibrilar.

fine tremor temblor fino.

flapping tremor temblor aleteante, temblor de aleteo.

head tremor temblor de la cabeza.

hereditary essential tremor temblor esencial, temblor esencial benigno, temblor esencial hereditario.

heredofamilial tremor temblor heredofamiliar.

hysterical tremor temblor histérico.

induced tremor temblor inducido.

intentional tremor temblor de intención, temblor intencional.

intermittent tremor temblor intermitente.

kinetic tremor temblor cinético.

mercurial tremor temblor mercurial.

metallic tremor temblor metálico.

muscular tremor temblor muscular.

Parkinsonian tremor temblor parkinsoniano.

passive tremor temblor pasivo.

perioral tremor temblor perioral.

persistent tremor temblor persistente.

physiologic tremor temblor fisiológico.

postural tremor temblor postural.

progressive cerebellar tremor temblor cerebeloso progresivo.

purring tremor temblor de ronroneo.

rest tremor temblor de reposo.

resting tremor temblor de reposo.

saturnine tremor temblor saturnino.

senile tremor temblor senil.

static tremor temblor estático.

toxic tremor temblor tóxico.

tremor cordis temblor cardíaco.

tremor linguae temblor lingual.

tremor opiophagorum temblor opiophago-rum, temblor por opio.

tremor tendinum temblor de los tendones, temblor tendinoso.

trombone tremor of the tongue temblor en trombón de la lengua.

volitional tremor temblor volicional, temblor volitivo.

tremorgram *n.* tremorgrama.

tremostable *adj.* tremoestable.

tremulor *n.* tremulor.

tremulous *adj.* tembloroso, -sa, trémulo, -la.

trend *n.* tendencia.

curvilinear trend tendencia curvilínea.

trend of thought tendencia de pensamiento.

trendscriber *n.* trendscriber.

trendscription *n.* trenscription.

trepan *n.* trépano.

trepanation *n.* trepanación.

corneal trepanation trepanación corneal, trepanación de la córnea.

corneoscleral trepanation trepanación esclerocorneal.

dental trepanation trepanación dental.

trepanation of the cornea trepanación corneal, trepanación de la córnea.

trepanner *n.* trepanador, -ra.

trephination *n.* trefinación.

trephine[1] *n.* trefina.

trephine[2] *v.* trepanar.

trephocyte *n.* trefocito.

trepidant *adj.* trepidante.

trepidatio *n.* trepidación.

trepidatio cordis trepidación del corazón.

trepidation *n.* trepidación.

Treponema Treponema.

treponemal *adj.* treponemal, treponémico, -ca.

treponematosis *n.* treponematosis.

treponemiasis *n.* treponemiasis, treponemosis.

treponemicidal *adj.* treponemicida.

trepopnea *n.* trepopnea.

treppe *n.* treppe.

tresis *n.* tresis.

triad *n.* tríada.

acute compression triad tríada de compresión aguda.

adrenomedullary triad tríada adrenomedular.

Andersen's triad tríada de Andersen.

Beck's triad tríada de Beck.

Bezold's triad tríada de Bezold.

buccolinguomasticatory triad tríada buco-linguomasticatoria.

Charcot's triad tríada de Charcot.

childhood triad tríada infantil.

Dieulafoy's triad tríada de Dieulafoy.

Fallot's triad tríada de Fallot.

Grancher's triad tríada de Grancher.

Hull's triad tríada de Hull.

Hutchinson's triad tríada de Hutchinson.

Kartagener's triad tríada de Kartagener.

knee triad tríada desgraciada de la rodilla.

pathologic triad tríada patológica.

primary triad tríada primaria.

Saint's triad tríada de Saint.

triad of Luciani tríada de Luciani.

triad of Schultz tríada de Schultz.

triad of the retinal cone tríada del cono retiniano.

Whipple's triad tríada de Whipple.
triaditis *n.* triaditis.
triage *n.* triage.
　neonatal triage triage neonatal.
trial *n.* ensayo.
　Bernoulli trial ensayo de Bernoulli.
　clinical trial ensayo clínico.
　crossover trial ensayo cruzado.
　double antibody sandwich trial ensayo de doble anticuerpo en sandwich.
　drug trial ensayo de un fármaco.
triangle *n.* triángulo.
　Burger's scalene triangle triángulo escaleno de Burger.
　Burow's triangle triángulo de Burow.
　Garland's triangle triángulo de Garland.
　Gerhardt's triangle triángulo de Gerhardt.
　Jackson's safety triangle triángulo de seguridad de Jackson.
　Koch's triangle triángulo de Koch.
　Minor's triangle triángulo de Minor.
　surgical triangle triángulo quirúrgico.
　Tweed triangle triángulo de Tweed.
triangular *adj.* triangular.
triangularis *adj.* triangular.
triangulum triángulo, triangulum.
triantebrachia *n.* triantebraquia.
triatomic *adj.* triatómico, -ca.
Triatominae Triatominae.
tribade *n.* tríbada.
tribadism *n.* tribadismo.
tribady *n.* tribadía.
tribasic *adj.* tribásico, -ca.
tribasilar *adj.* tribasilar.
tribe *n.* tribu.
tribology *n.* tribología.
triboluminiscence *n.* triboluminiscencia.
tribrachia *n.* tribraquia.
tribrachius *n.* tribraquio.
tricalcic *adj.* tricálcico, -ca.
tricelullar *adj.* tricelular.
tricephalus *n.* tricéfalo.
triceps *adj.* tríceps.
trichalgia *n.* tricalgia.
trichatrophia *n.* tricatrofia.
trichauxis *n.* tricauxis.
trichiasis *n.* triquiasis.
　anal trichiasis triquiasis anal.
trichilemmal *adj.* triquilémico, -ca.
trichilemmoma *n.* triquilemoma.
Trichina Trichina.
Trichinella Trichinella.
　Trichinella spiralis Trichinella spiralis.
trichinelliasis *n.* triquineliasis.
trichinellosis *n.* triquinelosis.
trichiniasis *n.* triquiniasis.
trichinipherous *adj.* triquinífero, -ra.
trichinization *n.* triquinización.
trichinoscope *n.* triquinoscopio.
trichinosis *n.* triquinosis.
trichinous *adj.* triquinoso, -sa.
trichion *n.* triquión.
trichitis *n.* triquitis.
trichoanesthesia *n.* tricoanestesia.
trichobacteria *n.* tricobacteria.
trichobezoar *n.* tricobezoar.
trichocephaliasis *n.* tricocefaliasis.
trichocephalosis *n.* tricocefalosis.
trichoclasia *n.* tricoclasia.
trichoclasis *n.* tricoclasia, tricoclasis, tricoclastia.
trichocryptosis *n.* tricocriptosis.
trichocyst *n.* tricocisto.
trichodynia *n.* tricodinia.
trichoepithelioma *n.* tricoepitelioma.

　desmoplastic trichoepithelioma tricoepitelioma desmoplásico.
　hereditary multiple trichoepithelioma tricoepitelioma múltiple hereditario.
　trichoepithelioma papillosum multiplex tricoepitelioma papiloso múltiple.
trichoesthesia *n.* tricoestesia.
trichoesthesiometer *n.* tricoestesiómetro.
trichofibroacanthoma *n.* tricofibroacantoma.
trichofibroepithelioma *n.* tricofibroepitelioma.
trichofolliculoma *n.* tricofoliculoma.
trichogen *n.* tricógeno.
trichogenous *adj.* tricogenoso, -sa.
trichoglossia *n.* tricoglosia.
trichographism *n.* tricografismo.
trichohyalin *n.* tricohialina.
trichoid *adj.* tricoide, tricoideo, -a.
tricholeukocyte *n.* tricoleucocito.
tricholith *n.* tricolito.
trichomadesis *n.* tricomadesis.
trichomania *n.* tricomanía.
trichomatosis *n.* tricomatosis.
trichomatous *adj.* tricomatoso, -sa.
trichome *n.* tricoma.
trichomegaly *n.* tricomegalia.
trichomonacidal *adj.* tricomonicida.
trichomonad *n.* tricomona.
trichomonadicidal *adj.* tricomonadicida.
Trichomonadida Trichomonadida.
trichomonal *adj.* tricomonal.
Trichomonas Trichomonas.
trichomoniasis *n.* tricomoniasis.
　trichomoniasis vaginitis tricomoniasis vaginitis.
trichomycetosis *n.* tricomicetosis.
trichomycosis *n.* tricomicosis.
　trichomycosis axillaris tricomicosis axilar.
　trichomycosis chromatica tricomicosis cromática, tricomicosis púbica.
　trichomycosis nodosa tricomicosis nodular, tricomicosis nudosa.
　trichomycosis nodularis tricomicosis nodular, tricomicosis nudosa.
　trichomycosis palmellina tricomicosis palmellina.
　trichomycosis pustulosa tricomicosis pustulosa.
trichonocardiosis *n.* triconocardiasis.
trichonodosis *n.* triconodosis.
trichonosis *n.* triconosis.
　versicolor trichonosis triconosis versicolor.
trichopathic *adj.* tricopático, -ca.
trichopathy *n.* tricopatía.
trichophagy *n.* tricofagia.
trichophytic *adj.* tricofítico, -ca.
trichophytid *n.* tricofítide.
Trichophyton Trichophyton.
trichophytosis *n.* fitoalopecia, tricofitosis.
　rural trichophytosis tricofitosis crural.
　trichophytosis barbae tricofitosis de la barba.
　trichophytosis capitis tricofitosis de la cabeza.
　trichophytosis corporis tricofitosis del cuerpo.
　trichophytosis unguium tricofitosis de las uñas.
trichopoliosis *n.* tricopoliosis.
Trichoptera Trichoptera.
trichoptilosis *n.* tricoptilosis.
trichorrhea *n.* tricorrea.
trichorrhexis *n.* tricorrexia, tricorrexis.
　trichorrhexis invaginata tricorrexis invaginada.
　trichorrhexis nodosa tricorrexis nudosa.

trichoschisis *n.* tricosquisis.
trichoscopy *n.* tricoscopia.
trichosis *n.* tricosis.
　trichosis carunculae tricosis caruncular, tricosis de la carúncula.
　trichosis sensitiva tricosis sensitiva.
　trichosis setosa tricosis setosa.
Trichosporon Trichosporon, Trichosporum.
trichosporosis *n.* tricosporia, tricosporosis.
Trichosporum Trichosporon, Trichosporum.
trichostasis spinulosa *n.* tricostasis espinulosa.
Trichostomatida Trichostomatida.
Trichostronglyade Trichostronglyade.
trichostrongyliasis *n.* tricostrongiliasis.
Trichostrongylus Trichostrongylus.
trichothiodystrophy *n.* tricotiodistrofia.
trichotillomania *n.* tricotilomanía.
trichotomous *adj.* tricotomoso, -sa.
trichotomy *n.* tricotomía.
trichotrophy *n.* tricotrofia.
trichroic *adj.* tricroico, -ca.
trichroism *n.* tricroísmo.
trichromasy *n.* tricromasia.
　anomalous trichromasy tricromasia anómala.
trichromatic *adj.* tricromático, -ca.
trichromatism *n.* tricromatismo, tricromía.
　anomalous trichromatism tricromatismo anómalo.
trichromatopsia *n.* tricromatopsia.
trichromic *adj.* tricrómico, -ca.
trichrotic *adj.* tricrótico, -ca, tricroto, -ta.
trichrotism *n.* tricrotismo.
trichuriasis *n.* trichuriasis, tricuriasis.
Trichuris Trichuris.
Trichuroidea Trichuroidea.
tricipital *adj.* tricipital, tricípite.
tricorn *adj.* tricorne.
tricornute *adj.* tricorne.
tricuspid *adj.* tricúspide.
tricuspidal *adj.* tricúspide.
tricuspidalization *n.* tricuspidalización.
tricuspidate *adj.* tricúspide.
tricyclic *adj.* tricíclico, -ca.
tridactylism *n.* tridactilia.
tridactylous *adj.* tridáctilo, -la.
tridemogenesis *n.* tridermogénesis.
trident *adj.* tridente.
tridentate *adj.* tridentado, -da, tridente.
tridermic *adj.* tridérmico, -ca.
tridermona *n.* tridermona.
tridigitate *adj.* tridigitado, -da.
trielcon *n.* trielcón.
triencephalous *adj.* triencéfalo, -la.
trifid *adj.* trífido, -da.
trifilocephalia *n.* trifilocefalia.
trifocal *adj.* trifocal.
trifurcation *n.* trifurcación.
trigastric *adj.* trigástrico, -ca.
trigeminal *adj.* trigeminal.
trigeminus *n.* trigémino.
trigeminy *n.* trigeminismo.
trigenic *adj.* trigénico, -ca.
trigger *n.* desencadenante, gatillo[2].
triglyceride *n.* triglicérido.
trigocephalus *n.* trigocéfalo, -la.
trigonal *adj.* trigonal.
trigone *n.* trígono.
trigonitis *n.* trigonitis.
trigonocephalia *n.* trigonocefalia.
trigonocephalus *n.* trigonocéfalo.
trigonocephaly *n.* trigonocefalia.
trigonodephalic *adj.* trigonocefálico, -ca.
trigonotome *n.* trigonótomo.

trigonum trígono, trigonum.
trihybrid *adj.* trihíbrido, -da.
triiniodymus *n.* triiniodimo.
triiodothyronine *n.* triyodotironina.
trilabe *n.* trilabo.
trilaminar *adj.* trilaminar.
trilateral *adj.* trilateral.
trilobate *adj.* trilobulado, -da.
trilobectomy *n.* trilobectomía.
trilocular *adj.* trilocular.
trilogy *n.* trilogía.
  Fallot's trilogy trilogía de Fallot.
trilostane *n.* trilostano.
trimensual *adj.* trimensual, trimestral.
trimer *n.* trímero.
trimeric *adj.* trimérico, -ca.
trimester *n.* trimestre.
trimethylaminuria *n.* trimetilaminuria.
trimorphism *n.* trimorfismo.
trimorphous *adj.* trimórfico, -ca, trimorfo, -fa.
trinegative *adj.* trinegativo, -va.
trineural *adj.* trineural, trinéurico, -ca.
trinucleate *adj.* trinucleado, -da.
trinucleotide *n.* trinucleótido.
triocephalus *n.* triocéfalo.
triolism *n.* triolismo.
trionym *n.* triónimo.
triophthalmos *n.* trioftalmo.
triopodymus *adj.* triopódimo, -ma.
triorchid *adj.* triárquido, -da, triorquio, -a.
triorquidism *n.* triorquidia, triorquidismo.
trioxde *n.* trióxido.
tripara *n.* trípara.
tripartite *adj.* tripartito, -ta.
triphalangeal *adj.* trifalángico, -ca.
triphalangia *n.* trifalangia.
triphalangism *n.* trifalangismo.
triphasic *adj.* trifásico, -ca.
triphthemia *n.* triftemia.
triplegia *n.* triplejía.
triplet *n.* triplete.
triplets *adj.* trillizo, -za.
triplex *adj.* triple, triplex.
triploblastic *adj.* triploblástico, -ca.
triploid *adj.* triploide.
triploidy *n.* triploidía.
triplokoria *n.* triplocoria.
triplopia *n.* triplopía, triplopsia.
tripod *n.* trípode.
  tripod of life trípode de la vida, trípode vital.
  vital tripod trípode de la vida, trípode vital.
tripodia *n.* tripodia.
tripoding *n.* tripodismo.
tripositive *adj.* tripositivo, -va.
triprosopus *n.* triprósopo.
triptokoria *n.* triptocoria.
triptus *adj.* trioto, -ta.
tripus tripus.
triradial *adj.* trirradial.
triradiate *adj.* trirradiado, -da.
triradiation *n.* trirradiación.
triradius *n.* trirradio.
trischiasis *n.* trisquiasis.
trismic *adj.* trísmico, -ca.
trismoid *n.* trismoide.
trismus trismo, trismus.
  trismus capistratus trismo capistratus.
  trismus dolorificus trismo doloroso.
  trismus nascentium trismo del nacimiento.
  trismus neonatorum trismo del recién nacido, trismo neonatal.
  trismus sardonicus trismo cómico, trismo sardónico.
trisomia *n.* trisomía.
trisomic *adj.* trisómico, -ca.

trisomy *n.* trisomía.
trisplanchnic *adj.* triesplácnico, -ca.
tristichia *n.* tristiquia.
trisulcate *adj.* trisurcado, -da.
tritan *adj.* tritánico, -ca.
tritanomal *adj.* tritanomalo, -la.
tritanomalopia *n.* tritanomalopía.
tritanomaly *n.* tritanomalía.
tritanope *adj.* tritánope.
tritanopia *n.* tritanopía.
tritanopic *adj.* tritanópico, -ca.
tritanopsia *n.* tritanopsia.
tritocone *n.* tritócono.
tritoconid *n.* tritocónide.
triturate *v.* triturar.
trituration *n.* trituration [2].
triturator *n.* triturador.
trivalence *n.* trivalencia.
trivalent *adj.* trivalente.
trivalve *adj.* trivalvo, -va, trivalvulado, -da.
trizonal *adj.* trizonal.
trocar *n.* trócar.
  Duchenne's trocar trócar de Duchenne.
  Durham's trocar trócar de Durham.
  piloting trocar trócar piloto.
trochanter *n.* trocánter.
trochin *n.* troquín.
trochinus *n.* troquín.
trochiter *n.* troquíter.
trochiterian *adj.* troquiteriano, -na.
trochlea *n.* tróclea.
trochlear *adj.* troclear.
trochleariform *adj.* trocleariforme.
trochocardia *n.* trococardia.
trochocephalia *n.* trococefalia.
trochocephaly *n.* trococefalia.
trochoid *n.* trocoide, trocoideo, -a.
trochoides *n.* trocoides.
trocorizocardia *n.* trocorrizocardia.
tromboblast *n.* tromboblasto.
tropesis *n.* tropesis.
trophectoderm *n.* trofectodermo.
trophedema *n.* trofedema, trofoedema.
trophesial *adj.* trofesial.
trophesic *adj.* trofésico, -ca.
trophesy *n.* trofesia.
trophic *adj.* trófico, -ca.
trophicity *n.* troficidad.
trophism *n.* trofismo.
trophoblast *n.* trofoblasto.
trophoblastoma *n.* trofoblastoma.
trophochromatin *n.* trofocromatina.
trophochromidia *n.* trofocromidia.
trophocyte *n.* trofocito.
trophoderm *n.* trofodermo.
trophodermatoneurosis *n.* trofodermatoneurosis.
trophodynamics *n.* trofodinámica.
tropholecithal *adj.* trofolecítico, -ca.
tropholecithus *n.* trofolecito.
trophology *n.* trofología.
trophoneurosis *n.* trofoneurosis.
  facial trophoneurosis trofoneurosis facial.
  lingual trophoneurosis trofoneurosis lingual.
  muscular trophoneurosis trofoneurosis muscular.
  Romberg's trophoneurosis trofoneurosis de Romberg.
trophoneurotic *adj.* trofoneurótico, -ca.
trophonosis *n.* trofonosis.
trophonucleus *n.* trofonúcleo.
trophopathy *n.* trofopatía.
trophoplast *n.* trofoplasto.
trophospongia *n.* trofospongia, trofospongio.

trophotaxis *n.* trofotaxia, trofotaxis.
trophotherapy *n.* trofoterapia.
trophotropism *n.* trofotropismo.
tropia *n.* tropía.
tropicopolitan *adj.* tropicopolita.
tropism *n.* tactismo, tropismo.
tropochrome *adj.* tropocromo, -ma.
tropocollagen *n.* tropocolágena.
tropometer *n.* tropómetro.
trough *n.* hondonada.
true *adj.* real.
truncal *adj.* truncal.
truncate *v.* truncado, -da, truncar.
truncatus *adj.* truncado, -da.
truncus *n.* tronco.
trunk *n.* tronco.
trusion *n.* trusión.
  bodily trusion trusión corporal.
  mandibular trusion trusión maxilar inferior.
  maxillary trusion trusión maxilar superior.
truss *n.* braguero [2].
  nasal truss braguero nasal.
  yarn truss braguero de hilaza.
trychostrongylosis *n.* tricoestrongilosis.
trypanid *n.* tripánide.
trypanocidal *adj.* tripanocida [2].
trypanocide *n.* tripanocida [1].
trypanolysis *n.* tripanólisis.
trypanolytic *adj.* tripanolítico, -ca.
Trypanosoma Trypanosoma.
trypanosomal *adj.* tripanosomíaco, -ca, tripanosómico, -ca.
trypanosomatic *adj.* tripanosomático, -ca.
Trypanosomatidae Trypanosomatidae.
Trypanosomatina Trypanosomatina.
trypanosomatosis *n.* tripanosomatosis.
trypanosomatotropic *adj.* tripanosomatotrópico, -ca.
trypanosome *n.* tripanosoma.
trypanosomiasis *n.* tripanosomiasis, tripnosomiosis.
  acute trypanosomiasis tripanosomiasis aguda.
  African trypanosomiasis tripanosomiasis africana.
  Brazilian trypanosomiasis tripanosomiasis americana, tripanosomiasis brasileña.
  chronic trypanosomiasis tripanosomiasis crónica.
  Cruz trypanosomiasis tripanosomiasis de Cruz.
  East African trypanosomiasis tripanosomiasis del África Oriental.
  Gambian trypanosomiasis tripanosomiasis gambiense.
  Rhodesian trypanosomiasis tripanosomiasis rhodesiense.
  South American trypanosomiasis tripanosomiasis sudamericana.
  West African trypanosomiasis tripanosomiasis del África Occidental.
trypanosomic *adj.* tripanosómico, -ca.
trypanosomid *n.* tripanosómide.
trypesis *n.* tripesis.
trypsinize *v.* tripsinizar.
trypsinogen *n.* tripsinógeno.
trypsogen *n.* tripsógeno.
tryptic *adj.* tríptico, -ca.
tryptolysis *n.* triptólisis.
tryptolytic *adj.* triptolítico, -ca.
tryptonemia *n.* triptonemia.
tryptophanuria *n.* triptofanuria.
  tryptophanuria with dwarfism triptofanuria con enanismo.
Tsa *n.* Tsa.

tsetse *n.* tsetsé.
tsutsugamushi tsutsugamushi.
tuba *n.* trompa.
tubal *adj.* tubárico, -ca, tubario, -ria.
tube *n.* sonda, trompa, tubo.
  Abbott-Miller tube sonda de Abbott-Miller.
  Abbott's tube tubo de Abbott.
  Abbott-Rawson tube sonda de Abbott-Rawson.
  Blakemore-Sengstaken tube sonda de Blakemore-Sengstaken.
  Bouchut's tube sonda de Bouchut, tubo de Bouchut.
  Bourdon tube tubo de Bourdon.
  Bowman's tube tubo de Bowman.
  Cantor tube sonda de Cantor, tubo de Cantor.
  Carlen's tube tubo de Carlen.
  Carrel tube sonda de Carrel.
  cathode-ray tube tubo de rayos catódicos.
  Celestin tube sonda de Celestín, tubo de Celestin.
  Chaoul tube tubo de Chaoul.
  Coolidge tube tubo de Coolidge.
  Crookes' tube tubo de Crookes.
  Devine's tube sonda de Devine.
  Diamond's tube sonda de Diamond.
  discharge tube tubo de descarga.
  drainage tube sonda de drenaje, tubo de drenaje.
  dressed tube sonda forrada.
  duodenal tube sonda duodenal.
  Durham tube sonda de Durham, tubo de Durham.
  empyema tube sonda de empiema, tubo de empiema.
  endobronchial tube sonda endobronquial.
  endotracheal tube sonda endotraqueal.
  Esmarch's tube tubo de Esmarch.
  esophageal tube sonda esofágica.
  Ewald tube sonda de Ewald.
  feeding tube sonda de alimentación, tubo de alimentación.
  fermentation tube tubo de fermentación.
  fusion tube tubo de fusión.
  gaz tube tubo de gas.
  Geissler-Pluecker tube tubo de Geissler, tubo de Geissler-Pluecker.
  Geissler's tube tubo de Geissler, tubo de Geissler-Pluecker.
  Harris tube sonda de Harris.
  Hittorf tube tubo de Hittorf.
  hot-cathode tube tubo catódico caliente.
  intubation tube sonda de intubación.
  jejunal feeding tube sonda de alimentación yeyunal.
  Killian's tube sonda de Killian.
  Leonard tube tubo de Leonard.
  Levin tube sonda de Levin, tubo de Levin.
  Martin's tube tubo de Martin.
  McCollum tube sonda de McCollum.
  Mett's tube tubo de Mett.
  Miller-Abbott tube sonda de Miller-Abbott, tubo de Miller-Abbott.
  Moss tube tubo de Moss.
  multiple-lumen tube sonda de luz múltiple.
  nasogastric tube sonda nasogástrica.
  nasojejunal tube sonda yeyunal.
  nasotracheal tube sonda nasotraqueal.
  nephrostomy tube sonda de nefrostomía.
  Neuber's tube sonda de Neuber.
  O'Dwyer's tube sonda de O'Dwyer, tubo de O'Dwyer.
  orotracheal tube tubo orotraqueal.
  Paul-Mixter tube sonda de Paul-Mixter, tubo de Pault-Mixter.

  photomultiplier tube tubo fotomultiplicador.
  rectal tube sonda rectal.
  Rehfuss stomach tube sonda gástrica de Rehfuss.
  Rehfuss tube sonda de Rehfuss, tubo de Rehfuss.
  Roida's tube tubo de Roida.
  roll tube tubo de rollo.
  Ryle's tube sonda de Ryle, tubo de Ryle.
  Sengstaken-Blakemore tube sonda de Sengstaken-Blakemore, tubo de Sengstaken-Blakemore.
  Shiner's tube sonda de Shiner.
  Souttar's tube tubo de Souttar.
  sputum tube tubo de esputo.
  stomach tube sonda gástrica.
  T tube sonda en T.
  tampon tube sonda de taponamiento.
  test tube tubo de ensayo.
  thoracostomy tube sonda de toracostomía.
  Thunberg tube tubo de Thunberg.
  tracheotomy tube tubo de traqueotomía.
  vacuum tube tubo al vacío, tubo de vacío.
  valve tube tubo de válvula.
  Veillon tube tubo de Veillon.
  vertical tube tubo vertical.
  Voltolini's tube sonda de Voltolini.
  Wangensteen tube sonda de Wangensteen, tubo de Wangensteen.
  X-ray tube tubo de rayos X.
tubectomy *n.* tubectomía.
tuber *n.* tuber.
tubercle *n.* tubérculo.
tubercular *adj.* tubercular.
tuberculate *adj.* tuberculado, -da.
tuberculated *adj.* tuberculado, -da.
tuberculation *n.* tuberculación.
tuberculid *n.* tubercúlide.
tuberculigenous *adj.* tuberculígeno, -na.
tuberculin *n.* tuberculina.
tuberculination *n.* tuberculinación.
tuberculinization *n.* tuberculinización.
tuberculinotherapy *n.* tuberculinoterapia.
tuberculitis *n.* tuberculitis.
tuberculocele *n.* tuberculocele.
tuberculocidal *adj.* tuberculocida[2].
tuberculocide *n.* tuberculocida[1].
tuberculoderma *n.* tuberculoderma.
tuberculofibroid *n.* tuberculofibroide.
tuberculofibrosis *n.* tuberculofibrosis.
tuberculoid *adj.* tuberculoide.
tuberculoidin *n.* tuberculoidina.
tuberculoma *n.* tuberculoma.
  tuberculoma en plaque tuberculoma en placa.
tuberculo-opsonic *adj.* tuberculoopsónico, -ca.
tuberculosilicosis *n.* tuberculosilicosis.
tuberculosis *n.* tuberculosis.
  acute miliary tuberculosis tuberculosis miliar, tuberculosis miliar aguda.
  acute tuberculosis tuberculosis aguda.
  adrenal tuberculosis tuberculosis suprarrenal.
  adult tuberculosis tuberculosis del adulto.
  aerogenic tuberculosis tuberculosis aérogena.
  anthracotic tuberculosis tuberculosis antracótica.
  attenuated tuberculosis tuberculosis atenuada.
  atypical tuberculosis tuberculosis atípica.
  basal tuberculosis tuberculosis basal.
  cerebral tuberculosis tuberculosis cerebral.
  cestodic tuberculosis tuberculosis cestódica.
  childhood tuberculosis tuberculosis de la infancia.

  childhood type tuberculosis tuberculosis de tipo infantil.
  cutaneous tuberculosis tuberculosis cutánea.
  dermal tuberculosis tuberculosis dérmica.
  enteric tuberculosis tuberculosis entérica.
  exudative tuberculosis tuberculosis exudativa.
  general tuberculosis tuberculosis general.
  genital tuberculosis tuberculosis genital.
  genitourinary tuberculosis tuberculosis genitourinaria.
  hematogenous tuberculosis tuberculosis hematógena.
  hilus tuberculosis tuberculosis hilial, tuberculosis hiliar.
  inhalation tuberculosis tuberculosis por inhalación.
  miliary tuberculosis tuberculosis miliar, tuberculosis miliar aguda.
  open tuberculosis tuberculosis abierta.
  oral tuberculosis tuberculosis bucal.
  orificial tuberculosis tuberculosis orificial.
  papulonecrotic tuberculosis tuberculosis papulonecrótica.
  postprimary tuberculosis tuberculosis posprimaria.
  primary inoculation tuberculosis tuberculosis primaria de inoculación.
  primary tuberculosis tuberculosis primaria.
  pulmonar tuberculosis tuberculosis pulmonar.
  reinfection tuberculosis tuberculosis de reinfección.
  secondary tuberculosis tuberculosis secundaria.
  spinal tuberculosis tuberculosis espinal, tuberculosis raquídea.
  tracheobronchial tuberculosis tuberculosis traqueobronquial.
  tuberculosis cutis tuberculosis cutis.
  tuberculosis cutis colliquativa tuberculosis cutánea colicuativa.
  tuberculosis cutis follicularis disseminata tuberculosis cutis folicular diseminada.
  tuberculosis cutis lichenoides tuberculosis cutánea liquenoide.
  tuberculosis cutis luposa tuberculosis cutis luposa.
  tuberculosis cutis miliaris disseminata tuberculosis cutánea miliar diseminada.
  tuberculosis cutis orificialis tuberculosis cutánea orificial.
  tuberculosis cutis verrucosa tuberculosis cutis verrugosa.
  tuberculosis lichenoides tuberculosis liquenoide.
  tuberculosis miliaris disseminata tuberculosis miliar diseminada.
  tuberculosis of bones and joints tuberculosis de huesos y articulaciones.
  tuberculosis of the intestines tuberculosis intestinal.
  tuberculosis of the larynx tuberculosis laríngea.
  tuberculosis of the lymph nodes tuberculosis de los ganglios linfáticos, tuberculosis linfoide.
  tuberculosis of the skin tuberculosis de la piel.
  tuberculosis of the spine tuberculosis raquídea.
  tuberculosis ulcerosa tuberculosis ulcerosa.
  tuberculosis verrucosa cutis tuberculosis verrucosa, tuberculosis verrucosa cutánea.
  warty tuberculosis tuberculosis verrucosa, tuberculosis verrucosa cutánea.

tuberculostatic *adj.* tuberculostático, -ca.
tuberculotic *adj.* tuberculótico, -ca.
tuberculous *adj.* tuberculoso, -sa.
tuberculum *n.* tubérculo, tuberculum.
tuberositas tuberosidad, tuberositas.
tuberosity *n.* tuberosidad.
tuberosus *adj.* tuberoso, -sa.
tuberous *adj.* tuberoso, -sa.
tuboabdominal *adj.* tuboabdominal.
tuboadnexopexy *n.* tuboanexopexia.
tuboligamentous *adj.* tuboligamentario, -ria, tuboligamentoso, -sa.
tubo-ovarian *adj.* tuboovárico, -ca.
tubo-ovariotomy *n.* tuboovariotomía.
tubo-ovaritis *n.* tuboovaritis.
tuboperitoneal *adj.* tuboperitoneal.
tuboplasty *n.* tuboplastia.
tuborrhea *n.* tuborrea.
tubotorsion *n.* tubotorsión.
tubotympanal *adj.* tubotimpánico, -ca.
tubotympanum *n.* tubotímpano.
tubouterine *adj.* tubouterino, -na.
tubovaginal *adj.* tubovaginal.
tubular *adj.* tubular.
tubule *n.* túbulo.
tubuloacinar tubuloacinar.
tubulocyst *n.* tubulocisto.
tubuloracemose *adj.* tubulorracemoso, -sa.
tubulosaccular *adj.* tubulosacular.
tubulous *adj.* tubulado, -da, tubuloso, -sa.
tubulus *n.* túbulo.
tubus tubo, tubus.
tugging *n.* tiro.
  tracheal tugging tiro traqueal.
tularemia *n.* tularemia.
  gastrointestinal tularemia tularemia gastrointestinal.
  glandular tularemia tularemia ganglionar.
  oculoglandular tularemia tularemia oculoganglionar.
  oropharyngeal tularemia tularemia orofaríngea.
  pulmonary tularemia tularemia pulmonar.
  typhoidal tularemia tularemia tifoídica.
  ulceroglandular tularemia tularemia ulceroganglionar.
tumefacient *adj.* tumefaciente.
tumefaction *n.* tumefacción.
tumescence *n.* tumescencia.
tumid *adj.* tumescente, túmido, -da.
tumidus *adj.* tumescente, túmido, -da.
tumor *n.* tumor.
  Abrikosov's tumor tumor de Abrikosov.
  acinar cell tumor tumor de células acinares.
  acoustic nerve tumor tumor del nervio acústico.
  acute splenic tumor tumor agudo esplénico, tumor esplénico agudo.
  adenoid tumor tumor adenoide, tumor adenoideo.
  adenomatoid odontogenic tumor tumor odontogénico adenomatoide.
  adenomatoid tumor tumor adenomatoide, tumor adenomatoideo.
  adipose tumor tumor adiposo.
  adrenal rest tumor tumor de restos suprarrenales.
  ameloblastic adenomatoid tumor tumor adenomatoide ameloblástico.
  amiloid tumor tumor amiloide.
  aortic body tumor tumor del cuerpo aórtico.
  Bednar tumor tumor de Bednar.
  benign tumor tumor benigno.
  blood tumor tumor sanguíneo.
  Brenner tumor tumor de Brenner.

  Brooke's tumor tumor de Brooke.
  brown tumor tumor pardo.
  Burkitt's tumor tumor de Burkitt.
  calcifying epithelial odontogenic tumor tumor odontogénico epitelial calcificado.
  carcinoid tumor tumor carcinoide.
  carcinoid tumor of the bronchus tumor carcinoide bronquial.
  carotid body tumor tumor del cuerpo carotídeo.
  cartilaginous tumor tumor cartilaginoso.
  cavernous tumor tumor cavernoso.
  cellular tumor tumor celular.
  cerebellopontine angle tumor tumor del ángulo pontocerebeloso.
  chemoreceptor tumor tumor de quimiorreceptores.
  chromaffin tumor tumor cromafín.
  chromaffin-cell tumor tumor de células cromafines.
  Codman's tumor tumor de Codman.
  collision tumor tumor de colisión.
  colloid tumor tumor coloide.
  connective tumor tumor conectivo.
  connective-tissue tumor tumor del tejido conectivo, tumor del tejido conjuntivo.
  cystic tumor tumor quístico.
  dermal duct tumor tumor de conductos dérmicos.
  dermoid tumor tumor dermoide.
  desmoid tumor tumor desmoide.
  dumb-bell tumor tumor en campana.
  eighth nerve tumor tumor del octavo par.
  embryonal tumor tumor embrionario.
  embryonic tumor tumor embrionario.
  embryoplastic tumor tumor embrioplástico.
  encysted tumor tumor enquistado.
  endodermal sinus tumor tumor endodérmico.
  endometrioid tumor tumor endometrioide.
  Erdhein tumor tumor de Erdhein.
  erectile tumor tumor eréctil.
  Ewing's tumor tumor de Ewing.
  false tumor tumor falso.
  fatty tumor tumor grasoso.
  fecal tumor tumor fecal.
  fibrocellular tumor tumor fibrocelular.
  fibroid tumor tumor fibroide.
  fibroplastic tumor tumor fibroplástico.
  fluid tumor tumor líquido.
  fungating tumor tumor micótico.
  gelatinous tumor tumor gelatinoso.
  germinal tumor tumor germinal.
  giant cell tumor of bone tumor de células gigantes del hueso, tumor óseo de células gigantes.
  giant cell tumor of tendon sheath tumor de células gigantes de la vaina tendinosa.
  glomus jugulare tumor tumor del glomo yugular.
  glomus tumor tumor del glomo.
  Godwin tumor tumor de Godwin.
  granular cell tumor tumor de células granulares, tumor de células granulosas.
  granulosa cell tumor tumor de células de la granulosa.
  granulosa tumor tumor de granulosa.
  granulosa-theca tumor tumor de células de granulosa y teca.
  Grawitz's tumor tumor de Grawitz.
  Gubler's tumor tumor de Gubler.
  gummy tumor tumor gomoso.
  heterologous tumor tumor heterólogo.
  heterotypic tumor tumor heterotípico.
  hilar cell tumor tumor de celulas hiliares.
  hilar cell tumor of the ovary tumor de células hiliares del ovario.
  histioid tumor tumor histioide.

  homoiotypic tumor tumor homotípico.
  homologous tumor tumor homólogo.
  Hortega cell tumor tumor de células de Hortega.
  hourglass tumor tumor en reloj de arena.
  Hürthle cell tumor tumor de células de Hürthle.
  hylic tumor tumor hílico.
  infiltrating tumor tumor infiltrante, tumor infiltrativo.
  innocent tumor tumor inocente.
  insterstitial cell tumor of testis tumor de células intersticiales de los testículos.
  islet cell tumor tumor de células insulares.
  ivory-like tumor tumor de dureza de marfil.
  Koenen's tumor tumor de Koenen.
  Krukenberg's tumor tumor de Krukenberg.
  lacteal tumor tumor lácteo.
  Leydig cell tumor tumor de células de Leydig.
  Lindau's tumor tumor de Lindau.
  lipoid cell tumor of the ovary tumor de células lipoides del ovario.
  luteinized granulosa-theca cell tumor tumor de células luteinizadas de granulosa y teca.
  malignant tumor tumor maligno.
  march tumor tumor de marcha.
  mast cell tumor tumor de mastocitos.
  melanotic neuroectodermal tumor tumor melanótico neuroectodérmico.
  melanotic neuroectodermic tumor tumor neuroectodérmico melanótico.
  Merkel cell tumor tumor de células de Merkel.
  mesonephroid tumor tumor mesonefroide.
  mixed tumor tumor mixto.
  mixed tumor of the salivary gland tumor mixto de la glándula salival.
  mixed tumor of the skin tumor mixto de la piel.
  mucous tumor tumor mucoso.
  muscular tumor tumor muscular.
  Nélaton's tumor tumor de Nélaton.
  Nelson tumor tumor de Nelson.
  neuroepithelial tumor tumor neuroepitelial.
  oil tumor tumor oleoso.
  oncocytic hepatocelular tumor tumor hepatocelular oncocítico.
  organoid tumor tumor organoide.
  oxyphil cell tumor tumor de células oxífilas.
  Pancoast's tumor tumor de Pancoast.
  papillary tumor tumor papilar.
  paraffin tumor tumor parafín.
  phantom tumor tumor fantasma.
  phyllodes tumor tumor filoide.
  pilar tumor of the scalp tumor piloso del cuero cabelludo.
  Pindborg tumor tumor de Pindborg.
  pontine angle tumor tumor del ángulo protuberancial.
  potato tumor tumor de patata.
  Pott's puffy tumor tumor hinchado de Pott.
  pregnancy tumor tumor de embarazo, tumor del embarazo.
  pulmonary sulcus tumor tumor del surco pulmonar.
  ranine tumor tumor ranino.
  Rathke's pouch tumor tumor de la bolsa de Rathke.
  Rathke's tumor tumor de Rathke.
  Recklinghausen's tumor tumor de Recklinghausen.
  retinal anlage tumor tumor del primordio retiniano.
  sacrococcygeal tumor tumor sacrococcígeo.
  sand tumor tumor arenoso.
  Schmincke's tumor tumor de Schmincke.
  Schwann-cell tumor tumor de células de Schwann.

Sertoli cell tumor tumor de células de Sertoli.
Sertoli-Leydig cell tumor tumor de células de Sertoli y Leydig.
squamous odontogenic tumor tumor odontogénico escamoso.
stercoral tumor tumor estercoráceo.
sugar tumor tumor de azúcar.
superior pulmonary sulcus tumor tumor del surco pulmonar superior.
superior sulcus tumor tumor del surco superior.
teratoid tumor tumor teratoide.
theca cell tumor tumor de células de la teca, tumor de células de teca.
tridermic tumor tumor tridérmico.
true tumor tumor verdadero.
tumor albus tumor blanco.
tumor albus pyogenes tumor blanco piógeno.
tumor colli tumor cervical.
tumor lienis tumor lienal.
turban tumor tumor en turbante.
vascular tumor tumor vascular.
villous tumor tumor velloso.
Warthin's tumor tumor de Warthin.
warty cicatricial tumor tumor verrucoso cicatricial.
white tumor tumor blanco.
Wilms' tumor tumor de Wilms.
yolk sac tumor tumor del saco vitelino.
Zollinger-Ellison tumor tumor de Zollinger-Ellison.
tumoraffin *adj.* tumorafin.
tumoricidal *n.* tumoricida.
tumorigenesis *n.* tumorigénesis.
tumorigenic *adj.* tumorígeno, -na.
tumorous *adj.* tumoroso, -sa.
tungiasis *n.* tungiasis.
tunic *n.* túnica.
tunica *n.* túnica.
  tunica intima vasorum endangio.
  tunica mucosa tubae uterinae endosálpinx.
tunnel *n.* túnel.
turbid *adj.* túrbido, -da, turbio, -bia.
turbidimeter *n.* turbidímetro.
turbidimetry *n.* turbidimetría.
turbidity *n.* enturbiamiento, turbiedad.
turbinal *adj.* turbinal.
turbinate *adj.* turbinado, -da.
turbinectomy *n.* turbinectomía.
turbinotome *n.* turbinótomo.
turbinotomy *n.* turbinotomía.
turgescence *n.* turgencia.
turgescent *adj.* turgente.
turgid *adj.* túrgido, -da.
turgidization *n.* turgidización.
turgidus *adj.* túrgido, -da.
turn *v.* girar.
turricephaly *n.* turricefalia.
tussal *adj.* tusivo, -va.
tussicula *n.* tusícula.
tussiculation *n.* tusiculación.
tussigenic *adj.* tusígeno, -na, tusíparo, -ra.
tussis tos, tussis.
  aneurismal tussis tos aneurismática.
tussive *adj.* tusivo, -va.
tweezers *n.* tenacillas.
twig *n.* ramita.
twilight *n.* crepúsculo.
twin *n.* gemelo, -la.
  acardiac twin gemelo acardíaco.
  allantoidoangiopagous twin gemelo alantoidoangiópago.
  asymmetrical conjoined twin gemelo unidos asimétrico.
  binovular twin gemelo binovular, gemelo biovular.

conjoined twin gemelo unido.
  dichorial twin gemelo dicoriales, gemelo dicoriónico.
  dichorionic twin gemelo dicoriales, gemelo dicoriónico.
  diovular twin gemelo binovular, gemelo biovular.
  dissimilar twin gemelo disimilar.
  dizygotic twin gemelo dicigótico.
  enzygotic twin gemelo encigótico.
  equal conjoined twin gemelo unidos igual.
  false twin gemelo falso.
  fraternal twin gemelo fraterno.
  heterologous twin gemelo heterólogo.
  hetero-ovular twin gemelo heteroovular.
  identical twin gemelo idéntico.
  impacter twin gemelo en impacción.
  incomplete conjoined twin gemelo unidos incompleto.
  monoamniotic twin gemelo monoamniótico.
  monochorial twin gemelo monocigótico, gemelo monocorial, gemelo monocoriónico, gemelo monoovular.
  monochorionic twin gemelo monocigótico, gemelo monocorial, gemelo monocoriónico, gemelo monoovular.
  mono-ovular twin gemelo monocigótico, gemelo monocorial, gemelo monocoriónico, gemelo monoovular.
  monovular twin gemelo monocigótico, gemelo monocorial, gemelo monocoriónico, gemelo monoovular.
  monozygotic twin gemelo monocigótico, gemelo monocorial, gemelo monocoriónico, gemelo monoovular.
  omphaloangiopagous twin gemelo onfaloangiópago.
  one-egg twin gemelo de un huevo.
  parasitic twin gemelo parásito.
  placental parasitic twin gemelo parásito placentario.
  polyzygotic twin gemelo policigótico.
  Siamese twin gemelo siamés.
  similar twin gemelo similar.
  symmetrical conjoined twin gemelo unidos simétrico.
  true twin gemelo verdadero.
  two-egg twin gemelo de dos huevos.
  unequal conjoined twin gemelo unidos desigual.
  unequal twin gemelo desigual.
  uniovular twin gemelo uniovular.
  unlike twin gemelo distinto.
twinge *n.* punzada.
twinning *n.* gemelación, gemeliparidad, gemelización.
  experimental twinning gemelación experimental.
  spontaneous twinning gemelación espontánea.
twitch *n.* contracción.
  fascicular twitch contracción fascicular espasmódica.
tylectomy *n.* tilectomía.
tylion *n.* tilión.
tyloma *n.* tiloma.
  tyloma conjuntivae tiloma conjuntival.
tylosis *n.* tilosis.
  tylosis ciliaris tilosis ciliar.
  tylosis linguae tilosis lingual.
  tylosis palmaris et plantaris tilosis palmar y plantar.
tylotic *adj.* tilótico, -ca.
tympanal *adj.* timpanal.
tympanectomy *n.* timpanectomía.
tympania *n.* timpania.

  bell tympania timpania de campana.
tympanic *adj.* timpánico, -ca.
tympanicity *n.* timpanicidad.
tympanism *n.* timpanismo.
  Skoda's tympanism timpanismo de Skoda.
  uterine tympanism timpanismo uterino.
tympanitic *adj.* timpanítico, -ca.
tympanitis *n.* timpanitis.
tympanoacryloplasty *n.* timpanoacriloplastia.
tympanocentesis *n.* timpanocentesis.
tympanoeustachian *adj.* timpanoeustaquiano, -na.
tympanogenic *adj.* timpánógeno, -na.
tympanogram *n.* timpanograma.
tympanohyal *adj.* timpanohial.
tympanomalleal *adj.* timpanomalear, timpanomáleo, -a.
tympanomandibular *adj.* timpanomandibular.
tympanomastoid *adj.* timpanomastoideo, -a.
tympanomastoiditis *n.* timpanomastoiditis.
tympanometric *adj.* timpanométrico, -ca.
tympanometry *n.* timpanometría.
tympanoplastic *adj.* timpanoplástico, -ca.
tympanoplasty *n.* timpanoplastia.
tympanosclerosis *n.* timpanoesclerosis, timpanosclerosis.
tympanosquamosal *adj.* timpanoescamoso, -sa, timpanoscamoso, -sa.
tympanostapedial *adj.* timpanoestapédico, -ca, timpanostapédico, -ca.
tympanosympathectomy *n.* timpanosimpatectomía.
tympanotemporal *adj.* timpanotemporal.
tympanotomy *n.* timpanotomía.
tympanous *adj.* timpanoso, -sa.
tympanum *n.* tímpano.
tympany *n.* timpania.
tyndallization *n.* tindalización, tyndalización.
type *n.* tipo.
  amyostatic-kinetic type tipo amiostático y acinético.
  asthenic type tipo asténico, tipo leptosómico.
  athletic type tipo atlético.
  Aztec type tipo azteca.
  bird's head type tipo de cabeza de pájaro.
  blood type tipo sanguíneo.
  buffalo type tipo de búfalo.
  constitutional type tipo constitucional.
  Jaeger's test type tipo de prueba de Jaeger.
  Lorain type tipo de Lorain.
  overactive type tipo hiperactivo.
  phage type tipo fágico.
  phthinoid type tipo tinoide.
  pyknic type tipo pícnico.
  scapulohumeral type tipo escapulohumeral.
  schizoid type tipo esquizoide, tipo esquizotímico.
  Snellen's test type tipo de prueba de Snellen.
  sthenic type tipo esténico.
  suspicious type tipo sospechoso.
  test type optotipo.
  unstable type tipo inestable.
  wild type tipo salvaje.
typhemia *n.* tifemia, tifohemia.
typhia *n.* tifia.
typhic *adj.* tífico, -ca.
typhlectasis *n.* tiflectasia, tifloectasia.
typhlectomy *n.* tiflectomía, tifloectomía.
typhlenteritis *n.* tiflenteritis.
typhlitis *n.* tiflitis.
typhlocele *n.* tiflocele.
typhlocolitis *n.* tiflocolitis.
typhlodicliditis *n.* tiflodicliditis.

typhloempyema *n.* tifloempiema.
typhloenteritis *n.* tiflenteritis, tifloenteritis.
typhlolithiasis *n.* tiflolitiasis.
typhlology *n.* tiflología.
typhlomegaly *n.* tiflomegalia.
typhlon *n.* tiflón.
typhlopexy *n.* tiflopexia.
typhloptosis *n.* tifloptosis.
typhlorrhaphy *n.* tiflorrafia.
typhlosis *n.* tiflosis.
typhlostenosis *n.* tifloestenosis, tiflostenosis.
typhlostomy *n.* tiflostomía.
typhloteritis *n.* tifloteritis.
typhlotomy *n.* tiflotomía.
typhloureterostomy *n.* tifloureterostomía.
typhobacillosis *n.* tifobacilosis.
typhoid *adj.* tifoideo, -a.
typhoidal *adj.* tifoidal.
typhomalarial *adj.* tifomalárico, -ca, tifopalúdico, -ca.
typhopaludism *n.* tifopaludismo.
typhopneumonia *n.* tifoneumonía.
typhosepsis *n.* tifosepsis.
typhous *adj.* tifoídico, -ca, tifoso, -sa.
typhus *n.* tifo, tifus.
  abdominal typhus tifus abdominal.
  African tick typhus tifus transmitido por garrapatas africanas.
  amarillic typhus tifus amarillo.
  Australian tick typhus tifus australiano por garrapatas.
  classic typhus tifus clásico.
  endemic typhus tifus endémico.

  epidemic typhus tifus epidémico.
  European typhus tifus europeo.
  exanthematous typhus tifus exantemático.
  flea-borne typhus tifus por pulgas, tifus transmitido por pulgas.
  KT typhus tifus KT.
  louse-borne typhus tifus transmitido por piojos.
  Manchurian typhus tifus de Manchuria.
  Mexican typhus tifus mexicano.
  mite-borne typhus tifus por ácaros.
  mitior typhus tifus mitior.
  murine typhus tifus murino.
  North Asian tick typhus tifus del norte de Asia por garrapata.
  North Queensland tick typhus tifus de North Queensland por garrapatas.
  petechial typhus tifus petequial.
  Queensland tick typhus tifus de Queensland por garrapata.
  rat typhus tifus de la rata.
  recrudescent typhus tifus recrudescente.
  rural typhus tifus rural.
  Sao Paulo typhus tifus de Sao Paulo.
  scrob typhus tifus de las malezas, tifus de los matorrales.
  shop typhus tifus de las tiendas.
  Siberian tick typhus tifus de Siberia por garrapata.
  tick typhus tifus por garrapatas.
  tropical typhus tifus de los trópicos, tifus tropical.
  urban typhus tifus urbano.
typing *n.* tipificación.

  bacteriophage typing tipificación por bacteriófagos.
  blood typing tipificación de la sangre, tipificación de los grupos sanguíneos.
  HLA typing tipificación de los HLA.
  phage typing tipificación fágica, tipificación por fagos.
  primed lymphocyte typing (PLT) tipificación de linfocitos preparados (TLP).
  tissue typing tipificación tisular.
typology *n.* tipología.
typoscope *n.* tipioscopio, tiposcopio.
tyrannism *n.* tiranismo.
tyremesis *n.* tiremesis.
tyroma *n.* tiroma.
tyromatosis *n.* tiromatosis.
tyrosinemia *n.* tirosinemia.
  hereditary tyrosinemia tirosinemia hereditaria.
tyrosinosis *n.* tirosinosis.
tyrosinurea *n.* tirosinurea.
tyrosinuria *n.* tirosinuria.
tyrosis *n.* tirosis.
tyrosyluria *n.* tirosiluria.
tyrotoxicon *n.* tirotoxicón.
tyrotoxicosis *n.* tirotoxicosis.
tyrotoxism *n.* tirotoxismo.
tyroxine *n.* tiroxina.
  free tyroxine tiroxina libre.
  radioactive tyroxine tiroxina radiactiva.
  tyroxine sodium tiroxina sódica.
tysonitis *n.* tisonitis.
tzetze *n.* tzetzé.

uarthritis *n.* uartritis.
uberous *adj.* uberoso, -sa.
ubihydroquinone *n.* ubihidroquinona.
ubiquinol *n.* ubiquinol.
ubiquinone *n.* ubiquinona.
ubiquitin *n.* ubicuitina, ubiquitina.
ubiquitous *adj.* ubiquista.
ulaganactesis *n.* ulaganactesis.
ulalgia *n.* ulalgia.
ulatrophy *n.* ulatrofia.
  afunctional ulatrophy ulatrofia afuncional.
  atrophic ulatrophy ulatrofia atrófica.
  calcic ulatrophy ulatrofia cálcica.
  ischemic ulatrophy ulatrofia isquémica.
  traumatic ulatrophy ulatrofia traumática.
ulcer *n.* llaga, úlcera, ulcus.
  chronic leg ulcer ulcus cruris.
  gastric ulcer ulcus gástrico.
  hard ulcer ulcus durum.
  leg ulcer ulcus cruris.
  rodent ulcer ulcus rodens.
  serpiginous ulcer ulcus serpens.
  tropical ulcer ulcus tropicum.
ulcerate *v.* ulcerar.
ulcerated *adj.* ulcerado, -da.
ulceration *n.* ulceración.
  lips and leg ulceration ulceración de labios
  pierna.
  tracheal ulceration ulceración traqueal.
  ulceration of Daguet ulceración de Daguet.
ulcerative *adj.* ulcerativo, -va.
ulcerocancer *n.* ulcerocáncer.
ulcerogangrenous *adj.* ulcerogangrenoso, -sa.
ulcerogenic *adj.* ulcerógeno, -na.
ulceroglandular *adj.* ulceroglandular.
ulcerogranuloma *n.* ulcerogranuloma.
ulceromembranous *adj.* ulceromembranoso, -sa.
ulcerous *adj.* ulceroso, -sa.
ulcus *n.* ulcus.
  ulcus ambulans ulcus ambulans.
  ulcus cruris ulcus cruris.
  ulcus exedens ulcus exedens.
  ulcus molle ulcus molle.
  ulcus rodens ulcus rodens.
  ulcus tropicum ulcus tropicum.
  ulcus ventriculi ulcus ventriculi.
  ulcus vulvae acutum ulcus vulvae acutum.
ulectomy *n.* ulectomía.
ulegyria *n.* ulegiria.
ulemorrhagia *n.* ulemorragia.
ulerythema *n.* uleritema.
  ulerythema centrifugum uleritema centrífugo.
  ulerythema ophryogenes uleritema ofriógeno.
  ulerythema sycosiforme uleritema sicosiforme.
uliginous *adj.* uliginoso, -sa.
ulitis *n.* ulitis.
  fungus ulitis ulitis micótica.
ullen *n.* ullen.
ulna *n.* cúbito, cubitus, ulna.

ulnad cubitad.
ulnar *adj.* ulnar.
ulnocarpal *adj.* ulnocarpal, ulnocarpiano, -na.
ulnoradial *adj.* ulnorradial.
ulocace *n.* ulocace.
ulocarcinoma *n.* ulocarcinoma.
ulodermatitis *n.* ulodermatitis.
uloglossitis *n.* uloglositis.
uloid *adj.* uloide.
uloncus *n.* uloma, ulonco.
ulorrhagia *n.* ulorragia.
ulorrhea *n.* ulorrea.
ulotic *adj.* ulótico, -ca.
ulotomy *n.* ulotomía.
ulotrichous *adj.* ulotrico, -ca.
ulotripsis *n.* ulotripsis.
ultimisternal *adj.* ultimisternal, ultimoesternal.
ultimobranchial *adj.* ultimobranquial.
ultimum moriens ultimum moriens.
ultrabrachycephalic *adj.* ultrabraquicefálico, -ca,
ultrabraquicéfalo, -la.
ultracentrifugation *n.* ultracentrifugación.
ultracentrifuge *n.* ultracentrífuga.
ultradian *adj.* ultradiano, -na.
ultradolichocephalic *adj.* ultradolicocefálico, -ca,
ultradolicocéfalo, -la.
ultrafilter *n.* ultrafiltro.
ultrafiltrate *n.* ultrafiltrado.
ultrafiltration *n.* ultrafiltración.
ultraligation *n.* ultraligadura.
ultramicrochemistry *n.* ultramicroquímica.
ultramicron *n.* ultramicro, ultramicrón.
ultramicropipet *n.* ultramicropipeta.
ultramicroscopic *adj.* ultramicroscópico, -ca.
ultramicroscopy *n.* ultramicroscopía.
ultramicrotome *n.* ultramicrotomo, ultramicrótomo.
ultramicrotomy *n.* ultramicrotomía.
ultraphagocytosis *n.* ultrafagocitosis.
ultraprophylaxis *n.* ultraprofilaxis.
ultra-red *adj.* ultrarrojo, -ja.
ultrasonic *adj.* ultrasónico, -ca.
ultrasonics *n.* ultraacústica, ultrasónica.
ultrasonogram *n.* ultrasonograma.
ultrasonographic *adj.* ultrasonográfico, -ca.
ultrasonography *n.* ultrasonografía.
  Doppler ultrasonography ultrasonografía
  Doppler.
  endoscopic ultrasonography ultrasonografía endoscópica.
  renal ultrasonography ultrasonografía renal.
ultrasonometry *n.* ultrasonometría.
ultrasonotherapy *n.* ultrasonoterapia.
ultrasound *n.* ultrasonido.
ultrastructure *n.* ultraestructura.
ultratherm *n.* ultratermo.
ultraviolet *adj.* ultravioleta.
  far ultraviolet ultravioleta lejana.
  near ultraviolet ultravioleta cercana.

ultravisible *adj.* ultravisible.
ultromotivity *n.* ultromotilidad, ultromovilidad.
ululation *n.* ululación.
umbilectomy *n.* umbilectomía.
umbilical *adj.* umbilical.
umbilicate *adj.* umbilicado[1], -da.
umbilicated *adj.* umbilicado[2], -da.
umbilication *n.* umbilicación.
umbilicus *n.* ombligo.
  amniotic umbilicus ombligo amniótico.
  decidual umbilicus ombligo decidual.
umbo *n.* umbo.
  umbo membranae tympani umbo de la
  membrana timpánica.
  umbo of the tympanic membrane umbo de
  la membrana timpánica.
umbonate *adj.* umbonado, -da.
umbrascopy *n.* umbrascopia.
unazotized *adj.* inazotizado, -da.
uncal *adj.* uncal.
uncarthrosis *n.* uncartrosis.
unciform *adj.* unciforme.
uncinal *adj.* uncinal.
Uncinaria Uncinaria.
  Uncinaria americana Uncinaria americana.
  Uncinaria duodenalis Uncinaria duodenalis.
uncinariasis *n.* uncinariasis.
uncinariatic *adj.* uncinariático, -ca.
uncinariosis *n.* uncinariosis.
uncinate *adj.* uncinado, -da.
uncipressure *n.* uncipresión.
uncomplemented *adj.* incomplementado,
-da.
unconscious *n.* inconsciente.
  collective unconscious inconsciente colectivo.
  familial unconscious inconsciente familiar.
  individual unconscious inconsciente individual.
  irreflective unconscious inconsciente irreflexivo.
  mnemic unconscious inconsciente mnémico.
  personal unconscious inconsciente personal.
  racial unconscious inconsciente racial.
  repressed unconscious inconsciente reprimido.
  SUBliminal unconscious inconsciente SU-
Bliminal.
  vital unconscious inconsciente vital.
unconsciousness *n.* inconsciencia.
unco-ossified *adj.* incoosificado, -da, uncoosificado, -da.
uncovertebral *adj.* uncovertebral.
unction *n.* unción.
uncus uncus.
  uncus corporis apófisis uncinada.
  uncus of the hamate bone uncus del hueso
ganchoso.
underachievement *n.* SUBlogro.

underbite *n.* SUBmordida.
underdamping *n.* SUBamortiguamiento.
underdrive pacing *n.* SUBestimulación con marcapaso.
undernutrition *n.* SUBnutrición.
understain *n.* hipotinción.
underventilation *n.* SUBventilación.
underweight *n.* bajo peso.
undifferentiated *adj.* indiferenciado, -da.
undine *n.* ondina.
undinism *n.* ondinismo.
undulant *adj.* ondulante.
undulate *adj.* ondulado, -da.
undulation *n.* ondulación.
  jugular undulation ondulación yugular.
  respiratory undulation ondulación respiratoria.
undulatory *adj.* ondulatorio, -ria.
ungual *adj.* ungueal, ungular.
unguent *n.* ungüento, unguentum.
unguiculate *adj.* unguiculado, -da.
unguiculus *n.* unguícula.
unguinal *adj.* unguinal.
unguis *n.* uña, unguis², unguis3.
  unguis aduncus uña encarnada, uña incardinada, uñero.
  unguis incarnatus uña encarnada, uña incardinada, uñero.
ungulate *adj.* ungulado, -da.
unhurt *adj.* ileso, -sa.
uniarticular *adj.* uniarticular.
uniaural *adj.* uniaural.
uniaxial *adj.* uniaxial, uniaxil.
unibasal *adj.* unibasal, unibásico, -ca.
unicameral *adj.* unicameral.
unicellular *adj.* unicelular.
unicentral *adj.* unicentral.
unicentric *adj.* unicéntrico, -ca.
uniceps *adj.* uniceps.
uniceptor *n.* uniceptor.
unicism *n.* unicismo.
unicollis unicollis.
unicorn *adj.* unicornio, -nia.
unicornis *adj.* unicornio, -nia.
unicornous *adj.* unicornio, -nia.
unicuspid *adj.* unicúspide.
unicuspidate *adj.* unicuspidado, -da.
unidirectional *adj.* unidireccional.
uniflagellate *adj.* uniflagelado, -da.
unifocal *adj.* unifocal.
uniforate *adj.* uniforado, -da, uniperforado, -da.
unigeminal *adj.* unigeminal, unigémino, -na.
unigerminal *adj.* unigerminal.
uniglandular *adj.* uniglandular.
unigravida *adj.* unigrávida.
unilaminar *adj.* unilaminar.
unilateral *adj.* unilateral.
unilobar *adj.* unilobar, unilobular.
unilocular *adj.* unilocular.
unimodal *adj.* unimodal.
unimolecular *adj.* unimolecular.
uninephrectomized *adj.* uninefrectomizado, -da.
uninuclear *adj.* uninuclear.
uninucleate *adj.* uninucleado, -da.
uniocular *adj.* uniocular.
union *n.* reunión, unión3.
  autogenous union unión autógena.
  faulty union unión defectuosa.
  fibrous union unión fibrosa.
  primary union unión primaria.
  secondary union unión secundaria.
  vicious union unión viciosa.
uniovular *adj.* uniovular.
unipara *adj.* unípara.

uniparental *adj.* uniparental.
uniparous *adj.* uníparo, -ra.
unipolar *adj.* unipolar.
unipotency *n.* unipotencia.
unipotent *adj.* unipotente.
unipotential *adj.* unipotencial.
unipuncture *n.* unipunción, unipuntura.
uniseptate *adj.* uniseptado, -da, unitabicado, -da.
unisexual *adj.* unisexual.
unit *n.* unidad.
  absolute unit unidad absoluta.
  Allen-Doisy unit unidad de Allen-Doisy.
  amboceptor unit unidad amboceptora.
  American Drug Manufacturers' Association unit unidad de la American Drug Manufacturers Association.
  Angström unit unidad Angström, unidad de Angström.
  Ansbacher unit unidad Ansbacher, unidad de Ansbacher.
  antigen unit unidad de antígeno.
  antitoxic unit unidad inmunizante.
  antitoxin unit unidad antitóxica.
  atomic mass unit unidad de masa atómica.
  atomic weight unit unidad de peso atómico.
  base unit unidad SI.
  Bethesda unit unidad Bethesda.
  Bodansky unit unidad Bodansky, unidad de Bodansky.
  CGS unit unidad cgs, unidad CGS.
  Clauberg unit unidad de Clauberg.
  clinical unit unidad clínica.
  Collip unit unidad Collip, unidad de Collip.
  colony-forming unit unidad de formación de colonias.
  complement unit unidad de complemento.
  Corner-Allen unit unidad Corner-Allen, unidad de Corner-Allen.
  coronary care unit unidad coronaria (UCC), unidad de cuidados coronarios.
  coronary intensive care unit (CCU) unidad coronaria (UCC), unidad de cuidados coronarios.
  Dam unit unidad de Dam.
  dental unit unidad dental.
  electromagnetic unit unidad eléctrica, unidad electromagnética, unidad electrostática.
  electrostatic unit unidad eléctrica, unidad electromagnética, unidad electrostática.
  enzyme unit unidad enzimática.
  exposure unit unidad de exposición.
  Felton's unit unidad de Felton, unidad Felton.
  Florey unit unidad de Florey.
  Hampson's unit unidad de Hampson, unidad Hampson.
  heat unit unidad de calor.
  hemolytic unit unidad hemolítica.
  Hounsfield unit unidad de Hounsfield, unidad Hounsfield.
  inpatient care unit unidad de cuidados hospitalarios.
  intensive care unit (ICU) unidad de cuidados intensivos (UCI).
  international insulin unit unidad internacional de insulina.
  international unit unidad internacional.
  international unit of enzime activity unidad internacional de actividad enzimática.
  international unit of estrogenic activity unidad internacional de actividad estrógena.
  international unit of gonadotropic activity unidad internacional de actividad gonadotrófica.
  King unit unidad de King, unidad de King-Armstrong.

  King-Armstrong unit unidad de King, unidad de King-Armstrong.
  light unit unidad luz.
  Mache's unit unidad de Mache, unidad Mache.
  map unit unidad de mapeo.
  meter-kilogram-second (MKS) unit unidad MKS.
  Montevideo unit unidad de actividad uterina, unidad de Álvarez Caldeiro.
  Montevideo unit of uterine activity unidad Montevideo.
  motor unit unidad motora, unidad motriz.
  mouse unit unidad ratón.
  neonatal intensive care unit (NICU) unidad de cuidados intensivos neonatales (UCIN).
  neonatal unit unidad neonatal.
  Noon pollen unit unidad de polen de Noon.
  Oxford unit unidad Oxford.
  pepsin unit unidad de pepsina.
  peripheral resistance unit unidad de resistencia periférica.
  pilosebaceous unit unidad pilosebácea.
  psychiatric inpatient unit unidad de ingreso psiquiátrico.
  quantum unit unidad quantum.
  rat unit unidad rata.
  resistance unit unidad de resistencia.
  roentgen unit unidad roentgen.
  SI unit unidad SI.
  skin test unit unidad de prueba cutánea.
  Somogyi unit unidad de Somogyi.
  specific smell unit unidad específica de olfato.
  Steenbock unit unidad de Steenbock, unidad Steenbock de vitamina D.
  Steenbock unit of vitamin D unidad de Steenbock, unidad Steenbock de vitamina D.
  Svedberg flotation unit unidad de flotación de Svedberg.
  tuberculin unit unidad de tuberculina.
  unit of current unidad de corriente.
  unit of heat unidad de calor.
unitage unitage.
unitary *adj.* unitario, -ria.
uniterminal *adj.* uniterminal.
univalence *n.* univalencia.
univalent *adj.* univalente.
universal *adj.* universal.
univitelline *adj.* univitelino, -na.
unorganized *adj.* no organizado, -da.
unphysiologic *adj.* no fisiológico, -ca.
unrest *n.* inquietud.
  peristaltic unrest inquietud peristáltica.
unsaturated *adj.* insaturado, -da.
unsex *v.* asexar, desexualizar.
unstriated *adj.* no estriado, -da.
uprighting *n.* enderezamiento².
upsiloide *adj.* upsiloide.
uptake *n.* captación.
urachal *adj.* uracal.
urachovesical *adj.* uracovesical.
urachus *n.* uraco.
uracil *n.* uracilo.
uracrasia *n.* uracrasia.
uracratia *n.* uracratia.
uragenetic *adj.* ureagénico, -ca.
uragogue *n.* uragogo, -ga.
uranalysis *n.* uranálisis.
uranianism *n.* uranianismo.
uraniscochasma *n.* uraniscocasma.
uraniscolalia *n.* uraniscolalia.
uranisconitis *n.* urasconitis.
uraniscoplasty *n.* uraniscoplastia.
uraniscorrhaphy *n.* uraniscorrafia.
uraniscus *n.* uranisco.

uranism *n.* uranismo.
uranist *adj.* uranista.
uranophobia *n.* uranofobia.
uranoplastic *adj.* uranoplástico, -ca.
uranoplasty *n.* uranoplastia.
uranoplegia *n.* uranoplejía.
uranorrhaphy *n.* uranorrafia.
uranoschisis *n.* uranosquisis.
uranoschism *n.* uranosquismo.
uranostaphyloplasty *n.* uranoestafiloplastia, uranostafiloplastia.
uranostaphylorrhaphy *n.* uranoestafilorrafia, uranostafilorrafia.
uranostaphyloschisis *n.* uranoestafilosquisis, uranostafilosquisis.
uranosteoplasty *n.* uranosteoplastia.
uranoveloschisis *n.* uranovelosquisis.
urapostema *n.* urapostema.
uraroma *n.* uraroma.
urarthritis *n.* urartritis.
uratemia *n.* uratemia.
uratic *adj.* urático, -ca.
uratohistechia *n.* uratohistequia.
uratolysis *n.* uratólisis.
uratolytic *adj.* uratolítico, -ca.
uratoma *n.* uratoma.
uratosis *n.* uratosis.
uraturia *n.* uraturia.
urceiform *adj.* urceiforme.
urceolate *adj.* urceolado, -da.
urea *n.* urea.
ureagenesis *n.* ureagénesis.
ureal *adj.* ureal, ureico, -ca.
ureameter *n.* ureámetro.
ureametry *n.* ureametría.
Ureaplasma Ureaplasma.
  Ureaplasma urealyticum Ureaplasma urealyticum.
ureapoiesis *n.* ureapoyesis.
urecchysis *n.* urequisis.
uredema *n.* uredema.
uredo *n.* uredo.
urein *n.* ureína.
urelcosis *n.* urelcosis.
uremia *n.* uremia, uroemia.
  extrarenal uremia uremia extrarrenal.
  hypercalcemic uremia uremia hipercalcémica.
  prerenal uremia uremia prerrenal.
  retention uremia uremia de retención.
uremic *adj.* urémico, -ca.
uremide *n.* urémide.
uremigenic *adj.* uremígeno, -na.
ureogenesis *n.* ureogénesis.
ureolysis *n.* ureólisis.
ureolytic *adj.* ureolítico, -ca.
ureometer *n.* ureómetro.
ureometry *n.* ureometría.
ureotelic *adj.* ureotélico, -ca.
uresiesthesia *n.* uresiestesia.
uresiesthesis *n.* uresiestesia.
uresis *n.* uresis.
ureter *n.* uréter.
  circumcaval ureter uréter circuncaval.
  curlicue ureter uréter enroscado.
  ectopic ureter uréter ectópico.
  postcaval ureter uréter poscaval.
  retrocaval ureter uréter retrocaval.
  retroiliac ureter uréter retroiliaco.
ureteral *adj.* ureteral.
ureteralgia *n.* ureteralgia.
uretercystoscope *n.* ureteristoscopio.
ureterectasia *n.* ureterectasia.
ureterectasis *n.* ureterectasia.
ureterectomy *n.* ureterectomía.

ureteric *adj.* uretérico, -ca.
ureteritis *n.* ureteritis.
  ureteritis cystica ureteritis quística.
  ureteritis glandularis ureteritis glandular.
ureterocele *n.* ureterocele.
  ectopic ureterocele ureterocele ectópico.
ureterocelectomy *n.* ureterocelectomía.
ureterocelorrhaphy *n.* ureterocelorrafia.
ureterocervical *adj.* ureterocervical.
ureterocolic *adj.* ureterocólico, -ca.
ureterocolostomy *n.* ureterocolostomía.
ureteroctasia *n.* ureteroctasia.
ureterocutaneostomy *n.* ureterocutaneostomía.
ureterocystanastomosis *n.* ureterocistanastomosis.
ureterocystoscope *n.* ureterocistoscopio.
ureterocystostomy *n.* ureterocistostomía.
ureteroduodenal *adj.* ureteroduodenal.
ureterodyalisis *n.* ureterodiálisis.
ureteroenteric *adj.* ureteroentérico, -ca.
ureteroenteroanastomosis *n.* ureteroenteroanastomosis.
ureteroenterostomy *n.* ureteroentcrostomía.
ureteroesicoplasty *n.* ureterovesicoplastia.
ureterogram *n.* ureterograma.
ureterography *n.* ureterografía.
ureteroheminephrectomy *n.* ureteroheminefrectomía.
ureterohydronephrosis *n.* ureterohidronefrosis.
ureteroileostomy *n.* ureteroileostomía.
ureterointestinal *adj.* ureterointestinal.
ureterolith *n.* ureterolito.
ureterolithiasis *n.* ureterolitiasis.
ureterolithotomy *n.* ureterolitotomía.
ureterolysis *n.* ureterólisis.
ureteromeatotomy *n.* ureteromeatotomía.
ureteroneocystostomy *n.* ureterocistoneostomía, ureteroneocistostomía.
ureteroneopyelostomy *n.* ureteroneopielostomía.
ureteronephrectomy *n.* ureteronefrectomía.
ureteropathy *n.* ureteropatía.
ureteropelvic *adj.* ureteropélvico, -ca.
ureteropelvioneostomy *n.* ureteropelvioneostomía.
ureteropelvioplasty *n.* ureteropelvioplastia.
  Culp de Weerd ureteropelvioplasty ureteropelvioplastia de Culp de Weerd.
  Foley Y-V ureteropelvioplasty ureteropelvioplastia de Foley en Y-V.
  Scardino-Prince ureteropelvioplasty ureteropelvioplastia de Scardino-Prince.
ureterophlegma *n.* ureteroflegma, ureteroflema.
ureteroplasty *n.* ureteroplastia.
ureteroproctostomy *n.* ureteroproctostomía.
ureteropyelitis *n.* ureteropielitis.
ureteropyeloneostomy *n.* ureteropieloneostomía.
ureteropyelonephritis *n.* ureteropielonefritis.
ureteropyelonephrostomy *n.* ureteropielonefrostomía.
ureteropyeloplasty *n.* ureteropieloplastia.
ureteropyelostomy *n.* ureteropielostomía.
ureteropyosis *n.* ureteropiosis.
ureterorectal *adj.* ureterorrectal.
ureterorectoneostomy *n.* ureterorrectoneostomía.
ureterorectostomy *n.* ureterorrectostomía.
ureterorenoscope *n.* ureterorrenoscopio.
ureterorenoscopy *n.* ureterorrenoscopia.
ureterorrhagia *n.* ureterorragia.
ureterorrhaphy *n.* ureterorrafia.

ureterosigmoid *adj.* ureterosigmoideo, -a.
ureterosigmoidostomy *n.* ureterosigmoidostomía.
ureterostegnosis *n.* ureterostegnosis.
ureterostenoma *n.* ureterostenoma.
ureterostenosis *n.* ureteroestenosis.
ureterostoma *n.* ureterostoma.
ureterostomosis *n.* ureterostomosis.
ureterostomy *n.* ureterostomía.
  cutaneous ureterostomy ureterostomía cutánea.
  lumbar SUBarachnoid ureterostomy ureterostomía lumbar SUBaracnoidea.
ureterostonoma *n.* ureterostonoma.
ureterotomy *n.* ureterotomía.
ureterotrigonoenterostomy *n.* ureterotrigonoenterostomía.
ureterotrigonosigmoidostomy *n.* ureterotrigonosigmoidostomía.
ureteroureteral *adj.* ureteroureteral.
ureteroureterostomy *n.* ureteroureterostomía.
ureterouterine *adj.* ureterouterino, -na.
ureterovaginal *adj.* ureterovaginal.
ureterovesical *adj.* ureterovesical.
ureterovesicostomy *n.* ureterovesicostomía.
urethra *n.* uretra.
  anterior urethra uretra anterior.
  double urethra uretra doble.
  female urethra uretra de la mujer, uretra muliebris.
  male urethra uretra del hombre.
  membranous urethra uretra membranosa.
  penile urethra uretra peneana.
  posterior urethra uretra posterior.
  prostatic urethra uretra prostática.
  spongy urethra uretra esponjosa.
  urethra feminina uretra femenina.
  urethra masculina uretra masculina.
  urethra virilis uretra virilis.
urethral *adj.* uretral.
urethralgia *n.* uretralgia.
urethrameter *n.* uretrámetro.
urethrascope *n.* uretrascopio.
urethratresia *n.* uretratresia.
urethrectomy *n.* uretrectomía.
urethremorrhagia *n.* uretremorragia.
urethremphraxis *n.* uretrenfraxis.
urethreurynter *n.* uretreurínter.
urethrism *n.* uretrismo.
urethrismus *n.* uretrismo.
urethritis *n.* uretritis.
  anterior urethritis uretritis anterior.
  follicular urethritis uretritis folicular.
  gonococcal urethritis uretritis gonocócica, uretritis gonorreica.
  gonococcic urethritis uretritis gonocócica, uretritis gonorreica.
  gonorrheal urethritis uretritis gonocócica, uretritis gonorreica.
  gouty urethritis uretritis gotosa.
  granular urethritis uretritis granular.
  non-gonococcal urethritis uretritis no gonocócica.
  non-specific urethritis (NSU) uretritis inespecífica (UNE).
  posterior urethritis uretritis posterior.
  prophylactic urethritis uretritis profiláctica.
  simple urethritis uretritis simple.
  specific urethritis uretritis específica.
  urethritis cystica uretritis quística.
  urethritis glandularis uretritis glandular.
  urethritis granulosa uretritis granulosa.
  urethritis orificii externi uretritis del orificio externo.

urethritis petrificans uretritis petrificante.
urethritis venerea uretritis venérea.
urethrobalanoplasty *n.* uretrobalanoplastia.
urethroblennorrhea *n.* uretroblenorrea.
urethrobulbar *adj.* uretrobulbar.
urethrocele *n.* uretrocele.
urethrocystitis *n.* uretrocistitis.
urethrocystogram *n.* uretrocistograma.
urethrocystography *n.* uretrocistografía.
urethrocystometrography *n.* uretrocistometrografía.
urethrocystometry *n.* uretrocistometría.
urethrocystopexy *n.* uretrocistopexia.
urethrodynia *n.* uretrodinia.
urethrography *n.* uretrografía.
voiding urethrography uretrografía de evacuación.
urethrometer *n.* uretrómetro.
urethrometry *n.* uretrometría.
urethropenile *adj.* uretropeneal, uretropeneano, -na, uretropeniano, -na.
urethroperineal *adj.* uretroperineal.
urethroperineoscrotal *adj.* uretroperineoscrotal.
urethropexy *n.* uretropexia.
urethrophraxis *n.* uretrofraxis.
urethrophyma *n.* uretrofima.
urethroplasty *n.* uretroplastia.
urethroprostatic *adj.* uretroprostático, -ca.
urethrorectal *adj.* uretrorrectal.
urethrorrhagia *n.* uretrorragia.
urethrorrhaphy *n.* uretrorrafia.
urethrorrhea *n.* uretrorrea.
urethroscope *n.* uretroscopio.
urethroscopic *adj.* uretroscópico, -ca.
urethroscopy *n.* uretroscopia.
urethroscrotal *adj.* uretroescrotal.
urethrospasm *n.* uretroespasmo, uretrospasmo.
urethrostaxis *n.* uretrostaxis.
urethrostenosis *n.* uretroestenosis, uretrostenosis.
urethrostomy *n.* uretrostomía.
perineal urethrostomy uretrostomía perineal.
urethrotome *n.* uretrótomo.
Maisonneuve's urethrotome uretrótomo de Maisonneuve.
urethrotomy *n.* uretrotomía.
external urethrotomy uretrotomía externa.
internal urethrotomy uretrotomía interna.
perineal urethrotomy uretrotomía perineal.
urethrotrigonitis *n.* uretrotrigonitis.
urethrovaginal *adj.* uretrovaginal, vaginouretral.
urethrovesical *adj.* uretrovesical.
urethrovesicopexy *n.* uretrovesicopexia.
uretic *adj.* urético, -ca.
urgency *n.* urgencia[2].
motor urgency urgencia motora.
sensory urgency urgencia sensorial.
urhidrosis *n.* urhidrosis, urinhidrosis, urohidrosis.
urhidrosis crystallina urhidrosis cristalina.
uric *adj.* úrico, -ca.
uricacidemia *n.* uricacidemia.
uricaciduria *n.* uricaciduria.
uricemia *n.* uricemia.
uricocholia *n.* uricocolia.
uricolysis *n.* uricólisis.
uricolytic *adj.* uricolítico, -ca.
uricometer *n.* uricómetro.
Ruhemann's uricometer uricómetro de Ruhemann.
uricopoiesis *n.* uricopoyesis.
uricosuria *n.* uricosuria.
uricosuric *adj.* uricosúrico, -ca.

uricotelic *adj.* uricotélico, -ca.
uridrosis *n.* uridrosis.
uriesthesis *n.* uriestesia.
urina *n.* orina.
urina potus orina de la bebida.
urinable *adj.* urinable.
urinacidometer *n.* orinacidómetro.
urinal *n.* orinal.
urinalysis *n.* urinálisis.
urinary *adj.* urinario, -ria.
urinate *v.* orinar.
urination *n.* micción, urinación.
precipitant urination micción precipitante.
stuttering urination micción tartamuda, micción tartamudeante.
urine *n.* orina, urina.
ammoniacal urine orina amoniacal.
black urine orina azul, orina negra.
brick dust urine orina en polvo de ladrillo.
chylous urine orina quilosa.
cloudy urine orina turbia.
crude urine orina bruta, orina cruda.
diabetic urine orina diabética.
dyspeptic urine orina dispéptica.
febrile urine orina febril.
feverish urine orina febril.
gouty urine orina gotosa.
maple syrup urine orina en jarabe de arce.
milky urine orina lechosa.
nebulous urine orina nebulosa.
residual urine orina residual.
urinemia *n.* urinemia.
urinidrosis *n.* urinhidrosis.
uriniferous *adj.* urinífero, -ra.
urinific *adj.* urinífico, -ca.
uriningism *n.* uriningismo.
uriniparous *adj.* uriníparo, -ra.
urinocryoscopy *n.* urinocrioscopia.
urinogenital *adj.* urinogenital.
urinogenous *adj.* urinógeno, -na.
urinoglucosometer *n.* urinoglucosómetro.
urinologist *n.* urinólogo, -ga.
urinology *n.* urinología.
urinoma *n.* urinoma.
urinometer *n.* urinómetro, urodensímetro.
urinometry *n.* urinometría.
urinophilous *adj.* urinófilo, -la.
urinoscopy *n.* urinoscopia.
urinosexual *adj.* urinosexual.
urinous *adj.* urinoso, -sa.
uriposia *n.* uriposia.
urisolvent *adj.* urisolvente.
urningism *n.* urningismo.
urnism *n.* urnismo.
uroacidimeter *n.* uroacidímetro, uroacidómetro.
uroammoniac *adj.* uroamoniacal, uroamónico, -ca.
uroanthelone *n.* uroantelona.
uroazotometer *n.* uroazómetro, uroazotómetro.
urobilin *n.* urobilina.
urobilinemia *n.* urobilinemia.
urobilinogen *n.* urobilinógeno.
urobilinogenemia *n.* urobilinogenemia.
urobilinogenuria *n.* urobilinogenuria.
urobilinoid *adj.* urobilinoide, urobilinoideo, -a.
urobilinoiden *n.* urobilinoideno.
urobilinuria *n.* urobilinuria.
urocele *n.* urocele.
urocheras *n.* uroqueras.
urochesia *n.* uroquesia.
urochezia *n.* uroquesia.
urochrome *n.* urocromo.
urochromogen *n.* urocromógeno.

uroclepsia *n.* uroclepsia.
urocoproporphyria *n.* urocoproporfiria.
urocrisia *n.* urocrisia.
urocrisis *n.* urocrisia, urocrisis.
urocriterion *n.* urocriterio.
urocyanin *n.* urocianina.
urocyanogen *n.* urocianógeno.
urocyanosis *n.* urocianosis.
urocyst *n.* urocisto.
urocystic *adj.* urocístico, -ca.
urocystis *n.* urocistis.
urocystitis *n.* urocistitis.
urodeum *n.* urodeo.
urodochium *n.* urodoquio.
urodyalisis *n.* urodiálisis.
urodynamic *adj.* urodinámico, -ca.
urodynamics *n.* urodinamia, urodinámica.
urodynia *n.* urodinia.
uroedema *n.* uroedema.
uroenterone *n.* uroenterona.
uroerythrin *n.* uroeritrina.
uroflavin *n.* uroflavina.
uroflometer *n.* uroflómetro.
urofluometer *n.* urofluómetro.
urofuscin *n.* urofuscina.
urofuscohematin *n.* urofuscohematina.
urogaster *n.* urogáster.
urogastrone *n.* urogastrona.
urogenesis *n.* urogénesis.
urogenital *adj.* urogenital.
urogenous *adj.* urógeno, -na.
uroglaucina *n.* uroglaucina.
urogram *n.* urograma.
urography *n.* urografía.
anterograde urography urografía anterógrada.
ascending urography urografía ascendente.
cystoscopyc urography urografía cistoscópica.
descending urography urografía descendente.
excretion urography urografía de excreción, urografía excretora, urografía excretoria.
excretory urography urografía de excreción, urografía excretora, urografía excretoria.
intravenous urography urografía intravenosa.
oral urography urografía bucal.
retrograde urography urografía retrógrada.
urogravimeter *n.* urogravímetro.
urohematin *n.* urohematina.
urohematonephrosis *n.* urohematonefrosis.
urohematoporphyrin *n.* urohematoporfirina.
uroheparin *n.* uroheparina.
urohypertensin *n.* urohipertensina.
urokinase *n.* urocinasa, uroquinasa.
urokinetic *adj.* urocinético, -ca, uroquinético, -ca.
urolagnia *n.* urolagnia.
urolith *n.* urolito.
urolithiasis *n.* urolitiasis.
urolithic *adj.* urolítico, -ca.
urolithology *n.* urolitología.
urologic *adj.* urológico, -ca.
urologist *n.* urólogo, -ga.
urology *n.* urología.
urolutein *n.* uroluteína.
uromancy *n.* uromancia, uromancía.
uromelanin *n.* uromelanina.
uromelus *n.* uromelo.
urometer *n.* urómetro.
urometric *adj.* urométrico, -ca.
urometry *n.* urometría.
uromucoid *n.* uromucoide.
uroncus *n.* uronco.
uronephrosis *n.* uronefrosis.
uronology *n.* uronología.
urononcometry *n.* urononcometría.

uronophile *adj.* uronófilo, -la.
uronoscopy *n.* uronoscopia.
uropathogen *n.* uropatógeno.
uropathy *n.* uropatía.
  obstructive uropathy uropatía obstructiva.
uropenia *n.* uropenia.
uropepsin *n.* uropepsina.
uropepsinogen *n.* uropepsinógeno.
urophanic *adj.* urofánico, -ca.
urophein *n.* urofeína.
urophilia *n.* urofilia.
urophobia *n.* urofobia.
urophosphometer *n.* urofosfómetro.
uroplania *n.* uroplania.
uropod *n.* urópodo.
uropoiesis *n.* uropoyesis.
uropoietic *adj.* uropoyético, -ca.
uroporphyria *n.* uroporfiria.
  erythropoietic uroporphyria uroporfiria eritropoyética.
uroporphyrin *n.* uroporfirina.
uropsammus *n.* uropsamo.
uropterin *n.* uropterina.
uropurpurin *n.* uropurpurina.
uropyonephrosis *n.* uropionefrosis.
uropyoureter *n.* uropiouréter.
uroradiology *n.* urorradiología.
urorectal *adj.* urorrectal.
urorhythmography *n.* urorritmografía.
urorosein *n.* urorroseína.
uroroseinogen *n.* urorroseinógeno.
urorrhagia *n.* urorragia.
urorrhea *n.* urorrea.
urorrhodin *n.* urorrodina.
urorrhodinogen *n.* urorrodinógeno.
urorubin *n.* urorrubina.
urorubinogen *n.* urorrubinógeno.
urorubrohematin *n.* urorrubrohematina.
urosaccharometry *n.* urosacarimetría.
urosacin *n.* urosacina.
uroscheocele *n.* urosqueocele.
uroschesis *n.* urosquesis.
uroscopic *adj.* uroscópico, -ca.
uroscopy *n.* uroscopia.
urosemiology *n.* urosemiología.
urosepsin *n.* urosepsina, uroseptina.
urosepsis *n.* urosepsis, urotoxemia.
uroseptic *adj.* uroséptico, -ca.
urosis *n.* urosis.
urospectrin *n.* uroespectrina, urospectrina.
urostalagmometry *n.* urostalagmia, urostalagmometría.
urostealith *n.* urostealito.
urostomy *n.* urostomía.
urothelial *adj.* urotelial.
urothelium *n.* urotelio.
urothorax *n.* urotórax.
urotoxia *n.* urotoxia.
urotoxic *adj.* urotóxico, -ca.
urotoxicity *n.* urotoxicidad.
urotoxin *n.* urotoxina.
urotoxy *n.* urotoxia.
uroureter *n.* urouréter.
uroxanthin *n.* uroxantina.
urrhodin *n.* urrodina.
urticant *adj.* urticante.
urticaria *n.* urticaria.
  acute urticaria urticaria aguda.
  aquagenic urticaria urticaria acuogénica.
  bullous urticaria urticaria ampollar, urticaria ampollosa, urticaria bullosa.
  cholinergic urticaria urticaria colinérgica.
  chronic urticaria urticaria crónica.
  cold urticaria urticaria fría, urticaria por frío.
  congelation urticaria urticaria por congelación.

  contact urticaria urticaria de contacto.
  factitious urticaria urticaria facticia.
  febril urticaria urticaria febril.
  giant urticaria urticaria gigante.
  heat urticaria urticaria por calor.
  hemorrhagic urticaria urticaria hemorrágica.
  juvenile urticaria pigmentosa urticaria pigmentosa juvenil.
  light urticaria urticaria fotógena.
  papular urticaria urticaria papular, urticaria papulosa.
  pressure urticaria urticaria por compresión, urticaria por presión.
  solar urticaria urticaria solar.
  urticaria acuta urticaria aguda.
  urticaria bullosa urticaria ampollar, urticaria ampollosa, urticaria bullosa.
  urticaria chronica urticaria crónica.
  urticaria conferta urticaria confluyente.
  urticaria endemica urticaria endémica, urticaria epidémica.
  urticaria epidemica urticaria endémica, urticaria epidémica.
  urticaria factitia urticaria facticia.
  urticaria febrilis urticaria febril.
  urticaria hemorrhagica urticaria hemorrágica.
  urticaria maculosa urticaria macular, urticaria maculosa.
  urticaria medicamentosa urticaria medicamentosa.
  urticaria multiformis endemica urticaria multiforme endémica.
  urticaria papulosa urticaria papular, urticaria papulosa.
  urticaria perstans urticaria persistente.
  urticaria pigmentosa urticaria pigmentosa.
  urticaria solaris urticaria solar.
  urticaria SUBcutanea urticaria SUBcutánea.
  urticaria tuberosa urticaria tuberosa.
  urticaria vesiculosa urticaria vesicular.
  vibratory urticaria urticaria vibratoria.
urticarial *adj.* urticarial.
urticariogenic *adj.* urticariógeno, -na.
urticarious *adj.* urticarioso, -sa.
urtication *n.* urticación.
ustilaginism *n.* ustilaginismo.
Ustilago Ustilago.
  Ustilago maydis Ustilago maydis.
ustion *n.* ustión.
ustulation *n.* ustulación.
ustus ustus.
usual *adj.* habitual.
uta *n.* uta.
uterine *adj.* uterino, -na.
uterismus *n.* uterismo.
uteroabdominal *adj.* uteroabdominal.
uterocele *n.* uterocele.
uterocervical *adj.* uterocervical.
uterocystostomy *n.* uterocistostomía.
uterodynia *n.* uterodinia.
uterofixation *n.* uterofijación.
uterogenic *adj.* uterógeno, -na.
uterogestation *n.* uterogestación.
uteroglobulin *n.* uteroglobulina.
uterography *n.* uterografía.
uterolith *n.* uterolito.
uterometer *n.* uterómetro.
uterometry *n.* uterometría.
utero-ovarian *adj.* uteroovárico, -ca.
uteroparietal *adj.* uteroparietal.
uteropelvic *adj.* uteropelviano, -na, uteropélvico, -ca.
uteropexy *n.* uteropexia.
uteroplacental *adj.* uteroplacentario, -ria.
uteroplasty *n.* uteroplastia.

uterorectal *adj.* uterorrectal.
uterosacral *adj.* uterosacro, -cra.
uterosalpingography *n.* uterosalpingografía.
uterosclerosis *n.* uterosclerosis.
uteroscope *n.* uteroscopio.
uteroscopy *n.* uteroscopia.
uterothermometry *n.* uterotermometría.
uterotomy *n.* uterotomía.
uterotonic *adj.* uterotónico, -ca.
uterotropic *adj.* uterotrópico, -ca.
uterotubal *adj.* uterotubárico, -ca, uterotubario, -ria.
uterotubography *n.* uterotubografía.
uterovaginal *adj.* uterovaginal, vaginouterino, -na.
uteroventral *adj.* uteroventral.
uterovesical *adj.* uterovesical.
uterus *n.* útero, uterus.
  anomalous uterus útero anómalo.
  arcuate uterus útero arcuato, útero arqueado, uterus arcuatus.
  bicornate uterus útero bicorne.
  bifid uterus útero bífido.
  biforate uterus útero biorificial.
  bipartite uterus útero bipartido, uterus bipartitus.
  capped uterus útero recubierto.
  cochleate uterus útero cocleado.
  cordiform uterus útero cordiforme.
  Couvelaire uterus útero de Couvelaire.
  double uterus útero doble, uterus duplex separatus.
  double-mouthed uterus útero de doble boca.
  duplex uterus útero doble, uterus duplex separatus.
  fetal uterus útero fetal.
  gravid uterus útero grávido.
  heart-shaped uterus útero en forma de corazón.
  hour-glass uterus útero en reloj de arena.
  incudiform uterus útero incudiforme.
  infantile uterus útero infantil.
  masculine uterus útero masculino.
  pubescent uterus útero pubescente.
  ribbon uterus útero en cinta.
  saddle-shaped uterus útero en silla de montar.
  septate uterus útero septado, útero tabicado.
  triangular uterus útero triangular.
  unicorn uterus útero unicorne.
  uterus acollis útero acervical, útero acólico, uterus acollis.
  uterus arcuatus útero arcuato, útero arqueado, uterus arcuatus.
  uterus bicameratus vetularum útero bicameral sellado, útero bicameral senil, uterus bicameratus vetularum.
  uterus bicornis útero bicorne.
  uterus bicornis bicollis útero bicorne bicervical.
  uterus bicornis unicollis útero bicorne unicervical.
  uterus bifidus útero bífido.
  uterus biforis útero biorificial.
  uterus bilocularis útero bilocular.
  uterus bipartitus útero bipartido, uterus bipartitus.
  uterus cordiformis útero cordiforme.
  uterus didelphys útero didelfo.
  uterus duplex útero doble, uterus duplex separatus.
  uterus incudiformis útero incudiforme.
  uterus masculinus útero masculino.
  uterus parvicollis útero parvicólico, uterus parvicollis.
  uterus planifundalis útero planifúndico.
  uterus rudimentarius útero rudimentario.

uterus septus útero septado, útero tabicado.
uterus simplex útero simple.
uterus SUBseptus útero SUBseptado, útero SUBtabicado.
uterus triangularis útero triangular.
uterus unicornis útero unicorne.
utricle *n.* utrículo.
  prostatic utricle utrículo prostático.
  urethral utricle utrículo uretral.
utricular *adj.* utricular.
utriculitis *n.* utriculitis.
utriculosaccular *adj.* utriculosacular.
utriculus *n.* utrículo.
  utriculus masculinus utrículo masculino.
  utriculus prostaticus utrículo prostático.
  utriculus vestibuli utrículo del oído, utrículo del vestíbulo, utrículo vestibular.
utriform *adj.* utriforme.
uvea *n.* úvea.
uveal *adj.* uveal.
uveitic *adj.* uveítico, -ca.
uveitis *n.* uveítis.
  anterior uveitis uveítis anterior.
  endogenous uveitis uveítis endógena.
  exogenous uveitis uveítis exógena.
  Förster's uveitis uveítis de Förster.

  Fuchs' uveitis uveítis de Fuchs.
  granulomatous uveitis uveítis granulomatosa.
  heterochromic uveitis uveítis heterocrómica.
  intermediate uveitis uveítis intermedia.
  lens-induced uveitis uveítis inducida por el cristalino.
  non-granulomatous uveitis uveítis no granulomatosa.
  phacoanaphylactic uveitis uveítis facoanafiláctica.
  phacoantigenic uveitis uveítis facoantigénica.
  phacogenic uveitis uveítis facogénica.
  phacotoxic uveitis uveítis facotóxica.
  posterior uveitis uveítis posterior.
  sympathetic uveitis uveítis simpática.
  total uveitis uveítis total.
  tuberculous uveitis uveítis tuberculosa.
uveoencephalitis *n.* uveoencefalitis.
uveolabyrinthitis *n.* uveolaberintitis.
uveomeningitis *n.* uveomeningitis.
uveoneuraxitis *n.* uveoneuraxitis.
uveoparotid *adj.* uveoparotídeo, -a.
uveoparotitis *n.* uveoparotitis.
uveoplasty *n.* uveoplastia.
uveoscleritis *n.* uveoescleritis, uveoscleritis.
uviform *adj.* uviforme.

uvula *n.* úvula.
  bifid uvula úvula bífida.
  cleft uvula úvula hendida.
  forked uvula úvula bifurcada.
  Lieutaud's uvula úvula de Lieutaud.
  palatine uvula úvula palatina.
  split uvula úvula hendida.
  uvula cerebelli úvula cerebelosa, úvula de cerebelo.
  uvula fissa úvula fisurada.
  uvula of the bladder úvula vesical.
  uvula of the cerebellum úvula cerebelosa, úvula de cerebelo.
  uvula palatina úvula palatina.
  uvula vermis úvula del vermis, úvula vermis.
uvulaptosis *n.* uvulaptosis.
uvular *adj.* uvular.
uvulatome *adj.* uvulátomo, -ma.
uvulatomy *n.* uvulatomía.
uvulectomy *n.* cionectomía, uvulectomía.
uvulitis *n.* uvulitis.
uvulopalatopharyngoplasty *n.* uvulopalatofaringoplastia.
uvuloptosis *n.* uvuloptosis.
uvulotome *n.* uvulótomo.
uvulotomy *n.* uvulotomía.

V v

vaccigenous *adj.* vaccígeno, -na.
vaccina *n.* vaccina.
vaccinable *adj.* vacunable.
vaccinal *adj.* vaccinal, vacunal.
vaccinate *v.* vacunar.
vaccination *n.* vacunación.
  smallpox vaccination vacunación contra la viruela.
vaccinationist *n.* vacunacionista.
vaccinator *n.* vacunador, vacunador, -ra.
vaccine *n.* vacuna.
  (bacillus) Calmette-Guérin (BCG) vaccine vacuna del bacilo de Calmette-Guérin (BCG).
  adjuvant vaccine vacuna auxiliar, vacuna coadyuvante.
  adsorbed diphtheria and tetanus toxoids and pertussis (DTP) vaccine vacuna absorbida de toxoide diftérico y tetánico y de la tos ferina (DTP).
  adsorbed pertussis vaccine vacuna absorbida de la tos ferina.
  anthrax vaccine vacuna del carbunco.
  antirabic vaccine vacuna antirrábica.
  antityphoid vaccine vacuna antitífica, vacuna antitifoidea, vacuna antitifus.
  aqueous vaccine vacuna acuosa.
  attenuated vaccine vacuna atenuada.
  autogenous vaccine vacuna autógena.
  bacterial vaccine vacuna bacteriana, vacuna bactérica.
  bovine vaccine vacuna bovina.
  Calmette-Guérin vaccine vacuna de Calmette-Guérin.
  Calmette's vaccine vacuna de Calmette.
  caprinized vaccine vacuna caprinizada.
  cholera vaccine vacuna anticólera, vacuna anticolérica, vacuna del cólera.
  combined vaccine vacuna polivalente.
  Cox vaccine vacuna de Cox.
  crystal violet vaccine vacuna de violeta cristal.
  Dakar vaccine vacuna de Dakar.
  diphtheria and tetanus toxoids and pertussis (DTP) vaccine tetánico y de la tos ferina (DTP), vacuna de toxoide diftérico.
  diphtheria vaccine vacuna antidiftérica, vacuna de la difteria.
  duck embryo origin vaccine (DEV) vacuna de embrión de pato.
  duck embryo vaccine vacuna de embrión de pato.
  Haffkine's vaccine vacuna de Haffkine.
  hepatitis B vaccine vacuna contra la hepatitis B, vacuna de la hepatitis B.
  heterologous vaccine vacuna heteróloga.
  homologous vaccine vacuna homóloga.
  human diploid cell rabies vaccine (HDRV) vacuna antirrábica preparada de células diploides humanas, vacuna antirrábica preparada en células diploides humanas (HDRV).

  hydrophobia vaccine vacuna contra la hidrofobia.
  inactivated poliovirus vaccine (IPV) vacuna antipoliomielítica inactivada (IPV).
  inactivated vaccine vacuna de virus inactivados, vacuna inactivada.
  inactived measles virus vaccine vacuna de virus del sarampión inactivado.
  inactived mumps virus vaccine vacuna de virus inactivado de la parotiditis.
  influenza virus vaccine vacuna antigripal, vacuna de virus de influenza, vacuna de virus de la influenza.
  killed vaccine vacuna de organismos muertos.
  live attenuated measles virus vaccine vacuna de virus vivos atenuados de sarampión.
  live measles and rubella virus vaccine vacuna de virus vivos de sarampión y rubéola.
  live measles virus vaccine vacuna de virus vivos de sarampión.
  live mumps virus vaccine vacuna de virus vivos de parotiditis.
  live rubella and mumps virus vaccine vacuna de virus vivos de rubéola y parotiditis.
  live rubella virus vaccine vacuna antirrubeólica de virus vivos, vacuna de virus de la rubéola vivos, vacuna de virus de rubéola vivos.
  live vaccine vacuna viva.
  measles vaccine vacuna antisarampión, vacuna antisarampionosa, vacuna del sarampión.
  measles virus vaccine vacuna antisarampión, vacuna antisarampionosa, vacuna de virus sarampionoso, vacuna del sarampión.
  meningococcal polysaccharide vaccine vacuna antimeningocócica de polisacáridos.
  mixed vaccine vacuna mixta.
  multivalent vaccine vacuna multivalente.
  measles, mumps and rubella (MMR) vaccine vacuna contra el sarampión, la parotiditis y la rubéola (MMR).
  mumps virus vaccine vacuna antiparotidítica, vacuna antiparotiditis, vacuna de virus de las paperas.
  oil vaccine vacuna de aceite.
  oral poliovirus vaccine (OPV) vacuna antipoliomielítica oral (OPV).
  Pasteur vaccine vacuna de Pasteur.
  pertussis vaccine vacuna anticoqueluchosa, vacuna antipertussis, vacuna antitosferinosa, vacuna contra la tos ferina, vacuna de la tos ferina.
  plague vaccine vacuna antipeste, vacuna de la peste.
  pneumococcal polysaccharide vaccine vacuna de polisacáridos neumocócicos.
  pneumococcal vaccine vacuna antineumocócica.
  poliovirus vaccine vacuna antipoliomielítica, vacuna antipoliomielitis, vacuna de la poliomielitis, vacuna de poliovirus.

  polyvalent vaccine vacuna polivalente.
  rabies vaccine vacuna de la rabia.
  recombinant hepatitis B vaccine vacuna recombinante de la hepatitis B.
  replicative vaccine vacuna duplicativa.
  rickettsia attenuated vaccine vacuna de rickettsias atenuadas.
  Rocky Mountain spotted fever vaccine vacuna anti-fiebre manchada de las Montañas Rocosas.
  rubella virus vaccine vacuna antirrubéola, vacuna antirrubeólica.
  Sabin's oral vaccine vacuna antipoliomielítica de Sabin, vacuna de Sabin bucal.
  Sabin's vaccine vacuna de Sabin.
  Salk vaccine vacuna antipoliomielítica de Salk, vacuna de Salk.
  Sauer's vaccine vacuna de Sauer.
  Semple's vaccine vacuna de Semple.
  sensitized vaccine vacuna sensibilizada, vacuna sensibilizada viva.
  smallpox vaccine vacuna antivariólica, vacuna de la viruela.
  Spencer-Parker vaccine vacuna de Spencer-Parker.
  split virus vaccine vacuna de fracciones virales.
  staphylococcus vaccine vacuna de estafilococo, vacuna estafilocócica.
  stock vaccine vacuna de stock.
  streptococcic vaccine vacuna de estreptococos, vacuna estreptocócica.
  subunit vaccine vacuna de subunidades, vacuna de subunidades virales.
  subvirion vaccine vacuna subviral.
  TAB vaccine vacuna TAB.
  tetanus toxoids and pertussis (DTP) vaccine tetánico y antipertussis (DTP), vacuna de toxoide diftérico.
  tetanus vaccine vacuna antitetánica.
  triple vaccine vacuna triple, vacuna triple vírica.
  trivalent vaccine vacuna triple, vacuna triple vírica.
  tuberculosis vaccine vacuna antituberculosa, vacuna de la tuberculosis.
  typhoid vaccine vacuna contra el tifus, vacuna de la tifoidea, vacuna del tifo, vacuna del tifus.
  typhus vaccine vacuna contra el tifus, vacuna de la tifoidea, vacuna del tifo, vacuna del tifus.
  whooping cough vaccine vacuna contra la tos ferina, vacuna de la tos ferina.
  yellow fever vaccine vacuna antiamarílica, vacuna anti-fiebre amarilla, vacuna de Aragão, vacuna de la fiebre amarilla.
vaccinia *n.* vaccinia.
  fetal vaccinia vaccinia fetal.
  generalized vaccinia vaccinia generalizada.
  progressive vaccinia vaccinia progresiva.

vaccinia gangrenosa vaccinia gangrenosa.
vaccinial *adj.* vaccinial.
vacciniculturist *n.* vacciniculturista.
vaccinid *n.* vaccínide.
vaccinifer *adj.* vaccinífero, vacunífero, -ra.
vacciniform *adj.* vacciniforme, vacuniforme.
vaccinin *n.* vaccinina.
vacciniola *n.* vacciniola, vaccinola.
vaccinist *n.* vacunador, -ra.
vaccinization *n.* vaccinización, vacunización.
vaccinogen *n.* vaccinógeno.
vaccinogenous *adj.* vaccinógeno, -na, vacunógeno, -na.
vaccinoid *adj.* vaccinoide, vacunoide.
vaccinostyle *n.* vaccinostilo, vacunostilo.
vaccinotherapy *n.* vacunoterapia.
vaccinum vaccinum.
vacuolar *adj.* vacuolar².
vacuolate *adj.* vacuolado, -da, vacuolar¹.
vacuolated *adj.* vacuolado, -da.
vacuolation *n.* vacuolación, vacuolización.
vacuole *n.* vacuola.
 autophagic vacuole vacuola autofágica.
 condensing vacuole vacuola de condensación.
 contractile vacuole vacuola contráctil, vacuola pulsátil.
 digestive vacuole vacuola digestiva.
 food vacuole vacuola alimenticia.
 parasitophorous vacuole vacuola parasitófora.
 plasmocrine vacuole vacuola plasmocrina.
 rhagiocrine vacuole vacuola ragiocrina.
 water vacuole vacuola acuosa.
vacuome *n.* vacuoma.
vacutome *n.* vacútomo.
vacuum *n.* vacío, vacuum.
 high vacuum gran vacío.
 Torricellian vacuum vacío de Torricelli, vacío torricelliano.
 vacuum extractor vacuoextractor.
vadum vadum.
vagal *adj.* vagal.
vagectomy *n.* vaguectomía.
vagina *n.* vagina, vaina.
 bipartite vagina vagina bipartida.
 septate vagina vagina septada, vagina tabicada.
 spiral vagina vaina espiral.
 vagina masculina vagina masculina.
vaginal *adj.* vaginal.
vaginalectomy *n.* vaginalectomía.
vaginalitis *n.* vaginalitis.
 plastic vaginalitis vaginalitis plástica.
vaginapexy *n.* vaginapexia.
vaginate¹ *adj.* vaginado, -da.
vaginate² *v.* vaginar.
vaginectomy *n.* vaginectomía.
vaginiperineotomy *n.* vaginoperineotomía.
vaginismus *n.* vaginismo.
 mental vaginismus vaginismo mental.
 perineal vaginismus vaginismo perineal.
 posterior vaginismus vaginismo posterior.
 vulvar vaginismus vaginismo anterior, vaginismo vulvar.
vaginitis *n.* vaginitis.
 adhesive vaginitis vaginitis adhesiva.
 amebic vaginitis vaginitis amebiana, vaginitis amébica.
 atrophic vaginitis vaginitis atrófica.
 Candida vaginitis vaginitis por Candida.
 desquamative inflammatory vaginitis vaginitis inflamatoria descamativa, vaginitis inflamatoria exfoliativa.
 diphtheritic vaginitis vaginitis diftérica.

emphysematous vaginitis vaginitis enfisematosa, vaginitis gaseosa.
Gardnerella vaginalis vaginitis vaginitis por Gardnerella vaginalis.
granular vaginitis vaginitis granulosa, vaginitis verrugosa.
pinworm vaginitis vaginitis por oxiuros.
postmenopausal vaginitis vaginitis posmenopáusica.
senile vaginitis vaginitis senil.
trichomonas vaginitis vaginitis tricomoniásica.
vaginitis adhaesiva vaginitis adhesiva.
vaginitis cystica vaginitis quística.
vaginitis emphysematosa vaginitis enfisematosa, vaginitis gaseosa.
vaginitis senilis vaginitis senil.
vaginitis testis vaginitis testicular, vaginitis testis.
vaginoabdominal *adj.* vaginoabdominal.
vaginocele *n.* vaginocele.
vaginocutaneous *adj.* vaginocutáneo, -a.
vaginodynia *n.* vaginodinia.
vaginofixation *n.* vaginofijación.
vaginogram *n.* vaginograma.
vaginography *n.* vaginografía.
vaginohysterectomy *n.* vaginohisterectomía.
vaginolabial *adj.* vaginolabial.
vaginometer *n.* vaginómetro.
vaginomycosis *n.* vaginomicosis.
vaginopathy *n.* vaginopatía.
vaginoperineal *adj.* vaginoperineal.
vaginoperineoplasty *n.* vaginoperineoplastia.
vaginoperineorrhaphy *n.* vaginoperineorrafia.
vaginoperineotomy *n.* vaginoperineotomía.
vaginoperitoneal *adj.* vaginoperitoneal.
vaginopexy *n.* vaginopexia.
vaginoplasty *n.* vaginoplastia.
vaginoscope *n.* vaginoscopio.
vaginoscopy *n.* vaginoscopia.
vaginosis *n.* vaginosis.
 bacterial vaginosis vaginosis bacteriana.
vaginotomy *n.* vaginotomía.
vaginovesical *adj.* vaginovesical.
vaginovulvar *adj.* vaginovulvar.
vagitus vagido, vagitus.
 vagitus uterinus vagido uterino.
 vagitus vaginalis vagido vaginal.
vagoaccessorius *n.* vagoaccesorio, vagoespinal.
vagoglossopharyngeal *adj.* vagoglosofaríngeo, -a.
vagogram *n.* vagograma.
vagolysis *n.* vagólisis.
vagolytic *adj.* vagolítico, -ca.
vagomimetic *adj.* vagomimético, -ca.
vagosplanchnic *adj.* vagoesplácnico, -ca, vagosplácnico, -ca.
vagosympathetic *adj.* vagosimpático, -ca.
vagotomy *n.* vagotomía.
 bilateral vagotomy vagotomía bilateral.
 highly selective vagotomy vagotomía muy selectiva, vagotomía selectiva total (VST), vagotomía supraselectiva.
 medical vagotomy vagotomía médica.
 parietal cell vagotomy vagotomía de células parietales.
 pharmacologic vagotomy vagotomía farmacológica.
 selective proximal vagotomy vagotomía selectiva proximal (VSP).
 selective vagotomy vagotomía selectiva.
 surgical vagotomy vagotomía quirúrgica.

truncal vagotomy vagotomía troncal (VT), vagotomía troncular.
vagotonia *n.* vagotonía.
vagotonic *adj.* vagotónico, -ca.
vagotonin *n.* vagotonina.
vagotony *n.* vagotonía.
vagotrope *adj.* vagotropo, -pa.
vagotropic *adj.* vagotrópico, -ca.
vagotropism *n.* vagotropismo.
vagovagal *adj.* vagovagal.
vagrant *adj.* vagrante.
vagus *n.* vago.
valence *n.* valencia.
 antigenic valence valencia antigénica.
 chemical valence valencia química.
 ecological valence valencia ecológica.
 negative valence valencia negativa.
 positive valence valencia positiva.
valency *n.* valencia.
valent *adj.* valente.
valetudinarian *adj.* valetudinario, -ria.
valetudinarianism *n.* valetudinarianismo.
valgoid *adj.* valgoide.
valgus *adj.* valgo, -ga, valgus.
valid *adj.* válido, -da.
validation *n.* validación.
 consensual validation validación consensuada, validación consensual.
 data validation validación de datos.
 model validation validación de un modelo.
 nomenclatural validation validación de la nomenclatura.
validity *n.* validez.
 concurrent validity validez concurrente, vigencia concurrente.
 constructive validity validez de construcción.
 content validity validez de contenido.
 criterion-related validity validez relacionada con un criterio.
 predictive validity validez predictiva.
 replicative validity validez replicativa.
 structural validity validez estructural.
valinemia *n.* valinemia.
vallate *adj.* valado, -da.
vallecula valécula, vallecula.
vallecular *adj.* valecular.
valley *n.* valle.
vallum vallum.
 vallum unguis vallum ungueal, vallum unguis.
value *n.* valor.
 % AT value valor % AT, valor AT.
 %GC value valor %GC, valor GC.
 acetyl value valor acetilo.
 acid value valor de ácido.
 additive value valor aditivo.
 AT value valor % AT, valor AT.
 biological value valor biológico.
 breakdown value valor de ruptura.
 breeding value valor de mejora.
 buffer value valor amortiguador, valor buffer.
 buffer value of the blood valor buffer de la sangre.
 C value valor C.
 caloric value valor calórico, valor calorífico de los alimentos.
 conventional value of a magnitude valor convencional de una magnitud.
 cryocrit value valor de criócrito.
 D value valor D.
 extreme value of a distribution valor extremo de una distribución.
 fuel value valor de combustible.
 GC value valor %GC, valor GC.
 genotypic value valor genotípico.

globular value valor globular.
Hehner value valor de Hehner.
homing value valor de base.
iodine value valor yodo.
liminal value valor liminal.
magnitude value valor de una magnitud.
maturation value valor de maduración.
mean clinical value valor clínico medio.
mean square value valor medio cuadrático.
mean value valor medio.
normal value valor normal.
numeric value of a quantity valor numérico de una magnitud.
P value valor P.
phenotypic value valor fenotípico.
physiological energetic value valor energético fisiológico.
predictive value valor de predicción, valor predictivo.
reference value valor de referencia.
threshold value valor umbral.
true value valor verdadero.
true value of a magnitude valor verdadero de una magnitud.
valva *n.* válvula.
valval *adj.* valvar.
valvar *adj.* valvar.
valvate *adj.* valvado, -da.
valve *n.* valva², válvula.
artificial cardiac valve válvula cardíaca artificial.
artificial heart valve válvula cardíaca artificial.
ball valve válvula esférica.
ball-type valve válvula de tipo de esfera.
Bjork-Shiley valve válvula de Bjork-Shiley.
Carpentier-Edwards valve válvula de Carpentier-Edwards.
Heyer-Pudenz valve válvula de Heyer-Pudenz.
non-rebreathing valve válvula sin respiración doble.
prosthetic heart valve válvula cardíaca protésica.
reducing valve válvula reductora.
tilting-disc valve válvula de disco cautivo.
valved *adj.* valvado, -da.
valviform *adj.* valviforme.
valvoplasty *n.* valvoplastia.
valvotome *n.* valvótomo.
valvotomy *n.* valvotomía.
mitral valvotomy valvotomía mitral.
pulmonar valvotomy valvotomía pulmonar.
rectal valvotomy valvotomía rectal.
transventricular closed valvotomy valvotomía transventricular cerrada.
valvular *adj.* valvular.
valvule *n.* válvula.
valvulitis *n.* valvulitis.
rheumatic valvulitis valvulitis reumática.
valvuloplasty *n.* valvuloplastia.
valvulotome *n.* valvulótomo.
valvulotomy *n.* valvulotomía.
vanadiumism *n.* vanadismo, vanadiumismo.
vanillism *n.* vainillismo, vanilismo.
vapocauterization *n.* vapocauterización.
vapor *n.* vapor.
anesthetic vapor vapor anestésico.
vaporarium *n.* vaporario.
vaporization *n.* vaporización.
vaporize *v.* vaporizar.
vaporizer *n.* vaporizador.
copper kettle vaporizer vaporizador de cobre.
flow-over vaporizer vaporizador de flujo.

temperature-compensated vaporizer vaporizador de temperatura compensada.
vaporthorax *n.* vaportórax.
vapotherapy *n.* vapoterapia.
variability *n.* variabilidad.
baseline variability of fetal heart rate variabilidad basal de la frecuencia cardíaca fetal.
variable *n.* variable.
Boolean variable variable binaria, variable booleana, variable lógica.
centered random variable variable aleatoria centrada.
complex variable variable compleja.
continuous random variable variable aleatoria continua.
continuous statistical variable variable estadística continua.
control variable variable de control, variable de decisión.
correlated random variable variable aleatoria correlacionada.
dependent variable variable dependiente.
design variable variable de diseño.
discrete random variable variable aleatoria discreta.
discrete statistical variable variable estadística discreta.
dynamic variable variable dinámica.
endogenous variable variable endógena.
equivalent random variable variable aleatoria equivalente.
exogenous variable variable exógena.
experimental variable variable experimental.
identically distributed random variable variable aleatoria idénticamente distribuida.
independent variable variable independiente.
input variable variable de entrada, variable de ingreso.
intervening variable variable interviniente.
latent variable variable latente.
model descriptive variable variable descriptiva del modelo.
non-controllable variable variable no controlable.
output variable variable de respuesta, variable de salida.
predictor variable variable predictiva.
random variable variable aleatoria, variable estocástica.
real variable variable real.
standardized random variable variable aleatoria tipificada, variable tipificada.
state variable variable de estado.
statistical variable variable estadística.
thermodynamic variable variable termodinámica.
uncorrelated random variable variable aleatoria incorrelacionada, variable aleatoria no correlacionada.
variance *n.* varianza.
variant *n.* variante.
inherited albumin variant variante hereditaria de albúmina.
I-phase variant variante de fase I.
variate *n.* variato.
variation *n.* variación.
allotypic variation variación alotípica.
antigenic variation variación antigénica.
bacterial variation variación bacteriana.
beat-to-beat variation of fetal heart rate variación latido a latido de la frecuencia cardíaca fetal.
circadian variation variación circadiana, variación diaria.

continuous variation variación continua.
discontinuous variation variación discontinua.
diurnal mood variation variación diurna del estado de ánimo.
idiotypic variation variación idiotípica.
impressed variation variación impresa.
inborn variation variación innata.
isotypic variation variación isotípica.
Lexis variation variación de Lexis.
meristic variation variación merística.
microbial variation variación microbiana.
phenotypic variation variación fenotípica.
quasi-continuous variation variación casi continua.
smooth-rough variation (S-R) variación lisarugosa (L-R).
varication *n.* varicación.
variceal *adj.* variceal.
varicella *n.* varicela.
pustular varicella varicela pustular, varicela pustulosa.
vaccination varicella varicela por vacunación.
varicella gangrenosa varicela gangrenosa.
varicella inoculata varicela inoculada.
varicella pustulosa varicela pustular, varicela pustulosa.
varicellation *n.* varicelación.
varicelliform *adj.* variceliforme.
varicellization *n.* varicelización.
varicelloid *adj.* variceloide.
variciform *adj.* variciforme.
varicoblepharon *n.* varicobléfaron.
varicocele *n.* varicocele.
ovarian varicocele varicocele ovárico, varicocele tubárico.
pelvic varicocele varicocele pélvico.
symptomatic varicocele varicocele sintomático.
tubo-ovarian varicocele varicocele tuboovárico.
utero-ovarian varicocele varicocele uteroovárico.
varicocelectomy *n.* varicocelectomía.
varicography *n.* varicografía.
varicoid *adj.* varicoide.
varicole *n.* varicole.
varicomphalus *n.* variconfalo, varicónfalo.
varicophlebitis *n.* varicoflebitis.
varicosclerosation *n.* varicosclerosación.
varicose *adj.* varicoso, -sa.
varicosis *n.* varicosis.
varicosity *n.* varicosidad.
varicotomy *n.* varicectomía, varicotomía.
varicula *n.* varícula.
variety *n.* variedad.
allogenic variety variedad alogénica.
syngenic variety variedad singénica.
xenogeneic variety variedad xenogénica.
variola *n.* variola, viruela.
variola benigna variola benigna.
variola crystallina variola crystallina.
variola hemorrhagica variola hemorrágica, variola hemorrhagica, viruela hemorrágica.
variola inserta variola inserta.
variola major variola major, variola mayor.
variola maligna variola maligna, viruela maligna.
variola miliaris variola miliar, variola miliaris, viruela miliar.
variola minor variola menor, variola minor.
variola mitigata variola mitigata.
variola pemphigosa variola pemphigosa, variola penfigosa, viruela penfigosa.
variola siliquosa variola silicuosa, variola siliquosa, viruela silicuosa.
variola sine eruptione variola sin erupción.

variola vaccine variola vaccinia.
variola vaccinia variola vaccinia.
variola vera variola vera, variola verdadera.
variola verrucosa variola verrucosa, variola verrugosa.
variolar *adj.* variolar.
variolate[1] *adj.* variolado, -da.
variolate[2] *v.* variolar.
variolation *n.* variolación.
variolic *adj.* variólico, -ca.
varioliform *adj.* varioliforme.
variolization *n.* variolización.
varioloid *adj.* varioloide.
variolous *adj.* varioloso, -sa.
variolovaccine *n.* variolovacuna.
varix *n.* varice, variz.
anastomotic varix variz anastomótica.
aneurysmal varix variz aneurismática.
aneurysmoid varix variz aneurismoide.
arterial varix variz arterial.
cirsoid varix variz cirsoide.
conjunctival varix variz conjuntival.
gelatinous varix variz gelatinosa.
lymph varix variz linfática.
turbinal varix variz turbinada.
varix anastomoticus variz anastomótica.
varix lymphaticus variz linfática.
varnish *n.* barniz.
cavity varnish barniz para cavidades.
dental varnish barniz dental.
varolian *adj.* varoliano, -na.
varus varo, -ra, varus.
vas vas, vaso.
vasal *adj.* vasal.
vasalgia *n.* vasalgia.
vascular *adj.* vascular.
vascularity *n.* vascularidad.
vascularization *n.* vascularización.
vascularize *v.* vascularizar.
vascularized *adj.* vascularizado, -da.
vasculature *n.* vasculatura.
vasculitic *adj.* vasculítico, -ca.
vasculitis *n.* vasculitis.
allergic cutaneous vasculitis vasculitis alérgica cutánea.
allergic vasculitis vasculitis alérgica.
cutaneous vasculitis vasculitis cutánea.
hypersensitivity vasculitis vasculitis de hipersensibilidad, vasculitis por hipersensibilidad.
leukocytoclastic vasculitis vasculitis leucocitoclástica.
livedo vasculitis vasculitis livedo.
necrotizing vasculitis vasculitis necrosante, vasculitis necrotizante.
nodular vasculitis vasculitis nodular.
segmented hyalinizing vasculitis vasculitis hialinizante segmentada, vasculitis hialinizante segmentaria.
umbilical vasculitis vasculitis umbilical.
vasculocardiac *adj.* vasculocardíaco, -ca.
vasculogenesis *n.* vasculogénesis.
vasculogenic *adj.* vasculógeno, -na.
vasculolymphatic *adj.* vasculolinfático, -ca.
vasculomotor *adj.* vasculomotor, -ra, vasculomotriz.
vasculomyelinopathy *n.* vasculomielinopatía.
vasculopathy *n.* vasculopatía.
diabetic vasculopathy vasculopatía diabética.
graft vasculopathy vasculopatía del injerto.
vasculotoxic *adj.* vasculotóxico, -ca.
vasculum vasculum.
vasectomized *adj.* vasectomizado, -da.

vasectomy *n.* vasectomía.
cross over vasectomy vasectomía cruzada.
vasifaction *n.* vasifacción.
vasifactive *adj.* vasifactivo, -va.
vasiform *adj.* vasiforme.
vasitis *n.* vasitis.
vasoactive *adj.* vasoactivo, -va.
vasoconstriction *n.* vasoconstricción.
active vasoconstriction vasoconstricción activa.
passive vasoconstriction vasoconstricción pasiva.
vasoconstrictive *adj.* vasoconstrictivo, -va, vasoconstrictor, -ra.
vasoconstrictor *adj.* vasoconstrictor, -ra.
vasocorona *n.* vasocorona.
vasodepression *n.* vasodepresión.
vasodepressor *n.* vasodepresor.
vasodilatation *n.* vasodilatación.
active vasodilatation vasodilatación activa.
passive vasodilatation vasodilatación pasiva.
reflex vasodilatation vasodilatación refleja.
vasodilative *adj.* vasodilatador, -ra, vasodilatativo, -va.
vasodilator *adj.* vasodilatador, -ra.
vasoepididymography *n.* vasoepididimografía.
vasoepididymostomy *n.* vasoepididimostomía.
vasofactive *adj.* vasofactivo, -va.
vasoformation *n.* vasoformación.
vasoformative *adj.* vasoformativo, -va.
vasography *n.* vasografía.
vasohypertonic *adj.* vasohipertónico, -ca.
vasohypotonic *adj.* vasohipotónico, -ca.
vasoinert *adj.* vasoinerte.
vasoinhibitor *n.* vasoinhibidor.
vasoinhibitory *adj.* vasoinhibidor, -ra, vasoinhibitorio, -ria.
vasolabile *adj.* vasolábil.
vasoligation *n.* vasoligadura.
vasoligature *n.* vasoligadura.
vasomotion *n.* vasomoción, vasomovimiento.
vasomotive *adj.* vasomotor, -ra.
vasomotorial *adj.* vasomotorio, -ria.
vasomotoricity *n.* vasomotricidad.
vasoneuropathy *n.* vasoneuropatía.
vasoneurosis *n.* vasoneurosis.
vaso-orchidostomy *n.* vasoorquidostomía.
vasoparalysis *n.* vasoparálisis.
vasoparesis *n.* vasoparesia, vasoparesis.
vasopermeability *n.* vasopermeabilidad.
vasopressin (VP) *n.* vasopresina (VP).
arginine vasopressin vasopresina arginina.
vasopressor *n.* vasopresor.
vasopuncture *n.* vasocentesis, vasopuntura.
vasoreflex *n.* vasorreflejo.
vasorelaxation *n.* vasorrelajación.
vasoresection *n.* vasorresección.
vasorrhaphy *n.* vasorrafia.
vasosection *n.* vasosección.
vasosensory *adj.* vasosensitivo, -va, vasosensorial.
vasospasm *n.* vasoespasmo, vasospasmo.
vasospasmolytic *adj.* vasoespasmolítico, -ca.
vasospastic *adj.* vasoespástico, -ca, vasospástico, -ca.
vasostimulant *adj.* vasoestimulante.
vasostomy *n.* vasostomía.
vasothrombin *n.* vasotrombina.
vasotocin *n.* vasotocina.
arginine vasotocin vasotocina arginina.
vasotomy *n.* vasotomía.
vasotonia *n.* vasotonía.
vasotonic *adj.* vasotónico, -ca.
vasotribe *n.* vasotribo.

vasotripsin *n.* vasotripsina.
vasotripsy *n.* vasotripsia.
vasotrophic *adj.* vasotrófico, -ca.
vasotropic *adj.* vasotrópico, -ca.
vasovagal *adj.* vasovagal.
vasovasostomy *n.* vasovasostomía.
vasovesiculectomy *n.* vasovesiculectomía.
vasovesiculitis *n.* vasovesiculitis.
vastus *n.* vasto.
vault *n.* bóveda.
vection *n.* vección.
vectocardiograph *n.* vectocardiógrafo.
vectocardiography *n.* vectocardiografía.
spatial vectocardiography vectocardiografía espacial.
vector *n.* vector.
axial vector vector axial.
bifunctional vector vector bifuncional.
biological vector vector biológico.
Burger's vector vector de Burger.
cloning vector vector clonal, vector de clonación.
expression vector vector de expresión.
instantaneous vector vector instantáneo.
manifest vector vector manifiesto.
mean vector vector medio.
mechanical vector vector mecánico pasivo.
polar vector vector polar.
position vector vector de posición.
recombinant vector vector recombinante.
shuttle vector vector transportador.
spatial vector vector espacial.
transmitter vector vector transmisor.
vectorcardiogram *n.* vectocardiograma.
vectorial *adj.* vectorial.
vectorscope *n.* vectoriscopio.
vegan *adj.* vegán.
veganism *n.* veganismo.
vegetans *adj.* vegetante.
vegetarian *n.* vegetariano, -na.
vegetarianism *n.* vegetarianismo, vegetarismo.
vegetation *n.* vegetación.
adenoid vegetation vegetación adenoide.
bacterial vegetation vegetación bacteriana.
vegetative *adj.* vegetante, vegetativo, -va.
vehicle *n.* vehículo.
veil *n.* velo, velum.
aqueduct veil velo del acueducto.
artificial veil velo artificial.
Fick's veil velo de Fick.
Jackson's veil velo de Jackson.
nursing veil velo de amamantamiento.
Sattler's veil velo de Sattler.
Veillonella Veillonella.
Veillonellaceae Veillonellaceae.
vein *n.* vena.
velamen *n.* velamen.
velamentous *adj.* velamentoso, -sa.
velamentum ve, velamentum.
velamentum cerebri ve cerebral.
velar *adj.* velar.
veliform *adj.* veliforme.
vellicate *v.* velicar.
vellication *n.* velicación, velificación.
vellus *n.* vello.
vellus olivae vello de la oliva.
vellus olivae inferioris vello de la oliva inferior.
velocimetry *n.* velocimetría.
laser-Doppler velocimetry velocimetría láser-Doppler.
velocity *n.* velocidad.
blood flow velocity velocidad circulatoria, velocidad de circulación.

conduction velocity velocidad de conducción.

linear flow velocity velocidad de flujo lineal.

maximum velocity velocidad máxima.

nerve conduction velocity velocidad de conducción nerviosa.

peak height velocity velocidad máxima de crecimiento.

sedimentation velocity velocidad de sedimentación.

velocity of ultrasound velocidad de ultrasonidos.

velogenic *adj.* velogénico, -ca.

velopharyngeal *adj.* velofaríngeo, -a.

velosynthesis *n.* velosíntesis.

velum *n.* velo, velum.

vena *n.* vena.

venacavogram *n.* venacavograma.

venacavography *n.* venacavografía.

venation *n.* venación.

venectasia *n.* venectasia.

venectomy *n.* venectomía.

veneer veneer.

venenation *n.* venenación.

veneniferous *adj.* venenífero, -ra.

venenific *adj.* venenífico, -ca.

venenosalivary *adj.* venenosalival.

venenosity *n.* venenosidad.

venenous *adj.* venenoso, -sa.

venepuncture *n.* venopunción.

venereal *adj.* venéreo, -a.

venereologist *n.* venereólogo, -ga.

venereology *n.* venereología.

venereophobia *n.* venereofobia.

venerupin *n.* venerrupina.

venesection *n.* venesección.

venesuture *n.* venisutura, venosutura.

venipuncture *n.* venepunción, venepuntura, venipuntura.

venisection *n.* venisección.

venisuture *n.* venisutura.

venoatrial *adj.* venoauricular.

venoauricular *adj.* venoauricular.

venoclysis *n.* venoclisis.

venofibrosis *n.* venofibrosis.

venogram *n.* venograma.

venography *n.* venografía.

splenic portal venography venografía esplenicoportal.

splenic venography venografía esplénica.

transosseous venography venografía transósea.

vertebral venography venografía vertebral.

venom *n.* veneno.

kokoi venom veneno kokoi.

Russell's viper venom veneno de víbora de Russell.

sedative venom veneno de fatiga, veneno hipostenizante, veneno sedante.

snake venom veneno de las serpientes.

spider venom veneno de araña.

viper venom veneno de víbora.

venomization *n.* venenización.

venomosalivary *adj.* venomosalival.

venomotor *adj.* venomotor, -ra.

venomous *adj.* venenoso, -sa.

veno-occlusive *adj.* venooclusivo, -va.

venoperitoneostomy *n.* venoperitoneostomía.

venopressor *adj.* venopresor, -ra.

venosclerosis *n.* venoesclerosis, venosclerosis.

venose *adj.* venoso, -sa.

venosinusal *adj.* venosinusal.

venosity *n.* venosidad.

venospasm *n.* venospasmo.

venostasia *n.* venoestasia.

venostasis *n.* venostasis.

venostat *n.* venóstato.

venotomy *n.* venotomía.

venous *adj.* venoso, -sa.

venous air trap burbuja de aire.

venovenostomy *n.* venovenostomía.

vent *n.* vent.

venter *n.* venter, vientre.

venter propendens vientre colgante, vientre en alforja, vientre propendens.

ventilate *v.* ventilar.

ventilation *n.* ventilación.

alveolar ventilation ventilación alveolar.

artificial ventilation ventilación artificial.

assist-control mode ventilation ventilación asistida de modalidad controlada.

assist-control ventilation ventilación asistida controlada.

assisted ventilation ventilación asistida.

collateral ventilation ventilación colateral.

constant positive pressure ventilation ventilación con presión positiva constante.

continous positive pressure ventilation (CPPV) ventilación con presión positiva continua (VPPC).

control mode ventilation ventilación de modalidad controlada.

controlled mechanical ventilation (CMV) ventilación mecánica controlada.

controlled ventilation ventilación controlada.

downward ventilation ventilación descendente.

exhausting ventilation ventilación de escape.

intermittent assisted ventilation (IAV) ventilación asistida intermitente (VAI).

intermittent mandatory ventilation (IMV) ventilación mandatoria intermitente, ventilación obligada intermitente (VOI).

intermittent positive pressure ventilation (IPPV) ventilación con presión positiva intermitente.

manual ventilation ventilación manual.

maximum voluntary ventilation (MVV) ventilación voluntaria máxima (VVM).

mechanical ventilation ventilación mecánica.

minute ventilation ventilación por minuto, ventilación-minuto.

plenum ventilation ventilación plena.

pressure support ventilation (PSV) ventilación con presión de soporte (VPS).

pulmonary ventilation ventilación pulmonar.

spontaneous intermittent mandatory ventilation (SIMV) ventilación mandatoria intermitente espontánea.

spontaneous ventilation ventilación espontánea.

synchronized intermittent mandatory ventilation (SIMV) ventilación mandatoria intermitente sincronizada, ventilación obligada intermitente sincronizada (VOIS).

upward ventilation ventilación ascendente.

wasted ventilation ventilación desperdiciada, ventilación residual.

ventilator *n.* ventilador.

bellows ventilator ventilador en fuelle.

combined cycling ventilator ventilador cíclico combinado.

fluidic ventilator ventilador fluídico.

pressure ventilator ventilador a presión.

volume ventilator ventilador de volumen.

venting *n.* descarga.

ventplant *n.* ventplante.

ventrad ventrad.

ventral *adj.* ventral.

ventral hernia repair *n.* eventrorrafia.

ventralis *adj.* ventral.

ventricle *n.* ventrículo, ventriculus.

ventricornu ventricornu, ventricuerno.

ventricornual *adj.* ventricornual.

ventricose *adj.* ventricoso, -sa.

ventricular *adj.* ventricular.

ventricularization *n.* ventricularización.

ventriculitis *n.* ventriculitis.

ventriculoatrial (V-A) *adj.* ventriculoauricular (V-A).

ventriculoatriostomy *n.* ventriculoauriculostomía.

ventriculocisternostomy *n.* ventriculocisternostomía.

ventriculocordectomy *n.* ventriculocordectomía.

ventriculogram *n.* ventriculograma.

isotope ventriculogram ventriculograma isotópico.

ventriculography *n.* ventriculografía.

isotope ventriculography ventriculografía isotópica.

ventriculomastoidostomy *n.* ventriculomastoidostomía.

ventriculometry *n.* ventriculometría.

ventriculomyotomy *n.* ventriculomiotomía.

ventriculoperitoneostomy *n.* ventriculoperitoneostomía.

ventriculophasic *adj.* ventrículofásico, -ca.

ventriculoplasty *n.* ventriculoplastia.

ventriculopuncture *n.* ventriculopunción, ventrículopuntura.

ventriculoscope *n.* ventriculoscopio.

ventriculoscopy *n.* ventriculoscopia.

ventriculostomy *n.* ventriculostomía.

third ventriculostomy ventriculostomía del tercer ventrículo.

ventriculosubarachnoid *adj.* ventriculosubaracnoideo, -a.

ventriculotomy *n.* ventriculotomía.

ventriculovenostomy *n.* ventriculovenostomía.

ventriculovenous *adj.* ventriculovenoso, -sa.

ventriculus *n.* ventrículo, ventriculus.

ventricumbent *adj.* ventricumbente.

ventriduct *v.* ventriducir.

ventriduction *n.* ventriducción.

ventrifixation *n.* ventrifijación.

ventriflexion *n.* ventriflexión.

ventrocystorrhaphy *n.* ventrocistorrafia.

ventrodorsad ventrodorsad.

ventrodorsal *adj.* ventrodorsal.

ventrofixation *n.* ventrofijación.

ventrohisteropexy *n.* ventrohisteropexia.

ventroinguinal *adj.* ventroinguinal.

ventrolateral *adj.* ventrolateral.

ventroposterior *adj.* ventroposterior.

ventroptosia *n.* ventroptosia.

ventroptosis *n.* ventroptosis.

ventroscopy *n.* ventroscopia.

ventrose *adj.* ventroso, -sa.

ventrosuspension *n.* ventrosuspensión.

ventrotomy *n.* ventrotomía.

ventrovesicofixation *n.* ventrovesicofijación.

venturimeter *n.* venturímetro.

venula *adj.* vénula, venular.

venule *n.* vénula.

venulous *adj.* venuloso, -sa.

verbiage *n.* verborrea.

verbigeration *n.* verbigeración.

verbomania *n.* verbomanía.

verdine *n.* verdina.
verdoglobin *n.* verdoglobina.
verdohemin *n.* verdohemina.
verdohemochrome *n.* verdohemocromo.
verdohemochromogen *n.* verdohemocromógeno.
verdohemoglobin *n.* verdohemoglobina.
verdoperoxidase *n.* verdoperoxidasa.
vergence *n.* vergencia.
  vergence of lens vergencia de una lente.
vermetoid *adj.* vermetoide.
vermian *adj.* vermiano, -na.
vermicidal *n.* vermicida.
vermicular *adj.* vermicular.
vermiculation *n.* vermiculación.
vermicule *n.* vermícula, vermículo.
  traveling vermicule vermícula viajera.
vermiculose *adj.* vermiculoso, -sa.
vermiculous *adj.* vermiculoso, -sa.
vermiculus *n.* vermículo.
vermiform vermiforme, vermoide.
vermifugal *adj.* vermífugo, -ga.
vermilion *n.* bermellón.
vermilionectomy *n.* bermellonectomía, vermilonectomía.
vermin *n.* vermina.
verminal *adj.* verminal.
vermination *n.* verminación.
verminosis *n.* verminosis.
verminotic *adj.* verminótico, -ca.
verminous *adj.* verminoso, -sa.
vermiphobia *n.* vermifobia.
vermis vermes, vermis.
  vermis cerebelli vermis cerebeloso, vermis del cerebelo.
  vermis inferior vermis inferior.
  vermis superior vermis superior.
vermix *n.* vérmix.
vermography *n.* vermografía.
vernier *n.* vernier.
vernix vérnix.
  vernix caseosa vérnix caseosa.
verruca *n.* verruca, verruga.
  seborrheic verruca verruga seborreica.
  verruca digitata verruga digitada.
  verruca filiformis verruga filiforme.
  verruca glabra verruga glabra.
  verruca mollusciformis verruga mollusciforme.
  verruca peruana verruga peruana.
  verruca peruviana verruga peruana.
  verruca plana verruga plana.
  verruca plana juvenilis verruga plana juvenil.
  verruca plantaris verruca plantaris, verruga plantar.
  verruca seborrheica verruga seborreica.
  verruca senilis verruga senil.
  verruca simplex verruga simple.
  verruca tuberculosa verruga tuberculosa.
  verruca vulgaris verruga vulgar.
verruciform *adj.* verruciforme.
verrucose *adj.* verrucoso, -sa, verrugoso, -sa.
verrucosis *n.* verrucosis.
  lymphostatic verrucosis verrucosis linfostática.
verrucous *adj.* verrucoso, -sa, verrugoso, -sa.
verruga *n.* verruca, verruga.
  verruga peruana verruga peruana.
versicolor *adj.* versicolor.
version *n.* versión.
  abdominal version versión abdominal.
  bimanual version versión bimanual.
  bipolar version versión bipolar.
  Braxton-Hicks version versión de Braxton-Hicks.

cephalic version versión cefálica.
  combined version versión combinada, versión mixta.
  Denman's spontaneous version versión espontánea de Denman.
  external version versión externa, versión por maniobras externas.
  Hicks version versión de Hicks.
  internal podalic version and total breech extraction versión podálica interna y extracción completa de nalgas.
  internal version versión interna, versión por maniobras internas.
  pelvic version versión pelviana.
  podalic version versión podálica.
  postural version versión postural.
  Potter's version versión de Potter.
  spontaneous version versión espontánea.
  version and extraction versión y extracción.
  Wright's version versión de Wright.
vertebra *n.* vértebra.
  hourglass vertebra vértebra en reloj de arena.
  vertebra plana vértebra plana.
vertebral *adj.* vertebral.
vertebrarterial *adj.* vertebrarterial.
vertebrated *adj.* vertebrado, -da.
vertebrectomy *n.* vertebrectomía.
vertebroarterial *adj.* vertebroarterial.
vertebrochondral *adj.* vertebrocondral.
vertebrocostal *adj.* vertebrocostal.
vertebrodidymus *adj.* vertebrodídimo, -ma.
vertebrodymus *n.* vertebrodimo.
vertebrofemoral *adj.* vertebrofemoral.
vertebrogenic *adj.* vertebrógeno, -na.
vertebroiliac *adj.* vertebroilíaco, -ca.
vertebromammary *adj.* vertebromamario, -ria.
vertebrosacral *adj.* vertebrosacro, -cra.
vertebrosternal *adj.* vertebroesternal, vertebrosternal.
vertex vertex, vértice.
vertical *adj.* vertical^1, vertical^2.
verticalis *adj.* vertical^2.
verticomental *adj.* verticomentoniano, -na.
vertiginous *adj.* vertiginoso, -sa.
vertigo *n.* vértigo.
  alternobaric vertigo vértigo alternobárico.
  angiopathic vertigo vértigo angiopático.
  auditory vertigo vértigo auditivo.
  aural vertigo vértigo aural, vértigo auricular.
  benign paroxysmal positional vertigo vértigo paroxístico posicional benigno, vértigo paroxístico postural benigno.
  benign paroxysmal postural vertigo vértigo paroxístico posicional benigno, vértigo paroxístico postural benigno.
  cardiovascular vertigo vértigo cardíaco, vértigo cardiovascular.
  central vertigo vértigo central.
  cerebral vertigo vértigo cerebral.
  Charcot's vertigo vértigo de Charcot.
  disabling positional vertigo vértigo posicional incapacitante.
  endemic paralytic vertigo vértigo endémico paralítico.
  epidemic vertigo vértigo epidémico.
  epileptic vertigo vértigo epiléptico.
  essential vertigo vértigo esencial.
  galvanic vertigo vértigo galvánico, vértigo voltaico.
  gastric vertigo vértigo estomacal, vértigo gástrico.
  height vertigo vértigo de altura.
  horizontal vertigo vértigo horizontal.
  hysterical vertigo vértigo histérico.

labyrinthine vertigo vértigo laberíntico.
  laryngeal vertigo vértigo laríngeo.
  lateral vertigo vértigo lateral.
  lithemic vertigo vértigo litémico.
  mechanical vertigo vértigo mecánico.
  nocturnal vertigo vértigo nocturno.
  objective vertigo vértigo objetivo.
  ocular vertigo vértigo ocular.
  organic vertigo vértigo orgánico.
  paralyzing vertigo vértigo paralizante.
  paroxysmal labyrinthine vertigo vértigo laberíntico paroxístico.
  peripheral vertigo vértigo periférico.
  pilot's vertigo vértigo de piloto aéreo.
  positional vertigo vértigo de posición, vértigo posicional.
  postural vertigo vértigo postural.
  rider's vertigo vértigo de los jinetes.
  rotary vertigo vértigo rotatorio.
  rotatory vertigo vértigo rotatorio.
  sham-movement vertigo vértigo de falso movimiento, vértigo de movimiento giratorio.
  special sense vertigo vértigo de los sentidos especiales.
  subjective vertigo vértigo subjetivo.
  systematic vertigo vértigo sistemático.
  toxemic vertigo vértigo toxémico, vértigo tóxico.
  vertical vertigo vértigo vertical.
  villous vertigo vértigo velloso.
verumontanitis *n.* verumontanitis.
verumontanum verum montanum, verumontanum.
vesalian *adj.* vesaliano, -na.
vesica *n.* vejiga, vesica.
  sacculated vesica vejiga saculada.
  vesica biliaris vejiga biliar.
  vesica fellea vesica fellea.
  vesica prostatica vejiga prostática, vesica prostatica.
  vesica urinaria vejiga urinaria, vesica urinalis, vesica urinaria.
vesical *adj.* vesical.
vesicant *adj.* vesicante.
vesication *n.* vesicación.
vesicatory *adj.* vesicatorio, -ria.
vesicle *n.* vesícula.
  acoustic vesicle vesícula acústica.
  allantoic vesicle vesícula alantoica, vesícula alantoidea.
  amniocardiac vesicle vesícula amniocardíaca.
  Ascherson's vesicle vesícula de Ascherson.
  auditory vesicle vesícula auditiva.
  blastodermic vesicle vesícula blastodérmica.
  brain vesicle vesícula cerebral.
  cephalic vesicle vesícula cefálica.
  cerebral vesicle vesícula cerebral.
  chorionic vesicle vesícula coriónica.
  coated vesicle vesícula recubiertas.
  compound vesicle vesícula compuesta, vesícula multilocular.
  encephalic vesicle vesícula encefálica.
  false spermatic vesicle vesícula espermática falsa.
  forebrain vesicle vesícula anterocerebral.
  germinal vesicle vesícula germinal.
  intraepidermal vesicle vesícula intraepidérmica.
  kerionic vesicle vesícula queriónica.
  lens vesicle vesícula del cristalino.
  lenticular vesicle vesícula lenticular.
  Malpighian vesicle vesícula de Malpighi.
  matrix vesicle vesícula de la matriz.
  ocular vesicle vesícula ocular.
  olfactory vesicle vesícula olfatoria.

ophthalmic vesicle vesícula oftálmica.
optic vesicle vesícula óptica.
otic vesicle vesícula ótica.
phagocytotic vesicle vesícula fagocítica.
pinocytotic vesicle vesícula pinocítica.
pituitary vesicle vesícula pituitaria.
plasmalemma vesicle vesícula plasmalémica.
primary brain vesicle vesícula cerebral primaria, vesícula encefálica primaria.
prostatic vesicle vesícula prostática.
secondary brain vesicle vesícula cerebral secundaria.
secretory vesicle vesícula de secreción.
seminal vesicle vesícula seminal.
sense vesicle vesícula de los sentidos.
synaptic vesicle vesícula sináptica.
transfer vesicle vesícula de transferencia.
transitional vesicle vesícula transicional.
transport vesicle vesícula de transporte.
umbilical vesicle vesícula umbilical.
water expulsion vesicle vesícula de excreción acuosa.
vesicoabdominal adj. vesicoabdominal.
vesicobullous adj. vesicoampollar.
vesicocavernous adj. vesicocavernoso, -sa.
vesicocele n. vesicocele.
vesicocervical adj. vesicocervical.
vesicoclysis n. vesicoclisis.
vesicocolic adj. vesicocólico, -ca.
vesicocolonic adj. vesicocólico, -ca.
vesicoenteric adj. vesicoentérico, -ca.
vesicofixation n. vesicofijación.
vesicointestinal adj. vesicointestinal.
vesicoperineal adj. vesicoperineal.
vesicoprostatic adj. vesicoprostático, -ca.
vesicopubic adj. vesicopubiano, -na, vesicopúbico, -ca.
vesicopustule n. vesicopústula.
vesicorectal adj. vesicorrectal.
vesicorenal adj. vesicorrenal.
vesicosigmoid adj. vesicosigmoideo, -a.
vesicosigmoidostomy n. vesicosigmoidostomía.
vesicospinal adj. vesicoespinal, vesicospinal.
vesicostomy n. vesicostomía.
vesicotomy n. vesicotomía.
vesicoumbilical adj. vesicoumbilical.
vesicourachal adj. vesicouracal.
vesicoureteral adj. vesicoureteral.
vesicoureteric adj. vesicoureteral.
vesicourethral adj. vesicouretral.
vesicouterine adj. vesicouterino, -na.
vesicouterovaginal adj. vesicouterovaginal.
vesicovaginal adj. vesicovaginal.
vesicovaginorectal adj. vesicovaginorrectal.
vesicula n. vesícula.
vesicula bilis vesícula biliar.
vesicula fellea vesícula biliar, vesícula fellea, vesícula fellis.
vesicula fellis vesícula fellea, vesícula fellis.
vesicula germinalis vesícula germinal.
vesicula ophthalmica vesícula oftálmica.
vesicula prostatica vesícula prostática.
vesicula seminalis vesícula seminal.
vesicula umbilicalis vesícula umbilical.
vesicular adj. vesicular.
vesiculase n. vesiculasa.
vesiculated adj. vesiculado, -da.
vesiculation n. vesiculación.
vesiculectomy n. vesiculectomía.
vesiculiform n. vesiculiforme.
vesiculitis n. vesiculitis.
seminal vesiculitis vesiculitis seminal.
vesiculobronchial adj. vesiculobronquial.
vesiculocavernous adj. vesiculocavernoso, -sa.

vesiculogram n. vesiculograma.
vesiculography n. vesiculografía.
vesiculopapular adj. vesiculopapuloso, -sa.
vesiculopostular adj. vesiculopostular.
vesiculoprostatitis n. vesiculoprostatitis.
vesiculopustular adj. vesiculopustuloso, -sa.
vesiculose adj. vesiculoso, -sa.
vesiculotomy n. vesiculotomía.
vesiculotubular adj. vesiculotubular.
vesiculotympanic adj. vesiculotimpánico, -ca.
vesiculous adj. vesiculoso, -sa.
Vesiculovirus Vesiculovirus.
vessel n. vaso.
vestibular adj. vestibular.
vestibulate adj. vestibulado, -da.
vestibule n. vestíbulo.
vestibuliferia vestibuliferia.
vestibulocerebellum n. vestibulocerebelo.
vestibulochoclear adj. vestibulococlear.
vestibulogenic adj. vestibulógeno, -na.
vestibulo-ocular adj. vestibulooocular.
vestibuloplasty n. vestibuloplastia.
vestibulospinal adj. vestibuloespinal.
vestibulotomy n. vestibulotomía.
vestibulourethral adj. vestibulouretral.
vestibulum n. vestíbulo.
vestige n. vestigio.
vestige of vaginal process vestigio del proceso vaginal.
vestigial adj. vestigial.
vestigium n. vestigio.
vestigium processus vaginalis vestigio del proceso vaginal.
veta n. veta.
veterinarian n. veterinario[1], -ria.
veterinary adj. veterinario[2], -ria.
via n. vía.
viability n. viabilidad.
viable adj. viable.
vial n. vial.
vibesate n. vibesato.
vibex n. víbice.
vibratile adj. vibrátil.
vibration n. vibración.
photoelectric vibration vibración fotoeléctrica.
vibrative adj. vibrante, vibrativo, -va.
vibratode n. vibrátodo.
vibrator n. vibrador.
vibratory adj. vibratorio, -ria.
Vibrio Vibrio.
Vibrio comma Vibrio comma.
Vibrio fluvialis Vibrio fluvialis.
Vibrio furnissii Vibrio furnissii.
Vibrio mimicus Vibrio mimicus.
Vibrio parahaemolyticus Vibrio parahaemolyticus.
Vibrio sputorum Vibrio sputorum.
Vibrio vulnificus Vibrio vulnificus.
vibrio n. vibrión.
vibriosis n. vibriosis.
vibrisal adj. vibrisal.
vibrissa n. vibrisa, vibriza.
vibrocardiogram n. vibrocardiograma.
vibromasseur n. vibromasajeador.
vibrometer n. vibrómetro.
vibrotherapeutics n. vibroterapéutica, vibroterapia.
vicarious adj. vicariante, vicario, -ria.
vice n. vicio.
vicious adj. vicioso, -sa.
videofluoroscopy n. videofluoroscopia.
videognosis n. videognosia.
videomicroscopy n. videomicroscopía.
videonystagmography n. videonistagmografía.

view n. vista.
vigilambulism n. vigilambulismo.
vigilance n. vigilia.
coma vigilance vigilia de coma.
vigintinormal adj. vigesimonormal.
vigor n. vigor.
hybrid vigor vigor híbrido.
villiferous adj. villífero, -ra.
villikinin n. villicinina.
villioma n. villioma.
villoma n. villoma.
villonodular adj. villonodular.
villose adj. velloso, -sa, velludo, -da.
villositis n. vellositis, villositis.
villosity n. vellosidad[2].
villous adj. velloso, -sa.
villus n. vellosidad[1], villus.
amniotic villus vellosidad amniotica.
anchoring villus vellosidad de anclaje, vellosidad de fijación.
floating villus vellosidad flotante.
free villus vellosidad libre.
lingual villus vellosidad lingual.
primary villus vellosidad primaria.
secondary villus vellosidad secundaria.
tertiary villus vellosidad terciaria.
villus of the small intestine vellosidad del intestino delgado.
villusectomy n. villosectomía, villusectomía.
vinculum n. vínculo, vinculum.
violaceous adj. violáceo, -a.
violation n. violación.
violescent adj. violescente.
violet n. violeta.
gentian violet violeta de genciana.
methyl violet violeta de metilo.
Paris violet violeta de París.
pentamethyl violet violeta de París.
viperid adj. vipérido, -da, viperino, -na.
vipoma n. vipoma.
viraginity n. viraginidad.
viral adj. viral, vírico, -ca, virósico, -ca, viroso, -sa.
viremia n. viremia.
virgin adj. virgen.
virginal adj. virginal.
virginity n. virginidad.
virgophrenia n. virgofrenia.
viricidal adj. viricida, virucida, virulicida.
virile adj. viril.
virilescence n. virilescencia, viriliscencia.
virilia virilia.
viriligenic adj. virilígeno, -na.
virilism n. virilismo.
adrenal virilism virilismo adrenal, virilismo suprarrenal.
prosopopilary virilism virilismo prosopopiloso.
virility n. virilidad.
virilization n. virilización.
virilizing adj. virilizador, -ra, virilizante.
virion n. virión.
viripotent adj. viripotente.
virocyte n. virocito.
viroid n. viroide.
virologist n. virólogo, -ga.
virology n. virología.
viropexis n. viropexis.
virosis n. virosis.
virtual adj. virtual.
virucidal n. virocida.
virulence n. virulencia.
virulent adj. virulento, -ta.
viruliferous adj. virulífero, -ra.
viruria n. viruria.
virus n. virus.

virusemia *n.* virusemia.
virustatic *adj.* virustático, -ca.
vis vis.
viscance *n.* viscancia.
viscera *n.* víscera.
viscerad viscerad.
visceral *adj.* visceral.
visceralgia *n.* visceralgia.
visceralism *n.* visceralismo.
viscerimotor *adj.* viscerimotor, -ra.
viscerocranium *n.* viscerocráneo.
viscerogenic *adj.* viscerogénico, -ca.
viscerograph *n.* viscerógrafo.
visceroinhibitory *adj.* visceroinhibidor, -ra, visceroinhibitorio, -ria.
visceromegaly *n.* visceromegalia.
visceromotor *adj.* visceromotor, -ra.
visceroneurotomy *n.* evisceroneurotomía.
visceroparietal *adj.* visceroparietal.
visceroperitoneal *adj.* visceroperitoneal.
visceropleural *adj.* visceropleural.
visceroptosia *n.* visceroptosia.
visceroptosis *n.* visceroptosia, visceroptosis.
viscerosensory *adj.* viscerosensitivo, -va, viscerosensorial.
visceroskeletal *adj.* visceroesquelético, -ca, viscerosquelético, -ca.
visceroskeleton *n.* visceroesqueleto.
viscerosomatic *adj.* viscerosomático, -ca.
viscerotome *n.* viscerótomo.
viscerotomy *n.* viscerotomía.
viscerotonia *n.* viscerotonía.
viscerotrophic *adj.* viscerotrófico, -ca.
viscerotropic *adj.* viscerotrópico, -ca.
viscid *adj.* viscido, -da.
viscidity *n.* viscidez.
viscidosis *n.* viscidosis.
viscoelasticity *n.* viscoelasticidad.
viscogel *n.* viscogel.
viscometer *n.* viscómetro.
viscosaccharose *n.* viscosacarosa.
viscose *n.* viscosa.
viscosimeter *n.* viscosímetro.
viscosimetry *n.* viscosimetría.
viscosity *n.* viscosidad.
  absolute viscosity viscosidad absoluta.
  anomalous viscosity viscosidad anómala.
  apparent viscosity viscosidad aparente.
  bulk viscosity viscosidad de dilatación, viscosidad volumétrica.
  dynamic viscosity viscosidad dinámica.
  kinematic viscosity viscosidad cinemática.
  Newtonian viscosity viscosidad newtoniana.
  relative viscosity viscosidad relativa.
viscous *adj.* viscoso, -sa.
viscus víscera, viscus.
visibility *n.* visibilidad.
visible *adj.* visible.
vision *n.* visión.
  achromatic vision visión acromática.
  binocular vision visión binocular.
  blue vision visión azul.
  central vision visión central.
  chromatic vision visión cromática.
  color vision visión de color.
  cone vision visión cónica.
  dichromatic vision visión dicromática.
  direct vision visión directa.
  double vision visión doble.
  facial vision visión facial.
  finger vision visión digital.
  foveal vision visión foveal.
  green vision visión verde.
  halo vision visión en aureola, visión en halo, visión iridiscente.

haploscopic vision visión haploscópica.
indirect vision visión indirecta.
low vision visión baja.
monocular vision visión monocular.
multiple vision visión múltiple.
night vision visión nocturna.
old vision visión de la vejez.
oscillating vision visión oscilante.
peripheral vision visión periférica.
photopic vision visión fotópica.
Pick's vision visión de Pick.
pseudoscopic vision visión pseudoscópica.
rainbow vision visión en arco iris.
red vision visión roja.
rod vision visión de bastones.
scoterythrous vision visión escoteritrosa.
scotopic vision visión escotópica.
stereoscopic vision visión estereoscópica.
subjective vision visión subjetiva.
triple vision visión triple.
tubular vision visión tubular.
tunnel vision visión en túnel.
twilight vision visión crepuscular.
word vision visión de las palabras.
yellow vision visión amarilla, visión amarillenta.
visit *n.* visita.
visoauditory *adj.* visoauditivo, -va, visuauditivo, -va.
visual *adj.* visual.
visualization *n.* visualización.
  double contrast visualization visualización de doble contraste.
visualize *v.* visualizar.
visuognosis *n.* visuognosis.
visuolexic *adj.* visuoléxico, -ca.
visuometer *n.* visuómetro.
visuomotor *adj.* visuomoto, -ra.
visuopsychic *adj.* visuopsíquico, -ca.
visuoscope *n.* visuoscopio.
visuosensory *adj.* visuosensitivo, -va, visuosensorial.
visuospatial *adj.* visuespacial, visuoespacial.
vitagonist *adj.* vitagonista.
vital *adj.* vital.
vitalism *n.* vitalismo.
vitalistic *adj.* vitalístico, -ca.
vitality *n.* vitalidad.
vitalize *v.* vitalizar.
vitalometer *n.* vitalómetro.
vitamer *n.* vitámero.
vitameter *n.* vitámetro.
vitamin *n.* vitamina, vitazima.
vitaminogenic *adj.* vitaminógeno, -na.
vitaminoid *adj.* vitaminoide.
vitaminology *n.* vitaminología.
vitaminoscope *n.* vitaminoscopio.
vitanition *n.* vitanición.
vitellary *adj.* vitelar.
vitelliform *adj.* viteliforme.
vitelline *adj.* vitelina, vitelino, -na.
vitellogenesis *n.* vitelogénesis.
vitellolutein *n.* viteloluteína.
vitellorubin *n.* vitelorrubina.
vitellose *n.* vitelosa.
vitellus *n.* vitellus, vitelo.
  ovi vitellus vitelo del huevo.
vitiatin *n.* vitiatina.
vitiation *n.* viciación, viciamiento.
vitiligines *n.* vitilígines.
vitiliginous *adj.* vitiliginoso, -sa.
vitiligo *n.* vitíligo.
  Cazenave's vitiligo vitíligo de Cazenave.
  Celsus' vitiligo vitíligo de Celsus.
  circumnevic vitiligo vitíligo circumnévico, vitíligo perinévico, vitíligo perinevoide.

vitiligo capitis vitíligo de la cabeza.
vitiligo iridis vitíligo del iris, vitíligo iridis.
vitiligoidea *adj.* vitiligoide.
vitium vicio, vitium.
  vitium conformationis vicio de conformación.
  vitium cordis vicio cardíaco.
  vitium primae formationis vicio de primera formación.
vitochemical *adj.* vitoquímico, -ca.
vitrectomy *n.* vitrectomía.
  anterior vitrectomy vitrectomía anterior.
  posterior vitrectomy vitrectomía posterior.
vitrein *n.* vitreína.
vitreitis *n.* vitreítis.
vitreocapsulitis *n.* vitreocapsulitis.
vitreodentin *n.* vitreodentina.
vitreoretinal *adj.* vitreorretiniano, -na.
vitreoretinopathy *n.* vitreorretinopatía.
  familial exudative vitreoretinopathy vitreorretinopatía familiar exudativa.
vitreous *adj.* vítreo, -a.
  vitreous loss vitreorragia.
vitreum vitreum.
vitrification *n.* vitrificación.
vitrina *n.* vitrina.
  vitrina oculi vitrina ocular.
vitriol *n.* vitriolo.
  blue vitriol vitriolo azul.
  green vitriol vitriolo verde.
  white vitriol vitriolo blanco.
  zinc vitriol vitriolo cínico.
vitriolated *adj.* vitriolado, -da.
vitriolation *n.* vitriolaje.
vitritis *n.* vitritis.
vitropression *n.* vitropresión.
vitrosin *n.* vitrosina.
vivarium *n.* vivario.
vividialysis *n.* vividiálisis.
vividiffusion *n.* vividifusión.
vivificatio *n.* vivificación^2.
vivification *n.* vivificación^2.
viviparition *n.* viviparición.
viviparity *n.* viviparidad.
viviparous *adj.* vivíparo, -ra.
viviperception *n.* vivipercepción.
vivisection *n.* vivisección.
vivisectionist *n.* viviseccionista.
vivisector *n.* vivisector, -ra.
vocal *adj.* vocal.
voice *n.* voz.
  amphoric voice voz anfórica.
  bronchial voice voz bronquial.
  cavernous voice voz cavernosa.
  double voice voz doble.
  epigastric voice voz epigástrica.
  eunuchoid voice voz de falsete, voz eunucoide.
  myxedema voice voz mixedematosa.
  whispered voice voz susurrada.
voix *n.* voz.
volar *adj.* volar.
volardorsal *adj.* volardorsal.
volatile *adj.* volátil.
volatilization *n.* volatilización.
volatilize *v.* volatilizar.
volatilizer *n.* volatilizador.
volition *n.* volición.
volitional *adj.* volitivo, -va.
volsella volsella.
voltage *n.* voltaje.
voltaic *adj.* voltaico, -ca.
voltaism *n.* voltaísmo.
voltameter *n.* voltámetro.
voltampere *n.* voltamperio.

voltmeter *n.* voltímetro.
volume *n.* volumen.
atomic volume volumen atómico.
blood volume volumen sanguíneo.
circulation volume volumen circulatorio, volumen de circulación.
closing volume (CV) volumen de cierre.
critical volume volumen crítico.
distribution volume volumen de distribución.
end-diastolic volume volumen de fin de diástole, volumen diastólico final, volumen telediastólico.
end-systolic volume volumen de fin de sístole, volumen sistólico final.
expiratory reserve volume (ERV) volumen de reserva espiratoria (VRE), volumen espiratorio de reserva (VER).
forced expiratory volume (FEV) volumen espiratorio forzado (VEF).
functional residual volume volumen funcional pulmonar.
inspiratory reserve volume (IRV) volumen de reserva aspiratoria (VRA), volumen de reserva inspiratoria, volumen inspiratorio de reserva (VIR).
mean cell volume (MCV) volumen celular medio (VCM).
mean corpuscular volume (MCV) volumen corpuscular medio (VCM).
minute output volume volumen minuto cardíaco.
minute volume (MV) volumen minuto (VM), volumen por minuto (VM).
packed-cell volume (PCV) volumen de células aglomeradas, volumen eritrocítico concentrado.
partial volume volumen parcial.
plasma volume volumen plasmático.
red cell volume volumen eritrocítico.
residual volume (RV) volumen residual (VR).
respiratory minute volume volumen minuto respiratorio.
resting tidal volume volumen corriente en reposo, volumen de ventilación pulmonar en reposo.
specific volume volumen específico.
standard volume volumen estándar.
stroke volume volumen por contracción.
systolic volume volumen sistólico.
target volume volumen blanco, volumen diana.
tidal volume (Vt) volumen corriente, volumen corriente pulmonar, volumen de ventilación pulmonar, volumen tidal (Vt).
volume of circulation volumen circulatorio, volumen de circulación.

volume of packed red cells (VPRC) volumen eritrocítico concentrado.
volumenometer *n.* volumenómetro.
volumetric *adj.* volumétrico, -ca.
volumetry *n.* volumetría.
volumette volumette.
volumination *n.* voluminación.
volumometer *n.* volumómetro.
voluntary *adj.* voluntario, -ria.
voluntomotory *adj.* voluntomotor, -ra.
voluptuous *adj.* voluptuoso, -sa.
voluptuousness *n.* voluptuosidad.
volute *n.* voluta.
volutin *n.* volutina.
volvulate *v.* volvular.
volvulosis *n.* volvulosis.
volvulus *n.* vólvulo.
gastric volvulus vólvulo gástrico.
volvulus neonatorum vólvulo neonatal.
vomer *n.* vómer.
vomerine *adj.* vomeriano, -na, vomerino, -na.
vomerobasilar *adj.* vomerobasilar.
vomeronasal *adj.* vomeronasal.
vomica *n.* vómica.
vomicose *adj.* vomicoso, -sa.
vomicus *n.* vómica.
vomit[1] *n.* vómito[1].
acetonemic vomit vómito acetonémico.
Barcoo vomit vómito de Barcoo.
bilious vomit vómito bilioso.
black vomit vómito negro.
coffee-ground vomit vómito de borra de café, vómito en posos de café.
vomit[2] *v.* vomitar, vómito[1].
vomiting *n.* vomición, vómito[2].
cerebral vomiting vómito cerebral.
cyclic vomiting vómito cíclico.
dry vomiting vómito seco.
epidemic vomiting vómito epidémico.
fecal vomiting vómito fecal, vómito fecaloideo.
hysterical vomiting vómito electivo, vómito histérico.
incoercible vomiting vómito incoercible.
morning vomiting vómito matinal.
nervous vomiting vómito nervioso.
periodic vomiting vómito periódico.
pernicious vomiting vómito pernicioso.
projectile vomiting vómito en escopetazo.
psychogenic vomiting vómito psicógeno.
recurrent vomiting vómito recurrente.
retention vomiting vómito por retención.
stercoraceous vomiting vómito estercoráceo.
vomiting of pregnancy vómito del embarazo.
vomition *n.* vomición.
vomitive *adj.* vomitivo, -va.
vomitory *n.* vomitivo, vomitorio.
vomiturition *n.* vomiturición.

vomitus vómito, vomitus.
vomitus cruentus vómito cruento, vomitus cruentus.
vomitus gravidarum vomitus gravidarum.
vomitus marinus vómito marino.
vomitus matutinus potatorum vomitus matutinus potatorum.
vomitus niger vómito negro.
vortex vortex, vórtice.
vorticose *adj.* vorticoso, -sa.
voussure *n.* voussure.
vox vox, voz.
vox choleraica voz colérica.
vox cholerica voz colérica.
voxel *n.* voxel.
voyeur *n.* voyeur.
voyeurism *n.* voyeurismo.
vuerometer *n.* vuerómetro.
vulcanize *v.* vulcanizar.
vulgaris *adj.* vulgar.
vulnerability *n.* vulnerabilidad.
vulnerable *adj.* vulnerable.
vulnerant *adj.* vulnerante.
vulnerary *n.* vulnerario, -ria.
vulnerate *v.* vulnerar.
vulsella vulsela, vulsella, vulsellum.
vulsellum *n.* vulsela.
vulva *n.* vulva.
vulval *adj.* vulvar.
vulvar *adj.* vulvar.
vulvectomy *n.* vulvectomía.
vulvismus *n.* vulvismo.
vulvitis *n.* vulvitis.
chronic atrophic vulvitis vulvitis atrófica crónica.
chronic hypertrophic vulvitis vulvitis hipertrófica crónica.
diabetic vulvitis vulvitis diabética.
diphtheritic vulvitis vulvitis diftérica.
eczematiform vulvitis vulvitis eccematiforme, vulvitis eccematosa.
erosive vulvitis vulvitis erosiva.
follicular vulvitis vulvitis folicular.
gonorrheal vulvitis vulvitis blenorrágica.
leukoplakic vulvitis vulvitis leucoplásica.
phlegmonous vulvitis vulvitis flemonosa.
plasma cell vulvitis vulvitis de células plasmáticas.
pseudoleukoplakic vulvitis vulvitis pseudoleucoplásica.
vulvitis plasmocellularis vulvitis plasmocelular.
vulvocrural *adj.* vulvocrural.
vulvorectal *adj.* vulvorrectal.
vulvouterine *adj.* vulvouterino, -na.
vulvovaginal *adj.* vulvovaginal.
vulvovaginitis *n.* vulvovaginitis.
senile vulvovaginitis vulvovaginitis senil.

W w

wadding *n.* guata.
wafer *n.* oblea.
wagaga *n.* wagaga.
waist *n.* cintura, talle.
wakamba *n.* wakamba.
wakefulness *n.* vigilia.
walk *n.* marcha.
  duck walk marcha de pato.
wall *n.* pared.
  cavity wall pared cavitaria.
  cell wall pared celular.
  splanchnic wall pared esplácnica.
wall-eye *n.* walleye.
wandering *adj.* errante, vagabundo, -da.
wanganga *n.* wanganga.
warblefly *n.* tábano.
ward *n.* sala.
  isolation ward sala de aislamiento.
warm *adj.* templado, -da.
wart *n.* verruca, verruga.
  acuminate wart verruga acuminada.
  asbestos wart verruga de amianto.
  common wart verruga común.
  digitate wart verruga digitada.
  fig wart verruga en higo.
  filiform wart verruga filiforme.
  flat wart verruga plana.
  fugitive wart verruga fugaz.
  genital wart verruga genital.
  Hassall-Henle wart verruga de Hassall-Henle.
  Henle's wart verruga de Henle.
  infectious wart verruga infecciosa.
  juvenile wart verruga juvenil.
  moist wart verruga húmeda.
  mosaic wart verruga en mosaico.
  mother wart verruga madre.
  mucocutaneous wart verruga mucocutánea.
  periungual wart verruga periungueal.
  Peruvian wart verruga peruana.
  pitch wart verruga de alquitrán.
  plane wart verruga plana.
  plantar wart verruca plantaris, verruga plantar.
  pointed wart verruga en punta.
  printed wart verruga de punto.
  prosector wart verruga de prosector.
  seborrheic wart verruga seborreica.
  seed wart verruga de semilla.
  senile wart verruga senil.
  simple wart verruga simple.
  soot wart verruga del deshollinador, verruga del hollín.
  telangiectatic wart verruga telangiectásica.
  tuberculous wart verruga tuberculosa.
  venereal wart verruga venérea.
  viral wart verruga viral.
wartpox *n.* wartpox.
waste *n.* mengua.
water *n.* agua.
waterpox *n.* waterpox.
watershed *n.* cuenca, divisoria de aguas.

  abdominal watershed cuenca abdominal.
wattage *n.* wattage.
wattmeter *n.* vatímetro.
wave *n.* onda.
  a wave onda a.
  acid wave onda ácida.
  alkaline wave onda alcalina.
  alpha wave onda alfa.
  anacrotic wave onda anacrótica, onda anadicrótica.
  anadicrotic wave onda anacrótica, onda anadicrótica.
  arterial wave onda arterial.
  beta wave onda beta.
  biphasic wave onda bifásica.
  brain wave onda cerebral.
  c wave onda c.
  cannon wave onda cañón, onda de cañón.
  catacrotic wave onda catacrótica, onda catadicrótica.
  catadicrotic wave onda catacrótica, onda catadicrótica.
  contraction wave onda de contracción.
  delta wave onda delta.
  dicrotic wave onda dicrótica.
  electrocardiographic wave onda electrocardiográfica.
  electroencephalographic wave onda electroencefalográfica.
  electromagnetic wave onda electromagnética.
  excitation wave onda de excitación.
  F wave onda F.
  fibrillary wave onda fibrilares.
  flat top wave onda de tope plano.
  fluid wave onda líquida.
  flutter wave onda F.
  flutter-fibrillation wave onda de aleteo-fibrilación.
  h wave onda h.
  intracraneal pressure wave onda en el registro de presión intracraneal.
  Liesegang's wave onda de Liesegang.
  light wave onda luminosa.
  longitudinal wave onda longitudinal.
  overflow wave onda de repleción.
  P wave onda P.
  papillary wave onda papilar.
  percussion wave onda de percusión.
  phrenic wave onda frénicas.
  postextrasystolic T wave onda T posextrasistólica.
  pulse wave onda de pulso, onda del pulso.
  Q wave onda Q.
  R wave onda R.
  radio wave onda de radio.
  random wave onda al azar.
  recoil wave onda de rebote, onda de retroceso.
  retrograde P wave onda P retrógrada.
  S wave onda S.
  sharp wave onda aguda.

  short wave onda corta.
  sine wave onda seno.
  sonic wave onda sónica, onda sonora.
  stimulus wave onda de estímulo.
  supersonic wave onda supersónicas.
  T wave onda T.
  theta wave onda teta, onda theta.
  tidal wave onda de marea, onda de marejada.
  transverse wave onda transversa.
  Traube-Hering wave onda de Traube-Hering.
  tricrotic wave onda tricrótica.
  triphasic wave onda trifásica.
  U wave onda U.
  ultrashort wave onda ultracorta.
  ultrasonic wave onda ultrasónica.
  V wave onda V.
  ventricular wave onda ventricular.
  X wave onda X.
  Y wave onda Y.
way *n.* vía.
weakening *n.* debilitación, depauperación.
weakness *n.* debilidad.
wean *v.* destetar.
weaning *n.* destete.
weanling *n.* destetado, -da.
wear *n.* desgaste.
  occlusal wear desgaste occlusal.
weather *n.* clima.
webbed *adj.* membranoso, -sa.
webbing *n.* palmatura.
weber *n.* weber.
wedge *n.* cuña.
  dental wedge cuña dental.
  step wedge cuña graduada.
weightlessness *n.* ingravidez.
Weismannism *n.* weismanismo.
well-being *n.* bienestar.
  well-being of the patient bienestar del enfermo.
wellness *n.* bienestar.
  high-level wellness bienestar de alto nivel.
wen *n.* lupia.
whartonitis *n.* whartonitis.
wheal *n.* roncha.
wheel *n.* rueda.
  Burlew wheel rueda de Burlew.
wheeze *n.* jadeo, sibilancia.
  asthmatoid wheeze jadeo asmatoide.
whey *n.* suero.
whim *n.* antojo[1].
whiplash *n.* latigazo.
whisper *n.* cuchicheo.
whistle *n.* silbato, silbido.
  Galton's whistle silbato de Galton.
white *n.* blanco, -ca[2].
  visual white blanco visual.
  white of the eye blanco del ojo.
  white with pressure blanco con presión.
  white without pressure blanco sin presión.

whoop *n.* gallo.

whorl *n.* bidelto, espira, vórtice.

whorled *adj.* espiralado, -da.

wick *n.* mecha.

will *n.* voluntad.

windage *n.* windage.

windigo *n.* wihtigo, windigo, witigo.

window *n.* ventana.

  aortic window ventana aórtica.

  aortopulmonary window ventana aortopulmonar.

  cochlear window fenestra cochleae, ventana coclear, ventana de la cóclea.

  oval window fenestra ovalis, ventana oval.

  round window ventana redonda.

  skin window ventana cutánea.

  tachycardia window ventana de taquicardia.

  vestibular window fenestra vestibuli, ventana del vestíbulo, ventana vestibular.

  window of the cochlea fenestra cochleae, ventana coclear, ventana de la cóclea.

  window of the vestibule fenestra vestibuli, ventana del vestíbulo, ventana vestibular.

wing *n.* ala.

wink *n.* guiñada, guiño.

winking *n.* guiñada, guiño.

wire[1] *n.* alambre.

  arch wire alambre de arco, alambre de la arcada.

  embolization wire alambre de embolización.

  full-arch wire alambre de arcada completa.

  ideal arch wire alambre de arco ideal.

  Kirschner's wire alambre de Kirschner.

  ligature wire alambre de ligadura.

  orthodontic wire alambre de ortodoncia.

  sectional arch wire alambre de arcada regional.

  separating wire alambre de separación, alambre separador.

wire[2] *v.* alambrar.

wiring *n.* alambrado.

  circumferential wiring alambrado circunferencial, alambrado en circunferencia.

  continuous loop wiring alambrado de asa continua.

  craniofacial suspension wiring alambrado craneofacial de suspensión.

  Ivy loop wiring alambrado de asa de Ivy, alambrado de Ivy.

  perialveolar wiring alambrado perialveolar.

  pyriform aperture wiring alambrado de la abertura piriforme.

  Stout's wiring alambrado de Stout continuo.

witzelsucht *n.* witzelsucht.

wobble *v.* tambalearse.

Wohlfahrtia Wohlfahrtia.

  Wohlfahrtia magnifica Wohlfahrtia magnifica.

  Wohlfahrtia opaca Wohlfahrtia opaca.

  Wohlfahrtia vigil Wohlfahrtia vigil.

wohlfahrtiosis *n.* wohlfahrtiosis.

Wolffian *adj.* wolffiano, -na.

wolfsbane *n.* luparia.

Wolinella Wolinella.

  Wolinella recta Wolinella recta.

word salad *n.* ensalada de palabras.

work *n.* trabajo.

  breathing work trabajo respiratorio.

  dream work trabajo del sueño.

  dynamic cardiac work trabajo cardíaco dinámico.

  static cardiac work trabajo cardíaco estático.

  work of mourning trabajo del duelo.

worm *n.* gusano[1], gusano[2].

wound *n.* herida, herir.

  aseptic wound herida aséptica.

  avulsed wound herida avulsa.

  blowing wound herida soplante.

  blunt wound herida contusa, herida por contusión.

  cold weapon wound herida por arma blanca.

  contused wound herida contusa, herida por contusión.

  crease wound herida acanalada.

  crushing wound herida por aplastamiento.

  glancing wound herida de refilón.

  gunshot wound herida por arma de fuego.

  gutter wound herida en gotiera.

  incised wound herida de incisión, herida incisa.

  incisional wound herida de incisión, herida incisa.

  non-penetrating wound herida no penetrante.

  open wound herida abierta.

  penetrating abdominal wound herida abdominal penetrante.

  penetrating wound herida penetrante.

  perforating wound herida perforante.

  poisoned wound herida emponzoñada, herida envenenada.

  puncture wound herida por punción, herida punzante.

  septic wound herida séptica.

  seton wound herida en sedal.

  stab wound herida por arma blanca.

  subcutaneous wound herida subcutánea.

  sucking wound herida aspirante, herida por aspiración.

  tangential wound herida tangencial.

  traumatopneic wound herida traumatopneica.

  tunnel wound herida en túnel.

  wound by firearm herida por arma de fuego.

W-plasty *n.* W-plastia.

wrinkle *n.* arruga.

wrinkled *adj.* rugoso, -sa.

wrist *n.* muñeca.

  tennis wrist muñeca de tenis.

Wuchereria Wuchereria.

  Wuchereria bancrofti Wuchereria bancrofti.

  Wuchereria malayi Wuchereria malayi.

wuchereriasis *n.* wuchereriasis.

xanchromatic *adj.* xancromático, -ca.
xanthelasma *n.* xantelasma.
  generalized xanthelasma xantelasma generalizado.
  xanthelasma palpebrarum xantelasma palpebral, xantelasma palpebrarum.
xanthelasmatosis *n.* xantelasmatosis.
xanthematin *n.* xantematina, xanthematina.
xanthemia *n.* xantemia.
xanthic *adj.* xántico, -ca, xántixo, -xa.
xanthin *n.* xantina.
xanthine *n.* xantina.
xanthine oxidase *n.* xantinoxidasa.
xanthinuria *n.* xantinuria.
xanthinuric *adj.* xantinúrico, -ca.
xanthism *n.* xantismo.
xanthiuria *n.* xantiuria.
xanthochroia *n.* xantocroia.
xanthochromatic *adj.* xancrómico, -ca.
xanthochromia *n.* xantocromía.
  xanthochromia striata palmaris xantocromía estriada palmar.
xanthochromic *adj.* xantocrómico, -ca.
xanthochroous *adj.* xantocroo, -a, xantodermo, -ma.
xanthocyanopsia *n.* xantocianopsia.
xanthocystine *n.* xantocistina.
xanthocyte *n.* xantocito, xantoxito.
xanthoderma *n.* xantoderma.
xanthodermia *n.* xantodermia.
xanthodont *adj.* xantodonte.
xanthoerythrodermia *n.* xantoeritrodermia.
xanthofibroma thecocellulare *n.* xantofibroma tecocelular.
xanthogranuloma *n.* xantogranuloma.
  choroidal plexus xanthogranuloma xantogranuloma de plexos coroideos.
  juvenile xanthogranuloma xantogranuloma juvenil.
  necrobiotic xanthogranuloma xantogranuloma necrobiótico.
xanthogranulomatosis *n.* xantogranulomatosis.
xanthogranulomatous *adj.* xantogranulomatoso, -sa.
xanthokyanopy *n.* xantocianopía.
xanthoma *n.* xantoma.
  craniohypophyseal xanthoma xantoma craneohipofisario.
  diabetic xanthoma xantoma de los diabéticos, xantoma diabético.
  disseminated xanthoma xantoma diseminado.
  eruptive xanthoma xantoma eruptivo.
  multiple xanthoma xantoma múltiple.
  normolipemic xanthoma planum xantoma plano normolipémico.
  planar xanthoma xantoma planar, xantoma plano.
  plane xanthoma xantoma planar, xantoma plano.

  tendinous xanthoma xantoma tendinoso.
  tuberoeruptive xanthoma xantoma tuberoeruptivo.
  tuberous xanthoma xantoma tuberoso, xantoma tuberoso múltiple.
  verrucous xanthoma xantoma verrugoso.
  xanthoma diabeticorum xantoma de los diabéticos, xantoma diabético.
  xanthoma disseminatum xantoma diseminado.
  xanthoma eruptivum xantoma eruptivo.
  xanthoma multiplex xantoma múltiple.
  xanthoma palpebrarum xantoma de los párpados, xantoma palpebral.
  xanthoma planum xantoma planar, xantoma plano.
  xanthoma striatum palmare xantoma estriado palmar.
  xanthoma tendinosum xantoma tendinoso.
  xanthoma tuberosum xantoma tuberoso, xantoma tuberoso múltiple.
  xanthoma tuberosum multiplex xantoma tuberoso, xantoma tuberoso múltiple.
xanthomasarcoma *n.* xantomasarcoma.
xanthomatosis *n.* xantomatosis.
  biliary hypercholesterolemic xanthomatosis xantomatosis biliar hipercolesterolémica.
  cerebrotendinous xanthomatosis xantomatosis cerebrotendinosa.
  chronic idiopathic xanthomatosis xantomatosis idiopática crónica.
  familial hypercholesterolemic xanthomatosis xantomatosis hipercolesterémica familiar.
  normal cholesteremic xanthomatosis xantomatosis colesterémica normal.
  primary familial xanthomatosis xantomatosis familiar primaria.
  Wolman xanthomatosis xantomatosis de Wolman.
  xanthomatosis bulbi xantomatosis bulbar.
  xanthomatosis corneae xantomatosis corneal.
  xanthomatosis generalisata ossium xantomatosis ósea generalizada.
  xanthomatosis iridis xantomatosis del iris.
xanthomatous *adj.* xantomatoso, -sa.
xanthopathy *n.* xantopatía.
xanthophane *n.* xantófano.
xanthophose *n.* xantofosia, xantofosis.
xanthopia *n.* xantopía.
xanthoproteic *adj.* xantoproteico, -ca.
xanthoprotein *n.* xantoproteína.
xanthopsia *n.* xantopsia.
xanthopsis *n.* xantopsis.
xanthopsydracia *n.* xantopsidracia.
xanthorubin *n.* xantorrubina.
xanthorubin *n.* xantorrubina.
xanthosarcoma *n.* xantosarcoma.
xanthosis *n.* xantosis.

  xanthosis of the septum nasi xantosis del tabique nasal.
xanthous *adj.* xantoso, -sa.
xanthuria *n.* xanturia.
xanthylic *adj.* xantílico, -ca.
xenembole *n.* xenembolia.
xenenthesis *n.* xenentesis.
xenoantigen *n.* xenoantígeno.
xenobiotic *adj.* xenobiótico, -ca.
xenocythophilic *adj.* xenocitófilo, -la.
xenodiagnosis *n.* xenodiagnosis, xenodiagnóstico.
xenodiagnostic *adj.* xenodiagnóstico, -ca.
xenogeneic *adj.* xenogeneico, -ca.
xenogenesis *n.* xenogénesis, xenogenia.
xenogenic *adj.* xenogénico[1], -ca.
xenogenous *adj.* xenogénico[2], -ca, xenógeno, -na.
xenograft *n.* xenograft, xenoinjerto.
xenology *n.* xenología.
xenomenia *n.* xenomenia.
xenoparasite *n.* xenoparásito.
xenoparasitism *n.* xenoparasitismo.
xenophobia *n.* xenofobia.
xenophonia *n.* xenofonía.
xenophthalmia *n.* xenoftalmía.
Xenopsylla Xenopsylla.
  Xenopsylla astia Xenopsylla astia.
  Xenopsylla brasiliensis Xenopsylla brasiliensis.
  Xenopsylla cheopis Xenopsylla cheopis.
xenorexia *n.* xenorexia.
xeransia *n.* xeransia.
xeransis *n.* xeransia, xeransis.
xerantic *adj.* xerántico, -ca.
xerasia *n.* xerasia.
xerasial *adj.* xerasial.
xerocheilia *n.* xeroqueilia.
xerochilia *n.* xeroqueilia, xeroquilia.
xerocollyrium *n.* xerocolirio.
xeroderma *n.* xeroderma, xerodermia.
  xeroderma pigmentosum xerodermia pigmentosa.
xerodermatic *adj.* xerodérmico, -ca.
xerodermoid *n.* xerodermoide.
  pigmented xerodermoid xerodermoide pigmentado.
xerogel *n.* xerogel.
xerogram *n.* xerograma.
xerography *n.* xerografía.
xeroma *n.* xeroma.
xeromammography *n.* xeromamografía.
xeromenia *n.* xeromenia.
xeromycteria *n.* xeromicteria.
xerophagia *n.* xerofagia.
xerophagy *n.* xerofagia.
xerophobia *n.* xerofobia.
xerophthalmia *n.* xeroftalmía.
xerophthalmus *n.* xeroftalmo.
xeroradiography *n.* xerorradiografía.

xerosis *n.* xerosis.
  conjunctival xerosis xerosis conjuntival.
  corneal xerosis xerosis corneal.
  xerosis conjuctivae xerosis conjuntival.
  xerosis corneae xerosis corneal.
  xerosis cutis xerosis cutánea, xerosis del cutis.
  xerosis parenchymatosa xerosis parenquimatosa.
  xerosis superficialis xerosis superficial.
xerostomia *n.* xerostomía.

xerotic *adj.* xerótico, -ca.
xerotocia *n.* xerotocia.
xerotomography *n.* xerotomografía.
xerotripsis *n.* xerotipia, xerotripsis.
xeroxialography *n.* xerosialografía.
xiphisternal *adj.* xifisternal.
xiphocostal *adj.* xifocostal.
xiphodidymus *n.* xifodídimo, xifodimo.
xiphodynia *n.* xifodinia.
xiphoid *adj.* xifoide, xifoides.
xiphoidalgia *n.* xifoidalgia.

xiphoiditis *n.* xifoiditis.
xiphopagotomy *n.* xifopagotomía.
xiphopagus *n.* xifópago.
xyloketose *n.* xilocetosa.
xyloketosuria *n.* xilocetosuria.
xylose *n.* xilosa.
xylosuria *n.* xilosuria.
xylotherapy *n.* xiloterapia.
xyrospasm *n.* xirospasmo.
xysma *n.* xisma.
xyster *n.* xister.

Y y

yaw *n.* yaw.
  mother yaw yaw madre.
yawey *n.* yawey.
yawn¹ *n.* bostezo.
yawn² *v.* bostezar.
yaws *n.* frambesia, yaws.
  crab yaws frambesia del cangrejo.
  foot yaws frambesia del pie.
  Guinea corn yaws frambesia de maíz, yaws maíz de Guinea.
  mother yaws frambesia madre, yaws madre.
  ringworm yaws frambesia tiñosa, yaws circinada.
yeast *n.* levadura.

yellow *n.* amarillo.
Yersinia Yersinia.
  Yersinia enterocolitica Yersinia enterocolítica.
  Yersinia frederiksenii Yersinia frederiksenii.
  Yersinia intermedia Yersinia intermedia.
  Yersinia kristensenii Yersinia kristensenii.
  Yersinia pestis Yersinia pestis.
  Yersinia pseudotuberculosis Yersinia seudotuberculosis.
  Yersinia ruckeri Yersinia ruckeri.
yersiniosis *n.* yersiniosis.
  pseudotubercular yersiniosis yersiniosis seudotuberculosa.

yin-yang *n.* yin-yang.
yodobrassid *n.* yodobrásido.
yoke *n.* junta, yugo.
  alveolar yoke of the mandible yugo alveolar del maxilar inferior.
  alveolar yoke of the maxilla yugo alveolar del maxilar superior.
  sphenoidal yoke yugo esfenoidal.
yolk *n.* vitelo.
yperite *n.* yperita.
ypsiliform *adj.* ipsiliforme.
ypsiloid *adj.* ipsiloide.

Z z

zaire *n.* zaire.
zaranthan *n.* zarantán.
z-cap cap-z.
zeiosis *n.* zeiosis.
zeism *n.* zeísmo.
Zeissian *adj.* zeisiano, -na.
zelophobia *n.* celofobia.
zelotypia *n.* celotipia.
zenkerism *n.* zenkerismo.
zenkerize *v.* zenkerizar.
zetacrit *n.* zetácrito.
zigzagplasty *n.* zigzagplastia.
zincalism *n.* cincalismo.
zinciferous *adj.* cincífero, -ra, cinquífero, -ra.
zincoid *adj.* cincoide.
zoacanthosis *n.* zoacantosis.
zoanthropic *adj.* zoantrópico, -ca.
zoanthropy *n.* zoantropía.
zoescope *n.* zoescopio.
zoetic *adj.* zoético, -ca.
zoetrope *n.* zoétropo.
zoic *adj.* zoico, -ca.
zoite *n.* zoíto.
zomidin *n.* zomidina.
zomotherapy *n.* zomoterapia.
zona *n.* zona.
  zona corona zona coronal.
  zona denticulata zona denticulada.
  zona dermatica zona dermática.
  zona epithelioserosa zona de epitelio seroso, zona epithelioserosa.
  zona ignea zona ígnea.
  zona ophthalmica zona oftálmica.
zonal *adj.* zonal.
zonary *adj.* zonal.
zonate *adj.* zonado, -da.
zone *n.* zona.
  androgenic zone zona andrógena, zona androgénica.
  anelectronic zone zona anelectrónica.
  anelectrotinic zone zona anelectrotínica.
  apical zone zona apical.
  biokinetic zone zona biocinética.
  border zone zona límite, zona limítrofe.
  Charcot's zone zona de Charcot.
  combining zone zona combinante.
  comfort zone zona confortable, zona de bienestar, zona de comodidad.
  cornuradicular zone zona cornurradicular.
  coronal zone zona coronal.
  denticulate zone zona denticulada.
  dentofacial zone zona dentofacial.
  dolorogenic zone zona dolorígena, zona dolorógena, zona dolorogénica.
  dorsal zone of His zona dorsal de His.
  entry zone zona de entrada.
  epileptogenic zone zona epileptógena.
  epileptogenous zone zona epileptógena.
  equivalence zone zona de equivalencia.
  erogenous zone zona erógena, zona erotógena.

  erotogenic zone zona erógena, zona erotógena.
  extravisual zone zona extravisual.
  fetal zone zona fetal.
  Flechsig's primordial zone zona primordial de Flechsig.
  focal zone zona focal.
  Fraunhofer zone zona de Fraunhofer.
  Fresnel zone zona de Fresnel.
  gliding zone zona de deslizamiento.
  Head's zone zona de Head.
  hyperesthetic zone zona hiperestésica.
  hypnogenic zone zona hipnógena.
  hypnogenous zone zona hipnógena.
  hysterogenic zone zona histerógena.
  hysterogenous zone zona histerógena.
  inhibition zone zona de inhibición.
  intermediate zone zona intermedia.
  isoelectric zone zona isoeléctrica.
  language zone zona del lenguaje.
  latent zone zona latente.
  Looser's zone zona de Looser.
  marginal zone zona marginal.
  nucleolar zone zona nucleolar.
  placental zone zona placentaria.
  polar zone zona polar.
  proagglutinoid zone zona proaglutinoide.
  pupillary zone zona pupilar.
  reflexogenic zone zona reflexógena.
  respiratory zone zona respiratoria.
  segmental zone zona segmentaria.
  thymus-dependent zone zona dependiente del timo, zona timodependiente.
  trigger zone zona desencadenante, zona gatillo.
  visual zone zona visual.
  zone of antibody excess zona de exceso de anticuerpo.
  zone of antigen excess zona de exceso de antígeno.
  zone of discontinuity zona de discontinuidad.
  zone of equivalence zona de equivalencia.
  zone of optimal proportions zona de proporciones óptimas.
zonesthesia *n.* zonestesia.
zonifugal *adj.* zonífugo, -ga.
zoning *n.* zonificación.
zonipetal *adj.* zonípeto, -ta.
zonula *n.* zonula, zónula.
  zonula adherens zónula adherente.
  zonula occludens zónula de oclusión, zonula occludens, zónula ocluyente.
zonular *adj.* zonular.
zonule *n.* zonula, zónula.
zonulitis *n.* zonulitis.
zonulolysis *n.* zonulólisis.
zonulotomy *n.* zonulotomía.
zonulysis *n.* zonulólisis.
zoo-agglutinin *n.* zooaglutinina.

zooanaphylactogen *n.* zooanafilactógeno.
zooanthroponosis *n.* zooantroponosis.
zoobiology *n.* zoobiología.
zoobiotism *n.* zoobiotismo.
zoochemical *adj.* zooquímico, -ca.
zoochemistry *n.* zooquímica.
zoodermic *adj.* zoodérmico, -ca.
zoodetritus *n.* zoodesecho.
zoodynamic *adj.* zoodinámico, -ca.
zoodynamics *n.* zoodinámica.
zooerastia *n.* zooerastia.
zooesteroid *n.* zooesteroide.
zoogenesis *n.* zoogénesis.
zoogenous *adj.* zoógeno, -na.
zoogeny *n.* zoogenia.
zoogeography *n.* zoogeografía.
zoograft *n.* zooinjerto.
zoografting *n.* zooinjerto.
zoography *n.* zoografía.
zoohormone *n.* zoohormona.
zookinase *n.* zoocinasa, zooquinasa.
zoolagnia *n.* zoolagnia.
zoology *n.* zoología.
  experimental zoology zoología experimental.
zoom *n.* zoom.
zoomania *n.* zoomanía.
zoomylus *n.* zoomilo.
zoonomy *n.* zoonomía.
zoonosis *n.* zoonosis.
  direct zoonosis zoonosis directa.
zoonotic *adj.* zoonótico, -ca.
zooparasite *n.* zooparásito.
zooparasitic *adj.* zooparasitario, -ria.
zooperal *adj.* zooperal.
zoopery *n.* zooperia.
zoophagus *n.* zoófago, -ga.
zoophile *adj.* zoófilo, -la.
zoophilia *n.* zoofilia.
zoophilic *adj.* zoofílico, -ca.
zoophilism *n.* zoofilismo.
zoophobia *n.* zoofobia.
zoophysiology *n.* zoofisiología.
zooplasty *n.* zooplastia.
zooprecipitins *n.* zooprecipitinas.
zooprophylaxis *n.* zooprofilaxis.
zoopsia *n.* zoopsia.
zoosadism *n.* zoosadismo.
zooscopy *n.* zooscopia.
zoosensitinogen *n.* zoosensitinógeno.
zoosis *n.* zoosis.
zoosmosis *n.* zoósmosis.
zoosperm *n.* zoosperma.
zoospermia *n.* zoospermia.
zoosterol *n.* zooesterol.
zootic *adj.* zoótico, -ca.
zootomist *n.* zootomista.
zootomy *n.* zootomía.
zootoxin *n.* zootoxina.
zootrophic *adj.* zootrófico, -ca.

zootrophotixism *n.* zootrofotoxismo.
zoster *n.* zoster.
  geniculate zoster zoster geniculado.
  ophthalmic zoster zoster oftálmico.
  zoster sine eruptione zoster sine eruptione, zoster sine herpete.
zosteriform *adj.* zosteriforme.
zosteroid *adj.* zosteroide.
Z-plasty *n.* zetaplastia, Z-plastia.
zwitterion *n.* zwiterión, zwitterion.
zwitterionic *adj.* zwiteriónico, -ca.
zygal *adj.* cigal.
zygapophyseal *adj.* cigapofisario, -ria.
zygapophysial *adj.* cigapofisario, -ria.
zygapophysis *n.* cigapófisis.
zygion *n.* cigión, zigion, zygion.

zygodactyly *n.* cigodactilia.
zygoma *n.* cigoma, zigoma.
zygomatic *adj.* cigomático, -ca.
zygomaticofacial *adj.* cigomaticofacial.
zygomaticofrontal *adj.* cigomaticofrontal.
zygomaticomaxillary *adj.* cigomaticomaxilar.
zygomatico-orbital *adj.* cigomaticoorbitario, -ria.
zygomaticosphenoid *adj.* cigomaticoesfenoidal.
zygomaticotemporal *adj.* cigomaticotemporal.
zygomaxillare *n.* cigomaxilar.
zygomycosis *n.* cigomicosis.
zygon *n.* cigón.
zygonema *n.* cigonema.
zygopodium *n.* cigopodio.
zygosis *n.* cigosis.
zygosity *n.* cigosidad.

zygote *n.* cigoto.
zygotene *n.* cigoteno.
zygotic *adj.* cigótico, -ca.
zyme *n.* zima.
zymin *n.* zimina.
zymodene *n.* cimodemo.
zymogen *n.* cimógeno, zimógeno.
zymogenesis *n.* cimogénesis, zimogénesis.
zymogenic *adj.* cimogénico, -ca, zimógeno, -na.
zymogenous *adj.* zimógeno, -na.
zymogic *adj.* zimógeno, -na.
zymogram *n.* cimograma.
zymolisis *n.* cimohidrólisis, cimólisis.
zymoscope *n.* cimoscopio[2].
zymosthenic *adj.* cimosténico, -ca, cimostético, -ca.

Spanish grammar

Main spelling difficulties

The letters *b* and *v*

These two letters are pronounced in exactly the same way. The letter b is used in all words in which this sound is followed by a consonant: bruma, blanco, abstenerse, but the letter v is used after b, d and n: obvio, advertir, convencer. Apart from this there are no general rules which govern their use; in case of doubt check in the dictionary.

The letters *c*, *k* and *q*

These three letters are used to represent the sound [k]. Before the vowels a, o, u, before a consonant, and in some cases at the end of a word c is used: casa, color, cuna, frac. Before the vowels e or i, qu is written: querer, quitar. The letter k is used in words of foreign origin in which the original spelling has been maintained: kitsch.

The letters *c* and *z*

These two letters are used to represent the sound [θ]. Before the vowels e and i the letter c is used; before the vowels a, o, u and at the end of a word z is used: cero, cima, zapato, azote, zurra, pez. There are a few exceptions to this rule: zigzag, zipizape, ¡zis, zas! Some words may also be written with either c or z: ácimo/ázimo, acimut/azimut, eccema/eczema, ceta/zeta, cinc/zinc.

Note that a final z changes to c in the plural: pez ⟶ peces.

The letters *g* and *j*

The letter j is always pronounced [x] (as in the Scottish "loch").

The letter g is pronounced [x] when it is followed by the vowels e and i, but [g] (as in "golf", "get") when it is followed by the vowels a, o or u.

In the group gu + e/i the u is silent and the pronunciation is [g], but when gu is followed by a or o the u is pronounced giving the sound [gw].

The group gü, with a dieresis over the u, is written only before e or i, and is pronounced [gw].

To summarize:

the sound [x] is written	j	before a, o and u
	j or g	before e and i
the sound [g] is written	g	before a, o, u
	gu	before i and e
the sound [gw] is written	gu	before a and o
	gü	before e and i.

The letters *r* and *rr*

The letter r is used to represent two different sounds: the one-tap [r] sound when it appears either in the middle of a word or in the final position: carta, ardor; and the multiple vibrant [rr] when it appears in initial position or follows the consonants l, n or s: roca, honra.

The double rr always represents the multiple vibrant [rr] sound and is written only between vowels: barro, borrar.

Stress in Spanish

The written accent

Words stressed on the final syllable require a written accent on that syllable when they end in a vowel or the consonants n or s:

    vendrá, café, jabalí, miró, tabú, sillón, Tomás, chochín

but   calor, carril, merced, sagaz, carcaj.

Words stressed on the penultimate syllable require a written accent on that syllable whenever the word does not end in a vowel or the consonants n or s:

    árbol, inútil, fémur, Gómez, fútbol

but   cosa, venden, acento, examen, pisos.

Words stressed on the antepenultimate syllable or earlier always require a written accent on the stressed syllable:

    pájaro, carámbano, cómpratelo, pagándoselas.

Generally speaking, monosyllabic words do not require written accents, but in some cases one is used to distinguish two different words with the same spelling: él (he, him) - el (the); té (tea) - te (the letter 'T'). These will be found in the dictionary.

Note that in the case of adverbs ending in -mente any written accent in the root adjective is retained:

    fácil ⟶ fácilmente; económico ⟶ económicamente

Diphthongs, triphthongs and hiatus

A group of two vowels that make one syllable is called a diphthong; a group of three is called a triphthong. A diphthong is formed by one weak vowel (i or u) in combination with one strong vowel (a, e or o). A triphthong is one strong vowel be tween two weak ones. As far as stress is concerned the general rules apply, with both diphthongs and triphthongs being treated as if they were one syllable. If a stressed dipthong or triphthong requires a written accent (following the rules above), this is placed above the strong vowel:

    miércoles, acariciéis.

Hiatus occurs when groups of consecutive vowels do not form diphthongs or triphthongs. In these cases the group is usually made up of strong vowels; the stressed vowel will carry a written accent or not in accordance with the rules above: neón, tebeo, traéis. However, when the stressed vowel is a weak vowel, it is the weak vowel which carries the written accent in order to distinguish the group from a diphthong or triphthong:

    María, reían, frío.

The combination ui is always considered a diphthong: contribuir, ruin.

The article

	definite		indefinite	
	masculine	femenine	masculine	masculine
singular	el	la	un	una
plural	los	las	unos	unas

Observations

With reflexive verbs the definite article is equivalent to an English possessive adjective in sentences such as:

    me lavo la cara *(I wash my face)*
    cámbiate de ropa *(change your clothes)*

The definite article may acquire the pronominal value of the English "the one" or "the ones": el del traje azul *(the one in the blue suit)*.

The masculine article (el, un) is used with feminine nouns which begin with a stressed a- or ha-, when these are used in the singular: el agua, un hacha. Note however that the plural forms are regular: las aguas, unas hachas. Nouns which behave in this way are marked in the dictionary.

The prepositions a and de and the article el contract to give the forms al and del.

There is also a neuter article lo which may be used with an adjective to signify a general quality:

    me gusta lo bello *(I like all that is beautiful)*
    lo extraño es que... *(what is strange is that ...,*
        the strange thing is that ...)

The noun

Gender indication in the dictionary

Unlike their English counterparts, Spanish nouns have grammatical gender. In this dictionary the gender of every Spanish headword is given, but in the translations on the English-Spanish side, unmarked nouns ending in -o are to be taken to be masculine and those ending in -a are to be taken to be feminine; gender is marked in those cases where this does not apply.

Masculine and feminine forms

In many cases gender is shown by the ending which is added to the root. Nouns denoting men or male animals commonly end in -o while their counterparts denoting women and female animals end in -a:

> chico → chica, gato → gata.

Masculine nouns ending in a consonant add -a to form the feminine:

> señor → señora.

Some nouns denoting persons have the same form for both sexes. In these cases the gender is indicated only by the article used: un pianista (*a male pianist*); una pianista (*a female pianist*).

In the case of some nouns denoting animals gender is not indicated by the article but by placing the word macho or hembra after the noun: una serpiente (*a snake*); una serpiente macho (*a male snake*); una serpiente hembra (*a female snake*).

In some cases a change in gender signifes a change in meaning. For example, la cólera means "anger" and el cólera, "cholera". Such changes of meaning will be found in the dictionary. However there are a very few words which are either masculine or feminine with no change in meaning whatever. Two examples are mar and azúcar; one may say el mar está agitado or la mar está agitada. Words of this type are marked *nm & nf* in the dictionary.

Formation of the plural

Nouns whose plural is formed by adding -s are:

- — those ending in an unstressed vowel: pluma, plumas.
- — those ending in a stressed -é: bebé, bebés.

Nouns whose plural is formed by adding -es are:

- — the names of vowels: a, aes; i, íes; o, oes; u, úes.
- — nouns ending in a consonant or stressed -í: color → colores; anís → anises.

When a compound noun is written as separate elements only the first element indicates the plural:

> ojos de buey, patas de gallo.

All irregular plurals are indicated at the appropriate entries in the dictionary.

The adjective

The adjective usually goes after the noun, and agrees with it in gender and number:

> un coche rojo; las chicas guapas.

However, indefinite, interrogative and exclamative adjectives are placed before the noun, as are adjectives expressing cardinal numbers:

> ¡qué vergüenza!; ¿cuántos leones hay?; hay treinta leones.

Formation of the masculine and feminine

Most adjectives have a double ending, one for the feminine and one for the masculine. The common are those ending in -o/-a, -or/-ora and those ending in or -és/-esa formed from place names: guapo,-a, trabajador,-ra, barcelonés,-esa.

Some, however, have a single ending: those which end in -a, -e, -i, -í, -n, -l, -r, -s, -z and -ista:

> alegre, marroquí, común, fiel, familiar, cortés, capaz.

Formation of the plural

The adjective follows the same rules as are given for the noun above.

Comparative and superlative

The comparative is formed with más ... que or menos ... que:

> Pedro es más alto que Alberto
> los perros corren menos que los tigres.

When que in a comparative expression is followed by a verb, it is replaced by de lo que:

> esto es más complicado de lo que parece.

The English comparative phrases "as ... as" and "so ... as" are rendered by tan ... como:

> mi patio es tan grande como el tuyo.

The superlative is formed with el más ... de or el menos ... de:

> el chico más listo de la clase.

The absolute superlative is formed by placing muy before the adjective or by adding the suffix -ísimo/-ísima:

> muy preocupado, preocupadísimo.

Observations

A few adjectives have special forms for the comparative and superlative:

	comparative	superlative
bueno,-a	mejor	óptimo
malo,-a	peor	pésimo,-a
grande	mayor	mayor

Comparative and superlative forms ending in -or do not change when forming the feminine singular:

> la mejor solución.

Demonstrative adjectives

		near me	near you	away from both
masculine	singular	este	ese	aquel
	plural	estos	esos	aquellos
femenine	singular	esta	esa	aquella
	plural	estas	esas	aquellas

Possessive adjectives

one possessor		yo		tú		él, ella, usted	
masculine possession	singular plural	mi mis	mío míos	tu tus	tuyo tuyos	su sus	suyo suyos
femenine possession	singular plural	mi mis	mía mías	tu tus	tuya tuyas	su sus	suya suyas

Note that the forms on the left are those which precede the noun; those on the right follow it:

> es mi pariente ⟶ es pariente mía
> son sus problemas ⟶ son problemas suyos

several possessors		nosotros,-as	vosotros,-as	ellos,-as, ustedes	
masculine possession	singular plural	nuestro nuestros	vuestro vuestros	su sus	suyo suyos
femenine possession	singular plural	nuestra nuestras	vuestra vuestras	su sus	suya suyas

The pronoun

Demonstrative pronouns

		near me	near you	away from both
masculine	singular plural	éste éstos	ése ésos	aquél aquellos
femenine	singular plural	ésta éstas	ésa ésas	aquélla aquéllas
neuter	singular	esto	eso	aquello

These are used to convey the distance between the person or thing they represent and the speaker or speakers: no viajaré en este coche, viajaré en aquél.

Possessive pronouns

one possessor		yo	tú	él, ella, usted
masculine possession	singular plural	mío míos	tuyo tuyos	suyo suyos
femenine possession	singular plural	mía mías	tuya tuyas	suya suyas

Like the adjective, the possessive pronoun agrees with the noun denoting the thing possessed: esta camisa es mía, la tuya está en el armario.

several possessors		nosotros,-as	vosotros,-as	ellos,-as, ustedes
masculine possession	singular plural	nuestro nuestros	vuestro vuestros	suyo suyos
femenine possession	singular plural	nuestra nuestras	vuestra vuestras	suya suyas

Personal pronouns

The following table shows recommended use, although in colloquial Spanish variations will be encountered.

subject	strong object	weak object	
		direct	indirect
yo	mí	me	me
tú	ti	te	te
él	él	lo	le
ella	ella	la	le
usted *m*	usted	lo	le
usted *f*	usted	la	le
nosotros,-as	nosotros,-as	nos	nos
vosotros,-as	vosotros,-as	os	os
ellos	ellos	los	les
ellas	ellas	las	les
ustedes *m pl*	ustedes	las	les
ustedes *f pl*	ustedes	las	les

Use

The Spanish subject pronoun is used only for emphasis or to prevent ambiguity as the person of the subject is already conveyed by the verb.

When neither of these reasons for its use exists, its presence in the sentence renders the style heavy and is to be avoided.

The strong object pronouns are always used as complements or objects preceded by a preposition:

> esta carta es para ti, aquélla es para mí
> ¿son de ustedes estos papeles?

Weak object pronouns precede a verb or are suffixed to an infinitive, imperative or gerund:

> lo tienes que hacer; tienes que hacerlo; haciéndolo así se gana tiempo; ¡hazlo ya!

When several weak pronouns accompany the verb, whether preceding or following it, the second and first person pronouns come before the third: póntelo; se lo ha dicho. The pronoun se always precedes the others: pónselo.

Note that while it is considered acceptable to use le as a weak object pronoun instead of lo when a man is being referred to, this is incorrect when referring to women or to objects of either gender, the same is true of les instead of los:

	direct object	indirect object
(el jarrón)	lo tiró a la basura	le quitó el asa
(Domingo)	acabo de conocerlo/le	le di mil pesetas
(María)	la vimos ayer	le dio un abrazo
(la botella)	la he descorchado	le he sacado el tapón
(los niños)	hay que escucharlos/les	les compraron muchos juguetes
(Pepe y Jaime)	los/les invitó a cenar	les concedieron un premio
(las plantas)	estaba regándolas	tendría que quitarles las hojas secas
(Ana y Bea)	las llamé por teléfono	les pediré disculpas

Se may also be an impersonal subject equivalent to the English "one", "you", "they", "people" or the passive voice:

> hay tantos accidentes porque se conduce demasiado rápido.

When le and les precede another third person pronoun they are replaced by se as in se lo mandaron. It is incorrect to say le lo mandaron.

Usted and ustedes are the second person pronouns used for courtesy. The accompanying verb is in the third person.

Vos is used in several Latin American countries instead of tú.

The preposition

General

The most usual Spanish prepositions are: a, ante, bajo, cabe, con, contra, de, desde, en, entre, hacia, hasta, para, por, según, sin, so, sobre, tras. Consult the dictionary for their use.

Uses of *por* and *para*

The basic difference between these prepositions is that por looks back to the roots, origins or causes of a thing, while para looks forwards to the result, aim, goal or destination.

por is used to express:

— cause, reason, motive (usually to say why something has happened): lo hizo por amor.
— the period in which the action takes place: vendrán por la mañana.
— the place where the action takes place: pasean por la calle.
— the means: lo enviaron por avión.
— the agent of the passive voice: el incendio fue provocado por el portero.
— substitution, equivalence: aquí puedes comer por mil pesetas.
— distribution, proportion: cinco por ciento; trescientas pesetas por persona.
— multiplication and measurements: cinco por dos son diez.
— "in search of" with verbs of movement (ir, venir ...): voy por pan.
— estar + por + infinitive expresses:
  – an action still to be performed: la cena está por hacer.
  – an action on the point of being performed: estaba por llamarte.
— tener/dar + por expresses opinion: lo dieron por perdido.

para is used to express:

— purpose: esto sirve para limpiar los cristales
— finality, destiny (often in the future): es para tu padre, compra pescado para la cena.
— direction of movement, i.e. "towards": salen para Valencia.
— deadlines: lo quiero para mañana.
— comparison: es muy alta para la edad que tiene.
— estar + para + infinitive expresses imminence: está para llegar.

The adverb

Position of the adverb

As a rule, when the word to be qualified is an adjective or an adverb, the adverb is placed immediately before it: un plato bien cocinado.

When the word to be qualified is a verb, the adverb may be placed before or after it:

> hoy iré al mercado; iré al mercado hoy.

Negative adverbs are always placed before the verb:

> no lo he visto; nunca volverás a verme.

Very rarely, adverbs may be placed between the auxiliary verb and the principal verb:

> ha llegado felizmente a su destino.

The verb

Moods

Spanish verbs have three moods, the *indicative*, *subjunctive* and *imperative*.

The indicative is generally used to indicate real actions. It is mainly used in independent statements:

> los coches circulan por la calzada.

The subjunctive is mainly used in subordinate statements where the actions are considered to be potential or doubtful, but not real: es posible que venga; or else necessary or desired:

> ¡ojalá venga!

The imperative is used to express orders:

> ¡Ven!; ¡Venid pronto!.

In negative imperatives the subjunctive is used:
> ¡No vengas!

Person

The endings of verbs vary according to whether the subject is the first, second or third person, singular or plural (see *Personal pronouns*). While in English it is not possible to omit the subject, this is quite common in Spanish since the ending of the verb indicates the subject.

Formation of tenses

For the formation of all tenses of both regular and irregular verbs see the Spanish verb conjugation tables at the end of this section.

Pronominal or reflexive verbs

Pronominal or reflexive verbs are those which are conjugated with a personal pronoun functioning as a complement, coinciding in person with the subject: for example the verb cambiar has a pronominal form which is cambiarse:

> cambia moneda; se cambia de ropa.

The personal pronouns (me, te, se, nos, os, se) are placed before the verb in all tenses and persons of the indicative and subjunctive moods, but are suffixed onto the infinitive, gerund and imperative.

In compound tenses the pronoun is placed immediately before the auxiliary verb.

The passive voice

The passive voice in Spanish is formed with the auxiliary verb ser and the past participle of the conjugating verb:

> el cazador hirió al jabalí → el jabalí fue herido por el cazador.

The use of this form of passive statement is less frequent than in English. However, another construction the reflexive (or impersonal) passive is quite common:

> se vende leña; se alquilan apartamentos; se habla inglés.

Uses of *ser* and estar

The English verb "to be" may be rendered in Spanish by two verbs: ser and estar.

When followed by a noun:

— ser is used without a preposition to indicate occupation or profession:

Jaime es el director de ventas (*Jaime is the sales manager*)
Eduardo es médico (*Eduardo is a doctor*).

— ser with the preposition de indicates origin or possession:

soy de Salamanca (*I am from Salamanca*).
es de Alberto (*it is Alberto's*)

— ser with para indicates destination:

el disco es para Pilar (*the record is for Pilar*).

— estar cannot be followed directly by a noun, it always takes a preposition and the meaning is dictated by the preposition. It is worth noting, however, its special use with de to indicate that someone is performing a function which they do not usually perform:

Andrés está de secretario (*Andrés is acting as secretary*)

Where the verb is followed by an adjective:

— ser expresses a permanent or inherent quality:

Jorge es rubio; sus ojos son grandes.

— estar expresses a quality which is neither permanent nor inherent:

Mariano está resfriado; el cielo está nublado.

Sometimes both verbs may be used with the same adjective, but there is a change of meaning. For example, Lorenzo es bueno means that Lorenzo is a good man but Lorenzo está bueno means either that he is no longer ill or, colloquially, that he is good-looking.

Finally, estar is used to indicate position and geographical location:

tu cena está en el microondas; Tafalla está en Navarra.

Spanish verbs

Spanish verbs are conjugated in three moods: the indicative, the subjunctive and the imperative. In the indicative and subjunctive there are simple tenses and compound tenses. Compound tenses for all verbs are formed with the auxiliary verb *haber*, which accompanies the invariable participle of the verb to be conjugated.

The following table shows the conjugation of compound tenses, which is, as stated above, the same for all verbs, the only difference being the participle which follows the auxiliary. Following on from that come the simple tenses; firstly the three regular conjugations and then the models for the conjugation of the irregular verbs.

Compound tenses

AMAR / TEMER / PARTIR					
INDICATIVE			**SUBJUNCTIVE**		
Present Perfect	he	*amado / temido /partido*	**Present Perfect**	haya	*amado / temido /partido*
	has	*amado / temido /partido*		hayas	*amado / temido /partido*
	ha	*amado / temido /partido*		haya	*amado / temido /partido*
	hemos	*amado / temido /partido*		hayamos	*amado / temido /partido*
	habéis	*amado /temido /partido*		hayáis	*amado / temido /partido*
	han	*amado / temido /partido*		hayan	*amado / temido /partido*
Pluperfect	había	*amado / temido / partido*			
	habías	*amado / temido / partido*	**Pluperfect**	hubiera	
	había	*amado / temido / partido*		*o hubiese*	*amado / temido /partido*
	habíamos	*amado / temido / partido*		hubieras	
	habíais	*amado / temido /partido*s		*o hubieses*	*amado / temido /partido*
	habían	*amado / temido / partido*		hubiera	
				o hubiese	*amado / temido /partido*
Past Anterior	hube	*amado / temido / partido*		hubiéramos	
	hubiste	*amado / temido / partido*		*o hubiésemos*	*amado / temido /partido*
	hubo	*amado / temido / partido*		hubierais	
	hubimos	*amado / temido / partido*		*o hubieseis*	*amado / temido /partido*
	hubisteis	*amado / temido / partido*		hubieran	
	hubieron	*amado / temido / partido*		*o hubiesen*	*amado / temido /partido*
Future Perfect	habré	*amado / temido / partido*			
	habrás	*amado / temido / partido*	**Future Perfect**	hubiere	*amado / temido /partido*
	habrá	*amado / temido / partido*		hubieres	*amado / temido /partido*
	habremos	*amado / temido / partido*		hubiere	*amado / temido /partido*
	habréis	*amado / temido / partido*		hubiéremos	*amado / temido /partido*
	habrán	*amado / temido / partido*		hubiereis	*amado / temido /partido*
				hubieren	*amado / temido /partido*
Conditional	habría	*amado / temido /partido*			
	habrías	*amado / temido /partido*			
	habría	*amado / temido /partido*			
	habríamos	*amado / temido /partido*			
	habríais	*amado / temido /partido*			
	habría	*amado / temido /partido*l			

Simple tenses
Models for the conjugation of regular verbs

AMAR

INDICATIVE		SUBJUNCTIVE	
Present	am-**o**	**Present**	am-**e**
	am-**as** / (vos) am-**ás**		am-**es**
	am-**a**		am-**e**
	am-**amos**		am-**emos**
	am-**áis**		am-**éis**
	am-**an**		am-**en**
Imperfect	am-**aba**		
	am-**abas**	**Imperfect**	am-**ara**
	am-**aba**		*o* am-**ase**
	am-**ábamos**		am-**aras**
	am-**abais**		*o* am-**ases**
	am-**aban**		am-**ara**
			o am-**ase**
Preterite	am-**é**		am-**áramos**
	am-**aste**		*o* am-**ásemos**
	am-**ó**		am-**arais**
	am-**amos**		*o* am-**aseis**
	am-**asteis**		am-**aran**
	am-**aron**		*o* am-**asen**
Future	am-**aré**		
	am-**arás**	**Future**	am-**are**
	am-**ará**		am-**ares**
	am-**aremos**		am-**are**
	am-**aréis**		am-**áremos**
	am-**arán**		am-**aréis**
			am-**aren**
Conditional	am-**aría**		
	am-**arías**		
	am-**aría**		
	am-**aríamos**		
	am-**aríais**		
	am-**arían**		

IMPERATIVE		NON-PERSONAL FORMS	
Imperative	am-**a** (tú)	**Infinitive**	am-**ar**
	am-**e** (él/Vd.)		
	am-**emos** (nos.)	**Gerund**	am-**ando**
	am-**ad** (vos.)		
	am-**en** (ellos/Vds.)	**Past participle**	am-**ado**

TEMER

INDICATIVE		SUBJUNCTIVE	
Present	tem-o	**Present**	tem-a
	tem-es / (vos) tem-és		tem-as
	tem-e		tem-a
	tem-emos		tem-amos
	tem-éis		tem-áis
	tem-en		tem-an
Imperfect	tem-ía		
	tem-ías	**Imperfect**	tem-iera
	tem-ía		*o* tem-iese
	tem-íamos		tem-ieras
	tem-íais		*o* tem-ieses
	tem-ían		tem-iera
			o tem-iese
Preterite	tem-í		tem-iéramos
	tem-iste		*o* tem-iésemos
	tem-ió		tem-ierais
	tem-imos		*o* tem-ieseis
	tem-isteis		tem-ieran
	tem-ieron		*o* tem-iesen
Future	tem-eré		
	tem-erás	**Future**	tem-iere
	tem-erá		tem-ieres
	tem-eremos		tem-iere
	tem-eréis		tem-iéremos
	tem-erán		tem-iereis
			tem-ieren
Conditional	tem-ería		
	tem-erías		
	tem-ería		
	tem-eríamos		
	tem-eríais		
	tem-erían		

IMPERATIVE		NON-PERSONAL FORMS	
Imperative	tem-e (tú)	**Infinitive**	tem-er
	tem-a (él/Vd.)		
	tem-amos (nos.)	**Gerund**	tem-iendo
	tem-ed (vos.)		
	tem-an (ellos/Vds.)	**Past participle**	tem-ido

PARTIR

INDICATIVE		SUBJUNCTIVE	
Present	part-o	**Present**	parta
	part-es / (vos) part-ís		partas
	part-e		parta
	part-imos		partamos
	part-ís		partáis
	part-en		partan
Imperfect	part-ía		
	part-ías	**Imperfect**	part-iera
	part-ía		*o* part-iese
	part-íamos		part-ieras
	part-íais		*o* part-ieses
	part-ían		part-iera
			o part-iese
Preterite	part-í		part-iéramos
	part-iste		*o* part-iésemos
	part-ió		part-ierais
	part-imos		*o* part-ieseis
	part-isteis		part-ieran
	part-ieron		*o* part-iesen
Future	part-iré		
	part-irás	**Future**	part-iere
	part-irá		part-ieres
	part-iremos		part-iere
	part-iréis		part-iéremos
	part-irán		part-iereis
			part-ieren
Conditional	part-iría		
	part-irías		
	part-iría		
	part-iríamos		
	part-iríais		
	part-irían		

IMPERATIVE		NON-PERSONAL FORMS	
Imperative	part-e (tú)	**Infinitive**	part-ir
	part-a (él/Vd.)		
	part-amos (nos.)	**Gerund**	part-iendo
	part-id (vos.)		
	part-an (ellos/Vds.)	**Past participle**	part-ido

Models for the conjugation of irregular verbs

	1 SACAR	**2** MECER	**3** ZURZIR		**1** SACAR	**2** MECER	**3** ZURZIR
	INDICATIVE				**SUBJUNCTIVE**		
Present	saco	mezo	zurzo	**Present**	saque	meza	zurza
	sacas	meces	zurces		saques	mezas	zurzas
	(vos) sacás	(vos) mecés	(vos) zurcís		saque	meza	zurza
	saca	mece	zurce		saquemos	mezamos	zurzamos
	sacamos	mecemos	zurcimos		saquéis	mezáis	zurzáis
	sacáis	mecéis	zurcís		saquen	mezan	zurzan
	sacan	mecen	zurcen				
Imperfect	sacaba	mecía	zurcía	**Imperfect**	sacara	meciera	zurciera
	sacabas	mecías	zurcías		o sacase	o meciese	o zurciese
	sacaba	mecía	zurcía		sacaras	mecieras	zurcieras
	sacábamos	mecíamos	zurcíamos		o sacases	o mecieses	o zurcieses
	sacabais	mecíais	zurcíais		sacara	meciera	zurciera
	sacaban	mecían	zurcían		o sacase	o meciese	o zurciese
					sacáramos	meciéramos	zurciéramos
Preterite	saqué	mecí	zurcí		o sacásemos	o meciésemos	o zurciésemos
	sacaste	meciste	zurciste		sacarais	mecierais	zurcierais
	sacó	meció	zurció		o sacaseis	o mecieseis	o zurcieseis
	sacamos	mecimos	zurcimos		sacaran	mecieran	zurcieran
	sacasteis	mecisteis	zurcisteis		o sacasen	o meciesen	o zurciesen
	sacaron	mecieron	zurcieron				
Future	sacaré	meceré	zurciré	**Future**	sacare	meciere	zurciere
	sacarás	mecerás	zurcirás		sacares	mecieres	zurcieres
	sacará	mecerá	zurcirá		sacare	meciere	zurciere
	sacaremos	meceremos	zurciremos		sacáremos	meciéremos	zurciéremos
	sacaréis	meceréis	zurciréis		sacareis	meciereis	zurciereis
	sacarán	mecerán	zurcirán		sacaren	mecieren	zurcieren
Conditional	sacaría	mecería	zurciría				
	sacarías	mecerías	zurcirías				
	sacaría	mecería	zurciría				
	sacaríamos	meceríamos	zurciríamos				
	sacaríais	meceríais	zurciríais				
	sacarían	mecerían	zurcirían				
	IMPERATIVE				**NON-PERSONAL FORMS**		
Imperative	saca	mece	zurce	**Infinitive**	sacar	mecer	zurcir
	(vos) sacá	(vos) mecé	(vos) zurcí	**Gerund**	sacando	meciendo	zurciendo
	saque	meza	zurza	**Past participle**	sacado	mecido	zurcido
	saquemos	mezamos	zurzamos				
	sacad	meced	zurcid				
	saquen	mezan	zurzan				

	4 REALIZAR	**5** PROTEGER		**4** REALIZAR	**5** PROTEGER
	INDICATIVE			**SUBJUNCTIVE**	
Present	realizo	protejo	**Present**	realice	proteja
	realizas	proteges		realices	protejas
	(vos) realizáis			realice	proteja
	realiza	protege		realicemos	protejamos
	realizamos	protegemos		realicéis	protejáis
	realizáis	protegéis		realicen	protejan
	realizan	protegen			
Imperfect	realizaba	protegía	**Imperfect**	realizara	protegiera
	realizabas	protegías		o realizase	o protegiese
	realizaba	protegía		realizaras	protegieras
	realizábamos	protegíamos		o realizases	o protegieses
	realizabais	protegíais		realizara	protegiera
	realizaban	protegían		o realizase	o protegiese
				realizáramos	protegiéramos
Preterite	realicé	protegí		o realizásemos	o protegiésemos
	realizaste	protegiste		realizarais	protegierais
	realizó	protegió		o realizaseis	o protegieseis
	realizamos	protegimos		realizaran	protegieran
	realizasteis	protegisteis		o realizasen	o protegiesen
	realizaron	protegieron			
Future	realizaré	protegeré	**Future**	realizare	protegiere
	realizarás	protegerás		realizares	protegieres
	realizará	protegerá		realizare	protegiere
	realizaremos	protegeremos		realizáremos	protegiéremos
	realizaréis	protegeréis		realizareis	protegiereis
	realizarán	protegerán		realizaren	protegieren
Conditional	realizaría	protegería			
	realizarías	protegerías			
	realizaría	protegería			
	realizaríamos	protegeríamos			
	realizaríais	protegeríais			
	realizarían	protegerían			
	IMPERATIVE			**NON-PERSONAL FORMS**	
Imperative	realiza	protege	**Infinitive**	realizar	protegerr
	(vos) realizá	(vos) protegé	**Gerund**	realizando	protegiendo
	realice	proteja	**Past participle**	realizado	protegido
	realicemos	protejamos			
	realizad	proteged			
	realicen	protejan			

6 DIRIGIR — 7 LLEGAR — 8 DISTINGUIR

INDICATIVE

	6 DIRIGIR	7 LLEGAR	8 DISTINGUIR
Present	dirijo	llego	distingo
	diriges	llegas	distingues
		(vos) llegás	(vos) distinguís
	dirige	llega	distingue
	dirigimos	llegamos	distinguimos
	dirigís	llegáis	distinguís
	dirigen	llegan	distinguen
Imperfect	dirigía	llegaba	distinguía
	dirigías	llegabas	distinguías
	dirigía	llegaba	distinguía
	dirigíamos	llegábamos	distinguíamos
	dirigíais	llegabais	distinguíais
	dirigían	llegaban	distinguían
Preterite	dirigí	llegué	distinguí
	dirigiste	llegaste	distinguiste
	dirigió	llegó	distinguió
	dirigimos	llegamos	distinguimos
	dirigisteis	llegasteis	distinguisteis
	dirigieron	llegaron	distinguieron
Future	dirigiré	llegaré	distinguiré
	dirigirás	llegarás	distinguirás
	dirigiré	llegará	distinguirá
	dirigiremos	llegaremos	distinguiremos
	dirigiréis	llegaréis	distinguiréis
	dirigirán	llegarán	distinguirán
Conditional	dirigiría	llegaría	distinguiría
	dirigirías	llegarías	distinguirías
	dirigiría	llegaría	distinguiría
	dirigiríamos	llegaríamos	distinguiríamos
	dirigiríais	llegaríais	distinguiríais
	dirigirían	llegarían	distinguirían

SUBJUNCTIVE

	6 DIRIGIR	7 LLEGAR	8 DISTINGUIR
Present	dirija	llegue	distinga
	dirijas	llegues	distingas
	dirija	llegue	distinga
	dirijamos	lleguemos	distingamos
	dirijáis	lleguéis	distingáis
	dirijan	lleguen	distingan
Imperfect	dirigiera	llegara	distinguiera
	o dirigiese	o llegase	o distinguiese
	dirigieras	llegaras	distinguieras
	o dirigieses	o llegases	o distinguieses
	dirigiera	llegara	distinguiera
	o dirigiese	o llegase	o distinguiese
	dirigiéramos	llegáramos	distinguiéramos
	o dirigiésemos	o llegásemos	o distinguiésemos
	dirigierais	llegarais	distinguierais
	o dirigieseis	o llegaseis	o distinguieseis
	dirigieran	llegaran	distinguieran
	o dirigiesen	o llegasen	o distinguiesen
Future	dirigiere	llegare	distinguiere
	dirigieres	llegares	distinguieres
	dirigiere	llegare	distinguiere
	dirigiéremos	llegáremos	distinguiéremos
	dirigiereis	llegareis	distinguiereis
	dirigieren	llegaren	distinguieren

IMPERATIVE

	6 DIRIGIR	7 LLEGAR	8 DISTINGUIR
Imperative	dirige	llega	distingue
	(vos) dirigí	(vos) llegá	(vos) distinguí
	dirija	**llegue**	**distinga**
	dirijamos	**lleguemos**	**distingamos**
	dirigid	llegad	distinguid
	dirijan	**lleguen**	**distingan**

NON-PERSONAL FORMS

	6 DIRIGIR	7 LLEGAR	8 DISTINGUIR
Infinitive	dirigir	llegar	distinguir
Gerund	dirigiendo	llegando	distinguiendo
Past participle	dirigido	llegado	distinguido

9 DELINQUIR — 10 ADECUAR

INDICATIVE

	9 DELINQUIR	10 ADECUAR
Present	delinco	adecuo o adecúo
	delinques	adecuas o adecúas
	(vos) delinquís	
	delinque	adecua o adecúa
	delinquimos	adecuamos
	delinquís	adecuáis
	delinquen	adecuan o adecúan
Imperfect	delinquía	adecuaba
	delinquías	adecuabas
	delinquía	adecuaba
	delinquíamos	adecuábamos
	delinquíais	adecuabais
	delinquían	adecuaban
Preterite	delinquí	adecué
	delinquiste	adecuaste
	delinquió	adecuó
	delinquimos	adecuamos
	delinquisteis	adecuasteis
	delinquieron	adecuaron
Future	delinquiré	adecuaré
	delinquirás	adecuarás
	delinquirá	adecuará
	delinquiremos	adecuaremos
	delinquiréis	adecuaréis
	delinquirán	adecuarán
Conditional	delinquiría	adecuaría
	delinquirías	adecuarías
	delinquiría	adecuaría
	delinquiríamos	adecuaríamos
	delinquiríais	adecuaríais
	delinquirían	adecuarían

SUBJUNCTIVE

	9 DELINQUIR	10 ADECUAR
Present	delinca	adecue o adecúe
	delincas	adecues o adecúes
	delinca	adecue o adecúe
	delincamos	adecuemos
	delincáis	adecuéis
	delincan	adecuen o adecúen
Imperfect	delinquiera	adecuara
	o delinquiese	o adecuase
	delinquieras	adecuaras
	o delinquieses	o adecuases
	delinquiera	adecuara
	o delinquiese	o adecuase
	delinquiéramos	adecuáramos
	o delinquiésemos	o adecuásemos
	delinquierais	adecuarais
	o delinquieseis	o adecuaseis
	delinquieran	adecuaran
	o delinquiesen	o adecuasen
Future	delinquiere	adecuare
	delinquieres	adecuares
	delinquiere	adecuare
	delinquiéremos	adecuáremos
	delinquiereis	adecuareis
	delinquieren	adecuaren

IMPERATIVE

	9 DELINQUIR	10 ADECUAR
Imperative	delinque	adecua o adecúa
	(vos) delinquí	
	delinca	adecue o adecúe
	delincamos	adecuemos
	delinquid	adecuad
	delincan	adecuen o adecúen

NON-PERSONAL FORMS

	9 DELINQUIR	10 ADECUAR
Infinitive	delinquir	adecuar
Gerund	delinquiendo	adecuando
Past participle	delinquido	adecuado

	11 ACTUAR	12 CAMBIAR	13 DESVIAR		11 ACTUAR	12 CAMBIAR	13 DESVIAR
INDICATIVE				**SUBJUNCTIVE**			
Present	actúo	cambio	desvío	Present	actúe	cambie	desvíe
	actúas	cambias	desvías		actúes	cambies	desvíes
	(vos) actuás	(vos) cambiás	(vos) desviás		actúe	cambie	desvíe
	actúa	cambia	desvía		actuemos	cambiemos	desviemos
	actuamos	cambiamos	desviamos		actuéis	cambiéis	desviéis
	actuáis	cambiáis	desviáis		actúen	cambien	desvíen
	actúan	cambian	desvían				
Imperfect	actuaba	cambiaba	desviaba	Imperfect	actuara	cambiara	desviara
	actuabas	cambiabas	desviabas		o actuase	o cambiase	o desviase
	actuaba	cambiaba	desviaba		actuaras	cambiaras	desviaras
	actuábamos	cambiábamos	desviábamos		o actuases	o cambiases	o desviases
	actuabais	cambiabais	desviabais		actuara	cambiara	desviara
	actuaban	cambiaban	desviaban		o actuase	o cambiase	o desviase
					actuáramos	cambiáramos	desviáramos
Preterite	actué	cambié	desvié		o actuásemos	o cambiásemos	o desviásemos
	actuaste	cambiaste	desviaste		actuarais	cambiarais	desviarais
	actuó	cambió	desvió		o actuaseis	o cambiaseis	o desviaseis
	actuamos	cambiamos	desviamos		actuaran	cambiaran	desviaran
	actuasteis	cambiasteis	desviasteis		o actuasen	o cambiasen	o desviasen
	actuaron	cambiaron	desviaron				
Future	actuaré	cambiaré	desviaré	Future	actuare	cambiare	desviare
	actuarás	cambiarás	desviarás		actuares	cambiares	desviares
	actuará	cambiará	desviará		actuare	cambiare	desviare
	actuaremos	cambiaremos	desviaremos		actuáremos	cambiáremos	desviáremos
	actuaréis	cambiaréis	desviaréis		actuareis	cambiareis	desviareis
	actuarán	cambiarán	desviarán		actuaren	cambiaren	desviaren
Conditional	actuaría	cambiaría	desviaría				
	actuarías	cambiarías	desviarías				
	actuaría	cambiaría	desviaría				
	actuaríamos	cambiaríamos	desviaríamos				
	actuaríais	cambiaríais	desviaríais				
	actuarían	cambiarían	desviarían				
IMPERATIVE				**NON-PERSONAL FORMS**			
Imperative	actúa	cambia	desvía	Infinitive	actuar	cambiar	desviar
	(vos) actuá	(vos) cambiá	(vos) desviá	Gerund	actuando	cambiando	desviando
	actúe	cambie	desvíe	Past participle	actuado	cambiado	desviado
	actuemos	cambiemos	desviemos				
	actuad	cambiad	desviad				
	actúen	cambien	desvíen				

	14 AUXILIAR	15 AISLAR		14 AUXILIAR	15 AISLAR
INDICATIVE			**SUBJUNCTIVE**		
Present	auxilío o auxilio	aíslo	Present	auxilíe o auxilie	aísle
	auxilías o auxilias	aíslas		auxilíes o auxilies	aísles
		(vos) aislás		auxilíe o auxilie	aísle
	auxilía o auxilia	aísla		auxiliemos	aislemos
	auxiliamos	aislamos		auxiliéis	aisléis
	auxiliáis	aisláis		auxilíen o auxilien	aíslen
	auxilían o auxilian	aíslan			
Imperfect	auxiliaba	aislaba	Imperfect	auxiliara	aislara
	auxiliabas	aislabas		o auxiliase	o aislase
	auxiliaba	aislaba		auxiliaras	aislaras
	auxiliábamos	aislábamos		o auxiliases	o aislases
	auxiliabais	aislabais		auxiliara	aislara
	auxiliaban	aislaban		o auxiliase	o aislase
				auxiliáramos	aisláramos
Preterite	auxilié	aislé		o auxiliásemos	o aislásemos
	auxiliaste	aislaste		auxiliarais	aislarais
	auxilió	aisló		o auxiliaseis	o aislaseis
	auxiliamos	aislamos		auxiliaran	aislaran
	auxiliasteis	aislasteis		o auxiliasen	o aislasen
	auxiliaron	aislaron			
Future	auxiliaré	aislaré	Future	auxiliare	aislare
	auxiliarás	aislarás		auxiliares	aislares
	auxiliará	aislará		auxiliare	aislare
	auxiliaremos	aislaremos		auxiliáremos	aisláremos
	auxiliaréis	aislaréis		auxiliareis	aislareis
	auxiliarán	aislarán		auxiliaren	aislaren
Conditional	auxiliaría	aislaría			
	auxiliarías	aislarías			
	auxiliaría	aislaría			
	auxiliaríamos	aislaríamos			
	auxiliaríais	aislaríais			
	auxiliarían	aislarían			
IMPERATIVE			**NON-PERSONAL FORMS**		
Imperative	auxilía o auxilia	aísla	Infinitive	auxiliar	aislar
	(vos) auxiliá	(vos) aislá	Gerund	auxiliando	aislando
	auxilíe o auxilie	aísle	Past participle	auxiliado	aislado
	auxiliemos	aislemos			
	auxiliad	aislad			
	auxilíen o auxilien	aíslen			

	16 AUNAR	17 DESCAFEINAR	18 REHUSAR		16 AUNAR	17 DESCAFEINAR	18 REHUSAR
INDICATIVE				**SUBJUNCTIVE**			
Present	aúno	descafeíno	rehúso	**Present**	aúne	descafeíne	rehúse
	aúnas	descafeínas	rehúsas		aúnes	descafeínes	rehúses
	(vos) aunás				aúne	descafeíne	rehúse
	aúna	descafeína	rehúsa		aunemos	descafeinemos	rehusemos
	aunamos	descafeinamos	rehusamos		aunéis	descafeinéis	rehuséis
	aunáis	descafeináis	rehusáis		aúnen	descafeínen	rehúsen
	aúnan	descafeínan	rehúsan				
Imperfect	aunaba	descafeinaba	rehusaba	**Imperfect**	aunara	descafeinara	rehusara
	aunabas	descafeinabas	rehusabas		o aunase	o descafeinase	o rehusase
	aunaba	descafeinaba	rehusaba		aunaras	descafeinaras	rehusaras
	aunábamos	descafeinábamos	rehusábamos		o aunases	o descafeinases	o rehusases
	aunabais	descafeinabais	rehusabais		aunara	descafeinara	rehusara
	aunaban	descafeinaban	rehusaban		o aunase	o descafeinase	o rehusase
					aunáramos	descafeináramos	rehusáramos
Preterite	auné	descafeiné	rehuse		o aunásemos	o descafeinásemos	o rehusásemos
	aunaste	descafeinaste	rehusaste		aunarais	descafeinaráis	rehusarais
	aunó	descafeinó	rehusó		o aunaseis	o descafeinaseis	o rehusaseis
	aunamos	descafeinamos	rehusamos		aunaran	descafeinaran	rehusaran
	aunasteis	descafeinasteis	rehusasteis		o aunasen	o descafeinasen	o rehusasen
	aunaron	descafeinaron	rehusaron				
Future	aunaré	descafeinaré	rehusaré	**Future**	aunare	descafeinare	rehusare
	aunarás	descafeinarás	rehusarás		aunares	descafeinares	rehusares
	aunará	descafeinará	rehusará		aunare	descafeinare	rehusare
	aunaremos	descafeinaremos	rehusaremos		aunáremos	descafeináremos	rehusáremos
	aunaréis	descafeinaréis	rehusaréis		aunareis	descafeinareis	rehusareis
	aunarán	descafeinarán	rehusarán		aunaren	descafeinaren	rehusaren
Conditional	aunaría	descafeinaría	rehusaría				
	aunarías	descafeinarías	rehusarías				
	aunaría	descafeinaría	rehusaría				
	aunaríamos	descafeinaríamos	rehusaríamos				
	aunaríais	descafeinaríais	rehusaríais				
	aunarían	descafeinarían	rehuarían				
IMPERATIVE				**NON-PERSONAL FORMS**			
Imperative	aúna	descafeína	rehúsa	**Infinitive**	aunar	descafeinar	rehusar
	(vos) auná	(vos) **descafeiná**	(vos) rehusá	**Gerund**	aunando	descafeinando	rehusando
	aúne	descafeíne	rehúse	**Past participle**	aunado	descafienado	rehusado
	aunemos	descafeinemos	rehusemos				
	aunad	descafeinad	rehusad				
	aúnen	descafeínen	rehúsen				

	19 REUNIR	20 AMOHINAR		19 REUNIR	20 AMOHINAR
INDICATIVE			**SUBJUNCTIVE**		
Present	reúno	amohíno	**Present**	reúna	amohíne
	reúnes	amohínas		reúnas	amohínes
	(vos) reunís	(vos) **amohinás**		reúna	amohíne
	reúne	amohína		reunamos	amohinemos
	reunimos	amohinamos		reunáis	amohinéis
	reunís	amohináis		reúnan	amohínen
	reúnen	amohínan			
Imperfect	reunía	amohinaba	**Imperfect**	reuniera	amohinara
	reunías	amohinabas		o reuniese	o amohinase
	reunía	amohinaba		reunieras	amohinara
	reuníamos	amohinábamos		o reunieses	o amohinase
	reuníais	amohinabais		reuniera	amohinaras
	reunían	amohinaban		o reuniese	o amohinases
				reuniéramos	amohináramos
Preterite	reuní	amohiné		o reuniésemos	o amohinásemos
	reuniste	amohinaste		reunierais	amohinarais
	reunió	amohinó		o reunieseis	o amohinaseis
	reunimos	amohinamos		reunieran	amohinaran
	reunisteis	amohinasteis		o reuniesen	o amohinasen
	reunieron	amohinaron			
Future	reuniré	amohinaré	**Future**	reuniere	amohinare
	reunirás	amohinarás		reunieres	amohinares
	reunirá	amohinará		reuniere	amohinare
	reuniremos	amohinaremos		reuniéremos	amohináremos
	reuniréis	amohinaréis		reuniereis	amohinareis
	reunirán	amohinarán		reunieren	amohinaren
Conditional	reuniría	amohinaría			
	reunirías	amohinarías			
	reuniría	amohinaría			
	reuniríamos	amohinaríamos			
	reuniríais	amohinaríais			
	reunirían	amohinarían			
IMPERATIVE			**NON-PERSONAL FORMS**		
Imperative	reúne	amohína	**Infinitive**	reunir	amohinar
	(vos) reuní	(vos) **amohiná**	**Gerund**	reuniendo	amohinando
	reúna	amohíne	**Past participle**	reunido	amohinado
	reunamos	amohinemos			
	reunid	amohinad			
	reúnan	amohínen			

21 PROHIBIR · 22 AVERIGUAR · 23 AHINCAR

INDICATIVE

	21 PROHIBIR	22 AVERIGUAR	23 AHINCAR
Present	prohíbo	averiguo	ahínco
	prohíbes	averiguas	ahíncas
	(vos) prohibís	(vos) averiguás	(vos) ahincás
	prohíbe	averigua	ahínca
	prohibimos	averiguamos	ahincamos
	prohibís	averiguais	ahincáis
	prohíben	averiguan	ahíncan
Imperfect	prohibía	averiguaba	ahincaba
	prohibías	averiguabas	ahincabas
	prohibía	averiguaba	ahincaba
	prohibíamos	averiguábamos	ahincábamos
	prohibíais	averiguabais	ahincabais
	prohibían	averiguaban	ahincaban
Preterite	prohibí	averigüé	ahinqué
	prohibiste	averiguaste	ahincaste
	prohibió	averiguó	ahincó
	prohibimos	averiguamos	ahincamos
	prohibisteis	averiguasteis	ahincasteis
	prohibieron	averiguaron	ahincaron
Future	prohibiré	averiguaré	ahincaré
	prohibirás	averiguarás	ahincarás
	prohibirá	averiguará	ahincará
	prohibiremos	averiguaremos	ahincaremos
	prohibiréis	averiguaréis	ahincaréis
	prohibirán	averiguarán	ahincarán
Conditional	prohibiría	averiguaría	ahincaría
	prohibirías	averiguarías	ahincarías
	prohibiría	averiguaría	ahincaría
	prohibiríamos	averiguaríamos	ahincaríamos
	prohibiríais	averiguaríais	ahincaríais
	prohibirían	averiguarían	ahincarían

SUBJUNCTIVE

	21 PROHIBIR	22 AVERIGUAR	23 AHINCAR
Present	prohíba	averigüe	ahínque
	prohíbas	averigües	ahínques
	prohíba	averigüe	ahínque
	prohibamos	averigüemos	ahinquemos
	prohibáis	averigüéis	ahinquéis
	prohíban	averigüen	ahínquen
Imperfect	prohibiera	averiguara	ahincara
	o prohibiese	o averiguase	o ahincase
	prohibieras	averiguaras	ahincaras
	o prohibieses	o averiguases	o ahincases
	prohibiera	averiguara	ahincara
	o prohibiese	o averiguase	o ahincase
	prohibiéramos	averiguáramos	ahincáramos
	o prohibiésemos	o averiguásemos	o ahincásemos
	prohibierais	averiguarais	ahincarais
	o prohibieseis	o averiguaseis	o ahincaseis
	prohibieran	averiguaran	ahincaran
	o prohibiesen	o averiguasen	o ahincasen
Future	prohibiere	averiguare	ahincare
	prohibieres	averiguares	ahincares
	prohibiere	averiguare	ahincare
	prohibiéremos	averiguáremos	ahincáremos
	prhibierais	averiguaseis	ahincareis
	prohibieren	averiguasen	ahincaren

IMPERATIVE

	21 PROHIBIR	22 AVERIGUAR	23 AHINCAR
Imperative	prohíbe	averigua	ahínca
	(vos) prohibí	(vos) averiguá	(vos) ahincá
	prohíba	averigüe	ahínque
	prohibamos	averigüemos	ahinquemos
	prohibid	averiguad	ahincad
	prohíban	averigüen	ahínquen

NON-PERSONAL FORMS

	21 PROHIBIR	22 AVERIGUAR	23 AHINCAR
Infinitive	prohibir	averiguar	ahincar
Gerund	prohibiendo	averiguando	ahincando
Past participle	prohibido	averiguado	ahincado

24 ENRAIZAR · 25 CABRAHIGAR

INDICATIVE

	24 ENRAIZAR	25 CABRAHIGAR
Present	enraízo	cabrahígo
	enraízas	cabrahígas
	(vos) enraizás	(vos) cabrahigás
	enraíza	cabrahíga
	enraizamos	cabrahigamos
	enraizáis	cabrahigáis
	enraízan	cabrahígan
Imperfect	enraizaba	cabrahigaba
	enraizabas	cabrahigabas
	enraizaba	cabrahigaba
	enraizábamos	cabrahigábamos
	enraizabais	cabrahigabais
	enraizaban	cabrahigaban
Preterite	enraicé	cabrahigué
	enraizaste	cabrahigaste
	enraizó	cabrahigó
	enraizamos	cabrahigamos
	enraizasteis	cabrahigasteis
	enraizaron	cabrahigaron
Future	enraizaré	cabrahigaré
	enraizarás	cabrahigarás
	enraizará	cabrahigará
	enraizaremos	cabrahigaremos
	enraizaréis	cabrahigaréis
	enraizarán	cabrahigarán
Conditional	enraizaría	cabrahigaría
	enraizarías	cabrahigarías
	enraizaría	cabrahigaría
	enraizaríamos	cabrahigaríamos
	enraizaríais	cabrahigaríais
	enraizarían	cabrahigarían

SUBJUNCTIVE

	24 ENRAIZAR	25 CABRAHIGAR
Present	enraíce	cabrahígue
	enraíces	cabrahígues
	enraíce	cabrahígue
	enraicemos	cabrahiguemos
	enraizad	cabrahiguéis
	enraícen	cabrahíguen
Imperfect	enraizara	cabrahigara
	o enraizase	o cabrahigase
	enraizaras	cabrahigaras
	o enraizases	o cabrahigases
	enraizara	cabrahigara
	o enraizase	o cabrahigase
	enraizáramos	cabrahigáramos
	o enraizásemos	o cabrahigásemos
	enraizarais	cabrahigarais
	o enraizaseis	o cabrahigaseis
	enraizaran	cabrahigaran
	o enraizasen	o cabrahigasen
Future	enraizare	cabrahigare
	enraizases	cabrahigares
	enraizare	cabrahigare
	enraizáremos	cabrahigáremos
	enraizareis	cabrahigareis
	enraizaren	cabrahigaren

IMPERATIVE

	24 ENRAIZAR	25 CABRAHIGAR
Imperative	enraíza	cabrahíga
	(vos) enraizá	(vos) cabrahigá
	enraíce	cabrahígue
	enraicemos	cabrahiguemos
	enraizad	cabrahigad
	enraícen	cabrahíguen

NON-PERSONAL FORMS

	24 ENRAIZAR	25 CABRAHIGAR
Infinitive	enraizar	cabrahigar
Gerund	enraizando	cabrahigando
Past participle	enraizado	cabrahigar

First table

	26 HOMOGENEIZAR	27 ACERTAR	28 ENTENDER		26 HOMOGENEIZAR	27 ACERTAR	28 ENTENDER
INDICATIVE				**SUBJUNCTIVE**			
Present	homogeneízo	acierto	entiendo	**Present**	homogeneíce	acierte	entienda
	homogeneízas	aciertas	entiendes		homogeneíces	aciertes	entiendas
	(vos) homogeneizás	(vos) acertás	(vos) entendés		homogeneíce	acierte	entienda
	homogeneíza	acierta	entiende		homogeneicemos	acertemos	entendamos
	homogeneizamos	acertamos	entendemos		homogeneicéis	acertéis	entendáis
	homogeneizáis	acertáis	entendéis		homogeneícen	acierten	entiendan
	homogeneízan	aciertan	entienden				
Imperfect	homogeneizaba	acertaba	entendía	**Imperfect**	homogeneizara	acertara	entendiera
	homogeneizabas	acertabas	entendías		o homogeneizase	o acertase	o entendiese
	homogeneizaba	acertaba	entendía		homogeneizaras	acertaras	entendieras
	homogeneizábamos	acertábamos	entendíamos		o homogeneizases	o acertases	o entendieses
	homogeneizabais	acertabais	entendíais		homogeneizara	acertara	entendiera
	homogeneizaban	acertaban	entenían		o homogeneizase	o acertase	o entendiese
					homogeneizáramos	acertáramos	entendiéramos
Preterite	homogeneicé	acerté	entendí		o homogeneizásemos	o acertásemos	o entendiésemos
	homogeneizaste	acertaste	entendiste		homogeneizarais	acertarais	entendierais
	homogeneizó	acertó	entendió		o homogeneizaseis	o acertaseis	o entendieseis
	homogeneizamos	acertamos	entendimos		homogeneizaran	acertaran	entendieran
	homogeneizasteis	acertasteis	entendisteis		o homogeneizasen	o acertasen	o entendiesen
	homogeneizaron	acertaron	entendieron				
Future	homogeneizaré	acertaré	entenderé	**Future**	homogeneizare	acertare	entendiere
	homogeneizarás	acertarás	entenderás		homogeneizares	acertares	entendieres
	homogeneizará	acertará	entenderá		homogeneizare	acertare	entendiere
	homogeneizaremos	acertaremos	entenderemos		homogeneizáremos	acertáremos	entendiéremos
	homogeneizareis	acertaréis	entenderéis		homogeneizareis	acertareis	entendiereis
	homogeneizarán	acertarán	entenderán		homogeneizaren	acertaren	entendieren
Conditional	homogeneizaría	acertaría	entendería				
	homogeneizarías	acertarías	entenderías				
	homogeneizaría	acertaría	entendería				
	homogeneizaríamos	acertaríamos	entenderíamos				
	homogeneizaríais	acertaríais	entenderíais				
	homogeneizarían	acertarían	entenderían				
IMPERATIVE				**NON-PERSONAL FORMS**			
Imperative	homogeneíza	acierta	entiende	**Infinitive**	homogeneizar	acertar	entender
	(vos) homogeneizá	(vos) acertá	(vos) entendé	**Gerund**	homogeneizando	acertando	entendiendo
	homogeneíce	acierte	entienda	**Past participle**	homogeneizado	acertado	entendido
	homogeneicemos	acertemos	entendamos				
	homogeneizad	acertad	entended				
	homogeneícen	acierten	entiendan				

Second table

	29 DISCERNIR	30 ADQUIRIR		29 DISCERNIR	30 ADQUIRIR
INDICATIVE			**SUBJUNCTIVE**		
Present	discierno	adquiero	**Present**	discierna	adquiera
	disciernes	adquieres		disciernas	adquieras
	(vos) discernís	(vos) adquirís		discierna	adquiera
	discierne	adquiere		discernamos	adquiramos
	discernimos	adquirimos		discernáis	adquiráis
	discernís	adquirís		disciernan	adquieran
	disciernen	adquieren			
Imperfect	discernía	adquiría	**Imperfect**	discerniera	adquiriera
	discernías	adquirías		o discerniese	o adquiriese
	discernía	adquiría		discernieras	adquirieras
	discerníamos	adquiríamos		o discernieses	o adquirieses
	discerníais	adquiríais		discerniera	adquiriera
	discernían	adquirían		o discerniese	o adquiriese
				discerniéramos	adquiriéramos
Preterite	discerní	adquirí		o discerniésemos	o adquiriésemos
	discerniste	adquiriste		discernierais	adquirierais
	discernió	adquirió		o discernieseis	o adquirieseis
	discernimos	adquirimos		discernieran	adquirieran
	discernisteis	adquiristeis		o discerniesen	o adquiriesen
	discernieron	adquirieron			
Future	discerniré	adquiriré	**Future**	discerniere	adquiriere
	discernirás	adquirirás		discernieres	adquirieres
	discernirá	adquirirá		discerniere	adquiriere
	discerniremos	adquiriremos		discerniéremos	adquiriéremos
	discerniréis	adquiriréis		discerniereis	adquiriereis
	discernirán	adquirirán		discernieren	adquirieren
Conditional	discerniría	adquiriría			
	discernirías	adquirirías			
	discerniría	adquiriría			
	discerniríamos	adquiriríamos			
	discerniríais	adquiriríais			
	discernirían	adquirirían			
IMPERATIVE			**NON-PERSONAL FORMS**		
Imperative	discierne	adquiere	**Infinitive**	discernir	adquirir
	(vos) discerní	(vos) adquirí	**Gerund**	discerniendo	adquiriendo
	discierna	adquiera	**Past participle**	discernido	adquirido
	discernamos	adquiramos			
	discernid	adquirid			
	disciernan	adquieran			

31 CONTAR · 32 MOVER · 33 DORMIR

INDICATIVE

	31 CONTAR	32 MOVER	33 DORMIR
Present	cuento	muevo	duermo
	cuentas	mueves	duermes
	(vos) contás	(vos) movés	(vos) dormís
	cuenta	mueve	duerme
	contamos	movemos	dormimos
	contáis	movéis	dormís
	cuentan	mueven	duermen
Imperfect	contaba	movía	dormía
	contabas	movías	dormías
	contaba	movía	dormía
	contábamos	movíamos	dormíamos
	contabais	movíais	dormíais
	contaban	movían	dormían
Preterite	conté	moví	dormí
	contaste	moviste	dormiste
	contó	movió	durmió
	contamos	movimos	dormimos
	contasteis	movisteis	dormisteis
	contaron	movieron	durmieron
Future	contaré	moveré	dormiré
	contarás	moverás	dormirás
	contará	moverá	dormirá
	contaremos	moveremos	dormiremos
	contaréis	moveréis	dormiréis
	contarán	moverán	dormirán
Conditional	contaría	movería	dormiría
	contarías	moverías	dormirías
	contaría	movería	dormiría
	contaríamos	moveríamos	dormiríamos
	contaríais	moveríais	dormiríais
	contarían	moverían	dormirían

SUBJUNCTIVE

	31 CONTAR	32 MOVER	33 DORMIR
Present	cuente	mueva	duerma
	cuentes	muevas	duermas
	cuente	mueva	duerma
	contemos	movamos	durmamos
	contéis	mováis	durmáis
	cuenten	muevan	duerman
Imperfect	contara	moviera	durmicra
	o contase	o moviese	o durmiese
	contaras	movieras	durmieras
	o contases	o movieses	o durmieses
	contara	moviera	durmiera
	o contase	o moviese	o durmiese
	contáramos	moviéramos	durmiéramo
	o contásemos	o moviésemos	o durmiésemos
	contarais	movierais	durmicrais
	o contaseis	o movieseis	o durmieseis
	contaran	movieran	durmieran
	o contasen	o moviesen	o durmiesen
Future	contare	moviere	durmiere
	contares	movieres	durmieres
	contare	moviere	durmiere
	contáremos	moviéremos	durmiéremos
	contareis	moviereis	durmiereis
	contaren	movieren	durmieren

IMPERATIVE

	31 CONTAR	32 MOVER	33 DORMIR
Imperative	cuenta	mueve	duerme
	(vos) contá	(vos) mové	(vos) dormí
	cuente	mueva	duerma
	contemos	movamos	durmamos
	contad	moved	dormid
	cuenten	muevan	duerman

NON-PERSONAL FORMS

	31 CONTAR	32 MOVER	33 DORMIR
Infinitive	contar	mover	dormir
Gerund	contando	moviendo	durmiendo
Past participle	contando	movido	dormido

34 SERVIR · 35 HERVIR

INDICATIVE

	34 SERVIR	35 HERVIR
Present	sirvo	hiervo
	sirves	hierves
	(vos) servís	(vos) hervís
	sirve	hierve
	servimos	hervimos
	servís	hervís
	sirven	hierven
Imperfect	servía	hervía
	servías	hervías
	servía	hervía
	servíamos	hervíamos
	servíais	herviais
	servían	hervian
Preterite	serví	herví
	serviste	herviste
	sirvió	hirvió
	servimos	hervimos
	servisteis	hervisteis
	sirvieron	hirvieron
Future	serviré	herviré
	servirás	hervirás
	servirá	hervirá
	serviremos	herviremos
	serviréis	herviréis
	servirán	hervirán
Conditional	serviría	herviría
	servirías	hervirías
	serviría	herviría
	serviríamos	herviríamos
	serviríais	herviríais
	servirían	hervirían

SUBJUNCTIVE

	34 SERVIR	35 HERVIR
Present	sirva	hierva
	sirvas	hiervas
	sirva	hierva
	sirvamos	hirvamos
	sirváis	hirváis
	sirvan	hiervan
Imperfect	sirviera	hirviera
	o sirviese	o hirviese
	sirvieras	hirvieras
	o sirvieses	o hirvieses
	sirviera	hirviera
	o sirviese	o hirviese
	sirviéramos	hirviéramos
	o sirviésemos	o hirviésemos
	sirvierais	hirvierais
	o sirvieseis	o hirvieseis
	sirvieran	hirvieran
	o sirviesen	o hirviesen
Future	sirviere	hirviere
	sirvieres	hirvieres
	sirviere	hirviere
	sirviéremos	hirviéremos
	sirviereis	hirviereis
	sirvieren	hirvieren

IMPERATIVE

	34 SERVIR	35 HERVIR
Imperative	sirve	hierve
	(vos) serví	(vos) herví
	sirva	hierva
	sirvamos	hirvamos
	servid	hervid
	sirvan	hiervan

NON-PERSONAL FORMS

	34 SERVIR	35 HERVIR
Infinitive	servir	hervir
Gerund	sirviendo	hirviendo
Past participle	servido	hervido

36 CEÑIR · 37 REÍR · 38 TAÑER

	36 CEÑIR	37 REÍR	38 TAÑER		36 CEÑIR	37 REÍR	38 TAÑER
INDICATIVE				**SUBJUNCTIVE**			
Present	ciño	río	taño	**Present**	ciña	ría	taña
	ciñes	ríes	tañes		ciñas	rías	tañas
	(vos) ceñís	(vos) reís	(vos) tañés		ciña	ría	taña
	ciñe	ríe	tañe		ciñamos	riamos	tañamos
	ceñimos	reímos	tañemos		ciñáis	riáis	tañáis
	ceñís	reís	tañéis		ciñan	rían	tañan
	ciñen	ríen	tañen				
Imperfect	ceñía	reía	tañía	**Imperfect**	ciñera	riera	tañera
	ceñías	reías	tañías		o ciñese	o riese	o tañese
	ceñía	reía	tañía		ciñeras	rieras	tañeras
	ceñíamos	reíamos	tañíamos		o ciñeses	o rieses	o tañeses
	ceñíais	reíais	tañíais		ciñera	riera	tañera
	ceñían	reían	tañían		o ciñese	o riese	o tañese
Preterite	ceñí	reí	tañí		ciñéramos	riéramos	tañéramos
	ceñiste	reíste	tañiste		o ciñésemos	o riésemos	o tañésemos
	ciñó	rió	tañó		ciñerais	rierais	tañerais
	ceñimos	reímos	tañimos		o ciñeseis	o rieseis	o tañeseis
	ceñisteis	reísteis	tañisteis		ciñeran	rieran	tañeran
	ciñeron	rieron	tañeron		o ciñesen	o riesen	o tañesen
Future	ceñiré	reiré	tañeré	**Future**	ciñere	riere	tañere
	ceñirás	reirás	tañerás		ciñeres	rieres	tañeres
	ceñirá	reirá	tañerá		ciñere	riere	tañere
	ceñiremos	reiremos	tañeremos		ciñéremos	riéremos	tañéremos
	ceñiréis	reiréis	tañeréis		ciñereis	riereis	tañereis
	ceñirán	reirán	tañerán		ciñeren	rieren	tañeren
Conditional	ceñiría	reiría	tañería				
	ceñirías	reirías	tañerías				
	ceñiría	reiría	tañería				
	ceñiríamos	reiríamos	tañeríamos				
	ceñiríais	reiríais	tañeríais				
	ceñirían	reirían	tañerían				
IMPERATIVE				**NON-PERSONAL FORMS**			
Imperative	ciñe	ríe	tañe	**Infinitive**	ceñir	reír	tañer
	(vos) ceñí	(vos) reí	(vos) tañé	**Gerund**	ciñendo	riendo	tañendo
	ciña	ría	taña	**Past participle**	ceñido	reido	tañido
	ciñamos	riamos	tañamos				
	ceñid	reíd	tañed				
	ciñan	rían	tañan				

39 EMPELLER · 40 MUÑIR

	39 EMPELLER	40 MUÑIR		39 EMPELLER	40 MUÑIR
INDICATIVE			**SUBJUNCTIVE**		
Present	empello	muño	**Present**	empelle	muña
	empelles	muñes		empelles	muñas
	(vos) empellés	(vos) muñís		empelle	muña
	empelle	muñe		empellemos	muñamos
	empellemos	muñimos		empelléis	muñáis
	empelleis	muñis		empellen	muñan
	empellen	muñen			
Imperfect	empellía	muñía	**Imperfect**	empellera	muñera
	empellías	muñías		o empellese	o muñese
	empellía	muñía		empelleras	muñeras
	empellíamos	muñíamos		o empelleses	o muñeses
	empellíais	muñíais		empellera	muñera
	empellían	muñían		o empellese	o muñese
Preterite	empellí	muñí		empelléramos	muñéramos
	empelliste	muñiste		o empellésemos	o muñésemos
	empelló	muñó		empellerais	muñcais
	empellimos	muñimos		o empelleseis	o muñeseis
	empellisteis	muñisteis		empelleran	muñeran
	empelleron	muñeron		o empellesen	o muñesen
Future	empelleré	muñiré	**Future**	empellere	muñere
	empellerás	muñirás		empelleres	muñeres
	empellerá	muñirá		empellere	muñere
	empelleremos	muñiremos		empelléremos	muñéremos
	empelleréis	muñiréis		empellereis	muñereis
	empellerán	muñirán		empelleren	muñeren
Conditional	empellería	muñiría			
	empellerías	muñirías			
	empellería	muñiría			
	empelleríamos	muñiríamos			
	empelleríais	muñiríais			
	empellerían	muñirían			
IMPERATIVE			**NON-PERSONAL FORMS**		
Imperative	empelle	muñe	**Infinitive**	empeller	muñir
	(vos) empellé	(vos) muñí	**Gerund**	empellendo	muñendo
	empelle	muña	**Past participle**	empellido	muñido
	empellemos	muñamos			
	empelled	muñid			
	empellen	muñan			

41 MULLIR · 42 NACER · 43 AGRADECER

	41 MULLIR	42 NACER	43 AGRADECER		41 MULLIR	42 NACER	43 AGRADECER
INDICATIVE				**SUBJUNCTIVE**			
Present	mullo	**nazco**	**agradezco**	**Present**	mulla	nazca	agradezca
	mulles	naces	agradeces		mullas	nazcas	agradezcas
	(vos) mullís	(vos) nacés	(vos) agradecés		mulla	nazca	agradezca
	mulle	nace	agradece		mullamos	nazcamos	agradezcamos
	mullimos	nacemos	agradecemos		mulláis	nazcáis	agradezcáis
	mullís	nacéis	agradecéis		mullan	nazcan	agradezcan
	mullen	nacen	agradecen				
Imperfect	mullía	nacía	agradecía	**Imperfect**	mullera	naciera	agradeciera
	mullías	nacías	agradecías		o mullese	o naciese	o agradeciese
	mullía	nacía	agradecía		mulleras	nacieras	agradecieras
	mullíamos	nacíamos	agradecíamos		o mulleses	o nacieses	o agradecieses
	mullíais	nacíais	agradecíais		mullera	naciera	agradeciera
	mullían	nacían	agradecían		o mullese	o naciese	o agradeciese
					mulléramos	naciéramos	agradeciéramos
Preterite	mullí	nací	agradecí		o mullésemos	o naciésemos	o agradeciésemos
	mulliste	naciste	agradeciste		mullerais	nacierais	agradecierais
	mulló	nació	agradeció		o mulleseis	o nacieseis	o agradecieseis
	mullimos	nacimos	agradecimos		mulleran	nacieran	agradecieran
	mullisteis	nacisteis	agradecisteis		o mullesen	o naciesen	o agradeciesen
	mulleron	nacieron	agradecieron				
Future	mulliré	naceré	agradeceré	**Future**	mullere	naciere	agradeciere
	mullirás	nacerás	agradecerás		mulleres	nacieres	agradecieres
	mullirá	nacerá	agradecerá		mullere	naciere	agradeciere
	mulliremos	naceremos	agradeceremos		mulléremos	naciéremos	agradeciéremos
	mulliréis	naceréis	agradeceréis		mullereis	naciereis	agradeciereis
	mullirán	nacerán	agradecerán		mulleren	nacieren	agradecieren
Conditional	mulliría	nacería	agradecería				
	mullirías	nacerías	agradecerías				
	mulliría	nacería	agradecería				
	mulliríamos	naceríamos	agradeceríamos				
	mulliríais	naceríais	agradeceríais				
	mullirían	nacerían	agradecerían				
IMPERATIVE				**NON-PERSONAL FORMS**			
Imperative	mulle	nace	agradece	**Infinitive**	mullir	nacer	agradecer
	(vos) mullí	(vos) nacé	(vos) agradecé	**Gerund**	**mullendo**	naciendo	agradeciendo
	mulla	**nazca**	**agradezca**	**Past participle**	mullido	nacido	agradecido
	mullamos	**nazcamos**	**agradezcamos**				
	mullid	naced	agradezed				
	mullan	**nazcan**	**agradezcan**				

44 CONOCER · 45 LUCIR

	44 CONOCER	45 LUCIR		44 CONOCER	45 LUCIR
INDICATIVE			**SUBJUNCTIVE**		
Present	**conozco**	**luzco**	**Present**	**conozca**	**luzca**
	conoces	luces		**conozcas**	**luzcas**
	(vos) conocés	(vos) lucís		**conozca**	**luzca**
	conoce	luce		**conozcamos**	**luzcamos**
	conocemos	lucimos		**conozcáis**	**luzcáis**
	conocéis	lucís		**conozcan**	**luzcan**
	conocen	lucen			
Imperfect	conocía	lucía	**Imperfect**	conociera	luciera
	conocías	lucías		o conociese	o luciese
	conocía	lucía		conocieras	lucieras
	conocíamos	lucíamos		o conocieses	o lucieses
	conocíais	lucíais		conociera	luciera
	conocían	lucían		o conociese	o luciese
				conociéramos	luciéramos
Preterite	conocí	lucí		o conociésemos	o luciésemos
	conociste	luciste		conocierais	lucierais
	conoció	lució		o conocieseis	o lucieseis
	conocimos	lucimos		conocieran	lucieran
	conocisteis	lucisteis		o conociesen	o luciesen
	conocieron	lucieron			
Future	conoceré	luciré	**Future**	conociere	luciere
	conocerás	lucirás		conocieres	lucieres
	conocerá	lucirá		conociere	luciere
	conoceremos	luciremos		conociéremos	luciéremos
	conoceréis	luciréis		conociereis	luciereis
	conocerán	lucirán		conocieren	lucieren
Conditional	conocería	luciría			
	conocerías	lucirías			
	conocería	luciría			
	conoceríamos	luciríamos			
	conoceríais	luciríais			
	conocerían	lucirían			
IMPERATIVE			**NON-PERSONAL FORMS**		
Imperative	conoce	luce	**Infinitive**	conocer	lucir
	(vos) conocé	(vos) lucí	**Gerund**	conociendo	luciendo
	conozca	**luzca**	**Past participle**	conocido	lucido
	conozcamos	**luzcamos**			
	conoced	lucid			
	conozcan	**luzcan**			

	46 CONDUCIR	**47** EMPEZAR	**48** REGAR		**46** CONDUCIR	**47** EMPEZAR	**48** REGAR
INDICATIVE				**SUBJUNCTIVE**			
Present	conduzco	empiezo	riego	**Present**	conduzca	empiece	riegue
	conduces	empiezas	riegas		conduzcas	empieces	riegues
	(vos) conducís	(vos) empezás	(vos) regás		conduzca	empiece	riegue
	conduce	empieza	riega		conduzcamos	empecemos	reguemos
	conducimos	empezamos	regamos		conduzcáis	empecéis	reguéis
	conducís	empezáis	regáis		conduzcan	empiecen	rieguen
	conducen	empiezan	riegan				
Imperfect	conducía	empezaba	regaba	**Imperfect**	condujera	empezara	regara
	conducías	empezabas	regabas		o condujese	o empezase	o regase
	conducía	empezaba	regaba		condujeras	empezaras	regaras
	conducíamos	empezábamos	regábamos		o condujeses	o empezases	o regases
	conducíais	empezabais	regabais		condujera	empezara	regara
	conducían	empezaban	regaban		o condujese	o empezase	o regase
					condujéramos	empezáramos	regáramos
Preterite	conduje	empecé	regué		o condujésemos	o empezásemos	o regásemos
	condujiste	empezaste	regaste		condujerais	empezarais	regarais
	condujo	empezó	regó		o condujeseis	o empezaseis	o regaseis
	condujimos	empezamos	regamos		condujeran	empezaran	regaran
	condujisteis	empezasteis	regasteis		o condujesen	o empezasen	o regasen
	condujeron	empezaron	regaron				
Future	conduciré	empezaré	regaré	**Future**	condujere	empezare	regare
	conducirás	empezarás	regarás		condujeres	empezares	regares
	conducirá	empezará	regará		condujere	empezare	regare
	conduciremos	empezaremos	regaremos		condujéremos	empezáremos	regáremos
	conduciréis	empezaréis	regaréis		condujereis	empezareis	regareis
	conducirán	empezarán	regarán		condujeren	empezaren	regaren
Conditional	conduciría	empezaría	regaría				
	conducirías	empezarías	regarías				
	conduciría	empezaría	regaría				
	conduciríamos	empezaríamos	regaríamos				
	conduciríais	empezaríais	regaríais				
	conducirían	empezarían	regarían				
IMPERATIVE				**NON-PERSONAL FORMS**			
Imperative	conduce	empieza	riega	**Infinitive**	conducir	empezar	regar
	(vos) conducí	(vos) empezá	(vos) regá	**Gerund**	conduciendo	empezando	regando
	conduzca	empiece	riegue	**Past participle**	conducido	empezado	regado
	conduzcamos	empecemos	reguemos				
	conducid	empezad	regad				
	conduzcan	empiecen	rieguen				

	49 TROCAR	**50** FORZAR		**49** TROCAR	**50** FORZAR
INDICATIVE			**SUBJUNCTIVE**		
Present	trueco	fuerzo	**Present**	trueque	fuerce
	truecas	fuerzas		trueques	fuerces
	(vos) trocás	(vos) forzás		trueque	fuerce
	trueca	fuerza		troquemos	forcemos
	trocamos	forzamos		troquéis	forcéis
	trocáis	forzáis		truequen	fuercen
	truecan	fuerzan			
Imperfect	trocaba	forzaba	**Imperfect**	trocara	forzara
	trocabas	forzabas		o trocase	o forzase
	trocaba	forzaba		trocaras	forzaras
	trocábamos	forzábamos		o trocases	o orzases
	trocabais	forzabais		trocara	forzara
	trocaban	forzaban		o trocase	o forzase
				trocáramos	forzáramos
Preterite	troqué	forcé		o trocásemos	o forzásemos
	trocaste	forzaste		trocarais	forzarais
	trocó	forzó		o trocaseis	o forzaseis
	trocamos	forzamos		trocaran	forzaran
	trocasteis	forzasteis		o trocasen	o forzasen
	trocaron	forzaron			
Future	trocaré	forzaré	**Future**	trocare	forzare
	trocarás	forzarás		trocares	forzares
	trocará	forzará		trocare	forzare
	trocaremos	forzaremos		trocáremos	forzáremos
	trocaréis	forzaréis		trocareis	forzareis
	trocarán	forzarán		trocaren	forzaren
Conditional	trocaría	forzaría			
	trocarías	forzarías			
	trocaría	forzaría			
	trocaríamos	forzaríamos			
	trocaríais	forzaríais			
	trocarían	forzarían			
IMPERATIVE			**NON-PERSONAL FORMS**		
Imperative	trueca	fuerza	**Infinitive**	trocar	forzar
	(vos) trocá	(vos) forzá	**Gerund**	trocando	forzando
	trueque	fuerce	**Past participle**	trocado	forzado
	troquemos	forcemos			
	trocad	forzad			
	truequen	fuercen			

	51 AVERGONZAR	52 COLGAR	53 JUGAR		51 AVERGONZAR	52 COLGAR	53 JUGAR
INDICATIVE				**SUBJUNCTIVE**			
Present	avergüenzo	cuelgo	juego	Present	avergüence	cuelgue	juegue
	avergüenzas	cuelgas	juegas		avergüences	cuelgues	juegues
	(vos) avergonzás	(voz) colgás	(vos) jugás		avergüence	cuelgue	juegue
	avergüenza	cuelga	juega		avergoncemos	colguemos	juguemos
	avergonzamos	colgamos	jugamos		avergoncéis	colguéis	juguéis
	avergonzáis	colgáis	jugáis		avergüencen	cuelguen	jueguen
	avergüenzan	cuelgan	juegan				
Imperfect	avergonzaba	actuaba	jugaba	Imperfect	avergonzara	colgara	jugara
	avergonzabas	actuabas	jugabas		o avergonzase	o colgase	o jugase
	avergonzaba	actuaba	jugaba		avergonzaras	colgaras	jugaras
	avergonzábamos	actuábamos	jugábamos		o avergonzases	o colgases	o jugases
	avergonzabais	actuabais	jugabais		avergonzara	colgara	jugara
	avergonzaban	actuaban	jugaban		o avergonzase	o colgase	o jugase
					avergonzáramos	colgáramos	jugáramos
Preterite	avergoncé	colgué	jugué		o avergonzásemos	o colgásemos	o jugásemos
	avergonzaste	colgaste	jugaste		avergonzarais	colgarais	jugarais
	avergonzó	colgó	jugó		o avergonzaseis	o colgaseis	o jugaseis
	avergonzamos	colgamos	jugamos		avergonzaran	colgaran	jugaran
	avergonzasteis	colgasteis	jugasteis		o avergonzasen	o colgasen	o jugasen
	avergonzaron	colgaron	jugaron				
Future	avergonzaré	actuaré	jugaré	Future	avergonzare	colgare	jugare
	avergonzarás	actuarás	jugarás		avergonzares	colgares	jugares
	avergonzará	actuará	jugará		avergonzare	colgare	jugare
	avergonzaremos	actuaremos	jugaremos		avergonzáremos	colgáremos	jugáremos
	avergonzaréis	actuaréis	jugaréis		avergonzareis	colgareis	jugareis
	avergonzarán	actuarán	jugarán		avergonzaren	colgaren	jugaren
	avergonzaría	actuaría	jugaría				
	avergonzarías	actuarías	jugarías				
Conditional	avergonzaría	actuaría	jugaría				
	avergonzaríamos	actuaríamos	jugaríamos				
	avergonzaríais	actuaríais	jugaríais				
	avergonzarían	actuarían	jugarían				
IMPERATIVE				**NON-PERSONAL FORMS**			
Imperative	avergüenza	cuelga	juega	Infinitive	avergonzar	colgar	jugar
	(vos) avergonzá	(vos) colgá	(vos) jugá	Gerund	avergonzando	colgando	jugando
	avergüence	cuelgue	juegue	Past participle	avergonzado	colgado	jugado
	avergoncemos	colguemos	juguemos				
	avergonzad	colgad	jugad				
	avergüencen	cuelguen	jueguen				

	54 COCER	55 ELEGIR		54 COCER	55 ELEGIR
INDICATIVE			**SUBJUNCTIVE**		
Present	cuezo	elijo	Present	cueza	elija
	cueces	eliges		cuezas	elijas
	(vos) cocés	(vos) elegís		cueza	elija
	cuece	elige		cozamos	elijamos
	cocemos	elegimos		cozáis	elijáis
	cocéis	elegís		cuezan	elijan
	cuecen	eligen			
Imperfect	cocía	elegía	Imperfect	cociera	eligiera
	cocías	elegías		o cociese	o eligiese
	cocía	elegía		cocieras	eligieras
	cocíamos	elegíamos		o cocieses	o eligieses
	cocíais	elegíais		cociera	eligiera
	cocían	elegían		o cociese	o eligiese
				cociéramos	eligiéramos
Preterite	cocí	elegí		o cociésemos	o eligiésemos
	cociste	elegiste		cocierais	eligierais
	coció	eligió		o cocieseis	o eligieseis
	cocimos	elegimos		cocieran	eligieran
	cocisteis	elegisteis		o cociesen	o eligiesen
	cocieron	eligieron			
Future	coceré	elegiré	Future	cociere	eligiere
	cocerás	elegirás		cocieres	eligieres
	cocerá	elegirá		cociere	eligiere
	coceremos	elegiremos		cociéremos	eligiéremos
	coceréis	elegiréis		cociereis	eligiereis
	cocerán	elegirán		cocieren	eligieren
Conditional	cocería	elegiría			
	cocerías	elegirías			
	cocería	elegiría			
	coceríamos	elegiríamos			
	coceríais	elegiríais			
	cocerían	elegirían			
IMPERATIVE			**NON-PERSONAL FORMS**		
Imperative	cuece	elige	Infinitive	cocer	elegir
	(vos) cocé	(vos) elegí	Gerund	cociendo	eligiendo
	cueza	elija	Past participle	cocido	elegido
	cozamos	elijamos			
	coced	elegid			
	cuezan	elijan			

	56 SEGUIR	**57** ERRAR	**58** AGORAR		**56** SEGUIR	**57** ERRAR	**58** AGORAR
	INDICATIVE				**SUBJUNCTIVE**		
Present	sigo	yerro	agüero	Present	siga	yerre	agüere
	sigues	yerras	agüeras		sigas	yerres	agüeres
	(vos) seguís	(vos) errás	(vos) agorás		siga	yerre	agüere
	sigue	yerra	agüera		sigamos	erremos	agoremos
	seguimos	erramos	agoramos		sigáis	erréis	agoréis
	seguís	erráis	agoráis		sigan	yerren	agüeren
	siguen	yerran	agüeran				
Imperfect	seguía	erraba	agoraba	Imperfect	siguiera	errara	agorara
	seguías	errabas	agorabas		o siguiese	o errase	o agorase
	seguía	erraba	agoraba		siguieras	erraras	agoraras
	seguíamos	errábamos	agorábamos		o siguieses	o errases	o agorases
	seguíais	errabais	agorabais		siguiera	errara	agorara
	seguían	erraban	agoraban		o siguiese	o errase	o agorase
Preterite	seguí	erré	agoré		siguiéramos	erráramos	agoráramos
	seguiste	erraste	agoraste		o siguiésemos	o errásemos	o agorásemos
	siguió	erró	agoró		siguierais	errarais	agorarais
	seguimos	erramos	agoramos		o siguieseis	o erraseis	o agoraseis
	seguisteis	errasteis	agorasteis		siguieran	erraran	agoraran
	siguieron	erraron	agoraron		o siguiesen	o errasen	o agorasen
Future	seguiré	erraré	agoraré	Future	siguiere	errare	agorare
	seguirás	errarás	agorarás		siguieres	errares	agorares
	seguirá	errará	agorará		siguiere	errare	agorare
	seguiremos	erraremos	agoraremos		siguiéremos	erráremos	agoráremos
	seguiréis	erraréis	agoraréis		siguiereis	errareis	agorareis
	seguirán	errarán	agorarán		siguieren	erraren	agoraren
Conditional	seguiría	erraría	agoraría				
	seguirías	errarías	agorarías				
	seguiría	erraría	agoraría				
	seguiríamos	erraríamos	agoraríamos				
	seguiríais	erraríais	agoraríais				
	seguirían	errarían	agorarían				
	IMPERATIVE				**NON-PERSONAL FORMS**		
Imperative	sigue	yerra	agüera	Infinitive	seguir	errar	agorar
	(vos) seguí	(vos) errá	(vos) agorá				
	siga	yerre	agüere	Gerund	siguiendo	errando	agorando
	sigamos	erremos	agoremos				
	seguid	errad	agorad	Past participle	seguido	errado	agorado
	sigan	yerren	agüeren				

	59 DESOSAR	**60** OLER		**59** DESOSAR	**60** OLER
	INDICATIVE			**SUBJUNCTIVE**	
Present	deshueso	huelo	Present	deshuese	huela
	deshuesas	hueles		deshueses	huelas
	(vos) deshuesás	(vos) olés		deshuese	huela
	deshuesa	huele		desosemos	olamos
	desosamos	olemos		desoséis	oláis
	desosáis	oléis		deshuesen	huelan
	deshuesan	huelen			
Imperfect	desosaba	olía	Imperfect	desosara	oliera
	desosabas	olías		o desosase	u oliese
	desosaba	olía		desosaras	olieras
	desosábamos	olíamos		o desosases	u olieses
	desosabais	olíais		desosara	oliera
	desosaban	olían		o desosase	u oliese
Preterite	desosé	olí		desosáramos	oliéramos
	desosaste	oliste		o desosásemos	u oliésemos
	desosó	olió		desosarais	olierais
	desosamos	olimos		o desosaseis	u olieseis
	desosasteis	olisteis		desosaran	olieran
	desosaron	olieron		o desosasen	u oliesen
Future	desosaré	oleré	Future	desosare	oliere
	desosarás	olerás		desosares	olieres
	desosará	olerá		desosare	oliere
	desosaremos	oleremos		desosáremos	oliéremos
	desosaréis	oleréis		desosareis	oliereis
	desosarán	olerán		desosaren	olieren
Conditional	desosaría	olería			
	desosarías	olerías			
	desosaría	olería			
	desosaríamos	oleríamos			
	desosaríais	oleríais			
	desosarían	olerían			
	IMPERATIVE			**NON-PERSONAL FORMS**	
Imperative	deshuesa	huele	Infinitive	desosar	oler
	(vos) deshuesá	(vos) olé			
	deshuese	huela	Gerund	desosando	oliendo
	desosemos	olamos			
	desosad	oled	Past participle	desosado	olido
	deshuesen	huelan			

	61 LEER	**62** HUIR	**63** ARGÜIR		**61** LEER	**62** HUIR	**63** ARGÜIR
	INDICATIVE				**SUBJUNCTIVE**		
Present	leo	huyo	arguyo	**Present**	lea	huya	arguya
	lees	huyes	arguyes		leas	huyas	arguyas
	(vos) leés	(vos) huís	(vos) argüís		lea	huya	arguya
	lee	huye	arguye		leamos	huyamos	arguyamos
	leemos	huimos	argüimos		leáis	huyáis	arguyáis
	leéis	huís	argüís		lean	huyan	arguyan
	leen	huyen	arguyen				
Imperfect	leía	huía	argüía	**Imperfect**	leyera	huyera	arguyera
	leías	huías	argüías		o leyese	o huyese	o arguyese
	leía	huía	argüía		leyeras	huyeras	arguyeras
	leíamos	huíamos	argüíamos		o leyeses	o huyeses	o arguyeses
	leíais	huíais	argüíais		leyera	huyera	arguyera
	leían	huían	argüían		o leyese	o huyese	o arguyese
					leyéramos	huyéramos	arguyéramos
Preterite	leí	huí	argüí		o leyésemos	o huyésemos	o arguyésemos
	leíste	huiste	argüiste		leyerais	huyerais	arguyerais
	leyó	huyó	arguyó		o leyeseis	o huyeseis	o arguyeseis
	leímos	huimos	argüimos		leyeran	huyeran	arguyeran
	leísteis	huisteis	argüisteis		o leyesen	o huyesen	o arguyesen
	leyeron	huyeron	arguyeron				
Future	leeré	huiré	argüiré	**Future**	leyere	huyere	arguyere
	leerás	huirás	argüirás		leyeres	huyeres	arguyeres
	leerá	huirá	argüirá		leyere	huyere	arguyere
	leeremos	huiremos	argüiremos		leyéremos	huyéremos	arguyéremos
	leeréis	huiréis	argüiréis		leyereis	huyereis	arguyereis
	leerán	huirán	argüirán		leyeren	huyeren	arguyeren
Conditional	leería	huiría	argüiría				
	leerías	huirías	argüirías				
	leería	huiría	argüiría				
	leeríamos	huiríamos	argüiríamos				
	leeríais	huiríais	argüiríais				
	leerían	huirían	argüirían				
	IMPERATIVE				**NON-PERSONAL FORMS**		
Imperative	lee	huye	arguye	**Infinitive**	leer	huir	argüir
	(vos) leé	(vos) huí	(vos) argüí	**Gerund**	leyendo	huyendo	arguyendo
	lea	huya	arguya	**Past participle**	leido	huido	argüido
	leamos	huyamos	arguyamos				
	leed	huid	argüid				
	lean	huyan	arguyan				

	64 ANDAR	**65** ASIR		**64** ANDAR	**65** ASIR
	INDICATIVE			**SUBJUNCTIVE**	
Present	ando	asgo	**Present**	ande	asga
	andas	ases		andes	asgas
	(vos) andás	(vos) asís		ande	asga
	anda	ase		andemos	asgamos
	andamos	asimos		andéis	asgáis
	andáis	asís		anden	asgan
	andan	asen			
Imperfect	andaba	asía	**Imperfect**	anduviera	asiera
	andabas	asías		o anduviese	o asiese
	andaba	asía		anduvieras	asieras
	andábamos	asíamos		o anduvieses	o asieses
	andabais	asíais		anduviera	asiera
	andaban	asían		o anduviese	o asiese
				anduviéramos	asiéramos
Preterite	anduve	así		o anduviésemos	o asiésemos
	anduviste	asiste		anduvierais	asierais
	anduvo	asió		o anduvieseis	o asieseis
	anduvimos	asimos		anduvieran	asieran
	anduvisteis	asisteis		o anduviesen	o asiesen
	anduvieron	asieron			
Future	andaré	asiré	**Future**	anduviere	asiere
	andarás	asirás		anduvieres	asieres
	andará	asirá		anduviere	asiere
	andaremos	asiremos		anduviéremos	asiéremos
	andaréis	asiréis		anduviereis	asiereis
	andarán	asirán		anduvieren	asieren
Conditional	andaría	asiría			
	andarías	asirías			
	andaría	asiría			
	andaríamos	asiríamos			
	andaríais	asiríais			
	andarían	asirían			
	IMPERATIVE			**NON-PERSONAL FORMS**	
Imperative	anda	ase	**Infinitive**	andar	asir
	(vos) andá	(vos) así	**Gerund**	andando	asiendo
	ande	asga	**Past participle**	andado	asido
	andemos	asgamos			
	andad	asid			
	anden	asgan			

	66 CABER	**67** CAER	**68** DAR		**66** CABER	**67** CAER	**68** DAR
	INDICATIVE				**SUBJUNCTIVE**		
Present	quepo	caigo	doy	**Present**	quepa	caiga	dé
	cabes	caes	das		quepas	caigas	des
	(vos) cabés	(vos) caés	(vos) das		quepa	caiga	dé
	cabe	cae	da		quepamos	caigamos	demos
	cabemos	caemos	damos		quepáis	caigáis	deis
	cabéis	caéis	dais		quepan	caigan	den
	caben	caen	dan				
Imperfect	cabía	caía	daba	**Imperfect**	cupiera	cayera	diera
	cabías	caías	dabas		*o* cupiese	*o* cayese	*o* diese
	cabía	caía	daba		cupieras	cayeras	dieras
	cabíamos	caíamos	dábamos		*o* cupieses	*o* cayeses	*o* dieses
	cabíais	caíais	dabais		cupiera	cayera	diera
	cabían	caían	daban		*o* cupiese	*o* cayese	*o* diese
					cupiéramos	cayéramos	diéramos
Preterite	cupe	caí	di		*o* cupiésemos	*o* cayésemos	*o* diésemos
	cupiste	caíste	diste		cupierais	cayerais	dierais
	cupo	cayó	dio		*o* cupieseis	*o* cayeseis	*o* dieseis
	cupimos	caímos	dimos		cupieran	cayeran	dieran
	cupisteis	caísteis	disteis		*o* cupiesen	*o* cayesen	*o* diesen
	cupieron	cayeron	dieron				
Future	cabré	caeré	daré	**Future**	cupiere	cayere	diere
	cabrás	caerás	darás		cupieres	cayeres	dieres
	cabrá	caerá	dará		cupiere	cayere	diere
	cabremos	caeremos	daremos		cupiéremos	cayéremos	diéremos
	cabréis	caeréis	daréis		cupiereis	cayereis	diereis
	cabrán	caerán	darán		cupieren	cayeren	dieren
Conditional	cabría	caería	daría				
	cabrías	caerías	darías				
	cabría	caería	daría				
	cabríamos	caeríamos	daríamos				
	cabríais	caeríais	daríais				
	cabrían	caerían	darían				
	IMPERATIVE				**NON-PERSONAL FORMS**		
Imperative	cabe	cae	da	**Infinitive**	caber	caer	dar
	(vos) cabé	(vos) caé	(vos) da	**Gerund**	cabiendo	cayendo	dando
	quepa	caiga	dé	**Past participle**	cabido	caído	dado
	quepamos	caigamos	demos				
	cabed	caed	dad				
	quepan	caigan	den				

	69 DECIR	**70** ERGUIR		**69** DECIR	**70** ERGUIR
	INDICATIVE			**SUBJUNCTIVE**	
Present	digo	irgo *o* yergo	**Present**	diga	irga *o* yerga
	dices	irgues *o* yergues		digas	irgas *o* yergas
	(vos) decís	(vos) erguís		diga	irga *o* yerga
	dice	irgue *o* yergue		digamos	irgamos
	decimos	erguimos			*o* yergamos
	decís	erguís		digáis	irgáis *o* yergáis
	dicen	irguen *o* yerguen		digan	irgan *o* yergan
Imperfect	decía	erguía	**Imperfect**	dijera	irguiera
	decías	erguías		*o* dijese	*o* irguiese
	decía	erguía		dijeras	irguieras
	decíamos	erguíamos		*o* dijeses	*o* irguieses
	decíais	erguíais		dijera	irguiera
	decían	erguían		*o* dijese	*o* irguiese
Preterite	dije	erguí		dijéramos	irguiéramos
	dijiste	erguiste		*o* dijésemos	*o* irguiésemos
	dijo	irguió		dijerais	irguierais
	dijimos	erguimos		*o* dijeseis	*o* irguieseis
	dijisteis	erguisteis		dijeran	irguieran
	dijeron	irguieron		*o* dijesen	*o* irguiesen
Future	diré	erguiré	**Future**	dijere	irguiere
	dirás	erguirás		dijeres	irguieres
	dirá	erguirá		dijere	irguiere
	diremos	erguiremos		dijéremos	irguiéremos
	diréis	erguiréis		dijereis	irguiereis
	dirán	erguirán		dijeren	irguieren
Conditional	diría	erguiría			
	dirías	erguirías			
	diría	erguiría			
	diríamos	erguiríamos			
	diríais	erguiríais			
	dirían	erguirían			
	IMPERATIVE			**NON-PERSONAL FORMS**	
Imperative	di / (vos) decí	irgue *o* yergue / (vos) erguí	**Infinitive**	decir	erguir
	diga	irga *o* yerga	**Gerund**	diciendo	irguiendo
	digamos	irgamos *o* yergamos	**Past participle**	dicho	erguido
	decid	erguid			
	digan	irgan *o* yergan			

	71 ESTAR	**72** HABER	**73** HACER		**71** ESTAR	**72** HABER	**73** HACER
	INDICATIVE				**SUBJUNCTIVE**		
Present	estoy	he	hago	**Present**	esté	haya	haga
	estás	has	haces		estés	hayas	hagas
	(vos) estás	(vos) habés	(vos) hacés		esté	haya	haga
	está	ha (hay)	hace		estemos	hayamos	hagamos
	estamos	hemos	hacemos		estéis	hayáis	hagáis
	estáis	habéis	hacéis		estén	hayan	hagan
	están	han	hacen				
Imperfect	estaba	había	hacía	**Imperfect**	estuviera	hubiera	hiciera
	estabas	habías	hacías		o estuviese	o hubiese	o hiciese
	estaba	había	hacía		estuvieras	hubieras	hicieras
	estábamos	habíamos	hacíamos		o estuvieses	o hubieses	o hicieses
	estabais	habíais	hacíais		estuviera	hubiera	hiciera
	estaban	habían	hacían		o estuviese	o hubiese	o hiciese
					estuviéramos	hubiéramos	hiciéramos
Preterite	estuve	hube	hice		o estuviésemos	o hubiésemos	o hiciésemos
	estuviste	hubiste	hiciste		estuvierais	hubierais	hicierais
	estuvo	hubo	hizo		o estuvieseis	o hubieseis	o hicieseis
	estuvimos	hubimos	hicimos		estuvieran	hubieran	hicieran
	estuvisteis	hubisteis	hicisteis		o estuviesen	o hubiesen	o hiciesen
	estuvieron	hubieron	hicieron				
Future	estaré	habré	haré	**Future**	estuviere	hubiere	hiciere
	estarás	habrás	harás		estuvieres	hubieres	hicieres
	estará	habrá	hará		estuviere	hubiere	hiciere
	estaremos	habremos	haremos		estuviéremos	hubiéremos	hiciéremos
	estaréis	habréis	haréis		estuviereis	hubiereis	hiciereis
	estarán	habrán	harán		estuvieren	hubieren	hicieren
Conditional	estaría	habría	haría				
	estarías	habrías	harías				
	estaría	habría	haría				
	estaríamos	habríamos	haríamos				
	estaríais	habríais	haríais				
	estarían	habrían	harían				
	IMPERATIVE				**NON-PERSONAL FORMS**		
Imperative	está	he	haz	**Infinitive**	estar	haber	hacer
	(vos) está	(vos) habé	(vos) hacé	**Gerund**	estando	habiendo	haciendo
	esté	haya	haga	**Past participle**	estado	habido	hecho
	estemos	hayamos	hagamos				
	estad	habed	haced				
	estén	hayan	hagan				

	74 IR	**75** OÍR		**74** IR	**75** OÍR
	INDICATIVE			**SUBJUNCTIVE**	
Present	voy	oigo	**Present**	vaya	oiga
	vas	oyes		vayas	oigas
	(vos) vas	(vos) oís		vaya	oiga
	va	oye		vayamos	oigamos
	vamos	oímos		vayáis	oigáis
	vais	oís		vayan	oigan
	van	oyen			
Imperfect	iba	oía	**Imperfect**	fuera	oyera
	ibas	oías		o fuese	u oyese
	iba	oía		fueras	oyeras
	íbamos	oíamos		o fueses	u oyeses
	ibais	oíais		fuera	oyera
	iban	oían		o fuese	u oyese
				fuéramos	oyéramos
Preterite	fui	oí		o fuésemos	u oyésemos
	fuiste	oíste		fuerais	oyerais
	fue	oyó		o fueseis	u oyeseis
	fuimos	oímos		fueran	oyeran
	fuisteis	oísteis		o fuesen	u oyesen
	fueron	oyeron			
Future	iré	oiré	**Future**	fuere	oyere
	irás	oirás		fueres	oyeres
	irá	oirá		fuere	oyere
	iremos	oiremos		fuéremos	oyéremos
	iréis	oiréis		fuereis	oyereis
	irán	oirán		fueren	oyeren
Conditional	iría	oiría			
	irías	oirías			
	iría	oiría			
	iríamos	oiríamos			
	iríais	oiríais			
	irían	oirían			
	IMPERATIVE			**NON-PERSONAL FORMS**	
Imperative	ve	oye	**Infinitive**	ir	oyendo
	(vos) andá	(vos) oí	**Gerund**	yendo	oído
	vaya	oiga	**Past participle**	ido	
	vayamos	oigamos			
	id	oíd			
	vayan	oigan			

	76 PLACER	77 PODER	78 PONER		76 PLACER	77 PODER	78 PONER
	INDICATIVE				**SUBJUNCTIVE**		
Present	plazco	puedo	pongo	**Present**	plazca	pueda	ponga
	places	puedes	pones		plazcas	puedas	pongas
	(vos) placés	(vos) podés	(vos) ponés		plazca	pueda	ponga
	place	puede	pone		*o* plegue		
	placemos	podemos	ponemos		plazcamos	podamos	pongamos
	placéis	podéis	ponéis		plazcáis	podáis	pongáis
	placen	pueden	ponen		plazcan	puedan	pongan
Imperfect	placía	podía	ponía	**Imperfect**	placiera	pudiera	pusiera
	placías	podías	ponías		*o* placiese	*o* pudiese	*o* pusiese
	placía	podía	ponía		placieras	pudieras	pusieras
	placíamos	podíamos	poníamos		*o* placieses	*o* pudieses	*o* pusieses
	placíais	podíais	poníais		placiera	pudiera	pusiera
	placían	podían	ponían		*o* placiese,	*o* pudiese	*o* pusiese
Preterite	plací	pude	puse		*o* pluguiera		
	placiste	pudiste	pusiste		*o* pluguiese		
	plació *o* plugo	pudo	puso		placiéramos	pudiéramos	pusiéramos
	placimos	pudimos	pusimos		*o* placiésemos	*o* pudiésemos	*o* pusiésemos
	placisteis	pudisteis	pusisteis		placierais	pudierais	pusierais
	placieron *o* pluguieron	pudieron	pusieron		*o* placieseis	*o* pudieseis	*o* pusieseis
Future	placeré	podré	pondré		placieran	pudieran	pusieran
	placerás	podrás	pondrás		*o* placiesen	*o* pudiesen	*o* pusiesen
	placerá	podrá	pondrá				
	placeremos	podremos	pondremos	**Future**	placieres	pudiere	pusiere
	placeréis	podréis	pondréis		placiere *o* pluguiere	pudieres	pusieres
	placerán	podrán	pondrán		placiéremos	pudiere	pusiere
Conditional	placería	podría	pondría		placiereis	pudiéremos	pusiéremos
	placerías	podrías	pondrías		placieren	pudiereis	pusiereis
	placería	podría	pondría			pudieren	pusieren
	placeríamos	podríamos	pondríamos				
	placeríais	podríais	pondríais				
	placerían	podrían	pondrían				
	IMPERATIVE				**NON-PERSONAL FORMS**		
Imperative	place	puede	pon	**Infinitive**	placer	poder	poner
	(vos) placé	(vos) podé	(vos) poné	**Gerund**	placiendo	pudiendo	poniendo
	plazca *o* plegue	pueda	ponga	**Past participle**	placido	podido	**puesto**
	plazcamos	podamos	pongamos				
	placed	poded	poned				
	plazcan	puedan	pongan				

	79 PREDECIR	80 QUERER		79 PREDECIR	80 QUERER
	INDICATIVE			**SUBJUNCTIVE**	
Present	predigo	quiero	**Present**	prediga	quiera
	predices	quieres		predigas	quieras
	(vos) **predecís**	(vos) querés		prediga	quiera
	predice	quiere		predigamos	queramos
	predecimos	queremos		predigáis	queráis
	predecís	queréis		predigan	quieran
	predicen	quieren			
Imperfect	predecía	quería	**Imperfect**	predijera	quisiera
	predecías	querías		*o* predijese	*o* quisiese
	predecía	quería		predijeras	quisieras
	predecíamos	queríamos		*o* predijeses	*o* quisieses
	predecíais	queríais		predijera	quisiera
	predecían	querían		*o* predijese	*o* quisiese
Preterite	predije	quise		predijéramos	quisiéramos
	predijiste	quisiste		*o* predijésemos	*o* quisiésemos
	predijo	quiso		predijerais	quisierais
	predijimos	quisimos		*o* predijeseis	*o* quisieseis
	predijisteis	quisisteis		predijeran	quisieran
	predijeron	quisieron		*o* predijesen	*o* quisiesen
Future	predeciré	querré	**Future**	predijere	quisiere
	predecirás	querrás		predijeres	quisieres
	predecirá	querrá		predijere	quisiere
	predeciremos	querremos		predijéremos	quisiéremos
	predeciréis	querréis		predijereis	quisiereis
	predecirán	querrán		predijeren	quisieren
Conditional	predeciría	querría			
	predecirías	querrías			
	predeciría	querría			
	predeciríamos	querríamos			
	predeciríais	querríais			
	predecirían	querrían			
	IMPERATIVE			**NON-PERSONAL FORMS**	
Imperative	predice	quiere	**Infinitive**	predecir	querer
	(vos) predecí	(vos) queré	**Gerund**	prediciendo	queriendo
	prediga	quiera	**Past participle**	predecido	querido
	predigamos	queramos			
	predecid	quered			
	predigan	quieran			

81 RAER   82 ROER   83 SABER

INDICATIVE

	81 RAER	82 ROER	83 SABER
Present	rao/raigo/rayo	roo/roigo/	sé
	raes	royo	sabes
	(vos) raés	roes	(vos) sabés
	rae	roe	sabe
	raemos	roemos	sabemos
	raéis	roéis	sabéis
	raen	roen	saben
Imperfect	raía	roía	sabía
	raías	roías	sabías
	raía	roía	sabía
	raíamos	roíamos	sabíamos
	raíais	roíais	sabíais
	raían	roían	sabían
Preterite	raí	roí	supe
	raíste	roíste	supiste
	rayó	royó	supo
	raímos	roímos	supimos
	raísteis	roísteis	supisteis
	rayeron	royeron	supieron
Future	raeré	roeré	sabré
	raerás	roerás	sabrás
	raerá	roerá	sabrá
	raeremos	roeremos	sabremos
	raeréis	roeréis	sabréis
	raerán	roerán	sabrán
Conditional	raería	roería	sabría
	raerías	roerías	sabrías
	raería	roería	sabría
	raeríamos	roeríamos	sabríamos
	raeríais	roeríais	sabríais
	raerían	roerían	sabrían

IMPERATIVE

	81 RAER	82 ROER	83 SABER
Imperative	rae	roe	sabe / (vos) sabé
	raiga, raya	roa, roiga, roya	sepa
	raigamos, rayamos	roamos, roigamos, royamos	sepamos
	raed	roed	sabed
	raigan, rayan	roan, roigan, royan	sepan

SUBJUNCTIVE

	81 RAER	82 ROER	83 SABER
Present	raiga	roa, roiga,	sepa
	o raya	roya	
	raigas	roas, roigas,	sepas
	o rayas	royas	
	raiga	roa, roiga,	sepa
	o raya	roya	
	raigamos	roamos, roigamos,	sepamos
	o rayamos	royamos	
	raigáis	roáis, roigáis,	sepáis
	o rayáis	royáis	
	raigan	roan, roigan,	sepan
	o rayan	royan	
Imperfect	rayera	royera	supiera
	o rayese	o royese	o supiese
	rayeras	royeras	supieras
	o rayeses	o royeses	o supieses
	rayera	royera	supiera
	o rayese	o royese	o supiese
	rayéramos	royéramos	supiéramos
	o rayésemos	o royésemos	o supiésemos
	rayerais	royerais	supierais
	o rayeseis	o royeseis	o supieseis
	rayeran	royeran	supieran
	o rayesen	o royesen	o supiesen
Future	rayere	royere	supiere
	rayeres	royeres	supieres
	rayere	royere	supiere
	rayéremos	royéremos	supiéremos
	rayereis	royereis	supiereis
	rayeren	royeren	supieren

NON-PERSONAL FORMS

	81 RAER	82 ROER	83 SABER
Infinitive	raer	roer	saber
Gerund	rayendo	royendo	sabiendo
Past participle	raído	roído	sabido

84 SALIR   85 SATISFACER

INDICATIVE

	84 SALIR	85 SATISFACER
Present	salgo	satisfago
	sales	satisfaces
	(vos) salís	(vos) satisfacés
	sale	satisface
	salimos	satisfacemos
	salís	satisfacéis
	salen	satisfacen
Imperfect	salía	satisfacía
	salías	satisfacías
	salía	satisfacía
	salíamos	satisfacíamos
	salíais	satisfacíais
	salían	satisfacían
Preterite	salí	satisfice
	saliste	satisficiste
	salió	satisfizo
	salimos	satisficimos
	salisteis	satisficisteis
	salieron	satisficieron
Future	saldré	satisfaré
	saldrás	satisfarás
	saldrá	satisfará
	saldremos	satisfaremos
	saldréis	satisfaréis
	saldrán	satisfarán
Conditional	saldría	satisfaría
	saldrías	satisfarías
	saldría	satisfaría
	saldríamos	satisfaríamos
	saldríais	satisfaríais
	saldrían	satisfarían

SUBJUNCTIVE

	84 SALIR	85 SATISFACER
Present	salga	satisfaga
	salgas	satisfagas
	salga	satisfaga
	salgamos	satisfagamos
	salgáis	satisfagáis
	salgan	satisfagan
Imperfect	saliera	satisficiera
	o saliese	o satisficiese
	salieras	satisficieras
	o salieses	o satisficieses
	saliera	satisficiera
	o saliese	o satisficiese
	saliéramos	satisficiéramos
	o saliésemos	o satisficiésemos
	salierais	satisficierais
	o salieseis	o satisficieseis
	salieran	satisficieran
	o saliesen	o satisficiesen
Future	saliere	satisficiere
	salieres	satisficieres
	saliere	satisficiere
	saliéremos	satisficiéremos
	saliereis	satisficiereis
	salierenn	satisficieren

IMPERATIVE

	84 SALIR	85 SATISFACER
Imperative	sal	satisfaz, satisface
	(vos) salí	
	salga	satisfaga
	salgamos	satisfagamos
	salid	satisfaced
	salgan	satisfagan

NON-PERSONAL FORMS

	84 SALIR	85 SATISFACER
Infinitive	salir	satisfacer
Gerund	saliendo	satisfaciendo
Past participle	salido	satisfecho

	86 SER	87 TENER	88 TRAER		86 SER	87 TENER	88 TRAER
	INDICATIVE				**SUBJUNCTIVE**		
Present	soy	tengo	traigo	Present	sea	tenga	traiga
	eres	tienes	traes		seas	tengas	traigas
	(vos) **sos**	(vos) tenés	(vos) traés		sea	tenga	traiga
	es	tiene	trae		seamos	tengamos	traigamos
	somos	tenemos	traemos		seáis	tengáis	traigáis
	sois	tenéis	traéis		sean	tengan	traigan
	son	tienen	traen				
Imperfect	era	tenía	traía	Imperfect	fuera	tuviera	trajera
	eras	tenías	traías		o fuese	o tuviese	o trajese
	era	tenía	traía		fueras	tuvieras	trajeras
	éramos	teníamos	traíamos		o fueses	o tuvieses	o trajeses
	erais	teníais	traíais		fuera	tuviera	trajera
	eran	tenían	traían		o fuese	o tuviese	o trajese
					fuéramos	tuviéramos	trajéramos
Preterite	fui	tuve	rraje		o fuésemos	o tuviésemos	o trajésemos
	fuiste	tuviste	trajiste		fuerais	tuvierais	trajerais
	fue	tuvo	trajo		o fueseis	o tuvieseis	o trajeseis
	fuimos	tuvimos	trajimos		fueran	tuvieran	trajeran
	fuisteis	tuvisteis	trajisteis		o fuesen	o tuviesen	o trajesen
	fueron	tuvieron	trajeron				
Future	seré	tendré	traeré	Future	fuere	tuviere	trajere
	serás	tendrás	traerás		fueres	tuvieres	trajeres
	será	tendrá	traerá		fuere	tuviere	trajere
	seremos	tendremos	traeremos		fuéremos	tuviéremos	trajéremos
	seréis	tendréis	traeréis		fuereis	tuviereis	trajereis
	serán	tendrán	traerán		fueren	tuvieren	trajeren
Conditional	sería	tendría	traería				
	serías	tendrías	traerías				
	sería	tendría	traería				
	seríamos	tendríamos	traeríamos				
	seríais	tendríais	traeríais				
	serían	tendrían	traerían				
	IMPERATIVE				**NON-PERSONAL FORMS**		
Imperative	sé	ten	trae	Infinitive	ser	tener	traer
	(vos) sé	(vos) tené	(vos) traé	Gerund	siendo	teniendo	trayendo
	sea	tenga	traiga	Past participle	sido	tenido	traído
	seamos	tengamos	traigamos				
	sed	tened	traed				
	sean	tengan	traigan				

	89 VALER	90 VENIR		89 VALER	90 VENIR
	INDICATIVE			**SUBJUNCTIVE**	
Present	valgo	vengo	Present	valga	venga
	vales	vienes		valgas	vengas
	(vos) valés	(vos) venís		valga	venga
	vale	viene		valgamos	vengamos
	valemos	venimos		valgáis	vengáis
	valéis	venís		valgan	vengan
	valen	vienen			
Imperfect	valía	venía	Imperfect	valiera	viniera
	valías	venías		o valiese	o viniese
	valía	venía		valieras	vinieras
	valíamos	veníamos		o valieses	o vinieses
	valíais	veníais		valiera	viniera
	valían	venían		o valiese	o viniese
				valiéramos	viniéramos
Preterite	valí	vine		o valiésemos	o viniésemos
	valiste	viniste		valierais	vinierais
	valió	vino		o valieseis	o vinieseis
	valimos	vinimos		valieran	vinieran
	valisteis	vinisteis		o valiesen	o viniesen
	valieron	vinieron			
Future	valdré	vendré	Future	valiere	viniere
	valdrás	vendrás		valieres	vinieres
	valdrá	vendrá		valiere	viniere
	valdremos	vendremos		valiéremos	viniéremos
	valdréis	vendréis		valiereis	viniereis
	valdrán	vendrán		valieren	vinieren
Conditional	valdría	vendría			
	valdrías	vendrías			
	valdría	vendría			
	valdríamos	vendríamos			
	valdríais	vendríais			
	valdrían	vendrían			
	IMPERATIVE			**NON-PERSONAL FORMS**	
Imperative	vale	ven	Infinitive	valer	venir
	(vos) valé	(vos) vení	Gerund	valiendo	viniendo
	valga	venga	Past participle	valido	venido
	valgamos	vengamos			
	valed	venid			
	valgan	vengan			

	91 VER	**92** YACER	**93** AGRIAR		**91** VER	**92** YACER	**93** AGRIAR
INDICATIVE				**SUBJUNCTIVE**			
Present	veo	yazco, yazgo *o* yago	agrío	**Present**	vea	yazca, yazga *o* yaga	agrie
	ves	yaces	agrías		veas	yazcas, yazgas *o* yagas	agries
	(vos) ves	(vos) yacés	(vos) agriás		vea	yazca, yazga *o* yaga	agrie
	ve	yace	agría		veamos	yazcamos, yazgamos *o* yagamos	agriemos
	vemos	yacemos	agriamos		veáis	yazcáis, yazgáis *o* yagáis	agriéis
	veis	yacéis	agriáis		vean	yazcan, yazgan *o* yagan	agrien
	ven	yacen	agrían				
Imperfect	veía	yacía	agriaba	**Imperfect**	viera *o* viese	yaciera *o* yaciese	agriara *o* agriase
	veías	yacías	agriabas		vieras *o* vieses	yacieras *o* yacieses	agriaras *o* agriases
	veía	yacía	agriaba		viera *o* viese	yaciera *o* yaciese	agriara *o* agriase
	veíamos	yacíamos	agriábamos		viéramos *o* viésemos	yaciéramos *o* yaciésemos	agriáramos *o* agriásemos
	veíais	yacíais	agriabais		vierais *o* vieseis	yacierais *o* yacieseis	agriarais *o* agriaseis
	veían	yacían	agriaban		vieran *o* viesen	yacieran *o* yaciesen	agriaran *o* agriaseis
Preterite	vi	yací	agrié	**Future**	viere	yaciere	agriare
	viste	yaciste	agriaste		vieres	yacieres	agriares
	vio	yació	agrió		viere	yaciere	agriare
	vimos	yacimos	agriamos		viéremos	yaciéremos	agriáremos
	visteis	yacisteis	agriasteis		viereis	yaciereis	agriareis
	vieron	yacieron	agriaron		vieren	yacieren	agriaren
Future	veré	yaceré	agriaré				
	verás	yacerás	agriarás				
	verá	yacerá	agriará				
	veremos	yaceremos	agriaremos				
	veréis	yaceréis	agriaréis				
	verán	yacerán	agriarán				
Conditional	vería	yacería	agriaría				
	verías	yacerías	agriarías				
	vería	yacería	agriaría				
	veríamos	yaceríamos	agriaríamos				
	veríais	yaceríais	agriaríais				
	verían	yacerían	agriarían				
IMPERATIVE				**NON-PERSONAL FORMS**			
Imperative	ve / (vos) ve	yace *o* yaz / (vos) yacé	agría / (vos) agriá	**Infinitive**	ver	yacer	agriar
	vea	yazca, yazga *o* yaga	agríe	**Gerund**	viendo	yaciendo	agriando
	veamos	yazcamos, yazgamos *o* yagamos	agriemos	**Past participle**	visto	yacido	agriado
	ved	yaced	agriad				
	vean	yazcan, yazgan *o* yagan	agríen				

Spanish-English
Español-Inglés

A*a*

abacteriano, -na *adj.* abacterial.
abandono *m.* abandonment.
 abandono infantil child neglect.
abapical *adj.* abapical.
abaptista *m.* abaptiston.
abaptiston *m.* abaptiston.
abarognosia *f.* abarognosis.
abarognosis *f.* abarognosis.
abarticulación *f.* abarticulation.
abarticular *adj.* abarticular.
abartrosis *f.* abarthrosis.
abasia *f.* abasia.
 abasia astasia abasia astasia.
 abasia atáctica, abasia atáxica atactic abasia,
 ataxic abasia.
 abasia coreica choreic abasia.
 abasia espástica spastic abasia.
 abasia paralítica paralytic abasia.
 abasia paroxística trepidante paroxysmal
 trepidant abasia.
 abasia trepidans abasia trepidans.
abásico, -ca *adj.* abasic, abatic.
abático, -ca *adj.* abatic.
abatimiento *m.* depression.
abaxial *adj.* abaxial, abaxile.
abaxil *adj.* abaxial, abaxile.
abdomen *m.* abdomen.
 abdomen agudo acute abdomen.
 abdomen aquillado carinate abdomen.
 abdomen en acordeón accordion abdomen.
 abdomen en batea boat-shaped abdomen.
 abdomen en bote boat-shaped abdomen.
 abdomen carinado carinate abdomen.
 abdomen en ciruela pasa prune belly.
 abdomen colgante venter propendens.
 abdomen escafoide, abdomen escafoideo
 scaphoid abdomen.
 abdomen navicular navicular abdomen.
 abdomen obstipum abdomen obstipum.
 abdomen péndulo pendulous abdomen.
 abdomen protuberante protuberant abdomen.
 abdomen quirúrgico surgical abdomen.
 abdomen en tabla abdominal splinting,
 wooden belly.
abdominal *adj.* abdominal.
abdominalgia *f.* abdominalgia.
abdominocentesis *f.* abdominocentesis.
abdominociesis *f.* abdominocyesis.
abdominocístico, -ca *adj.* abdominocystic.
abdominoescrotal *adj.* abdominoscrotal.
abdominogenital *adj.* abdominogenital.
abdominohisterotomía *f.* abdominohysterotomy.
abdominoperineal *adj.* abdominoperineal.
abdominoplastia *f.* abdominoplasty.
abdominoscopia *f.* abdominoscopy.
abdominoscrotal *adj.* abdominoscrotal.
abdominotorácico, -ca *adj.* abdominothoracic.

abdominovaginal *adj.* abdominovaginal.
abdominovesical *adj.* abdominovesical.
abducción *f.* abduction.
abducens abducens.
abducente *adj.* abducent, abducens.
abducir *v.* abduce, abduct.
abductor *adj.* abductor.
abembrionario, -ria *adj.* abembryonic.
abepitimia *f.* abepithemia, abepithymia.
aberración *f.* aberration, aberratio.
 aberración cromática chromatic aberration.
 aberración del color chromatic aberration.
 aberración cromosómica chromosomal aberration, chromosome aberration.
 aberración de curvatura curvature aberration.
 aberración dióptrica dioptric aberration.
 aberración distancial distantial aberration.
 *aberración esférica, aberración de esferici-
 dad* spherical aberration.
 aberratio lactis aberratio lactis.
 aberración lateral lateral aberration.
 aberración longitudinal longitudinal aberration.
 aberratio mensium aberratio mensium.
 aberración mental mental aberration.
 aberración meridional meridional aberration.
 aberración monocromática monochromatic aberration.
 aberración newtoniana Newtonian aberration.
 aberratio testis aberratio testis.
 aberración ventricular ventricular aberration.
aberrante *adj.* aberrant.
aberratio aberratio.
aberrómetro *m.* aberrometer.
abertura *f.* apertura, aperture, opening, ostium.
 abertura angular angular aperture.
abetalipoproteinemia *f.* abetalipoproteinemia.
abiofisiología *f.* abiophysiology.
abiogenesia *f.* abiogenesis.
abiogénesis *f.* abiogenesis.
abiogenético, -ca *adj.* abiogenetic.
abiogenia *f.* abiogenesis.
abiógeno, -na *adj.* abiogenous.
abiología *f.* abiology.
abiológico, -ca *adj.* abiologic, abiological.
abionergia *f.* abionergy.
abiosis *f.* abiosis.
abiótico, -ca *adj.* abiotic.
abiotrofia *f.* abiotrophia, abiotrophy.
 abiotrofia retinal, abiotrofia retiniana retinal abiotrophia.
abiotrófico, -ca *adj.* abiotrophic.
abiurético, -ca *adj.* abiuretic.
ablación *f.* ablatio.
 ablación placentaria ablatio placentae.
 ablación retiniana ablatio retinae.

ablactación *f.* ablactation.
ablatio *f.* ablatio.
 ablatio placentae ablatio placentae.
 ablatio retinae ablatio retinae.
ablefaria *f.* ablephary.
abléfaro, -ra *adj.* ablepharous.
ablepsia *f.* ablepsia, ablepsy.
ablución *f.* ablution.
abluente *adj.* abluent.
abluminal *adj.* abluminal.
ablutomanía *f.* ablutomania.
abocamiento *m.* abouchement.
aboclusión *f.* abocclusion.
aboral *adj.* aboral.
abordaje *m.* approach.
abortante *adj.* abortient, abortigenic.
abortar *v.* abort.
abortifaciente *adj.* abortifacient, abortigenic.
abortista *m., f.* abortionist.
abortivo, -va *adj.* abortive.
aborto *m.* abortion, abortus.
 aborto accidental accidental abortion.
 aborto afebril afebrile abortion.
 aborto ampollar, aborto ampular ampullar
 abortion.
 aborto artificial artificial abortion.
 aborto cervical cervical abortion.
 aborto en curso abortion in progress.
 aborto diferido missed abortion.
 aborto electivo elective abortion.
 aborto espontáneo spontaneous abortion.
 aborto febril septic abortion.
 aborto habitual habitual abortion.
 aborto idiopático idiopathic abortion.
 aborto ilegal illegal abortion.
 aborto incompleto incomplete abortion.
 aborto inevitable inevitable abortion.
 aborto infectado infected abortion.
 aborto inminente imminent abortion.
 aborto justificable justifiable abortion.
 aborto provocado induced abortion.
 aborto recurrente recurrent abortion.
 aborto retenido missed abortion.
 aborto séptico septic abortion.
 aborto terapéutico therapeutic abortion.
 aborto tubárico tubal abortion.
abortus abortus.
abraquia *f.* abrachia, abrachiatism.
abraquio *m.* abrachius.
abraquiocefalia *f.* abrachiocephalia, abrachiocephaly.
abraquiocéfalo *m.* abrachiocephalus.
abrasio abrasion, grinding, abrasio.
 abrasio corneae corneal abrasion, abrasio
 corneae.
 abrasio dentium tooth abrasion, abrasion of
 the teeth, abrasio dentium.
abrasión *f.* abrasion, grinding, abrasio.
 abrasión corneal corneal abrasion, abrasio
 corneae.

abrasión dental, abrasión dentaria tooth abrasion, abrasion of the teeth, abrasio dentium.

abrasión puntual spot grinding.

abrasión selectiva selective grinding.

abrasividad *f.* abrasiveness.

abrasivo, -va *adj.* abrasive, abradant.

abrasor *m.* abrasor.

abrazadera *f.* brace.

abrazadera de desrotación derotation brace.

abrazadera de Griswald Griswald brace.

abrazadera de Taylor Taylor's back brace.

abreacción *f.* abreaction.

abreacción motriz motor abreaction.

abreaccionar *v.* abreact.

abrebocas *m.* gag.

abrismo *m.* abrism.

abrosia *f.* abrosia.

abrupción *f.* abruption, abruptio.

abrupción placentaria abruptio placentae.

abruptio abruption, abruptio.

abruptio placentae abruptio placentae.

absceso *m.* abscess.

absceso abdominal abdominal abscess.

absceso agudo acute abscess.

absceso alveolar alveolar abscess.

absceso amebiano amebic abscess.

absceso amigdalino tonsillar abscess.

absceso anorrectal anorectal abscess.

absceso anular ring abscess.

absceso apendicular appendicular abscess, appendiceal abscess.

absceso apical apical abscess.

absceso artrifluente arthrifluent abscess.

absceso ateromatoso atheromatous abscess.

absceso axilar axillary abscess.

absceso de Bartholin, absceso de Bartolino Bartholinian abscess.

absceso de Bezold Bezold's abscess.

absceso bicameral bicameral abscess.

absceso bilharziásico, absceso bilharziótico bilharziasis abscess.

absceso biliar biliary abscess.

absceso de Brodie Brodie's abscess.

absceso en botón de camisa shirt-stud abscess.

absceso en botón de cuello collar-button abscess.

absceso bursal bursal abscess.

absceso caliente hot abscess.

absceso canalicular canalicular abscess.

absceso carniforme carniform abscess.

absceso caseoso caseous abscess, cheese abscess.

absceso cerebeloso cerebellar abscess.

absceso cerebral brain abscess, cerebral abscess.

absceso circunscrito circumscribed abscess.

absceso colangítico cholangitic abscess.

absceso de conductos biliares bile duct abscess.

absceso constitucional submastoid abscess.

absceso críptico crypt abscess.

absceso crónico chronic abscess.

absceso de Delpech Delpech's abscess.

absceso dental, absceso dentoalveolar dental abscess, dentoalveolar abscess.

absceso difundido, absceso difuso diffuse abscess.

absceso de Douglas Douglas' abscess.

absceso de Dubois Dubois' abscess.

absceso embólico embolic abscess.

absceso emigrante migrating abscess.

absceso enfisematoso emphysematous abscess.

absceso enquistado encysted abscess.

absceso epidural epidural abscess.

absceso epiploico epiploic abscess.

absceso errante wandering abscess.

absceso escrofuloso scrofulous abscess.

absceso espermático spermatic abscess.

absceso espirilar spirillar abscess.

absceso esplénico splenic abscess.

absceso estercoráceo stercoraceous abscess, stercoral abscess.

absceso estéril sterile abscess.

absceso estrellado stellate abscess.

absceso estreptocócico streptococcal abscess.

absceso estrumoso strumous abscess.

absceso extradural extradural abscess.

absceso fecal fecal abscess.

absceso fénix phoenix abscess.

absceso de fijación fixation abscess.

absceso filariásico filarial abscess.

absceso de Fochier Fochier's abscess.

absceso folicular follicular abscess, follicular collar-stud abscess.

absceso frío cold abscess.

absceso frontal frontal abscess.

absceso ganglionar glandular abscess.

absceso gangrenoso gangrenous abscess.

absceso gaseoso gas abscess.

absceso gástrico gastric abscess.

absceso gingival gingival abscess, gumboil abscess.

absceso gomatoso gummatous abscess.

absceso de gravitación, absceso por gravedad gravitation abscess, gravity abscess.

absceso helmíntico helminthic abscess.

absceso hemorrágico hemorrhagic abscess.

absceso hepático hepatic abscess, abscess of the liver.

absceso hipostático hypostatic abscess.

absceso idiopático idiopathic abscess.

absceso ilíaco iliac abscess.

absceso interdigital web-space abscess.

absceso intraamigdalino intratonsillar abscess.

absceso intradural intradural abscess.

absceso intramamario intramammary abscess.

absceso intramastoideo intramastoid abscess.

absceso intramedular medullary abscess.

absceso isquiorrectal ischiorectal abscess.

absceso lácteo milk abscess.

absceso lacunar, absceso lagunar lacunar abscess.

absceso lagrimal lacrimal abscess.

absceso lateral, absceso lateral alveolar lateral abscess, lateral alveolar abscess.

absceso de leche milk abscess.

absceso del ligamento ancho broad ligament abscess.

absceso linfático lymphatic abscess.

absceso lumbar lumbar abscess.

absceso madre mother abscess.

absceso mamario mammary abscess.

absceso marginal marginal abscess.

absceso mastoideo mastoid abscess.

absceso mediastínico mediastinal abscess.

absceso metastásico metastatic abscess.

absceso micótico fungal abscess.

absceso migratorio migrating abscess.

absceso miliar miliary abscess.

absceso de Munro Munro's abscess.

absceso múltiple multiple abscess.

absceso mural mural abscess.

absceso nocardiásico nocardial abscess.

absceso orbitario orbital abscess.

absceso óseo bone abscess.

absceso osifluente ossifluent abscess.

absceso de Paget Paget's abscess.

absceso palatino palatal abscess.

absceso pancreático pancreatic abscess.

absceso parafaríngeo parapharyngeal abscess.

absceso parafrenular parafrenal abscess.

absceso parametrial, absceso paramétrico parametrial abscess, parametric abscess.

absceso paranéfrico paranephric abscess.

absceso parapancreático parapancreatic abscess.

absceso paravertebral paravertebral abscess.

absceso parietal parietal abscess.

absceso parotídeo parotid abscess.

absceso de Pautrier Pautrier's abscess.

absceso pélvico pelvic abscess.

absceso pelvirrectal pelvirectal abscess.

absceso periamigdalino peritonsillar abscess.

absceso perianal perianal abscess.

absceso periapical periapical abscess.

absceso pericemental pericemental abscess.

absceso pericoronario, absceso pericoronal pericoronal abscess.

absceso peridental, absceso periodontal, absceso periodóntico peridental abscess, periodontal abscess.

absceso perinéfrico, absceso perinefrítico perinephric abscess.

absceso peripleural, absceso peripleurítico peripleuritic abscess.

absceso perirrectal perirectal abscess.

absceso peritoneal peritoneal abscess.

absceso peritonsilar circumtonsillar abscess, peritonsillar abscess.

absceso periureteral periureteral abscess.

absceso periuretral periurethral abscess.

absceso perivesical perivesical abscess.

absceso poscecal postcecal abscess.

absceso de Pott Pott's abscess.

absceso premamario premammary abscess.

absceso profundo deep abscess, deep-seated abscess.

absceso de psoas, absceso del psoas psoas abscess.

absceso pulmonar pulmonary abscess.

absceso pulpar pulp abscess, pulpar abscess.

absceso radicular root abscess.

absceso renal renal abscess.

absceso residual residual abscess.

absceso retroamigdalino retrotonsillar abscess.

absceso retrocecal retrocecal abscess.

absceso retrofaríngeo retropharyngeal abscess.

absceso retromamario retromammary abscess.

absceso retroperitoneal retroperitoneal abscess.

absceso sacrococcígeo sacrococcygeal abscess.

absceso satélite satellite abscess.

absceso seco dry abscess.

absceso secundario secondary abscess.

absceso septal septal abscess.

absceso septicémico septicemic abscess.

absceso sifilítico syphilitic abscess.

absceso simpático sympathetic abscess.

absceso subaponeurótico subfascial abscess, subaponeurotic abscess.

absceso subareolar subareolar abscess.

absceso subdiafragmático subdiaphragmatic abscess.

absceso subdural subdural abscess.

absceso subescapular subscapular abscess.

absceso subfrénico subphrenic abscess.
absceso subgaleal subgaleal abscess.
absceso subhepático subhepatic abscess.
absceso submamario submammary abscess.
absceso subpectoral subpectoral abscess.
absceso subperióstico subperiosteal abscess.
absceso subperitoneal subperitoneal abscess.
absceso sudoríparo sudoriparous abscess.
absceso superficial superficial abscess.
absceso suprahepático suprahepatic abscess.
absceso de sutura stitch abscess.
absceso tecal thecal abscess.
absceso de Thornwaldt Thornwaldt abscess.
absceso tímico thymus abscess, thymic abscess.
absceso timpánico, absceso timpanítico tympanitic abscess.
absceso timpanocervical tympanocervical abscess.
absceso timpanomastoideo tympanomastoid abscess.
absceso traumático traumatic abscess.
absceso tropical tropical abscess.
absceso tuberculoso tuberculous abscess.
absceso tuberculoso metastático metastatic tuberculous abscess.
absceso tuboovárico tuboovarian abscess.
absceso uretral urethral abscess.
absceso urinario urinary abscess.
absceso urinoso urinous abscess.
absceso verminoso verminous abscess.
absceso vítreo vitreous abscess.
absceso de Welch Welch's abscess.
abscesografía *f.* abscessography.
abscindir *v.* abscise.
abscisión *f.* abscission.
abscisión corneal corneal abscission.
absconsio *m.* absconsio.
Absidia Absidia.
absoluto, -ta *adj.* absolute.
absorbancia *f.* absorbance.
absorbefaciente *adj.* absorbefacient.
absorbente *adj.* absorbent.
absorber *v.* absorb.
absorciometría *f.* absorptiometry.
absorciómetro *m.* absorptiometer.
absorción *f.* absorption.
absorción cutánea cutaneous absorption.
absorción disyuntiva disjunctive absorption.
absorción excrementicia absorption excrementitia.
absorción de aglutinina agglutinin absorption.
absorción de fármaco drug absorption.
absorción externa external absorption.
absorción interna internal absorption.
absorción intersticial interstitial absorption.
absorción intestinal intestinal absorption.
absorción neta absorption neta.
absorción parenteral parenteral absorption.
absorción patológica pathologic absorption, pathological absorption.
absorción percutánea percutaneous absorption.
absortividad *f.* absortivity.
absortividad molar molar absortivity.
absortividad específica specific absortivity.
absortivo, -va *adj.* absorptive.
abstención *f.* abstention.
abstergente *adj.* abstergent.
abstinencia *f.* abstinence.
abstinencia alimentaria alimentary abstinence.
abstinencia de sustancias substance abstinence.

abstracción *f.* abstraction.
abstracto *m.* abstract.
abterminal *adj.* abterminal.
abtorsión *f.* abtorsion.
abtropfung *m.* abtropfung.
abulia *f.* abulia.
abúlico, -ca *adj.* abulic.
abuso *m.* abuse.
abuso de ancianos abuse of the elderly, elder abuse.
abuso de medicamentos drug abuse.
abuso del niño child abuse.
abuso de sustancias, abuso de sustancias psicoactivas substance abuse, psychoactive substance abuse.
abuso sexual del adulto sexual abuse of an adult.
abuso sexual del niño sexual child abuse.
acalasia *f.* acalasia.
acalasia del cardias achalasia of the cardia.
acalasia esfinteriana sphincteral achalasia.
acalasia esofágica esophageal achalasia, achalasia of the esophagus.
acalasia pelvirrectal pelvirectal achalasia.
acalcerosis *f.* acalcerosis.
acalcicosis *f.* acalcicosis.
acalculia *f.* acalculia.
acampsia *f.* acampsia.
acanaladura *f.* guttering.
acantamebiasis *f.* acanthamebiasis.
acantestesia *f.* acanthesthesia.
Acanthamoeba Acanthamoeba.
acantión *m.* acanthion, akanthion.
acanto *m.* acantha.
acantocefaliasis *f.* acanthocephaliasis.
acantocéfalos *m.* thorny headed worms, acanthocephalus.
acantocefalosis *f.* acanthocephaliasis.
acanthocephalus acanthocephalus.
acantocito *m.* acanthocyte.
acantocitosis *f.* acanthocytosis.
acantoide *adj.* acanthoid.
acantólisis *f.* acantholysis.
acantólisis ampollar, acantólisis bullosa acantholysis bullosa.
acantolítico, -ca *adj.* acantholytic.
acantoma *m.* acanthoma.
acantoma adenoideo, acantoma adenoquístico acanthoma adenoides cysticum.
acantoma de células claras clear cell acanthoma, Degos' acanthoma.
acantopélix *f.* acanthopelvis.
acantopelvis *f.* acanthopelvis.
acantoqueilonemiasis *f.* acanthocheilonemiasis.
acantoqueratodermia *f.* acanthokeratoderma.
acantorrexis *f.* acanthorrhexis.
acantosis *f.* acanthosis.
acantosis nigricans acanthosis nigricans.
acantosis seborreica acanthosis seborrhoeica.
acantosis verrugosa acanthosis verrucosa.
acapnia *f.* acapnia.
acápnico, -ca *adj.* acapnial, acapnic.
acarbia *f.* acarbia.
acardia *f.* acardia.
acardíaco, -ca *adj.* acardiac.
acardiacus acardiacus.
acardio *m.* acardius.
acardiotrofia *f.* acardiotrophia.
acariano, -na *adj.* acarian.
acariasis *f.* acariasis.
acariasis demodéctica demodectic acariasis.
acariasis soróptica psoroptic acariasis.

acariasis sarcóptica sarcoptic acariasis.
acaricida *m.* acaricide, miticide.
Acaridae Acaridae.
acarídeos *m.* Acaridae.
acárides *m.* Acaridae.
acaridiasis *f.* acaridiasis.
acáridos *m.* Acaridae.
Acarina Acarina.
acarino, -na *adj.* acarine.
acarinosis *f.* acarinosis.
acariocito *m.* akaryocyte.
acarionte *m.* akaryote.
acariota *m.* akaryota.
acariosis *f.* acarinosis.
ácaro *m.* mite.
acarodermatitis *f.* acarodermatitis.
acarodermatitis urticaroide acarodermatitis urticaroides.
acaroide *adj.* acaroid.
acaroideo, -a *adj.* acaroid.
acarología *f.* acarology.
acarotóxico, -ca *adj.* acarotoxic.
Acarus Acarus.
acatafasia *f.* acataphasia.
acatalasemia *f.* acatalasemia.
acatalasia *f.* acatalasia.
acatama *f.* akatama.
acatamatesia *f.* acatamathesia, akatamathesia.
acataposis *f.* acataposis.
acatastasia *f.* acatastasia.
acatastático, -ca *adj.* acatastatic.
acatexia *f.* acathexia, acathexis.
acatisia *f.* acathisia, akathisia.
acaudado, -da *adj.* acaudate.
acaudal *adj.* acaudal.
acáudeo, -a *adj.* acaudate.
acesión *f.* accession.
acceso¹ *m.* access.
acceso² *m.* attack, crisis, seizure.
accesorio *m.* accessorius.
accesorio, -ria *adj.* accessory.
accidental *adj.* accidental.
accidentalismo *m.* accidentalism.
accidente *m.* accident.
accidente cerebrovascular (ACV) cerebrovascular accident (CVA).
accidente laboral occupational accident, professional accident.
accidente de tráfico highway accident, traffic accident.
accidente de trabajo industrial accident.
acción *f.* action.
acción acumulativa cumulative action.
acción amortiguadora buffer action, buffering action.
acción braquial brachiation action.
acción calorígena calorigenic action.
acción capilar capillary action.
acción desencadenante trigger action.
acción descontrolada del corazón (DAH) disordered action of the heart.
acción dinámica específica, acción dinamicoespecífica, acción dinamicospecífica specific dynamic action.
acción específica specific action.
acción farmacológica drug action.
acción de pinza lateral lateral pinch action.
acción refleja reflex action.
acción tampón tampon action.
acción termogénica thermogenic action.
acción trófica trophic action.
acción valvular, acción de válvula esférica ball-valve action.
accípiter *m.* accipiter.
accomplice accomplice.

accretio accretio.
acedia *f.* acedia.
acedías *f.* brash.
  acedías acuosas water brash.
  acedías del destete weaning brash.
acefalia *f.* acephalia, acephaly.
acefalismo *m.* acephalism.
acéfalo *m.* acephalus.
  acéfalo dibraquio acephalus dibrachius.
  acéfalo dípodo acephalus dipus.
  acéfalo monobraquio acephalus monobrachius.
  acéfalo monópodo acephalus monopus.
  acéfalo paracéfalo acephalus paracephalus.
  acéfalo simpódico acephalus simpus.
acéfalo, -la *adj.* acephalous.
acefalobraquia *f.* acephalobrachia.
acefalocardia *f.* acephalocardia.
acefalocisto *m.* acephalocyst.
acefalogasteria *f.* acephalogasteria.
acefalogastria *f.* acephalogastria.
acefalogastro *m.* acephalogaster.
acefalopodia *f.* acephalopodia.
acefalópodo *m.* acephalopodius.
acefaloquiria *f.* acephalochiria.
acefaloquiro *m.* acephalochirus.
acefalorraquia *f.* acephalorachia.
acefalostomía *f.* acephalostomia.
acefalóstomo *m.* acephalostomus.
acefalotoracia *f.* acephalothoracia.
acephalus *m.* acephalus.
  acephalus dibrachius acephalus dibrachius.
  acephalus dipus acephalus dipus.
  acephalus monobrachius acephalus monobrachius.
  acephalus monopus acephalus monopus.
  acephalus paracephalus acephalus paracephalus.
  acephalus simpus acephalus simpus.
aceite *m.* oil.
acelerador *m.* accelerator.
  acelerador lineal linear accelerator.
acelerómetro *m.* accelerometer.
acelomado, -da *adj.* acelomate.
acelomatoso, -sa *adj.* acelomatous.
acelular *adj.* acellular.
acenestesia *f.* acenesthesia.
acéntrico, -ca *adj.* acentric.
acephalus acephalus.
aceptación *f.* acceptance.
aceptor *m.* acceptor.
aceratosis *f.* aceratosis.
acérvulo *m.* acervulus.
acescencia *f.* acescence.
acescente *adj.* acescent.
acesodino, -na *adj.* acesodyne.
acestoma *m.* accstoma.
acetabular *adj.* acetabular.
acetabulectomía *f.* acetabulectomy.
acetábulo *m.* acetabulum.
acetabuloplastia *f.* acetabuloplasty.
acetabulum acetabulum.
acético, -ca *adj.* acetic.
acetímetro *m.* acetimeter, acetometer.
acetólisis *f.* acetolysis.
acetómetro *m.* acetometer.
acetona *f.* acetone.
acetonemia *f.* acetonemia.
acetonémico, -ca *adj.* acetonemic.
acetonglucosuria *f.* acetonglycosuria.
acetonumerador *m.* acetonumerator.
acetonuria *f.* acetonuria.
acetosoluble *adj.* acetosoluble.
acianoblepsia *f.* acyanoblepsia.
acianopsia *f.* acyanoblepsia.

acianótico, -ca *adj.* acyanotic.
aciclia *f.* acyclia.
acicular *adj.* acicular.
acidalbúmina *f.* acidalbumin.
acidaminuria *f.* acidaminuria.
acidemia *f.* acidemia.
acidez *f.* acidity.
  acidez del estómago acidity of the stomach.
acídico, -ca *adj.* acidic.
acidificable *adj.* acidifiable.
acidificación *f.* acidification.
acidificador *m.* acidifier.
acidificar *v.* acidify.
acidimetría *f.* acidimetry.
acidímetro *m.* acidimeter.
acidismo *m.* acidism, acidismus.
acidismus acidism, acidismus.
ácido *m.* acid, acidum.
acidocetosis *f.* ketoacidosis.
acidofilia *f.* acidophilia.
acidofílico, -ca *adj.* acidophilic.
acidofilismo *m.* acidophilism.
acidógeno, -na *adj.* acidogenic.
acidorresistencia *f.* acidoresistance.
acidorresistente *adj.* acid-fast.
acidósico, -ca *adj.* acidosic.
acidosis *f.* acidosis.
  acidosis por anhidrido carbónico carbon dioxide acidosis.
  acidosis compensada compensated acidosis.
  acidosis descompensada uncompensated
  acidosis.
  acidosis diabética diabetic acidosis.
  acidosis hipercápnica hypercapnic acidosis.
  acidosis hiperclorémica hyperchloremic acidosis.
  acidosis láctica lactic acidosis.
  acidosis metabólica metabolic acidosis.
  acidosis metabólica compensada compensated metabolic acidosis.
  acidosis por diálisis acidosis dialysis.
  acidosis por inanición starvation acidosis.
  acidosis renal renal acidosis.
  acidosis no respiratoria non-respiratory acidosis.
  acidosis renal hiperclorémica renal hyperchloremic acidosis.
  acidosis renal tubular renal tubular acidosis.
  acidosis renal tubular distal distal renal tubular acidosis.
  acidosis renal tubular proximal proximal
  renal tubular acidosis.
  acidosis respiratoria respiratory acidosis.
  acidosis respiratoria compensada compensated respiratory acidosis.
  acidosis urémica uremic acidosis.
acidosteofito *m.* acidosteophyte.
acidótico, -ca *adj.* acidotic.
acidulado, -da *adj.* acidulated.
acidular *v.* acidulate.
acídulo, -la *adj.* acidulous.
acidum acidum.
aciduria *f.* aciduria.
  aciduria acetoacética acetoacetic aciduria.
  aciduria argininosuccínica argininosuccinic
  aciduria.
  aciduria beta-aminoisobutírica beta-aminoisobutyric aciduria.
  aciduria beta-hidroxiisovalérica beta-hydroxyisovaleric aciduria.
  aciduria glutárica glutaric aciduria.
  aciduria metilmalónica methylmalonic aciduria.
  aciduria orótica orotic aciduria.
acidúrico, -ca *adj.* aciduric.

aciesis *f.* acyesis.
acigografía *f.* azygography.
acigograma *m.* azygogram.
ácigos *adj.* azygos.
acinar *adj.* acinar.
acinesia *f.* akinesia.
  acinesia álgera akinesia algera.
  acinesia amnéstica akinesia amnestica.
  acinesia de O'Brien O'Brien akinesia.
  acinesia refleja reflex akinesia.
acinesis *f.* akinesia.
acinestesia *f.* akinesthesia.
acinético, -ca *adj.* akinetic.
Acinetobacter Acinetobacter.
acínico, -ca *adj.* acinic.
aciniforme *adj.* aciniform.
acinitis *f.* acinitis.
ácino *m.* acinus.
acinoso, -sa *adj.* acinous, acinose.
acinotubular *adj.* acinotubular.
acinus acinus.
acistia *f.* acystia.
acistineuria *f.* acystinervia.
acistinervia *f.* acystinervia.
acladiosis *f.* acladiosis.
aclarador *m.* clarifier, clearer, clearing agent.
aclaramiento *m.* clearance.
  aclaramiento de agua libre free water clearance.
  aclaramiento de fármaco drug clearance.
  aclaramiento de creatinina creatinine clearance.
  aclaramiento de inulina inulin clearance.
  aclaramiento de urea urea clearance.
  aclaramiento osmolar osmolarity clearance.
aclasia *f.* aclasis.
  aclasia diafisiaria diaphyseal aclasis.
  aclasia tarsoepifisaria tarsoepiphyseal aclasis.
aclástico, -ca *adj.* aclastic.
acleistocardia *f.* acleistocardia.
aclimatación *f.* acclimation, acclimatation, acclimatization.
aclínico, -ca *adj.* aclinic.
aclorhidria *f.* achlorhydria.
aclorhídrico, -ca *adj.* achlorhydric.
acloroblepsia *f.* achloroblepsia.
aclorófilo, -la *adj.* achlorophyllous.
acloropsia *f.* achloropsia.
acmástico, -ca *adj.* acmastic.
acmé *f.* acme.
acmestesia *f.* acmesthesia.
acné, acne *f.* acne.
  acné adolescentium acne adoslescentium.
  acné por alquitrán tar acne.
  acné artificial acne artificialis.
  acné por asbestos asbestos acne.
  acné atrófica acne atrophica.
  acné brómica bromide acne.
  acné caquéctica, acné de los caquécticos
  acne cachecticorum.
  acné ciliar acne ciliaris.
  acné clórica chlorine acne.
  acné común common acne.
  acné conglobata conglobate acne, acne conglobata.
  acné por contacto contact acne.
  acné cosmética cosmetic acne.
  acné decalvans acne decalvans.
  acné detergicans detergicans acne.
  acné diseminada acne disseminata.
  acné epidémica epidemic acne.
  acné eritematosa acne erythematosa.
  acné escorbútica acne scorbutica.
  acné esteroidea steroid acne.

acné estival acne estivalis.
acné excoriada, acné excoriada de las jovencitas excoriated acne, acne excoriée des jeunes filles.
acné frontal, acné frontalis acne frontalis.
acné fulminante acne fulminans.
acné general acne generalis.
acné halógena halogen acne.
acné hipertrófica acne hypertrophica.
acné hordeolaris acne hordeolaris.
acné indurada acne indurata.
acné infantil infantile acne.
acné luposa acne lupoides.
acné Mallorca Mallorca acne.
acné mecánica mechanical acne, acne mechanica.
acné medicamentoso acne medicamentosa.
acné necrótica miliar acne necrotica miliaris.
acné neonatal neonatal acne, acne neonatorum.
acné ocupacional occupational acne.
acné papulosa acne papulosa.
acné picealis acne picealis.
acné por petróleo petroleum acne.
acné pomada, acné por pomadas pomade acne.
acné premenstrual premenstrual acne.
acné punctata acne punctata.
acné pustulosa pustulosa acne.
acné queloide keloid acne.
acné queratosa acne keratosa.
acné quística cystic acne.
acné del recolector picker's acne.
acné rodens acne rodens.
acné rosácea acne rosacea.
acné sebácea acne sebacea.
acné sifilítica acne syphilitica.
acné simple simple acne, acne simplex.
acné tarsi acne tarsi.
acné telangiectásico, acné telangiectodes acne telangiectodes.
acné tropical, acné tropicalis tropical acne, acne tropicalis.
acné urticata acne urticata.
acné varioliforme acne varioliformis.
acné venenata acne venenata.
acné vulgar acne vulgaris.
acné yódica, acné por yodo, acné por yoduro iodide acne.
acnegénico, -ca *adj.* acnegenic.
acneiforme *adj.* acneform, acneiform.
acnemia *f.* acnemia.
acnitis *f.* acnitis.
acoasma *f.* acoasma, acousma.
acodado, -da *adj.* elbowed.
acodadura *f.* kink.
 acodadura de Lane ileal kink, Lane's kink.
acodamiento *m.* kink.
acognosia *f.* acognosy.
acolia *f.* acholia.
acólico, -ca *adj.* acholic.
acoluria *f.* acholuria.
acolúrico, -ca *adj.* acholuric.
acomia *f.* acomia.
acomodación *f.* accommodation.
acomodación absoluta absolute accommodation.
acomodación binocular binocular accommodation.
acomodación excesiva excessive accommodation.
acomodación histológica histologic accommodation.
acomodación negativa negative accommodation.

acomodación del nervio, acomodación nerviosa nerve accommodation.
acomodación del ojo accommodation of the eye.
acomodación positiva positive accommodation.
acomodación relativa relative accommodation.
acomodación subnormal subnormal accommodation.
acomodación visual visual accommodation.
acomodativo, -va *adj.* accommodative.
acomodómetro *m.* accommodometer.
acompañante *adj.* companion.
aconativo, -va *adj.* aconative.
acondicionar *v.* condition.
acondrogénesis *f.* achondrogenesis.
acondroplasia *f.* achondroplasia, achondroplasty.
acondroplásico, -ca *adj.* achondroplastic.
acondroplástico, -ca *adj.* achondroplastic.
acopado, -da *adj.* cupped.
acoplamiento *m.* coupling.
 acoplamiento fijo fixed coupling.
acoprosis *f.* acoprosis.
acoproso, -sa *adj.* acoprous.
acor *m.* achor, acor.
acorea *f.* acorea.
acoresis *f.* achoresis.
acormo *m.* acormus.
acosmia *f.* acosmia.
acoso sexual *m.* sexual harassment.
acousma *f.* acousma.
acral *adj.* acral.
acraneal *adj.* acranial.
acrania *f.* acrania.
acrasia *f.* acrasia.
acraturesis *f.* acraturesis.
acre *adj.* acrid.
acrecentamiento *m.* enhancement.
acreción *f.* accretion.
acrementación *f.* accrementition.
acremoniosis *f.* acremoniosis.
acrencéfalo *m.* akrencephalon, achrencephalon.
acribómetro *m.* acribometer.
acrilaldehído *m.* acrylaldehyde.
acrílico, -ca *adj.* acrylic.
acrimonia *f.* acrimonia, acrimony.
acrinia *f.* acrinia.
acrisia *f.* acrisia.
acrisis *f.* acrisia.
acrítico, -ca *adj.* acritical.
acritocromacia *f.* acritochromacy.
acritud *f.* acrimony.
acroagnosia *f.* acroagnosis.
acroagnosis *f.* acroagnosis.
acroanestesia *f.* acroanesthesia.
acroartritis *f.* acroarthritis.
acroasfixia *f.* acroasphyxia.
 acroasfixia crónica chronic acroasphyxia.
acrobistiolito *m.* acrobystiolith.
acrobistitis *f.* acrobystitis.
acroblasto *m.* acroblast.
acrobraquicefalia *f.* acrobrachycephaly.
acrocefalia *f.* acrocephaly.
 acrocefalia sindactilia acrocephaly syndactyly.
acrocefálico, -ca *adj.* acrocephalic.
acrocéfalo, -la *adj.* acrocephalous.
acrocefalopolisindactilia (ACPS) *f.* acrocephalopolysyndactyly.
 acrocefalopolisindactilia (ACPS) tipo I acrocephalopolysyndactyly type I.
 acrocefalopolisindactilia (ACPS) tipo II type II acrocephalopolysyndactyly.

 acrocefalopolisindactilia (ACPS) tipo III acrocephalopolysyndactyly type III.
 acrocefalopolisindactilia (ACPS) tipo IV acrocephalopolysyndactyly type IV.
acrocefalosindactilia *f.* acrocephalosyndactyly.
 acrocefalosindactilia tipo I acrocephalosyndactyly type I.
 acrocefalosindactilia tipo II acrocephalosyndactyly type II.
 acrocefalosindactilia tipo III acrocephalosyndactyly type III.
 acrocefalosindactilia tipo V acrocephalosyndactyly type V.
acrocéntrico, -ca *adj.* acrocentric.
acrocianosis *f.* acrocyanosis.
 acrocianosis periférica del recién nacido peripheral acrocyanosis of the newborn.
acrocianótico, -ca *adj.* acrocyanotic.
acrocontractura *f.* acrocontracture.
acrocordón *m.* acrochordon.
acrodermatitis *f.* acrodermatitis.
 acrodermatitis continua continuous acrodermatitis, acrodermatitis continua.
 acrodermatitis crónica atrófica, acrodermatitis crónica atrofiante acrodermatitis chronica atrophicans.
 acrodermatitis crónica de las extremidades acrodermatitis chronica atrophicans.
 acrodermatitis enteropática, acrodermatitis enteropática de Danbolt y Closs acrodermatitis enteropathica.
 acrodermatitis infantil infantile acrodermatitis.
 acrodermatitis invernal acrodermatitis hiemalis.
 acrodermatitis papular de la niñez, acrodermatitis papulosa infantum infantile papular acrodermatitis, papular acrodermatitis of childhood, acrodermatitis papulosa infantum.
 acrodermatitis perstans acrodermatitis perstans.
acrodermatosis *f.* acrodermatosis.
acrodinia *f.* acrodynia.
acrodisestesia *f.* acrodysesthesia.
acrodisostosis *f.* acrodysostosis.
acrodolicomelia *f.* acrodolichomelia.
acrodonte *m.* acrodont.
acrodonto *m.* acrodont.
acroedema *m.* acroedema.
acroesclerodermia *f.* acroscleroderma.
acroesclerosis *f.* acroscleroderma.
acroespiroma *m.* acrospiroma.
acrofobia *f.* acrophobia.
acrogeria *f.* acrogeria.
acrohiperhidrosis *f.* acrohyperhidrosis.
acrohipotermia *f.* acrohypothermy.
acroleína *f.* acrolein.
acroleucopatía *f.* acroleukopathy.
acroma *m.* achroma.
acromacria *f.* acromacria.
acromanía *f.* acromania.
acromaquia *f.* achromachia.
acromasia *f.* achromasia.
acromastitis *f.* acromastitis.
acromata *m., f.* achromate.
acromático, -ca *adj.* achromatic.
acromatismo *m.* achromatism.
acromatizar *v.* achromatize.
acromatofilia *f.* achromatophilia.
acromatófilo, -la *adj.* achromatophil.
acromatopia *f.* achromatopia.
acromatópico, -ca *adj.* achromatopic.
acromatopsia *f.* achromatopsia, achromatopsy, achromatopia.

acromatopsia atípica atypical achromatopsia.
acromatopsia completa complete achromatopsia.
acromatopsia incompleta incomplete achromatopsia.
acromatopsia ligada al cromosoma X X-linked achromatopsia.
acromatopsia típica typical achromatopsia.
acromatosis *f.* achromatosis.
acromatoso, -sa *adj.* achromatous.
acromaturia *f.* achromaturia.
acromegalia *f.* acromegalia, acromegaly.
acromegálico, -ca *adj.* acromegalic.
acromegalogigantismo *m.* acromegalogigantism.
acromegaloidismo *m.* acromegaloidism.
acromelalgia *f.* acromelalgia.
acromelia *f.* acromelia.
acromélico, -ca *adj.* acromelic.
acrometagénesis *f.* acrometagenesis.
acromia *f.* achromia, achroma.
 acromia cortical cortical achromia.
 acromia parasitaria achromia parasitica.
acromial *adj.* acromial.
acrómico, -ca *adj.* achromic.
acromicosis *f.* achromycosis.
acromicria *f.* acromicria.
acromioclavicular *adj.* acromioclavicular.
acromiocoracoide *adj.* acromiocoracoid.
acromiocoracoideo, -a *adj.* acromiocoracoid.
acromioescapular *adj.* acromioscapular.
acromiohumeral *adj.* acromiohumeral.
acromion *m.* acromion.
acromionectomía *f.* acromionectomy.
acromiotonía *m.* acromyotonia, acromyotonus.
acromiotono *m.* acromyotonus.
acromiotorácico, -ca *adj.* acromiothoracic.
acromofílico, -ca *adj.* achromophilic.
acromófilo, -la *adj.* achromophilous.
acromotriquia *f.* achromotrichia.
acronarcótico, -ca *adj.* acronarcotic.
acroneurosis *f.* acroneurosis.
acrónfalo *m.* acromphalus.
acronix *m.* acronyx.
acroosteólisis *f.* acroosteolysis.
acropaquia *f.* acropachy.
acropaquidermia *f.* acropachyderma.
acroparálisis *f.* acroparalysis.
acroparestesia *f.* acroparesthesia.
acropatía *f.* acropathy.
acropatología *f.* acropathology.
acrópeto, -ta *adj.* acropetal.
acropigmentación *f.* acropigmentation.
acropostitis *f.* acroposthitis.
acropúrpura *f.* acropurpura.
acropustulosis *f.* acropustulosis.
 acropustulosis infantil infantile acropustulosis.
acroqueratoelastoidosis *f.* acrokeratoelastoidosis.
acroqueratosis *f.* acrokeratosis.
 acroqueratosis paraneoplásica paraneoplastic acrokeratosis.
 acroqueratosis verruciforme acrokeratosis verruciformis.
acrosclerodermia *f.* acroscleroderma.
acrosclerosis *f.* acrosclerosis.
acrosfacelo *m.* acrosphacelus.
acrosfenosindactilia *f.* acrosphenosyndactylia.
acrosindactilia *f.* acrosyndactyly.
acrosoma *m.* acrosome.
acrospiroma *m.* acrospiroma.
 acrospiroma ecrino eccrine acrospiroma.
acrostealgia *f.* acrostealgia.

acrotérico, -ca *adj.* acroteric.
acrótico, -ca *adj.* acrotic.
acrotismo *f.* acrotism.
acrotrofodinia *f.* acrotrophodynia.
acrotrofoneurosis *f.* acrotrophoneurosis.
actina *f.* actin.
acting out acting out.
actinicidad *f.* actinicity.
actinidad *f.* actinicity.
actínico, -ca *adj.* actinic.
actinina *f.* actinine.
actinismo *m.* actinism.
actinobacilosis *f.* actinobacillosis.
Actinobacillus Actinobacillus.
actinodermatosis *f.* actinodermatosis.
actinófago *m.* actinophage.
actinofitosis *f.* actinophytosis.
actinogénesis *f.* actinogenesis.
actinogénico, -na *adj.* actinogenic.
actinología *f.* actinology.
Actinomadura Actinomadura.
actinometría *f.* actinometry.
actinómetro *m.* actinometer.
actinomicelial *adj.* actinomycelial.
actinomicético, -ca *adj.* actinomycelial.
actinomiceto *m.* actinomycete.
actinomicetoma *m.* actinomycetoma.
actinomicoma *m.* actinomycoma.
actinomicosis *f.* actinomycosis.
actinomicótico, -ca *adj.* actinomycotic.
Actinomyces Actinomyces.
actinoneuritis *f.* actinoneuritis.
actinoquímica *f.* actinochemistry.
actinoterapia *f.* actinotherapy.
actinotoxemia *f.* actinotoxemia.
actitud *f.* attitude.
 actitud antálgica antalgic attitude.
 actitud apasionada passionate attitude.
 actitud de boxeador pugilistic attitude.
 actitud de combate attitude of combat.
 actitud de crucifijo, actitud de crucifixión cruxifixion attitude.
 actitud de deflexión deflexion attitude.
 actitud de discóbolo discobolus attitude.
 actitud de Devergie Devergie's attitude.
 actitud emocional emotional attitude.
 actitud estereotipada stereotyped attitude.
 actitud fetal fetal attitude.
 actitud forzada forced attitude.
 actitud glacial frozen attitude.
 actitud ilógica illogical attitude.
 actitud pasional passional attitude.
 actitud de Wernicke-Mann Wernicke-Mann's attitude.
activación *f.* activation.
 activación de linfocitos lymphocyte activation.
 activación del aminoácido amino acid activation.
 activación del complemento complement activation.
 activación del espermatozoide sperm activation.
 activación monoclonal monoclonal activation.
 activación del óvulo, activación ovular ovum activation, ovular activation.
 activación del plasma, activación plasmática plasma activation.
 activación policlonal polyclonal activation.
activador *m.* activator.
 activador funcional functional activator.
 activador monobloque monoblock activator.
 activador del plasminógeno tisular tissue plasminogen activator.

 activador policlonal polyclonal activator.
activar *v.* activate.
actividad *f.* activity.
 actividad biológica biological activity.
 actividad colinérgica cholinergic activity.
 actividad de bloqueo blocking activity.
 actividad de renina plasmática plasma renin activity.
 actividad de la vida diaria activity of daily living.
 actividad desencadenada triggered activity.
 actividad enfocada focussed activity.
 actividad enzimática enzyme activity.
 actividad específica specific activity.
 actividad inhibitoria relacionada con la leucemia leukemia associated inhibitory activity.
 actividad intencional purposeful activity.
 actividad motora fina fine motor skill.
 actividad no suprimible non-suppressible activity.
 actividad óptica optical activity.
 actividad parecida a la insulina insulin-like activity.
 actividad-pasividad activity-passivity.
 actividad seudoinsulínica insulin-like activity.
 actividad simpaticoadrenal sympathoadrenal activity.
 actividad simpaticomimética intrínseca intrinsic sympathomimetic activity (ISA).
activo, -va *adj.* active.
 activo ópticamente optically active.
acto *m.* act.
 acto compulsivo compulsive act.
 acto experiencial experiential act.
 acto fallido faulty act, failed activity, mis-action, freudian slip.
 acto imperativo imperious act.
 acto impulsivo impulsive act.
 acto indiferente indifferent act.
 acto instintivo instinctive act.
 acto inteligente intelligent act.
 acto de inversión de roles role reversal act.
 acto neutro neutral act.
 acto reflejo reflex act.
 acto voluntario voluntary act.
actómetro *m.* actometer.
actomiosina *f.* actomyosin.
Actonia Actonia.
acuapuntura *f.* aquapuncture.
acuático, -ca *adj.* aquatic.
acuagénico, -ca *adj.* aquagenic.
acueducto *m.* aqueduct, aqueductus.
aqueductus *m.* aqueduct, aqueductus.
acúfeno *m.* tinnitus.
acufilopresión *f.* acufilopressure.
acufonía *f.* acuophonia.
acuidad *f.* acuity.
acuíparo, -ra *adj.* acuiparous.
aculado, -da *adj.* aculeate.
aculeado, -da *adj.* aculeate.
aculturación *f.* acculturation.
acumetría *f.* acoumetry.
acúmetro *m.* acoumeter.
acuminado, -da *adj.* acuminate.
acumulación *f.* accummulation.
acumulado, -da *adj.* accumulated.
acumulador *m.* accumulator.
acumulativo, -va *adj.* cumulative.
acuocapsulitis *f.* aquocapsulitis.
acuofonía *f.* acuophonia.
acuosidad *f.* aquosity.
acuoso, -sa *adj.* aqueous.
acupresión *f.* acupressure.
acupunto *m.* acupoint.

acupuntor, -ra *m., f.* acupuncturist.
acupuntura *f.* acupuncture.
acusección *m.* acusection.
acusector *m.* acusector.
acusia *f.* acusis.
acusma *f.* acousma.
acusmatamnesia *f.* acousmatamnesia.
acústica *f.* acoustics.
acústico, -ca *adj.* acoustic.
acusticofobia *f.* acousticophobia.
acustografía *f.* acoustogram.
acutómetro *m.* acoutometer.
acutorsión *f.* acutorsion.
achaque *f.* ailment, infirmity.
adacria *f.* adacrya.
adactllla *f.* adactylia, adactyly.
adactilismo *m.* adactylism.
adáctilo, -la *adj.* adactylous.
adamantino, -na *adj.* adamantine.
adamantinocarcinoma *m.* adamantinocarcinoma.
adamantinoma *m.* adamantinoma.
  adamantinoma pituitario pituitary adamantinoma.
adamantoblasto *m.* adamantoblast.
adamantoblastoma *m.* adamantoblastoma.
adamantoma *m.* adamantoma.
adaptabilidad *f.* compliance.
adaptable *adj.* adaptive.
adaptación *f.* adaptation.
  adaptación auditiva auditory adaptation.
  adaptación celular cellular adaptation.
  adaptación cromática color adaptation.
  adaptación enzimática enzymatic adaptation.
  adaptación escotópica scotopic adaptation.
  adaptación fenotípica phenotypic adaptation.
  adaptación fotópica photopic adaptation.
  adaptación a la luz light adaptation.
  adaptación a la oscuridad dark adaptation.
  adaptación a la realidad reality adaptation.
  adaptación retiniana retinal adaptation.
  adaptación social social adaptation.
adaptador *m.* adapter, adaptor.
  adaptador de bandas band adapter.
adaptometría *f.* adaptometry.
adaptómetro *m.* adaptometer.
  adaptómetro cromático color adaptometer.
adaxial *adj.* adaxial.
addisoniano, -na *adj.* Addisonian.
addisonismo *m.* Addisonism.
adducción *f.* adduction.
adducir *v.* adduct.
adductor, -ra *adj.* adductor.
adecuación *f.* adequacy.
  adecuación velofaríngea velopharyngeal adequacy.
adelfia *f.* adelphia.
adelomórfico, -ca *adj.* adelomorphic.
adelomorfo, -fa *adj.* adelomorphous.
adenalgia *f.* adenalgia.
adenasa *f.* adenase.
adenastenia *f.* adenasthenia.
  adenastenia gástrica adenasthenia gastrica.
adendrítico, -ca *adj.* adendric, adendritic.
adenectomia *f.* adenectomy.
adenectopía *f.* adenectopia.
adenenfraxis *f.* adenemphraxis.
adenia *f.* adenia.
adénico, -ca *adj.* adenic.
adeniforme *adj.* adeniform.
adenílico, -ca *adj.* adenylic.
adenina *f.* adenine.
adenitis *f.* adenitis.

adenitis aguda infecciosa epidémica acute epidemic infectious adenitis.
adenitis cervical cervical adenitis.
adenitis flemonosa phlegmonous adenitis.
adenitis mesentérica aguda mesenteric lymph-adenitis.
adenitis salival aguda acute salivary adenitis.
adenitis vulvovaginal vulvovaginal adenitis.
adenización *f.* adenization.
adenoacantoma *m.* adenoacanthoma.
adenoameloblastoma *f.* adenoameloblastoma.
adenoamigdalectomía *f.* adenotonsillectomy, tonsilloadenoidectomy.
adenocancroide *m.* adenocancroid.
adenocarcinoma *m.* adenocarcinoma.
  adenocarcinoma acinar, adenocarcinoma acinoso acinar adenocarcinoma, acinous adenocarcinoma.
  adenocarcinoma alveolar alveolar adenocarcinoma.
  adenocarcinoma bronquiolar bronchiolar adenocarcinoma.
  adenocarcinoma de células acinosas acinic cell adenocarcinoma.
  adenocarcinoma folicular follicular adenocarcinoma.
  adenocarcinoma hipofisario hypophyseal adenocarcinoma.
  adenocarcinoma in situ adenocarcinoma in situ.
  adenocarcinoma mucinoso mucinous adenocarcinoma.
  adenocarcinoma papilar papillary adenocarcinoma.
  adenocarcinoma polipoide polypoid adenocarcinoma.
  adenocarcinoma renal adenocarcinoma of the kidney, renal adenocarcinoma.
adenocele *m.* adenocele.
adenocelulitis *f.* adenocellulitis.
adenocistoma *m.* adenocystoma.
  adenocistoma papilar linfomatoso papillary adenocystoma lymphomatosum.
adenocondroma *m.* adenochondroma.
adenocondrosarcoma *m.* adenochondrosarcoma.
adenodiastasis *f.* adenodiastasis.
adenodinia *f.* adenodynia.
adenoepitelioma *m.* adenoepithelioma.
adenofaringitis *f.* adenopharyngitis.
adenofibroma *m.* adenofibroma.
  adenofibroma edematoso, adenofibroma edematodes adenofibroma edematodes.
adenofibromioma *m.* adenofibromyoma.
adenofibrosis *f.* adenofibrosis.
adenofima *f.* adenophyma.
adenoflemón *m.* adenophlegmon.
adenoftalmía *f.* adenophthalmia.
adenogénesis *f.* adenogenesis.
adenógeno, -na *adj.* adenogenous.
adenografía *f.* adenography.
adenográfico, -ca *adj.* adenographic.
adenograma *m.* lymph node differential cell count.
adenohiperestenia *f.* adenohypersthenia.
adenohipófisis *f.* adenohypophysis.
adenohipofisitis *f.* adenohypophysitis.
adenoide *adj.* adenoid.
adenoides *f.* adenoids.
adenoidectomía *f.* adenoidectomy.
adenoidismo *m.* adenoidism.
adenoiditis *f.* adenoiditis.
adenoleiomiofibroma *m.* adenoleiomyofibroma.

adenolinfitis *f.* adenolymphitis.
adenolinfocele *m.* adenolymphocele.
adenolinfoma *m.* adenolymphoma.
adenolipoma *m.* adenolipoma.
adenolipomatosis *f.* adenolipomatosis.
  adenolipomatosis simétrica symmetric adenolipomatosis.
adenólisis *f.* adenolysis.
adenologaditis *f.* adenologaditis.
adenología *f.* adenology.
adenoma *m.* adenoma.
  adenoma acidófilo acidophilic adenoma.
  adenoma adamantino adamantine adenoma.
  adenoma adrenal adrenal adenoma.
  adenoma adrenocortical adrenocortical adenoma.
  adenoma alveolar adenoma alveolare.
  adenoma anexial adnexal adenoma.
  adenoma apocrino apocrine adenoma.
  adenoma basófilo basophil adenoma, basophilic adenoma.
  adenoma bronquial bronchial adenoma.
  adenoma de células basales basal cell adenoma.
  adenoma de células de Hürthle Hürthle cell adenoma.
  adenoma de células nulas null cell adenoma.
  adenoma de células oxífilas granulosas oxyphilic granular cell adenoma.
  adenoma de células principales chief cell adenoma.
  adenoma coloide colloid adenoma.
  adenoma cortical cortical adenoma.
  adenoma cromófilo chromophil adenoma.
  adenoma cromófobo chromophobe adenoma.
  adenoma diverticular umbilical adenoma.
  adenoma embrionario embryonal adenoma.
  adenoma eosinofílico eosinophilic adenoma.
  adenoma fetal fetal adenoma.
  adenoma fibroso fibroid adenoma, adenoma fibrosum.
  adenoma folicular follicular adenoma.
  adenoma gelatinoso adenoma gelatinosum.
  adenoma hepático hepatic adenoma.
  adenoma hipofisario hypophyseal adenoma, pituitary adenoma.
  adenoma insular islet adenoma.
  adenoma de la lactación lactating adenoma.
  adenoma de Langerhans, adenoma langerhansiano langerhansian adenoma.
  adenoma macrofolicular macrofollicular adenoma.
  adenoma maligno malignant adenoma.
  adenoma microfolicular microfollicular adenoma.
  adenoma monomórfico monomorphic adenoma.
  adenoma mucinoso mucinous adenoma.
  adenoma nefrogénico nephrogenic adenoma.
  adenoma oxífilo oxyphil adenoma.
  adenoma papilar papillary adenoma.
  adenoma pleomorfo pleomorphic adenoma.
  adenoma polipoide polypoid adenoma.
  adenoma prostático prostatic adenoma.
  adenoma quístico papilar papillary cystic adenoma.
  adenoma renal adenoma of the kidney.
  adenoma sebáceo sebaceous adenoma.
  adenoma sudoríparo apocrine sweat gland adenoma.
  adenoma tóxico toxic adenoma.

adenoma tubular tubular adenoma.

adenoma tubular de Pick Pick's tubular adenoma.

adenoma tubular ovárico ovarian tubular adenoma.

adenoma tubular testicular testicular tubular adenoma.

adenoma tubular testicular del ovario adenoma tubulare testiculare ovarii.

adenoma velloso villous adenoma.

adenomalacia *f.* adenomalacia.

adenomatoide *adj.* adenomatoid.

adenomatoideo, -a *adj.* adenomatoid.

adenomatosis *f.* adenomatosis.

adenomatosis bucal adenomatosis oris.

adenomatosis erosiva del pezón erosive adenomatosis of the nipple.

adenomatosis fibrosante fibrosing adenomatosis.

adenomatosis múltiple endocrina multiple endocrine adenomatosis.

adenomatosis poliendocrina polyendocrine adenomatosis.

adenomatosis pluriglandular pluriglandular adenomatosis.

adenomatosis pulmonar pulmonary adenomatosis.

adenomatoso, -sa *adj.* adenomatous.

adenomectomía *f.* adenomectomy.

adenomegalia *f.* adenomegaly.

adenómero *m.* adenomere.

adenomioepitelioma *m.* adenomyoepithelioma.

adenomioepitelioma del estómago adenomyoepithelioma of the stomach.

adenomiofibroma *m.* adenomyofibroma.

adenomioma *m.* adenomyoma.

adenomiomatosis *f.* adenomyomatosis.

adenomiomatoso, -sa *adj.* adenomyomatous.

adenomiometritis *f.* adenomyometritis.

adenomiosarcoma *m.* adenomyosarcoma.

adenomiosarcoma embrionario embryonal adenomyosarcoma.

adenomiosis *f.* adenomyosis.

adenomiosis del estroma stromal adenomyosis.

adenomiosis externa external adenomyosis, adenomyosis externa.

adenomiosis tubaria adenomyosis tubae.

adenomiosis uterina adenomyosis of the uterus, adenomyosis uteri.

adenomiositis *f.* adenomyositis.

adenomixoma *m.* adenomyxoma.

adenomixosarcoma *m.* adenomyxosarcoma.

adenoncosis *f.* adenoncus.

adenoneural *adj.* adenoneural.

adenopatía *f.* adenopathy.

adenopituicito *m.* adenopituicyte.

adenoquiste *m.* adenocyst.

adenosalpingitis *f.* adenosalpingitis.

adenosarcoma *m.* adenosarcoma.

adenosarcorrabdomioma *m.* adenosarcorhabdomyoma.

adenosclerosis *f.* adenosclerosis.

adenosina *f.* adenosine.

adenosis *f.* adenosis.

adenosis de conductos romos u obstruidos blunt duct adenosis.

adenosis esclerosante sclerosing adenosis.

adenosis fibrosante fibrosing adenosis.

adenosis microglandular microglandular adenosis.

adenosis vaginal adenosis vaginae.

adenoso, -sa *adj.* adenous, adenose.

adenotifus *m.* adenotyphus.

adenotomía *f.* adenotomy.

adenótomo *m.* adenotome.

adenoviral *adj.* adenoviral.

adenovírico, -ca *adj.* adenoviral.

Adenoviridae Adenoviridae.

adenovirus *m.* adenovirus.

adermia *f.* adermia.

adermogénesis *f.* adermogenesis.

adesternal *adj.* adsternal.

adherencia *f.* adherence, adhesion.

adherencia abdominal abdominal adhesion.

adherencia amniótica amniotic adhesion.

adherencia inmunitaria immune adherence.

adherencia pericárdica pericardial adhesion.

adherencia primaria primary adherence.

adherencia secundaria secondary adherence.

adherencia serológica serological adherence.

adherencia sublabial sublabial adherence.

adherencia traumática uterina traumatic uterine adhesion.

adherente *adj.* adherent.

adherir *v.* adhere.

adherenciotomía *f.* adhesiotomy.

adhesio adhesion, adhesio.

adhesión *f.* adhesion, adhesio.

adhesión abdominal abdominal adhesion.

adhesión amniótica amniotic adhesion.

adhesión fibrinosa fibrinous adhesion.

adhesión fibrosa fibrous adhesion.

adhesión intertalámica interthalamic adhesion, adhesio interthalamica.

adhesión pericárdica pericardial adhesion.

adhesión de las plaquetas platelet adhesion.

adhesión primaria primary adhesion.

adhesión secundaria secondary adhesion.

adhesividad *f.* adhesiveness.

adhesividad plaquetaria platelet adhesiveness.

adhesiotomía *f.* adhesiotomy.

adhesivo, -va *adj.* adhesive.

adiabático, -ca *adj.* adiabatic.

adiactínico, -ca *adj.* adiactinic.

adiadococinesia *f.* adiadochocinesia, adiadochokinesia, adiadokokinesis, adiadochocinesis, adiadochokinesis.

adiaforesis *f.* adiaphoresis.

adiaforético, -ca *adj.* adiaphoretic.

adiaforia *f.* adiaphoria.

adiapneustia *f.* adiapneustia.

adiaspiromicosis *f.* adiaspiromycosis.

adiaspora *f.* adispore.

adiastolia *f.* adiastole, adiastolia.

adiatermancia *f.* adiathermance, adiathermancy.

adiatermia *f.* adiathermancy, adiathermance.

adiatérmico, -ca *adj.* adiathermic.

adlatésico, -ca *adj.* adiathetic.

adicción *f.* addiction.

adiemorrisis *f.* adiemorrhysis.

adiente *adj.* adient.

adiestrable *adj.* trainable.

adiestramiento *m.* training.

adiestramiento asertivo assertive training.

adiestramiento expresivo expressive training.

adiestramiento en habilidades sociales social skills training.

adimensional *adj.* dimensionless.

adinamia *f.* adynamia.

adinamia episódica hereditaria adynamia episodica hereditaria.

adinámico, -ca *adj.* adynamic.

ad integrum ad integrum.

ad libitum ad libitum.

ad nauseam ad nauseam.

adipectomía *f.* adipectomy.

adipocele *m.* adipocele.

adipocelular *adj.* adipocellular.

adipocera *f.* adipocere.

adipoceratoso, -sa *adj.* adipoceratous.

adipocinesia *f.* adipokinesis.

adipocinético, -ca *adj.* adipokinetic.

adipocinesis *f.* adipokinesis.

adipocira *f.* adipocere.

adipocito *m.* adipocyte.

adipofibroma *m.* adipofibroma.

adipogénesis *f.* adipogenesis.

adipogenia *f.* adipogenesis.

adipogénico, -ca *adj.* adipogenic.

adipógeno, -na *adj.* adipogenous.

adipoide *m.* adipoid.

adipólisis *f.* adipolysis.

adipolítico, -ca *adj.* adipolytic.

adipoma *m.* adipoma.

adipomastia *f.* adipomastia.

adipómetro *m.* adipometer.

adiponecrosis *f.* adiponecrosis.

adiponecrosis subcutánea de los recién nacidos, adiponecrosis subcutánea neonatal adiponecrosis subcutanea neonatorum.

adipopéctico, -ca *adj.* adipopectic, adipopexic.

adipopexia *f.* adipopexia, adipopexis.

adipopexis *f.* adipopexia, adipopexis.

adiposalgia *f.* adiposalgia.

adiposidad *f.* adiposity, adipositas.

adiposidad cerebral cerebral adiposity, adipositas cerebralis.

adiposidad hipofisaria pituitary adiposity.

adiposis *f.* adiposis.

adiposis cerebral adiposis cerebralis.

adiposis dolorosa adiposis dolorosa.

adiposis hepática adiposis hepatica.

adiposis órquica, adiposis orchalis adiposis orchica.

adiposis tuberosa simple adiposis tuberosa simplex.

adiposis universal adiposis universalis.

adipositas adipositas.

adipositas abdominis adipositas abdominis.

adipositas cordis adipositas cordis.

adipositas ex vacuo adipositas ex vacuo.

adipositas cerebralis cerebral adiposity, adipositas cerebralis.

adiposo, -sa *adj.* adipose.

adiposuria *f.* adiposuria.

adipsia *f.* adipsia, adipsy.

adisoniano, -na *adj.* Addisonian.

adisonismo *m.* Addisonism.

aditividad *f.* additivity.

aditivo, -va *adj.* additive.

aditivo alimentario food additive.

aditivo intencional intentional additive.

aditus *m.* aditus.

adleriano, -na *adj.* Adlerian.

admaxilar *adj.* admaxillary.

admedial *adj.* admedial.

admediano, -na *adj.* admedian.

admitancia *f.* admittance.

administración *f.* administration.

administración bucal de la medicación buccal administration of medication.

administración de fármacos drug administration.

administración de líquidos parenterales administration of parenteral fluids.

administración de medicación mediante inhalación inhalation administration of medication.

administración oftálmica de medicamentos ophthalmic administration of medication.

adnerval *adj.* adnerval.
adneural *adj.* adneural.
adnexa adnexa.
adolescencia *f.* adolescence.
adolescente *m., f. y adj.* adolescent.
adoral *adj.* adoral.
adormecimiento *m.* numbness.
adquirido, -da *adj.* acquired.
adrenal *adj.* adrenal.
adrenalectomía *f.* adrenalectomy.
adrenalina *f.* adrenaline.
adrenalinemia *f.* adrenalinemia.
adrenalinogénesis *f.* adrenalinogenesis.
adrenalinuria *f.* adrenalinuria.
adrenalismo *m.* adrenalism.
adrenalitis *f.* adrenalitis.
adrenalopatía *f.* adrenalopathy.
adrenalotrópico, -ca *adj.* adrenalotropic.
adrenarca *f.* adrenarche.
adrenarquia *f.* adrenarche.
adrenérgico, -ca *adj.* adrenergic.
adrenitis *f.* adrenitis.
adrenoceptivo, -va *adj.* adrenoceptive.
adrenocinético, -ca *adj.* adrenokinetic.
adrenocortical *adj.* adrenocortical.
adrenocorticomimético, -ca *adj.* adrenocorticomimetic.
adrenocorticotrófico, -ca *adj.* adrenocorticotrophic, adrenocorticotropic.
adrenocorticotrópico, -ca *adj.* adrenocorticotrophic, adrenocorticotropic.
adrenocorticotropo, -pa *adj.* adrenocorticotrophic, adrenocorticotropic.
adrenocromo *m.* adrenochrome.
adrenodoncia *f.* adrenodontia.
adrenodoxina *f.* adrenodoxin.
adrenogénico, -ca *adj.* adrenogenic.
adrenógeno, -na *adj.* adrenogenous.
adrenoglomerulotropina *f.* adrenoglomerulotropin.
adrenoleucodistrofia *f.* adrenoleukodystrophy.
adrenolítico, -ca *adj.* adrenolytic.
adrenolutina *f.* adrenolutin.
adrenomedulotrópico, -ca *adj.* adrenomedullotropic.
adrenomegalia *f.* adrenomegaly.
adrenomimético, -ca *adj.* adrenomimetic.
adrenopatía *f.* adrenopathy.
adrenopausia *f.* adrenopausia.
adrenoprivo, -va *adj.* adrenoprival.
adrenorreactivo, -va *adj.* adrenoreactive.
adrenostático, -ca *adj.* adrenostatic.
adrenosterona *f.* adrenosterone.
adrenotoxina *f.* adrenotoxin.
adrenotrófico, -ca *adj.* adrenotrophic, adrenotropic.
adrenotrópico, -ca *adj.* adrenotrophic, adrenotropic.
adrenotropina *f.* adrenotropin.
adrenotropismo *m.* adrenotropisme.
adromia *f.* adromia.
adsorbente *adj.* adsorbent.
adsorbido, -da *adj.* adsorbed.
adsorber *v.* adsorb.
adsorción *f.* adsorption.
  adsorción inmunitaria immune adsorption.
adsternal *adj.* adsternal.
adterminal *adj.* adterminal.
aducción *f.* adduction.
aducente *adj.* adducent.
aducir *v.* adduct.
aductor, -ra *adj.* adductor.
adulteración *f.* adulteration.
adultez *f.* adulthood.

adulto, -ta *m., f. y adj.* adult.
adventicia *f.* adventitia.
adventicio, -cia *adj.* adventitious.
adyacente *adj.* adjacent.
adyuvante *m. y adj.* adjuvant.
  adyuvante completo de Freund Freund's complete adjuvant.
  adyuvante incompleto de Freund Freund's incomplete adjuvant.
adyuvanticidad *f.* adjuvanticity.
Aedes Aedes.
aedocéfalo *m.* aedoeocephalus.
aeluropsis *f.* aeluropsis.
aereación *f.* aeration.
aerendocardia *f.* aerendocardia.
aerenterectasia *f.* aerenterectasia.
aerífero, -ra *adj.* aeriferous.
aéreo, -a *adj.* aerial.
aeriforme *adj.* aeriform.
aeróbico, -ca *adj.* aerobic.
aerobio, -bia *adj.* aerobe.
  aerobio estricto strict aerobe.
  aerobio facultativo facultative aerobe.
  aerobio obligado obligate aerobe.
aerobiología *f.* aerobiology.
  aerobiología extramural extramural aerobiology.
  aerobiología intramural intramural aerobiology.
aerobioscopio *m.* aerobioscope.
aerobiosis *f.* aerobiosis.
aerobiótico, -ca *adj.* aerobiotic.
aerobullosis *f.* aerobullosis.
aerocele *m.* aerocele.
aerocistoscopia *f.* aerocystoscopy.
aerocistoscopio *m.* aerocystoscope.
aerocolia *f.* aerocolia, aerocoly.
aerocolpos *m.* aerocolpos.
aerodermectasia *f.* aerodermectasia.
aerodinámica *f.* aerodynamics.
aerodoncia *f.* aerodontia.
aerodontalgia *f.* aerodontalgia, aeroodontalgia.
aerodóntica *f.* aerodontia.
aerodontodinia *f.* aeroodontodynia.
aerodromofobia *f.* aerodromophobia.
aeroembolia *m.* aeroembolism.
aeroembolismo *m.* aeroembolism.
aeroenfisema *m.* aeroemphysema.
aerofagia *f.* aerophagia, aerophagy, air swallowing.
aerofílico, -ca *adj.* aerophilic, aerophilous.
aerófilo, -la *adj.* aerophil, aerophile.
aeróforo, -ra *adj.* aerophore.
aerogastria *f.* aerogastria.
  aerogastria por bloqueo blocked aerogastria.
aerogastrocolia *f.* erogastrocolia.
aerogénesis *f.* aerogenesis.
aerogénico, -ca *adj.* aerogenic.
aerógeno, -na *adj.* aerogenous.
aerohidroterapia *f.* aerohydrotherapy.
aeroionoterapia *f.* aeroionotherapy.
aeromedicina *f.* aeromedicine.
aerómetro *m.* aerometer.
Aeromonas Aeromonas.
aerootitis media *f.* aerootitis media.
aeropatía *f.* aeropathy.
aeroperitoneo *m.* aeroperitonia, aeroperitoneum.
aeropiecismo *m.* aeropiesism.
aeropiesoterapia *f.* aeropiesotherapy.
aeroplancton *m.* aeroplankton.
aeropletismógrafo *m.* aeroplethysmograph.
aeroporotomía *f.* aeroporotomy.

aerosialofagia *f.* aerosialophagy.
aerosinusitis *f.* aerosinusitis.
aerosis *f.* aerosis.
aerosol *m.* aerosol.
aerotaxis *f.* aerotaxis.
aeroterapia *f.* aerotherapeutics, aerotherapy.
aerotitis media *f.* aerotitis media.
aerotolerante *adj.* aerotolerant.
aerotonometría *f.* aerotonometry.
aerotonómetro *m.* aerotonometer.
aerotransportado, -da *adj.* airborne.
aerotropismo *m.* aerotropism.
  aerotropismo negativo negative aerotropism.
  aerotropismo positivo positive aerotropism.
aerouretroscopia *f.* aerourethroscopy.
aerouretroscopio *m.* aerorethroscope.
afaco, -ca *m., f.* aphakic.
afagia *f.* aphagia.
  afagia álgera, afagia dolorosa aphagia algera.
afagopraxia *f.* aphagopraxia.
afalangia *f.* aphalangia.
afalangiasis *f.* aphalangia.
afaquia *f.* aphakia.
afaquial *adj.* aphakial.
afáquico, -ca *adj.* aphakic.
afasia *f.* aphasia.
  afasia acústica acoustic aphasia.
  afasia amnemónica aphasia lethica.
  afasia amnésica amnestic aphasia, amnesic aphasia, dysnomic aphasia.
  afasia anómica anomic aphasia.
  afasia anósmica anosmic aphasia.
  afasia asociativa associative aphasia.
  afasia atáxica ataxic aphasia.
  afasia auditiva auditory aphasia.
  afasia de Broca Broca's aphasia.
  afasia central central aphasia.
  afasia combinada combined aphasia.
  afasia comisural commisural aphasia.
  afasia completa complete aphasia.
  afasia de conducción conduction aphasia.
  afasia epiléptica adquirida acquired epileptic aphasia.
  afasia expresiva expressive aphasia.
  afasia fluente, afasia fluida fluent aphasia.
  afasia funcional functional aphasia.
  afasia global global aphasia.
  afasia gráfica, afasia grafomotora graphic aphasia, graphomotor aphasia.
  afasia impresiva impressive aphasia.
  afasia infantil childhood aphasia.
  afasia jergal, afasia en jeringonza jargon aphasia.
  afasia de Kussmaul Kussmaul's aphasia.
  afasia lética aphasia lethica.
  afasia mixta mixed aphasia.
  afasia motora motor aphasia.
  afasia nominal nominal aphasia.
  afasia óptica optic aphasia.
  afasia patemática pathematic aphasia.
  afasia pictórica pictorial aphasia.
  afasia psicosensitiva, afasia psicosensorial psychosensory aphasia.
  afasia receptiva receptive aphasia.
  afasia semántica semantic aphasia.
  afasia sensitiva, afasia sensorial sensory aphasia.
  afasia sintáctica syntactical aphasia.
  afasia subcortical subcortical aphasia.
  afasia temporoparietal temporoparietal aphasia.
  afasia transcortical transcortical aphasia.
  afasia verbal verbal aphasia.

afasia visual visual aphasia.
afasia de Wernicke Wernicke's aphasia.
afásico, -ca[1] *m., f.* aphasiac.
afásico, -ca[2] *adj.* aphasic.
afasiología *f.* aphasiology.
afasiólogo, -ga *m., f.* aphasiologist.
afebril *adj.* afebrile.
afección *f.* affection.
afectado, -da *adj.* affected.
afectividad *f.* affectivity.
afecto *m.* affect.
  afecto aplanado flat affect.
  afecto constreñido constricted affect.
  afecto embotado blunted affect.
  afecto inapropiado inappropiate affect.
  afecto negativo negative affect.
  afecto plano flat affect.
  afecto positivo positive affect.
  afecto restringido restricted affect.
afecto, -ta *adj.* affected.
afectomotor, -ra *adj.* affectomotor.
afefobia *f.* aphephobia.
afemia *f.* aphemia.
aferente *adj.* afferent.
aféresis *f.* apheresis.
afetal *adj.* afetal.
afibrilar *adj.* afibrillar.
afibrinogenemia *f.* afibrinogenemia.
afiláctico, -ca *adj.* aphylactic.
afilaxia *f.* aphylaxis.
afilaxis *f.* aphylaxis.
afiliación *f.* affiliation.
afín *adj.* affinous.
afinidad *f.* affinity.
  afinidad electiva elective affinity, selective affinity.
  afinidad genética genetic affinity.
  afinidad química chemical affinity.
  afinidad residual residual affinity.
afirmación *f.* affirmation.
  afirmación de la capacidad capacity affirmation.
aflicción *f.* grief, bereavement.
aflujo *m.* afflux.
afonía *f.* aphonia.
  afonía de los clérigos aphonia clericorum.
  afonía espástica spastic aphonia.
  afonía histérica hysterical aphonia.
  afonía paralítica aphonia paralytica.
afónico, -ca *adj.* aphonic.
áfono, -na *adj.* aphonous.
afonogelia *f.* aphonogelia.
aforesis *f.* aphoresis.
afosfágeno, -na *adj.* aphosphagenic.
afosforosis *f.* aphosphorosis.
afosia *f.* aphose.
afotestesia *f.* aphotesthesia.
afótico, -ca *adj.* aphotic.
afrasia *f.* aphrasia.
afrodisia *f.* aphrodisia.
afrodisíaco, -ca *adj.* aphrodisiac.
afrodisiomanía *f.* aphrodisiomania.
afrontamiento *m.* coping.
  afrontamiento defensivo defensive coping.
  afrontamiento comprometido compromised coping.
  afrontamiento familiar ineficaz ineffective family coping.
afta *f.* aphtha.
aftoide *adj.* aphthoid.
aftongía *f.* aphthongia.
aftosis *f.* aphthosis.
aftoso, -sa *adj.* aphthous.
afusión *f.* affusion.
agalactia *f.* agalactia.

agaláctico, -ca *adj.* agalactous.
agalacto, -ta *adj.* agalactous.
agalactorrea *f.* agalactorrhea.
agalactosis *f.* agalactosis.
agalactosuria *f.* agalactosuria.
agalaxia *f.* agalactia.
agalorrea *f.* agalorrhea.
agameto *m.* agamete.
agamético, -ca *adj.* agametic.
agamia *f.* agamogenesis.
agámico, -ca *adj.* agamic.
agammaglobulinemia *f.* agammaglobulinemia.
  agammaglobulinemia adquirida acquired agammaglobulinemia.
  agammaglobulinemia de Bruton Bruton's agammaglobulinemia.
  agammaglobulinemia congénita congenital agammaglobulinemia.
  agammaglobulinemia congénita ligada al sexo X-linked agammaglobulinemia.
  agammaglobulinemia con linfocitopenia, agammaglobulinemia linfopénica lymphopenic agammaglobulinemia.
  agammaglobulinemia tipo Suiza Swiss type agammaglobulinemia.
agamobio *m.* agamobium.
agamogénesis *f.* agamogenesis.
agamogenético, -ca *adj.* agamogenetic.
agamogonia *f.* agamogony.
agamonte *m.* agamont.
aganglionar *adj.* aglangionic.
aganglionosis *f.* aganglionosis.
agar, agar-agar *m.* agar, agar-agar.
agarosa *f.* agarose.
agástrico, -ca *adj.* agastric.
agastroneuria *f.* agastroneuria.
agenesia *f.* agenesia, agenesis.
  agenesia callosa callosal agenesis.
  agenesia cortical agenesia corticalis.
  agenesia del cuerpo calloso agenesia of the corpus callosum.
  agenesia gonadal gonadal agenesis.
  agenesia nuclear nuclear agenesia.
  agenesia ovárica ovarian agenesis.
  agenesia renal renal agenesis.
  agenesia del septum pellucidum septum pellucidum agenesia.
  agenesia tímica thymic agenesia.
  agenesia vaginal vaginal agenesis.
agenésico, -ca *adj.* agenesic.
agénesis *f.* agenesis.
ageniocefalia *f.* ageniocephaly.
agenitalismo *m.* agenitalism.
agenosoma *m.* agenosomus.
agenosomía *f.* agenosomia.
agente *m.* agent.
  agente de aclaramiento clearing agent.
  agente activador activating agent.
  agente alquilante alkylating agent.
  agente ansiolítico, agente antiansiedad antianxiety agent.
  agente antineoplásico antineoplastic agent.
  agente antipsicótico antipsychotic agent.
  agente bloqueador, agente bloqueante blocking agent.
  agente bloqueador de los canales del calcio calcium channel blocking agent.
  agente bloqueador de los canales lentos slow channel blocking agent.
  agente bloqueador de los receptores beta-adrenérgicos beta-adrenergic receptor blocking agent.
  agente bloqueador neuromuscular neuromuscular blocking agent.
  agente bloqueador neuromuscular despo-

larizante depolarizing neuromuscular blocking agent.
  agente bloqueador neuromuscular no despolarizante non-depolarizing neuromuscular blocking agent.
  agente de bloqueo adrenérgico adrenergic blocking agent.
  agente de bloqueo adrenérgico alfa alpha-adrenergic blocking agent.
  agente de bloqueo adrenérgico beta beta-adrenergic-blocking agent.
  agente de bloqueo colinérgico cholinergic blocking agent.
  agente de bloqueo de neuronas adrenérgicas, agente de bloqueo neural adrenérgico adrenergic neuron blocking agent, adrenergic neuronal blocking agent.
  agente de bloqueo ganglionar ganglionic blocking agent.
  agente de cambio change agent.
  agente caudalizante caudalizing agent.
  agente ceruminolítico ceruminolytic agent.
  agente de coriza de chimpancé chimpanzee coryza agent.
  agente diluyente diluting agent.
  agente dispersante dispersing agent.
  agente dorsalizante dorsalizing agent.
  agente de levigación levigating agent.
  agente embolizador embolization agent.
  agente enmascarador masking agent.
  agente farmacológico pharmacological agent.
  agente fijadores fixing agent.
  agente mesodermalizador mesodermalizing agent.
  agente midriático y ciclopéjico mydriatic and cyclopegic agent.
  agente naranja agent orange.
  agente neuroléptico neuroleptic agent.
  agente oxidante oxidizing agent.
  agente progestacional progestational agent.
  agente quelante chelating agent.
  agente químico chemical agent.
  agente quimioterápico chemotherapeutic agent.
  agente reductor reducing agent.
  agente sinérgico synergistic agent.
  agente sulfatante sulfiting agent.
  agente tensioactivo surfactant agent.
  agente teratógeno teratogenic agent.
  agente transformador, agente transformante transforming agent.
agerasia *f.* agerasia.
agiria *f.* agyria.
agírico, -ca *adj.* agyric.
agitación *f.* agitation.
  agitación psicomotriz pyschomotor agitation.
agitado, -da *adj.* agitated.
aglaucopsia *f.* aglaucopsia, aglaukopsia.
aglicosuria *f.* aglycosuria.
aglicosúrico, -ca *adj.* aglycosuric.
aglobulia *f.* aglobulia.
aglobulismo *f.* aglobulism.
aglomeración *f.* agglomeration.
aglomerado, -da *adj.* agglomerated, agglomerate.
aglosia *f.* aglossia.
aglosostomía *f.* aglossostomia.
aglucemia *f.* aglycemia.
aglutinable *adj.* agglutinable.
aglutinación *f.* agglutination.
  aglutinación ácida acid agglutination.
  aglutinación bacteriógena bacteriogenic agglutination.
  aglutinación cruzada cross agglutination.

aglutinación fría, aglutinación de frío cold agglutination.

aglutinación de grupo group agglutination.

aglutinación H H agglutination.

aglutinación inmune immune agglutination.

aglutinación no inmune non-immune agglutination.

aglutinación O O agglutination.

aglutinación plaquetaria platelet agglutination.

aglutinación perceptiva perceptive agglutination.

aglutinación salina salt agglutination.

aglutinación somática somatic agglutination.

aglutinador, -ra *adj.* agglutinating.

aglutinante *adj.* agglutinant.

aglutinativo, -va *adj.* agglutinative.

aglutinina *f.* agglutinin.

aglutinina anti-RH anti-RH agglutinin.

aglutinina caliente warm agglutinin.

aglutinina completa complete agglutinin.

aglutinina específica major agglutinin.

aglutininas esperada expected aglutinin.

aglutinina flagelar flagellar agglutinin.

aglutinina fría cold agglutinin.

aglutinina de grupo group agglutinin.

aglutinina incompleta incomplete agglutinin.

aglutinina inesperada unexpected agglutinin.

aglutinina inmune immune agglutinin.

aglutinina de Leptospira Leptospira agglutinin.

aglutinina leucocitaria leukocyte agglutinin.

aglutinina mayor major agglutinin.

aglutinina menor minor agglutinin.

aglutinina MG MG agglutinin.

aglutinina normal normal agglutinin.

aglutinina parcial partial agglutinin.

aglutinina principal chief agglutinin.

aglutinina de reacción cruzada cross-reacting agglutinin.

aglutinina salina saline agglutinin.

aglutinina somática somatic agglutinin.

aglutinina T T agglutinin.

aglutinogénico, -ca *adj.* agglutinogenic.

aglutinógeno *m.* agglutinogen.

aglutinoscopio *m.* agglutinoscope.

aglutogénico, -ca *adj.* agglutogenic.

agmantina *f.* agmantine.

agminado, -da *adj.* agminated.

agnacia *f.* agnathia.

agnatia *f.* agnathia.

agnato, -ta *adj.* agnathous.

agnogénico, -ca *adj.* agnogenic.

agnosia *f.* agnosia.

agnosia auditiva acoustic agnosia, auditory agnosia.

agnosia cronológica time agnosia.

agnosia de fisionomías agnosia for faces.

agnosia de ideación ideational agnosia.

agnosia de la imagen corporal body-image agnosia.

agnosia digital finger agnosia.

agnosia óptica optic agnosia.

agnosia de reacción cruzada cross-reacting agnosia.

agnosia táctil tactile agnosia.

agnosia temporal time agnosia.

agnosia visual visual agnosia.

agnosia visuoespacial visual-spatial agnosia, visuospatial agnosia.

agónada *f.* agonad.

agonadal *adj.* agonadal.

agonadismo *m.* agonadism.

agonfiasis *f.* agomphiasis.

agonfo, -fa *adj.* agomphious.

agonfosis *f.* agomphosis.

agonía *f.* agony.

agónico, -ca *adj.* agonal.

agonista *adj.* agonist.

agorafilia *f.* agoraphilia.

agorafobia *f.* agoraphobia.

agorafóbico, -ca *adj.* agoraphobic.

agotamiento *m.* exhaustion.

agotamiento de combate combat exhaustion.

agotamiento nervioso nervous exhaustion.

agotamiento por calor heat exhaustion.

agotamiento por calor anhidrótico, agotamiento por calor del tipo II anhidrotic heat exhaustion, heat exhaustion type II.

agotar *v.* deplete.

agrafia *f.* agraphia.

agrafia absoluta absolute agraphia.

agrafia amnemónica agraphia amnemonica.

agrafia atáctica, agrafia atáxica agraphia atactica.

agrafia auditiva acoustic agraphia.

agrafia cerebral cerebral agraphia.

agrafia de desarrollo developmental agraphia.

agrafia jergal jargon agraphia.

agrafia literal literal agraphia.

agrafia mental mental agraphia.

agrafia motora motor agraphia.

agrafia musical musical agraphia.

agrafia verbal verbal agraphia.

agráfico, -ca *adj.* agraphic.

agrafoestesia *f.* agraphesthesia.

agramática *f.* agrammatica.

agramatismo *m.* agrammatism.

agrandamiento *m.* enlargement.

agrandamiento cervical cervical enlargement.

agrandamiento gingival gingival enlargement.

agranulocito *m.* agranulocyte.

agranulocitosis *f.* agranulocytosis.

agranulocitosis infantil genética infantile genetic agranulocytosis.

agranulocitosis de Kostman Kostman's disease.

agranuloplásico, -ca *adj.* agranuloplastic.

agranuloplástico, -ca *adj.* agranuloplastic.

agranulosis *f.* agranulosis.

agravante *adj.* aggravating.

agravar *v.* aggravate.

agregación *f.* aggregation.

agregación de hematíes red cell aggregation.

agregación familiar familial aggregation.

agregación plaquetaria aggregation of platelets, platelet aggregation.

agregado, -da *adj.* aggregated.

agregar *v.* aggregate.

agregometría *f.* aggregometry.

agregómetro *m.* aggregometer.

agremia *f.* agremia.

agresión *f.* aggression.

agresión autodestructiva inward aggression.

agresión constructiva constructive aggression.

agresión destructiva destructive aggression.

agresión instrumental instrumental aggression.

agresión interna inward aggression.

agresión pasiva passive aggression.

agresión sexual sexual assault.

agresividad *f.* aggressivity, aggressiveness.

agresivo, -va *adj.* aggressive.

agresología *f.* agressology.

agrio, -a *adj.* sour.

agripnia *f.* agrypnia.

agrumar *v.* clump.

agrupación *f.* assortment.

agrupamiento *m.* grouping.

agrupamiento sanguíneo blood grouping.

agrura *f.* acor.

agua *f.* water.

agudeza *f.* acuity.

agudeza de resolución resolution acuity.

agudeza de Vernier Vernier acuity.

agudeza visual visual acuity.

agudo, -da *adj.* acute.

ague *m.* ague.

ague agitante shaking ague.

ague cotidiano quotidian ague.

ague cuartano quartan ague.

ague de los fundidores de latón brass-founder's ague, brass foundry worker ague.

ague quintano quintan ague.

ague terciano tertian ague.

aguja *f.* needle.

aguja de Abraham Abram's needle.

aguja de aneurisma aneurysm needle.

aguja aspiradora, aguja aspirante, aguja de aspiración aspirating needle, aspiration needle.

aguja atraumática atraumatic needle.

aguja de Babcock Babcock's needle.

aguja para biopsia biopsy needle.

aguja de bisturí knife needle.

aguja de Brockenbrough Brockenbrough's needle.

aguja de catarata cataract needle.

aguja de Chiba Chiba's needle.

aguja cilíndrica round needle.

aguja de Colapinto Colapinto's needle.

aguja de Cope Cope's needle.

aguja de corte biopsy needle.

aguja-cuchilla knife needle.

aguja cutánea skinny needle.

aguja de Deschamps Deschamps needle.

aguja de doble acceso double entry needle.

aguja de Emmet Emmet's needle.

aguja endovenosa intravenous needle.

aguja en espátula spatula needle.

aguja exploradora exploring needle.

aguja fina fine needle.

aguja de Francke Francke's needle.

aguja de Frazier Frazier's needle.

aguja de Gillmore Gillmore needle.

aguja gruesa biopsy needle.

aguja de Hagedorn Hagedorn needle.

aguja hipodérmica hypodermic needle.

aguja intramuscular intramuscular needle.

aguja intravenosa intravenous needle.

aguja de Kopan Kopan's needle.

aguja de ligadura ligature needle.

aguja de Menghini Menghini needle.

aguja para punción lumbar lumbar puncture needle.

aguja de radio radium needle.

aguja recta straight needle.

aguja redonda round needle.

aguja de Reverdin Reverdin's needle.

aguja de Salah para punción esternal Salah's sternal puncture needle.

aguja de stop stop needle.

aguja con tope stop needle.

aguja triangular triangular needle.

aguja de Tuohy Tuohy's needle.

aguja para vena del cuero cabelludo scalp vein needle.

aguja de Vim-Silverman Vim-Silverman needle.

agujero *m.* foramen.

agujetas *f.* stitch.

agutí *m.* agouti.
ahaptoglobinemia *f.* ahaptoglobinemia.
ahistidasia *f.* ahistidasia.
ahogamiento *m.* drowning.
 ahogamiento incompleto near drowning.
 ahogamiento secundario secondary drowning.
ahogamiento *m.* suffocation.
ahogo *m.* choke.
ainhum *m.* ainhum.
aire *m.* air.
 aire alveolar alveolar air.
 aire comprimido compressed air.
 aire confinado stale air.
 aire estacionario stationary air.
 aire facticio factitious air.
 aire líquido liquid air.
 aire de reserva reserve air.
airear *v.* aerate.
aislado, -da *adj.* isolated.
aislamiento[1] *m.* insulation.
aislamiento[2] *m.* isolation.
 aislamiento conductal behavioral isolation.
 aislamiento de actitud attitudinal isolation.
 aislamiento genético genetic isolate.
 aislamiento infeccioso infectious isolation.
 aislamiento inverso reversed isolation.
 aislamiento protector protective isolation.
 aislamiento social social isolation.
aislante *m.* insulator, isolator.
 aislante quirúrgico surgical isolator.
ajuste *m.* adjustment.
 ajuste falángico phalangeal adjustment.
akantion *m.* akanthion.
akatama *f.* akatama.
akatamatesia akatamathesia.
akathisia *f.* akathisia.
ala *f.* wing, ala.
alacestesia *f.* allachesthesia.
alacrima *f.* alacrima.
alactasia *f.* alactasia.
alactasis *f.* alactasia.
alalia *f.* alalia.
 alalia cófica alalia cophica.
 alalia fisiológica alalia physiologica.
 alalia orgánica alalia organica.
 alalia prolongada alalia prolongata.
alálico, -ca *adj.* alalic.
alambrar *v.* wire.
alambrado *m.* wiring.
 alambrado de la abertura piriforme pyriform aperture wiring.
 alambrado de asa continua continuous loop wiring.
 alambrado de asa de Ivy Ivy loop wiring.
 alambrado circunferencial, alambrado en circunferencia circumferential wiring.
 alambrado craneofacial de suspensión craniofacial suspension wiring.
 alambrado de Ivy Ivy loop wiring.
 alambrado perialveolar perialveolar wiring.
 alambrado de Stout continuo Stout's wiring.
alambre *m.* wire.
 alambre de arcada completa full-arch wire.
 alambre de arcada regional sectional arch wire.
 alambre de arco, alambre de la arcada arch wire.
 alambre de arco ideal ideal arch wire.
 alambre de embolización embolization wire.
 alambre de Kirschner Kirschner's wire.
 alambre de ligadura ligature wire.
 alambre de ortodoncia orthodontic wire.
 alambre de separación, alambre separador separating wire.

alanina *f.* alanine.
alantiasis *f.* allantiasis.
alantocorion *m.* allantochorion.
alantogénesis *f.* allantogenesis.
alantoico, -ca *adj.* allantoic.
alantoide *adj.* allantoid.
alantoideo, -a *adj.* allantoidean.
alantoides *f.* allantois.
alantoidoangiópago *m.* allantoidoangiopagus.
alantoína *f.* allantoin.
alantoinuria *f.* allantoinuria.
alantotoxina *f.* allantotoxicon.
alar *adj.* alar.
alarma *f.* alarm.
alasoterapia *f.* allassotherapy.
alastrim *m.* alastrim.
alastrímico, -ca *adj.* alastrimic.
alaxis *f.* allaxis.
alba *adj.* alba.
albedo *m.* albedo.
 albedo retinae albedo retinae.
álbido, -da *adj.* albidus.
albidus albidus.
albinismo *m.* albinism.
 albinismo ocular ocular albinism.
 albinismo ocular autosómico recesivo (AROA) autosomal recessive ocular albinism (AROA).
 albinismo ocular tipo Forsius-Erikson ocular-type Forsius-Erikson albinism.
 albinismo oculocutáneo oculocutaneous albinism.
 albinismo oculocutáneo tirosinasa negativo (ty-neg) tyrosinase-negative oculocutaneous albinism.
 albinismo oculocutáneo tirosinasa positivo (ty-pos) tyrosinase-positive oculocutaneous albinism.
 albinismo parcial partial albinism.
 albinismo punctata oculocutáneo punctate oculocutaneous albinism.
 albinismo total, albinismo universal total albinism.
albino, -na *adj.* albino.
albinoidismo *m.* albinoidism.
albinótico, -ca *adj.* albinotic.
albocinéreo, -a *adj.* albocinereous.
albopapuloide *adj.* albopapuloide.
albugínea *f.* albuginea.
 albugínea penis albuginea penis.
albugíneo, -a *adj.* albugineous.
albugineotomía *f.* albugineotomy.
albuginitis *f.* albuginitis.
albugo *m.* albugo.
albumen *m.* albumen.
albumímetro *m.* albumimeter.
albúmina *f.* albumin.
 albúmina A albumin A.
 albúmina acetosoluble acetosoluble albumin.
 albúmina ácida acid albumin.
 albúmina alcalina alkali albumin.
 albúmina de Bence Jones Bence Jones albumin.
 albúmina circulante circulating albumin.
 albúmina derivada derived albumin.
 albúmina hematina hematin albumin.
 albúmina de huevo egg albumin.
 albúmina humana human albumin.
 albúmina muscular muscle albumin.
 albúmina nativa native albumin.
 albúmina normal del suero humano normal human serum albumin.
 albúmina orgánica organ albumin.

 albúmina de Patein Patein's albumin.
 albúmina sanguínea blood albumin.
 albúmina sérica serum albumin.
 albúmina sérica humana normal normal human serum albumin.
 albúmina sérica humana yodada 131 I iodinated 131 I human serum albumin.
 albúmina sérica radioyodada radioiodinated serum albumin (RISA).
 albúmina sérica yodada con 125 I iodinated 125 I serum albumin.
 albúmina vegetal vegetable albumin.
albuminato *m.* albuminate.
albuminaturia *f.* albuminaturia.
albuminemia *f.* albuminemia.
albuminífero, -ra *adj.* albuminiferous.
albuminimetría *f.* albuminimetry.
albuminímetro *m.* albuminimeter.
albuminíparo, -ra *adj.* albuminiparous.
albuminocitológico, -ca *adj.* albuminocytological.
albuminocolia *f.* albuminocholia.
albuminógeno, -na *adj.* albuminogenous.
albuminoide *m. y adj.* albuminoid.
albuminolisina *f.* albuminolysin.
albuminólisis *f.* albuminolysis.
albuminómetro *m.* albuminometer.
albuminona *f.* albuminone.
albuminoptisis *f.* albuminoptysis.
albuminorrea *f.* albuminorrhea.
albuminorreacción *f.* albuminoreaction.
albuminosa *f.* albuminose.
albuminoscopio *m.* albumoscope.
albuminosis *f.* albuminosis.
albuminoso, -sa *adj.* albuminous.
albuminurético, -ca *adj.* albuminuretic.
albuminuria *f.* albuminuria.
 albuminuria accidental accidental albuminuria.
 albuminuria de la adolescencia, albuminuria de los adolescentes adolescent albuminuria.
 albuminuria adventicia adventitious albuminuria.
 albuminuria alimentaria dietetic albuminuria.
 albuminuria de los atletas albuminuria of athletes.
 albuminuria benigna benign albuminuria.
 albuminuria cardíaca cardiac albuminuria.
 albuminuria cíclica cyclic albuminuria.
 albuminuria clinostática hypostatic albuminuria.
 albuminuria colicuativa colliquative albuminuria.
 albuminuria dietética dietetic albuminuria.
 albuminuria digestiva digestive albuminuria.
 albuminuria esencial essential albuminuria.
 albuminuria espontánea adventitious albuminuria.
 albuminuria espuria adventitious albuminuria.
 albuminuria falsa false albuminuria.
 albuminuria febril febrile albuminuria.
 albuminuria fisiológica physiologic albuminuria, physiological albuminuria.
 albuminuria funcional functional albuminuria.
 albuminuria hematógena hematogenous albuminuria.
 albuminuria hémica hemic albuminuria.
 albuminuria hematógena de Bamberger Bamberger's albuminuria, Bamberger's hematogenic albuminuria.

albuminuria hipostática hypostatic albuminuria.

albuminuria intermitente intermittent albuminuria.

albuminuria intrínseca intrinsic albuminuria.

albuminuria lordótica lordotic albuminuria.

albuminuria neuropática neuropathic albuminuria.

albuminuria ortostática, albuminuria ortótica orthostatic albuminuria.

albuminuria palpatoria palpatory albuminuria.

albuminuria paroxismal paroxysmal albuminuria.

albuminuria posrenal postrenal albuminuria.

albuminuria postural postural albuminuria.

albuminuria prerrenal prerenal albuminuria.

albuminuria recurrente recurrent albuminuria.

albuminuria residual residual albuminuria.

albuminuria sérica serous albuminuria.

albuminuria tóxica toxic albuminuria.

albuminuria transitoria transient albuminuria.

albuminuria verdadera true albuminuria.

albuminurofobia *f.* albuminurophobia.

albumoide *m.* alumoid.

albumosa *f.* albumose.

albumosa de Bence Jones Bence Jones albumose.

albumoscopio *m.* albumoscope.

albumosemia *f.* albumosemia.

albumosuria *f.* albumosuria.

albumosuria de Bence Jones Bence Jones albumosuria.

albumosuria de Bradshaw Bradshaw's albumosuria.

alcalemia *f.* alkalemia.

alcalescencia *f.* alkalescence.

alcalescente *adj.* alkalescent.

álcali *m.* alkali.

Alcaligenes Alcaligenes.

alcalígeno, -na *adj.* alkaligenous.

alcalimetría *f.* alkalimetry.

alcalímetro *m.* alkalimeter.

alcalinidad *f.* alkalinity.

alcalinización *f.* alkalinization.

alcalinizador *m.* alkalizer, alkalinizing.

alcalinizar *v.* alkalify, alkalinize, alkalize.

alcalino, -na *adj.* alkaline.

alcalinuria *f.* alkalinuria.

alcalipenia *f.* alkalipenia.

alcaliterapia *f.* alkalitherapy.

alcalización *f.* alkalization.

alcalizador *m.* alkalizer.

alcalógeno, -na *adj.* alkalogenic.

alcaloide *m.* alkaloid.

alcalometría *f.* alkalometry.

alcalosis *f.* alkalosis.

alcalosis por acapnia respiratory alkalosis.

alcalosis por la altura altitude alkalosis.

alcalosis compensada compensated alkalosis.

alcalosis descompensada decompensated alkalosis.

alcalosis hipopotasémica hypokalemic alkalosis.

alcalosis hipocaliémica, alcalosis hipokaliémica hypokalemic alkalosis.

alcalosis hipoclorémica hypochloremic alkalosis.

alcalosis metabólica metabolic alkalosis.

alcalosis respiratoria respiratory alkalosis.

alcaloterapia *f.* alkalitherapy.

alcalótico, -ca *adj.* alkalotic.

alcaluria *f.* alkaluria.

alcanfor *m.* camphor.

alcanforáceo, -a *adj.* camphoraceous.

alcanforado, -da *adj.* camphorated.

alcanforismo *m.* camphorism.

alcanina *f.* alkanin.

alcanzadores *m.* reachers.

alcaptona *f.* alcapton, alkapton.

alcaptonuria *f.* alkaptonuria.

alcaptonúrico, -ca *adj.* alkaptonuric.

alcohol *m.* alcohol.

alcoholemia *f.* alcoholemia.

alcohólico, -ca *adj.* alcoholic.

alcohólisis *f.* alcoholysis.

alcoholismo *m.* alcoholism.

alcoholismo agudo acute alcoholism.

alcoholismo alfa alpha alcoholism.

alcoholismo beta beta alcoholism.

alcoholismo crónico chronic alcoholism.

alcoholismo delta delta alcoholism.

alcoholismo gamma gamma alcoholism.

alcoholización *f.* alcoholization.

alcoholizar *v.* alcoholize.

alcohología *f.* alcohology.

alcoholómetro *m.* alcoholometer.

alcoholresistente *adj.* alcohol-fast.

alcoholuria *f.* alcoholuria.

aldehído *m.* aldehyde.

aldosterona *f.* aldosterone.

aldosteronemia *f.* aldosteronemia.

aldosteronismo *m.* aldosteronism.

aldosteronismo idiopático idiopathic.

aldosteronismo primario primary aldosteronism.

aldosteronismo secundario secondary aldosteronism.

aldosteronismo seudoprimario pseudoprimary aldosteronism.

aldosteronogénesis *f.* aldosteronogenesis.

aldosteronoma *m.* aldosteronoma.

aldosteronopenia *f.* aldosteronopenia.

aldosteronuria *f.* aldosteronuria.

alecia *f.* alethia.

alélico, -ca *adj.* allelic.

alelismo *m.* allelism.

alelo *m.* allele.

alelo amorfo silent allele.

alelo codominante codominant allele.

alelo dominante dominant allele.

alelo isomorfo codominant allele.

alelo múltiple multiple allele.

alelo recesivo recessive allele.

alelo silencioso silent allele.

alelocatálisis *f.* allelocatalysis.

alelognatia *f.* allelognathia.

alelomórfico, -ca *adj.* allelomorphic.

alelomorfismo *m.* allelomosphism.

alelomorfo *m.* allelomorph.

aleloquímica *f.* allelochemics.

alelotaxia *f.* allelotaxy.

alelotaxis *f.* allelotaxy.

alemal *adj.* alemmal.

alentesis *f.* allenthesis.

alergénico, -ca *adj.* allergenic.

alergeno *m.* allergen.

alergeno del polen pollen allergen.

alergia *f.* allergy.

alergia alimentaria food allergy.

alergia atópica atopic allergy.

alergia bacteriana bacterial allergy.

alergia bronquial bronchial allergy.

alergia de contacto, alergia por contacto contact allergy.

alergia espontánea spontaneous allergy.

alergia a fármacos drug allergy.

alergia física physical allergy.

alergia fisiológica induced allergy.

alergia al frío cold allergy.

alergia hereditaria hereditary allergy.

alergia inmediata immediate allergy.

alergia a la insulina insulin allergy.

alergia latente latent allergy.

alergia medicamentosa drug allergy.

alergia normal induced allergy.

alergia al polen pollen allergy.

alergia polivalente multiple allergy, polyvalent allergy.

alergia provocada induced allergy.

alergia retardada delayed allergy.

alergia tardía delayed allergy.

alérgico, -ca *adj.* allergic.

alérgide *m.* allergid.

alergista *m., f.* allergist.

alergización *f.* allergization.

alergizado, -da *adj.* allergized.

alergizar *v.* allergize.

alergodermia *f.* allergodermia.

alergoide *m.* allergoid.

alergología *f.* allergology.

alergológico, -ca *adj.* allergological.

alergólogo, -ga *m., f.* allergologist.

alergometría *f.* allergometry.

alergosis *f.* allergosis.

alestesia *f.* allesthesia, alloesthesia.

aleta *f.* flange.

aleta bucal buccal flange.

aleta labial labial flange.

aleta lingual lingual flange.

aleta de mordida bite-wing.

aleteo *m.* flutter.

aleteo atrial atrial flutter.

aleteo auricular auricular flutter.

aleteo diafragmático diaphragmatic flutter.

aleteo impuro impure flutter.

aleteo nasal nasal flaring, flaring of the nostrils.

aleteo ocular ocular flutter.

aleteo ventricular ventricular flutter.

aleteo-fibrilación flutter-fibrillation.

aletia *f.* alethia.

aletocito *m.* aletocyte.

aletia *f.* alethia.

aleucemia *f.* aleucemia, aleukemia.

aleucemia alimentaria tóxica alimentary toxic aleucemia.

aleucemia hemorrágica aleucemia hemorrhagica.

aleucémico, -ca *adj.* aleukemic.

aleucia *f.* aleukia.

aleucocítico, -ca *adj.* aleukocytic.

aleucocitosis *f.* aleukocytosis.

aleuronoide *adj.* aleuronoid.

alexetérico, -ca *adj.* alexeteric.

alexia *f.* alexia.

alexia cortical cortical alexia.

alexia incompleta incomplete alexia.

alexia motora motor alexia.

alexia musical musical alexia.

alexia subcortical subcortical alexia.

aléxico, -ca *adj.* alexic.

alexifármaco, -ca *m. y adj.* alexipharmic.

alexínico, -ca *adj.* alexinic.

alexipirético, -ca *adj.* alexipyretic.

alexitimia *f.* alexithymia.

aleydigismo *m.* aleydigism.

alfa1-antitripsina *f.* alpha1-antitrypsin.

alfa-beta-bloqueante *f.* alpha-beta-blocker.

alfabloqueador *m.* alpha-blocker.

alfa-fetoproteína (AFP) *f.* alpha-fetoprotein (AFP).

alfa-globulina *f.* alpha-globulin.

alfahipofamina *f.* alpha-hypophamine.

alfa-lipoproteína *f.* alpha-lipoprotein.
alfalítico, -ca *adj.* alphalytic.
alfa2-macroglobulina *f.* alpha2-macroblogulin.
alfa-metildopa *f.* alpha-methyl dopa.
alfamimético, -ca *adj.* alphamimetic.
alfonsino *m.* alphonsin.
alfos *m.* alphos.
alganestesia *f.* alganesthesia.
algefaciente *adj.* algefacient.
algeoscopia *f.* algeoscopy.
algesia *f.* algesia.
algésico, -ca *adj.* algesic, algetic.
algesicronómetro *m.* algesichronometer.
algesidistrofia *f.* algesidystrophy.
algesimetría *f.* algesimetry.
algesímetro *m.* algesimeter.
algesiogénico, -ca *adj.* algesiogenic.
algesiógeno, -na *adj.* algesiogenic.
algestesia *f.* algesthesia, algesthesis.
algestesis *f.* algesthesis.
algestona acetofenida *f.* algestone acetophenide.
algético, -ca *adj.* algesic, algetic.
algia *f.* pain.
  algia facial atípica atypical facial pain.
algidez *f.* algidity.
álgido, -da *adj.* algid.
algina *f.* algin.
alginuresis *f.* dysuria.
algioglandular *adj.* algioglandular.
algiometabólico, -ca *adj.* algiometabolic.
algiomotor, -ra *adj.* algiomotor.
algiomuscular *adj.* algiomuscular.
algiovascular *adj.* algiovascular.
algodistrofia *f.* algodystrophy.
algodón *m.* cotton.
algodoncillo *m.* thrush.
algofobia *f.* algophobia.
algogenesia *f.* algogenesia, algogenesis.
algogénesis *f.* algogenesia, algogenesis.
algogenia *f.* algogenesia.
algogénico, -ca *adj.* algogenic.
algolagnia *f.* algolagnia.
  algolagnia activa active algolagnia.
  algolagnia pasiva passive algolagnia.
algología *f.* algology.
algólogo, -ga *m., f.* algologist.
algomenorrea *f.* algomenorrhea.
algometría *f.* algometry.
algómetro *m.* algometer.
algoparálisis *f.* painful paralysis.
algoparesia *f.* painful paresis.
algopareunia *f.* algopareunia.
algopsicalia *f.* algopsychalia.
algor *m.* algor.
algoscopia *f.* algoscopy.
algosis *f.* algosis.
algospasmo *m.* algospasm.
algovascular *adj.* algovascular.
aliáceo, -a *adj.* alliaceous.
alianza *f.* alliance.
  alianza terapéutica therapeutic alliance.
  alianza de trabajo working alliance.
alible *adj.* alible.
alices *f.* alices.
alicíclico, -ca *adj.* alicyclic.
alicuorrea *f.* aliquorrhea.
alienación *f.* alienation.
alienación mental *f.* insanity.
alienia *f.* alienia.
alienismo *m.* alienism.
alienista *m., f.* alienist.
aliento *m.* breath.
  aliento fétido bad breath.

  aliento hepático liver breath.
  mal aliento bad breath.
  aliento plúmbico lead breath.
  aliento urémico uremic breath.
alifático, -ca *adj.* aliphatic.
aliforme *adj.* aliform.
aligeramiento *m.* lightening.
alimentación *f.* alimentation, feeding.
  alimentación al pecho breast feeding.
  alimentación artificial artificial alimentation, artificial feeding.
  alimentación con biberón bottle feeding.
  alimentación complementaria complementary feeding.
  alimentación de Finkelstein Finkelstein's feeding.
  alimentación del lactante infant feeding.
  alimentación extrabucal extrabuccal feeding.
  alimentación ficticia fictitious feeding.
  alimentación forzada forced alimentation, forcible feeding, forced feeding.
  alimentación gástrica gastric feeding.
  alimentación intravenosa intravenous feeding.
  alimentación mediante gastrostomía gastrostomy feeding.
  alimentación nasogástrica nasogastric feeding.
  alimentación parenteral parenteral alimentation.
  alimentación parenteral total total parenteral alimentation.
  alimentación por sonda tube feeding.
  alimentación rectal rectal alimentation.
  alimentación simulada sham feeding.
alimentario, -ria *adj.* alimentary.
alimenticio, -cia *adj.* nutritive.
alimento *m.* food.
  alimento dietético dietetic food.
  alimento equivalentes food exchange list.
  alimento formador de bases base-forming food.
  alimento orgánico organic food.
alimentología *f.* alimentology.
alimentoterapia *f.* alimentotherapy.
alinasal *adj.* alinasal.
alineación *f.* alignment.
  alineación del haz beam alignment.
alineamiento *m.* alignment.
  alineamiento defectuoso malalignment.
  alineamiento dental tooth alignment.
alinfia *f.* alymphia.
alinfocitosis *f.* alymphocytosis.
alinfoplasia *f.* alymphoplasia.
  alinfoplasia tímica thymic alymphoplasia.
  alinfoplasia tímica de tipo Nezelof Nezelof type of thymic alymphoplasia.
alinfopotente *adj.* alymphopotent.
alipogenético, -ca *adj.* alipogenic, alipogenetic.
alipotrópico, -ca *adj.* alipotropic.
alisfenoide *adj.* alisphenoid.
aliviar *v.* relieve.
aliviadero interdentario interdental spillway.
alivio *m.* relief.
almidón *m.* starch.
almohadilla *f.* pad.
  almohadilla abdominal abdominal pad.
  almohadilla adiposa fat pad.
  almohadilla adiposa de Bichat Bichat's fat pad.
  almohadilla de agua waterpad.
  almohadilla de alimentación dinner pad.
  almohadilla para callo corn pad.

  almohadilla en donut donut pad.
  almohadilla grasa fat pad.
  almohadilla grasa bucal buccal fat pad.
  almohadilla grasa infrarrotuliana infrapatellar fat pad.
  almohadilla de Kelly Kelly's pad.
  almohadilla de laparotomía laparotomy pad.
  almohadilla navicular navicular pad.
  almohadilla de los nudillos knuckle pad.
  almohadilla de Passavant Passavant's pad.
  almohadilla pélvica girdle pad.
  almohadilla periarterial periarterial pad.
  almohadilla renal kidney pad.
  almohadilla retromolar retromolar pad.
  almohadilla de succión sucking pad, suctorial pad.
almorrana *f.* pile.
aloalbúmina *f.* alloalbumin.
aloalbuminemia *f.* alloalbuminemia.
aloanticuerpo *m.* alloantibody.
aloantígeno *m.* alloantigen.
alobiosis *f.* allobiosis.
alocéntrico, -ca *adj.* allocentric.
alocinesia *f.* allocinesia, allokinesia.
alocinético, -ca *adj.* allokinetic.
alocitófilo, -la *adj.* allocytophilic.
alocoloide *m.* allocolloid.
alocorteza *f.* allocortex.
alocroísmo *m.* allochroism.
alocromasia *f.* allochromasia.
alodinia *f.* allodynia.
alodiploide *adj.* allodiploid.
alodiploidia *f.* allodiploidy.
alodromia *f.* allodromy.
aloeroticismo *m.* alloeroticism.
aloerotismo *m.* alloerotism.
aloestesia *f.* alloesthesia.
alofanamida *f.* allophanamide.
alóforo, -ra *adj.* allophore.
aloftalmia *f.* allophtalmia.
alogamia *f.* allogamia.
alogénico, -ca *adj.* allogeneic, allogenic.
alogotrofia *f.* allogotrophia.
alogrupo *m.* allogroup.
aloinjerto *m.* allograft.
aloinmune *adj.* alloimmune.
aloinmunización *f.* alloimmunization.
alomería *f.* allomerism.
alomerismo *m.* allomerism.
alometría *f.* allometry.
alométrico, -ca *adj.* allometric.
alomorfismo *m.* allomorphism.
alónomo, -ma *adj.* allonomous.
alópata *m., f.* allopath, allopathist.
alopatía *f.* allopathy.
alopático, -ca *adj.* allopathic.
alopecia *f.* alopecia.
  alopecia adnata alopecia adnata.
  alopecia androgénica androgenetic alopecia, androgenic alopecia, alopecia androgenetica.
  alopecia apolillada moth-eaten alopecia.
  alopecia areata alopecia areata.
  alopecia capitis totalis alopecia capitis totalis.
  alopecia celsi alopecia celsi.
  alopecia cicatricial, alopecia cicatrisata cicatricial alopecia.
  alopecia circunscrita alopecia circumscripta.
  alopecia comida por polilla moth-eaten alopecia.
  alopecia por compresión pressure alopecia.
  alopecia congénita congenital alopecia, alopecia congenitalis.
  alopecia de distribución masculina male pattern alopecia.

alopecia de estrés stress alopecia.
alopecia farmacológica drug alopecia.
alopecia fisiológica physiologic alopecia.
alopecia generalizada alopecia generalisata.
alopecia hereditaria alopecia hereditaria.
alopecia de Jonston Jonston's alopecia.
alopecia liminar alopecia liminaris.
alopecia liminaris frontalis alopecia liminaris frontalis.
alopecia marginal, alopecia marginalis alopecia marginalis.
alopecia marginal traumática marginal traumatic alopecia.
alopecia medicamentosa alopecia medicamentosa.
alopecia mucinosa alopecia mucinosa.
alopecia orbicular alopecia orbicularis.
alopecia pitiroides, alopecia pityrodes alopecia pityroides, alopecia pityrodes.
alopecia de patrón masculino male pattern alopecia.
alopecia posparto postpartum alopecia.
alopecia prematura premature alopecia, alopecia prematura.
alopecia por presión pressure alopecia.
alopecia psicógena psychogenic alopecia.
alopecia por radiación radiation alopecia.
alopecia por rayos X X-ray alopecia.
alopecia seborreica alopecia seborrheica.
alopecia senil senile alopecia, alopecia senilis.
alopecia sifilítica syphilitic alopecia, alopecia syphilitica.
alopecia sintomática symptomatic alopecia, alopecia symptomatica.
alopecia de tipo masculino male pattern alopecia.
alopecia total alopecia totalis.
alopecia tóxica alopecia toxica.
alopecia traumática traumatic alopecia.
alopecia traumática marginal traumatic marginal alopecia.
alopecia universal alopecia universalis.
alopécico, -ca *adj.* alopecic.
alopentaploide *adj.* allopentaploid.
aloplasia *f.* alloplasia.
aloplastia *f.* alloplasty.
aloplástico, -ca *adj.* alloplastic.
aloplasto *m.* alloplast.
aloploide *adj.* alloploid.
alopoliploide *adj.* allopolyploid.
alopoliploidía *f.* allopolyploidy.
alopsíquico, -ca *adj.* allopsychic.
aloquecia *f.* allochetia, allochezia.
aloqueratoplastia *f.* allokeratoplasty.
aloquia *f.* alochia.
alorrítmico, -ca *adj.* allorhythmic.
alosensibilización *f.* allosensitization.
alosoma *m.* allosome.
alosteria *f.* allostery.
alostérico, -ca *adj.* allosteric.
alosterismo *m.* allosterism.
alotetraploide *adj.* allotetraploid.
alotipia *f.* allotypy.
alotípico, -ca *adj.* allotypic.
alotipo *m.* allotype.
  alotipo Am Am allotype.
  alotipo Gm Gm allotype.
  alotipo Inv Inv allotype.
  alotipo Km Km allotype.
  alotipo Oz Oz allotype.
alotopia *f.* allotopia.
alotópico, -ca *adj.* allotopic.
alotoxina *f.* allotoxin.
alotrasplante *m.* allotransplantation.
alotrílico, -ca *adj.* allotrylic.

alotriodoncia *f.* allotriodontia.
alotriodontia *f.* allotriodontia.
alotriolito *m.* allothriolith.
alotriploide *adj.* allotriploid.
alotriuria *f.* allotriuria.
alotrófico, -ca *adj.* allotrophic.
alotropía *f.* allotropy.
alotropismo *m.* allotropism.
aloxina *f.* alloxin.
aloxuremia *f.* alloxuremia.
aloxuria *f.* alloxuria.
aloxúrico, -ca *adj.* alloxuric.
alta *f.* discharge.
  alta definitiva absolute discharge.
  alta involuntaria involuntary discharge.
  alta sin permiso (ASP) absent without leave (AWOL).
alteración *f.* alteration.
  alteración cualitativa qualitative alteration.
  alteración cuantitativa quantitative alteration.
  alteración modal modal alteration.
  alteración nerviosa nervous breakdown.
  alteración del nivel de consciencia (ANC) altered state of consciousness (ASC).
alteregoísmo *m.* alteregoism.
alternación *f.* alternation.
  alternación cardiaca cardiac alternation.
  alternación concordante concordant alternation.
  alternación discordante discordant alternation.
  alternación mecánica mechanical alternation.
alternancia *f.* alternans.
  alternancia auditiva auditory alternans.
  alternancia auscultatoria auscultatory alternans.
  alternancia eléctrica electrical alternans.
  alternancia de generaciones alternation of generations.
  alternancia del pulso pulsus alternans.
alternante *adj.* alternating.
altruismo *m.* altruism.
altura *f.* height.
  altura apical apex height.
  altura del contorno height of contour.
  altura cuspídea cusp height.
  altura facial facial height.
  altura facial anterior anterior facial height.
  altura facial inferior lower facial height.
  altura facial posterior posterior facial height.
  altura facial superior upper facial height.
  altura del fondo del útero fundal height.
  altura límite del contorno surveyed height of contour.
  altura nasal nasal height.
  altura orbitaria orbital height.
alucinación *f.* hallucination.
  alucinación alcohólica alcoholic hallucination.
  alucinación auditiva auditory hallucination.
  alucinación cenestésica kinesthetic hallucination.
  alucinación consciente hallucinosis.
  alucinación gustativa gustatory hallucination.
  alucinación háptica haptic hallucination.
  alucinaciónhipnagógica hypnagogic hallucination.
  alucinación hipnopómpica hypnopompic hallucination.
  alucinación liliputiense Lilliputian hallucination.
  alucinación del muñón stump hallucination.

  alucinación olfatoria olfactory hallucination.
  alucinación somática somatic hallucination.
  alucinación táctil tactile hallucination.
  alucinación visual visual hallucination.
  alucinación visual formada formed visual hallucination.
  alucinación visual no formada unformed visual hallucination.
alucinante *adj.* hallucinotic.
alucinógeno *m.* hallucinogen.
alucinosis *f.* hallucinosis.
  alucinosis aguda acute hallucinosis.
  alucinosis orgánica organic hallucinosis.
alumbramiento *m.* accouchement.
alumbre *m.* alum.
alumbre-hematoxilina alum-hematoxylin.
aluminosis *f.* aluminosis.
alveobronquiolitis *f.* alveobronchiolitis.
alveolectomía *f.* alveolectomy.
alveólisis *f.* alveolysis.
alveolitis *f.* alveolitis.
  alveolitis alérgica, alveolitis alérgica extrínseca allergic alveolitis, extrinsic allergic alveolitis.
  alveolitis pulmonar aguda acute pulmonary alveolitis.
  alveolitis seca dolorosa alveolitis sicca dolorosa.
alvéolo, alveolo *m.* socket, alveolus.
  alvéolo seco dry socket.
alveolobronquiolitis *f.* alveolobronchiolitis.
alveoloclasia *f.* alveoloclasia.
alveolodental *adj.* alveolodental.
alveololabial *adj.* alveololabial.
alveololingual *adj.* alveololingual.
alveolomerotomía *f.* alveolomerotomy.
alveolonasal *adj.* alveolonasal.
alveolopalatino, -na *adj.* alveolopalatal.
alveolotomía *f.* alveolotomy.
alvino, -na *adj.* alvine.
alvinolito *m.* alvinolith.
amacia *f.* amazia.
amacrina *adj.* amakrine.
amalgama *f.* amalgam.
  amalgama dental, amalgama dentaria dental amalgam.
amalgamable *adj.* amalgamable.
amalgamación *f.* amalgamation.
amalgamar *v.* amalgamate.
amamantar *v.* suckle.
Amanita Amanita.
amargo, -ga *adj.* bitter.
amarílico, -ca *adj.* amarilic.
amarillo *m.* yellow.
amartritis *f.* amarthritis.
amasado de píldoras pill-rolling.
amasamiento *m.* kneading.
amasesis *f.* amasesis.
amasténico, -ca *adj.* amasthenic.
amastia *f.* amastia.
amastigote *m.* amastigote.
amaurosis *f.* amaurosis.
  amaurosis central central amaurosis, amaurosis centralis, cerebral amaurosis.
  amaurosis por compresión pressure amaurosis.
  amaurosis congénita congenital amaurosis, amaurosis congenita.
  amaurosis congénita de Leber Leber's congenital amaurosis.
  amaurosis diabética diabetic amaurosis.
  amaurosis fugaz amaurosis fugax.
  amaurosis histérica hysteric amaurosis.
  amaurosis de ojo de gato cat's eye amaurosis.
  amaurosis parcial fugaz amaurosis partialis fugax.

amaurosis refleja reflex amaurosis.
amaurosis saburral saburral amaurosis.
amaurosis tóxica intoxication amaurosis, toxic amaurosis.
amaurótico, -ca *adj.* amaurotic.
ambageusia *f.* ambageusia.
ambidestreza *f.* ambidexterity.
ambidextrismo *m.* ambidextrality, ambidextrism.
ambidextro, -tra *adj.* ambidexter.
ambiente *m.* environment.
ambilateral *adj.* ambilateral.
ambilevo, -va *adj.* ambilevous.
ambilevosidad *f.* ambilevosity.
ambiopía *f.* ambiopia.
ambisexual *adj.* ambisexual.
ambisexualidad *f.* bisexuality.
ambivalencia *f.* ambivalence.
amblicromasia *f.* amblychromasia.
ambliopía *f.* amblyopia.
ambliopía alcohólica alcoholic amblyopia.
ambliopía anisométrica anisometropic amblyopia.
ambliopía arsenical arsenic amblyopia.
ambliopía axil axial amblyopia.
ambliopía de color color amblyopia.
ambliopía cromática color amblyopia.
ambliopía cruzada crossed amblyopia, amblyopia cruciata.
ambliopía por eclipse eclipse amblyopia.
ambliopía estrabísmica strabismic amblyopia.
ambliopía funcional functional amblyopia.
ambliopía histérica hysterical amblyopia.
ambliopía índice index amblyopia.
ambliopía nocturna nocturnal amblyopia.
ambliopía nutricional deficiency amblyopia, nutritional amblyopia.
ambliopía por privación deprivation amblyopia.
ambliopía por la quinina, ambliopía quínica quinine amblyopia.
ambliopía refleja reflex amblyopia.
ambliopía refractiva refractive amblyopia.
ambliopía relativa relative amblyopia.
ambliopía reversible reversible amblyopia.
ambliopía sensorial sensory amblyopia.
ambliopía tabáquica tobacco amblyopia.
ambliopía tóxica toxic amblyopia.
ambliopía traumática traumatic amblyopia.
ambliopía urémica uremic amblyopia.
ambliopiatría *f.* amblyopiatrics.
ambiópico, -ca *f.* amblyopic.
ambliocospio *m.* amblyoscope.
Amblyomma Amblyomma.
ambo *m.* ambo.
ambomaleal *adj.* ambomalleal.
ambón *m.* ambo.
ambulancia *f.* ambulance.
ambulatorio, -a *adj.* ambulant, ambulatory.
ambustión *f.* ambustion.
ameba *f.* ameba.
amebiasis *f.* amebiasis.
amebiasis cutis amebiasis cutis.
amebiasis hepática hepatic amebiasis.
amebiasis intestinal intestinal amebiasis.
amebiasis pulmonar pulmonary amebiasis.
amebicida *adj.* amebicidal.
amébico, -ca *adj.* amebic.
amebismo *m.* amebismo.
ameboide *adj.* ameboid.
ameboidismo *m.* ameboidismo.
ameboma *m.* ameboma.
ameburia *f.* ameburia.
amelanosis *f.* amelanosis.

amelanótico, -ca *adj.* amelanotic.
amelia *f.* amelia.
amelificación *f.* amelification.
amelo *m.* amelus.
ameloblasto *m.* ameloblast.
ameloblastoma *m.* adamantinoma.
ameloblastoma hipofisario pituitary adamantinoma.
ameloblastoma pigmentado pigmented adamantinoma.
amelogénesis *f.* amelogenesis.
amelogénesis imperfecta amelogenesis imperfecta.
amenia *f.* amenia.
amenorrea *f.* amenorrhea.
amenorrea alimentaria dietary amenorrhea.
amenorrea dietaria dietary amenorrhea.
amenorrea disponderal dysponderal amenorrhea.
amenorrea emocional emotional amenorrhea.
amenorrea por estrés stress amenorrhea.
amenorrea fisiológica physiologic amenorrhea.
amenorrea hiperprolactinémica hyperprolactinemic amenorrhea.
amenorrea hipofisaria hypophyseal amenorrhea.
amenorrea hipotalámica hypothalamic amenorrhea.
amenorrea de la lactación lactation amenorrhea.
amenorrea nutricional nutritional amenorrhea.
amenorrea ovárica ovarian amenorrhea.
amenorrea patológica pathologic amenorrhea.
amenorrea posparto amenorrhea postpartum.
amenorrea pospildora postpill amenorrhea.
amenorrea premenopáusica premenopausal amenorrhea.
amenorrea primaria primary amenorrhea.
amenorrea relativa relative amenorrhea.
amenorrea secundaria secondary amenorrhea.
amenorrea traumática traumatic amenorrhea.
amenorrea de las trotadoras jogger's amenorrhea.
amenorreico, -ca *adj.* amenorrheal, amenorrheic.
amensalismo *m.* amensalismo.
amerismo *m.* amerism.
amerístico, -ca *adj.* ameristic.
ametábolo, -la *adj.* ametabolon, ametabolous.
ametacromófilo, -la *adj.* ametachromophil.
ametaneutrófilo, -la *adj.* ametaneutrophil.
ametria *f.* ametria.
ametrómetro *m.* ametrometer.
ametropía *f.* ametropia.
ametropía axil axial ametropia.
ametropía de curvatura curvature ametropia.
ametropía de posición position ametropia.
ametropía de refracción refractive ametropia.
ametrópico, -ca *adj.* ametropic.
amiastenia *f.* amyasthenia.
amiasténico, -ca *f.* amyasthenic.
amiba *f.* ameba.
amifocito *m.* amebocyte.
amicrobiano, -na *adj.* amicrobic.
amicróbico, -ca *adj.* amicrobic.
amíctico, -ca *adj.* amyctic.

amículo *m.* amiculum.
amielencefalia *f.* amyelencephalia.
amielia *f.* amyelia.
amielínico, -ca *adj.* amyelinic.
amielo *m.* amyelus.
amielotrofia *f.* amyelotrophia.
amígdala *f.* amygdala, tonsil.
amigdalectomía *f.* amygdalectomy.
amigdalino, -na *adj.* amygdaline.
amigdalitis *f.* tonsillitis.
amigdalitis aguda acute tonsillitis.
amigdalitis caseosa caseous tonsillitis.
amigdalitis diftérica diphtheritic tonsillitis.
amigdalitis estreptocócica streptococcal tonsillitis.
amigdalitis folicular follicular tonsillitis.
amigdalitis herpética herpetic tonsillitis.
amigdalitis lacunar lacunar tonsillitis.
amigdalitis lenta tonsillitis lenta.
amigdalitis lingual lingual tonsillitis.
amigdalitis micótica mycotic tonsillitis.
amigdalitis parenquimatosa aguda acute parenchymatous tonsillitis.
amigdalitis preglótica preglottic tonsillitis.
amigdalitis superficial superficial tonsillitis.
amigdalitis supurativa suppurative tonsillitis.
amigdalitis de Vincent Vincent's tonsillitis.
amigdalohemisporosis *f.* tonsillohemisporosis.
amigdaloide *adj.* amygdaloid.
amigdalolito *m.* amygdalolith.
amigdaloidiosis *f.* tonsillooidiosis.
amigdaloprivo, -va *adj.* tonsilloprive.
amigdalopatía *f.* amygdalopathy.
amigdalotomía *f.* tonsillotomy.
amigdalótomo *m.* tonsillotome.
amiláceo, -a *adj.* amylaceous.
amilemia *f.* amylemia.
amilismo *m.* amylism.
amiloclástico, -ca *adj.* amyloclastic.
amilodispepsia *f.* amylodyspepsia.
amilofagia *f.* amylophagia.
amilogénesis *f.* amylogenesis.
amilogenia *f.* amylogenesis.
amilohidrólisis *f.* amylohydrolysis.
amiloide *m.* amyloid.
amiloidemia *f.* amyloidemia.
amiloidosis *f.* amyloidosis.
amiloidosis AA AA amyloidosis.
amiloidosis AL AL amyloidosis.
amiloidosis cutánea, amiloidosis cutis cutaneous amyloidosis, amyloidosis cutis.
amiloidosis de la edad amyloidosis of aging.
amiloidosis familiar familial amyloidosis.
amiloidosis focal focal amyloidosis.
amiloidosis hereditaria, amiloidosis heredofamiliar hereditary amyloidosis, heredofamilial amyloidosis.
amiloidosis idiopática idiopathic amyloidosis.
amiloidosis inmunoderivada immuno-cyte-derived amyloidosis.
amiloidosis inmunocítica inmunocytic amyloidosis.
amiloidosis en liquen lichen amyloidosis.
amiloidosis macular macular amyloidosis.
amiloidosis del mieloma múltiple amyloidosis of multiple myeloma.
amiloidosis neuropática hereditaria hereditary neuropathic amyloidosis.
amiloidosis nodular nodular amyloidosis.
amiloidosis pericolágena pericollagen amyloidosis.
amiloidosis primaria primary amyloidosis.
amiloidosis relacionada con cadenas lige-

ras light chain-related amyloidosis.
amiloidosis renal renal amyloidosis.
amiloidosis secundaria secondary amyloidosis.
amiloidosis senil senile amyloidosis.
amiloidosis sistémica reactiva reactive systemic amyloidosis.
amiloidosis de la vejez amyloidosis of aging.
amilólisis *f.* amylolysis.
amilolítico, -ca *adj.* amylolytic.
amilopeptinosis *f.* amylopeptinosis.
amiloplástico, -ca *adj.* amyloplastic.
amilorrea *f.* amylorrhea.
amilosíntesis *f.* amylosinthesis.
amilosis *f.* amylosis.
amilosuria *f.* amylosuria.
amiluria *f.* amyluria.
amimia *f.* amimie.
  amimia amnésica, amimia receptiva amnesic amimie.
aminoacidemia *f.* aminoacidemia.
aminoácido *m.* aminoacid.
  aminoácido esencial essential aminoacid.
  aminoácido no esencial non-essential aminoacid.
aminoacidopatía *f.* aminoacidopathy.
aminoaciduria *f.* aminoaciduria.
aminograma *f.* aminogram.
aminolípido *m.* aminolipid.
aminolipina *f.* aminolipin.
aminólisis *f.* aminolysis.
aminosis *f.* aminosis.
aminosuria *f.* aminosuria.
aminuria *f.* aminuria.
amiocardia *f.* amyocardia.
amioestesia *f.* amyoesthesis.
amioplasia *f.* amyoplasia.
  amioplasia congénita amyoplasia congenita.
amioso, -sa *adj.* amyous.
amiostasia *f.* amyostasia.
amiostenia *f.* amyosthenia.
amiosténico, -ca *adj.* amyosthenic.
amiotonía *f.* amyotonia.
  amiotonía congénita amyotonia congenita.
amiotrofia *f.* amyotrophy.
  amiotrofia diabética diabetic amyotrophy.
  amiotrofia espinal progresiva amyotrophy spinalis progressiva.
  amiotrofia hemipléjica hemiplegic amyotrophy.
  amiotrofia neurálgica neuralgic amyotrophy, amyotrophy neuralgica.
amiotrófico, -ca *adj.* amyotrophic.
amitosis *f.* amitosis.
amitótico, -ca *adj.* amitotic.
amixorrea *f.* amyxorrhea.
  amixorrea gástrica amyxorrhea gastrica.
amnemónico, -ca *adj.* amnemonic.
amnesia *f.* amnesia.
  amnesia anterógrada anterograde amnesia.
  amnesia auditiva auditory amnesia.
  amnesia circunscrita circumscribed amnesia.
  amnesia continua continuous amnesia.
  amnesia disociativa dissociative amnesia.
  amnesia emocional emotional amnesia.
  amnesia episódica episodic amnesia.
  amnesia generalizada generalized amnesia.
  amnesia global transitoria transient amnesia.
  amnesia infantil infantile amnesia.
  amnesia lacunar, amnesia lagunar lacunar amnesia.
  amnesia localizada localized amnesia.
  amnesia orgánica organic amnesia.
  amnesia poscontusional postcontussional amnesia.

amnesia posthipnótica posthypnotic amnesia.
  amnesia postraumática post-traumatic amnesia.
  amnesia retroanterógrada retroanterograde amnesia.
  amnesia retrógada retrograde amnesia.
  amnesia selectiva selective amnesia.
  amnesia táctil tactile amnesia.
  amnesia traumática traumatic amnesia.
  amnesia verbal verbal amnesia.
  amnesia visual visual amnesia.
amnésico, -ca *adj.* amnesic.
amniocentesis *f.* amniocentesis.
amniocorial *adj.* amniochorial.
amniocoriónico, -ca *adj.* amniochorial.
amniogénesis *f.* amniogenesis.
amnioma *m.* amnioma.
amnionitis *f.* amnionitis, amniotitis.
amniorrea *f.* amniorrhea.
amniorrexis *f.* amniorrhexis.
amnios *m.* amnion.
amnioscopia *f.* amnioscopia.
amnioscopio *m.* amnioscope.
amniótico, -ca *adj.* amniotic.
amniotitis *f.* anmiotitis.
amniotomía *f.* amniotomy.
amniótomo *m.* amniotome.
amoaciduria *f.* ammoaciduria.
Amoeba Amoeba.
amok *m.* amok.
amoniaco, amoníaco *m.* ammonia.
amoniatado, -da *adj.* ammoniate.
amoniatar *v.* ammoniate.
amoniemia *f.* ammoniemia.
amoniuria *f.* ammoniuria.
amorfa *f.* amorpha.
amorfia *f.* amorphia.
amorfismo *m.* amorphism.
amorfo *m.* amorphus.
amorfo, -fa *adj.* amorphous.
amorfognosia *f.* tactile agnosia.
amortiguación *f.* damping.
amortiguador *m.* buffer.
amortiguamiento[1] *m.* buffering.
amortiguamiento[2] *m.* damping.
amoterapia *f.* ammotherapy.
amperaje *m.* amperage.
amperímetro *m.* amperemeter.
Amphistoma Amphistoma.
  Amphistoma hominis Amphistoma hominis.
ampleción *f.* amplexation.
amplexación *f.* amplexation.
amplificación *f.* amplification.
amplitud *f.* amplitude.
  amplitud de acomodación amplitude of accommodation.
  amplitud de convergencia amplitude of convergence.
ampolla[1] *f.* ampoule, ampule.
ampolla[2] *f.* ampulla.
ampolla[3] *f.* bleb, blister.
ampollar *adj.* ampular, ampullary.
ámpula *f.* ampoule, ampule.
ampúlula *f.* ampullula.
ampullitis *f.* ampullitis.
amputación *f.* amputation.
  amputación abdominoperineal del recto abdominoperineal resection amputation.
  amputación abierta open amputation.
  amputación de Abrashanow Abrashanow's amputation.
  amputación de Alanson Alanson's amputation.
  amputación de Alouette Alouette's amputation.

amputación amniótica amniotic amputation.
  amputación aperióstica aperiosteal amputation.
  amputación de Béclard Beclard's amputation.
  amputación de Bier Bier's amputation.
  amputación de Bunge Bunge's amputation.
  amputación de Callander Callander's amputation.
  amputación de Carden Carden's amputation.
  amputación central central amputation.
  amputación cerrada closed amputation.
  amputación cervical cervical amputation.
  amputación de Chopart Chopart's amputation.
  amputación cinemática cinematic amputation.
  amputación cineplástica cineplastic amputation, kineplastic amputation.
  amputación circular cirular amputation, circus amputation.
  amputación con colgajos, amputación de colgajo flap amputation.
  amputación sin colgajos flapless amputation.
  amputación completa complete amputation.
  amputación congénita congenital amputation.
  amputación en (la) contiguidad amputation in contiguity.
  amputación en (la) continuidad amputation in continuity.
  amputación cuádruple quadruple amputation.
  amputación por debajo de la rodilla (B-K) below-knee (B-K) amputation.
  amputación de Dieffenbach Dieffenbach's amputation.
  amputación de doble colgajo double flap amputation.
  amputación de Dupuytren Dupuytren's amputation.
  amputación elíptica elliptic amputation, elliptical amputation.
  amputación por encima de la rodilla (A-K) above-knee (A-K) amputation.
  amputación espontánea spontaneous amputation.
  amputación excéntrica eccentric amputation.
  amputación falangofalángica phalangophalangeal amputation.
  amputación de Farabeuf Farabeuf's amputation.
  amputación de Forbes Forbes' amputation.
  amputación galvanocaústica galvanocaustic amputation.
  amputación de Gritti Gritti's amputation.
  amputación de Gritti-Stokes Gritti-Stokes amputation.
  amputación de Guyon Guyon's amputation.
  amputación en guillotina guillotine amputation.
  amputación de Hancock Hancock's amputation.
  amputación de Hey Hey's amputation.
  amputación incruenta bloodless amputation.
  amputación inmediata immediate amputation.
  amputación interabdominopelviana interpelviabdominal amputation.
  amputación interilioabdominal interilioabdominal amputation, interinnominoabdominal amputation.

amputación intermedia, amputación intrapirética intermediary amputation, intermediate amputation.

amputación intrauterina intrauterine amputation.

amputación intrapirética intrapyretic amputation.

amputación de Jaboulay Jaboulay's amputation.

amputación de Kirk Kirk's amputation.

amputación de Langenbeck Langenbeck's amputation.

amputación de Larrey Larrey's amputation.

amputación de Le Fort Le Fort's amputation.

amputación lineal linear amputation.

amputación de Lisfranc Lisfranc's amputation.

amputación de Mackenzie Mackenzie's amputation.

amputación de Maisonneuve Maisonneuve's amputation.

amputación de Malgaigne Malgaigne's amputation.

amputación en manga de camisa coat-sleeve amputation.

amputación mayor major amputation.

amputación mediata mediate amputation.

amputación mediotarsiana mediotarsal amputation.

amputación menor minor amputation.

amputación musculocutánea musculocutaneous amputation.

amputación natural natural amputation, birth amputation.

amputación oblicua oblique amputation.

amputación operatoria operative amputation.

amputación osteoplástica osteoplastic amputation.

amputación oval oval amputation.

amputación parcial partial amputation.

amputación patológica pathologic amputation.

amputación de Pirogoff Pirogoff's amputation.

amputación primaria primary amputation.

amputación pulpar pulp amputation.

amputación radicular, amputación de la raíz root amputation.

amputación en raqueta racket amputation.

amputación rectangular rectangular amputation.

amputación de Ricard Ricard's amputation.

amputación seca dry amputation.

amputación secundaria secondary amputation.

amputación sin colgajos flapless amputation.

amputación sincrónica synchronous amputation.

amputación de Stokes Stokes amputation.

amputación subastragalina subastragalar amputation.

amputación subperióstica subperiosteal amputation.

amputación de Syme Syme's amputation.

amputación de Teale Teale's amputation.

amputación terciaria tertiary amputation.

amputación traumática traumatic amputation.

amputación de Tripier Tripier's amputation.

amputación de Vladimiroff-Mikulicz Vladimiroff-Mikulicz amputation.

amputado, -da *m., f.* amputee.

amusia *f.* amusia.

amusia instrumental instrumental amusia.

amusia motriz vocal vocal motor amusia.

amusia sensorial sensory amusia.

anabiosis *f.* anabiosis.

anabiótico, -ca *adj.* anabiotic.

anabolina *f.* anabolin.

anabolismo *m.* anabolism.

anabolito *m.* anabolite.

anabrosis *f.* anabrosis.

anabrótico, -ca *adj.* anabrotic.

anacamptómetro *m.* anacamptometer.

anacatadidimo *m.* anacatadidymus, anakatadidymus.

anacatestesia *f.* anacatesthesia.

anacidez *f.* anacidity.

anacidez gástrica gastric anacidity.

anaclasímetro *m.* anaclasimeter.

anaclasis *f.* anaclasis.

anaclisis *f.* anaclisis.

anaclítico, -ca *adj.* anaclitic.

anacmesis *f.* anacmesis, anakmesis.

anacoresis *f.* anachoresis.

anacorético, -ca *adj.* anachoretic.

anacrótico, -ca *adj.* anacrotic.

anacrotismo *m.* anacrotism.

anacultivo *m.* anaculture.

anacusia *f.* anakusis.

anacusis *f.* anakusis.

anadenia *f.* anadenia.

anadenia ventricular anadenia ventriculi.

anadicrótico, -ca *adj.* anadicrotic.

anadicrotismo *m.* anadicrotism.

anadídimo *m.* anadidymus.

anadipsia anadipsia.

anadrenalismo *m.* anadrenalism.

anadrenia *m.* anadrenia.

anaerobio, -a *adj.* anaerobe.

anaerobiosis *m.* aerobiosis.

anaerobiótico, -ca *adj.* anaerobiotic.

anaerógeno, -na *adj.* anaerogenic.

anaeroplastia *f.* anaeroplasty.

anafalantiasis *f.* anaphalantiasis.

anafase *f.* anaphase.

anafia *f.* anaphia, anhaphia.

anafiláctico, -ca *adj.* anaphylactic.

anafilactina *f.* anaphilactin.

anafilactogénesis *f.* anaphylactogenesis.

anafilactógeno *m.* anaphylactogen.

anafilaxia *f.* anaphylaxis.

anafilaxia activa active anaphylaxis.

anafilaxia adquirida acquired anaphylaxis.

anafilaxia de agregación, anafilaxia agregada aggregate anaphylaxis.

anafilaxia de antisuero antiserum anaphylaxis.

anafilaxia citotóxica cytotoxic anaphylaxis.

anafilaxia cutánea activa active cutaneous anaphylaxis.

anafilaxia cutánea pasiva (ACP) passive cutaneous anaphylaxis (PCA).

anafilaxia generalizada generalized anaphylaxis.

anafilaxia heteróloga heterologous anaphylaxis.

anafilaxia homóloga homologous anaphylaxis.

anafilaxia indirecta indirect anaphylaxis.

anafilaxia inversa inverse anaphylaxis.

anafilaxia invertida reversed anaphylaxis.

anafilaxia local local anaphylaxis.

anafilaxia pasiva passive anaphylaxis.

anafilaxia sistémica systemic anaphylaxis.

anafilaxis *f.* anaphylaxis.

anafilodiagnóstico *m.* anaphylodiagnosis.

anafilotoxina *f.* anaphylatoxin, anaphylotoxin.

anaforesis *f.* anaphoresis.

anaforia *f.* anaphoria.

anafrodisia *f.* anaphrodisia.

anafrodisíaco, -ca *adj.* anaphrodisiac.

anagénesis *f.* anagenesis.

anagen *m.* anagen.

anágeno *m.* anagen.

anahormona *f.* anahormone.

anal *adj.* anal.

analbuminemia *f.* analbuminemia.

analéptico, -ca *adj.* analeptic.

analérgico, -ca *adj.* anallergic.

analfalipoproteinemia *f.* analphalipoproteinemia.

analgesia *f.* analgesia.

analgesia álgera, analgesia álgica analgesia algera.

analgesia auditiva audio analgesia.

analgesia caudal continua continuous caudal analgesia.

analgesia dolorosa analgesia dolorosa.

analgesia epidural epidural.

analgesia por infiltración infiltration analgesia.

analgesia por inhalación inhalation analgesia.

analgesia narcolocal narcolocal analgesia.

analgesia parética paretic analgesia.

analgesia por penetración permeation analgesia.

analgesia superficial surface analgesia.

analgésico, -ca *adj.* analgesic.

analgia *f.* analgia.

análisis *m.* analysis.

análisis de activación activation analysis.

análisis antigénico antigenic analysis.

análisis bradicinético bradykinetic analysis.

análisis biocromático biochromatic analysis.

análisis de carácter character analysis.

análisis cefalométrico cephalometric analysis.

análisis cinético kinetic analysis.

análisis colorimétrico colorimetric analysis.

análisis de conjunto cluster analysis.

análisis de contenido content analysis.

análisis cromatográfico chromatographic analysis.

análisis cualitativo qualitative analysis, qualitive analysis.

análisis cuantitativo quantitative analysis, quantive analysis.

análisis de datos data analysis.

análisis de densidad óptica delta delta optical density analysis.

análisis densimétrico densimetric analysis.

análisis distributivo distributive analysis.

análisis de Downs Downs' analysis.

análisis del yo ego analysis.

análisis espectroscóspico spectroscopic analysis, spectrum analysis.

análisis estratográfico stratographic analysis.

análisis de gases sanguíneos blood gas analysis.

análisis gasométrico gasometric analysis.

análisis gástrico gastric analysis.

análisis gravimétrico gravimetric analysis.

análisis de grupo terminal end-group analysis.

análisis de imagen imaging analysis.

análisis de impedancia bioeléctrica (AIB) bioelectrical impedance analysis (BIA).

análisis de inhibición inhibition assay.

análisis de inmunoabsorción ligado a enzimas (ELISA) enzyme-linked immunosorbent assay.

análisis de orina urinalysis.

análisis radioquímico radiochemical analysis.

análisis de radiorreceptores de HCG HCG radioreceptor assay.

análisis secuencial sequential analysis.

análisis secuencial múltiple (ASM) sequential multiple analysis (SMA).

análisis de tétrada tetrad analysis.

análisis último ultimate analysis.

análisis de la varianza (ANOVA) analysis of variance.

análisis vectorial vector analysis.

análisis volumétrico volumetric analysis.

analista *m.* analyst.

analítico, -ca *adj.* analytic.

analizador *m.* analyzer.

analizador de aliento breath analyzer.

analogía *f.* analogy.

análogo, -ga *adj.* analog.

anamnésico, -ca *adj.* anamnestic.

anamnesis *f.* anamnesis.

anamniótico, -ca *adj.* amniotic.

anamorfosis *f.* anamorphosis.

ananastasia *f.* ananastasia.

anancastia *f.* anancastia.

anaplasia *f.* anaplasia.

anaplásico, -ca *adj.* anaplastic.

anaplerosis *f.* anaplerosis.

anapnógrafo *m.* anapnograph.

anapnoterapia *f.* anapnotherapy.

anapófisis *f.* anapophysis.

anaraxia *f.* anaraxia.

anárico, -ca *adj.* anaric.

anarrexis *f.* anarrhexis.

anarritmia *f.* anarithmia.

anartria *f.* anarthria.

anasarca *f.* anasarca.

anastalsis *f.* anastalsis.

anastigmático, -ca *adj.* anastigmatic.

anastomosar *v.* anastomose.

anastomosis *f.* anastomosis.

anastomosis arteriolovenular simple anastomosis arteriovenularis simplex.

anastomosis arteriovenosa arteriovenous anastomosis.

anastomosis arteriovenosa glomeriforme, anastomosis arteriovenular glomeriforme, anastomosis arteriolovenularis glomeriformis anastomosis arteriolovenularis glomeriformis.

anastomosis de Billroth I y II Billroth I and II anastomosis.

anastomosis de Braun Braun anastomosis.

anastomosis heterocládica heterocladic anastomosis.

anastomosis homocládica homocladic anastomosis.

anastomosis iliorrectal iliorectal anastomosis.

anastomosis isoperistáltica isoperistaltic anastomosis.

anastomosis microneurovascular microneurovascular.

anastomosis microvascular microvascular anastomosis.

anastomosis pieloileocutánea pyeloileocutaneous anastomosis.

anastomosis de Potts Potts' anastomosis.

anastomosis Schmidel Schmidel's anastomosis.

anastomosis terminoterminal termino-terminal anastomosis.

anastomosis transureteroureteral transureteroureteral anastomosis.

anastomosis ureteroileocutánea ureteroileocutaneous anastomosis.

anastomosis ureteroureteral ureteroureteral anastomosis.

anastomótico, -ca *adj.* anastomotic.

anastral *adj.* anastral.

anatomía *f.* anatomy.

anatomía aplicada applied anatomy.

anatomía artificial artificial anatomy.

anatomía artística artistic anatomy.

anatomía clástica clastic anatomy.

anatomía clínica clinical anatomy.

anatomía comparada comparative anatomy.

anatomía por corrosión corrosion anatomy.

anatomía dental dental anatomy.

anatomía de desarrollo developmental anatomy.

anatomía descriptiva descriptive anatomy.

anatomía especial special anatomy.

anatomía fisiológica physiological anatomy.

anatomía fisionómica physiognomic anatomy.

anatomía funcional functional anatomy.

anatomía general general anatomy.

anatomía histológica histological anatomy.

anatomía homológica homological anatomy.

anatomía macroscópica gross anatomy, macroscopic anatomy.

anatomía médica medical anatomy.

anatomía microscópica microscopic anatomy, minute anatomy.

anatomía patológica pathological anatomy.

anatomía plástica plastic anatomy.

anatomía práctica practical anatomy.

anatomía quirúrgica surgical anatomy.

anatomía radiológica radiological anatomy.

anatomía regional regional anatomy.

anatomía sistemática systematic anatomy.

anatomía de superficie surface anatomy.

anatomía topográfica topographic anatomy.

anatomía in vivo living anatomy.

anatómico, -ca *adj.* anatomic, anatomical.

anatomopatológico, -ca *adj.* anatomicopathological.

anatomista *m., f.* anatomist.

anatoxina *f.* anatoxin.

anatricrótico, -ca *adj.* anatricrotic.

anatropia *f.* anatropia.

anaxón *m.* anaxone.

anazoúria *f.* anazoturia.

anclaje *m.* anchorage.

anclaje cervical cervical anchorage.

anclaje compuesto compound anchorage.

anclaje estacionario stationary anchorage.

anclaje extramaxilar extramaxillary anchorage.

anclaje extraoral extraoral anchorage.

anclaje intermaxilar intermaxillary.

anclaje intramaxilar intramaxillary anchorage.

anclaje intraoral intraoral anchorage.

anclaje múltiple multiple anchorage.

anclaje occipital occipital anchorage.

anclaje recíproco reciprocal anchorage.

anclaje reforzado reinforced anchorage.

anclaje simple simple anchorage.

anconagra *f.* anconagra.

ancóneo, -a *adj.* anconal, anconeal.

anconitis *f.* anconitis.

Ancylostoma Ancylostoma.

andreioma *m.* andreioma.

andreoblastoma *m.* andreoblastoma.

androblastoma *m.* androblastoma, andreoblastoma.

androfobia *f.* androphobia.

androgalactocemia *f.* androgalactozemia.

androgénesis *f.* androgenesis.

androgenización *f.* androgenization.

andrógeno *m.* androgen.

androgineidad *f.* androgyneity.

androginia *f.* androgyny.

androide *adj.* android.

andrología *f.* andrology.

androma *f.* androma.

andromorfo, -fa *adj.* andromorphous.

andropatía *f.* androphathy.

androstano *m.* androstane.

androstanodiona *m.* androstanedione.

androstendiol *m.* androstenediol.

androstendiona *f.* androstenedione.

androsterona *f.* androsterone.

anedonia *f.* anhedonia.

anéfrico, -ca *adj.* anephric.

anefrogénesis *f.* anephrogenesis.

anelectrotono *m.* anelectrotonus.

anejos *m.* adnexa.

anemia *f.* anemia.

anemia aclorhídrica achlorhydric anemia.

anemia acréstica achrestic anemia.

anemia de Addison, anemia de Addison-Biermer, anemia addisoniana Addisonian anemia.

anemia aguda acute anemia.

anemia anhematopoyética, anemia anhemopoyética anhematopoietic anemia, anhemopoietic anemia.

anemia aplásica aplastic anemia.

anemia arregenerativa aregenerative anemia.

anemia arregenerativa crónica congénita chronic congenital aregenerative anemia.

anemia asiderótica asiderotic anemia.

anemia por Bartonella Bartonella anemia.

anemia de Biermer, anemia de Biermer-Ehrlich Biermer's anemia.

anemia de Blackfan-Diamond Blackfan-Diamond anemia.

anemia cameloide cameloid anemia.

anemia carencial deficiency anemia.

anemia de células diana target cell anemia.

anemia de células en espolón spur cell anemia.

anemia de células falciformes sickle cell anemia.

anemia de células globosas globe cell anemia.

anemia clorótica chlorotic anemia.

anemia congénita del neonato congenital anemia of the newborn.

anemia de Cooley Cooley's anemia.

anemia de cuerpos de Heinz Heinz body anemia.

anemia por deficiencia de ácido fólico folic acid deficiency anemia.

anemia por deficiencia de hierro iron deficiency anemia.

anemia por deficiencia de glucosa-6-fosfato-deshidrogenasa glucose-6-phosphate-dehydrogenase deficiency anemia.

anemia deficitaria deficiency anemia.

anemia por dilución dilution anemia.

anemia dimórfica dimorphic anemia.

anemia drepanocítica sickle cell anemia.

anemia de Ehrlich Ehrlich anemia.

anemia eliptocitaria, anemia eliptocítica elliptocitary anemia, elliptocytotic anemia.

anemia eritroblástica de la infancia erythroblastic anemia of childhood.

anemia eritroblástica familiar familial erythroblastic anemia.

anemia eritrocítica pura pure red cell anemia.

anemia escorbútica scorbutic anemia.

anemia esferocítica spherocytic anemia.

anemia esplénica splenic anemia, anemia splenica.

anemia de Fanconi Fanconi's anemia.

anemia por fenilhidracina phenylhydrazine anemia.

anemia ferropénica iron deficiency anemia.

anemia fisiológica physiologic anemia.

anemia de glóbulos rojos puros pure red cell anemia.

anemia hemolítica hemolytic anemia.

anemia hemolítica aguda acute hemolytic anemia.

anemia hemolítica autoinmune autoimmune hemolytic anemia (AIHS).

anemia hemolítica congénita congenital hemolytic anemia.

anemia hemolítica congénita no esferocítica congenital non-spherocytic hemolytic anemia.

anemia hemolítica infecciosa infectious hemolytic anemia.

anemia hemolítica inmune immune hemolytic anemia, immunohemolytic anemia.

anemia hemolítica inmune inducida por fármacos drug-induced immune hemolytic anemia.

anemia hemolítica microangiopática microangiopathic hemolytic anemia.

anemia hemolítica tóxica toxic hemolytic anemia.

anemia hemorrágica hemorrhagic anemia.

anemia hipercroma, anemia hipercrómica, anemia hipercromática hyperchromic anemia, hyperchromatic anemia.

anemia hipocroma, anemia hipocrómica hypochromic anemia.

anemia hipocrómica microcítica hypochromic microcytic anemia.

anemia hipocrómica sideroacréstica hereditaria anemia hypochromica sidroachrestica hereditaria.

anemia hipoférrica hypoferric anemia.

anemia hipoplásica hypoplastic anemia.

anemia hipoplásica congénita congenital hypoplastic anemia.

anemia hipoplásica familiar familial hypoplastic anemia.

anemia icterohemolítica icterohemolytic anemia.

anemia infantil seudoleucémica anemia infantum pseudoleukemiaca.

anemia intertropical intertropical anemia.

anemia isocrómica isochromic anemia.

anemia por leche de cabra goat's milk anemia.

anemia por leche de vaca cow's milk anemia.

anemia de Lederer Lederer's anemia.

anemia de Leishman Leishman's anemia.

anemia leucoeritroblástica leukoerythroblastic anemia.

anemia linfática anemia lymphatica.

anemia local local anemia.

anemia macrocítica macrocytic anemia.

anemia macrocítica del embarazo macrocytic anemia of pregnancy.

anemia macrocítica nutricional nutritional macrocytic anemia.

anemia maligna malignant anemia.

anemia de Marchiafava-Micheli Marchiafava-Micheli anemia.

anemia megaloblástica megaloblastic anemia.

anemia megaloblástica familiar familial megaloblastic anemia.

anemia megalocítica megalocytic anemia.

anemia metaplásica metaplastic anemia.

anemia microangiopática microangiopathic anemia.

anemia microcítica microcytic anemia.

anemia mielopática myelopathic anemia.

anemia mieloptísica myelophthisic anemia.

anemia de los mineros miners' anemia.

anemia de las montañas mountain anemia.

anemia neonatal anemia neonatorum.

anemia normocítica normocytic anemia.

anemia normocrómica normochromic anemia.

anemia nutricional nutritional anemia.

anemia osteoesclerótica osteosclerotic anemia.

anemia ovalocítica ovalocytic anemia.

anemia perniciosa pernicious anemia.

anemia perniciosa juvenil juvenile pernicious anemia.

anemia pizarrosa slaty anemia.

anemia polar polar anemia.

anemia poshemorrágica posthemorrhagic anemia.

anemia poshemorrágica neonatal posthemorrhagic anemia of the newborn.

anemia rebelde refractory anemia.

anemia refractaria refractory anemia.

anemia saturnina lead anemia.

anemia sideroacréstica sideroachrestic anemia.

anemia sideroblástica sideroblastic anemia.

anemia sideropénica sideropenic anemia.

anemia susceptible a la primaquina primaquine sensitive anemia.

anemia traumática traumatic anemia.

anemia tropical tropical anemia.

anémico, -ca *adj.* anemic.

anemómetro *m.* anemometer.

anemonismo *m.* anemonism.

anemotrofía *f.* anemotrophy.

anemotropismo *m.* anemotropism.

anencefalia *f.* anencephalia.

anencefalia parcial partial anencephalia.

anencefálico, -ca *adj.* anencephalic, anencephalous.

anencéfalo *m.* anencephalus.

anentero, -ra *adj.* anenterous.

anenzimia *f.* anenzimia.

anenzimia catalasia anenzimia catalasia.

anepiploico, -ca *adj.* anepiploic.

anergasia *f.* anergasia.

anergástico, -ca *adj.* anergastic.

anergia *f.* anergy.

anergia caquéctica cachectic anergy.

anergia específica specific anergy.

anergia inespecífica non-specific anergy.

anergia negativa negative anergy.

anergia positiva positive anergy.

anérgico, -ca *adj.* anergic.

aneritroblepsia *f.* anerythroblepsia.

aneritroplasia *f.* anerythroplasia.

aneritroplásico, -ca *adj.* anerythroplastic.

aneritropoyesis *f.* anerythropoiesis.

aneritropsia *f.* anerythropsia.

aneritrorregenerativo, -va *adj.* anerythroregenerative.

aneroide *adj.* aneroid.

anestecinesia *f.* anesthecinesia, anesthekinesia.

anestequinesia *f.* anesthecinesia, anesthekinesia.

anestesia *f.* anesthesia.

anestesia abierta open anesthesia.

anestesia de aceite etéreo de Gwathmey Gwathmey oil-ether anesthesia.

anestesia angioespástica angiospastic anesthesia.

anestesia balanceada balanced anesthesia.

anestesia basal basal anesthesia.

anestesia bloqueante, anestesia bloqueo block anesthesia.

anestesia bulbar bulbar anesthesia.

anestesia en cabeza de muñeca doll's head anesthesia.

anestesia caudal caudal anesthesia.

anestesia central central anesthesia.

anestesia cerrada closed anesthesia.

anestesia en cinturón girdle anesthesia.

anestesia cólica colonic anesthesia.

anestesia completa total anesthesia.

anestesia por compresión compression anesthesia.

anestesia por conducción conduction anesthesia.

anestesia por congelación frost anesthesia.

anestesia crepuscular twilight anesthesia.

anestesia cruzada crossed anesthesia.

anestesia disociada dissociated anesthesia.

anestesia dolorosa anesthesia dolorosa.

anestesia eléctrica electric anesthesia.

anestesia epidural epidural anesthesia.

anestesia epidural lumbar lumbar epidural anesthesia.

anestesia espinal spinal anesthesia.

anestesia esplácnica splanchnic anesthesia.

anestesia facial facial anesthesia.

anestesia faríngea pharyngeal anesthesia.

anestesia general general anesthesia.

anestesia en guante glove anesthesia.

anestesia en guantelete gauntlet anesthesia.

anestesia gustatoria gustatory anesthesia.

anestesia hiperestética talámica thalamic hyperesthetic anesthesia.

anestesia hipnótica hypnosis anesthesia.

anestesia con hipotensión, anestesia hipotensora hypotensive anesthesia.

anestesia hipotérmica hypothermic anesthesia.

anestesia histérica hysterical anesthesia.

anestesia por infiltración infiltration anesthesia.

anestesia por inhalación inhalation anesthesia.

anestesia por insuflación insufflation anesthesia.

anestesia intercostal intercostal anesthesia.

anestesia intrabucal intraoral anesthesia.

anestesia intranasal intranasal anesthesia.

anestesia intraósea intraosseous anesthesia.

anestesia intrapulpar intrapulpal anesthesia.

anestesia intraspinal intraspinal anesthesia.

anestesia intravenosa intravenous anesthesia.

anestesia local local anesthesia.

anestesia mixta mixed anesthesia.

anestesia muscular muscular anesthesia.

anestesia de la náusea nausea anesthesia.

anestesia olfatoria olfactory anesthesia.

anestesia paraneural paraneural anesthesia.

anestesia paravertebral paravertebral anesthesia.

anestesia peridural peridural anesthesia.

anestesia periférica peripheral anesthesia.

anestesia perineural perineural anesthesia.

anestesia por presión pressure anesthesia.

anestesia quirúrgica surgical anesthesia.

anestesia raquídea spinal anesthesia.

anestesia rectal rectal anesthesia.

anestesia por refrigeración refrigeration anesthesia.

anestesia regional regional anesthesia.
anestesia sacra sacral anesthesia.
anestesia segmentaria segmental anesthesia.
anestesia en silla de montar saddle block anesthesia.
anestesia subaracnoidea subarachnoid anesthesia.
anestesia de superficie surface anesthesia.
anestesia táctil tactile anesthesia.
anestesia térmica thermal anesthesia, thermic anesthesia.
anestesia tópica topical anesthesia.
anestesia transacra transsacral anesthesia.
anestesia traumática traumatic anesthesia.
anestesia unilateral unilateral anesthesia.
anestesia visceral visceral anesthesia.
anestesiar *v.* anesthetize.
anestésico, -ca *m. y adj.* anesthetic.
anestésico endovenoso intravenous anesthetic.
anestésico general general anesthetic.
anestésico local local anesthetic.
anestésico raquídeo spinal anesthetic.
anestésico tópico topical anesthetic.
anestesímetro *m.* anesthesimeter.
anestesióforo *m.* anesthesiophore.
anestesiología *f.* anesthesiology.
anestesiólogo, -ga *m., f.* anesthesiologist.
anestesista *m., f.* anesthetist.
anestro *m.* anestrus.
anetodermia *f.* anetoderma, anetodermia.
anetodermia de Jadassohn, anetodermia de Jadassohn-Pellizari Jadassohn's anetoderma, Jadassohn-Pellizari anetoderma.
anetodermia perifolicular perifollicular anetoderma.
anetodermia posinflamatoria postinflammatory anetoderma.
anetodermia de Schweninger-Buzzi Schweninger-Buzzi anetoderma.
aneugamia *f.* aneugamy.
aneumia *f.* apneumia.
aneuploide *adj.* aneuploid.
aneuploidia *f.* aneuploidy.
aneural *adj.* abneural.
aneurisma *m.* aneurysm.
aneurisma abdominal abdominal aneurysm.
aneurisma ampular ampullary aneurysm.
aneurisma anastomático, aneurisma por anastomosis aneurysm by anastomosis.
aneurisma aórtico aortic aneurysm.
aneurisma aórtico sinusal aortic sinusal aneurysm.
aneurisma arterioesclerótico atherosclerotic aneurysm.
aneurisma arteriovenoso arteriovenous aneurysm.
aneurisma arteriovenoso pulmonar arteriovenous pulmonary aneurysm.
aneurisma axial axial aneurysm.
aneurisma axilar axillary aneurysm.
aneurisma bacteriano bacterial aneurysm.
aneurisma braquiocefálico innominate aneurysm.
aneurisma cardíaco cardiac aneurysm.
aneurisma cerebral cerebral aneurysm.
aneurisma cerebral congénito congenital cerebral aneurysm.
aneurisma cerebral saculado berry aneurysm.
aneurisma de Charcot-Bouchard Charcot-Bouchard aneurysm.
aneurisma cilindroideo, aneurisma cilíndrico cylindroid aneurysm.
aneurisma cirsoideo cirsoid aneurysm.

aneurisma cistógeno cystogenic aneurysm.
aneurisma compuesto compound aneurysm.
aneurisma disecante dissecting aneurysm.
aneurisma ectático ectatic aneurysm.
aneurisma embólico embolic aneurysm.
aneurisma embolomicótico embolomycotic aneurysm.
aneurisma espúreo, aneurisma espurio spurious aneurysm.
aneurisma falso false aneurysm.
aneurisma fantasma phantom aneurysm.
aneurisma fusiforme fusiform aneurysm.
aneurisma herniario hernial aneurysm.
aneurisma infectado infected aneurysm.
aneurisma intracraneal intracranial aneurysm.
aneurisma lateral lateral aneurysm.
aneurisma micótico mycotic aneurysm.
aneurisma miliar miliary aneurysm.
aneurisma orbitario orbital aneurysm.
aneurisma óseo benigno benign bone aneurysm.
aneurisma de Park Park's aneurysm.
aneurisma pélvico pelvic aneurysm.
aneurisma de Pott Pott's aneurysm.
aneurisma racemoso racemous aneurysm.
aneurisma de Rasmussen Rasmussen's aneurysm.
aneurisma renal renal aneurysm.
aneurisma de Richet Richet's aneurysm.
aneurisma de Rodrigues Rodrigues' aneurysm.
aneurisma saculado, aneurisma sacular sacculated aneurysm, saccular aneurysm.
aneurisma serpentino serpentine aneurysm.
aneurisma sifilítico syphilitic aneurysm.
aneurisma suprasillar suprasellar aneurysm.
aneurisma torácico thoracic aneurysm.
aneurisma por tracción traction aneurysm.
aneurisma traumático traumatic aneurysm.
aneurisma tubular tubular aneurysm.
aneurisma varicoso varicose aneurysm.
aneurisma ventricular ventricular aneurysm.
aneurisma verdadero true aneurysm.
aneurismático, -ca *adj.* aneurysmal.
aneurismectomía *f.* aneurysmectomy.
aneurismoplastia *f.* aneurysmoplasty.
aneurismorrafia *f.* aneurysmorrhaphy.
aneurismotomía *f.* aneurysmotomy.
aneurógeno, -na *adj.* aneurogenic.
aneurolémico, -ca *adj.* aneurolemmic.
anexectomía *f.* adnexectomy.
anexitis *f.* adnexitis.
anexogénesis *f.* adnexogenesis.
anexopexia *f.* adnexopexy.
anexos *m.* adnexa.
anfanfoterodiplopía *f.* amphamphoterodiplopia.
anfeclexis *f.* amphclexis.
anfémero, -ra *adj.* amphemerous.
anfiartrodial *adj.* amphiarthrodial.
anfiartrosis *f.* amphiarthrosis.
anfiáster *m.* amphiaster.
anfiblástico, -ca *adj.* amphiblastic.
anfiblástula *f.* amphiblastula.
anfiblestritis *f.* amphiblestritis.
anfibolia *f.* amphibolia.
anfibólico, -ca *adj.* amphibolic.
anficarcinogénico, -ca *adj.* amphicarcinogenic.
anficelo, -la *adj.* amphicelous.
anficéntrico, -ca *adj.* amphicentric.
anficito *m.* amphicyte.
anficroico, -ca *adj.* amphicroic.
anficromático, -ca *adj.* amphichromatic.

anfidiartrosis *f.* amphidiarthrosis.
anfigástrula *f.* amphigastrula.
anfigenético, -ca *adj.* amphigenetic.
anfigonia *f.* amphigony.
anfileucémico, -ca *adj.* amphileukemic.
anfimicrobiano, -na *adj.* amphimicrobian.
anfimixis *f.* amphiymixis.
anfimórula *f.* amphimorula.
anfinúcleo *m.* amphinucleus.
anfipático, -ca *adj.* amphipathic.
anfipirenina *f.* amphipyrenin.
anfistomiasis *f.* amphistomiasis.
anfiteno, -na *m.* amphitene.
anfitipia *f.* amphitypy.
anfítrico, -ca *adj.* amphitrichous.
anfocito *m.* amphocite.
anfocromatófilo, -la *adj.* amphochromatophil.
anfocromófilo, -la *adj.* amphochromophil.
anfodiplopía *f.* amphodiplopy.
anfofílico, -ca *adj.* amphophilic.
anfofílico basófilo amphophilic basofil.
anfofílico oxifilo amphophilic oxyphil.
anfófilo, -la *adj.* amphophil.
anfogénico, -ca *adj.* amphogenic.
anfólito *m.* apholyte.
anfórico, -ca *adj.* amphoric.
anforiloquia *f.* amphoriloquy.
anforofonía *f.* amphorophony.
anfotericidad *f.* amphotericity.
anfotérico, -ca *adj.* amphoteric.
anfoterismo *m.* amphoterism.
anfótero, -ra *adj.* amphoteric.
anfoterodiplopía *f.* amphoterodiplopia.
anfotonía *f.* amphotony.
anfractuosidad *f.* anfractuosity.
angeitis *f.* angiitis.
angialgia *f.* angialgia.
angiastenia *f.* angiasthenia.
angiectasia *f.* angiectasis, angiectasia.
angiectasis *f.* angiectasis, angiectasia.
angiectasis displásica congénita congenital dysplastic angiectasis.
angiectomía *f.* angiectomy.
angiectopía *f.* angiectopia.
anglenfraxls *f.* angiemphraxis.
angiitis *f.* angiitis, angitis.
angiitis alérgica cutánea allergic cutaneous angiitis.
angiitis consecutiva consecutive angiitis.
angiitis granulomatosa alérgica allergic granulomatous angiitis.
angiitis leucocitoclástica leukocytoclastic angiitis.
angiitis necrosante necrotizing angiitis.
angiitis nodular cutánea nodular cutaneous angiitis.
angina *f.* angina.
angina abdominal abdominal angina, angina abdominalis, angina abdominis.
angina agranulocítica agranulocytic angina.
angina aguda angina acuta.
angina de Bretonneau Bretonneau's angina.
angina catarral angina catarrhalis.
angina cordis angina cordis.
angina crural angina cruris.
angina de decúbito angina decubitus.
angina diftérica angina diphtheritica.
angina dispéptica angina dyspeptica.
angina epiglótica, angina epiglotídea angina epiglottidea.
angina espuria angina spuria.
angina exudativa exudative angina.
angina falsa false angina.
angina folicular angina follicularia.

angina gangrenosa angina gangrenosa.
angina hipocrática hippocratic angina.
angina histérica hysteric angina.
angina intestinal intestinal angina.
angina inversa angina inversa.
angina lacunar lacunar angina.
angina laríngea angina laryngea.
angina de Ludwig Ludwig's angina.
angina maligna malignant angina.
angina membranosa angina membranacea.
angina monocítica monocytic angina.
angina neutropénica neutropenic angina.
angina de pecho angina pectoris.
angina de pecho vasomotora angina pectoris vasomotora.
angina de Prinzmetal Prinzmetal's angina.
angina reumática angina rheumatica.
angina seudomembranosa de Plaut pseudomembranous Plaut's angina, Plaut's angina, pseudomembranous angina.
angina sine dolore angina sine dolore.
angina de Schultz Schultz's angina.
angina traqueal angina trachealis.
angina vasomotora, angina vasomotriz vasomotor angina, angina vasomotora.
angina de Vincent Vincent's angina.
anginiforme *adj.* anginiform.
anginosis *f.* anginosis.
angioacceso *m.* angioaccess.
angioastenia *f.* angioasthenia.
angioataxia *f.* angioataxia.
angioblástico, -ca *adj.* angioblastic.
angioblasto *m.* angioblast.
angioblastoma *f.* angioblastoma.
angiocardiocinético, -ca *adj.* angiocardiokinetic.
angiocardiografía *f.* angiocardiography.
angiocardiograma *f.* angiocardiogram.
angiocardiopatía *f.* angiocardiopathy.
angiocarditis *f.* angiocarditis.
angiocavernoso, -sa *adj.* angiocavernous.
angioceratoma *m.* angiokeratoma.
angiocinesis *f.* angiokinesis.
angiocinético, -ca *adj.* angiokinetic.
angioclasto *m.* angioclast.
angiocolecistitis *f.* angiocholecistitis.
angiocondroma *m.* angiochondroma.
angiocolitis *f.* angiocholitis.
angiocrino, -na *adj.* angiocrine.
angiocrinosis *f.* angiocrinosis.
angiodermatitis *f.* angiodermatitis.
angiodiascopia *f.* angiodiascopy.
angiodinia *f.* angiodynia.
angiodisplasia *f.* angiodysplasia.
angiodistrofia *f.* angiodystrophy, angiodystrophia.
angiodistrofia ovárica angiodystrophia ovarii.
angioedema *m.* angioedema.
angioedema hereditario hereditary angioedema.
angioedema vibratorio vibratory angioedema.
angioedematoso, -sa *adj.* angioedematous.
angioelefantiasis *f.* angioelephantiasis.
angioendotelioma *f.* angioendothelioma.
angioescotoma *m.* angioscotoma.
angioespasmo *m.* angiospasm.
angioespástico, -ca *adj.* angiospastic.
angiofacomatosis *f.* angiophacomatosis, angiophakomatosis.
angiofibroma *f.* angiofibroma.
angiofibroma contagioso de los trópicos angiofibroma contagiosum tropicum.
angiofibroma juvenil angiofibroma juvenile.

angiofibroma nasofaríngeo nasopharyngeal angiofibroma.
angiofibrosis *f.* angiofibrosis.
angiogénesis *f.* angiogenesis.
angiogénico, -ca *adj.* angiogenic.
angioglioma *m.* angioglioma.
angiogliomatosis *f.* angiogliomatosis.
angiografía *f.* angiography.
angiografía cerebral cerebral angiography.
angiografía coronaria coronary angiography.
angiografía espinal spinal angiography.
angiohemofilia *f.* angiohemophilia.
angiohialinosis *f.* angiohyalinosis.
angiohipertonía *f.* angiohypertonia.
angiohipotonía *f.* angiohypotonia.
angioide *adj.* angioid.
angioleiomioma *m.* angioleiomyoma.
angioleucitis *f.* angioleucitis, angioleukitis.
angiolinfangioma *m.* angiolymphangioma.
angiolipoma *m.* angiolipoma.
angiólisis *f.* angiolysis.
angiolito *m.* angiolith.
angiología *f.* angiologia, angiology.
angiolupoide *m.* angiolupoid.
angioma *m.* angioma.
angioma aracnoideo, angioma arácneo spider angioma.
angioma arterial racemoso angioma arteriale racemosum.
angioma arteriovenoso del cerebro arteriovenous angioma of the brain.
angioma capilar capillary angioma.
angioma cavernoso cavernous angioma, angioma cavernosum.
angioma en cereza cherry angioma.
angioma del cutis angioma cutis.
angioma fisural fissural angioma.
angioma en fresa strawberry angioma.
angioma hipertrófico hypertrophic angioma.
angioma linfático angioma lymphaticum.
angioma pigmentoso atrófico angioma pigmentosum atrophicum.
angioma senil angioma senile.
angioma serpiginoso angioma serpiginosum.
angioma telangiectásico telangiectatic angioma.
angioma venoso racemoso angioma venosum racemosum.
angiomatosis *f.* angiomatosis.
angiomatosis cerebrorretiniana cerebroretinal angiomatosis.
angiomatosis encefalofacial, angiomatosis encefalotrigeminal encephalofacial angiomatosis, encephalotrigeminal angiomatosis.
angiomatosis hepática hepatic angiomatosis.
angiomatosis retiniana angiomatosis of the retina.
angiomatosis retinocerebral retinocerebral angiomatosis.
angiomatoso, -sa *adj.* angiomatous.
angiomegalia *f.* angiomegaly.
angiómetro *m.* angiometer.
angiomiocardíaco, -ca *adj.* angiomyocardiac.
angiomiofibroma *f.* angiomyofibroma.
angiomiolipoma *m.* angiomyolipoma.
angiomioma *m.* angiomyoma.
angiomioma cutáneo angiomyoma cutis.
angiomioneuroma *f.* angiomyoneuroma.
angiomiopatía *f.* angiomyopathy.
angiomiosarcoma *m.* angiomyosarcoma.
angiomixoma *m.* angiomyxoma.

angionecrosis *f.* angionecrosis.
angioneoplasia *f.* angioneoplasm.
angioneuralgia *f.* angioneuralgia.
angioneurectomía *f.* angioneurectomy.
angioneuroedema *m.* angioneuroedema.
angioneuroma *m.* angioneuroma.
angioneuromioma *m.* angioneuromyoma.
angioneuropatía *f.* angioneuropathy.
angioneuropático, -ca *adj.* angioneuropathic.
angioneurosis *f.* angioneurosis.
angioneurótico, -ca *adj.* angioneurotic.
angioneurotomía *f.* angioneurotomy.
angionoma *m.* angionoma.
angiopancreatitis *f.* angiopancreatitis.
angioparálisis *f.* angioparalysis.
angioparesia *f.* angioparesis.
angioparesis *f.* angioparesis.
angiopatía *f.* angiopathy.
angiopatía amiloide cerebral cerebral amyloid angiopathy.
angiopatía congofílica congophilic angiopathy.
angiopático, -ca *adj.* angiopathic.
angiopatología *f.* angiopathology.
angioplania *f.* angioplany.
angioplastia *f.* angioplasty.
angioplastia coronaria transluminal percutánea (ACTP) percutaneous transluminal coronary angioplasty (PTCA).
angioplastia transluminal percutánea percutaneous transluminal angioplasty.
angiopoyesis *f.* angiopoioesis.
angiopoyético, -ca *adj.* angiopoietic.
angiopresión *f.* angiopressure.
angioqueiloscopio *m.* angiocheiloscope.
angioqueratoma *m.* angiokeratoma.
angioqueratoma circunscrito angiokeratoma circumscriptum.
angioqueratoma corporal difuso, angioqueratoma corporis diffusum angiokeratoma corporis diffusum.
angioqueratoma difuso diffuse angiokeratoma.
angioqueratoma del escroto angiokeratoma of the scrotum.
angioqueratoma de Fordyce Fordyce's angiokeratoma.
angioqueratoma del Mibelli Mibelli's angiokeratoma.
angioqueratoma solitario solitary angiokeratoma.
angioqueratosis *f.* angiokeratosis.
angioquiste *m.* angiocyst.
angiorrafia *f.* angiorrhaphy.
angiorrafia arteriovenosa arteriovenous angiorrhaphy.
angiorreticuloendotelioma *m.* angioreticuloendothelioma.
angiorreticuloma *m.* angioreticuloma.
angiorrexis *f.* angiorrhexis.
angiosarcoma *m.* angiosarcoma.
angiosclerosis *f.* angiosclerosis.
angiosclerótico, -ca *adj.* angiosclerotic.
angioscopia *f.* angioscopy.
angioscopio *m.* angioscope.
angioscotoma *m.* angioscotoma.
angioscotometría *f.* angioscotometry.
angiosialitis *f.* angiosialitis.
angiosis *f.* angiosis.
angiospasmo *m.* angiospasm.
angiospástico, -ca *adj.* angiospastic.
angiostenia *f.* angiosthenia.
angiostenosis *f.* angiostenosis.
angiosteosis *f.* angiosteosis.

angiostomía *f.* angiostomy.
angiostrofia *f.* angiostrophy.
angiostrongiliasis *f.* angiostrongyliasis.
angiostrongilosis *f.* angiostrongylosis.
Angiostrongylus Angiostrongylus.
angiotelectasia *f.* angiotelectasia, angiotelectasis.
angiotelectasis *f.* angiotelectasia, angiotelectasis.
angiotensina *f.* angiotensin.
angiotensinógeno *m.* angiotensinogen.
angiotomía *f.* angiotomy.
angiótomo *m.* angiotome.
angiotonía *f.* angiotony.
angiotónico, -ca *adj.* angiotonic.
angiotonina *f.* angiotonin.
angiotribo *m.* angiotribe.
angiotripsia *f.* angiotripsy.
angiotrófico, -ca *adj.* angiotrophic.
angiotrofoneurosis *f.* angiotrophoneurosis.
angitis *f.* angitis.
angor angor.
  angor animis angor animis.
  angor pectoris angor pectoris.
angulación *f.* angulation.
angular *adj.* angular.
ángulo *m.* angle, angulus.
  ángulo de aberración angle of aberration.
  ángulo de abertura angle of aperture.
  ángulo de alcance carrying angle.
  ángulo alfa alpha angle.
  ángulo de anomalía angle of anomaly.
  ángulo de apertura, ángulo de abertura angle of aperture.
  ángulo apical apical.
  ángulo axial axial angle.
  ángulo cefalométrico cephalometric angle.
  ángulo de convergencia angle of convergence.
  ángulo craneométrico cephalometric angle.
  ángulo crítico critical angle.
  ángulo de desviación angle of deviation.
  ángulo de dirección angle of direction.
  ángulo de disparidad disparity angle.
  ángulo de excentricidad angle of eccentricity.
  ángulo de exposición exposure angle.
  ángulo horizontal horizontal angle.
  ángulo de impedancia impedance angle.
  ángulo de incidencia angle of incidence.
  ángulo métrico meter angle.
  ángulo metro meter angle.
  ángulo mínimo separable minimum separable angle.
  ángulo mínimo visible minimum visible angle, minimum visual angle.
  ángulo de reflexión angle of reflection.
  ángulo de refracción angle of refraction.
  ángulo de refracción de un prisma refracting angle of a prism.
  ángulo somatosplácnico somatosplanchnic angle.
  ángulo de Treitz Treitz angle.
angustia *f.* anxiety.
  angustia automática automatic anxiety.
  angustia real reality anxiety.
anhafia *f.* anaphia, anhaphia.
anhedonia *f.* anhedonia.
anhematopoyesis *f.* anhematopoiesis.
anhidratación *f.* anhydration.
anhidremia *f.* anhydremia.
anhídrido *m.* anhydride.
anhidro, -dra *adj.* anhydrous.
anhidrosis *f.* anhidrosis.
  anhidrosis termógena thermogenic anhidrosis.

anhidrótico, -ca *adj.* anhidrotic.
aniacinamidosis *f.* aniacinamidosis.
aniacinosis *f.* aniacinosis.
aniantinopsia *f.* anianthinopsy.
aniaquintinopsia *f.* anianthinopsy.
anictérico, -ca *adj.* anicteric.
anidación *f.* innidation.
anideano, -na *adj.* anidean.
anídeo *m.* anideus.
  anídeo embriónico, anídeo embrionario embryonic anideus.
anidrosis *f.* anidrosis.
anidrótico, -ca *adj.* anidrotic.
anilingus *m.* anilingus.
anilinismo *m.* anilinism, anilism.
anilinofilo, -la *adj.* anilinophil.
anilismo *m.* anilinism, anilism.
anillo *m.* ring, annulus.
  anillo de Albl Albl's ring.
  anillo de Bandl Bandl's ring.
  anillo de Cabot Cabot's ring.
  anillo carbocíclico carbocyclic ring.
  anillo cervical cervical loop, neck ring.
  anillo constrictor, anillo de constricción constriction ring, constrictive ring.
  anillo de contacto contact ring.
  anillo contráctil contractile ring.
  anillo corneal de Kayser-Fleischer Kayser-Fleischer ring.
  anillo de Donders Donders' ring.
  anillo de Fleischer, anillo de Fleischer-Strümpell Fleischer ring, Fleischer-Strümpell ring.
  anillo Flieringa Flieringa's ring.
  anillo germinal germ ring.
  anillo glaucomatoso glaucomatous ring.
  anillo de Graefenberg Graefenberg ring.
  anillo heterocíclico heterocyclic ring.
  anillo homocíclico homocyclic ring.
  anillo isocíclico isocyclic ring.
  anillo lenticular de Vossius Vossius ring.
  anillo de Liesegang Liesegang ring.
  anillo de Löwe Löwe's ring.
  anillo de Lyon Lyon's ring.
  anillo de Maxwell Maxwell's ring.
  anillo mordedor teething ring.
  anillo neonatal neonatal ring.
  anillo de retracción retraction ring.
  anillo de retracción fisiológica physiologic retraction ring.
  anillo de retracción patológica pathologic retraction ring.
  anillo de Soemmering ring of Soemmering.
  anillo timpánico tympanic ring, annulus tympanicus.
  anillo umbilical umbilical ring, annulus umbilicalis.
  anillo vascular vascular ring.
ánima *f.* anima.
animación *f.* animation.
  animación suspendida suspended animation.
animal *m.* animal.
  animal de control control animal.
  animal descerebrado decerebrate animal.
  animal espinal spinal animal.
  animal experimental experimental animal.
  animal hiperfágico hyperphagic animal.
  animal de Houssay Houssay animal.
  animal de Long-Lukens Long-Lukens animal.
  animal normal normal animal.
  animal de sangre caliente warm-blooded animal.
  animal talámico thalamic animal.

animalidad *f.* animality.
animismo *m.* animism.
anincretinosis *f.* anincretinosis.
anión *m.* anion.
aniónico, -ca *adj.* anionic.
aniquilación *f.* annihilation.
aniridia *f.* aniridia.
anisakiasis *f.* anisakiasis.
Anisakis Anisakis.
  Anisakis marina Anisakis marina.
anisaquiasis *f.* anisakiasis.
aniseiconía *f.* aniseikonia, anisoiconia.
aniseicónico, -ca *adj.* aniseikonic.
anisoacomodación *f.* anisoaccommodation.
anisocariosis *f.* anisokaryosis.
anisocitosis *f.* anisocytosis.
anisocoria *f.* anisocoria.
anisocromasia *f.* anisochromasia.
anisocromático, -ca *adj.* anisochromatic.
anisocromía *f.* anisochromia.
anisodactilia *f.* anisodactyly.
anisodáctilo, -la *adj.* anisodactylous.
anisodiamétrico, -ca *adj.* anisodiametric.
anisodonto, -ta *m., f.* anisodont.
anisoforia *f.* anisophoria.
anisogamético, -ca *adj.* anisogametic.
anisogameto *m.* anisogamete.
anisogamia *f.* anisogamy.
anisognato, -ta *adj.* anisognathous.
anisoiconía *f.* anisoiconia.
anisomastia *f.* anisomastia.
anisomelia *f.* anisomelia.
anisómero, -ra *adj.* anisomeric.
anisométrope *adj.* anisometrope.
anisometropía *m.* anisometropia.
anisometrópico, -ca *adj.* anisometropic.
anisomiopía *f.* anisomyopia.
anisoosmótico, -ca *adj.* anisosmotic.
anisopía *f.* anisopia.
anisopiesis *f.* anisopiesis.
anisopoiquilocitosis *f.* anisopoikilocytosis.
anisopsia *f.* anisopia.
anisorritmia *f.* anisorrhythmia.
anisosfigmia *f.* anisosphygmia.
anisosténico, -ca *adj.* anisosthenic.
anisotónico, -ca *adj.* anisotonic.
anisotropía *f.* anisotropy.
anisotrópico, -ca *adj.* anisotropic.
anisotropo, -pa *adj.* anisotropic.
anisuria *f.* anisuria.
anitrogenado, -da *adj.* anitrogenous.
anlaje *m.* anlage.
annulus annulus.
ano *m.* anus.
  ano artificial, ano contra natura artificial anus.
  ano ectópico ectopic anus.
  ano imperforado imperforate anus.
  ano tibiarum anus tibiarum.
  ano vesical anus vesicalis.
  ano vestibular, ano vulvovaginal vestibular anus, vulvovaginal anus.
anococcígeo, -a *adj.* anococcygeal.
anocoxígeo, -a *adj.* anococcygeal.
anocromasia *f.* anochromasia.
anodal *adj.* anodal.
anodermo *m.* anoderm.
anódico, -ca *adj.* anodic.
anodinia *f.* anodynia.
anodino, -na *adj.* anodyne.
ánodo *m.* anode.
  ánodo con capucha hooded anode.
  ánodo rotatorio rotating anode.
anodoncia *f.* anodontia.
  anodoncia falsa false anodontia.

anodoncia parcial partial anodontia.
anodoncia total total anodontia.
anodoncia verdadera true anodontia.
anodontia *f.* anodontia.
anodontismo *m.* anodontism.
anoespinal *adj.* anospinal.
anoético, -ca *adj.* anoetic.
anofelicida *adj.* anophelicide.
anofelífugo, -ga *adj.* anophelifuge.
anofelismo *m.* anophelism.
anoforia *f.* anophoria.
anoftalmía *f.* anophthalmia.
  anoftalmía consecutiva consecutive anophthalmia.
  anoftalmía primaria primary anophthalmia.
  anoftalmía secundaria secondary anophthalmia.
anoftalmo, -ma *m., f.* anophthalmus.
anogenital *adj.* anogenital.
anomalía *f.* anomaly.
  anomalía de Alder, anomalía de Alder-Reilly Alder's anomaly, Alder-Reilly anomaly.
  anomalía de Axenfeld Axenfeld's anomaly.
  anomalía en campanilla morning glory anomaly.
  anomalía cardíaca congénita congenital cardiac anomaly.
  anomalía de Chédiak-Steinbrinck-Higashi Chédiak-Steinbrinck-Higashi anomaly.
  anomalía congénita congenital anomaly.
  anomalía constitucional de la granulación de Alder Alder's constitutional granulation anomaly.
  anomalía cromosómica chromosomal anomaly, chromosome anomaly.
  anomalía de desarrollo developmental anomaly.
  anomalía de Ebstein Ebstein's anomaly.
  anomalía eugnásica eugnathic anomaly.
  anomalía de Freund Freund's anomaly.
  anomalía gestante gestant anomaly.
  anomalía de Hegglin Hegglin's anomaly.
  anomalía de May-Hegglin May-Hegglin's anomaly.
  anomalía Pelger-Hüet Pelger-Hüet anomaly.
  anomalía de Peters Peters' anomaly.
  anomalía de Poland Poland's anomaly.
  anomalía de Rieger Rieger's anomaly.
  anomalía de Shone Shone's anomaly.
  anomalía de Uhl Uhl's anomaly.
  anomalía de Undritz Undritz anomaly.
anomalopia *f.* anomalopia.
anomalopsia *f.* anomalopia.
anomaloscopio *m.* anomaloscope.
anomalotrofia *f.* anomalotrophy.
anomia *f.* anomia, anomie.
anonicosis *f.* anonychosis, anonychia.
anoniquia *f.* anonychosis, anonychia.
anoopsia *f.* anoopsia, anopsia.
anoperineal *adj.* anoperineal.
Anopheles Anopheles.
anopia *f.* anopia.
anoplastia *f.* anoplasty.
anopsia *f.* anoopsia, anopsia.
anorexia *f.* anorexia.
  anorexia falsa false anorexia.
  anorexia nerviosa anorexia nervosa.
anoréxico, -ca *adj.* anoretic, anorexic.
anorexígeno *m.* anorexiant.
anorexígeno, -na *adj.* anorexigenic.
anorgánico, -ca *adj.* anorganic.
anorganología *f.* anorganology.
anorgasmia *f.* anorgasmy, anorgasmia.
anormal *adj.* abnormal.
anormalidad *f.* abnormality.
anorquia *f.* anorchia, anorchidism.

anorquidia *f.* anorchia, anorchidism.
anórquidico, -ca *adj.* anorchidic.
anórquido, -da *adj.* anorchid.
anorquismo *m.* anorchism.
anorrectal *adj.* anorectal.
anortografía *f.* anorthography.
anortopia *f.* anorthopia.
anortosis *f.* anorthosis.
anorrectitis *f.* anorectitis.
anorrecto *m.* anorectum.
anorrectocólico, -ca *adj.* anorectocolonic.
anoscopia *f.* anoscopy.
anoscopio *m.* anoscope.
anosigmoidoscopia *f.* anosigmoidoscopy.
anosigmoidoscópico, -ca *adj.* anosigmoidoscopic.
anosmático, -ca *adj.* anosmatic.
anosmia *f.* anosmia.
  anosmia gustatoria anosmia gustatoria.
  anosmia preferencial preferential anosmia.
  anosmia respiratoria anosmia respiratoria.
anósmico, -ca *adj.* anosmic.
anosognosia *f.* anosognosia.
anosognósico, -ca *adj.* anosognosic.
anospinal *adj.* anospinal.
anosteoplasia *f.* anosteoplasia.
anostosis *f.* anostosis.
anotia *f.* anotia.
anoto *m.* anotus.
anotropía *f.* anotropia.
anovaginal *adj.* anovaginal.
anovaria *f.* anovaria.
anovarianismo *m.* anovarianism.
anovarismo *m.* anovarism.
anovesical *adj.* anovesical.
anovulación *f.* anovulation.
anovular *adj.* anovular.
anovulatorio, -a *adj.* anovulatory.
anovulomenorrea *f.* anovulomenorrhea.
anoxemia *f.* anoxemia.
anoxémico, -ca *adj.* anoxemic.
anoxihemia *f.* anoxemia.
anoxia *f.* anoxia.
  anoxia por afinidad con el oxígeno oxygen affinity anoxia.
  anoxia de altitud, anoxia de altura altitude anoxia.
  anoxia anémica anemic anoxia.
  anoxia anóxica anoxic anoxia.
  anoxia por difusión diffusion anoxia.
  anoxia por estancamiento, anoxia estasis stagnant anoxia.
  anoxia histotóxica histotoxic anoxia.
  anoxia del neonato anoxia neonatorum.
anóxico, -ca *adj.* anoxic.
anquilobléfaron *m.* ankyloblepharon.
  anquilobléfaron filiforme congénito ankyloblepharon filiforme adnatum.
anquilocolpos *m.* ankylocolpos.
anquilodactilia *f.* ankylodactyly, ankylodactylia.
anquilofobia *f.* ankylophobia.
anquiloglosia *f.* ankyloglossia.
  anquiloglosia completa complete ankyloglossia.
  anquiloglosia parcial partial ankyloglossia.
anquilómelo *m.* ankylomele.
anquilopoyético, -ca *adj.* ankylopoietic.
anquiloquilia *f.* ankylocheilia.
anquilorrafia *f.* anchillorrhaphy.
anquilorrinia *f.* ankylorrhinia.
anquilosado, -da *adj.* ankylosed.
anquilosis *f.* ankylosis.
  anquilosis de la articulación cricoaritenoidea cricoarytenoid joint ankylosis.

  anquilosis artificial artificial ankylosis.
  anquilosis dental dental ankylosis.
  anquilosis espuria spurious ankylosis.
  anquilosis del estribo stapedial ankylosis.
  anquilosis extracapsular extracapsular ankylosis.
  anquilosis falsa false ankylosis.
  anquilosis fibrosa fibrous ankylosis.
  anquilosis intracapsular intracapsular ankylosis.
  anquilosis ósea bony ankylosis.
  anquilosis verdadera true ankylosis.
anquilostoma *m.* ancylostome.
anquilostomático, -ca *adj.* ancylostomatic.
anquilostomiasis *f.* ancylostomiasis.
  anquilostomiasis cutánea, anquilostomiasis cutis cutaneous ancylostomiasis, ancylostomiasis cutis.
anquilótico, -ca *adj.* ankylotic.
anquilotomía *f.* ankylotomy.
anquilouretria *f.* ankylurethria.
anquiluretria *f.* ankylurethria.
ansa *f.* ansa.
ansado, -da *adj.* ansate.
ansiedad *f.* anxiety.
  ansiedad ante los extraños stranger anxiety.
  ansiedad anticipatoria anticipatory anxiety.
  ansiedad básica basic anxiety.
  ansiedad de castración castration anxiety.
  ansiedad circunstancial situational anxiety.
  ansiedad flotante free-floating anxiety.
  ansiedad noética noetic anxiety.
  ansiedad presenil anxietas presenilis.
  ansiedad de señal anticipatory anxiety.
  ansiedad de separación separation anxiety.
  ansiedad de situación situation anxiety.
  ansiedad traumática traumatic anxiety.
ansiforme *adj.* ansiform.
ansiolítico, -ca *adj.* anxiolytic.
ansotomía *f.* ansotomy.
antagonismo *m.* antagonism.
  antagonismo bacteriano bacterial antagonism.
antagonista *adj.* antagonist.
  antagonista del ácido fólico folic acid antagonist.
  antagonista aldosterona aldosterone antagonist.
  antagonista asociado associated antagonist.
  antagonista del calcio calcium antagonist.
  antagonista competitivo competitive antagonist.
  antagonista directo direct antagonist.
  antagonista enzimático enzyme antagonist.
  antagonista de los narcóticos, antagonista narcótico narcotic antagonist.
antálgico, -ca *adj.* antalgic, antalgesic.
antebrachium forearm, antebrachium.
antebraquial *adj.* antebrachial.
antebrazo *m.* forearm, antebrachium.
antecardio *m.* antecardium.
antecedente *m.* antecedent.
antecedentes *m.* background, history.
  antecedentes médicos past health.
  antecedentes personales y sociales personal and social history.
ante cibum ante cibum.
antecubital *adj.* antecubital.
antecurvatura *f.* antecurvature.
antefebril *adj.* antefebrile.
anteflexio anteflexion, anteflexio.
anteflexión *f.* anteflexion, anteflexio.
  anteflexión del iris anteflexion of the iris.
  anteflexión uterina, anteflexio uteri uterine anteflexion.

anteflexo, -xa *adj.* anteflex.
antehélix *m.* anthelix, antihelix.
antehipófisis *f.* antehypophysis.
antelocación *f.* antelocation.
antelona *f.* anthelone.
antelótico, -ca *adj.* anthelotic.
antema *m.* anthema.
antemético, -ca *adj.* antiemetic.
ante mortem ante mortem.
antemuro *m.* claustrum.
antenatal *adj.* antenatal.
anteojeras *f.* goggles.
anteojos *m.* spectacles.
 anteojos de armazón de alambre wire frame spectacles.
 anteojos de Bartels Bartels' spectacles.
 anteojos bifocales bifocal spectacles.
 anteojos de buzo divers' spectacles.
 anteojos de clérigo clerical spectacles.
 anteojos compuestos compound spectacles.
 anteojos descentrados decentered spectacles.
 anteojos divididos divided spectacles.
 anteojos entintados tinted spectacles.
 anteojos estenopeicos stenopeic spectacles, stenopaic spectacles.
 anteojos fotocrómicos photochromic spectacles.
 anteojos industriales industrial spectacles.
 anteojos de Masselon Masselon's spectacles.
 anteojos de media lente half-glass spectacles.
 anteojos de mica mica spectacles.
 anteojos de muleta crutch spectacles.
 anteojos ortoscópicos orthoscopic spectacles.
 anteojos pantoscópicos pantoscopic spectacles.
 anteojos periscópicos periscopic spectacles.
 anteojos de predicador clerical spectacles.
 anteojos prismáticos prismatic spectacles.
 anteojos protectores protective spectacles.
 anteojos de púlpito pulpit spectacles.
 anteojos de seguridad safety spectacles.
 anteojos trifocales trifocal spectacles.
anteparto *adj.* antepartum.
ante partum antepartum.
antepié *m.* forefoot.
antepirético, -ca *adj.* antepyretic.
anteposición *f.* anteposition.
antepróstata *f.* anteprostate.
anteprostatitis *f.* anteprostatitis.
antergia *f.* antergia.
antérgico, -ca *adj.* antergic.
anterior *adj.* anterior.
anteroclusión *f.* anteroclusion.
anteroexterno, -na *adj.* anteroexternal.
anterógrado, -ra *adj.* anterograde.
anteroinferior *adj.* anteroinferior.
anterointerno, -na *adj.* anterointernal.
anterolateral *adj.* anterolateral.
anteromediano, -na *adj.* anteromedian.
anteromedio, -dia *adj.* anteromedial.
anteroposterior *adj.* anteroposterior.
anteroseptal *adj.* anteroseptal.
anterosuperior *adj.* anterosuperior.
anteroventral *adj.* anteroventral.
antesistole *f.* antesystole.
anteversión *f.* anteversion.
antevertido, -da *adj.* anteverted.
anthélix *m.* anthelix.
antiabortivo *m.* antiabortifacient.
antiácido, -da *m. y adj.* antacid, antiacid.
antiadrenérgico, -ca *m. y adj.* antiadrenergic.
antiaglutinante *adj.* antiagglutinating.
antialcalino, -na *adj.* antalkaline.

antialérgico, -ca *adj.* antiallergic.
antialéxico, -ca *adj.* antialexic.
antialgesia *f.* antalgesia.
antiálgico, -ca *adj.* antalgic, antalgesic.
antiamilasa *f.* antiamylase.
antianabólico, -ca *adj.* antianabolic.
antianafilaxia *f.* antianaphylaxis.
antianafilaxis *f.* antianaphylaxis.
antiandrógeno *m.* antiandrogen.
antiandrógeno, -na *adj.* antiandrogenic.
antianémico, -ca *adj.* antianemic.
antianofelina *f.* antianopheline.
antianticuerpo *m.* antiantibody.
antiantídoto *m.* antiantidote.
antiantitoxina *f.* antiantitoxin.
antlapoplético, -ca *adj.* antapoplectic, antiapoplectic.
antiaracnolisina *f.* antiarachnolysin.
antiarina *f.* antiarin.
antiarrítmico, -ca *adj.* antiarrhythmic.
antiarsenina *f.* antiarsenin.
antiartrítico, -ca *adj.* antiarthritic, antarthritic.
antiasmático, -ca *adj.* antiasthmatic, antasthmatic.
antiasténico, -ca *adj.* antasthenic.
antiaterógeno, -na *adj.* antiatherogenic.
antiatrófico, -ca *adj.* antatrophic.
antiautolisina *f.* antiautolysin.
antibacteriano, -na *adj.* antibacterial.
antibactérico, -ca *adj.* antibacterial.
antibacteriolítico, -ca *adj.* antibacteriolytic.
antibéquico, -ca *adj.* antibechic.
antibiograma *m.* antibiogram.
antibiótico, -ca *adj.* antibiotic.
antibioticograma *m.* antibiogram.
antibioticorresistente *adj.* antibiotic-resistant.
antibiotina *f.* antibiotin.
antiblástico, -ca *adj.* antiblastic.
antiblenorrágico, -ca *adj.* antiblennorrhagic.
antibociógeno, -na *adj.* antigoitrogenic.
antibrómico, -ca *adj.* antibromic.
antibubónico, -ca *adj.* antibubonic.
anticalculoso, -sa *adj.* anticalculous.
anticanceroso, -sa *adj.* anticancer.
anticaquéctico, -ca *adj.* anticachectic.
anticarcinogénico, -ca *adj.* anticarcinogenic.
anticarcinógeno, -na *adj.* anticarcinogen.
anticariogénico, -ca *adj.* anticariogenic.
anticarioso, -sa *adj.* anticarious.
anticatafiláctico, -ca *adj.* anticataphylactic, antikataphylactic.
anticatalizador, -ra *adj.* anticatalyzer.
anticatarral *adj.* anticatarrhal.
anticátodo *m.* anticathode.
anticáustico, -ca *adj.* anticaustic.
anticefalálgico, -ca *adj.* anticephalalgic.
anticetogénesis *f.* antiketogenesis.
anticetogénico, -ca *adj.* antiketogenetic.
anticetógeno, -na *adj.* antiketogenic.
anticimohexasa *f.* antizymohexase.
anticimótico, -ca *adj.* antizymotic.
anticinasa *f.* antikinase.
anticipación *f.* anticipation.
anticipado, -da *adj.* anticipatory.
anticitolisina *f.* anticytolysin.
anticitotoxina *f.* anticytotoxin.
anticlorótico, -ca *adj.* antichlorotic.
anticnemion *m.* anticnemion.
anticoagulación *f.* anticoagulation.
anticoagulante *adj.* anticoagulant.
 anticoagulante circulante circulating anticoagulant.
anticoagulina *f.* anticoagulin.

anticodón *m.* anticodon.
anticolagenasa *f.* anticollagenase.
anticolagogo, -ga *adj.* anticholagogue.
anticolinérgico, -ca *adj.* anticholinergic.
anticolinesterasa *f.* anticholinesterase.
anticoloidoclástico, -ca *adj.* anticolloidoclastic.
anticomplemento *m.* anticomplement.
anticomplementario, -ria *adj.* anticomplementary.
anticoncepción *f.* contraception.
anticonceptivo, -va *adj.* contraceptive.
 anticonceptivo de barrera barrier contraceptive.
 anticonceptivo oral oral contraceptive.
 anticonceptivo oral combinado combination oral contraceptive.
 anticonceptivo oral secuencial sequential oral contraceptive.
anticontagioso, -sa *adj.* anticontagious.
anticonvulsivo, -va *adj.* anticonvulsive.
anticrecimiento *adj.* antigrowth.
anticrítico, -ca *adj.* anticritical.
anticuerpo *m.* antibody.
 anticuerpo aglutinante agglutinating antibody.
 anticuerpo alocitófilo allocytophilic antibody.
 anticuerpo anafiláctico anaphylactic antibody.
 anticuerpo anti-D anti-D antibody.
 anticuerpo anti-ADN anti-DNA antibody.
 anticuerpo antigliadina antigliadin antibody.
 anticuerpo antiidiotipo anti-idiotype antibody.
 anticuerpo antimembrana basal anti-basement membrane antibody.
 anticuerpo antimembrana basal glomerular (anti-MBG) anti-glomerular basement membrane antibody.
 anticuerpo antimicrosomal antimicrosomal antibody.
 anticuerpo antimitocóndrico, anticuerpo antimitocondrial antimitochondrial antibody.
 anticuerpo antinuclear (ANA) antinuclear antibody (ANA).
 anticuerpo antirreceptor antireceptor antibody.
 anticuerpo antirreceptor de acetilcolina antiacetylcholine receptor antibody.
 anticuerpo antitiroglobulina antithyroglobulin antibody.
 anticuerpo antitiroideo antithyroid antibody.
 anticuerpo antitreponema treponema-immobilizing antibody.
 anticuerpo autoantiidiotípico auto-anti-idiotypic antibody.
 anticuerpo autólogo antologous antibody.
 anticuerpo biespecífico bispecific antibody.
 anticuerpo bivalente bivalent antibody.
 anticuerpo bloqueante blocking antibody.
 anticuerpo caliente, anticuerpo caliente-reactivo warm antibody, warm-reactive antibody.
 anticuerpo circulante detectable circulating antibody.
 anticuerpo citófilo cytophilic antibody.
 anticuerpo citotóxico cytotoxic antibody.
 anticuerpo citotrópico cytotropic antibody.
 anticuerpo completo complete antibody.
 anticuerpo desespeciado despeciated antibody.

anticuerpo inhibidor de la TSH (TDA) TSH-displacing antibody (TDA).

anticuerpo fijador del complemento complement-fixing antibody.

anticuerpo fijo a célula, anticuerpo ligado a la célula cell-fixed antibody, cell-bound antibody.

anticuerpo fluorescente fluorescent antibody.

anticuerpo de Forssman Forsmann antibody.

anticuerpo frío, anticuerpo frío-reactivo cold antibody, cold-reactive antibody.

anticuerpo heterocitotrópico heterocytotropic antibody.

anticuerpo heteroclítico heteroclitic antibody.

anticuerpo heterófilo heterophil antibody, heterophile antibody.

anticuerpo heterogenético heterogenetic antibody.

anticuerpo híbrido hybrid antibody.

anticuerpo homocitotrópico homocytotropic antibody.

anticuerpo idiotipo idiotype antibody.

anticuerpo incompleto incomplete antibody.

anticuerpo inhibidor inhibiting antibody.

anticuerpo inmunitario immune antibody.

anticuerpo isófilo isophil antibody.

anticuerpo linfocitotóxico lymphocytotoxic antibody.

anticuerpo mitocondrial mitochondrial antibody.

anticuerpo monoclonal monoclonal antibody.

anticuerpo natural natural antibody.

anticuerpo neutralizante neutralizing antibody.

anticuerpo normal normal antibody.

anticuerpo policlonal polyclonal antibody.

anticuerpo de Prausnitz-Küstner Prausnitz-Küstner antibody.

anticuerpo protector protective antibody.

anticuerpo de reacción cruzada cross-reacting antibody.

anticuerpo reagínico reaginic antibody.

anticuerpo Rh Rh antibody.

anticuerpo salino saline antibody.

anticuerpo sensibilizante sensitizing antibody.

anticuerpo de tipo equino horse-type antibody.

anticuerpo treponémico treponemal antibody.

anticuerpo univalente univalent antibody.

anticuerpo Wassermann Wassermann antibody.

anticurare *m.* anticurare.

antidepresivo, -va *adj.* antidepressant.

antidiabético, -ca *adj.* antidiabetic.

antidiarreico, -ca *adj.* antidiarrheal, antidiarrheic.

antidiastasa *f.* antidiastase.

antidisentérico, -ca *adj.* antidysenteric.

antidisrítmico, -ca *adj.* antidysrhythmic.

antidisúrico, -ca *adj.* antidysuric.

antidiuresis *f.* antidiuresis.

antidiurético, -ca *adj.* antidiuretic.

antidiuretina *f.* antidiuretin.

antidotal *adj.* antidotal.

antidoto *m.* antidote.

antídoto fisiológico physiologic antidote.

antídoto mecánico mechanical antidote.

antídoto químico chemical antidote.

antídoto universal universal antidote.

antidrómico, -ca *adj.* antidromic.

antieccemático, -ca *adj.* antieczematic.

antieccematoso, -sa *adj.* antieczematous.

antiedematoso, -sa *adj.* antiedematous, antiedemic.

antiemético, -ca *adj.* antiemetic.

antiemulsina *f.* antiemulsin.

antiendotóxico, -ca *adj.* antiendotoxic.

antiendotoxina *f.* antiendotoxin.

antienérgico, -ca *adj.* antienergic.

antienzima *f.* antienzyme.

antiepiléptico, -ca *adj.* antiepileptic.

antiepitelial *adj.* antiepithelial.

antierótico, -ca *adj.* anterotic.

antiescabioso, -sa *adj.* antiscabietic.

antiescabiético, -ca *adj.* antiscabietic.

antiescarlatinoso, -sa *adj.* antiscarlatinal.

antiescorbútico, -ca *adj.* antiscorbutic.

antiespasmódico *m.* antispasmodic.

antiespasmódico biliar billiary antispasmodic.

antiespasmódico bronquial bronchial antispasmodic.

antiespasmódico, -ca *adj.* antispasmodic.

antiespástico, -ca *adj.* antispastic.

antiespermotoxina *f.* antispermotoxin.

antiespiroquético, -ca *adj.* antispirochetic.

antiesquistosómico, -ca *adj.* antischistosomal.

antiestafilocócico, -ca *adj.* antistaphylococcic.

antiestafilohemolisina *f.* antistaphylohemolysin.

antiestafilolisina *f.* antistaphylolysin.

antiesteapsina *f.* antisteapsin.

antiesterasa *f.* antiesterase.

antiestreptocinasa *f.* antistreptokinase.

antiestreptocócico, -ca *adj.* antistreptococcic.

antiestreptolisina *f.* antistreptolysin.

antiestreptoquinasa *f.* antistreptokinase.

antiestrógeno *m.* antiestrogen.

antifagina *f.* antiphagin.

antifagocítico, -ca *adj.* antiphagocytic.

antifebril *adj.* antifebrile.

antifermento *m.* antiferment.

antifibrilatorio, -ria *adj.* antifibrillatory.

antifibrinolisina *f.* antifibrinolysin.

antifibrinolítico, -ca *adj.* antifibrinolytic.

antifilárico, -ca *adj.* antifilarial.

antiflatulento, -ta *adj.* antiflatulent.

antiflogístico, -ca *adj.* antiphlogistic.

antifóbico, -ca *adj.* antiphobic.

antifol *m.* antifol.

antifolato *m.* antifolate.

antifólico, -ca *adj.* antifolic.

antifrinolisina *f.* antiphrynolysin.

antiftiríaco, -ca *adj.* antipediculotic.

antifúngico, -ca *adj.* antifungal.

antigalactagogo, -ga *adj.* antigalactagogue.

antigaláctico, -ca *adj.* antigalactic.

antigametocítico, -ca *adj.* antigametocytic.

antigelatinasa *f.* antigelatinase.

antigenemia *f.* antigenemia.

antigenémico, -ca *adj.* antigenemic.

antigenicidad *f.* antigenicity.

antigénico, -ca *adj.* antigenic.

antígeno *m.* antigen.

antígeno alogénico allogenic antigen.

antígeno asociado a hepatitis hepatitis associated antigen (HAA).

antígeno asociado a las leucemias humanas human leukemia-associated antigen.

antígeno asociado a tumor tumor associated antigen.

antígeno Australia Australia antigen.

antígeno Boivin Boivin's antigen.

antígeno capsular capsular antigen.

antígeno carbohidrato C C carbohydrate antigen.

antígeno carcinoembrionario (CEA) carcinoembryonic antigen.

antígeno central de la hepatitis B hepatitis B core antigen.

antígeno clase I class I antigen.

antígeno clase II class II antigen.

antígeno clase III class III antigen.

antígeno colesterinizado cholesterinized antigen.

antígeno completo complete antigen.

antígeno común common antigen.

antígeno conjugado conjugated antigen.

antígeno corazón de vacuno beef heart antigen.

antígeno core del virus de la hepatitis B hepatitis B core antigen.

antígeno de cubierta envelope antigen.

antígeno delta delta antigen.

antígeno específico de especie species-specific antigen.

antígeno específico de órgano organ-specific antigen.

antígeno específico de tejido tissue-specific antigen.

antígeno específico de tumor tumor-specific antigen (TSA).

antígeno específico specific antigen.

antígeno F F antigen.

antígeno febril febrile antigen.

antígeno flagelar flagellar antigen.

antígeno Forssman Forssman antigen.

antígeno Gm Gm antigen.

antígeno de grupo group antigen.

antígeno de grupo sanguíneo blood group antigen.

antígeno H H antigen.

antígeno de hepatitis hepatitis antigen.

antígeno de hepatitis sérica serum-hepatitis antigen (SH antigen).

antígeno heterófilo heterophil antigen.

antígeno heterogénico heterogenetic antigen.

antígeno heterógeno heterogenetic antigen.

antígeno heterólogo heterologous antigen.

antígeno hidrocarbonado carbohydrate antigen.

antígeno de histocompatibilidad histocompatibility antigen.

antígeno de histocompatibilidad mayor histocompatibility major antigen.

antígeno de histocompatibilidad menor histocompatibility minor antigen.

antígeno homólogo homologous antigen.

antígeno H-Y H-Y antigen.

antígeno Ia Ia antigen.

antígeno isófilo isophile antigen.

antígeno isogénico isogenic antigen.

antígeno K K antigen.

antígeno Km Km antigen.

antígeno Kveim Kveim antigen.

antígeno LD LD antigen.

antígeno de la leucemia linfoblástica aguda común (calla) common acute lymphoblastic leukemia antigen (calla).

antígeno leucocitario común common leukocyte antigen.

antígeno leucocitario humano, antígeno de los linfocitos humanos (hla) human lymphocyte antigen (HLA).

antígeno linfocito-definido (ld) lymphocyte-defined (ld) antigen.

antígeno Ly, antígeno Lyt Ly antigen, Lyt antigen.

antígeno Lyb Lyb antigen.

antígeno m estreptocócico streptococcus m antigen.

antígeno nuclear nuclear antigen.

antígeno nuclear extraíble (ena) extractable nuclear antigen (ena).

antígeno o o antigen.

antígeno oncofetal oncofetal antigen.

antígeno oncofetal pancreático (ofp) pancreatic oncofetal antigen (poa).

antígeno Oz Oz antigen.

antígeno parcial partial antigen.

antígeno del polen pollen antigen.

antígeno privado private antigen.

antígeno propio self-antigen.

antígeno prostático específico (psa) prostate specific antigen.

antígeno de proteína agregada por calor heat-aggregated protein antigen.

antígeno para la prueba cutánea de la parotiditis mumps skin test antigen.

antígeno público public antigen.

antígeno r R antigen.

antígeno de reacción cruzada cross-reacting antigen.

antígeno de recuerdo recall antigen.

antígeno Rhus toxicodendron Rhus toxicodendron antigen.

antígeno Rhus venenata Rhus venenata antigen.

antígeno s S antigen.

antígeno secuestrado sequestered antigen.

antígeno sensibilizado sensitized antigen.

antígeno serodefinido (sd) sero-defined antigen, serologically defined antigen.

antígeno de shock shock antigen.

antígeno Sm Sm antigens.

antígeno soluble soluble antigen.

antígeno somático somatic antigen.

antígeno SS-a SS-a antigen.

antígeno SS-b SS-b antigen.

antígeno de superficie del virus de la hepatitis b hepatitis b surface antigen (hbsag).

antígeno t t antigen.

antígeno Tac Tac antigen.

antígeno T-dependiente T-dependent antigen.

antígeno Thy, antígeno theta Thy antigen, theta antigen.

antígeno t-independiente t-independent antigen.

antígeno tl tl antigen.

antígeno de trasplante transplantation antigen.

antígeno de trasplante específico del tumor tumor-specific transplantation antigen (ttet).

antígeno tumoral tumor antigen.

antígeno Vi Vi antigen.

antígeno xenógeno xenogeneic antigen.

antigenófilo, -la *adj.* antigenophil, antigentophil.

antigenoterapia *f.* antigenotherapy, antigentotherapy.

antiglobulina *f.* antiglobulin.

antigonadotrópico, -ca *adj.* antigonadotrophic.

antigonorreico, -ca *adj.* antigonorrheic.

anti-hbc *m.* anti-hbc.

anti-hbs *m.* anti-hbs.

antihélix *m.* anthelix.

antihelmíntico, -ca *adj.* anthelmintic, antihelminthic, anthelminthic.

antihelótico, -ca *adj.* anthelotic.

antihemaglutinina *f.* antihemagglutinin.

antihemolisina *f.* antihemolysin.

antihemolítico, -ca *adj.* antihemolytic.

antihemorrágico, -ca *adj.* anthemorrhagic, antihemorrhagic.

antiherpético, -ca *adj.* antherpetic, antiherpetic.

antiheterolisina *f.* antiheterolysin.

antihidrofóbico, -ca *adj.* antihydrophobic.

antihidrópico, -ca *adj.* antihydropic.

antihidrótico, -ca *adj.* antihydrotic.

antihigiénico, -ca *adj.* insanitary.

antihipercolesterolémico, -ca *adj.* antihypercholesteronemic.

antihiperglucémico, -ca *adj.* antihyperglycemic.

antihiperlipoproteico, -ca *adj.* antihyperlipoproteinemic.

antihipertensivo, -va *adj.* antihypertensive.

antihipnótico, -ca *adj.* antihypnotic.

antihipotensor, -ra *adj.* antihypotensive.

antihistamina *f.* antihistamine.

antihistamínico, -ca *adj.* antihistaminic.

antihormona *f.* antihormone.

antictérico, -ca *adj.* anti-icteric.

antiictérico, -ca *adj.* anti-icteric.

antiidiotipo *m.* anti-idiotype.

antiinfeccioso *m.* anti-infective.

antiinfeccioso, -sa *adj.* anti-infectious.

antiinflamatorio, -ria *adj.* anti-inflammatory.

antiiniciador *m.* antiinitiator.

antiinión *m.* antinion.

antiinmune *adj.* anti-immune.

antiinsulina *f.* anti-insulin.

antiisolisina *f.* anti-isolysin.

antilactosuero *m.* antilactoserum.

antileishmaniásico, -ca *adj.* antileishmanial.

antilémico, -ca *adj.* antilemic.

antileproso, -sa *adj.* antileprotic.

antileucocidina *f.* antileukocidin.

antileucocito *m.* antileukocytic.

antileucotoxina *f.* antileukotoxin.

antilipasa *f.* antilipase.

antilipémico, -ca *adj.* antilipemic.

antilipoide *m.* antilipoid.

antilipotrópico, -ca *adj.* antilipotropic.

antilipotropismo *m.* antilipotropism.

antilísico, -ca *adj.* antilysic.

antilisina *f.* antilysin.

antilisis *f.* antilysis.

antilítico, -ca[1] *adj.* antilytic.

antilítico, -ca[2] *adj.* antilithic.

antilobium *m.* antilobium.

antiluético, -ca *adj.* antiluetic.

antiluteogénico, -ca *adj.* antiluteogenic.

antimalárico, -ca *adj.* antimalarial.

antimaníaco, -ca *adj.* antimaniacal.

antimefítico, -ca *adj.* antimephitic.

antímero *m.* antimere, antimer.

antimesentérico, -ca *adj.* antimesenteric.

antimetabolito *m.* antimetabolite.

antimetahemoglobinémico, -ca *adj.* antimethemoglobinemic.

antimetropía *f.* antimetropia.

antimiasmático, -ca *adj.* antimiasmatic.

antimiasténico, -ca *adj.* antimyasthenic.

antimicótico, -ca *adj.* antimycotic.

antimicrobiano, -na *adj.* antimicrobial, antimicrobic.

antimidriásico, -ca *adj.* antimydriatic.

antimineralocorticoide *m.* antimineralocorticoid.

antimitótico, -ca *adj.* antimitotic.

antimongolismo *m.* antimongolism.

antimórfico, -ca *adj.* antimorphic.

antimorfo *m.* antimorph.

antimuscarínico, -ca *adj.* antimuscarinic.

antimutagénico, -ca *adj.* antimutagenic.

antimutágeno *m.* antimutagen.

antinarcótico, -ca *adj.* antinarcotic.

antinatriférico, -ca *adj.* antinatriferic.

antinatriuresis *f.* antinatriuresis.

antinauseante *adj.* antinauseant.

antinauseoso, -sa *adj.* antinauseant.

antinefrítico, -ca *adj.* antinephritic.

antineoplásico, -ca *adj.* antineoplastic.

antineoplaston *m.* antineoplaston.

antineumocócico, -ca *adj.* antipneumococcic.

antineurálgico, -ca *adj.* antineuralgic.

antineurítico, -ca *adj.* antineuritic.

antineurotoxina *f.* antineurotoxin.

antiníade *m.* antiniad.

antinial *adj.* antinial.

antinión *m.* antinion.

antinomia *f.* antinomy.

antinuclear *adj.* antinuclear.

antiodontálgico, -ca *adj.* antiodontalgic.

antioftálmico, -ca *adj.* antophthalmic.

antiofídico, -ca *adj.* antivenom.

antioncogen *m.* antioncogene.

antioncótico, -ca *adj.* antioncotic.

antiopsonina *f.* antipsonin.

antiorgástico, -ca *adj.* antiorgastic.

antiovulatorio, -ria *adj.* antiovaluatory.

antioxidación *f.* antioxidation.

antioxidante *m.* antioxidant.

antioxidasa *f.* antioxidase.

antipalúdico, -ca *adj.* antipaludial.

antiparalelo, -la *adj.* antiparallel.

antiparalítico, -ca *adj.* antiparalytic.

antiparasitario, -ria *adj.* antiparasitic.

antiparastata *f.* antiparastata.

antiparasimpaticomimético, -ca *adj.* antiparasympathomimetic.

antiparastitis *f.* antiparastitis.

antiparkinsoniano, -na *adj.* antiparkinsonian.

antipedicular *adj.* antipedicular.

antipediculoso, -sa *adj.* antipedicular.

antipediculótico, -ca *adj.* antipediculotic.

antiperiódico, -ca *adj.* antiperiodic.

antiperistáltico, -ca *adj.* antiperistaltic.

antiperistalsis *f.* antiperistalsis.

antiperistaltismo *f.* antiperistalsis.

antiperspirante *adj.* antiperspirant.

antipestoso, -sa *adj.* antiplague.

antipiogénico, -ca *adj.* antipyogenic.

antipiógeno, -na *adj.* antipyogenic.

antipiresis *f.* antipyresis.

antipirético, -ca *adj.* antipyretic.

antipirótico, -ca *adj.* antipyrotic.

antiplaquetario, -ria *adj.* antiplatelet.

antiplásico, -ca *adj.* antiplastic.

antiplasmina *f.* antiplasmin.

antiplasmódico, -ca *adj.* antiplasmodial.

antiplástico, -ca *adj.* antiplastic.

antpneumocócico, -ca *adj.* antipneumococcal, antipneumococcic.

antipoda *f.* antipode.

antípoda óptica optical antipode.

antipodágrico, -ca *adj.* antipodagric.

antipodal *adj.* antipodal.

antipolicitémico, -ca *adj.* antipolycythemic.

antiponzoñoso, -sa *adj.* antivenin.

antiportador, -ra *adj.* antiporter.

antiporte *m.* antiport.

antiprecipitina *f.* antiprecipitin.

antiprogestágeno *m.* antiprogestin.

antipróstata *f.* antiprostate.

antiprostatitis *f.* antiprostatitis.
antiprotozoario, -ria *adj.* antiprotozoal.
antiprotrombina *f.* antiprothrombin.
antipruriginoso, -sa *adj.* antipruritical.
antiprurítico, -ca *adj.* antipruritical.
antipruritoso, -sa *adj.* antipruritical.
antipsicótico, -ca *adj.* antipsychotic.
antipsoriásico, -ca *adj.* antipsoriatic.
antipsórico, -ca *adj.* antipsoric.
antiptírico, -ca *adj.* antiphthiriac.
antipútrido, -da *adj.* antiputrefactive.
antiqueirotonía *f.* anticherotonus.
antiquenotoxina *f.* antikenotoxin.
antiquetógeno, -na *adj.* antiketogenic.
antiquimosina *f.* antichymosin.
antirrábico, -ca *adj.* antirabic.
antirraquítico, -ca *adj.* antirachitic.
antirreumático, -ca *adj.* antirheumatic.
antirrickettsiásico, -ca *adj.* antirickettsial.
antirrumiante *m.* antiruminant.
antisaluresis *f.* antisaluresis.
antiscólico, -ca *adj.* anthelmintic.
antiseborreico, -ca *adj.* antiseborrheic.
antisecretor, -ra *adj.* antisecretory.
antisecretorio, -ria *adj.* antisecretory.
antisentido *f.* antisense.
antisepsia *f.* antisepsis.
antisepsis *f.* antisepsis.
antisepticismo *m.* antisepticism.
antiséptico, -ca *adj.* antiseptic.
antiserotonina *f.* antiserotonin.
antisialagogo, -ga *adj.* antisialagogue.
antisiálico, -ca *adj.* antisialic.
antisidérico, -ca *adj.* antisideric.
antisifilítico, -ca *adj.* antisyphilitic.
antisimpático, -ca *adj.* antisympathetic.
antisocial *adj.* antisocial.
antisocialismo *m.* antisocialism.
antispasmódico, -ca *adj.* antispasmodic.
antistático, -ca *adj.* antagonist.
antisteapsina *f.* antisteapsin.
antisudoral *adj.* antisudoral.
antisudorífico, -ca *adj.* antisudorific.
antisudoríparo, -ra *adj.* antiperspirant.
antisuero *m.* antiserum.
  antisuero Erysipelothrix rhusiopathiae Erysipelothrix rhusiopathiae antiserum.
  antisuero específico specific antiserum.
  antisuero contra el factor de crecimiento nervioso nerve growth factor antiserum.
  antisuero de grupos sanguíneos blood group antiserum.
  antisuero heterólogo heterologous antiserum.
  antisuero homólogo homologous antiserum.
  antisuero monovalente monovalent antiserum.
  antisuero polivalente polyvalent antiserum.
  antisuero Rh Rh antiserum.
antitenar *adj.* antithenar.
antitérmico, -ca *adj.* antithermic.
antitetánico, -ca *adj.* antitetanic.
antitífico, -ca *adj.* antityphoid.
antitifoideo, -a *adj.* antityphoid.
antitifoídico, -ca *adj.* antityphoid.
antitíptico, -ca *adj.* antiperiodic.
antitiroideo, -a *adj.* antithyroid.
antitirotóxico, -ca *adj.* antithyrotoxic.
antitirotrópico, -ca *adj.* antithyrotropic.
antitísico, -ca *adj.* antiphthisic.
antitónico, -ca *adj.* antitonic.
antitóxico, -ca *adj.* antitoxic.
antitoxígeno *m.* antitoxigen.
antitoxina *f.* antitoxin, antivenin.
  antitoxina contra la araña viuda negra black widow spider antivenin.

antitoxina bivalente de la gangrena gaseosa bivalent gas gangrene antitoxin.
antitoxina botrófica bothropic antitoxin, bothrops antitoxin.
antitoxina botulínica botulism antitoxin, botulinum antitoxin.
antitoxina bovina bovine antitoxin.
antitoxina crotalus crotalus antitoxin.
antitoxina despeciada despeciated antitoxin.
antitoxina diftérica diphtheria antitoxin.
antitoxina disentérica dysentery antitoxin.
antitoxina de la escarlatina scarlet fever antitoxin.
antitoxina del estafilococo staphylococcus antitoxin.
antitoxina de la gangrena gaseosa gas gangrene antitoxin.
antitoxina normal normal antitoxin.
antitoxina pentavalente de la gangrena gaseosa pentavalent gas gangrene antitoxin.
antitoxina tetánica tetanus antitoxin.
antitoxina tetánica y de la gangrena gaseosa tetanus and gas gangrene antitoxin.
antitoxina tetánica perfringens tetanus-perfringens antitoxin.
antitoxina vegetal plant antitoxin.
antitoxinógeno *m.* antitoxinogen.
antitrago *m.* antitragus.
antitragus *m.* antitragus.
antitreponémico, -ca *adj.* antitreponemal.
antitricomoniásico, -ca *adj.* antitrichomonal.
antitripanosomásico, -ca *adj.* antitrypanosomal.
antitrípsico, -ca antitríptico, -ca *adj.* antitrypsic.
antitripsina *f.* antitrypsin.
antitríptico, -ca *adj.* antitryptic.
antitrismo *m.* antitrismus.
antitrombina *f.* antithrombin.
  antitrombina normal normal antithrombin.
antitromboplastina *f.* antithromboplastin.
antitrombótico, -ca *adj.* antithrombotic.
antitrópico, -ca *adj.* antitropic.
antitropina *f.* antitropin.
antítrope *m.* antitrope.
antítropo *m.* antitrope.
antituberculina *f.* antituberculin.
antituberculoso, -sa *adj.* antitubercular, antituberculous.
antitubulina *f.* antitubulin.
antitumorigénesis *f.* antitumorigenesis.
antitumorígeno, -na *adj.* antitumorigenic.
antitusígeno, -na *adj.* antitussive.
antitusivo, -va *adj.* antitussive.
antiulceroso, -sa *adj.* antiulcerative.
antiurático, -ca *adj.* antiuratic.
antiureasa *f.* antiurease.
antiurocinasa *f.* antiurokinase.
antiveneno *m.* antivenene, antivenin.
  antiveneno de araña viuda negra black widow spider antivenin.
antivenenoso, -sa *adj.* antivenomous.
antivenéreo, -a *adj.* antivenereal.
antivermicular *adj.* antihelminthic.
antiverminoso, -sa *adj.* antihelminthic.
antiviral *adj.* antiviral.
antivírico, - ca *adj.* antiviral.
antivirósico, -ca *adj.* antivirotic.
antivirulina *f.* antivirulin.
antivirus *m.* antivirus.
antivitamina *f.* antivitamin.
antivivisección *f.* antivivisection.
antixeroftálmico, -ca *adj.* antixerophthalmic.
antixerótico, -ca *adj.* antixerotic.

antocianidina *f.* anthocyanidin.
antocianinas *f.* anthocyanins.
antocianinemia *f.* anthocyaninemia.
antocianinuria *f.* anthocyaninuria.
antofobia *f.* anthophobia.
antojo[1] *m.* whim.
antojo[2] *m.* birthmark.
antorisma *m.* anthorisma.
antracele *m.* antrocele.
antracemia *f.* anthracemia.
antracia *f.* anthracia.
antrácico, - ca *adj.* anthracic, anthracidal.
antracoide *adj.* anthracoid.
antracómetro *m.* anthracometer.
antraconecrosis *f.* anthraconecrosis.
antracosilicosis *f.* anthracosilicosis.
antracosis *f.* anthracosis.
  antracosis lingual anthracosis linguae.
antracótico, -ca *adj.* anthracotic.
antral *adj.* antral.
antranecrosis *f.* anthraconecrosis.
antrapurpurina *f.* anthrapurpurin.
ántrax *m.* carbuncle.
  ántrax renal renal carbuncle.
antrectomía *f.* antrectomy.
ántrico, -ca *adj.* antral.
antritis *f.* antritis.
antro *m.* antrum.
antroaticotomía *f.* antroatticotomy.
antrobucal *adj.* antrobuccal.
antrocele *m.* antrocele.
antrodinia *f.* antrodynia.
antroduodenectomía *f.* antroduodenectomy.
antróforo *m.* antrophore.
antrofosia *f.* antrophose.
antronalgia *f.* antronalgia.
antronasal *adj.* antronasal.
antroneurólisis *f.* antroneurolysis.
antropilórico, -ca *adj.* antropyloric.
antropobiología *f.* anthropobiology.
antropocéntrico, -ca *adj.* anthropocentric.
antropocinética *f.* anthropokinetics.
antropocracia *f.* anthropocracy.
antropofílico, -ca *adj.* anthropophilic.
antropófilo, -la *adj.* anthropophilic.
antropofobia *f.* anthropophobia.
antropogénesis *f.* anthropogeny.
antropogenia *f.* anthropogeny.
antropogénico, -ca *adj.* anthropogenic, anthropogenetic.
antropografía *f.* anghrography.
antropoide *adj.* anthropoid.
antropología *f.* anthropology.
  antropología aplicada applied anthropology.
  antropología criminal criminal anthropology.
  antropología cultural cultural anthropology.
  antropología física physical anthropology.
antropometría *f.* anthropometry.
antropométrico, -ca *adj.* anthropometric.
antropometrista *m., f.* anthropometrist.
antropómetro *m.* anthropometer.
antropomórfico, -ca *adj.* anthropomorphic.
antropomorfismo *m.* anthropomorphism.
antropomorfo, -fa *adj.* anthropomorphic.
antroponomía *f.* anthroponomy.
antropopatía *f.* anthropopathy.
antroposcopia *f.* anthroposcopy.
antroposofia *f.* anthroposophy.
antroposomatología *f.* anthroposomatology.
antropozoófilo, -la *adj.* anthropozoophilic.
antropozoonosis *f.* anthropozoonosis.
antroscopia *f.* antroscopy.
antroscopio *m.* antroscope.
antrostomía *f.* antrostomy.
antrotimpánico, -ca *adj.* antrotympanic.

antrotimpanitis *f.* antrotympanitis.
antrotomía *f.* antrotomy.
antrótomo *m.* antrotome.
antrotonía *f.* antrotonia.
antrum antrum.
anuclear *adj.* anuclear.
anular[1] *m.* ring finger.
anular[2] *adj.* annular.
anuloplastia *f.* annuloplasty.
anulorrafia *f.* annulorrhaphy.
anuresis *f.* anuresis.
anuria *f.* anuria.
   anuria angioneurótica angioneurotic anuria.
   anuria calculosa calculus anuria.
   anuria obstructiva obstructive anuria.
   anuria posrenal postrenal anuria.
   anuria prerrenal prerenal anuria.
   anuria renal renal anuria.
   anuria por supresión suppressive anuria.
anurético, -ca *adj.* anuretic.
anúrico, -ca *adj.* anuric.
anuro, -ra *adj.* anurous.
anus anus.
anusitis *f.* anusitis.
anxietas tibiarum anxietas tibiarum.
añadido *m.* overlay.
aorta *f.* aorta.
aortal *adj.* aortal.
aortalgia *f.* aortalgia.
aortactia *f.* aortactia.
aortectasia *f.* aortectasis.
aortectasis *f.* aortectasis.
aortectomía *f.* aortectomy.
aórtico, -ca *adj.* aortic.
aorticorrenal *adj.* aorticorenal.
aortismo *m.* aortismus.
   aortismo abdominal, aortismus abdominalis aortismus abdominalis.
aortismus aortismus.
aortitis *f.* aortitis.
   aortitis gigantocelular giant cell aortitis.
   aortitis luética luetic aortitis.
   aortitis reumática rheumatic aortitis.
   aortitis sifilítica syphilitic aortitis.
aortocoronario, -ria *adj.* aortocoronary.
aortoesclerosis *f.* aortosclerosis.
aortoestenosis *f.* aortostenosis.
aortografía *f.* aortography.
   aortografía abdominal abdominal aortography.
   aortografía retrógrada retrograde aortography.
   aortografía translumbar translumbar aortography.
aortograma *m.* aortogram.
aortopatía *f.* aortopathy.
aortoplastia *f.* aortoplasty.
aortoptosis *f.* aortoptosia.
aortorrafia *f.* aortorrhaphy.
aortosclerosis *f.* aortosclerosis.
aortostenosis *f.* aortostenosis.
aortotomía *f.* aortotomy.
aosmia *f.* aosmia.
apálico, -ca *adj.* apallic.
apancreático, -ca *adj.* apancreatic.
apancria *f.* apancrea.
apantropía *f.* apanthropia, apanthropy.
aparalítico, -ca *adj.* aparalytic.
aparatireosis *f.* aparathyreosis.
aparatiroidismo *m.* aparathyroidism.
aparatirosis *f.* aparathyrosis.
aparato[1] *m.* apparatus.
   aparato de Abbé-Zeiss Abbé-Zeiss apparatus.
   aparato de aspiración de moco con válvula mucus trap suction apparatus.
   aparato de Barcroft, aparato de Barcroft-

Warburg Barcroft's apparatus, Barcroft-Warburg apparatus.
   aparato de Beckmann Beckmann's apparatus.
   aparato de descompresión abdominal de Heyns Heyns' abdominal decompression apparatus.
   aparato digestivo digestive apparatus, apparatus digestorius.
   aparato de Fell-O'Dwyer Fell-O'Dwyer apparatus.
   aparato de fijación attachment apparatus.
   aparato de Kirschner Kirschner's apparatus.
   aparato locomotor locomotor system.
   aparato masticatorio masticatory apparatus.
   aparato reproductor reproductive system.
   aparato respiratorio respiratory apparatus, apparatus respiratorius.
   aparato de Sayre Sayre's apparatus.
   aparato de Soxhlet Soxhlet's apparatus.
   aparato de Taylor Taylor's apparatus.
   aparato de Tiselius Tiselius apparatus.
   aparato de Tobold Tobold's apparatus.
   aparato urinario urinary apparatus.
   aparato de Wangestgeen Wangenstgeen's apparatus.
   aparato de Warburg Warburg's apparatus.
aparato[2] *m.* appliance.
   aparato de alambre liviano light wire appliance.
   aparato de arco de goma ribbon arch appliance.
   aparato craneofacial craniofacial appliance.
   aparato de canto edgewise appliance.
   aparato extraíble de ortodoncia removable orthodontic appliance.
   aparato de fijación con pernos de Roger Anderson Roger Anderson pin fixation appliance.
   aparato de fractura extraoral extraoral fracture appliance.
   aparato de fractura intraoral intraloral fracture appliance.
   aparato de Jackson Jackson crib.
   aparato labiolingual labiolingual appliance.
   aparato obturador obturator appliance.
   aparato ortodóncico orthodontic appliance.
   aparato ortodóncico extraoral cervical de Kloehn Kloehn cervical extraoral orthodontic appliance.
   aparato ortodóncico fijo con alambres gemelos twin-wire fixed orthodontic appliance.
   aparato ortodóncico fijo con alambre recto straight wire fixed orthodontic appliance.
   aparato ortodóncico fijo con clavijas y tubos pin and tube fixed orthodontic appliance.
   aparato ortodóncico labiolingual fijo labiolingual fixed orthodontic appliance.
   aparato ortodóncico de retención retaining orthodontic appliance.
apareamiento *m.* mating, pairing.
   apareamiento al azar random pairing.
   apareamiento de bases base pairing.
   apareamiento concordante assortative mating, assorted mating, assortive mating.
   apareamiento de los cromosomas chromosome pairing.
   apareamiento selectivo assortative mating, assorted mating, assortive mating.
apareunia *f.* apareunia.
apariencia *f.* appearance.
apartrosis *f.* aparthrosis.
apatía *f.* apathy.
apático, -ca *adj.* apathetic, apathic.
apatismo *m.* apathism.

apatita *f.* apatite.
apectomía *f.* apicectomy.
apeidosis *f.* apeidosis.
apelación al buen juicio *f.* judgement call.
apelo, -la *adj.* apellous.
apeloso, -sa *adj.* apellous.
apendalgia *f.* appendalgia.
apendectomía *f.* appendectomy.
apendicalgia *f.* appendalgia.
apéndice *m.* appendage, appendix.
apendicectasia *f.* appendicectasis.
apendicectomía *f.* appendicectomy.
apendicismo *m.* appendicism.
apendicitis *f.* appendicitis.
   apendicitis actinomicótica actinomycotic appendicitis.
   apendicitis aguda acute appendicitis.
   apendicitis bilharzial bilharzial appendicitis.
   apendicitis crónica chronic appendicitis.
   apendicitis por cuerpo extraño foreign-body appendicitis.
   apendicitis destructiva perforating appendicitis.
   apendicitis estercorácea stercoreal appendicitis, stercoral appendicitis.
   apendicitis focal focal appendicitis.
   apendicitis fulminante fulminating appendicitis.
   apendicitis gangrenosa gangrenous appendicitis.
   apendicitis izquierda left-sided appendicitis.
   apendicitis lumbar lumbar appendicitis.
   apendicitis obstructiva obstructive appendicitis.
   apendicitis perforante, apendicitis perforativa perforating appendicitis.
   apendicitis por contigüedad appendicitis by contiguity.
   apendicitis purulenta purulent appendicitis.
   apendicitis recurrente recurrent appendicitis.
   apendicitis segmentaria segmental appendicitis.
   apendicitis subperitoneal subperitoneal appendicitis.
   apendicitis supurada, apendicitis supurativa suppurative appendicitis.
   apendicitis traumática traumatic appendicitis.
   apendicitis verminosa verminous appendicitis.
apendiclausia *f.* appendiclausis.
apendiclausis *f.* appendiclausis.
apendicocecostomía *f.* appendicocecostomy.
apendicocele *m.* appendicocele.
apendicoenterostomía *f.* appendicoenterostomy.
apendicólisis *f.* appendicolysis.
apendicolitiasis *f.* appendicolithiasis, appendolithiasis.
apendicolito *m.* appendicolith.
apendicopatía *f.* appendicopathia, appendicopathy.
apendicosis *f.* appendicopathy.
apendicostomía *f.* appendicostomy.
apendicotomía *f.* appendicotomy.
apendicular *adj.* appendiceal, appendicular, appendical.
apentérico, -ca *adj.* apenteric.
apepsia *f.* apepsia.
apepsinia *f.* apepsinia.
apercepción *f.* apperception.
aperceptivo, -va *adj.* apperceptive.
aperiódico, -ca *adj.* aperiodic.
aperistalsis *f.* aperistalsis.

aperistaltismo *m.* aperistalsis.
apertognatia *f.* apertognathia.
apertómetro *m.* apertometer.
apertura *f.* aperture.
apestato *m.* appestat.
apetencia *f.* appetition.
apetitivo, -va *adj.* appetitive.
apetito *m.* appetite.
    apetito pervertido perverted appetite.
ápex, apex *m.* apex.
apexicardiografia *f.* apexcardiography.
apexcardiograma *m.* apexcardiogram, apex cardiogram.
apexiano, -na *adj.* apical.
apexicardiograma *m.* apexcardiogram, apex cardiogram.
apexificación *f.* apexification.
apexígrafo *m.* apexigraph.
apexógrafo *m.* apexigraph.
Aphiochaeta Aphiochaeta.
    Aphiochaeta ferruginea Aphiochaeta ferruginea.
Aphtovirus *m.* Aphthovirus.
apical *adj.* apical.
ápice *m.* Apex.
apicectomía *f.* apicectomy, apicoectomy.
apiceotomía *f.* apiceotomy.
apicitis *f.* apicitis.
apicoectomía *f.* apicoectomy.
apicólisis *f.* apicolysis.
apicolocalizador *m.* apicolocator.
apicostomía *f.* apicostomy.
apicóstomo *m.* apicostome.
apicotomía *f.* apicotomy.
apiculado, -da *adj.* apiculate.
apicuretaje *m.* apicurettage.
apinealismo *m.* apinealism.
apinoide *adj.* apinoid.
apiñamiento *m.* crowding.
apiógeno, -na *adj.* apyogenous.
apirético, -ca *adj.* apyretic, apyrexial.
apirexia *f.* apyrexia.
apirógeno, -na *adj.* apyrogenic.
apisinación *f.* apisination.
apiterapia *f.* apiotherapy.
apitoxina *f.* apitoxin.
apituitarismo *m.* apituitarism.
aplacentario, -ria *adj.* aplacental.
aplanación *f.* applanation.
aplanamiento[1] *m.* saucerization.
aplanamiento[2] *m.* planing.
aplanático, -ca *adj.* aplanatic.
aplanatismo *m.* aplanatism.
aplasia *f.* aplasia.
    aplasia congénita extracortical axial aplasia axialis extracorticalis congenita.
    aplasia congénita del timo congenital aplasia of the thymus.
    aplasia congénita del cutis aplasia cutis congenita.
    aplasia cutis congénita aplasia cutis congenita.
    aplasia eritrocitaria pura, aplasia eritrocítica pura pure red cell aplasia.
    aplasia germinal, aplasia germinativa germinal aplasia.
    aplasia gonadal gonadal aplasia.
    aplasia nuclear nuclear aplasia.
    aplasia ovárica ovarian aplasia, aplasia of the ovary.
    aplasia pilorum propia aplasia pilorum propia.
    aplasia tímica thymic aplasia.
aplásico, -ca *adj.* aplastic.
aplásmico, -ca *adj.* aplasmic.

aplastamiento *m.* crush.
aplastar *v.* crush.
apleuria *f.* apleuria.
aplicador *m.* applicator.
apnea *f.* apnea.
    apnea cardíaca cardiac apnea.
    apnea central central apnea.
    apnea central del sueño central sleep apnea.
    apnea de deglución deglutition apnea.
    apnea inducida induced apnea.
    apnea inducida por el sueño sleep-induced apnea.
    apnea neonatal apnea neonatorum.
    apnea obstructiva obstructive apnea.
    apnea obstructiva del sueño (SAOS) obstructive sleep apnea.
    apnea periférica peripheral apnea.
    apnea periódica del recién nacido periodic apnea of the newborn.
    apnea primaria primary apnea.
    apnea refleja reflex apnea.
    apnea secundaria secondary apnea.
    apnea del sueño sleep apnea.
    apnea del sueño mixta mixed sleep apnea.
    apnea tardía late apnea.
    apnea verdadera, apnea vera true apnea, apnea vera.
apneico, -ca *adj.* apneic.
apneumático, -ca *adj.* apneumatic.
apneumatosis *f.* apneumatosis.
apneumia *f.* apneumia.
apneusia *f.* apneusis.
apneusis *f.* apneusis.
apneustia *f.* apnea.
apneústico, -ca *adj.* apneustic.
apobiosis *f.* apobiosis.
apocamnosis *f.* apocamnosis, apokamnosis.
apocenosis *f.* apocenosis.
apócope *m.* apocope.
apocóptico, -ca *adj.* apocoptic.
apocrinitis *f.* apocrinitis.
apocrino, -na *adj.* apocrine.
apocromático, -ca *adj.* apochromatic.
apodal *adj.* apodal.
apodia *f.* apodia, apody.
ápodo, -da *adj.* apodous, apodal.
apoenzima *f.* apoenzyme.
apoferritina *f.* apoferritin.
apofiláctico, -ca *adj.* apophylactic.
apofilaxis *f.* apophylaxis.
apofisario, -ria *adj.* apophysary.
apofisial *adj.* apophysial, apophyseal.
apófisis *f.* apophysis.
apofisitis *f.* apophysitis.
    apofisitis tibial de los adolescentes apophysitis tibialis adolescentium.
apofisopatía *f.* apophyseopathy.
apoflemático, -ca *adj.* apophlegmatic.
apogeo *m.* apogee.
apolar *adj.* apolar.
apolegamia *f.* apolegamy.
apolegámico, -ca *adj.* apolegamic.
apolepsia *f.* apolepsis.
apolepsis *f.* apolepsis.
apolipoproteína *f.* apolipoprotein.
apomixia *f.* apomixia, apomixis.
apomixis *f.* apomixis.
aponeurectomía *f.* aponeurectomy.
aponeurología *f.* aponeurology.
aponeurorrafia *f.* aponeurorrhaphy.
aponeurosis *f.* aponeurosis.
aponeurositis *f.* aponeurositis.
aponeurótico, -ca *adj.* aponeurotic.
aponeurotomía *f.* aponeurotomy.
aponeurótomo *m.* aponeurotome.

aponia *f.* aponia.
apónico, -ca *adj.* aponic.
apoplasmia *f.* apoplasmia.
apopléctico, -ca *adj.* apoplectic.
apoplectiforme *adj.* apoplectiform.
apoplectoide *adj.* apoplectoid.
apoplejía *f.* apoplexy, apoplexia.
    apoplejía abdominal abdominal apoplexy.
    apoplejía de Broadbent Broadbent's apoplexy.
    apoplejía bulbar bulbar apoplexy.
    apoplejía por calor heat apoplexy.
    apoplejía cerebelar, apoplejía cerebelosa cerebellar apoplexy.
    apoplejía cerebral cerebral hemorrhage.
    apoplejía cutánea cutaneous apoplexy.
    apoplejía embólica embolic apoplexy.
    apoplejía espasmódica spasmodic apoplexy.
    apoplejía funcional functional apoplexy.
    apoplejía hipofisaria pituitary apoplexy.
    apoplejía ingravescente ingravescent apoplexy.
    apoplejía intestinal intestinal apoplexy.
    apoplejía medular spinal apoplexy.
    apoplejía neonatorum neonatal apoplexy.
    apoplejía pancreática pancreatic apoplexy.
    apoplejía placentaria placental apoplexy.
    apoplejía pituitaria pituitary apoplexy.
    apoplejía pontina pontile apoplexy, pontil apoplexy.
    apoplejía renal renal apoplexy.
    apoplejía serosa serous apoplexy.
    apoplejía suprarrenal adrenal apoplexy.
    apoplejía tardía delayed apoplexy.
    apoplejía tipo Raymond Raymond's apoplexy.
    apoplejía trombótica thrombotic apoplexy.
    apoplejía uterina apoplexia uterina.
    apoplejía uteroplacentaria uteroplacental apoplexy.
apoplético, -ca *adj.* apoplectic.
apoproteína *f.* apoprotein.
apoptosis *f.* apoptosis.
aporrepresor *m.* aporepressor.
aporte dietético *m.* dietary allowance.
aposia *f.* aposia.
aposición *f.* apposition.
apósito *m.* dressing.
apostasis *f.* apostasis.
apostaxia *f.* apostaxis.
apostia *f.* aposthia.
apotanasia *f.* apothanasia.
apotoxina *f.* apotoxin.
apotripsis *f.* apotripsis.
apoxemena *f.* apoxemena.
apoxesis *f.* apoxesis.
apoyo[1] *m.* rest.
    apoyo incisal incisal rest.
    apoyo oclusal occlusal rest.
apoyo[2] *m.* support.
    apoyo medio midstance support.
apractagnosia *f.* apractagnosia.
apráctico, -ca *adj.* apractic.
apragmatismo *m.* apragmatism.
apraxia *f.* apraxia.
    apraxia acinética akinetic apraxia.
    apraxia amnésica amnestic apraxia.
    apraxia de Bruns de la marcha Bruns' apraxia of gait.
    apraxia cinética kinetic apraxia.
    apraxia cinética de las extremidades limb-kinetic apraxia.
    apraxia clásica ideokinetic apraxia.
    apraxia constructiva, apraxia de construcción constructional apraxia.

apraxia cortical cortical apraxia.
apraxia del desarrollo developmental apraxia.
apraxia ideatoria, apraxia de ideación, apraxia ideomotriz ideational apraxia.
apraxia ideocinética idiokinetic apraxia.
apraxia ideomotora ideomotor apraxia.
apraxia de inervación, apraxia inervatoria innervation apraxia.
apraxia limbocinética limb-kinetic apraxia.
apraxia de la marcha gait apraxia.
apraxia motora, apraxia motriz motor apraxia.
apraxia oculomotora (de Cogan) ocular motor apraxia.
apraxia sensitiva sensory apraxia.
apraxia transcortical transcortical apraxia.
apraxia del vestido apraxia for dressing.
apráxico, -ca *adj.* apraxic.
aprehensión *f.* apprehension.
aprendizaje *m.* learning.
aprendizaje afectivo affective learning.
aprendizaje dependiente del estado state-dependent learning.
aprendizaje y estrés learning and stress.
aprendizaje de hábito habit training.
aprendizaje y humor learning and humor.
aprendizaje latente latent learning.
aprendizaje psicomotor psychomotor learning.
aprendizaje sexual en los niños sexual learning in children.
aprocia *f.* aproctia.
aproctia *f.* aproctia.
aprosexia *f.* aprosexia.
aprosodia *f.* aprosody.
aprosopia *f.* aprosopia.
aprósopo *m.* aprosopus.
aprotinina *f.* aprotinin.
aproximación *f.* approximation.
apselafesia *f.* apselaphesia.
apsitiria *f.* apsithyria.
aptialia *f.* aptyalia.
aptialismo *m.* aptyalism.
aptitud *f.* aptness, aptitude.
apudoma *m.* apudoma.
apulmonismo *m.* apulmonism.
aqueductus aqueductus.
aqueilia *f.* acheilia.
aqueilo, -la *adj.* acheilous, achilous.
aqueiria *f.* acheiria, achiria.
aqueiropodia *f.* acheiropody, achiropody.
aqueratosis *m.* akeratosis.
aquilia *f.* achylia.
aquilia gástrica hemorrágica achylia gastrica haemorrhagica.
aquilia pancreática achylia pancreatica.
aquílico, -ca *adj.* achylous.
aquilobursitis *f.* achillobursitis.
aquilodinia *f.* achillodynia.
aquilorrafia *f.* achillorrhaphy.
aquiloso, -sa *adj.* achylous.
aquilotenotomía *f.* achillotenotomy.
aquilotenotomía plástica plastic achillotenotomy.
aquilotomía *f.* achillotomy.
aquimia *f.* achymia, achymosis.
aquinesia *f.* akinesia, akinesis.
aquinésico, -ca *adj.* akinesic.
aquinesis *f.* akinesis.
aquiral *adj.* achiral.
aquiria *f.* achiria.
aquiro, -ra¹ *adj.* acheirous, achirous.
aquiro, -ra² *m., f.* acheirus.
aquiropodia *f.* achiropody.
arabinosis *f.* arabinosis.
arabinosuria *f.* arabinosuria.

aracnidismo *m.* arachnidism, arachnoidism.
arácnidos *m.* arachnids.
aracnitis *f.* arachnitis.
aracnodactilia *f.* arachnodactyly.
aracnoidal *adj.* arachnoidal.
aracnoide *adj.* arachnoid.
aracnoides *f.* arachnoidea.
aracnoidismo *m.* arachnoidism.
aracnoiditis *f.* arachnoiditis.
aracnoiditis crónica adhesiva chronic adhesive arachnoiditis.
aracnolisina *f.* arachnolysin.
aracnopía *f.* arachnopia.
aracnorrinitis *f.* arachnorhinitis.
araneísmo *m.* araneism.
araña *f.* spider.
araña arterial arterial spider.
araña vascular vascular spider.
árbol *m.* arbor.
árbor *m.* arbor.
arbóreo, -a *adj.* arboreal.
arborescente *adj.* arborescent.
arborización *f.* arborization.
arboviral *adj.* arboviral.
Arbovirus Arbovirus.
arcada *f.* arcade.
arcada Alveolar, arcada dentaria dental arcade.
arcaico, -ca *adj.* archaic.
arciforme *adj.* arciform.
arco *m.* arch, arcus.
arco de Birnberg Birnberg bow.
arco faríngeo pharyngeal arch.
arco reflejo reflex arch.
arco senil arcus senilis.
arcocele *m.* archocele.
arcocistosirinx *m.* archocystosyrinx.
arcoptoma *m.* archoptoma.
arcoptosis *f.* archoptosis.
arcorragia *f.* archorrhagia.
arcorrea *f.* archorrhea.
arcosirinx *f.* archosyrinx.
arcostenosis *f.* archostenosis.
arctación *f.* arctation.
arcuato, -ta *adj.* arcuate.
arcual *adj.* arcual.
arcus arcus.
ardanestesia *f.* ardanesthesia.
ardiente *adj.* ardent.
ardor *m.* ardor.
ardor epigástrico heartburn ardor.
área *f.* area.
área de alivio relief area.
área de Cohnheim Cohnheim's area.
área de descanso rest area.
área embrionaria embryonal area, embryonic area.
área germinal, área germinativa germinal area, area germinativa.
área motora del habla de Broca Broca's (motor speech) area, motor speech area of Broca.
área opaca area opaca.
área parolfatoria, área paraolfatoria de Broca parolfactory area, paraolfactory area of Broca.
área pelúcida area pellucida.
área silenciosa silent area of the brain.
área somatosensitiva somatic sensory area, somatosensory area, general sensory area.
área de soporte supporting area.
área de soporte de tensión stress-bearing area.
área de sostén de dentadura denture-bearing area, denture foundation area, denture-supporting area.

área vascular area vasculosa.
areata *adj.* areata.
arenación *f.* arenation.
Arenaviridae Arenaviridae.
Arenavirus *m.* Arenavirus.
areola, aréola *f.* areola.
areola de Chaussier Chaussier's areola.
areola de la mama, areola del pezón areola mammae, areola of mammary gland, areola of the nipple.
areola papilar areola papillaris.
areola secundaria second areola.
areola umbilical umbilical areola, areola umbilicus.
areola vacunal vaccinal areola.
areolar *adj.* areolar.
areolitis *f.* areolitis.
areometría *f.* areometry.
areométrico, -ca *adj.* areometric.
areómetro *m.* areometer.
argambliopía *f.* argamblyopia.
Argas Argas.
argasino *m.* argasid.
argema *f.* argema.
argentación *f.* argentation.
argentafinoma *m.* argentaffinoma.
argentafinoma bronquial argentaffinoma of the bronchus.
angentoproteína *f.* argentoproteinum.
arginuria *f.* arginuria.
argipresina *f.* argipresssin.
argiremia *f.* argyremia.
argiria *f.* argyria.
argiria nasal argyria nasalis.
argiriasis *f.* argyriasis.
argírico, -ca *adj.* argyric.
argirismo *m.* argyrism.
argirosis *f.* argyrosis.
aridura *f.* atrophy.
ariepiglótico, -ca *adj.* aryepiglottic, aryepiglottidean.
aristogénesis *f.* aristogenesis.
aristogenia *f.* aristegenics.
aristogénica *f.* aristegenics.
aristolóquico, -ca *adj.* aristolochic.
aritenectomia *f.* arytenoidectomy.
aritenoepiglótico, -ca *adj.* arytenoepiglottic.
aritenoidectomía *f.* arytenoidectomy.
aritenoides *adj.* arytenoid.
aritenoiditis *f.* arytenoiditis.
aritenoidopexia *f.* arytenoidopexy, arytenoidopexia.
aritmomanía *f.* arithmomania.
armadura *f.* armature.
armazón *m.* frame.
armazón de calentamiento electric frame, heat frame.
armazón de ensayo trial frame.
armazón de hielo ice frame.
Armigeres Armigeres.
Armillifer Armillifer.
aroma *m.* aroma.
aromático, -ca *adj.* aromatic, aromaticus.
aromatización *f.* aromatization.
arpón *m.* harpoon.
arqueado, -da *adj.* arcuate.
arquecéntrico, -ca *adj.* archecentric.
arquencéfalo *m.* archencephalon.
arquenterón *m.* archenteron.
arqueocinético, -ca *adj.* archeokinetic, archeokinetic.
arqueocito *m.* archeocyte.
arquepion *m.* archepyon.
arquetipo *m.* archetype.
arquiblástico, -ca *adj.* archiblastic.

arquiblasto *m.* archiblast.
arquicerebelo *m.* archicerebellum, archeocerebellum.
arquicórtex *f.* archicortex, archeocortex.
arquicorteza *f.* archicortex, archeocortex.
arquigastro *m.* archigaster.
arquinefros *m.* archinephros.
arquipalio *m.* archipallium.
arquiplasma *m.* archiplasm.
arquistoma *m.* archistoma, archistome.
arquitectura ósea *f.* bone architecture.
arquitis *f.* architis.
arrafia *f.* arrhaphia.
arrancamiento *m.* arrachement.
arrastre *m.* drag.
arrector, -ra *adj.* arrector.
arreflexia *f.* areflexia.
arregenerativo, -va *adj.* aregenerative.
arrenoblastoma *m.* arrhenoblastoma.
arrenogénico, -ca *adj.* arrhenogenic.
arrenoma *m.* arrhenoma.
arriboflavinosis *f.* ariboflavinosis.
arrinencefalia *f.* arrhinencephaly, arrhinencephalia.
arrinia *f.* arrhinia.
arritmia *f.* arrhythmia.
  arritmia cardiaca cardiac arrhythmia.
  arritmia continua continuous arrhythmia.
  arritmia fásica phasic arrhythmia.
  arritmia juvenil juvenile arrhythmia.
  arritmia perpetua perpetual arrhythmia.
  arritmia respiratoria respiratory arrhythmia.
  arritmia de seno, arritmia sinusal sinus arrhythmia.
arrítmico, -ca *adj.* arrhythmic.
arritmocinesis *f.* arrhythmokinesis.
arritmogénico, -ca *adj.* arrhythmogenic.
arruga *f.* wrinkle, ruga.
  arruga palatina ruga palatina.
  arruga vaginal ruga vaginale.
arseniasis *f.* arseniasis.
arsenicalismo *m.* arsenicalism.
arseniciasis *m.* arsenicalism.
arsenicismo *m.* arsenicalism.
arsenicofagia *f.* arsenicophagy.
arsenicorresistente *adj.* arsenic-fast.
arsenismo *m.* arsenism.
arsenización *f.* arsenization.
arsenoactivación *f.* arsenoactivation.
arsenoautohematoterapia *f.* arsenoautohemotherapy.
arsenoautohemoterapia *f.* arsenoatohemotherapy.
arsenofagia *f.* arsenophagy.
arsenorrecidiva *f.* arsenorelapsing.
arsenorresistente *adj.* arsenoresistant.
arsenoterapla *f.* arsenotherapy.
arsonvalismo *f.* arsonvalization.
arsonvalización *f.* arsonvalization.
artación *f.* arctation.
artefacto *m.* artefact.
arteralgia *f.* arteralgia.
arterectomía *f.* arteriectomy, arterectomy.
arteria *f.* artery, arteria.
arteriactia *f.* arteriactia.
arterial *adj.* arterial.
arterialización *f.* arterialization.
arteriectasia *f.* arteriectasia.
arteriectasis *f.* arteriectasis, arteriectasia.
arteriectomía *f.* arteriectomy, arterectomy.
arteriectopía *f.* arteriectopia.
arterioatonía *f.* arterioatony.
arteriocapilar *adj.* arteriocapillary, arterocapillary.
arteriodilatación *f.* arteriodilating.

arterioesclerosis *f.* arteriosclerosis.
  arterioesclerosis cerebral cerebral arteriosclerosis.
  arterioesclerosis coronaria coronary arteriosclerosis.
  arterioesclerosis difusa diffuse arteriosclerosis.
  arterioesclerosis hialina hyaline arteriosclerosis.
  arterioesclerosis hipertensiva hypertensive arteriosclerosis.
  arterioesclerosis infantil infantile arteriosclerosis.
  arterioesclerosis medial medial arteriosclerosis.
  arterioesclerosis de Mönckeberg Mönckeberg's arteriosclerosis.
  arterioesclerosis nodular, arterioesclerosis nudosa nodular arteriosclerosis.
  arterioesclerosis obliterante arteriosclerosis obliterans.
  arterioesclerosis periférica peripheral arteriosclerosis.
  arterioesclerosis presenil presenile arteriosclerosis.
  arterioesclerosis senil senile arteriosclerosis.
  arterioesclerosis de la túnica media medial arteriosclerosis.
arterioesclerótico *adj.* arteriosclerotic.
arterioespasmo *m.* arteriospasm.
arterioespástico, -ca *adj.* arteriospastic.
arterioestenosis *f.* arteriostenosis.
arteriogénesis *f.* arteriogenesis.
arteriografía *f.* arteriography.
  arteriografía cerebral cerebral arteriography.
  arteriografía espinal spinal arteriography.
  arteriografía selectiva coronaria selective coronary arteriography.
  arteriografía por sonda catheter arteriography.
arteriográfico, -ca *adj.* arteriographic.
arteriograma *m.* arteriogram.
arteriola *f.* arteriola, arteriole.
arteriolar *adj.* arteriolar.
arteriolitis *f.* arteriolitis.
  arteriolitis necrosante necrotizing arteriolitis.
arteriolito *m.* arteriolith.
arteriología *f.* arteriology.
arteriolonecrosis *f.* arteriolonecrosis.
arteriolonefroesclerosis *f.* arteriolonephrosclerosis.
arteriolosclerosis *f.* arteriolosclerosis.
arteriolosclerótico, -ca *adj.* arteriolosclerotic.
arteriolovenoso, -sa *adj.* arteriolovenous.
arteriolovenular *adj.* arteriolovenular.
arteriomalacia *f.* arteriomalacia.
arteriómetro *m.* arteriometer.
arteriomiomatosis *f.* arteriomyomatosis.
arteriomotor, -ra *adj.* arteriomotor.
arterionecrosis *f.* arterionecrosis.
arterionefroesclerosis *f.* arterionephrosclerosis.
arteriopalmus *m.* arteriopalmus.
arteriopatía *f.* arteriopathy.
  arteriopatía hipertensiva hypertensive arteriopathy.
  arteriopatía pulmonar plexogénica plexogenic pulmonary arteriopathy.
arterioperisia *f.* arterioperissia.
arterioplania *f.* arterioplania.
arterioplastia *f.* arterioplasty.
arteriopresor, -ra *adj.* arteriopressor.
arteriorrafia *f.* arteriorrhaphy.

arteriorragia *f.* arteriorrhagia.
arteriorrenal *adj.* arteriorenal.
arteriorrexis *f.* arteriorrhexis.
arteriosclerosis *f.* arteriosclerosis.
arteriosclerótico, -ca *adj.* arteriosclerotic.
arteriosimpatectomía *f.* arteriosympathectomy.
arterioso, -sa *adj.* arterious.
arteriospasmo *m.* arteriospasm.
arteriospástico, -ca *adj.* arteriospastic.
arteriostenosis *f.* arteriostenosis.
arteriosteogénesis *f.* arteriosteogenesis.
arteriosteosis *f.* arteriosteose, arteriostosis.
arteriostosis *f.* arteriosteose, arteriostosis.
arteriostrepsia *f.* arteriostrepsis, arteriotrepsis.
arteriostripsia *f.* arteriostrepsis, arteriotrepsis.
arteriotomía *f.* arteriotomy.
arteriótomo *m.* arteriotome.
arteriotonía *f.* arteriotony.
arteriotrepsia *f.* arteriostrepsis, arteriotrepsis.
arteriovenoso, -sa *adj.* arteriovenous, arteriovenosus.
arteritis *f.* arteritis.
  arteritis coronaria coronary arteritis.
  arteritis craneal cranial arteritis.
  arteritis deformante arteritis deformans.
  arteritis gigantocelular, arteritis de células gigantes giant cell arteritis.
  arteritis granulomatosa granulomatous arteritis.
  arteritis hiperplásica arteritis hyperplastica.
  arteritis de Horton Horton's arteritis.
  arteritis infantil infantile arteritis.
  arteritis obliterante obliterating arteritis, arteritis obliterans.
  arteritis reumática rheumatic arteritis.
  arteritis reumatoidea rheumatoid arteritis.
  arteritis sifilítica syphilitic arteritis.
  arteritis temporal temporal arteritis.
  arteritis tuberculosa tuberculous arteritis.
  arteritis umbilical arteritis umbilicalis.
  arteritis verrugosa arteritis verrucosa.
  arteritis visceral localizada localized visceral arteritis.
arterización *f.* arterialization.
articulación *f.* articulation, articulatio.
articulado, -da *adj.* articulated.
articulador *m.* articulator.
  articulador ajustable adjustable articulator.
  articulador en bisagra hinge articulator.
  articulador dental dental articulator.
  articulador en plano plain articulator, line articulator.
  articulador semiajustable semiadjustable articulator.
articular *v.* articulate.
articular *adj.* articulate.
articulare *m.* articulare.
articulatio articulatio.
articulatorio, -ria *adj.* articulatory.
artículo *m.* articulus.
articulóstato *m.* articulostat.
articulus articulus.
artificial *adj.* artificial.
artificio *m.* artifact.
artiodáctilo, -la *adj.* artiodactylous.
artragra *f.* arthragra.
artral *adj.* arthral.
artralgia *f.* arthralgia.
  artralgia intermitente intermittent arthralgia.
  artralgia periódica periodic arthralgia.
  artralgia saturnina arthralgia saturnina.
artrálgico, -ca *adj.* arthralgic.
artrectomía *f.* arthrectomy.

artrempiesis *f.* arthrempyesis.
artrestesia *f.* arthresthesia.
artrífugo, -ga *adj.* arthrifuge.
artrítico, -ca *adj.* arthritic.
artritide *f.* arthritide.
artritis *f.* arthritis.
  artritis aguda acute arthritis.
  artritis aguda supurativa acute suppurative arthritis.
  artritis atrófica atrophic arthritis.
  artritis bacteriana bacterial arthritis.
  artritis de Bechterew Bechterew's arthritis.
  artritis blenorrágica gonoccocal arthritis.
  artritis clamidial chlamydial arthritis.
  artritis climatérica climactic arthritis.
  artritis cricoaritenoidea cricoarytenoid joint arthritis.
  artritis deformante arthritis deformans.
  artritis degenerativa degenerative arthritis.
  artritis disentérica dysenteric arthritis.
  artritis exudativa exudative arthritis.
  artritis filarial filarial arthritis.
  artritis fúngica, artritis fungosa fungal arthritis, arthritis fungosa.
  artritis gonocócica, artritis gonorreica gonoccocal arthritis.
  artritis gotosa gouty arthritis.
  artritis gotosa aguda acute gouty arthritis.
  artritis hiemal, artritis hiemalis arthritis hiemalis.
  artritis infecciosa infectious arthritis.
  artritis inflamatoria crónica chronic inflammatory arthritis.
  artritis juvenil, artritis juvenil crónica juvenile arthritis, juvenile chronic arthritis.
  artritis de lyme lyme arthritis.
  artritis menopáusica menopausal arthritis.
  artritis micótica mycotic arthritis.
  artritis mutilante arthritis mutilans.
  artritis neuropática neuropathic arthritis.
  artritis nudosa arthritis nodosa.
  artritis ocronótica ochronotic arthritis.
  artritis proliferante proliferative arthritis.
  artritis psoriásica psoriatic arthritis.
  artritis reumática aguda acute rheumatic arthritis.
  artritis reumatoide rheumatoid arthritis.
  artritis reumatoide juvenil juvenile rheumatoid arthritis.
  artritis reumatoide del raquis rheumatoid arthritis of the spine.
  artritis seca arthritis sicca.
  artritis séptica septic arthritis.
  artritis sifilítica syphilitic arthritis.
  artritis supurada suppurative arthritis.
  artritis tuberculosa tuberculous arthritis.
  artritis urática uratic arthritis, arthritis uratica.
  artritis uretral urethral arthritis.
  artritis uretrítica arthritis urethritica.
  artritis vellosa crónica chronic villous arthritis.
  artritis venérea venereal arthritis.
  artritis vertebral vertebral arthritis.
  artritis virica viral arthritis.
artritismo *m.* arthritism.
Artrobacteria *f.* Arthrobacter.
artrobacterium arthrobacterium.
artrocace *m.* arthrocace.
artrocalasia *f.* arthrochalasis.
  artrocalasia múltiple congénita arthrochalasis multiplex congenita.
artrocatadisis *f.* arthrokatadysis.
artrocele *m.* arthrocele.
artrocentelleografía *f.* arthroscintigraphy.

artrocentelleograma *m.* arthroscintigram.
artrocentesis *f.* arthrocentesis.
artroclasia *f.* arthroclasia.
artrocleisis *f.* arthroclisis, arthrokleisis.
artroclisis *f.* arthroclisis, arthrokleisis.
artrocondritis *f.* arthrochondritis.
artrodesis *f.* arthrodesis.
  artrodesis triple triple arthrodesis.
artrodia *f.* arthrodia.
artrodial *adj.* arthrodial.
artrodinia *f.* arthrodynia.
artrodínico, -ca *adj.* arthrodynic.
artrodisplasia *f.* arthrodysplasia.
artroempiesis *f.* arthroempyesis.
artroendoscopia *f.* arthroendoscopy.
artroereisis *f.* arthroereisis.
artrofima *f.* arthrophyma.
artrofito *m.* arthrophyte.
artroflisis *f.* arthrophlysis.
artrógeno, -na *adj.* arthrogenous.
artrografía *f.* arthrography.
artrograma *m.* arthrogram.
artrogriposis *f.* arthrogriposis.
  artrogriposis congénita múltiple congenital multiple arthrogriposis, arthrogriposis multiplex congenita.
artrólisis *f.* arthrolysis.
artrolito *f.* arthrolith.
artrología *f.* arthrology, arthrologia.
artrometría *f.* arthrometry.
artrómetro *m.* arthrometer.
artronalgia *f.* arthralgia.
artroneumografía *f.* arthropneumography.
artroneumorradiografía *f.* arthropneumoroentgenography.
artroneuralgia *f.* arthroneuralgia.
artroonicodisplasia *f.* arthroonychodysplasia.
artropatía *f.* arthropathy, arthropathia.
  artropatía de Charcot Charcot's arthropathy.
  artropatía condrocalcificada chondrocalcific arthropathy.
  artropatía diabética diabetic arthropathy.
  artropatía estática static arthropathy.
  artropatía inflamatoria inflammatory arthropathy.
  artropatía neurógena neurogenic arthropathy.
  artropatía neuropática neuropathic arthropathy.
  artropatía osteopulmonar osteopulmonary arthropathy.
  artropatía ovariopriva arthropathia ovariopriva.
  artropatía psoriásica arthropathia psoriasica.
  artropatía sifilítica syphilitic arthropathy.
  artropatía tabética tabetic arthropathy.
artropático, -ca *adj.* arthropathic.
artropatología *f.* arthropathology.
artropiosis *f.* arthropyosis.
artroplastia *f.* arthroplasty.
artroplástico, -ca *adj.* arthroplastic.
artropodiasis *f.* arthropodiasis.
artropódico, -ca *adj.* arthropodan, arthropodic, arthropodous.
artrópodo *m.* arthropod.
artrorrafia *f.* arthrorrhaphy.
artrorreumatismo *m.* arthrorheumatism.
artrosclerosis *f.* arthrosclerosis.
artroscopia *f.* arthroscopy.
artroscopio *m.* arthroscope.
artrosinovitis *f.* arthrosynovitis.
artrosis *f.* arthrosis.
  artrosis deformante, artrosis deformans arthrosis deformans.
  artrosis temporomandibular temporomandibular arthrosis.

artrospora *m.* arthrospore.
artrosteítis *f.* arthrosteitis.
artrostomía *f.* arthrostomy.
artrotomía *f.* arthrotomy.
artrótomo *m.* arthrotome.
artrotropía *f.* arthrotropy.
artrotrópico, -ca *adj.* arthrotropic.
asa *f.* loop, ansa.
asacria *f.* asacria.
asafia *f.* asaphia.
asbestosis *f.* asbestosis.
ascariasis *f.* ascariasis.
  ascariasis sarcóptica sarcoptic ascariasis.
ascaricida[1] *m.* ascaricide.
ascaricida[2] *adj.* ascaricidal.
ascáride *m.* ascarid.
ascaridiasis *f.* ascaridiasis, ascaridosis.
ascaridosis *f.* ascaridiasis, ascaridosis.
ascaridol *m.* ascaridole.
Ascaris Ascaris.
ascetospora ascetospora.
ascia *m.* ascia.
ascítico, -ca *adj.* ascitic.
ascitis *f.* ascites.
  ascitis adiposa ascites adiposus.
  ascitis exudativa exudative ascites.
  ascitis grasa fatty ascites.
  ascitis hemorrágica hemorrhagic ascites.
  ascitis hidrémica hydremic ascites.
  ascitis lechosa milky ascites.
  ascitis preagónica preagonal ascites.
  ascitis precoz ascites praecox.
  ascitis quiliforme chyliform ascites.
  ascitis quilosa chylous ascites, ascites chylosus.
  ascitis sanguinolenta bloody ascites.
  ascitis seudoquilosa pseudochylous ascites.
  ascitis transudativa transudative ascites.
ascitógeno, -na *adj.* ascitogenous.
Ascobolus Ascobolus.
ascorbemia *f.* ascorbemia.
ascorbicemia *f.* ascorbemia.
ascorburia *f.* ascorburia.
asecretorio, -ria *adj.* asecretory.
asecuencia *f.* asequence.
asemasia *f.* asemasia.
asemia *f.* asemia.
  asemia gráfica asemia graphica.
  asemia mímica asemia mimica.
  asemia verbal asemia verbalis.
asepsia *f.* asepsis.
  asepsia integral integral asepsis.
asepsis *f.* asepsis.
asepticismo *m.* asepticism.
aséptico, -ca *adj.* aseptic.
asexar *v.* unsex.
asexual *adj.* asexual.
asexualidad *f.* asexuality.
asexualización *f.* asexualization.
asfictico, -ca *adj.* asphyxial.
asfigmia *f.* asphygmia.
asfixia *f.* asphyxia.
  asfixia azul blue asphyxia.
  asfixia blanca white asphyxia.
  asfixia carbónica asphyxia carbonica.
  asfixia cianótica cyanotic asphyxia.
  asfixia fetal fetal asphyxia.
  asfixia lívida asphyxia livida.
  asfixia local local asphyxia.
  asfixia neonatal, asfixia neonatorum asphyxia neonatorum.
  asfixia pálida asphyxia pallida.
  asfixia reticular asphyxia reticularis.
  asfixia secundaria secondary asphyxia.
  asfixia traumática traumatic asphyxia.

asfixiante *adj.* asphyxiant.
asfixiar *v.* asphyxiate.
asialia *f.* asialia.
asiaticósido *m.* asiaticoside.
asiderosis *f.* asiderosis.
asiento *m.* seat.
  asiento basal basal seat.
asilo *m.* asylum.
asimbolia *f.* asymbolia.
  asimbolia dolorosa pain asymbolia.
asimetría *f.* asymmetry.
  asimetría cromática chromatic asymmetry.
asimétrico, -ca *adj.* asymmetric, asymmetrical.
asimetropía *f.* anisometropia.
asimiento *m.* grip.
  asimiento de fuerza power grip.
  asimiento en gancho hook grip.
  asimiento de precisión precision grip.
asimilable *adj.* assimilable.
asimilación *f.* assimilation.
  asimilación cultural cultural assimilation.
  asimilación social social assimilation.
asinapsis *f.* asynapsis.
asinclitismo *m.* asynclitism.
  asinclitismo anterior anterior asynclitism.
  asinclitismo posterior posterior asynclitism.
asincronía *f.* asynchrony.
asincronismo *m.* asynchronism.
asindesis *f.* asyndesis.
asinequia *f.* asynechia.
asinérgico, -ca *adj.* asynergic, asynertic.
asinergia *f.* asynergia, asynergy.
asinesia *f.* asynesia, asynesis.
asínfitos *adj.* asymphytous.
asinovia *f.* asynovia.
asintomático, -ca *adj.* asymptomatic.
asistemático, -ca *adj.* asystematic.
asistolia *f.* asystole, asystolia.
asistólico, -ca *adj.* asystolic.
asitia *f.* asitia.
asjike *m.* asjike.
asma *f.* asthma.
  asma abdominal abdominal asthma.
  asma alérgica allergic asthma.
  asma de los alfareros potter's asthma.
  asma alimentaria food asthma.
  asma alveolar alveolar asthma.
  asma atópica atopic asthma.
  asma bacteriana bacterial asthma.
  asma bronquial bronchial asthma.
  asma bronquítica bronchitic asthma.
  asma catarral catarrhal asthma.
  asma caballar horse asthma.
  asma cardíaca cardiac asthma.
  asma convulsiva asthma convulsivum.
  asma por diisocianato diisocyanate asthma.
  asma enfisematosa Heberden's asthma.
  asma equina horse asthma.
  asma esencial essential asthma.
  asma espasmódica spasmodic asthma.
  asma extrínseca extrinsic asthma.
  asma de los gatos cat asthma.
  asma de Heberden Heberden's asthma.
  asma del heno hay asthma.
  asma húmeda humid asthma.
  asma infecciosa infective asthma.
  asma intrínseca intrinsic asthma.
  asma por isocianato isocyanate asthma.
  asma de Kopp Kopp's asthma.
  asma de Millar Millar's asthma.
  asma de los mineros miner's asthma.
  asma nerviosa nervous asthma.
  asma por polen pollen asthma.
  asma por polvo dust asthma.

  asma por polvo de algodón cotton dust asthma.
  asma refleja reflex asthma.
  asma renal renal asthma.
  asma sexual sexual asthma.
  asma tímica thymic asthma.
  asma de verano summer asthma.
  asma verdadera true asthma.
  asma de Wichmann Wichmann's asthma.
asmático, -ca *adj.* asthmatic.
asmógeno, -na *adj.* asthmatogenic, asthmogenic.
asociación *f.* association.
  asociación controlada controlled association.
  asociación dirigida controlled association.
  asociación genética genetic association.
  asociación de ideas association of ideas.
  asociación libre free association.
  asociación onírica dream association.
  asociación de sueño dream association.
asociado, -da *adj.* associated.
asocial *adj.* asocial.
asoma *m.* asoma.
asonancia *f.* assonance.
asonia *f.* amusia.
aspalasoma *m.* aspalosoma.
aspartilglucosaminuria *f.* aspartylglycosaminuria.
aspecto *m.* aspect.
  aspecto dorsal dorsal aspect.
aspergilar *adj.* aspergillar.
Aspergillus *m.* aspergillus.
aspergiloma *m.* aspergilloma.
aspergilosis *f.* aspergillosis.
  aspergilosis aural, aspergilosis auricular aural aspergillosis.
  aspergilosis bronconeumónica bronchopneumonic aspergillosis.
  aspergilosis broncopulmonar bronchopulmonary aspergillosis.
  aspergilosis diseminada disseminated aspergillosis.
  aspergilosis invasiva invasive aspergillosis.
  aspergilosis pulmonar pulmonary aspergillosis.
aspergilomicosis *f.* aspergillomycosis.
aspergilotoxicosis *f.* aspergillustoxicosis.
aspermia *f.* aspermia, aspermatism.
aspersión *f.* aspersion.
aspiración *f.* aspiration.
  aspiración broncoscópica bronchoscopic aspiration.
  aspiración meconial, aspiración de meconio meconium aspiration.
  aspiración postusiva post-tussive aspiration.
  aspiración al vacío vacuum aspiration.
aspirado, -da *adj.* aspirate.
aspirador *m.* aspirator.
  aspirador de vacío vacuum aspirator.
aspirar *v.* aspirate.
aspirómetro *m.* inspirometer.
asplenia *f.* asplenia.
asplénico, -ca *adj.* asplenic.
asporógeno, -na *adj.* asporogenous.
asporogénico, -ca *adj.* asporogenic.
asporoso, -sa *adj.* asporous.
asporulado, -da *adj.* asporulate.
asquelminto *m.* aschelminth.
astasia *f.* astasia.
  astasia abasia astasia-abasia.
astático, -ca *adj.* astatic.
asteatosis *f.* asteatosis.
  asteatosis del cutis asteatosis cutis.
astenia *f.* asthenia.

astenia anhidrótica tropical tropical anhidrotic asthenia.
astenia grave hipofisiógena asthenia gravis hypophyseogenea.
astenia miálgica myalgic asthenia.
astenia muscular myasthenia.
astenia nerviosa neurasthenia.
astenia neurocirculatoria neurocirculatory asthenia.
astenia pigmentosa Addison's disease.
asténico, -ca *adj.* asthenic.
astenobiosis *f.* asthenobiosis.
astenocoria *f.* asthenocoria.
astenofobia *f.* asthenophobia.
astenómetro *m.* asthenometer.
asténope *m., f.* asthenope.
astenopía *f.* asthenopia.
  astenopía acomodativa accommodative asthenopia.
  astenopía muscular muscular asthenopia.
  astenopía nerviosa nervous asthenopia.
  astenopía neurasténica neurasthenic asthenopia.
  astenopía retinal nervous asthenopia.
astenópico, -ca *adj.* asthenopic.
astenospermia *f.* asthenospermia.
astenoxia *f.* asthenoxia.
áster *m.* aster.
  áster espermático sperm aster.
astereognosia *f.* astereognosis, astereognosy.
astereognosis *f.* astereognosis, astereognosy.
asterión *m.* asterion.
asterixis *f.* asterixis.
asternal *adj.* asternal.
asternia *f.* asternia.
asteroide *m.* asteroid.
astigmágrafo *m.* astigmagraph.
astigmático, -ca *adj.* astigmatic.
astigmatismo *m.* astigmatism.
  astigmatismo adquirido acquired astigmatism.
  astigmatismo anormal astigmatism against the rule.
  astigmatismo compuesto compound astigmatism.
  astigmatismo congénito congenital astigmatism.
  astigmatismo corneal corneal astigmatism.
  astigmatismo directo direct astigmatism.
  astigmatismo fisiológico physiological astigmatism.
  astigmatismo hipermetrópico, astigmatismo hiperópico hypermetropic astigmatism, hyperopic astigmatism.
  astigmatismo inverso inverse astigmatism.
  astigmatismo irregular irregular astigmatism.
  astigmatismo lenticular lenticular astigmatism.
  astigmatismo miópico myopic astigmatism.
  astigmatismo miópico compuesto compound myopic astigmatism.
  astigmatismo miópico simple simple myopic astigmatism.
  astigmatismo mixto mixed astigmatism.
  astigmatismo normal, astigmatismo de regla astigmatism with the rule.
  astigmatismo oblicuo oblique astigmatism.
  astigmatismo de regla astigmatism with the rule.
  astigmatismo regular regular astigmatism.
  astigmatismo revertido reversed astigmatism.
astigmatometría *f.* astigmatometry.
astigmatómetro *m.* astigmatometer.

astigmatoscopia *f.* astigmatoscopy.
astigmatoscopio *m.* astigmatoscope.
astigmometría *f.* astigmometry.
astigmómetro *m.* astigmometer.
astigmoscopia *f.* astigmoscopy.
astigmoscopio *m.* astigmoscope.
astilla *f.* splinter.
  astilla ósea bone splinter.
astillar *v.* splinter.
astomatida astomatida.
astomatoso, -sa *adj.* astomatous.
astomia *f.* astomia.
ástomo, -ma *adj.* astomous.
astragalectomia *f.* astragalectomy.
astragalino, -na *adj.* astragalar.
astrágalo *m.* astragalus.
astragalocalcáneo, -a *adj.* astragalocalcanean.
astragalocrural *adj.* astragalocrural.
astragaloescafoide *adj.* astragaloscaphoid.
astragaloperoneo, -a *adj.* astragalofibular.
astragalotibial *adj.* astragalotibial.
astral *adj.* astral.
astricción *f.* astriction.
astringencia *f.* astriction.
astringente *m. y adj.* astringent.
astroblasto *m.* astroblast.
astroblastoma *m.* astroblastoma.
astrocinético, -ca *adj.* astrocinetic, astrokinetic.
astrocitina *f.* astrocytin.
astrocito *m.* astrocyte.
  astrocito fibroso fibrous astrocyte.
  astrocito protoplasmático astrocyte protoplasmaticum.
  astrocito protoplásmico protoplasmic astrocyte.
  astrocito reactivo reactive astrocyte.
astrocitoma *m.* astrocytoma.
  astrocitoma anaplásico anaplastic astrocytoma.
  astrocitoma fibrilar astrocytoma fibrillare.
  astrocitoma de grado I grade I astrocytoma.
  astrocitoma de grado II grade II astrocytoma.
  astrocitoma de grado III grade III astrocytoma.
  astrocitoma de grado IV grade IV astrocytoma.
  astrocitoma pilocítico pilocytic astrocytoma.
  astrocitoma piloide piloid astrocytoma.
  astrocitoma protoplasmático astrocytoma protoplasmaticum.
astrocitosis *f.* astrocytosis.
astroependimoma *m.* astroependymoma.
astroglia *f.* astroglia.
astroide *adj.* astroid.
astroma *m.* astroma.
astrosfera *f.* astrosphere.
astrostático, -ca *adj.* astrostatic.
asulfurosis *f.* asulfurosis.
atacador *m.* plugger.
atáctico, -ca *adj.* atactic.
atactiforme *adj.* atactiform.
ataque *m.* attack, stroke.
  ataque de calor heat stroke.
  ataque cardíaco heart attack.
  ataque isquémico transitorio transient ischemic attack.
  ataque de pánico panic attack.
  ataque salutatorio salaam attack.
  ataque de sol sunstroke.
  ataque de sueño sleep attack.
  ataque vagal vagal attack.
  ataque vasovagal vasovagal attack.
ataráctico, -ca *adj.* ataractic.
ataragelsia ataralgesia.
ataraxia *f.* ataraxia.

ataráxico, -ca *adj.* ataraxic.
atávico, -ca *adj.* atavic, atavistic.
atavismo *m.* atavism.
ataxafasia *f.* ataxaphasia, ataxiaphasia.
ataxia *f.* ataxia.
  ataxia aguda acute ataxia.
  ataxia alcohólica alcoholic ataxia.
  ataxia autónoma autonomic ataxia.
  ataxia de Briquet Briquet's ataxia.
  ataxia de Broca Broca's ataxia.
  ataxia cardíaca, ataxia cordis ataxia cordis.
  ataxia central central ataxia.
  ataxia cerebelosa cerebellar ataxia.
  ataxia cerebelosa aguda acute cerbellar ataxia.
  ataxia cerebelosa hereditaria hereditary cerebellar ataxia.
  ataxia cerebral cerebral ataxia.
  ataxia cinética kinetic ataxia.
  ataxia dinámica kinetic ataxia.
  ataxia espinal spinal ataxia.
  ataxia espinal hereditaria hereditary spinal ataxia.
  ataxia espinocerebelosa spinocerebellar ataxia.
  ataxia estática static ataxia.
  ataxia familiar de Friedreich Friedreich's ataxia.
  ataxia de Ferguson y Critchley Ferguson and Critchley's ataxia.
  ataxia de Friedreich Friedreich's ataxia.
  ataxia frontal frontal ataxia.
  ataxia hereditaria hereditary ataxia.
  ataxia histérica hysterical ataxia.
  ataxia intrapsíquica intrapsychic ataxia.
  ataxia laberíntica labyrinthic ataxia.
  ataxia de Leyden Leyden's ataxia.
  ataxia locomotora, ataxia locomotriz locomotor ataxia.
  ataxia de Marie Marie's ataxia.
  ataxia motora, ataxia motriz motor ataxia.
  ataxia ocular ocular ataxia.
  ataxia óptica optic ataxia.
  ataxia de sanger brown Sanger Brown ataxia.
  ataxia sensitiva sensory ataxia.
  ataxia telangiectasia ataxia telangiectasia.
  ataxia térmica thermal ataxia.
  ataxia troncal truncal ataxia.
  ataxia vasomotora vasomotor ataxia.
  ataxia vestibular vestibular ataxia.
  ataxia vestibulocerebelosa vestibulocerebellar ataxia.
atáxico, -ca *adj.* ataxic.
ataxiadinamia *f.* ataxoadynamia, ataxiadynamia.
ataxiofemia *f.* ataxiophemia.
ataxiofobia *f.* ataxiophobia, ataxophobia.
ataxoadinamia *f.* ataxoadynamia.
ataxofemia *f.* ataxiophemia.
ataxofobia *f.* ataxophobia.
atelectasia *f.* atelectasis.
  atelectasia por absorción adquirida acquired absorption atelectasis.
  atelectasia adquirida acquired atelectasis.
  atelectasia compresiva compression atelectasis.
  atelectasia congénita congenital atelectasis.
  atelectasia inicial initial atelectasis.
  atelectasia irregular patchy atelectasis.
  atelectasia lobular lobular atelectasis.
  atelectasia obstructiva obstructive atelectasis.
  atelectasia primaria primary atelectasis.
  atelectasia por relajación relaxation atelectasis.

  atelectasia por resorción resorption atelectasis.
  atelectasia secundaria secondary atelectasis.
  atelectasia segmentaria segmental atelectasis.
atelectásico, -ca *adj.* atelectatic.
atelencefalia *f.* atelencephalia.
atelia¹ *f.* atelia.
atelia² *f.* athelia.
atelocardia *f.* atelocardia.
atelocefalia *f.* atelocephaly.
atelocéfalo, -la *adj.* atelocephalous.
ateloencefalia *f.* ateloencephalia.
ateloglosia *f.* ateloglossia.
atelognatia *f.* atelognathia.
atelomielia *f.* atelomyelia.
atelopodia *f.* atelopodia.
ateloprosopia *f.* ateloprosopia.
ateloqueilia *f.* atelocheilia.
ateloquiria *f.* atelocheiria.
atelorraquidia *f.* atelorachidia.
atelostomía *f.* atelostomia.
atención *f.* attention.
atenuación *f.* attenuation.
atenuador *m.* attenuator.
atenuador, -ra *adj.* attenuant.
atenuante *adj.* attenuant.
atenuar *v.* attenuate.
atermal *adj.* athermal.
atermancia *f.* athermancy.
atérmano, -na *adj.* athermanous.
atérmico, -ca *adj.* athermic.
aterminal *adj.* abterminal.
atermosistáltico, -ca *adj.* athermosystaltic.
ateroembolia *m.* atheroembolism.
ateroembolismo *m.* atheroembolism.
ateroémbolo *m.* atheroembolus.
aterogénesis *f.* atherogenesis.
aterogenético, -ca *adj.* atherogenic.
aterogénico, -ca *adj.* atherogenic.
ateroma *m.* atheroma.
ateromatosis *f.* atheromatosis.
ateromatoso, -sa *adj.* atheromatous.
ateronecrosis *f.* atheronecrosis.
aterosclerosis *f.* atherosclerosis.
aterosclerótico, -ca *adj.* atherosclerotic.
aterosis *f.* atherosis.
aterotrombosis *f.* atherothrombosis.
aterotrombótico, -ca *adj.* atherothrombotic.
atesia *f.* athetosis.
atetoide *adj.* athetoid.
atetósico, -ca *adj.* athetosic, athetotic.
atetótico, -ca *adj.* athetosic, athetotic.
atetosis *f.* athetosis.
  atetosis congénita doble double congenital athetosis.
  atetosis poshemipléjica posthemiplegic athetosis.
  atetosis pupilar pupillary athetosis.
atiaminosis *f.* athiaminosis.
aticitis *f.* atticitis.
ático *m.* attic.
aticoantrotomía *f.* atticoantrotomy.
aticomastoideo, -a *adj.* atticomastoid.
aticotomía *f.* atticotomy.
atimia *f.* athymia.
atimismo *m.* athymism.
atipia *f.* atypia.
atípico, -ca *adj.* atypical.
atipismo *m.* atypism.
atirea *f.* athyrea.
atireosis *f.* athyreosis, athyrosis.
atireótico, -ca *adj.* athyrotic, athyreotic.
atiria *f.* athyria.
atiroidemia *f.* athyroidemia.

atiroidia *f.* athyroidosis.
atiroidismo *m.* athyroidism.
atiroidosis *f.* athyroidosis.
atiroismo *m.* athyroidism.
atirosis *f.* athyreosis, athyrosis.
atirótico, -ca *adj.* athyrotic, athyreotic.
atlantal *adj.* atlantal.
atlantoaxil *adj.* atlantoaxial.
atlantodídimo *m.* atlantodidymus.
atlantomastoideo, -a *adj.* atlantomastoid.
atlantooccipital *adj.* atlanto-occipital.
atlantoodontoideo, -a *adj.* atlanto-odontoid.
atlas *m.* atlas.
atlético, -ca *adj.* athletic.
atloaxoide *adj.* atloaxoid.
atlódimo *m.* atlodidymus.
atloideo, -a *adj.* atloid.
atloidoaxoideo, -a *adj.* atlantoaxoid.
atloidoepistrófico, -ca *adj.* atlantoepistrophic.
atloidooccipital *m. y adj.* atloido-occipital.
atmiatría *f.* atmiatrics, atmiatry.
atmidiatría *f.* atmiatrics, atmiatry.
atmocausis *f.* atmocausis.
atmocauterio *m.* atmocautery.
atmógrafo *m.* atmograph.
atmólisis *f.* atmolysis.
atmómetro *m.* atmometer.
atmoterapia *f.* atmotherapy.
atocia *f.* atocia.
atomización *f.* atomization.
atomizador *m.* atomizer.
átomo *m.* atom.
  átomo excitado excited atom.
  átomo ionizado ionized atom.
  átomo radiactivo radioactive atom.
atonía *f.* atony.
atonicidad *f.* atonicity.
atónico, -ca *adj.* atonic.
atopeno *m.* atopen.
atopia *f.* atopia.
atópico, -ca *adj.* atopic.
atopognosia *f.* atopognosia.
atoquia *f.* atocia.
atóxico, -ca *adj.* atoxic.
atracción *f.* attraction.
  atracción capilar capillary attraction.
  atracción eléctrica electric attraction.
  atracción magnética magnetic attraction.
  atracción química chemical attraction.
atransferrinemia *f.* atransferrinemia.
atraumático, -ca *adj.* atraumatic.
atremia *f.* atremia.
atrepsia *f.* athrepsia.
atresia *f.* atresia.
  atresia del ano anal atresia.
  atresia aórtica aortic atresia.
  atresia aural aural atresia.
  atresia biliar biliary atresia.
  atresia de las coanas choanal atresia.
  atresia duodenal duodenal atresia.
  atresia esofágica esophageal atresia.
  atresia folicular follicular atresia.
  atresia intestinal intestinal atresia.
  atresia irídica, atresia del iris atresia iridis.
  atresia mitral mitral atresia.
  atresia prepilórica prepyloric atresia.
  atresia pulmonar pulmonary atresia.
  atresia tricúspide, atresia tricuspídea tricuspid atresia.
  atresia vaginal vaginal atresia.
atrésico, -ca *adj.* atresic.
atrético, -ca *adj.* atresic.
atretoblefaria *f.* atretoblepharia.
atretocéfalo *m.* atretocephalus.

atretocistia *f.* atretocystia.
atretocormo *m.* atretocormus.
atretogastria *f.* atretogastria.
atretolemia *f.* atretolemia.
atretometría *f.* atretometria.
atretopsia *f.* atretopsia.
atretorrinia *f.* atretorrhinia.
atretostomía *f.* atretostomia.
atreturetria *f.* atreturethria.
atrial *adj.* atrial.
atrición *f.* attrition.
atricosis *f.* atrichosis.
atricoso, -sa *adj.* atrichous.
atrio *m.* atrium.
atriocomisuropexia *f.* atriocommissuropexy.
atriomegalia *f.* atriomegaly.
atriopeptina *f.* atriopeptin.
atriopeptinógeno *m.* atriopeptigen.
atrioseptopexia *f.* atrioseptopexy.
atrioseptoplastia *f.* atrioseptoplasty.
atrioseptostomía *f.* atrioseptostomy.
atriotomía *f.* atriotomy.
atriótomo *m.* atriotome.
atrioventricular *adj.* atrioventricular.
atrioventricularis comunis atrioventricularis comunis.
atriplicismo *m.* atriplicism.
atriquia *f.* atrichia.
  atriquia universal congénita universal congenital atrichia.
atriquiasis *f.* atrichia.
atrium atrium.
atrocitosis *f.* athrocytosis.
atrofagocitosis *f.* athrophagocytosis.
atrofedema *f.* athrophedema.
atrofia *f.* atrophy, atrophia.
  atrofia adiposa fatty atrophy.
  atrofia por agotamiento exhaustion atrophy.
  atrofia amarilla aguda del hígado acute yellow atrophy of the liver.
  atrofia amarilla cicatrizada healed yellow atrophy.
  atrofia amarilla subaguda del hígado subacute yellow atrophy of the liver.
  atrofia anular de la coroides y la retina gyrate atrophy of choroid and retina.
  atrofia artrítica arthritic atrophy.
  atrofia azul blue atrophy.
  atrofia blanca white atrophy.
  atrofia de Buchwald Buchwald's atrophy.
  atrofia cerebelosa cerebellar atrophy.
  atrofia cerebral circunscrita circumscribed cerebral atrophy.
  atrofia de Charcot-Marie-Tooth Charcot-Marie-Tooth type peroneal muscular atrophy.
  atrofia cianótica cyanotic atrophy.
  atrofia cianótica hepática cyanotic atrophy of the liver.
  atrofia compensadora, atrofia compensatoria compensatory atrophy.
  atrofia por compresión pressure atrophy, compression atrophy.
  atrofia concéntrica concentric atrophy.
  atrofia coroidea progresiva progressive choroidal atrophy.
  atrofia coroidea retiniana atrophy choroideae et retinae.
  atrofia correlativa correlated atrophy.
  atrofia corticostriatospinal atrophy corticostriatospinal.
  atrofia de Cruveilhier Cruveilhier's atrophy.
  atrofia cutis atrophy cutis.
  atrofia degenerativa degenerative atrophy.
  atrofia de Déjerine-Sottas Déjerine-Sottas type atrophy.

  atrofia de Déjerine-Thomas Dejerine-Thomas atrophy.
  atrofia dérmica idiopática atrophy cutis idiopathica.
  atrofia por desuso atrophy of disuse.
  atrofia de Eichhort Eichhort's atrophy.
  atrofia endocrina endocrine atrophy.
  atrofia endometrial endometrial atrophy.
  atrofia escapulohumeral scapulohumeral atrophy.
  atrofia esencial del iris essential atrophy of the iris.
  atrofia espinal spinal atrophy.
  atrofia estriada y maculosa atrophy striata et maculosa.
  atrofia excéntrica eccentric atrophy.
  atrofia facial unilateral progresiva progressive unilateral facial atrophy.
  atrofia fascioescapulohumeral facioscapulohumeral atrophy.
  atrofia de Fazio-Londe Fazio-Londe atrophy.
  atrofia fisiológica physiologic atrophy.
  atrofia de Fuchs Fuchs' atrophy.
  atrofia gástrica gastric atrophy.
  atrofia gingival gingival atrophy.
  atrofia girada de la coroides y la retina gyrate atrophy of choroid and retina.
  atrofia del globo ocular atrophy bulbi.
  atrofia granular del riñón, atrofia granulosa del riñón granular atrophy of the kidney.
  atrofia grasa fatty atrophy.
  atrofia gris gray atrophy.
  atrofia hemifacial hemifacial atrophy.
  atrofia hemilingual hemilingual atrophy.
  atrofia de Hoffmann Hoffmann's muscular atrophy.
  atrofia de Hunt Hunt's atrophy.
  atrofia por inacción atrophy of disuse.
  atrofia infantil infantile atrophy.
  atrofia inflamatoria inflammatory atrophy.
  atrofia intersticial interstitial atrophy.
  atrofia de Kienböck Kienböck's atrophy.
  atrofia de la lactación lactation atrophy.
  atrofia lineal linear atrophy.
  atrofia lobular lobar atrophy.
  atrofia maculosa varioliformis cutis atrophy maculosa varioliformis cutis.
  atrofia maculosa de Jadassohn Jadassohn's macular atrophy.
  atrofia maculosa cutánea atrophy maculosa cutis.
  atrofia maculosa de Schweninger-Buzzi Schweninger-Buzzi macular atrophy.
  atrofia marántica marantic atrophy.
  atrofia mesentérica atrophy mesenterica.
  atrofia miopática myopathic muscular atrophy.
  atrofia muscular muscular atrophy.
  atrofia muscular de Aran-Duchenne, atrofia muscular de Duchenne-Aran Aran-Duchenne muscular atrophy, Duchenne-Aran muscular atrophy.
  atrofia muscular por denervación denervated muscle atrophy.
  atrofia muscular espinal spinal muscular atrophy.
  atrofia muscular espinal familiar familial spinal muscular atrophy.
  atrofia muscular espinal de Werdnig-Hoffmann Werdnig-Hoffmann spinal muscular atrophy.
  atrofia muscular idiopática idiopathic muscular atrophy.
  atrofia muscular isquémica ischemic muscular atrophy.

atrofia muscular juvenil juvenile muscular atrophy.

atrofia muscular lipomatosa atrophy muscularum lipomatosa.

atrofia muscular mielopática myelopathic muscular atrophy.

atrofia muscular neurítica neuritic muscular atrophy.

atrofia muscular peronea neuropática progresiva progressive neuropathic peroneal muscular atrophy.

atrofia muscular progresiva progressive muscular atrophy.

atrofia neurítica neuritic atrophy.

atrofia neurogénica neurogenic atrophy.

atrofia neuropatica neuropathic atrophy.

atrofia neurótica neurotic atrophy.

atrofia neurotrófica neurotrophic atrophy.

atrofia numérica numeric atrophy.

atrofia olivopontocerebelosa olivopontocerebellar atrophy.

atrofia óptica optic atrophy.

atrofia óptica de Leber Leber's hereditary optic atrophy.

atrofia óptica primaria primary optic atrophy.

atrofia óptica secundaria secondary optic atrophy.

atrofia ósea bone atrophy.

atrofia ósea de Sudeck Sudeck's atrophy.

atrofia pálida pallidal atrophy.

atrofia parda brown atrophy.

atrofia de Parrot del neonato, atrofia de Parrot de los recién nacidos Parrot atrophy of the newborn.

atrofia patológica pathologic atrophy.

atrofia periodontal periodontal atrophy.

atrofia de Pick de las circunvoluciones Pick's convolutional atrophy.

atrofia pigmentaria pigmentary atrophy.

atrofia postraumática de los huesos posttraumatic atrophy of bone.

atrofia de la pulpa, atrofia pulpar pulp atrophy.

atrofia receptora receptoric atrophy.

atrofia reumática rheumatic atrophy.

atrofia roja red atrophy.

atrofia saltatoria leaping atrophy.

atrofia senil senile atrophy.

atrofia senil cutánea, atrofia senil de la piel senile atrophy of the skin.

atrofia serosa serous atrophy.

atrofia simple simple atrophy.

atrofia de Sudeck Sudeck's atrophy.

atrofia tóxica toxic atrophy.

atrofia por tracción traction atrophy.

atrofia transneuronal transneuronal atrophy.

atrofia trofoneurótica trophoneurotic atrophy.

atrofia ungueal atrophy unguium.

atrofia vascular vascular atrophy.

atrofia de von Leber von Leber's atrophy.

atrofia de Vulpian Vulpian's atrophy.

atrofia de Werdnig-Hoffmann Werdnig-Hoffmann atrophy.

atrofia de Zimmerlin Zimmerlin's atrophy.

atrofiado, -da *adj.* atrophied.

atrófico, -ca *adj.* atrophic.

atrofodermatosis *f.* atrophodermatosis.

atrofoderma *f.* atrophoderma.

atrofoderma biotripticum atrophoderma biotripticum.

atrofoderma neuriticum atrophoderma neuriticum.

atrofoderma reticulatum simetricum faciei atrophoderma reticulatum symmetricum faciei.

atrofodermia *f.* atrophoderma.

atrofodermia álbida atrophoderma albidum.

atrofodermia biotríptica atrophoderma biotripticum.

atrofodermia difusa atrophoderma diffussum.

atrofodermia neurítica atrophoderma neuriticum.

atrofodermia pigmentoso atrophoderma pigmentosum.

atrofodermia reticular simétrica facial atrophoderma reticulatum symmetricum faciei.

atrofodermia senil senile atrophoderma, atrophoderma senile.

atrofodermia vermicular atrophoderma vermiculare.

atrombasis *f.* athrombia.

atrombia *f.* athrombia.

atropinismo *m.* atropinism.

atropinización *f.* atropinization.

atropismo *m.* atropinism.

aturdimiento *m.* dizziness.

au-antigenemia *f.* au-antigenemia.

audible *adj.* audible.

audición *f.* audition.

audición coloreada, audición cromática chromatic audition.

audición gustativa, audición gustatoria gustatory audition.

audífono *m.* hearing aid.

audimutismo *m.* audimutitas.

audioanalgesia *f.* audioanalgesia.

audiogénico, -ca *adj.* audiogenic.

audiograma *m.* audiogram.

audiología *f.* audiology.

audiólogo, -ga *m., f.* audiologist.

audiometría *f.* audiometry.

audiometría de Békésy Békésy audiometry.

audiometría cortical cortical audiometry.

audiometría diagnóstica diagnostic audiometry.

audiometría electrococleográfica electrocochleographic audiometry.

audiometría electrodérmica electrodermal audiometry.

audiometría de grupo group audiometry.

audiometría del habla, audiometría del lenguaje speech audiometry.

audiometría de localización localization audiometry.

audiometría de respuesta evocada del tronco encefálico brainstem evoked response audiometry (BSER).

audiometría de tonos puros pure tone audiometry.

audiométrico, -ca *adj.* audiometric.

audiometrista *m., f.* audiometrist, audiometrician.

audiómetro *m.* audiometer.

audiómetro automático automatic audiometer.

audiómetro de Békésy Békésy audiometer.

audiómetro de grupo group audiometer.

audiómetro de lenguaje speech audiometer.

audiómetro de rango amplio wide range audiometer.

audiómetro de rango limitado limited range audiometer.

audiómetro de respuesta evocada evoked response audiometer.

audiómetro de tonos puros pure tone audiometer.

auditivo, -va *adj.* auditive, auditory.

auditognosis *f.* auditognosis.

augnato *m.* augnathus.

auliplexo *m.* auliplexus.

aumentador, -ra *adj.* augmentor.

aura *f.* aura.

aura asmática aura asthmatica.

aura auditiva auditory aura.

aura cinestésica kinesthetic aura.

aura eléctrica electric aura.

aura epigástrica epigastric aura.

aura epiléptica epileptic aura.

aura histérica aura hysterica.

aura intelectual intellectual aura.

aura reminiscente reminiscent aura.

aura vertiginosa vertiginous aura.

aural *adj.* aural.

auramina *f.* auramine.

aurantlasls *f.* aurantlasls.

auriasis *f.* auriasis.

aúrico, -ca *adj.* auric.

aurícula *f.* atrium.

auricular *adj.* auricular.

auricular *m.* auricular finger, little finger.

auriculocraneal *adj.* auriculocranial.

auriculotemporal *adj.* auriculotemporal.

auriculoterapia *f.* auriculotherapy.

auriculoventricular *adj.* auriculoventricular.

auriforme *adj.* auriform.

aurinasal *adj.* aurinasal.

auripuntura *f.* auripuncture.

auriscalpo *m.* auriscalpium.

auriscopio *m.* auriscope.

aurocromodermia *f.* aurochromoderma.

aurómetro *m.* aurometer.

auroterapia *f.* aurotherapy.

auscultación *f.* auscultation.

auscultación directa direct auscultation.

auscultación inmediata immediate auscultation.

auscultación de Korányi Korányi's auscultation.

auscultación mediata mediate auscultation.

auscultación obstétrica obstetric auscultation.

auscultar *v.* auscultate, auscult.

auscultatorio, -ria *adj.* auscultatory.

auscultoscopio *m.* auscultoscope.

ausencia *f.* absence.

ausencia atípica atypical absence.

ausencia atónica atonic absence.

ausencia compleja complex absence.

ausencia enurética enuretic absence.

ausencia epiléptica epileptic absence.

ausencia estornutatoria sternutatory absence.

ausencia hipertónica hypertonic absence.

ausencia mioclónica myoclonic absence.

ausencia pura pure absence.

ausencia retrocursiva retrocursive absence.

ausencia simple simple absence.

ausencia subclínica subclinical absence.

ausencia típica typical absence.

ausencia tusígena tussive absence.

ausencia vasomotora vasomotor absence.

autacoide *m.* autacoid.

autarcesiología *f.* autarcesiology.

autarcesis *f.* autarcesis.

autarcético, -ca *adj.* autarcetic.

autécico, -ca *adj.* autecic.

autemesia *f.* autemesia.

autismo *m.* autism.

autista *adj.* autistic.

autoactivación *f.* autoactivation.

autoaglutinación *f.* autoagglutination.

autoaglutinina *f.* autoagglutinin.

autoalergia *f.* autoallergy.

autoalérgico, -ca *adj.* autoallergic.

autoalergización *f.* autoallergization.
autoamputación *f.* autoamputation.
autoanafilaxia *f.* autoanaphylaxis.
autoanafilaxis *f.* autoanaphylaxis.
autoanálisis *m.* autoanalysis.
autoanalizador *m.* autoanalyzer.
autoanamnesis *f.* autoanamnesis.
autoanticomplemento *m.* autoanticomplement.
autoanticuerpo *m.* autoantibody.
　autoanticuerpo caliente warm autoantibody.
　autoanticuerpo frío cold autoantibody.
autoantígeno *m.* autoantigen.
autoantisepsia *f.* autoantisepsis.
autoantitoxina *f.* autoantitoxin.
autoaudible *adj.* autoaudible.
autobacteriófago *m.* autobacteriophage.
autocatálisis *f.* autocatalysis.
autocatalítico, -ca *adj.* autocatalytic.
autocatarsis *f.* autocatharsis.
autocateterismo *m.* autocatheterism.
autocinesis *f.* autocinesis, autokinesis.
autocinético, -ca *adj.* autokinetic.
autocistoplastia *f.* autocystoplasty.
autocitolisina *f.* autocytolysin.
autocitólisis *f.* autocytolysis.
autocitolítico, -ca *adj.* autocytolytic.
autocitotoxina *f.* autocytotoxin.
autoclasia *f.* autoclasia.
autoclasis *f.* autoclasis, autoclasia.
autoclave *m.* autoclave.
autocolecistectomía *f.* autocholecystectomy.
autoconciencia *f.* self-awareness.
autoconducción *f.* autoconduction.
autoconocimiento *m.* self-knowledge.
autocontrol *m.* self-control.
autodérmico, -ca *adj.* autodermic.
autodescubrimiento *m.* self-discovery.
autodiferenciación *f.* self-differentiation.
autodigestión *f.* autodigestion, self-digestion.
autodrenaje *m.* autodrainage.
autoecolalia *f.* autoecholalia.
autoensayo *m.* autoassay.
autoenvenenamiento *m.* self-poisoning.
autoeritrofagocitosis *f.* autoerythrophagocytosis.
autoerótico, -ca *adj.* autoerotic.
autoeroticismo *m.* autoerotism, autoeroticism.
autoerotismo *m.* autoerotism, autoeroticism.
autoesplenectomía *f.* autosplenectomy.
autoesterilización *f.* autosterilization.
autoestimulación *f.* autostimulation, self-stimulation.
autofagia *f.* autophagia.
autofágico, -ca *adj.* autophagic.
autofagolisosoma *f.* autophagolysosome.
autofagosoma *m.* autophagosome.
autofecundación *f.* self-fertilization.
autofilia *f.* autophilia.
autófilo, -la *adj.* autophil.
autofonía *f.* autophonia.
autofonometría *f.* autophonometry.
autofundoscopia *f.* autofundoscopy.
autofundoscopio *m.* autofundoscope.
autogénesis *f.* autogenesis.
autogenético, -ca *adj.* autogenetic.
autogénico, -ca *adj.* autogenic.
autógeno, -na *adj.* autogenous.
autognosia *f.* autognosis, autognosia.
autognosis *f.* autognosis, autognosia.
autognóstico, -ca *adj.* autognostic.

autografismo *m.* autographism.
autohemoaglutinación *f.* autohemoagglutination.
autohemólisis *f.* autohemolysis.
autohemolítico, -ca *adj.* autohemolytic.
autohemoterapia *f.* autohemotherapy.
autohemotransfusión *f.* autohemotransfusion.
autoinfección *f.* autoinfection.
autoinjerto *m.* autograft.
autoinmune *adj.* autoimmune.
autoinmunidad *f.* autoimmunity.
autoinmunitario, -ria *adj.* autoimmune.
autoinmunización *f.* autoimmunization.
autoinmunocitopenia *f.* autoimmunocytopenia.
autoinoculable *adj.* autoinoculable.
autoinoculación *f.* autoinoculation.
autointoxicación *f.* autointoxication.
autointoxicante *adj.* autointoxicant.
autolaringoscopia *f.* autolaryngoscopy.
autolesión *f.* autolesion.
autoleucocitoterapia *f.* autoleukocytotherapy.
autolimitado, -da *adj.* self-limited.
autolisado *m.* autolysate.
autolisina *f.* autolysin.
autólisis *f.* autolysis.
autólogo, -ga *adj.* autologous.
automatismo *m.* automatism.
　automatismo ambulatorio ambulatory automatism.
　automatismo deambulante ambulatory automatism.
　automatismo de orden command automatism.
　automatismo postraumático inmediato immediate post-traumatic automatism.
automatógrafo *m.* automatograph.
automutilación *f.* autolesion.
autonefrectomía *f.* autonephrectomy.
autonomía *f.* autonomy.
autonómico, -ca *adj.* autonomic.
autónomo, -ma *adj.* autonomous.
autonomotrópico, -ca *adj.* autonomotropic.
autooftalmoscopio *m.* autophthalmoscope.
autopatografía *f.* autopathography.
autopepsia *f.* autopepsia.
autoplasmoterapia *f.* autoplasmotherapy.
autoplastia *f.* autoplasty.
autoplástico, -ca *adj.* autoplastic.
autoplasto *m.* autoplast.
autoploide *m.* autoploid.
autopoliploide *adj.* autopolyploid.
autopoliploidia *f.* autopolyploidy.
autoprotección *f.* autoprotection.
autoproteólisis *f.* autoproteolysis.
autopsia *f.* autopsy, autopsia.
　autopsia psicológica psychological autopsy.
autoqueratoplastia *f.* autokeratoplasty.
autorrafia *f.* autorrhaphy.
autorreactivo, -va *adj.* autoreactive.
autorregulación *f.* autoregulation.
　autorregulación heterométrica heterometric autoregulation.
　autorregulación homeométrica homeometric autoregulation.
autorreinfección *f.* autoreinfection.
autorreinfusión *f.* autoreinfusion.
autoscopia *f.* autoscopy.
autosensibilización *f.* autosensitization.

autosepticemia *f.* autosepticemia.
autoseroterapia *f.* autoserotherapy.
autosítico, -ca *adj.* autositic.
autósito *m.* autosite.
autosmia *f.* autosmia.
autosoma *m.* autosome.
autosomatognosis *f.* autosomatognosis.
autosomatognóstico, -ca *adj.* autosomatognostic.
autosómico, -ca *adj.* autosomal.
autosuero *m.* autoserum.
autosueroterapia *f.* autoserotherapy.
autoterapia *f.* autotherapy.
autotolerancia *f.* self-tolerance.
autotomía *f.* autotomia, autotomy.
autotopagnosia *f.* autotopagnosia.
autotóxico, -ca *adj.* autotoxic.
autotransfusión *f.* autotransfusion.
autotrasplante *m.* autotransplantation.
autovacuna *f.* autovaccine.
auxanología *f.* auxanology.
auxesia *f.* auxesis.
auxético, -ca *adj.* auxetic.
auxocardia *f.* auxocardia.
auxohormona *f.* auxohormone.
auxología *f.* auxology.
auxometría *f.* auxometry.
auxoneurotrópico, -ca *adj.* auxoneurotropic.
avalvular *adj.* avalvular.
avariosis *f.* avariosis.
avascular *adj.* avascular.
avascularización *f.* avascularization.
avidina *f.* avidin.
avirulento, -ta *adj.* avirulent.
avitaminosis *f.* avitaminosis.
avivamiento *m.* avivement.
avulsión *f.* avulsion.
axantopsia *f.* axanthopsia.
axénico, -ca *adj.* axenic.
axila *f.* axilla, armpit.
axilar *adj.* axillary.
axioversión *f.* axioversion.
axis *m.* axis.
axófugo, -ga *adj.* axofugal, axifugal.
axoide *adj.* axoid, axoidean.
axoideo, -a *adj.* axoid, axoidean.
axólisis *f.* axolysis.
axón *m.* axon.
axonal *adj.* axonal.
axonapraxia *adj.* axonapraxia.
axónico, -ca *adj.* axonal.
axonografía *f.* axonography.
axonotmesis *f.* axonotmesis.
axópeto, -ta *adj.* axopetal.
axoplasma *m.* axoplasm.
axoplásmico, -ca *adj.* axoplasmic.
axosomático, -ca *adj.* axosomatic.
axotomía *f.* axotomy.
azimia *f.* azimia.
azoemia *f.* azotemia.
azoémico, -ca *adj.* azotemic.
azoospermia *f.* azoospermia, azoospermatism.
azorrea *f.* azotorrhea.
azotermia *f.* azothermia.
azoturia *f.* azoturia.
azotúrico, -ca *adj.* azoturic.
azouria *f.* azoturia.
azoúrico, -ca *adj.* azoturic.
azúcar *m.* sugar.
azurofilia *f.* azurophilia.
azurófilo, -la *adj.* azurophilic.

B b

baba *f.* slaver.
Babesia Babesia.
babesiasis *f.* babesiasis, babesiosis.
Babesiidae Babesiidae.
babesiosis *f.* babesiosis.
bacciforme *adj.* bacciform.
bacía *f.* basin.
  bacía de pus pus basin.
  bacía renal kidney basin.
  bacía para vómitos emesis basin.
bacciforme *adj.* baccate, bacciform.
bacilar *adj.* bacillar, bacillary.
bacilemia *f.* bacillemia.
bacilicultivo *m.* bacilliculture.
bacilicultura *f.* bacilliculture.
bacilífero, -ra *adj.* bacilleferous.
baciliforme *adj.* bacilliform.
baciligénico, -ca *adj.* bacilligenic, bacillogenic.
bacilíparo, -ra *adj.* bacilliparous.
Bacillaceae Bacillaceae.
Bacillus Bacillus.
bacilo *m.* bacillus.
bacilógeno, -na *adj.* bacillogenous.
baciloscopia *f.* bacilloscopy.
bacilosis *f.* bacillosis.
baciloterapia *f.* bacillotherapy.
baciluria *f.* bacilluria.
backscatter backscatter.
bacteremia *f.* bacteremia.
bacteria *f.* bacterium.
bacteriano, -na *adj.* bacterial.
bactericida¹ *m.* bactericide, bacteriocide.
  bactericida específico specific bactericide.
bactericida² *adj.* bactericidal, bacteriocidal.
bactericidina *f.* bactericidin.
bactericina *f.* bacteriocin.
bactericolia *f.* bactericholia.
bactéride bacterid.
  bactéride pustulosa pustular bacterid.
bacteriemia *f.* bacteriemia.
bacteriforme *adj.* bacteriform.
bacterina *f.* bacterin.
  toxoide de bacterina bacterin-toxoide.
bacterinia *f.* bacterinia.
bacterioaglutinina *f.* bacterioaglutinin.
bacteriocidina *f.* bacteriocidin.
bacteriocina *f.* bacteriocin.
bacteriocinogénico, -ca *adj.* bacteriocinogenic.
bacteriocinógeno *m.* bacteriocinogen.
bacterioclasis *f.* bacterioclasis.
bacterioclorofila *f.* bacteriochlorophyll.
bacteriofagia *f.* bacteriophagia.
bacteriofágico, -ca *adj.* bacteriophagic.
bacteriófago *m.* bacteriophage.
  bacteriófago atemperado, bacteriófago
  de plantilla temperate bacteriophage.
  bacteriófago defectuoso defective bacteriophage.
  bacteriófago filamentoso filamentous bacteriophage.

bacteriófago maduro mature bacteriophage.
bacteriófago tifoideo typhoid bacteriophage.
bacteriófago vegetativo vegetative bacteriophage.
bacteriófago virulento virulent bacteriophage.
bacteriofagología *f.* bacteriophagology.
bacteriofeofitina *f.* bacteriopheophytin.
bacteriofitoma *f.* bacteriophytoma.
bacteriofluoresceína *f.* bacteriofluorescin.
bacteriofobia *f.* bacteriophobia.
bacteriogénico, -ca *adj.* bacteriogenic.
bacteriógeno, -na *adj.* bacteriogenous.
bacteriohemaglutinina *f.* bacterial hemagglutinin.
bacteriohemolisina *f.* bacteriohemolysin.
bacterioide *m. y adj.* bacterioid.
bacteriolisante *m.* bacteriolysant.
bacteriolisina *f.* bacteriolysin.
bacteriólisis *f.* bacteriolysis.
bacteriolítico, -ca *adj.* bacteriolytic.
bacteriología *f.* bacteriology.
  bacteriología clínica clinical diagnostic bacteriology.
  bacteriología higiénica public health bacteriology.
  bacteriología médica medical bacteriology.
  bacteriología sanitaria sanitary bacteriology.
  bacteriología sistemática systematic bacteriology.
bacteriológico, -ca *adj.* bacteriologic, bacteriological.
bacteriólogo, -ga *m., f.* bacteriologist.
Bacterionema Bacterionema.
  Bacterionema matruchotii Bacterionema
  matruchotii.
bacterioopsonina *f.* bacterio-opsonin.
bacteriopexia *f.* bacteriopexy, bacteriopexia.
bacterioplasmina *f.* bacterioplasmin.
bacterioprecipitina *f.* bacterioprecipitin.
bacterioproteína *f.* bacterioprotein.
bacteriopsónico, -ca *adj.* bacteriopsonic.
bacteriopsonina *f.* bacteriopsonin.
bacteriorrodopsina *f.* bacteriorhodopsin.
bacterioscopia *f.* bacterioscopy.
bacterioscópico, -ca *adj.* bacterioscopic.
bacteriosis *f.* bacteriosis.
bacteriospermia *f.* bacteriospermia.
bacteriostasis *f.* bacteriostasis.
bacteriostático, -ca *adj.* bacteriostatic.
bacterioterapia *f.* bacteriotherapy.
bacteriotoxemia *f.* bacteriotoxemia.
bacteriotóxico, -ca *adj.* bacteriotoxic.
bacteriotoxina *f.* bacteriotoxin.
bacteriotrópico, -ca *adj.* bacteriotropic.
bacteriotropina *f.* bacteriotropin.
bacterítico, -ca *adj.* bacteritic.
bacteriuria *f.* bacteriuria, bacteruria.
  bacteriuria asintomática asymptomatic bacteriuria.
  bacteriuria gravídica pregnancy bacteriuria.

bacteriuria significativa significant bacteriuria.
bacteriúrico, -ca *adj.* bacteriuric.
Bacteroidaceae Bacteroidaceae.
bacteroide *m. y adj.* bacteroid.
Bacteroides Bacteroides.
bacteroides *m.* bacteroides.
bacteroidosis *f.* bacteroidosis.
baculiforme *adj.* baculiform.
bagazo *m.* marc.
bagazosis *f.* bagasscosis, bagassosis.
bahía *f.* bay.
  bahía celómica celomic bay.
baile de San Vito *m.* Saint Vitus' dance.
baja estatura *f.* short stature.
baja visión *f.* low vision.
bajo peso *m.* underweight.
balance *m.* balance.
  balance acidobásico acid-base balance.
  balance cálcico calcium balance.
  balance calórico energy balance.
  balance electrolítico electrolyte balance.
  balance energético energy balance.
  balance enzimático enzyme balance.
  balance genético genic balance.
  balance glomérulo-tubular glomerulotubular balance.
  balance hídrico water balance.
  balance de inhibición y acción inhibition-
  action balance.
  balance líquido fluid balance.
  balance nitrogenado, balance de nitróge-
  no nitrogen balance.
  balance oclusal occlusal balance.
balanceo *m.* body rocking.
  balanceo cefálico head bobbing.
  balanceo lateral lateral rocking.
balancín¹ *m.* beam.
balancín² *m.* swing.
balánico, -ca *adj.* balanic.
balanitis *f.* balanitis.
  balanitis candidiásica candidal balanitis.
  balanitis de células plasmáticas plasma cell
  balanitis.
  balanitis circinada, balanitis circinata balanitis circinata.
  balanitis circunscrita plasmocelular, bala-
  nitis circunscripta plasmacelular balanitis
  circumscripta plasmacellularis.
  balanitis diabética balanitis diabetica.
  balanitis erosiva erosive balanitis.
  balanitis fagedénica phagadenic balanitis.
  balanitis de Follmann Follmann's balanitis.
  balanitis gangrenosa gangrenous balanitis,
  balanitis gangrenosa.
  balanitis plasmocelular, balanitis plasmo-
  citaria, balanitis de plasmocitos balanitis
  plasmocellularis, balanitis plasmocellulare.
  balanitis xerótica obliterante, balanitis xe-
  rotica obliterans balanitis xerotica obliterans.
  balanitis de Zoon balanitis of Zoon.

balanoblenorrea *f.* balanoblennorrhea.
balanocele *m.* balanocele.
balanoclamiditis *f.* balanochlamyditis.
balanoplastia *f.* balanoplasty.
balanopostitis *f.* balanoposthitis.
  balanopostitis gangrenosa y ulcerativa específica specific gangrenous and ulcerative balanoposthitis.
  balanopostitis crónica circunscrita plasmocelular chronic circumscribed plasmocytic balanoposthitis, balanoposthitis chronica circumscripta plasmocellularis.
  balanopostitis plasmocítica circunscrita crónica chronic circumscribed plasmocytic balanoposthitis, balanoposthitis chronica circumscripta plasmocellularis.
balanopostomicosis *f.* balanoposthomycosis.
balanoprepucial *adj.* balanopreputial.
balantidiasis *f.* balantidiasis, balantidosis.
balantidiosis *f.* balantidiasis, balantidosis.
Balantidium Balantidium.
  Balantidium coli Balantidium coli.
balanus balanus.
balanza *f.* balance.
  balanza de torsión torsion balance.
  balanza de Wilhelmy Wilhelmy balance.
balata *f.* balata.
balbuceo[1] *m.* babbling.
balbuceo[2] *m.* stammering.
balismo *m.* ballism, ballismus.
balística *f.* ballistics.
  balística de las heridas wound ballistics.
  balística médico-legal forensic ballistics.
balístico, -ca *adj.* ballistic.
balistocardiografía *f.* ballistocardiography.
balistocardiógrafo *m.* ballistocardiograph.
balistocardiograma *m.* ballistocardiogram.
balistofobia *f.* ballistophobia.
ballet cardíaco *m.* cardiac ballet.
ballottement *m.* ballottement.
  ballottement renal renal ballottement.
balneología *f.* balneology.
balneoterapia *f.* balneotherapeutics, balneotherapy.
balón[1] *m.* balloon.
  angioplastia con balón balloon angioplasty.
  balón antral de Shea-Anthony Shea-Anthony antral balloon.
  balón bezoar balloon bezoar.
  balón de Fogarty Fogarty's catheter.
  balón de Sengstaken-Blakemore Sengstaken-Blakemore's tube.
  balón sinusal sinus balloon.
balón[2] *m.* flask.
  balón coronal crown flask.
  balón dental denture flask.
  balón de Dewar Dewar flask.
  balón de Erlenmeyer Erlenmeyer flask.
  balón de Fernbach Fernbach flask.
  balón de Florence Florence flask.
  balón de inyección injection flask.
  balón de moldeo casting flask.
  balón refractario refractory flask.
  balón de vacío vacuum flask.
  balón volumétrico volumetric flask.
balonizar *v.* balloon.
balopticón *m.* balopticon.
balotable *adj.* ballottable.
balotamiento *m.* ballottement.
balsámico, -ca *adj.* balsamic.
bálsamo[1] *m.* balm.
bálsamo[2] *m.* balsam.
balsámico, -ca *adj.* balsamic.
banco *m.* bank.
  banco de embriones embryo bank.

banco de esperma sperm bank.
banco de genes gene bank.
banco de ojos eye bank.
banco de sangre blood bank.
banco de semen semen bank.
banco de suero serum bank.
bancroftiasis *f.* bancroftiasis, bancroftosis.
bancroftosis *f.* bancroftiasis, bancroftosis.
banda *f.* band, bundle, stripe.
  banda abdominal belly band.
  banda aberrantes aberrant bundles.
  banda abrazadera clamp band.
  banda de absorción absorption band.
  banda amniótica amniotic band.
  banda de anclaje anchor band.
  banda anogenital anogenital band.
  banda anular annular band.
  banda de Bechterew Bechterew's band.
  banda de Büngner Büngner's bands.
  banda C C band.
  bandas celulares de Essick Essick's cell bands.
  banda de Clado Clado's band.
  banda clamp clamp band.
  banda contorneada contoured band.
  banda de contracción contraction band.
  banda córnea horny band.
  banda cromosómica chromosome band.
  banda elástica elastic band.
  banda estriada furrowed band.
  banda G G band.
  banda de Gennari band of Gennari, stripe of Gennari.
  banda de Harris Harris' band.
  banda de Henle Henle's band.
  banda de Kaes-Bechterew band of Kaes-Bechterew.
  banda de Lane Lane's bands.
  banda límbicas limbic bands.
  banda M M band.
  banda de Mach Mach's band.
  banda de Matas Matas' band.
  banda matriz matrix band.
  banda molar molar band.
  banda de Montgomery Montgomery strap.
  banda N N band.
  banda ortodóntica, banda ortodóncica orthodontic band.
  banda ortodóncica ajustable adjustable orthodontic band.
  banda de Parham Parham band.
  banda del pecten pecten band.
  banda Q Q band.
  banda R R band.
  banda de Soret Soret band.
  banda de Streeter Streeter's band.
  banda T T band.
  banda de Vicq d'Azyr Vicq d'Azyr band, Vicq d'Azyr bundle.
bandaje *m.* banding.
bandaleta *f.* band, bandaletta, bandelette.
bandeja *f.* tray.
  bandeja de impresión, bandeja para impresiones impression tray.
  bandeja de recocido annealing tray.
  bandeja de resina acrílica acrylic resin tray.
bandeleta *f.* band, bandaletta, bandelette.
bandeo *m.* banding.
  bandeo de alta resolución high resolution banding.
  bandeo de la arteria pulmonar pulmonary artery banding.
  bandeo BrDU BrDU banding.
  bandeo C, bandeo centromérico (de la heterocromatina céntrica) C banding, centromeric banding.

bandeo de cinacrina quinacrine banding.
bandeo de cromosomas, bandeo cromosómico chromosome banding.
bandeo dental tooth banding.
bandeo G, bandeo de Giemsa G banding, Giemsa banding.
bandeo inverso reverse banding.
bandeo NOR NOR banding.
bandeo de profase prophase banding.
bandeo de prometafase prometaphase banding.
bandeo Q Q banding.
bandeo R R banding.
bandicoot *m.* bandicoot.
banding *m.* banding.
baño *m.* bath.
  baño de aceite oil bath.
  baño ácido acid bath.
  baño de agua water bath.
  baño de agua de mar seawater bath.
  baño de agujas needle bath.
  baño de aire air bath.
  baño de aire caliente hot-air bath.
  baño alcalino alkaline bath.
  baño de alcanfor, baño alcanforado camphor bath.
  baño de alcohol alcohol bath.
  baño de alumbre alum bath.
  baño antipirético antipyretic bath.
  baño antiséptico antiseptic bath.
  baño de arena sand bath.
  baño aromático aromatic bath.
  baño de asiento sitz bath, hip bath.
  baño astringente astringent bath.
  baño de barro mud bath, mood bath.
  baño boratado, baño de bórax borax bath.
  baño de Brand Brand's bath.
  baño de burbujas bubble bath.
  baño en cabina cabinet bath.
  baño caliente hot bath.
  baño de cera wax bath.
  baño cinesiterapéutico, baño cinetoterapéutico kinetotherapeutic band.
  baño coloidal, baño coloide, baño de coloide colloid bath.
  baño completo full bath.
  baño completo en la cama complete bed bath.
  baño continuo, baño continuo en bañera continuous bath, continuous tub bath.
  baño de contraste contrast bath.
  baño de creosota creosote bath.
  baño de dióxido de carbono carbon dioxide bath.
  baño Dowsing Dowsing bath.
  baño de ducha douche bath.
  baño eléctrico electric bath.
  baño electroterapéutico electrotherapeutic bath.
  baño emoliente emollient bath.
  baño de envoltura pack bath.
  baño con esponja, baño de esponja sponge bath.
  baño de espuma, baño espumoso foam bath.
  baño estimulante stimulant bath.
  baño de fango mood bath.
  baño ferruginoso iron bath.
  baño finlandés Finnish bath.
  baño de Finsen Finsen bath.
  baño frío cold bath, cool bath.
  baño de gabinete cabinet bath.
  baño de gelatina gelatin bath.
  baño de glicerina glycerin bath.
  baño de grasa grease bath.

baño de Greville Greville bath.
baño hafussi hafussi bath.
baño hidroeléctrico hydroelectric bath.
baño de hierbas herb bath.
baño de hierro iron bath.
baño hipertérmico hyperthermal bath.
baño de inmersión immersion bath.
baño de inmersión lumínica Dowsing bath.
baño de leche milk bath.
baño de limo mood bath.
baño de linaza linseed bath.
baño de lodo mood bath.
baño de luz light bath.
baño con manta blanket bath.
baño de mar sea bath.
baño de María water bath.
baño medicado en bañera medicated tub bath.
baño medicamentoso medicamented bath.
baño de Nauheim Nauheim bath.
baño neumático balneum pneumaticum.
baño oleoso grease bath.
baño de parafina paraffin bath.
baño de remolino whirlpool bath.
baño ruso Russian bath.
baño de sábana sheet bath.
baño de salvado bran bath.
baño de Sandor foam bath.
baño de sauna sauna bath.
baño sedante sedative bath.
baño de sol sun bath.
baño de sudor sweat bath.
baño templado lukewarm bath.
baño tibio tepid bath.
baño de tierra earth bath.
baño de torbellino whirlpool bath.
baño de turba peat bath.
baño de vapor vapor bath.
baragnosis *f.* baragnosis.
barba *f.* beard, barba.
barbaralalia *f.* barbaralalia.
barbeiro *m.* barbeiro.
barbilla *f.* chin.
barbitalismo *m.* barbitalism.
barbitúrico *m.* barbiturate.
barbiturismo *m.* barbituism, barbiturism.
barbotaje *m.* barbotage.
barbula hirci barbula hirci.
barestesia *f.* baresthesia.
barestesiómetro *m.* baresthesiometer.
bariatría *f.* bariatrics.
bariátrico, -ca *adj.* bariatric.
baricidad *f.* baricity.
bárico, -ca *adj.* baric.
bariestesia *f.* baryesthesia.
bariglosia *f.* baryglossia.
barilalia *f.* barylalia.
barimastia *f.* barymazia.
barimazia *f.* barymazia.
bario *m.* barium.
 sulfato de bario barium sulfate.
baritosis *f.* baritosis, barytosis.
barniz *m.* varnish.
 barniz para cavidades cavity varnish.
 barniz dental dental varnish.
baroagnosis *f.* baroagnosis.
baroceptor *m.* baroceptor.
barodontalgia *f.* barodontalgia.
baroelectroestesiómetro *m.* baroelectroesthesiometer.
barofílico, -ca *adj.* barophilic.
barófilo, -la *adj.* barophilic.
barognosis *f.* barognosis.
barógrafo *m.* barograph.
baromacrómetro *m.* baromacrometer.

barométrico, -ca *adj.* barometric.
barómetro *m.* barometer.
barometrógrafo *m.* barometrograph.
barootitis *f.* barootitis.
barorreceptor *m.* baroreceptor.
barorreflejo *m.* baroreflex.
baroscopio *m.* baroscope.
barosinusitis *f.* barosinusitis.
barospirador *m.* barospirator.
baróstato *m.* barostat.
barotaxis *f.* barotaxis.
barotitis *f.* barotitis.
 barotitis media barotitis media.
barotrauma *m.* barotrauma.
barotraumatismo *m.* barotrauma.
 **barotraumatismo otítico, barotraumatis-
mo ótico** otic barotrauma, otitic barotrauma.
 barotraumatismo sinusal sinus barotrauma.
barotropismo *m.* barotropism.
barra *f.* bar.
 **barra de la arcada, barra de arco, barra en
arco** arch bar.
 barra bucal buccal bar.
 barra conectora connector bar.
 barra cromatoide chromatoid bar.
 barra de Erich Erich arch bar.
 barra esternal sternal bar.
 barra hioidea hyoid bar.
 barra de Kennedy Kennedy bar.
 barra labial labial bar.
 barra lingual lingual bar.
 barra media median bar.
 barra palatina palatal bar.
 barra de Passavant Passavant's bar.
 barra prismática prism bar.
 barra de resto oclusal occlusal rest bar.
 barra en T de Kazanjian Kazanjian T bar.
 barra tensora spreader bar.
 barra terminales terminal bars.
barrera *f.* barrier.
 barrera arquitectónica architectural barrier.
 barrera cutánea skin barrier.
 barrera de filtración filtration barrier.
 barrera hematoacuosa blood-aqueous barrier.
 barrera hematoaérea blood-air barrier.
 barrera hematogaseosa blood-gas barrier.
 barrera hematocerebral blood-brain barrier
(BBB), blood-cerebral barrier.
 barrera hematocerebroespinal blood-cerebrospinal fluid barrier.
 barrera hematoencefálica (BHE) blood-
brain barrier (BBB), blood-cerebral barrier.
 barrera hemato-LCR blood-CSF barrier.
 barrera hematotesticular blood-testis barrier.
 barrera hematotímica blood-thymus barrier.
 barrera histohemática de tejido conectivo
histohematic connective tissue barrier.
 barrera incestuosa incest barrier.
 **barrera mucosa, barrera de la mucosa gás-
trica** gastric mucosal barrier.
 barrera placentaria placental barrier.
 barrera protectora protective barrier.
 barrera protectora primaria primary protective barrier.
 barrera protectora secundaria secondary
protective barrier.
 barrera de radiación radiation barrier.
 barrera sinovial synovial barrier.
barrido *m.* scanning.
 barrido isotópico isotopic scan.
barro *m.* sludge.
bartholinitis *f.* bartholinitis.
bartolinitis *f.* bartolinitis.
bartoneliasis *f.* bartonelliasis.

bartonelosis *f.* bartonellosis.
Bartonella Bartonella.
 Bartonella bacilliformis Bartonella bacilliformis.
Bartonellaceae Bartonellaceae.
bartonellosis *f.* bartonellosis.
basal *adj.* basal.
basalioma *m.* basalioma, basaloma, basiloma.
basaloide *adj.* basaloid.
basaloma *m.* basaloma.
base[1] *f.* base.
 base acidificable acidifiable base.
 base de ácidos nucleicos nucleic acid base.
 base aloxúrica alloxuris base.
 base apical apical base.
 base de apoyo dental tooth-borne base.
 base de Brønsted Brønsted base.
 base de Brønsted-Lowry Brønsted-Lowry
base.
 base de cemento cement base.
 base conjugada conjugate base.
 base de datos database.
 **base dental, base de dentadura, base de la
dentadura artificial** denture base.
 **base dental coloreada, base dental teñida,
base de dentadura teñida** tinted denture
base.
 base de goma laca shellac base.
 base de hexona hexone bases.
 base de histona histone bases.
 base de Lewis Lewis base.
 base metálica metal base.
 base nitrogenada nitrogenous base.
 base de película film base.
 base pirimidínica pyrimidine base.
 base plástica plastic base.
 base de pomada ointment base.
 base de preparación cavitaria cavity preparation base.
 base presora pressor base.
 base púrica, base purínica purine base.
 base queoplástica cheoplastic base.
 base de resina acrílica acrylic resin base.
 base de Schiff Schiff's base.
 base vegetal vegetable base.
base[2] *f.* base, basis.
basedoide *adj.* basedoid.
basedovoide *adj.* basedowoïde.
basedowiano, -na *adj.* basedowian.
basedowiforme *adj.* basedowiform.
basial *adj.* basial, basialis.
basialveolar *adj.* basialveolar.
basiaracnitis *f.* basiarachnitis.
basiaracnoiditis *f.* basiarachnoiditis.
basicidad *f.* basicity.
básico, -ca *adj.* basic.
basicraneal *adj.* basicranial.
basidio *m.* basidium.
Basidiobolus Basidiobolus.
 Basidiobolus haptosporus Basidiobolus
haptosporus.
 Basidiobolus meristoporus Basidiobolus
meristoporus.
basidiocarpo *m.* basidiocarp.
basidiomiceto *m.* basidiomycetous.
Basidiomycetes Basidiomycetes.
basidiospora *f.* basidiospore.
basidium basidium.
basiesfenoides *m.* basisphenoid.
basifacial *adj.* basifacial.
basifobia *f.* basiphobia, basophobia.
basihial *m.* basihyal.
basihioide *m.* basihyoid.
basihioides *m.* basihyoid.
basilar *adj.* basilar, basilaris.

basilaris basilaris.
  basilaris cranii basilaris cranii.
basilateral *adj.* basilateral.
Basilea Nomina Anatomica Basel Nomina Anatomica.
basilema *m.* basilemma.
basílico, -ca *adj.* basilic.
basílico *m.* basilicus.
basiloma *m.* basiloma.
basinasial *adj.* basinasal.
basioccipital *adj.* basioccipital.
basiogloso *m.* basioglossus.
basión *m.* basion.
basiotribo *m.* basiotribe.
basiotripsia *f.* basiotripsy.
basipeto, -ta *adj.* basipetal.
basirrino, -na *adj.* basirhinal.
basis basis.
basisfenoides *m.* basisphenoid.
basitemporal *adj.* basitemporal.
basivertebral *adj.* basivertebral.
basocito *m.* basocyte.
basocitopenia *f.* basocytopenia.
basocitosis *f.* basocytosis.
basoeritrocito *m.* basoerythrocyte.
basoeritrocitosis *f.* basoerythrocytosis.
basofilia *f.* basophilia.
  basofilia de Grawitz Grawitz' basophilia.
  basofilia punteada punctate basophilia.
basofílico, -ca *adj.* basophile, basophilic.
basofilismo *m.* basophilism.
  basofilismo de Cushing Cushing's basophilism.
  basofilismo hipofisario, basofilismo pituitario pituitary basophilism.
basófilo, -la *m., f.* basophil.
  basófilo beta beta basophil.
  basófilo de Crooke-Russell Crooke-Russell basophil.
  basófilo delta delta basophil.
  basófilo hístico tissue basophil.
basofilocito *m.* basophilocyte.
basofobia *f.* basiphobia, basophobia.
basógrafo *m.* basograph.
basolateral *adj.* basolateral.
basometacromófilo, -la *adj.* basometachromophil, basometachromophile.
basopenia *f.* basopenia.
basoplasma *m.* basoplasm.
bastidor *m.* cassette.
bastión *m.* rampart.
  bastión maxilar maxillary rampart.
bastón *m.* cane.
  bastón ajustable adjustable cane.
  bastón cuadrípode quadripod cane.
  bastón de Esculapio staff of Aesculapius.
  bastón inglés English cane.
  bastón trípode tripod cane.
bastoncillo *m.* rod.
  bastoncillo analizador analyzing rod.
  bastoncillo de Auer Auer rods.
  bastoncillo basal basal rod.
  bastoncillo del esmalte enamel rod.
  bastoncillo germinal germinal rod.
  bastoncillo de Heidenhain rod of Heidenhain.
  bastoncillo de König König's rod.
  bastoncillo de Maddox Maddox's rod.
  bastoncillo muscular muscle rod.
  bastoncillo olfatorio olfactory rod.
  bastoncillo de Reichmann Reichmann's rod.
  bastoncillo retiniano retinal rod.
batarismo *m.* battarism, battarismus.
bateína *f.* batteyin.
batería *f.* battery.

batería estandarizada de tests de afasia standardized aphasia battery.
  batería de Halstead-Reitan Halstead-Reitan battery.
  batería de Kaufman Kaufman battery.
  batería neuropsicológica de Luria-Nebraska Luria-Nebraska neuropsychological battery.
  batería de pruebas battery of tests.
  batería de Reitan-Indiana Reitan-Indiana battery.
  batería de Woodcock-Johnson Woodcock-Johnson battery.
batianestesia *f.* bathyanesthesia.
baticardia *f.* bathycardia.
batiestesia *f.* bathyesthesia.
batigastria *f.* bathygastry.
batihiperestesia *f.* bathyhyperesthesia.
batihipoestesia *f.* bathyhypesthesia.
batipnea *f.* bathypnea.
batmotrópico, -ca *adj.* bathmotropic.
  batmotrópico negativamente, batmotrópico negativo negatively bathmotropic.
  batmotrópico positivamente, batmotrópico positivo positively bathmotropic.
batmotropismo *m.* bathmotropism.
batocromia *f.* bathochromy.
batocrómico, -ca *adj.* bathochromic.
batocromo *m.* bathochrome.
batoflora *f.* bathoflore.
batofobia *f.* bathophobia.
batomórfico, -ca *adj.* bathomorphic.
batracoplastia *f.* batrachoplasty.
batracotoxina *f.* batrachotoxin.
batrocefalia *f.* bathrocephaly.
bayoneta *f.* bayonet.
bazo *m.* spleen, splen, lien.
  bazo accesorio accessory spleen, lien accessorius, splen accesorius.
  bazo aumentado de tamaño enlarged spleen.
  bazo azucarado sugar-coated spleen.
  bazo céreo waxy spleen.
  bazo céreo difuso diffuse waxy spleen.
  bazo cianótico cyanotic spleen.
  bazo durococido hard-baked spleen.
  bazo errante wandering spleen.
  bazo flotante floating spleen.
  bazo Gandy-Gamna Gandy-Gamna spleen.
  bazo jaspeado sago spleen.
  bazo lardáceo lardaceous spleen.
  bazo moteado speckled spleen.
  bazo moteado de Feitis flecked spleen of Feitis.
  bazo movible, bazo móvil movable spleen, lien mobilis.
  bazo porfídico, bazo de porfiria porphyria spleen, prophyry spleen.
  bazo recubierto de azúcar sugar-coated spleen.
  bazo sagú sago spleen.
  bazo de tocino bacon spleen.
bazuqueo *m.* capotement.
Bdella Bdella.
  Bdella cardinalis Bdella cardinalis.
Bdellovibrio Bdellovibrio.
bdellovibrión *m.* bdellovibrio.
bebé *m.* baby.
  bebé azul blue baby.
  bebé de colodión collodion baby.
  bebé inmaduro immature baby.
  bebé maltratado battered baby.
  bebé probeta test-tube baby.
bebedero de molde *m.* sprue.
Bedsonia Bedsonia.
behaviorismo *m.* behaviorism.

bejel *m.* bejel.
Belascaris Belascaris.
belemnoide *adj.* belemnoid.
belonefobia *f.* belonephobia.
belonoide *adj.* belonoid.
belonosquiascopia *f.* belonoskiascopy.
benceno *m.* benzene.
bencenoide *adj.* benzenoid.
bends *m.* bends.
beneficio *m.* gain.
  beneficio primario de la enfermedad primary gain.
  beneficio secundario de la enfermedad secondary gain.
benigno, -na *adj.* benign.
bentiromida *f.* bentiromide.
benzolismo *m.* benzolism.
benzopireno *m.* benzopyrene, benzapyrene.
benzopurpurina 4-B *f.* benzopurpurin 4B.
benzoterapia *f.* benzotherapy.
béquico, -ca *adj.* bechic.
beriberi *m.* beriberi.
  beriberi atrófico atrophic beriberi.
  beriberi de los barcos ship beriberi.
  beriberi cerebral cerebral beriberi.
  beriberi húmedo wet beriberi.
  beriberi infantil infantile beriberi.
  beriberi de los navíos ship beriberi.
  beriberi paralítico paralytic beriberi.
  beriberi seco dry beriberi.
beribérico, -ca *adj.* beriberic.
beriliosis *f.* berylliosis.
bermellón *m.* vermilion.
bermellonectomía *f.* vermilionectomy.
berrinche *m.* tantrum.
bertieliasis *f.* bertielliasis, bertiellosis.
Bertiella Bertiella.
  Bertiella satyri, Bertiella studeri Bertiella satyri, Bertiella studeri.
bertielosis *f.* bertielliasis, bertiellosis.
bertillonaje *m.* Bertillon's system.
besiclómetro *m.* besiclometer.
bestialidad *f.* bestiality.
bestialismo *m.* bestiality.
beta *f.* beta.
  beta fetoproteína *f.* beta fetoprotein.
  beta oxidación *f.* beta oxidation.
betaalaninemia *f.* beta-alaninemia.
betabloqueante *m.* beta-blocker.
betacaroteno *m.* beta-carotene.
betacianinuria *f.* beeturia, betacyaninuria.
betacismo *m.* betacism.
betaglobulina *f.* beta globulin.
  betaglobulina específica de embarazo pregnancy-specific beta globulin.
beta-lipoproteína *f.* beta-lipoprotein.
betalisina *f.* beta-lysine.
betaoxibutiria *f.* beta-oxibutyria.
betapropiolactona *f.* betapropiolactone.
betatromboglobulina *f.* betathromboglobulin.
betatrón *m.* betatron.
bête rouge *f.* bête rouge.
bezo *m.* proud flesh.
bezoar *m.* bezoar.
bhang *m.* bhang.
biacromial *adj.* bisacromial.
biamniótico *adj.* biamniotic.
biangular[1] *m.* binangle.
biangular[2] *adj.* biangular.
biarticulado, -da *adj.* biarticulate.
biarticular *adj.* biarticular.
biastérico, -ca *adj.* biasteric.
biasteriónico, -ca *adj.* biasterionic.
biauricular[1] *adj.* biauricular.

biauricular² *adj.* binaural.
biaxilar *adj.* biaxillary.
bibásico, -ca *adj.* bibasic.
biberón *m.* nursing bottle.
bibliocleptomanía *f.* bibliokleptomania.
bibliofobia *f.* bibliophobia.
bibliomanía *f.* bibliomania.
biblioteca genética *f.* gene library.
biblioterapia *f.* bibliotherapy.
bíbulo, -la *adj.* bibulous.
bicamaral *adj.* bicameral.
bicameral *adj.* bicameral.
bicapa lipídica *f.* lipid bilayer.
bicapsular *adj.* bicapsular.
bicarbonatemia *f.* bicarbonatemia.
bicarbonato *m.* bicarbonate.
  bicarbonato estándar standard bicarbonate.
  bicarbonato del plasma plasma bicarbonate.
  bicarbonato sanguíneo blood bicarbonate.
  bicarbonato sódico, bicarbonato de sodio sodium bicarbonate.
  bicarbonato de sosa bicarbonate of sosa.
bicaudado, -da *adj.* bicaudate.
bicaudal *adj.* bicaudal.
bicéfalo *m.* bicephalus.
bicelular *adj.* bicellular.
bíceps *m.* biceps.
bicho *m.* bicho.
bicigomático, -ca *adj.* bizygomatic.
biciliado, -da *adj.* biciliate.
bicipital *adj.* bicipital.
biclonal *adj.* biclonal.
biclonalidad *f.* biclonality.
bicóncavo, -va *adj.* biconcave.
biconvexo, -xa *adj.* biconvex.
bicorne *adj.* bicornate, bicornous, bicornuate.
bicoronal *adj.* bicoronal.
bicorporal *adj.* bicorporate.
bicúspide *m. y adj.* bicuspid.
bicuspidización *f.* bicuspidization.
bicuspoide *adj.* bicuspoid.
bidactilia *f.* bidactyly.
bidé *m.* bidet.
bidelto *m.* bidelt, whorl.
bidentado, -da *adj.* bidentate.
bidet *m.* bidet.
bidermoma *m.* bidermoma.
bidial *adj.* biduous.
bidimensional *adj.* bidimensional.
bidiscoide *adj.* bidiscoidal.
biduoterciana *f.* biduotertian.
bienestar *m.* well-being, wellness.
  bienestar del enfermo well-being of the patient.
  bienestar de alto nivel high-level wellness.
biestefánico, -ca *adj.* bistephanic.
biestratificado, -da *adj.* bistratal.
bifascicular *adj.* bifascicular.
bifásico, -ca *adj.* biphasic.
bifenotipia *f.* biphenotypy.
bifenotípico, -ca *adj.* biphenotypic.
bífero, -ra *adj.* bisferient, bisferious.
bífido, -da *adj.* bifid, bifidus.
bifidobacteria *f.* bifidobacterium.
Bifidobacterium Bifidobacterium.
bifocal *adj.* bifocal.
biforado, -da *adj.* biforate.
bifurcación *f.* bifurcation, bifurcatio.
  bifurcación de la aorta, bifurcación aórtica bifurcation of the aorta, bifurcatio aortae, bifurcatio aortica.
  bifurcación de la carótida carotid bifurcation, bifurcatio carotidis.
  bifurcación de la tráquea bifurcation of trachea, bifurcatio tracheae.

bifurcación del tronco pulmonar bifurcation of the pulmonary trunk, bifurcatio trunci pulmonalis.
  bifurcación radicular root furcation.
bifurcado, -da *adj.* bifurcate, bifurcated.
bifurcatio *m.* bifurcatio.
  bifurcatio aortae bifurcation of the aorta, bifurcatio aortae, bifurcatio aortica.
  bifurcatio carotidis carotid bifurcation, bifurcatio carotidis.
  bifurcatio trunci pulmonalis bifurcation of the pulmonary trunk, bifurcatio trunci pulmonalis.
bigemina *f.* bigemina.
bigeminado, -da *adj.* bigeminal.
bigeminal *adj.* bigeminal.
bigeminia *f.* bigeminy.
bigeminidad *f.* bigeminy.
bigeminismo *m.* bigeminy.
  bigeminismo auricular atrial bigeminy.
  bigeminismo de escape-captura escape-capture bigeminy.
  bigeminismo nodal, bigeminismo nodal auriculoventricular nodal bigeminy, atrioventricular nodal bigeminy.
  bigeminismo recíproco reciprocal bigeminy.
  bigeminismo ventricular ventricular bigeminy.
bigerminal *adj.* bigerminal.
bigonial *adj.* bigonial.
bilabio *m.* bilabe.
bilabo *m.* bilabe.
bilaminar *adj.* bilaminar.
bilateral *adj.* bilateral.
bilateralismo *m.* bilateralism.
Bilharzia Bilharzia.
bilharzial *adj.* bilharzial.
bilharziasis *f.* bilharziasis, bilharziosis.
  bilharziasis vesical bilharzial bladder.
bilharzioma *m.* bilharzioma.
bilharziosis *f.* bilharziosis.
biliar *adj.* biliary.
bilicianina *f.* bilicyanin.
bilidigestivo, -va *adj.* bilidigestive.
bilifacción *f.* bilifaction.
bilífero, -ra *adj.* biliferous.
bilificación *f.* bilification.
biliflavina *f.* biliflavin.
biligénesis *f.* biligenesis.
biligenético, -ca *adj.* biligenetic.
biligenia *f.* biligenesis.
biligénico, -ca *adj.* biligenic.
biligulado, -da *adj.* biligulate.
bilihumina *f.* bilihumin.
bilina *f.* bilin, biline.
biliosidad *f.* biliousness.
bilioso, -sa *adj.* bilious.
biliprasina *f.* biliprasin.
biliptisis *f.* biliptysis.
bilirraquia *f.* bilirachia.
bilirrubina *f.* bilirubin.
  bilirrubina conjugada conjugated bilirubin.
  bilirrubina directa direct bilirubin.
  bilirrubina indirecta indirect bilirubin.
  bilirrubina libre free bilirubin.
  bilirrubina no conjugada unconjugated bilirubin.
  bilirrubina de reacción directa direct reacting bilirubin.
  bilirrubina de reacción indirecta indirect reacting bilirubin.
  bilirrubina total total bilirubin.
bilirrubinemia *f.* bilirubinemia.
bilirrubínico, -ca *adj.* bilirubinic.
bilirrubinglobulina *f.* bilirubinglobulin.

bilirrubinoides *m.* bilirubinoids.
bilirrubinuria *f.* bilirubinuria.
bilis *f.* bile.
  bilis A A bile.
  bilis B B bile.
  bilis blanca white bile.
  bilis C C bile.
  bilis caliza limy bile.
  bilis cística cystic bile.
  bilis cristalizada de Platner Platner's crystalized bile.
  bilis de la vesícula biliar gall-bladder bile.
biliuria *f.* biliuria.
biliverdina *f.* biliverdin, biliverdine.
biliverdinglobina *f.* biliverdinglobin.
bilobulado, -da *adj.* bilobate, bilobed.
bilobular *adj.* bilobed.
bilobulillado, -da *adj.* bilobular, bilobulate.
biloculado, -da *adj.* biloculate.
bilocular *adj.* bilocular.
bilofodonte *adj.* bilophodont.
biloma *m.* biloma.
bimanual *adj.* bimanual.
bimastoideo, -a *adj.* bimastoid.
bimaxilar *adj.* bimaxillary.
bimetro *m.* bimeter.
bimodal *adj.* bimodal.
bimolecular *adj.* bimolecular.
binario, -ria *adj.* binary.
binauricular *adj.* binauricular.
binegativo *m.* binegative.
binocular *adj.* binocular.
binóculo *m.* binoculus.
binoftalmoscopio *m.* binophthalmoscope.
binomial *adj.* binomial.
binoscopio *m.* binoscope.
binótico, -ca *adj.* binotic.
binucleación *f.* binucleation.
binucleado, -da *adj.* binucleate.
binuclear *adj.* binuclear.
binucleolado, -da *adj.* binucleolate.
bioactividad *f.* bioactivity.
bioactivo, -va *adj.* bioactive.
bioacústica *f.* bioacoustics.
bioaereación *f.* bioaeration.
bioaminérgico, -ca *adj.* bioaminergic.
bioanálisis *m.* bioassay.
bioastronáutica *f.* bioastronautics.
bioblasto *m.* bioblast.
biocatalizador *m.* biocatalyst.
biocenosis *f.* biocenosis.
biocenótico, -ca *adj.* biocenotic.
biocibernética *f.* biocybernetics.
biociclo *m.* biocycle.
biocida¹ *m.* biocide.
biocida² *adj.* biocidal.
biociencia *f.* bioscience.
biocinética *f.* biokinetics.
biocitina *f.* biocytin.
bioclimatología *f.* bioclimatology.
bioclimatólogo, -ga *m., f.* bioclimatologist.
biocoloide *m.* biocolloid.
biocompatibilidad *f.* biocompatibility.
biocompatible *adj.* biocompatible.
biodegradabilidad *f.* biodegradability.
biodegradable *adj.* biodegradable.
biodegradación *f.* biodegradation.
biodetritus *m.* biodetritus.
biodinámica *f.* biodynamics.
biodinámico, -ca *adj.* biodynamic.
biodisponibilidad *f.* bioavailability.
bioecología *f.* bioecology.
bioelectricidad *f.* bioelectricity.
bioelectrónica *f.* bioeletronics.
bioelemento *m.* bioelement.

bioenergética *f.* bioenergetics.
bioenergía *f.* bioenergy.
bioensayo *m.* bioassay.
bioequivalencia *f.* bioequivalence.
bioequivalente *adj.* bioequivalent.
bioespectrometría *f.* biospectrometry.
bioespectroscopia *f.* biospectroscopy.
bioespeleología *f.* biospeleology.
bioestadística *f.* biostatistics.
bioestadístico, -ca *m., f.* biostatistician.
bioestática *f.* biostatics.
bioestereométrica *f.* biostereometrics.
bioética *f.* bioethics.
biofagia *f.* biophagy.
biofagismo *f.* biophagism.
biófago, -ga[1] *m., f.* biophage.
biófago, -ga[2] *adj.* biophagous.
biofarmacéutica *f.* biopharmaceutics.
biofarmacia *f.* biopharmacy.
biofase *f.* biophase.
biofiláctico, -ca *adj.* biophylactic.
biofilaxis *f.* biophylaxis.
biofilia *f.* biophilia.
biofísica *f.* biophysics.
  biofísica dental dental biophysics.
biofísico, -ca *adj.* biophysical.
biofisiografía *f.* biophysiography.
biofisiología *f.* biophysiology.
bioflavonoide *m.* bioflavonoid.
biofotómetro *m.* biophotometer.
biogénesis *f.* biogenesis.
biogenético, -ca *adj.* biogenetic.
biogenia *f.* biogeny.
biogénico, -ca *adj.* biogenic.
biógeno, -na *adj.* biogenous.
biogeografía *f.* biogeography.
biogeoquímica *f.* biogeochemistry.
biógrafo *m.* biograph.
biogravedad *f.* biogravics.
biohidráulico, -ca *adj.* biohydraulic.
bioimplante *m.* bioimplant.
bioincompatibilidad *f.* bioincompatibility.
bioingeniería *f.* bioengineering.
bioinstrumento *m.* bioinstrument.
biólisis *f.* biolysis.
biolítico, -ca *adj.* biolytic.
biología *f.* biology.
  biología bucal oral biology.
  biología celular cellular biology.
  biología molecular molecular biology.
  biología de la radiación, biología de radiación radiation biology.
biológico, -ca *adj.* biologic, biological.
biólogo, -ga *m., f.* biologist.
bioluminiscencia *f.* bioluminiscence.
bioma *m.* biome.
biomarcador *m.* biomarker.
biomasa *f.* biomass.
biomatemáticas *f.* biomathematics.
biomaterial *m.* biomaterial.
biomecánica *f.* biomechanics.
  biomecánica dental dental biomechanics.
biomedicina *f.* biomedicine.
biomédico, -ca *adj.* biomedical.
biomembrana *f.* biomembrane.
biomembranoso, -sa *adj.* biomembranous.
biometeorología *f.* biometeorology.
biometeorólogo, -ga *m., f.* biometeorologist.
biómetra *m., f.* biometrician.
biometría *f.* biometrics, biometry.
biómetro *m.* biometer.
biomicroscopia *f.* biomicroscopy.
biomicroscopio *m.* biomicroscope.
  biomicroscopio de lámpara de hendidura slit-lamp biomicroscope.

biomo *m.* biome.
biomolécula *f.* biomolecule.
biomotor *m.* biomotor.
Biomphalaria Biomphalaria.
bion *m.* bion.
bionecrosis *f.* bionecrosis.
biónica *f.* bionics.
biónico, -ca *adj.* bionic.
bionomía *f.* bionomy.
bionómica *f.* bionomics.
bionosis *f.* bionosis.
bionucleónica *f.* bionucleonics.
bioosmótico, -ca *adj.* bio-osmotic.
biopiocultivo *m.* biopyoculture.
bioplasia *f.* bioplasia.
biopolímero *m.* biopolymer.
biopoyesis *f.* biopoiesis.
bioprótesis *f.* bioprosthesis.
biopsia *f.* biopsy.
  biopsia por aguja needle biopsy.
  biopsia por aspiración aspiration biopsy.
  biopsia por cepillado, biopsia por cepillo brush biopsy.
  biopsia cerebral cerebral biopsy.
  biopsia a cielo abierto open biopsy.
  biopsia citológica cytological biopsy.
  biopsia cónica, biopsia de cono cone biopsy.
  biopsia coriónica chorionic biopsy.
  biopsia del cuello uterino cervix uterinic biopsy.
  biopsia en cuña wedge biopsy.
  biopsia del endometrio endometrium biopsy.
  biopsia endoscópica endoscopic biopsy.
  biopsia por escisión, biopsia escisional excision biopsy.
  biopsia con esponja sponge biopsy.
  biopsia esternal sternal biopsy.
  biopsia exfoliativa surface biopsy.
  biopsia de exploración exploratory biopsy.
  biopsia fraccionaria bite biopsy.
  biopsia hepática liver biopsy.
  biopsia incisional incision biopsy.
  biopsia muscular muscular biopsy.
  biopsia negativa negative biopsy.
  biopsia ósea bone biopsy.
  biopsia percutánea percutaneous biopsy.
  biopsia positiva positive biopsy.
  biopsia por punción needle biopsy.
  biopsia por punción-aspiración con aguja fina fine-needle aspiration biopsy.
  biopsia quirúrgica surgical biopsy.
  biopsia renal renal biopsy.
  biopsia renal percutánea percutaneous renal biopsy.
  biopsia renal transvenosa transvenous renal biopsy.
  biopsia con sacabocados, biopsia de sacabocado punch biopsy.
  biopsia superficial, biopsia de superficie surface biopsy.
  biopsia por trepanación trephine biopsy.
  biopsia de vellosidad coriónica (BVC) chorionic villus biopsy (CVB).
biopsicología *f.* biopsychology.
biopsicosocial *adj.* biopsychosocial.
biopsíquico, -ca *adj.* biopsychic.
biopterina *f.* biopterin.
bioquemórfico, -ca *adj.* biochemorphic.
bioquemorfología *f.* biochemorphology.
bioquímica *f.* biochemistry.
bioquímico, -ca *adj.* biochemical.
bioquimórfico, -ca *adj.* biochemorphic.
bioquimorfología *f.* biochemorphology.
biorbital *adj.* biorbital.
biorbitario, -ria *adj.* biorbital.

biórgano *m.* biorgan.
biorracional *adj.* biorational.
biorreología *f.* biorheology.
biorretroalimentación *f.* biofeedback.
  biorretroalimentación alfa alpha biofeedback.
biorreversible *adj.* bioreversible.
biorriesgo *m.* biohazard.
biorritmo *m.* biorhythm.
bios *m.* bios.
bioscopia *f.* bioscopy.
biosfera *f.* biosphere.
biosíntesis *f.* biosynthesis.
biosintético, -ca *adj.* biosynthetic.
biosis *f.* biosis.
biosistema *m.* biosystem.
biósmosis *f.* biosmosis.
biosocial *adj.* biosocial.
biostática *f.* biostatics.
biota *f.* biota.
biotaxia *f.* biotaxy.
biotaxis *f.* biotaxis.
biotecnología *f.* biotechnology.
  biotecnología médica medical biotechnology.
  biotecnología mejorativa improvement biotechnology.
biotelemetría *f.* biotelemetry.
bioterapia *f.* biotherapy.
biotesiómetro *m.* biothesiometer.
biótica *f.* biotics.
biótico, -ca *adj.* biotic.
biotina *f.* biotin.
biotínidos *m.* biotinides.
biotinilisina *f.* biotinyllysine.
biotipo *m.* biotype.
biotipología *f.* biotypology.
biotomía *f.* biotomy.
biotomo *m.* biotome.
biotopo *m.* biotope.
biotoxicación *f.* biotoxication.
biotoxicología *f.* biotoxicology.
biotoxina *f.* biotoxin.
biotransfomación *f.* biotransformation.
biotropismo *m.* biotropism.
biovar *m.* biovar.
biovular *adj.* biovular, binovular.
bipalatinoide *adj.* bipalatinoid.
biparasitismo *m.* biparasitism.
biparásito, -ta *adj.* biparasitic.
biparental *adj.* biparental.
biparietal *adj.* biparietal.
bíparo, -a *adj.* biparous.
bipartido, -da *adj.* bipartite.
bipedal *adj.* bipedal.
bipedestación *f.* orthostatism.
bipédico, -ca *adj.* bipedal.
bípedo, -da *m., f.* biped.
bipenato, -ta *adj.* bipennate.
bipeniforme *adj.* bipenniform.
bipenniforme *adj.* bipenniform.
biperforado, -da *adj.* biperforate.
bipolar *adj.* bipolar.
bipositivo, -va *adj.* bipositive.
bipotencial *adj.* bipotential.
bipotencialidad *f.* bipotentiality.
  bipotencialidad de la gónada bipotentiality of the gonad.
birramoso, -sa *adj.* biramous.
birrefringencia *f.* birefringence.
  birrefringencia de corriente streaming birefringence.
  birrefringencia cristalina crystalline birefringence.
  birrefringencia de flujo flow birefringence.
  birrefringencia de forma form birefringence.

birrefringencia intrínseca intrinsic birefringence.

birrefringencia de tensión strain birefringence.

birrefringente *adj.* birefringent.

birrotación *f.* birotation.

bisacromial *adj.* bisacromial.

bisalbuminemia *f.* bisalbuminemia.

bisección *f.* bisection.

bisegmentectomía *f.* bisegmentectomy.

bisel[1] *m.* bevel.

 bisel cavosuperficial, bisel de cavosuperficie cavosurface bevel.

 bisel inverso reverse bevel.

bisel[2] *m.* chamfer.

biselar *v.* bevel.

biseptado, -da *adj.* biseptate.

bisexual *adj.* bisexual.

bisexualidad *f.* bisexuality.

bisferiens *adj.* bisferient, bisferious.

bisilíaco, -ca *adj.* bisiliac.

bisinosis *f.* byssinosis.

bisinótico, -ca *adj.* byssinotic.

bismutia *f.* bismuthia.

bismutosis *f.* bismuthosis.

bisocausis *f.* byssocausis.

bisque *m.* bisque.

 bisque bajo low bisque.

 bisque alto high bisque.

 bisque medio medium bisque.

bisteroide *m.* bisteroid.

Biston betularia Biston betularia.

bisturí[1] *m.* bistoury.

bisturí[2] *m.* knife.

 bisturí en anillo ring knife, spoke-shave knife.

 bisturí de banco buck knife.

 bisturí eléctrico cautery knife, electric knife, electrocautery knife.

 bisturí de Goldman-Fox Goldman-Fox knife.

 bisturí de Joseph Joseph knife.

 bisturí de Kirkland Kirkland knife.

 bisturí de Liston Liston's knife.

 bisturí de Merrifield Merrifield's knife.

 bisturí a pulso free-hand knife.

bitemporal *adj.* bitemporal.

biterminal *adj.* biterminal.

Bithynia Bithynia.

bitrocantéreo, -a *adj.* bitrochanteric.

bitrocantérico, -ca *adj.* bitrochanteric.

bitrópico, -ca *adj.* bitropic.

bituminosis *f.* bituminosis.

biuret *m.* biuret.

bivalencia *f.* bivalence, bivalency.

bivalente *adj.* bivalent.

bivalvo, -va *adj.* bivalve.

biventer *m.* biventer.

biventral *adj.* biventral.

biventricular *adj.* biventricular.

bivitelino, -na *adj.* bivitelline.

bizarro, -rra *adj.* bizarre.

bizco, -ca *adj.* cross-eyed.

bizcocho *m.* biscuit.

 bizcocho blando soft biscuit.

 bizcocho duro hard biscuit.

 bizcocho medio medium biscuit.

bizquear *v.* squint.

bizqueo *m.* squint.

 bizqueo de la acomodación accommodative squint.

 bizqueo concomitante comitant squint, concomitant squint.

 bizqueo convergente convergent squint.

 bizqueo divergente divergent squint.

 bizqueo hacia arriba y hacia abajo upward and downward squint.

bizquera *f.* squint.

blanco[1] *m.* target.

blanco, -ca[2] *m. y adj.* white.

 blanco del ojo white of the eye.

 blanco con presión white with pressure.

 blanco sin presión white without pressure.

 blanco visual visual white.

blanco, -ca[3] *adj.* blank.

blando, -da *adj.* bland.

blanqueamiento *m.* bleaching.

 blanqueamiento coronal coronal bleaching.

blanqueo gingival *m.* gingival blanching.

blasón *m.* escutcheon.

blast *m.* blast.

blastación *f.* blastation.

blastema *m.* blastema.

 blastema néfrico nephric blastema.

blastémico, -ca *adj.* blastemic.

blástico, -ca *adj.* blastic.

blástida *f.* blastid, blastide.

blástide *f.* blastid, blastide.

blastina *f.* blastin.

blasto *m.* blast.

blastocele *m.* blastocele, blastocoele.

blastocélico, -ca *adj.* blastocelic, blastocoelic.

blastocinina *f.* blastokinin.

blastocisto *m.* blastocyst.

blastocito *m.* blastocyte.

blastocitoma *m.* blastocytoma.

blastodermal *adj.* blastodermal.

blastodérmico, -ca *adj.* blastodermic.

blastodermo *m.* blastoderm, blastoderma.

 blastodermo bilaminar bilaminar blastoderm.

 blastodermo embrionario embryonic blastoderm.

 blastodermo extraembrionario extraembryonic blastoderm.

 blastodermo trilaminar trilaminar blastoderm.

blastodisco *m.* blastodisc, blastodisk.

blastófilo *m.* blastophyllum.

blastóforo *m.* blastophore.

blastoftoria *f.* blastophthoria.

blastoftórico, -ca *adj.* blastophthoric.

blastogénesis *f.* blastogenesis.

blastogenético, -ca *adj.* blastogenetic.

blastogenia *f.* blastogeny.

blastogénico, -ca *adj.* blastogenic.

blastólisis *f.* blastolysis.

blastolítico, -ca *adj.* blastolytic.

blastoma *m.* blastoma.

 blastoma autóctono autochthonous blastoma.

 blastoma heteróctono heterochthonous blastoma.

 blastoma pluricéntrico, blastoma pluricentro pluricentric blastoma.

 blastoma teratógeno heterochthonous blastoma.

 blastoma unicéntrico unicentric blastoma.

blastomatoide *adj.* blastomatoid.

blastomatosis *f.* blastomatosis.

blastomatoso, -sa *adj.* blastomatous.

blastómera *f.* blastomere.

blastómero *m.* blastomere.

blastomerotomía *f.* blastomerotomy.

blastomices *m.* blastomyces.

blastomiceto *m.* blastomycete.

blastomicosis *f.* blastomycosis.

 blastomicosis brasileña Brazilian blastomycosis.

 blastomicosis cutánea cutaneous blastomycosis.

 blastomicosis europea European blastomycosis.

 blastomicosis generalizada systemic blastomycosis.

 blastomicosis norteamericana North American blastomycosis.

 blastomicosis queloide keloidal blastomycosis.

 blastomicosis sudamericana South American blastomycosis.

blastomogénico, -ca *adj.* blastomogenic.

blastomógeno, -na *adj.* blastomogenous.

Blastomyces Blastomyces.

blastoneuroporo *m.* blastoneuropore.

blastoporo *m.* blastopore.

blastoquilo *m.* blastochyle.

blastosfera *f.* blastosphere.

blastostroma *m.* blastostroma.

blastotomía *f.* blastotomy.

blastozoide *m.* blastozooid.

blástula *f.* blastula.

blastulación *f.* blastulation.

blastular *adj.* blastular.

blefaradenitis *f.* blepharadenitis, blepharoadenitis.

blefarectomía *f.* blepharectomy.

blefaredema *m.* blepharedema.

blefarelosis *f.* blepharelosis.

blefárico, -ca *adj.* blepharal.

blefarismo *m.* blepharism.

blefaritis *f.* blepharitis.

 blefaritis acárica blepharitis acarica.

 blefaritis angular blepharitis angularis.

 blefaritis ciliar ciliary blepharitis, blepharitis ciliaris.

 blefaritis demodéctica demodectic blepharitis.

 blefaritis escamosa blepharitis squamosa.

 blefaritis estafilocócica staphylococcic blepharitis.

 blefaritis folicular blepharitis follicularis.

 blefaritis ftiriásica blepharitis phthiriatica.

 blefaritis marginal marginal blepharitis, blepharitis marginalis.

 blefaritis meibomiana Meibomian blepharitis.

 blefaritis no ulcerativa, blefaritis no ulcerosa non-ulcerative blepharitis.

 blefaritis oleosa blepharitis oleosa.

 blefaritis parasitaria blepharitis parasitica.

 blefaritis pediculosa pediculous blepharitis.

 blefaritis pustular pustular blepharitis.

 blefaritis rosácea blepharitis rosacea.

 blefaritis seborreica seborrheic blepharitis.

 blefaritis seborreica escamosa squamous seborrheic blepharitis.

 blefaritis seca blepharitis sicca.

 blefaritis ulcerosa ulcerative blepharitis, blepharitis ulcerosa.

blefaroadenitis *f.* blepharoadenitis.

blefaroadenoma *m.* blepharoadenoma.

blefaroateroma *m.* blepharoatheroma.

blefarocalasia *f.* blepharochalasis.

blefaroclono *m.* blepharoclonus.

blefarocoloboma *m.* blepharocoloboma.

blefaroconjuntivitis *f.* blepharoconjunctivitis.

blefarocromidrosis *f.* blepharochromidrosis.

blefarodermatitis *f.* blepharodermatitis.

blefarodiastasis *f.* blepharodiastasis.

blefaroedema *m.* blepharoedema.

blefaroespasmo *m.* blepharospasm, blepharospasmus.

 blefaroespasmo esencial essential blepharospasm.

blefaroespasmo reflejo reflex blepharospasm.
blefaroespasmo simpático sympathetic blepharospasm.
blefaroespasmo sintomático symptomatic blepharospasm.
blefarofima *f.* blepharophyma.
blefarofimosis *f.* blepharophimosis.
blefaromelasma *f.* blepharomelasma.
blefaron *m.* blepharon.
blefaroncosis *f.* blepharoncus.
blefaropaquinsis *f.* blepharopachynsis.
blefaropiorrea *f.* blepharopyorrhea.
blefaroplastia *f.* blepharoplasty.
blefaroplástico, -ca *adj.* blepharoplastic.
blefaroplasto *m.* blepharoplast.
blefaroplejía *f.* blepharoplegia.
blefaroptosis *f.* blepharoptosia, blepharoptosis.
  blefaroptosis adiposa blepharoptosia adiposa.
  blefaroptosis falsa false blepharoptosia.
blefaroqueratoconjuntivitis *f.* blepharokeratoconjunctivitis.
blefarorrafia *f.* blepharorrhaphy.
blefarosfinterectomía *f.* blepharosphincterectomy.
blefarosinequia *f.* blepharosynechia.
blefarospasmo *m.* blepharospasm.
blefaróstato *m.* blepharostat.
blefarostenosis *f.* blepharostenosis.
blefarotomía *f.* blepharotomy.
blenadenitis *f.* blennadenitis.
blenemesis *f.* blennemesis.
blenoftalmia, blenoftalmía *f.* blennophthalmia.
blenogénico, -ca *adj.* blennogenic.
blenógeno, -na *adj.* blennogenous.
blenoide *adj.* blennoid.
blenorragia *f.* blennorrhagia.
blenorrágico, -ca *adj.* blennorrhagic.
blenorrea *f.* blennorrhea.
  blenorrea conjuntival blennorrhea conjunctivalis.
  blenorrea de inclusión inclusion blennorrhea.
  blenorrea de los recién nacidos, blenorrea del neonato, blenorrea neonatorum blennorrhea neonatorum.
  blenorrea de Stoerk Stoerk's blennorrhea.
blenorreico, -ca *adj.* blennorrheal.
blenostasis *f.* blennostasis.
blenostático, -ca *adj.* blennostatic.
blenotórax *m.* blennothorax.
blenuria *f.* blennuria.
blindaje *m.* shielding.
blister *m.* blister.
  blíster hemorrágico blood blister.
blocaje *m.* blockage.
blockout *m.* block-out.
bloque *m.* block.
  bloque de Bunnel Bunnel block.
  bloque de mano handblock.
  bloque de mordida bite-block.
bloqueador, -ra *adj.* blocking[1].
bloqueante *m.* blocker.
  bloqueante alfa-adrenérgico alpha-adrenergic antagonist, alpha-blocker.
  bloqueante beta-adrenérgico beta-adrenergic antagonist, beta-blocker.
  bloqueante de los canales de calcio, bloqueante de la vía del calcio calcium channel blocker.
bloquear *v.* block.
bloqueo[1] *m.* block.
  bloqueo de aire air block.
  bloqueo alveolar-capilar, bloqueo alvéo-

locapilar alveolar-capillary block.
bloqueo anterógrado anterograde block.
bloqueo anestésico anesthetic block.
bloqueo de arborización arborization block.
bloqueo auditivo ear block.
bloqueo auriculoventricular bloqueo A-V) atrioventricular block, A-V block.
bloqueo auriculoventricular de primer grado first degree atrioventricular block, first degree heart block.
bloqueo auriculoventricular de segundo grado second degree atrioventricular block, second degree heart block.
bloqueo auriculoventricular completo, bloqueo auriculoventricular de tercer grado complete atrioventricular block, third degree heart block.
bloqueo de Bier Bier's block, intravenous block (I-V block).
bloqueo de campo field block.
bloqueo cardíaco heart block.
bloqueo cardíaco auriculoventricular atrioventricular heart block.
bloqueo cardíaco completo (BCC) complete heart block (CHB).
bloqueo cardíaco congénito congenital heart block, congenital complete heart block.
bloqueo cardíaco incompleto incomplete heart block.
bloqueo cardíaco parcial partial heart block.
bloqueo cardíaco de rama bundle branch block.
bloqueo cardíaco sinoauricular (SA) sinoatrial block, sinoatrial exit block, sinus exit block (SA block).
bloqueo cardíaco de tipo Mobitz I Mobitz type I heart block.
bloqueo cardíaco de tipo Mobitz II Mobitz type II heart block.
bloqueo cardíaco de Wenckebach Wenckebach heart block.
bloqueo caudal caudal block.
bloqueo del corazón heart block.
bloqueo criogénico, bloqueo criógeno cryogenic block.
bloqueo de despolarización depolarization block, depolarizing block.
bloqueo dinámico dynamic block.
bloqueo de entrada entrance block.
bloqueo epidural epidural block.
bloqueo espinal spinal block.
bloqueo espinal subaracnoideo spinal-subarachnoid block.
bloqueo esplácnico splanchnic block.
bloqueo estrellado stellate block.
bloqueo fascicular fascicular block.
bloqueo de fase I phase I block.
bloqueo de fase II phase II block.
bloqueo fenólico phenol block.
bloqueo infranodal infranodal block.
bloqueo de huesos bone block.
bloqueo intercostal intercostal block.
bloqueo intraauricular intra-atrial block.
bloqueo intraespinal intraspinal block.
bloqueo intranasal intranasal block.
bloqueo intraventricular intraventricular block.
bloqueo metabólico metabolic block.
bloqueo de los nervios intercostales intercostal nerve block.
bloqueo nervioso nerve block.
bloqueo neuromuscular neuromuscular block.
bloqueo no despolarizante non-depolarizing block.

bloqueo paracervical paracervical block.
bloqueo paraneural paraneural block.
bloqueo parasacro parasacral block.
bloqueo paravertebral paravertebral block.
bloqueo periinfarto peri-infarction block.
bloqueo perineural perineural block.
bloqueo presacro presacral block.
bloqueo protector protective block.
bloqueo pudendo pudendal block.
bloqueo de rama (BR) bundle-branch block (BBB), interventricular block.
bloqueo de rama derecha right bundle branch block (RBBB).
bloqueo retrógrado retrograde block.
bloqueo sacro sacral block.
bloqueo de salida exit block.
bloqueo en silla de montar saddle block.
bloqueo simpático sympathetic block.
bloqueo sinoauricular sinoauricular block.
bloqueo sinoatrial sinotrial block.
bloqueo sinusal sinus block.
bloqueo subaracnoideo subarachnoid block.
bloqueo suprahisiano suprahisian block.
bloqueo tipo Mobitz Mobitz block.
bloqueo tipo Mobitz I Mobitz type I heart block.
bloqueo tipo Mobitz II Mobitz type II heart block.
bloqueo trans-sacro trans-sacral block.
bloqueo tubárico tubal block.
bloqueo unidireccional unidirectional block.
bloqueo uterosacro uterosacral block.
bloqueo ventricular ventricular block.
bloqueo de Wenckebach Wenckebach block.
bloqueo de Wilson Wilson block.
bloqueo de Wolff-Chaikoff Wolff-Chaikoff block.
bloqueo[2] *m.* blockade.
bloqueo adrenérgico adrenergic blockade.
bloqueo adrenérgico alfa alpha-adrenergic blockade, alpha-blockade.
bloqueo adrenérgico beta "beta-adrenergic blockade; beta-blockade".
bloqueo colinérgico cholinergic blockade.
bloqueo ganglionar ganglionic blockade.
bloqueo por metadona methadone blockade.
bloqueo mioneural myoneural blockade.
bloqueo narcótico narcotic blockade.
bloqueo de neurona adrenérgica adrenergic neuron blockade.
bloqueo neuromuscular neuromuscular blockade.
bloqueo renal renal blockade.
bloqueo simpático sympathetic blockade.
bloqueo vagal vagal blockade, vagus nerve blockade.
bloqueo viral virus blockade.
bloqueo[3] *m.* blockage.
bloqueo de tendón tendon blockage.
bloqueo[4] *m.* blocking[2].
bloqueo afectivo affective blocking.
bloqueo emocional affective blocking.
bloqueo mental mental blocking.
bloqueo del pensamiento thought blocking.
bloqueo[5] *m.* block-out, block out.
bobbing ocular *m.* ocular bobbing.
bobina *f.* coil.
boca *f.* mouth, os.
  boca blanca white mouth.
  boca de carpa carp mouth.
  boca lastimada por prótesis denture sore mouth.
  boca saburral saburral mouth.
  boca seca dry mouth.

boca de los sopladores de vidrio glass-blowers' mouth.
boca de tapir tapir mouth.
boca de trinchera trench mouth.
boca ulcerada sore mouth.
boca ulcerada de Ceylán Ceylon sore mouth.
boca ulcerada por dentadura denture sore mouth.
bocado *m.* bite.
bocio *m.* goiter.
bocio aberrante aberrant goiter.
bocio adenomatoso adenomatous goiter.
bocio agudo acute goiter.
bocio de Basedow Basedow's goiter.
bocio buceador, bocio buzo diving goiter.
bocio coloidal, bocio coloide colloid goiter.
bocio congénito congenital goiter.
bocio difuso diffuse goiter.
bocio ectópico ectopic goiter.
bocio endémico endemic goiter.
bocio errante wandering goiter.
bocio esternal sternal goiter.
bocio exoftálmico exophthalmic goiter.
bocio familiar familial goiter.
bocio fibroso fibrous goiter.
bocio folicular follicular goiter.
bocio intratorácico intrathoracic goiter.
bocio linfadenoide lymphadenoid goiter.
bocio lingual lingual goiter.
bocio microfolicular microfollicular goiter.
bocio móvil diving goiter.
bocio multinodular multinodular goiter.
bocio multinodular tóxico toxic multinodular goiter.
bocio nodular nodular goiter.
bocio nodular tóxico toxic nodular goiter.
bocio no tóxico non-toxic goiter.
bocio parenquimatoso parenchymatous goiter.
bocio perivascular perivascular goiter.
bocio quístico cystic goiter.
bocio retrosternal substernal goiter.
bocio retrovascular retrovascular goiter.
bocio simple simple goiter.
bocio sofocante suffocative goiter.
bocio subesternal substernal goiter.
bocio torácico thoracic goiter.
bocio tóxico toxic goiter.
bocio vascular vascular goiter.
bocio por yoduro iodide goiter.
bocio zambullidor plunging goiter.
bociogenicidad *f.* goitrogenicity.
bociogénico, -ca *adj.* goitrogenic, goitrogenous.
bociógeno *m.* goitrogen.
bocioso, -sa *adj.* goitrous.
Bodo Bodo.
bola *f.* ball.
bola adiposa de Bichat fatty ball of Bichat, buccal fat pad.
bola alimentaria, bola de alimento food ball.
bola de condrina chondrin ball.
bola fúngica fungus ball.
bola grasa de Bichat fatty ball of Bichat, buccal fat pad.
bola de Marchi Marchi ball.
bola micótica fungus ball.
bola pleural de fibrina pleural fibril ball.
Boletus satanas Boletus satanas.
bolo *m.* bolus.
bolo alimenticio, bolo alimentario alimentary bolus.
bolo de condrina chondrin bolus.
bolo endovenoso intravenous bolus.

bolo fecal fecal bolus.
bolo fúngico fungus bolus.
bolo histérico globus hystericus.
bolo intravenoso intravenous bolus.
bolómetro *m.* bolometer.
boloscopio *m.* boloscope.
bolsa¹ *f.* bag.
bolsa de aguas bag of waters, forewaters bag.
bolsa Ambu Ambu bag.
bolsa de Barnes Barnes' bag.
bolsa de Bunyan Bunyan bag.
bolsa de Champetier de Ribes Champetier de Ribes bag.
bolsa de colostomía colostomy bag.
bolsa de Douglas Douglas bag.
bolsa de Hagner Hagner bag.
bolsa de hielo ice bag, ice pack.
bolsa de ileostomía ileostomy bag.
bolsa para micción micturition bag.
bolsa nuclear nuclear bag.
bolsa de Perry Perry bag.
bolsa de Petersen Petersen's bag.
bolsa de Pilcher Pilcher bag.
bolsa de Plummer Plummer's bag.
bolsa Politzer Politzer's bag.
bolsa de reserva, bolsa de reservorio reservoir bag.
bolsa de reinspiración rebreathing bag.
bolsa de respiración breathing bag.
bolsa testicular testicular bag.
bolsa de Voorhees Voorhees' bag.
bolsa² *f.* bursa.
bolsa³ *f.* pocket.
bolsa gingival gingival pocket.
bolsa infraósea infrabony pocket.
bolsa intraalveolar intra-alveolar pocket.
bolsa intraósea intrabony pocket.
bolsa periodontal periodontal pocket.
bolsa de Rathke Rathke's pocket.
bolsa de Seessel Seessel's pocket.
bolsa subcrestal subcrestal pocket.
bolsa⁴ *f.* pouch.
bolsa antral antral pouch.
bolsa branquial branchial pouch.
bolsa de Broca Broca's pouch.
bolsa celómica celomic pouch.
bolsa de Douglas Douglas's pouch, pouch of Douglas.
bolsa endodérmica endodermal pouch.
bolsa faríngea pharyngeal pouch.
bolsa de Hartmann Hartmann's pouch.
bolsa de Heidenhain Heidenhain pouch.
bolsa de Indiana Indiana pouch.
bolsa en J J-pouch.
bolsa Kock Kock's pouch.
bolsa de Mainz Mainz's pouch.
bolsa de Mainz 2 Mainz's pouch 2.
bolsa paracística paracystic pouch.
bolsa pararrectal pararectal pouch.
bolsa paravesical paravesical pouch.
bolsa de Pavlov Pavlov pouch.
bolsa de Physick Physick's pouch.
bolsa de Prussak Prussak's pouch.
bolsa de Rathke Rathke's pouch.
bolsa rectouterina rectouterine pouch.
bolsa de Seessel Seessel's pouch.
bolsa ultimobranquial ultimobranchial pouch.
bolsa⁵ *f.* sac.
bolsa amniótica amniotic sac.
bolseo *m.* bagging.
bomba *f.* pump.
bomba de aire air pump.
bomba de Abbott Abbott pump.
bomba de Alvegniat Alvegniat's pump.
bomba de aminas amine pump.

bomba-balón intraaórtico, bomba con balón intraaórtico intra-aortic balloon pump (IABP).
bomba de calcio calcium pump.
bomba cardíaca de balón cardiac balloon pump.
bomba de Carrel-Lindbergh Carrel-Lindbergh pump.
bomba dental dental pump.
bomba estomacal, bomba del estómago stomach pump.
bomba eyectora a chorro jet ejector pump.
bomba gástrica stomach pump.
bomba de Harvard Harvard pump.
bomba de infusión infusion pump.
bomba para infusión constante constant infusion pump.
bomba de infusión y extracción infusion-withdrawal pump.
bomba de infusión de insulina insulin infusion pump.
bomba de insulina insulin pump.
bomba intravenosa de pistón intravenous piston pump.
bomba iónica ionic pump.
bomba de jeringa intravenosa intravenous syringe pump.
bomba de Lindbergh Lindbergh's pump.
bomba mamaria, bomba para mamas breast pump.
bomba de morfina morphine pump.
bomba oxigenadora pump-oxygenator.
bomba peristáltica peristaltic pump.
bomba peristáltica intravenosa intravenous peristaltic pump.
bomba de protones proton pump.
bomba rápida de sangre slip-on blood pump.
bomba sacaleches breast pump.
bomba para saliva saliva pump.
bomba de sangre, bomba sanguínea blood pump.
bomba de sodio sodium pump.
bomba de sodio-potasio, bomba de Na y K sodium-potassium pump.
bomba de cobalto *f.* cobalt bomb.
bombardear *v.* bombard.
bombear *v.* pump.
bombeo *m.* barbotage.
bombesina *f.* bombesin.
boquera *f.* perlèche.
boratado, -da *adj.* borated.
borborigmo *m.* borborygmus.
borde¹ *m.* border.
borde bermellón vermilion border.
borde en cepillo brush border.
borde de dentadura, borde dentado, borde dental denture border.
borde estriado striated border.
borde² *m.* brim.
borde³ *m.* edge.
borde conductor leading edge.
borde cortante cutting edge.
borde de dentadura, borde dentado, borde dental denture edge.
borde incisal, borde incisivo incisal edge, margo incisalis.
resistencia del borde edge-strength.
borde⁴ *m.* margin, margo.
borde⁵ *m.* ridge.
borde primitivo primitive ridge.
borde⁶ *m.* rim.
borde de mordedura bite rim.
borde de oclusión occlusal rim, occlusion rim.

borde de registro record rim.
borderline *m.* borderline.
Bordetella Bordetella.
  Bordetella parapertussis Bordetella parapertussis.
  Bordetella pertussis Bordetella pertussis.
borismo *m.* borism.
boro *m.* boron.
borradura *f.* effacement.
borramiento *m.* effacement.
Borrelia Borrelia.
borreliosis *f.* borreliosis.
borrosidad *f.* blurring.
  borrosidad cinética kinetic blurring.
  borrosidad de foco focus blurring.
  borrosidad fotográfica photographic blurring.
  borrosidad geométrica focus blurring.
boselado, -da *adj.* bosselated.
bostezar *v.* yawn.
bostezo *m.* yawn.
bota *f.* boot.
  bota abductora abduction boot.
  bota de Gibney Gibney's boot.
  bota de Junod Junod's boot.
  bota de pasta de Unna Unna's paste boot.
  bota de Unna Unna's boot.
botánica *f.* botany.
  botánica médica medical botany.
botánico, -ca *adj.* botanic.
botella *f.* bottle.
  botella de Castaneda Castaneda bottle.
  botella de espiración blow bottle.
  botella para lavado wash bottle.
  botella de Mariotte Mariotte bottle.
  botella de Spritz Spritz bottle.
  botella de Woulfe Woulfe's bottle.
botiquín *m.* first-aid kit.
botón¹ *m.* boil.
  botón de Aleppo Aleppo boil.
  botón de Bagdad Baghdad boil.
  botón de Biskra Biskra boil.
  botón oriental, botón de Oriente Oriental boil.
botón² *m.* bouton.
  botón de Bagdad Baghdad bouton.
  botón de Biskra Biskra bouton.
  botón de camisa bouton en chemise.
  botón oriental, botón de Oriente bouton d'Orient.
  botón sináptico synaptic bouton.
  botón terminal terminal bouton, bouton terminale.
  botón terminal axónico axonal terminal bouton.
botón³ *m.* button.
  botón de Amboina Amboyna button.
  botón de Biskra Biskra button.
  botón de bromuro bromide button.
  botón cutáneo skin button.
  botón dérmico, botón intradérmico dermal button.
  botón gustativo taste button.
  botón de Jaboulay Jaboulay button.
  botón mamario mammary button.
  botón de mescal, botón de mezcal mescal button.
  botón de Murphy Murphy's button.
  botón oriental, botón de Oriente Oriental button.
  botón peritoneal peritoneal button.
  botón de yoduro iodide button.
botrio *m.* bothrium.
botriocefaliasis *f.* bothriocephaliasis.
botriocéfalo *m.* bothriocephalus.

botrioide *adj.* botryoid.
botriomicoma *m.* botryomycoma.
botriomicosis *f.* botryomycosis.
botriomicótico, -ca *adj.* botryomycotic.
Botryomyces Botryomyces.
botritimicosis *f.* botrytimycosis.
botuliforme *adj.* botuliform.
botulina *f.* botulin.
botulínico, -ca *adj.* botulinal.
botulinogénico, botulogénico, -ca *adj.* botulinogenic.
botulinógeno, -na *adj.* botulinogenic.
botulismo *m.* botulism.
  botulismo en heridas, botulismo por herida wound botulism.
  botulismo infantil infant botulism.
  botulismo del lactante infant botulism.
botulismotoxina *f.* botulismotoxin.
botulogénico, -ca *adj.* botulogenic.
bouba *f.* bouba.
bouche de tapir *f.* bouche de tapir.
bougienage *m.* bougienage.
bouquet *m.* bouquet.
  bouquet de Riolan bouquet de Riolan.
bouton *m.* bouton.
  bouton terminale terminal bouton, bouton terminale.
boutonnière *f.* boutonnière.
bóveda *f.* vault.
bovovacuna *f.* bovovaccine.
bovovacunación *f.* bovovaccination.
bowenoide *adj.* bowenoid.
boxel *m.* boxel.
braceo *m.* arm swing.
brachium brachium.
bracket *m.* bracket.
bradiacusia *f.* bradyacusia.
bradiarritmia *f.* bradyarrhythmia.
bradiartria *f.* bradyarthria.
bradiauxesis *f.* bradyauxesis.
bradicardia *f.* bradycardia.
  bradicardia de Branham Branham's bradycardia.
  bradicardia cardiomuscular cardiomuscular bradycardia.
  bradicardia central central bradycardia.
  bradicardia esencial essential bradycardia.
  bradicardia fetal fetal bradycardia.
  bradicardia idiopática idiopathic bradycardia.
  bradicardia nodal nodal bradycardia.
  bradicardia postinfecciosa, bradicardia posinfecciosa postinfectious bradycardia, postinfective bradycardia.
  bradicardia sinoauricular sinoatrial bradycardia.
  bradicardia sinusal sinus bradycardia.
  bradicardia vagal vagal bradycardia.
  bradicardia ventricular ventricular bradycardia.
bradicárdico, -ca *adj.* bradycardiac, bradycardic.
bradicinesia *f.* bradycinesia, bradykinesia.
bradicinético, -ca *adj.* bradykinetic.
bradicrótico, -ca *adj.* bradycrotic.
bradidiastalsis *f.* bradydiastalsis.
bradidiástole *f.* bradydiastole.
bradiecoia *f.* bradyecoia.
bradiespermatismo *m.* bradyspermatism.
bradiestesia *f.* bradyesthesia.
bradifagia *f.* bradyphagia.
bradifasia *f.* bradyphasia.
bradifemia *f.* bradyphemia.
bradifrasia *f.* bradyphrasia.
bradifrenia *f.* bradyphrenia.

bradigénesis *f.* bradygenesis.
bradiglosia *f.* bradyglossia.
bradilalia *f.* bradylalia.
bradilexia *f.* bradylexia.
bradilogia *f.* bradylogia.
bradipepsia *f.* bradypepsia.
bradipnea *f.* bradypnea.
bradipragia *f.* bradypragia.
bradipraxia *f.* bradypragia.
bradipsiquia *f.* bradypsychia.
bradiquinesia *f.* bradykinesia.
bradirritmia *f.* bradyrhythmia.
bradisfigmia *f.* bradysphygmia.
bradispermatismo *m.* bradyspermatism.
bradistalsia *f.* bradystalsis.
bradistalsis *f.* bradystalsis.
braditaquicardia *f.* bradytachycardia.
braditeleocinesia *f.* bradyteleocinesia, bradyteleokinesis.
braditeleocinesis *f.* bradyteleocinesia, bradyteleokinesis.
braditeleoquinesia *f.* bradyteleocinesia, bradyteleokinesis.
braditocia *f.* bradytocia.
braditrofia *f.* braditrophia.
braditrófico, -ca *adj.* bradytrophic.
bradiuria *f.* bradyuria.
bradizoíto *m.* bradyzoite.
braguero¹ *m.* brace.
  braguero dorsal de Taylor Taylor's back brace.
braguero² *m.* truss.
  braguero de hilaza yarn truss.
  braguero nasal nasal truss.
braidismo *m.* braidism.
braille *m.* braille.
Branhamella Branhamella.
branquia *f.* branchia.
branquial *adj.* branchial.
branquiogénico, -ca *adj.* branchiogenic.
branquiógeno, -na *adj.* branchiogenous.
branquioma *f.* branchioma.
branquiomérico, -ca *adj.* branchiomeric.
branquiomerismo *m.* branchiomerism.
branquiómero *m.* branchiomere.
branquiomotor, -ra *adj.* branchiomotor.
braquial *adj.* brachial.
braquialgia *f.* brachialgia.
  braquialgia estática parestésica brachialgia statica paresthestica.
braquiametacarpia *f.* brachiametacarpia.
braquimetacarpia *f.* brachiametacarpia.
braquiametatarsia *f.* brachiametatarsia.
braquimetatarsia *f.* brachiametatarsia.
braquibasia *f.* brachybasia.
braquibasocamptodactilia *f.* brachybasocamptodactyly.
braquibasofalangia *f.* brachybasophalangia.
braquicardia *f.* brachycardia.
braquicefalia *f.* brachycephalia, brachycephaly.
braquicefálico, -ca *adj.* brachycephalic.
braquicefalismo *m.* brachycephalism.
braquicéfalo, -la *adj.* brachicephalous.
braquicérquico, -ca *adj.* brachykerkic.
braquicnémico, -ca *adj.* brachycnemic, brachyknemic.
braquicránico, -ca *adj.* brachycranic.
braquicranio, -nia *adj.* brachycranial.
braquicrónico, -ca *adj.* brachychronic.
braquidactilia *f.* brachydactylia, brachydactyly.
braquidactílico, -ca *adj.* brachydactylic.
braquiesófago *m.* brachyesophagus.
braquifacial *adj.* brachyfacial.

braquifalangia *f.* brachyphalangia.
braquigloso, -sa *f.* brachyglossal.
braquignatia *f.* brachygnathia, bird face.
braquignato, -ta *adj.* brachygnathous.
braquimelia *f.* brachymelia.
braquimesofalangia *f.* brachymesophalangia.
braquimetacarpia *f.* brachymetacarpia, brachymetacarpalia, brachymetacarpalism.
braquimetapodia *f.* brachymetapody.
braquimetatarsia *f.* brachymetatarsia.
braquimétrope *adj.* brachymetropic.
braquimetropía *f.* brachymetropia.
braquimórfico, -ca *adj.* brachymorphic.
braquimorfo, -fa *adj.* brachymorphic.
braquimotrópico, -ca *adj.* brachymetropic.
braquiocefálico, -ca *adj.* brachiocephalic.
braquiocilosis *f.* brachiocyllosis.
braquiocirtosis *m.* brachiocyrtosis.
braquiocrural *adj.* brachiocrural.
braquiocubital *adj.* brachiocubital.
braquiodonte *adj.* brachyodont.
braquiofaciolingual *adj.* brachiofaciolingual.
braquiograma *f.* brachiogram.
braquioplastia *f.* brachioplasty.
braquipélvico, -ca *adj.* brachypellic, brachypelvic.
braquípodo, -da *adj.* brachypodous.
braquiprosópico, -ca *adj.* brachyprosopic.
braquiqueilia *f.* brachycheilia, brachychilia.
braquiquilia *f.* brachycheilia, brachychilia.
braquiquérquico, -ca *adj.* brachykerkic.
braquirrinco *m.* brachyrhynchus.
braquirrinia *f.* brachyrhinia.
braquisindactilia *f.* brachysyndactyly.
braquisquélico, -ca *adj.* brachyskelic.
braquisquelo, -la *adj.* brachyskelous.
braquistafilino, -na *adj.* brachystaphyline.
braquistasis *f.* brachystasis.
braquitelefalangia *f.* brachytelephalangia.
braquiterapia *f.* brachytherapy.
braquitípico, -ca *adj.* brachytypical.
braquitipo *m.* brachytype.
braquiuránico, -ca *adj.* brachyuranic.
brasileína *f.* brazilein.
brasilina *f.* brazilin.
brazal *m.* cuff.
brazalete *m.* bracelet.
brazalete de Nageotte Nageotte's bracelet.
brazalete de Nussbaum Nussbaum's bracelet.
brazo[1] *m.* arm.
brazo en barra bar clasp arm.
brazo en broche clasp arm.
brazo en broche circunferencial circumferential clasp arm.
brazo en broche circunferencial estabilizante stabilizing circumferential clasp arm.
brazo en broche circunferencial retentivo retentive circumferential clasp arm.
brazo cromosoma chromosome arm.
brazo de dineína dynein arm.
brazo estabilizador stabilizing arm.
brazo de golfista golf arm.
brazo de Krukenberg Krukenberg's arm.
brazo musculoso brawny arm.
brazo recíproco reciprocal arm.
brazo de retención retention arm, .
brazo retentivo retentive arm.
brazo sujetador de barra bar clasp arm.
brazo sujetador circunferencial circumferential clasp arm.
brazo de tenista lawn tennis arm.
brazo de vidrio glass arm.
brazo[2] *m.* arm, brachium.
brea *f.* tar.
brea de enebro juniper tar.

brea de pino pine tar.
brecha *f.* gap.
brecha de ADN DNA gap.
brecha aire-hueso air-bone gap.
brecha auscultatoria auscultatory gap.
brecha cromosómica chromosomal gap.
brecha de DNA DNA gap.
brecha silenciosa silent gap.
bréfico, -ca *adj.* brephic.
brefoplástico, -ca *adj.* brephoplastic.
brefotrópico, -ca *adj.* brephotropic.
bregma *f.* bregma.
bregmático, -ca *adj.* bregmatic.
bregmatodimia *f.* bregmatodymia.
brei *m.* brei.
bremsstrahlung *m.* bremsstrahlung.
Brevibacteriaceae Brevibacteriaceae.
Brevibacterium Brevibacterium.
brevicollis brevicollis.
brevilíneo, -a *adj.* brevilineal.
brevirradiado, -da *adj.* breviradiate.
bricomanía *f.* brychomania.
brida *f.* bridle.
bríctico, -ca *adj.* brightic.
brinolasa *f.* brinolase.
brisement forcé *m.* brisement forcé.
broca *f.* broach.
broca barbada barbed broach.
broca lisa smooth broach.
broche *m.* buttonhook.
bromado, -da *adj.* bromated, brominated, brominized, bromized.
bromatología *f.* bromatology.
bromatólogo, -ga *m., f.* bromatologist.
bromatoterapia *f.* bromatherapy, bromatotherapy.
bromatotoxina *f.* bromatotoxin.
bromatotoxismo *m.* bromatotoxismus.
bromatoxismo *m.* bromatoxism.
bromhidrosifobia *f.* bromhidrosiphobia, bromidrosiphobia.
bromhidrosis *f.* bromhidrosis, bromidrosis, fetid sweat.
brómico, -ca *adj.* bromic.
brómide *m.* bromide.
bromidrosifobia *f.* bromhidrosiphobia, bromidrosiphobia.
bromidrosis *f.* bromhidrosis, bromidrosis, fetid sweat.
brominismo *m.* brominism.
bromismo *m.* bromism.
bromoderma *f.* bromoderma.
bromodermia *f.* bromoderma.
bromofenol *m.* bromphenol.
bromohiperhidrosis *f.* bromohyperhidrosis.
bromomanía *f.* bromomania.
bromopnea *f.* bromopnea.
bromoyodismo *m.* bromoiodism.
bromuración *f.* bromization.
bronceado *m.* tanning.
bronchus bronchus.
broncoadenitis *f.* bronchoadenitis, bronchadenitis.
broncoalveolar *f.* bronchoalveolar.
broncoalveolitis *f.* bronchoalveolitis.
broncoaspergilosis *f.* bronchoaspergillosis.
broncoaspiración *f.* bronchoaspiration.
broncoblastomicosis *f.* bronchoblastomycosis.
broncoblenorrea *f.* bronchoblennorrhea.
broncocandidiasis *f.* bronchocandidiasis.
broncocaverноso, -sa *adj.* bronchocavernous.
broncocefalitis *f.* bronchocephalitis.
broncocele *m.* bronchocele.

broncoconstricción *f.* bronchoconstriction.
broncoconstrictor *m. y adj.* bronchoconstrictor.
broncodilación *m.* bronchodilation.
broncodilatación *m.* bronchodilatation.
broncodilatador *m. y adj.* bronchodilator.
broncodilatador activo sobre el sistema autónomo autonomic-active bronchodilator.
broncodilatador adrenérgico adrenergic bronchodilator.
broncodilatador simpaticomimético sympathomimetic bronchodilator.
broncoedema *f.* bronchoedema.
broncoegofonía *f.* bronchoegophony.
broncoesofágico, -ca *adj.* bronchoesophageal.
broncoesofagología *f.* bronchoesophagology.
broncoesofagoscopia *f.* bronchoesophagoscopy.
broncoespasmo *m.* bronchismus, bronchospasm.
broncoespasmo paradójico paradoxical bronchismus.
broncoespirografía, broncospirografía *f.* bronchospirography.
broncoespirometría *f.* bronchospirometry.
broncoespirómetro *m.* bronchospirometer.
broncoespiroquetosis *m.* bronchospirochetosis.
broncoestenosis *m.* bronchostenosis.
broncofibroscopia *f.* bronchofiberscopy, bronchofibroscopy.
broncofibroscopio *m.* bronchofiberscope, bronchofibroscope.
broncofonía *f.* bronchophony.
broncofonía de murmullo, broncofonía de susurro, broncofonía en susurro whispered bronchophony.
broncofonía con pectoriloquia pectoriloquous bronchophony.
broncofonía ruidosa sniffling bronchophony.
broncogénico, -ca *adj.* bronchogenic.
broncógeno, -na *adj.* bronchogenic.
broncografía *f.* bronchography.
broncográfico, -ca *adj.* bronchographic.
broncograma *m.* bronchogram.
broncograma aéreo air bronchogram.
broncolitiasis *f.* broncholithiasis.
broncolito *m.* broncholith.
broncología *f.* bronchology.
broncológico, -ca *adj.* bronchologic.
broncomalacia *f.* bronchomalacia.
broncomicosis *f.* bronchomycosis.
broncomoniliasis *f.* bronchomoniliasis.
broncomotor *m. y adj.* bronchomotor.
broncomucotrópico, -ca *adj.* bronchomucotropic.
bronconeumonía *f.* bronchopneumonia.
bronconeumonía postoperatoria postoperative bronchopneumonia.
bronconeumonía subaguda subacute bronchopneumonia.
bronconeumonía tuberculosa tuberculous bronchopneumonia.
bronconeumonía por virus virus bronchopneumonia.
bronconeumónico, -ca *adj.* bronchopneumonic.
bronconeumonitis *f.* bronchopneumonitis.
bronconeumopatía *f.* bronchopneumopathy.
bronconocardiosis *f.* bronchonocardiosis.
broncooidosis *f.* broncho-oidosis.
broncopancreático, -ca *adj.* bronchopancreatic.

broncopatía *f.* bronchopathy.
broncoplastia *f.* bronchoplasty.
broncoplejía *f.* bronchoplegia.
broncopleural *adj.* bronchopleural.
broncopleuroneumonía *f.* bronchopleuropneumonia.
broncopulmonar *adj.* bronchopulmonary.
broncorrafia *f.* bronchorrhaphy.
broncorragia *f.* bronchorrhagia.
broncorrea *f.* bronchorrhea.
broncoscopia *f.* bronchoscopy.
  broncoscopia de fibra óptica, broncoscopia fibroóptica fiberoptic bronchoscopy.
  broncoscopia láser laser bronchoscopy.
broncoscópico, -ca *adj.* bronchoscopic.
broncoscopio *m.* bronchoscope.
  broncoscopio fibroóptico fiberoptic bronchoscope.
broncosinusitis *m.* bronchosinusitis.
broncospasmo *m.* bronchospasm.
broncospirografía *f.* bronchospirography.
broncospirometría *f.* bronchospirometry.
broncospirómetro *m.* bronchospirometer.
broncospiroquetosis *m.* brochospirochetosis.
broncostaxis *f.* bronchostaxis.
broncostenosis *m.* bronchiostenosis, bronchostenosis.
broncostomía *f.* bronchostomy.
broncotifus *m.* bronchotyphus.
broncotomía *f.* bronchotomy.
broncótomo *m.* bronchotome.
broncotomograma *f.* bronchotomogram.
broncotraqueal *adj.* bronchotracheal.
broncovesicular *adj.* bronchovesicular.
bronquial *adj.* bronchial.
bronquiarctia *f.* bronchiarctia.
bronquiectasis *f.* bronchiectasia, bronchiectasis.
  bronquiectasia capilar capillary bronchiectasia.
  bronquiectasia cilíndrica cylindrical bronchiectasia.
  bronquiectasia folicular follicular bronchiectasia.
  bronquiectasia quística cystic bronchiectasia.
  bronquiectasia sacular saccular bronchiectasia.
  bronquiectasia seca, bronquiectasia sicca dry bronchiectasia, bronchiectasis sicca.
bronquiectasis *f.* bronchiectasia, bronchiectasis.
bronquiectásico, -ca *adj.* bronchiectasic.
bronquiectático, -ca *adj.* bronchiectatic.
bronquiloquia *f.* bronchiloquy.
bronquio *m.* bronchus.
  bronquio fuente, bronquio de sostén stem bronchus.
  bronquio traqueal tracheal bronchus.
bronquioalveolitis *f.* alveobronchitis.
bronquiocele *m.* bronchiocele.
bronquioestenosis *f.* bronchiostenosis.
bronquiogénico, -ca *adj.* bronchiogenic.
bronquiolectasia *f.* bronchiolectasia, bronchiolectasis.
bronquiolectasis *f.* bronchiolectasia, bronchiolectasis.
bronquiolitis *f.* bronchiolitis.
  bronquiolitis aguda obliterante acute obliterating bronchiolitis.
  bronquiolitis exudativa exudative bronchiolitis, bronchiolitis exudativa.
  bronquiolitis fibrosa obliterante bronchiolitis fibrosa obliterans.

bronquiolitis obliterante bronchiolitis obliterans.
bronquiolitis proliferativa proliferative bronchiolitis.
bronquiolitis vesicular vesicular bronchiolitis.
bronquiolo, bronquíolo *m.* bronchiole, bronchiolus.
  bronquiolo respiratorios alveolar bronchioles, respiratory bronchioles, bronchioli respiratorii.
  bronquiolo lobulillar lobular bronchiole.
  bronquiolo terminal terminal bronchiole, bronchiolus terminalis.
bronquiolopulmonar *adj.* bronchiolopulmonary.
bronquiospasmo *m.* bronchiospasm.
bronquítico, -ca *adj.* bronchitic.
bronquitis *f.* bronchitis.
  bronquitis aguda acute bronchitis.
  bronquitis asmática infecciosa infectious asthmatic bronchitis.
  bronquitis asmatiforme asthmatic bronchitis.
  bronquitis capilar capillary bronchitis.
  bronquitis capilar epidémica epidemic capillary bronchitis.
  bronquitis caseosa cheesy bronchitis.
  bronquitis de Castellani Castellani's bronchitis.
  bronquitis catarral catarrhal bronchitis.
  bronquitis crónica chronic bronchitis.
  bronquitis crupal croupous bronchitis.
  bronquitis epidémica epidemic bronchitis.
  bronquitis epidémica capilar epidemic capillary bronchitis.
  bronquitis estafilocócica staphylococcus bronchitis.
  bronquitis estreptocócica streptococcal bronchitis.
  bronquitis por éter ether bronchitis.
  bronquitis exudativa exudative bronchitis.
  bronquitis fétida putrid bronchitis.
  bronquitis fibrinosa fibrinous bronchitis.
  bronquitis ftinoide phthinoid bronchitis.
  bronquitis hemorrágica hemorrhagic bronchitis.
  bronquitis laringotraqueal aguda acute laryngotracheal bronchitis.
  bronquitis mecánica mechanic bronchitis.
  bronquitis membranosa membranous bronchitis.
  bronquitis obliterante obliterative bronchitis, bronchitis obliterans.
  bronquitis plástica plastic bronchitis.
  bronquitis polipoide polypoid bronchitis.
  bronquitis pútrida putrid bronchitis.
  bronquitis productiva productive bronchitis.
  bronquitis seca dry bronchitis.
  bronquitis secundaria secondary bronchitis.
  bronquitis seudomembranosa pseudomembranous bronchitis.
  bronquitis sofocante suffocative bronchitis.
  bronquitis verminosa verminous bronchitis.
  bronquitis vesicular vesicular bronchitis.
brontofobia *f.* brontophobia.
brote¹ *m.* bout.
brote² *m.* bud.
  brote bronquial bronchial bud.
  brote caudal tail bud.
  brote dental tooth bud.
  brote de la extremidad limb bud.
  brote hepático liver bud.
  brote metanéfrico metanephric bud.

brote de los miembros limb bud.
brote perióstico periosteal bud.
brote pulmonar lung bud.
brote terminal end bud.
brote ureteral ureteric bud.
brote vascular vascular bud.
brote³ *m.* sprout.
  brote sincitial syncytial sprout.
brucelar *adj.* brucellar.
brucelergina *f.* brucellergin.
brucelina *f.* brucellin.
brucella *f.* brucella.
Brucella Brucella.
Brucellaceae Brucellaceae.
brucelosis *f.* brucellosis.
Brugia Brugia.
  Brugia malayi Brugia malayi.
  Brugia pahangi Brugia pahangi.
bruissement *m.* bruissement.
brunneroma *m.* brunneroma.
brunnerosis *f.* brunnerosis.
bruñido *m.* burnishing.
bruñidor *m.* burnisher.
bruxismo *m.* bruxism.
  bruxismo céntrico centric bruxism.
bruxomanía *f.* bruxomania.
Bryobia Bryobia.
  Bryobia praetiosa Bryobia praetiosa.
buaki *m.* buaki.
buba *f.* buba, bubas.
  buba madre buba madre.
bubas *f.* buba, bubas.
bubón *m.* bubo.
  bubón en bala, bubón en forma de bala bullet bubo.
  bubón chancroidal, bubón chancroide chancroid bubo, chancroidal bubo.
  bubón climático climatic bubo.
  bubón d'emblée bubo d'emblée.
  bubón gonorreico gonorrheal bubo.
  bubón indolente indolent bubo.
  bubón maligno malignant bubo.
  bubón parotídeo parotid bubo.
  bubón pestilencial pestilential bubo.
  bubón primario primary bubo.
  bubón primitivo primary bubo.
  bubón protopático primary bubo.
  bubón sifilítico syphilitic bubo.
  bubón simpático, bubón simple sympathetic bubo.
  bubón tropical tropical bubo.
  bubón venéreo venereal bubo.
  bubón virulento virulent bubo.
bubas *f.* bubas.
bubonalgia *f.* bubonalgia.
bubónico, -ca *adj.* bubonic.
bubonocele *m.* bubonocele.
bubónulo *m.* bubonulus.
bucal *adj.* buccal.
bucca cavi oris bucca cavi oris.
bucky *m.* bucky.
buckyterapia *f.* buckytherapy.
bucle *m.* loop.
  bucle de flujo-volumen flow-volume loop.
  bucle-r r-loop.
bucnemia *f.* bucnemia.
bucoaxial *adj.* buccoaxial.
bucoaxil *adj.* buccoaxial.
bucoaxiocervical *adj.* buccoaxiocervical.
bucoaxiogingival *adj.* buccoaxiogingival.
bucocervical *adj.* buccocervical.
bucoclinación *f.* buccoclination.
bucoclusal *adj.* buccoclusal.
bucoclusión *f.* buccoclusion.
bucodistal *adj.* buccodistal.

bucofaríngeo, -a *adj.* buccopharyngeal.
bucogingival *adj.* buccogingival.
bucoglosofaringitis *f.* buccoglossopharyngitis.
  bucoglosofaringitis seca buccoglossopharyngitis sicca.
bucolabial *adj.* buccolabial.
bucolingual *adj.* buccolingual.
bucomaxilar *adj.* buccomaxillary.
bucomesial *adj.* buccomesial.
bucooclusal *adj.* bucco-oclusal.
bucooclusión *m.* bucco-oclusion.
bucopulpar *adj.* buccopulpal.
bucorregresión *f.* buccoplacement.
bucoversión *f.* buccoversion.
buffer *m.* buffer.
bufoterapia *f.* bufotherapy.
bufotoxina *f.* bufotoxin.
buftalmía *f.* buphthalmia, buphthalmus.
buftalmos *m.* buphthalmos.
bujía[1] *f.* bougie.
  bujía acodada elbowed bougie.
  bujía agregada following bougie.
  bujía ahusada tapered bougie.
  bujía auditiva ear bougie.
  bujía cáustica caustic bougie.
  bujía de cera wax bougie.
  bujía cilíndrica cylindrical bougie.
  bujía cónica conic bougie.
  bujía dilatable dilating bougie.
  bujía elástica elastic bougie.
  bujía con extremo cubierto de cera wax-tipped bougie.
  bujía filiforme filiform bougie.
  bujía fusiforme fusiform bougie.
  bujía de Hurst Hurst's bougie.
  bujía en látigo whip bougie.
  bujía de Maloney Maloney's bougie.
  bujía móvil whip bougie.
  bujía con punta de cera wax-tipped bougie.
  bujía con punta de oliva olive-tipped bougie.
bujía[2] *f.* candela, candle.
bulbar *adj.* bulbar.
bulbiforme *adj.* bulbiform.
bulbitis *f.* bulbitis.
bulbo *m.* bulb, bulbus.
bulboauricular *adj.* bulboatrial.

bulboespinal *adj.* bulbospinal.
bulbogastrona *f.* bulbogastrone.
bulboide *adj.* bulboid.
bulboideo, -a *adj.* bulboid.
bulbonuclear *adj.* bulbonuclear.
bulbopontino, -na *adj.* bulbopontine.
bulbosacro *adj.* bulbosacral.
bulboso, -sa *adj.* bulbous.
bulbospinal *adj.* bulbospinal.
bulbouretral *adj.* bulbourethral.
bulbus *m.* bulb, bulbus.
bulesis *f.* bulesis.
bulimia *f.* bulimia.
  bulimia nerviosa bulimia nervosa.
bulímico, -ca *adj.* bulimic.
bulla *f.* bulla.
  bulla enfisematosa emphysematous bulla.
  bulla etmoidal ethmoid bulla, ethmoidal bulla, bulla ethmoidalis.
  bulla ossea bulla ossea.
  bulla pulmonar pulmonary bulla.
bullosis *f.* bullosis.
  bullosis diabética diabetic bullosis.
bulloso, -sa *adj.* bullous.
bungarotoxina *f.* bungarotoxin.
buniectomía *f.* bunioectomy.
buninoide *adj.* buninoid.
bunio *m.* bunion.
  bunio de sastre tailor's bunion.
bunionectomía *f.* bunionectomy.
  bunionectomía de Keller Keller bunionectomy.
  bunionectomía de Mayo Mayo bunionectomy.
bunionete *m.* bunionette.
bunodonte *adj.* bunodont.
bunoselenodonte *adj.* bunoselenodont.
Bunyaviridae Bunyaviridae.
burbuja *f.* life island.
burbuja de aire *f.* venous air trap.
buret *f.* buret, burette.
bureta *f.* buret, burette.
burette *f.* buret, burette.
burquismo *m.* burquism.
bursa *f.* bursa.
bursal *adj.* bursal.
bursalogía *f.* bursalogy.
bursectomía *f.* bursectomy.
bursitis *f.* bursitis.

bursitis adhesiva adhesive bursitis.
bursitis anserina anserine bursitis.
bursitis aquilea, bursitis aquiliana Achilles bursitis.
bursitis aquilea anterior anterior Achilles bursitis.
bursitis aquilea posterior posterior Achilles bursitis.
bursitis calcaneana calcaneal bursitis.
bursitis calcificada calcific bursitis.
bursitis epiploica omental bursitis.
bursitis escapulohumeral scapulohumeral bursitis.
bursitis faríngea pharyngeal bursitis.
bursitis isquioglútea ischiogluteal bursitis.
bursitis oleocraniana, bursitis del olécranon olecranal bursitis.
bursitis omental omental bursitis.
bursitis poplítea popliteal bursitis.
bursitis prerrotuliana prepatellar bursitis.
bursitis radiohumeral radiohumeral bursitis.
bursitis retrocalcánea retrocalcaneal bursitis.
bursitis subacromial subacromial bursitis.
bursitis subdeltoidea subdeltoid bursitis.
bursitis de Thornwaldt, bursitis de Tornwaldt Tornwaldt's bursitis, Thornwaldt's bursitis.
bursografía *f.* bursography.
bursográfico, -ca *adj.* bursographic.
bursograma *m.* bursogram.
bursolito *m.* bursolith.
bursopatía *f.* bursopathy.
bursotomía *f.* bursotomy.
bursotomografía *f.* bursotomography.
burst-supression *m.* burst-supression.
bursula bursula.
  bursula testium bursula testium.
buserelina *f.* buserelin.
BUT *m.* BUT.
butiráceo, -a *adj.* butyraceous.
butiroide *adj.* butyroid.
butirómetro *m.* butyrometer.
butiroscopio *m.* butyroscope.
butiroso, -sa *adj.* butyrous.
Buttiauxella Buttiauxella.
Butyribacterium Butyribacterium.
by-pass *m.* by-pass.

cabalgamiento *m.* overriding.
  cabalgamiento del dedo gordo overtoe.
cabeceo *m.* head-nodding.
cabello *m.* hair, capillus, pilus.
capillus *m.* hair, capillus, pilus.
cabestrillo *m.* sling.
cabeza *f.* head, caput.
  cabeza de bulldog bulldog head.
  cabeza cuadrada square head, caput quadratum.
  cabeza de medusa medusa head, caput medusae.
  cabeza en reloj de arena hourglass head.
  cabeza en silla de montar saddle head.
cacaerómetro *m.* cacaerometer.
cachectomía *f.* lumpectomy.
cachet cachet.
cacoético, -ca *adj.* cacoethic.
cacogénesis *f.* cacogenesis.
cacogénico, -ca *adj.* cacogenic.
cacogeusia *f.* cacogeusia.
cacomelia *f.* cacomelia.
cacomorfosis *f.* cacomorphosis.
cacoplásico, -ca *adj.* cacoplastic.
cacorrítmico, -ca *adj.* cacorhythmic.
cacosmia *f.* cacosmia.
cacostomía *f.* cacostomia.
cacotrofia *f.* cacotrophy.
cacumen *m.* cacumen.
cacuminal *adj.* cacuminal.
cadáver *m.* cadaver.
cadavérico, -ca *adj.* cadaveric, cadaverous.
cadena *f.* chain.
cadera *f.* hip, coxa.
  cadera de resorte snapping hip.
cadherinas *f.* cadherins.
cadmiosis *f.* cadmiosis.
caduca *f.* caduca.
caduceo *m.* caduceus.
caecum caecum, cecum.
caecus caecus.
cafeinismo *m.* caffeinism.
cafeísmo *m.* caffeinism.
caída de espaldas *f.* swayback.
caja *f.* box.
  caja de CAAT CAAT box.
  caja de CENP-B CENP-B box.
  caja de Skinner Skinner box.
  caja superior cope.
  caja tata tata box.
calacio *m.* chalazion.
calambre *m.* cramp.
  calambre accesorio accessory cramp.
  calambre por calor heat cramp.
  calambre de camarero waiter's cramp.
  calambre de las costureras seamstress' cramp.
  calambre por decúbito recumbency cramp.
  calambre de los escritores writers' cramp.
  calambre de fogonero stoker's cramp.
  calambre intermitente intermittent cramp.

  calambre de minero miner's cramp.
  calambre de músico musician's cramp.
  calambre de pianista pianist's cramp.
  calambre de relojero watchmaker's cramp.
  calambre de los sastres tailor's cramp.
  calambre de violinista violinist's cramp.
cálamo *m.* calamus.
calasia *f.* chalasia, chalasis.
calasis *f.* chalasis.
calastodermia *f.* chalastodermia.
calcaneítis *f.* calcaneitis.
calcáneo *m.* calcaneus.
calcáneo, -a *adj.* calcaneal, calcanean.
calcaneoapofisitis *f.* calcaneoapophysitis.
calcaneoastragalino, -na *adj.* calcaneoastragaloid.
calcaneoastragaloide *adj.* calcaneoastragaloid.
calcaneoastragaloideo, -a *adj.* calcaneoastragaloid.
calcaneocavo *m.* calcaneocavus.
calcaneocuboide *adj.* calcaneocuboid.
calcaneocuboideo, -a *adj.* calcaneocuboid.
calcaneodinia *f.* calcaneodynia, calcanodynia.
calcaneoescafoideo, -a *adj.* calcaneoscaphoid.
calcaneonavicular *adj.* calcaneonavicular.
calcaneoperoneo, -a *adj.* calcaneofibular.
calcaneoplantar *adj.* calcaneoplantar.
calcaneoscafoideo, -a *adj.* calcaneoscaphoid.
calcaneotibial *adj.* calcaneotibial.
calcanodinia *f.* calcanodynia.
calcar calcar.
calcáreo, -a *adj.* calcareous.
calcarino, -na *adj.* calcarine.
calcariuria *f.* calcariuria.
calcaroide *adj.* calcaroid.
calcemia *f.* calcemia.
calcergia *f.* calcergy.
calcibilia *f.* calcibilia.
cálcico, -ca *adj.* calcic.
calcicosilicosis *f.* calcicosilicosis.
calcicosis *f.* calcicosis.
calcifames *f.* calcifames.
calcifero, -ra *adj.* calciferous.
calcificación *f.* calcification.
  calcificación en cáscara de huevo eggshell calcification.
  calcificación distrófica dystrophic calcification.
  calcificación medial de Mönckeberg Mönckeberg's medial calcification.
  calcificación metastásica metastatic calcification.
  calcificación de Mönckeberg Mönckeberg's calcification.
  calcificación patológica pathologic calcification.
  calcificación de la pulpa pulp calcification.
calcificar *v.* calcify.
calcifiláctico, -ca *adj.* calciphylactic.
calcifilaxia *f.* calciphylaxis.

  calcifilaxia general systemic calciphylaxis.
  calcifilaxia tópica topical calciphylaxis.
  calcifilaxia sistémica systemic calciphylaxis.
calcifilia *f.* calciphilia.
calcígero, -ra *adj.* calcigerous.
calcímetro *m.* calcimeter.
calcinación *f.* calcination.
calcinosis *f.* calcinosis.
  calcinosis circunscrita calcinosis circumscripta.
  calcinosis cutánea calcinosis cutis.
  calcinosis distrófica dystrophic calcinosis.
  calcinosis intersticial calcinosis interstitialis.
  calcinosis intervertebral calcinosis intervertebralis.
  calcinosis reversible reversible calcinosis.
  calcinosis tumoral tumoral calcinosis.
  calcinosis universal calcinosis universalis.
calcio *m.* calcium.
calciocinesis *f.* calciokinesis.
calciocinético, -ca *adj.* calciokinetic.
calcioglóbulo *m.* calcioglobule.
calciorraquia *f.* calciorrhachia.
calciotropismo *m.* calciotropism.
calcipéctico, -ca *adj.* calcipectic.
calcipenia *f.* calcipenia.
calcipénico, -ca *adj.* calcipenic.
calcipexia *f.* calcipexia, calcipexis, calcipexy.
calcipéxico, -ca *adj.* calcipexic.
calcipexis *f.* calcipexis, calcipexy.
calciprivia *f.* calciprivia.
calciprivo, -va *adj.* calciprivic.
calciterapia *f.* calcitherapy.
calciuria *f.* calciuria.
calcoglobulina *f.* calcoglobulin.
calcodinia *f.* calcodynia.
calcóforo, -ra *adj.* calcophorous.
calcosferito *m.* calcospherite.
calcosis *f.* chalcosis.
  calcosis del cristalino chalcosis lentis.
calcular *adj.* calculary.
cálculo *m.* gallstone, calculus.
  cálculo de ácido úrico uric acid calculus.
  cálculo alternante alternating calculus.
  cálculo alvino alvine calculus.
  cálculo amigdalino tonsillar calculus.
  cálculo de apatita apatite calculus.
  cálculo articular articular calculus.
  cálculo artrítico arthritic calculus.
  cálculo en asta de ciervo staghorn calculus.
  cálculo biliar biliary calculus.
  cálculo biliar opacificador opacifying gallstone.
  cálculo biliar silencioso silent gallstone.
  cálculo bronquial bronchial calculus.
  cálculo cardíaco cardiac calculus.
  cálculo cerebral cerebral calculus.
  cálculo de cistina cystine calculus.
  cálculo de colesterol cholesterol calculus.
  cálculo combinado, cálculo compuesto combination calculus.

cálculo coraliforme, cálculo coralino coral calculus.
cálculo por decúbito decubitus calculus.
cálculo dendrítico dendritic calculus.
cálculo dental, cálculo dentario dental calculus.
cálculo embolsado pocketed calculus.
cálculo enquistado encysted calculus.
cálculo espermático spermatic calculus.
cálculo de estruvita struvite calculus.
cálculo faríngeo pharyngeal calculus.
cálculo de fibrina fibrin calculus.
cálculo fosfático, cálculo de fosfato phosphate calculus, phosphatic calculus.
cálculo gástrico gastric calculus, stomachic calculus.
cálculo gonecquístico, cálculo gonoquístico gonecystic calculus.
cálculo hematógeno, cálculo hémico hematogenic calculus, hemic calculus.
cálculo hepático hepatic calculus.
cálculo de índigo indigo calculus.
cálculo de infección, cálculo infeccioso infection calculus.
cálculo intestinal intestinal calculus.
cálculo lácteo lacteal calculus.
cálculo mamario mammary calculus.
cálculo de matriz matrix calculus.
cálculo metabólico metabolic calculus.
cálculo en mora, cálculo moriforme mulberry calculus.
cálculo nasal nasal calculus.
cálculo de oxalato oxalate calculus.
cálculo pancreático pancreatic calculus.
cálculo pleural pleural calculus.
cálculo prepucial preputial calculus.
cálculo prostático prostatic calculus.
cálculo pulmonar lung calculus.
cálculo de la pulpa pulp calculus.
cálculo ramificado branched calculus.
cálculo renal renal calculus.
cálculo renal primario primary renal calculus.
cálculo renal secundario secondary renal calculus.
cálculo salival salivary calculus.
cálculo sanguíneo blood calculus.
cálculo serumal, cálculo seruminal serumal calculus.
cálculo subgingival subgingival calculus.
cálculo submorfo submorphous calculus.
cálculo supragingival supragingival calculus.
cálculo tonsilar tonsillar calculus.
cálculo de urato urate calculus.
cálculo de la uretra, cálculo uretral urethral calculus.
cálculo urinario urinary calculus.
cálculo uterino uterine calculus.
cálculo de la vejiga bladder calculus.
cálculo vesical vesical calculus.
cálculo vesicoprostático vesicoprostatic calculus.
cálculo de wedelita Weddellite calculus.
cálculo de whewelita Whewellite calculus.
cálculo xantínico xanthic calculus.
calculosis f. calculosis.
calculoso, -sa adj. calculous.
calculus calculus.
caldo m. bouillon, broth.
calefaciente calefacient.
calentura f. calentura, calenture.
calibeado, -da adj. chalybeate.
calibración f. calibration.
calibrador m. gauge.
calibrador de Boley Boley gauge.
calibrador de catéteres catheter gauge.

calibrador de mordida bite gauge.
calibrador de tensiones strain gauge.
calibrador de zonas retentivas undercut gauge.
calicectasia f. caliectasis, caliectasis, calyectasis.
calicectasis f. caliectasis, caliectasis, calyectasis.
calicectomía f. caliectomy, calycectomy, caliectomy.
caliciforme adj. caliciform, calyciform.
Caliciviridae Caliciviridae.
Calicivirus Calicivirus.
calicoplastia f. calioplasty, calycoplasty, calyoplasty.
calicosis f. chalicosis.
calicotomía f. calicotomy, caliotomy, calycotomy.
calicreinógeno m. kallikreinogen.
calículo m. calycle, caliculus.
caliculus m. calycle, caliculus.
caliectasia f. caliectasis, calyectasis.
caliectasis f. caliectasis, calyectasis.
caliectomía f. caliectomy.
caliemia f. kaliemia.
caligación f. caligation.
calígeno, -na adj. kaligenous.
caligo m. caligo.
calinoplastia f. chalinoplasty.
caliopenia f. kaliopenia.
caliopénico, -ca adj. kaliopenic.
calioplastia f. calioplasty, calyoplasty.
caliorrafia f. caliorrhaphy.
caliotomía f. caliotomy.
caliuresis f. kaliuresis.
caliurético, -ca adj. kaliuretic.
cáliz m. calyx.
calyx m. calyx.
cáliz glaucomatoso glaucomatous cup.
Callimastix Callimastix.
Calliphora Calliphora.
Calliphoridae Calliphoridae.
callo m. callus.
callo de amianto asbestos callus.
callo blando soft callus.
callo central central callus.
callo definitivo definitive callus.
callo duro hard callus.
callo envainante ensheathing callus.
callo externo external callus.
callo exuberante exuberant callus.
callo intermedio intermediate callus.
callo interno inner callus, internal callus.
callo invaginante ensheathing callus.
callo medular medullary callus.
callo mielógeno myelogenous callus.
callo óseo bony callus.
callo permanente permanent callus.
callo provisional provisional callus.
callo de semilla seed callus.
callo temporal temporary callus.
callosidad f. callosity, callositas.
calloso, -sa¹ adj. callous.
calloso, -sa² adj. callosal.
callosomarginal adj. callosomarginal.
calmante m. calmative.
calmodulina f. calmodulin.
calor m. heat, calor.
calor de combustión heat of combustion.
calor de compresión heat of compression.
calor de conducción, calor conductivo conductive heat.
calor de convección, calor convectivo convective heat.
calor de conversión conversive heat.
calor de cristalización heat of crystallization.
calor de disociación heat of dissociation.

calor específico specific heat.
calor de evaporación heat of evaporation.
calor febril calor febrilis.
calor fervens calor fervens.
calor de formación heat of formation.
calor de fusión heat of fusion.
calor inicial initial heat.
calor innato innate heat, calor innatus.
calor interno calor internus.
calor latente latent heat.
calor latente de fusión latent heat of fusion.
calor latente de sublimación latent heat of sublimation.
calor latente de vaporización latent heat of vaporization.
calor molecular molecular heat.
calor mordente calor mordax, calor mordicans.
calor radiante radiant heat.
calor de recuperación recovery heat.
calor de relajación delayed heat.
calor seco dry heat.
calor sensible sensible heat.
calor de sublimación heat of sublimation.
calor de vaporización heat of vaporization.
calorescencia f. calorescence.
caloría f. calorie.
calórico, -ca adj. caloric.
calorifaciente adj. calorifacient.
calorificación f. caloricity.
calorífico, -ca adj. calorific.
calorígeno, -na adj. calorigenetic, calorigenic.
calorimetría f. calorimetry.
calorimetría directa direct calorimetry.
calorimetría indirecta indirect calorimetry.
calorimétrico, -ca adj. calorimetric.
calorímetro m. calorimeter.
calorímetro a bomba, calorímetro de bomba bomb calorimeter.
calorímetro compensado compensating calorimeter.
calorímetro respiratorio respiration calorimeter.
caloripuntura f. caloripuncture.
caloriscopio m. caloriscope.
caloritrópico, -ca adj. caloritropic.
calostración f. colostration.
calóstrico, -ca adj. colostric.
calostro m. colostrum.
calostro gravídico colostrum gravidum.
calostro puerperal colostrum puerperarum.
calostrorrea f. colostrorrhea.
calostroso, -sa adj. colostrous.
calota f. calotte.
calquitis f. chalkitis.
calsecuestrina f. calsequestrin.
calvaria f. calvaria.
calvárico, -ca adj. calvarial.
calvario m. calvaria.
Calvatia Calvatia.
calvicie f. baldness, calvities.
calvicie congénita congenital baldness.
calvicie de distribución masculina male pattern baldness.
calvicie masculina común common male baldness.
calvicie del pubis pubic baldness.
calvo, -va adj. bald.
Calymmatobacteria Calymmatobacterium.
Calymmatobacteria granulomatis Calymmatobacterium granulomatis.
cámara f. chamber, camera.
cámara acústica acoustic camera, acoustic chamber.
cámara aérea de ionización equivalente

air-equivalent ionization camera, air-equivalent ionization chamber.

cámara de altitud, cámara de altura altitude camera, altitude chamber.

cámara anecoica anechoic chamber.

cámara de Anger Anger camera.

cámara de Boyden Boyden chamber.

cámara de burbujas bubble camera.

cámara de centelleos scintillation camera.

cámara contadora de Abbé-Zeiss, cámara cuentaglóbulos de Abbé-Zeiss Abbé-Zeiss counting camera, Abbé-Zeiss counting chamber.

cámara contadora de Thoma-Zeiss, cámara cuentaglóbulos de Thoma-Zeiss Thoma's counting chamber, Thoma-Zeiss counting chamber.

cámara contadora de Zappert Zappert counting chamber.

cámara cuentaglóbulos counting camera.

cámara dedal thimble camera.

cámara de descompresión decompression chamber.

cámara detonante detonating camera.

cámara de difusión diffusion camera, diffusion chamber.

cámara estándar de ionización standard ionization camera.

cámara gamma gamma camera.

cámara gástrica magenblase.

cámara de gran altitud high altitude chamber.

cámara de Haldane Haldane chamber, Haldane camera.

cámara hiperbárica hyperbaric chamber, hyperbaric camera.

cámara de ionización ionization chamber, ionization camera.

cámara de ionización de aire libre free-air ionization camera, free-air ionization chamber.

cámara letal lethal camera.

cámara lúcida, cámara clara camera lucida.

cámara de nube cloud camera.

cámara de Petroff-Hauser Petroff-Hauser counting camera.

cámara pulpar pulp camera, pulp chamber.

cámara sinoauricular sinuatrial chamber.

cámara de Storm Van Leeuwen Storm Van Leeuwen camera, Storm Van Leeuwen chamber.

cámara de Zappert Zappert's chamber.

cambiador *m.* exchanger.

cambiador de calor heat exchanger.

cambio *m.* change.

cambio de Armanni-Ebstein Armanni-Ebstein change.

cambio de Baggenstoss Baggenstoss change.

cambio en color de arlequín harlequin color change.

cambio de Crooke, cambio de Crooke-Russel Crooke's change, Crooke-Russel change.

cambio graso fatty change.

cambio hialino de Crooke Crooke's hyaline change.

cambio trófico trophic change.

cambium cambium.

camecefalia *f.* chamecephaly.

camecefálico, -ca *adj.* chamecephalic.

camecéfalo, -la *adj.* chamecephalous.

cameprosopia *f.* chameprosopy.

cameprosópico, -ca *adj.* chameprosopic.

cameprósopo, -pa *adj.* chameprosopic.

camilla *f.* litter, stretcher.

campana *f.* bell.

campilobacteriosis *f.* campylobacteriosis.

campilodactilia *f.* campylodactyly.

campilognatia *f.* campylognathia.

campimetría *f.* campimetry.

campímetro *m.* campimeter.

campo *m.* field.

campo auditivo auditory field.

campo de Broca Broca's field.

campo de Cohnheim Cohnheim's field.

campo citoarquitectónico de Brodmann, campo cortical de Brodmann Brodmann's field.

campo de fijación field of fixation.

campo de Flechsig Flechsig's field.

campo gamma gamma field.

campo de gran aumento high-power field.

campo de individualización individuation field.

campo magnético magnetic field.

campo microscópico, campo de un microscopio microscopic field.

campo mielogenético myelinogenetic field.

campo morfogenético morphogenetic field.

campo nervioso nerve field.

campo de poco aumento low-power field.

campo ungueal primario primary nail field.

campo de visión, campo visual visual field.

campo de visión cribriforme cribriform field of vision.

campoespasmo *m.* campospasm.

campotomía *f.* campotomy.

camptocormia *f.* camptocormia, camptocormy.

camptodactilia *f.* camptodactylia, camptodactylism, camptodactyly.

camptoespasmo *m.* camptospasm.

camptospasmo *m.* camptospasm.

camptomelia *f.* camptomelia.

camptomélico, -ca *adj.* camptomelic.

Campylobacter Campylobacter.

campylobacteriosis *f.* campylobacteriosis.

canabismo *m.* cannabism.

canal *m.* canal, canalis.

canal auriculoventricular persistente persistent atrioventricular canal.

canal iónico ion channel.

canal de irrupción irruption canal.

canal transnexo transnexus channel.

canalicular *adj.* canalicular.

canaliculitis *f.* caniculitis.

canaliculización *f.* canaliculization.

canalículo *m.* canaliculus.

canalículo biliar bile canaliculus, biliary canaliculus.

canaliculus *m.* canaliculus.

canaliculodacriocistostomía *f.* canaliculodacryocystostomy.

canaliculorrinostomia *f.* canaliculorhinostomy.

canalización *f.* canalization.

canalón *m.* through.

canasta *f.* canister.

canceloso, -sa *adj.* cancellated, cancellous.

cáncer *m.* cancer.

cáncer acinoso acinar cancer, acinous cancer.

cáncer acuático, cáncer de agua water cancer.

cáncer adenoideo epithelial cancer.

cáncer por alquitrán, cáncer por brea pitch-worker's cancer, tar cancer.

cáncer alveolar alveolar adenocarcinoma.

cáncer por anilina aniline cancer.

cáncer apinoide apinoid cancer.

cáncer atrófico atrophicans cancer.

cáncer de betel, cáncer por betel betel cancer.

cáncer blando soft cancer.

cáncer del buyo del carrillo buyo cheek cancer.

cáncer canalicular duct cancer.

cáncer de células fusiformes spindle cell cancer.

cáncer cerebriforme cerebrifom cancer.

cáncer en chaleco jacket cancer.

cáncer cicatricial scar cancer.

cáncer cicatricial de los pulmones scar cancer of the lungs.

cáncer coloidal, cáncer coloide colloid cancer, colloidal cancer.

cáncer por contacto contact cancer.

cáncer conyugal conjugal cancer.

cáncer en coraza cancer en cuirasse.

cáncer en corsé corset cancer.

cáncer dendrítico dendritic cancer.

cáncer de deshollinador chimney-sweep's cancer.

cáncer de a dos cancer à deux.

cáncer duro hard cancer.

cáncer endotelial endothelial cancer.

cáncer epidérmico, cáncer epidermoide epidermoid cancer.

cáncer epitelial epithelial cancer.

cáncer escirroso scirrhous cancer.

cáncer en escudo cancer en cuirasse.

cáncer familiar familial cancer.

cáncer de los fumadores de pipa pipe-smoker's cancer.

cáncer fungoso fungous cancer.

cáncer de hígado liver cancer.

cáncer in situ cancer in situ.

cáncer kang, cáncer kangri kang cancer, kangri cancer.

cáncer latente latent cancer.

cáncer de mama breast cancer.

cáncer medular medullary cancer.

cáncer melanótico melanotic cancer.

cáncer mucinoso mucinous cancer.

cáncer del muñón stump cancer.

cáncer negro black cancer.

cáncer oculto occult cancer.

cáncer óseo bone cancer.

cáncer papilar papillary carcinoma.

cáncer de parafina, cáncer por parafina paraffin cancer.

cáncer por pipa de arcilla claypipe cancer.

cáncer quístico cystic cancer.

cáncer de pulmón lung cancer.

cáncer de los radiólogos roetgenologist's cancer.

cáncer solanoide scirrhous carcinoma.

cáncer telangiectásico telangiectatic cancer.

cáncer de los tejedores mule-spinner's cancer.

cáncer terebrante boring cancer.

cáncer de los trabajadores de anilina aniline cancer, dye worker's cancer.

cáncer tubular tubular cancer.

canceremia *f.* canceremia.

cancericida *adj.* cancericidal, cancerocidal.

cancerígeno, -na *adj.* cancerigenic, cancerogenic.

cancerismo *m.* cancerism.

cancerización *f.* canceration, cancerization.

cancerocida *adj.* cancerocidal.

cancerofobia *f.* cancerphobia.

cancerología *f.* cancerology.

canceroso, -sa *adj.* cancerous.

cancriforme *adj.* cancriform.

cancroide *m. y adj.* cancroid.

cancrum cancrum.

cancrum nasi cancrum nasi.

cancrum oris cancrum oris.

candela *f.* candle, candela.

candicans *adj.* candicans.

Candida *f.* Candida.
candidemia *f.* candidemia.
candidiasis *f.* candidiasis.
  candidiasis cutánea cutaneous candidiasis.
  candidiasis endocárdica endocardial candidiasis.
candídide *f.* candidid.
candidiosis *f.* candidiasis.
candidosis *f.* candidosis.
candiduria *f.* candiduria.
canescente *adj.* canescent.
canforismo *m.* camphorism.
canicie *f.* canities.
  canicie canities canities canities.
  canicie circunscrita canities circumscripta.
  canicie rápida rapid canities.
  canicie ungular canities unguium.
canilla *f.* spool.
  canilla de Carassini Carassini's spool.
caniniforme *adj.* caniniform.
canino *m.* canine.
cannabis *m.* cannabis.
cannabismo *m.* cannabism.
canon *m.* canon.
cantariasis *f.* canthariasis.
cantárida *f.* cantharis.
cantaridina *f.* cantharidin.
cantaridismo *m.* cantharidism.
cantectomía *f.* canthectomy.
cantitis *f.* canthitis.
canto *m.* canthus.
cantólisis *f.* cantholisis.
cantoplastia *f.* canthoplasty.
cantorrafia *f.* canthorrhaphy.
cantotomía *f.* canthotomy.
cantus galli cantus galli.
cánula *f.* cannula.
  cánula de doble corriente perfusion cannula.
  cánula de granulación granulation cannula.
  cánula de Karman Karman cannula.
  cánula de Kuhn Kuhn's cannula.
  cánula para lavado de arrastre washout cannula.
  cánula de Lindemann Lindemann's cannula.
  cánula de perfusión perfusion cannula.
  cánula de traqueostomía tracheostomy cannula.
canulación *f.* cannulation.
canulización *f.* cannulization.
caolinosis *f.* kaolinosis.
capa¹ *f.* coat.
capa² *f.* layer.
capacidad *f.* capacity.
  capacidad buffer buffer capacity.
  capacidad contractual contractual capacity.
  capacidad de difusión diffusion capacity.
  capacidad de fijación de hierro (CFH) iron-binding capacity (IBC).
  capacidad hipnótica hypnotic capacity.
  capacidad inspiratoria inspiratory capacity.
  capacidad de oxígeno oxygen capacity.
  capacidad pulmonar total (CPT) total lung capacity (TLC).
  capacidad residual residual capacity.
  capacidad residual funcional (CRF) functional residual capacity (FRC).
  capacidad respiratoria respiratory capacity.
  capacidad térmica heat capacity, thermal capacity.
  capacidad vital (CV), capacidad vital forzada (CVF) vital capacity (VC), forced vital capacity (FVC).
capacitación *f.* capacitation.
capacitancia *f.* capacitance.
cap-z z-cap.

capelina *f.* capeline.
capilar *m.* capillary.
capilarectasia *f.* capillarectasia.
capilariasis *f.* capillariasis.
  capilariasis intestinal intestinal capillariasis.
capilaridad *f.* capillarity.
capilarioscopia *f.* capillarioscopy.
capilaritis *f.* capillaritis.
capilaropatía *f.* capillaopathy.
capilarioscopia *f.* capillaroscopy, capillarioscopy.
capilaroscopia *f.* capillaroscopy, capillarioscopy.
Capillaria philippinensis Capillaria philippinensis.
capistración *f.* capistration.
capitado, -da *adj.* capitate.
capital *adj.* capital.
capitellum capitellum.
capitonaje *m.* capitonnage.
capitopedal *adj.* capitopedal.
capitular *adj.* capitular.
capitulum capitulum.
Capnocytophaga Capnocytophaga.
capnófilo, -la *adj.* capnophilic.
capnógrafo *m.* capnograph.
capnograma *m.* capnogram.
capriloquia *f.* capriloquism.
capriloquismo *m.* capriloquism.
caprizante *adj.* caprizant.
cápsida *f.* capsid.
cápside *m.* capsid.
capsitis *f.* capsitis.
capsómero *m.* capsomer, capsomere.
cápsula, capsula *f.* capsule, capsula.
  cápsula adherente adherent capsule.
  cápsula auditiva auditory capsule.
  cápsula bacteriana bacterial capsule.
  cápsula de Bowman Bowman's capsule.
  cápsula de Crosby Crosby capsule.
  cápsula lenticular vascular, capsula vasculosa lentis capsula vasculosa lentis.
  cápsula nasal nasal capsule.
  cápsula óptica optic capsule.
  cápsula ótica otic capsule.
  cápsula radiotelemétrica radiotelemetering capsule.
capsulación *f.* capsulation.
capsular *adj.* capsular.
capsulectomía *f.* capsulectomy.
capsulitis *f.* capsulitis.
  capsulitis adhesiva adhesive capsulitis.
  capsulitis hepática hepatic capsulitis.
capsulolenticular *adj.* capsulolenticular.
capsuloplastia *f.* capsuloplasty.
capsulorrafia *f.* capsulorrhaphy.
capsulotomía *f.* capsulotomy.
  capsulotomía renal renal capsulotomy.
capsulótomo *m.* capsulotome.
captación *f.* captation, uptake.
captura *f.* capture.
  captura auricular atrial capture.
  captura de electrones electron capture.
  captura k k capture.
  captura ventricular ventricular capture.
capuchón *m.* cap.
caput caput.
  caput quadratum square head, caput quadratum.
  caput medusae medusa head, caput medusae.
caquéctico, -ca *adj.* cachectic.
caquexia *f.* cachexia.
  caquexia acuosa cachexia aquosa.
  caquexia africana geophagia, geophagy.
  caquexia aftosa cachexia aphthosa.

  caquexia cancerosa cancerous cachexia.
  caquexia estrumipriva cachexia strumipriva.
  caquexia exoftálmica cachexia exophthalmica.
  caquexia fluórica fluoric cachexia.
  caquexia hipofisaria pituitary cachexia.
  caquexia hipofisopriva cachexia hypophyseopriva.
  caquexia mercurial cachexia mercurialis.
  caquexia de los negros geophagia, geophagy.
  caquexia nerviosa anorexia nervosa.
  caquexia palúdica malarial cachexia.
  caquexia pituitaria pituitary cachexia.
  caquexia suprarrenal cachexia suprarrenalis.
  caquexia tiroidea cachexia thyroidea.
  caquexia tiropriva cachexia thyropriva.
  caquexia verminosa verminous cachexia.
caquidrosis *f.* kakidrosis.
cara *f.* face.
  cara articular facies articularis.
  cara hipocrática hippocratic face.
  cara de luna llena moon face.
  cara de máscara masklike face.
  cara de pájaro bird face.
  cara de plato dish face.
  cara de sapo frog face.
  cara de vaca cow face.
caracol *m.* cochlea.
carácter *m.* character.
  carácter compuesto compound character.
  carácter dominante dominant character.
  carácter hereditario inherited character.
  carácter ligado al sexo sex-linked character.
  carácter mendeliano Mendelian character.
  carácter recesivo recessive character.
  carácter sexual primario primary sex character.
  carácter sexual secundario secondary sex character.
característica *f.* characteristic.
  característica operativa receptora (ROC) receiver operating characteristic (ROC).
característico, -ca *adj.* characteristic.
caracterización *f.* characterization.
  caracterización protésica denture characterization.
carata *f.* carate.
carateas *f.* carate.
carbohemia *f.* carbohemia.
carbohemoglobina *f.* carbhemoglobin, carbohemoglobin.
carbohidraturia *f.* carbohydraturia.
carbolismo *m.* carbolism.
carboluria *f.* carboluria.
carbometría *f.* carbometry.
carbómetro *m.* carbometer.
carbonemia *f.* carbohemia.
carbono *m.* carbon.
carbonometría *f.* carbonometry.
carbonómetro *m.* carbonometer.
carbonuria *f.* carbonuria.
carboxihemoglobina *f.* carboxyhemoglobin.
carboxihemoglobinemia *f.* carboxyhemoglobinemia.
carboxilación *f.* carboxylation.
carbunco *m.* anthrax.
  carbunco cerebral cerebral anthrax.
  carbunco cutáneo cutaneous anthrax.
  carbunco gastrointestinal gastrointestinal anthrax.
  carbunco por inhalación inhalational anthrax.
  carbunco intestinal intestinal anthrax.
  carbunco meníngeo meningeal anthrax.
  carbunco pulmonar pulmonary anthrax.

carcinoembrionario, -ria *adj.* carcinoembryonic.

carcinelcosis *f.* carcinelcosis.

carcinemia *f.* carcinemia.

carcinofilia *f.* carcinophilia.

carcinofobia *f.* carcinophobia.

carcinogénesis *f.* carcinogenesis.

carcinogenia *f.* carcinogenesis.

carcinogénico, -ca *adj.* carcinogenic.

carcinógeno *m.* carcinogen.

  carcinógeno completo complet carcinogen.

carcinoide *m.* carcinoid.

carcinolítico, -ca *adj.* carcinolytic.

carcinólisis *f.* carcinolysis.

carcinología *f.* cancerology.

carcinoma *m.* carcinoma.

  carcinoma acinar, carcinoma acinoso acinar carcinoma, acinous carcinoma.

  carcinoma acinocelular acinic cell carcinoma.

  carcinoma adenoide escamocelular adenoid squamous cell carcinoma.

  carcinoma adenoide quístico adenoid cystic carcinoma.

  carcinoma alveolar alveolar cell carcinoma.

  carcinoma anaplásico anaplastic carcinoma.

  carcinoma anexal adnexal carcinoma.

  carcinoma apocrino apocrine carcinoma.

  carcinoma basaloide basaloid carcinoma.

  carcinoma basiescamoso basosquamous carcinoma.

  carcinoma basocelular basal cell carcinoma.

  carcinoma basoescamocelular basal squamous cell carcinoma.

  carcinoma broncoalveolar bronchioalveolar carcinoma.

  carcinoma broncogénico bronchogenic carcinoma.

  carcinoma bronquiolar bronchiolar carcinoma.

  carcinoma de células de anillo de sello signet-ring cell carcinoma.

  carcinoma de células claras del riñón clear cell carcinoma of the kidney.

  carcinoma de células gigantes giant cell carcinoma.

  carcinoma de células grandes large cell carcinoma.

  carcinoma de células en grano de arena, carcinoma de células pequeñas oat cell carcinoma, small cell carcinoma.

  carcinoma de células de la granulosa del ovario granulosa-theca cell tumor.

  carcinoma de células hepáticas liver cell carcinoma.

  carcinoma de células hepáticas fibrolaminillares fibrolamellar liver cell carcinoma.

  carcinoma de células de Hürthle Hürthle cell carcinoma.

  carcinoma de células renales renal cell carcinoma.

  carcinoma de células de transición transitional cell carcinoma.

  carcinoma cicatricial scar carcinoma.

  carcinoma cilindromatoso cylindromatous carcinoma.

  carcinoma coloide colloid carcinoma.

  carcinoma del conducto de Wolff Wolffian duct carcinoma.

  carcinoma corticosuprarrenal adrenal cortical carcinoma.

  carcinoma ductal duct carcinoma, ductal carcinoma.

  carcinoma embrionario embryonal carcinoma.

  carcinoma encefaloide encephaloid cancer.

  carcinoma endometrioide endometrioid carcinoma.

  carcinoma epidermoide epidermoid carcinoma.

  carcinoma epitelial epithelial cancer.

  carcinoma escamocelular squamous cell carcinoma.

  carcinoma escamoso squamous cell carcinoma.

  carcinoma escirroso scirrhous carcinoma.

  carcinoma ex adenoma pleomórfico carcinoma ex pleomorphic adenoma.

  carcinoma exofítico exophytic carcinoma.

  carcinoma folicular follicular carcinoma.

  carcinoma fusocelular spindle cell carcinoma.

  carcinoma gigantocelular del tiroides giant cell carcinoma of the thyroid gland.

  carcinoma de glándulas sudoríparas sweat gland carcinoma.

  carcinoma hepatocelular hepatocellular carcinoma.

  carcinoma inflamatorio inflammatory carcinoma.

  carcinoma in situ carcinoma in situ.

  carcinoma intraductal intraductal carcinoma.

  carcinoma intraepidérmico intraepidermal carcinoma.

  carcinoma intraepitelial intraepithelial carcinoma.

  carcinoma invasor invasive carcinoma.

  carcinoma juvenil juvenile carcinoma.

  carcinoma latente latent carcinoma.

  carcinoma leptomeníngeo leptomeningeal carcinoma.

  carcinoma lobular lobular carcinoma.

  carcinoma lobular in situ lobular carcinoma in situ.

  carcinoma lobular no infiltrativo noninfiltrating lobular carcinoma.

  carcinoma medular medullary carcinoma.

  carcinoma meníngeo meningeal carcinoma.

  carcinoma mesometanéfrico mesometanephric carcinoma.

  carcinoma metaplásico metaplastic carcinoma.

  carcinoma metastásico metastatic carcinoma.

  carcinoma microinvasor microinvasive carcinoma.

  carcinoma mucinoso, carcinoma mucoso mucinous carcinoma.

  carcinoma mucocelular carcinoma mucocellulare.

  carcinoma mucoepidermoide mucoepidermoid carcinoma.

  carcinoma oculto occult carcinoma.

  carcinoma papilar papillary carcinoma.

  carcinoma preinvasivo preinvasive carcinoma.

  carcinoma primario primary carcinoma.

  carcinoma primario neuroendocrino de la piel primary neuroendocrine carcinoma of the skin.

  carcinoma de quemadura kangri kangri burn carcinoma.

  carcinoma quístico cystic carcinoma.

  carcinoma sarcomatoide sarcomatoid carcinoma.

  carcinoma secretor secretory carcinoma.

  carcinoma secundario secondary carcinoma.

  carcinoma tiroideo aberrante lateral lateral aberrant thyroid carcinoma.

  carcinoma trabecular trabecular carcinoma.

  carcinoma tubular tubular carcinoma.

  carcinoma velloso villous carcinoma.

  carcinoma verrugoso verrucous carcinoma.

carcinomatosis *f.* carcinomatosis.

  carcinomatosis leptomeníngea leptomeningeal carcinomatosis.

  carcinomatosis meníngea meningeal carcinomatosis.

carcinomatoso, -sa *adj.* carcinomatous.

carcinosarcoma *m.* carcinosarcoma.

  carcinosarcoma embrionario embryonal carcinosarcoma.

carcinosis *f.* carcinosis.

carcinoso, -sa *adj.* cancerous.

carcinostático, -ca *adj.* carcinostatic.

cardíaco, -ca *adj.* cardiac.

cardialgia *f.* cardialgia.

cardias *m.* cardia.

cardiasma *f.* cardiasthma.

cardiastenia *f.* cardiasthenia.

cardiataxia *f.* cardiataxia.

cardiatelia *f.* cardiatelia.

cardiectasia *f.* cardiectasia.

cardiectomía *f.* cardiectomy.

cardiectomizado *m.* cardiectomized.

cardiectopia *f.* cardiectopia.

cardinal *adj.* cardinal.

cardioacelerador, -ra *adj.* cardioaccelerator.

cardioactivo, -va *adj.* cardioactive.

cardioangiografía *f.* cardioangiography.

cardioangiología *f.* cardioangiology.

cardioaórtico, -ca *adj.* cardioaortic.

cardioarterial *adj.* cardioarterial.

Cardiobacterium cardiobacterium.

  cardiobacterium hominis cardiobacterium hominis.

cardiocairógrafo *m.* cardiocairograph.

cardiocalasia *f.* cardiochalasia.

cardiocele *m.* cardiocele.

cardiocentesis *f.* cardiocentesis.

cardiocinético, -ca *adj.* cardiokinetic.

cardiocirrosis *f.* cardiocirrhosis.

cardioclasia *f.* cardioclasia.

cardiodilatador *m.* cardiodilator.

cardiodinámica *f.* cardiodynamics.

cardiodinia *f.* cardiodynia.

cardiodiosis *f.* cardiodiosis.

cardioesofágico, -ca *adj.* cardioesophageal.

cardioespasmo *m.* cardiospasm.

cardiofobia *f.* cardiophobia.

cardiófono *m.* cardiophone.

cardiogénesis *f.* cardiogenesis.

cardiogénico, -ca *adj.* cardiogenic.

cardiografía *f.* cardiography.

cardiógrafo *m.* cardiograph.

cardiograma *m.* cardiogram.

  cardiograma esofágico esophageal cardiogram.

cardiohemotrombo *m.* cardiohemothrombus.

cardiohepático, -ca *adj.* cardiohepathic.

cardiohepatomegalia *f.* cardiohepatomegaly.

cardioide *adj.* cardioid.

cardioinhibitorio, -ria *adj.* cardioinhibitory.

cardiólisis *f.* cardiolysis.

cardiolito *m.* cardiolith.

cardiología *f.* cardiology.

cardiólogo, -ga *m., f.* cardiologist.

cardiomalacia *f.* cardiomalacia.

cardiomegalia *f.* cardiomegaly.

  cardiomegalia glucógena, cardiomegalia glucogénica glycogen cardiomegaly, glycogenic cardiomegaly.

cardiomentopexia *f.* cardiomentopexy.

cardiometría *f.* cardiometry.
cardiomioliposis *f.* cardiomyoliposis.
cardiomiopatía *f.* cardiomyopathy.
 cardiomiopatía alcohólica alcoholic cardiomyopathy.
 cardiomiopatía congestiva congestive cardiomyopathy.
 cardiomiopatía de dilatación dilated cardiomyopathy.
 cardiomiopatía familiar hereditaria hipertrófica familial hypertrophic cardiomyopathy.
 cardiomiopatía hipertrófica hypertrophic cardiomyopathy.
 cardiomiopatía idiopática idiopathic cardiomyopathy.
 cardiomiopatía posparto, cardiomiopatía postpartum postpartum cardiomyopathy.
 cardiomiopatía primaria primary cardiomyopathy.
 cardiomiopatía restrictiva restrictive cardiomyopathy.
 cardiomiopatía secundaria secondary cardiomyopathy.
cardiomioplastia *f.* cardiomyoplasty.
cardiomiopexia *f.* cardiomyopexy.
cardiomiotomía *f.* cardiomyotomy.
cardiomotilidad *f.* cardiomotility.
cardiomuscular *adj.* cardiomuscular.
cardionecrosis *f.* cardionecrosis.
cardionector *m.* cardionector.
cardionéfrico, -ca *adj.* cardionephric.
cardioneumático, -ca *adj.* cardiopneumatic.
cardioneural *adj.* cardioneural.
cardiopaludismo *m.* cardiopaludism.
cardiópata *m., f.* cardiopath.
cardiopatía *f.* cardiopathy, cardiopathia.
 cardiopatía negra cardiopathia nigra.
cardiopericardiopexia *f.* cardiopericardiopexy.
cardiopericarditis *f.* cardiopericarditis.
cardiopilórico, -ca *adj.* cardiopyloric.
cardioplastia *f.* cardioplasty.
cardioplejia *f.* cardioplegia.
cardiopléjico, -ca *adj.* cardioplegic.
cardioptosis *f.* cardioptosis.
cardiopulmonar *adj.* cardiopulmonary.
cardioquimografía *f.* cardiokymography.
cardioquimógrafo *m.* cardiokymograph.
cardioquimograma *m.* cardiokymogram.
cardiorrafia *f.* cardiorrhaphy.
cardiorrenal *adj.* cardiorenal.
cardiorrexis *f.* cardiorrhexis.
cardiosclerosis *f.* cardiosclerosis.
cardioscopio *m.* cardioscope.
cardioselectividad *f.* cardioselectivity.
cardioselectivo, -va *adj.* cardioselective.
cardiosfigmógrafo *m.* cardiosphygmograph.
cardiosinfisis *f.* cardiosymphysis.
cardiospasmo *m.* cardiospasm.
cardiosquisis *f.* cardioschisis.
cardiotacómetro *m.* cardiotachometer.
cardiotaquímetro *m.* cardiotachometer.
cardioterapia *f.* cardiotherapy.
cardiotireosis *f.* cardiothyrotoxicosis.
cardiotirotoxicosis *f.* cardiothyrotoxicosis.
cardiotomía *f.* cardiotomy.
cardiotónico, -ca *adj.* cardiotonic.
cardiotopometría *f.* cardiotopometry.
cardiotóxico, -ca *adj.* cardiotoxic.
cardiotrombo *m.* cardiothrombus.
cardiovalvulitis *f.* cardiovalvulitis.
cardiovalvulotomía *f.* cardiovalvulotomy.
cardiovalvulótomo *m.* cardiovalvulotome.
cardiovascular *adj.* cardiovascular.
cardiovasculorrenal *adj.* cardiovasculorenal.

cardioversión *f.* cardioversion.
cardioversor *m.* cardioverter.
carditis *f.* carditis.
 carditis reumática rheumatic carditis.
carebaria *f.* carebaria.
carencia *f.* deficiency.
carfología *f.* carphology.
carga *f.* burden.
 carga corporal body burden.
 carga salina salt loading.
 carga tumoral tumor burden.
cariapsis *f.* karyapsis.
caribi *m.* caribi.
caries *f.* caries.
 caries activa active caries.
 caries bucal buccal caries.
 caries cementaria cemental caries.
 caries central central caries.
 caries compuesta compound caries.
 caries dental detenida arrested dental caries.
 caries dentaria dental caries.
 caries distal distal caries.
 caries de fisura fissure caries.
 caries de fosa pit caries.
 caries de fosa y fisura pit and fissure caries.
 caries incipiente incipient caries.
 caries interdentaria interdental caries.
 caries lisa smooth surface caries.
 caries mesial mesial caries.
 caries necrótica necrotic caries.
 caries oclusal occlusal caries.
 caries primaria primary caries.
 caries proximal proximal caries.
 caries por radiación radiation caries.
 caries radicular root caries.
 caries recurrente recurrent caries.
 caries seca dry caries, caries sicca.
 caries secundaria secondary caries.
 caries senil senile dental caries.
 caries vertebral spinal caries.
carilla *f.* facing.
carina *f.* carina.
carinado, -da *adj.* carinate.
cariocinesis *f.* karyokinesis.
 cariocinesis asimétrica asymmetrical karyokinesis.
carioclasis *f.* karyoklasis.
cariocromatófilo, -la *adj.* karyochromatophil.
cariocromófilo, -la *adj.* karyochromatophil.
cariogamia *f.* karyogamy.
cariogénesis¹ *f.* karyogenesis.
cariogénesis² *adj.* cariogenesis.
cariogenicidad *f.* cariogenicity.
cariogénico, -ca¹ *adj.* karyogenic.
cariogénico, -ca² *adj.* caryogenic.
cariolinfa *f.* karyolymph.
cariólisis *f.* karyolysis.
cariolítico, -ca *adj.* karyolitic.
cariología *f.* karyology.
cariómera *f.* karyomere.
cariomitosis *f.* karyomitosis.
cariomitótico, -ca *adj.* karyomitotic.
cariomorfismo *m.* karyomorphism.
cariopicnosis *f.* karyopyknosis.
carioplasma *m.* karyoplasm.
cariorrexis *f.* karyorrhexis.
cariosoma *m.* karyosome.
cariostasis *f.* karyostasis.
cariostático, -ca *adj.* cariostatic.
carioteca *f.* karyotheca, caryotheca.
cariotipo *m.* karyotype.
carmalum *m.* carmalum.
carnificación *f.* carnification.

carnívoro, -ra *adj.* carnivorous.
carnosidad *f.* carnosity.
carnosinemia *f.* carnosinemia.
carnoso, -sa *adj.* carneous.
carotenemia *f.* carotenemia.
carotenosis *f.* carotenosis, carotinosis cutis.
caroteno *m.* carotene.
carótico, -ca *adj.* carotic.
caroticotimpánico, -ca *adj.* caroticotympanic.
carótida *f.* carotid.
carotídeo, -a *adj.* carotid.
⊕ **carotidinia** *f.* carotidynia.
carotina *f.* carotin.
carotinemia *f.* carotenemia, carotinemia.
carotinosis *f.* carotinosis cutis.
carpectomía *f.* carpectomy.
carpiano, -na *adj.* carpal.
carpo *m.* carpus.
 carpo curvo carpus curvus.
carpocarpiano, -na *adj.* carpocarpal.
carpocifosis *f.* carpus curvus.
carpofalángico, -ca *adj.* carpophalangeal.
carpometacarpiano, -na *adj.* carpometacarpal.
carpopedal *adj.* carpopedal.
carpoptosia *f.* carpoptosia, carpoptosis.
carpoptosis *f.* carpoptosis.
carrillo *m.* cheek.
cartilaginificación *f.* cartilaginification.
cartilaginiforme *adj.* cartilaginiform.
cartilaginoideo, -a *adj.* cartilaginoid.
cartilaginoso, -a *adj.* cartilaginous.
cartílago *m.* cartilage, cartilago.
 cartílago branquial branchial cartilage.
 cartílago calcificado calcified cartilage.
 cartílago de crecimiento metaphyseal cartilage.
 cartílago metafisario metaphyseal cartilage.
 cartílago de osificación ossifying cartilage.
 cartílago precursor precursory cartilage.
 cartílago primordial primordial cartilage.
 cartílago de Reichert Reichert's cartilage.
 cartílago temporal temporary cartilage.
carúncula *f.* caruncle, caruncula.
 carúncula himenal hymenal caruncle.
 carúncula uretral urethral caruncle.
casco cefálico *m.* headgear.
caseificación *f.* caseation.
caseinógeno *m.* caseinogen.
caseoso, -sa *adj.* caseous.
caso *m.* case.
 caso de ensayo trial case.
 caso dudoso borderline case.
 caso índice index case.
caspa *f.* dandruff.
casquillo *m.* ferrule.
castración *f.* castration.
 castración funcional functional castration.
castrar¹ *v.* castrate.
castrar² *v.* spay.
casuística *f.* casuistics.
catabasial *adj.* catabasial.
catabasis *f.* catabasis.
catabiosis *f.* catabiosis.
catabiótico, -ca *adj.* catabiotic.
catabólico, -ca *adj.* catabolic.
catabolismo *m.* catabolism.
catabolito *m.* catabolite.
catacrótico, -ca *adj.* catacrotic.
catacronobiología *f.* catachronobiology.
catacrotismo *m.* catacrotism.
catadicrotismo *m.* catadicrotism.
catadicrótico, -ca *adj.* catadicrotic.
catadídimo *m.* catadidymus.

catadióptrico, -ca *adj.* catadioptric.
catafilaxis *f.* cataphylaxis.
cataforesis *f.* cataphoresis.
cataforético, -ca *adj.* cataphoretic.
cataforia *f.* cataphoria.
catagénesis *f.* catagenesis.
catágeno *m.* catagen.
catalepsia *f.* catalepsy.
cataléptico, -ca *adj.* cataleptic.
cataleptiforme *adj.* caleptiform.
cataleptoide *adj.* cataleptoid.
catálisis *f.* catalysis.
   catálisis de superficie surface catalysis.
   catálisis por contacto contact catalysis.
catalizador *m.* catalyst, catalyzer.
   catalizador inorgánico inorganic catalyst.
   catalizador negativo negative catalyst.
   catalizador orgánico organic catalyst.
   catalizador positivo positive catalyst.
catamenia *f.* catamenia.
catamenial *adj.* catamenial.
catamenógeno, -na *adj.* catamenogenic.
catamnesis *f.* catamnesis.
catamnésico, -ca *adj.* catamnestic.
catapasma *m.* catapasm.
cataplasia *f.* cataplasia, cataplasis.
cataplasma *f.* cataplasm.
catapléctico, -ca *adj.* cataplectic.
cataplejía *f.* cataplexy.
cataplexia *f.* cataplexy.
catarata *f.* cataract, cataracta.
   catarata adiposa cataracta adiposa.
   catarata anular annular cataract.
   catarata arborescente arborescent cataract.
   *catarata aridosiliculosa, catarata aridosili-
cuada* siliculose cataract, siliquose cataract.
   catarata atópica atopic cataract.
   catarata axial axial cataract.
   catarata axilar axillary cataract.
   catarata azul blue cataract.
   catarata por azúcar sugar cataract.
   catarata blanda soft cataract.
   catarata brunescens cataracta brunescens.
   catarata calcárea calcareous cataract.
   catarata capsular capsular cataract.
   catarata capsulolenticular capsulolenticular
cataract.
   catarata central central cataract.
   catarata cerúlea cerulean cataract, cataracta
cerulea.
   catarata por cobre copper cataract.
   catarata completa complete cataract.
   catarata complicada complicated cataract.
   catarata por concusión concussion cataract.
   catarata congénita congenital cataract.
   catarata coraliforme coralliform cataract.
   catarata coronaria coronary cataract.
   catarata cortical cortical cataract.
   catarata cristalina crystalline cataract.
   catarata cuneiforme cuneiform cataract.
   catarata cupuliforme cupuliform cataract.
   catarata dendrítica dendritic cataract.
   catarata dermatógena cataracta dermatogenes.
   catarata diabética diabetic cataract.
   catarata dura hard cataract.
   catarata eléctrica electric cataract.
   catarata embrionaria embryonic cataract.
   catarata embriopática embryopathic cataract.
   catarata estacionaria stationary cataract.
   catarata estrellada stellate cataract.
   catarata fibroide, catarata fibrosa fibroid
cataract, fibrinous cataract, cataracta fibrosa.
   catarata floriforme floriform cataract.
   catarata de los fogoneros furnacemen's cataract.

catarata en forma de disco disk-shaped cataract.
catarata en forma de gancho hook-shaped
cataract.
catarata en forma de platillo saucer-shaped
cataract.
catarata fusiforme fusiform cataract.
catarata por galactosa galactose cataract.
catarata general complete cataract.
catarata glaucomatosa glaucomatous cataract.
catarata gris gray cataract.
catarata hipermadura hypermature cataract.
catarata hipocalcémica hypocalcemic cataract.
catarata en huso spindle cataract.
catarata incipiente incipient cataract.
catarata infantil infantile cataract.
catarata infrarroja infrared cataract.
catarata inmadura immature cataract.
catarata intumescente intumescent cataract.
catarata juvenil juvenile cataract.
catarata lamelar, catarata laminar lamellar
cataract.
catarata madura mature cataract, ripe cataract.
catarata membranácea accreta cataracta membranacea accreta.
catarata membranosa membranous cataract.
catarata miotónica myotonic cataract.
catarata de Morgagni Morgagni's cataract.
catarata negra black cataract.
catarata neurodérmica cataracta neurodermica.
catarata nodular cataracta nodiformis.
catarata nuclear nuclear cataract.
catarata ósea cataract ossea.
catarata periférica peripheral cataract.
catarata perinuclear perinuclear cataract.
catarata piramidal pyramidal cataract.
catarata pisciforme pisciform cataract.
catarata polar polar cataract.
catarata progresiva progresssive cataract.
catarata punteada punctate cataract.
catarata por radiación radiation cataract.
catarata reduplicada reduplicated cataract.
catarata por rubéola rubella cataract.
catarata en salvavidas life-belt cataract.
catarata secundaria secondary cataract.
catarata sedimentaria sedimentary cataract.
catarata senil senile cataract.
catarata siderótica siderotic cataract.
catarata siliculosa, catarata silicuosa siliculose cataract, siliquose cataract.
catarata sindermatótica syndermatotic cataract.
catarata subcapsular subcapsular cataract.
catarata subcapsular posterior posterior
subcapsular cataract.
catarata supermadura overripe cataract.
catarata sutural sutural cataract.
catarata tetánica tetany cataract.
catarata total total cataract.
catarata tóxica toxic cataract.
catarata traumática traumatic cataract.
catarata umbilicada umbilicated cataract.
catarata vascular vascular cataract.
catarata de los vidrieros glassworker's cataract.
catarata zonular zonular cataract.
cataratogénesis *f.* cataractogenesis.
cataratogénico, -ca *adj.* cataractogenic.
catarral *adj.* catarrhal.
catarro *m.* catarrh.
   catarro atrófico atrophic catarrh.
   catarro bronquial bronchitis.
   catarro de Bostock Bostock's catarrh.
   catarro hipertrófico hypertrophic catarrh.

   catarro intestinal endoenteritis.
   catarro laríngeo laryngitis.
   catarro pituitoso de Laennec Laennec's catarrh.
   catarro sofocante suffocative catarrh.
catarsis *f.* catharsis.
catártico, -ca *adj.* cathartic.
catastalsis *f.* catastalsis.
catastáltico, -ca *adj.* catastaltic.
catástasis *f.* catastasis.
catatermómetro *m.* katathermometer.
catatonía *f.* catatonia.
   catatonía estuporosa stuporous catatonia.
   catatonía excitada excited catatonia.
catatónico, -ca *adj.* catatonic.
catatricrótico, -ca *adj.* catatricrotic.
catatricrotismo *m.* catatricrotism.
catatriquia *f.* catatrichy.
cataxia *f.* cataxia.
catecolaminas *f.* catecholamine.
catenario, -ria *adj.* catenating.
catenoide *adj.* catenoid.
catequina *f.* catechin.
catéresis *f.* catheresis.
caterético, -ca *adj.* catheretic.
catéter *m.* catheter.
   catéter acodado elbowed catheter, catheter
coudé.
   catéter alado winged catheter.
   catéter autorretentivo self-retaining catheter.
   catéter de balón balloon catheter.
   catéter biacodado bicoudate catheter, catheter bicoudé.
   catéter de Braasch Braasch catheter.
   catéter cardíaco cardiac catheter.
   catéter en cepillo brush catheter.
   catéter cónico conical catheter.
   catéter de doble canal double-channel catheter.
   catéter de dos vías two-way catheter.
   catéter de Drew-Smythe Drew- Smythe
catheter.
   catéter de eustaquio eustachian catheter.
   catéter de Fogarty Fogarty's catheter.
   catéter de Foley Foley's catheter.
   catéter de Gouley Gouley's catheter.
   catéter hembra female catheter.
   catéter intracardíaco intracardiac catheter.
   catéter de Malecot Malecot catheter.
   catéter marcapaso pacing catheter.
   catéter de Nélaton Nélaton's catheter.
   catéter permanente indwelling catheter.
   catéter de Pezzer Pezzer catheter.
   catéter de Philips Phillips' catheter.
   catéter prostático prostatic catheter.
   catéter de punta en balón balloon-tip catheter.
   catéter de punta en bellota acorn-tipped
catheter.
   catéter de punta en espiral spiral-tip catheter.
   catéter de punta en oliva olive-tip catheter.
   catéter de punta en silbato whistle-tip catheter.
   catéter de Robinson Robinson catheter.
   catéter de Swan-Ganz Swan-Ganz catheter.
   catéter venoso central central venous catheter.
   catéter vertebrado vertebrated catheter.
cateterismo *m.* catheterization.
   cateterismo cardiovascular cardiac catheterization.
   cateterismo retrouretral retrourethral catheterization.
cateterización *f.* catheterization.
cateteróstato *m.* catheterostat.

catexis *f.* cathexis.
catgut *m.* catgut.
 catgut crómico, catgut cromado chromic catgut.
 catgut iki iki catgut.
 catgut plateado silvered catgut.
cathemoglobina *f.* cathemoglobin.
catión *m.* cation.
catódico, -ca *adj.* cathodic, cathodal.
cátodo *m.* cathode.
católisis *f.* catholysis.
catóptrico, -ca *adj.* catoptric.
cauda cauda.
caudado, -da *adj.* caudate.
caudal *adj.* caudal.
caudocefalad caudocephalad.
caudolenticular *adj.* caudolenticular, caudatolenticular.
caumestesia *f.* caumesthesia.
causa *f.* cause.
 causa causante precipitating cause.
 causa constitucional constitutional cause.
 causa específica specific cause.
 causa excitante exciting cause.
 causa inmediata immediate cause.
 causa local local cause.
 causa necesaria necessary cause.
 causa predisponente predisposing cause.
 causa primaria primary cause.
 causa próxima proximate cause.
 causa remota remote cause.
 causa secundaria secondary cause.
 causa suficiente sufficient cause.
 causa última ultimate cause.
causalgia *f.* causalgia.
cáustico, -ca *adj.* caustic.
cauterio *m.* cautery.
cauterización *f.* cauterization.
cauterizante *adj.* cauterant.
cauterizar *v.* cauterize.
cavagrama *m.* cavagram.
caval *adj.* caval.
cavascopio *m.* cavascope.
cavéola *f.* caveola.
caveolina *f.* caveolin.
caverna *f.* cavern.
caverniloquia *f.* caverniloquy.
cavernitis *f.* cavernitis.
 cavernitis fibrosa fibrous cavernitis.
cavernoscopia *f.* cavernoscopy.
cavernoscopio *m.* cavernoscope.
cavernoso, -sa *adj.* cavernous.
cavernostomía *f.* cavernostomy.
cavidad *f.* cavity, cavitas.
 cavidad amniótica amniotic cavity.
 cavidad cariosa, cavidad de caries tooth-decay cavity.
 cavidad celómica celomic cavity.
 cavidad esplácnica splanchnic cavity.
 cavidad perivisceral perivisceral cavity.
 cavidad perivisceral primitiva primitive perivisceral cavity.
 cavidad de tensión tension cavity.
cavitación *f.* cavitation.
cavitario, -ria *adj.* cavitary.
cavitis *f.* cavitis.
cavografía *f.* cavography.
cavograma *m.* cavogram.
cavum cavum.
cebocefalia *f.* cebocephalia.
cecal *adj.* cecal.
cecectomía *f.* cecectomy.
ceceo *m.* lisping.
cecitis *f.* cecitis.
cecocele *m.* cecocele.

cecocolon *m.* cecocolon.
cecocolostomía *f.* cecocolostomy.
cecofijación *f.* ceofixation.
cecoileostomía *f.* cecoileostomy.
cecopexia *f.* cecopexy.
cecoplicación *f.* cecoplication.
cecorrafia *f.* cecorrhaphy.
cecosigmoidostomía *f.* cecosigmoidostomy.
cecostomía *f.* cecostomy.
cecotomía *f.* cecotomy.
cecum Cecum.
cefalalgia *f.* cephalalgia.
 cefalalgia de Horton Horton's cephalalgia.
cefalea *f.* headache.
 cefalea acuminada cluster headache.
 cefalea espinal spinal headache.
 cefalea en grupo cluster headache.
 cefalea histamínica histaminic headache.
 cefalea de Horton Horton's headache.
 cefalea migrañosa migraine headache.
 cefalea por efecto del vacío sinusal vacuum headache.
 cefalea en racimo cluster headache.
 cefalea tensional tension headache, tension-type headache.
cefalemia *f.* cephalemia.
cefálico, -ca *adj.* cephalic.
cefalina *f.* cephalin.
cefalitis *f.* cephalitis.
cefalización *f.* cephalization.
cefalocatártico, -ca *adj.* cephalocathartic.
cefalocaudal *adj.* cephalocaudal.
cefalocele *m.* cephalocele.
cefalocentesis *f.* cephalocentesis.
cefalocordio *m.* cephalochord.
cefalodídimo *m.* cephalodidymus.
cefalodiprosopo *m.* cephalodiprosopus.
cefalogénesis *f.* cephalogenesis.
cefalógiro, -ra *adj.* cephalogyric.
cefalohematocele *m.* cephalohematocele, cephalhematocele.
 cefalohematocele de Stromeyer Stromeyer's cephalohematocele.
cefalohematoma *m.* cephalohematoma, cephalhematoma.
cefalohemómetro *m.* cephalohemometer.
cefalohidrocele *m.* cephalohydrocele.
cefalomegalia *f.* cephalomegaly.
cefalómelo *m.* caphalomelus.
cefalomenia *f.* cephalomenia.
cefalomeningitis *f.* cephalomeningitis.
cefalometría *f.* cephalometry.
 cefalometría ultrasónica ultrasonic cephalometry.
cefalómetro *m.* cephalometer.
cefalomotor, -ra *adj.* cephalomotor.
cefalonía *f.* cephlonia.
cefalópago *m.* cephalopagus.
cefalopatía *f.* cephalopathy.
cefalopélvico, -ca *adj.* cephalopelvic.
cefalopelvimetría *f.* cephalomelvimetry.
cefaloplejía *f.* cephaloplegia.
cefaloquiste *m.* cephalocyst.
cefalorraquídeo, -a *adj.* cephalorrhachidian.
cefalóstato *m.* cephalostat.
cefalostilo *m.* cephalostyle.
cefalotomía *f.* cephalotomy.
cefalótomo *m.* cephalotome.
cefalotorácico, -ca *adj.* cephalothoracic.
cefalotoracópago *m.* cephalothoracopagus.
 cefalotoracópago asimétrico cephalothoracopagus asymmetros.
 cefalotoracópago disimétrico cephalothoracopagus disymmetros.
 cefalotoracópago monosimétrico cephalotho-

racopagus monosymmetros.
ceguera *f.* blindness.
 ceguera de Bright Bright's blindness.
 ceguera para los colores color blindness.
 ceguera cortical cortical blindness.
 ceguera por eclipse eclipse blindness.
 ceguera para el gusto taste blindness.
 ceguera histérica hysterical blindness.
 ceguera literal letter blindness.
 ceguera mental mind blindness.
 ceguera musical music blindness.
 ceguera de la nieve snow blindness.
 ceguera nocturna night blindness.
 ceguera objetiva object blindness.
 ceguera para el olfato smell blindness.
 ceguera psíquica psychic blindness.
 ceguera de los ríos river blindness.
 ceguera para los signos sign blindness.
 ceguera verbal text blindness, word blindness.
 ceguera verde green blindness.
 ceguera de vuelo flight blindness.
ceja *f.* eyebrow.
celario *m.* celarium.
celda *f.* cella.
 celda de Nageotte Nageotte cell.
celdilla *f.* cella.
celíaco, -ca *adj.* celiac.
celiagra *f.* celiagra.
celialgia *f.* celialgia.
celiaquía *f.* celiac disease.
celiectomía *f.* celiectomy.
celiocentesis *f.* celiocentesis.
celiocolpotomía *f.* celiocolpotomy.
celioenterotomía *f.* celioenterotomy.
celiogastrostomía *f.* celiogastrostomy.
celiohisterectomía *f.* celiohysterectomy.
celiohisterotomía *f.* celiohysterotomy.
celioma *m.* celioma.
celiomialgia *f.* celiomyalgia.
celiomiomectomía *f.* celiomyomectomy.
celioparacentesis *f.* celioparacentesis.
celiorrafia *f.* celiorrhaphy.
celiosalpingectomía *f.* celiosalpingectomy.
celiosalpingotomía *f.* celiosalpingotomy.
celioscopia *f.* celioscopy.
celioscopio *m.* celioscope.
celiotomía *f.* celiotomy.
 celiotomía vaginal vaginal celiotomy.
celofán *m.* cellophane.
celofobia *f.* zelophobia.
celoidina *f.* celloidin.
celoma *m.* celom, coelom.
 celoma extraembrionario extraembryonic coelom.
 celoma intraembrionario intraembryonic coelom.
celómico, -ca *adj.* celomic.
celoniquia *f.* celonychia, coilonychia, koilonychia.
celosomía *f.* celosomia.
celosomo *m.* celosomus.
celotipia *f.* zelotypia.
celotomía *f.* celotomy.
celozoico, -ca *adj.* celozoic.
célula *f.* cell.
 célula A A cell.
 célula absorbente del intestino absorptive cell of the intestine.
 célula acidófila acidophil cell.
 célula acidófila del lóbulo anterior de la hipófisis acidophil cell of anterior lobe of the hypophysis.
 célula acinar, célula acinosa, célula del ácino acinar cell, acinous cell.
 célula adiposa adipose cell.

célula adiposa blanca white adipocyte.
célula adiposa parda brown adipocyte.
célula adventicia adventitial cell.
célula alfa alpha cell.
célula alfa del lóbulo anterior de la hipófisis alpha cell of anterior lobe of the hypophysis.
célula alfa del páncreas alpha cell of the pancreas.
célula almacenadora de grasa del hígado fat-storing cell.
célula alveolare alveolar cell.
célula alveolar grande great alveolar cell.
célula de Alzheimer Alzheimer's cell.
célula amacrina amacrine cell.
célula ameboide ameboid cell.
célula anabiótica anabiotic cell.
célula anaplásica anaplastic cell.
célula angioblástica angioblastic cell.
célula en anillo de sello signet ring cell.
célula de Anitschkow Anitschkow cell.
célula antigenosensible antigen-sensitive cell.
célula apoptósica apoptotic cell.
célula APUD APUD cell.
célula argentafín argentaffin cell.
célula argirófila argyrophilic cell.
célula de Armanni-Ebstein Armanni-Ebstein cell.
célula de Aschoff Aschoff cell.
célula asesina killer cell.
célula de Askanazy Askanazy cell.
célula del asta anterior de la médula espinal anterior horn cell.
célula de astroglia astroglia cell.
célula atrófica atrophyc cell.
célula en avena oat cell.
célula B B-cell.
célula de balón, célula en balón balloon cell.
célula en banda band cell.
célula en banda de Schilling Schilling's band cell.
célula basal, célula basilar basal cell.
célula basófila basophil cell.
célula basófila de la hipófisis anterior basophil cell of anterior lobe of the hypophysis.
célula en bastón rod cell.
célula en bastón de la retina rod cell or retina.
célula de Beale Beale's cell.
célula de Berger Berger cell.
célula de Bergmann Bergmann cell.
célula beta beta cell.
célula beta del lóbulo anterior de la hipófisis beta cell of the anterior lobe of the hypophysis.
célula beta del páncreas beta cell of the pancreas.
célula de Betz Betz cell.
célula bipenachada bitufted cell.
célula bipolar bipolar cell.
célula bipolar de la retina bipolar retinal cell.
célula blástica blast cell.
célula de Boettcher Boettcher cell.
célula de Boll Boll's cell.
célula de Bowen Bowen's cell.
célula bronquial bronchic cell.
célula bronquiolar exocrina bronchiolar exocrine cell.
célula C C cell.
célula de Cajal-Retzius Cajal-Retzius's cell.
célula caliciforme, célula en cáliz caliciform cell, chalice cell, globet cell.
célula cardionectora, célula cardiovectora cell of the impulse-conducting system.
célula cartilaginosa cartilage cell.

célula de castración castration cell, castrate cell.
célula en cayado stab cell, staff cell.
célula cebada mast cell.
célula en cesto basket cell.
célula cigoto egg cell.
célula ciliada ciliated cell.
célula ciliada externa outer hair cell.
célula ciliada interna inner hair cell.
célula ciliada de tipo 1 y de tipo 2 hair cell.
célula cilíndrica columnar cell.
célula cimógena zymogenic cell.
célula citomegálica cyomegalic cell.
célula citotóxica cytotoxic cell.
célula citotóxica natural natural killer cell.
célula citotrofoblástica cytotrophoblastic cell.
célula clara clear cell.
célula de Clara Clara cell.
célula clara del tiroides light cell of the thyroid.
célula de Clarke Clarke cell.
célula de Claudius Claudius' cell.
célula colaboradora helper cell.
célula comisural commissural cell.
célula conjuntiva connective cell.
célula en cono de la retina cone cell of the retina, retinal rod cell.
célula contráctil contractile cell.
célula contrasupresora contrasuppressor cell.
célula cordonal column neuron.
célula córnea, célula corneal cell of the corneal epithelium.
célula en correa strap cell.
célula de Corti Corti's cell.
célula cromafín chromaffin cell.
célula cromófoba chromophobe cell.
célula cúbica, célula cuboidea cuboidal cell.
célula de Custer Custer cell.
célula D D cell.
célula decidual decidual cell.
célula de Deiters Deiters' cell.
célula delta del lóbulo anterior de la hipófisis delta cell of the anterior lobe of the hypophysis.
célula delta del páncreas delta cell of the pancreas.
célula dendrítica dendritic cell.
célula diana target cell.
célula en diana target cell.
célula de Dogiel Dogiel's cell.
célula de Downey Downey cell.
célula de Drysdale Drysdale cell.
célula en duela splenic endothelial cell.
célula EC EC cell.
célula ECL ECL cell.
célula efectora effector cell.
célula de Ehrlich Ehrlich cell.
célula del embarazo pregnancy cell.
célula embrionaria embryonic cell.
célula emigrante migrant cell.
célula endodérmica, célula entodérmica endodermal cell, entodermal cell.
célula endotelial endothelial cell.
célula endotelioide endothelioid cell.
célula enterocromafina enterochromaffin cell.
célula enteroendocrinas enteroendocrine cell.
célula ependimaria ependymal cell.
célula epidérmica epidermic cell.
célula epitelial epithelial cell.
célula epitelial folicular follicular epithelial cell.

célula epitelial de Golgi Golgi epithelial cell.
célula del epitelio del amnios amnion cell.
célula del epitelio pigmentario de la retina retinal pigment epithelium cell.
célula epitelioide epithelioid cell.
célula eritroide erythroid cell.
célula errante wandering cell.
célula escamosa squamous cell.
célula del esmalte enamel cell.
célula espermática sperm cell.
célula espinosa prickle cell, spine cell.
célula esplénica splenic cell.
célula espumosa foam cell.
célula estrelladas de la corteza cerebral stellate cell of the cerebral cortex.
célula fagocitica, célula fagocitaria phagocytic cell.
célula faja strap cell.
célula falángica phalangeal cell.
célula falángica externa outer phalangeal cell.
célula falángica interna inner phalangeal cell.
célula falciforme sickle cell.
célula fantasma ghost cell.
célula de Fañanás Fañanás cell.
célula fasciculada fasciculata cell.
célula fascicular column cell.
célula feocroma pheochrome cell.
célula de Ferrata Ferrata's cell.
célula fisalífera physaliphorous cell.
célula flagelada cell with flagellum.
célula folicular follicular cell.
célula del folículo tiroideo thyroid follicular cell.
célula formadora de rosetas rosette forming cell.
célula fotorreceptora photoreceptor cell.
célula foveolar del estómago foveolar cell of the stomach.
célula fucsinófila fuchsinophil cell.
célula funicular suprasegmental neuron.
célula fusiforme spindle cell.
célula fusiforme de la corteza cerebral fusiform cell of the cerebral cortex.
célula G G cell.
célula gametoide gametoid cell.
célula ganglionar ganglion cell.
célula ganglionar de los ganglios craneoespinales craneospinal ganglion neuron cell.
célula ganglionar de los ganglios del sistema nervioso autónomo autonomic ganglion neuron.
célula ganglionar de la retina ganglion cell of the retina.
célula de Gaucher Gaucher cell.
célula germinal germinal cell.
célula germinativa stem cell.
célula de Gierke Gierke cell.
célula gigante giant cell.
célula gigante de cuerpo extraño foreign body giant cell.
célula gigante de Touton Touton giant cell.
célula gitter gitter cell.
célula glial glia cell.
célula globoide globoid cell.
célula globosa balloon cell.
célula glomerular glomerulous cell.
célula glómica glomus cell.
célula de Golgi Golgi's cell.
célula de los granos granule cell.
célula grasa fat cell.
célula gustativa taste cell, gustatory cell.
célula hecatómera hecatomeral cell.

célula HeLa HeLa cell.
célula HEMPAS HEMPAS cell.
célula hendida cleaved cell.
célula hendida pequeña small cleaved cell.
célula de Hensen Hensen's cell.
célula hepática hepatocyte.
célula heterómera, célula heteromérica heteromeric cell.
célula hija daughter cell.
célula hiliar hilus cell.
célula hipercromática hyperchromatic cell.
célula hipertrófica hypertrophic cell.
célula de Höfbauer Höfbauer cell.
célula homómera, célula homomérica homomeric cell.
célula horizontal de Cajal horizontal cell of Cajal, Cajal's cell.
célula horizontal de la retina horizontal cell of the retina.
célula en hoz sickle cell.
célula huevo egg cell.
célula de Hürthle Hürthle cell.
célula en imagen de espejo mirror image cell.
célula indiferenciada undifferentiated cell.
célula inductora inducer cell.
célula de la insuficiencia cardíaca congestiva heart failure cell.
célula intercalar intercalary cell.
célula intercapilar intercapillary cell.
célula interplexiforme interplexiform cell.
célula intersticial del ovario ovarian interstitial cell.
célula intersticial del riñón interstitial cell of the kidney.
célula intersticial del testículo interstitial testicular cell.
célula de los islotes islet cell.
célula de Ito Ito cell.
célula juvenil juvenile cell.
célula de Kulchitsky Kulchitsky cell.
célula de Kupffer Kupffer cell.
célula lábil, célula en división continua continuously renewing cell.
célula de Lacis Lacis cell.
célula lactotropa lactotroph cell.
célula lacunar lacunar cell.
célula de Langerhans Langerhans' cell.
célula de Langhans Langhans' cell.
célula LE LE cell.
célula de Leishman Leishman's chrome cell.
célula de la lepra lepra cell.
célula de Leydig Leydig's cell.
célula linfoide lymphoid cell.
célula de Lipschütz Lipschütz cell.
célula de lupus eritematoso lupus erythematosus cell.
célula luteínica luteal cell, lutein cell.
célula luteínica de la granulosa granulosa lutein cell.
célula luteínica de la teca theca lutein cell.
célula de macroglia macroglia cell.
célula madre brood cell, mother cell.
célula de Malpighi Malpighian cell.
célula mamotropa mamotroph cell.
célula de Marchand Marchand's wandering cell.
célula de Martinotti Martinotti's cell.
célula de Max-Clara Max-Clara cell.
célula en media luna crescent cell.
célula de memoria B-memory cell.
célula mesangial mesangial cell.
célula mesenquimal, célula mesenquimática mesenchymal cell.
célula mesotelial mesothelial cell.
célula metaplásica metaplasic cell.

célula de Meynert Meynert's cell.
célula de microglia microglia cell, microglial cell.
célula mieloidea myeloid cell.
célula migratoria, célula migrante migratory cell, wandering cell.
célula de Mikulicz Milkulicz's cell.
célula miocárdica cardiac muscle cell of the myocardium.
célula mioepitelial myoepithelial cell.
célula mioide myoid cell.
célula mitral mitral cell.
célula mucosa mucous cell.
célula mucosas cervical, célula mucosa del cuello mucous neck cell.
célula de Müller Müller cell.
célula multipolar multipolar cell.
célula multipolar de la corteza cerebral multipolar neuron of the cerebral cortex.
célula mural mural cell.
célula muscular estriada striated muscle cell.
célula muscular estriada cardíaca cardiac muscle cell.
célula muscular estriada esquelética skeletal muscle cell.
célula muscular lisa smooth muscle cell.
célula necrótica necrotic cell.
célula nerviosa nerve cell.
célula neuroepitelial neuroepithelial cell.
célula de neuroglia neuroglia cell.
célula neurogliforme neurogliform cell.
célula neurosecretora neurosecretory cell.
célula de nevo nevus cell.
célula NK NK cell.
célula de Niemann-Pick Niemann-Pick cell.
célula noble noble cell.
célula no clonógena nonclonogenic cell.
célula nodal nodal cell.
célula nodriza nurse cell.
célula nodriza del timo epithelial reticular cell.
célula nucleada nucleated cell.
célula olfatoria olfactory cell.
célula de oligodendroglia oligodendroglia cell.
célula oscura dark cell.
célula oscura de los botones gustativos sustentacular cell of the taste buds.
célula ósea osseous cell, bone cell.
célula osteógena osteogenic cell.
célula osteoprogenitora osteoprogenitor cell.
célula ovárica folicular follicular ovarian cell.
célula oxífila oxyphil cell.
célula oxíntica oxyntic cell.
célula de Paget Paget's cell.
célula pagetoide Pagetoid cell.
célula de Paneth Paneth cell.
célula parafolicular parafollicular cell.
célula paraluteínica paraluteal cell.
célula parenquimatosa parenchymal cell.
célula parenquimatosa del cuerpo pineal parenchymatous cell of the corpus pineale.
célula parietal parietal cell.
célula pavimentosa squamous cell.
célula en penacho tufted cell.
célula péptica peptic cell.
célula pericapilar pericapillary cell.
célula permisiva permissive cell.
célula en pesario pessary cell.
célula de Pick Pick cell.
célula pigmentada pigmented cell.
célula pigmentaria pigment cell.
célula pigmentaria de la piel pigment cell of the skin.

célula pigmentaria de la retina pigment cell of the retina.
célula pigmentaria del iris pigment cell of the iris.
célula de los pilares pillar cell.
célula de los pilares externos outer pillar cell.
célula de los pilares internos inner pillar cell.
célula pilosa vestibular vestibular hair cell.
célula pineal pineal cell.
célula piramidal pyramidal cell.
célula de pirrol pyrrhol cell, pyrrol cell.
célula plana squamous cell.
célula plasmática plasma cell.
célula de plata silver cell.
célula de los plexos coroideos choroid plexus epithelial cell.
célula pluripotencial pluripotent cell.
célula policromatófila polychromatophil cell.
célula del polvo dust cell.
célula PP PP cell.
célula pregranulosa pregranulosa cell.
célula presentadora del antígeno antigen-presenting cell.
célula primordial primordial cell.
célula principal clara de la paratiroides water clear cell of the parathyroid gland, wasserhelle cell.
célula principal del cuerpo pineal chief cell of the corpus pineale.
célula principal del estómago chief cell of the stomach.
célula principal oscura de la paratiroides chief cell of the parathyroid gland.
célula prolactínica prolactin cell.
célula protectora protective cell.
célula de Purkinje Purkinje's cell.
célula de pus pus cell.
célula queratinizada keratinized cell.
célula radial de Müller Müller's radial cell.
célula radicular root neuron.
célula de Raji Raji cell.
célula receptora auditiva auditory receptor cell.
célula receptora del sentido del equilibrio hair vestibular cell.
célula receptora olfatoria olfactory receptor cell.
célula receptora visual visual receptor cell.
célula recolectora scavenger cell.
célula redonda spherical cell.
célula de Reed Reed cell.
célula de Reed-Sternberg Reed-Sternberg cell.
célula de Renshaw Renshaw cell.
célula en reposo quiescent cell.
célula reticular reticular cell.
célula reticular epitelial del timo epithelial reticular cell.
célula reticularis cell reticularis.
célula reticuloendotelial reticuloendothelial cell.
célula de revestimiento lining cell.
célula de Rieder Rieder cell.
célula de Rindfleisch Rindfleisch's cell.
célula roja de la sangre red blood cell.
célula de Rolando Rolando's cell.
célula de Rouget Rouget cell.
célula sanguínea blood cell.
célula sanguínea humana centrifugada packed human blood cell.
célula satélite satellite cell.
célula satélite del músculo esquelético satellite cell of skeletal muscle.

célula de Schultze Schultze's cell.
célula de Schwann Schwann cell.
célula de segmentación cleavage cell.
célula segmentada segmented cell.
célula semilunar crescent cell.
célula sensitiva cell of somatic senses.
célula sensibilizada sensitized cell.
célula sensorial sensory cell.
célula señuelo decoy cell.
célula septal septal cell.
célula de Sertoli Sertoli's cell.
célula seudo-Gaucher pseudo-Gaucher cell.
célula seudounipolar, célula seudomonopolar pseudounipolar cell.
célula de seudoxantoma pseudoxanthoma cell.
célula de Sezary-Lutzner Sézary-Lutzner cell.
célula siderófila siderophil cell.
célula simpaticocromafín sympathochromaffin cell.
célula sinovial synovial cell.
célula del sistema APUD APUD cell.
célula somática somatic cell.
célula somatotropa somatotroph cell.
célula de sostén supporting cell.
célula de Sternberg Sternberg cell.
célula de Sternberg-Reed Sternberg-Reed cell.
célula de la superficie mucosa del estómago surface mucous cell of the stomach.
célula supresora suppressor cell.
célula sustentacular sustentacular cell.
célula T T cell.
célula T citotóxica, célula TC T cytotoxic cell, TC cell.
célula T colaboradora, célula TH T-helper cell, TH cell.
célula T supresora, célula TS T-suppressor cell, TS cell.
célula táctil tactile cell.
célula en tarta tart cell.
célula de la teca thecal cell.
célula del tejido conjuntivo connective tissue cell.
célula tipo I type I cell.
célula tipo II type II cell.
célula tirotropa thyrotroph cell.
célula totipotencial, célula totipotente totipotent cell.
célula transductora transducer cell.
célula transductora neuroendocrina neuroendocrine transducer cell.
célula transformada por virus transformed virus cell, transformed cell.
célula de transición transitional cell.
célula transportadora carrier cell.
célula triangular triangular-shape cell.
célula trofoblástica trophoblast cell.
célula del túnel de Corti tunnel cell.
célula de Türck Türck cell.
célula de Tzanck Tzanck cell.
célula unipolar unipolar cell.
célula velada veil cell, veiled cell.
célula vellosa hairy cell.
célula de Virchow Virchow's cell.
célula vítrea vitreous cell.
célula de Warthin-Finkeldey Warthin-Finkeldey cell.
célula wic. 38 wic. 38 cell.
célula yuxtaglomerulare juxtaglomerular cell.
celular *adj.* cellular.
celularidad *f.* cellularity.
celulicida *adj.* cellulicidal.
celulífugo, -ga *adj.* cellulifugal.
celulípeto, -ta *adj.* cellulipetal.

celulitis *f.* cellulitis.
celulitis aguda del cuero cabelludo acute scalp cellulitis.
celulitis anaeróbica anaerobic cellulitis.
celulitis disecante dissecting cellulitis.
celulitis flemosa phlegmonous cellulitis.
celulitis gangrenosa gangrenous cellulitis.
celulitis necrotizante necrotizing cellulitis.
celulitis orbitaria orbital cellulitis.
celulitis pélvica pelvic cellulitis.
celulito *m.* cellulite.
celuloide *m.* celluloid.
celuloneuritis *f.* celluloneuritis.
celulotóxico, -ca *adj.* cellulitoxic.
cementación *f.* cementation.
cementiculo *m.* cementicle.
cementificación *f.* cementification.
cementitis *f.* cementitis.
cemento *m.* cement, cementum.
cemento afibrilar afibrillar cement.
cemento dental dental cement, tooth cement.
cemento dental compuesto composite dental cement.
cemento dental inorgánico inorganic dental cement.
cemento de fosfato de cinc zinc phosphate cement.
cemento de fosfato de cobre copper phosphate cement.
cemento de óxido de cinc, cemento eugenol modificado modified zinc oxide cement, eugenol cement.
cemento de policarboxilato polycarboxylate cement.
cemento de resina resin cement.
cemento de silicato silicate cement.
cementoblasto *m.* cementoblast.
cementoblastoma *m.* cementoblastoma.
cementoblastoma benigno benign cementoblastoma.
cementocito *m.* cementocyte.
cementoclasia *f.* cementoclasia.
cementoclasto *m.* cementoclast.
cementoexostosis *f.* cemento-exostosis.
cementoma *m.* cementome.
cementoma gigantiforme gigantiform cementome.
cementoma verdadero true cementome.
cementosis *f.* cementosis.
cementum *m.* cementum.
cenadelfo *m.* cenadelphus.
cenencefalocele *m.* cenencephalocele.
cenestesia *f.* cenesthesia.
cenestésico, -ca *adj.* cenesthesic, cenesthetic.
cenestesiopatía *f.* cenesthesiopathy.
cenestopatia *f.* cenesthopathy.
cenocítico, -ca *adj.* cenocytic.
cenocito *m.* cenocyte.
cenogénesis *f.* cenogenesis.
cenosito *m.* cenosite.
coenosito *m.* cenosite.
cenotoxina *f.* cenotoxin.
censura *f.* censorship.
centelleador *m.* scintillator.
centelleo *m.* scintillation.
centellobarrido *m.* scintiscan.
centellocisternografía *f.* scinticisternography.
centellofotografía *f.* scintiphotography.
centellografía *f.* scintigraphy.
centellográfico, -ca *adj.* scintigraphic.
centellograma *m.* scintigram.
centellómetro *m.* scintillometer.
centelloscopio *m.* scintillascope.

centesis *f.* centesis.
centraje *m.* centrage.
central *adj.* central.
centrecefálico, -ca *adj.* centrecephalic.
céntrico, -ca *adj.* centric.
centrifugacion *f.* centrifugation, centrifugalization.
centrifugacion por bandas band centrifugation.
centrifugacion por gradiente de densidad density gradient centrifugation.
centrifugacion por zonas zone centrifugation.
centrifugador *m.* centrifuge.
centrifuga *f.* centrifuge.
centrifugo, -ga *adj.* centrifugal.
centrilobular *adj.* centrilobular.
centríolo, centriolo *m.* centriole.
centriolo distal distal centriole.
centriolo proximal proximal centriole.
centrípeto, -ta *adj.* centripetal.
centro *m.* center, centrum.
centro activo active center.
centro de la alimentación feeding center.
centro anospinal anospinal center.
centro atómico atomic core.
centro de Broca Broca's center.
centro catalítico catalytic center.
centro celular cell center.
centro ciliospinal ciliospinal center.
centro de condrificación chondrification center.
centro dentario dentary center.
centro diafisario diaphysial center.
centro epiótico epiotic center.
centro esfenótico sphenotic center.
centro espiratorio expiratory center.
centro germinal de Flemming germinal center of Flemming.
centro inspiratorio inspiratory center.
centro de kerckring Kerckring's center.
centro del lenguaje speech center.
centro medular medullary center, centrum medulare.
centro motor del habla motor speech center.
centro de osificación ossific center, center of ossification.
centro oval centrum ovale.
centro oval de Vieussens Vieussens' centrum.
centro primario de osificación primary centrum of ossification.
centro de reacción reaction center.
centro del reborde center of ridge.
centro respiratorio respiratory center.
centro de rotación rotation center, center of rotation.
centro de la saciedad satiety center.
centro secundario de osificación secondary center of ossification.
centro semioval semioval center, centrum semiovale.
centro semioval de Vicq d'Azyr Vicq d'Azyr centrum semiovale.
centro sensitivo del habla sensory speech center.
centro vasomotor vasomotor center.
centro vitales vital center.
centro de wernicke Wernicke's center.
centroblasto *m.* centroblast.
Centrocesto Centrocestus.
centrocinesia *f.* centrokinesia.
centrocinético, -ca *adj.* centrokinetic.
centrocito *m.* centrocyte.
centrolecítico, -ca *adj.* centrolecithal.

centrómero *m.* centromere.
centroplasma *m.* centroplasm.
centrosfera *f.* centrosphere.
centrosoma *m.* centrosome.
centrostáltico, -ca *adj.* centrostaltic.
centrum centrum.
cenuro *m.* cenuris.
cenurosis *f.* cenurosis, cenuriasis, coenurasis.
cenuriasis *f.* cenuriasis, coenurasis.
cepa *f.* strain.
  cepa auxotrófica auxotrophic strain.
  cepa celular cell strain.
  cepa congénica congenic strain.
  cepa isogénica isogenic strain.
  cepa lisógena lysogenic strain.
  cepa media hipotética (CMH) hypothetical mean strain (HMS).
  cepa neotipo neotype strain.
  cepa portadora carrier strain.
  cepa prototrófica prototrophic strain.
  cepa de reserva stock strain.
  cepa seudolisogénica pseudolysogenic strain.
  cepa tipo type strain.
  cepa tipo salvaje wild type strain.
cepillo *m.* brush.
  cepillo de Ayre Ayre brush.
  cepillo broncoscópico bronchoscopic brush.
  cepillo dental denture brush.
  cepillo de Kruse Kruse's brush.
  cepillo de pulimento polishing brush.
ceptor *m.* ceptor.
  ceptor a distancia distance ceptor.
  ceptor de contacto contact ceptor.
  ceptor químico chemical ceptor.
ceramida *f.* ceramide.
cerasina *f.* cerasin.
ceratocricoides *adj.* ceratocricoid.
ceratohial *adj.* ceratohyal.
cercaria *f.* cercaria.
cercenamiento *m.* retrenchment.
cerclaje *m.* cerclage.
cercocisto *m.* Cercocystis.
Cercocystis *m.* Cercocystis.
cercómero *m.* cercomer.
cercomónada *f.* cercomonad.
cercomonas *f.* cercomonas.
cerebelar *adj.* cerebellar.
cerebelífugo, -ga *adj.* cerebellifugal.
cerebelina *f.* cerebellin.
cerebelípeto, -ta *adj.* cerebellipetal.
cerebelitis *f.* cerebellitis.
cerebelo *m.* cerebellum.
cerebelobulbar *adj.* cerebellomedullary.
cerebeloespinal *adj.* cerebellospinal.
cerebelolenticular *adj.* cerebellolental.
cerebeloolivar *adj.* cerebello-olivary.
cerebelopontino, -na *adj.* cerebellopontine.
cerebelorrúbrico, -ca *adj.* cerebellorubral.
cerebeloso -sa *adj.* cerebellar.
cerebración *f.* cerebration.
cerebral *adj.* cerebral.
cerebralgia *f.* cerebralgia.
cerebrastenia *f.* cerebrasthenia.
cerebriforme *adj.* cerebriform.
cerebrífugo, -ga *adj.* cerebrifugal.
cerebrípeto, -ta *adj.* cerebripetal.
cerebritis *f.* cerebritis.
  cerebritis supurativa suppurative cerebritis.
cerebro *m.* brain, cerebrum.
  cerebro anterior forebrain.
  cerebro medio midbrain.
  cerebro posterior hindbrain.
cerebrocardíaco, -ca *adj.* cerebrocardiac.
cerebroesclerosis *f.* cerebrosclerosis.
cerebroespinal *adj.* cerebrospinal.

cerebrogalactósido *m.* cerebrogalactoside.
cerebroide *adj.* cerebroid.
cerebroma *m.* cerebroma.
cerebromalacia *f.* cerebromalacia.
cerebromedular *adj.* cerebrospinal.
cerebromeníngeo, -a *adj.* cerebromeningeal.
cerebromeningitis *f.* cerebromeningitis.
cerebropatía *f.* cerebropathia, cerebropathy.
cerebrorraquídeo, -a *adj.* cerebrospinal.
cerebrosclerosis *f.* cerebrosclerosis.
cerebrósido *m.* cerebroside.
cerebrosidosis *f.* cerebrosidosis.
cerebrosis *f.* cerebrosis.
cerebrospinal *adj.* cerebrospinal.
cerebrosterol *m.* cerebrosterol.
cerebrostomía *f.* cerebrostomy.
cerebrotomía *f.* cerebrotomy.
cerebrotonía *f.* cerebrotonia.
cerebrovascular *adj.* cerebrovascular.
cerebrum *m.* cerebrum.
cero absoluto *m.* absolute zero.
ceroide *m.* ceroid.
ceroma *m.* ceroma.
ceroplastia *f.* ceroplasty.
certificación *f.* certification.
ceruleína *f.* cerulein.
ceruloplasmina *f.* ceruloplasmin.
cerumen *m.* cerumen.
  cerumen espesado inspissated cerumen, cerumen inspissatum.
ceruminal *adj.* ceruminal.
ceruminolítico, -ca *adj.* ceruminolytic.
ceruminoma *m.* ceruminoma.
ceruminosis *f.* ceruminosis.
ceruminoso, -sa *adj.* ceruminous.
cervical *adj.* cervical.
cervicectomía *f.* cervicectomy.
cervicitis *f.* cervicitis.
cervicoaxilar *adj.* cervicoaxillary.
cervicobraquial *adj.* cervicobrachial.
cervicobucal *adj.* cervicobuccal.
cervicodinia *f.* cervicodynia.
cervicodorsal *adj.* cervicodorsal.
cervicoescapular *adj.* cervicoscapular.
cervicofacial *adj.* cervicofacial.
cervicografía *f.* cervicography.
cervicolabial *adj.* cervicolabial.
cervicolingual *adj.* cervicolingual.
cervicolinguoaxial *adj.* cervicolinguoaxial.
cervicooccipital *adj.* cervico-occipital.
cervicoplastia *f.* cervicoplasty.
cervicoscapular *adj.* cervicoscapular.
cervicotorácico, -ca *adj.* cervicothoracic.
cervicovesical *adj.* cervicovesical.
cérvix *m.* cervix.
cesárea *f.* cesarean.
cestodiasis *f.* cestodiasis.
cestodos *m.* cestode.
cestoideo, -a *adj.* cestoid.
cetoacidosis *f.* ketoacidosis.
cetoaciduria *f.* ketoaciduria.
  cetoaciduria de cadena ramificada branched chain ketoaciduria.
cetogénesis *f.* ketogenesis.
cetogenético, -ca *adj.* ketogenetic.
cetogénico, -ca *adj.* ketogenic.
cetólisis *f.* ketolysis.
cetolítico, -ca *adj.* ketolytic.
cetona *f.* ketone.
cetonemia *f.* ketonemia.
cetónico, -ca *adj.* ketonic.
cetonización *f.* ketonization.
cetonuria *f.* ketonuria.
  cetonuria de cadena ramificada branched chain ketonuria.

cetosis *f.* ketosis.
cetosteroide *m.* ketosteroid.
chagoma *m.* chagoma.
chalazión *m.* chalazion.
  chalazión agudo acute chalazion.
  chalazión en botón de camisa collar-stud chalazion.
chaleco *m.* jacket.
  chaleco Minerva Minerva jacket.
  chaleco de Sayre Sayre's jacket.
chancro *m.* chancre.
  chancro blando soft chancre.
  chancro duro hard chancre.
  chancro esporotricótico sporotrichositic chancre.
  chancro mixto mixed chancre.
  chancro monorrecidivante monorecidive chancre.
  chancro redux redux chancre.
  chancro sifilítico hard chancre.
chancroide *m.* chancroid.
chancroideo, -a *adj.* chancroidal.
chancroso, -sa *adj.* chancrous.
chapa *f.* chappa.
chapoteo *m.* clapotement.
Chilomastix Chilomastix.
chiufa *f.* chiufa.
Chlamydia *f.* Chlamydia.
Chlamydiaceae Chlamydiaceae.
choque *m.* shock.
  choque anafiláctico anaphylactic shock.
  choque anafilactoide anaphylactoid shock.
  choque por anestesia, choque anestésico anesthetic shock.
  choque bacteriémico bacteriemic shock.
  choque cardiogénico cardiogenic shock.
  choque crónico chronic shock.
  choque cultural cultural shock.
  choque delirante delirious shock.
  choque por descompresión declamping shock.
  choque diferido deferred shock, delayed shock.
  choque eléctrico electric shock.
  choque por endotoxinas endotoxin shock.
  choque endotóxico endotoxic shock.
  choque eretístico erethistic shock.
  choque espinal spinal shock.
  choque por exceso de rapidez speed shock.
  choque hematogénico hematogenic shock.
  choque hemorrágico hemorrhagic shock.
  choque hipovolémico hypovolemic shock.
  choque histamínico histamine shock.
  choque húmedo wet shock.
  choque insulínico insulin shock.
  choque por interrupción break shock.
  choque irreversible irreversible shock.
  choque medular spinal shock.
  choque neurogénico neurogenic shock.
  choque nitroide nitroid shock.
  choque oligohémico oligemic shock.
  choque osmótico osmotic shock.
  choque primario primary shock.
  choque proteico protein shock.
  choque quirúrgico surgical shock.
  choque reversible reversible shock.
  choque secundario secondary shock.
  choque séptico septic shock.
  choque sérico serum shock.
  choque traumático traumatic shock.
  choque vasogénico vasogenic shock.
Chrysomya Chrysomya.
Chrysops Chrysops.
Chrysosporium parvum Chrysosporium parvum.

cianefridrosis *f.* cyanephidrosis.
cianobacterias *f.* Cyanobacteria.
cianófilo *m.* cyanophil, cyanophile.
cianófilo, -la *adj.* cyanophilous.
cianogénico, -ca *adj.* cyanogenic.
cianopía *f.* cyanopia, cyanopsia.
cianopsia *f.* cyanopsia.
cianosado, -da *adj.* cyanosed.
cianosis *f.* cyanosis.
  cianosis por compresión compression cyanosis.
  cianosis enterógena enterogenous cyanosis.
  cianosis falsa false cyanosis.
  cianosis hereditaria metahemoglobinúrica hereditary methemoglobinemic cyanosis.
  cianosis por movimiento shunt cyanosis.
  cianosis de la retina cyanosis retinae.
  cianosis tardía late cyanosis, tardive cyanosis.
  cianosis tóxica toxic cyanosis.
cianótico, -ca *adj.* cyanotic.
cianuria *f.* cyanuria.
cianurina *f.* cyanurin.
ciática *f.* sciatica.
ciático, -ca *adj.* isciatic.
cibernética *f.* cybernetics.
cibofobia *f.* cibophobia.
cíbrido *m.* cybrid.
cicatrectomía *f.* cicatrectomy.
cicatricial *adj.* cicatrizal.
cicatricotomía *f.* cicatricotomy, cicatrisotomy.
cicatrisotomía *f.* cicatrisotomy.
cicatriz *f.* scar, cicatrix.
  cicatriz en chelín shilling scar.
  cicatriz cerebral brain cicatrix.
  cicatriz filtrante filtering cicatrix.
  cicatriz hipertrófica hypertrophic scar.
  cicatriz meningocerebral meningocerebral cicatrix.
  cicatriz en papel de cigarrillo cigarette-paper scar.
  cicatriz papirácea papyraceous scar.
  cicatriz viciosa vicious cicatrix.
cicatrización *f.* cicatrization.
cicatrizal *adj.* cicatricial.
cicatrizante *adj.* cicatrizant.
ciclartrodial *adj.* cyclarthrodial.
ciclartrosis *f.* cyclarthrosis.
ciclectomía *f.* cyclectomy.
ciclencefalia *f.* cyclencephalia, cyclencephaly.
cíclico, -ca *adj.* cyclic.
ciclicotomía *f.* cyclicotomy.
ciclitis *f.* cyclitis.
  ciclitis heterocrómica heterochromic cyclitis.
  ciclitis plástica plastic cyclitis.
  ciclitis purulenta purulent cyclitis.
ciclo *m.* cycle.
  ciclo del ácido cítrico citric acid cycle.
  ciclo del ácido cítrico citric acid cycle.
  ciclo del ácido dicarboxílico dicarboxylic acid cycle.
  ciclo del ácido succínico succinic acid cycle.
  ciclo del ácido tricarboxílico tricarboxilic acid cycle.
  ciclo del anhídrido carbónico, ciclo del carbono carbon dioxide cycle, carbon cycle.
  ciclo anovulatorio anovulatory cycle.
  ciclo cardíaco cardiac cycle.
  ciclo celular cell cycle.
  ciclo de cori cori cycle.
  ciclo endógeno endogenous cycle.
  ciclo estrual estrous cycle.
  ciclo exoeritrocítico exoerythrocytic cycle.
  ciclo exógeno exogenous cycle.
  ciclo forzado force cycle.
  ciclo genésico genesial cycle.

  ciclo de Krebs Krebs cycle.
  ciclo de Krebs-Henseleit Krebs-Henseleit cycle.
  ciclo masticatorio chewing cycle.
  ciclo menstrual menstrual cycle.
  ciclo del nitrógeno nitrogen cycle.
  ciclo de las ondas cerebrales brain wave cycle.
  ciclo oogenético, ciclo ovárico ovarian cycle.
  ciclo de la ornitina ornithine cycle.
  ciclo de oxidación de ácidos grasos fatty acid oxidation cycle.
  ciclo del pelo hair cycle.
  ciclo de las pentosa fosfato pentose phosphate cycle.
  ciclo reproductivo reproductive cycle.
  ciclo restaurado restored cycle.
  ciclo de retorno returning cycle.
  ciclo de Ross Ross cycle.
  ciclo por segundo cycle per second.
  ciclo de la urea urea cycle.
  ciclo visual visual cycle.
  ciclo vital life cycle.
ciclocefalla *f.* cyclocephalia, cyclocephaly.
ciclocoroiditis *f.* cyclochoroiditis.
ciclocrioterapia *f.* cyclocryotherapy.
ciclodiálisis *f.* cyclodialysis.
ciclodiatermia *f.* cyclodiathermy.
cicloducción *f.* cycloduction.
cicloelectrólisis *f.* cycloelectrolysis.
cicloespasmo *m.* cyclospasm.
cicloforia *f.* cyclophoria.
cicloforómetro *m.* cyclophorometer.
ciclofotocoagulación *f.* cyclophotocoagulation.
ciclofrenia *f.* cyclophrenia.
ciclogenia *f.* cyclogeny.
ciclograma *m.* cyclogram.
cicloide *m.* cycloid.
ciclomastopatía *f.* cyclomastopathy.
cíclope, ciclope *adj.* cyclops.
ciclopea *f.* cyclopea.
ciclopentanofenantreno *m.* cyclopentenophenanthrene.
ciclópeo, -a *adj.* cyclopean.
ciclopía *f.* cyclopia, cyclopea.
ciclopiano, -na *adj.* cyclopian.
cicloplejía *f.* cycloplegia.
ciclopléjico, -ca *adj.* cycloplegic.
cicloqueratitis *f.* cyclokeratitis.
ciclosis *f.* cyclosis.
ciclospasmo *m.* cyclospasm.
ciclóstato *m.* cyclostat.
ciclotimia *f.* cyclothymia.
ciclotímico, -ca *adj.* cyclothymiac, cyclotymic.
ciclotomía *f.* cyclotomy.
ciclótomo *m.* cyclotome.
clotorsión *f.* cyclotorsion.
ciclotrón *m.* cyclotron.
ciclotropía *f.* cyclotropia.
ciego *m.* caecum.
ciego, -ga *adj.* blind.
cierre *m.* closure.
  cierre de la mufla flask closure.
  cierre velofaríngeo velopharyngeal closure.
ciesis *f.* cyesis.
cifoescoliosis *f.* kyphoscoliosis.
cifoscoliosis *f.* kyphoscoliosis.
cifosis *f.* kyphosis.
  cifosis de Scheuermann Scheuermann's kyphosis.
cigal *adj.* zygal.
cigapofisario, -ria *adj.* zygapophysial, zygapophyseal.
cigapófisis *f.* zygapophysis.

cigión *m.* zygion.
cigodactilia *f.* zygodactyly.
cigoma *m.* zygoma.
cigomático, -ca *adj.* zygomatic.
cigomaticoesfenoidal *adj.* zygomaticosphenoid.
cigomaticofacial *adj.* zygomaticofacial.
cigomaticofrontal *adj.* zygomaticofrontal.
cigomaticomaxilar *adj.* zygomaticomaxillary.
cigomaticoorbitario, -ria *adj.* zygomaticoorbital.
cigomaticotemporal *adj.* zygomaticotemporal.
cigomaxilar *m.* zygomaxillare.
cigomicosis *f.* zygomycosis.
cigón *m.* zygon.
cigonema *m.* zygonema.
cigopodio *m.* zygopodium.
cigosidad *f.* zygosity.
cigosis *f.* zygosis.
cigoteno *m.* zygotene.
cigótico, -ca *adj.* zygotic.
cigoto *m.* zygote.
ciguatera *f.* ciguatera.
ciguatoxina *f.* ciguatoxin.
ciliado *m.* ciliate.
ciliado, -da *adj.* ciliate.
ciliar *adj.* ciliary.
ciliaroscopio *m.* ciliaroscope.
ciliarotomía *f.* ciliarotomy.
ciliastático, -ca *adj.* ciliastatic.
ciliectomía *f.* ciliectomy.
cilindrartrosis *f.* cylindrarthrosis.
cilíndrico, -ca *adj.* cylindrical.
cilindriforme *adj.* cylindriform.
cilindro *m.* cast, cylinder.
  cilindro bacteriano bacterial cast.
  cilindro de Bence Jones Bence Jones cylinder.
  cilindro capilar hair cast.
  cilindro de células blancas de la sangre white blood cell cast.
  cilindro de células rojas, cilindro de células rojas de la sangre red cell cast, red blood cell cast.
  cilindro céreo waxy cast.
  cilindro del coma coma cast.
  cilindro cruzado crossed cylinder.
  cilindro decidual decidual cast.
  cilindro ensayado en halo halo cast.
  cilindro epitelial epithelial cast.
  cilindro espurio spurious cast.
  cilindro falso false cast.
  cilindro fibrinoso fibrinous cast.
  cilindro granular granular cast.
  cilindro graso fatty cast.
  cilindro hemático blood cast.
  cilindro hialino hyaline cast.
  cilindro de Külz Külz's cylinder.
  cilindro modelo dental dental cast.
  cilindro modelo diagnóstico diagnostic cast.
  cilindro modelo patrón master cast.
  cilindro modelo refractario refractory cast.
  cilindro modelo de revestimiento investment cast.
  cilindro mucoso mucous cast.
  cilindro renal renal cast.
  cilindro en tubo tube cast.
  cilindro urinario urinary cast.
cilindroadenoma *m.* cylindroadenoma.
cilindrocelular *adj.* cylindrocellular.
cilindroeje *m.* axis cylinder, cylindraxis.
cilindroide *m. y adj.* cylindroid.
cilindroma *m.* cylindroma.
cilindruria *f.* cylindruria.
cilio *m.* cilium.

cilioescleral *adj.* cilioscleral.
cilioespinal *adj.* ciliospinal.
ciliogénesis *f.* ciliogenesis.
ciliorretiniano, -na *adj.* cilioretinal.
ciliospinal *adj.* ciliospinal.
ciliotomía *f.* ciliotomy.
ciliotoxicidad *f.* ciliotoxicity.
cilium *m.* cilium.
cilosis *f.* cillosis.
cilósomo *m.* cyllosomus.
cilosoma *m.* cyllosoma.
cimba *f.* cymba conchae.
cimbocefalia *f.* cymbocephalia.
cimbocefálico, -ca *adj.* cymbocephalic, cymbocephalous.
cimex cimex.
cimicida *m.* cimicid.
cimodemo *m.* zymodene.
cimogénesis *f.* zymogenesis.
cimogénico, -ca *adj.* zymogenic.
cimógeno *m.* zymogen.
cimografía *f.* kymography.
cimógrafo *m.* kymograph.
cimograma *f.* zymogram.
cimohidrólisis *f.* zymolisis.
cimólisis *f.* zymolisis.
cimoscopio¹ *m.* kymoscope.
cimoscopio² *m.* zymoscope.
cimosténico, -ca *adj.* zymosthenic.
cimostético, -ca *adj.* zymosthenic.
cinanestesia *f.* cinanesthesia, kinanesthesia.
cinanquia *f.* cynanche.
cinantropía *f.* cynanthropy.
cincalismo *m.* zincalism.
cincífero, -ra *adj.* zinciferous.
cinquífero, -ra *adj.* zinciferous.
cinclisis *f.* cinclisis.
cincoide *adj.* zincoid.
cinconismo *m.* cinchonism.
cineangiocardiografía *f.* cineangiocardiography.
cineangiografía *f.* cineangiography.
cinedensigrafía *f.* cinedensigraphy.
cinefluorografía *f.* cinefluorography.
cinefluoroscopia *f.* cinefluoroscopy.
cinegastroscopia *f.* cinegastroscopy.
cinemática *f.* cinematics, kinematics.
cinematización *f.* cinematization.
cinematografía *f.* cinematography.
cinematorradiografía *f.* cinematoradiography.
cinemicrofotografía *f.* cinephotomicrography.
cinemómetro *m.* kinemometer.
cineplastia *f.* cineplasty, cineplastics, kineplastics.
cinérea *f.* cinerea.
cinéreo, -a *adj.* cinereal, cineritious.
cinerradiografía *f.* cineradiography.
cinerroentgenografía *f.* cincrocntgcnography.
cinesalgia *f.* cinesalgia, kinesalgia.
cinescopio *m.* kinescopy.
cinesia *f.* kinesia, kinesis.
cinesialgia *f.* cinesalgia.
cinesiatría *f.* kinesitherapy.
cinesiestesiómetro *m.* kinesiestesiometer.
cinesímetro *m.* kinesimeter, kinesiometer.
cinesiología *f.* kinesiology.
cinesiómetro *m.* kinesiometer.
cinesioneurosis *f.* kinesioneurosis.
cinesis *f.* kinesia, kinesis.
cinesismografía *f.* cinesismography.
cinesiterapia *f.* kinesiotherapy, kinesitherapy, kinetotherapy.
cinesódico, -ca *adj.* kinesodic.
cinesofobia *f.* kinesophobia.
cinestesia *f.* kinesthesia.
cinestésico, -ca *adj.* kinesthetic.

cinestesiómetro, kinestesiómetro *m.* kinesthesiometer.
cinesioterapia *f.* kinesiotherapy, kinesitherapy, kinetotherapy.
cinética *f.* kinetics.
  cinética química chemical kinetics.
cinético, -ca *adj.* kinetic.
cinetismo *m.* kinetism.
cinetocardiógrafo *m.* kinetocardiograph.
cinetocardiograma *m.* kinetocardiogram.
cinetocoro *m.* kinetochore.
cinetogénico -ca *adj.* kinetogenic.
cinetógeno, -na *adj.* kinetogenic.
cinetonúcleo *m.* kinetonucleus.
cinetoplasto *m.* kinetoplast.
cinetoscopia *f.* kinetoscopy.
cinetoscopio *m.* kinetoscope.
cinetosis *f.* kinetosis.
cinetosoma *m.* kinetosome.
cinetoterapia *f.* kinetotherapy.
cineurografía *f.* cineurography.
cingulado, -da *adj.* cingulate.
cingular *adj.* cingulate.
cingulectomía *f.* cingulectomy.
cíngulo *m.* cingulum.
cingulotomía *f.* cingulotomy.
cininógeno *m.* kininogen.
cinocefalia *f.* cynocephaly.
cinocéfalo *m.* cynocephalus.
cinodonto *m.* cynodont.
cinofobia *f.* kynophobia, cynophobia.
cinohapto *m.* kinohapt.
cinomómetro *m.* kinomometer.
cinorexia *f.* cynorexia.
cinoxato *m.* cinoxate.
cinta *f.* ribbon, tape.
  cinta adhesiva adhesive tape.
  cinta dental dental tape.
cintilla *f.* band.
cintura *f.* girdle, waist.
  cintura de Hitzig Hitzig's girdle.
  cintura de Neptuno Neptune's girdle.
  cintura escapular shoulder girdle.
  cintura torácica thoracic girdle.
cionectomía *f.* uvulectomy.
cionitis *f.* cionitis.
cionoptosis *f.* cionoptosis.
cionorrafia *f.* cionorrhaphy.
cionotomía *f.* cionotomy.
cipridofobia *f.* cypridophobia.
ciprifobia *f.* cypridophobia.
circadiano, -na *adj.* circadian.
circellus *m.* circellus.
circinado, -ca *adj.* circinate.
circuito *m.* circuit.
  circuito anestésico anesthetic circuit.
  circuito gamma gamma circuit.
  circuito de Granit Granit's circuit.
  circuito de memoria memory circuit.
  circuito de Papez Papez circuit.
  circuito reflejo reflex circuit.
  circuito reverberante reverberating circuit.
  circuito vector vector circuit.
circulación *f.* circulation.
  circulación alantoidea allantoic circulation.
  circulación asistida assisted circulation.
  circulación capilar capillary circulation.
  circulación colateral collateral circulation.
  circulación compensadora, circulación compensatoria compensatory circulation.
  circulación coronaria coronary circulation.
  circulación cruzada cross circulation.
  circulación derivativa derivative circulation.
  circulación embrionaria embryonic circulation.

  circulación enterohepática enterohepatic circulation.
  circulación extracorpórea extracorporeal circulation.
  circulación fetal fetal circulation.
  circulación general systemic circulation.
  circulación linfática lymph circulation.
  circulación mayor greater circulation.
  circulación menor lesser circulation.
  circulación onfalomesentérica omphalomesenteric circulation.
  circulación placentaria placental circulation.
  circulación portal portal circulation.
  circulación portal hipotalamohipofisaria hypothalamohypophyseal portal circulation.
  circulación pulmonar pulmonary circulation.
  circulación sanguínea bloodstream.
  circulación sinusoidal sinusoidal circulation.
  circulación sistémica systemic circulation.
  circulación de la vena porta portal circulation.
  circulación vitelina vitelline circulation.
circulatorio, -ria *adj.* circulatory.
circular *adj.* circular.
círculo *m.* circle, circulus.
  círculo cerrado closed circle.
  círculo de Berry Berry's circle.
  círculo defensivo defensive circle.
  círculo de menor difusión least diffusion circle.
  círculo de Pagenstecher Pagenstecher's circle.
  círculo semicerrado semi-closed circle.
  círculo vicioso vicious circle.
circumanal *adj.* circumanal.
circumaxilar *adj.* circumaxillary.
circumbulbar *adj.* circumbulbar.
circumoral *adj.* circumoral.
circumpolarización *f.* circumpolarization.
circunanal *adj.* circumanal.
circunarticular *adj.* circumarticular.
circuncidar *v.* circumcise.
circuncisión *f.* circumcision.
  circuncisión faraónica pharaonic circumcision.
circuncorneal *adj.* circumcorneal.
circunducción *f.* circumduction.
circunferencia *f.* circumference.
circunflejo, -ja *adj.* circumflex.
circungemal *adj.* circumgemmal.
circunintestinal *adj.* circumintestinal.
circunmandibular *adj.* circummandibular.
circunoral *adj.* circumoral.
circunnuclear *adj.* circumnuclear.
circunocular *adj.* circumocular.
circunorbitario, -ria *adj.* circumorbital.
circunrenal *adj.* circumrenal.
circunscrito, -ta *adj.* circumscribed, circumscriptus.
circunscripto, -ta *adj.* circumscriptus.
circunstancialidad *f.* circumstantiality.
circunvalado, -da *adj.* circumvallate.
circunvascular *adj.* circumvascular.
circunventricular *adj.* circumventricular.
circunvolución *f.* convolution.
circunvolutivo *adj.* circumvolute.
cirro *m.* cirrus.
cirrogénico, -ca *adj.* cirrhogenic.
cirrógeno, -na *adj.* cirrhogenous.
cirronosis *f.* cirrhonosus.
cirrosis *f.* cirrhosis.
  cirrosis alcohólica alcoholic cirrhosis.
  cirrosis atrófica atrophic cirrhosis.
  cirrosis biliar biliary cirrhosis.
  cirrosis biliar de los niños biliary cirrhosis of children.
  cirrosis biliar primaria primary biliary cirrhosis.

cirrosis de Budd Budd's cirrhosis.
cirrosis capsular, cirrosis capsular del hígado capsular cirrhosis, capsular cirrhosis of the liver.
cirrosis cardíaca cardiac cirrhosis.
cirrosis colangiolítica cholangiolitic cirrhosis.
cirrosis congestiva congestive cirrhosis.
cirrosis criptogénica cryptogenic cirrhosis.
cirrosis por estasis stasis cirrhosis.
cirrosis de Glisson Glisson's cirrhosis.
cirrosis grasa fatty cirrhosis.
cirrosis de Hanot Hanot's cirrhosis.
cirrosis hipertrófica hypertrophic cirrhosis.
cirrosis juvenil juvenile cirrhosis.
cirrosis de Laennec Laennec cirrhosis.
cirrosis necrótica necrotic cirrhosis.
cirrosis nutricional nutritional cirrhosis.
cirrosis periportal periportal cirrhosis.
cirrosis de pigmento, cirrosis pigmentaria pigment cirrhosis, pigmentary cirrhosis.
cirrosis portal portal cirrhosis.
cirrosis poshepática posthepatitic cirrhosis.
cirrosis posnecrótica postnecrotic cirrhosis.
cirrosis pulmonar pulmonary cirrhosis.
cirrosis sifilítica syphilitic cirrhosis.
cirrosis de Todd Todd's cirrhosis.
cirrosis tóxica toxic cirrhosis.
cirrosis unilobulillar unilobular cirrhosis.
cirroso, -sa *adj.* cirrose, cirrous.
cirrótico, -ca *adj.* cirrhotic.
cirsectomía *f.* cirsectomy.
cirsenquisis *f.* cirsenchysis.
cirsocele *m.* cirsocele.
cirsodesia *f.* cirsodesis.
cirsodesis *f.* cirsodesis.
cirsoftalmia *f.* cirsophthalmia.
cirsoide *adj.* cirsoid.
cirsoideo, -a *adj.* cirsoid.
cirsónfalo *m.* cirsomphalos.
cirsotomía *f.* cirsotomy.
cirsótomo *m.* cirsotome.
cirtógrafo *m.* cyrtograph.
cirtómetro *m.* cyrtometer.
cirtosis *f.* cyrtosis.
cirugía *f.* surgery.
  cirugía a corazón abierto open heart surgery.
  cirugía abdominal abdominal surgery.
  cirugía ambulatoria ambulatory surgery.
  cirugía antiséptica antiseptic surgery.
  cirugía aséptica aseptic surgery.
  cirugía bucal oral surgery.
  cirugía cardíaca cardiac surgery.
  cirugía cerrada closed surgery.
  cirugía cineplástica cineplastic surgery.
  cirugía clínica clinical surgery.
  cirugía conservadora conservative surgery.
  cirugía cosmética cosmetic surgery.
  cirugía craneofacial craniofacial surgery.
  cirugía de las facciones featural surgery.
  cirugía dental dental surgery.
  cirugía dentofacial dentofacial surgery.
  cirugía estereotáctica, cirugía estereotáxica stereotactic surgery, stereotaxic surgery.
  cirugía estética esthetic surgery.
  cirugía estructural structural surgery.
  cirugía general general surgery.
  cirugía maxilofacial maxillofacial surgery.
  cirugía mayor major surgery.
  cirugía menor minor surgery.
  cirugía operatoria operative surgery.
  cirugía oral oral surgery.
  cirugía ortognática orthognathic surgery.
  cirugía ortopédica orthopedic surgery.
  cirugía ótica, cirugía otológica aural surgery.

  cirugía plástica plastic surgery.
  cirugía radical radical surgery.
  cirugía reconstructora, cirugía reconstructiva reconstructive surgery.
  cirugía transexual transsexual surgery.
cirujano, -na *m., f.* surgeon.
cistadenocarcinoma *m.* cystadenocarcinoma.
cistadenoma *m.* cystadenoma, cystoadenoma.
  cistadenoma mucinoso mucinous cystadenoma.
  cistadenoma papilar papillary cystadenoma.
  cistadenoma papilar linfomatoso papillary cystadenoma lymphomatosum.
  cistadenoma seroso serous cystadenoma.
  cistadenoma seudomucinoso pseudomucinous cystadenoma.
cistalgia *f.* cystalgia.
cistatrofia *f.* cystatrophia.
cistationinuria *f.* cystathioninuria.
cistauquenitis *f.* cystauchenitis.
cistauquenotomía *f.* cystauchenotomy.
cistectasia *f.* cystectasia, cystectasy.
cistectomía *f.* cystectomy.
  cistectomía de Bartholin Bartholin's cystectomy.
  cistectomía parcial partial cystectomy.
  cistectomía radical radical cystectomy.
  cistectomía total total cystectomy.
cistelcosis *f.* cystelcosis.
cistendesis *f.* cystendesis.
cisterna *f.* cistern, cisterna.
cisternal *adj.* cisternal.
cisternografía *f.* cisternography.
  cisternografía cerebelopontina cerebellopontine cisternography.
  cisternografía con radionúclidos radionuclide cisternography.
cisticerco *m.* Cysticercus.
cisticercoide *m.* cysticercoid.
cisticercosis *f.* cysticercosis.
cístico, -ca *adj.* cystic, cystous.
cisticolitectomía *f.* cysticolithectomy.
cisticolitotripsia *f.* cysticolithotripsy.
cisticotomía *f.* cysticotomy.
cisticotraquelotomía *f.* cysticotrachelotomy.
cistifeleotomía *f.* cystifelleotomy.
cistifelotomía *f.* cystifelleotomy.
cistífero, -ra *adj.* cystigerous, cystygerous, cystopherous, cystophorous.
cistiforme *adj.* cystiform.
cistíforo, -ra *adj.* cystiphorous.
cistígero, -ra *adj.* cystigerous.
cistinemia *f.* cystinemia.
cistinosis *f.* cystinosis.
cistinuria *f.* cystinuria.
  cistinuria familiar familial cystinuria.
cistirragia *f.* cystirrhagia.
cististaxis *f.* cystistaxis, cystostaxis.
cistitis *f.* cystitis.
  cistitis aguda acute catarrhal cystitis.
  cistitis alérgica allergic cystitis.
  cistitis bacteriana bacterial cystitis.
  cistitis del cuello, cistitis cervical cystitis colli.
  cistitis crupal croupous cystitis.
  cistitis diftérica diphtheritic cystitis.
  cistitis enfisematosa emphysematous cystitis.
  cistitis eosinófila eosinophilic cystitis.
  cistitis exfoliativa exfoliative cystitis.
  cistitis folicular follicular cystitis.
  cistitis glandular cystitis glandularis.
  cistitis hemorrágica hemorrhagic cystitis.
  cistitis incrustada incrusted cystitis.
  cistitis intersticial crónica interstitial cystitis.

  cistitis papilomatosa cystitis papillomatosa.
  cistitis quística cystitis cystica.
  cistitis senil cystitis senilis.
  cistitis vírica viral cystitis.
cistitomía *f.* cystitomy.
cistítomo *m.* cystitome.
cistoadenoma *m.* cystoadenoma.
cistoblasto *m.* cystoblast.
cistocarcinoma *m.* cystocarcinoma.
cistocele *m.* cystocele.
cistocolostomía *f.* cystocolostomy.
cistocromoscopia *f.* cystochromoscopy.
cistodinia *f.* cystodynia.
cistodivertículo *m.* cystodiverticulum.
cistoduodenostomía *f.* cystoduodenostomy.
cistoelitroplastia *f.* cystoelytroplasty.
cistoenterocele *m.* cystoenterocele.
cistoenterostomía *f.* cystoenterostomy.
cistoepiplocele *m.* cystoepiplocele.
cistoepitelioma *m.* cystoepithelioma.
cistoesclerosis *f.* cystosclerosis.
cistoespasmo *m.* cystospasm.
cistófero, -ra *adj.* cystopherous.
cistofibroma *m.* cystofibroma.
cistóforo, -ra *adj.* cystophorous.
cistofotografía *f.* cystophotography.
cistogastrostomía *f.* cystogastrostomy.
cistografía *f.* cystography.
cistograma *m.* cystogram.
  cistograma de evacuación voiding cystogram.
cistoide *m. y adj.* cystoid.
cistolitectomía *f.* cystolithectomy.
cistolitiasis *f.* cystolithiasis.
cistolítico, -ca *adj.* cystolithic.
cistolito *m.* cystolith.
cistolitotomía *f.* cystolithotomy.
cistoma *m.* cystoma.
  cistoma seroso simple cystoma serosum simplex.
cistometría *f.* cystometry.
cistómetro *m.* cystometer.
cistometrografía *f.* cystometrography.
cistometrograma *m.* cystometrogram.
cistomioma *m.* cystomyoma.
cistomixoadenoma *m.* cystomyxoadenoma.
cistomixoma *m.* cystomyxoma.
cistomorfo, -fa *adj.* cystomorphous.
cistonefrosis *f.* cystonephrosis.
cistoneuralgia *f.* cystoneuralgia.
cistopanendoscopia *f.* cystopanendoscopy.
cistoparálisis *f.* cystoparalysis.
cistopexia *f.* cystopexy.
cistopielitis *f.* cystopyelitis.
cistopielografía *f.* cystopielography.
cistopielonefritis *f.* cystopyelonephritis.
cistoplastia *f.* cystoplasty.
cistoplejía *f.* cystoplegia.
cistoproctostomía *f.* cystoproctostomy.
cistoptosis *f.* cystoptosis.
cistorradiografía *f.* cystoradiography.
cistorrafia *f.* cystorraphy.
cistorragia *f.* cystorrhagia, cystirrhagia.
cistorrea *f.* cystorrhea.
cistorrectostomía *f.* cystorectostomy.
cistosarcoma *m.* cystosarcoma.
  cistosarcoma filoides cystosarcoma phylloides, cystosarcoma phylloides of the breast.
cistosclerosis *f.* cystosclerosis.
cistoscopia *f.* cystoscopy.
cistoscopio *m.* cystoscope.
cistoscópico, -ca *adj.* cystoscopic.
cistospasmo *m.* cystospasm.
cistosquisis *f.* cystoschisis.
cistostaxis *f.* cystostaxis.

cistostomía *f.* cystostomy.
cistotomía *f.* cystotomy.
  cistotomía hipogástrica suprapubic cystotomy.
  cistotomíasuprapúbica suprapubic cystotomy.
cistótomo *m.* cystotome.
cistotraquelotomía *f.* cystotrachelotomy.
cistoureteritis *f.* cystoureteritis.
cistoureterografía *f.* cystoureterography.
cistoureterograma *m.* cystoureterogram.
cistoureteropielitis *f.* cystoureteropyelitis.
cistouretritis *f.* cystourethritis.
cistouretrocele *m.* cystourethrocele.
cistouretrografía *f.* cystourethrography.
cistouretrograma *m.* cystourethrogram.
cistouretroscopio *m.* cystourethroscope.
cistrón *m.* cistron, cystron.
cisura *f.* fissure, scissura.
citaféresis *f.* cytapheresis.
citemia *f.* cytemia.
citemólisis *m.* cythemolysis.
citoarquitectónico, -ca *adj.* cytoarchitectural, cytoarchitectonic.
citoarquitectura *f.* cytoarchitecture, cytoarchitectonics.
citobiología *f.* cytobiology.
citobiotaxis *f.* cytobiotaxis.
citocalasinas *f.* cytochalasins.
citocentro *m.* cytocentrum.
citocida¹ *m.* cytocide.
citocida² *adj.* cytocidal.
citocima *f.* cytozyme.
citocina *f.* cytokine.
citocinesis *f.* cytocinesis.
citoclasia *f.* cytoclasis.
citoclasis *f.* cytoclasis.
citoclástico, -ca *adj.* cytoclastic.
citodiagnóstico *m.* cytodiagnosis.
citodiéresis *f.* cytodieresis.
citoesqueleto *m.* cytoskeleton.
citofagia *f.* cytophagy.
citófago, -ga *adj.* cytophagous.
citofiláctico, -ca *adj.* cytophylactic.
citofilaxis *f.* cytophilaxis.
citofilético, -ca *adj.* cytophiletic.
citofílico, -ca *adj.* cytophilic.
citófilo, -la *adj.* cytophil.
citofotometría *f.* cytophotometry.
citofrotis *m.* cytosmear.
citogénesis *f.* cytogenesis.
citogenética *f.* cytogenetics.
citogenetista *m., f.* cytogeneticist.
citogenia *f.* cytogenesis.
citogénico, -ca *adj.* cytogenic.
citógeno, -na *adj.* cytogenous.
citoglucopenia *f.* cytoglycopenia.
citoide *adj.* cytoid.
citolisina *f.* cytolysin.
citólisis *f.* cytolysis.
citolisosoma *m.* cytolysosome.
citolítico, -ca *adj.* cytolytic.
citología *f.* cytology.
  citología biópsica por aspiración aspiration biopsy cytology.
  citología cervicovaginal cervicovaginal cytology.
  citología exfoliativa exfoliative cytology.
citológico, -ca *adj.* cytologic.
citólogo, -ga *m., f.* cytologist.
citomegálico, -ca *adj.* cytomegalic.
citomegaloviruria *f.* cytomegaloviruria.
citomegalovirus *m.* cytomegalovirus.
citomembrana *f.* cytomembrane.
citómera *f.* cytomere.

citómero *f.* cytomere.
citometaplasia *f.* cytometaplasia.
citometría *f.* cytometry.
  citometría de flujo flow cytometry.
citómetro *m.* cytometer.
citomicosis *f.* cytomycosis.
citomorfología *f.* cytomorphology.
citomorfosis *f.* cytomorphosis.
citopatía *f.* cytopathy.
citopático, -ca *adj.* cytopathic.
citopatógénico, -ca *adj.* cytopathogenic.
citopatología *f.* cytopathology.
citopatológico, -ca *adj.* cytopathologic, cytopathological.
citopatólogo, -ga *m., f.* cytopathologist.
citopempsis *f.* cytopempsis.
citopenia *f.* cytopenia.
citopipeta *f.* cytopipette.
citoplasma *m.* cytoplasm.
citoplasmático, -ca *adj.* cytoplasmic.
citopoyesis *f.* cytopoiesis.
citopreparación *f.* cytopreparation.
citoquímica *f.* cytochemistry.
citoscopia *f.* cytoscopy.
citosis *f.* cytosis.
citosoma *m.* cytosome.
citostasis *f.* cytostasis.
citotáctico, -ca *adj.* cytotactic.
citotaxia *f.* cytotaxia, cytotaxis.
citotaxis *f.* cytotaxis.
citoterapia *f.* cytotherapy.
citotesis *f.* cythothesis.
citotoxicidad *f.* cytotoxicity.
  citotoxicidad celular anticuerpo-dependiente, citotoxicidad celular dependiente de anticuerpo antibody dependent cell-mediated cytotoxicity.
  citotoxicidad mediada por linfocitos lymphocyte-mediated cytotoxicity.
citotóxico, -ca *adj.* cytotoxic.
citotoxina *f.* cytotoxin.
citotrofoblasto *m.* cytotrophoblast.
citotropismo *m.* cytotropism.
citozima *f.* cytozyme.
citozoario *m.* cytozoon.
citozoico, -ca *adj.* cytozoic.
citozoo *m.* cytozoon.
Citrobacter Citrobacter.
citrulinemia *f.* citrullinemia.
citrulinuria *f.* citrullinuria.
cituria *f.* cyturia.
cladiosis *f.* cladiosis.
cladosporiosis *f.* cladosporiosis.
  cladosporiosis cerebral cerebral cladosporiosis.
  cladosporiosis cutánea cutaneous cladosporiosis.
Cladosporium Cladosporium.
clamidia *f.* Chlamydia.
clamidial *adj.* chlamydial.
clamidiasis *f.* chlamydiosis.
clamp *m.* clamp.
  clamp de Cope Cope's clamp.
  clamp de Crawford Crawford clamp.
  clamp de Crile Crile's clamp.
  clamp para dique de goma rubber dam clamp.
  clamp de Doyen Doyen's clamp.
  clamp de Fogarty Fogarty clamp.
  clamp de Gant Gant's clamp.
  clamp de Gaskell Gaskell's clamp.
  clamp gingival gingival clamp.
  clamp de Goldblatt Goldblatt's clamp.
  clamp de Gussenbauer Gussenbauer's clamp.
  clamp de Joseph Joseph's clamp.

  clamp de Kelly Kelly clamp.
  clamp de Kocher Kocher clamp.
  clamp de Mikulicz Mikulicz clamp.
  clamp Mogen Mogen clamp.
  clamp mosquito mosquito clamp.
  clamp de Ochsner Ochsner clamp.
  clamp de Payr Payr's clamp.
  clamp para pedículos pedicle clamp.
  clamp de Potts Potts clamp.
  clamp de Rankin Rankin's clamp.
  clamp de Willet Willet's clamp.
  clamp de Yellen Yellen clamp.
clapoteo *m.* clapotage, clapotement.
clarificación *f.* clarification.
clarificador, -ra *adj.* clarificant.
clarividencia *f.* clear-sightedness, clairvoyance.
clase *f.* class.
clasificación *f.* classification.
clasmatosis *f.* clasmatosis.
clástico, -ca *adj.* clastic.
clastogénico, -ca *adj.* clastogenic.
clastógeno *m.* clastogen.
clastotrix *m.* clastothrix.
claudicación *f.* claudication.
  claudicación cerebral cerebral claudication.
  claudicación intermitente intermittent claudication.
  claudicación venosa venous claudication.
  claudicación del tríceps sural triceps surae claudication.
claudicante *adj.* claudicatory.
claudicatorio, -ria *adj.* claudicatory.
claustral *adj.* claustral.
claustro *m.* claustrum.
claustrofilia *f.* claustrophilia.
claustrofobia *f.* claustrophobia.
claustrofóbico, -ca *adj.* claustrophobic.
claustrum claustrum.
clava *f.* clava.
claval *adj.* claval.
clavar *v.* nailing.
clavicotomía *f.* clavicotomy.
clavícula *f.* clavicle, clavicula.
clavicular *adj.* clavicular.
claviculo *m.* claviculus.
claviforme *adj.* clavate.
clavija *f.* peg.
clavipectoral *adj.* clavipectoral.
clavo¹ *m.* clavus.
clavo² *m.* nail.
cleidagra *f.* cleidagra, clidagra.
cleidal *adj.* cleidal, clidal.
cleidartritis *f.* cleidarthritis.
cleidocostal *adj.* cleidocostal.
cleidocraneal *adj.* cleidocranial.
cleidomastoideo, -a *adj.* cleidomastoid.
cleidorrexis *f.* cleidorrhexis.
cleidotomía *f.* cleidotomy.
cleidotripsia *f.* cleidotripsy.
cleoide *m.* cleoid.
cleptofobia *f.* kleptophobia.
cleptolagnia *f.* kleptolagnia.
cleptomanía *f.* kleptomania.
cleptomaníaco *m.* kleptomaniac.
cleptómano *m.* kleptomaniac.
clidagra *f.* clidagra.
clidal *adj.* clidal.
clidocostal *adj.* clidocostal.
clidocraneal *adj.* clidocranial.
clima *m.* climate, weather.
climacofobia *f.* climacophobia.
climaterio *m.* climacterium.
climático, -ca *adj.* climatic.
climatología *f.* climatology.

climatoterapia *f.* climatotherapy.
clímax *m.* climax.
climógrafo *m.* climograph.
clínica *f.* clinic.
clínico, -ca[1] *adj.* clinical.
clínico, -ca[2] *m., f.* clinician.
clinicopatológico, -ca *adj.* clinicopathologic.
clino *m.* cline.
clinocefalia *f.* clinocephaly.
clinocefalismo *m.* clinocephaly.
clinocéfalo, -la *adj.* clinocephalic, clinocephalous.
clinodactilia *f.* clinodactyly.
clinografía *f.* clinography.
clinoide *adj.* clinoid.
clinología *f.* clinology.
clinomanía *f.* clinomania.
clinómetro *m.* clinometer.
clinoscopio *m.* clinoscope.
clinostático, -ca *adj.* clinostatic.
clinostatismo *m.* clinostatism.
clinoterapia *f.* clinotherapy.
clíster *m.* clyster.
clitión *m.* clition.
clitorectomía *f.* clitorectomy.
clitoridectomía *f.* clitoridectomy.
clitorídeo, -a *adj.* clitoral, clitoridean.
clitoriditis *f.* clitoriditis.
clitoridotomía *f.* clitoridotomy.
clítoris *m.* clitoris.
clitorismo *m.* clitorism.
clitoritis *f.* clitoritis.
clitoromegalia *f.* clitoromegaly.
clitorotomía *f.* clitorotomy.
clitrofobia *f.* clithrophobia.
clivus clivus.
cloaca *f.* cloaca.
cloacal *adj.* cloacal.
cloasma *m.* chloasma.
  cloasma broncíneo chloasma bronzinum.
clon *m.* clone.
clonación *f.* cloning.
clonal *adj.* clonal.
clonar *v.* clone.
clonicidad *f.* clonicity.
clónico, -ca *adj.* clonic.
clonicotónico, -ca *adj.* clonicotonic.
clonismo *m.* clonism.
clono *m.* clone.
clonoespasmo *m.* clonospasm.
clonogénico, -ca *adj.* clonogenic.
clonógeno, -na *adj.* clonogenic.
clonógrafo *m.* clonograph.
Clonorchis sinensis Clonorchis sinensis.
clonorquiasis *f.* clonorchiasis, clonchiosis.
clonorquiosis *f.* clonorchiosis.
clonospasmo *m.* clonospasm.
clonus *m.* clonus.
  clonus de apertura catódica cathodal opening clonus.
  clonus de los dedos del pie toe clonus.
  clonus de la muñeca wrist clonus.
  clonus rotuliano patellar clonus.
  clonus del tobillo ankle clonus.
cloracné *f.* chloracne.
clorado, -da *adj.* chlorinated.
cloranemia *f.* chloranemia.
cloremia *f.* chloremia.
clorhidria *f.* chlorhydria.
cloridemia *f.* chloridemia.
cloridimetría *f.* chloridimetry.
cloridímetro *m.* chloridimeter.
cloriduria *f.* chloriduria.
clorinado, -da *adj.* chlorinated.
clorófano *m.* chlorophane.

cloroformismo *m.* chloroformism.
cloroformización *f.* chloroformization.
cloroformo *m.* chloroform.
clorolabe *m.* chlorable.
cloroleucemia *f.* chloroleukemia.
cloroleucosarcomatosis *f.* chloroma.
clorolinfosarcoma *m.* chloroma.
cloroma *m.* chloroma.
clorometría *f.* chlorometry.
cloromieloma *m.* chloromyeloma.
cloromielosarcomatosis *f.* chloromyeloma.
cloronaftaleno *m.* chloronaftalene.
cloropenia *f.* chloropenia.
cloropexia *f.* chloropexia.
cloropía *f.* chloropsia.
cloroplasto *m.* chloroplast.
cloroprivo, -va *adj.* chloroprivic.
cloropsia *f.* chloropsia.
clorosarcolinfadenia *f.* chlorosarcolymphadeny.
clorosis *f.* chlorosis.
cloroso, -sa *adj.* chlorous.
clorótico, -ca *adj.* chlorotic.
cloroyodado, -da *adj.* chloroiodized.
cloruresis *f.* chloruresis, chlouresis.
clorurémico, -ca *adj.* chloruremic.
clorurético, -ca *adj.* chloruretic, chlouretic.
cloruria *f.* chloruria.
clorurometría *f.* chloridimetry.
clorurómetro *m.* chloridimeter.
clostridial *adj.* chlostridial.
clostridio *m.* clostridium.
Clostridium Clostridium.
clounismo *m.* clownism.
clouresis *f.* chlouresis.
clourético, -ca *adj.* chlouretic.
clownismo *m.* clownism.
clubbing *m.* clubbing.
clubhand *m.* clubhand.
cnemial *adj.* cnemial.
cnémico, -ca *adj.* cnemial.
cnemis *f.* cnemis.
cnemitis *f.* cnemitis.
cnemoscoliosis *f.* cnemoscoliosis.
cnidosis *f.* cnidosis.
cnismogénico, -ca *adj.* knismogenic.
cnismolagnia *f.* knismolagnia.
coadaptación *f.* coadaptation.
coadunación *f.* coadunation, coadunition.
coadyuvante *adj.* adjuvant.
coaglutinación *f.* coagglutination.
coaglutinina *f.* coagglutinin.
coagulabilidad *f.* coagulability.
coagulable *adj.* coagulable.
coagulación *f.* coagulation.
  coagulación cerrada closing coagulation.
  coagulación intravascular difusa diffuse intravascular coagulation.
  coagulación intravascular diseminada (CID) disseminated intravascular coagulation (DIC).
  coagulación masiva massive coagulation.
  coagulación plasmática plasmatic coagulation.
  coagulación sanguínea blood clotting.
coagulador *m.* coagulator.
coagulante *adj.* coagulant.
coagulativo, -va *adj.* coagulative.
coágulo *m.* clot, coagulum.
  coágulo agónico, coágulo de la agonía agonal clot, agony clot.
  coágulo ante mortem antemortem clot.
  coágulo blanco white clot.
  coágulo cardíaco heart clot.
  coágulo de cierre closing clot.
  coágulo distal distal clot.

  coágulo estratificado stratified clot.
  coágulo externo external clot.
  coágulo en grasa de pollo chicken fat clot.
  coágulo interno internal clot.
  coágulo en jalea de grosella, coágulo en gelatina de grosella currant jelly clot.
  coágulo laminado laminated clot.
  coágulo lavado washed clot.
  coágulo maránico marantic clot.
  coágulo pasivo passive clot.
  coágulo plástico plastic clot.
  coágulo post mortem post mortem clot.
  coágulo proximal proximal clot.
  coágulo sanguíneo blood clot.
  coágulo de Schede Schede's clot.
  coágulo en telaraña spider web clot.
coagulograma *f.* coagulogram.
coagulopatía *f.* coagulopathy.
  coagulopatía por consumo de factores consumption coagulopathy.
coalescencia *f.* coalescence.
coalescente *adj.* coalescent.
coana *f.* choana.
  coana primaria, coana primitiva primary choana, primitive choana.
  coana secundaria secondary choana.
coanado, -da *adj.* choanate.
coanal *adj.* choanal.
coanoide *adj.* choanoid.
coaptación *f.* coaptation.
coartación *f.* coarctation.
  coartación de la aorta, coartación aórtica coarctation of the aorta.
  coartación aórtica de tipo adulto adult type coarctation of the aorta.
  coartación aórtica de tipo infantil infantile type coarctation of the aorta.
  coartación invertida reversed coarctation.
coartado, -da *adj.* coarctate.
coarticulación *f.* coarticulation.
coartotomía *f.* coarctotomy.
cobaltosis *f.* cobaltosis.
cobaltoso, -sa *adj.* cobaltous.
cobaya *f.* guinea pig.
cobayo *m.* guinea pig.
cobertura funcional *f.* functional overlay.
cobraísmo *m.* cobraism.
cocaína *f.* cocaine, cocain.
cocainismo *m.* cocainism.
cocainización *f.* cocainization.
cocainomanía *f.* cocainism.
cocaínómano, -na *m., f.* cocainist.
cocarcinogénesis *f.* cocarcinogenesis.
cocarcinógeno *m.* cocarcinogen.
cocardiforme *adj.* cocardiform.
coccialgia *f.* coccyalgia, coccygalgia.
coccicefalia *f.* coccycephaly.
Coccidia Coccidia.
coccidial *adj.* coccidial.
coccidiano, -na *adj.* coccidian.
coccidinia *f.* coccydinia.
coccidio *m.* coccidium.
coccidioide *adj.* coccidioidal.
coccidioideo, -a *adj.* coccidioidial.
Coccidioides Coccidioides.
coccidioidina *f.* coccidioidina.
coccidioidoma *m.* coccidioidoma.
coccidioidomicosis *f.* coccidioidomycosis.
  coccidioidomicosis asintomática asymptomatic coccidioidomycosis.
  coccidioidomicosis diseminada disseminate coccidioidomycosis.
  coccidioidomicosis extrapulmonar primaria primary extrapulmonary coccidioidomycosis.

coccidioidomicosis latente latent coccidioidomycosis.

coccidioidomicosis primaria primary coccidioidomycosis.

coccidioidomicosis secundaria secondary coccidioidomycosis.

coccidioidosis *f.* coccidioidosis.

coccidiosis *f.* coccidiosis.

coccidiostático, -ca *adj.* coccidiostatic.

Coccidium Coccidium.

coccigalgia *f.* coccygalgia.

coccigectomía *f.* coccygectomy.

coccigénico, -ca *adj.* coccigenic.

coccígeno, -na *adj.* coccigenic.

coccígeo, -a *adj.* coccygeal.

coccigodinia *f.* coccygodynia, coccyodynia.

coccigotomía *f.* coccygotomy.

cocciodinia *f.* coccyodinia.

cóccix *m.* coccyx.

cóxis *m.* coccyx.

Coccobacillus Coccobacillus.

cócico, -ca *adj.* coccal.

cociente *m.* quotient.

cocktail *m.* cocktail.

cóclea *f.* cochlea.

coclear *adj.* cochlear.

cocleariforme *adj.* cochleariform.

cocleítis *f.* cochleitis.

cocleotópico, -ca *adj.* cochleotopic.

cocleosaculotomía *f.* cochleosacculotomy.

cocleovestibular *adj.* cochleovestibular.

coclitis *f.* cochlitis.

cocobacilo *m.* coccobacillus.

cocobacilar *adj.* coccobacillary.

cocobacteria *f.* coccobacteria.

cocógeno, -na *adj.* coccogenic, coccogenous.

cocoideo, -a *adj.* coccoid.

coconsciencia *f.* coconsciousness.

coconsciente *adj.* coconscious.

cocontracción *f.* cocontraction.

coco *m.* coccus.

cóctel *m.* cocktail.

coctoantígeno *m.* coctoantigen.

coctoestable *adj.* coctostabile, coctostable.

coctoinmunógeno *m.* coctoimmunogen.

coctolábil *adj.* coctolabile.

coctoprecipitina *f.* coctoprecipitin.

coctoproteína *f.* coctoprotein.

coctostable *adj.* coctostable.

cocultivo *m.* cocultivation.

Cochliomyia Cochliomyia.

codificación *f.* coding, encoding.

código *m.* code.

código analógico analogical code.

código digital digital code.

código genético genetic code.

codivilla *f.* fibrous release.

codo *m.* elbow.

codo dislocado pulled elbow.

codo del estudiante student elbow.

codo de golfista golfer's elbow.

codo de lanzador baseball pitcher's elbow.

codo de Little Leaguer Little Leaguer's elbow.

codo de los mineros miner's elbow.

codo de las niñeras nursemaid's elbow.

codo péndulo dropped elbow.

codo de tenista tennis elbow.

codocito *m.* codocyte.

codominancia *f.* codominance.

codominante *adj.* codominant.

codón *m.* codon.

codón de iniciación initiating codon, initiation codon.

codón de terminación termination codon.

coeficiente *m.* coefficient.

Coenerus Coenerus.

coenocito *m.* cenocyte.

coenzima *f.* coenzyme.

coenzimómetro *m.* coenzymometer.

coetáneo, -a *adj.* coetaneous.

coexcitación *f.* coexcitation.

cofactor *m.* cofactor.

cofemia *f.* kophemia.

cofia *f.* caul.

cofosis *f.* deafness.

cognición *f.* cognition.

cognitivo, -va *adj.* cognitive.

coherencia *f.* coherence.

cohesión *f.* cohesion.

cohesividad *f.* cohesiveness.

cohesivo, -va *adj.* cohesive.

cohorte *f.* cohort.

coilocito *m.* koilocyte.

coilocitosis *f.* koilocytosis.

coiloniquia *f.* koilonychia.

coinervación *f.* coinnervation.

coilosternia *f.* koilosternia.

coinonía *f.* koinonia.

coinosito *m.* coinosite.

coinotropía *f.* koinotropy.

coisogénico, -ca *adj.* coisogenic.

coital *adj.* coital.

coitalgia *f.* coitalgia.

coito *m.* coitus.

coitofobia *f.* coitophobia.

cojera *f.* lameness, limp.

cojo -ja *adj.* lame.

col *f.* col.

cola *f.* tail.

colado *m.* casting.

colado funda de oro gold casting.

coladura *f.* colation.

colágena *f.* collagen.

colagenación *f.* collagenation.

colagénico, -ca *adj.* collagenic.

colagenitis *f.* collagenitis.

colagenización *f.* collagenation.

colágeno *m.* collagen.

colágeno tipo I type I collagen.

colágeno tipo II type II collagen.

colágeno tipo III type III collagen.

colágeno tipo IV type IV collagen.

colágeno, -na *adj.* collagenous.

colagenogénico, -ca *adj.* collagenogenic.

colagenólisis *f.* collagenolysis.

colagenolítico, -ca *adj.* collagenolytic.

colagenosis *f.* collagenosis.

colagenosis perforante activa reactive perforating collagenosis.

colálico, -ca *adj.* cholalic.

colaligénico, -ca *adj.* cholaligenic.

colaneresis *f.* cholaneresis.

colangeítis *f.* cholangeitis.

colangia *f.* cholangia.

colangiectasia *f.* cholangiectasis.

colangiocarcinoma *m.* cholangiocarcinoma.

colangiocolecistocoledocectomía *f.* cholangiocholecystocholedochectomy.

colangiocolecistografía *f.* cholangiocholecystography.

colangiocolecistografía intravenosa intravenous cholangiocholecystography.

colangiocolecistografía retrógada retrogressive cholangiocholecystography.

colangiocolecistografía TC CT cholangiocholecystography.

colangioenterostomía *f.* cholangioenterostomy.

colangiofibrosis *f.* cholangiofibrosis.

colangiogastrostomía *f.* cholangiogastrostomy.

colangiografía *f.* cholangiography.

colangiografía del conducto cístico cystic duct cholangiography.

colangiografía endoscópica retrógrada endoscopic retrograde cholangiography.

colangiografía intravenosa intravenous cholangiography.

colangiografía percutánea percutaneous cholangiography.

colangiografía retrógrada endoscópica (CPRE) endoscopic retrograde cholangiography.

colangiografía transhepática transhepatic cholangiography.

colangiografía transhepática percutánea percutaneous transhepatic cholangiography.

colangiografía transparietohepática transparietohepatic cholangiography.

colangiografía transyugular transjugular cholangiography.

colangiografía tubular en T T tubule cholangiography.

colangiograma *m.* cholangiogram.

colangiohepatitis *f.* cholangiohepatitis.

colangiohepatoma *m.* cholangiohepatoma.

colangiolar *adj.* cholangiolar.

colangiolitis *f.* cholangiolitis.

colangiolo *m.* cholangiole.

colangioma *m.* cholangioma.

colangiopancreatografía *f.* cholangiopancreatography.

colangiopancreatografía endoscópica retrógrada, colangiopancreatografía retrógrada endoscópica (CPRE) ERCP, endoscopic retrograde cholangiopancreatography (ERCP).

colangioscopia *f.* cholangioscopy.

colangiostomía *f.* cholangiostomy.

colangiotomía *f.* cholangiotomy.

colangioyeyunostomía *f.* cholangiojejunostomy.

colangitis *f.* cholangitis, cholangeitis.

colangitis aguda acute cholangitis.

colangitis destructiva crónica no supurada chronic nonsuppurative destructive cholangitis.

colangitis esclerosante sclerosing cholangitis.

colangitis esclerosante primaria primary sclerosing cholangitis.

colangitis progresiva no supurada progressive nonsuppurative cholangitis.

colangitis lenta cholangitis lenta.

colanopoyesis *f.* cholanopoiesis.

colanopoyético, -ca *adj.* cholanopoietic.

colapso *m.* collapse.

colapso por absorción absorption collapse.

colapso del arco dentario collapse of the dental arch.

colapso bronquiolar bronchiolar collapse.

colapso circulatorio circulatory collapse.

colapso masivo massive collapse.

colapso nervioso nervous breakdown.

colapso por presión pressure collapse.

colapso pulmonar pulmonary collapse, collapse of the lung.

colapso pulmonar hipostático hypostatic lung collapse.

colapso pulmonar pasivo passive lung collapse.

colapsoterapia *f.* collapsotherapy.

colascos *m.* cholascos.

colastina *f.* collastin.

colateral *adj.* collateral.
colateralización *f.* collateralization.
  colateralización coronaria coronary collateralization.
colaturo *m.* colature.
colebilirrubina *f.* cholebilirubin.
colecistagógico, -ca *adj.* cholecystagogic.
colecistagogo, -ga *adj.* cholecystagogue.
colecistalgia *f.* cholecystalgia.
colecistatonía *f.* cholecystanony.
colecistectasia *f.* cholecystectasia.
colecistectomía *f.* cholecystectomy.
  colecistectomía laparoscópica laparoscopic cholecystectomy.
colecistendisis *f.* cholecystendysis.
colecistentérico, -ca *adj.* cholecystenteric.
colecistenteroanastomosis *f.* cholecystenteroanastomosis.
colecistenterorrafia *f.* cholecystenterorrhaphy.
colecistenterostomía *f.* cholecystenterostomy.
colecístico, -ca *adj.* cholecystic.
colecistitis *f.* cholecystitis.
  colecistitis aguda acute cholecystitis.
  colecistitis crónica chronic cholecystitis.
  colecistitis enfisematosa emphysematous cholecystitis.
  colecistitis folicular follicular cholecystitis.
  colecistitis gaseosa gaseous cholecystitis.
  colecistitis glandular proliferativa cholecystitis glandularis proliferans.
  colecistitis xantogranulomatosa xanthogranulomatous cholecystitis.
colecisto *m.* cholecyst.
colecistocinético, -ca *adj.* cholecystokinetic.
colecistocinina *f.* cholecystokinin.
colecistocolangiograma *m.* cholecystocholangiogram.
colecistocólico, -ca *adj.* cholecystocolonic.
colecistocolostomía *f.* cholecystocolostomy.
colecistocolotomía *f.* cholecystocolotomy.
colecistoduodenostomía *f.* cholecystoduodenostomy.
colecistoentérico, -ca *adj.* cholecystenteric.
colecistoenteroanastomosis *f.* cholecystenteroanastomosis.
colecistoenterorrafia *f.* cholecystenterorrhaphy.
colecistoenterostomía *f.* cholecystenterostomy.
colecistogástrico, -ca *adj.* cholecystogastric.
colecistogastrostomía *f.* cholecystogastrostomy.
colecistogógico, -ca *adj.* cholecystogogic.
colecistografía *f.* cholecystrography.
colecistograma *m.* cholecystogram.
colecistoileostomía *f.* cholecystoileostomy.
colecistointestinal *adj.* cholecystointestinal.
colecistoliatiasis *f.* cholecystolithiasis.
colecistolitotripsia *f.* cholecystolithotripsy.
colecistonefrostomía *f.* cholecystonephrostomy.
colecistopatía *f.* cholecystopathy.
colecistopexia *f.* cholecystopexy.
colecistopielostomía *f.* cholecystopyelostomy.
colecistoplastia *f.* cholecystoplasty.
colecistoptosis *f.* cholecystoptosis.
colecistoquinina *f.* cholecystokinin.
colecistorrafia *f.* cholecystorrhaphy.
colecistosonografía *f.* cholecystosonography.
colecistosis *f.* cholecystosis.
colecistostomía *f.* cholecystostomy.
colecistotifoidea *adj.* cholecystotyphoid.

colecistotomía *f.* cholecystotomy.
colecistoyeyunostomía *f.* cholecystojejunostomy.
colecromopoyesis *f.* cholechromopoiesis.
colectasia *f.* colectasia.
colectomía *f.* colectomy.
  colectomía subtotal subtotal colectomy.
  colectomía total total colectomy.
  colectomía transversa transverse colectomy.
colector *m.* collector.
coledocal *adj.* choledocal.
coledocectomía *f.* choledochectomy.
coledocele *m.* choledochocele.
coledocendisis *f.* choledochendysis.
coledociano, -na *adj.* choledochal.
coledociartia *f.* choledochiartia.
coledocitis *f.* choledochitis.
colédoco *m.* choledoch.
coledocócico, -ca *adj.* choledochal.
coledococoledocostomía *f.* choledochocholedochostomy.
coledocoduodenostomía *f.* choledochoduodenostomy.
coledocoenterostomía *f.* choledochoenterostomy.
coledocogastrostomía *f.* choledochogastrostomy.
coledocografía *f.* choledochography.
coledocograma *m.* choledochogram.
coledocohepatostomía *f.* choledochohepatostomy.
coledocoileostomía *f.* choledochoileostomy.
coledocolitiasis *f.* choledocholithiasis.
coledocolito *m.* choledocholith.
coledocolitotomía *f.* choledocholithotomy.
coledocolitotricia *f.* choledocholithotripsy.
coledocolitotripsia *f.* choledocholithotripsy.
coledocoplastia *f.* choledochoplasty.
coledocorrafia *f.* choledochorrhaphy.
coledocoso, -sa *adj.* choledochous.
coledocostomía *f.* choledochostomy.
coledocotomía *f.* choledochotomy.
coledocoyeyunostomía *f.* choledochojejunostomy.
coledoquectomía *f.* choledochectomy.
coledoquendisis *f.* choledochendysis.
coledoscopio *m.* choledoscope.
coleglobina *f.* choleglobin.
colehemia *f.* cholehemia.
coleico, -ca *adj.* choleic.
colelitiasis *f.* cholelithiasis.
colelítico, -ca *adj.* cholelithic.
colelito *m.* cholelith, cholelith.
colelitomía *f.* cholelithomy.
colelitotricia *f.* cholelithotripsy.
colelitotripsia *f.* cholelithotripsy.
colemesis *f.* cholemesis.
colemia *f.* cholemia, cholehemia.
colémico, -ca *adj.* cholemic.
colemimetría *f.* cholemimetry.
coleocele *m.* coleocele.
coleoptosis *f.* coleoptosis.
coleotomía *f.* coleotomy.
colepatía *f.* cholepathia.
  colepatía espástica cholepathia spastica.
coleperitoneo *m.* choleperitoneum.
coleperitonitis *f.* choleperitonitis.
colepoyesis *f.* cholepoiesis, cholopoiesis.
colepoyético, -ca *adj.* cholepoietic.
coleprasina *f.* choleprasin.
cólera *m.* cholera.
  cólera asiático Asiatic cholera.
  cólera fulminante dry cholera, cholera sicca.
  cólera infantil cholera infantum.
  cólera morbo cholera morbus.

  cólera seco dry cholera, cholera sicca.
  cólera tífico, cólera tifoídico typhoid cholera.
coleráfago *m.* choleraphage.
colerágeno *m.* cholerangen.
coleraico, -ca *adj.* choleraic.
colereico, -ca *adj.* cholereic.
coleresis *f.* choleresis.
colerético, -ca *adj.* choleretic.
coleriforme *adj.* choleriform.
colerigénico, -ca *adj.* cholerogenic.
colerígeno, -na *adj.* cholerigenous.
colerina *f.* cholerine.
colerización *f.* cholerization.
coleroide *adj.* choleroid.
colerragia *f.* cholerrhagia.
colerrágico, -ca *adj.* cholerrhagic.
coles *m.* coles.
colescintigrafía *f.* cholescintigraphy.
colescintigrama *m.* cholescintigram.
colestanol *m.* cholestanol.
colestasia *f.* cholestasia, cholestasis.
colestasis *f.* cholestasis.
colestático -ca *adj.* cholestatic.
colesteatoma *m.* cholesteatoma.
  colesteatoma timpánico cholesteatoma tympani.
colesteatomatoso, -sa *adj.* cholesteatomatous.
colesteatosis *f.* cholesteatosis.
colesterasa *f.* cholesterase.
colesteremia *f.* cholesteremia.
colesterinemia *f.* cholesterinemia.
colesterinosis *f.* cholesterinosis.
  colesterinosis cerebrotendinosa cerebrotendinous cholesterinosis.
colesterinuria *f.* cholesterinuria.
colesterodermia *f.* cholesteroderma.
colesterogénesis *f.* cholesterogenesis.
colesterohidrotórax *m.* cholesterohydrothorax.
colesterohistequia *f.* cholesterohistechia.
colesterol *m.* cholesterol.
colesterolemia *f.* cholesterolemia.
colesteroléresis *f.* cholesteroleresis.
colesterologénesis *f.* cholesterologenesis.
colesterolosis *f.* cholesterolosis.
  colesterolosis extracelular extracellular cholesterolosis.
colesteroluria *f.* cholesteroluria.
colesteropoyesis *f.* cholesteropoiesis.
colesterosis *f.* cholesterosis.
  colesterosis cutis cholesterosis cutis.
  colesterosis cutánea cholesterosis cutis.
  colesterosis extracelular extracellular cholesterolosis.
coleterapia *f.* choletherapy.
coleuria *f.* choleuria, choluria.
colgajo *m.* flap.
  colgajo de Abbe Abbe's flap.
  colgajo abierto open flap.
  colgajo arterial arterial flap.
  colgajo de avance advacement flap.
  colgajo axial axial flap.
  colgajo en bandera flag flap.
  colgajo bilobulado bilobed flap.
  colgajo bipediculado bipedicle flap.
  colgajo en bisagra hinged flap.
  colgajo celulocutáneo cellulocutaneous flap.
  colgajo de cobertura envelope flap.
  colgajo compuesto composite flap, compound flap.
  colgajo con configuración axial axial pattern flap.
  colgajo en cordel rope flap.

colgajo cruzado cross flap.
colgajo de cuerda rope flap.
colgajo cutáneo skin flap.
colgajo deltopectoral deltopectoral flap.
colgajo por deslizamiento, colgajo deslizante sliding flap.
colgajo diferido delayed flap.
colgajo directo direct flap.
colgajo a distancia, colgajo distante distant flap.
colgajo de distribución al azar random pattern flap.
colgajo doblado turnover flap.
colgajo de doble cabo double pedicle flap.
colgajo de envoltura envelope flap.
colgajo de Eloesser Eloesser flap.
colgajo de espesor completo full thickness flap.
colgajo de espesor parcial partial thickness flap, split thickness flap.
colgajo de Estlander Estlander flap.
colgajo falciforme sickle flap.
colgajo fascial fascial flap.
colgajo de Filatov, colgajo de Filatov-Gillies Filatov flap, Filatov-Gillies flap.
colgajo francés French flap.
colgajo de Gillies Gillies' flap.
colgajo gingival gingival flap.
colgajo de guantelete gauntlet flap.
colgajo indio Indian flap.
colgajo inguinal groin flap.
colgajo inmediato immediate flap.
colgajo insular, colgajo en isla island flap.
colgajo italiano Italian flap.
colgajo interpolado interpolated flap.
colgajo libre free flap.
colgajo libre microquirúrgico michrochirurgic free flap.
colgajo libre vascularizado free flap.
colgajo de Limberg Limberg's flap.
colgajo lingual tongue flap.
colgajo linguopalatino lingual tongue flap.
colgajo local local flap.
colgajo miocutáneo myocutaneous flap.
colgajo modificado de Widman modified Widman flap.
colgajo mucopericondral mucoperichondral flap.
colgajo mucoperióstico mucoperiosteal flap.
colgajo mucoperióstico bipendiculado de Langebeck Langebeck pedicle mucoperiosteal flap.
colgajo muscular muscular flap.
colgajo de músculo recto abdominal rectus abdominis muscle flap.
colgajo musculocutáneo musculocutaneous flap.
colgajo neurovascular neurovascular flap.
colgajo en oruga caterpillar flap.
colgajo óseo bone flap.
colgajo óseo libre free bone flap.
colgajo osteomiocutáneo osteomiocutaneous flap.
colgajo parabiótico parabiotic flap.
colgajo de pectoral pectoralis muscle flap.
colgajo pediculado pedicle flap.
colgajo pediculado permanente permanent pedicle flap.
colgajo de pedículo doble double pedicle flap.
colgajo pediculado tubular tubed flap.
colgajo pericoronal pericoronal flap.
colgajo de piel skin flap.
colgajo plano flat flap.
colgajo radial radial forearm flap.
colgajo randomizado random pattern flap.

colgajo por rotación, colgajo de rotación rotation flap.
colgajo en salto jump flap.
colgajo sepultado buried flap.
colgajo subcutáneo subcutaneous flap.
colgajo tapizado lined flap.
colgajo TRAM TRAM flap.
colgajo de transferencia directa, colgajo de transferencia inmediata direct transfer flap, immediate transfer flap.
colgajo de transferencia tardía delayed transfer flap.
colgajo de traslación translation flap.
colgajo de tubo tubed flap.
colgajo tubular tubed flap.
colgajo de túnel tunnel flap.
colgajo vesical bladder flap.
colgajo VRAM VRAM flap.
colgajo en V-Y V-Y flap.
colgajo en Z Z flap.
colibacilemia *f.* colibacillemia.
colibacilo *m.* colibacillus.
colibacilosis *f.* colibacillosis.
colibacilosis gravídica colibacillosis gravidarum.
colibaciluria *f.* colibacilluria.
colicele *m.* cholicele.
colicinogenia *f.* colicinogeny.
colicinogénico, -ca *adj.* colicinogenic.
colicinógeno *m.* colicinogen.
colicistitis *f.* colicystitis.
colicistopielitis *f.* colicystopyelitis.
cólico *m.* colic.
cólico apendicular appendicular colic.
cólico biliar, cólico bilioso biliary colic.
cólico por cálculo biliar gallstone colic.
cólico cíncico, cólico por cinc zinc colic.
cólico colelitiásico gallstone colic.
cólico cúprico copper colic.
cólico de Devonshire Devonshire colic.
cólico endémico endemic colic.
cólico estercoráceo stercoral colic.
cólico flatulento flatulent colic.
cólico gaseoso flatulent colic.
cólico gástrico gastric colic.
cólico hepático hepatic colic.
cólico intestinal intestinal colic.
cólico del lactante infantile colic.
cólico meconial meconial colic.
cólico menstrual menstrual colic.
cólico nefrítico nephritic colic.
cólico ovárico ovarian colic.
cólico pancreático pancreatic colic.
cólico de los pintores painter's colic.
cólico de plomo, cólico plúmbico lead colic.
cólico renal renal colic.
cólico salival salivary colic.
cólico saturnino saturnine colic.
cólico tubárico, cólico tubario tubal colic.
cólico ureteral ureteral colic.
cólico uterino uterine colic.
cólico ventoso flatulent colic.
cólico vermicular vermicular colic.
cólico verminoso verminous colic.
cólico -ca *adj.* colic.
colicodinia *f.* colonalgia.
colicolitis *f.* colitis.
colicoplejía *f.* colicoplegia.
colicuación *f.* colliquation.
colicuación balón, colicuación en globo ballooning colliquation.
colicuación reticular reticulating colliquation.
colicuativo, -va *adj.* colliquative.
coliculectomía *f.* colliculectomy.

coliculitis *f.* colliculitis.
colículo *m.* colliculus.
colifijación *f.* colifixation.
coliforme *adj.* coliform.
coligación *f.* colligation.
coligativo, -va *adj.* colligative.
colimación *f.* collimation.
colimación del haz beam collimation.
colimador *m.* collimator.
colina *f.* choline.
colinealidad *f.* colinearity, collinearity.
colinefritis *f.* cholinephritis.
colinérgico, -ca *adj.* cholinergic.
colinoceptivo, -va *adj.* cholinoceptive.
colinoceptor *m.* cholinoceptor, cholinoreceptor.
colinomimético, -ca *adj.* cholinomimetic.
colinorreactivo, -va *adj.* cholinoreactive.
colinorreceptor *m.* cholinoreceptor.
coliotomía *f.* colliotomy.
colipasa *f.* colipase.
colipéptico, -ca *adj.* colypeptic, kolypeptic.
coliplicación *f.* coliplication, coloplication.
colipuntura *f.* colipuncture.
colisepsis *f.* colisepsis.
colisión *f.* collision.
colítico, -ca *adj.* kolytic.
colitis *f.* colitis.
colitis amebiana amebic colitis.
colitis balantidiásica balantidial colitis.
colitis colagenosa collagenous colitis.
colitis granulomatosa granulomatous colitis.
colitis grave colitis gravis.
colitis hemorrágica hemorrhagic colitis.
colitis isquémica ischemic colitis.
colitis mixomembranosa myxomembranous colitis.
colitis mucosa mucous colitis.
colitis poliposa colitis polyposa.
colitis quística profunda colitis cystica profunda.
colitis quística superficial colitis cystica superficialis.
colitis regional regional colitis.
colitis segmentaria segmental colitis.
colitis seudomembranosa pseudomembranous colitis.
colitis transmural transmural colitis.
colitis ulcerosa ulcerative colitis, colitis ulcerativa.
colitis urémica uremic colitis.
colitoxemia *f.* colitoxemia.
colitoxicosis *f.* colitoxicosis.
colitoxina *f.* colitoxin.
coliuria *f.* coliuria.
collar *m.* collar.
collar de Biett, collarete de Biett Biett's necklace.
collar de Casal Casal's collar, Casal's necklace.
collar español Spanish collar.
collar de hueso perióstico periosteal bone collar.
collar ortopédico cervical collar.
collar de perlas collar of pearls.
collar de Stokes collar of Stokes.
collar de Venus, collar venéreo venereal collar, collar of Venus, necklace of Venus.
collarete *m.* collarette.
collarín cervical *m.* cervical collar.
colliculus colliculus.
collodium collodion, collodium.
collum *m.* collum.
collum distortum collum distortum.
colmillo *m.* canine tooth, fang, dens caninus.
coloboma *m.* coloboma.

coloboma atípico atypical coloboma.
coloboma completo complete coloboma.
coloboma de la coroides coloboma of the choroid, choroidal coloboma.
coloboma del cristalino coloboma of the lens, coloboma lentis.
coloboma del cuerpo ciliar coloboma of the ciliary body.
coloboma del disco óptico, coloboma del nervio óptico coloboma of the optic disc, coloboma of the optic nerve.
coloboma en la entrada del nervio óptico coloboma at optic nerve entrance.
coloboma del fundus coloboma of the fundus.
coloboma de Fuch Fuch's coloboma.
coloboma del humor vítreo coloboma of the vitreous humor.
coloboma del iris coloboma of the iris, coloboma iridis.
coloboma lobular coloboma lobuli.
coloboma macular macular coloboma.
coloboma de la retina, coloboma retiniano coloboma of the retina, coloboma retinae.
coloboma en puente bridge coloboma.
coloboma palpebral palpebral coloboma, coloboma palpebrale.
coloboma vítreo coloboma of the vitreous humor.
coloboma peripapilar peripapillary coloboma.
coloboma retinocoroidal retinochoroidal coloboma.
coloboma típico typical coloboma.
colocación *f.* placement.
colocación de un catéter percutáneo percutaneous catheter placement.
colocación lingual lingual placement.
colocador de bandas *m.* band pusher.
colocecostomía *f.* colocecostomy.
colocentesis *f.* colocentesis.
colocianina *f.* cholecyanin, cholocyanin.
coloclisis *f.* coloclysis.
coloclister *m.* coloclyster.
colocolecistostomía *f.* cholocholecystostomy.
colocólico, -ca *adj.* colocolic.
colocolostomía *f.* colocolostomy.
colocromo *m.* cholochrome.
colocutáneo, -a *adj.* colocutaneous.
colodiafisario, -ria *adj.* collodiaphyseal.
colodión *m.* collodion, collodium.
colodión de ácido salicílico salicylic acid collodion.
colodión ampollante blistering collodion.
colodión cantarídeo cantharidal collodion.
colodión elástico collodion elastique.
colodión estíptico styptic collodion.
colodión flexible flexible collodion.
colodión hemostático hemostatic collodion.
colodión vesicante collodium vesicans.
colodión yodado iodized collodion.
colodispepsia *f.* colodyspepsia.
coloenteritis *f.* coloenteritis.
colofijación *f.* colofixation.
cologénico, -ca *adj.* chologenetic.
colohematina *f.* cholehematin, cholohematin.
colohemotórax *m.* cholohemothorax.
colohepatopexia *f.* colohepatopexy.
coloidal *adj.* colloidal.
coloide *m.* colloid.
coloideo, -a *adj.* colloidal.
coloidina *f.* colloidin.
coloidoclasia *f.* colloidoclasia, colloidoclasis.
coloidoclasis *f.* colloidoclasis.
coloidoclástico, -ca *adj.* colloidoclastic.
coloidofagia *f.* colloidophagia, colloidophagy.

coloidógeno *m.* colloidogen.
coloidopexia *f.* colloidopexy.
coloidoquímica *f.* collochemistry.
coloileal *f.* coloileal.
colólisis *f.* cololysis.
cololitiasis *f.* cholelithiasis, chololithiasis.
cololítico, -ca *adj.* cholelithic, chololithic.
cololito *m.* chololith.
coloma *m.* colloma.
colometrómetro *m.* colometrometer.
colon *m.* colon.
colon en caño de plomo lead-pipe colon.
colon gigante giant colon.
colon inactivo inactive colon.
colon irritable irritable colon.
colon pelviano pelvic colon, colon pelvinum.
colon perezoso lazy colon.
colonalgia *f.* colonalgia.
colonia *f.* colony.
colónico, -ca *adj.* colonic.
colonitis *f.* colonitis.
colonización *f.* colonization.
colonización genética genetic colonization.
colonograma *m.* colonogram.
colonómetro *m.* colonometer.
colonopatía *f.* colonopathy.
colonorragia *f.* colonorrhagia.
colonorrea *f.* colonorrhea.
colonoscopia *f.* colonoscopy.
colonoscopio *m.* colonoscope.
colopatía *f.* colopathy.
colopexia *f.* colpexia, colpexy.
colopexostomía *f.* colopexostomy.
colopexotomía *f.* colopexotomy.
coloplania *f.* choloplania.
coloplicación *f.* coloplication.
coloplicatura *f.* coloplication.
colopoyesis *f.* cholopoiesis.
coloproctectomía *f.* coloproctectomy.
coloproctia *f.* coloproctia.
coloproctitis *f.* coloproctitis.
coloproctostomía *f.* coloproctostomy.
coloptosia *f.* coloptosia.
coloptosis *f.* coloptosis.
colopunción *f.* colopuncture.
colopuntura *f.* colopuncture.
coloquintidismo *m.* colocynthidism.
color *m.* color.
color de arlequín harlequin color.
color complementario complementary color.
color de confusión confusion color.
color de contraste contrast color.
color extrínseco extrinsic color.
color gingival gingival color.
color incidental incidental color.
color intrínseco intrinsic color.
color metamérico metameric color.
color de Munsell Munsell's color.
color oponente opponent color.
color primario primary color.
color puro pure color.
color reflejado reflected color.
color de saturación, color saturado saturated color, saturation color.
color seudoisocromático pseudoisochromatic color.
color simple simple color.
color sólido solid color.
color del tono tone color.
coloración *f.* staining.
colorante[1] *adj.* staining, dyeing.
colorante[2] *m.* stain, dye.
colorimetría *f.* colorimetry.
colorimétrico, -ca *adj.* colorimeter.
colorímetro *m.* colorimeter.

colorímetro de Duboscq Duboscq's colorimeter.
colorímetro de titulación titration colorimeter.
colorrafia *f.* colorrhaphy.
colorragia *f.* colorrhagia.
colorrea *f.* colorrhea.
colorrectal *adj.* colorectal.
colorrectitis *f.* colorectitis.
colorrectostomía *f.* colorectostomy.
coloscopia *f.* choloscopy.
coloscopio *m.* colonoscope.
colosigmoidoscopia *f.* colosigmoioddoscopy.
colosigmoidostomía *f.* colosigmoidostomy.
colostomía *f.* colostomy.
colostomia en asa loop colostomy.
colostomia húmeda wet colostomy.
colostomia ileotransversa ileotransverse colostomy.
colostomia lateral lateral colostomy.
colostomia seca dry colostomy.
colostomia terminal terminal colostomy.
colostomizado, -da *adj.* colostomate.
colotifoidea *adj.* colotyphoid.
colotomía *f.* colotomy.
colotórax *m.* cholothorax.
colovaginal *adj.* colovaginal.
colovesical *adj.* colovesical.
colpalgia *f.* colpalgia.
colpatresia *f.* colpatresia.
colpectasia *f.* colpectasia.
colpectomía *f.* colpectomy.
colpeurinter *m.* colpeurynter.
colpeurisis *f.* colpeurisis.
colpismo *m.* colpismus.
colpítico, -ca *adj.* colpitic.
colpitis *f.* colpitis.
colpitis enfisematosa emphysematous colpitis, colpitis emphysematosa.
colpitis micótica colpitis mycotica.
colpitis senil, colpitis vetularum colpitis senile.
colpocele *m.* colpocele, coleocele.
colpoceliocentesis *f.* colpoceliocentesis.
colpocistitis *f.* colpocystitis.
colpocistocele *m.* colpocystocele.
colpocistoplastia *f.* colpocystoplasty.
colpocistotomía *f.* colpocystotomy.
colpocistoureterotomía *f.* colpocystoureterotomy.
colpocitograma *m.* colpocytogram.
colpocitología *f.* colpocytology.
colpocleisis *f.* colpocleisis.
colpodinia *f.* colpodynia.
colpoepisiorrafia *f.* colpoepisiorrhaphy.
colpografía *f.* colpography.
colpohiperplasia *f.* colpohyperplasia.
colpohiperplasia quística colpohyperplasia cystica.
colpohiperplasia enfisematosa colpohyperplasia emphysematosa.
colpohisterectomía *f.* colpohysterectomy.
colpohisteropexia *f.* colpohysteropexy.
colpohisterorrafia *f.* colpohysterorrhaphy.
colpohisterotomía *f.* colpohysterotomy.
colpomicosis *f.* colpomycosis.
colpomicroscopia *f.* colpomicroscopy.
colpomicroscópico, -ca *adj.* colpomicroscopic.
colpomicroscopio *m.* colpomicroscope.
colpomiomectomía *f.* colpomyomectomy.
colpomiotomía *f.* colpomyomectomy.
colpopatía *f.* colpopathy.
colpoperineoplastia *f.* colpoperineoplasty.
colpoperineorrafia *f.* colpoperineorrhaphy.

colpopexia *f.* colpopexy.
colpoplastia *f.* colpoplasty.
colpoptosis *f.* colpoptosis.
colporrafia *f.* colporrhaphy.
colporragia *f.* colporrhagia.
colporrectopexia *f.* colporectopexy.
colporrexis *f.* colporrhexis.
colposcopia *f.* colposcopy.
colposcópico, -ca *adj.* colposcopic.
colposcopio *m.* colposcope.
colpospasmo *m.* colpospasm.
colpóstato *m.* colpospat.
colpostenosis *f.* colposteonosis.
colpostenotomía *f.* colpostenotomy.
colposuspensión *f.* colposuspension.
colpotermo *m.* colpotherm.
colpotomía *f.* colpotomy.
  colpotomía posterior posterior colpotomy.
colpoureterocistotomía *f.* colpoureterocystotomy.
colpoureterotomía *f.* colpoureterotomy.
colpoxerosis *f.* colpoxerosis.
columella *f.* columella.
columna *f.* column, columna.
  columna aferente somática especial special
  somatic afferent column.
  columna aferente somática general general
  somatic afferent column.
  *columna aferente visceral esplácnica ge-
  neral* general visceral splanchnic afferent column.
  columna de afinidad affinity column.
  columna de Bertin Bertin's column.
  columna branquial eferente branchial efferent column.
  columna gris de la médula espinal colum-
  nae griseae medulla spinalis.
  columna vertebral vertebral column.
columnela *f.* columnella.
columnización *f.* columnization.
colunario *m.* collunarium.
coluria *f.* choluria.
colúrico, -ca *adj.* choluric.
colutorio *m.* collutory, mouthwash, collutorium.
  colutorio de Miller Miller's collutory.
coma *m.* coma.
  coma agripnótico agrypnodal coma.
  coma alcohólico alcoholic coma.
  coma alfa alpha coma.
  coma apoplético apoplectic coma.
  coma por barbitúricos barbiturate coma.
  coma carcinomatoso carcinomatous coma.
  coma diabético diabetic coma.
  coma hepático hepatic coma, coma hepaticum.
  coma hiperosmolar hyperosmolar coma.
  *coma hiperosmolar hiperglucémico no ce-
  tónico* hyperosmolar hyperglycemic non-ketonic coma.
  coma hiperosmolar no cetósico hyperosmolar nonketotic coma.
  coma hipoclorémico coma hypochloraemicum.
  coma hipoglucémico hypoglycemic coma.
  coma irreversible irreversible coma.
  coma de Kussmaul Kussmaul's coma.
  coma de Kussmaul Kussmaul's coma.
  coma metabólico metabolic coma.
  coma tirotóxico thyrotoxic coma.
  coma de trance trance coma.
  coma urémico uremic coma.
  coma vigil coma vigil.
comadrona *f.* midwife.
comasculación *m.* comasculation.

comatoso, -sa *adj.* comatose.
combinación *f.* combination.
  combinación binaria binary combination.
  combinación nueva new combination.
combustible *adj.* combustible.
combustión *f.* combustion.
  combustión espontánea spontaneous combustion.
comedocarcinoma *m.* comedocarcinoma.
comedogeneidad *f.* comedogenecity.
comedogénico, -ca *adj.* comedogenic.
comedógeno, -na *adj.* comedogenic.
comedomastitis *adj.* comedomastitis.
comedón *m.* comedo.
  comedón abierto open comedo.
  comedón blanco whitehead comedo.
  comedón cerrado closed comedo.
comensal *m.* commensal.
comensalismo *m.* commensalism.
comes *m.* comes.
comezón *m.* itch.
comida *f.* food, meal.
comisura *f.* commissura, commisure.
comisural *adj.* commisural.
comisurorrafia *f.* commissurorrhaphy.
comisurotomía *f.* comissurotomy, commissurotomy.
  comisurotomía mitral mitral comissurotomy.
comorbilidad *f.* comorbidity.
compacción *f.* compaction.
compacta *f.* compacta.
compacto, -ta *adj.* compact.
comparador *m.* comparator.
comparascopio *m.* comparascope.
compartimentación *f.* compartmentalization,
gating.
compartimento *m.* compartment.
compás *m.* calipers.
  compás de espesor dérmico skinfold calipers.
  compás de pliegue cutáneo skinfold calipers.
compatibilidad *f.* compatibility.
compatible *adj.* compatible.
compensación *f.* compensation.
  compensación de dosis dosage compensation.
  compensación en profundidad depth compensation.
compensador, -ra *adj.* compensatory.
competencia *f.* competence.
  competencia cardíaca cardiac competence.
  competencia embrionaria embryonic competence.
  competencia inmunológica immunological
  competence.
competición *f.* competition.
complejo, -ja *m. y adj.* complex.
  complejo aberrante aberrant complex.
  complejo anómalo anomalous complex.
  complejo antigénico antigenic complex.
  complejo antigeno-anticuerpo antigen-antibody complex.
  complejo apical apical complex.
  complejo de ataque de membrana membrane attack complex.
  complejo auricular atrial complex, auricular
  complex.
  complejo bifásico diphasic complex.
  complejo de Caín Cain complex.
  complejo de castración castration complex.
  complejo demencia SIDA (CDS) AIDS dementia complex (ADC).
  complejo de Diana Diana complex.

  complejo EAFH EAHF complex.
  complejo de Edipo Oedipus complex.
  complejo de Eisenmenger Eisenmenger's
  complex.
  complejo de Electra Electra complex.
  complejo electrocardiográfico electrocardiographic complex.
  complejo equifásico equiphasic complex.
  complejo de espiga y onda spike and wave
  complex.
  complejo de factor IX factor IX complex.
  complejo faríngeo caudal caudal pharyngeal complex.
  complejo de femineidad femininity complex.
  complejo fraternal brother complex.
  complejo de Gohn Gohn's complex.
  complejo de Golgi Golgi complex.
  complejo hapteno-portador hapten-carrier
  complex.
  complejo hemoglobina-haptoglobina hemoglobin-haptoglobin complex.
  complejo hierro-dextrán iron-dextran complex.
  complejo HLA HLA complex.
  complejo de inclusión inclusion complex.
  complejo de inferioridad inferiority complex.
  complejo inmune, complejo inmunológico
  immune complex.
  complejo isobifásico isodiphasic complex.
  complejo K K complex.
  complejo de Lear Lear complex.
  complejo de madre superiora mother superior complex.
  complejo materno mother complex.
  *complejo mayor de histocompatibilidad
  (CMH)* major histocompatibility complex
  (MHC).
  complejo de Meyemburg Meyemburg's complex.
  complejo monofásico monophasic complex.
  complejo de ondas cerebrales brain wave.
  *complejo de parkinsonismo, demencia y
  esclerosis lateral amiotrófica* amyotrophic-
  lateral-sclerosis-parkinsonism-demential
  complex.
  complejo paterno father complex.
  *complejo perihipogloso, perihipogloso
  nuclear* perhypoglossal complex, perihypoglossal nuclear complex.
  complejo del poro pore complex.
  complejo primario de inoculación primary
  inoculation complex.
  complejo principal de histocompatibilidad
  major histocompatibility complex.
  complejo QRS QRS complex.
  complejo QRST QRST complex.
  complejo relacionado con el SIDA (CRS)
  AIDS related complex (ARC).
  complejo ribosoma-laminilla ribosome-lamella complex.
  complejo sexual sex complex.
  complejo sicca sicca complex.
  complejo sinaptonémico synaptonemal complex.
  complejo de Steidele Steidele's complex.
  complejo de superioridad superiority complex.
  complejo Tacaribe de virus Tacaribe complex of viruses.
  complejo ternario ternary complex.
  complejo transferencia de carga charge transfer complex.
  complejo triple de síntomas triple symptom
  complex.

complejo tuberculoso primario primary tuberculous complex.

complejo de unión junctional complex.

complejo ureterotrigonal ureterotrigonal complex.

complejo VATER VATER complex.

complejo ventricular ventricular complex.

complejo vitamínico B vitamin B complex.

complejo de Yocasta Jocasta complex.

complejo yuxtaglomerular, complejo Y-G juxtaglomerular complex, J-G complex.

complementación *f.* complementation.

complementación interalélica interallelic complementation.

complementación intergénica intergenic complementation.

complementado, -da *adj.* complemented.

complementariedad *f.* complementarity.

complementario, - ria *adj.* complementary.

complemento *m.* complement.

complemento cromosómico chromosome complement.

complemento dominante dominant complement.

complementófilo, -la *adj.* complementophil.

complementoide *m.* complementoid.

complementos de la anestesia adjunct to anesthesia.

complexión *f.* complexion.

compliance *f.* compliance.

compliancia *f.* compliance.

compliancia cerebral brain compliance.

compliancia del corazón compliance of the heart.

compliancia dinámica del pulmón dynamic compliance of the lung.

compliancia eficaz effective compliance.

compliancia específica specific compliance.

compliancia estática static compliance.

compliancia pulmonar lung compliance.

compliancia torácica thoracic compliance.

compliancia ventilatoria ventilatory compliance.

complianza *f.* compliance.

complicación *f.* complication.

complicación médica medical complication.

complicación quirúrgica surgical complication.

complicación vascular vascular complication.

complicado, -da *adj.* complicated.

componente *m.* constituent.

componente anterior, componente anterior de fuerza anterior constituent, anterior constituent of force.

componente del complemento constituent of complement.

componente específico del grupo group specific constituent.

componente esplácnico motor splanchnic motor constituent.

componente esplácnico sensitivo splanchnic sensory constituent.

componente de fuerza constituent of force.

componente M M constituent.

componente de la masticación constituent of mastication.

componente metabólico metabolic constituent.

componente de la oclusión constituent of occlusion.

componente respiratorio respiratory constituent.

componente secretor secretory constituent.

componente somático motor somatic motor constituent.

componente somático sensitivo somatic sensory constituent.

componente visceral motor splanchnic motor constituent.

componente visceral sensitivo splanchnic sensory constituent.

componer *v.* compound.

comportamiento *m.* behavior.

comportamiento impulsivo acting out.

comportamiento sexual sexual behavior.

composición *f.* composition.

composición de bases base composition.

composición para modelar modeling composition.

comprensión *f.* comprehension.

compresa *f.* compress.

compresa caliente hot compress.

compresa fría cold compress.

compresa ginecológica gynecologic compress.

compresa graduada graduated compress.

compresa húmeda wet compress.

compresa perineal perinal compress.

compresibilidad *f.* compressibility.

compresión *f.* compression.

compresión cardíaca cardiac compression.

compresión cerebral, compresión del cerebro cerebral compression, compression of the brain.

compresión digital digital compression.

compresión espinal spinal compression.

compresión instrumental instrumental compression.

compresión de la médula espinal spinal cord compression.

compresión medular medullar compression.

compresión nerviosa nerve compression.

compresión raquídea spinal compression.

compresor *m.* compressor.

compresor de aire air compressor.

compresor de Deschamps Deschamps' compressor.

compresor de perdigón shot compressor.

comprimido *m.* tablet.

comprimido recubierto coated tablet.

comprobación *f.* ascertainment.

comprobación completa complete ascertainment.

comprobación incompleta incomplete ascertainment.

comprobación múltiple multiple ascertainment.

comprobación única single ascertainment.

comprobación truncada truncate ascertainment.

compuesto, -ta *adj.* compound.

compulsión *f.* compulsion.

compulsión a la repetición repetition compulsion.

compulsivo *adj.* compulsive.

comunicable *adj.* communicable.

comunicación *f.* communication.

comunicación congruente congruent communication.

comunicación disfuncional dysfunctional communication.

comunicación incongruente incongruent communication.

comunicación interpersonal diádica dyadic interpersonal communication.

comunicación verbal alterada impaired verbal communication.

comunicante *adj.* communicans.

comunidad *f.* community.

comunidad biótica biotic community.

comunidad clímax climax community.

comunidad terapéutica therapeutic community.

conación *f.* conation.

conamen *m.* intention of suicide.

conario *m.* conarium.

conativo, -va *adj.* conative.

conato *m.* conatus.

concameración *f.* concameration.

concatenación *f.* concatenation.

concatenado, -da *adj.* concatenate.

concavidad *f.* concavity.

cóncavo, -va *adj.* concave.

concavocóncavo, -va *adj.* concavoconcave.

concavoconvexo, -xa *adj.* concavoconvex.

concebir *v.* conceive.

concentración *f.* concentration.

concentración alveolar mínima (anestésica) minimal alveolar concentration (anesthetic).

concentración bactericida mínina minimal bactericidal concentration.

concentración celular máxima (CM) maximum cell concentration (MC).

concentración de hemodiálisis hemodialysate concentration.

concentración de hemoglobina celular media mean cell hemoglobin concentration.

concentración de hidrogeniones hydrogen ion concentration.

concentración inhibitoria mínima minimum inhibitory concentration.

concentración iónica ionic concentration.

concentración isorreica limitante (CIL) limiting isorrheic concentration (LIC).

concentración letal mínima (MCL) minimal lethal concentration (MLC).

concentración de masa mass concentration.

concentración M M concentration.

concentración máxima peak concentration.

concentración molar molar concentration.

concentración normal normal concentration.

concentración sérica de oxigeno oxygen concentration in blood.

concentración de la solución ratio solution.

concentración urinaria máxima (CUM) maximum urinary concentration (MUC).

concentrado, -da *adj.* concentrated.

concentrado *m.* concentrate.

concentrado celular packed cell concentrate.

concentrado complejo protrombínico prothrombin concentrate.

concentrado de hematíes red blood cell concentrate.

concentrado de hematíes congelados frozen red blood concentrate.

concentrado de hematíes lavados washed red blood concentrate.

concentrado de hematíes pobre en leucocitos red blood concentrate leucocytes removed.

concentrado de hígado liver concentrate.

concentrado de plaquetas platelet concentrate.

concentrado de proteasa vegetal plant protease concentrate.

concentrado vitamínico vitamin concentrate.

concentrar *v.* concentrate.

concéntrico, -ca *adj.* concentric.

concepción *f.* conception.

concepción imperativa imperative conception.

conceptivo, -va *adj.* conceptive.

concepto *m.* concept.

concepto de no umbral no-threshold concept.
conceptual adj. conceptual.
conceptus conceptus.
concha f. shell, concha.
conchiforme adj. conchiform.
conchitis f. conchitis.
conciencia f. consciousness.
  conciencia doble double consciousness, dual consciousness.
  conciencia moral moral consciousness.
  conciencia nublada clouding consciousness.
  conciencia de la realidad reality awareness.
conclinación f. conclination.
concocción f. concoction.
concoideo, -a adj. conchoidal.
concomitancia f. concomitance.
concomitante adj. concomitant.
conconsciente m. conconscious.
concordancia f. concordance.
concordante adj. concordant.
concoscopio m. conchoscope.
concotomía f. conchotomy.
concótomo m. conchotome.
concreción f. concretion, concretio.
  concreción alvina alvine concretion.
  concreción calculosa calculous concretion.
  concreción cardiaca concretio cordis.
  concreción prostástica prostatic concretion.
  concreción tofácea, concreción tófica tophic concretion.
concrescencia f. concrescence.
concretio concretio.
concretización f. concretization.
concusión f. concussion.
  concusión abdominal abdominal concussion.
  concusión del cerebro, concusión cerebral concussion of the brain.
  concusión espinal spinal concussion.
  concusión hidráulica hydraulic concussion.
  concusión del laberinto concussion of the labyrinth.
  concusión de la médula espinal concussion of the spinal cord.
  concusión pulmonar pulmonary concussion.
  concusión de la retina concussion of the retina.
concusor m. concussor.
condensación f. condensation.
condensador m. condenser.
  condensador de Abbé Abbé's condenser.
  condensador de acción retorno back-action condenser.
  condensador amalgama amalgam condenser.
  condensador automático automatic condenser.
  condensador en bayoneta bayonet condenser.
  condensador de campo oscuro darkfield condenser.
  condensador cardioide cardioid condenser.
  condensador Hollenback Hollenback condenser.
  condensador de mano hand condenser.
  condensador de martillo automático automatic mallet condenser.
  condensador de martillo eléctrico electromallet condenser.
  condensador mecánico mechanical condenser.
  condensador neumático pneumatic condenser.
  condensador de oro gold condenser.
  condensador parabólico paraboloid condenser.
  condensador paralelogramo parallelogram condenser.
  condensador de pie foot condenser.
condición f. condition.

condición basal basal condition.
condicionamiento m. conditioning.
  condicionamiento asertivo assertive conditioning.
  condicionamiento aversivo aversive conditioning.
  condicionamiento clásico classical conditioning, classic conditioning.
  condicionamiento de escape escape conditioning.
  condicionamiento de evitación avoidance conditioning.
  condicionamiento instrumental instrumental conditioning.
  condicionamiento operante, condicionamiento operativo operant conditioning.
  condicionamiento de orden superior high order conditioning.
  condicionamiento de Pavlov, condicionamiento pavloviano Pavlovian conditioning.
  condicionamiento de respuesta respondent conditioning.
  condicionamiento de segundo orden second-order conditioning.
  condicionamiento de Skinner Skinnerian conditioning.
  condicionamiento de traza trace conditioning.
condilar adj. condylar.
condíleo, -a adj. condylar.
condilectomía f. condylectomy.
condilión m. condylion.
cóndilo m. condyle.
condiloartrosis f. condylarthrosis.
condiloide adj. condyloid.
condiloideo, -a adj. condyloid.
condiloma m. condyloma.
  condiloma acuminado, condiloma acuminatum condyloma acuminatum.
  condiloma gigante giant condyloma.
  condiloma lato condyloma latum.
  condiloma plano flat condyloma.
  condiloma puntiagudo pointed condyloma.
condilomatoide adj. condylomatoid.
condilomatosis f. condylomatosis.
condilomatoso, -sa adj. condylomatous.
condilotomía f. condylotomy.
condón m. condom.
condrosqueleto m. chondroskeleton.
condral adj. chondral.
condralgia f. chondralgia.
condraloplasia f. chondralloplasia.
condrectomía f. chondrectomy.
cóndrico, -ca adj. chondric.
condrificación f. chondrification.
condrígeno m. chondrogen.
condrina f. chondrin.
condrioconto m. chondriocont.
condriosoma m. chondriosome.
condritis f. chondritis.
  condritis costal costal chondritis.
  condritis invertebral calcárea chondritis intervertebralis calcarea.
condroadenoma m. chondroadenoma.
condroangioma m. chondroangioma.
condroblasto m. chondroblast, chondroplast.
condroblastoma m. chondroblastoma.
condrocalcinosis f. chondrocalcinosis.
condrocarcinoma m. chondrocarcinoma.
condrocele m. chondroma.
condrocito m. chondrocyte.
  condrocito isógeno isogenous chondrocyte.
condroclasto m. chondroclast.
condrocostal adj. chondrocostal.
condrocráneo m. chondrocranium.

condrodermatitis f. chondrodermatitis.
  condrodermatitis nodular crónica helical chondrodermatitis nodularis chronica helicis.
condrodinia f. chondrodynia.
condrodisplasia f. chondrodysplasia.
  condrodisplasia deformante hereditaria hereditary deforming chondrodysplasia.
  condrodisplasia punteada, condrodisplasia puntiforme, condrodisplasia punctata chondrodysplasia punctata.
condrodistrofia f. chondrodystrophia, chondrodistrophy.
  condrodistrofia calcificante congénita chondrodystrophia calcificans congenita.
  condrodistrofia congénita puntiforme chondrodystrophia calcificans congenita.
  condrodistrofia familiar familial chondrodystrophia.
  condrodistrofia fetal calcificada chondrodystrophia calcificans congenita.
  condrodistrofia fetal hipoplásica hypoplastic fetal chondrodystrophia.
  condrodistrofia hiperplásica hyperplastic chondrodystrophia.
  condrodistrofia hipoplásica hypoplastic chondrodystrophia.
  condrodistrofia malácica chondrodystrophia malacia.
  condrodistrofia punteada congénita chondrodystrophia congenita punctata.
  condrodistrofia torácica asfixiante asphyxiating thoracic chondrodystrophia.
condroectodérmico, -ca adj. chondroectodermal.
condroendotelioma m. chondroendothelioma.
condroepifisario, -ria adj. chondroepiphyseal.
condroepifisitis f. chondroepiphysitis.
condroesqueleto m. chondroskeleton.
condroesternal adj. chondrosternal.
condroesternoplastia f. chondrosternoplasty.
condrofibroma m. chondrofibroma.
condrofima m. chondrophyte.
condrofito m. chondrophyte.
condrogénesis f. chondrogenesis.
condrógeno, -na adj. chondrogenic.
condrogloso, -sa adj. chondroglossous.
condrografía f. chondrography.
condrohipoplasia f. chondrohypoplasia.
condroide adj. chondroid.
condroítico, -ca adj. chondroitic.
condroitinuria f. chondroitinuria.
condrolipoma m. chondrolipoma.
condrólisis f. chondrolysis.
condrología f. chondrology.
condroma m. chondroma.
  condroma articular joint chondroma.
  condroma extraesquelético extraskeletal chondroma.
  condroma sarcomatoso chondroma sarcomatosum.
  condroma sinovial synovial chondroma.
  condroma verdadero true chondroma.
condromalacia f. chondromalacia.
  condromalacia fetal chondromalacia fetalis.
  condromalacia generalizada generalized chondromalacia.
  condromalacia de la laringe chondromalacia of the larynx.
  condromalacia patelar, condromalacia rotuliana chondromalacia patellae.
  condromalacia sistémica systemic chondromalacia.
condromatosis f. chondromatosise.
  condromatosis múltiple multiple chondromatosise.

condromatosis sinovial synovial chondromatosise.

condromatoso, -sa *adj.* chondromatous.

condrómera *f.* chondromere.

condrometaplasia *f.* chondrometaplasia.

condrometaplasia sinovial synovial chondrometaplasia.

condrometaplasia tenosinovial tenosynovial chondrometaplasia.

condromioma *m.* chondromyoma.

condromixofibroma *m.* chondromyxofibroma.

condromixoide *adj.* chondromyxoid.

condromixoma *m.* chondromyxoma.

condromixosarcoma *m.* chondromyxosarcoma.

condromucina *f.* chondromucin.

condromucoproteína *f.* chondromucoprotein.

condronecrosis *f.* chondronecrosis.

condroóseo, -a *adj.* chondro-osseous.

condroosteodistrofia *f.* chondro-osteodystrophy.

condropatía *f.* chondropathia.

condropatía tuberosa chondropathia tuberosa.

condropatología *f.* chondropathology.

condroplasia *f.* chondroplasia.

condroplasia puntiforme chondroplasia punctata.

condroplastia *f.* chondroplasty.

condroplástico, -ca *adj.* chondroplastic.

condroplasto *m.* chondroplast.

condroporosis *f.* chondroporosis.

condroproteína *f.* chondroprotein.

condrosarcoma *m.* chondrosarcoma.

condrosarcoma central central chondrosarcoma.

condrosarcoma mesenquimatoso mesenchymal chondrosarcoma.

condrosarcomatosis *f.* chondrosarcomatosis.

condrosarcomatoso, -sa *adj.* chondrosarcomatous.

condroseptum *m.* chondroseptum.

condrosis *f.* chondrosis.

condrosteodistrofia *f.* Morquio's disease.

condrosteoma *m.* chondrosteoma.

condrosternal *adj.* chondrosternal.

condrosternoplastia *f.* chondrosternoplasty.

condrotomía *f.* chondrotomy.

condrótomo *m.* chondrotome.

condrotrófico, -ca *adj.* chondrotrophic.

condroxifoide *adj.* chondroxiphoid.

condroxifoideo, -a *adj.* chondroxiphoid.

conducción *f.* conduction.

conducción acelerada accelerated conduction.

conducción aérea aerial conduction, air conduction.

conducción aerotimpánica aerotympanal conduction.

conducción anterior forward conduction.

conducción anterógrada anterograde conduction.

conducción antidrómica antidromic conduction.

conducción en alud avalanche conduction.

conducción anómala anomalous conduction.

conducción auriculoventricular (A-V) atrioventricular conduction (A-V).

conducción en avalancha avalanche conduction.

conducción craneal cranial conduction.

conducción decreciente decremental conduction.

conducción demorada delayed conduction.

conducción del impulso nervioso conduction of the nervous impulse.

conducción intraventricular intraventricular conduction.

conducción nerviosa nerve conduction.

conducción oculta concealed conduction.

conducción ortodrómica orthodromic conduction.

conducción ósea bone conduction.

conducción osteotimpánica osteotympanic conduction.

conducción de Purkinje Purkinje's conduction.

conducción retardada delayed conduction.

conducción retrógrada retrograde conduction.

conducción saltatoria saltatory conduction.

conducción sináptica synaptic conduction.

conducción supranormal supranormal conduction.

conducción ventricular ventricular conduction.

conducción ventricular aberrante aberrant ventricular conduction.

conducción ventriculoauricular (V-A) ventriculoatrial conduction (V-A).

conducta *f.* behavior.

conductismo *m.* behaviorism.

conductista *adj.* behaviorist.

conducto *m.* duct, ductus.

conducto aberrante aberrant duct, ductus aberrans.

conducto de Cuvier Cuvier's duct.

conducto de Hannover Hannover's canal.

conducto hipofisario hypophyseal duct.

conducto de Müller Müller's canal.

conducto neural neural canal.

conducto neuroentérico neurenteric canal.

conducto de Nuck canal of Nuck.

conducto pronéfrico pronephric duct.

conducto tirogloso thyroglossal duct.

conducto tirolingual thyrolingual duct.

conducto tubotimpánico tubotympanic canal.

conducto urogenital urogenital canal.

conductor, -ra *adj.* conductive.

conductor *m.* conductor.

conductor bipolar bipolar lead.

conduplicado, -da *adj.* conduplicate.

conduplicato corpore conduplicato-corpore.

conecondrosternón *m.* chonechondrosternon.

conectinas *f.* connectins.

conectivo, -va *adj.* connective.

conectivopatía *f.* connective tissue disease.

conector *m.* connector.

conector mayor major connector.

conector menor minor connector.

conector secundario minor connector.

conespecífico, -ca *adj.* conespecific.

conexión *f.* connection, connexus.

conexión de catéter catheter hub.

conexión de pinza clamp connection.

conexión en vivo quick connect.

conexón *m.* connexon.

confabulación *f.* confabulation.

conferto *m.* confertus.

confertus confertus.

confianza *f.* confidence.

confianza básica, confianza fundamental basic confidence, fundamental confidence.

confidencialidad *f.* confidentiality.

configuración *f.* configuration.

conflicto *m.* conflict.

conflicto de acercamiento-acercamiento approach-approach conflict.

conflicto de acercamiento-evitación approach-avoidance conflict.

conflicto doble double conflict.

conflicto de doble acercamiento double approach conflict.

conflicto de doble evitación double-avoidance conflict.

conflicto de enfoque-enfoque approach-approach conflict.

conflicto enfoque-evitación approach-avoidance conflict.

conflicto de evitación-evitación avoidance-avoidance conflict.

conflicto extrapsíquico extrapsychic conflict.

conflicto de función paterna paternal role conflict.

conflicto intrapersonal intrapsychic conflict.

conflicto intrapsíquico intrapsychic conflict.

conflicto motivación motivational conflict.

conflicto de rol role conflict.

confluente *adj.* confluent.

conformación *f.* conformation.

conformador, -ra *adj.* conformer.

confricación *f.* confrication.

confrontación *f.* confrontation.

congelación¹ *f.* congelation, freezing.

congelación gástrica gastric freezing.

congelación² *f.* frostbite.

congelación profunda deep frostbite.

congelación superficial superficial frostbite.

congelación-desecación *f.* freeze-drying.

congelación-sustitución *f.* freeze-substitution.

congénere *m.* congener.

congenérico, -ca *adj.* congeneric.

congénito, -ta *adj.* congenital.

congestión *f.* congestion.

congestión activa active congestion.

congestión bronquial bronchial congestion.

congestión cerebral brain congestion.

congestión esplácnica splanchnic engorgement.

congestión fisiológica physiologic congestion.

congestión funcional functional congestion.

congestión hipostática hypostatic congestion.

congestión mamaria caked breast.

congestión neurotónica neurotonic congestion.

congestión ocular bloodshot.

congestión pasiva passive congestion.

congestión pulmonar pulmonary congestion.

congestión de rebote rebound congestion.

congestión venosa venous congestion.

congestionado, -da *adj.* congested.

congestivo, -va *adj.* congestive.

conglobación *f.* conglobation.

conglobado, -da *adj.* conglobate.

conglomerado, -da *m. y adj.* conglomerate.

conglutinación *f.* conglutination, conglutinatio.

conglutinatio *f.* conglutination, conglutinatio.

congófilo, -la *adj.* congophilic.

congruente *adj.* congruent.

cónico, -ca *adj.* conic, conical.

Conidiobolus Conidiobolus.

conidióforo *m.* conidiophore.

conidióforo tipo Phialophora Phialophore-type conidiophore.

conidiógeno, -na *adj.* conidiogenous.

conímetro *m.* coniometer, konimeter, konometer.

coniocorteza *f.* koniocortex.

coniolinfestasia *f.* coniolymphestasis.

coniología *f.* coniology.

coniómetro *m.* coniometer, konimeter, konometer.

coniosis *f.* coniosis.
coniosporosis *f.* coniosporosis.
coniotomía *f.* coniotomy, coniotomia.
coniotoxicosis *f.* coniotoxicosis.
conización *f.* conization.
  conización cervical cervical conization.
  conización por cauterio cautery conization.
  conización en frío cold conization.
conjugación *f.* conjugation.
conjugado *m.* conjugate.
conjugado, -da *adj.* conjugate.
conjugón *m.* conjugon.
conjuntiva *f.* conjunctiva.
  conjuntiva bulbar bulbar conjunctiva.
  conjuntiva palpebral palpebral conjunctiva.
conjuntival *adj.* conjunctival.
conjuntiviplastia *f.* conjunctiviplasty, conjunctivoplasty.
conjuntivitis *f.* conjunctivitis.
  conjuntivitis actínica actinic conjunctivitis.
  conjuntivitis aguda acute conjunctivitis.
  conjuntivitis aguda contagiosa epidemic conjunctivitis.
  conjuntivitis alérgica allergic conjunctivitis.
  conjuntivitis anafiláctica allergic conjunctivitis.
  conjuntivitis angular angular conjunctivitis.
  conjuntivitis arco luminoso actinic conjunctivitis.
  conjuntivitis árida conjunctivitis arida.
  conjuntivitis de los astilleros shipyard conjunctivitis.
  conjuntivitis atópica atopic conjunctivitis.
  conjuntivitis atropínica atropine conjunctivitis.
  conjuntivitis bacteriana bacterial conjunctivitis.
  conjuntivitis de Béal Béal's conjunctivitis.
  conjuntivitis blenorrágica blenorrheal conjunctivitis.
  conjuntivitis calcárea calcareous conjunctivitis.
  conjuntivitis catarral, conjuntivitis catarral aguda catarrhal conjunctivitis, acute catarrhal conjunctivitis.
  conjuntivitis cicatricial, conjuntivitis cicatrizal cicatricial conjunctivitis.
  conjuntivitis contagiosa aguda acute contagious conjunctivitis.
  conjuntivitis crupal croupous conjunctivitis.
  conjuntivitis por destello de arco arc-flash conjunctivitis.
  conjuntivitis diftérica diphtheritic conjunctivitis.
  conjuntivitis diplobacilar diplobacillary conjunctivitis.
  conjuntivitis eccematosa eczematous conjunctivitis.
  conjuntivitis egipcia Egyptian conjunctivitis.
  conjuntivitis epidémica epidemic conjunctivitis.
  conjuntivitis epidémica aguda acute epidemic conjunctivitis.
  conjuntivitis escrofulosa phlyctenular conjunctivitis.
  conjuntivitis flictenular phlyctenular conjunctivitis.
  conjuntivitis folicular follicular conjunctivitis.
  conjuntivitis folicular aguda acute follicular conjunctivitis.
  conjuntivitis folicular crónic chronic follicular conjunctivitis.
  conjuntivitis gonocócica gonococcal conjunctivitis.

  conjuntivitis gonorreica gonorrheal conjunctivitis.
  conjuntivitis granular, conjuntivitis granulosa granular conjunctivitis.
  conjuntivitis granular contagiosa contagious granular conjunctivitis.
  conjuntivitis hemorrágica aguda acute hemorrhagic conjunctivitis.
  conjuntivitis hemorrágica epidémica epidemic hemorrhagic conjunctivitis.
  conjuntivitis de inclusión inclusion conjunctivitis.
  conjuntivitis infantil purulenta infantile purulent conjunctivitis.
  conjuntivitis infecciosa necrótica necrotic infectious conjunctivitis.
  conjuntivitis de Koch-Weeks Koch-Weeks conjunctivitis.
  conjuntivitis lagrimal lacrimal conjunctivitis.
  conjuntivitis larval larval conjunctivitis.
  conjuntivitis leñosa ligneous conjunctivitis.
  conjuntivitis litiásica lithiasis conjunctivitis.
  conjuntivitis medicamentosa conjunctivitis medicamentosa.
  conjuntivitis de Meibomio Meibomian conjunctivitis.
  conjuntivitis membranosa membranous conjunctivitis.
  conjuntivitis meningocócica meningococcus conjunctivitis.
  conjuntivitis del molusco, conjuntivitis por molusco molluscum conjunctivitis.
  conjuntivitis de Morax-Axenfeld Morax-Axenfeld conjunctivitis.
  conjuntivitis mucopurulenta mucopurulent conjunctivitis.
  conjuntivitis necrótica infecciosa necrotic infectious conjunctivitis.
  conjuntivitis neonatal neonatal conjunctivitis.
  conjuntivitis de la nieve snow conjunctivitis.
  conjuntivitis de Parinaud Parinaud's conjunctivitis.
  conjuntivitis de Pascheff Pascheff's conjunctivitis.
  conjuntivitis de la peste de las ardillas squirrel plague conjunctivitis.
  conjuntivitis petrificante conjunctivitis petrificans.
  conjuntivitis de las piscinas swimming pool conjunctivitis.
  conjuntivitis de las praderas prairie conjunctivitis.
  conjuntivitis primaveral spring conjunctivitis.
  conjuntivitis purulenta purulent conjunctivitis.
  conjuntivitis purulenta infantil infantile purulent conjunctivitis.
  conjuntivitis química chemical conjunctivitis.
  conjuntivitis del recién nacido, conjuntivitis de los recién nacidos conjunctivitis of the newborn.
  conjuntivitis seudomembranosa pseudomembranous conjunctivitis.
  conjuntivitis simple simple conjunctivitis.
  conjuntivitis de soldador welder's conjunctivitis.
  conjuntivitis toxicogénica toxicogenic conjunctivitis.
  conjuntivitis tracomatosa trachomatous conjunctivitis.
  conjuntivitis tularémica, conjuntivitis tularensis tularemic conjunctivitis, conjunctivitis tularensis.
  conjuntivitis urática uratic conjunctivitis.
  conjuntivitis vacunal vaccinial conjunctivitis.

  conjuntivitis vernal vernal conjunctivitis.
  conjuntivitis vírica viral conjunctivitis.
  conjuntivitis de Widmark Widmark's conjunctivitis.
conjuntivo, -va *adj.* conjunctive.
conjuntivodacriocistorrinostomía *f.* conjunctivodacryocystorhinostomy.
conjuntivodacriocistostomía *f.* conjunctivodacryocystostomy.
conjuntivoma *m.* conjunctivoma.
conjuntivoplastia *f.* conjunctivoplasty.
conjuntivorrinostomía *f.* conjunctivorhinostomy.
conminución *f.* comminution.
conminuto, -ta *adj.* comminuted.
conmoción *f.* commotio.
  conmoción cerebral commotio cerebri.
  conmoción espinal commotio spinalis.
  conmoción medular medullar commotio.
  conmoción de la retina commotio retinae.
  conmoción del laberinto commotio of the labyrinth.
connatal *adj.* connatal.
cono *m.* cone, conus.
  cono acrosómico achrosomal cone.
  cono antípoda, cono antipódico antipodal cone.
  cono arterial, cono arterioso arterial cone.
  cono axónico axonic cone.
  cono de bifurcación bifurcation cone.
  cono congénito congenital cone.
  cono corto short cone.
  cono de crecimiento growth cone.
  cono de distracción distraction cone.
  cono de éter, para éter ether cone.
  cono de fecundación, cono de fertilización fertilization cone.
  cono gutapercha gutta-percha cone.
  cono de implantación implantation cone.
  cono l l-cone.
  cono largo long cone.
  cono luminoso, cono luminoso de Politzer cone of light, Politzer's luminous cone.
  cono m m-cone.
  cono miópico myopic cone.
  cono de Politzer Politzer's cone.
  cono de presión, cono de presión cerebelosa pressure cone, cerebellar pressure cone.
  cono primitivo primitive cone.
  cono plata silver cone.
  cono pulmonar pulmonary cone.
  cono queratósico, cono queratótico keratosic cone.
  cono de la retina, cono retinal retinal cone.
  cono-s s-cone.
  cono de supertracción supertraction cone.
  cono de la teca interna theca interna cone.
  cono de Tyndall Tyndall cone.
conoftalmía *f.* conophthalmus.
conoide *adj.* conoid.
conoideo, -a *adj.* conoid.
conómetro *m.* konometer.
conos *m.* cones.
  conos y bastones rods and cones.
conquiolinosteomielitis *f.* conchiolinosteomyelitis.
conquitis *f.* conchitis.
consanguíneo, -a *adj.* consanguineous.
consanguinidad *f.* consanguinity, sibship.
consciencia *f.* conscience.
consciente *adj.* conscious.
consecutivo, -va *adj.* consecutive.
consensual *adj.* consensual.
consentimiento informado *m.* informed consent.

conservación *f.* conservation, preservation.
conservación de la energía conservation of energy.
conservación en frío cold preservation.
conservación en máquina perfusion system.
conservación de la materia conservation of matter.
conservador, -ra *adj.* conservative.
conservante *m.* preservative.
consistencia *f.* consistence.
consistencia gingival gingival consistence.
consolidación *f.* consolidation.
consolidación viciosa malunion.
consolidado, -da *adj.* consolidate.
consolidante *adj.* consolidant.
consonación *m.* consonation.
consonancia *f.* consonance.
conspicuo, -cua *adj.* conspicuous.
constancia *f.* constancy.
constancia celular cell constancy.
constancia del objeto, constancia de los objetos object constancy.
constancia perceptiva, constancia perceptual perceptive constancy, perceptual constancy.
constante *f. y adj.* constant.
constante de asociación association constant.
constante de Avogadro Avogadro's constant.
constante de conjugación binding constant.
constante cuántica Planck's constant.
constante de desactivación desintegration constant.
constante de desintegración desintegration constant.
constante dieléctrica dielectric constant.
constante de difusión diffusion constant.
constante de disociación dissociation constant.
constante de equilibrio equilibrium constant.
constante de Faraday Faraday's constant.
constante de los gases gas constant.
constante gravitacional, constante de gravitación gravitational constant, constant of gravitation.
constante de ionización ionization constant.
constante de Lapicque Lapicque's constant.
constante de Michaelis Michaelis constant.
constante newtoniana de gravitación Newtonian constant of gravitation.
constante de Planck Planck's constant.
constante radiactiva, constante de radiactividad radioactive constant.
constante de Rohrer Rohrer constant.
constante de sedimentación sedimentation constant.
constante de tasa de absorción absorption rate constant.
constante de velocidad velocity constant.
constelación *f.* constellation.
constitución *f.* constitution.
constitución cromosómica chromosome set.
constitución linfática lymphatic constitution.
constitucional *adj.* constitutional.
constricción *f.* constriction.
constricción duodenopilórica duodenopyloric constriction.
constricción primaria primary constriction.
constricción secundaria secondary constriction.
constrictivo, -va constrictive.
constrictor *m.* constrictor.
constructivo, -va *adj.* constructive.
consumo *m.* consumption.
consumo de oxígeno oxygen consumption.

consumo pasivo de tabaco passive smoking consumption.
consumo perjudicial damaging consumption.
consumo sistémico de oxígeno systemic oxygen consumption.
consunción *f.* consumption.
consuntivo, -va *adj.* consumptive.
contactante *adj.* contactant.
contacto *m.* contact.
contacto de balance, contacto balanceado balancing contact.
contacto céntrico centric contact.
contacto completo complete contact.
contacto débil weak contact.
contacto deflectivo deflective contact.
contacto directo direct contact.
contacto indirecto mediate contact.
contacto inicial initial contact.
contacto inmediato immediate contact.
contacto oclusal occlusal contact.
contacto oclusal deflectivo deflective occlusal contact.
contacto oclusal inicial initial occlusal contact.
contacto oclusal interceptiva interceptive occlusal contact.
contacto prematuro premature contact.
contacto proximal, contacto próximo proximal contact, proximate contact.
contacto con la realidad contact with reality.
contacto de trabajo working contact.
contador *m.* counter.
contador automático diferencial de leucocitos automated differential leukocyte counter.
contador de centelleo scintillation counter.
contador de colonias colony counter.
contador de Coulter Coulter counter.
contador electrónico celular electronic cell counter.
contador de flujo compensado compensated flow meter counter.
contador gamma gamma counter.
contador de Geiger, contador Geiger-Müller Geiger counter, Geiger-Müller counter.
contador proporcional proportional counter.
contador para todo el cuerpo whole-body counter.
contagio *m.* contagion.
contagio directo, contagio inmediato immediate contagion.
contagio indirecto mediate contagion.
contagio mental psychic contagion.
contagio psíquico psychic contagion.
contagiosidad *f.* contagiosity.
contagioso, -sa *adj.* contagious.
contaminación *f.* contamination.
contaminante *adj.* contaminant.
contención *f.* fixation.
contenido *m.* content.
contenido de anhídrido carbónico carbon dioxide content.
contenido de información del polimorfismo (PIC) polymorphism information content.
contenido latente del sueño latent content.
contenido manifiesto del sueño manifest content.
contexto *m.* context.
contiguo, -a *adj.* contiguous.
continencia *f.* continence.
continencia fecal fecal continence.
continencia urinaria urinary continence.
continente *adj.* continent.

contorneado, -da *adj.* contoured.
contorneo *m.* contourning.
contorno *m.* contour.
contorno de la aleta flange contour.
contorno bucal buccal contour.
contorno de la encía gum contour.
contorno gingival gingival contour.
contorno de restauración restoration contour.
contorsión *f.* contortion.
contraabertura *f.* contra-aperture, counteropening.
contraángulo *m.* contra-angle.
contraapertura *f.* contra-aperture, counteropening.
contrabalanceo *m.* counterbalancing.
contrabisel *m.* contrabevel.
contracatexis *f.* anticathexis.
contracción *f.* contraction, twitch.
contracción de abertura, contracción de apertura opening contraction.
contracción de abertura anódica opening contraction, anodal opening contraction.
contracción de abertura catódica cathodal opening contraction.
contracción anodal anodal contraction.
contracción de apertura anódica opening contraction, anodal opening contraction.
contracción de apertura catódica cathodal opening contraction.
contracción auricular prematura premature atrial contraction.
contracción automática automatic contraction.
contracción Braxton Hicks Braxton-Hicks contraction.
contracción carpopedia, contracción carpopedal carpopedal contraction.
contracción de cierre closing contraction.
contracción de cierre anódico anodal closure contraction.
contracción de cierre catódico cathodal closure contraction.
contracción concéntrica concentric contraction.
contracción de Dupuytren Dupuytren's contraction.
contracción de dupuytren falsa false Dupuytren's contraction.
contracción de escape, contracción de escape ventricular escaped contraction escaped ventricular contraction.
contracción espasmódica twiching contraction.
contracción espasmódica de Trousseau Trousseau's contraction.
contracción excéntrica eccentric contraction.
contracción fascicular espasmódica fascicular twitch.
contracción fibrilar fibrillary contraction.
contracción de golpe delantero front-tap contraction.
contracción de Gowers Gowers' contraction.
contracción de hambre hunger contraction.
contracción idiomuscular idiomuscular contraction.
contracción isométrica isometric contraction.
contracción isotónica isotonic contraction.
contracción isovolumétrica isovolumetric contraction.
contracción miotática myotatic contraction.
contracción paradójica paradoxical contraction.

contracción postural postural contraction.

contracción prematura premature contraction.

contracción en reloj de arena hourglass contraction.

contracción de sacudida twich contraction.

contracción tetánica tetanic contraction.

contracción tónica tonic contraction.

contracción uterina uterine contraction.

contracción ventricular automática automatic ventricular contraction.

contracción ventricular de escape escaped ventricular contraction.

contracción ventricular prematura (CVP) premature ventricular contraction (PVC).

contracepción *f.* contraception.

contracepción hormonal hormonal contraception.

contracepción intrauterina intrauterine contraception.

contraceptivo *m.* contraceptive.

contracolorante *m.* counterstain.

contracondicionamiento *m.* counterconditioning.

contracorriente *f.* countercurrent.

contráctil *adj.* contractile.

contractilidad *f.* contractility.

contractilidad cardíaca cardiac contractility.

contractilidad galvánica galvanic contractility.

contractilidad idiomuscular idiomuscular contractility.

contractura *f.* contracture.

contractura de defensa defense contracture.

contractura dolorosa painful contracture.

contractura de Dupuytren Dupuytren's contracture.

contractura fisiológica physiologic contracture.

contractura funcional functional contracture.

contractura hipertónica hypertonic contracture.

contractura histérica hysterical contracture.

contractura isquémica ischemic contracture.

contractura isquémica del ventrículo izquierdo ischemic contracture of the left ventricle.

contractura pospoliomielítica postpoliomyelitic contracture.

contractura por veratrina veratrin contracture.

contractura de Volkmann Volkmann's contracture.

contrachoque *m.* countershock.

contradepresor *adj.* counterdepressant.

contraestimulante *adj.* contrastimulant.

contraestimulismo *m.* contrastimulism.

contraestímulo *m.* contrastimulus.

contraextensión *f.* counterextension.

contrafisura *f.* contrafissure.

contrafobia *f.* counterphobia.

contrafóbico, -ca *adj.* counterphobic.

contrafuerte *m.* abutment.

contrafuerte del implante implant abutment.

contrafuerte primario primary abutment.

contragolpe *m.* contrecoup.

contraincisión *f.* contraincision, counterincision.

contraindicación *f.* contraindication.

contraindicado, -da *adj.* contraindicated.

contraindicar *v.* contraindicate.

contrainmunoelectroforesis *f.* counterimmunoelectrophoresis.

contrainsular *adj.* contrainsular.

contrairritación *f.* counterirritation.

contrairritante *adj.* counterirritant.

contralateral *adj.* contralateral.

contraorden *f.* counterinjunction.

contraparético, -ca *adj.* contraparetic.

contrapulsación *f.* counterpulsation.

contrapulsación por balón intraaórtico intra-aortic balloon.

contrapulsación externa external counterpulsation.

contrapunción *f.* counterpunture.

contrarregulación *f.* counterregulation.

contraste *m.* contrast.

contraste baritado baric contrast.

contraste doble double contrast.

contraste ferromagnético ferromagnetic contrast.

contraste hidrosoluble hydrosoluble contrast.

contraste hiperosmolar hyperosmolar contrast.

contraste iónico ionic contrast.

contraste isoosmolar iso-osmolar contrast.

contraste liposoluble liposoluble contrast.

contraste negativo negative contrast.

contraste no iónico non-ionic contrast.

contraste norosmolar normo-osmolar contrast.

contraste objetivo objective contrast.

contraste paramagnético paramagnetic contrast.

contraste de la película film contrast.

contraste positivo positive contrast.

contraste radiográfico radiographic contrast.

contraste subjetivo subjective contrast.

contraste yodado, contraste iodado iodate contrast.

contrasugestión *f.* countersuggestion.

contratracción *f.* counteraction.

contratransferencia *f.* countertransference.

contratransporte *m.* countertransport.

contraveneno *m.* counterpoison.

contravolitivo, -va *adj.* contravolitional.

control *m.* control.

control automático automatic control.

control aversivo aversive control.

control biológico biological control.

control de calidad quality control.

control del estímulo, control de estímulos stimulus control.

control del estrés stress management.

control de ganancia tiempo-variada time-varied gain control.

control de la hemorragia control of hemorrhage.

control idiodinámico idiodynamic control.

control local local control.

control natal, control de la natalidad birth control.

control del niño sano well baby care.

control con placebo en investigación control with placebo in investigation.

control por presión nudge control.

control propio own control.

control reflejo reflex control.

control regional regional control.

control respiratorio respiratory control.

control por retroalimentación feedback control.

control del sexo sex control.

control sinérgico synergic control.

control social social control.

control tónico tonic control.

control vestibuloequilibratorio vestibuloequilibratory control.

control volitivo, control voluntario volitional control, voluntary control.

controlado, -da por el sexo sex-controlled.

controlador intravenoso intravenous controller.

controversia *f.* controversy.

contusión *f.* contusion.

contusión aérea wind contusion.

contusión cerebral brain contusion.

contusión del cuero cabelludo scalp contusion.

contusión por contragolpe countercoup contusion.

contusión del lóbulo temporal temporal lobe contusion.

contusión de la médula espinal contusion of the spinal cord.

contusión medular medullar contusion.

contusión por piedra stone contusion.

contusión renal renal contusion.

conular *adj.* conular.

conus conus.

convalecencia *f.* convalescence.

convaleciente *adj.* convalescent.

convencional *adj.* conventional.

convergencia *f.* convergence.

convergencia de acomodación, convergencia acomodativa accommodative convergence.

convergencia de fusión fusional convergence.

convergencia negativa negative convergence.

convergencia positiva positive convergence.

convergiómetro *m.* convergiometer.

conversión *f.* conversion.

conversión en base libre freebasing conversion.

conversor *m.* converter.

conversor analógico-digital *m.* analog-digital converter.

conversor D-A *m.* D-A converter.

conversor digital-analógico *m.* digital-to-analog converter.

convexidad *f.* convexity.

convexidad cortical cortical convexity.

convexo, -xa *adj.* convex.

convexobasia *f.* convexobaxia.

convexocóncavo, -va *adj.* convexoconcave.

convexoconvexo, -xa *adj.* convexoconvex.

convoluto, -ta *adj.* convolute, convoluted.

convulsión *f.* convulsion, seizure.

convulsión acinética akinetic seizure.

convulsión clónica clonic convulsion, clonic seizure.

convulsión coordinada coordinate convulsion.

convulsión estática static convulsion.

convulsión por éter ether convulsion.

convulsión febril febrile convulsion, febrile seizure.

convulsión focal focal seizure.

convulsión histérica, convulsión histeroide hysterical convulsion, hysteroid convulsion, hysterical seizure.

convulsión infantil infantile convulsion.

convulsión mímica mimetic convulsion, mimic convulsion.

convulsión neonatal neonatal seizure.

convulsión parcial partial convulsion, partial seizure.

convulsión parcial compleja complex partial convulsion.

convulsión postraumática inmediata immediate post-traumatic convulsion.

convulsión puerperal puerperal convulsion.

convulsión en "salaam" salaam convulsion.

convulsión tetánica tetanic convulsion.

convulsión tónica tonic convulsion, tonic seizure.

convulsión tónico-clónica generalizada generalized tonic-clonic convulsion, generalized tonic-clonic seizure.

convulsionante *adj.* convulsant.

convulsivante *adj.* convulsivant.

convulsivo, -va *adj.* convulsive.

convulsoterapia *f.* convulsotherapy.

coordenada *f.* coordenate.

coordinación *f.* coordination.

coordinación motora motor coordination.

coordinación visualmotora visual-motor coordination.

coosificación *f.* co-ossification.

copa *f.* cup, poculum.

copa de Diógenes Diogenes cup, poculum diogenis.

copa fisiológica physiologic cup.

copa glaucomatosa glaucomatous cup.

copa ocular eye cup, eyecup.

copépodo *m.* copepod.

copiopía *f.* copiopia.

copiopsia *f.* copiopia.

copofobia *f.* kopophobia.

copolímero *m.* copolymer.

copracrasia *f.* copracrasia.

coprecipitación *f.* coprecipitation.

coprecipitina *f.* coprecipitin.

copremesis *f.* copremesis.

copremia *f.* copremia.

coproanticuerpo *m.* coproantibody.

coprocultivo *m.* coproculture.

coprófago, -ga *adj.* coprofagous.

coprofagia *f.* coprophagy.

coprofemia *f.* coprophemie.

coprofílico, -ca *adj.* coprophilic, coprophil.

coprofilia *f.* coprophilia.

coprófilo, -la *adj.* coprophilic, coprophil.

coprofrasia *f.* coprophrasia.

coprolagnia *f.* coprolagnia.

coprolalia *f.* coprolalia.

coprolito *m.* coprolith.

coprología *f.* coprology.

coproma *m.* coproma.

copromimia *f.* copromimia.

coproplanesia *f.* coproplanesia.

coproporfiria *f.* coproporphyria.

coproporfirina *f.* coproporphyrin.

coproporfirinuria *f.* coproporphyrinuria.

coprostanol *m.* coprostanol.

coprostasia *f.* coprostasis.

coprostasis *f.* coprostasis.

coprostasofobia *f.* coprostasophobia.

coprosterina *f.* coprosterin.

coprostenol *m.* coprostenol.

coprozoarios *m.* coprozoa.

coprozoico, -ca *adj.* coprozoic.

coptosis *f.* coptosis.

coptosístole *f.* coptosystole.

cópula *f.* copula.

copulación *f.* copulation.

cor cor.

cor adiposum fat heart, fatty heart, cor adiposum.

cor mobile movable heart, cor mobile.

cor pulmonale pulmonary heart, cor pulmonale.

cor triloculare three-chambered heart, cor triloculare.

coracoacromial *adj.* coracoacromial.

coracoideo, -a *adj.* coracoid.

coracoiditis *f.* coracoiditis.

coraliforme *adj.* coralliform.

coraloide *adj.* coralloid.

corasma *m.* corasthma.

coraza *f.* curiass.

coraza analgésica analgesic curiass.

coraza tabética tabetic curiass.

corazón *m.* heart, cor.

corazón adiposo fat heart, fatty heart, cor adiposum.

corazón en armadura armor heart.

corazón artificial artificial heart.

corazón de atleta, corazón atlético athlete's heart, athletic heart.

corazón de bebedor de cerveza beer heart.

corazón blindado armored heart.

corazón caído drop heart.

corazón de cerveza beer heart.

corazón colgante hanging heart.

corazón congelado frosted heart.

corazón cutáneo skin heart.

corazón derecho right heart.

corazón en forma de lágrima teardrop heart.

corazón errante wandering heart.

corazón graso fat heart, fatty heart.

corazón graso de Quain Quain's fatty heart.

corazón de hielo icing heart.

corazón hipoplásico hypoplastic heart.

corazón horizontal horizontal heart.

corazón intermedio intermediate heart.

corazón irritable irritable heart.

corazón izquierdo left heart.

corazón en matriz flask-shaped heart.

corazón militar soldier's heart.

corazón mixedematoso myxedema heart.

corazón móvil movable heart, cor mobile.

corazón navicular boat-shaped heart.

corazón óseo bony heart.

corazón en pecho de tordo tabby cat heart.

corazón de pergamino parchment heart.

corazón de piedra stone heart.

corazón piloso hairy heart.

corazón piriforme pear-shaped heart.

corazón pulmonar pulmonary heart, cor pulmonale.

corazón recubierto frosted heart.

corazón redondeado round heart.

corazón semihorizontal semihorizontal heart.

corazón semivertical semivertical heart.

corazón sistémico systemic heart.

corazón de soldado soldier's heart.

corazón suspendido suspended heart.

corazón tabáquico tobacco heart.

corazón de tigre, corazón tigroide tiger heart.

corazón de tres cavidades three-chambered heart, cor triloculare.

corazón venoso venous heart.

corazón vertical vertical heart.

corazón en zueco sabot heart.

corbata *f.* necklace.

corbata de Casal Casal's necklace.

corcova *f.* humpback.

cordabrasión *f.* cordabrasion.

cordal *adj.* chordal.

cordamesodermo *m.* chorda-mesoderm.

cordectomía *f.* cordectomy.

cordencéfalo *m.* chordencephalon.

cordial cordial, cordiale.

cordiforme *adj.* cordiform.

cordilobiasis *f.* cordylobiasis.

corditis *f.* chorditis, corditis.

corditis de los cantantes chorditis cantorum.

corditis fibrinosa chorditis fibrinosa.

corditis nudosa chorditis nodosa.

corditis tuberosa chorditis tuberosa.

corditis vocal chorditis vocalis.

corditis vocal inferior chorditis vocalis inferior.

cordoblastoma *m.* chordoblastoma.

cordocarcinoma *m.* chordocarcinoma.

cordoepitelioma *m.* chordoepithelioma.

cordoesqueleto *m.* chordoskeleton.

cordoide *adj.* chordoid.

cordoma *m.* chordoma.

cordón *m.* cord, funiculus.

cordón dental dental cord.

cordón de esmalte enamel cord.

cordón genital genital cord.

cordón germinal germinal cord.

cordón gonadal gonadal cord.

cordón medular medullary cord.

cordón nefrógeno, cordón nefrogénico nephrogenic cord.

cordón nucal nuchal cord.

cordón ovígero ovigerous cord.

cordón de la rete rete cord.

cordón sexual sex cord, sexual cord.

cordón umbilical umbilical cord, funiculus umbilicalis.

cordón vitelino vitelline cord.

cordopexia *f.* cordopexy.

cordosarcoma *m.* chordosarcoma.

cordotomía *f.* cordotomy.

cordotomía abierta open cordotomy.

cordotomía anterolateral anterolateral cordotomy.

cordotomía espinotalámica spinothalamic cordotomy.

cordotomía estereotáctica stereotactic cordotomy.

cordotomía del haz posterior posterior column cordotomy.

cordura *f.* sanity.

corea *f.* chorea.

corea aguda acute chorea.

corea automática automatic chorea.

corea cardíaca chorea cordis.

corea crónica chronic chorea.

corea crónica progresiva, corea crónica progresiva hereditaria chronic progressive chorea, chronic progressive hereditary chorea.

corea crónica progresiva no hereditaria chronic progressive nonhereditary chorea.

corea danzante dancing chorea.

corea degenerativa degenerative chorea.

corea diafragmática diaphragmatic chorea.

corea dimidiata chorea dimidiata.

corea eléctrica electric chorea.

corea epidémica epidemic chorea.

corea de fabricantes de botones button maker's chorea.

corea festinante chorea festinans.

corea fibrilar fibrillary chorea.

corea fláccida limp chorea.

corea gravídica, corea gravidarum chorea gravidarum.

corea habitual habit chorea.

corea hemilateral hemilateral chorea.

corea de Henoch Henoch's chorea.

corea hereditaria hereditary chorea.

corea por hioscina hyoscine chorea.

corea histérica hysteric chorea, hysterical chorea.

corea de Huntington Huntington's chorea.

corea juvenil juvenile chorea.

corea laríngea laryngeal chorea.

corea mayor, corea major chorea major.
corea menor, corea minor chorea minor.
corea metódica methodic chorea.
corea mimética mimetic chorea.
corea de Morvan Morvan's chorea.
corea nutans chorea nutans.
corea paralítica paralytic chorea.
corea poshemipléjica posthemiplegic chorea.
corea prehemipléjica prehemiplegic chorea.
corea procursiva procursive chorea.
corea reumática rheumatic chorea.
corea rítmica rhythmic chorea.
corea rotatoria rotary chorea.
corea saltatoria saltatory chorea.
corea senil senile chorea.
corea de Sydenham Sydenham's chorea.
corea tetanoide tetanoid chorea.
corea unilateral onesided chorea.
corea-acantocitosis *f.* chorea-acanthocytosis.
coreal *adj.* choreal.
coreclisis *f.* coreclisis, corenclisis.
corectasia *f.* corectasis.
corectasis *f.* corectasis.
corectomediálisis *f.* corectomedialysis, coretomedialysis.
corectomía *f.* corectomy.
corectopia *f.* corectopia.
corediastasis *f.* corediastasis, corodiastasis.
coreico, -ca *adj.* choreic.
coreiforme *adj.* choreiform.
corélisis *f.* corelysis.
coremorfosis *f.* coremorphosis.
corenclisis *f.* corenclisis.
coreoatetoide *adj.* choreoathetoid.
coreoatetosis *f.* choreoathetosis.
coreofrasia *f.* choreophrasia.
coreoide *adj.* choreoid.
coreometría *f.* coreometry.
coreómetro *m.* coreometer, corometer.
coreoplastia *f.* coreoplasty, coroplasty.
corepexia *f.* corepexy.
corepraxia *f.* corepraxy.
corestenoma *m.* corestenoma.
  corestenoma congénito corestenoma congenitum.
coretomediálisis *f.* coretomedialysis.
coretomía *f.* coretomy.
coriáceo, -a *adj.* coriaceous.
corial *adj.* chorial.
coribantismo *m.* corybantism.
corificación *f.* corification.
corimbiforme *adj.* corymbiform.
corinebacteria *f.* corynebacterium.
corineforme *adj.* coryneform.
corioadenoma *m.* chorioadenoma.
  corioadenoma destructivo, corioadenoma destruens chorioadenoma destruens.
corioalantoico, -ca *adj.* chorioallantoic.
corioalantoideo, -a *adj.* chorioallantoic.
corioalantoides *f.* chorioallantois.
corioamnionitis *f.* chorioamnionitis.
corioamniótico, -ca *adj.* chorioamnionic.
corioangiofibroma *m.* chorioangiofibroma.
corioangioma *m.* chorioangioma.
corioangiomatosis *f.* chorioangiomatosis.
corioangiosis *f.* chorioangiosis.
corioblastoma *m.* chorioblastoma.
corioblastosis *f.* chorioblastosis.
coriocarcinoma *m.* choriocarcinoma.
coriocele *m.* choriocele.
corioepitelioma *m.* chorioepithelioma.
coriogonadotropina *f.* choriogonadotropin.
coriogénesis *f.* choriogenesis.
corioideo, - a *adj.* chorioid.

corioma *m.* chorioma.
coriomeningitis *f.* choriomeningitis.
  coriomeningitis linfocítica lymphocytic choriomeningitis.
corion *m.* chorion, corium.
  corion frondoso corium frondosum.
  corion gingival gingival chorion.
  corion hirsuto shaggy chorion.
  corion leve corium laeve.
  corion liso smooth chorion.
  corion prevelloso previllous chorion.
  corion primitivo primitive chorion.
  corion velloso shaggy chorion.
coriónico, -ca *adj.* chorionic.
corioplacentario, -ria *adj.* chorioplacental.
coriorretiniano, -na *adj.* chorioretinal.
coriorretinitis *f.* chorioretinitis.
  coriorretinitis esclopetaria chorioretinitis sclopetaria.
coriorretinopatía *f.* chorioretinopathy.
  coriorretinopatía serosa central central serous chorioretinopathy.
coristo *m.* chorista.
coristoblastoma *m.* choristoblastoma.
coristoma *m.* choristoma.
corium corium.
  corium laeve corium laeve.
coriza *f.* coryza.
  coriza alérgica allergic coryza.
  coriza espasmódica coryza spasmodica.
  coriza del polen pollen coryza.
córnea *f.* cornea.
  córnea cónica conical cornea.
  córnea farinácea cornea farinata.
  córnea guttata guttate cornea.
  córnea plana congénita familiar cornea plana congenita familiaris.
  córnea úrica cornea urica.
  córnea verticilada, córnea verticillata cornea verticillata.
corneal *adj.* corneal.
corneano, -na *adj.* corneal.
corneítis *f.* corneitis.
córneo, -a *adj.* corneous, horny.
corneobléfaron *m.* corneoblepharon.
corneocito *m.* corneocyte.
corneoescleral *adj.* corneoscleral.
corneoesclerótica *f.* corneosclera.
corneoiritis *f.* corneoiritis.
cornete *m.* concha.
corniculado, -da *adj.* corniculate.
cornículo *m.* corniculum.
cornificación *f.* cornification.
cornificado, -da *adj.* cornified.
cornucomisural *adj.* cornucommissural.
cornucopia *f.* cornucopia.
corodiastasis *m.* coriodiastasis.
coroidal *adj.* choroidal.
coroidectomía *f.* choroidectomy.
coroideo, -a *adj.* choroidal.
coroideremia *f.* choroideremia.
coroides *f.* choroidea.
coroiditis *f.* choroiditis.
  coroiditis anterior anterior choroiditis.
  coroiditis areolar areolar choroiditis.
  coroiditis difusa, coroiditis diseminada diffuse choroiditis, disseminated choroiditis.
  coroiditis exudativa exudative choroiditis.
  coroiditis metastásica metastatic choroiditis.
  coroiditis multifocal multifocal choroiditis.
  coroiditis posterior posterior choroiditis.
  coroiditis proliferante proliferative choroiditis.
  coroiditis senil maculosa exudativa senile macular exudative choroiditis.

  coroiditis serosa serous choroiditis.
  coroiditis serpiginosa serpiginous choroiditis.
  coroiditis supurativa, coroiditis supurada suppurative choroiditis.
  coroiditis yuxtapupilar juxtapupillary choroiditis.
coroidociclitis *f.* choroidocyclitis.
coroidoiritis *f.* choroidoiritis.
coroidopatía *f.* choroidopathy.
  coroidopatía areolar areolar choroidopathy.
  coroidopatía de Doyne en panal Doyne's honeycomb choroidopathy.
  coroidopatía geográfica geographic choroidopathy.
  coroidopatía guttata guttate choroidopathy.
  coroidopatía guttata senil senile guttate choroidopathy.
  coroidopatía helicoidal helicoid choroidopathy.
  coroidopatía miópica myopic choroidopathy.
  coroidopatía serosa central central serous choroidopathy.
  coroidopatía serpiginosa serpiginous choroidopathy.
coroidorretinitis *f.* choroidoretinitis.
coroidosis *f.* choroidosis.
  coroidosis miópica myopic choroidosis.
corología *f.* chorology.
corómetro *m.* corometer.
corona *f.* crown, corona.
  corona acampanada bell-shaped crown.
  corona artificial artificial crown.
  corona estática static crown.
  corona funda jacket crown.
  corona parcial partial crown.
  corona radiada, corona radiante radiate crown, corona radiata.
  corona seborreica corona seborrheica.
  corona de Venus, corona venérea, corona veneris corona veneris.
coronal *adj.* coronal, coronale.
coronale coronale.
coronamiento *m.* crowning.
coronario, -ria *adj.* coronary.
coronariografía *f.* coronariography.
coronariopatía *f.* coronary artery disease.
coronarismo *m.* coronarism.
coronaritis *f.* coronaritis.
Coronavirus Coronavirus.
coronión *m.* coronion.
coronoide *adj.* coronoid.
coronoidectomía *f.* coronoidectomy.
coronoideo, -a *adj.* coronoid.
coroparelcisis *f.* coroparelcysis.
coroparelquisis *f.* coroparelcysis.
coroplastia *f.* coroplasty.
coroscopia *f.* coroscopy.
corotomía *f.* corotomy.
corporal *adj.* corporeal.
corporectomía *f.* corporectomy.
corpóreo, -a *adj.* corporeal.
corpus corpus.
  corpus albicans corpus albicans.
  corpus luteum corpus luteum.
corpuscular *adj.* corpuscular.
corpúsculo *m.* corpuscle, corpusculum.
  corpúsculo amiláceo, corpúsculo amiloide amylaceous corpuscle, amyloid corpuscle.
  corpúsculo de Barr Barr's corpuscle.
  corpúsculo basal basal corpuscle.
  corpúsculo de Bizzozero Bizzozero's corpuscle.
  corpúsculo blanco white corpuscle.

corpúsculo bulboide, corpúsculo bulboideo bulboid corpuscle.
corpúsculo del calostro colostrum corpuscle.
corpúsculo de cemento cement corpuscle.
corpúsculo concéntrico, corpúsculo concéntrico de Hassall concentric corpuscle, Hassall's concentric corpuscle.
corpúsculo de la corea, corpúsculo de corea chorea corpuscle.
corpúsculo corneal corneal corpuscle.
corpúsculo cromófilo chromophil corpuscle.
corpúsculo de Dogiel Dogiel's corpuscle.
corpúsculo de Donné Donne's corpuscle.
corpúsculo de Drysdale Drysdale's corpuscle.
corpúsculo de Eichhorst Eichhorst's corpuscle.
corpúsculo de exudación exudation corpuscle.
corpúsculo fantasma phantom corpuscle.
corpúsculo genital genital corpuscle.
corpúsculo de Gierke Gierke's corpuscle.
corpúsculo de Gluge Gluge's corpuscle.
corpúsculo de Golgi Golgi's corpuscle.
corpúsculo de Golgi-Mazzoni Golgi-Mazzoni corpuscle.
corpúsculo de Grandy, corpúsculo de Grandy-Merkel Grandy's corpuscle.
corpúsculo de Guarnieri Guarnieri's corpuscle.
corpúsculo gustativo, corpúsculo del gusto gustatory corpuscle, taste corpuscle.
corpúsculo de Hassall Hassall's corpuscle.
corpúsculo inflamatorio inflammatory corpuscle.
corpúsculo Jaworski Jaworski's corpuscle.
corpúsculo de Krause Krause's corpuscle.
corpúsculo de Leber Leber's corpuscle.
corpúsculo de la leche milk corpuscle.
corpúsculo de la linfa, corpúsculo linfático, corpúsculo linfoide lymph corpuscle, lymphatic corpuscle, lymphoid corpuscle.
corpúsculo de Lostorfer Lostorfer's corpuscle.
corpúsculo de Malpighi Malpighian corpuscle.
corpúsculo de Mazzoni Mazzoni's corpuscle.
corpúsculo meconales, corpúsculo del meconio meconium corpuscle.
corpúsculo de Meissner Meissner's corpuscle.
corpúsculo de Merkel Merkel corpuscle.
corpúsculo mucoso mucous corpuscle.
corpúsculo de Negri Negri's corpuscle.
corpúsculo de Nissl Nissl corpuscle.
corpúsculo de Norris Norris' corpuscle.
corpúsculo óseo bone corpuscle.
corpúsculo oval oval corpuscle.
corpúsculo de Pacini Pacini's corpuscle.
corpúsculo de Pacchioni Pacchionian corpuscle.
corpúsculo de Paschen Paschen's corpuscle.
corpúsculo pequeño de Bennet Bennet's small corpuscle.
corpúsculo en pesario pessary corpuscle.
corpúsculo plástico plastic corpuscle.
corpúsculo en puente bridge corpuscle.
corpúsculo de Purkinje Purkinje's corpuscle.
corpúsculo de pus pus corpuscle.
corpúsculo del quilo chyle corpuscle.
corpúsculo renal renal corpuscle.
corpúsculo reticulado reticulated corpuscle.
corpúsculo rojo de la sangre red corpuscle.
corpúsculo de Ruffini Ruffini's corpuscle.
corpúsculo salival salivary corpuscle.
corpúsculo sanguíneo blood corpuscle.

corpúsculo sanguíneo rojo humano concentrado concentrated human red blood corpuscle.
corpúsculo de Schwalbe Schwalbe's corpuscle.
corpúsculo en sombrero mexicano Mexican hat corpuscle.
corpúsculo táctil, corpúsculo táctil de Meissner tactile corpuscle of Meissner.
corpúsculo del tacto touch corpuscle.
corpúsculo tendinoso tendon corpuscle.
corpúsculo tercero third corpuscle.
corpúsculo tífico typhic corpuscle.
corpúsculo tímico, corpúsculo del timo thymus corpuscle, thymic corpuscle.
corpúsculo de Timofeew Timofeew's corpuscle.
corpúsculo de Toynbee Toynbee's corpuscle.
corpúsculo de Traube Traube's corpuscle.
corpúsculo Tröltsch Tröltsch's corpuscle.
corpúsculo de Valentin Valentin's corpuscle.
corpúsculo de Vater, corpúsculo de Vater-Pacini Vater's corpuscle, Vater-Pacini corpuscle.
corpúsculo de Virchow Virchow's corpuscle.
corpúsculo de Zimmermann Zimmermann's corpuscle.
corrección f. correction.
corrección de Allen Allen correction.
corrección espontánea de la placenta previa spontaneous correction of the placenta previa.
corrección oclusal occlusal correction.
corrector, -ra adj. corrective.
corrector m. corrector.
corrector de función function corrector.
corredera f. groove.
correlación f. correlation.
correspondencia f. correspondence.
correspondencia anómala anomalous correspondence.
correspondencia armoniosa harmonious correspondence.
correspondencia inarmónica dysharmonious correspondence.
correspondencia retiniana retinal correspondence.
correspondencia retiniana anómala anomalous retinal correspondence.
correspondencia retiniana anormal anormal retinal correspondence.
correspondencia retiniana normal normal retinal correspondence.
corriente f. current.
corrosión f. corrosion.
corrosivo, -va adj. corrosive.
corrugador m. corrugator.
corrupción f. corruption.
corsé m. brace, jacket, corset.
corsé de flexión flexion jacket.
corsé en forma de pañal diaper restraint jacket.
corsé de Milwaukee Milwaukee brace.
corsé de Minerva Minerva's corset.
corsé de restricción restraint jacket.
corsé de Riser Riser jacket.
corsé de Sayre Sayre's jacket.
corsé de Taylor Taylor brace.
corte m. cut, section.
corte congelado, corte por congelación frozen cut, frozen section.
corte cónico cone cut.
corte coronal coronal cut.
corte frontal frontal section.
corte medio midsection.

corte de parafina, corte en parafina paraffin cut, paraffin section.
corte de Pitres Pitres' section.
corte sagital saggital cut.
corte en serie serial section.
corte transversal transversal cut, transversal section.
corteza f. cortex.
corteza fetal fetal cortex.
corteza provisional provisional cortex.
corticado, -da adj. corticate.
cortical adj. cortical.
corticalización f. corticalization.
corticalosteotomía f. corticalosteotomy.
corticectomía f. corticectomy.
corticífugo, -ga adj. corticifugal.
corticípeto, -ta adj. corticipetal.
corticoaferente adj. corticoafferent.
corticoautónomo, -ma adj. corticoautonomic.
corticobulbar adj. corticobulbar.
corticocerebelo m. corticocerebellum.
corticocerebral adj. corticocerebral.
corticodiencefálico, -ca adj. corticodiencephalic.
corticoeferente adj. corticoefferent.
corticoespinal adj. corticospinal.
corticoesteroide m. corticosteroid.
corticófugo, -ga adj. corticofugal, corticifugal.
corticoide m. corticoid.
corticomedial adj. corticomedial.
corticomedular adj. corticospinal.
corticomesencefálico, -ca adj. corticomesencephalic.
corticopeduncular adj. corticopeduncular.
corticópeto, -ta adj. corticopetal, corticipetal.
corticopleuritis f. corticopleuritis.
corticopontino, -na adj. corticopontine.
corticorresistencia f. steroid-resistance.
corticospinal adj. corticospinal.
corticosteroide m. corticosteroid.
corticosterona f. corticosterone.
corticosuprarrenal adj. adrenocortical, corticoadrenal.
corticosuprarrenaloma m. corticosuprarenaloma.
corticosuprarrenoma m. corticosuprarenoma.
corticotalámico, -ca adj. corticothalamic.
corticotrofo m. corticotroph.
corticotrofo-lipotrofo m. corticotroph-lipotroph.
corticotropa f. corticotrope.
corticotrópico, -ca adj. corticotropic.
corticotropinoma f. corticotropinoma.
cortilinfa f. cortilymph.
cortisol m. cortisol.
cortisolemia f. cortisolemia.
cortisoluria f. cortisoluria.
coruscación f. coruscation.
costa f. rib, costa.
costal adj. costal.
costalgia f. costalgia.
costectomía f. costectomy.
costicartílago m. costicartilage.
costicervical adj. costicervical.
costífero, -ra adj. costiferous.
costiforme adj. costiform.
costilla, costa f. rib, costa.
costilla cervical cervical rib, costa cervicalis.
costilla deslizada, costilla deslizante slipping rib.
costoabdominal adj. costoabdominal.
costocentral adj. costocentral.
costocervical adj. costicervical.
costoclavicular adj. costoclavicular.

costocondral *adj.* costochondral.
costocondritis *f.* costochondritis.
costocoracoideo, -a *adj.* costocoracoid.
costoescapular *adj.* costoscapular.
costoespinal *m.* costospinal.
costoesternal *adj.* costosternal.
costoesternoplastia *f.* costosternoplasty.
costofrénico, -ca *adj.* costophrenic.
costogénico, -ca *adj.* costogenic.
costoinferior *adj.* costoinferior.
costoneumopexia *f.* costopneumopexy.
costopleural *adj.* costopleural.
costopúbico, -ca *adj.* costopubic.
costoscapular *adj.* costoscapular.
costospinal *m.* costospinal.
costosternal *adj.* costosternal.
costosuperior *adj.* costosuperior.
costotomía *f.* costotomy.
costótomo *m.* costotome.
costotransversectomía *f.* costotransversectomy.
costotransverso, -sa *adj.* costotransverse.
costovertebral *adj.* costovertebral.
costoxifoideo, -a *adj.* costoxiphoid.
costra *f.* crust, crusta.
  costra flogística crusta phlogistica.
  costra inflamatoria crusta inflammatoria.
  costra láctea, costra de leche milk crust, crusta lactea.
costroso, -sa *adj.* costrous, crustal.
costura *f.* seam.
  costura de pigmento pigment seam.
cotidiana *adj.* quotidian.
cotiledón *m.* cotyledon.
cótilo *m.* cotyle.
cotiloide *adj.* cotyloid.
cotiloideo, -a *adj.* cotyloid.
cotilopúbico, -ca *adj.* cotylopubic.
cotilosacro, -cra *adj.* cotylosacral.
cotransporte *m.* cotransport.
cotromboplastina *f.* cothromboplastin.
couvercle *f.* couvercle.
cowdriosis *f.* cowdriosis.
cowperiano, -na *adj.* Cowperian.
cowperitis *f.* cowperitis.
cowpox *m.* cowpox.
coxa *f.* coxa.
  coxa adducta coxa adducta.
  coxa flexa coxa flexa.
  coxa magna coxa magna.
  coxa plana coxa plana.
  coxa valga coxa valga.
  coxa valga subluxans coxa valga subluxans.
  coxa vara coxa vara.
  coxa vara falsa false coxa vara.
  coxa vara luxante, coxa vara luxans coxa vara luxans.
coxalgia *f.* coxalgia.
  coxalgia fugaz coxalgia fugax.
coxartria *f.* coxarthria.
coxartritis *f.* coxarthritis.
coxartrocace *m.* coxarthrocace.
coxartropatía *f.* coxarthropathy, hip-joint disease.
coxartrosis *f.* coxarthrosis.
Coxiella Coxiella.
  Coxiella burnetii Coxiella burnetii.
coxitis *f.* coxitis.
  coxitis fugaz fugitive coxitis, coxitis fugax.
  coxitis senil coxitis senile.
  coxitis tuberculosa tuberculous coxitis.
coxodinia *f.* coxodynia.
coxofemoral *adj.* coxofemoral.
coxotomía *f.* coxotomy.
coxotuberculosis *f.* coxotuberculosis.

Coxsackie Coxsackie.
Coxsackievirus Coxsackievirus.
craneal *adj.* cranial.
craneano, -na *adj.* cranial.
craneítis *f.* cranitis.
cráneo *m.* skull, cranium.
  cráneo bífido, cranium bifidum bifid skull, cranium bifidum.
  cráneo bífido oculto cranium bifidum occultum.
  cráneo en campanario steeple skull.
  cráneo en mapa maplike skull.
  cráneo natiforme natiform skull.
  cráneo en torre tower skull.
craneoacromial *adj.* cranioacromial.
craneoanfitomía *f.* cranioamphitomy.
craneoaural *adj.* cranioaural.
craneobucal *adj.* craniobucal.
craneocaudal *adj.* craniocaudal.
craneocele *m.* craniocele.
craneocerebral *adj.* craniocerebral.
craneocervical *adj.* craniocervical.
craneocleidodisostosis *f.* craniocleidodysostosis.
craneodídimo *m.* craniodidymus.
craneoesclerosis *f.* craniosclerosis.
craneoespinal *adj.* craniospinal.
craneoestenosis *f.* craniostenosis.
craneofacial *adj.* craniofacial.
craneofaríngeo, -a *adj.* craniopharyngeal.
craneofaringioma *m.* craniopharyngioma.
  craneofaringioma papilomatoso quístico cystic papillomatous craniopharyngioma.
craneofenestria *f.* craniofenestria.
craneóforo *m.* craniophore.
craneognomía *f.* craniognomy.
craneografía *f.* craniography.
craneógrafo *m.* craniograph.
craneolacunia *f.* craniolacunia.
craneología *f.* craniology.
craneomalacia *f.* craneomalacia.
  craneomalacia circunscrita circumscribed craneomalacia.
craneomeningocele *m.* craniomeningocele.
craneometría *f.* craniometry.
craneométrico, -ca *adj.* craniometric.
craneómetro *m.* craniometer.
craneópago *m.* craniopagus.
  craneópago occipital craniopagus occipitalis.
  craneópago parásito craniopagus parasiticus.
  craneópago parietal craniopagus parietalis.
craneopatía *f.* craniopathy.
  craneopatía metabólica metabolic craniopathy.
craneoplastia *f.* cranioplasty.
craneopuntura *f.* craniopuncture.
craneorraquídeo, -a *adj.* craniorrhachidian.
craneorraquisquisis *f.* craniorachischisis.
craneosacral *adj.* craniosacral.
craneosacro, -cra *adj.* craniosacral.
craneosclerosis *f.* craniosclerosis.
craneoscopia *f.* cranioscopy.
craneosinostosis *f.* craniosynostosis.
craneospinal *adj.* craniospinal.
craneosquisis *f.* cranioschisis.
craneostenosis *f.* craniostenosis.
craneostosis *f.* craniostosis.
craneotabes *f.* craniotabes.
craneotimpánico, -ca *adj.* craniotympanic.
craneotomía *f.* craniotomy.
  craneotomía osteoplástica osteoplastic craniotomy.
  craneotomía separada detached craniotomy.
  craneotomía unida attached craniotomy.
craneótomo *m.* craniotome.

craneotonoscopia *f.* craniotonoscopy.
craneotopografía *f.* craniotopography.
craneotripesis *f.* craniotrypesis.
craniad craniad.
cranianfitomía *f.* craniamphitomy.
craniectomía *f.* craniectomy.
  craniectomía lineal linear craniectomy.
cranium cranium.
crapulento, -ta *adj.* crapulent.
crapuloso, -sa *adj.* crapulous.
crasis *f.* crasis.
cráter *m.* crater.
  cráter gingival gingival crater.
  cráter interdental interdental crater.
crateriforme *adj.* crateriform.
craterización *f.* craterization.
cratomanía *f.* cratomania.
cratómetro *m.* kratometer.
craunología *f.* craunology.
craunoterapia *f.* craunotherapy.
crauomanía *f.* krauomania.
craurosis *f.* kraurosis.
  craurosis del pene kraurosis penis.
  craurosis vulvar kraurosis vulvae.
craw-craw *m.* craw-craw.
creatina *f.* creatine.
creatinemia *f.* creatinemia.
creatinina *f.* creatinin, creatinine.
  creatinina de 24 horas creatinine height index.
creatinuria *f.* creatinuria.
creatorrea *f.* creatorrhea.
creatotoxismo *m.* creatotoxism.
creciente *adj.* crescent.
crecimiento *m.* growth.
  crecimiento absoluto absolute growth.
  crecimiento acrecionario, crecimiento por acreción accretionary growth.
  crecimiento alométrico allometric growth.
  crecimiento por aposición appositional growth.
  crecimiento auxético auxetic growth.
  crecimiento compensador catch-up growth.
  crecimiento condíleo condylar growth.
  crecimiento diferencial differential growth.
  crecimiento gingival hormonal gingival hormonal enlargement.
  crecimiento heterógono heterogonous growth.
  crecimiento histiotípico histiotypic growth.
  crecimiento interno ingrowth.
  crecimiento intersticial interstitial growth.
  crecimiento intrauterino retardado intrauterine retarded growth.
  crecimiento isométrico isometric growth.
  crecimiento de multiplicación multiplicative growth.
  crecimiento nuevo new growth.
  crecimiento organotípico organotypic growth.
  crecimiento relativo relative growth.
crema *f.* cream.
cremastérico, -ca *adj.* cremasteric.
crematorio *m.* crematorium.
cremación *f.* cremation.
cremnofobia *f.* cremnophobia.
crenación *f.* crenation.
crenado, -da *adj.* crenate, crenated.
crenocito *m.* crenocyte.
crenocitosis *f.* crenocytosis.
crenología *f.* crenology, craunology.
crenoterapia *f.* crenotherapy, craunotherapy.
crenulación *f.* crenulation.
creofagia *f.* creophagism, creophagy.
creotoxina *f.* creotoxin, kreotoxin.
creotoxismo *m.* creotoxism, kreotoxism.
crepitación *m.* crepitation, crepitus.

crepitación articular, crépito articular articular crepitus, joint crepitus.

crepitación dolorosa de los tendones painful tendon crepitus.

crepitación falsa false crepitus.

crepitus indux crepitus indux.

crepitación ósea, crépito óseo bony crepitus.

crepitación de retorno, crepitus redux crepitus redux.

crepitación de seda silken crepitus.

crepitante adj. crepitant.

crépito m. crepitus.

crepitus m. crepitus.

crepuscular adj. crepuscular.

crepúsculo m. twilight.

crescógrafo m. crescograph.

cresofucsina f. kresofuchsin.

cresomanía f. cresomania.

crista f. crest, crista.

cresta f. crest, crista.

  cresta acusticofacial acousticofacial crest.

  cresta de gallo cockscomb.

cretinismo m. cretinism.

  cretinismo atireótico athyreotic cretinism.

  cretinismo bocioso goitrous cretinism.

  cretinismo espontáneo, cretinismo esporádico spontaneous cretinism, sporadic cretinism.

  cretinismo esporádico bocioso sporadic goitrous cretinism.

  cretinismo familiar familial cretinism.

cretino, -na[1] m., f. cretin.

cretino, -na[2] adj. cretinous.

cretinoide adj. cretinoid.

crialgesia f. cryalgesia.

crianalgesia f. cryanalgesia.

crianestesia f. cryanesthesia.

criba f. crib.

  criba de Jackson Jackson crib.

  criba lingual tongue crib.

cribado m. cribration.

cribado, -da adj. cribrate.

cribiforme adj. cribriform.

cribrum m. cribrum.

cricoaritenoideo, -a adj. cricoarytenoid.

cricofaríngeo, -a adj. cricopharyngeal.

cricoide adj. cricoid.

cricoidectomía f. cricoidectomy.

cricoideo, -a adj. cricoid.

cricoidinia f. cricoidynia.

cricotireotomía f. cricothyreotomy.

cricotiroideo, -a adj. cricothyroid.

cricotiroidotomía f. cricothyroidotomy.

cricotirotomía f. cricothyrotomy.

cricotomía f. cricotomy.

cricotraqueotomía f. cricotracheotomy.

criestesia f. cryesthesia.

criminología f. criminology.

crimoanestesia f. crymoanesthesia.

crimodinia f. crymodinia.

crimófilo, -la adj. crymophilic.

crimoterapia f. crymotherapy.

crinofagia f. crinophagy.

crinogénico, -ca adj. crinogenic.

crinógeno, -na crinogenic.

crinología f. crinology.

crioaglutinina f. cryoagglutinine.

crioanalgesia f. cryoanalgesia.

crioanestesia f. cryoanesthesia.

crioaspersión f. cryospray.

crioautoaglutinina f. cold autoagglutinin.

criobanco m. cryobank.

criobiología f. cryobiology.

criocardioplejía f. cryocardioplegia.

criocauterio m. cryocautery.

criocauterización f. cryocautery.

criocirugía f. cryosurgery.

crioconización f. cryoconization.

crioconservación f. cryopreservation.

criodesecación f. freeze-drying.

crioespasmo m. cryospasm.

crioestilete m. cryostylet, cryostylette.

crioextracción f. cryoextraction.

crioextractor m. cryoextractor.

criofibrinogenemia f. cryofibrinogenemia.

criofibrinógeno m. cryofibrinogen.

criofiláctico, -ca adj. cryophylactic.

criófilo, -la adj. cryophile.

criofractura f. freeze-fracturing.

criogammaglobulina f. cryogammaglobulin.

criogénico, -ca adj. cryogenic.

criógeno m. cryogen.

crioglobulina f. cryoglobulin.

crioglobulinemia f. cryoglobulinemia.

  crioglobulinemia cristalina crystal cryoglobulinemia.

criohipofisectomía f. cryohypophysectomy.

criólisis f. cryolysis.

criómetro m. cryometer.

criopalidectomía f. cryopallidectomy.

criopatía f. cryopathy.

criopexia f. cryopexy.

crioprecipitabilidad f. cryoprecipitability.

crioprecipitación f. cryoprecipitation.

crioprecipitado m. cryoprecipitate.

criopreservación f. cryopreservation.

crioprostatectomía f. cryoprostatectomy.

crioprotector m. cryoprotective.

crioproteína f. cryoprotein.

criopulvinectomía f. cryopulvinectomy.

criórito m. cryorit.

crioscopia f. cryoscopy.

crioscópico, -ca adj. cryoscopical.

crioscopio m. cryoscope.

crióstato m. cryostat.

criosombreado m. freeze-etching.

criosonda f. cryoprobe.

criotalamectomía f. cryothalamectomy.

crioterapia f. cryotherapy, crymotherapy.

criotolerante adj. cryotolerant.

criounidad f. cryounit.

cripta f. crypt.

criptanamnesia f. cryptanamnesia.

criptectomía f. cryptectomy.

criptestesia f. cryptesthesia.

críptico, -ca adj. cryptic.

criptitis f. cryptitis.

criptocéfalo m. cryptocephalus.

criptocigo, -ga adj. cryptozygous.

criptococoma cryptococcoma.

criptococosis f. cryptococcosis.

criptocristalino, -na adj. cryptocrystalline.

criptodeterminante adj. cryptodeterminant.

criptodídimo m. cryptodidymus.

criptoempiema m. cryptoempyema.

criptoftalmía f. cryptophthalmia.

criptoftalmos m. cryptophthalmus.

criptogénico, -ca adj. cryptogenetic, cryptogenic.

criptógeno, -na adj. cryptogenic.

criptoglioma m. cryptoglioma.

criptolito m. cryptolith.

criptomenorrea f. cryptomenorrhea.

criptómero m. cryptomere.

criptomerorraquisquisis f. cryptomerorachischisis.

criptomnesia f. cryptomnesia.

criptomnésico, -ca adj. cryptomnesic.

criptopiosis f. cryptopiosis.

criptoplásmico, -ca adj. cryptoplasmic.

criptopodia f. cryptopodia.

criptopsíquico, -ca adj. cryptopsychic.

criptopsiquismo m. cryptopsychism.

criptorquidectomía f. cryptorchidectomy.

criptorquidia f. cryptorchidy.

criptorquídico, -ca adj. cryptorchid.

criptorquidismo m. cryptorchidism.

criptorquidopexia f. cryptorchidopexy.

criptorquismo m. cryptorchism.

criptorradiómetro m. cryptoradiometer.

criptorrea f. cryptorrhea.

criptorreico, -ca adj. cryptorrheic.

criptoscopia f. cryptoscopy.

criptoscopio m. cryptoscope.

criptosporidiosis f. cryptosporidiosis.

criptotia f. criptotia.

criptotóxico, -ca adj. cryptotoxic.

criptozoíto m. cryptozoite.

crisiasis f. chrysiasis, chrysosis.

crisis[1] f. seizure.

  crisis anosognósica anosognosic seizure.

  crisis de ansiedad anxiety attack.

  crisis atónica atonic seizure.

  crisis de ausencia absence seizure.

  crisis convulsiva convulsive seizure.

  crisis epiléptica epileptic seizure.

  crisis jacksoniana Jacksonian seizure.

  crisis generalizada generalized seizure.

  crisis generalizada secundaria secondarily generalized seizure.

  crisis generalizada tónico-clónica tonic-clonic seizure.

  crisis de gran mal grand mal seizure.

  crisis mioclónica myoclonic seizure.

  crisis motora motor seizure.

  crisis parcial partial seizure.

  crisis parcial compleja partial complex seizure.

  crisis parcial simple partial simple seizure.

  crisis de pequeño mal petit mal seizure.

crisis[2] f. crisis.

  crisis de Adam Stokes Adam-Stokes syndrome.

  crisis de Addison, crisis addisoniana Addison crisis, Addisonian crisis.

  crisis de adolescencia adolescent crisis.

  crisis adrenal adrenal crisis.

  crisis adventicia adventitious crisis.

  crisis con agotamiento salino salt depletion crisis.

  crisis anafilactoide anaphylactoid crisis.

  crisis aplásica aplastic crisis.

  crisis blástica, crisis de blastos blast crisis.

  crisis bronquial bronchial crisis.

  crisis cardíaca cardiac crisis.

  crisis de catatimia catathymic crisis.

  crisis celíaca celiac crisis.

  crisis clitoridea clitoris crisis.

  crisis colinérgica colinergic crisis.

  crisis del desarrollo developmental crisis.

  crisis de desglobulinización desglobulinization crisis.

  crisis de Dietl Dietl's crisis.

  crisis drepanocítica sickle cell crisis.

  crisis de la mediana edad midlife crisis.

  crisis falsa false crisis.

  crisis faríngea pharyngeal crisis.

  crisis febril febrile crisis.

  crisis gástrica gastric crisis.

  crisis genital del neonato genital crisis of the newborn.

  crisis glaucomatociclítica glaucomatocyclitic crisis.

  crisis hepática hepatic crisis.

crisis hipertensiva hypertensive crisis.
crisis de identidad identity crisis.
crisis intestinal intestinal crisis.
crisis laríngea laryngeal crisis.
crisis de maduración maturational crisis.
crisis de miastenia, crisis miasténica myasthenic crisis.
crisis mielocítica myelocytic crisis.
crisis nefasta nefast crisis.
crisis nefrálgica nephralgic crisis.
crisis ocular ocular crisis.
crisis oculógira oculogiric crisis.
crisis con pérdida salina salt-losing crisis.
crisis puberal puberal crisis.
crisis de rechazo rejection crisis.
crisis renal renal crisis.
crisis sanguínea blood crisis.
crisis de situación situational crisis.
crisis suprarrenal adrenal crisis.
crisis tabética tabetic crisis.
crisis terapéutica therapeutic crisis.
crisis tiroidea, crisis tirotóxica thyroid crisis, thyrotoxic crisis.
crisis torácica thoracic crisis.
crisis visceral visceral crisis.
crisocianosis *f.* chrysocianosis.
crisodermia *m.* chrysoderma.
crisoforesis *f.* chrysophoresis.
crisoidina *f.* chrysoidin.
crisol *m.* crucible.
crisosis *f.* chrysosis.
crisoterapia *f.* chrysotheraphy.
crispación *f.* crispation.
crista crista.
cristal[1] *m.* glass.
cristal[2] *m.* crystal.
cristal de asma asthma crystal.
cristal de Böttcher Böttcher's crystal.
cristal de Charcot-Leyden Charcot-Leyden crystal.
cristal de Charcot-Neumann Charcot-Neumann crystal.
cristal de Charcot-Robin Charcot-Robin crystal.
cristal en erizo hedgehog crystal.
cristal de esperma sperm crystal.
cristal de espermina spermin crystal.
cristal de estramonio thorn apple crystal.
cristal de Florence Florence crystal.
cristal gemelo twin crystal.
cristal del halterio dumbell crystal.
cristal hemático blood crystal.
cristal de hematoidina hematoidin crystal.
cristal de hidrato hydrate crystal.
cristal leucocítico leukocytic crystal.
cristal de Leyden Leyden's crystal.
cristal líquido liquid crystal.
cristal de Lubarsch Lubarsch's crystal.
cristal en mango de cuchillo knife-rest crystal.
cristal del oído ear crystal.
cristal en piedra de afilar whetstone crystal.
cristal quiral chiral crystal.
cristal de Reinke crystal of Reinke.
cristal de roca rock crystal.
cristal en tapa de ataúd coffin lid crystal.
cristal de Teichmann Teichmann's crystal.
cristal de Virchow Virchow's crystal.
cristal de Wood Wood's glass crystal.
cristalbúmina *f.* crystalbumin.
cristalina *f.* crystallin.
cristalina gamma gamma crystallin.
cristalino *m.* lens.
cristalino, -na *adj.* crystalline.
cristalización *f.* crystallization.

cristalización en hojas de helecho fern-leaf crystallization.
cristalofobia *f.* crystallophobia.
cristalografía *f.* crystallography.
cristalograma *m.* crystallogram.
cristaloide *m. y adj.* crystalloid.
cristaloide de Charcot-Böttcher Charcot-Böttcher crystalloid.
cristaloide de Reinke crystalloid of Reinke.
cristaluria *f.* crystalluria.
criterio *m.* criterion.
criterio de anormalidad abnormality criterion.
criterio de Jones Jones' criterion.
criterio de normalidad normality criterion.
criterio de normalidad de frecuencia frequency normality criterion.
criterio de normalidad funcional functional normality criterion.
criterio de normalidad ideal ideal normality criterion.
criterio de normalidad social social normality criterion.
criterio de normalidad subjetivo subjective normality criterion.
criterio de Spiegelberg Spiegelberg's criterion.
crítico, -ca *adj.* critical.
croceína *f.* crocein.
crocidismo *m.* crocidismus.
cromafílico, -ca *adj.* chromaphil.
cromáfilo, -la *adj.* chromaphil.
cromafín *adj.* chromaffin.
cromafínico, -ca *adj.* chromaffin.
cromafinidad *f.* chromaffinity.
cromafinoma *m.* chromaffinoma.
cromafinopatía *f.* chromaffinopathy.
cromargentafin *m.* chromargentaffin.
cromatelopsia *f.* chromatelopsia.
cromático, -ca *adj.* chromatic.
cromátida *f.* chromatid.
cromátide *f.* chromatid.
cromatina *f.* chromatin.
cromatina asociada al núcleo nucleolar-associated chromatin, nucleus-associated chromatin.
cromatina heteropicnótica heteropyknotic chromatin.
cromatina nuclear nucleolar chromatin, nucleous chromatin.
cromatina oxifílica oxyphil chromatin.
cromatina sexual sex chromatin.
cromatínico, -ca *adj.* chromatinic.
cromatín-negativo *adj.* chromatin-negative.
cromatinólisis *f.* chromatinolysis.
cromatinorrexis *f.* chromatinorrhexis.
cromatín-positivo *adj.* chromatin-positive.
cromatismo *m.* chromatism.
cromatocinesis *f.* chromatokinesis.
cromatodisopía *f.* chromatodysopia.
cromatófago, -ga *adj.* chromophage.
cromatofilia *f.* chromatophilia.
cromatofílico ca *adj.* chromatophilic.
cromatófilo, -la *adj.* chromatophil, chromatophile.
cromatofobia *f.* chromatophobia.
cromatoforoma *m.* chromatophoroma.
cromatógeno, -na *adj.* chromatogenous.
cromatografía *f.* chromatography.
cromatografía por adsorción adsorption chromatography.
cromatografía de afinidad affinity chromatography.
cromatografía bidimensional two-dimensional chromatography.

cromatografía en capa fina thin layer chromatography.
cromatografía en columna column chromatography.
cromatografía por exclusión exclusion chromatography.
cromatografía de filtración en gel gel filtration chromatography, gel permeation chromatography.
cromatografía de gases gas chromatography.
cromatografía de gas y líquido gas-liquid chromatography.
cromatografía de gas y sólido gas-solid chromatography.
cromatografía de intercambio iónico ion exchange chromatography.
cromatografía de líquido de alta presión high pressure liquid chromatography.
cromatografía líquido-gaseosa gas-liquid chromatography.
cromatografía de líquido y líquido, cromatografía líquido-líquida liquid-liquid chromatography.
cromatografía sobre papel paper chromatography.
cromatografía de partición partition chromatography.
cromatografía de tamiz molecular molecular sieve chromatography.
cromatográfico, -ca *adj.* chromatographic.
cromatógrafo *m.* chromatograph.
cromatograma *m.* chromatogram.
cromatoide *adj.* chromatoid.
cromatólisis *f.* chromatolysis.
cromatólisis central central chromatolysis.
cromatólisis retrógrada retrograde chromatolysis.
cromatolítico, -ca *adj.* chromatolytic.
cromatología *f.* chromatology.
cromatómetro *m.* chromatometer.
cromatopatía *f.* chromatopathy.
cromatopéctico, -ca *adj.* chromatopectic.
cromatopexia *f.* chromatopexis.
cromatoplasma *m.* chromatoplasm.
cromatopsia *f.* chromatopsia.
cromatoptometría *f.* chromatoptometry.
cromatoptómetro *m.* chromatoptometer.
cromatoscopia *f.* chromatoscopy.
cromatoscopia gástrica gastric chromatoscopy.
cromatoscopio *m.* chromatoscope.
cromatoseudopsis *f.* chromatopseudopsis.
cromatosis *f.* chromatosis.
cromatosquiámetro *m.* chromatoskiameter.
cromatotropismo *m.* chromatotropism.
cromaturia *f.* chromaturia.
cromestesia *f.* chromesthesia.
cromhidrosis *f.* chromhidrosis.
cromhidrosis apocrina apocrine chromhidrosis.
cromidiación *f.* chromidiation.
cromidial *adj.* chromidial.
cromidiosis *f.* chromidiosis.
cromidrosis *f.* chromhidrosis.
cromobacteriosis *f.* chromobacteriosis.
cromoblasto *m.* chromoblast.
cromoblastomicosis *f.* chromoblastomycosis.
cromocentro *m.* chromocenter.
cromocistoscopia *f.* chromocystoscopy.
cromocoloscopia *f.* chromocholoscopy.
cromocrinia *f.* chromocrinia.
cromodacriorrea *f.* chromadacryorrhea.
cromodiagnosis *f.* chromodiagnosis.
cromodiagnóstico *m.* chromodiagnosis.
cromófago *m.* chromophage.

cromófano *m.* chromophane.
cromofílico, -ca *adj.* chromophilic, chromophilous.
cromófilo *m.* cromophilus.
cromofobia *f.* chromophobia.
cromofóbico, -ca *adj.* chromophobic.
cromófobo *m.* chromophobe.
cromofórico, -ca *adj.* chromophoric.
cromóforo *m.* chromophore.
cromofosia *f.* chromophose.
cromofototerapia *f.* chromophototherapy.
cromogénesis *f.* chromogenesis.
cromogénico, -ca *adj.* chromogenic.
cromógeno *m.* chromogen.
  cromógeno de Porter-Silber Porter-Silber chromogen.
cromohidrosis *f.* chromhidrosis.
cromoisomería *f.* chromoisomerism.
cromolipoide *m.* chromolipoid.
cromólisis *f.* chromolysis.
cromómero *m.* chromomere.
cromómetro *m.* chromometer.
cromomicosis *f.* chromomycosis.
cromonema *m.* chromonema.
cromonémico, -ca *adj.* chromonemal.
cromoniquia *f.* chromonychia.
cromopárico, -ca *adj.* chromoparic.
cromopatía *f.* chromopathy.
cromopéctico *adj.* chromopectic, chromopexic.
cromoperturbación *f.* chromoperturbation.
cromopexia *f.* chromopexy.
cromopéxico, -ca *adj.* chromopexic.
cromoproteína *f.* chromoprotein.
cromopsia *f.* chromopsia.
cromoptómetro *m.* chromoptometer.
cromorradiómetro *m.* chromoradiometer.
cromorretinografía *f.* chromoretinography.
cromorrinorrea *f.* chromorhinorrhea.
cromosantonina *f.* chromosantonin.
cromoscopia *f.* chromoscopy.
  cromoscopia gástrica gastric chromoscopy.
cromoscopio *m.* chromoscope.
cromosoma *m.* chromosome.
  cromosoma accesorio accessory chromosome.
  cromosoma acéntrico acentric chromosome.
  cromosoma acrocéntrico acrocentric chromosome.
  cromosoma en anillo, cromosoma anular ring chromosome.
  cromosoma artificial de levaduras yeast artificial chromosome.
  cromosoma bivalente bivalent chromosome.
  cromosoma de Christchurch Christchurch chromosome.
  cromosoma derivativo derivative chromosome.
  cromosoma dicéntrico dicentric chromosome.
  cromosoma de Filadelfia Philadelphia chromosome.
  cromosoma gamético gametic chromosome.
  cromosoma gigante giant chromosome.
  cromosoma heterotípico heterotypical chromosome.
  cromosoma heterólogo heterologous chromosome.
  cromosoma hijo daughter chromosome.
  cromosoma homólogo homologous chromosome.
  cromosoma ligado a X X-linked chromosome.
  cromosoma ligado a Y Y-linked chromosome.
  cromosoma M M-chromosome.
  cromosoma metacéntrico metacentric chromosome.

  cromosoma no apareado unpaired chromosome.
  cromosoma no homólogo nonhomologous chromosome.
  cromosoma nucleolar nucleolar chromosome.
  cromosoma Ph[1] Ph1 chromosome.
  cromosoma recombinante recombinant chromosome.
  cromosoma replicativo tardío late replicative chromosome.
  cromosoma sexual sex chromosome.
  cromosoma somático somatic chromosome.
  cromosoma submetacéntrico submetacentric chromosome.
  cromosoma supernumerario supernumerary chromosome.
  cromosoma telocéntrico telocentric chromosome.
  cromosoma de translocación translocation chromosome.
  cromosoma X X chromosome.
  cromosoma Y Y chromosome.
  cromosoma X frágil fragile X chromosome.
cromosómico, -ca *adj.* chromosomal.
cromospermia *f.* chromospermism.
cromoterapia *f.* chromotherapy.
cromotóxico, -ca *adj.* chromatotoxic.
cromotriquia *f.* chromotrichia.
cromotriquial *adj.* chromotrichial.
cromotrópico, -ca *adj.* chromotropic.
cromótropo *m.* chromotrope.
cromótropo 2R *m.* chromotrope 2R.
cromoureteroscopia *f.* chromoureteroscopy.
cromourinografía *f.* chromourinography.
cronaxia *f.* chronaxia, chronaxie, chronaxis, chronaxy.
cronaximetría *f.* chronaximetry.
cronaximétrico, -ca *adj.* chronaximetric.
cronaxímetro *m.* chronaximeter.
cronicidad *f.* chronicity.
crónico, -ca *adj.* chronic.
croniosepsis *f.* chroniosepsis.
croniosepticemia *f.* chroniosepsis.
cronobiología *f.* chronobiology.
cronobiológico, -ca *adj.* chronobiologic, chronobiological.
cronobiólogo, -ga *m., f.* chronobiologist.
cronoesfigmógrafo *m.* chronosphygmograph.
cronofarmacología *f.* chronopharmacology.
cronofobia *f.* chronophobia.
cronofotografía *f.* chronophotograph.
cronognosis *f.* chronognosis.
cronógrafo *m.* chronograph.
cronológico, -ca *adj.* chronologic.
cronometría *f.* chronometry.
  cronometría mental mental chronometry.
  cronometría psíquica mental chronometry.
cronómetro *m.* timer.
cronomiómetro *m.* chronomyometer.
cronooncología *f.* chrono-oncology.
cronopsicofisiología *f.* chronopsychophysiology.
cronoscopio *m.* chronoscope.
cronotanatodiagnóstico *m.* chronothanatodiagnosis.
cronotaraxia *f.* chronotaraxis.
cronotaraxis *f.* chronotaraxis.
cronotrópico, -ca *adj.* chronotropic.
cronotropismo *m.* chronotropism.
  cronotropismo negativo negative chronotropism.
  cronotropismo positivo positive chronotropism.
cross-match cross-match.

crossing-over crossing-over.
crotafión *m.* crotaphion.
croup *m.* croup.
cruce *m.* cross.
  cruce dihíbrido dihybrid cross.
  cruce de dos factores two-factor cross.
  cruce de fago phage cross.
  cruce monohíbrido monohybrid cross.
  cruce polihíbrido polyhybrid cross.
  cruce reversivo back cross.
  cruce reversivo doble double back cross.
  cruce trihíbrido trihybrid cross.
crucial *adj.* crucial.
crucíbulo *m.* crucible.
cruciforme *adj.* cruciform.
cruentación *f.* cruentation.
crujido *m.* crackle.
  crujido de pergamino parchment crackling.
cruomanía *f.* cruomania.
crúor *m.* cruor.
crup *m.* croup.
  crup catarral catarrhal croup.
  crup diftérico diphtheritic croup.
  crup espasmódico, crup espástico spasmodic croup.
  crup fibrinoso membranous croup.
  crup membranoso membranous croup.
  crup seudomembranoso pseudomembranous croup.
crupal *adj.* croupous, croupy.
cruposo, -sa *adj.* croupous, croupy.
crural *adj.* crural.
cruris *adj.* cruris.
cruropelvímetro *m.* cruropelvimeter.
crusotomía *f.* crusotomy.
crusta crusta.
  crusta lactea milk crust, crusta lactea.
cruz *f.* cross.
  cruz argéntica silver cross.
  cruz del corazón cross of the heart.
  cruz clavicular clavicular cross.
  cruz del pelo hair cross.
  cruz de Ranvier Ranvier's cross.
cruzado, -da[1] *adj.* crossed.
cruzado, -da[2] *adj.* crossbreed.
cruzamiento *m.* crossover, crossing over.
Cryptococcus Cryptococcus.
Cryptosporidium Cryptosporidium.
cryptosporidiosis *f.* cryptosporidiosis.
Ctenocephalides Ctenocephalides.
Ctenus Ctenus.
cuadrángulo *m.* quadrangle.
cuadrantanopia *f.* quadrantanopia.
cuadrantanopsia *f.* quadrantanopsia, quadrantanopia.
cuadrante *m.* quadrant.
  cuadrante abdominal abdominal quadrant.
cuádriceps *adj.* quadriceps.
cuadricepsplastia *f.* quadricepsplasty.
cuadriceptor *m.* quadriceptor.
cuadricúspide *adj.* quadricuspid.
cuadridentado, -da *adj.* quadridentate.
cuadridigitado, -da *adj.* quadridigitate.
cuadrigeminia *f.* quadrigeminy.
cuadrigémino, -na *adj.* quadrigeminal.
cuadrilátero *m.* quadrilateral, tetragonum.
  cuadrilátero de Celso Celsus' quadrilateral.
  cuadrilátero lumbar tetragonum lumbale.
cuadrilocular *adj.* quadrilocular.
cuadrípara *f.* quadripara.
cuadriparesia *f.* quadriparesis.
cuadripartito, -ta *adj.* quadripartite.
cuadriplejía *f.* quadriplegia.
cuadripléjico, -ca *adj.* quadriplegic.
cuadripolar *adj.* quadripolar.

cuadrisección *f.* quadrisection.
cuadrisectar *v.* quadrisect.
cuadritubercular *adj.* quadritubercular.
cuadrivalente *adj.* quadrivalent.
cuadro *m.* chart.
cualidad *f.* quality.
  cualidad del haz beam quality.
cualímetro *m.* qualimeter.
cualitativo, -va *adj.* qualitative.
cuantímetro *m.* quantimeter.
cuantitativo, -va *adj.* quantitative.
cuarentena *f.* quarantine.
cuartana *f.* quartan.
  cuartana doble double quartan.
  cuartana triple triple quartan.
cuartil *m.* quartile.
cuartípara *f.* quartipara.
cuartisectar *v.* quartisect.
cuasidominancia *f.* quasidominance.
cuasidominante *adj.* quasidominant.
cuaternario, -ria *adj.* quaternary.
cuatrillizo, -za *m., f.* quadruplet.
cubeta *f.* bowl.
cubierta *f.* envelope.
cubitad ulnad.
cubital *adj.* cubital.
cúbito *m.* cubitus, ulna.
  cúbito valgo cubitus valgus.
  cúbito varus cubitus varus.
cubitocarpal *adj.* cubitocarpal.
cubitocarpiano, -na *m.* cubitocarpal.
cubitopalmar *adj.* cubitopalmar.
cubitorradial *adj.* cubitorradial.
cubitus *m.* cubitus, ulna.
  cubitus valgus cubitus valgus.
  cubitus varus cubitus varus.
cuboide *adj.* cuboid, cuboidal.
cuboideo, -a *adj.* cuboid, cuboidal.
cuboides *m.* cuboid.
cubreobjeto *m.* cover-slip, coverglass.
cubrir *v.* capping.
cuclillas *f.* squatting.
cuchara *f.* spoon.
  cuchara afilada sharp spoon.
  cuchara para cataratas cataract spoon.
  cuchara cortante sharp spoon.
  cuchara de Daviel Daviel's spoon.
  cuchara de Volkmann Volkmann's spoon.
cucharilla *f.* scoop.
cuchicheo *m.* whisper.
cuchilla *f.* knife.
  cuchilla de Fox Fox knife.
  cuchilla de Goldman-Fox Goldman-Fox knife.
  cuchilla de oro gold knife.
cuchillo *m.* knife.
  cuchillo de amputación amputation knife.
  cuchillo balancín rocker knife.
  cuchillo de banco buck knife.
  cuchillo de Beer Beer's knife.
  cuchillo de botón button knife.
  cuchillo de catarata cataract knife.
  cuchillo para cartílago cartilage knife.
  cuchillo de cauterización cautery knife.
  cuchillo eléctrico electric knife.
  cuchillo electrodo electrode knife.
  cuchillo endotérmico endotermic knife.
  cuchillo falciforme de Ramsbotham Ramsbotham's sickle knife.
  cuchillo de Goldman-Fox Goldman-Fox knife.
  cuchillo de Graefe Graefe's knife.
  cuchillo de hernia hernia knife.
  cuchillo de Hymby Hymby knife.
  cuchillo de Kirkland Kirkland knife.
  cuchillo lenticular lenticular knife.
  cuchillo de Liston Liston's knife.

  cuchillo de Merrifield Merrifield's knife.
  cuchillo químico chemical knife.
cuello *m.* neck, cervix, collum.
  cuello dentario neck of a tooth.
  cuello incompetente incompetent cervix.
  cuello de Madelung Madelung's neck.
  cuello membranoso webbed neck.
  cuello rígido wry neck.
  cuello torcido collum distortum.
  cuello de toro bullneck, bull neck.
cuenca *f.* watershed.
  cuenca abdominal abdominal watershed.
  cuenca del ojo eyesocket.
cuentagotas *m.* dropper.
cuentamonedas *f.* coin-counting.
cuerda *f.* cord, chorda.
  cuerda vocal vocal cord.
cuerdo, -da *m., f.* sane.
cuerno *m.* horn, cornu.
  cuerno cicatricial, cuerno cicatrizal cicatricial horn.
  cuerno cutáneo cutaneous horn.
  cuerno de la pulpa, cuerno pulpar pulp horn.
  cuerno sebáceo sebaceous horn.
  cuerno ungular nail horn.
cuero cabelludo scalp.
cuerpo *m.* body, corpus.
  cuerpo albicans corpus albicans.
  cuerpo alcaptónico alkapton body.
  cuerpo de Alder Alder body.
  cuerpo amarillo yellow body.
  cuerpo amarillo atrésico atretic luteum body.
  cuerpo amarillo del ovario yellow body of the ovary.
  cuerpo de amianto asbestos body.
  cuerpo amiláceo, cuerpo amiloide amylaceous body amyloid body.
  cuerpo amiloide de la próstata amyloid body of the prostate.
  cuerpo anular de Cabot Cabot's ring body.
  cuerpo apoptótico apoptotic body.
  cuerpo arenáceo, cuerpo de arena sand body.
  cuerpo de Arnold Arnold's body.
  cuerpo de arroz rice body.
  cuerpo de asbestosis asbestos body, asbestosis body.
  cuerpo de Aschoff Aschoff body.
  cuerpo asteroide asteroid body.
  cuerpo de Auer Auer body.
  cuerpo azul de Koch Koch's blue body.
  cuerpo de Babès-Ernst Babès-Ernst body.
  cuerpo de Balbiani Balbiani's body.
  cuerpo de bambú bamboo body.
  cuerpo de Barr Barr body.
  cuerpo basal, cuerpo basal del cilio basal body, basal body of the cilia.
  cuerpo de Behla Behla's body.
  cuerpo bigémino bigeminal body.
  cuerpo de Bracht-Wächter Bracht-Wächter body.
  cuerpo bronceado brassy body.
  cuerpo de Call-Exner Call-Exner body.
  cuerpo del calostro colostrum body.
  cuerpo de cáncer cancer body.
  cuerpo carotídeo carotid body.
  cuerpo de cebra zebra body.
  cuerpo celular cell body.
  cuerpo cetónico ketone body.
  cuerpo citoide cytoid body.
  cuerpo citoplasmático de inclusión cytoplasmic inclusion body.
  cuerpo de Civatte Civatte body.
  cuerpo cocoide X coccoid X body.
  cuerpo coloide colloid body.
  cuerpo concoidal conchoidal body.

  cuerpo de Councilman Councilman body.
  cuerpo de criollo creola body.
  cuerpo cromafín, cuerpo cromafínico chromaffin body.
  cuerpo de cromatina, cuerpo cromatínico chromatin body, chromatinic body.
  cuerpo de cromatina de Barr Barr chromatin body.
  cuerpo cromatoide chromatoid body.
  cuerpo cromófilo chromophilous body.
  cuerpo de Deetjen Deetjen's body.
  cuerpo denso dense body.
  cuerpo de Döhle Döhle body.
  cuerpo de Donné Donné's body.
  cuerpo de Dutcher Dutcher body.
  cuerpo elemental elementary body.
  cuerpo elemental de Gordon Gordon's elementary body.
  cuerpo de Elschnig Elschnig body.
  cuerpo esclerótico sclerotic body.
  cuerpo esférico spherical body.
  cuerpo extraño foreign body.
  cuerpo extraño auditivo foreign body in the ear.
  cuerpo extraño corneal corneal foreign body.
  cuerpo en la garganta foreign body in the throat.
  cuerpo extraño esofágico foreign body in the esophagus.
  cuerpo extraño intraocular intraocular foreign body.
  cuerpo extraño laríngeo foreign body in the larynx.
  cuerpo extraño ocular foreign body in the eye.
  cuerpo extraño subtarsal subtarsal foreign body.
  cuerpo feocromo pheochrome body.
  cuerpo ferruginoso ferruginous body.
  cuerpo fibroso corpus fibrosum.
  cuerpo final end body.
  cuerpo de fucsina fuchsin body.
  cuerpo gamma de Favre gamma-Favre body.
  cuerpo de Gamma-Gandy, cuerpo de Gandy-Gamma Gamma-Gandy body, Gandy-Gamma body.
  cuerpo glómico, cuerpo de glomus glomus body.
  cuerpo de Guarnieri Guarnieri body.
  cuerpo habenular habenular body.
  cuerpo de Halberstaedter-Prowazek Halberstaedter-Prowazek body.
  cuerpo Harting Harting body.
  cuerpo de Hassall Hassall's body.
  cuerpo de Hassall-Henle Hassall-Henle body.
  cuerpo de Heinz Heinz body.
  cuerpo de Heinz-Ehrlich Heinz-Ehrlich body.
  cuerpo hematoxifílico, cuerpo hematoxilínico hematoxyphil body, hematoxylin body.
  cuerpo hemorrágico corpus hemorrhagicum.
  cuerpo de Hensen Hensen's body.
  cuerpo de Herring Herring body.
  cuerpo hialino hyaline body.
  cuerpo hialino alcohólico alcoholic hyaline body.
  cuerpo hialino de la hipófisis hyaline body of the pituitary.
  cuerpo hialoideo hyaloid body.
  cuerpo de Howell Howell's body.
  cuerpo de Howell, cuerpo de Howell-Jolly Howell body, Howell-Jolly body.
  cuerpo de inclusión, cuerpo de inclusión nuclear inclusion body, nuclear inclusion body.
  cuerpo de inclusión de la psitacosis psittacosis inclusion body.

cuerpo de inclusión tipo A de Cowdry Cowdry's type A inclusion body.
cuerpo de inclusión tipo B de Cowdry Cowdry's type B inclusion body.
cuerpo inicial de Lindner Lindner's initial body.
cuerpo inmune immune body.
cuerpo intermedio de Flemming midbody of Flemming.
cuerpo interno inner body.
cuerpo internos de Ehrlich Ehrlich's inner body.
cuerpo de Jaworski Jaworski's body.
cuerpo de Joest Joest body.
cuerpo de Jolly Jolly's body.
cuerpo de Lafora Lafora body.
cuerpo de Landolt Landolt's body.
cuerpo LE LE body.
cuerpo de Leishman-Donovan, cuerpo LD Leishman-Donovan body, LD body.
cuerpo de Levinthal-Coles-Lillie, cuerpo LCL Levinthal-Coles-Lillie body, LCL body.
cuerpo de Lewy Lewy body.
cuerpo de Lindner Lindner's body.
cuerpo de Lipschütz Lipschütz body.
cuerpo de Lostorfer Lostorfer's body.
cuerpo de Luschka Luschka's body.
cuerpo de Luse Luse body.
cuerpo lúteo corpus luteum.
cuerpo de Mallory Mallory's body.
cuerpo de Malpighi Malpighian body.
cuerpo de Marchal Marchal body.
cuerpo de Masson Masson body.
cuerpo de Michaleis-Gutman Michaelis-Gutman body.
cuerpo de mielina myelin body.
cuerpo de Miyagawa Miyagawa body.
cuerpo de Mooser Mooser body.
cuerpo de Mott Mott body.
cuerpo multilaminar multilamellar body.
cuerpo de Negri Negri body.
cuerpo de Neill-Mooser Neill-Mooser body.
cuerpo neuroepitelial neuroepithelial body.
cuerpo neuronal nerve cell body.
cuerpo de Nissl Nissl body.
cuerpo nodular nodular body.
cuerpo de Nothnagel Nothnagel's body.
cuerpo de Odland Odland body.
cuerpo de Pacchioni Pacchionian body.
cuerpo de Pappenheimer Pappenheimer body.
cuerpo paraaórtico paraaortic body.
cuerpo parafisiario paraphyseal body.
cuerpo paranéfrico paranephric body.
cuerpo de Paschen Paschen body.
cuerpo de Pick Pick's body.
cuerpo picnótico pyknotic body.
cuerpo de Plimmer Plimmer's body.
cuerpo presegmentae presegmenting body.
cuerpo de Prowazek, cuerpo de Prowazek-Greef Prowazek body, Prowazek-Greef body.
cuerpo de psamoma psamoma body.
cuerpo redondo corps ronds.
cuerpo de Reilly Reilly body.
cuerpo de Renaut Renaut body.
cuerpo residual residual body.
cuerpo residual de Regaud residual body of Regaud.
cuerpo restiforme restiform body.
cuerpo riciforme rice body.
cuerpo de Ross Ross's body.
cuerpo de Russell Russell body.
cuerpo de Schaumann Schaumann body.
cuerpo de Schmorl Schmorl body.
cuerpo segmentante segmenting body.
cuerpo de semilla de melón melon-seed body.

cuerpo suelto loose body.
cuerpo tigroide tigroid body.
cuerpo tobáceo tuffstone body.
cuerpo de Torres-Teixeira Torres-Teixeira body.
cuerpo de tracoma trachoma body.
cuerpo ultimobranquial ultimobranchial body.
cuerpo de Verocay Verocay body.
cuerpo vermiforme vermiform body.
cuerpo vítreo vitreous body.
cuerpo de Virchow-Hassall Virchow-Hassall body.
cuerpo vitelino vitelline body.
cuerpo vítreo vitreous body.
cuerpo de Weibel-Palade Weibel-Palade body.
cuerpo de Winkler Winkler's body.
cuerpo de Wolff Wolffian body, corpus Wolffi.
cuerpo de Wolff-Orton Wolff-Orton body.
cuerpo yuxtaglomerular yuxtaglomerular body.
cueva *f.* cave.
cuidado *m.* care.
cuidado crítico critical care.
cuidado intensivo intensive care.
cuidado médico medical care.
cuidado médico primario primary medical care.
cuidado médico secundario secondary medical care.
cuidado médico terciario tertiary medical care.
cuidado médico total comprehensive medical care.
cuidado paliativo palliative care.
cuidado posparto postpartal care.
cuidado posterior aftercare.
cuidado posoperatorio postoperative care.
cuidado preoperatorio preoperative care.
cuidado terminal terminal care.
cul-de-sac *m.* cul-de-sac.
culdocentesis *f.* culdocentesis.
culdoplastia *f.* culdoplasty.
culdoscopia *f.* culdoscopy.
culdoscopio *m.* culdoscope.
culdotomía *f.* culdotomy.
Culex Culex.
culicifugo, -ga *adj.* culicifuge.
Culicoides Culicoides.
culicosis *f.* culicosis.
culmen *m.* culmen.
cultivar *v.* harvest.
cultivo *m.* culture.
cúmulo *m.* cumulus.
cúmulo proligero cumulus oophorus.
cumulus cumulus.
cuna *f.* cradle.
cuneiforme *m. y adj.* cuneiform.
cuneocuboide *adj.* cuneocuboid.
cuneoescafoide *adj.* cuneoscaphoid.
cuneonavicular *adj.* cuneonavicular.
cuneoscafoide *adj.* cuneoscaphoid.
cuneus cuneus.
cunículo *m.* cuniculus.
cuniculus cuniculus.
cuña *f.* wedge, cuneus.
cuña dental dental wedge.
cuña graduada step wedge.
cuperosis *f.* couperose.
cupremia *f.* cupremia.
cúprico, -ca *adj.* cupric.
cupriuresis *f.* cupriuresis, cupruresis.
cupriuria *f.* cupriuria.
cuproso, -sa *adj.* cuprous.
cupruresis *f.* cupruresis.
cuprurético, -ca *adj.* cupruretic.
cúpula *f.* cupola, cupula.
cupular *adj.* cupular.

cupuliforme *adj.* cupuliform.
cupulograma *m.* cupulogram.
cupulolitiasis *f.* cupulolithiasis.
cupulometría *f.* cupulometry.
cura *f.* cure.
curación *f.* healing.
curación por primera intención healing by first intention.
curación por segunda intención healing by second intention.
curación por tercera intención healing by third intention.
curativo, -va *adj.* curative.
cureta *f.* curet.
cureta de Hartmann Hartmann's curet.
curetaje *m.* curettage.
curiegrama *m.* curiegram.
curieterapia *f.* curietherapy.
curtosis *f.* kurtosis.
curva *f.* curve.
curva de aclaramiento clearance curve.
curva de alineación aligment curve.
curva anti-Monson anti-Monson curve.
curva atenuación attenuation curve.
curva de audibilidad audibility curve.
curva de Barnes Barnes curve.
curva de Bragg Bragg curve.
curva bucal buccal curve.
curva de camello camel curve.
curva característica characteristic curve.
curva de compensación compensating curve.
curva contorneada milled-in curve.
curva de crecimiento growth curve.
curva de crecimiento intrauterino intrauterine growth curve.
curva de Damoiseau Damoiseau curve.
curva dental dental curve.
curva de dilución de colorante dye-dilution curve.
curva de dilución de indicador indicator-dilution curve.
curva de disociación del oxigeno, curva de disociación oxígeno-hemoglobina, curva de disociación de oxihemoglobina oxygen dissociation curve, oxyhemoglobin dissociation curve.
curva de distribución distribution curve.
curva de distribución normal normal curve of distribution.
curva dorsal dorsal flexure.
curva de dosis-efecto, curva de dosis-reacción, curva de dosis-respuesta dose-effect, curve dose-response curve.
curva epidémica epidemic curve.
curva de flujo-volumen flow-volume curve.
curva de Frank-Starling Frank-Starling curve.
curva de frecuencia frequency curve.
curva de Friedman Friedman curve.
curva de fuerza-duración strength-duration curve.
curva de Gauss, curva gaussiana Gaussian curve.
curva inversa, curva invertida reverse curve.
curva de isodosis isodose curve.
curva isovolumétrica de presión-flujo isovolume pressure-flow curve.
curva labial labial curve.
curva de lavado del nitrógeno nitrogen washout curve.
curva logística logistic curve.
curva de luminiscencia glow curve.
curva de Monson Monson curve.
curva muscular muscle curve.
curva normal de distribución normal curve of distribution.

curva de oclusión curve of occlusion.

curva de pleasure pleasure curve.

curva de pulso pulse curve.

curva de presión intracardíaca intracardiac pressure curve.

curva de presión-volumen volume-pressure curve.

curva de Price-Jones Price-Jones curve.

curva de probabilidad probability curve.

curva de pulso pulse curve.

curva de Spee curve of Spee.

curva de Starling Starling's curve.

curva de supervivencia survival curve.

curva de supervivencia de Kaplan-Meier Kaplan-Meier survival curve.

curva térmica, curva de temperatura temperature curve.

curva de tensión tension curve.

curva de tensión-esfuerzo stress-strain curve.

curva de titulación del dióxido de carbono carbon dioxide titration curve.

curva de titulación de todo el cuerpo whole-body titration curve.

curva de Traube, curva de Traube-Hering Traube-Hering curve.

curva de visibilidad visibility curve.

curva de von Spee von Spee's curve.

curvado, -da *adj.* curvated.

curvatura *f.* curvature.

curvatura angular angular curvature.

curvatura anterior anterior curvature.

curvatura de compensación compensating curvature.

curvatura de Ellis-Daimoseau Ellis-Daimoseau's curvature.

curvatura espinal spinal curvature.

curvatura lateral lateral curvature.

curvatura posterior backward curvature.

curvatura de Pott Pott's curvature.

curvatura protuberancial pontine curvature.

curvatura vertebral spinal curvature.

curvatura vertebral angular angular spinal curvature.

curvatura vertebral lateral lateral spinal curvature.

curvilíneo, -a *adj.* curvilinear.

cuspad *adv.* cuspad.

cushingoide *adj.* Cushingoid.

cuspidado, -da *adj.* cuspidate.

cúspide *f.* cusp, cuspis.

cuspídeo, -a *adj.* cuspid.

cuspis *f.* cuspis.

cutáneo, -a *adj.* cutaneous.

cutaneomucoso, -sa *adj.* cutaneomucosal.

Cuterebra Cuterebra.

cutícula *f.* cuticle, cuticula.

cutícula dentaria dental cuticle, cuticula dentis.

cutícula del esmalte enamel cuticle.

cutícula de Nasmyth Nasmyth's cuticle.

cutícula del pelo, cutícula pilosa cuticle of the hair, cuticula pili.

cutícula queratosa keratose cuticle.

cutícula de la vaina del folículo piloso cuticle of the root sheath.

cutícula de la vaina de la raíz cuticle of the root sheath.

cuticularización *f.* cuticularization.

cutinización *f.* cutinization, cutization.

cutirreacción *f.* cutireaction.

cutis *m.* cutis.

cutis anserina cutis anserina.

cutis hiperelástico cutis hyperelastica.

cutis laxa cutis laxa.

cutis marmóreo, cutis marmorata marble skin, cutis marmorata.

cutis romboidal de la nuca cutis rhomboidalis nuchae.

cutis testácea cutis unctuosa.

cutis untuosa cutis unctuosa.

cutis verdadero, cutis vera cutis vera.

cutis verticis gyrata cutis verticis gyrata.

cutisector *m.* cutisector.

cutización *f.* cutization.

Cynomya Cynomya.

Cysticercus Cysticercus.

D d

dacriadenalgia *f.* dacryadenalgia.
dacriadenectomia *f.* dacryoadenectomy.
dacriadenitis *f.* dacryadenitis.
dacriagogatresia *f.* dacryagogatresia.
dacriagógico, -ca *adj.* dacryagogic.
dacrielcosis *f.* dacryelcosis, dacryohelcosis.
dacrihelcosis *f.* dacryelcosis, dacryohelcosis.
dacriohelcosis *f.* dacryelcosis, dacryohelcosis.
dacriadenalgia *f.* dacryodenalgia, dacryadenalgia.
dacrioadenalgia *f.* dacryodenalgia, dacryadenalgia.
dacriadenitis *f.* dacryoadenitis.
dacrioadenitis *f.* dacryoadenitis.
dacrioblenorrea *f.* dacryoblennorrhea.
dacriocanaliculitis *f.* dacryocanaliculitis.
dacriocele *m.* dacryocele.
dacriocentellografía *f.* dacryoscintigraphy.
dacriocistalgia *f.* dacryocystalgia.
dacriocistectasia *f.* dacryocystectasia.
dacriocistestomía *f.* dacryocystectomy.
dacriocistitis *f.* dacryocystitis.
dacriocistítomo *m.* dacryocistitome, dacryocystotome.
dacriocistótomo *m.* dacryocistitome, dacryocystotome.
dacriocisto *m.* dacryocyst, dacryocystis.
dacriocistoblenorrea *f.* dacryocystoblennorrhea.
dacriocistocele *m.* dacryocystocele.
dacriocistoetmoidostomía *f.* dacryocystoethmoidostomy.
dacriocistograma *m.* dacryocystogram.
dacriocistografía *f.* dacryocystograph.
dacriocistoptosia *f.* dacrycystoptosia.
dacriocistoptosia *f.* dacryocystoptosis, dacrycystoptosia.
dacriocistoptosis *f.* dacryocystoptosis, dacrycystoptosia.
dacriocistorrinoestenosis *f.* dacryocystorhinostenosis.
dacriocistorrinostomía *f.* dacryocystorhinostomy.
dacriocistorrinotomía *f.* dacryocystorhinotomy.
dacriocistosiringotomía *f.* dacryocystosyringotomy.
dacriocistostenosis *f.* dacryocystostenosis.
dacriocistostomía *f.* dacryocystostomy.
dacriocistótomo *m.* dacryocystotome.
dacrioestenosis *f.* dacryostenosis.
dacriógeno, -na *adj.* dacryogenic.
dacriogógico, -ca *adj.* dacryagogic.
dacriohelcosis *f.* dacryohelcosis.
dacriohemorragia *f.* dacryohemorrhea.
dacriohemorrea *f.* dacryohemorrhea.
dacriolitiasis *f.* dacryolithiasis.
dacriolito *m.* dacryolith.
  dacriolito de Desmarres Desmarres' dacryolith.
dacrioma *m.* dacryoma.
dacrión *m.* dacryon.

dacrionoma *m.* dacryelcosis.
dacriooptosis *f.* dacryocystoptosis.
dacriopiorrea *f.* dacryopyorrhea.
dacriopiosis *f.* dacryopyosis.
dacriops *m.* dacryops.
dacriorrea *f.* dacryorrhea.
dacriorrinocistotomía *f.* dacryorhinocystotomy.
dacriorrisis *f.* dacryorrhea.
dacriosinusitis *f.* dacryosinusitis.
dacriosirinx *m.* dacryosyrinx.
dacriosolenitis *f.* dacryosolenitis.
dacriostenosis *f.* dacryostenosis.
dactilagra *f.* dactylagra.
dactilalgia *f.* dactylalgia.
dactilar *adj.* dactilar.
dactiledema *m.* dactyledema.
dactilia *f.* dactylia.
dactiliforme *adj.* dactiliform.
dactilio *m.* dactylion, dactylium.
dactilión *m.* dactylion, dactylium.
dactilitis *f.* dactylitis.
  dactilitis drepanocítica sickle cell dactylitis.
  dactilitis estrumosa strumous dactylitis.
  dactilitis sifilítica syphilitic dactylitis.
  dactilitis tuberculosa tuberculous dactylitis.
dáctilo *m.* dactyl.
dactilocampsia *f.* dactylocampsis, dactylocampsiasis.
dactilocampsis *f.* dactylocampsis, dactylocampsiasis.
dactilocampsodinia *f.* dactylocampsodynia.
dactilodinia *f.* dactylodinia.
dactiloespasmo *m.* dactylospasm.
dactilofasia *f.* dactylophasia.
dactilografía *f.* dactylography.
dactilograma *m.* dactylogram.
dactilogriposis *f.* dactylogryposis.
dactilolalia *f.* dactylology.
dactilólisis *f.* dactylolysis.
  dactilólisis espontánea dactylolysis spontanea.
dactilología *f.* dactylology.
dactilomegalia *f.* dactylomegaly.
dactiloscopia *f.* dactyloscopy.
dactilospasmo *m.* dactylospasm.
dactylium dactylium.
Dactylomyia Dactylomyia.
dador *m.* donor.
daltónico, -ca *adj.* daltonian.
daltonismo *m.* daltonism.
danza *f.* dance.
  danza espacial spatial dance.
  danza hiliar hilar dance.
  danza del hilio hilus dance.
  danza humeral brachial dance.
  danza de san Antonio Saint Anthony's dance.
  danza de san Juan Saint John's dance.
  danza de san Vito Saint Vitus dance.
dartoico, -ca *adj.* dartoic.

dartoideo, -a *adj.* dartoid.
dartos *m.* dartos.
  dartos femenino dartos muliebris.
dartros *m.* dartre.
dartroso, -sa *adj.* dartrous.
darwiniano, -na *adj.* Darwinian.
darwinismo *m.* Darwinism.
dato aberrante *m.* outlier.
daturismo *m.* daturism.
deacuación *f.* deaquation.
dealbación *f.* dealbation.
debilidad *f.* debility, weakness.
  debilidad mental mental debility, feeblemindedness, mild mental retardation.
debilitación *f.* debilitation, weakening.
debilitante *m. y adj.* debilitant.
decaimiento *m.* decline, decay.
decalaje *m.* rotational deformity, displacement.
decalcificación *f.* decalcification.
decalcificante *m.* decalcifying.
decalvante *m.* decalvant, decalvans.
decantación *f.* decantation.
decantar *v.* decant.
decapitación *f.* decapitation.
decapitado, -da *adj.* decapitate.
decapitar *v.* decapitate.
decapsulación *f.* decapsulation.
decentración *f.* decentration.
decerebración *f.* decerebration.
deceso *m.* decease, death.
decidua *f.* decidua, membranae deciduae.
  decidua basal basal decidua, decidua basalis.
  decidua capsular capsular decidua, decidua capsularis.
  decidua ectópica ectopic decidua.
  decidua esponjosa decidua spongiosa.
  decidua menstrual decidua menstrualis.
  decidua parietal parietal decidua, decidua parietalis.
  decidua poliposa decidua polyposa.
  decidua refleja decidua reflexa.
  decidua serotina decidua serotina.
  decidua verdadera, decidua vera true decidua, decidua vera.
deciduación *f.* deciduation.
deciduado, -da *adj.* deciduate.
decidual *adj.* decidual.
deciduitis *f.* deciduitis.
deciduo, -a *adj.* deciduo, deciduous.
deciduoma *m.* deciduoma.
  deciduoma de Loeb Loeb's deciduoma.
deciduomatosis *f.* deciduomatosis.
deciduosarcoma *m.* deciduosarcoma.
deciduosis *f.* deciduosis.
décimo par craneal *m.* tenth cranial nerve.
declinación *f.* declination.
declive *m.* slop.
decolorante[1] *adj.* bleaching.
decolorante[2] *m.* bleaching agent.

decolorar *v.* decolorize.
decoluración *f.* dechloridation.
decocción *f.* decoction.
decolación *f.* decollation.
decoloración *f.* decoloration.
decorticación *f.* decortication, decortization.
  decorticación cerebral brain decortication.
  decorticación pulmonar decortication of the lung.
  decorticación renal renal decortication.
  decorticación reversible reversible decortication.
decortización *f.* decortization.
decrecimiento *m.* degrowth.
decremento *m.* decrement, decrementum.
decrepitación *f.* decrepitation.
decrepitar *v.* decrepitate.
decrudescencia *f.* decrudescence.
decubación *f.* decubation.
decúbito *m.* decubitus.
  decúbito agudo acute decubitus.
  decúbito de Andral Andral's decubitus.
  decúbito dorsal dorsal decubitus.
  decúbito lateral lateral decubitus.
  decúbito prono prone position.
  decúbito supino supine decubitus position.
decupelación *f.* decantation.
decurso *m.* course.
decurrente *adj.* decurrent.
decusación *f.* decussation, decussatio.
decusado, -da *adj.* decussate.
decusorio *m.* decussorium.
dedentición *f.* dedentition.
dedo[1] *m.* finger.
  dedo acolchado bolster finger.
  dedo de araña, dedo arácnido spider finger.
  dedo de cera, dedo céreo waxy finger.
  dedo en gatillo trigger finger.
  dedo de jugador de béisbol baseball finger.
  dedo en llave lock finger.
  dedo de Madonna Madonna's finger.
  dedo en martillo hammer finger.
  dedo en maza mallet finger.
  dedo en pala spade finger.
  dedo en palillo de tambor drumstick finger.
  dedo en resorte spring finger.
  dedo en salchicha sausage finger.
  dedo trabado lock finger.
dedo[2] *m.* toe.
  dedo caído toe drop.
  dedo doloroso painful toe.
  dedo hipocrático hippocratic toe.
  dedo de Hong Kong Hong Kong toe.
  dedo en martillo hammer toe.
  dedo de Morton Morton's toe.
  dedo de paloma pigeon toe.
  dedo palmado webbed toe.
  dedo del pie de tenista tennis toe.
  dedo rígido stiff toe.
  dedo valgo digitus valgus.
  dedo varo digitus varus.
dedolación *f.* dedolation.
dedolar *v.* dedolate.
defecación *f.* defecation.
defecografía *f.* defecography.
defecto *m.* defect.
  defecto adquirido acquired defect.
  defecto de las almohadillas endocárdicas endocardial cushion defect.
  defecto de campo politrópico polytropic field defect.
  defecto del campo visual visual field defect.
  defecto congénito birth defect.
  defecto congénito acianótico acyanotic congenital defect.

defecto de conducción cardíaca cardiac conduction defect.
defecto de conducción intraventricular (DCI) intraventricular conduction defect (ICD).
defecto cortical fibroso fibrous cortical defect.
defecto cortical fibroso metafisario metaphysial fibrous cortical defect.
defecto de difusión diffusion defect.
defecto ectodérmico congénito congenital ectodermal defect.
defecto de Embden-Meyerhof Embden-Meyerhof defect.
defecto de la fase luteínica luteal phase defect.
defecto genético genetic defect.
defecto de llenado filling defect.
defecto de nacimiento birth defect.
defecto de ostium primum ostium primum defect.
defecto de ostium secundum ostium secundum defect.
defecto perceptual, defecto de percepción perceptual defect.
defecto de relieve endocárdico endocardial cushion defect.
defecto de relleno filling defect.
defecto de retención retention defect.
defecto septal septal defect.
defecto septal aórtico aortic septal defect.
defecto septal aorticopulmonar aorticopulmonary septal defect.
defecto septal ventricular ventricular septal defect.
defecto septal auricular atrial septal finger, atroseptal finger.
defecto del tabique septal defect.
defecto del tubo neural neural-tube defect.
defecto de ventilación-perfusión ventilation-perfusion defect.
defectuoso, -sa *adj.* defective.
defeminación *f.* defeminization.
defeminización *f.* defeminization.
defensa *f.* defense.
  defensa abdominal abdominal guarding.
  defensa muscular muscular defense.
  defensa táctil tactile defensiveness.
deferencial *f.* deferential.
deferente *adj.* deferent.
deferentectomía *f.* deferentectomy.
deferentitis *f.* deferentitis.
defervescencia *f.* defervescence.
deficiencia *f.* deficiency.
  deficiencia de anticuerpo secundario secondary antibody deficiency.
  deficiencia de antitripsina antitrypsin deficiency.
  deficiencia dependiente del timo thymus-dependent deficiency.
  deficiencia desramificante debrancher deficiency.
  deficiencia familiar de lipoproteínas familial lipoprotein deficiency.
  deficiencia familiar de lipoproteínas de alta densidad (HDL) familial high-density lipoprotein deficiency, HDL deficiency.
  deficiencia de la fase luteínica luteal phase deficiency.
  deficiencia focal femoral proximal proximal femoral focal deficiency (PFFD).
  deficiencia de fosfohexosa isomerasa phosphohexose isomerase deficiency.
  deficiencia de galactoquinasa galactokinase deficiency.

deficiencia de glucosafosfato isomerasa glucosephosphate isomerase deficiency.
deficiencia de G6PD leucocitaria leukocyte G6PD deficiency.
deficiencia de 17-hidroxilasa 17-hydroxylase deficiency.
deficiencia de IgA aislada isolated IgA deficiency.
deficiencia de IgA selectiva selective IgA deficiency.
deficiencia inmune inmune deficiency.
deficiencia de inmunidad, deficiencia inmunitaria, deficiencia inmunológica inmune deficiency.
deficiencia de lactasa en el adulto adult lactase deficiency.
deficiencia de lactasa lactase deficiency.
deficiencia de lactasa intestinal intestinal lactase deficiency.
deficiencia de LCAT LCAT deficiency.
deficiencia de oxígeno oxygen deficiency.
deficiencia de piruvato quinasa pyruvate kinase deficiency.
deficiencia de riboflavina riboflavin deficiency.
deficiencia de seudocolinesterasa pseudocholinesterase deficiency.
deficiencia congénita de sucrasa isomaltasa congenital sucrase-isomaltase deficiency.
deficiencia de sulfatasa placentaria placental sulfatase deficiency.
deficiencia de yodotirosina deyodinasa iodotyrosine deiodinase defect.
déficit *m.* deficit.
  déficit de base base deficit.
  déficit de oxígeno oxygen deficit.
  déficit de piruvatocinasa pyruvate kinase deficit.
  déficit del pulso pulse deficit.
  déficit de saturación saturation deficit.
  déficit sensitivo sensory deficit.
  déficit vitamínico vitamin deficit.
definición *f.* definition.
definitivo, -va *adj.* definitive.
deflexión *f.* deflection.
  deflexión H H deflection.
  deflexión V (EFH) V deflection (HBE).
deflujo *f.* defluxion.
defluvium defluvium.
  defluvium capillorum defluvium capillorum.
defluxión *f.* defluxion.
deformación *f.* deformation.
deformante *adj.* deforming.
deformidad *f.* deformity.
  deformidad de Akerlund Akerlund deformity.
  deformidad en aleta de foca seal-fin deformity.
  deformidad anterior lordosis.
  deformidad de Arnold-Chiari Arnold-Chiari deformity.
  deformidad en caja de escopeta gunstock deformity.
  deformidad en caja de fusil gunstock deformity.
  deformidad por contractura contracture deformity.
  deformidad craneal en trébol cloverleaf skull deformity.
  deformidad en cuello de cisne swan-neck deformity.
  deformidad en dorso de tenedor silver-fork deformity.
  deformidad en frasco de Erlenmeyer Erlenmeyer flask deformity.

deformidad de Haglund Haglund's deformity.

deformidad de Ilfeld-Holder Ilfeld-Holder deformity.

deformidad de Madelung Madelung's deformity.

deformidad en ojal boutonnière deformity.

deformidad en ojo de cerradura keyhole deformity.

deformidad en pinza de langosta lobster-claw deformity.

deformidad por reducción reduction deformity.

deformidad selar en J J-sella deformity.

deformidad en pseudopinza de langosta pseudolobster-claw deformity.

deformidad en silbato, deformidad en silbido whistling deformity.

deformidad de sirena mermaid deformity.

deformidad de Sprengel Sprengel's deformity.

deformidad de Velpeau Velpeau's deformity.

deformidad de Volkmann Volkmann's deformity.

deformidad de Whitehead Whitehead deformity.

defurfuración *f.* defurfuration.

degeneración *f.* degeneration, degeneratio.

degeneración de Abercrombie Abercombie's degeneration.

degeneración adiposa adipose degeneration.

degeneración adiposogenital adiposogenital degeneration.

degeneración amiloidea amyloid degeneration.

degeneración angiolítica angiolithic degeneration.

degeneración de Armanni-Ebstein Armanni-Ebstein's degeneration.

degeneración ascendente ascending degeneration.

degeneración ateromatosa atheromatous degeneration.

degeneración en balón ballooning degeneration.

degeneración blastoftórica blastophthoric degeneration.

degeneración calcárea calcareous degeneration.

degeneración cárnea carneous degeneration.

degeneración caseosa caseous degeneration.

degeneración celulosa cellulose degeneration.

degeneración cérea waxy degeneration.

degeneración cerebelosa primaria progresiva primary progressive cerebelar degeneration.

degeneración cerebromacular (CMD) cerebromacular degeneration (CMD).

degeneración cerebrorretiniana cerebroretinal degeneration.

degeneración combinada combined degeneration.

degeneración combinada subaguda de la médula espinal subacute combined degeneration of the spinal cord.

degeneración de conos cone degeneration.

degeneración corneal marginal marginal corneal degeneration.

degeneración descendente descending degeneration.

degeneración disciforme macular macular disciform degeneration.

degeneración ectásica marginal de la córnea ectatic marginal degeneration of the cornea.

degeneración elastoidea elastoid degeneration.

degeneración elastósica elastotic degeneration.

degeneración esclerótica sclerotic degeneration.

degeneración esponjosa spongy degeneration.

degeneración fascicular fascicular degeneration.

degeneración fibrinoide fibrinoid degeneration, fibroid degeneration.

degeneración fibrosa, degeneración fibroide fibrous degeneration.

degeneración glucógena glycogenic degeneration.

degeneración grasa fatty degeneration.

degeneración gris gray degeneration.

degeneración de Haab-Biber-Dimmer Biber-Haab-Dimmer degeneration.

degeneración hematohialoidea hematohyaloid degeneration.

degeneración hepatolenticular, degeneración hepatolenticular de Kinnear Wilson hepatolenticular degeneration.

degeneración heredomacular heredomacular degeneration.

degeneración hialina hyaline degeneration.

degeneración hialina de Crooke Crooke's hyaline degeneration.

degeneración hialoidea granuliforme degeneratio hyaloidea granuliformis.

degeneración hialoideorretiniana hyaloideoretinal degeneration.

degeneración hidrópica hydropic degeneration.

degeneración de Holmes Holmes degeneration.

degeneración de Horn Horn degeneration.

degeneración de Kuhnt-Junius Kuhnt-Junius degeneration.

degeneración lardácea lardaceous degeneration.

degeneración lenticular progresiva lenticular progressive degeneration.

degeneración por licuefacción liquefaction degeneration.

degeneración lipoidea lipoidal degeneration.

degeneración macular macular degeneration.

degeneración macular cistoidea cystoid macular degeneration.

degeneración macular congénita congenital macular degeneration.

degeneración macular disciforme disciform macular degeneration.

degeneración macular exudativa senil senile exudative macular degeneration.

degeneración macular de Sorsby Sorsby's macular degeneration.

degeneración macular seudoinflamatoria familiar familial pseudoinflamatory macular degeneration.

degeneración de Maragliano Maragliano degeneration.

degeneración marginal de Terrien Terrien's marginal degeneration.

degeneración mielínica myelinic degeneration.

degeneración mixoide, degeneración mixomatosa myxoid degeneration, myxomatous degeneration.

degeneración de Mönkeberg Mönkeberg's degeneration.

degeneración mucinosa mucinoid degeneration.

degeneración mucoide medial mucoid medial degeneration.

degeneración mucoidea mielínica myelin mucoid degeneration.

degeneración neurofibrilar neurofibrillary degeneration.

degeneración neuronal infantil infantile neuronal degeneration.

degeneración neuronal primaria primary neuronal degeneration.

degeneración de Nissl Nissl degeneration.

degeneración olivopontocerebelosa olivopontocerebellar degeneration.

degeneración ortógrada orthograde degeneration.

degeneración de Paschutin Paschutin's degeneration.

degeneración pigmentaria pigmentary degeneration.

degeneración pigmentaria primaria de la retina primary pigmentary degeneration of the retina.

degeneración polipoide polypid degeneration.

degeneración de Quain Quain's degeneration.

degeneración queratoidea keratoid degeneration.

degeneración quística cystic degeneration.

degeneración quitinosa chitinous degeneration.

degeneración reticular reticular degeneration.

degeneración retrógrada retrograde degeneration.

degeneración roja red degeneration.

degeneración de Rosenthal Rosenthal's degeneration.

degeneración secundaria secondary degeneration.

degeneración senil senile degeneration.

degeneración serosa serous degeneration.

degeneración seudotubular pseudotubular degeneration.

degeneración tapetorretiniana tapetoretinal degeneration.

degeneración trabecular trabecular degeneration.

degeneración traumática traumatic degeneration.

degeneración de Türck Türck's degeneration.

degeneración urática, degeneración úrica uratic degeneration.

degeneración vacuolar vacuolar degeneration.

degeneración de Virchow Virchow's degeneration.

degeneración viteliforme viteliform degeneration.

degeneración vitelirruptiva vitelliruptive degeneration.

degeneración vítrea vitreous degeneration.

degeneración de Waller, degeneración walleriana Wallerian degeneration.

degeneración xerótica xerotic degeneration.

degeneración de Zenker Zenker's degeneration.

degenerado, -da *adj.* degenerate.

degenerar *v.* degenerate.

degeneratio degeneratio.

degenerativo, -va *adj.* degenerative.

deglución *f.* deglutition.

deglutir *v.* swallow.
deglutivo, -va *adj.* deglutitive.
degradación *f.* degradation.
degustación *f.* degustation.
dehidración *f.* dehydration.
dehiscencia *f.* dehiscence.
  dehiscencia de una herida wound dehiscence.
  dehiscencia del iris iris dehiscence.
  dehiscencia radicular root dehiscence.
  dehiscencia del útero dehiscence of the uterus.
  dehiscencia de Zuckerkandl Zuckerkandl's dehiscence.
déjà entendu déjà entendu.
déjà pensé déjà pensé.
déjà vécu déjà vécu.
déjà vu déjà vu.
delactación *f.* delactation.
deleción *f.* deletion.
  deleción cromosómica chromosomal deletion.
  deleción intersticial interstitial deletion.
  deleción parcial gene deletion.
  deleción terminal terminal deletion.
deletéreo, -a *adj.* deleterious.
delgadez *f.* leanness, thinness.
delicuescencia *f.* deliquescence.
delicuescente *adj.* deliquescent.
delimitación *f.* delimitation.
delirante *adj.* deliriant.
delirio *m.* delusion.
  delirio agudo acute delusion.
  delirio de autoacusación delusion of self-accusation.
  delirio bajo low delusion.
  delirio de celos delusion of jealousy.
  delirio congruente con el estado de ánimo mood-congruent delusion.
  delirio de control delusion of control.
  delirio crónico chronic delusion.
  delirio febril febrile delusion.
  delirio furioso furious delusion.
  delirio de grandeza delusion of grandeur.
  delirio incongruente con el estado de ánimo mood-incongruent delusion.
  delirio de infidelidad delusion of infidelity.
  delirio místico mystic delusion.
  delirio de negación delusion of negation.
  delirio nihilista nihilistic delusion.
  delirio onírico oneiric delusion.
  delirio paranoico, delirio paranoide paranoiac delusion.
  delirio de persecución delusion of persecution.
  delirio polimorfo polymorphic delusion.
  delirio postraumático postraumatic delusion.
  delirio de referencia delusion of reference.
  delirio senil senile delusion.
  delirio sintomático symptomatic delusion.
  delirio sistematizado systematized delusion.
  delirio somático somatic delusion.
  delirio de transformación delusion of transformation.
  delirio traumático traumatic delusion.
delirium delirium.
  delirium tremens delirium tremens.
delitescencia *f.* delitescence.
delomórfico, -ca *adj.* delomorphous.
delomorfo, -fa *adj.* delomorphous.
delta *f.* delta.
  delta de Galton Galton's delta.
  delta mesoscapular delta mesoscapulae.
deltoideo, -a, deltoide *adj.* deltoide.
deltoide *adj.* deltoid.
deltoiditis *f.* deltoiditis.
demacración *f.* emaciation.

demafito *m.* dermatophyte.
demanda *f.* request.
demarcación *f.* demarcation.
demencia *f.* dementia.
  demencia de Alzheimer Alzheimer's dementia.
  demencia de Binswanger Binswanger's dementia.
  demencia catatónica catatonic dementia.
  demencia por diálisis dyalisis dementia.
  demencia epiléptica epileptic dementia.
  demencia hebefrénica hebephrenic dementia.
  demencia mioclónica myoclonic dementia, dementia myoclonica.
  demencia multiinfarto multi-infarct dementia.
  demencia paralítica paralytic dementia, dementia paralytica.
  demencia parética paretic dementia.
  demencia presenil presenile dementia.
  demencia postraumática post-traumatic dementia.
  demencia primaria primary dementia.
  demencia secundaria secondary dementia.
  demencia senil senile dementia.
  demencia tóxica toxic dementia.
  demencia vascular vascular dementia.
demente *adj.* demented.
demografía *f.* demography.
demonomanía *f.* demonomania.
demulcente *adj.* demulcent.
dendriforme *adj.* dendriform.
dendrita *f.* dendrite.
dendrodendrítico, -ca *adj.* dendrodendritic.
dendrofagocitosis *f.* dendrophagocytosis.
dendroide *adj.* dendroid.
dendrón *m.* dendron.
denegación *f.* denial.
dengue *m.* dengue.
  dengue hemorrágico hemorrhagic dengue.
denidación *f.* denidation.
desnidación *f.* denidation.
dens dens.
densidad *f.* density.
  densidad de flujo flux density.
  densidad de fotones photon density.
  densidad óptica optical density.
  densidad de protones proton density.
  densidad de recuento count density.
  densidad urinaria urine specific gravity.
densímetro *m.* densimeter.
densitometría *f.* densitometry.
  densitometría ósea bone densitometry.
densitómetro *m.* densitometer.
dentado, -da *adj.* dentatum.
dentadura *f.* denture.
  dentadura artificial artificial denture.
  dentadura felina feline denture.
dental *adj.* dental.
dentalgia *f.* dentalgia.
dentario, -ria *adj.* dental.
dentellada *f.* bite.
dentibucal *adj.* dentibucal.
dentición *f.* dentition, teething.
  dentición mixta mixed dentition.
  dentición primaria, primera dentición primary dentition, first dentition.
  dentición secundaria, segunda dentición secondary dentition.
denticulado, -da *adj.* denticulate, denticulated.
dentículo *m.* denticle.
dentificación *f.* dentification.
dentiforme *adj.* dentiform.

dentífrico *m.* dentifrice.
dentígero, -ra *adj.* dentigerous.
dentilabial *adj.* dentilabial.
dentilingual *adj.* dentilingual.
dentímetro *m.* dentimeter.
dentina *f.* dentin.
  dentina adventicia adventitious dentin.
  dentina hipersensible hypersensitive dentin.
  dentina primaria primary dentin.
  dentina secundaria secondary dentin.
  dentina sensible sensitive dentin.
  dentina terciaria tertiary dentin.
  dentina transparente transparent dentin.
dentinal *adj.* dentinal.
dentinario, -ria *adj.* dentinal.
dentinificación *f.* dentinification.
dentinoide *adj.* dentinoid.
dentíparo, -ra *adj.* dentiparous.
dentista *m., f.* dentist.
dentoalveolitis *f.* dentoalvelolitis.
dentofacial *adj.* dentofacial.
dentografía *f.* dentography.
dentoide *adj.* dentoid.
dentoliva *f.* dentoliva.
dentología *f.* deontology.
dentoma *m.* dentoma.
dentonomía *f.* dentonomy.
denudación *f.* denudation.
deontología *f.* deontology.
deorsum *adv.* deorsum.
deorsumducción *f.* deorsumduction.
deorsumversión *f.* deorsumversion.
depauperación *f.* weakening.
dependencia *f.* dependence.
depigmentación *f.* depigmentation.
depilación *f.* depilation.
  depilación electrica electric depilation.
depilatorio, -ria *m. y adj.* depilatory.
depleción *f.* depletion.
  depleción de plasma plasma depletion.
deposición *f.* stool.
depósito *m.* deposit.
  depósito de polvo de ladrillo brickdust deposit.
depravación *f.* depravation, depravity.
depresión *f.* depression.
  depresión anaclítica anaclitic depression.
  depresión atípica atypical depression.
  depresión auricular auricular depression.
  depresión de la catarata cataract depression.
  depresión involuntaria late depression.
  depresión mental mental depression.
  depresión neurótica neurotic depression.
  depresión posparto postnatal depression.
  depresión reactiva reactive depression.
  depresión secundaria secondary depression.
  depresión sintomática symptomatic depression.
depresomotor, -ra *adj.* depressomotor.
depresor, -ra *m. y adj.* depressant.
  depresor de la lengua tongue depressant.
  depresor de Sims Sims' depressant.
deprimens oculi deprimens oculi.
deprimido, -da *adj.* depressed.
depuración *f.* depuration.
depurador, -ra *adj.* depurant.
depurante *adj.* depurant.
deradelfo *m.* deradelphus.
deranencefalia *f.* deranencephaly.
desmasculinización *f.* demasculinization.
dereísmo *m.* dereism, dereistic thinking.
dereístico, -ca *adj.* dereistic.
derencefalia *f.* derencephalia, derencephaly.
derencéfalo *m.* derencephalus.
derencefalocele *m.* derencephalocele.

derismo *m.* derism.

deriva *f.* drift.

deriva antigénica antigenic drift.

deriva genética genetic drift, random genetic drift.

derivación[1] *f.* by pass.

derivación aortocoronaria aortocoronary by pass, coronary artery by pass.

derivación aortofemoral aortofemoral by pass.

derivación aortoiliaca aortoiliac by pass.

derivación aortorrenal aortorenal by pass.

derivación de arteria mamaria interna internal mammary artery by pass.

derivación biliar biliary by pass.

derivación cardíaca derecha right heart by pass, right heart derivation.

derivación cardíaca izquierda left heart by pass, left heart derivation.

derivación cardiopulmonar cardiopulmonary by pass, cardiopulmonary derivation.

derivación coronaria coronary by pass.

derivación extracraneal-intracraneal extracranial-intracranial by pass.

derivación femoropoplítea femoropopliteal by pass.

derivación gástrica gastric by pass.

derivación ileal ileal by pass.

derivación ileal parcial partial ileal by pass.

derivación intestinal bowel by pass, intestinal by pass.

derivación parcial partial by pass.

derivación yeyunoileal jejunoileal by pass, jejunoileal shunt.

derivación[2] *f.* derivation, revulsion.

derivación[3] *f.* lead.

derivación ABC ABC lead.

derivación aVF aVf lead.

derivación aVL aVl lead.

derivación aVR aVr lead.

derivación bipolar bipolar lead.

derivación CB CB lead.

derivación CF CF lead.

derivación CL CL lead.

derivación CR CR lead.

derivación directa direct lead.

derivación electrocardiográfica electrocardiograph lead.

derivación esofágica esophageal lead.

derivación estándar standard lead.

derivación de las extremidades limb lead.

derivación indirecta indirect lead.

derivación intracardíaca intracardiac lead.

derivación del miembro, derivación de los miembros limb lead.

derivación precordial precordial lead.

derivación semidirecta semidirect lead.

derivación torácica chest lead.

derivación unipolar unipolar lead.

derivación V V lead.

derivación de Wilson Wilson's lead.

derivación[4] *f.* referral.

derivación[5] *f.* shunt.

derivación arteriovenosa (AV) arteriovenous (A-V) shunt.

derivación cardiovascular cardiovascular shunt.

derivación de Denver Denver shunt.

derivación de derecha a izquierda right-to-left shunt.

derivación para diálisis dialysis shunt.

derivación de Dickens Dickens shunt.

derivación espinotubárica spinofallopian tube shunt.

derivación esplenorrenal, derivación es-

plenorrenal distal splenorenal shunt, distal splenorenal shunt.

derivación externa external shunt.

derivación de Glenn Glenn shunt, Glenn's shunt.

derivación de la hexosa monofosfato hexose monophosphate shunt.

derivación intrapulmonar intrapulmonary shunt.

derivación invertida reversed shunt.

derivación desde izquierda hacia derecha left to right shunt.

derivación de LeVeen LeVeen shunt.

derivación lumboperitoneal lumboperitoneal shunt.

derivación mesocava mesocaval shunt.

derivación del monofosfato de hexosa hexose monophosphate shunt.

derivación de pentosa pentose shunt.

derivación peritoneovenosa, derivación periventosa de LeVeen peritoneovenous shunt, LeVeen peritonovenous shunt.

derivación portocava, derivación poscava portacaval shunt, portocaval shunt, postcaval shunt.

derivación de Rapoport-Luebering Rapoport-Luebering shunt.

derivación traqueoesofágica tracheoesophageal shunt.

derivación venosa renal-esplénica renal-splenic venous shunt.

derivación ventriculoauricular ventriculoatrial shunt.

derivación ventriculoperitoneal ventriculoperitoneal shunt.

derivación ventriculopleural ventriculopleural shunt.

derivación ventriculotubárica ventriculofallopian tube shunt.

derivación ventriculovenosa ventriculovenous shunt.

derivación de Warren Warren shunt.

derivación de Warburg-Lipmann-Dickens Warburg Lipmann Dickens shunt.

derivaciónde Waterson Waterson shunt.

derivativo, -va *adj.* derivative.

derma *f.* derma.

dermabrasión *f.* dermabrasion.

Dermacentor Dermacentor.

dermad *adv.* dermad.

dermahemia *f.* dermahemia.

dermal *adj.* dermal.

dermalaxia *f.* dermalaxia.

dermalgia *f.* dermalgia.

dermametropatismo *m.* dermametropathism.

dermanaplastia *f.* dermanaplasty.

dermatalgia *f.* dermatalgia.

dermatergosis *f.* dermatergosis.

dermático, -ca *adj.* dermatic.

dermatitis *f.* dermatitis.

dermatitis por ácaro de la cebolla onion mite dermatitis.

dermatitis del ácaro de la rata, dermatitis por ácaros de la rata rat-mite dermatitis.

dermatitis por aceite de corte cutting oil dermatitis.

dermatitis actínica actinic dermatitis.

dermatitis alérgica allergic dermatitis.

dermatitis por ambustión, dermatitis ambustionis dermatitis ambustionis.

dermatitis amoniacal, dermatitis por amoniaco ammonia dermatitis.

dermatitis anquilostomiásica, dermatitis por anquilostomiasis ancylostoma dermatitis.

dermatitis del área del pañal napkin dermatitis.

dermatitis artefacta, dermatitis artificial dermatitis artefacta.

dermatitis atópica atopic dermatitis.

dermatitis atrófica dermatitis atrophicans.

dermatitis autofítica dermatitis autophytica.

dermatitis de berloque berlock dermatitis, berloque dermatitis.

dermatitis por betún para calzado shoe dye dermatitis.

dermatitis blastomicética, dermatitis blastomicótica blastomycetic dermatitis, dermatitis blastomycotica.

dermatitis brucelósica brucella dermatitis.

dermatitis bullosa striata pratensis dermatitis bullosa striata pratensis.

dermatitis calórica dermatitis calorica.

dermatitis cercarial cercarial dermatitis.

dermatitis por césped grass dermatitis.

dermatitis por combustión dermatitis combustionis.

dermatitis por congelación dermatitis congelationis.

dermatitis de contacto, dermatitis por contacto contact dermatitis.

dermatitis por contacto alérgica allergic contact dermatitis.

dermatitis por contacto fotoalérgico photoallergic contact dermatitis.

dermatitis por correas de sandalias sandal strap dermatitis.

dermatitis por cosméticos, dermatitis cosmética cosmetic dermatitis.

dermatitis dhobie dhobie mark dermatitis.

dermatitis eccematosa eczematous dermatitis.

dermatitis eccematoide infecciosa, dermatitis eccematoidea infecciosa, dermatitis eccematosa infecciosa infectious eczematous dermatitis, infectious eczematoid dermatitis.

dermatitis eccematosa numular nummular eczematous dermatitis.

dermatitis esquistosomiásica, dermatitis esquistosómica schistosomal dermatitis, schistosome dermatitis, swimmer's itch.

dermatitis por estasis stasis dermatitis.

dermatitis estival dermatitis aestivalis.

dermatitis estriada pratense ampollosa dermatitis striata pratensis bullosa.

dermatitis exfoliativa exfoliative dermatitis, dermatitis exfoliativa.

dermatitis exfoliativa infantil, dermatitis exfoliativa neonatal, dermatitis exfoliativa del neonato, dermatitis exfoliativa de los niños, dermatitis exfoliativa del recién nacido dermatitis exfoliativa infantum, dermatitis exfoliativa neonatorum.

dermatitis exudativa discoide y liquenoide exudative discoid and lichenoid dermatitis.

dermatitis facticia, dermatitis ficticia factitial dermatitis.

dermatitis fitofototóxica phytophototoxicity dermatitis.

dermatitis fotoalérgica de contacto photoallergic contact dermatitis.

dermatitis por fotocontacto photocontact dermatitis.

dermatitis fototóxica, dermatitis fototóxica de contacto phototoxic dermatitis, phototoxic contact dermatitis.

dermatitis gangrenosa infantil, dermatitis gangrenosa infantum dermatitis gangrenosa infantum.

dermatitis por goma de mascar bubble gum dermatitis.

dermatitis gravídica dermatitis gestationis.

dermatitis herpetiforme dermatitis herpetiformis.

dermatitis por hiedra venenosa rhus dermatitis.

dermatitis hiemal, dermatitis hiemalis dermatitis hiemalis.

dermatitis de la hierba de las praderas meadow-grass dermatitis.

dermatitis húmeda weeping dermatitis.

dermatitis industrial industrial dermatitis.

dermatitis infecciosa eccematoide, dermatitis infecciosa eccematoidea, dermatitis infecciosa eccematosa infectious eczematous dermatitis.

dermatitis por insectos insect dermatitis.

dermatitis invernal dermatitis hiemalis.

dermatitis por irritante, dermatitis por irritante primario irritant dermatitis, primary irritant dermatitis.

dermatitis de Jacquet Jacquet's dermatitis.

dermatitis del lavandero dhobie mark dermatitis.

dermatitis liquenoide crónica atrófica dermatitis lichenoides chronica atrophicans.

dermatitis liquenoide purpúrica pigmentada pigmented purpuric lichenoid dermatitis.

dermatitis livedoide livedoid dermatitis.

dermatitis del mango mango dermatitis.

dermatitis marina marine dermatitis.

dermatitis medicamentosa dermatitis medicamentosa.

dermatitis micropapulosa, eritematosa e hiperhidrótica de la nariz dermatitis micropapulosa, erythematosa et hyperhidrotica nasi.

dermatitis por molusco dermatitis moluscum contagiosum.

dermatitis multiforme dermatitis multiformis.

dermatitis de los nadadores swimmer's dermatitis.

dermatitis por níquel nickel dermatitis.

dermatitis nodular necrótica dermatitis nodularis necrotica.

dermatitis nudosa dermatitis nodosa.

dermatitis numular nummular dermatitis.

dermatitis ocupacional occupational dermatitis.

dermatitis de Oppenheim Oppenheim's dermatitis.

dermatitis por orugas caterpillar dermatitis.

dermatitis del pañal diaper dermatitis.

dermatitis papilar capilar, dermatitis papillaris capillitii dermatitis papillaris capillitii.

dermatitis papulosa del embarazo papular dermatitis of pregnancy.

dermatitis pediculoides ventricosus dermatitis pediculoides ventricosus.

dermatitis por perfume, dermatitis por perfumes perfume dermatitis.

dermatitis peribucal, dermatitis perioral perioral dermatitis.

dermatitis pigmentada purpúrica liquenoide pigmented purpuric lichenoid dermatitis.

dermatitis por plantas del género Rhus rhus dermatitis.

dermatitis por polilla moth dermatitis.

dermatitis por polilla de cola parda brown-tail moth dermatitis.

dermatitis por polilla io io-moth dermatitis.

dermatitis de los prados meadow dermatitis.

dermatitis precancerosa precancerous dermatitis.

dermatitis primaria primary dermatitis.

dermatitis primaria irritante primary irritant dermatitis.

dermatitis profesional professional dermatitis.

dermatitis purpúrica pigmentada liquenoide pigmented purpuric lichenoid dermatitis.

dermatitis pustulosa contagiosa contagious pustular dermatitis.

dermatitis pustulosa subcorneal subcorneal pustular dermatitis.

dermatitis química chemical dermatitis.

dermatitis por radiación radiation dermatitis.

dermatitis por rayos X Roentgen ray dermatitis.

dermatitis repens dermatitis repens.

dermatitis por rhus rhus dermatitis.

dermatitis de Schamberg Schamberg's dermatitis.

dermatitis seborreica seborrheic dermatitis, dermatitis seborrheica.

dermatitis simple dermatitis simplex.

dermatitis solar solar dermatitis.

dermatitis por tinta de marcar dhobie mark dermatitis.

dermatitis del tintorero dhobie mark dermatitis.

dermatitis traumática traumatic dermatitis.

dermatitis uncinariásica uncinarial dermatitis.

dermatitis por vainilla vanilla dermatitis.

dermatitis vegetal plant dermatitis.

dermatitis vegetante dermatitis vegetans.

dermatitis venenata, dermatitis venenosa dermatitis venenata.

dermatitis verrugosa verrucous dermatitis, dermatitis verrucosa.

dermatitis por el viento, dermatitis por viento windburn.

dermatitis por zumaque venenoso poison ivy dermatitis.

dermatoartritis f. dermatoarthritis.

dermatoartritis lípida, dermatoartritis lipoide lipid dermatoarthritis, lipoid dermatoarthritis.

dermatoautoplastia f. dermatoautoplasty.

Dermatobia Dermatobia.

dermatobiasis f. dermatobiasis.

dermatocalasia f. dermatochalasia, dermatochalasis, dermatochalazia.

dermatocalasis f. dermatochalasia, dermatochalasis, dermatochalazia.

dermatocandidiasis f. dermatocandidiasis.

dermatocele m. dermatocele.

dermatocelulitis f. dermatocellulitis.

dermatocisto m. dermatocyst.

dermatoconiosis f. dermatoconiosis.

dermatoconjuntivitis f. dermatoconjunctivitis.

dermatodinia f. dermatodynia.

dermatodisplasia f. dermatodysplasia.

dermatoesclerosis f. dermatosclerosis.

dermatoesqueleto m. dermatoskeleton.

dermatofarmacología f. dermatopharmacology.

dermatofibroma m. dermatofibroma.

dermatofibroma protuberans dermatofibroma protuberans.

dermatofibrosarcoma m. dermatofibrosarcoma.

dermatofibrosarcoma protuberans, dermatofibrosarcoma protuberante dermatofibrosarcoma protuberans.

dermatofibrosarcoma protuberante pig-

mentado pigmented dermatofibrosarcoma protuberans.

dermatofibrosis f. dermatofibrosis.

dermatofibrosis lenticular diseminada, dermatofibrosis lenticularis disseminata dermatofibrosis lenticularis disseminata.

dermatofiliasis f. dermatophiliasis.

dermatofilosis f. dermatophilosis.

dermatofítide f. dermatophytid.

dermatofito m. dermatophyte.

dermatofitosis f. dermatophytosis.

dermatofobia f. dermatophobia.

dermatófono m. dermatophone.

dermatoglifia f. dermatoglyphics.

dermatografía f. dermatographia, dermatography.

dermatográfico, -ca adj. dermatographic.

dermatografismo m. dermatographism.

dermatografismo blanco white dermatographism.

dermatografismo negro black dermatographism.

dermatógrafo m. dermatograph.

dermatoheteroplastia f. dermatoheteroplasty.

dermatohistopatología f. dermatohistopathology.

dermatoide adj. dermatoid.

dermatólisis f. dermatolysis.

dermatólisis de los párpados, dermatólisis palpebral dermatolysis palpebrarum.

dermatología f. dermatology.

dermatológico, -ca adj. dermatologic.

dermatólogo, -ga m., f. dermatologist.

dermatoma¹ m. dermatoma.

dermatoma² m. dermatome.

dermatomegalia f. dermatomegaly.

dermatómera f. dermatomere.

dermatomices f. dermatomyces.

dermatomicina f. dermatomycin.

dermatómico, -ca adj. dermatomic.

dermatomicosis dermatomycosis.

dermatomicosis del pie dermatomycosis pedis.

dermatomioma m. dermatomyoma.

dermatomiositis f. dermatomyositis.

dermátomo m. dermatome.

dermátomo de Brown Brown dermatome.

dermátomo de Castroviejo Castroviejo dermatome.

dermátomo eléctrico electric dermatome.

dermátomo de Padgett Padgett dermatome.

dermátomo de Reese Reese dermatome.

dermatoneurología f. dermatoneurology.

dermatoneurosis f. dermatoneurosis.

dermatonosología f. dermatonosology.

dermatooftalmitis f. dermato-ophthalmitis.

dermatopatía f. dermatopathia, dermatopathy.

dermatopático, -ca adj. dermatopathic.

dermatopatología f. dermatopathlogy.

dermatoplastia f. dermoplasty.

dermatoplástico, -ca adj. dermatoplastic.

dermatopolineuritis f. dermatopolyneuritis.

dermatoquelidosis f. dermatokelidoisis.

dermatoquiste m. dermatocyst.

dermatorrea f. dermatorrhea.

dermatorrexis f. dermatorrhexis.

dermatosclerosis f. dermatosclerosis.

dermatoscopia f. dermatoscopy.

dermatosis f. dermatosis.

dermatosis acantolítica pasajera, dermatosis acantolítica transitoria transient acantholytic dermatosis (TAD).

dermatosis acarina acarine dermatosis.

dermatosis ampollar crónica benigna de la

niñez benign chronic bullous dermatosis of childhood.

dermatosis ampollosa dermatolítica dermatolytic bullous dermatosis.

dermatosis de Auspitz Auspitz's dermatosis.

dermatosis cenicienta, dermatosis cenicienta de Ramírez ashy dermatofibrosarcoma protuberans of Ramirez, dermatosis cenicienta.

dermatosis dermolítica ampollar dermolytic bullous dermatosis.

dermatosis industrial industrial dermatosis, dermatosis industrialis.

dermatosis liquenoide lichenoid dermatosis.

dermatosis liquenoide purpúrica pigmentada pigmented purpuric lichenoid dermatosis.

dermatosis medicamentosa dermatosis medicamentosa.

dermatosis neutrófila aguda, dermatosis neutrófila febril aguda acute neutrophilic dermatosis, acute febrile neutrophilic dermatosis.

dermatosis papulosa negra, dermatosis papulosa nigra dermatosis papulosa nigra.

dermatosis pigmentada progresiva, dermatosis pigmentaria progresiva progressive pigmentary dermatosis.

dermatosis profesional professional dermatosis.

dermatosis pustular subcorneal, dermatosis pustulosa subcorneal subcorneal pustular dermatosis.

dermatosis por radiación radiation dermatosis.

dermatosis de Schamberg, dermatosis purpúrica pigmentada progresiva de Schamberg Schamberg's dermatosis, Schamberg's progressive pigmented purpuric dermatosis.

dermatosis seborreica seborrheic dermatosis.

dermatosis ulcerosa ulcerative dermatosis.

dermatosparaxis *f.* dermatosparaxis.

dermatoterapia *f.* dermatotherapy.

dermatótomo *m.* dermatotome.

dermatotrópico, -ca *adj.* dermatotropic.

dermatoxenoplastia *f.* dermatoxenoplasty.

dermatoxerasia *f.* dermatoxerasia.

dermatozoiasis *f.* dermatozoiasis.

dermatozoario *m.* dermatozoon.

dermatozoo *m.* dermatozoon.

dermatozoonosis *f.* dermatozoonosis.

dermatrofia *f.* dermatrophia, dermatrophy.

dermenquisis *f.* dermenchysis.

dérmico, -ca *adj.* dermic.

dermis *f.* dermis.

dermoabrador *m.* dermabrader.

dermoabrasión *f.* dermabrasion.

dermoanergia *f.* dermoanergy.

dermoblasto *m.* dermoblast.

dermócimo *m.* dermocyma, dermocymus.

dermoepidérmico, -ca *adj.* dermoepidermal.

dermoesqueleto *m.* dermoskeleton.

dermoestenosis *f.* dermostenosis.

dermófito *m.* dermophyte.

dermoflebitis *f.* dermophlebitis.

dermografía *f.* dermographia, dermography.

dermográfico, -ca *adj.* dermographic.

dermografismo *m.* dermographism.

dermógrafo *m.* dermograph.

dermohigrómetro *m.* dermohygrometer.

dermoide *m. y adj.* dermoid.

dermoide de implantación implantation dermoid.

dermoide de inclusión inclusion dermoid.

dermolde de secuestro sequestration dermoid.

dermoidectomía *f.* dermodeictomy.

dermolipectomía *f.* dermolipectomy.

dermolipoma *m.* dermolipoma.

dermolisina *f.* dermolysin.

dermólisis *f.* dermolysis.

dermometría *f.* dermometry.

dermómetro *m.* dermometer.

dermomicosis *f.* dermomycosis.

dermomiotoma *m.* dermomyotome.

dermonecrótico, -ca *adj.* dermonecrotic.

dermoneurosis *f.* dermoneurosis.

dermoneurotrópico, -ca *adj.* dermoneurotropic.

dermonosología *f.* dermonosology.

dermopatía *f.* dermopathy.

dermopatía diabética diabetic dermopathy.

dermopatía pigmentaria reticular dermatopathia pigmentosa reticularis.

dermopático, -ca *adj.* dermopathic.

dermoplastia *f.* dermoplasty.

dermosifilopatía *f.* dermosyphilopathy.

dermosinovitis *f.* dermosynovitis.

dermosqueleto *m.* dermoskeleton.

dermostenosis *f.* dermostenosis.

dermotáctil *adj.* dermotactile.

dermotoxina *f.* dermotoxin.

dermotrópico, -ca *adj.* dermotropic.

dermótropo, -pa *adj.* dermotropic.

dermovacuna *f.* dermovaccine.

dermovascular *adj.* dermovascular.

dermovirus *m.* dermovirus.

derodídimo *m.* derodidymus.

derodimo *m.* derodidymus.

derramadero *m.* spillway.

derramamiento *m.* spill.

derrame *m.* effusion.

derrame abdominal abdominal effusion.

derrame articular articular effusion, joint effusion.

derrame cerebral cerebral effusion.

derrame hemorrágico hemorrhagic effusion.

derrame pericárdico pericardial effusion, pericardium effusion.

derrame peritoneal peritoneum effusion.

derrame pleural, derrame pleurítico pleural effusion.

derrame purulento purulent effusion.

derrame sanguíneo sanguineous effusion.

derrame seroso serous effusion.

derrame sinovial joint effusion.

desaceleración *f.* deceleration.

desaceleración inicial early deceleration.

desaceleración tardía late deceleration.

desaceleración variable variable deceleration.

desacidificación *f.* deacidification.

desacidificar *v.* disacidify.

desacondicionamiento *m.* deconditioning.

desadaptación *f.* dysadaptation, dysaptation.

desaferenciación *f.* deafferentation.

desaferentación *f.* deafferentation.

desagotar *v.* strip.

desagregación *f.* disaggregation.

desalcoholización *f.* dealcoholization.

desalergización *f.* deallergization.

desalergizar *v.* deallergize.

desalinación *f.* desalination.

desalivación *f.* desalivation.

desamidación *f.* deamidation.

desamidización *f.* deamidization.

desamidizar *v.* deamidize, desamidize.

desaminación *f.* deamination.

desaminización *f.* deaminization.

desaminizar *v.* deaminize.

desangramiento *m.* bleeding.

desarreglo *m.* derangement.

desarreglo interno de Hey Hey's internal derangement.

desarrollo *m.* development.

desarrollo cognitivo cognitive development.

desarrollo detenido arrested development.

desarrollo físico y psicomotor de los lactantes psychomotor and physical development of infants.

desarrollo infantil child development.

desarrollo libidinal libidinal development.

desarrollo en mosaico mosaic development.

desarrollo embrionario embryologic development.

desarrollo posnatal postnatal development.

desarrollo prenatal prenatal development.

desarrollo psicomotor psychomotor development.

desarrollo psicosexual psychosexual development.

desarrollo psicosocial psychosocial development.

desarrollo puberal onset of puberty.

desarrollo regulador regulative development.

desarrollo de por vida life-span development.

desarterialización *f.* dearterialization.

desarticulación *f.* disarticulation.

desarticulación de Chopart Chopart's disarticulation.

desarticulación de Larrey Larrey's disarticulation.

desarticulación de Mackenzie Mackenzie's disarticulation.

desarticulación de Malgaigne Malgaigne's disarticulation.

desarticulación de Syme Syme's disarticulation.

desarticulación de Tripier Tripier's disarticulation.

desarticular *v.* disjoint.

desasimilación *f.* dissimilation.

desasimilar *v.* dissimilate.

desatar *v.* debanding.

desaturación *f.* desaturation.

desaturar *v.* desaturate.

desbandamiento *m.* debanding.

desbridamiento *m.* débridement, wound excision.

desbridamiento enzimático enzymatic débridement.

desbridamiento epitelial epithelial débridement.

desbridamiento quirúrgico surgical débridement.

desbridar *v.* débride.

descalabradura *f.* head injury, head wound.

descalcificación *f.* decalcification.

descalcificante[1] *adj.* decalcifying.

descalcificante[2] *m.* decalcifying agent, decalcifier.

descalcificar *v.* decalcify.

descamación *f.* desquamation.

descamación furfurácea furfuraceous desquamation.

descamación en salvado branny desquamation.

descamar *v.* desquamate, scale.

descamativo, -va *adj.* desquamative.

descanso *m.* rest.

descanulación *f.* decannulation.

descapacitación *f.* decapacitation.

descapsulación *f.* decapsulation.

descapsulación renal decapsulation of the kidney.

descarbonización *f.* decarbonization.
descarboxilación *f.* decarboxylation.
descarga[1] *f.* discharge.
  descarga de cepillo brush discharge.
  descarga de desorganización disruptive discharge.
  descarga electrica electric discharge.
  descarga epiléptica epileptic discharge.
  descarga nerviosa nervous discharge.
  descarga sistólica systolic discharge.
descarga[3] *f.* venting.
descarrilamiento *m.* derailment.
descemetitis *f.* descemetitis.
descemetocele *m.* descemetocele.
descendencia *f.* lineage.
descendens descendens.
descendente *adj.* descending.
descenso *m.* descent, descensus.
  descenso aberrante del testículo descensus aberrans testis.
  descensus funiculi umbilicalis descensus funiculi umbilicalis.
  descenso paradójico del testículo descensus paradoxus testis.
  descenso de la presión de vapor vapor pressure lowering descent.
  descenso testicular, descenso del testículo descent of the testis, descensus testis.
  descenso uterino, descenso del útero descensus uteri.
  descenso vaginal vaginal descent.
  descenso ventricular, descenso ventriculi, descenso del vientre descensus ventriculi.
descensus descensus.
descentración *f.* decentration.
descentramiento lateral *m.* lateral decentering.
descentrar *v.* decenter.
desceración *f.* deceration.
descerebelación *f.* decerebellation.
descerebración *f.* decerebration.
  descerebracion exangüe bloodless decerebration.
  descerebracion incruenta bloodless decerebration.
descerebrado, -da *adj.* decerebrate.
descloruración *f.* dechloridation, dechlorination, dechloruration.
descloruración *f.* dechloridation, dechlorination, dechloruration.
desclorurante *m.* dechlorurant.
descoagulante *m.* decoagulant.
descolesterinización *f.* decholesterinization.
descolesterolización *f.* decholesterolization.
descoloración *f.* decoloration.
descolorante *adj.* bleaching agent.
descolorar *v.* decolorize.
descompensación *f.* decompensation.
  descompensación corneal corneal decompensation.
descomplementar *v.* decomplementize.
descomposición[1] *f.* abbau.
descomposición[2] *f.* decay.
descomposición[3] *f.* decomposition.
  descomposición anaerobia anaerobic decomposition.
  descomposición del movimiento decomposition of movement, movement decomposition.
descomposición[4] *f.* rot.
  descomposición de Barcoo Barcoo rot.
  descomposición negra black rot.
descompresión *f.* decompression.
  descompresión abdominal abdominal decompression.

descompresión cardíaca cardiac decompression.
descompresión cerebral cerebral decompression.
descompresión del corazón decompression of the heart.
descompresión espinal spinal decompression.
descompresión explosiva explosive decompression.
descompresión interna internal decompression.
descompresión de la médula espinal decompression of the spinal cord.
descompresión nerviosa nerve decompression.
descompresión orbitaria orbital decompression.
descompresión pericárdica pericardial decompression, decompression of the pericardium.
descompresión rápida rapid decompression.
descompresión suboccipital suboccipital decompression.
descompresión subtemporal subtemporal decompression.
descompresión trigeminal trigeminal decompression.
descongestionante *m. y adj.* decongestant.
descongestivo *m.* decongestant.
  descongestivo nasal nasal decongestant.
descongestivo, -va *adj.* decongestant, decongestive.
descontaminación *f.* decontamination.
descontrol *m.* dyscontrol.
descostramiento *m.* decrustation.
descoyuntamiento *m.* dislocation.
descuido unilateral *m.* unilateral neglect.
desdiferenciación[1] *f.* dedifferentation.
desdiferenciación[2] *f.* splitting.
desdoblamiento *m.* splitting.
  desdoblamiento de la personalidad split personality.
  desdoblamiento de los ruidos cardíacos splitting of heart sounds.
  desdoblamiento sagital de la mandíbula sagittal splitting of the mandible.
desecación[1] *f.* desiccation, exsiccation.
  desecación eléctrica electric desiccation.
desecación[2] *f.* exsiccation.
desecador *m.* desiccator, exsiccant.
  desecador al vacío vacuum desiccator.
desecante[1] *adj.* desiccant.
desecante[2] *m.* desiccant, desiccator, exsiccant.
desecar *v.* desiccate, exsiccate.
desecativo, -va *adj.* desiccative.
desecho[1] *m.* débris.
desecho[2] *m.* detritus.
deseferentación *f.* de-efferentation.
desemanación *f.* deemanate.
desembocadura[1] *f.* débouchement.
desembocadura[2] *f.* embouchement.
desencadenante *m.* trigger.
desenguantamiento *m.* degloving.
desensibilización *f.* desensitization.
  desensibilización fóbica phobic desensitization.
  desensibilización general systemic desensitization.
  desensibilización heteróloga heterologous desensitization.
  desensibilización homóloga homologous desensitization.
  desensibilización sistemática systematic desensitization.

desensibilizar *v.* desensitize.
desepicardialización *f.* de-epicardialization.
desequilibrado, -da *adj.* imbalanced.
desequilibrio[1] *m.* imbalance, disequilibrium.
  desequilibrio autónomo autonomic imbalance.
  desequilibrio binocular binocular imbalance.
  desequilibrio de cromosomas sexuales sex chromosome imbalance.
  desequilibrio de enlace linkage disequilibrium.
  desequilibrio genético genetic disequilibrium.
  desequilibrio por ligadura, desequilibrio de ligamiento linkage disequilibrium.
  desequilibrio oclusivo occlusal imbalance.
  desequilibrio vasomotor vasomotor imbalance.
desequilibrio[2] *m.* disequilibrium, dysequilibrium.
desesperanza *f.* hopelessness.
desexualizar *v.* desexualize, unsex.
desfallecimiento *m.* faint.
desfatigación *f.* defatigation.
desfeminación *f.* defemination.
desfeminización *f.* defeminization.
desfibración *f.* defibrillation.
desfibrilación *f.* defibrillation.
desfibrilador *m.* defibrillator.
  desfibrilador automático implantable automatic implantable cardioverter defibrillator.
  desfibrilador externo external defibrillator.
desfibrinación *f.* defibrination.
desfibrinado, -da *adj.* defibrinated.
desflexión *f.* deflection.
desfloración *f.* defloration.
desfluoridación *f.* defluoridation.
desfurfuración *f.* defurfuration.
desganglionar *v.* deganglionate.
desgarramiento *m.* tear.
desgarro *m.* tear.
  desgarro en asa de cubo bucket-handle tear.
  desgarro de Mallory-Weiss Mallory-Weiss tear.
  desgarro del cemento cemental tear, cementum tear.
  desgarro ligamentoso ligamental tear.
  desgarro perineal, desgarro del perineo tear of the perineum.
  desgarro vaginal vaginal tear.
desgasificación *f.* degassing.
desgaste *m.* detrition, fretting, grinding, wear.
  desgaste occlusal occlusal wear.
  desgaste selectivo selective grinding.
desgenitalizar *v.* degenitalize.
desgerminar *v.* degerm.
desgranulación *f.* degranulation.
desgrasado, -da *adj.* defatted.
deshabituación *f.* deprivation.
deshematizar *v.* dehematize.
deshemoglobinizar *v.* dehemoglobinize.
deshidratación *f.* dehydration.
  deshidratación absoluta absolute dehydration.
  deshidratación de las encías dehydration of gingivae.
  deshidratación hipernatrémica hypernatremic dehydration.
  deshidratación intersticial interstitial dehydration.
  deshidratación intracelular intracellular dehydration.
  deshidratación intravascular intravascular dehydration.

deshidratación relativa relative dehydration.

deshidratación voluntaria voluntary dehydration.

deshidratante *adj.* dehydrant.

deshidratar *v.* dehydrate.

deshidremia *f.* deshydremia.

deshidrogenación *f.* dehydrogenation.

deshidrogenar *v.* dehydrogenate.

deshidrogenasa *f.* dehydrogenase.

deshipnotizar *v.* dehypnotize.

deshumanización *f.* dehumanization.

deshumectante *m.* dehumidifier.

desimpactación *f.* disimpaction.

desinfección *f.* disinfection.

desinfección concomitante, desinfección concurrente concomitant disinfection, concurrent disinfection.

desinfección terminal terminal disinfection.

desinfección del termómetro thermometer disinfection.

desinfectante *m.* disinfectant.

desinfectante completo complete disinfectant.

desinfectante incompleto incomplete disinfectant.

desinfectar *v.* disinfect.

desinfestación *f.* disinfestation.

desinhibición *f.* disinhibition.

desinmune *adj.* disimmune.

desinmunidad *f.* disimmunity.

desinmunizar *v.* disimmunize.

desinsectación *f.* disinsection.

desinsectado, -da *adj.* disinsected.

desinsectización *f.* disinsectization.

desinserción *f.* disinsertion.

desintegración[1] *f.* disintegration.

desintegración alfa alpha disintegration.

desintegración beta beta disintegration.

desintegración radiactiva radioactive disintegration.

desintegración[2] *f.* decay.

desintegrante *m.* disintegrant.

desintoxicación *f.* detoxication, detoxification.

desintoxicar *v.* detoxicate, detoxify.

desinvaginación *f.* disinvagination.

desinvaginación radiológica radiologic disinvagination.

desionización *f.* deionization.

deslactación *f.* delactation.

deslagrimación *f.* delacrimation.

deslizamiento *m.* glide.

deslizamiento de la epífisis femoral slipped femoral epiphysis glide.

deslizamiento mandibular mandibular glide.

deslizamiento del maxilar inferior mandibular glide.

deslizamiento oclusal occlusal glide.

deslumbramiento[1] *m.* glare.

deslumbramiento cegador blinding glare.

deslumbramiento directo direct glare.

deslumbramiento especular specular glare.

deslumbramiento indirecto indirect glare.

deslumbramiento ofuscador dazzling glare.

deslumbramiento periférico peripheral glare.

deslumbramiento velador veiling glare.

deslumbramiento[2] *m.* halation.

desmalgia *f.* desmalgia.

desmasculinización *f.* demasculinization.

desmayo *m.* blackout, faint.

desmayo visual visual blackout.

desmectasia *f.* desmectasia.

desmectasis *f.* desmectasis.

desmedular[1] *v.* emedullate.

desmedular[2] *v.* pith.

desmembramiento *m.* dismemberment.

desmenuzar *v.* tease.

desmepitelio *m.* desmepithelium.

desmielinación *f.* demyelination.

desmielinación segmentaria segmentary demyelination.

desmielinización *f.* demyelinization.

desmielinizar *v.* demyelinate.

desmina *f.* desmin.

desmineralización *f.* demineralization.

desmiognato *m.* desmiognathus.

desmitis *f.* desmitis.

desmocitoma *m.* desmocytoma.

desmocráneo *m.* desmocranium.

desmodinia *f.* desmodynia.

desmodontio *m.* desmodontium.

Desmodus Desmodus.

desmógeno, -na *adj.* desmogenous.

desmografia *f.* desmography.

desmohemoblasto *m.* desmohemoblast.

desmoide *m. y adj.* desmoid.

desmoide extraabdominal extra-abdominal desmoid.

desmolasa *f.* desmolase.

desmólisis *f.* desmolysis.

desmología *f.* desmology.

desmoma *m.* desmoma.

desmoneoplasia *f.* desmoneoplasm.

desmopatía *f.* desmopathy.

desmopexia *f.* desmopexia.

desmopicnosis *f.* desmopyknosis.

desmoplaquina *f.* desmoplakin.

desmoplasia *f.* desmoplasia.

desmoplásico, -ca *adj.* desmoplastic.

desmoplastia *f.* desmoplasia.

desmoplástico, -ca *adj.* desmoplastic.

desmopresina *f.* desmopressin.

desmorfinización *f.* demorphinization.

desmorrexia *f.* desmorrhexis.

desmorrexis *f.* desmorrhexis.

desmosis *f.* desmosis.

desmosoma *m.* desmosome.

desmosterol *m.* desmosterol.

desmotomía *f.* desmotomy.

desmotropía *f.* desmotropism.

desmucosación *f.* demucosation.

desmutización *f.* demutization.

desnarcotizar *v.* denarcotize.

desnatalidad *f.* denatality.

desnaturalización *f.* denaturation.

desnaturalización de proteínas protein denaturation.

desnaturalizado, -da *adj.* denatured.

desnaturalizante *m.* denaturant.

desnervación *f.* denervation.

desnicotinizado, -da *adj.* denicotinized.

desnidación *f.* denidation.

desnitratación *f.* denitration.

desnitrificación *f.* denitrification.

desnitrificante *adj.* denitrifier.

desnitrificar *v.* denitrify.

desnitrogenación *f.* denitrogenation.

desnucleado, -da *adj.* denucleated.

desnutrición *f.* denutrition, malnutrition.

desnutrición maligna malignant malnutrition.

desobstruyente *adj.* deobstruent.

desodorante *m.* deodorant.

desodorizante *m.* deodorizer.

desodorizar *v.* deodorize.

desopilación *f.* deoppilation.

desopilativo, -va *adj.* deoppilative.

desorber *v.* desorb.

desorción *f.* desorption.

desorden *m.* disorder.

desorganización *f.* disorganization.

desorientación *f.* disorientation.

desorientación espacial spatial disorientation.

desosificación *f.* deossification.

desoxicolaneresis *f.* deoxycholaneresis.

desoxidación[1] *f.* deoxidation.

desoxidación[2] *f.* pickling.

desoxidar *v.* deoxidize.

desoxigenación *f.* deoxygenation.

desosirribonucleico, -ca *m.* deoxyribonucleic.

ácido desosirribonucleico (ADN) *m.* deoxyribonucleic acid (DNA).

desoxirribonucleósido *m.* deoxyribonucleoside.

desoxirribonucleótido *m.* deoxyribonucleotide.

desoxivirus *m.* deoxyvirus.

desozonizar *v.* deozonize.

despancreatizar *v.* depancratize.

despeciación *f.* despeciation.

despeciar *v.* despeciate.

despecificación *f.* despecification.

despegamiento *m.* décollement.

despersonalización *f.* depersonalization.

despertar[1] *m.* arousal.

despertar[2] *m.* emergence.

despigmentación *f.* depigmentation.

despiojamiento *m.* delousing.

desplasmólisis *f.* deplasmolysis.

desplazabilidad *f.* displaceability.

desplazabilidad de tejidos tissue displaceability.

desplazamiento[1] *m.* displacement.

desplazamiento del afecto affect displacement.

desplazamiento en anzuelo fish-hook displacement.

desplazamiento de carácter character displacement.

desplazamiento competitivo competitive displacement.

desplazamiento condíleo condylar displacement.

desplazamiento fetal fetal displacement.

desplazamiento hístico tissue displacement.

desplazamiento pélvico lateral lateral pelvic displacement.

desplazamiento tisular tissue displacement.

desplazamiento vesicular gallbladder displacement.

desplazamiento[2] *m.* drift.

desplazamiento antigénico antigenic drift.

desplazamiento genético genetic drift.

desplazamiento[3] *m.* drifting.

desplazamiento[4] *m.* shift.

desplazamiento axial axis shift.

desplazamiento de cloruros chloride shift.

desplazamiento hacia la derecha shift to the right.

desplazamiento de Doppler Doppler shift.

desplazamiento hacia la izquierda shift to the left.

desplazamiento de Purkinje Purkinje shift.

desplazamiento del umbral threshold shift.

desplomar *v.* de-lead.

despoblación *f.* depopulation.

despolarización *f.* depolarization.

despolarización dendrítica dendritic depolarization.

despolarización diastólica lenta slow diastolic depolarization.

despolarizador *m.* depolarizer.

despolarizar *v.* depolarize.
despolimerización *f.* depolymerization.
despolimerizar *v.* depolymerize.
desprendimiento *m.* detachment.
 desprendimiento de coroides choroidal detachment.
 desprendimiento epifisario epiphytical detachment.
 desprendimiento del epitelio pigmentario retinal pigment epithelium detachment.
 desprendimiento exudativo de la retina exudative retinal detachment.
 desprendimiento de los miembros detachment of members.
 desprendimiento de la placenta, desprendimiento placentario detachment of the placenta, placental detachment.
 desprendimiento posterior del vítreo posterior vitreous detachment.
 desprendimiento regmatógeno de la retina rhegmatogenous retinal detachment.
 desprendimiento de la retina, desprendimiento de retina, desprendimiento retiniano detachment of the retina, retinal detachment.
 desprendimiento de retina exudativo exudative retinal detachment.
 desprendimiento vítreo vitreous detachment.
desproporción *f.* disproportion.
 desproporción cefalopélvica (DCP) cephalopelvic disproportion (CPD).
desproteinización *f.* deproteinization.
despulpado, -da *adj.* pulpless.
desrealización *f.* derealization.
desreflexión *f.* dereflection.
desrepresión *f.* derepression.
desrotación *f.* derotation.
destello *m.* flicker.
desternalización *f.* desternalization.
destetado, -da *m., f.* weanling.
destetar *v.* wean.
destete *m.* weaning.
destilación *f.* distillation.
 destilación destructiva destructive distillation.
 destilación fraccionada, destilación fraccional fractional distillation.
 destilación molecular molecular distillation.
 destilación seca dry distillation.
 destilación al vacío, destilación en el vacío vacuum distillation.
destilado *m.* distillate.
destilar *v.* distill.
destino *m.* fate.
 destino prospectivo prospective fate.
destorsión *f.* detorsion.
destoxicación *f.* detoxication.
destoxificación *f.* detoxification.
destoxicar *v.* detoxicate.
destoxificar *v.* detoxify.
destreza *f.* skill.
destructivo, -va *adj.* destructive.
destrudo *m.* destrudo.
destubación *f.* detubation.
Desulfomonas Desulfomonas.
desvanecimiento *m.* dizziness.
desvascularización *f.* devascularization.
desvenador *m.* stripper.
desvenamiento *m.* strip.
desviación[1] *f.* bias.
desviación[2] *f.* deviance, deviation.
desviación[3] *f.* deviation.
 desviación animal animal deviation.
 desviación de la columna vertebral spinal column deviation.

 desviación del complemento complement deviation.
 desviación conjugada, desviación conjugada de los ojos conjugate deviation, conjugate deviation of the eyes.
 desviación a la derecha, desviación hacia la derecha deviation to the right.
 desviación derecha del eje right axis deviation (RAD).
 desviación de los dientes deviation of the teeth.
 desviación del eje, desviación del eje eléctrico axis deviation.
 desviación estándar (DE) standard deviation (SD).
 desviación estándar de una muestra sample standard deviation.
 desviación estrábica strabismal deviation, strabismic deviation, squint deviation.
 desviación de Hering-Hellebrand Hering-Hellebrand deviation.
 desviación inmunitaria, desviación inmunológica immune deviation.
 desviación a la izquierda, desviación hacia la izquierda deviation to the left.
 desviación izquierda del eje left axis deviation (LAD).
 desviación latente latent deviation.
 desviación de la lengua deviation of the tongue.
 desviación manifiesta manifest deviation.
 desviación mínima minimal deviation, minimum deviation.
 desviación de la norma deviation from normal.
 desviación oblicua skew deviation.
 desviación del ojo eye deviation.
 desviación orgánica organic deviation.
 desviación primaria primary deviation.
 desviación secundaria secondary deviation.
 desviación sesgada skew deviation.
 desviación sexual sexual deviation.
 desviación social social deviation.
 desviación uterina uterine deviation.
 desviación vertical disociada dissociated vertical deviation.
desviación[4] *f.* drift.
 desviación antigénica antigenic drift.
 desviación cubital ulnar drift.
 desviación genética genetic drift.
desviación[5] *f.* shift.
 desviación axial axis shift.
 desviación de cloruros chloride shift.
 desviación hacia la derecha shift to the right.
 desviación hacia la izquierda shift to the left.
 desviación luteoplacentaria luteoplacental shift.
 desviación de Purkinje Purkinje shift.
 desviación química chemical shift.
 desviación sanguínea regenerativa regenerative blood shift.
desviado, -da *adj.* deviant.
 desviado sexual sexual deviant.
desviómetro *m.* deviometer.
desvisceración *f.* devisceration.
desvitalización *f.* devitalization.
 desvitalización pulpar pulp devitalization.
desvitalizado, -da *adj.* devitalized.
desvitalizar *v.* devitalize.
desyodación *f.* deiodination.
detección *f.* counting, detection, screening.
 detección por coincidencia coincidence counting.
 detección de heterocigotos heterozygote detection.

 detección selectiva genética genetic screening.
 detección selectiva multifásica multiphasic screening.
detectar *v.* detect.
detector *m.* detector.
 detector de aire air detector.
 detector automático de infiltración automatic infiltration detector.
 detector de centelleo scintillation detector.
 detector cerámico ceramic detector.
 detector de mentiras lie detector.
 detector proporcional de gas proportional gas detector.
 detector de radiación radiation detector.
detergente *adj.* detergent.
deterioro *m.* deterioration, impairment, loss.
 deterioro alcohólico alcoholic deterioration.
 deterioro auditivo hearing loss.
 deterioro mental mental impairment.
 deterioro senil senile deterioration.
determinación[1] *f.* ascertainment.
 determinación aislada single ascertainment.
 determinación completa complete ascertainment.
 determinación incompleta incomplete ascertainment.
 determinación trunca truncate ascertainment.
determinación[2] *f.* determination, measurement.
 determinación directa de la tensión arterial direct measurement of blood pressure.
 determinación embrionaria embryonic determination.
 determinación de gases en sangre blood gas determination.
 determinación en serie serial determination.
 determinación del sexo, determinación sexual sex determination.
determinante *m. y adj.* determinant.
 determinante alotípico allotypic determinant.
 determinante anterior de la cúspide anterior determinant of cusp.
 determinante antigénico antigenic determinant.
 determinante antigénico idiotípico idiotypic antigenic determinant.
 determinante de enfermedad disease determinant.
 determinante genético genetic determinant.
 determinante inmunogénico immunogenic determinant.
 determinante isoalotípico isoallotypic determinant.
 determinante de la marcha gait determinant.
 determinante de oclusión determinant of occlusion.
 determinante oculto hidden determinant.
 determinante psíquico psychic determinant.
 determinante secuencial sequential determinant.
determinismo *m.* determinism.
 determinismo psíquico psychic determinism.
detersivo *m.* detersive.
detiroidismo *m.* dethyroidism.
detiroidizar *v.* dethyroidize.
detonación *f.* detonation.
detorsión *f.* detorsion.
detoxificar *v.* detoxify.
detrición *f.* detrition.
detrito *m.* detritus.
detritos *m.* débris.
detritus *m.* detritus.
detrusor *adj.* detrusor.

detumescencia *f.* detumescence.
deturgescencia *f.* deturgescence.
deuda *f.* debt.
   deuda de oxígeno oxygen debt.
   deuda de oxígeno aláctico alactic oxygen debt.
   deuda de oxígeno lactácido lactacid oxygen debt.
deutan *adj., m., f.* deutan.
deutencéfalo *m.* deutencephalon.
deuteranomalía *f.* deuteranomaly.
deuteranómalo, -la¹ *adj.* deuteranomalous.
deuteranómalo, -la² *m., f.* deutan, deuteranomal.
deuteranomalopía *f.* deuteranomalopia.
deuteranope *m., f.* deuteranope.
deuteranopía *f.* deuteranopia.
deuteranópico, -ca *adj.* deuteranopic.
deuteranopsia *f.* deuteranopsia.
deuterograsa *f.* deuterofat.
deuterohemina *f.* deuterohemin.
deuterohemofilia *f.* deuterohemophilia.
deuteromerito *m.* deuteromerite.
deuteromiceto *m.* deuteromycete.
Deuteromyces Deuteromycetes.
Deuteromycetae Deuteromycetes.
Deuteromycetes Deuteromycetes.
deuteronomalopsia *f.* deuteronomalopsia.
deuteropatía *f.* deuteropathy.
deuteropático, -ca *adj.* deuteropathic.
deuteroplasma *m.* deuteroplasm.
deuterosoma *m.* deuterosome.
deuterotocia *f.* deuterotoky.
deuterotoquia *f.* deuterotoky.
deutogénico, -ca *adj.* deutogenic.
deutomerito *m.* deutomerite.
deutoplasma *m.* deutoplasm.
deutoplasmático, -ca *adj.* deutoplasmic.
deutoplasmígeno, -na *adj.* deutoplasmigenon.
deutoplasmólisis *f.* deutoplasmolysis.
devolución *f.* devolution.
devolutivo, -va *adj.* devolutive.
dewar *m.* dewar.
dexiocardia *f.* dexiocardia.
dexiotrópico, -ca *adj.* dexiotropic.
dextrad *adj.* dextrad.
dextralidad *f.* dextrality.
dextraural *adj.* dextraural.
dextrinosis *f.* dextrinosis.
   dextrinosis límite, dextrinosis límite por deficiencia de desramificación *f.* debranching deficiency limit dextrinosis.
dextrinuria *f.* dextrinuria.
dextrocardia *f.* dextrocardia.
   dextrocardia aislada isolated dextrocardia.
   dextrocardia corregida corrected dextrocardia.
   dextrocardia falsa false dextrocardia.
   dextrocardia en imagen en espejo mirror-image dextrocardia.
   dextrocardia secundaria secondary dextrocardia.
   dextrocardia con situs inversus dextrocardia with situs inversus.
   dextrocardia tipo 1 type 1 dextrocardia.
   dextrocardia tipo 2 type 2 dextrocardia.
   dextrocardia tipo 3 type 3 dextrocardia.
   dextrocardia tipo 4 type 4 dextrocardia.
dextrocardiograma *m.* dextrocardiogram.
dextrocerebral *adj.* dextrocerebral.
dextrocicloducción *f.* dextrocycloduction.
dextroclinación *f.* dextroclination.
dextrocular *adj.* dextrocular, right-eyed.
dextrocularidad *f.* dextrocularity.

dextroducción *f.* dextroduction.
dextrogastria *f.* dextrogastria.
dextrogiración *f.* dextrogyration.
dextrógiro, -ra *adj.* dextrogyral.
dextrograma *m.* dextrogram.
dextromano, -na *adj.* dextromanual, right-handed.
dextromanual *adj.* dextromanual.
dextroocular *adj.* dextrocular.
dextropedal *adj.* dextropedal, right-footed.
dextroposición *f.* dextroposition.
   dextroposición del corazón dextroposition of the heart.
dextrorrotación *f.* dextrorotation.
dextrorrotatorio, -ria *adj.* dextrorotary, dextrorotatory.
dextrosinistro, -tra *adj.* dextrosinistral.
dextrosuria *f.* dextrosuria.
dextrotrópico, -ca *adj.* dextrotropic.
dextrotorsión *f.* dextrotorsion.
dextroversión *f.* dextroversion.
   dextroversión del corazón dextroversion of the heart.
dextrovertido, -da *adj.* dextroverted.
deyección *f.* dejection.
diabetes *f.* diabetes.
   diabetes del adulto type II diabetes.
   diabetes albuminúrica diabetes albuminurinicus.
   diabetes alimentaria alimentary diabetes.
   diabetes aloxánica, diabetes por aloxano alloxan diabetes.
   diabetes artificial artificial diabetes.
   diabetes azucarada diabetes mellitus.
   diabetes bronceada bronze diabetes.
   diabetes calcinúrica calcinuric diabetes.
   diabetes cerebroespinal cerebrospinal diabetes.
   diabetes clínica clinical diabetes.
   diabetes de comienzo en el crecimiento growth-onset diabetes.
   diabetes de comienzo en la edad adulta adult-onset diabetes.
   diabetes de comienzo en la juventud juvenile onset diabetes.
   diabetes de comienzo en la madurez maturity-onset diabetes.
   diabetes de comienzo en la madurez de la juventud maturity-onset diabetes of youth (MODY).
   diabetes cutánea skin diabetes.
   diabetes con deficiencia de insulina insulin-deficient diabetes.
   diabetes por derramamiento overflow diabetes.
   diabetes disimulada masked diabetes.
   diabetes del embarazo pregnancy diabetes.
   diabetes esteroide, diabetes esteroidea steroid diabetes.
   diabetes experimental experimental diabetes.
   diabetes floricínica phlorhizin diabetes.
   diabetes fosfatúrica phosphate diabetes.
   diabetes frágil brittle diabetes.
   diabetes frustrada subclinical diabetes.
   diabetes glucémica diabetes mellitus.
   diabetes iatrogénica iatrogenic diabetes.
   diabetes idiopática idiopathic diabetes.
   diabetes por inanición starvation diabetes.
   diabetes inestable brittle diabetes.
   diabetes inocente diabetes innocens.
   diabetes inositus diabetes inositus.
   diabetes insípida diabetes insipidus.
   diabetes insípida nefrogénica nephrogenic diabetes insipidus.

   diabetes insulinodependiente insulin-dependent diabetes.
   diabetes intermitente diabetes intermittens.
   diabetes no insulinodependiente non-insulin dependent diabetes.
   diabetes juvenil juvenile diabetes.
   diabetes de Lancereaux pancreatic diabetes.
   diabetes latente latent diabetes.
   diabetes lipoatrófica lipoatrophic diabetes.
   diabetes lipógena lipogenous diabetes.
   diabetes lipopletórica lipoplethoric diabetes.
   diabetes lipúrica lipuric diabetes.
   diabetes manifiesta overt diabetes.
   diabetes mellitus (DM) diabetes mellitus (DM).
   diabetes mellitus endocrina endocrine diabetes mellitus.
   diabetes mellitus gestacional (DMG) gestational diabetes mellitus (GDM).
   diabetes mellitus insulinodependiente (DMID) insulin-dependent diabetes mellitus (IDDM).
   diabetes mellitus no insulinodependiente (DMNID) non-insulin-dependent diabetes mellitus (NIDDM).
   diabetes de Mosler Mosler's diabetes.
   diabetes nefrogénica nephrogenic diabetes.
   diabetes nerviosa neurogenous diabetes.
   diabetes neurógena neurogenous diabetes.
   diabetes no insulinodependiente (DNID) non-insulin dependent diabetes (NIDD).
   diabetes pancreática pancreatic diabetes.
   diabetes pasajera temporary diabetes.
   diabetes potencial potencial diabetes.
   diabetes preclínica preclinic diabetes.
   diabetes por punción puncture diabetes.
   diabetes química chemical diabetes.
   diabetes renal renal diabetes.
   diabetes resistente a la cetosis ketosis-resistant diabetes.
   diabetes sacarina diabetes mellitus.
   diabetes simple simple diabetes.
   diabetes subclínica subclinical diabetes.
   diabetes temporal temporary diabetes.
   diabetes con tendencia a la cetosis ketosis-prone diabetes.
   diabetes por tiazida thiazide diabetes.
   diabetes tipo I type I diabetes.
   diabetes tipo II type II diabetes.
   diabetes tóxica toxic diabetes.
   diabetes verdadera true diabetes.
diabético, -ca *adj.* diabetic.
diabétide *m.* diabetid.
diabetogénico, -ca *adj.* diabetogenic.
diabetógeno, -na *adj.* diabetogenous.
diabetógrafo *m.* diabetograph.
diabetología *f.* diabetology.
diabetómetro *m.* diabetometer.
diabolepsia diabolepsy.
diabrosis *f.* diabrosis.
diabrótico, -ca *adj.* diabrotic.
diacetemia *f.* diacetemia.
diaceticaciduria *f.* diaceticaciduria.
diacetonuria *f.* diacetonuria.
diaceturia *f.* diaceturia.
diácido *m.* diacid.
diacinesis *f.* diakinesis.
diaclasia *f.* diaclasia, diaclasis.
diaclasis *f.* diaclasia, diaclasis.
diaclasto *m.* diaclast.
diaclismosis *f.* enteroclysis.
diacrino, -na *adj.* diacrinous.
diacrisis *f.* diacrisis.
diacrítico, -ca *adj.* diacritic, diacritical.

diacrónico, -ca *adj.* diachronic.
diactínico, -ca *adj.* diactinic.
diactinismo *m.* diactinism.
díada *f.* dyad.
diadérmico, -ca *adj.* diadermic.
diadermo *m.* diaderm.
diadococinesia *f.* diadochokinesia.
diadococinético, -ca *adj.* diadochokinesis.
diafanidad *f.* diaphaneity.
diáfano, -na *adj.* diaphane.
diafanometría *f.* diaphanometry.
diafanómetro *m.* diaphanometer.
diafanoscopia *f.* diaphanoscopy.
diafanoscopio *m.* diaphanoscope.
diáfisis *f.* diaphysis, shaft.
diafemétrico, -ca *adj.* diaphemetric.
diafiláctico, -ca *adj.* prophylactic.
diafisario, -ria *adj.* diaphyseal.
diafisectomía *f.* diaphysectomy.
diafisistis *f.* diaphysitis.
diaforesis *f.* diaphoresis.
diaforético, -ca *adj.* diaphoretic.
diafragma¹ *m.* diaphragm.
diafragma² *m.* diaphragm.
  diafragma de Akerlund Akerlund diaphragm.
  diafragma anticonceptivo contraceptive diaphragm.
  diafragma anticonceptivo de espiral arcing spring contraceptive diaphragm.
  diafragma anticonceptivo de muelle espiral coil-spring contraceptive diaphragm.
  diafragma anticonceptivo de resorte plano flat spring contraceptive diaphragm.
  diafragma de Bucky, diafragma de Bucky-Potter Bucky diaphragm, Bucky-Potter diaphragm.
  diafragma de Potter-Bucky Potter-Bucky diaphragm.
  diafragma vaginal vaginal diaphragm.
diafragmalgia *f.* diaphragmalgia.
diafragmático, -ca *adj.* diaphragmatic.
diafragmatitis *f.* diaphragmitis.
diafragmatocele *m.* diaphragmatocele.
diafragmodinia *f.* diaphragmodynia.
diagnosticador, -ra *m., f.* diagnostician.
diagnosticar *v.* diagnose.
diagnóstico *m.* diagnosis.
  diagnóstico antenatal antenatal diagnosis.
  diagnóstico biológico biological diagnosis.
  diagnóstico citológico, diagnóstico cito-histológico cytohistologic diagnosis.
  diagnóstico clínico clinical diagnosis.
  diagnóstico diferencial differencial diagnosis.
  diagnóstico directo direct diagnosis.
  diagnóstico ex juvantibus diagnosis ex-juvantibus.
  diagnóstico por exclusión diagnosis by exclusion.
  diagnóstico de Ficker Ficker diagnosis.
  diagnóstico físico physical diagnosis.
  diagnóstico de laboratorio laboratory diagnosis.
  diagnóstico neonatal neonatal diagnosis.
  diagnóstico de nivel niveau diagnosis.
  diagnóstico patológico pathologic diagnosis.
  diagnóstico prenatal prenatal diagnosis.
  diagnóstico provocado provocative diagnosis.
  diagnóstico serológico serum diagnosis.
  diagnóstico topográfico topographic diagnosis.
diagnosticum diagnosticum.
diágrafo *m.* diagraph.

diagrama *m.* diagram.
  diagrama de Punnet Punnett square.
  diagrama de Werner Werner diagram.
diagramático, -ca *adj.* diagrammatic.
dial *m.* dial.
dialectolisis *f.* ionization.
dialisancia *f.* dialysance.
diálisis *f.* dialysis.
  diálisis cruzada cross dialysis.
  diálisis por equilibrio equilibrium dialysis.
  diálisis extracorpórea extracorporeal dialysis.
  diálisis de linfa lymph dialysis.
  diálisis peritoneal peritoneal dialysis.
  diálisis peritoneal ambulatoria continua (DPAC) continuous ambulatory peritoneal dialysis (CAPD).
  diálisis renal renal dialysis.
  diálisis de la retina, diálisis retiniana dialysis retinae.
dializable *adj.* dialyzable.
dialización *f.* dialysance.
dializador, -ra *m., f.* dialysate.
dializador *m.* dialyzer.
dializar *v.* dialyze.
diamagnético, -ca *adj.* diamagnetic.
diamagnetismo *m.* diamagnetism.
diámetro *m.* diameter.
diaminuria *f.* diaminuria.
diamnótico, -ca *adj.* diamnotic.
diamorfosis *f.* diamorphosis.
diandria *f.* diandry, diandria.
dianoético, -ca *adj.* dianoetic.
Diantamoeba Diantamoeba.
diantebraquia *f.* diantebrachia.
diapasón *m.* diapason.
diapausa *f.* diapause.
  diapausa embrionaria embryonic diapause.
diapédesis *f.* diapedesis.
diaphragma *f.* diaphragma.
diapiesis *f.* diapyesis.
diapiético, -ca *adj.* diapyetic.
diapiresis *f.* diapiresis.
diaplacentario, -ria *adj.* diaplacenta.
diaplasis *f.* diaplasis.
diaplástico, -ca *adj.* diaplastic.
diaplex *m.* diaplexus.
diaplexo *m.* diaplexus.
diapnoico, -ca *adj.* diapnoic.
diapnótico, -ca *adj.* diapnotic.
diapófisis *f.* diapophysis.
diarrea *f.* diarrhea.
  diarrea ablactorum diarrhea ablactorum.
  diarrea acuosa watery diarrhea.
  diarrea aguda acute diarrhea.
  diarrea alba diarrhea alba.
  diarrea por alimentación dietética dietetic food diarrhea.
  diarrea de las alturas hill diarrhea.
  diarrea blanca white diarrhea.
  diarrea por chicle chewing gum diarrhea.
  diarrea coleraica, diarrea coleriforme choleraic diarrhea.
  diarrea colicuativa colliquative diarrhea.
  diarrea de las colinas hill diarrhea.
  diarrea congénita con cloruro congenital chloride diarrhea.
  diarrea crítica critical diarrhea.
  diarrea del destete diarrhea ablactatorum.
  diarrea disentérica dysentric diarrhea.
  diarrea entérica enteral diarrhea.
  diarrea epidémica del neonato, diarrea epidémica del recién nacido epidemic diarrhea of the newborn.
  diarrea estercorácea stercoral diarrhea.

  diarrea estival summer diarrhea.
  diarrea familiar con cloruro familial chloride diarrhea.
  diarrea fermentativa fermental diarrhea, fermentative diarrhea.
  diarrea por flagelados flagellate diarrhea.
  diarrea gastrógena gastrogenous diarrhea.
  diarrea grasa fatty diarrhea.
  diarrea infantil infantile diarrhea.
  diarrea intestinal enteral diarrhea.
  diarrea irritativa irritative diarrhea.
  diarrea lientérica lienteric diarrhea.
  diarrea matinal morning diarrhea.
  diarrea mecánica mecanical diarrhea.
  diarrea membranosa membranous diarrhea.
  diarrea mucosa mucous diarrhea.
  diarrea neonatal neonatal diarrhea.
  diarrea nocturna nocturnal diarrhea.
  diarrea osmótica osmotic diarrhea.
  diarrea pancreatógena pancreatogenous diarrhea.
  diarrea paradójica paradoxical diarrhea.
  diarrea parenteral parenteral diarrhea.
  diarrea promontoria promontory diarrhea.
  diarrea purulenta purulent diarrhea.
  diarrea putrefactiva putrefactive diarrhea.
  diarrea quilosa diarrhea chylosa.
  diarrea serosa serous diarrhea.
  diarrea simple simple diarrhea.
  diarrea de las trincheras trench diarrhea.
  diarrea tropical tropical diarrhea.
  diarrea tubular diarrhea tubular.
  diarrea urémica uremic diarrhea.
  diarrea del viajero traveler's diarrhea.
  diarrea viral, diarrea virósica, diarrea por virus virus diarrhea.
diarreico, -ca *adj.* diarrheal, diarrheic.
diarreógeno, -na *adj.* diarrheogenic.
diarticular *v.* diarticular.
diártrico, -ca *adj.* diarthric.
diartrodial *adj.* diarthrodial.
diartrosis *f.* diarthrosis.
  diartrosis rotatoria rotatory diarthrosis.
diascopia *f.* diascopy].
diascopio *m.* diascope.
diaspironecrosis *f.* diaspironecrosis.
diasquisis *f.* diaschisis.
diastalsis *f.* diastalsis.
diastáltico, -ca *adj.* diastaltic.
diastásico, -ca *adj.* diastasic.
diastasimetría *f.* diastasimetry.
diastasis *f.* diastasis.
  diastasis cardiaca, diastasis cordis diastasis cordis.
  diastasis del iris iris diastasis.
  diastasis recti abdominis diastasis recti abdominis.
diastasuria *f.* diastasuria.
diastático, -ca, diastásico, -ca *adj.* diastatic.
diastema *m.* diastema.
diastematocrania *f.* diastematocrania.
diastematomielia *f.* diastematomyelia.
diastematopielia *f.* diastematopyelia.
diáster *m.* diaster.
diástole *f.* diastole.
  diástole cardiaca cardiac diastole.
diastólico, -ca *adj.* diastolic.
diastrofia *f.* diastrophism.
diastrofismo *m.* diastrophism.
diataxia *f.* diataxia.
  diataxia cerebral cerebral diataxia.
diatela *f.* diatela.
diatermancia *f.* diathermancy.
diatermia *f.* diathermy.
  diatermia de onda corta short wave diathermy.

diatermia por ondas ultracortas ultrashort wave diathermy.
diatermia quirúrgica surgical diathermy.
diatérmico, -ca *adj.* diathermal.
diatermocoagulación *f.* diathermocoagultion.
diatésico, -ca *adj.* diathetic.
diátesis *f.* diathesis.
diátesis aneurismática aneurysmal diathesis.
diátesis artrítica arthritic diathesis.
diátesis asténica asthenic diathesis.
diátesis biliosa bilious diathesis.
diátesis catarral catharral diathesis.
diátesis de contractura contractural diathesis.
diátesis de Czerny Czerny's diathesis.
diátesis diastrófica gouty diathesis.
diátesis espasmódica, diátesis espasmofílica spasmodic diathesis, spasmophilic diathesis.
diátesis exudativa exudative diathesis.
diátesis exudativa linfática Czerny's diathesis.
diátesis fibroplástica fibroplastic diathesis.
diátesis gotosa gouty diathesis.
diátesis hemorrágica hemorrhagic diathesis.
diátesis hemorrágica del neonato hemorrhagic diathesis of the newborn.
diátesis inopéctica inopectic diathesis.
diátesis lupoide lupus diathesis.
diátesis neuropática neuropathic diathesis.
diátesis osificante ossifying diathesis.
diátesis oxálica oxalic diathesis.
diátesis psicopática psychopathic diathesis.
diátesis quística cystic diathesis.
diátesis reumática rheumatic diathesis.
diátesis tuberculosa tuberculous diathesis.
diátesis úrica urica diathesis.
diatómico, -ca *adj.* diatomic.
diatórico *m.* diatoric.
diauqueno *m.* diauchenos.
diazona *m.* diazone.
diazonal *adj.* diazonal.
dibásico, -ca *adj.* dibasic.
dibraquia *f.* dibrachia.
dibraquio *m.* dibrachius.
dicefalia *f.* dicephaly.
dicéfalo, -la *m.* dicephalus.
dicéfalo diauqueno dicephalus diauchenos.
dicéfalo monauqueno dicephalus monauchenos.
dicéfalo dipus dibrachius dicephalus dipus dibrachius.
dicéfalo dipus tetrabrachius dicephalus dipus tetrabrachius.
dicéfalo dipygus dicephalus dipygus.
dicéfalo parásito dicephalus parasiticus.
dicelo, -la *adj.* dicelous.
dicéleo, -a *adj.* dicelous.
dicéntrico, -ca *adj.* dicentric.
dicigótico, -ca *adj.* dizygotic, dizygous.
dicigoto, -ta *adj.* dizygotic, dizygous.
diclidistosis *f.* diclodostosis.
diclidistis *f.* dicliditis.
diclidostosis *f.* diclodostosis.
diclidotomia *f.* diclodotomy.
dicogenia *f.* dichogeny.
dicoria *f.* dicoria.
dicorial *adj.* dichorial.
dicoriónico, -ca *adj.* dichorionic.
dicotomía *f.* dichotomy.
dicotomización *f.* dichotomization.
dicroico, -ca *adj.* dichroic.
dicroísmo *m.* dichroism.
dicromasia *f.* dichromasy.

dicrómata *adj.* dichromat.
dicromático, -ca *adj.* dichromatic.
dicromatismo *m.* dichromatism.
dicromatopsia *f.* dichromatopsia.
dicrómico, -ca *adj.* dichromic.
dicromodermia *f.* dyschromia.
dicromofilia *f.* dichromophilism.
dicromófilo, -la *adj.* dichromophil, dichromophile.
dicrótico, -ca *adj.* dicrotic.
dicrotismo *m.* dicrotism.
dictiocinesis *f.* dictyokinesis.
dictioma *m.* diktyoma.
dictiosoma *m.* dictyosome.
dictiotene *m.* dictyotene.
dictioteno *m.* dictyotene.
dictitis *f.* retinitis.
dichuchwa *f.* dichuchwa.
didactilismo *m.* didactylism.
didactilo, -la *adj.* didactylous.
didelfia *f.* didelphia.
didélfico, -ca *adj.* didelphic.
didimalgia *f.* didymalgia.
didimitis *f.* didymitis.
dídimo *m.* didymus.
didimodinia *f.* didymodinia.
diecoscopio *m.* diechoscope.
dieléctrico, -ca *adj.* dielectric.
dielectrolisis *f.* dielectrolysis.
diembrionía *f.* diembryony.
diencefálico, -ca *adj.* diancephalic.
diencéfalo *m.* diencephalon.
diencefalohipofisiario, -ria *adj.* diencephalohypophyseal.
Dientamoeba Dientamoeba.
diente *m.* tooth, dens.
diente de acrílico acrylic resin tooth.
diente anatómico anatomic tooth.
diente no anatómico non-anatomic tooth.
diente artificial artificial tooth.
diente de clavillos cruzados cross-pin tooth.
diente complementario supplemental tooth.
diente decidual deciduous tooth.
diente despulpado pulpless tooth.
diente en destornillador screwdriver tooth.
diente desvitalizado devitalized tooth.
diente no erupcionado unerupted tooth.
diente errante wandering of a tooth.
diente esclerótico sclerotic tooth.
diente espaciado spaced tooth.
diente de espiga recta straightpin tooth.
diente extruido extruded tooth.
diente fantasma ghost tooth.
diente fluorado fluoridated tooth.
diente de Fournier Fournier tooth.
diente fuera de lugar snaggle tooth.
diente fusionado fused tooth.
diente geminado geminated tooth.
diente de Goslee Goslee tooth.
diente de grado cero zero degree tooth.
diente de Horner Horner's tooth.
diente de Hutchinson screwdriver tooth.
diente impactado impacted tooth.
diente con inserción de metal metal insert tooth.
diente intruido embedded tooth.
diente del juicio wisdom tooth.
diente de leche milk tooth, dens lacteus.
diente malacótico malacotic tooth.
diente en malposición malposed tooth.
diente manchado mottled tooth.
diente migratorio migrating tooth.
diente en mora mulberry tooth.
diente en mordida cruzada crossbite tooth.
diente muerto dead tooth.

diente con muescas notched tooth.
diente natal natal tooth.
diente neonatal neonatal tooth.
diente no anatómico non-anatomic tooth.
diente no vital non-vital tooth.
diente permanente permanent tooth.
diente de plástico plastic tooth.
diente en posición normal normally posed tooth.
diente prelácteo premilk tooth.
diente prematuro premature tooth.
diente primario primary tooth.
diente prominente buck tooth.
diente protruido protruding tooth.
diente queoplástico cheoplastic tooth.
diente en rastrillo rake tooth.
diente de resina acrílica acrylic resin tooth.
diente salido buck tooth.
diente secundario second tooth.
diente serotino dens serotinus.
diente sifilítico syphilitic tooth.
diente sumergido submerged tooth.
diente supernumerario supernumerary tooth.
diente temporal temporary tooth.
diente en tubo tube tooth.
diente de Turner Turner's tooth.
diente verde green tooth.
diente vital vital tooth.
diéresis *f.* dieresis.
diéresis espontánea spontaneous dieresis.
dierético, -ca *adj.* dieretic.
diesófago *m.* diesophagus.
diestro, -tra *adj.* dextromanual.
dieta *f.* diet.
dieta absoluta absolute diet.
dieta ácida acid-ash diet.
dieta adecuada adequate diet.
dieta de adelgazamiento reduction diet.
dieta alcalina alkali-ash diet.
dieta animal animal diet.
dieta de arroz rice diet.
dieta baja en calorías low calorie diet.
dieta baja en purinas purine-low diet.
dieta basal basal diet.
dieta básica basic diet.
dieta blanda soft diet.
dieta de Cantani Cantani's diet.
dieta de cenizas ácidas acid-ash diet.
dieta de cenizas alcalinas alkali-ash diet.
dieta cetógenica ketogenic diet.
dieta completa full diet.
dieta de conservación de proteínas protein sparing diet.
dieta desencadenante provocative diet.
dieta diabética, dieta para diabéticos diabetic diet.
dieta de Duke Duke diet.
dieta elemental elemental diet.
dieta de eliminación elimination diet.
dieta equilibrada balanced diet.
dieta de Feingold Feingold diet.
dieta fibrosa fiber diet.
dieta de Giordano-Giovanneti Giordano-Giovannetti diet.
dieta para gotosos gouty diet.
dieta hídrica clear liquid diet.
dieta hipocalórica low-caloric diet.
dieta hiposódica low salt diet.
dieta de Keith Keith's low ionic diet.
dieta de Kempner Kempner's diet.
dieta láctea milk diet.
dieta libre de gluten gluten-free diet.
dieta libre de purinas ligera light diet.
dieta ligera light diet.
dieta líquida liquid diet.

dieta líquida clara clear liquid diet.
dieta líquida completa full liquid diet.
dieta macrobiótica macrobiotic diet.
dieta mixta mixed diet.
dieta de Moro-Heisler Moro-Heisler diet.
dieta óptima optimal diet.
dieta pobre en calcio low-calcium diet.
dieta pobre en calorías low calorie diet.
dieta pobre en colesterol low-cholesterol diet.
dieta pobre en grasas low fat diet.
dieta pobre en grasas saturadas low-saturated-fat diet.
dieta pobre en oxalato low oxalate diet.
dieta pobre en purina low purine diet.
dieta pobre en residuos low residue diet.
dieta de provocación challenge diet.
dieta raquítica rachitic diet.
dieta reductora reducing diet.
dieta regular regular diet.
dieta con restricción de purina purine restricted diet.
dieta rica en calorías high calorie diet.
dieta rica en fibra high fiber diet.
dieta rica en grasas high fat diet.
dieta rica en potasio high-potassium diet.
dieta rica en proteínas high protein diet.
dieta rica en vitaminas high-vitamin diet.
dieta sin gluten gluten-free diet.
dieta sin sal salt-free diet.
dieta de Schemm Schemm diet.
dieta de Schmidt, dieta Schmidt-Strassburger Schmidt diet, Schmidt-Strassburger diet.
dieta de Sippy Sippy diet.
dieta suave smooth diet.
dieta de subsistencia subsistence diet.
dieta de Taylor Taylor's diet.
dietética *f.* dietetics.
dietético, -ca *adj.* dietetic.
dietetista *m.* dietitian.
dietista *m.* dietitian.
dietogenética *f.* dietogenetics.
dietoterapia *f.* dietotherapy.
dietotoxicidad *f.* dietotoxicity.
difalia *f.* diphalia.
difalia *m.* diphallus.
difásico, -ca *adj.* diphasic.
diferencia *f.* difference.
diferencia arteriovenosa de dióxido de carbono arteriovenous carbon dioxide difference.
diferencia arteriovenosa de oxígeno arteriovenous oxygen difference.
diferencia individual individual difference.
diferencia luminosa light difference.
diferencia de oxígeno alveolar-arterial alveolar-arterial oxygen difference.
diferenciación *f.* differentiation.
diferenciación correlativa correlative differentiation.
diferenciación dependiente dependent differentiation.
diferenciación funcional functional differentiation.
diferenciación invisible invisible differentiation.
diferenciación propia self differentiation.
diferenciación regional regional differentiation.
diferenciado, -da *adj.* differentiated.
diferencial *adj.* differential.
diferenciar *v.* differentiate.
difonía *f.* diphonia.
difracción *f.* diffraction.
difracción de rayos X X-ray diffraction.

difteria *f.* diphtheria.
difteria aviaria avian diphtheria.
difteria de Bretonneau Bretonneau diphtheria.
difteria circunscrita circumscribed diphtheria.
difteria cutánea cutaneous diphtheria.
difteria dérmica cutaneous diphtheria.
difteria falsa false diphtheria.
difteria faríngea pharyngeal diphtheria.
difteria faucial faucial diphtheria.
difteria gangrenosa gangrenous diphtheria.
difteria grave diphtheria gravis.
difteria de las heridas wound diphtheria.
difteria laríngea laryngeal diphtheria.
difteria maligna malignant diphtheria.
difteria nasal nasal diphtheria.
difteria nasofaríngea nasopharyngeal diphtheria.
difteria quirúrgica surgical diphtheria.
difteria séptica septic diphtheria.
difteria umbilical umbilical diphtheria.
difterial *adj.* diphterial.
diftérico, -ca *adj.* diphtheritic.
difteritis *f.* diphtheritis.
difteroide *adj.* diphtheroid.
diftongia *f.* diphthongia.
difundido, -ca *adj.* diffuse.
difundir *v.* diffuse.
difusible *adj.* diffusible.
difusiómetro *m.* diffusiometer.
difusión *f.* diffusion.
difusión doble double diffusion.
difusión doble unidimensional double diffusion in one dimension.
difusión doble bidimensional double diffusion in two dimensions.
difusión facilitada facilitated diffusion.
difusión en gel, difusión de geles gel diffusion.
difusión impedida impeded diffusion.
difusión libre free diffusion.
difusión del pensamiento thought broadcasting.
difusión de recambio exchange diffusion.
difusión simple single diffusion.
difusión simple radial single radial diffusion.
difuso, -sa *adj.* diffuse.
difusograma *m.* scattergram.
digamético, -ca *adj.* digametic.
digástrico, -ca *adj.* digastric.
digenea *f.* digenea.
digenesia *f.* digenesis.
digerir *v.* digest.
digestión *f.* digestion.
digestión artificial artificial digestion.
digestión biliar bile digestion.
digestión del cieno sludge digestion.
digestión gástrica gastric digestion.
digestión gastrointestinal gastrointestinal digestion.
digestión intercelular intercellular digestion.
digestión intestinal intestinal digestion.
digestión intracelular intracellular digestion.
digestión laboriosa difficult digestion.
digestión lipolítica lipolytic digestion.
digestión pancreática pancreatic digestion.
digestión parenteral parenteral digestion.
digestión péptica peptic digestion.
digestión primaria primary digestion.
digestión salival salivary.
digestión secundaria secondary digestion.
digestivo, -va *adj.* digestant.
diginia *f.* digynia, digyny.
digitación *f.* digitation.

digitado, -da *adj.* digitate.
digital *adj.* digital.
digital *f.* digitalis.
digitalgia parestésica *f.* digitalgia paresthetica.
digitalismo *m.* digitalism.
digitalización *f.* digitalization.
digitatio digitatio.
digitiforme *adj.* digitiform.
dígito *m.* digit, digitus.
dígito claviforme clubbed digit.
digitoplantar *adj.* digitoplantar.
digitoxicidad *f.* digitoxicity.
digitus *m.* digitus.
digitus valgus digitus valgus.
digitus varus digitus varus.
diglosia *f.* diglossia.
dignato *m.* dignathus.
diheterocigoto *m.* diheterozygote.
dihíbrido *m.* dihybrid.
dihidratado, -da *adj.* dihydrated.
dihídrico, -ca *adj.* dihydric.
dihisteria *f.* dihysteria.
dihisterismo *m.* dihysteria.
dilaceración *f.* dilaceration.
dilaceración radicular radicular dilaceration, root dilaceration.
dilatación *f.* dilatation, dilation.
dilatación ab ingestis ab ingestis dilatation, ab ingestis dilation.
dilatación de los bronquios bronchiectasia, bronchiectasis.
dilatación cardíaca cardiac dilatation, cardiac dilation.
dilatación cervical cervical dilatation, cervical dilation.
dilatación cirsoidea cirsoid aneurysm.
dilatación congénita del colón congenital megacolon.
dilatación digital digital dilatation, digital dilation.
dilatación del estómago dilatation of the stomach, dilation of the stomach.
dilatación gástrica gastric dilatation, gastric dilation.
dilatación idiopática idiopathic dilatation, idiopathic dilation.
dilatación y legrado dilatation and curettage (D & C), dilation and curettage (D & C).
dilatación y legrado fraccionados fractional dilatation and curettage, fractional dilation and curettage.
dilatación postestenótica post-stenotic dilatation, post-stenotic dilation.
dilatación prognática, dilatación del prognatión prognathic dilatation, prognathic dilation.
dilatación tóxica del colon toxic dilatation of the colon, toxic dilation of the colon.
dilatación de la uretra, dilatación uretral urethral dilatation, urethral dilation.
dilatador *m.* dilator.
dilatador anal anal dilator.
dilatador de Arnott Arnott's dilator.
dilatador de Einhorn Einhorn's dilator.
dilatador de Goodell Goodell's dilator.
dilatador de Hanks Hanks' dilator.
dilatador de Hegar Hegar's dilator.
dilatador hidrostático hydrostatic dilator.
dilatador de Kollmann Kollmann's dilator.
dilatador laríngeo laryngeal dilator.
dilatador de Plummer Plummer's dilator.
dilatador de Seigneux Seigneux's dilator.
dilatador de Starck Starck's dilator.
dilatador de Tubbs Tubbs' dilator.

dilatador de Walther Walther's dilator.
dilatancia f. dilatancy.
dildo m. dildo.
dilecanus m. dilecanus.
dilución f. dilution.
 dilución de duplicación doubling dilution.
 dilución de nitrógeno nitrogen dilution.
 dilución seriada serial dilution.
diluente adj. diluent.
diluido, -da adj. dilute, diluted.
diluir v. dilute.
diluyente m. diluent.
dimelia f. dimelia.
dimelo m. dimelus.
dimensión f. dimension.
 dimensión bucolingual buccolingual dimension.
 dimensión de postura postural dimension.
 dimensión vertical vertical dimension.
 dimensión vertical oclusal occlusal vertical dimension.
 dimensión vertical en reposo rest vertical dimension.
dimetria f. dimetria.
dimidiado, -da adj. hemilateral.
dimidiar v. dimidiate.
dimorfobiótico, -ca adj. dimorphobiotic.
dinámica f. dynamics.
 dinámica de grupo group dynamics.
dinámico, -ca adj. dynamic.
dinamismo m. dynamism.
dinamización f. dynamization.
dinamogenia f. dynamogeny.
dinamogénesis f. dynamogenesis.
dinamogénico, -ca adj. dynamogenic.
dinamógeno, -na adj. dynamogenic.
dinamógrafo m. dynamograph.
dinamómetro m. dynamometer.
dinamopático, -ca adj. dynamopathic.
dinamoscopia f. dynamoscopy.
dinamoscopio m. dynamoscope.
dineína f. dynein.
dinérico, -ca adj. dineric.
dinéurico, -ca adj. dineuric.
dínico, -ca adj. dinical.
dinitrorresorcinol m. dinitroresorcinol.
dinofobia f. dinophobia.
diocele m. diocoele.
dionisíaco, -ca adj. dyonisiac.
dionismo m. dyonism.
diopsímetro m. diopsimeter.
dioptometría f. dioptometry.
dioptómetro m. dioptometer.
dioptría f. diopter.
 dioptría prismática prism diopter.
dióptrica f. dioptrics.
dióptrico, -ca adj. dioptric.
dioptrometría f. dioptometry.
dioptrómetro m. dioptometer.
dioptroscopia f. dioptroscopy.
diortosis f. diorthosis.
diótico, -ca adj. biauricular.
diovular adj. diovular.
diovulatorio, -a adj. diovulatory.
dióxido m. dioxide.
dip m. dip.
dipetalonemiasis f. dipetalonemiasis.
Diphyllobothriidae Diphyllobothriidae.
dipigo m. dipygus.
diplacusia f. diplacusis.
 diplacusia biaural diplacusis binauralis.
 diplacusia diaural disarmónica diplacusis binauralis dysharmonica.
 diplacusia disarmónica diplacusis dysharmonica.

diplacusia ecoica diplacusis echoica.
diplacusia monoaural diplacusis monauralis.
diplejía f. diplegia.
 diplejía atónica atonic diplegia.
 diplejía cerebral infantil cerebral infantile diplegia.
 diplejía espástica spastic diplegia.
 diplejía facial facial diplegia.
 diplejía facial congénita congenital facial diplegia.
 diplejía masticatoria masticatory diplegia.
dipléjico, -ca adj. diplegic.
diploalbuminuria f. diploalbuminuria.
diplobacilo m. diplobacillus.
 diplobacilo de Morax- Axenfeld Morax-Axenfeld diplobacillus.
diplobacteria f. diplobacteria.
diploblástico, -ca adj. diploblastic.
diplocardia f. diplocardia.
diplocefalia f. diplocephaly.
diplocéfalo m. diplocephalus.
diplococemia f. diplococcemia.
diplocócico, -ca adj. diplococcoid.
diplococo m. diplococcus.
diplococoide adj. diplococcoid.
diplocoria f. diplocoria.
diplodiatoxicosis f. diplodiatoxicosis.
diploe m. diploë.
diploético, -ca adj. diploetic.
diplofase f. diplophase.
diplofonia f. diplophonia.
diplogénésis f. diplogenesis.
diplograma m. diplogram.
diploico, -ca adj. diploic.
diploide adj. diploid.
diploidía f. diploidy.
diplomelituria f. diplomelituria.
diplomielia f. diplomyelia.
diploneural adj. diploneural.
diplonte m. diplont.
diplópago, -ga adj. diplopagus.
diplopía f. diplopia.
 diplopía binocular binocular diplopia.
 diplopía cruzada crossed diplopia.
 diplopía directa direct diplopia.
 diplopía estereoscópica stereoscopic diplopia.
 diplopía fisiológica physiological diplopia.
 diplopía heterónima heteronymous diplopia.
 diplopía homónima homonymous diplopia.
 diplopía horizontal horizontal diplopia.
 diplopía monocular monocular diplopia.
 diplopía paradójica paradoxical diplopia.
 diplopía simple simple diplopia.
 diplopía de torsión torsional diplopia.
 diplopía unicular monocular diplopia.
 diplopía vertical vertical diplopia.
diplopiomietro m. diplopiometer.
diplopodia f. diplopodia.
diploqueiria f. diplocheiria, diplochiria.
diploquiria f. diplocheiria, diplochiria.
diploscopía f. diploscopia.
diploscopio m. diploscope.
diplosoma m. diplosome.
diplosomancia f. diplosomatia.
diplosomía f. diplosomia.
diplotene m. diplotene.
diploteno m. diplotene.
dipo m. dipus.
dipodia f. dipodia.
diprósopo m. diprosopus.
 diprósopo tetroftalmo diprosopus tetrophthalmus.
diprotrizoato m. diprotrizoate.
dipséptico, -ca adj. dipsetic.

dipsesis f. dipsesis.
dipsógeno m. dipsogen.
dipsogénico, -ca adj. dipsogenic.
dipsomanía f. dipsomania.
diposis f. dipsosis.
dipsoterapia f. dipsotherapy.
dipygus m. dipygus.
dique m. dam.
 dique de goma, dique de hule rubber dam.
 dique posterior post dam.
diqueilia f. dicheilia, dichilia.
diquiria f. dicheiria, dichiria.
diquiro, -ra m., f. dicheirus.
directo, -ta adj. direct.
director, -ra m., f. director.
 director acanalado grooved director.
 director médico medical director.
directoscopio m. directoscope.
dirigación f. dirigation.
dirigomotor, -ra adj. dirigomotor.
dirrínico, -ca adj. dirhinic.
disacariduria f. disacchariduria.
disacusia f. dysacousia, dysacusia, dysacusis, auditory dyscsthesia.
disacusis f. dysacousia, dysacusia, dysacusis, auditory dysesthesia.
disacusma f. dysacousia, dysacusia, dysacusis, auditory dysesthesia.
disadrenalismo m. dysadrenalism.
disadrenia f. dysadrenia.
disafia f. dysaphia.
disáfico, -ca adj. dysaphic.
disalelognatia f. dysallilognathia.
disanagnosia f. dysanagnosia.
disantigrafía f. dysantigraphia.
disaptación f. dysaptation.
disarmonía f. disharmony.
 disarmonía oclusal occlusal disharmony.
disarteriotonía f. dysarteriotony.
disartria f. dysarthria.
 disartria espástica rigid dysarthria, spastic dysarthria.
 disartria literal dysarthria literalis.
 disartria silábica espasmódica dysarthria syllabaris spasmodica.
disártrico, -ca adj. dysarthric.
disartrosis f. dysarthrosis.
disasociación f. disassociation.
disautonomía f. dysautonomia.
 disautonomía familiar familial dysautonomia.
disbarismo m. dysbarism.
disbasia f. dysbasia.
 disbasia angioesclerótica, disbasia angiosclerótica, angiosclerótica intermitente dysbasia angiosclerotica, dysbasia intermittens angiosclerotica.
 disbasia angioespástica dysbasia angiospastica.
 disbasia lordótica progresiva dysbasia lordotica progressiva.
 disbasia neurasténica intermitente dysbasia neurasthenica intermittens.
disbetalipoproteinemia f. dysbetalipoproteinemia.
disbolismo m. dysbolism.
disbulia f. dysboulia, dysbulia.
disbúlico, -ca adj. dysboulic, dysbulic.
discalculia f. dyscalculia.
discaliemia f. dyskaliemia.
discapacidad f. disability.
 discapacidad para el aprendizaje learning disability.
 discapacidad de desarrollo (DD) developmental disability (DD).

discapacidad profesional occupational disability.

discariosis *f.* dyskaryosis.

discariótico, -ca *adj.* dyskaryotic.

discectomía *f.* discectomy, diskectomy.

discectomía percutánea percutaneous discectomy.

discefalia *f.* dyscephalia, dyscephaly.

discefalia mandibulooculofacial mandibulo-oculofacial dyscephaly, dyscephalia mandibulo-oculofacialis.

disciforme *adj.* disciform.

discinesia *f.* dyscinesia.

discinético, -ca *adj.* dyskinetic.

discisión *f.* discission.

discisión de la catarata cataract discission.

discisión del cuello uterino discission of the cervix uteri.

discisión de la pleura discission of the pleura.

discisión posterior posterior discission.

discitis *f.* discitis, diskitis.

disclinación *f.* disclination.

disco *m.* disc, disk, discus.

disco abrasivo abrasive disc.

disco de Bardeen Bardeen's disc.

disco de Blake Blake's disc.

disco blastodérmico blastodermic disc, blastodisk.

disco de Burlew Burlew disc.

disco de carborundo carborundum disc.

disco de las células de los bastones rod disc.

disco cónico conic disc.

disco cortante cutting disc.

disco dental dental disc.

disco de diamante diamond disc.

disco ectodérmico ectodermal disc.

disco embrionario embryonic disc.

disco de esmeril emery disc.

disco estenopeico, disco estenopaico stenopeic disc, stenopaic disc.

disco estroboscópico stroboscopic disc.

disco en forma de copa cupped disc.

disco de gelatina gelatin disc.

disco germinal, disco germinativo germ disc, germinal disc.

disco herniado herniated disc.

disco intercalado intercalated disc.

disco interpúbico interpubic disc, discus interpubicus.

disco intraarticular intra-articular disc.

disco de Merkel Merkel's disc.

disco micrométrico micrometer disc.

disco de Newton Newton's disc.

disco obstruido choked disc.

disco de papel de lija sandpaper disc.

disco de Plácido Plácido's disc.

disco primitivo de Bardeen Bardeen's primitive disc.

disco prolígero proligerous disc, discus proligerus.

disco protruido protruded disc.

disco pulidor polishing disc.

disco de Rekoss Rekoss disc.

disco roto, disco rupturado ruptured disc.

disco sacrococcígeo sacrococcygeal disc.

disco sanguíneo blood disc.

disco de Schiefferdecker Schiefferdecker's disc.

disco de sepia cuttlefish disc.

disco de tela cloth disc.

discoblástico, -ca *adj.* discoblastic.

discoblástula *f.* discoblastula.

discocito *m.* discocyte.

discóforo, -ra *adj.* discophorous.

discogástrula *f.* discogastrula.

discogenético, -ca *adj.* discogenetic.

discogénico, -ca *adj.* discogenic.

discografía *f.* discography, diskography.

discograma *m.* discogram, diskogram.

discoide *m. y adj.* discoid.

discoidectomía *f.* discoidectomy.

discolia *f.* dyscholia.

discondrogenésis *f.* dyschondrogenesis.

discondroplasia *f.* dyschondroplasia.

discondroplasia con hemangiomas dyschondroplasia with hemangiomas.

discondroplasia de Ollier Ollier's dyschondroplasia.

discondrosteosis *f.* dyschondrosteosis.

discontinuo, -a *adj.* discontinuous.

discopatía *f.* discopathy.

discopatía cervical traumática traumatic cervical discopathy.

discoplasma *m.* discoplasm.

discordancia *f.* discordance.

discordante *adj.* discordant.

discoria¹ *f.* discoria.

discoria² *f.* dyscoria.

discorticismo *m.* dyscorticism.

discrasia *f.* dyscrasia.

discrasia de las células plasmáticas plasma cell dyscrasia.

discrasia sanguínea blood dyscrasia.

discrásico, -ca *adj.* dyscrasic, dyscratic.

discrepancia *f.* discrepancy.

discrepancia de las dimensiones dentales tooth size discrepancy.

discreto, -ta *adj.* discrete.

discriminación *f.* discrimination.

discriminación táctil tactile discrimination.

discriminador *m.* discriminator.

discriminador de alto nivel (DAN) upper level discriminator (ULD).

discriminador de bajo nivel (DBN) lower level discriminator (LLD).

discroa *f.* dyschroa, dyschroia.

discroia *f.* dyschroa, dyschroia.

discromasia *f.* dyschromasia.

discromatopsia *f.* dyschromatopsia.

discromatopsia cromática chromatic dyschromatopsia.

discromatopsia discromática dyschromatic dyschromatopsia.

discromatosis *f.* dyschromatosis.

discromía *f.* dyschromia.

discronación *f.* dischronation.

discronismo *m.* dyschronism.

discronometría *f.* dyschronometry.

discus *m.* discus.

disdiaclasto *m.* disdiaclast.

disdiadococinesia *f.* dysdiadochokinesia.

disdiadococinético, -ca *adj.* dysdiadochokinetic.

disdipsia *f.* dysdipsia.

disecar *v.* dissect.

disección *f.* dissection.

disección aórtica aortic dissection.

disección cervical neck dissection.

disección cervical funcional functional neck dissection.

disección cervical radical radical neck dissection.

disección cortante sharp dissection.

disección de los ganglios linfáticos retroperitoneales retroperitoneal lymph node dissection.

disección radical radical dissection.

disección radical de cuello radical neck dissection.

disección roma blunt dissection.

disecoia *f.* dysecoia.

disector *m.* dissector.

disector, -a *adj.* dissecting.

disembrioma *m.* dysembryoma.

disembrioplasia *f.* dysembryoplasia.

disemia *f.* dysemia.

diseminación *f.* dissemination.

diseminado, -da *adj.* disseminated.

disencefalia esplacnoquística *f.* dysencephalia splanchnocystica.

disendografía *f.* dysendography.

diseneia *f.* dysenia.

disentería *f.* dysentery.

disentería amebiana, disentería amibiana amebic dysentery.

disentería de los asilos asylum dysentery.

disentería bacilar bacillary dysentery.

disentería balantidiana, disentería balantidiásica balantidial dysentery.

disentería bilharziana bilharzial dysentery.

disentería catarral catharral dysentery.

disentería por ciliados, disentería ciliar ciliary dysentery, ciliate dysentery.

disentería crónica chronic dysentery.

disentería epidémica epidemic dysentery.

disentería escorbútica scorbutic dysentery.

disentería espiralar spirillar dysentery.

disentería esporádica sporadic dysentery.

disentería esquistosomiásica schistosoma dysentery.

disentería por flagelados flagellate dysentery.

disentería de Flexner Flexner's dysentery.

disentería fulminante fulminating dysentery.

disentería giardiásica giardiasis dysentery.

disentería helmíntica helminthic dysentery.

disentería de las instituciones institutional dysentery.

disentería japonesa Japanese dysentery.

disentería maligna malignant dysentery.

disentería palúdica malarial dysentery.

disentería por protozoarios protozoal dysentery.

disentería de Sonne Sonne dysentery.

disentería viral, disentería virósica viral dysentery.

disentérico, -ca *adj.* dysenteric.

disenteriforme *adj.* dysenteriform.

diseño *m.* design.

diseño del asiento basal basal seat outline.

diseño experimental experimental design.

diseño sin barreras barrier-free design.

disepimiento *m.* dissepiment.

diseretesia *f.* dyserethesia.

diseretismo *m.* dyserethism.

disergia *f.* dysergia.

disespondilismo *m.* dysspondylism.

disestasia *f.* dysstasia, dystasia.

disestático, -ca *adj.* dysstatic.

disestesia *f.* dysesthesia.

disestesia auditiva auditory dysesthesia.

disestésico, -ca *adj.* dysesthetic.

disestético, -ca *adj.* dysesthetic.

disfagia *f.* dysphagy, dysphagia.

disfagia por anillo contráctil contractile ring dysphagy.

disfagia de Bayford-Autenrieth Bayford-Autenrieth's dysphagy.

disfagia espástica dysphagia spastica.

disfagia inflamatoria dysphagia inflammatoria.

disfagia lusoria dysphagia lusoria.

disfagia nerviosa nervous dysphagy, dysphagia nervosa.

disfagia paralítica dysphagia paralytica.
disfagia sideropénica sideropenic dysphagy.
disfagia valecular vallecular dysphagy.
disfagia de Valsalva Valsalva's dysphagy, dysphagia valsalviana.
disfagocitosis *f.* dysphagocytosis.
disfagocitosis congénita congenital dysphagocytosis.
disfasia *f.* dysphasia.
disfemia *f.* dysphemia.
disfibrinogenemia *f.* dysfibrinogenemia.
disfonía *f.* dysphonia.
disfonía de los clérigos dysphonia clericorum.
disfonía de las cuerdas vocales falsas dysphonia plicae ventricularis.
disfonía displástica dysplastic dysphonia.
disfonía espasmódica, disfonía espástica spasmodic dysphonia, spastic dysphonia, dysphonia spastica.
disfonía funcional functional dysphonia.
disfonía puberal, disfonía de los púberes dysphonia puberum.
disfónico, -ca *adj.* dysphonic.
disforético, -ca *adj.* dysphoretic.
disforia *f.* dysphoria.
disforia postcoital postcoitus dysphoria.
disforia premenstrual premenstrual syndrome.
disforiante *adj.* dysphoriant.
disfórico, -ca *adj.* dysphoric.
disfunción *f.* dysfunction.
disfunción de la articulación temporomandibular temporomandibular joint dysfunction (TMD, TMJ).
disfunción cerebral mínima minimal brain dysfunction.
disfunción constitucional del hígado constitutional hepatic dysfunction.
disfunción dentaria dental dysfunction.
disfunción por dolor miofascial myofascial pain dysfunction.
disfunción eréctil erectile dysfunction.
disfunción hepática constitucional constitutional hepatic dysfunction.
disfunción de la integración sensitiva sensory integrative dysfunction.
disfunción del lenguaje speech dysfunction.
disfunción esofágica esophageal dysfunction.
disfunción muscular papilar papillary muscle dysfunction.
disfunción orgásmica orgastic dysfunction.
disfunción placentaria placental dysfunction.
disfunción sexual sexual dysfunction.
disfunción sexual femenina female sexual dysfunction.
disfunción sexual masculina male sexual dysfunction.
disfunción sexual no orgánica non-organic sexual dysfunction.
disfunción temporomandibular temporomandibular dysfunction.
disfunción ventricular ventricular dysfunction.
disfuncional *adj.* dysfunctional.
disgalactia *f.* dysgalactia.
disgammaglobulinemia *f.* dysgammaglobulinemia.
disgenesia¹ *f.* dysgenesia.
disgenesia² *f.* dysgenesis.
disgenesia cerebral brain dysgenesis.
disgenesia epifisaria epiphyseal dysgenesis.
disgenesia gonadal gonadal dysgenesis.

disgenesia gonadal mixta mixed gonadal dysgenesis.
disgenesia gonadal pura pure gonadal dysgenesis.
disgenesia mesodérmica iridocorneal iridocorneal mesodermal dysgenesis.
disgenesia reticular reticular dysgenesis.
disgenesia de los túbulos seminíferos seminiferous tubule dysgenesis.
disgenitalismo *m.* dysgenitalism.
disgenopatía *f.* gysgenopathy.
disgerminoma *m.* dysgerminoma.
disgeusia *f.* dysgeusia.
disglandular *adj.* dysglandular.
disglobulinemia *f.* dysglobulinemia.
disglucemia *f.* dysglycemia.
disgnatia *f.* dysgnathia.
disgnático, -ca *adj.* dysgnathic.
disgnosia *f.* dysgnosia.
disgónico, -ca *adj.* dysgonic.
disgrafia *f.* dysgraphia.
disgramatismo *m.* dysgrammatism.
disgregación *f.* disaggregation.
dishematopoyesis *f.* dyshematopoiesis.
dishematopoyético, -ca *adj.* dyshematopoietic.
dishemopoyesis *f.* dyshemopoiesis.
dishemopoyético, -ca *adj.* dyshemopoietic.
dishepatia *f.* dyshepatia.
dishepatia lipogénica lipogenic dyshepatia.
dishesión *f.* dyshesion.
dishidria *f.* dyshidria, dyshidrosis.
dishidrosis *f.* dyshidria, dyshidrosis.
dishormonal *adj.* dyshormonal.
dishormónico, -ca *adj.* dyshormonic.
dishormonismo *m.* dyshormonism.
dishormonogénesis *f.* dyshormonogenesis.
disidria *f.* dyshidria, dyshidrosis.
disidrosis *f.* dyshidria, dyshidrosis.
disimbolia *f.* dyssymbolia, dyssymboly.
disimetría *f.* dyssymmetry.
disimilación *f.* dissimilation.
disimulo *f.* dissimulation.
disinergia *f.* dyssynergia.
disinergia biliar biliary dyssynergia.
disinergia cerebelosa mioclónica dyssynergia cerebellaris myoclonica.
disinergia cerebelosa progresiva dyssynergia cerebellaris progressiva.
disinergia detrusor-esfínter detrusor sphincter dyssynergia.
disinergia mioclónica cerebelosa dyssynergia cerebellaris myoclonica.
disinmunidad *f.* dysimmunity.
disistolia *f.* dyssystole.
dislaceración *f.* dilaceration.
dislalia *f.* dyslalia.
dislexia *f.* dyslexia.
disléxico, -ca *adj.* dyslexic.
dislipidemia *f.* dyslipidemia.
dislipidosis *f.* dyslipidosis, dyslipoidosis.
dislipoproteinemia *f.* dyslipoproteinemia.
dislocación *f.* dislocation, dislocatio.
dislocación erecta dislocatio erecta.
dismadurez *f.* dysmaturity.
dismadurez pulmonar pulmonary dysmaturity.
dismaduro, -ra *adj.* dysmature.
dismasesis *f.* dysmasesis.
dismegalopsia *f.* dysmegalopsia.
dismelia *f.* dysmelia.
dismenorrea *f.* dysmenorrhea.
dismenorrea adquirida acquired dysmenorrhea.
dismenorrea congestiva congestive dysmenorrhea.

dismenorrea esencial essential dysmenorrhea.
dismenorrea espasmódica spasmodic dysmenorrhea.
dismenorrea funcional functional dysmenorrhea.
dismenorrea inflamatoria inflammatory dysmenorrhea.
dismenorrea intermenstrual dysmenorrhea intermenstrualis.
dismenorrea intrínseca intrinsic dysmenorrhea.
dismenorrea mecánica mechanical dysmenorrhea.
dismenorrea membranosa membranous dysmenorrhea.
dismenorrea nerviosa nervous dysmenorrhea.
dismenorrea obstructiva obstructive dysmenorrhea.
dismenorrea ovárica ovarian dysmenorrhea.
dismenorrea primaria primary dysmenorrhea.
dismenorrea uretérica ureteric dysmenorrhea.
dismenorrea psicógena psychogenic dysmenorrhea.
dismenorrea secundaria secondary dysmenorrhea.
dismenorrea tubaria, dismenorrea tubárica tubal dysmenorrhea.
dismenorrea uretérica ureteric dysmenorrhea.
dismenorrea uterina uterine dysmenorrhea.
dismenorrea vaginal vaginal dysmenorrhea.
dismetabolismo *m.* dysmetabolism.
dismetría *f.* dysmetria.
dismetría ocular ocular dysmetria.
dismetropsia *f.* dysmetropsia.
dismielinación *f.* dysmyelination.
dismimia *f.* dysmimia.
disminución *f.* decrease.
dismiotonía *f.* dysmyotonia.
dismnesia *f.* dysmnesia.
dismnésico, -ca *adj.* dysmnesic.
dismorfia *f.* dysmorphia.
dismorfia craneofacial craniofacial dysmorphia.
dismorfia mandibulo-oculofacial mandibulo-oculofacial dysmorphia.
dismórfico, -ca *adj.* dysmorphic.
dismorfismo *m.* dysmorphism.
dismorfofobia *f.* dysmorphophobia.
dismorfogénesis *f.* dysmorphogenesis.
dismorfología *f.* dysmorphology.
dismorfologista *m.* dysmorphologist.
dismorfosis *f.* dysmorphosis.
disnea *f.* dyspnea.
disnea cardíaca cardiac dyspnea.
disnea de ejercicio exertional dyspnea.
disnea de esfuerzo exertional dyspnea.
disnea espiratoria expiratory dyspnea.
disnea funcional functional dyspnea.
disnea inspiratoria inspiratory dyspnea.
disnea nocturna nocturnal dyspnea.
disnea nocturna paroxística paroxysmal nocturnal dyspnea (PND).
disnea no expansiva non-expansional dyspnea.
disnea ortostática orthostatic dyspnea.
disnea paroxística nocturna (DPN) paroxysmal nocturnal dyspnea (PND).
disnea renal renal dyspnea.
disnea de reposo dyspnea at rest.
disnea suspirosa sighing dyspnea.
disneico, -ca *adj.* dyspneic.
disnistaxis *f.* dysnystaxis.
disnomia *f.* dysnomia.
disnomia para los colores color dysnomia.

disociable *adj.* dissociable.
disociación *f.* dissociation.
　disociación albuminocelular, disociación albuminocitológica albuminocytologic dissociation.
　disociación auricular atrial dissociation.
　disociación auriculoventricular (AV) atrioventricular dissociation.
　disociación auriculoventricular completa complete atrioventricular dissociation, complete AV dissociation.
　disociación auriculoventricular incompleta incomplete atrioventricular dissociation, incomplete AV dissociation.
　disociación bacteriana bacterial dissociation.
　disociación electromecánica electromechanical dissociation.
　disociación de interferencia interference dissociation, dissociation by interference.
　disociación iónica ionic dissociation.
　disociación isorrítmica isorhythmic dissociation.
　disociación longitudinal longitudinal dissociation.
　disociación microbiana microbic dissociation.
　disociación periférica peripheral dissociation.
　disociación siringomiélica syringomyelic dissociation.
　disociación del sueño sleep dissociation.
　disociación tabética tabetic dissociation.
　disociación termoalgésica thermoalgesic dissociation.
disociado, -da *adj.* dissociated.
disocluir *v.* disocclude.
disodontiasis *f.* dysodontiasis.
disoemia *f.* dysoemia.
disolución *f.* dissolution.
　disolución salina salting dissolution.
disolvente[1] *m. y adj.* dissolvent.
disolvente[2] *m. y adj.* discutient, discussive.
disoma *m.* disome.
disomia *f.* disomy.
　disomía uniparental uniparental disomy.
disómico, -ca *adj.* disomic.
disomnia *f.* dyssomnia.
disomo *m.* disomus.
disonancia *f.* dissonance.
　disonancia cognitiva cognitive dissonance.
disontogénesis *f.* dysontogenesis.
disontogenético, -ca *adj.* dysontogenetic.
disontogenia *f.* dysontogenesis.
disontogénico, -ca *adj.* dysontogenetic.
disontología *f.* dysonthology.
disopía *f.* dysopia.
　disopía álgera dysopia algera.
disopsia *f.* dysopsia.
disorexia *f.* dysorexia.
disorganoplasia *f.* dysorganoplasia.
disoria *f.* dysoria.
disórico, -ca *adj.* dysoric.
disosmia *f.* dysosmia.
disosteogénesis *f.* dysosteogenesis.
disostosis *f.* dysostosis.
　disostosis acrofacial, disostosis acrofacial de Nager acrofacial dysostosis, Nager's acrofacial dysostosis.
　disostosis cleidocraneal, disostosis cleidocraneal congénita cleidocranial dysostosis, clidocranial dysostosis, dysostosis cleidocranialis congenita.
　disostosis craneofacial, disostosis craneofacial hereditaria craniofacial dysostosis, craniofacial hereditary dysostosis.
　disostosis craneometafisaria craniometaphyseal dysostosis.

　disostosis encondral epifisaria dysostosis enchondralis epiphysaria.
　disostosis mandibuloacral mandibuloacral dysostosis.
　disostosis mandibulofacial mandibulofacial dysostosis.
　disostosis mandibulofacial con dermoides epibulbares mandibulofacial dysostosis with epibulbar dermoids.
　disostosis maxilofacial mandibulofacial dysostosis.
　disostosis metafisaria metaphyseal dysostosis, metaphysial dysostosis.
　disostosis múltiple dysostosis multiplex.
　disostosis orodigitofacial orodigitofacial dysostosis.
　disostosis otomandibular otomandibular dysostosis.
　disostosis periférica peripheral dysostosis.
disoxidativo, -va *adj.* dysoxidative.
dispalia *f.* dyspallia.
dispancreatismo *m.* dyspancreatism.
dispar *adj.* dispar.
disparatiroidismo *m.* dysparathyroidism.
dispareunia *f.* dispareunia.
　dispareunia orgánica organic dispareunia.
disparidad *f.* disparity.
　disparidad conjugada conjugate disparity.
　disparidad de fijación fixation disparity.
　disparidad retinal retinal disparity.
dispepsia *f.* dyspepsia.
　dispepsia ácida acid dyspepsia.
　dispepsia por adherencia adhesion dyspepsia.
　dispepsia apendicular appendicular dyspepsia, appendix dyspepsia.
　dispepsia atónica atonic dyspepsia.
　biliar dispepsia biliary dyspepsia.
　dispepsia catarral catarrhal dyspepsia.
　dispepsia colelítica, dispepsia colelitiásica cholelithic dyspepsia.
　dispepsia cólica colon dyspepsia.
　dispepsia fermentativa fermentative dyspepsia.
　dispepsia flatulenta flatulent dyspepsia.
　dispepsia funcional functional dyspepsia.
　dispepsia gástrica gastric dyspepsia.
　dispepsia idiopática idiopathic dyspepsia.
　dispepsia intestinal intestinal dyspepsia.
　dispepsia nerviosa nervous dyspepsia.
　dispepsia ovárica ovarian dyspepsia.
　dispepsia refleja reflex dyspepsia.
　dispepsia salival salivary dyspepsia.
　dispepsia sulfhídrica sulphuretted dyspepsia.
dispéptico, -ca *adj.* dyspeptic.
disperistalsis *f.* dysperistalsis.
dispermia[1] *f.* dispermia, dispermy.
dispermia[2] *f.* dysspermia.
dispersión[1] *f.* dispersion.
　dispersión cromática chromatic dispersion.
　dispersión óptica rotatoria (DOR) optical rotatory dispersion (ORD).
　dispersión relámpago flash dispersal.
　dispersión temporal temporal dispersion.
dispersión[2] *f.* scatter, scattering.
　dispersión de Compton Compton scatter.
　dispersión de Thompson Thompson scatter.
dispersograma *m.* scattergram.
dispersoide *m.* dispersoid.
dispigmentación *f.* dyspigmentation.
dispira *f.* dispira.
dispirema *m.* dispireme.
dispituitarismo *m.* dyspituitarism.
displasia *f.* dysplasia.
　displasia anterofacial, displasia antero-

posterior, displasia anteroposterior facial anterofacial dysplasia, anteroposterior dysplasia, anteroposterior facial dysplasia.
　displasia auriculodigital atriodigital dysplasia.
　displasia broncopulmonar bronchopulmonary dysplasia.
　displasia de cadera de Namaqualand Namaqualand hip dysplasia.
　displasia cemental periapical periapical cemental dysplasia.
　displasia cerebral cerebral dysplasia.
　displasia cervical cervical dysplasia.
　displasia cleidocraneal, displasia clidocraneal cleidocranial dysplasia, clidocranial dysplasia.
　displasia condroectodérmica chondroectodermal dysplasia.
　displasia craneocarpotarsiana craniocarpotarsal dysplasia.
　displasia craneodiafisaria craniodiaphyseal dysplasia, craniodiaphysial dysplasia.
　displasia craneometafisaria craniometaphyseal dysplasia, craniometaphysial dysplasia.
　displasia cretinoide cretinoid dysplasia.
　displasia del cuello uterino dysplasia of the cervix.
　displasia dental dental dysplasia.
　displasia de la dentina, displasia dentinaria dentin dysplasia, dentinal dysplasia.
　displasia dentoalveolar dentoalveolar dysplasia.
　displasia diafisaria, displasia diafisaria progresiva diaphyseal dysplasia, diaphysial dysplasia, progressive diaphyseal dysplasia.
　displasia ectodérmica ectodermal dysplasia.
　displasia ectodérmica anhidrótica anhidrotic ectodermal dysplasia.
　displasia ectodérmica congénita congenital ectodermal dysplasia.
　displasia ectodérmica hidrótica hidrotic ectodermal dysplasia.
　displasia ectodérmica hipohidrótica hypohidrotic ectodermal dysplasia.
　displasia encefalooftálmica encephalo-ophthalmic dysplasia.
　displasia epifisaria epiphyseal dysplasia.
　displasia epifisaria hemimelia, displasia epifisaria hemimélica dysplasia epiphysealis hemimelica, dysplasia epiphysialis hemimelia.
　displasia epifisaria múltiple multiple epiphysial dysplasia, dysplasia epiphysealis multiplex, dysplasia epiphysialis multiplex.
　displasia epifisaria punteada dysplasia epiphysealis punctata, dysplasia epiphysialis punctata.
　displasia epitelial epithelial dysplasia.
　displasia del esmalte enamel dysplasia.
　displasia espondiloepifisaria spondyloepiphyseal dysplasia, spondyloepiphysial dysplasia.
　displasia espondiloepifisaria seudoacondroplásica pseudoachondroplastic spondyloepiphysial dysplasia.
　displasia del esqueleto skeletal dysplasia.
　displasia esqueletodental skeletodental dysplasia.
　displasia facial anteroposterior anteroposterior facial dysplasia.
　displasia faciodigitogenital faciodigitogenital dysplasia.
　displasia faciogenital faciogenital dysplasia.
　displasia familiar de pliegues blancos familial white folded mucosal dysplasia.
　displasia fibromuscular fibromuscular dysplasia.

displasia fibrosa fibrous dysplasia.

displasia fibrosa familiar de los maxilares, displasia fibrosa mandibular familial fibrous dysplasia of the jaws.

displasia fibrosa de los huesos, displasia fibrosa ósea fibrous dysplasia of bone.

displasia fibrosa monostótica monostotic fibrous dysplasia.

displasia fibrosa poliostótica polyostotic dysplasia.

displasia hereditaria de los huesos hereditary bone dysplasia.

displasia linguofacial dysplasia linguofacialis.

displasia mamaria mammary dysplasia.

displasia maxilofacial mandibulofacial dysplasia.

displasia metafisaria metaphyseal dysplasia, metaphysial dysplasia.

displasia de Mondini Mondini dysplasia.

displasia mucoepitelial mucoepithelial dysplasia.

displasia oculoauricular, displasia oculoauriculovertebral (OAV) oculoauricular dysplasia, oculoauriculovertebral dysplasia (OAV dysplasia).

displasia oculodentodigital (ODD), displasia oculodentoóseo (ODOD) oculodentodigital dysplasia (ODD), oculodento-osseous dysplasia (ODOD).

displasia oculovertebral oculovertebral dysplasia.

displasia odontogénica odontogenic dysplasia.

displasia oftalmomandibulomélica (OMM) ophthalmomandibulomelic dysplasia.

displasia ósea hereditaria hereditary bone dysplasia.

displasia renal renal dysplasia.

displasia renal-retiniana hereditaria hereditary renal-retinal dysplasia.

displasia retiniana retinal dysplasia.

displasia septoóptica septo-optic dysplasia.

displasia de Streeter Streeter's dysplasia.

displasia tímica thymic dysplasia.

displasia tímica linfopénica lymphopenic thymic dysplasia.

displasia torácica asfixiante asphyxiating thoracic dysplasia.

displasia ureteral neuromuscular ureteral neuromuscular dysplasia.

displasia ventriculorradial ventriculoradial dysplasia.

displásico, -ca *adj.* dysplastic.

disponderal *adj.* dysponderal.

disposición *f.* arrangement.

disposición de dientes tooth arrangement.

dispositivo¹ *m.* appliance.

dispositivo de alambre gemelo, dispositivo de alambre gemelo de Johnson twin wire appliance, Johnson twin wire appliance.

dispositivo de Andresen Andresen appliance.

dispositivo de arco de cinta ribbon arch appliance.

dispositivo Begg Begg appliance.

dispositivo de Bimler Bimler appliance.

dispositivo de borde edgewise appliance.

dispositivo de Crozat Crozat appliance.

dispositivo de Denholz Denholz appliance.

dispositivo extrabucal extraoral appliance.

dispositivo fijo fixed appliance.

dispositivo de Jackson Jackson appliance.

dispositivo de Kesling Kesling appliance.

dispositivo de Kingsley Kingsley appliance.

dispositivo labiolingual labiolingual appliance.

dispositivo monobloque monoblock appliance.

dispositivo ortodóncico orthodontic appliance.

dispositivo ortodóncico extraoral extraoral orthodontic appliance.

dispositivo ortodóncico fijo fixed orthodontic appliance.

dispositivo ortodóncico intraoral intraoral orthodontic appliance.

dispositivo permanente permanent appliance.

dispositivo de placa dividida split plate appliance.

dispositivo de placa expansiva expansion plate appliance.

dispositivo rompe hábito habit-braking appliance.

dispositivo de saltamordida jumping-the-bite appliance.

dispositivo de Schwarz Schwarz appliance.

dispositivo universal universal appliance.

dispositivo de Walker Walker appliance.

dispositivo² *m.* device.

dispositivo de acceso vascular (DAV) vascular access device (DAV).

dispositivo de acceso venoso venous access device.

dispositivo de adaptación adaptive device.

dispositivo anticonceptivo contraceptive device.

dispositivo de apoyo central central-bearing device.

dispositivo de asistencia ventricular izquierda (DAVI) left-ventricular assist device (LVAD).

dispositivo de ayuda pulsátil (DAP) pulsatile assist device (PAD).

dispositivo de compresión fluoroscópica fluoroscopic compression device.

dispositivo contraceptivo contraceptive device.

dispositivo de entrada input device.

dispositivo de flotación flotation device.

dispositivo intraaórtico en balón intra-aortic balloon device.

dispositivo intrauterino (DIU), dispositivo intrauterino anticonceptivo (DIUA) intrauterine device (IUD), intrauterine contraceptive device.

dispositivo manual de velocidad ultrarrápida ultra-high-speed handpiece.

dispositivo de salida output device.

dispositivo de soporte central central-bearing device.

dispositivo de soporte central trazador central-bearing tracing device.

dispositivo trazador de apoyo central central-bearing tracing device.

disposición *f.* disposition.

dispoyesis *f.* dyspoiesis.

dispragia *f.* dyspragia.

dispragia intermitente angioesclerótica intestinal dyspragia intermittens angioesclerotica intestinalis.

dispraxia *f.* dyspraxia.

dispraxia del desarrollo developmental dyspraxia.

disprosodia *f.* dysprosody.

disprosodia de Monrod-Krohn Monrod-Krohn's dysprosody.

disproteinemia *f.* dysproteinemia.

disproteinémico, -ca *adj.* dysproteinemic.

disquecia *f.* dyschesia, dyschezia.

disqueratoma *m.* dyskeratoma.

disqueratoma verrugoso warty dyskeratoma.

disqueratósico, -ca *adj.* diskeratotic.

disqueratosis *f.* diskeratosis.

disqueratosis benigna benign diskeratosis.

disqueratosis congénita congenital diskeratosis, diskeratosis congenita.

disqueratosis folicular aislada isolated diskeratosis follicularis.

disqueratosis intraepitelial intraepithelial diskeratosis.

disqueratosis intraepitelial hereditaria benigna hereditary benign intraepithelial diskeratosis.

disqueratosis maligna malignant diskeratosis.

disquesia *f.* dyschesia.

disquezia *f.* dyschezia.

disquilia *f.* dyschilia, dyschylia.

disquinesia *f.* dyskinesia, dyscinesia.

disquinesia álgera dyskinesia algera.

disquinesia biliar biliary dyskinesia.

disquinesia bucofacial orofacial dyskinesia.

disquinesia ciliar ciliar dyskinesia.

disquinesia extrapiramidales extrapiramidal dyskinesia.

disquinesia intermitente dyskinesia intermittens.

disquinesia oral tardía tardive oral dyskinesia.

disquinesia tardía tardive dyskinesia.

disquinesia traqueobronquial tracheobronchial dyskinesia.

disquiria *f.* dyscheiria, dyschiria.

disquirial *adj.* dyscheiral, dyschiral.

disquitis *f.* diskitis.

disrafia *f.* dysraphia, dysrhaphia.

disrafia raquídea spinal dysraphia.

disrafia vertebral oculta occult spinal dysraphia.

disrafismo *m.* dysraphism, dysrhaphism.

disreflexia *f.* dysreflexia.

disreflexia autonómica autonomic dysreflexia.

disritmia *f.* dysrhythmia.

disritmia cardíaca cardiac dysrhythmia.

disritmia cerebral cerebral dysrhythmia.

disritmia cerebral paroxística paroxysmal cerebral dysrhythmia.

disritmia circadiana circadian dysrhythmia.

disritmia electroencefalográfica electroencephalographic dysrhythmia.

disritmia esofágica esophageal dysrhythmia.

disrupción *f.* disruption.

disruptivo, -va *adj.* disruptive.

dissemia *f.* dysemia.

distal *adj.* distal, distalis.

distalis *adj.* distal, distalis.

distancia *f.* distance.

distancia angular angular distance.

distancia blanco-piel target-skin distance.

distancia cono-superficie cone-surface distance.

distancia focal focal distance.

distancia fuente-cono source-cone distance.

distancia grande interarcos large interarch distance.

distancia infinita infinite distance.

distancia interarcos interarch distance.

distancia interarcos reducida reduced interarch distance.

distancia interoclusal interocclusal distance.

distancia interocular interocular distance.

distancia interpedicular interpediculate distance.

distancia interpupilar interpupillary distance.

distancia interrebordes interridge distance.

distancia de mapa, distancia de mapeo map distance.

distancia objeto-pelicula object-film distance.

distancia pequeña interarcos small interarch distance.

distancia pupilar pupillary distance.

distancia sociométrica sociometric distance.

distancia de trabajo working distance.

distasia *f.* dystasia, dystassia.

distasia arrefléxica hereditaria hereditary areflexic dystasia.

distasia atáxica hereditaria, distasia de Roussy-Lévy hereditary ataxic dystasia, Roussy-Lévy hereditary ataxic dystasia.

distásico, -ca *adj.* dysstatic.

distasis *f.* dystasia, dystassia.

distaxia *f.* dystaxia.

distectia *f.* dystectia.

distelefalangia *f.* dystelephalangy.

disteleología *f.* dysteleology.

distender[1] *v.* distend.

distender[2] *v.* strain.

distensibilidad *f.* distensibility.

distensibilidad dinámica dynamic compliance.

distensión[1] *f.* distension, distention.

distensión gaseosa gas distension.

distensión[2] *f.* strain.

distensión abdominal abdominal strain.

distensión ocular eye strain.

distensión de los saltadores de altura high-jumper's strain.

dístico, -ca *adj.* distichous.

distimia *f.* dysthymia.

distímico, -ca *adj.* dysthymic.

distimismo *m.* dysthymism.

distiquia *f.* distichia.

distiquia adquirida acquired distichia.

distiquiasis *f.* distichiasis.

distireosis *f.* dysthyreosis.

distiroideo, -a *adj.* dysthyroid, dysthyroidal.

distiroidismo *m.* dysthyroidism.

distitia *f.* dystitia.

distoaxiogingival *adj.* distoaxiogingival.

distoaxioincisal *adj.* distoaxioincisal.

distoaxiooclusal *adj.* distoaxio-occlusal.

distobucal *adj.* distobuccal.

distobucooclusal *adj.* distobucco-occlusal.

distobucopulpar *adj.* distobuccopulpal.

distocervical *adj.* distocervical.

distocia *f.* dystocia.

distocia por anillo de constricción constriction ring dystocia, contraction ring dystocia.

distocia cervical cervical dystocia.

distocia fetal fetal dystocia.

distocia materna maternal dystocia.

distocia placentaria placental dystocia.

distoclinación *f.* distoclination.

distoclusión *f.* distoclusion.

distocolocación *f.* distoplacement.

distogingival *adj.* distogingival.

distoincisal *adj.* distoincisal.

distolabial *adj.* distolabial.

distolabioincisal *adj.* distolabioincisal.

distolabiopulpar *adj.* distolabiopulpal.

distolingual *adj.* distolingual.

distolinguoincisal *adj.* distolinguoincisal.

distolinguooclusal *adj.* distolinguo-occlusal.

distolinguopulpar *adj.* distolinguopulpar.

Distoma Distoma.

distomatosis *f.* distomatosis.

distomia *f.* distomia.

distomiasis *f.* distomiasis.

distomiasis hémica hemic distomiasis.

distomiasis hepática hepatic distomiasis.

distomiasis pulmonar pulmonary distomiasis.

distomiasis sanguínea hemic distomiasis.

distomo *m.* distomus.

distomolar *m.* distomolar.

distonía *f.* dystonia.

distonía deformante muscular, distonía deformante progresiva dystonia deformans progressiva, dystonia musculorum deformans.

distonía kinesigénica kinesigenic dystonia.

distonía lenticular dystonia lenticularis.

distonía muscular deformante dystonia musculorum deformans.

distonía paroxística paroxysmal dystonia.

distonía tardía tardive dystonia.

distonía de torsión, distonía por torsión torsion dystonia.

distónico, -ca *adj.* dystonic.

distooclusal *adj.* distoclusal, disto-occlusal.

distooclusión *f.* disto-occlusion, distoclusion.

distopia *f.* dystopia.

distopia de los cantos dystopia canthorum.

distopia testis dystopia testis.

distópico, -ca *adj.* dystopic.

distopulpar *adj.* distopulpal.

distopulpolabial *adj.* distopulpolabial.

distopulpolingual *adj.* distopulpolingual.

distorsión *f.* distortion.

distorsión cognitiva cognitive distortion.

distorsión oris distortion oris.

distorsión paratáxica parataxic distortion.

distorsión perceptiva perceptive distortion.

distoversión *f.* distoversion.

distracción *f.* distraction.

distracción ósea bone distraction.

distractibilidad *f.* distractibility.

distraibilidad *f.* distractibility.

distractor *m.* distractor.

distrés *m.* distress.

distrés respiratorio del adulto adult respiratory distress.

distrés respiratorio del recién nacido tipo I idiopathic respiratory distress of the newborn (type I).

distrés respiratorio del recién nacido tipo II transient tachypnea.

distribución *f.* distribution.

distribución aleatoria randomization.

distribución de Bernouilli Bernouilli distribution.

distribución bimodal bimodal distribution.

distribución binomial binomial distribution.

distribución chi-cuadrado chi-square distribution, chi-squared distribution.

distribución por contracorriente countercurrent distribution.

distribución de dosis dose distribution.

distribución exponencial exponential distribution.

distribución F F distribution.

distribución del fármaco drug distribution.

distribución de frecuencia frequency distribution.

distribución de Gauss, distribución gausiana Gaussian distribution.

distribución independiente independent assortment.

distribución normal normal distribution.

distribución normal estándar standard normal distribution.

distribución oligoclonal oligoclonal banding.

distribución de Poisson Poisson distribution.

distribución de probabilidad probability distribution.

distribuidor *m.* spreader.

distribuidor para conductos radiculares root canal distribution.

distribuidor de gutapercha gutta-percha spreader.

distripsia *f.* dystrypsia.

distriquia *f.* districhiasis.

distriquiasis *f.* districhiasis.

distrix distrix.

distrofia *f.* dystrophy, dystrophia.

distrofia adiposa de la córnea dystrophia adiposa corneae.

distrofia adiposogenital adiposogenital dystrophy, dystrophia adiposogenitalis.

distrofia de Albright Albright's dystrophy.

distrofia anular de la córnea ring-like corneal dystrophy.

distrofia asfíctica torácica asphyxiating thoracic dystrophy (ATD).

distrofia de Barnes Barnes' dystrophy.

distrofia de Becker Becker's dystrophy.

distrofia de Biber-Haab-Dimmer Biber-Haab-Dimmer dystrophy.

distrofia brevicollis dystrophia brevicollis.

distrofia canaliforme mediana dystrophia mediana canaliformis.

distrofia canaliforme mediana de la uña dystrophia unguis mediana canaliformis.

distrofia cleidocraneal cleidocranial dystrophy.

distrofia de los conos cones dystrophy.

distrofia corneal corneal dystrophy.

distrofia corneal granular (de Groenouw tipo I) granular corneal dystrophy (Groenouw's type I).

distrofia corneal macular (de Groenouw tipo II) macular corneal dystrophy (Groenouw's type II).

distrofia corneal nodular de Salzmann Salzmann's nodular corneal dystrophy.

distrofia craneocarpotarsiana craniocarpotarsal dystrophy.

distrofia de Déjerine-Landouzy Déjerine-Landouzy dystrophy.

distrofia difusa dystrophia diffusa.

distrofia de Duchenne Duchenne's dystrophy.

distrofia de Duchenne-Landouzy Duchenne-Landouzy dystrophy.

distrofia en encaje (de la córnea) lattice dystrophy(of cornea).

distrofia endotelial de la córnea endothelial dystrophy of the cornea, dystrophia endothelialis corneae.

distrofia en enrejado de la córnea lattice corneal dystrophy.

distrofia epitelial epithelial dystrophy.

distrofia epitelial de la córnea dystrophia epithelialis corneae.

distrofia epitelial de Fuchs Fuchs' epithelial dystrophy.

distrofia epitelial juvenil juvenile epithelial dystrophy.

distrofia epitelial microquística microcystic epithelial dystrophy.

distrofia de Erb Erb's dystrophy.

distrofia de Favre Favre's dystrophy.

distrofia de Fuchs Fuchs' dystrophy.

distrofia en gotera de la córnea gutter dystrophy of the cornea.

distrofia granular de la estroma granular stromal dystrophy.

distrofia de heridas wound dystrophy.

distrofia hipofisaria hypophyseal dystrophy.

distrofia hipofiseopriva crónica, distrofia hipofisopriva crónica dystrophia hypophysopriva chronica.

distrofia en huellas dactilares, distrofia como impresiones digitales fingerprint dystrophy.

distrofia de Landouzy-Déjerine Landouzy-Déjerine type dystrophy.

distrofia de Leyden-Möbius Leyden-Möbius muscular dystrophy.

distrofia macular de la estroma macular stromal dystrophy.

distrofia manchada de la córnea fleck dystrophy of the cornea.

distrofia mapa-puntos-impresiones digitales map-dot-fingerprint dystrophy.

distrofia de Meesman Meesman dystrophy.

distrofia mesodérmica congénita hiperplástica dystrophia mesodermalis congenita hyperplastica.

distrofia microquística de Cogan Cogan's microcystic dystrophy.

distrofia miotónica myotonic dystrophy, dystrophia myotonica.

distrofia muscular muscular dystrophy.

distrofia muscular de Becker Becker's muscular dystrophy, Becker type muscular dystrophy.

distrofia muscular benigna seudohipertrófica benign pseudohypertrophic muscular dystrophy.

distrofia muscular de las cinturas de las extremidades, distrofia muscular de las cinturas escapulohumeral o pélvica limb-girdle muscular dystrophy.

distrofia muscular distal distal muscular dystrophy.

distrofia muscular de Duchenne Duchenne's muscular dystrophy.

distrofia muscular de Erb Erb's muscular dystrophy.

distrofia muscular escapulohumeral scapulohumeral muscular dystrophy.

distrofia muscular facioescapulohumeral, distrofia muscular fascioscapulohumeral facioscapulohumeral muscular dystrophy.

distrofia muscular de Gowers Gowers muscular dystrophy.

distrofia muscular infantil childhood muscular dystrophy.

distrofia muscular de Leyden-Möbius Leyden-Möbius muscular dystrophy.

distrofia muscular miotónica myotonic muscular dystrophy.

distrofia muscular oculofaríngea oculopharyngeal muscular dystrophy.

distrofia muscular pelvifemoral pelvofemoral muscular dystrophy.

distrofia muscular progresiva progressive muscular dystrophy.

distrofia muscular seudohipertrófica pseudohypertrophic muscular dystrophy.

distrofia muscular seudohipertrófica adulta adult pseudohypertrophic muscular dystrophy.

distrofia muscular de Steinert Steinert's muscular dystrophy.

distrofia muscular tardía tipo Becker Becker type tardive muscular dystrophy.

distrofia muscular tipo Welander Welander's muscular dystrophy.

distrofia oculocerebrorrenal oculocerebrorenal dystrophy.

distrofia ósea familiar familial osseous dystrophy.

distrofia papilar y pigmentaria papillary and pigmentary dystrophy.

distrofia perióstica hiperplástica familiar dystrophia periostalis hyperplastica familiar.

distrofia polimorfa posterior posterior polymorphous dystrophy.

distrofia refleja simpática sympathetic reflex dystrophy.

distrofia de Reis-Bucklers Reis-Bucklers' dystrophy.

distrofia reticular de la córnea reticular dystrophy of the cornea.

distrofia de Salzmann Salzmann's dystrophy.

distrofia de Simmerlin Simmerlin's dystrophy.

distrofia simpática refleja sympathetic reflex dystrophy.

distrofia tapetocoroidea, distrofia taperocoroidea progresiva tapetochoroidal dystrophy, progressive tapetochoroidal dystrophy.

distrofia tironeural, distrofia tironerviosa thyroneural dystrophy.

distrofia torácica-pélvica-falángica thoracic-pelvic-phalangeal dystrophy.

distrofia ungueal, distrofia ungular dystrophia unguium.

distrofia ungueal mediana canaliforme dystrophia unguis mediana canaliformis.

distrofia de las veinte uñas twenty-nail dystrophy.

distrofia viteliforme vitelliform dystrophy.

distrofia viteliforme hereditaria hereditary vitelliform dystrophy.

distrofia vitreotapetorretiniana vitreo-tapetoretinal dystrophy.

distrófico, -ca *adj.* dystrophic.

distrofina *f.* dystrophin.

distrofinopatía *f.* dystrophinopathy.

distrofoneurosis *f.* dystrophoneurosis.

disuresia *f.* dysuresia.

disuria *f.* dysuria, dysury.

disuria espasmódica, disuria espástica spasmodic dysuria, spastic dysuria.

disuria psíquica psychic dysuria.

disúrico, -ca *adj.* dysuric, dysuriac.

disvitaminosis *f.* dysvitaminosis.

disyunción *f.* disjunction.

disyunción de la coordinación coodination disjunction.

disyunción craneofacial craniofacial disjunction.

diszoospermia *f.* dyszoospermia.

diurea *f.* diurea.

diuresis *f.* diuresis.

diuresis acuosa water diuresis.

diuresis alcohólica alcohol diuresis.

diuresis osmótica osmotic diuresis.

diuresis tubular osmotic diuresis.

diurético, -ca *m. y adj.* diuretic.

diurético ahorrador de potasio potassium-sparing diuretic.

diurético del asa, diurético del asa ascendente loop diuretic, high-ceiling diuretic.

diurético cardiaco cardiac diuretic.

diurético directo direct diuretic.

diurético indirecto indirect diuretic.

diurético mercurial, diurético de mercurio mercurial diuretic.

diurético osmótico osmotic diuretic.

diurético de recambio de potasio potassium-sparing diuretic.

diurético tiacídico thiazide diuretic.

diuria *f.* diuria.

diúrnula *f.* diurnule.

divagación *f.* divagation.

divalencia *f.* divalence, divalency.

divalente *adj.* divalent.

divaricación *f.* divarication.

divergencia *f.* divergence.

divergencia vertical negativa negative vertical divergence.

divergencia vertical positiva positive vertical divergence.

divergente *adj.* divergent.

diverticular *adj.* diverticular.

diverticulectomía *f.* diverticulectomy.

diverticulitis *f.* diverticulitis.

diverticulización *f.* diverticulization.

divertículo *m.* diverticulum.

divertículo adquirido acquired diverticulum.

divertículo cervical cervical diverticulum.

divertículo funcional functional diverticulum.

divertículo de ganglión ganglion diverticulum.

divertículo de Ganser Ganser's diverticulum.

divertículo de Graser Graser's diverticulum.

divertículo hepático hepatic diverticulum.

divertículo ilei verum diverticulum ilei verum.

divertículo de Meckel Meckel's diverticulum.

divertículo pancreático pancreatic diverticula.

divertículo de Pertik Pertik's diverticulum.

divertículo de presión, divertículo por presión pressure diverticulum.

divertículo de pulsión, divertículo por pulsión pulsion diverticulum.

divertículo Rokitansky Rokitansky's diverticulum.

divertículo sinovial synovial diverticulum.

divertículo tirogloso, divertículo tiroideo thyroglossal diverticulum, thyroid diverticulum.

divertículo por tracción traction diverticulum.

divertículo traqueal tracheal diverticula, diverticula of the trachea.

divertículo uretral urethral diverticulum.

divertículo ventricular ventricular diverticulum.

divertículo verdadero true diverticulum.

divertículo vesical vesical diverticulum.

diverticulograma *m.* diverticulogram.

diverticuloma *m.* diverticuloma.

diverticulopexia *f.* diverticulopexy.

diverticulosis *f.* diverticulosis.

diverticulum *m.* diverticulum.

divieso *m.* boil.

división *f.* division, divisio.

división celular cell division.

división celular directa direct cell division.

división celular indirecta indirect cell division.

división conjugada conjugate division.

división craneosacra craniosacral division.

división por ecuación equation division.

división ecuacional equational division.

división de maduración maturation division.

división meiótica meiotic division.

división mitótica mitotic division.

división multiplicativa multiplicative division.

división nuclear directa direct nuclear division.

división nuclear indirecta indirect nuclear division.

división nuclear de Remak Remak's nuclear division.

división quirúrgica surgical sectioning.

división de reducción, división por reducción, división reduccional reduction division.

división por segmentación cleavage division.

divisoria de aguas *f.* watershed.

divulsión *f.* divulsion.

divulsor *m.* divulsor.

doble *adj.* double.

doble ciego double-mind.

doble micción double-void.

doblete *m.* doublet.

doblete de Wollaston Wollaston's doublet.

docimasia *f.* docimasia.

docimasia de la agonía agony docimasia.

docimasia alimenticia nutritional docimasia.

docimasia bacteriológica bacteriological docimasia.

docimasia diafragmática diaphragmatic docimasia.

docimasia gastrointestinal gastrointestinal docimasia.

docimasia hepática hepatic docimasia.

docimasia hidrostática hydrostatic docimasia.

docimasia ótica otic docimasia.

docimasia pulmonar pulmonary docimasia.

docimasia radiológica radiologic docimasia.

docimasia siálica sialic docimasia.

docimasia suprarrenal suprarenal docimasia.

docimásico, -ca *adj.* docimastic.

doctor, -ra *m., f.* doctor.

doctrina *f.* doctrine.

doctrina humoral humoral doctrine.

doctrina de Monro, doctrina de Monro-Kellie Monro's doctrine, Monro-Kellie doctrine.

doctrina neuronal neuron doctrine.

doigt mort doigt mort.

dolabrado, -da *adj.* dolabrate.

dolabriforme *adj.* dolabriform.

dolencia *f.* ache, infirmity.

dolencia gástrica stomach ache.

dolencia ósea bone ache.

dolicocefalia *f.* dolichocephaly.

dolicocefálico, -ca *adj.* dolichocephalic.

dolicocefalismo *m.* dolichocephalism.

dolicocéfalo, -la *adj.* dolichocephalous.

dolicocérquico, -ca *adj.* dolichokerkic.

dolicocnémico, -ca *adj.* dolichoknemic.

dolicocolon *m.* dolichocolon.

dolicocraneal *adj.* dolichocranial.

dolicodero *m.* dolichoderus.

dolicoestenomelia *f.* dolichostenomelia.

dolicofacial *adj.* dolichofacial.

dolicogastria *f.* dolichogastry.

dolicohiérico, -ca *adj.* dolichohieric.

dolicomorfo, -fa *adj.* dolichomorphic.

dolicopélico, -ca *adj.* dolichopellic.

dolicopélvico, -ca *adj.* dolichopelvic.

dolicoprosópico, -ca *adj.* dolichoprosopic.

dolicoprosopo, -pa *adj.* dolichoprosopous.

dolicostenomelia *f.* dolichostenomelia.

dolicouránico, -ca *adj.* dolichouranic, dolichuranic.

dolicuránico, -ca *adj.* dolichouranic, dolichuranic.

dolor *m.* pain, dolor.

dolor "para abajo" bearing-down pain.

dolor abdominal abdominal pain.

dolor agudo acute pain.

dolor de apendicitis appendicitis pain.

dolor de cabeza, dolor capitis headache, dolor capitis.

dolor de cabeza postcoital postcoitus headache.

dolor cardíaco cardiac pain.

dolor central central pain.

dolor en cinturón girdle pain.

dolor de coxis dolor coxae.

dolor de crecimiento, dolor del crecimiento growing pain.

dolor crónico chronic pain.

dolor crónico resistente al tratamiento chronic intractable pain.

dolor de dilatación dilating pain.

dolor epigástrico epigastric pain.

dolor errante, dolor errático wandering pain.

dolor de espalda backache.

dolor de expulsión, dolor expulsivo expulsive pain.

dolor de la extremidad fantasma phantom limb pain.

dolor fulgurante fulgurant pain.

dolor de gas gas pain.

dolor de hambre hunger pain.

dolor heterotópico heterotopic pain.

dolor homotópico homotopic pain.

dolor ideógeno ideogenous pain.

dolor imperativo imperative pain.

dolor intermenstrual intermenstrual pain.

dolor intratable intractable pain.

dolor isquémico ischemic pain.

dolor lancinante lightning pain.

dolor en manchas spot pains.

dolor mental, dolor de la mente mind pain.

dolor nervioso nerve pain.

dolor nocturno night pain.

dolor orgánico organic pain.

dolor osteocópico osteocopic pain.

dolor parietal parietal pain.

dolor de parto labor pain.

dolor pélvico pelvic pain.

dolor posprandial postprandial pain.

dolor precordial precordial pain.

dolor presagiente dolor praesagiente.

dolor premonitorio premonitory pain.

dolor psicogénico psychogenic pain.

dolor psicosomático psychosomatic pain.

dolor psíquico psychic pain.

dolor de pujos bearing-down pain.

dolor de raíz root pain.

dolor referido referred pain.

dolor de la región inferior de la espalda low back pain.

dolor de reposo, dolor en reposo rest pain.

dolor resistente al tratamiento intractable pain.

dolor saltante jumping pain.

dolor sobresaltante starting pain.

dolor sordo dull pain.

dolor en sueños dream pain.

dolor terebrante boring pain.

dolor torácico chest pain.

dolor traqueal tracheal pain.

dolor urente burning pain.

dolor vagus dolor vagus.

dolor visceral visceral pain.

dolorífico, -ca *adj.* dolorific.

dolorimiento *m.* ache.

dolorimetría *f.* dolorimetry.

dolorímetro *m.* dolorimeter.

dolorógeno, -na *adj.* dolorogenic.

dolorología *f.* dolorology.

doloroso, -sa *adj.* dolorific.

doloroso a la presión tender.

domaria *f.* domaria.

domiciliario, -ria *adj.* domiciliary.

dominancia *f.* dominance.

dominancia cerebral cerebral dominance.

dominancia falsa false dominance.

dominancia genética genetic dominance.

dominancia incompleta incomplete dominance.

dominancia lateral lateral dominance.

dominancia ocular eye dominance, ocular dominance.

dominancia parcial partial dominance.

dominancia unilateral one-sided dominance.

dominante *adj.* dominant.

dominio *m.* domain.

donador, -ra *m.* donor.

donante *m.* donor.

donante de cadáver cadaveric donor.

donante F F donor.

donante general general donor.

donante de hidrógeno hydrogen donor.

donante de sangre blood donor.

donante universal universal donor.

donante vivo living donor.

donante xenogénico xenogenic donor.

Donovania granulomatis Donovania granulomatis.

donovanosis *f.* donovanosis.

dopar *v.* dope.

Doppler Doppler.

Doppler color color Doppler.

Doppler continuo continuous Doppler.

Doppler dúplex duplex Doppler.

Doppler pulsado pulsed Doppler.

Doppler transcraneal transcranial Doppler.

dormancia *f.* dormancy.

dormifaciente *adj.* dormifacient.

dorsal *adj.* dorsal, dorsalis.

dorsalgia *f.* dorsalgia, backache.

dorsalgia benigna benign dorsalgia.

dorsalis *adj.* dorsal, dorsalis.

dorsalización *f.* dorsalization.

dorsiductor, -ra *adj.* dorsiduct.

dorsiescapular *adj.* dorsiscapular.

dorsiespinal *adj.* dorsispinal.

dorsiflexión *f.* dorsiflexion.

dorsiflexionar *v.* dorsiflect.

dorsimesial *adj.* dorsimesial.

dorso *m.* back, dorsum.

dorso de tenedor silver fork deformity.

dorsoabdominal *adj.* dorsabdominal.

dorsoacromial *adj.* dorsiacromial.

dorsoanterior *adj.* dorsoanterior.

dorsocefálico, -ca *adj.* dorsocephalad.

dorsocervical *adj.* dorsicervical.

dorsodinia *f.* dorsodynia.

dorsoescapular *adj.* dorsoscapular.

dorsointercostal *adj.* dorsointercostal.

dorsolateral *adj.* dorsolateral.

dorsolumbar *adj.* dorsolumbar.

dorsomedial *adj.* dorsomedian.

dorsomesial *adj.* dorsomesial.

dorsonasal *adj.* dorsonasal.

dorsonucal *adj.* dorsonuchal.

dorsoposterior *adj.* dorsoposterior.

dorsorradial *adj.* dorsoradial.

dorsotraqueliano, -na *adj.* trachelodorsal.

dorsoventrad *adv.* dorsoventrad.

dorsoventral *adj.* dorsoventral.

dorsum *m.* dorsum.

dosificación *f.* dosage.

dosificación pediátrica pediatric dosage.

dosimetría *f.* dosimetry.

dosimetría fotográfica photographic dosimetry.

dosimetría hidrostática hydrostatic dosimetry.

dosimetría de rayos X X-ray dosimetry.

dosimetría de termoluminiscencia, dosimetría por termoluminiscencia thermoluminiscence dosimetry.

dorsimétrico, -ca *adj.* dorsimetric.

dosimetrista *m., f.* dosimetrist.

dosímetro *m.* dosimeter.

  dosímetro de área area dosimeter.

  dosímetro dúplex duplex dosimeter.

  dosímetro de Fricke Fricke dosimeter.

  dosímetro individual individual dosimeter.

  dosímetro integrador integrating dosimeter.

  dosímetro de película film dosimeter.

  dosímetro de placa film badge.

dosis *f.* dose, dosis.

  dosis absorbida, dosis absorbida de radiación absorbance dose, absorbed dose, radiation absorbed dose.

  dosis acumulada, dosis acumulativa cumulative dose.

  dosis de ataque loading dose.

  dosis de cebamiento priming dose.

  dosis de choque intravenosa intravenous push.

  dosis curativa curative dose, dosis curativa.

  dosis curativa mediana median curative dose.

  dosis cutánea skin dose.

  dosis de depilación epilation dose.

  dosis dérmica skin dose.

  dosis diaria daily dose.

  dosis dividida divided dose.

  dosis de duplicación doubling dose.

  dosis efectiva, dosis eficaz, dosis efficax (DE) effective dose (ED), dosis efficax.

  dosis eficaz media, dosis eficaz mediana (DE50) median effective dose (ED50).

  dosis equianalgésica equianalgesic dose.

  dosis equivalente equivalent dose.

  dosis equivalente acumulada accumulated dose equivalent.

  dosis eritema erythema dose.

  dosis fetal fetal dose.

  dosis fraccionada fractional dose.

  dosis genéticamente significativa (DGS) genetically significant dose (GSD).

  dosis génica gene dosage.

  dosis gonadal gonadal dose.

  dosis infectante infective dose.

  dosis infectante media en cultivo de tejidos median tissue culture infective dose.

  dosis infectante mediana median infective dose.

  dosis inicial initial dose.

  dosis integral, dosis integral absorbida integral dose, integral absorbed dose.

  dosis intoxicante intoxicating dose.

  dosis L L dose.

  dosis L+d L+d dose.

  dosis L D limes nul dose, limes zero dose.

  dosis letal (DL) lethal dose (LD).

  dosis letal media (DL50) median lethal dose (LD50).

  dosis letal mínima (DLM) minimal lethal dose (MLD).

  dosis Lf Lf dose.

  dosis limes nul, dosis limes cero limes nul dose, limes zero dose.

  dosis Lo Lo dose.

  dosis Lr Lr dose.

  dosis de mantenimiento maintenance dose.

  dosis máxima maximal dose, maximal dose.

  dosis máxima permisible, dosis máxima permitida (DMP) maximal permissible dose, maximum permissible dose (MPD).

  dosis mínima minimal dose, minimum dose.

  dosis mínima infecciosa (DMI) minimal infecting dose (MID).

  dosis mínima reactiva (DMR) minimal reacting dose (MRD).

  dosis mortal lethal dose (LD).

  dosis mortal media, dosis mortal mediana median lethal dose.

  dosis mortal mínima minimal lethal dose, minimum lethal dose.

  dosis óptima optimal dose, optimum dose.

  dosis oral oral dosage.

  dosis permisible permissible dose.

  dosis personal personal dose.

  dosis en piel dose to skin.

  dosis preventiva preventive dose.

  dosis profunda, dosis de profundidad depth dose.

  dosis prolongada protracted dose.

  dosis promedio average dose.

  dosis de radiación acumulativa cumulative radiation dose.

  dosis reactiva reacting dose.

  dosis refracta dosis refracta.

  dosis de refuerzo booster dose.

  dosis de salida exit dose.

  dosis sensibilizante sensitizing dose.

  dosis de shock shocking dose.

  dosis subletal sublethal dose.

  dosis superficial superficial dose.

  dosis terapéutica therapeutic dose.

  dosis tisular tissue dose.

  dosis tolerada, dosis de tolerancia tolerance dose.

  dosis de tolerancia de órganos organ tolerance dose.

  dosis tolerata dosis tolerata.

  dosis tóxica (DT) toxic dose (TD).

  dosis tóxica media (DT50) median toxic dose (TD50).

  dosis umbral threshold dose.

  dosis umbral de eritema threshold erythema dose.

  dosis unitaria unit dose.

  dosis de urgencia emergency dose.

  dosis de volumen volume dose.

dotación cromosómica *f.* chromosomic complement.

douglascele *m.* douglascele.

douglasitis *f.* douglasitis.

dracontiasis *f.* dracontiasis.

dracuncular *adj.* dracuncular.

dracunculiasis *f.* dracunculiasis.

dracunculosis *f.* dracunculosis.

Dracunculus Dracunculus.

  Dracunculus medinensis Dracunculus medinensis.

dramatismo *m.* dramatism.

dramatización *f.* dramatization.

drástico *m.* drastic purgative.

drástico, -ca *adj.* drastic.

dren *m.* drain.

  dren en cigarrillo cigarette drain.

  dren por contraabertura stab wound drain.

  dren controlado controlled drain.

  dren de cuarentena quarantine drain.

  dren de Mikulicz Mikulicz's drain.

  dren de Penrose Penrose's drain.

  dren transfixión stab drain.

drenaje[1] *m.* drain.

drenaje[2] *m.* drainage.

  drenaje abierto open drainage.

  drenaje por aspiración, drenaje aspirativo suction drainage.

  drenaje de Barraya Barraya's drainage.

  drenaje basal basal drainage.

  drenaje con botón, drenaje en botón button drainage.

  drenaje bronquial bronchial drainage.

  drenaje de Bülau Bülau's drainage.

  drenaje capilar capillary drainage.

  drenaje cerrado closed drainage.

  drenaje en cigarrillo cigarette drain.

  drenaje continuo por aspiración continuous suction drainage.

  drenaje por contraabertura stab drainage.

  drenaje definitivo definitive drainage.

  drenaje por gravedad gravity drainage.

  drenaje de una herida cerrada closed-wound suction drainage.

  drenaje hermético bajo agua underwater seal drainage.

  drenaje por infusión-aspiración infusion-aspiration drainage.

  drenaje por irrigación through-and-through drainage.

  drenaje de Mikulicz Mikulicz's drainage.

  drenaje de Monaldi Monaldi's drainage.

  drenaje de Penrose Penrose's drainage.

  drenaje periódico tidal drainage.

  drenaje pleural cerrado closed pleural drainage.

  drenaje postural postural drainage.

  drenaje de Redon Redon's drainage.

  drenaje por succión suction drainage.

  drenaje total through drainage.

  drenaje de Wagensteen Wagensteen's drainage.

drenar *v.* drain.

drepanocitemia[1] *f.* drepanocytemia.

drepanocitemia[1] *f.* sicklemia.

drepranocítico, -ca *adj.* drepanocytic.

drepanocito *m.* drepanocyte, sickle cell.

drepanocitosis[1] *f.* drepanocytosis.

drepanocitosis[2] *f.* sickling.

droga *f.* drug.

  droga antagonista antagonistic drug.

  droga bruta crude drug.

  droga cruda crude drug.

  droga de diseño designer drug.

  droga nefrotóxica nephrotoxic drug.

  droga que produce hábito habit-forming drug.

drogadicto, -ta *adj.* drug addict.

drogar *v.* drug.

drogarresistente *m.* drug-fast.

drogodependencia *f.* drug dependence.

drómico, -ca *adj.* dromic.

dromógrafo *m.* dromograph.

dromotrópico, -ca *adj.* dromotropic.

dromotropismo *m.* dromotropism.

  dromotropismo negativo negative dromotropism.

  dromotropismo positivo positive dromotropism.

dropacismo *m.* dropacism.

drop attack drop attack.

Drosophila melanogaster Drosophila melanogaster.

drusa *f.* drusen.

  drusa gigantes giant drusen.

  drusa del nervio óptico optic nerve drusen.

  drusa de la papila óptica drusen of the optic disk.

drüsen drusen.

dualidad de control del SNC *f.* duality of CNS control.

dualismo *m.* dualism.

ducción *f.* duction.

  ducción forzada forced duction.

  ducción pasiva passive duction.

ducha *f.* douche, shower.

  ducha en abanico fan douche.

  ducha de aire air douche.

  ducha alternante transition douche.

ducha escocesa Scotch douche.
ductal *adj.* ductal.
dúctil *adj.* ductile.
dúctulo *m.* ductulus.
ductulus *m.* ductulus.
ductus ductus.
duela *f.* fluke.
  duela hepática, duela hepática humana liver fluke, human liver fluke.
  duela intestinal intestinal fluke.
  duela pulmonar lung fluke.
  duela sanguínea blood fluke.
duelo *m.* bereavement, grief, mourning.
  duelo anticipatorio anticipatory grieving.
  duelo normal normal bereavement.
  duelo patológico pathological bereavement.
duocrinina *f.* duocrinin.
duodécimo par craneal *m.* twelfth cranial nerve.
duodenal *adj.* duodenal.
duodenectomía *f.* duodenectomy.
duodenitis *f.* duodenitis.
duodeno *m.* duodenum.
duodenocistostomía *f.* duodenocystostomy.
duodenocolangeítis *f.* duodenocholangeitis.
duodenocolangitis *f.* duodenocholangeitis.
duodenocolecistostomía *f.* duodenocholecystostomy.
duodenocoledocotomía *f.* duodenocholedochotomy.

duodenocólico, -ca *adj.* duodenocolic.
duodenoduodenostomía *f.* duodenoduodenostomy.
duodenoenterostomía *f.* duodenoenterostomy.
duodenografía *f.* duodenography.
duodenograma *m.* duodenogram.
duodenohepático, -ca *adj.* duodenohepatic.
duodenoileostomía *f.* duodenoileostomy.
duodenólisis *f.* duodenolysis.
duodenorrafia *f.* duodenorrhaphy.
duodenoscopia *f.* duodenoscopy.
duodenoscopio *m.* duodenoscope.
duodenostomía *f.* duodenostomy.
duodenotomía *f.* duodenotomy.
duodenoyeyunostomía *f.* duodenojejunostomy.
duoparental *adj.* duoparental.
duovirus *m.* duovirus.
duplicación *f.* duplication.
  duplicación conservadora conservative duplication.
  duplicación cromosómica duplication of chromosomes.
  duplicación dispersora dispersive duplication.
  duplicación semiconservadora semiconservative duplication.
duplicidad *f.* duplicitas.
  duplicidad anterior duplicitas anterior.
  duplicidad asimétrica duplicitas asymmetros.

  duplicidad completa duplicitas completa.
  duplicidad cruzada duplicitas cruciata.
  duplicidad incompleta duplicitas incompleta.
  duplicidad inferior duplicitas inferior.
  duplicidad media duplicitas media.
  duplicidad paralela duplicitas parallela.
  duplicidad posterior duplicitas posterior.
  duplicidad simétrica duplicitas symmetros.
  duplicidad superior duplicitas superior.
dupp dupp.
dura *f.* dura.
duración *f.* duration.
  duración del pulso pulse duration.
  duración de semiamplitud del pulso half amplitude pulse duration.
dural *adj.* dural, duramatral.
duraluminio *m.* duralumin.
duramadre *f.* dura mater.
duramater dura mater.
duraplastia *f.* duraplasty.
dureza *f.* hardness.
  dureza de indentación indentation hardness.
  dureza permanente permanent hardness.
  dureza de la pirámide del diamante diamond pyramid hardness.
  dureza temporal temporary hardness.
  dureza de los rayos X hardness of X-rays.
duro, -ra *adj.* hard.
duroaracnitis *f.* duroarachnitis.

E e

ebonación *f.* ebonation.
ébranlement *m.* ébranlement.
ebriedad *f.* ebriety.
ebrio, -a *adj.* ebrious.
ebullición *f.* ebullition.
ebullismo *m.* ebullism.
ebur *m.* ebur.
  ebur dentis ebur dentis.
eburnación *f.* eburnation.
  eburnación de la dentina eburnation of dentin.
ebúrneo, -a *adj.* eburneous.
eburnitis *f.* eburnitis.
écarteur *m.* écarteur.
ecaudado, -da *adj.* ecaudate.
ecbólico, -ca *adj.* ecbolic.
ECBOvirus, ecbovirus *m.* ecbovirus (Enteric Cytopathic Bovine Orphan).
eccema *m.* eczema.
  eccema de las amas de casa housewives' eczema.
  eccema agrietado eczema craquelé.
  eccema agudo acute eczema.
  eccema alérgico allergic eczema.
  eccema asteatótico asteatotic eczema.
  eccema atópico atopic eczema.
  eccema capitis eczema capitis.
  eccema constitucional atopic eczema.
  eccema de contacto contact eczema.
  eccema crónico chronic eczema.
  eccema depilatorio eczema epilans.
  eccema diabético eczema diabeticorum.
  eccema epilante eczema epilans.
  eccema eritematoso erythematous eczema, eczema erythematosum.
  eccema escamoso eczema squamosum.
  eccema por estasis stasis eczema.
  eccema de estrés neurodermatitis.
  eccema exudativo weeping eczema.
  eccema flexural flexural eczema.
  eccema folicular follicular eczema.
  eccema herpético eczema herpeticum.
  eccema hipertrófico eczema hypertrophicum.
  eccema húmedo moist eczema.
  eccema impetiginizado, eccema impetiginoso impetiginous eczema.
  eccema infantil infantile eczema.
  eccema intertriginoso intertrigo.
  eccema invernal winter eczema.
  eccema liquenoide lichenoid eczema.
  eccema madidans eczema madidans.
  eccema de las manos hand eczema.
  eccema marginado, eccema marginatum eczema marginatum.
  eccema microbiano microbic eczema.
  eccema de la niñez infantile eczema.
  eccema numular nummular eczema, eczema nummulare.
  eccema orbicular orbicular eczema.
  eccema de los panaderos baker's eczema.

eccema papuloso eczema papulosum.
eccema parasitario eczema parasiticum.
eccema de los pliegues de flexión flexural eczema.
eccema pustuloso eczema pustulosum.
eccema rezumante weeping eczema.
eccema rojo eczema rubrum.
eccema seborreico seborrheic eczema.
eccema seborreico seco dry seborrheic eczema.
eccema simple eczema vesiculosum.
eccema solar solar eczema.
eccema tilótico eczema tyloticum.
eccema tropical tropical eczema.
eccema vacunal eczema vaccinatum.
eccema varicoso varicose eczema.
eccema verrugoso eczema verrucosum.
eccema vesiculoso eczema vesiculosum.
eccema xerótico xerotic eczema.
eccemátide *f.* eczematid.
eccematización *f.* eczematization.
eccematogénico, -ca *adj.* eczematogenic.
eccematógeno, -na *adj.* eczematogenic.
eccematoide *adj.* eczematoid.
eccematosis *f.* eczematosis.
eccematoso, -sa *adj.* eczematous.
eccemógeno, -na *adj.* eczematogenic.
eccentrocondroplasia *f.* eccentrochondroplasia.
eccentroosteocondrodisplasia *f.* eccentroosteochondrodysplasia.
ecciesis *f.* eccyesis.
ecdémico, -ca *adj.* ecdemic.
ecfiadectomía *f.* ecphyadectomy.
ecfiaditis *f.* ecphyaditis.
ecfiláctico, -ca *adj.* ecphylactic.
ecfilaxis *f.* ecphylaxis.
ecfima *m.* ecphyma.
Echinococcus Echinococcus.
ECHOvirus, echovirus *m.* echo virus, echovirus (Enteric Cytopathic Human Orphan).
eclabio *m.* eclabium.
eclampsia *f.* eclampsia.
  eclampsia puerperal puerperal eclampsia.
  eclampsia urémica uremic eclampsia.
eclámpsico, -ca *adj.* eclamptic.
eclampsismo *m.* eclampsism, eclamptism.
eclámptico, -ca *adj.* eclamptic.
eclamptismo *m.* eclampsism, eclamptism.
eclamptogénico, -ca *adj.* eclamptogenic.
eclamptógeno, -na *adj.* eclamptogenous.
eclipse *f.* eclipse.
eclisis *f.* eclysis.
ecmetropía *f.* ametropia.
ecmnesia *f.* ecmnesia.
ecmofobia *f.* aichmophobia.
eco *m.* echo.
  eco anfórico amphoric echo.
  eco auricular atrial echo.
  eco del latido beat echo.
  eco metálico metallic echo.

eco del nódulo sinoauricular echo nodus sinuatrialis.
eco del pensamiento thought hearing echo.
ecoacusia *f.* echoacousia.
ecoaortografía *f.* echoaortography.
ecocardiografía *f.* echocardiography.
  ecocardiografía bidimensional B-mode two dimensional echocardiography.
  ecocardiografía transesofágica transesophageal echocardiography.
  ecocardiografía Doppler Doppler echocardiography.
  ecocardiografía de sección transversal cross-sectional echocardiography.
ecocardiograma *m.* echocardiogram.
ecocinesia *f.* echokinesia, echokinesis.
ecocinesis *f.* echokinesia, echokinesis.
ecocleación *f.* ecochleation.
ecoencefalografía *f.* echoencephalography.
ecoencefalógrafo *m.* echoencephalograph.
ecoencefalograma *m.* echoencephalogram.
ecoestructura *f.* echostructure.
ecofonía *f.* echophony, echophonia.
ecofonocardiografía *f.* echophonocardiography.
ecofotonía *f.* echophotony.
ecofrasia *f.* echophrasia.
ecogenética *f.* ecogenetics.
ecogenético, -ca *adj.* ecogenetic.
ecogenicidad *f.* echogenicity.
ecogénico, -ca *adj.* echogenic.
ecógeno, -na *adj.* echogenic.
ecografía *f.* echography.
ecografía *f.* echography.
  ecografía Doppler Doppler echography.
  ecografía estática static echography.
  ecografía en modo A A mode echography.
  ecografía en modo B B mode echography.
  ecografía en modo M M mode echography.
  ecografía en tiempo real real time echography.
  ecografía renal renal ultrasonography.
  ecografía tiroidea thyroid ultrasonography.
ecográfico, -ca *adj.* echographic.
ecografista *m., f.* echographist.
ecógrafo *m.* echographer.
ecograma *m.* echogram.
ecolalia *f.* echolalia, echo speech.
  ecolalia tardía delayed echolalia.
ecología *f.* ecology.
  ecología humana human ecology.
ecólogo, -ga *m., f.* ecologist.
ecolúcido, -da *adj.* echolucent.
ecomatismo *m.* echomatism, echomotism.
ecomotismo *m.* echomatism, echomotism.
ecomimia *f.* echomimia.
econdroma *m.* ecchondroma.
  econdroma fisaliforme ecchondroma physaliphora.
econdrótomo *m.* ecchondrotome.
economía *f.* economy.

economía animal animal economy.
economía simbólica token economy.
económico, -ca *adj.* economic.
ecoparásito *m.* ecosite.
ecopatía *f.* echopathy.
ecopraxia *f.* echopraxis, echopraxia.
ecoquinesis *f.* echokinesia, echokinesis.
ecoscopio *m.* echoscope.
ecosistema *m.* ecosystem.
ecósito *m.* ecosite.
ecotaxis *f.* ecotaxis.
ecotono *m.* ecotone.
ecovirus *m.* echovirus.
ecrino, -na *adj.* eccrine.
ecrinología *f.* eccrinology.
ecrisiología *f.* eccrisiology.
ecrisis *f.* eccrisis.
ecrítico, -ca *adj.* eccritic.
ecsomática *f.* ecsomatics.
ectacolia *f.* ectacolia.
ectal *adj.* ectal.
ectasia, *f.* ectasia, ectasis.
   ectasia alveolar alveolar ectasia.
   ectasia anuloaórtica annuloaortic ectasia.
   ectasia arterial difusa diffuse arterial ectasia.
   ectasia cardíaca ectasia cordis.
   ectasia de conductos mamarios mammary duct ectasia.
   ectasia corneal corneal ectasia.
   ectasia escleral, ectasia de la esclerótica scleral ectasia.
   ectasia hipostática hypostatic ectasia.
   ectasia papilar papillary ectasia.
   ectasia paradójica del vientre ectasia ventriculi paradoxa.
   ectasia senil senile ectasia.
   ectasia tubular tubular ectasia.
   ectasia ureteral ureteral ectasia.
ectásico, -ca *adj.* ectatic.
ectasis *f.* ectasia, ectasis.
ectático, -ca *adj.* ectatic.
ectental *adj.* ectental, ectoental.
ecterógrafo *m.* ecterograph.
ectetmoides *m.* ectethmoid.
ectima *m.* ecthyma.
   ectima contagioso contagious ecthyma.
   ectima gangrenoso ecthyma gangrenosum.
   ectima sifilítico ecthyma shyphiliticum.
ectimatiforme *adj.* ecthymatiform.
ectimiforme *adj.* ecthymiform.
ectimosis *f.* ecthyma.
ectipia *f.* ectypia.
ectireosis *f.* ecthyreosis.
ectiris *f.* ectiris.
ectobiología *f.* ectobiology.
ectoblasto *m.* ectoblast.
ectocardia *f.* ectocardia.
ectocardíaco, -ca *adj.* ectocardiac, ectocardial.
ectocervical *adj.* ectocervical.
ectocérvix *m.* ectocervix.
ectocinérea *f.* ectocinerea.
ectocítico, -ca *adj.* ectocytic.
ectocolon *f.* ectocolon.
ectocóndilo *m.* ectocondyle.
ectocórnea *f.* ectocornea.
ectocoroides *f.* ectochoroidea.
ectodermatosis *f.* ectodermatosis.
ectodérmico, -ca *adj.* ectodermic.
ectodermo *m.* ectoderm.
   ectodermo amniótico amniotic ectoderm.
   ectodermo basal basal ectoderm.
   ectodermo coriónico chorionic ectoderm.
   ectodermo extraembrionario extraembryonic ectoderm.
   ectodermo neural neural ectoderm.

ectodermo epitelial epithelial ectoderm.
ectodermo superficial superficial ectoderm.
ectodermosis *f.* ectodermosis.
   ectodermosis erosiva pluriorificial ectodermosis erosiva pluriorificialis.
ectoental *adj.* ectental, ectoental.
ectoesqueleto *m.* ectoskeleton.
ectógeno, -na *adj.* ectogenous, ectogenic.
ectoglia *f.* ectoglia.
ectoglobular *adj.* ectoglobular.
ectogonia *f.* ectogony.
ectolecito, -ta *adj.* ectolecithal.
ectólisis *f.* ectolysis.
ectomeninge *f.* ectomeninx.
ectómera *f.* ectomere.
ectómero *f.* ectomere.
ectomerogonia *f.* ectomerogony.
ectomesoblasto *m.* ectomesoblast.
ectonuclear *adj.* ectonuclear.
ectópago *m.* ectopagus.
ectoparasiticida *m.* ectoparasiticide.
ectoparasitismo *m.* ectoparasitism.
ectoparásito *m.* ectoparasite.
ectoperitoneal *adj.* ectoperitoneal.
ectoperitonitis *f.* ectoperitonitis.
ectopia *f.* ectopy, ectopia.
   ectopia cervical cervical ectopy.
   ectopia de la cloaca ectopia cloacae.
   ectopia congénita de la pupila ectopia pupillae congenita.
   ectopia cordis, ectopia cardiaca ectopia cordis.
   ectopia cordis abdominalis ectopia cordis abdominalis.
   ectopia cordis pectoral pectoral ectopia cordis.
   ectopia del iris ectopia iridis.
   ectopia lentis, ectopia del cristalino ectopia lentis.
   ectopia macular ectopia maculae.
   ectopia pupilar pupillary ectopy, ectopia pupillae.
   ectopia renal renal ectopy, ectopia renis.
   ectopia renal cruzada crossed renal ectopy.
   ectopia testicular ectopia testis.
   ectopia de la vejiga, ectopia vesical ectopia vesicae.
ectópico, -ca *adj.* ectopic.
ectoplacenta *f.* ectoplacenta.
ectoplacentario, -ria *adj.* ectoplacental.
ectoplasma *m.* ectoplasm.
ectoplasmático, -ca *adj.* ectoplasmatic.
ectoplásmico, -ca *adj.* ektoplasmic.
ectoplástico, -ca *adj.* ectoplastic, ektoplastic.
ectoplasto *m.* ectoplast.
ectopotomía *f.* ectopotomy.
ectoquiste *m.* ectocyst.
ectorretina *f.* ectoretina.
ectoscopia *f.* ectoscopy.
ectosqueleto *m.* ectoskeleton.
ectósito *m.* ectosite.
ectósteo, -a *adj.* ectosteal.
ectóstico, -ca *adj.* ectosteal.
ectostosis *f.* ectostosis.
ectosugestión *f.* ectosuggestion.
ectotrix *m.* ectothrix.
ectozoario *m.* ectozoon.
ectozoo, -a *adj.* ectozoon.
ectrodactilia *f.* ectrodactylia, ectrodactyly.
ectrodactilismo *m.* ectrodactylism.
ectrofalangia *f.* ectrophalangia.
ectrogenia *f.* ectrogeny.
ectrogénico, -ca *adj.* ectrogenic.
ectromelia *f.* ectromelia.
ectromélico, -ca *adj.* ectromelic.
ectromelo *m.* ectromelus.

ectrometacarpia *f.* ectrometacarpia.
ectrometatarsia *f.* ectrometatarsia.
ectropía *f.* ectropion.
ectropión *m.* ectropion.
   ectropión atónico atonic ectropion.
   ectropión de la capa pigmentaria ectropion of pigment layer.
   ectropión cervical cervical ectropion.
   ectropión cicatrizal cicatricial ectropion.
   ectropión espástico spastic ectropion.
   ectropión fláccido flaccid ectropion.
   ectropión lujuriante ectropion luxurians.
   ectropión paralítico paralytic ectropion.
   ectropión sarcomatoso ectropion sarcomatosum.
   ectropión senil senile ectropion.
   ectropión uveal uveal ectropion, ectropion uveae.
ectropionizar *v.* ectropionize.
ectropodia *f.* ectropody.
ectroqueiria *f.* ectrocheiry, ectrochiry.
ectroquiria *f.* ectrocheiry, ectrochiry.
ectrosindactilia *f.* ectrosyndactyly, ectrosyndactylia.
ectrosis *f.* ectrosis.
ectrótico, -ca *adj.* ectrotic.
ecuación *f.* equation.
ecuador *m.* equator.
   ecuador de la célula equator of the cell.
ecualización *f.* equalization.
ecuatorial *adj.* equatorial.
eczema *m.* eczema.
edad *f.* age.
   edad de adquisición del lenguaje acquisition of language age.
   edad adulta adulthood.
   edad anatómica anatomical age.
   edad de Binet Binet age.
   edad cronológica chronological age.
   edad de desarrollo development age.
   edad esquelética skeletal age.
   edad estatural statural age.
   edad fértil childbearing age.
   edad de fertilización fertilization age.
   edad fetal fetal age.
   edad física physical age.
   edad fisiológica physiologic age, physiological age.
   edad funcional functional age.
   edad gestacional gestational age.
   edad de la menarquia menarcheal age, menarchial age.
   edad menstrual menstrual age.
   edad mental mental age.
   edad de la obstinación obstinacy age.
   edad ósea bone age.
   edad posovulatoria postovulatory age.
   edad de realización achievement age.
   edad de rendimiento achievement age.
edema *m.* edema.
   edema agudo circunscrito acute circumscribed edema.
   edema agudo esencial acute essential edema.
   edema agudo paroxístico acute paroxysmal edema.
   edema alimentario alimentary edema.
   edema de altitud high-altitude edema.
   edema alveolar alveolar edema.
   edema ampollar bullous edema.
   edema ampollar de la vejiga, edema ampolloso vesical bullous vesicae edema, edema bullosum vesicae.
   edema angioneurótico angioneurotic edema.
   edema angioneurótico hereditario hereditary angioneurotic edema.

edema azul blue edema.
edema de Berlín Berlin's edema.
edema de Calabar Calabar edema.
edema cálido edema calidum.
edema por calor heat edema.
edema caquéctico cachectic edema.
edema cardíaco cardiac edema.
edema cerebral, edema del cerebro cerebral edema, brain edema.
edema cíclico idiopático cyclic idiopathic edema.
edema circunscrito circumscribed edema.
edema compresible pitting edema.
edema corneal corneal edema.
edema de la conjuntiva, edema conjuntival conjunctival edema.
edema por declive dependent edema.
edema depresible pitting edema.
edema del disco óptico edema of the optic disk.
edema errante wandering edema.
edema del escroto scrotal edema.
edema frígido edema frigidum.
edema fugaz edema fugax.
edema gaseoso gaseous edema.
edema gestacional gestational edema.
edema de la glotis edema of the glottis.
edema de guerra war edema.
edema de hambre famine edema, hunger edema.
edema hepático hepatic edema.
edema histérico hysterical edema.
edema inflamatorio inflammatory edema.
edema por insulina insulin edema.
edema intradérmico local local intracutaneous edema.
edema linfático lymphatic edema.
edema macular diabético macular diabetic edema.
edema macular quístico cystoid macular edema.
edema maligno malignant edema.
edema marántico marantic edema.
edema menstrual menstrual edema.
edema migratorio migratory edema.
edema de Milton Milton's edema.
edema mucoso mucous edema.
edema nefrótico nephrotic syndrome.
edema neonatal, edema neonatorum edema neonatorum.
edema neuropático neuropathic edema.
edema no inflamatorio non-inflammatory edema.
edema nutricional nutritional edema.
edema palpebral palpebral edema.
edema de papila papilar edema.
edema pardo brown edema.
edema pasivo passive edema.
edema periódico periodic edema.
edema periorbitario periorbital edema.
edema perirretiniano periretinal edema.
edema de Pirogoff malignant edema.
edema placentario placental edema.
edema postural dependent edema.
edema prehepático prehepatic edema.
edema premenstrual premenstrual edema.
edema por presión pressure edema.
edema de pulmón, edema pulmonar edema of the lung, pulmonary edema.
edema pulmonar de las grandes alturas high-altitude pulmonary edema.
edema pulmonar paroxístico paroxysmal pulmonary edema.
edema purulento purulent edema.
edema de Quincke Quincke's edema.

edema de Reinke Reinke's edema.
edema renal renal edema.
edema reumático rheumatic edema.
edema salino salt edema.
edema sólido solid edema.
edema sólido de los pulmones solid edema of the lungs.
edema terminal terminal edema.
edema tóxico toxic edema.
edema traumático de la retina traumatic edema of the retina.
edema vasógeno vasogenic edema.
edema venoso venous edema.
edema vernal del pulmón vernal edema of the lung.
edema Yangtze Yangtze edema.
edemágeno *m.* edemagen.
edematígeno, -na *adj.* edematigenous, edematogenic.
edematógeno, -na *adj.* edematigenous, edematogenic.
edematización *f.* edematization.
edematoso, -sa *adj.* edematous.
edemígeno, -na *adj.* edemarigenous.
edencia *f.* edentia.
edeocéfalo *m.* edeocephalus.
educción *f.* eduction.
efapsis *f.* ephapse.
efáptico, -ca *adj.* ephaptic.
efébico, -ca *adj.* ephebic.
efectividad *f.* effectiveness.
efectividad de un programa effectiveness of a program.
efecto *m.* effect.
efecto abscopal abscopal effect.
efecto acumulativo cumulative effect.
efecto aditivo additive effect.
efecto anacorético anachoretic effect.
efecto anódico anodic effect.
efecto de Anrep Anrep effect.
efecto de Arias-Stella Arias Stella effect.
efecto autocinético autokinetic effect.
efecto autocrino autocrine effect.
efecto de Bernoulli Bernoulli effect.
efecto biológico biologic effect.
efecto de Bohr Bohr effect.
efecto citopático cytopathic effect.
efecto colateral side effect.
efecto de Compton Compton effect, Compton scatter.
efecto contrario contrary effect.
efecto de Cotton Cotton effect.
efecto de Crabtree Crabtree effect.
efecto de Cushing Cushing effect.
efecto de Danysz Danysz effect.
efecto de Deelman Deelman effect.
efecto dinámico específico specific dynamic effect.
efecto Doppler Doppler effect.
efecto de dosificación genética gene dosage effect.
efecto electrofónico electrophonic effect.
efecto de Emerson Emerson effect.
efecto enfriador del viento wind chill effect.
efecto del entrenamiento training effect.
efecto de espacio muerto dead space effect.
efecto del experimentador experimenter's effect.
efecto de Fahraeus-Lindqvist Fahraeus-Lindqvist effect.
efecto farmacológico adverso adverse drug effect.
efecto de Fenn Fenn effect.
efecto de formación de pares pair formation effect.

efecto fotéquico, efecto fotéxico photechic effect.
efecto fotográfico photographic effect.
efecto fundador founder effect.
efecto gonadal de la radioterapia gonadal effect of radiation.
efecto Haldane Haldane effect.
efecto de Hallwachs Hallwachs effect.
efecto Hawthorne Hawthorne effect.
efecto hematológico hematologic effect.
efecto de ionización ionization effect.
efecto isomórfico isomorphic effect.
efecto de Mierzejewski Mierzejewski effect.
efecto de Nagler Nagler effect.
efecto de Orbeli Orbeli effect.
efecto oxígeno oxygen effect.
efecto de Pasteur Pasteur effect.
efecto piezoeléctrico piezoelectric effect.
efecto placebo placebo effect.
efecto de presión pressure effect.
efecto de la privación del sueño effect of sleep deprivation.
efecto psicológico del aborto psychological effect of abortion.
efecto de posición position effect.
efecto de Purkinje Purkinje effect.
efecto radiactivo radioactive effect.
efecto Rivero-Carvallo Rivero-Carvallo effect.
efecto de Russell Russell effect.
efecto secundario secundary effect.
efecto secundario extrapiramidal extrapyramidal sideffect.
efecto del segundo gas second gas effect.
efecto sigma sigma effect.
efecto de Somogyi Somogyi effect.
efecto de Soret Soret effect.
efecto de Staub-Traugott Staub-Traugott effect.
efecto de Stiles-Crawford Stiles-Crawford effect.
efecto de talón heel effect.
efecto de Tyndall Tyndall effect.
efecto de Venturi Venturi effect.
efecto velo curtain effect.
efecto de Vulpian Vulpian's effect.
efecto de Wedensky Wedensky effect.
efecto de Wolff-Chaikoff Wolff-Chaikoff effect.
efecto de Zeeman Zeeman effect.
efector *m.* effector.
efélide *f.* ephelides.
eferente *adj.* efferent.
efervescencia *f.* effervescence.
efervescente *adj.* effervescent.
eficacia *f.* effectiveness.
eficacia anticonceptiva contraceptive effectiveness.
eficacia biológica biologic effectiveness.
eficacia biológica relativa relative biological effectiveness.
eficacia de costes cost effectiveness.
eficacia teórica theoretic effectiveness.
eficacia de uso use effectiveness.
eficiencia *f.* efficiency.
eficiencia visual visual efficiency.
efidrosis *f.* ephidrosis.
efímero, -ra *adj.* ephemeral.
eflorescencia *f.* efflorescence.
efluvio *m.* effluve, effluvium.
efluvio ácido acid flush.
efluvio anágeno anagen effluve.
efluvio telógeno telogen effluve.
efracción *f.* effraction.
efumabilidad *f.* effumability.

efusión *f.* effusion.
egagrópilo *m.* egagropilus.
egílope *m.* egilops.
egilops *m.* egilops.
eglanduloso, -sa *adj.* eglandulous.
ego *m.* ego.
egobroncofonía *f.* egobronchophony.
egocéntrico, -ca *adj.* egocentric.
egocentrismo *m.* egocentricity, egocentrism.
egodistónico, -ca *adj.* ego-dystonic.
egofonía *f.* egophony.
egofónico, -ca *adj.* egophonic.
egoísmo *m.* egoism, egotism.
egomanía *f.* egomania.
egosintónico, -ca *adj.* ego-syntonic.
Ehrlichia Ehrlichia.
Ehrlichieae Ehrlichieae.
ehrliquiosis *f.* ehrlichiosis.
eiconómetro *m.* eikonometer, eiconometer.
eideísmo *m.* eidetic imagery.
eidético, -ca *adj.* eidetic.
eidógeno *m.* eidogen.
eidopometría *f.* eidoptometry, eidopometry.
eidoptometría *f.* eidoptometry, eidopometry.
Eikenella Eikenella.
eiloide *adj.* eiloid.
eisantema *m.* eisanthema.
eisódico, -ca *adj.* eisodic.
eje *m.* axis.
　eje eléctrico del corazón cardiac electrical axis, electrical axis of the heart.
　eje eléctrico instantáneo instantaneous electrical axis.
　eje embrionario embryonic axis.
　eje normal normal axis.
　eje óptico optic axis.
　eje principal principal axis.
　eje sagital del ojo sagittal axis of the eye.
　eje secundario secondary axis.
ejecución *f.* implementing.
ejercicio *m.* exercise.
　ejercicio activo active exercise.
　ejercicio activo asistido active assisted exercise.
　ejercicio activo contra resistencia active resistive exercise.
　ejercicio aeróbico aerobic exercise.
　ejercicio anaeróbico anaerobic exercise.
　ejercicio de arco de movilidad range of motion exercise.
　ejercicio asistido progresivo progressive assistive exercise.
　ejercicio bajo el agua underwater exercise.
　ejercicio de Codman Codman's exercise.
　ejercicio correctivo corrective exercise.
　ejercicio con resistencia progresiva progressive resistance exercise.
　ejercicio estático muscle-setting exercise.
　ejercicio físico physical exercise.
　ejercicio de Frenkel Frenkel exercise.
　ejercicio isocinético isokinetic exercise.
　ejercicio isométrico isometric exercise.
　ejercicio isotónico isotonic exercise.
　ejercicio de Kegel Kegel's exercise.
　ejercicio de leñador chopping exercise.
　ejercicio libre free exercise.
　ejercicio pasivo passive exercise.
　ejercicio posmastectomía postmastectomy exercise.
　ejercicio postural de Buerger Buerger postural exercise.
　ejercicio de preparación muscular muscle-setting exercise.
　ejercicio pubococcígeo pubococcygeous exercise.

　ejercicio reduccionista de la medicina reductionist practice of medicine.
　ejercicio de resistencia activa active resistance exercise.
　ejercicio de resistencia graduada graduated resistance exercise.
　ejercicio de resistencia progresiva de ajuste diario daily adjusted progressive resistance exercise.
　ejercicio de respiración profunda y de tos deep breathing and coughing exercise.
　ejercicio terapéutico therapeutic exercise.
elaboración *f.* elaboration.
　elaboración secundaria secondary elaboration.
elaiómetro *m.* elaiometer.
elaioplasto *m.* elaioplast.
elaiopatía *f.* elaiopathy.
elastancia *f.* elastance.
　elastancia cerebral cerebral elastance.
elasticidad *f.* elasticity, resilience.
　elasticidad física del músculo physical elasticity of muscle.
　elasticidad fisiológica del músculo physiologic elasticity of muscle.
　elasticidad psicobiológica psychobiologic resilience.
　elasticidad total del músculo total elasticity of muscle.
elasticina *f.* elasticin.
elástico, -ca *m. y adj.* elastic.
elastina *f.* elastin.
elastofibroma *m.* elastofibroma.
　elastofibroma dorsal elastofibroma dorsi.
elastogénesis *f.* elastogenesis.
elastoidosis *f.* elastoidosis.
　elastoidosis nodular nodular elastoidosis.
elastólisis *f.* elastolysis.
　elastólisis generalizada generalized elastolysis.
elastolítico, -ca *adj.* elastolytic.
elastoma *m.* elastoma.
　elastoma juvenil juvenile elastoma.
　elastoma de Miescher Miescher's elastoma.
elastometría *f.* elastometry.
elastómetro *m.* elastometer.
elastopatía *f.* elastopathy.
elastorrexis *f.* elastorrhexis.
elastosis *f.* elastosis.
　elastosis actínica actinic elastosis.
　elastosis coloidal conglomerada elastosis colloidalis conglomerata.
　elastosis distrófica elastosis dystrophica.
　elastosis nodular de Favre-Racouchot nodular elastosis of Favre and Racouchot.
　elastosis perifolicular perifollicular elastosis.
　elastosis posinflamatoria postinflammatory elastosis.
　elastosis reactiva perforante perforating elastosis, elastosis perforans serpiginosa.
　elastosis senil senile elastosis.
　elastosis serpiginosa perforante perforating elastosis, elastosis perforans serpiginosa.
　elastosis solar solar elastosis.
elección *f.* choice.
　elección de objeto object choice.
electivo, -va *adj.* elective.
electricidad *f.* electricity.
electrización *f.* electrization.
electroacupuntura *f.* electroacupuncture.
electroanalgesia *f.* electroanalgesia.
electroánalisis *m.* electroanalysis.
electroanestesia *f.* electroanesthesia.
electroapendicectomía *f.* electroappendectomy.

electroaxonografía *f.* electroaxonography.
electrobasografía *f.* electrobasography.
electrobasógrafo *m.* electrobasograph.
electrobiología *f.* electrobiology.
electrobioscopia *f.* electrobioscopy.
electrocardiofonografía *f.* electrocardiophonography.
electrocardiofonógrafo *m.* electrocardiophonograph.
electrocardiofonograma *m.* electrocardiophonogram.
electrocardiografía *f.* electrocardiography.
　electrocardiografía fetal fetal electrocardiography.
　electrocardiografía intracardíaca intracardiac electrocardiography.
　electrocardiografía precordial precordial electrocardiography.
electrocardiógrafo *m.* electrocardiograph.
electrocardiograma (ECG) *m.* electrocardiogram (ECG).
　electrocardiograma (ECG) escalar scalar electrocardiogram (ECG).
　electrocardiograma (ECG) de esfuerzo stress electrocardiogram (ECG).
　electrocardiograma (ECG) unipolar unipolar electrocardiogram (ECG).
electrocardioscopia *f.* electrocardioscopy.
electrocatálisis *f.* electrocatalysis.
electrocauterio *m.* electrocautery.
electrocauterización *f.* electrocauterization.
electrochoque *m.* electroshock.
electrocinético, -ca *adj.* electrokinetic.
electrocirugía *f.* electrosurgery.
electrocistografía *f.* electrocystography.
electrocoagulación *f.* electrocoagulation.
electrococleografía *f.* electrocochleography.
electrococleográfico, -ca *adj.* electrocochleographic.
electrococleograma *m.* electrocochleogram.
electrocolecistectomía *f.* electrocholecystectomy.
electrocolecistocausis *f.* electrocholecystocausis.
electrocontractilidad *f.* electrocontractility.
electroconvulsivo, -va *adj.* electroconvulsive.
electrocorticografía *f.* electrocorticography.
electrocorticograma *m.* electrocorticogram.
electrocriptectomía *f.* electrocryptectomy.
electrocromatografía *f.* electrochromatography.
electrocución *f.* electrocution.
electrodermátomo *m.* electrodermatome.
electrodérmico, -ca *adj.* electrodermal.
electrodesecación *f.* electrodesiccation.
electrodiagnóstico *m.* electrodiagnosis.
electrodiálisis *f.* electrodialysis.
electrodializador *m.* electrodialyzer.
electrodinámico, -ca *adj.* electrodynamic.
electrodinógrafo *m.* electrodynograph.
electrodo *m.* electrode.
electroencefalografía *f.* electroencephalography.
electroencefalografista *m., f.* electroencephalographer, electroencephalograph technologist.
electroencefalógrafo *m.* electroencephalograph.
electroencefalograma *m.* electroencephalogram.
　electroencefalograma isoeléctrico plano flat isoelectric electroencephalogram.
electroencefaloscopio *m.* electroencephaloscope.
electroendósmosis *f.* electroendosmosis.
electroescisión *f.* electroscission.

electroespectrografía *f.* electrospectrography.
electroespectrograma *m.* electroespectrogram.
electroespinografía *f.* electrospinography.
electroespinograma *m.* electrospinogram.
electroestenólisis *f.* electrostenolysis.
electroestetógrafo *m.* electrostethograph.
electroestimulación *f.* electrostimulation.
electroferograma *m.* electropherogram, electrophoregram.
electrofílico, -ca *adj.* electrophilic.
electrófilo, -la *adj.* electrophil, electrophile.
electrofisiología *f.* electrophysiology.
electrofisiológico, -ca *adj.* electrophysiologic, electrophysiological.
electroforegrama *m.* electropherogram, electrophoregram.
electroforesis *f.* electrophoresis.
  electroforesis en capas delgadas thin-layer electrophoresis (TLE).
  electroforesis capilar capillary electrophoresis.
  electroforesis de disco disc electrophoresis.
  electroforesis de fronteras móviles moving boundary electrophoresis.
  electroforesis en gel gel electrophoresis.
  electroforesis de gradiente en un campo de pulsos pulsed field gradient electrophoresis, PFG.
  electroforesis de hemoglobina hemoglobin electrophoresis.
  electroforesis de isoenzimas isoenzyme electrophoresis.
  electroforesis de lipoproteínas lipoprotein electrophoresis.
  electroforesis en papel paper electrophoresis.
  electroforesis de proteína protein electrophoresis.
  electroforesis de zona zone electrophoresis.
electroforético, -ca *adj.* electrophoretic.
electroforetograma *m.* electrophoretogram.
electróforo *m.* electrophorus.
electrofotómetro *m.* electrophotometer.
electrofototerapia *f.* electrophototherapy.
electrofrénico, -ca *adj.* electrophrenic.
electrogastrografía *f.* electrogastrography.
electrogastrógrafo *m.* electrogastrograph.
electrogastrograma *m.* electrogastrogram.
electrografía *f.* electrography.
  electrografía del haz de His His bundle electrography.
electrograma *m.* electrogram.
  electrograma del haz de His His bundle electrogram.
electrogustometría *f.* elctrogustometry.
electrohemodinámica *f.* electrohemodynamics.
electrohemostasia *f.* electrohemostasis.
electrohemostasis *f.* electrohemostasis.
electrohisterografía *f.* electrohysterography.
electrohisterógrafo *m.* electrohysterograph.
electrohisterograma *m.* electrohysterogram.
electroimán *m.* electromagnet.
electroinmunodifusión *f.* electroimmunodiffusion.
electrólisis *f.* electrolysis.
electrolítico, -ca *adj.* electrolytic.
electrolito *m.* electrolyte.
  electrolito anfótero amphoteric electrolyte.
  electrolito coloidal colloidal electrolyte.
electrolitotricia *f.* electrolithotrity.
electrolizador *m.* electrolyzer.
electromagnético, -ca *adj.* electromagnetic.
electromagnetismo *m.* electromagnetism.
electromanómetro *m.* electromanometer.

electromasaje *m.* electromassage.
electrómetro *m.* electrometer.
electrometrografía *f.* electrometrography.
electrometrograma *m.* electrometrogram.
electromicción *f.* electromicturation.
electromigratorio, -ria *adj.* electromigratory.
electromiografía *f.* electromyography.
  electromiografía cinesiológica kinesiologic electromyography.
  electromiografía ureteral ureteral electromyography.
electromiografista *m., f.* electromyographer.
electromiógrafo *m.* electromyograph.
electromiograma *m.* electromyogram.
electromorfo, -fa *adj.* electromorph.
electrón *m.* electron.
  electrón de Auger Auger electron.
  electrón de conversión, electrón de conversión interna internal conversion electron.
  electrón de emisión emission electron.
  electrón de valencia valence electron.
  electrón positivo positive electron.
electronarcosis *f.* electronarcosis.
electronegatividad *f.* electronegativity.
electronegativo, -va *adj.* electronegative.
electroneumógrafo *m.* electropneumograph.
electroneurografía *f.* electroneurography.
electroneurólisis *f.* electroneurolysis.
electroneuromiografía *f.* electroneuromyography.
electrónica *f.* electronics.
electrónico, -ca *adj.* electronic.
electronistagmografía (ENG) *f.* electronystagmography (ENG).
electronistagmógrafo *m.* electronystagmograph.
electronistagmograma *m.* electronystagmogram.
electronógrafo *m.* electronograph.
electrooculografía *f.* electro-oculography.
electrooculograma *m.* electro-oculogram.
electroolfatograma *m.* electro-olfactogram.
electroparacentesis *f.* electroparacentesis.
electropatología *f.* electropathology.
electroporación *f.* electroporation.
electropositivo, -va *adj.* electropositive.
electropuntura *f.* electropuncture.
electroquímica *f.* electrochemistry.
electroquímico, -ca *adj.* electrochemical.
electrorradiología *f.* electroradiology.
electrorradiómetro *m.* electroradiometer.
electrorradioscopia *f.* electroradioscopy.
electrorresección *f.* electroresection.
electrorretinografía *f.* electroretinography.
electrorretinógrafo *m.* electroretinograph.
electrorretinograma *m.* electroretinogram.
electroscopio *m.* electroscope.
electrosección *f.* electrosection.
electroshock *m.* electroshock.
electrosialograma *m.* electrosalivograma.
electrosíntesis *f.* electrosynthesis.
electrosistolia *f.* electropacing.
electrosmosis *f.* electro-osmosis.
electrospinograma *m.* electrospinogram.
electrostático, -ca *adj.* electrostatic.
electrostenólisis *f.* electrostenolysis.
electrostriatograma *m.* electrostriatogram.
electrostricción *f.* electrostriction.
electrosueño *m.* electrosleep.
electrotanasia *f.* electrothanasia.
electrotaxis *f.* electrotaxis.
  electrotaxis negativa negative electrotaxis.
  electrotaxis positiva positive electrotaxis.
electroterapia *f.* electrotherapeutics, electrotherapy.

  electroterapia cerebral cerebral electrotherapeutics, (CET).
electrotermo *m.* electrotherm.
electrotomía *f.* electrotomy.
electrótomo *m.* electrotome.
electrotónico, -ca *adj.* electrotonic.
electrotono *m.* electrotonus.
electrotrépano *m.* electrotrephine.
electrotropismo *m.* electrotropism.
  electrotropismo negativo negative electrotropism.
  electrotropismo positivo positive electrotropism.
electroultrafiltración *f.* electroultrafiltration.
electroureterografía *f.* electroureterography.
electroureterograma *m.* electroureterogram.
electrovagograma *m.* electrovagogram.
electrovalencia *f.* electrovalence.
electrovalente *adj.* electrovalent.
electroversión *f.* electroversion.
elefantiásico, -ca *adj.* elephantiasic.
elefantiasis *f.* elephantiasis.
  elefantiasis angiomatosa congénita elephantiasis congenita angiomatosa.
  elefantiasis asturiensis pellagra.
  elefantiasis congénita congenital elephantiasis.
  elefantiasis del escroto, elefantiasis escrotal elephantiasis scroti.
  elefantiasis filariásica elephantiasis filariensis.
  elefantiasis gingival gingival elephantiasis, elephantiasis gingivae.
  elefantiasis de los griegos, elefantiasis griega elephantiasis graecorum.
  elefantiasis linfangiectásica, elefantiasis linfangiectodes lymphangiectatic elephantiasis.
  elefantiasis neuromatosa elephantiasis neuromatosa.
  elefantiasis nevoide nevoid elephantiasis.
  elefantiasis nostras elephantiasis nostras.
  elefantiasis ocular elephantiasis oculi.
  elefantiasis quirúrgica elephantiasis chirurgica.
  elefantiasis telangiectoide telangiectodes elephantiasis.
  elefantiasis tubárica elephantiasis neuromatosa.
  elefantiasis vulvar elephantiasis vulvae.
elefantiásico, -ca *adj.* elephantiasic.
elefantoide *adj.* elephantoid.
elefantoideo, -a *adj.* elephantoid.
eleidina *f.* eleidin.
elemental *adj.* elementary.
elemento *m.* element, elementum.
eleómetro *m.* eleometer, elaiometer.
eleopatía *f.* eleopathy, elaiopathy.
eleoplasto *m.* eleoplast, elaioplast.
eleoterapia *f.* eleotherapy.
elevador *m.* elevator, levator.
  elevador angular angular elevator.
  elevador apical apical elevator.
  elevador de barra cruzada cross bar elevator.
  elevador de barra en T T-bar elevator.
  elevador de Cryer Cryer elevator.
  elevador en cuña wedge elevator.
  elevador dental wedge elevator.
  elevador perióstico periosteal elevator, elevator periosteum.
  elevador de raíz root elevator.
  elevador recto straight elevator.
  elevador a tornillo screw elevator.
eliminación *m.* elimination.
  eliminación de dióxido de carbono carbon dioxide elimination.

eliminación inmunitaria immune elimination.

eliminación urinaria urinary output.

eliminador, -ra *adj.* eliminant.

eliminante *adj.* eliminant.

elinguación *f.* elinguation.

elinina *f.* elinin.

elipse *f.* ellipsis.

elipsis *f.* ellipsis.

elipsoide *adj.* ellipsoid, ellipsoidal.

eliptocitario, -ria *adj.* elliptocytary.

elipocítico, -ca *adj.* elypocytic.

eliptocito *m.* elliptocyte.

eliptocitosis *f.* elliptocytosis.

eliptocitótico, -ca *adj.* elliptocytotic.

elitrocele *m.* colpocele.

ELISA ELISA.

elixir *m.* elixir.

ello *m.* it.

elongación *f.* elongation.

elución *f.* elution.

eluir *v.* elute.

elutriación *f.* elutriation.

elutriación por centrifugación centrifugal elutriation.

elutriar *v.* elutriate.

emaciación *f.* emaciation.

emaculación *f.* emaculation.

emanación *f.* emanation.

emanador *m.* emanator.

emanatorio *m.* emanatorium.

emancipación *f.* emancipation.

emanoterapia *f.* emanotherapy.

emarginación *f.* emargination.

emarginado, -da *adj.* emarginate.

emasculación *f.* emasculation.

Embadomonas Embadomonas.

embalsamamiento *m.* embalming.

embalsamar *v.* embalm.

embarazada *adj.* pregnant.

embarazo *m.* pregnancy.

embarazo abdominal abdominal pregnancy.

embarazo abdominal secundario secondary abdominal pregnancy.

embarazo afetal molar pregnancy.

embarazo ampollar, embarazo ampular ampullar pregnancy.

embarazo bigémino bigeminal pregnancy.

embarazo cervical cervical pregnancy.

embarazo combinado combined pregnancy.

embarazo cornual cornual pregnancy.

embarazo ectópico ectopic pregnancy.

embarazo ectópico abortado aborted ectopic pregnancy.

embarazo espurio spurious pregnancy.

embarazo eutópico uterine pregnancy.

embarazo extraamniótico extra-amniotic pregnancy.

embarazo extracorial extrachorial pregnancy.

embarazo extramembranoso extramembranous pregnancy.

embarazo extrauterino extrauterine pregnancy.

embarazo falopiano, embarazo de Falopio fallopian pregnancy.

embarazo falso false pregnancy.

embarazo fantasma phantom pregnancy.

embarazo gemelar twin pregnancy.

embarazo heterotópico heterotopic pregnancy.

embarazo hidatídico hydatid pregnancy.

embarazo intersticial interstitial pregnancy.

embarazo intraligamentario, embarazo intraligamentoso intraligamentary pregnancy.

embarazo intramural intramural pregnancy.

embarazo intraperitoneal intraperitoneal pregnancy.

embarazo en el ligamento ancho broad ligament pregnancy.

embarazo molar molar pregnancy.

embarazo múltiple multiple pregnancy.

embarazo de muñón stump pregnancy.

embarazo mural mural pregnancy.

embarazo ovárico ovarian pregnancy.

embarazo ovaricoabdominal, embarazo ovarioabdominal ovarioabdominal pregnancy.

embarazo plural plural pregnancy.

embarazo posmaduro postdate pregnancy.

embarazo prolongado prolonged pregnancy.

embarazo sarcofetal sarcofetal pregnancy.

embarazo tubárico tubal pregnancy.

embarazo tubárico ampular ampullary tubal pregnancy.

embarazo tuboabdominal tuboabdominal pregnancy.

embarazo tuboovárico tubo-ovarian pregnancy.

embarazo tubouterino tubouterine pregnancy.

embarazo uterino uterine pregnancy.

embarazo uteroabdominal uteroabdominal pregnancy.

embarazo uteroovárico utero-ovarian pregnancy.

embarazo uterotubárico uterotubal pregnancy.

embolemia *f.* embolemia.

embolia¹ *f.* embole, emboly.

embolia² *f.* embolism.

embolia adiposa fat embolism.

embolia aérea air embolism.

embolia amniótica amniotic fluid embolism.

embolia arterial arterial embolism.

embolia por ateroma atheroma embolism.

embolia bacilar bacillary embolism.

embolia cabalgante riding embolism.

embolia capilar capillary embolism.

embolia celular cellular embolism.

embolia cerebral cerebral embolism.

embolia por colesterol cholesterol embolism.

embolia coronaria coronary embolism.

embolia cruzada crossed embolism.

embolia cutis medicamentosa embolism cutis medicamentosa.

embolia directa direct embolism.

embolia espinal spinal embolism.

embolia por fibras de algodón cotton-fiber embolism.

embolia gaseosa gas embolism.

embolia grasa fat embolism.

embolia hematógena hematogenous embolism.

embolia a horcajadas straddling embolism.

embolia infecciosa infective embolism.

embolia linfática, embolia linfógena lymph embolism, lymphogenous embolism.

embolia de médula ósea bone marrow embolism.

embolia miliar, embolia múltiple miliary embolism, multiple embolism.

embolia obturante obturating embolism.

embolia oleosa oil embolism.

embolia en pantalón pantaloon embolism.

embolia paradójica paradoxical embolism.

embolia piémica pyemic embolism.

embolia por plasmodios plasmodium embolism.

embolia pulmonar pulmonary embolism.

embolia de la retina retinal embolism.

embolia retrógrada retrograde embolism.

embolia en silla de montar saddle embolism.

embolia triquinosa trichinous embolism.

embolia tumoral tumor embolism.

embolia venosa venous embolism.

embolia séptica septic embolism, septical embolism.

embólico, -ca *adj.* embolic.

emboliectomía *f.* embolectomy.

emboliforme *adj.* emboliform.

embolización *f.* embolization.

embolización percutánea percutaneous embolization.

émbolo *m.* embolus.

émbolo adiposo fat embolus.

émbolo cabalgante riding embolus.

émbolo canceroso cancer embolus.

émbolo de catéter catheter embolus.

émbolo celular cell embolus.

émbolo espumoso foam embolus.

émbolo gaseoso air embolus.

émbolo obturador obturating embolus.

émbolo en silla de montar saddle embolus.

embolomicótico, -ca *adj.* embolomycotic.

emboloterapia *f.* embolotherapy.

embotamiento *m.* dullness.

embotamiento afectivo emotional dullness.

embriaguez *f.* drunkenness, inebriation.

embriaguez ligera light inebriation.

embriaguez grave serious inebriation.

embriaguez subclínica subclinical inebriation.

embrioblasto *m.* embryoblast.

embriocardia *f.* embryocardia.

embriocardia yugular jugular embryocardia.

embriocárdico, -ca *adj.* embryocardial.

embriogénesis *f.* embryogenesis.

embriogenético, -ca *adj.* embryogenetic.

embriogenia *f.* embryogeny.

embriogénico, -ca *adj.* embryogenic.

embrioide *adj.* embryoid.

embriología *f.* embryology.

embriología causal causal embryology.

embriología comparada comparative embryology.

embriología descriptiva descriptive embryology.

embriología experimental experimental embryology.

embriólogo, -ga *m., f.* embryologist.

embrioma *m.* embryoma.

embrioma del riñón embryoma of the kidney.

embriomorfo, -fa *adj.* embryomorphous.

embrión *m.* embryo.

embrión heterogamético heterogametic embryo.

embrión homogamético homogametic embryo.

embrión de Janösik Janösik's embryo.

embrión presomita presomite embryo.

embrión prevelloso previllous embryo.

embrión somita somite embryo.

embrión de Spee Spee's embryo.

embrionado, -da *adj.* embryonate.

embrionario, -ria *adj.* embryonal, embryonic.

embrionia *f.* embryony.

embrioniforme *adj.* embryoniform.

embrionismo *m.* embryonism, embryoism.

embrionización *f.* embryonization.

embrionoide *adj.* embryonoid.

embriopatía *f.* embryopathia, embriopathy.

embriopatía rubeolar, embriopatía rubeólica rubella embryopathy.

embriopatología *f.* embryopathology.

embrioplásico, -ca *adj.* embryoplastic.

embriotomía *f.* embryotomy.
embriótomo *m.* embryotome.
embriotoxicidad *f.* embryotoxicity.
embriotóxico, -ca *adj.* embryotoxic.
embriotoxon *m.* embryotoxon.
embriotoxon posterior posterior embryo-toxon.
embriotrofia *f.* embryotrophy.
embriotrófico, -ca *adj.* embryotrophic.
embriotrofo *m.* embryotroph.
emedular *v.* emedullate.
emeiocitosis *f.* emeiocytosis.
emenagógico, -ca *adj.* emmenagogic.
emenagogo *m.* emmenagogue.
emenagogo directo direct emmenagogue.
emenagogo indirecto indirect emmena-gogue.
emenia *f.* emmenia.
eménico, -ca *adj.* emmenic.
emeniopatia *f.* emmeniopathy.
emenología *f.* emmenology.
emenopatía *f.* emmeniopathy.
emergencia *f.* emergency.
emergente *adj.* emergent.
emesia *f.* emesia, emesis.
emesia gravídica, emesia gravidarum eme-sis gravidarum.
emesia gástrica gastric emesia.
emesia nerviosa nervous emesia.
emesis *f.* emesia, emesis.
emetatrofia *f.* emetatrophia.
emético, -ca *m. y adj.* emetic.
emético central central emetic.
emético directo direct emetic.
emético indirecto indirect emetic.
emético mecánico mechanical emetic.
emético sistémico systemic emetic.
emeticología *f.* emeticology.
emetizante *adj.* emetic.
emetocatártico, -ca *adj.* emetocathartic.
emetofobia *f.* emetophobia.
emetología *f.* emetology.
emétrope *adj.* emmetrope.
emetropía *f.* emmetropia.
emetrópico, -ca *adj.* emmetropic.
emetropización *f.* emmetropization.
emigración *f.* emigration.
eminencia *f.* eminence, eminentia.
eminentia *f.* eminence, eminentia.
emiocitosis *f.* emiocytosis.
emisaria *f.* emissarium.
emisario, -ria *adj.* emissary.

emissarium *f.* emissarium.
emoción expresada expressed emotionality.
emocional *adj.* emotional.
emoliente *adj.* emollient.
emotividad *f.* emotivity.
empacador *m.* packer.
empacamiento *m.* packing.
empacamiento protésico denture packing.
empacho *m.* empacho.
empalizada *f.* palisade.
empalme *m.* splicing.
emparejamiento *m.* coupling.
emparejamiento aleatorio random mating.
empatía *f.* empathy.
empatía generativa generative empathy.
empático, -ca *adj.* empathic.
empatizar *v.* empathize.
empeine *m.* instep.
emperiopolesis *f.* emperipolesis.
emperipolesis *f.* emperipolesis.
empiema *m.* empyema.
empiema benigno empyema benignum.

empiema epidural epidural empyema.
empiema estreptocócico streptococcal em-pyema.
empiema interlobular interlobar empyema.
empiema latente latent empyema.
empiema loculado loculated empyema.
empiema mastoideo mastoid empyema.
empiema metaneumónico metapneumonic empyema.
empiema de necesidad, empiema necessi-tatis empyema necessitatis.
empiema neumocócico pneumococcal em-pyema.
empiema pericárdico, empiema del peri-cardio empyema of the pericardium.
empiema pulsátil pulsating empyema.
empiema pútrido putrid empyema.
empiema sinneumónico sypneumonic em-pyema.
empiema subdural subdural empyema.
empiema torácico empyema of the chest, thoracic empyema.
empiema tuberculoso tuberculous empy-ema.
empiema vesicular gallbladder empyema, empyema of the gallblader.
empiémico, -ca *adj.* empyiemic.
empiesis *f.* empyesis.
empiocele *m.* empyocele.
empireuma *m.* empyreuma.
empireumático, -ca *adj.* empyreumatic.
empírico, -ca *adj.* empirical, empiric.
emplasto *m.* plaster.
emprostótonos *m.* emprosthotonos, empros-thotonus.
emptisis *f.* emptysis.
emulgente *m. y adj.* emulgent.
emulsión *f.* emulsion.
emulsionante *m.* emulsifier.
emulsionar *v.* emulsify.
emulsivo, -va *adj.* emulsive.
emulsoide *m.* emulsoid.
emuntorio, -ria *adj.* emunctory.
enajenación *f.* abalienation.
enajenación mental mental abalienation.
enamelogénesis *f.* enamelogenesis.
enamelogénesis imperfecta enamelogene-sis imperfecta.
enameloma *m.* enameloma.
enanismo *m.* dwarfism.
enanismo acondroplásico achondroplastic dwarfism.
enanismo acromélico acromelic dwarfism.
enanismo aórtico aortic dwarfism.
enanismo de Brissaud Brissaud's dwarfism.
enanismo camptomélico camptomelic dwarfism.
enanismo condrodistrófico chondrodystro-phic dwarfism.
enanismo carencial deprivation dwarfism.
enanismo diastrófico diastrophic dwarfism.
enanismo fisiológico physiologic dwarfism.
enanismo focomélico phocomelic dwarfism.
enanismo hipofisario hypophyseal dwarfism.
enanismo hipotiroideo hypothyroid dwarf-ism.
enanismo infantil infantile dwarfism.
enanismo de Laron, enanismo tipo Laron Laron type dwarfism.
enanismo de Lorain-Lévi Lorain-Lévi dwarf-ism.
enanismo mesomélico mesomelic dwarfism.
enanismo metatrófico metatropic dwarfism.
enanismo micromélico micromelic dwarf-ism.

enanismo mortal lethal dwarfism.
enanismo mulibrey mulibrey dwarfism.
enanismo de nariz respingada snub-nose dwarfism.
enanismo pituitario pituitary dwarfism.
enanismo primordial primordial dwarfism.
enanismo senil senile dwarfism.
enanismo de Silver-Russell Silver-Russell dwarfism.
enanismo tanatofórico thanatophoric dwarfism.
enanismo verdadero true dwarfism.
enanismo de Walt Disney Walt Disney dwarfism.
enano, -na *m., f.* dwarf, midget.
enano acondroplásico achondroplasic dwarf.
enano asexual asexual dwarf.
enano ateliótico ateliotic dwarf.
enano de Brissaud Brissaud's dwarf.
enano con cabeza de pájaro, enano con ca-beza de pájaro de Seckel bird-headed dwarf, bird-headed dwarf of Seckel.
enano cretino cretin dwarf.
enano diastrófico diastrophic dwarf.
enano fisiológico physiologic dwarf.
enano focomélico phocomelic dwarf.
enano de Fröhlich Fröhlich's dwarf.
enano geleofísico geleophysic dwarf.
enano hipofisario hypophyseal dwarf.
enano hipotiroideo hypothyroid dwarf.
enano idiopático idiopathic dwarf.
enano infantil infantile dwarf.
enano micromélico micromelic dwarf.
enano normal normal dwarf.
enano de Paltauf Paltauf's dwarf.
enano pituitario pituitary dwarf.
enano primordial primordial dwarf.
enano puro pure dwarf.
enano raquítico rachitic dwarf.
enano renal renal dwarf.
enano rizomélico rhizomelic dwarf.
enano de Russell Russell dwarf.
enano de Seckel Seckel dwarf.
enano sexual sexual dwarf.
enano tanatofórico thanatophoric dwarf.
enano verdadero true dwarf.
enantema *m.* enanthem, enanthema.
enantematoso, -sa *adj.* enanthematous.
enantesis *f.* enanthesis.
enantiobiosis *f.* enantiobiosis.
enantrópico, -ca *adj.* enanthrope.
enartritis *f.* enarthritis.
enartrodia *f.* enarthrosis.
enartrodial *adj.* enarthrodial, enarthrodial.
enartrosis *f.* enarthrosis.
encadenamiento *m.* chaining.
encadenante *adj.* catenating.
encajamiento *m.* engagement.
encaje *m.* emboitement.
encaje cefálico headgear emboitement.
encapsulación *f.* encapsulation.
encapsulado, -da *adj.* encapsulated, encap-suled.
encarcelado, -da *adj.* incarcerated.
encarditis *f.* encarditis.
encarnadura *f.* incarnation.
encarnamiento *m.* incarnation, incarnatio.
encarnante *adj.* incarnant.
encatarrafia *f.* enkatarrhaphy, encatarrhaphy.
encefalalgia *f.* encephalalgia.
encefalatrofia *f.* encephalatrophy.
encefalatrófico, -ca *adj.* encephalatrophic.
encefalauxa *f.* encephauxe.
encefalauxia *f.* encephauxe.
encefalemia *f.* encephalemia.

encefálico, -ca *adj.* encephalic.
encefalina *f.* enkephalin.
encefalinérgico, -ca *adj.* enkephalinergic.
encefalítico, -ca *adj.* encephalitic.
encefalitis *f.* encephalitis.
  encefalitis aguda diseminada acute disseminated encephalitis.
  encefalitis aguda necrosante acute necrotizing encephalitis.
  encefalitis alérgica experimental experimental allergic encephalitis.
  encefalitis australiana X Australian X encephalitis.
  encefalitis B B encephalitis.
  encefalitis de Binswanger Binswanger's encephalitis.
  encefalitis del bosque Semliki Semliki forest encephalitis.
  encefalitis por Bunyavirus Bunyavirus encephalitis.
  encefalitis C encephalitis C.
  encefalitis de California California encephalitis.
  encefalitis cortical cortical encephalitis, encephalitis corticalis.
  encefalitis por Coxsackie Coxsackie encephalitis.
  encefalitis por cuerpos de inclusión inclusion body encephalitis.
  encefalitis chikungunya chikungunya encephalitis.
  encefalitis de Dawson Dawson's encephalitis.
  encefalitis epidémica epidemic encephalitis, encephalitis epidemica.
  encefalitis estival summer encephalitis.
  encefalitis de Europa Central Central European encephalitis.
  encefalitis hemorrágica, encefalitis hemorrágica aguda hemorrhagic encephalitis, acute hemorrhagic encephalitis.
  encefalitis hemorrágica por arsfenamina hemorrhagic arsphenamine encephalitis.
  encefalitis hemorrágica superior encephalitis hemorrhagica superior.
  encefalitis herpética herpes simplex encephalitis, herpetic encephalitis.
  encefalitis hiperérgica hyperergic encephalitis.
  encefalitis hiperplásica encephalitis hyperplastica.
  encefalitis Ilhéus, encefalitis de Ilheus Ilheus encephalitis.
  encefalitis por influenza influenzal encephalitis.
  encefalitis japonesa B Japanese B encephalitis.
  encefalitis japonesa, encefalitis japonica Japanese encephalitis, encephalitis japonica.
  encefalitis del leñador woodcutter's encephalitis.
  encefalitis letárgica lethargic encephalitis.
  encefalitis Mengo Mengo encephalitis.
  encefalitis miálgica benigna benign myalgic encephalitis.
  encefalitis de Murray-Valley Murray-Valley encephalitis.
  encefalitis necrosante necrotizing encephalitis.
  encefalitis necrosante aguda acute necrotizing encephalitis.
  encefalitis neonatal encephalitis neonatorum.
  encefalitis periaxial, encefalitis periaxil concéntrica encephalitis periaxialis, encephalitis periaxialis concentrica.
  encefalitis periaxial difusa encephalitis periaxialis diffusa.
  encefalitis piógena, encefalitis piogénica pyogenic encephalitis.

  encefalitis por plomo lead encephalitis.
  encefalitis posinfecciosa postinfectious encephalitis.
  encefalitis posvacunal postvaccinal encephalitis.
  encefalitis de Powassan Powassan encephalitis.
  encefalitis primaveral de los bosques forest-spring encephalitis.
  encefalitis purulenta purulent encephalitis.
  encefalitis rusa endémica Russian endemic encephalitis.
  encefalitis rusa otoñal Russian autumn encephalitis.
  encefalitis rusa primaveral de los bosques, encefalitis rusa de primavera y verano Russian forest-spring encephalitis, Russian spring-summer encephalitis.
  encefalitis rusa transmitida por garrapatas Russian tick-borne encephalitis.
  encefalitis rusa vernoestival (subtipo oriental) Russian spring-summer encephalitis (Eastern subtype).
  encefalitis de San Luis St Louis encephalitis.
  encefalitis secundaria secondary encephalitis.
  encefalitis subaguda por cuerpos de inclusión subacute inclusion body encephalitis.
  encefalitis supurada, encefalitis supurativa suppurative encephalitis.
  encefalitis toxoplásmica toxoplasmic encephalitis.
  encefalitis transmitida por garrapatas (subtipo oriental) tick-borne encephalitis (Eastern subtype).
  encefalitis vacunal vaccinal encephalitis.
  encefalitis de van Bogaert van Bogaert's encephalitis.
  encefalitis de la varicela varicella encephalitis.
  encefalitis vernal vernal encephalitis.
  encefalitis vernoestival vernoestival encephalitis.
  encefalitis de Viena Vienna encephalitis.
  encefalitis de von Economo von Economo's encephalitis.
encefalitogénico, -ca *adj.* encephalitogenic.
encefalitógeno *m.* encephalitogen.
encefalización *f.* encephalization.
encéfalo *m.* brain, encephalon.
encefaloarteriografía *f.* encephalo-arteriography.
encefalocele *m.* encephalocele.
encefalocistocele *m.* encephalocystocele.
encefaloclástico, -ca *adj.* encephaloclastic.
encefalodiálisis *f.* encephalodyalisis.
encefalodinia *f.* encephalodynia.
encefalodisplasia *f.* encephalodysplasia.
encefaloesclerosis *f.* encephalosclerosis.
encefaloespinal *adj.* encephalospinal.
encefalofima *m.* encephalophyma.
encefalografía *f.* encephalography.
  encefalografía gamma gamma encephalography.
encefalograma *m.* encephalogram.
encefaloide *adj.* encephaloid.
encefalolito *m.* encephalolith.
encefalología *f.* encephalology.
encefaloma *f.* encephaloma.
encefalomalacia *f.* encephalomalacia.
encefalomeningitis *f.* encephalomeningitis.
encefalomeningocele *m.* encephalomeningocele.
encefalomeningopatía *f.* encephalomeningopathy.
encefalómero *m.* encephalomere.

encefalométrico, -ca *adj.* encephalometric.
encefalómetro *m.* encephalometer.
encefalomielitis *f.* encephalomyelitis.
  encefalomielitis aguda diseminada acute disseminated encephalomyelitis.
  encefalomielitis alérgica experimental experimental allergic encephalomyelitis.
  encefalomielitis diseminada aguda acute disseminated encephalomyelitis.
  encefalomielitis equina equine encephalomyelitis.
  encefalomielitis equina del Este Eastern equine encephalomyelitis.
  encefalomielitis equina del Oeste Western equine encephalomyelitis.
  encefalomielitis equina venezolana Venezuelan equine encephalomyelitis.
  encefalomielitis granulomatosa granulomatous encephalomyelitis.
  encefalomielitis posinfecciosa postinfectious encephalomyelitis.
  encefalomielitis posvacunal postvaccinal encephalomyelitis.
  encefalomielitis toxoplásmica toxoplasmic encephalomyelitis.
  encefalomielitis viral, encefalomielitis virósica, encefalomielitis por virus viral encephalomyelitis, virus encephalomyelitis.
  encefalomielitis zoster zoster encephalomyelitis.
encefalomielocele *m.* encephalomyelocele.
encefalomieloneuropatía *f.* encephalomyeloneuropathy.
  encefalomieloneuropatía inespecífica non-specific encephalomyeloneuropathy.
encefalomielopatía *f.* encephalomyelopathy.
  encefalomielopatía carcinomatosa carcinomatous encephalomyelopathy.
  encefalomielopatía miálgica epidémica epidemic myalgic encephalomyelopathy.
  encefalomielopatía mitocondrial mitochondrial encephalomyelopathy.
  encefalomielopatía necrosante, encefalomielopatía necrosante subaguda subacute necrotizing encephalomyelopathy.
  encefalomielopatía paracarcinomatosa paracarcinomatous encephalomyelopathy.
  encefalomielopatía posinfecciosa postinfection encephalomyelopathy.
  encefalomielopatía posvacunal postvaccinial encephalomyelopathy.
encefalomielorradiculitis *f.* encephalomyeloradiculitis.
encefalomielorradiculoneuritis *f.* encephalomyeloradiculoneuritis.
encefalomielorradiculopatía *f.* encephalomyeloradiculopathy.
encefalomiocarditis *f.* encephalomyocarditis.
encefalopatía *f.* encephalopathy, encephalopathia.
  encefalopatía de Addison Addisonian encephalopathy.
  encefalopatía arteriosclerótica subcortical subcortical arteriosclerotic encephalopathy.
  encefalopatía biliar biliary encephalopathy.
  encefalopatía por bilirrubina, encefalopatía bilirrubínica bilirubin encephalopathy.
  encefalopatía de Binswanger Binswanger's encephalopathy.
  encefalopatía de los boxeadores punch-drunk encephalopathy.
  encefalopatía desmielinizante demyelinating encephalopathy.
  encefalopatía de diálisis, encefalopatía por diálisis dialysis encephalopathy.

encefalopatía espongiforme spongiform encephalopathy.

encefalopatía espongiforme bovina bovine spongiform encephalopathy.

encefalopatía espongiforme subaguda subacute spongiform encephalopathy.

encefalopatía espongiforme transmisible transmissible spongiform encephalopathy.

encefalopatía familiar familial encephalopathy.

encefalopatía hepática hepatic encephalopathy.

encefalopatía hipernatrémica hypernatremic encephalopathy.

encefalopatía hipertensiva hypertensive encephalopathy.

encefalopatía hipoglucemica hypoglycemic encephalopathy.

encefalopatía metabólica metabolic encephalopathy.

encefalopatía mioclónica infantil myoclonic encephalopathy of childhood.

encefalopatía necrosante subaguda subacute necrotizing encephalopathy.

encefalopatía necrosante hemorrágica aguda acute necrotizing hemorrhagic encephalopathy.

encefalopatía palindrómica palindromic encephalopathy.

encefalopatía pancreática pancreatic encephalopathy.

encefalopatía por plomo lead encephalopathy.

encefalopatía portal sistemática, encefalopatía portosistemática portal-systemic encephalopathy.

encefalopatía posanóxica postanoxic encephalopathy.

encefalopatía recurrente recurrent encephalopathy.

encefalopatía saturnina saturnine encephalopathy.

encefalopatía subcortical progresiva progressive subcortical encephalopathy.

encefalopatía tirotóxica thyrotoxic encephalopathy.

encefalopatía transmisible del visón transmissible encephalopathy of mink.

encefalopatía transmisible por virus espongiforme transmissible spongiform virus encephalopathy.

encefalopatía traumática progresiva traumatic progressive encephalopathy.

encefalopatía urémica uremic encephalopathy.

encefalopático, -ca *adj.* encephalopathic.
encefalopiosis *f.* encephalopyosis.
encefalopsia *f.* encephalopsy.
encefalopuntura *f.* encephalopuncture.
encefalorradiculitis *f.* encephaloradiculitis.
encefalorragia *f.* encephalorrhagia.
encefalorraquídeo, -a *adj.* encephalorachidian.
encefalosclerosis *f.* encephalosclerosis.
encefaloscopia *f.* encephaloscopy.
encefaloscopio *m.* encephaloscope.
encefalosepsis *f.* encephalosepsis.
encefalosis *f.* encephalosis.
encefalospinal *adj.* encephalospinal.
encefalosquisis *f.* encephaloschisis.
encefalotlipsis *f.* encephalothlipsis.
encefalotomía *f.* encephalotomy.
encefalótomo *m.* encephalotome.
encelialgia *f.* encelialgia.
encelitis *f.* encelitis, enceliitis.

encerado *m.* cerecloth.
encía *f.* gum, gingiva.

encía adherida attached gingiva.

encía alveolar alveolar gingiva.

encía areolar areolar gingiva.

encía bucal buccal gingiva.

encía cemental cemental gingiva.

encía interdental, encía interdentaria interdental gingiva.

encía interproximal interproximal gingiva.

encía papilar papillary gingiva.

encía labial labial gingiva.

encía libre free gingiva.

encía lingual lingual gingiva.

encía no adherida free gingiva.

encía septal septal gingiva.

enciesis *f.* encyesis.
encigótico, -ca *adj.* enzygotic.
enciopielitis *f.* encyopyelitis.
enclavamiento *m.* nailing.

enclavamiento intramedular intramedullary nailing.

enclavamiento medular medullary nailing.

enclave *m.* enclave.
encolpitis *f.* encolpitis.
encondral *adj.* enchondral.
encondroma *m.* enchondroma.

encondroma congénito múltiple multiple congenital enchondroma.

encondromatosis *f.* enchondromatosis.

encondromatosis esquelética skeletal enchondromatosis.

encondromatosis múltiple multiple enchondromatosis.

encondromatoso, -sa *adj.* enchondromatous.
encondrosarcoma *m.* enchondrosarcoma.
encondrosis *f.* enchondrosis.
encopresis *f.* encopresis.

encopresis no órganica non-organic encopresis.

encordamiento *m.* chordee.
encostración *f.* incrustation.
encostradura *f.* incrustation.
encraneal *adj.* encranial.
encráneo *m.* encranius.
endadelfo *m.* endadelphos.
endamebiasis *f.* endamoebiasis.
Endamoeba Endamoeba.
endamoebiasis *f.* endamoebiasis.
endangio *m.* endangium, tunica intima vasorum.
endangeítis *f.* endangeitis, endangiitis, endangitis, endoangiitis, endoangitis.

endangeítis obliterante endangeitis obliterans.

endangiitis *f.* endangeitis, endangiitis, endangitis, endoangiitis, endoangitis.
endangitis *f.* endangeitis, endangiitis, endangitis, endoangiitis, endoangitis.
endeíctico, -ca *adj.* endeictic.
endemia *f.* endemia, endemy.
endémico, -ca *adj.* endemic.
endemoepidémico, -ca *adj.* endemoepidemic.
enderezamiento[1] *m.* redressement.

enderezamiento forzado redressement forcé.

enderezamiento[2] *m.* uprighting.
endermático, -ca *adj.* endermatic.
endérmico, -ca *adj.* endermic.
endermismo *m.* endermism.
endermosis *f.* endermosis.
enderón *m.* enderon.
enderónico, -ca *adj.* enderonic.
endima *f.* endyma.
endoabdominal *adj.* endoabdominal.

endoaneurismoplastia *f.* endoaneurysmoplasty.
endoantitoxina *f.* endoantitoxin.
endoaórtico, -ca *adj.* endaortic, endoaortic.
endoaortitis *f.* endaortitis, endoaortitis.

endoaortitis bacteriana bacterial endaortitis.

endoapendicitis *f.* endoappendicitis.
endoarteria *f.* endarterium.
endoarterial *adj.* endarterial.
endoarteriectomía *f.* endarterectomy.

endoarteriectomía carotídea carotid endarterectomy.

endoarteriectomía coronaria coronary endarterectomy.

endoarteriectomía por gas gas endarterectomy.

endoarteriopatía *f.* endarteropathy.

endoarteriopatía digital digital endarteropathy.

endoarteritis *f.* endarteritis, endoarteritis.

endoarteritis bacteriana bacterial endarteritis.

endoarteritis deformante endarteritis deformans.

endoarteritis específica de Heubner Heubner's specific endarteritis.

endoarteritis obliterante endarteritis obliterans.

endoarteritis proliferante endarteritis proliferans.

endoauscultación *f.* endoauscultation.
endobacilar *adj.* endobacillary.
endobasión *m.* endobasion.
endobiótico, -ca *adj.* endobiotic.
endoblástico, -ca *adj.* endoblastic.
endoblasto *m.* endoblast, entoblast.
endobronquial *adj.* endobronchial.
endobronquitis *f.* endobronchitis.
endocardíaco, -ca *adj.* endocardiac.
endocárdico, -ca *adj.* endocardial.
endocardio *m.* endocardium.
endocardiografía *f.* endocardiography.
endocardítico, -ca *adj.* endocarditic.
endocarditis *f.* endocarditis.

endocarditis abacteriana trombótica abacterial thrombotic endocarditis.

endocarditis bacteriana subacute bacterial endocarditis.

endocarditis bacteriana aguda bacterial endocarditis.

endocarditis bacteriana subaguda acute bacterial endocarditis.

endocarditis caquéctica cachectic endocarditis.

endocarditis constrictiva constrictive endocarditis.

endocarditis cordal endocarditis chordalis.
endocarditis crónica chronic endocarditis.
endocarditis derecha right-sided endocarditis.

endocarditis fibroplásica parietal de Löffler Löffler's parietal fibroplastic endocarditis.

endocarditis por hongos fungal endocarditis.

endocarditis infecciosa infectious endocarditis, infective endocarditis.

endocarditis lenta endocarditis lenta.

endocarditis de Libman-Sacks Libman-Sacks endocarditis.

endocarditis de Löffler Löffler's endocarditis.

endocarditis lúpica lupus endocarditis.
endocarditis maligna malignant endocarditis.

endocarditis marántica marantic endocarditis.

endocarditis micótica mycotic endocarditis.

endocarditis mural mural endocarditis.

endocarditis de Osler Osler's endocarditis.

endocarditis parietal parietal endocarditis.

endocarditis parietal aislada isolated parietal endocarditis.

endocarditis poliposa polypous endocarditis.

endocarditis pulmonar pulmonic endocarditis.

endocarditis pustulosa pustulous endocarditis.

endocarditis reumática rheumatic endocarditis.

endocarditis rickettsiana rickettsial endocarditis.

endocarditis séptica septic endocarditis.

endocarditis sifilítica syphilitic endocarditis.

endocarditis terminal terminal endocarditis.

endocarditis trombótica no bacteriana non-bacterial thrombotic endocarditis.

endocarditis tuberculosa tuberculous endocarditis.

endocarditis ulcerativa, endocarditis ulcerada ulcerative endocarditis.

endocarditis por válvula de prótesis prosthetic valve endocarditis.

endocarditis valvular valvular endocarditis.

endocarditis vegetante, endocarditis vegetativa vegetative endocarditis.

endocarditis verrugosa, endocarditis verrucosa verrucous endocarditis.

endocarditis verrugosa atípica, endocarditis verrugosa no bacteriana atypical verrucous endocarditis, non-bacterial verrucous endocarditis.

endocelíaco, -ca *adj.* endoceliac.

endocelular *adj.* endocellular.

endocervical *adj.* endocervical.

endocervicitis *f.* endocervicitis.

endocérvix *m.* endocervix.

endocíclico, -ca *adj.* endocyclic.

endocistitis *f.* endocystitis.

endocito *m.* endocyte.

endocitosis *f.* endocytosis.

  endocitosis mediada por receptor receptor-mediated endocytosis.

endocolitis *f.* endocolitis.

endocolpitis *f.* endocolpitis.

endocomensal *m.* endocommensal.

endocondral *adj.* endochondral.

endoconidiotoxicosis *f.* endoconidiotoxicosis.

endocorion *m.* endochorion.

endocorpuscular *adj.* endocorpuscular.

endocraneal *adj.* endocranial, entocranial.

endocráneo *m.* endocranium, entocranium.

endocraneosis *f.* endocraniosis.

endocranitis *f.* endocranitis.

endocría *f.* inbreeding.

endocriado, -da *adj.* inbred.

endocrinismo *m.* endocrinism.

endocrino, -na *adj.* endocrine, endocrinous.

endocrinología *f.* endocrinology.

  endocrinología reproductora reproductive endocrinology.

endocrinólogo, -a *m., f.* endocrinologist.

endocrinoma *m.* endocrinoma.

  endocrinoma múltiple multiple endocrinoma.

endocrinópata *m., f.* endocrinopath.

endocrinopatía *f.* endocrinopathy.

  endocrinopatía múltiple multiple endocrinopathy.

endocrinopático, -ca *adj.* endocrinopathic.

endocrinosis *f.* endocrinosis.

endocrinoterapia *f.* endocrinotherapy.

endocromo *m.* endochrome.

endodérmico, -ca *adj.* endodermal, entodermal, entodermic.

endodermo *m.* endoderm, entoderm.

  endodermo del saco vitelino yolk-sac endoderm.

endodermorreacción *f.* endodermoreaction.

endodiascopia *f.* endodiascopy.

endodiascopio *m.* endodiascope.

endodoncia *f.* endodontics, endodontia.

endodoncista *m., f.* endodontist.

endodontista *m., f.* endodontist.

endodontitis *f.* endodontitis.

endodonto *m.* endodontium.

endodontología *f.* endodontology.

endodontólogo, -ga *m., f.* endodontologist.

endoenteritis *f.* endoenteritis.

endoenzima *f.* endoenzyme.

endoepidérmico, -ca *adj.* endoepidermal.

endoepitelial *adj.* endoepithelial.

endoesofagitis *f.* endoesophagitis.

endoesqueleto *m.* endoskeleton.

endoestetoscopio *m.* endostethoscope.

endoexotérico, -ca *adj.* endoexoteric.

endofaradismo *m.* endofaradism.

endofilaxis *f.* endophylaxination.

endoflebitis *f.* endophlebitis.

endoforia *f.* endophoria.

endoftalmía *f.* endophthalmitis, entophtalmia.

endoftalmitis *f.* endophthalmitis.

  endoftalmitis bacteriana bacterial endophthalmitis.

  endoftalmitis estéril sterile endophthalmitis.

  endoftalmitis facoalérgica phacoallergic endophthalmitis.

  endoftalmitis facoanafiláctica phacoanaphylactic endophthalmitis, endophthalmitis phacoanaphylactica.

  endoftalmitis por gérmenes lentos retarded endophthalmitis.

  endoftalmitis granulomatosa granulomatous endophthalmitis.

  endoftalmitis nudosa endophthalmitis ophthalmia nodosa.

endogalvanismo *m.* endogalvanism.

endogamia *f.* endogamy, inbreeding.

endógamo, -ma *adj.* endogamous.

endogástrico, -ca *adj.* endogastric.

endogastritis *f.* endogastritis.

endogenético, -ca *adj.* endogenetic.

endogénico, -ca *adj.* endogenic.

endógeno, -na *adj.* endogenous.

endogenota *m.* endogenote.

endogenoto *m.* endogenote.

endoglobular *adj.* endoglobular, endoglobar.

endognatio *m.* endognathion.

endognation *m.* endognathion.

endoherniorrafia *f.* endoherniorrhaphy.

endointoxicación *f.* endointoxication.

Endolaberintitis *f.* endolabyrinthitis.

endolaringe *f.* endolarynx.

endolaríngeo, -a *adj.* endolaryngeal.

endolinfa *f.* endolymph, endolympha.

endolinfático, -ca *adj.* endolymphatic.

endolínfico, -ca *adj.* endolymphic.

endolisina *f.* endolysin.

  endolisina leucocítica, endolisina leucocitaria leukocytic endolysin.

endólisis *f.* endolysis.

endolisosoma *m.* endolysosome.

endolito *m.* endolith.

endomastoiditis *f.* endomastoiditis.

endomeninge *f.* endomeninx.

endomesodermo *m.* endomesoderm, entomesoderm.

endometrectomía *f.* endometrectomy.

endometria *f.* endometry.

endometrial *adj.* endometrial.

endometrio *m.* endometrium.

  endometrio en queso suizo, endometrio gruyère Swiss cheese endometrium.

endometrioide *adj.* endometrioid.

endometrioma *m.* endometrioma.

endometriosis *f.* endometriosis.

  endometriosis directa direct endometriosis.

  endometriosis del estroma stromal endometriosis.

  endometriosis externa endometriosis externa.

  endometriosis de implantación implantation endometriosis.

  endometriosis interna endometriosis interna.

  endometriosis metastásica metastatic endometriosis.

  endometriosis ovárica ovarian endometriosis, endometriosis ovarii.

  endometriosis peritoneal peritoneal endometriosis.

  endometriosis primaria primary endometriosis.

  endometriosis transplantada transplantation endometriosis.

  endometriosis uterina endometriosis uterina.

  endometriosis tuberculosa tuberculous endometriosis.

  endometriosis vesical endometriosis vesicae.

endometritis *f.* endometritis.

  endometritis bacteriotóxica bacteriotoxic endometritis.

  endometritis cervical cervical endometritis.

  endometritis decidual decidual endometritis.

  endometritis disecante endometritis dissecans.

  endometritis exfoliativa endometritis dissecans.

  endometritis glandular glandular endometritis.

  endometritis hiperplásica hyperplastic endometritis.

  endometritis membranosa membranous endometritis.

  endometritis puerperal puerperal endometritis.

  endometritis sincicial syncytial endometritis.

  endometritis tuberculosa tuberculous endometritis.

  endometritis tuberosa papulosa endometritis tuberosa papulosa.

endometrópico, -ca *adj.* endometropic.

endomiocárdico, -ca *adj.* endomyocardial.

endomiocarditis *f.* endomyocarditis.

endomiometritis *f.* endomyometritis.

endomisio *m.* endomysium.

endomitosis *f.* endomitosis.

endomitótico, -ca *adj.* endomitotic.

endomixis *f.* endomixis.

endomorfia *f.* endomorphy.

endomórfico, -ca *adj.* endomorphic.

endomorfo, -fa *m., f.* endomorph.

endomotorsonda *f.* endomotorsonde.

endonasal *adj.* endonasal.

endonefritis *f.* endonephritis.

endoneural *adj.* endoneural.

endonéurico, -ca *adj.* endoneural.
endoneurio *m.* endoneurium.
endoneuritis *f.* endoneuritis.
endoneuro *m.* endoneurium.
endoneurólisis *f.* endoneurolysis.
endonuclear *adj.* endonuclear.
endonucléolo *m.* endonucleolus.
endoparasitismo *m.* endoparasitism.
endoparásito *m.* endoparasite.
endopélvico, -ca *adj.* endopelvic.
endoperiarteritis *f.* endoperiarteritis.
endopericardíaco, -ca *adj.* endopericardiac.
endopericárdico, -ca *adj.* endopericardial.
endopericarditis *f.* endopericarditis.
endoperimiocarditis *f.* endoperimyocarditis.
endoperineuritis *f.* endoperineuritis.
endoperitoneal *adj.* endoperitoneal.
endoperitonitis *f.* endoperitonitis.
endoplasma *m.* endoplasm, entoplasm.
endoplasmático, -ca *adj.* endoplasmatic.
endoplásmico, -ca *adj.* endoplasmic.
endopoligenia *f.* endopolygeny.
endopoliploide *adj.* endopolyploid.
endopoliploidía *f.* endoplyploidy.
endoprótesis *f.* stent, endoprothesis.
endoquiste *m.* endocyst.
endorfina *f.* endorphin.
endorfinérgico, -ca *adj.* endorphinergic.
endorradiosonda *f.* endoradiosonde.
endorraquis *m.* endorrhachis.
endorreduplicación *f.* endoreduplication.
endorrinitis *f.* endorhinitis.
endosalpingiosis *f.* endosalpingiosis, endosalpingosis.
endosalpingitis *f.* endosalpingitis.
endosalpingosis *f.* endosalpingosis.
endosálpinx *f.* endosalpinx, tunica mucosa tubae uterinae.
endosarco *m.* endosarc.
endoscopia *f.* endoscopy.
  endoscopia perbucal peroral endoscopy.
  endoscopia transcólica transcolonic endoscopy.
endoscópico, -ca *adj.* endoscopic.
endoscopio *m.* endoscope.
endoscopista *m.*, *f.* endoscopist.
endosecretorio, -ria *adj.* endosecretory.
endosepsis *f.* endosepsis.
endosimbiosis *f.* endosymbiosis.
endósito *m.* endosite.
endosmómetro *m.* endosmometer.
endósmosis *f.* endosmosis.
endosmótico, -ca *adj.* endosmotic.
endosoma *m.* endosome.
endosonoscopia *f.* endosonoscopy.
endosqueleto *m.* endoskeleton.
endosteoma *m.* endosteoma, endostoma.
endostetoscopio *m.* endostethoscope.
endóstico, -ca *adj.* endosteal.
endostio *m.* endosteum.
endostitis *f.* endosteitis, endostitis.
endostoma *m.* endostoma.
endostosis *f.* endostosis.
endotelial *adj.* endothelial.
endotelio *m.* endothelium.
endotelioblastoma *m.* endothelioblastoma.
endoteliocito *m.* endotheliocyte.
endoteliocitosis *f.* endotheliocytosis.
endoteliocorial *adj.* endotheliochorial.
endotelioide *adj.* endothelioid.
endoteliolisina *f.* endotheliolysin.
endoteliolítico, -ca *adj.* endotheliolytic.
endotelioma *m.* endothelioma.
  endotelioma angiomatoso endothelioma angiomatosum.

endotelioma capitis endothelioma capitis.
  endotelioma cutis endothelioma cutis.
  endotelioma difuso diffuse endothelioma.
  endotelioma dural dural endothelioma.
endoteliomatosis *f.* endotheliomatosis.
endoteliosarcoma *m.* endotheliosarcoma.
endoteliosis *f.* endotheliosis.
endoteliotoxina *f.* endotheliotoxin.
endotelitis *f.* endothelitis.
endotelización *f.* endothelization.
endotendón *m.* endotenon, endotendineum.
endotermia *f.* endothermy.
endotérmico, -ca *adj.* endothermic.
endotermo *m.* endotherm.
endotiroidopexia *f.* endothyropexy.
endotiropexia *f.* endothyropexy.
endotoscopio *m.* endotoscope.
endotoxinemia *f.* endotoxemia.
endotóxico, -ca *adj.* endotoxic.
endotoxicosis *f.* endotoxicosis.
Endotoxina *f.* endotoxin.
endotraqueal *adj.* endotracheal.
endotrix *m.* endothrix.
endovasculitis *f.* endovasculitis.
  endovasculitis hemorrágica hemorrhagic endovasculitis.
endovenitis *f.* endovenitis.
endovenoso, -sa *adj.* endovenous.
endurecimiento *m.* hardening.
enema *m.* enema.
  enema alto high enema.
  enema analéptico analeptic enema.
  enema de bario barium enema.
  enema baritado barium enema.
  enema ciego blind enema.
  enema de contraste contrast enema.
  enema de doble contraste double contrast enema.
  enema nutriente nutrient enema, nutritive enema.
  enema opaco contrast enema.
  enema para flato flatus enema.
  enema de trementina turpentine enema.
energía *f.* energy.
energómetro *m.* energometer.
enervación *f.* enervation.
enfermedad *f.* disease, illness, sickness.
  enfermedad aaa aaa disease.
  enfermedad de Acosta Acosta's disease.
  enfermedad por acumulación accumulation disease.
  enfermedad de Adams-Stokes Adams-Stokes disease.
  enfermedad de Addison Addison's disease.
  enfermedad de Addison-Biermer Addison-Biermer disease.
  enfermedad adenoidea adenoid disease.
  enfermedad del aire airsickness.
  enfermedad akamushi akamushi disease.
  enfermedad de los albañiles stone-masons' disease.
  enfermedad de Albers-Schönberg Albers-Schönberg disease.
  enfermedad de Albert Albert's disease.
  enfermedad de Albright Albright's disease.
  enfermedad de Alexander Alexander's disease.
  enfermedad por almacenamiento storage disease.
  enfermedad por almacenamiento de cistina cystine storage disease.
  enfermedad por almacenamiento de ésteres de colesterol cholesterol ester storage disease.
  enfermedad por almacenamiento de glucógeno glycogen-storage disease.

  enfermedad por almacenamiento de hierro iron-storage disease.
  enfermedad de Alpers Alpers disease.
  enfermedad de las alturas altitude sickness.
  enfermedad de Alzheimer Alzheimer's disease.
  enfermedad amarilla yellow disease.
  enfermedad ampollar de IgA lineal en niños linear IgA bullous disease in children.
  enfermedad anartrítica reumatoidea anarthritic rheumatoid disease.
  enfermedad de Anders Anders' disease.
  enfermedad aortoilíaca oclusiva aortoiliac occlusive disease.
  enfermedad de Apert acrocephalopolysyndactyly.
  enfermedad de Aran-Duchenne Aran-Duchenne disease.
  enfermedad por arañazo de gato cat-scratch disease.
  enfermedad de Armstrong Armstrong's disease.
  enfermedad de Arrillaga-Ayerza Ayerza's disease.
  enfermedad articular degenerativa degenerative joint disease.
  enfermedad de Aujeszky Aujeszky's disease.
  enfermedad autoinmune autoimmune disease.
  enfermedad autoinmune sistémica systemic autoimmune disease.
  enfermedad de los aviadores aviator's disease.
  enfermedad de Ayerza Ayerza's disease.
  enfermedad azul blue disease.
  enfermedad de Baelz Baelz's disease.
  enfermedad de Ballet Ballet's disease.
  enfermedad de Baló Baló's disease.
  enfermedad de Bamberger Bamberger's disease.
  enfermedad de Bamberger-Marie Bamberger-Marie disease.
  enfermedad de Bannister Bannister's disease.
  enfermedad de Barclay-Baron Barclay-Baron disease.
  enfermedad de Barlow Barlow's disease.
  enfermedad de Barraquer, enfermedad de Barraquer-Simons Barraquer's disease.
  enfermedad de Basedow Basedow's disease.
  enfermedad de Batten-Mayou Batten-Mayou disease.
  enfermedad de Bazin Bazin's disease.
  enfermedad de Beauvais Beauvais' disease.
  enfermedad de Bechterew Bechterew's disease.
  enfermedad de Begbie Begbie's disease.
  enfermedad de Béguez César Béguez César disease.
  enfermedad de Behçet Behçet's disease.
  enfermedad de Behr Behr's disease.
  enfermedad de Benson Benson's disease.
  enfermedad de Bernhardt, enfermedad de Bernhardt-Roth Bernhardt's disease.
  enfermedad de Besnier-Boeck-Schaumann Besnier-Boeck-Schaumann disease.
  enfermedad del beso infectious mononucleosis.
  enfermedad de Best Best's disease.
  enfermedad de Bielschowsky Bielschowsky's disease.
  enfermedad de Binswanger Binswanger's disease.
  enfermedad de Bloch-Sulzberger Bloch-Sulzberger disease.

enfermedad de Blocq Blocq's disease.

enfermedad de Blount, enfermedad de Blount-Barber Blount's disease, Blount-Barber disease.

enfermedad de Bornholm Bornholm disease.

enfermedad de Bouchard Bouchard's disease.

enfermedad de Bouillaud Bouillaud's disease.

enfermedad de Bourneville Bourneville's disease.

enfermedad de Bourneville-Pringle Bourneville-Pringle disease.

enfermedad de Bowen Bowen's disease.

enfermedad Brailsford-Morquio Brailsford-Morquio disease.

enfermedad de Breda Breda's disease.

enfermedad de Bright Bright's disease.

enfermedad de Brill-Symmers Brill-Symmers disease.

enfermedad de Brill, enfermedad de Brill-Zinsser Brill's disease, Brill-Zinsser disease.

enfermedad de Brocq Brocq's disease.

enfermedad de Brodie Brodie's disease.

enfermedad de Brooke Brooke's disease.

enfermedad bronceada bronzed disease.

enfermedad de Bruck Bruck's disease.

enfermedad de Brushfield-Wyatt Brushfield-Wyatt disease.

enfermedad de Bruton Bruton's disease.

enfermedad de Buerger Buerger's disease.

enfermedad de Bury Bury's disease.

enfermedad de Buschke Buschke's disease.

enfermedad de Busquet Busquet's disease.

enfermedad de Busse-Buschke Busse-Buschke disease.

enfermedad de Bürger-Grütz Bürger-Grütz disease.

enfermedad de Byler Byler's disease.

enfermedad de cabello ensortijado kinky-hair disease.

enfermedad de cadena L L-chain disease.

enfermedad de cadera quieta quiet hip disease.

enfermedad de Caffey Caffey's disease.

enfermedad de la caída falling sickness.

enfermedad de los cajones caisson disease.

enfermedad de Calvé-Perthes Calvé-Perthes disease.

enfermedad de cambios mínimos minimal-change disease.

enfermedad de Canavan Canavan's disease.

enfermedad cardíaca reumática rheumatic heart disease.

enfermedad de Caroli Caroli's disease.

enfermedad de Carrión Carrión's disease.

enfermedad cegadora blinding disease.

enfermedad celíaca celiac disease.

enfermedad de células I I-cell disease.

enfermedad cerebrovascular cerebrovascular disease.

enfermedad de Chagas, enfermedad de Chagas-Cruz Chagas' disease, Chagas-Cruz disease.

enfermedad de Charcot Charcot's disease.

enfermedad de Charcot-Marie-Tooth Charcot-Marie-Tooth disease.

enfermedad de Charlouis Charlouis' disease.

enfermedad de Cheadle Cheadle's disease.

enfermedad de Chiari Chiari's disease.

enfermedad de Chicago Chicago disease.

enfermedad de Christian Christian's disease.

enfermedad de Christmas Christmas disease.

enfermedad de los círculos circling disease.

enfermedad de Coats Coats' disease.

enfermedad de Cockayne Cockayne's disease.

enfermedad colágena, enfermedad colagenovascular collagen-vascular disease.

enfermedad comunicable communicable disease.

enfermedad de Conradi Conradi's disease.

enfermedad constitucional constitutional disease.

enfermedad contagiosa contagious disease.

enfermedad de Cori Cori's disease.

enfermedad de Corrigan Corrigan's disease.

enfermedad de Cotugnof, enfermedad de Cotunnius Cotunnius disease.

enfermedad de Cowden Cowden's disease.

enfermedad de Creutzfeldt-Jakob Creutzfeldt-Jakob disease.

enfermedad de Crigler-Najjar Crigler-Najjar disease.

enfermedad de Crocq Crocq's disease.

enfermedad de Crohn Crohn's disease.

enfermedad crónica de la montaña chronic mountain disease.

enfermedad de Crouzon Crouzon's disease.

enfermedad de Cruveilhier Cruveilhier's disease.

enfermedad de Cruveilhier-Baumgarten Cruveilhier-Baumgarten disease.

enfermedad de Csillag Csillag's disease.

enfermedad de cuerpos de inclusión inclusion body disease.

enfermedad de cuerpos de Lafora Lafora body disease.

enfermedad de Curschmann Curschmann's disease.

enfermedad de Cushing Cushing's disease.

enfermedad de Czerny Czerny's disease.

enfermedad danzante dancing disease.

enfermedad de Darier Darier's disease.

enfermedad de Darling Darling's disease.

enfermedad de Davies Davies' disease.

enfermedad de De Quervain De Quervain's disease.

enfermedad por deficiencia deficiency disease.

enfermedad por deficiencia de anticuerpos antibody deficiency disease.

enfermedad por deficiencia de grasas fat-deficiency disease.

enfermedad de Degos Degos' disease.

enfermedad Déjerine, enfermedad Déjerine-Sottas Déjerine's disease, Déjerine-Sottas disease.

enfermedad con depósitos densos dense-deposit disease.

enfermedad de Dercum Dercum's disease.

enfermedad por descompresión decompression disease, decompression sickness.

enfermedad de Deutschländer Deutschländer's disease.

enfermedad de Devic Devic's disease.

enfermedad de Di Guglielmo Di Guglielmo's disease.

enfermedad de Döhle Döhle disease.

enfermedad de Donders Donders' glaucoma.

enfermedad de Donohue Donohue's disease.

enfermedad drepanocítica sickle cell disease.

enfermedad de Dubini Dubini's disease.

enfermedad de Dubois Dubois' disease.

enfermedad de Duchenne Duchenne's disease.

enfermedad de Duhring Duhring's disease.

enfermedad de Dukes, enfermedad de Dukes-Filatov Dukes' disease.

enfermedad de Duncan Duncan's disease.

enfermedad de Duplay Duplay's disease.

enfermedad de Durand-Nicolas-Favre Durand-Nicolas-Favre disease.

enfermedad de Duroziez Duroziez's disease.

enfermedad de Eales Eales' disease.

enfermedad de Ebstein Ebstein's disease.

enfermedad de Eisenmenger Eisenmenger's disease.

enfermedad emocional emotional disease.

enfermedad de Engelmann Engelmann's disease.

enfermedad de Epstein Epstein's disease.

enfermedad de Erb Erb's disease.

enfermedad de Erb-Charcot Erb-Charcot disease.

enfermedad de Erb-Goldflam Erb-Goldflam disease.

enfermedad de Erdheim Erdheim disease.

enfermedad escleroquística del ovario sclerocystic disease of the ovary.

enfermedad específica specific disease.

enfermedad de Eulenburg Eulenburg's disease.

enfermedad exantemática exanthematous disease.

enfermedad extramamaria de Paget extramammary Paget's disease.

enfermedad extrapiramidal extrapyramidal disease.

enfermedad de Fabry Fabry's disease.

enfermedad de Fahr Fahr's disease.

enfermedad de Fahr-Volhard Fahr-Volhard disease.

enfermedad de Farber Farber's disease.

enfermedad de Favre-Durand-Nicolas Favre-Durand-Nicolas disease.

enfermedad febril sistémica systemic-febrile disease.

enfermedad de Feer Feer's disease.

enfermedad femoropoplítea oclusiva femoropopliteal occlusive disease.

enfermedad de Fenwick Fenwick's disease.

enfermedad fibroquística de la mama fibrocystic disease of the breast.

enfermedad fibroquística del páncreas fibrocystic disease of the pancreas.

enfermedad de Fiedler Fiedler's disease.

enfermedad de Filatov, enfermedad de Filatow Filatov's disease.

enfermedad de Flajani Flajani disease.

enfermedad de Flatau-Schilder Flatau-Schilder disease.

enfermedad de Flegel Flegel's disease.

enfermedad de Fleischner Fleischner's disease.

enfermedad de Folling Folling's disease.

enfermedad de Forbes Forbes' disease.

enfermedad de Fordyce Fordyce's disease.

enfermedad de Forrestier Forrestier's disease.

enfermedad de Fothergill Fothergill's disease.

enfermedad de Fournier Fournier's disease.

enfermedad de Fox-Fordyce Fox-Fordyce disease.

enfermedad de Francis Francis' disease.

enfermedad de Frei Frei disease.

enfermedad de Freiberg Freiberg's disease.

enfermedad de Friedländer Friedländer disease.

enfermedad de Friedmann Friedmann's disease.

enfermedad de Friedreich Friedreich's disease.

enfermedad de Frommel Frommel's disease.

enfermedad de Fuerstner Fuerstner's disease.

enfermedad funcional functional sickness, functional illness.

enfermedad fusoespiroquetal fusospirochetal disease.

enfermedad de Gaisböck Gaisböck's disease.

enfermedad de Gamma Gamma's disease.

enfermedad de Gamstorp Gamstorp's disease.

enfermedad de Gandy-Nanta Gandy-Nanta disease.

enfermedad de las garrapatas garapata disease.

enfermedad de Garré Garré's disease.

enfermedad de Gaucher Gaucher's disease.

enfermedad de Gee, enfermedad de Gee-Herter, enfermedad de Gee-Herter-Heubner, enfermedad de Gee-Thaysen Gee's disease, Gee-Herter disease, Gee-Herter-Heubner disease, Gee-Thaysen disease.

enfermedad de Gerhardt Gerhardt's disease.

enfermedad de Gerlier Gerlier's disease.

enfermedad de Gibney Gibney's disease.

enfermedad de Gierke Gierke's disease.

enfermedad de Gilbert Gilbert's disease.

enfermedad de Gilchrist Gilchrist's disease.

enfermedad de Gilles de la Tourette Gilles de la Tourette's disease.

enfermedad de Glanzmann Glanzmann's disease.

enfermedad de Goldflam Goldflam disease.

enfermedad de Gorham Gorham's disease.

enfermedad de Gougerot y Blum Gougerot and Blum disease.

enfermedad de Gougerot-Ruiter Gougerot-Ruiter disease.

enfermedad de Gougerot-Sjögren Gougerot-Sjögren disease.

enfermedad de Gowers Gowers disease.

enfermedad de Graefe Graefe's disease.

enfermedad de Graves Graves' disease.

enfermedad de Gross Gross disease.

enfermedad de Grover Grover's disease.

enfermedad de Guinon Guinon's disease.

enfermedad del gusano de arena sandworm disease.

enfermedad del gusano del arenque herring-worm disease.

enfermedad H H disease.

enfermedad de Haff Haff disease.

enfermedad de Haglund Haglund's disease.

enfermedad de Hailley y Hailley Hailley and Hailley disease.

enfermedad de Hallervorden-Spatz Hallervorden-Spatz disease.

enfermedad de Hansen Hansen's disease.

enfermedad de Harada Harada's disease.

enfermedad de Hartnup Hartnup disease.

enfermedad de Hashimoto Hashimoto's disease.

enfermedad de Heberden Heberden's disease.

enfermedad de Hebra Hebra's disease.

enfermedad de Heck Heck's disease.

enfermedad de Heine-Medin Heine-Medin disease.

enfermedad hemorrágica del neonato, enfermedad hemorrágica del recién nacido hemorrhagic disease of the newborn.

enfermedad hepática crónica activa chronic active liver disease.

enfermedad hepatolenticular hepatolenticular disease.

enfermedad hereditaria hereditary disease.

enfermedad de Herlitz Herlitz's disease.

enfermedad de Hers Hers' disease.

enfermedad de Heubner Heubner's disease.

enfermedad hidatídica hydatic disease.

enfermedad hipertensiva crónica chronic hypertensive disease.

enfermedad de Hippel, enfermedad de Hippel-Lindau Hippel's disease, Hippel-Lindau disease.

enfermedad de Hirschprung Hirschsprung's disease.

enfermedad de histiocitos de color azul marino sea-blue histiocyte disease.

enfermedad de His-Werner His disease, His-Werner disease.

enfermedad de Hodgkin Hodgkin's disease.

enfermedad de Hodgson Hodgson's disease.

enfermedad de Hoffa Hoffa's disease.

enfermedad de Hoppe-Goldflam Hoppe-Goldflam disease.

enfermedad de Horton Horton's disease.

enfermedad de Huchard Huchard's disease.

enfermedad de hueso de mármol marble bone disease.

enfermedad de hueso desaparecido disappearing bone disease.

enfermedad de Hunt Hunt's disease.

enfermedad de Huntington Huntington's disease.

enfermedad de Hutchinson-Gilford Hutchinson-Gilford disease.

enfermedad de Hutinel Hutinel's disease.

enfermedad de Hyde Hyde's disease.

enfermedad idiopática de Bamberger-Marie idiopathic Bamberger-Marie disease.

enfermedad de inclusiones citomegálicas cytomegalic inclusion disease.

enfermedad india Indian sickness.

enfermedad inducida por fármacos drug-induced disease.

enfermedad industrial industrial disease.

enfermedad infecciosa infectious disease, infective disease.

enfermedad inflamatoria de la pelvis pelvic inflammatory disease.

enfermedad de injerto versus huésped graft versus host disease.

enfermedad de inmunodeficiencia immunodeficiency disease.

enfermedad de inmunocomplejos immune complex disease.

enfermedad inmunoproliferativa del intestino delgado immunoproliferative small intestinal disease.

enfermedad intersticial interstitial disease.

enfermedad de Islandia Iceland disease.

enfermedad de las islas island disease.

enfermedad IVH GVH disease.

enfermedad de Jacquet Jacquet's dermatitis.

enfermedad de Jaffe-Lichtenstein Jaffe-Lichtenstein disease.

enfermedad de Jakob, enfermedad de Jakob-Creutzfeldt Jakob-Creuzfeldt disease.

enfermedad de Jansky-Bielschowsky Jansky-Bielschowsky disease.

enfermedad de Jensen Jensen's disease.

enfermedad de Johnson-Stevens Johnson-Stevens disease.

enfermedad de Jüngling Jüngling's disease.

enfermedad de Katayama Katayama disease.

enfermedad de Kawasaki Kawasaki disease.

enfermedad de Kienböck Kienböck's disease.

enfermedad de Kimmelstiel-Wilson Kimmelstiel-Wilson disease.

enfermedad de Kimura Kimura's disease.

enfermedad de Kinnier-Wilson Kinnier-Wilson disease.

enfermedad de Kirkland Kirkland's disease.

enfermedad de Köhler Köhler's disease.

enfermedad de Köhlmeier-Degos Köhlmeier-Degos disease.

enfermedad de Krabbe Krabbe's disease.

enfermedad de Krishaber Krishaber's disease.

enfermedad de Kufs Kufs disease.

enfermedad de Kugelberg-Welander Kugelberg-Welander disease.

enfermedad de Kuhnt-Junius Kuhnt-Junius disease.

enfermedad de Kümmel Kümmel's disease.

enfermedad de Kyrle Kyrle's disease.

enfermedad de Laënnec Laënnec's disease.

enfermedad de Lafora Lafora's disease.

enfermedad de Landouzy Landouzy's disease.

enfermedad de La Peyronie La Peyronie's disease.

enfermedad de Legg, enfermedad de Legg-Calvé-Perthes, enfermedad de Legg-Perthes Legg disease, Calvé-Perthes disease, Legg-Perthes disease.

enfermedad de los legionarios legionnaires' disease.

enfermedad lisosomal lysosomal disease.

enfermedad de Little Little's disease.

enfermedad de Lyme Lyme disease.

enfermedad de Madelung Madelung's disease.

enfermedad de Malassez Malassez's disease.

enfermedad de Malherbe Malherbe's disease.

enfermedad del mar seasickness.

enfermedad de Marchiafava-Micheli Marchiafava-Micheli disease.

enfermedad de Marie-Strümpell Marie-Strümpell disease.

enfermedad del martillo neumático Kienböck's disease.

enfermedad matinal morning sickness.

enfermedad del mar seasickness.

enfermedad de Marsh Marsh's disease.

enfermedad de McArdle McArdle's disease.

enfermedad mediterránea-hemoglobina Mediterranean-hemoglobin E disease.

enfermedad de Meige Meige's disease.

enfermedad de la membrana hialina hyaline membrane disease.

enfermedad de Ménétrier Ménétrier's disease.

enfermedad de Ménière Ménière's disease.

enfermedad mental mental disease, mental illness.

enfermedad de Meyer Meyer's disease.

enfermedad miasmática miasmatic disease.

enfermedad micrometastásica micrometastatic disease.

enfermedad microquística de la médula renal microcystic disease of the renal medulla.

enfermedad de Miller Miller's disease.

enfermedad de Milroy Milroy's disease.

enfermedad de Milton Milton's disease.

enfermedad de Minamata Minamata disease.

enfermedad de los mineros miner's disease.

enfermedad mixta del tejido conjuntivo mixed connective-tissue disease.

enfermedad molecular molecular disease.

enfermedad de Monge Monge's disease.

enfermedad de la montaña mountain sickness.

enfermedad por mordedura de gato cat-bite disease.

enfermedad de Morgagni Morgagni's disease.

enfermedad de Morquio Morquio's disease.

enfermedad de Morton Morton's disease.

enfermedad de Morvan Morvan's disease.

enfermedad del movimiento motion sickness.

enfermedad multifocal multicore disease.

enfermedad de las neuronas motoras motor neuron disease.

enfermedad de Nicolas-Favre Nicolas-Favre disease.

enfermedad de Niemann-Pick Niemann-Pick disease.

enfermedad nil, enfermedad nula nil disease.

enfermedad de Nonne-Milroy Nonne-Milroy disease.

enfermedad notificable notifiable disease.

enfermedad del núcleo central central core disease.

enfermedad ocupacional occupational disease.

enfermedad de Ollier Ollier's disease.

enfermedad de Oppenheim Oppenheim disease.

enfermedad orgánica organic disease.

enfermedad de la orina en jarabe de arce maple syrup urine disease.

enfermedad de Ormond Ormond's disease.

enfermedad ósea de Recklinghausen Recklinghausen's disease of the bone.

enfermedad de Osler Osler's disease.

enfermedad de Paget Paget's disease.

enfermedad de Paget extramamaria extramammary Paget's disease.

enfermedad parasitaria parasitic disease.

enfermedad de Parkinson Parkinson's disease.

enfermedad de Parrot Parrot's disease.

enfermedad de Parry Parry's disease.

enfermedad de Pauzat Pauzat's disease.

enfermedad de Pavy Pavy's disease.

enfermedad de Paxton Paxton's disease.

enfermedad de Payr Payr's disease.

enfermedad de pedernal flint disease.

enfermedad de Pel-Ebstein Pel-Ebstein disease.

enfermedad de Pelizaeus-Merzbacher Pelizaeus-Merzbacher disease.

enfermedad de Pellegrini, enfermedad de Pellegrini-Stieda Pellegrini's disease, Pellegrini-Stieda disease.

enfermedad periódica periodic disease.

enfermedad perna perna disease.

enfermedad de Perthes Perthes disease.

enfermedad de Peyronie Peyronie's disease.

enfermedad de Pfeiffer Pfeiffer's disease.

enfermedad de Pick Pick's disease.

enfermedad del pie de Dupuytren Dupuytren's disease of the foot.

enfermedad de la piel endurecida hidebound disease, skinbound disease.

enfermedad de Plummer Plummer's disease.

enfermedad poliquística del hígado polycystic liver disease.

enfermedad poliquística de los riñones polycystic disease of the kidneys.

enfermedad de Pompe Pompe's disease.

enfermedad de los porquerizos swineherd's disease.

enfermedad de Posada-Wernicke Posada-Wernicke disease.

enfermedad de Pott Pott's disease.

enfermedad de Potter Potter's disease.

enfermedad de Preiser Preiser's disease.

enfermedad primaria primary disease.

enfermedad de Pringle Pringle's disease.

enfermedad de Profichet Profichet's disease.

enfermedad pulmonar obstructiva crónica (EPOC) chronic obstructive pulmonary disease (COPD).

enfermedad de Purtscher Purtscher's disease.

enfermedad de Pyle Pyle's disease.

enfermedad de Quincke Quincke's disease.

enfermedad de Quinquaud Quinquaud's disease.

enfermedad quinta fifth disease.

enfermedad quística de la mama cystic disease of the breast.

enfermedad quística de la médula renal cystic disease of renal medulla.

enfermedad por radiaciones radiation disease.

enfermedad de Raynaud Raynaud's disease.

enfermedad de Recklinghausen Recklinghausen's disease.

enfermedad de Reed-Hodgkin Reed-Hodgkin disease.

enfermedad de Refsum Refsum's disease.

enfermedad de Reiter Reiter's disease.

enfermedad de Rendu-Osler-Weber Rendu-Osler-Weber disease.

enfermedad reumática rheumatic disease.

enfermedad reumatoidea rheumatoid disease.

enfermedad de Riedel Riedel's disease.

enfermedad de Riga-Fede Riga-Fede disease.

enfermedad del riñón pulposo pulpy kidney disease.

enfermedad de la risa laughing disease, laughing sickness.

enfermedad de Ritter Ritter's disease.

enfermedad de Robinson Robinson's disease.

enfermedad de Robles Robles' disease.

enfermedad de Rokitansky Rokitansky's disease.

enfermedad de Romberg Romberg's disease.

enfermedad rosada pink disease.

enfermedad de Rose Rose disease.

enfermedad de Rosenbach Rosenbach's disease.

enfermedad de Rossbach Rossbach's disease.

enfermedad de Roth, enfermedad de Roth-Bernhardt Roth's disease, Roth-Bernhardt disease.

enfermedad de Rougnon-Heberden Rougnon-Heberden disease.

enfermedad de Roussy-Lévy Roussy-Lévy disease.

enfermedad de Sandhoff Sandhoff's disease.

enfermedad de Saunders Saunders disease.

enfermedad de Schamberg Schamberg's disease.

enfermedad de Schaumann Schaumann's disease.

enfermedad de Schaumberg Schaumberg's disease.

enfermedad de Schenck Schenck's disease.

enfermedad de Scheuermann Scheuermann's disease.

enfermedad de Schilder Schilder's disease.

enfermedad de Schimmelbusch Schimmelbusch's disease.

enfermedad de Schlatter, enfermedad de Schlatter-Osgood Schlatter's disease, Schlatter-Osgood disease.

enfermedad de Schönlein Schönlein's disease.

enfermedad de Schottmüller Schottmüller's disease.

enfermedad de Schroeder Schroeder's disease.

enfermedad de Schultz Schultz's disease.

enfermedad de Schwediauer Schwediauer's disease.

enfermedad secundaria secondary disease.

enfermedad de Selter Selter's disease.

enfermedad de Senear-Usher Senear-Usher disease.

enfermedad sexta sixth disease.

enfermedad sexta venérea sixth venereal disease.

enfermedad de Shaver Shaver's disease.

enfermedad de Shimamushi shimamushi disease.

enfermedad Siemerling-Creutzfeldt Siemerling-Creutzfeldt disease.

enfermedad de los silos silo-filler's disease.

enfermedad de Simon Simon's disease.

enfermedad de Simmonds Simmonds' disease.

enfermedad de sistemas combinados combined system disease.

enfermedad de Sjögren Sjögren's disease.

enfermedad de Sneddon-Wilkinson Sneddon-Wilkinson disease.

enfermedad de Spencer Spencer's disease.

enfermedad de Spielmeyer-Sjögren Spielmeyer-Sjögren disease.

enfermedad Spielmeyer-Stock Spielmeyer-Stock disease.

enfermedad de Spielmeyer-Vogt Spielmeyer-Vogt disease.

enfermedad de Stargardt Stargardt's disease.

enfermedad de Steele-Richardson-Olszewski Steele-Richardson-Olszewski disease.

enfermedad de Steinert Steinert's disease.

enfermedad de Sternberg Sternberg's disease.

enfermedad de Sticker Sticker's disease.

enfermedad de Stieda Stieda's disease.

enfermedad de Still Still's disease.

enfermedad de Stokes-Adams Stokes-Adams disease.

enfermedad de Strümpell-Marie Strümpell-Marie disease.

enfermedad de Sturge Sturge's disease.

enfermedad de Stuttgart Stuttgart disease.

enfermedad de Sudeck Sudeck's disease.

enfermedad del sueño sleeping sickness.

enfermedad del sueño africano African sleeping sickness.

enfermedad del suero serum sickness.

enfermedad de Sulzberger-Garbe Sulzberger-Garbe disease.

enfermedad de Sutton Sutton's disease.

enfermedad de Swediauer Swediauer's disease.

enfermedad de Sweet Sweet's disease.

enfermedad de Swift, enfermedad de Swift-Feer Swift's disease, Swift-Feer disease.

enfermedad de Sydenham Sydenham's disease.

enfermedad de Sylvest Sylvest's disease.

enfermedad de Takahara Takahara's disease.

enfermedad de Takayasu Takayasu's disease.

enfermedad de talasemia drepanocítica sickle cell-thalassemia disease.

enfermedad de Talma Talma's disease.

enfermedad de Tánger Tangier disease.

enfermedad de Taussig-Bing Taussig-Bing disease.

enfermedad de Tay-Sachs Tay-Sachs disease.

enfermedad de Taylor Taylor's disease.

enfermedad tercera third disease.

enfermedad terrestre car sickness.

enfermedad de Thiemann Thiemann's disease.

enfermedad de Thomsen Thomsen's disease.

enfermedad de Thygeson Thygeson's disease.

enfermedad de Tietze Tietze's disease.

enfermedad de Tillaux Tillaux's disease.

enfermedad tirocardiaca thyrocardiac disease.

enfermedad de Tommaselli Tommaselli's disease.

enfermedad de Tornwaldt Tornwaldt's disease.

enfermedad de Tourette Tourette's disease.

enfermedad de los trabajadores de bauxita bauxite worker's disease.

enfermedad de los trabajadores de fábricas de papel paper mill worker's disease.

enfermedad de los que trabajan con perlas pearl-worker's disease.

enfermedad de transmisión sexual (ETS) sexually transmitted disease (STD).

enfermedad de los traperos ragpicker's disease, ragsorter's disease.

enfermedad de tsutsugamushi tsutsugamushi disease.

enfermedad de uncinarias hookworm disease.

enfermedad de Underwood Underwood's disease.

enfermedad de Unna Unna's disease.

enfermedad de Unverricht Unverricht's disease.

enfermedad de Urbach-Wiethe Urbach-Wiethe disease.

enfermedad del vagabundo vagabond's disease.

enfermedad de van Buren van Buren's disease.

enfermedad de Vaquez, enfermedad de Vaquez-Osler Vaquez's disease, Vaquez-Osler disease.

enfermedad venérea venereal disease.

enfermedad venooclusiva del hígado veno-occlusive disease of the liver.

enfermedad verde green sickness.

enfermedad de Vidal Vidal's disease.

enfermedad de Vincent Vincent's disease.

enfermedad de Virchow Virchow's disease.

enfermedad por virus de Marburg Marburg virus disease.

enfermedad de Vogt-Spielmeyer Vogt-Spielmeyer disease.

enfermedad de von Gierke von Gierke's disease.

enfermedad de von Hippel-Lindau von Hippel-Lindau disease.

enfermedad de von Meyenburg von Meyenburg's disease.

enfermedad de von Recklinghausen von Recklinghausen's disease.

enfermedad de von Willebrand von Willebrand's disease.

enfermedad de Voorhoeve Voorhoeve's disease.

enfermedad de Vrolik Vrolik's disease.

enfermedad de Wagner Wagner's disease.

enfermedad de Wardrop Wardrop's disease.

enfermedad de Wartenberg Wartenberg disease.

enfermedad de Weber Weber's disease.

enfermedad de Weber-Christian Weber-Christian disease.

enfermedad de Wegner Wegner's disease.

enfermedad de Weil Weil's disease.

enfermedad de Weir-Mitchell Weir-Mitchell's disease.

enfermedad de Werdnig-Hoffmann Werdnig-Hoffmann disease.

enfermedad de Werlhoff Werlhof's disease.

enfermedad de Werner-His Werner-His disease.

enfermedad de Werner-Schultz Werner-Schultz disease.

enfermedad de Wernicke Wernicke's disease.

enfermedad de Werther Werther's disease.

enfermedad de Westphal Wesphal's disease.

enfermedad de Whipple Whipple's disease.

enfermedad de Whitmore Whitmore's disease.

enfermedad de Whytt Whytt's disease.

enfermedad de Wilkie Wilkie's disease.

enfermedad de Wilson Wilson's disease.

enfermedad de Winckel Winckel's disease.

enfermedad de Winiwarter-Buerger Winiwarter-Buerger disease.

enfermedad de Winkelman Winkelman's disease.

enfermedad de Winkler Winkler's disease.

enfermedad de Wolman Wolman's disease.

enfermedad de Woringer-Kolopp Woringer-Kolopp disease.

enfermedad X X disease.

enfermedad X australiana Australian X disease.

enfermedad de Ziehen-Oppenheim Ziehen-Oppenheim disease.

enfermeria *f.* nursing.

enfermero, -ra *m., f.* male nurse, nurse.

enfermizo, -za *adj.* infirm.

enfermo, -ma *adj.* ill, sick.

enfermo, -ma *m., f.* ill person, sick person.

enfisema *m.* emphysema.

enfisema alveolar alveolar emphysema.

enfisema atrófico atrophic emphysema.

enfisema centriacinar, enfisema centriacinoso centriacinar emphysema.

enfisema centrilobulillar centrilobular emphysema.

enfisema compensador, enfisema compensatorio compensating emphysema, compensatory emphysema.

enfisema cutáneo cutaneous emphysema.

enfisema difuso diffuse emphysema.

enfisema ectásico ectatic emphysema.

enfisema falso false emphysema.

enfisema familiar familial emphysema.

enfisema gangrenoso gangrenous emphysema.

enfisema generalizado generalized emphysema.

enfisema interlobulillar interlobular emphysema.

enfisema intersticial interstitial emphysema.

enfisema mediastínico mediastinal emphysema.

enfisema panacinar, enfisema panacinoso panacinar emphysema.

enfisema panlobulillar panlobular emphysema.

enfisema paraseptal paraseptal emphysema.

enfisema pulmonar pulmonary emphysema.

enfisema quirúrgico surgical emphysema.

enfisema senil senile emphysema.

enfisema subcutáneo subcutaneous emphysema.

enfisema subgaleal subgaleal emphysema.

enfisema suplementario compensating emphysema, compensatory emphysema.

enfisema traumático traumatic emphysema.

enfisema vesicular vesicular emphysema.

enfisema vicariante compensating emphysema, compensatory emphysema.

enfisematoso, -sa *adj.* emphysematous.

enflisis *f.* emphlysis.

enfráctico, -ca *adj.* emphractic.

enfraxis *f.* emphraxis.

enfriamiento *m.* cold.

engastrio *m.* engastrius.

englobamiento *m.* englobement.

engrafia *f.* engraphia.

engrama *m.* engram.

enhematospora *f.* enhematospore.

enhemospora *f.* enhemospore.

enlace *m.* bond.

enmascarado, -da *adj.* masked.

enmascaramiento *m.* masking.

enoftalmía *f.* enophthalmus.

enoftalmos *m.* enophthalmos.

enorquia *f.* enorchia.

enósmosis *f.* endosmosis.

enostasis *f.* enostosis, entostosis.

enostosis *f.* enostosis, entostosis.

enquima *f.* enchima.

enquiresis *f.* encheiresis.

enquistado, -da *adj.* encysted, saccate.

enquistamiento *m.* encystment.

enranciarse *v.* rancidify.

enrarecimiento *m.* rarefaction.

enriquecimiento *m.* enrichment.

enrojecimiento *m.* flare.

ensalada de palabras *f.* word salad.

ensambladura *f.* compages.

ensanchador *m.* reamer.

ensanchador de costillas rib spreader reamer.

ensanchador intramedular intramedullary reamer.

ensanchador a motor engine reamer.

ensayo *m.* assay, trial.

ensayo aleatorio aleatory assay.

ensayo de Bernoulli Bernoulli trial.

ensayo de blastogénesis blastogenesis assay.

ensayo de célula Raji Raji cell assay.

ensayo CH50 CH50 assay.

ensayo clínico clinical trial.

ensayo clínico de medicamentos clinical drug assay.

ensayo clonogénico clonogenic assay.

ensayo cognitivo cognitive rehearsal.

ensayo de la conducta behavioral rehearsal.

ensayo cruzado crossover trial.

ensayo de doble anticuerpo en sandwich double antibody sandwich trial.

ensayo clínico doble ciego double blind clinical assay.

ensayo de un fármaco drug trial.

ensayo de Grunstein-Hogness Grunstein-Hogness assay.

ensayo de inmunoadsorción ligado a enzimas enzyme-linked immunosorbent assay.

ensayo indirecto indirect assay.

ensayo enzimoinmunoensayo enzyme-linked immunosorbent assay.

ensayo de hemaglutinación por treponema pallidum (EHTP) Treponema pallidum hemagglutination assay (TPHA).

ensayo inmunoquímico immunochemical assay.

ensayo inmunorradiométrico immunoradiometric assay.

ensayo de microtoxicidad microtoxicity assay.

ensayo de microhemaglutinación-Treponema pallidum (MHATO) microhemagglutination assay for Treponema pallidum (MHA-TP).

ensayo de placa hemolítica hemolytic plaque assay.

ensayo de la placa de Jerne Jerne plaque assay.

ensayo de proliferación linfocitaria lymphocyte proliferation assay.

ensayo de radiorreceptores radioreceptor assay.

ensayo de radioligando radioligand assay.

ensayo de roseta rosette assay.

ensayo de roseta EAC EAC rosette assay.

ensayo de unión por competencia competitive binding assay.

ensayo por unión del complemento complement binding assay.

ensisternón *m.* ensisternum.

ensisternum *m.* ensisternum.

ensónfalo *m.* ensomphalus.

ensoñación *f.* fantasy.

enstrofia *f.* enstrophe.

ensueño *m.* dream.

  ensueño clarividente clairvoyant dream.

  ensueño diurno day dream.

entablillado *m.* splinting.

entalpía *f.* enthalpy.

entamebiasis *f.* entamebiasis.

Entamoeba Entamoeba.

entasia *f.* entasia, entasis.

éntasis *f.* entasis.

entático, -ca *adj.* entatic.

entepicóndilo *m.* entepicondyle.

enteradenitis *f.* entaredinitis.

enteradeno *m.* enteraden.

enteral *adj.* enteral.

enteralgia *f.* enteralgia.

enterangienfraxis *f.* enterangiemphraxis.

enterauxa *f.* enterauxe.

enterectasia *f.* enterectasis.

enterectasis *f.* enterectasis.

enterectomía *f.* enterectomy.

enterelcosis *f.* enterelcosis.

entérico, -ca *adj.* enteric.

entericoide *adj.* entericoid.

enteritis *f.* enteritis.

  enteritis alérgica, enteritis anafiláctica anaphylactic enteritis.

  enteritis cicatricial, enteritis cicatrizante crónica chronic cicatrizing enteritis.

  enteritis coleriforme choleriform enteritis.

  enteritis diftérica diphtheritic enteritis.

  enteritis felina, enteritis felina específica, enteritis felina infecciosa feline enteritis, specific feline enteritis, feline infectious enteritis.

  enteritis flemonosa phlegmonous enteritis.

  enteritis granulomatosa granulomatous enteritis.

  enteritis membranosa, enteritis mucomembranosa mucomembranous enteritis.

  enteritis mucosa mucous enteritis.

  enteritis necrosante, enteritis necrótica, enteritis necrotizante necrotizing enteritis, enteritis necroticans.

  enteritis nodular enteritis nodularis.

  enteritis poliposa enteritis polyposa.

  enteritis protozoaria, enteritis por proto-

zoarios protozoan enteritis.

  enteritis quística crónica enteritis cystica chronica.

  enteritis regional regional enteritis.

  enteritis segmentaria segmental enteritis.

  enteritis seudomembranosa pseudomembranous enteritis.

  enteritis terminal terminal enteritis.

  enteritis tuberculosa tuberculous enteritis.

entero *m.* entire.

enteroanastomosis *f.* enteroanastomosis.

enteroantígeno *m.* enteroantigen.

enteroapocleisis *f.* enteroapocleisis.

Enterobacter Enterobacter.

Enterobacteriaceae Enterobacteriaceae.

enterobacteriano, -na *adj.* enterobacterial.

enterobiasis *f.* enterobiasis.

enterobiliar *adj.* enterobiliary.

Enterobius Enterobius.

enterobrosia *f.* enterobrosia, enterobrosis.

enterobrosis *f.* enterobrosia, enterobrosis.

enterocele *m.* enterocele, enterocoele.

enterocelo *m.* enterocele, enterocoele.

enterocentesia *f.* enterocentesis.

enterocinesis *f.* enterocinesia, enterocinesis, enterokinesia, enterokinesis.

enterocinesis *f.* enterocinesia, enterocinesis, enterokinesia, enterokinesis.

enterocinético, -ca *adj.* enterocinetic, enterokinetic.

enterocinina *f.* enterokinin.

enterocistocele *m.* enterocystocele.

enterocito *m.* enterocyte.

enterocleisis *f.* enterocleisis.

  enterocleisis epiploica, enterocleisis del epiplón omental enterocleisis.

enteroclisis *f.* enteroclysis.

enteroclisma *m.* enteroclysis.

Enterococcus Enterococcus.

enterococemia *f.* enterococcemia.

enterococo *m.* Enterococcus.

enterocolecistostomía *f.* enterocholecystostomy.

enterocolectomía *f.* enterocolectomy.

enterocolitis *f.* enterocolitis.

  enterocolitis antibiótica antibiotic enterocolitis.

  enterocolitis hemorrágica hemorrhagic enterocolitis.

  enterocolitis necrosante necrotizing enterocolitis.

  enterocolitis regional regional enterocolitis.

  enterocolitis seudomembranosa pseudomembranous enterocolitis.

  enterocolitis relacionada con antibióticos antibiotic-associated enterocolitis.

enterocolostomía *f.* enterocolostomy.

enterocromafin *adj.* enterochromaffin.

enterocutáneo, -a *adj.* enterocutaneous.

enterodinia *f.* enterodynia.

enteroenterostomía *f.* enteroenterostomy.

enteroepiplocele *m.* enteroepiplocele.

enteroespasmo *m.* enterospasm.

enteroestenosis *f.* enterostenosis.

enterogástrico, -ca *adj.* enterogastric.

enterogastritis *f.* enterogastritis.

enterógeno, -na *adj.* enterogenous.

enterografía *f.* enterography.

enterógrafo *m.* enterograph.

enterograma *m.* enterogram.

enterohepatitis *f.* enterohepatitis.

  enterohepatitis infecciosa infectious enterohepatitis.

enterohepatocele *m.* enterohepatocele.

enterohidrocele *m.* enterohydrocele.

enteroide *adj.* enteroidea.

enteroidea *adj.* enteroidea.

enterointestinal *adj.* enterointestinal.

enterólisis *f.* enterolysis.

enterolitiasis *f.* enterolithiasis.

enterolito *m.* enterolith.

enterología *f.* enterology.

enteromegalia *f.* enteromegaly, enteromegalia.

enteromenia *f.* enteromenia.

enterómera *f.* enteromere.

enteromerocele *m.* enteromerocele.

enterómetro *m.* enterometer.

enteromicodermitis *f.* enteromycodermitis.

enteromicosis *f.* enteromycosis.

  enteromicosis bacteriana enteromycosis bacteriacea.

enteromiiasis *f.* enteromyiasis.

Enteromonas Enteromonas.

  Enteromonas hominis Enteromonas hominis.

enteron *m.* enteron.

enteroneuritis *f.* enteroneuritis.

enteronitis *f.* enteronitis.

enteroparálisis *f.* enteroparesis.

enteroparesia *f.* enteroparesis.

enteropatía *f.* enteropathy.

  enteropatía eosinofílica eosinophilic enteropathy.

  enteropatía exudativa exudative enteropathy.

  enteropatía con pérdida de proteínas, enteropatía con pérdida proteínica protein-losing enteropathy.

  enteropatía por gluten gluten enteropathy.

enteropatogenia *f.* enteropathogenesis.

enteropatogénico, -ca *adj.* enteropathogenic.

enteropatógeno *m.* enteropathogen.

enteropexia *f.* enteropexy, enteroplexy.

enteroplastia *f.* enteroplasty.

enteroplejía *f.* enteroplegia.

enteroplex *m.* enteroplex.

enteroplexia *f.* enteroplexy.

enteroproccia *f.* enteroproctia.

enteroproctia *f.* enteroproctia.

enteroptiquia *f.* enteroptychia, enteroptychy.

enteroptósico, -ca *adj.* enteroptotic.

enteroptosis *f.* enteroptosia, enteroptosis.

enteroquinesia *f.* enterocinesia, enterocinesis, enterokinesia, enterokinesis.

enteroquinesis *f.* enterocinesia, enterocinesis, enterokinesia, enterokinesis.

enteroquinético, -ca *adj.* enterokinetic.

enteroquiste *m.* enterocyst.

enteroquistoma *m.* enterocystoma.

enterorrafia *f.* enterorrhaphy.

  enterorrafia circular circular enterorrhaphy.

  enterorrafia terminoterminal circular enterorrhaphy.

enterorragia *f.* enterorrhagia.

enterorrea *f.* enterorrhea.

enterorrenal *adj.* enterorenal.

enterorrexia *f.* enterorrhexis.

enterorrexis *f.* enterorrhexis.

enteroscopio *m.* enteroscope.

enterosepsis *f.* enterosepsis.

enterósito *m.* enterosite.

enterosorción *f.* enterosorption.

enterospasmo *m.* enterospasm.

enterostasis *f.* enterostasis.

enterostaxis *f.* enterostaxis.

enterostenosis *f.* enterostenosis.

enterostomía *f.* enterostomy.

  enterostomía doble double enterostomy.

enterostomía en cañón de escopeta gunbarrel enterostomy.
enterostómico, -ca *adj.* enterostomal.
enterotifus *m.* enterotyphus.
enterotomía *f.* enterotomy.
enterótomo *m.* enterotome.
enterótomo de Dupuytren Dupuytren's enterotome.
enterotoxemia *f.* enterotoxemia.
enterotoxicación *f.* enterotoxication.
enterotoxigénico, -ca *adj.* enterotoxigenic.
enterotoxígeno, -na *adj.* enterotoxigenic.
enterotoxina *f.* enterotoxin.
enterotoxina citotónica cytotonic enterotoxin.
enterotoxina del cólera cholera enterotoxin.
enterotoxina de Escherichia coli Escherichia coli enterotoxin.
enterotoxina estafilocócica staphylococcal enterotoxin.
enterotoxismo *m.* enterotoxism.
enterotrópico, -ca *adj.* enterotropic.
enterovaginal *adj.* enterovaginal.
enterovenoso, -sa *adj.* enterovenous.
enterovesical *adj.* enterovesical.
enterovirósico, -ca *adj.* enteroviral.
enterovirus *m.* enterovirus.
enteroxintina *f.* entero-oxyntin.
enterozoico, -ca *adj.* enterozoic.
enterozoo *m.* enterozoon.
enteruria *f.* enteruria.
entésico, -ca *adj.* enthetic.
entesis *f.* enthesis.
entesitis *f.* enthesitis.
entesopatía *f.* enthesopathy.
entesopático, -ca *adj.* enthesopathic.
entético, -ca *adj.* enthetic.
entetobiosis *f.* enthetobiosis.
entidad *f.* entity.
entipia *f.* entypy.
entiris *f.* entiris.
entlasis *f.* enthlasis.
entoblasto *m.* endoblast, entoblast.
entocele *m.* entocele.
entocito *m.* entocyte.
entocnémico, -ca *adj.* entocnemial.
entocóndilo *m.* entocondyle.
entocondrostosis *f.* entochondrostosis.
entoconida *f.* entoconid.
entoconidio *m.* entoconid.
entocono *m.* entocone.
entocórnea *f.* entocornea.
entocoroides *f.* entochoroidea.
entocraneal *adj.* endocranial, entocranial.
entocráneo *m.* endocranium, entocranium.
entodérmico, -da *adj.* endodermal, entodermal, entodermic.
entodermo *m.* endoderm, entoderm.
entófito *m.* entophyte.
entoftalmía *f.* entophtalmia.
entómera *f.* entomere.
entomesodermo *m.* entomesoderm.
entomión *m.* entomion.
entomo *m.* entomo.
entomofobia *f.* entomophobia.
entomoftoramicosis *f.* entomophthoramycosis.
entomoftoramicosis basidiobolae entomophthoramycosis basidiobolae.
entomoftoramicosis conidiobolae entomophthoramycosis conidiobolae.
entomología *f.* entomology.
entomología cadavérica cadaveric entomology.
entomólogo, -a *m., f.* entomologist.

Entomophthoraceae Entomophthoraceae.
entonación *f.* toning.
entópico, -ca *adj.* entopic.
entoplásico, -ca *adj.* entoplastic.
entoplasma *f.* entoplasm.
entóptico, -ca *adj.* entoptic.
entoptoscopia *f.* entoptoscopy.
entoptoscopio *m.* entoptoscope.
entorretina *f.* entoretina.
entostosis *f.* enostosis, entostosis.
entótico, -ca *adj.* entotic.
entotimpánico, -ca *adj.* entotympanic.
entozoario *m.* entozoon.
entozoo *m.* entozoon.
entrada *f.* inlet.
entrecruzamiento *m.* crossing-over, intercross.
entrecruzamiento de genes, entrecruzamiento genético genetic crossing-over, genetic crossover.
entrecruzamiento desigual uneven crossing-over, unequal crossing-over.
entrecruzamiento somático somatic crossing-over.
entrenamiento *m.* training.
entrenamiento aeróbico aerobic training.
entrenamiento afirmativo assertive training.
entrenamiento asertivo assertive training.
entrenamiento aversivo aversive training.
entrenamiento en habilidades sociales social skills training.
entrenamiento en hábitos higiénicos hygienic habit training.
entrenamiento de resistencia activa (ERA) active resistance training (ART).
entrenamiento muscular con resistencia a la inspiración inspiratory resistance muscle training.
entrenamiento ortópico orthopic training.
entrenar *v.* train.
entretejido *m.* knitting.
entrevista *f.* interview.
entrevista abierta open interview.
entrevista cerrada enclosed interview.
entrevista clínica clinical interview.
entrevista descriptiva descriptive interview.
entrevista directa direct interview.
entrevista directiva directive interview.
entrevista estandarizada standardized interview.
entrevista estructurada structured interview.
entrevista indirecta indirect interview.
entrevista no directiva non-directive interview.
entrevista no estructurada unstructured interview.
entrevista de preguntas directas direct-question interview.
entrevista psiquiátrica psychiatric interview.
entrevista terapéutica therapeutic interview.
entrevista en urgencias emergency interview.
entropía *f.* entropy.
entropión *m.* entropion.
entropión atónico atonic entropion.
entropión cicatricial, entropión cicatrizal cicatricial entropion.
entropión congénito congenital entropion.
entropión espasmódico spasmodic entropion.
entropión espástico spastic entropion.
entropión involutivo involutive entropion.
entropión senil senile entropion.
entropión uveal uvea entropion.

entropionizar *v.* entropionize.
entuertos *m.* afterpains.
entumecimiento *m.* numbness.
entumecimiento al despertar waking numbness.
enturbiamiento *m.* turbidity.
enucleación *f.* enucleation.
enucleación ocular enucleation of the eyeball.
enucleado, -da *adj.* enucleated.
enucleador *m.* enucleator.
enula *f.* enula.
enuresis *f.* enuresis.
enuresis diurna diurnal enuresis.
enuresis nocturna nocturnal enuresis.
enurético, -ca *adj.* enuretic.
envainado, -da *adj.* insheathed.
envejecimiento *m.* aging.
envenenamiento *m.* poisoning.
envergadura *f.* span.
envidia *f.* envy.
envidia del pene penis envy.
envoltura¹ *f.* envelope.
envoltura nuclear nuclear envelope.
envoltura virósica viral envelope.
envoltura² *f.* pack.
enyesado *m.* cast.
enyesado en halo halo cast.
enyesado colgante hanging cast.
enzima *f.* enzyme.
enzimático, -ca *adj.* enzymatic.
enzimohistoquímica *f.* enzymohistochemistry.
enzimoinmunoensayo *m.* enzyme-immunoassay.
enzimólisis *f.* enzymolysis.
enzimosis *f.* enzymolysis.
enzimología *f.* enzymology.
enzimólogo, -a *m., f.* enzymologist.
enzimopatía *f.* enzymopathy.
enzimuria *f.* enzymuria.
eosinocito *m.* eosinocyte.
eosinofilia *f.* eosinophilia.
eosinofilia asmática asthmatic eosinophilia.
eosinofilia con infiltración pulmonar pulmonary infiltration eosinophilia.
eosinofilia de Löffler Löffler's eosinophilia.
eosinofilia pulmonar simple, eosinofilia de Löffler simple pulmonary eosinophilia, Löffler's eosinophilia.
eosinofilia tropical, eosinofilia tropical pulmonar tropical eosinophilia, tropical pulmonary eosinophilia.
eosinofílico, -ca *adj.* eosinophilic.
eosinófilo *m.* eosinophil, eosinophile.
eosinofilopoyetina *f.* eosinophylopoietin.
eosinofilosis *f.* eosinophilosis.
eosinofilotáctico, -ca *adj.* eosinophilotactic.
eosinofiluria *f.* eosinophiluria.
eosinopenia *f.* eosinopenia.
eosinotáctico, -ca *adj.* eosinotactic.
eosinotaxis *f.* eosinotaxis.
epacmástico, -ca *adj.* epacmastic.
epacmo *m.* epacme.
epalobiosis *f.* epallobiosis.
epamniótico, -ca *adj.* epamniotic.
eparsalgia *f.* eparsalgia, epersalgia.
eparterial *adj.* eparterial.
epaxial *adj.* epaxial.
epaxil *adj.* epaxial.
epencefálico, -ca *adj.* epencephalic.
epencéfalo *m.* epencephalon.
ependimario, -ria *adj.* ependymal.
ependimitis *f.* ependymitis.
epéndimo *m.* ependyma.
ependimoblasto *m.* ependymoblast.

ependimoblastoma *m.* ependymoblastoma.
ependimocito *m.* ependymocyte.
ependimocitoma *m.* ependimocytoma.
ependimoma *m.* ependymoma.
 ependimoma intramedular intramedullary ependymoma.
 ependimoma mixopapilar myxopapillary ependymoma.
ependimopatía *f.* ependymopathy.
ependopatía *f.* ependopathy.
eperitrozoonosis *f.* eperythrozoonosis.
epersalgia *f.* eparsalgia, epersalgia.
Ephemerida Ephemerida.
epiblástico, -ca *adj.* epiblastic.
epiblasto *m.* epiblast.
epibléfaron *m.* epiblepharon.
epibolia *f.* epiboly, epibole.
epibulbar *adj.* epibulbar.
epicántico, -ca *adj.* epicanthal, epicanthic.
epicanto *m.* epicanthus.
 epicanto Invertido epicanthus inversus.
epicardial *adj.* epicardial.
epicardias *m.* epicardia.
epicárdico, -ca *adj.* epicardial.
epicardiectomía *f.* epicardiectomy.
epicardio *m.* epicardium.
epicardiólisis *f.* epicardiolysis.
epicarditis *f.* epicarditis.
epicauma *m.* epicauma.
epiceloma *m.* epicoeloma.
epicentral *adj.* epicentral.
epicistitis *f.* epicystitis.
epicistotomía *f.* epicystotomy.
epicito *m.* epicyte.
epicomo *m.* epicomus.
epicondialgia *f.* epicondylalgia.
 epicondialgia externa externa epicondylalgia.
epicondilalgia *f.* epicondylalgia.
epicondilar *adj.* epicondylian, epicondylic.
epicondíleo, -a *adj.* epicondylian, epicondylic.
epicondilitis *f.* epicondylitis.
 epicondilitis humeral externa, epicondilitis humeral lateral lateral humeral epicondylitis.
epicóndilo *m.* epicondyle, epicondylus.
epicoracoideo, -a *adj.* epicoracoid.
epicorion *f.* epichorion.
epicorneoescleritis *f.* epicorneoscleritis.
epicostal *adj.* epicostal.
epicráneo *m.* epicranium, epicranius.
epicrisis *f.* epicrisis.
epicrítico, -ca *adj.* epicritic.
epidemia *f.* epidemic.
 epidemia puntual point epidemic.
epidemicidad *f.* epidemicity.
epidémico, -ca *adj.* epidemic.
epidemiografía *f.* epidemiography.
epidemiología *f.* epidemiology.
 epidemiología analítica analytic epidemiology.
 epidemiología descriptiva descriptive epidemiology.
 epidemiología experimental experimental epidemiology.
 epidemiología observacional descriptive epidemiology.
 epidemiología sustantiva substantive epidemiology.
epidemiólogo, -a *m., f.* epidemiologist.
epidermalización *f.* epidermalization.
epidermático, -ca *adj.* epidermatic.
epidermatitis *f.* epidermatitis.
epidermatoplastia *f.* epidermatoplasty.
epidérmico, -ca *adj.* epidermic.

epidermícula *f.* epidermicula.
epidermidosis *f.* epidermidosis.
epidermis *f.* epiderm, epidermis.
epidermitis *f.* epidermitis.
epidermización *f.* epidermization, epidermidalization.
epidermo *m.* epiderm, epidermis.
epidermodisplasia *f.* epidermodysplasia.
 epidermodisplasia verruciforme epidermodysplasia verruciformis.
epidermofítide *f.* epidermophytid.
epidermofitosis *f.* epidermophytosis.
 epidermofitosis cruris epidermophytosis cruris.
 epidermofitosis interdigital epidermophytosis interdigitale.
epidermoide *adj.* epidermoid.
epidermólisis *f.* epidermolysis.
 epidermólisis adquirida epidermolysis acquisita.
 epidermólisis ampollar epidermolysis bullosa.
 epidermólisis ampollar adquirida acquired epidermolysis bullosa, epidermolysis bullosa acquisita.
 epidermólisis ampollar de las articulaciones junctional epidermolysis bullosa.
 epidermólisis ampollar distrófica epidermolysis bullosa dystrophica.
 epidermólisis ampollar distrófica albopapuloide albopapuloid epidermolysis bullosa dystrophica.
 epidermólisis ampollar distrófica displásica dysplastic epidermolysis bullosa dystrophica.
 epidermólisis ampollar distrófica dominante dominant epidermolysis bullosa dystrophica.
 epidermólisis ampollar distrófica hiperplásica hyperplastic epidermolysis bullosa dystrophica.
 epidermólisis ampollar distrófica polidisplásica polydysplastic epidermolysis bullosa dystrophica.
 epidermólisis ampollar distrófica recesiva recessive epidermolysis bullosa dystrophica.
 epidermólisis ampollar hereditaria epidermolysis bullosa hereditaria.
 epidermólisis ampollar hiperplásica hyperplastic epidermolysis bullosa.
 epidermólisis ampollar letal, epidermólisis ampollar mortal epidermolysis bullosa lethalis.
 epidermólisis ampollar polidisplásica polydysplastic epidermolysis bullosa.
 epidermólisis ampollar simple, epidermólisis ampollar simple generalizada epidermolysis bullosa simplex, generalized epidermolysis bullosa simplex.
 epidermólisis ampollar tóxica toxic bullous epidermolysis.
 epidermólisis ampollar de Weber-Cockayne bullous epidermolysis of Weber-Cockayne.
epidermolítico, -ca *adj.* epidermolytic.
epidermoma *m.* epidermoma.
epidermomicosis *f.* epidermomycosis.
Epidermophyton Epidermophyton.
epidermosis *f.* epidermosis.
epidermotrófico, -ca *adj.* epidermotropic.
epidermotrópico, -ca *adj.* epidermotropic.
epidermotropismo *m.* epidermotropism.
epidiálisis *f.* epidialysis.
epidiascopio *m.* epidiascope.
epididimal *adj.* epididymal.
epididimario, -ria *adj.* epididymal.
epididimectomía *f.* epididymectomy.

epididimisoplastia *f.* epididymisoplasty.
epididimitis *f.* epididymitis.
 epididimitis inespecífica acute epididymitis.
 epididimitis tuberculosa tuberculous epididymitis.
epidídimo *m.* epididymis.
epididimodeferencial *adj.* epididymodeferential.
epididimodeferentectomía *f.* epididymodeferentectomy.
epididimoorquitis *f.* epididymo-orchitis.
epididimoplastia *f.* epididymoplasty.
epididimotomía *f.* epididymotomy.
epididimovasectomía *f.* epididymovasectomy.
epididimovasostomía *f.* epididymovasostomy.
epididimovesiculografía *f.* epididymovesiculography.
epidural *adj.* epidural.
epidurografía *f.* epidurography.
epiescleral *adj.* episcleral.
epiescleritis *f.* episcleritis.
 epiescleritis multinodular episcleritis multinodularis.
 epiescleritis nodular episcleritis nodular.
 epiescleritis periódica fugaz episcleritis periodica fugax.
epiesclerótica *f.* episclera.
epiesclerótico, -ca *adj.* episcleral.
epiesclerotitis *f.* episcleritis.
epiespinal *adj.* epispinal.
epiesplenitis *f.* episplenitis.
epiesternal *adj.* episternal.
epiesternón *m.* episternum.
epifaringitis *f.* epipharingitis.
epifascial *adj.* epifascial.
epifenómeno *m.* epiphenomenon.
epifilaxis *f.* epiphylaxis.
epifisario, -ria *adj.* epiphyseal, epiphysial.
epifisectomía *f.* pinealectomy.
epifisiodesis *f.* epiphyseodesis, epiphysiodesis.
epifisioide *adj.* epiphysioid.
epifisiólisis *f.* epiphysiolysis.
epifisiómetro *m.* epiphysiometer.
epifisiopatía *f.* epiphysiopathy.
epífisis *f.* epiphysis.
 epífisis desprendida slipped epiphysis.
 epífisis femoral femoral epiphysis.
 epífisis punteada stippled epiphysis.
 epífisis por presión pressure epiphysis.
 epífisis por tracción traction epiphysis.
epifisitis *f.* epiphysitis.
 epifisitis vertebral vertebral epiphysitis.
epífora *f.* epiphora.
 epífora atónica atonic epiphora.
epigámico, -ca *adj.* epigamic.
epigáster *m.* epigaster.
epigastralgia *f.* epigastralgia.
epigástrico, -ca *adj.* epigastric.
epigastrio *m.* epigastrium.
epigastrios *m.* epigastrius.
epigastrius *m.* epigastrius.
epigastrocele *m.* epigastrocele.
epigastrorrafia *f.* epigastrorrhaphy.
epigénesis *f.* epigenesis, epigeny.
epigenética *f.* epigenetics.
epigenético, -ca *adj.* epigenic, epigenetic.
epiglectomía *f.* epiglottectomy.
epiglotectomía *f.* epiglottectomy.
epiglótico, -ca *adj.* epiglottic.
epiglotidectomía *f.* epiglottidectomy.
epiglotídeo, -a *adj.* epiglottidean.
epiglotis *f.* epiglottis.
epiglotitis *f.* epiglottitis.
 epiglotitis aguda acute epiglottitis.
epignato *m.* epignathus.

epihial *adj.* epihyal.
epihioideo, -a *adj.* epihyoid.
epilamelar *adj.* epilamellar.
epilaminillar *adj.* epilamellar.
epilema *m.* epilemma.
epilémico, -ca *adj.* epilemmal.
epilepidoma *m.* epilepidoma.
epilepsia *f.* epilepsy, epilepsia.
  epilepsia abdominal abdominal epilepsy.
  epilepsia acinética akinetic epilepsy.
  epilepsia activada activated epilepsy.
  epilepsia adquirida acquired epilepsy.
  epilepsia anosognósica anosognosic epilepsy.
  epilepsia astática mioclónica myoclonic astatic epilepsy.
  epilepsia atónica atonic epilepsy.
  epilepsia audiogénica audiogenic epilepsy.
  epilepsia automática automatic epilepsy.
  epilepsia autónoma autonomic epilepsy.
  epilepsia benigna infantil, epilepsia benigna del niño benign childhood epilepsy.
  epilepsia de Bravais-Jackson Jacksonian epilepsy.
  epilepsia centroencefálica centrencephalic epilepsy.
  epilepsia cortical cortical epilepsy.
  epilepsia criptogenética, epilepsia criptogénica cryptogenic epilepsy.
  epilepsia demorada late epilepsy.
  epilepsia del despertar matutinal epilepsy.
  epilepsia diencefálica diencephalic epilepsy.
  epilepsia diurna diurnal epilepsy.
  epilepsia enmascarada masked epilepsy.
  epilepsia esencial essential epilepsy.
  epilepsia espinal spinal epilepsy.
  epilepsia familiar familial epilepsy.
  epilepsia fisiológica physiologic epilepsy.
  epilepsia focal focal epilepsy.
  epilepsia focal crónica chronic focal epilepsy.
  epilepsia focal menor minor focal epilepsy.
  epilepsia fótica photic epilepsy.
  epilepsia fotógena, epilepsia fotogénica photogenic epilepsy.
  epilepsia fotosensible photosensitive epilepsy.
  epilepsia generalizada generalized epilepsy.
  epilepsia generalizada en flexión generalized flexion epilepsy.
  epilepsia generalizada primaria primary generalized epilepsy.
  epilepsia generalizada secundaria, epilepsia secundaria generalizada secondary generalized epilepsy.
  epilepsia de grand mal, epilepsia de gran mal grand mal epilepsy.
  epilepsia histérica hysterical epilepsy.
  epilepsia idiopática idiopathic epilepsy.
  epilepsia infantil con paroxismos occipitales benign childhood epilepsy with occipital paroxysms.
  epilepsia jacksoniana Jacksonian epilepsy.
  epilepsia de Kojewnikoff Kojewnikoff's epilepsy.
  epilepsia laríngea laryngeal epilepsy.
  epilepsia larvada larval epilepsy.
  epilepsia latente latent epilepsy.
  epilepsia del lóbulo temporal temporal lobe epilepsy.
  epilepsia local, epilepsia localizada local epilepsy, localized epilepsy.
  epilepsia matutina matutinal epilepsy.
  epilepsia mayor, epilepsia major major epilepsy.
  epilepsia menor, epilepsia minor minor epilepsy.

  epilepsia mioclónica myoclonic epilepsy.
  epilepsia mioclónica juvenil juvenile myoclonic epilepsy.
  epilepsia mioclónica progresiva, epilepsia mioclónica progresiva familiar progressive myoclonic epilepsy, progressive familial myoclonic epilepsy.
  epilepsia musicógena, epilepsia musicogénica musicogenic epilepsy.
  epilepsia nocturna nocturnal epilepsy.
  epilepsia nutatoria epilepsia nutans.
  epilepsia orgánica organic epilepsy.
  epilepsia parcial partial epilepsy.
  epilepsia parcial continua epilepsia partialis continua.
  epilepsia de petit mal, epilepsia de pequeño mal petit mal epilepsy.
  epilepsia por comida eating epilepsy.
  epilepsia postraumática post-traumatic epilepsy.
  epilepsia postraumática precoz early post-traumatic epilepsy.
  epilepsia precipitada compleja complex precipitated epilepsy.
  epilepsia precipitada sensorial sensory precipitated epilepsy.
  epilepsia primaria generalizada primary generalized epilepsy.
  epilepsia primaria de la lectura reading epilepsy.
  epilepsia procursiva procursive epilepsy.
  epilepsia psicomotora psychomotor epilepsy.
  epilepsia con punta-onda continuada del sueño continuous spike-and wave epilepsy during sleep.
  epilepsia refleja reflex epilepsy.
  epilepsia rolándica rolandic epilepsy.
  epilepsia sensible a un patrón pattern sensitive epilepsy.
  epilepsia sensitiva, epilepsia sensorial sensory epilepsy.
  epilepsia seriada serial epilepsy.
  epilepsia sobresalto, epilepsia por sobresalto startle epilepsy.
  epilepsia del sonámbulo somnambulic epilepsy.
  epilepsia del sueño sleep epilepsy.
  epilepsia tardía late epilepsy.
  epilepsia tónica tonic epilepsy.
  epilepsia tonico-clónica generalizada generalized tonic-clonic epilepsy.
  epilepsia en tornado tornado epilepsy.
  epilepsia traumática traumatic epilepsy.
  epilepsia uncinada uncinate epilepsy.
  epilepsia vasomotora vasomotor epilepsy.
  epilepsia vasovagal vasovagal epilepsy.
  epilepsia visceral visceral epilepsy.
epiléptico, -ca *adj.* epileptic.
epileptiforme *adj.* epileptiform.
epileptógeno, -ca *adj.* epileptogenic.
epileptógeno, -na *adj.* epileptogenous.
epileptoide *adj.* epileptoid.
epileptología *f.* epileptology.
epileptólogo, -ga *m., f.* epileptologist.
epileptosis *f.* epileptosis.
epilesional *adj.* epilesional.
epiloia *f.* epiloia.
epimandibular *adj.* epimandibular.
epimastical *adj.* epimastical.
epimastigote *m.* epimastigote.
epimastigoto *m.* epimastigote.
epimenorragia *f.* epimenorrhagia.
epimenorrea *f.* epimenorrhea.
epimerización *f.* epimerization.

epímero *m.* epimer.
epimicroscopio *m.* epimicroscope.
epimisio *m.* epimysium.
epimisiotomía *f.* epimysiotomy.
epimórfico, -ca *adj.* epimorphic.
epimorfosis *f.* epimorphosis.
epinefrina *f.* epinephrine.
epinefrinemia *f.* epinephrinemia.
epinefritis *f.* epinephritis.
epinefros *m.* epinephros.
epineural¹ *adj.* epineural.
epineural² *adj.* epineurial.
epineurio *m.* epineurium.
epineuro *m.* epineurium.
epinósico, -ca *adj.* epinosic.
epinosis *f.* epinosis.
epiótico, -ca *adj.* epiotic.
epiparoniquia *f.* epiparonychia.
epipástico, -ca *adj.* epipastic.
epipericárdico, -ca *adj.* epipericardial.
epipial *adj.* epipial.
epípigo *m.* epipygus.
epipiramidal *m.* epipyramis.
epiplectomía *f.* epiploectomy.
epiplenterocele *m.* epiploenterocele.
epiplocele *m.* epiplocele.
epiploectomía *f.* epiploectomy.
epiploenterocele *m.* epiploenterocele.
epiploico, -ca *adj.* epiploic.
epiploítis *f.* epiploitis.
epiplomerocele *m.* epiplomerocele.
epiplón *m.* epiploon, omentum.
epiplonfalocele *m.* epiplomphalocele.
epiplopexia *f.* epiplopexy.
epiploplastia *f.* epiploplasty.
epiplorrafia *f.* epiplorrhaphy.
epiplosarconfalocele *m.* epiplosarcomphalocele.
epiplosqueocele *m.* epiploscheocele.
epiptérico, -ca *adj.* epipteric.
epiqueratofaquia *f.* epikeratophakia.
epiqueratoprótesis *f.* epikeratoprosthesis.
epirrotuliano, -na *adj.* epirotulian.
episclera *f.* episclera.
episcleral *adj.* episcleral.
escleritis *f.* episcleritis.
epiesclerótica *f.* episclera.
epiesclerótico, -ca *adj.* episcleral.
epiesclerotitis *f.* episclerotitis.
episiotomía *f.* episiotomy.
episodio *m.* episode.
  episodio afectvo affective episode.
  episodio depresivo depressive episode.
  episodio depresivo grave major depressive episode.
  episodio depresivo grave sin síntomas psicóticos major depressive episode without psychotic symptoms.
  episodio depresivo grave con síntomas psicóticos major depressive episode with psychotic symptoms.
  episodio esquizofrénico agudo acute schizophrenic episode.
  episodio hipomaníaco hypomaniac episode.
  episodio maníaco manic episode.
  episodio mixto mixed episode.
  episodio psicoléptico psycholeptic episode.
episoma *m.* episome.
  episoma que transfiere resistencia resistance-transferring episome.
espispadias *m.* epispadia, epispadias.
  epispadias balánico balanic epispadia, balanitic epispadia.
  epispadias clitorídeo clitoric epispadia.
  epispadias completo complete epispadia.

epispadias glandular balanic epispadia.
epispadias peniano penile epispadia.
epispadias penopubiano penopubic epispadia.
epispadias subsinfisario subsymphyseal epispadia.
epispádico, -ca *adj.* epispadiac.
epispástico, -ca *adj.* epispastic.
epispinal *adj.* epispinal.
episplenitis *f.* episplenitis.
epistasia *f.* epistasis, epistasy.
epistasis *f.* epistasis, epistasy.
epistático, -ca *adj.* epistatic.
epistaxis *f.* epistaxis, nosebleed.
  epistaxis renal renal epistaxis.
epistemología *f.* epistemology.
  epistemología evolutiva evolutive epistemology.
  epistemología genética genetic epistemology.
episternón *m.* episternum.
epistótonos *m.* epistothonos.
epistrofeo *m.* epistropheus.
epitalámico, -ca *adj.* epithalamic.
epitálamo *m.* epithalamus.
epitalaxia *f.* epithalaxia.
epitalaxis *f.* epithalaxia.
epitaxia *f.* epitaxy.
epitaxis *f.* epitaxy.
epitela *f.* epitela.
epitelial *adj.* epithelial.
epitelio *m.* epithelium.
  epitelio anterior de la córnea anterior epithelium of the cornea, anterius epithelium
corneae.
  epitelio capsular capsular epithelium.
  epitelio ciliado ciliated epithelium.
  epitelio cilíndrico cylindrical epithelium.
  epitelio columnar columnar epithelium.
  epitelio de la cornea, epitelio corneal corneal epithelium, epithelium corneae.
  epitelio cúbico simple cubical epithelium,
cuboidal epithelium.
  epitelio del cristalino epithelium of the lens,
epithelium lentis.
  epitelio escamoso squamous epithelium.
  epitelio del esmalte enamel epithelium.
  epitelio estratificado stratified epithelium.
  *epitelio externo dental, epitelio externo
del esmalte* external dental epithelium, external enamel epithelium.
  epitelio germinal masculino seminiferous
epithelium.
  epitelio glandular glandular epithelium.
  epitelio laminado laminated epithelium.
  epitelio de la membranas serosas mesothelium.
  epitelio multiestratificado stratified epithelium.
  epitelio muscular muscle epithelium.
  epitelio de las mucosas epithelium mucosae.
  epitelio no queratinizado epithelium mucosae.
  epitelio olfatorio olfactory epithelium.
  epitelio pigmentado del iris pigmented epithelium of the iris, epithelium pigmentosum
iridis.
  epitelio pigmentario de la retina retinal pigmentary epithelium.
  epitelio poliestratificado stratified epithelium.
  epitelio respiratorio respiratory epithelium.
  epitelio seminífero seminiferous epithelium.
  epitelio sensorial sense epithelium, sensory
epithelium.
  epitelio seudoestratificado pseudostrafied
epithelium.

epitelio simple simple epithelium.
epitelio subcapsular subcapsular epithelium.
epitelio de superficies húmedas epithelium
mucosae.
epitelio transicional, epitelio de transición
transitional epithelium.
epitelio vascular endothelium.
epitelioblastoma *m.* epithelioblastoma.
epitelioceptor *m.* epithelioceptor.
epiteliocito *m.* epitheliocyte.
epiteliocorial *adj.* epitheliochorial.
epiteliofibrilla *f.* epitheliofibril.
epiteliogenético, -ca *adj.* epitheliogenic.
epitelioglandular *adj.* epithelioglandular.
epitelioide *adj.* epithelioid.
epiteliólisis *f.* epitheliolysis.
epiteliolítico, -ca *adj.* epitheliolytic.
epitelioma *m.* epithelioma.
  epitelioma adamantino epithelioma adamantinum.
  *epitelioma adenoide quístico, epitelioma
adenoideo quístico* epithelioma adenoides
cysticum.
  *epitelioma basocelular, epitelioma de cé-
lulas basales* basal cell epithelioma.
  epitelioma calcificante de Malherbe Malherbe's calcifying epithelioma.
  epitelioma ciliar maligno malignant ciliary
epithelioma.
  epitelioma cilíndrico columnar epithelioma,
cylindrical epithelioma.
  epitelioma coriónico chorionic epithelioma.
  epitelioma cuniculado epithelioma cuniculatum.
  *epitelioma escamoso de involución espon-
tánea, epitelioma escamoso múltiple autocicatrizante, epitelioma escamoso múltiple autocurable, epitelioma escamoso
múltiple de involución espontánea* multiple self-healing squamous epithelioma.
  epitelioma espinocelular prickle cell epithelioma.
  *epitelioma intraepidérmico tipo Borst-Ja-
dassohn* Borst-Jadassohn type intraepidermal epithelioma.
  epitelioma maligno carcinoma.
  epitelioma quístico benigno múltiple multiple benign cystic epithelioma.
  epitelioma sebáceo sebaceous epithelioma.
epiteliomatosis *f.* epitheliomatosis.
epiteliomatoso, -sa *adj.* epitheliomatous.
epiteliomuscular *adj.* epitheliomuscular.
epiteliopatía *f.* epitheliopathy.
  epiteliopatía pigmentaria pigment epitheliopathy.
epiteliosis *f.* epitheliosis.
  *epiteliosis descamativa de la conjuntiva,
epiteliosis exfoliativa conjuntival* epitheliosis desquamativa conjunctivae.
epiteliotoxina *f.* epitheliotoxin.
epitelitis *f.* epithelitis.
epitelito *m.* epithelite.
epitelización *f.* epithelialization, epithelization.
epítema *f.* epithem.
epitendineo *m.* epitendineum.
epitendineum *m.* epitendineum.
epitenón *m.* epitenon.
epítesis *f.* epithesis.
epithelium *m.* epithelium.
epitiflitis *f.* epityphlitis.
epitimpánico, -ca *adj.* epitympanic.
epitímpano *m.* epitympanum, recessus epitympanicus.
epitónico, -ca *adj.* epitonic.

epitopo *m.* epitope.
epitriquial *adj.* epitrichial.
epitriquio *m.* epitrichium.
epitróclea *f.* epitrochlea.
epitrocleano, -na *adj.* epitrochlear.
epitroclear *adj.* epitrochlear.
epitrocleítis *f.* epitrochleytis.
epituberculosis *f.* epituberculosis.
epizoario *m.* epizoo, epizoon.
epizoicida *adj.* epizoicide.
epizoico, -ca *adj.* epizoic.
epizoo *m.* epizoo, epizoon.
epizoonosis *f.* epizoonosis.
eponímico, -ca *adj.* eponymic.
epónimo *m.* eponym.
epónimo, -ma *adj.* eponymous.
eponiquia *f.* eponychia.
eponiquio *m.* eponychium.
epooforectomía *f.* epoophorectomy.
épulis *m.* epulis.
  épulis de células gigantes giant cell epulis.
  *épulis congénito, épulis congénito del re-
cién nacido* congenital epulis, congenital epulis of the newborn.
  épulis del embarazo epulis gravidarum.
  épulis fibromatoso epulis fibromatosa.
  épulis fisurado epulis fissurata.
  épulis gigantocelular giant cell epulis.
  épulis granulomatoso epulis granulomatosa.
  épulis del neonato epulis of the newborn.
  épulis pigmentado pigmented epulis.
  épulis telangiectásico telangiectatic epulis.
epulofibroma *m.* epulofibroma.
epuloide *adj.* epuloid.
epuloideo, -a *adj.* epuloid.
epulosis *f.* epulosis.
epulótico, -ca *adj.* epulotic.
equiaxial *adj.* equiaxial.
equiaxil *adj.* equiaxial.
equicalórico, -ca *adj.* equicaloric.
equilibración *f.* equilibration.
  equilibración mandibular mandibular equilibration.
  equilibración oclusal occlusal equilibration.
equilibrador *m.* equilibrator.
equilibrio *m.* balance, equilibrium.
  *equilibrio ácido-base, equilibrio acidobá-
sico* acid-base equilibrium, acid-base balance.
  equilibrio de acople arbitrario random mating equilibrium.
  equilibrio del carbono carbon equilibrium.
  equilibrio coloide colloid equilibrium.
  equilibrio corporal body equilibrium.
  equilibrio dinámico dynamic equilibrium.
  equilibrio de Donnan Donnan equilibrium.
  equilibrio electrolítico electrolyte balance.
  equilibrio de enlace linkage equilibrium.
  equilibrio estable stable equilibrium.
  equilibrio estático static equilibrium.
  equilibrio fisiológico physiologic equilibrium.
  equilibrio genético genetic equilibrium.
  equilibrio de Gibbs-Donnan Gibbs-Donnan
equilibrium.
  equilibrio de Hardy-Weinberg Hardy-
Weinberg equilibrium.
  equilibrio hídrico fluid equilibrium.
  equilibrio homeostático homeostatic equilibrium.
  equilibrio inestable unstable equilibrium.
  equilibrio líquido cero zero fluid balance.
  equilibrio de membrana membrane equilibrium.
  equilibrio metabólico metabolic balance.
  equilibrio nitrogenado, equilibrio nitróge-

no nitrogen equilibrium, nitrogen balance, nitrogenous equilibrium.

equilibrio nutritivo nutritive equilibrium.

equilibrio oclusal occlusal balance.

equilibrio proteínico protein equilibrium.

equilibrio radiactivo radioactive equilibrium.

equimolar *adj.* equimolar.

equimolecular *adj.* equimolecular.

equimoma *m.* ecchymoma.

equimosado, -da *adj.* ecchymosed.

equimosis *f.* ecchymosis.

equimosis cadavérica cadaveric ecchymosis.

equimosis palpebral palpebral ecchymosis.

equimosis de Tardieu Tardieu's ecchymosis.

equimótico, -ca *adj.* ecchymotic.

equinación *f.* equination.

equinado, -da *adj.* echinate.

equinenona *f.* echinenone.

equinia *f.* equinia.

equinocito *m.* echinocyte.

equinococo *m.* echinococcus.

equinococosis *f.* echinococciasis, echinococcosis.

equinococosis renal renal echinococciasis.

equinococosis retrovesical retrovesical echinococciasis.

equinococotomía *f.* echinococcotomy.

equinoftalmia *f.* echinophthalmia.

equinosis *f.* echinosis.

equinostomiasis *f.* echinostomiasis.

equinovalgo, -ga *adj.* equinovalgus.

equinovalgus *m.* equinovalgus.

equinovaro, -ra *adj.* equinovarus.

equinovarus *adj.* equinovarus.

equinulado, -da *adj.* echinulate.

equipo[1] *m.* equipment.

equipo[2] *m.* team.

equipo de reanimación code team.

equipotencial *adj.* equipotential.

equitóxico, -ca *adj.* equitoxic.

equivalencia *f.* equivalence, equivalency.

equivalente *m. y adj.* equivalent.

Eratyrus Eratyrus.

erección *f.* erection.

erección peneana penile erection.

eréctil *adj.* erectile.

erector *adj.* erector.

eremacausia *f.* eremacausis.

Erethmapodites Erethmapodites.

eretismo *m.* erethism.

ergastoplasma *m.* ergastoplasm.

ergodinamógrafo *m.* ergodynamograph.

ergoestesiógrafo *m.* ergoesthesiograph.

ergogénico, -ca *adj.* ergogenic.

ergográfico, -ca *adj.* ergographic.

ergógrafo *m.* ergograph.

ergógrafo de Mosso Mosso's ergograph.

ergograma *m.* ergogram.

ergómetro *m.* ergometer.

ergómetro de bicicleta bicycle ergometer.

ergonomía *f.* ergonomics.

ergoplasma *m.* ergoplasm.

ergosoma *m.* ergosome.

ergóstato *m.* ergostat.

ergoterapia *f.* ergotherapy.

ergotioneína *f.* ergothioneine.

ergotismo *m.* ergotism.

ergotizado, -da *adj.* ergotized.

ergotoxicosis *f.* ergotoxicosis.

ergotropía *f.* ergotropy.

ergotrópico, -ca *adj.* ergotropic.

erina *f.* dissecting hook.

eriometría *f.* eriometry.

erisífaco *m.* erisiphake, erisophake.

erisipela *f.* erysipelas.

erisipela ambulante ambulant erysipelas.

erisipela blanca white erysipelas.

erisipela de la costa coast erysipelas.

erisipela crónica erysipeloid erysipelas.

erisipela errante wandering erysipelas.

erisipela facial facial erysipelas.

erisipela flemonosa phlegmonous erysipelas.

erisipela gangrenosa gangrenous erysipelas.

erisipela grave interna erysipelas grave internum.

erisipela interna erysipelas internum.

erisipela linfática white erysipelas.

erisipela maligna malignant erysipelas.

erisipela migratoria erysipelas migrans.

erisipela necrosante necrotizing erysipelas.

erisipela perstans, erisipela perstans facial erysipelas perstans, erysipelas perstans faciei.

erisipela pustulosa erysipelas pustulosum.

erisipela quirúrgica surgical erysipelas.

erisipela recurrente recurrent erysipelas.

erisipela verrugosa erysipelas verrucosum.

erisipela zoonótica zoonotic erysipelas.

erisipelatoso, -sa *adj.* erysipelatous.

erisipeloide *f.* erysipeloid.

erisófaco *m.* erisophake.

eritema *m.* erythema.

eritema ab igne erythema ab igne.

eritema acrodínico acrodynic erythema.

eritema amoniacal diaper erythema.

eritema ampollar erythema bullosum.

eritema anular erythema annulare.

eritema anular centrífugo erythema annulare centrifugum.

eritema anular reumático erythema annulare rheumaticum.

eritema calórico erythema caloricum.

eritema chromicum melanodermicum erythema chromicum melanodermicum.

eritema circinado erythema circinatum.

eritema crónico migratorio erythema chronicum migrans.

eritema discrómico persistente, eritema dyschromicum perstans erythema dyschromicum perstans.

eritema elevado, eritema elevatum, eritema elevatum diutinum erythema elevatum diutinum.

eritema epidémico epidemic erythema.

eritema epidémico artrítrico epidemic arthritic erythema.

eritema escarlatiniforme, eritema escarlatinoide scalatiniform erythema, erythema ecarlatinoides.

eritema estreptógeno erythema streptogenes.

eritema exfoliativo erythema exfoliativa.

eritema exudativo hemorrágico hemorrhagic exudative erythema.

eritema figurado perstans, eritema figuratum perstans erythema figuratum perstans.

eritema figuratum figurate erythema, erythema figuratum.

eritema del frío cold erythema.

eritema fugaz erythema fugax.

eritema generalizado generalized erythema.

eritema glúteo gluteal erythema.

eritema gyratum, eritema gyratum perstans gyrate erythema, equilibrium gyratum, equilibrium gyratum perstans.

eritema indurado erythema induratum.

eritema indurado de Bazin Bazin's indurative erythema.

eritema infeccioso erythema infectiosum.

eritema intertrigo erythema intertrigo.

eritema iris, eritema en iris erythema iris.

eritema de Jacquet Jacquet's erythema.

eritema leproso nudoso erythema nodosum leprosum.

eritema macular macular erythema.

eritema marginado reumático erythema marginatum, erythema marginatum rheumaticum.

eritema migratorio erythema migrans.

eritema migratorio crónico erythema chronicum migrans.

eritema migratorio de la lengua erythema migrans linguae.

eritema migratorio necrolítico necrolytic migratory erythema.

eritema de Milian Milian's erythema.

eritema multiforme erythema multiforme.

eritema multiforme ampollar erythema multiforme bullosum.

eritema multiforme exudativo erythema multiforme exudativum.

eritema multiforme mayor erythema multiforme major.

eritema multiforme menor erythema multiforme minor.

eritema necrolítico migratorio necrolytic migratory erythema.

eritema necroticans erythema necroticans.

eritema neonatal erythema neonatorum.

eritema neonatal tóxico erythema neonatorum toxicum.

eritema nodoso, eritema nudoso erythema nodosum.

eritema nudoso leproso erythema nodosum leprosum.

eritema nudoso migratorio erythema nodosum migrans.

eritema nudoso sifilítico erythema nodosum syphiliticum.

eritema palmar palmar erythema, erythema palmare.

eritema palmar hereditario erythema palmare hereditarium.

eritema por pañal napkin erythema.

eritema papuloso erythema papulatum, erythema papulosum.

eritema paratrimma erythema paratrimma.

eritema pernio erythema pernio.

eritema persistente erythema perstans.

eritema polimorfo polymorphe erythema.

eritema queratoide erythema keratodes.

eritema del recién nacido erythema neonatorum.

eritema simple, eritema simplex erythema simplex.

eritema sintomático symptomatic erythema.

eritema solar erythema solare.

eritema tóxico toxic erythema, erythema toxicum.

eritema tóxico del neonato, eritema tóxico del recién nacido erythema toxicum neonatorum, erythema toxicum of the newborn.

eritema traumático erythema traumaticum.

eritema tuberculatum erythema tuberculatum.

eritema venenatum toxic erythema, erythema toxicum.

eritematogénico, -ca *adj.* erythematogenic.

eritematopultáceo, -a *adj.* erythematopultaceous.

eritematoso, -sa *adj.* erythematous.

eritematovesicular *adj.* erythematovesicular.

eritemógeno, -na *adj.* erythemogenic.

eritralgia *f.* erythralgia.

eritrasma *m.* erythrasma.

eritredema *m.* erythredema.
eritredermia *f.* erythrederma.
eritremia *f.* erythremia.
  eritremia de altura altitude erythremia.
eritremomelalgia *f.* erythremomelalgia.
eritrismo *m.* erythrism.
eritrístico, -ca *adj.* erythristic.
eritroblastemia *f.* erythroblastemia.
eritroblástico, -ca *adj.* erythroblastic.
eritroblasto *m.* erythroblast.
  eritroblasto acidófilo acidophilic erythroblast.
  eritroblasto basófilo basophilic erythroblast.
  eritroblasto definitivo definitive erythroblast.
  eritroblasto eosinófilo eosinophilic erythroblast.
  eritroblasto intermedio intermediate erythroblast.
  eritroblasto ortocromático orthochromatic erythroblast.
  eritroblasto oxífilo oxyphilic erythroblast.
  eritroblasto policromático polychromatic erythroblast.
  eritroblasto primitivo primitive erythroblast.
  eritroblasto tardío late erythroblast.
  eritroblasto temprano early erythroblast.
eritroblastoma *m.* erythroblastoma.
eristroblastomatosis *f.* erythroblastomatosis.
eritroblastopenia *f.* erythroblastopenia.
eritroblastósico, -ca *adj.* eyrtroblastotic.
eritroblastosis *f.* erythroblastosis.
  eritroblastosis fetal erythroblastosis fetalis.
  eritroblastosis neonatal erythroblastosis neonatorum.
eritrocatálisis *f.* erythrocatalysis.
eritrocianosis *f.* erythrocyanosis.
eritrocinética *f.* erythrokinetics.
eritrocitaféresis *f.* erythrocytapheresis.
eritrocitario, -ria *adj.* erythrocytic.
eritrocitemia *f.* erythrocythemia.
eritrocítico, -ca *adj.* erythrocytic.
eritrocito *m.* erythrocyte.
  eritrocito acrómico achromic erythrocyte.
  eritrocito básofilo basophilic erythrocyte, stippled erythrocyte.
  eritrocito crenado crenated erythrocyte.
  eritrocito en diana target erythrocyte.
  eritrocito falciforme sickled erythrocyte.
  eritrocito hipocrómico hypochromic erythrocyte.
  eritrocito inmaduro immature erythrocyte.
  eritrocito normocrómico normochromic erythrocyte.
  eritrocito nucleado nucleated erythrocyte.
  eritrocito ortocromático orthochromatic erythrocyte.
  eritrocito policromático, eritrocito policromatófilo, eritrocito policromatofílico polychromatic erythrocyte, polychromatophilic erythrocyte.
  eritrocito en sombrero mexicano Mexican hat erythrocyte.
eritrocitoblasto *m.* erythrocytoblast.
eritrocitofagia *f.* erythrocytophagy.
eritrocitófago, -ga *adj.* erythrocytophagous.
eritrocitolisina *f.* erythrocytolysin.
eritrocitólisis *f.* erythrocytolisis.
eritrocitómetro *m.* erythrocytometer.
eritrocitopenia *f.* erythrocytopenia.
eritrocitopoyesis *f.* erythrocytopoiesis.
eritrocitorrexia *f.* erythrocytorrhexis.
eritrocitorrexis *f.* erythrocytorrhexis.
eritrocitosis *f.* erythrocytosis.
  eritrocitosis leucémica leukemic erythrocytosis.

eritrocitosquisis *f.* erythrocytoschisis.
eritrocituria *f.* erythrocyturia.
eritroclasia *f.* erythroclasis.
eritroclasis *f.* erythroclasis.
eritroclástico, -ca *adj.* erythroclastic.
eritroclasto *m.* erythroclast.
eritrocromía *f.* erythrochromia.
eritrodegenerativo, -va *adj.* erythrodegenerative.
eritrodermatitis *f.* erythrodermatitis.
eritrodermia *f.* erythroderma.
  eritrodermia descamativa erythroderma desquamativum.
  eritrodermia exfoliativa exfoliative erythroderma.
  eritrodermia ictiosiforme, eritrodermia ictiosiforme congénito ichthyosiform erythroderma, congenital ichthyosiform erythroderma.
  eritrodermia ictiosiforme congénito bulloso bullous congenital ichthyosiform erythroderma.
  eritrodermia ictiosiforme congénito no bulloso non-bullous congenital ichthyosiform erythroderma.
  eritrodermia linfomatoso lymphomatous erythroderma.
  eritrodermia psoriásica erythroderma psoriaticum.
  eritrodermia de Sézary Sézary erythroderma.
eritrodermitis *f.* erythrodermatitis.
eritrodoncia *f.* erythrodontia.
eritroedema *f.* erythredema.
eritrofagia *f.* erythrophagia.
eritrófago *m.* erythrophage.
eritrofagocito *m.* erythrophagocyte.
eritrofagocitosis *f.* erythrophagocytosis.
eritroféresis *f.* erythropheresis.
eritrofílico, -ca *adj.* erythrophilic.
eritrófilo *m.* erythrophil.
eritrófilo, -la *adj.* erythrophilous.
eritrófilo³ *m.* erythrophyll.
eritrófobo, -ba *adj.* erythrophobic.
eritróforo *m.* erythrophore.
eritrofosia *f.* erythophose.
eritrogénesis *f.* erythrogenesis.
  eritrogénesis imperfecta erythrogenesis imperfecta.
eritrogenia *f.* erythrogenesis.
eritrogénico, -ca *adj.* erythrogenic.
eritrógeno, -na *adj.* erythrogenic.
eritrogonio *m.* erythrogonium.
eritroide *adj.* erythroid.
eritrolabo *m.* erythrolabe.
eritrolabo *m.* erythrolabe.
eritroleucemia *f.* erythroleukemia.
eritroleucoblastosis *f.* erythroleukoblastosis.
eritroleucosis *f.* erythroleukosis.
eritroleucotrombocitemia *f.* erythroleukothrombocythemia.
eritrólisis *f.* erythrolysis.
eritromelalgia *f.* erythromelalgia.
  eritromelalgia de la cabeza erythromelalgia of the head.
eritromelia *f.* erythromelia.
eritrómetro *m.* erythrometer.
eritrón *m.* erythron.
eritroneocitosis *f.* erythroneocytosis.
eritronoclástico, -ca *adj.* erythronoclastic.
eritroparásito *m.* erythroparasite.
eritropenia *f.* erythropenia.
eritropía *f.* erythropia, erythropsia.
eritropicnosis *f.* erythropyknosis.
eritroplaquia *f.* erythroplakia.

  eritroplaquia moteada speckled erythroplakia.
eritroplasia *f.* erythroplasia.
  eritroplasia de Queyrat erythroplasia of Queyrat.
  eritroplasia de Zoon Zoon's erythroplasia.
eritroplástide *f.* erythroplastid.
eritropoyesis *f.* erythropoiesis.
eritropoyético, -ca *adj.* erythropoietic.
eritroprosopalgia *f.* erythroprosopalgia.
eritropsia *f.* erythropsia.
eritroqueratoderma *f.* erythrokeratoderma.
  eritroqueratodermia variable erythrokeratoderma variabilis.
eritrorrexia *f.* erythrorrhexis.
eritrorrexis *f.* erythrorrhexis.
eritrosa *f.* erythrosis, érythrose.
  eritrosa peribucal pigmentaria de Brocq érythrose péribuccale pigmentaire of Brocq.
eritrosedimentación *f.* erythrosedimentation.
eritrosis *f.* erythrosis, érythrose.
  eritrosis peribucal pigmentaria erythrosis pigmentata faciei, érythrose peribuccale pigmentaire.
  eritrosis pigmentaria facial erythrosis pigmentata faciei.
eritrostasis *f.* erythrostasis.
eritrotioneína *f.* erythrothioneine.
eritruria *f.* erythruria.
erogeneidad *f.* erogeneity.
erógeno, -na *adj.* erogenous.
eros *m.* eros.
erosión *f.* erosion.
  erosión cervical cervical erosion.
  erosión corneal recurrente recurrent corneal erosion.
  erosión dental, erosión dentaria dental erosion.
  erosión de Dieulafoy Dieulafoy's erosion.
erosionar *v.* erode.
erosivo, -va *adj.* erosive.
eroticismo *m.* eroticism.
erótico, -ca *adj.* erotic.
erotismo *m.* erotism.
  erotismo anal anal erotism.
  erotismo oral oral erotism.
  erotismo muscular muscle erotism.
  erotismo uretral urethral erotism.
erotización *f.* erotization.
erotizar *v.* erotize.
erotofobia *f.* erotophobia.
erotogénesis *f.* erotogenesis.
erotogénico, -ca *adj.* erotogenic.
erotógeno, -na *adj.* erotogenic.
erotomanía *f.* erotomania.
erotomaniaco, -ca *adj.* erotomaniac.
erotómano, -na *adj.* erotomaniac.
errante *adj.* wandering.
errático, -ca *adj.* erratic.
error *m.* error.
  error aleatorio random error.
  error cognitivo cognitive equilibrium.
  error congénito del metabolismo inborn equilibrium of the metabolism.
  error estándar standard error.
  error innato del metabolismo inborn equilibrium of the metabolism.
  error de laboratorio laboratory error.
  error de medicacion medication error.
  error médico medical error.
  error permisible allowable error.
  error de refracción refractive error.
  error sistemático systematic error, systemic error.

error de tipo I type I error.
error de tipo II type II error.
erubescencia *f.* erubescence.
erubescente *adj.* erubescent.
eructar *v.* belch.
eructación *f.* eructation.
eructo *m.* belch, ructus.
erupción *f.* eruption.
  erupción acelerada accelerated eruption.
  erupción activa active eruption.
  erupción ampollosa bullous eruption.
  erupción de los bañistas seabather's eruption.
  erupción clínica clinical eruption.
  erupción continua continuous eruption.
  erupción demorada delayed eruption.
  erupción dentaria, erupción del diente eruption of the teeth, tooth eruption.
  erupción por drogas drug eruption.
  erupción eritematosa erythematous eruption.
  erupción farmacológica drug eruption.
  erupción farmacológica acneiforme acneiform drug eruption.
  erupción fija fixed eruption.
  erupción fija medicamentosa fixed drug eruption.
  erupción fingida feigned eruption.
  erupción luminosa polimorfa polymorphic light eruption.
  erupción macular, erupción maculosa macular eruption.
  erupción maculopapulosa maculopapular eruption.
  erupción medicamentosa, erupción medicinal medicinal eruption.
  erupción medicamentosa fija fixed drug eruption.
  erupción pasiva passive eruption.
  erupción petequial petechial eruption.
  erupción polimorfa polymorphous eruption.
  erupción polimorfa lumínica polymorphous light eruption.
  erupción pustulosa pustular eruption.
  erupción quirúrgica surgical eruption.
  erupción reptante creeping eruption.
  erupción retardada delayed eruption.
  erupción sérica, erupción por suero serum eruption.
  erupción serpiginosa creeping eruption.
  erupción variceliforme de Kaposi Kaposi's varicelliform eruption.
  erupción vesiculosa vesicobullous eruption.
  erupción por yodo iodine eruption.
eruptivo, -va *adj.* eruptive.
esbozo embrionario *m.* anlage.
escabético, -ca *adj.* scabetic, scabietic.
escabiasis *f.* scabies.
  escabiasis costrosa crusted scabies.
  escabiasis de Noruega Norway scabies.
escabicida *adj.* scabicide, scabicidal.
escabieticida *m.* scabieticide.
escabiético, -ca *adj.* scabetic, scabietic.
escabioso, -sa *adj.* scabetic, scabietic.
escafocefalia *f.* scaphocephaly.
escafocefálico, -ca *adj.* scaphocephalic.
escafocefalismo *m.* scaphocephalism.
escafocéfalo, -la *adj.* scaphocephalous.
escafohidrocefalia *f.* scaphohydrocephaly.
escafohidrocéfalo *m.* scaphohydrocephalus.
escafoide *adj.* scaphoid.
escafoideo, -a *adj.* scaphoid.
escafoides *m.* scaphoid.
escafoiditis *f.* scaphoiditis.
escala *f.* scale.

escalar *adj.* scalar.
escaldadura *f.* scald.
escalenectomía *f.* scalenectomy.
escalenotomía *f.* scalenotomy.
escalofrío *m.* chill.
  escalofrío de cinc zinc chill.
  escalofrío congestivo congestive chill.
  escalofrío de los fundidores brass chill, brazier chill.
  escalofrío nervioso nervous chill.
  escalofrío reptante creeping chill.
  escalofrío uretral urethral chill.
escalpelo *m.* scalpel.
escalpriforme *adj.* scalpriform.
escalpro *m.* scalprum.
escama¹ *f.* squame, squama.
escama² *f.* scale.
escamado, -da *adj.* squamate.
escamatización *f.* squamatization.
escamización *f.* squamatization.
escamocelular *adj.* squamocellular.
escamocigomático, -ca *adj.* squamozygomatic.
escamoesfenoidal *adj.* squamosphenoid.
escamoesfenoideo, -a *adj.* squamosphenoid.
escamofrontal *m.* squamofrontal.
escamomastoideo, -a *adj.* squamomastoid.
escamooccipital *adj.* squamo-occipital.
escamoparietal *adj.* squamoparietal.
escamopetroso, -sa *adj.* squamopetrosal.
escamoso, -sa *adj.* scaly, squamate, squamous.
escamosoparietal *adj.* squamosoparietal.
escamotemporal *adj.* squamotemporal.
escáner *m.* scanner.
escanografía *f.* scanography.
escape *m.* escape.
  escape de aldosterona aldosterone escape.
  escape nodal nodal escape.
  escape vagal vagal escape.
  escape ventricular ventricular escape.
escápula *f.* scapula.
  escápula alada, escápula alata alar scapula, winged scapula, scapula alata.
  escápula escafoide, escápula escafoidea scaphoid scapula.
  escápula flotante floating scapula.
  escápula de Graves Graves' scapula.
escapulalgia *f.* scapulalgia.
escapular *adj.* scapular.
escapulario *m.* scapulary.
escapulectomía *f.* scapulectomy.
escapuloanterior *adj.* scapuloanterior.
escapuloclavicular *adj.* scapuloclavicular.
escapulodinia *f.* scapulodynia.
escapulohumeral *adj.* scapulohumeral.
escapulopexia *f.* scapulopexy.
escapuloposterior *adj.* scapuloposterior.
escara¹ *f.* eschar.
escara² *f.* scab.
escariador *m.* broach.
  escariador barbado barbed broach.
  escariador del conducto radicular root canal broach.
  escariador de exploración pathfinder broach.
  escariador liso smooth broach.
escarificación¹ *f.* scarification.
escarificación² *f.* scaling.
  escarificación profunda deep scaling.
  escarificación ultrasónica ultrasonic scaling.
escarificador¹ *m.* scarificator.
escarificador² *m.* scaler.
  escarificador en ala wing scaler.
  escarificador de azada hoe scaler.
  escarificador de doble filo double-ended scaler.

  escarificador en hoz sickle scaler.
  escarificador profundo deep scaler.
  escarificador superficial superficial scaler.
  escarificador ultrasónico ultrasonic scaler.
escarlatina *f.* scarlatina, scarlet fever.
  escarlatina anginosa anginose scarlatina, scarlatina anginosa.
  escarlatina frustrada latent scarlatina, scarlatina latens.
  escarlatina latente latent scarlatina, scarlatina latens.
  escarlatina hemorrágica scarlatina hemorrhagica.
  escarlatina maligna scarlatina maligna.
  escarlatina pruriginosa urticaria.
  escarlatina puerperal puerperal scarlatina.
  escarlatina reumática scarlatina rheumatica.
  escarlatina simple scarlatina simplex.
escarlatinela *f.* scarlatinella.
escarlatínico, -ca *adj.* scarlatinal.
escarlatiniforme *adj.* scarlatiniform.
escarlatinoide *adj.* scarlatinoid.
escarótico, -ca *adj.* escharotic.
escarotomía *f.* escharotomy.
escatemia *f.* scatemia.
escatofagia *f.* scatophagy.
escatofilia *f.* scatophilia.
escatología *f.* scatologia, scatology.
  escatología telefónica telephone scatology.
escatológico, -ca *adj.* scatologic.
escatoma *m.* scatoma.
escatoscopia *f.* scatoscopy.
escayola *f.* cast.
  escayola de cuatro apoyos four-poster cast.
  escayola de yeso plaster cast.
escayolar *v.* casting.
escelalgia *f.* scelalgia, skelalgia.
escelotirba *f.* scelotyrbe.
escelotirbe *f.* scelotyrbe.
esceptofilaxis *f.* skeptophylaxis.
escialiscopio *m.* scialyscope.
esciametría *f.* skiametry.
escíbalo *m.* scybalum.
escibaloso, -sa *adj.* scybalous.
escieropía *f.* scieropia.
escififorme *adj.* scyphiform.
escifoide *adj.* scyphoid.
escindir *v.* excise.
escintigrafía *f.* scintigraphy, scyntography.
escintigrama *m.* scintigram.
escintilación *f.* scintillation.
escintilascopio *m.* scintillascope.
esciopodia *f.* sciopody.
escirrencantis *m.* scirrhencanthis.
escirro *m.* scirrhus.
escirroftalmía *f.* scirrhopthalmia.
escirroide *adj.* scirrhoid.
escirroma *m.* scirrhoma.
escirrosarca *m.* scleroderma.
escirrosidad *f.* scirrhosity.
escirroso, -sa *adj.* scirrhous.
escisión¹ *f.* cleavage.
  escisión meridional meridional cleavage.
escisión² *f.* scission, excision.
escisión³ *f.* split, splitting.
escitoblastema *m.* scytoblastema.
escleradenitis *f.* scleradenitis.
esclera *f.* sclera.
escleral *adj.* scleral.
escleratitis *f.* scleratitis.
escleratógeno, -na *adj.* scleratogenous.
esclerectasia *f.* sclerectasia.
esclerectoiridectomía *f.* sclerectoiridectomy.
esclerectoiridodiálisis *f.* sclerectoiridodialysis.

esclerectomía *f.* sclerectomy.
escleréctomo *m.* sclerectome.
escleredema *m.* scleredema.
  escleredema del adulto scleredema adultorum.
esclerema *m.* sclerema.
  esclerema adiposo sclerema adiposum.
  esclerema neonatal sclerema neonatorum.
  esclerema de los recién nacidos sclerema neonatorum.
escleremia *f.* scleroderma.
esclerencefalia *f.* sclerencephaly.
escleriasis *f.* scleriasis.
escleriritomía *f.* scleriritomy.
esclerismo *m.* sclerosis.
escleritis *f.* scleritis.
  escleritis anterior anterior scleritis.
  escleritis anular annular scleritis.
  escleritis difusa diffuse scleritis.
  escleritis gelatinosa gelatinous scleritis.
  escleritis maligna malignant scleritis.
  escleritis marginal brawny scleritis.
  escleritis necrosante, escleritis necrotizante necrotizing scleritis.
  escleritis necrosante anterior anterior necrotizing scleritis.
  escleritis nodular nodular scleritis.
  escleritis posterior posterior scleritis.
  escleritis profunda deep scleritis.
escleroadiposo, -sa *adj.* scleroadipose.
escleroatrofia *f.* scleroatrophy.
escleroblastema *f.* scleroblastema.
escleroblastémico, -ca *adj.* scleroblastemic.
esclerocatarata *f.* sclerocataracta.
escleroconjuntival *adj.* scleroconjunctival.
escleroconjuntivitis *f.* scleroconjunctivitis.
esclerocórnea *f.* sclerocornea.
esclerocorneal *adj.* sclerocorneal.
esclerocoroideo, -a *adj.* sclerochoroidal.
esclerocoroiditis *f.* sclerochoroiditis.
  esclerocoroiditis anterior anterior sclerochoroiditis.
  esclerocoroiditis posterior posterior sclerochoroiditis.
esclerodactilia *f.* sclerodactylia, sclerodactyly.
esclerodermatitis *f.* sclerodermatitis.
esclerodermatoso, -sa *adj.* sclerodermatous.
esclerodermia *f.* scleroderma.
  esclerodermia circunscrita circumscribed scleroderma.
  esclerodermia difusa diffuse scleroderma.
  esclerodermia generalizada generalized scleroderma.
  esclerodermia lineal linear scleroderma.
  esclerodermia localizada localized scleroderma.
  esclerodermia sistémica systemic scleroderma.
esclerodermitis *f.* sclerodermatitis.
esclerodermoide *adj.* sclerodermoid.
esclerodesmia *f.* sclerodesmia.
escleroesqueleto *m.* scleroskeleton.
escleroestenosis *f.* sclerostenosis.
escleroftalmía *f.* sclerophthalmia.
esclerogénico, -ca *adj.* sclerogenic.
esclerógeno, -na *adj.* sclerogenous.
esclerogomatoso, -sa *adj.* sclerogummatous.
esclerogomoso, -sa *adj.* sclerogummatous.
escleroide *adj.* scleroid.
escleroiritis *f.* scleroiritis.
escleroiritomía *f.* scleriritomy.
escleroma *m.* scleroma.
  escleroma respiratorio respiratory scleroma.
escleromalacia *f.* scleromalacia.
  escleromalacia perforante scleromalacia perforans.

esclerómero *m.* scleromere.
esclerómetro *m.* sclerometer.
escleromixedema *m.* scleromyxedema.
escleroniquia *f.* scleronychia.
escleronixis *f.* scleronyxis.
esclero-ooforitis *f.* sclero-ophoritis.
esclerooftalmía *f.* sclerophthalmia.
esclerootecitis *f.* sclero-oothecitis.
escleropatía *f.* sclerosis.
escleroplastia *f.* scleroplasty.
escleroproteína *f.* scleroprotein.
escleroqueratitis *f.* sclerokeratitis.
escleroqueratoiritis *f.* sclerokeratoiritis.
escleroqueratosis *f.* sclerokeratosis.
esclerosado, -da *adj.* sclerosed.
esclerosante *adj.* sclerosant, sclerosing.
esclerosarcoma *m.* sclerosarcoma.
escleroscopio *m.* scleroscope.
esclerosis *f.* sclerosis.
  esclerosis de Alzheimer Alzheimer's sclerosis.
  esclerosis anterolateral anterolateral sclerosis.
  esclerosis arterial, esclerosis arteriocapilar arterial sclerosis, arteriocapillary sclerosis.
  esclerosis arteriolar arteriolar sclerosis.
  esclerosis de Canavan Canavan's sclerosis.
  esclerosis centrolobulillar familiar familial centrolobar sclerosis.
  esclerosis combinada combined sclerosis.
  esclerosis coriónica sclerosis corii.
  esclerosis coroidal areolar central central areolar choroidal sclerosis.
  esclerosis cortical laminar laminar cortical sclerosis.
  esclerosis cutánea sclerosis cutanea.
  esclerosis dentinal, esclerosis dentinaria dentinal sclerosis.
  esclerosis diafisaria diaphyseal sclerosis.
  esclerosis difusa diffuse sclerosis.
  esclerosis diseminada disseminated sclerosis.
  esclerosis endocárdica endocardial sclerosis.
  esclerosis de Erb Erb's sclerosis.
  esclerosis espinal lateral lateral spinal sclerosis.
  esclerosis espinal posterior posterior spinal sclerosis.
  esclerosis familiar centrolobulillar familial centrolobar sclerosis.
  esclerosis familiar infantil difusa diffuse infantile familial sclerosis.
  esclerosis fisiológica physiologic sclerosis.
  esclerosis focal focal sclerosis.
  esclerosis gástrica gastric sclerosis.
  esclerosis glomerular glomerular sclerosis.
  esclerosis glomerular focal focal glomerular sclerosis.
  esclerosis hipercalcémica idiopática infantil idiopathic hypercalcemic sclerosis of infants.
  esclerosis hiperplásica hyperplastic sclerosis.
  esclerosis hipocámpica hippocampal sclerosis.
  esclerosis insular insular sclerosis.
  esclerosis de la íntima intimal sclerosis.
  esclerosis lateral lateral sclerosis.
  esclerosis lateral amiotrófica (ELA) amyotrophic lateral sclerosis (ALS).
  esclerosis lateral primaria primary lateral sclerosis.
  esclerosis lateral simétrica amyotrophic lateral sclerosis.
  esclerosis lobular lobar sclerosis.
  esclerosis del lóbulo temporal mesial temporal sclerosis.

  esclerosis del manto mantle sclerosis.
  esclerosis de Marie Marie's sclerosis.
  esclerosis menstrual menstrual sclerosis.
  esclerosis miliar miliary sclerosis.
  esclerosis de Mönckeberg Mönckeberg's sclerosis.
  esclerosis múltiple (EM) multiple sclerosis (MS).
  esclerosis nodular nodular sclerosis.
  esclerosis nuclear nuclear sclerosis.
  esclerosis ósea bone sclerosis.
  esclerosis ovulatoria ovulational sclerosis.
  esclerosis de Pelizaeus-Merzbacher Pelizaeus-Merzbacher sclerosis.
  esclerosis en placas sclérose en plaques.
  esclerosis posterior posterior sclerosis.
  esclerosis posterolateral posterolateral sclerosis.
  esclerosis renal renal sclerosis.
  esclerosis sistémica systemic sclerosis.
  esclerosis sistémica progresiva (ESP) progressive systemic sclerosis (PSS).
  esclerosis sistémica difusa diffuse systemic sclerosis.
  esclerosis subendocárdica subendocardial sclerosis.
  esclerosis de la sustancia blanca sclerosis of white matter.
  esclerosis tuberosa tuberous sclerosis.
  esclerosis unicelular unicellular sclerosis.
  esclerosis valvular valvular sclerosis.
  esclerosis vascular vascular sclerosis.
  esclerosis venosa venous sclerosis.
  esclerosis ventrolateral ventrolateral sclerosis.
escleroso, -sa *adj.* sclerosal, sclerous.
esclerostenosis *f.* sclerostenosis.
esclerostomía *f.* sclerostomy.
escleroterapia *f.* sclerotherapy.
esclerótica *f.* sclerotica.
  esclerótica azul blue sclera.
escleroticectomía *f.* scleroticectomy.
esclerótico, -ca *adj.* sclerotic.
escleroticocoroiditis *f.* scleroticochoroiditis.
escleroticonixis *f.* scleroticonyxis.
escleroticopunción *f.* scleroticopuncture.
escleroticotomía *f.* sclerotycotomy.
esclerotilosis *f.* sclerotylosis.
esclerotitis *f.* sclerotitis, scleratitis.
esclerotoma *f.* sclerotome.
esclerotomía *f.* sclerotomy.
  esclerotomía anterior anterior sclerotomy.
  esclerotomía posterior posterior sclerotomy.
esclerótomo *m.* sclerotome.
esclerotonixis *f.* scleronychia.
esclerotriquia *f.* sclerotrichia.
esclerotrix *f.* sclerothrix.
esclerozona *f.* sclerozone.
escoleciasis *f.* scoleciasis.
escoleciforme *adj.* scoleciform.
escolecoide *adj.* scolecoid.
escólex *m.* scolex.
escoliocifosis *f.* scoliokyphosis.
escoliometría *f.* scoliometry.
escoliómetro *m.* scoliometer.
escoliosis *f.* scoliosis.
  escoliosis antálgica, escoliosis antiálgica antalgic scoliosis, pain scoliosis.
  escoliosis de Brissaud Brissaud's scoliosis.
  escoliosis ciática sciatic scoliosis.
  escoliosis cicatricial, escoliosis cicatrizal cicatricial scoliosis.
  escoliosis congénita congenital scoliosis.
  escoliosis coxítica coxitic scoliosis.
  escoliosis empiemática, escoliosis empiémica empyemic scoliosis.

escoliosis esencial essential scoliosis.
escoliosis estática static scoliosis.
escoliosis estructurada structured scoliosis.
escoliosis por hábito, escoliosis habitual habit scoliosis.
escoliosis idiopática idiopathic scoliosis.
escoliosis inflamatoria inflammatory scoliosis.
escoliosis isquiática coxitic scoliosis.
escoliosis miopática myopathic scoliosis.
escoliosis neuropática neuropathic scoliosis.
escoliosis ocular, escoliosis oftálmica ocular scoliosis, ophthalmic scoliosis.
escoliosis osteopática osteopathic scoliosis.
escoliosis paralítica paralytic scoliosis.
escoliosis postural postural scoliosis.
escoliosis raquítica rachitic scoliosis.
escoliosis reumática rheumatic scoliosis.
escoliosis siringomiélica syringomyelic scoliosis.
escoliótico, -ca *adj.* scoliotic.
escoliótono *m.* scoliotone.
escolopsia *f.* scolopsia.
escoplo *m.* chisel.
escoplo blangulado binangle chisel.
escopofilia *f.* scopophilia.
escopofobia *f.* scopophobia, scoptophobia.
escopometría *f.* scopometry.
escopómetro *m.* scopometer.
escoptofilia *f.* scoptophilia, escopophilia.
escoptofobia *f.* scoptophobia.
escoptolagnia *f.* scoptolagnia.
escorbútico, -ca *adj.* scorbutic.
escorbutigénico, -ca *adj.* scorbutigenic.
escorbutígeno, -na *adj.* scorbutigenic.
escorbuto *m.* scurvy.
escorbuto de los Alpes, escorbuto alpino Alpine scurvy.
escorbuto hemorrágico hemorrhagic scurvy.
escorbuto infantil infantile scurvy.
escorbuto marino sea scurvy.
escorbuto marítimo sea scurvy.
escorbuto terrestre land scurvy.
escordinema *f.* scordinema.
escoretemia *f.* scatemia.
escorpionismo *m.* scorpionism.
escotado, -da *adj.* notched.
escotadura *f.* notch.
escotamiento *m.* nicking.
escotobacteria *f.* scotobacterium.
escotocromogenicidad *f.* scotochromogenicity.
escotoma *m.* scotoma.
escotoma absoluto absolute scotoma.
escotoma anular annular scotoma, ring scotoma.
escotoma arqueado arcuate scotoma.
escotoma auditivo, escotoma aural, escotoma auricular aural scotoma, scotoma auris.
escotoma de Bjerrum Bjerrum's scotoma.
escotoma cecocentral cecocentral scotoma.
escotoma centelleante scintillating scotoma.
escotoma central central scotoma.
escotoma centrocecal centrocecal scotoma.
escotoma de color color scotoma.
escotoma cuadrántico quadrantic scotoma.
escotoma eclíptico eclipse scotoma.
escotoma falciforme sickle scotoma.
escotoma fluctuante flittering scotoma.
escotoma glaucomatoso de haces de fibras nerviosas glaucomatous nerve-fiber-bundle scotoma.
escotoma hemianópico hemianopic scotoma.
escotoma insular insular scotoma.
escotoma móvil motile sclerose.

escotoma negativo negative scotoma.
escotoma paracentral paracentral scotoma.
escotoma pericentral pericentral scotoma.
escotoma periférico peripheral scotoma.
escotoma peripapilar peripapillary scotoma.
escotoma positivo positive scotoma.
escotoma relativo relative scotoma.
escotoma de Seidel Seidel's scotoma.
escotoma zonular zonular scotoma.
escotomatógrafo *m.* scotomagraph.
escotomatoso, -sa *adj.* scotomatous.
escotometría *f.* scotometry.
escotómetro *m.* scotometer.
escotomización *f.* scotomization.
escotopía *f.* scotopia.
escotópico, -ca *adj.* scotopic.
escotopsia *f.* scotopia.
escototerapia *f.* scototherapy.
escozor *m.* ardor.
escrobiculado, -da *adj.* scrobiculate.
escrobículo *m.* scrobilulus.
escrofúlide *f.* scrofulide.
escrofulodermia *f.* scrofuloderma.
escrofulodermia gomosa scrofuloderma gummosa.
escrofulodermia papulosa papular scrofuloderma.
escrofulodermia tuberculosa tuberculous scrofuloderma.
escrofulodermia ulcerosa ulcerative scrofuloderma.
escrofulodermia verrugosa verrucous scrofuloderma.
escrofulosis *f.* scrofulosis.
escrofulotuberculosis *f.* scrofulotuberculosis.
escrolalia *f.* eschrolalia.
escrotal *adj.* scrotal.
escrotectomía *f.* scrotectomy.
escrotiforme *adj.* scrotiform.
escrotitis *f.* scrotitis.
escroto *m.* scrotum.
escrotocele *m.* scrotocele.
escrotoplastia *f.* scrotoplasty.
escrupulosidad *f.* scrupulosity.
escudo¹ *m.* scute.
escudo² *m.* shield.
escudo bucal oral shield.
escudo de Büller Buller's shield.
escudo de contacto contact shield.
escudo embrionario embryonic shield.
escudo de estrés stress shielding.
escudo fálico phallic shield.
escudo ocular eye shield.
escudo orale oral shield.
escudo de pezón, escudo para el pezón nipple shield.
escudo de plomo lead shield.
escupidera *f.* spittoon.
escutado, -da *adj.* scutate.
escutiforme *adj.* scutiform.
escútula *f.* scutulum.
escutular *adj.* scutular.
Escherichia Escherichia.
esencia *f.* essence.
esencial *adj.* essential.
eseptado, -da *adj.* eseptate.
esfacelación *f.* sloughing, sphacelation.
esfacelado, -da *adj.* sloughing, sphacelous.
esfacelo *m.* slough, sphacelus.
esfacelodermia *f.* sphaceloderma.
esfagitis *f.* sphagitis.
esfenión *f.* sphenion.
esfenobasilar *adj.* sphenobasilar.
esfenocefalia *adj.* sphenocephaly.
esfenocéfalo *m.* sphenocephalus.

esfenocigomático, -ca *adj.* sphenozygomatic.
esfenoescamoso, -sa *adj.* sphenosquamosal.
esfenoetmoidal *adj.* sphenoethmoid.
esfenoetmoides *adj.* sphenoethmoid, sphenetmoid.
esfenofrontal *adj.* sphenofrontal.
esfenoidal *adj.* sphenoidal.
esfenoideo, -a *adj.* sphenoid.
esfenoiditis *f.* sphenoiditis.
esfenoides *m.* sphenoid.
esfenoiditis *f.* sphenoiditis.
esfenoidostomía *f.* sphenoidostomy.
esfenoidotomía *f.* sphenoidotomy.
esfenomalar *adj.* sphenomalar.
esfenomaxilar *adj.* sphenomaxillary.
esfenómetro *m.* sphenometer.
esfenooccipital *adj.* spheno-occipital.
esfenoorbital *adj.* sphenorbital.
esfenoorbitario, - ria *adj.* sphenorbital.
esfenópago *m.* sphenopagus.
esfenopalatino, -na *adj.* sphenopalatine.
esfenoparietal *adj.* sphenoparietal.
esfenopetroso, -sa *adj.* sphenopetrosal.
esfenoscamoso, -sa *adj.* sphenosquamosal.
esfenotemporal *adj.* sphenotemporal.
esfenótico, -ca *adj.* sphenotic.
esfenotresia *f.* sphenotresia.
esfenotribo *m.* sphenotribe.
esfenotripsia *f.* sphenotripsy.
esfenoturbinal *adj.* sphenoturbinal.
esfenoturbinal *m.* sphenoturbinal ossicle.
esfenovomeriano, -na *adj.* sphenovomerine.
esfenovomerino, -na *adj.* sphenovomerine.
esfera *f.* sphere.
esfera de atracción attraction sphere.
esfera embriótica embryotic sphere.
esfera de Morgagni Morgagni's sphere.
esfera de segmentación segmentation sphere.
esfera vitelina vitelline sphere, yolk sphere.
esférico, -ca *adj.* spherical.
esferocilindro *m.* spherocylinder.
esferocítico, -ca *adj.* spherocytic.
esferocito *m.* spherocyte.
esferocitosis *f.* spherocytosis.
esferocitosis hereditaria hereditary spherocytosis.
esferofaquia *f.* spherophakia.
esferoidal *adj.* spheroidal.
esferoide *adj.* spheroid.
esferolito *m.* spherolith.
esferómetro *m.* spherometer.
esferoplasto *m.* spheroplast.
esferoprisma *m.* spheroprism.
esferospermia *f.* spherospermia.
esférula *f.* spherule.
esférula de Fulci spherule of Fulci.
esferulina *f.* spherulin.
esfígmico, -ca *adj.* sphygmic.
esfigmobolograma *m.* sphigmobologram.
esfigmobolometría *f.* sphygmobolometry.
esfigmobolómetro *m.* sphygmobolometer.
esfigmocardiógrafo *m.* sphygmocardiograph.
esfigmocardiograma *m.* sphygmocardiogram.
esfigmocardioscopio *m.* sphygmocardioscope.
esfigmocronógrafo *m.* sphygmochronograph.
esfigmodinamómetro *m.* sphygmodynamometer.
esfigmófono *m.* sphygmophone.
esfigmogenina *f.* sphygmogenin.
esfigmografía *f.* sphygmography.
esfigmográfico, -ca *adj.* sphygmographic.
esfigmógrafo *f.* sphygmograph.
esfigmograma *m.* sphygmogram.
esfigmoide *adj.* sphygmoid.
esfigmoideo, -a *adj.* sphygmoid.

esfigmología *f.* sphygmology.
esfigmomanometría *f.* sphygmomanometry.
esfigmomanómetro *m.* sphygmomanometer.
  esfigmomanómetro de Mosso Mosso's sphygmomanometer.
  esfigmomanómetro de Rogers Rogers' sphygmomanometer.
esfigmometroscopio *m.* sphygmometroscope.
esfigmometría *f.* sphygmometry.
esfigmómetro *m.* sphygmometer.
esfigmometrógrafo *m.* sphygmometrograph.
esfigmometroscopio *m.* sphygmometroscope.
esfigmooscilómetro *m.* sphygmo-oscillometer.
esfigmopalpación *f.* sphygmopalpation.
esfigmopletismógrafo *m.* sphygmoplethysmograph.
esfigmoscopia *f.* sphygmoscopy.
esfigmoscopio *m.* sphygmoscope.
  esfigmoscopio de Bishop Bishop's sphygmoscope.
esfigmosístole *f.* sphygmosystole.
esfigmotonógrafo *m.* sphygmotonograph.
esfigmotonómetro *m.* sphygmotonometer.
esfigmoviscosimetría *f.* sphygmoviscosimetry.
esfingogalactósido *m.* sphingogalactoside.
esfingolípido *m.* sphingolipid.
esfingolipidosis *f.* sphingolipidosis.
  esfingolipidosis cerebral cerebral sphingolipidosis.
  esfingolipidosis cerebral infantil infantile cerebral sphingolipidosis.
esfingolipodistrofia *f.* sphingolipodystrophy.
esfingomielina *f.* sphingomyelin.
esfingomielinosis *f.* sphingomyelinosis.
esfínter *m.* sphincter.
  esfínter artificial artificial sphincter.
  esfínter artificial AMS-800 AMS-800 artificial sphincter.
  esfínter extrínseco extrinsic sphincter.
  esfínter microscópico microscopic sphincter.
  esfínter de Nélaton Nélaton's sphincter.
  esfínter de Oddi Oddi's sphincter.
  esfínter ostial ostial sphincter.
  esfínter patológico pathologic sphincter.
esfinteralgia *f.* sphincteralgia.
esfinteriano, -na *adj.* sphincterial.
esfinterismo *m.* sphincterismus.
esfinteritis *f.* sphincteritis.
esfinteroide *adj.* sphincteroid.
esfinterólisis *f.* sphincterolysis.
esfinteroplastia *f.* sphincteroplasty.
esfinteroscopia *f.* sphincteroscopy.
esfinteroscopio *m.* sphincteroscope.
esfinterotomía *f.* sphincterotomy.
  esfinterotomía endoscópica endoscopic sphincterotomy.
  esfinterotomía lateral interna lateral sphincterotomy.
  esfinterotomía transduodenal transduodenal sphincterotomy.
  esfinterotomía uretral urethral sphincterotomy.
esfinterectomía *f.* sphincterectomy.
esfinterótomo *m.* sphincterotome.
esfuerzo¹ *m.* strain.
  esfuerzo expulsivo bearing down.
esfuerzo² *m.* effort.
  esfuerzo distribuido distributed effort.
esguince *m.* sprain.
  esguince cervical cervical sprain.
  esguince de espalda sprain of the back.
  esguince del jinete, esguince de los jinetes rider's sprain.

esguince lumbar lumbar sprain.
esguince de tobillo o de pie sprain of the ankle or foot.
esmalte *m.* enamel.
  esmalte enano, esmalte enanoide dwarfed enamel, nanoid enamel.
  esmalte dental dental enamel.
  esmalte hipoplásico hypoplastic enamel.
  esmalte marrón hereditario hereditary brown enamel.
  esmalte moteado mottled enamel.
  esmalte nanoide nanoid enamel.
  esmalte nudoso gnarled enamel.
  esmalte pardo hereditario hereditary brown enamel.
  esmalte recto straight enamel.
  esmalte con remolinos whorled enamel.
  esmalte rizado curled enamel.
esmaltoblasto *m.* enameloblast.
esmaltoblastoma *m.* enameloblastoma.
esmaltoma *m.* enameloma.
esmegma *m.* smegma.
  esmegma del clítoris smegma clitoridis.
  esmegma del prepucio smegma preputii.
esmegmalito *m.* smegmalith, smegmolith.
esmegmático, -ca *adj.* smegmatic.
esmegmolito *m.* smegmalith, smegmolith.
esocataforia *f.* esocataphoria.
esodesviación *f.* esodeviaton.
esódico, -ca *adj.* esodic.
esoetmoiditis *f.* esoethmoiditis.
esofagalgia *f.* esophagalgia.
esofagectasia *f.* esophagectasia, esophagectasis.
esofagectasis *f.* esophagectasia, esophagectasis.
esofagectomía *f.* esophagectomy.
esofágico, -ca *adj.* esophageal.
esofagismo *m.* esophagism.
  esofagismo hiatal cardiospasm.
esofagitis *f.* esophagitis.
  esofagitis cáustica caustic esophagitis.
  esofagitis disecante superficial esophagitis dissecans superficialis.
  esofagitis péptica crónica chronic peptic esophagitis.
  esofagitis de reflujo, esofagitis por reflujo reflux esophagitis.
esófago *m.* esophagus.
  esófago cascanueces, esófago en cascanueces nutcracker esophagus.
  esófago en sacacorchos corkscrew esophagus.
esofagocardioplastia *f.* esophagocardioplasty.
esofagocele *m.* esophagocele.
esofagectomía *f.* esophagectomy.
  esofagectomía subtotal subtotal esophagectomy.
  esofagectomía total total esophagectomy.
esofagocologastrostomía *f.* esophagocologastrostomy.
esofagocoloplastia *f.* esophagocoloplasty.
esofagodinia *f.* esophagodynia.
esofagoduodenostomía *f.* esophagoduodenostomy.
esofagoectasia *f.* esophagectasia, esophagectasis.
esofagoectomía *f.* esophagectomy.
esofagoenterostomía *f.* esophagoenterostomy.
esofagoespasmo *m.* esophagospasm.
esofagoestenosis *f.* esophagostenosis.
esofagofaringe *f.* esophagopharynx.
esofagofibroscopio *m.* esophagofiberscope.
esofagogastrectomía *f.* esophagogastrectomy.

esofagogástrico, -ca *adj.* esophagogastric.
esofagogastroanastomosis *f.* esophagogastroanastomosis.
esofagogastromiotomía *f.* esophagogastromyotomy.
esofagogastroplastia *f.* esophagogastroplasty.
esofagogastroscopia *f.* esophagogastroscopy.
esofagogastrostomía *f.* esophagogastrostomy.
esofagogastroyeyunostomía *f.* esophagogastrojejunostomy.
esofagografía *f.* esophagography.
esofagograma *m.* esophagogram, esophagram.
esofagolaringectomía *f.* esophagolaryngectomy.
esofagología *f.* esophagology.
esofagomalacia *f.* esophagomalacia.
esofagomicosis *f.* esophagomycosis.
esofagomiotomía *f.* esophagomyotomy.
esofagoplastia *f.* esophagoplasty.
esofagoplicación *f.* esophagoplication.
esofagoplicatura *f.* esophagoplication.
esofagoptosis *f.* esophagoptosis.
esofagoscopia *f.* esophagoscopy.
esofagoscopio *m.* esophagoscope.
esofagospasmo *m.* esophagospasm.
esofagostenosis *f.* esophagostenosis.
esofagostoma *m.* esophagostoma.
esofagostomía *f.* esophagostomy.
esofagostomiasis *f.* esophagostomiasis, oesophagostomiasis.
esofagotomía *f.* esophagotomy.
esofagótomo *m.* esophagotome.
esofagotraqueal *adj.* esophagotracheal.
esofagoyeyunogastrostomía *f.* esophagojejunogastrostomy.
esofagoyeyunogastrostomosis *f.* esophagojejunogastrostomosis.
esofagoyeyunoplastia *f.* esophagojejunoplasty.
esofagoyeyunostomía *f.* esophagojejunostomy.
esoforia *f.* esophoria.
  esoforia no acomodativa non-accommodative esophoria.
  esoforia acomodativa no refractiva non-refractive accommodative esophoria.
  esoforia acomodativa refractiva refractive accommodative esophoria.
  esoforia básica basic esophoria.
  esoforia consecutiva consecutive esophoria.
  esoforia mixta mixed esophoria.
esofórico, -ca *adj.* esophoric.
esotropía *f.* esotropia.
esotrópico, -ca *adj.* esotropic.
espaciador *m.* spreader.
  espaciador del empaste del conducto radicular root canal filling spreader.
espacial *adj.* spatial.
espacio *m.* space, spatium.
  espacio aéreo mecánico muerto mechanical dead air space.
  espacio de Blessig Blessig's space.
  espacio celulares cell spaces.
  espacio de Crookes Crookes' space.
  espacio de Czermak Czermak's space.
  espacio de escape escapement spaces.
  espacio extracelular extracellular compartment.
  espacio de Havers Haversian space.
  espacio intercrestal intercristal space.
  espacio interglobulares spatia interglobularia.
  espacio interoclusal de reposo, espacio interoclusal en reposo interocclusal rest space.
  espacio interóseo interosseous space.
  espacio intracelular intracellular compartment.

espacio K K space.
espacio de la membrana mitocondrial mitochondrial membrane space.
espacio muerto anatómico anatomical dead space.
espacio muerto fisiológico physiologic dead space.
espacio perineural perineuronal space.
espacio perinuclear perinuclear space.
espacio perivascular perivascular space.
espacio de Poiseuille Poiseuille's space.
espacio presacro presacral space.
espacio del quilo chyle space.
espacio de tiocianato thiocyanate space.
espacio de vía libre freeway space.
espalda *f.* back.
espalda curvada juvenil adolescent round back.
espalda funcional functional back.
espalda hueca hollow back.
espalda jorobada hump back, hunch back.
espalda de jugador de póquer poker back.
espalda plana flat back.
espalda en silla de montar saddle back.
espanomenorrea *f.* spaniomenorrhea.
espanopnea *f.* spanopnea.
esparadrapo *m.* adhesive tape, strap.
esparcido, -da *adj.* effuse.
esparganosis *f.* sparganosis.
esparganosis ocular ocular sparganosis.
espasmo *m.* spasm, spasmus.
espasmo de acomodación spasm of accommodation.
espasmo afectivos affect spasm.
espasmo anorrectal anorectal spasm.
espasmo arterial coronario coronary artery spasm.
espasmo atetoide athetoid spasm.
espasmo de Bell Bell's spasm.
espasmo bronquial bronchial spasm.
espasmo cadavérico cadaveric spasm.
espasmo canino canine spasm.
espasmo carpopedal, espasmo carpopédico carpopedal spasm.
espasmo cerebral cerebral spasm.
espasmo cervical cervical spasm.
espasmo cínico cynic spasm.
espasmo clónico clonic spasm.
espasmo coordinado spasmus coordinatus.
espasmo coreiforme choreiform spasm.
espasmo de las costureras sewing spasm.
espasmo de danza, espasmo danzante dancing spasm.
espasmo dentario tooth spasm.
espasmo diafragmático transitorio epidémico epidemic transient diaphragmatic spasm.
espasmo de los escritores writer's spasm.
espasmo esofágico, espasmo esofágico difuso esophageal spasm, diffuse esophageal spasm.
espasmo facial facial spasm.
espasmo de fatiga functional spasm.
espasmo fijo fixed spasm.
espasmo fonatorio phonatory spasm, phonic spasm.
espasmo funcional functional spasm.
espasmo glótico glottic spasm.
espasmo de la glotis spasmus glottidis.
espasmo de guiños winking spasm.
espasmo por hábito, espasmo habitual habit spasm.
espasmo hemifacial hemifacial spasm.
espasmo infantil, espasmo infantil masivo infantile spasm, infantile massive spasm.
espasmo intencional intention spasm.

espasmo maleatorio malleatory spasm.
espasmo masticatorio masticatory spasm.
espasmo mímico mimic spasm.
espasmo miopático myopathic spasm.
espasmo mixto mixed spasm.
espasmo móvil mobile spasm.
espasmo muscular twitch spasm.
espasmo del músculo ciliar ciliary muscle spasm.
espasmo nictitante nictitating spasm.
espasmo nutans spasmus nutans.
espasmo ocupacional occupation spasm, occupational spasm.
espasmo de parpadeo winking spasm.
espasmo perineal perineal spasm.
espasmo pilórico pyloric spasm.
espasmo profesional professional spasm.
espasmo progresivo de torsión progressive torsion spasm.
espasmo respiratorio respiratory spasm.
espasmo retrocervical retrocollic spasm.
espasmo retrocólico retrocollic spasm.
espasmo de Romberg Romberg's spasm.
espasmo rotatorio rotatory spasm.
espasmo salaam salaam spasm.
espasmo saltatorio saltatory spasm.
espasmo salutatorio salaam spasm.
espasmo de los sastres tailors' spasm.
espasmo sinclónico synclonic spasm.
espasmo tetánico tetanic spasm.
espasmo tónico tonic spasm.
espasmo tonicoclónico tonoclonic spasm.
espasmo de torsión torsion spasm.
espasmo de torsión progresiva progressive torsion spasm.
espasmo tóxico toxic spasm.
espasmo de trabamiento lock spasm.
espasmo vaginal vaginal spasm.
espasmo vasomotor vasomotor spasm.
espasmódico, -ca *adj.* spasmodic.
espasmofilia *f.* spasmophilia.
espasmofílico, -ca *adj.* spasmophilic.
espasmófilo, -a *adj.* spasmophile.
espasmogénico, -ca *adj.* spasmogenic.
espasmógeno *m.* spasmogen.
espasmoligmo *m.* spasmolygmus.
espasmolisante *adj.* spasmolysant.
espasmólisis *f.* spasmolysis.
espasmolítico, -ca *adj.* spasmolytic.
espasmología *f.* spasmology.
espasticidad *f.* spasticity.
espástico, -ca *adj.* spastic.
espátula *f.* spatula.
especialista *m., f.* specialist.
especie *f.* species.
especie tipo type species.
especificidad *f.* specificity.
especificidad de asociación specificity of association.
especificidad diagnóstica diagnostic specificity.
especificidad enzimática enzymatic specificity.
especificidad de estereoisomérica stereoisomer specificity.
especificidad de órgano organ specificity.
especificidad relativa relative specificity.
especificidad de unión bond specificity.
específico, -ca *m. y adj.* specific.
especilo *m.* specillum.
espécimen *m.* specimen.
espectral *adj.* spectral.
espectro *m.* spectrum.
espectro de absorción absorption spectrum.
espectro de acción action spectrum.

espectro amplio broad spectrum, wide spectrum.
espectro antimicrobiano antimicrobial spectrum.
espectro calorífico thermal spectrum.
espectro de color color spectrum.
espectro continuo continuous spectrum.
espectro cromático chromatic spectrum.
espectro de difracción diffraction spectrum.
espectro electromagnético electromagnetic spectrum.
espectro de fortificación fortification spectrum.
espectro gaseoso gaseous spectrum.
espectro infrarrojo infrared spectrum.
espectro invisible invisible spectrum.
espectro ocular ocular spectrum.
espectro prismático prismatic spectrum.
espectro químico chemical spectrum.
espectro de rayos X X-ray spectrum.
espectro de rayos X continuo continuous X-ray spectrum.
espectro solar solar spectrum.
espectro térmico thermal spectrum.
espectro de toxinas toxin spectrum.
espectro visible visible spectrum.
espectrocolorímetro *f.* spectrocolorimeter.
espectrofluorómetro *m.* spectrofluorometer.
espectrofobia *f.* spectrophobia.
espectrofotofluorimetría *f.* spectrophotofluorimetry.
espectrofotofluorómetro *m.* spectrophotofluorometer.
espectrofotometría *f.* spectrophotometry.
espectrofotometría por absorción atómica atomic absorption spectrophotometry.
espectrofotometría por emisión de llama flame emission spectrophotometry.
espectrofotómetro *m.* spectrophotometer.
espectrografía *f.* spectrography.
espectrógrafo *m.* spectrograph.
espectrógrafo de masa mass spectrograph.
espectrograma *m.* spectrogram.
espectrometría *f.* spectrometry.
espectrómetro *m.* spectrometer.
espectrómetro de masa mass spectrometer.
espectrómetro de Mössbauer Mössbauer spectrometer.
espectropireliómetro *m.* spectropyrheliometer.
espectropolarímetro *m.* spectropolarimeter.
espectroquímica *f.* spectrochemistry.
espectroscopia *f.* spectroscopy.
espectroscopia infrarroja infrared spectroscopy.
espectroscopia por resonancia magnética magnetic resonance spectroscopy.
espectroscópico, -ca *adj.* spectroscopic.
espectroscopio *m.* spectroscope.
espectroscopio de visión directa direct vision spectroscope.
espéculo *m.* speculum.
espéculo bivalvo bivalve speculum.
espéculo de Bozeman Bozeman's speculum.
espéculo de Brinkerhoff Brinkerhoff's speculum.
espéculo de Cook, espéculo Cooke Cook's speculum, Cooke's speculum.
espéculo de detención stop speculum.
espéculo de Fergusson Fergusson's speculum.
espéculo de Fränkel Fränkel speculum.
espéculo graduado stop speculum.
espéculo de Gruber Gruber's speculum.
espéculo de Hartmann Hartmann's speculum.

espéculo de Kelly Kelly's speculum.
espéculo de Martin, espéculo de Martin y Davy Martin's speculum, Martin and Davy speculum.
espéculo de Mathews Mathews speculum.
espéculo metálico bivalvo wire bivalve speculum.
espéculo nasal nasal speculum.
espéculo ocular eye speculum.
espéculo de oído ear speculum.
espéculo de Pedersen Pedersen's speculum.
espéculo de pico de pato, espéculo en pico de pato duckbill speculum, duck-billed speculum.
espéculo de Politzer Politzer's speculum.
espéculo rectal de Kelly Kelly's rectal speculum.
espéculo de Sims Sims' speculum.
espéculo con tope stop speculum.
espejismo *m.* mirage.
espejo *m.* mirror.
espejo bucal mouth mirror.
espejo cóncavo concave mirror.
espejo convexo convex mirror.
espejo dental dental mirror.
espejo de frente, espejo frontal frontal mirror, head mirror.
espejo de Glatzel Glatzel's mirror.
espejo laríngeo laryngeal mirror.
espejo nasográfico nasographic mirror.
espejo plano plane mirror.
espelencefalia *f.* spelencephaly.
espeleostomía *f.* speleostomy.
esperma *m.* sperm.
espermacrasia *f.* spermacrasia.
espermaglutinación *f.* spermagglutination.
espermalista *m.* spermalist.
espermatenfraxis *f.* spermatemphraxis.
espermaticida¹ *m.* spermaticide, spermatocide.
espermaticida² *adj.* spermaticidal, spermatocidal.
espermático, -ca *adj.* spermatic.
espermátide *f.* spermatid.
espermatitis *f.* spermatitis.
espermatocele *m.* spermatocele, spermatocyst.
espermatocelectomía *f.* spermatocelectomy.
espermatocida¹ *m.* spermaticide, spermatocide.
espermatocida² *adj.* spermaticidal, spermatocidal.
espermatocistectomía *f.* spermatocystectomy.
espermatocistitis *f.* spermatocystitis.
espermatocisto *m.* spermatocyst.
espermatocistotomía *f.* spermatocystotomy.
espermatocítico, -ca *adj.* spermatocytal.
espermatocito *m.* spermatocyte.
espermatocito primario primary spermatocyte.
espermatocito secundario secondary spermatocyte.
espermatocitogénesis *f.* spermatocytogenesis.
espermatocitoma *m.* spermatocytoma.
espermatofobia *f.* spermatophobia.
espermatogénesis *f.* spermatogenesis.
espermatogenético, -ca *adj.* spermatogenetic.
espermatogenia *f.* spermatogeny.
espermatogénico, -ca *adj.* spermatogenic.
espermatógeno, -na *adj.* spermatogenous.
espermatogonia *m.* spermatogonium.
espermatogonio *m.* spermatogonium.

espermatoide *adj.* spermatoid.
espermatólisis *f.* spermatolysis.
espermatolítico, -ca *adj.* spermatolytic.
espermatopatía *f.* spermatopathia, spermatopathy.
espermatopoyético, -ca *adj.* spermatopoietic.
espermatorrea *f.* spermatorrhea.
espermatosquesis *f.* spermatoschesis.
espermatotoxina *f.* spermatotoxin.
espermatozoico, -ca *adj.* spermatozoal.
espermatozoide *m.* spermatozoid.
espermatozoo *m.* spermatozoon.
espermaturia *f.* spermaturia.
espermectomía *f.* spermectomy.
espermiación *f.* spermiation.
espermicida¹ *m.* spermicide.
espermicida² *adj.* spermicidal.
espermiducto *m.* spermiduct.
espermio *m.* spermium.
espermiocito *m.* spermiocyte.
espermiogénesis *f.* spermiogenesis.
espermiograma *f.* spermiogram.
espermoblasto *m.* spermoblast.
espermocitoma *m.* spermocytoma.
espermoespora *f.* spermospore.
espermoflebectasia *f.* spermophleboectasia.
espermogonio *m.* spermogonium.
espermólisis *f.* spermolysis.
espermolítico, -ca *adj.* spermolytic.
espermolito *m.* spermolith.
espermoloropexia *f.* spermoloropexy.
espermoloropexis *f.* spermoloropexis.
espermoneuralgia *f.* spermoneuralgia.
espermospora *f.* spermospore.
espermoteliosis *f.* spermioteleosis.
espermoteliótico, -ca *adj.* spermioteleotic.
espermotóxico, -ca *adj.* spermotoxic.
espermotoxina *f.* spermotoxin.
espesado, -da *adj.* inspissated, spissated.
espesador *m.* inspissator.
espícula *f.* spicule, spiculum.
espicular *adj.* spicular.
espilo *m.* spilus.
espiloma *m.* spiloma.
espiloplaxia *f.* spiloplaxia.
espina *f.* spine, spina.
espina de bambú bamboo spine.
espina bífida bifid spine, spina bifida.
espina bífida abierta spina bifida aperta.
espina bífida anterior spina bifida anterior.
espina bífida manifiesta spina bifida manifesta.
espina bífida oculta spina bifida occulta.
espina bífida posterior spina bifida posterior.
espina bífida quística spina bifida cystica.
espina de Civinni Civinni's spine.
espina dendrítica dendritic spine.
espina dividida cleft spine.
espina dorsal dorsal spine.
espina dorsal rígida poker spine.
espina de ferrocarril railway spine.
espina hendida cleft spine.
espina ventosa spina ventosa.
espinado, -da *adj.* spinate.
espinal *adj.* spinal.
espinalgia *f.* spinalgia.
espinazo *m.* backbone.
espinífugo, -ga *adj.* spinifugal.
espinilla *f.* shin.
espinilla en pepino cucumber shin.
espinilla en férula shin splints.
espinilla en sable saber shin.
espinilla tostada toasted shin.
espinípeto, -ta *adj.* spinipetal, spinopetal.

espinobulbar *adj.* spinobulbar.
espinocelular *adj.* spinocellular.
espinocerebeloso, -sa *adj.* spinocerebellar.
espinocolicular *adj.* spinocollicular.
espinocortical *adj.* spinocortical.
espinocostal *m.* spinocostalis.
espinogalvanización *f.* spinogalvanization.
espinoglenoideo, -a *adj.* spinoglenoid.
espinomuscular *adj.* spinomuscular.
espinoneural *adj.* spinoneural.
espinoolivar *adj.* spino-olivar.
espinópeto, -ta *adj.* spinipetal, spinopetal.
espinorreticular *adj.* spinoreticular.
espinotalámico, -ca *adj.* spinothalamic.
espinotectal *adj.* spinotectal.
espintaricón *m.* spintharicon.
espintariscopio *m.* spinthariscope.
espinterismo *f.* spintherism.
espinterómetro *m.* spintherometer.
espinteropía *f.* spintherism.
espinteropsia *f.* spintherism.
espinteroscopio *m.* spinthariscope.
espira *f.* whorl.
espiración *f.* expiration.
espiración activa active expiration.
espiración pasiva passive expiration.
espiradenitis *f.* spiradenitis.
espiradenoma *m.* spiradenoma.
espiradenoma cilindromatoso cylindromatous spiradenoma.
espiradenoma ecrino eccrine spiradenoma.
espirador, -ra *adj.* coil.
espiral *f. y adj.* spiral.
espiral de Curschmann Curschmann's spiral.
espiral de Tillaux spiral of Tillaux.
espiralado, -da *adj.* whorled.
espiratorio, -ria *adj.* expiratory.
espirilar *adj.* spirillar.
espirilemia *f.* spirillemia.
espirilicida *adj.* spirillicidal.
espirilicidina *f.* spirillicidin.
espirilo *m.* spirillum.
espirilosis *f.* spirillosis.
espirilotrópico, -ca *adj.* spirilotropic.
espiróforo *m.* spirophore.
espirografía *f.* spirography.
espirógrafo *m.* spirograph.
espirograma *m.* spirogram.
espiroidal *adj.* spiroid.
espiroideo *m.* spiroid.
espiro-índice *m.* spiro-index.
espiroma *m.* spiroma.
espirometría *f.* spirometry.
espirometría broncoscópica bronchoscopic spirometry.
espirometría incentivada incentive spirometry.
espirométrico, -ca *adj.* spirometric.
espirómetro *m.* spirometer.
espirómetro compensado por una cadena chain-compensated spirometer.
espirómetro en cuña wedge spirometer.
espirómetro de Krogh Krogh spirometer.
espirómetro de Tissot Tissot's spirometer.
espiroqueta *f.* spirochaeta, spirochete.
espiroquetal *adj.* spirochetal.
espiroquetemia *f.* spirochetemia.
espiroqueticida *adj.* spirocheticidal.
espiroquetógeno, -na *adj.* spirochetogenous.
espiroquetolisina *f.* spirochetolysin.
espiroquetólisis *f.* spirochetolysis.
espiroquetósico, -ca *adj.* spirochetotic.
espiroquetosis *f.* spirochetosis.
espiroquetosis artrítica spirochetosis arthritica.

espiroquetosis broncopulmonar broncho-pulmonary spirochetosis.
espiroqueturia *f.* spirocheturia.
espiroscopia *f.* spiroscopy.
espiroscopio *m.* spiroscope.
espirosoma *m.* spirochete.
esplacnapofisario, -ria *adj.* splanchnapophyseal, splanchnapophysial.
esplacnapófisis *f.* splachnapophysis.
esplacnectopia *f.* splanchnectopia.
esplacnenfraxis *f.* splanchnemphraxis.
esplacnestesia *f.* splanchnesthesia.
esplacnestésico, -ca *adj.* splanchnesthetic.
esplacnicectomía *f.* splanchnicectomy.
esplácnico, -ca *adj.* splanchnic.
esplacnicotomía *f.* splanchnicotomy.
esplacnoapofisario, -ria *adj.* splanchnapophyseal, splanchnapophysial.
esplacnoapófisis *f.* splanchnapophysis.
esplacnoblasto *m.* splanchnoblast.
esplacnocele *m.* splanchnocele.
esplacnocráneo *m.* splanchnocranium.
esplacnodermo *m.* splanchnoderm.
esplacnodiastasis *f.* splanchnodiastasis.
esplacnoesclerosis *f.* splanchnosclerosis.
esplacnoesquelético, -ca *adj.* splanchnoskelctal.
esplacnoesqueleto *m.* splanchnoskeleton.
esplacnografía *f.* splanchnography.
esplacnolito *m.* splanchnolith.
esplacnología *f.* splanchnology.
esplacnomegalia *f.* splanchnomegalia, splanchnomegaly.
esplacnomicria *f.* splanchnomicria.
esplacnopatía *f.* splanchnopathy.
esplacnopleura *f.* splanchnopleura, splanchnopleure.
esplacnopleural *adj.* splanchnopleural.
esplacnopléurico, -ca *adj.* splanchnopleuric.
esplacnoptosis *f.* splanchnoptosia, splanchnoptosis.
esplacnosclerosis *f.* splanchnosclerosis.
esplacnoscopia *f.* splanchnoscopy.
esplacnosomático, -ca *adj.* splanchnosomatic.
esplacnosqueleto *m.* splanchnoskeleton.
esplacnotomía *f.* splanchnotomy.
esplacnotopia *f.* splanchnectopia.
esplacnotribo *m.* splanchnotribe.
esplenadenoma *m.* splenadenoma.
esplenalgia *f.* splenalgia.
esplenatrofia *f.* splenatrophy.
esplenauxa *f.* splenauxe.
esplénculo *m.* splenculus.
esplenectasia *f.* splenectasis.
esplenectomia *f.* splenectomy.
 esplenectomía parcial partial splenectomy.
esplenectopia *f.* splenectopia, splenectopy.
esplenelcosis *f.* splenelcosis.
esplenemia *f.* splenemia.
esplenenfraxis *f.* splenemphraxis.
esplenéolo *m.* spleneolus.
esplenético, -ca *adj.* splenetic.
esplenial *adj.* splenial.
esplénico, -ca *adj.* splenic.
esplenicterus *m.* splenicterus.
espleniculo *m.* spleniculus, splenunculus.
esplenificación *f.* splenification.
espleniforme *adj.* spleniform.
esplenio *m.* splenium.
espleniserrato, -ta *adj.* spleniserrate.
esplenitis *f.* splenitis.
 esplenitis espodógena spodogenous splenitis.
esplenización *f.* splenization.
 esplenización hipostática hypostatic splenization.

esplenoadenoma *f.* splenadenoma.
esplenoblasto *m.* splenoblast.
esplenocele *m.* splenocele.
esplenoceratosis *f.* splenceratosis, splenoceratosis.
esplenocito *m.* splenocyte.
esplenocitoma *m.* splenoma.
esplenocleisis *f.* splenocleisis.
esplenocólico, -ca *adj.* splenocolic.
esplenodinia *f.* splenodynia.
esplenoectasia *f.* splenectasis.
esplenofrénico, -ca *adj.* splenophrenic.
esplenógeno, -na *adj.* splenogenous.
esplenografía *f.* splenography.
esplenograma *m.* splenogram.
esplenohemia *f.* splenemia.
esplenohepatomegalia *f.* splenohepatomegalia, splenohepatomegaly.
esplenoide *adj.* splenoid.
esplenoideo, -a *adj.* splenoid.
esplenolaparotomía *f.* splenolaparotomy.
esplenolinfático, -ca *adj.* splenolymphatic.
esplenólisis *f.* splenolysis.
esplenología *f.* splenology.
esplenoma *m.* splenoma.
esplenomalacia *f.* splenomalacia.
esplenomedular *adj.* splenomedullary.
esplenomegalia *f.* splenomegaly.
 esplenomegalia congestiva congestive splenomegaly.
 esplenomegalia egipcia Egyptian splenomegaly.
 esplenomegalia de Gaucher Gaucher splenomegaly.
 esplenomegalia hemolítica hemolytic splenomegaly.
 esplenomegalia infecciosa infectious splenomegaly, infective splenomegaly.
 esplenomegalia mielotísica myelopthisic splenomegaly.
 esplenomegalia de Niemann Niemann splenomegaly.
 esplenomegalia palúdica hiperreactiva hyperreactive malarious splenomegaly.
 esplenomegalia siderótica siderotic splenomegaly.
 esplenomegalia tromboflebítica thrombophlebitic splenomegaly.
 esplenomegalia tropical, esplenomegalia tropical febril tropical splenomegaly, febrile tropical splenomegaly.
esplenomielógeno, -na *adj.* splenomyelogenous.
esplenomielomalacia *f.* splenomyelomalacia.
esplenonco *m.* splenoncus.
esplenonéfrico, -ca *adj.* splenonephric.
esplenonefroptosis *f.* splenonephroptosis.
esplenoneumonia *f.* splenopneumonia.
esplenometría *f.* splenometry.
esplenopancreático, -ca *adj.* splenopancreatic.
esplenoparectasia *f.* splenoparectasis.
esplenopatía *f.* splenopathy.
esplenopexia *f.* splenopexia, splenopexis, splenoplexy.
esplenoportografía *f.* splenoportography.
 esplenoportografía directa direct splenoportography.
 esplenoportografía indirecta indirect splenoportography.
esplenoportograma *m.* splenoportogram.
esplenoptosia *f.* splenoptosis, splenoptosia.
esplenoptosis *f.* splenoptosis, splenoptosia.
esplenopulmonitis *f.* splenopneumonia.
esplenoqueratosis *f.* splenokeratosis.

esplenorrafia *f.* splenorrhaphy.
esplenorragia *f.* splenorrhagia.
esplenorrenal *adj.* splenorenal.
esplenorrenopexia *f.* splenorenopexia.
esplenosis *f.* splenosis.
 esplenosis pericárdica pericardial splenosis.
esplenotomía *f.* splenotomy.
esplenotoxina *f.* splenotoxin.
esplénulo *m.* splenule, splenulus.
esplenúnculo *m.* spleniculus, splenunculus.
espliceosoma *f.* spliceosome.
espodóforo, -ra *adj.* spodophorous.
espodógeno, -na *adj.* spodogenous.
espondilalgia *f.* spondylalgia.
espondilartritis *f.* spondylarthritis.
 espondilartritis anquilopoyética spondylarthritis ankylopoietica.
espondilartrosis *f.* spondylarthrosis.
espondíleo, -a *adj.* spodylous.
espondilicema *f.* spondylizema, spondylozema.
espondilítico, -ca *adj.* spondyliric.
espondilitis *f.* spondylitis.
 espondilitis anquilopoyética spondylitis ankylopoietica.
 espondilitis anquilosante ankylosing spondylitis, spondylitis ankylosans.
 espondilitis de Bechterew Bechterew's spondylitis.
 espondilitis brucelósica spondylitis brucella.
 espondilitis deformante spondylitis deformans.
 espondilitis hipertrófica hypertrofic spondylitis.
 espondilitis infecciosa spondylitis infectiosa.
 espondilitis de Kümmell Kümmell's spondylitis.
 espondilitis de Marie-Strümpell Marie-Strümpell spondylitis.
 espondilitis muscular muscular spondylitis.
 espondilitis postraumática postraumatic spondylitis.
 espondilitis reumatoide, espondilitis reumatoidea rheumatoid spondylitis.
 espondilitis rizomélica rhizomelic spondylitis, spondylitis rhizomelica.
 espondilitis tífica, espondilitis tifosa spondylitis typhosa.
 espondilitis traumática traumatic spondylitis.
 espondilitis tuberculosa tuberculous spondylitis, spondylitis tuberculosa.
 espondilitis vertebral vertebral spondylitis.
espondiloartritis *f.* spondylarthritis.
espondiloartrografía *f.* spondyloarthrography.
espondiloartropatía *m.* spondyloarthropathy.
espondilocace *m.* spondylocace.
espondilocema *f.* spondylizema, spondylozema.
espondiloclisis *f.* spondyloclisis.
espondilodidimia *f.* spondylodidymia.
espondilodinia *f.* spondylodynia.
espondilólisis *f.* spondylolysis.
espondilolistésico, -ca *adj.* spondylolisthetic.
espondilolistesis *f.* spondylolisthesis.
 espondilolistesis congénita congenital spondylolisthesis.
 espondilolistesis degenerativa degenerative spondylolisthesis.
 espondilolistesis displásica dysplasic spondylolisthesis.
 espondilolistesis ístmica isthmic spondylolisthesis.

espondilomalacia *f.* spondylomalacia.
  espondilomalacia traumática spondylomalacia traumatica.
espondilomielitis *f.* spondylomyelitis.
espondilopatía *f.* spondylopathy.
  espondilopatía traumática traumatic spondylopathy.
espondilopiosis *f.* spondylopyosis.
espondiloptosis *f.* spondyloptosis.
espondilosindesis *f.* spondylosyndesis.
espondilosis *f.* spondylosis.
  espondilosis cervical cervical spondylosis.
  espondilosis crónica anquilopoyética spondylosis chronica ankylopoietica.
  espondilosis hiperostótica hyperostotic spondylosis.
  espondilosis lumbar lumbar spondylosis.
  espondilosis uncovertebral spondylosis uncovertebralis.
espondiloso, -sa *adj.* spondylous.
espondilosquisis *f.* spondyloschisis.
espondilótico, -ca *adj.* spondylotic.
espondilotomía *f.* spondylotomy.
espondilotorácico, -ca *adj.* spondylothoracic.
espongeítis *f.* spongeitis, spongiitis.
espongiforme *adj.* spongiform.
espongiítis *f.* spongeitis, spongiitis.
espongioblasto *m.* spongioblast.
espongioblastoma *m.* spongioblastoma.
  espongioblastoma multiforme multiform spongioblastoma.
  espongioblastoma polar polar spongioblastoma, spongioblastoma polare.
  espongioblastoma unipolar unipolar spongioblastoma.
espongiocito *m.* spongiocyte.
espongiocitoma *m.* spongiocytoma.
espongioide *adj.* spongioid.
espongioideo, -a *adj.* spongioid.
espongioplastia *f.* spongioplasty.
espongiosis *f.* spongiosis.
espongiositis *f.* spongiositis.
espongiótico, -ca *adj.* spongiotic.
esponja *f.* sponge, spongia.
  esponja abdominal abdominal sponge.
  esponja absorbible de gelatina, esponja gelatinada absorbible absorbable gelatin sponge.
  esponja anticonceptiva contraceptive sponge.
  esponja de Bernays Bernays' sponge.
  esponja broncoscópica bronchoscopic sponge.
  esponja comprimida compressed sponge.
  esponja de fibrina fibrin sponge.
  esponja de gasa gauze sponge.
  esponja de gelatina, esponja de gelatina absorbible gelatin sponge, absorbable gelatin sponge.
  esponja vaginal vaginal sponge.
esponjoso, -sa *adj.* spongiose, spongy.
espontáneo, -a *adj.* spontaneous.
espora *f.* spore.
esporación *f.* sporulation.
esporádico, -ca *adj.* sporadic.
esporadina *m.* sporadin.
esporadino *m.* sporadin.
esporángico, -ca *adj.* sporangial.
esporangio *m.* sporangium.
esporangioespora *f.* sporangiospore.
esporangióforo *m.* sporangiophore.
esporicida *adj.* sporicidal.
esporífero, -ra *adj.* sporiferous.
esporíparo, -ra *adj.* sporiparous.
esporoaglutinación *f.* sporoagglutination.
esporoblasto *m.* sporoblast.
esporocisto *m.* sporocyst.

esporoducto *m.* sporoduct.
esporóforo *m.* sporophore.
esporogénesis *f.* sporogenesis.
esporogenia *f.* sporogeny.
esporogénico, -ca *adj.* sporogenic.
esporógeno, -na *adj.* sporogenic.
esporogonia *f.* sporogony.
esporonticida *f.* sporonticide.
esporonto *m.* sporonto.
esporotricosis *f.* sporotrichosis.
esporotricótico, -ca *adj.* sporotrichotic.
esporozoario *m.* sporozoon.
esporozoide *adj.* sporozooid.
esporozoíto *m.* sporozoite.
esporozoo *m.* sporozoon.
esporozooide *m.* sporozooid.
esporozoosis *f.* sporozoosis.
esporulación *f.* sporulation.
esprue *f.* sprue.
  esprue celíaco celiac sprue.
  esprue refractario refractory sprue.
  esprue no tropical non-tropical sprue.
  esprue tropical tropical sprue.
espuma *m.* foam.
espurio, -ria *adj.* spurious.
esputo *m.* sputum.
espúreo, -a *adj.* spurious.
esquelastenia *f.* skelasthenia.
esquelético, -ca *adj.* skeletal.
esqueletización *f.* skeletization.
esqueleto *m.* framework, skeleton.
  esqueleto apendicular appendicular framework, skeleton appendiculare.
  esqueleto articulado articulated framework.
  esqueleto axial, esqueleto axil axial framework, skeleton axiale.
  esqueleto cardíaco, esqueleto del corazón cardiac framework.
  esqueleto cartilaginoso cartilaginous skeleton.
  esqueleto de la esclerótica sclera framework.
  esqueleto de la extremidad inferior libre skeleton of free inferior limb.
  esqueleto de la extremidad superior libre skeleton of free superior limb.
  esqueleto fibroso del corazón fibrous skeleton of the heart.
  esqueleto libre de los miembros inferiores skeleton membri inferioris liberi.
  esqueleto libre de los miembros superiores skeleton membri superioris liberi.
  esqueleto maxilar jaw framework.
  esqueleto torácico thoracic skeleton, skeleton of the thorax.
  esqueleto visceral visceral framework.
esqueletogenia *f.* skeletogeny.
esqueletógeno, -na *adj.* skeletogenous.
esqueletopia *f.* skeletopia, skeletopy.
esquema *m.* schema, scheme.
esquemático, -ca *adj.* schematic.
esquematógrafo *m.* schematograph.
esqueneoscopio *m.* skenoscope, skeneoscope.
esquenitis *f.* skeneitis, skenitis.
esquenoscopio *m.* skenoscope, skeneoscope.
esqueocitosis *f.* skeocytosis.
esqueroma *m.* scheroma.
esquiámetro *m.* skiameter.
esquiascopia *f.* skiascopy.
esquiascopio *m.* skiascope.
esquiascotometría *f.* skiascotometry.
esquiencefalia *f.* schiencephaly.
esquilectomía *f.* esquillectomy.
esquinancia *f.* esquinancea.
esquinencia *f.* esquinancea.

esquindilesis *f.* schindylesis.
esquirla *f.* chip, splinter.
esquistasis *f.* schistasis.
esquistocéfalo *m.* schistocephalus.
esquistocelia *f.* schistocelia.
esquistocistis *f.* schistocystis.
esquistocito *m.* schistocyte.
esquistocitosis *f.* schistocytosis.
esquistocormia *f.* schistocormia.
esquistocormo *m.* schistocormus.
esquistoglosia *f.* schistoglossia.
esquistomelia *f.* schistomelia.
esquistomelo *m.* schistomelus.
esquistómetro *m.* schistometer.
esquistoprosopia *f.* schistoprosopia.
esquistoprosopo *m.* schistoprosopus.
esquistorraquis *m.* schistorhachis.
esquistosis *f.* schistosis.
esquistosoma *m.* schistosome.
esquistosomia *f.* schistosomia.
esquistosomiásico, -ca *adj.* schistosomal.
esquistosomiasis *f.* schistosomiasis.
  esquistosomiasis asiática asiatic schistosomiasis.
  esquistosomiasis cutánea cutaneous schistosomiasis.
  esquistosomiasis ectópica ectopic schistosomiasis.
  esquistosomiasis haematobia, esquistosomiasis haematobium schistosomiasis haematobium.
  esquistosomiasis intercalatum schistosomiasis intercalatum.
  esquistosomiasis hepática hepatic schistosomiasis.
  esquistosomiasis japonesa, esquistosomiasis japonica Japanese schistosomiasis, schistosomiasis japonica.
  esquistosomiasis intestinal intestinal schistosomiasis.
  esquistosomiasis de Manson, esquistosomiasis mansoni Manson's schistosomiasis, schistosomiasis mansoni.
  esquistosomiasis del Mekong schistosomiasis mekongi.
  esquistosomiasis oriental Oriental schistosomiasis.
  esquistosomiasis pulmonar pulmonary schistosomiasis.
  esquistosomiasis urinaria urinary schistosomiasis.
  esquistosomiasis vesical bladder schistosomiasis.
  esquistosomiasis visceral visceral schistosomiasis.
esquistosomicida *adj.* schistosomicidal.
esquistosomo *m.* schistosomus.
esquistosómula *m.* schistosomulum.
esquistosternia *f.* schistosternia.
esquistotórax *m.* schistothorax.
esquistotraquelo *m.* schistotrachelus.
esquizencefalia *f.* schizencephaly.
esquizencefálico, -ca *adj.* schizencephalic.
esquizoafectivo, -va *adj.* schizoaffective.
esquizocefalia *f.* schizocephalia.
esquizocinesia *f.* schizokinesis.
esquizocitosis *f.* schizocytosis.
esquizencefalia *f.* schizoencephalia.
esquizofasia *f.* schizophasia.
esquizofrenia *f.* schizophrenia.
  esquizofrenia aguda acute schizophrenia.
  esquizofrenia catatónica catatonic schizophrenia.
  esquizofrenia desorganizada disorganized schizophrenia.

esquizofrenia hebefrénica hebephrenic schizophrenia.

esquizofrenia indiferenciada undifferentiated schizophrenia.

esquizofrenia infantil childhood schizophrenia.

esquizofrenia latente latent schizophrenia.

esquizofrenia paranoide paranoid schizophrenia.

esquizofrenia residual residual schizophrenia.

esquizofrenia seudoneurótica pseudoneurotic schizophrenia.

esquizofrenia simple simple schizophrenia.

esquizofrénico, -ca *adj.* schizophrenic.

esquizofreniforme *adj.* schizophreniform.

esquizogénesis *f.* schizogenesis.

esquizógeno, -na *adj.* schizogenous.

esquizogiria *f.* schizogyria.

esquizogonia *f.* schizogony.

esquizoide *adj.* schizoid.

esquizomiceto *m.* schizomycete.

esquizomicosis *f.* schizomycosis.

esquizoniquia *f.* schizonychia.

esquizonte *m.* schizont.

esquizonticida *m.* schizonticide.

esquizotimia *f.* schizothymia.

esquizotípico, -ca *adj.* schizotypal.

esquizotórax *m.* schizothorax.

esquizotripanosomiasis *f.* schizotrypanosomiasis.

esquizotriquia *f.* schizotrichia.

esquizotrópico, -ca *adj.* schizotropic.

esquizozoito *m.* schizozoite.

estabilidad *f.* stability.

estabilidad dimensional dimensional stability.

estabilidad endémica endemic stability.

estabilidad enzoótica enzootic stability.

estabilidad de una prótesis dental denture stability.

estabilidad de suspensión suspension stability.

estabilímetro *m.* stabilimeter.

estabilización *f.* stabilization.

estabilización de la escayola cast stabilization.

estabilizador *m.* stabilizer.

estabilizador endodóntico endodontic stabilizer.

estabilógrafo *m.* stabilograph.

estable *adj.* stabile, stable.

estación¹ *f.* season.

estación² *f.* station.

estación de trabajo workstation.

estacionario, -a *adj.* stationary.

estadificación *m.* staging.

estadificación del cáncer cancer staging.

estadificación de Jewett y Strong Jewett and Strong staging.

estadificación TNM TNM staging.

estadificación del linfoma lymphoma staging.

estadio *m.* stage.

estadio de Arneth Arneth stage.

estadio defervescente defervescent stage.

estadio embrionario embryonic stage.

estadio fetal fetal stage.

estadio germinal germinal stage.

estadio madurativo de Tanner Tanner's stage.

estadio de las operaciones formales formal operation stage.

estadio de las operaciones concretas concrete operations stage.

estadio preoperacional preoperational stage.

estadio sensoriomotor sensoriomotor stage.

estadio de Tanner Tanner's stage.

estadio terminal end stage.

estadio tumoral tumor stage.

estadiómetro *m.* stadiometer.

estadística *f.* statistics.

estadística bayesiana Bayesian statistics.

estadística descriptiva descriptive statistics.

estadística inferencial inferential statistics.

estadística de la morbididad morbidity statistics.

estadística paramétrica parametric statistics.

estadística vital vital statistics.

estadístico, -ca *adj.* statistic.

estado *m.* state, status.

estado de agregación aggregation state.

estado de alerta alertness.

estado alfa alpha state.

estado anginoso status anginosus.

estado de ánimo mood state.

estado de ánimo disfórico dysphoric state.

estado de ánimo elevado elevated state.

estado de ánimo eutímico eutimic state.

estado de ánimo expansivo expansive state.

estado de ánimo irritable irritable state.

estado de ansiedad anxiety state, anxiety tension state.

estado apálico apallic state.

estado del arte state of the art.

estado artrítico status arthriticus.

estado asmático, estado asthmaticus status asthmaticus.

estado de ausencia absence state, absent state.

estado basal ground state.

estado catelectrotónico catelectrotonic state.

estado coleraico, estado colérico status choleraicus.

estado confusional confusional state.

estado confusional agudo acute confusional state.

estado de contacto inicial del apoyo initial contact stance state.

estado convulsivo convulsive state, status convulsivus.

estado coreico status choreicus.

estado crepuscular crepuscular state, twilight state.

estado criboso status cribrosus.

estado crítico status criticus.

estado desmielinizado status dysmyelinisatus.

estado diabetógeno diabetogenic state.

estado disráfico status dysraphicus.

estado de ensoñación dreamy state.

estado epiléptico status epilepticus.

estado de equilibrio equilibrium state.

estado esponjoso status spongiosus.

estado estable steady state.

estado estornutatorio status sternuens.

estado excitado excited state.

estado excitador central central excitatory state.

estado excitador local local excitatory state.

estado eunucoide eunuchoid state.

estado de fatiga fatigue state.

estado febril febrile state.

estado fóbico phobic state.

estado hemicraneal status hemicranicus.

estado hipnagógico hypnagogic state.

estado hipnoide hypnoid state.

estado hipnótico hypnotic state, status hypnoticus.

estado hipometabólico hypometabolic state.

estado iatrógeno iatrogenic state.

estado intersexual intersexual state.

estado lacunar lacunar state, status lacunaris.

estado limítrofe borderline state.

estado linfático status lymphaticus.

estado de mal epiléptico status epilepticus.

estado marmóreo status marmoratus.

estado mental mental status.

estado metaestable metastable state.

estado nervioso nervous state.

estado onírico dreamy state.

estado paranoide paranoid state.

estado pluripotente pluripotent state.

estado de portador carrier state.

estado preesquizofrénico preschizophrenic state.

estado prototáxico prototaxic mode state.

estado refractario refractory state.

estado de reposo resting stage.

estado singulete singlet state.

estado subliminal subliminal self state.

estado tifoso status typhosus.

estado tímico, estado timicolinfático, estado timolinfático status thymicus, status thymicolymphaticus.

estado triplete, estado de triplete triplet state.

estado vegetativo vegetative state.

estado vegetativo crónico chronic vegetative state.

estado vegetativo persistente persistent vegetative state.

estado verrucoso status verrucosum.

estado vertiginoso status vertiginosus.

estafilagra *f.* staphylagra.

estafilectomía *f.* staphylectomy.

estafiledema *m.* staphyledema, staphyloedema.

estafilematoma *f.* staphylematoma.

estafilhematoma *m.* staphylematoma.

estafilino, -na *adj.* staphyline.

estafilión *m.* staphylion.

estafilitis *f.* staphylitis.

estafiloangina *f.* staphyloangina.

estafilobacterina *f.* staphylobacterin.

estafilocemia *f.* staphylococcemia.

estafilococia *f.* staphylococcia.

estafilocócico, -ca *adj.* staphylococcal, staphylococcic.

estafilococida *m.* staphylococcide.

estafilococo *m.* staphylococcus.

estafilococosis *f.* staphylococcosis.

estafilococolisina *f.* staphylococcolysin.

estafilococólisis *f.* staphylococcolysis.

estafilodermatitis *f.* staphylodermatitis.

estafilodermia *f.* staphyloderma.

estafilodiálisis *f.* staphylodialysis.

estafiloedema *m.* staphyledema, staphyloedema.

estafilofaringorrafia *f.* staphylopharyngorrhaphy.

estafilohemia *f.* staphylohemia.

estafilohemolisina *f.* staphylohemolysin.

estafiloleucocidina *f.* staphyloleukocidin.

estafilolisina *f.* staphylolysin.

estafiloma *m.* staphyloma.

estafiloma anterior anterior staphyloma.

estafiloma anular annular staphyloma.

estafiloma ciliar ciliary staphyloma.

estafiloma de la córnea, estafiloma corneal corneal staphyloma.

estafiloma corneal racemoso staphyloma corneae racemosum.

estafiloma escleral, estafiloma de la escle-

rótica scleral staphyloma.
estafiloma ecuatorial equatorial staphyloma.
estafiloma intercalar intercalary staphyloma.
estafiloma posterior posterior staphyloma.
estafiloma proyectado, estafiloma proyectante projecting staphyloma.
estafiloma retiniano retinal staphyloma.
estafiloma de Scarpa Scarpa's staphyloma.
estafiloma uveal uveal staphyloma.
estafilomatoso, -sa *adj.* staphylomatous.
estafilonco *m.* staphyloncus.
estafiloplastia *f.* staphyloplasty.
estafiloptosia *f.* staphyloptosia, staphyloptosis.
estafiloptosis *f.* staphyloptosia, staphyloptosis.
estafilorrafia *f.* staphylorrhaphy.
estafilosquisis *f.* staphyloschisis.
estafilotomía *f.* staphylotomy.
estafilótomo *m.* staphylotome.
estafilotoxina *f.* staphylotoxin.
estafilotrópico, -ca *adj.* staphylotropic.
estalagmón *m.* stalagmon.
estáltico, -ca *adj.* staltic.
estallido *f.* spallation.
estallido renal kidney rupture.
estampador *m.* swager.
estampar *v.* swage.
estancamiento *m.* stagnation.
estándar *m.* standard.
estándar de aire ambiental ambient air standard.
estándar interno internal standard.
estándar NBS NBS standard.
estandarización *f.* standardization.
estandarización de una prueba standardization of a test.
estannífero, -ra *adj.* stanniferous.
estanosis *f.* stannosis.
estapedectomía *f.* stapedectomy.
estapedial *adj.* stapedial.
estapédico, -ca *adj.* stapedial.
estapedio *m.* stapedius.
estapediólisis *f.* stapediolysis.
estapedioplastia *f.* stapedioplasty.
estapediotenotomía *f.* stapediotenotomy.
estapediovestibular *adj.* stapediovestibular.
estar en fase *v.* be in phase.
estasia *f.* stasis.
estasia del colon colon stasis.
estasia ileal ileal stasis.
estasia intestinal intestinal stasis.
estasia papilar papillary stasis.
estasia por presión pressure stasis.
estasia urinaria urinary stasis.
estasia venosa venous stasis.
estasimorfia *f.* stasimorphia, stasimorphy.
estasis *f.* stasis.
estática equilibrio *m.* stance.
estático, -ca *adj.* static.
estatoacústico, -ca *adj.* statoacoustic.
estatocinesis *f.* statokinetics.
estatocinético, -ca *adj.* statokinetic.
estatoconios *m.* statoconia.
estatolito *m.* statolith.
estatómetro *m.* statometer.
estatoquiste *f.* statocyst.
estatura *f.* height, stature.
estatural *adj.* statural.
estaurión *m.* staurion.
estauroplejia *f.* stauroplegia.
estaxis *f.* staxis.
esteafanión *m.* stephanion.
esteariforme *adj.* steariform.
estearrea *f.* stearrhea.
esteatitis *f.* steatitis.
esteatocele *m.* steatocele.

esteatocistoma *m.* steatocystoma.
esteatocistoma múltiple steatocystoma multiplex.
esteatogénesis *f.* steatogenesis.
esteatógeno, -na *adj.* steatogenous.
esteatohepatitis *f.* steatohepatitis.
esteatólisis *f.* steatolysis.
esteatolítico, -ca *adj.* steatolytic.
esteatomatosis *f.* steatomatosis.
esteatomeria *f.* steatomery.
esteatonecrosis *f.* steatonecrosis.
esteatopigia *f.* steatopygia.
esteatopígico, -ca *adj.* steatopygous.
esteatópigo, -ga *adj.* steatopygous.
esteatorrea *f.* steatorrhea.
esteatorrea biliar biliary steatorrhea.
esteatorrea idiopática idiopathic steatorrhea.
esteatorrea intestinal intestinal steatorrhea.
esteatorrea pancreática pancreatic steatorrhea.
esteatorrea simple steatorrhea simplex.
esteatosis *f.* steatosis.
esteatosis cardiaca, esteatosis cordis steatosis cardiaca, steatosis cordis.
esteatosis hepática hepatic steatosis.
estefanión *m.* stephanion.
estegnosis *f.* stegnosis.
estegnótico, -ca *adj.* stegnotic.
estelectomía *f.* stellectomy.
estenia *f.* sthenia.
esténico, -ca *adj.* sthenic.
estenión *m.* stenion.
estenobregmático, -ca *adj.* stenobregmatic.
estenobregmato, -ta *adj.* stenobregmatic.
estenocardia *f.* stenocardia.
estenocefalia *f.* stenocephalia, stenocephaly.
estenocefálico, -ca *adj.* stenocephalic.
estenocéfalo, -la *adj.* stenocephalous.
estenocompresor *m.* stenocompressor.
estenocoria *f.* stenochoria.
estenocoriasis *f.* stenocoriasis.
estenocrotafia *f.* stenocrotaphy, stenocrotaphia.
estenoestenosis *f.* stenostenosis.
estenofótico, -ca *adj.* sthenophotic, stenophotic.
estenómetro *m.* sthenometer.
estenopaico, -ca *adj.* pinhole, stenopeic, stenopaic.
estenopeico, -ca *adj.* pinhole, stenopeic, stenopaic.
estenosado, -da *adj.* stenosed.
estenosis *f.* stenosis.
estenosis del acueducto de Silvio aqueductal stenosis.
estenosis anal anal stenosis.
estenosis anorrectal anorectal stricture.
estenosis aórtica aortic stenosis.
estenosis aórtica doble double aortic stenosis.
estenosis aórtica nodular calcificada calcific nodular aortic stenosis.
estenosis arterial renal renal artery stenosis.
estenosis del canal lumbar lumbar stenosis.
estenosis aórtica subvalvular subvalvular aortic stenosis.
estenosis cardiaca cardiac stenosis.
estenosis caroticovertebral caroticovertebral stenosis.
estenosis cervical cervical stenosis.
estenosis cicatricial, estenosis cicatrizal cicatricial stenosis.
estenosis del conducto lateral recess stenosis.
estenosis coronaria ostial coronary ostial stenosis.

estenosis de Dittrich Dittrich's stenosis.
estenosis espasmódica spasmodic stricture.
estenosis por granulación granulation stenosis.
estenosis infundibular infundibular stenosis.
estenosis laríngea laryngeal stenosis.
estenosis mitral mitral stenosis.
estenosis mitral en boca de pez fish-mouth mitral stenosis.
estenosis en ojal buttonhole stenosis.
estenosis pélvica outlet contracture.
estenosis pilórica pyloric stenosis.
estenosis pilórica congénita congenital pyloric stenosis.
estenosis pilórica hipertrófica hypertrophic pyloric stenosis.
estenosis posdiftérica postdiphtheritic stenosis.
estenosis pulmonar pulmonary stenosis.
estenosis raquidea spinal stenosis.
estenosis subaórtica subaortic stenosis.
estenosis subaórtica hipertrófica idiopática idiopathic hypertrophic subaortic stenosis.
estenosis subaórtica muscular muscular subaortic stenosis.
estenosis subvalvular subvalvular stenosis.
estenosis supravalvular supravalvular stenosis.
estenosis tricuspídea tricuspid stenosis.
estenosis uretral urethral stricture.
estenosis de la válvula mitral mitral valve stenosis.
estenosis valvular valvular stenosis.
estenostomía *f.* stenostomia.
estenotérmico, -ca *adj.* stenothermic.
estenotermo, -ma *adj.* stenothermic.
estenótico, -ca *adj.* stenosal, stenotic.
estenotórax *m.* stenothorax.
estenoxeno *m.* stenoxenous.
estepaje *m.* steppage.
estequiología *f.* stechiology, stoichiology.
estequiometría *f.* stechiometry, stoichiometry.
estequiométrico, -ca *adj.* stechiometric, stoichiometric.
éster *m.* ester.
estercolito *m.* stercolith.
estercoráceo, -a *adj.* stercoraceous.
estercoral *adj.* stercoral.
estercoraria *f.* stercorarian.
estercoremia *f.* stercoremia.
estercorolito *m.* stercorolith.
estercoroma *m.* stercorome, stercoroma.
estercoroso, -sa *adj.* stercorous.
estereoagnosia *f.* stereoagnosis.
estereoanestesia *f.* stereoanesthesia.
estereoartrólisis *f.* stereoarthrolysis.
estereoauscultación *f.* steroauscultation.
estereocampimetría *f.* stereocampimetry.
estereocampímetro *m.* stereocampimeter.
estereocilio *m.* stereocilium.
estereocognosia *f.* stereocognosy.
estereocognosis *f.* stereocognosy.
estereocolpograma *m.* stereocolpogram.
estereocolposcopio *m.* stereocolposcope.
estereoelectroencefalografía *f.* stereoelectroencephalography.
estereoencefalometría *f.* stereoencephalometry.
estereoencefalotomía *f.* stereoencephalotomy.
estereoencefálotomo *m.* stereoencephalotome.
estereoespecífico *m.* stereospecific.
estereofluoroscopia *f.* stereofluoroscopy.

estereoforómetro *m.* stereophorometer.
estereoforoscopio *m.* stereophoroscope.
estereofotografía *f.* stereophotography.
estereofotomicrografía *f.* stereophotomicrograph.
estereoftalmoscopio *m.* stereo-ophthalmoscope.
estereognosia *f.* stereognosis.
estereognósico, -ca *adj.* stereognostic.
estereognosis *f.* stereognosis.
estereognóstico, -ca *adj.* stereognostic.
estereografía *f.* stereography.
estereógrafo *m.* stereograph.
estereograma *m.* stereogram.
estereometría *f.* stereometry.
estereómetro *m.* stereometer.
estereoortóptero *m.* stereo-orthopter.
estereopantoscopio *m.* stereophantoscope.
estereopatía *f.* stereopathy.
estereopsia *f.* stereopsis.
estereopsis *f.* stereopsis.
estereorradiografía *f.* stereoradiography.
estereorroentgenografía *f.* stereoroentgenography.
estereoscopia *f.* stereoscopy.
estereoscópico, -ca *adj.* stereoscopic.
estereoscopio *m.* stereoscope.
estereotáctico, -ca *adj.* stereotactic.
estereotaxia *f.* stereotaxis, stereotaxy.
estereotáxico, -ca *adj.* stereotaxic, stereotactic.
estereotaxis *f.* stereotaxis, stereotaxy.
estereotipia *f.* stereotypy.
  estereotipia oral oral stereotypy.
estereotipo *m.* stereotype.
  estereotipo disfuncional dysfunctional stereotype.
estereotrópico, -ca *adj.* stereotropic.
estereotropismo *m.* stereotropism.
esterigma *m.* sterigm.
estéril *adj.* sterile.
esterilidad *f.* sterility, sterilitas.
  esterilidad absoluta absolute sterility.
  esterilidad adquirida acquired sterility.
  esterilidad femenina female sterility.
  esterilidad de un hijo, esterilidad de un solo hijo, esterilidad de un niño one-child sterility.
  esterilidad masculina male sterility.
  esterilidad normoespermatogénica normospermatogenic sterility.
  esterilidad primaria primary sterility.
  esterilidad relativa relative sterility.
esterilización *f.* sterilization.
  esterilización por calor seco dry heat sterilization.
  esterilización coactiva coercive sterilization.
  esterilización concurrente concurrent sterilization.
  esterilización de deficientes sterilization of deficient persons.
  esterilización eugénica eugenic sterilization.
  esterilización fraccionada, esterilización fraccional fractional sterilization.
  esterilización gaseosa gas sterilization.
  esterilización intermitente intermittent sterilization.
  esterilización involuntaria involuntary sterilization.
  esterilización laparoscópica laparoscopic sterilization.
  esterilización por vapor steam sterilization.
  esterilización voluntaria voluntary sterilization.
esterilizador *m.* sterilizer.

  esterilizador de perlas de vidrio glass bead sterilizer.
  esterilizador de sal caliente hot salt sterilizer.
esternal *adj.* sternal.
esternalgia *f.* sternalgia.
esternebra *f.* sternebra.
esternoclavicular *adj.* sternoclavicular.
esternocleidal *f.* sternocleidal.
esternocleido, -da *adj.* sternocleidal.
esternocleidomastoideo, -a *adj.* sternocleidomastoid.
esternocostal *m.* sternocostal.
esternodimia *f.* sternodymia.
esternódimo *m.* sternodymus.
esternodinia *f.* sternodynia.
esternoescapular *adj.* sternoscapular.
esternogloso, -sa *adj.* sternoglossal.
esternogoniómetro *m.* sternogoniometer.
esternohioideo, -a *adj.* sternohyoid.
esternoide *adj.* sternoid.
esternomastoideo, -a *adj.* sternomastoid.
esternón *m.* sternum.
esternopagia *f.* sternopagia.
esternópago *m.* sternopagus.
esternopericárdico, -ca *adj.* sternopericardial.
esternosquisis *f.* sternoschisis.
esternotiroideo, -a *adj.* sternothyroid.
esternotomía *f.* sternotomy.
  esternotomía media median sternotomy.
esternotraqueal *adj.* sternotracheal.
esternotripesis *f.* sternotrypesis.
esternovertebral *adj.* sternovertebral.
esteroidal *adj.* steroidal.
esteroide *m.* steroid.
  esteroide anabólicos, esteroide anabolizante anabolic steroid.
  esteroide hidroxilasa steroid hydroxylase.
  esteroide monoxigenasa steroid monoxygenase.
esteroidogénesis *f.* steroidogenesis.
esteroidógeno, -na *adj.* steroidogenic.
estertor *m.* rattle, stertor.
  estertor agónico death-rattle.
  estertor anfórico amphoric rattle.
  estertor atelectásico atelectatic rattle.
  estertor del borde border rattle.
  estertor bronquial bronchial rattle.
  estertor de burbujas, estertor burbujeante bubbling rattle.
  estertor cavernoso cavernous rattle.
  estertor de celofán cellophane rattle.
  estertor de chasquido clicking rattle.
  estertor en cloqueo de gallina hen-cluck stertor.
  estertor de colapso collapse rattle.
  estertor consonante consonating rattle.
  estertor crepitante crepitant rattle.
  estertor de crujido cracking rattle.
  estertor extratorácico guttural rattle.
  estertor de gorgoteo gurgling rattle.
  estertor gutural guttural rattle.
  estertor húmedo moist rattle.
  estertor marginal marginal rattle.
  estertor metálico metallic rattle.
  estertor mortal death-rattle.
  estertor mucoso mucous rattle.
  estertor palpable palpable rattle.
  estertor redux stertor redux.
  estertor de retorno stertor de retour.
  estertor ronco dry rattle.
  estertor seco dry rattle.
  estertor sibilante sibilant rattle.
  estertor de silbido whistling rattle.
  estertor de Skoda Skoda's rattle.
  estertor sonoro sonorous rattle.

  estertor subcrepitante subcrepitant rattle.
  estertor traqueal tracheal rattle.
  estertor vesicular vesicular rattle.
estertoroso, -sa *adj.* stertorous.
estesia *f.* esthesia.
estésico, -ca *adj.* esthesic.
estesiódico, -ca *adj.* esthesiodic, esthesodic.
estesiofisiología *f.* esthesiophysiology.
estesiogénesis *f.* esthesiogenesis.
estesiogénico, -ca *adj.* esthesiogenic.
estesiógeno, -na *adj.* esthesiogenic.
estesiografía *f.* esthesiography.
estesiometría *f.* esthesiometry.
estesiómetro *m.* esthesiometer.
estesioneuroblastoma *m.* esthesioneuroblastoma.
  estesioneuroblastoma olfatorio olfactory esthesioneuroblastoma.
estesioneurocitoma *m.* esthesioneurocytoma.
estesioscopia *f.* esthesioscopy.
estesódico, -ca *adj.* esthesodic.
estetalgia *f.* stethalgia.
estetarteritis *f.* stetharteritis.
estetemia *f.* stethemia.
estetoacústico, -ca *adj.* stethoacoustic.
estetocirtógrafo *m.* stethocyrtograph, stethokyrtograph.
estetocirtómetro *m.* stethocyrtometer.
estetoendoscopio *m.* stethendoscope.
estetoespasmo *m.* stethospasm.
estetófono *m.* stethophone.
estetofonómetro *m.* stethophonometer.
estetogoniómetro *m.* stethogoniometer.
estetografía *f.* stethography.
estetógrafo *m.* stethograph.
estetómetro *m.* stethometer.
estetomiítis *f.* stethomyitis.
estetomimético, -ca *adj.* stethomimetic.
estetomiositis *f.* stethomyositis.
estetomitis *f.* stethomyitis.
estetoparálisis *f.* stethoparalysis.
estetopoliscopio *m.* stethopolyscope.
estetoquirtógrafo *m.* stethokyrtograph.
estetoscopia *f.* stethoscopy.
estetoscópico, -ca *adj.* stethoscopic.
estetoscopio *m.* stethoscope.
  estetoscopio biauricular binaural stethoscope.
  estetoscopio de Cammann Cammann's stethoscope.
  estetoscopio diafragmático diaphragm stethoscope.
  estetoscopio diferencial differential stethoscope.
  estetoscopio electrónico electronic stethoscope.
  estetoscopio esofágico esophageal stethoscope.
estibiación *f.* stibiation.
estibiado, -da *adj.* stibiated.
estibialismo *m.* stibialism.
estibismo *m.* stibialism.
esticosis *f.* stycosis.
estigma *m.* stigma.
  estigma folicular, estigma del folículo de De Graaf follicular stigma.
  estigma de Malpighi, estigma de Malpigio Malpighian stigma.
estigmático, -ca *adj.* stigmatic.
estigmatismo *m.* stigmatism.
estigmatización *f.* stigmatization.
estigmatómetro *m.* stigmatometer.
estigmatoscopia *f.* stigmatoscopy.
estigmatoscopio *m.* stigmatoscope.
estilete *m.* stilet, stilette, style, stylet, stylette, stylus.

estilete endotraqueal endotracheal stylet.
estilicidio *m.* stillicidium.
  estilicidio de la orina, estilicidio urinario stillicidium urinae.
  estilicidio nasal stillicidium narium.
estiliforme *adj.* styliform.
estilisco *m.* styliscus.
estiloestafilino, -na *adj.* stylostaphyline.
estilogloso, -sa *adj.* styloglossus.
estilohioideo, -a *adj.* stylohyal, stylohyoid.
estiloide *adj.* styloid.
estiloideo, -a *adj.* styloid.
estiloiditis *f.* styloiditis.
estilomandibular *adj.* stylomandibular.
estilomastoideo, -a *adj.* stylomastoid.
estilomaxilar *adj.* stylomaxillary.
estilomiloideo, -a *adj.* stylomyloid.
estilopodio *m.* stylopodium.
estilosteófito *m.* stylosteophyte.
estilostixis *f.* stylostixis.
estimación *f.* estimate.
  estimación consistente consistent estimate.
  estimación en un intervalo interval estimate.
  estimación del límite del producto product-limit estimate.
  estimación puntual point estimate.
  estimación del riesgo para la salud health risk appraisal.
  estimación sesgada biased estimate.
  estimación no sesgada unbiased estimate.
estimatosis *f.* stymatosis.
estimulación *f.* stimulation.
  estimulación de área area stimulation.
  estimulación audiovisual y táctil audio-visual-tactile stimulation.
  estimulación cardíaca con marcapasos pacing stimulation.
  estimulación del cerebelo cerebellar stimulation.
  estimulación eléctrica en el dolor electrical stimulation for pain.
  estimulación eléctrica galvánica galvanic electric stimulation.
  estimulación de los fascículos dorsales dorsal column stimulation.
  estimulación fótica photic stimulation.
  estimulación Ganzfeld Ganzfeld stimulation.
  estimulación del lactante infant stimulation.
  estimulación magnética cortical cortical magnetic stimulation.
  estimulación del nervio vago vagal stimulation.
  estimulación nerviosa eléctrica transcutánea (TENS) transcutaneous electric nerve stimulation (TENS).
  estimulación nerviosa transcutánea transcutaneous nerve stimulation.
  estimulación percutánea perctaneous stimulation.
  estimulación de punto punctual stimulation.
  estimulación repetitiva repetitive stimulation.
estimulador *m.* stimulator.
  estimulador de la adenilatociclasa tiroidea humana (HTACS) human thyroid adenylate cyclase stimulator.
  estimulador de Bimler Bimler stimulator.
  estimulador palidal pallidal stimulator.
  estimulador talámico thalamic stimulator.
  estimulador tiroideo de acción prolongada long-acting thyroid stimulator.
estimulante *m. y adj.* stimulant.
  estimulante central central stimulant.
  estimulante difusivo, estimulante difusi-

ble diffusible stimulant.
  estimulante general general stimulant.
  estimulante local local stimulant.
  estimulante del sistema nervioso central central nervous system stimulant.
  estimulante tópico local stimulant.
  estimulante uterino uterine stimulant.
estímulo *m.* stimulus.
  estímulo adecuado adequate stimulus.
  estímulo aversivo aversive stimulus.
  estímulo condicionado conditioned stimulus.
  estímulo eléctrico electric stimulus.
  estímulo discriminante discriminant stimulus.
  estímulo discriminativo discriminative stimulus.
  estímulo heterólogo heterologous stimulus.
  estímulo heterotópico heterotopic stimulus.
  estímulo hipóxico hypoxic drive stimulus.
  estímulo homólogo homologous stimulus.
  estímulo inadecuado inadequate stimulus.
  estímulo incondicionado unconditioned stimulus.
  estímulo liberador releasing stimulus.
  estímulo liminal liminal stimulus.
  estímulo máximo maximal stimulus.
  estímulo mecánico mechanical stimulus.
  estímulo mínimo liminal stimulus.
  estímulo nociceptivo nociceptive stimulus.
  estímulo no condicionado unconditioned stimulus.
  estímulo nomotópico nomotopic stimulus.
  estímulo de onda cuadrada square wave stimulus.
  estímulo subliminal subliminal stimulus.
  estímulo subumbral subthreshold stimulus.
  estímulo supraliminal supraliminal stimulus.
  estímulo supramáximo supramaximal stimulus.
  estímulo umbral, estímulo de umbral threshold stimulus.
estíptico, -ca *adj.* styptic.
estiramiento *m.* stretching.
  estiramiento de las contracturas stretching of contractures.
  estiramiento facial facelift.
  estiramiento pasivo passive stretching.
estirpe *f.* strain.
  estirpe celular cellular strain.
estirpicultivo *m.* stirpiculture.
estirpicultural *adj.* stirpicultural.
estivación *f.* estivation, stivation.
estocástico, -ca *adj.* stochastic.
estoma *m.* stoma.
  estoma en asa loop stoma.
  estoma de Fuchs Fuchs' stoma.
estomacace *m.* stomacace.
estomacal *adj.* stomachal.
estomacalgia *f.* stomachalgia.
estomacitosis *f.* stomatocytosis.
estomacodinia *f.* stomachodynia.
estomacoscopia *f.* stomachoscopy.
estómago *m.* stomach.
  estómago en billetera wallet stomach.
  estómago bilocular bilocular stomach.
  estómago en bota de vino leather-bottle stomach.
  estómago en caída de agua cascade stomach.
  estómago en cascada cascade stomach.
  estómago de copa y derrame cup and spill stomach.
  estómago esclerótico sclerotic stomach.
  estómago en reloj de arena hourglass stomach.

estómago torácico thoracic stomach.
  estómago en trampa de agua water-trap stomach.
  estómago en trampa de drenaje drain-trap stomach.
  estómago trífido trifid stomach.
  estómago umbilical aberrante aberrant umbilical stomach.
  estómago de vaciamiento rápido dumping stomach.
estomal *adj.* stomal.
estomalgia *f.* stomalgia.
estomáquico, -ca *adj.* stomachic.
estomatal *adj.* stomatal.
estomatalgia *f.* stomatalgia.
estomático, -ca *adj.* stomatic.
estomatitis *f.* stomatitis.
  estomatitis aftosa aphthous stomatitis, stomatitis aphthosa.
  estomatitis aftosa recurrente recurrent aphthous stomatitis.
  estomatitis de agua water stomatitis.
  estomatitis alérgica allergic stomatitis.
  estomatitis angular angular stomatitis.
  estomatitis arsenical, estomatitis por arsénico arsenic stomatitis.
  estomatitis por Atabrine Atabrine stomatitis.
  estomatitis por bismuto bismuth stomatitis.
  estomatitis candidiásica stomatitis parasitica.
  estomatitis catarral catarrhal stomatitis.
  estomatitis de contacto contact stomatitis.
  estomatitis por dentadura denture stomatitis.
  estomatitis por escarlatina stomatitis scarlatina.
  estomatitis eritematopultácea erythematopultaceous stomatitis.
  estomatitis escorbútica stomatitis scorbutica.
  estomatitis exantemática stomatitis exantematica.
  estomatitis folicular aphthous stomatitis, stomatitis aphthosa.
  estomatitis fusoespiroquetósica fusospirochetal stomatitis.
  estomatitis gangrenosa gangrenous stomatitis.
  estomatitis gonocócica gonococcal stomatitis.
  estomatitis gonorreica gonorrheal stomatitis.
  estomatitis herpética herpetic stomatitis.
  estomatitis herpética primaria primary herpetic stomatitis.
  estomatitis herpética recurrente recurrent herpetic stomatitis.
  estomatitis medicamentosa medicamentous stomatitis, stomatitis medicamentosa.
  estomatitis membranosa membranous stomatitis.
  estomatitis mercurial mercurial stomatitis.
  estomatitis micótica mycotic stomatitis.
  estomatitis por nicotina stomatitis nicotina.
  estomatitis por plomo lead stomatitis.
  estomatitis seudomembranosa pseudomembranous stomatitis.
  estomatitis sifilítica syphilitic stomatitis.
  estomatitis simple simple stomatitis.
  estomatitis tropical tropical stomatitis.
  estomatitis ulcerativa, estomatitis ulcerosa, estomatitis ulcerosa recurrente ulcerative stomatitis, recurrent ulcerative stomatitis.
  estomatitis urémica uremic stomatitis.
  estomatitis venenosa, estomatitis venenata stomatitis venenata.
  estomatitis vesicular vesicular stomatitis.
  estomatitis de Vincent Vincent's stomatitis.

estomatocatarsis *f.* stomatocatharsis.
estomatocito *m.* stomatocyte.
estomatocitosis *f.* stomatocytosis.
estomatodeo *m.* stomatodeum.
estomatodinia *f.* stomatodynia.
estomatodisodia *f.* stomatodysodia.
estomatogástrico, -ca *adj.* stomatogastric.
estomatoglositis *f.* stomatoglossitis.
estomatognático, -ca *adj.* stomatognathic.
estomatografía *f.* stomatography.
estomatolalia *f.* stomatolalia.
estomatología *f.* stomatology.
estomatológico, -ca *adj.* stomatologic, stomatological.
estomatólogo, -ga *m., f.* stomatologist.
estomatomalacia *f.* stomatomalacia.
estomatomía *f.* stomatomy.
estomatomicosis *f.* stomatomycosis.
estomatonecrosis *f.* stomatonecrosis.
estomatonoma *m.* stomatonoma.
estomatopatía *f.* stomatopathy.
estomatoplastia *f.* stomatoplasty.
estomatoplástico, -ca *adj.* stomatoplastic.
estomatorragia *f.* stomatorrhagia.
estomatoscopio *m.* stomatoscope.
estomatosis *f.* stomatosis.
estomatosquisis *f.* stomatoschisis.
estomatotifo *m.* stomatotyphus.
estomatotomía *f.* stomatotomy.
estomatoterapeuta *m., f.* stomatotherapist.
estomatoterapia *f.* stomatotherapy.
estomencéfalo *m.* stomocephalus.
estomocéfalo *m.* stomocephalus.
estomodeal *adj.* stomodeal.
estomodeo *m.* stomodeum.
estomosquisis *f.* stomoschisis.
estoriforme *adj.* storiform.
estornudo *m.* sneeze, sternutatio, sternutation.
estrábico, -ca *adj.* strabismal.
estrabísmico, -ca *adj.* strabismic.
estrabismo *m.* cross-eye, strabismus.
  estrabismo absoluto absolute strabismus.
  estrabismo de acomodación, estrabismo acomodativo accommodative strabismus.
  estrabismo alternado, estrabismo alternante alternating strabismus.
  estrabismo bilateral bilateral strabismus.
  estrabismo binocular bilateral strabismus.
  estrabismo cicatricial mechanical strabismus.
  estrabismo cíclico cyclic strabismus.
  estrabismo cinético kinetic strabismus.
  estrabismo concomitante comitant strabismus, concomitant strabismus.
  estrabismo constante constant strabismus.
  estrabismo convergente convergent strabismus.
  estrabismo deorsum vergens strabismus deorsum vergens.
  estrabismo en días alternados alternate day strabismus.
  estrabismo divergente divergent strabismus.
  estrabismo espástico spastic strabismus.
  estrabismo externo external strabismus.
  estrabismo intermitente intermittent strabismus.
  estrabismo interno internal strabismus.
  estrabismo latente latent strabismus.
  estrabismo manifiesto manifest strabismus.
  estrabismo mecánico mechanical strabismus.
  estrabismo monocular monocular strabismus.
  estrabismo monolateral monolateral strabismus.
  estrabismo muscular concomitant strabismus.

  estrabismo no concomitante non-concomitant strabismus.
  estrabismo paralelo divergent strabismus.
  estrabismo paralítico paralytic strabismus.
  estrabismo sursum vergens strabismus sursum vergens.
  estrabismo unilateral monolateral strabismus.
  estrabismo uniocular monolateral strabismus.
  estrabismo vertical vertical strabismus.
estrabismología *f.* strabismology.
estrabismometría *f.* strabismometry.
estrabismómetro *m.* strabismometer.
estrabometría *f.* strabometry.
estrabómetro *m.* strabometer.
estrabotomía *f.* strabotomy.
estrabótomo *m.* strabotome.
estrangalestesia *f.* strangalesthesia.
estrangulación *f.* strangle, strangulation.
  estrangulación interna internal strangulation.
  estrangulación intestinal intestinal strangulation.
estrangulado, -da *adj.* strangulated.
estranguria *f.* stranguria, strangury.
estrategia *f.* strategy.
  estrategia de afrontamiento coping strategy.
  estrategia cognitiva cognitive strategy.
estratificación *f.* stratification.
estratificado, -da *adj.* stratified.
estratigrafía *f.* stratigraphy.
estratiforme *adj.* stratiform.
estrato *m.* stratum.
estreblomicrodactilia *f.* streblomicrodactyly.
estrechamiento *m.* stricturization.
estrechez *f.* stricture.
  estrechez anastomótica anastomotic stricture.
  estrechez anular annular stricture.
  estrechez en brida bridle stricture.
  estrechez cicatricial cicatricial stricture.
  estrechez contráctil contractile stricture.
  estrechez espasmódica, estrechez espástica spasmodic stricture, spastic stricture.
  estrechez falsa false stricture.
  estrechez funcional functional stricture.
  estrechez de Hunner Hunner's stricture.
  estrechez impermeable impassable stricture, impermeable stricture.
  estrechez irritable irritable stricture.
  estrechez orgánica organic stricture.
  estrechez permanente permanent stricture.
  estrechez recurrente recurrent stricture.
  estrechez temporal temporary stricture.
estrecho *m.* strait.
estrefenopodia *f.* strephenopodia.
estrefexopodia *f.* strephexopodia.
estrefopodia *f.* strephopodia.
estrefosimbolia *f.* strephosymbolia.
estrella *f.* star.
estrellado, -da *adj.* stellate.
estrema *f.* stremma.
estremecimiento[1] *m.* shiver.
estremecimiento[2] *m.* shudder.
estreñido, -da *adj.* constipated, costive.
estreñimiento *m.* constipation, costiveness.
  estreñimiento por atonía, estreñimiento atónico atonia constipation.
  estreñimiento colónico colonic constipation.
  estreñimiento espástico spastic constipation.
  estreñimiento gastroyeyunal gastrojejunal constipation.

  estreñimiento obstructivo obstructive constipation.
  estreñimiento rectal rectal constipation.
  estreñimiento subjetivo perceived constipation.
estrépito *m.* strepitus.
estrepticemia *f.* strepticemia.
estreptobacilo *m.* streptobacillus.
estreptobacterias *f.* streptobacteria.
estreptobacterina *f.* streptobacterin.
estreptocercosis *f.* streptocerciasis.
estreptococemia *f.* streptococcemia.
estreptococia *f.* streptococcosis.
estreptococicida *m.* streptococcicide.
estreptocócico, -ca *adj.* streptococcic, streptococcal.
estreptococicosis *f.* streptococcosis.
estreptococito *m.* streptococcus.
estreptococo *m.* streptococcus.
estreptocosis *f.* streptococcosis.
estreptodermatitis *f.* streptodermatitis.
estreptodermia *f.* streptoderma.
estreptomiceto *m.* streptomycete.
estreptomicrodactilia *f.* streptomicrodactyly.
estreptosepticemia *f.* streptosepticemia.
estreptotricosis *f.* streptotrichosis.
estreptotriquiasis *f.* streptotrichiasis.
estrés *m.* stress.
  estrés laboral occupational stress.
  estrés postraumático post-traumatic stress.
  estrés psicosocial psychosocial stress.
  estrés de rendimiento yield stress.
estresante *adj.* stressor.
estresor *m.* stressor.
  estresor psíquico psychic stressor.
estría *f.* streak, stria.
  estría angioide angioid streak.
  estría atrófica stria atrophica.
  estría cutánea distendida stria cutis distensa.
  estría cutis cutaneous stria.
  estría de distensión stria distensa.
  estría del embarazo pregnancy streak, stria gravidarum.
  estría gravídica gravidic streak.
  estrías de Wickham Wickham's striae.
estriación *f.* striation.
  estriación gatuna tabby cat striation.
  estriación tigroide tigroid striation.
estriado, -da *adj.* striate, striated.
estriascopio *m.* striascope.
estriatonigro, -gra *adj.* striatonigral, strionigral.
estriatonígrico, -ca *adj.* striatonigral, strionigral.
estribo *m.* stapes.
estricturoplastia *f.* stricturoplasty.
estricturotomía *f.* stricturotomy.
estricturótomo *m.* stricturotome.
estridente *adj.* strident.
estridor *m.* stridor.
  estridor convulsivo whoop stridor.
  estridor dentario stridor dentium.
  estridor espiratorio expiratory stridor.
  estridor inspiratorio inspiratory stridor.
  estridor laríngeo laryngeal stridor.
  estridor laríngeo congénito congenital laryngeal stridor.
  estridor serrático stridor serraticus.
  estridor sistólico systolic stridor.
estriduloso, -sa *adj.* stridulous.
estrina *f.* estrin.
estriocelular *adj.* striocellular.
estriocerebeloso, -sa *adj.* striocerebellar.
estriol *m.* estriol.

estriomotor, -ra *adj.* striomotor.
estriomuscular *adj.* striomuscular.
estróbila *m., f.* strobila, strobilus.
estróbilo *m.* strobilus.
estrobiloide *adj.* strobiloid.
estrobiloideo, -a *adj.* strobiloid.
estroboscopia *f.* stroboscopy.
estroboscópico, -ca *adj.* stroboscopic.
estroboscopio *m.* stroboscope.
estrofilina *f.* strophilin.
estrofocefalia *f.* strophocephaly.
estrofocéfalo, -la *adj.* strophocephalus.
estrofosomía *f.* strophosomia.
estrófulo *m.* strophulus.
  estrófulo cándido, estrófulo candidus strophulus candidus.
  estrófulo intertinto, estrófulo intertinctus strophulus intertinctus.
  estrófulo pruriginoso, estrófulo pruriginosus strophulus pruriginosus.
estrogénico, -ca *adj.* estrogenic.
estrógeno *m.* estrogen.
estrogenoterapia *f.* estrogen therapy.
estroma *m.* stroma.
estromal *adj.* stromal, stromic.
estromático, -ca *adj.* stromatic.
estromatógeno, -na *adj.* stromatogenous.
estromatólisis *f.* stromatolysis.
estromatosis *f.* stromatosis.
estronciouresis *f.* strontiuresis.
estronciourético, -ca *adj.* strontiuretic.
estrongiliasis *f.* strongyliasis, strongylosis.
estrongiloidiasis *f.* strongyloidiasis, strongyloidosis.
estrongiloidiosis *f.* strongyloidiasis, strongyloidosis.
estrongiloidosis *f.* strongyloidiasis, strongyloidosis.
estrongilosis *f.* strongyliasis, strongylosis.
estruación *f.* estruation.
estructura *f.* structure.
  estructura antigénica antigenic structure.
  estructura colaboradora de poder collaborative power structure.
  estructura cristalina crystal structure.
  estructura cuaternaria quaternary structure.
  estructura de ADN DNA structure.
  estructura familiar family structure.
  estructura fina fine structure.
  estructura de gel gel structure.
  estructura mental mental structure.
  estructura en cerdas de cepillo brush heap structure.
  estructura primaria primary structure.
  estructura de la proteína protein structure.
  estructura secundaria secondary structure.
  estructura de soporte protésico denture-supporting structure.
  estructura de sostén de dentadura dentine-supporting structure.
  estructura terciaria tertiary structure.
  estructura tuborreticular tuboreticular structure.
estructuración cognitiva *f.* cognitive structuring.
estructural *adj.* structural.
estructuralismo *m.* structuralism.
estruma *m.* struma.
  estruma aberrante struma aberrata.
  estruma coloidal, estruma coloide struma colloides.
  estruma coloide quístico struma calculosa.
  estruma fibroso struma fibrosa.
  estruma folicular struma parenchymatosa.
  estruma gelatinoso struma colloides.

  estruma de Hashimoto Hashimoto's struma.
  estruma leñoso, estruma lígneo ligneous struma.
  estruma linfático struma lymphatica.
  estruma linfomatoso struma lymphomatosa.
  estruma maligno struma maligna.
  estruma medicamentoso struma medicamentosa.
  estruma de molde de hierro Riedel's struma.
  estruma ovárico ovaric s, struma ovarii.
  estruma parenquimatoso struma parenchymatosa.
  estruma de Riedel Riedel's struma.
  estruma vasculoso struma vasculosa.
estrumectomía *f.* strumectomy.
  estrumectomía mediana median strumectomy.
estrumiforme *adj.* strumiform.
estrumiprivo, -va *adj.* strumiprivous.
estrumitis *f.* strumitis.
estrumoso, -sa *adj.* strumous.
estudio *m.* study.
  estudio de búsqueda de factores factor-search study.
  estudio ciego blind study.
  estudio de cohortes cohort study.
  estudio de control de casos case-control study.
  estudio controlado aleatorio random controlled trial.
  estudio diacrónico diachronic study.
  estudio diagnóstico workup study.
  estudio dinámico de imagen dynamic image study.
  estudio doble ciego double blind study.
  estudio Doppler Doppler scanning study.
  estudio electrofisiológico electrophysiologic testing study.
  estudio en fase uno phase one study.
  estudio en fase dos phase two study.
  estudio en fase tres phase three study.
  estudio de fibra óptica fiberoptic study.
  estudio longitudinal longitudinal study.
  estudio longitudinal de Duke Duke longitudinal study.
  estudio longitudinal del envejecimiento de Baltimore Baltimore Longitudinal Study of Anging.
  estudio multivariados multivariate study.
  estudio prospectivo prospective study.
  estudio retrospectivo retrospective study.
  estudio simple ciego single-blind study.
  estudio sincrónico synchronic study.
  estudio transversal cross sectional study, cross-selectional study.
estufa *f.* stove.
estupefaciente *adj.* stupefacient, stupefactive.
estupidez *f.* stupidity.
estupor *m.* stupor.
  estupor benigno benign stupor.
  estupor catatónico catatonic stupor.
  estupor depresivo depressive stupor.
  estupor disociativo dissociative stupor.
estuporoso, -sa *adj.* stuporous.
etanol *m.* ethanol.
etanolismo *m.* ethanolism.
etapa *f.* stage.
  etapa anal, etapa anal-sádica anal stage, anal-sadistic stage.
  etapa fálica phallic stage.
  etapa genital genital stage.
  etapa oral oral stage.
  etapa proliferativa proliferative stage.
éter *m.* ether.
etéreo, -a *adj.* ethereal.

eterificación *f.* etherification.
eterismo *m.* etherism.
eterización *f.* etherization.
eteromanía *f.* etheromania.
eterómetro *m.* etherometer.
ética *f.* ethics.
  ética biomédica biomedical ethics.
  ética de consenso agreement ethics.
  ética descriptiva descriptive ethics.
  ética empírica empiric ethics.
  ética médica medical ethics.
etilación *f.* ethylation.
etilismo *m.* ethylism.
etiolación *f.* etiolation.
etiolado, -da *adj.* etiolated.
etiología *f.* etiology.
etiológico, -ca *adj.* etiologic, etiological.
etiopático, -ca *adj.* etiopathic.
etiopatogenia *f.* etiopathogenesis, etiology and pathogenesis.
etiotrópico, -ca *adj.* etiotropic.
etiquetado, -da *adj.* labeling.
etmocarditis *f.* ethmocarditis.
etmocefalia *f.* ethmocephalia.
etmocéfalo *m.* ethmocephalus.
etmocraneal *adj.* ethmocranial.
etmoesfenoidal *adj.* ethmosphenoid.
etmoesfenoideo, -a *adj.* ethmosphenoid.
etmofrontal *adj.* ethmofrontal.
etmoidal *adj.* ethmoidal, ethmoidale.
etmoide *adj.* ethmoid.
etmoidectomía *f.* ethmoidectomy.
etmoideo, -a *adj.* ethmoid.
etmoides *m.* ethmoid bone.
etmoiditis *f.* ethmoiditis.
etmoidotomía *f.* ethmoidotomy.
etmolagrimal *adj.* ethmolacrimal.
etmomaxilar *adj.* ethmomaxillary.
etmonasal *adj.* ethmonasal.
etmopalatino, -na *adj.* ethmopalatal.
etmoturbinal *adj.* ethmoturbinal.
etmovomeriano, -na *adj.* ethmovomerine.
etmovomerino, -na *adj.* ethmovomerine.
etnobiología *f.* ethnobiology.
etnografía *f.* etnography.
etnología *f.* ethnology.
etofarmacología *f.* ethopharmacology.
etología *f.* ethology.
etológico, -ca *adj.* ethological.
etólogo, -ga *m., f.* ethologist.
euadrenocorticismo *m.* euadrenocorticism.
eubacteria *f.* eubacterium.
Eubacterium Eubacterium.
eubiótica *f.* eubiotics.
eucapnia *f.* eucapnia.
eucariocito, -ta *adj.* eukaryocyte.
eucarion *m.* eucarion, eukarion.
eucarión *m.* eucarion, eukarion.
eucariosis *f.* eucaryosis, eukaryosis.
eucariota *m.* eucaryote, eukaryote.
eucariótico, -ca *adj.* eucaryotic, eukaryotic.
eucinesia *f.* eukinesia.
eucinético, -ca *adj.* eukinetic.
euclorhidria *f.* euchlorhydria.
eucolia *f.* eucholia.
eucorticalismo *m.* eucorticalism.
eucromático, -ca *adj.* euchromatic.
eucromatina *f.* euchromatin.
eucromatopsia *f.* euchromatopsy.
eudiaforesis *f.* eudiaphoresis.
eudiemorrisis *f.* eudiemorrhysis.
eudiómetro *m.* eudiometer.
eudipsia *f.* eudipsia.
euergasia *f.* euergasis.
Euestesia *f.* euesthesia.

euestrés *m.* eustress.
eufenia *f.* euphenics.
eufénico, -ca *adj.* euphenic.
euforético, -ca *adj.* euphoretic.
euforia *f.* euphoria.
  euforia del corredor runner's high.
eufórico, -ca *adj.* euphoric.
euforigeno, -na *adj.* euphorigenic.
euforizante *adj.* euphoriant.
eugamia *f.* eugamy.
eugenesia *f.* eugenics, eugenetics.
  eugenesia negativa negative eugenics.
  eugenesia positiva positive eugenics.
eugénesis *f.* eugenics.
eugenética *f.* eugenetics.
eugenia *f.* eugenics.
eugenotenia *f.* eutenothenics.
euglucemia *f.* euglycemia.
euglucémico, -ca *adj.* euglycemic.
eugnatia *f.* eugnathia.
eugnático, -ca *adj.* eugnathic.
eugnosia *f.* eugnosia.
eugnóstico, -ca *adj.* eugnostic.
eugónico, -ca *adj.* eugonic.
euhidratación *f.* euhydratation.
eumastia *f.* eumastia.
eumelanosoma *m.* eumelanosome.
eumenorrea *f.* eumenorrhea.
eumetría *f.* eumetria.
eumicetoma *m.* eumycetoma.
eumorfia *f.* eumorphics.
eumorfismo *m.* eumorphism.
eunuco *m.* eunuch.
eunucoide *m. y adj.* eunuchoid.
eunucoidismo *m.* eunuchoidism.
  eunucoidismo femenino female eunuchoidism.
  eunucoidismo hipergonadotrópico hypergonadotropic eunuchoidism.
  eunucoidismo hipogonadotrópico hypogonadotropic eunuchoidism.
eunuquismo *m.* eunuchism.
  eunuquismo hipofisario pituitary eunuchism.
euosmia *f.* euosmia.
eupancreatismo *m.* eupancreatism.
eupepsia *f.* eupepsia, eupepsy.
eupéptico, -ca *adj.* eupeptic.
euperistalsis *f.* euperistalsis.
eupireno *m.* eupyrene.
eupirexia *f.* eupirexia.
euplasia *f.* euplasia.
euplásico, -ca *adj.* euplastic.
euploide *adj.* euploid.
euploidia *f.* euploidy.
eupnea *f.* eupnea.
eupneico, -ca *adj.* eupneic.
eupráctico, -ca *adj.* eupraxic, eupractic.
eupraxia *f.* eupraxia.
eupráxico, -ca *adj.* eupraxic, eupractic.
euquilia *f.* euchylia.
euricraneal *adj.* eurycranial.
eurifótico, -ca *adj.* euryphotic.
eurignático, -ca *adj.* eurygnathic.
eurignatismo *m.* eurygnathism.
eurignato, -ta *adj.* eurygnathous.
eurion *m.* euryon.
euriopia *f.* euryopia.
eurisomático, -ca *adj.* eurysomatic.
euritérmico, -ca *adj.* eurythermic.
euritermo, -ma *adj.* eurythermal.
eurritmia *f.* eurhythmia.
eusístole *f.* eusystole.
eusistolia *f.* eusystole.
eusistólico, -ca *adj.* eusystolic.
eusitia *f.* eusitia.

eusplacnia *f.* eusplanchnia.
eustaquitis *f.* eustachitis.
eustenia *f.* eusthenia.
eustenuria *f.* eusthenuria.
eutanasia *f.* euthanasia.
  eutanasia activa active euthanasia.
  eutanasia involuntaria involuntary euthanasia.
  eutanasia legal legal euthanasia.
  eutanasia neonatal neonatal euthanasia.
  eutanasia pasiva passive euthanasia.
  eutanasia voluntaria voluntary euthanasia.
eutéctico, -ca *adj.* eutectic.
eutelegenesia *f.* eutelegenesis.
eutelegénesis *f.* eutelegenesis.
euterapéutico, -ca *adj.* eutherapeutic.
eutérmico, -ca *adj.* euthermic.
eutiforia *f.* euthyphoria.
eutimia *f.* euthymia.
eutímico, -ca *adj.* euthymic.
eutimismo *m.* euthymism.
eutireosis *f.* euthyroidism.
eutiroideo, -a *adj.* euthyroid.
eutiroidismo *m.* euthyroidism.
eutocia *f.* eutocia.
eutónico, -ca *adj.* eutonic.
eutópico, -ca *adj.* eutopic.
eutricosis *f.* eutrichosis.
eutrofia *f.* eutrophia.
eutroficación *f.* eutrophication.
eutrófico, -ca *adj.* eutrophic.
euvolia *f.* euvolia.
evacuación *f.* evacuation.
evacuador *m.* evacuator.
  evacuador de Ellik Ellik evacuator.
evacuar *v.* evacuate.
evaginación *f.* evagination.
evaluación *f.* evaluation.
  evaluación cognitiva cognitive evaluation.
  evaluación prelaboral prevocational evaluation.
  evaluación neuropsicológica neuropsychological evaluation.
  evaluación psicosocial psychosocial assessment.
evanescente *adj.* evanescent.
evaporación *f.* evaporation.
evasión *f.* evasion.
eventración *f.* eventration.
  eventración del diafragma, eventración eventration of the diaphragm.
  eventración umbilical umbilical eventration.
eventrorrafia *f.* ventral hernia repair.
eversión *f.* eversion.
eviración *f.* eviration.
evisceración *f.* evisceration, exenteration.
  evisceración orbitaria orbital evisceration.
  evisceración pélvica pelvic evisceration.
  evisceración pélvica anterior anterior pelvic evisceration.
  evisceración pélvica posterior posterior pelvic evisceration.
  evisceración pélvica total total pelvic evisceration.
evisceroneurotomía *f.* visceroneurotomy.
evitación *f.* avoidance.
evitativo, -va *adj.* evitative.
evocación *f.* evocation.
evocador *m.* evocator.
evolución *f.* evolution.
  evolución bátmica bathmic evolution.
  evolución biológica biological evolution.
  evolución convergente convergent evolution.
  evolución determinante determinant evolution.

  evolución emergente emergent evolution.
  evolución espontánea spontaneous evolution.
  evolución espontánea de Denman Denman's spontaneous evolution.
  evolución del infarto evolution of infarction.
  evolución orgánica organic evolution.
  evolución ortogénica orthogenic evolution.
  evolución paralela parallel evolution.
  evolución saltatoria saltatory evolution.
evolutivo, -va *adj.* evolutive.
evulsión *f.* evulsion, evulsio.
exacerbación *f.* exacerbation.
exactitud *f.* accuracy.
exairesis *f.* exeresis, exairesis.
exaltación *f.* exaltation.
examen *m.* examination.
  examen bacteriológico de esputo bacteriologic sputum examination.
  examen cardiovascular cardiovascular assessment.
  examen citológico cytologic examination.
  examen citológico del esputo cytologic sputum examination.
  examen directo fresh examination.
  examen con doble contraste double contrast examination.
  examen del estado mental mental status examination.
  examen físico physical examination.
  examen de huevos y parásitos ova and parasites test.
  examen de mama breast examination.
  examen mental mental examination.
  examen neurológico neurologic examination.
  examen de Papanicolaou Papanicolaou examination.
  examen post mortem postmortem examination.
  examen de salud health assessment.
exangia *f.* exangia.
exangüe *adj.* exsanguine.
exanguinación *f.* exsanguination.
exanguinado, -da *adj.* exsanguinate.
exanguinotransfusión *f.* exsanguinotransfusion.
exania *f.* exania.
exanimación *f.* exanimation.
exantema *m.* rash, exanthema.
  exantema en alas de mariposa butterfly rash.
  exantema arthrosia exanthema arthrosia.
  exantema de Boston Boston rash.
  exantema por calor heat rash.
  exantema equimótico ecchymotic rash.
  exantema errante wandering rash.
  exantema fijo medicamentoso fixed-drug eruption.
  exantema macular macular rash.
  exantema maculopapuloso maculopapular rash.
  exantema en mariposa butterfly rash.
  exantema medicamentoso drug rash.
  exantema por ortigas nettle rash.
  exantema del pañal diaper rash.
  exantema queratoide keratoid rash.
  exantema sifilítico syphilitic rash.
  exantema súbito exanthema subitum.
exantemático, -ca *adj.* exanthematous.
exantematoso, -sa *adj.* exanthematous.
exantesis *f.* exanthesis.
  exantesis rosalia artrodinia dengue.
exantrópico, -ca *adj.* exanthropic.
exántropo, -pa *adj.* exanthrope.
exarteritis *f.* exarteritis.

exarticulación *f.* exarticulation.
excalación *f.* excalation.
excarnación *f.* excarnation.
excavación *f.* excavation, excavatio.
  excavación atrófica atrophic excavation.
  excavación dental dental excavation.
  excavación glaucomatosa glaucomatous excavation.
excavador *m.* excavator.
  excavador en azada hoe excavator.
  excavador en cucharilla spoon excavator.
  excavador dental dental excavator.
excefalosis *f.* eccephalosis.
excementosis *f.* excementosis.
excéntrico, -ca *adj.* eccentric, excentric.
excentricidad *f.* eccentricity.
excentrocondroplasia *f.* eccentrochondroplasia.
excentropiesis *f.* eccentropiesis.
excerebración *f.* excerebration.
excernente *adj.* excernent.
exceso *m.* excess.
  exceso de anticuerpos antibody excess.
  exceso de antígeno antigen excess.
  exceso de base base excess.
  exceso de base negativo negative base excess.
  exceso de convergencia convergence excess.
excicloducción *f.* excycloduction.
excicloforia *f.* excyclophoria.
exciclotropía *f.* excyclotropia.
exciclovergencia *f.* excyclovergence.
exciesis *f.* eccyesis.
excindir *v.* excise.
excipiente *m.* excipient.
excisión *f.* excision.
excitabilidad *f.* excitability.
  excitabilidad nerviosa nerve excitability.
  excitabilidad supranormal supernormal excitability, supranormal excitability.
excitable *adj.* excitable.
excitación[1] *f.* excitation.
  excitación auriculoventricular anómala anomalous atrioventricular excitation.
  excitación directa direct excitation.
  excitación indirecta indirect excitation.
  excitación protónica proton excitation.
excitación[2] *f.* excitement.
  excitación catatónica catatonic excitement.
  excitación maníaca maniac excitement.
excitante *adj.* excitant.
excitativo, -va *adj.* excitatory.
excitoanabólico, -ca *adj.* excitoanabolic.
excitocatabólico, -ca *adj.* excitocatabolic.
excitoglandular *adj.* excitoglandular.
excitometabólico, -ca *adj.* excitometabolic.
excitomotor, -ra *adj.* excitomotor, excitomotory.
excitomuscular *adj.* excitomuscular.
excitonutritivo, -va *adj.* excitonutrient.
excitosecretor, -ra *adj.* excitosecretory.
excitosecretorio, -ria *adj.* excitosecretory.
excitovascular *adj.* excitovascular.
exclusión *f.* exclusion.
  exclusión alélica allelic exclusion.
  exclusión competitiva competitive exclusion.
  exclusión de Devine Devine exclusion.
  exclusión de la pupila exclusion of the pupil.
excocleación *f.* excochleation.
excondroma *m.* ecchondroma.
excondrosis *f.* ecchondrosis.
  excondrosis fisaliforme, excondrosis fisalifora ecchondrosis physaliformis, ecchondrosis physaliphora.
excondrótomo *m.* ecchondrotome.

excoriación *f.* excoriation.
  excoriación neurótica neurotic excoriation.
excrecencia *f.* excrescence.
  excrecencia en coliflor cauliflower excrescence.
  excrecencia cutánea skin tag excrescence.
  excrecencia fungosa fungating excrescence, fungous excrescence.
excreción *f.* excretion.
  excreción de seudouridina pseudouridine excretion.
  excreción de yodo radiactivo radioactive iodine excretion.
excrementicio, -cia *adj.* excrementitious.
excremento *m.* egesta, excrement, excreta, stool.
excretor, -ra *adj.* excretory.
excursión *f.* excursion.
  excursión lateral lateral excursion.
  excursión protrusiva protrusive excursion.
  excursión retrusiva retrusive excursion.
exemia *f.* exemia.
exencefalia *f.* exencephalia, exencephaly.
exencefálico, -ca *adj.* exencephalic.
exencéfalo *m.* exencephalus.
exencefalocele *m.* exencephalocele.
exenteración *f.* exenteration.
exenteritis *f.* exenteritis.
exéresis *f.* exeresis, exairesis.
exérgico, -ca *adj.* exergic, exoergic.
exergónico, -ca *adj.* exergonic.
exesión *f.* exesion.
exfoliación *f.* exfoliation.
  exfoliación areata de la lengua exfoliation areata linguae.
  exfoliación del cristalino exfoliation of the lens.
  exfoliación laminar del neonato, exfoliación laminar del recién nacido lamellar exfoliation of the newborn.
exfoliativo, -va *adj.* exfoliative.
exhalación *f.* exhalation.
exhausto, -ta *adj.* exhausted.
exhibicionismo *m.* exhibitionism.
exhibicionista *m., f.* exhibitionist.
exicosis *f.* exsiccosis.
exocardia *f.* exocardia.
exocardíaco, -ca *adj.* exocardial.
exocataforia *f.* exocataphoria.
exocele *m.* exocele.
exoceloma *m.* exocoelom, exocoeloma.
exocelular *adj.* exocellular.
exocérvix *f.* exocervix.
exocitosis *f.* exocytosis.
exocolitis *f.* exocolitis.
exocorion *m.* exochorion.
exocrino, -na *adj.* exocrin, exocrine.
exocrinología *f.* exocrinology.
exodoncia[1] *f.* exodontics.
exodoncia[2] *f.* exodontia.
exodontista *m., f.* exodontist.
exoeritrocítico, -ca *adj.* exoerythrocytic.
exoesqueleto *m.* exoskeleton.
exosqueleto *m.* exoskeleton.
exofilaxis *f.* exophylaxis.
exofítico, -ca *adj.* exophytic.
exoforia *f.* exophoria.
exofórico, -ca *adj.* exophoric.
exoftalmía *f.* exophthalmia.
  exoftalmía endocrina endocrine exophthalmia.
  exoftalmía maligna malignant exophthalmia.
  exoftalmía pulsátil pulsating exophthalmia.
exoftálmico, -ca *adj.* exophthalmic.
exoftalmógeno, -na *adj.* exophthalmogenic.

exoftalmometría *f.* exophthalmometry.
exoftalmométrico, -ca *adj.* exophthalmometric.
exoftalmómetro *m.* exophthalmometer.
exoftalmos *m.* exophthalmos, exophtalmus.
  exoftalmos tirotóxico thyrotoxic exophthalmos.
  exoftalmos tirotrópico thyrotropic exophthalmos.
exogamia *f.* exogamy.
exogástrico, -ca *adj.* exogastric.
exogastritis *f.* exogastritis.
exógeno, -na *adj.* exogenic, exogenous.
exognatia *f.* exognathia.
exognatio *m.* exognathion.
exognation *m.* exognathion.
exohemofilaxia *f.* exohemophylaxis.
exómetro *m.* exometer.
exón *m.* exon.
exónfalo *m.* exomphalos.
exonfalocele *m.* exomphalos.
exopalanca *f.* exolever.
exopatía *f.* exopathy.
exopático, -ca *adj.* exopathic.
exoplasma *m.* exoplasm.
exorbitis *m.* exorbitism.
exorbitismo *m.* exorbitism.
exormía *f.* exormia.
exoserosis *f.* exoserosis.
exosmosis *f.* exosmosis.
exósmosis *f.* exosmosis.
exosplenopexia *f.* exosplenopexy.
exostectomía *f.* exostectomy.
exostosectomía *f.* exostosectomy.
exostosis *f.* exostosis.
  exostosis bursata exostosis bursata.
  exostosis cartilaginosa exostosis cartilaginea.
  exostosis dental, exostosis dentaria dental exostosis.
  exostosis ebúrnea ivory exostosis.
  exostosis múltiple, exostosis múltiple hereditaria multiple exostosis, hereditary multiple exostosis.
  exostosis osteocartilaginosa, exostosis osteocartilaginosa solitaria osteocartilaginous exostosis, solitary osteocartilaginous exostosis.
exostóxico, -ca *adj.* exostotic.
exotelioma *m.* exothelioma.
exotérico, -ca *adj.* exoteric.
exotermia *f.* exothermy.
exotérmico, -ca *adj.* exothermic, exothermal.
exótico, -ca *adj.* exotic.
exotimopexia *f.* exothymopexy.
exotiropexia *f.* exothyropexy.
exotropía *f.* exotropia.
  exotropía básica basic exotropia.
  exotropía por exceso de divergencia divergence excess exotropia.
  exotropía por insuficiencia de divergencia divergence insufficiency exotropia.
exotrópico, -ca *adj.* exotropic.
expansión *f.* expansion.
  expansión del arco expansion of the arch.
  expansión de cera wax expansion.
  expansión clonal clonal expansion.
  expansión cúbica cubical expansion.
  expansión de fraguado setting expansion.
  expansión higroscópica hygroscopic expansion.
  expansión del maxilar maxillary expansion.
  expansión perceptual perceptual expansion.
  expansión térmica thermal expansion.
  expansión del volumen extracelular extracellular volume expansion.
expansividad *f.* expansiveness.

expansor *m.* expander.
  expansor del plasma plasma expander.
  expansor tisular tissue expander.
expectoración *f.* expectoration.
expectorante *m. y adj.* expectorant.
  expectorante colicuativo liquefying expectorant.
  expectorante estimulante stimulant expectorant.
expediente *m.* dossier.
experiencia *f.* experience.
experimentación *f.* experimentation.
  experimentación clínica clinical experimentation.
experimental *adj.* experimental.
experimento *m.* experiment.
expiración *f.* expiration.
expirar *v.* expire.
exploración *f.* exploration.
  exploración bucodental oral examination.
  exploración física physical exploration.
  exploración ginecológica gynecological exploration.
  exploración muscular muscle testing.
  exploración ortóptica orthoptic examination.
  exploración pélvica pelvic examination.
  exploración post mortem postmortem examination.
  exploración psicológica psychologic exploration.
  exploración selectiva screening.
explorador[1] *m.* explorer.
explorador[2] *m.* searcher.
explorador, -ra *adj.* exploratory.
explosión[1] *f.* explosion.
explosión[2] *f.* burst.
  explosión en araña spider burst.
  explosión metabólica metabolic burst.
  explosión respiratoria respiratory burst.
explosivo, -va *adj.* explosive.
exponencial *adj.* exponential.
exponente *m.* exponent.
exposición *f.* exposure.
  exposición aguda, exposición aguda a la radiación acute exposure, acute radiation exposure.
  exposición automática automatic exposure.
  exposición crónica, exposición crónica a la radiación chronic exposure, chronic radiation exposure.
  exposición de entrada entrance exposure.
  exposición a la radiación radiation exposure.
expresión *f.* expression.
  expresión temprana early expression.
expresividad *f.* expressivity.
exprimir *v.* strip.
expulsión *f.* expulsion.
expulsivo, -va *adj.* expulsive.
exquistación *f.* excystation.
exquistamiento *m.* excystation.
exsomatizar *v.* exsomatize.
exsuflación *f.* exsufflation.
exsuflador *f.* exsufflator.
éxtasis *m.* ecstasy.
extático, -ca *adj.* ecstatic.
extensión *f.* extension.
  extensión bucal buccal smear.
  extensión de Buck Buck's extension.
  extensión del clavo nail extension.
  extensión de Codivilla Codivilla's extension.
  extensión por contigüidad extension per contiguitatem.
  extensión continua extension per continuitatem.

  extensión esquelética skeletal extension.
  extensión del infarto infarct extension.
  extensión marginal ridge extension.
  extensión paraselar parasellar extension.
  extensión del reborde alveolar, extensión de rebordes ridge extension.
  extensión saltatoria extension per saltam.
  extensión de sangre blood smear.
  extensión supraselar suprasellar extension.
  extensión de la vida life extension.
extensómetro *m.* extensometer.
extensor, -ra *adj.* extensor.
extenuación *f.* exhaustion.
exterior *m. y adj.* exterior.
externalidad *f.* externality.
externalización *f.* externalization.
externalizar *v.* externalize.
externo, -na *adj.* external.
exteroceptivo, -va *adj.* exteroceptive.
exteroceptor *m.* exteroceptor.
exterofección *f.* exterofection.
exterofectivo, -va *adj.* exterofective.
extinción *f.* extinction, quenching.
  extinción específica specific extinction.
  extinción de fluorescencia, extinción por fluorescencia fluorescence quenching.
  extinción sensitiva sensory extinction.
extirpación *f.* extirpation.
extirpar *v.* ablate, excise.
extorsión *f.* extorsion.
extraantrópico, -ca *adj.* extra-anthropic.
extraarticular *adj.* extra-articular.
extraaxial *adj.* extraxial.
extrabronquial *adj.* extrabronchial.
extrabucal *adj.* extrabuccal.
extrabulbar *adj.* extrabulbar.
extracaliceal *adj.* extracaliceal.
extracapsular *adj.* extracapsular.
extracardíaco, -ca *adj.* extracardiac, extracardial.
extracarpiano, -na *adj.* extracarpal.
extracción *f.* extraction, delivery.
  extracción abdominal abdominal delivery.
  extracción de una catarata cataract extraction.
  extracción dental tooth extraction.
  extracción expontánea spontaneous delivery.
  extracción extracapsular de una catarata extracapsular cataract extraction.
  extracción extracapsular del cristalino extracapsular extraction of the lens.
  extracción fetal fetal extraction.
  extracción con fórceps forceps delivery.
  extracción homogeneizadora baffling.
  extracción intracapsular de una catarata intracapsular cataract extraction.
  extracción intracapsular del cristalino intracapsular extraction of the lens.
  extracción de nalgas breech delivery, breech extraction.
  extracción del pensamiento thought withdrawal.
  extracción podálica podalic extraction.
  extracción post morten postmortem delivery.
  extracción seriada, extracción en serie progressive extraction, selected extraction serial extraction.
extracelular *adj.* extracellular.
extracerebral *adj.* extracerebral.
extracístico, -ca *adj.* extracystic.
extracorporal *adj.* extracorporal, extracorporeal, extracorpored.
extracorpóreo, -a *adj.* extracorporeal, extracorpored.

extracorticoespinal *adj.* extracorticospinal.
extracraneal *adj.* extracranial.
extracraneano, -na *adj.* extracranial.
extracromósico, -ca *adj.* extrachromosomal.
extractivo, -va *adj.* extractive.
extracto *m.* extract.
extractor *m.* extractor.
extradural *adj.* extradural.
extraembrionario, -ria *adj.* extraembryonic.
extraepifisario, -ria *adj.* extraepiphyseal, extraepiphysial.
extraer *v.* extract.
extragénico, -ca *adj.* extragenic.
extragenital *adj.* extragenital.
extrahepático, -ca *adj.* extrahepatic.
extraligamentoso, -sa *adj.* extraligamentous.
extramarginal *adj.* extramarginal.
extramastoiditis *f.* extramastoiditis.
extramedular *adj.* extramedullary.
extrameníngeo, -a *adj.* extrameningeal.
extramural *adj.* extramural.
extranuclear *adj.* extranuclear.
extraño, -ña[1] *adj.* extraneous, foreign.
extraño, -ña[2] *adj.* foreign.
extraocular *adj.* extraocular.
extraoculograma *m.* extraoculogram.
extraoral *adj.* extraoral.
extraóseo, -a *adj.* extraosseous.
extraovular *adj.* extraovular.
extrapapilar *adj.* extrapapillary.
extraparenquimático, -ca *adj.* extraparenchymal.
extraparenquimatoso, -sa *adj.* extraparenchymal.
extrapélvico, -ca *adj.* extrapelvic.
extrapericárdico, -ca *adj.* extrapericardial.
extraperineal *adj.* extraperineal.
extraperióstico, -ca *adj.* extraperiosteal.
extraperitoneal *adj.* extraperitoneal.
extrapiramidal *adj.* extrapyramidal.
extraplacentario, -ria *adj.* extraplacental.
extraplantar *adj.* extraplantar.
extrapleural *adj.* extrapleural.
extrapolación *f.* extrapolation.
extraprostático, -ca *adj.* extraprostatic.
extraprostatitis *f.* extraprostatitis.
extrapsíquico, -ca *adj.* extrapsychic.
extrapulmonar *adj.* extrapulmonary.
extrasensorial *adj.* extrasensory.
extraseroso, -sa *adj.* extraserous.
extrasistolia *f.* extrasystole.
extrasístole *f.* extrasystole.
  extrasístole auricular atrial extrasystole, auricular extrasystole.
  extrasístole auriculoventricular atrioventricular extrasystole, auriculoventricular extrasystole, extrasystole atrioventriculare.
  extrasístole infranodular infranodal extrasystole.
  extrasístole interpolada interpolated extrasystole.
  extrasístole mesonodular midnodal extrasystole.
  extrasístole nodular nodal extrasystole.
  extrasístole nodular auriculoventricular atrioventricular nodal extrasystole.
  extrasístole nodular inferior lower nodal extrasystole.
  extrasístole nodular superior upper nodal extrasystole.
  extrasístole de retorno return extrasystole.
  extrasístole retrógada retrograde extrasystole.
  extrasístole supraventricular supraventricular extrasystole.

extrasístole de la unión junctional extrasystole.

extrasístole de la unión oculta concealed junctional extrasystole.

extrasístole ventricular ventricular extrasystole.

extrasomático, -ca *adj.* extrasomatic.

extrasuprarrenal *adj.* extra-adrenal.

extratarsal *adj.* extratarsal.

extratensivo, -va *adj.* extratensive.

extratimpánico, -ca *adj.* extratympanic.

extratorácico, -ca *adj.* extrathoracic.

extratraqueal *adj.* extratracheal.

extratubárico, -ca *adj.* extratubal.

extratubario, -ria *adj.* extratubal.

extravaginal *adj.* extravaginal.

extrauterino, -na *adj.* extrauterine.

extravasación *f.* extravasation.

extravasación puntiforme extravasation punctiforme.

extravasado *m.* extravasate.

extravascular *adj.* extravascular.

extraventricular *adj.* extraventricular.

extraversión *f.* extraversion.

extravisual *adj.* extravisual.

extrayección *f.* extrajection.

extremidad *f.* extremity, limb.

extremo *m.* end, extreme.

extremo amino amino extreme.

extremo cohesivo cohesive end, sticky end.

extrínseco, -ca *adj.* extrinsic.

extrofia *f.* ecstrophe, ecstrophy, exstrophy, extrophia.

extrofia de la cloaca cloacal exstrophy, exstrophy of the cloaca.

extrofia de la vejiga, extrofia vesical exstrophy of the bladder.

extrogastrulación *f.* extrogastrulation.

extrospección *f.* extrospection.

extroversión *f.* extroversion, extraversion.

extrudir *v.* extrude.

extrudoclusión *f.* extrudoclusion.

extrusión *f.* extrusion.

extrusión dentaria extrusion of a tooth.

extubación *f.* extubation.

extubar *v.* extubate.

exuberante *adj.* exuberant.

exudación *f.* exudation.

exudado *m.* exudate.

exudado algodonoso cotton-wool exudate.

exudativo, -va *adj.* exudative.

exulceración *f.* exulceratio.

exulceración simple exulceratio simplex.

exulcerante *adj.* exulcerans.

exumbilicación *f.* exumbilication.

exutorio *m.* exutory, issue.

exuviación *f.* exuviation.

eyaculación *f.* ejaculation, ejaculatio.

eyaculación deficiente ejaculatio deficiens.

eyaculación precoz ejaculatio praecox.

eyaculación prematura premature ejaculation.

eyaculación retardada retarded ejaculation, ejaculatio retardata.

eyaculación retrógrada retrograde ejaculation.

eyaculado, -da *adj.* ejaculate.

eyaculador, -ra *adj.* ejaculator.

eyaculatorio, -ria *adj.* ejaculatory.

eyección *f.* ejection.

eyección de la leche milk ejection.

eyección ventricular ventricular ejection.

eyecta *f.* ejecta.

eyector *m.* ejector.

eyector de saliva saliva ejector.

F f

fabela *f.* fabella.
fabulación *f.* fabulation.
faceta *f.* facet, facette.
  faceta articular articular facet.
  faceta clavicular clavicular facet.
  faceta corneal corneal facet.
  faceta trabada locked facet.
facetectomía *f.* facetectomy.
facialis *adj.* facial, facialis.
facialis *adj.* facial, facialis.
facies face, facies.
  facies abdominal facies abdominalis.
  facies acromegálica acromegalic face.
  facies adenoide, facies adenoidea adenoid face.
  facies agónica hippocratic face, facies hippocratica.
  facies angélica cherubic face.
  facies aórtica aortic face.
  facies bovina cow face, facies bovina.
  facies de Corvisart Corvisart's face.
  facies descompósita hippocratic face, facies hippocratica.
  facies dolorosa facies dolorosa.
  facies de duende elfin face.
  facies escafoidea facies scaphoidea.
  facies hepática facies hepatica.
  facies hipocrática hippocratic face, facies hippocratica.
  facies de Hutchinson Hutchinson's face.
  facies leonina leonine face, facies leonina.
  facies de luna, facies lunar moon face.
  facies marmórea Parkinson's face.
  facies de Marshall Hall Marshall Hall's face.
  facies de máscara masklike face.
  facies miasténica myasthenic face.
  facies miopática myopathic face.
  facies mitral mitral face.
  facies de Parkinson, facies parkinsoniana Parkinson's face, Parkinsonian face.
  facies de Potter Potter's face.
  facies querúbica cherubic face.
  facies de sabueso hound-dog face.
  facies uterina facies uterina.
  facies de vaca cow face, facies bovina.
facilitación *f.* facilitation.
facilitatorio, -ria *adj.* facilitative.
faciobraquial *adj.* faciobrachial.
faciocefalalgia *f.* faciocephalalgia.
faciocervical *adj.* faciocervical.
facioescapulohumeral *adj.* facioscapulo-humeral.
facioestenosis *f.* faciostenosis.
faciolingual *adj.* faciolingual.
facioplastia *f.* facioplasty.
facioplejía *f.* facioplegia.
faciostenosis *f.* faciostenosis.
facoanafilaxia *f.* phacoanaphylaxis.
facocele *m.* phacocele.
facocistectomía *f.* phacocystectomy.

facocistitis *f.* phacocystitis.
facocisto *m.* phacocyst.
facodonesis *f.* phacodonesis.
facoemulsión *f.* phacoemulsification.
facoemulsificación *f.* phacoemulsification.
facoéresis *f.* phacoerysis.
facoerisis *f.* phacoerysis.
facoesclerosis *f.* phacosclerosis.
facofragmentación *f.* phacofragmentation.
facoglaucoma *m.* phacoglaucoma.
facohimenitis *f.* phacohymenitis.
facoide *adj.* phacoid.
facoidoscopio *m.* phacoidoscope.
facolisina *f.* phacolysin.
facólisis *f.* phacolysis.
facolítico, -ca *adj.* phacolytic.
facoma *m.* phacoma, phakoma.
facomalacia *f.* phacomalacia.
facomatosis *f.* phacomatosis, phakomatosis.
facometacoresis *f.* phacometachoresis.
facometecesis *f.* phacometecesis.
facopalingénesis *f.* phacopalingenesis.
facoplanesis *f.* phacoplanesis.
facosclerosis *f.* phacosclerosis.
facoscopia *f.* phacoscopy.
facoscopio *m.* phacoscope.
facoscotasmo *m.* phacoscotasmus.
facoterapia *f.* phacotherapy.
facotóxico, -ca *adj.* phacotoxic.
facticio, -cia *adj.* factitious, factitial.
factor *m.* factor.
factorial *f.* factorial.
facultad *f.* faculty.
  facultad de fusión fusion faculty.
facultativo *m.* doctor, physician, surgeon.
facultativo, -va *adj.* facultative.
fagedena *m.* phagedena.
  fagedena esfacelante sloughing phagedena.
  fagedena gangrenosa phagedena gangrenosa.
  fagedena nosocomial phagedena nosocomialis.
  fagedena tropical phagedena tropica.
fagedénico, -ca *adj.* phagedenic.
fagedeno *m.* phagedena.
fago *m.* phage.
fagocariosis *f.* phagokaryosis.
fagocitar *v.* phagocytize.
fagocitario, -ria *adj.* phagocytic.
fagocítico, -ca *adj.* phagocytic.
fagocitina *f.* phagocytin.
fagocito *m.* phagocyte.
fagocitólisis *f.* phagocytolysis.
fagocitolítico, -ca *adj.* phagocytolytic.
fagocitosis *f.* phagocytosis.
  fagocitosis espontánea spontaneous phagocytosis.
  fagocitosis inducida induced phagocytosis.
fagodinamómetro *m.* phagodynamometer.
fagólisis *f.* phagolysis.

fagolisosoma *m.* phagolysosome.
fagolítico, -ca *adj.* phagolytic.
fagopirismo *m.* phagopyrism.
fagosoma *m.* phagosome.
faja¹ *f.* binder.
  faja abdominal abdominal binder.
faja² *f.* strap.
  faja T, faja en T T strap.
fajar *v.* strap.
falacrosis *f.* phalacrosis.
falalgia *f.* phallalgia.
falange *f.* phalanx.
falangectomia *f.* phalangectomy.
falangeta *f.* phalangeta.
falángico, -ca *adj.* phalangeal.
falangosis *f.* phalangosis.
falcado, -da *adj.* falcate.
falcial *adj.* falcial.
falcicular *adj.* falciform.
falciforme *adj.* falciform.
falcino, -na *adj.* falcine.
fálcula *f.* falcula.
falcular *adj.* falcular.
falectomía *f.* phallectomy.
fálico, -ca *adj.* phallic.
faliforme *adj.* phalliform.
faltIs *f.* phallitis.
fallo *f.* failure.
falo *m.* phallus.
falocampsia *f.* phallocampsis.
falocampsis *f.* phallocampsis.
falocripsis *f.* phallocrypsis.
falodinia *f.* phallodynia.
faloide *adj.* phalloid.
falonco *m.* phalloncus.
faloplastia *f.* phalloplasty.
falorragia *f.* phallorrhagia.
falorrea *f.* phallorrhea.
falotomía *f.* phallotomy.
falsete *m.* falsetto.
falsificación *f.* falsification.
  falsificación retrospectiva retrospective falsification.
falso, -sa *adj.* false.
falsonegativo *m.* false negative.
falsopositivo *m.* false positive.
falx falx.
familia *f.* family.
  familia de cáncer cancer family.
  familia nuclear nuclear family.
familiar *adj.* familial.
fanerogénico, -ca *adj.* phanerogenic.
fanerógeno, -na *adj.* phanerogenic.
faneroscopio *m.* phaneroscope.
fanerosis *f.* phanerosis.
  fanerosis grasa fatty phanerosis.
fanerozoíto *m.* phanerozoite.
fantascopio *m.* fantascope.
fantasía *f.* fantasy, phantasy.
fantasma *m.* phantasm.

fantasmagoría *f.* phantasmagoria.
fantasmatomoria *f.* phantasmatomoria.
fantasmoscopia *f.* phantasmoscopia, phantasmoscopy.
faquitis *f.* phakitis.
farádico, -ca *adj.* faradaic, faradic.
faradímetro *m.* faradimeter.
faradismo *m.* faradism.
faradización *f.* faradization.
faradocontractilidad *f.* faradocontractility.
faradomuscular *adj.* faradomuscular.
faradopalpación *f.* faradopalpation.
faradoterapia *f.* faradotherapy.
farcinosis *f.* farcy.
fardo *m.* fardel.
farfulla *f.* jabbering.
faringalgia *f.* pharyngalgia.
faringe *f.* pharynx.
faringectasia *f.* pharyngectasia.
faringectomía *f.* pharyngectomy.
faringenfraxis *f.* pharyngemphraxis.
faríngeo, -a *adj.* pharyngeal.
faringismo *m.* pharyngism, pharyngismus.
faringítico, -ca *adj.* pharyngitic.
faringitis *f.* pharyngitis.
 faringitis aguda acute pharyngitis.
 faringitis apostemática phlegmonous pharyngitis.
 faringitis atrófica atrophic pharyngitis.
 faringitis catarral catarrhal pharyngitis.
 faringitis crónica chronic pharyngitis.
 faringitis crupal, faringitis cruposa croupous pharyngitis.
 faringitis diftérica diphtheritic pharyngitis.
 faringitis flemonosa phlegmonous pharyngitis.
 faringitis folicular follicular pharyngitis.
 faringitis gangrenosa gangrenous pharyngitis.
 faringitis glandular glandular pharyngitis.
 faringitis granulosa, faringitis granular granular pharyngitis.
 faringitis herpética pharyngitis herpetica.
 faringitis hipertrófica lateral pharyngitis hypertrophica lateralis.
 faringitis linfonodular aguda acute lymphonodular pharyngitis.
 faringitis membranosa membranous pharyngitis.
 faringitis queratosa pharyngitis keratosa.
 faringitis seca pharyngitis sicca.
 faringitis ulceromembranosa ulceromembranous pharyngitis.
 faringitis ulcerosa ulcerative pharyngitis.
faringoamigdalitis *f.* pharyngoamygdalitis.
faringobucal *adj.* pharyngo-oral.
faringocele *m.* pharyngocele.
faringodinia *f.* pharyngodynia.
faringoepiglótico, -ca *adj.* pharyngoepiglottic.
faringoesofágico, -ca *adj.* pharyngoesophageal.
faringoesofagoplastia *f.* pharyngoesophagoplasty.
faringoespasmo *m.* pharyngospasm.
faringoestenosis *f.* pharyngostenosis.
faringogloso, -sa *adj.* pharyngoglossal.
faringolaríngeo, -a *adj.* pharyngolaryngeal.
faringolaringitis *f.* pharyngolaryngitis.
faringolito *m.* pharyngolith.
faringología *f.* pharyngology.
faringomaxilar *adj.* pharyngomaxillary.
faringomicosis *f.* pharyngomycosis.
faringonasal *adj.* pharyngonasal.
faringopalatino, -na *adj.* pharyngopalatine.

faringoparálisis *f.* pharyngoparalysis.
faringopatía *f.* pharyngopathy, pharyngopathia.
faringoperístole *m.* pharyngoperistole.
faringoplastia *f.* pharyngoplasty.
faringoplejía *f.* pharyngoplegia.
faringoqueratosis *f.* pharyngokeratosis.
faringorragia *f.* pharyngorrhagia.
faringorrinitis *f.* pharyngorhinitis.
faringosalpingitis *f.* pharyngosalpingitis.
faringoscleroma *m.* pharyngoscleroma.
faringoscopia *f.* pharyngoscopy.
faringoscopio *m.* pharyngoscope.
faringospasmo *m.* pharyningospasm.
faringostenosis *f.* pharyngostenosis.
faringoterapia *f.* pharyngotherapy.
faringotifoidea *f.* pharyngotyphoid.
faringotomía *f.* pharyngotomy.
 faringotomía externa external pharyngotomy.
 faringotomía interna internal pharyngotomy.
 faringotomía subhioidea subhyoid pharyngotomy.
faringótomo *m.* pharyngotome.
faringotonsilitis *f.* pharyngotonsillitis.
faringoxerosis *f.* pharyngoxerosis.
farmaceútico, -ca[1] *m., f.* pharmaceutist, pharmacist.
farmacéutico, -ca[2] *adj.* pharmaceutic, pharmaceutical.
farmacia *f.* pharmaceutics, pharmacy.
 farmacia clínica clinical pharmaceutics.
 farmacia galénica Galenic pharmaceutics.
fármaco *m.* drug.
farmacocinética *f.* pharmacokinetics.
farmacocinético, -ca *adj.* pharmacokinetic.
farmacodiagnóstico *m.* pharmacodiagnosis.
farmacodinamia *f.* pharmacodynamics.
farmacodinámico, -ca *adj.* pharmacodynamic.
farmacoendocrinología *f.* pharmacoendocrinology.
farmacogenética *f.* pharmacogenetics.
farmacognosia *f.* pharmacognosy.
farmacognosista *m., f.* pharmacognosist.
farmacografía *f.* pharmacography.
farmacología *f.* pharmacology.
 farmacología clínica clinical pharmacology.
farmacológico, -ca *adj.* pharmacologic, pharmacological.
farmacólogo, -ga *m., f.* pharmacologist.
 farmacólogo clínico clinical pharmacologist.
farmacopea *f.* pharmacopoeia.
farmacopeico, -ca *adj.* pharmacopeial.
farmacoquímica *f.* pharmacochemistry.
farmacoterapia *f.* pharmacotherapy.
fascia *f.* fascia.
fasciagrafía *f.* fasciagraphy.
fascial *adj.* fascial.
fasciculación *f.* fasciculation.
fasciculado, -da *adj.* fasciculate, fasciculated.
fascicular *adj.* fascicular.
fascículo *m.* bundle, fascicle, fasciculus.
fasciodesis *f.* fasciodesis.
Fasciola Fasciola.
fascioliasis *f.* fascioliasis.
fasciólido *m.* fasciolid.
fasciolopsiasis *f.* fasciolopsiasis.
fascioplastia *f.* fascioplasty.
fasciorrafia *f.* fasciorrhaphy.
fasciotomía *f.* fasciotomy.
fascitis *f.* fasciitis.
 fascitis eosinofílica eosinophilic fasciitis.
 fascitis exudativa calcificante exudative calcifying fasciitis.

fascitis necrosante necrotizing fasciitis.
fascitis nodular nodular fasciitis.
fascitis paróstica parosteal fasciitis.
fascitis perirrenal perirenal fasciitis.
fascitis proliferativa proliferative fasciitis.
fascitis seudosarcomatosa pseudosarcomatous fasciitis.
fase *f.* phase, stage.
fase 0 phase 0.
fase 1 phase 1.
fase 2 phase 2.
fase 3 phase 3.
fase 4 phase 4.
fase de aceleración acceleration phase.
fase de acoplamiento coupling phase.
fase acuosa aqueous phase.
fase de la agonía stage of dying.
fase alfa alpha phase.
fase álgida algid stage.
fase anal, fase anal-sádica anal stage, anal-sadistic stage.
fase de la anestesia stage of anesthesia.
fase anfibólica amphibolic stage.
fase de anillo ring stage.
fase apofiláctica negative phase.
fase de apoyo de la marcha stance phase of gait.
fase de asfixia asphyxial stage.
fase autista autistic phase.
fase de balanceo de la marcha swing phase of gait.
fase de bipedestación previa al balanceo preswing stance stage.
fase beta beta phase.
fase caliente hot stage.
fase cis cis phase.
fase continua continuous phase.
fase de crecimiento radial radial growth phase.
fase de crecimiento vertical vertical growth phase.
fase cuarta (del trabajo del parto) fourth stage.
fase de declinación phase of decline.
fase de defervescencia defervescent stage.
fase demorada lag phase.
fase de desaceleración deceleration phase.
fase de descanso rest phase, resting stage.
fase de eclipse eclipse phase.
fase edípica oedipal stage.
fase eruptiva eruptive phase.
fase en escalera stepladder stage.
fase del espejo mirror stage.
fase espiratoria expiration phase.
fase estacionaria stationary phase.
fase de estrina proliferative stage.
fase estrogénica follicular phase.
fase exponencial logarithmic phase.
fase de expulsión expulsive stage.
fase externa external phase.
fase fálica phallic phase.
fase de fervescencia stage of fervescence.
fase folicular follicular phase.
fase fría cold stage.
fase genital genital phase.
fase imperfecta imperfect stage.
fase de incubación incubative stage.
fase de inducción[1] inductive phase.
fase de inducción[2] induction phase.
fase de intervalo bacteriano log phase.
fase de latencia latency stage.
fase latente latent phase.
fase logarítmica logarithmic phase.
fase luteínica luteal phase.
fase de máxima pendiente phase of maximum slope.

fase meiótica meiotic phase.
fase menstrual menstrual phase.
fase motofaciente motofacient phase.
fase negativa negative phase.
fase oral oral phase.
fase oral sádica oral-sadistic stage.
fase de patito feo ugly duckling stage.
fase de pensamiento preoperativo preoperational thought phase.
fase perfecta perfect stage.
fase piretógena pyretogenic stage.
fase pirógena pyrogenic stage.
fase placentaria placental stage.
fase positiva positive phase.
fase preconceptual preconceptual stage.
fase preedípica preoedipical phase.
fase preeruptiva preeruptive stage.
fase pregenital pregenital phase.
fase premeiótica premeiotic phase.
fase premenstrual premenstrual stage.
fase primera (del trabajo de parto) first stage.
fase prodrómico prodromal stage.
fase progestacional progestational stage.
fase proliferativa proliferative stage.
fase de la pulpa transicional transitional pulp stage.
fase de Ranke Ranke's stage.
fase de recuperación supernormal supernormal recovery phase.
fase de reducción reduction phase.
fase de reposo resting phase, rest stage.
fase S S phase.
fase secretora secretory phase.
fase segunda (del trabajo del parto) second stage.
fase sensitivomotora sensorimotor phase.
fase de sudación sweating stage.
fase tercera (del trabajo del parto) third stage.
fase trans trans phase.
fase vegetativa vegetative stage.
fase vulnerable vulnerable phase.
fastigio *m.* fastigium.
fastigium fastigium.
fatal *adj.* fatal.
fatalidad *f.* fatality.
fatiga *f.* fatigue.
fatiga auditiva auditory fatigue.
fatiga de batalla, fatiga de las batallas battle fatigue.
fatiga de combate combat fatigue.
fatiga de estimulación stimulation fatigue.
fatiga de seudocombate pseudocombat fatigue.
fatigabilidad *f.* fatigability.
fatigable *adj.* fatigable.
fatnorragia *f.* phatnorrhagia.
fauces *f.* fauces.
faucial *adj.* faucial.
faucitis *f.* faucitis.
faveolado, -da *adj.* faveolate.
faveolar *adj.* faveolate.
fávide *f.* favid.
favo *m.* favus.
favus *m.* favus.
faz *f.* face.
febricante *adj.* febricant.
febricida *m.* febricide.
febricidad *f.* febricity.
febrícula *f.* febricula.
febrifaciente *adj.* febrifacient.
febrífero, -a *adj.* febriferous.
febrífico, ca *adj.* febrific.
febrífugo *m.* febrifuge.

febrífugo, -ga *adj.* febrifugal.
febril *adj.* febrile.
febris *adj.* febris.
fecal *adj.* fecal.
fecalito *m.* fecalith.
fecaloide *adj.* fecaloid.
fecaloma *m.* fecaloma.
fecaluria *f.* fecaluria.
feculento, -ta *adj.* feculent.
fecundación *f.* fecundation, fecundatio.
fecundación artificial artificial fecundation.
fecundación ab extra fecundatio ab extra.
fecundación externa external fecundation.
fecundación interna internal fecundation.
fecundación in vitro in vitro fecundation.
fecundar *v.* fecundate.
fecundidad *f.* fecundity.
fecundo, -da *adj.* fecund.
feedback *m.* feedback.
femenino, -na *adj.* femenine.
feminismo *m.* feminism.
feminización *f.* feminization.
feminización testicular testicular feminization.
femoral *adj.* femoral.
femorocele *m.* femorocele.
femoroilíaco, -ca *adj.* femoroiliac.
femorotibial *adj.* femorotibial.
fémur *m.* femur.
fenestra *f.* fenestra.
fenestra novovalis fenestra novovalis.
fenestración *f.* fenestration.
fenestración apical apical fenestration.
fenestración de la placa alveolar alveolar plate fenestration.
fenestración traqueal tracheal fenestration.
fenestrado, -da *adj.* fenestrated.
fenestrar *v.* fenestrate.
fenetidinuria *f.* phenetidinuria.
fenilalaninemia *f.* phenylalaninemia.
fenilcetonuria (FCU) *f.* phenylketonuria (FKU).
fenilcetonuria (FCU) maternal maternal phenylketonuria (FKU).
feno *m.* phene.
fenoanómalo, -la *adj.* phenodeviant.
fenobutiodil *m.* phenobutiodil.
fenocigo, -ga *adj.* phenozygous.
fenocopia *f.* phenocopy.
fenodesviado, -da *adj.* phenodeviant.
fenogenética *f.* phenogenetics.
fenolemia *f.* phenolemia.
fenolización *f.* phenolization.
fenología *f.* phenology.
fenologista *m., f.* phenologist.
fenoluria *f.* phenoluria.
fenoma *f.* phenom.
fenómeno *m.* phenomenon.
fenómeno de abstinencia abstinence phenomenon.
fenómeno de adherencia de eritrocitos erythrocyte adherence phenomenon.
fenómeno de adherencia de glóbulos rojos red cell adherence phenomenon.
fenómeno de adhesión adhesion phenomenon.
fenómeno de alejamiento breakaway phenomenon, breakoff phenomenon.
fenómeno del alba dawn phenomenon.
fenómeno del amanecer dawn phenomenon.
fenómeno anafilactoide pseudoanaphylaxis.
fenómeno de anderson Anderson's phenomenon.
fenómeno Anrep Anrep phenomenon.
fenómeno de Arias-Stella Arias-Stella phenomenon.

fenómeno de Aschner Aschner's phenomenon.
fenómeno Ashman Ashman's phenomenon.
fenómeno de Aubert Aubert's phenomenon.
fenómeno de Austin-Flint Austin-Flint phenomenon.
fenómeno autocinético de luz visible autokinetic visible light phenomenon.
fenómeno autoscópico autoscopic phenomenon.
fenómeno de Babinski Babinski's phenomenon.
fenómeno de Bell Bell's phenomenon.
fenómeno de bercker Bercker's phenomenon.
fenómeno de blanqueamiento blanching phenomenon.
fenómeno de Bordet-Gengou Bordet-Gengou phenomenon.
fenómeno del brazo arm phenomenon.
fenómeno de Brücke-Bartley Brücke-Bartley phenomenon.
fenómeno de la cabeza de la muñeca doll's head phenomenon.
fenómeno de caída y elevación fall and rise phenomenon.
fenómeno cervicolumbar cervicolumbar phenomenon.
fenómeno de Collie Collie phenomenon.
fenómeno de constancia constancy phenomenon.
fenómeno de Cushing Cushing phenomenon.
fenómeno de Danysz Danysz phenomenon.
fenómeno de Debré Debré phenomenon.
fenómeno de "declamping" declamping phenomenon.
fenómeno del dedo finger phenomenon.
fenómeno del dedo gordo toe phenomenon.
fenómeno de los dedos de Souques Souques' phenomenon.
fenómeno de "déjà vu" déjà vu phenomenon.
fenómeno de Déjérine-Lichtheim Déjérine-Lichtheim phenomenon.
fenómeno de Denys-Leclef Denys-Leclef phenomenon.
fenómeno de d'Hérelle d'Hérelle phenomenon.
fenómeno del diafragma, fenómeno diafragmático diaphragm phenomenon, diaphragmatic phenomenon.
fenómeno diafragmático de Litten Litten's diaphragm phenomenon.
fenómeno en dirección errada misdirection phenomenon.
fenómeno de donath Donath phenomenon.
fenómeno de Donath-Landsteiner Donath-Landsteiner phenomenon.
fenómeno de Doppler Doppler phenomenon.
fenómeno de Duckworth Duckworth's phenomenon.
fenómeno de Ehret Ehret's phenomenon.
fenómeno de Erben Erben's phenomenon.
fenómeno de la escalera staircase phenomenon.
fenómeno de escape escape phenomenon.
fenómeno de la extinción de la erupción rash-extinction phenomenon.
fenómeno de fermentación simbiótica symbiotic fermentation phenomenon.
fenómeno fi phi phenomenon.
fenómeno de Fick Fick's phenomenon.

fenómeno de fijación fixation phenomenon.

fenómeno de flexión de la cadera hipflexion phenomenon.

fenómeno frénico phrenic phenomenon.

fenómeno frénico cruzado crossed phrenic phenomenon.

fenómeno de freno broke phenomenon.

fenómeno de Friedreich Friedreich's phenomenon.

fenómeno de Gallavardin Gallavardin's phenomenon.

fenómeno gap gap phenomenon.

fenómeno de Gärtner Gärtner phenomenon.

fenómeno de Gengou Gengou phenomenon.

fenómeno de Gengou-Bordet Gengou-Bordet phenomenon.

fenómeno de Gerhardt Gerhardt's phenomenon.

fenómeno de Goldblatt Goldblatt phenomenon.

fenómeno de Gowers Gowers' phenomenon.

fenómeno de Grasset Grasset's phenomenon.

fenómeno de Grasset-Gaussel Grasset-Gaussel phenomenon.

fenómeno de guiño maxilar jaw-winking phenomenon.

fenómeno de Gunn Gunn phenomenon.

fenómeno de halistéresis halisteresis phenomenon.

fenómeno de Hamburger Hamburger's phenomenon.

fenómeno de hammerschlag Hammerschlag phenomenon.

fenómeno de Hata Hata phenomenon.

fenómeno de Hecht Hecht phenomenon.

fenómeno de Hektoen Hektoen phenomenon.

fenómeno hemodinámico de intercambio borrowing-lending hemodynamic phenomenon.

fenómeno de Hering Hering's phenomenon.

fenómeno de Hertwig-Magendie Hertwig-Magendie phenomenon.

fenómeno de Hecht Hecht phenomenon.

fenómeno de Hochsinger Hochsinger's phenomenon.

fenómeno de Hoffmann Hoffmann's phenomenon.

fenómeno de Holmes Holmes' phenomenon.

fenómeno de Holmes-Stewart Holmes-Stewart phenomenon.

fenómeno de Houssay Houssay phenomenon.

fenómeno de Hunt Hunt's paradoxical phenomenon.

fenómeno de influjo acuoso aqueous influx phenomenon.

fenómeno de influjo de sangre blood influx phenomenon.

fenómeno de inmersión dip phenomenon.

fenómeno de inmunoadherencia immune adherence phenomenon.

fenómeno de interferencia interference phenomenon.

fenómeno de interrupción breakoff phenomenon.

fenómeno de intervalo gap phenomenon.

fenómeno de Jod-Basedow Jod-Basedow phenomenon.

fenómeno de Kienböck Kienböck's phenomenon.

fenómeno de Köbner Köbner's phenomenon.

fenómeno de Koch Koch's phenomenon.

fenómeno de Kohnstamm Kohnstamm's phenomenon.

fenómeno le le phenomenon.

fenómeno de Leede-Rumpel Leede-Rumpel phenomenon.

fenómeno de Le Grand Geblewics Le Grand Geblewics phenomenon.

fenómeno leproso de Lucio Lucio's leprosy phenomenon.

fenómeno de lewis Lewis' phenomenon.

fenómeno de Liacopoulus Liacopoulus phenomenon.

fenómeno de liberación release phenomenon.

fenómeno de liesegang Liesegang's phenomenon.

fenómeno lingual tongue phenomenon.

fenómeno de Litten Litten's phenomenon.

fenómeno de lucio Lucio's phenomenon.

fenómeno de Lust Lust's phenomenon.

fenómeno de Marcus-Gunn Marcus-Gunn phenomenon.

fenómeno maxilar de parpadeo jaw-winking phenomenon.

fenómeno de Meirowsky Meirowsky phenomenon.

fenómeno de la mejilla cheek phenomenon.

fenómeno de Mills-Reincke Mills-Reincke phenomenon.

fenómeno de Mitzuo Mitzuo's phenomenon.

fenómeno de Moreschi complement fixation.

fenómeno muscular de Kühne Kühne's muscular phenomenon.

fenómeno negativo de la varilla de cristal de Ascher Ascher's negative glass rod phenomenon.

fenómeno de Negro Negro's phenomenon.

fenómeno de Neisser-Wechsberg Neisser-Wechsberg phenomenon.

fenómeno de no reflujo no reflow phenomenon.

fenómeno on-off on-off phenomenon.

fenómeno de Orbeli Orbeli phenomenon.

fenómeno orbicular, fenómeno del orbicular orbicularis phenomenon.

fenómeno paradójico del diafragma paradoxical diaphragm phenomenon.

fenómeno paradójico de distonia paradoxical phenomenon of dystonia.

fenómeno paradójico de Hunt Hunt's paradoxical phenomenon.

fenómeno paradójico de la pupila paradoxical pupil phenomenon.

fenómeno peroneo peroneal phenomenon.

fenómeno de Pfeiffer Pfeiffer's phenomenon.

fenómeno de la pierna leg phenomenon.

fenómeno de Piltz-Westphal Piltz-Westphal phenomenon.

fenómeno de Pool Pool's phenomenon.

fenómeno de Porret Porret's phenomenon.

fenómeno positivo de la varilla de cristal de ascher Ascher's positive glass rod phenomenon.

fenómeno de prezona, fenómeno de prozona prezone phenomenon, prozone phenomenon.

fenómeno psi psi phenomenon.

fenómeno pupilar de Gunn Gunn's pupillary phenomenon.

fenómeno pupilar paradójico paradoxical pupillary phenomenon.

fenómeno de Purkinje Purkinje's phenomenon.

fenómeno de Queckenstedt Queckenstedt's phenomenon.

fenómeno radial radial phenomenon.

fenómeno de Raynaud Raynaud's phenomenon.

fenómeno de rebote rebound phenomenon.

fenómeno de recoagulación reclotting phenomenon.

fenómeno de reentrada reentry phenomenon.

fenómeno de Rieger Rieger's phenomenon.

fenómeno de Ritter-Rollet Ritter-Rollet phenomenon.

fenómeno de R sobre T R-on-T phenomenon.

fenómeno de rueda dentada cogwheel phenomenon.

fenómeno de Rumpel-Leede Rumpel-Leede phenomenon.

fenómeno de Rust Rust's phenomenon.

fenómeno satélite satellite phenomenon.

fenómeno de Schellong-Strisower Schellong-Strisower phenomenon.

fenómeno de Schlesinger Schlesinger's phenomenon.

fenómeno de Schramm Schramm's phenomenon.

fenómeno de Schultz-Charlton Schultz-Charlton phenomenon.

fenómeno de Schüller Schüller's phenomenon.

fenómeno de seda tornasolada shotsilk phenomenon.

fenómeno de separación breakoff phenomenon, breakaway phenomenon.

fenómeno seudo-Graefe pseudo-Graefe's phenomenon.

fenómeno de Sherrington Sherrington phenomenon.

fenómeno de Somogyi Somogyi phenomenon.

fenómeno de Soret Soret's phenomenon.

fenómeno de Souques Souques' phenomenon.

fenómeno de Splendore-Hoeppli Splendore-Hoeppli phenomenon.

fenómeno de Staub-Traugott Staub-Traugott phenomenon.

fenómeno de Strassmann Strassmann's phenomenon.

fenómeno de Strümpell Strümpell's phenomenon.

fenómeno tibial tibial phenomenon.

fenómeno de tornasol shotsilk phenomenon.

fenómeno de Tournay Tournay's phenomenon.

fenómeno de Trousseau Trousseau's phenomenon.

fenómeno de Twort Twort phenomenon.

fenómeno de Twort-d'Hérelle Twort-d'Hérelle phenomenon.

fenómeno de Tyndall Tyndall phenomenon.

fenómeno de varilla de vidrio de Ascher Ascher's glassrod phenomenon.

fenómeno venoso de Gärtner Gärtner's vein phenomenon.

fenómeno de Wedensky Wedensky's phenomenon.

fenómeno de Wenckebach Wenckebach phenomenon.

fenómeno de Westphal-Piltz Westphal-Piltz phenomenon.

fenómeno de Williams Williams' phenomenon.

fenómeno de zambullida dip phenomenon.

fenómeno de zona zone phenomenon.

fenomenología *f.* phenomenology.

fenotípico, -ca *adj.* phenotypic.

fenotipo *m.* phenotype.

fenotipo de bombay Bombay phenotype.

feocromo, -ca *adj.* pheochrome.
feocromoblasto *m.* pheochromoblast.
feocromocito *m.* pheochromocyte.
feocromocitoma *m.* pheochromocytoma.
feohifomicosis *f.* phaeohyphomycosis.
feomelanina *f.* pheomelanin.
feomelanogénesis *f.* pheomelanogenesis.
feomelanosoma *m.* pheomelanosome.
feral *adj.* feral.
féresis *f.* pheresis.
fermentable *adj.* fermentable.
fermentación *f.* fermentation.
   fermentación acética, fermentación acetosa acetic fermentation, acetous fermentation.
   fermentación alcohólica alcoholic fermentation.
   fermentación de almacenamiento storing fermentation.
   fermentación amílica amylic fermentation.
   fermentación amoniacal ammoniacal fermentation.
   fermentación butírica butyric fermentation.
   fermentación caseosa caseous fermentation.
   fermentación diastásica diastatic fermentation.
   fermentación láctica lactic acid fermentation.
   fermentación viscosa viscous fermentation.
fermentativo, -va *adj.* fermentative.
fermento *m.* ferment, fermentum.
fermentoide *m.* fermentoid.
fermentum fermentum.
feromonas *f.* pheromone.
ferrialbumínico, -ca *adj.* ferrialbuminic.
ferricitocromo *m.* ferricytochrome.
ferrihemoglobina *f.* ferrihemoglobin.
ferriprivo, -va *adj.* sideropenic.
ferritina *f.* ferritin.
ferrocinética *f.* ferrokinetics.
ferrocinético, -ca *adj.* ferrokinetic.
ferrocitocromo *m.* ferrocytochrome.
ferrohemocromo *m.* ferrohemochrome.
ferropexia *f.* ferropexy.
ferroporfirina *f.* ferroporphyrin.
ferroproteínas *f.* ferroproteins.
ferroprotoporfirina *f.* ferroprotoporphyrin.
ferroterapia *f.* ferrotherapy.
ferruginación *f.* ferrugination.
ferruginoso, -sa *adj.* ferruginous.
ferrum ferrum.
fértil *adj.* fertile.
fertilicina *f.* fertilizin.
fertilidad *f.* fertility.
fertilisina *f.* fertilizin.
fertilización *f.* fertilization.
férula *f.* splint.
   férula en abducción airplane splint.
   férula activa active splint.
   férula en aeroplano airplane splint.
   férula de Agnew Agnew's splint.
   férula de aire air splint.
   férula de alambre wire splint.
   férula de alambre de Cramer Cramer wire splint.
   férula de alambre de Kirschner Kirschner wire splint.
   férula de almohada de Frejka Frejka pillow splint.
   férula en ancla anchor splint.
   férula de Anderson Anderson splint.
   férula de Angle Angle's splint.
   férula de Asch Asch splint.
   férula de Ashhurst Ashhurst's splint.
   férula bávara Bavarian splint.
   férula de Böhler Böhler's splint.

férula de Bond Bond's splint.
férula bucal buccal splint.
férula de Cabot Cabot's splint.
férula en capuchón cap splint.
férula cementada por grabado en ácido acid etch cemented splint.
férula de Charfield-Girdleston Charfield-Girdleston splint.
férula de coaptación coaptation splint.
férula de contacto contact splint.
férula de Cramer Cramer's splint.
férula de Denis Browne Denis Browne splint.
férula dental cap splint.
férula dinámica dynamic splint.
férula dorsal backboard splint.
férula escalonada, férula en escalera ladder splint.
férula de Essig Essig splint.
férula de Frejka Frejka splint.
férula de fijación anchor splint.
férula de Fox Fox's splint.
férula de fractura fracture splint.
férula funcional functional splint.
férula de Gilmer Gilmer's splint.
férula de Gordon Gordon's splint.
férula de Gunning Gunning splint.
férula de Hodgen Hodgen splint.
férula de incrustación inlay splint.
férula inflable inflatable splint.
férula interdental, férula interdentaria interdental splint.
férula intranasal de Carter Carter's intranasal splint.
férula invertida de Kingsley reverse Kingsley splint.
férula de Keller-Blake Keller-Blake splint.
férula de Kingsley Kingsley splint.
férula labial labial splint.
férula de levantamiento de Kanavel Kanavel cockup splint.
férula de Levis Levis' splint.
férula de lindero abutment splint.
férula lingual lingual splint.
férula de Liston Liston's splint.
férula de marcha de Gibson Gibson's walking splint.
férula de Mason Mason's splint.
férula de Mclintire Mclintire splint.
férula de muñeca cockup splint.
férula nasal de Jones Jones nasal splint.
férula neumática air splint.
férula nocturna night splint.
férula oponente opponens splint.
férula palatina lingual splint.
férula de plástico plastic splint.
férula poroplástica poroplastic splint.
férula de Porzett Porzett splint.
férula posterior backboard splint.
férula posterior de Thomas Thomas posterior splint.
férula de protección de la mordida biteguard splint.
férula quirúrgica surgical splint.
férula de rodilla de Thomas Thomas knee splint.
férula de Roger Anderson Roger Anderson splint.
férula de Sayre Sayre's splint.
férula de Simpson Simpson's splint.
férula de sostén abutment splint.
férula de Staeder Staeder splint.
férula de stromeyer Stromeyer's splint.
férula en T T splint.
férula de Taylor Taylor's splint.
férula terapéutica therapeutic splint.

férula de thomas Thomas splint.
férula de tipo de Essig Essig-type splint.
férula de Tobruk Tobruk splint.
férula Toronto Toronto splint.
férula de trabas bracketed splint.
férula de tracción de banjo banjo traction splint.
férula de Valentine Valentine's splint.
férula vestibular labial splint.
férula viva live splint.
férula de Volkman Volkman splint.
férula de Wertheim Wertheim splint.
férula de yeso plaster splint.
ferulización *f.* splinting.
fervescencia *f.* fervescence.
festinación *f.* festination.
festinante *adj.* festinant.
festón *m.* festoon.
   festón gingival gingival festoon.
   festón de mcCall McCall festoon.
festoneado, -da *adj.* festooning.
fetal *adj.* fetal.
fetalismo *m.* fetalism.
fetalización *f.* fetalization.
fetiche *m.* fetish.
fetichismo *m.* fetishism.
   fetichismo travestido transvestic fetishism.
feticidio *m.* feticide.
fetidez *f.* mephitis.
fétido, -da *adj.* fetid.
feto *m.* fetus.
   feto acardio, feto acardíaco fetus acardius.
   feto amorfo fetus amorphus.
   feto arlequín harlequin fetus.
   feto calcificado calcified fetus.
   feto compressus fetus compressus.
   feto in fetu fetus in fetu.
   feto momificado mummified fetus.
   feto papiráceo papyraceous fetus.
   feto parásito parasitic fetus.
   feto retenido impacted fetus.
   feto sanguinolento fetus sanguinolentus.
   feto viable viable fetus.
fetoglobulina *f.* fetoglobulin.
fetología *f.* fetology.
fetometría *f.* fetometry.
fetopatía *f.* fetopathy.
   fetopatía diabética diabetic fetopathy.
fetoplacentario, -ria *adj.* fetoplacental.
fetoproteína *f.* fetoprotein.
fetor *m.* fetor.
   fetor exoris fetor exoris.
   fetor hepaticus fetor hepaticus.
   fetor oris fetor oris.
fetoscopia *f.* fetoscopy.
fetoscopio *m.* fetoscope.
fetotoxicidad *f.* fetotoxicity.
fetotóxico, -ca *adj.* fetotoxic.
fiabilidad *f.* reliability.
fial *m.* phial.
fibra *f.* fiber.
   fibra de Sharpey Sharpey's fiber.
fibremia *f.* fibremia.
fibriforme *adj.* fibroid.
fibrilación *f.* fibrillation.
   fibrilación auricular atrial fibrillation, auricular fibrillation.
   fibrilación ventricular ventricular fibrillation.
fibrilado, -da *adj.* fibrillated.
fibrilar[1] *v.* fibrillate.
fibrilar[2] *adj.* fibrillar, fibrillary.
fibrilla *f.* fibril.
fibriloblasto *m.* fibrilloblast.
fibriloflúter *m.* fibrilloflutter.

fibrilogénesis *f.* fibrillogenesis.
fibrilólisis *f.* fibrillolysis.
fibrilolítico, -ca *adj.* fibrillolytic.
fibrina *f.* fibrin.
  fibrina del estroma stroma fibrin.
fibrinemia *f.* fibrinemia.
fibrinocelular *adj.* fibrinocellular.
fibrinogenemia *f.* fibrinogenemia.
fibrinogénesis *f.* fibrinogenesis.
fibrinogénico, -ca *adj.* fibrinogenic.
fibrinógeno *m.* fibrinogen.
  fibrinógeno humano human fibrinogen.
fibrinógeno, -na *adj.* fibrinogenous.
fibrinogenólisis *f.* fibrinogenolysis.
fibrinogenolítico, -ca *adj.* fibrinogenolytic.
fibrinogenopenia *f.* fibrinogenopenia.
fibrinogenopénico, -ca *adj.* fibrinogenopenic.
fibrinoide *m. y adj.* fibrinoid.
fibrinólisis *f.* fibrinolysis.
fibrinolítico, -ca *adj.* fibrinolytic.
fibrinopenia *f.* fibrinopenia.
fibrinopéptido *m.* fibrinopeptide.
fibrinoplásico, -ca *adj.* fibrinoplastic.
fibrinoplastina *f.* fibrinoplastin.
fibrinoplasto *m.* fibrinoplastin.
fibrinopurulento, -ta *adj.* fibrinopurulent.
fibrinorrea *f.* fibrinorrhea.
fibrinoscopia *f.* fibrinoscopy.
fibrinoso, -sa *adj.* fibrinous.
fibrinuria *f.* fibrinuria.
fibroadenia *f.* fibroadenia.
fibroadenoma *m.* fibroadenoma.
  fibroadenoma gigante giant fibroadenoma.
  fibroadenoma gigante de las mamas giant fibroadenoma of the breast.
  fibroadenoma intracanalicular intracanalicular fibroadenoma.
  fibroadenoma pericanalicular pericanalicular fibroadenoma.
fibroadenosis *f.* fibroadenosis.
fibroadiposo, -sa *adj.* fibroadipose.
fibroangioma *m.* fibroangioma.
  fibroangioma nasofaríngeo nasopharyngeal fibroangioma.
fibroareolar *adj.* fibroareolar.
fibroatrofia *f.* fibroatrophy.
fibroblástico, -ca *adj.* fibroblastic.
fibroblasto *m.* fibroblast.
fibroblastoma *m.* fibroblastoma.
  fibroblastoma aracnoide meningioma.
  fibroblastoma perineural perineural fibroblastoma.
fibrobronquitis *f.* fibrobronchitis.
fibrocalcificado, -da *adj.* fibrocalcific.
fibrocarcinoma *m.* fibrocarcinoma.
fibrocartilaginoso, -sa *adj.* fibrocartalaginous.
fibrocartílago *m.* fibrocartilage.
fibrocaseoso, -sa *adj.* fibrocaseous.
fibrocelular *adj.* fibrocellular.
fibrocistoma *m.* fibrocystoma.
fibrocito *m.* fibrocyte.
fibrocitogénesis *f.* fibrocytogenesis.
fibrocolágeno, -na *adj.* fibrocollagenous.
fibrocolonoscopio *m.* fibercolonoscope.
fibrocondritis *f.* fibrochondritis.
fibrocongestivo, -va *adj.* fibrocongestive.
fibrodisplasia *f.* fibrodysplasia.
fibroelástico, -ca *adj.* fibroelastic.
fibroelastosis *f.* fibroelastosis.
  fibroelastosis endocárdica endocardial fibroelastosis.
  fibroelastosis endomiocárdica endomyocardial fibroelastosis.
fibroencondroma *m.* fibroenchondroma.
fibroepitelioma *m.* fibroepithelioma.

fibrofascitis *f.* fibrositis.
fibrofoliculoma *m.* fibrofolliculoma.
fibrogastroscopio *m.* fibergastroscope.
fibrogénesis *f.* fibrogenesis.
fibrogénico, -ca *adj.* fibrogenic.
fibroglia *f.* fibroglia.
fibroglioma *m.* fibroglioma.
fibrogliosis *f.* fibrogliosis.
fibrograso, -sa *adj.* fibrofatty.
fibrohemorrágico, -ca *adj.* fibrohemorrhagic.
fibrohistiocítico, -ca *adj.* fibrohistiocytic.
fibroide *adj.* fibroid.
fibroidectomía *f.* fibroidectomy.
fibroleiomioma *m.* fibroleiomyoma.
fibrolipoma *m.* fibrolipoma.
fibrolipomatoso, -sa *adj.* fibrolipomatous.
fibroma *m.* fibroma.
  fibroma ameloblástico ameloblastic fibroma.
  fibroma aponeurótico aponeurotic fibroma.
  fibroma blando fibroma molle.
  fibroma blando del embarazo fibroma molle gravidarum.
  fibroma cavernoso fibroma cavernosum.
  fibroma cimentante central cementifying fibroma.
  fibroma concéntrico concentric fibroma.
  fibroma condromixoide chondromyxoid fibroma.
  fibroma desmoplásico desmoplastic fibroma.
  fibroma digital recurrente de la infancia recurring digital fibroma of childhood.
  fibroma intracanalicular intracanalicular fibroma.
  fibroma mixomatodes, fibroma mixomatoide, fibroma mixomatoso fibroma myxomatodes.
  fibroma molle fibroma molle.
  fibroma nasofaríngeo juvenil juvenile nasopharyngeal fibroma.
  fibroma no osteogénico non-osteogenic fibroma.
  fibroma odontogénico, fibroma odontógeno odontogenic fibroma.
  fibroma osificante ossifying fibroma.
  fibroma osificante periférico peripheral ossifying fibroma.
  fibroma péndulo, fibroma pendulum fibroma pendulum.
  fibroma periungueal periungual fibroma.
  fibroma quístico cystic fibroma.
  fibroma sarcomatoso fibrosarcoma.
  fibroma tecocelular xantomatodes fibroma thecocellulare xanthomatodes.
  fibroma xantoma fibroxanthoma.
fibromatogénico, -ca *adj.* fibromatogenic.
fibromatoide *adj.* fibromatoid.
fibromatosis *f.* fibromatosis.
  fibromatosis abdominal abdominal fibromatosis.
  fibromatosis cervical fibromatosis colli.
  fibromatosis congénita generalizada congenital generalized fibromatosis.
  fibromatosis digital, fibromatosis digital infantil infantile digital fibromatosis.
  fibromatosis gingival gingival fibromatosis, fibromatosis gingivae.
  fibromatosis infantil digital infantile digital fibromatosis.
  fibromatosis palmar palmar fibromatosis.
  fibromatosis peniana penile fibromatosis.
  fibromatosis plantar plantar fibromatosis.
  fibromatosis subcutánea seudosarcomatosa subcutaneous pseudosarcomatous fibromatosis.

  fibromatosis ventricular fibromatosis ventriculi.
fibromatoso, -sa *adj.* fibromatous.
fibromectomía *f.* fibromectomy.
fibromembranoso, -sa *adj.* fibromembranous.
fibromiectomía *f.* fibromyectomy.
fibromiítis *f.* fibromyitis.
fibromioma *f.* fibromyoma.
fibromiomectomía *f.* fibromyomectomy.
fibromiositis *f.* fibromyositis.
  fibromiositis nodular nodular fibromyositis.
fibromiotomía *f.* fibromyotomy.
fibromixoma *m.* fibromyxoma.
fibromixosarcoma *m.* fibromyxosarcoma.
fibromuscular *adj.* fibromuscular.
fibronectina *f.* fibronectin.
  fibronectina plasmática plasma fibronectin.
fibroneuroma *m.* fibroneuroma.
fibronuclear *adj.* fibronuclear.
fibroóptica *f.* fiberoptics.
fibroóptico, -ca *adj.* fiberoptic.
fibrosteoma *m.* fibro-osteoma, fibrosteoma.
fibropapiloma *m.* fibropapilloma.
fibropericarditis *f.* fibrinous pericarditis.
fibroplasia *f.* fibroplasia.
  fibroplasia retrolenticular retrolental fibroplasia (RLF), retrolenticular fibroplasia.
fibroplástico, -ca *adj.* fibroplastic.
fibroplastina *f.* fibroplastin.
fibropólipo *m.* fibropolypus.
fibropsamoma *m.* fibropsamoma.
fibróptica *f.* fiberoptics.
fibróptico, -ca *adj.* fiberoptics.
fibropurulento, -ta *adj.* fibropurulent.
fibroqueratoma *m.* fibrokeratoma.
fibroquiste *m.* fibrocyst.
fibroquístico, -ca *adj.* fibrocystic.
fibrorreticulado, -da *adj.* fibroreticulate.
fibrosarcoma *m.* fibrosarcoma.
fibroscopio *m.* fiberscope.
fibroseroso, -sa *adj.* fibroserous.
fibrosis *f.* fibrosis.
  fibrosis endomiocárdica, fibrosis endomiocárdica africana endomyocardial fibrosis, African endomyocardial fibrosis.
  fibrosis hepática congénita congenital hepatic fibrosis.
  fibrosis del mediastino mediastinal fibrosis.
  fibrosis neoplásica proliferative fibrosis.
  fibrosis nodular subepidérmica nodular subepidermal fibrosis.
  fibrosis panmural de la vejiga panmural fibrosis of the bladder.
  fibrosis pericentral pericentral fibrosis.
  fibrosis perimuscular perimuscular fibrosis.
  fibrosis periureteral periureteric fibrosis.
  fibrosis posfibrinosa postfibrinous fibrosis.
  fibrosis proliferativa proliferative fibrosis.
  fibrosis pulmonar idiopática idiopathic pulmonary fibrosis.
  fibrosis quística, fibrosis quística del páncreas cystic fibrosis, cystic fibrosis of the pancreas.
  fibrosis retroperitoneal, fibrosis retroperitoneal idiopática retroperitoneal fibrosis, idiopathic retroperitoneal fibrosis.
  fibrosis subadventicia subadventitial fibrosis.
  fibrosis de sustitución replacement fibrosis.
fibrositis *f.* fibrositis.
fibroso, -sa *adj.* fibrous.
fibrótico, -ca *adj.* fibrotic.
fibrotórax *m.* fibrothorax.
fibrovascular *adj.* fibrovascular.
fibroxantoma *m.* fibroxanthoma.

fíbula *f.* fibula.
fibular *adj.* fibular.
fibulocalcáneo, -a *adj.* fibulocalcaneal.
ficomicetosis *f.* phycomycetosis.
ficomicetoso, -sa *adj.* phycomycetous.
ficomicosis *f.* phycomycosis.
  ficomicosis entomóftora phycomycosis entomophthorae.
  ficomicosis subcutánea subcutaneous phycomycosis.
ficosis *f.* ficosis.
fiebre *f.* fever.
  fiebre de absorción, fiebre por absorción absorption fever.
  fiebre de aclimatación acclimating fever.
  fiebre de Adén Aden fever.
  fiebre adinámica adynamic fever.
  fiebre africana por garrapatas African tick fever.
  fiebre aftosa aphthous fever.
  fiebre de aguas negras blackwater fever.
  fiebre álgida perniciosa algid pernicious fever.
  fiebre amarilla yellow fever.
  fiebre amarilla del mediterráneo Weil's disease.
  fiebre amarilla de la jungla, fiebre amarilla de las selvas jungle yellow fever.
  fiebre por arañazo de gato catscratch fever.
  fiebre argentina hemorrágica Argentine hemorrhagic fever, Argentinian hemorrhagic fever.
  fiebre de los arrozales rice-field fever.
  fiebre artificial artificial fever.
  fiebre aséptica aseptic fever.
  fiebre de assam Assam fever.
  fiebre asténica asthenic fever.
  fiebre australiana Q Australian Q fever.
  fiebre azul blue fever.
  fiebre biliosa hematúrica hemoglobinuric fever.
  fiebre biliosa perniciosa yellow fever.
  fiebre blanca chlorosis.
  fiebre botonosa boutonneuse fever.
  fiebre de Bullis Bullis fever.
  fiebre Bwamba Bwamba fever.
  fiebre cacoquímica hectic fever.
  fiebre de los campamentos, fiebre castrense camp fever.
  fiebre de los campos field fever.
  fiebre de los campos de arroz rice-field fever.
  fiebre de los campos de azúcar cane-field fever.
  fiebre canícola canicola fever.
  fiebre caquéctica cachectic fever, cachexial fever.
  fiebre de las cárceles prison fever.
  fiebre catarral epidémica influenza fever.
  fiebre central central fever.
  fiebre cerebral cerebrospinal fever.
  fiebre cerebroespinal cerebrospinal fever.
  fiebre de Chagres Chagres fever.
  fiebre de Charcot Charcot's fever.
  fiebre de Chipre Cyprus fever.
  fiebre de chitral pappataci fever.
  fiebre del cieno slime fever.
  fiebre del cinc zinc fever.
  fiebre de los cinco días five-day fever.
  fiebre colicuativa hectic fever.
  fiebre colombiana por garrapata Colombian tick fever.
  fiebre de los conejos rabbit fever.
  fiebre consecutiva hectic fever.
  fiebre contagiosa de los barcos ship fever.
  fiebre continua continuous fever.

  fiebre continuada continued fever.
  fiebre cotidiana quotidian fever.
  fiebre crónica intermittent fever.
  fiebre cuadrilátera Q fever.
  fiebre cuartana quartan fever.
  fiebre cuartana doble double quartan fever.
  fiebre dandy dandy fever.
  fiebre dengue dengue fever.
  fiebre por deshidratación dehydration fever.
  fiebre del desierto desert fever.
  fiebre digestiva digestive fever.
  fiebre disociada de Jaccoud Jaccoud's dissociated fever.
  fiebre Dumdum Dumdum fever.
  fiebre efímera ephemeral fever.
  fiebre elefantoidea elephantoid fever.
  fiebre entérica, fiebre entericoide enteric fever, entericoid fever.
  fiebre eruptiva eruptive fever.
  fiebre eruptiva eruptive fever.
  fiebre por espirilos spirillum fever.
  fiebre esplénica splenic fever.
  fiebre estival de tres días three-day fever.
  fiebre exantemática exanthematous fever.
  fiebre exantemática brasileña Brazilian spotted fever.
  fiebre exantemática del mediterráneo Mediterranean fever.
  fiebre exantemática de las montañas rocosas Rocky Mountain spotted fever.
  fiebre de fatiga, fiebre por fatiga fatigue fever.
  fiebre faringoconjuntival pharyngoconjunctival fever.
  fiebre flava yellow fever.
  fiebre flebotoma, fiebre por flebotomos phlebotomus fever.
  fiebre fluvial japonesa Japanese flood fever, Japanese river fever.
  fiebre de fractura traumatic fever.
  fiebre de Fuerte Bragg Fort Bragg fever.
  fiebre de los fundidores brass founders' fever.
  fiebre de las garrapatas, fiebre por garrapatas tick fever.
  fiebre gástrica yellow fever.
  fiebre de Gibraltar Gibraltar fever.
  fiebre por hambre famine fever.
  fiebre de Hankow Hankow fever.
  fiebre de Hasami Hasami fever.
  fiebre héctica hectic fever.
  fiebre hemoglobinúrica hemoglobinuric fever.
  fiebre hemorrágica, fiebre hemorrágica aguda epidémica hemorrhagic fever.
  fiebre hemorrágica dengue dengue hemorrhagic fever.
  fiebre hemorrágica epidémica epidemic hemorrhagic fever.
  fiebre hemorrágica vírica viral hemorrhagic fever.
  fiebre del heno hay fever.
  fiebre hepática intermitente intermittent hepatic fever.
  fiebre herpética herpetic fever.
  fiebre de los hospitales hospital fever.
  fiebre de los humos de metales, fiebre de los humos metálicos metal fume fever.
  fiebre ictérica, fiebre icterohemorrágica Weil's disease.
  fiebre de inanición inanition fever.
  fiebre de inundación inundation fever.
  fiebre intermenstrual intermenstrual fever.
  fiebre intermitente intermittent fever.
  fiebre de las inundaciones inundation fever.

  fiebre japonesa de los siete días nanukayami fever.
  fiebre de Junín Junin fever.
  fiebre de Katayama Katayama fever.
  fiebre de Korin Korin fever.
  fiebre láctea, fiebre láctica milk fever.
  fiebre de Lassa Lassa fever.
  fiebre lenta hectic fever.
  fiebre de las letrinas cesspool fever.
  fiebre del lodo mud fever.
  fiebre malárica malarial fever.
  fiebre de Malta Malta fever.
  fiebre de Manchuria Manchurian fever.
  fiebre de Marsella Marseille fever.
  fiebre medicamentosa drug fever.
  fiebre mediterránea familiar familial Mediterranean fever.
  fiebre del Mediterráneo Mediterranean fever.
  fiebre de las montañas rocosas Rocky Mountain spotted fever.
  fiebre por mordedura de gato cat-bite fever.
  fiebre por mordedura de rata rat-bite fever.
  fiebre de Mossman Mossman fever.
  fiebre de Murchinson-Pel-Ebstein Murchinson-Pel-Ebstein fever.
  fiebre nanukayami nanukayami fever.
  fiebre napolitana Malta fever.
  fiebre negra black fever.
  fiebre nodular erythema nodosum.
  fiebre de las nueve millas ninemile fever.
  fiebre ondulante undulant fever.
  fiebre de o'nyong-nyong o'nyong-nyong fever.
  fiebre de origen desconocido (FOD) fever of unknown origin (FUO).
  fiebre ortigosa urticaria.
  fiebre de Oroya Oroya fever.
  fiebre oscilante undulant fever.
  fiebre otoñal autumn fever.
  fiebre palúdica paludal fever.
  fiebre de los pantanos swamp fever.
  fiebre de Panamá Chagres fever.
  fiebre papataci pappataci fever.
  fiebre paratifoidea paratyphoid fever.
  fiebre parenteral parenteric fever.
  fiebre de las parturientas parturient fever.
  fiebre de Pel-Ebstein Pel-Ebstein fever.
  fiebre periódica periodic fever.
  fiebre perniciosa malarial fever.
  fiebre petequial petechial fever.
  fiebre de Pfeiffer Pfeiffer's glandular fever.
  fiebre de pinta pinta fever.
  fiebre pitogénica typhoid fever.
  fiebre poliléptica polyleptic fever.
  fiebre de Pomona Pomona fever.
  fiebre pretibial pretibial fever.
  fiebre de las prisiones prison fever.
  fiebre de proteínas, fiebre por proteínas protein fever.
  fiebre puerperal puerperal fever.
  fiebre pulmonar pulmonary fever.
  fiebre purpúrea de Brasil Brazilian purpuric fever.
  fiebre Q Q fever.
  fiebre de Queensland Q fever.
  fiebre quintana quintan fever.
  fiebre recidivante relapsing fever.
  fiebre recurrente recurrent fever.
  fiebre recurrente de Dutton Dutton's relapsing fever.
  fiebre remitente remittent fever.
  fiebre roja del Congo Congolian red fever.
  fiebre rompehuesos dengue fever.
  fiebre de rose rose fever.

figura 624

fiebre por sal salt fever.
fiebre de San Joaquín San Joaquin fever.
fiebre de schee trench fever.
fiebre de Schottmüller Schottmüller fever.
fiebre de las selvas jungle fever.
fiebre séptica septic fever.
fiebre de los siete días seven-day fever.
fiebre sifilítica syphilitic fever.
fiebre Sindbis Sindbis fever.
fiebre solar dengue fever.
fiebre de Songo Songo fever.
fiebre sudafricana por garrapatas South African tickbite fever.
fiebre supurativa suppurative fever.
fiebre telúrica malaria.
fiebre terciana tertian fever.
fiebre térmica thermic fever.
fiebre tibiálgica trench fever.
fiebre tifoidea typhoid fever.
fiebre de Tobia Tobia fever.
fiebre traumática traumatic fever.
fiebre de los tres días three-day fever.
fiebre de las trincheras trench fever.
fiebre tsutsugamushi tsutsugamushi fever.
fiebre de un día ephemeral fever.
fiebre uretral urethral fever.
fiebre urinaria, fiebre urinosa urinary fever.
fiebre uveoparotídea uveoparotid fever.
figura *f.* figure.
figura de fortificación fortification figure.
figura en llama flame figure.
figura mitótica mitotic figure.
figura de Purkinje Purkinje's figure.
figura de Stifel Stifel's figure.
figura de Zöllner Zöllner's figure.
fijación *f.* fixation.
fijación de alexina complement fixation.
fijación autotrófica autotrophic fixation.
fijación por banda elástica elastic band fixation.
fijación bifoveal bifoveal fixation.
fijación binocular binocular fixation.
fijación circunalveolar circumalveolar fixation.
fijación circunmandibular circummandibular fixation.
fijación del complemento complement fixation.
fijación craneofacial craneofacial fixation.
fijación cruzada crossed fixation.
fijación del diente tooth fixation.
fijación del dióxido de carbono carbon dioxide fixation.
fijación esquelética skeletal fixation.
fijación externa external fixation.
fijación externa por clavos external pin fixation.
fijación intermaxilar intermaxillary fixation.
fijación interna internal fixation.
fijación intraósea intraosseous fixation.
fijación mandibulomaxilar mandibulomaxillary fixation.
fijación maxilomandibular maxilomandibular fixation.
fijación de nitrógeno nitrogen fixation.
fijado, -da *adj.* bound.
fijador *m.* fixative.
fijador, -ra *adj.* fixative.
filacagogo, -ga *adj.* phylacagogic.
filáceo, -a *adj.* filaceous.
filáctico, -ca *adj.* phylactic.
filactotransfusión *f.* phylactotransfusion.
filagrina *f.* filaggrin.
filagripnia *f.* phylagrypnia.
filamen *m.* filamen.

filamento *m.* filament, filamentum.
filamento de Billroth Billroth's filament.
filamento de citoqueratina cytokeratin filament.
filamento espermático spermatic filament.
filamento intermedio intermediate filament.
filamento lateral del esmalte lateral enamel filament.
filamento linfático de anclaje lymphatic anchoring filament.
filamento de miosina myosin filament.
filamento polar polar injecting filament.
filamento de queratina keratin filament.
filamento Z Z filament.
filamentoso, -sa *adj.* filamentous.
filamentum *m.* filament, filamentum.
filar *adj.* filar.
Filaria Filaria.
filarial *adj.* filarial.
filariasis *m.* filariasis.
filariasis de Bancroft, filariasis brancrofti, filariasis bancroftiana Bancroftian filariasis, filariasis bancrofti.
filariasis de Brug Brug's filariasis, Brugian filariasis.
filariasis malaya Malayan filariasis, filariasis malayi.
filariasis oculta occult filariasis.
filariasis de Ozzard Ozzard's filariasis.
filaricida¹ *m.* filaricide.
filaricida² *adj.* filaricidal.
filariforme *adj.* filariform.
Filarioidea Filarioidea. .
filariosis *m.* filariasis.
filaxis *f.* phylaxis.
filaxiología *f.* phylaxiology.
filete *m.* fillet.
filético, -ca *adj.* phyletic.
filiación *f.* filiation.
filial *adj.* filial.
filiforme *adj.* filiform.
filipunción *f.* filipuncture.
filogenia *f.* phylogeny.
filogénesis *f.* phylogenesis.
filogenético, -ca *adj.* phylogenetic.
filogenia *f.* phylogeny.
filogénico, -ca *adj.* phylogenic.
filoide *adj.* phyllode.
filoideo, -a *adj.* phyllode.
filopresión *f.* filopressure.
filovaricosis *f.* filovaricosis.
filtrable *adj.* filtrable, filterable.
filtración *f.* filtration.
filtración en gel gel filtration.
filtrado *m.* filtrate.
filtrar *v.* filter.
filtro *m.* filter.
filum filum.
fima *m.* phyma.
fimatología *f.* phymatology.
fimatorrisina *f.* phymatorrhysin.
fimbria *f.* fimbria.
fimbriación *f.* fimbriation.
fimbriado, -da *adj.* fimbriate, fimbriated.
fimbriectomía *f.* fimbriectomy.
fimbriocele *m.* fimbriocele.
fimbroplastia *f.* fimbrioplasty.
fimosiectomía *m.* phymosiectomy.
fimosis *f.* phimosis.
fimótico, -ca *adj.* phimotic.
fisalífero, -ra *adj.* physaliferous, physaliphore.
fisaliforme *adj.* physaliform.
fisalíforo, -ra *adj.* physaliphore.
fisalis *f.* physalis.
fisalización *f.* physalization.

fisalopteriasis *f.* physalopteriasis.
fisario, -ria *adj.* physeal.
fiseal *adj.* physeal.
fisiatra *m., f.* physiatrist.
fisiatría *f.* physiatrics.
física *f.* physics.
físico, -ca *adj.* physical.
fisicogénico, -ca *adj.* physicogenic.
fisicógeno, -na *adj.* physicogenic.
fisicoquímico, -ca *adj.* physicochemical.
fisiocracia *f.* physiocracy.
fisiofilia *f.* physiophyly.
fisiogénesis *f.* physiogenesis.
fisiogenia *f.* physiogenesis.
fisiogénico, -ca *adj.* physiogenic.
fisiognomía *f.* physiognosis.
fisiognómica *f.* physiognosis.
fisiognosis *f.* physiognosis.
fisiólisis *f.* physiolysis.
fisiología *f.* physiology.
fisiología animal animal physiology.
fisiología celular cellular physiology.
fisiología comparada comparative physiology.
fisiología dental dental physiology.
fisiología especial special physiology.
fisiología evolutiva developmental physiology.
fisiología experimental experimental physiology.
fisiología general general physiology.
fisiología humana human physiology.
fisiología mórbida morbid physiology.
fisiología patológica pathologic physiology.
fisiología perinatal perinatal physiology.
fisiológico, -ca *adj.* physiologic, physiological.
fisiologicoanatómico, -ca *adj.* physiologicoanatomical.
fisiólogo, -ga *m., f.* physiologist.
fisiometría *f.* physiometry.
fisión *f.* fission.
fisión atómica nuclear fission.
fisión binaria binary fission.
fisión celular cellular fission.
fisión múltiple multiple fission.
fisión nuclear nuclear fission.
fisonomía *f.* physiognomy.
fisiopatología *f.* physiopathology.
fisiopatológico, -ca *adj.* physiopathologic.
fisiopirexia *f.* physiopyrexia.
fisioquímica *f.* physiochemistry.
fisioquímico, -ca *adj.* physiochemical.
fisioterapeuta *m., f.* physiotherapeutist, physiotherapist.
fisioterapéutico, -ca *adj.* physiotherapeutic.
fisioterapia *f.* physiotherapy.
fisis *f.* physis.
fisocefalia *f.* physocephaly.
fisocele *m.* physocele.
fisohematometra *f.* physohematometra.
fisohidrómetra *f.* physohydrometra.
fisómetra *m.* physometra.
fisonomía *f.* physiognomy.
fisopiosálpinx *m.* physopyosalpinx.
fisostigmina *f.* physostigmine.
fisostigminismo *m.* physostigminism.
fístula *f.* fistula.
fístula abdominal abdominal fistula.
fístula alveolar dental fistula.
fístula anal, fístula del ano anal fistula, fistula in ano.
fístula arterial coronaria coronary artery fistula.
fístula arteriovenosa arteriovenous fistula.

fístula arteriovenosa coronaria coronary arteriovenous fistula.
fístula arteriovenosa pulmonar congénita congenital pulmonary arteriovenous fistula.
fístula biliar biliary fistula.
fístula bimucosa fistula bimucosa.
fístula branquial branchial fistula.
fístula broncoesofágica bronchoesophageal fistula.
fístula broncopleural bronchopleural fistula.
fístula carotídea cavernosa carotid-cavernous fistula.
fístula cervical cervical fistula.
fístula cervicovaginal, fístula cervicovaginal laqueática fistula cervicovaginalis laqueatica.
fístula ciega blind fistula.
fístula coccígea coccygeal fistula.
fístula colecistoduodenal cholecystoduodenal fistula.
fístula cólica, fístula colónica colonic fistula.
fístula coloileal coloileal fistula.
fístula colovaginal colovaginal fistula.
fístula colovesical colovesical fistula.
fístula completa complete fistula.
fístula congénita cervical branchial fistula.
fístula corneal fistula corneae.
fístula craniosinus craniosinus fistula.
fístula dental, fístula dentaria dental fistula.
fístula de Eck Eck's fistula.
fístula de Eck invertida Eck's fistula in reverse.
fístula enterocutánea enterocutaneous fistula.
fístula enterovaginal enterovaginal fistula.
fístula enterovesical enterovesical fistula.
fístula espermática spermatic fistula.
fístula estercorácea stercoral fistula.
fístula externa external fistula.
fístula faríngea pharyngeal fistula.
fístula fecal fecal fistula.
fístula gástrica gastric fistula.
fístula gastrocólica, fístula gastrocolónica gastrocolic fistula.
fístula gastroduodenal gastroduodenal fistula.
fístula gastrointestinal gastrointestinal fistula.
fístula genitourinaria genitourinary fistula.
fístula gingival gingival fistula.
fístula hepática hepatic fistula.
fístula en herradura horseshoe fistula.
fístula histeroperitoneal metroperitoneal fistula.
fístula incompleta incomplete fistula.
fístula interna internal fistula.
fístula intestinal intestinal fistula.
fístula lacrimal, fístula lagrimal lacrimal fistula.
fístula láctea lacteal fistula.
fístula linfática lymphatic fistula, fistula lymphatica.
fístula de Mann-Bollman Mann-Bollman fistula.
fístula onfaloentérica umbilical fistula.
fístula oroantral oroantral fistula.
fístula orofacial orofacial fistula.
fístula oronasal oronasal fistula.
fístula parietal parietal fistula.
fístula perineovaginal perineovaginal fistula.
fístula pilonidal pilonidal fistula.
fístula preauricular congénita congenital preauricular fistula.
fístula pulmonar pulmonary fistula.

fístula rectolabial rectolabial fistula.
fístula rectouretral rectourethral fistula.
fístula rectovaginal rectovaginal fistula.
fístula rectovesical rectovesical fistula.
fístula rectovestibular rectovestibular fistula.
fístula rectovulvar rectovulvar fistula.
fístula sacrococcígea pilonidal fistula.
fístula salival salivary fistula.
fístula submentoniana submental fistula.
fístula de Thiry Thiry's fistula.
fístula de Thiry-Vella Thiry-Vella fistula.
fístula torácica thoracic fistula.
fístula traqueal tracheal fistula.
fístula traqueoesofágica tracheoesophageal fistula.
fístula umbilical umbilical fistula.
fístula umbilicourinaria urachal fistula.
fístula uracal, fístula del uraco urachal fistula.
fístula ureterocutánea ureterocutaneous fistula.
fístula ureterovaginal ureterovaginal fistula.
fístula urinaria urinary fistula.
fístula urogenital urogenital fistula.
fístula uteroperitoneal uteroperitoneal fistula.
fístula vesical vesical fistula.
fístula vesicocólica, fístula vesicolónica vesicocolic fistula.
fístula vesicocutánea vesicocutaneous fistula.
fístula vesicointestinal vesicointestinal fistula.
fístula vesicouterina vesicouterine fistula.
fístula vesicovaginal vesicovaginal fistula.
fístula vitelina vitelline fistula.
fistulátomo *m.* fistulatome.
fistulectomía *f.* fistulectomy.
fistulización *f.* fistulization.
fistuloenterostomía *f.* fistuloenterostomy.
fistuloso, -sa *adj.* fistulous.
fistulotomía *f.* fistulotomy.
fistulótomo *m.* fistulatome.
fisura *f.* fissure, fissura.
fisura de ammon Ammon's fissure.
fisura anal, fisura del ano, fisura in ano anal fissure.
fisuración *f.* fissuration.
fisural *adj.* fissural.
fitoalopecia *f.* trichophytosis.
fitobezoar *m.* phytobezoar.
fitofodermatitis *f.* phytophotodermatitis.
fitofotodermatitis *f.* phytophotodermatitis.
fitoflictodermatitis *f.* phytophlyctodermatitis.
fitohemaglutinina *f.* phytohemagglutinin.
fitoide *adj.* phytoid.
fitonosis *f.* phytonosis.
fitoparásito *m.* phytoparasite.
fitopatía *f.* phytopathy.
fitosis *f.* phytosis.
fitoterapia *f.* phytotherapy.
flabelo *m.* flabellum.
fláccido, -da *adj.* flaccid.
flácido, -da *adj.* flaccid.
flagelación *f.* flagellation.
flagelado, -da *adj.* flagellate, flagellated.
flagelar *adj.* flagellar.
flageliforme *adj.* flagelliform.
flagelo *m.* flagellum.
flagelosis *f.* flagellosis.
flamear *v.* flame.
flanco *m.* flank.
flato *m.* flatus.

flatulencia *f.* flatulence.
flatulento, -ta *adj.* flatulent.
flavectomía *f.* flavectomy.
flavedo *m.* flavedo.
flavescente *adj.* flavescent.
flavismo *m.* flavism.
Flavivirus Flavivirus.
Flavobacterium Flavobacterium.
flavoproteína *f.* flavoprotein.
flebalgia *f.* phlebalgia.
flebanestesia *f.* phlebanesthesia.
flebangioma *m.* phlebangioma.
flebarteriectasia *f.* phlebarteriectasia.
flebastenia *f.* phlebasthenia.
flebectasia *f.* phlebectasia.
flebectasis *f.* phlebectasis.
flebectomía *f.* phlebectomy, strip.
flebectopia *f.* phlebectopia, phlebectopy.
flebenfraxis *f.* phlebemphraxis.
flebepatitis *f.* phlebepatitis.
flebeurismo *m.* phlebeurysm.
flebexairesis *f.* phlebexairesis.
flebismo *m.* phlebismus.
flebítico, -ca *adj.* phlebitic.
flebitis *f.* phlebitis.
flebitis adhesiva adhesive phlebitis.
flebitis anémica anemic phlebitis.
flebitis azul blue phlebitis.
flebitis clorótica chlorotic phlebitis.
flebitis esclerosante sclerosing phlebitis.
flebitis gotosa gouty phlebitis.
flebitis migratoria migrating phlebitis, phlebitis migrans.
flebitis necrótica phlebitis nodularis necrotisans.
flebitis nodular, flebitis nodular necrosante phlebitis nodularis necrotisans.
flebitis obliterante, flebitis obliterativa obliterating phlebitis.
flebitis obstructiva obstructive phlebitis.
flebitis plástica plastic phlebitis.
flebitis productiva productive phlebitis.
flebitis proliferativa proliferative phlebitis.
flebitis puerperal puerperal phlebitis.
flebitis séptica septic phlebitis.
flebitis sinusal sinus phlebitis.
flebitis supurativa suppurative phlebitis.
fleboanestesia *f.* phlebanesthesia.
fleboclisis *f.* phleboclysis.
fleboclisis gota a gota, fleboclisis por goteo drip phleboclysis.
fleboclisis lenta slow phleboclysis.
flebodinamia *f.* phlebodynamics.
fleboesclerosis *f.* phlebosclerosis.
fleboestenosis *f.* phlebostenosis.
fleboestrepsis *f.* phleboestrepsis.
flebofibrosis *f.* phlebofibrosis.
fleboflebostomía *f.* phlebophlebostomy.
fleboftalmotomía *f.* phlebophthalmotomy.
flebógeno, -na *adj.* phlebogenous.
flebografía *f.* phlebography.
flebógrafo *m.* phlebograph.
flebograma *m.* phlebogram.
fleboide *adj.* phleboid.
flebolitiasis *f.* phlebolithiasis.
flebolito *m.* phlebolith.
flebología *f.* phlebology.
flebomanómetro *m.* phlebomanometer.
flebometritis *f.* phlebometritis.
flebomiomatosis *f.* phlebomyomatosis.
flebonarcosis *f.* phlebonarcosis.
flebopexia *f.* phlebopexy.
flebopiezometría *f.* phlebopiezometry.
fleboplastia *f.* phleboplasty.
fleborrafia *f.* phleborrhaphy.

fleborragia *f.* phleborrhagia.
fleborrexis *f.* phleborrhexis.
flebosclerosis *f.* phlebosclerosis.
flebosis *f.* phlebosis.
flebostasia, *f.* phlebostasis.
flebostasis *f.* phlebostasis.
flebostenosis *f.* phlebostenosis.
flebotomía *f.* phlebotomy.
flebotomista *m., f.* phlebotomist.
flebotomizar *v.* phlebotomize.
flebótomo *m.* phlebotome.
flebotrombosis *f.* phlebothrombosis.
flegmasía *f.* phlegmasia.
  flegmasía alba dolens phlegmasia alba dolens.
  flegmasía celulítica cellulitic phlegmasia.
  flegmasía cerulea dolens phlegmasia cerulea dolens.
  flegmasía trombótica thrombotic phlegmasia.
flema *f.* phlegm.
flemón *m.* phlegmon.
  flemón difuso diffuse phlegmon.
  flemón enfisematoso emphysematous phlegmon.
  flemón gaseoso gas phlegmon.
  flemón pancreático pancreatic phlegmon.
flemonosis *f.* phlegmonosis.
flemonoso, -sa *adj.* phlegmonous.
flemoso, -sa *adj.* phlegmonous.
fletcherismo *m.* fletcherism.
flexibilidad *f.* flexibility.
flexible *adj.* flexible.
flexímetro *m.* fleximeter.
flexión¹ *f.* flexion.
flexión² *f.* flexure, flexura.
  flexión cefálica cephalic flexure.
  flexión cerebral cerebral flexure.
  flexión craneal cranial flexure.
  flexión mesencefálica mesencephalic flexure.
flexionar *v.* flex.
flexoplastia *f.* flexoplasty.
flexor, -ra *adj.* flexor.
flexura *f.* flexura.
flexural *adj.* flexural.
flictena *f.* phlyctena.
flictenar *adj.* phlyctenar.
flictenoide *adj.* phlyctenoid.
flictenosis *f.* phlyctenosis.
flictenoso, -sa *adj.* phlyctenous.
flictenoterapia *f.* phlyctenotherapy.
flicténula *f.* phlyctenule.
flictenular *adj.* phlyctenular.
flictenulosis *f.* phlyctenulosis.
floc *m.* floc.
flocculus *m.* flocculus.
flocoso, -sa *adj.* floccose.
floculable *adj.* flocculable.
floculación *f.* flocculation.
flocular¹ *v.* flocculate.
flocular² *adj.* flocular.
floculencia *f.* flocculence.
floculento, -ta *adj.* flocculent.
flóculo *m.* flocculus.
  flóculo accesorio accessory flocculus.
  flóculo secundario accessory flocculus.
floculorreacción *f.* flocculoreaction.
flogístico, -ca *adj.* phlogistic.
flogisticozimoide *f.* phlogisticozymoid.
flogocito *m.* phlogocyte.
flogocitosis *f.* phlogocytosis.
flogogénico, -ca *adj.* phlogogenic.
flogósico, -ca *adj.* phlogotic.
flogosis *f.* phlogosis.

flogoterapia *f.* phlogotherapy.
flora *f.* flora.
  flora intestinal intestinal flora.
florescencia *f.* bloom.
florido, -da *adj.* florid.
flotación *f.* flotation.
floxina *f.* phloxine.
flucrilato *m.* flucrylate.
fluctuación *f.* fluctuation.
fluctuante *adj.* fluctuant.
fluente *adj.* fluent.
fluidez *f.* fluidity.
fluidificar *v.* thin.
fluido *m.* fluid.
flujo¹ *m.* flow.
  flujo axoplasmático axoplasmic flow.
  flujo espiratorio forzado forced expiratory flow (FEF).
  flujo espiratorio máximo peak expiratory flow.
  flujo genético gene flow.
  flujo plasmático renal (RPF) renal plasma flow (RPF).
  flujo plasmático renal efectivo (ERPF) effective renal plasma (ERPF).
  flujo retrógrado retrograde flow.
  flujo sanguíneo cerebral local (FSCL) local cerebral blood flow (LCBF).
  flujo sanguíneo renal total (FSRT) total renal blood flow (TRBF).
flujo² *m.* flux.
  flujo albino diarrhea.
  flujo blanco leukorrhea.
  flujo catamenial menstruation.
  flujo celíaco celiac flux.
  flujo iónico ionic flux.
  flujo luminoso luminous flux.
  flujo menstrual menstrual flux.
  flujo newtoniano newtonian flux.
  flujo vaginal vaginal discharge.
flujómetro *m.* flowmeter.
flumina pilorum flumina pilorum.
fluor albus leukorrhea.
fluoración *f.* fluoridation.
fluoresceína *f.* fluorescein.
fluoresceinuria *f.* fluoresceinuria.
fluorescencia *f.* fluorescence.
fluorescente *adj.* fluorescent.
fluoridización *f.* fluoridization.
fluorimetría *f.* fluorimetry.
fluorocito *m.* fluorocyte.
fluorocromación *f.* fluorochroming.
fluorocromo *m.* fluorochrome.
fluorofotometría *f.* fluorometry.
fluorografía *f.* fluorography.
fluoroinmunoensayo *m.* fluoroimmunoassay.
fluorometría *f.* fluorometry.
fluorómetro *m.* fluorometer.
fluoronefelómetro *m.* fluoronephelometer.
fluororradiografía *f.* fluororoentgenography.
fluoroscopia *f.* fluoroscopy.
fluoroscópico, -ca *adj.* fluoroscopic.
fluoroscopio *m.* fluoroscope.
  fluoroscopio biplano biplane fluoroscope.
fluorosis *f.* fluorosis.
  fluorosis dental dental fluorosis.
  fluorosis endémica crónica chronic endemic fluorosis.
fluorroentgenografía *f.* fluororoentgenography.
flúter *m.* flutter.
  flúter auricular atrial flutter.
  flúter diafragmático diaphragmatic flutter.
  flúter impuro impure flutter.

  flúter mediastínico mediastinal flutter.
  flúter puro pure flutter.
  flúter ventricular ventricular flutter (VFI).
fluxión *f.* fluxion.
fobia *f.* phobia.
fóbico, -ca *adj.* phobic.
fobodipsia *f.* hydrophobia.
focal *adj.* focal.
foco *m.* focus.
  foco aplanático aplanatic focus.
  foco de Assmann Assmann focus.
  foco conjugado conjugate focus.
  foco epileptógeno epileptogenic focus.
  foco de Gohn Gohn's focus.
  foco natural de infección natural focus of infection.
  foco principal principal focus.
  foco real real focus.
  foco de Simon Simon focus.
  foco virtual virtual focus.
focomelia *f.* phocomelia.
focomelo *m.* phocomelus.
focómetro *m.* focimeter.
folicular *adj.* follicular.
foliculitis *f.* folliculitis.
  foliculitis abscedens et suffodiens folliculitis abscedens et suffodiens.
  foliculitis agminada agminate folliculitis.
  foliculitis de la barba folliculitis barbae.
  foliculitis blenorrágica folliculitis gonorrheica.
  foliculitis decalvante folliculitis decalvans.
  foliculitis externa folliculitis externa.
  foliculitis gonorreica folliculitis gonorrheica.
  foliculitis gramnegativa gram-negative folliculitis.
  foliculitis interna folliculitis interna.
  foliculitis perforante perforating folliculitis.
  foliculitis perforante de la nariz folliculitis nares perforans.
  foliculitis pustulosa eosinofílica eosinophilic pustular folliculitis.
  foliculitis queloide keloidal folliculitis, folliculitis keloidalis.
  foliculitis uleritematosa reticulada folliculitis ulerythematosa reticulata.
  foliculitis varioliformis folliculitis varioliformis.
folículo *m.* follicle.
foliculoma *m.* folliculoma.
  foliculoma lipoídico lipidic folliculoma.
foliculosis *f.* fulliculosis.
folitropina *f.* follitropin.
fomentación *f.* fomentation.
fomite *f.* fomite.
fonación *f.* phonation.
fonacoscopia *f.* phonacoscopy.
fonacoscopio *m.* phonacoscope.
fonastenia *f.* phonasthenia.
fonatorio, -ria *adj.* phonatory.
fonautógrafo *m.* phonautograph.
fondo *m.* fundus.
  fondo albinótico albinotic fundus.
  fondo albipunctatus fundus albipunctatus.
  fondo del conducto auditivo interno fundus of internal acoustic meatus.
  fondo diabético fundus diabeticus.
  fondo de estómago fundus of stomach, fundus gastricus.
  fondo flavimaculatus fundus flavimaculatus.
  fondo en leopardo leopard fundus.
  fondo del meato auditivo interno fundus meatus acustici interni.
  fondo en mosaico tesellated fundus.
  fondo de ojo fundus oculi.

fondo de saco cul de sac.
fondo teselado tesselated fundus.
fondo tigroide tigroid fundus, fundus tigre.
fondo timpánico fundus tympani.
fondo uterino, fondo del útero fundus of the uterus, fundus uteri.
fondo de la vagina fundus of the vagina, fundus vaginae.
fondo vesical, fondo de la vejiga urinaria fundus of the urinary bladder, fundus vesicae urinariae.
fonendoscopio *m.* phonendoscope.
fonendosquiascopio *m.* phonendoskiascope.
foniatra *m., f.* phoniatrician.
foniatría *f.* phoniatrics.
fónico, -ca *adj.* phonic.
fonismo *m.* phonism.
fonoangiografía *f.* phonoangiography.
fonoarteriografía *f.* phonarteriography.
fonoarteriográfico, -ca *adj.* phonarteriographic.
fonoarteriograma *m.* phonarteriogram.
fonoauscultación *f.* phonoauscultation.
fonocardiografía *f.* phonocardiography.
fonocardiográfico, -ca *adj.* phonocardiographic.
fonocardiógrafo *m.* phonocardioagraph.
fonocardiograma *m.* phonocardiogram.
fonocatéter *m.* phonocatheter.
fonocateterismo *m.* phonocatheterization.
fonocateterismo intracardiaco intracardiac phonocatheterization.
fonoelectrocardioscopio *m.* phonoelectrocardioscope.
fonoestetógrafo *m.* phonostethograph.
fonofobia *f.* phonophobia.
tonóforo *m.* phonophore.
fonofotografía *f.* phonophotography.
fonógrafo *m.* phonograph.
fonograma *m.* phonogram.
fonomanía *f.* phonomania.
fonómetro *m.* phonometer.
fonomioclonía *f.* phonomyoclonus.
fonomioclono *m.* phonomyoclonus.
fonomiografía *f.* phonomyography.
fonopatía *f.* phonopathy.
fonopsia *f.* phonopsia.
fonorreceptor *m.* phonoreceptor.
fonorrenograma *m.* phonorenogram.
fonoscopia *f.* phonoscopy.
fonoscopio *m.* phonoscope.
fonoselectoscopio *m.* phonoselectoscope.
fonostetógrafo *m.* phonostethograph.
fontactoscopio *m.* phontactoscope.
fontanela *f.* fontanel.
fontículo *m.* fonticulus.
foración *f.* foration.
forage *m.* forage.
foramen *m.* foramen.
foraminífero, -ra *adj.* foraminiferous, foraminiferal.
foraminotomía *f.* foraminotomy.
fórceps *m.* forceps.
  fórceps aligátor alligator forceps.
  fórceps de Allis Allis forceps.
  fórceps alto high forceps.
  fórceps de Asch Asch forceps.
  fórceps de Bailey-Williamson Bailey-Williamson forceps.
  fórceps bajo low forceps.
  fórceps de Barton Barton forceps.
  fórceps de DeLee DeLee forceps.
  fórceps dental dental forceps.
  fórceps de Elliot Elliot forceps.
  fórceps de Garrison Garrison's forceps.

  fórceps de Hawks-Dennen Hawks-Dennen forceps.
  fórceps de Kielland Kielland's forceps.
  fórceps de Kjelland Kjelland's forceps.
  fórceps de Kocher Kocher forceps.
  fórceps de Koeberlé Koeberlé forceps.
  fórceps de Levret Levret's forceps.
  fórceps de Luikart Luikart forceps.
  fórceps obstétrico obstetrical forceps.
  fórceps de Piper Piper forceps.
  fórceps de salida outlet forceps.
  fórceps de Simpson Simpson's forceps.
  fórceps de Tarnier Tarnier's forceps.
  fórceps de tracción axial axis-traction forceps.
  fórceps de Tucker-McLean Tucker-McLean forceps.
  fórceps de Walsham Walsham's forceps.
  fórceps de Willett Willett forceps.
forcipresión *f.* forcipressure.
forense[1] *m., f.* forensic scientist.
forense *adj.* forensic.
foriascopio *m.* phoriascope.
forma *f.* form.
forma accolée accollé form, forme accolée.
forma de anillo ring form.
forma appliquée appliqué form, forme appliquée.
forma de arco, forma arqueada arch form.
forma de bote boat form.
forma cérea wax form.
forma de contorno outline form.
forma dental tooth form.
forma de diente posterior posterior tooth form.
forma de extensión extension form.
forma facial face form.
forma frustrada forme frustre.
forma de involución involution form.
forma joven, forma juvenil young form, juvenile form.
forma L L form.
forma en media silla half-chair form.
forma oclusal occlusal form.
forma de onda wave form.
forma de preparación cavitaria cavity preparation form.
forma Q Q-sort.
forma replicativa replicative form.
forma de resistencia resistance form.
forma de retención retencion form.
forma retorcida twist form.
forma sesgada skew form.
forma de silla chair form.
formación *f.* formation.
formación de compromiso compromise formation.
formación en empalizada palisade formation.
formación de esporas sporulation.
formador de masa *m.* bulkage.
formalinizar *v.* formalinize.
formicación *f.* formication.
formiciasis *f.* formiciasis.
fórmula *f.* formula.
formular *v.* formulate.
fórnix *m.* fornix.
forocitosis *f.* phorocytosis.
forología *f.* phorology.
forólogo, -ga *m., f.* phorologist.
forometría *f.* phorometry.
forómetro *m.* phorometer.
foronte *m.* phoront.
forooptómetro *m.* phoro-optometer.
foróptero *m.* phoroptor.

foroptómetro *m.* phoro-optometer.
foroscopio *m.* phoroscope.
forótono *m.* phorotone.
forúnculo *m.* foruncle.
forzar *v.* strain.
fosa *f.* fosso.
foseta *f.* fossula.
fosfagénico, -ca *adj.* phosphagenic.
fosfágeno *m.* phosphagen.
fosfastat *m.* phosphastat.
fosfatado, -da *adj.* phosphated.
fosfatemia *f.* phosphatemia.
fosfatidosis *f.* phosphatidosis.
fosfatoptosis *f.* phosphatoptosis.
fosfaturia *f.* phosphaturia.
fosfógeno *m.* phosphagen.
fosfoglicérido *m.* phosphoglyceride.
fosfoglucomutasa *f.* phosphoglucomutase.
fosfoglucoproteina *f.* phosphoglucoprotein.
fosfolipidemia *f.* phospholipidemia.
fosfolípido *m.* phospholipid.
fosfonecrosis *f.* phosphonecrosis.
fosfopenia *f.* phosphopenia.
fosfoproteína *f.* phosphoprotein.
fosforescencia *f.* phosphorescence.
fosforescente *adj.* phosphorescent.
fosforilación *f.* phosphorylation.
fosforismo *m.* phosphorism.
fosforizado, -da *adj.* phosphorized.
fosforólisis *f.* phosphorolysis.
fosforonecrosis *f.* phosphonecrosis.
fosforopenia *f.* phosphopenia.
fosforoscopio *m.* phosphoroscope.
fosforuria *f.* phosphoruria.
fosfuresis *f.* phosphuresis.
fosfurético, -ca *adj.* phosphuretic.
fosgénico, -ca *adj.* phosgenic.
fosia *f.* phose.
fosis *f.* phosis.
fosita *f.* fossula.
fotalgia *f.* photalgia.
fotalocromia *f.* photallochromy.
fotequia *f.* photechy.
fotestesia *f.* photesthesis.
fótico, -ca *adj.* photic.
fotismo *m.* photism.
fotoablación *f.* photoablation.
fotoactínico, -ca *adj.* photoactinic.
fotoactivo, -va *adj.* photoactive.
fotoalergia *f.* photoallergy.
fotoautotrófico, -ca *adj.* photoautotrophic.
fotobacteria *f.* photobacteria.
fotobiología *f.* photobiology.
fotocatálisis *f.* photocatalysis.
fotocentelleo *m.* photoscan.
fotocentelleografía *f.* photoscan.
fotoceptor *m.* photoceptor.
fotocinesia *f.* photokinesis.
fotocinesis *f.* photokinesis.
fotocinética *f.* photokinetics.
fotocinético, -ca *adj.* photokinetic.
fotocoagulación *f.* photocoagulation.
fotocoagulador *m.* photocoagulator.
fotocoagulador de arco de xenón xenon-arc photocoagulator.
fotocoagulador de láser laser photocoagulator.
fotocromógena *f.* photochromogen.
fotodermatitis *f.* photodermatitis.
fotodermatosis *f.* photodermatosis.
fotodinamia *f.* photodynamics.
fotodinámico, -ca *adj.* photodynamic.
fotodinia *f.* photodynia.
fotodistribución *f.* photodistribution.
fotoelectrómetro *m.* photoelectrometer.

fotoeléctrico, -ca *adj.* photoelectric.
fotoelectrón *m.* photoelectron.
fotoelemento *m.* photoelement.
fotoeritema *m.* photoerythema.
fotoestable *adj.* photostable.
fotoestético, -ca *adj.* photosthetic.
fotoestetoscopio *m.* photostethoscope.
fotoestrés *m.* photostress.
fotofarmacología *f.* photopharmacology.
fotofílico, -ca *adj.* photophilic.
fotofluorografía *f.* photofluorography.
fotofluorograma *f.* photofluorogram.
fotofluoroscopia *f.* photofluoroscopy.
fotofobia *f.* photophobia.
fotofóbico, -ca *adj.* photophonic.
fotoftalmia *f.* photophthalmia.
fotogastroscopio *m.* photogastroscope.
fotogénico, -ca *adj.* photogenic, photogenous.
fotógeno *m.* photogen.
fotograma *m.* photogram.
fotohemotacómetro *m.* photohematachometer.
fotoinactivación *f.* photoinactivation.
fotólisis *f.* photolysis.
fotolítico, -ca *adj.* photolitic.
fotolito *m.* photolyte.
fotología *f.* photology.
fotoluminiscencia *f.* photoluminiscence.
fotoluminiscente *adj.* photoluminescent.
fotoma *m.* photoma.
fotomacrografía *f.* photomacrography.
fotomagnetismo *m.* photomagnetism.
fotometría *f.* photometry.
fotómetro *m.* photometer.
  fotómetro de Förster Förster photometer.
fotomicrografía *f.* photomicrography.
fotomicroscopia *f.* photomicroscopy.
fotomioclono *m.* photomyoclonus.
fotón *m.* photon.
fotoncia *f.* photoncia.
fotonosis *f.* photonosus.
fotopatía *f.* photopathy.
fotoperceptivo, -va *adj.* photoperceptive.
fotoperiodicidad *f.* photoperiod.
fotopía *f.* photopia.
fotópico, -ca *adj.* photopic.
fotopsia *f.* photopsia.
fotopsina *f.* photopsin.
fotoptarmosis *f.* photoptarmosis.
fotoptometría *f.* photoptometry.
fotoptómetro *m.* photoptometer.
fotoquímica *f.* photochemistry.
fotoquímico, -ca *adj.* photochemical.
fotoquimioterapia *f.* photochemotherapy.
fotoquimógrafo *m.* photokymograph.
fotorradiación *f.* photoradiation.
fotorradiografía *f.* photofluorography.
fotorradiómetro *m.* photoradiometer.
fotorreacción *f.* photoreaction.
fotorreactivación *f.* photoreactivation.
fotorreceptivo, -va *adj.* photoreceptive.
fotorreceptor, -ra *m.* photoreceptor.
fotorretinitis *f.* photoretinitis.
fotorretinopatía *f.* photoretinopathy.
fotoscopia *f.* photoscopy.
fotosensibilización *f.* photosensitization.
fotosensor *m.* photosensor.
fotosíntesis *f.* photosynthesis.
fotostable *adj.* photostable.
fotostetoscopio *m.* photostethoscope.
fototactismo *m.* phototaxis.
fototaxia *f.* phototaxis.
fototaxis *f.* phototaxis.
fototerapia *f.* phototherapy.
fototermia *f.* photothermy.

fototérmico, -ca *adj.* photothermal.
fototono *m.* phototonus.
fototóxico, -ca *adj.* phototoxic.
fototoxis *f.* phototoxis.
foturia *f.* photuria.
fóvea *f.* fovea.
foveación *f.* foveation.
foveado, -da *adj.* foveate, foveated.
foveola *f.* foveola.
foveolar, -da *adj.* foveolate.
foveolar *adj.* foveolar.
fracción *f.* fraction.
  fracción amorfa de la corteza suprarrenal amorphous fraction of adrenal cortex.
  fracción de eyección (FE), fracción de eyección sistólica ejection fraction (EF), systolic ejection fraction.
  fracción de filtración (FF) filtration fraction (FF).
  fracción molar mole fraction.
  fracción del plasma blood plasma fraction.
  fracción proteica del plasma humano desecado dried human plasma protein fraction.
  fracción proteica del plasma humano human plasma protein fraction.
  fracción de recombinación recombination fraction.
  fracción de regurgitación regurgitant fraction.
fraccionamiento *m.* fractionation.
fraccionario, -ria *adj.* fractional.
fractura *f.* fracture.
  fractura abierta open fracture.
  fractura abierta de cráneo open skull fracture.
  fractura apofisaria apophysial fracture.
  fractura articular articular fracture, joint fracture.
  fractura astillada splintered fracture.
  fractura por avulsión avulsion fracture.
  fractura de Barton Barton's fracture.
  fractura de la base del cráneo basal skull fracture.
  fractura en bayoneta Colles' fracture.
  fractura de Bennett Bennett's fracture.
  fractura en bisel chisel fracture.
  fractura del boxeador, fractura de los boxeadores boxer fracture, boxer's fracture.
  fractura en canaleta gutter fracture.
  fractura en caña verde greenstick fracture, hickory-stick fracture.
  fractura capilar hairline fracture, capillary fracture.
  fractura centinela de la apófisis espinosa sentinel spinous process fracture.
  fractura cerrada closed fracture.
  fractura de Chance Chance fracture.
  fractura de chófer chauffeur's fracture.
  fractura de Colles Colles' fracture.
  fractura completa complete fracture.
  fractura complicada complicated fracture.
  fractura compuesta compound fracture.
  fractura congénita congenital fracture.
  fractura conminuta comminuted fracture.
  fractura por contragolpe fracture by contrecoup.
  fractura de cráneo skull fracture.
  fractura de cráneo cerrada closed skull fracture.
  fractura de cráneo conminuta comminuted skull fracture.
  fractura de cráneo deprimida depressed skull fracture.
  fractura de cráneo desplazada expressed skull fracture.

  fractura de cráneo diastásica diastatic skull fracture.
  fractura de cráneo estrellada stellate skull fracture.
  fractura de cráneo lineal linear skull fracture.
  fractura de cráneo simple simple skull fracture.
  fractura en crecimiento growing fracture.
  fractura en cuña wedge fracture.
  fractura curva bending fracture.
  fractura dentada dentate fracture.
  fractura directa direct fracture.
  fractura discrásica dyscrasic fracture.
  fractura con disyunción craneofacial craniofacial dysjunction fracture.
  fractura doble double fracture.
  fractura en dorso de tenedor silver-fork fracture.
  fractura de Dupuytren Dupuytren's fracture.
  fractura de Duverney Duverney's fracture.
  fractura epifisaria epiphyseal fracture.
  fractura por esguince sprain fracture.
  fractura espiral, fractura espiroidea spiral fracture.
  fractura espontánea spontaneous fracture.
  fractura estable stable fracture.
  fractura estrellada stellate fracture.
  fractura extracapsular extracapsular fracture.
  fractura por fatiga fatigue fracture.
  fractura fetal fetal fracture.
  fractura fisurada fissured fracture.
  fractura de Galeazzi Galeazzi's fracture.
  fractura de Gosselin Gosselin's fracture.
  fractura de Guérin Guérin's fracture.
  fractura incompleta incomplete fracture.
  fractura indirecta indirect fracture.
  fractura impactada, fractura con impacto impacted fracture.
  fractura inestable unstable fracture.
  fractura intraarticular intraarticular fracture.
  fractura intracapsular intracapsular fracture.
  fractura intraperióstica intraperiosteal fracture.
  fractura intrauterina intrauterine fracture.
  fractura en laguna pond fracture.
  fractura de Le Fort Le Fort's fracture.
  fractura de Le Fort tipo I Le Fort I fracture.
  fractura de Le Fort tipo II Le Fort II fracture.
  fractura de Le Fort tipo III Le Fort III fracture.
  fractura lineal, fractura longitudinal linear fracture, longitudinal fracture.
  fractura por luxación dislocation fracture.
  fractura de la marcha march fracture.
  fractura en mariposa butterfly fracture.
  fractura de Monteggia Monteggia's fracture.
  fractura de Moore Moore's fracture.
  fractura múltiple multiple fracture.
  fractura neurógena neurogenic fracture.
  fractura oblicua oblique fracture.
  fractura oculta occult fracture.
  fractura en ojal buttonhole fracture.
  fractura en paila dishpan fracture.
  fractura parcial incomplete fracture.
  fractura del parto birth fracture.
  fractura patológica pathologic fracture.
  fractura perforante perforating fracture.
  fractura pertrocantérea pertrochanteric fracture.
  fractura en ping-pong ping-pong fracture.
  fractura piramidal pyramidal fracture.
  fractura por plegamiento folding fracture.
  fractura de Pott Pott's fracture.
  fractura en rama verde greenstick fracture, hickory stick fracture.

fractura secundaria secondary fracture.
fractura segmentaria segmental fracture.
fractura de Shepherd Sheperd fracture.
fractura simple simple fracture.
fractura de Skilldern Skilldern's fracture.
fractura de Smith Smith's fracture.
fractura en sombrero hongo derby hat fracture.
fractura de Stieda Stieda's fracture.
fractura subcapital subcapital fracture.
fractura subcutánea subcutaneous fracture.
fractura subperióstica subperiosteal fracture.
fractura supracondílea supracondylar fracture.
fractura en tallo verde greenstick fracture, hickory stick fracture.
fractura en tenedor silver-fork fracture.
fractura por tensión stress fracture.
fractura por torsión torsion fracture.
fractura torus torus fracture.
fractura por tos cough fracture.
fractura transcervical transcervical fracture.
fractura transcondílea transcondylar fracture.
fractura transversa transverse fracture.
fractura transversa facial transverse facial fracture.
fractura trimaleolar trimalleolar fracture.
fractura trófica trophic fracture.
fractura en V V fracture.
fractura en T T fracture.
fractura en Y Y fracture.
fractura del verdugo hangman's fracture.
fractura de Wagstaffe Wagstaffe's fracture.
fragiforme *adj.* fragiform.
fragilidad *f.* fragility, fragilitas.
fragilidad capilar capillary fragility, fragilitas crinium.
fragilidad de la sangre erythrocyte fragility, fragility of the blood.
fragilidad de los huesos fragility of bone, fragilitas ossium.
fragilitas fragility, fragilitas.
fragilitas crinium capillary fragility, fragilitas crinium.
fragilitas ossium fragility of bone, fragilitas ossium.
fragilocito *m.* fragilocyte.
fragilocitosis *f.* fragilocytosis.
fragmentación *f.* fragmentation.
fragmento *m.* fragment.
fragmento acéntrico acentric fragment.
fragmento de un carbono one-carbon fragment.
fragmento de dos carbonos two-carbon fragment.
fragmento Fab Fab fragment.
fragmento Fc Fc. fragment.
fragmento en mariposa butterfly fragment.
fragmento de Spengler Spengler's fragment.
frambesia *f.* yaws.
frambesia del cangrejo crab yaws.
frambesia madre mother yaws.
frambesia de maíz Guinea corn yaws.
frambesia del pie foot yaws.
frambesia tiñosa ringworm yaws.
frambesiforme *adj.* frambesiform.
frambesioma *m.* frambesioma.
Francisella Francisella.
franclínico, -ca *adj.* franklinic.
franco, -ca *adj.* frank.
franja *f.* fringe, fimbria.
franja cervical cervical fringe.
franja costal costal fringe.
franklinización *f.* franklinization.

frasco *m.* bottle.
frasco lavador wash bottle.
frasco de Mariotte Mariotte bottle.
frasco volumétrico volumetric bottle.
frecuencia *f.* frequency.
frecuencia cardiaca heart rate.
frecuencia cardiaca fetal fetal heart rate.
frecuencia cardiaca fetal basal baseline fetal heart rate.
frecuencia fundamental fundamental frequency.
frecuencia de fusión crítica de destellos critical flicker fusion frequency.
frecuencia genética gene frequency.
frecuencia de micción frequency of micturition.
frecuencia de repetición repetition rate.
frecuencia de la respiración breathing respiration frequency.
frémito *m.* fremitus.
frémito bronquial bronchial fremitus.
frémito diastólico diastolic thrill.
frémito por fricción friction fremitus.
frémito hidatídico hydatid thrill.
frémito pericárdico pericardial fremitus.
frémito pleural pleural fremitus.
frémito presistólico presystolic thrill.
frémito rónquico rhonchal fremitus.
frémito sistólico systolic thrill.
frémito subjetivo subjective fremitus.
frémito táctil tactile fremitus.
frémito tusígeno tussive fremitus.
frémito vocal vocal fremitus.
frenalgia *f.* phrenalgia.
frenectomía *f.* phrenicectomy.
frenenfraxis *f.* phrenemphraxis.
frenético, -ca *adj.* phrenetic.
frenesí *m.* frenzy.
frenicectomía *f.* phrenicectomy.
freniclasia *f.* phreniclasia, phreniclasis.
freniclasis *f.* phreniclasia, phreniclasis.
frénico, -ca *adj.* phrenic.
frenicoexéresis *f.* phrenicoexeresis.
freniconeurectomía *f.* phreniconeurectomy.
frenicotomía *f.* phrenicotomy.
frenicotripsia *f.* phrenicotripsy.
frenillo *m.* frenulum.
frenitis *f.* phrenitis.
freno *m.* frenum.
frenocólico, -ca *adj.* phrenocolic.
frenocolopexia *f.* phrenocolopexy.
frenodinia *f.* phrenodynia.
frenoespasmo *m.* phrenospasm.
frenoesplénico, -ca *adj.* phrenosplenic.
frenogástrico, -ca *adj.* phrenogastric.
frenoglótico, -ca *adj.* phrenoglottic.
frenógrafo *m.* phrenograph.
frenohepático, -ca *adj.* phrenohepatic.
frenoparálisis *f.* phrenoplegia.
frenoplastia *f.* phrenoplasty.
frenoplejía *f.* phrenoplegia.
frenoptosis *f.* phrenoptosis.
frenospasmo *m.* phrenospasm.
frenosplénico, -ca *adj.* phrenosplenic.
frenotomía *f.* frenotomy.
frente *f.* forehead.
frente olímpica Olympian forehead.
fresa *f.* bur, fraise.
fresa con borde cortante end-cutting bur.
fresa en cono invertido inverted cone bur.
fresa de corte transversal cross-cut bur.
fresa para fisuras fissure bur.
fresa redonda round bur.
fresa de terminación finishing bur.
freudiano, -na *adj.* Freudian.

friabilidad *f.* friability.
friable *adj.* friable.
fricasmo *m.* cutis anserina.
fricativo, -va *adj.* fricative.
fricción *f.* friction.
fricción dinámica dynamic friction.
fricción estática static friction.
fricción de iniciación starting friction.
frictopático, -ca *adj.* phrictopathic.
friega *f.* friction.
frigidez *f.* frigidity.
frígido, -da *adj.* frigid.
frigoestable *adj.* frigostable.
frigolábil *adj.* figolabile.
frigoterapia *f.* frigotherapy.
frinodermia *f.* phrynoderma.
frío *m.* cold.
frito *m.* frit.
fronda *f.* sling.
frontal *adj.* frontal.
frontípeto, -ta *adj.* frontipetal.
frontocigomático, -ca *adj.* frontozygomatic.
frontofocómetro *m.* frontofocometer.
frontomalar *adj.* frontomalar.
frontomaxilar *adj.* frontomaxillary.
frontonasal *adj.* frontonasal.
frontooccipital *adj.* fronto-occipital.
frontoparietal *adj.* frotoparietal.
frontotemporal *adj.* frontotemporal.
frotamiento *m.* frottement.
frotis *m.* smear.
frotis bucal buccal smear.
frotis cervical cervical smear.
frotis citológico cytologic smear.
frotis citológico FGT FGT cytologic smear.
frotis colónico colonic smear.
frotis duodenal duodenal smear.
frotis ectocervical ectocervical smear.
frotis endocervical endocervical smear.
frotis endometrial endometrial smear.
frotis esofágico esophageal smear.
frotis de esputo sputum smear.
frotis del fondo de saco cul-de-sac smear.
frotis gástrico gastric smear.
frotis oral oral smear.
frotis pancervical pancervical smear.
frotis de Pap, frotis de Papanicolaou Pap smear.
frotis de la pared vaginal lateral lateral vaginal wall smear.
frotis rápido fast smear.
frotis sanguíneo blood smear.
frotis del tracto alimentario alimentary tract smear.
frotis del tracto respiratorio inferior lower respiratory tract smear.
frotis urinario urinary smear.
frotis vaginal vaginal smear.
fructosemia *f.* fructosemia.
fructosuria *f.* fructosuria.
fructosuria esencial essential fructosuria.
frustración *f.* frustration.
ftiriasis *f.* phthiriasis.
fucosidosis *f.* fucosidosis.
fucsina *f.* fuchsin.
fucsinofilia *f.* fuchsinophilia.
fucsinofílico, -ca *adj.* fuchsinophilic.
fucsinófilo *m.* fuchsinophil.
fucsinófilo, -la *adj.* fuchsinophil.
fuera de fase *adj.* out of phase.
fuerza[1] *f.* force.
fuerza animal animal force.
fuerza catabólica catabolic force.
fuerza centrífuga centrifugal force.
fuerza centrífuga relativa (FCR) relative centrifugal force (RCF).

fuerza centrípeta centripetal force.
fuerza coercitiva de los músculos coercitive force.
fuerza electromotriz (FEM) electromotive force (EMF).
fuerza extrabucal extraoral force.
fuerza de fricción frictional force.
fuerza de Londres London force.
fuerza de masticación, fuerza de masticación force of mastication.
fuerza de mordida bite force.
fuerza nerviosa nerve force, nervous force.
fuerza oclusal occlusal force.
fuerza radical reserve force.
fuerza de reposo rest force.
fuerza de reserva reserve force.
fuerza de van der Waals van der Waals' force.
fuerza vital vital force.
fuerza² *f.* strength.
fuerza asociativa associative strength.
fuerza iónica ionic strength.
fuerza tensil tensile strength.
fuga *f.* fugue.
fuga epiléptica epileptic fugue.
fuga de ideas psychogenic fugue.
fugacidad *f.* fugacity.
fugaz *adj.* fugitive.
fuguismo *m.* fuguism.
fulcro *m.* fulcrum.
fulguración *f.* fulguration.
fulgurante *adj.* fulgurant.
fuliginosidad *f.* sordes.
fulminante *adj.* fulminant.
fumigación *f.* fumigation.
fumigar *v.* fumigate.
función *f.* function.
función alomérica allomeric function.
función de densidad de probabilidad probability density function.
función de despertar arousal function.
función discriminante discriminant function.
función de distribución distribution function.

función de distribución acumulable cumulative distribution function.
función isomérica isomeric function.
función de mapeo mapping function.
función de transferencia de modulación modulation transfer function.
función de transporte auricular atrial transport function.
funcional *adj.* functional.
funda *f.* jacket.
fundación *f.* foundation.
fundación dental denture foundation.
fundador, -ra *m., f.* founder.
fundamental *adj.* fundamental.
fundamento *m.* fundament.
fundectomía *f.* fundectomy.
fúndico, -ca *adj.* fundic.
fundiforme *adj.* fundiform.
fundir *v.* fuse.
fundisectomía *f.* fundusectomy.
fundoplicación *f.* fundoplication.
fundoscopia *f.* funduscopy.
fundoscopio *m.* funduscope.
fundosectomía *f.* fundectomy.
fundus *m.* fundus.
fundusectomía *f.* fundectomy.
fungal *adj.* fungal.
fungemia *f.* fungemia.
fungicida *m.* funcigide.
fungifitóxico, -ca *adj.* fungitoxic.
fungiforme *adj.* fungiforme.
fungiliforme *adj.* fungiliform.
fungistasis *f.* fungistasis.
fungistático, -ca *adj.* fungistatic.
fungitoxicidad *f.* fungitoxicity.
fungitóxico, -ca *adj.* fungitoxic.
fungoide *adj.* fungoid.
fungosidad *f.* fungosity.
fungoso, -sa *adj.* fungous.
fungus *m.* fungus.
fúnico, -ca *adj.* funic.
funiculalgia *f.* funiculalgia.

funicular *adj.* funicular.
funiculitis *f.* funiculitis.
funiculitis endémica endemic funiculitis.
funiculitis filariásica filarial funiculitis.
funículo, funiculus *m.* funicle, funiculus.
funiculopexia *f.* funiculopexy.
funiculus funicle, funiculus.
funiforme *adj.* funiform.
funis *m.* funis.
functio laesa functio laesa.
furcación *f.* furcation.
fúrfura *f.* furfur.
furfuráceo, -a *adj.* furfuraceous.
furuncular *adj.* furuncular.
furúnculo *m.* furuncle, boil.
furúnculo ciego blind boil.
furúnculo de Delhi Delhi boil.
furúnculo de Jericó Jericho boil.
furúnculo tropical tropical boil.
furúnculo oriental cutaneous leishmaniasis.
furunculoide *adj.* furunculoid.
furunculosis *f.* furunculosis.
furunculosis blastomicética furunculosis blastomycetica.
furunculosis criptocócica furunculosis cryptococcica.
furunculosis oriental furunculosis orientalis.
furunculoso, -sa *adj.* furunculous.
Fusarium Fusarium.
fuscina *f.* fuscin.
fusiforme *adj.* fusiform.
fusimotor, -ra *adj.* fusimotor.
fusión *f.* fusion.
fusión celular cell fusion.
fusión céntrica centric fusion.
fusión nuclear nuclear fusion.
Fusobacterium Fusobacterium.
fusocelular *adj.* fusocellular.
fusoespirilosis *f.* fusospirillosis.
fusoespiroquetosis *f.* fusospirochetosis.
fututrix *f.* fututrix.

G g

Gaba *m.* Gaba.
gabaminérgico, -ca *adj.* gabaergic, Gabaergic.
gabinete *m.* cabinet.
  gabinete neumático pneumatic cabinet.
  gabinete de Sauerbruch Sauerbruch's cabinet.
gafas *f.* glasses, spectacles.
  gafas bifocales bifocal glasses, Franklin glasses.
  gafas nasales nasal strip.
  gafas de seguridad safety glasses.
gafedad *f.* griffin claw.
galactacrasia *f.* galactacrasia.
galactagogo *m.* galactagogue.
galactemia *f.* galactemia.
galacthidrosis *f.* galactidrosis.
galactia *f.* galactorrhea.
galáctico, -ca *adj.* galactic.
galactidrosis *f.* galactidrosis.
galactisquia *f.* galactischia.
galactoblasto *m.* galactoblast.
galactobólico, -ca *adj.* galactobolic.
galactocele *m.* galactocele.
galactocinasa *f.* galactokinase.
galactocrasia *f.* galactocrasia.
galactófago, -ga *adj.* galactophagous.
galactófigo, -ga *adj.* galactophygous.
galactoflebitis *f.* galactophlebitis.
galactóflisis *f.* galactophlysis.
galactoforitis *f.* galactophoritis.
galactóforo *m.* galactophore.
galactóforo, -ra *adj.* galactophorous.
galactógeno *m.* galactogen.
galactógeno, -na *adj.* galactogenous.
galactogogo, -ga *m. y adj.* galactogogue.
galactografía *f.* galactography.
galactohidrosis *f.* galactidrosis.
galactolípido *m.* galactolipid.
galactolipina *f.* galactolipin.
galactoma *m.* galactoma.
galactometástasis *f.* galactometastasis.
galactómetro *m.* galactometer.
galactopexia *f.* galactopexy.
galactópira *f.* galactopyra.
galactoplania *f.* galactoplania.
galactopoyesis *f.* galactopoiesis.
galactopoyético, -ca *adj.* galactopoietic.
galactoquinasa *f.* galactokinase.
galactorrea *f.* galactorrhea.
galactosa *f.* galactose.
galactoscopio *m.* galactoscope.
galactosemia *f.* galactosemia.
  galactosemia congénita classic galactosemia, congenital galactosemia.
  galactosemia por déficit de galactocinasa galactokinase deficiency galactosemia.
galactósido *m.* galactoside.
galactosilceramidasa *f.* galactosylceramidase.
galactosis *f.* galactosis.
galactosquesis *f.* galactoschesis.
galactostasia *f.* galactostasis.
galactostasis *f.* galactostasis.

galactosurla *f.* galactosuria.
galactoterapia *f.* galactotherapy.
galactotoxina *f.* galactotoxin.
galactotoxismo *m.* galactotoxism.
galactoxismo *m.* galactoxism.
galactotrofia *f.* galactotrophy.
galacturia *f.* galacturia.
galea *f.* galea.
  galea aponeurótica galea aponeurotica.
  galea capitis galea capitis.
galeado, -da *adj.* galeatus.
galeatomía *f.* galeatomy.
galeína *f.* gallein.
galenicales *m.* galenicals, galenics, galenica.
galénicos *m.* galenicals, galenics, galenica.
galeropía *f.* galeropia.
galeropsia *f.* galeropsia.
galope *m.* gallop.
  galope auricular atrial gallop.
  galope presistólico presystolic gallop.
  galope protodiastólico protodiastolic gallop.
  galope sistólico systolic gallop.
  galope de sumación summation gallop.
galvánico, -ca *adj.* galvanic.
galvanismo *m.* galvanism.
  galvanismo dental dental galvanism.
galvanización *f.* galvanization.
galvanocaustia *f.* galvanocaustia.
  galvanocaustia química chemical galvanocaustia.
  galvanocaustia térmica thermal galvanocaustia.
galvanocauterio *m.* galvanocautery.
galvanocirugía *f.* galvanosurgery.
galvanocontractilidad *f.* galvanocontractility.
galvanofaradización *f.* galvanofaradization.
galvanogustómetro *m.* galvanogustometer.
galvanoionización *f.* galvanoionization.
galvanólisis *f.* galvanolysis.
galvanómetro *m.* galvanometer.
  galvanómetro de d'Arsonval, galvanómetro de bovina móvil, galvanómetro de cuadro móvil d'Arsonval galvanometer.
  galvanómetro de Einthoven, galvanómetro de filamento, galvanómetro de hilo Einthoven's galvanometer, Einthoven's string galvanometer.
galvanomuscular *adj.* galvanomuscular.
galvanonarcosis *f.* galvanonarcosis.
galvanonervioso, -sa *adj.* galvanonervous.
galvanopalpación *f.* galvanopalpation.
galvanopuntura *f.* electropuncture.
galvanoquímico, -ca *adj.* galvanochemical.
galvanoscopio *m.* galvanoscope.
galvanotaxia *f.* galvanotaxis.
galvanotaxis *f.* galvanotaxis.
galvanoterapia *f.* galvanotherapeutics, galvanotherapy.

galvanotonía *f.* galvanotonus.
galvanotono *m.* galvanotonus.
galvanotropismo *m.* galvanotropism.
gallo *m.* whoop.
gama *f.* range, scale.
gamacismo *m.* gammacism.
gamético, -ca *adj.* gametic.
gameto *m.* gamete, germ cell.
gametocida[1] *m.* gametocide.
gametocida[2] *adj.* gametocydal.
gametocinético, -ca *adj.* gametokinetic.
gametocitemia *f.* gametocytemia.
gametocito *f.* gametocyte.
gametofagia *f.* gametophagia.
gametogénesis *f.* gametogenesis.
gametogenia *f.* gametogenesis.
gametogénico, -ca *adj.* gametogenic.
gametogonia *f.* gametogonia, gametogony.
gametoide *adj.* gametoid.
gametología *f.* gametology.
gametólogo, -ga *m., f.* gametologist.
gametopatía *f.* gametopathy.
gametoquiste *m.* gametocyst.
gametotrópico, -ca *adj.* gametotropic.
gámico, -ca *adj.* gamic.
gamma-angiocardiografía *f.* radioisotope angiocardiography.
gamma-angioencefalografía *f.* radioisotope cerebral angiography.
gamma-angiografía *f.* radioisotope angiography.
gammacámara *f.* radioisotope cineangiocardiography.
gammacardiografía *f.* gammacardiography.
gammacardiograma *m.* gammacardiogram.
gammacismo *f.* gammacism.
gammaencefalografía *f.* gammagraphy of the brain, isotopic brain scintigraphy.
gammaencefalograma *m.* gammaencephalogram.
gammaflebografía *f.* gammavenography.
gammaglobulina *f.* gammaglobulin.
gammaglobulinopatía *f.* gammaglobulinopathy.
gammaglobulinoprofilaxis *f.* prophylactic therapy by gammablobulin.
gammaglutamiltransferasa *f.* gammaglutamyltranspeptidase.
gammaglutamiltranspeptidasa *f.* gammaglutamyltranspeptidase.
gammagrafía *f.* gammagraphy.
  gammagrafía cardíaca gammacardiography.
  gammagrafía hepática liver scan, radioisotope scanning of the liver.
  gammagrafía pancreática pancreas scan.
  gammagrafía renal radioisotope scanning of the kidney, renal scan.
gammagráfico, -ca gammagraphic.
gammagrama *m.* gammagram.
gammaorbitografía *f.* gamma-orbitography.

gammapatía *f.* gammopathy.
gammapatía monoclonal, gammapatía monoclónica monoclonal gammopathy.
gammapatía monoclonal benigna, gammapatía monoclónica benigna benign monoclonal gammopathy.
gammapatía policlonal, gammapatía policlónica polyclonal gammopathy.
gammaterapia *f.* gammatherapy.
gammatomografía *f.* gammatomography.
gamobio *m.* gamobium.
gamofagia *f.* gamophagia.
gamofobia *f.* gamophobia.
gamogénesis *f.* gamogenesis.
gamogonia *f.* gamogony.
gamonte *m.* gamont.
gamonto *m.* gamont.
gampsodactilia *f.* gampsodactyly.
ganancia *f.* gain.
ganancia de antígeno antigen gain.
ganancia en brillo brightness gain.
ganancia de compensación de tiempo time-compensated gain, time compensation gain (TCG).
ganancia primaria primary gain.
ganancia secundaria secondary gain.
ganancia terapéutica therapeutic gain.
ganancia tiempo-variada time-varied gain (TVG)]).
gancho¹ *m.* clasp.
gancho de Adams Adams' clasp.
gancho de barra, gancho en barra bar clasp.
gancho circunferencial circumferential clasp.
gancho continuo continuous clasp, continuous lingual clasp.
gancho extendido extended clasp.
gancho de Roach Roach's clasp.
gancho² *m.* hook, hamulus.
gancho de la apófisis pterigoides pterygoid hook, hamulus pterygoideus.
gancho de Bose Bose's hook.
gancho de Braun Braun's hook.
gancho calvárico calvarial hook.
gancho deslizable sliding hook.
gancho de Dujarier Dujarier's hook.
gancho de estrabismo squint hook.
gancho del hueso ganchoso hook of the hamate bone.
gancho lagrimal lacrimal hook, hamulus lacrimalis.
gancho de llave blunt hook.
gancho de Loughnane Loughnane's hook.
gancho de Malpaigne Malpaigne's hook.
gancho muscular muscle hook.
gancho obtuso obtuse hook.
gancho de Pajot Pajot's hook.
gancho del paladar, gancho palatino palate hook.
gancho del páncreas pancreas hook.
gancho de la pterigoides pterygoid hook.
gancho de Ramsbotham Ramsbotham's hook.
gancho romo blunt hook.
gancho para traqueotomía tracheotomy hook.
gancho de Tyrrell Tyrrell's hook.
gancho del unguis lacrimal hook.
ganchoso, -sa hamate.
gangliado, -da *adj.* gangliate, gangliated.
gangliastenia *f.* gangliasthenia.
gangliectomía *f.* gangliectomy.
gangliitis *f.* gangliitis.
ganglio *m.* ganglion.
ganglioblasto *m.* ganglioblast.
gangliocito *m.* gangliocyte.
gangliocitoma *m.* gangliocytoma.
ganglioforme *adj.* ganglioform.
ganglioglioma *m.* ganglioglioma.

ganglioglioneuroma *m.* ganglioglioneuroma.
gangliólisis *f.* gangliolysis.
gangliólisis percutánea por radiofrecuencia percutaneous radiofrequency gangliolysis.
gangliolítico, -ca *adj.* gangliolytic.
ganglioma *m.* ganglioma.
ganglioma embrionario simpático sympathetic embryonic ganglioma.
ganglión *m.* ganglion.
ganglión de Acrel Acrel's ganglion.
ganglión compuesto compound ganglion.
ganglión difuso diffuse ganglion.
ganglión primario primary ganglion.
ganglión simple simple ganglion.
ganglión sinovial synovial ganglion.
ganglionado, -da *adj.* ganglionated.
ganglionar *adj.* ganglionic.
ganglionectomía *f.* ganglionectomy.
ganglioneuroblastoma *m.* ganglioneuroblastoma.
ganglioneurofibroma *m.* ganglioneurofibroma.
ganglioneuroma *m.* ganglioneuroma.
ganglioneuroma central central ganglioneuroma.
ganglioneuroma en pesa de gimnasia dumbbell ganglioneuroma.
ganglioneuromatosis *f.* ganglioneuromatosis.
ganglionitis *f.* ganglionitis.
ganglionitis de Gasser Gasserian ganglionitis.
ganglionitis posterior aguda acute posterior ganglionitis.
ganglionostomía *f.* ganglionostomy.
gangliopléjico, -ca *adj.* ganglioplegic.
gangliósido *m.* ganglioside.
gangliósido GM1 ganglioside GM1.
gangliósido GM2 ganglioside GM2.
gangliosidosis *f.* gangliosidosis, gangliosialidosis.
gangliosidosis generalizada generalized gangliosidosis.
gangliosidosis GM1 GM1 gangliosidosis.
gangliosidosis GM1 del adulto, gangliosidosis GM1 tipo 3 adult GM1 gangliosidosis, type 3 GM1 gangliosidosis.
gangliosidosis GM1 infantil, gangliosidosis GM1 tipo 1 infantile GM1 gangliosidosis, type 1 GM1 gangliosidosis.
gangliosidosis GM1 juvenil, gangliosidosis GM1 tipo 2 juvenile GM1 gangliosidosis, type 2 GM1 gangliosidosis.
gangliosidosis GM2 GM2 gangliosidosis.
gangliosidosis GM2 del adulto adult GM2 gangliosidosis.
gangliosidosis GM2 infantil, gangliosidosis GM2 tipo 1 infantile GM2 gangliosidosis, type 1 GM2 gangliosidosis.
gangliosidosis GM2 juvenil, gangliosidosis GM2 tipo 3 juvenile GM2 gangliosidosis, type 3 GM2 gangliosidosis.
gangliosidosis GM2 variante 0, gangliosidosis GM2 tipo 2 variant 0 GM2 gangliosidosis, type 2 GM2 gangliosidosis.
gangliosimpatectomía *f.* gangliosympathectomy.
ganglitis *f.* gangliitis.
gangosa *f.* gangosa.
gangrena *f.* gangrene.
gangrena anémica anemic gangrene.
gangrena angioesclerótica angiosclerotic gangrene.
gangrena arterioesclerótica arteriosclerotic gangrene.

gangrena bacteriana sinergística progresiva progressive bacterial synergistic gangrene.
gangrena benigna de los párpados eyelid benign gangrene.
gangrena blanca white gangrene.
gangrena de la boca, gangrena bucal gangrenous stomatitis.
gangrena caliente hot gangrene.
gangrena carbólica carbolic gangrene.
gangrena circunscrita circumscribed gangrene.
gangrena cutánea cutaneous gangrene.
gangrena cutánea diseminada disseminated cutaneous gangrene.
gangrena por decúbito decubital gangrene.
gangrena diabética diabetic gangrene.
gangrena diftérica diphtheritic gangrene.
gangrena embólica embolic gangrene.
gangrena enfisematosa emphysematous gangrene.
gangrena epidémica epidemic gangrene.
gangrena espontánea del recién nacido spontaneous gangrene of the newborn.
gangrena estática, gangrena por estasis static gangrene.
gangrena de Fournier Fournier's gangrene.
gangrena fría cold gangrene.
gangrena fulminante fulminant gangrene.
gangrena fulminante de los órganos genitales fulminant gangrene in the genital member.
gangrena gaseosa gas gangrene, gaseous gangrene.
gangrena glucémica glycemic gangrene.
gangrena hemorrágica hemorrhagic gangrene.
gangrena húmeda humid gangrene, moist gangrene, wet gangrene.
gangrena inflamatoria inflammatory gangrene.
gangrena de Lasègue Lasègue's gangrene.
gangrena mefítica mephitic gangrene.
gangrena de Meleney Meleney's gangrene.
gangrena mixta mixed gangrene.
gangrena molecular molecular gangrene.
gangrena múltiple multiple gangrene.
gangrena neurótica neurotic gangrene.
gangrena oral oral gangrene.
gangrena de Pott Pott's gangrene.
gangrena presenil presenile gangrene.
gangrena presenil espontánea presenile spontaneous gangrene.
gangrena por presión pressure gangrene.
gangrena primaria primary gangrene.
gangrena progresiva progressive gangrene.
gangrena pulmonar pulmonary gangrene.
gangrena de Raynaud Raynaud's gangrene.
gangrena seca dry gangrene.
gangrena secundaria secondary gangrene.
gangrena senil senile gangrene.
gangrena simétrica symmetrical gangrene.
gangrena simétrica de las extremidades symmetrical gangrene on both sides.
gangrena simpática sympathetic gangrene.
gangrena sinérgica, gangrena sinérgica de Meleney, gangrena sinergística de Meleney Meleney's synergistic gangrene.
gangrena sinérgica bacteriana progresiva, gangrena sinergística progresiva progressive bacterial synergistic gangrene, progressive synergistic gangrene.
gangrena traumática traumatic gangrene.
gangrena trófica trophic gangrene.
gangrena trombótica thrombotic gangrene.
gangrena venosa venous gangrene.
gangrenosis *f.* gangrenosis.

gangrenoso, -sa *adj.* gangrenous.
ganoblasto *m.* ganoblaste.
Gardnerella Gardnerella.
gargajeo *m.* spitting.
gargalanestesia *f.* gargalanesthesia.
gargalestesia *f.* gargalesthesia.
gargalestésico, -ca *adj.* gargalesthetic.
garganta *f.* throat.
  garganta dolorida sore throat.
  garganta dolorida séptica septic sore throat.
  garganta pútrida putrid throat.
gárgaras *f.* gargle.
gargarismo *m.* gargarism, mouthwash.
gargarizar *v.* gargle.
gargoilismo *m.* gargoylysm.
gargolismo *m.* gargoylysm.
garra *f.* claw.
  garra cubital claw hand.
garrapata *f.* tick.
garrotillo *m.* laryngeal diphtheria.
garrulitas vulvae flatus vaginalis.
gas *m.* gas.
  gas ácido marino marine acid gas.
  gas de albañal, gas de las alcantarillas sewer gas.
  gas del alumbrado coal gas.
  gas alveolar alveolar gas.
  gas amoniaco ammoniac gas.
  gas asfixiante suffocating gas.
  gas aspirado inspired gas.
  gas de Clayton Clayton's gas.
  gas deletéreo deleterious gas.
  gas del estómago gas in the stomach.
  gas espirado expired gas.
  gas estornutatorio sneezing gas, sternutatory gas.
  gas de guerra war gas.
  gas hemolítico hemolytic gas.
  gas hepático liver gas.
  gas hilarante laughing gas.
  gas inerte inert gas.
  gas intestinal intestinal gas.
  gas lacrimógeno tear gas.
  gas mostaza mustard gas.
  gas nitroso nitrous gas.
  gas noble noble gas.
  gas olefiante, gas oleificante olefiant gas.
  gas de los pantanos marsh gas.
  gas silvestre wild gas.
  gas sanguíneo blood gas.
  gas sofocante suffocating gas.
  gas vesicante vesicating gas.
  gas vomitivo vomiting gas.
gasa *f.* gauze.
  gasa absorbente absorbent gauze.
  gasa absorbente estéril sterile absorbent gauze.
  gasa absorbible absorbable gauze.
  gasa hidrófila hydrophile gauze.
  gasa impregnada en gelatina de cinc zinc gelatin impregnated gauze.
  gasa vaselinada petrolatum gauze.
gaseiforme *adj.* gasiform.
gaseoso, -sa *adj.* gaseous.
gasiforme *adj.* gasiform.
gasógeno, -na *adj.* gasogenic.
gasometría *f.* gasometry.
  gasometría sanguínea blood gas analysis.
gasométrico, -ca *adj.* gasometric.
gasómetro *m.* gasometer.
gasserectomía *f.* gasserectomy.
gasseriano, -na *adj.* Gasserian.
Gasterophilus hemorrhoidalis Gasterophilus hemorrhoidalis.
gasto *m.* output.

gasto cardíaco cardiac output.
gasto por contracción stroke output.
gasto de energía energy output.
gasto urinario urinary output.
gastralgia *f.* gastralgia.
  gastralgia apendicular appendicular gastralgia.
gastralgocenocis *f.* gastralgokenosis.
gastralgoquenosis *f.* gastralgokenosis.
gastratrofia *f.* gastric atrophy.
gastrectasia *f.* gastrectasia.
  gastrectasia aguda acute gastrectasia.
gastrectasis *f.* gastrectasis.
gastrectomía *f.* gastrectomy.
  gastrectomía parcial, gastrectomía subtotal partial gastrectomy, subtotal gastrectomy.
  gastrectomía de Pólya Pólya gastrectomy.
  gastrectomía total total gastrectomy.
gástrico, -ca *adj.* gastric.
gastrina *f.* gastrine.
gastrinemia *f.* gastrinaemia.
gastrinoma *m.* gastrinoma.
gastrinosis *f.* gastrinosis.
gastrítico, -ca *adj.* gastritic.
gastritis *f.* gastritis.
  gastritis antral, gastritis del antro antrum gastritis, antral gastritis.
  gastritis atrófica atrophic gastritis.
  gastritis atrófica hiperplásica atrophic hyperplastic gastritis.
  gastritis catarral catarrhal gastritis.
  gastritis cirrótica cirrhotic gastritis.
  gastritis corrosiva corrosive gastritis.
  gastritis eosinófila eosinophilic gastritis.
  gastritis erosiva erosive gastritis.
  gastritis esclerótica sclerotic gastritis.
  gastritis exfoliativa exfoliative gastritis.
  gastritis fibroplástica gastritis fibroplastica.
  gastritis flemonosa phlegmonous gastritis.
  gastritis folicular follicular gastritis.
  gastritis folicular crónica chronic follicular gastritis.
  gastritis hemorrágica hemorrhagic gastritis.
  gastritis hiperpéptica hyperpeptic gastritis.
  gastritis hipertrófica hypertrophic gastritis.
  gastritis hipertrófica gigante giant hypertrophic gastritis.
  gastritis intersticial interstitial gastritis.
  gastritis micótica mycosis gastritis.
  gastritis poliposa polypous gastritis.
  gastritis poliposa quística gastritis cystica poliposa.
  gastritis química chemical gastritis.
  gastritis quística crónica chronic cystic gastritis.
  gastritis por radiación radiation gastritis.
  gastritis seudomembranosa pseudomembranous gastritis.
  gastritis tóxica toxic gastritis.
gastroacéfalo *m.* gastroacephalus.
gastroadenitis *f.* gastradenitis.
gastroadinámico, -ca *adj.* gastrodynamic.
gastroalbumorrea *f.* gastroalbumorrhea.
gastroamorfo *m.* gastramorphus.
gastroanastomosis *f.* gastroanastomosis.
gastroatrofia *f.* gastroatrophy.
gastrobiopsia *f.* gastric biopsy.
gastroblenorrea *f.* gastroblennorrhea.
gastrocámara *f.* gastrocamera.
gastrocardíaco, -ca *adj.* gastrocardiac.
gastrocele *m.* gastrocele.
gastrocelo *m.* gastrocoele.
gastrocinesiógrafo *m.* gastrokinesograph.
gastrocnemio *m.* gastrocnemius.
gastrocólico, -ca *adj.* gastrocolic.

gastrocolitis *f.* gastrocolitis.
gastrocolostomía *f.* gastrocolostomy.
gastrocolotomía *f.* gastrocolotomy.
gastrocutáneo, -a *adj.* gastrocutaneous.
gastrodiafania *f.* gastrodiaphany.
gastrodiafanoscopia *f.* gastrodiaphany.
gastrodiálisis *f.* gastrodialysis.
gastrodídimo *m.* gastrodidymus.
gastrodinia *f.* gastrodynia.
gastrodisciasis *f.* gastrodisciasis.
Gastrodiscoides hominis Gastrodiscoides hominis.
gastroduodenal *adj.* gastroduodenal.
gastroduodenectomía *f.* gastroduodenectomy.
gastroduodenltls *f.* gastroduodenitis.
gastroduodenoenterostomía *f.* gastroduodenoenterostomy.
gastroduodenoscopia *f.* gastroduodenoscopy.
gastroduodenostomía *f.* gastroduodenostomy.
gastroenteralgia *f.* gastroenteralgia.
gastroentérico, -ca *adj.* gastroenteric.
gastroenteritis *f.* gastroenteritis.
  gastroenteritis eosinófila eosinophilic gastroenteritis.
  gastroenteritis infantil, gastroenteritis infantil no bacteriana endémica infantile gastroenteritis, endemic infectious non-bacterial infantile gastroenteritis.
  gastroenteritis infecciosa aguda acute infectious gastroenteritis.
  gastroenteritis infecciosa no bacteriana aguda acute infectious non-bacterial gastroenteritis.
  gastroenteritis no bacteriana epidémica epidemic non-bacterial gastroenteritis.
  gastroenteritis de Norwalk Norwalk gastroenteritis.
  gastroenteritis paratifosa B, gastroenteritis paratifosa tipo B Salmonella paratyphi B gastroenteritis.
  gastroenteritis tifosa Salmonella typhosa gastroenteritis.
  gastroenteritis viral viral gastroenteritis.
gastroenteroanastomosis *f.* gastroenteroanastomosis.
gastroenterocolitis *f.* gastroenterocolitis.
gastroenterocolostomía *f.* gastroenterocolostomy.
gastroenterología *f.* gastroenterology.
gastroenterólogo, -ga *m.*, *f.* gastroenterologist.
gastroenteropatía *f.* gastroenteropathy.
gastroenteroplastia *f.* gastroenteroplasty.
gastroenteroptosis *f.* gastroenteroptosis.
gastroenterostomía *f.* gastroenterostomy.
gastroenterotomía *f.* gastroenterotomy.
gastroepiploico, -ca *adj.* gastroepiploic.
gastroesofagectomía *f.* gastroesophagectomy.
gastroesofágico, -ca *adj.* gastroesophageal.
gastroesofagitis *f.* gastroesophagitis.
gastroesofagostomía *f.* gastroesophagostomy.
gastroespasm *m.* gastrospasm.
gastroesplénico, -ca *adj.* gastrosplenic.
gastroestenosis *f.* gastrostenosis.
gastrofibroscopia *f.* gastrofiberscopy.
gastrofibroscopio *m.* gastrofiberscope.
gastrofotografía *f.* gastrophotography.
gastrofrénico, -ca *adj.* gastrophrenic.
gastrogastrostomía *f.* gastrogastrostomy.
gastrogavaje *m.* gastrogavage.

gastrogénico, -ca *adj.* gastrogenic.
gastrógrafo *m.* gastrograph.
gastrohepático, -ca *adj.* gastrohepatic.
gastrohepatitis *f.* gastrohepatitis.
gastrohipertonía *f.* gastrohypertony.
gastrohipertónico, -ca *adj.* gastrohypertonic.
gastroileítis *f.* gastroileitis.
gastroileostomía *f.* gastroileostomy.
gastroilíaco, -ca *adj.* gastroileac.
gastrointestinal *adj.* gastrointestinal.
gastrolavado *m.* gastrolavage.
gastrolienal *adj.* gastrolienal.
gastrólisis *f.* gastrolysis.
gastrolitiasis *f.* gastrolithiasis.
gastrolito *m.* gastrolith.
gastrología *f.* gastrology.
gastrólogo, -ga *m., f.* gastrologist.
gastromalacia *f.* gastromalacia.
gastromegalia *f.* gastromegaly.
gastromelo *m.* gastromelus.
gastromicosis *f.* gastromycosis.
gastromiotomía *f.* gastromyotomy.
gastromixorrea *f.* gastromyxorrhea.
gastrona *f.* gastrone.
gastronesteostomía *f.* gastronesteostomy.
gastroneumónico, -ca *adj.* gastropneumonic.
gastropancreatitis *f.* gastropancreatitis.
gastroparálisis *f.* gastroparalysis.
 gastroparálisis diabética gastroparalysis diabeticorum.
gastroparásito *m.* gastroparasitus.
gastroparesia *f.* gastroparesis.
gastroparesis *f.* gastroparesis.
gastroparietal *adj.* gastroparietal.
gastropatía *f.* gastropathy.
 gastropatía hipertrófica hipersecretoria hypertrophic hypersecretory gastropathy.
gastropático, -ca *adj.* gastropathic.
gastroperiodinia *f.* gastroperiodynia.
gastroperitonitis *f.* gastroperitonitis.
gastropexia *f.* gastropexy.
 gastropexia posterior de Hill Hill posterior gastropexy.
Gastrophilus hemorrhoidalis Gastrophilus hemorrhoidalis.
gastropilorectomía *f.* gastropylorectomy.
gastropilórico, -ca *adj.* gastropyloric.
gastropilorospasmo del recién nacido *m.* pyloric spasm of the newborn.
gastroplastia *f.* gastroplasty.
 gastroplastia en banda vertical vertical banded gastroplasty.
 gastroplastia de Collis Collis gastroplasty.
gastroplejía *f.* gastroplegia, gastroplegy.
gastroplicación *f.* gastroplication, gastroplicature.
gastroptixis *f.* gastroptyxis.
gastroptosi *f.* gastroptosia, gastroptosis.
gastroptosis *f.* gastroptosis.
gastropulmonar *adj.* gastropulmonary.
gastrorradiculitis *f.* gastroradiculitis.
gastrorrafia *f.* gastrorrhaphy.
gastrorragia *f.* gastrorrhagia.
gastrorrea *f.* gastrorrhea.
gastrorrexis *f.* gastrorrhexis.
gastroscopia *f.* gastroscopy.
gastroscópico, -ca *adj.* gastroscopic.
gastroscopio *m.* gastroscope.
 gastroscopio fibróptico fiberoptic gastroscope.
gastroselectivo, -va *adj.* gastroselective.
gastrosia *f.* gastrosia, gastrosis.
 gastrosia micótica gastrosia fungosa.
gastrosis *f.* gastrosis.
gastrospasmo *m.* gastrospasm.
gastrospiria *f.* gastrospiry.

gastrosplénico, -ca *adj.* gastrosplenic.
gastrosquisis *f.* gastroschisis.
gastrostaxis *f.* gastrostaxis.
gastrostenosis *f.* gastrostenosis.
gastrostogavaje *m.* gastrostogavage.
gastrostolavado *m.* gastrostolavage.
gastrostoma *m.* gastrostoma.
gastrostomía *f.* gastrostomy.
 gastrostomía de Beck Beck's gastrostomy.
 gastrostomía de Glassman Glassman's gastrostomy.
 gastrostomía de Stamm Stamm's gastrostomy.
 gastrostomía de Witzel Witzel's gastrostomy.
gastrostomosis *f.* gastrostomy.
gastrosucorrea *f.* gastrosuccorrhea.
 gastrosucorrea digestiva digestive gastrosuccorrhca.
gastrotimpanitis *f.* gastrotympanites.
gastrotisis *f.* gastrophthisis.
gastrotomía *f.* gastrotomy.
gastrótomo *m.* gastrotome.
gastrotonometría *f.* gastrotonometry.
gastrotonómetro *m.* gastrotonometer.
gastrotoracópago *m.* gastrothoracopagus.
gastrotóxico, -ca *adj.* gastrotoxic.
gastrotoxina *f.* gastrotoxin.
gastrotraquelotomía *f.* gastrotrachelotomy.
gastrotrópico, -ca *adj.* gastrotropic.
gastroxia *f.* gastroxia.
gastroxinsis *f.* gastroxynsis.
gastroyeyunocólico, -ca *adj.* gastrojejunocolic.
gastroyeyunoesofagostomía *f.* gastrojejunoesophagostomy.
gastroyeyunostomía *f.* gastrojejunostomy.
gástrula *f.* gastrula.
gastrulación *f.* gastrulation.
gatillo¹ *m.* ferrule.
gatillo² *m.* trigger.
gatismo *m.* gatism.
gato *m.* jackscrew.
 gato de tornillo jackscrew.
gaussiano, -na *adj.* Gaussian.
gavaje *m.* gavage.
gavilla *f.* leash.
gay *m., f.* gay.
gaznate *m.* gullet.
Gedoelstia Gedoelstia.
gedoelstiosis *f.* gedoelstiosis.
gefirofobia *f.* gephyrophobia.
gegenhalten *f.* gegenhalten.
gel *m.* gel.
 gel coloidal colloidal gel.
 gel farmacopeico pharmacopeial gel.
gelación *f.* gelation.
gelar *v.* gelate.
gelasa *f.* gelase.
gelasma *m.* gelasmus.
gelasmo *m.* gelasmus.
gelástico, -ca *adj.* gelastic.
gelatificación *f.* gelatification.
gelatígeno, -na *adj.* gelatigenous.
gelatina *f.* gelatin, jelly.
 gelatina cardíaca cardiac jelly.
 gelatina de cinc zinc gelatin.
 gelatina de Elsner Elsner's jelly.
 gelatina de esmalte enamel jelly.
 gelatina de glicerina, gelatina glicerinada glycerin jelly, glycerinated gelatin.
 gelatina medicada medicated gelatin.
 gelatina mineral mineral jelly.
 gelatina de musgo de Irlanda Irish moss gelatin.
 gelatina nutriente nutrient jelly.
 gelatina peptona peptone.

 gelatina de Piorkowski Piorkowski's gelatin.
 gelatina de Stilling Stilling's jelly.
 gelatina vegetal vegetable gelatin, vegetable jelly.
 gelatina de Wharton Wharton's jelly, gelatin of Wharton.
gelatinífero, -ra *adj.* gelatiniferous.
gelatiniforme *adj.* gelatinous.
gelatinización *f.* gelatification.
gelatinizar *v.* gelatinize.
gelatinoide *adj.* gelatinoid.
gelatinolítico, -ca *adj.* gelatinolytic.
gelatinoso, -sa *adj.* gelatinous.
gelatión *f.* gelation.
gelcromatografía *f.* gel filtration.
gelificación *f.* gelification.
gelificar *v.* gelate.
gelómetro *m.* gelometer.
gelosis *f.* gelosis.
geloterapia *f.* gelotherapy, gelotothérapy.
gelotripsia *f.* gelotripsy.
gelsolina *f.* gelsolin.
gema *f.* gemma.
gemación *f.* budding, gemmation.
gemangioma *m.* gemmangioma.
gemelación *f.* twinning.
 gemelación espontánea spontaneous twinning.
 gemelación experimental experimental twinning.
gemelar *adj.* gemellary.
gemelípara *f.* gemellipara.
gemeliparidad *f.* twinning.
gemelización *f.* twinning.
gemelo, -la *m., f.* twin, geminus.
 gemelo acardíaco acardiac twin.
 gemelo alantoidoangiópago allantoidoangiopagous twin.
 gemelo binovular, gemelo biovular binovular twin, diovular twin.
 gemelo desigual unequal twin.
 gemelo dicigótico dizygotic twin.
 gemelo dicoriales, gemelo dicoriónico dichorial twin, dichorionic twin.
 gemelo disimilar dissimilar twin.
 gemelo distinto unlike twin.
 gemelo de dos huevos two-egg twin.
 gemelo encigótico enzygotic twin.
 gemelo falso false twin.
 gemelo fraterno fraternal twin.
 gemelo heterólogo heterologous twin.
 gemelo heteroovular hetero-ovular twin.
 gemelo idéntico identical twin.
 gemelo en impacción impacter twin.
 gemelo monoamniótico monoamniotic twin.
 gemelo monocigótico, gemelo monocorial, gemelo monocorlónico, gemelo monoovular monozygotic twin, monochorial twin, monochorionic twin, monovular twin, mono-ovular twin.
 gemelo onfaloangiópago omphaloangiopagous twin.
 gemelo parásito parasitic twin.
 gemelo parásito placentario placental parasitic twin.
 gemelo policigótico polyzygotic twin.
 gemelo siamés Siamese twin.
 gemelo similar similar twin.
 gemelo de un huevo one-egg twin.
 gemelo unido conjoined twin.
 gemelo unidos asimétrico asymmetrical conjoined twin.
 gemelo unidos desigual unequal conjoined twin.
 gemelo unidos igual equal conjoined twin.

gemelo unidos incompleto incomplete conjoined twin.
gemelo unidos simétrico symmetrical conjoined twin.
gemelo uniovular uniovular twin.
gemelo verdadero true twin.
gemelología *f.* gemellology.
Gemella haemolysans Gemella haemolysans.
geminación *f.* gemination.
geminado, -da *adj.* geminate.
gémino, -na *m., f.* geminus.
geminoso, -sa *adj.* geminous.
gemistocítico, -ca *adj.* gemistocytic.
gemistocito *m.* gemistocyte.
gemistocitoma *m.* gemistocytoma.
gémula *f.* gemmule.
gen *m.* gene.
  gen alélico allelic gene.
  gen autosómico autosomal gene.
  gen CI CI gene.
  gen codominante codominant gene.
  gen complementario complementary gene.
  gen condicionado por el sexo sex-conditioned gene.
  gen de control control gene.
  gen desreprimido derepressed gene.
  gen dividido split gene.
  gen dominante dominant gene.
  gen estructural structural gene.
  gen de fuga leaky gene.
  gen H, gen de histocompatibilidad H gene, histocompatibility gene.
  gen holándrico holandric gene.
  gen influido por el sexo sex-influenced gene.
  gen de inmunoglobulinas inmunoglobulin gene.
  gen de inmunorrespuesta immune response gene.
  gen de interacción celular cell interaction gene.
  gen Ir Ir gene.
  gen Is Is gene.
  gen letal lethal gene.
  gen ligado al sexo sex-linked gene.
  gen ligado a X X-linked gene.
  gen ligado a Y Y-linked gene.
  gen limitado por el sexo sex-limited gene.
  gen mayor major gene.
  gen mímico mimic gene.
  gen mitocondrial mitochondrial gene.
  gen mutante mutant gene.
  gen operador operator gene.
  gen penetrante penetrant gene.
  gen pleyotrópico, gen pleiotrópico pleiotropic gene.
  gen de reacción inmunitaria immune response gene.
  gen recesivo recessive gene.
  gen recíproco reciprocal gene.
  gen regulador regulator gene, regulatory gene.
  gen represor repressor gene.
  gen reprimido repressed gene.
  gen silencioso silent gene.
  gen sinténicos syntenic gene.
  gen subletal sublethal gene.
  gen de tipo salvaje wild-type gene.
  gen supresor inmunitario immune suppressor gene.
  gen de transferencia transfer gene.
gena *f.* gena.
genal *adj.* genal.
gencianina *f.* gentianin.
gencianofílico, -ca *adj.* gentianophilic, gentianophilous.

gencianófilo, -la[1] *m., f.* gentianophil.
gencianófilo, -la[2] *adj.* gentianophilic, gentianophilous.
gencianófobo, -ca *adj.* gentianophobic, gentianophobous.
gendarme *m.* policeman.
genealogía *f.* genealogy.
generación *f.* generation.
  generación alternada, generación alternante alternate generation.
  generación asexual asexual generation.
  generación directa direct generation.
  generación espontánea spontaneous generation.
  generación filial primera first filial generation, F1 generation.
  generación filial segunda second filial generation, F2 generation.
  generación no sexual non-sexual generation.
  generación paterna, generación parental parental generation.
  generación saltada skipped generation.
  generación sexual sexual generation.
  generación virgen virgin generation.
  generación vivípara viviparous generation.
generador *m.* generator.
  generador de aerosoles aerosol generator.
  generador de pulso pulse generator.
  generador de pulso asincrónico asynchronous pulse generator.
  generador de pulso de demanda demand pulse generator.
  generador de pulso desencadenado auricular atrial triggered pulse generator.
  generador de pulso de frecuencia fija fixed rate pulse generator.
  generador de pulso inhibido ventricular ventricular inhibited pulse generator.
  generador de pulso sincrónico auricular atrial synchronous pulse generator.
  generador de pulso sincrónico ventricular ventricular synchronous pulse generator.
  generador de pulso standby standby pulse generator.
  generador de radionúclido radionuclide generator.
general *adj.* general.
generalista *m., f.* general practitioner.
generalización *f.* generalization.
generalizado, -da *adj.* generalized.
generativo, -va *adj.* generative.
genérico, -ca *adj.* generic.
género[1] *m.* genus.
género[2] *m.* gender.
genesíaco, -ca *adj.* genesial.
genésico, -ca *adj.* genesic.
genesiología *f.* genesiology.
génesis *f.* genesis.
genesistasia *f.* genesistasis.
genesistasis *f.* genesistasis.
genestático, -ca *adj.* genestatic.
genética *f.* genetics.
  genética bacteriana bacterial genetics.
  genética bioquímica biochemical gene.
  genética clínica clinical genetics.
  genética de la conducta behavior genetics.
  genética cuantitativa quantitative genetics.
  genética estadística statistical genetics.
  genética galtoniana Galtonian genetics.
  genética humana human genetics.
  genética inversa reverse genetics.
  genética matemática mathematical genetics.
  genética médica medical genetics.
  genética mendeliana Mendelian genetics.
  genética microbiana microbial genetics.

  genética molecular molecular genetics.
  genética de población, genética poblacional population genetics.
  genética de trasplantes transplantation genetics.
genético, -ca *adj.* genetic.
genetista *m., f.* geneticist.
genetotrófico, -ca *adj.* genetotrophic.
geniano, -na *adj.* genial, genian.
geniantralgia *f.* genyantralgia.
geniantritis *f.* genyantritis.
geniantro *m.* genyantrum.
génico, -ca *adj.* genic.
geniculado, -da *adj.* geniculate, geniculated.
genicular *adj.* genicular.
genículo *m.* geniculum.
geniculum *m.* geniculum.
geniohioideo, -a *adj.* geniohyoid.
genión *m.* genion.
genioplastia *f.* genioplasty.
geniplastia *f.* genyplasty.
geniquelloplastia *f.* geniocheiloplasty, genycheiloplasty.
geniquiloplastia *f.* geniocheiloplasty, genycheiloplasty.
genital *adj.* genital.
genitales *m.* genitals, genitalia.
  genitales externos external genitalia.
  genitales externos ambiguos ambiguous external genitalia.
  genitales indiferentes indifferent genitalia.
  genitales internos internal genitalia.
genitalia *f.* genitals, genitalia.
genitaloide *adj.* genitaloid.
genitaloideo, -a *adj.* genitaloid.
genitocrural *adj.* genitocrural.
genitofemoral *adj.* genitofemoral.
genitoinfeccioso, -sa *adj.* genitoinfectious.
genitoplastia *f.* genitoplasty.
genitourinario, -ria *adj.* genitourinary.
genoblasto *m.* genoblast.
genodermatología *f.* genodermatology.
genodermatosis *f.* genodermatosis.
genoespecie *f.* genospecies.
genofobia *f.* genophobia.
genoma *m.* genome.
  genoma humano human genome.
genómico, -ca *adj.* genomic.
genoneurodermatosis *f.* genoneurodermatosis.
genoplastia *f.* genyplasty.
genoteca *f.* gene library.
genotípico, -ca *adj.* genotypic, genotypical.
genotipo *m.* genotype.
genoto *m.* genote.
genotoxicidad *f.* genotoxicity.
genotóxico, -ca *adj.* genotoxic.
genu genu.
  genu recurvatum genu recurvatum.
  genu valgo, genu valgum genu introrsum, genu valgum.
  genu varo, genu varum genu extrorsum, genu varum.
genual *adj.* genual.
genucubital *adj.* genucubital.
genufacial *adj.* genufacial.
genulna *adj.* genuine.
genupectoral *adj.* genupectoral.
genus *m.* genus.
geocancerología *f.* geocarcinology.
geocarcinología *f.* geocarcinology.
geoda *f.* geode.
geofagia *f.* geophagia, geophagy.
geofagismo *m.* geophagism.
geofagista *m., f.* geophagist.

geófago, -ga *m., f.* geophagist.
geofílico, -ca *adj.* geophilic.
geomedicina *f.* geomedicine.
geopatología *f.* geopathology.
Geophilus Geophilus.
geoquímica *f.* geochemistry.
geotáctico, -ca *adj.* geotactic.
geotactismo *m.* geotaxis.
geotaxia *f.* geotaxis.
geotaxis *f.* geotaxis.
geotragia *f.* geotragia.
Geotrichum candidum Geotrichum candidum.
geotricosis *f.* geotrichosis.
geotrópico, -ca *adj.* geotropic.
geotropismo *m.* geotropism.
  geotropismo positivo positive geotropism.
  geotropismo negativo negative geotropism.
gerático, -ca *adj.* geratic.
geratología *f.* geratology.
gerbo *m.* gerbil.
gereología *f.* gereology.
geriatra *m., f.* geriatrician.
geriatría *f.* geriatrics.
  geriatría dental dental geriatrics.
geriátrico, -ca *adj.* gerontal, geriatric.
geriodóntica *f.* geriodontics.
geriodontista *m., f.* geriodontist.
germectomía *f.* dental germectomy.
germen *m.* germ.
  germen dental, germen dental de reserva, germen dentario, germen del diente dental germ, tooth germ, reserve tooth germ.
  germen del esmalte enamel germ.
  germen del pelo hair germ.
germicida¹ *m.* germicide.
germicida² *adj.* germicidal.
germinación *f.* germination.
germinal *adj.* germinal.
germinativo, -va *adj.* germinative.
germinoma *m.* germinoma.
germógeno *m.* germogen.
gerocomia *f.* gerocomia, gerocomy, gerokomy.
gerodermia *f.* geroderma.
  gerodermia osteodisplásica geroderma osteodysplastica.
gerodoncia *f.* gerodontics.
gerodóntico, -ca *adj.* gerodontic.
gerodontista *m., f.* gerodontist.
gerodontología *f.* gerodontology.
geromarasmo *m.* geromarasmus.
geromorfismo *m.* geromosphism.
  geromorfismo cutáneo cutaneous geromosphism.
geróntico, -ca *adj.* gerontal.
gerontofilia *f.* gerontophilia.
gerontófilo *m.* gerontophile.
gerontofobia *f.* gerontophobia.
gerontología *f.* gerontology.
gerontólogo, -ga *m., f.* gerontologist.
gerontopía *f.* gerontopia.
gerontopsia *f.* gerontopia.
gerontopsiquiatría *f.* geropsychiatry.
gerontoterapéutica *f.* gerontotherapeutics.
gerontoterapia *f.* gerontotherapy.
gerontotoxón *m.* gerontotoxon.
  gerontotoxón lenticular gerontoxon lentis.
gerontoxón *m.* gerontoxon.
geruestmark *f.* geruestmark.
gestación *f.* gestation.
gestacional *adj.* gestational.
gestágeno *m.* gestagen.
gestágeno, -na *adj.* gestagenic.
gestaltismo *m.* gestaltism.
gestosis *f.* gestosis.
Giardia Giardia.

Giardia intestinalis Giardia intestinalis.
Giardia lamblia Giardia lamblia.
giardiasis *f.* giardiasis.
giba *f.* boss, gibbus, hump.
  giba de Hampton Hampton's hump.
  giba parietal parietal boss.
gibosidad *f.* gibbosity, humpback, hunchback.
giboso, -sa *adj.* bosselated, gibbous.
gigante *m., f.* giant.
gigantismo *m.* gigantism.
  gigantismo acromegálico acromegalic gigantism.
  gigantismo cerebral cerebral gigantism.
  gigantismo eunucoide, gigantismo eunucoideo eunuchoid gigantism.
  gigantismo fetal fetal gigantism.
  gigantismo hiperhipofisario hyperpituitary gigantism.
  gigantismo hipofisario pituitary gigantism.
  gigantismo normal, gigantismo primordial normal gigantism, primordial gigantism.
gigantoblasto *m.* gigantoblast, gigantochromoblast.
gigantocito *m.* gigantocyte.
gigantomastia *f.* gigantomastia.
gigantosoma *m.* gigantosoma.
gikiyami *f.* gikiyami.
gimnasia *f.* gymnastics.
  gimnasia ocular ocular gymnastics.
  gimnasia sueca Swedish gymnastics.
gimnobacteria *f.* gymnobacterium.
gimnocito *m.* gymnocyte.
gimnofobia *f.* gymnophobia.
gimnoplasto *m.* gymnoplast.
gimnoscópico, -ca *adj.* gymnoscopic.
gimnosofía *f.* gymnosophy.
ginandria *f.* gynandria, gynandry.
ginandrismo *m.* gynandrism.
ginandro *m.* gynander.
ginandroblastoma *m.* gynandroblastoma.
ginandroide *m.* gynandroid.
ginandromorfismo *m.* gynandromorphism.
ginandromorfo *m.* gynandromorph.
ginandromorfo, -fa *adj.* gynandromorphous.
ginantropía *f.* gynanthropia.
ginantropismo *m.* gynanthropism.
ginatresia *f.* gynatresia.
ginecogénico, -ca *adj.* gynecogenic.
ginecógeno *m.* gynecogen.
ginecoide *adj.* gynecoid, gynoid.
ginecoideo, -a *adj.* gynecoid.
ginecología *f.* gynecology.
ginecológico, -ca *adj.* gynecologic, gynecological.
ginecólogo, -ga *m., f.* gynecologist.
ginecomanía *f.* gynecomania.
ginecomastia *f.* gynecomastia.
  ginecomastia nutricional nutritional gynecomastia.
  ginecomastia de realimentación refeeding gynecomastia.
  ginecomastia de rehabilitación rehabilitation gynecomastia.
ginecomatismo *m.* gynecomastism.
ginecopatía *f.* gynecopathy.
ginecotocología *f.* gynecotocology.
gineducto *m.* gyneduct.
ginefilia *f.* gynephilia.
ginefobia *f.* gynephobia.
gineplastia *f.* gyneplasty.
giniva *f.* gingiva.
gingival *adj.* gingival.
gingivalgia *f.* gingivalgia.
gingivectomía *f.* gingivectomy.
gingivitis *f.* gingivitis.

gingivitis atrófica senil atrophic senile gingivitis.
gingivitis por bismuto bismuth gingivitis.
gingivitis descamativa desquamative gingivitis.
gingivitis descamativa crónica chronic desquamative gingivitis.
gingivitis por difenilhidantoína diphenylhydantoin gingivitis.
gingivitis por Dilantin Dilantin gingivitis, dilantin gingivitis.
gingivitis del embarazo pregnancy gingivitis.
gingivitis eruptiva eruptive gingivitis.
gingivitis escorbútica scorbutic.
gingivitis estreptocócica streptococcal gingivitis.
gingivitis fagedénica phagedenic gingivitis.
gingivitis fusoespirilar, gingivitis fusospiroquetósica fusospirillary gingivitis, fusospirochetal gingivitis.
gingivitis de la gravidez gingivitis gravidarum.
gingivitis hemorrágica hemorrhagic gingivitis.
gingivitis herpética herpetic gingivitis.
gingivitis hiperplásica hyperplastic gingivitis.
gingivitis hormonal hormonal gingivitis.
gingivitis leucémica hiperplásica hyperplastic leukemic gingivitis.
gingivitis marginal marginal gingivitis.
gingivitis marginal generalizada generalized marginal gingivitis.
gingivitis marginal simple simple marginal gingivitis.
gingivitis marginal supurativa suppurative marginal gingivitis, gingivitis marginalis suppurativa.
gingivitis necrosante aguda acute necrotizing gingivitis.
gingivitis proliferativa proliferative gingivitis.
gingivitis supurante suppurating gingivitis.
gingivitis por rollos de algodón cotton-roll gingivitis.
gingivitis tuberculosa tuberculous gingivitis.
gingivitis ulceromembranosa, gingivitis ulceromembranosa aguda, gingivitis ulcerosa aguda, gingivitis ulcerosa necrosante ulceromembranous gingivitis, acute ulceromembranous gingivitis, acute ulcerative gingivitis, necrotizing ulcerative gingivitis.
gingivitis ulcerosa necrosante aguda acute necrotizing ulcerative gingivitis (ANUG).
gingivitis de Vincent Vincent's gingivitis.
gingivoaxial *adj.* gingivoaxial.
gingivoaxil *adj.* gingivoaxial.
gingivobucoaxil *adj.* gingivobuccoaxial.
gingivoestomatitis *f.* gingivostomatitis.
  gingivoestomatitis herpética herpetic gingivostomatitis.
  gingivoestomatitis ulcerosa necrosante necrotizing ulcerative gingivostomatitis.
gingivoglositis *f.* gingivoglossitis.
gingivolabial *adj.* gingivolabial.
gingivolinguoaxial *adj.* gingivolinguoaxial.
gingivolinguoaxil *adj.* gingivolinguoaxial.
gingivoóseo, -a *adj.* gingivo-osseous.
gingivoperiodontis *f.* gingivoperiodontis.
  gingivoperiodontis ulcerosa necrosante necrotizing ulcerative gingivoperiodontis.
gingivoplastia *f.* gingivoplasty.
gingivorragia *f.* gingivorrhagia.
gingivosis *f.* gingivosis.

gingliforme *adj.* ginglyform.
gínglimo *m.* ginglymus.
ginglimoartrodial *adj.* ginglymoarthrodial.
ginglimoide *adj.* ginglymoid.
ginglimoideo, -a *adj.* ginglymoid.
giniatría *f.* gyniatrics, gyniatry.
ginofobia *f.* gynophobia.
ginogénesis *f.* gynogenesis.
ginomerogonia *f.* gynomerogony.
ginomerogono *m.* gynomerogon.
ginopatía *f.* gynopathy.
ginopático, -ca *adj.* gynopathic.
ginoplastia *f.* gynoplastics, gynoplasty.
girar *v.* gyrate, turn.
girectomía *f.* gyrectomy.
   girectomía frontal frontal gyrectomy.
girencefálico, -ca *adj.* gyrencephalic.
girencéfalo, -la *adj.* gyrencephalic.
giro *m.* gyrus.
giromagnético, -ca *adj.* gyromagnetic.
girómetro *m.* gyrometer.
girosa *f.* gyrosa.
girosis *f.* gyrosa.
giroespasmo *m.* gyrospasm.
girospasmo *m.* gyrospasm.
girotropo *m.* gyrotrope.
gitagismo *m.* githagism.
glabela *f.* glabella, glabellum.
glabro, -bra *adj.* glabrous.
glacial *adj.* glacial.
   glacial ácido acético glacial acetic acid.
gladiado, -da *adj.* gladiate.
gladiomanubrial *adj.* gladiomanubrial.
glairidina *f.* glairin.
glairina *f.* glairin.
glande *m.* glans.
   glande del clítoris, glans clitoridis glans clitoridis.
   glande del pene, glans penis glans penis.
glandilema *m.* glandilemma.
glándula *f.* gland, glandula.
   glándula abierta exocrine gland.
   glándula absorbente absorbent gland.
   glándula accesoria accessory gland.
   glándula ácida acid gland.
   glándula acinar, glándula acinosa acinar
gland, acinous gland.
   glándula acinotubular acinotubular gland.
   glándula admaxilar admaxillary gland.
   glándula adrenal, glándula adrenalis adrenal gland, glandula adrenalis.
   glándula adrenal accesoria accessory adrenal gland.
   glándula agregada aggregate gland.
   glándula de Albarrán Albarran's gland.
   glándula albuminosa albuminous gland.
   glándula alveolar alveolar gland.
   glándula anacrina exocrine gland.
   glándula anal anal gland.
   glándula anómala endocrine gland.
   glándula anteprostática anteprostatic gland.
   *glándula apical, glándula apicas de la len-
gua* apical gland, apical gland of the tongue.
   glándula apocrina apocrine gland.
   glándula apórica aporic gland.
   glándula areolar areolar gland, glandulae
areolares.
   glándula aritenoidea, glándula aritenoide
arytenoid gland.
   glándula arterial arterial gland.
   glándula de Aselli Aselli's gland.
   glándula atrabiliar, glándula atrabiliaria
glandula atrabiliaris.
   glándula de Bartholin Bartholin's gland,
glandula vestibularis major.

   glándula basilar glandula basilaris.
   glándula de Bauhin Bauhin's gland.
   glándula de Baumgarten Baumgarten's gland.
   glándula blanco target gland.
   *glándula de Blandin, glándula de Blandin y
Nuhn* Blandin's gland, Blandin and Nuhn's
gland.
   glándula de la boca gland of the mouth.
   glándula de Boerhaave Boerhaave's gland.
   glándula de Bowman Bowman's gland.
   glándula bronquial bronchial gland, glandula bronchiale.
   glándula de Bruch Bruch's gland.
   glándula de Brunner Brunner's gland.
   glándula bucale buccal gland, glandula buccale.
   glándula bulbocavernosa bulbocavernous
gland.
   glándula bulbouretral bulbourethral gland,
glandula bulbo-urethralis, glandula bulbourethralis (Cowperii).
   glándula cardial, glándula del cardias cardiac gland.
   glándula cardial del esófago cardiac gland
of the esophagus.
   glándula carotídea carotid gland.
   glándula celiaca celiac gland.
   glándula centinela sentinel gland.
   glándula cerrada closed gland.
   glándula ceruminosa ceruminous gland, glandula ceruminosa.
   *glándula cervical, glándula cervical del úte-
ro* cervical gland of the uterus, cervical gland,
glandulae cervicales uteri.
   glándula de Ciaccio Ciaccio's gland.
   *glándula ciliar, glándula ciliar de la conjun-
tiva* ciliary gland, ciliary gland of the conjunctiva, glandulae ciliares conjunctivales, glandulae ciliares (Molli).
   glándula circumanal circumanal gland, glandulae circumanales.
   glándula cística de Luschka Luschka's cystic
gland.
   glándula clausa closed gland.
   glándula de Cobelli Cobelli's gland.
   glándula compuesta compound gland.
   glándula conglobada conglobate gland.
   glándula conglomerada compound gland.
   glándula conjuntival conjunctival gland,
glandulae conjunctivales.
   glándula contorneada convoluted gland.
   glándula de Cowper Cowper's gland.
   glándula cutáne cutaneous gland, glandulae
cutis.
   glándula duodenal duodenal gland, glandulae duodenales.
   glándula de Duverney Duverney's gland.
   glándula de Ebner Ebner's gland.
   glándula ecrina eccrine gland.
   glándula endocrina endocrine gland, glandulae endocrinae.
   glándula enroscada coil gland.
   glándula esofágica esophageal gland, glandulae esophageae, glandulae oesophageae.
   glándula estafilina staphyline gland.
   glándula excretoria excretory gland.
   glándula exocrina exocrine gland.
   glándula faríngea pharyngeal gland, gland
of the pharynx.
   glándula fúndica fundic gland of the stomach, fundus gland, proper gastric gland, glandula gastrica propria.
   glándula de Galeati (duodenal) Galeati's
gland, glandulae duodenales.
   glándula gástrica gastric gland, glandulae

gastricae.
   glándula de Gay Gay's gland.
   glándula genal, glándula geniana genal
gland.
   glándula genital genital gland.
   glándula gingival gingival gland.
   glándula de Gley Gley's gland.
   glándula gustatoria gustatory gland.
   glándula de Havers Havers' gland, Haversian
gland.
   glándula hemática hemal gland.
   glándula hematopoyética hematopoietic gland.
   glándula hemolinfática hemolymph gland, hemal lymph gland.
   glándula de Henle Henle's gland.
   glándula heterocrina heterocrine gland.
   glándula holocrina holocrine gland.
   glándula intercarotídea intercarotid gland.
   glándula intersticial interstitial gland.
   glándula intestinal intestinal gland, glandulae intestinales.
   glándula de Krause Krause's gland, glandulae conjunctivales, glandulae mucosae conjunctivae (Krausei).
   glándula labiales de la boca labial gland of
the mouth, labial gland, glandulae labiales oris,
glandulae labiales.
   glándula lagrimal lacrimal gland, glandula
lacrimalis.
   glándula laríngea laryngeal gland, gland of
larynx, glandulae laryngeae.
   glándula de Lieberkühn gland of Lieberkühn, Lieberkühn's gland, glandulae intestinales.
   glándula linfática lymph gland, lymphatic
gland.
   glándula lingual anterior anterior lingual
gland (of Blandin and Nuhn), glandulae lin-
guales anteriores.
   glándula de Littre Littre's gland.
   glándula de Luschka Luschka's gland.
   glándula mamaria mammary gland, lactiferous gland, milk gland, glandula mammaria.
   glándula de Meibomio Meibomian gland.
   glándula merocrina merocrine gland.
   glándula mixta mixed gland.
   glándula molar molar gland, retromolar
gland, glandulae molares.
   glándula de Moll Moll's gland, glandulae ciliares (Molli).
   glándula monoptíquica monoptychic gland.
   glándula de Montgomery Montgomery's
gland.
   glándula de Morgagni Morgagni's gland.
   glándula mucípara, glándula mucosa muciparous gland, mucous gland, glandula mucosa.
   glándula de la mucosa biliar gland of the
biliary mucosa, glandula mucosae biliosae.
   glándula de Nuhn Nuhn's gland.
   glándula odorífica odoriferous gland.
   glándula olfatoria olfactory gland.
   glándula oral gland of the mouth, glandulae
oris.
   glándula oxíntica oxyntic gland.
   glándula de Pacchioni pacchionian gland.
   glándula palatina palatine gland, glandulae
palatinae.
   glándula palpebral palpebral gland, glandulae tarsales.
   glándula paratiroide parathyroid gland, glandulae parathyroideae.
   glándula parauretral paraurethral gland, ductus para-urethrales urethrae femininae, ductus
para-urethrales urethrae masculinae.

glándula parótida parotid gland, glandula parotidea, glandula parotis.

glándula parótida accesoria accessory parotid gland, glandula parotidea accesoria.

glándula péptica peptic gland, glandulae gastricae.

glándula perspiratoria perspiratory gland.

glándula pilórica pyloric gland, glandulae pyloricae.

glándula pilosa pileous gland.

glándula pituitaria pituitary gland, glandula pituitaria.

glándula poliptíquica polyptychic gland.

glándula prehioide prehyoid gland.

glándula prepucial preputial gland, odoriferous gland of the prepuce, glandulae preputiales.

glándula prostática prostate gland, glandula prostatica.

glándula racemosa racemose gland.

glándula de Rivinus Rivinus' gland.

glándula de Rosenmüller Rosenmüller's gland.

glándula sacular saccular gland.

glándula salival salivary gland, glandulae salivariae.

glándula salival mayor major salivary gland, glandulae salivariae majores.

glándula salival menor minor salivary gland, glandulae salivariae minores.

glándula de Sandström Sandström's gland.

glándula de Schüller Schüller's gland.

glándula sebácea sebaceous gland, oil gland, glandulae sebaceae.

glándula de secreción externa exocrine gland.

glándula de secreción interna gland of internal secretion.

glándula seromucosa seromucous gland, glandula seromucosa.

glándula serosa serous gland, glandula serosa.

glándula de Serres Serres' gland.

glándula sexual sexual gland.

glándula de Sigmund Sigmund's gland.

glándula simple simple gland.

glándula sinovial synovial gland.

glándula de Skene Skene's gland.

glándula sublingual sublingual gland, glandula sublingualis.

glándula submandibular submandibular gland, glandula submandibularis.

glándula submaxilar submaxillary gland, maxillary gland, glandula submaxillaris.

glándula sudorípara sudoriferous gland, sudoriparous gland, sweat gland, glandulae sudoriferae.

glándula suprarrenal suprarenal gland, glandula suprarenalis.

glándula suprarrenal accesoria accessory suprarenal gland, glandula suprarenales accessoriae.

glándula de Suzanne Suzanne's gland.

glándula tarsal tarsal gland, tarsoconjunctival gland, glandulae tarsales.

glándula de Theile Theile's gland.

glándula de Tiedemann Tiedemann's gland.

glándula timo thymus gland.

glándula tiroides thyroid gland, glandula thyroidea.

glándula tubular, glándula tubulosa tubular gland.

glándula tubuloacinar tubuloacinar gland.

glándula de Tyson gland of Tyson, Tyson's gland.

glándula unicelular unicellular gland.

glándula uretral urethral gland, glandulae urethrales (Littrei).

glándula uterina uterine gland, glandulae uterinae.

glándula vascular vascular gland.

glándula vestibular vestibular gland.

glándula vestibular mayor greater vestibular gland, glandula vestibularis major.

glándula vulvovaginal vulvovaginal gland.

glándula de Wasmann Wasmann's gland.

glándula de Weber Weber's gland.

glándula de Woelfler Woelfler's gland.

glándula de Wolfring gland of Wolfring.

glándula de Zeis gland of Zeis.

glándula de Zuckerkandl Zuckerkandl's gland.

glandular *adj.* glandular.

glandulilla *f.* glandule.

glanduloso, -sa *adj.* glandulous.

glans glans.

glarómetro *m.* glarometer.

glaseriano, -na *adj.* Glaserian.

glaucoma *m.* glaucoma.

glaucoma absoluto absolute glaucoma.

glaucoma afáquico aphakic glaucoma.

glaucoma agudo acute glaucoma.

glaucoma de ángulo abierto open-angle glaucoma.

glaucoma de ángulo amplio wide-angle glaucoma.

glaucoma de ángulo cerrado angle-closure glaucoma.

glaucoma de ángulo cerrado agudo acute angle-closure glaucoma.

glaucoma de ángulo cerrado crónico chronic angle-closure glaucoma.

glaucoma de ángulo cerrado intermitente intermittent angle-closure glaucoma.

glaucoma de ángulo cerrado latente latent angle-closure glaucoma.

glaucoma de ángulo estrecho narrow-angle glaucoma.

glaucoma apopléctico apoplectic glaucoma.

glaucoma auricular auricular glaucoma.

glaucoma de baja tensión glaucoma without hypertension, low-tension glaucoma.

glaucoma por bloqueo de aire air-block glaucoma.

glaucoma por bloqueo de humor vítreo vitreous block glaucoma.

glaucoma por bloqueo pupilar pupillary block glaucoma.

glaucoma capsular capsular glaucoma, glaucoma capsulare.

glaucoma capsular seudoexfoliativo pseudoexfoliative capsular glaucoma.

glaucoma por células fantasmas ghost cell glaucoma.

glaucoma de cierre de ángulo, glaucoma por cierre del ángulo closed-angle glaucoma.

glaucoma combinado combined glaucoma.

glaucoma compensado compensated glaucoma.

glaucoma congénito congenital glaucoma.

glaucoma congestivo congestive glaucoma.

glaucoma congestivo agudo acute congestive glaucoma.

glaucoma consumado glaucoma consummatum.

glaucoma por contusión contusion glaucoma.

glaucoma crónico chronic glaucoma.

glaucoma crónico de ángulo estrecho chronic narrow-angle glaucoma.

glaucoma crónico simple chronic simple glaucoma.

glaucoma de Donders Donders' glaucoma.

glaucoma por esteroides corticosteroid glaucoma, steroid glaucoma.

glaucoma enzimático enzyme glaucoma.

glaucoma facógeno, glaucoma facolítico, glaucoma facomórfico phacogenic glaucoma, phacolytic glaucoma, phacomorphic glaucoma.

glaucoma fulminante glaucoma fulminans.

glaucoma hemorrágico hemorrhagic glaucoma.

glaucoma por hipersecreción hypersecretion glaucoma.

glaucoma inducido por corticosteroides corticosteroid glaucoma.

glaucoma inducido por quimotripsina chymotrypsin-induced glaucoma.

glaucoma infantil infantile glaucoma.

glaucoma inflamatorio inflammatory glaucoma.

glaucoma juvenil juvenile glaucoma.

glaucoma lenticular lenticular glaucoma.

glaucoma maligno malignant glaucoma.

glaucoma melanomalítico melanomalytic glaucoma.

glaucoma neovascular neovascular glaucoma.

glaucoma no congestivo non-congestive glaucoma.

glaucoma obstructivo obstructive glaucoma.

glaucoma pigmentario pigmentary glaucoma.

glaucoma primario primary glaucoma.

glaucoma prodrómico prodromal glaucoma.

glaucoma por quimotripsina chymotrypsin-induced glaucoma.

glaucoma de recesión del ángulo angle-recession glaucoma.

glaucoma secundario secondary glaucoma.

glaucoma simple, glaucoma simplex simple glaucoma, glaucoma simplex.

glaucoma de tensión baja low-tension glaucoma.

glaucoma traumático traumatic glaucoma.

glaucomatociclítico, -ca *adj.* glaucomatocyclitic.

glaucomatoso, -sa *adj.* glaucomatous.

glaucosis *f.* glaucosis.

glaucosuria *f.* glaucosuria.

glenohumeral *adj.* glenohumeral.

glenoide *adj.* glenoid.

glenoideo, -a *adj.* glenoid.

glenoiditis *f.* osteitis of the glenoid cavity.

glía *f.* glia.

glía ameboide ameboid glia.

glía citoplásmica cytoplasmic glia.

glía de Fañanás glia of Fañanás.

glía fibrilar fibrillary glia.

gliacito *m.* gliacyte.

glial *adj.* glial.

glicemia *f.* glycemia, glykemia.

glicemina *f.* glycemin.

glicerado *m.* glycerate.

glicerato *m.* glycerate.

gliceridemia *f.* glyceridaemia.

glicerina *f.* glycerin, glycerinum.

glicerinado, -na *adj.* glycerinated.

glicerinum glycerinum.

glicerófilo, -la *adj.* glycerophilic.

glicerogel *m.* glycerogel.

glicerogelatina *f.* glycerogelatin.

glicerol *m.* glycerol.

glicerolizar *v.* glycerolize.

glicina *f.* glycine.

glicinemia *f.* glycinemia.

glicinuria *f.* glycinuria.

glicinuria familiar familial glycinuria.
glicocálix *m.* glycocalyx.
glicocola *f.* glycocoll.
glicocorticoide *m.* glycocorticoid.
glicogénesis *f.* glycogenesis.
glicogenético, -ca *adj.* glycogenetic.
glicogénico, -ca *adj.* glycogenic.
glicógeno *m.* glycogen.
glicólisis *f.* glycolysis.
glicoproteína *f.* glycoprotein.
glicosemia *f.* glycosemia.
glicurónido, -da *adj.* glycuronide.
gliobacteria *f.* gliobacteria.
glioblasto *m.* glioblast.
glioblastoma multiforme *m.* glioblastoma multiforme.
glioblastosis cerebral glioblastosis cerebri.
gliocito *m.* gliocyte.
gliocitoma *m.* gliocytoma.
gliococo *m.* gliococcus.
gliofagia *f.* gliophagia.
gliofibrilar *adj.* gliofibrillary.
gliógeno, -na *adj.* gliogenous.
glioma *m.* glioma.
 glioma astrocítico astrocytic glioma.
 glioma endofítico, glioma endófito glioma endophytum.
 glioma ependimario ependymal glioma.
 glioma exofítico, glioma exófito glioma exophytum.
 glioma ganglionar ganglionic glioma.
 glioma gigantocelular gigantocellular glioma.
 glioma de la médula espinal glioma of the spinal cord.
 glioma mixto mixed glioma.
 glioma nasal nasal glioma.
 glioma óptico optic nerve glioma, optic glioma.
 glioma periférico peripheral glioma.
 glioma del quiasma óptico glioma of optic chiasm.
 glioma de la retina, glioma retiniano glioma retinae.
 glioma telangiectásico, glioma telangiectodes telangiectatic glioma, glioma telangiectodes.
gliomatosis *f.* gliomatosis.
gliomatoso, -sa *adj.* gliomatous.
gliomioma *m.* gliomyoma.
gliomixoma *m.* gliomyxoma.
glioneuroma *m.* glioneurona.
gliosarcoma *m.* gliosarcoma.
gliosis *f.* gliosis.
 gliosis difusa diffuse gliosis.
 gliosis endometrial glioma endometrii.
 gliosis espinal spinal gliosis.
 gliosis hemisférica hemispheric gliosis.
 gliosis isomorfa, gliosis isomórfica isomorphic gliosis, isomosphous gliosis.
 gliosis nodular hipertrófica hypertrophic nodular gliosis.
 gliosis perivascular perivascular gliosis.
 gliosis piloide piloid gliosis.
 gliosis raquídea spinal gliosis.
 gliosis unilateral unilateral gliosis.
 gliosis uterina glioma uteri.
gliosoma *m.* gliosome.
glioxalasa *f.* glyoxalase.
gliscrina *f.* glischrin.
gliscruria *f.* glischruria.
glisonitis *f.* glissonitis.
glissade *m.* glissade.
glissonitis *f.* glissonitis.
globina *f.* globin.

globinómetro *m.* globinometer.
globo *m.* globus.
 globo histérico globus hystericus.
 globo ocular, globo del ojo bulb, eyeball, globus of the eye.
 globo pálido globus pallidus.
 globo pálido lateral globus pallidus lateralis.
 globo pálido medial globus pallidus medialis.
globoide *adj.* globoid.
globos *m.* globi.
globósido, -da *adj.* globoside.
globoso, -sa *adj.* globose.
globular *adj.* globular.
globulífero, -ra *adj.* globuliferous.
globulímetro *m.* globulimeter.
globulina *f.* globulin.
 globulina aceleradora del suero serum accelerator globulin.
 globulina alfa alpha globulin.
 globulina antidiftérica antidiphtheritic globulin.
 globulina antihumana anti-human globulin.
 globulina antihumana sérica anti-human serum globulin.
 globulina antilinfocito (ALG) antilymphocyte globulin (ALG).
 globulina antitimocito (ATG) antithymocyte globulin (ATG).
 globulina antitóxica antitoxic globulin.
 globulina beta beta globulin.
 globulina conjugadora de testosterona-estradiol testosterone-estradiol-binding globulin (TEBG).
 globulina conjugadora (fijadora) de tiroxina, globulina que conjuga tiroxina thyroxine-binding globulin (TBG).
 globulina gamma gamma globulin.
 globulina inmune, globulina inmunitaria immune globulin.
 globulina inmune de hepatitis B, globulina inmunitaria de hepatitis B hepatitis B immune globulin.
 globulina inmune de la tos, globulina Inmunitaria de la tos ferina pertussis immune human globulin.
 globulina inmune humana vacunal, globulina inmunitaria humana vacunal vaccinia immune human globulin.
 globulina Inmune de poliomielitis, globulina inmunitaria de poliomielitis poliomyelitis immune globulin.
 globulina inmune contra (de), globulina inmunitaria contra (de) la rabia rabies immune globulin.
 globulina inmune de RH0 (D), globulina inmunitaria de RH0 (D) RH0 (D) immune globulin.
 globulina inmune de sarampión, globulina inmunitaria de sarampión measles immune globulin.
 globulina inmune sérica específica, globulina inmunitaria sérica específica, globulina inmune específica, globulina inmunitaria específica specific immune serum globulin.
 globulina inmune tetánica humana, globulina inmunitaria tetánica humana tetanus immune human globulin.
 globulina inmune contra (de) la tos ferina, globulina inmunitaria contra (de) la tos ferina pertussis immune globulin.
 globulina inmune de la varicela humana, globulina inmunitaria de la varicela humana chickenpox immune (human) globulin.
 globulina inmune contra la varicela zóster,

 globulina inmunitaria contra la varicela zóster varicella-zoster immune globulin (VZIG).
 globulina inmune al zóster, globulina inmunitaria al zóster, globulina inmune antizóster, globulina inmunitaria antizóster zoster immune globulin.
 globulina sérica humana inmune, globulina sérica humana inmunitaria immune human serum globulin.
 globulina séricas serum globulin.
globulinemia *f.* globulinemia.
globulinuria *f.* globulinuria.
globulisis *f.* globulysis.
glóbulo *m.* globule.
 glóbulo blanco white blood cell.
 glóbulo de dentina dentin globule.
 glóbulo de Dobie Dobie's globule.
 glóbulo de leche milk globule.
 glóbulo de Marchi Marchi's globule.
 glóbulo de mielina myelin globule.
 glóbulo de Morgagni Morgagni's globule.
 glóbulo rojo red blood cell.
globulólisis *f.* globulolysis.
globulolítico, -ca *adj.* globulolytic.
globulosa *f.* globulose.
globus globus.
 globus pallidus globus pallidus.
glomangioma *m.* glomangioma.
glomangiosis *f.* glomangiosis.
 glomangiosis pulmonar pulmonary glomangiosis.
glomectomía *f.* glomectomy.
glomerado, -da *adj.* glomerate.
glomerular *adj.* glomerular.
glomerulitis *f.* glomerulitis.
glomérulo *m.* glomerule, glomerulus.
 glomérulo arterial coccígeo coccygeal arterial glomerulus.
 glomérulo arterioso coclear glomerulus arteriosi cochleae.
 glomérulo caudal caudal glomerulus.
 glomérulo de Malpighi, glomérulo de Malpigio Malpighian glomerulus.
 glomérulo del mesonefros glomerulus of mesonephros.
 glomérulo nervioso no encapsulado nonencapsulated nerve glomerulus.
 glomérulo olfatorio olfactory glomerulus.
 glomérulo del pronefros glomeruli of pronephros.
 glomérulo renal, glomérulo del riñón, glomérulo de Ruysch glomerulus of the kidney, renal glomerulus glomerulus renis, Ruysch's glomerulus.
glomeruloesclerosis *f.* glomerulosclerosis.
 glomeruloesclerosis diabética diabetic glomerulosclerosis, glomerulosclerosis diabetica.
 glomeruloesclerosis intercapilar intercapillary glomerulosclerosis.
 glomeruloesclerosis segmentada focal, glomeruloesclerosis segmentaria focal focal segmentary glomerulosclerosis.
glomerulonefritis *f.* glomerulonephritis.
 glomerulonefritis aguda (GNA) acute glomerulonephritis.
 glomerulonefritis antimembrana basal antibasement membrane glomerulonephritis.
 glomerulonefritis crónica chronic glomerulonephritis.
 glomerulonefritis difusa diffuse glomerulonephritis.
 glomerulonefritis embólica focal focal embolic glomerulonephritis.
 glomerulonefritis exudativa exudative glo-

merulonephritis.

glomerulonefritis focal focal glomerulonephritis.

glomerulonefritis focal de Berger Berger's focal glomerulonephritis.

glomerulonefritis hemorrágica aguda acute hemorrhagic glomerulonephritis.

glomerulonefritis hipocomplementémica hypocomplementemic glomerulonephritis.

glomerulonefritis hipocomplementémica crónica chronic hypocomplementemic glomerulonephritis.

glomerulonefritis por IgA IgA glomerulonephritis.

glomerulonefritis lobular lobular glomerulonephritis.

glomerulonefritis local local glomerulonephritis.

glomerulonefritis maligna malignant glomerulonephritis.

glomerulonefritis membranoproliferativa membranoproliferative glomerulonephritis.

glomerulonefritis membranosa membranous glomerulonephritis.

glomerulonefritis mesangiocapilar mesangiocapillary glomerulonephritis.

glomerulonefritis nodular nodular glomerulonephritis.

glomerulonefritis posestreptocócica aguda acute poststreptococcal glomerulonephritis.

glomerulonefritis de progresión rápida rapidly progressive glomerulonephritis.

glomerulonefritis proliferativa, glomerulonefritis proliferativa mesangial proliferative glomerulonephritis, mesangial proliferative glomerulonephritis.

glomerulonefritis rápidamente progresiva rapidly progressive glomerulonephritis.

glomerulonefritis segmentaria segmental glomerulonephritis.

glomerulonefritis semilunar aguda acute crescentic glomerulonephritis.

glomerulonefritis subaguda subacute glomerulonephritis.

glomerulonefropatía *f.* glomerulonephropathy.

glomerulopatía *f.* glomerulopathy.

glomerulopatía diabética diabetic glomerulopathy.

glomerulopatía esclerosante focal focal sclerosing glomerulopathy.

glomerulosclerosis *f.* glomerulosclerosis.

glomeruloso, -sa *adj.* glomerulose.

glomerulotropina *f.* glomerulotropin.

glómico, -ca *adj.* glomal, glomic.

glomo *m.* glomus.

glomo aórticos, glomera aortica glomera aortica.

glomo carotídeo, glomus carotídeo, glomus caroticum body glomus, carotid glomus, glomus caroticum.

glomo coccígeo, glomus coccygeum coccygeal glomus, glomus coccygeum.

glomo coroideo, glomus choroideum choroid glomus, glomus choroideum.

glomo cutáneo cutaneous glomus.

glomo digital digital glomus.

glomo intravagal intravagal glomus, glomus intravagale.

glomo neuromioarterial neuromyoarterial glomus.

glomo pulmonar pulmonary glomus, glomus pulmonale.

glomoide *adj.* glomoid.

glomus glomus.

glosagra *f.* glossagra.

glosal *adj.* glossal.

glosalgia *f.* glossalgia.

glosectomía *f.* glossectomy.

glositis *f.* glossitis.

glositis areata exfoliativa, glositis areata marginada, glositis exfoliativa glossitis areata exfoliativa.

glositis atrófica atrophic glossitis.

glositis desecante glossitis desiccans.

glositis flemonosa phlegmonous glossitis.

glositis de Hunter Hunter's glossitis.

glositis idiopática idiopathic glossitis.

glositis migratoria glossitis migrans.

glositis migratoria benigna benign migratory glossitis.

glositis de Möller Möller's glossitis.

glositis rómbica media, glositis romboidal media, glositis romboidal mediana, glositis romboidea media median rhomboid glossitis, glossitis rhomboidea mediana.

glosocele *m.* glossocele.

glosocinestésico, -ca *adj.* glossocinesthesic, glossokinesthetic.

glosocoma *m.* glossocoma.

glosodinamómetro *m.* glossodynamometer.

glosodinia *f.* glossodynia.

glosodinia exfoliativa glossodynia exfoliativa.

glosodiniotropismo *m.* glossodyniotropism.

glosodontotropismo *m.* glossodontotropism.

glosoepiglótico, -ca *adj.* glossoepiglottic, glossoepiglottidean.

glosoespasmo *m.* glossospasm.

glosoestéresis *f.* glossosteresis.

glosofaríngeo *m.* glossopharyngeus.

glosofaríngeo, -a *adj.* glossopharyngeal.

glosofitia *f.* glossophytia.

glosofobia *f.* glossophobia.

glosógrafo *m.* glossograph.

glosograma *m.* glottogram.

glosografía *f.* glottography.

glosohial *adj.* glossohyal.

glosohioideo, -a *adj.* glossohyal.

glosolabial *adj.* glossolabial.

glosolalia *f.* glossolalia.

glosólisis *f.* glossolysis.

glosología *f.* glossology, glottology.

glosomanía *f.* glossomania.

glosomantia *f.* glosomantia.

glosonco *m.* glossoncus.

glosopalatino *m.* glossopalatinus.

glosopalatino, -na *adj.* glossopalatine.

glosopatía *f.* glossopathy.

glosopexia *f.* glossopexy.

glosopirosis *f.* glossopyrosis.

glosoplastia *f.* glossoplasty.

glosoplejía *f.* glossoplegia.

glosoptosia *f.* glossoptosis.

glosoptosis *f.* glossoptosis.

glosorrafia *f.* glossorrhaphy.

glososcopia *f.* glossoscopy.

glosospasmo *m.* glossospasm.

glosostéresis *f.* glossosteresis.

glosotomía *f.* glossotomy.

glosotractor *m.* glossotilt.

glosotriquia *f.* glossotrichia.

Glossina Glossina.

Glossina morsitans Glossina morsitans.

Glossina pallidipes Glossina pallidipes.

Glossina palpalis Glossina palpalis.

glossy-skin *f.* glossy-skin.

glotal *adj.* glottal.

glótico, -ca *adj.* glottic.

glotidoespasmo *m.* glottidospasm.

glotis *f.* glottis.

glotis intercartilaginosa intercartilaginous glottis.

glotis respiratoria respiratory glottis, glottis respiratoria.

glotis vocal glottis vocalis.

glotitis *f.* glottitis.

glotología *f.* glottology.

glucación *f.* glycation.

glucagón *m.* glucagon.

glucagonoma *m.* glucagonoma.

glucasa *f.* glucase, glycase.

glucatonía *f.* glucatonia.

glucemia *f.* glycemia, glykemia.

glúcido *m.* glucide.

glucíforo *m.* gluciphore.

glucocálix *m.* glycocalyx.

glucocáliz *m.* glycocalyx.

glucocerebrosidasa *f.* glucocerebrosidase.

glucocerebrósido *m.* glucocerebroside.

glucociaminasa *f.* glycocyaminase.

glucocinasa *f.* glucokinase.

glucocinético, -ca *adj.* glucokinetic.

glucocorticoide *m.* glucocorticoid.

glucocorticotrófico, -ca *adj.* glucocorticotrophic.

glucofilia *f.* glycophilia.

glucoforina *f.* glycophorin.

glucóforo *m.* glucophore.

glucosfingolipidosis *f.* glycosphingolipidosis.

glucogenasa *f.* glycogenase.

glucogénesis *f.* glucogenesis.

glucogenético, -ca *adj.* glucogenetic.

glucogénico, -ca *adj.* glucogenic.

glucógeno *m.* glucogen.

glucogenogénesis *f.* glycogenesis.

glucogenólisis *f.* glycogenolysis.

glucogenolítico, -ca *adj.* glycogenolytic.

glucogenopexia *f.* glycogenopexy.

glucogenosis *f.* glycogenosis.

glucogenosis por deficiencia de enzima ramificante brancher deficiency glycogenosis.

glucogenosis por deficiencia de fosforilasa hepática hepatophosphorylase deficiency glycogenosis.

glucogenosis por deficiencia de miofosforilasa myophosphorylase deficiency glycogenosis.

glucogenosis generalizada generalized glycogenosis.

glucogenosis hepatorrenal de glucosa 6-fosfatasa glucose 6-phosphatase hepatorenal glycogenosis.

glucogenosis tipo I type I glycogenosis.

glucogenosis tipo II type II glycogenosis.

glucogenosis tipo III type III glycogenosis.

glucogenosis tipo IV type IV glycogenosis.

glucogenosis tipo V type V glycogenosis.

glucogenosis tipo VI type VI glycogenosis.

glucogenoso, -sa *adj.* glycogenous.

glucogeusia *f.* glycogeusia.

glucoglicinuria *f.* glycoglycinuria.

glucohemia *f.* glucohemia, glycohemia.

glucohemoglobina *f.* glycohemoglobin.

glucohistequia *f.* glycohistechia.

glucólisis *f.* glucolysis.

glucolítico, -ca *adj.* glucolytic, glycolytic.

glucometabólico, -ca *adj.* glycometabolic.

glucometabolismo *m.* glycometabolism.

gluconeogénesis *f.* gluconeogenesis, glyconeogenesis.

gluconeogénico, -ca *adj.* gluconeogenetic.

glucopenia *f.* glucopenia, glycopenia.

glucopexia *f.* glycopexis.

glucopéxico, -ca *adj.* glycopexic.
glucopoliuria *f.* glycopolyuria.
glucoprivo *m.* glycoprival.
glucoproteína *f.* glycoprotein.
glucoproteinasa *f.* glucoproteinase.
glucoptialismo *m.* glycoptyalism.
glucorraquia *f.* glycorrhachia.
glucorrea *f.* glycorrhea.
glucorregulación *f.* glycoregulation.
glucorregulatorio, -ria *adj.* glycoregulatory.
glucorónico, -ca *adj.* glycuronic.
glucosa *f.* glucose.
glucosecretorio, -ria *adj.* glycosecretory.
glucosemia *f.* glycosemia.
glucosialia *f.* glycosialia.
glucosialorrea *f.* glycosialorrhea.
glucosilación *f.* glycosylation.
glucosina *f.* glucosin.
glucosómetro *m.* glycosometer.
glucostático, -ca *adj.* glycostatic.
glucosuria *f.* glucosuria, glycosuria.
 glucosuria por adrenalina epinephrine glycosuria.
 glucosuria alimentaria alimentary glycosuria.
 glucosuria benigna benign glycosuria.
 glucosuria digestiva digestive glycosuria.
 glucosuria emocional emotional glycosuria.
 glucosuria por floridzina, glucosuria floricínica phloridzin glycosuria, phlorhizin glycosuria.
 glucosuria hiperglucémica hyperglycemic glycosuria.
 glucosuria por magnesio magnesium glycosuria.
 glucosuria nerviosa nervous glycosuria.
 glucosuria no diabética non-diabetic glycosuria.
 glucosuria no hiperglucémica non-hyperglycemic glycosuria.
 glucosuria normoglucémica normoglycemic glycosuria.
 glucosuria ortoglucémica orthoglycemic glycosuria.
 glucosuria patológica pathologic glycosuria.
 glucosuria renal renal glycosuria.
 glucosuria tóxica toxic glycosuria.
glucotaxis *f.* glycotaxis.
glucotialismo *m.* glucoptialism.
glucotrófico, -ca *adj.* glycotrophic.
glucotrópico, -ca *adj.* glycotropic.
glucuresis *f.* glycuresis.
glucuroconjugación *f.* glycuronic conjugation.
glucurónido *m.* glucuronide.
glucuronidoconjugación *f.* glucuronic acid conjugation, glycuronic acid conjugation.
glucuronuria *f.* glucuronuria, glycuronuria.
glutamil *m.* glutamyl.
 glutamil transferasa, glutamil transpeptidasa glutamyl transferase, glutamyl transpeptidase.
glutamilo *m.* glutamyl.
glutatión *m.* glutathione.
glutationemia *f.* glutathionemia, glutathionaemia.
glutationuria *f.* glutathionuria.
gluten *m.* gluten.
glúteo, -a *adj.* gluteal.
gluteofemoral *adj.* gluteofemoral.
gluteoinguinal *adj.* gluteoinguinal.
glutinoso, -sa *adj.* glutinous.
glutitis *f.* glutitis.
glutolina *f.* glutolin.
glutoscopio *m.* glutoscope.
Glycophagus Glycophagus.

gnatalgia *f.* gnathalgia.
Gnathostoma spinigerum Gnathostoma spinigerum.
gnático, -ca *adj.* gnathic.
gnatión *m.* gnathion.
gnatitis *f.* gnathitis.
gnatocéfalo *m.* gnathocephalus.
gnatodinámica *f.* gnathodynamics.
gnatodinamómetro *m.* gnathodynamometer.
gnatodinia *f.* gnathodynia.
gnatografía *f.* gnathography.
gnatología *f.* gnathology.
gnatológico, -ca *adj.* gnathologic, gnathological.
gnatopalatosquisis *f.* gnathopalatoschisis.
gnatoplastia *f.* gnathoplasty.
gnatosquisis *f.* gnathoschisis.
gnatostática *f.* gnathostatics.
gnatostato *m.* gnathostat.
gnatostomiasis *f.* gnathostomiasis.
gnosia *f.* gnosia.
gnotobiología *f.* gnotobiology.
gnotobiota *f.* gnotobiota.
gnotobiote *m.* gnotobiote.
gnotobiótica *f.* gnotobiotics.
gnotobiótico, -ca *adj.* gnotobiotic.
gnotobioto *m.* gnotobiote.
gnotoforesis *f.* gnotophoresis.
gnotofórico, -ca *adj.* gnotophoric.
gola *f.* gorget.
golfo de la vena yugular interna bulbus venae jugularis superior.
golgiocinesis *f.* golgiokinesis.
golgiosoma *m.* golgiosome.
goma[1] *f.* gum.
goma[2] *m.* gumma.
 goma tuberculosa tuberculous gumma.
gomatoso, -sa[1] *adj.* gummatous.
gomatoso, -sa[2] *adj.* gummy.
gomitoli *f.* gomitoli.
gomoso, -sa *adj.* gummatous, gummy.
gonacracia *f.* gonacratia.
gónada *f.* gonad.
 gónada indiferente indifferent gonad.
 gónada tercera third gonad.
 gónada en tiras streak gonad.
gonadal *adj.* gonadal.
gonadectomía *f.* gonadectomy.
gonádico, -da *adj.* gonadial.
gonadoblastoma *m.* gonadoblastoma.
gonadocinético, -ca *adj.* gonadokinetic.
gonadocrina *f.* gonadocrin.
gonadogénesis *f.* gonadogenesis.
gonadoinhibidor *adj.* gonadoinhibitory.
gonadoinhibitorio, -ria *adj.* gonadoinhibitory.
gonadopatía *f.* gonadopathy.
gonadopausia *f.* gonadopause.
gonadostimulina *f.* gonadostimuline.
gonadoterapia *f.* gonadotherapy.
gonadotrofa *f.* gonadotroph.
gonadotrofo *m.* gonadotroph.
gonadotrófico, -ca *adj.* gonadotrophic.
gonadotrofina *f.* gonadotrophin.
 gonadotrofina anterohipofisaria, gonadotrofina pituitaria anterior anterior pituitary gonadotrophin.
 gonadotrofina coriónica (CG) chorionic gonadotrophin (CG).
 gonadotrofina coriónica humana (HCG) human chorionic gonadotrophin, (HCG).
 gonadotrofina equina, gonadotrofina sérica de yegua preñada (PMSG) equine PMSG, pregnant mare serum gonadotrophin.
 gonadotrofina menopáusica humana (HMG) human menopausal gonadotrophin, (HMG).

gonadotropa *f.* gonadotrope.
gonadotrópico, -ca *adj.* gonadotropic.
gonadotropina *f.* gonadotropin.
gonaducto *m.* gonaduct.
gonagra *f.* gonagra.
gonalgia *f.* gonalgia.
gonangiectomía *f.* gonangiectomy.
gonano *m.* gonane.
gonartritis *f.* gonarthritis.
gonartrocace *m.* gonarthrocace.
gonartromeningitis *f.* gonarthromeningitis.
gonartrosis *f.* gonarthrosis.
gonartrotomía *f.* gonarthrotomy.
gonatagra *f.* gonatagra.
gonatocele *m.* gonatocele.
gonecistitis *f.* gonecystitis.
gonecisto *m.* gonecyst, gonecystis.
gonecistolito *m.* gonecystolith.
gonecistopiosis *f.* gonecystopyosis.
goneítis *f.* gonitis.
gonfiasis *f.* gomphiasis.
gonfosis *f.* gomphosis.
gongilonemiasis *f.* gongylonemiasis.
Gongylonema Gongylonema.
 Gongylonema pulchrum, Gongylonema scutatum Gongylonema pulchrum, Gongylonema scutatum, scutate threadworm.
gonia *f.* gonia.
goniacampsia *f.* gonycampsis.
gonial *adj.* gonial.
gonicampsis *f.* gonycampsis.
gonicrótesis *f.* gonycrotesis.
goniectíposis *f.* gonyectyposis.
goniocele *m.* gonyocele.
goniocraneometría *f.* goniocraniometry.
goniocraniometría *f.* goniocraniometry.
goniodisgenesia *f.* goniodysgenesis.
goniofotografía *f.* goniophotography.
gonioma *m.* gonioma.
goniómetro *m.* goniometer.
 goniómetro digital finger goniometer.
gonión *m.* gonion.
gonionco *m.* gonyoncus.
goniopunción *f.* goniopuncture.
gonioscopia *f.* gonioscopy.
gonioscópico, -ca *adj.* gonioscopic.
gonioscopio *m.* gonioscope.
goniosinequia *f.* goniosynechia.
goniospasis *f.* gonyspasis.
goniotomía *f.* goniotomy.
goniscopia *f.* gonioscopy.
gonitis *f.* gonitis.
gonoblenorrea *f.* gonoblennorrhea.
gonocampsis *f.* gonocampsis.
gonocele *m.* gonocele.
gonocida *m.* gonocide.
gonocito *m.* gonocyte.
gonocitoma *m.* gonocytoma.
gonococemia *f.* gonococcemia.
gonococia *f.* gonococcia.
gonococicida *adj.* gonococcocidal.
gonocócico, -ca *adj.* gonococcal, gonococcic.
gonococida *adj.* gonococcidal.
gonococo *m.* gonococcus.
gonocorismo *m.* gonochorism, gonochorismus.
gonófago *m.* gonophage.
gonóforo *m.* gonophore, gonophorus.
gonohemia *f.* gonohemia.
gonorrea *f.* gonorrhea.
gonorreacción *f.* gonoreaction.
gonorreico, -ca *adj.* gonorrheal.
gonótomo *m.* gonotome.
gonotoxemia *f.* gonotoxemia.
gonotoxina *f.* gonotoxin.

Gonyaulax catanella Gonyaulax catanella.
Gordius Gordius.
   Gordius aquaticus Gordius aquaticus.
gorgoteo *m.* gurgling.
gorjerete *m.* gorget.
   sonda gorjerete probe gorget.
gorondou *m.* gorondou.
gorondú *m.* gorondou.
gorro frigio *m.* Phrygian cap.
gota[1] *f.* drop.
   gota a gota drip feeding, guttatim.
   gota de esmalte enamel drop.
   gota colgante hanging drop.
   gota estomacal stomach drop.
   gota knock-out knock-out drop.
   gota nasal nose drop.
   gota para el oído ear drop.
   gota ocular, gota para los ojos eye drop.
gota[2] *f.* gout, gutta.
   gota abarticular abarticular gout.
   gota aguda acute gout.
   gota articular articular gout.
   gota cálcica, gota por calcio calcium gout.
   gota cretácea chalky gout.
   gota enmascarada masked gout.
   gota idiopática idiopathic gout.
   gota irregular irregular gout.
   gota latente latent gout.
   gota oxálica oxalic gout.
   gota por plomo lead gout.
   gota poliarticular polyarticular gout.
   gota primaria primary gout.
   gota regular regular gout.
   gota retrocedente, gota retropulsa retrocedent gout.
   gota reumática rheumatic gout.
   gutta rosácea gutta rosacea.
   gota saturnina saturnine gout.
   gota secundaria secondary gout.
   gota serena, gutta serena gutta serena.
   gota tofácea tophaceous gout.
goteo *m.* drip.
   goteo de leche alcalina, goteo de leche alcalinizada de Winkelstein alkaline milk drip, alkalinized milk drip of Winkelstein.
   goteo intravenoso intravenous drip.
   goteo de Murphy Murphy drip.
   goteo posnasal postnasal drip.
gotero *m.* dropper.
gotiera *f.* gutter.
gotita *f.* droplet.
gotoso, -sa *adj.* gouty.
goundou *m.* goundou.
graafiano, -na *adj.* Graafian.
grácil *adj.* gracile.
gracilis *adj.* gracilis.
gradiente *m.* gradient.
   gradiente auriculoventricular atrioventricular gradient.
   gradiente de densidad density gradient.
   gradiente electroquímico electrochemical gradient.
   gradiente mitral mitral gradient.
   gradiente sistólico systolic gradient.
   gradiente ventricular ventricular gradient.
grado[1] *m.* degree.
   grado de libertad degree of freedom.
   grado de validez validity degree.
grado[2] *m.* grade.
   grado tumoral de Gleason Gleason's tumor grade.
graduado, -da *adj.* graduated.
grafanestesia *f.* graphanesthesia.
grafestesia *f.* graphesthesia.
gráfica *f.* chart, graph.

gráfica de Amsler Amsler's chart.
gráfica de colores de Reuss Reuss color chart.
gráfica de control de calidad quality control chart.
gráfica de dispersión scatterplot.
gráfica de Guibor Guibor's chart.
gráfica de lectura reading chart.
gráfica de Walker Walker's chart.
graficación *f.* charting.
gráfico, -ca *adj.* graphic.
gráfico *m.* chart, graph.
grafito *m.* graphite.
grafitosis *f.* graphitosis.
grafoanálisis graphoanalysis.
grafocatarsis *f.* graphocatharsis.
grafocinestésico, -ca *adj.* graphokinesthetic.
grafoespasmo *m.* graphospasm.
grafofobia *f.* graphophobia.
grafología *f.* graphology.
grafomanía *f.* graphomania.
grafomotor, -ra *adj.* graphomotor.
grafopatología *f.* graphopathology.
graforrea *f.* graphorrhea.
grafoscopio *m.* graphoscope.
grafospasmo *m.* graphospasm.
gragea *f.* dragée, sugar-coated pill.
gramínea *f.* grass.
gramnegativo, -va *adj.* gram-negative.
grampositivo, -va *adj.* gram-positive.
grandiosidad *f.* grandiosity.
grandioso, -sa *adj.* grandiose.
granito *m.* pimple.
grano *m.* grain, granum.
granoplasma *m.* granoplasm.
granulación *f.* granulation, granulatio.
   granulación aracnoidea, granulación aracnoide arachnoidal granulation, granulationes arachnoideae, granulationes arachnoideales.
   granulación de Bayle Bayle's granulation.
   granulación de Bright Bright's granulation.
   granulación celular cell granulation.
   granulación cerebral cerebral granulation, granulationes cerebrales.
   granulación exuberante exuberant granulation.
   granulación gris phthisis nodes.
   granulación de Pacchioni pacchionian granulation.
   granulación pironinófila pyroninophilic granulation.
   granulación de Reilly Reilly granulation.
   granulación de Virchow Virchow's granulation.
granulado *m.* granulated.
granular *adj.* granular.
granulia *f.* granulitis.
granuliforme *adj.* granuliform.
gránulo *m.* granule.
   gránulo acidófilo acidophil granule.
   gránulo acrosómico acrosomal granule.
   gránulo albuminoso albuminous granule.
   gránulo aleuronoides aleuronoid granule.
   gránulo alfa alpha granule.
   gránulo de Altmann Altmann's granule.
   gránulo anfófilo amphophil granule.
   gránulo argentafin argentaffin granule.
   gránulo atrial atrial granule.
   gránulo auricular específico specific atrial granule.
   gránulo de azufre sulfur granule.
   gránulo azur, gránulo azurófilo azure granule, azurophilic granule, azurophil granule.
   gránulo de Babès-Ernst Babès-Ernst granule.
   gránulo basal basal granule.
   gránulo basófilo basophil granule.

gránulo beta beta granule.
gránulo de Birbeck Birbeck granule.
gránulo de Bollinger Bollinger granule.
gránulo de Bütschli Bütschli's granule.
gránulo de cimógeno zymogen granule.
gránulo citoplásmico cytoplasmic granule.
gránulo cromático, gránulo cromófilo chromatic granule, chromophil granule, chromophilic granule.
gránulo cromófobo chromophobe granule.
gránulo de Crooke Crooke's granule.
gránulo delta delta granule.
gránulo de Ehrlich, gránulo de Ehrlich-Heinz Ehrlich-Heinz granule.
gránulo eosinófilo eosinophil granule.
gránulo esférico sphere granule.
gránulo específico de Bensley Bensley's specific granule.
gránulo de Fordyce Fordyce's granule.
gránulo fucsinófilo fuchsinophil granule.
gránulo gamma gamma granule.
gránulo de Grawitz Grawitz's granule.
gránulo de Heinz Heinz granule.
gránulo intersticial de Kölliker Kölliker's interstitial granule.
gránulo de Isaacs Isaacs' granule.
gránulo kappa kappa granule.
gránulo de Kretz Kretz's granule.
gránulo de Langerhans Langerhans' granule.
gránulo de Langley Langley's granule.
gránulo con membrana recubierta membrane-coating granule.
gránulo meníngeo meningeal granule.
gránulo metacromático metachromatic granule.
gránulo de Much Much's granule.
gránulo de mucinógeno mucinogen granule.
gránulo de Neusser Neusser's granule.
gránulo neutrófilo neutrophil granule.
gránulo de Nissl Nissl granule.
gránulo oxífilo oxyphil granule.
gránulo de Palade Palade granule.
gránulo de Paschen Paschen granule.
gránulo de pigmento pigment granule.
gránulo de Plehn Plehn's granule.
gránulo proacrosómicos proacrosomal granule.
gránulo de prosecreción prosecretion granule.
gránulo proteínico protein granule.
gránulo de queratohialina, gránulo queratohialino keratohyalin granule.
gránulo riciforme melon seed body granule.
gránulo de Schrön-Much Schrön-Much granule.
gránulo de Schüffner Schüffner's granule.
gránulo de secreción secretion granule, secretory granule.
gránulo seminal seminal granule.
gránulo tóxico toxic granule.
gránulo vermiforme vermiform granule.
gránulo de volutina volutin granule.
gránulo yodófilo iodophil granule.
gránulo yuxtaglomerulares juxtaglomerular granule.
gránulo de Zimmermann Zimmermann's granule.
granuloadiposo, -sa *adj.* granuloadipose.
granulocitario, -ria *adj.* granulocytic.
granulocítico, -ca *adj.* granulocytic.
granulocito *m.* granulocyte.
   granulocito en banda band form granulocyte.
   granulocito inmaduro immature granulocyte.

granulocito segmentado segmented granulocyte.

granulocitopatía *f.* granulocytopathy.

granulocitopenia *f.* granulocytopenia.

granulocitopoyesis *f.* granulocytopoiesis.

granulocitopoyético, -ca *adj.* granulocytopoietic.

granulocitosis *f.* granulocytosis.

granulocorpúsculo *m.* granulocorpuscle.

granulograsoso, -sa *adj.* granular-fatty.

granuloma *m.* granuloma.

  granuloma de las albercas swimming pool granuloma.

  granuloma amebiano, granuloma amibiano amebic granuloma.

  granuloma anular granuloma annulare.

  granuloma apical apical granuloma.

  granuloma de los balnearios swimming pool granuloma.

  granuloma por berilio beryllium granuloma.

  granuloma bilharzial bilharzial granuloma.

  granuloma por candida, granuloma candidiásico candida granuloma, candidal granuloma.

  granuloma de células gigantes giant cell granuloma.

  granuloma de células plasmáticas plasma cell granuloma.

  granuloma central de reparación de células gigantes central giant cell reparative granuloma.

  granuloma por circonio zirconium granuloma.

  granuloma coccidioide, granuloma coccidioideo coccidioidal granuloma.

  granuloma por colesterol cholesterol granuloma.

  granuloma de cuerpo extraño foreign body granuloma.

  granuloma dental, granuloma dentario dental granuloma.

  granuloma del embarazo granuloma gravidarum.

  granuloma endémico granuloma endemicum, granuloma epidemicum.

  granuloma eosinofílico de los huesos, granuloma eosinófilo eosinophilic granuloma, eosinophilic granuloma of the bone.

  granuloma eosinófilo de Mignon Mignon's eosinophilic granuloma.

  granuloma de erizo de mar sea urchin granuloma.

  granuloma esquistosómico schistosome granuloma.

  granuloma facial, granuloma facial eosinofílico granuloma faciale.

  granuloma fisurado granuloma fissuratum.

  granuloma fungoide granuloma fungoides.

  granuloma gangrenoso granuloma gangraenescens.

  granuloma glúteo infantil granuloma gluteale infantum.

  granuloma de Hodgkin Hodgkin's granuloma.

  granuloma infeccioso infectious granuloma.

  granuloma inguinal granuloma inguinale.

  granuloma inguinal tropical granuloma in guinale tropicum.

  granuloma del iris granuloma iridis.

  granuloma laríngeo laryngeal granuloma.

  granuloma por licopodio lycopodium granuloma.

  granuloma de la línea media midline granuloma.

  granuloma lipofágico lipophagic granuloma.

  granuloma lipoide, granuloma lipoideo lipoid granuloma.

  granuloma de Majocchi Majocchi granuloma.

  granuloma maligno malignant granuloma.

  granuloma moniliásico monilial granuloma.

  granuloma mortal de la línea media lethal midline granuloma.

  granuloma multiforme granuloma multiforme.

  granuloma oleoso oily granuloma.

  granuloma palúdico malarial granuloma.

  granuloma parasitario parasitic granuloma.

  granuloma periapical periapical granuloma.

  granuloma piogénico, granuloma piógeno pyogenic granuloma, granuloma pyogenicum.

  granuloma de las piscinas swimming pool granuloma.

  granuloma pudendo granuloma pudendi.

  granuloma pudendo tropical granuloma pudens tropicum.

  granuloma radicular root end granuloma.

  granuloma de reparación de células gigantes giant cell reparative granuloma.

  granuloma reparador de células gigantes reparative giant cell granuloma.

  granuloma reparador de células gigantes, central giant cell reparative granuloma, central.

  granuloma reparador de células gigantes, periférico giant cell reparative granuloma, peripheral.

  granuloma reticulohistiocítico reticulohistiocytic granuloma.

  granuloma reumático rheumatic granuloma.

  granuloma sarcoide sarcoidal granuloma.

  granuloma seudopiogénico pseudopyogenic granuloma.

  granuloma telangiectásico granuloma telangiectaticum.

  granuloma tricofítico trichophytic granuloma, granuloma trichophyticum.

  granuloma tropical granuloma tropicum.

  granuloma ulcerativo de los genitales, granuloma ulceroso de las regiones pudendas ulcerating granuloma of the pudenda.

  granuloma umbilical umbilical granuloma.

  granuloma venéreo venereal granuloma, granuloma venereum.

  granuloma xantomatoso xanthomatous granuloma.

granulomatosis *f.* granulomatosis.

  granulomatosis alérgica allergic granulomatosis.

  granulomatosis broncocéntrica bronchocentric granulomatosis.

  granulomatosis de células de Langerhans Langerhans cell granulomatosis.

  granulomatosis disciforme crónica y progresiva granulomatosis disciformis progressiva et chronica.

  granulomatosis intestinal lipofágica lipophagic intestinal granulomatosis.

  granulomatosis linfomatoide, granulomatosis linfomatoidea lymphomatoid granulomatosis.

  granulomatosis lipídica, granulomatosis lipoide lipid granulomatosis, lipoid granulomatosis.

  granulomatosis maligna malignant granulomatosis.

  granulomatosis de Miescher Miescher granulomatosis.

  granulomatosis respiratoria necrosante necrotizing respiratory granulomatosis.

  granulomatosis siderótica granulomatosis siderotica.

  granulomatosis de Wegener Wegener's granulomatosis.

granulomatoso, -sa *adj.* granulomatous.

granulómero *m.* granulomere.

granulopenia *f.* granulopenia.

granulopexia *f.* granulopexis, granulopexy.

granuloplasma *m.* granuloplasm.

granuloplástico, -ca *adj.* granuloplastic.

granulopotente *adj.* granulopotent.

granulopoyesis *f.* granulopoiesis.

granulopoyético, -ca *adj.* granulopoietic.

granulopoyetina *f.* granulopoietin.

granulosa *f.* granulose.

granulosidad *f.* granulosity.

granulosis *f.* granulosis.

  granulosis nasal roja, granulosis rubra nasi granulosis rubra nasi.

granuloso, -sa *adj.* granulose.

granulovacuolar *adj.* granulovacuolar.

granum granum.

grapa *f.* clip.

grasa *f.* fat.

  grasa blanca white fat.

  grasa de cadáver, grasa cadavérica corpse fat, grave-wax fat.

  grasa conjugada bound fat.

  grasa desdoblada split fat.

  grasa disimulada masked fat.

  grasa fetal fetal fat.

  grasa grave grave fat.

  grasa insaturada unsaturated fat.

  grasa de la leche milk fat.

  grasa moruloide moruloid fat, mulberry fat.

  grasa multilocular multilocular fat.

  grasa neutra neutral fat.

  grasa parda brown fat.

  grasa poliinsaturada polyunsaturated fat.

  grasa del quilo chyle fat.

  grasa saturada saturated fat.

  grasa unilocular unilocular fat.

graso, -sa *adj.* fatty.

gratificación *f.* gratification.

grattage *m.* grattage.

grave *adj.* grave, gravis.

gravedad *f.* gravity.

  gravedad cero zerogravidity.

  gravedad estándar standard gravity.

gravedo *m.* gravedo.

gravela *f.* gravel.

grávida *f.* gravid, gravida.

gravidez *f.* gravidity, graviditas.

  gravidez examinal graviditas examnialis.

  gravidez excorial graviditas exochorialis.

gravídico, -ca *adj.* gravidic.

gravidismo *m.* gravidism.

graviditas graviditas.

  graviditas examnialis graviditas examnialis.

  graviditas exochorialis graviditas exochorialis.

gravidocardiaco, -ca *adj.* gravidocardiac.

gravidopuerperal *adj.* gravidopuerperal.

gravilla *f.* gravel.

gravimétrico, -ca *adj.* gravimetric.

gravímetro *m.* gravimeter.

gravirreceptores *m.* gravireceptors.

gravistático, -ca *adj.* gravistatic.

gravitación *f.* gravitation.

gravitómetro *m.* gravitometer.

graznido sistólico *m.* systolic honk.

grefótomo *m.* greffotome.

gregaloide *adj.* gregaloid.

gregarismo *m.* gregariousness.

gresión *f.* gression.

grieta *f.* chasma, crevice.

grieta gingival gingival crevice.
grifosis *f.* gryphosis.
grilla *f.* grid.
  grilla de Wetzel Wetzel grid.
griocromo *m.* gryochrome.
gripal *adj.* grippal.
gripe *f.* flu, influenza, grippe.
  gripe A swine flu.
  gripe aviar bird flu, avian flu.
  gripe áurica grippe aurique.
  gripe endémica endemic flu.
  gripe porcina swine flu.
griposis *f.* gryposis.
  griposis del pene gryposis penis.
  griposis ungueal, griposis ungulum gryposis ungulum.
gris *adj.* gray.
  gris de acero steel gray.
  gris de plata silver gray.
  gris perihipogloso perihypoglossal gray.
grito *m.* cry.
  grito artrítico, grito articular arthritic cry,
articular cry, joint cry.
  grito cefálico cephalic cry.
  grito epiléptico epileptic cry.
  grito nocturno night cry.
grueso, -sa *adj.* gross.
grumo *m.* clot.
  grumo de cromatina chromatin clot.
  grumo de Nissl Nissl clot.
grumoso, -sa *adj.* grumose, grumous.
grupo *m.* group.
  grupo aglutinación group agglutination.
  grupo de capacitación training group.
  grupo citófilo cytophil group.
  grupo CMN CMN group.
  *grupo colon-tifóidico-disentérico, grupo de
colon, tifoidea y disentería* colon-typhoid-
dysentery group.
  grupo de control control group.
  grupo determinante determinant group.
  *grupo de diagnósticos relacionados (GDR),
grupos relacionados por diagnóstico* diag-

nosis-related group (DRG).
  grupo E E group.
  grupo emparejado matched group.
  grupo de encuentro encounter group.
  grupo de entrenamiento training group.
  grupo de entrenamiento de la sensibilidad
sensitivity training group.
  grupo específico specific group.
  grupo experimental experimental group.
  grupo glucóforo glucophore group.
  grupo de Lancefield Lancefield group of
streptococci.
  grupo de ligamiento linkage group.
  *grupo de paratifoidea y enteritis, grupo
paratifoidenteritis Salmonella* paraty-
phoid-enteritis group.
  grupo sanguíneo blood group.
  grupo de sensibilidad sensitivity group.
  grupo de septicemia hemorrágica hemorrhagic-septicemia group.
  grupo T T group.
  grupo de tareas task oriented group.
  grupo terapéutico therapeutic group.
guanidina *f.* guanidine.
guanidinemia *f.* guanidinemia.
guanóforo *m.* guanophore.
guantelete *m.* gauntlet.
guarda *f.* guard.
  guarda bucal mouth guard.
  guarda de mordida bite guard.
  guarda nocturna night guard.
  guarda oclusal occlusal guard.
guardaboca *f.* mouth guard.
guata *f.* wadding.
guayacán *m.* guaiac, guiac.
guayaco *m.* guaiac, guiac.
gubernacular *adj.* gubernacular.
gubernáculo *m.* gubernaculum.
  gubernáculo del cordón chorda gubernaculum.
  gubernáculo dental, gubernáculo dentis
gubernaculum dentis.
  gubernáculo de Hunter, gubernáculo testi-

cular, gubernáculo testis Hunter's gubernaculum, gubernaculum testis.
gubia *f.* gouge.
  gubia de Kelley Kelley gouge.
guía *f.* guidance, guide, guideline.
  guía ajustable anterior adjustable anterior
guide.
  guía anterior anterior guide.
  guía de catéter catheter guidance.
  guía condílea condylar guidance, condylar
guide.
  guía incisal incisal guidance, incisal guide.
guillotina *f.* guillotine.
guiñada *f.* wink, winking.
guiño *m.* wink, winking.
gundo *m.* goundou.
gundú *m.* goundou.
gurgulio *m.* gurgulio.
gurney *m.* gurney.
gusano[1] *m.* worm.
gusano[2] *m.* worm.
gustación *f.* gustation.
  gustación coloreada colored gustation.
gustatismo *m.* gustatism.
gustativo, -va *adj.* gustatory.
gustina *f.* gustin.
gusto *m.* taste.
  ceguera al gusto taste blindness.
  gusto del color, gusto coloreado color taste.
  gusto de Franklin, gusto franklínico
Franklinic taste.
  gusto voltaico voltaic taste.
gustometría *f.* gustometry.
gustómetro *m.* gustometer.
gutada *f.* guttate.
gutapercha *f.* gutta-percha.
gutta gutta.
guttata *f.* guttate.
gutural *adj.* guttural.
guturofonía *f.* gutturophony.
guturotetania *f.* gutturotetany.
Gymnoascus Gymnoascus.
gyrus gyrus.

H h

habeas corpus habeas corpus.
habena *f.* habena.
habenal *adj.* habenal, habenar.
habenar *adj.* habenal, habenar.
habénula *f.* habenula.
habenular *adj.* habenular.
habilidad *f.* ability, skill.
  habilidad motora gross motor skill.
hábitat *m.* habitat.
hábito *m.* habit, habitus.
habituación *f.* habituation.
habitual *adj.* habitual, usual.
habla *f.* speech.
  habla adenoidea adenoid speech.
  habla alaríngea alaryngeal speech.
  habla apresurada, habla apremiante pressured speech.
  habla arrastrada slurring speech.
  habla cercenada clipped speech.
  habla cerebelosa cerebellar speech.
  habla confusa jumbled speech.
  habla ecolálica echo speech.
  habla entrecortada staccato speech.
  habla escándida scanning speech.
  habla esofágica esophageal speech.
  habla espástica spastic speech.
  habla en espejo mirror speech.
  habla explosiva explosive speech.
  habla incoherente incoherent speech.
  habla en meseta plateau speech.
  habla no espontánea non-spontaneous speech.
  habla silábica syllabic speech.
habón *m.* hive.
hacha *f.* hatchet.
  hacha esmalte enamel hatchet.
hachís *m.* hashish.
Haemagogus Haemagogus.
haemamoeba Haemamoeba.
Haemaphysalis Haemaphysalis.
Haementeria Haementeria.
Haemodipsus Haemodipsus.
Haemophilus Haemophylus, Hemophilus.
Haemosporidium Haemosporidium.
hafalgesia *f.* haphalgesia.
hafemetría *f.* esthesiometry.
Hafnia Hafnia.
halifagia *f.* haliphagia.
halistéresis *f.* halisteresis.
  halistéresis cérea halisteresis cerea.
halisterético, -ca *adj.* halisteretic.
hálito *m.* halitus.
halitosis *f.* halitosis.
halitoso, -sa *adj.* halituous.
hallux hallux.
  hallux dolorosus hallux dolorosus.
  hallux extensus hallux extensus.
  hallux flexus hallux flexus.
  hallux malleus hallux malleus.
  hallux rigidus hallux rigidus.

  hallux valgus hallux valgus.
  hallux varus hallux varus.
halmatogénesis *f.* halmatogenesis.
halo *m.* halo.
  halo anémico anemic halo.
  halo Fick Fick's halo.
  halo glaucomatoso glaucomatous halo, halo glaucomatosus.
  halo límbico blanco de Vogt Vogt's white limbal girdle.
  halo nevus halo nevus.
  halo senil senile halo.
Halobacteriaceae Halobacteriaceae.
Halobacterium Halobacterium.
Halococcus Halococcus.
halodermia *f.* halodermia.
halofílico, -ca *adj.* halophilic.
halófilo, -la *m.* halophil, halophile.
halogenación *f.* halogenation.
halógeno *m.* halogen.
haloide *adj.* haloid.
haloideo, -a *adj.* haloid.
halometría *f.* halometry.
halómetro *m.* halometer.
halostéresis *f.* halosteresis.
halterio *m.* dumbbell.
hamarcial *adj.* hamartial.
hamartia *f.* hamartia.
hamartial *adj.* hamartial.
hamartoblastoma *m.* hamartoblastoma.
hamartocondromatosis *f.* hamartochondromatosis.
hamartoma *m.* hamartoma.
  hamartoma epitelial fragmentario de la retina retinal pigment epithelium hamartoma.
  hamartoma fibroso del lactante fibrous hamartoma of infancy.
  hamartoma neuronal neuronal hamartoma.
  hamartoma neuronal hipotalámico neuronal hypothalamic hamartoma.
  hamartoma pulmonar pulmonary hamartoma.
  hamartoma renal renal hamartoma.
hamartomatosis *f.* hamartomatosis.
hamartomatoso, -sa *adj.* hamartomatous.
hamartoplasia *f.* hamartoplasia.
hamartritis *f.* hamarthritis.
hamatum *m.* hamatum, hamate bone.
hambre *f.* hunger.
hamelar *adj.* hamular.
hamular *adj.* hamular.
hamulus *m.* hamulus.
hapaloniquia *f.* hapalonychia.
haplodermatitis *f.* haplodermatitis.
haplodermitis *f.* haplodermatitis.
haplodonto, -ta *adj.* haplodont.
haplofase *f.* haplophase.
haploide *adj.* haploid.
haploidéntico, -ca *adj.* haploidentical.

haploidentidad *f.* haploidentity.
haploidía *f.* haploidy.
haplología *f.* haplology.
haplomicosis *f.* haplomycosis.
haplonto *m.* haplont.
haplopatía *f.* haplopathy.
haplopia *f.* haplopia.
haploscópico, -ca *adj.* haploscopic.
haploscopio *m.* haploscope.
  haploscopio en espejo mirror haploscope.
haplotipo *m.* haplotype.
hapténico, -ca *adj.* haptenic.
hapteno *m.* hapten, haptene.
  hapteno bacterial bacterial hapten.
  hapteno grupo A group A hapten.
háptica *f.* haptics.
háptico, -ca *adj.* haptic.
haptófilo, -la *adj.* haptophil, haptophile.
haptofórico, -ca *adj.* haptophoric, haptophorous.
haptóforo *m.* haptophore.
haptología *f.* haptics.
haptómetro *m.* haptometer.
haptotaxis *f.* thigmotaxis.
harara *f.* harara.
harmonia *f.* harmonia.
hartmanneliasis *f.* hartmannelliasis.
Hartmannella Hartmanella.
hauch *f.* Hauch.
haustrum *m.* haustrum.
haustración *f.* haustration.
haustral *adj.* austral.
Haverhillia multiformis Haverhillia multiformis.
hawkinsinuria *f.* hawkinsinuria.
haz¹ *m.* tract, tractus.
haz² *m.* beam.
  haz de rayos X X-ray beam.
  haz útil primary beam, useful beam.
heautoscopia *f.* autoscopic phenomenon.
hebefrenia *f.* hebephrenia.
hebético, -ca *adj.* hebetic.
hebetomía *f.* hebetomy, hebotomy.
hebotomía *f.* hebotomy.
hebra *f.* strand.
  hebra antisentido de ADN ADN antisense strand.
  hebra codificante de ADN DNA sense strand, DNA coding strand, DNA plus strand.
  hebra complementaria de ADN ADN complementary strand.
  hebra no codificante de ADN DNA noncoding strand.
  hebra molde de ADN DNA template strand, DNA minus strand.
  hebra sentido de ADN DNA sense strand, DNA plus strand.
hecatomérico, -ca *adj.* hecatomeral, hecatomeric.
hecatómero, -ra *adj.* hecatomeral.

heces *f.* feces, stool.
  heces grasas fatty stool.
  heces lientérica lienteric stool.
  heces mantecosas butter stool.
  heces mucosas mucous stool.
héctico, -ca *adj.* hectic.
hedatresia *f.* hedatresia, hedratresia.
hedonismo *m.* hedonia, hedonism.
hedónico, -ca *adj.* hedonic.
hedratresia *f.* hedratresia.
hedrocele *m.* hedrocele.
helcoide *adj.* helcoid.
helcología *f.* helcology.
helcoma *m.* helcoma.
helcomenia *f.* helcomenia.
helcoplastia *f.* helcoplasty.
helcosis *f.* helcosis.
Heleidae Heleidae.
hélice *f.* helix.
Helicobacter Helicobacter.
helicoide *adj.* helical, helicoid, helicoidal.
helicoidal *adj.* helical, helicoid, helicoidal.
helicopodia *f.* helicopodia.
helicópodo, -da *adj.* helicopod.
helicotrema *m.* helicotrema.
heliencefalitis *f.* heliencephalitis.
helioaeroterapia *f.* helioaerotherapy.
helioencefalitis *f.* helioencephalitis.
heliofobia *f.* heliophobia.
heliosis *f.* heliosis.
helioterapia *f.* heliotherapy.
hélix *m.* helix.
helmintagogo, -ga *adj.* helminthagogue.
helmintiasis *f.* helminthiasis.
helmíntico, -ca *adj.* helminthic, helminthous.
helmintismo *m.* helminthism.
helminto *m.* helminth.
helmintogénesis *f.* helminthiasis.
helmintoide *adj.* helminthoid.
helmintoma *m.* helminthoma.
heloma *m.* heloma.
  heloma blando, heloma molle heloma molle.
  heloma duro, heloma durum heloma durum.
Helophilus Helophilus.
helópira *f.* malaria.
helosis *f.* helosis.
helotomía *f.* helotomy.
hem *m.* hem.
hemabarómetro *m.* hemabarometer.
hemacito *m.* hemacyte.
hemactometría *f.* hemacytometry.
hemacitómetro *m.* hemacytometer.
hemacitopoyesis *f.* hemacytopoiesis.
hemacitozoo *m.* hemacytozoon.
hemacituria *f.* hematocyturia.
hemacromatosis *f.* hemachromatosis.
hemacromatósico, -ca *f.* hemachromatotic.
hemacromo *m.* hemachrome.
hemacrosis *f.* hemachrosis.
hemadeno *m.* hemaden.
hemadenología *f.* hemadenology.
hemadinamometría *f.* hemadynamometry.
hemadinamómetro *m.* hemadynamometer.
hemadostenosis *f.* hemadostenosis.
hemadsorbente *adj.* hemadsorbent.
hemadsorción *f.* hemadsorption.
hemafaciente *adj.* hemafacient.
hemafecia *f.* hemafecia.
hemafeico, -ca *adj.* hemapheic.
hemafeína *f.* hemaphein.
hemafeísmo *m.* hemapheism.
hemaféresis *f.* hemapheresis.
hemafotografía *f.* hemaphotograph.

hemaglutinación *f.* hemagglutination.
  hemaglutinación indirecta indirect hemagglutination.
  hemaglutinación pasiva passive hemagglutination.
  hemaglutinación virósica, hemaglutinación viral viral hemagglutination.
hemaglutinante *adj.* hemagglutinative.
hemaglutinina *f.* hemagglutinin.
hemagógico, -ca *adj.* hemagogic.
hemagogo *m.* hemagogue.
hemagonio *m.* hemagonium.
hemal *adj.* hemal.
hemalum *m.* hemalum.
hemalumbre *m.* hemalum.
hemamebiasis *f.* hemamebiasis.
hemanálisis *m.* hemanalysis.
hemangiectasia *f.* hemagiectasa, hemangiectasis.
hemangiectasis *f.* hemagiectasa, hemangiectasis.
hemangioameloblastoma *m.* hemangioameloblastoma.
hemangioblasto *m.* hemangioblasto.
hemangioblastoma *m.* hemangioblastoma.
hemangioendothelioblastoma *m.* hemangioendothelioblastoma.
hemangioendotelioma *m.* hemangioendothelioma.
  hemangioendotelioma benigno benign hemangioendothelioma.
  hemangioendotelioma maligno malignant hemangioendothelioma.
  hemangioendotelioma tuberoso múltiple hemangioendothelioma tuberosum multiplex.
hemangiofibroma *m.* hemangiofibroma.
  hemangiofibroma juvenil juvenile hemangiofibroma.
hemangioma *m.* hemangioma.
  hemangioma ameloblástico ameloblastic hemangioma.
  hemangioma arterial arterial hemangioma.
  hemangioma capilar capillary hemangioma.
  hemangioma cavernoso cavernous hemangioma.
  hemangioma congénito congenital hemangioma.
  hemangioma coroideo choroidal hemangioma.
  hemangioma esclerosante sclerosing hemangioma.
  hemangioma infantil superficial evanescente superficial fading infantile hemangioma.
  hemangioma en fresa strawberry hemangioma.
  hemangioma plano extenso hemangioma planum extensum.
  hemangioma racemoso racemose hemangioma.
  hemangioma senil senile hemangioma.
  hemangioma simple hemangioma simplex.
  hemangioma venoso venous hemangioma.
  hemangioma verrugoso verrucous hemangioma.
  hemangioma vertebral vertebral hemangioma.
hemangiomatosis *f.* hemangiomatosis.
hemangiomatoso, -sa *adj.* hemangiomatous.
hemangiopericito *m.* hemangiopericyte.
hemangiosarcoma *m.* hemangiosarcoma.
hemapófisis *f.* hemapophysis.
hemapoyesis *f.* hemapoiesis.
hemapoyético, -ca *adj.* hemapoietic.

hemartoma *m.* hemartoma.
hemartros *m.* hemarthros.
hemartrosis *f.* hemarthrosis.
hemastroncio *m.* hemastrontium.
hemataerómetro *m.* hemataerometer.
hematapostema *m.* hematapostema.
hemateína *f.* hematein.
  hemateína ácida de Baker Baker's acid hematein.
hematemesis *f.* hematemesis.
  hematemesis Goldstein Goldstein's hematemesis.
hematencéfalo *m.* hematencephalon.
hematerapia *f.* hematherapy.
hematérmico, -ca *adj.* hemathermous, hemathermal.
hematermo, -ma *adj.* hemathermous, hemathermal.
hemático, -ca *adj.* hematic.
hemathidrosis *f.* hemathidrosis, hematidrosis.
hematidrosis *f.* hemathidrosis, hematidrosis.
hematíe *m.* red blood cell.
  hematíe falciforme falciform red blood cell.
  hematíe nucleado nucleated erythrocyte.
hematimetría *f.* hematimetry.
hematina *f.* hematin.
hematinemia *f.* hematinemia.
hematínico, -ca *adj.* hematinic.
hematinógeno *m.* hematinogen.
hematinómetro *m.* hematinometer.
hematinuria *f.* hematinuria.
hematisquesis *f.* hematischesis.
hematobilia *f.* hematobilia.
hematobio *m.* hematobium.
hematoblasto *m.* hematoblast.
hematocatarsis *f.* hemocatharsis.
hematocefalia *f.* hematocephaly.
hematocéfalo *m.* hematocephalus.
hematocele *m.* hematocele.
  hematocele del escroto, hematocele escrotal scrotal hematocele.
  hematocele paramétrico, hematocele periuterino, hematocele retrouterino parametric hematocele, retrouterine hematocele.
  hematocele pudendo pudendal hematocele.
  hematocele vaginal vaginal hematocele.
hematocelia *f.* hematocelia, hematocoelia.
hematocisto *m.* hematocyst.
hematocito *m.* hematocyte.
hematocitoblasto *m.* hematocytoblast.
hematocitólisis *f.* hematocytolysis.
hematocitómetro *m.* hematocytometer.
hematocitopenia *f.* hematocytopenia.
hematocituria *f.* hematocyturia.
hematoclorina *f.* hematochlorin.
hematocolpómetra *f.* hematocolpometra.
hematocolpos *m.* hematocolpos, hematokolpos.
hematocórnea *f.* hematocornea.
hematocrito *m.* hematocrit, hematokrit.
  hematocrito corporal total, hematocrito de cuerpo entero total body hematocrit, whole body hematocrit.
  hematocrito de gran vaso large vessel hematocrit.
  hematocrito de Wintrobe Wintrobe hematocrit.
hematocromatosis *f.* hematochromatosis.
hematodiálisis *f.* hematodialysis.
hematodiscrasia *f.* hematodyscrasia.
hematodistrofia *f.* hematodystrophy.
hematoencefálico, -ca *adj.* hematoencephalic.
hematoesferinemia *f.* hematospherinemia.
hematoespectrofotómetro *m.* hematospectrophotometer.

hematoespectroscopia *f.* hematospectroscopy.

hematoespectroscopio *m.* hematospectroscope.

hematoespermatocele *m.* hematospermatocele.

hematoespermia *f.* hematospermia.

hematofagia *f.* hematophagy, hematophagia.

hematófago *m.* hematophage.

hematófago, -ga *adj.* hematophagous.

hematofagocito *m.* hematopahgocyte.

hematofilia *f.* hematophilia.

hematofítico, -ca *adj.* hematophytic.

hematofito *m.* hematophyte.

hematofobia *f.* hematophobia.

hematogénesis *f.* hematogenesis.

hematogénico, -ca *adj.* hematogenic.

hematógeno, -na *adj.* hematogenous.

hematoglobina *f.* hematoglobin.

hematoglobinuria *f.* hematoglobinuria.

hematoglobulina *f.* hematoglobulin.

hematogonia, *m.* hematogone.

hematógono *m.* hematogone.

hematohialoide *m.* hematohyaloid.

hematohidrosis *f.* hematohidrosis.

hematoide *adj.* hematoid.

hematoidina *f.* hematoidin.

hematolina *f.* hematolin.

hematolinfagioma *m.* hematolymphangioma.

hematólisis *f.* hematolysis.

hematolítico, -ca *adj.* hematolytic.

hematolito *m.* hematolith.

hematología *f.* hematology.

hematólogo, -ga *m., f.* hematologist.

hematoma *m.* hematoma.

   hematoma aneurismático aneurysmal hematoma.

   hematoma en antifaz periorbital hematoma.

   hematoma auricular, hematoma auris hematoma auris.

   hematoma de cerebelo cerebellum hematoma.

   hematoma del cuerpo amarillo corpus luteum hematoma.

   hematoma intracerebral espontáneo spontaneous cerebral hematoma.

   hematoma intracraneal intracranial hematoma.

   hematoma intraparenquimatoso intraparenchymatous hematoma.

   hematoma neonatorum cephalohematoma.

   hematoma pélvico pelvic hematoma.

   hematoma perianal perianal hematoma.

   hematoma perirrenal espontáneo, hematoma perirrenal traumático post-traumatic spontaneous hematoma, post-traumatic perirenal hematoma.

   hematoma pulsátil false aneurysm.

   hematoma retroplacentario retroplacental hematoma.

   hematoma retrouterino retrouterine hematoma.

   hematoma subcorial hematomole.

   hematoma subdural subdural hematoma.

   hematoma subgaleal subgaleal hematoma.

   hematoma subperióstico subperiostial hematoma.

   hematoma subungueal subungual hematoma.

   hematoma tuberoso subcoriónico subchorionic tuberous hematoma.

hematómetra *m.* hematometra.

hematometría *f.* hematometry.

hematomicosis *f.* hematomycosis.

hematomielia *f.* hematomyelia.

hematomielitis *f.* hematomyelitis.

hematomieloporosis *f.* hematomyelopore.

hematomola *f.* hematomole.

hematoncometría *f.* hematoncometry.

hematonefrosis *f.* hematonephrosis.

hematónfalo *m.* hematomphalus.

hematonfalocele *m.* hematomphalocele.

hematónico, -ca *adj.* hematonic.

hematonosis *f.* hematonosis.

hematopatía *f.* hematopathy.

hematopatología *f.* hematopathology.

hematopedesis *f.* hematopedesis.

hematopenia *f.* hematopenia.

hematopericardio *m.* hematopericardium.

hematoperitoneo *m.* hematoperitoneum.

hematopexis *f.* hematopexis.

hematopiesis *f.* hematopiesis.

hematoplania *f.* hematoplania.

hematoplásico, -ca *adj.* hematoplastic.

hematopneico, -ca *adj.* hematopneic.

hematoporfiria *f.* hematoporphyria.

hematoporfirina *f.* hematoporphyrin.

hematoporfirinemia *f.* hematoporphyrinemia.

hematoporfirinismo *m.* hematoporphyrinism.

hematoporfirinuria *f.* hematoporphyrinuria.

hematopoyesis *f.* hematopoiesis.

hematopoyético, -ca *adj.* hematopoietic.

hematopsia *f.* hematopsia.

hematoquecia *f.* hematochezia.

hematoquezia *f.* hematochezia.

hematoquiluria *f.* hematochyluria.

hematoquiste *m.* hematocyst.

hematórax *m.* hemathorax.

hematorraquis *m.* hematorrhachis.

hematorrea *f.* hematorrhea.

hematosalpinge *m.* hematosalphinx.

hematosálpinx *m.* hematosalphinx.

hematoscopia *f.* hematoscopy.

hematoscopio *m.* hematoscope.

hematosepsis *f.* hematosepsis.

hematósido *m.* hematoside.

hematosina *f.* hematosin.

hematosis *f.* hematosis.

hematospectrofotómetro *m.* hematospectrophotometer.

hematospermatocele *m.* hematospermatocele.

hematospermia *f.* hematospermia.

hematosporidios *m.* hematosporida.

hematosqueocele *m.* hematoscheocele.

hematostático, -ca *adj.* hemostatic.

hematostaxis *f.* hemotasis.

hematósteon *m.* hematosteon.

hematoterapia *f.* hematotherapy.

hematotérmico, -ca *adj.* hematothermal.

hematotímpano *m.* hematotympanum.

hematotórax *m.* hematothorax.

hematotóxico, -ca *adj.* hematotoxic.

hematotoxicosis *f.* hematotoxicosis.

hematotoxina *f.* hematotoxin.

hematotraquelo *m.* hematotrachelos.

hematotrópico *m.* hematotropic.

hematóxico, -ca *adj.* hematoxic.

hematoxilina *f.* hematoxylin.

hematoxina *f.* hematoxin.

hematozoico, -ca *adj.* hematozoic.

hematozoo *m.* hematozoon.

hematuresis *f.* hematuresis.

hematuria *f.* hematuria.

   hematuria dolorosa painful hematuria.

   hematuria egipcia Egyptian hematuria.

   hematuria endémica endemic hematuria.

   hematuria esencial essential hematuria.

   hematuria falsa false hematuria.

   hematuria familiar benigna benign familial hematuria.

   hematuria indolora painless hematuria.

   hematuria inicial initial hematuria.

   hematuria macroscópica macroscopic hematuria.

   hematuria microscópica microscopic hematuria.

   hematuria nefrológica nephrological hematuria.

   hematuria primaria primary hematuria.

   hematuria recurrente familiar benign recurrent hematuria.

   hematuria renal renal hematuria.

   hematuria terminal terminal hematuria.

   hematuria uretral urethral hematuria.

   hematuria vesical vesical hematuria.

hembra *f.* female.

hemelitrómetra lateralis *f.* hemelytrometra lateralis.

hemerálope *adj.* hemeralope.

hemeralopía *f.* hemeralopia.

hemeropía *f.* hemeralopia.

hemiablepsia *f.* hemiablepsia.

hemiacardio *m.* hemiacardius.

hemiacéfalo *m.* hemiacephalus.

hemiacromatopsia *f.* hemiachromatopsia.

hemiacrosomía *f.* hemiacrosomia.

hemiageusia *f.* hemiageusia, hemiageustia.

hemiageustia *f.* hemiageusia, hemiageustia.

hemialbúmina *f.* hemialbumin.

hemialbumosa *f.* hemialbumose.

hemialbumosuria *f.* hemialbumosuria.

hemialgia *f.* hemialgia.

hemiamaurosis *f.* hemiamaurosis.

hemiambliopía *f.* hemiamblyopia.

hemiamiostenia *f.* hemiamyosthenia.

hemianacusia *f.* hemianacusia.

hemianalgesia *f.* hemianalgesia.

hemianencefalia *f.* hemianencephaly.

hemianestesia *f.* hemianesthesia.

   hemianestesia alternada, hemianestesia alternante alternate hemianesthesia.

   hemianestesia cerebral cerebral hemianesthesia.

   hemianestesia cruzada crossed hemianesthesia, hemianesthesia cruciata.

   hemianestesia espinal spinal hemianesthesia.

   hemianestesia mesocefálica mesocephalic hemianesthesia, pontile hemianesthesia.

hemianopía *f.* hemianopsia, hemianopia.

hemianopsia *f.* hemianopsia, hemianopia.

   hemianopsia absoluta absolute hemianopsia.

   hemianopsia altitudinal altitudinal hemianopsia.

   hemianopsia bilateral bilateral hemianopsia.

   hemianopsia binasal binasal hemianopsia.

   hemianopsia binocular binocular hemianopsia.

   hemianopsia bitemporal bitemporal hemianopsia.

   hemianopsia completa complete hemianopsia.

   hemianopsia congruente congruous hemianopsia.

   hemianopsia cruzada crossed hemianopsia.

   hemianopsia cuadrántica, hemianopsia de cuadrantes quadrantic hemianopsia, quadrant hemianopsia.

   hemianopsia equilateral equilateral hemianopsia.

   hemianopsia heterónima heteronymous hemianopsia.

   hemianopsia homónima homonymous hemianopsia.

hemianopsia horizontal horizontal hemianopsia.
hemianopsia incompleta incomplete hemianopsia.
hemianopsia incongruente incongruous hemianopsia.
hemianopsia lateral lateral hemianopsia.
hemianopsia nasal nasal hemianopsia.
hemianopsia parcial incomplete hemianopsia.
hemianopsia relativa relative hemianopsia.
hemianopsia temporal temporal hemianopsia.
hemianopsia total complete hemianopsia.
hemianopsia unilateral unilateral hemianopsia.
hemianopsia uniocular uniocular hemianopsia.
hemianopsia verdadera true hemianopsia.
hemianopsia vertical heteronymous hemianopsia.
hemianopsis *f.* hemianopsia.
hemianóptico, -ca *adj.* hemianoptic, hemianopic.
hemianosmia *f.* hemianosmia.
hemiapraxia *f.* hemiapraxia.
hemiartroplastia *f.* hemiarthroplasty.
hemiartrosis *f.* hemiarthrhosis.
hemiasinergia *f.* hemiasynergia.
hemiataxia *f.* hemiataxy, hemiataxia.
hemiatetosis *f.* hemiathetosis.
hemiatrofia *f.* hemiatrophy.
hemiatrofia facial facial hemiatrophy.
hemiatrofia lingual progresiva progressive lingual hemiatrophy.
hemiautotrófico, -ca *adj.* hemiautotrophic.
hemiautótrofo *m.* hemiautotroph.
hemibalismo *m.* hemiballism, hemiballismus.
hemibloqueo *m.* hemiblock.
hemibloqueo ventricular ventricular hemiblock.
hemicanicie *f.* hemicanities.
hemicardia *f.* hemicardia.
hemicardia derecha, hemicardia dextra hemicardia dextra.
hemicardia izquierda, hemicardia sinistra hemicardia sinistra.
hemicardio *m.* hemicardius.
hemicarilla *f.* demifacet.
hemicarion *m.* hemikaryon.
hemicefalalgia *f.* meicephalalgia.
hemicefalia *f.* hemicephalia.
hemicéfalo *m.* hemicephalus.
hemicentro *m.* hemicentrum.
hemicerebro *m.* hemicerebrum.
hemicigosidad *f.* hemizygosity.
hemicigotia *f.* hemizygosity.
hemicigótico, -ca *adj.* hemizygotic, hemizygous.
hemicigoto *m.* hemizygote.
hémico, -ca *adj.* hemic.
hemicolectomía *f.* hemicolectomy.
hemicolectomía derecha right hemicolectomy.
hemicolectomía izquierda left hemicolectomy.
hemicorea *f.* hemichorea.
hemicorporectomía *f.* hemicorporectomy.
hemicorticectomía *f.* hemicorticectomy.
hemicránea *f.* hemicrania.
hemicraneal *adj.* hemicranial.
hemicrania *f.* hemicrania.
hemicraniectomía *f.* hemicraniectomy.
hemicraniosis *f.* hemicraniosis.
hemicromatopsia *f.* hemichromatopsia.

hemicromosoma *m.* hemichromosome.
hemidecorticación *f.* hemidecortication.
hemidesmosoma *m.* hemidesmosome.
hemidiaforesis *f.* hemidiaphoresis.
hemidiafragma *m.* hemidiaphragm.
hemidisergia *f.* hemidysergia.
hemidisestesia *f.* hemidysesthesia.
hemidistrofia *f.* hemidystrophy.
hemidrosis *f.* hemidrosis.
hemiectromelia *f.* hemiectromelia.
hemiencefalia *f.* hemicephalia.
hemiencéfalo *m.* hemiencephalus.
hemiepilepsia *f.* hemiepilepsy.
hemiespasmo *m.* hemispasm.
hemifacial *adj.* hemifacial.
hemifalangectomía *f.* hemiphalangectomy.
hemigastrectomía *f.* hemigastrectomy.
hemigigantismo *m.* hemigigantism.
hemiglosectomía *f.* hemiglossectomy.
hemiglósico, -ca *adj.* hemiglossal.
hemiglositis *f.* hemiglossitis.
hemidrosis *f.* hemihidrosis.
hemignatia *f.* hemignatia.
hemihepatectomía *f.* hemihepatectomy.
hemihidrosis *f.* hemihidrosis.
hemihipalgesia *f.* hemihypalgesia.
hemihiperestesia *f.* hemihyperesthesia.
hemihiperhidrosis *f.* hemihyperidrosis, hemihyperhidrosis.
hemihipermetría *f.* hemihypermetria.
hemihiperplasia *f.* hemihyperplasia.
hemihipertonía *f.* hemihypertonia.
hemihipertrofia *f.* hemihypertrophy.
hemihipertrofia facial facial hemihypertrophy.
hemihipoestesia *f.* hemihypoesthesia, hemihypesthesia.
hemihipofisectomía *f.* hemihypophysectomy.
hemihipometría *f.* hemihypometria.
hemihipoplasia *f.* hemihypoplasia.
hemihipotonía *f.* hemihypotonia.
hemilaminectomía *f.* hemilaminectomy.
hemilaringectomía *f.* hemilaryngectomy.
hemilateral *adj.* hemilateral.
hemilesión *f.* hemilesion.
hemilingual *adj.* hemilingual.
hemimacroglosia *f.* hemimacroglossia.
hemimandibulectomía *f.* hemimandibulectomy.
hemimaxilectomía *f.* hemimaxillectomy.
hemimegaloencefalia *f.* hemimegalencephaly.
hemimelia *f.* hemimelia.
hemimelia cubital cubital hemimelia, ulnar hemimelia.
hemimelia peronea, peroneal fibular hemimelia, peroneal hemimelia.
hemimelia radial radial hemimelia.
hemimelia tibial tibial hemimelia.
hemimelo *m.* hemimelus.
hemimembrana *f.* hemimembrane.
hemimielomeningocele *m.* hemimyelomeningocele.
heminefrectomía *f.* heminephrectomy.
heminefrourectomía *f.* heminephrourectomy.
hemineurastenia *f.* hemineurasthenia.
hemiobesidad *f.* hemiobesity.
hemiopalgia *f.* hemiopalgia.
hemiopía *f.* hemiopia.
hemiópico, -ca *adj.* hemiopic.
hemípago *m.* hemipagus.
hemipagos *m.* hemipagus.
hemiparálisis *f.* hemiparalysis.
hemiparanestesia *f.* paranesthesia.

hemiparaplejía *f.* hemiparaplegia.
hemiparesia *f.* hemiparesis.
hemiparestesia *f.* hemiparesthesia.
hemiparético, -ca *adj.* hemiparetic.
hemiparkinsonismo *m.* hemiparkinsonism.
hemipelvectomía *f.* hemipelvectomy.
hemipeptona *f.* hemipeptone.
hemipilorectomía *f.* hemipylorectomy.
hemipionefrosis *f.* hemipyonephrosis.
hemiplacenta *f.* hemiplacenta.
hemiplejía *f.* hemiplegia.
hemiplejía alterna, hemiplejía alternada alternate hemiplegia, alternating hemiplegia.
hemiplejía alterna oculocomotriz alternating oculomotor hemiplegia.
hemiplejía alternans hypoglossica hemiplegia alternans hypoglossica.
hemiplejía ascendente ascending hemiplegia.
hemiplejía capsular capsular hemiplegia.
hemiplejía cerebral cerebral hemiplegia.
hemiplejía contralateral contralateral hemiplegia.
hemiplejía cruzada crossed hemiplegia, hemiplegia cruciata.
hemiplejía espasmódica, hemiplejía espástica spastic hemiplegia.
hemiplejía espinal spinal hemiplegia.
hemiplejía facial facial hemiplegia.
hemiplejía faciobraquial faciobraquial hemiplegia.
hemiplejía faciolingual faciolingual hemiplegia.
hemiplejía fláccida flaccid hemiplegia.
hemiplejía infantil infantile hemiplegia.
hemiplejía puerperal puerperal hemiplegia.
hemipléjico, -ca *adj.* hemiplegic.
hemiprostatectomía *f.* hemiprostatectomy.
Hemiptera Hemiptera.
hemíptero, -ra *adj.* hemipterous.
hemirraquisquisis *f.* hemirachischisis.
hemisacralización *f.* hemisacralization.
hemiscotoma *m.* hemiscotoma.
hemiscotosis *f.* hemiscotosis.
hemisección *f.* hemisection.
hemisectomía *f.* hemisectomy.
hemisensorial *adj.* hemisensory.
hemisferectomía *f.* hemispherectomy.
hemisferio *m.* hemispherium.
hemisferio dominante dominant hemisphere.
hemisfigmia *f.* hemisphygmia.
hemisfinterectomía *f.* hemispherectomy.
hemisíndrome *m.* hemisyndrome.
hemisístole *f.* hemisystole.
hemisistolia *f.* hemisystole.
hemisoanticuerpo *m.* hemisoantibody.
hemisoma *m.* hemisomus.
hemisonambulismo *m.* hemisomnambulism.
hemisotónico, -ca *adj.* hemisotonic.
Hemispora stellata Hemispora stellata.
hemisporosis *f.* hemispore.
hemistrumectomía *f.* hemistrumectomy.
hemitemblor *m.* hemitremor.
hemiteria *f.* hemiteras.
hemitérico, -ca *adj.* hemiteratic.
hemitermoanestesia *f.* hemithermoanesthesia.
hemitetania *f.* hemitetany.
hemitiroidectomía *f.* hemithyroidectomy.
hemitonía *f.* hemitonia.
hemitórax *m.* hemithorax.
hemitoxina *f.* hemitoxin.
hemivagotonía *f.* hemivagotony.
hemivejiga *f.* hemibladder.

hemivértebra *f.* hemivertebra.
hemoacceso *m.* hemoaccess.
hemoaglutinación *f.* hemoagglutination.
hemoaglutinina *f.* hemoagglutinin.
hemoalcalímetro *m.* hemoalkalimeter.
hemoanálisis *f.* hemoanalysis.
hemoangioblasto *m.* hemangioblast.
hemoangiofibroma *m.* hemangiofibroma.
hemoantitoxina *f.* hemoantitoxin.
hemobilia *f.* hemobilia.
hemobilinuria *f.* hemobilinuria.
hemoblasto *m.* hemoblast.
hemoblastosis *f.* hemoblastosis.
hemocatarsis *f.* hemocatharsis.
hemocatéresis *f.* hemocatheresis.
hemocateretico, -ca *adj.* hemocatheretic.
hemocele *m.* hemocele.
hemoceloma *m.* hemocelom, hemocoelom, hemocoeloma.
hemocinesis *f.* hemokinesis.
hemocinético, -ca *adj.* hemokinetic.
hemocito *m.* hemocyte.
hemocitoblasto *m.* hemocytoblast.
hemocitoblastoma *m.* hemocytoblastoma.
hemocitocatéresis *f.* hemocytocatheresis.
hemocitofagia *f.* hemocytophagia, hemocytophagy.
hemocitofágico, -ca *adj.* hemocytophagic.
hemocitólisis *f.* hemocytolysis.
hemocitología *f.* hemocytology.
hemocitoma *m.* hemocytoma.
hemocitometría *f.* hemocytometry.
hemocitómetro *m.* hemocytometer.
hemocitopoyesis *f.* hemocytopoiesis.
hemocitotripsia *f.* hemocytotripsis.
hemocitozoo *m.* hemocytozoon.
hemoclasia *f.* hemoclasia, hemoclasis.
hemoclasis *f.* hemoclasia, hemoclasis.
hemoclástico, -ca *adj.* hemoclastic.
hemoclip *m.* hemoclip.
hemocoagulina *f.* hemocoagulin.
hemocolecistitis *f.* hemocholecystitis.
hemoconcentración *f.* hemoconcentration.
hemoconiosis *f.* hemoconiosis.
hemocorial *adj.* hemochorial.
hemocrinia *f.* hemocrinia.
hemocrino, -na *adj.* hemocrine.
hemocrinoterapia *f.* hemocrinotherapy.
hemocrioscopia *f.* hemocryoscopy.
hemocroína *f.* hematin.
hemocromatósico, -ca *adj.* hemochromatotic, hemachromatotic.
hemocromatosis *f.* hemochromatosis, hemachromatosis.
  hemocromatosis exógena exogenous hemochromatosis.
  hemocromatosis hereditaria hereditary hemochromatosis.
  hemocromatosis idiopática idiopathic hemochromatosis.
  hemocromatosis primaria primary hemochromatosis.
  hemocromatosis secundaria secondary hemochromatosis.
hemocromógeno *m.* hemochromogen.
hemocromometría *f.* hemochromometry.
hemocromómetro *m.* hemochromometer.
hemocultivo *m.* hemoculture.
hemodia *f.* hemodia.
hemodiagnóstico *m.* hemodiagnosis.
hemodiálisis *f.* hemodialysis.
  hemodiálisis domiciliaria home hemodialysis.
  hemodiálisis hospitalaria hospital hemodialysis.

hemodializador *m.* hemodialyzer.
hemodiapédesis *f.* hemodiapedesis.
hemodilución *f.* hemodilution.
hemodinámica *f.* hemodynamics.
  hemodinámica intrarrenal intrarenal hemodynamics.
hemodinámico, -ca *adj.* hemodynamic.
hemodinamometría *f.* hemodynamometry.
hemodinamómetro *m.* hemodynamometer.
hemodiscrasia *f.* hemodyscrasia.
hemodistrofia *f.* hemodystrophy.
hemoendotelial *adj.* hemoendothelial.
hemoendotelioma *m.* hemoendothelioma.
hemofagia *f.* hemophagia.
hemófago *m.* hemophage.
hemofagocito *m.* hemophagocyte.
hemofagocitosis *f.* hemophagocytosis.
hemofilia *f.* hemophilia.
  hemofilia A hemophilia A.
  hemofilia B hemophilia B.
  hemofilia C hemophilia C.
  hemofilia clásica classical hemophilia.
  hemofilia de Leyden Leyden hemophilia.
  hemofilia neonatal hemophilia neonatorum.
  hemofilia vascular vascular hemophilia.
hemofílico *m.* hemophiliac.
hemofílico, -ca *adj.* hemophilic.
hemofilioide *adj.* hemophilioid.
hemófilo, -la *adj.* hemophil, hemophile.
hemofiltración *f.* hemofiltration.
hemofiltro *m.* hemofilter.
hemoflagelado, -da *adj.* hemoflagellate.
hemafobia *f.* hemophobia.
hemofobia *f.* hemophobia.
hemoforesis *f.* hemophoresis.
hemofórico, -ca *adj.* hemophoric.
hemofotografía *f.* hemophotograph.
hemofotómetro *m.* hemophotometer.
hemoftalmia *m.* hemophtalmos, hemophthalmus.
hemoftalmos *m.* hemophtalmos, hemophthalmus.
hemogenesia *f.* hemogenesis.
hemogénesis *f.* hemogenesis.
hemoglobina *f.* hemoglobin, hemiglobin.
hemoglobinado, -da *adj.* hemoglobinated.
hemoglobinemia *f.* hemoglobinemia.
  hemoglobinemia puerperal puerperal hemoglobinemia.
hemoglobinífero, -ra *adj.* hemoglobiniferous.
hemoglobinobilia *f.* hemoglobinocholia.
hemoglobinocolia *f.* hemoglobinocholia.
hemoglobinofilia *f.* hemoglobinophilia.
hemoglobinofílico, -ca *adj.* hemoglobinophilic.
hemoglobinólisis *f.* hemoglobinolysis.
hemoglobinómetro *m.* hemoglobinometer.
hemoglobinopatía *f.* hemoglobinopathy.
hemoglobinopepsia *f.* hemoglobinopepsia.
hemoglobinorrea *f.* hemoglobinorrhea.
hemoglobinoso, -sa *adj.* hemoglobinous.
hemoglobinuria *f.* hemoglobinuria.
  hemoglobinuria bacilar bacillary hemoglobinuria.
  hemoglobinuria epidémica epidemic hemoglobinuria.
  hemoglobinuria al frío, hemoglobinuria por frío cold hemoglobinuria.
  hemoglobinuria intermitente paroxysmal hemoglobinuria.
  hemoglobinuria malárica malarial hemoglobinuria.
  hemoglobinuria de la marcha march hemoglobinuria.

  hemoglobinuria palúdica malarial hemoglobinuria.
  hemoglobinuria paroxistica "a trigore" paroxysmal hemoglobinuria.
  hemoglobinuria paroxística nocturna (HPN) paroxysmal nocturnal hemoglobinuria (PNH).
  hemoglobinuria tóxica toxic hemoglobinuria.
hemoglobinúrico, -ca *adj.* hemoglobinuric.
hemograma *m.* hemogram.
hemoide *adj.* hemoid.
hemolaminilla *f.* hemolamella.
hemoleucocitario, -ria *adj.* hemoleukocytic.
hemoleucocítico, -ca *adj.* hemoleukocytic.
hemoleucocito *m.* hemoleukocyte.
hemolinfa *f.* hemolymph.
hemolinfangioma *m.* hemolymphangioma.
hemolisado *m.* hemolysate.
hemolisina *f.* hemolysin.
hemólisis *f.* hemolysis.
  hemólisis alfa alpha hemolysis.
  hemólisis beta beta hemolysis.
  hemólisis biológica biologic hemolysis.
  hemólisis condicionada conditioned hemolysis.
  hemólisis por contacto contact hemolysis.
  hemólisis gamma gamma hemolysis.
  hemólisis inmune, hemólisis inmunitaria immune hemolysis.
  hemólisis pasiva passive hemolysis.
  hemólisis por veneno, hemólisis venenosa venom hemolysis.
  hemólisis viridans viridans hemolysis.
hemolisofílico, -ca *adj.* hemolysophilic.
hemolisoide *m.* hemolisoid.
hemolítico, -ca *adj.* hemolytic.
hemolito *m.* hemolith.
hemolizable *adj.* hemolyzable.
hemolización *f.* hemolization.
hemolizar *v.* hemolyze.
hemología *f.* hemology.
hemomediastino *m.* hemomediastium.
hemómetra *m.* hemometra.
hemometría *f.* hemometry.
hemómetro *m.* hemometer.
hemomielosis *f.* hemomyelosis.
hemonefrosis *f.* hemonephrosis.
hemoneumopericardio *m.* hemopneumopericardium.
hemoneumotórax *m.* hemopneumothorax.
hemonormoblasto *m.* erythroblast.
hemopatía *f.* hemopathy.
hemopatología *f.* hemopathology.
hemoperfusión *f.* hemoperfusion.
hemopericardio *m.* hemopericardium.
hemoperitoneo *m.* hemoperitoneum.
hemopexina *f.* hemopexin.
hemopexis *f.* hematopexis.
Hemophilus Hemophilus.
hemopielectasia *f.* hemopyelectasis.
hemopiesímetro *m.* hemopiezometer.
hemopiesómetro *m.* hemopiezometer.
hemopiezómetro *m.* hemopiezometer.
hemoplásico, -ca *adj.* hemoplastic.
hemoplasmodio *m.* hermoplasmodium.
hemopleura *f.* hemopleura.
hemoporfirina *f.* hemoporphyrin.
hemopoyésico, -ca *adj.* hemopoiesic.
hemopoyesis *f.* hemopoiesis.
hemopoyético, -ca *adj.* hemopoietic.
hemoprecipitina *f.* hemoprecipitin.
hemoproccia *f.* hemoproctia.
hemoproctia *f.* hemoproctia.
hemoproteína *f.* hemoprotein.
hemóptico, -ca *adj.* hemoptic.
hemoptísico, -ca *adj.* hemoptysic.

hemoptisis *f.* hemoptysis.
 hemoptisis cardiaca cardiac hemoptysis, cardiovascular hemoptysis.
 hemoptisis endémica endemic hemoptysis.
 hemoptisis de Goldstein Goldstein's hemoptysis.
 hemoptisis de Manson oriental hemoptysis.
 hemoptisis parasitaria parasitic hemoptysis.
hemorragénico, -ca *adj.* hemorrhagenic.
hemorrágeno, -na *adj.* hemorrhagenic.
hemorragia *f.* bleeding, hemorrhage, haemorrhagia.
 hemorragia alveolar alveolar hemorrhage.
 hemorragia anteparto antepartum hemorrhage.
 hemorragia arterial arterial bleeding.
 hemorragia en astilla splinter hemorrhage.
 hemorragia bronquial hemoptysis.
 hemorragia capsuloganglionar capsuloganglionic hemorrhage.
 hemorragia capilar capillary hemorrhage.
 hemorragia cerebelosa cerebellar hemorrhage.
 hemorragia cerebral cerebral hemorrhage, brain hemorrhage.
 hemorragia cerebral espontánea spontaneous cerebral hemorrhage.
 hemorragia digestiva digestive hemorrhage.
 hemorragia digestiva alta upper digestive hemorrhage.
 hemorragia digestiva baja lower digestive hemorrhage.
 hemorragia de disrupción breakthrough bleeding.
 hemorragia esencial essential hemorrhage.
 hemorragia espontánea spontaneous hemorrhage.
 hemorragia estival summer bleeding.
 hemorragia expulsiva expulsive hemorrhage.
 hemorragia extradural extradural hemorrhage.
 hemorragia externa external hemorrhage.
 hemorragia fetomaterna fetomaternal hemorrhage.
 hemorragia gástrica gastric hemorrhage.
 hemorragia en ganglios basales basal ganglia hemorrhage.
 hemorragia gastroesofágica gastroesophageal hemorrhage.
 hemorragia gastrointestinal gastrointestinal bleeding.
 hemorragia hemisférica hemispheric hemorrhage.
 hemorragia por implantación implantation bleeding.
 hemorragia inevitable unavoidable hemorrhage.
 hemorragia intermedia intermediate hemorrhage.
 hemorragia interna internal hemorrhage.
 hemorragia intracerebral intracerebral hemorrhage.
 hemorragia intestinal intestinal hemorrhage.
 hemorragia intracraneal intracranial hemorrhage.
 hemorragia intramedular intramedullary hemorrhage.
 hemorragia intraparenquimatosa intraparenchymatous hemorrhage.
 hemorragia intraparto intrapartum hemorrhage.
 hemorragia intraventricular intraventricular hemorrhage.
 hemorragia lobular lobar hemorrhage.
 hemorragia en llamas flame-shaped hemorrhage.

 hemorragia masiva massive hemorrhage.
 hemorragia de la médula espinal intramedullary hemorrhage.
 hemorragia nasal nasal hemorrhage, nosebleed.
 hemorragia oculta occult bleeding.
 hemorragia parenquimatosa parenchymatous hemorrhage.
 hemorragia petequial petechial hemorrhage.
 hemorragia plasmática plasma hemorrhage.
 hemorragia pontina pontine hemorrhage.
 hemorragia posparto postpartum hemorrhage.
 hemorragia posparto retardada delayed postpartum hemorrhage.
 hemorragia primaria primary hemorrhage.
 hemorragia primitiva primary hemorrhage.
 hemorragia por privación withdrawal bleeding.
 hemorragia puerperal puerperal hemorrhage.
 hemorragia pulmonar pulmonary hemorrhage.
 hemorragia puntiforme punctate hemorrhage.
 hemorragia recidivante recurring hemorrhage.
 hemorragia recurrente recurring hemorrhage.
 hemorragia renal renal hemorrhage.
 hemorragia en sábana oozing hemorrhage.
 hemorragia secundaria secondary hemorrhage.
 hemorragia siringomiélica syringomyelic hemorrhage.
 hemorragia subaracnoidea HSA subarachnoid hemorrhage.
 hemorragia subdural subdural hemorrhage.
 hemorragia subgaleal subgaleal hemorrhage.
 hemorragia traumática primary hemorrhage.
 hemorragia del tronco encefálico brainstem hemorrhage.
 hemorragia uterina uterine hemorrhage.
 hemorragia uterina disfuncional (HUD) dysfunctional uterine hemorrhage (DUB).
 hemorragia uterina esencial metropathia hemorrhagica.
 hemorragia vaginal vaginal hemorrhage.
 hemorragia vitrea vitreous hemorrhage.
hemorrágico, -ca *adj.* hemorrhagic.
hemorragíparo, -ra *adj.* hemorrhagiparous.
hemorraquis *m.* hemorrhachis.
hemorrea *f.* hemorrhea.
hemorreología *f.* hemorheology, hemorrheology.
hemorrepelente *adj.* hemorepellant.
hemorroidal *adj.* hemorrhoidal.
hemorroides *f.* hemorrhoids.
 hemorroides centinelas sentinel hemorrhoids.
 hemorroides combinadas combined hemorrhoids.
 hemorroldes cutáneas cutaneous hemorrhoids.
 hemorroides estranguladas strangulated hemorrhoids.
 hemorroides externas external hemorrhoids.
 hemorroides internas internal hemorrhoids.
 hemorroides mixtas mixed hemorrhoids.
 hemorroides mucocutáneas mucocutaneous hemorrhoids.
 hemorroides prolapsadas prolapsed hemorrhoids.
 hemorroides trombosadas thrombosed hemorrhoids.
hemorroidectomía *f.* hemorrhoidectomy.
hemorroidólisis *f.* hemorrhoidolysis.
hemosálpinx *f.* hemosalpinx.
hemoscopio *m.* hemoscope.
hemosialemesis *f.* hemosialemesis.
hemosiderinuria *f.* hemosiderinuria.
hemosiderosis *f.* hemosiderosis.

 hemosiderosis hepática hepatic hemosiderosis.
 hemosiderosis nutricional nutritional hemosiderosis.
 hemosiderosis pulmonar pulmonary hemosiderosis.
 hemosiderosis pulmonar idiopática idiopathic pulmonary hemosiderosis.
 hemosiderosis superficial del sistema nervioso central superficial hemorrhage of the CNS.
hemosideruria *f.* hemosiderinuria.
hemósito *m.* hemosite.
hemospasia *f.* hemospasia.
hemospermia *f.* hemospermia.
 hemospermia espúrea hemospermia espuria.
 hemospermia verdadera hemospermia vera.
hemosporidio *m.* haemosporidium, hemosporidium.
hemosqueocele *m.* hematoscheocele.
hemostasia *f.* hemostasia.
hemostático, -ca *adj.* hemostatic.
hemostasis *f.* hemostasia, hemostasis.
 hemostasis quirúrgica surgical hemostasia.
hemóstato *m.* hemostat.
hemostíptico, -ca *adj.* hemostyptic.
hemoterapia *f.* hematherapy, hemotherapy, hemotherapeutics.
hemotímpano *m.* hemotympanum.
hemotisis *f.* hemophthisis.
hemotórax *m.* hemothorax.
hemotóxico, -ca *adj.* hemotoxic.
hemotoxina *f.* hemotoxin.
hemotrófico, -ca *adj.* hemotrophic.
hemotrofo *m.* hemotroph, hemotrophe.
hemotrópico, -ca *adj.* hemotropic.
hemovítreo, -a *adj.* hemovitreous.
hemoxímetro *m.* hemoxometer.
hemoxómetro *m.* hemoxometer.
hemozoo *m.* hemozoon.
hemuresis *f.* hemuresis.
hender *v.* slit.
hendido, -da *adj.* cleft.
hendidura *f.* fissure, fissura.
henogenesia *f.* henogenesis.
henogenesis *f.* henogenesis.
henoma *m.* henoma.
henosis *f.* henosis.
hepaptosis *f.* hepaptosis.
heparina *f.* heparin.
 heparina cálcica heparin calcium.
 heparina sódica heparin sodium.
heparinemia *f.* heparinemia.
heparinización *f.* heparinization.
heparinizar *v.* heparinize.
hepatalgia *f.* hepatalgia.
hepatargia *f.* hepatargia, hepatargy.
hepatectomía *f.* hepatectomy.
 hepatectomía derecha right lobar hepatectomy.
 hepatectomía izquierda left lobar hepatectomy.
 hepatectomía total total hepatectomy.
hepatectomizar *v.* hepatectomize.
hepático, -ca *adj.* hepatic.
hepaticocolangioyeyunostomía *f.* hepaticocholangiojejunostomy.
hepaticocoledostomía *f.* hepatichodochotomy.
hepaticodocotomía *f.* hepatichodochotomy.
hepaticoduodenostomía *f.* hepaticoduodenostomy.
hepaticoenterostomía *f.* hepaticoenterostomy.

hepaticogastronomía *f.* hepaticogastronomy.
hepaticoliasis *f.* hepaticoliasis.
hepaticolitotomía *f.* hepaticolithotomy.
hepaticolitotripsia *f.* hepaticolithotripsy.
hepaticopulmonar *adj.* hepaticopulmonary.
hepaticorrafia *f.* hepatorrhaphy.
hepaticostomía *f.* hepaticostomy.
hepaticotomía *f.* hepaticotomy.
hepaticoyeyunostomía *f.* hepaticojejunostomy.
hepatismo *m.* hepatism.
hepatítico, -ca *adj.* hepatitic.
hepatitis *f.* hepatitis.
  hepatitis A hepatitis A.
  hepatitis por agente delta delta agent hepatitis.
  hepatitis alcohólica alcoholic hepatitis.
  hepatitis anictérica anicteric hepatitis.
  hepatitis anictérica aguda acute anicteric hepatitis.
  hepatitis B hepatitis B.
  hepatitis C hepatitis C.
  hepatitis de células gigantes giant cell hepatitis.
  hepatitis de células plasmáticas plasma cell hepatitis.
  hepatitis colestásica cholestatic hepatitis.
  hepatitis colangiolítica cholangitic hepatitis, cholangiolitic hepatitis.
  hepatitis crónica chronic hepatitis.
  hepatitis crónica activa chronic active hepatitis, active chronic.
  hepatitis crónica agresiva chronic agressive hepatitis.
  hepatitis crónica intersticial chronic interstitial hepatitis.
  hepatitis crónica persistente chronic persisting hepatitis, persistent chronic hepatitis.
  hepatitis D hepatitis D.
  hepatitis delta delta hepatitis.
  hepatitis E hepatitis E.
  hepatitis epidémica epidemic hepatitis.
  hepatitis externa hepatitis externa.
  hepatitis familiar familial hepatitis.
  hepatitis fulminante fulminant hepatitis, fulminating hepatitis.
  hepatitis por halotano halothane hepatitis.
  hepatitis de incubación breve short-incubation hepatitis.
  hepatitis de incubación prolongada long-incubation hepatitis.
  hepatitis inducida por tóxicos o fármacos drug-induced hepatitis.
  hepatitis infecciosa infectious hepatitis.
  hepatitis por inoculación inoculation hepatitis.
  hepatitis lupoide lupoid hepatitis.
  hepatitis MS-1 MS-1 hepatitis.
  hepatitis MS-2 MS-2 hepatitis.
  hepatitis neonatal neonatal hepatitis.
  hepatitis neonatal de células gigantes neonatal giant cell hepatitis.
  hepatitis no-A, no-B, NANB no-A, no-B, NANB hepatitis.
  hepatitis postransfusional post-transfusion hepatitis.
  hepatitis recrudescente recrudescent hepatitis.
  hepatitis sérica serum hepatitis.
  hepatitis subaguda subacute hepatitis.
  hepatitis por suero serum hepatitis.
  hepatitis por suero homólogo homologous serum hepatitis.
  hepatitis supurada suppurative hepatitis.
  hepatitis tóxica toxic hepatitis.

  hepatitis tranfusional, por transfusión transfusion hepatitis.
  hepatitis viral A, hepatitis viral de tipo A viral hepatitis type A.
  hepatitis viral B, hepatitis viral de tipo B viral hepatitis type B.
  hepatitis viral C, hepatitis viral de tipo C viral hepatitis type C.
  hepatitis viral D, hepatitis viral de tipo D delta agent hepatitis.
  hepatitis viral E, hepatitis viral de tipo E viral hepatitis type E.
  hepatitis viral, hepatitis vírica, hepatitis por virus viral hepatitis, virus hepatitis.
hepatización *f.* hepatization.
  hepatización amarilla yellow hepatization.
  hepatización gris gray hepatization.
  hepatización roja red hepatization.
hepatizado, -da *adj.* hepatized.
hepatobiliar *adj.* hepatobiliary.
hepatoblastoma *m.* hepatoblastoma.
hepatobronqulal *adj.* hepatobronchial.
hepatocarcinogénesis *f.* hepatocarcinogenesis.
hepatocarcinogenético, -ca *adj.* hepatocarcinogenetic.
hepatocarcinoma *m.* hepatocarcinoma.
hepatocele *m.* hepatocele.
hepatocelular *adj.* hepatocellular.
hepatocirrosis *f.* hepatocirrhosis.
hepatocístico, -ca *adj.* hepatocystic.
hepatocito *m.* hepatocyte.
hepatocolangiocistoduodenostomía *f.* hepatocholangiocystoduodenostomy.
hepatocolangioenterostomía *f.* hepatocholangioenterostomy.
hepatocolangiostomía *f.* hepatocholangiostomy.
hepatocolangitis *f.* hepatocholangitis.
hepatocólico, -ca *adj.* hepatocolic.
hepatodinia *f.* hepatodynia.
hepatodistrofia *f.* hepatodystrophy.
hepatoentérico, -ca *adj.* hepatoenteric.
hepatoesplénico, -ca *adj.* hepatolienal.
hepatoesplenitis *f.* hepatosplenitis.
hepatoesplenografía *f.* hepatosplenography.
hepatoesplenomegalia *f.* hepatosplenomegaly.
hepatosplenomegalia *f.* hepatosplenomegaly.
hepatófago *m.* hepatophage.
hepatoflebitis *f.* hepatophlebitis.
hepatófugo, -ga *adj.* hepatofugal.
hepatogénico, -ca *adj.* hepatogenic.
hepatógeno, -na *adj.* hepatogenous.
hepatografía *f.* hepatography.
hepatoide *adj.* hepatoid.
hepatolenticular *adj.* hepatolenticular.
hepatolienal *adj.* hepatolienal.
hepatolisina *f.* hepatolysin.
hepatólisis *f.* hepatolysis.
hepatolitectomía *f.* hepatolithectomy.
hepatolitiasis *f.* hepatolithiasis.
hepatolito *m.* hepatolith.
hepatolitotripsia *f.* hepatolithotripsy.
hepatoma *m.* hepatoma.
hepatomalacia *f.* hepatomalacia.
hepatomegalia *f.* hepatomegalia, hepatomegaly.
hepatomelanosis *f.* hepatomelanosis.
hepatonco *m.* hepatoma.
hepatonefromegalia *f.* hepatonephromegaly.
hepatónfalo *m.* hepatomphalos.
hepatonfalocele *m.* hepatomphalocele.
hepatopatía *f.* hepatopathy.

hepatópeto, -ta *adj.* hepatopetal.
hepatopexia *f.* hepatopexy.
hepatoptosis *f.* hepatoptosis.
hepatorrafia *f.* hepatorrhaphy.
hepatorragia *f.* hepatorrhagia.
hepatorrea *f.* hepatorrhea.
hepatorrenal *adj.* hepatorenal.
hepatorrexis *f.* hepatorrhexis.
hepatoscopia *f.* hepatoscopy.
hepatosis *f.* hepatosis.
hepatostomía *f.* hepatostomy.
hepatoterapia *f.* hepatotherapy.
hepatotomía *f.* hepatotomy.
  hepatotomía transtorácica transthoracic hepatotomy.
hepatotoxemia *f.* hepatotoxemia.
hepatotoxicidad *f.* hepatotoxicity.
hepatotóxico, -ca *adj.* hepatotoxic.
hepatotoxina *f.* hepatotoxin.
hepatotrofia *f.* hepatotrophia, hepatotrophy.
hepatotrópico, -ca *adj.* hepatotropic.
hepatoyugular *adj.* hepatojugular.
heptacrómico, -ca *adj.* heptachromic.
heptosa *f.* heptose.
heptosuria *f.* heptosuria.
heredabilidad *f.* hereditability, heritability.
hereditario, -ria *adj.* hereditary.
heredoataxia *f.* heredoataxia, heredotaxia.
heredodegeneración *f.* heredodegeneration.
heredofamiliar *adj.* heredofamilial.
heredoinfección *f.* heredoinfection.
heredoinmunidad *f.* heredoimmunity.
heredolúes *f.* heredolues.
heredoluético, -ca *adj.* heredoluetic.
heredopatía *f.* heredopathia.
  heredopatía atáxica polineuritiforme heredopathia atactica polyneuritiformis.
heredorretinopatía congénita *f.* heredoretinopathia congenita.
heredosífilis *f.* heredosyphilis.
heredosifilítico, -ca *adj.* heredosyphilitic.
heredosifilología *f.* heredosyphilology.
herencia[1] *f.* heritability.
herencia[2] *f.* heredity, inheritance.
  herencia alternativa alternative inheritance.
  herencia anfígona amphigenous inheritance.
  herencia autosómica autosomal heredity, autosomal inheritance.
  herencia autosómica dominante autosomal dominant inheritance.
  herencia autosómica recesiva autosomal recessive inheritance.
  herencia biparenteral biparental inheritance.
  herencia citoplasmática, herencia citoplásmica cytoplasmic inheritance.
  herencia colateral collateral heredity.
  herencia complementaria complemental inheritance.
  herencia cruzada crisscross inheritance.
  herencia cuantitativa quantitative inheritance.
  herencia cuasidominante quasidominant inheritance.
  herencia doble duplex inheritance.
  herencia dominante ligada al cromosoma X X-linked dominant inheritance.
  herencia extracromosómica extrachromosomal heredity.
  herencia extranuclear extranuclear heredity.
  herencia galtoniana Galtonian heredity.
  herencia holándrica holandric inheritance.
  herencia hologínica hologynic inheritance.
  herencia homócrona homochronous inheritance.
  herencia homotrópica homotropic inheritance.

herencia influida por el sexo sex-influenced heredity.

herencia intermedia intermediate inheritance.

herencia ligada al sexo sex-linked heredity.

herencia ligada al cromosoma X X-linked heredity, X-linked inheritance.

herencia ligada al cromosoma Y Y-linked heredity.

herencia limitada por el sexo sex-limited heredity.

herencia materna maternal inheritance.

herencia mendeliana Mendelian heredity.

herencia mezclada blending inheritance.

herencia mitocondrial mitochondrial inheritance.

herencia monofactorial monofactorial inheritance.

herencia mosaica, herencia en mosaico mosaic heredity.

herencia multifactorial multifactorial inheritance.

herencia poligénica polygenic inheritance.

herencia recesiva recessive heredity.

herencia recesiva ligada al cromosoma X X-linked recessive inheritance.

herencia suplementaria supplemental inheritance.

herida *f.* wound.

herida abdominal penetrante penetrating abdominal wound.

herida abierta open wound.

herida acanalada crease wound.

herida por aplastamiento crushing wound.

herida por arma blanca cold weapon wound, stab wound.

herida por arma de fuego gunshot wound, wound by firearm.

herida aséptica aseptic wound.

herida por aspiración, herida aspirante sucking wound.

herida avulsa avulsed wound.

herida contusa, herida por contusión blunt wound, contused wound.

herida envenenada, herida emponzoñada poisoned wound.

herida en gotiera gutter wound.

herida incisa, herida de incisión incised wound, incisional wound.

herida no penetrante non-penetrating wound.

herida penetrante penetrating wound.

herida perforante perforating wound.

herida por pinchazo de aguja needle-stick injury.

herida por punción puncture wound.

herida punzante puncture wound.

herida de refilón glancing wound.

herida en sedal seton wound.

herida séptica septic wound.

herida soplante blowing wound.

herida subcutánea subcutaneous wound.

herida tangencial tangential wound.

herida traumatopneica traumatopneic wound.

herida en túnel tunnel wound.

herir *v.* wound.

hermafrodita *m. y adj.* hermaphrodite.

hermafrodita verdadero true hermaphrodite.

hermafrodismo *m.* hermaphrodism.

hermafroditismo *m.* hermaphroditism.

hermafroditismo alterno lateral hermaphroditism.

hermafroditismo bilateral bilateral hermaphroditism.

hermafroditismo completo true hermaphroditism.

hermafroditismo externo lateral hermaphroditism.

hermafroditismo dimidiado dimidiate hermaphroditism.

hermafroditismo espurio spurious hermaphroditism.

hermafroditismo falso false hermaphroditism.

hermafroditismo femenino female hermaphroditism.

hermafroditismo masculino male hermaphroditism.

hermafroditismo lateral lateral hermaphroditism.

hermafroditismo partido dimidiate hermaphroditism.

hermafroditismo suprarrenal adrenal hermaphroditism.

hermafroditismo transverso transverse hermaphroditism.

hermafroditismo unilateral unilateral hermaphroditism.

hermafroditismo verdadero true hermaphroditism.

Hermetia illucens Hermetia illucens.

hermético, -ca *adj.* hermetic.

hernia *f.* hernia.

hernia abdominal abdominal hernia.

hernia adiposa hernia adiposa.

hernia adquirida acquired hernia.

hernia anteroexterna lateral ventral hernia.

hernia de asa doble double loop hernia.

hernia de Barth Barth's hernia.

hernia de Béclard Béclard's hernia.

hernia bilocular femoral bilocular femoral hernia.

hernia de Birkett Birkett's hernia.

hernia de Bochdaleck Bochdaleck's hernia.

hernia cecal cecal hernia.

hernia cerebral cerebral hernia, hernia cerebri.

hernia ciática sciatic hernia.

hernia cística cystic hernia.

hernia de Cloquet Cloquet's hernia.

hernia coercible reducible hernia.

hernia completa complete hernia.

hernia congénita congenital hernia.

hernia de Cooper Cooper's hernia.

hernia crural crural hernia.

hernia por deslizamiento, hernia deslizante, hernia deslizada sliding hernia, slipped hernia.

hernia diafragmática diaphragmatic hernia.

hernia diafragmática congénita congenital diaphragmatic hernia.

hernia directa direct hernia.

hernia discal, hernia de disco herniated disk.

hernia diverticular diverticular hernia.

hernia en doble saco hernia en bissac.

hernia duodenoyeyunal duodenojejunal hernia.

hernia del elevador levator hernia.

hernia encarcelada incarcerated hernia.

hernia enquistada encysted hernia.

hernia epigástrica epigastric hernia.

hernia epiploica omental hernia.

hernia escrotal scrotal hernia.

hernia estrangulada strangulated hernia.

hernia externa external hernia.

hernia extrasacular extrasacular hernia.

hernia fascial fascial hernia.

hernia femoral femoral hernia.

hernia femoral bilocular bilocular femoral hernia.

hernia foraminal foraminal hernia.

hernia funicular funicular hernia.

hernia gastroesofágica gastroesophageal hernia.

hernia glútea gluteal hernia.

hernia grasa fatty hernia.

hernia de Gruber Gruber's hernia.

hernia de Grynfelt Grynfelt hernia.

hernia de Hesselbach Hesselbach's hernia.

hernia de Hey Hey's hernia.

hernia hiatal, hernia de hiato hiatal hernia, hiatus hernia.

hernia hiatal axial axial hiatal hernia.

hernia hiatal por deslizamiento, hernia hiatal deslizante sliding hiatal hernia.

hernia hiatal esofágica deslizante sliding esophageal hiatal hernia.

hernia de hiato esofágico hiatal hernia.

hernia de Holthouse Holthouse's hernia.

hernia iliacosubfascial iliacosubfascial hernia.

hernia incarcerada incarcerated hernia.

hernia incisional incisional hernia.

hernia incompleta incomplete hernia.

hernia indirecta indirect hernia.

hernia infantil infantile hernia.

hernia inguinal inguinal hernia.

hernia inguinal directa direct inguinal hernia.

hernia inguinal externa indirect inguinal hernia.

hernia inguinal indirecta indirect inguinal hernia.

hernia inguinal interna direct inguinal hernia.

hernia inguinal properitoneal properitoneal inguinal hernia.

hernia inguinocrural inguinocrural hernia.

hernia inguinoescrotal inguinoescrotal hernia.

hernia inguinofemoral inguinofemoral hernia.

hernia inguinolabial inguinolabial hernia.

hernia inguinoproperitoneal properitoneal inguinal hernia.

hernia inguinosuperficial inguinosuperficial hernia.

hernia intermuscular intermuscular hernia.

hernia interna internal hernia.

hernia interparietal interparietal hernia.

hernia intersigmoidea intersigmoid hernia.

hernia intersticial interstitial hernia.

hernia intrapelviana intrapelvic hernia.

hernia del iris hernia of the iris.

hernia irreductible irreducible hernia.

hernia isquiática ischiatic hernia.

hernia isquiorrectal ischiorectal hernia.

hernia de Krönlein Krönlein's hernia.

hernia de Küster Küster's hernia.

hernia labial labial hernia.

hernia labial posterior posterior labial hernia.

hernia de Laugier Laugier's hernia.

hernia del ligamento ancho uterino hernia of the broad ligament of the uterus.

hernia de Littré Littré's hernia.

hernia lumbar lumbar hernia.

hernia de Malgaigne Malgaigne's hernia.

hernia meningea meningeal hernia.

hernia mesentérica mesenteric hernia.

hernia mesocólica mesocolic hernia.

hernia de Morgagni Morgagni's hernia.

hernia mucosa mucosal hernia.

hernia muscular muscular hernia.

hernia oblicua oblique hernia.

hernia obturatriz, hernia del obturador obturator hernia.

hernia oculta concealed hernia.

hernia omental omental hernia.

hernia orbitaria orbital hernia.

hernia ovárica ovarian hernia.

hernia panicular pannicular hernia.

hernia paraesofágica paraesophageal hernia.

hernia paraestomal stomal hernia.

hernia parahiatal parahiatal hernia.

hernia paraperitoneal paraperitoneal hernia.

hernia parasacular parasaccular hernia.

hernia parietal parietal hernia.

hernia pectínea pectineal hernia.

hernia perineal perineal hernia.

hernia de Petit Petit's hernia.

hernia prevascular prevascular hernia.

hernia prevesical antevesical hernia.

hernia properitoneal properitoneal hernia.

hernia pudenda pudendal hernia.

hernia por pulsión pulsion hernia.

hernia rectovaginal rectovaginal hernia.

hernia reducible, hernia reductible reducible hernia.

hernia retrocecal retrocecal hernia.

hernia retrógrada retrograde hernia.

hernia retroperitoneal retroperitoneal hernia.

hernia retropubiana retropubic hernia.

hernia retrosternal retrosternal hernia.

hernia retrovascular retrovascular hernia.

hernia de Richter Richter's hernia.

hernia de Rieux Rieux' hernia.

hernia por rodamiento rolling hernia.

hernia de Rokitansky Rokitansky's hernia.

hernia seca dry hernia.

hernia de Serafini Serafini's hernia.

hernia sinovial synovial hernia.

hernia de Spiegel Spiegelian hernia.

hernia subpúbica subpubic hernia.

hernia de Treitz Treitz's hernia.

hernia umbilical umbilical hernia.

hernia uterina uterine hernia.

hernia vaginal vaginal hernia.

hernia vaginal posterior posterior vaginal hernia.

hernia vaginolabial vaginolabial hernia.

hernia de la vejiga vesical hernia.

hernia de Velpeau Velpeau's hernia.

hernia ventral ventral hernia.

hernia vesical vesical hernia.

hernia vesiculosa vesicle hernia.

hernia del vítreo vitreous hernia.

hernia de von Bergmann von Bergmann's hernia.

hernia en W W hernia.

herniación *f.* herniation.

herniación amigdalina tonsillar herniation.

herniación central central herniation.

herniación cerebral cerebral herniation.

herniación del cíngulo cingulate herniation.

herniación de disco intervertebral herniation of the intervertebral disk.

herniación esfenoidal sphenoidal herniation.

herniación foraminal foraminal herniation.

herniación del núcleo pulposo herniation of the nucleus pulposus.

herniación subfacial subfacial herniation.

herniación tentorial tentorial herniation.

herniación tonsilar tonsillar herniation.

herniación transtentorial transtentorial herniation.

herniación transtentorial caudal caudal transtentorial herniation.

herniación transtentorial rostral rostral transtentorial herniation.

herniación uncal, herniación del uncus uncal herniation.

herniado, -da *adj.* herniated.

herniario, -ria *adj.* herniary.

hernioapendicectomía *f.* hernioappendectomy.

hernioenterotomía *f.* hernioenterotomy.

herniografía *f.* herniography.

hernioide *adj.* hernioid.

herniolaparotomía *f.* herniolaparotomy.

herniología *f.* herniology.

hernioplastia *f.* hernioplasty.

herniopunción *f.* herniopuncture.

herniopuntura *f.* herniopuncture.

herniorrafia *f.* herniorrhaphy.

herniorrafia inguinal inguinal herniorrhaphy.

herniotomía *f.* herniotomy.

herniotomía de Petit Petit's herniotomy.

herniótomo *m.* herniotome.

herniótomo de Cooper Cooper's herniotome.

heroinomanía *f.* heroin addiction.

heroinómano, -na *m., f.* heroin addict.

herpangina *f.* herpangina.

herpes *m.* herpes.

herpes auricular posterior herpes zoster auricularis.

herpes catarral herpes catarrhalis.

herpes circinado ampolloso herpes circinatus bullosus.

herpes corneal herpes corneae.

herpes descamativo herpes desquamans.

herpes digital herpes digitalis.

herpes facial herpes facialis.

herpes febril herpes febrilis.

herpes generalizado herpes generalisatus.

herpes genital genital herpes, herpes genitalis.

herpes gestacional, herpes gravídico herpes gestationis.

herpes de los gladiadores herpes gladiatorum.

herpes del iris, herpes iris iris herpes.

herpes labial herpes labialis.

herpes de los luchadores wrestler's herpes.

herpes menstrual herpes menstrualis.

herpes neonatal neonatal herpes.

herpes oral oral herpes.

herpes progenital herpes progenitalis.

herpes recidivante relapsing herpes.

herpes recurrente recurrent herpes, herpes recurrens.

herpes simple herpes simplex.

herpes traumático traumatic herpes.

herpes zoster herpes zoster.

herpes zoster oftálmico herpes zoster ophthalmicus.

herpes zoster ótico herpes zoster oticus.

herpes zoster variceloso herpes zoster varicellosus.

herpesencefalitis *f.* herpes simplex encephalitis.

Herpesviridae Herpesviridae.

herpesvirus *m.* herpesvirus.

herpesvirus hominis herpesvirus hominis.

herpesvirus suis herpesvirus suis.

herpético, -ca *adj.* herpetic.

herpetiforme *adj.* herpetiform.

herpetoide *adj.* herpetoide.

Herpetoviridae Herpetoviridae.

herpetovirus *m.* herpetovirus.

hersaje *m.* hersage.

herzstoss *m.* herzstoss.

hesperanopía *f.* hesperanopia.

hesperanopsia *f.* hesperanopia.

heteradelfia *f.* heteradelphia.

heteradelfo *m.* heteradelphus.

heteradenia *f.* heteradenia.

heteradénico, -ca *adj.* heteradenic.

heteralio *m.* heteralius.

heteralo *m.* heteralius.

heterauxesia *f.* heterauxesis.

heterauxesis *f.* heterauxesis.

heterauxia *f.* heterauxesis.

heteraxial *adj.* heteraxial.

heteraxil *adj.* heteraxial.

heterecio, -cia *adj.* heterecious.

heterecismo *m.* hetericism.

heterérgico, -ca *adj.* heterergic.

heterestesia *f.* heteresthesia.

heteroaglutinación *f.* heteroagglutination.

heteroaglutinina *f.* heteroagglutinin.

heteroalbuminosuria *f.* heteroalbuminosuria.

heteroalbumosa *f.* heteroalbumose.

heteroalelo *m.* heteroallele.

heteroanticuerpo *m.* heteroantibody.

heteroantígeno *m.* heteroantigen.

heteroantisuero *m.* heteroantiserum.

heteroátomo *m.* heteroatom.

Heterobilharzia Heterobilharzia.

heteroblásico, -ca *adj.* heteroblastic.

heterocarion *m.* heterokaryon.

heterocariosis *f.* heterokaryosis.

heterocariótico, -ca *adj.* heterokaryotic.

heterocéfalo *m.* heterocephalus.

heterocelular *adj.* heterocellular.

heterocéntrico, -ca *adj.* heterocentric.

heterocíclico, -ca *adj.* heterocyclic.

heterocigosidad *f.* heterozygosity.

heterocigosis *f.* heterozygosis.

heterocigotia *f.* heterozygosity.

heterocigótico, -ca *adj.* heterozygous.

heterocigoto *m.* heterozygote.

heterocigoto compuesto compound heterozygote.

heterocigoto doble double heterozygote.

heterocigoto manifiesto manifesting heterozygote.

heterocigoto obligado obligate heterozygote.

heterocinesia *f.* heterokinesia.

heterocinesis *f.* heterokinesis.

heterocitolisina *f.* heterocytolysin.

heterocitotoxina *f.* heterocytotoxin.

heterocitotrópico, -ca *adj.* heterocytotropic.

heterocládico, -ca *adj.* heterocladic.

heterocomplemento *m.* heterocomplement.

heterocrinia *f.* heterocrinia.

heterocrino, -na *adj.* heterocrine.

heterocromático, -ca *adj.* heterochromatic.

heterocromatina *f.* heterochromatin.

heterocromatina constitutiva constitutive heterochromatin.

heterocromatina facultativa facultative heterochromatin.

heterocromatina rica en satélite satellite-rich heterochromatin.

heterocromatinización *f.* heterochromatinization.

heterocromatización *f.* heterochromatization.

heterocromatosis *f.* heterochromatosis.

heterocromía *f.* heterochromia.

heterocromía atrófica atrophic heterochromia.

heterocromía binocular binocular heterochromia.

heterocromía del iris iris heterochromia.

heterocromía simpática sympathetic heterochromia.

heterocromía simple simple heterochromia.
heterocrómico, -ca *adj.* heterochromous.
heterocromo, -ma *adj.* heterochromous.
heterocromosoma *m.* heterochromosome.
heterocronia *f.* heterochronia.
heterocrónico, -ca *adj.* heterochronic, heterochronous.
heterócrono, -na *adj.* heterochron.
Heterodera radicicola Heterodera radicicola.
heterodérmico, -ca *adj.* heterodermic.
heterodesmótico, -ca *adj.* heterodesmotic.
heterodídimo *m.* heterodidymus.
heterodímero *m.* heterodimer.
heterodisperso, -sa *adj.* heterodisperse.
heterodonto, -ta *adj.* heterodont.
heteródromo, -ma *adj.* heterodromous.
heterodúplex *m.* heteroduplex.
heteroecio, -cia *adj.* heteroecious.
heteroerótico, -ca *adj.* heteroerotic.
heteroerotismo *m.* heteroerotism, heteroeroticism.
heteroespecífico, -ca *adj.* heterospecific.
heterofagia *f.* heterophagy.
heterofermentación *f.* heterofermentation.
heterofermentador *m.* heterofermenter.
heterofiasis *f.* heterophyasis.
heterofidiasis *f.* heterophydiasis.
heterófido *m.* heterophyd.
heterofílico, -ca *adj.* heterophilic.
heterófilo *m. y adj.* heterophil, heterophile.
heterofonía *f.* heterophonia.
heteroforia *f.* heterophoria.
heterofórico, -ca *adj.* heterophoric.
heteroftalmía *f.* heterophthalmia.
heteroftalmos *m.* heterophthalmos.
heteroftongia *f.* heterophtongia.
heterogamético, -ca *adj.* heterogametic.
heterogametismo *m.* heterogamety.
heterogameto *m.* heterogamete.
heterogamia *f.* heterogamy.
heterogámico, -ca *adj.* heterogamous.
heterógamo, -ma *adj.* heterogamous.
heteroganglionar *adj.* heteroganglionic.
heterogeneidad *f.* heterogeneity.
heterogeneidad genética genetic heterogeneity.
heterogeneidad genética alélica allelic genetic heterogeneity.
heterogeneidad genética de locus locus genetic heterogeneity.
heterogéneo, -a *adj.* heterogeneous, heterogenous.
heterogénesis *f.* heterogenesis.
heterogenético, -ca *adj.* heterogenetic.
heterogenia *f.* heterogeny.
heterogenicidad *f.* heterogeneity.
heterogénico, -ca *adj.* heterogenic, heterogeneic, heterogenous.
heterógeno, -na *adj.* heterogenous.
heterogenoto *m.* heterogenote.
heteroglobulosa *f.* heteroglobulose.
heterogonia *f.* heterogony.
heterografía *f.* heterography.
heterohemaglutinación *f.* heterohemagglutination.
heterohemaglutinina *f.* heterohemagglutinin.
heterohipnosis *f.* heterohypnosis.
heteroinfección *f.* heteroinfection.
heteroinjerto *m.* heterograft.
heteroinmune *adj.* heteroimmune.
heteroinmunidad *f.* heteroimmunity.
heteroinoculable *adj.* hetroinoculable.
heteroinoculación *f.* heteroinoculation.
heterolateral *adj.* heterolateral.
heterolípidos *m.* heterolipids.

heterolisina *f.* heterolysin.
heterólisis *f.* heterolysis.
heterolítico, -ca *adj.* heterolytic.
heterolito *m.* heterolith.
heterología *f.* heterology.
heterólogo, -ga *adj.* heterologous.
heteromastigoto, -ta *adj.* heteromastigote.
hetéromérico, -ca *adj.* heteromeric.
heterómero, -ra *adj.* heteromerous.
heterometaplasia *f.* heterometaplasia.
heterometropía *f.* heterometropia.
heteromorfismo *m.* heteromorphism.
heteromorfo, -fa *adj.* heteromorphous.
heteromorfosis *f.* heteromorphosis.
heterónimo, -ma *adj.* heteronymous.
heteronomía *f.* heteronomy.
heterónomo, -ma *adj.* heteronomous.
heteroosteoplastia *f.* hetero-osteoplasty.
heterópago *m.* heteropagus.
heteropancreatismo *m.* heteropancreatism.
Heterophyes Heterophyes.
Heterophyidae Heterophyidae.
heteropía *f.* heteropsia.
heteropicnosis *f.* heteropyknosis.
heteropicnosis negativa negative heteropyknosis.
heteropicnosis positiva positive heteropyknosis.
heteroplasia *f.* heteroplasia.
heteroplasma *m.* heteroplasm.
heteroplastia *f.* heteroplasty.
heteroplástico, -ca *adj.* heteroplastic.
heteroplástido *m.* heteroplastid.
heteroploide *adj.* heteroploid.
heteroploidía *f.* heteroploidy.
heterópodo, -da *adj.* heteropodal.
heteropolimérico, -ca *adj.* heteropolymeric.
heteropolímero, -ra *adj.* heteropolymer.
heteroprosopus *m.* heteroprosopus.
heteropsia *f.* heteropsia.
heteroqueratoplastia *f.* heterokeratoplasty.
heteroquilia *f.* heterochylia.
heteróquiro, -ra *adj.* heterochiral, heterocheiral.
heterosacárido *m.* heterosaccharide.
heteroscopia *f.* heteroscopy.
heteroscopio *m.* heteroscope.
heterosexismo *m.* heterosexism.
heterosexual *adj.* heterosexual.
heterosexualidad *f.* heterosexuality.
heterosis *f.* heterosis.
heterosmia *f.* heterosmia.
heterosoma *m.* heterosome.
heterosueroterapia *f.* heteroserotherapy.
heterosugestión *f.* heterosuggestion.
heterotaxia *f.* heterotaxia, heterotaxis, heterotaxy.
heterotaxis *f.* heterotaxia, heterotaxis, heterotaxy.
heterotaxia cardíaca cardiac heterotaxia.
heterotáxico, -ca *adj.* heterotaxic.
heterotaxis *f.* heterotaxis.
heteroterapia *f.* heterotherapy.
heterotermia *f.* heterothermy.
heterotérmico, -ca *adj.* heterothermic.
heterotermo, -ma *adj.* heterotherm.
heterótico, -ca *adj.* heterotic.
heterotípico, -ca *adj.* heterotypic.
heterotonía *f.* heterotonia.
heterotónico, -ca *adj.* heterotonic.
heterotopia *f.* heterotopia, heterotopy.
heterotopia macular heterotopia maculae.
heterotopia neuronal neuronal heterotopia.
heterotópico, -ca *adj.* heterotopic.
heterotoxina *f.* heterotoxin.

heterotrasplante[1] *m.* heterotransplant.
heterotrasplante[2] *m.* heterotransplantation.
heterótrico, -ca *adj.* heterotrichous.
heterotricosis *f.* heterotrichosis.
heterotricosis superciliar heterotrichosis superciliorum.
heterotrofia *f.* heterotrophia, heterotrophy.
heterotrófico, -ca *adj.* heterotrophic.
heterótrofo *m.* heterotroph.
heterotropía *f.* heterotropia, heterotropy.
heterovacuna *f.* heterovaccine.
heteroxenia *f.* heteroxeny.
heteroxénico, -ca *adj.* heteroxenous.
heteroxeno, -na *adj.* heteroxenous.
heterozigoto *m.* heterozygote.
heterozoico, -ca *adj.* heterozoic.
heurístico, -ca *adj.* heuristic.
hexabásico, -ca *adj.* hexabasic.
hexacanto *m.* hexacanth.
hexacrómico, -ca *adj.* hexachromic.
héxada *f.* hexad.
hexadactilia *f.* hexadactylia, hexadactyly.
hexadactilismo *m.* hexadactylism.
Hexagenia bilineata Hexagenia bilineata.
hexámero *m.* hexamer.
hexaploide *adj.* hexaploid.
hexaploidía *f.* hexaploidy.
hexatómico, -ca *adj.* hexatomic.
hexavacuna *f.* hexavaccine.
hexenmilch hexenmilch.
hexiología *f.* hexiology.
hialina *f.* hyalin.
hialina alcohólica alcoholic hyalin.
hialina de Crooke Crooke's hyalin.
hialina hematógena hematogenous hyalin.
hialinización *f.* hyalinization.
hialino, -na *adj.* hyaline.
hialinosis *f.* hyalinosis.
hialinosis cutis et mucosae hyalinosis cutis et mucosae.
hialinuria *f.* hyalinuria.
hialitis *f.* hyalitis.
hialitis asteroide asteroid hyalosis.
hialitis punctata punctate hyalitis, hyalitis punctata.
hialitis supurativa suppurative hyalitis, hyalitis suppurativa.
hialocito *m.* hyalocyte.
hialofagia *f.* hyalophagia, hyalophagy.
hialógeno, -na *m., f.* hyalogen.
hialohifomicosis *f.* hyalohyphomycosis.
hialoide *adj.* hyaloid.
hialoideo, -a *adj.* hyaloid.
hialoiditis *f.* hyaloiditis.
hialómera *f.* hyalomere.
hialómero *f.* hyalomere.
hialomitoma *m.* hyalomitome.
hialomucoide *adj.* hyalomucoid.
hialonixis *f.* hyalonyxis.
hialoplasma *m.* hyaloplasm, hyaloplasma.
hialoplasma nuclear nuclear hyaloplasm.
hialoserositis *f.* hyaloserositis.
hialoserositis múltiple progresiva progressive multiple hyaloserositis.
hialosis *f.* hyalosis.
hialosis asteroide asteroid hyalosis.
hialosis punteada punctate hyalosis.
hialosoma *m.* hyalosome.
hiatal *adj.* hiatal.
hiato *m.* hiatus.
hibaroxia *f.* hybaroxia.
hibernación *f.* hibernation.
hibernación artificial artificial hibernation.
hibernoma *m.* hibernoma.
hibridación *f.* hybridization.

hibridación de ácidos nucleicos nucleic acid hybridization.

hibridación celular cell hybridization.

hibridación de células somáticas somatic cell hybridization.

hibridación de ADN DNA hybridization.

hibridación in situ fluorescente fluorescence in situ hybridization.

hibridez *f.* hybridity.

hibridismo *m.* hybridism.

híbrido, -da *m. y adj.* hybrid.

híbrido falso false hybrid.

híbrido SV40-adenovirus SV40-adenovirus hybrid.

hibridoma *m.* hybridoma.

hidátide *f.* hydatid.

hidatidiforme *adj.* hydatidiform.

hidatidocele *m.* hydatidocele.

hidatidoma *m.* hydatodoma.

hidatidosis *f.* hydatidosis.

hidatidostomía *f.* hydatidostomy.

hidatiduria *f.* hydatiduria.

hidatiforme *adj.* hydatiform.

hidatismo *m.* hydatism.

hidatoide *m. y adj.* hydatoid.

hidatoides *m.* hydatoid.

hidradenitis *f.* hidradenitis.

hidradenitis axilar hidradenitis axillaris.

hidradenitis axilar de Verneuil hidradenitis axillaris of Verneuil.

hidradenitis supurada, hidradenitis supurativa hidradenitis suppurativa.

hidradenoide *adj.* hidradenoid.

hidradenoma *m.* hidradenoma.

hidradenoma de células claras clear cell hidradenoma.

hidradenoma eruptivo hidradenoma eruptivum.

hidradenoma nodular nodular hidradenoma.

hidradenoma papilar papillary hidradenoma, hidradenoma papilliferum.

hidragogo, -ga *adj.* hydragog.

hidramnios *m.* hydramnios, hydramnion.

hidranencefalia *f.* hydranencephaly.

hidrangiografía *f.* hydrangiography.

hidrangiología *f.* hydrangiology.

hidrangiotomía *f.* hydrangiotomy.

hidrargiria *f.* hydrargyria.

hidrargirismo *m.* hydrargyrism.

hidrargiromanía *f.* hydrargyromania.

hidrargirosis *f.* hydrargirosis.

hidrartrosis *f.* hydrarthrosis.

hidrartrosis intermitente, hidrartrosis periódica intermittent hydrarthrosis.

hidrartródico, -ca *adj.* hydrarthrodial.

hidrartrósico, -ca *adj.* hydrarthrodial.

hidratación *f.* hydration.

hidratado, -da *adj.* hydrous, hydrated.

hidrato *m.* hydrate.

hidráulica *f.* hydraulics.

hidremia *f.* hydremia.

hidrencefalia *f.* hydranencephaly.

hidrencéfalo *m.* hydrencephalus.

hidrencefalocele *m.* hydrencephalocele.

hidrencefalomeningocele *m.* hydrencephalomeningocele.

hidrepigastrio *m.* hydrepigastrium.

hidriático, -ca *adj.* hydriatic, hydriatric.

hidriatría *f.* hydriatrics.

hidriátrico, -ca *adj.* hydriatric.

hídrico, -ca *adj.* hydric.

hidroa *f.* hydroa.

hidroadenoma *m.* hidroadenoma.

hidroaeroperitoneo *m.* hydraeroperitoneum.

hidroanencefalia *f.* hydroanencephalia.

hidroapéndice *m.* hydroappendix.

hidrobléfaron *m.* hydroblepharon.

hidrocalicosis *f.* hydrocalicosis.

hidrocáliz *m.* hydrocalyx.

hidrocarburismo *m.* hydrocarburism.

hidrocarburo *m.* hydrocarbon.

hidrocardia *f.* hydrocardia.

hidrocefalia *f.* hydrocephalia.

hidrocefalia de compartimento doble double compartment hydrocephalia.

hidrocefalia comunicante communicating hydrocephalia.

hidrocefalia ex vacuo ex vacuo hydrocephalia.

hidrocefalia congénita congenital hydrocephalia.

hidrocefalia externa external hydrocephalia.

hidrocefalia hiperproductiva hyperproductive hydrocephalia.

hidrocefalia hiporreabsortiva hyporeabsortive hydrocephalia.

hidrocefalia interna internal hydrocephalia.

hidrocefalia no comunicante non-communicating hydrocephalia.

hidrocefalia normotensa normal-pressure hydrocephalia.

hidrocefalia obstructiva obstructive hydrocephalia.

hidrocefalia oculta, hidrocefalia oculta a presión normal occult hydrocephalia, normal pressure occult hydrocephalia.

hidrocefalia otítica otitic hydrocephalia.

hidrocefalia posmeningítica postmeningitic hydrocephalia.

hidrocefalia postraumática post-traumatic hydrocephalia.

hidrocefalia a presión normal normal pressure hydrocephalia.

hidrocefalia primaria primary hydrocephalia.

hidrocefalia secundaria secondary hydrocephalia.

hidrocefalia tóxica toxic hydrocephalia.

hidrocefalia trombótica thrombotic hydrocephalia.

hidrocefálico, -ca *adj.* hydrocephalic.

hidrocéfalo, -la *m., f.* hydrocephalus.

hidrocefalocele *m.* hydrocephalocele.

hidrocefaloide *adj.* hydrocephaloid.

hidrocele *m.* hydrocele.

hidrocele agudo acute hydrocele.

hidrocele cervical, del cuello cervical hydrocele, hydrocele of the neck.

hidrocele comunicante communicating hydrocele.

hidrocele congénito congenital hydrocele.

hidrocele difuso diffused hydrocele.

hidrocele de Dupuytren Dupuytren's hydrocele.

hidrocele enquistado encysted hydrocele.

hidrocele escrotal externo scrotal hydrocele.

hidrocele espinal spinal hydrocele.

hidrocele femenino hydrocele feminae.

hidrocele filiriásico filarial hydrocele.

hidrocele funicular funicular hydrocele.

hidrocele herniario hernial hydrocele.

hidrocele del lactante infantile hydrocele.

hidrocele de Maunoir Maunoir's hydrocele.

hidrocele muliebris hydrocele feminae.

hidrocele de Nuck Nuck's hydrocele.

hidrocele quiloso chylous hydrocele.

hidrocele renal hydrocele renalis.

hidrocelectomía *f.* hydrocelectomy.

hidrocenosis *f.* hydrocenosis.

hidrocianismo *m.* hydrocyanism.

hidrocinesiterapia *f.* hydrokinesitherapy.

hidrocinética *f.* hydrokinetics.

hidrocinético, -ca *adj.* hydrokinetic.

hidrocirsocele *m.* hydrocirsocele.

hidrocistadenoma *m.* hydrocystadenoma.

hidrocistoma *m.* hydrocystoma.

hidrocolecisto *m.* hydrocholecystis.

hidrocoleresis *f.* hydrocholeresis.

hidrocolerético, -ca *adj.* hydrocholeretic.

hidrocolesterol *m.* hydrocholesterol.

hidrocoloide *m.* hydrocolloid.

hidrocoloide irreversible irreversible hydrocolloid.

hidrocoloide reversible reversible hydrocolloid.

hidrocolpocele *m.* hydrocolpocele.

hidrocolpos *m.* hydrocolpos.

hidroconión *m.* hydroconion.

hidrocortisona *f.* hydrocortisone.

hidrodictiotomía *f.* hydrodictiotomy.

hidrodifusión *f.* hydrodiffusion.

hidrodiuresis *f.* hydrodiuresis.

hidroeléctrico, -ca *adj.* hydroelectric.

hidroencefalocele *m.* hydroencephalocele.

hidroencefalomeningocele *m.* hydroencephalomeningocele, hydrencephalomeningocele.

hidroesfigmógrafo *m.* hydrosphygmograph.

hidroespirómetro *m.* hydrospirometer.

hidroestable *m.* hydrostable.

hidrofagocitosis *f.* hydrophagocytosis.

hidrofilia *f.* hydrophilia.

hidrofílico, -ca *adj.* hydrophilic.

hidrofilismo *m.* hydrophilism.

hidrófilo, -la *adj.* hydrophil, hydrophile.

hidrofisómetra *m.* hydrophysometra.

hidrofobia *f.* hydrophobia.

hidrofóbico, -ca *adj.* hydrophobic.

hidrofobofobia *f.* hydrophobophobia.

hidroforógrafo *m.* hydrophorograph.

hidroftalmía *f.* hydrophthalmia.

hidroftalmos *m.* hydrophthalmus.

hidroftalmos anterior hydrophthalmus anterior.

hidroftalmos posterior hydrophthalmus posterior.

hidroftalmos total hydrophthalmus totalis.

hidrogenación *f.* hydrogenation.

hidrogenar *v.* hydrogenate.

hidrógeno *m.* hydrogen.

hidrogenoide *m.* hydrogenoid.

hidrohematonefrosis *f.* hydrohematonephrosis.

hidrohepatosis *f.* hydrohepatosis.

hidrohimenitis *f.* hydrohymenitis.

hidrolaberinto *m.* hydrolabyrinth.

hidrolábil *adj.* hydrolabile.

hidrolabilidad *f.* hydrolability.

hidrólisis *f.* hydrolysis.

hidrolítico, -ca *adj.* hydrolytic.

hidrólito *m.* hydrolite.

hidrolizado, -da *m.* hydrolysate.

hidrolizar *v.* hydrolyze.

hidroma *m.* hydroma.

hidromasaje *m.* hydromassage.

hidromeningitis *f.* hydromeningitis.

hidromeningocele *m.* hydromeningocele.

hidrómetra *m.* hydrometra.

hidrometría *f.* hydrometry.

hidrométrico, -ca *adj.* hydrometric.

hidrómetro *m.* hydrometer.

hidrometrocolpos *m.* hydrometrocolpos.

hidromicrocefalia *f.* hydromicrocephaly.

hidromielia *f.* hydromyelia.

hidromielocele *m.* hydromyelocele.
hidromielomeningocele *m.* hydromyelomeningocele.
hidromioma *m.* hydromyoma.
hidronefrosis *f.* hydronephrosis.
 hidronefrosis abierta open hydronephrosis.
 hidronefrosis cerrada closed hydronephrosis.
hidronefrótico, -ca *adj.* hydronephrotic.
hidroneumatosis *f.* hydropneumatosis.
hidroneumogonia *f.* hydropneumogony.
hidroneumopericardio *m.* hydropneumopericardium.
hidroneumoperitoneo *m.* hydropneumoperitoneum.
hidroneumotórax *m.* hydropneumothorax.
hidrónfalo *m.* hydromphalus.
hidroosqueocele *m.* hydroscheocele.
hidroovario *m.* hydrovarium.
hidroparasálpinx *m.* hydroparasalpinx.
hidroparotitis *f.* hydroparotitis.
hidropenia *f.* hydropenia.
hidropénico, -ca *adj.* hydropenic.
hidropepsia *f.* dropsy, hydrops.
hidropericardio *m.* hydropericardium.
hidropericarditis *f.* hydropericarditis.
hidroperinefrosis *f.* hydroperinephrosis.
hidroperion *m.* hydroperion.
hidroperitoneo *m.* hydroperitoneum.
hidropesia *f.* dropsy, hydrops.
 hidropesia abdominal abdominal dropsy.
 hidropesia ad matulam hydrops ad matulam.
 hidropesia del amnios dropsy of the amnion.
 hidropesia anémica aguda acute anemic dropsy.
 hidropesia articular articular dropsy, hydrops articuli.
 hidropesia asmática beriberi.
 hidropesia de la cabeza dropsy of the head.
 hidropesia cardiaca cardiac dropsy.
 hidropesia cerebral hydrocephalia.
 hidropesia cutánea cutaneous dropsy.
 hidropesia endolinfática endolymphatic hydrops.
 hidropesia epidémica epidemic dropsy.
 hidropesia fetal fetal hydrops, hydrops fetalis.
 hidropesia fetal inmune immune fetal hydrops.
 hidropesia fetal no inmune non-immune fetal hydrops.
 hidropesia folicular hydrops folliculi.
 hidropesia gravídica hydrops gravidarum.
 hidropesia hepática hepatic dropsy.
 hidropesia de guerra war dropsy.
 hidropesia del hambre famine dropsy.
 hidropesia húmeda wet dropsy.
 hidropesia hipostrófica angioneurotic edema.
 hidropesia del laberinto, hidropesia laberíntica labyrinthine hydrops.
 hidropesia meníngea meningeal hydrops.
 hidropesia ovárica hydrops ovarii.
 hidropesia del pericardio dropsy of the pericardium.
 hidropesia peritoneal peritoneal dropsy.
 hidropesia renal renal dropsy.
 hidropesia del tórax dropsy of the chest.
 hidropesia tubárica hydrops tubae.
 hidropesia tubárica intermitente, hidropesia tubae profluens hydrops tubae profluens.
hidropexia *f.* hydropexia, hydropexis.
hidropéxico, -ca *adj.* hydropexic.
hidropexis *f.* hydropexis.
hidrópico, -ca *adj.* dropsical, hydropic.

hidropígeno, -na *adj.* hydropigenous.
hidropionefrosis *f.* hydropyonephrosis.
hidroplasma *m.* hydroplasma.
hidropoterapia *f.* hydropotherapy.
hidropoyesis *f.* hydropoiesis.
hidropoyético, -ca *adj.* hydropoietic.
hidroquiste *m.* hydrocyst.
hidrorraquis *m.* hydrorachis.
hidrorraquitis *f.* hydrorachitis.
hidrorrea *f.* hydrorrhea.
 hidrorrea gravídica hydrorrhea gravidarum.
 hidrorrea nasal nasal hydrorrhea.
hidrosadenitis *f.* hidrosadenitis.
hidrosálpinx *m.* hydrosalpinx.
 hidrosálpinx folicular hydrosalpinx follicularis.
 hidrosálpinx intermitente intermittent hydrosalpinx.
 hidrosálpinx simple hydrosalpinx simplex.
hidrosarcocele *m.* hydrosarcocele.
hidroscopio *m.* hydroscope.
hidrosfigmógrafo *m.* hydrosphygmograph.
hidrosíntesis *f.* hydrosynthesis.
hidrosiringomielia *f.* hydrosyringomyelia.
hidrosis *f.* hidrosis.
hidroso, -sa *adj.* hydrous.
hidrosolubilidad *f.* hydrosolubility.
hidrosoluble *adj.* hydrosoluble.
hidrospirómetro *m.* hydrospirometer.
hidrosquesis *f.* hydroschesis.
hidrostática *f.* hydrostatics.
hidrostático, -ca *adj.* hydrostatic.
hidróstato *m.* hydrostat.
hidrotaxia *f.* hydrotaxis.
hidrotaxis *f.* hydrotaxis.
hidroterapéutico, -ca *adj.* hydrotherapeutic.
hidroterapia *f.* hydrotherapy, hydrotherapeutics.
hidroterápico, -ca *adj.* hydrotherapeutic.
hidrotérmico, -ca *adj.* hydrothermal.
hidrótico, -ca *adj.* hidrotic.
hidrotionamonemia *f.* hydrothionammonemia.
hidrotionemia *f.* hydrothionemia.
hidrotionuria *f.* hydrothionuria.
hidrotomía *f.* hydrotomy.
hidrotórax *m.* hydrothorax.
 hidrotórax quiloso chylous hydrothorax.
hidrotropismo *m.* hydrotropism.
hidrotubación *f.* hydrotubation.
hidrouréter *m.* hydroureter.
hidroureteronefrosis *f.* hydroureteronephrosis.
hidroureterosis *f.* hydroureter.
hidrouria *f.* hydrouria.
hidrovario *m.* hydrovarium.
hidroxifeniluria *f.* hydroxyphenyluria.
hidroxiprolinemia *f.* hydroxyprolinemia.
hidroxiquinurreninuria *f.* hydroxykynereninuria.
hidruria *f.* hydruria, hydrouria.
hidrúrico, -ca *adj.* hydruric.
hiemal *adj.* hiemal.
hieralgia *f.* hieralgia.
hierolistesis *f.* hierolisthesis.
hierro *m.* iron, ferrum.
hifa *f.* hypha.
hifomiceto *m.* hyphomycetes.
hifomicosis *f.* hyphomycosis.
hígado *m.* liver, hepar.
 hígado adiposo fatty liver.
 hígado albuminoide albuminoid liver.
 hígado amiloide amyloid liver.
 hígado de bronce bronze liver.
 hígado cardíaco cardiac liver.

 hígado céreo waxy liver.
 hígado cirrótico cirrhotic liver.
 hígado cirrótico biliar biliary cirrhotic liver.
 hígado claveteado hobnail liver.
 hígado degradado degraded liver.
 hígado espumoso foamy liver.
 hígado de estasis stasis liver.
 hígado errante wandering liver.
 hígado flotante wandering liver.
 hígado graso fatty liver.
 hígado infantil infantile liver.
 hígado lardáceo lardaceous liver.
 hígado de nuez moscada nutmeg liver.
 hígado pigmentado pigmented liver.
 hígado poliquístico polycystic liver.
higiene *f.* hygiene.
 higiene broncopulmonar bronchopulmonary hygiene.
 higiene bronquial bronchial hygiene.
 higiene bucal mouth hygiene.
 higiene dental dental hygiene.
 higiene mental mental hygiene.
 higiene oral oral hygiene.
higiénico, -ca *adj.* hygienic.
higienista *m., f.* hygienist.
higienización *f.* cleaning.
hígrico, -ca *adj.* hygric.
higroblefárico, -ca *adj.* hygroblepharic.
higroma *m.* hygroma, hydroma.
 higroma axilar hygroma axillare.
 higroma cervical hygroma colli cystum.
 higroma mesotelial mesothelial hygroma.
 higroma prepatelar hygroma praepatellare.
 higroma prerrotuliano hygroma praepatellare.
 higroma quístico cystic hygroma, hygroma cysticum.
 higroma subdural subdural hygroma.
higromatoso, -sa *adj.* hygromatous.
higrometría *f.* hygrometry.
higrométrico, -ca *adj.* hygrometric.
higrómetro *m.* hygrometer.
higroscópico, -ca *adj.* hygroscopic.
hijo de madre adicta *m.* infant of an addicted mother.
hijo de madre diabética *m.* infant of a diabetic mother.
hila *f.* hyla.
hilergografía *f.* hylergography.
hiliar *adj.* hilar.
hilio *m.* hilum.
hilitis *f.* hilitis.
hilo *m.* thread.
hilogénesis *f.* hylogeny.
hilogenia *f.* hylogeny.
hilología *f.* hylology.
hiloma *m.* hyloma.
 hiloma mesenquimático mesenchymal hyloma.
 hiloma mesotelial mesothelial hyloma.
hilotropía *f.* hylotropy.
hilotrópico, -ca *adj.* hylotropic.
himantosis *f.* himantosis.
himen *m.* hymen.
 himen anular annular hymen.
 himen bifenestrado hymen bifenestratus, hymen biforis.
 himen circular circular hymen.
 himen cribriforme cribriform hymen.
 himen denticulado, himen denticular denticulate hymen, denticular hymen.
 himen esculpido hymen sculptatus.
 himen falciforme falciform hymen.
 himen fenestrado fenestrated hymen.
 himen franjeado denticular hymen.

himen imperforado imperforated hymen.

himen infundibuliforme infundibuliform hymen.

himen septado septate hymen, hymen septus.

himen subseptus hymen subseptus.

himen subtabicado hymen subseptus.

himen tabicado hymen septate.

himen vertical vertical hymen.

himenal *adj.* hymenal.

himenectomía *f.* hymenectomy.

himenitis *f.* hymenitis.

himenolepiasis *f.* hymenolepiasis.

himenolépido, -da *adj.* hymenolepidid.

himenopterismo *m.* hymenopterism.

himenorrafia *f.* hymenorrhaphy.

hlmenotomía *f.* hymenotomy.

hioepiglótico, -ca *adj.* hyoepiglottic, hyoepiglottidean.

hiofaríngeo, -a *adj.* hyopharyngeal.

hiogloso, -sa *adj.* hyoglossal.

hioide *adj.* hyoid.

hioideo, -a *adj.* hyoid.

hioides *m.* hyoid.

hiotiroide *adj.* hyothyroid.

hiotiroideo, -a *adj.* hyothyroid.

hipacidemia *f.* hypacidemia.

hipacusia *f.* hypacusia.

hipacusis *f.* hypacusis.

hipalbuminemia *f.* hypalbuminemia.

hipalbuminosis *f.* hypoalbuminosis.

hipalgesia *f.* hypalgesia.

hipalgésico, -ca *adj.* hypalgesic, hypalgetic.

hipamnios *m.* hypamnios.

hiparterial *adj.* hyparterial.

hipaxial *adj.* hypaxial.

hipaxil *adj.* hypaxial.

hipazouria *f.* hypoazoturia.

hipema *f.* hyphema.

hipencéfalo *m.* hypencephalon.

hipénquima *m.* hypenchime.

hiperabsorción *f.* hyperabsorption.

hiperacantosis *f.* hyperacanthosis.

hiperacidaminuria *f.* hyperacidaminuria.

hiperacidez *f.* hyperacidity.

  hiperacidez gástrica gastric hyperacidity.

hiperácido, -da *adj.* hyperacid.

hiperactividad *f.* hyperactivity.

hiperactivo, -va *adj.* hyperactive.

hiperacusia *f.* hyperacuity, hyperacusia.

hiperacusis *f.* hyperacusis.

hiperadenosis *f.* hyperadenosis.

hiperadiposidad *f.* hyperadiposity.

hiperadiposis *f.* hyperadiposis.

hiperadrenalinemia *f.* hyperadrenalinemia.

hiperadrenalismo *m.* hyperadrenalism.

hiperadrenia *f.* hyperadrenalism.

hiperadrenocorticalismo *m.* hyperadrenocorticalism, hyperadrenalcorticalism.

hiperadrenocorticismo *m.* hyperadrenocorticism.

hiperafia *f.* hyperaphia.

hiperáfico, -ca *adj.* hyperaphic.

hiperagudo, -da *adj.* hyperacute.

hiperalantoinuria *f.* hyperallantoinuria.

hiperalbuminemia *f.* hyperalbuminemia.

hiperalbuminosis *f.* hyperalbuminosis.

hiperalcalescencia *f.* hyperalkalescence.

hiperalcalinidad *f.* hyperalkalinity.

hiperaldosteronemia *f.* hyperaldosteronemia.

hiperaldosteronismo *m.* hyperaldosteronism.

hiperalfalipoproteinemia *f.* hyperalphalipoproteinemia.

hiperalgesia *f.* hyperalgesia.

  hiperalgesia auditiva auditory hyperalgesia.

hiperalgesia muscular muscular hyperalgesia.

hiperalgésico, -ca *adj.* hyperalgesic.

hiperalgético, -ca *adj.* hyperalgetic.

hiperalgia *f.* hyperalgia.

hiperalimentación *f.* hyperalimentation.

hiperalimentación parenteral parenteral hyperalimentation.

hiperalimentosis *f.* hyperalimentosis.

hiperalonemia *f.* hyperalonemia.

hiperamilasemia *f.* hyperamylasemia.

hiperaminoacidemia *f.* hyperaminoacidemia.

hiperaminoaciduria *f.* hyperaminoaciduria.

hiperamonemia *f.* hyperammonemia.

hiperamonemia cerebroatrófica cerebroatrophic hyperammonemia.

hiperamonemia congénita tipo I type I congenital hyperammonemia.

hiperamonemia congénita tipo II type II congenital hyperammonemia.

hiperamoniemia *f.* hyperammonemia.

hiperamonurla *f.* hyperammonuria.

hiperandrogenemia *f.* hyperandrogenemia.

hiperandrogenismo *m.* hyperandrogenism.

hiperargininemia *f.* hyperargininemia.

hiperazoemia *f.* hyperazotemia, azotemia.

hiperazoemia cloropénica chloropenic azotemia.

hiperazoemia extrarrenal extrarenal azotemia.

hiperazoemia hipoclorémica hypochloremic azotemia.

hiperazoemia prerrenal prerenal azotemia.

hiperazoturia *f.* hyperazoturia.

hiperbárico, -ca *adj.* hyperbaric.

hiperbarismo *m.* hyperbarism.

hiperbasofílico, -ca *adj.* hyperbasophilic.

hiperbetalipoproteinemia *f.* hyperbetalipoproteinemia.

hiperbetalipoproteinemia familiar familial hyperbetalipoproteinemia.

hiperbetalipoproteinemia familiar e hiperprebetalipoproteinemia familial hyperbetalipoproteinemia and hyperprebetalipoproteinemia.

hiperbicarbonatemia *f.* hyperbicarbonatemia.

hiperbilirrubinemia *f.* hyperbilirubinemia.

hiperbilirrubinemia congénita congenital hyperbilirubinemia.

hiperbilirrubinemia conjugada conjugated hyperbilirubinemia.

hiperbilirrubinemia neonatal neonatal hyperbilirubinemia.

hiperbilirrubinemia no conjugada unconjugated hyperbilirubinemia.

hiperbilirrubinemia del recién nacido hyperbilirubinemia of the newborn.

hiperblastosis *f.* hyperblastosis.

hiperbradicinemia *f.* hyperbradykinemia.

hiperbradicininismo *m.* hyperbradykininism.

hiperbraquicefalia *f.* hyperbrachycephaly.

hiperbraquicefálico, -ca *adj.* hyperbrachycephalic.

hipercalcemia *f.* hypercalcemia.

hipercalcemia hipocalciúrica familiar familial hypocalciuric hypercalcemia.

hipercalcemia idiopática, hipercalcemia idiopática del lactante idiopathic hypercalcemia, idiopathic hypercalcemia of infants.

hipercalcinemia *f.* hypercalcinemia.

hipercalcinuria *f.* hypercalcinuria.

hipercalcipexia *f.* hypercalcipexy.

hipercalciuria *f.* hypercalciuria.

hipercalciuria absortiva absortive hypercalciuria.

hipercalciuria idiopática idiopathic hypercalciuria.

hipercalciuria renal renal hypercalciuria.

hipercalcuria *f.* hypercalcuria.

hipercalemia *f.* hyperpotassemia.

hipercaliemia *f.* hyperkalemia, hyperkaliemia.

hipercaliuresis *f.* hyperkaluresis.

hipercapnia *f.* hypercapnia.

hipercápnico, -ca *adj.* hypercapnic.

hipercarbia *f.* hypercarbia.

hipercardia *f.* hypercardia.

hipercarotinemia *f.* hypercarotenemia, hypercarotinemia.

hipercatarsis *f.* hypercatharsis.

hipercatártico, -ca *adj.* hypercathartic.

hipercelular *adj.* hypercellular.

hipercelularidad *f.* hypercellularity.

hipercementosis *f.* hypercementosis.

hipercetonemia *f.* hyperketonemia.

hipercetonuria *f.* hypercetonuria, hyperketonuria.

hiperquetonuria *f.* hypercetonuria, hyperketonuria.

hipercetosis *f.* hyperketosis.

hiperquetosis *f.* hyperketosis.

hipercianótico, -ca *adj.* hypercyanotic.

hiperciesis *f.* hypercyesis.

hipercinemia *f.* hyperkinemia.

hipercinémico, -ca *adj.* hyperkinemic.

hipercinesia *f.* hyperkinesia, hyperkinesis.

hipercinesis *f.* hyperkinesis.

hipercinético, -ca *adj.* hyperkinetic.

hipercitemia *f.* hypercythemia.

hipercitocromía *f.* hypercytochromia.

hipercitosis *f.* hypercytosis.

hipercloremia *f.* hyperchloremia.

hiperclorémico, -ca *adj.* hyperchloremic.

hiperclorhidria *f.* hyperchlorhydria.

hipercloruración *f.* hyperchloruration.

hipercloruria *f.* hyperchloruria.

hipercoagulabilidad *f.* hypercoagulability.

hipercoagulable *adj.* hypercoagulable.

hipercolesteremia *f.* hypercholesteremia.

hipercolesterémico, -ca *adj.* hypercholesteremic.

hipercolesterinemia *f.* hypercholesterinemia.

hipercolesterolemia *f.* hypercholesterolemia.

hipercolesterolemia familiar familial hypercholesterolemia.

hipercolesterolemia familiar con hiperlipemia familial hypercholesterolemia with hyperlipemia.

hipercolesterolémico, -ca *adj.* hypercholesterolemic.

hipercolesterolia *f.* hypercholesterolia.

hipercolia *f.* hypercholia.

hipercondroplasia *f.* hyperchondroplasia.

hipercoria *f.* hypercoria, hyperkoria.

hipercorticalismo *m.* hypercorticalism.

hipercorticismo *m.* hypercorticism.

hipercorticoidismo *m.* hypercorticoidism.

hipercortisolemia *f.* hypercortisolemia.

hipercortisolismo *m.* hypercortisolism.

hipercreatinemia *f.* hypercreatinemia.

hipercrialgesia *f.* hypercryalgesia.

hipercriestesia *f.* hypercryesthesia.

hipercrinia *f.* hypercrinia.

hipercrinismo *m.* hypercrinia.

hipercrino, -na *adj.* hypercrine.

hipercrisia *f.* hypercrisia.

hipercromafinismo *m.* hyperchromaffinism.

hipercromasia *f.* hyperchromasia.

hipercromático, -ca *adj.* hyperchromatic.

hipercromatismo *m.* hyperchromatism.
hipercromatopsia *f.* hyperchromatopsia.
hipercromatosis *f.* hyperchromatism.
hipercromemia *f.* hyperchromemia.
hipercromia *f.* hyperchromia.
hipercrómico, -ca *adj.* hyperchromic.
hipercupremia *f.* hypercrupremia.
hipercupriuria *f.* hypercupriuria.
hiperdactilia *f.* hyperdactyly.
hiperdactilismo *m.* hyperdactylism.
hiperdensidad *f.* hyperdensity.
hiperdenso, -sa *adj.* hyperdens.
hiperdiástole *f.* hyperdiastole.
hiperdicrótico, -ca *adj.* hyperdicrotic.
hiperdicrotismo *m.* hyperdicrotism.
hiperdinamia *f.* hyperdynamia.
  hiperdinamia uterina hyperdynamia uteri.
hiperdinámico, -ca *adj.* hyperdynamic.
hiperdiploide *adj.* hyperdiploid.
hiperdipsia *f.* hyperdipsia.
hiperdistensión *f.* hyperdistension.
hiperdiuresis *f.* hyperdiuresis.
hiperdontia *f.* hyperdontia.
hiperecogenicidad *f.* hyperechogenicity.
hiperecogénico, -ca *adj.* hyperechogenic.
hiperecoico, -ca *adj.* hyperechoic.
hiperecrisia *f.* hypereccrisia.
hiperecrisis *f.* hypereccrisis.
hiperecrítico, -ca *adj.* hypereccritic.
hiperefidrosis *f.* hyperephidrosis.
hiperelectrolitemia *f.* hyperelectrolytemia.
hiperemesis *f.* hyperemesis.
  hiperemesis del embarazo, hiperemesis gravídica hyperemesis gravidarum.
  hiperemesis de la lactancia, hiperemesis lactentium hyperemesis lactentium.
hiperemético, -ca *adj.* hyperemetic.
hiperemia *f.* hyperemia.
  hiperemia activa, hiperemia arterial active hyperemia, arterial hyperemia.
  hiperemia de Bier Bier's hyperemia.
  hiperemia colateral collateral hyperemia.
  hiperemia congestiva fluxionary hyperemia.
  hiperemia por constricción constriction hyperemia.
  hiperemia fluxionaria fluxionary hyperemia.
  hiperemia leptomeníngea leptomeningeal hyperemia.
  hiperemia pasiva passive hyperemia.
  hiperemia peristática peristatic hyperemia.
  hiperemia reactiva reactive hyperemia.
  hiperemia venosa venous hyperemia.
hiperémico, -ca *adj.* hyperemic.
hiperemización *f.* hyperemization.
hiperencefalia *f.* hyperencephaly.
hiperencéfalo *m.* hyperencephalus.
hiperendémico, -ca *adj.* hyperendemic.
hiperendocrinismo *m.* hyperendocrinism.
hipereosinofilia *f.* hypereosinophilia.
  hipereosinofilia filarial filarial hypereosinophilia.
hiperepinefrinemia *f.* hyperepinephrinemia.
hiperepitemia *f.* hyperepithymia.
hiperepitimia *f.* hyperepithymia.
hiperequema *f.* hyperechema.
hiperequilibrio *m.* hyperequilibrium.
hipereretismo *m.* hypererethism.
hiperergasia *f.* hyperergasia.
hiperergia *f.* hyperergia, hyperergy.
hiperérgico, -ca *adj.* hyperergic.
hipereritrocitemia *f.* hypererytrocythemia.
hiperesfixia *f.* hypersphyxia.
hiperesoforia *f.* hyperesophoria.
hiperespadias *f.* hyperspadias.
hiperesplenia *f.* hypersplenia.

hiperesplenismo *m.* hypersplenism.
hiperesqueocitosis *f.* hyperskeocytosis.
hiperesteatosis *f.* hypersteatosis.
hiperestenia *f.* hypersthenia.
hiperesténico, -ca *adj.* hypersthenic.
hiperestenuria *f.* hypersthenuria.
hiperestereorroentgenografía *f.* hypersthereoroentgenography.
hiperestesia *f.* hyperesthesia.
  hiperestesia acústica, hiperestesia auditiva auditory hyperesthesia.
  hiperestesia cerebral cerebral hyperesthesia.
  hiperestesia cervical cervical hyperesthesia.
  hiperestesia gustatoria gustatory hyperesthesia.
  hiperestesia muscular muscular hyperesthesia.
  hiperestesia onírica oneiric hyperesthesia.
  hiperestesia óptica hyperesthesia optica.
  hiperestesia táctil tactile hyperesthesia.
hiperestésico, -ca *adj.* hyperesthetic.
hiperestrinemia *f.* hyperestrinemia.
hiperestrinismo *m.* hyperestrinism.
hiperestrogenemia *f.* hyperestrogenemia.
hiperestrogenismo *m.* hyperestrogenism.
hipereuriopía *f.* hypereuryopia.
hipereuropía *f.* hypereuryopia.
hiperevolutismo *m.* hyperevolutism.
hiperexcretorio, -ria *adj.* hyperexcretory.
hiperexoforia *f.* hyperexophoria.
hiperexplexia *f.* hyperexplesia.
hiperextensión *f.* hyperextension.
hiperfagia *f.* hyperphagia.
hiperfalangia *f.* hyperphalangia.
hiperfalangismo *m.* hyperphalangism.
hiperfasia *f.* hyperphasia.
hiperfenilalaninemia *f.* hyperphenylalaninemia.
hiperferremia *f.* hyperferremia.
hiperferrémico, -ca *adj.* hyperferremic.
hiperferricemia *f.* hyperferricemia.
hiperfibrinogenemia *f.* hyperfibrinogenemia.
hiperfibrinólisis *f.* hyperfibrinolysis.
hiperfiltración glomerular *f.* glomerular hyperfiltration.
hiperflexión *f.* hyperflexion.
hiperfoliculinemia *m.* hyperfolliculinemia.
hiperfoliculinuria *f.* hyperfolliculinuria.
hiperfoliculismo *m.* hyperfolliculinism.
hiperfoliculoidismo *m.* hyperfolliculoidism.
hiperfonesis *f.* hyperphonesis.
hiperfonía *f.* hyperphonia.
hiperforia *f.* hyperphoria.
hiperfosfatasemia *f.* hyperphosphatasemia.
  hiperfosfatasemia idiopática congénita crónica chronic congenital idiopathic hyperphosphatascmia.
  hiperfosfatasemia tardía hyperphosphatasemia tarda.
hiperfosfatasia *f.* hyperphosphatasia.
hiperfosfatemia *f.* hyperphosphatemia.
hiperfosfaturia *f.* hyperphosphaturia.
hiperfosforemia *f.* hyperphosphoremia.
hiperfunción *f.* hyperfunction.
  hiperfunción suprarrenal adrenal hyperfunction.
hiperfuncionamiento *m.* hyperfunctioning.
hipergalactia *f.* hypergalactia.
hipergalactosis *f.* hypergalactosis.
hipergammaglobulinemia *f.* hypergammaglobulinemia.
  hipergammaglobulinemia monoclonal monoclonal hypergammaglobulinemia.
hipergastrinemia *f.* hypergastrinemia.
hipergénesis *f.* hypergenesis.

hipergenético, -ca *adj.* hypergenetic.
hipergenitalismo *m.* hypergenitalism.
hipergeusestesia *f.* hypergeusesthesia.
hipergeusia *f.* hypergeusia.
hiperginecosmia *f.* hypergynecosmia.
hiperglandular *adj.* hyperglandular.
hiperglicemia *f.* hyperglycemia.
hipergliceridemia *f.* hyperglyceridemia.
  hipergliceridemia endógena endogenous hyperglyceridemia.
  hipergliceridemia exógena exogenous hyperglyceridemia.
hipergliceridémico, -ca *adj.* hyperglyceridemic.
hiperglicinemia *f.* hyperglycinemia.
hiperglicinuria *f.* hyperglycinuria.
  hiperglicinuria con hiperglicinemia hyperglycinuria with hyperglycinemia.
hiperglicistia *f.* hyperglycistia.
hiperglioxilemia *f.* hyperglyoxylemia.
hiperglobulinemia *f.* hyperglobulinemia.
hiperglucagonemia *f.* hyperglucagonemia.
hiperglucemia *f.* hyperglycemia.
  hiperglucemia no cetósica non-ketotic hyperglycemia.
  hiperglucemia poshipoglucémica posthypoglycemic hyperglycemia.
hiperglucogenólisis *f.* hyperglucogenolysis.
hiperglucorraquia *f.* hyperglycorrhachia.
hiperglucosemia *f.* hyperglycosemia.
hiperglucosuria *f.* hyperglycosuria.
hipergonadismo *m.* hypergonadism.
hipergonadotrópico, -ca *adj.* hypergonadotropic.
hipergranulosis *f.* hypergranulosis.
hiperguanidinemia *f.* hyperguanidinemia.
hiperhemoglobinemia *f.* hyperhemoglobinemia.
hiperheparinemia *f.* hyperheparinemia.
hiperhepatía *f.* hyperhepathia.
hiperhidratación *f.* overhydration.
hiperhidrocloria *f.* hyperhydrochloria.
hiperhidropexia *f.* hyperhydropexy, hyperhydropexis.
hiperhidrosis *f.* hyperhidrosis.
  hiperhidrosis gustatoria gustatory hyperhidrosis.
  hiperhidrosis lateral hyperhidrosis unilateralis.
  hiperhidrosis oleosa hyperhidrosis oleosa.
hiperhidrótico, -ca *adj.* hyperhidrotic.
hiperhidroxiprolinemia *f.* hyperhydroxyprolinemia.
hiperhipofisismo *m.* hyperhypophysism.
hiperhormonismo *m.* hyperhormonism.
hiperidrosis *f.* hyperhidrosis.
hiperimidodipeptiuria *f.* hyperimidodipeptiuria.
hiperinclusividad *f.* overinclusiveness.
hiperindicanemia *f.* hyperindicanemia.
hiperinfección *f.* hyperinfection.
hiperingestión *f.* hyperingestion.
hiperinmune *adj.* hyperimmune.
hiperinmunidad *f.* hyperimmunity.
hiperinmunización *f.* hyperimmunization.
hiperinmunoglobulinemia *f.* hyperimmunoglobulinemia.
  hiperinmunoglobulinemia E hyperimmunoglobulinemia E.
hiperinosemia *f.* hyperinosemia.
hiperinosis *f.* hyperinosis.
hiperinsuflación *f.* hyperinsuflation.
  hiperinsuflación periódica periodic hyperinsuflation.
hiperinsular *adj.* hyperinsular.

hiperinsulinemia *f.* hyperinsulinemia.
hiperinsulinismo *m.* hyperinsulinism.
  hiperinsulinismo alimentario alimentary hyperinsulinism.
hiperintensidad *f.* hyperintensity.
hiperintenso, -sa *adj.* hyperintense.
hiperirritabilidad *f.* hyperirritability.
hiperisotonia *f.* hyperisotonia.
hiperisotónico, -ca *adj.* hyperisotonic.
hiperlactacidemia *f.* hyperlactacidemia.
hiperlactación *f.* hyperlactation.
hiperlaxitud *f.* hyperlaxicity.
hiperlecitinemia *f.* hyperlecithinemia.
hiperleucocitosis *f.* hyperleukocytosis.
hiperlexia *f.* hyperlexia.
hiperleydigismo *m.* hyperleydigism.
hiperlipemia *f.* hyperlipemia.
  hiperlipemia combinada inducida por grasas y carbohidratos combined fat-and carbohydrate-induced hyperlipemia.
  hiperlipemia familiar esencial essential familial hyperlipemia.
  hiperlipemia idiopática idiopathic hyperlipemia.
  hiperlipemia inducida por carbohidratos carbohydrate-induced hyperlipemia.
  hiperlipemia inducida por grasas fat-induced hyperlipemia.
  hiperlipemia mixta mixed hyperlipemia.
  hiperlipemia provocada por carbohidratos carbohydrate-induced hyperlipemia.
  hiperlipemia provocada por grasas fat-induced hyperlipemia.
hiperlipidemia *f.* hyperlipidemia, hyperlipoidemia.
hiperlipoidemia *f.* hyperlipoidemia.
hiperlipoproteinemia *f.* hyperlipoproteinemia.
  hiperlipoproteinemia adquirida acquired hyperlipoproteinemia.
  hiperlipoproteinemia combinada familiar combined hyperlipoproteinemia, familial.
  hiperlipoproteinemia familiar familial hyperlipoproteinemia.
  hiperlipoproteinemia familiar de tipo I type I familial hyperlipoproteinemia.
  hiperlipoproteinemia familiar de tipo II type II familial hyperlipoproteinemia.
  hiperlipoproteinemia familiar de tipo IIa type IIa familial hyperlipoproteinemia.
  hiperlipoproteinemia familiar de tipo IIb type IIb familial hyperlipoproteinemia.
  hiperlipoproteinemia familiar de tipo III type III familial hyperlipoproteinemia.
  hiperlipoproteinemia familiar de tipo IV type IV familial hyperlipoproteinemia.
  hiperlipoproteinemia familiar de tipo V type V familial hyperlipoproteinemia.
  hiperlipoproteinemia mixta mixed hyperlipoproteinemia.
hiperliposis *f.* hyperliposis.
hiperlisinemia *f.* hyperlysinemia.
hiperlisinuria *f.* hyperlysinuria.
hiperlitemia *f.* hyperlithemia.
hiperlítico, -ca *adj.* hyperlithic.
hiperlituria *f.* hyperlithuria.
hiperlordosis *f.* hyperlordosis.
hiperlucencia *f.* hyperlucency.
hiperlucente *adj.* hyperlucent.
hiperluteinización *f.* hyperluteinization.
hipermaduro, -ra *adj.* hypermature.
hipermagnesemia *f.* hypermagnesemia.
hipermastia *f.* hypermastia.
hipermastigoto *m.* hypermastigote.
hipermelanótico, -ca *adj.* hypermelanotic.

hipermenorrea *f.* hypermenorrhea.
hipermetabólico, -ca *adj.* hypermetabolic.
hipermetabolismo *m.* hypermetabolism.
  hipermetabolismo extratiroideo extrathyroidal hypermetabolism.
hipermetaplasia *f.* hypermetaplasia.
hipermetría *f.* hypermetria.
hipermétrope *m.* hypermetrope.
hipermetropía *f.* hypermetropia, hypermetropy.
  hipermetropía absoluta absolute hypermetropia.
  hipermetropía axial, hipermetropía axil axial hypermetropia.
  hipermetropía de curvatura curvature hypermetropia.
  hipermetropía facultativa facultative hypermetropia.
  hipermetropía latente latent hypermetropia.
  hipermetropía manifiesta manifest hypermetropia.
  hipermetropía relativa relative hypermetropia.
  hipermetropía total total hypermetropia.
hipermiestesia *f.* hypermyesthesia.
hipermimia *f.* hypermimia.
hipermineralización *f.* hypermineralization.
hipermiotonía *f.* hypermyotonia.
hipermiotrofia *f.* hypermyotrophy.
hipermnesia *f.* hypermnesia.
hipermnésico, -ca *adj.* hypermnesic.
hipermodal *adj.* hypermodal.
hipermorfo, -fa *m., f.* hypermorph.
hipermotilidad *f.* hypermotility.
hipermovilidad *f.* hypermobility.
hipernasalidad *f.* hypernasality.
hipernatremia *f.* hypernatremia.
  hipernatremia hipodípsica hypodipsic hypernatremia.
hipernatrémico, -ca *adj.* hypernatremic.
hipernatronemia *f.* hypernatronemia.
hipernefroide *adj.* hypernephroid.
hipernefroma *m.* hypernephroma.
hiperneocitosis *f.* hyperneocytosis.
hipernitremia *f.* hypernitremia.
hipernutrición *f.* hypernutrition.
hiperoncótico, -ca *adj.* hyperoncotic.
hiperonicosis *f.* hyperonychosis.
hiperoniquia *f.* hyperonychosis.
hipérope *m.* hyperope.
hiperopía *f.* hyperopia.
hiperópico, -ca *adj.* hyperopic.
hiperorexia *f.* hyperorexia.
hiperornitinemia *f.* hyperornithinemia.
hiperorquidismo *m.* hyperorchidism.
hiperortocitosis *f.* hyperorthocytosis.
hiperosmolalidad *f.* hyperosmolality.
hiperosmolaridad *f.* hyperosmolarity.
hiperosmótico, -ca *adj.* hyperosmotic.
hiperosteogenia *f.* hyperosteogeny.
hiperosteoidosis *f.* hyperosteoidosis.
hiperostósico, -ca *adj.* hyperostotic.
hiperostosis *f.* hyperostosis.
  hiperostosis anquilosante ankylosing hyperostosis.
  hiperostosis anquilosante senil del raquis senile ankylosing hyperostosis of the spine.
  hiperostosis confluente flowing hyperostosis.
  hiperostosis cortical deformante hyperostosis corticalis deformans.
  hiperostosis cortical juvenil deformante hyperostosis corticalis deformans juvenilis.
  hiperostosis cortical generalizada generalized cortical hyperostosis.

  hiperostosis cortical infantil child cortical hyperostosis.
  hiperostosis cortical del lactante infantile cortical hyperostosis.
  hiperostosis craneal hyperostosis cranii.
  hiperostosis esquelética idiopática difusa diffuse idiopathic skeletal hyperostosis.
  hiperostosis de flujo flowing hyperostosis.
  hiperostosis frontal interna frontal internal hyperostosis, hyperostosis frontalis interna.
  hiperostosis de Morgagni frontal internal hyperostosis, hyperostosis frontalis interna.
  hiperostosis vertebral senil anquilosante ankylosing age-related vertebral hyperostosis.
  hiperostosis veteada streak hyperostosis.
hiperostótico, -ca *adj.* hyperostotic.
hiperovarismo *m.* hyperovarianism, hyperovarism.
hiperoxaluria *f.* hyperoxaluria.
  hiperoxaluria entérica enteric hyperoxaluria.
  hiperoxaluria primaria primary hyperoxaluria.
  hiperoxaluria primaria y oxalosis primary hyperoxaluria and oxalosis.
  hiperoxaluria primaria tipo I type I primary hyperoxaluria.
  hiperoxaluria primaria tipo II type II primary hyperoxaluria.
hiperoxemia *f.* hyperoxemia.
hiperoxia *f.* hyperoxia.
hiperóxico, -ca *adj.* hyperoxic.
hiperoxidación *f.* hyperoxidation.
hiperoxigenación *f.* hyperoxygenation.
hiperpalestesia *f.* hyperpallesthesia.
hiperpancreatismo *m.* hyperpancreatism.
hiperpancreorrea *f.* hyperpancreorrhea.
hiperparasitismo *m.* hyperparasitism.
hiperparásito *m.* hyperparasite.
  hiperparásito de segundo grado second degree hyperparasite.
hiperparatiroidismo *m.* hyperparathyroidism.
  hiperparatiroidismo primario primary hyperparathyroidism.
  hiperparatiroidismo secundario secondary hyperparathyroidism.
  hiperparatiroidismo terciario tertiary hyperparathyroidism.
hiperparotidismo *m.* hyperparotidism.
hiperpatía *f.* hyperpathia.
hiperpepsia *f.* hyperpepsia.
hiperpepsinemia *f.* hyperpepsinemia.
hiperpepsinia *f.* hyperpepsinia.
hiperpepsinuria *f.* hyperpepsinuria.
hiperperistalsis *f.* hyperperistalsis.
hiperperistaltismo *m.* hyperperistalsis.
hiperpermeabilidad *f.* hyperpermeability.
hiperpexia *f.* hyperpexia, hyperpexy.
hiperpiesia *f.* hyperpiesia.
hiperpiesis *f.* hyperpiesis.
hiperpiético, -ca *adj.* hyperpietic.
hiperpigmentación *f.* hyperpigmentation.
hiperpinealismo *m.* hyperpinealism.
hiperpipecolatemia *f.* hyperpipecolatemia.
hiperpirático, -ca *adj.* hyperpyrexial.
hiperpiremia *f.* hyperpyremia.
hiperpirético, -ca *adj.* hyperpyretic.
hiperpirexia *f.* hyperpyrexia.
  hiperpirexia por calor heat hyperpyrexia.
  hiperpirexia fulminante fulminant hyperpyrexia.
  hiperpirexia maligna malignant hyperpyrexia.
hiperpiréxico, -ca *adj.* hyperpyrexial.
hiperpituitarismo *m.* hyperpituitarism.

hiperplasia *f.* hyperplasia.

hiperplasia adenoidea adenoid hyperplasia.

hiperplasia adrenal congénita congenital adrenal hyperplasia.

hiperplasia angiolinfoide, hiperplasia angiolinfoide con eosinofilia angiolymphoid hyperplasia, angiolymphoid hyperplasia with eosinophilia.

hiperplasia basocelular basal cell hyperplasia.

hiperplasia canalicular ductal hyperplasia.

hiperplasia de células yuxtaglomerulares juxtaglomerular cell hyperplasia.

hiperplasia del cemento hyperplasia cementum.

hiperplasia corticosuprarrenal adrenocortical hyperplasia.

hiperplasia corticotropa corticotroph hyperplasia.

hiperplasia de la dentadura denture hyperplasia.

hiperplasia por Dilantín Dilantin hyperplasia.

hiperplasia del endometrio, hiperplasia endometrial endometrial hyperplasia.

hiperplasia endotelial papilar intravascular intravascular papillary endothelial hyperplasia.

hiperplasia epitelial focal focal epithelial hyperplasia.

hiperplasia fibromuscular fibromuscular hyperplasia.

hiperplasia fibrosa inflamatoria inflammatory fibrous hyperplasia.

hiperplasia folicular gigante giant follicular hyperplasia.

hiperplasia ganglionar mediastínica angiofolicular angiofollicular lymph node hyperplasia.

hiperplasia ganglionar mediastínica benigna benign mediastinal lymph node hyperplasia.

hiperplasia gingival gingival hyperplasia.

hiperplasia hipofisaria pituitary hyperplasia.

hiperplasia inflamatoria, hiperplasia inflamatoria fibrosa inflammatory hyperplasia, fibrous inflammatory hyperplasia.

hiperplasia lactótropa lactotroph hyperplasia.

hiperplasia linfoide cutánea cutaneous lymphoid hyperplasia.

hiperplasia linfoide nodular nodular lymphoid hyperplasia.

hiperplasia lipoide lipoid hyperplasia.

hiperplasia medular suprarrenal adrenal medullary hyperplasia.

hiperplasia melanocítica atípica atypical melanocytic hyperplasia.

hiperplasia neoplásica neoplastic hyperplasia.

hiperplasia nodular de próstata nodular hyperplasia of the prostate.

hiperplasia ovárica del estroma ovarian stromal hyperplasia.

hiperplasia papilar inflamatoria inflammatory papillary hyperplasia.

hiperplasia paratiroidea parathyroid hyperplasia.

hiperplasia perforante crónica de la pulpa chronic perforating pulp hyperplasia.

hiperplasia polar polar hyperplasia.

hiperplasia prostática benigna (HBP) benign prostatic hyperplasia.

hiperplasia quística cystic hyperplasia.

hiperplasia quística de la mama cystic hyperplasia of the breast.

hiperplasia regenerativa nodular nodular regenerative hyperplasia.

hiperplasia seudocarcinomatosa pseudocarcinomatous hyperplasia.

hiperplasia seudoepiteliomatosa pseudoepitheliomatous hyperplasia.

hiperplasia suprarrenal congénita congenital adrenal hyperplasia.

hiperplasia tireotropa thyrotroph hyperplasia.

hiperplasia verrugosa verrucous hyperplasia.

hiperplásico, -ca *adj.* hyperplastic.

hiperplasmia *f.* hyperplasmia.

hiperploide *adj.* hyperploid.

hiperploidía *f.* hyperploidy.

hiperpnea *f.* hyperpnea.

hiperpneico, -ca *adj.* hyperpneic.

hiperpolarización *f.* hyperpolarization.

hiperpolipeptidemia *f.* hyperpolypeptidemia.

hiperponesis *f.* hyperponesis.

hiperponético, -ca *adj.* hyperponetic.

hiperposia *f.* hyperposia.

hiperpotasemia *f.* hyperpotassemia.

hiperpragia *f.* hyperpragia.

hiperprebetalipoproteinemia *f.* hyperprebetalipoproteinemia.

hiperprebetalipoproteinemia familiar familial hyperprebetalipoproteinemia.

hiperpresbiopía *f.* hyperpresbyopia.

hiperproinsulinemia *f.* hyperproinsulinemia.

hiperprolactinemia *f.* hyperprolactinemia.

hiperprolactinémico, -ca *adj.* hyperprolactinemic.

hiperprolinemia *f.* hyperprolinemia.

hiperprosexia *f.* hyperprosexia.

hiperproteinemia *f.* hyperproteinemia.

hiperproteosis *f.* hyperproteosis.

hiperpselafesia *f.* hyperpselaphesia.

hiperptialismo *m.* hyperptyalism.

hiperqueratinización *f.* hyperkeratinization.

hiperqueratomicosis *f.* hyperkeratomycosis.

hiperqueratosis *f.* hyperkeratosis.

hiperqueratosis congénita hyperkeratosis congenita.

hiperqueratosis congénita palmar y plantar hyperkeratosis of palms and soles.

hiperqueratosis distrófica progresiva progressive dystrophic hyperkeratosis.

hiperqueratosis epidermolítica epidermolytic hyperkeratosis.

hiperqueratosis excéntrica eccentric hyperkeratosis.

hiperqueratosis figurada centrífuga atrófica hyperkeratosis figurata centrifuga atrophica.

hiperqueratosis folicular follicular hyperkeratosis, hyperkeratosis follicularis.

hiperqueratosis folicular y parafolicular hyperkeratosis follicularis et parafollicularis.

hiperqueratosis follicularis in cutem penetrans, hiperqueratosis follicularis et parafollicularis in cutem penetrans hyperkeratosis follicularis in cutem penetrans, hyperkeratosis follicularis et parafollicularis in cutem penetrans.

hiperqueratosis lacunar, hiperqueratosis lagunar hyperkeratosis lacunaris.

hiperqueratosis lenticularis perstans hyperkeratosis lenticularis perstans.

hiperqueratosis palmar y plantar hyperkeratosis of palms and soles.

hiperqueratosis penetrante, hiperqueratosis penetrans hyperkeratosis penetrans.

hiperqueratosis subungueal hyperkeratosis subungualis.

hiperquetonuria *f.* hyperketonuria.

hiperquetosis *f.* hyperketosis.

hiperquilia *f.* hyperchylia.

hiperquilomicronemia *f.* hyperchylomicronemia.

hiperquilomicronemia familiar familial hyperchylomicronemia.

hiperquilomicronemia familiar con hiperprebetalipoproteinemia familial hyperchylomicronemia with hyperprebetalipoproteinemia.

hiperquinesia *f.* hyperkinesia.

hiperreflexia *f.* hyperreflexia.

hiperreflexia autónoma autonomic hyperreflexia.

hiperreactividad *f.* hyperreactivity.

hiperreactividad bronquial bronchial hyperreactivity.

hiperreactivo, -va *adj.* hyperreactive.

hiperreninemia *f.* hyperreninemia.

hiperreninémico, -ca *adj.* hyperreninemic.

hipersalemia *f.* hypersalemia.

hipersalino, -na *adj.* hypersaline.

hipersalivación *f.* hypersalivation.

hipersarcosinemia *f.* hypersarcosinemia.

hipersecreción *f.* hypersecretion.

hipersecreción gástrica gastric hypersecretion.

hipersegmentación *f.* hypersegmentation.

hipersensibilidad *f.* hypersensitivity.

hipersensibilidad anafiláctica anaphylactic hypersensitivity.

hipersensibilidad basófila cutánea cutaneous basophil hypersensitivity.

hipersensibilidad citotóxica cytotoxic hypersensitivity.

hipersensibilidad por contacto contact hypersensitivity.

hipersensibilidad inmediata immediate hypersensitivity.

hipersensibilidad por inmunocomplejos immune complex hypersensitivity.

hipersensibilidad de lápiz pencil hypersensitivity.

hipersensibilidad de rebote rebound hypersensitivity.

hipersensibilidad retardada (HR), de tipo retardado (HTR) delayed hypersensitivity (DH), delayed-type hypersensitivity (DTH).

hipersensibilidad tipo tuberculina tuberculin-type hypersensitivity.

hipersensibilidad de tipo I type I hypersensitivity.

hipersensibilidad de tipo II type II hypersensitivity.

hipersensibilidad de tipo III type III hypersensitivity.

hipersensibilización *f.* hypersensitization.

hiperserotonemia *f.* hyperserotonemia.

hipersexualidad *f.* hypersexuality.

hipersimpaticotonía *f.* hypersympathicotonus.

hipersistole *f.* hypersystole.

hipersistolia *f.* hypersystole.

hipersistólico, -ca *adj.* hypersystolic.

hipersomatotropismo *m.* hypersomatotropism.

hipersomia *f.* hypersomia.

hipersomnia *f.* hypersomnia.

hipersomnolencia *f.* hypersomnolence.

hipersomnolencia primaria primary hypersomnolence.

hipersuprarrenalemia *f.* hypesuprarenalemia.

hipersuprarrenalismo *m.* hypersuprarenalism.

hipersusceptibilidad *f.* hypersusceptibility.

hipertaraquia *f.* hypertarachia.

hipertaurodontismo *m.* hypertaurodontism.

hipertecosis *f.* hyperthecosis.

  hipertecosis estromal stromal hyperthecosis.

  hipertecosis ovárico ovarian hyperthecosis.

  hipertecosis testoide testoid hyperthecosis.

hipertelia *f.* hyperthelia.

hipertelorismo *m.* hypertelorism.

  hipertelorismo cántico canthal hypertelorism.

  hipertelorismo ocular ocular hypertelorism.

  hipertelorismo orbitario orbital hypertelorism.

hipertensión *f.* hypertension, high blood pressure.

  hipertensión acelerada accelerated hypertension.

  hipertensión arterial arterial hypertension.

  hipertensión arterial de bata blanca white coat arterial hypertension.

  hipertensión arterial benigna benign arterial hypertension.

  hipertensión arterial esencial essential arterial hypertension.

  hipertensión arterial hiperreninémica hyperreninemic arterial hypertension.

  hipertensión arterial lábil labile arterial hypertension.

  hipertensión arterial limítrofe border-line arterial hypertension.

  hipertensión arterial maligna malignant arterial hypertension.

  hipertensión arterial nefrógena renal parenchymal arterial hypertension.

  hipertensión arterial paroxística hypertensive crisis hypertension.

  hipertensión arterial pulmonar pulmonary arterial hypertension.

  hipertensión arterial secundaria secondary arterial hypertension.

  hipertensión arterial sistémica systemic arterial hypertension.

  hipertensión arterial transitoria del embarazo mild pregnancy-induced arterial hypertension.

  hipertensión arterial vasculorrenal renovascular arterial hypertension.

  hipertensión benigna benign hypertension.

  hipertensión esencial essential hypertension.

  hipertensión esplenoportal splenoportal hypertension.

  hipertensión de Goldblatt Goldblatt's hypertension.

  hipertensión idiopática idiopathic hypertension.

  hipertensión intracraneal intracranial hypertension.

  hipertensión intracraneal benigna benign intracranial hypertension.

  hipertensión lábil labile hypertension.

  hipertensión en los límites labile hypertension.

  hipertensión maligna malignant hypertension.

  hipertensión ocular ocular hypertension.

  hipertensión pálida pale hypertension.

  hipertensión portal portal hypertension.

  hipertensión posparto postpartum hypertension.

  hipertensión primaria primary hypertension.

  hipertensión pulmonar pulmonary hypertension.

  hipertensión renal renal hypertension.

  hipertensión con renina baja low-renin hypertension.

  hipertensión renovascular renovascular hypertension.

  hipertensión roja benign hypertension.

  hipertensión secundaria secondary hypertension.

  hipertensión sintomática symptomatic hypertension.

  hipertensión suprarrenal adrenal hypertension.

  hipertensión vascular vascular hypertension.

  hipertensión vasculorrenal renovascular arterial hypertension.

  hipertensión venosa sistémica systemic venous hypertension.

hipertensivo, -va *adj.* hypertensive.

hipertenso, -sa *adj.* hypertensive.

hipertensor, -ra *adj.* hypertensor.

hipertermalgesia *f.* hyperthermalgesia.

hipertermestesia *f.* hyperthermesthesia.

hipertermia *f.* hyperthermia.

  hipertermia de la anestesia hyperthermia of anesthesia.

  hipertermia de las extremidades limb hyperthermia.

  hipertermia habitual habitual hyperthermia.

  hipertermia intraoperatoria intraoperative hyperthermia.

  hipertermia maligna (HM) malignant hyperthermia (MH).

  hipertermia regional regional hyperthermia.

  hipertermia terapéutica therapeutic hyperthermia.

hipertermestesia *f.* hyperthermoesthesia, hypertermesthesia.

hipertermoestesia *f.* hyperthermoesthesia, hypertermesthesia.

hipertestoidismo *m.* hypertestoidism.

hipertetraploide *adj.* hypertetraploid.

hipertimia *f.* hyperthymia.

hipertimico, -ca *adj.* hyperthymic.

hipertimismo *m.* hyperthymism.

hipertireosis *m.* hyperthyreosis.

hipertiroide *adj.* hyperthyroid.

hipertiroideo, -a *adj.* hyperthyroid.

hipertiroidismo *m.* hyperthyroidism.

  hipertiroidismo apático apathetic hyperthyroidism.

  hipertiroidismo enmascarado masked hyperthyroidism.

  hipertiroidismo inducido por yodo iodine-induced hyperthyroidism.

  hipertiroidismo oftálmico ophthalmic hyperthyroidism.

  hipertiroidismo primario primary hyperthyroidism.

  hipertiroidismo secundario secondary hyperthyroidism.

hipertiroidosis *f.* hyperthyroidosis.

hipertiroxinemia *f.* hyperthyroxinemia.

  hipertiroxinemia disalbuminémica familiar familial dysalbuminemic hyperthyroxinemia.

hipertonía *f.* hypertonia.

  hipertonía ocular glaucoma.

  hipertonía policitémica hypertonia polycythemica.

  hipertonía simpática sympathetic hypertonia.

hipertonicidad *f.* hypertonicity.

hipertónico, -ca *adj.* hypertonic.

hipertoxicidad *f.* hypertoxicity.

hipertóxico, -ca *adj.* hypertoxic.

hipertricofridia *f.* hypertrichophrydia.

hipertricosis *f.* hypertrichosis.

  hipertricosis lanuginosa hypertrichosis lanuginosa.

  hipertricosis lanuginosa adquirida hypertrichosis lanuginosa acquisita.

  hipertricosis nevoide nevoid hypertrichosis.

  hipertricosis del pabellón auricular hypertrichosis pinae auris.

  hipertricosis parcial hypertrichosis partialis.

  hipertricosis universal hypertrichosis universalis.

hipertrigliceridemia *f.* hypertryglyceridemia.

  hipertrigliceridemia familiar familial hypertryglyceridemia.

  hipertrigliceridemia inducida por carbohidratos carbohydrate-induced hypertryglyceridemia.

hipertriploide *adj.* hypertriploid.

hipertriquiasis *f.* hypertrichiasis.

hipertrofia *f.* hypertrophy.

  hipertrofia de adaptación, hipertrofia adaptativa adaptative hypertrophy.

  hipertrofia adenoide adenoid hypertrophy.

  hipertrofia de Billroth Billroth hypertrophy.

  hipertrofia cardíaca cardiac hypertrophy.

  hipertrofia compensadora compensatory hypertrophy.

  hipertrofia compensadora del corazón compensatory hypertrophy of the heart.

  hipertrofia complementaria complementary hypertrophy.

  hipertrofia concéntrica concentric hypertrophy.

  hipertrofia del corazón hypertrophy of the heart.

  hipertrofia cuantitativa quantitative hypertrophy.

  hipertrofia excéntrica eccentric hypertrophy.

  hipertrofia falsa false hypertrophy.

  hipertrofia fisiológica physiologic hypertrophy.

  hipertrofia funcional functional hypertrophy.

  hipertrofia gigante de la mucosa gástrica giant hypertrophy of the gastric mucosa.

  hipertrofia hemangiectásica hemangiectatic hypertrophy.

  hipertrofia hemifacial hemifacial hypertrophy.

  hipertrofia lipomatosa lipomatous hypertrophy.

  hipertrofia mamaria mammary hypertrophy.

  hipertrofia de Marie Marie's hypertrophy.

  hipertrofia numérica numerical hypertrophy.

  hipertrofia prostática prostatic hypertrophy.

  hipertrofia prostática benigna benign prostatic hypertrophy.

  hipertrofia renal, hipertrofia renal compensadora renal hypertrophy, compensatory renal hypertrophy.

  hipertrofia septal asimétrica asimmetrical septal hypertrophy.

  hipertrofia seudomuscular pseudomuscular hypertrophy.

  hipertrofia simple simple hypertrophy.

  hipertrofia unilateral unilateral hypertrophy.

  hipertrofia ventricular ventricular hypertrophy.

  hipertrofia verdadera true hypertrophy.

  hipertrofia vicaria, hipertrofia vicariante vicarious hypertrophy.

hipertrófico, -ca *adj.* hypertrophic.

hipertrofo *m.* hypertroph.

hipertrombinemia *f.* hyperthrombinemia.
hipertropía *f.* hypertropia.
hiperuresis *f.* hyperuresis.
hiperuricemia *f.* hyperuricemia.
 hiperuricemia hereditaria hereditary hyperuricemia.
hiperuricémico, -ca *adj.* hyperuricemic.
hiperuricosuria *f.* hyperuricosuria.
hiperuricuria *f.* hyperuricuria.
hipervalinemia *f.* hypervalinemia.
hiperventilación *f.* hyperventilation.
 hiperventilación neurógena central neurogenic central hyperventilation.
hipervigilancia *f.* hypervigilance.
hiperviscosidad *f.* hyperviscosity.
hipervitaminósico, -ca *adj.* hypervitaminotic.
hipervitaminosis *f.* hypervitaminosis.
 hipervitaminosis A hypervitaminosis A.
 hipervitaminosis D hypervitaminosis D.
hipervolemia *f.* hypervolemia.
hipervolémico, -ca *adj.* hypervolemic.
hipervolia *f.* hypervolia.
hiperyodemia *f.* hyperiodemia.
hipestesia *f.* hypesthesia.
hipidrosis *f.* hyphidrosis.
hipnagógico, -ca *adj.* hypnagogic.
hipnagogo *m.* hypnagogue.
hipnalgia *f.* hypnalgia.
hipnapagógico, -ca *adj.* hypnapagogic.
hípnico, -ca *adj.* hypnic.
hipnoanálisis *m.* hypnoanalysis.
hipnoanalítico, -ca *adj.* hypnoanalytic.
hipnoanestesia *f.* hypoanesthesia.
hipnocatarsis *f.* hypnocatharsis.
hipnocinematógrafo *m.* hypnocinematogrph.
hipnodóntica *f.* hypnodontics.
hipnogénico, -ca *adj.* hypnogenic.
hipnógeno, -na *adj.* hypnogenous.
hipnoideo, -a *adj.* hypnoid.
hipnoidización *f.* hypnoidization.
hipnología *f.* hypnology.
hipnólogo, -ga *m., f.* hypnologist.
hipnonarcoanálisis *m.* hypnonarcoanalysis.
hipnonarcosis *f.* hypnonarcosis.
hipnopómpico, -ca *adj.* hypnopompic.
hipnosia *f.* hypnosia.
hipnosis *f.* hypnosis.
 hipnosis letárgica lethargic hypnosis.
 hipnosis mayor major hypnosis.
 hipnosis menor minor hypnosis.
hipnosofia *f.* hypnosophy.
hipnoterapia *f.* hypnotherapy.
hipnótico, -ca *adj.* hypnotic.
hipnotismo *m.* hypnotism.
hipnotización *f.* hypnotization.
hipnotizador, -ra *m.* hypnotist.
hipnotizar *v.* hypnotize.
hipo *m.* hiccough, hiccup.
hipoacidemia *f.* hypoacidemia.
hipoacidez *f.* hypoacidity.
hipoactividad *f.* hypoactivity.
hipoactivo, -va *adj.* hypoactive.
hipoacusia *f.* hypoacusia, hypoacusis, hypacusia, hypacusis.
 hipoacusia conductiva conductive hypoacusia.
 hipoacusia mixta mixed hypoacusia.
 hipoacusia neurosensorial sensorineural hypoacusia.
 hipoacusia súbita sudden hypoacusia.
hipoacusis *f.* hypoacusia, hypoacusis, hypacusia, hypacusis.
hipoadenia *f.* hypoadenia.
hipoadrenalismo *m.* hypoadrenalism.

hipoadrenia *f.* hypoadrenia.
hipoadrenocorticismo *m.* hypoadrenocorticism.
hipoalbuminemia *f.* hypoalbuminemia, hypalbuminemia.
hipoalbuminosis, *f.* hypoalbuminosis, hypalbuminosis.
hipoalcalinidad *f.* hypoalkalinity.
hipoalcalino, -na *adj.* hypoalkaline.
hipoaldosteronemia *f.* hypoaldosteronemia.
hipoaldosteronismo *m.* hypoaldosteronism.
 hipoaldosteronismo aislado isolated hypoaldosteronism.
 hipoaldosteronismo hiporreninémico hyporeninemic hypoaldosteronism.
 hipoaldosteronismo selectivo selective hypoaldosteronism.
hipoaldosteronuria *f.* hypoaldosteronuria.
hipoalérgenico, -ca *adj.* hypoallergenic.
hipoalgesia, hipalgesia *f.* hypalgesia.
hipoalgésico, -ca *adj.* hypalgesic, hypalgetic.
hipoalgia *f.* hypalgia.
hipoalimentación *f.* hypoalimentation.
hipoalonemia *f.* hypoalonemia.
hipoaminoacidemia *f.* hypoaminoacidemia.
hipoamnesia *f.* hypamnesia.
hipoamnios *m.* hypamnion, hypamnios.
hipoanacinesia *f.* hypoanakinesia.
hipoanacinesis *f.* hypoanakinesis.
hipoandrogenismo *m.* hypoandrogenism.
hipoarterial *adj.* hyparterial.
hipoaxial *adj.* hypaxial.
hipoazoturia *f.* hypoazoturia.
hipobaria *f.* hypobaria.
hipobárico, -ca *adj.* hypobaric.
hipobarismo *m.* hypobarism.
hipobaropatía *f.* hypobaropathy.
hipobasemia *f.* hypobasemia.
hipobetalipoproteinemia *f.* hypobetalipoproteinemia.
 hipobetalipoproteinemia familiar familial hypobetalipoproteinemia.
hipobilirrubinemia *f.* hypobilirubinemia.
hipoblástico, -ca *adj.* hypoblastic.
hipoblasto *m.* hypoblast.
hipobranquial *adj.* hypobranchial.
hipocalcemia *f.* hypocalcemia.
hipocalcia *f.* hypocalcia.
hipocalcificación *f.* hypocalcification.
 hipocalcificación del esmalte enamel hypocalcification.
hipocalcipéctico, -ca *adj.* hypocalcipectic.
hipocalcipexia *f.* hypocalcipexy.
hipocalciuria *f.* hypocalciuria.
hipocalemia *f.* hypokalemia.
hipocaliemia *f.* hypokaliemia, hypokalemia.
hipocaliémico, -ca *adj.* hypokalemic.
hipocámpico, -ca *adj.* hippocampal.
hipocampo *m.* hippocampus.
hipocapnia *f.* hypocapnia.
hipocápnico, -ca *adj.* hypocapnic.
hipocarbia *f.* hypocarbia.
hipoceloma *m.* hypocelom, hypocoelom.
hipocelular *adj.* hypocellular.
hipocelularidad *f.* hypocellurarity.
hipociclosis *f.* hypocyclosis.
hipocinemia *f.* hypokinemia.
hipocinesia *f.* hypokinesia, hypokinesis.
hipocinesis *f.* hypokinesis.
hipocistotomía *f.* hypocystotomy.
hipocitemia *f.* hypocythemia.
 hipocitemia progresiva progressive hypocythemia.
hipocitosis *f.* hypocytosis.
hipocitraturia *f.* hypocitraturia.

hipocitremia *f.* hypocitremia.
hipocitruria *f.* hypocitruria.
hipocloremia *f.* hypochloremia.
hipoclorémico, -ca *adj.* hypochloremic.
hipoclorhidria *f.* hypochlorhydria.
hipocloridación *f.* hypochloridation.
hipocloridemia *f.* hypochloridemia.
hipoclorización *f.* hypochlorization.
hipocloruración *f.* hypochlorization.
hipocloruria *f.* hypochloruria.
hipocoagulabilidad *f.* hypocoagulability.
hipocoagulable *adj.* hypocoagulable.
hipocolasia *f.* hypokolasia.
hipocolesterinemia *f.* hypocholesterinemia.
hipocolesterémico, -ca *adj.* hypocholesteremic.
hipocolesterolemia *f.* hypocholesterolemia.
hipocolesterolémico, -ca *adj.* hypocholesterolemic.
hipocolia *f.* hypocholia.
hipocoluria *f.* hypocholuria.
hipocomplementemia *f.* hypocomplementemia.
hipocomplementémico, -ca *adj.* hypocomplementemic.
hipocondíleo, -a *adj.* hypocondylar.
hipocondría *f.* hypochondria.
hipocondríaco, -ca¹ *m., f.* hypochondriac.
hipocondríaco, -ca² *adj.* hypochondriacal.
hipocondriasis *f.* hypochondriasis.
hipocondroplasia *f.* hypochondroplasia.
hipocónido *m.* hypoconid.
hipocono *m.* hypocone.
hipoconúlido *m.* hypoconulid.
hipocónulo *m.* hypoconule.
hipocordal *adj.* hypochordal.
hipocorticalismo *m.* hypocorticalism.
hipocorticismo *m.* hypocorticoidism.
hipocrático, -ca *adj.* hippocratic.
hipocratismo *m.* hippocratism.
hipocromasia *f.* hypochromasia.
hipocromatemia *f.* hypochromemia.
hipocromático, -ca *adj.* hypochromatic.
hipocromatismo *m.* hypochromatism.
hipocromatosis *f.* hypochromatosis.
hipocromemia *f.* hypochromemia.
hipocromía *f.* hypochromia.
hipocrómico, -ca *adj.* hypochromic.
hipocrosis *f.* hypochrosis.
hipocupremia *f.* hypocupremia.
hipodactilia *f.* hypodactyly, hypodactylia.
hipodactilismo *m.* hypodactylism.
hipodensidad *f.* hypodensity.
hipodenso, -sa *adj.* hypodense.
hipodermatoclisis *f.* hypodermatoclysis.
hipodermatomía *f.* hypodermatomy.
hipodermatosis *f.* hypodermatosis.
hipodérmico, -ca *adj.* hypodermic.
hipodermis *f.* hypoderm, hypodermis.
hipodermoclisis *f.* hypodermoclysis.
hipodermolitiasis *f.* hypodermolithiasis.
hipodiafragmático, -ca *adj.* hypodiaphragmatic.
hipodinamia *f.* hypodinamia.
 hipodinamia cordis hypodinamia cordis.
 hipodinamia uterina uterine hypodinamia.
 hipodinamia uterina primaria primary uterine hypodinamia.
 hipodinamia uterina secundaria secondary uterine hypodinamia.
hipodinámico, -ca *adj.* hypodynamic.
hipodiploide *adj.* hypodiploid.
hipodipsia *f.* hypodipsia.
hipodípsico, -ca *adj.* hypodipsic.
hipodontia *f.* hypodontia.

hipoecogenicidad *f.* hypoechogenicity.
hipoecogénico, -ca *adj.* hypoechogenic.
hipoecoico, -ca *adj.* hypoechois.
hipoecrisia *f.* hypoeccrisia, hypoeccrisis.
hipoecrisis *f.* hypoeccrisis.
hipoecrítico, -ca *adj.* hypoeccritic.
hipoelectrolitemia *f.* hypoelectrolytemia.
hipoendocrinia *f.* hypoendocrinia.
hipoendocrinismo *m.* hypoendocrinial.
hipoeosinofilia *f.* hypoeosinophilia.
hipoergasia *f.* hypoergasia.
hipoergia *f.* hypoergy, hypoergia, hypergia.
hipoérgico, -ca *adj.* hypoergic.
hipoescleral *adj.* hyposcleral.
hipoesclerótico, -ca *adj.* hyposcleral.
hipoestixia *f.* hyposphyxia.
hipoesoforia *f.* hypoesophoria.
hipoesplenismo *m.* hyposplenism.
hipoesqueocitosis *f.* hyposkeocytosis.
hipoesteatosis *f.* hyposteatosis.
hipoestenia *f.* hyposthenia.
hipoesténico, -ca *adj.* hyposthenic.
hipoestenizante *adj.* hypostheniant.
hipoestenuria *f.* hyposthenuria.
  hipoestenuria tubular tubular hyposthenuria.
hipoestesia *f.* hypoesthesia, hypesthesia.
  hipoestesia acústica, hipoestesia auditiva hypoacusis.
  hipoestesia gustatoria hypogeusesthesia.
  hipoestesia olfatoria hyposmia.
hipoestrinemia *f.* hypoestrinemia.
hipoestrogenemia *f.* hypoestrogenemia.
hipoestrogenismo *m.* hypoestrogenism.
hipoevolutismo *m.* hypoevolutism.
hipoexoforia *f.* hypoexophoria.
hipoexposición *f.* hypoexposition.
hipofalangismo *m.* hypophalangism.
hipofaringe *f.* hypopharynx.
hipofaríngeo, -a *adj.* hypopharyngeal.
hipofaringoscopia *f.* hypopharyngoscopy.
hipofaringoscopio *m.* hypopharyngoscope.
hipoferremia *f.* hypoferremia.
hipoferrismo *m.* hypoferrism.
hipofértil *adj.* hypofertile.
hipofertilidad *f.* hypofertility.
hipofibrinogenemia *f.* hypofibrinogenemia.
hipofisario, -ria *adj.* hypophyseal, hypophysial.
hipofisectomía *f.* hypophysectomy.
hipofisectomizar *v.* hypophysectomize.
hipofisioportal *adj.* hypophysioportal.
hipofisioprivo, -va *adj.* hypophyseoprivic, hypophysioprivic.
hipofisiotrópico, -ca *adj.* hypophyseotropic, hypophysiotropic.
hipófisis *f.* hypophysis, pituitary gland.
hipofisitis *f.* hypophysitis.
  hipofisitis linfoide lymphocytic hypophysitis.
hipofisógeno, -na *adj.* pituitarigenic.
hipofisoma *m.* hypophysoma.
hipofisoportal *adj.* hypophyseoportal.
hipofisoprivo, -va *adj.* hypophyseoprivic.
hipofisotrópico, -ca *adj.* hypophyseotropic, hypophysiotropic.
hipofonesis *f.* hypophonesis.
hipofonía *f.* hypophonia.
hipoforia *f.* hypophoria.
hipofosfatasemia *f.* hypophosphatasemia.
hipofosfatasia *f.* hypophosphatasia.
hipofosfatemia *f.* hypophosphatemia.
  hipofosfatemia familiar familial hypophosphatemia.
hipofosfatémico, -ca *adj.* hypophosphatemic.

hipofosfaturia *f.* hypophosphaturia.
hipofosforemia *f.* hypophosphoremia.
hipofrenio *m.* hypophrenium.
hipofunción *f.* hypofunction.
hipofuncionamiento *m.* hypofunction.
hipogalactia *f.* hypogalactia.
hipogalactoso, -sa *adj.* hypogalactous.
hipogammaglobinemia *f.* hypogammaglobinemia.
hipogammaglobulinemia *f.* hypogammaglobulinemia.
  hipogammaglobulinemia adquirida acquired hypogammaglobulinemia.
  hipogammaglobulinemia congénita congenital hypogammaglobulinemia.
  hipogammaglobulinemia fisiológica physiologic hypogammaglobulinemia.
  hipogammaglobulinemia ligada a X, hipogammaglobulinemia infantil ligada a X linked-X hypogammaglobulinemia, X-linked infantile hypogammaglobulinemia.
  hipogammaglobulinemia pasajera transient hypogammaglobulinemia.
  hipogammaglobulinemia primaria primary hypogammaglobulinemia.
  hipogammaglobulinemia secundaria secondary hypogammaglobulinemia.
  hipogammaglobulinemia transitoria de la infancia transient hypogammaglobulinemia of infancy.
hipoganglionosis *f.* hypoganglionosis.
hipogástrico, -ca *adj.* hypogastric.
hipogastrio *m.* hypogastrium.
hipogastrocele *m.* hypogastrocele.
hipogastrodídimo *m.* hypogastropagus.
hipogastrópago *m.* hypogastropagus.
hipogastrosquisis *f.* hypogastroschisis.
hipogénesis *f.* hypogenesis.
  hipogénesis polar polar hypogenesis.
hipogenético, -ca *adj.* hypogenetic.
hipogenia *f.* hypogenesis.
hipogenitalismo *m.* hypogenitalism.
hipogeusestesia *f.* hypogeusesthesia.
hipogeusia *f.* hypogeusia.
hipoglandular *adj.* hypoglandular.
hipogloso, -sa *adj.* hypoglossus, hypoglossal.
hipoglotis *f.* hippoglottis.
hipoglucagonemia *f.* hypoglucagonemia.
hipoglucemia *f.* hypoglycemia.
  hipoglucemia en ayunas fasting hypoglycemia.
  hipoglucemia cetósica ketotic hypoglycemia.
  hipoglucemia facticia factitial hypoglycemia.
  hipoglucemia inducida por leucina leucine-induced hypoglycemia.
  hipoglucemia mixta mixed hypoglycemia.
  hipoglucemia neonatal neonatal hypoglycemia.
  hipoglucemia reactiva reactive hypoglycemia.
hipoglucemiante *m.* hypoglycemic agent.
hipoglucémico, -ca *adj.* hypoglycemic.
hipoglucogenólisis *f.* hypoglycogenolysis.
hipoglucorraquia *f.* hypoglycorrhachia.
hipognato, -ta *adj.* hypognathous.
hipogonadía *f.* hypogonadism.
hipogonadismo *m.* hypogonadism.
  hipogonadismo con anosmia hypogonadism with anosmia.
  hipogonadismo eugonadotrópico eugonadotropic hypogonadism.
  hipogonadismo hipergonadotrópico hypergonadotropic hypogonadism.
  hipogonadismo hipogonadotrópico hypogonadotropic hypogonadism.

  hipogonadismo hipogonadotrópico familiar familial hypogonadotropic hypogonadism.
  hipogonadismo masculino male hypogonadism.
  hipogonadismo primario primary hypogonadism.
  hipogonadismo secundario secondary hypogonadism.
hipogonadotrópico, -ca *adj.* hypogonadotropic.
hipogranulocitosis *f.* hypogranulocytosis.
hipohemia *f.* hyphemia.
  hipohemia intertropical intertropical hyphemia.
  hipohemia tropical tropical hyphemia.
hipohepatia *f.* hypohepathia.
hipohidremia *f.* hypohydremia.
hipohidrocloria *f.* hypohydrochloria.
hipohidrosis *f.* hypohidrosis.
hipohidrótico, -ca *adj.* hypohidrotic.
hipohiloma *m.* hypohyloma.
hipohipnótico, -ca *adj.* hypohypnotic.
hipohipofisismo *m.* hypohypophisism.
hipohormonal *adj.* hypohormonal.
hipohormónico, -ca *adj.* hypohormonic.
hipoinmunidad *f.* hypoimmunity.
hipoinsulinemia *f.* hypoinsulinemia.
hipoinsulinismo *m.* hypoinsulinism.
hipointensidad *f.* hypointensity.
hipointenso, -sa *adj.* hypointense.
hipoisotónico, -ca *adj.* hypoisotonic.
hipolactasia *f.* hypolactasia.
hipolaringe *f.* hypolarynx.
hipolemal *adj.* hypolemmal.
hipolepidoma *m.* hypolepidoma.
hipoletal *adj.* hypolethal.
hipoleucemia *f.* hypoleukemia.
hipoleydigismo *m.* hypoleydigism.
hipolicuorrea *f.* hypoliquorrhea.
hipolinfemia *f.* hypolymphemia.
hipolipemia *f.* hypolipemia.
hipolipémico, -ca *adj.* hypolipidemic.
hipolipidemia *f.* hypolipemia.
hipolipidemiante *m.* lipid reducer.
hipolipoproteinemia *f.* hypolipoproteinemia.
hipoliposis *f.* hypoliposis.
hipolucencia *f.* hypolucency.
hipolucente *adj.* hypolucent.
hipomacia *f.* hypomazia.
hipomagnesemia *f.* hypomagnesemia.
hipomagnesuria *f.* hypomagnesuria.
hipomanía *f.* hypomania.
hipomaníaco, -ca *m., f.* hypomaniac.
hipomastia *f.* hypomastia.
hipomastia *f.* hypomastia.
hipomelanismo *m.* hypomelanosis.
hipomelanosis *f.* hypomelanosis.
  hipomelanosis idiopática guttata idiopathic guttate hypomelanosis.
  hipomelanosis de Ito Ito's hypomelanosis.
hipomelia *f.* hypomelia.
hipomenorrea *f.* hypomenorrhea.
hipómera *f.* hypomere.
hipometabólico, -ca *adj.* hypometabolic.
hipometabolismo *m.* hypometabolism.
  hipometabolismo eutiroideo euthyroid hypometabolism.
hipometria *f.* hypometria.
hipomicrosomía *f.* hypomicrosoma.
hipomielinización *f.* hypomyelination.
hipomielinogénesis *f.* hypomyelinogenesis.
hipomimia *f.* hypomimia.
hipomineralización *f.* hypomineralization.
hipomiotonía *f.* hypomyotonia.
hipomixia *f.* hypomyxia.

hipomixis *m.* hypomyxia.
hipomodal *adj.* hypomodal.
hipomorfo, -fa *m., f.* hypomorph.
hipomotilidad *f.* hypomotility.
hipomovilidad *f.* hypomobility.
hiponanosomía *f.* hyponanosoma.
hiponasalidad *f.* hyponasality.
hiponatremia *f.* hyponatremia.
  hiponatremia por depleción depletional hyponatremia.
  hiponatremia por dilución dilutional hyponatremia.
  hiponatremia hiperlipémica hyperlipemic hyponatremia.
hiponatruria *f.* hyponatruria.
hiponeocitosis *f.* hyponeocytosis.
hiponicón *m.* hyponychon.
hiponiquial *adj.* hyponychial.
hiponiquio *m.* hyponychium.
hiponitremia *f.* hyponitremia.
hipooncótico, -ca *adj.* hypooncotic.
hipoorquidia *f.* hypoorchidia.
hipoorquidismo *m.* hypoorchidism.
hipoortocitosis *f.* hypoorthocytosis.
hipoosmolalidad *f.* hypoosmolality.
hipoosmolar *adj.* hypoosmolar.
hipoosmolaridad *f.* hypoosmolarity.
hipoósmosis *f.* hyposmosis.
hipoosmótico, -ca *adj.* hyposmotic.
hipoovarismo *m.* hypoovarinism, hypovarism.
hipopancreatismo *m.* hypopancreatism.
hipopancreorrea *f.* hypopancreorrhea.
hipoparatireosis *f.* hypoparathyreosis.
hipoparatiroidia *f.* hypoparathyroidism.
hipoparatiroidismo *m.* hypoparathyroidism.
  hipoparatiroidismo familiar familial hypoparathyroidism.
hipopepsia *f.* hypopepsia.
hipopepsinia *f.* hypopepsinia.
hipoperfusión *f.* hypoperfusion.
  hipoperfusión renal renal hypoperfusion.
hipoperistalsis *f.* hypoperistalsis.
hipoperistaltismo *m.* hypoperistalsis.
hipopexia *f.* hypopexia, hypopexy.
hipopiesis *f.* hypopiesis.
  hipopiesis ortostática orthostatic hypopiesis.
hipopiético, -ca *adj.* hypopietic.
hipopigmentación *f.* hypopigmentation.
hipopinealismo *m.* hypopinealism.
hipopión *m.* hypopyon.
  hipopión recurrente recurrent hypopyon.
hipopituitarismo *m.* hypopituitarism.
hipoplasia *f.* hypoplasia, hypoplasty.
  hipoplasia de cartílago y pelo cartilage-hair hypoplasia.
  hipoplasia dérmica-focal focal dermal hypoplasia.
  hipoplasia del esmalte enamel hypoplasia.
  hipoplasia hereditaria del esmalte hereditary enamel hypoplasia.
  hipoplasia del mesénquima hypoplasia of the mesenchyme.
  hipoplasia del nervio óptico optic nerve hypoplasia.
  hipoplasia renal renal hypoplasia.
  hipoplasia renal oligomeganefrónica oligomeganephronic renal hypoplasia.
  hipoplasia renal segmentaria segmental renal hypoplasia.
  hipoplasia renal simple true hypoplasia.
  hipoplasia tímica thymic hypoplasia.
  hipoplasia de Turner Turner's hypoplasia.
  hipoplasia del ventrículo derecho right ventricular hypoplasia.
hipoplásico, -ca *adj.* hypoplastic.

hipoploide *m. y adj.* hypoploid.
hipoploidía *f.* hypoploidy.
hipopnea *f.* hypopnea.
hipopneico, -ca *adj.* hypopneic.
hipoponesis *f.* hypoponesis.
hipoporosis *f.* hypoporosis.
hipoposia *f.* hypoposia.
hipopotasemia *f.* hypopotassemia.
hipopotasémico, -ca *adj.* hypopotassemic.
hipopotencia *f.* hypopotentia.
hipopraxia *f.* hypopraxia.
hipopraxis *f.* hypopraxia.
hipoproacelerinemia *f.* hypoproaccelerinemia.
hipoproconvertinemia *f.* hypoproconvertinemia.
hipoprolactinemia *f.* hypoprolactinemia.
hipoprolanemia *f.* hypoprolanemia.
hipoprosexia *f.* hypoprosexia.
hipoprosodia *f.* hypoprosody.
hipoproteinemia *f.* hypoproteinemia.
  hipoproteinemia prehepática prehepatic hypoproteinemia.
hipoproteinia *f.* hypoproteinia.
hipoproteínico, -ca *adj.* hypoproteinic.
hipoproteinosis *f.* hypoproteinosis.
hipoprotrombinemia *f.* hypoprothrombinemia.
hipopselafesia *f.* hypopselaphesia.
hipoptialismo *m.* hypoptyalism.
hipoquilia *f.* hypochylia.
hipoquinesia *f.* hypokinesia.
hiporrea *f.* hyporrhea.
hiporreactivo, -va *adj.* hyporeactive.
hiporreflexia *f.* hyporeflexia.
hiporreninemia *f.* hyporeninemia.
hiporreninémico, -ca *adj.* hyporeninemic.
hiporreninismo *m.* hyporreninism.
hiporriboflavinosis *f.* hyporiboflavinosis.
hiposalemia *f.* hyposalemia.
hiposalivación *f.* hyposalivation.
hiposecreción *f.* hyposecretion.
hiposensibilidad *f.* hyposensitivity.
hiposensibilización *f.* hyposensitization.
hiposensitivo, -va *adj.* hyposensitive.
hiposexualidad *f.* hyposexuality.
hiposfresia *f.* hyposphresia.
hiposialadenitis *f.* hyposialadenitis.
hiposialosis *f.* hyposialosis.
hiposimpaticotonía *m.* hyposympathicotonous.
hiposinergia *f.* hyposynergia.
hiposístole *f.* hyposystole.
hiposistolia *f.* hyposystole.
hiposmia *f.* hyposmia.
hiposomatotropismo *m.* hyposomatotropism.
hiposomía *f.* hyposomia.
hiposomnia *f.* hyposomnia.
hipospadia *m.* hypospadias.
hipospadias *m.* hypospadias.
  hipospadia balánico, hipospadia balanítico balanic hypospadias, anterior hypospadias.
  hipospadia balanoprepucial balanopreputial hypospadias.
  hipospadia femenino female hypospadias.
  hipospadia glandular glandular hypospadias.
  hipospadia peneano penile hypospadias.
  hipospadia peneano-escrotal penoscrotal hypospadias.
  hipospadia perineal perineal hypospadias, posterior hypospadias.
  hipospadia seudovaginal pseudovaginal hypospadias.

hipospádico *m.* hypospadiac.
hiposplenismo *m.* hyposplenism.
hiposqueotomía *f.* hyposcheotomy.
hipostasis *f.* hypostasis.
  hipostasis post morten post morten hypostasis.
  hipostasis pulmonar pulmonary hypostasis.
hipostático, -ca *adj.* hypostatic.
hiposteatólisis *f.* hyposteatolysis.
hipostoma *m.* hypostome.
hipostomía *f.* hypostomia.
hipostomial *adj.* hypostomial.
hipostosis *f.* hypostosis.
hiposudoración *f.* deficiency of sweating.
hiposuprarrenalemia *f.* hyposuprarenalism.
hiposuprarrenalismo *m.* hyposuprarenalism.
hipotalamia *f.* hypothalamia.
hipotalámico, -ca *adj.* hypothalamic.
hipotálamo *m.* hypothalamus.
hipotalamohipofisario, -ria *adj.* hypothalamohypophyseal.
hipotalamotomía *f.* hypothalamotomy.
hipotaxia *f.* hypotaxia.
hipotelorismo *m.* hypotelorism.
  hipotelorismo ocular ocular hypotelorism.
  hipotelorismo orbitario orbital hypotelorism.
hipotenar *m.* hypothenar.
hipotensión *f.* hypotension.
  hipotensión arterial arterial hypotension.
  hipotensión controlada controlled hypotension.
  hipotensión deliberada controlled hypotension.
  hipotensión inducida induced hypotension.
  hipotensión intracraneal intracranial hypotension.
  hipotensión ortostática orthostatic hypotension.
  hipotensión ortostática crónica, hipotensión ortostática idiopática crónica chronic orthostatic hypotension, chronic idiopathic orthostatic hypotension.
  hipotensión postural postural hypotension.
  hipotensión sintomática symtomatic hypotension.
  hipotensión en supino supine hypotension.
  hipotensión vascular vascular hypotension.
hipotensivo, -va *adj.* hypotensive.
hipotenso, -sa *adj.* hypotensive.
hipotensor, -ra *adj.* hypotensor.
hipotermia *f.* hypothermia.
  hipotermia accidental accidental hypothermia.
  hipotermia corporal total total body hypothermia.
  hipotermia endógena endogenous hypothermia.
  hipotermia local local hypothermia.
  hipotermia moderada moderate hypothermia.
  hipotermia profunda profound hypothermia.
  hipotermia regional regional hypothermia.
hipotérmico, -ca *adj.* hypothermal.
hipótesis *f.* hypothesis.
  hipótesis alternativa alternative hypothesis.
  hipótesis de las aminas biógenas biogenic amine hypothesis.
  hipótesis autocrina autocrine hypothesis.
  hipótesis de Avogadro Avogadro's hypothesis.
  hipótesis del balanceo wobble hypothesis.
  hipótesis de la causa social social cause hypothesis.

hipótesis científica scientific hypothesis.

hipótesis del control de compuerta gate-control hypothesis.

hipótesis de la deriva drift hypothesis.

hipótesis de la dopamina en la esquizofrenia dopamine hypogammaglobulinemia of schizophrenia.

hipótesis de Dreyer y Bennet Dreyer and Bennet hypothesis.

hipótesis de filamentos deslizantes sliding filament hypothesis.

hipótesis de Gad Gad's hypothesis.

hipótesis un gen-una cadena polipeptídica one gen-one polypeptide chain hypothesis.

hipótesis un gen-una enzima one gene-one enzyme hypothesis.

hipótesis de Gompertz Gompertz's hypothesis.

hipótesis de la inestabilidad wobble hypothesis.

hipótesis insular insular hypothesis.

hipótesis de Lyon Lyon's hypothesis.

hipótesis de Makeham Makeham's hypothesis.

hipótesis de Michaelis-Menten Michaelis-Menten hypothesis.

hipótesis nula null hypothesis.

hipótesis permisiva permissive hypothesis.

hipótesis predictiva predictive hypothesis.

hipótesis quimiosmótica chemiosmotic hypothesis.

hipótesis de rollo de jalea jelly roll hypothesis.

hipótesis de la segregación segregation hypothesis.

hipótesis de Starling Starling's hypothesis.

hipótesis unitaria unitarian hypothesis.

hipótesis zwitter zwitter hypothesis.

hipotetraploide *adj.* hypotetraploid.

hipotimia *f.* hypothymia.

hipotímico, -ca *adj.* hypothymic.

hipotimismo *m.* hypothymism.

hipotímpano *m.* hypotympanum.

hipotimpanotomía *f.* hypotympanotomy.

hipotinción *f.* understain.

hipotireosis *f.* hypothyreosis.

hipotiroidación *f.* hyppothyroidation.

hipotiroideo, -a *adj.* hypothyroid.

hipotiroidía *f.* hypothyroidism.

hipotiroidismo *m.* hypothyroidism.

hipotiroidismo del lactante infantile hypothyroidism.

hipotiroidismo secundario secondary hypothyroidism.

hipotiroxinemia *f.* hypothyroxinemia.

hipotonía *f.* hypotonia, hypotony.

hipotonía congénita benigna benign congenital hypotonia.

hipotonía ocular hypotonia oculi.

hipotonicidad *f.* hypotonicity.

hipotónico, -ca *adj.* hypotonic.

hipotono *m.* hypotonus.

hipotoxicidad *f.* hypotoxicity.

hipotrepsia *f.* hypothrepsia.

hipotricosis *f.* hypotrichosis.

hipotricoso, -sa *adj.* hypotrichous.

hipotriploide *adj.* hypotriploid.

hipotriquiasis *f.* hypotrichiasis.

hipotrofia *f.* hypotrophy.

hipotrombinemia *f.* hypothrombinemia.

hipotromboplastinemia *f.* hypothromboplastinemia.

hipotropía *f.* hypotropia.

hipouremia *f.* hypouremia.

hipouresis *f.* hypouresis.

hipouricemia *f.* hypouricemia.

hipouricosuria *f.* hypouricuria.

hipouricuria *f.* hypouricuria.

hipourocrinia *f.* hypourocrinia.

hipovarismo *m.* hypovarism.

hipovenosidad *f.* hypovenosity.

hipoventilación *f.* hypoventilation.

hipovigilancia *f.* hypovigilance.

hipovitaminosis *f.* hypovitaminosis.

hipovolemia *f.* hypovolemia.

hipovolémico, -ca *adj.* hypovolemic.

hipovolia *f.* hypovolia.

hipoxemia *f.* hypoxemia.

hipoxia *f.* hypoxia.

hipoxia por afinidad con el oxígeno oxygen affinity hypoxia.

hipoxia aguda acute hypoxia.

hipoxia anémica anemic hypoxia.

hipoxia crónica chronic hypoxia.

hipoxia por difusión diffusion hypoxia.

hipoxia estancada stagnant hypoxia.

hipoxia por estasis stagnant hypoxia.

hipoxia hipóxica hypoxic hypoxia.

hipoxia histotóxica histotoxic hypoxia.

hipoxia isquémica ischemic hypoxia.

hipóxico, -ca *adj.* hypoxic.

hipoxidosis *f.* hypoxidosis.

hippocampus *m.* hippocampus.

hippus *m.* hippus.

hippus pupilar pupillar hippus.

hippus respiratorio respiratory hippus.

hipsarritmia *f.* hypsarrhythmia.

hipsicefalia *f.* hypsicephaly.

hipsicefálico, -ca *adj.* hypsicephalic.

hipsiloide *adj.* hypsiloid.

hipsistafilia *f.* hypsistaphylia.

hipsitenocefálico, -ca *adj.* hypsitenocephalic.

hipsobraquicefalia *f.* hypsibrachycephaly.

hipsobraquicefálico, -ca *adj.* hypsibrachycephalic.

hipsocefalia *f.* hypsicephaly.

hipsocefálico, -ca *adj.* hypsicephalic.

hipsocinesia *f.* hypsokinesis.

hipsocinesis *f.* hypsokinesis.

hipsocromía *f.* hypsochromy.

hipsocrómico, -ca *adj.* hypsochromic.

hipsodonto *m.* hypsodont.

hipsoterapia *f.* hypsotherapy.

hipurgia *f.* hypurgia.

hipuria *f.* hippuria.

hircismo *m.* hircismus.

hirsutismo *m.* hirsutism.

hirsutismo de Apert Apert's hirsutism.

hirsutismo constitucional constitutional hirsutism.

hirsutismo idiopático idiopathic hirsutism.

hirsuto, -ta *adj.* hirsute.

hirudicida[1] *m.* hirudicide.

hirudicida[2] *adj.* hirudicidal.

hirudiniasis *f.* hirudiniasis.

hirudinización *f.* hirudinization, leeching.

hirudinizar *v.* hirudinize.

hisiograma *m.* His electrogram.

histamina *f.* histamine.

histaminemia *f.* histaminemia.

histaminérgico, -ca *adj.* histaminergic.

histaminuria *f.* histaminuria.

histanoxia *f.* histanoxia.

histeralgia *f.* hysteralgia.

histeratresia *f.* hysteratresia.

histerectomía *f.* hysterectomy.

histerectomía abdominal abdominal hysterectomy.

histerectomía abdominovaginal abdominovaginal hysterectomy.

histerectomía cesárea cesarean hysterectomy.

histerectomía completa complete hysterectomy.

histerectomía paravaginal paravaginal hysterectomy.

histerectomía parcial partial hysterectomy.

histerectomía de Porro Porro hysterectomy.

histerectomía radical radical hysterectomy.

histerectomía radical modificada modified radical hysterectomy.

histerectomía subtotal subtotal hysterectomy.

histerectomía supracervical supracervical hysterectomy.

histerectomía supravaginal supravaginal hysterectomy.

histerectomía total total hysterectomy.

histerectomía vaginal vaginal hysterectomy.

histéresis *f.* hysteresis.

histéresis estática static hysteresis.

histéresis protoplásmica protoplasmic hysteresis.

histereurisis *f.* hystereurysis.

histeria *f.* hysteria.

histeria de angustia anxiety hysteria.

histeria de conversión conversion hysteria.

histeria hipnoide hypnoid hysteria.

histeria traumática traumatic hysteria.

histérico, -ca *adj.* hysteric, hysterical.

histeriforme *adj.* hysteriform.

histeritis *f.* hysteritis.

histerobubonocele *m.* hysterobubonocele.

histerocele *m.* hysterocele.

histerocístico, -ca *adj.* hysterocystic.

histerocistocleisis *f.* hysterocystocleisis.

histerocistopexia *f.* hysterocystopexy.

histerocleisis *f.* hysterocleisis.

histerocolposcopio *m.* hysterocolposcope.

histerodinia *f.* hysterodynia.

histeroepilepsia *f.* hysteroepilepsy.

histeróforo *m.* hysterophore.

histerografía *f.* hysterography.

histerógrafo *m.* hysterograph.

histerograma *m.* hysterogram.

histeroide *adj.* hysteroid.

histerolaparotomía *f.* hysterolaparotomy.

histerólisis *f.* hysterolysis.

histerolito *m.* hysterolith.

histerología *f.* hysterology.

histerometría *f.* hysterometry.

histerómetro *m.* hysterometer.

histeromioma *m.* hysteromyoma.

histeromiomectomía *f.* hysteromyomectomy.

histeromiotomía *f.* hysteromyotomy.

histeronarcolepsia *f.* hysteronarcolepsy.

histeroneurastenia *f.* hysteroneurasthenia.

histerooforectomía *f.* hystero-oophorectomy.

histeropatía *f.* hysteropathy.

histeropexia *f.* hysteropexy.

histeropexia abdominal abdominal hysteropexy.

histeropexia vaginal vaginal hysteropexy.

histeropía *f.* hysteropia.

histeroplastia *f.* hysteroplasty.

histeroptosia *f.* hysteroptosis.

histeroptosis *f.* hysteroptosis.

histerorrafia *f.* hysterorrhaphy.

histerorrea *f.* hysterorrhea.

histerorrexis *f.* hysterorrhexis.

histerosalpingectomía *f.* hysterosalpingectomy.

histerosalpingografía *f.* hysterosalpingography.

histerosalpingograma *m.* hysterosalpingogram.

histerosalpingooforectomía *f.* hysterosalpingo-oophorectomy.

histerosalpingostomía *f.* hysterosalpingostomy.

histerosalpinguectomía *f.* hysterosalpingectomy.

histeroscopia *f.* hysteroscopy.

histeroscopio *m.* hysteroscope.

histerosístole *f.* hysterosystole.

histeróstato *m.* hysterostat.

histerostomatocleisis *f.* hysterostomatocleisis.

histerotabetismo *m.* hysterotabetism.

histerotermometría *f.* hysterothermometry.

histerotomía *f.* hysterotomy.

   histerotomía abdominal abdominal hysterotomy.

   histerotomía vaginal vaginal hysterotomy.

histerótomo *m.* hysterotome.

histerotraquelectasia *f.* hysterotrachelectasia.

histerotraquelectomía *f.* hysterotrachelectomy.

histerotraqueloplastia *f.* hysterotracheloplasty.

histerotraquelorrafia *f.* hysterotrachelorrhaphy.

histerotraquelotomía *f.* hysterotrachelotomy.

histerotubografía *f.* hysterotubography.

histerovaginoenterocele *m.* hysterovaginoenterocele.

hístico, -ca *adj.* histic.

histidinemia *f.* histidinemia.

histidinuria *f.* histidinuria.

histioblasto *m.* histioblast.

histiocítico, -ca *adj.* histiocytic.

histiocito *m.* histiocyte.

   histiocito azul marino sea-blue histiocyte.

histiocitoma *m.* histiocytoma, histocytoma.

   histiocitoma eruptivo generalizado generalized eruptive histiocytoma.

   histiocitoma fibroso fibrous histiocytoma.

   histiocitoma fibroso maligno malignant fibrous histiocytoma.

   histiocitoma lipoide lipoid histiocytoma.

histiocitomatosis *f.* histyocytomatosis.

histiocitosis *f.* histiocytosis, histocytosis.

   histiocitosis acumulativa accumulative histiocytosis.

   histiocitosis atípica con regresión regressing atypical histiocytosis.

   histiocitosis de células de Langerhans Langerhans cell histiocytosis.

   histiocitosis lipídica, histiocitosis lipoídica lipid histiocytosis.

   histiocitosis maligna malignant histiocytosis.

   histiocitosis nodular no X nodular non-X histiocytosis.

   histiocitosis sinusal sinus histiocytosis.

   histiocitosis X X histiocytosis.

   histiocitosis Y Y histiocytosis.

histiogénico, -ca *adj.* hystiogenic.

histioide *adj.* histioid, histoid.

histioideo, -a *adj.* histioid.

histioirritante *adj.* histio-irritative.

histioma *m.* histioma, histoma.

histiónico, -ca *adj.* histionic.

histioángico, -ca *adj.* histoangic.

histoblasto *m.* histoblast.

histocinesis *f.* histokinesis.

histocito *m.* histocyte.

histocitoma *m.* histocytoma.

histocitosis *f.* histocytosis.

histoclástico, -ca *adj.* histoclastic.

histoclínico, -ca *adj.* histoclinical.

histocompatibilidad *f.* histocompatibility.

histocompatible *adj.* histocompatible.

histocromatosis *f.* histochromatosis.

histodiagnosis *f.* histodiagnosis.

histodiálisis *f.* histodialysis.

histodiferenciación *f.* histodifferentiation.

histófago *m.* histophagus.

histofisiología *f.* histophysiology.

histofluorescencia *f.* histofluorescence.

histogénesis *f.* histogenesis.

histogenético, -ca *adj.* histogenetic.

histogenia *f.* histogeny.

histógeno, -na *adj.* histogenous.

histografía *f.* histography.

histograma *m.* histogram.

histohematógeno, -na *adj.* histohematogenous.

histohidria *f.* histohydria.

histohipoxia *f.* histohypoxia.

histoide *adj.* histoid.

histoideo, -a *adj.* histoid.

histoincompatibilidad *f.* histoincompatibility.

histoincompatible *adj.* histoincompatible.

histolisado *m.* histolysate.

histólisis *f.* hystolisis.

histolítico, -ca *adj.* histolytic.

histología *f.* histology.

   histología normal normal histology.

   histología patológica pathologic histology.

histológico, -ca *adj.* histological, histologic.

histólogo, -ga *m., f.* histologist.

histoma *m.* histoma.

histometaplásico, -ca *adj.* histometaplastic.

histomorfología *f.* histomorphology.

histomorfometría *f.* histomorphometry.

histona *f.* histone.

   histona nucleinato de histone nucleinate.

histonectomía *f.* histonectomy.

histoneurología *f.* histoneurology.

histonomía *f.* histonomy.

histonuria *f.* histonuria.

histopatogenia *f.* histopathogenesis.

histopatología *f.* histopathology.

Histoplasma Histoplasma.

histoplasmona *m.* histoplasmona.

histoplasmosis *f.* histoplasmosis.

   histoplasmosis africana African histoplasmosis.

   histoplasmosis ocular ocular histoplasmosis.

   histoplasmosis ocular presunta presumed ocular histoplasmosis.

histoquímica *f.* histochemistry.

histoquímico, -ca *adj.* histochemical.

historia *f.* history.

   historia actual history of present illness.

   historia clínica clinical history, health history.

   historia clínica completa complete health history.

   historia de la enfermedad actual history of present illness.

   historia familiar family history.

   historia laboral occupational history.

   historia personal y familiar case history.

   historia psiquiátrica psychiatric history.

   historia sexual sexual history.

historradiografía *f.* historadiography.

historretención *f.* historetention.

historrexis *f.* historrhexis.

histotanatología *f.* histothanatology.

histoteliosis *f.* histoteliosis.

histoterapia *f.* histotherapy.

histotomía *f.* histotomy.

histótomo *m.* histotome.

histotóxico, -ca *adj.* histotoxic.

histotrófico, -ca *adj.* histotrophic.

histotrofo *m.* histotroph, histotrophe.

histotrombina *f.* histothrombin.

histotrópico, -ca *adj.* histotropic.

histozoico, -ca *adj.* histozoic.

histriónico, -ca *adj.* histrionic.

histrionismo *m.* histrionism.

histriquiasis *f.* hystriciasis.

hodoneurómera *f.* hodoneuromere.

hojuela *f.* leaflet.

holándrico, -ca *adj.* holandric.

holartritis *f.* holarthritis.

holoacardio *m.* holoacardius.

   holoacardio acéfalo holoacardius acephalus.

   holoacardio acórmico holoacardius acormus.

   holoacardio amorfo holoacardius amorphus.

holoacrania *f.* holoacrania.

holoanencefalia *m.* holoanencephaly.

holoantígeno *m.* holoantigen.

holoartrítico, -ca *adj.* holarthritic.

holoartritis *f.* holoarthritis.

holoblástico, -ca *adj.* holoblastic.

holocefálico, -ca *adj.* holocephalic.

holocéfalo, -la *adj.* holocephalic.

holocordón *m.* holocord.

holocrino, -na *adj.* holocrine.

holoendémico, -ca *adj.* holoendemic.

holofítico, -ca *adj.* holophytic.

hologamia *f.* hologamy.

hologastrosquisis *f.* hologastroschisis.

hologénesis *f.* hologenesis.

hologínico, -ca *adj.* hologynic.

holografía *f.* holography.

   holografía acústica acoustical holography.

holograma *m.* hologram.

holomastigoto, -ta *adj.* holomastigote.

holomiarial *adj.* holomyarial.

holomorfosis *f.* holomorphosis.

holoprosencefalia *f.* holoprosencephaly.

   holoprosencefalia familiar alobular familial alobar holoprosencephaly.

holorraquisquisis *f.* holorachischisis.

holosistólico, -ca *adj.* holosystolic.

holosquisis *f.* holoschisis.

holotelencefalia *f.* holotelencephaly.

Holothyrus Holothyrus.

holotipo *m.* holotype.

holotonía *f.* holotonia.

holotónico, -ca *adj.* holotonic.

holotopia *f.* holotopy.

holotrico, -ca *adj.* holotrichous.

holozoico, -ca *adj.* holozoic.

holoxénico, -ca *adj.* holoxenic.

holter *m.* holter monitoring.

homalocéfalo, -la *m., f.* homalocephalous.

homalografía *f.* homalography.

Homalomyia Homalomyia.

homaluria *f.* homaluria.

homaxil *adj.* homaxial.

hombro *m.* shoulder.

   hombro caído drop shoulder.

   hombro congelado frozen shoulder.

   hombro flojo loose shoulder.

   hombro en tocón stubbed shoulder.

   hombro trabado knocked-down shoulder.

homeocinesia *f.* homeokinesis.

homeocinesis *f.* homeokinesis.

homeocromo, -ma *adj.* homeochrome.

homeodinámica *f.* homeodynamics.

homeométrico, -ca *adj.* homeometric.

homeomorfo, -fa *adj.* homeomorphous.

homeópata *m., f.* homeopathist, homeopath.

homeopatía *f.* homeopathy.

homeopático, -ca *adj.* homeopathic.

homeoplasia *f.* homeoplasia.

homeoplásico, -ca *adj.* homeoplastic.

homeorrexis *f.* homeorrhexis.

homeosis *f.* homeosis, homoeosis.

homeostasia *f.* homeostasis.
homeostasis *f.* homeostasis.
  homeostasis Bernard-Cannon Bernard-Cannon homeostasis.
  homeostasis fisiológica physiological homeostasis.
  homeostasis genética genetic homeostasis.
  homeostasis de Lerner Lerner homeostasis.
  homeostasis ontogénica ontogenic homeostasis.
  homeostasis waddingtoniana Waddingtonian homeostasis.
homeostático, -ca *adj.* homeostatic.
homeosteoplastia *f.* homeoosteoplasty.
homeoterapéutico, -ca *adj.* homeotherapeutic.
homeoterapia *f.* homeotherapy, homeotherapeutics.
homeotermia *f.* homeothermy.
homeotérmico, -ca *adj.* homeothermic, homothermal, homothermic.
homeotermismo *m.* homeothermism.
homeotermo, -ma *adj.* homeotherm, homotherm.
homeótico, -ca *adj.* homeotic.
homeotípico, -ca *adj.* homeotypic, homeotypical.
homeotransplante *m.* homeotransplant, homeotransplantation.
homeotrasplante *m.* homeotransplant, homeotransplantation.
homicidio *m.* homicide.
  homicidio simple simple homicide.
Hominidae Hominidae.
hominido, -da *adj.* hominid.
hominoide *adj.* hominoid.
Hominoidea Hominoidea.
Homo Homo.
  Homo sapiens Homo sapiens.
homoblástico, -ca *adj.* homoblastic.
homocarion *m.* homokaryon.
homocariótico, -ca *adj.* homokaryotic.
homocarnosinosis *f.* homocarnosinosis.
homocéntrico, -ca *adj.* homocentric.
homocíclico, -ca *adj.* homocyclic.
homocigosidad *f.* homozygosity.
homocigosis *f.* homozygosis.
homocigótico, -ca *adj.* homozygous.
homocigoto, -ta *adj.* homozygote.
  homocigoto por descendencia homozygote by descent.
homocistinemia *f.* homocystinemia.
homocistinuria *f.* homocystinuria.
homocitotrópico, -ca *adj.* homocytotropic.
homocládico, -ca *adj.* homocladic.
homócrono, -na *adj.* homochronous.
homocuerpo *m.* homobody.
homodesmótico, -ca *adj.* homodesmotic.
homodímero *m.* homodimer.
homodonto, -ta *m., f.* homodont.
homódromo, -ma *adj.* homodromous.
homoeosis *f.* homoeosis.
homoerótico, -ca *adj.* homoerotic.
homoerotismo *m.* homoeroticism, homoerotism.
homoestimulación *f.* homostimulation.
homoestimulante *adj.* homostimulant.
homofermentación *f.* homofermentation.
homofermentador *m.* homofermenter.
homofílico, -ca *adj.* homophilic.
homófilo *m.* homophil.
homofobia *f.* homophobia.
homogamético, -ca *adj.* homogametic.
homogameto *m.* homogamete.
homogamia *f.* homogamy.

homógamo, -ma *adj.* homogamous.
homogenado *m.* homogenate.
homogeneidad *f.* homogeneity.
homogeneización *f.* homogeneization, shimming.
homogeneizado, -da *adj.* homogenized.
homogeneizar *v.* homogenize.
homogéneo, -a *adj.* homogeneous.
homogenesia *f.* homogenesis.
homogénesis *f.* homogenesis.
homogenético, -ca *adj.* homogenetic.
homogenia *f.* homogeny.
homogenicidad *f.* homogenicity.
homogénico, -ca *adj.* homogenic.
homogenoto *m.* homogenote.
homogentisinuria *f.* homogentisuria.
homogentisuria *f.* homogentisuria.
homoglandular *adj.* homoglandular.
homoinjerto *m.* homograft.
homoiostasis *f.* homoiostasis.
homoláctico, -ca *adj.* homolactic.
homolateral *adj.* homolateral.
homolípidos *m.* homolipids.
homolisina *f.* homolysin.
homólisis *f.* homolysis.
homólogo, -ga *adj.* homolog, homologous.
homomórfico, -ca *adj.* homomorphic.
homomorfosis *f.* homomorphosis.
homónimo, -ma *adj.* homonymous.
homónomo, -ma *adj.* homonomous.
homonuclear *adj.* homonuclear.
homoorgánico, -ca *adj.* homorganic.
homoplastia *f.* homoplasty.
homoplástico, -ca *adj.* homoplastic.
homoqueratoplastia *f.* homokeratoplasty.
homorgánico, -ca *adj.* homorganic.
homosexual *adj.* homosexual.
homosexualidad *f.* homosexuality.
  homosexualidad egodistónica ego-dystonia homosexuality.
  homosexualidad femenina female homosexuality.
  homosexualidad inconsciente unconscious homosexuality.
  homosexualidad latente latent homosexuality.
  homosexualidad manifiesta overt homosexuality.
homotálico, -ca *adj.* homothallic.
homotalismo *m.* homothallism.
homotérmico, -ca *adj.* homothermal, homothermic.
homotermo *m.* homotherm.
homotípico, -ca *adj.* homotypic, homotypical.
homotipo *m.* homotype.
homotónico, -ca *adj.* homotonic.
homotópico, -ca *adj.* homotopic.
homotrasplante *m.* homotransplant, homotransplantation.
homotropismo *m.* homotropism.
homoyopódico, -ca *adj.* homoiopodal.
homoxénico, -ca *adj.* homoxenous.
homozigoto *m.* homozygote.
homozoico, -ca *adj.* homozoic.
homúnculo *m.* homunculus.
hondonada *f.* trough.
hongo *m.* fungus.
horizonte *m.* horizon.
  horizonte clínico clinical horizon.
  horizonte del desarrollo developmental horizon.
hormesis *f.* hormesis.
hormigueo *m.* formication, tingling.
hormión *m.* hormion.

hormona *f.* hormone.
hormonagogo, -ga *adj.* hormonagogue.
hormonal *adj.* hormonal.
hormónico, -ca *adj.* hormonic.
hormonogénesis *f.* hormonogenesis.
hormonogenia *f.* hormonogenic.
hormonogénico, -ca *adj.* hormonogenic.
hormonología *f.* hormonology.
hormonopéxico, -ca *adj.* hormonopexic.
hormonopoyesis *f.* hormonopoiesis.
hormonopoyético, -ca *adj.* hormonopoietic.
hormonoprivia *f.* hormonoprivia.
hormonosis *f.* hormonosis.
hormopoyesis *f.* hormonopoiesis.
hormonoterapia *f.* hormonotherapy.
horripilación *f.* horripilation.
horror *m.* horror.
hospedador *m.* host.
hospital *m.* hospital.
  hospital general general hospital.
  hospital geriátrico de día geriatric day care hospital.
  hospital de maternidad, hospital materno maternity hospital.
  hospital psiquiátrico psychiatric hospital.
hospitalización *f.* hospitalization.
  hospitalización parcial partial hospitalization.
hospitalizado, -da *adj.* inpatient.
hospitalizar *v.* institutionalize.
hostilidad *f.* hostility.
hoyo¹ *m.* pockmark.
hoyo² *m.* hollow, pit.
hoyuelo *m.* dellen, dimple.
hoz *f.* falx.
hueco *m.* hollow, pit.
huella AV *f.* AV nicking.
huella digital *f.* fingerprint.
huella palmar *f.* palmprint.
huesecillo *m.* bonelet, ossicle.
hueso *m.* bone, os.
huésped *m.* host.
huevo *m.* ovum.
humectación *f.* humectation.
humectante *adj.* humectant.
humedad *f.* humidity.
  humedad absoluta absolute humidity.
  humedad relativa relative humidity.
húmedo, -da *adj.* moist.
humeral *adj.* humeral.
húmero *m.* humerus.
humerocubital *adj.* humeroulnar.
humeroescapular *adj.* humeroscapular.
humerorradial *adj.* humerorradial.
humeroscapular *adj.* humeroscapular.
humidificación *f.* humidification.
humidificador *m.* humidifier.
  humidificador en cascada cascade humidifier.
  humidificador de chorro jet humidifier.
  humidificador de difusión de burbujas bubble diffusion humidifier.
  humidificador higroscópico hygroscopic humidifier.
  humidificador de mecha wick humidifier.
humor *m.* humor.
  humor acuoso humor aquosus.
  humor cristalino humor cristallinus, crystalline humor.
  humor ocular ocular humor.
  humor plasmoide plasmoid humor.
  humor vítreo humor vitreus, vitreous humor.
humoral *adj.* humoral.
hundimiento craneal *m.* depressed cranial fracture.

huso *m.* spindle.

  huso aórtico aortic spindle.

  huso central central spindle.

  huso del esmalte enamel spindle.

  huso de His His spindle.

  huso de Krukenberg, huso de Axenfeld-Krukenberg Axenfeld-Krukenberg spindle.

  huso de Kühne Kühne's spindle.

  huso mitótico mitotic spindle.

  huso muscular muscle spindle, muscular spindle.

  huso neuromuscular neuromuscular spindle.

  huso neurotendinoso neurotendinous spindle.

  huso nuclear nuclear spindle.

  huso de segmentación cleavage spindle.

  huso tigroide tigroid spindle.

  huso urinaria urine spindle.

Hyalomma Hyalomma.

Hydatigena Hydatigena.

I i

iatergia *f.* iathergy.
iatraléptica *f.* iatraliptics.
iataléptico, -ca *adj.* iatraliptic.
iatraliptica *f.* iatraliptics.
iatralíptico, -ca *adj.* iatraliptic.
iatreusiología *f.* iatreusiology.
iatreusis *f.* iatreusis.
iátrico, -ca *adj.* iatric.
iatrofisica *f.* iatrophysics.
iatrogenia *f.* iatrogenia.
iatrogénico, -ca *adj.* iatrogenic.
iatrógeno, -na *adj.* iatrogenic.
iatrología, *f.* iatrology.
iatrotécnica *f.* iatrotechnics, iatrotechnique.
icnograma *m.* ichnogram.
iconomanía *f.* iconomania.
icor *m.* ichor.
icoremia *f.* ichoremia.
icoroide *adj.* ichoroid.
icoroso, -sa *adj.* ichorous.
icorrea *f.* ichorrea.
Icorremia *f.* ichorrhemia.
icosaédrico, -ca *adj.* icosahedral.
ictal *adj.* ictal.
icterepatitis *f.* icterohepatitis.
ictericia *f.* jaundice, icterus.
　ictericia por ácido pícrico picric acid jaundice.
　ictericia acolúrica acholuric jaundice.
　ictericia acolúrica crónica chronic acholuric jaundice.
　ictericia acolúrica familiar acholuric familial jaundice, familial acholuric jaundice.
　ictericia anhepática, ictericia anhepatógena anhepatic jaundice, anhepatogenous jaundice.
　ictericia de la arsfenamina post-arsphenamine jaundice.
　ictericia de Budd Budd's jaundice.
　ictericia catarral catarrhal jaundice.
　ictericia catarral epidémica epidemic catarrhal icterus.
　icterus citohemolítico cythemolytic icterus.
　ictericia colestática cholestatic jaundice.
　ictericia colérica choleric jaundice.
　ictericia congénita congenital jaundice.
　ictericia de Crigler-Najjar Crigler-Najjar jaundice.
　ictericia epidémica epidemic jaundice.
　ictericia esferocítica spherocytic jaundice.
　ictericia espiroquetósica spirochetal jaundice.
　icterus familiar benigno benign familial icterus.
　ictericia familiar congénita congenital familial jaundice, congenital familial icterus.
　ictericia familiar crónica, icterus familiar crónico chronic familial jaundice, chronic familial icterus.
　ictericia febril febrile jaundice.
　ictericia fisiológica, icterus fisiológico physiologic jaundice, physiologic icterus.

　ictericia grave, icterus gravis icterus gravis.
　ictericia grave del recién nacido icterus gravis neonatorum.
　ictericia gravídica gravidic jaundice.
　ictericia hematógena hematogenous jaundice.
　ictericia hemolítica hemolytic jaundice.
　icterus hemolítico adquirido acquired hemolytic icterus.
　ictericia hemolítica congénita, icterus hemolítico congénito congenital hemolytic jaundice, congenital hemolytic icterus.
　ictericia hemorrágica hemorrhagic jaundice.
　ictericia hepatocelular hepatocellular jaundice.
　ictericia hepatógena hepatogenic jaundice, hepatogenous jaundice.
　ictericia idiopática crónica chronic idiopathic jaundice.
　ictericia indolora painless jaundice.
　ictericia infecciosa, icterus infeccioso infectious jaundice, infective jaundice, infectious icterus.
　ictericia latente latent jaundice.
　ictericia por leche materna breast milk jaundice.
　ictericia por leptospiras leptospiral jaundice.
　ictericia maligna malignant jaundice.
　ictericia mecánica mechanical jaundice.
　icterus melas icterus melas.
　ictericia negra black jaundice.
　ictericia neonatal, icterus neonatal neonatal jaundice, icterus neonatorum.
　ictericia neonatal grave icterus gravis neonatorum.
　ictericia del neonato icterus neonatorum.
　ictericia no hemolítica non-hemolytic jaundice.
　ictericia no hemolítica congénita, ictericia No hemolítica congénito familiar congenital nonhemolytic jaundice, congenital familial non-hemolytic jaundice.
　ictericia no hemolítica familiar familial non-hemolytic jaundice.
　ictericia no obstructiva non-obstructive jaundice.
　ictericia nuclear nuclear jaundice, nuclear icterus.
　ictericia obstructiva obstructive jaundice.
　ictericia posthepática posthepatic jaundice.
　ictericia precoz, icterus praecox icterus praecox.
　ictericia del recién nacido jaundice of the newborn.
　ictericia de regurgitación regurgitation jaundice.
　ictericia de retención retention jaundice.
　ictericia de Schmorl Schmorl's jaundice.
　ictericia por suero homólogo, por suero humano homologous serum jaundice, human serum jaundice.

　ictericia de Sumatra Sumatra jaundice.
　ictericia toxémica toxemic jaundice.
　ictericia tóxica toxic jaundice.
ictérico, -ca *adj.* icteric.
icteroanemia *f.* icteroanemia.
　icteroanemia hemolítica hemolytic icteroanemia.
icterogenicidad *f.* icterogenicity.
icterogénico, -ca *adj.* icterogenic.
icterohematuria *f.* icterohematuria.
icterohematúrico, -ca *adj.* icterohematuric.
icterohemoglobinuria *f.* icterohemoglobinuria.
icterohepatitis *f.* icterohepatitis.
icteroide *adj.* icteroid.
icterus *m.* icterus.
ictioacantotoxina *f.* ichthyoacanthotoxin.
ictioacantotoxismo *m.* ichthyoacanthotoxism.
ictiocola *f.* ichthyocolla.
ictiofagia *f.* ichthyophagia.
ictiófago, -ga *adj.* ichthyophagous.
ictiofobia *f.* ichthyophobia.
ictiohemotoxina *f.* ichthyohemotoxin.
ictiohemotoxismo *m.* ichthyhemotoxism.
ictioide *adj.* ichthyoid.
ictiología *f.* ichthyology.
ictiootoxina *f.* ichthyootoxin.
ictiootoxismo *m.* ichthyootoxism.
ictiosarcotoxina *f.* ichthyosarcotoxin.
ictiosarcotoxismo *m.* ichthyosarcotoxism.
ictiosiforme *adj.* ichthyosiform.
ictiósico, -ca *adj.* ichthyotic.
ictiosis *f.* ichthyosis.
　ictiosis adquirida acquired ichthyosis.
　ictiosis congénita congenital ichthyosis, ichthyosis congenita.
　ictiosis congénita neonatal ichthyosis congenita neonatorum.
　ictiosis córnea ichthyosis corneae.
　ictiosis escutiforme ichthyosis scutulata.
　ictiosis espinosa ichthyosis spinosa.
　ictiosis fetal ichthyosis fetalis.
　ictiosis folicular ichthyosis follicularis.
　ictiosis hystrix ichthyosis hystrix.
　ictiosis intrauterina ichthyosis intrauterina.
　ictiosis lamelar, ictiosis laminar, ictiosis laminillar lamellar ichthyosis.
　ictiosis ligada al cromosoma X X-linked ichthyosis.
　ictiosis ligada al sexo sex-linked ichthyosis.
　ictiosis lineal circunfleja ichthyosis linearis circumflexa.
　ictiosis lineal circunscripta ichthyosis linearis circumscripta.
　ictiosis nacarada, ictiosis nácrea nacreous ichthyosis.
　ictiosis palmar y plantar ichthyosis palmaris et plantaris.
　ictiosis sauroderma, ictiosis saurodérmica ichthyosis sauroderma.
　ictiosis sebácea ichthyosis sebacea.

ictiosis sebácea córnea ichthyosis sebacea cornea.
ictiosis simple ichthyosis simplex.
ictiosis vulgar ichthyosis vulgaris.
ictiosismo *m.* ichthyosismus.
ictiosismo exantemático ichthyosismus exanthematicus.
ictiótico, -ca *adj.* ichthyotic.
ictiotóxico, -ca *adj.* ichthyotoxic.
ictiotoxicología *f.* ichthyotoxicology.
ictiotoxicon *m.* ichthyotoxicon.
ictiotoxina *f.* ichthyotoxin.
ictiotoxismo *m.* ichthyotoxism.
ictismo *m.* ichthyism.
ictómetro *m.* ictometer.
ictus *m.* ictus.
ictus cordis ictus cordis.
ictus epiléptico ictus epilepticus.
ictus hemorrágico ictus sanguinis.
ictus paralyticus ictus paralyticus.
ictus solis ictus solis.
id *m.* id.
ide id.
idea *f.* idea.
idea autóctona autochthonous idea.
idea compulsiva compulsive idea.
idea delirante delirious idea.
idea delirante primaria primary delirious idea.
idea delirante secundaria secondary delirious idea.
idea deliroide deliroid idea.
idea fija fixed idea, idée fixe.
idea imperativa, idea imperiosa imperative idea.
idea obsesiva obsessional idea.
idea de persecución idea of persecution.
idea de referencia, idea referencial idea of reference, referential idea.
idea sobrevalorada overvalued idea.
ideación *f.* ideation.
ideación paranoide paranoid ideation.
ideación suicida suicidal ideation.
ideacional *adj.* ideational.
ideal *m.* ideal.
ideal del ego, ideal del yo ego ideal.
idealización *f.* idealization.
idealización primitiva primitive idealization.
ideatum ideatum.
identidad *f.* identity.
identidad básica de grupo basic group identity.
identidad del ego ego identity.
identidad de género gender identity, core gender identity.
identidad negativa negative identity.
identidad personal personal identity.
identidad sexual sexual identity.
identidad del yo ego identity.
identificación *f.* identification.
identificación con el agresor aggressor identification.
identificación competitiva competitive identification.
identificación cósmica cosmic identification.
identificación dental dental identification.
identificación positiva positive identification.
identificación proyectiva projective identification.
ideocinético, -ca *adj.* idiokinetic.
ideodinamismo *m.* ideodynamism.
ideofobia *f.* ideophobia.
ideofrenia *f.* ideophrenia.
ideofrénico, -ca *adj.* ideophrenic.

ideógeno, -na *adj.* ideogenetic.
ideoglandular *adj.* ideoglandular.
ideología *f.* ideology.
ideometabólico, -ca *adj.* ideometabolic.
ideometabolismo *m.* ideometabolism.
ideomoción *f.* ideomotion.
ideomotor, -ra *adj.* ideomotor.
ideomuscular *adj.* ideomuscular.
ideoplastia *f.* ideoplastia.
ideovascular *adj.* ideovascular.
idioaglutinina *f.* idioagglutinin.
idioblapsis *f.* idioblapsis.
idiobláptico, -ca *adj.* idioblaptic.
idioblasto *m.* idioblast.
idiocia *f.* idiocy.
idiocia amaurotica familiar amaurotic idiocy, amaurotic familial idiocy.
idiocia azteca Aztec idiocy.
idiocia cretinoide cretinoid idiocy.
idiocia eretística erethistic idiocy.
idiocia familiar amaurótica amaurotic familial idiocy.
idiocia microcefálica microcephalic idiocy.
idiocia de Kalmuk Kalmuk idiocy.
idiocia mongólica Mongolian idiocy.
idiocia moral moral idiocy.
idiocrasia *f.* idiocrasy.
idiocrático, -ca *adj.* idiocratic.
idiocromatina *f.* idiochromatin.
idiocromidio *m.* idiochromidia.
idiocromosoma *m.* idiochromosome.
idiodinámico, -ca *adj.* idiodynamic.
idioespasmo *m.* idiospasm.
idióforo *m.* idiophore.
idiogénesis *f.* idiogenesis.
idioglosia *f.* idioglossia.
idioglótico, -ca *adj.* idioglottic.
idiográfico, -ca *adj.* idiographic.
idiograma *m.* idiogram.
idioheteroaglutinina *f.* idioheteroagglutinin.
idioheterolisina *f.* idioheterolysin.
idiohipnotismo *m.* idiohypnotism.
idioisoaglutinina *f.* idioisoagglutinin.
idioisolisina *f.* idioisolysin.
idiolalia *f.* idiolalia.
idiolisina *f.* idiolysin.
idiologismo *m.* idiologism.
idiólogo *m.* idiolog.
idiómero *m.* idiomere.
idiomuscular *adj.* idiomuscular.
idionodal *adj.* idionodal.
idiopatético, -ca *adj.* idiopathetic.
idiopatía *f.* idiopathy.
idiopático, -ca *adj.* idiopathic.
idiopsicológico, -ca *adj.* idiopsychologic.
idiorreflejo *m.* idioreflex.
idiorretinal *adj.* idioretinal.
idiosincrasia *f.* idiosyncrasy.
idiosincrasia a un fármaco idiosyncrasy to a drug.
idiosincrático, -ca *adj.* idiosyncratic.
idiosoma *m.* idiosoma, idiosome.
idiospasmo *m.* idiospasm.
idiota *m., f. y adj.* idiot.
idiota-prodigio idiot-prodigy.
idiota-sabio, idiota sabio idiot-savant, idiot savant.
idiota sapiente idiot-savant, idiot savant.
idiotez *f.* idiocy.
idiotípico, -ca *adj.* idiotypic.
idiotipo *m.* idiotype.
idiotopía *f.* idiotopy.
idiótopo *m.* idiotope.
idiotoxina *f.* idiotoxin.
idiotrófico, -ca *adj.* idiotrophic.

idiotrópico, -ca *adj.* idiotropic.
idiovariación *f.* idiovariation.
idioventricular *adj.* idioventricular.
iduronato-2-sulfatasa *f.* iduronate-2-sulfatase.
igniextirpación *f.* igniextirpation.
ignioperación *f.* ignioperation.
ignipedites *f.* ignipedites.
ignipuntura *f.* ignipuncture.
ignis infernalis ignis infernalis.
ignización *f.* ignisation.
igualar *v.* equate.
ikota *f.* ikota.
ilaqueación *f.* illaqueation.
iléaco, -ca *adj.* ileac.
ileadelfo *m.* ileadelphus.
ileal *adj.* ileal.
ileectomía *f.* ileectomy.
ileítis *f.* ileitis.
ileítis distal distal ileitis.
ileítis regional regional ileitis.
ileítis terminal terminal ileitis.
ileítis retrógrada backwash ileitis.
íleo *m.* ileus.
íleo adinámico adynamic ileus.
íleo biliar biliary ileus.
íleo por cálculos biliares gallstone ileus.
íleo dinámico dynamic ileus.
íleo espástico spastic ileus.
íleo hiperdinámico hyperdynamic ileus.
íleo mecánico mechanical ileus.
íleo meconial meconial ileus, meconium ileus.
íleo oclusivo occlusive ileus.
íleo paralítico paralytic ileus, ileus paralyticus.
íleo postoperatorio postoperative ileus.
íleo subparto icterus subparta.
íleo terminal terminal ileus.
íleo verminoso verminous ileus.
ileocecal *adj.* ileocecal.
ileocecostomía *f.* ileocecostomy.
ileociego *m.* ileocecum.
ileocistoplastia *f.* ileocystoplasty.
ileocistostomía *f.* ileocystostomy.
ileocólico, -ca *adj.* ileocolic.
ileocolitis *f.* ileocolitis.
ileocolitis tuberculosa tuberculous ileocolitis.
ileocolitis ulcerosa crónica ileocolitis ulcerosa chronica.
ileocolónico, -ca *adj.* ileocolonic.
ileocolostomía *f.* ileocolostomy.
ileocolotomía *f.* ileocolotomy.
ileoentectropia *f.* ileoentrectropy.
ileografía *f.* ileography.
ileoileostomía *f.* ileoileostomy.
íleon *m.* ileum.
íleon doble duplex ileum.
ileopexia *f.* ileopexy.
ileoproctostomía *f.* ileoproctostomy.
ileorrafia *f.* ileorrhaphy.
ileorrectal *adj.* ileorectal.
ileorrectostomía *f.* ileorectostomy.
ileosigmoide *adj.* ileosigmoid.
ileosigmoidostomía *f.* ileosigmoidostomy.
ileostomía *f.* ileostomy.
ileostomía de Brooke Brooke ileostomy.
ileostomía de continencia continent ileostomy.
ileostomía de Kock Kock ileostomy.
ileostomía urinaria urinary ileostomy.
ileostomizado, -da *adj.* ileostomate.
ileotomía *f.* ileotomy.
ileotransversostomía *f.* ileotransversostomy.
ileoyeyunitis *f.* ileojejunitis.
ileso, -sa *adj.* unhurt.

íleus *m.* ileus.
ilíaco *m.* iliacus.
ilíaco, -ca *adj.* Iliac.
iliadelfo *m.* iliadelphus.
ilinación *f.* illinition.
ilinición *f.* illinition.
iliocapsular *adj.* iliocapsular.
iliociático, -ca *adj.* iliosciatic.
iliococcígeo, -a *adj.* iliococcygeal.
iliocolotomía *f.* iliocolotomy.
iliocostal *adj.* iliocostal.
ilioespinal *adj.* iliospinal.
iliofemoral *adj.* iliofemoral.
iliofemoroplastia *f.* iliofemoroplasty.
iliohipogástrico, -ca *adj.* iliohypogastric.
ilioinguinal *adj.* ilioinguinal.
ilioisquiático, -ca *adj.* iliosciatic.
iliolumbar *adj.* iliolumbar.
iliolumbocostoabdominal *adj.* iliolumbocostoabdominal.
iliómetro *m.* iliometer.
ilion *m.* ilium.
iliópago *m.* iliopagus.
iliopectíneo, -a *adj.* iliopectineal.
iliopélvico, -ca *adj.* iliopelvic.
iliopubiano, -na *adj.* iliopubic.
iliosacro, -cra *adj.* iliosacral.
iliospinal *adj.* iliospinal.
iliotibial *adj.* iliotibial.
iliotoracópago *m.* iliothoracopagus.
iliotrocantéreo, -a *adj.* iliotrocanteric.
ilioxifópago *m.* ilioxiphopagus.
ilium *m.* ilium.
iluminación *f.* illumination.
　iluminación axial, iluminación axil axial illumination.
　iluminación de campo oscuro, iluminación en campo oscuro dark-field illumination.
　iluminación central central illumination.
　iluminación de contacto, iluminación por contacto contact illumination.
　iluminación crítica critical illumination.
　iluminación directa direct illumination.
　iluminación erecta erect illumination.
　iluminación focal focal illumination.
　iluminación en fondo oscuro dark-ground illumination.
　iluminación de Köhler Köhler illumination.
　iluminación de lado a lado through illumination.
　iluminación lateral lateral illumination.
　iluminación oblicua oblique illumination.
　iluminación vertical vertical illumination.
iluminador *m.* illuminator.
　iluminador de Abbe Abbe's illuminator.
ilusión *f.* illusion.
　ilusión catatímica catatimic illusion.
　ilusión de dobles illusion of doubles.
　ilusión por inatención illusion for inattention.
　ilusión de movimiento illusion of movement.
　ilusión oculógira oculogyral illusion.
　ilusión oculográvica oculogravic illusion.
　ilusión óptica optical illusion.
　ilusión pareidólica paraeidolic illusion.
ilusional *adj.* illusional.
ilusivo, -va *adj.* illusional.
ilustrador médico *m., f.* medical illustrator.
ilutación *f.* illutation.
ima ima.
imagen *f.* image.
　imagen accidental accidental image.
　imagen de adición further image.
　imagen alucinoide hallucinoid image.
　imagen amorfa amorphous image.

imagen analógica analogic image.
imagen aséptica del cuerpo aseptic body image.
imagen catatrópica catatropic image.
imagen consecutiva consecutive image.
imagen corporal body image.
imagen corporal de compromiso compromise body image.
imagen de descompresión decompression image.
imagen digital digital image.
imagen dinámica dynamic image.
imagen directa direct image.
imagen en donuts doughnut image.
imagen eidética eidetic image.
imagen electrostática electrostatic image.
imagen de energía dual dual-energy image.
imagen erecta, imagen erguida erect image.
imagen especular specular image.
imagen de espejo mirror image.
imagen en espejo de Purkinje-Sanson Purkinje-Sanson mirror image.
imagen falsa false image.
imagen fantasma phantom image.
imagen funcional functional image.
imagen guiada guided image.
imagen heterónima heteronymous image.
imagen hipnagógica hypnagogic image.
imagen hipnopómpica hypnopompic image.
imagen homónima homonymous image.
imagen idealizada idealized image.
imagen incidental incidental image.
imagen invertida inverted image.
imagen latente latent image.
imagen localizadora localizer image.
imagen matriz image matrix.
imagen de memoria memory image.
imagen mental mental image.
imagen mnémica mnemic image.
imagen motora motor image.
imagen en nevada snowfall image.
imagen en ojo de buey bull's-eye image.
imagen óptica optical image.
imagen paterna parent image.
imagen primordial primordial image.
imagen de Purkinje Purkinje image.
imagen de Purkinje-Sanson Purkinje-Sanson image.
imagen de radioisótopo radioisotope image.
imagen real real image.
imagen por resonancia magnética (IRM) magnetic resonance image (MRI).
imagen retinal, imagen retiniana retinal image.
imagen retiniana desigual unequal retinal image.
imagen de Sanson Sanson's image.
imagen sensitiva sensory image.
imagen sensorial sensory image.
imagen de sustracción subtraction image.
imagen táctil tactile image.
imagen en tiempo real real-time image.
imagen de transformación de Fourier Fourier transform image.
imagen de uno mismo self-image.
imagen virtual virtual image.
imagen visual visual image.
imaginación *f.* imagination.
　imaginación creadora creative imagination.
　imaginación productiva productive imagination.
　imaginación reproductiva reproductive imagination.
imaginal *adj.* imaginal.
imaginería¹ *f.* imagery.

imaginería² *f.* imaging.
imago imago.
imagocida *adj.* imagocide.
imán *m.* magnet.
　imán de dentadura denture magnet.
　imán de Grüning, imán de Haab, imán de Hirschberg Grüning's magnet, Haab's magnet, Hirschberg's magnet.
　imán permanente permanent magnet.
　imán resistivo resistive magnet.
　imán superconductivo superconducting magnet.
　imán temporal temporary magnet.
imbalance *m.* imbalance.
imbécil *m., f. y adj.* imbecile.
imbecilidad *f.* Imbecility.
　imbecilidad moral moral imbecility.
imbibición *f.* imbibition.
　imbibición de hemoglobina hemoglobin imbibition.
imbricación *f.* imbrication.
　imbricación horizontal horizontal imbrication.
imbricado, -da *adj.* imbricate, imbricated.
imbricar *v.* imbricate.
iminoácido *m.* imino acid.
iminoglicinuria *f.* iminoglycinuria.
iminohidrolasa *f.* iminohydrolase.
iminourea *f.* iminourea.
impacción¹ *f.* impaction.
　impacción de alimentos food impaction.
　impacción de cerumen ceruminal impaction.
　impacción dental, impacción dentaria dental impaction.
　impacción fecal fecal impaction.
　impacción por inercia inertial impaction.
　impacción mucosa mucus impaction.
impacción² *f.* rabbeting.
impactación *f.* rabbeting.
impacto *m.* impact.
impalpable *adj.* impalpable.
impaludación *f.* impaludation.
impaludismo *m.* impaludation.
impar *adj.* impar.
impardigitado, -da *adj.* impardigitate.
impatencia *f.* impatency.
impatente *adj.* impatent.
impedancia *f.* impedance.
　impedancia acústica acoustic impedance.
impedimento *m.* handicap.
impenetrable *adj.* impervious.
imperativo, -va *adj.* imperative.
impercepción *f.* imperception.
imperforación *f.* imperforation.
imperforado, -da *adj.* imperforate.
imperioso, -sa *adj.* imperious.
impermeabilidad *f.* impermeability.
impermeable *adj.* impermeable.
impermeante *adj.* impermeant.
impersistencia *f.* impersistence.
　impersistencia motora motor impersistence.
impervio, -via *adj.* impervious.
impetiginización *f.* impetiginization.
impetiginoso, -sa *adj.* impetiginous.
impétigo *m.* impetigo.
　impétigo ampollar impetigo bullosa.
　impétigo ampollar del recién nacido bullous impetigo of the newborn.
　impétigo de Bockhart Bockhart's impetigo.
　impétigo bulloso impetigo bullosa.
　impétigo circinado impetigo circinata.
　impétigo contagioso impetigo contagiosa.
　impétigo contagioso bulloso impetigo contagiosa bullosa.
　impétigo eccematodes, impétigo eccematoide impetigo eczematodes.

impétigo estafilocócico staphylococcal impetigo.

impétigo estreptocócico streptococcal impetigo.

impétigo folicular follicular impetigo.

impétigo herpetiforme impetigo herpetiformis.

impétigo neonatal impetigo neonatorum.

impétigo vulgar impetigo vulgaris impetigo.

ímpetu *m.* impetus.

implantación *f.* implantation.

implantación central central implantation.

implantación circunferencial circumferential implantation.

implantación cortical cortical implantation.

implantación dental dental implant.

implantación endometrial endometrial implant.

implantación endoósea endo-osseous implant.

implantación excéntrica eccentric implantation.

implantación hipodérmica hypodermic implantation.

implantación intersticial interstitial implantation.

implantación de nervio, implantación nerviosa nerve implantation.

implantación de pellet pellet implantation.

implantación perióstica periosteal implantation.

implantación subcutánea subcutaneous implantation.

implantación subperióstica subperiosteal implantation.

implantación superficial superficial implantation.

implantar *v.* implant.

implante *m.* implant.

implante de bolsa-gel bag-gel implant.

implante carcinomatoso carcinomatous implant.

implante de células cell implant.

implante coclear cochlear implant.

implante de cristalino lens implant.

implante dental dental implant.

implante de endodoncia endodontic implant.

implante endometrial endometrial implant.

implante endoóseo endo-osseous implant, endosseous implant.

implante endóstico endosteal implant.

implante hipodérmico hypodermic implant.

implante inflable inflatable implant.

implante intraocular intraocular implant.

implante intraóseo endosseous implant.

implante intramucoso intramucosal implant.

implante intraperióstico intraperiosteal implant.

implante magnético magnetic implant.

implante mucoso mucosal insert.

implante orbitario orbital implant.

implante osteointegrado osseointegrated implant.

implante peniano penile implant.

implante a perno pin implant.

implante en poste post implant.

implante submucoso submucosal implant.

implante subperióstico subperiosteal implant.

implante supraperióstico supraperiosteal implant.

implante de tejidos tissue implant.

implante triplante triplant.

implantodoncia *f.* implantodontics.

implantodoncista *m., f.* implantodontist.

implantodontología *f.* implantodontology.

implantología *f.* implantology.

implantología dental, implantología oral dental implantology, oral implantology.

implantólogo, -ga *m., f.* implantologist.

implosión *f.* implosion.

impotencia *f.* impotence, impotency, impotentia.

impotencia aprendida learned impotence.

impotencia atónica atonic impotence, neurogenic impotence.

impotentia coeundi impotence, impotency.

impimpotentiaotentia erigendi impotence, impotency.

impotencia funcional functional impotence.

impotencia hormonal hormonal impotence.

impotencia medicamentosa medicamentous impotence.

impotencia neurológica neurogenic impotence.

impotencia psicógena psychogenic impotence.

impotencia vasculogénica vasculogenic impotence.

impotencia venosa venous impotence.

impotentia *f.* impotence, impotency, impotentia.

impregnación *f.* impregnation.

impregnar *v.* impregnate.

impresión *f.* impression, impressio.

impresión anatómica anatomic impression.

impresión angular para el ganglio de Gasser trigeminal impression of the temporal bone.

impresión basilar basilar impression.

impresión cardiaca cardiac impression.

impresión cardiaca del hígado cardiac impression of the liver, impressio cardiaca hepatis.

impresión cardiaca del pulmón cardiac impression of the lung, impressio cardiaca pulmonis.

impresión cólica, impresión cólica del hígado colic impression, colic impression of the liver, impressio colica, impressio colica hepatis.

impresión deltoidea, impresión deltoidea del húmero deltoid impression, deltoid impression of the humerus.

impresión de dentadura completa o total complete denture impression.

impresión definitiva final impression.

impresión de dentadura parcial partial denture impression.

impresión dental dental impression.

impresión digástrica digastric impression.

impresión digital fingerprint.

impresión digitada, impresión digital digital impression, digitate impression.

impresión duodenal, impresión duodenal del hígado duodenal impression, duodenal impression of the liver, impressio duodenalis, impressio duodenalis hepatis.

impresión esofágica, impresión esofágica del hígado esophageal impression, esophageal impression of the liver, impressio esophagea, impressio esophagea hepatis.

impresión final final impression.

impresión de fisura paladar cleft palate impression.

impresión gástrica gastric impression, impressio gastrica.

impresión gástrica del hígado gastric impression of the liver, impressio gastrica hepatis.

impresión gástrica del riñón impressio gastrica renis.

impresiones gyrorum gyrate impression, impressiones gyrorum.

impresión hepática, impresión hepática del riñón renal impression of the liver, impressio hepatica renis.

impresión hidrocoloide hydrocolloid impression.

impresión de huellas digitales thumbprinting.

impresión inferior lower impression.

impresión del ligamento costoclavicular impression for costoclavicular ligament, impressio ligamenti costoclavicularis.

impresión del maxilar inferior mandibular impression.

impresión maxilar superior maxillary impression.

impresión mental mental impression.

impresión muscular renal impressio muscularis renis.

impresión ósea directa direct bone impression.

impresión de paladar hendido cleft palate impression.

impresión petrosa, impresión petrosa del palio petrosal impression of the pallium, impressio petrosa pallii.

impresión preliminar preliminary impression.

impresión primaria primary impression.

impresión para prótesis parcial partial denture impression.

impresión para prótesis completa o total complete denture impression.

impresión de puente bridge impression.

impresión renal, impresión renal del hígado renal impression, renal impression of the liver, impressio renalis, impressio renalis hepatis.

impresión romboidea, impresión romboidea de la clavícula rhomboid impression, rhomboid impression of the clavicle.

impresión seccional sectional impression.

impresión secundaria secondary impression.

impresión superior upper impression.

impresión suprarrenal, impresión suprarrenal del hígado suprarenal impression, suprarenal impression of the liver, impressio suprarenalis, impressio suprarenalis hepatis.

impresión trigémina, impresión trigémina del hueso temporal trigeminal impression, trigeminal impression of the temporal bone, impressio trigeminalis, impressio trigeminalis ossis temporalis, impressio trigemini ossis temporalis.

imprimación *f.* imprinting.

imprimador *m.* primer.

imprimador de cavidad cavity primer.

impronta[1] *f.* imprinting.

impronta[2] *f.* imprint.

impúber *adj.* impuberal.

impulsión[1] *f.* driving.

impulsión fótica photic driving.

impulsión[2] *f.* impulsion.

impulsividad *f.* impulsivity, impulsiveness.

impulsivo, -va *adj.* impulsive.

impulso[1] *m.* drive.

impulso adquirido acquired drive.

impulso agresivo aggressive drive.

impulso aprendido learned drive.

impulso exploratorio exploratory drive.

impulso fisiológico physiological drive.

impulso meiótico meiotic drive.

impulso primario primary drive.

impulso secundario secondary drive.

impulso sexual sexual drive.
impulso[2] *m.* impulse.
impulso apical apex impulse, apical impulse.
impulso cardíaco cardiac impulse.
impulso cinético kinetic impulse.
impulso ectópico ectopic impulse.
impulso epiesternal epiesternal impulse.
impulso de escape escape impulse.
impulso irresistible irresistible impulse.
impulso morboso morbid impulse.
impulso nervioso nerve impulse.
impulso neural neural impulse.
impulso paraesternal derecho right parasternal impulse.
impulso paraesternal izquierdo left parasternal impulse.
impulso prematuro premature impulse.
impulsor cardíaco neumático *m.* pneumatic heart driver.
imu *f.* imu.
in articulo mortis in articulo mortis.
in extremis in extremis.
in loco parentis in loco parentis.
in situ in situ.
in utero in utero.
in vacuo in vacuo.
in vitro in vitro.
in vivo in vivo.
inacción *f.* inaction.
inacidez *f.* inacidity.
inactivación *f.* inactivation.
inactivación por calor heat inactivation.
inactivación del complemento, inactivación del suero complement inactivation, inactivation of complement.
inactivación X X inactivation.
inactivador *m.* inactivator.
inactivar *v.* inactivate.
inadaptación *f.* maladjustment.
inadaptación social social maladjustment.
inaglutinable *adj.* inagglutinable.
inanición[1] *f.* inanition.
inanición[2] *f.* starvation.
inanimado, -da *adj.* inanimate.
inaparente *adj.* inapparent.
inapetencia *f.* inappetence.
inarticulado, -da *adj.* inarticulate.
inasimilable *adj.* inassimilable.
inatención *f.* inattention.
inatención selectiva selective inattention.
inatención sensitiva sensory inattention.
inatención visual visual inattention.
inaxón *m.* inaxon.
inazotizado, -da *adj.* unazotized.
incandescencia *f.* incandescence, incandescency.
incasdescente *adj.* incandescent.
incapacidad *f.* disability.
incapacidad del desarrollo developmental disability.
incapacidad para mantener la ventilación espontánea disability to sustain spontaneous ventilation.
incapacidad mental mental disability.
incarceración *f.* incarceration.
incarcerado, -da *adj.* incarcerated.
incarnativo, -va *adj.* incarnative.
incendiarismo *m.* incendiarism.
incentivo *m.* incentive.
incertae sedis incertae sedis.
incesto *m.* incest.
incestuoso, -sa *adj.* incestuous.
incicloducción *f.* incycloduction.
incicloforia *f.* incyclophoria.
inciclotropía *f.* incyclotropia.

incidencia *f.* incidence.
incidente *adj.* incident.
incidir *v.* incise.
incineración *f.* incineration.
incipiente *adj.* incipient.
incisal *adj.* incisal.
incisión *f.* incision.
incisión abdominal transversa transverse abdominal incision.
incisión de Agnew-Verhoeff Agnew-Verhoeff incision.
incisión de alivio relief incision.
incisión en asa de cubo bucket-handle incision.
incisión de Battle Battle's incision.
incisión de Battle-Jalaguier-Kammerer Battle-Jalaguier-Kammerer incision.
incisión de Bevan Bevan's incision.
incisión en cabrio chevron incision.
incisión de celiotomía celiotomy incision.
incisión de Cherney Cherney incision.
incisión de Deaver Deaver's incision.
incisión de Dührssen Dührssen's incision.
incisión endaural endaural incision.
incisión de Fergusson Fergusson's incision.
incisión del flanco flank incision.
incisión de Kammerer-Battle Kammerer-Battle incision.
incisión de Kocher Kocher's incision.
incisión de Maylard Maylard incision.
incisión de McBurney McBurney's incision.
incisión de Munro-Kerr Munro-Kerr incision.
incisión de Nagamatsu Nagamatsu incision.
incisión paramedia, paramediana paramedian incision.
incisión paravaginal paravaginal incision.
incisión de Pfannenstiel Pfannenstiel's incision.
incisión de Rockey-Davis Rockey-Davis incision.
incisión de Schuchardt Schuchardt's incision.
incisión de Warren Warren's incision.
incisivo *m.* incisor.
incisivo en ala winged incisor.
incisivo central central incisor.
incisivo en forma de ala shovel-shaped incisor.
incisivo de Hutchinson Hutchinson's incisor.
incisivo lateral lateral incisor.
incisivo medial medial incisor.
incisivo primero first incisor.
incisivo segundo second incisor.
incisivo, -va *adj.* incisive.
incisolabial *adj.* incisolabial.
incisolingual *adj.* incisolingual.
incisoproximal *adj.* incisoproximal.
incisor *adj.* incisor.
incisura *f.* incisure, incisura.
incitante *adj.* incitant.
incitograma *m.* incitogram.
inclinación *f.* inclination, incline, slant, inclinatio.
inclinación condílea lateral lateral condylar inclination.
inclinación dental dental inclination.
inclinación de guía condílea condylar guidance inclination, condylar guide inclination.
inclinación lingual lingual inclination.
inclinación pélvica, inclinación de la pelvis pelvic inclination, inclination of the pelvis, pelvic incline, incline of the pelvis, inclinatio pelvis.
inclinación del plano oclusal slant of the occlusal plane.

inclinación de los prismas del esmalte enamel rod inclination.
inclinómetro *m.* inclinometer.
inclusión *f.* inclusion.
inclusión celular cell inclusion.
inclusión de Döhle Döhle inclusion.
inclusión dental dental inclusion.
inclusión fetal fetal inclusion.
inclusión de Guarnieri Guarnieri's inclusion.
inclusión intranuclear intranuclear inclusion.
inclusión leucocitaria, inclusión leucocítica leukocyte inclusion.
inclusión nuclear nuclear inclusion.
inclusión de Walthard Walthard's inclusion.
incoagulabilidad *f.* incoagulability.
incoagulable *adj.* incoagulable.
incoercible *adj.* incoercible.
incoestapedio, -dia *adj.* incostapedial.
incoherencia *f.* incoherence.
incoherente *adj.* incoherent.
incompatibilidad *f.* incompatibility.
incompatibilidad fisiológica physiologic incompatibility.
incompatibilidad HLA HLA mismatching.
incompatibilidad Rh Rh incompatibility.
incompatibilidad química chemical incompatibility.
incompatibilidad terapéutica therapeutic incompatibility.
incompatible *adj.* incompatible.
incompetencia *f.* incompetence, incompetency.
incompetencia aórtica aortic incompetence.
incompetencia cardíaca cardiac incompetence.
incompetencia mitral mitral incompetence.
incompetencia muscular muscular incompetence.
incompetencia pilórica pyloric incompetence.
incompetencia pulmonar pulmonary incompetence, pulmonic incompetence.
incompetencia tricúspidea tricuspid incompetence.
incompetencia valvular valvular incompetence.
incompetente *adj.* incompetent.
incomplementado, -da *adj.* uncomplemented.
inconsciencia *f.* unconsciousness.
inconsciente *m.* unconscious.
inconsciente colectivo collective unconscious.
inconsciente familiar familial unconscious.
inconsciente individual individual unconscious.
inconsciente irreflexivo irreflective unconscious.
inconsciente mnémico mnemic unconscious.
inconsciente personal personal unconscious.
inconsciente racial racial unconscious.
inconsciente reprimido repressed unconscious.
inconsciente subliminal subliminal unconscious.
inconsciente vital vital unconscious.
inconstante *adj.* inconstant.
incontinencia *f.* incontinence, incontinentia.
incontinencia activa active incontinence.
incontinencia afectiva affective incontinence.
incontinencia alva incontinentia alvi.
incontinencia anal anal incontinence.
incontinencia continua continuous incontinence.
incontinencia de esfuerzo stress incontinence.

incontinencia de excremento incontinence of the feces.

incontinencia fecal fecal incontinence.

incontinencia de orina de esfuerzo genuina stress urinary incontinence.

incontinencia de orina por rebosamiento overflow incontinence.

incontinencia paradójica paradoxical incontinence.

incontinencia paralítica paralytic incontinence.

incontinencia pigmentaria, incontinencia de pigmento, incontinentia pigmenti incontinence of pigment, incontinentia pigmenti.

incontinencia pigmentaria acrómica incontinentia pigmenti achromians.

incontinencia pigmentaria de Bloch-Sulzberger Bloch-Sulzberger incontinentia pigmenti.

incontinencia pigmentaria de Naegeli Naegeli's incontinentia pigmenti.

incontinencia rebosamiento overflow incontinence.

incontinencia rectal rectal incontinence.

incontinencia por tensión stress incontinence.

incontinencia con urgencia miccional urge incontinence, urgency incontinence.

incontinencia urinaria urinary incontinence, incontinence of urine, incontinentia urinae.

incontinencia urinaria por esfuerzo urinary exertional incontinence.

incontinencia urinaria por estrés urinary stress incontinence.

incontinente *adj.* incontinent.

incontinentia *f.* incontinentia.

incoordinación *f.* incoordination.

incoordinación cricofaríngea cricopharyngeal incoordination.

incoosificado, -da *adj.* unco-ossified.

incorporación *f.* incorporation.

incostración *f.* incrustation.

incremento *m.* increment.

increscencia *f.* ingrowth.

increscencia epitelial epithelial ingrowth.

incretodiagnóstico *m.* incretodiagnosis.

incretógeno, -na *adj.* incretogenous.

incretología *f.* incretology.

incretopatía *f.* incretopathy.

incretoterapia *f.* incretotherapy.

incruento, -ta *adj.* bloodless.

incrustación[1] *f.* incrustation.

incrustación[2] *f.* inlay.

incrustación de cera wax inlay.

incrustación epitelial epithelial inlay.

incrustación de oro gold inlay.

incrustación de porcelana porcelain inlay.

incubación *f.* incubation.

incubado *m.* incubate.

incubadora *f.* incubator.

incubadora de aislamiento isolation incubator.

íncubo *m.* incubus.

incubus *m.* incubus.

incudal *adj.* incudal.

incudectomía *f.* incudectomy.

incúdeo, -a *adj.* incudal.

incudiforme *adj.* incudiform.

Incudoestapedio, -dia *adj.* incudostapedial.

incudomaleolar *adj.* incudomalleal.

incudostapedio, -dia *adj.* incudostapedial.

incumplimiento *m.* non-compliance.

incurable *adj.* incurable.

incus *m.* incus.

inchacao *m.* inchacao.

indagación *f.* ascertainment.

indagación completa complete ascertainment.

indagación truncada truncate ascertainment.

indagación única single ascertainment.

indefensión aprendida *f.* learned helplessness.

indenización *f.* indenization.

indentación *f.* indentation.

indentación escleral scleral indentation.

independencia *f.* independence.

independencia profesional professional independence.

index index.

indicación *f.* indication, indicatio.

indicación causal indicatio causalis.

indicación curativa indicatio curativa.

indicación mórbida indicatio morbi.

indicación morbosa indicatio morbi.

indicación operatoria indication for surgery.

indicación quirúrgica indication for surgery.

indicación sintomática indicatio symptomatica.

indicador, -ra *m. y adj.* indicator.

indicador de alizarina alizarin indicator.

indicador anaerobio anaerobic indicator.

indicador de Andrade Andrade's indicator.

indicador de oxidación-reducción oxidation-reduction indicator.

indicador químico chemical indicator.

indicador radiactivo radioactive indicator.

indicador redox redox indicator.

indicador de Schneider Schneider's indicator.

indicador de temperatura de condensación dew point indicator.

indicán *m.* indican.

indicán metabólico metabolic indican.

indicanemia *f.* indicanemia.

indicanhidrosis *f.* indicanidrosis.

indicanidrosis *f.* indicanidrosis.

indicánmetro *m.* indicanmeter.

indicano *m.* indican.

indicanorraquia *f.* indicanorachia.

indicante *m. y adj.* indicant.

indicanuria *f.* indicanuria.

índice *m.* rate, index.

índice de abortos abortion rate.

índice de absorbancia absorbancy index.

índice de absorbancia molar molar absorbancy index.

índice ACH ACH index.

índice de altura height index, altitudinal index.

índice de altura-largo height-length index.

índice alveolar alveolar index.

índice anestésico anesthetic index.

índice de antebrazo y mano forearm-hand index.

índice antitrípico antitryptic index.

índice de Apgar Apgar index.

índice de Arneth Arneth index.

índice de ataque attack rate.

índice de ataque secundario secondary attack rate.

índice auricular auricular index.

índice auriculoparietal auriculoparietal index.

índice auriculovertical auriculovertical index.

índice bárico baric index.

índice de Barthel (IB) Barthel index (BI).

índice basilar basilar index.

índice de Becker-Lennhoff Becker-Lennhoff index.

índice de Bödecker Bödecker index.

índice de Bouchard Bouchard's index.

índice braquial braquial index.

índice de Brugsch Brugsch's index.

índice bruto crude rate.

índice buffer buffer index.

índice cálcico, de calcio calcium index.

índice de calidad de vida quality of life index.

índice cardíaco cardiac index.

índice cardíaco fetal basal baseline fetal heart index.

índice cardiotorácico cardiothoracic index.

índice de caries en raíces root caries index.

índice cariopicnótico karyopyknotic index.

índice carioplásmico karyoplasmic rate.

índice de casos case rate.

índice de casos fatales case fatality rate, fatality rate.

índice de casos de mortalidad case fatality rate.

índice cefálico, index cefálico cephalic index.

índice cefaloespinal cephalospinal index.

índice cefaloorbitario cephalo-orbital index.

índice cefalorraquídeo cephalorachidian index.

índice centromérico centromeric index.

índice cerebral cerebral index.

índice cerebrospinal cerebrospinal index.

índice cigomaticoauricular zygomaticoauricular index.

índice del color (IC) color index (CI).

índice colorimétrico color index (CI).

índice de comprensión de los sentimientos empathy index.

índice de concordancia concordance rate.

índice coronofrontal corofrontal index.

índice de corrección adjusted rate.

índice de corte shear rate.

índice craneal cranial index.

índice de crecimiento growth rate.

índice crítico critical rate.

índice DEF, índice def de caries, índice DEF de caries def caries index, DEF caries index, DEF rate.

índice degenerativo degenerative index.

índice dental, índice dentario, index dental dental index.

índice dental de Flower Flower's dental index.

índice de depuración metabólica de los esteroides steroid metabolic clearance rate (MCR).

índice DF, índice df de caries, índice DF de caries df caries index, DF caries index.

índice DMF, índice dmf de caries, índice DMF de caries dmf caries index, DMF caries index, DMF rate.

índice DMS, índice dmfs de caries, índice DMFS de caries dmfs caries index, DMFS caries index.

índice de dosis dose rate.

índice efectivo de temperatura effective temperature index.

índice de empatía, índice empático empathic index, empathy index.

índice endémico endemic index.

índice de enfermedad sickness rate.

índice de enfermedad periodontal periodontal disease index, (PDI).

índice eritrocitario erythrocyte index, red cell index.

índice eritrocítico erythrocyte index, red cell index.

índice de eritrosedimentación erythrocyte sedimentation rate (ESR).

índice específico specific rate.

índice esplénico spleen index, splenic index.

índice esplenométrico splenometric index.

índice de esporozoítos sporozoite rate.

índice estafiloopsónico staphylo-opsonic index.

índice estandarizado standarized rate.

índice de excreción de urea urea excretion rate.

índice de exposición a las irradiaciones output exposure rate.

índice facial facial index.

índice fagocitario, i fagocítico phagocytic index.

índice femorohumeral femorohumeral index.

índice de filtración glomerular (GFR) glomerular filtration rate (GFR).

índice fisiognomónico de la parte superior de la cara physiognomonic upper face index.

índice de Flower Flower's index.

índice de flujo de micción voiding flow index.

índice de fluorosis de Dean Dean's fluorosis index.

índice de frío del aire wind chill index.

índice gingival gingival index.

índice gingivo-periodontal gingival-periodontal index.

índice gnático gnathic index.

índice de hábito habitus index.

índice de hematíes red cell index.

índice hematopneico hematopneic index.

índice hemorrenal hemorenal index.

índice hemorrenal de sal hemorenal salt index.

índice de higiene oral oral hygiene index.

índice de higiene oral simplificado simplified oral hygiene index.

índice ictérico, índice de icterus icteric index, jaundice index, icterus index.

índice de incremento corto de la sensibilidad short increment sensitivity index (SISI).

índice de incidencia incidence rate.

índice inferior de pierna y pie lower leg-foot index.

índice de Kaup Kaup index.

índice largo-altura length-height index.

índice largo-ancho length-breadth index.

índice de Lennhoff Lennhoff's index.

índice de letalidad lethality rate.

índice leucopénico leukopenic index.

índice de longitud y altura length-height index.

índice entre longitud y anchura length-breadth index.

índice de maduración maturation index.

índice de la mano hand index.

índice de masa corporal body mass index.

índice maxiloalveolar maxilloalveolar index.

índice mendeliano Mendelian rate.

índice metabólico metabolic rate.

índice metabólico basal basal metabolic rate (BMR).

índice metacarpiano metacarpal index.

índice mitótico mitotic index.

índice de morbilidad morbidity rate.

índice de morbilidad estandarizada (SMR) standarized morbidity rate (SMR).

índice de mortalidad mortality rate.

índice de mortalidad infantil infant mortality rate.

índice de mortalidad materna maternal mortality rate.

índice de mortalidad neonatal neonatal mortality rate.

índice de mortalidad perinatal perinatal mortality rate, postnatal mortality rate.

índice de mortalidad proporcionada (PMR) proportionate mortality rate (PMR).

índice de mortalidad puerperal, index de mortalidad puerperal puerperal mortality rate.

índice de mortinatos stillbirth rate.

índice de muertes death rate.

índice de muertes fetales fetal death rate.

índice de muerte materna maternal death rate.

índice de mutación mutation rate.

índice nasal nasal index.

índice de natalidad birth rate.

índice nucleocitoplásmico nucleocytoplasmic index.

índice nucleoplásmico nucleoplasmic index.

índice nutritivo nutritive rate.

índice de obesidad obesity index.

índice de oocistos oocyst rate.

índice opsónico opsonic index.

índice orbitario (de Broca) orbital index (of Broca).

índice orbitonasal orbitonasal index.

índice palatino palatal index, palatine index.

índice palatomaxilar palatomaxillary index.

índice parasitario parasite index.

índice de pelo hair index.

índice pélvico pelvic index.

índice periodontal periodontal index.

índice de Pirquet Pirquet's index.

índice de placa plaque index.

índice PMA PMA index.

índice ponderal ponderal index.

índice de presión-volumen pressure-volume index.

índice de prevalencia prevalence rate.

índice de producción de esteroides steroid production index.

índice de pulso pulse index.

índice de Quetelet Quetelet's index.

índice quimioterapéutico chemotherapeutic index.

índice radiohumeral radiohumeral index.

índice de refracción refraction index, refractive index.

índice de Reid Reid index.

índice de repetición repetition index.

índice respiratorio respiration index.

índice de retraso holdaway.

índice de Robinson Robinson index.

índice de Röhrer Röhrer's index.

índice del sacro sacral index.

índice de saturación saturation index.

índice de saturación de la hemoglobina saturation index of hemoglobin.

índice de Schilling Schilling's index.

índice secretorio de esteroides steroid secretory index.

índice de sedimentación sedimentation index.

índice de sedimentación de eritrocitos, índice de sedimentación eritrocítica (ESR) erythrocyte sedimentation rate (ESR).

índice de sedimentación zeta (ZSR) zeta sedimentation rate (ZSR).

índice sexual sex rate.

índice de shock shock index.

índice de superficie de cálculos Calculus Surface index.

índice de supervivencia a cinco años five-year survival rate.

índice de temperatura efectiva effective temperature index.

índice terapéutico therapeutic index.

índice tibiofemoral tibiofemoral index.

índice tibiorradial tibioradial index.

índice de Tiffeneau Tiffeneau's index.

índice de tiroxina libre free thyroxine index.

índice torácico, index torácico thoracic index.

índice torácico de Fourmentin Fourmentin's thoracic index.

índice de torsión slew index.

índice de trabajo sistólico stroke work index.

índice transversovertical transversovertical index.

índice del tronco trunk index.

índice tuberculoopsónico tuberculo-opsonic index.

índice uricolítico uricolytic index.

índice vertical vertical index.

índice vital vital index.

índice de volumen volume index.

índice de volumen sistólico stroke volume index.

índice yuxtaglomerular juxtaglomerular index.

indicofosia *f.* indicophose.

indiferencia *f.* indifference.

indiferencia afectiva affective flattening.

indiferencia atencional attentional indifference.

indiferencia bella belle indifference.

indiferenciación *f.* indifferentiation.

indiferenciado, -da *adj.* undifferentiated.

indígena *m., f. y adj.* indigenous.

indigencia *f.* indigence.

indigencia médica medical indigence.

indigerible *adj.* indigestible.

indigestión *f.* indigestion.

indigestión ácida acid indigestion.

indigestión de azúcares sugar indigestion.

indigestión gástrica gastric indigestion.

indigestión grasa fat indigestion.

indigestión intestinal intestinal indigestion.

indigestión nerviosa nervous indigestion.

indigitación *f.* indigitation.

índigo *m.* indigo.

indigógeno *m.* indigogen.

indigopurpurina *f.* indigopurpurine.

indigotina *f.* indigotin.

indigouria *f.* indigouria.

indiguria *f.* indiguria.

indirecto, -ta *adj.* indirect.

indirrubina *f.* indirubin.

indirrubinuria *f.* indirubinuria.

indiscriminado, -da *adj.* indiscriminate.

indisposición *f.* indisposition.

indiversión *f.* indiversion.

individuación *f.* individuation.

individualidad *f.* individuality.

individualismo *m.* individualism.

individualización *f.* individuation.

individuo ciclotímico *m.* cyclothymic personality.

indol *m.* indole.

indolaceturia *f.* indolaceturia.

indolente *adj.* indolent.

indológeno, -na *adj.* indologenous.

indoloro, -ra *adj.* indolent.

indoluria *f.* indoluria.

indoxilemia *f.* indoxylemia.

indoxilo *m.* indoxyl.

indoxilsulfato *m.* indoxyl-sulfate.

indoxiluria *f.* indoxyluria.

inducción *f.* induction.

inducción de la anestesia induction of anesthesia.

inducción autónoma autonomous induction.
inducción complementaria complementary induction.
inducción electiva del parto elective induction of labor.
inducción electromagnética electromagnetic induction.
inducción enzimática enzyme induction.
inducción espinal spinal induction.
inducción lisogénica lysogenic induction.
inducción médica del parto medical induction of labor.
inducción del parto induction of labor.
inducción raquídea spinal induction.
inducción de Spemann Spemann's induction.
inducido, -da *adj.* induced.
inducir *v.* induce.
inductancia *f.* inductance.
inductor, -ra *m., f.* inductor.
inductor *m.* inductorium.
inductora *f.* inducer.
inductotermia *f.* inductothermy.
inductotermo *m.* inductotherm.
indulina *f.* indulin.
indulinófilo *m.* indulinophil, indulinophile.
indulinófilo, -la *adj.* indulinophilic.
induración *f.* induration.
induración carnosa brawny induration.
induración cianótica cyanotic induration.
induración fibroide fibrous induration.
induración de Froriep Froriep's induration.
induración granular, induración granulosa granular induration.
induración gris gray induration.
induración laminada, induración laminar laminate induration.
induración marrón del pulmón brown induration of the lung.
induración negra black induration.
induración en parche parchment induration.
induración parda brown induration.
induración del pene penile induration.
induración pigmentaria del pulmón pigment induration of the lung.
induración plástica, induración plástica del pene plastic induration.
induración roja red induration.
indurado, -da *adj.* indurated.
indurativo, -va *adj.* indurative.
inebriación *f.* inebriation.
inebriante *adj.* inebriant.
inebriativo, -va *adj.* inebriant.
inedia *f.* inedia.
inelástico, -ca *adj.* inelastic.
inemia *f.* inemia.
inercia *f.* inertia.
inercia del colon colonic inertia.
inercia inmunológica immunological inertia.
inercia magnética magnetic inertia.
inercia psíquica psychic inertia.
Inermicapsifer Inermicapsifer.
inerte *adj.* inert.
inervación *f.* innervation.
inervación doble double innervation.
inervación recíproca reciprocal innervation.
inespecífico, -ca *adj.* non-specific.
inestabilidad *f.* instability.
inestabilidad articular joint instability.
inestabilidad atencional attentional instability.
inestabilidad genética genetic instability.
inestabilidad tumoral tumor instability.
inestabilidad vertebral cervical vertebral cervical instability.

infancia *f.* babyhood, childhood, infancy.
infanticida *m., f.* infanticide.
infanticidio *m.* infanticide.
infantil *adj.* infantile.
infantilismo *m.* infantilism.
infantilismo de Brissaud Brissaud's infantilism.
infantilismo caquéctico cachectic infantilism.
infantilismo celíaco celiac infantilism.
infantilismo distiroideo, infantilismo distiróidico dysthyroidal infantilism.
infantilismo estático static infantilism.
infantilismo hepático hepatic infantilism.
infantilismo de Herter Herter's infantilism.
infantilismo hipofisario hypophyseal infantilism, pituitary infantilism.
infantilismo hipotiroideo hypothyroid infantilism.
infantilismo idiopático idiopathic infantilism.
infantilismo intestinal intestinal infantilism.
infantilismo de Lévi-Lorain Lévi-Lorain infantilism.
infantilismo linfático lymphatic infantilism.
infantilismo de Lorain Lorain's infantilism.
infantilismo de Lorain-Lévi Lorain-Lévi infantilism.
infantilismo mixedematoso myxedematous infantilism.
infantilismo pancreático pancreatic infantilism.
infantilismo parcial partial infantilism.
infantilismo pituitario pituitary infantilism.
infantilismo proporcionado proportionate infantilism.
infantilismo regresivo regressive infantilism.
infantilismo renal renal infantilism.
infantilismo reversivo regressive infantilism.
infantilismo del sexo, infantilismo sexual sexual infantilism.
infantilismo sintomático symptomatic infantilism.
infantilismo tardío regressive infantilism.
infantilismo universal universal infantilism.
infartectomía *f.* infarctectomy.
infarto *m.* infarct, infarction.
infarto de ácido úrico uric acid infarct.
infarto agudo de miocardio (IAM) acute myocardial infarction (AMI).
infarto anémico anemic infarct.
infarto anterior del miocardio anterior myocardial infarction.
infarto anteroinferior del miocardio anteroinferior myocardial infarction.
infarto anterolateral del miocardio anterolateral myocardial infarction.
infarto anteroseptal del miocardio anteroseptal myocardial infarction.
infarto auricular atrial infarction.
infarto de bilirrubina bilirubin infarct.
infarto blanco white infarct.
infarto blando bland infarct.
infarto de Brewer Brewer's infarct.
infarto calcáreo calcareous infarct.
infarto cardiaco cardiac infarction.
infarto cerebral cerebral infarction.
infarto del cuero cabelludo scalp infarct.
infarto diafragmático del miocardio diaphragmatic myocardial infarction.
infarto embólico embolic infarct.
infarto hemorrágico hemorrhagic infarct.
infarto hepático hepatic infarction, liver infarction.
infarto inferior del miocardio inferior myocardial infarction.

infarto inferolateral del miocardio inferolateral myocardial infarction.
infarto intestinal intestinal infarction.
infarto lacunar lacunar infarction.
infarto lateral del miocardio lateral myocardial infarction.
infarto del lóbulo anterior de la hipófisis anterior pituitary lobe infarction.
infarto mesentérico mesenteric infarction.
infarto a través del miocardio through-and-through myocardial infarction.
infarto del miocardio (IM) myocardial infarction (MI).
infarto del miocardio en forma de H myocardial infarction in H-form.
infarto no transmural del miocardio nontransmural myocardial infarction.
infarto óseo bone infarct.
infarto pálido pale infarct.
infarto posterior del miocardio posterior myocardial infarction.
infarto pulmonar (IP) pulmonary infarction (PI).
infarto quístico cystic infarct.
infarto renal renal infarction.
infarto rojo red infarct.
infarto septal del miocardio septal myocardial infarction.
infarto séptico septic infarct.
infarto silencioso del miocardio silent myocardial infarction.
infarto subendocárdico, infarto subendocárdico del miocardio subendocardial infarction, subendocardial myocardial infarction.
infarto transmural, infarto transmural del miocardio transmural infarction, transmural myocardial infarction.
infarto trombótico thrombotic infarct.
infarto en vertiente watershed infarction.
infarto de Zahn Zahn's infarct.
infausto, -ta *adj.* infaust.
infección *f.* infection.
infección adquirida en el hospital hospital-acquired infection.
infección aérea airborne infection.
infección aerógena aerogenous infection.
infección agonal, infección agónica agonal infection.
infección por anaerobios anaerobic infection.
infección apical apical infection.
infección colonizadora colonization infection.
infección concurrente concurrent infection.
infección criptógena, infección criptogénica, criptogenética cryptogenic infection.
Infección cruzada cross infection.
infección de las derivaciones de LCR LCR shunts infection.
infección ectógena ectogenous infection.
infección endógena endogenous infection.
infección epidural epidural infection.
infección estafilocócica staphylococcal infection.
infección estreptocócica streptococcal infection.
infección exógena exogenous infection.
infección extracraneal extracanial infection.
infección extradural extradural infection.
infección extrahospitalaria community-acquired infection.
infección focal focal infection.
infección fúngica fungal infection.
infección gastrointestinal gastrointestinal infection.

infección germinal germinal infection.
infección por gotillas droplet infection.
infección iatrogénica iatrogenic infection.
infección intestinal enteric infection.
infección intraventricular intraventicular infection.
infección latente latent infection.
infección leve low-grade infection.
infección local local infection.
infección masiva mass infection.
infección mixta mixed infection.
infección nosocomial nosocomial infection.
infección oportunista opportunistic infection.
infección periapical periapical infection.
infección piógena pyogenic infection.
infección polimicrobiana polymicrobic infection.
infección protozoaria protozoal infection.
infección psíquica psychic infection.
infección raquimedular spinal infection.
infección retrógrada retrograde infection.
infección secundaria secondary infection.
infección secundaria a esplenectomía infection following splenectomy.
infección sistémica systemic infection.
infección subaguda subacute infection.
infección subclínica subclinical infection.
infección subdural subdural infection.
infección terminal terminal infection.
infección del tracto respiratorio respiratory tract infection.
infección del tracto urinario (ITU) urinary tract infection (UTI).
infección transmitida por agua water-borne infection.
infección transmitida por el aire airborne infection.
infección transmitida por gotitas droplet infection.
infección transmitida por un vector vector-borne infection.
infección transportada por polvo dust-borne infection.
infección del trayecto del clavo pin track infection.
infección tripanosómica trypanosomal infection.
infección urinaria urinary infection.
infección urinaria complicada complicated urinary infection.
infección urinaria no complicada uncomplicated infection.
infección de las vías respiratorias superiores upper respiratory infection.
infección de Vincent Vincent's infection.
infección vírica viral infection.
infección yatrogénica iatrogenic infection.
infección zoonótica zoonotic infection.
infección-inmunidad *f.* infection-immunity.
infecciosidad *f.* infectiosity, infectiousness.
infeccioso, -sa *adj.* infectious.
infectable *adj.* infectible.
infectar *v.* infect.
infectividad *f.* infectivity.
infectivo, -va *adj.* infective.
inferencia arbitraria *f.* arbitrary inference.
inferente *adj.* inferent.
inferior *adj.* inferior.
inferioridad *f.* inferiority.
inferoexterno, -na *adj.* inferolateral.
inferointerno, -na *adj.* inferomedial.
inferolateral *adj.* inferolateral.
inferomedial *adj.* inferomedian.
inferomediano, -na *adj.* inferomedian.

inferonasal *adj.* inferonasal.
inferoposterior *adj.* inferoposterior.
inferotemporal *adj.* inferotemporal.
infertilidad *f.* infertility.
infertilidad primaria primary infertility.
infertilidad secundaria secondary infertility.
infestación *f.* infestation.
infestar *v.* infest.
infibulación *f.* infibulation.
infiltración *f.* infiltration.
infiltración adiposa adipose infiltration.
infiltración calcárea calcareous infiltration.
infiltración cálcica calcium infiltration.
infiltración celular cellular infiltration.
infiltración epituberculosa epituberculous infiltration.
infiltración gelatinosa gelatinous infiltration.
infiltración de glucógeno, infiltración glucogénica glycogen infiltration.
infiltración grasa fatty infiltration.
infiltración grasa del corazón fatty infiltration of the heart.
infiltración gris gray infiltration.
infiltración inflamatoria inflammatory infiltration.
infiltración linfocítica de la piel lymphocytic infiltration of the skin.
infiltración lipomatosa lipomatous infiltration.
infiltración de orina urinous infiltration.
infiltración paraneural paraneural infiltration.
infiltración perineural perineural infiltration.
infiltración sanguínea sanguineous infiltration.
infiltración serosa serous infiltration.
infiltración de los tejidos tissular infiltration.
infiltración tuberculosa tuberculous infiltration.
infiltración urinaria urinous infiltration.
infiltración urinosa urinous infiltration.
infiltrado *m.* infiltrate.
infiltrado de Assmann Assmann's tuberculous infiltrate.
infiltrado infraclavicular infraclavicular infiltrate.
infiltrado tuberculoso de Assmann Assmann's tuberculous infiltrate.
infiltrar *v.* infiltrate.
infinito *m.* infinity.
infirme *adj.* infirm.
inflación *f.* inflation.
inflador *m.* inflator.
inflamación *f.* inflammation.
inflamación adherente adhesive inflammation.
inflamación adhesiva adhesive inflammation.
inflamación aguda acute inflammation.
inflamación alérgica allergic inflammation.
inflamación alterante alterative inflammation.
inflamación atrófica atrophic inflammation.
inflamación bacteriana bacterial inflammation.
inflamación catarral catarrhal inflammation.
inflamación cirrótica cirrhotic inflammation.
inflamación crónica chronic inflammation.
inflamación crupal croupous inflammation.
inflamación cruposa croupous inflammation.
inflamación degenerativa degenerative inflammation.

inflamación difusa diffuse inflammation.
inflamación diseminada disseminated inflammation.
inflamación esclerosante sclerosing inflammation.
inflamación específica specific inflammation.
inflamación exudativa exudative inflammation.
inflamación fibrinosa fibrinous inflammation.
inflamación fibrinopurulenta fibrinopurulent inflammation.
inflamación fibroide fibroid inflammation, fibrosing inflammation.
inflamación focal focal inflammation.
inflamación granulomatosa granulomatous inflammation.
inflamación del hígado inflammation of the liver.
inflamación hiperplásica, inflamación hiperplástica hyperplastic inflammation.
hipertrófica hypertrophic inflammation.
inflamación inmune immune inflammation.
inflamación intersticial interstitial inflammation.
inflamación metastásica, inflamación metastática metastatic inflammation.
inflamación necrosante necrotizing inflammation.
inflamación necrótica necrotic inflammation.
inflamación obliterante obliterative inflammation.
inflamación obliterativa obliterative inflammation.
inflamación parenquimatosa parenchymatous inflammation.
inflamación plásica, inflamación plástica plastic inflammation.
inflamación productiva productive inflammation.
inflamación proliferante proliferous inflammation.
inflamación proliferativa proliferative inflammation.
inflamación purulenta purulent inflammation.
inflamación reactiva reactive inflammation.
inflamación serofibrinosa serofibrinous inflammation.
inflamación seroplásica, inflamación seroplástica seroplastic inflammation.
inflamación serosa serous inflammation.
inflamación serótica serous inflammation.
inflamación seudomembranosa pseudomembranous inflammation.
inflamación simple simple inflammation.
inflamación subaguda subacute inflammation.
inflamación supurativa suppurative inflammation.
inflamación tóxica toxic inflammation.
inflamación traumática traumatic inflammation.
inflamación ulcerativa ulcerative inflammation.
inflamación ulcerosa ulcerative inflammation.
inflamágeno *m.* inflammagen.
inflamatorio, -ria *adj.* inflammatory.
inflexibilidad *f.* inflexibility.
inflexión *f.* inflection, inflexion.
influenza *f.* influenza.
influenza a influenza A.

influenza asiática Asian influenza.
influenza B influenza B.
influenza C influenza C.
influenza endémica endemic influenza.
influenza española Spanish influenza.
influenza de Hong Kong Hong Kong influenza.
influenza nostras influenza nostras.
influenza rusa Russian influenza.
influenzal *adj.* influenzal.
Influenzavirus Influenzavirus.
influido, -da por el sexo *adj.* sex-influenced.
informatividad *f.* informativeness.
informe *m.* report.
informe de alta discharge summary.
informe BEIR-III BEIR-III report.
informe de incidencias incident report.
informe radiológico radiological report.
informe Remmelink Remmelink report.
informe uniforme uniform reporting.
informe Warnock Warnock's report.
informosoma *m.* informosome.
infraamigdalino, -na *adj.* infratonsillar.
infraaxilar *adj.* infra-axillary.
infracardíaco, -ca *adj.* infracardiac.
infracción *f.* infraction.
infracción de Freiberg Freiberg's infraction.
infracerebral *adj.* infracerebral.
infraciliatura *f.* infraciliature.
infraclase *f.* infraclass.
infraclavicular *adj.* infraclavicular.
infraclusión *f.* infraclusion.
infraconstrictor, -ra *adj.* infraconstrictor.
infracortical *adj.* infracortical.
infracostal *adj.* infracostal.
infracotiloideo, -a *adj.* infracotyloid.
infracrestal *adj.* infracristal.
infractura *m.* infracture.
infradental *m.* infradentale.
infradiafragmático, -ca *adj.* infradiaphragmatic.
infradiano, -na *adj.* infradian.
infraducción *f.* infraduction.
infraescapular *adj.* infrascapular.
infraespinoso, -sa *adj.* infraspinous.
infraesplénico, -ca *adj.* infrasplenic.
infraesternal *adj.* infrasternal.
infraestructura *f.* infrastructure.
infraglenoideo, -a *adj.* infraglenoid.
infraglótico, -ca *adj.* infraglottic.
infrahepático, -ca *adj.* infrahepatic.
infrahioideo, -a *adj.* infrahyoid.
infrainguinal *adj.* infrainguinal.
inframamario, -ria *adj.* inframammary.
inframamilar *adj.* inframamillary.
inframandibular *adj.* inframandibular.
inframarginal *adj.* inframarginal.
inframaxilar *adj.* inframaxillary.
infranuclear *adj.* infranuclear.
infraoclusión *f.* infraocclusion.
infraorbital *adj.* infraorbital.
infraorbitario, -ria *adj.* infraorbital.
infrapatelar *adj.* infrapatellar.
infrapsíquico, -ca *adj.* infrapsychic.
infrarrojo, -ja *adj.* infrared.
infrarrojo cercano near infrared.
infrarrojo distante far infrared.
infrarrojo de onda corta short-wave infrared.
infrarrojo de onda larga long-wave infrared.
infrarrotuliano, -na *adj.* infrapatellar.
infrascapular *adj.* infrascapular.
infrasónico, -ca *adj.* infrasonic.
infrasonido *m.* infrasound.
infraspinoso, -sa *adj.* infraspinous.
infrasplénico, -ca *adj.* infrasplenic.

infrasternal *adj.* infrasternal.
infrasubespecífico, -ca *adj.* infrasubspecific.
infratemporal *adj.* infratemporal.
infratentorial *adj.* infratentorial.
infratonsilar *adj.* infratonsillar.
infratorácico, -ca *adj.* infrathoracic.
infratraqueal *adj.* infratracheal.
infratroclear *adj.* infratrochlear.
infratubárico, -ca *adj.* infratubal.
infraturbinal *adj.* infraturbinal.
infraumbilical *adj.* infraumbilical.
infravergencia *f.* infravergence.
infraversión *f.* infraversion.
infricción *f.* infriction.
infundibular *adj.* infundibular.
infundibulectomía *f.* infundibulectomy.
infundibulectomía de Brock Brock's infundibulectomy.
infundibuliforme *adj.* infundibuliform.
infundibulina *f.* infundibulin.
infundíbulo *m.* infundibulum.
infundibulofoliculitis *f.* infundibulofolliculitis.
infundibulofoliculitis diseminada recurrente disseminated recurrent infundibulofolliculitis.
infundiboloma *m.* infundibuloma.
infundibulopélvico, -ca *adj.* infundibulopelvic.
infundibulum infundibulum.
infundido, -da *adj.* infusate.
infusible *adj.* infusible.
infusión *f.* infusion.
infusión de carne meat infusion.
infusión endovenosa intravenous infusion.
infusión fría cold infusion.
infusión intersticial interstitial infusion.
infusión intraósea intraosseous infusion.
infusión intravenosa intravenous infusion.
infusión salina saline infusion.
infusión subcutánea subcutaneous infusion.
infusodecocción *f.* infusodecoction.
ingeniería *f.* engineering.
ingeniería biomédica biomedical engineering.
ingeniería dental dental engineering.
ingeniería genética genetic engineering.
ingeniería médica medical engineering.
ingénito, -ta *adj.* inborn.
ingesta *f.* intake, ingesta.
ingesta calórica caloric intake.
ingesta diaria permisible (IDP) acceptable daily intake (ADI).
ingesta de líquidos fluid intake.
ingesta de sal salt dietary intake.
ingestante *m.* ingestant.
ingestión *f.* ingestion.
ingestivo, -va *adj.* ingestive.
ingle *f.* groin, inguen.
ingravescente *adj.* ingravescent.
ingravidez *f.* weightlessness.
ingrediente *m.* ingredient.
ingreso *m.* intake.
inguinal *adj.* inguinal.
inguinoabdominal *adj.* inguinoabdominal.
inguinocrural *adj.* inguinocrural.
inguinodinia *f.* inguinodynia.
inguinoescrotal *adj.* inguinoscrotal.
inguinolabial *adj.* inguinolabial.
inguinoperitoneal *adj.* inguinoperitoneal.
inguinoscrotal *adj.* inguinoscrotal.
ingurgitación *f.* engorgement.
ingurgitado, -da *adj.* engorged.
inhalación *f.* inhalation.
inhalación de humo smoke inhalation.

inhalación de solventes solvent inhalation.
inhalación de sulfato de isoproterenol isoproterenol sulfate inhalation.
inhalador *m.* inhaler.
inhalador de dosis fija metered dose inhaler.
inhalador de éter ether inhaler.
inhalador H.H H.H. inhaler.
inhalante *m. y adj.* inhalant.
inhalante antiespumante antifoaming inhalant.
inhalar *v.* inhale.
inherente *adj.* inherent.
inhibición *f.* inhibition.
inhibición alogénica allogeneic inhibition, allogenic inhibition.
inhibición alostérica allosteric inhibition.
inhibición central central inhibition.
inhibición competitiva competitive inhibition.
inhibición de contacto contact inhibition.
inhibición enzimática inhibition of enzymes.
inhibición de hemaglutinación (IH, IHA) hemagglutination inhibition.
inhibición no competitiva non-competitive inhibition.
inhibición latente latent inhibition.
inhibición por potasio potassium inhibition.
inhibición de precipitación por hapteno hapten inhibition of precipitation.
inhibición proactiva proactive inhibition.
inhibición de producto terminal endproduct inhibition.
inhibición recíproca reciprocal inhibition.
inhibición refleja, inhibición de reflejos reflex inhibition, inhibition of the reflexes.
inhibición residual residual inhibition.
inhibición retroactiva retroactive inhibition.
inhibición de retroalimentación, inhibición por retroalimentación feedback inhibition.
inhibición selectiva selective inhibition.
inhibición social social inhibition.
inhibición suicida suicide inhibition.
inhibición de Wedensky Wedensky inhibition.
inhibidor *m.* inhibitor.
inhibidor del activador del plasminógeno-1 (PAI-1) plasminogen activator inhibitor (PAI-1).
inhibidor de alfa1 proteinasa humana human alpha1 proteinase inhibitor.
inhibidor de alpha1-tripsina alpha1-trypsin inhibitor.
inhibidor de la anhidrasa carbónica carbonic anhydrase inhibitor.
inhibidor del apetito appetite inhibitor.
inhibidor de C1 (C1 INH), inhibidor de C1 esterasa C1 inhibitor (C1 INH), C1 esterase inhibitor.
inhibidor de carbonato deshidratasa carbonate dehydratase inhibitor.
inhibidor del colesterol cholesterol inhibitor.
inhibidor de la colinesterasa cholinesterase inhibitor.
inhibidor competitivo competitive inhibitor.
inhibidor de la enzima de conversión angiotensin converting enzyme inhibitor (ACE).
inhibidor de la enzima de conversión de la angiotensina (ECA) angiotensin converting enzyme inhibitor (ACE).
inhibidor de la enzima convertidora de angiotensina angiotensin converting enzyme inhibitor (ACE).
inhibidor de la esterasa C1 C1 esterase inhibitor.

inhibidor mitótico mitotic inhibitor.
inhibidor de la monoaminaoxidasa, inhibidor de la monoaminooxidasa (IMAO) monoamine oxidase inhibitor (MAOI).
inhibidor no competitivo uncompetitive inhibitor.
inhibidor no reversible non-reversible inhibitor.
inhibidor residual residual inhibitor.
inhibidor de tripsina trypsin inhibitor.
inhibidor, -ra *adj.* inhibitive, inhibitory.
inhibina *f.* inhibin.
inhibir *v.* inhibit.
inhibitorio, -ria *adj.* inhibitory.
inhibítropo, -pa *adj.* inhibitrope.
inhomogeneidad *f.* inhomogeneity.
inhomogéneo, -a *adj.* inhomogeneous.
iniaco, -ca *adj.* iniac.
iniad iniad.
inial *adj.* inial.
iniciación *f.* initiation.
iniciador *m.* initiator.
inicial *adj.* initial.
inicio de la acción *m.* onset of action.
inidiación *f.* innidiation.
iniencefalia *f.* iniencephaly.
iniencéfalo *m.* iniencephalus.
inigurgitación *f.* engorgement.
iniodimo *m.* iniodymus.
inión *m.* inion.
iniópago *m.* iniopagus.
iniope *m.* iniops.
iniops *m.* iniops.
initis *f.* initis.
injertar *v.* graft.
injerto *m.* graft.
injerto en acordeón accordion graft.
injerto activado activated graft.
injerto adipodérmico adipodermal graft.
injerto adiposo fat graft.
injerto alogénico, injerto alógeno allogeneic graft.
injerto anastomosado anastomosed graft.
injerto animal animal graft.
injerto aponeurótico aponeurotic graft.
injerto arterial arterial graft.
injerto de aumento augmentation graft.
injerto autóctono autochthonous graft.
injerto autodérmico autodermic graft.
injerto autoepidérmico autoepidermic graft.
injerto autógeno autogenous graft.
injerto autólogo autologous graft.
injerto autoplástico autoplastic graft.
injerto avascular avascular graft.
injerto de Blair-Brown Blair-Brown graft.
injerto blanco white graft.
injerto brefoplástico brephoplastic graft.
injerto en cable cable graft.
injerto de cadáver cadaver graft.
injerto de cartílago cartilage graft.
injerto de columela columellar graft.
injerto compuesto compound graft, composite graft.
injerto corioalantoico chorioallantoic graft.
injerto corioalantoideo chorioallantoic graft.
injerto corneal corneal graft.
injerto costal rib graft.
injerto en criba sieve graft.
injerto en cubitos de cartílago diced cartilage graft.
injerto cutáneo skin graft.
injerto cutáneo parcial split-skin graft.
injerto cutáneo primario primary skin graft.
injerto de cutis cutis graft.
injerto de Davis Davis graft.

injerto dérmico dermal graft, dermic graft.
injerto dermoadiposo dermal-fat graft.
injerto dermograso dermal-fat graft.
injerto diferido delayed graft.
injerto directo onlay graft.
injerto de Douglas Douglas graft.
injerto epidérmico epidermic graft.
injerto epiploico, injerto epiplónico omental graft.
injerto de espesor completo full-thickness graft.
injerto de espesor dividido split-thickness graft.
injerto de espesor parcial partial-thickness graft.
injerto de espesor total full-thickness graft.
injerto de esponjosa spongeous graft.
injerto de Esser Esser graft.
injerto expansivo spreader graft.
injerto de fascia fascia graft.
injerto fascicular fascicular graft.
injerto funicular funicular graft.
injerto de grasa fat graft.
injerto H H graft.
injerto heterodérmico heterodermic graft.
injerto heteroespecífico heterospecific graft.
injerto heterólogo heterologous graft.
injerto heteroplástico heteroplastic graft.
injerto heterotópico heterotopic.
injerto hiperplásico, injerto hiperplástico hyperplastic graft.
injerto homólogo homologous graft.
injerto homoplástico homoplastic graft.
injerto de hueso bone graft.
injerto de implantación implantation graft.
injerto de incrustación inlay graft.
injerto de infusión infusion graft.
injerto interespecífico interspecific graft.
injerto isogeneico, injerto isogénico isogeneic graft.
injerto isólogo isologous graft.
injerto isoplástico isoplastic graft.
injerto de Krause, injerto de Krause-Wolfe Krause graft, Krause-Wolfe graft.
injerto laminar lamellar graft.
injerto libre free graft.
injerto en malla mesh graft.
injerto en manga sleeve graft.
injerto en manguito sleeve graft.
injerto mucoso mucosal graft.
injerto de nervio, injerto nervioso, injerto neural nerve graft.
injerto ortotópico orthotopic graft.
injerto óseo osseous graft.
injerto óseo sobrepuesto onlay bone graft.
injerto osteoarticular osteoarticular graft.
injerto osteocondral osteochondral graft.
injerto osteoperiostal, injerto osteoperióstico osteoperiosteal graft.
injerto osteoperióstico de Delagenière Delagenière's osteoperiostic graft.
injerto "outlay" outlay graft.
injerto en parche patch graft.
injerto parcial grueso thick-split graft.
injerto pediculado pedicle graft.
injerto de pelo hair graft, scalp graft.
injerto de pellizco pinch graft.
injerto penetrante penetrating graft.
injerto perióstico periosteal graft.
injerto de peroné fibula graft.
injerto de Phemister Phemister graft.
injerto de piel skin graft.
injerto de piel dividida split-skin graft.
injerto porcino porcine graft.
injerto en red mesh graft.

injerto de relleno filler graft.
injerto retrasado delayed graft.
injerto de Reverdin Reverdin graft.
injerto de revestimiento onlay graft.
injerto de sacabocados punch graft.
injerto saltón jump graft.
injerto en sello de correos postage stamp graft.
injerto singeneico, injerto singénico syngeneic graft.
injerto de Stent Stent graft.
injerto en tablero de ajedrez chessboard graft.
injerto tendinoso tendinous graft, tendon graft.
injerto de Thiersch Thiersch graft.
injerto en trocitos chip graft.
injerto en tubo tube graft.
injerto en túnel tunnel graft.
injerto vascularizado vascularized graft.
injerto de vena autóloga autologous venous graft.
injerto venoso venous graft.
injerto de Wolfe Wolfe's graft.
injerto de Wolfe-Krause Wolfe-Krause graft.
injerto xenogénico xenogeneic graft.
injerto zooplástico zooplastic graft.
injuria *f.* injury.
inlay *m.* inlay.
inmadurez *f.* immaturity.
inmadurez afectiva affective immaturity.
inmadurez psicomotriz psychomotor immaturity.
inmaduro, -ra *adj.* immature.
inmediato, -ta *adj.* immediate.
inmersión *f.* immersion.
inmersión en aceite oil immersion.
inmersión en agua water immersion.
inmersión homogénea homogeneous immersion.
inmiscible *adj.* immiscible.
inmitancia *f.* immitance.
inmortalización *f.* immortalization.
inmovilidad *f.* immobility.
inmovilización *f.* immobilization.
inmovilización con férula splinting.
inmovilizar *v.* immobilize.
inmune *adj.* immune.
inmunidad *f.* immunity.
inmunidad activa active immunity.
inmunidad activa artificial artificial active immunity.
inmunidad activa específica specific active immunity.
inmunidad adoptiva adoptive immunity.
inmunidad adquirida acquired immunity.
inmunidad antibacteriana antibacterial immunity.
inmunidad antitóxica antitoxic immunity.
inmunidad antiviral, inmunidad antivírica, inmunidad antivirósica antiviral immunity.
inmunidad a bacteriófagos bacteriophage immunity.
inmunidad bacteriolítica antibacterial immunity.
inmunidad celular cellular immunity.
inmunidad colectiva herd immunity.
inmunidad de comunidad community immunity.
inmunidad concomitante concomitant immunity.
inmunidad congénita congenital immunity.
inmunidad cruzada cross immunity.
inmunidad de especie species immunity.
inmunidad específica specific immunity.

inmunidad al *estrés* stress immunity.
inmunidad *familiar* familial immunity.
inmunidad *general* general immunity.
inmunidad *genética* genetic immunity.
inmunidad de *grupo* group immunity.
inmunidad *hereditaria* inherited immunity.
inmunidad *humoral* humoral immunity.
inmunidad *individual* individual immunity.
inmunidad *inespecífica* non-specific immunity.
inmunidad *inespecífica natural* natural non-specific immunity.
inmunidad a la *infección* infection immunity.
inmunidad *inherente* inherent immunity.
inmunidad *innata* innate immunity.
inmunidad *intrauterina* intrauterine immunity.
inmunidad *local* local immunity.
inmunidad *materna* maternal immunity.
inmunidad de *mediación celular, inmunidad mediada por células (IMC), inmunidad mediada por células T (IMCT)* cell-mediated immunity (CMI), T cell-mediated immunity (TCMI).
inmunidad *nativa* native immunity.
inmunidad *pasiva* passive immunity.
inmunidad *pasiva artificial* artificial passive immunity.
inmunidad *pasiva específica* specific passive immunity.
inmunidad *racial* racial immunity.
inmunidad de *rebaño* herd immunity.
inmunidad *relativa* relative immunity.
inmunidad *tisular* tissue immunity.
inmunisina *f.* immunisin.
inmunización *f.* immunization.
inmunización *activa* active immunization.
inmunización *pasiva* passive immunization.
inmunizador, -ra *adj.* immunizator.
inmunizante *adj.* immunizator.
inmunizar *v.* immunize.
inmunoadsorbente *m.* immunoadsorbent.
inmunoadsorción *f.* immunoadsorption.
inmunoadyuvante *adj.* immunoadjuvant.
inmunoaglutinación *f.* immunoagglutination.
inmunoanálisis *m.* immunoassay.
inmunobiología *f.* immunobiology.
inmunoblástico, -ca *adj.* immunoblastic.
inmunoblasto *m.* immunoblast.
inmunocatálisis *f.* immunocatalysis.
inmunocirugía *f.* immunosurgery.
inmunocito *m.* immunocyte.
inmunocitoadherencia *f.* immunocytoadherence.
inmunocitoquímica *f.* immunocytochemistry.
inmunocoadyuvante *m.* immunocoadjuvant.
inmunocompetencia *f.* immunocompetence.
inmunocompetente *adj.* immunocompetent.
inmunocomplejo *m.* immunocomplex.
inmunocomprometido, -da *adj.* immunocompromised.
inmunoconglutinina *f.* immunoconglutinin.
inmunodeficiencia *f.* immunodeficiency.
inmunodeficiencia *asociada a timoma* immunodeficiency with thymoma.
inmunodeficiencia con *aumento de IgM* immunodeficiency with elevated IgM.
inmunodeficiencia *celular con síntesis anormal de inmunoglobulinas* cellular immunodeficiency with abnormal immunoglobulin synthesis.
inmunodeficiencia *combinada* combined immunodeficiency.
inmunodeficiencia *combinada grave, inmunodeficiencia combinada severa (IDCG)* severe combined immunodeficiency (SCID.

inmunodeficiencia *común variable* common variable immunodeficiency.
inmunodeficiencia con *enanismo de miembros cortos* immunodeficiency with short-limbed dwarfism.
inmunodeficiencia con *hiper IgM* immunodeficiency with hyper-IgM.
inmunodeficiencia con *hiperproducción de IgM* hyper IgM syndrome immunodeficiency.
inmunodeficiencia con *hipoparatiroidismo* immunodeficiency with hypoparathyroidism.
inmunodeficiencia *primaria* primary immunodeficiency.
inmunodeficiencia *secundaria* secondary immunodeficiency.
inmunodeficiencia *variable común* common variable immunodeficiency.
inmunodeficiencia *variable común inclasificable* common variable unclassifiable immunodeficiency.
inmunodeficiente *adj.* immunodeficient.
inmunodepresión *f.* immunodepression.
inmunodepresor, -ra *adj.* immunodepressive.
inmunodermatología *f.* immunodermatology.
inmunodiagnosis *f.* immunodiagnosis.
inmunodiagnóstico *m.* immunodiagnosis.
inmunodifusión *f.* immunodiffusion.
inmunodifusión *doble* double immunodiffusion.
inmunodifusión *radial (IDR)* radial immunodiffusion.
inmunodifusión *simple* single immunodiffusion.
inmunodominancia *f.* immunodominance.
inmunodominante *adj.* immunodominant.
inmunoelectrodifusión *f.* immunoelectrodiffusion.
inmunoelectroforesis *f.* immunoelectrophoresis.
inmunoelectroforesis *bidimensional* two-dimensional immunoelectrophoresis.
inmunoelectroforesis en *cohete* rocket immunoelectrophoresis.
inmunoelectroforesis *contra corriente* counter immunoelectrophoresis, countercurrent immunoelectrophoresis.
inmunoelectroforesis *cruzada* crossed immunoelectrophoresis.
inmunoensayo *m.* immunoassay.
inmunoensayo en *capa delgada* thin-layer immunoassay.
inmunoensayo *enzimático* enzyme immunoassay.
inmunoensayo en *fase sólida* solid phase immunoassay.
inmunoensayo *multiplicado por enzimas* enzyme-multiplied immunoassay (EMIT).
inmunoestimulación *f.* immunostimulation.
inmunoestimulador *m.* immunoenhancer.
inmunoestimulante *adj.* immunostimulant.
inmunoferritina *f.* immunoferritin.
inmunofiltración *f.* immunofiltration.
inmunofisiología *f.* immunophysiology.
inmunofluorescencia *f.* immunofluorescence.
inmunofluorescencia *directa* direct immunofluorescence.
inmunofluorescencia *indirecta* indirect immunofluorescence.
inmunofomento *m.* immunoenhancement.
inmunogenética *f.* immunogenetics.
inmunogenético, -ca *adj.* immunogenetic.
inmunogenicidad *f.* immunogenicity.
inmunogénico, -ca *adj.* immunogenic.
inmunógeno *m.* immunogen.

inmunógeno por *conducta* behavioral immunogen.
inmunoglobulina *f.* immunoglobulin.
inmunoglobulina *A (IgA)* immunoglobulin A (IgA).
inmunoglobulina *A deficitaria* immunoglobulin A deficiency.
inmunoglobulina *A secretoria* secretory immunoglobulin A.
inmunoglobulina *anti-D* anti-D immunoglobulin.
inmunoglobulina *antirrábica* rabies immunoglobulin.
inmunoglobulina *D (IgD)* immunoglobulin D (IgD).
inmunoglobulina *E (IgE)* immunoglobulin E (IgE).
inmunoglobulina *específica* specific immunoglobulin.
inmunoglobulina *estimulantes del crecimiento del tiroides* thyroid growth stimulating immunoglobulin.
inmunoglobulina *estimulantes del tiroides (TSI)* thyroid-stimulating immunoglobulin.
inmunoglobulina *G (IgG)* immunoglobulin G (IgG).
inmunoglobulina *contra la hepatitis B (IgHB)* hepatitis B immunoglobulin (HBIG).
inmunoglobulina *humana normal* human normal immunoglobulin.
inmunoglobulina *inhibitoria de fijación del tiroides* thyroid-binding inhibitory immunoglobulin (TBII).
inmunoglobulina *inhibitoria de la fijación de la TSH (TBII)* TSH-binding inhibitory immunoglobulin (TBII).
inmunoglobulina *M (IgM)* immunoglobulin M (IgM).
inmunoglobulina *M deficitaria* immunoglobulin M deficiency.
inmunoglobulina *monoclonal* monoclonal immunoglobulin.
inmunoglobulina *del pertussis* pertussis immunoglobulin.
inmunoglobulina *de la poliomielitis* poliomyelitis immunoglobulin.
inmunoglobulina *de la rabia* rabies immunoglobulin.
inmunoglobulina *Rh0 (D)* Rh0 immunoglobulin (DD).
inmunoglobulina *del sarampión* measles immunoglobulin.
inmunoglobulina *tetánica, inmunoglobulina del tétanos (IGT)* tetanus immunoglobulin TIG).
inmunoglobulina *contra la tos ferina* pertussis immunoglobulin.
inmunoglobulina *de la varicela* chickenpox immunoglobulin.
inmunoglobulina *de la varicela zoster (IGVZ)* varicellazoster immunoglobulin (VZIG).
inmunoglobulina *zoster (ZIG)* zoster immunoglobulin (ZIG).
inmunoglobulinopatía *f.* immunoglobulinopathy.
inmunohematología *f.* immunohematology.
inmunohemolisina *f.* hemolysin immune.
inmunohemólisis *f.* hemolysis immune.
inmunoheterogeneidad *f.* immunoheterogeneity.
inmunoheterogéneo, -a *adj.* immunoheterogeneous.
inmunohistofluorescencia *f.* immunohistofluorescence.

inmunohistoquímica *f.* immunohistochemistry.
inmunohistoquímico, -ca *adj.* immunohistochemical.
inmunoinsuficiente *adj.* immunoincompetent.
inmunología *f.* immunology.
inmunológico, -ca *adj.* immunologic, immunological.
inmunólogo, -ga *m., f.* immunologist.
inmunomarcaje *m.* immunostaining.
inmunomodulación *f.* immunomodulation.
inmunomodulador *m.* immunomodulator.
inmunoparálisis *f.* immunoparesis.
inmunoparasitología *f.* immunoparasitology.
inmunopatogenia *f.* immunopathogenesis.
inmunopatología *f.* immunopathology.
inmunopatológico, -ca *adj.* immunopathologic.
inmunoperoxidasa *f.* immunoperoxidase.
inmunopotencia *f.* immunopotency.
inmunopotenciación *f.* immunopotentiation.
inmunopotenciador *m.* immunopotentiator.
inmunoprecipitación *f.* immunoprecipitation.
inmunoprofilaxis *f.* immunoprophylaxis.
inmunoproliferativo, -va *adj.* immunoproliferative.
inmunoproteína *f.* immunoprotein.
inmunoquímica *f.* immunochemistry.
inmunoquímico, -ca *adj.* immunochemical.
inmunoquimioterapia *f.* immunochemotherapy.
inmunorradiometría *f.* immunoradiometry.
inmunorradiométrico, -ca *adj.* immunoradiometric.
inmunorreacción *f.* immunoreaction.
inmunorreactivo, -va *adj.* immunoreactant, immunoreactive.
   inmunorreactivo de glucagón glucagon immunoreactant.
inmunorregulación *f.* immunoregulation.
inmunoselección *f.* immunoselection.
inmunosenectud *f.* immunosenescence.
inmunosorbente *adj.* immunosorbent.
inmunosuficiencia *f.* immunocompetence.
inmunosuficiente *adj.* immunocompetent.
inmunosupresión *f.* immunosuppression.
inmunosupresivo, -va *adj.* immunosuppresive.
inmunosupresor *m.* immunosuppresant.
inmunoterapia *f.* immunotherapy.
   inmunoterapia adoptiva adoptive immunotherapy.
   inmunoterapia específica activa active specific immunotherapy.
   inmunoterapia con veneno venom immunotherapy.
inmunotolerancia *f.* immunotolerance.
inmunotoxina (IT) *f.* immunotoxin (IT).
inmunotransfusión *f.* immunotransfusion.
inmunotrópico, -ca *adj.* immunotropic.
inmunovaloración *f.* immunoassay.
inmunovigilancia *f.* immunosurveillance.
innato, -ta *adj.* innate.
innidación *f.* innidation.
innocuo, -cua *adj.* innocuous, innoxious.
innominado, -da *adj.* innominate.
innominático, -ca *adj.* innominatal.
inocente *adj.* innocent.
inocondritis *f.* inochondritis.
inoculabilidad *f.* inoculability.
inoculable *adj.* inoculable.
inoculación *f.* inoculation.
   inoculación de estrés, inoculación para estrés stress inoculation.
   inoculación protectora protective inoculation.
inocular *v.* inoculate.
inóculo *m.* inoculum.
inocuo, -cua *adj.* innocuous.

inoesclerosis *f.* inosclerosis.
inofragma *m.* inophragma.
inogénesis *f.* inogenesis.
inoglia *f.* inoglia.
inohimenitis *f.* inohymenitis.
inolito *m.* inolith.
inomiositis *f.* inomyositis.
inoperable *adj.* inoperable.
inorgánico, -ca *adj.* inorganic.
inosa *f.* inose.
inosclerosis *f.* inosclerosis.
inoscopia *f.* inoscopy.
inosculación *f.* inosculation.
inoscular *v.* inosculate.
inose *m.* inose.
inosemia *f.* inosemia.
inosita *f.* inosite.
inositis *f.* inositis.
inositol *m.* inositol.
   inositol 1-4-5-trisfosfato (IP3) inositol-1-4-5-triphosphate.
inositoluria *f.* inositoluria.
inosituria *f.* inosituria.
inostosis *f.* inostosis.
inosuria *f.* inosuria.
inotagma *f.* inotagma.
inotrópico, -ca *adj.* inotropic.
   inotrópico negativo negatively inotropic.
   inotrópico positivo positively inotropic.
inótropo, -pa *adj.* inotropic.
inotropismo *m.* inotropism.
inquietud *f.* unrest.
   inquietud peristáltica peristaltic unrest.
inquilino *m.* inquiline.
inructación *f.* inructation.
insaciable *adj.* insatiable.
insalivación *f.* insalivation.
insalivar *v.* insalivate.
insalubre *adj.* insalubrious.
insania *f.* insanity.
   insania de Basedow Basedowian insanity.
insanitario, -ria *adj.* insanitary.
insano, -na *m., f.* insane.
insaturado, -da *adj.* unsaturated.
inscripción *f.* inscription, inscriptio.
   inscripción tendinosa tendinous inscription, inscriptio tendinea.
   inscripción tendinosa del músculo rectoabdominal tendinous inscription of the rectus abdominis muscle.
Insecta Insecta.
insectario *m.* insectarium.
insectarium *m.* insectarium.
insecticida *m. y adj.* insecticide.
insectífugo, -ga *m. y adj.* insectifuge.
insecto *m.* insect.
inseminación *f.* insemination.
   inseminación artificial artificial insemination.
   inseminación artificial del cónyuge (IAC) artificial insemination-husband (AIH).
   inseminación artificial de donante (IAD) artificial insemination-donor (AID).
   inseminación de donador donor insemination.
   inseminación heteróloga heterologous insemination.
   inseminación homóloga homologous insemination.
insenescencia *f.* insenescence.
insensibilidad *f.* insensibility.
insensible *adj.* insensible.
inserción *f.* attachment, insert, insertion, insertio.
   inserción epitelial (de Gottlieb) epithelial attachment (of Gottlieb).

   inserción de fricción interna, inserción de fricción paralela internal friction attachment, parallel friction attachment.
   inserción intramucosa intramucosal insert, mucosal insert.
   inserción del pensamiento thinking insertion, thought insertion.
   inserción de precisión precision attachment.
   inserción de radio radium insertion.
   inserción velamentosa velamentous insertion, insertio velamentosa.
insertar *v.* insert.
insidioso, -sa *adj.* insidious.
insight *m.* insight.
insolación *f.* insolation.
   insolación astictica asphyxial insolation.
   insolación hiperpiréxica hyperpyrexial insolation.
insoluble *adj.* insoluble.
insomne *adj.* insomniac, insomnic.
insomnio *m.* insomnia.
   insomnio familiar fatal familial fatal insomnia.
insorción *f.* insorption.
inspección *f.* inspection.
inspeccionismo *m.* inspectionism.
inspersión *f.* inspersion.
inspiración *f.* inspiration.
   inspiración en forma de silbido áspero crowing inspiration.
   inspiración forzada forced inspiration, forcible inspiration.
   inspiración mantenida inspiration hold.
   inspiración profunda periódica periodic deep inspiration.
inspirar *v.* inspirate.
inspiratorio, -ria *adj.* inspiratory.
inspirómetro *m.* inspirometer.
inspisación *f.* inspissation.
instilación *f.* instillation.
   instilación de gotas óticas eardrop instillation.
   instilación nasal de medicamentos nasal instillation of medication.
   instilación rectal de medicamentos rectal instillation of medication.
   instilación vaginal de fármacos vaginal instillation of medication.
   instilación vesical con BCG BCG instillation in bladder cancer.
   instilación vesical con tiotepa thiotepa instillation in bladder cancer.
instilador *m.* instillator.
instintivo, -va *adj.* instinctive, instinctual.
instinto *m.* instinct.
   instinto agresivo aggressive instinct.
   instinto del ego ego instinct.
   instinto de grupo herd instinct.
   instinto materno mother instinct.
   instinto mortal, instinto de muerte death instinct.
   instinto de rebaño herd instinct.
   instinto sexual sexual instinct.
   instinto social social instinct.
   instinto de vida, instinto vital life instinct.
   instinto del yo ego instinct.
instrucción *f.* directive.
   instrucción previa advance directive.
instructor, -ra del parto *m., f.* labor coach.
instrumentación *f.* instrumentation.
   instrumentación de Dwyer Dwyer instrumentation.
   instrumentación de Harrigton Harrington instrumentation.
instrumental[1] *adj.* instrumental.

**instrumental² ** *m.* instrumentarium.
instrumentario *m.* instrumentarium.
instrumento *m.* instrument.
  instrumento cortante de diamantes diamond cutting instrument.
  instrumento estereotáxico stereotactic instrument, stereotaxic instrument.
  instrumento de investigación research instrument.
  instrumento de mango de prueba test handle instrument.
  instrumento para obturar plugging instrument.
  instrumento para sutura en tabaquera purse-string instrument.
  instrumento tope de Krueger Krueger instrument stop.
insucación *f.* insucation.
insudación *f.* insudation.
insuficiencia *f.* failure, insufficiency.
  insuficiencia activa active insufficiency.
  insuficiencia acomodativa accommodative insufficiency.
  insuficiencia aórtica aortic insufficiency.
  insuficiencia arterial arterial insufficiency.
  insuficiencia arterial de las extremidades inferiores arterial insufficiency of the lower extremities.
  insuficiencia capsular adrenal insufficiency.
  insuficiencia cardíaca cardiac insufficiency, heart failure.
  insuficiencia cardíaca anterógrada forward heart insufficiency.
  insuficiencia cardíaca compensada compensated heart failure.
  insuficiencia cardíaca congestiva (ICC) congestive heart failure (CHF).
  insuficiencia cardíaca derecha, insuficiencia cardíaca ventricular derecha right-heart failure.
  insuficiencia cardíaca izquierda, insuficiencia cardíaca ventricular izquierda left-heart failure.
  insuficiencia cardíaca retrógrada backward heart insufficiency.
  insuficiencia circulatoria circulatory insufficiency, circulatory failure.
  insuficiencia circulatoria aguda acute circulatory failure.
  insuficiencia por convergencia convergence insufficiency.
  insuficiencia coronaria coronary insufficiency.
  insuficiencia corticosuprarrenal adrenocortical insufficiency.
  insuficiencia corticosuprarrenal aguda acute adrenocortical insufficiency.
  insuficiencia corticosuprarrenal crónica chronic adrenocortical insufficiency.
  insuficiencia corticosuprarrenal latente latent adrenocortical insufficiency.
  insuficiencia corticosuprarrenal parcial partial adrenocortical insufficiency.
  insuficiencia corticosuprarrenal primaria primary adrenocortical insufficiency.
  insuficiencia corticosuprarrenal secundaria secondary adrenocortical insufficiency.
  insuficiencia por divergencia divergence insufficiency.
  insuficiencia eléctrica electric insufficiency.
  insuficiencia gástrica gastric insufficiency.
  insuficiencia gastromotora gastromotor insufficiency.
  insuficiencia gonadal gonadal insufficiency.
  insuficiencia hepática hepatic insufficiency, liver failure.

  insuficiencia hipofisaria pituitary insufficiency.
  insuficiencia de IgA IgA deficiency.
  insuficiencia ileocecal ileocecal insufficiency.
  insuficiencia del miocardio myocardial insufficiency.
  insuficiencia mitral mitral failure, mitral insufficiency.
  insuficiencia muscular muscular insufficiency.
  insuficiencia de los músculos externos insufficiency of the externi.
  insuficiencia de los músculos internos insufficiency of the interni.
  insuficiencia palpebral insufficiency of the eyelids.
  insuficiencia pancreática pancreatic insufficiency.
  insuficiencia paratiroidea parathyroid insufficiency.
  insuficiencia de los párpados insufficiency of the eyelids.
  insuficiencia pilórica pyloric insufficiency.
  insuficiencia placentaria placental insufficiency.
  insuficiencia prerrenal prerenal failure.
  insuficiencia pulmonar pulmonary insufficiency.
  insuficiencia renal renal insufficiency, renal failure.
  insuficiencia renal aguda acute renal failure.
  insuficiencia renal aguda poliúrica polyuric acute renal failure.
  insuficiencia renal aguda posrenal postrenal acute renal failure.
  insuficiencia renal crónica chronic renal failure.
  insuficiencia renal crónica terminal end-stage renal failure.
  insuficiencia respiratoria respiratory insufficiency, respiratory failure.
  insuficiencia respiratoria aguda (IRA) acute respiratory failure (ARF).
  insuficiencia suprarrenal adrenal insufficiency.
  insuficiencia tiroidea thyroid insufficiency.
  insuficiencia tricuspídea tricuspid insufficiency.
  insuficiencia uterina uterine insufficiency.
  insuficiencia valvular valvular insufficiency, insufficiency of the valves.
  insuficiencia vascular vascular insufficiency.
  insuficiencia velofaríngea velopharyngeal insufficiency.
  insuficiencia venosa venous insufficiency.
  insuficiencia ventricular derecha right ventricular failure.
  insuficiencia ventricular izquierda left ventricular failure.
  insuficiencia vertebrobasilar vertebrobasilar insufficiency, basilar insufficiency.
insuflación *f.* insufflation.
  insuflación craneal cranial insufflation.
  insuflación endotraqueal endotracheal insufflation.
  insuflación intratraqueal endotracheal insufflation.
  insuflación perirrenal perirenal insufflation.
  insuflación presacra presacral insufflation.
  insuflación pulmonar, de los pulmones insufflation of the lungs.
  insuflación tubaria, insuflación tubárica tubal insufflation.
insuflador *m.* insufflator.
insuflar *v.* insufflate.
ínsula *f.* insula.

insular *adj.* insular.
insularpancreatotrópico, -ca *adj.* insular-pancreatotropic.
insulina *f.* insulin.
  insulina de acción corta short-acting insulin.
  insulina de acción intermedia intermediate-acting insulin.
  insulina de acción lenta slow-acting insulin.
  insulina de acción prolongada long-acting insulin.
  insulina de acción rápida rapid-acting insulin.
  insulina atípica atypical insulin.
  insulina bifásica biphasic insulin.
  insulina con cinc y globina, insulina cíncica globina globin zinc insulin, globin zinc injection.
  insulina de componente único single component insulin.
  insulina globina globin insulin.
  insulina humana human insulin.
  insulina inmunorreactiva immunoreactive insulin.
  insulina isofánica isophane insulin.
  insulina lenta lente insulin.
  insulina lispro lyspro insulin.
  insulina NPH (Neutral Protamine Hagedorn) NPH (Neutral Protamine Hagedorn) insulin.
  insulina protamina cinc, insulina protamina cíncica protamine zinc insulin.
  insulina regular regular insulin.
  insulina semilenta semilente insulin.
  insulina sintética synthetic insulin.
  insulina de tres a uno three-to-one insulin.
insulinasa *f.* insulinase.
insulinemia *f.* insulinemia.
insulinismo *m.* insilinism.
insulinocinasa *f.* insulin kinase.
insulinogénesis *f.* insulinogenesis.
insulinogénico, -ca *adj.* insulinogenic.
insulinoide *adj.* insulinoid.
insulinolipodistrofia *f.* insulinolipodystrophy.
insulinoma *m.* insulinoma.
insulinopénico, -ca *adj.* insulinopenic.
insulinoterapia *f.* insulin therapy.
insulitis *f.* insulitis.
insulogénico, -ca *adj.* insulogenic.
insuloma *m.* insuloma.
insulopático, -ca *adj.* insulopathic.
insulto *m.* insult.
insusceptibilidad *f.* insusceptibility.
integración *f.* integration.
  integración biológica biological integration.
  integración estructural structural integration.
  integración de la personalidad personality integration.
  integración sensitiva sensory integration.
integrador *m.* integrator.
integrasa *f.* integrase.
integridad marginal de la amalgama marginal integrity of amalgam.
integrina *f.* integrin.
integumento *m.* integument, integumentum.
integumentum *m.* integument, integumentum.
  integumento común, integumentum commune integumentum commune.
intelección *f.* intellection.
intelecto *m.* intellect.
intelectualización *f.* intellectualization.
inteligencia *f.* intelligence.
  inteligencia abstracta abstract intelligence.
  inteligencia artificial (IA) artificial intelligence (AI).

inteligencia cristalizada crystallized intelligence.

inteligencia fluida fluid intelligence.

inteligencia mecánica mechanical intelligence.

inteligencia medida measured intelligence.

inteligencia social social intelligence.

intemperancia *f.* intemperance.

intención *f.* intention.

intención paradójica paradoxical intention.

intensidad *f.* intensity, strength.

intensidad de asociación strength of association.

intensidad del campo eléctrico electric intensity, electric field strength.

intensidad luminosa luminous intensity.

intensidad de los rayos roentgen intensity of x-rays.

intensidad de señal signal intensity.

intensidad del sonido intensity of sound.

intensificación *f.* enhancement.

intensificación de sombras shadow casting enhancement.

intensificador de imagen *m.* image intensifier.

intensímetro *m.* intensimeter.

intensionómetro *m.* intensionometer.

intensivo, -va *adj.* intensive.

interaccesorio, -ria *adj.* interaccessory.

interacción *f.* interaction.

interacción entre alimentos y fármacos food and drug interaction.

interacción enfermero-paciente nurse-client interaction.

interacción fármaco-alimentos, interacciones entre alimentos y fármacos drug-food interaction.

interacción medicamentosa drug-drug interaction.

interacción rodilla-tobillo knee-ankle interaction.

interacinar *adj.* interacinar.

interacinoso, -sa *adj.* interacinous.

interaglutinación *f.* interagglutination.

interalveolar *adj.* interalveolar.

interangular *adj.* interangular.

interanular *adj.* interannular.

interarcos *m.* interarch.

interaritenoideo, -a *adj.* interarytenoid.

interarticular *adj.* interarticular.

interastérico, -ca *adj.* interasteric.

interatrial *adj.* interatrial.

interauricular *adj.* interauricular.

intercadencia *f.* intercadence.

intercadente *adj.* intercadent.

intercalación *f.* intercalation.

intercalado, -da *adj.* intercalary.

intercalar *v.* intercalate.

intercambiador iónico *m.* ionic exchanger.

intercambio *m.* exchange, interchange, intercourse.

intercambio de cromátides hermanas sister chromatid exchange.

intercambio gaseoso gaseous exchange.

intercambio gaseoso alterado impaired gas exchange.

intercambio de Hamburger Hamburger interchange.

intercambio sexual sexual intercourse.

intercanalicular *adj.* intercanalicular.

intercapilar *adj.* intercapillary.

intercarotídeo, -a *adj.* intercarotic, intercarotid.

intercarpal *adj.* intercarpal.

intercarpiano, -na *adj.* intercarpal.

intercartilaginoso, -sa *adj.* intercartilaginous.

intercavernoso, -sa *adj.* intercavernous.

intercelular *adj.* intercellular.

intercentral *adj.* intercentral.

intercepción *f.* interception.

intercerebral *adj.* intercerebral.

intercerebro *m.* interbrain.

interciático, -ca *adj.* intersciatic.

intercilium *m.* intercilium.

intercinesia *f.* interkinesis.

intercinesis *f.* interkinesis.

interclavicular *adj.* interclavicular.

interclinoide *adj.* interclinoid.

intercoccígeo, -a *adj.* intercoccygeal.

intercolumnar *adj.* intercolumnar.

intercolumnario, -ria *adj.* intercolumnar.

intercondllar *adj.* intercondylar.

intercondíleo, -a *adj.* intercondylous.

intercondiloideo, -a *adj.* intercondyloid.

intercondral *adj.* interchondral.

interconsulta de salud mental *f.* mental health consultation.

interconsulta médica *f.* medical consulta-consultationtion.

intercostal *adj.* intercostal.

intercostohumeral *adj.* intercostohumeral.

intercrestal *adj.* intercrristal.

intercricotirotomía *f.* intercricothyrotomy.

intercristal *adj.* intercristal.

intercrítico, -ca *adj.* intercritical.

intercrural *adj.* intercrural.

intercuerpos *adj.* interbody.

intercurrente *adj.* intercurrent.

intercuspación *f.* intercuspation.

intercuspidación *f.* intercusping.

intercutaneomucoso, -sa *adj.* intercutaneomucous.

interdeferencial *adj.* interdeferential.

interdental *adj.* interdental.

interdentario, -ria *adj.* interdental.

interdentium *m.* interdentium.

interdicto *m.* injunction.

interdigitación *f.* interdigitation.

interdigital *adj.* interdigital.

interdigitar *v.* interdigitate.

interdígito *m.* interdigit.

interdisciplinario, -ria *adj.* interdisciplinary.

interescapular *adj.* interscapular.

interespacio *m.* interspace.

interespacio dinérico dineric interspace.

interespinal *adj.* interspinal.

interespinoso, -sa *adj.* interspinous.

interesternal *adj.* intersternal.

interfacial *adj.* interfacial.

interfalángico, -ca *adj.* interphalangeal.

interfascicular *adj.* interfascicular.

interfase *f.* interface, interphase.

interfase cristalina crystalline interface.

interfase dermoepidérmica dermoepidermal interface.

interfase estructural structural interface.

interfase metálica metal interface.

interfeminium *m.* interfeminium.

interfemoral *adj.* interfemoral.

interferencia *f.* interference.

interferencia bacteriana bacterial interference.

interferencia constructiva constructive interference.

interferencia de las cúspides cuspal interference.

interferencia destructiva destructive interference.

interferencia oclusal occlusal interference.

interferencia proactiva proactive interference.

interferencia retroactiva retroactive interference.

interferometría *f.* interferometry.

interferometría electrónica electron interferometry.

interferómetro *m.* interferometer.

interferómetro electrónico electron interferometer.

interferón (IFN, INF) *m.* interferon (IFN, INF).

interfibrilar *adj.* interfibrillar.

interfibroso, -sa *adj.* interfibrous.

interfilamentoso, -sa *adj.* interfilamentous.

interfilar *adj.* interfilar.

interfilético, -ca *adj.* interphyletic.

interfrontal *adj.* interfrontal.

interganglionar *adj.* interganglionic.

intergemal *adj.* intergemmal.

intergénico, -ca *adj.* intergenic.

intergiral *adj.* intergyral.

interglobular *adj.* interglobular.

interglúteo, -a *adj.* intergluteal.

intergonial *adj.* intergonial.

intergradación *f.* intergradation.

intergrado *m.* intergrade.

intergranular *adj.* intergranular.

intergranuloso, -sa *adj.* intergranular.

interhemicerebral *adj.* interhemicerebral.

interhemisférico, -ca *adj.* interhemispheric.

interhorquilla *f.* interfurca.

interictal *adj.* interictal.

interior *adj.* interior.

interiorización *f.* internalization.

interisquiático, -ca *adj.* interischiadic.

interlabial *adj.* interlabial.

interlamelar *adj.* interlamellar.

interlaminillar *adj.* interlamellar.

Interleucina (IL) *f.* interleukin (IL).

interleuquina (IL) *f.* interleukin (IL).

interligamentario, -ria *adj.* interligamentary.

interligamentoso, -sa *adj.* interligamentous.

interlobar *adj.* interlobar.

interlobitis *f.* interlobitis.

interlobular *adj.* interlobar.

interlobulillar *adj.* interlobular.

interlobulitis *f.* interlobitis.

Interludio *m.* intermission.

intermaleolar *adj.* intermalleolar.

intermamario, -ria *adj.* intermammary.

intermamilar *adj.* intermamillary.

intermatrimonio *m.* intermarriage.

intermaxila *f.* intermaxilla.

intermaxilar *adj.* intermaxillary.

intermediario, -ria *m., f. y adj.* intermediary, intermediate.

intermedio, -dia *adj.* intermediary, intermediate.

intermedio *m.* intermediate.

intermediolateral *adj.* intermediolateral.

intermembranoso, -sa *adj.* intermembranous.

intermeníngeo, -a *adj.* intermeningeal.

intermenstrual *adj.* intermenstrual.

intermenstruo *m.* intermenstruum.

intermetacarpiano, -na *adj.* intermetacarpal.

intermetamérico, -ca *adj.* intermetameric.

intermetatarsiano, -na *adj.* intermetatarsal.

intermisión *f.* intermission.

intermitencia *f.* intermittence, intermittency.

intermitente *adj.* intermittent.

intermitir *v.* intermit.

intermitótico, -ca *adj.* intermitotic.

intermolecular *adj.* intermolecular.

intermural *adj.* intermural.

intermuscular *adj.* intermuscular.

internación *f.* internation.

internado *m.* internship.

internalización *f.* internalization.
internamiento *m.* commitment.
internarinal *adj.* internarial.
internasal *adj.* internasal.
interneuromérico, -ca *adj.* interneuromeric.
interneurona *f.* interneuron.
internista *m., f.* internist.
interno, -na *adj.* internal.
interno, -na *m., f.* intern, interne.
internodal *adj.* internodal.
internodo *m.* internode.
internodular *adj.* internodular.
internuclear *adj.* internuclear.
internudo *m.* internode.
  internudo de Ranvier internode of Ranvier.
internuncial *adj.* internuncial.
interoceptivo, -va *adj.* interoceptive.
interoceptor *m.* interoceptor.
interoclusal *adj.* interocclusal.
interofección *f.* interofection.
interofectivo, -va *adj.* interofective.
interoinferior *adj.* interoinferior.
interolivar *adj.* interolivary.
interorbitario, -ria *adj.* interorbital.
interóseo, -a *adj.* interosseal, interosseous.
interpalpebral *adj.* interpalpebral.
interparietal *adj.* interparietal.
interparoxismal *adj.* interparoxysmal.
interparoxísmico, -ca *adj.* interparoxysmal.
interparoxístico, -ca *adj.* interparoxysmal.
interpediculado, -da *adj.* interpediculate.
interpedicular *adj.* interpediculate.
interpeduncular *adj.* interpeduncular.
interpersonal *adj.* interpersonal.
interpial *adj.* interpial.
interplantación *f.* interplanting.
interplante *m.* interplant.
interpleural *adj.* interpleural.
interpolación *f.* interpolation.
interpolar[1] *adj.* interpolar.
Interpolar[2] *v.* interpolate.
interposición *f.* interposition.
interpretación *f.* interpretation.
  interpretación catastrofista doomwatcher interpretation.
  interpretación de los sueños interpretation of dreams.
interprotometámera *f.* interprotometamere.
interprotometamérico, -ca *adj.* interprotometamere.
interproximal *adj.* interproximal.
interpúbico, -ca *adj.* interpubic.
interpupilar *adj.* interpupillary.
interradial *adj.* interradial.
interrenal *adj.* interrenal.
interrumpido, -da *adj.* interrupted.
interruptor *m.* switch.
  interruptor de exposición exposure switch.
interscapulum interscapulum.
intersección *f.* intersection, intersectio.
  intersección tendinosa tendinous intersection, intersectio tendinea.
  intersección tendinosas del músculo rectoabdominal intersectiones tendineae musculi recti abdominis.
intersegmentario, -ria *adj.* intersegmental.
intersegmento *m.* intersegment.
interseptal *adj.* interseptal.
interseptovalvular *adj.* interseptovalvular.
interseptum interseptum.
intersexual[1] *m.* intersex.
  intersexual femenino female intersex.
  intersexual masculino male intersex.
  intersexual verdadero true intersex.
intersexual[2] *adj.* intersexual.

intersexualidad *f.* intersexuality.
intersístole *f.* intersystole.
intersticial *adj.* interstitial.
intersticio *m.* interstice, interstitium.
  intersticio renal interstice of the kidney.
intertalámico, -ca *adj.* interthalamic.
intertarsal *adj.* intertarsal.
intertarsiano, -na *adj.* intertarsal.
intertransverso, -sa *adj.* intertransverse.
intertriginoso, -sa *adj.* intertriginous.
intertrigo *m.* intertrigo.
  intertrigo labial intertrigo labialis.
intertrocantéreo, -a *adj.* intertrochanteric.
intertubercular *adj.* intertubercular.
intertuberculoso, -sa *adj.* intertubercular.
intertubular *adj.* intertubular.
interureteral *adj.* interureteral.
interuretérico, -ca *adj.* interureteric.
intervaginal *adj.* intervaginal.
intervalo *m.* interval, gap.
  intervalo 1 (G 1) 1 interval (G 1).
  intervalo 2 (G 2) 2 interval (G 2).
  intervalo de acoplamiento, intervalo de acople coupling interval.
  intervalo A-H A-H interval.
  intervalo A-N A-N interval.
  intervalo aniónico anion gap.
  intervalo auriculocarotídeo (a-c) atriocarotid interval (a-c).
  intervalo auriculoventricular auriculoventricular interval.
  intervalo A-V A-V interval.
  intervalo BH BH interval.
  intervalo cardioarterial (c-a) cardioarterial interval (c-a), cardioarterious interval.
  intervalo ectópico interectopic interval.
  intervalo de escape escape interval.
  intervalo esfígmico sphygmic interval.
  intervalo fijo (IF) de refuerzo fixed interval (FI) of reinforcement.
  intervalo focal, intervalo focal de Sturm focal interval.
  intervalo H-V H-V interval.
  intervalo isométrico isometric interval.
  intervalo lúcido lucid interval.
  intervalo osmolal osmolal gap.
  intervalo P-A P-A interval.
  intervalo pasivo passive interval.
  intervalo P-J P-J.
  intervalo posesfígmico, intervalo postesfigmico postsphygmic interval.
  intervalo P-P P-P interval.
  intervalo P-Q P-Q interval.
  intervalo P-R P-R interval.
  intervalo preesfígmico, intervalo presfigmico presphygmic interval.
  intervalo Q-R Q-R interval.
  intervalo Q-RB Q-RB interval.
  intervalo Q-RS Q-RS interval.
  intervalo Q-RST Q-RST interval.
  intervalo Q-S Q-S interval.
  intervalo Q-T Q-T interval.
  intervalo de referencia reference interval.
  intervalo R-R R-R interval.
  intervalo S-T S-T interval.
  intervalo de Sturm Sturm's interval.
  intervalo de tiempo sistólico systolic time interval.
  intervalo de tolerancia tolerance interval.
intervalvular *adj.* intervalvular.
intervascular *adj.* intervascular.
intervelloso, -sa *adj.* intervillous.
intervención *f.* intervention, procedure.
  intervención de crisis, intervención en crisis crisis intervention.

  intervención dependiente dependent intervention.
  intervención directiva directive intervention.
  intervención no directiva no directive intervention.
  intervención de Duhamel Duhamel's procedure.
  intervención de enfermería nursing intervention.
  intervención de Friederich Friederich's procedure.
  intervención de Hartmann Hartmann's procedure.
  intervención de Kaplan Kaplan's procedure.
  intervención de Kasai Kasai's procedure.
  intervención de Ladd Ladd's procedure.
  intervención neurorreflejoterápica (NRT) neuroreflexotherapy intervention (NRT).
  intervención psicológica psychological intervention.
  intervención de Puestow Puestow's procedure.
  intervención de Senning Senning intervention.
  intervención de Sugiura Sugiura's procedure.
  intervención de Warren Warren's procedure.
  intervención de Whipple Whipple's procedure.
interventricular *adj.* interventricular.
intervertebral *adj.* intervertebral.
intestinal *adj.* intestinal.
intestino *m.* gut, intestine, intestinum.
  intestino anterior foregut intestine.
  intestino ciego blindgut, blind gut, blind intestine, intestinum caecum, intestinum cecum.
  intestino de la cola tail gut.
  intestino congelado iced intestine, zuckergussdarm.
  intestino delgado small intestine, intestinum tenue.
  intestino delgado mesenterial, intestino delgado mesentérico jejunoileal intestine, intestinum tenue mesenteriale.
  intestino faríngeo foregut.
  intestino grueso large intestine, intestinum crassum.
  intestino íleon ileum intestine, intestinum ileum.
  intestino medio midgut.
  intestino mesenterial mesenterial intestine.
  intestino posanal postanal gut.
  intestino posterior hindgut.
  intestino primitivo primitive gut.
  intestino recto rectum intestine, straight intestine, intestinum rectum.
  intestino terminal endgut.
  intestino vacío empty intestine.
  intestino yeyuno jejunum intestine, intestinum jejunum.
intestinotoxina *f.* intestinotoxin.
intestinum *m.* gut, intestine, intestinum.
íntima *adj.* intima.
intimidad *f.* intimacy.
  intimidad afectiva affective intimacy.
intimitis *f.* intimitis.
  intimitis proliferativa proliferative intimitis.
intolerancia *f.* intolerance.
  intolerancia al acetato acetate intolerance.
  intolerancia a la actividad activity intolerance.
  intolerancia congénita a la lisina congenital lysine intolerance.
  intolerancia congénita a la sacarosa congenital sucrose intolerance.
  intolerancia a los disacáridos disaccharide intolerance.
  intolerancia a fármacos drug intolerance.

intolerancia a la fructosa fructose intolerance.

intolerancia a la glucosa (IGT) glucose intolerance (IGT).

intolerancia al gluten gluten intolerance.

intolerancia hereditaria a la fructosa hereditary fructose intolerance.

intolerancia hidrocarbonada impaired glucose tolerance.

intolerancia congénita a la lactosa congenital lactose intolerance.

intolerancia a la lactosa lactose intolerance.

intolerancia a la lisina lysine intolerance.

intolerancia proteínica con lisinuria lysinuric protein intolerance.

intorsión *f.* intorsion.

intorsor *m.* intorter.

intoxación *f.* intoxation.

intoxicación *f.* intoxication, poisoning.

intoxicación ácida, intoxicación por ácidos acid intoxication.

intoxicación por ácido acetilsalicílico acetylsalicylic acid poisoning.

intoxicación por ácido carbólico carbolic acid poisoning.

intoxicación acuosa, intoxicación por agua water intoxication.

intoxicación aguda debida al consumo de alcohol acute alcohol intoxication.

intoxicación alcalina, intoxicación por álcalis alkali poisoning.

intoxicación por alcanfor camphor poisoning.

intoxicación alcohólica idiosincrática alcohol idiosyncratic intoxication.

intoxicación alimentaria, intoxicación alimenticia food poisoning.

intoxicación alimentaria bacteriana bacterial food poisoning.

intoxicación por almejas clamp poisoning.

intoxicación por aluminio aluminum intoxication.

intoxicación anafiláctica anaphylactic intoxication.

intoxicación por anfeteminas amphetamine poisoning.

intoxicación por anhídrido carbónico carbon dioxide poisoning.

intoxicación por antimonio antimony poisoning.

intoxicación por arsénico arsenic poisoning.

intoxicación por arsenito de sodio sodium arsenite poisoning.

intoxicación por aspirina aspirin poisoning.

intoxicación por benceno benzene poisoning.

intoxicación por bongkrek bongkrek intoxication, tempeh poisoning.

intoxicación por cadmio cadmium poisoning.

intoxicación por cafeína caffeine poisoning.

intoxicación por carne meat poisoning.

intoxicación por cáusticos caustic poisoning.

intoxicación por cianuro cyanide poisoning.

intoxicación por ciguatera ciguatera poisoning.

intoxicación con citrato citrate intoxication.

intoxicación por clordano chlordane poisoning.

intoxicación por clorhidrato de cocaína cocaine hydrochloride poisoning.

intoxicación por cornezuelo del centeno ergot poisoning.

intoxicación crónica por fluoruro, crónica por flúor chronic fluoride poisoning, chronic fluorine poisoning.

intoxicación por crustáceos shellfish poisoning.

intoxicación por DDT DDT poisoning.

intoxicación por destilados del petróleo petroleum distillate poisoning.

intoxicación por dicloruro de etileno ethylene dichloride poisoning.

intoxicación por digitálicos digitalis poisoning.

intoxicación escombroide scombroid poisoning.

intoxicación por estricnina strychnine poisoning.

intoxicación por etilenglicol ethylene glycol poisoning.

intoxicación por fenol phenol poisoning.

intoxicación por fluoruro sódico sodium fluoride poisoning.

intoxicación por fluoruros fluoride poisoning.

intoxicación por fósforo phosphorus poisoning.

intoxicación por gasolina gasoline poisoning.

intoxicación por guayacol guaiacol poisoning.

intoxicación por heptaclor heptachlor poisoning.

intoxicación por herbicida herbicide poisoning.

intoxicación hídrica water intoxication.

intoxicación por hierro iron poisoning.

intoxicación con hipoclorito hypochlorite poisoning.

intoxicación por insecticidas organoclorados chlorinated organic insecticide poisoning.

intoxicación intestinal intestinal intoxication.

intoxicación por malatión malathion poisoning.

intoxicación por marisco shellfish poisoning.

intoxicación por mercurio mercury poisoning.

intoxicación por metales pesados heavy metal poisoning.

intoxicación por monóxido de carbono carbon monoxide poisoning.

intoxicación por naftaleno naphtalene poisoning.

intoxicación por naftol naphthol poisoning.

intoxicación por narcóticos narcotic poisoning.

intoxicación por nicotina nicotine poisoning.

intoxicación nicotínica aguda acute nicotine poisoning.

intoxicación por nitrobenceno nitrobenzene poisoning.

intoxicación opiácea opiate poisoning.

intoxicación por paracetamol acetaminophen poisoning.

intoxicación por paracuat paraquat poisoning.

intoxicación por paradiclorobenceno paradichlorobenzene poisoning.

intoxicación paralizante por marisco paralytic shellfish poisoning.

intoxicación por paratión parathion poisoning.

intoxicación patológica pathological intoxication.

intoxicación por peces escombroides scombroid poisoning.

intoxicación por pescado fish poisoning.

intoxicación por pesticidas pesticide poisoning.

intoxicación por plomo lead poisoning.

intoxicación por queroseno kerosene poisoning.

intoxicación por raticida rodenticide poisoning.

intoxicación por sal de zinc zinc salt poisoning.

intoxicación por sales de hierro iron salts poisoning.

intoxicación por sales de plata silver salts poisoning.

intoxicación por salicilatos salicylate poisoning.

intoxicación saturnina saturnine intoxication.

intoxicación séptica blood poisoning, septic intoxication.

intoxicación por setas mushroom poisoning.

intoxicación por sulfato de atropina atropine sulfate poisoning.

intoxicación por talio thallium poisoning.

intoxicación por tetracloruro de carbono carbon tetrachloride poisoning.

intoxicación por venerupina venerupin poisoning.

intoxicación por warfarina warfarin poisoning.

intoxicación por yodo iodine poisoning.

intoxicación por zumaque venenoso ivy poisoning.

intoxicante *adj.* intoxicant.

intraabdominal *adj.* intra-abdominal.

intraacinoso, -sa *adj.* intra-acinous.

intraadenoideo, -a *adj.* intra-adenoidal.

intraamigdalino, -na *adj.* intratonsillar.

intraapendicular *adj.* intra-apendicular.

intraaracnoideo, -a *adj.* intra-arachnoid.

intraarterial *adj.* intra-arterial.

intraarticular *adj.* intra-articular.

intraatómico, -ca *adj.* intra-atomic.

intraaural *adj.* intra-aural.

intraauricular *adj.* intra-atrial.

intrabronquial *adj.* intrabronchial.

intrabucal *adj.* intrabuccal.

intrabulbar *adj.* intramedullary.

intracanalicular *adj.* intracanalicular.

intracapsular *adj.* intracapsular.

intracardíaco, -ca *adj.* intracardiac.

intracarpal *adj.* intracarpal.

intracarpiano, -na *adj.* intracarpal.

intracartilaginoso, -sa *adj.* intracartilaginous.

intracatéter *m.* intracatheter.

intracavitario, -ria *adj.* intracavitary.

intracefálico, -ca *adj.* intracephalic.

intracelíaco, -ca *adj.* intracelial.

intracelial *adj.* intracelial.

intracelular *adj.* intracellular.

intracerebelar *adj.* intracerebellar.

intracerebeloso, -sa *adj.* intracerebellar.

intracerebral *adj.* intracerebral.

intracervical *adj.* intracervical.

intracisternal *adj.* intracisternal.

intracístico, -ca *adj.* intracystic.

intracistrónico, -ca *adj.* intracistronic.

intracitoplasmático, -ca *adj.* intracytoplasmic.

intracólico, -ca *adj.* intracolic.

intracondral *adj.* intrachondral.

intracondrial *adj.* intrachondrial.

intraconducto *m.* intraduct.

intracordal *adj.* intrachordal.

intracordial *adj.* intracordal.

intracoronal *adj.* intracoronal.

intracorporal *adj.* intracorporal.

intracorpóreo, -a *adj.* intracorporeal.

intracorpuscular *adj.* intracorpuscular.

intracostal *adj.* intracostal.

intracraneal *adj.* intracranial.

intracutáneo, -a *adj.* intracutaneous.

intrad intrad.
intradérmico, -ca *adj.* intradermal.
intradermorreacción *f.* intradermoreaction.
intraductal *adj.* intraductal.
intraduodenal *adj.* intraduodenal.
intradural *adj.* intradural.
intraembrionario, -ria *adj.* intraembryonic.
intraepidérmico, -ca *adj.* intraepidermal.
intraepifisario, -ria *adj.* intraepiphyseal.
intraepitelial *adj.* intraepithelial.
intraeritrocítico, -ca *adj.* intraerythrocytic.
intraescleral *adj.* intrascleral.
intraesclerótico, -ca *adj.* intrascleral.
intraescrotal *adj.* intrascrotal.
intraespinal *adj.* intraspinal.
intraesplénico, -ca *adj.* intrasplenic.
intraesternal *adj.* intraesternal.
intraestromático, -ca *adj.* intrastromal.
intraestrómico, -ca *adj.* intrastromal.
intrafaradización *f.* intrafaradization.
intrafascicular *adj.* intrafascicular.
intrafebril *adj.* intrafebrile.
intrafetación *f.* intrafetation.
intrafilar *adj.* intrafilar.
intrafistular *adj.* intrafistular.
intrafistuloso, -sa *adj.* intrafistular.
intrafisural *adj.* intrafissural.
intrafolicular *adj.* intrafollicular.
intrafusal *adj.* intrafusal.
intragalvanización *f.* intragalvanization.
intragástrico, -ca *adj.* intragastric.
intragemal *adj.* intragemmal.
intragemario, -ria *adj.* intragemmal.
intragénico, -ca *adj.* intragenic.
intragiral *adj.* intragyral.
intragírico, -ca *adj.* intragyral.
intraglandular *adj.* intraglandular.
intraglobular *adj.* intraglobular.
intragraso, -sa *adj.* intrafat.
intrahepático, -ca *adj.* intrahepatic.
intrahioideo, -a *adj.* intrahyoid.
intraictal *adj.* intraictal.
intraintestinal *adj.* intraintestinal.
intralaminar *adj.* intralamellar.
intralaríngeo, -a *adj.* intralaryngeal.
intralesional *adj.* intralesional.
intraleucocitario, -ria *adj.* intraleukocytic.
intraleucocítico, -ca *adj.* intraleukocytic.
intraligamentario, -ria *adj.* intraligamentous.
intraligamentoso, -sa *adj.* intraligamentous.
intralingual *adj.* intralingual.
intralobar *adj.* intralobar.
intralobular *adj.* intralobar.
intralobulillar *adj.* intralobular.
intralocular *adj.* intralocular.
intraluminal *adj.* intraluminal.
intramamario, -ria *adj.* intramammary.
intramarginal *adj.* intramarginal.
intramastoiditis *f.* intramastoiditis.
intramedular *adj.* intramedullary.
intramembranoso, -sa *adj.* intramembranous.
intrameníngeo, -a *adj.* intrameningeal.
intramiocardíaco, -ca *adj.* intramyocardial.
intramiometrial *adj.* intramyometrial.
intramolecular *adj.* intramolecular.
intramural *adj.* intramural.
intramuscular *adj.* intramuscular.
intranasal *adj.* intranasal.
intranatal *adj.* intranatal.
intraneural *adj.* intraneural.
intranuclear *adj.* intranuclear.
intraocular *adj.* intraocular.
intraoperatorio, -ria *adj.* intraoperative.
intraoral *adj.* intraoral.

intraorbital *adj.* intraorbital.
intraorbitario, -ria *adj.* intraorbital.
intraóseo, -a *adj.* intraosseous.
intraosteal *adj.* intraosteal.
intraótico, -ca *adj.* intra-aural.
intraovárico, -ca *adj.* intraovarian.
intraovular *adj.* intraovular.
intraparenquimatoso, -sa *adj.* intraparenchymatous.
intraparietal *adj.* intraparietal.
intraparto intrapartum.
intrapélvico, -ca *adj.* intrapelvic.
intrapericárdico, -ca *adj.* intrapericardiac, intrapericardial.
intraperineal *adj.* intraperineal.
intraperitoneal *adj.* intraperitoneal.
intrapersonal *adj.* intrapersonal.
intrapial *adj.* intrapial.
intrapirético, -ca *adj.* intrapyretic.
intraplacentario, -ria *adj.* intraplacental.
intrapleural *adj.* intrapleural.
intrapontino, -na *adj.* intrapontine.
intraprostático, -ca *adj.* intraprostatic.
intraprotoplasmático, -ca *adj.* intraprotoplasmic.
intraprotoplásmico, -ca *adj.* intraprotoplasmic.
intrapsíquico, -ca *adj.* intrapsychic, intrapsychical.
intrapulmonar *adj.* intrapulmonary.
intraquístico, -ca *adj.* intracystic.
intrarraquídeo, -a *adj.* intrarachidian.
intrarrectal *adj.* intrarectal.
intrarrenal *adj.* intrarenal.
intrarretiniano, -na *adj.* intraretinal.
intrascleral *adj.* intrascleral.
intrasclerótico, -ca *adj.* intrascleral.
intrascrotal *adj.* intrascrotal.
intraselar *adj.* intrasellar.
intraseroso, -sa *adj.* intraserous.
intrasillar *adj.* intrasellar.
intrasinovial *adj.* intrasynovial.
intraspinal *adj.* intraspinal.
intrasplénico, -ca *adj.* intrasplenic.
intrasticial *adj.* intrastitial.
intrastromático, -ca *adj.* intrastromatic.
intrastrómico, -ca *adj.* intrastromic.
intratable *adj.* intractable.
intratarsal *adj.* intratarsal.
intratarsiano, -na *adj.* intratarsal.
intratecal *adj.* intrathecal.
intratenar *adj.* intrathenar.
intratesticular *adj.* intratesticular.
intratimpánico, -ca *adj.* intratympanic.
intratonsilar *adj.* intratonsillar.
intratorácico, -ca *adj.* intrathoracic.
intratrabecular *adj.* intratrabecular.
intratraqueal *adj.* intratracheal.
intratubárico, -ca *adj.* intratubal.
intratubario, -ria *adj.* intratubal.
intratubular *adj.* intratubular.
intraural *adj.* intra-aural.
intraureteral *adj.* intraureteral.
intrauretral *adj.* intraurethral.
intrauterino, -na *adj.* intrauterine.
intravaginal *adj.* intravaginal.
intravasación *f.* intravasation.
intravascular *adj.* intravascular.
intravelloso, -sa *adj.* intravillous.
intravenación *f.* intravenation.
intravenoso, -sa *adj.* intravenous.
intraventricular *adj.* intraventicular.
intravertebral *adj.* intravertebral.
intravesical *adj.* intravesical.
intravital *adj.* intravital.

intravitelino, -na *adj.* intravitelline.
intravítreo, -a *adj.* intravitreous.
intrayugular *adj.* intrajugular.
intrínseco, -ca *adj.* intrinsic.
introductor *m.* introducer.
introflexión *f.* introflexion.
introgástrico, -ca *adj.* introgastric.
introgresión *f.* introgression.
introito *m.* introitus.
   introito vaginal introitus vaginae.
intromisión *f.* intromission.
intromitente *adj.* intromittent.
intrón *m.* intron.
introspección *f.* introspection, insight.
introspectivo, -va *adj.* introspective.
introsuscepción *f.* introsusception.
introversión *f.* introversion.
introvertido, -da *adj.* introvert.
introvertir *v.* introvert.
introyección *f.* introjection.
intrusión *f.* intrusion.
intrusismo profesional *m.* professional intrusism.
intubación *f.* intubation.
   intubación acueductal aqueductal intubation.
   intubación altercursiva altercursive intubation.
   intubación bucal oral intubation.
   intubación bucotraqueal orotracheal intubation.
   intubación endotraqueal endotracheal intubation.
   intubación intratraqueal intratracheal intubation.
   intubación nasal nasal intubation.
   intubación nasogástrica nasogastric intubation.
   intubación nasotraqueal nasotracheal intubation.
   intubación nasotraqueal ciega blind nasotracheal intubation.
   intubación oral oral intubation.
   intubación orotraqueal orotracheal intubation.
intubacionista *m., f.* intubationist.
intubador *m.* intubador.
intubar *v.* intubate.
intuición *f.* intuition.
   intuición delirante delirious intuition.
   intuición psicótica psychotic insight.
intumecer *v.* intumesce.
intumescencia *f.* intumescence, intumescentia.
   intumescencia cervical cervical intumescence, intumescentia cervicalis.
   intumescencia lumbar lumbar intumescence, intumescentia lumbalis.
   intumescencia lumbosacra intumescentia lumbosacralis.
intumescente *adj.* intumescent.
intumescentia *f.* intumescence, intumescentia.
intumescer *v.* intumesce.
intussusceptum intussusceptum.
intussuscipiens intussuscipiens.
intususcepción *f.* intussusception.
   intususcepción agónica agonic intussusception.
   intususcepción cólica colic intussusception.
   intususcepción doble double intussusception.
   intususcepción ileal ileal intussusception.
   intususcepción iliocecal ileocecal intussusception.

intususcepción intestinal intestinal intussusception.
intususcepción postmortem postmortem intussusception.
intususcepción retrógrada retrograde intussusception.
intususcepción yeyunogástrica jejunogastric intussusception.
intususceptum intussusceptum.
intususcipiens intussuscipiens.
intususceptivo, -va *adj.* intussusceptive.
inulación *f.* swarming.
inulasa *f.* inulase.
inulina *f.* inulin.
inulinasa *f.* inulinase.
inunción *f.* inunction.
inundación *f.* flooding.
invacunación *f.* invaccination.
invaginación *f.* invagination.
invaginación basilar basilar invagination.
invaginador *m.* invaginator.
invaginar *v.* invaginate.
invalidez *f.* invalidism.
inválido, -da *adj.* invalid, handicapped.
invasibilidad *f.* invasiveness.
invasión *f.* invasion.
invasividad *f.* invasiveness.
invasivo, -va *adj.* invasive.
invasor, -ra *adj.* invasive.
inventario *m.* inventory.
inventario clínico multiaxial de Millón (MCMI) Millon clinical multiaxial inventory (MCMI).
inventario diagnóstico de Beck (IDB) Beck's diagnostic inventory (BDI).
inventario multifásico de la personalidad de Minnesota, Minnesota multiphasic personality inventory (MMPI).
inventario de personalidad personality inventory.
inverminación *f.* invermination.
invernación *f.* overwintering.
inversión *f.* inversion.
inversión de adrenalina adrenaline inversion, epinephrine inversion.
inversión de carbohidratos carbohydrate inversion.
inversión cromosómica chromosome inversion.
inversión narcótica narcotic inversion.
inversión paracéntrica paracentric inversion.
inversión pericéntrica pericentric inversion.
inversión por presión pressure inversion.
inversión sexual sexual inversion.
inversión térmica thermic inversion.
inversión uterina, inversión del útero uterine inversion, inversion of the uterus.
inversión visceral visceral inversion.
inversor *m.* invertor.
invertasa *f.* invertase.
invertebrado, -da *m., f.* invertebrate.
invertido, -da *m., f. y adj.* invert.
invertina *f.* invertin.
investigación *f.* investigation, research, searching.
investigación científica scientific investigation.
investigación científica en animales investigation in animals.
investigación clínica clinical investigation, clinical research.
investigación clínica en el tercer mundo clinical investigation in the third world.
investigación de enfermería nursing research.
investigación de relación relation searching.

investigación no terapéutica non-therapeutic investigation.
investigación terapéutica therapeutic investigation.
inveterado, -da *adj.* inveterate.
inviable *adj.* non-viable.
inviscación *f.* inviscation.
involución *f.* involution.
involución senil senile involution.
involución uterina, involución del útero uterine involution, involution of the uterus.
involucional *adj.* involutional.
involucrina *f.* involucrin.
involucro *m.* involucre, involucrum.
involuntario, -ria *adj.* involuntary.
involuntomotor, -ra *adj.* involuntomotory.
involutivo, -va *adj.* involutional.
inyección *f.* injection.
inyección de albúmina marcada con^{125} I iodinated I125 albumin injection.
inyección de albúmina marcada con^{131} I iodinated I131 albumin injection.
inyección anatómica anatomical injection.
inyección burda coarse injection.
inyección circuncorneal circumcorneal injection.
inyección a chorro, inyección de chorro jet injection.
inyección de cloruro de sodio sodium chloride injection.
inyección de cloruro de sodio y dextrosa, inyección de cloruro sódico y dextrosa dextrose and sodium chloride injection.
inyección por depósito, inyección depot depot injection.
inyección endodérmica endermic injection.
inyección epifascial epifascial injection.
inyección esclerosante sclerosing injection.
inyección fina fine injection.
inyección de fructosa fructose injection.
inyección gaseosa gaseous injection.
inyección gelatinosa gelatin injection.
inyección de hidrolizado proteico protein hydrolysate injection.
inyección de hierro dextrán iron dextran injection.
inyección de hierro sorbitex iron sorbitex injection.
inyección hipodérmica hypodermic injection.
inyección de hipófisis posterior posterior pituitary injection.
inyección de insulina insulin injection.
inyección intraarticular intraarticular injection.
inyección intracutánea intracutaneous injection.
inyección intradermal, inyección intradérmica intradermal injection, intradermic injection.
inyección intramuscular intramuscular injection.
inyección intratecal intrathecal injection.
inyección intravascular intravascular injection.
inyección intravenosa intravenous injection.
inyección intraventricular intraventricular injection.
inyección de lactato sódico sodium lactate injection.
inyección lactada de Ringer, inyección de lactato de Ringer lactated Ringer's injection.
inyección opacificante opacifying injection.
inyección paraperióstica paraperiosteal injection.

inyección parenquimatosa parenchymatous injection.
inyección de pertenectato de sodio marcado con Tc99m sodium pertenechtate Tc99m injection.
inyección preservativa preservative injection.
inyección de radiocromato de sodio sodium radiochromate injection.
inyección de recuerdo booster injection.
inyección regular de insulina regular insulin injection.
inyección de Ringer Ringer's injection.
inyección sensibilizadora, inyección sensibilizante sensitizing injection.
inyección subcutánea subcutaneous injection.
inyección de sulfato de protamina protamine sulfate injection.
inyección de vasopresina vasopressin injection.
inyección en Z Z-tract injection.
inyectable *m. y adj.* injectable.
inyectado, -da *adj.* injected.
inyectar *v.* inject.
inyector *m.* injector.
inyector a chorro jet injector.
iodado, -da *adj.* iodate.
iodemia *f.* iodemia.
iodermia *m.* ioderma.
iodo *m.* iodine.
iodocolesterol *m.* iodocholesterol.
iodotironinas *f.* iodothyronines.
iodotirosinas *f.* iodotyrosines.
iofobia *f.* iophobia.
iohexol *m.* iohexol.
ión *m.* ion.
ión amonio ion ammonium.
ión bipolar, ión dipolar dipolar ion.
ión espectador spectator ion.
ión gramo gram-ion.
ión de hidrógeno hydrogen ion.
ión de hidronio, ión hidronio hydronium ion.
ión hidruro hydride ion.
ión oxonio oxonium ion.
ión sulfonio sulfonium ion.
iónico, -ca *adj.* ionic.
ionización *f.* ionization.
ionización en avalancha avalanche ionization.
ionización de Townsend Townsend ionization.
ionizar *v.* ionize.
ionocolorímetro *m.* ionocolorimeter.
ionoferograma *m.* ionopherogram.
ionoforesis *f.* ionophoresis.
ionoforético, -ca *adj.* ionophoretic.
ionóforo *m.* ionophore.
ionofosia *f.* ionophose.
ionógeno, -na *adj.* ionogenic.
ionograma *m.* ionogram.
ionómero *m.* iometer.
ionómetro *m.* ionometer.
ionoscopio *m.* ionoscope.
ionósfera *f.* ionosphere.
ionoterapia *f.* ionotherapy.
ión-proteína *f.* ion-protein.
iontocuantímetro *m.* iontoquantimeter.
iontoforesis *f.* iontophoresis.
iontoforético, -ca *adj.* iontophoretic.
iontorradiómetro *m.* iontoradiometer.
iontoterapia *f.* iontotherapy.
iopamidol *m.* iopamidol.
iotacismo *m.* iotacism.
iotalamato *m.* iothalamate.

iotalamato meglumina iothalamate meglumine.

iotalamato sódico iothalamate sodium.

ioxaglato *m.* ioxaglate.

ipodato sódico *m.* sodium ipodate.

ipsación *f.* ipsation.

ipsilateral *adj.* ipsilateral.

ipsiliforme *adj.* ypsiliform.

ipsiloide *adj.* ypsiloid.

ipsismo *m.* ipsism.

ipsolateral *adj.* ipsilateral.

ira *f.* anger, rage.

ira falsa, ira fingida sham rage.

irascibilidad *f.* irascibility.

iridal *adj.* iridal.

iridalgia *f.* iridalgia.

iridauxesis *f.* iridauxesis.

iridectasia *f.* iridectasis.

iridectomesodiálisis *f.* iridectomesodialysis.

iridectomía *f.* iridectomy.

iridectomía basal basal iridectomy.

iridectomía completa complete iridectomy.

iridectomía estenopeica stenopeic iridectomy.

iridectomía en ojal buttonhole iridectomy.

iridectomía óptica optic iridectomy, optical iridectomy.

iridectomía periférica peripheral iridectomy.

iridectomía preliminar preliminary iridectomy.

iridectomía preparatoria preparatory iridectomy.

iridectomía en sector, iridectomía sectorial sector iridectomy.

iridectomía terapéutica therapeutic iridectomy.

iridectomizar *v.* iridectomize.

iridéctomo *m.* iridectome.

iridectopia *f.* iridectopia.

iridectropión *m.* iridectropium.

iridemia *f.* iridemia.

iridencleisis *f.* iridencleisis.

iridenclisis *f.* iridencleisis.

iridentropión *m.* iridentropium.

irideremia *f.* irideremia.

iridescencia *f.* iridescence.

iridescente *adj.* iridescent.

iridesis *f.* iridesis.

iridiagnosis *f.* iridiagnosis.

iridial *adj.* iridial.

iridiano, -na *adj.* iridian.

irídico, -ca *adj.* iridic.

iridiscencia *f.* iridescence.

iridiscente *adj.* iridescent.

iridización *f.* iridization.

iridoavulsión *f.* iridoavulsion.

iridocapsulitis *f.* iridocapsulitis.

iridocele *m.* iridocele.

iridociclectomía *f.* iridocyclectomy.

iridociclitis *f.* iridocyclitis.

iridociclitis Heterocrómica, iridociclitis Heterocrómica de Fuchs heterochromic iridocyclitis, Fuchs' heterochromic iridocyclitis.

iridociclitis hipertensiva hypertensive iridocyclitis.

iridociclitis séptica iridocyclitis septica.

iridociclocoroiditis *f.* iridocyclochoroiditis.

iridocinesia *f.* iridokinesia, iridokinesis.

iridocinesis *f.* iridokinesis.

iridocinético, -ca *adj.* iridokinetic.

iridocistectomía *f.* iridocystectomy.

iridocoloboma *m.* iridocoloboma.

iridoconstrictor, -ra *m. y adj.* iridoconstrictor.

iridocorneal *adj.* iridocorneal.

iridocorneoscleréctomia *f.* iridocorneosclerectomy.

iridocoroiditis *f.* iridochoroiditis.

iridodesis *f.* iridodesis.

iridodiagnosis *f.* iridodiagnosis.

iridodiagnóstico *m.* iridodiagnosis.

iridodiálisis *f.* iridodialyisis.

iridodiastasis *f.* iridodiastasis.

iridodilatador, -ra *m. y adj.* iridodilator.

iridodonesis *f.* iridodonesis.

iridoesclerotomía *f.* iridosclerotomy.

iridoleptinsis *f.* iridoleptynsis.

iridólisis *f.* iridolysis.

iridología *f.* iridology.

iridomalacia *f.* iridomalacia.

iridomesodiálisis *f.* iridomesodialysis.

iridomotor, -ra *adj.* iridomotor.

iridonco *m.* iridoncus.

iridoncosis *f.* iridoncosis.

iridoparálisis *f.* iridoparalysis.

iridopatía *f.* iridopathy.

iridoperifacitis *f.* iridoperiphakitis.

iridoperifaquitis *f.* iridoperiphakitis.

iridoplejía *f.* iridoplegia.

iridoplejía de acomodación accommodation iridoplegia.

iridoplejía completa complete iridoplegia.

iridoplejía refleja reflex iridoplegia.

iridoplejía simpática sympathetic iridoplegia.

iridoptosis *f.* iridoptosis.

iridopupilar *adj.* iridopupillary.

iridoqueratitis *f.* iridokeratitis.

iridorrexis *f.* iridorhexis.

iridosclerotomía *f.* iridosclerotomy.

iridosquisis *f.* iridoschisis.

iridosquisma *m.* iridoschisma.

iridostéresis *f.* iridosteresis.

iridotasis *f.* iridotasis.

iridotomía *f.* iridotomy.

iris *m.* iris.

iris abombado, iris bombé iris bombé.

iris en meseta plateau iris.

iris separado detached iris.

iris en sombrilla umbrella iris.

iris tremulans, iris trémulo tremulous iris.

irisopsia *f.* irisopsia.

irítico, -ca *adj.* iritic.

iritis *f.* iritis.

iritis blenorrágica con recaídas iritis blennorrhagique à rechutes.

iritis catamenial iritis catamenialis.

iritis diabética diabetic iritis.

iritis esponjosa spongy iritis.

iritis estafilococoalérgica recidivante iritis recidivans staphylococcoallergica.

iritis fibrinosa fibrinous iritis.

iritis folicular follicular iritis.

iritis glaucomatosa iritis glaucomatosa.

iritis gotosa gouty iritis.

iritis guttata de Doyne Doyne's guttate iritis.

iritis hemorrágica hemorrhagic iritis.

iritis nodular nodular iritis.

iritis obturante iritis obturans.

iritis papulosa iritis papulosa.

iritis plásica, iritis plástica plastic iritis.

iritis primaria primary iritis.

iritis purulenta purulent iritis.

iritis secundaria secondary iritis.

iritis serosa serous iritis.

iritis silenciosa quiet iritis.

iritis simpática sympathetic iritis.

iritis tranquila quiet iritis.

iritis urática uratic iritis.

iritoectomía *f.* iritectomy.

iritomía *f.* iritomy.

irotomía *f.* iritomy.

irradiación *f.* irradiation.

irradiación corporal total total body irradiation.

irradiación linfoide total (ILT) total lymphoid irradiation (TLI).

irradiación local del injerto local graft irradiation.

irradiado, -da *adj.* irradiate.

irradiar¹ *v.* irradiate.

irradiar² *v.* radiate.

irreal *adj.* dereistic.

irreducible *adj.* irreducible.

irregular *adj.* irregular.

irregularidad *f.* irregularity.

irregularidad del pulso irregularity of the pulse.

irreinoculabilidad *f.* irreinoculability.

irrespirable *adj.* irrespirable.

irresponsabilidad *f.* irresponsibility.

irresponsabilidad criminal criminal irresponsibility.

irresucitable *adj.* irresucitable.

irreversible *adj.* irreversible.

irrigación *f.* irrigation.

irrigación de ácido acético acetic acid irrigation.

irrigación de ácido aminoacético aminoacetic acid irrigation.

irrigación de cloruro sódico sodium chloride irrigation.

irrigación colónica colonic irrigation.

irrigación de la colostomía colostomy irrigation.

irrigación continua continuous irrigation.

irrigación fría cold caloric irrigation.

irrigación gingival gingival blood irrigation.

irrigación goteo-aspiración drip-suck irrigation.

irrigación de una herida wound irrigation.

irrigación mediata mediate irrigation.

irrigación de la ostomía ostomy irrigation.

irrigación de Ringer Ringer's irrigation.

irrigación salina saline irrigation.

irrigación vaginal vaginal irrigation.

irrigación vesical bladder irrigation.

irrigador *m.* irrigator.

irrigar *v.* irrigate.

irrigorradioscopia *f.* irrigoradioscopy.

irrigoscopia *f.* irrigoscopy.

irritabilidad *f.* irritability.

irritabilidad eléctrica electric irritability.

irritabilidad del estómago irritability of the stomach.

irritabilidad mecánica mechanical irritability.

irritabilidad miotática myotatic irritability.

irritabilidad muscular muscular irritability.

irritabilidad nerviosa nervous irritability.

irritabilidad química chemical irritability.

irritabilidad táctil tactile irritability.

Irritabilidad vesical irritability of the bladder.

irritable *adj.* irritable.

irritación *f.* irritation.

irritación directa direct irritation.

irritación funcional functional irritation.

irritación peritoneal peritoneal tenderness, abdominal tenderness, peritoneal sign.

irritación simpática sympathetic irritation.

irritante *m. y adj.* irritant.

irritante primario primary irritant.

irritativo, -va *adj.* irritative.

isauxesis *f.* isauxesis.

ischias *f.* ischias.

ischium *m.* ischium.

iscogiria *f.* ischogyria.

iscuria *f.* ischuria.

iscuria espasmódica, iscuria espástica ischuria spastica.

iscuria paradójica ischuria paradoxa.

iscúrico, -ca *adj.* ischuretic.
iseiconía *f.* iseiconia.
iseicónico, -ca *adj.* iseiconic.
isla *f.* island.
   isla de Calleja island of Calleja.
   isla de Langerhans island of Langerhans.
   isla olfatoria olfactory island.
   isla ósea bone island.
   isla del páncreas, isla pancreática island of the pancreas, pancreatic island.
   isla de Pander Pander's island.
   isla sanguínea blood island.
islote *m.* islet.
   islote de Calleja islet of Calleja.
   islote de Langerhans islet of Langerhans.
   islote pancreático pancreatic islet.
   islote sanguíneo blood islet.
   islote de Walthard Walthard's islet.
isoadrenocorticismo *m.* isoadrenocorticism.
isoaglutinación *f.* isoagglutination.
isoaglutinina *f.* isoagglutinin.
isoaglutinógeno, -na *m.* isoagglutinogen.
isoalelismo *m.* isoallelism.
isoalelo *m.* isoallele.
isoamilasa *f.* isoamylase.
isoanafilaxia *f.* isoanaphylaxis.
isoanafilaxis *f.* isoanaphylaxis.
isoanticuerpo *m.* isoantibody.
isoantígeno *m.* isoantigen.
isóbaro *m.* isobar.
isobárico, -ca *adj.* isobaric.
isobolismo *m.* isobolism.
isocalórico, -ca *adj.* isocaloric.
isocapnia *f.* isocapnia.
isocápnico, -ca *adj.* isocapnic.
isocelular *adj.* isocellular.
isocéntrico, -ca *adj.* isocentric.
isocentro *m.* isocenter.
isocíclico, -ca *adj.* isocyclic.
isocinético, -ca *adj.* isokinetic.
isocitolisina *f.* isocytolysin.
isocitosis *f.* isocytosis.
isocitotoxina *f.* isocytotoxin.
isoclina *f.* isocline.
isocoagulasa *f.* isocoagulase.
isocomplemento *m.* isocomplement.
isocomplementófilo, -la *adj.* isocomplementophilic.
isocoria *f.* isochoria.
isocórico, -ca *adj.* isochoric.
isocórtex *m.* isocortex.
isocorteza *f.* isocortex.
isocromático, -ca *adj.* isochromatic.
isocromatófilo, -la *adj.* isochromatophil, isochromatophile.
isocromosoma *m.* isochromosome.
isocronal *adj.* isochronal.
isocronía *f.* isochronia.
isocrónico, -ca *adj.* isochronic.
isocronismo *m.* isochronism.
isócrono, -na *adj.* isochron, isochronous.
isocroo, -a *adj.* isochrous.
isocuerpo *m.* isobody.
isodactilia *f.* isodactylism.
isodactilismo *m.* isodactylism.
isodenso, -sa *adj.* isodense.
isodiamétrico, -ca *adj.* isodiametric.
isodinámico, -ca *adj.* isodynamic.
isodinamógeno, -na *adj.* isodynamogenic.
isodonto, -ta *adj.* isodontic.
isodosis *f.* isodose.
isoecogénico, -ca *adj.* isoechogenic.
isoefecto *m.* isoeffect.
isoeléctrico, -ca *adj.* isoelectric.
isoenergético, -ca *adj.* isoenergetic.

isoenzima *f.* isoenzyme.
   isoenzima CPK fraction isoenzyme CPK.
   isoenzima de Regan Regan isoenzyme.
isoeritrólisis *f.* isoerythrolysis.
   isoeritrólisis neonatal neonatal isoerythrolysis.
isoestimulación *f.* isostimulation.
isofagia *f.* isophagy.
isofenolización *f.* isophenolization.
isoflujo *m.* isoflows.
isoforia *f.* isophoria.
isofotómetro *m.* isophotometer.
isogametía *f.* isogamety.
isogamético, -ca *adj.* isogametic.
isogameto *m.* isogamete.
Isogamla *f.* isogamy.
isógamo *m.* isogamus.
isogeneico, -ca *adj.* isogeneic.
isogenérico, -ca *adj.* isogeneric.
isogénesis *f.* isogenesis.
isogenia *f.* isogenesis.
isogénico, -ca *adj.* isogenic.
isógeno, -na *adj.* isogenous.
isognato, -ta *adj.* isognathous.
isohemaglutinación *f.* isohemagglutination.
isohemaglutinina *f.* isohemagglutinin.
isohemolisina *f.* isohemolysin.
isohemólisis *f.* isohemolysis.
isohemolítico, -ca *adj.* isohemolytic.
isohídrico, -ca *adj.* isohydric.
isohidruria *f.* isohydruria.
isohipercitosis *f.* isohypercytosis.
isohipocitosis *f.* isohypocytosis.
isoiconía *f.* isoiconia.
isoicónico, -ca *adj.* isoiconic.
isoinjerto *m.* isograft.
isoinmunización *f.* isoimmunization.
   isoinmunización Rh Rh isoimmunization.
isointenso, -sa *adj.* isointense.
isolecítico, -ca *adj.* isolecithal.
isolecito, -ta *adj.* isolecithal.
isoleucina *f.* isoleucine.
isoleucoaglutinina *f.* isoleukoagglutinin.
isolisina *f.* isolysin.
isólisis *f.* isolysis.
isolítico, -ca *adj.* isolytic.
isólogo, -ga *m.* isologous.
isomastigoto, -ta *adj.* isomastigote.
isomerasa *f.* isomerase.
isomérico, -ca *adj.* isomeric.
isomerismo *m.* isomerism.
isomerización *f.* isomerization.
isómero, -ra *adj.* isomer.
isometría *f.* isometry.
isométrico, -ca *adj.* isometric.
isometropía *f.* isometropia.
isomicrogameto *m.* isomicrogamete.
isomórfico, -ca *adj.* isomorphic.
isomorfismo *m.* isomorphism.
isomorfo, -fa *adj.* isomorphous.
isoncótico, -ca *adj.* isoncotic.
isooncótico, -ca *adj.* iso-oncotic.
isoosmótico, -ca *adj.* iso-osmotic.
isopatía *f.* isopathy.
isopía *f.* isopia.
isopícnico, -ca *adj.* isopyknic.
isopicnosis *f.* isopyknosis.
isopicnótico, -ca *adj.* isopyknotic.
isoplasontes *m.* isoplassonts.
isoplastia *f.* isoplasty.
isoplástico, -ca *adj.* isoplastic.
isopleta *f.* isopleth.
isopotencial *m.* isopotential.
isoprecipitina *f.* isoprecipitin.
isóptero *m.* isopter.

isorrea *f.* isorrhea.
isorreico, -ca *adj.* isorrheic.
isorrópico, -ca *adj.* isorrhopic.
isoscopio *m.* isoscope.
isosensibilización *f.* isosensitization.
isosexual *adj.* isosexual.
isosmoticidad *f.* isosmoticity.
isosmótico, -ca *adj.* isosmotic.
isospermotoxina *f.* isospermotoxin.
Isospora Isospora.
   Isospora belli Isospora belli.
   Isospora hominis Isospora hominis.
isosporiasis *f.* isosporiasis.
isostenuria *f.* isosthenuria.
isóstero *m.* isostere.
isosuero *m.* isoserum.
isosueroterapia *f.* isoserotherapy.
isoterapia *f.* isotherapy.
isotérmico, -ca *adj.* isothermic.
isotípico, -ca *adj.* isotypical.
isotipo *m.* isotype.
isotonía *f.* isotonia.
isotonicidad *f.* isotonicity.
isotónico, -ca *adj.* isotonic.
isotono *m.* isotone.
isotópico, -ca *adj.* isotopic.
isotopo *m.* isotope.
   isótopo radiactivo radioactive isotope.
isotopología *f.* isotopology.
isotóxico, -ca *adj.* isotoxic.
isotoxina *f.* isotoxin.
isotrasplantación *f.* isotransplantation.
isotrasplante *m.* isotransplantation.
isotrimorfismo *m.* isotrimorphism.
isotrimorfo, -fa *adj.* isotrimorphous.
isotrón *m.* isotron.
isotropía *f.* isotropy.
isotrópico, -ca *adj.* isotropic.
isótropo, -pa *adj.* isotropous.
isovolumen *m.* isovolume.
isovolumétrico, -ca *adj.* isovolumetric.
isovolúmico, -ca *adj.* isovolumic.
isozima *f.* isozyme.
isquemia *f.* ischemia.
   isquemia cerebral cerebral ischemia.
   Isquemia intestinal crónica chronic intestinal ischemia.
   isquemia del miocardio, isquemia miocardíaca myocardial ischemia.
   isquemia postural postural ischemia.
   isquemia renal renal ischemia.
   isquemia retiniana ischemia retinae.
   isquemia silenciosa silent ischemia.
   isquemia subclínica silent ischemia.
   isquemia uterina uterine ischemia.
isquémico, -ca *adj.* ischemic.
isquesis *f.* ischesis.
isquiaco, -ca *adj.* ischiac.
isquiadelfo *m.* ischiadelphus.
isquiádico, -ca *adj.* ischiadic, ischiadicus, ischial, ischiatic.
isquial *adj.* ischial.
isquialgia *f.* ischialgia.
isquiático, -ca *adj.* ischiatic.
isquidrosis *f.* ischidrosis.
isquiectomía *f.* ischiectomy.
isquioanal *adj.* ischioanal.
isquiobulbar *adj.* ischiobulbar.
isquiocapsular *adj.* ischiocapsular.
isquiocavernoso, -sa *adj.* ischiocavernous.
isquiocele *m.* ischiocele.
isquiococcígeo, -a *adj.* ischiococcygeal.
isquiodídimo *m.* ischiodidymus.
isquiodimia *f.* ischiodymia.
isquiodinia *f.* ischiodynia.

isquiofemoral *adj.* ischiofemoral.
isquiohebotomía *f.* ischiohebotomy.
isquiómelo *m.* ischiomelus.
isquion *m.* ischium.
isquioneuralgia *f.* ischioneuralgia.
isquionitis *f.* ischionitis.
isquiopagia *f.* ischiopagia, ischiopagy.
isquiópago *m.* ischiopagus.
isquioperineal *adj.* ischioperineal.
isquioperoneo, -a *adj.* ischiofibular.
isquiopúbico, -ca *adj.* ischiopubic.
isquioquimia *f.* ischiochimia.
isquiorrectal *adj.* ischiorectal.
isquiosacral *adj.* ischiosacral.
isquiosacro, -cra *adj.* ischiosacral.
isquiotibial *adj.* ischiotibial.
isquiotoracópago *m.* ischiothoracopagus.
isquiovaginal *adj.* ischiovaginal.
isquiovertebral *adj.* ischiovertebral.

isquiurético, -ca *m. y adj.* ischiuretic.
isquiuria *f.* ischiuria.
  isquiuria espástica ischiuria spastica.
istmectomía *f.* isthmectomy.
ístmico, -ca *adj.* isthmian, isthmic.
istmitis *f.* isthmitis.
istmo *m.* isthmus.
istmoespasmo *m.* isthmospasm.
istmoparálisis *f.* isthmoparalysis.
istmoplejía *f.* isthmoplegia.
isuria *f.* isuria.
iter iter.
  iter ad infundibulum iter ad infundibulum.
  iter chordae anterius iter chordae anterius.
  iter chordae posterius iter chordae posterius.
  iter dentis, iter dentium iter dentium.
  iter de Silvio iter of Sylvius.
iteración *f.* iteration.
iteral *adj.* iteral.

iteroparidad *f.* iteroparity.
iteróparo, -ra *adj.* iteroparous.
Ixodes Ixodes.
  Ixodes bicornis Ixodes bicornis.
  Ixodes cavipalpus Ixodes cavipalpus.
  Ixodes dammini Ixodes dammini.
  Ixodes frequens Ixodes frequens.
  Ixodes pacificus Ixodes pacificus.
  Ixodes persulcatus Ixodes persulcatus.
  Ixodes ricinus Ixodes ricinus.
  Ixodes scapularis Ixodes scapularis.
ixodiasis *f.* ixodiasis.
ixódico, -ca *adj.* ixodic.
Ixodidae Ixodidae.
Ixodides Ixodides.
ixódido *m.* ixodid.
ixodismo *m.* ixodism.
Ixodoidea Ixodoidea.
ixomielitis *f.* ixomyelitis.

J j

jabón *m.* soap, sapo.
  jabón de agua salada salt water soap.
  jabón animal animal soap.
  jabón blando soft soap, sapo mollis.
  jabón de Castilla Castile soap.
  jabón de cinc zinc soap.
  jabón de cuajada curd soap.
  jabón doméstico domestic soap, sapo domesticus.
  jabón duro hard soap.
  jabón fenicado carbolic soap.
  jabón insoluble insoluble soap.
  jabón líquido de hexaclorofeno hexachlorophene liquid soap.
  jabón marino marine soap.
  jabón medicinal blando medicinal soft soap, sapo mollis medicinalis.
  jabón de potasa potash soap.
  jabón de sebo tallow soap.
  jabón soluble soluble soap.
  jabón supergraso superfatted soap.
  jabón verde green soap, sapo viridis.
jabonadura *f.* mollin.
jabonoso, -sa *adj.* saponatus.
jactación *f.* jactatio.
  jactación cefálica nocturna jactatio capitis nocturna.
jactitación *f.* jactitation.
jaculífero, -ra *adj.* jaculiferous.
jadear *v.* pant.
jadeo *m.* panting, wheeze.
  jadeo asmatoide asthmatoid wheeze.
jalea *f.* jelly.
  jalea anticonceptiva contraceptive jelly.
  jalea cardíaca cardiac jelly.
  jalea de clorhidrato de lidocaína lidocaine hydrochloride jelly.
  jalea de clorhidrato de pramoxina pramoxine hydrochloride jelly.
  jalea contraceptiva contraceptive jelly.
  jalea de glicerina glycerin jelly.
  jalea vaginal vaginal jelly.
  jalea de Wharton Wharton's jelly.
janicéfalo *m.* janiceps.
  janicéfalo asimétrico janiceps assymmetrus.
  janicéfalo parásito janiceps parasiticus.
janiceps *m.* janiceps.
jaqueca *f.* migraine.
  jaqueca abdominal abdominal migraine.
  jaqueca confusional aguda acute confusional migraine.
  jaqueca fulgurante fulgurating migraine.
  jaqueca hemipléjica hemiplegic migraine.
  jaqueca oftálmica ophthalmic migraine.
  jaqueca oftalmopléjica ophthalmoplegic migraine.
jaquecoso, -sa *adj.* migranoid, migranous.
jarabe *m.* syrup.
  jarabe de ácido cítrico citric acid syrup.
  jarabe de ácido yodhídrico hydriodic acid syrup.

jarabe aromático de yerba santa aromatic eriodictyon syrup.
  jarabe de bálsamo de tolú tolu balsam syrup.
  jarabe de bitartrato de dihidrocodeinona dihydrocodeinone bitartrate syrup.
  jarabe de cacao cacao syrup.
  jarabe de cereza cherry syrup.
  jarabe de cereza silvestre wild cherry syrup.
  jarabe de citrato de piperacina piperazine citrate syrup.
  jarabe de clorhidrato de ciproheptadina cyproheptadine hydrochloride syrup.
  jarabe de clorhidrato de diciclomina dicyclomine hydrochloride syrup.
  jarabe de clorhidrato de metdilacina methdilazine hydrochloride syrup.
  jarabe de clorhidrato de prometacina promethazine hydrochloride syrup.
  jarabe de cocoa cocoa syrup.
  jarabe compuesto de pino blanco compound white pine syrup.
  jarabe compuesto de pino blanco con codeína compound white pine syrup with codeine.
  jarabe de ditartrato de hidrocodona hydrocodone bitartrate syrup.
  jarabe de frambuesa raspberry syrup.
  jarabe de goma arábiga acacia syrup.
  jarabe de guayacolato de glicerilo glyceryl guaiacolate syrup.
  jarabe de hoja sen senna syrup.
  jarabe de ipecacuana syrup of ipecac.
  jarabe de naranja orange syrup.
  jarabe de orozuz glycirrhiza syrup.
  jarabe de regaliz licorice syrup.
  jarabe simple simple syrup.
  jarabe de tolú syrup of tolu.
jargonafasia *f.* jargonaphasia, jargon aphasia.
jarra *f.* jar.
  jarra en campana bell jar.
  jarra de Leyden Leyden jar.
jaula *f.* cage.
  jaula de Faraday Faraday's cage.
  jaula de población population cage.
  jaula torácica thoracic cage.
jecorizar *v.* jecorize.
jején *m.* gnat, midge.
jeneriano, -na *adj.* Jennerian.
jenerización *f.* jennerization.
jennerización *f.* jennerization.
jerarquía *f.* hierarchy.
  jerarquía de Maslow, jerarquía de necesidades de Maslow Maslow's hierarchy, Maslow's hierarchy of need.
  jerarquía de respuesta response hierarchy.
jerga *f.* jargon.
jeringa *f.* syringe.
  jeringa de agua water syringe.
  jeringa de aire air syringe.
  jeringa de Anel Anel's syringe.

  jeringa anular ring syringe.
  jeringa de aspiración aspiration syringe.
  jeringa con bulbo de goma rubber-bulb syringe.
  jeringa de control control syringe.
  jeringa de Davidson Davidson syringe.
  jeringa dental dental syringe.
  jeringa de fragmentillos chip syringe.
  jeringa de fuente, jeringa fuente fountain syringe.
  jeringa hipodérmica hypodermic syringe.
  jeringa de Luer, jeringa de Luer-Lok Luer's syringe, Luer-Lok syringe.
  jeringa de Neisser Neisser's syringe.
  jeringa de Pitkin Pitkin syringe.
  jeringa sonda probe syringe.
jeringuilla *f.* syringe.
jet lag *m.* jet lag.
jitter *m.* jitter.
joroba *f.* hump, humpback.
  joroba de búfalo buffalo hump.
juanete *m.* bunion.
juccuya *f.* juccuya.
jucuya *f.* juccuya.
juego *m.* game, play.
  juego activo active play.
  juego amoroso foreplay.
  juego de azar gamble.
  juego compulsivo compulsive game.
  juego controlado controlled game.
  juego cooperativo cooperative play.
  juego de habilidad skill play.
  juego modelo model game.
  juego paralelo parallel play.
  juego patológico pathologic game.
jugo *m.* juice, succus.
  jugo del apetito appetite juice, appetite succus.
  jugo de cáncer, jugo canceroso cancer juice.
  jugo de cereza cherry juice, succus cerasi.
  jugo de exprimido press juice.
  jugo de frambuesa raspberry juice.
  jugo gástrico gastric juice, succus gastricus.
  jugo intestinal intestinal juice, succus entericus.
  jugo nuclear nuclear sap.
  jugo pancreático pancreatic juice, succus pancreaticus.
  jugo prostático prostatic juice, succus prostaticus.
jugulum jugulum.
jugum jugum.
juicio *m.* judgment.
Jukes *m.* Jukes.
jumentoso, -sa *adj.* jumentous.
jungiano, -na *adj.* Jungian.
junta *f.* yoke.
juramento *m.* oath, pledge.
  juramento de Hipócrates, juramento hipo-

crático oath of Hippocrates, hippocratic oath.

juramento de Nightingale Nightingale oath.

jurisprudencia *f.* jurisprudence.

jurisprudencia dental dental jurisprudence.

jurisprudencia médica medical jurisprudence.

justo justo.

justo major justo major.

justo minor justo minor.

juvenil *adj.* juvenile.

k *k*

kabure *m.* kabure.
kafindo *m.* kafindo.
kaif *m.* kaif.
kakke, kakké *m.* kakke, kakke disease.
kala-azar *f.* kala-azar.
kalicreína *f.* kallikrein.
kalímetro *m.* kalimeter.
kaliopenia *f.* kaliopenia.
kaliopénico, -ca *adj.* kaliopenic.
kalium kalium.
kaliuresis *f.* kaliuresis, kaluresis.
kaliurético, -ca *adj.* kaliuretic, kaluretic.
kallak *m.* kallak.
Kallikak *m.* Kallikak.
kaniemba *f.* kaniemba, kanyemba.
kanyemba *f.* kaniemba, kanyemba.
kansasina *f.* kansasiin.
kaodzera *f.* kaodzera.
kappacismo *m.* kappacism.
karnofsky *m.* karnofsky.
kasai *m.* kasai.
katal *m.* katal.

keratectomía *f.* keratectomy.
kerión *m.* kerion.
kermes *m.* kermes.
kernel *m.* kernel.
kerníctero *m.* kernicterus.
kernicterus *m.* kernicterus.
kimputu *m.* kimputu.
kinesialgia *f.* kinesialgia, kinesalgia.
kinesiatría *f.* kinesiatrics.
kinésica *f.* kinesics.
kinesímetro *m.* kinesimeter.
kinesiología *f.* kinesiology.
kinesiólogo, -ga *m., f.* kinesiologist.
kinesiómetro *m.* kinesimeter.
kinesiópata *m., f.* kinesipathist.
kinesiopatía *f.* kinesipathy.
kinesioterapeuta *m., f.* kinesipathist.
kinesioterapia *f.* kinesitherapy.
kinesis *f.* kinesis.
kinesiterapeuta *m., f.* kinesipathist.
kinesiterapia *f.* kinesitherapy.
kinesofobia *f.* kinesophobia.

kinestesia *f.* kinesthesia.
kinestésico, -ca *adj.* kinesthetic.
kinestesiómetro *m.* kinesthesiometer.
kinetoplasma *m.* kinetoplasm.
Kingella Kingella.
kinomómetro *m.* kinomometer.
kinotoxina *f.* kinotoxin.
Klebsiella Klebsiella.
Klebsielleae Klebsielleae.
klexografía *f.* klexography.
Kluyvera Kluyvera.
kneippismo *m.* kneippism.
kocherización *f.* kocherization.
koro *m.* koro.
kra-kra *m.* kra-kra.
kubisagari *m.* kubisagari, kubisagaru, kubisgari.
kubisagaru *m.* kubisagari, kubisagaru, kubisgari.
kubisgari *m.* kubisagari, kubisagaru, kubisgari.
Kurthia Kurthia.
kuru *m.* kuru.
kwashiorkor *m.* kwashiorkor.
kwaski *m.* kwaski.

L l

laberintectomía *f.* labyrinthectomy.
laberíntico, -ca *adj.* labyrinthine.
laberintitis *f.* labyrinthitis.
laberinto *m.* labyrinth, labyrinthus.
laberintotomía *f.* labyrinthotomy.
labiación *f.* lipping.
labiado, -da *adj.* liplike.
labial *adj.* labial.
labialismo *m.* labialism.
labialmente *adv.* labially.
lábil *adj.* labile.
labilidad *f.* lability.
labio *m.* lip, labium.
 labio fisurado cleft lip.
 labio hendido cleft lip.
 labio leporino harelip.
labioalveolar *adj.* labioalveolar.
labioaxiogingival *adj.* labioaxiogingival.
labiocervical *adj.* labiocervical.
labiocolocación *f.* labioplacement.
labiocorea *f.* labiochorea.
labiodental *adj.* labiodental.
labiogingival *adj.* labiogingival.
labioglosofaríngeo, -a *adj.* labioglossopharyngeal.
labioglosolaríngeo, -a *adj.* labioglossolaryngeal.
labiógrafo *m.* labiograph.
labioincisal *adj.* labioincisal.
labioinclinación *f.* labioclination.
labiolingual *adj.* labiolingual.
labiología *f.* labiology.
labiológico, -ca *adj.* labiologic.
labiomentoniano, -na *adj.* labiomental.
labiomicosis *f.* labiomycosis.
labionasal *adj.* labionasal.
labiopalatino, -na *adj.* labiopalatine.
labioplastia *f.* labioplasty.
labioposición *f.* labioplacement.
labiotenáculo *m.* labiotenaculum.
labioversión *f.* labioversion.
labítomo *m.* labitome.
laboratorio *m.* laboratory.
 laboratorio clínico clinical laboratory.
laborterapia *f.* worktherapy.
labrale labrale.
labrum labrum.
lacado *m.* lake.
lacar *v.* lake.
lacerable *adj.* lacerable.
laceración *f.* laceration.
 laceración cerebral brain laceration.
 laceración del cuero cabelludo scalp laceration.
 laceración vaginal vaginal laceration.
lacerado, -da *adj.* lacerated.
lacertus lacertus.
lacocistorrinostomía *f.* lacocystorhinostomy.
lacrimación *f.* lacrimation, lachrymation.
lacrimal *adj.* lachrymal, lacrimal.
lacrimalina *f.* lacrimalin.

lacrimatorio, -a *adj.* lacrimatory.
lacrimógeno, -na *adj.* lacrimator.
lacrimonasal *adj.* lacrimonasal.
lacrimotomía *f.* lacrimotomy.
lacrimótomo *m.* lacrimotome.
lactacidemia *f.* lactacidemia.
lactacidosis *f.* lactacidosis.
lactaciduria *f.* lactaciduria.
lactación *f.* lactation.
lactacional *adj.* lactational.
lactagogo, -ga *adj.* lactagogue.
lactancia¹ *f.* lactation.
lactancia² *f.* infancy.
lactancia materna *f.* breast-feeding.
 lactancia materna materna eficaz effective breast-feeding.
 lactancia materna materna ineficaz ineffective breast-feeding.
 lactancia materna materna interrumpida interrumpted breast-feeding.
lactante *m.* infant, nursing infant.
lactar *v.* lactate.
lácteo, -a *adj.* lacteal.
lactescencia *f.* lactescence.
lactescente *adj.* lactescent.
lacticacidemia *f.* lacticacidemia.
lacticemia *f.* lacticemia.
láctico, -ca *adj.* lactic.
lactífero, -ra *adj.* lactiferous.
lactífugo, -ga *adj.* lactifuge, lactifugal.
lactígeno, -na *adj.* lactigenous.
lactígero, -ra *adj.* lactigerous.
lactina *f.* lactin.
lactívoro, -ra *adj.* lactivorous.
lactobacilina *f.* lactobacillin.
lactobacilo *m.* lactobacillus.
Lactobacillaceae Lactobacillaceae.
Lactobacilleae Lactobacilleae.
Lactobacillus Lactobacillus.
 Lactobacillus acidophilus Lactobacillus acidophilus.
 Lactobacillus bifidus Lactobacillus bifidus.
 Lactobacillus bulgaricus Lactobacillus bulgaricus.
lactobutirómetro *m.* lactobutyrometer.
lactocele *m.* lactocele.
lactocrito *m.* lactocrit.
lactodensímetro *m.* lactodensimeter.
lactofarináceo, -a *adj.* lactofarinaceous.
lactoferrina *f.* lactoferrin.
lactogénesis *f.* lactogenesis.
lactogénico, -ca *adj.* lactogenic.
lactógeno *m.* lactogen.
 lactógeno placentario humano (HPL) human placental lactogen (HPL).
lactógeno, -na *adj.* lactogenic.
lactoglobulina *f.* lactoglobulin.
lactómetro *m.* lactometer.
lactoovovegetariano, -na *adj.* lacto-ovovegetarian.

lactoprecipitina *f.* lactoprecipitin.
lactoproteína *f.* lactoprotein.
lactorrea *f.* lactorrhea.
lactosa *f.* lactose.
lactoscopio *m.* lactoscope.
lactósido *m.* lactoside.
lactosidosis *f.* lactosidosis.
 lactosidosis de ceramida ceramide lactosidosis.
lactosil *m.* lactosyl.
lactosil-ceramida *f.* lactosyl ceramide.
lactosil-ceramidasa *f.* lactosyl ceramidase.
lactosilceramidosis *f.* lactosyl ceramidosis.
lactosuria *f.* lactosuria.
lactoterapia *f.* lactotherapy.
lactotoxina *f.* lactotoxin.
lactotropina *f.* lactotropin.
lactótropa *f.* lactotrope.
lactovegetariano, -na *adj.* lactovegetarian.
lacunar *adj.* lacunar.
lacus lacus.
ladilla *f.* crab, crablouse.
lado *m.* side.
lagena *f.* lagena.
lageniforme *adj.* lageniform.
lagneomanía *f.* lagnesis.
lagnesis *f.* lagnesis.
lagnosis *f.* lagnosis.
lago *m.* lake, lacus.
lagoftalmía *f.* lagophthalmos, lagophthalmus.
lagoftalmos *m.* lagophthalmos.
lágrima *f.* tear.
 lágrima artificial artificial tear.
 lágrima de cocodrilo crocodile tear.
lagrimación *f.* lacrimation, lachrymation.
lagrimal¹ *m.* lacrimal, lachrymal.
lagrimal² *adj.* lacrimal, lachrymal.
lagrimeo *m.* delacrimation, lacrimation, tearing.
laguna *f.* lacuna.
 laguna de absorción resorption lacuna.
 laguna de Blessig Blessig's lacunae.
 laguna cerebral cerebral lacuna.
 laguna de Howship Howship's lacuna.
 laguna de reabsorción resorption lacuna.
lagunar *adj.* lacunar.
lagunilla *f.* lacunule.
lagúnula *f.* lacunule.
lalación *f.* lallation.
laliatría *f.* laliatry.
lalofobia *f.* lalophobia.
lalognosis *f.* lalognosis.
laloneurosis *f.* laloneurosis.
lalopatía *f.* lalopathy.
lalopatología *f.* lalopathology.
laloplejía *f.* laloplegia.
laloquecia *f.* lalochezia.
lalorrea *f.* lalorrhea.
lambda *f.* lambda.
lambdacismo *m.* lambdacism, lambdacismus.

lambdoideo, -a *adj.* lamboloid.
lambliasis *f.* lambliasis, lambliosis.
lamelar *adj.* lamellar.
lameliforme *adj.* lamelliform.
lamelipodio *m.* lamellipodia.
lamella *f.* lamella.
lámina *f.* lamina.
laminación *f.* lamination.
   laminación de la membrana fascial fascial membrane lamination.
laminado, -da *adj.* laminated.
laminagrafía *f.* laminagraphy.
laminágrafo *m.* laminagraph.
laminagrama *m.* laminagram.
laminal *adj.* lamellar.
laminar *adj.* laminar.
laminectomía *f.* laminectomy.
laminilla¹ *f.* lamella.
   laminilla anulares annulate lamellae.
   laminilla del esmalte enamel lamellae.
   laminilla glandoprepucial glandulopreputial lamella.
   laminilla ósea bone lamella.
laminilla² *f.* slide.
   laminilla portaobjetos slide.
laminillar *adj.* lamellar.
laminina *f.* laminin.
laminitis *f.* laminitis.
laminografía *f.* laminography.
laminógrafo *m.* laminograph.
laminograma *m.* laminogram.
laminoso, -sa *adj.* laminated.
laminotomía *f.* laminotomy.
lámpara *f.* lamp.
   lámpara de alcohol spirit lamp.
   lámpara de arco arc lamp.
   lámpara de arco carbónico carbon arc lamp.
   lámpara de arco de tungsteno tungsten arc lamp.
   lámpara de calor heat lamp.
   lámpara catódica hueca hollow cathode lamp.
   lámpara de cuarzo quartz lamp.
   lámpara de diagnóstico diagnostic lamp.
   lámpara de Eldridge-Green Eldridge-Green lamp.
   lámpara de Finsen Finsen lamp.
   lámpara de Gullstrand Gullstrand's slit lamp.
   lámpara de hendidura slit lamp.
   lámpara mignon mignon lamp.
   lámpara de recocción annealing lamp.
   lámpara ultravioleta ultraviolet lamp.
   lámpara de vapor de mercurio mercury vapor lamp.
   lámpara de Wood Wood's lamp.
lamprofonía *f.* lamprophonia.
lamprofónico, -ca *adj.* lamprophonic.
lanceolado, -da *adj.* lanceolate.
lanceta *f.* lancet.
   lanceta de absceso abscess lancet.
   lanceta de acné acne lancet.
   lanceta gingival gum lancet.
   lanceta laringea laryngeal lancet.
   lanceta de muelle spring lancet.
   lanceta en pulgar thumb lancet.
   lanceta con resorte spring lancet.
lancinante *adj.* lancinating.
languidez *f.* asthenia.
laniario, -ria *adj.* laniary.
lantalgia *f.* lantalgy.
lantánico, -ca *adj.* lanthanic.
lanuginoso, -sa *adj.* lanuginous.
lanugo *m.* lanugo.
lapáctico, -ca *adj.* lapactic.
laparectomía *f.* laparectomy.

laparocele *m.* laparocele.
laparocistectomía *f.* laparocystectomy.
laparocistotomía *f.* laparocystostomy.
laparocolecistotomía *f.* laparocholecystotomy.
laparocolectomía *f.* laparocolectomy.
laparocolostomía *f.* laparocolostomy.
laparocolotomía *f.* laparocolotomy.
laparoenterostomía *f.* laparoenterostomy.
laparoenterotomía *f.* laparoenterotomy.
laparoesplenectomía *f.* laparosplenectomy.
laparoesplenotomía *f.* laparosplenotomy.
laparogastroscopia *f.* laparogastroscopy.
laparogastrostomía *f.* laparogastrostomy.
laparogastrotomía *f.* laparogastrotomy.
laparohepatotomía *f.* laparohepatotomy.
laparohisterectomía *f.* laparohysterectomy.
laparohisterooforectomía *f.* laparohysterooophorectomy.
laparohisteropexia *f.* laparohysteropexy.
laparohisterosalpingooforectomía *f.* laparohysterosalpingo-oophorectomy.
laparohisterotomía *f.* laparohysterotomy.
laparoileotomía *f.* laparoileotomy.
laparomiitis *f.* laparomyitis.
laparomiomectomía *f.* laparomyomectomy.
laparomiositis *f.* laparomyositis.
laparomonodídimo *m.* laparomonodidymus.
laparonefrectomía *f.* laparonephrectomy.
laparorrafia *f.* laparorrhaphy.
laparosalpingectomía *f.* laparosalpingectomy.
laparosalpingooforectomía *f.* laparosalpingo-oophorectomy.
laparosalpingotomía *f.* laparosalpingotomy.
laparoscopia *f.* laparoscopy.
laparoscopio *m.* laparoscope.
laparosplenectomía *f.* laparosplenectomy.
laparosplenotomía *f.* laparosplenotomy.
laparostato *m.* abdominal retractor.
laparotiflotomía *f.* laparotyphlotomy.
laparotomafilia *f.* laparotomaphilia.
laparotomía *f.* laparotomy.
   laparotomía de estadiaje staging laparotomy.
   laparotomía exploradora exploration laparotomy.
   laparotomía media midline laparotomy.
   laparotomía pararrectal pararectal laparotomy.
   laparotomía de Pfannestiel Pfannestiel's laparotomy.
   laparotomía subcostal subcostal laparotomy.
   laparotomía transversa transverse laparotomy.
laparótomo *m.* laparotome.
lapsus *m.* lapsus.
   lapsus calami lapsus calami.
   lapsus linguae lapsus linguae.
   lapsus memoriae lapsus memoriae.
lardaceína *f.* lardacein.
laringalgia *f.* laryngalgia.
laringe *f.* larynx.
   laringe artificial artificial larynx.
laringenfraxis *f.* laryngemphraxis.
laríngeo, -a *adj.* laryngeal.
laringísmico, -ca *adj.* laryngismal.
laringítico, -ca *adj.* laryngytic.
laringitis *f.* laryngitis.
   laringitis aguda acute catarrhal laryngitis.
   laringitis atrófica atrophic laryngitis.
   laringitis catarral aguda acute catarrhal laryngitis.
   laringitis catarral crónica chronic catarrhal laryngitis.

   laringitis crupal, laringitis cruposa croupous laryngitis.
   laringitis diftérica diphtheritic laryngitis.
   laringitis espasmódica spasmodic laryngitis.
   laringitis estridulosa laryngitis stridulosa.
   laringitis flemonosa phlegmonous laryngitis.
   laringitis membranosa membranous laryngitis.
   laringitis seca laryngitis sicca.
   laringitis sifilítica syphilitic laryngitis.
   laringitis subglótica, laringitis subglótica crónica subglottic laryngitis, chronic subglottic laryngitis.
   laringitis tuberculosa tuberculous laryngitis.
   laringitis vestibular vestibular laryngitis.
laringocele *m.* laryngocele.
   laringocele ventricular ventricular laryngocele, laryngocele ventricularis.
laringocentesis *f.* laryngocentesis.
laringodinia *f.* laryngalgia.
laringoendoscopio *m.* laryngendoscope.
laringoescleroma *m.* laryngoscleroma.
laringoespasmo *m.* laryngospasm.
laringoestasis *f.* laryngostasis.
laringoestenosis *f.* laryngostenosis.
laringoestroboscopio *m.* laryngostroboscope.
laringofantoma *m.* laryngophantom.
laringofaringe *f.* laryngopharynx.
laringofaríngeo, -a *adj.* laryngopharyngeal.
laringofaringitis *f.* laryngopharyngitis.
laringofisión *f.* laryngofission.
laringofisura *f.* laryngofissure.
laringofonía *f.* laryngophony.
laringófono *m.* laryngophone.
laringografía *f.* laryngography.
laringógrafo *m.* laryngograph.
laringograma *m.* laryngogram.
laringohipofaringe *f.* laryngohypopharynx.
laringología *f.* laryngology.
laringomalacia *f.* laryngomalacia.
laringometría *f.* laryngometry.
laringoparálisis *f.* laryngoparalysis.
laringopatía *f.* laryngopathy.
laringopiocele *f.* laryngopyocele.
laringoplastia *f.* laryngoplasty.
laringoplejía *f.* laryngoplegia.
laringoptosis *f.* laryngoptosis.
laringorrafia *f.* laryngorrhaphy.
laringorragia *f.* laryngorrhagia.
laringorrea *f.* laryngorrhea.
laringorrinología *f.* laryngorhinology.
laringoscleroma *f.* laryngoscleroma.
laringoscopia *f.* laryngoscopy.
   laringoscopia directa direct laryngoscopy.
   laringoscopia de espejo indirect laryngoscopy.
   laringoscopia indirecta indirect laryngoscopy.
   laringoscopia por suspensión suspension laryngoscopy.
laringoscópico, -ca *adj.* laryngoscopic.
laringoscopio *m.* laryngoscope.
   laringoscopio de Bullard Bullard's laryngoscope.
   laringoscopio de Miller Miller's laryngoscope.
laringoscopista *f.* laryngoscopist.
laringospasmo *m.* laryngospasm.
laringostasis *f.* laryngostasis.
laringóstato *m.* laryngostat.
laringostenosis *f.* laryngostenosis.
laringostomía *f.* laryngostomy.
laringostroboscopio *m.* laryngostroboscope.
laringotisis *f.* laryngophthisis.
laringotomía *f.* laryngotomy.
   laringotomía inferior inferior laryngotomy.
   laringotomía mediana median laryngotomy.

laringotomía subhioidea subhyoid laryngotomy.

laringotomía superior superior laryngotomy.

laringotomía tirohioidea thyrohyoid laryngotomy.

laringotomía total complete laryngotomy.

laringótomo *m.* laryngotome.

laringótomo de dilatación dilating laryngotome.

laringotraqueal *adj.* laryngotracheal.

laringotraqueitis *f.* laryngotracheitis.

laringotraqueobroncoscopia *f.* laryngotracheobronchoscopy.

laringotraqueobronquitis *f.* laryngotracheobronchitis.

laringotraqueobronquitis aguda acute laryngotracheobronchitis.

laringotraqueoscopia *f.* laryngotracheoscopy.

laringotraqueotomía *f.* laryngotracheotomy.

laringoxerosis *f.* laryngoxerosis.

laringuectomía *f.* laryngectomy.

laringuectomía supraglótica supraglottic laryngectomy.

laringuectomía total total laryngectomy.

laringuectomizado, -da[1] *adj.* laryngectomized.

Olaringuefaringectomía *f.* laryngopharyngectomy.

larva *f.* larva.

larváceo, -a *adj.* larvaceous.

larvado, -da *adj.* larvate.

larval *adj.* larval.

larvicida *adj.* larvacide.

larviposición *f.* larviposition.

lasánum *m.* lasanum.

lascivia *f.* lascivia.

láser *m.* laser.

láser de alta potencia high power laser.

láser de argón argon laser.

láser de arseniuro de galio galium-arsenide laser.

láser de CO2 CO2 laser.

láser de colorante dye laser.

láser de criptón krypton laser.

láser de dióxido de carbono carbon-dioxide laser.

láser de excímero excimer laser.

láser de helio y neón helium-neon laser.

láser iónico ion laser.

láser de neodimio: itrio-alumino-granate (Nd: YAG) neodymium: yttrium-aluminium-garnet (Nd: YAG) laser.

láser quirúrgico surgical laser.

Lasiohelea Lasiohelea.

lasitud *f.* lassitude.

lastre genético *m.* genetic load.

latencia *f.* latency.

latencia distal distal latency.

latenciación *f.* latenciation.

latente[1] *adj.* latent.

latente[2] *adj.* throbbing.

lateral *adj.* lateral.

lateralidad *f.* laterality.

lateralidad cruzada crossed laterality.

lateralidad dominante dominant laterality.

lateralización *f.* lateralization.

lateroabdominal *adj.* lateraabdominal.

laterodesviación *f.* laterodeviation.

lateroducción *f.* lateroduction.

lateroflexión *f.* lateroflexion.

lateroposición *f.* lateroposition.

lateropulsión *f.* lateropulsion.

laterotorsión *f.* laterotorsion.

laterotrusión *f.* laterotrusion.

lateroversión *f.* lateroversion.

latido *m.* beat.

latido acoplado coupled beat.

latido por agregado summation beat.

latido apareado paired beat.

latido apexiano apex beat.

latido automático automatic beat.

latido de captura capture beat.

latido cardíaco heart beat.

latido ciliar ciliary beat.

latido de combinación combination beat.

latido dependiente dependent beat.

latido de Dressler Dressler beat.

latido eco echo beat.

latido ectópico ectopic beat.

latido ectópico complejo complex ectopic beat.

latido de escape escape beat, escaped beat.

latido extra extra beat.

latido fallido dropped beat.

latido forzado forced beat.

latido de fusión fusion beat.

latido de fusión auricular atrial fusion beat.

latido de fusión ventricular ventricular fusion beat.

latido de interferencia interference beat.

latido mixto mixed beat.

latido omitido dropped beat.

latido parasistólico parasystolic beat.

latido prematuro premature beat.

latido de la punta apex beat.

latido recíproco reciprocal beat.

latido retrógrado retrograde beat.

latigazo *m.* whiplash.

latir *v.* beat, throb, pulsate.

latírico, -ca *adj.* lathyritic.

latirismo *m.* lathyrism.

latirógeno, -na *adj.* lathyrogen.

latitud *f.* latitude.

Latrodectus Latrodectus.

latrodectismo *m.* latrodectism.

laudable *adj.* laudabilis.

lavado *m.* lavage.

lavado broncopulmonar bronchopulmonary lavage.

lavado bronquial bronchial lavage.

lavado del estómago gastric lavage.

lavado gástrico gastric lavage, gastrolavage.

lavado general blood lavage.

lavado peritoneal peritoneal lavage.

lavado pleural pleural lavage.

lavado quirúrgico surgical scrub.

lavado de la sangre, lavado sanguíneo blood lavage.

lavado vesical vesical lavage.

lavador *m.* laveur.

lavaojos *m.* eyecup.

lavativa *f.* enema.

laxación *f.* laxation.

laxador, -ra *adj.* laxator.

laxante *m.* laxative.

laxitud *f.* laxity.

laxo, -xa *adj.* lax.

layosa *f.* laiose.

lecanópago *m.* lecanopagus.

lechada *f.* slurry.

leche *f.* milk.

lecho *m.* bed.

lecho capilar capillary bed.

lecho ungueal nail bed.

lecopira *f.* lechopyra.

lectotipo *m.* lectotype.

lectura *f.* reading.

lectura de labios, lectura del habla lip reading, speech reading.

legaña *f.* rheum.

legionelosis *f.* legionellosis.

Legionella Legionella.

Legionellaceae Legionellaceae.

legra *f.* curet, scoop.

legra de Hartmann Hartmann's curet.

legra de Mulles Mulles' scoop.

legrado *m.* curettage.

legrado uterino *m.* curettage.

legrar *v.* curet.

leguminívoro, -ra *adj.* leguminivorous.

leiastenia *f.* leiasthenia.

leiodermia *f.* leiodermia.

leiodistonía *f.* leiodystonia.

leiomioblastoma *m.* leiomyoblastoma.

leiomiofibroma *m.* leiomyofibroma.

leiomioma *m.* leiomyoma.

leiomioma cutis, leiomioma cutáneo leiomyoma cutis.

leiomioma epitelioide epithelioid leiomyoma.

leiomioma parasitario parasitic leiomyoma.

leiomioma uterino leiomyoma uteri.

leiomioma vascular vascular leiomyoma.

leiomiomatosis *f.* leiomyomatosis.

leiomiosarcoma *m.* leiomyosarcoma.

leiótrico, -ca *adj.* leiotrichous.

Leishmania Leishmania.

leishmaniasis *f.* leishmaniasis.

leishmanicida *adj.* leishmanicidal.

leishmánide *f.* leishmanid.

leishmanina leishmanin.

leishmaniosis *f.* leishmaniosis, leishmaniasis.

leishmaniosis americana American leishmaniosis, leishmaniosis americana.

leishmaniosis anérgica, anérgica cutánea anergic leishmaniosis, cutaneous anergic leishmaniosis.

leishmaniosis canina canine leishmaniosis.

leishmaniosis cutánea cutaneous leishmaniosis.

leishmaniosis cutánea aguda acute cutaneous leishmaniosis.

leishmaniosis cutánea antroponótica anthroponotic cutaneous leishmaniosis.

leishmaniosis cutánea crónica chronic cutaneous leishmaniosis.

leishmaniosis cutánea difusa diffuse cutaneous leishmaniosis.

leishmaniosis cutánea diseminada disseminated cutaneous leishmaniosis.

leishmaniosis cutánea húmeda wet cutaneous leishmaniosis.

leishmaniosis cutánea mexicana chiclero's ulcer.

leishmaniosis cutánea rural rural cutaneous leishmaniosis.

leishmaniosis cutánea seca dry cutaneous leishmaniosis.

leishmaniosis cutánea urbana urban cutaneous leishmaniosis.

leishmaniosis cutánea zoonótica zoonotic cutaneous leishmaniosis.

leishmaniosis cutaneomucosa mucocutaneous leishmaniosis.

leishmaniosis dérmica cutaneous leishmaniosis.

leishmaniosis dérmica ulterior a kala-azar post-kala-azar dermal leishmaniosis.

leishmaniosis infantil infantile leishmaniosis.

leishmaniosis lupoide lupoid leishmaniosis.

leishmaniosis mucocutánea mucocutaneous leishmaniosis.

leishmaniosis nasobucal nasopharyngeal leishmaniosis.

leishmaniosis nasofaríngea nasopharyngeal leishmaniosis.

leishmaniosis nasooral nasopharyngeal leishmaniosis.

leishmaniosis del Nuevo Mundo New Word leishmaniosis.
leishmaniosis recidivante leishmaniosis recidivans.
leishmaniosis seudolepromatosa pseudolepromatous leishmaniosis.
leishmaniosis tegumentaria difusa leishmaniosis tegumentaria diffusa.
leishmaniosis urbana urban leishmaniosis.
leishmaniosis del Viejo Mundo Old Word leishmaniosis.
leishmaniosis visceral visceral leishmaniosis.
leishmanoide *f.* leishmanoid.
leishmanoide dérmica, leishmanoide dérmica post-kala-azar dermal leishmanoid, post-kala-azar dermal leishmanoid.
lema *m.* lema.
lémico, -ca *adj.* lemic.
lemnisco *m.* lemniscus.
lemoestenosis *f.* lemostenosis.
lemografía *f.* lemography.
lemología *f.* lemology.
lemoparálisis *f.* lemoparalysis.
lengua *f.* tongue, lingua.
lengua adherente adherent tongue.
lengua aframbuesada raspberry tongue.
lengua amiloide amyloid tongue.
lengua de antibióticos antibiotic tongue.
lengua arrugada fissured tongue.
lengua bífida bifid tongue.
lengua blanca white tongue.
lengua calva bald tongue.
lengua cerebriforme cerebriform tongue.
lengua claveteada hobnail tongue.
lengua de cocodrilo crocodile tongue.
lengua cuarteada crocodile tongue.
lengua de color magenta magenta tongue.
lengua cubierta coated tongue.
lengua disecada geographic tongue.
lengua doble double tongue.
lengua escrotal scrotal tongue.
lengua fisurada, lingua fissurata fissured tongue, lingua fissurata.
lengua en frambuesa strawberry tongue.
lengua en frambuesa blanca white strawberry tongue.
lengua en frambuesa roja red strawberry tongue.
lengua frenada tie tongue.
lengua en fresa strawberry tongue.
lengua de los fumadores smoker's tongue.
lengua geográfica, lingua geographica geographic tongue, lingua geographica.
lengua graneada dotted tongue, stippled tongue.
lengua en guijarro cobble-stone tongue.
lengua hendida cleft tongue.
lengua en hoja de helecho fern leaf tongue.
lengua horneada baked tongue.
lengua ligada tie tongue.
lengua lobulada lobulated tongue.
lengua de loro parrot tongue.
lengua de magenta magenta tongue.
lengua en mapa geographic tongue.
lengua negra, lengua negra vellosa black tongue, black hairy tongue.
lengua partida bifid tongue.
lengua de perico parrot tongue.
lengua pilosa hairy tongue.
lengua plana flat tongue.
lengua plegada grooved tongue.
lengua punteada dotted tongue, stippled tongue.
lengua quemante burning tongue.
lengua saburral furred tongue.

lengua surcada sulcated tongue.
lengua tragada swallowing tongue.
lengua vellosa hairy tongue.
lengua vellosa negra black hairy tongue.
lenguaje[1] *m.* language.
lenguaje corporal body language.
lenguaje sensitivo sensory-based language.
lenguaje de signos sign language.
lenguaje verbal verbal language.
lenguaje[2] *m.* speech.
lenguaje afónico aphonic speech.
lenguaje atáxico ataxic speech.
lenguaje automático automatic speech.
lenguaje cercenado clipped speech, scamping speech.
lenguaje cerebeloso cerebellar speech.
lenguaje escándido scanning speech.
lenguaje esofágico esophageal speech.
lenguaje especular, en espejo mirror speech.
lenguaje explosivo explosive speech.
lenguaje paralelo parallel talk.
lenguaje resonante clanging.
lenguaje seriado serial speech.
lenguaje en staccato staccato speech.
lenitivo, -va *adj.* lenitive.
lensectomía *f.* lensectomy.
lente *f.* lens.
lente de acrílico acrylic lens.
lente acromática achromatic lens.
lente adherente adherent lens.
lente anastigmática anastigmatic lens.
lente aniseicónica aniseikonic lens.
lente aplanática, lente aplanética aplanatic lens.
lente apocromática apochromatic lens.
lente asférica aspheric lens.
lente astigmática astigmatic lens.
lente bicilíndrica bicylindrical lens.
lente bicóncava biconcave lens.
lente biconvexa biconvex lens.
lente biesférica bispherical lens.
lente bifocal bifocal lens.
lente de Brücke Brücke lens.
lente de catarata cataract lens.
lente cilíndrica cylindrical lens.
lente compuesta compound lens.
lente cóncava concave lens.
lente concavocóncava concavoconcave lens.
lente concavoconvexa concavoconvex lens.
lente condensadora condensing lens.
lente de contacto contact lens.
lente de contacto blanda soft contact lens.
lente de contacto corneal corneal contact lens.
lente de contacto dura hard contact lens.
lente de contacto permeable al gas gas permeable contact lens.
lente de contacto escleral scleral contact lens.
lente convergente convergent lens.
lente convexa lens convex lens.
lente convexocóncava convexoconcave lens.
lente convexoconvexa convexoconvex lens.
lente de Coquille coquille lens.
lente corneal corneal lens.
lente cristalina crystalline lens, lens crystallina.
lente de Crookes Crookes' lens.
lente cruzada crossed lens.
lente descentrada decentered lens.
lente divergente diverging lens.
lente dividida slab-off lens.
lente doble cóncava double concave lens.
lente doble convexa double convex lens.
lente esférica spherical lens.

lente esferocilíndrica spherocylindrical lens.
lente estigmática stigmatic lens.
lente fotosensible photosensitive lens.
lente de Franklin Franklin's lens.
lente de inmersión immersion lens.
lente iseicónica iseikonic lens.
lente de menisco meniscus lens.
lente en menisco convergente converging meniscus lens.
lente en menisco divergente diverging meniscus lens.
lente en menisco negativa negative meniscus lens.
lente en menisco positiva positive meniscus lens.
lente metro meter lens.
lente minus minus lens.
lente multifocal multifocal lens.
lente nivelada plane lens, plano lens.
lente ocular ocular lens.
lente ojo de abeja honeybee lens.
lente omnifocal omnifocal lens.
lente ortoscópica orthoscopic lens.
lente periscópica periscopic lens.
lente periscópica cóncava periscopic concave lens.
lente periscópica convexa periscopic convex lens.
lente plana flat lens.
lente planocóncava planoconcave lens.
lente planoconvexa planoconvex lens.
lente plus plus lens.
lente de prueba trial lens.
lente puntal punktal lens.
lente de seguridad safety lens.
lente de tamaño size lens.
lente tórica toric lens.
lente trifocal trifocal lens.
lentectomía *f.* lentectomy.
lentectomizar *v.* lentectomize.
lenticono *m.* lenticonus.
lentícula *f.* lenticula.
lenticular *adj.* lenticular.
lentículo *m.* lenticulus.
lenticuloestríado, -da *adj.* lenticulostriate.
lenticuloóptico, -ca *adj.* lenticulo-optic.
lenticulopapular *adj.* lenticulopapular.
lenticulotalámico, -ca *adj.* lenticulothalamic.
lentiforme *adj.* lentiform.
lentiginosis *f.* lentiginosis.
lentiginosis cardiomiopática progresiva progressive cardiomyopathic lentiginosis.
lentiginosis centrofacial centrofacial lentiginosis.
lentiginosis generalizada generalized lentiginosis.
lentiginosis periorificial periorificial lentiginosis.
lentiginoso, -sa *adj.* lentiginous.
lentiglobo *m.* lentiglobus.
léntigo *m.* lentigo.
léntigo de Hutchinson Hutchinson's freckle.
léntigo juvenil juvenile lentigo.
léntigo maligno lentigo maligna, malignant lentigo.
léntigo nevoide nevoid lentigo.
léntigo senil senile lentigo.
léntigo simplex lentigo simplex.
léntigo solar solar lentigo.
lentigomelanosis *f.* lentigomelanosis.
lentilla *f.* contact lens.
lentinas *f.* cottonoids.
lentitis *f.* lentitis.
lentivirus *m.* lentivirus.
lentómetro *m.* lensometer.

lentoptosis *f.* lentoptosis.
léntula *f.* lentula.
leñoso, -sa *adj.* ligneous.
leontiasis *f.* leontiasis.
  leontiasis ósea leontiasis ossea.
leotrópico, -ca *adj.* leotropic.
lepídico, -ca *adj.* lepidic.
lepidosis *f.* lepidosis.
lepotrix *m.* lepothrix.
lepra *f.* lepra, leprosy.
  lepra cutánea cutaneous leprosy.
  lepra dimorfa dimorphous leprosy.
  lepra difusa de Lucio diffuse leprosy of Lucio.
  lepra fronteriza borderline leprosy.
  lepra histoide histoid leprosy.
  lepra indeterminada indeterminate leprosy.
  lepra intermedia intermediate leprosy.
  lepra lazarina Lazarine leprosy.
  lepra lepromatosa lepromatous leprosy.
  lepra limítrofe borderline leprosy.
  lepra limítrofe lepromatosa borderline lepromatous leprosy.
  lepra limítrofe tuberculoide borderline tuberculous leprosy.
  lepra lisa smooth leprosy.
  lepra de Lucio Lucio's leprosy.
  lepra macular, maculoanestésica macular leprosy.
  lepra de Malabar Malabar leprosy.
  lepra neural neural leprosy.
  lepra no característica uncharacteristic leprosy.
  lepra nodular nodular leprosy.
  lepra reaccional reactional leprosy.
  lepra tuberculoide tuberculoid leprosy.
leprechaunismo *m.* leprechaunism.
lépride *f.* leprid.
leprología *f.* leprology.
leprólogo, -ga *f.* leprologist.
leproma *m.* leproma, leprosy nodule.
lepromatoso, -sa *adj.* lepromatous.
lepromina *f.* lepromin.
leprosario *m.* leprosarium.
leprosería *f.* leprosary.
leproso, -sa *adj.* leper, leprose, leprous.
leprostático, -ca *adj.* leprostatic.
leprótico, -ca *adj.* leprotic.
leptocefalia *f.* leptocephaly.
leptocefálico, -ca *adj.* leptocephalic, leptocephalous.
leptocéfalo, -la *adj.* leptocephalus.
leptocito *m.* leptocyte.
leptocitosis *f.* leptocytosis.
Leptoconops Leptoconops.
leptocromático, -ca *adj.* leptochromatic.
leptodactilia *f.* leptodactyly.
leptodáctilo, -la *adj.* leptodactylous.
leptodermia *f.* leptodermia.
leptodérmico, -ca *adj.* leptodermic.
leptodonto, -ta *adj.* leptodontus.
leptoestafilino, -na *adj.* leptostaphyline.
leptofonía *f.* leptophonia.
leptofónico, -ca *adj.* leptophonic.
leptomeníngeo, -a *adj.* leptomeningeal.
leptomeninges *f.* leptomeninges.
leptomeningioma *m.* leptomeningioma.
leptomeningitis *f.* leptomeningitis.
  leptomeningitis basilar basilar leptomeningitis.
  leptomeningitis sarcomatosa sarcomatous leptomeningitis.
leptomeningopatía *f.* leptomeningopathy.
leptopélvico, -ca *adj.* leptopellic.
leptopiélico, -ca *adj.* leptopellic.
leptopodia *f.* leptopodia.

leptoprosopia *f.* leptoprosopia.
leptoprosópico, -ca *adj.* leptoprosopic.
leptoprosopo, -pa *adj.* leptoprosope.
Leptopsylla Leptopsylla.
  Leptopsylla segnis Leptopsylla segnis.
leptorrino, -na *adj.* leptorrhine.
leptoscopio *m.* leptoscope.
leptosomático, -ca *adj.* leptosomatic.
Leptospira Leptospira.
leptospira *f.* leptospire.
Leptospiraceae Leptospiraceae.
leptospirósico, -ca *adj.* leptospiral.
leptospirosis *f.* leptospirosis.
  leptospirosis anictérica anicteric leptospirosis.
  leptospirosis benigna benign leptospirosis.
  leptospirosis equina equine leptospirosis.
  leptospirosis icterohemorrágica leptospirosis icterohaemorrhagica.
leptospiuria *f.* leptospiruria.
leptotene *m.* leptotene.
leptoteno *m.* leptotene.
leptotrix leptothrix.
Leptotrichia Leptotrichia.
  Leptotrichia buccalis Leptotrichia buccalis.
leptotricosis *f.* leptotrichosis.
  leptotricosis de la conjuntiva leptotrichosis conjunctivae.
leresis *f.* leresis.
lesbiana *adj.* lesbian.
lesbianismo *m.* lesbianism.
lesión *f.* injury, lesion.
  lesión en anillo de pared, lesión anular de pared ring-wall lesion.
  lesión de Armanni-Ebstein Armanni-Ebstein lesion.
  lesión en asa, lesión en asa de alambre wire-loop lesion.
  lesión axonal difusa diffuse axonal lesion.
  lesión de Baehr-Löhlein Baehr-Löhlein lesion.
  lesión de Bankart Bankart's lesion.
  lesión de Blumenthal Blumenthal lesion.
  lesión de Bracht-Wächter Bracht-Wächter lesion.
  lesión de la cabeza head injury.
  lesión en cáscara de cebolla onion scale lesion, onionskin lesion.
  lesión en caviar caviar lesion.
  lesión cefálica abierta open head lesion.
  lesión cefálica cerrada closed head lesion.
  lesión central central lesion.
  lesión de clara de huevo egg-white injury.
  lesión por contragolpe contrecoup injury, counter-coup lesion.
  lesión en contragolpe del cerebro contrecoup injury of the brain.
  lesión de Councilman Councilman's lesion.
  lesión degenerativa degenerative lesion.
  lesión por desaceleración deceleration injury.
  lesión de descarga discharging lesion.
  lesión destructiva destructive lesion.
  lesión difusa y coma diffuse lesion and coma.
  lesión difusa, lesión diseminada diffuse lesion.
  lesión del disco intervertebral injury of the intervertebral disk.
  lesión de Duret Duret's lesion.
  lesión de Ebstein Ebstein's lesion.
  lesión esclerosante radial radial sclerosing lesion.
  lesión estructural structural lesion.
  lesión por explosión blast injury.
  lesión por explosión roindage injury.

  lesión focal focal lesion.
  lesión por frío cold injury.
  lesión glomerular glomerular lesion.
  lesión en golpe del cerebro coup injury of the brain.
  lesión de Goyrand Goyrand's injury.
  lesión de Hill-Sachs Hill-Sachs lesion.
  lesión de hiperextensión-hiperflexión hyperextension-hyperflexion injury.
  lesión histológica histologic lesion.
  lesión por impacción impaction lesion.
  lesión interna internal injury.
  lesión irritativa irritative lesion.
  lesión de Janeway Janeway lesion.
  lesión en látigo whiplash lesion.
  lesión de Lennert Lennert's lesion.
  lesión linfoepitelial benigna benign lymphoepithelial lesion.
  lesión local local lesion.
  lesión macroscópica gross lesion.
  lesión de Mallory-Weiss Mallory-Weiss lesion.
  lesión manifiesta gross lesion.
  lesión de la médula espinal spinal cord injury.
  lesión medular medullar lesion.
  lesión molecular molecular lesion.
  lesión de nacimiento birth lesion.
  lesión de nervios periféricos peripheral nerve damage.
  lesión por un neumático pneumatic lesion.
  lesión de la neurona motora superior upper motor neuron lesion.
  lesión en nido de pájaro birds' nest lesion.
  lesión numular de los pulmones coin lesion of the lungs.
  lesión numular solitaria solitary coin lesion.
  lesión orgánica organic lesion.
  lesión parcial partial lesion.
  lesión de parto birth injury.
  lesión periférica peripheral lesion.
  lesión posradiación postradiation damage.
  lesión precancerosa precancerous lesion.
  lesión primaria primary lesion.
  lesión primaria de Ghon Ghon's primary lesion.
  lesión puntual point lesion.
  lesión por radiación ionizante ionizing radiation injury.
  lesión sistémica systemic lesion.
  lesión supranuclear supranuclear lesion.
  lesión total total lesion.
  lesión traumática traumatic lesion.
  lesión trófica trophic lesion.
  lesión vital vital injury.
lesionar *v.* injure.
letal *adj.* lethal.
letalidad *f.* lethality.
letargia *f.* lethargy.
  letargia histérica hysteric lethargy.
letargo *m.* lethargy.
  letargo africano African lethargy.
  letargo histérico hysteric lethargy.
  letargo inducido induced lethargy.
  letargo lúcido lucid lethargy.
letología *f.* lethologica.
letra de prueba *f.* test letter.
leucaféresis *f.* leucapheresis, leukapheresis.
leucemia *f.* leukemia.
  leucemia aguda acute leukemia.
  leucemia aguda indiferenciada undifferentiated cell leukemia.
  leucemia aguda infantil acute childhood leukemia.
  leucemia aguda no linfocítica acute non-lymphocytic leukemia.

leucemia aguda mieloblástica myeloblastic acute leukemia.

leucemia aleucémica, leucemia aleucocitémica aleukemic leukemia, aleukocythemic leukemia.

leucemia basófila, leucemia basofilica basophilic leukemia, basophilocytic leukemia.

leucemia de células blásticas stem cell leukemia.

leucemia de células cebadas mast cell leukemia.

leucemia de células indiferenciadas undifferentiated cell leukemia.

leucemia de células de linfosarcoma lymphosarcoma cell leukemia.

leucemia de células madre stem cell leukemia.

leucemia de células maduras mature cell leukemia.

leucemia de células mixtas mixed cell leukemia.

leucemia de células peludas, leucemia de células pilosas, leucemia de células vellosas hairy-cell leukemia.

leucemia de células plasmáticas plasma cell leukemia.

leucemia de células de Rieder Rieder's cell leukemia.

leucemia de células T en adultos adult T-cell leukemia.

leucemia cutánea leukemia cutis.

leucemia embrionaria embryonal leukemia.

leucemia eosinofílica eosinophilic leukemia.

leucemia eritroide erythroleukemia.

leucemia eritromieloblástica erythromyeloblastic leukemia.

leucemia esplénica splenic leukemia.

leucemia granulocítica granulocytic leukemia.

leucemia granulocítica crónica chronic granulocytic leukemia.

leucemia granulocítica mieloide myeloid granulocytic leukemia.

leucemia de Gross Gross' leukemia.

leucemia hemoblástica, leucemia hemocitoblástica hemoblastic leukemia, hemocytoblastic leukemia.

leucemia histiocítica histiocytic leukemia.

leucemia leucémica leukemic leukemia.

leucemia leucopénica leukopenic leukemia.

leucemia linfática lymphatic leukemia.

leucemia linfoblástica lymphoblastic leukemia.

leucemia linfoblástica aguda acute lymphoblastic leukemia.

leucemia linfocítica lymphocytic leukemia.

leucemia linfocítica aguda acute lymphocytic leukemia.

leucemia linfocítica crónica (LLC) chronic lymphocytic leukemia (LLC).

leucemia de linfocitos grandes granulares (LLG) large granular lymphocytes leukemia.

leucemia linfógena lymphogenous leukemia.

leucemia linfoide lymphoid leukemia.

leucemia linfoidocítica lymphoidocytic leukemia.

leucemia de mastocitos, leucemia mastocítica mast cell leukemia.

leucemia megacarioblástica aguda acute megakaryoblastic leukemia.

leucemia megacariocítica megakarycytic leukemia.

leucemia meníngea meningeal leukemia.

leucemia micromieloblástica micromyeloblastic leukemia.

leucemia mieloblástica myeloblastic leukemia.

leucemia mielocítica myelocytic leukemia.

leucemia mielocítica aguda (LMA) acute myelocytic leukemia (AML).

leucemia mielocítica crónica chronic myelocytic leukemia.

leucemia mielógena myelogenous leukemia.

leucemia mieloide aguda acute myeloid leukemia.

leucemia mieloide aguda diferenciada differentiated acute myeloid leukemia.

leucemia mieloide aguda indiferenciada (M1) undifferentiated acute myeloid leukemia.

leucemia mieloide crónica (LMC) chronic myelocytic leukemia.

leucemia mielomonocítica myelomonocytic leukemia.

leucemia mielomonocítica aguda (M4) acute myelomonocytic leukemia.

leucemia mielomonocítica crónica chronic myelomonocytic leukemia.

leucemia mixta mixed leukemia.

leucemia monoblástica monoblastic leukemia.

leucemia monoblástica aguda (M5) acute monoblastic leukemia.

leucemia monocítica monocytic leukemia.

leucemia monocítica aguda acute monocytic leukemia.

leucemia de Naegeli Naegeli's leukemia.

leucemia neutrófila neutrophilic leukemia.

leucemia no linfoblástica aguda acute non-lymphoblastic leukemia.

leucemia plasmática plasmacytic leukemia.

leucemia polimorfocítica polymorphocytic leukemia.

leucemia prolinfocítica prolymphocytic.

leucemia prolinfocítica de origen B B-prolymphocytic leukemia.

leucemia prolinfocítica de origen T T-prolymphocytic leukemia.

leucemia promielocítica, leucemia promielocítica aguda promyelocytic leukemia, acute promyelocytic leukemia.

leucemia de Schilling Schilling's leukemia.

leucemia subleucémica subleukemic leukemia.

leucémico, -ca *adj.* leukemic.

leucémide *f.* leukemid.

leucemogénesis *f.* leukemogenesis.

leucemogénico, -ca *adj.* leukemogenic.

leucemógeno, -na *adj.* leukemogen.

leucemoide *adj.* leukemoid.

leucencefalitis *f.* leukencephalitis.

leucilo *m.* leucyl.

leucina *f.* leucine, leukina.

leukina *f.* leucine, leukina.

leucinosis *f.* leucinosis.

leucinuria *f.* leucinuria.

leucismo *m.* leucismus.

leucitis *f.* leucitis.

leucoaglutinina *f.* leukoagglutinin.

leucoaraiosis *f.* leukoaraiosis.

leucoblasto *m.* leukoblast.

leucoblasto granuloso granular leukoblast.

leucoblastosis *f.* leukoblastosis.

leucocidina *f.* leukocidin.

leucocidina de Panton-Valentine (P-V) Panton-Valentine (P-V) leukocidin.

leucocinesia *f.* leukokinesis.

leucocinética *f.* leukokinetics.

leucocinético, -ca *adj.* leukokinetic.

leucocinina *f.* leukokinin.

leucocitario, -a *adj.* leukocytic, leukocytal.

leucocitaxia *f.* leukocytaxia, leukocytaxis.

leucocitaxis *f.* leukocytaxis.

leucocitemia *f.* leukocythemia.

leucocítico, -ca *adj.* leukocytal, leukocytic, leukocytic.

leucocito *m.* leukocyte.

leucocito acidófilo acidophilic leukocyte.

leucocito agranuloso agranular leukocyte.

leucocito basófilo basophilic leukocyte.

leucocito cebado mast leukocyte.

leucocito cistonótico cystonotic leukocyte.

leucocito eosinófilo eosinophilic leukocyte.

leucocito granuloso granular leukocyte.

leucocito heterófilo heterophilic leukocyte.

leucocito inmóvil non-motile leukocyte.

leucocito linfoide lymphoid leukocyte.

leucocito marcados labeled leukocyte.

leucocito móvil motile leukocyte.

leucocito multinuclear multinuclear leukocyte.

leucocito neutrófilo neutrophilic leukocyte.

leucocito neutrófilo polinuclear polynuclear neutrophilic leukocyte.

leucocito no granulosos non-granular leukocyte.

leucocito no mótil non-motile leukocyte.

leucocito oxífilo oxyphilic leukocyte.

leucocito polimorfonuclear polymorphonuclear leukocyte.

leucocito polimorfonuclear filamentoso filament polymorphonuclear leukocyte.

leucocito polimorfonuclear no filamentoso non-filament polymorphonuclear leukocyte.

leucocito polinuclear polynuclear leukocyte.

leucocito segmentado segmented leukocyte.

leucocitoblasto *m.* leukocytoblast.

leucocitofagia *f.* leukocytophagy.

leucocitoclasia *f.* leukocytoclasis.

leucocitogénesis *f.* leukocytogenesis.

leucocitoide *adj.* leukocytoid.

leucocitoideo, -a *adj.* leukocytoid.

leucocitolisina *f.* leukocytolisin.

leucocitólisis *f.* leukocytolysis.

leucocitólisis venenosa venom leukocytolysis.

leucocitolítico, -ca *adj.* leukocytolytic.

leucocitoma *m.* leukocytoma.

leucocitómetro *m.* leukocytometer.

leucocitopenia *f.* leukocytopenia.

leucocitoplania *f.* leukocytoplania.

leucocitopoyesis *f.* leukocytopoiesis.

leucocitosis *f.* leukocytosis.

leucocitosis absoluta absolute leukocytosis.

leucocitosis agonal, leucocitosis agónica agonal leukocytosis.

leucocitosis basófila basophilic leukocytosis.

leucocitosis digestiva digestive leukocytosis.

leucocitosis de distribución distribution leukocytosis.

leucocitosis emocional emotional leukocytosis.

leucocitosis eosinófila eosiniphilic leukocytosis.

leucocitosis fisiológica physiologic leukocytosis.

leucocitosis gravídica digestive leukocytosis.

leucocitosis linfocítica lymphocytic leukocytosis.

leucocitosis monocítica monocytic leukocytosis.

leucocitosis mononuclear mononuclear leukocytosis.

leucocitosis del neonato leukocytosis of the newborn.

leucocitosis neutrófila neutrophilic leukocytosis.

leucocitosis patológica pathologic leukocytosis.
leucocitosis pura pure leukocytosis.
leucocitosis relativa relative leukocytosis.
leucocitosis terminal terminal leukocytosis.
leucocitosis tóxica toxic leukocytosis.
leucocitotáctico, -ca *adj.* leukocytotactic.
leucocitotaxia *f.* leukocytotaxis.
leucocitotaxis *f.* leukocytotaxis.
leucocitoterapia *f.* leukocytotherapy.
leucocitotoxina *f.* leukocytotoxin.
leucocitotrópico, -ca *adj.* leukocytotropic.
leucocituria *f.* leukocyturia.
leucocloroma *m.* leukochloroma.
leucocoria *f.* leucocoria.
leucocraurosis *f.* leukokraurosis.
leucócrito *m.* leukocrit.
leucodermatoso, -sa *adj.* leukodermatous.
leucodermia *f.* leukoderma, leukodermia.
  leucodermia adquirida acquired leukoderma.
  leucodermia centrífuga adquirida leukoderma acquisitum centrifugum.
  leucodermia cervical leukoderma colli.
  leucodermia congénita congenital leukoderma.
  leucodermia del cuello leukoderma colli.
  leucodermia postinflamatoria postinflammatory leukoderma.
  leucodermia profesional occupational leukoderma.
  leucodermia sifilítica syphilitic leukoderma.
leucodistrofia *f.* leukodystrophy.
  leucodistrofia de células globosas globoid cell.
  leucodistrofia cerebral hereditaria hereditary cerebral leukodystrophy.
  leucodistrofia cerebral progresiva leukodystrophy cerebri progressiva.
  leucodistrofia espongiforme spongiform leukodystrophy.
  leucodistrofia globoide, leucodistrofia de células globoides globoid leukodystrophy, globoid cell leukodystrophy.
  leucodistrofia de Krabbe Krabbe's leukodystrophy.
  leucodistrofia metacromática metachromatic leukodystrophy.
  leucodistrofia sudanófila sudanophilic leukodystrophy.
leucodontia *f.* leukodontia.
leucoencefalia *f.* leukoencephaly.
  leucoencefalia metacromática metachromatic leukoencephaly.
leucoencefalina *f.* leukoenkephalin.
leucoencefalitis *f.* leukencephalitis.
  leucoencefalitis epidémica aguda acute epidemic leukencephalitis.
  leucoencefalitis esclerosante subaguda subacute sclerosing leukencephalitis.
  leucoencefalitis esclerosante de Van Bogaert van Bogaert's sclerosing leukencephalitis.
  leucoencefalitis hemorrágica aguda acute hemmorrhagic leukencephalitis.
  leucoencefalitis periaxial concéntrica leukencephalitis periaxialis concentrica.
leucoencefalopatía *f.* leukoencephalopathy.
  leucoencefalopatía esclerosante subaguda subacute sclerosing leukoencephalopathy.
  leucoencefalopatía metacromática metachromatic leukoencephalopathy.
  leucoencefalopatía multifocal progresiva progressive multifocal leukoencephalopathy.
leucoeritroblastosis *f.* leukoerythroblastosis.
leucofagocitosis *f.* leukophagocytosis.

leucoféresis *f.* leukapheresis.
leucoflegmasía *f.* leukophlegmasia, milk-leg.
  leucoflegmasía dolens leukophlegmasia dolens.
leucoforesis *f.* leukophoresis.
leucograma *m.* leukogram.
leucolinfosarcoma *m.* leukolymphosarcoma.
leucolisina *f.* leukolysin.
leucólisis *f.* leukolysis.
leucolítico, -ca *adj.* leukolytic.
leucoma *m.* leukoma.
  leucoma adherente adherent leukoma.
leucomaína *f.* leukomaine.
leucomainemia *f.* leukomainemia.
leucomaínico, -ca *adj.* leukomainic.
leucomalacia *f.* leukomalacia.
leucomatoso, -sa *adj.* leukomatous.
leucomielitis *f.* leukomyelitis.
leucomielopatía *f.* leukomyelopathy.
leucomioma *m.* leukomyoma.
leuconecrosis *f.* leukonecrosis.
leuconiquia *f.* leukonychia.
leucopatía *f.* leukopathia.
  leucopatía adquirida acquired leukopathia.
  leucopatía congénita congenital leukopathia.
  leucopatía punteada reticular simétrica leukopathia punctata reticularis symmetrica.
  leucopatía ungueal, leucopatía de las uñas leukopathia unguis.
leucopédesis *f.* leukopedesis.
leucopenia *f.* leukopenia.
  leucopenia basófila basophilic leukopenia.
  leucopenia congénita congenital leukopenia.
  leucopenia eosinófila eosinophilic leukopenia.
  leucopenia maligna malignant leukopenia.
  leucopenia perniciosa pernicious leukopenia.
  leucopenia monocítica monocytic leukopenia.
  leucopenia neutrófila neutrophilic leukopenia.
leucopénico, -ca *adj.* leukopenic.
leucoplaquia *f.* leukoplakia.
leucoplasia *f.* leukoplasia.
  leucoplasia bucal leukoplasia buccalis.
  leucoplasia de cuello cervical leukoplasia.
  leucoplasia lingual leukoplasia lingualis.
  leucoplasia moteada speckled leukoplasia.
  leucoplasia oral oral leukoplasia.
  leucoplasia peluda hairy leukoplasia.
  leucoplasia pilosa hairy leukoplasia.
  leucoplasia vocal laryngeal leukoplasia.
  leucoplasia de vulva vulval leukoplasia, leukoplasia vulvae.
leucopoyesis *f.* leukopoiesis.
leucopoyético, -ca *adj.* leukopoietic.
leucopoyetina *f.* leukopoietin.
leucoprecipitina *f.* leukoprecipitin.
leucoprofilaxis *f.* leukoprophylaxis.
leucoproteasa *f.* leukoprotease.
leucopsina *f.* leukopsin.
leucoqueratosis *f.* leukokeratosis.
leucorrea *f.* leukorrhea.
  leucorrea menstrual, leucorrea periódica menstrual leukorrhea.
leucorreico, -ca *adj.* leukorrheal.
leucosarcoma *m.* leukosarcoma.
leucoscopio *m.* leukoscope.
leucosina *f.* leucosin.
leucosis *f.* leukosis.
  leucosis aguda acute leukosis.
  leucosis cutánea skin leukosis.
  leucosis linfoide lymphoid leukosis.
  leucosis mieloblástica myeloblastic leukosis.

  leucosis mielocítica myelocytic leukosis.
leucotáctico, -ca *adj.* leukotactic.
leucotaxia *f.* leukotaxia.
leucotaxina *f.* leukotaxine.
leucotaxis *f.* leukotaxis, leukotaxis.
leucoterapia *f.* leukotherapy.
  leucoterapia preventiva preventive leukotherapy.
leucótico, -ca *adj.* leukotic.
leucotomía *f.* leukotomy.
  leucotomía transorbitaria transorbital leukotomy.
leucótomo *m.* leukotome.
leucotóxico, -ca *adj.* leukotoxic.
leucotoxina *f.* leukotoxin.
leucotrico, -ca *adj.* leukotrichous.
leucotriquia *f.* leukotrichia.
  leucotriquia anular leukotrichia annularis.
leucotrombina *f.* leukothrombin.
leucourobilina *f.* leukourobilin.
Leukothrix Leucothrix, Leukothrix.
leuquina *f.* leukin.
levadura *f.* yeast.
levadúrido *m.* levuride.
levantamiento del cadáver *m.* removal of the body.
levator *m.* levator.
leve[1] *adj.* laeve.
leve[2] *adj.* mild.
levigación *f.* levigation.
levitación *m.* levitation.
levocardia *f.* levocardia.
  levocardia aislada isolated levocardia.
  levocardia mixta mixed levocardia.
levocardiograma *m.* levocardiogram.
levocicloducción *f.* levocycloduction.
levoclinación *f.* levoclination.
levoducción *f.* levoduction.
levofobia *f.* levophobia.
levoforma *f.* levoform.
levogiración *f.* levogiration.
levógiro, -ra *adj.* levogyral, levogyrate, levogyrous.
levograma *m.* levogram.
levorrotación *f.* levorotation.
levorrotatorio, -a *adj.* levorotatory.
levotorsión *f.* levotorsion.
levoversión *f.* levoversion.
levulosemia *f.* levulosemia.
levulosuria *f.* levulosuria.
levúrido *f.* levuride.
ley *f.* law.
  ley de la acción de masas law of mass action.
  ley de Ambard Ambard's law.
  ley de Angström Angström's law.
  ley de Aran Aran's law.
  ley de Arndt-Schulz Arndt-Schutz's law.
  ley de articulación law of articulation.
  ley de asociación law of association.
  ley de Avogadro Avogadro's law.
  ley de Baer Baer's law.
  ley de Barfurth Barfurth's law.
  ley de Baruch Baruch's law.
  ley de Bastian, ley de Bastian-Bruns Bastian's law, Bartian-Bruns law.
  ley de Beer Beer's law.
  ley de Behring Behring's law.
  ley de Bell, ley de Bell-Magendie Bell's law.
  ley de Bergonié-Tribondeau Bergonié-Tribondeau law.
  ley biogenética biogenetic law.
  ley de Bowditch Bowditch's law.
  ley de Boyle Boyle's law.
  ley de Bunsen-Roscoe bunsen-Roscoe law.
  ley de Camerer Camerer's law.

ley de Charles Charles' law.
ley de la combinación independiente law of independent assortment.
ley de la conducción aislada law of isolated conduction.
ley de conservación de la energía law of conservation of energy.
ley de conservación de la materia law of conservation of matter.
ley de Cope Cope's law.
ley del corazón law of the heart.
ley del coseno de Lambert Lambert's cosine law.
ley de Coulomb Coulomb's law.
ley de Courvoiser Courvoisier's law.
ley de Coutard Coutard's law.
ley del cuadrado inverso de la distancia inverse square law.
ley de Dalton-Henry Dalton-Henry law.
ley de Dalton Dalton's law.
ley de denervación law of denervation.
ley de Descartes Descartes' law.
ley de Desmarres Desmarres' law.
ley de distribución de Maxwell-Boltzmann Maxwell-Boltzmann distibrution law.
ley del dolor referido law of referred pain.
ley de Dollo Dollo's law.
ley de Donders Donders' law.
ley de Draper Draper's law.
ley de Du Bois-Reymond Du Bois-Reymond's law.
ley de Dulong-Petit Dulong-Petit's law.
ley de Einstein-Starck Einstein-Starck law.
ley de Einthoven Einthoven's law.
ley de Elliot Elliot's law.
ley de Ewald Ewald's law.
ley de la excitación law of excitation.
ley de Fajans Fajans' law.
ley de Faraday Faraday's law.
ley de Farr Farr's law.
ley de la fatiga de Houghton Houghton's fatigue law.
ley de Fechner-Weber Fechner-Weber law.
ley de Ferry-Porter Ferry-Porter law.
ley de Flatau Flatau's law.
ley de Flint Flint's law.
ley de Flourens Flourens' law.
ley de Froriep Froriep's law.
ley de los gases perfectos ideal gas law.
ley de Gay-Lussac Gay-Lussac law.
ley de Giraud-Teulon Giraud-Teulon law.
ley de Godelier Godelier's law.
ley de Golgi Golgi's law.
ley de Gompertz Gompertz's law.
ley de Graham Graham's law.
ley de Grasset Grasset's law.
ley de la gravitación universal law of universal gravitation.
ley de Grotthus Grotthus' law.
ley de Grotthus-Draper Grotthus-Draper's law.
ley de Gudden Gudden's law.
ley de Guldberg-Waage Guldberg-Waage law.
ley de Gullstrand Gullstrand's law.
ley de Gull-Toynbee Gull-Toynbee law.
ley de Haeckel Haeckel's law.
ley de Hanau de la articulación Hanau's law of articulation.
ley de Hardy-Weinberg Hardy-Weinberg law.
ley de Heidenhain Heidenhain's law.
ley de Hellin, de Hellin-Zeleny Hellin's law.
ley de Henry Henry's law.
ley de Hering Hering's law.

ley de Hilton Hilton's law.
ley de la inervación contraria law of contrary innervation.
ley del intestino law of the intestine.
ley del isocronismo law of isochronism.
ley de la isodinamia isodynamic law.
ley de Jackson Jackson's law.
ley de Kahler Kahler's law.
ley de Knapp Knapp's law.
ley de Koch Koch's law.
ley de Küstner Küstner's law.
ley de Landouzy-Grasset Landouzy-Grasset law.
ley de Lapicque Lapicque's law.
ley de Laplace Laplace's law.
ley de Listing Listing's law.
ley de la localización promedio law of average localization.
ley de Louis Louis' law.
ley de Madgendie Madgendie's law.
ley de Malthus Malthusian law.
ley de Marey Marey's law.
ley de Marfan Marfan's law.
ley de Mariotte Mariotte's law.
ley de las masas mass law.
ley de Meltzer Meltzer's law.
ley de Mendel Mendel's law.
ley de Mendeleiev Mendeleiev's law.
ley de Meyer Meyer's law.
ley del mínimo law of the minimum.
ley de Müller-Haeckel Müller-Haeckel law.
ley de Nernst Nerst's law.
ley de Newland Newland's law.
ley de Newton Newton's law.
ley del número constante de ovulación law of constant numbers in ovulation.
ley de Nysten Nysten's law.
ley de Ochoa Ochoa's law.
ley de Ohm Ohm's law.
ley de Ollier Ollier's law.
ley de Pajot Pajot's law.
ley paradójica de Allen Allen's paradoxic law.
ley de Pascal Pascal's law.
ley periódica periodic law.
ley de Petit Petit's law.
ley de Pflueger Pflueger's law.
ley de las presiones parciales law of partial pressures.
ley de Prévost Prévost's law.
ley de Profeta Profeta's law.
ley de las proporciones múltiples law of multiple proportions.
ley de las proporciones recíprocas law of reciprocal proportions.
ley de Raoult Raoult's law.
ley de la recapitulación law of recapitulation.
ley de la reciprocidad reciprocity law.
ley de la refracción law of refraction.
ley de Ritter Ritter's law.
ley de Rosenbach Rosenbach's law.
ley de Rubner del crecimiento Rubner's law of growth.
ley de Schoeder van der Kolk Schoeder van der Kolk's law.
ley de Schütz, de Schütz-Borissov Schütz's law.
ley de la segregación law of segregation.
ley de Semon, de Semon-Rosenbach Semon's law, Semon-Rosenbach law.
ley de los senos law of sines.
ley de Sherrington Sherrington's law.
ley de Snell Snell's law.
ley de Spallanzani Spallanzani's law.
ley de Starling del corazón Starling's law of the heart.
ley de Stokes Stokes' law.

ley de Teevan Teevan's law.
ley del todo o nada all-or-none law.
ley de Toynbee Toynbee's law.
ley de la uniformidad uniformity principle.
ley del valor inicial law of initial value.
ley de van der Kolk van der Kolk's law.
ley de Van't Hoff Van't Hoff's law.
ley de las variantes múltiples law of multiple variants.
ley de Virchow Virchow's law.
ley de Waller Waller's law.
ley de Walton Walton's law.
ley de Weber Weber's law.
ley de Weber-Fechner Weber-Fechner law.
ley de Weigert Weigert's law.
ley de Wilder del valor inicial Wilder's law of initial value.
ley de Williston Williston's law.
ley de Wolff Wolff's law.
ley de Wund-Lamansky Wund-Lamansky law.
leydigarquia *f.* leydigarche.
liastenia *f.* leiasthenia.
liberación *f.* liberation, release.
liberación de membranas strip membranes.
liberación programada timed release.
liberación prolongada prolonged release.
liberación sostenida sustained release.
liberador *m.* liberator.
liberador de histamina histamine liberator.
liberomotor, -ra *adj.* liberomotor.
libidinal *adj.* libidinal.
libidinización *f.* libidinization.
libinidoso, -sa *adj.* libidinous.
líbido *f.* libido.
líbido bisexual bisexual libido.
líbido por el yo ego-libido.
libre elección de médico *f.* free choice of doctor.
licantropía *f.* lycanthropy.
licomanía *f.* lycomania.
licoperdonosis *f.* lycoperdonosis.
licor *m.* liquor.
licorexia *f.* lycorexia.
licuación *f.* liquefaction.
licuación de un gas gas liquefaction.
licuación vitrea synchisys senilis.
licuefacción *f.* liquefaction.
licuefaciente *adj.* liquefacient.
licuefactivo, -va *adj.* liquefactive.
licuescente *adj.* liquescent.
licuogel *m.* liquogel.
licuoral *adj.* liquoral.
licuorrea *f.* liquorrhea.
lien *m.* lien.
lienal *adj.* lienal.
liénculo *m.* lienculus.
liendre *f.* nit.
lienectomía *f.* lienectomy.
lienitis *f.* lienitis.
lienografía *f.* lienography.
lienomalacia *f.* lienomalacia.
lienomedular *adj.* lienomedullary.
lienomielógeno, -na *adj.* lienomyelogenous.
lienomielomalacia *f.* lienomyelomalacia.
lienopancreático, -ca *adj.* lienopancreatic.
lienopatía *f.* lienopathy.
lienorrenal *adj.* lienorenal.
lienotoxina *f.* lienotoxin.
lientería *f.* lientery.
lientérico, -ca *adj.* lienteric.
lienúnculo *m.* lienunculus.
lifting *m.* lifting.
lifting de las cejas brow lifting.
lifting facial facial lifting.
ligación *f.* ligation.

ligado, -da *adj.* linked.
  ligado al sexo sex-linked.
  ligado a X X-linked.
  ligado a Y Y-linked.
ligador *m.* linker.
ligadura[1] *f.* ligation.
  ligadura con banda elástica banding ligation, rubber-band ligation.
  ligadura de Barron Barron ligation.
  ligadura dental teeth ligation.
  ligadura tubaria, tubárica tubal ligation.
ligadura[2] *f.* ligature.
  ligadura en cadena, ligadura catenaria chain ligature.
  ligadura elástica elastic ligature.
  ligadura entrelazada interlacing ligature, interlocking ligature.
  ligadura con fibra vegetal grass-line ligature.
  ligadura de hilo elástico thread-elastic ligature.
  ligadura intravascular intravascular ligature.
  ligadura lateral lateral ligature.
  ligadura de Larrey Larrey's ligature.
  ligadura oclusiva occluding ligature.
  ligadura polar pole ligature.
  ligadura provisional provisional ligature.
  ligadura quirúrgica surgical ligature.
  ligadura soluble soluble ligature.
  ligadura suboclusiva suboccluding ligature.
  ligadura terminal terminal ligature.
  ligadura vascular vascular ligature.
ligamento *m.* ligament, ligamentum.
  ligamento periodontal periodontal ligament.
ligamentopexia *f.* ligamentopexis.
ligamentoso, -sa *adj.* ligamentous.
ligamentum *m.* ligamentum.
ligamiento *f.* linkage.
  ligamiento genético genetic linkage.
  ligamiento de registros clínicos medical record linkage.
  ligamiento sexual sex linkage.
ligando *m.* ligand.
ligar *v.* ligate.
ligofilia *f.* lygophilia.
lijado *m.* grinding.
  lijado dental grinding.
  lijado de punto spot grinding.
  lijado selectivo selective grinding.
lima[1] *f.* file.
  lima del conducto radicular root canal file.
  lima endodóntica endodontic file.
  lima de Hirschfeld-Dunlop Hirschfeld-Dunlop file.
  lima para hueso bone file.
  lima de oro gold file.
  lima periodontal periodontal file.
lima[2] *f.* lime.
limbal *adj.* limbal.
límbico, -ca *adj.* limbic.
limbo *m.* limbus.
limen *m.* limen.
liminal *adj.* liminal.
liminar *adj.* liminal.
liminómetro *m.* liminometer.
limitación *f.* limitation.
  limitación de la cadera hip limitation.
  limitación excéntrica eccentric limitation.
  limitación del movimiento limitation of motion.
limitado, -a por el sexo *adj.* sex-limited.
limitador del haz *m.* beam restrictor.
limitante *adj.* limitans.
límite *m.* limit.
  límite de asimilación assimilation limit.
  límite auditivo, límite de la audibilidad audibility limit.

límite de la confidencialidad limit of the confidentiality.
  límite elástico elastic limit.
  límite para exposición corta short-term exposure limit (STEL).
  límite de floculación limit of flocculation.
  límite de Hayflick Hayflick's limit.
  límite de percepción limit of perception.
  límite proporcional proportional limit.
  límite de saturación saturation limit.
  límite del trastorno de la personalidad personality disorder borderline.
  límite del yo ego-boundary.
limitisis *f.* limophthisis.
limítrofe *adj.* borderline.
limitrófico, -ca *adj.* limitrophic.
limnemia *f.* limnemia.
limnémico, -ca *adj.* limnemic.
limnología *f.* limnology.
limoptisis *f.* limophthisis.
limosis *f.* limosis.
limoterapia *f.* limotherapy.
limotisis *f.* limophthisis.
limpieza *f.* cleaning, clearance.
  limpieza ineficaz de la vía aérea *f.* ineffective airway clearance.
  limpieza con seda dental flossing.
  limpieza ultrasónica ultrasonic cleaning.
linaje *m.* lineage.
  linaje celular cell lineage.
lindero *m.* abutment.
línea *f.* line, linea.
  línea de absorción absorption line.
  línea de acreción accretion line.
  línea albicante linea albicantes.
  línea de Aldrich-Mees Aldrich-Mees line.
  línea de altura labial high lip line.
  línea argentina silver line.
  línea arterial arterial line.
  línea azul blue line.
  línea B de Kerley-B Kerley-B line.
  línea bala del labio low lip line.
  línea base baseline.
  línea base de Reid Reid's base line.
  línea entre base y vértice base-apex line.
  línea de Beau Beau's line.
  línea de Bechterew Bechterew's line.
  línea de Bismutia Bismuth's line.
  línea de bismuto bismuth line.
  línea de Borsieri Borsieri's line.
  línea de Burton Bruton's line.
  línea de calcificación de Retzius calcification line of Retzius.
  línea celular cell line.
  línea celular establecida established line.
  línea del cemento cementing line.
  línea de Clapton Clapton.
  línea de cobre copper line.
  línea de demarcación line of demarcation.
  línea de demarcación de la retina demarcation line of the retina.
  línea de Dennie Dennie's line.
  línea de desarrollo developmental line.
  línea digástrica digastric line.
  línea dinámica dynamic line.
  línea de Ebner line of Ebner.
  línea ectental ectental line.
  línea de Ehrlich-Türk Ehrlich-Türk line.
  línea de Ellis, línea de Ellis-Garland Ellis' line, Ellis-Garland line.
  línea embrionaria embryonic line.
  línea epifisaria epiphysial line.
  línea estabilizadora del fulcro stabilizing fulcrum line.
  línea de expresión line of expression.

línea de fijación line of fixation.
  línea de Fleischner Fleishner line.
  línea de fuerza magnética magnetic line of force.
  línea del fulcro fulcrum line.
  línea de Galton Galton's line.
  línea germinal germ line.
  línea de gravedad line of gravity.
  línea guía guideline, survey line.
  línea de Hampton Hampton line.
  línea de Harris Harris' line.
  línea de Head Head's line.
  línea de Hensen Hensen's line.
  línea de Hunter-Schreger Hunter-Schreger line.
  línea de imbricación del cemento imbrication line of cementum.
  línea de imbricación de von Ebner imbrication line of von Ebner.
  línea de incremento incremental line.
  línea incremental de Salter Salter's incremental line.
  línea de incremento del cemento incremental line of cementum.
  línea de incremento de Ebner incremental line of von Ebner.
  línea intraperiódica intraperiod line.
  línea de isoefecto isoeffect line.
  línea isoeléctrica isoelectric line.
  línea de Jadelot Jadelot's line.
  línea labial labial line.
  línea magnética de fuerza magnetic line of force.
  línea de McGregor McGregor's line.
  línea de Mees Mees' line.
  línea mercurial mercurial line.
  línea de Morgan Morgan's line.
  línea Muehrcke Muehrcke's line.
  línea nasal nasal line.
  línea negra black line.
  línea neonatal neonatal line.
  línea nigra linea nigra.
  línea de Obersteiner-Redlich Obersteiner-Redlich line.
  línea oblicua oblique line.
  línea de oclusión line of occlusion.
  línea oculocigomática oculozygomatic line.
  línea de Ogsten Ogsten line.
  línea de Ohngren Ohngren's line.
  línea orbitomeatal orbitolmeatal line.
  línea ortostática orthostatic line.
  línea de Owen Owen's line.
  línea de palanca fulcrum line.
  línea de palanca estabilizante stabilizing fulcrum line.
  línea de palanca de retención fulcrum retentive line.
  línea de París Paris line.
  línea de Pastia Pastia's line.
  línea periódica period line.
  línea periódica mayor major period line.
  línea pleuroesofágica pleuroesophageal line.
  línea de plomo lead line.
  línea de recesión recessional line.
  línea roja tiroidea thyroid red line.
  línea sagital sagittal line.
  línea de Salter Salter's line.
  línea de sangre blood line.
  línea de Schreger Schreger's line.
  línea suprarrenal blanca de Sergent Sergent's white adrenal line.
  línea surco del desarrollo developmental line.
  línea de tensión cleavage line.
  línea de tensión mínima line of minimal tension.

línea de tensión de la piel relajada relaxed skin tension line.

línea de Trümmerfeld Trümmerfeld line.

línea venosa venous line.

línea vibratoria vibrating line.

línea de la visión line of vision.

línea visual visual.

línea de Zahn line of Zahn.

línea de Zöllner Zöllner's line.

lineal *adj.* linear.

linfa *f.* lymph.

linfa aplástica aplastic lymph.

linfa corpuscular corpuscular lymph.

linfa cruposa croupous lymph.

linfa euplástica euplastic lymph.

linfa fibrinosa fibrinous lymph.

linfa hística tissue lymph.

linfa inflamatoria inflammatory lymph.

linfa intercelular intercellular lymph.

linfa intravascular intravascular lymph.

linfa plástica plastic lymph.

linfa sanguínea blood lymph.

linfa tisular tissue lymph.

linfa de vacuna, linfa de vaccinia vaccine lymph, vaccinia lymph.

linfadenectasia *f.* lymphadenectasis.

linfadenectomía *f.* lymphadenectomy.

linfadenehipertrofia *f.* lymphadenhypertrophy.

linfadenia *f.* lymphadenia.

linfadenitis *f.* lymphadenitis.

linfadenitis caseosa caseous lymphadenitis.

linfadenitis dermatopática dermatopathic lymphadenitis.

linfadenitis granulomatosa regional regional granulomatous lymphadenitis.

linfadenitis mesentérica mesenteric lymphadenitis.

linfadenitis paratuberculosa paratuberculous lymphadenitis.

linfadenitis regional regional lymphadenitis.

linfadenitis tuberculoide tuberculoid lymphadenitis.

linfadenitis tuberculosa tuberculous lymphadenitis.

linfadenocele *m.* lymphadenocele.

linfadenografía *f.* lymphadenography.

linfadenograma *f.* lymphadenogram.

linfadenoma *m.* lymphadenoma.

linfadenomatosis *f.* lymphadenomatosis.

linfadenopatía *f.* lymphadenopathy.

linfadenopatía angioinmunoblástica con disproteinemia (LAID) angioimmunoblastic lymphadenopathy with dysproteinemia (AILD).

linfadenopatía dermatopática dermatopathic lymphadenopathy.

linfadenopatía inmunoblástica immunoblastic lymphadenopathy.

linfadenopatía tuberculosa tuberculous lymphadenopathy.

linfadenoquiste *m.* lymphadenocyst.

linfadenosis *f.* lymphadenosis.

linfadenosis benigna benign lymphadenosis.

linfadenosis cutánea benigna lymphadenosis cutis benigna.

linfadenotomía *f.* lymphadenotomy.

linfadenovárice *f.* lymphadenovarix.

linfaféresis *f.* lymphapheresis.

linfagogo *m.* lymphagogue.

linfangeítis *f.* lymphangeitis.

linfangial *adj.* lymphangial.

linfangiectasia *f.* lymphangiectasia.

linfangiectasia cavernosa cavernous lymphangiectasia.

linfangiectasia intestinal intestinal lymphangiectasia.

linfangiectasia quística cystic lymphangiectasia.

linfangiectasia simple simple lymphangiectasia.

linfangiectásico, -ca *adj.* lymphangiectatic.

linfangiectodes *m.* lymphangiectodes.

linfangiectomía *f.* lymphangiectomy.

linfangiítis *f.* lymphangiitis.

linfangioadenografía *f.* lymphangioadenography.

linfangioadenograma *f.* lymphangioadenogram.

linfangioectomía *f.* lymphangiectomy.

linfangioendotelioblastoma *m.* lymphangioendothelioblastoma.

linfangioendotelioma *m.* lymphangioendothelioma.

linfangioflebitis *f.* lymphangiophlebitis.

linfangiografía *f.* lymphangiography.

linfangiograma *m.* lymphangiogram.

linfangioleiomiomatosis *f.* lymphangioleiomyomatosis.

linfangiología *f.* lymphangiology.

linfangioma *m.* lymphangioma.

linfangioma capilar capillary lymphangioma.

linfangioma capilar varicoso lymphangioma capillare varicosum.

linfangioma cavernoso lymphangioma cavernosum, cavernous lymphangioma.

linfangioma circunscrito lymphangioma circumscriptum.

linfangioma quístico cystic lymphangioma.

linfangioma simple simple lymphangioma, lymphangioma simplex.

linfangioma superficial simple lymphangioma superficium simplex.

linfangiomiomatosis *f.* lymphangiomyomatosis.

linfangiomatoso, -sa *adj.* lymphangiomatous.

linfangion *m.* lymphangion.

linfangioplastia *f.* lymphangioplasty.

linfangiosarcoma *m.* lymphangiosarcoma.

linfangiotomía *f.* lymphangiotomy.

linfangitis *f.* lymphangitis.

linfangitis carcinomatosa lymphangitis carcinomatosa.

linfangitis gomatosa gummatous lymphangitis.

linfático, -ca *adj.* lymphatic.

linfaticostomía *f.* lymphaticostomy.

linfatismo *m.* lymphatism.

linfatitis *f.* lymphatitis.

linfatógeno, -na *adj.* lymphatogenous.

linfatólisis *f.* lymphatolysis.

linfatolítico, -ca *adj.* lymphatolytic.

linfatología *f.* lymphatology.

linfatomo *m.* lymphatome, lymphotome.

linfectasia *f.* lymphectasia.

linfedema *m.* lymphedema.

linfedema congénito congenital lymphedema.

linfedema hereditario hereditary lymphedema.

linfedema precoz lymphedema praecox.

linfedema primario primary lymphedema.

linfemia *f.* lymphemia.

linfendotelioma *m.* lymphendothelioma.

linfenteritis *f.* lymphenteritis.

linfepitelioma *m.* lymphepithelioma.

linfización *f.* lymphization.

linfoadenoma *m.* lymphoadenoma.

linfoblástico, -ca *adj.* lymphoblastic.

linfoblasto *m.* lymphoblast.

linfoblastoma *m.* lymphoblastoma.

linfoblastoma folicular gigante giant follicular lymphoblastoma.

linfoblastomatosis *f.* lymphoblastomatosis.

linfoblastomatoso, -sa *adj.* lymphoblastomatous.

linfoblastómide *f.* lymphoblastomid.

linfoblastosis *f.* lymphoblastosis.

linfocele *m.* lymphocoele.

linfocina *f.* lymphokine.

linfocinesia *f.* lymphocinesia, lymphokinesis.

linfocinesis *f.* lymphokinesis.

linfocisto *m.* lymphocyst.

linfocitaféresis *f.* lymphocitapheresis.

linfocitemia *f.* lymphocythemia.

linfocítico, -ca *adj.* lymphocytic.

linfocito *m.* lymphocyte.

linfocito asesino killer lymphocyte.

linfocito B B lymphocyte.

linfocito dependiente del timo thymus-dependent lymphocyte.

linfocito granular grande large granular lymphocyte.

linfocito independiente del timo thymus independent lymphocyte.

linfocito de Rieder Rieder's lymphocyte.

linfocito T T lymphocyte.

linfocito T amplificador amplifier T lymphocyte.

linfocito T ayudador helper T lymphocyte.

linfocito T citotóxicos cytotoxic T lymphocyte.

linfocito transformado transformed lymphocyte.

linfocitoblasto *m.* lymphocytoblast.

linfocitoféresis *m.* lymphocytopheresis.

linfocitoma *m.* lymphocytoma.

linfocitoma benigno de la piel benign lymphocytoma cutis.

linfocitoma cutáneo, linfocitoma cutis lymphocytoma cutis.

linfocitomatosis *f.* lymphocytomatosis.

linfocitopenia *f.* lymphocytopenia.

linfocitopoyesis *f.* lymphocytopoiesis.

linfocitopoyético, -ca *adj.* lymphocytopoietic.

linfocitorrexis *f.* lymphocytorrhexis.

linfocitósico, -ca *adj.* lymphocytotic.

linfocitosis *f.* lymphocitosis.

linfocitosis infecciosa aguda acute infectious lymphocitosis.

linfocitotoxicidad *f.* lymphocytotoxicity.

linfocitotóxina *f.* lymphocytotoxin.

linfodermia *f.* lymphodermia.

linfoducto *m.* lymphoduct.

linfoepitelioma *m.* lymphoepithelioma.

linfoganglina *f.* lymphoganglin.

linfogenia *f.* lymphogenesis.

linfogénesis *f.* lymphogenesis.

linfogénico, -ca *adj.* lymphogenic.

linfógeno, -na *adj.* lymphogenous.

linfografía *f.* lymphography.

linfograma *m.* lymphogram.

linfogranuloma *m.* lymphogranuloma.

linfogranuloma benigno lymphogranuloma benignum.

linfogranuloma inguinal lymphogranuloma inguinale.

linfogranuloma venéreo venereal lymphogranuloma, lymphogranuloma venereum.

linfogranulomatosis *f.* lymphogranulomatosis.

linfogranulomatosis benigna benign lymphogranulomatosis.

linfogranulomatosis inguinal lymphogranulomatosis inguinalis.

linfogranulomatosis maligna de la piel lymphogranulomatosis cutis.

linfohistiocitosis *f.* lymphohistiocytosis.

linfohistioplasmático, -ca *adj.* lymphohistioplasmacytic.
linfoide *adj.* lymphoid.
linfoidectomía *f.* lymphoidectomy.
linfoideo, -a *adj.* lymphoid.
linfoidotoxemia *f.* lymphoidotoxemia.
linfólisis *f.* lympholysis.
linfolítico, -ca *adj.* lympholytic.
linfología *f.* lymphology.
linfoma *m.* lymphoma.
　linfoma africano African lymphoma.
　linfoma benigno del recto benign lymphoma of the rectum.
　linfoma de Burkitt Burkitt's lymphoma.
　linfoma de células B pequeñas small B-cell lymphoma.
　linfoma de células del centro folicular follicular center cell lymphoma.
　linfoma de células grandes large cell lymphoma.
　linfoma de células madre stem cell lymphoma.
　linfoma de células T T-cell lymphoma.
　linfoma de células T del adulto adult T cell lymphoma.
　linfoma de células T contorsionado convoluted T-cell lymphoma.
　linfoma de células T cutáneo cutaneous T-cell lymphoma.
　linfoma de células T de pequeños linfocitos small lymphocytic T-cell lymphoma.
　linfoma de células U (indefinido) U-cell (undefined) lymphoma.
　linfoma cutis lymphoma cutis.
　linfoma difuso diffuse lymphoma.
　linfoma folicular follicular lymphoma.
　linfoma folicular gigante giant follicle lymphoma.
　linfoma granulomatoso granulomatous lymphoma.
　linfoma histiocítico histiocytic lymphoma.
　linfoma histiocítico verdadero real histiocytic lymphoma.
　linfoma de Hodgkin Hodgkin's lymphoma.
　linfoma indiferenciado undifferentiated lymphoma.
　linfoma inmunoblástico inmunoblastic lymphoma.
　linfoma intestinal T intestinal T-cell lymphoma.
　linfoma de Lennert Lennert's lymphoma.
　linfoma linfoblástico lymphoblastic lymphoma.
　linfoma linfocítico lymphocytic lymphoma.
　linfoma linfocítico bien diferenciado well-differentiated lymphocytic lymphoma.
　linfoma linfocítico mal diferenciado poorly differentiated lymphocytic lymphoma.
　linfoma linfocítico maligno bien diferenciado well-differentiated lymphocytic malignant lymphoma.
　linfoma linfocítico maligno mal diferenciado poorly differentiated lymphocytic malignant lymphoma.
　linfoma linfocítico pequeño small lymphocytic lymphoma.
　linfoma linfocítico plasmacitoide plasmacytoid lymphocytic lymphoma.
　linfoma linfoepitelioide lymphoepithelioid cell lymphoma.
　linfoma linfoplasmocítico lymphoplasmocytic lymphoma.
　linfoma maligno malignant lymphoma.
　linfoma maligno indiferenciado undifferentiated malignant lymphoma.

　linfoma MALT MALT lymphoma.
　linfoma mediterráneo, linfoma del Mediterráneo Mediterranean lymphoma.
　linfoma mixto linfocítico e histiocítico mixed lymphocytic-histiocytic lymphoma.
　linfoma monocitoide monocytoid lymphoma.
　linfoma nodular nodular lymphoma.
　linfoma nodular histiocítico nodular histiocytic lymphoma.
　linfoma no de Hodgkin non-Hodgkin's lymphoma.
　linfoma pleomorfo pleomorphic lymphoma.
　linfoma tiroideo thyroid lymphoma.
　linfoma T periférico peripheral T-cell lymphoma.
linfomatoide *adj.* lymphomatoid.
linfomatoideo, -a *adj.* lymphomatoid.
linfomatosis *f.* lymphomatosis.
　linfomatosis neural neural lymphomatosis.
　linfomatosis ocular ocular lymphomatosis.
linfomatoso, -sa *adj.* lymphomatous.
linfomieloma *m.* lymphomyeloma.
linfomixoma *m.* lymphomyxoma.
linfonoditis *f.* lymphonoditis.
linfonódulo *m.* lymphonodulus.
linfopatía *f.* lymphopathy, lymphopathia.
　linfopatía atáxica ataxic lymphopathy.
　linfopatía venérea lymphopathy venereum.
linfopenia *f.* lymphopenia.
linfoplasia *f.* lymphoplasia.
　linfoplasia cutánea cutaneous lymphoplasia.
linfoplasma *m.* lymphoplasm.
linfoplasmaféresis *f.* lymphoplasmapheresis.
linfoplastia *f.* lymphoplasty.
linfopoyesis *f.* lymphopoiesis.
linfopoyético, -ca *adj.* lymphopoietic.
linfoproliferativo, -va *adj.* lymphoproliferative.
linfoquinesia *f.* lymphokinesis.
linforragia *f.* lymphorrhagia.
linforrea *f.* lymphorrhea.
linforreticular *adj.* lymphoreticular.
linforreticulosis *f.* lymphoreticulosis.
　linforreticulosis benigna (de inoculación) benign (inoculation) lymphoreticulosis.
linforroide *m.* lymphorrhoid.
linfosarcoma *m.* lymphosarcoma.
linfosarcomatosis *f.* lymphosarcomatosis.
linfoso, -sa *adj.* lymphous.
linfostasia *f.* lymphostasis.
linfostasis *f.* lymphotasis.
linfotaxis *f.* lymphotaxis.
linfotismo *m.* lymphotism.
linfotomo *m.* lymphotome.
linfotoxemia *f.* lymphotoxemia.
linfotoxina *f.* lymphotoxin.
linfotrofia *f.* lymphotrophy.
linfotrópico, -ca *adj.* lymphotropic.
linfovascular *adj.* lymph-vascular.
linfuria *f.* lymphuria.
lingua *f.* lingua.
lingual *adj.* lingual, lingualis.
linguale *m.* linguale.
Linguatula Linguatula.
linguatuliasis *f.* linguatuliasis, linguatulosis.
linguatulosis *f.* linguatulosis.
lingüiforme *adj.* linguiform.
língula *f.* lingula.
lingular *adj.* lingular.
lingulectomía *f.* lingulectomy.
linguoaxil *adj.* linguoaxial.
linguoaxiogingival *adj.* linguoaxiogingival.
linguocervical *adj.* linguocervical.
linguoclinación *f.* linguoclination.

linguoclusión *f.* linguoclusion.
linguodental *adj.* linguodental.
linguodistal *adj.* linguodistal.
linguogingival *adj.* linguogingival.
linguoincisal *adj.* linguoincisal.
linguomesial *adj.* linguomesial.
linguooclusal *adj.* linguo-occlusal.
linguopapilitis *f.* linguopapilitis.
linguopulpal *adj.* linguopulpal.
linguoubicación *f.* linguoplacement.
linguoversión *f.* linguoversion.
linimento *m.* liniment, linimentum.
linitis *f.* linitis.
　linitis plástica linitis plastica.
linkage linkage.
lioadsorción *f.* lyosorption.
liofílico, -ca *adj.* lyophilic.
liofilización *f.* lyophilization.
liofilizador *m.* lyophilizer.
liofilizar *v.* lyophilize.
liófilo, -la *adj.* lyophile.
liofóbico, -ca *adj.* lyophobic.
liófobo, -ba *adj.* lyophobe, lyophobic.
liomiofibroma *m.* leiomyofibroma.
liomioma *m.* leiomyoma.
　liomioma cutis, liomioma cutáneo cutis leiomyoma.
lionización *f.* lyonization.
lionizado, -da *adj.* lyonized.
liosorción *f.* lyosorption.
liotrópico, -ca *adj.* lyotropic.
lipacidemia *f.* lipacidemia.
lipaciduria *f.* lipaciduria.
liparodisnea *f.* liparodypnea.
liparoide *adj.* liparoid.
liparoideo, -a *adj.* liparoid.
liparónfalo *m.* liparomphalus.
lipartritis *f.* lipoarthritis.
lipasa *f.* lipase.
lipásico, -ca *adj.* lipasic.
lipasuria *f.* lipasuria.
lipectomía *f.* lipectomy.
　lipectomía por succión suction lipectomy.
lipedema *m.* lipedema.
lipemia *f.* lipemia.
　lipemia alimentaria alimentary lipemia.
　lipemia diabética diabetic lipemia.
　lipemia posprandial postprandial lipemia.
　lipemia retiniana lipemia retinalis.
lipidasa *f.* lipidase.
lipidemia *f.* lipidemia.
lipídico, -ca *adj.* lipidic.
lípido *m.* lipid.
　lípido compuesto compound lipid.
　lípido simple simple lipid.
lipidólisis *f.* lipidolysis.
lipidolítico, -ca *adj.* lipidolytic.
lipidosis *f.* lipidosis.
　lipidosis cerebral cerebral lipidosis.
　lipidosis por cerebrósidos cerebroside lipidosis.
　lipidosis de cerebrósidos glucosílicos glucosyl cerebroside lipidosis.
　lipidosis por esfingomielina sphingomyelin lipidosis.
　lipidosis de galactósido de ceramida, lipidosis galactosilceramida galactosylceramide lipidosis.
　lipidosis por gangliósidos ganglioside lipidosis.
　lipidosis por glucolípidos glycolipid lipidosis.
　lipidosis de glucósido de ceramida glucosylceramide lipidosis.
　lipidosis por sulfátidos sulfatide lipidosis.

lipiduria *f.* lipiduria, lipoiduria.
lipina *f.* lipin.
lipitud *f.* lippitude, lippitudo.
lipoadenoma *m.* lipoadenoma.
lipoartritis *f.* lipoarthritis.
lipoaspiración *f.* liposuction.
lipoatrofia *f.* lipoatrophia.
　lipoatrofia circunscrita lipoatrophia circumscripta.
　lipoatrofia por insulina insulin lipoatrophia.
　lipoatrofia parcial partial lipoatrophia.
lipoblasto *m.* lipoblast.
lipoblastoma *m.* lipoblastoma.
lipoblastomatosis *f.* lipoblastomatosis.
lipocaico *m.* lipocaic.
lipocardíaco, -ca *adj.* lipocardiac.
lipocatabólico, -ca *adj.* lipocatabolic.
lipocele *m.* lipocele.
lipocera *f.* lipocere.
lipoceratoso, -sa *adj.* lipoceratous.
lipocito *m.* lipocyte.
lipoclasis *f.* lipoclasis.
lipoclástico, -ca *adj.* lipoclastic.
lipocondrodistrofia *f.* lipochondrodystrophy.
lipocondroma *m.* lipochondroma.
lipócrito *m.* lipocrit.
lipocromo *m.* lipochrome.
lipodermoide *m.* lipodermoid.
lipodierético, -ca *adj.* lipodieretic.
lipodistrofia *f.* lipodystrophy, lipodystrophia.
　lipodistrofia bitrocantérea bitrochanteric lipodystrophy.
　lipodistrofia congénita generalizada congenital generalized lipodystrophy.
　lipodistrofia congénita progresiva congenital progressive lipodystrophy.
　lipodistrofia generalizada generalized lipodystrophy.
　lipodistrofia por insulina, lipodistrofia insulínica insulin lipodystrophy.
　lipodistrofia intestinal intestinal lipodystrophy, lipodystrophia intestinalis.
　lipodistrofia parcial partial lipodystrophy, progressive partial lipodystrophy.
　lipodistrofia progresiva lipodystrophia progressiva.
　lipodistrofia progresiva congénita progressive congenital lipodystrophy.
　lipodistrofia progresiva superior lipodystrophia progressiva superior.
　lipodistrofia total total lipodystrophy.
lipoedema *m.* lipoedema.
lipofagia *f.* lipophagy, lipophagia.
　lipofagia granulomatosa granulomatous lipophagy.
lipofágico, -ca *adj.* lipophagic.
lipófago, -ga *m.* lipophage.
lipofanerosis *f.* lipophanerosis.
lipófero, -ra *adj.* lipoferous.
lipoferoso, -sa *adj.* lipoferous.
lipofibroma *m.* lipofibroma.
lipofilia *f.* lipophilia.
lipófilo, -la *adj.* lipophilic, lipophil.
lipogenia *f.* lipogenesis.
lipogénesis *f.* lipogenesis.
lipogenético, -ca *adj.* lipogenetic.
lipogénico, -ca *adj.* lipogenic.
lipógeno, -na *adj.* lipogenic.
lipogranuloma *m.* lipogranuloma.
lipogranulomatosis *f.* lipogranulomatosis.
　lipogranulomatosis diseminada disseminated lipogranulomatosis.
　lipogranulomatosis de Farber Farber's lipogranulomatosis.
lipohemartrosis *f.* lipohemarthrosis.

lipohialina *f.* lipohyalin.
lipohipertrofia *f.* lipohyperprophy.
lipohistiodiéresis *f.* lipohistiodieresis.
lipoidal *adj.* lipoid.
lipoide *adj.* lipoid.
lipoidemia *f.* lipoidemia.
lipoídico, -ca *adj.* lipoidic.
lipoidoproteinosis *f.* lipoidproteinosis.
lipoidosiderosis *f.* lipoidsiderosis.
lipoidosis *f.* lipoidosis.
　lipoidosis arterial arterial lipoidosis.
　lipoidosis corneal lipoidosis corneae.
　lipoidosis cutis et mucosae lipoidosis cutis et mucosae.
　lipoidosis renal renal lipoidosis.
lipoiduria *f.* lipoiduria.
lipolipoidosis *f.* lipolipoidosis.
lipólisis *f.* lipolysis.
lipolítico, -ca *adj.* lipolytic.
lipoma *m.* lipoma.
　lipoma anular del cuello lipoma annulare colli.
　lipoma arborescente lipoma arborescens.
　lipoma atípico atypical lipoma.
　lipoma capsular lipoma capsulare.
　lipoma cavernoso lipoma cavernosum.
　lipoma de células fusiformes spindle cell lipoma.
　lipoma de células grasas, lipoma de células grasas fetales fat cell lipoma.
　lipoma difuso diffuse lipoma.
　lipoma difuso renal lipoma diffusu renis.
　lipoma doloroso lipoma dolorosa.
　lipoma fetal fetal lipoma.
　lipoma fibroso lipoma fibrosum.
　lipoma infiltrativo infiltrating lipoma.
　lipoma intradural intradural lipoma.
　lipoma lipoblástico lipoblastic lipoma.
　lipoma mixomatoso lipoma myxomatodes.
　lipoma osificante lipoma ossificans.
　lipoma pleomórfico pleomorphic lipoma.
　lipoma sarcomatoso lipoma sarcomatodes, lipoma sarcomatosum.
　lipoma telangiectásico telangiectatic lipoma, lipoma telangiectodes.
lipomatoide *adj.* lipomatoid.
lipomatoideo, -a *adj.* lipomatoid.
lipomatosis *f.* lipomatosis.
　lipomatosis atrófica lipomatosis atrophicans.
　lipomatosis congénita del páncreas congenital lipomatosis of the pancreas.
　lipomatosis difusa diffuse lipomatosis.
　lipomatosis dolorosa lipomatosis dolorosa.
　lipomatosis gigante lipomatosis gigantea.
　lipomatosis múltiple multiple lipomatosis.
　lipomatosis neurótica lipomatosis neurotica.
　lipomatosis nodular circunscrita nodular circumscribed lipomatosis.
　lipomatosis renal, lipomatosis renis renal lipomatosis, lipomatosis renis.
　lipomatosis de restitución del riñón renal lipomatosis, lipomatosis renis.
　lipomatosis simétrica symmetric lipomatosis, symmetrical lipomatosis.
　lipomatosis simétrica múltiple multiple symmetric lipomatosis.
lipomatoso, -sa *adj.* lipomatous.
lipomeningocele *m.* lipomeningocele.
lipomería *f.* lipomeria.
lipometabólico, -ca *adj.* lipometabolic.
lipometabolismo *m.* lipometabolism.
lipomicrón *m.* lipomicron.
lipomiohemangioma *m.* lipomyohemangioma.
lipomioma *m.* lipomyoma.

lipomixoma *m.* lipomyxoma.
lipomucopolisacaridosis *f.* lipomucopolysaccharidosis.
liponefrosis *f.* liponephrosis.
lipopatía *f.* lipopathy.
lipopéctico, -ca *adj.* lipopectic.
lipopenia *f.* lipopenia.
lipopénico, -ca *adj.* lipopenic.
lipopexia *f.* lipopexia.
lipopéxico, -ca *adj.* lipopexic.
lipopolisacárido *m.* lipopolysaccharide.
lipoproteína *f.* lipoprotein.
lipoproteinemia *f.* lipoproteinemia.
lipoproteinosis *f.* lipoproteinosis.
liposarcoma *m.* liposarcoma.
liposis *f.* liposis.
liposolubilidad *f.* liposolubility.
liposoluble *adj.* liposoluble.
liposoma *m.* liposome.
lipostomía *f.* lipostomy.
liposucción *f.* liposuction.
lipotimia *f.* lipothymia.
　lipotimia de los aviadores blackout.
lipotrofia *f.* lipotrophy.
lipotrófico, -ca *adj.* lipotrophic.
lipotropía *f.* lipotropy.
lipotrópico, -ca *adj.* lipotropic.
lipotropismo *m.* lipotropism.
lipovacuna *f.* lipovaccine.
lipovitelina *f.* lipovitellin.
lipoxenia *f.* lipoxeny.
lipoxidasa *f.* lipoxidase.
lipoxigenasa *f.* lipoxygenase.
lipoxismo *m.* lipoxysm.
lipresina *f.* lypressin.
lipsotriquia *f.* lipsotrichia.
lipuria *f.* lipuria.
lipúrico, -ca *adj.* lipuric.
liquen *m.* lichen.
　liquen acuminado lichen acuminatus.
　liquen agrio lichen agrius.
　liquen albo lichen albus.
　liquen amiloideo, liquen amiloidoso lichen amyloidosus.
　liquen anular lichen annularis.
　liquen córneo hipertrófico lichen corneus hypertrophicus.
　liquen crónico simple lichen simplex chronicus.
　liquen escleroatrófico lichen sclerosus et atrophicus.
　liquen escleroso lichen sclerosus.
　liquen escrofuloso lichen scrofulosus.
　liquen espinuloso lichen spinulosus.
　liquen estriado lichen striatus.
　liquen estrofuloso lichen strophulosus.
　liquen fibromucinoidoso lichen fibromucinoidosus.
　liquen hemorrágico lichen hemorrhagicus.
　liquen infantil lichen infantum.
　liquen iris lichen iris.
　liquen mixedematoso lichen myxedematosus.
　liquen nítido lichen nitidus.
　liquen de la nuca lichen nuchae.
　liquen obtuso lichen obtusus.
　liquen obtuso córneo lichen obtusus corneus.
　liquen pilar lichen pilaris.
　liquen plano lichen planus.
　liquen plano anular lichen planus annularis.
　liquen plano atrófico lichen planus atrophicus.
　liquen plano bucal erosivo oral erosive lichen.
　liquen plano bucal no erosivo oral non-erosive lichen.
　liquen plano bulloso lichen planus bullous.

liquen plano bulloso-vesicular lichen planus vesiculobullous.
liquen plano eritematoso lichen planus erythematosus.
liquen plano folicular lichen planus follicularis.
liquen plano hipertrófico lichen planus hypertrophicus.
liquen plano verrugoso lichen planus verrucosus.
liquen planopilar, liquen planopiloso lichen planopilaris.
liquen planus et acuminatus atrophicans lichen planus et acuminatus atrophicans.
liquen rojo moniliforme lichen ruber moniliformis.
liquen rojo plano lichen ruber planus.
liquen rojo verrugoso lichen ruber verrucosus.
liquen sifilítico lichen syphiliticus.
liquen simple crónico lichen simplex chronicus.
liquen tropical tropical lichen.
liquen trópico lichen tropicus.
liquen urticado lichen urticatus.
liquen variegatus lichen variegatus.
liquen de Wilson Wilson's lichen.
liquenificación *f.* lichenification.
liquenoide *adj.* lichenoid.
liquinoideo, -a *adj.* liquenoid.
líquido *m.* fluid, liquid, liquor.
líquido alantoico, líquido alantoideo allantoic fluid.
líquido amniótico amniotic fluid.
líquido ascítico ascitic fluid.
líquido cefalorraquídeo cerebrospinal fluid, liquor cerebrospinalis.
líquido cerebrospinal, liquor cerebrospinalis liquor cerebrospinalis.
líquido crevicular crevicular fluid.
líquido de Condy Condy's fluid.
líquido corporal body fluid.
líquido de Dakin Dakin's fluid.
líquido de Delafield Delafield's fluid.
líquido descalcificante decalcifying fluid.
líquido de diálisis, líquido dializador dialysis fluid.
líquido de dilución de Rees y Ecker Rees and Ecker diluting fluid.
líquido de Ecker Ecker's fluid.
líquido espinal spinal fluid.
líquido extravascular extravascular fluid.
líquido fijador de Flemming Flemming's fixing fluid.
líquido folicular, liquor folliculi follicular fluid, liquor folliculi.
líquido gingival gingival fluid.
líquido hístico tissue fluid.
líquido intersticial interstitial fluid.
líquido intracelular intracellular fluid.
líquido intraocular intraocular fluid.
líquido de Kaiserling Kaiserling's fluid.
líquido laberíntico labyrinthine fluid.
líquido de Lang Lang's fluid.
líquido de Locke Locke's fluid.
líquido de Müller Müller's fluid, Müller's liquid.
líquido pericárdico pericardial fluid.
líquido peritoneal peritoneal fluid.
líquido de Piazza Piazza's fluid.
líquido pleural pleural fluid.
líquido prostático prostatic fluid.
líquido de Rees-Ecker Rees-Ecker fluid.
líquido de Scarpa Scarpa's fluid.
líquido seminal seminal fluid.

líquido seroso serous fluid.
líquido sinovial synovial fluid.
líquido sulcular sulcular fluid.
líquido de Thoma Thoma's fluid.
líquido tisular tissue fluid.
líquido transcelular transcellular fluid.
líquido uterino uterine fluid.
líquido ventricular ventricular fluid.
líquido de Waldeyer Waldeyer's fluid.
líquido de Wickersheimer Wickersheimer's fluid.
líquido de Zenker Zenker's fluid.
líquido, -da *adj.* liquid.
liquiforme *adj.* liquiform.
liquor *m.* liquor.
liquor chorii liquor chorii.
liquor cotunnii liquor cotunnii.
liquor gastricus liquor gastricus.
liquor madre mother liquor.
liquor pancreaticus liquor pancreaticus.
liquor prostaticus liquor prostaticus.
liquor puris liquor puris.
liquor sanguinis liquor sanguinis.
liquor de Scarpa liquor of Scarpa, liquor scarpae.
liquor seminis liquor seminis.
lira *f.* lyra.
lisa *f.* lyssa, lyse.
lisado *m.* lysate.
lisado, -da *adj.* lysate.
lisar *v.* lyse.
lisemia *f.* lysemia.
lisencefalia *f.* lissencephaly, lissencephalia.
lisencefálico, -ca *adj.* lissencephalic.
lísico, -ca *adj.* lyssic.
lisímetro *m.* lysimeter.
lisina *f.* lysine, lysin.
lisinemia *f.* lysinemia.
lisiogenia *f.* lysogenesis.
lisinogénesis *f.* lysinogenesis.
lisinógeno, -na *adj.* lysinogen.
lisinosis *f.* lysinosis.
lisinuria *f.* lysinuria.
lisis *f.* lysis.
lisobacteria *f.* lysobacteria.
lisocinasa *f.* lysokinase.
lisocitina *f.* lysocythin.
lisodexia *f.* lyssodexis.
lisoesfínter *m.* lissosphincter.
lisofobia *f.* lyssophobia.
lisogénesis *f.* lysogenesis.
lisogenia *f.* lysogeny.
lisogenicidad *f.* lysogenicity.
lisogénico, -ca *adj.* lysogenic.
lisogenización *f.* lysogenization.
lisógeno, -na *adj.* lysogen.
lisoide *adj.* lyssoid.
lisorremoción *f.* lysotripping.
lisosoma *m.* lysosome.
lisosoma definitivo definitive lysosome.
lisosoma primario primary lysosome.
lisosoma secundario secondary lysosome.
lisosómico, -ca *adj.* lysosomal.
lisotipo *m.* lysotype.
lisótrico, -ca *adj.* lissotrichic, lissotrichous.
lisozima *f.* lysozyme.
lisozimuria *f.* lysozymuria.
listerelosis *f.* listerellosis.
Listerella Listerela.
Listeria Listeria.
Listeria monocytogenes Listeria monocytogenes.
listerial *adj.* Listerial.
listeriosis *f.* listeriosis.
listerismo *m.* listerism.

litagogectasia *f.* lithagogectasia.
litagogo, -ga *adj.* lithagogue.
litangiuria *f.* lithangiuria.
litecbolia *f.* lithecbole.
litectasia *f.* lithectasy.
litectomía *f.* lithectomy.
litemia *f.* lithemia.
litémico, -ca *adj.* lithemic.
litiásico, -ca *adj.* lithiasic.
litiasis *f.* lithiasis.
litiasis apendicular appendicular lithiasis.
litiasis conjuntival lithiasis conjunctivae.
litiasis pancreática pancreatic lithiasis.
litiasis urinaria urinary lithiasis.
lítico, -ca[1] *adj.* lytic.
lítico, -ca[2] *adj.* lithic.
litio *m.* lithium.
litocelifo *m.* lithokelyphos.
litocelifopedio *m.* lithokelyphopedion, lithokelyphopedium.
litocelifopedion *m.* lithokelyphopedium.
litocenosis *f.* lithocenosis.
litocistotomía *f.* lithocystotomy.
litoclasto *m.* lithoclast.
litoclisma *m.* lithoclysmia.
litoconion *m.* lithokonion.
litodiálisis *f.* lithodialysis.
litófono *m.* lithophone.
litogenia *f.* lithogeny.
litogénesis *f.* lithogenesis.
litógeno, -na *adj.* lithogenous, lithogenic.
litoide *adj.* lithoid.
litolabo *m.* litholabe.
litolapaxia *f.* litholapaxy.
litólisis *f.* litholysis.
litolítico, -ca *adj.* litholytic.
litolito *m.* litholyte.
litología *f.* lithology.
litómetro *m.* lithometer.
litómilo *m.* lithomil.
litonefria *f.* lithonephria.
litonefrosls *f.* lithonephria.
litonefritis *f.* lithonephritis.
litonefrotomía *f.* lithonephrotomy.
litontríptico, -ca *adj.* lithontriptic, lithotriptic.
litopedion *m.* lithopedion, lithopedium.
litoquelifopedion *m.* lithokelyphopedion.
litoquelifos *m.* lithokelyphos.
litoscopio *m.* lithoscope.
litoso, -sa *adj.* lithous.
litotomía *f.* lithotomy.
litotomía alta high lithotomy.
litotomía lateral lateral lithotomy.
litotomía mariana marian lithotomy.
litotomía mediana median lithotomy.
litotomía mediolateral mediolateral lithotomy.
litotomía perineal perineal lithotomy.
litotomía prerrectal prerectal lithotomy.
litotomía rectal, litotomía rectovesical rectal lithotomy, rectovesical lithotomy.
litotomía suprapúbica suprapubic lithotomy.
litotomía vaginal, litotomía vesicovaginal vaginal lithotomy, vesicovaginal lithotomy.
litotomía vesical vesical lithotomy.
litotomista *m.* lithotomist.
litótomo *m.* lithotome.
litotonía *f.* lithotony.
litotresis *f.* lithotresis.
litotresis ultrasónica ultrasonic lithotresis.
litotricia *f.* lithotrity.
litotripsia *f.* lithotripsy.
litotríptico, -ca *adj.* lithotriptic.

litotriptor *m.* lithotripter.
litotriptoscopia *f.* lithotriptoscopy.
litotriptoscopio *m.* lithotriptoscope.
litotritor *m.* lithotrite.
litoxiduria *f.* lithoxiduria.
litritis *f.* littritis.
littritis *f.* littritis.
lituresis *f.* lithuresis.
litureteria *f.* lithureteria.
lituria *f.* lithuria.
livedo *f.* livedo.
  livedo anular livedo racemosa.
  livedo post mortem livedo postmortem.
  livedo racemosa livedo racemosa.
  livedo reticular, livedo reticularis livedo reticularis.
  livedo reticular idiopática idiopathic livedo reticularis.
  livedo reticular sintomática symptomatic livedo reticularis.
  livedo telangiectásica livedo telangiectatica.
livedoide *adj.* livedoid.
livedoideo, -a *adj.* livedoid.
liviandad *f.* lightening.
lividez *f.* lividity.
  lividez cadavérica livor mortis.
  lividez postmortem postmortem lividity.
lívido, -da *adj.* livid.
livor *m.* livor.
  livor mortis livor mortis.
lixiviación *f.* lixiviation.
lixivio *m.* lixivium.
lixivium lixivium.
llaga *f.* sore.
  llaga por presión pressure sore.
lobado, -da *adj.* lobate.
lobar *adj.* lobar.
lobectomía *f.* lobectomy.
lobitis *f.* lobitis.
Loboa loboi Loboa loboi.
lobopodio *m.* lobopod, lobopodium.
lobópodo *m.* lobopod.
lobotomía *f.* lobotomy.
  lobotomía frontal frontal lobotomy.
  lobotomía prefrontal prefrontal lobotomy.
  lobotomía transorbitaria transorbital lobotomy.
lobulación *f.* lobulation, lobation.
  lobulación portal portal lobulation.
  lobulación renal renal lobulation.
lobulado, -da *adj.* lobulated.
lobular *adj.* lobular.
lobulillo *m.* lobule, lobulus.
lobulus *m.* lobule, lobulus.
lóbulo *m.* lobe, lobus.
lobus *m.* lobe, lobus.
lobuloso, -sa *adj.* lobulous, lobulose.
local *adj.* local.
localización *f.* localization.
  localización auditiva auditory localization.
  localización cerebral cerebral localization.
  localización espacial spatial localization.
  localización estereotáxica stereotaxic localization.
  localización germinal germinal localization.
  localización táctil tactile localization.
localizado, -da *adj.* localized.
localizador *m.* localizer, locator.
  localizador de Berman-Moorhead Berman-Moorhead localizer, Moorhead foreign body localizer.
  localizador de confín abutment localizer.
  localizador electroacústico electroacoustic localizer.
lochia *m.* lochia.

loci loci.
loción *f.* lotion, lotio.
loco, -ca *adj.* insane, mad.
locomoción *f.* locomotion.
  locomoción braquial braquial locomotion.
locomotor, -a *adj.* locomotor, locomotory, locomotive.
loculación *f.* loculation.
loculado, -da *adj.* loculate.
locular *adj.* locular.
lóculo *m.* loculus.
locura *f.* insanity, madness.
locus *m.* locus.
loemología *f.* loemology.
loempe *m.* loempe.
lofodonto, -ta *adj.* lophodont.
lofotrico, -ca *adj.* lophotrichous.
logadectomía *f.* logadectomy.
logaditis *f.* logaditis.
logafasia *f.* logaphasia.
logamnesia *f.* logamnesia.
logoafasia *f.* logaphasia.
logoagnosia *f.* logagnosia.
logoagrafía *f.* logagraphia.
logoamnesia *f.* logamnesia.
logoastenia *f.* logasthenia.
logoclonía *f.* logoclonia, logoklony.
logocofosia *f.* logokophasis.
logocofasis *f.* logokophasis.
logoespasmo *f.* logospasm.
logomanía *f.* logomania.
logoneurosis *f.* logoneurosis.
logopatía *f.* logopathy.
logopeda *m.* speech-language pathologist.
logopedia *f.* logopedia, logopedics, speech pathology.
logoplejía *f.* logoplegia.
logorrea *f.* logorrhea.
logospasmo *m.* logospasm.
logoterapia *f.* logotherapy.
loímico, -ca *adj.* loimic.
loimografía *f.* loimographia.
loimología *f.* loimology.
lolismo *f.* loliism.
lombriz *f.* lumbricus.
lomo *m.* loin.
longevidad *f.* longevity.
longilíneo, -a *adj.* longilineal.
longímano, -na *adj.* longimanous.
longípedo, -da *adj.* longipedate.
longirradiado, -da *adj.* longiradiate.
longitípico, -ca *adj.* longitypical.
longitud *f.* length.
  longitud de arco, longitud de la arcada arch length.
  longitud de arco disponible, longitud de arcada disponible available arch length.
  longitud basialveolar basialveolar length.
  longitud basinasal basinasal length.
  longitud efectiva de onda effective wave length, equivalent wave length.
  longitud focal focal length.
  longitud de onda wavelength.
  longitud truncal stem length.
  longitud vértex a rabadilla crown-rump length (CRL).
  longitud vértex a talón crown-heel length.
  longitud vértice-nalgas crown-rump length (CRL).
  longitud vértice-talón crown-heel length.
longitudinal *adj.* longitudinal, longitudinalis.
loquial *adj.* lochial.
loquiocolpos *m.* lochiocolpos.
loquioesquesis *f.* lochioschesis.
loquiómetra *m.* lochiometra.

loquiorrea *f.* lochiorrhea.
loquios *m.* lochia.
  loquios blancos lochia alba.
  loquios cruentos, lochia cruenta lochia cruenta.
  loquios purulentos lochia purulenta.
  loquios rojos lochia rubra.
  loquios sanguinolentos lochia sanguinolenta.
  loquios serosos lochia serosa.
loquiosquesis *f.* lochioschesis.
loquiostasis *f.* lochiostasis.
lordoescoliosis *f.* lordoscoliosis.
lordosis *f.* lordosis.
lordótico, -ca *adj.* lordotic.
loxartrosis *f.* loxarthrosis.
loxoftalmía *f.* loxophthalmus.
Loxosceles Loxosceles.
Loxoscelidae Loxoscelidae.
loxoscelismo *m.* loxoscelism.
  loxoscelismo viscerocutáneo viscerocutaneous loxoscelism.
loxotomía *f.* loxotomy.
loyasis *f.* loiasis.
lucidez *f.* lucidity.
lucidificación *f.* lucidification.
lúcido, -da *adj.* lucid.
lucífugo, -ga *adj.* lucifugal.
lucípeto, -ta *adj.* lucipetal.
ludopatía *f.* gambling.
ludoterapia *f.* play therapy.
lúe *f.* lues.
lúes *f.* lues.
  lúe venérea lues venerea.
luético, -ca *adj.* luetic.
lugar *m.* site, locus.
  lugar de infección locus of infection.
  lugar de inserción insertion site.
  lugar de unión binding site.
lujo *m.* luxus.
lujuriante *adj.* luxuriant.
lumbago *m.* lumbago.
  lumbago isquémico ischemic lumbago.
lumbalgia *f.* low back pain.
lumbar *adj.* lumbar.
lumbalización *f.* lumbarization.
lumbarización *f.* lumbarization.
lumbartria *f.* lambartry.
lumboabdominal *adj.* lumboabdominal.
lumbocolostomía *f.* lumbocolostomy.
lumbocolotomía *f.* lumbocolotomy.
lumbocostal *adj.* lumbocostal.
lumbocrural *adj.* lumbocrural.
lumbodinia *f.* lumbodynia.
lumbodorsal *adj.* lumbodorsal.
lumboilíaco, -ca *adj.* lumboiliac.
lumboinguinal *adj.* lumboinguinal.
lumboovárico, -ca *adj.* lumbo-ovarian.
lumbosacro, -cra *adj.* lumbosacral.
lumbricida *adj.* lumbricide.
lumbricoide *adj.* lumbricoid.
lumbricoideo, -a *adj.* lumbricoid.
lumbricosis *f.* lumbricosis.
lumen *m.* lumen.
  lumen residual residual lumen.
luminal *adj.* luminal.
luminífero, -ra *adj.* luminiferous.
luminiscencia *f.* luminescence, luminiscency.
luminóforo, -ra *adj.* luminophore.
luminoso, -sa *adj.* luminous.
lunatomalacia *f.* lunatomalacia.
lúnula *f.* lunula.
lupa *f.* loupe.
  lupa corneal corneal loupe.
luparia *f.* wolfsbane.

lupia *f.* wen.
lúpico, -ca *adj.* lupoid.
lupiforme *adj.* lupiform.
lupinosis *f.* lupinosis.
lupoide *adj.* lupoid.
luposo, -sa *adj.* lupous.
lupus *m.* lupus.
　lupus eritematoso lupus erythematosus (LE).
　lupus eritematoso cutáneo cutaneous lupus erythematosus.
　lupus eritematoso discoide, lupus eritematoso discoideo discoid lupus erythematosus.
　lupus eritematoso discoide crónico chronic discoid lupus erythematosus.
　lupus eritematoso diseminado disseminated lupus erythematosus.
　lupus eritematoso hipertrófico hypertrophic lupus erythematosus.
　lupus eritematoso profundo lupus erythematosus profundus.
　lupus eritematoso en sabañones chilblain lupus erythematosus, chilblain lupus.
　lupus eritematoso sistémico (LES) systemic lupus erythematosus (SLE).
　lupus eritematoso sistémico neonatal transitorio transient neonatal systemic lupus erythematosus.
　lupus eritematoso túmido lupus erythematosus tumidus.
　lupus eritematoso vulgar lupus vulgaris erythematoides.
　lupus hipertrófico lupus hypertrophicus.
　lupus inducido por fármacos drug-induced lupus.
　lupus lívido lupus livido.
　lupus miliar diseminado de la cara, lupus miliar diseminado facial lupus miliaris disseminatus faciei.
　lupus nefrítico lupus nephritis.
　lupus neonatal neonatal lupus.
　lupus papilomatoso lupus papillomatosus.
　lupus pernio lupus pernio.
　lupus psoriásico lupus psoriasis.
　lupus sebáceo lupus sebaceus.
　lupus serpiginoso lupus serpiginosus.
　lupus superficial lupus superficialis.
　lupus túmido, lupus tumidus lupus tumidus.
　lupus verrucoso, lupus verrugoso lupus verrucosus.
　lupus vulgar lupus vulgaris.
lura lura.
lusus naturae *m.* lusus naturae.
lutectomía *f.* luteectomy.

luteína *f.* lutein.
luteinización *f.* luteinization.
lúteo, -a *adj.* luteal.
luteogénico, -ca *adj.* luteogenic.
luteohormona *f.* luteohormone.
luteoide *adj.* luteoid.
luteoideo, -a *adj.* luteoid.
luteol *m.* luteol, luteole.
luteólisis *f.* luteolysis.
luteoma *m.* luteoma.
　luteoma del embarazo pregnancy luteoma.
luteotrofa *f.* luteotroph.
luteotropa *f.* luteotrope.
luteotrófico, -ca *adj.* luteotrophic.
luteotrofina *f.* luteotrophin.
luteotrópico, -ca *adj.* luteotropic.
luteotropina *f.* luteotropin.
lutropina *f.* lutropin.
Lutzomyia Lutzomyia.
lux lux.
luxación *f.* dislocation, luxation, luxatio.
　luxación abierta open dislocation.
　luxación antigua old dislocation.
　luxación de la articulación metacarpofalángica metacarpophalangeal joint dislocation.
　luxación de Bell-Dally Bell-Dally dislocation.
　luxación de cadera dislocation of the hip.
　luxación cerrada closed dislocation.
　luxación ciática sciatic dislocation.
　luxación de la clavícula dislocation of the clavicle.
　luxación completa complete dislocation.
　luxación complicada complicated luxation.
　luxación compuesta compound dislocation.
　luxación congénita congenital dislocation.
　luxación congénita de cadera congenital dislocation of the hip.
　luxación consecutiva consecutive dislocation.
　luxación del cristalino dislocation of the lens.
　luxación del dedo dislocation of the finger.
　luxación dentaria dental luxation.
　luxación divergente divergent dislocation.
　luxación erecta luxatio erecta.
　luxación y fractura fractura dislocation.
　luxación habitual habitual dislocation.
　luxación del hombro dislocation of the shoulder.
　luxación imperfecta luxatio imperfecta.
　luxación incompleta incomplete dislocation.
　luxación intrauterina intrauterine dislocation.

　luxación inveterada old dislocation.
　luxación iterativa habitual dislocation.
　luxación de Kienböck Kienböck's dislocation.
　luxación de Lisfranc Lisfranc dislocation.
　luxación de Malgaigne Malgaigne's dislocation.
　luxación de Monteggia Monteggia dislocation.
　luxación de Nélaton Nélaton's dislocation.
　luxación del obturador obturator dislocation.
　luxación parcial partial dislocation.
　luxación patológica pathologic dislocation.
　luxación perineal perineal dislocation.
　luxación primitiva primitive dislocation.
　luxación reciente recent dislocation.
　luxación recidivante habitual dislocation.
　luxación de la rodilla dislocation of the knee.
　luxación simple simple dislocation.
　luxación de Smith Smith dislocation.
　luxación subastragalina subastragalar dislocation.
　luxación subespinosa subspinous dislocation.
　luxación subpúbica subpubic dislocation.
　luxación traumática traumatic dislocation.
luxatio *f.* dislocation, luxation, luxatio.
luxus luxus.
lux *f.* light, lux.
luz *f.* light, lux.
　luz actínica actinic light.
　luz blanca white light.
　luz coherente coherent light.
　luz difusa diffused light, stray light.
　luz fría cold light.
　luz idiorretiniana idioretinal light.
　luz infrarroja infrared light.
　luz intrínseca intrinsic light.
　luz mínima light minimum.
　luz monocromática monochromatic light.
　luz negra black light.
　luz oblicua oblique light.
　luz polarizada polarized light.
　luz reflejada reflected light.
　luz refractada refracted light.
　luz transmitida transmitted light.
　luz de Tyndall Tyndall light.
　luz ultravioleta ultraviolet light.
　luz venosa vein light.
　luz visible visible light.
　luz de Wood Wood's light.
Lyponyssus Lyponyssus.

M m

maceración *f.* maceration.
macerado *m.* macerate.
macerar *v.* macerate.
macerativo, -va *adj.* macerative.
machismo *m.* machismo.
macho *m. y adj.* male.
mácico, -ca *adj.* mazic.
macies macies.
macrencefalia *f.* macrencephalia.
macroadenoso, -sa *adj.* macradenous.
macroagregado *m.* macroaggregate.
macroamilasa *f.* macroamylase.
macroamilasemia *f.* macroamylasemia.
macroamilasémico, -ca *adj.* macroamylasemic.
macroanálisis *m.* macroanalysis.
macroaneurisma *m.* macroaneurysm.
macroangiopatía *f.* macroangiopathy.
macrobacteria *f.* macrobacterium.
macrobiosis *f.* macrobiosis.
macrobiota *m.* macrobiote.
macrobiótico, -ca *adj.* macrobiotic.
macrobiótica *f.* macrobiotics.
macroblasto *m.* macroblast.
macroblefaria *f.* macroblepharia.
macrobraquia *f.* macrobrachia.
macrocardia *f.* macrocardia.
macrocardio *m.* macrocardius.
macrocefalia *f.* macrocephalia, macrocephaly.
macrocefálico, -ca *adj.* macrocephalic.
macrocéfalo *m.* macrocephalus.
macrocisto *m.* macrocyst.
macrocitemia *f.* macrocythemia.
macrocítico, -ca *adj.* macrocytic.
macrocito *m.* macrocyte.
macrocitosis *f.* macrocytosis.
macroclítoris *m.* macroclitoris.
macrocnemia *f.* macrocnemia.
macrococo *m.* macrococcus.
macrocolia *f.* macrocolon.
macrocolon *m.* macrocolon.
macrocórnea *f.* macrocornea.
macrocrania *f.* macrocrania.
macrocráneo *m.* macrocranium.
macrocrioglobulina *f.* macrocryoglobulin.
macrocrioglobulinemia *f.* macrocryoglobulinemia.
macrodactilia *f.* macrodactylia, macrodactyly.
macrodactilismo *m.* macrodactylism.
macrodiente *m.* macrotooth.
macrodistrofia *f.* macrodystrophia.
  macrodistrofia lipomatosa progresiva macrodystrophia lipomatosa progressiva.
macrodoncia *f.* macrodontia.
macrodonte *m.* macrodont.
macrodontia *f.* macrodontia.
macrodóntico, -ca *adj.* macrodontic.
macrodontismo *m.* macrodontism.
macrodonto *m.* macrodont.
macroelemento *m.* macroelement.

macroencefalia *f.* macroencephaly, macrencephaly, macrencephalia.
macroencéfalo *m.* macroencephalon.
macroencías *f.* macrogingivae.
macroeritroblasto *m.* macroerythroblast.
macroeritrocito *m.* macroerythrocyte.
macroesplácnico, -ca *adj.* macrosplanchnic.
macroestereognosia *f.* macrostereognosia, macrostereognosis.
macroestesia *f.* macroesthesia.
macroestructural *adj.* macrostructural.
macrófago *m.* macrophage.
  macrófago alveolar alveolar macrophage.
  macrófago fijo fixed macrophage.
  macrófago de Hansemann Hansemann macrophage.
  macrófago libre free macrophage.
  macrófago tisular tissue macrophage.
macrofagocito *m.* macrophagocyte.
macrofalia *f.* macrophallus.
macrofalo *m.* macrophallus.
macrofauna *f.* macrofauna.
macroflora *f.* macroflora.
macroftalmía *f.* macrophthalmia.
macroftálmico, -ca *adj.* macrophthalmous.
macrogameto *m.* macrogamete.
macrogametocito *m.* macrogametocyte.
macrogamonte *m.* macrogamont.
macrogamonto *m.* macrogamont.
macrogastria *f.* macrogastria.
macrogenesia *f.* macrogenesy.
macrogénesis *f.* macrogenesy.
macrogenia *f.* macrogenia, macrogeny.
macrogenitosomía *f.* macrogenitosomia.
  macrogenitosomía precoz macrogenitosomia precox.
macrogiria *f.* macrogyria.
macroglia *f.* macroglia.
macroglobulina *f.* macroglobulin.
macroglobulinas totales *f.* total macroglobulins.
macroglobulinemia *f.* macroglobulinemia.
  macroglobulinemia de Waldenström Waldenström's macroglobulinemia.
macroglosia *f.* macroglossia.
macrognatia *f.* macrognathia.
macrognatismo *m.* macrognathia.
macrogotero *m.* macrodrip.
macrografía *f.* macrographia.
macrolabia *f.* macrolabia.
macrolecito, -ta *adj.* macrolecithal.
macroleucoblasto *m.* macroleukoblast.
macrólido *m.* macrolide.
macrolinfocito *m.* macrolymphocyte.
macrolinfocitosis *f.* macrolymphocytosis.
macromanía *f.* macromania.
macromastia *f.* macromastia, macromazia.
macromelanosoma *m.* macromelanosome.
macromelia *f.* macromelia.
macrómera *f.* macromerus.

macrómero *m.* macromerus.
macromerozoíto *m.* macromerozoite.
macrométodo *m.* macromethod.
macromieloblasto *m.* macromyeloblast.
macromolécula *f.* macromolecule.
macromolecular *adj.* macromolecular.
macromonocito *m.* macromonocyte.
macroniquia *f.* macronychia.
macronodular *adj.* macronodular.
macronormoblasto *m.* macronormoblast.
macronormocromoblasto *m.* macronormochromoblast.
macronúcleo *m.* macronucleus.
macronutriente *m.* macronutrient.
macroorquidia *f.* macroorchidism.
macroorquidismo *m.* macroorchidism.
macroparásito *m.* macroparasite.
macropatología *f.* macropathology.
macropene *m.* macropenis.
macropenisomía *f.* macropenis.
macropía *f.* macropia.
macroplasia *f.* macroplasia, macroplastia.
macroplastia *f.* macroplastia.
macropodia *f.* macropodia.
macropolicito *m.* macropolycyte.
macropolocito *m.* macropolycyte.
macroprolactinoma *f.* macroprolactinoma.
macropromielocito *m.* macropromyelocyte.
macroprosopia *f.* macroprosopia.
macroprosópico, -ca *adj.* macroprosopous.
macropsia *f.* macropsia.
macroqueilia *f.* macrocheilia, macrochilia.
macroqueiria *f.* macrocheiria, macrochiria.
macroquilia *f.* macrochilia.
macroquilomicrón *m.* macrochylomicron.
macroquímica *f.* macrochemistry.
macroquímico, -ca *adj.* macrochemical.
macroquiria *f.* macrochiria.
macroquiste *m.* macrocyst.
macrorquidismo *m.* macroorchisdism.
macrorradiografía *f.* macroradiography.
macrorreentrada *f.* macroreentry.
macrorrinia *f.* macrorhinia.
macroscelia *f.* macroscelia.
macroscopia *f.* macroscopy.
macroscópico, -ca *adj.* macroscopic, macroscopical.
macrosigmoide *m.* macrosigmoid.
macrosis *f.* macrosis.
macrosmático, -ca *adj.* macrosmatic.
macrosomatia *f.* macrosomatia.
macrosomía *f.* macrosomia.
macrosplácnico, -ca *adj.* macrosplanchnic.
macrostereognosia *f.* macrostereognosis.
macrostereognosis *f.* macrostereognosis.
macrostesia *f.* macroesthesia.
macrostomía *f.* macrostomia.
macrotia *f.* macrotia.
macrótomo *m.* macrotome.
mácula, macula *f.* macula.

mácula acústica del sáculo macula acustica
sacculi.
mácula acústica del utrículo macula acustica
utriculi.
mácula adherente macula adherens.
mácula álbida macula albida.
mácula atrófica, macula atrophica macula
atrophica.
mácula blanca macula albida.
mácula blanca de la retina macula retinae.
mácula cerúlea, macula cerulea macula cerulea.
macula communicans communicans.
mácula común macula communis.
mácula corneal macula corneae.
mácula cribosa macula cribosa.
mácula cribosa inferior macula cribosa inferior.
mácula cribosa media macula cribosa media.
mácula cribosa superior macula cribosa superior.
mácula cribosa macula cribosa.
mácula densa densa.
mácula falsa false macula.
mácula flava macula flava.
mácula folicular macula folliculi.
mácula germinativa macula germinativa.
mácula gonorreica, macula gonorrhoica
macula gonorrhoica.
mácula láctea macula lactea.
mácula lútea macula lutea.
mácula lútea de la retina macula retinae.
mácula mongólica mongolian macula.
mácula en panal de abejas honeycomb.
macula pellucida macula pellucida.
mácula de la retina macula retinae.
mácula del sáculo macula sacculi.
mácula de Saenger Saenger's macula.
mácula solar freckle.
mácula tendínea macula tendinea.
mácula utriculi macula utriculi.
maculación *f.* maculation.
maculado, -da *adj.* maculate.
macular *adj.* macular.
maculocerebral *adj.* maculocerebral.
maculoeritematoso, -sa *adj.* maculoerythematous.
maculopápula *f.* maculopapule.
maculopapular *adj.* maculopapular.
maculopatía *f.* maculopathy.
 maculopatía diabética diabetic maculopathy.
maculovesicular *adj.* maculovesicular.
madarosis *f.* madarosis.
madescente *adj.* madescent.
madesis *f.* madarosis.
madidans *adj.* madidans.
madre *f. y adj.* mother.
 madre de alquiler surrogate mother.
 madre de nacimiento birth mother.
 madre sustituta surrogate mother.
 madre del vinagre mother of vinegar.
maduración *f.* maturation.
 maduración de afinidad affinity maturation.
 maduración cervical cervical maturation.
 maduración ósea bone maturation.
madurante *m.* maturant.
madurar *v.* mature.
Madurella Madurella.
madurez orgásmica *f.* orgasmic maturity.
maduro, -ra *adj.* mature.
maduromicosis *f.* maduromycosis.
mageírico, -ca *adj.* mageiric.
magenstrasse *f.* magenstrasse.
magistral *adj.* magistral.

magma *m.* magma.
magnesemia *f.* magnesemia.
magnesio *m.* magnesium.
magnesita *f.* magnesite.
magnesium *m.* magnesium.
magnético, -ca *adj.* magnetic.
magnetismo *m.* magnetism.
magnetización *f.* magnetization.
magnetocardiografía *f.* magnetocardiography.
magnetocardiógrafo *m.* magnetocardiograph.
magnetoconstricción *f.* magnetoconstriction.
magnetoelectricidad *f.* magnetoelectricity.
magnetoencefalografía *f.* magnetoencephalography.
magnetoencefalógrafo *m.* magnetoencephalograph.
magnetoencefalograma (MEG) *m.* magnetoencephalogram (MEG).
magnetología *f.* magnetology.
magnetómetro *m.* magnetometer.
magnetón *m.* magneton.
magnetoterapia *f.* magnetotherapy.
magnetrón *m.* magnetron.
magnetropismo *m.* magnetropism.
magnicelular *adj.* magnicellular.
magnificación *f.* magnification.
 magnificación radiográfica radiographic
 magnification.
magnificar *v.* magnify.
magnitud *f.* magnitude.
magulladura *f.* bruise.
mahamari *f.* mahamari.
MAID MAID.
maidismo *m.* maidism.
mal *m.* mal.
 mal de altura mountain sickness.
 mal de los aviadores airsickness, aviator's disease.
 mal azul pinta.
 mal de bazo malaria.
 mal de boca sore mouth.
 mal de cabeza headache.
 mal de Cayenne mal de Cayenne.
 mal de los clérigos clergyman's disease.
 mal comicial epilepsy.
 mal epidémico por estreptococos epidemic
 streptococcal disease.
 mal estreptocócico streptococcal disease.
 mal de garganta sore throat.
 mal de garganta séptica septic sore throat.
 mal manchado spotted disease.
 mal de las mandíbulas tetanus.
 mal de mar, mal marino mal de mer.
 mal de Meleda mal de Meleda, Meleda's disease, Meleda sickness.
 mal de miseria pellagra.
 mal de las montañas mountain sickness.
 mal morado mal morado.
 mal de Ondina Ondine's curse.
 mal pequeño petit mal.
 mal de Pinto, mal de los pintos mal del pinto.
 mal de Pott, mal vertebral de Pott Pott's disease.
 mal de riñones lumbago.
 mal rojo mal rouge.
 mal de San Juan epilepsy.
 mal de San Lázaro leprosy.
 mal de San Lázaro elephantiasis.
 mal de San Vito chorea.
 mal de Siam yellow fever.
 mal de los siete días nanukayami.
 mal del sol pellagra.
 mal de las vacas locas mad cow disease.
 mal venéreo syphilis.
 mal verde chlorosis.

malabsorción *f.* malabsorption.
 malabsorción congénita de lactosa congenital lactose malabsorption.
 *malabsorción congénita de sucrosa-isomal-
 tosa* congenital sucrose-isomaltose malabsorption.
 *malabsorción familiar de glucosa-galacto-
 sa* glucose-galactose malabsorption.
mala práctica *f.* malpractice.
malacia *f.* malacia.
 malacia metaplástica metaplastic malacia.
 malacia parótica parotic malacia.
 malacia traumática malacia traumatica.
malácico, -ca *adj.* malacic.
malacogastria *f.* gastromalacia.
malacoma *m.* malacoma.
malacoplaquia *f.* malacoplakia.
 malacoplaquia vesical malacoplakia vesicae.
malacoplasia *f.* malacoplakia.
malacosarcosis *f.* malacosarcosis.
malacosis *f.* malacosis.
malacosteon *m.* malacosteon.
malacótico, -ca *adj.* malacotic.
malacotomía *f.* malacotomy.
maláctico, -ca *adj.* malactic.
maladaptado, -da *adj.* maladjusted.
maladaptación *f.* maladjustment.
maladigestión *f.* maldigestion.
malaemisión *f.* malemission.
malaerupción *f.* maleruption.
malagma *m.* malagma.
malainterdigitación *f.* malinterdigitation.
malalineación *f.* malalignment.
malapresentación *f.* malpresentation.
malar *adj.* malar.
malaria *f.* malaria.
malariaterapia *f.* malariatherapy.
malaricida *adj.* malariacidal.
malárico, -ca *adj.* malarious.
malariología *f.* malariology.
malariólogo, -ga *m., f.* malariologist.
malariometría *f.* malariometry.
malarioterapia *f.* malariotherapy.
malarrotación *f.* malrotation.
malasimilación *f.* malassimilation.
malaunión *f.* malunion.
malaxación *f.* malaxation, malaxate.
maldesarrollo *m.* maldevelopment.
maldigestión *f.* maldigestion.
maleabilidad *f.* malleability.
maleable *adj.* malleable.
maleación *f.* malleation.
maleal *adj.* malleal.
malear *adj.* mallear.
malemisión *f.* malemission.
maleoincúdeo, -a *adj.* malleoincudal.
maleolar *adj.* malleolar.
maléolo *m.* malleolus.
maleotomía *f.* malleotomy.
malerupción *f.* maleruption.
malestar *m.* malaise.
 malestar general malaise.
 malestar gravídico matutino morning sickness.
malformación *f.* malformation.
 malformación de Arnold Chiari Arnold Chiari malformation.
 malformación congénita cianótica cyanotic
 congenital defect.
malfunción *f.* malfunction.
maliasmo *m.* maliasmus.
mali-mali *m.* mali-mali.
malignidad *f.* malignancy.
malignina *f.* malignin.
maligno, -na *adj.* malignant.

malignograma *m.* malignogram.
malinterdigitación *f.* malinterdigitation.
malla *f.* mesh.
  malla gingival gingival mat.
malnutrición *f.* malnutrition.
  malnutrición maligna malignant malnutrition.
  malnutrición de proteínas protein malnutrition.
  malnutrición proteicocalórica energy-protein malnutrition.
maloclusión *f.* malocclusion.
  maloclusión de mordida abierta open-bite malocclusion.
  maloclusión de mordida cerrada close-bite malocclusion.
  maloclusión en telescopio telescoping malocclusion.
malocorion *m.* mallochorion.
malogro *m.* miscarriage.
malos tratos *m.* abuse.
  malos tratos a menores child abuse.
  malos tratos al anciano abuse of the elderly, elder abuse.
  malos tratos emocionales emotional abuse.
  malos tratos físicos physical abuse.
  malos tratos sexuales sexual abuse.
malpighiano, -na *adj.* Malpighian.
malposición *f.* malposition.
malpraxis *f.* malpraxis.
malpuesto, -ta *adj.* malposed.
malrotado, -da *adj.* malturned.
malsexual *adj.* missexual.
maltósido *m.* maltoside.
maltosuria *f.* maltosuria.
maltrato *m.* maltreatment.
malunión *f.* malunion.
malleinización *f.* malleinization.
malleoidosis *f.* malleoidosis.
mama *f.* breast, mamma.
  mama accesorias (femeninas y masculinas) mammae accessoriae feminiae et masculinae.
  mama aréolada mamma aréolata.
  mama errática mamma erratica.
  mama masculina mamma masculina.
  mama supernumerarias supernumerary mammae.
  mama viril mamma masculina.
mamalgia *f.* mamalgia.
mamaplastia *f.* mammaplasty.
mamatrófico, -ca *adj.* mamatroph.
mamectomía *f.* mammectomy.
mamelón *m.* mamelon.
mamelonación *f.* mamelonation.
mamelonado, -da *adj.* mamelonated.
mamiforme *adj.* mammiform.
mamila *f.* mamilla.
mamilación *f.* mamillation.
mamilado, -da *adj.* mamillate, mamillated.
mamilar *adj.* mamillary.
mamiliforme *adj.* mamilliform, mammilliform.
mamilitis *f.* mamillitis, mammillitis.
mamiloplastia *f.* mamiloplasty, mamilliplasty.
mamitis *f.* mammitis.
mamogénesis *f.* mammogenesis.
mamógeno *m.* mammogen.
mamografía *f.* mammography.
  mamografía de barrido film screen mammography.
mamográfico, -ca *adj.* mammographic.
mamógrafo *m.* mammograph.
mamograma *m.* mammogram.
mamoplasia *f.* mammoplasty.
mamoplastia *f.* mammoplasty.

mamoplastia de Aries-Pitanguy Aries-Pitanguy mammoplasty.
mamoplastia de aumento augmentation mammoplasty.
mamoplastia de Biesenberger Biesenberger mammoplasty.
mamoplastia de Conway Conway mammoplasty.
mamoplastia de incremento augmentation mammoplasty.
mamoplastia reconstructiva reconstructive mammoplasty.
mamoplastia de reducción reduction mammoplasty.
mamoplastia de Strömbeck Strömbeck mammoplasty.
mamosomatotrofo *m.* mammosomatotroph.
mamotermografía *f.* mammothermography.
mamotomía *f.* mammotomy.
mamótrofa *m.* mammotroph.
mamotrófico, -ca *adj.* mammotrophic, mammotropic.
mamotrópico, -ca *adj.* mammotropic.
mamotropina *f.* mammotropin.
mancha *f.* dot, spot, tache.
  mancha algodonosa cotton-wool spot.
  mancha amarilla yellow spot.
  mancha azul blue spot, tache bleuâtre.
  mancha de Baelz Mongolian spot.
  mancha de Bitot Bitot's spot.
  mancha blanca tache blanche.
  mancha blanca frontal white frontal spot.
  mancha de Brushfield Brushfield's spot.
  mancha de café con leche café au lait spot.
  mancha caliente hot spot.
  mancha de Carleton Carleton's spot.
  mancha cerebral tache cérébrale.
  mancha cerúlea macula caerulea.
  mancha de Christopher Christopher's spot.
  mancha ciega blind spot.
  mancha de color rojo de cereza cherry-red spot.
  mancha de la córnea, mancha corneana corneal spot.
  mancha cribiforme, mancha cribosa cribiform spot.
  mancha de cromatina chromatin spot.
  mancha de De Morgan De Morgan's spot.
  mancha de Elschnig Elschnig's spot.
  mancha embrionaria embryonic spot.
  mancha epigástrica epigastric spot.
  mancha esclerótica de Sommer-Larcher Sommer-Larcher's spot.
  mancha espinal tache spinale.
  mancha focal focal spot.
  mancha de Fordyce Fordyce's spot.
  mancha de Forscheimer Forscheimer spot.
  mancha fría cold spot.
  mancha de Fuchs Fuchs' spot.
  mancha de Gaule Gaule's spot.
  mancha de Graefe Graefe's spot.
  mancha de Gunn Gunn's dot.
  mancha hepática liver spot.
  mancha hipnógena hypnogenic spot.
  mancha de Koplik Koplik's spot.
  mancha de leche, mancha láctea tache laitcuse.
  mancha en llama flame spot.
  mancha de luz light spot.
  mancha de Marcus Gunn Marcus Gunn's dot.
  mancha de Mariotte Mariotte's spot.
  mancha de Maurer Maurer's dot, Maurer's spot.
  mancha de Maxwell Maxwell's spot.
  mancha melánica pigmented nevus.

  mancha melanótica de Hutchinson Hutchinson's melanotic freckle.
  mancha meníngea tache cérébrale.
  mancha de Mittendorf Mittendorf's dot.
  mancha mongólica Mongolian spot.
  mancha en mora mulberry spot.
  mancha motriz tache motrice.
  mancha negra tache noire.
  mancha negra de Fuchs Fuchs' black spot.
  mancha pélvica pelvic spot.
  mancha perniciosa Maurer's spot.
  mancha de pimienta de Cayena Cayenne pepper spot.
  mancha raquídea tache spinale.
  mancha rojo cereza cherry-red spot.
  mancha de rosa, mancha rosáceas, mancha rosada rose spot.
  mancha de Roth Roth's spot.
  mancha rubí ruby spot.
  mancha sacra sacral spot.
  mancha sacular saccular spot.
  mancha de Schüffner Schüffner's dot.
  mancha de Soemmering Soemmering's spot.
  mancha de Tardieu Tardieu's spot.
  mancha de Tay Tay's spot.
  mancha de temperatura, mancha por temperatura temperature spot.
  mancha tendinosa tendinous spot.
  mancha tibial shin spot.
  mancha de tifoidea typhoid spot.
  mancha de Trantas Trantas' dot.
  mancha de Trousseau Trousseau's spot.
  mancha utricular utricular spot.
  mancha en vino de Oporto Port wine spot.
manchado *m.* spotting.
manchette *f.* manchette.
manco, -ca *adj.* one-armed, armless.
mandama mandama.
mandíbula *f.* mandible.
  mandíbula abultada lumpy mandible.
  mandíbula crujiente crackling mandible.
  mandíbula inferior lower mandible.
  mandíbula de loro parrot mandible.
  mandíbula superior upper mandible.
mandibular *adj.* mandibular.
mandibulectomía *f.* mandibulectomy.
mandibulofacial *adj.* mandibulofacial.
mandibulofaríngeo, -a *adj.* mandibulopharyngeal.
mandibulooculofacial *adj.* mandibulo-oculofacial.
mandril *m.* mandrel, mandril.
mandrina *f.* mandrel, mandril.
manerismo *m.* mannerism.
manganesismo *m.* manganism.
manganismo *m.* manganism.
mange *m.* mange.
  mange demodéctico, mange folicular demodectic mange, follicular mange.
  mange psoróptico psoroptic mange.
  mange sarcóptico sarcoptic mange.
mango *m.* handle.
manguito *m.* cuff.
  manguito de Dacron Dacron cuff.
  manguito musculotendinoso musculotendinous cuff.
  manguito de presión pressure cuff.
  manguito rotador del hombro rotator cuff.
manía *f.* mania.
  manía a potu mania à potu.
  manía megalomanía megalomania.
maníaco, -ca *adj.* maniac.
maniacodepresivo, -va *adj.* maniac-depressive.
manicia *f.* manicy.

manicomio *m.* mental hospital.
manidiestro, -tra *adj.* right-handed.
manierismo *m.* mannerism.
manifalange *f.* maniphalanx.
manifestación *f.* manifestation.
manilocuismo *m.* maniloquism.
maniobra *f.* maneuver.
  maniobra de acordeón accordion maneuver.
  maniobra de Allen Allen's maneuver.
  maniobra aloplástica alloplastic maneuver.
  maniobra de aspiración aspirant maneuver.
  maniobra autoplástica autoplastic maneuver.
  maniobra de Bill Bill's maneuver.
  maniobra de Bracht Bracht's maneuver.
  maniobra de Brandt-Andrews Brandt-Andrews maneuver.
  maniobra de Buzzard Buzzard's maneuver.
  maniobra de Credé Credé's maneuver.
  maniobra de DeLee DeLee's maneuver.
  maniobra de Ejrup Ejrup maneuver.
  maniobra de Fowler Fowler maneuver.
  maniobra de Gowers Gowers' maneuver.
  maniobra de Halstead Halstead's maneuver.
  maniobra de Hampton Hampton maneuver.
  maniobra de Heimlich Heimlich's maneuver.
  maniobra de Hoffmann Hoffmann's sign.
  maniobra de Hoguet Hoguet's maneuver.
  maniobra de Hueter Hueter's maneuver.
  maniobra de Jendrassik Jendrassik's maneuver.
  maniobra de Kocher Kocher maneuver.
  maniobra de Lasegue Lasegue's maneuver.
  maniobra de Leopold Leopold's maneuver.
  maniobra de la llave en el cerrojo key-in-lock maneuver.
  maniobra de Mauriceau Mauriceau's maneuver.
  maniobra de Mauriceau-Smellie-Vett Mauriceau-Smellie-Vett maneuver.
  maniobra de Mc Donald McDonald's maneuver.
  maniobra de Müller Müller's maneuver.
  maniobra de Munro Kerr Munro Kerr maneuver.
  maniobra de Nägeli Nägeli's maneuver.
  maniobra de Pajot Pajot's maneuver.
  maniobra de Phalen Phalen's maneuver.
  maniobra de Pinard Pinard's maneuver.
  maniobra de Praga Prague maneuver.
  maniobra de Pringle Pringle's maneuver.
  maniobra de Ritgen Ritgen's maneuver.
  maniobra de Saxtorph Pajot's maneuver.
  maniobra de Scanzoni Scanzoni's maneuver.
  maniobra de Schatz Schatz's maneuver.
  maniobra de Schreiber Schreiber's maneuver.
  maniobra de Sellick Sellick maneuver.
  maniobra de Toynbee Toynbee maneuver.
  maniobra de Valsalva Valsalva's maneuver.
manipulación *f.* manipulation.
  manipulación conjunta conjoined manipulation.
  manipulación genética genetic manipulation.
  manipulación vertebral spinal manipulation.
maniquí *m.* manikin.
mano *f.* hand, main, manus.
  mano ajena alien hand.
  mano en anteojo opera-glass hand.
  mano apostólica benediction hand.
  mano caída drop hand.
  mano de cangrejo crab hand.
  mano cava manus cava.
  mano de comadrón accoucheur's hand, main d'accoucheur.
  mano congelada frozen hand.
  mano dividida split hand.

  mano de escritor writing hand.
  mano en espejo mirror hand.
  mano esquelética, mano de esqueleto skeleton hand, main en squelette.
  mano extendida manus extensa.
  mano fantasma phantom hand.
  mano fisurada cleft hand.
  mano en flexión manus flexa.
  mano en garra claw hand.
  mano en gemelo, mano en gemelos de teatro opera-glass hand.
  mano en guantelete mitten hand.
  mano hendida cleft hand.
  mano en horquilla cleft hand.
  mano de Madelung Madelung's deformity.
  mano de mono monkey hand.
  mano muerta dead hand.
  mano obstétrica obstetrical hand.
  mano en pala spade hand.
  mano de partero accoucheur's hand, main d'accoucheur.
  mano péndula drop hand.
  mano en pimienta de Cayena Cayenne pepper spot.
  mano en pinzas de langosta lobster-claw hand.
  mano plana manus plana.
  mano de predicador benediction hand.
  mano radial Madelung's deformity.
  mano simiesca, mano de simio monkey hand.
  mano suculenta main succulente.
  mano suculenta de Marinesco Marinesco's succulent hand.
  mano superextendida manus superextensa.
  mano en tridente trident hand.
  mano de trinchera trench hand.
  mano valga manus valga.
  mano de vampiro ghoul hand.
  mano vara manus vara.
  mano zamba club hand.
manodinamómetro *m.* manudynamometer.
manometría *f.* manometry.
manométrico, -ca *adj.* manometric.
manómetro *m.* manometer.
  manómetro aneroide aneroid manometer.
  manómetro de dial dial manometer.
  manómetro diferencial differential manometer.
  manómetro mercurial, manómetro de mercurio mercurial manometer.
manoptoscopio *m.* manoptoscope.
manoscopia *f.* manoscopy.
manoscopio *f.* baroscope.
manosidosis *f.* mannosidosis.
mansoneliasis *f.* mansonelliasis.
Mansonella Mansonella.
mansonelosis *f.* mansonellosis.
Mansonia Mansonia.
manta *f.* blanket.
  manta de baño bath blanket.
  manta de hipotermia hypothermia blanket.
mantenedor *m.* maintainer.
  mantenedor de espacio space maintainer.
mantenimiento *m.* maintenance.
manto *m.* mantle.
manual *adj.* manual.
  manual de Bergey Bergey's manual.
manualidad *f.* handedness.
manubrio *m.* manubrium.
manudinamómetro *m.* manudynamometer.
manus manus.
mapa *m.* map.
  mapa de actividad eléctrica cerebral (MAEC) brain electric activity map (BEAM).

  mapa citológico cytologic map.
  mapa cognitivo cognitive map.
  mapa cromosómico chromosomal map.
  mapa físico physical map.
  mapa de ligadura, mapa de ligamiento linkage map.
  mapa óseo bone map.
mapeo *m.* mapping.
maqueta *f.* mock up.
machina *f.* machine, engine.
máquina *f.* machine, engine.
  máquina de alta velocidad high-speed engine.
  máquina de anestesia anesthesia machine.
  máquina cardiopulmonar heart-lung machine.
  máquina corazón-púlmón heart-lung machine.
  máquina dental dental engine.
  máquina quirúrgica surgical engine.
  máquina renal kidney machine.
  máquina rotativa panorámica panoramic rotating machine.
  máquina ultrarrápida ultraspeed engine.
marántico, -ca *adj.* marantic.
maraña *f.* tangle.
  maraña neurofibrilares neurofibrillary tangle.
marasmático, -ca *adj.* marasmatic.
marásmico, -ca *adj.* marasmic.
marasmo *m.* marasmus.
marasmoide *adj.* marasmoid.
marca *f.* mark.
  marca de belleza beauty mark.
  marca en frambuesa strawberry mark.
  marca de fresa strawberry mark.
  marca lineal scoring mark.
  marca de nacimiento birth mark, birthmark.
  marca de Pohl Pohl's mark.
  marca registrada trademark.
marcación *f.* marking.
marcador *m.* marker.
  marcador bioquímico biochemical marker.
  marcador celular de superficie cell-surface marker.
  marcador genético genetic marker.
  marcador radiactivo radioactive label.
  marcador tumoral tumor marker.
marcador *m.* marker.
marcaje *m.* label.
  marcaje radiactivo radioactive label.
marcapaso *m.* pacemaker.
marcapasos *m.* pacemaker.
  marcapaso artificial artificial pacemaker.
  marcapaso asincrónico asynchronous pacemaker.
  marcapaso auricular errante wandering atrial pacemaker.
  marcapaso auricular subsidiario subsidiary atrial pacemaker.
  marcapaso cardíaco cardiac.
  marcapaso cardíaco artificial artificial cardiac pacemaker.
  marcapaso cardíaco eléctrico electric cardiac pacemaker.
  catéter marcapaso transvenoso transvenous catheter pacemaker.
  marcapaso ciliar cilium pacemaker.
  marcapaso del corazón pacemaker of the heart.
  marcapaso de demanda, marcapaso por demanda demand pacemaker.
  marcapaso deslizante shifting pacemaker.
  marcapaso ectópico ectopic pacemaker.
  marcapaso errante wandering pacemaker.
  marcapaso externo external pacemaker.

marcapaso de frecuencia fija fixed-rate pacemaker.

marcapaso gástrico gastric pacemaker.

marcapaso implantado interno implanted internal pacemaker.

marcapaso migratorio wandering pacemaker.

marcapaso natural natural pacemaker.

marcapaso permanente permanent pacemaker.

marcapaso programable programmable pacemaker.

marcapaso de radiofrecuencia radiofrequency pacemaker.

marcapaso pervenoso pervenous pacemaker.

marcapaso de ritmo fijo fixed-rate pacemaker.

marcapaso sincrónico synchronous pacemaker.

marcapaso sinusal sinus pacemaker.

marcapaso transitorio temporary pacemaker.

marcapaso transtorácico transthoracic pacemaker.

marcha *f.* gait, walk.

marcha de ánade waddling gait.

marcha antálgica antalgic gait.

marcha arrastrada drag-to gait.

marcha de arrastre drag-to gait.

marcha atáxica ataxic gait.

marcha calcánea calcaneous gait.

marcha cautelosa cautious gait.

marcha cerebelosa cerebellar gait.

marcha con muletas crutch gait.

marcha del cuádriceps quadriceps gait.

marcha de cuatro puntos four-point gait.

marcha distrófica dystrophic gait.

marcha de dorsiflexión dorsiflexor gait.

marcha de dos apoyos, marcha de dos puntos two point gait.

marcha durante el sueño sleep walking.

marcha equina equine gait.

marcha espasmódica spastic gait.

marcha espástica spastic gait.

marcha en estepaje, marcha en estepaje alto high steppage gait.

marcha festinante festinating gait.

marcha gemelar gastrocnemius gait.

marcha glútea gluteal gait.

marcha glútea compensada compensated gluteal gait.

marcha glútea descompensada uncompensated gluteal gait.

marcha helicópoda helicopod gait.

marcha hemipléjica hemiplegic gait.

marcha miopática dystrophic gait.

marcha oscilante cerebellar gait.

marcha de paloma pigeon gait.

marcha de paso doble double step gait.

marcha parkinsoniana Parkinsonian gait.

marcha de pato duck walk.

marcha a pequeños pasos stepping gait.

marcha en pequeños pasos petit pas.

marcha de Petren Petren's gait.

marcha de pie caído drop foot gait.

marcha de segador hemiplegic gait.

marcha sobre los talones heel walking.

marcha tabética tabetic gait.

marcha de talón y dedos, marcha taloneante heel-toe gait, stamping gait.

marcha en tijeras scissors gait.

marcha de Trendelenburg Trendelenburg gait.

marcha en tres apoyos, marcha de tres puntos three-point gait.

marco *m.* frame.

marco de lectura reading frame.

marea *f.* tide.

marea ácida acid tide.

marea alcalina alkaline tide.

marea grasa fat tide.

marea roja red tide.

mareado, -da *adj.* sick.

mareo *m.* dizziness, giddiness.

mareo marino seasickness.

marfanoide *adj.* marfanoid.

marfil *m.* ivory.

margarita *f.* daisy.

margen *m.* margin, margo.

margen anterior anterior margin.

margen ciliar ciliary margin.

margen inferior inferior margin.

margen lateral lateral.

margen medial medial.

margen posterior posterior.

margen pupilar del iris pupillary margin of the iris.

margen de seguridad margin of safety.

margen social social margin.

margen superior superior margin.

marginación *f.* margination.

marginalis *adj.* marginal.

marginal *adj.* marginal.

marginoplastia *f.* marginoplasty.

margo *m.* margo.

marinoterapia *f.* medulla ossium rubra.

mariposa *f.* medulla ossium rubra.

mariposia *f.* mariposia.

mariscal *adj.* mariscal.

maritonúcleo *m.* maritonucleus.

marmóreo, -a *adj.* marmoreal, marble.

marmota *f.* marmot, marmotte.

marsupialización *f.* marsupialization.

martillo *m.* hammer.

martillo de reflejos reflex hammer.

massa *f.* mass, massa.

masa *f.* mass, massa.

masa acromática achromatic mass.

masa apendicular appendiceal mass, appendix mass.

masa atómica atomic mass.

masa celular cell mass.

masa celular interna inner cell mass.

masa de las células corporales body cell mass.

masa cementaria esclerótica sclerotic cemental mass.

masa excretoria tubular tubular excretory mass.

masa innominada massa innominata.

masa interfilar hyaloplasm.

masa intermedia intermediate cell mass.

masa de inyección injection mass.

masa lateral de atlas lateral mass of atlas, massa lateralis atlantis.

masa magra, masa magra corporal lean body mass.

masa de píldoras, masa pilular pill mass, pilular mass.

masa tigroide tigroid mass.

masa ventrolateral ventrolateral mass.

masa vertebral lateral mass lateralis vertebrae.

masaje *m.* massage.

masaje cardíaco cardiac massage, heart massage.

masaje cardíaco externo external cardiac massage.

masaje de vapor vapor massage.

masaje electrovibratorio electrovibratory massage.

masaje gingival gingival massage.

masaje prostático prostatic massage.

masaje sueco Swedish massage.

masaje a tórax abierto open chest massage.

masaje a tórax cerrado closed chest massage.

masaje vibratorio vibratory massage.

masajista *m., f.* masseur.

mascaladenitis *f.* maschaladenitis.

mascalefidrosis *f.* maschalephidrosis.

mascalhiperhidrosis *f.* maschalhyperhidrosis.

mascaloma *m.* maschaloncus.

mascalonco *m.* maschaloncus.

mascaloncus maschaloncus.

máscara *f.* mask.

máscara del embarazo mask of pregnancy.

máscara equimótica ecchymotic mask.

máscara luética luetic mask.

máscara de Parkinson Parkinson's mask.

máscara respiratoria única, máscara de sentido único non-rebreathing mask.

máscara tropical tropical mask.

mascarilla *f.* mask.

mascarilla de Boothby-Lovelace-Bulbulia, mascarilla BLB Boothby-Lovelace-Bulbulian mask, BLB mask.

mascarilla de Hutchinson Hutchinson's mask.

mascarilla laríngea laryngeal mask.

mascarilla de oxígeno oxygen mask.

mascarilla tabética tabetic mask.

mascarilla total de la cara full face mask.

mascarilla de Venturi Venturi's mask.

masculinidad *f.* masculinity.

masculinización *f.* masculinization.

masculinizar *v.* masculinize.

masculinovoblastoma *m.* masculinovoblastoma.

mascullamiento *m.* mumbling.

MASER *m.* MASER.

MASER óptico optic MASER.

maseterino, -na *adj.* masseteric.

masilla *f.* putty.

masoquismo *m.* masochism.

masoquista *m.* masochist.

masoquístico, -ca *adj.* masochistic.

masoterapia *f.* massotherapy.

mastadenitis *f.* mastadenitis.

mastadenoma *m.* mastadenoma.

Mastadenovirus Mastadenovirus.

mastalgia *f.* mastalgia.

mastatrofia *f.* mastatrophia, mastatrophy.

mastauxa *f.* mastauxe.

mastectomía *f.* mastectomy.

mastectomía de Halsted Halsted's mastectomy.

mastectomía lumpectomía mastectomy lumpectomy.

mastectomía de Meyer Meyer's mastectomy.

mastectomía radical radical mastectomy.

mastectomía radical ampliada extended radical mastectomy.

mastectomía radical modificada modified radical mastectomy.

mastectomía simple simple mastectomy.

mastectomía subcutánea subcutaneous mastectomy.

mastectomía total total mastectomy.

mastelcosis *f.* masthelcosis.

masticación *f.* mastication.

masticatorio, -ria *adj.* masticatory.

mastigoto *m.* mastigote.

mastitis *f.* mastitis.

mastitis aguda acute mastitis.

mastitis de células plasmáticas plasma cell mastitis.

mastitis estancada, mastitis de estancamiento stagnation mastitis.

mastitis flemonosa phlegmonous mastitis.
mastitis de Gargantúa, mastitis gigante gargantuan mastitis.
mastitis glandular glandular mastitis.
mastitis granulomatosa granulomatous mastitis.
mastitis intersticial interstitial mastitis.
mastitis neonatal mastitis neonatorum.
mastitis parenquimatosa, mastitis parenquimática parenchymatous mastitis.
mastitis periductal periductal mastitis.
mastitis plasmocítica, mastitis plasmocitaria plasma cell mastitis.
mastitis quística cystic mastitis.
mastitis quística crónica chronic cystic mastitis.
mastitis del recién nacido mastitis neonatorum.
mastitis retroareolar periductal mastitis.
mastitis retromamaria retromammary mastitis.
mastitis submamaria submammary mastitis.
mastitis supurativa suppurative mastitis.
mastitis tuberculosa crónica chronic tuberculous mastitis.
mastocarcinoma *m.* mastocarcinoma.
mastoccipital *adj.* mastooccipital.
mastocirrus *m.* mastoscirrhus.
mastocito *m.* mastocyte, mast-cell.
mastocitogénesis *f.* mastocytogenesis.
mastocitoma *m.* mastocytoma.
mastocitosis *f.* mastocytosis.
mastocitosis cutánea difusa diffuse cutaneous mastocytosis.
mastocitosis difusa diffuse mastocytosis.
mastocitosis sistémica systemic mastocytosis.
mastocondroma *m.* mastochondroma.
mastocondrosis *f.* mastochondroma.
mastodinia *f.* mastodynia.
mastoescamoso, -sa *adj.* mastosquamous.
mastografía *f.* mastography.
mastograma *m.* mastogram.
mastoidalgia *f.* mastoidalgia.
mastoidectomía *f.* mastoidectomy.
mastoidectomía radical radical mastoidectomy.
mastoidectomía radical modificada modified radical mastoidectomy.
mastoideo, -a *adj.* mastoid.
mastoideocentesis *f.* mastoideocentesis.
mastoiditis *f.* mastoiditis.
mastoiditis de Bezold Bezold's mastoiditis.
mastoiditis esclerosante sclerosing mastoiditis.
mastoiditis silenciosa silent mastoiditis.
mastoidocentesis *f.* mastoideocentesis.
mastoidotimpanectomía *f.* mastoidotympanectomy.
mastoidotomía *f.* mastoidotomy.
mastonco *m.* mastoncus.
mastoncus mastoncus.
mastooccipital *adj.* mastooccipital.
mastoparietal *adj.* mastoparietal.
mastopatía *f.* mastopathy.
mastopatía fibroquística fibrocystic disease.
mastopatía de Schimmelbusch Schimmelbusch's disease.
mastopexia *f.* mastopexy.
mastoplastia *f.* mastoplasty, mastoplastia.
mastoptosis *f.* mastoptosis, mastopsis.
mastorragia *f.* mastorrhagia.
mastoscamoso, -sa *adj.* mastosquamous.
mastoscirro *m.* mastoscirrhus.
mastosis *f.* mastosis.

mastosyrinx *f.* mastosyrinx.
mastótico, -ca *adj.* mastotic.
mastotomía *f.* mastotomy.
masturbación *f.* masturbation.
materia *f.* matter, materia.
materia blanca materia alba.
material *m.* material.
material aloplástico alloplastic material.
material de base base material.
material dental dental material.
material equivalente de tejido tissue equivalent material.
material genético genetic material.
material de impresión impression material.
material de placa base baseplate material.
material punzante sharp material.
material de reacción cruzada crossreacting material (CRM).
material de sutura suture material.
maternal *adj.* maternal.
maternidad *f.* motherhood, maternity.
maternidad de alquiler surrogate motherhood.
maternidad genética genetic motherhood.
maternidad gestacional gestational motherhood.
maternidad legal legal motherhood.
maternidad subrogada surrogate motherhood.
materno, -na *adj.* maternal.
matidez *m.* dullness.
matidez de Gerhardt Gerhardt's triangle.
matidez móvil shifting dullness.
matidez poscordial postcardial dullness.
matidez precordial precardial dullness.
matidez timpánica tympanitic dullness.
matiniosa *f.* matiniose.
matiz *m.* hue.
matlazáhuatl *m.* matlazahuatl.
matraz *m.* matrass.
matrical *adj.* matrical.
matricial *adj.* matricial, matrical.
matriclinoso, -sa *adj.* matriclinous.
matrilineal *adj.* matrilineal.
matriz¹ *f.* matrix.
matriz caída falling of the matrix.
matriz² *f.* matrix.
matriz de amalgama amalgam matrix.
matriz capsular capsular matrix.
matriz de cartílago cartilage matrix.
matriz celular cell matrix.
matriz citoplasmática cytoplasmic matrix.
matriz extracelular extracellular matrix.
matriz funcional functional matrix.
matriz interterritorial interterritorial matrix.
matriz intersticial interstitial matrix.
matriz de la uña nail matrix, matrix unguis.
matriz mitocondrial mitochondrial matrix.
matriz ósea bone matrix.
matriz de pelo hair matrix.
matriz sarcoplásmica sarcoplasmic matrix.
matriz territorial territorial matrix.
matriz ungueal nail matrix, matrix unguis.
matriz ungular nail matrix, matrix unguis.
matrona *f.* midwife.
matróclinia *f.* matrocliny.
matróclino, -na *adj.* matroclinous.
maxilar¹ *m.* jaw, maxilla.
maxilar² *adj.* maxillary.
maxilectomía *f.* maxillectomy.
maxilitis *f.* maxillitis.
maxilodental *adj.* maxillodental.
maxilodentario, -ria *adj.* maxillodental.
maxiloetmoidectomía *f.* maxilloethmoidectomy.

maxilofacial *adj.* maxillofacial.
maxilofaríngeo, -a *adj.* maxillopharyngeal.
maxilolabial *adj.* maxillolabial.
maxilomandibular *adj.* maxillomandibular.
maxilopalatino, -na *adj.* maxillopalatine.
maxilotomía *f.* maxillotomy.
maxiloyugal *adj.* maxillojugal.
máxima capacidad de concentración urinaria *f.* maximal urine concentration.
máximo *m.* maximum.
máximo transporte (Tm) transport maximum (Tm).
máximo transporte de glucosa glucose transport.
máximo tubular (Tm) tubular maximum (Tm).
mayidismo *m.* mayidism.
mazolisis *f.* mazolysis.
mazopatía *f.* mazopathy.
mazoplasia *f.* mazoplasia.
meatal *adj.* meatal.
meato *m.* meatus.
meatus *m.* meatus.
meatomastoidectomía *f.* meatomastoidectomy.
meatómetro *m.* meatometer.
meátomo *m.* meatome.
meatoplastia *f.* meatoplasty.
meatorrafia *f.* meatorrhaphy.
meatoscopia *f.* meatoscopy.
meatoscopio *m.* meatoscope.
meatotomía *f.* meatotomy.
meátomo *m.* meatotome.
mecánica *f.* mechanics.
mecánica animal animal mechanics.
mecánica corporal body mechanics.
mecánica cuántica quantum mechanics.
mecánica del desarrollo developmental mechanics.
mecánico, -ca *adj.* mechanical.
mecanicorreceptor *m.* mechanicoreceptor.
mecanicoterapéutica *f.* mechanicotherapeutics, mechanicotherapy.
mecanismo *m.* mechanism.
mecanismo a contra corriente countercurrent mechanism.
mecanismo de asociación association.
mecanismo de compuerta gating mechanism.
mecanismo de concentración urinaria mechanism of urine concentration.
mecanismo de defensa defense mechanism.
mecanismo de defensa del huésped host defense mechanism.
mecanismo de doble desplazamiento double displacement mechanism.
mecanismo del dolor pain mechanism.
mecanismo de Douglas Douglas mechanism.
mecanismo de Duncan Duncan's mechanism.
mecanismo de escape escape mechanism.
mecanismo de Frank-Starling Frank-Starling mechanism.
mecanismo inmunológico immunological mechanism.
mecanismo mental mental mechanism.
mecanismo oculógiro oculogyric mechanism.
mecanismo del parto mechanism of labor.
mecanismo de ping-pong ping-pong mechanism.
mecanismo presorreceptivo presoreceptive.
mecanismo propioceptivo proprioceptive mechanism.
mecanismo de reacción de ping-pong ping-pong reaction mechanism.
mecanismo reentrante reentrant mechanism.
mecanismo de Schultze Schultze's mechanism.
mecanocardiografía *f.* mechanocardiography.

mecanocito *m.* mechanocyte.
mecanofobia *f.* mechanophobia.
mecanogimnasia *f.* mechanogymnastics.
mecanorreceptor *m.* mechanoreceptor.
mecanorreflejo *m.* mechanoreflex.
mecanoterapia *f.* mecanotherapy, mechanotherapy.
mecanotermia *f.* mechanothermy.
mecismo *m.* mecism.
mecistasia *f.* mecystasis.
mecistocéfalo, -la *adj.* mecistocephalic, mecistocephalous.
meckelectomía *f.* meckelectomy.
mecocéfalo, -la *adj.* mecocephalic.
mecocefalia *f.* mecocephaly.
mecómetro *m.* mecometer.
meconio *m.* meconium.
meconiorrea *f.* meconiorrhea.
meconismo *m.* meconism.
mecha *f.* wick.
media *f.* mean.
 media aritmética arithmetic mean.
 media armónica harmonic.
 error estándar de la media standard error of the mean.
 media geométrica geometric mean.
 media muestral sample mean.
 media de la población population mean.
mediación *f.* mediation.
mediad mediad.
mediador *m.* mediator.
 mediador químico chemical.
medial *adj.* medial, medialis.
medialecital *adj.* medialecithal.
medialecito *m.* medialecithe.
medialuna *f.* crescent.
mediámetro *m.* mediameter.
mediana *f.* median.
mediano, -na *adj.* median.
mediar *v.* mediate.
medias antiembolia *f.* antiembolism hose.
mediastínico, -ca *adj.* mediastinal.
mediastinitis *f.* mediastinitis.
 mediastinitis fibrosa fibrous mediastinitis.
 mediastinitis fibrosa idiopática idiopathic fibrous mediastinitis.
 mediastinitis indurativa indurative mediastinitis.
mediastino *m.* mediastinum.
mediastinografía *f.* mediastinography.
mediastinograma *m.* mediastinogram.
mediastinopericarditis *f.* mediastinopericarditis.
mediastinoscopia *f.* mediastinoscopy.
mediastinoscópico, -ca *adj.* mediastinoscopic.
mediastinoscopio *m.* mediastinoscope.
mediastinotomía *f.* mediastinotomy.
medicable *adj.* medicable.
medicación *f.* medication.
 medicación arrénica arrhenic medication.
 medicación conservadora conservative medication.
 medicación derivativa substitutive medication.
 medicación hipodérmica hypodermic medication.
 medicación intravenosa intravenous medication.
 medicación iónica ionic medication.
 medicación preanestésica preanesthetic medication.
 medicación sublingual sublingual medication.
 medicación sustitutiva substitutive medication.
 medicación transduodenal transduodenal medication.

medicado, -da *adj.* medicated.
medicador *m.* medicator.
medicamento *m.* drug, medicine.
 medicamento compuesto compound medicine.
 medicamento patentado proprietary medicine.
 medicamento sin receta patent medicine.
medicamentoso, -sa *adj.* medicamentous.
medicina *f.* medicine.
 medicina aeroespacial, medicina aeronáutica aerospace medicine.
 medicina alopática allopathic medicine.
 medicina alternativa alternative medicine.
 medicina ambiental environmental medicine.
 medicina de aviación, medicina de la aviación aviation medicine.
 medicina basada en la evidencia evidence based medicine.
 medicina ciéntífica scientific medicine.
 medicina clínica clinical medicine.
 medicina comparada comparative medicine.
 medicina comunitaria medicine community.
 medicina de la conducta, medicina del comportamiento behavioral medicine.
 medicina defensiva defensive medicine.
 medicina del deporte, medicina deportiva sports medicine.
 medicina dosimétrica dosimetric medicine.
 medicina espacial space medicine.
 medicina estatal state medicine.
 medicina experimental experimental medicine.
 medicina de familia, medicina familiar family medicine.
 medicina fetal fetal medicine.
 medicina física physical medicine.
 medicina forense forensic medicine.
 medicina geriátrica geriatric medicine.
 medicina hiperbárica hyperbaric medicine.
 medicina holística holistic medicine.
 medicina iónica ionic medicine.
 medicina interna internal medicine.
 medicina legal legal medicine.
 medicina militar military medicine.
 medicina neonatal neonatal medicine.
 medicina nuclear nuclear medicine.
 medicina osteopática osteopathic medicine.
 medicina pediátrica pediatric medicine.
 medicina perinatal perinatal medicine.
 medicina preclínica preclinical medicine.
 medicina preventiva preventive medicine.
 medicina prospectiva prospective medicine.
 medicina psicosomática psychosomatic medicine.
 medicina racional rational medicine.
 medicina social social medicine.
 medicina socializada socialized medicine.
 medicina del trabajo occupational medicine.
 medicina tropical tropical medicine.
 medicina de urgencia emergency medicine.
medicinal *adj.* medicinal.
medición *f.* measurement.
médico, -ca *m., f.* physician.
 médico alopático allopathic physician.
 médico de atención primaria primary care physician.
 médico de cabecera general practitioner.
 médico de urgencia emergency physician.
 médico especialista specialist.
 médico de familia family physician.
 médico generalista general practitioner.
 médico osteópata osteopathic physician.
 médico de presencia física house physician.
 médico residente resident physician.

médico, -ca *adj.* medical.
medicobiológico, -ca *adj.* medicobiologic, medicobiological.
medicodental *adj.* medicodental.
medicolegal *adj.* medicolegal.
medicomecánico, -ca *adj.* medicomechanical.
medicoquirúrgico, -ca *adj.* medicochirurgical.
medicosocial *adj.* medicosocial.
medicotopográfico, -ca *adj.* medicotopographical.
medicozoológico, -ca *adj.* medicozoological.
medida *f.* measure.
medidor *m.* meter.
medidor de agudeza visual potencial *m.* potential acuimeter.
medidor de flujo *m.* flowmeter.
medidor de ritmo de dosis *m.* dose ratemeter.
medium *m.* average, medium.
medio *m.* average, medium.
 medio aclarador, medio aclarante clearing medium.
 medio activo active medium.
 medio completo complete medium.
 medio de contraste contrast medium.
 medio de contraste radiactivo radioactive contrast medium.
 medio de cultivo culture medium.
 medio de dispersión disperse medium, dispersion medium, dispersive medium.
 medio externo external medium, milieu extérieur.
 medio interno milieu intérieur.
 medio montador, medio de montaje mounting medium.
 medio para prueba de motilidad motility test medium.
 medio pasivo passive medium.
 medio radiolúcido radiolucent medium.
 medio radioopaco radiopaque medium.
 medio selectivo selective medium.
 medio separador, medio de separación separating medium.
 medio de soporte support medium.
 medio de transporte transport medium.
 medio de Wickersheimer Wickersheimer medium.
mediocarpiano, -na *adj.* mediocarpal, midcarpal.
mediocuerpo *m.* midbody.
mediodens *m.* mediodens.
mediofrontal *adj.* medifrontal, midfrontal.
mediolateral *adj.* mediolateral.
medimestrual *adj.* midmenstrual.
medionecrosis *f.* medionecrosis.
mediooccipital *adj.* medio-occipital, midoccipital.
mediotarsal *adj.* midtarsal.
mediotarsiano, -na *adj.* mediotarsal.
mediotipo *m.* mediotype.
mediotrusión *f.* mediotrusion.
medisección *f.* medisect.
mediseccionar *v.* medisect.
médula *f.* marrow, medulla.
 médula deprimida depressed marrow.
 médula gelatinosa gelatinous marrow.
 médula ósea amarilla yellow bone marrow.
 médula ósea roja red bone marrow.
 médula roja red marrow.
medulación *f.* medullation.
medulado, -da *adj.* medullated.
medular *adj.* medullary.
medulectomía *f.* medullectomy.
medulización *f.* medullization.
medulitis *f.* medullitis.

meduloadrenal *adj.* medulliadrenal, medulloadrenal.
meduloartritis *f.* medulloarthritis.
meduloblasto *m.* medulloblast.
meduloblastoma *m.* medulloblastoma.
medulocélula *f.* medullocell.
meduloencefálico, -ca *adj.* medulloencephalic.
meduloepitelioma *m.* medulloepithelioma.
meduloide *adj.* medulloid.
medulomioblastoma *m.* medullomyoblastoma.
medulosuprarrenoma *m.* medullosuprarenoma.
meduloterapia *f.* medullotherapy.
megabacteria *m.* megabacterium.
megacalicosis *f.* megacalycosis.
megacaliosis *f.* megacalycosis.
megacardia *f.* megacardia.
megacarioblasto *m.* megakaryoblast.
megacariocito *m.* megakaryocyte.
megacariocitopoyesis *f.* megakaryocytopoiesis.
megacariocitosis *f.* megakaryocytosis.
megacefalia *f.* megacephaly.
megacefálico, -ca *adj.* megacephalic.
megacéfalo, -la *adj.* megacephalous.
megaciego *m.* megacecum.
megacistis *m.* megacystis.
megaclítoris *f.* megaclitoris.
megacolédoco *m.* megacholedochus.
megacoco *m.* megacoccus.
megacolon *m.* megacolon.
   megacolon adquirido acquired megacolon.
   megacolon adquirido funcional acquired functional megacolon.
   megacolon aganglionar, megacolon aganglónico aganglionic megacolon.
   megacolon agudo acute megacolon.
   megacolon congénito congenital megacolon, megacolon congenitum.
   megacolon idiopático idiopathic megacolon.
   megacolon tóxico toxic megacolon.
megadactilia *f.* megadactylia, megadactyly, megadactylism.
megadolicocolon *f.* megadolichocolon.
megadoncia *f.* megadontia.
megadonte *m.* megadont.
megadonto *m.* megadont.
megadóntico, -ca *adj.* megadontic.
megadontismo *m.* megadontism.
megadosis *f.* megadose.
megaduodeno *m.* megaduodenum.
megaesófago *m.* megaesophagus.
megagameto *m.* megagamete.
megagnatia *m.* megagnathia.
megalacria *f.* megalakria.
megalecítico, -ca *adj.* megalecithal.
megalecito, -ta *adj.* megalecithal.
megalgia *f.* megalgia.
megaloblasto *m.* megaloblast.
megaloblastoide *adj.* megaloblastoid.
megalocardia *f.* megalocardia.
megalocariocito *m.* megakaryocyte.
megalocefalia *f.* megalocephaly.
megalocefálico, -ca *adj.* megalocephalic.
megalocéfalo, -la *m., f.* macrocephalus.
megalocisto *f.* megalocystis.
megalocitemia *f.* megalocythemia.
megalocito *m.* megalocyte.
megalocitosis *f.* megalocytosis.
megaloclítoris *f.* megaloclitoris.
megalocolia *f.* megalocolon.
megalocórnea *f.* megalocornea.
megalodactilia *f.* megalodactylia, megalodactyly.

megalodactilismo *m.* megalodactylism.
megalodoncia *f.* megalodontia.
megaloencefalia *f.* megalencephaly.
megaloencefálico, -ca *adj.* megaloencephalic.
megaloencéfalo *m.* megaloencephalon.
megaloenterón *m.* megaloenteron.
megaloesplácnico *m.* megalosplanchnic.
megaloesófago *m.* megaloesophagus.
megaloesplenia *f.* megalosplenia.
megalofalo *m.* megalophallus.
megaloftalmía *f.* megalophthalmos.
   megaloftalmía anterior anterior megalophthalmos.
megaloftalmo *m.* megalophtalmus.
megalogastria *f.* megalogastria.
megaloglosia *f.* megaloglossia.
megalografía *f.* megalographia, megalography.
megalomanía *f.* megalomania.
megalomaníaco, -ca *adj.* megalomaniac.
megalómano, -na *adj.* megalomaniac.
megalomelia *f.* megalomelia.
megalonicosis *f.* megalonychosis.
megaloniquia *f.* megalonychia.
megalopene *m.* megalopenis.
megalopía *f.* megalopia.
megalopodia *f.* megalopodia.
megalopsia *f.* megalopsia.
Megalopyge Megalopyge.
   Megalopyge opercularis Megalopyge opercularis.
megaloqueiria *f.* megalocheiria, megalochiria.
megaloquiria *f.* megalocheiria, megalochiria.
megaloscopio *m.* megaloscope.
megalosindactilia *f.* megalosyndactyly.
megalosplácnico, -ca *adj.* megalosplanchnic.
megalosplenia *f.* megalosplenia.
megalouréter *m.* megaloureter.
megalouretra *f.* megalourethra.
megamerozoíto *m.* megamerozoite.
meganúcleo *m.* meganucleus.
megaoftalmía *f.* megaophthalmos.
megaprosopia *f.* megaprosopia.
megaprosópico, -ca *adj.* megaprosopous.
megaprosopo, -pa *adj.* megaprosopous.
megarrecto *m.* megarectum.
Megaselia Megaselia.
megasema *f.* megaseme.
megasemo *m.* megaseme.
megasigmoide *m.* megasigmoid.
megasoma *m.* megasoma.
megasomía *f.* megasomia.
megatrombocito *m.* megathrombocyte.
megauréter *m.* megaureter.
megauretra *f.* megaurethra.
megavejiga *f.* megabladder.
megavitamina *f.* megavitamin.
megavoltaje *m.* megavoltage.
megoxicito *m.* megoxicyte.
megoxifilo *f.* megoxyphil.
mehlnährschaden *m.* mehlnährschaden.
mebiomianitis *f.* meibomianitis.
meibomitis *f.* meibomitis.
meiocito *m.* meiocyte.
meiogénico, -ca *adj.* meiogenic.
meiógeno, -na *adj.* meiogenic.
meiosis *f.* meiosis.
meiótico, -ca *adj.* meiotic.
mejilla *f.* cheek.
mejoría *f.* amelioration.
melagra *f.* melagra.
melalgia *f.* melalgia.
melanemesis *f.* melanemesis.
melanemia *f.* melanemia.
melanidrosis *f.* melanidrosis.
melanífero, -ra *adj.* melaniferous.

melanina *f.* melanin.
   melanina artificial, melanina ficticia artificial melanin, factitious melanin.
melanismo *m.* melanism.
melanístico, -ca *adj.* melanistic.
melano *m.* melano.
melanoacantoma *m.* melanoacanthoma.
melanoameloblastoma *m.* melanoameloblastoma.
melanoblasto *m.* melanoblast.
melanoblastoma *m.* melanoblastoma.
melanoblastosis *f.* melanoblastosis.
melanocarcinoma *m.* melanocarcinoma.
melanocítico, -ca *adj.* melanocytic.
melanocito *m.* melanocyte.
   melanocito dendrítico dendritic melanocyte.
melanocitoma *m.* melanocytoma.
   melanocitoma compuesto compound melanocytoma.
   melanocitoma dérmico dermal melanocytoma.
   melanocitoma del disco óptico melanocytoma of the optic disk.
melanocitosis *f.* melanocytosis.
   melanocitosis oculodérmica oculodermal melanocytosis.
   melanocitosis tóxica liquenoide melanocytosis toxica lichenoides.
melanocomo, -ca *adj.* melanocomous.
melanodendrocito *m.* melanodendrocyte.
melanodermatitis *f.* melanodermatitis.
   melanodermatitis tóxica liquenoide melanodermatitis toxica lichenoides.
melanodermia *f.* melanoderma.
   melanodermia caquéctica melanoderma cachecticorum.
   melanodermia chloasma chloasma.
   melanodermia parasitaria parasitic melanoderma.
   melanodermia racial racial melanoderma.
   melanodermia senil senile melanoderma.
melanodérmico, -ca *adj.* melanodermic.
melanodermo *m.* melanoderm.
melanoedema, -ma *m.* melanedema.
melanoepitelioma *m.* melanoepithelioma.
melanoescirro *m.* melanoscirrhus.
melanófago *m.* melanophage.
melanoforina *f.* melanophorin.
melanóforo *m.* melanophore.
melanogenemia *f.* melanogenemia.
melanogénesis *f.* melanogenesis.
melanogénico, -ca *adj.* melanogenic.
melanógeno *m.* melanogen.
melanoglosia *f.* melanoglossia.
melanohidrosis *f.* melanohidrosis.
melanoide *m.* melanoid.
Melanolestes Melanolestes.
   Melanolestes picipes Melanolestes picipes.
melanoleucodermia *f.* melanoleukoderma.
   melanoleucodermia cervical, melanoleucodermia colli melanoleukoderma colli.
melanoma *m.* melanoma.
   melanoma acral lentiginoso acral lentiginous melanoma.
   melanoma amelánico, melanoma amelanótico amelanic melanoma, amelanotic melanoma.
   melanoma de Cloudman Cloudman melanoma.
   melanoma coroideo maligno choroidal malignant melanoma.
   melanoma cutáneo primario primary cutaneous melanoma.
   melanoma con desviación mínima minimal deviation melanoma.

melanoma de extensión superficial superficial spreading melanoma.

melanoma de halo, melanoma de aureola halo melanoma.

melanoma de Harding-Passey Harding-Passey melanoma.

melanoma juvenil, melanoma juvenil benigno juvenile melanoma, benign juvenile melanoma.

melanoma lentiginoso acral acral lentiginous melanoma.

melanoma de léntigo maligno lentigo maligna melanoma.

melanoma maligno malignant melanoma.

melanoma maligno in situ in situ malignant melanoma.

melanoma nodular nodular melanoma.

melanoma S91 de Cloudman Cloudman's S 91 melanoma.

melanoma in situ in-situ melanoma.

melanoma subungueal, melanoma subungular subungual melanoma.

melanoma de úvea choroidal melanoma.

melanomatosis *f.* melanomatosis.

melanomatoso, -sa *adj.* melanomatous.

melanoniquia *f.* melanonichya.

melanopatía *f.* melanopathy.

melanoplaquia *f.* melanoplakia.

melanoplasia *f.* melanoplakia.

melanoprecipitación *f.* melanoprecipitation.

melanoqueratosis *f.* melanokeratosis.

melanorragia *f.* melanorrhagia.

melanorrea *f.* melanorrhea.

melanosarcoma *m.* melanosarcoma.

melanosarcomatosis *f.* melanosarcomatosis.

melanoscirro *m.* malignant melanoma.

melanosidad *f.* melanosity.

melanosis *f.* melanosis.

melanosis por alquitrán tar melanosis.

melanosis circunscrita precancerosa melanosis circumscripta precancerosa.

melanosis coli, melanosis de colon melanosis coli.

melanosis conjuntival conjunctival melanosis.

melanosis corii degenerativa melanosis corii degenerativa.

melanosis iridiana, melanosis del iris melanosis iridis, melanosis of the iris.

melanosis lenticular progresiva xeroderma pigmentosum.

melanosis neurocutánea neurocutaneous melanosis.

melanosis oculocutánea, melanosis oculodérmica oculocutaneous melanosis, oculodermal melanosis.

melanosis precancerosa circunscrita de Dubreuilh circumscribed precancerous melanosis of Dubreuilh.

melanosis precancerosa de Dubreuilh precancerous melanosis of Dubreuilh.

melanosis progresiva lenticular melanosis lenticularis progressiva.

melanosis pustulosa neonatal neonatal pustular melanosis.

melanosis de Riehl Riehl's melanosis.

melanosoma *m.* melanosome.

melanosoma de células gigantes giant melanosome.

melanótico, -ca *adj.* melanotic.

melanotonina *f.* melanotonin.

melanoptisis *f.* melanoptysis.

melanotrico, -ca *adj.* melanotrichous.

melanotriquia *f.* melanotrichia.

melanotrofina *f.* melanotropin.

melanotrofo *m.* melanotroph.

melanotrópico, -ca *adj.* melanotropic.

melanotropina *f.* melanotropin.

melanuresis *f.* melanuresis.

melanuria *f.* melanurie.

melanúrico, -ca *adj.* melanuric.

melanurina *f.* melanurin.

melasma *m.* melasma.

melasma de Addison, melasma addisoniano melasma addisonnii.

melasma gravídico, melasma uterino melasma gravidarum.

melasma suprarrenal melasma suprarenale.

melasma universal melasma universale.

melatonina *f.* melatonin.

melena *f.* melena.

melena espuria, melena falsa melena spuria.

melena neonatal, melena del recién nacido melena neonatorum.

melena verdadera melena vera.

melenémesis *f.* melenemesis.

melénico, -ca *adj.* melenic.

melicera *m.* melicera, meliceris.

meliceris *m.* meliceris.

melioidosis *f.* melioidosis.

melioidosis aguda acuta melioidosis.

melioidosis crónica chronic melioidosis.

melisofobia *f.* melissophobia.

melisoterapia *f.* melissotherapy.

melitis *f.* melitis.

melitoptialismo *m.* melitptyalism.

melitoptialón *m.* melitoptyalon.

mellizo *m.* sibling.

melocervicoplastia *f.* melocervicoplasty.

melodídimo *m.* melodidymus.

melomelia *f.* melomelia.

melómelo *m.* melomelus.

melonco *m.* meloncus.

meloplastia *f.* meloplasty.

melorreostosis *f.* melorheostosis.

melosalgia *f.* melosalgia.

melosquisis *f.* meloschisis.

melotia *f.* melotia.

membrana *f.* membrane, membrana.

membrana alveolocapilar alveolocapillary membrane.

membrana animal animal membrane.

membrana aponeurótica aponeurotic membrane.

membrana aracnoidea arachnoid membrane.

membrana celular cell membrane.

membrana de cierre closing membrane.

membrana ciclítica cyclitic membrane.

membrana cruposa croupous membrane.

membrana de dentina y esmalte dentinoenamel membrane.

membrana de diálisis biocompatible biocompatible membrane of dialysis.

membrana de diálisis semipermeable semipermeable membrane of dialysis.

membrana diftérica diphtheritic membrane.

membrana dismenorreica dysmenorrheal membrane.

membrana embrionaria embryonic membrane.

membrana endoneural endoneural membrane.

membrana epipapilar epipapillary membrane.

membrana epirretinal epiretinal membrane.

membrana extraembrionaria, membrana fetal extraembryonic membrane, fetal membrane.

membrana fundamental basement membrane.

membrana fusca fusca membrane.

membrana genitourinaria urogenital membrane.

membrana germinal, membrana germinativa germinal membrane.

membrana de gradocol gradocol membrane.

membrana de Haller Haller's membrane.

membrana de Heuser Heuser's membrane.

membrana hialina hyaline membrane.

membrana del huevo egg membrane.

membrana de Jackson Jackson's membrane.

membrana laríngea laryngeal web.

membrana limitante externa external limiting membrane, outer limiting membrane.

membrana limitante de Held blood-brain barrier.

membrana limitante interna internal limiting membrane.

membrana limitante del tubo neural limiting membrane of the neural tube.

membrana del nacimiento birth membrane.

membrana de Nitabuch Nitabuch's membrane.

membrana nuclear nuclear membrane.

membrana perforada membrana perforata.

membrana piofiláctica pyophylactic membrane.

membrana piógena pyogenic membrane.

membrana placentaria placental membrane.

membrana plasmática plasma membrane.

membrana pleuropericárdica pleuropericardial membrane.

membrana pleuroperitoneal pleuroperitoneal membrane.

membrana preformativa membrana preformativa.

membrana presináptica presynaptic membrane.

membrana pupilar membrana pupilaris.

membrana queratógena keratogenous membrane.

membrana urogenital urogenital membrane.

membrana urorrectal urorectal membrane.

membrana vitelina viteline membrane.

membrana de Volkmann Volkmann's membrane.

membranáceo, -a *adj.* membranaceous.

membranado, -da *adj.* membranate.

membranectomía *f.* membranectomy.

membranela *f.* membranella.

membraniforme *adj.* membraniform.

membranina *f.* membranin.

membranocartilaginoso, -sa *adj.* membranocartilaginous.

membranoide *adj.* membranoid.

membranólisis *f.* membranolysis.

membranoso, -sa *adj.* webbed, membranous.

memoria *f.* memory.

memoria de acceso aleatorio (RAM) random-access memory (RAM).

memoria de acceso directo direct-access memory.

memoria afectiva affect memory.

memoria anterógrada anterograde memory.

memoria cinestésica kinesthetic memory.

memoria a corto plazo (MCP) short-term memory (STM).

memoria ecoica echoic memory.

memoria inmunológica inmunologic memory.

memoria a largo plazo (MLP) long term memory (LTM).

memoria ocular eye memory.

memoria de pantalla screen memory.

memoria protectora screen memory.

memoria remota remote memory.

memoria retrógrada retrograde memory.
memoria selectiva selective memory.
memoria senil senile memory.
memoria sólo de lectura (ROM) read-only memory (ROM).
memoria subconsciente subconscious memory.
memoria visual visual memory.
menacma *m.* menacme.
menalgia *f.* menalgia.
menaquinona (MK) *f.* menaquinone (MK).
menarca *f.* menarche.
menarcal *adj.* menarchal.
menarquia, menarquía *f.* menarche.
menárquico, -ca *adj.* menarcheal, menarchial.
mendeliano, -na *adj.* Mendelian.
mendelismo *m.* Mendelism.
mendelizante *adj.* mendelizing.
mengua *f.* waste.
menhidrosis *f.* menhidrosis.
meninge *f.* meninx.
meninge primitiva meninx primitiva.
meníngeo, -a *adj.* meningeal.
meningeocortical *adj.* meningeocortical.
meningeoma *m.* meningeoma.
meningeorrafia *f.* meningeorrhaphy.
meninginitis *f.* meninginitis.
meningioma *m.* meningioma, meningeoma, meningoma.
meningioma angioblástico angioblastic meningioma.
meningioma cutáneo cutaneous meningioma.
meningioma intrarraquídeo spinal meningioma.
meningioma intraventricular ventricular meningioma.
meningioma del nervio óptico optic nerve meningioma.
meningioma orbitario orbit meningioma.
meningioma psamomatoso psammomatous meningioma.
meningioma raquídeo spinal meningioma.
meningiomatosis *f.* meningiomatosis.
meningismo *m.* meningism.
meningítico, -ca *adj.* meningitic.
meningitis *f.* meningitis.
meningitis africana trypanosomiasis.
meningitis aséptica, meningitis aséptica aguda aseptic meningitis, acute aseptic meningitis.
meningitis bacteriana bacterial meningitis.
meningitis basal, meningitis basilar basilar meningitis.
meningitis carcinomatosa carcinomatous meningitis.
meningitis cefalorraquídea cerebrospinal mcningitis.
meningitis cefalorraquídea epidémica epidemic cerebrospinal meningitis.
meningitis cerebral cerebral meningitis.
meningitis cerebroespinal cerebrospinal meningitis.
meningitis cerebroespinal epidémica epidemic cerebrospinal meningitis.
meningitis eosinófila eosinophilic meningitis.
meningitis espinal spinal meningitis.
meningitis estéril sterile meningitis.
meningitis gomatosa gummatous meningitis.
meningitis linfocítica, meningitis linfocítica benigna lymphocytic meningitis.
meningitis listeria listeria meningitis.
meningitis meningocócica meningococcal meningitis.
meningitis de Mollaret Mollaret's meningitis.

meningitis neoplásica neoplastic meningitis.
meningitis neumocócica pneumococcal meningitis.
meningitis oclusiva occlusive meningitis.
meningitis osificante meningitis ossificans.
meningitis otítica otitic meningitis.
meningitis por peste plague meningitis.
meningitis purulenta purulent meningitis.
meningitis de Quincke Quincke's meningitis.
meningitis serosa serous meningitis.
meningitis serosa circunscrita, meningitis serosa circunscrita quística meningitis serosa circumscripta.
meningitis simpática meningitis sympathica.
meningitis traumática traumatic meningitis.
meningitis tuberculosa tubercular meningitis, tuberculous meningitis.
meningitis viral, meningitis virásica viral meningitis.
meningoarteritis *f.* meningoarteritis.
meningoblastoma *m.* meningoblastoma.
meningocele *m.* meningocele.
meningocele craneal cranial meningocele.
meningocele espurio spurious meningocele.
meningocele raquídeo spinal meningocele.
meningocele traumático traumatic meningocele.
meningocerebritis *f.* meningocerebritis.
meningocistocele *m.* meningocystocele.
meningocito *m.* meningocyte.
meningococemia *f.* meningococcemia.
meningococemia fulminante aguda acute fulminating meningococcemia.
meningococia *f.* meningococcemia.
meningococo *m.* meningococci.
meningococosis *f.* meningococcosis.
meningocortical *adj.* meningocortical.
meningoencefalitis *f.* meningoencephalitis.
meningoencefalitis amebiana primaria primary amebic meningoencephalitis.
meningoencefalitis biondulante biundulant meningoencephalitis.
meningoencefalitis hemorrágica primaria aguda acute primary hemorrhagic meningoencephalitis.
meningoencefalitis herpética herpetic meningoencephalitis.
meningoencefalitis de las paperas, meningoencefalitis por parotiditis mumps meningoencephalitis.
meningoencefalitis sifilítica syphilitic meningoencephalitis.
meningoencefalocele *m.* meningoencephalocele.
meningoencefalomielitis *f.* meningoencephalomyelitis.
meningoencefalomielopatía *f.* meningoencephalomyelopathy.
meningoencefalopatía *f.* meningoencephalopathy.
meningofibroblastoma *m.* meningofibroblastoma.
meningógeno, -na *adj.* meningogenic.
meningohematoma *m.* meningematoma.
meningoma *m.* meningoma.
meningomalacia *f.* meningomalacia.
meningomielitis *f.* meningomyelitis.
meningomielocele *m.* meningomyelocele.
meningomieloencefalitis *f.* meningomyeloencephalitis.
meningomielorradiculitis *f.* meningomyeloradiculitis.
meningoosteoflebitis *f.* meningo-osteophlebitis.
meningopatía *f.* meningopathy.

meningorradicular *adj.* meningoradicular.
meningorradiculitis *f.* meningoradiculitis.
meningorrafia *f.* meningorrhaphy.
meningorragia *f.* meningorrhagia.
meningorraquídeo, -a *adj.* meningorachidian.
meningosis *f.* meningosis.
meningosteoflebitis *f.* meningo-osteophlebitis.
meningotelioma *m.* meningothelioma.
meningovascular *adj.* meningovascular.
meninguria *f.* meninguria.
meniscal *adj.* meniscal.
meniscectomía *f.* meniscectomy.
meniscitis *f.* meniscitis.
menisco *m.* meniscus.
meniscocito *m.* meniscocyte.
meniscocitosis *f.* meniscocytosis.
meniscorrafia *f.* meniscorrhaphy.
meniscosinovial *adj.* meniscosynovial.
meniscótomo *m.* meniscotome.
menisquesis *f.* menischesis.
menocelis *f.* menocelis.
menofanía *f.* menophania.
menometástasis *f.* menoplania.
menometrorragia *f.* menometrorrhagia.
menopausis *f.* menopause.
menopausia *f.* menopause.
menopausia artificial artificial menopause.
menopausia masculina male menopause.
menopausia precoz, menopausia prematura menopause praecox.
menopausia quirúrgica surgical menopause.
menopáusico, -ca *adj.* menopausal.
menoplanía *f.* menoplania.
menorragia *f.* menorrhagia.
menorralgia *f.* menorralgia.
menorrea *f.* menorrhea.
menorreico, -ca *adj.* menorrheal.
menosquesia *f.* menoschesis.
menosquesis *f.* menoschesis.
menostasia *f.* menostasia, menostasis.
menostasis *f.* menostasis.
menostaxis *f.* menostaxis.
menoxenia *f.* menoxenia.
menotropina *f.* menotropin.
menouria *f.* menouria.
mensajero *m.* messenger.
segundo mensajero second messenger.
menstruación *f.* menstruation.
menstruación anovular, menstruación anovulatoria anovular menstruation, anovulatory menstruation.
menstruación complementaria supplementary menstruation.
menstruación difícil difficult menstruation.
menstruación no ovulatoria non-ovulational menstruation.
menstruación retrasada delayed menstruation.
menstruación regurgitante, menstruación retrógrada regurgitant menstruation, retrograde menstruation.
menstruación sin ovulación non-ovulational menstruation.
menstruación suplementaria supplementary menstruation.
menstruación suprimida suppressed menstruation.
menstruación sustitutiva vicarious menstruation.
menstruación vicariante vicarious menstruation.
menstrualis *adj.* menstrual.
menstrual *adj.* menstrual.

menstruante *adj.* menstruant.

menstruar *v.* menstruate.

menstruo *m.* menstruum.

menstruoso, -sa *adj.* menstruous.

mentación *f.* mentation.

mental *adj.* mental.

mentalidad *f.* mentality.

mente *f.* mind.

  mente errante wandering mind.

menticida *m.* menticide.

mentímetro *m.* mentimeter.

mentoanterior *adj.* mentoanterior, anterior.

mentolabial *adj.* mentolabial.

mentón *m.* chin, menton, mentum.

mentonera *f.* chin cap.

mentoniano, -na *adj.* mental, mentalis.

mentoplastia *f.* mentoplasty.

mentoposterior *adj.* mentoposterior, posterior.

mentotransversa *adj.* mentotransverse.

méntula *f.* mentula.

mentulado *m.* mentulate.

mentulagra *f.* mentulagra.

meralgia *f.* meralgia.

  meralgia parestésica meralgia paresthetica.

mercurialismo *m.* mercurialism.

mercurialización *f.* mercurialization.

mercurializado, -da *adj.* mercurialized.

mercúrico, -ca *adj.* mercuric.

mercurio *m.* mercury.

mercurioso, -sa *adj.* mercurous.

merergasia *f.* merergasia.

merergástico, -ca *adj.* merergastic.

mericismo *m.* merycism.

merisis *f.* merisis.

merismo *m.* merism.

merístico, -ca *adj.* meristic.

meroacrania *f.* meroacrania.

meroanencefalia *f.* meroanencephaly.

meroblástico, -ca *adj.* meroblastic.

merocele *m.* merocele.

merocisto *m.* merocyst.

merocito *m.* merocyte.

merocoxalgia *f.* merocoxalgia.

merocrino, -na *adj.* merocrine.

merodiastólico, -ca *adj.* merodiastolic.

meroergasia *f.* meroergasia.

merogamia *f.* merogamy.

merogástrula *f.* merogastrula.

merogénesis *f.* merogenesis.

merogenético, -ca *adj.* merogenetic.

merogénico, -ca *adj.* merogenic.

merogonia *f.* merogony.

  merogonia diploide diploid merogony.

  merogonia partenogenética parthenogenetic merogony.

merogónico, -ca *adj.* merogonic.

merología *f.* merology.

meromelia *f.* meromelia.

meromicrosomia *f.* meromicrosomia.

meromiosina *f.* meromyosin.

meromorfosis *f.* meromorphosis.

meronecrobiosis *f.* meronecrobiosis.

meronecrosis *f.* meronecrosis.

meroosmia *f.* merosmia.

meropía *f.* meropia.

meropsia *f.* meropsia.

merorraquisquisis *f.* merorachischisis.

meroscopia *f.* meroscopy.

meroscopio *m.* meroscope.

merosteósico, -ca *adj.* merostotic.

merosistólico, -ca *adj.* merosystolic.

merosmia *f.* merosmia.

merotomía *f.* merotomy.

merozoíto *m.* merozoite.

merulius lacrymans Merulius lacrymans.

mesa *f.* table.

  mesa basculante tilt table.

  mesa de examen examining table.

  mesa inclinada tilt table.

  mesa de laparotomía lap-board.

  mesa de operaciones operating table.

mesad mesad, mesiad.

mesal *adj.* mesal.

mesangial *adj.* mesangial.

mesangio *m.* mesangium.

  mesangio extraglomerular extraglomerular mesangium.

mesangiocapilar *adj.* mesangiocapillary.

mesaortitis *f.* mesaortitis.

mesaraico, -ca *adj.* mesaraic.

mesareico, -ca *adj.* mesaraic.

mesarteritis *f.* mesarteritis.

mesaticefálico, -ca *adj.* mesaticephalic.

mesatipélico, -ca *adj.* mesatipellic.

mesatipélvico, -ca *adj.* mesatipelvic.

mesaxón *m.* mesaxon.

meséctico, -ca *adj.* mesectic.

mesectoblasto *m.* mesectoblast.

mesectodermo *m.* mesectoderm.

mesencefálico, -ca *adj.* mesencephalic.

mesencefalitis *f.* mesencephalitis.

mesencéfalo *m.* mesencephalon.

mesencefalohipofisiario, -ria *adj.* mesencephalohypophyseal.

mesencefalotomía *f.* mesencephalotomy.

mesénquima *m.* mesenchyma.

mesenquimático, -ca *adj.* mesenchymal.

mesenquimatoso, -sa *adj.* mesenchymal.

mesenquimoma *m.* mesenchymoma.

  mesenquimoma benigno benign mesenchymoma.

  mesenquimoma maligno malignant mesenchymoma.

mesenterectomía *f.* mesenterectomy.

mesentérico, -ca *adj.* mesenteric.

mesenterio *m.* mesentery, mesenterium.

  mesenterio común, mesenterio dorsal común mesenterium commune, mesenterium dorsale commune.

  mesenterio primitivo primitive mesentery.

  mesenterio ventral ventral mesentery.

mesenteriolo *m.* mesenteriolum.

mesenteriopexia *f.* mesenteriopexy.

mesenteriorrafia *f.* mesenteriorrhaphy.

mesenterioplicación *f.* mesenteriplication.

mesenteritis *f.* mesenteritis.

mesenterium mesenterium.

mesenteroblasto *m.* mesenteron.

mesénteron *m.* mesenteron.

mesentómero *m.* mesentomere.

mesentorrafia *f.* mesentorrhaphy.

meseta *m.* plateau.

mesiad mesiad.

mesial *adj.* mesial, mesially.

mesino, -na *adj.* mesien.

mesiobucal *adj.* mesiobuccal.

mesiobucooclusal *adj.* mesiobucco-occlusal.

mesiobucopulpal *adj.* mesiobuccopulpal.

mesiobucopulpar *adj.* mesiobuccopulpal.

mesiocervical *adj.* mesiocervical.

mesioclinación *f.* mesioclination.

mesioclusión *f.* mesiocclusion.

mesiocolocación *f.* mesiplacement.

mesiodens *m.* mesiodens.

mesiodiente *m.* mesiodens.

mesiodistal *adj.* mesiodistal.

mesiodistooclusal (MOD) *adj.* mesiodistocclusal (MOD).

mesiogingival *adj.* mesiogingival.

mesiognático, -ca *adj.* mesiognathic.

mesioincisal *adj.* mesioincisal.

mesioincisodistal *adj.* mesioincisodistal.

mesiolabial *adj.* mesiolabial.

mesiolabioincisal *adj.* mesiolabioincisal.

mesiolingual *adj.* mesiolingual.

mesiolinguoincisal *adj.* mesiolinguoincisal.

mesiolinguooclusal *adj.* mesiolinguo-occlusal.

mesiolinguopulpar *adj.* mesiolinguopulpal.

mesión *m.* mesion.

mesioclusal *adj.* mesio-occlusal.

mesiooclusión *f.* mesio-occlusion, mesiocclusion.

mesiooclusodistal *adj.* mesio-occlusodistal.

mesiopulpal *adj.* mesiopulpal.

mesiopulpar *adj.* mesiopulpal.

mesiopulpolabial *adj.* mesiopulpolabial.

mesiopulpolingual *adj.* mesiopulpolingual.

mesioversión *f.* mesioversion.

mesoaortitis *f.* mesoaortitis.

  mesoaortitis sifilítica mesoaortitis syphilitica.

mesoapéndice *m.* mesoappendix.

mesoapendicitis *f.* mesoappendicitis.

mesoarial *adj.* mesoarial.

mesoario *m.* mesoarium.

mesoarium *m.* mesoarium.

mesoblastema *m.* mesoblastema.

mesoblastémico, -ca *adj.* mesoblastemic.

mesoblástico, -ca *adj.* mesoblastic.

mesoblasto *m.* mesoblast.

mesobronquitis *f.* mesobronchitis.

mesocardia *f.* mesocardia.

mesocardio *m.* mesocardium.

  mesocardio arterial arterial mesocardium.

  mesocardio dorsal dorsal mesocardium.

  mesocardio lateral lateral mesocardium.

  mesocardio venoso venous mesocardium.

  mesocardio ventral ventral mesocardium.

mesocarpiano, -na *adj.* mesocarpal.

mesocárpico, -ca *adj.* mesocarpal.

mesocecal *adj.* mesocecal.

mesocefálico, -ca *adj.* mesocephalic.

mesocéfalo *m.* mesocephalon.

mesocéfalo, -la *adj.* mesocephalic.

mesociego *m.* mesocecum.

mesocisto *m.* mesocyst.

mesocitoma *m.* mesocytoma.

mesococo *m.* mesococcus.

mesocólico, -ca *adj.* mesocolic.

mesocolon *m.* mesocolon.

mesocolopexia *f.* mesocolopexy.

mesocoloplegadura *f.* mesocoloplication.

mesocoloplicación *f.* mesocoloplication.

mesocondrio *m.* mesochondrium.

mesocordio *m.* mesocord.

mesocordón *m.* mesocord.

mesocórnea *f.* mesocornea.

mesocoroides *f.* mesochoroidea.

mesocráneo, -a *adj.* mesocranic.

mesocuerpo *m.* midbody.

mesocuneiforme *adj.* mesocuneiform.

mesodérmico, -ca *adj.* mesodermic.

mesodermo *m.* mesoderm.

  mesodermo branquial branchial mesoderm.

  mesodermo esplácnico splanchnic mesoderm.

  mesodermo extraembrionario extraembryonic mesoderm.

  mesodermo gastral gastral mesoderm.

  mesodermo intermedio intermediate mesoderm.

  mesodermo intraembrionario intraembryonic mesoderm.

  mesodermo lateral lateral mesoderm.

  mesodermo paraxial paraxial mesoderm.

  mesodermo secundario secondary mesoderm.

mesodermo somático somatic mesoderm.
mesodermo visceral visceral mesoderm.
mesodiastólico, -ca *adj.* mesodiastolic.
mesodolor *m.* midpain.
mesodonte *m.* mesodont.
mesodóntico, -ca *adj.* mesodontic.
mesodontismo *m.* mesodontism.
mesodonto *m.* mesodont.
mesoduodenal *adj.* mesoduodenal.
mesoduodeno *m.* mesoduodenum.
mesoencéfalo *m.* mesencephalon.
mesoenteriolo *m.* mesoenteriolum.
mesoepidídimo *m.* mesoepididymis.
mesoepitelio *m.* mesoepithelium.
mesoesófago *m.* mesoesophagus.
mesoesternón *m.* mesosternum, midsternum.
mesoestroma *m.* mesostroma.
mesofaringe *f.* oropharynx.
mesofílico, -ca *adj.* mesophilic.
mesófilo *m.* mesophil, mesophile.
mesoflebitis *f.* mesophlebitis.
mesofragma *f.* mesophragma.
mesofrión *m.* mesophryon.
mesogaster *m.* mesogaster.
mesogástrico, -ca *adj.* mesogastric.
mesogastrio *m.* mesogastrium.
mesogenital *adj.* mesogenital.
mesoglia *f.* mesoglia.
mesoglioma *m.* mesoglioma.
mesoglúteo, -a *adj.* mesogluteal.
mesognático, -ca *adj.* mesognathous, mesognathic.
mesognation *m.* mesognathion.
Mesogonimus Mesogonimus.
mesográcil *adj.* midgracile.
mesohiloma *m.* mesohyloma.
mesoíleon *m.* mesoileum.
mesoiris *m.* mesiris.
mesolepidoma *m.* mesolepidoma.
mesolinfocito *m.* mesolymphocyte.
mesolobotomía *f.* mesolobotomy.
mesología *f.* mesology.
mesomelia *f.* mesomelia.
mesomélico, -ca *adj.* mesomelic.
mesomestrual *adj.* midmenstrual.
mesómera *f.* mesomere.
mesomérico, -ca *adj.* mesomeric.
mesomerismo *m.* mesomerism.
mesómero *m.* mesomere.
mesometrio *m.* mesometrium.
mesometritis *f.* mesometritis.
mesomorfia *f.* mesomorphy.
mesomórfico, -ca *adj.* mesomorphic.
mesomorfo *m.* mesomorph.
mesómula *f.* mesomula.
mesón *m.* meson.
mesonasal *adj.* mesonasal.
mesonéfrico, -ca *adj.* mesonephric.
mesonefroma *m.* mesonephroma.
mesonefros *m.* mesonephron, mesonephros.
mesoneumo *m.* mesopneumon.
mesoomento *m.* meso-omentum.
mesoneuritis *f.* mesoneuritis.
mesontomorfo *m.* meso-ontomorph.
mesooccipital *adj.* midoccipital.
mesoovario *m.* mesovarium.
mesopalio *m.* mesopallium.
mesopexia *f.* mesopexy.
mesopía *f.* mesopia.
mesópico, -ca *adj.* mesopic.
mesoprosópico, -ca *adj.* mesoprosopic.
mesopsíquico, -ca *adj.* mesopsychic.
mesopulmón *m.* mesopulmonum.
mesoróptero *m.* mesoropter.
mesorquial *adj.* mesorchial.

mesorquio *m.* mesorchium.
mesorrafia *f.* mesorrhaphy.
mesorrecto *m.* mesorectum.
mesorretina *f.* mesoretine.
mesorrino, -na *adj.* mesorrhine.
mesosálpinx *m.* mesosalpinx.
mesoscopio *m.* mesoscope.
mesosemo, -ma *adj.* mesoseme.
mesosífilis *f.* mesosyphilis.
mesosigmoide *m.* mesosigmoid.
mesosigmoides *m.* mesosigmoid.
mesosigmoiditis *f.* mesosigmoiditis.
mesosigmoidopexia *f.* mesosigmoidopexy.
mesosistólico, -ca *adj.* mesosystolic.
mesosoma *m.* mesosome.
mesosomatoso, -sa *adj.* mesosomatous.
mesosomía *f.* mesosomia.
mesosomo, -ma *adj.* mesosomatous.
mesosquélico, -ca *adj.* mesoskelic.
mesostenio *m.* mesostenium.
mesosternón *m.* midsternum, mesosternum.
mesotarsiano, -na *adj.* mesotarsal.
mesotaurodontismo *m.* mesotaurodontism.
mesotelial *adj.* mesothelial.
mesotelio *m.* mesothelium.
mesotelioma *m.* mesothelioma.
  mesotelioma benigno del tracto genital
  benign mesothelioma of the genital tract.
mesotendón *m.* mesotendon.
mesotenon *m.* mesotenon.
mesotímpano *m.* mesotympanum.
mesotrópico, -ca *adj.* mesotropic.
mesouránico, -ca *adj.* mesouranic, mesuranic.
mesovario *m.* mesovarium.
mesoyeyuno *m.* mesojejunum.
mestizo, -za *adj.* half-caste.
mesuránico, -ca *adj.* mesuranic.
meta *f.* goal.
metaaglutinina *f.* metagglutinin.
metaalbúmina *f.* metalbumin.
metaalergia *f.* metallergy.
metaapófisis *f.* metapophysis.
metaarteriola *f.* metarteriole.
metaartrítico, -ca *adj.* meta-arthritic.
metábasis *f.* metabasis.
metabiosis *f.* metabiosis.
metabólico, -ca *adj.* metabolic.
metabolimetría *f.* metabolimetry.
metabolímetro *m.* metabolimeter.
metabolina *f.* metabolin.
metabolismo *m.* metabolism.
  metabolismo acidobásico acid-base metabolism.
  metabolismo amonotélico ammonotelic metabolism.
  metabolismo anaeróbico anaerobic metabolism.
  metabolismo basal basal metabolism.
  metabolismo de carbohidratos carbohydrate metabolism.
  metabolismo del colesterol cholesterol metabolism.
  metabolismo constructivo anabolism.
  metabolismo destructivo catabolism.
  metabolismo de los electrólitos electrolyte metabolism.
  metabolismo endógeno endogenous metabolism.
  metabolismo energético energy metabolism.
  metabolismo exógeno exogenous metabolism.
  metabolismo farmacológico drug metabolism.
  metabolismo de las grasas, metabolismo graso fat metabolism.

  metabolismo de los hidratos de carbono carbohydrate metabolism.
  metabolismo del hierro iron metabolism.
  metabolismo intermediario intermediary metabolism.
  metabolismo proteico, metabolismo de las proteínas protein metabolism.
  metabolismo renal renal metabolism.
  metabolismo respiratorio respiratory metabolism.
  metabolismo ureotélico ureotelic metabolism.
  metabolismo uricotélico uricotelic metabolism.
metabolito *m.* metabolite.
metabolizable *adj.* metabolizable.
metabolizar *v.* metabolize.
metacarpectomía *f.* metacarpectomy.
metacarpiano, -na *adj.* metacarpal.
metacarpo *m.* metacarpus.
metacarpofalángico, -ca *adj.* metacarpophalangeal.
metacelio *m.* metacele, metacoele.
metacelo *m.* metacele.
metaceloma *m.* metacoeloma.
metacéntrico, -ca *adj.* metacentric.
metaciesis *f.* metacyesis.
metacinesia *f.* metakinesis.
metacinesis *f.* metakinesis.
mutacismo *m.* mytacism.
metacismo *m.* mytacism.
metacónido, -da *f.* metaconid.
metacono *m.* metacone.
metacontraste *m.* metacontrast.
metacónulo, -la *adj.* metaconule.
metacriptozoíto *m.* metacryptozoite.
metacromasia *f.* metachromasia.
metacromático, -ca *adj.* metachromatic.
metacromatina *f.* metachromatin.
metacromatismo *m.* metachromasia.
metacromatófilo, -la *adj.* metachromophil, metachromophile.
metacromía *f.* metachromia.
metacrómico, -ca *adj.* metachromic.
metacromófilo, -la *adj.* metachromophil, metacromophile.
metacromosoma *m.* metachromosome.
metacrónico, -ca *adj.* metachronous.
metacrono, -na *adj.* metachronous.
metadisentería *f.* metadysentery.
metadona *f.* methadone.
metaduodeno *m.* metaduodenum.
metaencefálico, -ca *adj.* metencephalic.
metaencéfalo *m.* metencephalon.
metaestable *adj.* metastable.
metaesternón *m.* metasternum.
metaestro *m.* metestrum, metestrus.
metafase *f.* metaphase.
metafisario, -ria *adj.* metaphyseal, metaphysial.
metáfisis *f.* metaphysis.
metafisitis *f.* metaphysitis.
metafrenia *f.* metaphrenia.
metagastrio *m.* metagaster.
metagástrula *f.* metagastrula.
metagenesia *f.* metagenesis.
metagénesis *f.* metagenesis.
metaglobulina *f.* metaglobulin.
metagonimiasis *f.* metagonimiasis.
Metagonimus Metagonimus.
  Metagonimus yokogawai Metagonimus yokogawai.
metagripal *adj.* metagrippal.
metahem *m.* metheme.
metahemalbúmina *f.* methemalbumin.

metahemalbuminemia *f.* methemalbuminemia.

metahemoglobina *f.* methemoglobin.

metahemoglobina reductasa (NADPH) methemoglobin reductase (NADPH).

metahemoglobinemia *f.* methemoglobinemia.

metahemoglobinemia adquirida acquired methemoglobinemia.

metahemoglobinemia congénita congenital methemoglobinemia.

metahemoglobinemia enterógena enterogenous methemoglobinemia.

metahemoglobinemia hereditaria hereditary methemoglobinemia.

metahemoglobinemia primaria primary methemoglobinemia.

metahemoglobinemia secundaria secondary methemoglobinemia.

metahemoglobinémico, -ca *adj.* methemoglobinemic.

metahemoglobinuria *f.* methemoglobinuria.

metaherpes *m.* metaherpes.

metaictérico, -ca *adj.* metaicteric.

metainfeccioso, -sa *adj.* metainfective.

metal *m.* metal.

metalaxia *f.* metallaxis.

metalergia *f.* metallergy.

metalestesia *f.* metallesthesia.

metálico, -ca *adj.* metallic.

metalización *f.* metallization.

metalizado, -da *adj.* metallized.

metalizante *adj.* metallizing.

metalofilia *f.* metallophilia.

metalófilo, -la *adj.* metallophilic.

metaloflavoproteína *f.* metalloflavoprotein.

metaloide *m.* metalloid.

metaloscopia *f.* metalloscopy.

metaloterapia *f.* metallotherapy.

metalotioneína *f.* metallothionein.

metalúes *f.* metasyphilis.

metaluético, -ca *adj.* metaluetic.

metámera *f.* metamer, metamere.

metamería *f.* metamerism.

metamérico, -ca *adj.* metameric.

metamerismo *m.* metamerism.

metámero *m.* metamer.

metamielocito *m.* metamyelocite.

metamioglobina *f.* metmyoglobin.

metamórfico, -ca *adj.* metamorphotic.

metamorfopsia *f.* metamorphopsia.

metamorfósico, -ca *adj.* metamorphotic.

metamorfótico, -ca *adj.* metamorphotic.

metamorfosis *f.* metamorphosis.

metamorfosis adiposa fatty metamorphosis.

metamorfosis estructural viscous metamorphosis.

metamorfosis grasa fatty metamorphosis.

metamorfosis plaquetaria platelet metamorphosis.

metamorfosis retrógrada, metamorfosis retrogresiva retrograde metamorphosis, retrogressive metamorphosis.

metamorfosis de revisión revisionary metamorphosis.

metamorfosis viscosa viscous metamorphosis.

metanéfrico, -ca *adj.* metanephric.

metanefrina *f.* metanephrine.

metanefrogénico, -ca *adj.* metanephrogenic.

metanefrógeno, -na *adj.* metanephrogenic.

metanefrón *m.* metanephro, metanephron, metanephros.

metanefros *m.* metanephros.

metaneumónico, -ca *adj.* metapneumonic.

metaneutrófilo, -la *adj.* metaneutrophil, metaneutrophile.

metanógeno *m.* methanogen.

metanógeno, -na *adj.* methanogenic.

metanólisis *f.* methanolysis.

metanúcleo *m.* metanucleus.

metapeptona *f.* metapeptone.

metapirético, -ca *adj.* metapyretic.

metaplasia *f.* metaplasia.

metaplasia apocrina apocrine metaplasia.

metaplasia escamosa squamous metaplasia.

metaplasia intestinal intestinal metaplasia.

metaplasia mieloide myeloid metaplasia.

metaplasia mieloide agnógena, metaplasia mieloide agnogénica agnogenic myeloid metaplasia.

metaplasia mieloide pospolicitémica postpolycythemic myeloid metaplasia.

metaplasia mieloide primaria primary myeloid metaplasia.

metaplasia mieloide secundaria secondary myeloid metaplasia.

metaplasia mieloide sintomática symptomatic myeloid metaplasia.

metaplasia seudopilórica pseudopyloric metaplasia.

metaplásico, -ca *adj.* metaplastic.

metaplasis *f.* metaplasis.

metaplasma *m.* metaplasm.

metaplexo *m.* metaplexus.

metapodalia *f.* metapodalia.

metapófisis *f.* metapophysis.

metaporo *m.* metapore.

metaproteína *f.* metaprotein.

metapsicología *f.* metapsychology.

metapsíquica *f.* metapsychics.

metaptosis *f.* metastasis.

metaquisis *f.* metachysis.

metarrubricito *m.* metarubricyte.

metarteriola *f.* metarteriole.

metasífilis *f.* metasyphilis.

metasifilítico, -ca *adj.* metasyphilitic.

metasinapsis *f.* metasynapsis.

metasincrisis *f.* metasyncrisis.

metasindesis *f.* metasyndesis.

metastable *adj.* metastable.

metastasectomía *f.* metastasectomy.

metastásico, -ca *adj.* metastatic.

metástasis *f.* metastasis.

metástasis bioquímica biochemical metastasis.

metástasis calcárea calcareous metastasis.

metástasis de contacto contact metastasis.

metástasis cruzada crossed metastasis.

metástasis directa direct metastasis.

metástasis paradójica paradoxical metastasis.

metástasis pulsátil pulsating metastasis.

metástasis retrógrada retrograde metastasis.

metástasis satélite satellite metastasis.

metastático, -ca *adj.* metastatic.

metasternón *m.* metasternum.

metatálamo *m.* metathalamus.

metatarsalgia *f.* metatarsalgia.

metatarsalgia de Morton Morton's toe.

metatarsectomía *f.* metatarsectomy.

metatarsiano, -na *adj.* metatarsal.

metatarso *m.* metatarsus.

metatarso aducido, metatarso aducto metatarsus adductus.

metatarso aducto cavo metatarsus adductocavus.

metatarso aducto varo metatarsus adductovarus.

metatarso ancho metatarsus latus, broad foot, spread foot.

metatarso atávico metatarsus atavicus.

metatarso breve metatarsus brevis.

metatarso valgo metatarsus valgus.

metatarso primo varo metatarsus primus varus.

metatarso varo metatarsus varus.

metatarsofalángico, -ca *adj.* metatarsophalangeal.

metatarsus *m.* metatarsus.

metatarsus latus metatarsus latus.

metatésico, -ca *adj.* metathetic.

metátesis *f.* metathesis.

metatípico, -ca *adj.* metatypic, metatypical.

metatrofia *f.* metatrophy.

metatrófico, -ca *adj.* metatrophic.

metatrófo *m.* metatroph.

metatrombina *f.* metathrombin.

metatrópico, -ca *adj.* metatropic.

metazonal *adj.* metazonal.

metazoonosis *f.* metazoonosis.

metecio *m.* metecious.

metéctico, -ca *adj.* methectic.

metencéfalo *m.* metencephalon.

metencefálico, -ca *adj.* metencephalic.

metencefalina *f.* metenkephalin.

metencefaloespinal *adj.* metencephalospinal.

meteorismo *m.* meteorism.

meteorolábil *adj.* meteorosensitive.

meteoropatía *f.* meteoropathy.

meteoropatología *f.* meteoropathology.

meteorresistente *adj.* meteororesistant.

meteorosensitivo, -va *adj.* meteorosensitive.

meteorotrópico, -ca *adj.* meteorotropic.

meteorotropismo *m.* meteorotropism.

metepencéfalo *m.* metepencephalon.

metergasia *f.* metergasia, metergasis.

metergasis *f.* metergasia, metergasis.

metilación *f.* methylation.

metilación de ADN DNA methylation.

metilado, -da *adj.* methylated.

metilar *v.* methylate.

metilcelulosa *f.* methylcellulose.

metilepsia *f.* methilepsia.

metílico, -ca *adj.* methylic.

método *m.* method.

método de Abbott Abbott's method.

método ABC alum, blood, charcoal method, ABC method.

método de Abell-Kendall Abell-Kendall.

método abortivo abortive method.

método de absorción absorption method.

método de la acetona acetone test.

método de achard-castaigne methylene blue test.

método para los ácidos grasos method for fatty acids.

método para el ácido oxálico Salkowski, Autenrieth and Barth method.

método para la actividad péptica method for peptic activity.

método de alineación controlada del contorno trocantérico en aducción contoured adducted trochanteric controlled alignment method.

método de Altmann-Gersh Altmann-Gersh method.

método aristotélico Aristotelian method.

método de Ashby Ashby's method.

método de Askenstedt Askenstedt's method.

método de autoclave autoclave method.

método auxanográfico auxanographic method.

método para los azúcares method for sugar.

método para el azufre total total method for sulfur.

método de Barger Barger's method.

método de barraquer Barraquer's method.

método de barrera barrier method.

método de Barsony-Koppenstein Barsony-Koppenstein's.

método para las bases fijas, método para las bases fijas totales fixed base method, method for total fixed base.

método de Baudelocque Baudelocque's method.

método de Beck Beck's method.

método de Benassi Benassi method.

método de Bertel Bertel's method.

método de bier Bier's treatment.

método de Billings Billings method.

método para el dióxido de carbono van Slyke and Cullen method.

método Blackett-Healy Blackett-Healy method.

método de Bloor, Pelkan y Allen Bloor, Pelkan and Allen's method.

método de Bock y Benedict Bock and Benedict's method.

método de Born de reconstrucción con placas de cera Born method of wax plate reconstruction.

método de Bradley Bradley's method.

método de Brandt-Andrews Brandt-Andrews maneuver.

método de Brasdor Brasdor's method.

método de Brehmer Brehmer's method.

método para el calcio method for calcium.

método del calibre caliper method.

método del calendario de planificación familiar calendar method of family planning.

método de Callahan Callahan's method.

método de Carrel Carrel's method.

método de Carrel-Dakin Carrel-Dakin method.

método de Castañeda Castañeda's method.

método de Charters Charters' method.

método de Chayes Chayes' method.

método de Chick-Martin Chick-Martin method.

método de Ciaccio Ciaccio's method.

método científico scientific method.

método de circuito abierto open circuit method.

método de circuito cerrado closed circuit method.

método de Clark-Collip Clark-Collip method.

método de la cloropercha chloropercha method.

método para los cloruros method for chlorides.

método para el colesterol method for cholesterol.

método comparativo comparative.

método para la concentración de huevecillos ova concentration method.

método de condensación lateral lateral condensation method.

método de condensación vertical vertical condensation method.

método de confrontación confrontation method.

método de confrontación marginal amplia broad marginal confrontation.

método del cono de plata silver cone method.

método de cono único single cone method.

método del cono múltiple multiple cone method.

método contraceptivo contraceptive method.

método de Converse Converse method.

método de Corley y Denis Corley and Denis' method.

método correlativo correlational method.

método de cortes transversales cross-sectional method.

método de Couette Couette method.

método de Coutard Coutard's method.

método para la creatina method for creatine.

método de Credé Credé's method.

método de Cronin Cronin method.

método de Cuignet Cuignet's method.

método de cultivo culture procedure.

método de Denis y Leche Denis and Leche's method.

método de Denman Denman's method.

método de la densidad óptica optical density method.

método para la dextrosa method for dextrose.

método de Dick-Read Dick-Read method.

método de Dieffenbach Dieffenbach's method.

método de difusión diffusion method.

método de difusión en disco disk diffusion method.

método de Dickinson Dickinson method.

método de dilución de helio en sistema cerrado closed system helium dilution method.

método directo direct method.

método directo para hacer incrustaciones direct method for making inlays.

método de doble anticuerpo double antibody method.

método de dosificación de fluctuación limitada limited fluctuation method of dosing.

método de dosificación máxima peak method of dosing.

método de Duke Duke's method.

método de Duncan autotherapy.

método de Eicken Eicken's method.

método de Ellinger Ellinger's method.

método empírico trial and error method.

método de Epstein Epstein's method.

método experimental experimental method.

método de expulsión de Leboyer Leboyer method of delivery.

método de Fahraeus Fahraeus method.

método de Faust Faust's method.

método de Fick Fick method.

método para el filtrado de sangre libre de proteínas method for protein-free blood filtrate.

método de Fiske Fiske's method.

método de Fiske y Subbarow Fiske and Subbarow's method.

método del flash flash method.

método de Fleischer Fleischer.

método de flotación flotation method.

método de Folin Folin's method.

método de Folin y Wu Folin and Wu's method.

método de Fone Fone's method.

método del formol y éter de Ritchie Ritchie's formol ether method.

método para los fosfatos inorgánicos method for inorganic phosphates.

método para el fósforo acidosoluble method for acid soluble phosphorus.

método de Fülleborn Fülleborn's method.

método de Gärtner Gärtner's method.

método de Gerota Gerota's method.

método de Givens Givens' method.

método para la glucosa method for glucose.

método de glucosa oxidasa glucose oxidase method.

método de Gräupner Gräupner's.

método Greulich-Pyle Greulich-Pyle method.

método de Gruber Gruber's method.

método para la guanidina method for guanidine.

método Gunson Gunson method.

método de Haas Haas method.

método de Hamilton Hamilton's method.

método de Hammerschlag Hammerschlag's method.

método de Handley lymphangioplasty.

método de Hartel Hartel's treatment.

método de Heintz Heintz's method.

método de la hematina ácida, método para la hemoglobina acid hematin method, hemoglobin method.

método de Henschen Henschen method.

método de Herter y Foster Herter and Foster method.

método de Heublein Heublein's method.

método de hexocinasa hexokinase method.

método para el hierro method for iron.

método de Hirschberg Hirschberg's method.

método de Hirschfeld Hirschfeld's method.

método de Holmgren Holmgren method.

método de Howell Howell's method.

método de Hung Hung's method.

método para el indicán method for indican.

método indirecto para hacer incrustaciones indirect method for making inlays.

método de indofenol indophenol method.

método para el indol Herter and Foster method.

método inductivo inductive approach.

método de infusión con torniquete tourniquet infusion method.

método de inmunofluorescencia immunofluorescence method.

método introspectivo introspective method.

método de Ivy Ivy's method.

método de Jaboulay Jaboulay's method.

método de Johnson Johnson's method.

método de Judd Judd method.

método de Karr Karr's method.

método de Kasabach Kasabach method.

método de Kendall Kendall's method.

método de Kenny Kenny's treatment.

método de Kety-Schmidt Kety-Schmidt method.

método de Killian bronchoscopy.

método de Kirstein Kirstein's method.

método de Kite Kite method.

método de Kjeldahl Kjedahl's method.

método de Klapp Klapp's method.

método de Krause Krause's.

método de Klüver-Barrera Klüver-Barrera method.

método de Knaus-Ogino Knaus-Ogino's method.

método Kuchendorf Kuchendorf method.

método de Laborde Laborde's method.

método de Lamaze Lamaze method.

método de Lane Lane method.

método de Lauenstein Lauenstein method.

método de Law Law method.

método de Leboyer Leboyer method.

método de Lee-White Lee-White method.

método de Ling Ling's method.

método de Lister Lister's.

método de localización de Sweet Sweet localization method.

método longitudinal longitudinal method.

método de Lyon Meltzer-Lyon test.

método de Lysholm Lysholm method.

método macro-Kjeldahl macro-Kjeldahl method.

método de Marchi Marchi's method.
método de Marshall Marshall's method.
método de McCrudden McCrudden method.
método de Meltzer Meltzer's method.
método de Meltzer-Lyon Meltzer-Lyon test.
método de Meyer Meyer's method.
método microbiológicos culture media method.
método micro-Kjeldahl micro-Kjeldahl method.
método del modelo dividido split cast method.
método de Mohr Mohr's method.
método del molde dividido split cast method.
método del molde de yeso cerrado[1] Orr treatment.
método del molde de yeso cerrado[2] Trueta treatment.
método de Moore Moore's method.
método de Murphy Murphy method.
método de Myers y Wardell Myers and Wardell's method.
método de Nägeli Nägeli's maneuver.
método natural natural method.
método de Needles del modelo dividido Needles' split cast method.
método de Nikiforoff Nikiforoff's method.
método para el nitrógeno de aminoácidos method for aminoacid nitrogen.
método para el nitrógeno de amoniaco method for amoniac nitrogen.
método del número de oro gold number method.
método de Ogata Ogata's method.
método de Ogino-Knaus Ogino-Knaus method.
método de ollier Ollier's graft.
método de Orr Orr method.
método de Orsi-Grocco Orsi-Grocco method.
método de Osborne y Folin Osborne and Folin's method.
método de la ovulación para planificación familiar ovulation method of family planning.
método de Paracelso Paracelsian method.
método de la parafina paraffin method.
método parallax parallax method.
método de Parker Parker's method.
método de Pavlov Pavlov method.
método de planificación familiar del moco cervical cervical mucus method of family planning.
método de planificación familiar mediante la temperatura basal basal body temperature method of family planning.
método de planificación familiar natural natural family planning method.
método de Porges Porges method.
método de la precipitación de plata de Home Home's silver precipitation method.
método de Price-Jones Price-Jones method.
método del punto de plata silver point method.
método para los cuerpos púrico method for purine bodies.
método de Purman Purman's method.
método de Read Read method.
método de Rehfuss Rehfuss method.
método para la reserva alcalina van Slyke and Cullen method, van Slyke and Fitz method.
método de la retirada withdrawal method.
método de Reverding Reverding's method.

método de Ritgen Ritgen's method.
método del ritmo rhythm method.
método de Roux Roux's method.
método de Sahli Sahli's method.
método de Saling Saling's method.
método de Salkowski, Autenrieth y Barth Salkowski, Autenrieth, and Barth's method.
método de Satterthwaite Satterthwaite method.
método de Scarpa Scarpa's method.
método de Schaffer Schaffer method.
método de Scherer Scherer's method.
método de Schick Schick's method.
método de Schmidt-Thannhauser Schmidt-Thannhauser method.
método de Schlösser Schlösser's treatment.
método de Schüller Schüller's method.
método de sección congelada frozen section method.
método seccional, método de segmentación sectional method, segmentation method.
método de sensibilidad por discos disk sensitivity method.
método de Shohl y Pedley Shohl and Pedley's method.
método de Siffert Siffert's method.
método sintotérmico de planificación familiar symptomthermal method of family planning.
método de Sluder Sluder's method.
método de Smellie Smellie's method.
método de Stas-Otto Stas-Otto method.
método de Stehle Stehle's method.
método de Stroganoff Stroganoff's method.
método subperióstico de Ollier Ollier's graft.
método del sulfato de cobre copper sulfate method.
método de Sumner Sumner's method.
método de suspensión suspension method.
método de temperatura basal basal temperature method.
método de Thane Thane's method.
método de Theden Theden's method.
método de Thiersch Thiersch's method.
método de tinción de Feulgen Feulgen stainning method.
método de tiocromo thiochrome method.
método del trazador depot tracer depot method.
método de Trueta Trueta treatment.
método ultraopaco ultropaque method.
método de van Gehuchten van Gehuchten's method.
método de van Slyke van Slyke's method.
método de van Slyke y Cullen Van Slyke and Cullen's method.
método de van Slyke y Fitz van Slyke and Fitz's method.
método de van Slyke y Meyer van Slyke and Meyer method.
método de van Slyke y Palmer van Slyke and Palmer method.
método de Walker Walker's method.
método de Waring Waring's method.
método de Weber Weber's method.
método de Welcker Welcker's method.
método de Welker Welker's method.
método de Westergren Westergren's method.
método de Wheeler Wheeler's method.
método de Whipple Whipple's method.
método Wiechowski y Handorsky Wiechowski and Handorsky's method.
método de Wilson Wilson's method.

método de Wintrobe Wintrobe method.
método de Wintrobe y Landsberg Wintrobe and Landsberg's method.
método de Wolfe Wolfe's method.
método de Wolter Wolter's method.
método de Wynn Wynn's method.
método para el yodo Kendall's method.
metodología f. methodology.
metomanía f. methomania.
metomioglobina f. metmyoglobin.
metonimia f. metonymy.
metópago m. metopagus, metopopagus.
metópico, -ca adj. metopic.
metopión m. metopion.
metopismo m. metopism.
metoplastia f. metoplasty.
metopodinia f. metopodynia.
metopón m. metopon.
metopoplastia f. metopoplasty.
metoposcopia f. metoposcopy.
metraatrofia f. metratrophy, metratrophia.
metralgia f. metralgia.
metratomía f. hysterotomy.
metratonía f. metratonia.
metratrofia f. metratrophia.
metrecoscopia f. metrechoscopy.
metrectasia f. metrectasia.
metrectomía f. metrectomy.
metrectopia f. metrectopia.
metrenfisema m. physometra.
metreurínter m. metreurynter.
metreurisis f. metreurysis.
metria f. metria.
metriocefálico, -ca adj. metriocephalic.
metritis f. metritis.
 metritis disecante dissecting metritis, metritis dissecans.
 metritis mucosa endometritis.
 metritis puerperal puerperal metritis.
metro m. meter.
 metro de flujo máximo peak flow meter.
 metro de luz light meter.
 metro de posología dosage meter.
metrocarcinoma m. metrocarcinoma.
metrocele m. metrocele.
metrocistosis f. metrocystosis.
metrocolpocele m. metrocolpocele.
metrodinia f. metrodynia.
metroendometritis f. metroendometritis.
metroestenosis f. metrostenosis.
metrofibroma m. metrofibroma.
metroflebitis f. metrophlebitis.
metrógeno, -na adj. metrogenous.
metrografia f. metrography.
metroleucorrea f. metroleukorrhea.
metrolinfangitis f. metrolymphangitis.
metrología f. metrology.
metromalacia f. metromalacia.
metromalacoma m. metromalacoma.
metromalacosis f. metromalacosis.
metromenorragia f. metromenorrhagia.
metronoscopio m. metronoscope.
metroparálisis f. metroparalysis.
metropatía f. metropathy.
 metropatía hemorrágica metropathy hemorrhagica.
metropático, -ca adj. metropathic.
metroperitoneal adj. metroperitoneal.
metroperitonitis f. metroperitonitis.
metropexia f. hysteropexy.
metroplastia f. metroplasty.
metroptosia f. metroptosis.
metroptosis f. metroptosis.
metrorragia f. metrorrhagia.
metrorrea f. metrorrhea.

metrorrexia *f.* metrorrhexis.
metrorrexis *f.* metrorrhexis.
metrosalpingitis *f.* metrosalpingitis.
metrosalpingografía *f.* metrosalpingography.
metroscopio *m.* metroscope.
metrostaxis *f.* metrostaxis.
metrostenosis *f.* metrostenosis.
metrotéresis *f.* hysterectomy.
metrotomía *f.* metrotomy.
metrotoxina *f.* metrotoxin.
metrotubografía *f.* metrotubography.
meyopragia *f.* miopragia.
mezcla *f.* mixture.
  mezcla extemporánea extemporaneous mixture.
mezclado *m.* mixing.
mialgia *f.* myalgia.
  mialgia abdominal myalgia abdominis.
  mialgia cefálica myalgia capitis.
  mialgia cervical myalgia cervicalis.
  mialgia craneal myalgia capitis.
  mialgia epidémica epidemic myalgia.
  mialgia lumbar lumbar myalgia.
  mialgia térmica myalgia thermica.
miana *f.* miana.
miasis *f.* myasis, myiasis.
  miasis dérmica tumbu tumbu myasis.
  miasis foruncular africana African furuncular myasis.
  miasis de heridas wound myasis.
  miasis intestinal intestinal myasis.
  miasis por moscardón humano human botfly myasis.
  miasis nasal nasal myasis.
  miasis ocular ocular myasis.
  miasis reptante creeping myasis.
  miasis subcutánea subcutaneous myasis.
  miasis traumática traumatic myasis.
miasma *m.* miasma.
miasmático, -ca *adj.* miasmatic.
miastenia *f.* myasthenia.
  miastenia gástrica myasthenia gastrica.
  miastenia grave, miastenia grave seudoparalítica myasthenia gravis, myasthenia gravis pseudoparalytica.
  miastenia laríngea myasthenia laryngis.
  miastenia neonatal neonatal myasthenia.
miasténico, -ca *adj.* myasthenic.
miasteniforme *adj.* myasteniform.
miatonía *f.* myatonia, myatony.
  miatonía congénita myatonia congenita.
miatrofia *f.* myatrophy, myoatrophy.
micáceo, -a *adj.* micaceous.
micación *f.* mication.
micatosis *f.* micatosis.
micciometría *f.* micciometry.
micción *f.* miction, urination.
  micción en dos tiempos pis en deux temps.
  micción involuntaria enuresis.
  micción precipitada precipitant urination.
  micción refleja enuresis.
  micción tartamuda, micción tartamudeante stuttering urination.
micela *f.* micella, micelle.
micelar *adj.* micellar.
miceliano, -na *adj.* mycelian.
micélico, -ca *adj.* mycelial.
micelio *m.* mycelium.
  micelio aéreo aerial mycelium.
  micelio septado, micelio tabicado septate mycelium.
  micelio no septado non-septate mycelium.
micelioide *adj.* mycelioid.
micesis *f.* myzesis.
micetemia *f.* mycethemia.

micetismo *m.* mycetismus.
  micetismo cerebral mycetismus cerebris.
  micetismo coleriforme mycetismus choleriformis.
  micetismo gastrointestinal mycetismus gastrointestinalis.
  micetismo nervioso mycetismus nervosus.
  micetismo sanguinario mycetismus sanguinarius.
miceto *m.* mycete.
micetogénico, -ca *adj.* mycetogenetic.
micetógeno, -na *adj.* mycetogenic, mycetogenous.
micetología *f.* mycology.
micetoma *m.* mycetoma.
  micetoma actinomicótico actimomycotic mycetoma.
  micetoma blanco de Bouffardi Bouffardi's white mycetoma.
  micetoma blanco de Brumpt Brumpt's white mycetoma.
  micetoma blanco de Nicolle Nicolle's white mycetoma.
  micetoma blanco de Vincent Vincent's white mycetoma.
  micetoma eumicótico eumycotic mycetoma.
  micetoma negro de Bouffardi Bouffardi's black mycetoma.
  micetoma negro de Carter Carter's black mycetoma.
micetosis *f.* mycosis.
mícide *adj.* mycid.
micoaglutinina *f.* mycoagglutinin.
micoangioneurosis *f.* mucous colitis.
micobacteria *f.* mycobacteria.
  micobacteria anónima, micobacteria atípica anonymous mycobacteria, atypical mycobacteria.
micobacteriosis *f.* mycobacteriosis.
micobactina *f.* mycobactin.
micocida *m.* mycocide.
micoderma *m.* mycoderma.
micodermatitis *f.* mycodermatitis.
micodermomicosis *f.* mycodermomycosis.
micodesmoide *m.* botryomycosis.
micoesteroles *m.* mycosterols.
micofagia *f.* mycophagy.
micófago *m.* mycophage.
micofibroma *m.* botryomycosis.
micogastritis *f.* mycogastritis.
micohemia *f.* mycohemia.
micología *f.* mycology.
  micología médica medical mycology.
micólogo, -ga *m.* mycologist.
micomiringitis *f.* mycomyringitis.
micopatología *f.* mycopathology.
micoplasma *m.* micoplasma.
  micoplasma de cepa T T-strain micoplasma.
micoplasmático, -ca *adj.* mycoplasmal.
micoprecipitina *f.* mycoprecipitin.
micoproteinación *f.* mycoproteination.
micopús *m.* mycopus.
micosis *f.* mycosis.
  micosis cutánea tinea.
  micosis crónica mycosis chronica.
  micosis de Posadas Posadas mycosis.
  micosis favosa favus.
  micosis framboesioides mycosis framboesioides.
  micosis fungoides mycosis fungoides.
  micosis interdigital athlete's foot.
  micosis intestinal, micosis intestinalis mycosis intestinalis.
  micosis leptótrica mycosis leptotrica.
micostasis *f.* mycostasis.

micostático, -ca *adj.* mycostatic.
micótico, -ca *adj.* mycotic.
micotoxicosis *f.* mycotoxicosis.
micotoxina *f.* mycotoxin.
micotoxinización *f.* mycotoxinization.
micovirus *m.* mycovirus.
micracústico, -ca *adj.* micracoustic.
micranatomía *f.* microanatomy.
micrangio *m.* micrangium.
micrangiopatía *f.* microangiopathy.
micrergia *f.* micrergy.
microabsceso *m.* microabscess.
  microabsceso de Munro Munro microabscess.
  microabsceso de Pautrier Pautrier's microabscess.
microacústico, -ca *adj.* microacoustic.
microadenoma *m.* microadenoma.
microadenopatía *f.* microadenopathy.
microaerobio *m.* microaerobion.
microaerófilo, -la *adj.* microaerophilic.
microaerosol *m.* microaerosol.
microaerotonómetro *m.* microaerotonometer.
microagregado *m.* microaggregate.
microaguja *f.* microneedle.
microalbuminuria *f.* microalbuminuria.
microambiente *m.* microenvironment.
microanálisis *f.* microanalysis.
microanastomosis *f.* microanastomosis.
microanatomía *f.* micranatomy.
microanatomista *m., f.* microanatomist.
microaneurisma *m.* microaneurysm.
microangiografía *f.* microangiography.
microangiopatía *f.* microangiopathy.
  microangiopatía trombótica thrombotic microangiopathy.
microangiopático, -ca *adj.* microangiopathic.
microangioscopia *f.* microangioscopy.
microarteriografía *f.* microarteriography.
microarteriográfico, -ca *adj.* microarteriographic.
microbacteria *f.* microbacterium.
Microbacterium Microbacterium.
microbalanza *f.* microbalance.
microbiano, -na *adj.* microbic, microbial, microbian.
microbicida[1] *m.* microbicide.
microbicida[1] *adj.* microbicidal.
micróbide *f.* microbid.
microbiemia *f.* microbiemia.
microbihemia *f.* microbiemia.
microbio *m.* microbe.
microbioensayo *m.* microbioassay.
microbiofotómetro *m.* microbiophotometer.
microbiohemia *f.* microbiemia.
microbioinvestigación *f.* microbioassay.
microbiología *f.* microbiology.
microbiológico, -ca *adj.* microbiological.
microbiólogo, -ga *m., f.* microbiologist.
microbiosis *f.* microbism.
microbiota *m.* microbiota.
microbiótico, -ca *adj.* microbiotic.
microbismo *m.* microbism.
microbívoro *m.* bacteriophage.
microblasto *m.* microblast.
microblefaria *f.* microblepharia.
microblefarismo *m.* microblepharism.
microbléfaron *m.* microblepharon.
microbraquia *f.* microbrachia.
microbraquio *m.* microbrachius.
microbrenner *m.* microbrenner.
microbureta *f.* microburet.
microcalcificación *f.* microcalcification.
microcáliz *m.* microcalix, microcalyx.
microcaloría *f.* microcalorie.
microcapsulación *f.* microencapsulation.

microcardia *f.* microcardia.
microcaulia *f.* microcaulia.
microcefalia *f.* microcephalia, microcephaly.
microcefálico, -ca *adj.* microcephalic, microcephalous.
microcefalismo *m.* microcephalism.
microcéfalo *m.* microcephalus.
microcentro *m.* microcentrum.
microcinematografía *f.* microcinematography, microkinematography.
microcirculación *f.* microcirculation.
microcircunvolución *f.* microcircunvolution.
microcirugía *f.* microsurgery.
microcistómetro *m.* microcystometer.
microcitemia *f.* microcythemia.
microcítico, -ca *adj.* microcytic.
microcito *m.* microcyte.
microcitosis *f.* microcytosis.
microcitotoxicidad *f.* microcytotoxicity.
microcnemia *f.* microcnemia.
micrococaceae Micrococaceae.
Micrococáceas *f.* Micrococaceae.
Micrococcus Micrococcus.
micrococo *m.* micrococcus.
microcolitis *f.* microcolitis.
microcolon *m.* microcolon.
microcolonia *f.* microcolony.
microconcentración *f.* microconcentration.
microconidio *m.* microconidium.
microcoria *f.* microcoria.
microcórnea *f.* microcornea.
microcrania *f.* microcrania.
microcristal *m.* microcrystal.
microcristalino, -na *adj.* microcrystalline.
microdactilia *f.* microdactilia, microdactyly.
microdáctilo, -la *adj.* microdactylous.
microdeleción *f.* microdeletion.
microdensitómetro *m.* microdensitometer.
microdentismo *m.* microdentism.
microdermatomo *m.* microdermatome.
microdeterminación *f.* microdetermination.
microdisección *f.* microdisection.
microdoncia *f.* microdontia.
microdontia *f.* microdontia.
microdóntico, -ca *adj.* microdontic.
microdontismo *m.* microdontism.
microdonto *m.* microdont.
microdosificación *f.* microdosage.
microdosis *f.* microdose.
microdrepanocitico, -ca *adj.* microdrepanocytic.
microdrepanocitosis *f.* microdrepanocytosis.
microecología *m.* microecology.
microelectrodo *m.* microelectrode.
microelectroforesis *f.* microelectrophoresis.
microelectroforético, -ca *adj.* microelectrophoretic.
microelemento *m.* microelement.
microémbolo *m.* microembolus.
microencefalia *f.* micrencephaly.
microencéfalo *m.* micrencephalon.
microencefálico, -ca *adj.* micrencephalous.
microeritrocito *m.* microerythrocyte.
microescintigrafía *f.* microscintigraphy.
microesferocito *m.* microspherocyte.
microesferocitosis *f.* microspherocytosis.
microespectrofotometría *f.* microspectrophotometry.
microespectrofotómetro *m.* microspectrophotometer.
microespectroscopio *m.* microspectroscope.
microesplácnico, -ca *adj.* microsplanchnic.
microesplenia *f.* microsplenia.
microesplénico, -ca *adj.* microsplenic.
microestetófono *m.* microstethophone.

microestetoscopio *m.* microstethoscope.
microestimación *f.* microestimation.
microestrabismo *m.* microstrabismus.
micrófago, -ga *m.* microphage.
microfagocito *m.* microphagocyte.
microfalia *f.* microphallus.
microfaquia *f.* microphakia.
microfasia *f.* microphakia.
microfauna *f.* microfauna.
microfibrilla *f.* microfibril.
microfilamento *m.* microfilament.
microfilaremia *f.* microfilaremia.
microfilaria *f.* microfilaria.
microfísica *f.* microphysics.
microfito *m.* microphyte.
microflora *f.* microflora.
microfluorometría *f.* microfluorometry.
microfonía *f.* microphonia, microphony.
microfónico, -ca *adj.* microphonic.
micrófono *m.* microphone.
microfotografía *f.* microphotograph.
microftalmía *f.* microphthalmos.
microftalmo *m.* microphthalmus.
microftalmos *m.* microphthalmos.
microftalmoscopio *m.* microphthalmoscope.
microfulgurador *m.* microbrenner.
microgameto *m.* microgamete.
microgametocito *m.* microgametocyte.
microgamia *f.* microgamy.
microgamonte *m.* microgamont.
microgamonto *m.* microgamont.
microgastria *f.* microgastria.
microgénesis *f.* microgenesis.
microgenia *f.* microgenia.
microgenitalia *f.* microgenitalism.
microgenitalismo *m.* microgenitalism.
microgiria *f.* microgyria.
microgiria esclerótica sclerotic microgyria.
microgiro *m.* microgyrus.
microglia *f.* microglia.
microgliacito *m.* microgliacyte.
microglial *adj.* microglial.
microgliocito *m.* microgliacyte, microgliocyte.
microglioma *m.* microglioma.
microgliomatosis *f.* microgliomatosis.
microgliosis *f.* microgliosis.
microglobulina *f.* microglobulin.
microglosia *f.* microglossia.
micrognatia *f.* micrognathia.
micrognacia *f.* micrognathia.
micrognacia con peromelia micrognathia with peromelia.
microgonioscopio *m.* microgonioscope.
microgotero *m.* microdrip.
micrografía *f.* micrography.
micrógrafo *m.* micrographer.
microhematocrito *m.* microhematocrit.
microhepatía *f.* microhepatia.
microhistología *f.* microhistology.
microincineración *f.* microincineration.
microincisión *f.* microincision.
microinfarto *m.* microinfarct.
microinjerto *m.* micrograft.
microinvasión *f.* microinvasion.
microinvasor, -ra *adj.* microinvasive.
microinyector *m.* microinjector.
microjeringa *f.* microsyringe.
microlaringoscopia *f.* microlaryngoscopy.
microlecito, -ta *adj.* microlecithal.
microlentia *f.* microlentia.
microlesión *f.* microlesion.
microleucoblasto *m.* microleukoblast.
microlinfoidocito *m.* microlymphoidocyte.
microlitiasis *f.* microlithiasis.

microlitiasis alveolar, microlitiasis alveolar pulmonar alveolar microlithiasis, pulmonary alveolar microlithiasis.
microlito *m.* microlith.
micromanía *f.* micromania.
micromanipulación *f.* micromanipulation.
micromanipulador *m.* micromanipulator.
micromanométrico, -ca *adj.* micromanometric.
micromanómetro *m.* micromanometer.
micromastia *f.* micromastia.
micromaxilia *f.* micromaxilla.
micromazia *f.* micromazia.
micromegalopsia *f.* micromegalopsia.
micromelia *f.* micromelia.
micromelo *m.* micromelus.
micrómera *f.* micromere.
micrómero *m.* micromere.
micromerozoíto *m.* micromerozoite.
micrometabolismo *m.* micrometabolism.
micrometástasis *f.* micrometastasis.
micrometastático, -ca *adj.* micrometastasic.
micrométodo *m.* micromethod.
micrometría *f.* micrometry.
micrómetro *m.* micrometer.
micrómetro a compás caliper micrometer.
micrómetro para portaobjetos slide micrometer.
micromielia *f.* micromyelia.
micromieloblasto *m.* micromyeloblast.
micromielolinfocito *m.* micromyelolymphocyte.
micromolar *adj.* micromolar.
micromolecular *adj.* micromolecular.
Micromonospora Micromonospora.
Micromonosporaceae Micromonosporaceae.
micromotoscopio *m.* micromotoscope.
micron *m.* micron.
micronema *m.* microneme.
microneurocirugía *f.* microneurosurgery.
micrónico, -ca *adj.* micronic.
micronicosis *f.* micronychosis.
microniquia *f.* micronychia.
micronistagmo *m.* mycronystagmus.
micronizar *v.* micronize.
micronodular *adj.* micronodular.
micronormoblasto *m.* micronormoblast.
micronúcleo *m.* micronucleus.
micronutriente *m.* micronutrient.
microorgánico, -ca *adj.* microorganic.
microorganismo *m.* microorganism.
microorquia *f.* microrchidia.
microorquidia *f.* microrchidia.
microorquidismo *m.* micro-orchidism.
microosmático, -ca *adj.* microsmatic.
microparásito *m.* microparasite.
micropatología *f.* micropathology.
micropene *m.* micropenis.
microperfusión *f.* microperfusion.
micropía *f.* micropia.
micropinocitosis *f.* micropinocytosis.
micropipeta *f.* micropipet.
microplasia *f.* microplasia.
micropletismografía *f.* microplethysmography.
micropodia *f.* micropodia.
micrópodo *m.* micropodus.
micropolariscopio *m.* micropolariscope.
micropoligiria *f.* micropolygyria.
microprecipitación *f.* microprecipitation.
microprolactinoma *f.* microprolactinoma.
microprosopia *f.* microprosopia.
microprosopo *m.* microprosopus.
microproyección *f.* microprojection.
microproyector *m.* microprojector.

micropsia *f.* micropsia.
micróptico, -ca *adj.* microptic.
micropunción *f.* micropuncture.
micropuntura *f.* micropuncture.
microqueilia *f.* microcheilia, microchilia.
microquilia *f.* microchilia.
microquímica *f.* microchemistry.
microquímico, -ca *adj.* microchemical.
microqueiria *f.* microcheiria, microchiria.
microquiria *f.* microchiria.
microquiste *m.* microcyst.
microrradiografía *f.* microradiography.
microrradiográfico, -ca *adj.* micorradiographic.
microrradiograma *m.* microradiogram.
microrreentrada *f.* microreentry.
microrrefractómetro *m.* microrefractometer.
microrrespirómetro *m.* microrespirometer.
microrrinia *f.* microrhinia.
microsacudidas *f.* microsaccades.
microscelia *f.* microscelia.
microscopía *f.* microscopy.
  microscopía clínica clinical microscopy.
  microscopía electrónica electron microscopy.
  microscopía electrónica de barrido scanning electron microscopy.
  microscopía electrónica de barrido de transmisión (MEBT) transmission scanning electron microscopy (TSEM).
  microscopía de fluorescencia, microscopía fluorescente fluorescence microscopy.
  microscopía de fondo, microscopía fúndica fundus microscopy.
  microscopía de inmersión immersion microscopy.
  microscopía inmunoelectrónica immune electron microscopy.
  microscopía de inmunofluorescencia, microscopía inmunofluorescente immunofluorescence microscopy.
  microscopía ultravioleta ultraviolet microscopy.
microscópico, -ca *adj.* microscopic, microscopical.
microscopio *m.* microscope.
  microscopio acústico acoustic microscope.
  microscopio de barrido scanning microscope.
  microscopio de campo oscuro dark-field microscope.
  microscopio capilar capillary microscope.
  microscopio centrífugo centrifuge microscope.
  microscopio de comparación, microscopio comparativo comparator microscope.
  microscopio compuesto compound microscope.
  microscopio de contraste de color color-contrast microscope.
  microscopio electrónico electron microscope.
  microscopio electrónico de barrido (MEG) scanning electron microscope (SEM).
  microscopio electrónico de barrido de transmisión transmission scanning electron microscope.
  microscopio eléctronico de centelleo scanning electron microscope.
  microscopio estereoscópico stereoscopic microscope.
  microscopio estroboscópico stroboscopic microscope.
  microscopio de fluorescencia, microscopio fluorescente fluorescence microscope.
  microscopio de Greenough Greenough microscope.

  microscopio hipodérmico hypodermic microscope.
  microscopio infrarrojo infrared microscope.
  microscopio de integración integrating microscope.
  microscopio de interferencia interference microscope.
  microscopio iónico ion microscope.
  microscopio de lámpara de hendidura slit lamp microscope.
  microscopio láser laser microscope.
  microscopio de luz light microscope.
  microscopio de luz polarizada polarizing microscope.
  microscopio opaco opaque microscope.
  microscopio de operaciones, microscopio operatorio operating microscope.
  microscopio de polarización, microscopio polarizante polarization microscope.
  microscopio de proyección de rayos X projection X ray microscope.
  microscopio quirúrgico operating microscope.
  microscopio de rayos beta beta ray microscope.
  microscopio de rayos X X-ray microscope.
  microscopio reflejante reflecting microscope.
  microscopio de Rheinberg Rheinberg microscope.
  microscopio trinocular trinocular microscope.
  microscopio ultrasónico acoustic microscope.
  microscopio ultravioleta ultraviolet microscope.
microscopista *m., f.* microscopist.
microsección *f.* microsection.
microsemo, -ma microseme.
microsferolito *m.* microspherolith.
microsfigmia *f.* microsphygmia, microsphygmy.
microsfixia *f.* microsphyxia.
microsoldadura *f.* microwelding.
microsoma *m.* microsoma.
microsomático, -ca *adj.* microsomal.
microsonda *f.* microprobe.
microspectroscopio *m.* microspectroscope.
microsplácnico, -ca *adj.* microsplanchnic.
microsplenia *f.* microsplenia.
microspora *f.* microspore.
Microspora Microspora.
Microsporasida Microsporasida.
Microsporida Microsporida.
microspóride *f.* microsporid.
microsporosis *f.* microsporosis.
Microsporum Microsporum.
microstato *m.* microstat.
microsténico, -ca *adj.* microsthenic.
microstomia *f.* microstomy.
microsutura *f.* microsuture.
microtelia *f.* microthelia.
microtermia *f.* microthermy.
microtia *f.* microtia.
microtítulo *m.* microtiter.
microto *m.* microtus.
microtomía *f.* microtomy.
microtomo *m.* microtome.
microtonómetro *m.* microtonometer.
microtransfusión *f.* microtransfusion.
microtrauma *m.* microtrauma.
Microtrombidium Microtrombidium.
microtrombo *m.* microthrombus.
microtrombosis *f.* microthrombosis.
microtropía *f.* microtropia.
microtúbulo *m.* microtubule.
microunidad *f.* microunit.
microvascular *adj.* microvascular.

microvasculatura *f.* microvasculature.
microvellosidad *f.* microvillus.
microvesícula *f.* microvesicle.
microviscosímetro *m.* microviscosimeter.
microvivisección *f.* microvivisection.
microvoltímetro *m.* microvoltimeter.
microxicito *m.* microxycyte.
microxifilo *m.* microxyphil.
microzoario *m.* microzoaria.
microzoo *m.* microzoon.
micrurgia *f.* micrurgy.
micrúrgico, -ca *adj.* micrurgic.
micruroides Micrurus.
Micrurus Micrurus.
mictérico, -ca *adj.* mycteric.
micteroxerosis *f.* mycteroxerosis.
micturición *f.* micturition.
midaleína *f.* mydaleine.
midatoxina *f.* mydatoxine.
midriasis *f.* mydriasis.
  midriasis alternante alternating mydriasis.
  midriasis amaurótica amaurotic mydriasis.
  midriasis artificial pharmacologic mydriasis.
  midriasis espasmódica spasmodic mydriasis.
  midriasis espástica spastic mydriasis.
  midriasis espinal spinal mydriasis.
  midriasis farmacológica pharmacologic mydriasis.
  midriasis paralítica paralytic mydriasis.
midriático, -ca *adj.* mydriatic.
miectomía *f.* miectomy.
miectopia *f.* myectopy, myectopia.
miedo *m.* fear.
miel *f.* honey.
mielacéfalo *m.* myelacephalus.
mielalgia *f.* myelalgia.
mielanalosis *f.* myelanalosis.
mielapoplejía *f.* myelapoplexy.
mielastenia *f.* myelasthenia.
mielatelia *f.* myelatelia.
mielatrofia *f.* myelatrophy.
mielauxa *f.* myelauxe.
mielemia *f.* myelemia.
mielencefalitis *f.* myelencephalitis.
mielencéfalo *m.* myelencephalon.
mielencefaloespinal *adj.* myelencephalospinal.
mieleterosis *f.* myeleterosis.
miélico, -ca *adj.* myelic.
mielina *f.* myelin.
mielinado, -da *adj.* myelinated.
mielínico, -ca *adj.* myelinic.
mielinización *f.* myelinization.
mielinizado, -da *adj.* myelinated.
mielinoclasia *f.* myelinoclasis.
mielinoclasis *f.* myelinoclasis.
mielinogénesis *m.* myelogenesis.
mielinogenético, -ca *adj.* myelogenetic.
mielinogenia *f.* myelogeny.
mielinolisina *f.* myelinolysin.
mielinólisis *f.* myelinolysis.
  mielinólisis central pontina central pontine myelinolysis.
mielinopatía *f.* myelinopathy.
mielinosis *f.* myelinosis.
mielinotoxicidad *f.* myelonotoxicity.
mielítico, -ca *adj.* myelitic.
mielitis *f.* myelitis.
  mielitis aguda acute myelitis.
  mielitis ascendente, mielitis ascendente aguda ascending myelitis, acute ascending myelitis.
  mielitis bulbar bulbar myelitis.
  mielitis central central myelitis.
  mielitis por compresión compression myelitis.

mielitis por concusión concussion myelitis.
mielitis por conmoción concussion myelitis.
mielitis cornual cornual myelitis.
mielitis crónica chronic myelitis.
mielitis descendente descending myelitis.
mielitis difusa diffuse myelitis.
mielitis diseminada disseminated myelitis.
mielitis de Foix-Alajouaine Foix-Alajouaine myelitis.
mielitis funicular funicular myelitis.
mielitis hemorrágica hemorrhagic myelitis.
mielitis necrosante subaguda subacute necrotizing myelitis.
mielitis neuroóptica neuro-optic myelitis.
mielitis periependimaria periependymal myelitis.
mielitis transversa, mielitis transversal transverse myelitis.
mielitis transversa aguda, mielitis transversal aguda acute transverse myelitis.
mielitis traumática traumatic myelitis.
mielitis por vacuna postvaccinal myelitis, myelitis vaccinia.
mieloarquitectura *f.* myeloarchitecture.
mieloblastemia *f.* myeloblastemia.
mieloblasto *m.* myeloblast.
mieloblastoma *m.* myeloblastoma.
mieloblastosis *f.* myeloblastosis.
mielocéfalo *m.* myelocephalus.
mielocele *m.* myelocele.
mielocelo *m.* myelocoele.
mielocéntrico, -ca *adj.* myelocentric.
mielocintigrama *m.* myeloscintogram.
mielocístico, -ca *adj.* myelocystic.
mielocisto *m.* myelocist.
mielocistocele *m.* myelocystele.
mielocistomeningocele *m.* myelocystomenyngocele.
mielocitemia *f.* myelocythemia.
mielocítico, -ca *adj.* myelocytic.
mielocito *m.* myelocyte.
mielocitoma *m.* myelocytoma.
mielocitomatosis *f.* myelocitomatosis.
mielocitosis *f.* myelocytosis.
mieloclasto *m.* myeloclast.
mielocono *m.* myelocone.
mielodiastasia *f.* myelodiastasis.
mielodiastasis *f.* myelodiastasia.
mielodisplasia *f.* myelodysplasia.
mieloencefálico, -ca *adj.* myeloencephalic.
mieloencefalitis *f.* myeloencephalitis.
mieloencefalitis eosinofílica eosinophilic myeloencephalitis.
mieloescintograma *m.* myeloscintogram.
mieloesclerosis *f.* myelosclerosis.
mieloespasmo *m.* myelospasm.
mielófago *m.* myelophage.
mielofibrosis *f.* myelofibrosis.
mielofibrosis osteoesclerótica osteosclerosis myclofibrosis.
mielófugo, -ga *adj.* myelofugal.
mielogénesis *f.* myelogenesis.
mielogenético, -ca *adj.* myelogenetic.
mielogenia *f.* myelogeny.
mielogénico, -ca *adj.* myelogenic.
mielógeno, -na *adj.* myelogenous.
mielogonia *f.* myelogone.
mielogónico, -ca *adj.* myelogonic.
mielografía *f.* myelography.
mielograma *m.* myelogram.
mieloico, -ca *adj.* myeloic.
mieloide *adj.* myeloid.
mieloideo, -a *adj.* myeloid.
mieloidina *f.* myeloidin.
mieloidosis *f.* myeloidosis.

mieloleucemia *f.* myeloleukemia.
mielolinfangioma *m.* myelolymphangioma.
mielolinfocito *m.* myelolymphocyte.
mielolipoma *m.* myelolipoma.
mielólisis *f.* myelolysis.
mielolítico, -ca *adj.* myelolytic.
mieloma *m.* myeloma.
mieloma de Bence Jones Bence Jones myeloma.
mieloma de cadena L L-chain myeloma.
mieloma de células plasmáticas plasma cell myeloma.
mieloma de células plasmáticas periféricas peripheral plasma cell myeloma.
mieloma endotelial endothelial myeloma.
mieloma extramedular extramedullary myeloma.
mieloma indolente indolent myeloma.
mieloma localizado localized myeloma.
mieloma múltiple multiple myeloma.
mieloma no secretorio non-secretory myeloma.
mieloma solitario solitary myeloma.
mielomalacia *f.* myelomalacia.
mielomatoide *adj.* myelomatoid.
mielomatosis *f.* myelomatosis.
mielomenia *f.* myelomenia.
mielomeningitis *f.* myelomeningitis.
mielomeningocele *m.* myelomeningocele.
mielómera *f.* myelomere.
mielómero *m.* myelomere.
mielomices *m.* myelomyces.
mielomonocito *m.* myelomonocyte.
mieloneuritis *f.* myeloneuritis.
mielónico, -ca *adj.* myelonic.
mieloopticoneuropatia *f.* myelo-opticoneuropathy.
mieloparálisis *f.* myeloparalysis.
mielopatía *f.* myelopathy.
mielopatía ascendente ascending myelopathy.
mielopatía cervical cervical myelopathy.
mielopatía cervical espondilótica cervical spondylotic myelopathy, spondylotic cervical myelopathy.
mielopatía carcinomatosa carcinomatous myelopathy.
mielopatía por compresión, mielopatía compresiva compressive myelopathy.
mielopatía por concusión concussion myelopathy.
mielopatía por conmoción concussion myelopathy.
mielopatía descendente descending myelopathy.
mielopatía diabética diabetic myelopathy.
mielopatía funicular funicular myelopathy.
mielopatía hemorrágica hemorrhagic myelopathy.
mielopatía paracarcinomatosa paracarcinomatous myclopathy.
mielopatía por radiaciones radiation myelopathy.
mielopatía transversa transverse myelopathy.
mielopatía traumática traumatic myelopathy.
mielopático, -ca *adj.* myelopathic.
mieloperoxidasa *f.* myeloperoxidase.
mielópeto, -ta *adj.* myelopetal.
mieloplaca *f.* myeloplaque.
mieloplasto *m.* myeloplast.
mieloplaxa *f.* myeloplax.
mieloplejía *f.* myeloplegia.
mieloporo *m.* myelopore.
mielopoyesis *f.* myelopoiesis.
mielopoyesis ectópica ectopic myelopoiesis.
mielopoyesis extramedular extramedullary myelopoiesis.

mielopoyético, -ca *adj.* myelopoietic.
mieloproliferativo, -va *adj.* myeloproliferative.
mieloquiste *m.* myelocyst.
mieloquístico, -ca *adj.* myelocystic.
mielorradiculitis *f.* myeloradiculitis.
mielorradiculodisplasia *f.* myeloradiculodysplasia.
mielorradiculopatía *f.* myeloradiculopathy.
mielorradiculopolineuronitis *f.* myeloradiculopolyneuronitis.
mielorrafia *f.* myelorrhaphy.
mielorragia *f.* myelorrhagia.
mielosarcoma *m.* myelosarcoma.
mielosarcomatosis *f.* myelosarcomatosis.
mielosclerosis *f.* myelosclerosis.
mielosífilis *f.* myelosyphilis.
mielosiringosis *f.* myelosyringosis.
mielosis *f.* myelosis.
mielosis aleucémica aleukemic myelosis.
mielosis crónica no leucémica chronic non-leukemic myelosis.
mielosis eritrémica erythremic myelosis.
mielosis funicular funicular myelosis.
mielosis leucémica leukemic myelosis.
mielosis leucopénica leukopenic myelosis.
mielosis no leucémica non-leukemic myelosis.
mielosis no leucémica crónica chronic non-leukemic myelosis.
mielosis subleucémica subleukemic myelosis.
mielospongio *m.* myelospongium.
mielosquisis *f.* myeloschisis.
mielosupresión *f.* myelosuppression.
mielosupresor, -ra *adj.* myelosuppressive.
mieloterapia *f.* myelotherapy.
mielotisis *f.* myelophthisis.
mielotísico, -ca *adj.* myelophthisic.
mielotomía *f.* myelotomy.
mielotomía de Bischof Bischof's myelotomy.
mielotomia comisural commissural myelotomy.
mielotomía de la línea media midline myelotomy.
mielotomía en T T myelotomy.
mielótomo *m.* myelotome.
mielotomografia *f.* myelotomography.
mielotoxicidad *f.* myelotoxicity.
mielotóxico, -ca *adj.* myelotoxic.
mielotoxina *f.* myelotoxin.
miembro *f.* limb, member, membrum.
miembro anacrótico anacrotic limb.
miembro catacrótico catacrotic limb.
miembro fantasma phantom member.
miembro inferior inferior limb, lower limb, membrum inferius.
miembro de la mujer membrum muliebre.
miembro sirena siren member.
miembro superior superior limb, upper limb, membrum superius.
miembro torácico thoracic limb.
miembro viril virile member, membrum virile.
mientérico, -ca *adj.* myenteric.
mienteron *m.* myenteron.
Miescheria Miescheria.
miestesia *f.* myesthesia.
migración *f.* migration.
migración anódica anodic migration.
migración catódica cathodic migration.
migración celular cellular migration.
migración dental fisiológica physiological tooth migration.
migración dental patológica pathologic tooth migration.

migración externa external migration.
migración interna internal migration.
migración del óvulo migration of the ovum.
migración retrógrada retrograde migration.
migración transperitoneal transperitoneal migration.
migraña *f.* migraine.
migraña abdominal abdominal migraine.
migraña acompañada accompanied migraine.
migraña con aura migraine with aura.
migraña sin aura migraine without aura.
migraña basilar basilar-artery migraine.
migraña clásica classic migraine.
migraña común common migraine.
migraña confusional aguda acute confusional migraine.
migraña fulgurante fulgurating migraine.
migraña de Harris Harris migraine.
migraña hemipléjica hemiplegic migraine.
migraña oftálmica ophthalmic migraine.
migraña oftalmopléjica ophthalmoplegic migraine.
migrañoso, -sa *adj.* migrainous.
miiasis *f.* myiasis.
miitis *f.* myitis.
miiodesopsia *f.* myodesopsia.
miiodopsia *f.* myodesopsia.
milámetro *m.* milammeter.
milfosis *f.* milphosis.
miliámetro *m.* milliammeter.
miliamperímetro *m.* milliamperemeter.
miliamperio *m.* milliampere.
miliar *adj.* miliary.
miliaria *f.* miliaria.
miliaria alba cristalina miliaria alba.
miliaria roja, miliaria rubra miliaria rubra.
miliequivalente *m.* milliequivalent.
milio *m.* millium.
milio coloidal colloid millium.
miliosis neonatal *f.* millia neonatorum.
milling-in milling-in.
millium millium.
milohioideo, -a *adj.* mylohyoid.
Mima Mima.
mimación *f.* mimmation.
mimesis *f.* mimesis.
mimético, -ca *adj.* mimetic.
mimetismo *m.* mimicry.
mímica *f.* mimic.
mímico, -ca *adj.* mimic.
mimmación *f.* mimmation.
mimosis *f.* mimosis.
mineral *m.* mineral.
mineralcorticoide *m.* mineralcorticoid.
mineralocorticoide *m.* mineralcorticoid.
mineralización *f.* mincralization.
mineralizado, -da *adj.* mineralized.
miniabdominoplastia *f.* miniabdominoplasty.
mini examen nervioso *m.* neurocheck.
mini examen del estado mental *m.* mini mental state examination.
minificar *v.* minify.
minilaparatomía *f.* minilaparatomy.
minilaparatomía pélvica pelvic minilaparatomy.
mínima *f.* minim.
minimización *f.* minimization.
mínimo *m.* minimum.
mínimo audible minimum audibile.
mínimo cognoscible minimum cognoscibile.
mínimo legible minimum legibile.
mínimo de luz light minimum.
mínimo separable minimum separabile.
mínimo visible visibile minimum.

minusvalía mental *f.* mental handicap.
minusválido, -da *adj.* handicapped.
minutesis *f.* minuthesis.
mioalbúmina *f.* myoalbumin.
mioadenilato desaminasa *m.* myoadenylate deaminase.
mioarquitectónico, -ca *adj.* myoarchitectonic.
mioastenia *f.* myoasthenia.
mioatrofia *f.* myoatrophy.
mioautonomía *f.* myoautonomy.
mioblástico, -ca *adj.* myoblastic.
mioblasto *m.* myoblast.
mioblastoma *m.* myoblastoma.
mioblastomioma *m.* myoblastomyoma.
miobradia *f.* myobradia.
miocardia *f.* myocardia.
miocárdico, -ca *adj.* myocardiac, myocardial.
miocardio *m.* myocardium.
miocardio aturdido stunned myocardium.
miocardiógrafo *m.* myocardiograph.
miocardiograma *m.* myocardiogram.
miocardiólisis *f.* myocardiolysis.
miocardiopatía *f.* myocardiopathy.
miocardiopatía alcohólica alcoholic myocardiopathy.
miocardiopatía del bebedor de cerveza beer-drinker myocardiopathy.
miocardiopatía chagásica chagasic myocardiopathy.
miocardiopatía congestiva congestive myocardiopathy.
miocardiopatía constrictiva constrictive myocardiopathy.
miocardiopatía diabética diabetic myocardiopathy.
miocardiopatía dilatada dilated myocardiopathy.
miocardiopatía hipertrófica hypertrophic myocardiopathy.
miocardiopatía hipertrófica obstructiva hypertrophic obstructive myocardiopathy.
miocardiopatía idiopática idiopathic myocardiopathy.
miocardiopatía infiltrante infiltrative myocardiopathy.
miocardiopatía periparto peripartum myocardiopathy.
miocardiopatía posparto post partum myocardiopathy.
miocardiopatía primaria primary myocardiopathy.
miocardiopatía restrictiva restrictive myocardiopathy.
miocardiopatía secundaria secondary myocardiopathy.
miocardiorrafia *f.* myocardiorrhaphy.
miocardiosis *f.* myocardiosis.
miocardítico, -ca *adj.* myocarditic.
miocarditis *f.* myocarditis.
miocarditis aguda aislada acute isolated myocarditis.
miocarditis aguda primaria acute primary myocarditis.
miocarditis aguda secundaria acute secondary myocarditis.
miocarditis aislada aguda acute isolated myocarditis.
miocarditis bacteriana aguda acute bacterial myocarditis.
miocarditis de células gigantes giant cell myocarditis.
miocarditis crónica chronic myocarditis.
miocarditis diftérica diphtheritic myocarditis.
miocarditis fibrosa fibrous myocarditis.

miocarditis de Fieldler Fieldler's myocarditis.
miocarditis de fragmentación fragmentation myocarditis.
miocarditis idiopática idiopathic myocarditis.
miocarditis indurativa indurative myocarditis.
miocarditis intersticial interstitial myocarditis.
miocarditis parenquimosa parenchymatous myocarditis.
miocarditis reumática rheumatic myocarditis.
miocarditis séptica aguda acute septic myocarditis.
miocarditis tóxica toxic myocarditis.
miocarditis tuberculosa tuberculous myocarditis.
miocardiosis *f.* myocardosis.
miocardosis *f.* myocardosis.
miocéfalo *m.* myocephalon.
miocele *m.* myocele.
miocelialgía *f.* myocelialgia.
miocelitis *f.* myocelitis.
miocelo *m.* myocoele.
miocelitis *f.* myocelitis.
miocelulitis *f.* myocellulitis.
mioceptor *m.* myoceptor.
miocerosis *f.* myocerosis.
miocimia *f.* myokimia.
miocinesímetro *m.* myokinesimeter.
miocito *m.* myocyte.
miocitólisis *f.* myocytolisis.
miocitoma *m.* myocytoma.
mioclonía *f.* myoclonia.
mioclonía cortical cortical myoclonia.
mioclonía epiléptica myoclonia epileptica.
mioclonía espinal spinal myoclonia.
mioclonía fibrilar fibrillary myoclonia.
mioclonía fibrilar múltiple myoclonia fibrillaris multiplex.
mioclonía focal focal myoclonia.
mioclonía generalizada disseminated myoclonia.
mioclonía múltiple multiplex myoclonia.
mioclonía palatina palatal myoclonia.
mioclonía parcelar segmental myoclonia.
mioclonía reticular reticular myoclonia.
mioclonía sensible a los estímulos stimulus sensitive myoclonia.
mioclonía seudoglótica pseudoglottic myoclonia.
mioclonía velopalatina palatal myoclonia.
mioclónico, -ca *adj.* myoclonic.
mioclono *m.* myoclonus.
mioclono nocturno nocturnal myoclonus.
miocolpitis *f.* myocolpitis.
miocorditis *f.* myochorditis.
miocrismo *m.* myocrismus.
miocromo *m.* myochrome.
miocronoscopio *m.* myochronoscopc.
mioculador *m.* myoculator.
miocutáneo, -a *adj.* myocutaneous.
mioctonina *f.* myoctonine.
miodegeneración *f.* myodegeneration.
miodemia *f.* myodemia.
miodesopsia *f.* myodesopsia.
miodiastasis *f.* myodiastasis.
miodídimo *m.* myodidymus.
miodinamia *f.* myodynamia.
miodinámica *f.* myodynamics.
miodinámico, -ca *adj.* myodynamic.
miodinamómetro *m.* myodynamometer.
miodinia *f.* myodynia.
miodioptría *f.* myodiopter.
miodistonía *f.* myodystonia, myodystony.
miodistrofia *f.* myodystrophy, myodystrophia.
miodistrofia fetal myodystrophia fetalis.
miodérmico, -ca *adj.* myodermal.

mioedema *m.* myoedema.
mioelástico, -ca *adj.* myoelastic.
mioeléctrico, -ca *adj.* myoelectric, myoelectrical.
mioendocarditis *f.* myoendocarditis.
mioepitelial *adj.* myoephitelial.
mioepitelio *m.* myoepithelium.
mioepitelioma *m.* myoepithelioma.
mioesclerosis *f.* myosclerosis.
mioesferulosis *f.* myospherulosis.
mioespasmia *f.* myospasmia.
mioespasmo *m.* myospasm.
mioestenómetro *m.* myosthenometer.
mioestesia *f.* myoesthesia.
mioestroma *m.* myostroma.
mioestromina *f.* myostromin.
miofascial *adj.* myofascial.
miofagia *f.* myophagism.
miofagismo *m.* myophagism.
miófago *m.* myophage.
miofascitis *f.* myofascitis.
miofibrilar *adj.* myofibrillar.
miofibrilla *f.* myofibril.
miofibroblasto *m.* myofibroblast.
miofibroma *m.* myofibroma.
miofibrosis *f.* miofibrosis.
  miofibrosis cardíaca miofibrosis cordis.
miofibrositis *f.* myofibrositis.
miófono *m.* myophone.
miofuncional *adj.* myofunctional.
miogelosis *f.* myogelosis.
miogénesis *f.* myogenesis.
miogenético, -ca *adj.* myogenetic.
miogénico, -ca *adj.* myogenic.
miógeno *m.* myogen.
miógeno, -na *adj.* myogenous.
mioglia *f.* myoglia.
mioglobina *f.* myoglobin.
mioglobinuria *f.* myoglobinuria.
mioglobulina *f.* myoglobulin.
mioglobulinuria *f.* myoglobulinuria.
miognato *m.* myognathus.
miografía *f.* myography.
miográfico, -ca *adj.* myographic.
miógrafo *m.* myograph.
miograma *m.* myogram.
miohematina *f.* myohematin.
miohemoglobina *f.* myohemoglobin.
miohipertrofia *f.* myohypertrophia.
mioide *adj.* myoid.
mioideo, -a *adj.* myoid.
mioidema *m.* myoidema.
mioidismo *m.* myoidism.
mioinositol *m.* myoinositol.
mioisquemia *f.* myoischemia.
miolecito, -ta *adj.* myolecithal.
miolema *f.* myolemma.
miolipoma *f.* myolipoma.
miólisis *f.* myolysis.
  miólisis cardiotóxica, miólisis cordis tóxica cardiotoxic myolysis, myolysis cardiotoxica.
miología *f.* myologia, myology.
mioma *m.* myoma.
  mioma estriocelular myoma striocellulare.
  mioma previo myoma previum.
  mioma sarcomatodes myoma sarcomatodes.
miomagénesis *f.* myomagenesis.
miomalacia *f.* myomalacia.
miomatectomía *f.* myomatectomy.
miomatosis *f.* myomatosis.
miomatoso, -sa *adj.* myomatous.
miomectomía *f.* myomectomy.
miomelanosis *f.* myomelanosis.
miómera *f.* myomere.
miometrial *adj.* myometrial.

miometrio *m.* myometrium.
miometritis *f.* myometritis.
miómetro *m.* myometer.
miomitocondria *f.* myomitochondrion.
miomohisterectomía *f.* myomohysterectomy.
miomotomía *f.* myomotomy.
mion *m.* myon.
mionecrosis *f.* myonecrosis.
  mionecrosis clostridial, mionecrosis por clostridios clostridial myonecrosis.
mionefropexia *f.* myonephropexy.
mionema *f.* myoneme.
mioneural *adj.* myoneural.
mioneura *f.* myoneure.
mioneurastenia *f.* myoneurasthenia.
mioneuro *m.* myoneure.
mioneuroma *m.* myoneuroma.
mionimia *f.* myonymy.
mionosis *f.* myonosus.
miopalmo *m.* myopalmus.
miopaquinsis *m.* myopachynsis.
mioparálisis *f.* myoparalysis.
mioparesis *f.* myoparesis.
miopatía *f.* myopathy.
  miopatía en la acromegalia acromegalic myopathy.
  miopatía alcohólica alcoholic myopathy.
  miopatía de bastoncillos rod myopathy.
  miopatía carcinomatosa carcinomatous myopathy.
  miopatía cardíaca myopathy cordis.
  miopatía central core central core myopathy.
  miopatía centronuclear centronuclear myopathy.
  miopatía con desproporción congénita de los tipos de fibras myopathy with fiber type disproportion.
  miopatía distal distal myopathy.
  miopatía esteroidea steroid myopathy.
  miopatía miotónica myotonic myopathy.
  miopatía miotubular myotubular myopathy.
  miopatía mitocondrial mitochondrial myopathy.
  miopatía nemalínica nemaline myopathy.
  miopatía ocular ocular myopathy.
  miopatía tirotóxica thyrotoxic myopathy.
miopático, -ca *adj.* myopathic.
miope *adj.* myope.
miopericarditis *f.* myopericarditis.
miopía *f.* myopia.
  miopía axil axial myopia.
  miopía cromática chromatic myopia.
  miopía de curvatura curvature myopia.
  miopía degenerativa degenerative myopia.
  miopía espacial space myopia.
  miopía de índice index myopia.
  miopía magna myopia magna.
  miopía maligna malignant myopia.
  miopía nocturna night myopia.
  miopía patológica pathologic myopia.
  miopía perniciosa malignant myopia.
  miopía prematura premature myopia.
  miopía primaria primary myopia.
  miopía prodrómica prodromal myopia.
  miopía progresiva progressive myopia.
  miopía simple simple myopia.
  miopia transitoria transient myopia.
miópico, -ca *adj.* myopic.
mioplasma *m.* myoplasm.
mioplastia *f.* myoplasty.
mioplástico, -ca *adj.* myoplastic.
miopo *m.* myopus.
miopolar *adj.* myopolar.
miopragia *f.* miopragia.
mioproteína *f.* myoprotein.

miopsia *f.* myopsis.
miopsicopatía *f.* myopsychopathy.
miopsicosis *f.* myopsychosis.
miopsíquico, -ca *adj.* myopsychic.
miopus *m.* myopus.
mioquinasa *f.* myokinase.
mioquinesia *f.* myokinesis.
mioquinesímetro *m.* myokinesemeter.
mioquinesis *f.* myokinesis.
mioquinético, -ca *adj.* myokinetic.
mioquinina *f.* myokinin.
miorrafia *f.* myorraphy.
miorreceptor *m.* myorreceptor.
miorrelajante *adj.* lissive.
miorrexis *f.* myorrhexis.
miosalgia *f.* myosalgia.
miosalpingitis *f.* myosalpingitis.
miosálpinx *m.* myosalpinx.
miosán *m.* myosan.
miosarcoma *m.* myosarcoma.
miosclerosis *f.* myosclerosis.
mioscopio *m.* myoscope.
mioseísmo *m.* myoseism.
miosfigmia *f.* myosphygmia.
miosina *f.* myosin.
miosinézesis *f.* myosynizesis.
miosinicesis *f.* myosynizesis.
miosinógeno *m.* myosinogen.
miosinosa *f.* myosinose.
miosinuria *f.* myosinuria.
miosis *f.* miosis, myosis.
  miosis espasmódica, miosis espástica spastic miosis.
  miosis irritativa irritative miosis.
  miosis paralítica paralytic miosis.
miosismia *f.* myoseism.
miositis *f.* myositis.
  miositis aguda diseminada acute disseminated myositis.
  miositis aguda progresiva acute progressive myositis.
  miositis anaeróbica anaerobic myositis.
  miositis bacteriana espontánea spontaneous bacterial myositis.
  miositis cervical cervical myositis.
  miositis fibrosa myositis fibrosa.
  miositis a frigore myositis a frigore.
  miositis infecciosa infectious myositis.
  miositis intersticial interstitial myositis.
  miositis múltiple multiple myositis.
  miositis orbitaria orbital myositis.
  miositis osificante myositis ossificans.
  miositis osificante circunscrita myositis ossificans circumscripta.
  miositis osificante progresiva myositis ossificans progressiva.
  miositis osificante traumática myositis ossificans traumatica.
  miositis parenquimatosa parenchymatous myositis.
  miositis primaria múltiple primary multiple myositis.
  miositis proliferativa, myositis proliferante proliferative myositis.
  miositis purulenta myositis purulenta.
  miositis reumatoidea rheumatoid myositis.
  miositis serosa myositis serosa.
  miositis supurativa myositis purulenta.
  miositis traumática traumatic myositis.
  miositis triquinosa myositis trichinosa.
  miositis tropical tropical myositis.
  miositis tropical purulenta myositis purulenta tropica.
miosítico, -ca *f.* myositic.
miospasia *f.* myospasia.

miospasmia *f.* myospasmia.
miospasmo *m.* myospasm.
miostasia *f.* myostasis.
miostático, -ca *adj.* myostatic.
miosténico, -ca *adj.* myosthenic.
miostenómetro *m.* myostenometer.
miosteoma *m.* myosteoma.
miostroma *m.* myostroma.
miosuero *m.* myoserum.
miosuria *f.* myosuria.
miosutura *f.* myosuture.
miotabique *m.* myoseptum.
miotáctico, -ca *adj.* myotactic.
miotaponamiento *f.* myotamponade.
miotasis *f.* myotasis.
miotático, -ca *adj.* myotatic.
miotenoplastia *f.* myotenoplasty.
miotenositis *f.* myotenositis.
miotenotomía *f.* myotenotomy.
miotérmico, -ca *adj.* myothermic.
miótico, -ca *adj.* myotic.
miotilidad *f.* myotility.
miotoma *m.* myotome.
miotomía *f.* myotomy.
miótomo *m.* myotome.
miotonía *f.* myotonia.
  miotonía adquirida myotonia acquisita.
  miotonía atrófica myotonia atrophica.
  miotonía distrófica myotonia dystrophica.
  miotonía neonatal myotonia neonatorum.
miotónico, -ca *adj.* myotonic.
miotono *m.* myotone, myotonus.
miotonoide *adj.* myotonoid.
miotonómetro *m.* myotonometer.
miotrofia *f.* myotrophy.
miotrófico, -ca *adj.* myotrophic.
miotrópico, -ca *adj.* myotropic.
mira *f.* mire.
miracidio *m.* miracidium.
miringe *f.* myrinx, myringa.
miringectomía *f.* myringodectomy.
miringitis *f.* myringitis.
  miringitis ampollar bullous myringitis, myringitis bullosa.
  miringitis infecciosa infectious myringitis.
  miringitis vesicular bullous myringitis, myringitis bullosa.
miringodectomía *f.* myringodectomy.
miringodermatitis *f.* myringodermatitis.
miringoestapediopexia *f.* myringostapediopexy.
miringomicosis *f.* myringomycosis.
  miringomicosis aspergilina myringomycosis aspergillina.
miringoplastia *f.* myringoplasty.
miringotomía *f.* myringotomy.
miringótomo *m.* myringotome.
miristicina *f.* myristicin.
mirmecia *f.* myrmecia.
mirtiforme *adj.* myrtiform.
misandria *f.* misanthropy.
misantropía *f.* misanthropia, misanthropy.
miscegenación *f.* miscegenation.
miscible *adj.* miscible.
miserotia *f.* miserotia.
misofilia *f.* mysophilia.
misofobia *f.* mysophobia.
misofóbico, -ca *adj.* mysophobic.
misófobo, -ba *m.* mysophobiac.
misogamia *f.* misogamy.
misoginia *f.* misogyny.
misología *f.* misologia.
misoneísmo *m.* misoneism.
misopedia *f.* misopedia, misopedy.
mitacismo *m.* mytacism.

mitapsis *f.* mitapsis.
mitela *f.* mitella.
miticida *adj.* miticidal.
mitigar *v.* mitigate.
mitilotoxina *f.* mytilotoxine.
mitilotoxismo *m.* mytilotoxism.
mitocinético, -ca *adj.* mitokinetic.
mitocondria *f.* mitochondria.
mitocondrial *adj.* mitochondrial.
mitofobia *f.* mythophobia.
mitogenético, -ca *adj.* mitogenetic.
mitogénesis *f.* mitogenesis.
mitogenia *f.* mitogenesis.
mitógeno *m.* mitogen.
mitoma *m.* mitome.
mitomanía *f.* mythomania.
mitoplasma *m.* mitoplasm.
mitor *m.* mittor, mitere.
mitosis *f.* mitosis.
  mitosis acinética akinetic mitosis.
  mitosis anastral anastral mitosis.
  mitosis astral astral mitosis.
  mitosis heterotípica heterotype mitosis.
  mitosis homeotípica homeotypic mitosis.
  mitosis multicéntrica multicentric mitosis.
  mitosis patológica pathologic mitosis.
  mitosis pluripolar pluripolar mitosis.
  mitosis somática somatic mitosis.
mitosoma *f.* mitosome.
mitosquisis *f.* mitoschisis.
mitótico, -ca *adj.* mitotic.
mitral *adj.* mitral.
mitralizacion *f.* mitralization.
mitridatismo *m.* mithridatism.
mittelschmerz *m.* mittelschmerz.
mixadenitis *f.* myxadenitis.
mixadenoma *m.* myxadenoma.
mixangitis *f.* myxangitis.
mixastenia *f.* myxasthenia.
mixedema *m.* myxedema.
  mixedema circunscrito circumscribed myxedema.
  mixedema congénito congenital myxedema.
  mixedema hipofisario pituitary myxedema.
  mixedema infantil childhood myxedema, infantile myxedema.
  mixedema nodular nodular myxedema.
  mixedema operatorio operative myxedema.
  mixedema papular papular myxedema.
  mixedema pretibial pretibial myxedema.
  mixedema secundario secondary myxedema.
mixedematoide *adj.* myxedematoid.
mixedematoideo, -a *adj.* myxedematoid.
mixedematoso, -sa *adj.* myxedematous.
mixemia *f.* myxemia.
mixidiocia *f.* myxidiocy.
mixoadenitis *f.* myxoadenitis.
mixoadenoma *m.* myxoadenoma.
mixoangoítis *f.* myxangoitis.
mixoblastoma *m.* myxoblastome.
mixocistoma *m.* myxocystoma.
mixocistitis *f.* myxocystitis.
mixocito *m.* myxocyte.
mixocondroma *m.* mixochondroma.
mixocondrofibrosarcoma *m.* myxochandrofibrosarcoma.
mixocondroma *m.* myxochondroma.
mixocondrosarcoma *m.* myxochondrosarcoma.
mixoencondroma *m.* myxoenchondroma.
mixoendotelioma *m.* myxoendothelioma.
mixofibroma *m.* myxofibroma.
mixofibrosarcoma *m.* myxofibrosarcoma.
mixoglioma *m.* myxogliomia.
mixoglobulosis *f.* myxoglobulosis.

mixoide *adj.* myxoid.
mixoinoma *m.* myxoinoma.
mixolipoma *m.* myxolipoma.
mixoma *m.* myxoma.
  mixoma auricular atrial myxoma.
  mixoma encondromatoso enchondromatous myxoma, myxoma enchondromatosum.
  mixoma eréctil erectile myxoma.
  mixoma fibroso myxoma fibrosum.
  mixoma lipomatoso lipomatous myxoma, myxoma lipomatosum.
  mixoma odontogénico, mixoma odontógeno ondontogenic myxoma.
  mixoma quístico cystic myxoma.
  mixoma sarcomatoso myxoma sarcomatosum.
  mixoma vascular vascular myxoma.
mixomatosis *f.* myxomatosis.
mixomatoso, -sa *adj.* myxomatous.
mixomioma *m.* myxomiome.
mixoneuroma *m.* myxoneuroma.
mixoneurosis *f.* myxoneurosis.
mixopapiloma *m.* myxopapilloma.
mixopoyesis *f.* myxopoiesis.
mixorrea *f.* myxorrhea.
  mixorrea gástrica myxorrhea gastrica.
  mixorrea intestinal myxorrhea intestinalis.
mixosarcoma *m.* myxosarcoma.
mixosarcomatoso, -sa *adj.* mysosarcomatous.
mixoscopia *f.* mixoscopia.
mixotrófico, -ca *adj.* mixotrophic.
mixótrofo *m.* mixotroph.
mixtura *f.* mixture.
mixto, -ta *adj.* mixed.
mneme *m.* mneme.
mnémico, -ca *adj.* mnemic.
mnemismo *m.* mnemism.
mnemónica *f.* mnemonics.
mnemónico, -ca *adj.* mnemic.
mnemotecnia *f.* mnemotechnics.
mnésico, -ca *adj.* mnemic.
mnéstico, -ca *adj.* mnemic.
moción *f.* motion.
moco *m.* mucus.
mocopús *m.* mucopus.
modalidad *f.* modality.
modelación *f.* shaping.
modelado *m.* modeling.
modelador *m.* carver.
modelar *v.* model.
modelo *m.* cast.
  modelo dental dental cast.
  modelo de diagnóstico diagnostic cast.
  modelo de estudio study cast.
  modelo gnatostático gnathostatic cast.
  modelo patrón master cast.
  modelo preoperatorio preoperative cast.
  modelo refractario refractory cast.
  modelo de revestimiento investment cast.
modelo *m.* model.
  modelo médico medical model.
modelo cinético de la urea *m.* urea kinetic modeling.
modificación *f.* modification.
  modificación de conducta behavior modification.
modioliforme *adj.* modioliform.
modiolo *m.* modiolus.
modo Schultze Schultze mode.
modorra *f.* drowsiness.
modulación *f.* modulation.
  modulación antigénica antigenic modulation.
modulador *m.* modulator.
mogiartria *f.* mogiarthria.

mogifonía *f.* mogiphonia.
mogigrafía *f.* mogigraphia.
mogilalia *f.* mogilalia.
moho *m.* mold.
mola *f.* mole.
  mola aracnoidea spider mole.
  mola de Breus Breus' mole.
  mola carnosa fleshy mole.
  mola falsa false mole.
  mola hidatídica, mole hidatiforme hydatid mole, hydatidiform mole.
  mola invasiva, mola invasora invasive mole.
  mola maligna malignant mole.
  mola metastatizante malignant mole.
  mola pétrea stone mole.
  mola quística cystic mole.
  mola sanguínea blood mole.
  mola tubaria tubal mole.
  mola verdadera true mole.
  mola vesicular vesicular mole.
molal *adj.* molal.
molalidad *f.* molality.
molar *adj.* molar.
molar *m. y adj.* molar.
  molar de los doce años twelfth-year molar.
  molar de Moon Moon's molar.
  molar en mora, molar moriforme mulberry molar.
  primer molar first molar.
  segundo molar second molar.
  molar de los seis años, molar del sexto años sixth-year molar.
  tercer molar third molar, molaris tertius.
  molar supernumerario supernumerary.
molaridad *f.* molarity.
molariforme *adj.* molariform.
molde *m.* cast.
  molde decidual decidual cast.
  molde diagnóstico diagnostic cast.
  molde fibrinoso fibrinous cast.
  molde gnatostático gnathostatic cast.
  molde granular granular cast.
  molde maestro master cast.
  molde del pelo hair cast.
  molde refractario refractory cast.
molde *m.* mold.
moldeado *m.* casting, molding.
  moldeado en vacío vacuum casting.
moldear *v.* cast, mold.
molécula *f.* molecule.
  molécula de adhesión adhesion molecule.
  molécula coestimuladora coestimulatory molecule.
  molécula media middle molecule.
  molécula proteica del complemento complement protein molecule.
  molécula señal signal molecule.
molecular *adj.* molecular.
moleta *f.* muller.
molibdénico, -ca *adj.* molybdenic.
molibdeno *m.* molybdenum.
molibdenosis *f.* molybdenosis.
molibdenoso, -sa *adj.* molybdenous.
molibdoproteína *f.* molybdoprotein.
molibdoso, -sa *adj.* molybdous.
molilalia *f.* molilalia.
mollmen *m.* molimen.
molismofobia *f.* molismophobia.
mollities mollities.
  mollities ossium mollities ossium.
molusco *m.* molluscum.
  molusco contagioso molluscum contagiosum.
  molusco fibroso molluscum fibrosum.
  molusco verrugoso molluscum verrucosum.

moluscocida *m.* molluscacide.
moluscocida *adj.* molluscacidal.
momia *m.* mummy.
momificación *f.* mummification.
monartritis *f.* monarthritis.
  monartritis deformante monarthritis deformans.
monáster *m.* monaster.
monauqueno *m.* monauchenos.
mónera *m.* moner.
monérula *f.* monerula.
monestésico, -ca *adj.* monesthetic.
mongolismo *m.* mongolism.
  mongolismo por traslocación translocation mongolism.
mongoloide *adj.* mongoloid.
monilado, -da *adj.* monilated.
monilétrix *m.* monilethrix.
Monilia Monilia.
monilial *adj.* monilial.
moniliasis *f.* moniliasis.
monílide *m.* monilid.
moniliforme *adj.* moniliform.
moniliosis *f.* moniliosis.
monismo *m.* monism.
monitor *m.* monitor.
  monitor cardíaco cardiac monitor.
  monitor fetal electrónico electronic fetal monitor.
  monitor Holter Holter monitor.
  monitor de presión arterial blood pressure monitor.
  monitor de presión venosa central central venous pressure monitor.
  monitor de PVC CVP monitor.
monitorizar *v.* monitor.
monoamella *f.* monoamelia.
monoamida *f.* monoamide.
monoamina *f.* monoamine.
monoaminérgico, -ca *adj.* monoaminergic.
monoaminooxidasa *f.* monamine oxidase.
monoaminuria *f.* monoaminuria.
monoamniótico, -ca *adj.* monoamniotic.
monoanestesia *f.* monoanesthesia.
monoangular *adj.* monangle.
monoángulo *m.* monangle.
monoarticular *adj.* monoarticular.
monoartritis *f.* monarthritis.
monoasociado, -da *adj.* monoassociated.
monoatetosis *f.* monoathetosis.
monoatómico, -ca *adj.* monatomic.
monoaural *adj.* monoaural.
monoavitaminosis *f.* monavitaminosis.
monoaxónico, -ca *adj.* monaxonic.
monobásico, -ca *adj.* monobasic.
monoblasto *m.* monoblast.
monoblastoma *m.* monoblastoma.
monobraquia *f.* monobrachia.
monobraquio *m.* monobrachius.
monobromado, -da *adj.* monobromated.
monocálcico, -ca *adj.* monocalcic.
monocapa *f.* monolayer.
monocardio, -a *adj.* monocardian.
monocariota *m.* monokaryote.
monocariótico, -ca *adj.* monokaryotic.
monocéfalo *m.* monocephalus.
  monocéfalo tetrápodo dibraquio monocephalus tetrapus dibrachius.
  monocéfalo trípodo dibraquio monocephalus tripus dibrachius.
monocelular *adj.* monocelled, monocellular.
monocíclico, -ca *adj.* monocyclic.
monociesis *f.* monocyesis.
monocigosidad *f.* monozygosity.
monocigótico, -ca *adj.* monozygotic.

monocigoto, -ta *adj.* monozygous.
monocina *f.* monokine.
monocítico, -ca *adj.* monocytic.
monocito *m.* monocyte.
monocitoide *adj.* monocytoid.
monocitopenia *f.* monocytopenia.
monocitopoiesis *f.* monocytopoiesis.
monocitosis *f.* monocytosis.
monoclonal *adj.* monoclonal.
monoclónico, -ca *adj.* monoclonal.
monocontaminación *f.* monocontamination.
monocontaminado, -da *adj.* monocontaminated.
monocordio *m.* monochord.
monocorditis *f.* monochorditis.
monocorea *f.* monochorea.
monocorial *adj.* monochorial.
monocorionico, -ca *adj.* monochorial.
monocroico, -ca *adj.* monochroic.
monocromasia *f.* monochromasia.
monocrómata *m.* monochromat.
monocromático, -ca *adj.* monochromatic.
monocromatismo *m.* monochromatism.
monocromatófilo *m.* monochromatophil.
monocrómico, -ca *adj.* monochromic.
monocromófilo, -la *adj.* monochromophil, monochromophile.
monocrótico, -ca *adj.* monocrotic.
monocrotismo *m.* monocrotism.
monocular *adj.* monocular.
monóculo *m.* monoculus.
monodactilia *f.* monodactylia, monodactyly.
monodactilismo *m.* monodactylism.
monodelto *m.* monodelt.
monodermoma *m.* monodermoma.
monodiplopía *f.* monodiplopia.
monodisperso, -sa *adj.* monodisperse.
monoescenismo *m.* monoscenism.
monoespasmo *m.* monospasm.
monoespecífico, -ca *adj.* monospecific.
monoespermia *f.* monospermy.
monoestético, -ca *adj.* monoesthetic.
monoestratal *adj.* monostratal.
monoestratificado, -da *adj.* monostratified.
monoestro, -ra *adj.* monoestrous.
monoestrual *adj.* monoestrous.
monofagia *f.* monophagia.
monofagismo *m.* monophagism.
monofasia *f.* monophasia.
monofásico, -ca *adj.* monophasic.
monofilamento *m.* monofilament.
monofilético, -ca *adj.* monophyletic.
monofiletismo *m.* monophyletism.
monofiletista *m.* monophyletist.
monofiodonto, -ta *adj.* monophyodont.
monofobia *f.* monophobia.
monoftalmo *m.* monophthalmos.
monogamético, -ca *adj.* monogametic.
monoganglionar *adj.* monoganglial.
monogástrico, -ca *adj.* monogastric.
monogénesis *f.* monogenesis.
monogenético, -ca *adj.* monogenetic.
monogenia *f.* monogenesis.
monogénico, -ca *adj.* monogenic.
monogerminal *adj.* monogerminal.
monohíbrido, -da *adj.* monohybrid.
monohidratado, -da *adj.* monohydrated.
monohídrico, -ca *adj.* monhydric.
monoideísmo *m.* monoideism.
monoinfección *f.* monoinfection.
monolepsis *f.* monolepsis.
monolocular *adj.* monolocular.
monomanía *f.* monomania.
monomaníaco *m., f. y adj.* monomaniac.
monomastigoto *m.* monomastigote.

monomaxilar *adj.* monomaxillary.
monomélico, -ca *adj.* monomelic.
monomérico, -ca *adj.* monomeric.
monómero *m.* monomer.
monometálico, -ca *adj.* monometallic.
monomicrobiano, -na *adj.* monomicrobic.
monomioplejía *f.* monomioplegia.
monomiositis *f.* monomyositis.
monomolecular *adj.* monomolecular.
monomórfico, -ca *adj.* monomorphic.
monomorfismo *m.* monomorphism.
monomorfo, -fa *adj.* monomorphous.
mononeural *adj.* mononeural.
mononeuralgia *f.* mononeuralgia.
mononéurico, -ca *adj.* mononeuric.
mononeuritis *f.* mononeuritis.
  mononeuritis diabética diabetic mononeuritis.
  mononeuritis múltiple mononeuritis multiplex.
mononeuropatía *f.* mononeuropathy.
monónfalo *m.* monomphalus.
mononte *m.* monont.
mononoea *f.* mononoea.
mononucleado, -da *adj.* mononucleate.
mononuclear *adj.* mononuclear.
mononucleosis *f.* mononucleosis.
  mononucleosis por citomegalovirus cytomegalovirus mononucleosis.
  mononucleosis infecciosa infectious mononucleosis.
  mononucleosis postransfusional posttransfusion mononucleosis.
mononucleótido *m.* mononucleotide.
monoosteítico, -ca *adj.* mono-osteitic.
monoovular *adj.* mono-ovular, monovular.
monoovulatorio, -a *adj.* monovulatory.
monooxigenasa *f.* monooxygenase.
monoparesia *f.* monoparesis.
monoparestesia *f.* monoparesthesia.
monopatía *f.* monopathy.
monopático, -ca *adj.* monopathic.
monopenia *f.* monopenia.
monoplasmático, -ca *adj.* monoplasmatic.
monoplástico, -ca *adj.* monoplastic.
monoplejía *f.* monoplegia.
monopléjico, -ca *adj.* monoplegic.
monopo *m.* monopus.
monopodia *f.* monopodia.
monopodial *adj.* monopodial.
monopoyesis *f.* monopoiesis.
monoptiquial *adj.* monoptychial.
monorquia *f.* monorchia.
monorquidia *f.* monorchism.
monorquídico, -ca *adj.* monorchidic.
monorquidismo *m.* monorchidism.
monorquísmo *adj.* monorchism.
monorrinico, -ca *adj.* monorhinic.
monosacárido *m.* monosaccharide.
monosacarosa *f.* monosaccharose.
monoscelo, -la *adj.* monoscelous.
monosifílide *f.* monosyfilide.
monosináptico, -ca *adj.* monosynaptic.
monosíntoma *m.* monosymptom.
monosintomático, -ca *adj.* monosymptomatic.
monosoma *m.* monosome.
monosomo *adj.* monosomous.
monosomía *f.* monosemia.
monosómico, -ca *adj.* monosomic.
monospasmo *m.* monospasm.
monospermia *f.* monospermy.
monostótico, -ca *adj.* monostotic.
monotermia *f.* monothermia.
monoterminal *adj.* monoterminal.
monótico, -ca *adj.* monotic.

monotoco, -ca *adj.* monotocous.
monotocoso, -sa *adj.* monotocous.
monotricado, -da *adj.* monotricate.
monotrico, -ca *adj.* monotrichous.
monovalente *adj.* monovalent.
monovular *adj.* monovular.
monoxénico, -ca *adj.* monoxenic, monoxenous.
monóxido *m.* monoxide.
monoxigenasa *f.* monoxygenase.
monoyodotirosina *f.* monoiodotyrosine.
monozoico, -ca *adj.* monozoic.
monstruicidio *m.* monstricide.
mons mons.
monstrum monstrum.
monstruo *m.* monster, monstrum.
monstruosidad *f.* monstrosity.
montaje *m.* mounting, setup.
montante *m.* mountant.
montar *v.* mount.
monte *m.* mount, mons.
  monte de venus mount of venus, mons veneris.
montículo *m.* monticulus.
morbididad *f.* morbidity.
mórbido, -da *adj.* morbid.
morbidostático, -ca *adj.* morbidostatic.
morbífico, -ca *adj.* morbific.
morbígeno, -na *adj.* morgibenous.
morbilia morbilli.
morbilidad *f.* morbility.
  morbilidad puerperal puerperal morbility.
morbiliforme *adj.* morbilliform.
morbilloso, -sa *adj.* morbillous.
morbosidad *f.* morbidity.
morboso, -sa *adj.* morbid.
morbus morbus.
  morbus Addisonii morbus Addisonii.
  morbus coxae senilis morbus coxae senilis.
  morbus moniliformis morbus moniliformis.
morcelación *f.* morcellation.
morcelamiento *m.* morcellement.
morcelar *v.* morcel.
mordaza *f.* gag.
  mordaza bucal de Davis-Crowe Davis-Crowe mouth gag.
mordedura *f.* bite.
mordente *m.* mordant.
mordida *f.* bite.
  mordida abierta open bite.
  mordida balanceada balanced bite.
  mordida borde a borde edge-to-edge bite.
  mordida sobre cera wax bite.
  mordida cerrada closed bite.
  mordida cruzada cross bite.
  mordida normal normal bite.
  mordida para registro check bite.
  mordida en reposo restbite.
  mordida sobresaliente underhung bite.
  mordida en tijera scissor bite.
mordiente *m.* mordant.
mordisco *m.* bite.
morfaláctico, -ca *adj.* morphallactic.
morfalaxia *f.* morphallaxis.
morfea *f.* morphea.
  morfea acrotérica morphea acroterica.
  morfea alba morphea alba.
  morfea generalizada generalized morphea.
  morfea gutada, morfea guttata guttate morphea, morphea guttata.
  morfea herpetiformis morphea herpetiformis.
  morfea lineal linear morphea, morphea linearis.
  morfea nigra morphea pigmentosa.
  morfea pigmentosa morphea pigmentosa.

morfina *f.* morphine.
morfínico, -ca *adj.* morphinic.
morfinismo *m.* morphinism.
morfinístico, -ca *adj.* morphinistic.
morfinización *f.* morphinization.
morfinomanía *f.* morphinomania, morphiomania.
morfinómano, -na *adj.* morphinist.
morfodiferenciación *f.* morphodifferentiation.
morfofilia *f.* morphophyly.
morfofísica *f.* morphophysics.
morfogénesis *f.* morphogenesis.
morfogenético, -ca *adj.* morphogenetic.
morfogenia *f.* morphogeny.
morfógeno *m.* morfogen.
morfografía *f.* morphography.
morfólisis *f.* morpholysis.
morfología *f.* morphology.
morfológico, -ca *adj.* morphological.
morfometría *f.* morphometry.
morfométrico, -ca *adj.* morphometric.
morfón *m.* morphon.
morfoplasma *m.* morphoplasm.
morfosis *f.* morphosis.
morfótico, -ca *adj.* morphotic.
Morganella Morganella.
morgue *f.* morgue.
moria *f.* moria.
moribundo, -da *adj.* moribund, dying.
morir *v.* die.
morón *m.* moron.
moronismo *f.* moronism, moronity.
morosis *f.* morosis.
morruina *f.* morrhuin.
morsal *adj.* morsal.
mortal *adj.* mortal.
mortalidad *f.* mortality.
  mortalidad fetal fetal mortality.
  mortalidad infantil infant mortality.
  mortalidad maternal maternal mortality.
  mortalidad neonatal neonatal mortality.
  mortalidad perinatal perinatal mortality.
  mortalidad prenatal prenatal mortality.
mortalograma *m.* mortalogram.
mortandad *f.* toll.
mortero *m.* mortar.
Mortierella Mortierella.
mortífero, -ra *adj.* deadly.
mortificación *f.* mortification.
mortificado, -da *adj.* mortified.
mortinatalidad *f.* mortinatalidad.
mortinato, -ta *adj.* stillborn.
mortuorio *m.* mortuary.
mortuorio, -a *adj.* mortuary.
mórula *f.* morula.
morulación *f.* morulation.
morular *adj.* morular.
moruloide *adj.* moruloid.
mosaicismo *m.* mosaicism.
  mosaicismo celular cellular mosaicism.
  mosaicismo cromosómico chromosome mosaicism.
  mosaicismo eritrocítico erythrocyte mosaicism.
  mosaicismo de genes gene mosaicism.
  mosaicismo germinal germinal mosaicism.
  mosaicismo gonadal gonadal mosaicism.
  mosaicismo de línea germinal germ line mosaicism.
mosaico *m.* mosaic.
  mosaico cervical colposcopic mosaic.
  mosaico de cromosomas sexuales sex chromosomic mosaic.
  mosaico sexual sex mosaic.

mosaiquismo *m.* mosaicism.
mosca *f.* fly, musca.
moscas volantes *f.* floaters.
moscardón *m.* botfly.
mosquito *m.* mosquito.
mosquitocida *m.* mosquitocide.
mota *f.* mote.
moteado *m.* mottling.
moteado, -da *adj.* mottled.
mótil *adj.* motile.
motilidad *f.* motility.
motilina *f.* motilin.
motivación *f.* motivation.
 motivación extrínseca extrinsic motivation.
 motivación fisiológica physiological motivation.
 motivación intrínseca intrinsic motivation.
 motivación de logro achievement motivation.
 motivación orgánica organic motivation.
 motivación personal personal motivation.
 motivación social social motivation.
motivo *adj.* motive.
 motivo de dominio mastery motive.
 motivo de éxito, motivo de logro achievement motive.
motoceptor *m.* motoceptor.
motofaciente *adj.* motofacient.
motoneurona *f.* motoneuron.
 motoneurona alfa alfa motoneuron.
 motoneurona central upper motoneuron.
 motoneurona gamma gamma motoneuron.
 motoneurona heterónima heteronymous motoneuron.
 motoneurona homónima homonymous motoneuron.
 motoneurona inferior lower motoneuron.
 motoneurona periférica peripheral motoneuron.
 motoneurona superior upper motoneuron.
motor *m.* motor.
motórico, -ca *adj.* motorial.
motorium *m.* motorium.
motormetro *m.* motormeter.
motorogerminativo, -va *adj.* motorogerminative.
motorpatía *f.* motorpathy.
motricidad *f.* motoricity.
movible *adj.* motile.
movilidad *f.* mobility.
 movilidad electroforética electrophoretic mobility.
móvil *adj.* motile.
movilización *f.* mobilization.
movilizar *v.* mobilize.
movilómetro *m.* mobilometer.
movimiento *m.* movement.
 movimiento de abertura, movimiento apertura opening movement.
 movimiento accesorio accessory movement.
 movimiento activo active movement.
 movimiento adversivo adversive movement.
 movimiento ameboide ameboid movement.
 movimiento angular angular movement.
 movimiento asistivo assistive movement.
 movimiento asociado associated movement.
 movimiento automático automatic movement.
 movimiento auxiliar assistive movement.
 movimiento balístico ballistic movement.
 movimiento de Bennett Bennett movement.
 movimiento en bisagra hinge movement.
 movimiento de bordes border movement.
 movimiento browniano, movimiento brunoniano Brownian movement.
 movimiento de Brown-Zsigmondy Brown-Zsigmondy movement.

 movimiento cardinal del parto cardinal movement of labor.
 movimiento ciliar ciliary movement.
 movimiento circular circus movement.
 movimiento de circo circus movement.
 movimiento conjugado de los ojos conjugate movement of the eyes.
 movimiento no conjugado de los ojos disconjugate movement of the eyes.
 movimiento contralateral asociado contralateral associated movement.
 movimiento coreico, movimiento coreiforme choreic movement.
 movimiento corporal body movement.
 movimiento de corriente streaming movement.
 movimiento de decorticación decorticated movement, decorticated posturing movement.
 movimiento deslizante gliding movement.
 movimiento distónico dystonic movement.
 movimiento espontáneo spontaneous movement.
 movimiento euglenoide euglenoid movement.
 movimiento de excursión excursive movement.
 movimiento fetal fetal movement.
 movimiento de flujo streaming movement.
 movimiento forzado forced movement.
 movimiento de Frenkel Frenkel's movement.
 movimiento funcional del maxilar functional mandibular movement.
 movimiento fusional fusional movement.
 movimiento hipocicloidal hypocycloidal motion.
 movimiento hístico de bordes, movimiento hístico de límites border tissue movement.
 movimiento intermediario, movimiento intermedio intermediary movement, intermediate movement.
 movimiento lateral lateral movement.
 movimiento libre del maxilar inferior free mandibular movement.
 movimiento de límites border movement.
 movimiento de Magnan Magnan's movement.
 movimiento mandibular jaw movement, mandibular movement.
 movimiento mandibular funcional functional mandibular movement.
 movimiento mandibular libre free mandibular movement.
 movimiento de masa mass movement.
 movimiento masticatorio masticatory movement.
 movimiento del maxilar inferior jaw movement, mandibular movement.
 movimiento molecular molecular movement.
 movimiento morfogenético morphogenetic movement.
 movimiento muscular muscular movement.
 movimiento neurobiotáctico neurobiotactic movement.
 movimiento nucleópeto nucleopetal movement.
 movimiento ocular de búsqueda uniforme smooth pursuit eye movement.
 movimiento ocular cardinal cardinal ocular movement.
 movimiento ocular de fijación fixational ocular movement.
 movimiento ocular inverso inverse ocular movement.
 movimiento ocular no rápido non-rapid eye movement.
 movimiento ocular pervertido perverted ocular movement.

 movimiento ocular de piñón cogwheel ocular movement movement.
 movimiento ocular rápido rapid eye movement (REM).
 movimiento paradójico de los párpados paradoxical movement of the eyelids.
 movimiento pasivo passive movement.
 movimiento pasivo continuo continuous passive movement.
 movimiento pendular pendular movement.
 movimiento precordial precordial movement.
 movimiento protoplasmático protoplasmatic movement.
 movimiento reflejo reflex movement.
 movimiento resistido, movimiento de resistencia resistive movement.
 movimiento sacádico, movimiento sacudido saccadic movement.
 movimiento de segmentación segmentation movement.
 movimiento sincinético synkinetic movement.
 movimiento sueco Swedish movement.
 movimiento en tijeras scissor movement.
 movimiento a tirones saccadic movement.
 movimiento traslatorio, movimiento de traslación translatory movement.
 movimiento de trombón de Magnan Magnan's trombone movement.
 movimiento vermicular vermicular movement.
moxa *f.* moxa.
moxibustión *f.* moxibustion.
moyamoya *f.* moyamoya.
mucicarmin *m.* mucicarmine.
múcido, -da *adj.* mucid.
mucífero, -ra *adj.* muciferous.
mucificación *f.* mucification.
muciforme *adj.* muciform.
mucígeno, -na *adj.* mucigenous.
mucilaginoso, -sa *adj.* mucilagenous.
mucílago *m.* mucilage.
mucina *f.* mucin.
mucinasa *f.* mucinase.
mucinemia *f.* mucinemia.
mucinoblasto *m.* mucinoblast.
mucinógeno *m.* mucinogen.
mucinoide *adj.* mucionoid.
mucinolítico, -ca *adj.* mucinolytic.
mucinosis *f.* mucinosis.
 mucinosis folicular follicular mucinosis.
 mucinosis papular papular mucinosis.
mucinoso, -sa *adj.* mucinous.
mucinuria *f.* mucinuria.
mucíparo, -ra *adj.* muciparous.
mucitis *f.* mucitis.
mucoanticuerpo *m.* mucoantibody.
mucocartílago *m.* mucocartilage.
mucocolpos *m.* mucocolpos.
mucocele *m.* mucocele.
mucocito *m.* mucocyte.
mucoclasia *f.* mucoclasis.
mucocutáneo, -a *adj.* mucocutaneous.
mucoderma *m.* mucoderm.
mucodérmico, -ca *adj.* mucodermal.
mucoepidermoide *adj.* mucoepidermoid.
mucofibroso, -sa *adj.* mucofibrous.
mucofloculento, -ta *adj.* mucoflocculent.
mucoglobulina *f.* mucoglobulin.
mucoide *adj.* mucoid.
 mucoide urinario urine mucoid.
mucolipidosis *f.* mucolipidosis.
mucolisis *f.* mucolysis.
mucolítico, -ca *adj.* mucolytic.

mucomembranoso, -sa *adj.* mucomembranous.
mucopéptido *m.* mucopeptide.
mucopericondrial *adj.* mucoperichondrial.
mucopericondrio *m.* mucoperichondrium.
mucoperióstico, -ca *adj.* mucoperiosteal.
mucoperiostio *m.* mucoperiosteum.
mucopolisacaridasa *f.* mucopolysaccharidase.
mucopolisacárido *m.* mucopolysaccharide.
mucopolisacaridosis *f.* mucopolysaccharidosis.
mucopolisacariduria *f.* mucopolysacchariduria.
 mucopolisacariduria de Tamm-Horsfall Tamm-Horsfall mucopolysaccachariduria.
mucoproteína *f.* mucoprotein.
mucopurulento, -ta *adj.* mucopurulent.
mucopús *m.* mucopus.
mucoquiste *m.* mucocyst.
mucormicosis *f.* mucormycosis.
mucosa *f.* mucosa.
mucosanguíneo, -a *adj.* mucoanguineous.
mucosectomía *f.* mucosectomy.
mucosedante *adj.* mucosedative.
mucoseroso, -sa *adj.* mucoserous.
mucosidad *f.* mucus.
mucosina *f.* mucosin.
mucositis *f.* mucositis.
mucoso, -sa *adj.* mucous.
mucosocutáneo, -a *adj.* mucosocutaneous.
mucótomo *m.* mucotome.
mucostático, -ca *adj.* mucostatic.
mucosulfatidosis *f.* mucosulfatidosis.
mucoviscidosis *f.* mucoviscidosis.
mucro *m.* mucro.
 mucro cardiaco mucro cordis.
 mucro esternal mucro sternis.
mucronato, -ta *adj.* mucronate.
mucroniforme *adj.* mucroniform.
mucus *m.* mucus.
muda *f.* moulting.
mudez *f.* dumbness.
mudo, -da *adj.* dumb, mute.
muela *f.* molar, tooth.
 muela del juicio wisdom tooth.
muermo *m.* glanders, farcy.
muerte *f.* death.
 muerte accidental accidental death.
 muerte aparente, mors putativa apparent death.
 muerte asistida assisted death.
 muerte cardíaca súbita sudden cardiac death.
 muerte celular cell death.
 muerte cerebral cerebral death.
 muerte en la cuna cot death.
 muerte encefálica brain death.
 muerte fetal fetal death.
 muerte fetal intermedia intermediate fetal death.
 muerte fetal tardía late fetal death.
 muerte fetal temprana early fetal death.
 muerte funcional functional death.
 muerte genética genetic death.
 muerte hepática liver death.
 muerte infantil infant death.
 muerte local local death.
 muerte a mano airada violent death.
 muerte materna maternal death.
 muerte molecular molecular death.
 muerte natural natural death.
 muerte negra black death.
 muerte neonatal neonatal death.
 muerte neocortical neocortical death.
 muerte perinatal perinatal death.
 muerte real true death.
 muerte sistémica systemic death.
 muerte somática somatic death.
 muerte súbita, mors subitanea sudden death unexpected death.
 muerte tímica mors thymica.
 muerte violenta violent death.
muerto, -ta *adj.* dead.
muesca *f.* notch.
muesca *f.* nick.
muestra *f.* sample.
 muestra al azar random sample.
 muestra sesgada biased sample.
muestra *f.* specimen.
 muestra citológica cytologic specimen.
 muestra de esputo sputum specimen.
 muestra miccional aleatoria random voided specimen.
 muestra no contaminada clean-catch specimen.
 muestra de orina de mitad de micción mid-stream-catch urine specimen.
muestreo *m.* sampling.
 muestreo aleatorio random sampling.
mufla *f.* muffle.
mufla *f.* flask.
muguet *m.* thrush.
mujer gestante *f.* pregnant woman.
mujer gestante incapaz *f.* incompetent pregnant woman.
mular *adj.* mular.
mulato, -ta *m., f. y adj.* mulatto.
muleta *f.* crutch.
muliebria *f.* muliebria.
muliebridad *f.* muliebrity.
multiangular *adj.* multiangular.
multialélico, -ca *adj.* multiallelic.
multiarticular *adj.* multiarticular.
multiaxial *adj.* multiaxial.
multibacilar *adj.* multibaccilary.
multicapsular *adj.* multicapsular.
multicélula *f.* multicell.
multicelular *adj.* multicellular.
multicelularidad *f.* multicellularity.
multicéntrico, -ca *adj.* multicentric.
multicontaminado, -da *adj.* multicontaminated.
multicorte *m.* multiscan.
multicúspide *adj.* multicuspid, multicuspidate.
multicuspídeo, -a *adj.* multicuspidate.
multidentado, -da *adj.* multidentate.
multidimensional *adj.* multidimensional.
multifactorial *adj.* multifactorial.
multifamiliar *adj.* multifamilial.
multifetación *f.* multifetation.
multifido, -da *adj.* multifidus.
multifocal *adj.* multifocal.
multiforme *adj.* multiform.
multiganglionar *adj.* multiganglionic.
multigesta *adj.* multigesta.
multiglandular *adj.* multiglandular.
multigrávida *adj.* multigravida.
multihalucalismo *m.* multihallucalism.
multihalucismo *m.* multihallucism.
multiinfección *f.* multi-infection.
multilobular *adj.* multilobar.
multilobulillar *adj.* multilobular.
multilocal *adj.* multilocal.
multilocular *adj.* multilocular.
multimamia *f.* multimammae.
multinodal *adj.* multinodal.
multinodular *adj.* multinodular.
multinuclear *adj.* multinuclear.
multípara *adj.* multipara.
multiparcial *adj.* multipartial.
multiparidad *f.* multiparity.
multíparo, -ra *adj.* multiparous.
multiplanar *adj.* multiplanar.
múltiple *adj.* multiple.
multiplicación *f.* multiplication.
 multiplicación bacteriana bacterial growth.
multiplicidad *f.* multiplicitas.
 multiplicidad cardíaca multiplicitas cordis.
multipolar *adj.* multipolar.
multipolicalismo *m.* multipollicalism.
multiquístico, -ca *adj.* multicystic.
multirradicular *adj.* multirooted.
multirrotación *f.* multirotation.
multisensibilidad *f.* multisensitivity.
multiterminal *adj.* multiterminal.
multituberculado, -da *adj.* multituberculate.
multivalente *adj.* multivalent.
müllerianoma *m.* müllerianoma.
munidad *f.* munity.
muñeca *f.* wrist.
 muñeca caída wristdrop.
 muñeca de tenis tennis wrist.
muñón *m.* stump.
 muñón cónico conical stump.
 muñón duodenal duodenal stump.
 muñón gástrico gastric stump.
 muñón rectal rectal stump.
mural *adj.* mural.
muramidasa *f.* muramidase.
mureína *f.* murein.
muriforme *adj.* muriform.
murmullo *m.* murmur.
 murmullo venoso venous hum.
 murmullo vesicular vesicular breath sound.
Musca Musca.
muscacida *m.* muscacide.
muscarina *f.* muscarinique.
muscarínico, -ca *adj.* muscarinic.
muscarinismo *m.* muscarinism.
muscicida *m.* muscicide.
muscular *adj.* muscular.
muscularidad *f.* muscularity.
musculatura *f.* musculature.
músculo *m.* muscle, musculus.
 músculo agonista agonistic muscle.
 músculo antagonista antagonistic muscle.
 músculo antigravitatorio antigravity muscle.
 músculo articular articular muscle.
 músculo estriado striated muscle, striped muscle.
 músculo extrínseco extrinsic muscle.
 músculo de fibra estriada striated muscle, strimped muscle.
 músculo de fibra lisa smooth muscle, non-striated muscle.
 músculo intrafusal intrafusal muscle.
 músculo intrínseco intrinsic muscle.
 músculo involuntario involuntary muscle.
 músculo isométrico isometric muscle.
 músculo liso smooth muscle, nonstriated muscle.
 músculo miotómico myotomic muscle.
 músculo principal prime muscle.
 músculo voluntario voluntary muscle.
 músculo sinérgico synergitic muscle.
musculoaponeurótico, -ca *adj.* musculoaponeurotic.
musculocutáneo, -a *adj.* musculocutaneous.
musculodérmico, -ca *adj.* musculodermic.
musculoelástico, -ca *adj.* musculoelastic.
musculoesquelético, -ca *adj.* musculoskeletal.
musculofrénico, -ca *adj.* musculophrenic.
musculointestinal *adj.* musculointestinal.
musculomembranoso, -sa *adj.* musculomembranous.
musculotendinoso, -sa *adj.* musculotendinous.

musculotónico, -ca *adj.* musculotonic.
musicogénico, -ca *adj.* musicogenic.
musicoterapia *f.* musicotherapy.
musitación *f.* mussitation.
muslo *m.* thigh.
  muslo de los conductores, muslo del chófer driver's thigh.
  muslo de cricket cricket thigh.
  muslo de Heilbronner Heilbronner's thigh.
mutación *f.* mutation.
  mutación alélica allelic mutation.
  mutación auxotrófica auxotrophic mutation.
  mutación bioquímica biochemical mutation.
  mutación por cambio de encuadre reading-frame-shift mutation.
  mutación condicional conditional mutation.
  mutación condicional mortal conditional lethal mutation.
  mutación constitutiva constitutive mutation.
  mutación corregida reverse mutation.
  mutación cromosómica chromosomal mutation.
  mutación de desviación de la estructura frameshift mutation.
  mutación de desviación de la estructura de la lectura reading-frame-shift mutation.
  mutación espontánea spontaneous mutation.

mutación genómica genomic mutation.
mutación germinal germinal mutation.
mutación hacia delante forward mutation.
mutación homeótica homeotic mutation.
mutación inducida induced mutation.
mutación por inserción-deleción addition-deletion mutation.
mutación inversa reverse mutation.
mutación letal lethal mutation.
mutación mortal lethal mutation.
mutación natural natural mutation.
mutación neutra neutral mutation.
mutación nutricional nutritional mutation.
mutación opalina opal mutation.
mutación en placa clara clear plaque mutation.
mutación puntiforme, mutación de punto point mutation.
mutación retrógrada back mutation.
mutación sensible al frío cold-sensitive mutation.
mutación sensible a la temperatura temperature-sensitive mutation.
mutación de sentido erróneo missense mutation.
mutación silente silent mutation.
mutación somática somatic mutation.

mutación supresora supressor mutation.
mutación visible visible mutation.
mutacional *adj.* mutational.
mutacismo *f.* mutacism.
mutagénesis *f.* mutagenesis.
  mutagénesis insercional insertional mutagenesis.
mutagenicidad *f.* mutagenicity.
mutagénico, -ca *adj.* mutagenic.
mutágeno *m.* mutagen.
mutante *m. y adj.* mutant.
mutarrotación *f.* mutarotation.
muteína *f.* mutein.
mutilación *f.* mutilation.
mutilar *v.* maim.
mutismo *m.* mutism.
  mutismo acinético akinetic mutism.
  mutismo electivo elective mutism.
  mutismo sordo deaf mutism.
mutón *m.* muton.
mutualismo *m.* mutualism.
mutualista *adj.* mutualist.
Mycobacteriaceae Mycobacteriaceae.
Mycobacterium Mycobacterium.
Mycoplasma Mycoplasma.
Mycoplasmataceae Mycoplasmataceae.
Myzorhynchus Myzorhynchus.

N n

nacarado, -da *adj.* nacreous.
nacela *f.* nacelle.
nacido, -da sin asepsia *adj.* born out of asepsis.
nacido, -da vivo, -va *adj.* liveborn.
naciente *adj.* nascent.
nacimiento *m.* birth.
 nacimiento completo complete birth.
 nacimiento múltiple multiple birth.
 nacimiento natural natural childbirth.
 nacimiento prematuro preterm birth.
 nacimiento pretérmino preterm birth.
 nacimiento con producto muerto dead birth.
 nacimiento tardío post-term birth.
 nacimiento transversal cross birth.
 nacimiento de vértice head birth.
nada por boca nothing per os (NPO).
nadir *m.* nadir.
Naegleria Naegleria.
naegleriasis *f.* naegleriasis.
naevus *m.* naevus.
naftilpararrosanilina *f.* naphthylpararosaniline.
naftolismo *m.* naphtolism.
nanismo *m.* nanism.
nanocefalia *f.* nanocephalia, nanocephaly.
nanocefálico, -ca *adj.* nanocephalic.
nanocéfalo, -la *adj.* nanocephalous.
nanocormia *f.* nanocormia.
nanoftalmia *f.* nanophthalmia.
nanoftalmos *m.* nanophthalmos.
nanoide *adj.* nanoid.
nanomelia *f.* nanomelia.
nanomelo *m.* nanomelus.
nanosomía *f.* nanosomia.
nanósomo, -ma *m., f.* nanosomus.
nanukayami *f.* nanukayami.
napiforme *adj.* napiform.
naprápata *m., f.* naprapath.
naprapatía *f.* naprapathy.
naranja *f.* orange.
naranjófilo, -la *adj.* orangeophil.
narcisismo *m.* narcissism.
narcisista *adj.* narcissistic.
narcismo *m.* narcism.
narcoácrido, -da *adj.* narcotico-acrid.
narcoanálisis *m.* narcoanalysis.
narcoanestesia *f.* narcoanesthesia.
narcocatarsis *f.* narcocatharsis.
narcodiagnóstico *m.* narcodiagnosis.
narcoestimulante *adj.* narcostimulant.
narcohipnia *f.* narcohypnia.
narcohipnosis *f.* narcohypnosis.
narcoirritante *adj.* narcotico-irritant.
narcolepsia *f.* narcolepsia, narcolepsy.
narcoléptico, -ca *adj.* narcoleptic.
narcoma *m.* narcoma.
narcomanía *f.* narcomania.
narcosíntesis *f.* narcosynthesis.
narcosis *f.* narcosis.
 narcosis basal basal narcosis, narcosis basis.
 narcosis bulbar medullary narcosis.

narcosis intravenosa intravenous narcosis.
narcosis medular medullary narcosis.
narcosis por nitrógeno nitrogen narcosis.
narcosis de Nussbaum Nussbaum's narcosis.
narcoso, -sa *adj.* narcose, narcous.
narcostimulante *adj.* narcostimulant.
narcoterapia *f.* narcotherapy.
narcótico, -ca *adj.* narcotic.
 narcótico anodino narcotic anodyne.
 narcótico hipnótico narcotic hypnoytic.
 narcótico sedante narcotic sedative.
narcotizar *v.* narcotize.
narina *f.* naris.
naris naris.
nariz *f.* nose, nasus.
 nariz de bebedor toper's nose.
 nariz de brandy brandy nose.
 nariz de cobre copper nose.
 nariz en dorso de silla de montar saddle-back nose.
 nariz hendida cleft nose.
 nariz en lomo equino swayback nose.
 nariz en martillo hammer nose.
 nariz en patata potato nose.
 nariz respingona upturned nose.
 nariz de perro dog nose.
 nariz de ron rum nose.
 nariz en silla de montar saddle nose.
nasal *adj.* nasal, nasalis.
nasalidad *f.* nasonnement.
nasalización *f.* snuffling.
nasioiníaco, -ca *adj.* nasioiniac.
nasioníaco, -ca *adj.* nasioiniac.
nasioiníaco, -ca *adj.* nasioiniac.
nasión *m.* nasion.
nasitis *f.* nasitis.
nasoantral *adj.* nasoantral.
nasoantritis *f.* rhinoantritis.
nasoantrostomía *f.* nasoantrostomy.
nasobronquial *adj.* nasobronchial.
nasobucal *adj.* naso-oral.
nasociliar *adj.* nasociliary.
nasofaringe *f.* nasopharynx.
nasofaríngeo, -a *adj.* nasopharyngeal.
nasofaringitis *f.* nasopharyngitis.
nasofaringografía *f.* nasopharyngography.
nasofaringolaringoscopio *m.* nasopharyngolaryngoscope.
nasofaringoscopia *f.* nasopharyngoscopy.
nasofaringoscopio *m.* nasopharyngoscope.
nasofrontal *adj.* nasofrontal.
nasogástrico, -ca *adj.* nasogastric.
nasógrafo *m.* nasograph.
nasolabial *adj.* nasolabial.
nasolacrimal *adj.* nasolacrimal.
nasolagrimal *adj.* nasolacrimal.
nasomanómetro *m.* nasomanometer.
nasooral *adj.* naso-oral.
nasopalatino, -na *adj.* nasopalatine.
nasopalpebral *adj.* nasopalpebral.

nasorrostral *adj.* nasorostral.
nasoscopio *m.* nasoscospe.
nasoseptal *adj.* nasoseptal.
nasoseptitis *f.* nasoseptitis.
nasosinusitis *f.* nasosinusitis.
nasoturbinal *adj.* nasoturbinal.
nasus nasus.
natal *adj.* natal.
natalidad *f.* natality.
nates nates.
naticefalia *f.* caput natiforme.
natimortalidad *f.* natimortality.
nativo, -va *adj.* native.
natremia *f.* natremia, natriemia.
natriférico, -ca *adj.* natriferic.
natrium natrium.
natriuresis *f.* natriuresis.
natruresis *f.* natruresis, natriuresis.
natriurético, -ca *adj.* natruretic, natriuretic.
natriuria *f.* natriuria.
natural *adj.* natural.
naturaleza *f.* nature.
naturalismo *m.* naturalism.
naturalización *f.* naturalization.
naturópata *m., f.* naturopath.
naturopatía *f.* naturopathy.
naturopático, -ca *adj.* naturopathic.
naupatía *f.* naupathia.
náusea *f.* nausea.
 náusea epidémica nausea epidemica.
 náusea gravídica nausea gravidarum.
 náusea marítima nausea marina.
 náusea naval nausea marina.
nauseabundo, -da *adj.* nauseant.
nauseado, -da *adj.* sick.
nauseante *adj.* nauseant.
nauseoso, -sa *adj.* nauseous.
navaja *f.* razor.
navicula *f.* navicula.
navicular *adj.* navicular.
naviculartritis *f.* naviculararthritis.
nealogía *f.* nealogy.
neartrosis *f.* nearthrosis.
nébula *f.* nebula.
nebulización *f.* spray, nebulization.
 nebulización de aguja needle spray.
 nebulización de éter ether spray.
 nebulización de Pickrell Pickrell's spray.
 nebulización de tirotricina tyrothricin spray.
 nebulización de Tucker Tucker's spray.
nebulizador *m.* nebulizer.
 nebulizador a chorro jet nebulizer.
 nebulizador de disco giratorio spinning disk nebulizer.
 nebulizador ultrasónico ultrasonic nebulizer.
nebulizar *v.* nebulize.
necatoriasis *f.* necatoriasis.
necesidad *f.* necessity, need.
 necesidad básica basic human necessity.
 necesidad compulsiva compulsion need.

necesidad de dependencia dependency necessity.

necesidad diaria mínima (NMD) minimum daily requirement (MDR).

necrectomía *f.* necrectomy.

necrobiosis *f.* necrobiosis.

necrobiosis lipídica, necrobiosis lipoídica necrobiosis lipoidica.

necrobiosis lipídica diabética, necrobiosis lipoídica diabética, necrobiosis lipoidea de los diabéticos necrobiosis lipoidica diabeticorum.

necrobiótico, -ca *adj.* necrobiotic.

necrocitosis *f.* necrocytosis.

necrocitotoxina *f.* necrocytotoxin.

necrocomio *m.* mortuary.

necrofagia *f.* necrophagia.

necrófago, -ga *adj.* necrophagous.

necrofilia *f.* necrophily, necrophilia.

necrofilismo *m.* necrophilism.

necrofílico, -ca *adj.* necrophilic.

necrófilo *m.* necrophile.

necrófilo, -la *adj.* necrophilous.

necrofobia *f.* necrophobia.

necrogénico, -ca *adj.* necrogenic.

necrógeno, -na *adj.* necrogenous.

necrogranulomatoso, -sa *adj.* necrogranulomatous.

necrólisis *f.* necrolysis.

necrólisis epidérmica tóxica (NET) toxic epidermal necrolysis (TEN).

necrología *f.* necrology.

necrológico, -ca *adj.* necrologic.

necrólogo, -ga *m., f.* necrologist.

necromanía *f.* necromania.

necrómetro *m.* necrometer.

necromimesis *f.* necromimesis.

necronectomía *f.* necronectomy.

necroneumonía *f.* necropneumonia.

necroparásito *m.* necroparasite.

necropatía *f.* necropathy.

necropsia *f.* necropsy.

necropsia médico-legal medicolegal necropsy.

necrosadismo *m.* necrosadism.

necrosante *adj.* necrotizing.

necroscopia *f.* necroscopy.

necrosis *f.* necrosis.

necrosis adiposa fat necrosis.

necrosis adiposa subcutánea del recién nacido subcutaneous fat necrosis of the newborn.

necrosis arteriolar arteriolar necrosis.

necrosis aséptica aseptic necrosis.

necrosis avascular avascular necrosis.

necrosis caseosa cheesy necrosis, caseous necrosis, caseation necrosis.

necrosis central central necrosis.

necrosis por coagulación, necrosis coagulativa coagulation necrosis.

necrosis colicuativa colliquative necrosis.

necrosis confluente bridging necrosis.

necrosis embólica embolic necrosis.

necrosis enfisematosa progresiva progressive emphysematous necrosis.

necrosis exantematosa exanthematous necrosis.

necrosis fibrinoide fibrinoid necrosis.

necrosis focal focal necrosis.

necrosis por fósforo phosphorus necrosis.

necrosis fragmentaria piecemeal necrosis.

necrosis gangrenosa gangrenous necrosis.

necrosis grasa fat necrosis.

necrosis grasa de Balser Balser's fatty necrosis.

necrosis hepática masiva massive hepatic necrosis.

necrosis hepática en puente bridging necrosis.

necrosis hialina hyaline necrosis.

necrosis húmeda moist necrosis.

necrosis isquémica ischemic necrosis.

necrosis isquémica epifisaria epiphyseal ischemic necrosis.

necrosis licuefactiva, necrosis por licuefacción liquefactive necrosis, liquefaction necrosis.

necrosis medial medial necrosis.

necrosis mercurial mercurial necrosis.

necrosis medial quística, necrosis medial quística de Erdheim cystic medial necrosis, Erdheim's cystic medial necrosis.

necrosis por momificación mummification necrosis.

necrosis ósea aséptica aseptic bone necrosis.

necrosis papilar renal, necrosis de las papilas renales renal papillary necrosis, necrosis of renal papillae.

necrosis periférica peripheral necrosis.

necrosis por presión pressure necrosis.

necrosis progresiva enfisematosa progressive emphysematous necrosis.

necrosis por radiación radiation necrosis.

necrosis por radio radium necrosis.

necrosis seca dry necrosis.

necrosis séptica septic necrosis.

necrosis sifilítica syphilitic necrosis.

necrosis silenciosa de Paget Paget's quiet necrosis.

necrosis superficial superficial necrosis.

necrosis total total necrosis.

necrosis supurativa suppurative necrosis.

necrosis tubular tubular necrosis.

necrosis tubular aguda (NTA) acute tubular necrosis (ATN).

necrosis de Zenker Zenker's necrosis.

necrosis zonal zonal necrosis.

necrospermia *f.* necrospermia.

necrotactismo *m.* necrotactism.

necrótico, -ca *adj.* necrotic.

necrotizante *adj.* necrotizing.

necrotomía *f.* necrotomy.

necrotomía osteoplástica osteoplastic necrotomy.

necrozoospermia *f.* necrozoospermia.

neencéfalo *m.* neencephalon.

nefeloide *adj.* nepheloid.

nefelometría *f.* nephelometry.

nefelométrico, -ca *adj.* nephelometric.

nefelómetro *m.* nephelometer.

nefelopía *f.* nephelopia.

nefelopsia *f.* nephelopia.

nefluorofotómetro *m.* nefluorophotometer.

nefradenoma *m.* nephradenoma.

nefralgia *f.* nephralgia.

nefrálgico, -ca *adj.* nephralgic.

nefrapostasis *f.* nephrapostasis.

nefrastenia *f.* nephrasthenia.

nefratonía *f.* nephratonia, nephratony.

nefrauxa *f.* nephrauxa, nephrauxe.

nefrectasia *f.* nephrectasia, nephrectasy, nephrectasis.

nefrectasis *f.* nephrectasis.

nefrectomía *f.* nephrectomy.

nefrectomía abdominal abdominal nephrectomy.

nefrectomía anterior anterior nephrectomy.

nefrectomía lumbar lumbar nephrectomy.

nefrectomía posterior posterior nephrectomy.

nefrectomía paraperitoneal paraperitoneal nephrectomy.

nefrectomía parcial partial nephrectomy.

nefrectomía radical radical nephrectomy.

nefrectomía subcapsular subcapsular nephrectomy.

nefrectomizar *v.* nephrectomize.

nefredema *m.* nephredema.

nefrelcosis *f.* nephrelcosis.

nefremia *f.* nephremia.

nefrenfraxis *f.* nephremphraxis.

nefria *f.* nephria.

néfrico, -ca *adj.* nephric.

nefridio *m.* nephridium.

nefridrosis *f.* nephrydrosis.

nefrismo *m.* nephrism.

nefrítico, -ca *adj.* nephritic.

nefrítides *f.* nephritides.

nefritis *f.* nephritis.

nefritis aguda acute nephritis.

nefritis por analgésicos analgesic nephritis.

nefritis antimembrana basal anti-basement membrane nephritis.

nefritis arteriosclerótica arteriosclerotic nephritis.

nefritis bacteriana bacterial nephritis.

nefritis de los Balcanes Balkan nephritis.

nefritis capsular capsular nephritis.

nefritis caseosa cheesy nephritis, nephritis caseosa, caseous nephritis.

nefritis congénita congenital nephritis.

nefritis crónica chronic nephritis.

nefritis crónica por pérdida de potasio potassium-losing nephritis.

nefritis cruposa crupous nephritis.

nefritis dolorosa nephritis dolorosa.

nefritis de Ellis, tipo 2 Ellis type 2 nephritis.

nefritis del embarazo nephritis of pregnancy.

nefritis escarlatínica, nefritis por escarlatina scarlatinal nephritis.

nefritis exudativa exudative nephritis.

nefritis fibrolipomatosa fibrolipomatous nephritis.

nefritis focal focal nephritis.

nefritis glomerular glomerular nephritis.

nefritis glomerulocapsular glomerulocapsular nephritis.

nefritis gravídica, nefritis de la gravidez nephritis gravidarum.

nefritis de guerra war nephritis.

nefritis hemorrágica hemorrhagic nephritis.

nefritis hereditaria hereditary nephritis.

nefritis hidrópica dropsical nephritis.

nefritis hiperazoémica azotemic nephritis.

nefritis indurativa indurative nephritis.

nefritis por inmunocomplejos immune complex nephritis.

nefritis intersticial interstitial nephritis.

nefritis intersticial aguda acute interstitial nephritis.

nefritis de Lancereaux Lancereaux's nephritis.

nefritis lipomatosa lipomatous nephritis.

nefritis lúpica, nefritis del lupus lupus nephritis.

nefritis de Masugi Masugi-type nephritis.

nefritis mesangial mesangial nephritis.

nefritis neumocócica neumococcus nephritis.

nefritis parenquimatosa parenchymatous nephritis.

nefritis parenquimatosa crónica chronic parenchymatous nephritis.

nefritis con pérdida de sal salt-losing nephritis.

nefritis productiva productive nephritis.

nefritis repentina nephritis repens.

nefritis saturnina saturnine nephritis.

nefritis sifilítica syphilitic nephritis.

nefritis subaguda subacute nephritis.

nefritis supurativa suppurative nephritis.

nefritis supurativa aguda acute suppurative nephritis.

nefritis supurativa crónica chronic suppurative nephritis.

nefritis por tartrato tartrate nephritis.
nefritis por transfusión transfusion nephritis.
nefritis de las trincheras trench nephritis.
nefritis tuberculosa tuberculous nephritis.
nefritis tubular tubular nephritis, tubal nephritis.
nefritis tubulointersticial tubulointerstitial nephritis.
nefritis tubulointersticial aguda acute tubulointerstitial nephritis.
nefritis tubulointersticial de los Balcanes Balkan tubulointerstitial nephritis.
nefritis tubulointersticial infecciosa infective tubulointerstitial nephritis.
nefritis por uranio uranium nephritis.
nefritogénico, -ca *adj.* nephritogenic.
nefritógeno, -na *adj.* nephritogenic.
nefroadenoma *m.* nephradenoma.
nefroabdominal *adj.* nephroabdominal.
nefroangioesclerosis *f.* nephroangiosclerosis.
nefroangiosclerosis *f.* nephroangiosclerosis.
nefrobiopsia *f.* nephrobiopsy.
nefroblastema *m.* nephroblastema.
nefroblastoma *m.* nephroblastoma.
nefroblastomatosis *f.* nephroblastomatosis.
nefrocalcinosis *f.* nephrocalcinosis.
nefrocapsectomía *f.* nephrocapsectomy.
nefrocardíaco, -ca *adj.* nephrocardiac.
nefrocarcinoma *m.* renal cell carcinoma, renal adenocarcinoma.
nefrocele *m.* nephrocele.
nefroceloma *m.* nephrocelom.
nefrocistanastomosis *f.* nephrocystanastomosis.
nefrocistitis *f.* nephrocystitis.
nefrocistoanastomosis *f.* nephrocystoanastomosis.
nefrocistosis *f.* nephrocystosis.
nefrocólico *m.* nephrocolic.
nefrocólico, -ca *m. y adj.* nephrocolic.
nefrocolopexia *f.* nephrocolopexy.
nefrocoloptosis *f.* nephrocoloptosis.
nefrodinia *f.* nephralgia.
nefroedema *m.* nephredema.
nefroepitelioma *m.* hypernephroma.
nefroerisipela *f.* nephroerysipelas.
nefroesclerosis *f.* nephrosclerosis, nephroscleria.
  nefroesclerosis arterial arterial nephrosclerosis.
  nefroesclerosis arteriolar arteriolar nephrosclerosis.
  nefroesclerosis arteriolar hialina hyaline arteriolar nephrosclerosis.
  nefroesclerosis arteriolar hiperplásica hyperplastic arteriolar nephrosclerosis.
  nefroesclerosis benigna benign nephrosclerosis.
  nefroesclerosis intercapilar intercapillary nephrosclerosis.
  nefroesclerosis maligna malignant nephrosclerosis.
  nefroesclerosis senil senile nephrosclerosis.
nefroesclerótico, -ca *adj.* nephrosclerotic.
nefroesplenografía *f.* nephrography with splenography.
nefroesplenopexia *f.* nephrosplenopexy.
nefrofagiasis *f.* nephrophagiasis.
nefrogástrico, -ca *adj.* nephrogastric.
nefrogenético, -ca *adj.* nephrogenetic.
nefrogénico, -ca *adj.* nephrogenetic.
nefrógeno, -na *adj.* nephrogenetic.
nefrografía *f.* nephrography.
nefrograma *m.* nephrogram.
sefrohelcosis *f.* nephrelcosis.

nefrohemia *f.* nephrohemia.
nefrohidrosis *f.* nephrohydrosis.
nefrohidrótico, -ca *adj.* nephrhydrotic, nephrydrotic.
nefrohipertrofia *f.* nephrohypertrophy.
nefroide *f.* nephroid.
nefroideo, -a *f.* nephroid.
nefrolisina *f.* nephrolysine.
nefrólisis *f.* nephrolysis.
nefrolitiasis *f.* nephrolithiasis.
nefrolítico, -ca *adj.* nephrolytic.
nefrolito *m.* nephrolith.
nefrolitotomía *f.* nephrolithotomy.
  nefrolitotomía percutánea percutaneous nephrolithotomy.
nefrología *f.* nephrology.
nefrólogo, -ga *m., f.* nephrologist.
nefroma *f.* nephroma.
  nefroma embrionario embryonal nephroma.
  nefroma mesoblástico mesoblastic nephroma.
nefromalacia *f.* nephromalacia.
nefromegalla *f.* nephromegaly.
nefrómera *f.* nephromere.
nefrón *m.* nephron.
nefrona *f.* nephron.
nefronoptisis *f.* nephronophthisis.
  nefronoptisis familiar juvenil familial juvenile nephronophthisis.
  nefronoptisis hereditaria del niño familial juvenile nephronophthisis.
nefroomentopexia *f.* nephro-omentopexy.
nefroparálisis *f.* nephroparalysis.
nefropatía *f.* nephropathy, nephropathia.
  nefropatía por analgésicos analgesic nephropathy.
  nefropatía balcánica, nefropatía de los Balcanes Balkan nephropathy.
  nefropatía crónica chronic nephropathy.
  nefropatía endémica balcánica endemic Balkan nephropathy.
  nefropatía epidémica epidemic nephropathy, nephropathia epidemica.
  nefropatía gotosa gouty nephropathy.
  nefropatía gravídica toxemia of pregnancy.
  nefropatía hematúrica familiar con sordera hereditary nephropathy, hereditary hematuria associated with nerve deafness and ocular changes.
  nefropatía hidropésica dropsical nephropathy.
  nefropatía hipercalcémica hypercalcemic nephropathy.
  nefropatía hipoazoúrica hypazoturic nephropathy.
  nefropatía hipoclorúrica hypochloruric nephropathy.
  nefropatía hipopotasémica hypokalemic nephropathy.
  nefropatía por IgA IgA nephropathy.
  nefropatía por IgM IgM nephropathy.
  nefropatía osmótica osmotic nephropathy.
  nefropatía con pérdida de potasio potassium-losing nephropathy.
  nefropatía con pérdida de sal salt-losing nephropathy.
  nefropatía postransfusional transfusion nephropathy.
  nefropatía de reflujo, nefropatía por reflujo reflux nephropathy.
  nefropatía tubular crónica chronic tubular nephropathy.
  nefropatía por virus de la hepatitis B hepatitis B virus related nephropathy.
  nefropatía por virus de la hepatitis C hepatitis C virus related nephropathy.

nefropático, -ca *adj.* nephropathic.
nefropexia *f.* nephropexy.
nefropielitis *f.* nephropyelitis.
nefropielografía *f.* nephropyelography.
nefropielolitotomía *f.* nephropyelolithotomy.
nefropieloplastia *f.* nephropyeloplasty.
nefropiosis *f.* nephropyosis.
nefropoyético, -ca *adj.* nephropoietic.
nefropoyetina *f.* nephropoietin.
nefroptisis *f.* nephrophthisis, nephroptosia, nephroptosis.
nefroptosia *f.* nephroptosia.
nefroptosis *f.* nephroptosis.
nefrorrafia *f.* nephrorrhaphy.
nefrorragia *f.* nephrorrhagia.
nefrosclerosis *f.* nephrosclerosis.
nefroscopia *f.* nephroscopy.
nefroscopio *m.* nephroscope.
  nefroscopio percutáneo percutaneous nephroscope.
nefrosialidosis *f.* nephrosialidosis.
nefrosis *f.* nephrosis.
  nefrosis aguda acute nephrosis.
  nefrosis amiloidea amyloid nephrosis.
  nefrosis colécmica cholemic nephrosis.
  nefrosis crónica chronic nephrosis.
  nefrosis de Epstein Epstein's nephrosis.
  nefrosis familiar familial nephrosis.
  nefrosis de glucógeno glycogen nephrosis.
  nefrosis hemoglobinúrica hemoglobinuric nephrosis.
  nefrosis hidrópica hydropic nephrosis.
  nefrosis hipopotasémica hypokalemic nephrosis.
  nefrosis hipóxica hypoxic nephrosis.
  nefrosis larvada larval nephrosis.
  nefrosis lípida, nefrosis lipoide, nefrosis lipoidea lipoid nephrosis.
  nefrosis necrosante necrotizing nephrosis.
  nefrosis de la nefrona inferior lower nephron nephrosis.
  nefrosis osmótica osmotic nephrosis.
  nefrosis tóxica toxic nephrosis.
  nefrosis vacuolar vacuolar nephrosis.
nefrosonografía *f.* nephrosonography.
nefrostograma *m.* nephrostogram.
nefrostolitotomía *f.* nephrostolithotomy.
nefrostoma *m.* nephrostoma, nephrostome.
nefrostomía *f.* nephrostomy.
  nefrostomía anatrófica anatrophic nephrostomy.
nefrótico, -ca *adj.* nephrotic.
nefrotifo *m.* nephrotyphus.
nefrotifoidea *adj.* nephrotyphoid.
nefrotifus nephrotyphus.
nefrotisis *f.* nephrothisis.
nefrotoma *m.* nephrotome.
nefrotomía *f.* nephrotomy.
  nefrotomía abdominal abdominal nephrotomy.
  nefrotomía lumbar lumbar nephrotomy.
nefrotómico, -ca *adj.* nephrotomic.
nefrótomo *m.* nephrotome.
nefrotomografía *f.* nephrotomography.
nefrotomograma *m.* nephrotomogram.
nefrotoxicidad *f.* nephrotoxicity.
nefrotóxico, -ca *adj.* nephrotoxic.
nefrotoxina *f.* nephrotoxin.
nefrotresis *f.* nephrotresis.
nefrotriesis *f.* nephrotresis.
nefrotrófico, -ca *adj.* nephrotrophic.
nefrotrópico, -ca *adj.* nephrotropic.
nefrotuberculosis *f.* nephrotuberculosis.
nefroureterectomía *f.* nephroureterectomy.

nefroureterocistectomía *f.* nephroureterocystectomy.
nefroureterolitiasis *f.* nefroureterolithiasis.
negación *f.* negation, denial.
negatividad *f.* negativity.
negativismo *m.* negativism.
negativo, -va *adj.* negative.
negatoscopio *m.* negatoscope, viewing box.
negligencia *f.* negligence.
negligencia motriz *f.* neglect syndrome.
negro, -gra *adj.* black.
Neisseria Neisseria.
Neisseriaceae Neisseriaceae.
neissérico, -ca *adj.* neisserial.
nelauna *m.* nelavan, nelavane.
nelavan *m.* nelavan, nelavane.
nelaván *m.* nelavan, nelavane.
nematelmintiasis *f.* nemathelminthiasis.
nematelminto *m.* nemathelminth.
nematicida *adj.* nematicide, nematocidal.
nematización *f.* nematization.
nematoblasto *m.* nematoblast.
nematocida[1] *m.* nematocide.
nematocida[2] *adj.* nematocidal.
Nematoda Nematoda.
nematodiasis *f.* nematodiasis.
nematodo *m.* nematode.
nematoide *adj.* nematoid.
nematoideo, -a *adj.* nematoid.
nematosis *f.* nematosis.
nematospermia *f.* nematospermia.
némico, -ca *adj.* nemic.
neoantígeno *m.* neoantigen.
neoartrosis *f.* neoarthrosis.
neobiogénesis *f.* neobiogenesis.
neoblástico, -ca *adj.* neoblastic.
neocerebelo *m.* neocerebellum.
neocinética *f.* neokinetics.
neocinético, -ca *adj.* neocinetic, neokinetic.
neocito *m.* neocyte.
neocitoféresis *f.* neocytopheresis.
neocitosis *f.* neocytosis.
neocistostomía *f.* neocystostomy.
neoconductismo *m.* neobehaviorism.
neocórtex *m.* neocortex.
neocorteza *f.* neocortex.
neodarvinismo *m.* neo-Darwinism.
neodarwinismo *m.* neo-Darwinism.
neodiatermia *f.* neodiathermy.
neencéfalo *m.* neencephalon.
neoencéfalo *m.* neoencephalon.
neoestriado, -da *adj.* neostriatum.
neofetal *adj.* neofetal.
neofeto *m.* neofetus.
neofilia *m.* neophilia.
neoformación *f.* neoformation.
neoformativo, -va *adj.* neoformative.
neogala *f.* neogala.
neogáster *m.* pneogaster.
neogénesis *f.* neogenesis.
neogenético, -ca *adj.* neogenetic.
neoglicogénesis *f.* neoglycogenesis.
neoglótico, -ca *adj.* neoglottic.
neoglotis *f.* neoglottis.
neoglucogénesis *f.* neoglycogenesis.
neógrafo *m.* pneograph.
neograma *m.* pneogram.
neohimen *m.* neohymen.
neolalia *f.* neolalia.
neolalismo *m.* neolalism.
neolipogénesis *f.* neolipogenesis.
neologismo *m.* neologism.
neomembrana *f.* neomembrane.
neómetro *m.* pneometer.
neomorfismo *m.* neomorphism.

neomorfo, -fa *adj.* neomorph.
neonatal *adj.* neonatal.
neonato *m.* baby, neonate.
  neonato azul blue baby.
  neonato en "bollito de arándanos" blueberry muffin baby.
  neonato de colodión collodion baby.
  neonato deficiente mentally handicapped neonate.
  neonato gigante giant baby.
  neonato malformado malformed neonate.
  neonato prematuro, neonato pretérmino premature infant, preterm infant.
neonatología *f.* neonatology.
neonatólogo, -ga *m., f.* neonatologist.
neonatómetro *m.* neonatometer.
neopalio *m.* neopallium.
neopallium neopallium.
neopatía *f.* neopathy.
neoplasia *f.* neoplasia.
  neoplasia benigna benign neoplasia.
  neoplasia endocrina múltiple multiple endocrine neoplasia.
  neoplasia endocrina múltiple, tipo I type I neoplasia.
  neoplasia endocrina múltiple, tipo II type II neoplasia.
  neoplasia endocrina múltiple, tipo III type III neoplasia.
  neoplasia histoide histoid neoplasia.
  neoplasia maligna malignant neoplasia.
  neoplasia mixta mixed neoplasia.
  neoplasia organoide organoid neoplasia.
neoplásico, -ca *adj.* neoplastic.
neoplasma *m.* neoplasm.
  neoplasma benigno benign neoplasm.
  neoplasma histoide histoid neoplasm.
  neoplasma maligno malignant neoplasm.
neoplastia *f.* neoplasty.
neoplástico, -ca *adj.* neoplastic.
neoplastigénico, -ca *adj.* neoplastigenic.
neorickettsiosa *f.* neorickettsious.
neoscopio *m.* pneoscope.
neostomía *f.* neostomy.
neostriado, -da *adj.* neostriatum.
neostriatal *adj.* neostriatal.
neostriatum neostriatum.
neostrófico, -ca *adj.* neostrophingic.
neotálamo *m.* neothalamus.
neovascularización *f.* neovascularization.
  neovascularización retiniana retinal neovascularization.
nepéntico, -ca *adj.* nepenthic.
nepiología *f.* nepiology.
neropatía *f.* neropathy.
nervimoción *f.* nervimotion.
nervimovilidad *f.* nervimotility.
nervimotilidad *f.* nervimotility.
nervimuscular *adj.* nervimuscular, nervomuscular.
nervino, -na *adj.* nervine.
nervio *m.* nerve, nervus.
nervios *m.* nerves.
nerviosidad *f.* nervosity.
nerviosismo *m.* nervosism, nervousness.
nervioso, -sa *adj.* nervous.
nervona *f.* nervone.
nervotabes *f.* nervotabes.
nervus nervus.
nesidiectomía *f.* nesidiectomy.
nesidioblasto *m.* nesidioblast.
nesidioblastoma *m.* nesidioblastoma.
nesidioblastosis *f.* nesidioblastosis.
nesslerización *f.* Nesslerization.
nesteostomía *f.* nesteostomy.

nestiatría *f.* nestiatria.
nestiterapia *f.* nestitherapy.
nestoterapia *f.* nestotherapy.
neumartrografía *f.* pneumarthography.
neumartrograma *m.* pneumarthrogram.
neumartrosis *f.* pneumarthrosis.
neumascopio *m.* pneumascope.
neumatemia *f.* pneumathemia.
neumática *f.* pneumatics.
neumático, -ca *adj.* pneumal.
neumatinuria *f.* pneumatinuria.
neumatipo *m.* pneumatype.
neumatización *f.* pneumatization.
neumatizado, -da *adj.* pneumatized.
neumatocardia *f.* pneumatocardia.
neumatocele *m.* pneumatocele.
  neumatocele craneal cranial pneumatocele, pneumatocele cranii.
  neumatocele extracraneal extracranial pneumatocele.
  neumatocele intracraneal intracranial pneumatocele.
neumatocefalia *f.* pneumatocephalus.
neumatodisnea *f.* pneumatodyspnea.
  neumatodisnea parotídeo parotid pneumatodyspnea.
neumatóforo *m.* pneumatophore.
neumatógrafo *m.* pneumatograph.
neumatograma *m.* pneumatogram.
neumatohemia *m.* pneumatohemia.
neumatometría *f.* pneumatometry.
neumatómetro *m.* pneumatometer.
neumatorraquis *m.* pneumatorrhachis.
neumatoscopio *m.* pneumatoscope.
neumatosis *f.* pneumatosis.
  neumatosis cistoide intestinal, neumatosis cystoides intestinalis pneumatosis cystoides intestinalis, pneumatosis cystoides intestinorum.
  neumatosis intestinal intestinal pneumatosis, pneumatosis intestinalis.
  neumatosis pulmonar pneumatosis pulmonum.
neumatoterapia *f.* pneumatotherapy.
neumatotórax *m.* pneumatothorax.
neumaturia *f.* pneumaturia.
neumectomía *f.* pneumectomy.
neumencefalografía *f.* pneumoencephalography.
neumoalveolografía *f.* pneumoalveolography.
neumoamnios *m.* pneumoamnios.
neumoangiografía *f.* pneumoangiography.
neumoangiograma *f.* pneumoangiogram.
neumoartrografía *f.* pneumoarthrography.
neumoartrograma *m.* pneumarthrogram.
neumoartrosis *f.* pneumarthrosis.
neumobacilo *m.* pneumobacillus.
  neumobacilo de Friedlander Friedlander's pneumobacillus.
neumobulbar *adj.* pneumobulbar.
neumobulboso, -sa *adj.* pneumobulbous.
neumocardíaco, -ca *adj.* pneumocardial.
neumocardiografía *f.* pneumocardiography.
neumocardiógrafo *m.* pneumocardiograph.
neumocefalia *f.* pneumocephalia.
neumocele *m.* pneumocele.
neumocentesis *f.* pneumocentesis.
neumocistiasis *f.* pneumocystiasis.
neumocístico, -ca *adj.* pneumocystic.
neumocistografía *f.* pneumocystography.
neumocistosis *f.* pneumocystosis.
neumocistotomografía *f.* pneumocystotomography.
neumocito *m.* pneumocyte.
neumococemia *f.* pneumococcemia.

neumocócico, -ca *adj.* pneumococcal, pneumococcic.
neumococida *adj.* pneumococcidal.
neumococo *m.* pneumococcus.
neumococólisis *f.* pneumococcolysis.
neumococosis *f.* pneumococcosis.
neumococosuria *f.* pneumococcosuria.
neumocolecistitis *f.* pneumocholecystitis.
neumocolon *m.* pneumocolon.
neumoconiosis *f.* pneumoconiosis.
 neumoconiosis de la bauxita, neumoconiosis por bauxita bauxite pneumoconiosis.
 neumoconiosis colagenosa collagenous pneumoconiosis.
 neumoconiosis de los mineros del carbón pneumoconiosis of coal workers.
 neumoconiosis siderótica pneumoconiosis siderotica.
neumocráneo *f.* pneumocranium, pneumocrania.
neumocrania *f.* pneumocrania.
neumodermia *f.* pneumoderma.
neumodinámica *f.* pneumodynamics.
neumodógrafo *m.* pneumodograph.
neumoectasia *f.* pneumonectasia, pneumonectasis.
neumoempiema *m.* pneumoempyema.
neumoencéfalo *m.* pneumoencephalus.
neumoencefalografía *f.* pneumoencephalography.
neumoencefalograma *f.* pneumoencephalogram.
neumoencefalomielografía *f.* pneumoencephalomyelography.
neumoencefalomielograma *f.* pneumoencephalomyelogram.
neumoenteritis *f.* pneumoenteritis.
neumoescroto *m.* pneumoscrotum.
neumofagia *f.* pneumophagia.
neumofasciografía *f.* neumofasciography.
neumofasciograma *m.* pneumofasciogram.
neumofonía *f.* pneumophonia.
neumogalactocele *m.* pneumogalactocele.
neumogástrico, -ca *adj.* pneumogastric.
neumogastrografía *f.* pneumogastrography.
neumogastroscopia *f.* pneumogastroscopy.
neumoginograma *m.* pneumogynogram.
neumografía *f.* pneumography.
 neumografía cerebral cerebral pneumography.
 neumografía retroperitoneal retroperitoneal pneumography.
neumógrafo *m.* pneumograph.
neumograma *m.* pneumogram.
neumohemia *f.* pneumohemia.
neumohemopericardio *m.* pneumohemopericardium.
neumohemotórax *m.* pneumohemothorax.
neumohidrómetra *m.* pneumohydrometra.
neumohidropericardio *m.* pneumohydropericardium.
neumohidroperitoneo *m.* pneumohydroperitoneum.
neumohidrotórax *m.* pneumohydrothorax.
neumohipodermia *m.* pneumohypoderma.
neumolitiasis *f.* pneumolithiasis.
neumolito *m.* pneumolith.
neumología *f.* pneumology.
neumomalacia *f.* pneumomalacia.
neumomasaje *m.* pneumomassage.
neumomastografía *f.* pneumomastography.
neumomediastino *m.* pneumomediastinum.
neumomediastinografía *f.* pneumomediastinography.
neumomediastinograma *m.* pneumomediastinogram.

neumomelanosis *f.* pneumomelanosis.
neumómetro *m.* pneumometer.
neumomicosis *f.* pneumomycosis.
neumomielografía *f.* pneumomyelography.
neumonectasia *f.* pneumonectasia.
neumonectasis *f.* pneumonectasis.
neumonectomía *f.* pneumonectomy.
neumonedema *m.* pneumonedema.
neumonemia *f.* pneumonedema.
neumonía *f.* pneumonia.
 neumonía abortiva abortive pneumonia.
 neumonía por aceites oil pneumonia.
 neumonía por agente de Eaton Eaton agent pneumonia.
 neumonía por aglutininas frías cold agglutinin pneumonia.
 neumonía aguda acute pneumonia.
 neumonía alba pneumonia alba.
 neumonía alcohólica alcoholic pneumonia.
 neumonía alérgica extrínseca extrinsic allergic pneumonia.
 neumonía amibiana amebic pneumonia.
 neumonía apical apical pneumonia, apex pneumonia.
 neumonía por aspiración aspiration pneumonia.
 neumonía por aspiración congénita congenital aspiration pneumonia.
 neumonía por aspiración de ácido gástrico Mendelsson's syndrome.
 neumonía atípica, neumonía atípica primaria atypical pneumonia, primary atypical pneumonia.
 neumonía bacteriana bacterial pneumonia.
 neumonía biliosa bilious pneumonia.
 neumonía blanca white pneumonia.
 neumonía bronquial bronchial pneumonia.
 neumonía bronquial atípica atypical bronchial pneumonia.
 neumonía por carbunco anthrax pneumonia.
 neumonía de los cardadores de lana woolsorter's pneumonia.
 neumonía caseosa caseous pneumonia, cheesy pneumonia.
 neumonía de células plasmáticas plasma cell pneumonia.
 neumonía central central pneumonia.
 neumonía de células gigantes giant cell pneumonia.
 neumonía central central pneumonia.
 neumonía cerebral cerebral pneumonia.
 neumonía congénita, neumonía congénita por aspiración congenital pneumonia, congenital aspiration pneumonia.
 neumonía por contusión contusion pneumonia.
 neumonía de Corrigan Corrigan's pneumonia.
 neumonía crónica chronic pneumonia.
 neumonía crónica eosinófila chronic eosinophilic pneumonia.
 neumonía cruposa croupous pneumonia.
 neumonía de la deglución, neumonía por deglución deglutition pneumonia.
 neumonía descamativa desquamative pneumonia.
 neumonía descamativa de Buhl Buhl's desquamative pneumonia.
 neumonía de Desnos Desnos' pneumonia.
 neumonía disecante pneumonia dissecans.
 neumonía doble double pneumonia.
 neumonía efímera ephemeral pneumonia.
 neumonía embólica embolic pneumonia.
 neumonía eosinófila, neumonía eosinofílica eosinophilic pneumonia.
 neumonía errante wandering pneumonia. .

 neumonía estafilocócica staphylococcal pneumonia.
 neumonía estreptocócica streptococcal pneumonia.
 neumonía fibrinosa fibrinous pneumonia.
 neumonía fibrosa fibrous pneumonia.
 neumonía fibrosa crónica chronic fibrous pneumonia.
 neumonía de Friedlander, neumonía por bacilo de Friedlander Friedlander's pneumonia, Friedlander's bacillus pneumonia.
 neumonía gangrenosa gangrenous pneumonia.
 neumonía generalizada generalized pneumonia.
 neumonía de Hecht Hecht's pneumonia.
 neumonía por hipersensibilidad hypersensitivity pneumonia.
 neumonía hipostática hypostatic pneumonia.
 neumonía indurativa indurative pneumonia.
 neumonía por inhalación inhalation pneumonia.
 neumonía interlobulillar purulenta pneumonia interlobularis purulenta.
 neumonía intersticial interstitial pneumonia.
 neumonía intersticial de células plasmáticas interstitial plasma cell pneumonia.
 neumonía intersticial descamativa desquamative interstitial pneumonia (DIP).
 neumonía intersticial linfoide lymphoid interstitial pneumonia.
 neumonía intrauterina intrauterine pneumonia.
 neumonía de Kaufmann Kaufmann's pneumonia.
 neumonía linfoide intersticial lymphoid interstitial pneumonia.
 neumonía lipida, neumonía lipoide, neumonía lipoidea lipoid pneumonia.
 neumonía lobular, neumonía lobulillar lobar pneumonia, lobular pneumonia.
 neumonía de Löffler Löffler's pneumonia.
 neumonía de Louisiana Louisiana pneumonia.
 neumonía maleosa pneumonia malleosa.
 neumonía masiva massive pneumonia.
 neumonía metastásica metastatic pneumonia.
 neumonía micoplasmática, neumonía por micoplasma mycoplasmal pneumonia, mycoplasma pneumonia.
 neumonía migratoria migratory pneumonia.
 neumonía neumocócica pneumococcal pneumonia.
 neumonía no resuelta unresolved pneumonia.
 neumonía nuclear core pneumonia.
 neumonía obstructiva obstructive pneumonia.
 neumonía parenquimatosa parenchymatous pneumonia.
 neumonía pestífera, neumonía pestosa, neumonía por peste plague pneumonia.
 neumonía de Pittsburgh Pittsburgh pneumonia.
 neumonía pleurítica pleuritic pneumonia.
 neumonía pleurógena pleurogenetic pneumonia, pleurogenic pneumonia.
 neumonía por Pneumocystis carinii Pneumocystis carinii pneumonia.
 neumonía primaria atípica primary atypical pneumonia.
 neumonía purulenta purulent pneumonia.

neumonía reumática rheumatic pneumonia.
neumonía de Riesman Riesman's pneumonia.
neumonía secundaria secondary pneumonia.
neumonía séptica septic pneumonia.
neumonía superficial superficial pneumonia.
neumonía supurativa suppurative pneumonia.
neumonía terminal terminal pneumonia.
neumonía tífica, neumonía tifoidica, neumonía tifoidea typhoid pneumonia.
neumonía toxémica toxemic pneumonia.
neumonía de los transplantes transplantation pneumonia.
neumonía traumática traumatic pneumonia.
neumonía tuberculosa tuberculous pneumonia.
neumonía tularémica tularemic pneumonia.
neumonía urémica uremic pneumonia.
neumonía vagal vagus pneumonia.
neumonía por varicela varicella pneumonia.
neumonía viral, neumonía vírica viral pneumonia.
neumonía por virus de la gripe influenzal pneumonia, influenza virus pneumonia.
neumónico, -ca *adj.* pneumonic.
neumonitis *f.* pneumonitis.
   neumonitis por aspiración aspiration pneumonitis.
   neumonitis de colesterol cholesterol pneumonitis.
   neumonitis granulomatosa granulomatous pneumonitis.
   neumonitis por hipersensibilidad hypersensitivity pneumonitis.
   neumonitis intersticial aguda acute interstitial pneumonitis.
   neumonitis intersticial linfocítica lymphocytic interstitial pneumonitis.
   neumonitis por Pneumocystis Pneumocystis pneumonitis.
   neumonitis palúdica malarial pneumonitis.
   neumonitis química chemical pneumonitis.
   neumonitis urémica uremic pneumonitis.
neumonocele *m.* pneumonocele.
neumonocentesis *f.* pneumonocentesis.
neumonocirrosis *f.* pneumonocirrhosis.
neumonocito *m.* pneumonocyte.
   neumonocito granuloso granular pneumonocyte.
   neumonocito membranoso membranous pneumonocyte.
neumonococo *m.* pneumonococcus.
neumonoconiosis *f.* pneumonoconiosis, pneumonokoniosis.
neumonoenteritis *f.* pneumonoenteritis.
neumonografía *f.* pneumonograph, pneumonography.
neumonolipoidosis *f.* pneumonolipoidosis.
neumonología *f.* pneumonology.
neumonomelanosis *f.* pneumonomelanosis.
neumonómetro *m.* pneumonometer.
neumonomicosis *f.* pneumonomycosis.
neumonopaludismo *m.* pneumonopaludism.
neumonopatía *f.* pneumonopathy.
neumonopexia *f.* pneumonopexy.
neumonopleuritis *f.* pneumonopleuritis.
neumonorrafia *f.* pneumorrhaphy.
neumonorragia *f.* pneumonorrhagia.
neumonorresección *f.* pneumonoresection.
neumonosis *f.* pneumonosis.
neumonoterapia *f.* pneumonotherapy.
neumonotisis *f.* pneumonophthisis.
neumonotomía *f.* pneumonotomy.
neumopaludismo *m.* pneumopaludism.
neumopatía *f.* pneumopathy.

neumopericardio *m.* pneumopericardium.
neumoperitoneal *adj.* pneumoperitoneal.
neumoperitoneo *m.* pneumoperitoneum.
neumoperitonitis *f.* pneumoperitonitis.
neumopexia *f.* pneumopexy.
neumopielografía *f.* pneumopyelography.
neumopiopericardio *m.* pneumopyopericardium.
neumopiotórax *m.* pneumopyothorax.
neumopleuritis *f.* pneumopleuritis.
neumopleuroparietopexia *f.* pneumopleuroparietopexy.
neumoprecordio *m.* pneumoprecordium.
neumopreperitoneo *m.* pneumopreperitoneum.
neumoquisis *f.* pneumochysis.
neumorradiografía *f.* pneumoradiography.
neumorrafia *f.* pneumorrhaphy.
neumorragia *f.* pneumorrhagia.
neumonorraquicentesis *f.* pneumonorachicentesis.
neumorraquis *m.* pneumorachis.
neumorresección *f.* pneumoresection.
neumorretroperitoneo *m.* pneumoretroperitoneum.
neumorriñón *m.* pneumokidney.
neumorroentgenografía *f.* pneumoroentgenonography.
neumosepticemia *f.* pneumosepticemia.
neumoserosa *f.* pneumoserosa.
neumoserotórax *m.* pneumoserothorax.
neumosilicosis *f.* pneumosilicosis.
neumotaquígrafo *m.* pneumotachygraph.
neumotacógrafo *m.* pneumotachograph, pneumotachygraph.
   neumotacógrafo de Fleich Fleich pneumotachograph.
   neumotacógrafo de Silverman-Lilly Silverman-Lilly pneumotachograph.
neumotacograma *m.* pneumotachogram.
neumotacómetro *m.* pneumotachometer.
neumoterapia *f.* pneumotherapy.
neumotermomasaje *m.* pneumothermomassage.
neumotifo *m.* pneumotyphus.
neumotifus *m.* pneumotyphus.
neumotímpano *m.* pneumotympanum.
neumotomía *f.* pneumotomy.
neumotomografía *f.* pneumotomography.
neumotórax *m.* pneumothorax.
   neumotórax abierto open pneumothorax, opening pneumothorax.
   neumotórax catamenial catamenial pneumothorax.
   neumotórax cerrado closed pneumothorax.
   neumotórax de chasquido clicking pneumothorax.
   neumotórax diagnóstico diagnostic pneumothorax.
   neumotórax espontáneo spontaneous pneumothorax.
   neumotórax extrapleural extrapleural pneumothorax.
   neumotórax hiperbárico tension pneumothorax.
   neumotórax a presión pressure pneumothorax.
   neumotórax a tensión tension pneumothorax.
   neumotórax valvular valvular pneumothorax.
neumotrópico, -ca *adj.* pneumotropic.
neumotropismo *m.* pneumotropism.
neumouria *f.* pneumouria.
neumoventrículo *f.* pneumoventricle.
neumoventriculografía *f.* pneumoventriculography.

neura *f.* neure.
neuradinamia *f.* neuradynamia.
neuragmia *f.* neuragmia.
neural *adj.* neural.
neuralgia *f.* neuralgia.
   neuralgia alucinatoria hallucinatory neuralgia.
   neuralgia de la articulación temporomaxilar mandibular joint neuralgia.
   neuralgia cardíaca cardiac neuralgia.
   neuralgia cervicobraquial cervicobrachial neuralgia.
   neuralgia cervicooccipital cervico-occipital neuralgia.
   neuralgia ciática sciatic neuralgia.
   neuralgia craneal cranial neuralgia.
   neuralgia craneal migrañosa migrainous cranial neuralgia.
   neuralgia degenerativa degenerative neuralgia.
   neuralgia esfenopalatina sphenopalatine neuralgia.
   neuralgia facial verdadera neuralgia facialis vera.
   neuralgia de Fothergill Fothergill's neuralgia.
   neuralgia geniculada geniculate neuralgia.
   neuralgia glosofaríngea glossopharyngeal neuralgia.
   neuralgia herpética herpetic neuralgia.
   neuralgia de Hunt Hunt's neuralgia.
   neuralgia idiopática idiopathic neuralgia.
   neuralgia intercostal intercostal neuralgia.
   neuralgia jaquecosa, neuralgia jaquecosa de Harris migrainous neuralgia, Harris' migrainous neuralgia.
   neuralgia mamaria mammary neuralgia.
   neuralgia del muñón stump neuralgia.
   neuralgia nasociliar nasociliary neuralgia.
   neuralgia ótica otic neuralgia.
   neuralgia periférica peripheral neuralgia.
   neuralgia plantar de Morton Morton's plantar neuralgia.
   neuralgia reminiscente reminiscent neuralgia.
   neuralgia roja red neuralgia.
   neuralgia sintomática symptomatic neuralgia.
   neuralgia de Sluder Sluder's neuralgia.
   neuralgia supraorbitaria supraorbital neuralgia.
   neuralgia trifacial trifacial neuralgia, trifocal neuralgia.
   neuralgia del trigémino trigeminal neuralgia.
   neuralgia vidiana vidian neuralgia.
   neuralgia visceral visceral neuralgia.
neurálgico, -ca *adj.* neuralgic.
neuralgiforme *adj.* neuralgiform.
neuranagénesis *f.* neuranagenesis.
neurangiosis *f.* neurangiosis.
neurapófisis *f.* neurapophysis.
neurapraxia *f.* neurapraxia.
neurarquia *f.* neurarchy.
neurartropatía *f.* neurarthropathy.
neurastenia *f.* neurasthenia.
neurasténico, -ca *adj.* neurasthenic.
neurataxia *f.* neurataxia, neurataxy.
neuratrofia *f.* neuratrophia, neuratrophy.
neuraxis *m.* neuraxis.
neuraxón *m.* neuraxon, neuraxone.
neurectasia *f.* neurectasia, neurectasy, neurectasis.
neurectasis *f.* neurectasis.
neurectomía *f.* neurectomy, neuroectomy.
   neurectomía gástrica gastric neurectomy.
neurectopia *f.* neurectopia, neurectopy.
neurentérico, -ca *adj.* neurenteric.
neurérgico, -ca *adj.* neurergic.

neurexéresis *f.* neurexeresis.
neuriatría *f.* neuriatry, neuratria.
neurilema *m.* neurilemma, neurolemma, neurolema.
neurilémico, -ca *adj.* neurilemmal.
neurilemitis *f.* neurilemmitis, neurolemmitis.
neurilemoma *m.* neurilemmoma, neurolemmoma.
   neurilemoma acústico acoustic neurilemoma.
neurilidad *f.* neurility.
neurimotilidad *f.* neurimotility.
neurinoma *m.* neurinoma.
   neurinoma acústico acoustic neurinoma.
   neurinoma benigno benign neurinoma.
   neurinoma del trigémino trigeminal neurinoma.
neurinomatosis *f.* neurinomatosis.
neurita *f.* neurite, neurit.
neurítico, -ca *adj.* neuritic.
neuritis *f.* neuritis.
   neuritis adventicia adventitial neuritis.
   neuritis alcohólica alcoholic neuritis.
   neuritis axial, neuritis axonal axial neuritis.
   neuritis braquial brachial neuritis.
   neuritis central central neuritis.
   neuritis de la cintura escapular shoulder-girdle neuritis.
   neuritis descendente descending neuritis.
   neuritis dietética dietetic neuritis.
   neuritis diseminada disseminated neuritis.
   neuritis endémica, neuritis endémica múltiple endemica neuritis, neuritis multiplex endemica.
   neuritis de Falopio Fallopian neuritis.
   neuritis de Gombault Gombault's neuritis.
   neuritis facial facial neuritis.
   neuritis intersticial interstitial neuritis.
   neuritis intersticial hipertrófica hypertrophic interstitial neuritis.
   neuritis intraocular intraocular neuritis.
   neuritis latente latent neuritis.
   neuritis leprosa leprous neuritis.
   neuritis migratoria migrating neuritis, neuritis migrans.
   neuritis múltiple multiple neuritis.
   neuritis nodosa neuritis nodosa.
   neuritis óptica optic neuritis.
   neuritis óptica orbitaria orbital optic neuritis.
   neuritis palúdica malarial neuritis.
   neuritis palúdica múltiple malarial multiple neuritis.
   neuritis parenquimatosa parenchymatous neuritis.
   neuritis periaxial periaxial neuritis.
   neuritis periférica peripheral neuritis.
   neuritis porfírica porphyric neuritis.
   neuritis posfebril postfebrile neuritis.
   neuritis postocular postocular neuritis.
   neuritis por presión pressure neuritis.
   neuritis puerperal traumática neuritis puerperalis traumatica.
   neuritis por radiación radiation neuritis.
   neuritis radicular radicular neuritis.
   neuritis retrobulbar retrobulbar neuritis.
   neuritis reumática rheumatic neuritis.
   neuritis saturnina neuritis saturnina.
   neuritis segmentaria segmental neuritis.
   neuritis senil senile neuritis.
   neuritis sérica serum neuritis.
   neuritis sifilítica syphilitic neuritis.
   neuritis tabética tabetic neuritis.
   neuritis tóxica toxic neuritis.
   neuritis traumática traumatic neuritis.
neuroalergia *f.* neuroallergy.
neuroamibiasis *f.* neuroamebiasis.

neuroamplificación *f.* neuroaugmentation.
neuroanastomosis *f.* neuroanastomosis.
neuroanatomía *f.* neuroanatomy.
neuroangiosis *f.* neurangiosis.
neuroapófisis *f.* neurapophysis.
neuroapraxia *f.* neurapraxia.
neuroartropatía *f.* neuroarthropathy.
neuroastrocitoma *m.* neuroastrocytoma.
neuroatrofia *f.* neuratrophia, neuratrophy.
neuroaxial *adj.* neuraxial.
neuroaxis *m.* neuraxis.
neuroaxón *m.* neuraxon, neuroaxone.
neurobiología *f.* neurobiology.
neurobiólogo, -ga *m.*, *f.* neurobiologist.
neurobiotaxis *f.* neurobiotaxis.
neuroblasto *m.* neuroblast.
neuroblastoma *m.* neuroblastoma.
neuroborreliosis *f.* neuroboreliosis.
neurocardíaco, -ca *adj.* neurocardiac.
neurocele *m.* neurocele.
neurocelo *m.* neurocele.
neurocentral *adj.* neurocentral.
neurocentro *m.* neurocentrum.
neuroceptor *m.* neuroceptor.
neurociencias *f.* neurosciences.
neurocientífico, -ca *m.*, *f.* y *adj.* neuroscientist.
neurocirugía *f.* neurosurgery.
   neurocirugía funcional functional neurosurgery.
neurocirujano *m.* neurosurgeon.
neurocito *m.* neurocyte.
neurocitólisis *f.* neurocytolysis.
neurocitología *f.* neurocytology.
neurocitoma *m.* neurocytoma.
neurocladismo *m.* neurocladism.
neuroclónico, -ca *adj.* neuroclonic.
neurocondrita *f.* neurochondrite.
neuroconductual *adj.* neurobehavioral.
neurocoriorretinitis *f.* neurochorioretinitis.
neurocoroiditis *f.* neurochoroiditis.
neurocraneal *adj.* neurocranial.
neurocráneo *m.* neurocranium.
   neurocráneo cartilaginoso cartilaginous neurocranium.
   neurocráneo membranoso membranous neurocranium.
neurocrinia *f.* neurocrinia.
neurocrino, -na *adj.* neurocrine.
neurocristopatía *f.* neurocristopathy.
neurocutáneo, -a *adj.* neurocutaneous.
neurodealgia *f.* neurodealgia.
neurodeatrofia *f.* neurodeatrophia.
neurodegenerativo, -va *adj.* neurodegenerative.
neurodendrita *f.* neurodendrite.
neurodendrón *m.* neurodendron.
neurodermatitis *f.* neurodermatitis.
   neurodermatitis crónica circunscrita circumscribed neurodermatitis.
   neurodermatitis diseminada disseminated neurodermatitis, neurodermatitis disseminata.
   neurodermatitis exudativa exudative neurodermatitis.
   neurodermatitis numular nummular neurodermatitis.
neurodermitis *f.* neurodermitis.
neurodermo *m.* neuroderm.
neurodiagnóstico *m.* neurodiagnosis.
neurodinámico, -ca *adj.* neurodynamic.
neurodinia *f.* neurodynia.
neurodocitis *f.* neurodocitis.
neuroectodérmico, -ca *adj.* neuroectodermal.
neuroectodermo *m.* neuroectoderm.
neuroectomía *f.* neuroectomy.

neuroefector, -ra *adj.* neuroeffector.
neuroeje *m.* brain stem.
neuroelectricidad *f.* neuroelectricity.
neuroelectroterapia *f.* neuroelectrotherapeutics, neuroelectrotherapy.
neuroemisor *m.* neuromittor.
neuroencefalomielopatía *f.* neuroencephalomyelopathy.
   neuroencefalomielopatía óptica optic neuroencephalomyelopathy.
neuroendarteriectomía *f.* neuroendarteriectomy.
neuroendocrino, -na *adj.* neuroendocrine.
neuroendocrinología *f.* neuroendocrinology.
neuroepidérmico, -ca *adj.* neuroepidermal.
neuroepitelial *adj.* neuroepithelial.
neuroepitelio *m.* neuroepithelium.
neuroepitelioma *m.* neuroepithelioma.
neuroesclerosis *f.* neurosclerosis.
neuroespasmo *m.* neurospasm.
neuroesplácnico, -ca *adj.* neurosplanchnic.
neuroespongio *m.* neurospongium.
neuroespongioma *m.* neurospongioma.
neuroesquelético, -ca *adj.* neuroskeletal.
neuroesqueleto *m.* neuroskeleton.
neuroestado *m.* neurostatus.
neuroestatus *m.* neurostatus.
neuroestimulación *f.* neurostimulation.
neuroestimulador *m.* neurostimulator.
neuroestimulante *m.* central nervous system stimulant.
neurofagia *f.* neuronophagia.
neurófago *m.* neurophage.
neurofarmacología *f.* neuropharmacology.
neurofarmacológico, -ca *adj.* neuropharmacological.
neurofibra *f.* neurofiber, neurofibra.
neurofibrilar *adj.* neurofibrillar.
neurofibrilla *f.* neurofibril.
neurofibroma *m.* neurofibroma.
   neurofibroma estoriforme storiform neurofibroma.
   neurofibroma plexiforme plexiform neurofibroma.
neurofibromatosis *f.* neurofibromatosis.
   neurofibromatosis abortiva abortive neurofibromatosis.
   neurofibromatosis incompleta incomplete neurofibromatosis.
neurofibrosarcomatosa *f.* neurofibrosarcomatosis.
neurofijación *f.* neurofixation.
neurofilamento *m.* neurofilament.
neurofilaxia *f.* neurophylaxy.
neurofílico, -ca *adj.* neurophilic.
neurófilo, -la *adj.* neurophilic.
neurofisiología *f.* neurophysiology.
neurofisiólogo, -ga *m.*, *f.* neurophysiologist.
neuroftalmología *f.* neurophthalmology, neuro-ophthalmology.
neuroganglitis *f.* neuroganglitis.
neurogástrico, -ca *adj.* neurogastric.
neurogénesis *f.* neurogenesis.
neurogenético, -ca *adj.* neurogenetic.
neurogénico, -ca *adj.* neurogenic.
neurógeno, -na *adj.* neurogenous.
neuroglía *m.* neuroglia.
   neuroglía interfascicular interfascicular neuroglia.
   neuroglía periférica peripheral neuroglia.
neuroglial *adj.* neuroglial, neurogliar.
neurogliar *adj.* neurogliar.
neurogliocito *m.* neurogliocyte.
neurogliocitoma *m.* neurogliocytoma.
neuroglioma *m.* neuroglioma.

neuroglioma ganglionar neuroglioma ganglionare.
neuroglucopenia f. neuroglycopenia.
neurografía f. neurography.
neurohemal adj. neurohemal.
neurohipnología f. neurohypnology.
neurohipofisario, -a adj. neurohypophyseal.
neurohipofisectomia f. neurohypophysectomy.
neurohipófisis f. neurohypophysis.
neurohistología f. neurohistology.
neurohormona f. neurohormone.
neurohormonal adj. neurohormonal.
neurohumor m. neurohumor.
neurohumoral adj. neurohumoral.
neuroide adj. neuroid.
neuroideo, -a adj. neuroid.
neuroinidia f. neuroinidia.
neuroinmunología f. neuroimmunology.
neuroinmunológico, -ca adj. neuroimmunologic.
neurolaberintitis f. neurolabyrinthitis.
neurolatirismo m. neurolathyrism.
neurolema m. neurolemma, neurolema.
neurolemitis f. neurolemmitis.
neurolemoma m. neurolemmoma.
neuroléptico, -ca adj. neuroleptic.
neuroleptoanalgesia f. neuroleptoanalgesia.
neuroleptoanalgésico, -ca adj. neuroleptanalgesic.
neuroleptoanestesia f. neuroleptanesthesia.
neuroleptoanestésico, -ca adj. neuroleptanesthetic.
neurolinfa f. neurolymph.
neurolinfomatosis f. neurolymphomatosis.
neurolinfomatosis periférica peripheral neurolymphomatosis.
neurolingüística f. neurolinguistics.
neurolipomatosis dolorosa f. neurolipomatosis dolorosa.
neurolisina f. neurolysin.
neurólisis f. neurolysis.
neurolítico, -ca adj. neurolytic.
neurolofoma m. neurolophoma.
neurología f. neurology.
neurología clínica clinical neurology.
neurológico, -ca adj. neurologic.
neurólogo, -ga m., f. neurologist.
neurolúes f. neurolues.
neuroma m. neuroma.
neuroma acústico acoustic neuroma.
neuroma amielínico amyelinic neuroma.
neuroma de amputación amputation neuroma.
neuroma cutáneo neuroma cutis.
neuroma falso false neuroma.
neuroma fascicular fascicular neuroma.
neuroma fibrilar fibrillary neuroma.
neuroma ganglionado, neuroma ganglionar, neuroma gangliónico ganglionated neuroma, ganglionar neuroma, ganglionic neuroma.
neuroma maligno malignant neuroma.
neuroma mielínico myelinic neuroma.
neuroma múltiple multiple neuroma.
neuroma del muñón stump neuroma.
neuroma nevoide nevoid neuroma.
neuroma plexiforme plexiform neuroma.
neuroma telangiectásico, neuroma telangiectodes neuroma telangiectodes.
neuroma traumático traumatic neuroma.
neuroma verdadero true neuroma.
neuroma de Verneuil Verneuil's neuroma.
neuromalacia f. neuromalacia, neuromalakia.
neuromarcapasos m. neuropacemaker.
neuromatosis f. neuromatosis.
neuromatoso, -sa adj. neuromatous.

neuromecanismo m. neuromechanism.
neuromelitococia f. neuromelitococcosis.
neuromeníngeo, -a adj. neuromeningeal.
neurómero m. neuromere.
neuromería f. neuromery.
neuromial adj. neuromyal.
neuromiastenia f. neuromyasthenia.
neuromiastenia epidémica epidemic neuromyasthenia.
neurómico, -ca adj. neuromyic.
neuromielitis f. neuromyelitis.
neuromielitis óptica neuromyelitis optica.
neuromimético, -ca adj. neuromimetic.
neuromiopatía f. neuromyopathy.
neuromiopatía carcinomatosa carcinomatous neuromyopathy.
neuromiopático, -ca adj. neuromyopathic.
neuromiositis f. neuromyositis.
neuromiotonía f. neuromyotonia.
neuromisor m. neuromittor.
neuromitor m. neuromittor.
neuromodulación f. neuromodulation.
neuromodulador m. neuromodulator.
neuromotor, -ra adj. neuromotor.
neuromuscular adj. neuromuscular.
neurona f. neuron, neurone.
neurona aferente afferent neuron.
neurona de asociación intercalary neuron, intercalated neuron.
neurona bipolar bipolar neuron.
neurona central central neuron.
neurona de conexión connector neuron.
neurona corta short neuron.
neurona de correlación correlation neuron.
neurona eferente efferent neuron.
neurona de Golgi del tipo I Golgi type I neuron.
neurona de Golgi del tipo II Golgi type II neuron.
neurona intercalar intercalary neuron, intercalated neuron.
neurona internuncial internuncial neuron.
neurona larga long neuron.
neurona motora motor neuron.
neurona motora periférica peripheral motor neuron.
neurona multiforme multiform neuron.
neurona multipolar multipolar neuron.
neurona polimórfica polymorphic neuron.
neurona posganglionar postganglionic neuron.
neurona preganglionar preganglionic neuron.
neurona premotora premotor neuron.
neurona de proyección projection neuron.
neurona sensitiva, neurona sensorial sensory neuron.
neurona sensitiva periférica, neurona sensorial periférica peripheral sensory neuron.
neurona seudounipolar pseudounipolar neuron.
neurona unipolar unipolar neuron.
neuronagénesis f. neuronagenesis.
neuronal adj. neuronal.
neuroncología f. neuroncology.
neuronéfrico, -ca adj. neuronephric.
neuronevo m. neuronevus.
neurónico, -ca adj. neuronic.
neuronimia f. neuronymy.
neuronina f. neuronin.
neuronitis f. neuronitis.
neuronixis f. neuronixis.
neuronoatrofia f. neuronoatrophy.
neuronofagia f. neuronophagia, neuronophagy.

neuronófago m. neuronophage.
neuronopatía f. neuronopathy.
neuronopatía sensorial sensory neuronopathy.
neuronosis f. neuronosis.
neuronotrópico, -ca adj. neuronotropic.
neurooftalmología f. neuro-ophthalmology.
neurootología f. neuro-otology.
neuropapilitis f. neuropapillitis.
neuroparálisis f. neuroparalysis.
neuroparalítico, -ca adj. neuroparalytic.
neurópata m., f. neuropath.
neuropatía f. neuropathy.
neuropatía alcohólica alcoholic neuropathy.
neuropatía amiloidea familiar familial amyloid neuropathy.
neuropatía anterior isquémica aguda acute anterior ischemic optic neuropathy.
neuropatía ascendente ascending neuropathy.
neuropatía de atrapamiento entrapment neuropathy.
neuropatía axonal glial glial axonal neuropathy.
neuropatía descendente descending neuropathy.
neuropatía diabética diabetic neuropathy.
neuropatía diftérica diphtheritic neuropathy.
neuropatía distal simétrica symmetric distal neuropathy.
neuropatía hipertrófica progresiva progressive hypertrophic neuropathy.
neuropatía intersticial hipertrófica progresiva progressive hypertrophic interstitial neuropathy.
neuropatía por isoniazida isoniazid neuropathy.
neuropatía leprosa leprous neuropathy.
neuropatía metabólica metabollic neuropathy.
neuropatía motora asimétrica asymmetric motor neuropathy.
neuropatía motora por dapsona motor dapsone neuropathy.
neuropatía óptica isquémica ischemic optic neuropathy.
neuropatía óptica hereditaria de Lieber Lieber's hereditary optic neuropathy, hereditary optic neuropathy, Lieber's optic neuropathy.
neuropatía paraneoplásica paraneoplastic neuropathy.
neuropatía del plexo braquial brachial plexus neuropathy.
neuropatía periaxial periaxial neuropathy.
neuropatía periférica peripheral neuropathy.
neuropatía por plomo lead neuropathy.
neuropatía radicular sensitiva hereditaria hereditary sensory radicular neuropathy.
neuropatía segmentaria segmental neuropathy.
neuropatía sérica serum neuropathy, serum sickness neuropathy.
neuropatía tomacular tomaculous neuropathy.
neuropático, -ca adj. neuropathic.
neuropatogénesis f. neuropathogenesis.
neuropatogenia f. neuropathogenesis.
neuropatogenicidad f. neuropathogenicity.
neuropatología f. neuropathology.
neuropatólogo, -ga m., f. neuropathologist.
neuropéptido m. neuropeptide.
neuropilema m. neuropilem.
neurópilo m. neuropil, neuropile.
neuroplasma m. neuroplasm.
neuroplásmico, -ca adj. neuroplasmic.

neuroplastia *f.* neuroplasty.
neuroplejia *f.* neuroplegia.
neuroplejía *f.* neuroplegia.
neuropléjico, -ca *adj.* neuroplegic.
neuroplexo *m.* neuroplexus.
neuropodio *m.* neuropodion.
neurópodo *m.* neuropodion.
neuroporo *m.* neuropore.
   neuroporo anterior anterior neuropore.
   neuroporo caudal caudal neuropore.
   neuroporo posterior posterior neuropore.
   neuroporo rostral rostral neuropore.
neuropotencial *m.* neuropotential.
neuropraxia *f.* neuropraxia.
neuroprobasia *f.* neuroprobasia.
neuroprobasis *f.* neuroprobasia.
neuropsicofarmacología *f.* neuropsychofarmacology.
neuropsicología *f.* neuropsychology.
neuropsicológico, -ca *adj.* neuropsychologic,
neuropsychological.
neuropsicoquimica *f.* neuropsychochemistry.
neuropsicosis *f.* neuropsychosis.
neuropsiquiatría *f.* neuropsychiatry.
neuropsiquiátrico, -ca *adj.* neuropsychiatric.
neuropsíquico, -ca *adj.* neuropsychic.
neuroptisis *f.* neurophthisis.
neuroquímica *f.* neurochemistry.
neuroquimo *m.* neurokyme.
neuroquineto *m.* neurokinet.
neurorradiología *f.* neuroradiology.
   neurorradiología intervencional interventional neuroradiology.
neurorradiólogo, -ga *m., f.* neuroradiologist.
neurorrafia *f.* neurorrhaphy.
neurorrecaída *f.* neurorelapse.
neurorreceptor *m.* neuroreceptor.
neurorrecidiva *f.* neurorecidive.
neurorrecurrencia *f.* neurorecurrence.
neurorrelapso *m.* neurorelapse.
neurorretinitis *f.* neuroretinitis.
neurorretinopatía *f.* neuroretinopathy.
   neurorretinopatía hipertensiva hypertensive neuroretinopathy.
neurorrexis *f.* neurorrhexis.
Neurorrhyctes hydrophobiae Neurorrhyctes hydrophobiae.
neurorroentgenografía *f.* neuroroentgenography.
neurosarcocleisis *f.* neurosarcocleisis.
neurosarcoidosis *f.* neurosarcoidosis.
neurosarcoma *m.* neurosarcoma.
neurosclerosis *f.* neurosclerosis.
neuroschwannoma *m.* neurosschwannoma.
neurosecreción *f.* neurosecretion.
neurosecretor, -ra *adj.* neurosecretory.
neurosecretorio, -ria *adj.* neurosecretory.
neurosegmentario, -ria *adj.* neurosegmental.
neurosensitivo, -va *adj.* neurosensory.
neurosensorial *adj.* neurosensory.
neurosífilis *f.* neurosyphilis.
   neurosífilis asintomática asymptomatic neurosyphilis.
   neurosífilis meningovascular meningovascular neurosyphilis.
   neurosífilis parenquimatosa parenchymatous
neurosyphilis.
   neurosífilis parética paretic neurosyphilis.
neurosis *f.* neurosis.
   neurosis de abandono neurosis of abandonment.
   neurosis actual actual neurosis.
   neurosis de angustia anxiety neurosis.
   neurosis de ansiedad anxiety neurosis.
   neurosis de carácter character neurosis.

   neurosis cardíaca cardiac neurosis.
   *neurosis compulsiva, neurosis de compul-
sión* compulsion neurosis.
   neurosis de combate combat neurosis.
   neurosis de conversión conversion neurosis.
   neurosis del corazón del soldado combat
neurosis.
   neurosis depresiva depressive neurosis.
   neurosis experimental experimental neurosis.
   neurosis familiar family neurosis.
   neurosis de fatiga fatigue neurosis.
   neurosis fóbica phobic neurosis.
   neurosis de fracaso failure neurosis.
   neurosis gástrica gastric neurosis.
   neurosis de guerra war neurosis.
   neurosis hipocondríaca hypochondriacal neurosis, hypochondrial neurosis.
   neurosis histérica hysterical neurosis.
   neurosis mixta mixed neurosis.
   neurosis narcisista narcissistic neurosis.
   neurosis neurasténica neurasthenic neurosis.
   neurosis obsesiva obsessional neurosis.
   neurosis obsesivo-compulsiva obsessional
neurosis.
   neurosis de transferencia transference neurosis.
   neurosis traumática traumatic neurosis.
   neurosis vegetativa vegetative neurosis.
neurosismo *m.* neurosism.
neurosoma *m.* neurosome.
neurospasmo *m.* neurospasm.
neurosplácnico, -ca *adj.* neurosplanchnic.
neurospongio *m.* neurospongium.
neurospongioma *m.* neurospongioma.
neurosquelético, -ca *adj.* neuroskeletal.
neurosqueleto *m.* neuroskeleton.
neurostenia *f.* neurosthenia.
neurosténico, -ca *adj.* neurosthenic.
neurosutura *f.* neurosuture.
neurotabes *f.* neurotabes.
neurotagma *m.* neurotagma.
neurotendinoso, -sa *adj.* neurotendinous.
neurotensión *f.* neurotension.
neurotequeoma *m.* neurothekeoma.
neuroterapia *f.* neurotherapeutics, neurotherapy.
neuroterminal *adj.* neuroterminal.
neuroticismo *m.* neuroticism.
neurótico, -ca *adj.* neurotic.
neurotismo *m.* neuroticism.
neurotización *f.* neurotization.
neurotizar *v.* neurotize.
neurotlipsia *f.* neurothlipsia, neurothlipsis.
neurotlipsis *f.* neurothlipsis.
neurotmesis *f.* neurotmesis.
neurotología *f.* neurotology, neuro-otology.
neurotoma *m.* neurotome.
neurotomía *f.* neurotomy.
   neurotomía opticociliar opticociliary neurotomy.
   neurotomía retrogasseriana retro-Gasserian
neurotomy.
   neurotomía por radiofrecuencia radiofrequency neurotomy.
neurótomo *m.* neurotome.
neurotomografía *f.* neurotomography.
neurotonía *f.* neurotonia, neurotony.
neurotónico, -ca *adj.* neurotonic.
neurotonómetro *m.* neurotonometer.
neurotoxia *f.* neurotoxia.
neurotoxicidad *f.* neurotoxicity.
neurotóxico, -ca *adj.* neurotoxic.
neurotransductor *m.* neurotransducer.

neurotransmisión *f.* neurotransmission.
neurotransmisor *m.* neurotransmitter.
   neurotransmisor falso false neurotransmitter.
neurotrauma *m.* neurotrauma.
neurotripsia *f.* neurotripsy.
neurotrofastenia *f.* neurotrophasthenia.
neurotrofia *f.* neurotrophy.
neurotrófico, -ca *adj.* neurotrophic.
neurotrofoastenia *f.* neurotrophastenia.
neurotropía *f.* neurotropy.
neurotrópico, -ca *adj.* neurotropic.
neurotropismo *m.* neurotropism.
neurotrosis *f.* neurotrosis.
neurotúbulo *m.* neurotubule.
neurovacuna *f.* neurovaccine.
neurovaricosidad *f.* neurovaricosity.
neurovaricosis *f.* neurovaricosis.
neurovariola *f.* neurovariola.
neurovascular *adj.* neurovascular.
neurovegetativo, -va *adj.* neurovegetative.
neurovirulencia *f.* neurovirulence.
neurovirulento, -ta *adj.* neurovirulent.
neurovirus *m.* neurovirus.
neurovisceral *adj.* neurovisceral.
néurula *f.* neurula.
neurulación *f.* neurulation.
neurúrgico, -ca *adj.* neururgic.
neusímetro *m.* pneusometer.
neusis *f.* pneusis.
neutral *adj.* neutral.
neutralidad *f.* neutrality.
neutralismo *m.* neutralism.
neutralización *f.* neutralization.
   neutralización ocular unicular suppression.
   neutralización viral viral neutralization.
neutralizar *v.* neutralize.
neutreto *m.* neutretto.
neutrino *m.* neutrino.
neutro, -tra *adj.* neutral.
neutrocito *m.* neutrocyte.
neutrocitofilia *f.* neutrocytophilia.
neutrocitopenia *f.* neutrocytopenia.
neutrocitosis *f.* neutrocytosis.
neutroclusión *f.* neutroclusion.
neutrofilia *f.* neutrophilia.
neutrofílico, -ca *adj.* neutrophilic.
neutrófilo *m.* neutrophil.
   neutrófilo en banca stab neutrophil.
   neutrófilo en banda band neutrophil.
   neutrófilo en bastoncillo rod neutrophil.
   neutrófilo filamentado filamented neutrophil.
   neutrófilo gigante giant neutrophil.
   neutrófilo hipersegmentado hypersegmented neutrophil.
   neutrófilo inmaduro immature neutrophil.
   neutrófilo juvenil juvenile neutrophil.
   neutrófilo maduro mature neutrophil.
   neutrófilo segmentado segmented neutrophil.
neutrófilo, -la *adj.* neutrophilous.
neutrofilopenia *f.* neutrophilopenia.
neutrografía *m.* neutrography.
neutrón *m.* neutron.
neutropenia *f.* neutropenia.
   neutropenia cíclica cyclic neutropenia.
   neutropenia congénita congenital neutropenia.
   neutropenia crónica benigna de la infancia
chronic benign neutropenia of childhood.
   neutropenia esplénica primaria primary splenic neutropenia.
   neutropenia familiar crónica benigna familial benign chronic neutropenia.

neutropenia hiperesplénica hypersplenic neutropenia.

neutropenia hipoplásica crónica chronic hypoplastic neutropenia.

neutropenia idiopática idiopathic neutropenia.

neutropenia de Kostmann Kostmann neutropenia.

neutropenia maligna malignant neutropenia.

neutropenia neonatal neonatal neutropenia.

neutropenia neonatal transitoria transitory neonatal neutropenia.

neutropenia periférica peripheral neutropenia.

neutropenia periódica periodic neutropenia.

neutropismo *m.* neutropism.

neutrotaxis *f.* neutrotaxis.

nevo *m.* nevus, naevus.

nevo acrómico achromic nevus.

nevo adquirido acquired nevus.

nevo amelanótico amelanotic nevus.

nevo ampolla de forma azul blue nevus.

nevo anémico naevus anemicus.

nevo angiectodeo naevus angiectodes.

nevo angiomatodieo naevus angiomatodes.

nevo arácneo, nevo aracnoideo naevus arachnoideus, naevus araneosus, naevus araneus.

nevo en araña spider nevus.

nevo azul blue nevus.

nevo azul celular cellular blue nevus.

nevo azul con flictenas de goma blue rubber bleb nevus.

nevo azul en pezón blue rubber bleb nevus.

nevo azul en tetina de goma blue rubber bleb nevus.

nevo azul de Jadassohn-Tièche Jadassohn-Tièche nevus.

nevo de Becker Becker's nevus.

nevo capilar capillary nevus.

nevo cavernoso naevus cavernosus.

nevo celular cellular nevus.

nevo celular azul cellular blue nevus.

nevo celular en balón, nevo celular baloniforme balloon cell nevus.

nevo de células basales basal cell nevus.

nevo de células epitelioides epithelioid cell nevus.

nevo de células fusiformes spindle cell nevus.

nevo de células fusiformes y epitelioides spindle and epithelioid cell nevus.

nevo de células névicas nevus-cell nevus.

nevo cola de fauno faun tail nevus.

nevo comedónico naevus comedonicus.

nevo compuesto compound nevus.

nevo congénito congenital nevus.

nevo cromatóforo de Naegeli chromatophore nevus of Naegeli.

nevo dérmico dermal nevus.

nevo dermoepidérmico epidermic-dermic nevus.

nevo despigmentado naevus despigmentosus.

nevo displásico dysplastic nevus.

nevo elástico naevus elasticus.

nevo elástico de Lewandowsky naevus elasticus of Lewandowsky.

nevo epidérmico epidermal nevus.

nevo epidérmico piloso pigmentado pigmented hairy epidermal nevus.

nevo epidérmico velloso pigmentado pigmented hairy epidermal nevus.

nevo epitelial epithelial nevus.

nevo epitelial oral oral epithelial nevus.

nevo esponjoso blanco white sponge nevus.

nevo estelar stellar nevus.

nevo flámeo naevus flammeus.

nevo flamígero naevus flammeus.

nevo folicular naevus follicularis.

nevo de los folículos pilosos hair follicle nevus.

nevo folicular queratoso naevus follicularis keratosis.

nevo en frambuesa, nevo en fresa strawberry nevus.

nevo fuscocerúleo acromiodeltoideo naevus fuscoceruleus acromiodeltoideus.

nevo gigante congénito pigmentado giant congenital pigmented nevus.

nevo gigante pigmentado giant pigmented nevus.

nevo gigante velloso giant hairy nevus.

nevo graso fatty nevus.

nevo en halo halo nevus.

nevo hepático hepatic nevus.

nevo intermedio junction nevus.

nevo intradérmico intradermal nevus.

nevo de Ito Ito's nevus, nevus of Ito.

nevo de Jadassohn Jadassohn's nevus.

nevo lineal linear nevus.

nevo lipomatoso naevus lipomatoides.

nevo lipomatoso cutáneo superficial naevus lipomatosus cutaneus superficialis.

nevo en llama flame nevus.

nevo melanocítico melanocytic nevus.

nevo neural neural nevus, neuroid nevus.

nevo nevocelular nevocellular nevus.

nevo nevocítico nevocytic nevus.

nevo nodular de tejido conjuntivo nodular connective tissue nevus.

nevo no pigmentado non-pigmented nevus.

nevo de la nuca nape nevus, nuchal nevus.

nevo organoide organoid nevus.

nevo de Ota Ota's nevus, nevus of Ota.

nevo papilomatoso naevus papillomatosus.

nevo pigmentado, nevo pigmentario, nevo pigmentoso pigmented nevus, naevus pigmentosus.

nevo pigmentado gigante giant pigmented nevus.

nevo piloso hairy nevus, pilose nevus, naevus pilosus.

nevo plano naevus spilus.

nevo plano tardío naevus spilus tardus.

nevo sanguíneo naevus sanguineus, nevus sanguineus.

nevo sebáceo, nevo sebáceo de Jadassohn naevus sebaceus, naevus sebaceus of Jadassohn.

nevo siringocistadenoso papilífero naevus syringocystadenosus papilliferus.

nevo siringoquístico adenomatoso papilífero naevus syringocystadenomatosus papilliferus.

nevo sistemizado systemized nevus.

nevo de Spitz Spitz nevus.

nevo de Sutton Sutton's nevus.

nevo de tejido conjuntivo connective tissue nevus.

nevo telangiectásico telangiectatic nevus.

nevo en traje de baño bathing trunk nevus.

nevo de transición junction nevus.

nevo unilateral, naevus unius lateris, nevus unius lateris naevus unius lateris.

nevo de unión junction nevus, junctional nevus.

nevo de Unna Unna's nevus.

nevo vascular vascular nevus, nevus vascularis, naevus vasculosus.

nevo velloso hairy nevus.

nevo venoso naevus venosus.

nevo verrucoide, nevo verrucoso, nevo verrugoso verrucous nevus, verrucoid nevus, naevus verrucosus.

nevoblasto *m.* nevoblast.

nevocáncer *m.* naevocancer.

nevocarcinoma *m.* nevocarcinoma.

nevocítico, -ca *adj.* nevocytic.

nevocito *m.* nevocyte.

nevofibroma miliar *m.* miliary nevofibroma.

nevoide *adj.* nevoid.

nevoideo, -a *adj.* nevoid.

nevolipoma *m.* nevolipoma.

nevomatosa basocelular *f.* Gorlin-Goltz syndrome.

nevoxantoendotelioma *m.* naevoxanthoendothelioma, nevoxanthoendothelioma.

nevus nevus.

nexo *m.* nexus.

nexus nexus.

niacinamida *f.* niacinamide.

nicho *m.* niche.

nicho de Barclay Barclay's niche.

nicho ecológico ecological niche, ecologic niche.

nicho del esmalte enamel niche.

nicho de Haudek Haudek's niche.

nicho de la ventana redonda niche of round window.

nicotina *f.* nicotine.

nicotinamida *f.* nicotinamide.

nicotinamidemia *f.* nicotinamidemia.

nicotinismo *m.* nicotinism.

nicotinolítico, -ca *adj.* nicotinolytic.

nicotinomimético, -ca *adj.* nicotinomimetic.

nictación *f.* nictation.

nictafonía *f.* nyctaphonia.

nictalgia *f.* nyctalgia.

nictálope *adj.* nyctalope.

nictalopía *f.* nyctalopia.

nictalopía con miopía congénita nyctalopia with congenital myopia.

nictanopía *f.* nyctanopia.

nictémero, -ra *adj.* nictemeral.

nicterino, -na *adj.* nycterine.

nicterohemeral *adj.* nycterohemeral.

nictificación *f.* nictitation.

nictitación *f.* nictitation.

nictitante *adj.* nictitating.

nictofilia *f.* nyctophilia.

nictofobia *f.* nyctophobia, noctiphobia.

nictofonía *f.* nictophonia.

nictohemeral *adj.* nyctohemeral.

nictotiflosis *f.* nyctotyphlosis.

nictotiplosis *f.* nyctotyphlosis.

nicturia *f.* nicturia, nycturia, nocturia.

nidación *f.* nidation.

nidal *adj.* nidal.

nido *m.* nest, nidus.

nido de ave miliar avis.

nido de cáncer cancer nidus.

nido epitelial epithelial nest.

nido epitelial de Brunn Brunn's epithelial nest.

nido de golondrina swallow nest, nidus hirundinis.

nido de Waltard Waltard cell nest.

nifablepsia *f.* niphablepsia.

nifotiflosis *f.* niphotyphlosis.

nigral *adj.* nigral.

nigrities nigrities.

nigrities linguae nigrities linguae.

nigroestriado, -da *adj.* nigrostriatal.

nigrosina *f.* nigrosin, nigrosine.

nigrosis rectal *f.* melanosis recti.

nihilismo *m.* nihilism.
  nihilismo terapéutico therapeutic nihilism.
ninfa *f.* nymph, nympha.
  ninfa de Krause nymph of Krause.
ninfal *adj.* nymphal.
ninfectomía *f.* nymphectomy.
ninfitis *f.* nymphitis.
ninfocaruncular *adj.* nymphocaruncular.
ninfohimenal *adj.* nymphohymeneal.
ninfohimeneal *adj.* nymphohymeneal.
ninfolabial *adj.* nympholabial.
ninfolepsia *f.* nympholepsy.
ninfómana *f.* nymphomaniac.
ninfomanía *f.* nymphomania.
ninfomaníaco, -ca *adj.* nymphomaniacal.
ninfonco *m.* nymphoncus.
ninfotomía *f.* nymphotomy.
niñez *f.* childhood.
niño, -ña *m., f.* child.
nistágmico, -ca *adj.* nystagmic.
nistagmiforme *adj.* nystagmiform.
nistagmo *m.* nystagmus.
  nistagmo adaptable resilient nystagmus.
  nistagmo amaurótico amaurotic nystagmus.
  nistagmo ambliópico amblyopic nystagmus.
  nistagmo atáxico ataxic nystagmus.
  nistagmo aural aural nystagmus.
  nistagmo calórico caloric nystagmus, nystagmus in caloric tests.
  nistagmo de Cheyne, nistagmo de Cheyne-Stokes Cheyne's nystagmus.
  nistagmo central central nystagmus.
  nistagmo congénito congenital nystagmus, congenital hereditary nystagmus.
  nistagmo conjugado conjugate nystagmus.
  nistagmo convergente convergence nystagmus.
  nistagmo desviacional deviational nystagmus.
  nistagmo disociado dissociated nystagmus.
  nistagmo disyuntivo dysjunctive nystagmus.
  nistagmo eléctrico electrical nystagmus.
  nistagmo espontáneo spontaneous nystagmus.
  nistagmo de fatiga fatigue nystagmus.
  nistagmo de ferrocarril railroad nystagmus.
  nistagmo de fijación fixation nystagmus.
  nistagmo galvánico galvanic nystagmus.
  nistagmo laberíntico labyrinthine nystagmus.
  nistagmo latente latent nystagmus.
  nistagmo lateral lateral nystagmus.
  nistagmo de los mineros miner's nystagmus.
  nistagmo mioclónico nystagmus myoclonus.
  nistagmo de la mirada gaze nystagmus.
  nistagmo ocular ocular nystagmus.
  nistagmo ondulatorio ondulatory nystagmus.
  nistagmo opticocinético, nistagmo opticinético, nistagmo optoquinético optokinetic nystagmus, opticokinetic nystagmus.
  nistagmo oscilante, nistagmo oscilatorio ondulatory nystagmus.
  nistagmo palatino palatal nystagmus.
  nistagmo parético paretic nystagmus.
  nistagmo pendular pendular nystagmus.
  nistagmo de posición final, nistagmo de posición terminal end-position nystagmus.
  nistagmo posicional positional nystagmus.
  nistagmo de retracción retraction nystagmus, nystagmus retractorius.
  nistagmo rítmico rhythmical nystagmus.
  nistagmo rotatorio rotatory nystagmus.
  nistagmo en sacudidas jerky nystagmus, jerk nystagmus.
  nistagmo secundario secondary nystagmus.
  nistagmo en sierra see-saw nystagmus.

  nistagmo unilateral unilateral nystagmus.
  nistagmo vertical vertical nystagmus.
  nistagmo vertical hacia abajo downbeat nystagmus.
  nistagmo vertical hacia arriba upbeat nystagmus.
  nistagmo vibratorio vibratory nystagmus.
  nistagmo vestibular vestibular nystagmus.
  nistagmo visual visual nystagmus.
  nistagmo voluntario voluntary nystagmus.
nistagmografía *f.* nystagmography.
nistagmógrafo *m.* nystagmograph.
nistagmograma *m.* nystagmogram.
nistagmoide *adj.* nystagmoid.
nistagmometría *f.* nystagmometry.
nistagmus nystagmus.
nistaxis *f.* nystaxis.
nitremia *f.* nitremia.
nitrificación *f.* nitrification.
nitrituria *f.* nitrituria.
nitrogenación *f.* nitrogen-fixing.
nitrogenado, -da *adj.* nitrogenous.
nitrogenización *f.* nitrogenization.
nitrógeno *m.* nitrogen.
nitrómetro *m.* nitrometer.
nitrón *m.* nitron.
nivel *m.* level.
  nivel auditivo hearing level.
  nivel de Clark Clark's level.
  nivel de consciencia level of consciousness.
  nivel de creatinina en suero serum creatinine level.
  nivel isoeléctrico isoelectric level.
  nivel máximo peak level.
  nivel operativo operant level.
  nivel plasmático de fenobarbitalfenitoína phenobarbitalphenytoin serum level.
  nivel de presión del sonido sound pressure level.
  nivel de referencia acústica acoustic reference level.
  nivel sanguíneo blood level.
  nivel sanguíneo de glucosa blood level of glucose.
  nivel de significación significance level.
  nivel de ventana window level.
nixis *f.* nyxis.
njovera *f.* njovera.
no adherente *adj.* non-adherent.
no antigénico, -ca *adj.* non-antigenic.
no cariogénico, -ca *adj.* non-cariogenic.
no celular *adj.* non-cellular.
no conductor, -ra *adj.* non-conductor.
no despolarizador, -ra *adj.* non-depolarizer.
no disyunción *f.* non-disjunction.
no electrolito *m.* non-electrolyte.
no enfermedad *f.* non-disease.
no estriado, -da *adj.* unstriated.
no fisiológico, -ca *adj.* unphysiologic.
no fotocromógeno *m.* non photochromogen.
no gustador, -ra *adj.* non-taster.
no hem *adj.* non-heme.
no infeccioso, -sa *adj.* non-infectious.
no inmune *adj.* non-immune.
no inmunidad *f.* non-immunity.
no intentar la reanimación (NIR) do not attempt resuscitation (DNAR).
no iónico, -ca *adj.* non-ionic.
no invasivo, -va *adj.* non-invasive.
no involución *f.* non-involution.
no mielínico, -ca *adj.* non-medullated, non-myelinic.
no neoplásico, -ca *adj.* non-neoplastic.
no nucleado, -da *adj.* non-nucleated.
no oclusión *f.* non-occlusion.

no oligúrico, -ca *adj.* non-oliguric.
no oncógeno, -na *adj.* non-oncogenic.
no opaco, -ca *adj.* non-opaque.
no organizado, -da *adj.* unorganized.
no penetrancia *f.* non-penetrance.
no polar *adj.* non-polar.
no radiable *adj.* non-radiable.
no respuesta (NR) *f.* no response (NR).
no rotación *f.* non-rotation.
no secretor, -ra *m., f.* non-secretor.
no septado, -da *adj.* non-septate.
no tóxico, -ca *adj.* non-toxic.
no unión *f.* non-union.
no valente *adj.* non-valent.
no vascular *adj.* non-vascular.
no verbal *adj.* non-verbal.
no viable *adj.* non-viable.
Nocardia Nocardia.
nocardial *adj.* nocardial.
nocardiasis *f.* nocardiasis.
Nocardiaceae Nocardiaceae.
nocardioforme *adj.* nocardioform.
nocardiosis *f.* nocardiosis.
  nocardiosis granulomatosa granulomatous nocardiosis.
Nocardiopsis Nocardiopsis.
nocebo *m.* nocebo.
nociasociación *f.* nociassociation.
nocicepción *f.* nociception.
nociceptivo, -va *adj.* nociceptive.
nociceptor *m.* nociceptor.
  nociceptor polimodal polymodal nociceptor.
nocifensor, -ra *adj.* nocifensor.
nociinfluencia *f.* noci-influence.
nocipercepción *f.* nociperception.
nocivo, -va *adj.* noxious.
noctalbuminuria *f.* noctalbuminuria.
noctambulación *f.* noctambulation.
noctambulismo *m.* noctambulism.
noctámbulo, -la *adj.* noctambulic.
noctifobia *f.* noctiphobia.
nocturia *f.* nocturia.
nocturno, -na *adj.* nocturnal.
nocuidad *f.* nocuity.
nodal *adj.* nodal.
nodriza *f.* wet nurse.
nodulación *f.* nodulation.
nodulado, -da *adj.* nodulate, nodulated.
nodular *adj.* nodular.
nodulectomía *f.* nodulectomy.
nodulitis *f.* nodulitis.
  nodulitis reumatoide rheumatoid nodulitis.
nódulo[1] *m.* nodule, nodulus.
nódulo[2] *m.* node.
  nódulo de Aschoff-Tawara Aschoff-Tawara's node.
  nódulo auriculoventricular atrioventricular node.
  nódulo de Bouchard Bouchard's node.
  nódulo de cantante singer's node.
  nódulo de Féréol Féréol's node.
  nódulo de Haygarth Haygarth's node.
  nódulo de Heberden Heberden's node.
  nódulo de Meynet Meynet's node.
  nódulo de Osler Osler's node.
  nódulo de profesor teacher's node.
  nódulo sifilítica syphilitic node.
  nódulo sinoauricular sinoatrial node, sinoauricular node.
  nódulo sinusal sinoatrial node, sinoauricular node.
  nódulo de Tawara Tawara's node.
nodulosis *f.* nodulosis.
  nodulosis reumatoide rheumatoid nodulosis.
noduloso, -sa *adj.* nodulous.

nodulus nodulus.
nodus nodus.
noematocómetro *m.* noematochometer.
noemático, -ca *adj.* noematic.
noesis *f.* noesis.
noético, -ca *adj.* noetic.
noma *m.* noma.
  noma de la vulva, noma pudendi noma pudendi, noma vulvae.
nómada *adj.* nomadic.
nomatofobia *f.* nomatophobia.
nombre *m.* name.
  nombre genérico generic name.
  nombre patentado proprietary name.
  nombre no patentado non-proprietary name.
  nombre registrado proprietary name.
  nombre no registrado non-proprietary name.
  nombre sistemático systematic name.
  nombre trivial trivial name.
  nombre vulgar trivial name.
nomenclatura *f.* nomenclature.
  nomenclatura binaria, nomenclatura binomial binary nomenclature, binomial nomenclature.
  nomenclatura cromosómica chromosomal nomenclature.
Nomina Anatomica (NA) *f.* Nomina Anatomica (NA).
nomogénesis *f.* nomogenesis.
nomografía *f.* nomography.
nomograma *m.* nomogram.
  nomograma cartesiano Cartesian nomogram.
  nomograma de Radford Radford nomogram.
  nomograma respiratorio breathing nomogram.
  nomograma de Siggard-Andersen Siggard-Andersen nomogram.
  nomograma del volumen sanguíneo blood volume nomogram.
  nomograma de West West nomogram.
nomotético, -ca *adj.* nomothetic.
nomotópico, -ca *adj.* nomotopic.
non compos mentis *adj.* non compos mentis.
nona *f.* nona.
nonana *adj.* nonan.
nooanaléptico, -ca *adj.* nooanaleptic.
noocleptia *f.* nookleptia.
norma¹ *f.* rule.
norma² *f.* norma.
normal *adj.* normal.
normalidad *f.* normality.
normalización *f.* normalization.
normalizar *v.* normalize.
normérgico, -ca *adj.* normergic.
normoblástico, -ca *adj.* normoblastic.
normoblasto *m.* normoblast.
  normoblasto acidófilo acidophilic normoblast.
  normoblasto basófilo basophilic normoblast.
  normoblasto eosinófilo eosinophilic normoblast.
  normoblasto intermedio intermediate normoblast.
  normoblasto ortocromático orthochromatic normoblast.
  normoblasto oxífilo oxyphilic normoblast.
  normoblasto policromático polychromatic normoblast.
  normoblasto tardío late normoblast.
  normoblasto temprano early normoblast.
normoblastosis *f.* normoblastosis.
normocalcemia *f.* normocalcemia.
normocalcémico, -ca *adj.* normocalcemic.
normocapnia *f.* normocapnia.
normocítico, -ca *adj.* normocytic.
normocito *m.* normocyte.
normocitosis *f.* normocytosis.

normocolesterolemia *f.* normocholesterolemia.
normocolesterolémico, -ca *adj.* normocholesterolemic.
normocromía *f.* normochromia.
normocrómico, -ca *adj.* normochromic.
normocromocito *m.* normochromocyte.
normodrómico, -ca *adj.* normodromous.
normoérgico, -ca *adj.* normergic.
normoeritrocito *m.* normoerythrocyte.
normoespermia *f.* normospermia.
normogénesis *f.* normogenesis.
normoglucemia *f.* normoglycemia.
normoglucémico, -ca *adj.* normoglycemic.
normolineal *adj.* normolineal.
normolipedemia *f.* normolipidemia.
normolipemia *f.* normolipidemia.
normonormocitosis *f.* normonormocytosis.
normoortocitosis *f.* normo-orthocytosis.
normoplasia *f.* normoplasia.
normopotasemia *f.* normokalemia, normokaliemia.
normosexualidad *f.* normosexuality.
normosqueocitosis *f.* normosqueocitosis.
normostenuria *f.* normosthenuria.
normotenso, -sa *adj.* normotensive.
normotermia *f.* normothermia.
normotonia *f.* normotonia.
normotónico, -ca *adj.* normotonic.
normotopo *f.* normotopic.
normovolemia *f.* normovolemia.
normoxemia *f.* normoxia.
normoxia *f.* normoxia.
nosemia *f.* nosohemia.
nosencéfalo *m.* nosencephalus.
nosetiología *f.* nosetiology.
nosocomio *m.* nosocomium.
nosocomial *adj.* nosocomial.
nosoctonografía *f.* nosochthonography.
nosofilia *f.* nosophilia.
nosófito *m.* nosophyte.
nosofobia *f.* nosophobia.
nosófobo, -ba *adj.* nosophobe.
nosogénesis *f.* nosogenesis.
nosogenia *f.* nosogeny.
nosogeografía *f.* nosogeography.
nosografía *f.* nosography.
nosográfico, -ca *adj.* nosographic.
nosógrafo, -fa *m., f.* nosographist.
nosohemia *f.* nosohemia.
nosointoxicación *f.* nosointoxication.
nosología *f.* nosology.
  nosología psiquiátrica psychiatric nosology.
nosológico, -ca *adj.* nosologic.
nosomania *f.* nosomania.
nosometría *f.* nosometry.
nosomicosis *f.* nosomycosis.
nosonomía *f.* nosonomy.
nosoparásito *m.* nosoparasite.
nosopoyético, -ca *adj.* nosopoietic.
nosotaxia *f.* nosotaxy.
nosoterapia *f.* nosotherapy.
nosotóxico, -ca *adj.* nosotoxic.
nosotoxicosis *f.* nosotoxicosis.
nosotoxina *f.* nosotoxin.
nosotrofia *f.* nosotrophy.
nosotrópico, -ca *adj.* nosotropic.
nostalgia *f.* nostalgia.
nostocitosis *f.* homing.
nostofobia *f.* nostophobia.
nostología *f.* nostology.
nostomanía *f.* nostomania.
nostrum *m.* nostrum.
notal *adj.* notal.
notancefalia *f.* notancephalia.

notanencefalia *f.* notanencephalia.
notencefalia *m.* notencephalocele.
notencefalocele *m.* notencephalocele.
notocorda *m.* notochord.
notocordal *adj.* notochordal.
notocordio *m.* notochord.
notocordodisrafia *f.* split notochord syndrome.
notocordoma *m.* notochordoma.
notogénesis *f.* notogenesis.
notomelia *f.* notomelia.
notomelo *m.* notomelus.
notomielitis *f.* notomyelitis.
noúmeno *m.* noumenon.
noxa *f.* noxa.
nuca *f.* nape, nucha.
nucal *adj.* nuchal.
nucleación *f.* nucleation.
nucleado, -da *adj.* nucleated.
nuclear *adj.* nuclear.
nucleido *m.* nucleide.
nucleiforme *adj.* nucleiform.
nucleína *f.* nuclein.
núcleo *m.* nucleus.
  núcleo de Béclard Béclard's nucleus.
  núcleo de Klein-Gumprecht Klein-Gumprecht shadow nucleus.
  núcleo de segmentación segmentation nucleus.
  núcleo vitelino yolk nucleus.
nucleoalbúmina *f.* nucleoalbumium.
nucleocápsida *f.* nucleocapsid.
nucleocápside *f.* nucleocapsid.
nucleofagocitosis *f.* nucleophagocytosis.
nucleofílico, -ca *adj.* nuclephilic.
nucleófilo, -la *adj.* nucleophil, nucleophile.
nucleofugal *adj.* nucleofugal.
nucleófugo, -ga *adj.* nucleofugal.
nucleohialoplasma *m.* nucleohyaloplasm.
nucleohistona *f.* nucleohistone.
nucleohuso *m.* nucleospindle.
nucleoide *adj.* nucleoid.
nucleolar *adj.* nucleolar.
nucleoliforme *adj.* nucleoliform.
nucleolina *f.* nucleolin.
nucleolino *m.* nucleolinus.
nucleólisis *f.* chemonucleolysis.
nucléolo *m.* nucleolus.
  nucléolo de cromatina chr°vomatin nucleolus.
  nucléolo falso false nucleolus.
  nucléolo nucleínico nucleinic nucleolus.
  nucléolo secundario secondary nucleolus.
nucleoloide *adj.* nucleoloid.
nucleólolo *m.* nucleololulus.
nucleolonema *m.* nucleolonema, nucleoloneme.
nucleomicrosoma *m.* nucleomicrosome.
nucleón *m.* nucleon.
nucleónico, -ca *adj.* nucleonic.
nucleópeto, -ta *adj.* nucleopetal.
nucleoplasma *m.* nucleoplasm.
nucleoproteido *m.* nucleoproteid.
nucleoproteína *f.* nucleoprotein.
nucleoquilema *m.* nucleochylema.
nucleoquima *f.* nucleochyme.
nucleorrexis *f.* nucleorrhexis.
nucleortesis *f.* nucleorthesis.
nucleosidasa *f.* nucleosidase.
nucleósido *m.* nucleoside.
nucleosoma *m.* nucleosome.
nucleoterapia *f.* nucleotherapy.
nucleótido *m.* nucleotide.
nucleotoxina *f.* nucleotoxin.
nucleus nucleus.
núclido *m.* nuclide.

nudillo *m.* knuckle.
  nudillo aórtico aortic knuckle.
  nudillo cervical aórtico cervical aortic knuckle.
nudo *m.* knot, node, nodus.
  nudo de ballestrinque clove-hitch knot.
  nudo de cirujano surgeon's knot.
  nudo cuadrado square knot.
  nudo cruzado reef knot.
  nudo doble double knot.
  nudo del esmalte enamel knot.
  nudo de fricción friction knot.
  nudo falso del cordón umbilical false knot of the umbilical cord.
  nudo de marinero sailor's knot.
  nudo quirúrgico surgical knot.
  nudo de redecilla ret knot.
  nudo de retén stay knot.
  nudo de rizo mal cruzado granny knot.
  nudo de Schmidt Schmidt's node.
  nudo de Schmorl Schmorl's node.
  nudo sincitial syncytial node.
  nudo verdadero del cordón umbilical true knot of the umbilical cord.
nudofobia *f.* nudophobia.
nudomanía *f.* nudomania.
nudosidad *f.* nodosity, nodositas.
nudoso, -sa *adj.* nodose, nodous.
nuligrávida *f.* nulligravida.
nulípara *f.* nullipara.
nuliparidad *f.* nulliparity.

numeración *f.* count.
  numeración de los huevos egg count.
  numeración globular blood count.
numérico, -ca *adj.* numerical.
número *m.* number.
  número acetilo acetyl number.
  número ácido acid number.
  número atómico (z) atomic number (z).
  número de Avogado Avogadro's number.
  número cromosómico chromosome number.
  número de dibucaína dibucaine number.
  número de dureza hardness number.
  número de dureza de Brinell Brinell hardness number.
  número de dureza de Knoop Knoop hardness number.
  número de dureza de Rockwell Rockwell hardness number.
  número electrónico electronic number.
  número de Hehner Hehner number.
  número de hidrógeno hydrogen number.
  número de Hittorf Hittorf number.
  número de Hübl, número de Huebl Hübl number, Huebl number.
  número isotópico isotopic number.
  número de Looschmidt Looschmidt's number.
  número de masa mass number.
  número másico mass number.
  número de oxidación oxidation number.
  número polar polar number.

  número de Polenske Polenske number.
  número de recambio turnorver number.
  número de Reichert-Meissl Reichert-Meissl number.
  número de saponificación saponification number.
  número de transporte transport number.
  número de yodo iodine number.
numiforme *adj.* nummiform.
numulación *f.* nummulation.
numular *adj.* nummular.
nunación *f.* nunnation.
nupcialidad *f.* nuptiality.
nutación *f.* nutation.
nutatorio, -ria *adj.* nutatory.
nutricio, -cia *adj.* nutritious.
nutrición *f.* nutrition.
  nutrición adecuada adequate nutrition.
  nutrición parenteral parenteral nutrition.
  nutrición parenteral total (npt) total parenteral nutrition (tpn).
nutricional *adj.* nutritional.
nutriente *m.* nutrient.
nutrimento *m.* nutriment.
nutriología *f.* nutriology.
nutripompa *f.* nutripump.
nutrista *m., f.* nutritionist.
nutritivo, -va *adj.* nutritive.
Nyctotherus Nyctotherus.
Nyssorhynchus Nyssorhynchus.

O o

oasis *m.* oasis.
obdormición *f.* obdormition.
obducción *f.* obduction.
obducente *adj.* obducent.
obelíaco, -ca *adj.* obeliac.
obeliad obeliad.
obelión *m.* obelion.
obesidad *f.* obesity.
  obesidad alimentaria alimentary obesity.
  obesidad armónica generalized obesity.
  obesidad cushingoide cushingoid obesity.
  obesidad endógena endogenous obesity.
  obesidad exógena exogenous obesity.
  obesidad hiperinsulínica hyperinsulinar obesity.
  obesidad hiperplásmica hyperplasmic obesity.
  obesidad hiperplásica e hipertrófica hyperplastic-hypertrophic obesity.
  obesidad hipersuprarrenal hyperadrenal obesity.
  obesidad hipertrófica hypertrophic obesity.
  obesidad hipogonádica hypogonad obesity.
  obesidad hipoplásmica hypoplasmic obesity.
  obesidad hipotalámica hypothalamic obesity.
  obesidad hipotiroidea hypothyroid obesity.
  obesidad de iniciación en la edad adulta adult-onset obesity.
  obesidad mórbida morbid obesity.
  obesidad simple simple obesity.
  obesidad de toda la vida lifelong obesity.
  obesidad troncular truncal obesity.
obeso, -sa *adj.* obese.
obesógeno, -na *adj.* obesogenous.
Obesumbacterium Obesumbacterium.
óbex *m.* obex.
obfuscación *f.* obfuscation.
óbito *m.* decease.
objetivo *m.* objective.
  objetivo acromático achromatic objective.
  objetivo apocromático apochromatic objective.
  objetivo de campo plano flat field objective.
  objetivo de fluorita fluorite objective.
  objetivo de inmersión immersion objective.
  objetivo seco dry objective.
  objetivo semiapocromático semiapochromatic objective.
objeto *m.* object.
  objeto de elección choice object.
  objeto de prueba test object.
  objeto sexual sex object.
  objeto transicional transitional object.
oblea *f.* wafer.
oblicuidad *f.* obliquity.
  oblicuidad de Litzmann Litzmann's obliquity.
  oblicuidad de Nägele Nägele's obliquity.
  oblicuidad de la pelvis obliquity of the pelvis.
oblicuo, -cua *adj.* oblique, obliquus.

obligado, -da *adj.* obligate.
obliteración *f.* obliteration.
  obliteración cortical cortical obliteration.
obliterans *adj.* obliterans.
oblongada *adj.* oblongata.
obnubilación de la conciencia *f.* obnubilation.
observador *m.* observer.
  observador no participante non-participant observer.
  observador participante participant observer.
observoscopio *m.* observoscope.
obsesión *f.* obsession.
  obsesión impulsiva impulsive obsession.
  obsesión inhibitoria inhibitory obsession.
obsesivo, -va *adj.* obsessive.
obsesivo-compulsivo, -va *adj.* obsessive-compulsive.
obsolescencia *f.* obsolescence.
obstetra *m.* obstetrician.
obstetricia *f.* obstetrics.
  obstetricia médico-legal medico-legal obstetrics.
obstétrico, -ca *adj.* obstetric, obstetrical.
obstinado, -da *adj.* obstinate.
obstipación *f.* obstipation.
obstrucción *f.* obstruction.
  obstrucción en ansa cerrada closed-loop obstruction.
  obstrucción de la arteria central de la retina retinal central arterial obstruction.
  obstrucción biliar biliary obstruction.
  obstrucción de bucle cerrado closed-loop obstruction.
  obstrucción crónica de las vías respiratorias chronic airway obstruction.
  obstrucción por cuerpo extraño foreign body obstruction.
  obstrucción y dilatación pilóricas pyloric obstruction and dilatation.
  obstrucción falsa del colon false colonic obstruction.
  obstrucción intestinal intestinal obstruction.
  obstrucción intestinal estrangulante strangulating intestinal obstruction.
  obstrucción intestinal mecánica mechanical intestinal obstruction.
  obstrucción nasal nasal obstruction.
  obstrucción de la vena central de la retina retinal central venous obstruction.
  obstrucción ventricular ventricular obstruction.
  obstrucción de la vía aérea airway obstruction.
  obstrucción de las vías respiratorias superiores (OVRS) upper airway obstruction (UAO).
  obstrucción ureteropelviana ureteropelvic obstruction.
  obstrucción ureterovesical ureterovesical obstruction.
obstructivo, -va *adj.* obstructive.

obstruyente *m. y adj.* obstruent.
obtundente *m. y adj.* obtundent.
obtundir *v.* obtund.
obtunción *f.* obtundation.
obturación¹ *f.* filling.
  obturación del conducto radicular root canal filling.
  obturación retrógrada retrograde filling.
  obturación temporal temporary filling.
obturación² *f.* obturation.
  obturación de un canal, obturación de un conducto canal obturation.
obturador¹ *m.* obturator.
  obturador de Cripp Cripp's obturator.
obturador² *m.* plugger.
  obturador de acción retrógrada back-action plugger.
  obturador de amalgama amalgam plugger.
  obturador automático automatic plugger.
  obturador de conductos radiculares root canal plugger.
  obturador en forma de pie foot plugger.
obtusión *f.* obtusion.
obtuso, -sa *adj.* obtuse.
occipital *adj.* occipital, occipitalis.
occipitalis *m.* occipitalis.
occipitalización *f.* occipitalization.
occipitoanterior *adj.* occipitoanterior.
occipitoatloideo, -a *adj.* occipitoatloid.
occipitoaxial *adj.* occipitoaxial.
occipitoaxoideo, -a *adj.* occipitoaxoid.
occipitobasilar *adj.* occipitobasilar.
occipitobregmático, -ca *adj.* occipitobregmatic.
occipitocalcarino, -na *adj.* occipitocalcarine.
occipitocervical *adj.* occipitocervical.
occipitofacial *adj.* occipitofacial.
occipitofrontal *adj.* occipitofrontal.
occipitomastoideo, -a *adj.* occipitomastoid.
occipitomentoniano, -na *adj.* occipitomental.
occipitoparietal *adj.* occipitoparietal.
occipitoposterior *adj.* occipitoposterior.
occipitotalámico, -ca *adj.* occipitothalamic.
occipitotemporal *adj.* occipitotemporal.
occipucio *m.* occiput.
occisión *f.* violent death.
ocelo *m.* ocellus.
ocena *f.* ozena.
  ozena laríngea ozena laryngis.
ocenoso, -sa *adj.* ozenous.
ocitocina *f.* ocytocin.
oclesis *f.* ochlesis.
oclofobia *f.* ochlophobia.
ocluido, -da *adj.* occluded.
ocluir *v.* occlude.
oclusal *adj.* occlusal.
oclusión *f.* occlusion.
  oclusión acéntrica acentric occlusion.
  oclusión afuncional afunctional occlusion.
  oclusión anatómica anatomic occlusion.

oclusión anormal abnormal occlusion.

oclusión anterior anterior occlusion.

oclusión de la arteria basilar basilar artery occlusion.

oclusión de la arteria mesentérica mesenteric artery occlusion.

oclusión balanceada balanced occlusion.

oclusión a borde, oclusión de borde, oclusión de borde a borde, oclusión borde con borde edge-to-edge occlusion.

oclusión bucal buccal occlusion.

oclusión central, oclusión céntrica centric occlusion.

oclusión congénita del esófago esophageal atresia.

oclusión coronaria coronary occlusion.

oclusión dental dental occlusion.

oclusión distal distal occlusion.

oclusión enteromesentérica enteromesenteric occlusion.

oclusión equilibrada balanced occlusion.

oclusión excéntrica eccentric occlusion.

oclusión extremo con extremo end-to-end occlusion.

oclusión fisiológica physiologic occlusion, physiological occlusion.

oclusión fisiológicamente balanceada physiologically balanced occlusion.

oclusión en forma esférica, forma esférica de oclusión spherical form of occlusion.

oclusión funcional functional occlusion.

oclusión habitual habitual occlusion.

oclusión hiperfuncional hyperfunctional occlusion.

oclusión ideal ideal occlusion.

oclusión intestinal intestinal occlusion.

oclusión labial labial occlusion.

oclusión lateral lateral occlusion.

oclusión lingual lingual occlusion.

oclusión mecánicamente balanceada mechanically balanced occlusion.

oclusión mesial mesial occlusion.

oclusión neutra neutral occlusion.

oclusión normal normal occlusion.

oclusión de los orificios respiratorios asphyxiation, suffocation.

oclusión patógena, oclusión patogénica pathogenic occlusion.

oclusión posnormal postnormal occlusion.

oclusión posterior posterior occlusion.

oclusión prenormal prenormal occlusion.

oclusión protrusiva protrusive occlusion.

oclusión protrusiva bimaxilar bimaxillary protrusive occlusion.

oclusión de la pupila occlusion of the pupil.

oclusión retrusiva retrusive occlusion.

oclusión terminal terminal occlusion.

oclusión terminoterminal end-to-end occlusion.

oclusión torsiva torsive occlusion.

oclusión de trabajo working occlusion.

oclusión traumática traumatic occlusion.

oclusión traumatógena, oclusión traumatogénica traumatogenic occlusion.

oclusional *adj.* occlusal.

oclusivo, -va *adj.* occlusive.

oclusocervical *adj.* occlusocervical.

oclusómetro *m.* occlusometer.

oclusor *m.* occluder.

ocrilato *m.* ocrylate.

ocrodermia *f.* ochrodermia.

ocrómetro *m.* ochrometer.

ocronosis *f.* ochronosis, ochronosus.

ocronosis exógena exogenous ochronosis.

ocronoso, -sa *adj.* ochronotic.

ocronótico, -ca *adj.* ochronotic.

octana *f.* octan.

octapéptido *m.* octapeptide.

octaploide *adj.* octaploid.

octaploidía *f.* octaploidy.

octaploídico, -ca *adj.* octaploidic.

octario *m.* octarius.

octavalente *adj.* octavalent.

octeto *m.* octet.

octigrávida *f.* octigravida.

octípara *f.* octipara.

octográvida *f.* octigravida.

Octomitidae Octomitidae.

Octomyces Octomyces.

Octomyces etiennei Octomyces etiennei.

octopamina *f.* octopamine.

octosa *f.* octose.

ocufilcón *m.* ocufilcon.

ocular[1] *adj.* ocular.

ocular[2] *m.* eyepiece, ocular.

ocular de amplio campo, ocular de campo amplio wide field eyepiece, wide field ocular.

ocular de comparación comparison eyepiece.

ocular de compensación, ocular compensador, ocular compensatorio compensating eyepiece, compensating ocular.

ocular de demostración demonstration eyepiece.

ocular de Huygens Huygens' eyepiece, Huyguenian eyepiece, Huygens' ocular.

ocular con el punto de mira elevado high-eyepoint eyepiece.

ocular negativo negative eyepiece.

ocular positivo positive eyepiece.

ocular de Ramsden Ramsden's eyepiece, Ramsden's ocular.

ocularista *m.* ocularist.

oculista *m., f.* oculist.

oculística *f.* oculistics.

oculoauriculovertebral *adj.* oculoauriculovertebral.

oculocardíaco, -ca *adj.* oculocardiac.

oculocefalógiro, -ra *adj.* oculocephalogyric.

oculocefalorrenal *adj.* oculocerebrorenal.

oculocigomático, -ca *adj.* oculozygomatic.

oculocutáneo, -a *adj.* oculocutaneous.

oculodentodigital *adj.* oculodentodigital.

oculodérmico, -ca *adj.* oculodermal.

oculodinia *f.* oculodynia.

oculoespinal *adj.* oculospinal.

oculofacial *adj.* oculofacial.

oculogiración *f.* oculogyration.

oculogiria *f.* oculogyria.

oculogírico, -ca *adj.* oculogyric.

oculógiro, -ra *adj.* oculogyric.

oculografía *f.* oculography.

oculografía fotosensora photosensor oculography.

oculomandibulodiscefalia *f.* oculomandibulodyscephaly.

oculometroscopio *m.* oculometroscope.

oculomicosis *f.* oculomycosis.

oculomotor, -ra *adj.* oculomotor, ocular motor.

oculonasal *adj.* oculonasal.

oculoneumopletismografía *f.* oculopneumoplethysmography.

oculopalpebral *adj.* oculopalpebral.

oculopatía *f.* oculopathy.

oculoplástico, -ca *adj.* oculoplastic.

oculopletismografía *f.* oculoplethysmography.

oculopupilar *adj.* oculopupillary.

oculosimpático, -ca *adj.* oculosympathetic.

oculospinal *adj.* oculospinal.

oculovertebral *adj.* oculovertebral.

oculto, -ta *adj.* occult.

oculus oculus.

ocupación *f.* occupancy.

odaxesmo *m.* odaxesmus.

odaxético, -ca *m. y adj.* odaxetic.

odditis *f.* odditis.

odinacusia *f.* odynacusis.

odinacusis *f.* odynacusis.

odinoacusia *f.* odynacusis.

odinofagia *f.* odynophagia, odynphagia.

odinofobia *f.* odynophobia.

odinofonía *f.* odynophonia.

odinólisis *f.* odynolysis.

odinómetro *m.* odynometer.

oditis *f.* odditis.

odogénesis *f.* odogenesis.

odon-eki *m.* odon-eki.

odondectomía *f.* odondectomy.

odontagra *f.* odontagra.

odontalgia *f.* odontalgia.

odontalgia dental odontalgia dentalis.

odontálgico, -ca *adj.* odontalgic.

odontectomía *f.* odontectomy.

odonterismo *m.* odonterism.

odontexesis *f.* odontexesis.

odontiasis *f.* odontiasis.

odontiatría *f.* odontiatria.

odontiatrogénico, -ca *adj.* odontiatrogenic.

odóntico, -ca *adj.* odontic.

odontinoide *m.* odontinoid.

odontitis *f.* odontitis.

odontoameloblastoma *m.* odontoameloblastoma.

odontoblasto *m.* odontoblast.

odontoblastoma *m.* odontoblastoma.

odontobotritis *f.* odontobothritis.

odontocia *f.* odontocia.

odontocisma *m.* odontoschism.

odontoclamis *f.* odontoclamis.

odontoclasto *m.* odontoclast.

odontodinia *f.* odontodynia.

odontodisplasia *f.* odontodysplasia.

odontofobia *f.* odontophobia.

odontogén *m.* odontogen.

odontogénesis *f.* odontogenesis.

odontogénesis imperfecta odontogenesis imperfecta.

odontogenético, -ca *adj.* odontogenetic.

odontogenia *f.* odontogeny.

odontogénico, -ca *adj.* odontogenic, odontogenous.

odontógeno, -na *adj.* odontogenic.

odontografía *f.* odontography.

odontógrafo *m.* odontograph.

odontograma *m.* odontogram.

odontoide *adj.* odontoid.

odontoides *adj.* odontoid.

odontólisis *f.* odontolysis.

odontolitiasis *f.* odontolithiasis.

odontolito *m.* odontolith.

odontología *f.* dentistry, odontology.

odontología comunitaria community dentistry.

odontología cosmética cosmetic dentistry.

odontología a cuatro four-handed odontology.

odontología estética esthetic dentistry.

odontología forense forensic dentistry, forensic odontology.

odontología geriátrica geriatric dentistry.

odontología legal legal dentistry.

odontología operatoria operative dentistry.

odontología pediátrica pediatric dentistry.

odontología preventiva preventive dentistry.

odontología psicosomática psychosomatic dentistry.

odontología de restauración, odontología restauradora restorative dentistry.
odontología de salud pública public health dentistry.
odontólogo, -ga *m.* odontologist.
odontoloxia *f.* odontoloxia, odontoloxy.
odontoma *m.* odontoma.
  odontoma adamantino odontoma adamantinum.
  odontoma ameloblástico ameloblastic odontoma.
  odontoma complejo complex odontoma.
  odontoma compuesto composite odontoma, compound odontoma.
  odontoma coronal, odontoma coronario coronal odontoma, coronary odontoma.
  odontoma embrioplásico embryoplastic odontoma.
  odontoma fibroso fibrous odontoma.
  odontoma mixto mixed odontoma.
  odontoma radicular radicular odontoma.
odontomía profiláctica *f.* prophylactic odontomy.
odontonecrosis *f.* odontonecrosis.
odontoneuralgía *f.* odontoneuralgia.
odontonimia *f.* odontonomy.
odontonomía *f.* odontonomy.
odontonosología *f.* odontonosology.
odontopatía *f.* odontopathy.
odontopático, -ca *adj.* odontopathic.
odontoperiostio *m.* odontoperiosteum.
odontoplastia *f.* odontoplasty.
odontoplasto *m.* odontoplast.
odontoplerosis *f.* odontoplerosis.
odontoprisis *f.* odontoprisis.
odontoptosis *f.* odontoptosis.
odontorradiografía *f.* odontoradiograph.
odontorragia *f.* odontorrhagia.
odontortosis *f.* odontorthosis.
odontoscopia *f.* odontoscopy.
odontoscopio *m.* odontoscope.
odontoseisis *f.* odontoseisis.
odontosis *f.* odontosis.
odontosquisis *f.* odontoschism.
odontoteca *f.* odontotheca.
odontotecnia *f.* odontotechny.
odontoterapia *f.* odontotherapy.
odontotomía *f.* odontotomy.
  odontotomía profiláctica prophylactic odontotomy.
odontotripsia *f.* odontotripsis.
odontotripsis *f.* odontotripsis.
odontoyatrógeno, -na *adj.* odontiatrogenic.
odor odor.
odorante *adj.* odorant.
odorífero, -ra *adj.* odoriferous.
odoríforo *m.* odoriphore.
odorimetría *f.* odorimetry.
odorímetro *m.* odorimeter.
odorivección *f.* odorivection.
odorivector, -ra *adj.* odorivector.
odorografía *f.* odorography.
Oeciacus hirudinis Oeciacus hirudinis.
oesófago *m.* oesophagus.
oesofagostomiasis *f.* oesophagostomiasis.
Oesophagostomum Oesophagostomum.
  Oesophagostomum apiostomum Oesophagostomum apiostomum.
  Oesophagostomum bifurcum Oesophagostomum bifurcum.
  Oesophagostomum brumpti Oesophagostomum brumpti.
oestriasis *f.* oestriasis.
Oestridae Oestridae.
oestro *m.* oestrum, oestrus, estrus.

oestrosis *f.* oestrosis.
Oestrus Oestrus.
  Oestrus hominis Oestrus hominis.
  Oestrus ovis Oestrus ovis.
ofiasis *f.* ophiasis.
oficial *adj.* official.
ofidiasis *f.* ophidiasis.
ofídico, -ca *adj.* ophidic.
ofidiofobia *f.* ophidiophobia.
ofidismo *m.* ophidism.
ofiotoxemia *f.* ophiotoxemia.
ofitoxemia *f.* ophitoxemia.
ofriítis *f.* ophryitis.
ofrio *m.* ophryon.
ofriogenes *f.* ophryogenes.
ofrión *m.* ophryon.
ofriosis *f.* ophryosis.
ofritis *f.* ophrytis.
oftalmagra *f.* ophthalmagra.
oftalmalgia *f.* ophthalmalgia.
oftalmatrofia *f.* ophthalmatrophia.
oftalmectomía *f.* ophthalmectomy.
oftalmencéfalo *m.* ophthalmencephalon.
oftalmía *f.* ophthalmia.
  oftalmía brasileña Brazilian ophthalmia.
  oftalmía catarral catarrhal ophthalmia.
  oftalmía del cosechador reaper's ophthalmia.
  oftalmía de destello flash ophthalmia.
  oftalmía eccematosa ophthalmia eczematosa.
  oftalmía egipcia, o de Egipto Egyptian ophthalmia.
  oftalmía eléctrica electric ophthalmia.
  oftalmía escrofulosa scrofulous ophthalmia.
  oftalmía estrumosa strumous ophthalmia.
  oftalmía flictenular phlyctenular ophthalmia.
  oftalmía gonorreica gonorrheal ophthalmia.
  oftalmía granular, oftalmía granulosa granular ophthalmia.
  oftalmía hepática hepatic ophthalmia, ophthalmia hepatica.
  oftalmía lenta ophthalmia lenta.
  oftalmía metastásica metastatic ophthalmia.
  oftalmía migratoria migratory ophthalmia.
  oftalmía mucosa mucous ophthalmia.
  oftalmía neonatal ophthalmia neonatorum.
  oftalmía neuroparalítica neuroparalytic ophthalmia.
  oftalmía de la nieve, oftalmía nivalis ophthalmia nivalis.
  oftalmía nodosa, oftalmía nudosa ophthalmia nodosa.
  oftalmía de pelo de oruga caterpillar ophthalmia, caterpillar-hair ophthalmia.
  oftalmía primaveral spring ophthalmia.
  oftalmía purulenta purulent ophthalmia.
  oftalmía por rayos actínicos actinic ray ophthalmia.
  oftalmía por rayos ultravioleta ultraviolet ray ophthalmia.
  oftalmía del recién nacido ophthalmia neonatorum.
  oftalmía seudotuberculosa pseudotuberculous ophthalmia.
  oftalmía simpática sympathetic ophthalmia.
  oftalmía transferida transferred ophthalmia.
  oftalmía varicosa varicose ophthalmia.
  oftalmía vegetal vegetable ophthalmia.
oftalmíaco, -ca *adj.* ophthalmiac.
oftalmiatría *f.* ophthalmiatrics.
oftálmico, -ca *adj.* ophthalmic.
oftalmítico, -ca *adj.* ophthalmitic.
oftalmitis *f.* ophthalmitis.
oftalmoblenorrea *f.* ophthalmoblennorrhea.
oftalmocele *m.* ophthalmocele.
oftalmocopia *f.* ophthalmocopia.

oftalmodesmitis *f.* ophthalmodesmitis.
oftalmodiafanoscopio *m.* ophthalmodiaphanoscope.
oftalmodiastímetro *m.* ophthalmodiastimeter.
oftalmodinamometría *f.* ophthalmodynamometry.
oftalmodinamómetro *m.* ophthalmodynamometer.
  oftalmodinamómetro de Bailliart Bailliart's ophthalmodynamometer.
  oftalmodinamómetro de succión suction ophthalmodynamometer.
oftalmodinia *f.* ophthalmodynia.
oftalmodonesis *f.* ophthalmodonesis.
oftalmoeiconómetro *m.* ophthalmoeikonometer.
oftalmoencéfalo *m.* ophthalmoencephalon.
oftalmoespectroscopia *f.* ophthalmospectroscopy.
oftalmoespectroscopio *m.* ophthalmospectroscope.
oftalmofacómetro *m.* ophthalmophacometer.
oftalmofantasma *m.* ophthalmophantom.
oftalmofantoma *m.* ophthalmophantom.
oftalmoflebotomía *f.* ophthalmophlebotomy.
oftalmoftisis *f.* ophthalmophthisis.
oftalmofundoscopio *m.* ophthalmofundoscope.
oftalmogírico, -ca *adj.* ophthalmogyric.
oftalmógiro, -ra *adj.* ophthalmogyric.
oftalmografía *f.* ophthalmography.
oftalmógrafo *m.* ophthalmograph.
oftalmograma *m.* ophthalmogram.
oftalmoleucoscopio *m.* ophthalmoleukoscope.
oftalmolito *m.* ophthalmolith.
oftalmología *f.* ophthalmology.
oftalmológico, -ca *adj.* ophthalmologic, ophthalmological.
oftalmólogo, -ga *m., f.* ophthalmologist.
oftalmomalacia *f.* ophthalmomalacia.
oftalmomelanosis *f.* ophthalmomelanosis.
oftalmometría *f.* ophthalmometry.
oftalmómetro *m.* ophthalmometer.
oftalmometroscopio *m.* ophthalmometroscope.
oftalmomiasis *f.* ophthalmomyiasis.
oftalmomicosis *f.* ophthalmomycosis.
oftalmomiiasis *f.* ophthalmomyiasis.
oftalmomiitis *f.* ophthalmomyitis.
oftalmomiositis *f.* ophthalmomyositis.
oftalmomitis *f.* ophthalmomyitis.
oftalmomiotomía *f.* ophthalmomyotomy.
oftalmoneuritis *f.* ophthalmoneuritis.
oftalmoneuromielitis *f.* ophthalmoneuromyelitis.
oftalmopatía *f.* ophthalmopathy.
  oftalmopatía endocrina endocrine ophthalmopathy.
  oftalmopatía externa external ophthalmopathy.
  oftalmopatía de Graves-Basedow Graves' ophthalmopathy, Graves-Basedow's ophthalmopathy.
  oftalmopatía interna internal ophthalmopathy.
  oftalmopatía tiroidea thyroid ophthalmopathy.
oftalmoplastia *f.* ophthalmoplasty.
oftalmoplejía *f.* ophthalmoplegia.
  oftalmoplejía basal, oftalmoplejía basilar basal ophthalmoplegia.
  oftalmoplejía dolorosa de Tolosa-Hunt Tolosa-Hunt's ophthalmoplegia.
  oftalmoplejía exoftálmica exophthalmic ophthalmoplegia.

oftalmoplejía externa external ophthalmoplegia.

oftalmoplejía fascicular fascicular ophthalmoplegia.

oftalmoplejía interna internal ophthalmoplegia.

oftalmoplejía internuclear internuclear ophthalmoplegia, ophthalmoplegia internuclearis.

oftalmoplejía nuclear nuclear ophthalmoplegia.

oftalmoplejía orbitaria orbital ophthalmoplegia.

oftalmoplejía parcial partial ophthalmoplegia, ophthalmoplegia partialis.

oftalmoplejía de Parinaud Parinaud's ophthalmoplegia.

oftalmoplejía progresiva progressive ophthalmoplegia.

oftalmoplejía progresiva externa progressive external ophthalmoplegia.

oftalmoplejía total total ophthalmoplegia, ophthalmoplegia totalis.

oftalmopléjico, -ca *adj.* ophthalmoplegic.

oftalmorragia *f.* ophthalmorrhagia.

oftalmorrea *f.* ophthalmorrhea.

oftalmorrexis *f.* ophthalmorrhexis.

oftalmoscopia *f.* ophthalmoscopy.

oftalmoscopia directa direct ophthalmoscopy.

oftalmoscopia indirecta indirect ophthalmoscopy.

oftalmoscopia con luz reflejada ophthalmoscopy with reflected light.

oftalmoscopia médica medical ophthalmoscopy.

oftalmoscopia métrica metric ophthalmoscopy.

oftalmoscópico, -ca *adj.* ophthalmoscopic.

oftalmoscopio *m.* ophthalmoscope.

oftalmoscopio binocular binocular ophthalmoscope.

oftalmoscopio de demostración demonstration ophthalmoscope.

oftalmoscopio directo direct ophthalmoscope.

oftalmoscopio indirecto indirect ophthalmoscope.

oftalmosinquisis *f.* ophthalmosynchysis.

oftalmospasmo *m.* ophthalmospasm.

oftalmostasis *f.* ophthalmostasis.

oftalmostato *m.* ophthalmostat.

oftalmostatómetro *m.* ophthalmostatometer.

oftalmostéresis *f.* ophthalmosteresis.

oftalmotermómetro *m.* ophthalmothermometer.

oftalmotomía *f.* ophthalmotomy.

oftalmotonometría *f.* ophthalmotonometry.

oftalmotonómetro *m.* ophthalmotonometer.

oftalmotoxina *f.* ophthalmotoxin.

oftalmótropo *m.* ophthalmotrope.

oftalmotropometría *f.* ophthalmotropometry.

oftalmotropómetro *m.* ophthalmotropometer.

oftalmovascular *adj.* ophthalmovascular.

oftalmoxerosis *f.* ophthtalmoxerosis.

oftalmoxistro *m.* ophthalmoxyster.

ofuscación *f.* obfuscation.

ofuscamiento *m.* obfuscation.

ogo *m.* ogo.

ohmámetro *m.* ohmammeter.

óhmetro *m.* ohmmeter.

ohne Hauch *m.* ohne Hauch.

oicosito *m.* oikosite.

oidiomicina *f.* oidiomycin.

oidiomicosis *f.* oidiomycosis.

oidiomicótico, -ca *adj.* oidiomycotic.

oído *m.* ear, auris.

oído de aviador aviator's ear.

oído externo, auris externa external ear, outer ear, auris externa.

oído de Hong Kong Hong Kong ear.

oído interno, auris interna internal ear, inner ear, auris interna.

oído medio, auris media middle ear, auris media.

oído de nadador swimmer's ear.

oído de playa beach ear.

oído de Singapur Singapore ear.

oído de tanque tank ear.

oído de tiempo caliente hot weather ear.

oído tropical tropical ear.

oinomanía *f.* oinomania.

oir *v.* hear.

ojal *m.* buttonhole.

ojal mitral mitral buttonhole.

ojete *m.* eyelet.

ojiva *f.* ogive.

ojo *m.* eye, oculus.

ojo adaptado a la luz light-adapted eye.

ojo adaptado a la oscuridad dark-adapted eye.

ojo afáquico aphakic eye.

ojo artificial artificial eye.

ojo de los astilleros shipyard eye.

banco de ojo bank eye.

ojo bizco squinting eye.

ojo blefarítico bleary eye.

ojo caliente hot eye.

ojo de cíclope cyclopean eye, cyclopian eye.

ojo de cinematógrafo cinema eye.

ojo desviado deviating eye.

ojo dominante dominant eye.

ojo errante following eye.

ojo escotópico scotopic eye.

ojo esquemático schematic eye.

ojo estrábico squinting eye.

ojo de excitación, ojo excitante exciting eye.

ojo fáquico phakic eye.

ojo de fijación, ojo fijador fixing eye, fixating eye.

ojo fotópico photopic eye.

ojo de gato amaurótico amaurotic cat's eye.

ojo de Klieg Klieg eye.

ojo legañoso bleary eye.

ojo de liebre hare's eye.

ojo maestro, ojo maestro dominante master eye, master-dominant eye.

ojo de mapache raccoon eye.

ojo mediano de Nairobi median eye.

ojo membranoso web eye.

ojo monocromático monochromatic eye.

ojo negro black eye.

ojo pesado heavy eye.

ojo primario primary eye.

ojo quístico cystic eye.

ojo reducido reduced eye.

ojo reducido de Listing Listing's reduced eye.

ojo rosado pink eye.

ojo secundario secondary eye.

ojo seudofáquico pseudophakic eye.

ojo simpatizante sympathizing eye.

ojo de Snellen Snellen's reform eye.

ojo sonrosado pink eye.

oleada *f.* rush.

oleaginoso, -sa *adj.* oleaginous.

oleandrina *f.* oleandrin.

oleandrismo *m.* oleandrism.

olecranartritis *f.* olecranarthritis.

olecranartrocace *m.* olecranarthrocace.

olecranartropatía *f.* olecranarthropaty.

olecraneal *adj.* olecranal.

olécrano *m.* olecranon.

olecranoide *adj.* olecranoid.

olécranon *m.* olecranon.

oleinitis *f.* oleinitis.

oleoartrosis *f.* oleoarthrosis.

oleocrisoterapia *f.* oleochrysotherapy.

oleogranuloma *m.* oleogranuloma.

oleoinfusión *f.* oleinfusion.

oleoma *m.* oleoma.

oleómetro *m.* oleometer, eleometer, elaiometer.

oleonucleoproteína *f.* oleonucleoprotein.

oleoperitoneografía *f.* oleoperitoneography.

oleoso, -sa *adj.* oily, oleosus.

oleoterapia *f.* oleotherapy, eleotherapy.

oleotórax *m.* oleothorax.

oleovitamina *f.* oleovitamin.

oler *v.* smell.

olfacción *f.* olfaction.

olfatía *f.* olfactie, olfacty.

olfatismo *m.* olfactism.

olfato *m.* olfact, olfactus.

olfatofobia *f.* olfactophobia.

olfatología *f.* olfactology.

olfatometría *f.* olfactometry.

olfatómetro *m.* olfactometer.

olfatorio, -ria *adj.* olfactory.

oligaquisuria *f.* oligakisuria.

oligemia *f.* oligemia.

olighidria *f.* olighidria.

oligidria *f.* oligidria.

oligoamnios *m.* oligoamnios.

oligoblasto *m.* oligoblast.

oligocardia *f.* oligocardia.

oligocístico, -ca *adj.* oligocystic.

oligocitemia *f.* oligocythemia.

oligocitémico, -ca *adj.* oligocythemic.

oligocitosis *f.* oligocytosis.

oligocolia *f.* oligocholia.

oligocromasia *f.* oligochromasia.

oligocromemia *f.* oligochromemia.

oligodactilia *f.* oligodactyly, oligodactylia.

oligodendria *f.* oligodendria.

oligodendroblasto *m.* oligodendroblast.

oligodendroblastoma *m.* oligodendroblastoma.

oligodendrocito *m.* oligodendrocyte.

oligodendroglia, oligodendroglía *f.* oligodendroglia.

oligodendroglioma *m.* oligodendroglioma.

oligodinámico, -ca *adj.* oligodynamic.

oligodipsia *f.* oligodipsia.

oligodoncia *f.* oligodontia.

oligodontia *f.* oligodontia.

oligoelemento *m.* trace element.

oligoencéfalo *m.* oligoencephalon.

oligofosfaturia *f.* oligophosphaturia.

oligofrenia *f.* oligophrenia.

oligofrenia fenilpirúvica phenylpyruvate oligophrenia, phenylpyruvic oligophrenia.

oligofrénico, -ca *adj.* oligophrenic.

oligogalactia *f.* oligogalactia.

oligogalia *f.* oligogalactia.

oligogénesis *f.* oligogenics.

oligogenia *f.* oligogenics.

oligogénico, -ca *adj.* oligogenic.

oligoglia *f.* oligoglia.

oligoglobulia *f.* oligoglobulia.

oligohemia *f.* oligohemia.

oligohémico, -ca *adj.* oligohemic.

oligohidramnios *m.* oligohydramnios.

oligohidria *f.* oligohidria.

oligohidruria *f.* oligohydruria.

oligohipermenorrea *f.* oligohypermenorrhea.

oligohipomenorrea *f.* oligohypomenorrhea.

oligolecito, -ta *adj.* oligolecithal.

oligoleucocitemia *f.* oligoleukocythemia.
oligoleucocitosis *f.* oligoleukocytosis.
oligomeganefronia *f.* oligomeganephronia.
oligomeganefrónico, -ca *adj.* oligomeganephronic.
oligomenorrea *f.* oligomenorrhea.
oligómero *m.* oligomer.
oligometálico, -ca *adj.* oligometallic.
oligomorfo, -fa *adj.* oligomorphic.
oligomúrfico, -ca *adj.* oligomorphic.
oligonatalidad *f.* oligonatality.
oligonecrospermia *f.* oligonecrospermia.
oligonefrónico, -ca *adj.* oligonephronic.
oligonitrófilo, -la *adj.* oligonitrophilic.
oligonucleótido *m.* oligonucleotide.
oligoovulación *f.* oligo-ovulation.
oligopepsia *f.* oligopepsia.
oligopéptido *m.* oligopeptide.
oligopirénico, -ca *adj.* oligopyrene.
oligopiroso, -sa *adj.* oligopyrous.
oligoplasmia *f.* oligoplasmia.
oligoplástico, -ca *adj.* oligoplastic.
oligopnea *f.* oligopnea.
oligoposia *f.* oligoposia.
oligopsiquia *f.* oligopsychia.
oligoptialismo *m.* oligoptyalism.
oligoquilia *f.* oligochylia.
oligoquimia *f.* oligochymia.
oligoquístico, -ca *adj.* oligocystic.
oligoria *f.* oligoria.
oligosacárido *m.* oligosaccharide.
oligosialia *f.* oligosialia.
oligosideremia *f.* oligosideremia.
oligosináptico, -ca *adj.* oligosynaptic.
oligosintomático, -ca *adj.* oligosymptomatic.
oligospermatismo *m.* oligospermatism.
oligospermia *f.* oligospermia.
oligotialismo *m.* oligoptyalism.
oligotimia *f.* oligothymia.
oligotricosis *f.* oligotrichosis.
oligotriquia *f.* oligotrichia.
oligotrofia *f.* oligotrophy, oligotrophia.
oligotrófico, -ca *adj.* oligotrophic.
oligozoospermia *f.* oligozoospermatism, oligozoospermia.
oliguresis *f.* oliguresia, oliguresis.
oliguria *f.* oliguria.
oligúrico, -ca *adj.* oliguric.
olistía *f.* olisthy.
oliva *f.* olive, oliva.
  oliva inferior inferior olive, oliva inferior.
olivar *adj.* olivary.
olivífugo, -ga *adj.* olivifugal.
olivípeto, -ta *adj.* olivipetal.
olivococlear *adj.* olivocochlear.
olivopontocerebeloso, -sa *adj.* olivopontocerebellar.
olofonía *f.* olophonia.
olor *m.* odor.
  olor corporal body odor.
  olor a carnicería butcher's shop odor.
  olor mínimo identificable minimal identifiable odor.
oloroso, -sa *adj.* odorous.
olvido *m.* forgetting.
omacéfalo *m.* omacephalus.
omagra *f.* omagra.
omalgia *f.* omalgia.
omartritis *f.* omarthritis.
ombligo *m.* navel, umbilicus.
  ombligo amniótico amniotic umbilicus.
  ombligo azul blue navel.
  ombligo decidual decidual umbilicus.
  ombligo del esmalte enamel navel.
  ombligo de la membrana timpánica, om-

bligo de la membrana del tímpano umbo of the tympanic membrane, umbo membranae tympani.
ombrofobia *f.* ombrophobia.
ombróforo *m.* ombrophore.
omega *f.* omega.
  omega melancólica omega melancholicum.
omental *adj.* omental.
omentectomía *f.* omentectomy.
omentitis *f.* omentitis.
omento *m.* omentum.
omentoesplenopexia *f.* omentosplenopexy.
omentofijación *f.* omentofixation.
omentopexia *f.* omentopexy.
omentoplastia *f.* omentoplasty.
omentoportografía *f.* omentoportography.
omentorrafia *f.* omentorrhaphy.
omentosplenopexia *f.* omentosplenopexy.
omentotomía *f.* omentotomy.
omentovólvulo *m.* omentovolvulus.
omentumectomía *f.* omentumectomy.
omisión *f.* omission.
omitis *f.* omitis.
omnipotencia *f.* omnipotence.
omnívoro, -ra *adj.* omnivorous.
omocéfalo *m.* omocephalus.
omoclavicular *adj.* omoclavicular.
omocromo *m.* ommochrome.
omodinia *f.* omodynia.
omoesternón *m.* omosternum.
omofagia *f.* omophagia.
omohioideo, -a *adj.* omohyoid.
omóplato, omoplato *m.* omoplata.
omotiroides *f.* omothyroid.
omotocia *f.* omotocia.
omunono *m.* omunono.
onanismo *m.* onanism.
onaya *f.* onaye.
Onchocerca Onchocerca, Oncocerca.
  Onchocerca caecutiens Onchocerca caecutiens.
  Onchocerca volvulus Onchocerca volvulus.
Oncocerca Oncocerca.
oncocerciasis *f.* onchocerciasis.
oncocercoma *m.* onchocercoma.
oncocercosis *f.* onchocercosis.
oncocítico, -ca *adj.* oncocytic.
oncocito *m.* oncocyte.
oncodnavirus *m.* oncodnavirus.
oncogén *m.* oncogene.
oncogene *m.* oncogene.
oncogenesia *f.* oncogenesis.
oncogénesis *f.* oncogenesis.
oncogenético, -ca *adj.* oncogenetic.
oncogenia *f.* oncogenia.
oncogenicidad *f.* oncogenicity.
oncogénico, -ca *adj.* oncogenic.
oncógeno, -na *adj.* oncogenous.
oncografía *f.* oncography.
oncógrafo *m.* oncograph.
oncoide *m. y adj.* oncoides.
oncoides *m. y adj.* oncoides.
oncólisis *f.* oncolysis.
oncolítico, -ca *adj.* oncolytic.
oncolizado *m.* oncolysate.
oncología *f.* oncology.
  oncología radioterápica radiation oncology.
oncológico, -ca *adj.* oncologic.
oncólogo, -ga *m.* oncologist.
  oncólogo radioterapeuta radiation oncologist.
oncoma *m.* oncoma.
Oncomelania Oncomelania.
oncometría *f.* oncometry.
oncométrico, -ca *adj.* oncometric.

oncómetro *m.* oncometer.
Oncornavirus Oncornavirus.
oncosfera *f.* oncosphere.
oncosis *f.* oncosis.
oncoterapia *f.* oncotherapy.
oncótico, -ca *adj.* oncotic.
oncotlipsis *f.* oncothlipsis.
oncotomía *f.* oncotomy.
oncotrópico, -ca *adj.* oncotropic.
oncovirus *m.* oncovirus.
onda *f.* wave.
  onda a a wave.
  onda ácida acid wave.
  onda aguda sharp wave.
  onda alcalina alkaline wave.
  onda de aleteo-fibrilación flutter fibrillation wave.
  onda alfa alpha wave.
  onda anacrótica, onda anadicrótica anacrotic wave, anadicrotic wave.
  onda arterial arterial wave.
  onda al azar random wave.
  onda beta beta wave.
  onda bifásica biphasic wave.
  onda c c wave.
  onda cañón, onda de cañón cannon wave.
  onda catacrótica, onda catadicrótica catacrotic wave, catadicrotic wave.
  onda cerebral brain wave.
  onda de contracción contraction wave.
  onda corta short wave.
  onda delta delta wave.
  onda dicrótica dicrotic wave.
  onda electrocardiográfica electrocardiographic wave.
  onda electroencefalográfica electroencephalographic wave.
  onda electromagnética electromagnetic wave.
  onda de estímulo stimulus wave.
  onda de excitación excitation wave.
  onda F F wave, flutter wave.
  onda fibrilares fibrillary wave.
  onda frénicas phrenic wave.
  onda h h wave.
  onda de Liesegang Liesegang's wave.
  onda líquida fluid wave.
  onda longitudinal longitudinal wave.
  onda luminosa light wave.
  onda de marea, onda de marejada tidal wave.
  onda P P wave.
  onda P retrógrada retrograde P wave.
  onda papilar papillary wave.
  onda de percusión percussion wave.
  onda de pulso, onda del pulso pulse wave.
  onda Q Q wave.
  onda R R wave.
  onda de radio radio wave.
  onda de rebote recoil wave.
  onda en el registro de presión intracraneal intracraneal pressure wave.
  onda de repleción overflow wave.
  onda de retroceso recoil wave.
  onda S S wave.
  onda seno sine wave.
  onda sónica, onda sonora sonic wave.
  onda supersónicas supersonic wave.
  onda T T wave.
  onda T posextrasistólica postextrasystolic T wave.
  onda theta, onda teta theta wave.
  onda de tope plano flat top wave.
  onda transversa transverse wave.
  onda de Traube-Hering Traube-Hering wave.
  onda tricrótica tricrotic wave.

onda trifásica triphasic wave.
onda U U wave.
onda ultracorta ultrashort wave.
onda ultrasónica ultrasonic wave.
onda V V wave.
onda ventricular ventricular wave.
onda X X wave.
onda Y Y wave.
ondina *f.* undine.
ondinismo *m.* undinism.
ondómetro *m.* ondometer.
ondulación *f.* undulation.
ondulación respiratoria respiratory undulation.
ondulación yugular jugular undulation.
ondulado, -da *adj.* undulate.
ondulante *adj.* undulant.
ondulatorio, -ria *adj.* undulatory.
oneirismo *m.* oneirism.
oneiroanálisis *m.* oneiroanalysis.
oneirodinia *f.* oneirodynia.
oneirofrenia *f.* oneirophrenia.
oneirógeno, -na *adj.* oneirogenic.
oneirogmo *m.* oneirogmus.
oneiroide *adj.* oneiroid.
onfalectomía *f.* omphalectomy.
onfalelcosis *f.* omphalelcosis.
onfálico, -ca *adj.* omphalic.
onfalitis *f.* omphalitis.
ónfalo *m.* omphalus.
onfaloangiópago *m.* omphaloangiopagus.
onfalocele *m.* omphalocele.
onfalocorion *m.* omphalochorion.
onfalodídimo *m.* omphalodidymus.
onfaloentérico, -ca *adj.* omphaloenteric.
onfaloespinoso, -sa *adj.* omphalospinous.
onfaloflebitis *f.* omphalophlebitis.
onfalogenesia *f.* omphalogenesis.
onfalogénesis *f.* omphalogenesis.
onfaloma *m.* omphaloma.
onfalomesaraico, -ca *adj.* omphalomesaraic.
onfalomesentérico, -ca *adj.* omphalomesenteric.
onfalomonodídimo *m.* omphalodidymus.
onfalonco *m.* omphaloncus.
onfalópago *m.* omphalopagus.
onfaloproptosis *f.* omphaloproptosis.
onfaloptosis *f.* omphaloproptosis.
onfalorragia *f.* omphalorrhagia.
onfalorrea *f.* omphalorrhea.
onfalorrexis *f.* omphalorrhexis.
onfalósito *m.* omphalosite.
onfalotomía *f.* omphalotomy.
onfalotribo *m.* omphalotribe.
onfalotricia *f.* omphalotripsy.
onfalotripsia *f.* omphalotripsy.
onfalovesical *adj.* omphalovesical.
onialai *f.* onyalai.
onicalgia *f.* onychalgia.
onicatrofia *f.* onychatrophia, onychatrophy.
onicauxis *f.* onychauxis.
onicectomía *f.* onychectomy.
onicoatrofia *f.* onychatrophia, onychatrophy.
onicoclasis *f.* onychoclasis.
onicocriptosis *f.* onychocryptosis.
onicodinia *f.* onychodynia.
onicodistrofia *f.* onychodystrophy.
onicoestroma *m.* onychostroma.
onicofagia *f.* onychophagy, onychophagia.
onicófag, -ga *m., f.* onychophagist.
onicofima *m.* onychophyma.
onicofosis *f.* onychophosis.
onicogénico, -ca *adj.* onychogenic.
onicógrafo *m.* onychograph.
onicograma *m.* onychogram.

onicogrifosis *f.* onychogryphosis.
onicogriposis *f.* onychogryposis, onychogryphosis.
onicoheterotopia *f.* onychoheterotopia.
onicoide *adj.* onychoid.
onicólisis *f.* onycholysis.
onicología *f.* onychology.
onicoma *m.* onychoma.
onicomadesis *f.* onychomadesis.
onicomalacia *f.* onychomalacia.
onicomicosis *f.* onychomycosis.
onicomicosis dermatofítica dermatophytic onychomycosis.
oniconosis *f.* onychonosis.
onicoosteodisplasia *f.* onycho-osteodysplasia.
onicopatía *f.* onychopathy.
onicopático, -ca *adj.* onychopathic.
onicopatología *f.* onychopathology.
onicoplastia *f.* onychoplasty.
onicoptosis *f.* onychoptosis.
onicorrexis *f.* onychorrhexis.
onicosis *f.* onychosis.
onicosquisis *f.* onychoschizia.
onicotilomanía *f.* onychotillomania.
onicotomía *f.* onychotomy.
onicotrofia *f.* onychotrophy.
oniomanía *f.* oniomania.
oniquectomía *f.* onychectomy.
oniquia *f.* onychia.
oniquia lateral onychia lateralis.
oniquia maligna onychia maligna.
oniquia periungueal onychia periunguealis.
oniquia seca onychia sicca.
oniquitis *f.* onychitis.
onírico, -ca *adj.* oneiric.
onirismo *m.* oneirism.
onirocrítico, -ca *adj.* oneirocritical.
onirodinia *f.* oneirodynia.
onirodinia activa oneirodynia activa.
onirodinia grave oneirodynia gravis.
onirofonía *f.* oneirophonia.
onirofrenia *f.* oneirophrenia.
onirógeno, -na *adj.* oneirogenic.
onirogma *f.* oneirogmus.
oniroide *adj.* oneiroid.
onirología *f.* oneirology.
oniroscopia *f.* oneiroscopy.
ónix *m.* onyx.
onixis *f.* onyxis.
onixitis *f.* onyxitis.
onlay *m.* onlay.
onomatofobia *f.* onomatophobia.
onomatomanía *f.* onomatomania.
onomatopoyesis *f.* onomatopoiesis.
onquinocele *m.* onkinocele.
ontogenesia *f.* ontogenesis.
ontogénesis *f.* ontogenesis.
ontogenético, -ca *adj.* ontogenetic.
ontogenia *f.* ontogeny.
ontogénico, -ca *adj.* ontogenic.
onyalai onyalai.
O'nyong-nyong O'nyong-nyong.
onyx onyx.
oocéfalo *m.* oocephalus.
oocéfalo, -la *adj.* oocephalous.
oocianina *f.* oocyanin.
ociano, -na *adj.* oocyan.
oociesis *f.* oocyesis.
oocinesis *f.* ookinesia, ookinesis, oocinesia.
oocineto *m.* oocinete.
oocisto *m.* oocyst.
oocitasa *f.* oocytase.
oocito *m.* oocyte.
oocito de primer orden primary oocyte.

oocito primario primary oocyte.
oocito secundario secondary oocyte.
oocito de segundo orden secondary oocyte.
oodeocele *m.* oodeocele.
oofagia *f.* oophagia, oophagy.
ooforalgia *f.* oophoralgia.
ooforectomía *f.* oophorectomy.
ooforectomizar *v.* oophorectomize.
ooforitis *f.* oophoritis.
ooforitis parotídea oophoritis parotidea.
ooforitis autoinmune auntoinmune oophoritis.
oóforo *m.* oophoron.
ooforocistectomía *f.* oophorocystectomy.
ooforocistosis *f.* oophorocystosis.
ooforógeno, -na *adj.* oophorogenous.
ooforohisterectomía *f.* oophorohysterectomy.
ooforoma *m.* oophoroma.
ooforoma folicular oophoroma folliculare.
ooforopatía *f.* oophoropathy.
ooforopexia *f.* oophoropexy.
ooforoplastia *f.* oophoroplasty.
oofororrafia *f.* oophororrhaphy.
oofororragia *f.* oophorrhagia.
ooforosalpingectomía *f.* oophorosalpingectomy.
ooforosalpingitis *f.* oophorosalpingitis.
ooforostomía *f.* oophorostomy.
ooforotomía *f.* oophorotomy.
oogamia *f.* oogamy.
oogamo, -ma *adj.* oogamous.
oogenesia *f.* oogenesis.
oogénesis *f.* oogenesis.
oogenético, -ca *adj.* oogenetic.
oogenia *f.* oogenesis.
oogénico, -ca *adj.* oogenic.
oógeno, -na *adj.* oogenic.
oogonia *f.* oogonium.
oolema *m.* oolemma.
ooplasma *m.* ooplasm.
ooporfirina *f.* ooporphyrin.
ooquiste *m.* oocyst.
oorrodeína *f.* oorhodein.
oospermo *m.* oosperm.
oospora *f.* oospore.
ooteca *f.* ootheca.
ooterapia *f.* ootherapy.
oótide *f.* ootid.
ootipo *m.* ootype.
ooxantina *f.* ooxanthine.
oozoide *m.* oozooid.
opacamiento *f.* opacification.
opacidad *f.* opacity.
opacidad anular de Caspar Caspar's ring opacity.
opacificación *f.* opacification.
opacificación de la cápsula posterior posterior capsule opacification.
opacificado, -da *adj.* opacified.
opaco, -ca *adj.* opaque.
opalescente *adj.* opalescent.
opalescina *f.* opalescin.
opalgia *f.* opalgia.
opalino, -na *adj.* opaline.
opalisina *f.* opalisin.
opeidoscopio *m.* opeidoscope.
operabilidad *f.* operability.
operable *adj.* operable.
operación *f.* operation.
operación de Abbe Abbe's operation.
operación de Abbé-Estlander Abbé-Estlander operation.
operación abdominal abdominal section.
operación abierta open operation.

operación de Adams Adam's operation for ectropion.
operación de Akin Akin operation.
operación de Albee Albee's operation.
operación de Albee-Delbet Albee-Delbet operation.
operación de Albert Albert's operation.
operación de Alexander Alexander's operation.
operación de Alexander-Adams Alexander-Adams operation.
operación de Alouette Alouette operation.
operación de Ammon Ammon's operation.
operación de Amussat Amussat's operation.
operación de Anagnostakis Anagnostakis' operation.
operación de Aries-Pitanguy Aries-Pitanguy operation.
operación de Arlt Arlt's operation.
operación de Asch Asch operation.
operación de Babcock Babcock's operation.
operación de Baldy Baldy's operation.
operación de Baldy-Webster Baldy-Webster operation.
operación de Ball Ball's operation.
operación de Barkan Barkan's operation.
operación de Barker Barker operation.
operación de Barraquer Barraquer's operation.
operación de Barsky Barsky's operation.
operación de Barton Barton's operation.
operación de Basset Basset's operation.
operación de Bassini Bassini's operation.
operación de Battle Battle's operation.
operación de Baudelocque Baudelocque's operation.
operación de Beer Beer's operation.
operación de Belsey Belsey operation.
operación de Belsey Mark IV Belsey Mark IV operation.
operación de Berger Berger's operation.
operación de Berke Berke operation.
operación de Bevan Bevan's operation.
operación de Bier Bier's operation.
operación de Biesenberger Biesenberger's operation.
operación de Billroth I Billroth's operation I.
operación de Billroth II Billroth's operation II.
operación de Blair-Brown Blair-Brown operation.
operación de Blalock-Hanlon Blalock-Hanlon operation.
operación de Blalock-Taussig Blalock-Taussig operation.
operación de Blaskovics Blaskovics' operation.
operación de Bonnet Bonnet's operation.
operación de Bowman Bowman's operation.
operación de Bozeman Bozeman's operation.
operación de Bricker Bricker's operation.
operación de Brock Brock operation.
operación de Brophy Brophy's operation.
operación de Browne Browne operation.
operación de Brunschwig Brunschwig's operation.
operación de Buck Buck's operation.
operación de Burow Burow's operation.
operación de Caldwell-Luc Caldwell-Luc operation.
operación de Carmody-Batson Carmody-Batson operation.
operación de Carpue Carpue's operation.
operación de Cecil Cecil's operation.
operación de Celso Celsian operation.
operación cesárea cesarean operation.
operación cesárea baja low cesarean section.

operación cesárea cervical cervical cesarean section.
operación cesárea clásica classic cesarean section.
operación cesárea corporal corporal cesarean section.
operación cesárea extraperitoneal extraperitoneal cesarean section.
operación cesárea de Latzko Latzko's cesarean section.
operación cesárea segmentaria lower segment cesarean section.
operación cesárea transperitoneal transperitoneal cesarean section.
operación cesárea vaginal vaginal cesarean section.
operación de Chopart Chopart's operation.
operación de colgajo flap operation.
operación de Colonna Colonna's operation.
operación de Commando Commando's operation.
operación con seton seton operation.
operación de Conway Conway operation.
operación de Cotte Cotte's operation.
operación de Cotting Cotting's operation.
operación de Dana Dana's operation.
operación de Dandy Dandy's operation.
operación de Daviel Daviel's operation.
operación de Denonvilliers Denonvilliers' operation.
operación de Dieffenbach Dieffenbach's operation.
operación de Doyle Doyle's operation.
operación de Duhamel Duhamel operation.
operación de Duplay Duplay's operation.
operación de Dupuy-Dutemps Dupuy-Dutemps operation.
operación de Dupuytren Dupuytren's operation.
operación de Elliot Elliot's operation.
operación de Emmet Emmet's operation.
operación equilibrante equilibrating operation.
operación de Esser Esser's operation.
operación de esterilización de Irving Irving's sterilization operation.
operación de Estes Estes' operation.
operación de Everbusch Eversbusch's operation.
operación exangüe bloodless operation.
operación exploradora, operación exploratoria exploratory operation.
operación de fenestración, operación de fenestración de Lempert fenestration operation, Lempert's fenestration operation.
operación de Fergusson Fergusson's operation.
operación de Filatov Filatov's operation.
operación filtrante filtering operation.
operación de Finney Finney's operation.
operación de Foley Foley operation.
operación de Fontan Fontan operation.
operación de Fothergill Fothergill's operation.
operación de Franco Franco's operation.
operación de Frank Frank's operation.
operación de Frazier-Spiller Frazier-Spiller operation.
operación de Fredet-Ramstedt Fredet-Ramstedt operation.
operación de Freund Freund's operation.
operación de Freyer Freyer's operation.
operación de Frost-Lang Frost-Lang's operation.
operación de Fukala Fukala's operation.
operación de Fuller Fuller's operation.

operación de Gifford Gifford's operation.
operación de Gigli Gigli's operation.
operación de Gil-Vernet Gil-Vernet operation.
operación de Gilliam Gilliam's operation.
operación de Gillies Gillies' operation.
operación de Girdlestone Girdlestone operation.
operación de Glenn Glenn's operation.
operación de Graefe Graefe's operation.
operación de Gritti Gritti's operation.
operación de Grondahl-Finney Grondahl-Finney operation.
operación de Guyon Guyon's operation.
operación de Halsted Halsted's operation.
operación de Hancock Hancock's operation.
operación de Hartmann Hartmann's operation.
operación de Haultain Haultain's operation.
operación de Heaney Heaney's operation.
operación de Heath Heath's operation.
operación de Heine Heine's operation.
operación de Heinecke-Mikulicz Heineke-Mikulicz operation.
operación de Heller Heller's operation.
operación de Herbert Herbert's operation.
operación de Hey Hey's operation.
operación de Hibbs Hibbs' operation.
operación de Hill Hill operation.
operación hindú Indian operation.
operación de Hoffa, operación de Hoffa-Lorenz Hoffa's operation, Hoffa-Lorenz operation.
operación de Hofmeister Hofmeister's operation.
operación de Holth Holth's operation.
operación de Horsley Horsley's operation.
operación de Hotz-Anagnostakis Hotz-Anagnostakis operation.
operación de Huggins Huggins' operation.
operación de Hummelsheim Hummelsheim's operation.
operación de Huntington Huntington's operation.
operación india de Smith Smith-Indian operation.
operación de interposición interposition operation.
operación de intervalo interval operation.
operación italiana Italian operation.
operación de Jaboulay Jaboulay's operation.
operación de Jacobaeus Jacobaeus operation.
operación de Jansen Jansen's operation.
operación de Juvara Juvara's operation.
operación de Kader Kader's operation.
operación de Kasai Kasai operation.
operación de Kazanjian Kazanjian's operation.
operación de Keen Keen's operation.
operación de Keller Keller operation.
operación de Kelly Kelly's operation.
operación de Killian Killian's operation.
operación de Killian-Freer Killian-Freer operation.
operación de King King's operation.
operación de Knapp Knapp's operation.
operación de Kocher Kocher's operation.
operación de Köerte-Ballance Köerte-Ballance operation.
operación de Kondoleon Kondoleon operation.
operación de Kraske Kraske's operation.
operación de Krimer Krimer's operation.
operación de Krogius Krogius' operation.
operación de Krönlein Krönlein operation.
operación de Kuhnt Kuhnt's operation.

operación de Küstner Küstner operation.
operación de Ladd Ladd's operation.
operación de Lagrange Lagrange's operation.
operación de Lambrinudi Lambrinudi operation.
operación de Landolt Landolt's operation.
operación de Lane Lane's operation.
operación de Lapidus Lapidus operation.
operación de Laroyenne Laroyenne's operation.
operación de Larrey Larrey's operation.
operación de Lash Lash's operation.
operación de le fort, operación de Le Fort-Neugebauer Le Fort's operation, Le Fort-Neugebauer operation.
operación de Leriche Leriche's operation.
operación de Lindner Lindner's operation.
operación de Lisfranc Lisfranc's operation.
operación de Liston Liston's operation.
operación de Lizars Lizars' operation.
operación de Longmire Longmire's operation.
operación de Lorenz Lorenz's operation.
operación de Luc Luc's operation.
operación de Macewen Macewen's operation.
operación de Madlener Madlener operation.
operación de Manchester Manchester operation.
operación de Marshall-Marchetti-Krantz Marshall-Marchetti-Krantz operation.
operación de Mason Mason's operation.
operación mastoides mastoid operation.
operación de Matas Matas' operation.
operación de Mayo Mayo's operation.
operación mayor major operation.
operación de McBride McBride operation.
operación de McBurney McBurney's operation.
operación de McReynolds McReynolds' operation.
operación de McVay McVay's operation.
operación de Meller Meller's operation.
operación menor minor operation.
operación de Mikulicz Mikulicz's operation.
operación de Miles Miles' operation.
operación de morcelación morcellation operation.
operación de Moschcowitz Moschcowitz's operation.
operación de Motais Motais' operation.
operación de movilización del estribo stapes mobilization operation.
operación de Mules Mules' operation.
operación de mustard mustard operation.
operación de Naffziger Naffziger operation.
operación de Nissen Nissen's operation.
operación de Norton Norton's operation.
operación de Ober Ober's operation.
operación de Ogston-Luc Ogston-Luc operation.
operación de Olshausen Olshausen's operation.
operación de Patey Patey's operation.
operación de Payne Payne operation.
operación perineal perineal section.
operación de Phelps Phelps' operation.
operación de Phemister Phemister operation.
operación plástica plastic operation, cosmetic operation.
operación de Pólya Pólya's operation.
operación de Pomeroy Pomeroy's operation.
operación de Porro Porro operation.
operación de Potts Potts operation.
operación de Puttio-Platt Puttio-Platt operation.

operación radical radical operation.
operación de Ramstedt Ramstedt operation.
operación de Rastelli Rastelli operation.
operación de Récamier Récamier's operation.
operación de reducción debulking operation.
operación de reexploración second-look operation.
operación de Regnoli Regnoli's operation.
operación de Ridell Ridell operation.
operación de Roux, operación de Roux en Y Roux operation, Roux-en-Y operation.
operación de Saemisch Saemisch's operation, Saemisch's section.
operación de Saenger Saenger's operation.
operación de Scanzoni Scanzoni's operation.
operación de Schauta Schauta's operation.
operación de Schede Schede's operation.
operación de Scheie Scheie's operation.
operación de Schönbein Schönbein's operation.
operación de Schröder Schröder's operation.
operación de Schuchardt Schuchardt's operation.
operación de Sédillot Sédillot's operation.
operación de Senning Senning operation.
operación de Serre Serre's operation.
operación de Sever Sever's operation.
operación de Silver Silver operation.
operación de Shirodkar Shirodkar's operation.
operación de Sistrunk Sistrunk's operation.
operación de Smith Smith's operation.
operación de Smith-Boyce Smith-Boyce's operation.
operación de Smith-Robinson Smith-Robinson's operation.
operación de Soave Soave operation.
operación de Sorrin Sorrin's operation.
operación de Spinelli Spinelli's operation.
operación de Ssabanejew-Frank Ssabanejew-Frank operation.
operación de State State operation.
operación de Stein Stein operation.
operación de Steindler Steindler operation.
operación de Stoffel Stoffel's operation.
operación de Stokes Stokes' operation.
operación de Strassmann Strassmann's operation.
operación de Stookey-Scarff Stookey-Scarff operation.
operación de Strömbeck Strömbeck operation.
operación de Sturmdorf Sturmdorf's operation.
operación subcutánea subcutaneous operation.
operación de Swenson Swenson's operation.
operación de Syme Syme's operation.
operación de Tagliacozzi, operación tagliacotiana Tagliacotian operation.
operación de Tanner Tanner's operation.
operación de Teale Teale's operation.
operación de TeLinde TeLinde operation.
operación de Thiersch Thiersch's operation.
operación de Torek Torek operation.
operación de Torkildsen Torkildsen's operation.
operación de Toti Toti's operation.
operación de Trendelenburg Trendelenburg's operation.
operación vaginal de Schauta Schauta vaginal operation.
operación de van Hook van Hook's operation.
operación de Vincentiis de Vincentiis operation.

operación de Vineberg Vineberg operation.
operación de Vladimiroff Vladimiroff operation.
operación de Waterston Waterston operation.
operación de Watkins Watkins' operation.
operación de Webster Webster's operation.
operación de Wertheim, operación de Wertheim-Meigs Wertheim's operation, Wertheim-Meigs' technique.
operación de Wheelhouse Wheelhouse's operation.
operación de White White's operation.
operación de Whitehead Whitehead's operation.
operación de Whitman Whitman's operation.
operación de Young Young's operation.
operación de Ziegler Ziegler's operation.
operacionalización de la conducta *f.* operationalization of behavior.
operador, -ra *m., f. y adj.* operator.
operante *adj.* operant.
operar *v.* operate.
operativo, -va *adj.* operative.
opercular *adj.* opercular.
operculectomía *f.* operculectomy.
operculitis *f.* operculitis.
opérculo *m.* operculum.
opérculo dental dental operculum, operculum dentale.
opérculo trofoblástico trophoblastic operculum.
operón *m.* operon.
opiáceo, -a *adj.* opiate.
opiado, -da *adj.* opiate.
opilação *f.* opilação.
opilación *f.* oppilation.
opilativo, -va *adj.* oppilative.
opio *m.* opium.
opio de Boston Boston opium.
opio de budín pudding opium.
opio bruto crude opium.
opio desnarcotizado denarcotized opium.
opio desodorizado deodorized opium, opium deodoratum.
opio granulado granulated opium, opium granulatum.
opio de lechuga lettuce opium.
opio en polvo powdered opium, opium pulveratum.
opiofagia *f.* opiophagy.
opiofagismo *m.* opiophagism.
opioide *m.* opioid.
opiomanía *f.* opiomania.
opiomaníaco, -ca *adj.* opiomaniac.
opiómano, -na *adj.* opiomaniac.
opiomelanocortina *f.* opiomelanocortin.
opistenar *m.* opisthenar.
opistencéfalo *m.* opisthencephalon.
Opisthorchiidae Opisthorchiidae.
Opisthorchis Opisthorchis.
opisthorchis felineus opisthorchis felineus.
opisthorchis sinensis opisthorchis sinensis.
opisthorchis viverrini opisthorchis viverrini.
opistiobasial *adj.* opisthiobasial.
opistión *m.* opisthion.
opistionasial *adj.* opisthionasial.
opistocráneo *m.* opisthocranion.
opistogenia *f.* opisthogenia.
opistognatismo *m.* opisthognathism.
opistoporeia *f.* opisthoporeia.
opistoqueilia *f.* opisthocheilia, opisthochilia.
opistoquilia *f.* opisthochilia.
opistorcosis *f.* opisthorchosis.

opistorquiasis *f.* opisthorchiasis.
opistórquido *m.* opisthorchid.
opistótico, -ca *adj.* opisthotic.
opistotónico, -ca *adj.* opisthotonic.
opistotonoide *adj.* opisthotonoid.
opistótonos *m.* opisthotonos, opisthotonus.
  opistótonos fetal opisthotonus fetalis.
opium opium.
opocéfalo *m.* opocephalus.
opocéfalo, -la *adj.* opocephalous.
opodídimo *m.* opodidymus.
opódimo *m.* opodymus.
oponente *adj.* opposing, opponens.
oportunista *adj.* opportunistic.
opositipolar *adj.* oppositipolar.
opoterapia *f.* opotherapy.
opresión *f.* suffocation.
opsialgia *f.* opsialgia.
opsígeno, -na *adj.* opsigenes.
opsina *f.* opsin.
opsinógeno *m.* opsinogen.
opsiómetro *m.* opsiometer.
opsiuria *f.* opsiuria.
opsoclonía *f.* opsoclonia.
opsoclono *m.* opsoclonus.
opsoclonus opsoclonus.
opsógeno *m.* opsogen.
opsomanía *f.* opsomania.
opsona *f.* opsone.
opsónico, -ca *adj.* opsonic.
opsonífero, -ra *adj.* opsoniferous.
opsonificación *f.* opsonification.
opsonificar *v.* opsonify.
opsonina *f.* opsonin.
  opsonina común common opsonin.
  opsonina específica specific opsonin.
  opsonina inmune immune opsonin.
  opsonina normal normal opsonin.
  opsonina termoestable thermostable opsonin.
  opsonina termolábil thermolabile opsonin.
opsoninopatía *f.* opsoninopathy.
  opsoninopatía por utilización consumptive opsoninopathy.
opsonización *f.* opsonization.
opsonizar *v.* opsonize.
opsonocitofágico, -ca *adj.* opsonocytophagic.
opsonofilia *f.* opsonophilia.
opsonófilo, -la *adj.* opsonophilic.
opsonóforo, -ra *adj.* opsonophoric.
opsonógeno *m.* opsonogen.
opsonología *f.* opsonology.
opsonometría *f.* opsonometry.
opsonoterapia *f.* opsonotherapy.
optestesia *f.* optesthesia.
óptica *f.* optics.
  óptica de fibras fiber optics.
  óptica de Nomarski Nomarski optics.
óptico, -ca¹ *adj.* optic, optical.
óptico, -ca² *m., f.* optician, opticist, optist.
opticociliar *adj.* opticociliary.
opticocinérea *f.* opticocinerea.
opticocinético, -ca *adj.* opticokinetic.
opticonasión *m.* opticonasion.
opticopupilar *adj.* opticopupillary.
opticoquiasmático, -ca *adj.* opticochiasmatic.
optímetro *m.* optimeter.
optimismo *m.* optimism.
  optimismo terapéutico therapeutic optimism.
óptimo, -ma *adj.* optimal.
óptimo *m.* optimum.
optimum optimum.
optoblasto *m.* optoblast.
optocinético, -ca *adj.* optokinetic.
optófono *m.* optophone.

optograma *m.* optogram.
optomeninge *f.* optomeninx.
optometría *f.* optometry.
optometrista *m.* optometrist.
optómetro *m.* optometer.
  optómetro objetivo objective optometer.
optomiómetro *m.* optomyometer.
optoquiasmático, -ca *adj.* optochiasmic.
optostriado, -da *adj.* optostriate.
optotipo *m.* optotype, test type.
  optotipo de Jaeger Jaeger's test type.
ora serrata, ora serrata retinae *f.* ora serrata, ora serrata retinae.
orad orad.
oral¹ *adj.* oral.
oral² *m.* orale.
oralidad *f.* orality.
orbicular¹ *adj.* orbicular.
orbicular² *m.* orbicularis.
orbiculare *m.* orbiculare.
orbicularis orbicularis.
orbículo *m.* orbiculus.
órbita *f.* orbit, orbita.
orbital¹ *m.* orbitale.
orbital² *adj.* orbital.
orbitario, -ria *adj.* orbitalis.
orbitectomía *f.* orbitectomy.
orbitoesfenoidal *adj.* orbitosphenoid.
orbitografía *f.* orbitography.
orbitonasal *adj.* orbitonasal.
orbitonometría *f.* orbitonometry.
orbitonómetro *m.* orbitonometer.
orbitópago *m.* orbitopagus.
orbitóstato *m.* orbitostat.
orbitotemporal *adj.* orbitotemporal.
orbitotomía *f.* orbitotomy.
orbivirus *m.* orbivirus.
orcaneta *f.* alkanet.
orceína *f.* orcein.
orcela *f.* orchella.
orchella *f.* orchella.
orchilla *f.* cudbear.
orchis orchis.
orcina *f.* orcin.
orcinol *m.* orcinol.
orcotomía *f.* orchotomy.
orden¹ *m.* order.
  orden forzado pecking order.
orden² *f.* order.
  orden de no reanimación, orden de no resucitar do-not-resuscitate order, DNR order.
  orden de no reanimación sin consentimiento do-not-resuscitate-without-consent order.
  orden de procedimiento order of procedure.
  orden de tratamiento medication order.
  orden de enfermería nursing order.
ordenada *f.* ordinate.
ordenador *m.* computer.
ordeño *m.* milking.
oréctico, -ca *adj.* orectic.
oreja *f.* ear.
  oreja en asa loop ear.
  oreja azteca Aztec ear.
  oreja de blainville Blainville ear.
  oreja de boxeador boxer's ear, prizefighter ear.
  oreja de Cagot Cagot ear.
  oreja caída lop ear.
  oreja de coliflor, oreja en coliflor cauliflower ear.
  oreja de darwin Darwin's ear.
  oreja de gato cat's ear.
  oreja de macaco, oreja de Morel Morel's ear.
  oreja de Mozart Mozart ear.
  oreja de murciélago bat ear.

  oreja en pergamino scroll ear.
  oreja pilosa hairy ear.
  oreja en punta de sátiro, oreja en punta, oreja de sátiro scroll ear.
  oreja de Stahl nº 1 Stahl ear, Nº 1.
  oreja de Stahl nº 2 Stahl ear, Nº 2.
  oreja en taza cup ear.
  oreja de Wildermuth Wildermuth's ear.
orejuela *f.* auricle, auricula.
orexia *f.* orexia, orexis.
orexigénico, -ca *adj.* orexigenic.
orexígeno, -na *adj.* orexigenic.
oreximanía *f.* oreximania.
orf *m.* orf.
organacidia *f.* organacidia.
organela *f.* organelle, organella.
  organela cristal de reloj, organela Lieberkühn holdfast organelle.
organelo *m.* organelle, organella.
organicismo *m.* organicism.
organicista *m., f.* organicist.
orgánico, -ca *adj.* organic.
organismo *m.* organism.
  organismo consumidor consumer organism.
  organismo exigente fastidious organism.
  organismo medio calculado calculated mean organism (CMO).
  organismo medio hipotético hypothetical mean organism (HMO).
  organismo nitrificante nitrifying organism.
  organismo nitrosificante nitrosifying organism.
  organismo tipo pleuroneumonía pleuropneumonia-like organism (PPLO).
organización *f.* organization.
  Organización Mundial de la Salud (OMS) World Health Organization (WHO).
  organización pregenital pregenital organization.
  organización de prestadores seleccionados (OPS) preferred provider organization (PPO).
  organización profesional professional organization.
organizador, -ra *m., f.* organizer.
  organizador nucleolar, organizador del nucléolo nucleolar organizer, nucleolus organizer.
  organizador primario, organizador principal primary organizer.
  organizador procentriolo, organizador de los procentriolos procentriole organizer.
  organizador secundario secondary organizer.
  organizador terciario tertiary organizer.
órgano *m.* organ, organon, organum.
  órgano accesorio accessory organ.
  órgano accesorio del ojo accessory organ of the eye, organa oculi accessoria.
  órgano acústico acoustic organ.
  órgano anuloespiral anulospiral organ.
  órgano de la audición organ of hearing.
  órgano auditivo organum auditus.
  órgano blanco target organ.
  órgano celular cell organ.
  órgano del cemento cement organ.
  órgano de Chievitz Chievitz's organ.
  órgano de choque organ of shock.
  órgano circunventricular circumventricular organ.
  órgano de Corti Corti's organ, organ of Corti.
  órgano crítico critical organ.
  órgano diana target organ.
  órgano digestivo digestive organ, apparatus digestorius.

órgano efector effector organ.
órgano errante wandering organ.
órgano esmalte, órgano del esmalte enamel organ.
órgano espiral spiral organ, organum spirale.
órgano extraperitoneal extraperitoneal organ, organum extraperitoneale.
órgano final end organ.
órgano flotante floating organ.
órgano genital organa genitalia.
órgano genital externo external genital organ, organa genitalia externa.
órgano genital femenino female genital organ.
órgano genital femenino externo organa genitalia femenina externa.
órgano genital femenino interno organa genitalia femenina interna.
órgano genital interno internal genital organ, organa genitalia interna.
órgano genital masculino male genital organ.
órgano genital masculino externo organa genitalia masculina externa.
órgano genital masculino interno organa genitalia masculina interna.
órgano de Giraldès organ of Giraldès.
órgano de Golgi organ of Golgi.
órgano gustativo, órgano gustatorio, órgano del gusto gustatory organ, taste organ, organ of taste, organon gustus, organum gustatorium, organum gustus.
órgano homólogo homologous organ.
órgano introductor intromittent organ.
órgano intromitente intromittent organ.
órgano de Jacobson Jacobson's organ.
órgano linfático lymphatic organ.
órgano linfoide lymphoid organ.
órgano linfoide primario primary lymphoid organ.
órgano linfoide secundario secondary lymphoid organ.
órgano de Meyer Meyer's organ.
órgano neurotendinoso neurotendinous organ.
órgano olfatorio, órgano del olfato olfactory organ, organ of smell, organon olfactus, organum olfactus, organum olfactorium.
órgano primitivo de grasa primitive fat organ.
órgano ptótico ptotic organ.
órgano en ramillete de Ruffini flower-spray organ of Ruffini.
órgano reproductor reproductive organ.
órgano reproductor femenino female reproductive organ.
órgano reproductor del varón male reproductive organ.
órgano retroperitoneal retroperitoneal organ, organum retroperitoneale.
órgano de Rosenmüller organ of Rosenmüller, Rosenmüller's organ.
órgano rudimentario rudimentary organ.
órgano de Ruffini organ of Ruffini, Ruffini's organ.
órgano segmentario segmental organ.
órgano sensitivo terminal sensory end organ.
órgano sensorial, órgano de los sentidos sense organ, sensory organ, organa sensoria, organa sensuum.
órgano de un sentido sense organ.
órgano subcomisural subcommissural organ, organum subcommissurale.
órgano subfornical subfornical organ, organum subfornicale.

órgano supernumerario supernumerary organ.
órgano del tacto organ of touch, touch receptor organ, organum tactus.
órgano tendinoso de Golgi Golgi's tendon organ.
órgano terminal end organ, terminal organ.
órgano urinario urinary organ, organa urinaria.
órgano uropoyético organa uropoietica.
órgano vestibular vestibular organ.
órgano vestibulococlear vestibulocochlear organ, organum vestibulocochleare.
órgano vestigial vestigial organ.
órgano de la visión, órgano visual organ of vision, visual organ, organum visuale, organum visus.
órgano vomeronasal vomeronasal organ, organum vomeronasale.
órgano de Weber Weber's organ.
organocloro *m.* organochlorine.
organoespecífico, -ca *adj.* organ-specific.
organofacción *f.* organofaction.
organoférrico, -ca *adj.* organoferric.
organofílico, -ca *adj.* organophilic.
organófilo, -la *adj.* organophilic.
organofosfato *m.* organophosphate.
organofosforado, -da *adj.* organophosphorated.
organofósforo *m.* organophosphorus.
organogel *m.* organogel.
organogenesia *f.* organogenesis.
organogénesis *f.* organogenesis.
organogenético, -ca *adj.* organogenetic.
organogenia *f.* organogeny.
organogénico, -ca *adj.* organogenic.
organógeno *m.* organogen.
organografía *f.* organography.
organoide *m. y adj.* organoid.
organoléptico, -ca *adj.* organoleptic.
organología *f.* organology.
organoma *m.* organoma.
organomegalia *f.* organomegaly.
organomercurial *adj.* organomercurial.
organometálico, -ca *adj.* organometallic.
organonimia *f.* organonymy.
organonomía *f.* organonomy.
organopatía *f.* organopathy.
organopexia *f.* organopexy, organopexia.
organoscopia *f.* organoscopy.
organosol *m.* organosol.
organotaxis *f.* organotaxis.
organoterapia *f.* organotherapy.
organoterapia heteróloga heterologous organotherapy.
organoterapia homóloga homologous organotherapy.
organotrófico, -ca *adj.* organotrophic.
organotropía *f.* organotropy.
organotrópico, -ca *adj.* organotropic.
organotropismo *m.* organotropism.
organótropo *m.* organotrope.
organulo *m.* organule.
orgásmico, -ca *adj.* orgasmic.
orgasmo *m.* orgasm.
orgástico, -ca *adj.* orgasmic.
oricenina *f.* oryzenin.
orientación *f.* orientation.
orientación personal personal orientation.
orientación de la realidad reality orientation.
orientación sexual sexual orientation.
orientar *v.* orient.
orificial *adj.* orificial.
orificialista *m., f.* orificialist.
orificio *m.* orifice, orificium.

origen *m.* origin.
orín *m.* rust.
orina *f.* urine, urina.
orina amoniacal ammoniacal urine.
orina azul black urine.
orina de la bebida urina potus.
orina bruta crude urine.
orina cruda crude urine.
orina diabética diabetic urine.
orina dispéptica dyspeptic urine.
orina febril febrile urine, feverish urine.
orina gotosa gouty urine.
orina en jarabe de arce maple syrup urine.
orina lechosa milky urine.
orina nebulosa nebulous urine.
orina negra black urine.
orina nebulosa nebulous urine.
orina en polvo de ladrillo brick dust urine.
orina quilosa chylous urine.
orina residual residual urine.
orina turbia cloudy urine.
orinacidómetro *m.* urinacidometer.
orinal *m.* urinal.
orinar *v.* urinate.
orinoterapia *f.* orinotherapy.
ornado *m.* ornate.
Ornithodoros Ornithodoros.
Ornithonyssu bacoti Ornithonyssu bacoti.
ornitina *f.* ornithine.
ornitina carbamiltransferasa, ornitina carbamoiltransferasa ornithine carbamoyltransferase.
ornitina descarboxilasa ornithine decarboxylase.
ornitina transcarbamoilasa ornithine transcarbamoylase.
ornitinemia *f.* ornithinemia.
ornitinuria *f.* ornithinuria.
ornitosis *f.* ornithosis.
oro *m.* gold.
oro blanco white gold.
oro cohesivo cohesive gold.
oro coloidal colloidal gold.
oro coloidal radiactivo colloidal radioactive gold.
oro directo direct gold.
oro fibroso fibrous gold.
oro laminado gold foil.
oro laminado no cohesivo non-cohesive gold foil.
oro laminado platinado platinized gold foil.
oro mate matt gold.
oro no cohesivo non-cohesive gold.
oro en polvo powdered gold.
oro radiactivo radioactive gold.
orodiagnóstico *m.* orodiagnosis.
orodigitofacial *adj.* orodigitofacial.
orofacial *adj.* orofacial.
orofaringe *f.* oropharynx.
orofaríngeo, -a *adj.* oropharyngeal.
orofaringolaringitis *f.* oropharyngolaryngitis.
orogranulocítico, -ca *adj.* orogranulocytic.
orogranulocito *m.* orogranulocyte.
oroinmunidad *f.* oroimmunity.
orolingual *adj.* orolingual.
oromaxilar *adj.* oromaxillary.
oromeningitis *f.* oromeningitis.
oronasal *adj.* oronasal.
Oropsylla Oropsylla.
Oropsylla idahoensis Oropsylla idahoensis.
Oropsylla silantiewi Oropsylla silantiewi.
oroquinasa *f.* orokinase.
orosomucoide *m.* orosomucoid.
orotato *m.* orotate.
oroterapia *f.* orotherapy.

oroticoaciduria *f.* orotic aciduria, oroticaciduria.

orotidilato *m.* orotidylato.

orotidina *f.* orotidine.

orquectomía *f.* orchectomy.

orquialgia *f.* orchialgia.

orquiatrofia *f.* orchiatrophy.

orquicatabasis *f.* orchicatabasis.

órquico, -ca *adj.* orchic.

orquicorea *f.* orchichorea.

orquidalgia *f.* orchidalgia.

orquidectomía *f.* orchidectomy.

orquídico, -ca *adj.* orchidic.

orquiditis *f.* orchiditis.

orquidoepididimectomía *f.* orchidoepididymectomy.

orquidoepididimitis *f.* orchiepididymitis.

orquidofuniculisis *f.* orchiofuniculisis.

orquidómetro *m.* orchidometer.

orquidonco *m.* orchidoncus.

orquidopatía *f.* orchidopathy.

orquidopexia *f.* orchidopexy.

orquidoplastia *f.* orchidoplasty.

orquidoptosis *f.* orchidoptosis.

orquidorrafia *f.* orchidorrhaphy.

orquidoterapia *f.* orchidotherapy.

orquidotomía *f.* orchidotomy.

orquiectomía *f.* orchiectomy.

orquectomía *f.* orchiectomy.

  orquiectomía por cáncer de testículo orchiectomy in testicular carcinoma.

  orquiectomía subalbugínea orchiectomy in prostate adenocarcinoma.

orquiepididimitis *f.* orchiepididymitis.

orquioepididimitis *f.* orchiepididymitis.

orquiolítico, -ca *adj.* orchilytic.

orquiocatabasis *f.* orchiocatabasis.

orquiocele *m.* orchiocele.

orquiodinia *f.* orchiodynia.

orquioescirro *m.* orchioscirrhus.

orquionco *m.* orchioncus.

orquioneuralgia *f.* orchioneuralgia.

orquiopatía *f.* orchiopathy.

orquiopexia *f.* orchiopexy.

orquioplastia *f.* orchioplasty.

orquioptosis *f.* orchidoptosis.

orquiorrafia *f.* orchiorrhaphy.

orquioscirro *m.* orchioscirrhus.

orquiosqueocele *m.* orchioscheocele.

orquioterapia *f.* orchiotherapy.

orquiotomía *f.* orchiotomy.

orquidotomía *f.* orchiotomy.

orquis *m.* orchis.

orquítico, -ca *adj.* orchitic.

orquitis *f.* orchitis.

  orquitis granulomatosa espermatógena spermatogenic granulomatous orchitis.

  orquitis metastática metastatic orchitis.

  orquitis parótida, orquitis parotídea, orquitis parotídica orchitis parotidea.

  orquitis traumática traumatic orchitis.

  orquitis variolosa orchitis variolosa.

orquitolítico, -ca *adj.* orchitolytic.

orrodiagnosis *f.* orrhodiagnosis.

orrodiagnóstico *m.* orrhodiagnosis.

orroinmunidad *f.* orrhoimmunity.

orrología *f.* orrhology.

orromeningitis *f.* orrhomeningitis.

orrorrea *f.* orrhorrhea.

orrorreacción *f.* orrhoreaction.

orroterapéutico, -ca *adj.* orrhotherapeutic.

orroterapia *f.* orrhotherapy.

orseilina BB *f.* orseillin BB.

ortergasia *f.* orthergasia.

ortésica *f.* orthetics.

ortésico, -ca *adj.* orthetic.

ortesis *f.* orthesis.

  Engen extensión ortesis Engen extension orthesis.

  ortesis de escayola cast brace.

  ortesis de Newington Newington orthesis.

  ortesis de pie de formato libre free-form foot orthesis.

  ortesis raquídea eléctrica electric spinal orthesis.

  ortesis tobillo-pie (OTP) ankle-foot orthesis (AFO).

ortética *f.* orthetics.

ortetista *m., f.* orthetist.

Orthomyxoviridae Orthomyxoviridae.

Orthopoxvirus Orthopoxvirus.

ortiga *f.* nettle.

ortoácido *m.* orthoacid.

ortoarteriotonía *f.* orthoarteriotony, orthoarteriotony.

ortobiosis *f.* orthobiosis.

ortocefálico, -ca *adj.* orthocephalic.

ortocéfalo, -la *adj.* orthocephalous.

ortocinética *f.* orthokinetics.

ortocitosis *f.* orthocytosis.

ortocorea *f.* orthochorea.

ortocresol *m.* orthocresol.

ortocromático, -ca *adj.* orthochromatic.

ortocromía *f.* orthochromia.

ortocromófilo, -la *adj.* orthochromophil, orthochromophile.

ortodáctilo, -la *adj.* orthodactylous.

ortodentina *f.* orthodentin.

ortodentista *m., f.* orthodontist.

ortodesoxia *f.* orthodeoxia.

ortodiagrafía *f.* orthodiagraphy.

ortodiágrafo *m.* orthodiagraph.

ortodiagrama *m.* orthodiagram.

ortodiametría *f.* orthodiametry.

ortodiascopio *m.* orthodiascope.

ortodiascopia *f.* orthodiascopy.

ortodigita *f.* orthodigita.

ortodoncia *f.* orthodontia, orthodontics, denturism.

  ortodoncia correctiva corrective orthodontics.

  ortodoncia interperceptiva interperceptive orthodontics.

  ortodoncia preventiva preventive orthodontics, prophylactic orthodontics.

  ortodoncia quirúrgica surgical orthodontics.

ortodóntico, -ca *adj.* orthodontic.

ortodoncista *adj.* orthodontist, denturist.

ortodontista *m., f.* orthodontist.

ortodontología *f.* orthodontology.

ortodrómico, -ca *adj.* orthodromic.

ortoestereoscopio *m.* orthostereoscope.

ortofonia *f.* orthophony.

ortoforia *f.* orthophoria.

ortofórico, -ca *adj.* orthophoric.

ortofosfato *m.* orthophosphate.

  ortofosfato inorgánico (pi) inorganic orthophosphate (pi).

ortofrenia *f.* orthophrenia.

ortogénesis *f.* orthogenesis.

ortogenia *f.* orthogenesis.

ortogénica *f.* orthogenics.

ortogénico, -ca *adj.* orthogenic.

ortoglucémico, -ca *adj.* orthoglycemic.

ortognatia *f.* orthognathia.

ortognática *f.* orthognathics.

ortognático, -ca *adj.* orthognathic.

ortognatismo *m.* orthognathism.

ortognato, -ta *adj.* orthognathous.

ortógrado, -da *adj.* orthograde.

ortomecánico, -ca *adj.* orthomechanical.

ortomecanoterapia *f.* orthomechanotherapy.

ortomélico, -ca *adj.* orthomelic.

ortómetro *m.* orthometer.

ortomixovirus *m.* orthomyxovus.

ortomolecular *adj.* orthomolecular.

ortomorfia *f.* orthomorphia.

ortoneutrófilo, -la *adj.* orthoneutrophil.

ortopantografía *f.* orthopantograph.

ortopantomografía *f.* orthopantomography.

ortopantomógrafo *m.* orthopantomograph.

ortopeda *m.* orthopod.

ortopedia *f.* orthopedics.

  ortopedia dental dental orthopedics.

  ortopedia funcional de los maxilares functional jaw orthopedics.

ortopédico, -ca *adj.* orthopedic.

ortopedista *m.* orthopedist.

ortopercusión *f.* orthopercussion.

ortopía *f.* orthopia.

ortoplastocito *m.* orthoplastocyte.

ortoplexímetro *m.* orthoplessimeter.

ortopnea *f.* orthopnea.

  ortopnea de dos almohadas two-pillow orthopnea.

ortopneico, -ca *adj.* orthopneic.

Ortopoxvirus Orthopoxvirus.

ortoprótesis *f.* orthoprosthesis.

ortopsia *f.* orthopia.

ortopsiquiatría *f.* orthopsychiatry.

ortóptica *f.* orthoptics.

ortóptico, -ca *adj.* orthoptic.

ortoptista *m., f.* orthoptist.

ortoptoscopio *m.* orthoptoscope.

ortorráquico, -ca *adj.* orthorrhachic.

ortorrómbico, -ca *adj.* orthorhombic.

ortoqueratología *f.* orthokeratology.

ortoqueratosis *f.* orthokeratosis.

ortoscopia *f.* orthoscopy.

ortoscópico, -ca *adj.* orthoscopic.

ortoscopio *m.* orthoscope.

ortosimpático, -ca *m.* orthosympathetic.

ortosis *f.* orthosis.

ortosquiagrafía *f.* orthoskiagraphy.

ortosquiágrafo *m.* orthoskiagraph.

ortostático, -ca *adj.* orthostatic.

ortostatismo *m.* orthostatism.

ortostereoscopio *m.* orthostereoscope.

ortotanasia *f.* orthothanasia.

ortotasto *m.* orthotast.

ortoterapia *f.* orthotherapy.

ortoterion *m.* orthoterion.

ortótica *f.* orthotics.

ortótico, -ca *adj.* orthotic.

ortotifoidea *f.* orthotyphoid.

ortotista *m., f.* orthotist.

ortotolidina *f.* orthotolidine.

ortótonos *m.* orthotonos, orthotonus.

ortotópico, -ca *adj.* orthotopic.

ortotrofia *f.* orthotrophy.

ortotrópico, -ca *adj.* orthotropic.

ortovoltaje *m.* orthovoltage.

ortropsia *f.* orthropsia.

orturia *f.* orthuria.

orzuelo *m.* sty, stye, hordeolum.

  orzuelo externo external sty, hordeolum externum.

  orzuelo interno internal sty, hordeolum internum.

  orzuelo meibomiano, orzuelo de Meibomio Meibomian sty, hordeolum meibomianum.

  orzuelo de Zeis, o zeisiano Zeisian sty.

os os.

osamenta *f.* ossature.

osamina *f.* osamine.
osazona *f.* osazone.
oscedo *f.* oscedo.
oscilación *f.* oscillation.
  oscilación bradicinética bradykinetic oscillation.
oscilador *m.* oscillator.
oscilatorio, -ria *adj.* oscillatory.
oscilografía *f.* oscillography.
oscilógrafo *m.* oscillograph.
oscilograma *m.* oscillogram.
oscilometría *f.* oscillometry.
oscilométrico, -ca *adj.* oscillometric.
oscilómetro *m.* oscillometer.
oscilopsia *f.* oscillopsia.
osciloscopio *m.* oscilloscope.
  osciloscopio de almacenamiento storage oscilloscope.
  osciloscopio de rayos catódicos cathode ray oscilloscope.
oscitación *m.* oscitation.
oscitar *v.* oscitate.
ósculo *m.* osculum.
osculum *m.* osculum.
oscuro, -ra *adj.* dark.
ose *f.* ose.
oseína *f.* ossein.
óseo, -a *adj.* osseous, bony.
oseocartilaginoso, -sa *adj.* osseocartilaginous.
oseomucina *f.* osseomucin.
oseomucoide *m.* osseomucoid.
oseosonometría *f.* osseosonometry.
oseosonómetro *m.* osseosonometer.
osfialgia *f.* osphyalgia.
osfiartrosis *f.* osphyarthrosis.
osfiomielitis *f.* osphyomyelitis.
osfiotomía *f.* osphyotomy.
osfresiofilia *f.* osphresiophilia.
osfresiofobia *f.* osphresiophobia.
osfresiolagnia *f.* osphresiolagnia.
osfresiología *f.* osphresiology.
osfresiológico, -ca *adj.* osphresiologic.
osfresiómetro *m.* osphresiometer.
osfresis *f.* osphresis.
osfrético, -ca *adj.* osphretic.
osicular *adj.* ossicular.
osiculectomía *f.* ossiculectomy.
osículo *m.* ossicle, ossiculum.
osiculotomía *f.* ossiculotomy.
osidesmosis *f.* ossidesmosis.
osífero, -ra *adj.* ossiferous.
osificación *f.* ossification.
  osificación accidental metaplastic ossification.
  osificación cartilaginosa cartilaginous ossification.
  osificación ectópica ectopic ossification.
  osificación encondral, osificación endocondral endochondral ossification.
  osificación heterotópica heterotopic ossification.
  osificación intramembranosa intramembranous ossification.
  osificación membranosa membranous ossification.
  osificación metaplásica metaplastic ossification.
  osificación pericondral perichondral ossification.
  osificación perióstica periosteal ossification.
osificante *adj.* ossifying.
osificar *v.* ossify.
osífico, -ca *adj.* ossific.
osífono *m.* ossiphone.

osiforme *adj.* ossiform.
osmático, -ca *adj.* osmatic.
osmato *m.* osmate.
osmesis *f.* osmesis.
osmestesia *f.* osmesthesia.
ósmica *f.* osmics.
osmicar *v.* osmicate.
osmidrosis *f.* osmidrosis.
osmificación *f.* osmication, osmification.
osmiófilo, -la *adj.* osmiophilic.
osmiófobo, -ba *adj.* osmiophobic.
osmoceptor *m.* osmoceptor.
osmodisforia *f.* osmodysphoria.
osmofílico, -ca *adj.* osmophilic.
osmófilo, -la *adj.* osmophilic.
osmofobia *f.* osmophobia.
osmóforo *m.* osmophore.
osmograma *f.* osmogram.
osmol *m.* osmol, osmole.
osmolagnia *f.* osmolagnia.
osmolalidad *f.* osmolality.
  osmolalidad calculada del suero calculated serum osmolality.
osmolar *adj.* osmolar.
osmolaridad *f.* osmolarity.
  osmolaridad de la orina, osmolaridad urinaria urine osmolarity.
  osmolaridad sanguínea blood osmolarity.
  osmolaridad del suero, osmolaridad sérica serum osmolarity.
osmología *f.* osmology.
osmoluto *m.* osmolute.
osmometría *f.* osmometry.
osmómetro *m.* osmometer.
  osmómetro de Hepp Hepp osmometer.
  osmómetro de membrana membrane osmometer.
  osmómetro de punto de congelación freezing point osmometer.
osmonosología *f.* osmonosology.
osmorreceptor *m.* osmoreceptor.
osmorregulación *f.* osmoregulation.
osmorregulador, -ra *adj.* osmoregulatory.
osmosar *v.* osmose.
osmoscopio *m.* osmoscope.
osmosidad *f.* osmosity.
osmosis, ósmosis *f.* osmosis.
  osmosis inversa reverse osmosis.
osmosología *f.* osmosology.
osmostato *m.* osmostat.
osmotaxis *f.* osmotaxis.
osmoterapia *f.* osmotherapy.
osmótico, -ca *adj.* osmotic.
osqueal *adj.* oscheal.
osqueítis *f.* oscheitis.
osqueocele *m.* oscheocele.
osqueoelefantiasis *f.* oschelephantiasis.
osqueohidrocele *m.* oscheohydrocele.
osqueolito *m.* oscheolith.
osqueoma *m.* oscheoma.
osqueonco *m.* oscheoncus.
osqueoplastia *f.* oscheoplasty.
osquitis *f.* oschitis.
ossiculum ossiculum.
ostalgia *f.* ostalgia.
ostameba *f.* osteameba.
ostartritis *f.* ostarthritis.
osteal *adj.* osteal.
ostealgia *f.* ostealgia.
osteálgico, -ca *adj.* ostealgic.
osteameba *f.* osteameba.
osteamiba *f.* osteameba.
osteanáfisis *f.* osteanaphysis.
osteanagenesia *f.* osteanagenesis.
osteanagénesis *f.* osteanagenesis.

osteartritis *f.* ostearthritis.
ostectomía *f.* ostectomy.
ostectopía *f.* ostectopy.
osteectomía *f.* osteectomy.
osteectopía *f.* osteectopia.
osteico, -ca *adj.* osteal.
osteína *f.* ostein, osteine.
osteítico, -ca *adj.* osteitic.
osteítis *f.* osteitis.
  osteítis aguda acute osteitis.
  osteítis albuminosa osteitis albuminosa.
  osteítis alveolar, osteítis alveolar localizada alveolar osteitis, localized alveolar osteitis.
  osteítis cariosa carious osteitis.
  osteítis carnosa osteitis carnosa.
  osteítis central central osteitis.
  osteítis condensante condensing osteitis.
  osteítis cortical cortical osteitis.
  osteítis condensante generalizada osteitis condensans generalisata.
  osteítis condensante ilíaca osteitis condensans ilii.
  osteítis cortical cortical osteitis.
  osteítis crónica chronic osteitis.
  osteítis crónica no supurativa de Garré Garré's chronic non-suppurative osteitis.
  osteítis deformante osteitis deformans.
  osteítis esclerosante sclerosing osteitis.
  osteítis fibrosaquística osteitis fibrosa cystica.
  osteítis fibroquística circunscripta osteitis fibrosa circumscripta.
  osteítis fibrosa diseminada osteitis fibrosa disseminata.
  osteítis fibrosa localizada localized osteitis fibrosa, osteitis fibrosa localisata.
  osteítis fibrosa multifocal multifocal osteitis fibrosa.
  osteítis fibrosa osteoplástica osteitis fibrosa osteoplastica.
  osteítis fibrosa quística osteitis fibrosa cystica.
  osteítis fibrosa quística generalizada osteitis fibrosa cystica generalisata.
  osteítis fibrosa renal renal osteitis fibrosa.
  osteítis formativa formative osteitis.
  osteítis fragilizante osteitis fragilitans.
  osteítis fungosa osteitis fungosa.
  osteítis gomatosa gommatous osteitis.
  osteítis granulosa osteitis granulosa.
  osteítis hematógena hematogenous osteitis.
  osteítis hiperplásica secundaria secondary hyperplastic osteitis.
  osteítis necrótica necrotic osteitis.
  osteítis no supurativa crónica chronic non-suppurative osteitis.
  osteítis osificante osteitis ossificans.
  osteítis paratiroidea parathyroid osteitis.
  osteítis productiva productive osteitis.
  osteítis púbica osteitis pubis.
  osteítis quística osteitis fibrosa cystica.
  osteítis rarefaciente, osteítis rareficante rarefying osteitis.
  osteítis tuberculosa quística múltiple osteitis tuberculosa multiplex cystica.
  osteítis vascular vascular osteitis.
osteíto *m.* osteite.
ostemia *f.* ostemia.
ostempiesis *f.* ostempyesis.
osteacusia *f.* osteoacusis.
osteoacusis *f.* osteoacusis.
osteoalbumoide *m.* osseoalbumoid, ostealbumoid.
osteoanagénesis *f.* osteoanagenesis.
osteoanestesia *f.* osteoanesthesia.

osteoaneurisma *m.* osteoaneurysm.

osteoaponeurótico, -ca *adj.* osseoaponeurotic.

osteoarticular *adj.* osteoarticular.

osteoartritis *f.* osteoarthritis.

  osteoartritis crónica chronic osteoarthritis.

  osteoartritis deformante osteoarthritis deformans.

  osteoartritis endémica endemic osteoarthritis.

  osteoartritis erosiva erosive osteoarthritis.

  osteoartritis hiperplásica, osteoartritis hiperplástica hyperplastic osteoarthritis.

  osteoartritis interfalángica interphalangeal osteoarthritis.

osteoartropatía *f.* osteoarthropathy.

  osteoartropatía hipertrófica idiopática idiopathic hypertrophic osteoarthropathy.

  osteoartropatía hipertrófica neumónica hypertrophic pneumic osteoarthropathy.

  osteoartropatía hipertrófica primaria primary hypertrophic osteoarthropathy.

  osteoartropatía hipertrófica pulmonar hypertrophic pulmonary osteoarthropathy.

  osteoartropatía hipertrófica secundaria secondary hypertrophic osteoarthropathy.

  osteoartropatía neumogénica pneumogenic osteoarthropathy.

  osteoartropatía neumónica hipertrófica hypertrophic pneumic osteoarthropathy.

  osteoartropatía pulmonar, osteoartropatía pulmonar hipertrófica pulmonary osteoarthropathy, hypertrophic pulmonary osteoarthropathy.

osteoartrosis *f.* osteoarthrosis.

osteoartrotomía *f.* osteoarthrotomy.

osteoblástico, -ca *adj.* osteoblastic.

osteoblasto *m.* osteoblast.

osteoblastoma *m.* osteoblastoma.

osteocalcina *f.* osteocalcin.

osteocampsia *f.* osteocampsia.

osteocampsis *f.* osteocampsis.

osteocaquéctico, -ca *adj.* osteocachectic.

osteocaquexia *f.* osteocachexia.

osteocarcinoma *m.* osteocarcinoma.

osteocartilaginoso, -sa *adj.* osteocartilaginous.

osteocele *m.* osteocele.

osteocemento *m.* osteocementum.

osteocistoma *m.* osteocystoma.

osteocito *m.* osteocyte.

osteoclasia *f.* osteoclasia.

osteoclasis *f.* osteoclasis.

osteoclastia *f.* osteoclasty.

osteoclástico, -ca *adj.* osteoclastic.

osteoclasto *m.* osteoclast.

osteoclastoma *m.* osteoclastoma.

osteocoma *m.* osteocomma.

osteocondensante *adj.* osteocondensans.

osteocondral *adj.* osteochondral.

osteocondritis *f.* osteochondritis.

  osteocondritis calcánea calcaneal osteochondritis.

  osteocondritis deformante juvenil, osteocondritis juvenil deformante osteochondritis deformans juvenilis.

  osteocondritis deformante juvenil dorsal osteochondritis deformans juvenilis dorsi.

  osteocondritis deformante metatarsofalángica juvenil juvenile deforming metatarsophalangeal osteochondritis.

  osteocondritis disecante osteochondritis dissecans.

  osteocondritis de los huesos metatarsianos y metacarpianos osteochondritis ossis metacarpi et metatarsi.

  osteocondritis isquiopúbica osteochondritis ischiopubica.

  osteocondritis juvenil deformante osteochondritis deformans juvenilis.

  osteocondritis necrosante osteochondritis necroticans.

  osteocondritis sifilítica syphilitic osteochondritis.

osteocondrodisplasia *f.* osteochondrodysplasia.

osteocondrodistrofia *f.* osteochondrodystrophy, osteochondrodystrophia.

  osteocondrodistrofia deformante osteochondrodystrophia deformans.

  osteocondrodistrofia familiar familial osteochondrodystrophy.

osteocondrofibroma *m.* osteochondrofibroma.

osteocondrófito *m.* osteochondrophyte.

osteocondrólisis *f.* osteochondrolysis.

osteocondroma *m.* osteochondroma.

  osteocondroma fibrosante fibrosing osteochondroma.

osteocondromatosis *f.* osteochondromatosis.

  osteocondromatosis sinovial synovial osteochondromatosis.

osteocondromixoma *m.* osteochondromyxoma.

osteocondropatía *f.* osteochodropathy, osteochondropathia.

  osteocondropatía cretinoide osteochondropathia cretinoidea.

  osteocondropatía inducida por sulfato de poliglucosa (dextrán) polyglucose (dextran) sulfate-induced osteochodropathy.

osteocondrosarcoma *m.* osteochondrosarcoma.

osteocondrósico, -ca *adj.* osteochondrous.

osteocondrosis *f.* osteochondrosis.

  osteocondrosis del escafoides navicular osteochondrosis.

  osteocondrosis del navicular navicular osteochondrosis.

  osteocondrosis tibial deformante osteochondrosis deformans tibiae.

  osteocondrosis de la tuberosidad de la tibia tibial tubercle osteochondrosis.

  osteocondrosis vertebral vertebral osteochondrosis.

osteocondroso, -sa *adj.* osteochondrous.

osteocondrótico, -ca *adj.* osteochondrous.

osteocópico, -ca *adj.* osteocopic.

osteócopo *m.* osteocope.

osteocráneo *m.* osteocranium.

osteocranium *m.* osteocranium.

osteodensitometría *f.* osteoradiodensitometry.

osteodensitómetro *m.* osteodensitometer.

osteodentina *f.* osteodentin.

osteodentinoma *m.* osteodentinoma.

osteodermatopoiquilosis *f.* osteodermatopoikilosis.

osteodermatoso, -sa *adj.* osteodermatous.

osteodermia *f.* osteodermia.

osteodiastasis *f.* osteodiastasis.

osteodinia *f.* osteodynia.

osteodisplasia *f.* osteodysplasty.

osteodistrofia *f.* osteodystrophy, osteodystrophia.

  osteodistrofia hereditaria de Albright Albright's hereditary osteodystrophy.

  osteodistrofia renal renal osteodystrophy.

osteoectasia *f.* osteoectasia.

  osteoectasia familiar familial osteoectasia.

osteoectomía *f.* osteoectomy.

osteoencondroma *m.* osteoenchondroma.

osteoepífisis *f.* osteoepiphysis.

osteoesclerosis *f.* osteosclerosis.

  osteoesclerosis congénita osteosclerosis congenita.

  osteoesclerosis diseminada disseminated osteosclerosis.

  osteoesclerosis endóstica pneumica de Faneras Faneras' osteosclerosis.

  osteoesclerosis del flúor fluor osteosclerosis.

  osteoesclerosis frágil osteosclerosis fragilis.

  osteoesclerosis frágil generalizada osteosclerosis fragilis generalisata.

  osteoesclerosis mielofibromatosa osteosclerosis myelofibrosis.

  osteoesclerosis osteopetrosis osteopetrosis osteosclerosis.

osteoesclerótico, -ca *adj.* osteosclerotic.

osteoespongioma *m.* osteospongioma.

osteoesteatoma *m.* osteosteatoma.

osteofagia *f.* osteophagia.

osteófago *m.* osteophage.

osteofibrocondrosarcoma *m.* osteofibrochondrosarcoma.

osteofibroma *m.* osteofibroma.

osteofibromatosis *f.* osteofibromatosis.

  osteofibromatosis quística cystic osteofibromatosis.

osteofibrosis *f.* osteofibrosis.

  osteofibrosis periapical periapical osteofibrosis.

osteofibroso, -sa *adj.* osteofibrous, osseofibrous.

osteofima *m.* osteophyma.

osteófito *m.* osteophyte.

osteofitosis *f.* osteophytosis.

osteoflebitis *f.* osteophlebitis.

osteofluorosis *f.* osteofluorosis.

osteofonía *f.* osteophony.

osteófono *m.* osteophone.

osteogenesia *f.* osteogenesis.

  osteogenesia estimulada eléctricamente electrically stimulated osteogenesis.

  osteogenesia imperfecta defective osteogenesis, osteogenesis imperfecta.

osteogénesis *f.* osteogenesis.

osteogenia *f.* osteogeny.

osteogenético, -ca *adj.* osteogenetic.

osteogénico, -ca *adj.* osteogenic.

osteógeno *m.* osteogen.

osteógeno, -na *adj.* osteogenous.

osteografía *f.* osteography.

osteograma *m.* osteogram.

osteohalistéresis *f.* osteohalisteresis.

osteohidatidosis *f.* osteohydatidosis.

osteohipertrofia *f.* osteohypertrophy.

osteoide *adj.* osteoid.

osteoinducción *f.* osteoinduction.

osteolipocondroma *m.* osteolipochondroma.

osteolipoma *m.* osteolipoma.

osteólisis *f.* osteolysis.

osteolítico, -ca *adj.* osteolytic.

osteología *f.* osteology, osteologia.

osteólogo, -ga *m., f.* osteologist.

osteoma *m.* osteoma.

  osteoma de los caballistas rider's bone.

  osteoma compacto compact osteoma.

  osteoma cutáneo osteoma cutis.

  osteoma dental dental osteoma.

  osteoma duro osteoma durum.

  osteoma ebúrneo ivory osteoma, osteoma eburneum.

  osteoma esponjoso spongy osteoma, osteoma spongiosum.

  osteoma del jinete rider's bone.

  osteoma medular osteoma medullare.

osteoma osteoide osteoid osteoma.

osteoma osteoide gigante giant osteoid osteoma.

osteoma sarcomatoso osteoma sarcomatosum.

osteoma de soldado de caballería cavalryman's osteoma.

osteomalacia *f.* osteomalacia.

osteomalacia hepática hepatic osteomalacia.

osteomalacia hipofosfatémica ligada al cromosoma X X-linked hypophosphatemic osteomalacia.

osteomalacia infantil infantile osteomalacia.

osteomalacia juvenil juvenile osteomalacia.

osteomalacia puerperal puerperal osteomalacia.

osteomalacia senil senile osteomalacia.

osteomalacia tubular renal renal tubular osteomalacia.

osteomalácico, -ca *adj.* osteomalacic.

osteomalacosis *m.* osteomalacosis.

osteomatoide *adj.* osteomatoid.

osteomatoideo, -a *adj.* osteomatoid.

osteomatosis *f.* osteomatosis.

osteómera *f.* osteomere.

osteómero *m.* osteomere.

osteomesopicnosis *f.* osteomesopyknosis.

osteometría *f.* osteometry.

osteomielítico, -ca *adj.* osteomyelitic.

osteomielitis *f.* osteomyelitis.

osteomielitis por conciolina conchiolin osteomyelitis.

osteomielitis craneal cranial osteomyelitis.

osteomielitis esclerosante no supurada sclerosing non-suppurative osteomyelitis.

osteomielitis de Garré Garré's osteomyelitis.

osteomielitis maligna malignant osteomyelitis.

osteomielitis salmonella salmonella osteomyelitis.

osteomielitis tifoidea typhoid osteomyelitis.

osteomielitis variolosa osteomyelitis variolosa.

osteomielitis vertebral vertebral osteomyelitis.

osteomielodisplasia *f.* osteomyelodysplasia.

osteomielografía *f.* osteomyelography.

osteomiositis *f.* osteomiositis.

osteomixocondroma *m.* osteomyxochondroma.

osteomucina *f.* osteomucin.

osteón *m.* osteon.

osteona *f.* osteone.

osteonco *m.* osteoncus.

osteonecrosis *f.* osteonecrosis.

osteoneuralgia *f.* osteoneuralgia.

osteonosis *f.* osteonosus.

osteoodontoma *m.* osteo-odontoma.

osteoonicodisplasia *f.* osteo-onychodysplasia.

osteópata *m.* osteopath.

osteopatía *f.* osteopathy, osteopathia.

osteopatía alimentaria alimentary osteopathy.

osteopatía condensante condensing osteopathy, osteopathia condensans.

osteopatía condensante diseminada disseminated condensing osteopathy, osteopathia condensans disseminata.

osteopatía condensante generalizada osteopathia condensans generalisata.

osteopatía estriada striated osteopathy, osteopathia striata.

osteopatía de hambre, osteopatía por hambre hunger osteopathy.

osteopatía hiperostótica congénita osteopathia hyperstotica congenita.

osteopatía hiperostótica múltiple infantil osteopathia hyperstotica multiplex infantilis.

osteopatía mielógena, osteopatía mielogénica myelogenic osteopathy.

osteopatía de pubis pubis osteopathy.

osteopático, -ca *adj.* osteopathic.

osteopatología *f.* osteopathology.

osteopecilia *f.* osteopecilia.

osteopedion *m.* osteopedion.

osteopenia *f.* osteopenia.

osteopénico, -ca *adj.* osteopenic.

osteoperióstico, -ca *adj.* osteoperiosteal.

osteoperiostitis *f.* osteoperiostitis.

osteopetrósico, -ca *adj.* osteopetrotic.

osteopetrosis *f.* osteopetrosis.

osteopetrosis acroosteolítica osteoporosis acro-osteolytica.

osteopetrótico, -ca *adj.* osteopetrotic.

osteoplaca *f.* osteoplaque.

osteoplasia *f.* osteoplasia.

osteoplastia *f.* osteoplasty.

osteoplástico, -ca *adj.* osteoplastic.

osteoplasto *m.* osteoplast.

osteopoiquilosis *f.* osteopoikilosis.

osteopoiquilótico, -ca *adj.* osteopoikilotic.

osteoporomalacia *f.* osteoporomalacia.

osteoporosis *f.* osteoporosis.

osteoporosis craneal circunscrita osteoporosis circumscripta cranii.

osteoporosis por desuso osteoporosis of disuse.

osteoporosis juvenil juvenile osteoporosis.

osteoporosis posmenopáusica postmenopausal osteoporosis.

osteoporosis postraumática post-traumatic osteoporosis.

osteoporosis por reposo excesivo osteoporosis of disuse.

osteoporosis senil senile osteoporosis.

osteoporótico, -ca *adj.* osteoporotic.

osteopsatirosis *f.* osteopsathyrosis.

osteorradionecrosis *f.* osteoradionecrosis.

osteorrafia *f.* osteorrhaphy.

osteorragia *f.* osteorrhagia.

osteosarcoma *m.* osteosarcoma.

osteosarcoma de células pequeñas small cell osteosarcoma.

osteosarcoma condroblástico chondroblastic osteosarcoma.

osteosarcoma extraesquelético extraskeletal osteosarcoma.

osteosarcoma fibroblástico fibroblastic osteosarcoma.

osteosarcoma multifocal multifocal osteosarcoma.

osteosarcoma osteoblástico osteoblastic osteosarcoma.

osteosarcoma perióstico periostic osteosarcoma.

osteosarcoma telangiectásico telangiectatic osteosarcoma.

osteosarcoma yuxtacortical juxtacortical osteosarcoma.

osteosarcomatoso, -sa *adj.* osteosarcomatous.

osteoscopio *m.* osteoscope.

osteosepto *m.* osteoseptum.

osteoseptum *m.* osteoseptum.

osteosinovitis *f.* osteosynovitis.

osteosíntesis *f.* osteosynthesis.

osteosis *f.* osteosis.

osteosis cutánea osteosis cutis.

osteosis eburnizante monomélica osteosis eburnisans monomelica.

osteosis fibroquística renal renal fibrocystic osteosis.

osteosis paratiroidea parathyroid osteosis.

osteospongioma *m.* osteospongioma.

osteostixis *f.* osteostixis.

osteosutura *f.* osteosuture.

osteotabes *f.* osteotabes.

osteotelangiectasia *f.* osteotelangiectasia.

osteotilo *m.* osteotylus.

osteotomía *f.* osteotomy.

osteotomía de abducción abduction osteotomy.

osteotomía abductora en cuña de apertura (OACA) opening abductory wedge osteotomy (OAWO).

osteotomía de adducción adduction osteotomy.

osteotomía alveolar segmentaria segmental alveolar osteotomy.

osteotomía de angulación angulation osteotomy.

osteotomía en bisagra hinge osteotomy.

osteotomía en bloque block osteotomy.

osteotomía de Chiari Chiari's osteotomy.

osteotomía cuneiforme cuneiform osteotomy.

osteotomía en cuña de apertura opening wedge osteotomy.

osteotomía deslizante en C sliding osteotomy.

osteotomía deslizante oblicua sliding oblique osteotomy.

osteotomía de desplazamiento displacement osteotomy.

osteotomía esférica cup-and-ball osteotomy.

osteotomía horizontal horizontal osteotomy.

osteotomía ilíaca iliac osteotomy, innominate osteotomy.

osteotomía lineal linear osteotomy.

osteotomía de Lorenz Lorenz's osteotomy.

osteotomía mandibular dividida sagital sagittal split mandibular osteotomy.

osteotomía pélvica, osteotomía púbica pelvic osteotomy.

osteotomía valguizante, osteotomía varizante valgus osteotomy, varus osteotomy.

osteotomía vertical vertical osteotomy.

osteótomo *m.* osteotome.

osteotomoclasia *f.* osteotomoclasia, osteotomoclasis.

osteotomoclasis *f.* osteotomoclasis.

osteotribo *m.* osteotribe.

osteotrito *m.* osteotrite.

osteotrofia *f.* osteotrophy.

osteotromboflebitis *f.* osteothrombophlebitis.

osteotrombosis *f.* osteothrombosis.

ostexia *f.* osthexia, osthexy.

ostial *adj.* ostial.

ostiario, -ria *adj.* ostiary.

ostítico, -ca *adj.* ostitic.

ostitis *f.* ostitis.

ostium *m.* ostium.

ostium primum ostium primum defect.

ostium secundum ostium secundum defect.

ostomado, -da *adj.* ostomate.

ostomía *f.* ostomy.

ostomizado, -da *adj.* ostomate.

ostosis *f.* ostosis.

ostráceo, -a *adj.* ostraceous.

ostracosis *f.* ostracosis.

ostreotoxismo *m.* ostreotoxism.

otáfono *m.* otaphone.

otagra *f.* otagra.

otalgia *f.* otalgia.

otalgia dental otalgia dentalis.

otalgia geniculada geniculate otalgia.

otalgia intermitente otalgia intermittens.

otalgia refleja reflex otalgia.

otalgia tabética secundaria secondary tabetic otalgia.

otálgico, -ca *adj.* otalgic.

otiatría *f.* otiatria, otiatrics.

ótico, -ca *adj.* otic, otor.

otítico, -ca *adj.* otitic.

otitis *f.* otitis.

otitis adhesiva adhesive otitis.

otitis de aviación, o del aviador, otitis de los aviadores aviation otitis.

otitis crupal, otitis cruposa otitis crouposa.

otitis descamativa otitis desquamativa.

otitis diabética diabetic ear.

otitis diftérica otitis diphtheritica.

otitis esclerótica otitis sclerotica.

otitis externa external otitis, otitis externa.

otitis externa circunscrita otitis externa circumscripta.

otitis externa difusa otitis externa diffusa.

otitis externa forunculosa otitis externa furunculosa.

otitis externa maligna malignant otitis externa.

otitis foruncular, o furunculosa furuncular otitis, otitis furunculosa.

otitis interna otitis interna.

otitis íntima otitis intima.

otitis laberíntica otitis labyrinthica.

otitis mastoidea otitis mastoidea.

otitis media otitis media.

otitis media adhesiva adhesive otitis media, otitis media adhesiva.

otitis media barotraumática barotraumatic otitis media.

otitis media catarral aguda otitis media catarrhalis acuta.

otitis media catarral crónica otitis media catarrhalis chronica.

otitis media esclerótica otitis media sclerotica.

otitis media fibroadhesiva fibroadhesive otitis media.

otitis media purulenta otitis media purulenta.

otitis media purulenta aguda otitis media purulenta acuta.

otitis media purulenta crónica otitis media purulenta chronica.

otitis media de reflujo reflux otitis media.

otitis media secretoria secretory otitis media.

otitis media serosa serous otitis media, otitis media serosa.

otitis media supurada, otitis media supurativa otitis media suppurativa.

otitis micótica otitis mycotica.

otitis mucosa mucosus otitis.

otitis serosa serous otitis.

otitis vasomotora otitis media vasomotorica.

otoantritis *f.* otoantritis.

otoblenorrea *f.* otoblennorrhea.

otocefalia *f.* otocephaly.

otocéfalo *m.* otocephalus.

otocerebritis *f.* otocerebritis.

otocisto *m.* otocyst.

otocleisis *f.* otocleisis.

otoconias *f.* otoconia.

otocraneal *adj.* otocranial.

otocráneo *m.* otocranium.

otodinia *f.* otodynia.

otoencefalitis *f.* otoencephalitis.

otoespongiosis *f.* otospongiosis.

otoesclerosis *f.* otosclerosis.

otoesclerótico, -ca *adj.* otosclerotic.

otofaríngeo, -a *adj.* otopharyngeal.

otófono *m.* otophone.

otoganglio *m.* otoganglion.

otogénico, -ca *adj.* otogenic.

otógeno, -na *adj.* otogenous.

otografía *f.* otography.

otohematoma *m.* othematoma.

otohemineurastenia *f.* otohemineurasthenia.

otohemorragia *f.* othemorrhagia.

otolaringología *f.* otolaryngology.

otolaringólogo, -ga *m., f.* otolaryngologist.

otolitiasis *f.* otolithiasis.

otolito *m.* otolith, otolite.

otología *f.* otology.

otológico, -ca *adj.* otologic.

otólogo, -ga *m., f.* otologist, aurist.

otomastoiditis *f.* otomastoiditis.

otomiasis *f.* otomyiasis.

otomiastenia *f.* otomyasthenia.

otomicosis *f.* otomycosis.

otomucormicosis *f.* otomucormycosis.

Otomyces Otomyces.

otoneuralgia *f.* otoneuralgia.

otoneurastenia *f.* otoneurasthenia.

otoneurología *f.* otoneurology.

otoneurológico, -ca *adj.* otoneurologic.

otopalatodigital *adj.* otopalatodigital.

otopatía *f.* otopathy.

otopiorrea *f.* otopyorrhea.

otopiosis *f.* otopyosis.

otoplastia *f.* otoplasty.

otopólipo *m.* otopolypus.

otorragia *f.* otorrhagia.

otorrea *f.* otorrhea.

otorrea de líquido cefalorraquídeo cerebrospinal fluid otorrhea.

otorrinolaringología *f.* otorhinolaryngology.

otorrinolaringólogo, -ga *m., f.* otorhinolaryngologist.

otorrinología *f.* otorhinology.

otosalpinge *m.* otosalpinx.

otosalpinx *m.* otosalpinx.

otosclerosis *f.* otosclerosis.

otosclerótico, -ca *adj.* otosclerotic.

otoscopia *f.* otoscopy.

otoscopio *m.* otoscope.

otoscopio de Brunton Brunton's otoscope.

otoscopio de Siegle Siegle's otoscope.

otoscopio de Toynbee Tonybee's otoscope.

otosis *f.* otosis.

otospongiosis *f.* otospongiosis.

ototomía *f.* ototomy.

ototoxicidad *f.* ototoxicity.

ototóxico, -ca *adj.* ototoxic.

oulectomía *f.* oulectomy.

oulitis *f.* oulitis.

oulonitis *f.* oulonitis.

oulorragia *f.* oulorrhagia.

oval *adj.* oval.

ovalado, -da *adj.* oval.

ovalbúmina *f.* ovalbumin.

ovalocitario, -ria *adj.* ovalocytary.

ovalocito *m.* ovalocyte.

ovalocitosis *f.* ovalocytosis.

ovarialgia *f.* ovarialgia.

ovárico, -ca *adj.* ovarian.

ovariectomía *f.* ovariectomy.

ovario *m.* ovary, ovarium.

ovario adenoquístico adenocystic ovary.

ovario bipartito ovarium bipartitum.

ovario lobulado ovarium lobatum.

ovario masculino ovarium masculinum.

ovario de ostra oyster ovary.

ovario poliquístico polycystic ovary.

ovariocele *m.* ovariocele.

ovariocentesis *f.* ovariocentesis.

ovariociesis *f.* ovariocyesis.

ovariodisneuria *f.* ovariodysneuria.

ovariogénico, -ca *adj.* ovariogenic.

ovariógeno, -na *adj.* ovariogenic.

ovariohisterectomía *f.* ovariohysterectomy.

ovariolítico, -ca *adj.* ovariolytic.

ovarionco *m.* ovarioncus.

ovariopatía *f.* ovariopathy.

ovariopexia *f.* ovariopexy.

ovariorrexis *f.* ovariorrhexis.

ovariosalpingectomía *f.* ovariosalpingectomy.

ovariosalpingitis *f.* ovariosalpingitis.

ovariostéresis *f.* ovariosteresis.

ovariostomía *f.* ovariostomy.

ovarioterapia *f.* ovariotherapy.

ovariotestis *m.* ovariotestis.

ovariotomía *f.* ovariotomy.

ovariotomía abdominal abdominal ovariotomy.

ovariotomía vaginal vaginal ovariotomy.

ovariotubárico, -ca *adj.* ovariotubal.

ovaritis *f.* ovaritis.

ovarium ovarium.

ovarium gyratum ovarium gyratum.

ovaroterapia *f.* ovarotherapy.

ovicida[1] *m.* ovicide.

ovicida[2] *adj.* ovicidal.

oviductal *adj.* oviductal, oviducal.

oviducto *m.* oviduct.

ovífero, -ra *adj.* oviferous.

oviforme *adj.* oviform.

ovigénesis *f.* ovigenesis.

ovigenético, -ca *adj.* ovigenetic.

ovigénico, -ca *adj.* ovigenic.

ovígeno, -na *adj.* ovigenous.

ovigermen *m.* ovigerm.

ovígero, -ra *adj.* ovigerous.

oviparidad *f.* oviparity.

oviposición *f.* oviposition.

ovipostura *f.* oviposition.

ovísaco *m.* ovisac.

ovocito *m.* ovocyte.

ovogenesia *f.* ovogenesis.

ovogénesis *f.* ovogenesis.

ovoglobulina *f.* ovoglobulin.

ovoide *m. y adj.* ovoid.

ovoide fetal fetal ovoid.

ovoide de Manchester Manchester ovoid.

ovolisina *f.* ovolysin.

ovolítico, -ca *adj.* ovolytic.

ovomucina *f.* ovomucin.

ovomucoide *m.* ovomucoid.

ovoplasma *m.* ovoplasm.

ovoprecipitina *f.* ovoprecipitin.

ovoprotógeno *m.* ovoprotogen.

ovoterapia *f.* ovotherapy.

ovotestículo *m.* ovotestis.

ovotestis *m.* ovotestis.

ovotransferrina *f.* ovotransferrin.

ovovitelina *f.* ovovitelin, ovovitellin.

ovulación *f.* ovulation.

ovulación amenstrual amenstrual ovulation.

ovulación complementaria supplementary ovulation.

ovulación paracíclica paracyclic ovulation.

ovular *adj.* ovular.

ovulasa *f.* ovulase.

ovulativo, -va *adj.* ovulatory.

ovulatorio, -ria *adj.* ovulatory.

ovulógeno, -na *adj.* ovulogenous.

óvulo, *m.* ovule, ovum.

óvulo fecundado fertilized ovum.

óvulo fertilizado fertilized ovum.

óvulo de Graaf Graafian ovule.

óvulo de Naboth Naboth's ovule.

óvulo de Peters Peter's ovule, Peter's ovum.

óvulo primitivo primitive ovule, primitive ovum.

óvulo primordial primordial ovule, primordial ovum.

óvulo vaginal vaginal ovum.

ovulocíclico, -ca *adj.* ovulocyclic.

ovum *m.* ovum.

oxalacetato *m.* oxaloacetate.

oxalación *f.* oxalation.

oxalatado, -da *adj.* oxalated.

oxalato *m.* oxalate.

oxalemia *f.* oxalemia.

oxalismo *m.* oxalism.

oxaloacetato *m.* oxaloacetate.

oxaloacético (ácido) *adj.* oxaloacetic acid.

oxalosis *f.* oxalosis.

oxaluria *f.* oxaluria.

oxalúrico (ácido) *adj.* oxaluric acid.

oxamida *f.* oxamide.

oxamniquina *f.* oxamniquine.

oxandrolona *f.* oxandrolone.

oxiacoia *f.* oxyacoia, oxyakoia.

oxiafia *f.* oxyaphia.

oxibarbitúrico *m.* oxybarbiturate.

oxiblepsia *f.* oxyblepsia.

oxiblepsis *f.* oxyblepsia.

oxibutiria *f.* oxybutyria.

oxibutiricacidemia *f.* oxybutyricacidemia.

oxibutírico (ácido) *adj.* oxybutyric acid.

oxibutiruria *f.* oxybutyria.

oxicalorímetro *m.* oxycalorimeter.

oxicefalia *f.* oxycephalia, oxycephaly.

oxicefálico, -ca *adj.* oxycephalic.

oxicéfalo, -la *adj.* oxycephalous.

oxicinesia *f.* oxycinesia.

oxicolina *f.* oxycholine.

oxicromático, -ca *adj.* oxychromatic.

oxicromatina *f.* oxychromatin.

oxidación *f.* oxidation.

oxidación de ácidos grasos fatty acid oxidation.

oxidación acoplada coupled oxidation.

oxidación beta beta oxidation.

oxidación biológica biological oxidation.

omega oxidación omega oxidation.

oxidación-reducción *f.* oxidation-reduction.

oxidado, -da *adj.* oxidized.

oxidante *adj.* oxidant.

oxidar *v.* oxidize.

oxidasis *f.* oxidasis.

oxidativo, -va *adj.* oxidative.

oxidización *f.* oxidization.

óxido *m.* oxide.

óxido de etileno ethylene oxide.

óxido de etilo ethyl oxide.

óxido indiferente indifferent oxide.

óxido mercúrico amarillo yellow mercuric oxide.

óxido mercúrico rojo red mercuric oxide.

óxido neutro neutral oxide.

óxido nítrico nitric oxide.

óxido nitroso nitrous oxide.

oxidorreducción *f.* oxidation-reduction.

oxidorreductasa *f.* oxidoreductase, oxydoreductase.

oxidosis *f.* oxidosis, oxyosis.

oxiecoia *f.* oxyecoia.

oxiestesia *f.* oxyesthesia.

oxifílico, -ca *adj.* oxyphilic, oxyphilous.

oxifilo, -la *adj.* oxiphil.

oxifonía *f.* oxiphonia, oxyphonia.

oxiforasa *f.* oxyphorase.

oxigenación *f.* oxygenation.

oxigenación apneica apneic oxygenation.

oxigenación hiperbárica hyperbaric oxygenation.

oxigenación extracorpórea extracorporeal oxygenation.

oxigenado, -da *adj.* oxygenated.

oxigenador *m.* oxygenator.

oxigenador de bomba pump-oxygenator.

oxigenador de disco, oxigenador de disco giratorio disk oxygenator, rotating disk oxygenator.

oxigenador de membrana membrane oxygenator.

oxigenador de pantalla screen oxygenator.

oxigenador de película film oxygenator.

oxigenar *v.* oxygenate.

oxigenasa *f.* oxygenase.

oxigénico, -ca *adj.* oxygenic.

oxigenizar *v.* oxygenize.

oxígeno *m.* oxygen.

oxígeno en exceso excess oxygen.

oxígeno hiperbárico, oxígeno de presión elevada hyperbaric oxygen, high pressure oxygen.

oxígeno molecular molecular oxygen.

oxígeno naciente nascent oxygen.

oxígeno pesado heavy oxygen.

oxígeno singlete, oxígeno singulete singlet oxygen.

oxígeno transtraqueal transtracheal oxygen.

oxigenoterapia *f.* oxygentherapy, oxygen therapy.

oxigenoterapia hiperbárica hyperbaric oxygen therapy.

oxigeusia *f.* oxigeusia.

oxihem *m.* oxyheme.

oxihemocromógeno *m.* oxyhemochromogen.

oxihemocianina *f.* oxyhemocyanine.

oxihemoglobina *f.* oxyhemoglobin.

oxihemoglobinómetro *m.* oxyhemoglobinometer.

oxihemógrafo *m.* oxyhemograph.

oxihemograma *m.* oxyhemogram.

oxihidrocéfalo *m.* oxyhydrocephalus.

oxilalia *f.* oxylalia.

oximetría *f.* oximetry.

oxímetro *m.* oximeter.

oxímetro de cubeta cuvette oximeter.

oxímetro auditivo ear oximeter.

oxímetro intracardíaco intracardiac oximeter.

oximioglobina *f.* oxymyoglobin.

oximinotransferasa *f.* oximinotransferase.

oxinervona *f.* oxynervon, oxynervone.

oxíntico, -ca *adj.* oxyntic.

oxiopía *f.* oxyopia.

oxiopsia *f.* oxyopia.

oxioptría *f.* oxyopter.

oxiosfresia *f.* oxyosphresia.

oxiosis *f.* oxyosis.

oxiosmia *f.* oxyosmia.

oxiparaplastina *f.* oxyparaplastin.

oxipatía *f.* oxypathia.

oxiperitoneo *m.* oxyperitoneum.

oxiplasma *m.* oxyplasm.

oxipurina *f.* oxypurine.

oxipurinasa *f.* oxypurinase.

oxirrino, -na *adj.* oxyrhine.

oxitalán *m.* oxytalan.

oxitalanólisis *f.* oxytalanolysis.

oxitocia *f.* oxytocia.

oxitócico, -ca *adj.* oxytocic.

oxitocina (OXT) *f.* oxytocin (OXT).

oxitoxina *f.* oxytoxin.

oxitropismo *m.* oxytropism.

oxituberculina *f.* oxytuberculin.

oxiuria *f.* oxyuria.

oxiuriasis *f.* oxyuriasis.

oxiuricida *m.* oxyuricide.

oxiúrido *m.* oxyurid.

oxiurifugo, -ga *adj.* oxyurifuge.

oxiuriosis *f.* oxyuriosis.

oxiuro *m.* oxyuris.

oxiuroide *m.* oxyuroid.

oxiyoduro *m.* oxyiodide.

oxonemia *f.* oxonemia.

oxonuria *f.* oxonuria.

oxozono *m.* oxozone.

5-oxoprolinuria *f.* 5-oxoprolinuria.

Oxymonadida Oxymonadida.

Oxyspirura Oxyspirura.

Oxyuroidea Oxyuroidea.

ozena *f.* ozena.

ozonador *m.* ozonator.

ozónido *m.* ozonide.

ozonizador *m.* ozonizer.

ozonizar *v.* ozonize.

ozono *m.* ozone.

ozonóforo *m.* ozonophore.

ozonólisis *f.* ozonolysis.

ozonómetro *m.* ozonometer.

ozonoscopio *m.* ozonoscope.

ozostomía *f.* ozostomia.

P *p*

pabellón *m.* pavilion.
pabular *adj.* pabular.
pábulo *m.* pabulum.
paciente *m., f.* patient.
pacómetro *m.* pachometer.
paculosis *m.* pachylosis.
padrastro *m.* hangnail.
pagetoide *adj.* pagetoid.
paidofilia *f.* pedophilia.
paladar *m.* palate, palatum.
   paladar artificial artificial palate.
   paladar caído falling palate.
   paladar del fumador smoker's palate.
   paladar fisurado cleft palate.
   paladar hendido cleft palate.
palanca *f.* lever.
   palanca dental dental lever.
palanestesia *f.* pallanesthesia, palmanesthesia.
palatal *adj.* palatal.
palatiforme *adj.* palatiform.
palatino, -na *adj.* palatine.
palatitis *f.* palatitis.
palatofaríngeo, -a *adj.* palatopharyngeal.
palatogloso, -sa *adj.* palatoglossal.
palatognato, -ta *adj.* palatognathous.
palatografía *f.* palatography.
palatomaxilar *adj.* palatomaxillary.
palatomiografía *f.* palatomyography.
palatonasal *adj.* palatonasal.
palatópago *m.* palatopagus.
palatoplastia *f.* palatoplasty.
palatoplejía *f.* palatoplegia.
palatopterigoideo, -a *adj.* pterygopalatine.
palatorrafia *f.* palatorrhaphy.
palatosalpíngeo, -a *m.* palatosalpingeus.
palatosquisis *f.* palatoschisis.
palatum palatum.
paleocinético, -ca *adj.* paleocinetic, paleokinetic.
paleocórtex *m.* paleocortex.
paleoestriado *m.* paleostriatum.
paleogénesis *f.* paleogenesis.
paleopalio *m.* paleocortex.
paleostriatum paleostriatum.
paleotálamo *m.* paleothalamus.
palescencia *f.* pallescense.
palestesia *f.* pallesthesia, palmesthesia.
palial *adj.* pallial.
paliar *v.* palliate.
paliativo, -va *adj.* palliative.
palidal *adj.* pallidal.
palidez *f.* pallor.
palifrasia *f.* paliphrasia.
palilalia *f.* palilalia.
palinestesia *f.* palinesthesia.
palingénesis *f.* palingenesis.
palinopsia *f.* palinopsia.
palio *m.* pallium.
pallium pallium.
palma *f.* palm.

palma de deportista hand ball palm.
palma hepática liver palm.
palma de la mano palma manus.
palmanestesia *f.* palmanesthesia.
palmar *adj.* palmar.
palmatura *f.* palmature, webbing.
palmestesia *f.* palmesthesia.
pálmico, -ca *adj.* palmic.
palmidactilia *f.* syndactyly.
palmo *m.* palmus.
palmus *m.* palmus.
palmoscopia *f.* palmoscopy.
palpable *adj.* palpable.
palpación *f.* palpation.
   palpación bimanual bimanual palpation.
palpatometría *f.* palpatometry.
palpatopercusión *f.* palpatopercussion.
palpebración *f.* palpebration.
palpebral *adj.* palpebral.
palpebritis *f.* palpebritis.
palpitación *f.* palpitation.
palúdico, -ca *adj.* paludal.
palúdide *f.* paludide.
paludismo *m.* malaria.
   paludismo álgido algid malaria.
   paludismo autóctono autochthonous malaria.
   paludismo bilioso remitente bilious remittent malaria.
   paludismo cerebral cerebral malaria.
   paludismo comatoso malaria comatosa.
   paludismo cotidiano quotidian malaria.
   paludismo cuartano quartan malaria.
   paludismo falciparum malaria falciparum.
   paludismo hemolítico hemolytic malaria.
   paludismo inducido induced malaria.
   paludismo intermitente intermittent malaria.
   paludismo nono nonan malaria.
   paludismo pernicioso pernicious malaria.
   paludismo oval, paludismo oval terciano ovale malaria, ovale tertian malaria.
   paludismo remitente remittent malaria.
   paludismo terapéutico induced malaria.
   paludismo terciano, paludismo terciano benigno tertian malaria, benign tertian malaria.
   paludismo terciano maligno malignant tertian malaria.
   paludismo vivax malaria vivax.
paludosis *f.* paludism.
panangeítis *f.* panangiitis.
panarteritis *f.* panarteritis.
panartritis *f.* panarthritis.
panastesia *f.* panasthesia.
pancarditis *f.* pancarditis.
pancistitis *f.* pancystitis.
pancitopenia *f.* pancytopenia.
   pancitopenia congénita congenital pancytopenia.
   pancitopenia de Fanconi Falconi's pancytopenia.
páncreas *m.* pancreas.

páncreas accesorio accessory pancreas, pancreas accessorium.
páncreas anular annular pancreas.
páncreas de Aselli Aselli's pancreas.
páncreas menor small pancreas, pancreas minus.
páncreas de Willis Willis' pancreas.
páncreas de Winslow Winslow's pancreas.
pancreatalgia *f.* pancreatalgia.
pancreatectomía *f.* pancreatectomy.
pancreatenfraxis *f.* pancreatemphraxis.
Pancreaticocolecistostomía *f.* pancreaticocholecistostomy.
pancreaticoduodenal *adj.* pancreaticoduodenal.
pancreaticoduodenostomía *f.* pancreaticoduodenostomy.
pancreaticoenterostomía *f.* pancreaticoenterostomy.
pancreaticoesplénico, -ca *adj.* pancreaticosplenic.
pancreaticotomía *f.* pancreatomy.
pancreaticoyeyunostomía *f.* pancreaticojejunostomy.
pancreatismo *m.* pancreatism.
pancreatitis *f.* pancreatitis.
   pancreatitis aguda acute pancreatitis.
   pancreatitis calcárea calcareous pancreatitis.
   pancreatitis centrilobular centrilobar pancreatitis.
   pancreatitis crónica chronic pancreatitis.
   pancreatitis intersticial interstitial pancreatitis.
   pancreatitis purulenta purulent pancreatitis.
   pancreatitis recidivante crónica chronic relapsing pancreatitis.
pancreatoduodenectomía *f.* pancreatoduodenectomy.
pancreatógeno, -na *adj.* pancreatogenic, pancreatogenous.
pancreatografía *f.* pancreatography.
pancreatólisis *f.* pancreatolysis.
pancreatolitectomía *f.* pancreatolithectomy.
pancreatolito *m.* pancreatolith.
pancreatolitotomía *f.* pancreatolithotomy.
pancreatomía *f.* pancreatomy.
pancreatonco *m.* pancreatoncus.
pancreatopatía *f.* pancreatopathy.
pancreatotomía *f.* pancreatotomy.
pancreatotrópico, -ca *adj.* pancreatotropic.
pancreatrópico, -ca *adj.* pancreatropic.
pancreectomía *f.* pancreectomy.
pancreólisis *f.* pancreolysis.
pancreolitotomía *f.* pancreatolithotomy.
pancreocimina *f.* pancreozymin.
pancreopatía *f.* pancreatopathy.
pancreoprivo, -va *adj.* pancreoprivic.
pancreoterapia *f.* pancreotherapy.
pandemia *f.* pandemia.
pandémico, -ca *adj.* pandemic.

pandiculación *f.* pandiculation.
panelectroscopio *m.* panelectroscope.
panencefalitis *f.* panencephalitis.
  panencefalitis esclerosante subaguda subacute sclerosing panencephalitis.
panesclerosis *f.* pansclerosis.
panespermatismo *m.* panspermatism.
panespermia *f.* panspermia.
panestesia *f.* panesthesia.
panfobia *f.* pamphobia.
pangénesis *f.* pangenesis.
pangenia *f.* pangenesis.
panglosia *f.* panglossia.
panhematopenia *f.* panhematopenia.
panhidrosis *f.* panhidrosis.
panhiperemia *f.* panhyperemia.
panhisterosalpingooforectomía *f.* panhystero-oophorectomy.
pánico *m.* panic.
paniculalgia *f.* panniculalgia.
paniculitis *f.* panniculitis.
  paniculitis nodular no supurativa, paniculitis nodular no supurativa recurrente febril relapsing febrile nodular non-suppurative panniculitis.
  paniculitis migratoria nodular subaguda subacute nodular migratory panniculitis.
  paniculitis de Weber-Christian Weber-Christian panniculitis.
paniculo *m.* panniculus.
panidrosis *f.* panhidrosis.
paninmunidad *f.* panimmunity.
panmielopatía *f.* panmyelopathy.
  panmielopatía constitucional infantil constitutional infantile panmyelopathy.
panmieloptisis *f.* panmyelophthisis.
panmielotisis *f.* panmyelophthisis.
panmixia *f.* panmixia.
panneuritis *f.* panneuritis.
panniculus panniculus.
pannus pannus.
panoftalmia *f.* panophthalmia.
panoftalmitis *f.* panophthalmitis.
panoptosis *f.* panoptosis.
panosteítis *f.* panosteitis.
panotitis *f.* panotitis.
panplejia *f.* panplegia.
pansinusitis *f.* pansinusitis.
pantacromático, -ca *adj.* pantachromatic.
pantalla *f.* screen.
  pantalla de Bjerrum Bjerrum screen.
  pantalla fluorescente fluorescent screen.
  pantalla intensificadora intensifying screen.
  pantalla tangente tangent screen.
pantamorfia *f.* pantamorphia.
pantanencefalia *f.* pantanencephaly, pantanencephalia.
pantatrofia *f.* pantatrophia, pantatrophy.
pantódico, -ca *adj.* panthodic.
pantofobia *f.* panphobia.
pantogamia *f.* pantogamy.
pantógrafo *m.* pantograph.
pantomografía *f.* pantomography.
pantomógrafo *m.* pantomograph.
pantomórfico, -ca *adj.* pantomorphic.
pantorrilla *f.* calf.
pantoscópico, -ca *adj.* pantoscopic.
pantrópico, -ca *adj.* pantropic.
panuveítis *f.* panuveitis.
paño *m.* pannus.
paperas *f.* mumps.
papila *f.* papilla.
  papila dentaria tooth bud.
papilar *adj.* papillary, papillate.
papilectomía *f.* papillectomy.

papiledema *m.* papilledema.
papilífero, -ra *adj.* papilliferous.
papiliforme *adj.* papilliform.
papilitis *f.* papillitis.
  papilitis necrosante necrotizing papillitis.
  papilitis renal necrosante necrotizing renal papillitis.
papiloadenocistoma *m.* papilloadenocystoma.
papilocarcinoma *m.* papillocarcinoma.
papiloma *m.* papilloma.
  papiloma acuminado papilloma acuminatum.
  papiloma córneo hornifying papilloma.
  papiloma de Hopmann Hopmann's papilloma.
  papiloma difuso papilloma diffusum.
  papiloma intracanicular intraductal papilloma.
  papiloma intracístico intracystic papilloma.
  papiloma mucoso condyloma.
  papiloma múltiple papilloma diffusum.
  papiloma neuropático papilloma neuropathicum.
  papiloma velloso villous papilloma.
  papiloma venéreo papilloma venereum.
papilomatosis *f.* papillomatosis.
  papilomatosis nigricans acanthosis nigricans.
papilorretinitis *f.* papilloretinitis.
papilotomía *f.* papillotomy.
papiráceo, -a *adj.* papyraceous.
pappus pappus.
pápula *f.* papule.
  pápula de Celso Celsus' papule.
papulación *f.* papulation.
papulífero, -ra *adj.* papuliferous.
papulización *f.* papulization.
papuloeritematoso, -sa *adj.* papuloerythematous.
papuloescamoso, -sa *adj.* papulosquamous.
papuloide *adj.* papuloid.
papulopustuloso, -sa *adj.* papulopostular.
papulosis *f.* papulosis.
  papulosis atrófica maligna malignant atrophic papulosis.
papulovesicular *adj.* papulovesicular.
paquiacria *f.* pachyacria.
paquibléfaron *f.* pachyblepharon.
paquicefalia *f.* pachycephaly.
paquicolia *f.* pachycholia.
paquicolpismo *m.* pachycolpismus.
paquicromático, -ca *adj.* pachychromatic.
paquidactilia *f.* pachydactylia.
paquidermatocele *m.* pachydermatocele.
paquidermatosis *f.* pachydermatosis.
paquidermia *f.* pachydermia.
  paquidermia laríngea pachydermia laryngis.
  paquidermia linfangiectásica pachydermia lymphangiectatica.
paquiemia *f.* pachyemia.
paquiglosia *f.* pachyglossia.
paquignato, -ta *adj.* pachygnatous.
paquihemia *f.* pachyhemia.
paquilosis *f.* pachylosis.
paquimenia *f.* pachymenia.
paquimeninge *f.* pachymeninx.
paquimeningitis *f.* pachymeningitis.
  paquimeningitis cervical hipertrófica hypertrophic cervical pachymeningitis.
  paquimeningitis hemorrágica interna hemorrhagic internal pachymeningitis.
  paquimeningitis intralaminar pachymeningitis intralamellaris.
  paquimeningitis purulenta purulent pachymeningitis.

  paquimeningitis serosa interna serous internal pachymeningitis.
paquímetro *m.* pachymeter, pachometer.
paquinema *m.* pachynema.
paquinsis *f.* pachynsis.
paquioniquia *f.* pachyonychia.
paquiotia *f.* pachyotia.
paquipelviperitonitis *f.* pachypelviperitonitis.
paquiperiosteodermia *m.* pachyperiosteoderma.
paquiperiostitis *f.* pachyperiostitis.
paquiperitonitis *f.* pachyperitonitis.
paquipleuritis *f.* pachypleuritis.
paquiqueilia *f.* pachycheilia.
paquiquilia *f.* pachychilia.
paquisalpingitis *f.* pachysalpingitis.
paquisalpingoovaritis *f.* pachysalpingo-ovaritis.
paquivaginalitis *f.* pachyvaginalitis.
paquivaginitis *f.* pachyvaginitis.
  paquivaginitis quística pachyvaginitis cystica.
paraanalgesia *f.* para-analgesia.
paraanestesia *f.* para-anesthesia.
paraapendicitis *f.* para-appendicitis.
parabiosis *f.* parabiosis.
  parabiosis dialítica dialytic parabiosis.
  parabiosis vascular vascular parabiosis.
parablepsia *f.* parablepsia.
paracantoma *m.* paracanthoma.
paracantosis *f.* paracanthosis.
paracardíaco, -ca *adj.* paracardiac.
paracarmín *m.* paracarmine.
paracéfalo *m.* paracephalus.
paracelo *m.* paracele.
paracenestesia *f.* paracoenesthesia.
paracentesis *f.* paracentesis.
  paracentesis abdominal abdominal paracentesis.
  paracentesis ocular paracentesis oculi.
  paracentesis timpánica tympanic paracentesis.
paracentral *adj.* paracentral.
paraceratosis *f.* parakeratosis.
paracinesia *f.* paracinesia, paracinesis.
paracinesis *f.* paracinesis.
paracistio *m.* paracystium.
paracistitis *f.* paracystitis.
paracmé *f.* paracme.
paracnemidion *m.* paracnemidion.
paracnemis *m.* paracnemis.
paracólera *m.* paracholera.
paracolitis *f.* paracolitis.
paracolpio *m.* paracolpium.
paracolpitis *f.* paracolpitis.
paracono *m.* paracone.
paracordal *adj.* parachordal.
paracoxalgia *f.* paracoxalgia.
paracroia *f.* parachroia.
paracromatismo *m.* parachromatism.
paracromatopsia *f.* parachromatopsia.
paracromatosis *f.* parachromatosis.
paracromía *f.* dyschromia.
paracusia *f.* paracusia, paracusis.
  paracusia acris paracusia acris.
  paracusia doble paracusia duplicata.
  paracusia falsa false paracusia.
  paracusia de Willis, paracusia willisiana Willis' paracusia.
paracusis *f.* paracusis.
paradenitis *f.* paradenitis.
paradental *adj.* paradental.
paradentitis *f.* paradentitis.
paradentosis *f.* paradentosis.
paradiabetes *f.* paradiabetes.

paradídimo *m.* paradidymis.
paradiftérico, -ca *adj.* paradiphtheritic.
paradisentería *f.* paradysentery.
paradoja *f.* paradox.
  paradoja de Opie Opie paradox.
  paradoja de Weber Weber's paradox.
paradójico, -ca *adj.* paradoxical.
paradontosis *m.* paradentosis.
paraecrisis *f.* paraeccrisis.
paraepicele *m.* paradidymis.
paraepilepsia *f.* paraepilepsy.
paraespecífico, -ca *adj.* paraspecific.
paraesteatosis *f.* parasteatosis.
paraesternal *adj.* parasternal.
paraestesia *f.* paraesthesia.
parafasia *f.* paraphasia.
  parafasia fonémica literal paraphasia.
  parafasia literal literal paraphasia.
  parafasia verbal verbal paraphasia.
parafemia *f.* paraphasia.
parafia *f.* paraphia.
parafilia *f.* paraphilia.
parafimosis *f.* paraphimosis.
parafinoma *m.* paraffinoma.
paráfisis *f.* paraphysis.
paraflagelo *m.* paraflagellum.
parafonía *f.* paraphonia.
  parafonía puberum paraphonia puberum.
parafrenia *f.* paraphrenia.
parafrenitis *f.* paraphrenitis.
parafuncional *adj.* parafunctional.
paraganglio *m.* paraganglion.
paraganglioma *m.* paraganglioma.
  paraganglioma medular medullary paraganglioma.
  paraganglioma no cromafín non-chromaffin paraganglioma.
parageusia *f.* parageusia.
paraglobina *f.* paraglobulin.
paraglobulina *f.* paraglobulin.
paraglobulinuria *f.* paraglobulinuria.
paraglosia *f.* paraglossa.
paraglosis *f.* paraglossa.
paraglositis *f.* paraglossitis.
paraglutinación *f.* paragglutination.
paragnato *m.* paragnatus.
paragrafia *f.* paragraphia.
paragramatismo *m.* paragrammatism.
paragripal *adj.* parainfluenza.
parahemoglobina *f.* parahemoglobin.
parahepático, -ca *adj.* parahepatic.
parahepatitis *f.* parahepatitis.
parahormona *f.* parahormone.
parainfección *f.* parainfection.
paralaje *m.* parallax.
  paralaje binocular binocular parallax.
paralalia *f.* paralalia.
paralambdacismo *m.* paralambdacism.
paralax *m.* parallax.
paralergia *f.* parallergia.
paralérgico, -ca *adj.* parallergic.
paralexia *f.* paralexia.
paralgesia *f.* paralgesia.
paralgia *f.* paralgia.
parálisis *f.* paralysis.
  parálisis de la acomodación paralysis of accommodation.
  parálisis acústica acoustic paralysis.
  parálisis agitante paralysis agitans.
  parálisis agitante juvenil (de Hunt) Hunt's juvenile paralysis agitans.
  parálisis alcohólica alcoholic paralysis.
  parálisis alterna alternate paralysis.
  parálisis ambiguoaccesoria ambiguo-accessorius paralysis.

  parálisis ambiguoaccesoriohipoglosa ambiguo-accessorius-hipoglossal paralysis.
  parálisis ambioguoespinotalámica ambiguous pinothalamic paralysis.
  parálisis ambioguohipoglosa ambiguous hypoglossal paralysis.
  parálisis de la anestesia anesthesia paralysis.
  parálisis arsenical arsenical paralysis.
  parálisis ascendente ascending paralysis.
  parálisis ascendente aguda acute ascending paralysis.
  parálisis de asociación association paralysis.
  parálisis astenobulboespinal asthenobulbospinal paralysis.
  parálisis de Bell Bell's paralysis.
  parálisis braquial brachial paralysis.
  parálisis braquiofacial brachifacial paralysis.
  parálisis de Brown-Séquard Brown-Séquard's paralysis.
  parálisis bulbar bulbar paralysis.
  parálisis bulbar aguda acute bulbar paralysis.
  parálisis bulbar asténica asthenic bulbar paralysis.
  parálisis bulbar espástica spastic bulbar paralysis.
  parálisis bulbar progresiva progressive bulbar paralysis.
  parálisis bulbar tegmentaria medullary tegmental paralysis.
  parálisis bulboespinal bulbospinal paralysis.
  parálisis de los buzos diver's paralysis.
  parálisis central central paralysis.
  parálisis centrocortical centrocortical paralysis.
  parálisis cerebral cerebral paralysis.
  parálisis circunfleja cincumflex paralysis.
  parálisis completa complete paralysis.
  parálisis por compresión compression paralysis.
  parálisis crural crural paralysis.
  parálisis cruzada crossed paralysis.
  parálisis por decúbito decubitus paralysis.
  parálisis del despertar waking paralysis.
  parálisis diftérica diphtheritic paralysis.
  parálisis de Duchenne Duchenne's paralysis.
  parálisis de Duchenne-Erb Duchenne-Erb paralysis.
  parálisis emocional emotional paralysis.
  parálisis de Erb-Duchenne Erb-Duchenne paralysis.
  parálisis de los escritores writer's paralysis.
  parálisis espasmódica, parálisis espástica spastic paralysis.
  parálisis espinal espasmódica spinal spastic paralysis.
  parálisis fláccida flaccid paralysis.
  parálisis falsa false paralysis.
  parálisis fonética phonetic paralysis.
  parálisis glosofaringolabial glossopharyngolabial paralysis.
  parálisis glosolabial glossolabial paralysis.
  parálisis de Gluber Gluber's paralysis.
  parálisis histérica hysterical paralysis.
  parálisis incompleta incomplete paralysis.
  parálisis infantil infantile paralysis.
  parálisis isquémica, parálisis isquémica de Volkmann ischemic paralysis, Volkmann's ischemic paralysis.
  parálisis de Klumpke, parálisis de Klumpke-Déjerine Klumpke's paralysis, Klumpke-Déjerine paralysis.
  parálisis labioglosofaringea glossolabiopharyngeal paralysis.
  parálisis labioglosolaríngea glossolabiolaryngeal paralysis.

  parálisis de Landry Landry's paralysis.
  parálisis de Lissauer Lissauer's paralysis.
  parálisis local local paralysis.
  parálisis de Millard-Gluber Millard-Gluber paralysis.
  parálisis mimética mimetic paralysis.
  parálisis miopática myopathic paralysis.
  parálisis nuclear nuclear paralysis.
  parálisis obstétrica obstetrical paralysis.
  parálisis ocular ocular paralysis.
  parálisis periférica peripheral paralysis.
  parálisis periódica familiar familial periodic paralysis.
  parálisis posdiftérica postdiphtheritic paralysis.
  parálisis psíquica psychic paralysis.
  parálisis de Ramsay Hunt Ramsay Hunt paralysis.
  parálisis refleja reflex paralysis.
  parálisis reptante creeping paralysis.
  parálisis seudobulbar pseudobulbar paralysis.
  parálisis seudohipertrófica pseudohypertrophic paralysis.
  parálisis del sueño sleep paralysis.
  parálisis supranuclear supranuclear paralysis.
  parálisis de Todd Todd's paralysis.
  parálisis del trigémino trigeminal paralysis.
  parálisis de Weber Weber's paralysis.
  parálisis de Werding-Hoffmann Werding-Hoffmann paralysis.
paralizador, -ra *m. y adj.* paralyzant.
paralizante *m. y adj.* paralyzant.
paramagnetismo *m.* paramagnetism.
paramastitis *f.* paramastitis.
paramastoiditis *f.* paramastoiditis.
paramediano, -na *adj.* paramedian.
paramesial *adj.* paramesial.
parametrio *m.* parametrium.
parametritis *f.* parametritis.
  parametritis anterior anterior parametritis.
  parametritis posterior posterior parametritis.
parámetro *m.* parameter.
paramimia *f.* paramimia.
paramioclonía *m.* paramyoclonus.
  paramioclonía múltiple paramyoclonus multiplex.
paramiosinógeno *m.* paramyosinogen.
paramiotonía *f.* paramyotonia.
  paramiotonía congénita congenital paramyotonia.
paramiotono *m.* paramyotonus.
paramiotoma *m.* hyaloplasm.
paramnesia *f.* paramnesia.
Paramoeba Paramoeba.
paramolar *m.* paramolar.
paramorfia *f.* paramorphia.
paranalgesia *f.* paranalgesia.
paranefritis *f.* paranephritis.
paranefroma *m.* paranephroma.
paranestesia *f.* paranesthesia.
paraneumonía *f.* parapneumonia.
paraneural *adj.* paraneural.
paranéurico, -ca *adj.* paraneural.
paranfistomlasis *f.* paramphistomiasis.
paranoia *f.* paranoia.
paranoico, -ca *adj.* paranoiac.
paranoide *adj.* paranoid.
paranormal *adj.* paranormal.
paranúcleo *m.* paranucleus.
paraonfálico, -ca *adj.* paraomphalic.
paraonfalocele *m.* paromphalocele.
paraoperatorio, -ria *adj.* paraoperative.

parapancreático, -ca *adj.* parapancreatic.
paraparesia *f.* paraparesis.
parapedésis *f.* parapedesis.
paraperitoneal *adj.* paraperitoneal.
parapeste *f.* parapestis.
paraplejía *f.* paraplegia.
 paraplejía alcohólica alcoholic paraplegia.
 paraplejía atáxica ataxic paraplegia.
 paraplejía cerebral cerebral paraplegia.
 paraplejía espástica spastic paraplegia.
 paraplejía espástica congénita congenital spastic paraplegia.
 paraplejía espástica infantil infantile spastic paraplegia.
 paraplejía fláccida flaccid paraplegia.
 paraplejía periférica peripheral paraplegia.
 paraplejía de Pott Pott's paraplegia.
 paraplejía superior paraplegia superior.
 paraplejía tóxica toxic paraplegia.
parapléjico, -ca *adj.* paraplectic, paraplegic.
paraplejiforme *adj.* paraplegiform.
parapleuritis *f.* parapleuritis.
paraplexo *m.* paraplexus.
parapófisis *f.* parapophysis.
parapraxia *f.* parapraxia.
paraproctio *m.* paraproctium.
paraproctitis *f.* paraproctitis.
paraproteína *f.* paraprotein.
paraproteinemia *f.* paraproteinemia.
parapsia *f.* parapsia.
parapsicología *f.* parapsychology.
parapsis *f.* parapsis.
parapsoriasis *f.* parapsoriasis.
paraqueratosis *f.* parakeratosis.
 paraqueratosis escutular parakeratosis scutularis.
 paraqueratosis psoriasiforme parakeratosis psoriasiformis.
pararreacción *f.* parareaction.
pararrectal *f.* pararectal.
pararreflexia *f.* parareflexia.
pararrenal *adj.* pararenal.
pararritmia *f.* pararrhythmia.
pararrizoclasia *f.* pararhizoclasia.
pararrotacismo *m.* pararhotacism.
parasacro, -cra *adj.* parasacral.
parasagital *adj.* parasagittal.
parasalpingitis *f.* parasalpingitis.
parasífilis *f.* parasyphilis.
parasifilosis *f.* parasyphilosis.
parasigmatismo *m.* parasigmatism.
parasimpático, -ca *adj.* parasympathetic.
parasimpaticolítico, -ca *adj.* parasympatholytic.
parasimpaticomimético, -ca *adj.* parasympathomimetic.
parasimpaticotonía *f.* parasympathicotonia.
parasinoidal *adj.* parasinoidal.
parasinovitis *f.* parasynovitis.
parasinusal *adj.* parasinoidal.
parasístole *f.* parasystole.
parasitario, -ria *adj.* parasitic.
parasitemia *f.* parasitemia.
parasiticida[1] *m.* parasiticide.
parasiticida[2] *adj.* parasiticidal.
parasítico, -ca *adj.* parasitic.
parasitífero *m.* parasitifer.
parasitismo *m.* parasitism.
parásito *m.* parasite.
 parásito accidental accidental parasite.
 parásito auxiliar auxiliary parasite.
 parásito comensal commensal parasite.
 parásito específico specific parasite.
 parásito facultativo facultative parasite.
 parásito incidental incidental parasite.

 parásito inquilino inquiline parasite.
 parásito obligado obligate parasite.
parasitofobia *f.* parasitophobia.
parasitogénico, -ca *adj.* parasitogenic.
parasitoide *adj.* parasitoid.
parasitología *f.* parasitology.
parasitólogo, -ga *m., f.* parasitologist.
parasitosis *f.* parasitosis.
parasitotropía *f.* parasitotropy.
parasitotropismo *m.* parasitotropy.
parasitótropo, -pa *adj.* parasitotrope.
parasomnia *f.* parasomnia.
paraspadias *m.* paraspadia, paraspadias.
parasplénico, -ca *adj.* parasplenic.
parastenia *f.* parasthenia.
parastruma *m.* parastruma.
paratarso *m.* paratarsium.
paratendón *m.* paratenon.
paratereseomanía *f.* paratereseomania.
paraterminal *adj.* paraterminal.
parathormona *f.* parathormone.
paratiflitis *f.* paratyphlitis.
paratifoide *f.* paratyphoid.
paratifoidea *f.* paratyhpoid.
paratimia *f.* parathymia.
paratípico, -ca *adj.* paratypical.
paratirina *f.* parathyrin.
paratiroidectomía *f.* parathyroidectomy.
paratiroideo, -a *adj.* parathyroid.
paratiroides *f.* parathyroid.
paratiroidoma *m.* parathyroidoma.
paratiroprivia *f.* parathyroprivia.
paratirotrópico, -ca *adj.* parathyrotropic.
paratonía *f.* paratonia.
paratormona *f.* parathormone.
paratricosis *f.* paratrichosis.
paratripsis *f.* paratripsis.
paratríptico, -ca *adj.* paratriptic.
paratrofia *f.* paratrophy.
paratuberculosis *f.* paratuberculosis.
paraumbilical *adj.* paraumbilical.
parauretra *f.* paraurethra.
parauretritis *f.* paraurethritis.
parauterino, -na *adj.* parauterine.
paravacuna *f.* paravaccinia.
paravaginal *adj.* paravaginal.
paravaginitis *f.* paravaginitis.
paravenoso, -sa *adj.* paravenous.
paravertebral *adj.* paravertebral.
paravesical *adj.* paravesical.
paravitaminosis *f.* paravitaminosis.
paraxial *adj.* paraxial.
paraxil *adj.* paraxial.
parazoo *m.* parazoon.
parcialismo *m.* partialism.
parectasia *f.* parectasia, parectasis.
parectasis *f.* parectasis.
parectropía *f.* parectropia.
pared *f.* wall.
 pared cavitaria cavity wall.
 pared celular cell wall.
 pared esplácnica splanchnic wall.
pareidolia *f.* pareidolia.
parelectrotomía *f.* parelectrotomy.
parencefalia *f.* parencephalia.
parencefalitis *f.* parencephalitis.
parencéfalo *m.* parencephalon.
parencefalocele *m.* parencephalocele.
parénquima *m.* parenchyma.
parenquimatitis *f.* parenchymatitis.
parental *adj.* parental.
parenteral *adj.* parenteral.
parentérico, -ca *adj.* parenteral.
parepicele *m.* parepicele.
parepitimia *f.* parepithymia.

parergasia *f.* parergasia.
paresia *f.* paresis.
 paresia estacionaria stationary paresis.
 paresia galopante galloping paresis.
 paresia general general paresis.
parestesia *f.* paresthesia.
 parestesia de Bernhardt Bernhardt's paresthesia.
parético, -ca *adj.* paretic.
pareunia *f.* pareunia.
paridad *f.* parity.
parahidrosis *f.* paridrosis.
paridrosis *f.* paridrosis.
parietal *adj.* parietal.
parietitis *f.* parietitis.
parietoescamoso, -sa *adj.* parietosquamosal.
parietoesfenoidal *adj.* parietosphenoid.
parietofrontal *adj.* parietofrontal.
parietooccipital *adj.* parieto-occipital.
parietosplácnico, -ca *adj.* parietosplanchnic.
parietotemporal *adj.* parietotemporal.
parietovisceral *adj.* parietovisceral.
parkinsonismo *m.* parkinsonism.
paradencio *m.* parodontium.
paradoncio *m.* parodontium.
parodontio *m.* parodontium.
parodontitis *f.* parodontitis.
parodontosis *f.* parodontosis.
paroftalmía *f.* parophthalmia.
paroftalmitis *f.* parophthalmia.
parolivar *adj.* parolivary.
paronicosis *f.* paronychosis.
paroniria *f.* paroneiria, paroniria.
paropsia *f.* paropsia, paropsis.
paropsis *f.* paropsis.
parorexia *f.* parorexia.
parorquidia *f.* parorchidium.
parosfresia *f.* parosphresia.
parosmia *f.* parosmia.
parosteitis *f.* parosteitis, parostitis.
parosteosis *f.* parosteosis, parostosis.
parostitis *f.* parostitis.
parostosis *f.* parostosis.
parótico, -ca *adj.* parotic.
parótida *f.* parotid.
parotidectomía *f.* parotidectomy.
parotídeo, -a *adj.* parotid.
parotiditis *f.* parotiditis.
 parotiditis contagiosa epidemic parotiditis.
 parotiditis epidémica epidemic parotiditis.
 parotiditis flemonosa parotiditis phlegmonosa.
 parotiditis posoperatoria postoperative parotiditis.
parotidoauricular *adj.* parotidoauricularis.
parotidoesclerosis *f.* parotidosclerosis.
parotitis *f.* parotitis.
parovariotomía *f.* parovariotomy.
parovaritis *f.* parovaritis.
paroxismal *adj.* paroxysmal.
paroxísmico, -ca *adj.* paroxysmal.
paroxismo *m.* paroxysm.
paroxístico, -ca *adj.* paroxysmal.
parpadeo *m.* blinking.
párpado *m.* eyelid, palpebra.
pars pars.
 pars planitis pars planitis.
parsimonia *f.* parsimony.
parte *f.* part, pars.
partenogénesis *f.* parthenogenesis.
partenoplastia *f.* parthenoplasty.
partícula *f.* particle.
 partícula alfa alpha particle.
 partícula beta beta particle.
 partícula coloide colloid particle.

partícula de Dane Dane particle.
partícula elemental de Zimmermann Zimmermann's elementary particle.
partícula F F particle.
partimutismo *m.* partimutism.
parto *m.* delivery, labor, partus.
parto abdominal abdominal delivery.
parto artificial artificial labor.
parto atónico atonic labor.
parto complicado complicated labor.
parto espontáneo spontaneous delivery.
parto eutícico spontaneous delivery.
parto eutócico spontaneous delivery.
parto falso false labor.
parto inducido induced labor.
parto instrumental instrumental labor.
parto múltiple multiple labor.
parto precipitado precipitate labor.
parto prematuro premature delivery.
parto prolongado prolonged labor.
parto provocado induced labor.
parto vaginal vaginal delivery.
parturienta *adj.* parturient.
parturifaciente *m. y adj.* parturifacient.
parturiómetro *m.* parturiometer.
párulis *m.* parulis.
paruria *f.* paruria.
parvicelular *adj.* parvicellular.
párvulo, -la *adj.* parvule.
pasión *f.* passion.
pasivo, -va *adj.* passive.
paso¹ *m.* step.
paso² *m.* passage.
pasta *f.* paste.
pasteurella *f.* pasteurella.
pasteurización *f.* pasteurization.
patefacción *f.* patefaction.
patela *f.* patella.
patelapexia *f.* patellapexy.
patelar *adj.* patellar.
patelectomía *f.* patellectomy.
pateliforme *adj.* patelliform.
patelofemoral *adj.* patellofemoral.
patema *f.* pathema.
patematología *f.* pathematology.
patergasia *f.* pathergasia.
patergia *f.* pathergy.
paternalismo *m.* paternalism.
paternidad *f.* fatherhood.
patético, -ca *adj.* pathetic.
patetismo *m.* pathetism.
patizambo, -ba *m., f.* knock-kneed.
patoanatomía *f.* pathoanatomy.
patobiología *f.* pathobiology.
patobolismo *m.* pathobolism.
patoclisis *f.* pathoclisis.
patocrinia *f.* pathocrinia.
patodoncia *f.* pathodontia.
patofilia *f.* pathophilia.
patofobia *f.* pathophobia.
patoforesis *f.* pathophoresis.
patogénesis *f.* pathogeny.
patogenia *f.* pathogeny.
patogenicidad *f.* pathogenicity.
patógeno *m.* pathogen.
patógeno, -na *adj.* pathogenic.
patognomía *f.* pathognomonia.
patognomónico, -ca *adj.* pathognomonic.
patognóstico, -ca *adj.* pathognostic.
patografía *f.* pathography.
patólisis *f.* patholysis.
patología *f.* pathology.
patología celular cellular pathology.
patología clínica clinical pathology.
patología comparada comparative pathology.

patología dental dental pathology.
patología especial special pathology.
patología experimental experimental pathology.
patología externa external pathology.
patología funcional functional pathology.
patología general general pathology.
patología geográfica geographical pathology.
patología humoral humoral pathology.
patología interna internal pathology.
patología médica medical pathology.
patología mental mental pathology.
patología quirúrgica surgical pathology.
patológico, -ca *adj.* pathologic, pathological.
patólogo, -ga *m., f.* pathologist.
patomciosis *f.* pathomciosis.
patometabolismo *m.* pathometabolism.
patomimesis *f.* pathomimesis.
patomorfismo *m.* pathomorphism.
patomorfología *f.* pathomorphism.
patomorfosis *f.* pathomorphosis.
patoneurosis *f.* pathoneurosis.
patonomía *f.* pathonomia, pathonomy.
patooclusión *f.* patho-occlusion.
patopsicología *f.* pathopsychology.
patopsicosis *f.* pathopsychosis.
patosis *f.* pathosis.
patotropismo *m.* pathotropism.
patrilineal *adj.* patrilineal.
patróclino, -na *adj.* patroclinous.
patrogénesis *f.* patrogenesis.
patrón *m.* pattern.
patrón de acción action pattern.
patrón de acción fija fixed action pattern.
patrón capsular capsular pattern.
patrón de cera wax pattern.
patrón combinado combined pattern.
patrón de conducta behavior pattern.
patrón de estimulo stimulus pattern.
patrón de flujo aéreo airflow pattern.
patrón de inhibición refleja (PIR) reflex inhibiting pattern (RIP).
patrón muscular muscle pattern.
patrón oclusal occlusal pattern.
patrón de reloj de arena hourglass pattern.
patrón de sobresalto startle pattern.
patuloso, -sa *adj.* patulous.
pauciarticular *adj.* pauciarticular.
paucibacilar *adj.* paucibacillary.
paucisináptico, -ca *adj.* paucisynaptic.
pausa *f.* pause.
pausa apneica apneic pause.
pausa compensatoria compensatory pause.
pausa posextrasistólica postextrasystolic pause.
pavimentación *f.* pavementing.
pavor *m.* pavor.
pavor nocturno pavor nocturnus.
P-congénita P-congenitale.
P-dextrocardial P-dextrocardiale.
peca *f.* freckle.
peca de Hutchinson Hutchinson's freckle.
peca del iris iris freckle.
peca melanótica melanotic freckle.
pecante *adj.* pecant.
peciolado, -da *adj.* petiolate, petiolated.
peciolo, peciolo *m.* petiolus.
peciolo epiglótico petiolus epiglottidis.
pectenitis *f.* pectenitis.
pectenosis *f.* pectenosis.
pectenotomía *f.* pectenotomy.
pectinado, -da *adj.* pectinate.
pectíneo, -a *adj.* pectineal.
pectiniforme *adj.* pectiniform.
pectoral *adj.* pectoral.
pectoralgia *f.* pectoralgia.

pectoriloquia *f.* pectoriloquy.
pectoriloquia afónica aphonic pectoriloquy.
pectoriloquia susurrante whispering pectoriloquy.
pectorofonía *f.* pectorophony.
pecho *m.* chest, pectus.
pedal *adj.* pedal.
paidoatrofia *f.* pedatrophia, pedatrophy.
pedartrocace *m.* pedarthrocace.
pedatrofia *f.* pedatrophia, pedatrophy.
pediadoncia *f.* pediadontia.
pediadontología *f.* pediadontology.
pediatra *m., f.* pediatrician.
pediatría *f.* pediatrics.
pediátrico, -ca *adj.* pediatric.
pedicelación *f.* pedicellation.
pedicelado, -da *adj.* pedicellate, pedicellated.
pedicelo *m.* pedicel.
pediculación *f.* pediculation.
pediculado, -da *adj.* pediculate.
pedicular *adj.* pedicular.
pediculicida *m.* pediculicide.
pedículo *m.* pedicle, pediculus.
pedículo óptico optic pedicle.
pediculosis *f.* pediculosis.
pediculosis capitis pediculosis capitis.
pediculosis corporis pediculosis corporis.
pediculosis palpebrarum pediculosis palpebrarum.
pediculosis pubis pediculosis pubis.
pediculoso, -sa *adj.* pediculous.
pediculus *m.* pediculus.
Pediculus Pediculus.
pedicura *f.* pedicure.
pediculría *f.* pedicure.
pedifalange *f.* pediphalanx.
pediluvio *m.* pediluvium.
pedodinamómetro *f.* pedodynamometer.
pedodoncia *f.* pedodontics.
pedofilia *f.* pedophilia.
pedofílico, -ca *adj.* pedophilic.
pedófilo, -la¹ *adj.* pedophilic.
pedófilo, -la² *m., f.* pedophile.
pedofobia *f.* pedophobia.
pedogamia *f.* pedogamy.
pedogénesis *f.* pedogenesis.
pedografía *f.* pedography.
pedógrafo *f.* pedograph.
pedograma *m.* pedogram.
pedómetro *m.* pedometer.
pedomórfico, -ca *adj.* pedomorphic.
pedomorfismo *m.* pedomorphism.
pedopatía *f.* pedopathy.
pedunculado, -da *adj.* pedunculated.
peduncular *adj.* peduncular.
pedúnculo *m.* peduncle, pedunculus.
pedunculotomía *f.* pedunculotomy.
peine *m.* pecten.
pelagismo *m.* pelagism.
pelagra *f.* pellagra.
pelagra infantil infantile pellagra.
pelagra secundaria secondary pellagra.
pelagra sin pelagra pellagra sine pellagra.
pelagra tifoidea typhoid pellagra.
pelagrágeno, -na *adj.* pellagragenic.
pelagral *adj.* pellagral.
pelagroide *adj.* pellagroid.
pelagrología *f.* pellagrology.
pelagrólogo, -ga *m., f.* pellagrologist.
pelagrosis *f.* pellagrosis.
pelagroso, -sa *adj.* pellagrous.
película¹ *f.* pellicle.
película adquirida acquired pellicle.
película de gelatina absorbible absorbable gelatin pellicle.

película lagrimal tear pellicle.
película marrón brown pellicle.
película parda brown pellicle.
película² *f.* film.
película de cine cine film.
película dental dental film.
película duplicadora duplicating film.
película de emulsión doble double-emulsion film.
película de exposición directa direct-exposure film.
película fluorográfica fluororoentgenography.
película de localización localization film.
película radiográfica panorámica panoramic X-ray film.
película de sangre fijada fixed blood film.
película de sulfa sulfa film.
pelicular *adj.* pellicular.
peliculoso, -sa *adj.* pelliculous.
pelidnoma *m.* pelidnoma.
peligro biológico *m.* biohazard.
pelioma *m.* pelioma.
peliosis *f.* peliosis.
peliosis hepática peliosis hepatis.
pelirrojo, -ja *adj.* ginger, red-haired, red-headed.
pelmático, -ca *adj.* pelmatic.
pelmatograma *m.* pelmatogram.
pelo *m.* hair.
pelo anular ringed hair.
pelo auditivo auditory hair.
pelo de bambú bamboo hair.
pelo canceroso de Schridde Schridde's cancer hair.
cilindro de pelo cast hair.
pelo claviforme club hair.
pelo encarnado ingrown hair.
pelo ensortijado kinky hair.
pelo estrellado stellate hair.
pelo gustativo taste hair.
pelo horadante burrowing hair.
pelo invaginado ingrown hair.
pelo irritantes de Frey Frey's irritation hair.
pelo lanudo woolly hair.
pelo lanugo lanugo hair.
pelo en signo de admiración exclamation point hair.
pelo urticante nettling hair.
pelota *f.* ball.
pelota de comida food ball.
pelota de condrina chondrin ball.
peloteo *m.* ballottement.
peloteo abdominal abdominal ballottement.
peloteo indirecto indirect ballottement.
peltación *f.* peltation.
peltado, -da *adj.* peltate.
pelúcido, -da *adj.* pellucid.
peludo, -da *adj.* hairy.
pelviano, -na *adj.* pelvic.
pelvicalicial *adj.* pelvicaliceal, pelvicalyceal.
pelvicefalometría *f.* pelvicephalometry.
pelvicelulitis *f.* pelvicellulitis.
pelvicilla renal *f.* renal pelvis, pelvis renalis.
pélvico, -ca *adj.* pelvic.
pelviesternón *m.* pelvisternum.
pelvifemoral *adj.* pelvifemoral.
pelvifijación *f.* pelvifixation.
pelvigrafía *f.* pelviography.
pelvígrafo *m.* pelvigraph.
pelvilitotomía *f.* pelvilithotomy.
pelvimetría *f.* pelvimetry.
pelvimetría clínica clinical pelvimetry.
pelvimetría con rayos X X-ray pelvimetry.
pelvimetría estereoscópica stereoscopic pelvimetry.

pelvimetría manual manual pelvimetry.
pelvimetría planográfica planographic pelvimetry.
pelvímetro *m.* pelvimeter.
pelviografía *f.* pelviography.
pelviógrafo *m.* pelviograph.
pelvioileoneocistostomía *f.* pelvioileoneocystostomy.
pelviolitotomía *f.* pelviolithotomy.
pelvioneostomía *f.* pelvioneostomy.
pelvioperitonitis *f.* pelviperitonitis.
pelvioplastia *f.* pelvioplasty.
pelviorradiografía *f.* pelvioradiography.
pelvioscopia *f.* pelvioscopy.
pelviotomía *f.* pelviotomy, pelvitomy.
pelviperitonitis *f.* pelviperitonitis.
pelvirradiografía *f.* pelviradiography.
pelvirrectal *adj.* pelvirectal.
pelvirroentgenografía *f.* pelviroentgenography.
pelvis *f.* pelvis.
pelvis androide android pelvis.
pelvis antropoide anthropoid pelvis.
pelvis asimilada assimilation pelvis.
pelvis braquipélica brachypellic pelvis.
pelvis de caucho caoutchouc pelvis.
pelvis cifoescoliótica kyphoscoliotic pelvis.
pelvis cifótica kyphotic pelvis.
pelvis congelada frozen pelvis.
pelvis contraida contracted pelvis.
pelvis cordiforme cordate pelvis, cordiform pelvis.
pelvis coxálgica coxalgic pelvis.
pelvis dolicopélica dolichopellic pelvis.
pelvis en embudo funnel-shaped pelvis.
pelvis enana dwarf pelvis.
pelvis endurecida hardened pelvis.
pelvis escoliótica scoliotic pelvis.
pelvis espinosa pelvis spinosa.
pelvis espondilolistética spondylolisthetic pelvis.
pelvis extrarrenal extrarenal pelvis.
pelvis en forma de corazón heart-shaped pelvis.
pelvis gigante justo major pelvis.
pelvis ginecoide gynecoid pelvis.
pelvis de goma caoutchouc pelvis.
pelvis hendida split pelvis.
pelvis infantil infantile pelvis.
pelvis infundibuliforme funnel-shaped pelvis.
pelvis invertida inverted pelvis.
pelvis juvenil juvenile pelvis.
pelvis lordótica lordotic pelvis.
pelvis masculina masculine pelvis.
pelvis mesatipélica mesatipellic pelvis.
pelvis de Nägele Nägele's pelvis.
pelvis oblicua Nägele's pelvis.
pelvis obtecta pelvis obtecta.
pelvis osteomalácica osteomalacic pelvis.
pelvis de Otto Otto pelvis.
pelvis oval longitudinal longitudinal oval pelvis.
pelvis oval transversa transverse oval pelvis.
pelvis en pico beaked pelvis.
pelvis plana flat pelvis.
pelvis platipélica platypellic pelvis.
pelvis de Praga Prague pelvis.
pelvis raquítica rachitic pelvis.
pelvis redonda round pelvis.
pelvis renal renal pelvis.
pelvis reniforme reniform pelvis.
pelvis de Robert Robert's pelvis.
pelvis de Rokitansky Rokitansky's pelvis.
pelvis rostrata rostrate pelvis.

pelvis seudoosteomalácica pseudo-osteomalacic pelvis.
pelvis de la vesícula biliar pelvis of the gallbladder.
pelvisacral *adj.* pelvisacral.
pelvisacro *m.* pelvisacrum.
pelviscopia *f.* pelvioscopy.
pelvioscopio *m.* pelviscope.
pelviscopio *m.* pelviscope.
pelvisección *f.* pelvisection.
pelvitermo *m.* pelvitherm.
pelvitomía *f.* pelvitomy.
pelviureterografía *f.* pelviureterography.
pelvoespondilitis osificante *f.* pelvospondylitis ossificans.
pena *f.* grief.
pendelluft pendelluft.
pendiente *f.* slant.
pendular *adj.* pendular.
pene *m.* penis.
pene claviforme clubbed penis.
pene doble double penis.
pene femenino femineus penis.
pene en masa clubbed penis.
pene membranoso webbed penis.
pene oculto concealed penis.
pene palmado penis palmatus.
pene plástico plastica penis.
peneano, -na *adj.* penial, penile.
penectomía *f.* penectomy.
penetrabilidad *f.* penetrability.
penetración *f.* penetration.
penetrancia *f.* penetrance.
penetrante *adj.* penetrating.
penetrología *f.* penetrology.
penetrómetro *m.* penetrometer.
pénfigo *m.* pemphigus.
pénfigo agudo pemphigus acutus.
pénfigo contagioso pemphigus contagiosus.
pénfigo cruposo, pénfigo crupal pemphigus crouposus.
pénfigo diftérico pemphigus diphtheriticus.
pénfigo eritematoso pemphigus erythematosus.
pénfigo familiar benigno crónico familial benign chronic pemphigus.
pénfigo foliáceo pemphigus foliaceus.
pénfigo gangrenoso pemphigus gangrenosus.
pénfigo leproso pemphigus leprosus.
pénfigo neonatal pemphigus neonatorum.
pénfigo ocular ocular pemphigus.
pénfigo vegetante pemphigus vegetans.
pénfigo vulgar pemphigus vulgaris.
penfigoide *m.* pemphigoid.
penfigoide ampollar bulbous pemphigoid.
penfigoide cicatricial cicatricial pemphigoid.
penfigoide mucoso benigno benign mucosal pemphigoid.
penfigoide ocular ocular pemphigoid.
peniciliado, -da *adj.* penicillate.
peniciliosis *f.* penicilliosis.
penicilio *m.* penicillus.
penisquisis *f.* penischisis.
penitis *f.* penitis.
penniforme *adj.* penniform.
penoescrotal *adj.* penoscrotal.
penotomía *f.* penotomy.
pensamiento *m.* thinking, thought.
pensamiento abstracto abstract thinking.
pensamiento animista animistic thinking.
pensamiento autista autistic thinking.
pensamiento automático automatic thought.
pensamiento concreto concrete thinking.
pensamiento creativo creative thinking.

pensamiento egocéntrico egocentric thinking.
pensamiento icónico iconic thinking.
pensamiento ilógico illogical thinking.
pensamiento hipotético-deductivo hypothetical-deductive thinking.
pensamiento operacional operatory thought.
pensamiento paleológico paleologic thinking.
pentacrómico, -ca *adj.* pentachromic.
pentadáctilo, -la *adj.* pentadactyl, pentadactyle.
pentalogía *f.* pentalogy.
pentalogía de Fallot pentalogy of Fallot.
pentámero *m.* pentamer.
pentaploide *adj.* pentaploid.
pentaploidía *f.* pentaploidy.
pentasomía *f.* pentasomy.
pentastomiasis *f.* pentastomiasis.
pentosa *f.* pentose.
pentosemia *f.* pentosemia.
pentosuria *f.* pentosuria.
pentosuria alimentaria alimentary pentosuria.
pentosuria esencial esential pentosuria.
pentosuria primaria primary pentosuria.
pentosúrico, -ca *adj.* pentosuric.
peotomía *f.* peotomy.
peplo *f.* peplos.
peplómero *m.* peplomer.
pepsinuria *f.* pepsinuria.
péptico, -ca *adj.* peptic.
Peptococcaceae Peptococcaceae.
Peptococcus Peptococcus.
peptocrinina *f.* peptocrinine.
peptogénico, -ca *adj.* peptogenic.
peptógeno, -na *adj.* peptogenous.
peptólisis *f.* peptolysis.
peptolítico, -ca *adj.* peptolytic.
peptonización *f.* peptonization.
peptonizar *v.* peptonize.
peptonuria *f.* peptonuria.
peptonuria enterógena enterogenous peptonuria.
peptonuria hepatógena hepatogenous peptonuria.
peptonuria nefrógena nephrogenic peptonuria.
peptonuria piógena pyogenic peptonuria.
peptonuria puerperal puerperal peptonuria.
Peptostreptococcus Peptostreptococcus.
pequeño mal *m.* petit mal.
pequiagra *f.* pechyagra.
peracéfalo *m.* peracephalus.
peracidez *f.* peracidity.
peragudo, -da *adj.* peracute.
peraxilar *adj.* peraxillary.
perbucal *adj.* peroral.
percentil *m.* percentile.
percepción *f.* perception.
percepción consciente conscious perception.
percepción extrasensorial (PES) extrasensory perception (ESP).
percepción facial facial perception.
percepción de la profundidad depth perception.
percepción simultánea simultaneous perception.
perceptividad *f.* perceptivity.
perceptivo, -va *adj.* perceptive.
percepto *m.* percept.
perceptor, -ra *adj.* percipient.
percusión *f.* percussion.
percusión auscultatoria auscultatory percussion.

percusión bimanual bimanual percussion.
percusión clavicular clavicular percussion.
percusión digital finger percussion.
percusión directa direct percussion.
percusión inmediata immediate percussion.
percusión mediata mediate percussion.
percusión palpatoria palpatory percussion.
percusión profunda deep percussion.
percusión umbral threshold percussion.
percusopuntor *m.* percussopunctator.
percusor *m.* percussor.
percutáneo, -a *adj.* percutaneous.
percutible *adj.* percussible.
pérdida *f.* deletion.
perencefalia *f.* perencephaly.
perenne *adj.* perennial.
perfeccionismo *m.* perfectionism.
perfil *m.* profile.
perfil antigénico antigenic profile.
perfil bioquímico biochemical profile.
perfil facial facial profile.
perfil de la personalidad personality profile.
perfil de presión uretral urethral pressure profile.
perfil de pruebas test profile.
perfilómetro *m.* perfilometer.
perflación *f.* perflation.
perforación *f.* perforation.
perforación de Bezold Bezold's perforation.
perforación dental dental perforation.
perforado, -da *adj.* perforated.
perforador *m.* perforator.
perforante *adj.* perforans.
perforar *v.* drill.
perfricación *f.* perfrication.
perfundido, -da *adj.* perfusate.
perfundir *v.* perfuse.
perfusión *f.* perfusion.
perfusión regional regional perfusion.
periacinal *adj.* periacinal.
periacinoso, -sa *adj.* periacinous.
periacueductal *adj.* periaqueductal.
periadenitis *f.* periadenitis.
periadenitis aftosa periadenitis aphtae.
periadenitis mucosa necrótica recurrente periadenitis mucosa necrotica recurrens.
periadventicio, -a *adj.* periadventitial.
perialienitis *f.* perialienitis.
periamigdalar *adj.* peritonsillar.
periamigdalitis *f.* peritonsillitis.
periampular *adj.* periampullary.
perianal *adj.* perianal.
periangeítis *f.* periangitis.
periangiocolitis *f.* periangiocholitis.
periangioma *m.* periangioma.
periaórtico, -ca *adj.* periaortic.
periaortitis *f.* periaortitis.
periapendicitis *f.* periappendicitis.
periapendicitis decidual periappendicitis decidualis.
periapendicular *adj.* periappendicular.
periapical *adj.* periapical.
periápice *m.* periapex.
periarterial *adj.* periarterial.
periarteritis *f.* periarteritis.
periarticular *adj.* periarticular.
periártrico, -ca *adj.* periarthric.
periartritis *f.* periarthritis.
periauricular *adj.* periauricular.
periaxial *adj.* periaxial.
periaxilar *adj.* periaxillary.
periaxónico, -ca *adj.* periaxonal.
periblasto *m.* periblast.
peribronquial *adj.* peribronchial.
peribronquiolar *adj.* peribronchiolar.

peribronquiolitis *f.* peribronchiolitis.
peribronquitis *f.* peribronchitis.
peribucal *adj.* peribuccal.
peribulbar *adj.* peribulbar.
peribursal *adj.* peribursal.
pericaliceo, -a *adj.* pericaliceal, perycaliceal.
pericalloso, -sa *adj.* pericallosal.
pericanalicular *adj.* pericanalicular.
pericapsular *adj.* pericapsular.
pericardectomía *f.* pericardectomy.
pericardíaco, -ca *adj.* pericardiac, pericardial.
pericardicentesis *f.* pericardicentesis.
pericárdico, -ca *adj.* pericardiac, pericardial.
pericardiectomía *f.* pericardiectomy.
pericardio *m.* pericardium.
pericardio adherente adherent pericardium.
pericardio de pan y mantequilla bread-and-butter pericardium.
pericardio peludo shaggy pericardium.
pericardiocentesis *f.* pericardiocentesis.
pericardiofrénico, -ca *adj.* pericardiophrenic.
pericardiólisis *f.* pericardiolysis.
pericardiomediastinitis *f.* pericardiomediastinitis.
pericardioperitoneal *adj.* pericardioperitoneal.
pericardiopleural *adj.* pericardiopleural.
pericardiorrafia *f.* pericardiorrhaphy.
pericardiostomía *f.* pericardiostomy.
pericardiotomía *f.* pericardiotomy.
pericardítico, -ca *adj.* pericarditic.
pericarditis *f.* pericarditis.
pericarditis adherente adhesive pericarditis.
pericarditis adherente interna internal adhesive pericarditis.
pericarditis amibiana amebic pericarditis.
pericarditis benigna aguda acute benign pericarditis.
pericarditis calculosa pericarditis calculosa.
pericarditis carcinomatosa carcinomatous pericarditis.
pericarditis con derrame pericarditis with effusion.
pericarditis constrictiva crónica chronic constrictive pericarditis.
pericarditis externa external pericarditis.
pericarditis fibrinosa fibrinous pericarditis.
pericarditis hemorrágica hemorrhagic pericarditis.
pericarditis idiopática idiopathic pericarditis.
pericarditis localizada localized pericarditis.
pericarditis obliterante pericarditis obliterans.
pericarditis purulenta purulent pericarditis.
pericarditis reumática rheumatic pericarditis.
pericarditis seca pericarditis sicca.
pericarditis serofibrinosa serofibrinous pericarditis.
pericarditis supurativa suppurative pericarditis.
pericarditis tuberculosa tuberculous pericarditis.
pericarditis urémica uremic pericarditis.
pericarditis vellosa pericarditis villosa.
pericardotomía *f.* pericardotomy.
pericarion *m.* perikaryon.
pericecal *adj.* pericecal.
pericecitis *f.* pecicecitis.
pericefálico, -ca *adj.* pericephalic.
pericelular *adj.* pericellular.
pericemental *adj.* pericemental.
pericementario, -ria *adj.* pericemental.
pericementitis *f.* pericementitis.

pericementitis apical apical pericementitis.
pericemento *m.* pericementum.
pericementoclasia *f.* pericementoclasia.
pericentral *adj.* pericentral.
pericentriolar *adj.* pericentriolar.
periciclo *m.* pericycle.
pericima *f.* perikyma.
pericístico, -ca *adj.* pericystic.
pericistio *m.* pericystium.
pericistitis *f.* pericystitis.
pericítico, -ca *adj.* pericytial.
pericito *m.* pericyte.
pericolangitis *f.* pericholangitis.
pericólico, -ca *adj.* pericolic.
pericolitis *f.* pericolitis.
pericolitis derecha pericolitis dextra.
pericolitis izquierda pericolitis sinistra.
pericolonitis *f.* pericolonitis.
pericolpitis *f.* pericolpitis.
pericondral *adj.* perichondral, perichondrial.
pericondrial *adj.* perichondral, perichondrial.
pericondrio *m.* perichondrium.
pericondritis *f.* perichondritis.
pericondritis periesternal peristernal perichondritis.
pericondritis recidivante relapsing perichondritis.
pericordal *adj.* perichordal.
pericordio *m.* perichord.
pericorneal *adj.* pericorneal.
pericoroidal *adj.* perichoroidal.
pericoronal *adj.* pericoronal.
pericoronitis *f.* pericoronitis.
pericraneal *adj.* pericranial.
pericráneo *m.* pericranium.
pericranitis *f.* pericranitis.
peridectomía *f.* peridectomy.
peridencio *m.* peridentium.
peridens *m.* peridens.
peridental *adj.* peridental.
peridérmico, -ca *adj.* peridermal, peridermic.
periderma *f.* periderm, periderma.
peridermo *m.* periderm, periderma.
peridésmico, -ca *adj.* peridesmic.
peridesmio *m.* peridesmium.
peridesmitis *f.* peridesmitis.
perididimitis *f.* periddidymitis.
peridídimo *m.* peridydymis.
peridiverticulitis *f.* peridiverticulitis.
periduodenitis *f.* periduodenitis.
peridural *adj.* peridural.
periencefalitis *f.* periencephalitis.
perientérico, -ca *adj.* perienteric.
perienteritis *f.* perienteritis.
periependimal *adj.* periependymal.
periesofagico, -ca *adj.* periesophageal.
periesofagitis *f.* pericsophagitis.
periespermatitis *f.* perispermatitis.
periespermatitis serosa perispermatitis serosa.
periesplácnico, -ca *adj.* perisplanchnic.
periesplacnitis *f.* perisplanchnitis.
periesplénico, -ca *adj.* perisplenic.
periesplenitis *f.* perisplenitis.
periespondílico, -ca *adj.* perispondylic.
periespondilitis *f.* perispondylitis.
periestafilitis *f.* peristaphylitis.
periestrumoso, -sa *adj.* peristrumous.
perifaríngeo, -a *adj.* peripharyngeal.
periferia *f.* periphery.
periférico, -ca *adj.* peripheral.
periferocentral *adj.* peripherocentral.
periflebítico, -ca *adj.* periphlebitic.
periflebitis *f.* periphlebitis.
perifocal *adj.* perifocal.

perifolicular *adj.* perifollicular.
perifoliculitis *f.* perifolliculitis.
perifoliculitis capitis abscedens et suffodiens perifolliculitis capitis abscedens et suffodiens.
perifoliculitis pustulosa superficial superficial pustular perifolliculitis.
perifundir *v.* perifuse.
perifusión *f.* perifusion.
periganglionar *adj.* periganglionic.
perigástrico, -ca *adj.* perigastric.
perigastritis *f.* perigastritis.
perigemal *adj.* perigemmal.
periglandulitis *f.* periglandulitis.
periglótico, -ca *adj.* periglottic.
periglotis *f.* periglottis.
perihepático, -ca *adj.* perihepatic.
perihepatitis *f.* perihepatitis.
perihernial *adj.* perihernial.
periimplantitis *f.* peri-implantitis.
periimplantoclasia *f.* peri-implantoclasia.
perilaberintitis *f.* perilabyrinthitis.
perilaríngeo, -a *adj.* perilaryngeal.
perilaringitis *f.* perilaryngitis.
perilenticular *adj.* perilenticular.
periligamentoso, -sa *adj.* periligamentous.
perilinfa *f.* perilympha.
perilinfangial *adj.* perilymphangial.
perilinfangeítis *f.* perilymphangitis.
perilinfático, -ca *adj.* perilymphatic.
perimeningitis *f.* perimeningitis.
perimetral *adj.* perimetric.
perimetría *f.* perimetry.
perimetría cinética kinetic perimetry.
perimetría computerizada computed perimetry.
perimetría cuantitativa quantitative perimetry.
perimetría escotópica scotopic perimetry.
perimetría estática static perimetry.
perimetría flicker flicker perimetry.
perimetría mesópica mesopic perimetry.
perimetría objetiva objective perimetry.
perimétrico, -ca *adj.* perimetric.
perimetrio *m.* perimetrium.
perimetrítico, -ca *adj.* perimetritic.
perimetritis *f.* perimetritis.
perímetro *m.* perimeter.
perímetro de arco arc perimeter.
perímetro de Goldmann Goldmann perimeter.
perímetro de proyección projection perimeter.
perímetro de Tubinga Tübingen perimeter.
perimielitis *f.* perimyelitis.
perimielo *m.* perimyelis.
perimioendocarditis *f.* perimyoendocarditis.
perimiositis *f.* perimyositis.
perimisial *adj.* perimysial.
perimisio *m.* perimysium.
perimisio externo perimysium externum.
perimisio interno perimysium internum.
perimisitis *f.* perimysiitis, perimysitis.
perinatal *adj.* perinatal.
perinatología *f.* perinatology.
perinatólogo, -ga *m., f.* perinatologist.
periné *m.* perineum.
perineal *adj.* perineal.
perinéfrico, -ca *adj.* perinephric.
perinefrio *m.* perinephrium.
perinefrítico, -ca *adj.* perinephritic.
perinefritis *f.* perinephritis.
perineo *m.* perineum.
perineo en regadera watering-can perineum.
perineocele *m.* perineocele.

perineómetro *m.* perineometer.
perineoplastia *f.* perineorrhaphy.
perineorrafia *f.* perineorrhaphy.
perineoescrotal *adj.* perineoscrotal.
perineosíntesis *f.* perineosynthesis.
perineostomía *f.* perineostomy.
perineotomía *f.* perineotomy.
perineovaginal *adj.* perineovaginal.
perineúrico, -ca *adj.* perineural.
perineurio *m.* perineurium.
perineuritis *f.* perineuritis.
perinuclear *adj.* perinuclear.
periocular *adj.* periocular.
periodicidad *f.* periodicity.
periodicidad diurna diurnal periodicity.
periodicidad filariásica filarial periodicity.
periodicidad lunar lunar periodicity.
periodicidad nocturna norturnal periodicity.
periodicidad palúdica malarial periodicity.
periodicidad subperiódica subperiodic periodicity.
periódico, -ca *adj.* periodic.
período *m.* period.
período de capuchón, período de casquete cap period.
período crítico critical period.
período de eclipse eclipse period.
período edípico oedipal period.
período de eyección ejection period.
período faltante missed period.
período fértil fertile period.
período de frío cold period.
período de incubación incubative period.
período de incubación extrínseca extrinsic incubation period.
período de inducción induction period.
período intersistólico intersystolic period.
período intraparto intrapartum period.
período de invasión period of invasion.
período isoeléctrico isoelectric period.
período isométrico isometric period.
período isométrico del ciclo cardíaco isometric period of cardiac cycle.
período de latencia, período latente latency period, latent period.
período menstrual menstrual period.
período mitótico mitotic period.
período de preeyección preejection period.
período prodrómico prodromal period.
período puerperal puerperal period.
período refractario refractory period.
período refractario absoluto absolute refractory period.
período refractario funcional functional refractory period.
período refractario del marcapaso electrónico refractory period of electronic pacemaker.
período refractario relativo relative refractory period.
período refractario total total refractory period.
período de reposo resting period.
período silencioso silent period.
período silencioso masticatorio masticatory silent period.
período vegetativo vegetative period.
período vulnerable (del corazón) vulnerable (of heart) period.
período de Wenckebach Wenckebach period.
periodoncia *f.* periodontics.
periodoncio *m.* periodontium.
periodoncista *m.* periodontist.
periodontal *adj.* periodontal.
periodontitis *f.* periodontitis.

periodontitis apical apical periodontitis.
periodontitis compleja complex periodontitis.
periodontitis complicada complicated periodontitis.
periodontitis leve light periodontitis.
periodontitis juvenil juvenile periodontitis.
periodontitis simple simple periodontitis.
periodontitis supurativa suppurative periodontitis.
periodonto *m.* periodontium.
periodontoclasia *f.* periodontoclasia.
periodontólisis *f.* periodontolysis.
periodontosis *f.* periodontosis.
perioftálmico, -ca *adj.* periophthalmic.
perioftalmitis *f.* periophthalmitis.
perionfálico, -ca *adj.* periomphalic.
perioniquia *f.* perionychia.
perioniquio *m.* perionychium.
periónix *m.* perionyx.
perionixis *f.* perionyxis.
periooforitis *f.* perioophoritis.
periooforosalpingitis *f.* perioophorosalpingitis.
perioperatorio, -ria *adj.* perioperative.
perioral *adj.* perioral.
periórbita *f.* periorbita.
periorbitario, -ria *adj.* periorbital.
periorquitis *f.* periorchitis.
periorquitis hemorrágica periorchitis hemorrhagica.
periosteítis *f.* periosteitis.
periosteofito *m.* periosteophyte.
periosteoma *m.* periosteoma.
periosteomedulitis *f.* periosteomedullitis.
periosteomielitis *f.* periosteomyelitis.
periosteopatía *f.* periosteopathy.
periosteosis *f.* periosteosis.
periosteotomía *f.* periosteotomy.
periosteótomo *m.* periosteotome.
perióstico, -ca *adj.* periosteal.
periostio *m.* periosteum.
periostio alveolar alveolar periosteum, periosteum alveolare.
periostio craneal periosteum cranii.
periostitis *f.* periostitis.
periostitis orbitaria orbital periostitis.
periostoma *m.* periostoma.
periostosis *f.* periostosis.
periostosteítis *f.* periostosteitis.
periostotomía *f.* periostotomy.
periostótomo *m.* periostotome.
periótico, -ca *adj.* periotic.
periovaritis *f.* periovaritis.
periovular *adj.* periovular.
peripancreatitis *f.* peripancreatitis.
peripapilar *adj.* peripapillary.
peripaquimeningitis *f.* peripachymeningitis.
peripeniano, -na *adj.* peripenial.
peripílico, -ca *adj.* peripylic.
peripiloflebitis *f.* peripylephlebitis.
peripilórico, -ca *adj.* peripyloric.
peripolar *adj.* peripolar.
peripolesis *f.* peripolesis.
periporitis *f.* periporitis.
periportal *adj.* periportal.
perlproctitis *f.* periproctitis.
periprostático, -ca *adj.* periprostatic.
periprostatitis *f.* periprostatitis.
periquerático, -ca *adj.* perikeratic.
periquístico, -ca *adj.* pericystic.
perirrectal *adj.* perirectal.
perirrectitis *f.* perirectitis.
perirrenal *adj.* perirenal.
perirrínico, -ca *adj.* perirhinal.

perirrizoclasia *f.* perirhizoclasia.
perisalpingitis *f.* perisalpingitis.
perisalpingoovaritis *f.* perisalpingo-ovaritis.
perisálpinx *m.* perisalpinx.
periscópico, -ca *adj.* periscopic.
perisigmoiditis *f.* perisigmoiditis.
perisinovial *adj.* perisynovial.
peristáltico, -ca *adj.* peristaltic.
peristaltismo *m.* peristalsis.
peristaltismo invertido reversed peristalsis.
peristaltismo masivo mass peristalsis.
peristaltismo retrógrado retrograde peristalsis.
peristasis *f.* peristasis.
perístole *f.* peristole.
peristólico, -ca *adj.* peristolic.
peristomatoso, -sa *adj.* peristomal, peristomatous.
peritectomía *f.* peritectomy, peridectomy.
peritelio *m.* perithelium.
peritelio de Eberth Eberth's perithelium.
peritendíneo *m.* peritendineum.
peritendinitis *f.* peritendinitis.
peritendinitis calcárea peritendinitis calcarea.
peritenón *m.* peritenon.
peritenontitis *f.* peritenontitis.
peritiflico, -ca *adj.* perityphlic.
peritiroiditis *f.* perithyroiditis.
peritomía *f.* peritomy.
peritomista *m.* peritomist.
peritoneal *adj.* peritoneal.
peritonealgia *f.* peritonealgia.
peritoneo *m.* peritoneum.
peritoneocentesis *f.* peritoneocentesis.
peritoneoclisis *f.* peritoneoclysis.
peritoneopatía *f.* peritoneopathy.
peritoneopericárdico, -ca *adj.* peritoneopericardial.
peritoneopexia *f.* peritoneopexy.
peritoneoplastia *f.* peritoneoplasty.
peritoneoscopia *f.* peritoneoscopy.
peritoneoscopio *m.* peritoneoscope.
peritoneotomía *f.* peritoneotomy.
peritonismo *m.* peritonism.
peritonitis *f.* peritonitis.
peritonitis adherente adhesive peritonitis.
peritonitis biliar bile peritonitis.
peritonitis circunscrita circumscribed peritonitis.
peritonitis deformante peritonitis deformans.
peritonitis diafragmática diaphragmatic peritonitis.
peritonitis difusa diffuse peritonitis.
peritonitis encapsulante peritonitis encapsulans.
peritonitis fibrocaseosa fibrocaseous peritonitis.
peritonitis gaseosa gas peritonitis.
peritonitis general general peritonitis.
peritonitis localizada localized peritonitis.
peritonitis por meconio meconium peritonitis.
peritonitis pélvica pelvic peritonitis.
peritonitis productiva productive peritonitis.
peritonitis quílica chyle peritonitis.
peritonitis química chemical peritonitis.
peritonitis tuberculosa tuberculous peritonitis.
peritorácico, -ca *adj.* perithoracic.
peritraqueal *adj.* peritracheal.
peritrocantérico, -ca *adj.* peritrochanteric.
periumbilical *adj.* periumbilical.
periungular *adj.* periungual.
periureteral *adj.* periureteral, periureteric.

periureteritis *f.* periureteritis.
periureteritis plástica periureteritis plastica.
periuretral *adj.* periurethral.
periuretritis *f.* periurethritis.
periuterino, -na *adj.* periuterine.
periuvular *adj.* periuvular.
perivaginitis *f.* perivaginitis.
perivascular *adj.* perivascular.
perivasculitis *f.* perivasculitis.
perivenoso, -sa *adj.* perivenous.
perivertebral *adj.* perivertebral.
perivesical *adj.* perivesical.
perivisceral *adj.* perivisceral.
perivisceritis *f.* perivisceritis.
perivitelino, -na *adj.* perivitelline.
periyeyunitis *f.* perijejunitis.
perla *f.* pearl.
perla de Elschnig Elschnig pearl.
perla epitelial epithelial pearl.
perla de Epstein Epstein's pearl.
perla escamosa squamous pearl.
perla de esmalte enamel pearl.
perla gotosa gouty pearl.
perla de queratina keratin pearl.
perlèche *m.* perlèche.
permanencia del objeto *f.* object permanence.
permeabilidad *f.* permeability.
permeable *adj.* permeable.
permeación *f.* permeation.
permeante *adj.* permeant.
permear *v.* permeate.
pernicioso, -sa *adj.* pernicious.
perniosis *f.* perniosis.
perno *m.* pin.
perno de Steinmann Steinmann pin.
perobraquio *m.* perobrachius.
perocéfalo *m.* perocephalus.
perodactilia *f.* perodactylia, perodactyly.
peroesplacnia *f.* perosplanchnia.
peromelia *f.* peromelia.
peroné *m.* fibula.
peroneo, -a *adj.* peroneal.
peroneocalcáneo, -a *adj.* peroneocalcaneal.
peroneotibial *adj.* peroneotibial.
peropo *m.* peropus.
peróquiro *m.* prochirus.
peroral *adj.* peroral, per os.
per os *adv.* per os.
peróseo, -a *adj.* perosseous.
perseveración *f.* perseveration.
persistencia *f.* persistence.
persistente *adj.* persistent.
persona *f.* persona.
personalidad *f.* personality.
personalidad anal anal personality.
personalidad epileptoide epileptic personality.
personalidad escindida split personality.
persuasión *f.* persuasion.
perversión *f.* perversion.
perversión polimorfa polymorphous perversion.
perversión sexual sexual perversion.
perverso, -sa *m., f.* pervert.
pervertido, -da *adj.* perverted.
pes pes.
pesadilla *f.* nightmare.
pesario *m.* pessary.
pesario de anillo ring pessary.
pesario de diafragma diaphragm pessary.
pesario de Gariel Gariel's pessary.
pesario de Hodge Hodge's pessary.
pesimismo *m.* pessimism.
pesimismo terapéutico therapeutic pessimism.
pestaña *f.* eyelash.

pestaña ectópica ectopic eyelash.
pestaña partialbina piebald eyelash.
peste *f.* plague, pestis.
  peste ambulante, peste ambulatoria ambulant plague, ambulatory plague.
  peste bubónica bubonic plague.
  peste glandular glandular plague.
  peste hemorrágica hemorrhagic plague.
  peste larval larval plague.
  peste negra black plague.
  peste neumónica pneumonic plague.
  peste septicémica septicemic plague.
  peste del valle de Pahvant Pahvant Valley plague.
  peste variolosa pestis variolosa.
pesticemia *f.* pesticemia.
pestífero, -ra *adj.* pestiferous.
pestilencia *f.* pestilence.
pestilente *adj.* pestilential.
petequia *f.* petechia.
  petequia de Tardieu Tardieu's petechia.
petequial *adj.* petechial.
petequiasis *f.* petechiasis.
pétreo, -a *adj.* petrous.
petroccipital *adj.* petroccipital.
petroescamoso, -sa *adj.* petrosquamosal, petrosquamous.
petroesfenoidal *adj.* petrosphenoid.
petromastoideo, -a *adj.* petromastoid.
petrooccipital *adj.* petro-occipital.
petrositis *f.* petrositis.
petrosomastoideo, -a *adj.* petrosomastoid.
pexis *f.* pexis.
pezón *m.* nipple.
pial *adj.* pial.
piamadre *f.* pia mater.
pian *m.* pian.
piaracnitis *f.* pia-arachnitis.
piartrosis *f.* pyarthrosis.
piblokto *m.* piblokto.
pica *f.* pica.
picadura *f.* sting.
picazón *f.* itching.
pícnico, -ca *adj.* picnic.
picnodisostosis *f.* pyknodysostosis.
picnofrasia *f.* pyknophrasia.
picnosis *f.* pyknosis.
picnótico, -ca *adj.* pyknotic.
pictógrafo *m.* pictograph.
pie *m.* foot, pes.
  pie abducto, pes abductus pes abductus.
  pie aducto, pes adductus pes adductus.
  pie ancho metatarsus latus.
  pie de atleta athlete's foot.
  pie caído drop foot.
  pie cavo, pes cavus clawfoot, pes cavus.
  pie de Charcot Charcot's foot.
  pie chupador perivascular foot.
  pie de cuervo corvinus pes.
  pie equino pes equinus.
  pie equinovalgo, pes equinovalgus pes equinovalgus.
  pie equinovaro, pes equinovarus pes equinovarus.
  pie en espátula spatula foot.
  pie extendido metatarsus latus.
  pie forzado forced foot.
  pie de Friedreich Friedreich's foot.
  pie en garra claw foot.
  pie gigante, pes gigas pes gigas.
  pie hendido cleft foot.
  pie de Hong-Kong Hong-Kong foot.
  pie de inmersión immersion foot.
  pie de madura madura foot.
  pie de marcha march foot.

  pie micótico fungous foot.
  pie de Morand Morand's foot.
  pie de Morton Morton's foot.
  pie musgoso mossy foot.
  pie perivascular perivascular foot.
  pie plano, pes planus flat foot, pes planus.
  pie plano espástico spastic flat foot.
  pie planovalgo, pes planovalgus pes planovalgus.
  pie en pronación, pes pronatus pes pronatus.
  pie en sandalia sandal foot.
  pie supino, pes supinatus pes supinatus.
  pie talo, pes talus pes talus.
  pie terminal end-foot.
  pie de trinchera trench foot.
  pie valgo, pes valgus pes valgus.
  pie varo, pes varus pes varus.
  pie zambo club foot, skewfoot.
piebaldismo *m.* piebaldness.
piedra *f.* piedra.
  piedra artificial artificial piedra.
  piedra blanca white piedra.
  piedra cutánea skin piedra.
  piedra lagrimal tear piedra.
  piedra pulpar pulp piedra.
  piedra venosa vein piedra.
piel *f.* skin.
  piel de agricultor farmer's skin.
  piel amarilla yellow skin.
  piel apergaminada parchment skin.
  piel brillante glossy skin.
  piel bronceada bronzed skin.
  piel de cerdo pig skin.
  piel de cocodrilo, piel de lagarto crocodile skin.
  piel decidua deciduous skin.
  piel de los dientes skin of the teeth.
  piel elástica elastic skin.
  escritura en la piel writing skin.
  piel lampiña glabrous skin.
  piel laxa loose skin.
  piel de marinero sailor's skin.
  piel multicolor piebald skin.
  piel de naranja peau d'orange.
  piel de pescado fish skin.
  piel de puercoespín porcupine skin.
  piel de sapo toad skin.
  piel de las uñas nail skin.
  piel de zapa shagreen skin.
pielectasia *f.* pyelectasia, pyelectasis.
pielectasis *f.* pyelectasis.
pielítico, -ca *adj.* pyelitic.
pielitis *f.* pyelitis.
pielocaliceal *adj.* pyelocalyceal.
pielocaliectasis *f.* pyelocaliectasis.
pielocistitis *f.* pyelocystitis.
pielofluoroscopia *f.* pyelofluoroscopy.
pielografía *f.* pyelography.
  pielografía antégrada antegrade pyelography.
pielograma *m.* pyelogram.
pielolinfático, -ca *adj.* pyelolymphatic.
pielolitotomía *f.* pyelolithotomy.
pielonefritis *f.* pyelonephritis.
  pielonefritis aguda acute pyelonephritis.
  pielonefritis ascendente ascending pyelonephritis.
  pielonefritis crónica chronic pyelonephritis.
  pielonefritis xantogranulomatosa xanthogranulomatous pyelonephritis.
pielonefrosis *f.* pyelonephrosis.
pieloplastia *f.* pyeloplasty.
  pieloplastia de Anderson-Hynes Anderson-Hynes pyeloplasty.

  pieloplastia de colgajo capsular capsular flap pyeloplasty.
  pieloplastia de colgajo vertical de Scardino Scardino vertical flap pyeloplasty.
  pieloplastia de Culp Culp pyeloplasty.
  pieloplastia desarticulada disjoined pyeloplasty.
  pieloplastia desmembrada dismembered pyeloplasty.
  pieloplastia en Y de Foley Foley Y-plasty pyeloplasty.
pieloscopia *f.* pyeloscopy.
pielostomía *f.* pyelostomy.
pielotomía *f.* pyelotomy.
  pielotomía extendida extended pyelotomy.
pieloureterectasis *f.* pyeloureterectasis.
pieloureterografía *f.* pyeloureterography.
pielovenoso, -sa *adj.* pyelovenous.
piemesis *f.* pyemesis.
piemia *f.* pyemia.
  piemia criptogénica cryptogenic pyemia.
piémico, -ca *adj.* pyemic.
piencéfalo *m.* pyencephalus.
pierna *f.* leg.
  pierna en arco bow leg.
  pierna de Barbados Barbados leg.
  pierna blanca white leg.
  pierna de elefante elephant leg.
  pierna inquietas restless leg.
  pierna del jinete rider's leg.
  pierna de leche milk leg.
  pierna de tenista tennis leg.
piesestesia *f.* piesesthesia.
piesímetro *m.* piesimeter, piesometer, piezometer.
  piesímetro de Hales Hales' piesimeter.
piesómetro *m.* piesometer.
piesis *f.* piesis.
pieza *f.* piece.
  pieza Fab Fab piece.
  pieza Fc Fc piece.
piezogénico, -ca *adj.* piezogenic.
piezómetro *m.* piezometer.
piezoquímica *f.* piezochemistry.
pigal *adj.* pygal.
pigmalionismo *m.* pygmalionism.
pigmentación *f.* pigmentation.
  pigmentación arsenical arsenic pigmentation.
  pigmentación exógena exogenous pigmentation.
pigmentado, -da *adj.* pigmented.
pigmentario, -ria *adj.* pigmentary.
pigmento *m.* pigment.
  pigmento biliar bile pigment.
  pigmento de desgaste wear-and-tear pigment.
  pigmento hematógeno hematogenous pigment.
  pigmento hepatógeno hepatogenous pigment.
  pigmento melanótico, pigmento melánico melanotic pigment.
  pigmento negro nigrum pigment.
  pigmento palúdico malarial pigment.
  pigmento respiratorio respiratory pigment.
  pigmento residual wear-and-tear pigment.
  pigmento visual visual pigment.
pigmentolisina *f.* pigmentolysin.
pigmeo, -a *m., f.* pygmy.
pigoamorfo *m.* pygoamorphus.
pigodídimo *m.* pygodidymus.
pigomelo *m.* pygomelus.
pigópago *m.* pygopagus.
pila *f.* pila.
pilar *m.* pillar.

pilas *f.* piles.
píldora *f.* pill.
pileflebectasia *f.* pylephlebectasia, pylephlebectasis.
pileflebectasis *f.* pylephlebectasis.
pileflebitis *f.* pylephlebitis.
pilenfraxis *f.* pylemphraxis.
piletromboflebitis *f.* pylethrombophlebitis.
piletrombosis *f.* pylethrombosis.
pílico, -ca *adj.* pylic.
pilimicción *f.* pilimiction.
pilobezoar *m.* pilobezoar.
piloerección *f.* piloerection.
piloide *adj.* piloid.
pilomatricoma *m.* pilomatrichoma.
pilómetro *m.* pilometer.
pilomotor, -ra *adj.* pilomotor.
pilonidal *adj.* pilonidal.
piloquístico, -ca *adj.* pilocystic.
piloralgia *f.* pyloralgia.
pilorectomía *f.* pylorectomy.
pilórico, -ca *adj.* pyloric.
piloritis *f.* pyloritis.
píloro *m.* pylorus.
pilorodiosis *f.* pylorodiosis.
piloroduodenitis *f.* pyloroduodenitis.
piloroespasmo *m.* pylorospasm.
piloroestenosis *f.* pylorostenosis.
pilorogastrectomía *f.* pylorogastrectomy.
piloromiotomía *f.* pyloromyotomy.
piloroplastia *f.* pyloroplasty.
  piloroplastia de Finney Finney pyloroplasty.
  piloroplastia de Heineke-Mikulicz Heineke-Mikulicz pyloroplasty.
  piloroplastia de Jaboulay Jaboulay pyloroplasty.
piloroptosia *f.* pyloroptosia, pyloroptosis.
piloroptosis *f.* pyloroptosis.
pilorostenosis *f.* pylorostenosis.
pilorostomía *f.* pylorostomy.
pilorotomía *f.* pylorotomy.
pilosebáceo, -a *adj.* pilosebaceous.
pilosis *f.* pilosis.
piloso, -sa *adj.* pilose.
piloyección *f.* pilojection.
pilular *adj.* pilular.
pimeloma *m.* pimeloma.
pimelopterigión *m.* pimelopterygium.
pimelorrea *f.* pimelorrhea.
pimelortopnea *f.* pimelorthopnea.
pimelosis *f.* pimelosis.
pimeluria *f.* pimeluria.
pinal *adj.* pinnal.
pincelación *f.* paint.
pineal *adj.* pineal.
pinealectomía *f.* pinealectomy.
pinealocito *m.* pinealocyte.
pinealoma *m.* pinealoma.
  pinealoma ectópico ectopic pinealoma.
  pinealoma extrapineal extrapineal pinealoma.
pinealopatía *f.* pinealopathy.
pineoblastoma *m.* pineoblastoma.
pinguécula *f.* pinguecula, pinguicula.
pinguícula *f.* pinguecula, pinguicula.
piniforme *adj.* piniform.
pinocito *m.* pinocyte.
pinocitosis *f.* pinocytosis.
pinosoma *m.* pinosome.
pinta *f.* pinta.
píntide *f.* pintid.
pintoide *adj.* pintoid.
pinzas *f.* forceps.
  pinzas de Adson Adson forceps.
  pinzas para agujas needle forceps.
  pinzas alligator alligator forceps.

pinzas de Arruga Arruga's forceps.
pinzas arterial arterial forceps.
pinzas para biopsias cup biopsy forceps.
pinzas de Brown-Adson Brown-Adson forceps.
pinzas bulldog bulldog forceps.
pinzas para cálculos, de Randall Randall stone forceps.
pinzas para cápsula capsule forceps.
pinzas para cortar cutting forceps.
pinzas dental dental forceps.
pinzas diente de ratón mouse-tooth forceps.
pinzas especular speculum forceps.
pinzas de Evans Evans forceps.
pinzas de extracción extracting forceps.
pinzas de Graefe Graefe forceps.
pinzas hemostática hemostatic forceps.
pinzas para huesos bone forceps.
pinzas de joyero jeweler's forceps.
pinzas Lahey Lahey forceps.
pinzas de Laplace Laplace's forceps.
pinzas de Löwenberg Löwenberg's forceps.
pinzas O'Hara O'Hara forceps.
pinzas para proyectiles bullet forceps.
pinzas tubular tubular forceps.
pinzas para vendajes dressing forceps.
pinzas vulsellum vulsellum forceps.
pinzas de Willett Willett forceps.
piocefalia *f.* pyocephalus.
  piocefalia circunscripta circumscribed pyocephalus.
piocele *m.* pyocele.
piocelia *f.* pyocelia.
piociánico, -ca *adj.* pyocyanic.
piocianógeno, -na *adj.* pyocyanogenic.
piocianolisina *f.* pyocyanolysin.
piocistitis *f.* pyocystitis.
piocito *m.* pyocyte.
piococo *m.* pyococcus.
piocolpocele *m.* pyocolpocele.
piocolpos *m.* pyocolpos.
piodermia *m.* pyoderma.
  piodermia chancriforme chancriform pyoderma.
  piodermia gangrenoso pyoderma gangrenosum.
  piodermia primario primary pyoderma.
  piodermia secundario secondary pyoderma.
  piodermia vegetante pyoderma vegetans.
piodermatitis *f.* pyodermatitis.
piodermatosis *f.* pyodermatosis.
pioepitelio *m.* piopithelium.
pioestomatitis *f.* pyostomatitis.
  pioestomatitis vegetante pyostomatitis vegetans.
piofisómetra *m.* pyophysometra.
pioftalmía *f.* pyophthalmia.
pioftalmitis *f.* pyophthalmitis.
piogénesis *f.* pyogenesis.
piogenético, -ca *adj.* pyogenetic.
piogénico, -ca *adj.* pyogenic.
piógeno *m.* pyogen.
piohemia *f.* pyohemia.
piohemotórax *m.* pyohemothorax.
pioide *adj.* pyoid.
piojo *m.* louse, pediculus.
piolaberintitis *f.* pyolabyrinthitis.
piómetra *m.* pyometra.
piometritis *f.* pyometritis.
piomiositis *f.* pyomyositis.
  piomiositis tropical tropical pyomyositis.
pionefritis *f.* pyonephritis.
pionefrolitiasis *f.* pyonephrolithiasis.
pionefrosis *f.* pyonephrosis.
pionefrótico, -ca *adj.* pyonephrotic.

pioneumocisto *m.* pyopneumocyst.
pioneumocolecistitis *f.* pyopneumocholecystitis.
pioneumohepatitis *f.* pyopneumohepatitis.
pioneumopericardio *m.* pyopneumopericardium.
pioneumoperitoneo *m.* pyopneumoperitoneum.
pioneumoperitonitis *f.* pyopneumoperitonitis.
pioneumotórax *m.* pyopneumothorax.
  pioneumotórax subdiafragmático, pioneumotórax subfrénico subdiaphragmatic pyopneumothorax, subphrenic pyopneumothorax.
pioombligo *m.* pyoumbilicus.
pioovario *m.* pyo-ovarium.
piopericardio *m.* pyopericardium.
piopericarditis *f.* pyopericarditis.
pioperitoneo *m.* pyoperitoneum.
pioperitonitis *f.* pyoperitonitis.
piopielectasis *f.* pyopyelectasis.
piopoyesis *f.* pyopoiesis.
piopoyético, -ca *adj.* pyopoietic.
pioptisis *f.* pyoptysis.
pioquecia *f.* pyochezia.
pioquiste *m.* pyocyst.
piorrea *f.* piorrea.
piortopnea *f.* piorthopnea.
piosalpingitis *f.* pyosalpingitis.
piosalpingooforitis *f.* pyosalpingo-oophoritis.
piosalpingootecitis *f.* pyosalpingo-oothecitis.
piosálpinx *m.* pyosalpinx.
piosemia *f.* pyosemia.
piosepticemia *f.* pyosepticemia.
piosis *f.* pyosis.
  piosis de Manson Manson's pyosis.
piospermia *f.* pyospermia.
piostático, -ca *adj.* pyostatic.
piotórax *m.* pyothorax.
piouraco *m.* pyourachus.
piouréter *m.* pyoureter.
pipeta *f.* pipette, pipet.
piramidal *adj.* pyramidal.
pirámide *f.* pyramid.
piramidotomía *f.* pyramitodomy.
  piramidotomía bulbar medullary pyramitodomy.
  piramidotomía espinal spinal pyramidotomy.
  piramidotomía medular medullary pyramitodomy.
  piramidotomía raquídea spinal pyramitodomy.
pirenemia *f.* pyrenemia.
pirético, -ca *adj.* pyrectic, pyretic.
piretogenético, -ca *adj.* pyretogenetic.
piretogénico, -ca *adj.* pyretogenic.
pirexia *f.* pyrexia.
piréxico, -ca *adj.* pyrexial.
piriforme *adj.* piriform.
pirogénico, -ca *adj.* pyrogenic.
pirógeno *m.* pyrogen.
piroglobulinemia *f.* pyroglobulinemia.
pirólisis *f.* pyrolysis.
piromanía *f.* pyromania.
pirómetro *m.* pyrometer.
pironina *f.* pyronine.
piroplasmosis *f.* piroplasmosis.
piroscopio *m.* pyroscope.
pirosis *f.* pyrosis.
piruvemia *f.* pyruvemia.
pitecoide *adj.* pitecoid.
pitiatismo *m.* pithiatism.
pitiriasis *f.* pityriasis.
  pitiriasis alba pityriasis alba.
  pitiriasis alba atrófica pityriasis alba atrophicans.

pitiriasis capitis pityriasis capitis.
pitiriasis circinada pityriasis circinata.
pitiriasis lingual pityriasis linguae.
pitiriasis manchada, pitiriasis maculata pityriasis maculata.
pitiriasis negra pityriasis nigra.
pitiriasis rosácea, pitiriasis rosada pityriasis rosea.
pitiriasis rubra pityriasis rubra.
pitiriasis rubra pilaris pityriasis rubra pilaris.
pitiriasis seca pityriasis sicca.
pitiriasis simple pityriasis simplex.
pitiriasis versicolor pityriasis versicolor.
pitode *m.* pithode.
pitogénesis *f.* pytogenesis.
pitógeno, -na *adj.* pythogenic, pythogenous.
pltoide *m.* pithode.
pituicito *m.* pituicyte.
pituitaria *f.* pituitarium.
pituitario, -ria *adj.* pituitary.
pituitarismo *m.* pituitarism.
pituitectomía *f.* pituitectomy.
pituitoso, -sa *adj.* pituitous.
Pityrosporum Pityrosporum.
Pityrosporum orbiculare Pityrosporum orbiculare.
piuria *f.* pyuria.
piuria miliar miliary pyuria.
placa¹ *f.* patch.
placa asalmonada salmon patch.
placa de Bitot Bitot's patch.
placa de los fumadores smoker's patch.
placa heráldica herald patch.
placa de Hutchinson Hutchinson's patch.
placa mucosa mucous patch.
placa de los soldados soldier's patch.
placa² *f.* plaque.
placa argirófila argyrophile plaque.
placa bacteriana bacterial plaque.
placa bacteriófaga bacteriophage plaque.
placa dentaria dental plaque.
placa fibromielínica fibromyelinic plaque.
placa Hollenhorst Hollenhorst plaque.
placa radiográfica radiographic film.
placa senil senile plaque.
placa³ *f.* plate.
placa cardiógena cardiogenic plate.
placa coriónica chorionic plate.
placa de cuentas counting plate.
placa ecuatorial equatorial plate.
placa de Egger Egger's plate.
placa de Kingsley Kingsley plate.
placa etmovomeriana ethmovomerine plate.
placa de lane Lane's plate.
placa de Moe Moe plate.
placa de mordedura bite plate.
placa de nefrotoma nephrotome plate.
placa neural neural plate.
placa ósea bone plate.
placa segmentaria segmental plate.
placa de tos cough plate.
placebo *m.* placebo.
placenta *f.* placenta.
placenta accesoria accessory placenta.
placenta adherente adherent placenta.
placenta anular annular placenta.
placenta bilobulada bilobate placenta, bilobed placenta.
placenta bipartida placenta bipartita.
placenta circunvalada placenta circunvallata.
placenta cirsoide cirsoid placenta, placenta cirsoides.
placenta dimidiada dimidiate placenta, placenta dimidiata.
placenta difusa placenta diffusa.

placenta doble placenta duplex.
placenta espuria placenta spuria.
placenta fenestrada placenta fenestrata.
placenta fetal fetal placenta, placenta fetalis.
placenta incarcerada incarcerated placenta.
placenta lobulada lobed placenta.
placenta materna maternal placenta.
placenta membranácea, placenta membranosa placenta membranacea.
placenta previa placenta previa.
placenta retenida retained placenta.
placenta de Schultze Schultze's placenta.
placenta succenturiada succenturiate placenta.
placenta triple triplex placenta.
placenta uterina placenta uterina.
placentación *f.* placentation.
placentario, -ria *adj.* placental.
placentitis *f.* placentitis.
placentografía *f.* placentography.
placentoide *adj.* placentoid.
placentología *f.* placentology.
placentoma *m.* placentoma.
placentoterapia *f.* placentotherapy.
placer *m.* pleasure.
placer de órgano organ pleasure.
placoda *f.* placode.
placoide *adj.* placoide.
pladaroma *m.* pladaroma.
pladarosis *f.* pladarosis.
plagiocefalia *f.* plagiocephaly.
plagiocefalismo *m.* plagiocephalism.
plagiocefálico, -ca *adj.* plagiocephalic.
planigrafía *f.* planigraphy.
planímetro *m.* planimeter.
plano *m.* plane, planum.
planocelular *adj.* planocellular.
planocito *m.* planocyte.
planocóncavo, -va *adj.* planoconcave.
planoconvexo, -xa *adj.* planoconvex.
planografía *f.* planography.
planta del pie *f.* planta pedis.
plantalgia *f.* plantalgia.
plantar *adj.* plantar.
plantilla *f.* template.
plantilla quirúrgica surgical template.
plánula *f.* planula.
plánula invaginada invaginate planula.
planum *m.* planum.
planuria *f.* planuria.
plaqueta *f.* platelet.
plaquetaféresis *f.* plateletpheresis.
plasma *m.* plasma.
plasma citratado citrated plasma.
plasma humano antihemofílico antihemophilic human plasma.
plasma mezclado pooled plasma.
plasma muscular muscle plasma.
plasma salado salt plasma.
plasma sanguíneo blood plasma.
plasma verdadero true plasma.
plasmacitoma *m.* plasmacytoma, plasmocytoma.
plasmaféresis *f.* plasmapheresis.
plasmalema *m.* plasmalemma.
plasmarrexis *f.* plasmarrhexis.
plasmatorrexis *f.* plasmatorrhexis.
plasmatosis *f.* plasmatosis.
plásmido *m.* plasmid.
plasmocito *m.* plasmacyte, plasmocyte.
plasmocitoma *m.* plasmocytoma.
plasmodial *adj.* plasmodial.
plasmodiblasto *m.* plasmodiblast.
plasmodicida¹ *m.* plasmodicide.
plasmodicida² *adj.* plasmodicidal.

plasmodio *m.* plasmodium.
Plasmodium Plasmodium.
plasmólisis *m.* plasmolysis.
plasmoma *m.* plasmoma.
plasmoptisis *f.* plasmoptysis.
plasmorrexis *f.* plasmorrhexis, plasmarrhexis.
plasmosquisis *f.* plasmoschisis.
plasmoterapia *f.* plasmatherapy.
plasmotisis *f.* plasmoptysis.
plasmotomía *f.* plasmotomy.
plasmotrópico, -ca *adj.* plasmotropic.
plasmotropismo *m.* plasmotropism.
plasteína *f.* plastein.
plástia *f.* plasty.
plástico, -ca *adj.* plastic.
plástida *f.* plastid.
plastocitopenia *f.* thrombocytopenia.
plastocitosis *f.* thrombocytolysis.
plastogamia *f.* plasmatogamy.
plastrón *m.* plastron.
platelminto *m.* platyhelminth.
platibasia *f.* platybasia.
platibasis *f.* platybasia.
platicefalia *f.* platycephaly.
platicéfalo, -la *adj.* platycephalic, platycephalous.
platicito *m.* platycyte.
platicnemia *f.* platycnemia.
platicnemismo *f.* platycnemia.
platicoria *f.* mydriasis.
platicrania *f.* platycrania.
platihiérico, -ca *adj.* platyhieric.
platimeria *f.* platymeria.
platimorfia *f.* platymorphia.
platina *f.* stage.
platiopia *f.* platyopia.
platipodia *f.* platypodia.
platirrinia *f.* platyrrhiny.
platispondilia *f.* platyspondylia.
platispondilisis *f.* platyspondylia.
platoniquia *f.* platyonychia.
plegafonía *f.* plegaphonia.
pleiocitosis *f.* pleiocytosis, pleocytosis.
pleiotropía *f.* pleiotropia.
pleiotrópico, -ca *adj.* pleiotropic.
pleocitosis *f.* pleiocytosis.
pleocolia *f.* pleocholia.
pleocroico, -ca *adj.* pleochromatic.
pleocroísmo *m.* pleochroism.
pleocromático, -ca *adj.* pleochromatic.
pleocromatismo *m.* pleochromatism.
pleocromia *f.* pleiochromy.
pleomastia *f.* pleomastia.
pleomería *f.* polymeria.
pleomorfia *f.* pleomorphism.
pleomorfismo *m.* pleomorphism.
pleonosteosis *f.* pleonosteosis.
pleóptica *f.* pleoptics.
pleotropía *f.* pleiotropy.
pleotrópico, -ca *adj.* pleiotropic.
plerosis *f.* plerosis.
plesestesia *f.* plessesthesia.
plesígrafo *m.* plexigraph.
plesimetría *f.* plessimetry.
plesímetro *m.* plessimeter.
Plesiomonas Plesiomonas.
plesiomonas shigelloides Plesiomonas shigelloides.
plesiomorfo, -fa *adj.* plesiomorphic.
plesor *m.* plessor.
pletismografía *f.* plethysmography.
pletismógrafo *m.* plethysmograph.
pletismógrafo corporal body plethysmograph.
pletismógrafo digital digital plethysmograph.

pletismógrafo a presión pressure plethysmograph.
pletismograma *m.* plethysmogram.
pletismometría *f.* plethysmometry.
plétora *f.* plethora.
  plétora hiperalbuminosa hyperalbuminosis.
  plétora policitémica polycythemia.
pleura *f.* pleura.
pleuracentesis *f.* pleuracentesis.
pleuralgia *f.* pleuralgia.
pleurapófisis *f.* pleurapophysis.
pleurectomía *f.* pleurectomy.
pleuresía *f.* pleurisy.
  pleuresía adhesiva adhesive pleurisy.
  pleuresía aguda acute pleurisy.
  pleuresía costal costal pleurisy.
  pleuresía crónica chronic pleurisy.
  pleuresía diafragmática diaphragmatic pleurisy.
  pleuresía doble double pleurisy.
  pleuresía enquistada encysted pleurisy.
  pleuresía exudativa pleurisy with effusion.
  pleuresía falsa pleurodynia.
  pleuresía fibrinosa fibrinous pleurisy.
  pleurisia hemorrágica hemorrhagic pleurisy.
  pleuresía húmeda wet pleurisy.
  pleuresía icorosa ichorous pleurisy.
  pleuresía interlobular interlobar pleurisy.
  pleuresía latente latent pleurisy.
  pleuresía mediastínica mediastinal pleurisy.
  pleuresía metaneumónica metapneumonic pleurisy.
  pleuresía proliferante proliferating pleurisy.
  pleuresía pulmonar pulmonary pleurisy.
  pleuresía pulsátil pulsating pleurisy.
  pleuresía purulenta purulent pleurisy.
  pleuresía quilosa chylous pleurisy.
  pleuresía saculada sacculated pleurisy.
  pleuresía seca dry pleurisy.
  pleuresía serofibrinosa serofibrinous pleurisy.
  pleuresía serosa serous pleurisy.
  pleuresía tífica typhoid pleurisy.
  pleuresía visceral visceral pleurisy.
pleuritis *f.* pleuritis.
pleuritógeno, -na *adj.* pleuritogenous.
pleurobronquitis *f.* pleurobronchitis.
pleurocele *m.* pleurocele.
pleurocentesis *f.* pleurocentesis.
pleurocentro *m.* pleurocentrum.
pleuroclisis *f.* pleuroclysis.
pleurocolecistitis *f.* pleurocholecystitis.
pleurocutáneo, -a *adj.* pleurocutaneous.
pleurodinia *f.* pleurodynia.
  pleurodinia diafragmática epidémica epidemic pleurodynia.
pleurógeno, -na *adj.* pleurogenous.
pleurografía *f.* pleurography.
pleurohepatitis *f.* pleurohepatitis.
pleurólisis *f.* pleurolysis.
pleurolito *m.* pleurolith.
pleuromelo *m.* pleuromelus.
pleuroneumólisis *f.* pleuropneumonolysis.
pleuroneumonía *f.* pleuropneumonia.
pleuroneumonólisis *f.* pleuropneumonolysis.
pleuroparietopexia *f.* pleuroparietopexy.
pleuropericarditis *f.* pleuropericarditis.
pleuroperineumonía *f.* pleuroneumonia.
pleuroperitoneal *adj.* pleuroperitoneal.
pleuropulmonar *adj.* pleuropulmonary.
pleurorrea *f.* pleurorrhea.
pleuroscopia *f.* pleuroscopy.
pleuroscopio *m.* pleuroscope.
pleurosomo *m.* pleurosomus.
pleurostótonos *m.* pleurothotonos, pleurothotonus.

pleurotifus *m.* pleurotyphoid.
pleurotomía *f.* pleurotomy.
pleurotótonos *m.* pleurothotonos.
pleurovisceral *adj.* pleurovisceral.
plexiforme *adj.* plexiform.
pleximetría *f.* pleximetry.
plexímetro *m.* pleximeter, plexometer.
plexitis *f.* plexitis.
plexo *m.* plexus.
plexómetro *m.* plexometer.
plexor *m.* plexor.
plicación *f.* plication.
plicotomía *f.* plicotomy.
pliegue *m.* fold.
  pliegue coroideo plica choroidea.
  pliegue de Jonnesco Jonnesco's fold.
  pliegue de Juvara Juvara's fold.
  pliegue de Rathke Rathke's fold.
  pliegue de Schultze Schultze's fold.
  pliegue genital genital fold.
plombaje *m.* plombage.
plomizo, -za *adj.* livid.
plumbismo *m.* plumbism.
plumoso, -sa *adj.* plumose.
plúmula *f.* plumula.
pluriglandular *adj.* pluriglandular.
plurigrávida *f.* plurigravida.
plurilocular *adj.* plurilocular.
plurinuclear *adj.* plurinuclear.
plurípara *f.* pluripara.
pluriparidad *f.* pluriparity.
pluripolar *adj.* pluripolar.
pluripotencial *adj.* pluripotential.
pluripotencialidad *f.* pluripotenciality.
pluripotente *adj.* pluripotent.
plutonismo *m.* plutonism.
Pneumovirus Pneumovirus.
podagra *f.* podagra.
podagrismo *m.* podagra.
podalgia *f.* podalgia.
podálico, -ca *adj.* podalic.
podartritis *f.* podarthritis.
podedema *m.* podedema.
podencéfalo *m.* podencephalus.
poder *m.* power.
podiatra *adj.* podiatrist.
podiatría *f.* podiatry.
pododinamómetro *m.* pododynamometer.
pododinia *f.* pododynia.
podograma *m.* podogram.
podología *f.* podology.
podólogo, -ga *m., f.* podologist.
pogoniasis *f.* pogoniasis.
pogonión *m.* pogonion.
poiquiloblasto *m.* poikiloblast.
poiquilocitemia *f.* poikilocythemia.
poiquilocito *m.* poikilocyte.
poiquilocitosis *f.* poikilocytosis.
poiquilodermia *f.* poikiloderma.
poiquiloploide *adj.* poikiloploid.
poiquiloploidía *f.* poikiloploidy.
poiquilósmosis *f.* poikilosmosis.
poiquilosmótico, -ca *adj.* poikilosmotic.
poiquilotermia *f.* poikilothermy.
poiquilotérmico, -ca *adj.* poikilothermic.
poiquilotrombocito *m.* poikilothrombocyte.
polaquidipsia *f.* pollakidipsia.
polaquisuria *f.* pollakisuria.
polaquiuria *f.* pollakiuria.
polar *f.* polar.
polaridad *f.* polarity.
polarímetro *m.* polarimeter.
polariscopio *m.* polariscope.
polaristrobómetro *m.* polaristrobometer.
polarización *f.* polarization.

polarizador, -ra *m. y adj.* polarizer.
polarografía *f.* polarogaphy.
polarograma *m.* polarogram.
polenogénico, -ca *adj.* pollenogenic.
polenógeno, -na *adj.* pollenogenic.
polenosis *f.* pollenosis.
poliadenia *f.* polyadenitis.
poliadenitis *f.* polyadenitis.
poliadenoma *m.* polyadenoma.
poliadenopatía *f.* polyadenopathy.
poliadenosis *f.* polyadenosis.
poliarteritis *f.* polyarteritis.
poliarticular *adj.* polyarticular.
poliartritis *f.* polyarthritis.
  poliartritis crónica vellosa chronic villous polyarthritis, polyarthritis chronica villosa.
  poliartritis deformante polyarthritis destruens.
  poliartritis tuberculosa tuberculous polyarthritis.
  poliartritis vertebral vertebral polyarthritis.
poliatómico, -ca *adj.* polyatomic.
poliauxotrófico, -ca *adj.* polyauxotrophic.
poliavitaminosis *f.* polyavitaminosis.
poliblenia *f.* polyblennia.
policardia *f.* polycardia.
policariocito *m.* polykaryocyte.
policelular *adj.* polycellular.
policéntrico, -ca *adj.* polycentric.
policíclico, -ca *adj.* polycyclic.
policiesis *f.* polycyesis.
policitemia *f.* polycythemia.
  policitemia crónica esplenomegálica splenomegalic polycythemia.
  policitemia espuria spurious polycythemia.
  policitemia de estrés stress polycythemia.
  policitemia mielopática myelopathic polycythemia.
  policitemia relativa relative polycythemia.
  policitemia roja, policitemia rubra polycythemia rubra.
  policitemia secundaria secondary polycythemia.
  policitemia verdadera, policitemia vera polycythemia vera.
policización *f.* pollicization.
policlínica *f.* polyclinic.
policlonía *f.* polyclonia.
policloruria *f.* polychloruria.
policolia *f.* polycholia.
policondritis *f.* polychondritis.
  policondritis atrófica crónica chronic atrophic polychondritis, polychondritis chronica atrophicans.
  policondritis recidivante relapsing polychondritis.
policondropatía *f.* polychondropathia.
policoria *f.* polycoria.
policromasia *f.* polychromasia.
policromático, -ca *adj.* polychromatic.
policromatocito *m.* polychromatocyte.
policromatocitosis *f.* polychromatocytosis.
policromatofilia *f.* polychromatophilia.
policromatófilo, -la *adj.* polychromatophil, polychromatophile.
policromatosis *f.* polychromatosis.
policromemia *f.* polychromemia.
policromo, -ma *adj.* polychromatic.
policromofilia *f.* polychromatophilia.
policrótico, -ca *adj.* polycrotic.
policrotismo *m.* polycrotism.
policroto, -ta *adj.* polycrotic.
polidactilia *f.* polydactylia, polydactyly.
polidactilismo *m.* polydactylism.
polideficiencia *f.* polyavitaminosis.

polidipsia *f.* polydipsia.
polidispersoide *m.* polydispersoid.
polidisplasia *f.* polydysplasia.
 polidisplasia ectodérmica hereditaria hereditary ectodermal polydysplasia.
poliembrionia *f.* polyembryony.
poliencefalitis *f.* poliencephalitis.
poliencefalomielitis *f.* polyencephalomyelitis.
poliendocrino, -na *adj.* polyendocrine.
poliendocrinoma *m.* polyendocrinoma.
poliendocrinopatía *f.* polyendocrinopathy.
poliérgico, -ca *adj.* polyergic.
poliespermia *f.* polyspermy.
polispermia *f.* polyspermy.
 poliespermia fisiológica physiological polyspermy.
 poliespermia patológica pathological polyspermy.
poliestesia *f.* polyesthesia.
poliestésico, -ca *adj.* polyesthetic.
polifagia *f.* polyphagia.
polifalangismo *m.* polyphalangism.
polifármacia *f.* polypharmacy.
polifásico, -ca *adj.* polyphasic.
polifiodonto, -ta *adj.* polyphyodont.
polifrasia *f.* polyphrasia.
poligalactia *f.* polygalactia.
poligalia *f.* polygalactia.
poliganglionar *adj.* polyganglionic.
poligénico, -ca *adj.* polygenic.
polígeno *m.* polygene.
poliginia *f.* polygyny.
poligiria *f.* polygyria.
poliglandular *f.* polyglandular.
poliglobulia *f.* polycythemia.
polignato *m.* polygnathus.
polígono *m.* polygon.
polígrafo *m.* polygraph.
polihíbrido, -da *adj.* polyhybrid.
polihidramnios *m.* polyhydramnios.
polihidrosis *f.* polyhidrosis.
polihidruria *f.* polyhydruria.
polihipermenorrea *f.* polyhypermenorrhea.
polihipomenorrea *f.* polyhypomenorrhea.
polihósido *m.* polysaccharide.
poliinfección *f.* polyinfection.
poliléptico, -ca *adj.* polyleptic.
polilogia *f.* polylogia.
polimastia *f.* polymastia.
polimazia *f.* polymazia.
polimelia *f.* polymelia.
polimería *f.* polymeria.
polimerismo *m.* polymeria.
polimerización *f.* polymerization.
polímero *m.* polymer.
polimetacarpia *f.* polymetacarpia.
polimetatarsia *f.* polymetatarsia.
polimicrobiano, -na *adj.* polymicrobial.
polimicrogiria *f.* polymicrogyria.
polimicrolipomatosis *f.* polymicrolipomatosis.
polimioclonía *f.* polymyoclonus.
polimiositis *f.* polymyositis.
 polimiositis triquinosa trichinous polymyositis.
polimórfico, -ca *adj.* polymorphic.
polimorfismo *m.* polymorphism.
polimorfo, -fa *m. y adj.* polymorphic, polymorphous.
polimorfocelular *adj.* polymorphocellular.
polimorfocito *m.* polymorphocyte.
polimorfonuclear *adj.* polymorphonuclear.
polineural *adj.* polyneural.
polineuralgia *f.* polyneuralgia.

polinéurico, -ca *adj.* polyneural.
polineuritis *f.* polyneuritis.
 polineuritis anémica anemic polyneuritis.
 polineuritis endémica endemic polyneuritis.
 polineuritis febril aguda acute febrile polyneuritis.
 polineuritis idiopática aguda acute idiopathic polyneuritis.
 polineuritis infecciosa, polineuritis infecciosa aguda infectious polyneuritis, acute infective polyneuritis.
 polineuritis posinfecciosa, polineuritis posinfecciosa aguda postinfectious polyneuritis, acute postinfectious polyneuritis.
polineurorradiculitis *f.* polyneuroradiculitis.
polinosis *f.* pollinosis.
polinucleado, -da *adj.* polynucleate, polynucleated.
polinuclear *adj.* polynuclear.
polinucleolar *adj.* polynucleolar.
polinucleosis *f.* polynucleosis.
polinucleótido *m.* polynucleotide.
polio *f.* polio.
poliocida *adj.* poliocidal.
polioclástico, -ca *adj.* polioclastic.
poliodistrofia *f.* poliodystrophy.
poliodoncia *f.* polyodontia.
polioencefalitis *f.* polioencephalitis.
polioencefalomielitis *f.* polioencephalomyelitis, polyencephalomyelitis.
polioencefalopatía *f.* polioencephalopathy.
poliomielencefalitis *f.* poliomyelencephalitis.
poliomielitis *f.* poliomyelitis.
 poliomielitis anterior aguda acute anterior poliomyelitis.
 poliomielitis anterior crónica chronic anterior poliomyelitis.
 poliomielitis ascendente ascending poliomyelitis.
 poliomielitis bulbar bulbar poliomyelitis.
 poliomielitis endémica endemic poliomyelitis.
 poliomielitis epidémica epidemic poliomyelitis.
 poliomielitis espinal paralítica spinal paralytic poliomyelitis.
 poliomielitis lateral aguda acute lateral poliomyelitis.
 poliomielitis posamigdalectomía post-tonsillectomy poliomyelitis.
 poliomielitis posinoculación postinoculation poliomyelitis.
 poliomielitis posvacunal postvaccinal poliomyelitis.
poliomieloencefalitis *f.* poliomyeloencephalitis.
poliomielopatía *f.* poliomyelopathy.
polioneurómera *f.* polioneuromere.
polioniquia *f.* polyonychia.
poliopía *f.* polyopia.
 poliopía monocular polyopia monophthalmica.
poliopsia *f.* polyopsia.
poliorquidismo *m.* polyorchidism.
poliórquido *m.* polyorchid.
poliorquismo *m.* polyorchism.
poliorromeningitis *f.* polyserositis.
poliosis *f.* poliosis.
poliotia *f.* polyotia.
poliotriquia *f.* poliosis.
poliovirus *m.* poliovirus.
poliovular *adj.* polyovular.
poliovulatorio, -ria *adj.* polyovulatory.
polipapiloma *m.* polypapilloma.
poliparasitismo *m.* polyparasitism.

polipatía *f.* polypathia.
polipectomía *f.* polypectomy.
polipeptidemia *f.* polypeptidemia.
polipéptido *m.* polypeptide.
polipeptidorraquia *f.* polypeptidorrhachia.
polipiforme *adj.* polypiform.
poliplástico, -ca *adj.* polyplastic.
poliplasmia *f.* polyplasmia.
poliplejia *f.* polyplegia.
poliploide *adj.* polyploid.
poliploidía *f.* polyploidy.
polipnea *f.* polypnea.
pólipo *m.* polyp.
 pólipo adenomatoso adenomatous polyp.
 pólipo bronquial bronchial polyp.
 pólipo cardiaco cardiac polyp.
 pólipo carnoso fleshy polyp.
 pólipo celular cellular polyp.
 pólipo coanal choanal polyp.
 pólipo fibrinoso fibrinous polyp.
 pólipo fibroso fibrous polyp.
 pólipo gingival gingival polyp.
 pólipo hidatídico hydatid polyp.
 pólipo hiperplásico hyperplastic polyp.
 pólipo de Hopmann Hopmann's polyp.
 pólipo inflamatorio inflammatory polyp.
 pólipo juvenil juvenile polyp.
 pólipo laríngeo laryngeal polyp.
 pólipo linfoide lymphoid polyp.
 pólipo lipomatoso lipomatous polyp.
 pólipo metaplásico metaplastic polyp.
 pólipo miomatoso myomatous polyp.
 pólipo mucoso mucous polyp.
 pólipo nasal nasal polyp.
 pólipo óseo osseous polyp.
 pólipo placentario placental polyp.
 pólipo pulpar pulp polyp.
 pólipo quístico cystic polyp.
 pólipo de retención retention polyp.
 pólipo sangrante bleeding polyp.
 pólipo vascular vascular polyp.
polipodia *f.* polypodia.
polipoide *adj.* polypoid.
poliporoso, -sa *adj.* polyporous.
poliposia *f.* polyposia.
poliposis *f.* polyposis.
 poliposis gástrica gastric polyposis.
 poliposis intestinal intestinal polyposis.
polipótomo *m.* polypotome.
polipotribo *m.* polypotrite.
polipotrito *m.* polypotrite.
poliqueiria *f.* polycheiria, polychiria.
poliquilia *f.* polychylia.
poliquiria *f.* polychiria.
poliquístico, -ca *adj.* polycystic.
polirradiculitis *f.* polyradiculitis.
polirradiculoneuritis *f.* polyradiculoneuritis.
polirrea *f.* polyrrhea.
polirribosoma *m.* polyribosome.
polisacárido *m.* polysaccharide.
polisarcia *f.* polysarcia.
poliscelia *f.* polyscelia.
poliscelo *m.* polyscelus.
poliscopio *m.* polyscope.
poliserositis *f.* polyserositis.
polisialia *f.* polysialia.
polisoma *m.* polysome.
polisomía *f.* polysomy.
polisómico, -ca *adj.* polysomic.
polisomo *m.* polysome.
polisquelia *f.* polyscelia.
polistiquia *f.* polystichia.
polisuspensoide *m.* polysuspensoid.
politelia *f.* polythelia.
politenia *f.* polyteny.

politeno *m.* polythene.
politricosis *f.* polytrichosis.
politriquia *f.* polytrichia.
politrofia *f.* polytrophy.
politrópico, -ca *adj.* polytropic.
politzeración *f.* politzerization.
  politzeración negativa negative politzerization.
poliuria *f.* polyuria.
polivalente *adj.* polyvalent.
polo *m.* pole.
  polo animal animal pole.
  polo germinativo germinal pole.
  polo negativo negative pole.
  polo positivo positive pole.
  polo vegetativo vegetative pole.
polocito *m.* polocyte.
poloplasto *f.* polyplastic.
polución *f.* pollution.
pomada *f.* ointment.
ponderable *adj.* ponderable.
ponderal *adj.* ponderal.
ponfo *m.* pomphus.
ponfólix *m.* pompholyx.
ponógrafo *m.* ponograph.
ponticular *adj.* ponticular.
pontículo *m.* ponticulus.
pontino, -na *adj.* pontile, pontine.
pontocerebeloso, -sa *adj.* pontocerebellar.
pool *m.* pool.
poples *m.* poples.
poplíteo, -a *adj.* popliteal.
poradenia *f.* poradenitis.
poradenitis *f.* poradenitis.
poradenolinfitis *f.* poradenolymphitis.
porción *f.* portion.
porencefalia *f.* porencephaly.
porfiria *f.* porphyria.
  porfiria cutánea tardía, porfiria cutanea tarda porphyria cutanea tarda (PCT).
  porfiria variegata variegata porphyria.
porfirinemia *f.* porphyrinemia.
porfirinuria *f.* porphyrinuria.
porfirización *f.* porphyrization.
porfiruria *f.* porphyruria.
porfobilinógeno *m.* porphobilinogen.
poriomanía *f.* poriomania.
porión *m.* porion.
poro *m.* pore.
  poro nuclear nuclear pore.
porocefaliasis *f.* porocephaliasis.
porocefalosis *f.* porocephaliasis.
porocele *m.* porocele.
Porocephalus Porocephalus.
poroencefalia *f.* porencephalia.
poroma *m.* poroma.
poroqueratosis *f.* porokeratosis.
porosis *f.* porosis.
  porosis cerebral cerebral porosis.
poroso, -sa *adj.* porous.
porótico, -ca *adj.* porotic.
porotomía *f.* porotomy.
pórrigo *m.* porrigo.
  pórrigo decalvante porrigo decalvans.
  pórrigo favoso porrigo favosa.
  pórrigo larval porrigo larvalis.
porropsia *f.* porropsia.
porta *m.* porta.
portaagujas *m.* needle-carrier, needle-driver, needle-holder.
portaamalgama *f.* amalgam carrier.
portador, - ra *m., f.* carrier.
  portador de amalgama amalgam carrier.
  portador de gametocitos gametocyte carrier.
  portador de hemofilia hemophilia carrier.

portaligaduras *m.* portligature.
portanudos *m.* knot-carrier.
portaobjetos *m.* slide.
portografía *f.* portography.
  portografía esplénica splenic portography.
posaxial *adj.* postaxial.
posbraquial *adj.* postbrachial.
posbucal *adj.* postbuccal.
posbulbar *adj.* postbulbar.
poscecal *adj.* postcecal.
poscentral *adj.* postcentral.
poscibal *adj.* postcibal.
poscisterna *f.* postcisterna.
posclavicular *adj.* postclavicular.
posclimatérico, -ca *adj.* postclimacteric.
poscondíleo, -a *adj.* postcondylar.
posconubial *adj.* postconnubial.
posconvulsivo, -va *adj.* postconvulsive.
poscordial *adj.* postcordial.
poscubital *adj.* postcubital.
posdiastólico, -ca *adj.* postdiastolic.
posdicrótico, -ca *adj.* postdicrotic.
posdiftérico, -ca *adj.* postdiphtheritic.
posdigestivo, -va *adj.* postdigestive.
posembrionario, -ria *adj.* postembryonic.
posencefálico, -ca *adj.* postencephalic.
posepiléptico, -ca *adj.* postepileptic.
posesfenoides *m.* postsphenoid.
posesfígmico, -ca *adj.* postsphygmic.
posesofágico, -ca *adj.* postesophageal.
posesplénico, -ca *adj.* postsplenic.
posetmoideo, -a *adj.* postethmoid.
posfaríngeo, -a *adj.* postpharyngeal.
posfebril *adj.* postfebrile.
posganglionar *adj.* postganglionic.
posglenoideo, -a *adj.* postglenoid.
posgripal *adj.* postinfluenzal.
poshemipléjico, -ca *adj.* posthemiplegic.
poshemorragia *f.* posthemorrhage.
poshemorrágico, -ca *adj.* posthemorrhagic.
poshepático, -ca *adj.* posthepatic.
poshioideo, -a *adj.* posthyoid.
poshipnótico, -ca *adj.* posthypnotic.
poshipófisis *f.* posthypophysis.
poshipoglucémico, -ca *adj.* posthypoglycemic.
poshipóxico, -ca *adj.* posthypoxic.
posición *f.* position.
  posición de Albert Albert's position.
  posición alemana Walcher's position.
  posición anatómica anatomical position.
  posición de Bonner Bonner's position.
  posición de Bozeman Bozeman's position.
  posición de Casselberry Casselberry's position.
  posición de decúbito dorsal dorsal recumbent position.
  posición de decúbito lateral lateral recumbent position.
  posición de decúbito prono prone position.
  posición de decúbito supino dorsal recumbent position.
  posición de Depage Depage's position.
  posición depresiva depressive position.
  posición de descerebración descerebrate position.
  posición dorsal dorsal position.
  posición dorsosacra dorsosacral position.
  posición de Duncan Duncan's position.
  posición de Edebohls Edebohls' position.
  posición de Elliot Elliot's position.
  posición escapular anterior, posición escapuloanterior scapula anterior position.
  posición escapular posterior, posición escapuloposterior scapula posterior position.

  posición esquizoparanoide paranoid-schizoid position.
  posición excéntrica eccentric position.
  posición fetal fetal position.
  posición de Fowler Fowler's position.
  posición frontal anterior, posición frontoanterior frontoanterior position.
  posición frontal posterior, posición frontoposterior frontoposterior position.
  posición frontal transversa, posición frontotransversa frontotransverse position.
  posición funcional de la mano functional position of the hand.
  posición genucubital genucubital position.
  posición genupectoral genupectoral position.
  posición de Jones Jones' position.
  posición de Kraske Kraske position.
  posición lateroabdominal lateral recumbent position.
  posición de litotomía lithotomy position.
  posición mentoniana anterior, posición mentoanterior mentum anterior position.
  posición mentoniana posterior, posición mentoposterior mentum posterior position.
  posición mentoniana transversa mentum transverse position.
  posición en navaja de bolsillo jackknife position.
  posición de Noble Noble's position.
  posición obstétrica obstetric position.
  posición occipital anterior, posición occipitoanterior occipitoanterior position.
  posición occipital posterior, posición occipitoposterior occipitoposterior position.
  posición occipital transversa, posición occipitotransversa occipitotransverse position.
  posición oclusal occlusal position.
  posición ortopneica orthopneic position.
  posición prona prone position.
  posición de referencia landmark position.
  posición rodilla-codo knee-elbow position.
  posición rodilla-tórax knee-chest.
  posición de Rose Rose's position.
  posición sacra anterior, posición sacroanterior sacroanterior position.
  posición sacra posterior, posición sacroposterior sacroposterior position.
  posición sacra transversa, posición sacrotransversa sacrotranverse position.
  posición del salto de rana leapfrog position.
  posición de Simon Simon's position.
  posición de Sims Sims' position.
  posición supina supine position.
  posición de Trendelenburg Trendelenburg's position.
  posición de trípode tripod position.
  posición de Valentine Valentine's position.
  posición de Walcher Walcher's position.
positivo, -va *adj.* positive.
positrón *m.* positron.
posmaduro, -ra *adj.* postmature.
posmalárico, -ca *adj.* postmalarial.
posmastoideo, -a *adj.* postmastoid.
posmediastínico, -ca *adj.* postmediastinal.
posmeiótico, -ca *adj.* postmeiotic.
posmenopáusico, -ca *adj.* postmenopausal.
posmesentérico, -ca *adj.* postmesenteric.
posnasal *adj.* postnasal.
posnatal *adj.* postnatal.
posnecrótico, -ca *adj.* postnecrotic.
posneumónico, -ca *adj.* postpneumonic.
posneurítico, -ca *adj.* postneuritic.
posología *f.* posology.
posológico, -ca *adj.* posologic.

posoperatorio, -ria *adj.* postoperative.
posoral *adj.* postbuccal.
posorbitario, -ria *adj.* postorbital.
pospalatino, -na *adj.* postpalatine.
pospalúdico, -ca *adj.* postmalarial.
posparalítico, -ca *adj.* postparalytic.
posparto *m.* post partum.
pospicnótico, -ca *adj.* postpyknotic.
posponente *adj.* postponent.
posprandial *adj.* postprandial.
pospúbero, -ra *adj.* postpubescent.
pospubescente *adj.* postpubescent.
posrolándico, -ca *adj.* postrolandic.
posterior, -ra *adj.* posterior.
posteroanterior *adj.* posteroanterior.
posteroinferior *adj.* posteroinferior.
posterointerno, -na *adj.* posterointernal.
posterolateral *adj.* posterolateral.
posteromediano, -na *adj.* posteromedian.
posteroparietal *adj.* posteroparietal.
posterosuperior, -ra *adj.* posterosuperior.
postérula *f.* posterula.
postetomía *f.* posthetomy.
postifoídico, -ca *adj.* post-typhoid.
postioplastia *f.* posthioplasty.
postitis *f.* posthitis.
post mortem post mortem.
post nares post nares.
postolito *m.* postholith.
post partum post partum.
postración *f.* prostration.
postraumático, -ca *adj.* post-traumatic.
postsilviano, -na *adj.* postsylvian.
postulado *m.* postulate.
 postulado de Koch Koch's postulate.
póstumo, -ma *adj.* posthumous.
postura *f.* posture.
postural *adj.* postural.
posuterino, -na *adj.* postuterine.
posvacunal *adj.* postvaccinal.
potable *adj.* potable.
potasemia *f.* potassemia.
potasio *m.* potassium.
potencia *f.* potency.
potenciación *f.* potentiation.
potencial *m. y adj.* potential.
potencialización *f.* potentialization.
potomanía *f.* potomania.
Poxviridae Poxviridae.
práctica *f.* practice.
prandial *adj.* prandial.
praxis *f.* praxis.
preagónico, -ca *adj.* preagonal.
preanal *adj.* preanal.
preanestesia *f.* preanesthesia.
preaórtico, -ca *adj.* preaortic.
preatáxico, -ca *adj.* preataxic.
preauricular *adj.* preauricular.
preaxial *adj.* preaxial.
preaxil *adj.* preaxial.
prebacilar *adj.* prebacillary.
prebase *f.* prebase.
precancerosis *f.* precancerosis.
precanceroso, -sa *adj.* precancerous.
precapilar *m.* precapillary.
precarcinomatoso, -sa *adj.* precarcinomatous.
precardíaco, -ca *adj.* precardiac.
precartílago *m.* precartilage.
precava *f.* precava.
precentral *adj.* precentral.
precigótico, -ca *adj.* prezygotic.
precimógeno *m.* prezymogen.
precipitable *adj.* precipitable.
precipitación *f.* precipitation.

precipitado *m. y adj.* precipitate.
precipitante *adj.* precipitant.
precipitinógeno *m.* precipitinogen.
precirrosis *f.* precirrhosis.
precisión *f.* accuracy.
preclavicular *adj.* preclavicular.
preclínico, -ca *adj.* preclinical.
precocidad *f.* precocity.
precoma *m.* precoma.
preconsciente *m.* preconscious.
precordal *m. y adj.* prechordal.
precordial *adj.* precordial.
precordialgia *f.* precordialgia.
precordio *m.* precordia.
precostal *adj.* precostal.
precoz *adj.* precocious.
precrítico, -ca *adj.* precritical.
precursor, -ra *adj.* precursor.
predentina *f.* predentin.
prediabetes *f.* prediabetes.
prediástole *f.* prediastole.
predigestión *f.* predigestion.
predisposición *f.* predisposition.
prediverticular *adj.* prediverticular.
preeclampsia *f.* pre-eclampsia.
preepiglótico, -ca *adj.* pre-epiglottic.
preeruptivo, -va *adj.* pre-eruptive.
preescapular *adj.* prescapular.
preesfenoides *m.* presphenoid.
preflagelado, -da *adj.* preflagellate.
preformación *f.* preformation.
prefrontal *adj.* prefrontal.
preganglionar *adj.* preganglionic.
pregenital *adj.* pregenital.
pregonio *m.* pregonium.
pregonium *m.* pregonium.
pregravídico, -ca *adj.* pregravidic.
prehallux *m.* prehallux.
prehemipléjico, -ca *adj.* prehemiplegic.
prehepático *m.* prehepaticus.
prehipófisis *f.* prehypophysis.
preinmunización *f.* preimmunization.
prelacrimal *adj.* prelacrimal.
prelácteo, -a *adj.* prelacteal.
prelagrimal *adj.* prelacrimal.
prelaríngeo, -a *adj.* prelaryngeal.
preleucemia *f.* preleukemia.
prelímbico, -ca *adj.* prelymbic.
premaligno, -na *adj.* premalignant.
premaníaco, -ca, premaniaco, -ca *adj.* premaniacal.
prematuro, -ra *m. y adj.* premature.
premaxilar *adj.* premaxillary.
premedicación *f.* premedication.
premenstrual *adj.* premenstrual.
premieloblasto *m.* premyeloblast.
premielocito *m.* premyelocyte.
premórbido, -da *adj.* premorbid.
premolar *m. y adj.* premolar.
premortal *adj.* premortal.
premunición *f.* premunition.
premunitivo, -va *adj.* premunitive.
prenarcosis *f.* prenarcosis.
prenasal *adj.* prenasal.
prenatal *adj.* prenatal.
preneoplásico, -ca *adj.* preneoplastic.
prensa *f.* torcula.
prensil *adj.* prehensile.
prensión *f.* prehension.
preoperatorio, -ria *adj.* preoperative.
preóptico, -ca *adj.* preoptic.
preoral *adj.* preoral.
prepalatino, -na *adj.* prepalatal.
preparación *f.* preparation.
prepatelar *adj.* prepatellar.

preperforativo, -va *adj.* preperforative.
preperitoneal *adj.* preperitoneal.
preplacentario, -ria *adj.* preplacental.
preponderancia *f.* preponderance.
prepsicosis *f.* prepsychosis.
prepubescente *adj.* prepubescent.
prepucial *adj.* prepucial.
prepucio *m.* preputium.
 prepucio del clítoris preputium clitoridis.
prepuciotomía *f.* preputiotomy.
prerrectal *adj.* prerectal.
prerrenal *adj.* prerenal.
prerrotuliano, -na *adj.* prepatellar.
presbiacusia *f.* presbyacusia.
presbiacusis *f.* presbyacusia.
presbiatría *f.* presbyatrics.
presbicia *f.* presbyopia.
presbiofrenia *f.* presbyophrenia.
presbíope *m., f.* presbyope.
presbiopía *f.* presbyopia.
présbita *f.* presbyopic.
présbite *m.* presbyopic.
presbitismo *m.* presbyopia.
prescripción *f.* prescription.
presenil *adj.* presenile.
presenilidad *f.* presenility.
presentación *f.* presentation.
 presentación anormal malpresentation.
 presentación de cara face presentation.
 presentación cefálica cephalic presentation.
 presentación compuesta compound presentation.
 presentación doble de nalgas double breech presentation.
 presentación facial face presentation.
 presentación de frente brow presentation.
 presentación funicular funis presentation.
 presentación de hombros shoulder presentation.
 presentación mentoanterior anterior presentation.
 presentación mentoposterior posterior presentation.
 presentación de nalgas breech presentation.
 presentación de nalgas completa breech complete presentation.
 presentación oblicua oblique presentation.
 presentación pelviana, presentación pélvica pelvic presentation.
 presentación de la placenta placental presentation.
 presentación podálica footing presentation.
 presentación de rodillas knee presentation.
 presentación transversa transverse presentation.
 presentación de tronco trunk presentation.
 presentación de vértice vertex presentation.
preservativo *m.* condom.
presilviano, -na *adj.* presylvian.
presináptico *m.* presynaptic.
presión *f.* pressure.
 presión de apertura opening pressure.
 presión de apertura alveolar alveolar distending pressure.
 presión arterial blood pressure.
 presión arterial diastólica diastolic blood pressure.
 presión atmosférica atmospheric pressure.
 presión capilar capillary pressure.
 presión cefalorraquídea cerebrospinal pressure.
 presión coloidosmótica colloid osmotic pressure.
 presión del cricoides cricoid pressure.
 presión crítica critical pressure.

presión de enclavamiento wedge pressure.
presión de enclavamiento de la arteria pulmonar pulmonary artery wedge pressure.
presión de enclavamiento pulmonar (PEP) pulmonary wedge pressure (PWP).
presión espiratoria final cero zero-end expiratory pressure (ZEEP).
presión espiratoria final negativa (PEFN) negative end-expiratory pressure (NEEP).
presión espiratoria final positiva (PEFP) positive end expiratory pressure (PEEP).
presión estática static pressure.
presión de fondo back pressure.
presión hidrostática hydrostatic pressure.
presión inspiratoria máxima (PIM) maximum inspiratory pressure (MIP).
presión intraabdominal intra-abdominal pressure.
presión intracraneal intracranial pressure.
presión intraocular intraocular pressure.
presión intraventricular intraventricular pressure.
presión de llenado filling pressure.
presión de llenado diastólico diastolic filling pressure.
presión negativa negative pressure.
presión oncótica oncotic pressure.
presión osmótica osmotic pressure.
presión parcial partial pressure.
presión parcial de anhídrido carbónico partial pressure of carbon dioxide.
presión de perfusión cerebral (PPC) cerebral perfusion pressure (CPP).
presión pleural pleural pressure.
presión positive positive pressure.
presión positiva continua de las vías respiratorias (PPCVR) continuous positive airway pressure (CPAP).
presión pulmonar pulmonary pressure.
presión del pulso pulse pressure.
presión retrógrada back pressure.
presión sistólica systolic pressure.
presión de solución solution pressure.
presión torácica negativa continua continuous negative chest wall pressure.
presión transpulmonar transpulmonary pressure.
presión venosa venous pressure.
presión venosa central (PVC) central venous pressure (CVP).
presión venosa yugular (PVY) jugular venous pressure (JVP).
presístole *f.* presystole.
presor, -ra *adj.* pressor.
presorreceptor, -ra *adj.* pressoreceptor.
presupurativo, -va *adj.* presuppurative.
pretarsal *adj.* pretarsal.
pretarsiano, -na *adj.* pretarsal.
pretibial *adj.* pretibial.
pretimpánico, -ca *adj.* pretympanic.
pretiroideo, -a *adj.* prethyroid, prethyroideal, prethyroidean.
pretremático, -ca *adj.* pretrematic.
pretuberculosis *f.* pretuberculosis.
preuretritis *f.* preurethritis.
prevalencia *f.* prevalence.
prevención *f.* prevention.
prevención primaria primary prevention.
prevención secundaria secondary prevention.
prevención terciaria tertiary prevention.
preventivo, -va *adj.* preventive.
prevertebral *adj.* prevertebral.
prevesical *adj.* prevesical.
previo, -via *adj.* previous.
previtamina *f.* previtamin.

priapismo *m.* priapism.
priapitis *f.* priapitis.
priapos *m.* priapus.
primario, -ria *adj.* primary.
primate *m.* primate.
primigrávida *f.* primigravida.
primípara *f.* primipara.
primiparidad *f.* primiparity.
primitivo, -va *adj.* primitive.
primordial *adj.* primordial.
primordio *m.* primordium.
primordium *m.* primordium.
principio *m.* principle.
principio de abstinencia abstinence principle.
principio activo active principle.
principio antianémico antianemia principle.
principio de cierre closure principle.
principio de constancia principle of constancy.
principio de conversión de protrombina prothrombin converting principle.
principio Doppler Doppler principle.
principio epigenético epigenetic principle.
principio de equilibrio de Hardy-Weinberg Hardy-Weinberg equilibrium principle.
principio de expectancia preparedness principle.
principio de Fick Fick principle.
principio inmediato proximate principle.
principio de inclusión inclusiveness principle.
principio de Le Chatelier Le Chatelier's principle.
principio de nirvana nirvana principle.
principio orgánico organic principle.
principio de Pascal Pascal's principle.
principio de placer pleasure principle.
principio de preparación preparedness principle.
principio de realidad reality principle.
prión *m.* prion.
prisma *m.* prism.
prismoesfera *f.* prismosphere.
prismoide *adj.* prismoid.
prismoptómetro *m.* prisoptometer.
prismosfera *f.* prismosphere.
prisoptómetro *m.* prisoptometer.
privación *f.* deprivation.
proacrosómico, -ca *adj.* proacrosomal.
proal *adj.* proal.
probacteriófago *m.* probacteriophage.
probacteriófago defectuoso defective probacteriophage.
probando *m.* proband.
probeta *f.* test tube.
probiótico, -ca *adj.* probiotic.
probóscide *f.* proboscis.
procariota *m.* prokaryote.
procariótico, -ca *adj.* prokaryotic.
procedimiento *m.* procedure.
procedimiento de Blalock-Taussing Blalock-Taussing procedure.
procedimiento de Commando Commando procedure.
procedimiento del estante shelf procedure.
procedimiento de Ewart Ewart's procedure.
procedimiento de Fontan Fontan procedure.
procedimiento de Girdlestone Girdlestone procedure.
procedimiento invasivo invasive procedure.
procedimiento de mustard mustard procedure.
procedimiento de Nicola Nicola procedure.
procedimiento de Nicholas Nicholas procedure.
procedimiento de Puestow Puestow's procedure.

procedimiento de Puttio-Platt Puttio-Platt procedure.
procedimiento de Rashkind Rashkind procedure.
procedimiento telescópico endorrectal endorrectal pull-through procedure.
procedimiento de Torkildsen Torkildsen's procedure.
procedimiento en V-Y V-Y procedure.
procedimiento W W-plastia procedure.
procedimiento z Z-plastia procedure.
procefálico, -ca *adj.* procephalic.
procesamiento de la información *f.* information processing.
proceso *m.* process.
procidencia *f.* procidentia.
procidencia del útero procidentia uteri.
procigosis *f.* prozygosis.
prozigosis *f.* prozygosis.
procolágeno *m.* procollagen.
procondral *adj.* prochondral.
procordal *adj.* prochordal.
procorion *m.* prochorion.
procreación *f.* procreation.
procrear *m.* procreate.
proctagra *f.* proctagra.
proctalgia *f.* proctalgia.
proctalgia fugaz proctalgia fugax.
proctatresia *f.* proctatresia.
proctectasia *f.* proctectasia.
proctectomía *f.* proctectomy.
procteurínter *m.* procteurynter.
proctitis *f.* proctitis.
proctitis epidémica gangrenosa, proctitis gangrenosa epidémica epidemic gangrenous proctitis.
proctitis idiopática idiopathic proctitis.
proctitis por radiación radiation proctitis.
proctitis ulcerosa crónica chronic ulcerative proctitis.
proctocele *m.* proctocele.
proctocistocele *m.* proctocystocele.
proctocistoplastia *f.* proctocystoplasty.
proctocistotomía *f.* proctocystotomy.
proctoclisis *f.* proctoclysis.
proctococcipexia *f.* proctococcypexy.
proctocolectomía *f.* proctocolectomy.
proctocolitis *f.* proctocolitis.
proctocolonoscopia *f.* proctocolonoscopy.
proctocolpoplastia *f.* proctocolpoplasty.
proctocoxipexia *f.* proctococcypexy.
proctodeico, -ca *adj.* proctodeal.
proctodeo *m.* proctodeum.
proctodinia *f.* proctodynia.
proctoelitroplastia *f.* proctoelytroplasty.
proctoespasmo *m.* proctospasm.
proctoestenosis *f.* proctostenosis.
proctogénico, -ca *adj.* proctogenic.
proctógeno, -na *adj.* proctogenic.
proctología *f.* proctology.
proctológico, -ca *adj.* proctologic.
proctólogo, -ga *m., f.* proctologist.
proctoparálisis *f.* proctoparalysis.
proctoperineoplastia *f.* proctoperineoplasty.
proctoperineorrafia *f.* proctoperineorrhaphy.
proctopexia *f.* proctopexy.
proctoplastia *f.* proctoplasty.
proctoplejía *f.* proctoplegia.
proctoptosia *f.* proctoptosia, proctoptosis.
proctoptosis *f.* proctoptosis.
proctorrafia *f.* proctorrhaphy.
proctorragia *f.* protorrhagia.
proctorrea *f.* proctorrhea.
proctoscopia *f.* proctoscopy.
proctoscopio *m.* proctoscope.

proctoscopio de Tuttle Tuttle's proctoscope.
proctosigmoidectomía *f.* proctosigmoidectomy.
proctosigmoiditis *f.* proctosigmoiditis.
proctosigmoidopexia *f.* proctosigmoidopexy.
proctosigmoidoscopia *f.* proctosigmoidoscopy.
proctosigmoidoscopio *m.* proctosigmoidoscope.
proctospasmo *m.* proctospasm.
proctostasis *f.* proctostasis.
proctóstato *m.* proctostat.
proctostenosis *f.* proctostenosis.
proctostomía *f.* proctostomy.
proctotomía *f.* proctotomy.
proctótomo *m.* proctotome.
proctotresia *f.* proctotresia.
proctovalvotomía *f.* proctovalvotomy.
procumbente *adj.* procumbent.
procursivo, -va *adj.* procursive.
procurvación *f.* procurvation.
prodrómico, -ca *adj.* prodromic, prodomous.
pródromo *m.* prodrome.
productivo, -va *adj.* productive.
producto *m.* product.
proencéfalo *m.* proencephalon.
proenzima *f.* proenzyme.
proeritroblasto *m.* proerythroblast.
proescólex *m.* proscolex.
proespermia *f.* prospermia.
proestro *m.* proestrum.
proestrógeno *m.* proestrogen.
proestrum proestrum.
profase *f.* prophase.
profiláctico, -ca *adj.* prophylactic.
profilaxis *f.* prophylaxis.
  profilaxis activa active prophylaxis.
  profilaxis bucal oral prophylaxis.
  profilaxis dental dental prophylaxis.
  profilaxis pasiva passive prophylaxis.
  profilaxis química chemical prophylaxis.
  profilaxis sérica serum prophylaxis.
profundidad *f.* depth.
  profundidad anestésica anesthetic depth.
profundo, -da *adj.* deep.
progenie *f.* progeny.
progenital *adj.* progenitalis.
progenitor, -ra *m., f.* progenitor.
progeria *f.* progeria.
progestacional *adj.* progestational.
progestágeno *m.* progestogen.
progesterona *f.* progesterone.
progestógeno *m.* progestogen.
proglosis *f.* proglossis.
proglotis *f.* proglottis.
proglótide *f.* proglottid.
prognatismo *m.* prognathism.
prognato, -ta *adj.* prognathic.
prognatómetro *m.* prognathometer.
progonoma *m.* progonoma.
  progonoma mandibular progonoma of the jaw.
progravido, -da *adj.* progravid.
progresión *f.* progression.
progresivo, -va *adj.* progressive.
progreso *m.* progress.
prohormona *f.* prohormone.
proinsulina *f.* proinsulin.
proiosístole *f.* proiosystole.
proiosistolia *f.* proiosystolia.
prolabial *adj.* prolabial.
prolabio *m.* prolabium.
prolactina *f.* prolactin.
prolapso *m.* prolapse.
  prolapso del ano anal prolapse, prolapse of the anus.

prolapso del cordón prolapse of the cord.
prolapso del cordón umbilical prolapse of the umbilical cord.
prolapso franco frank prolapse.
prolapso del iris prolapse of the iris.
prolapso rectal, prolapso del recto rectal prolapse, prolapse of the rectum.
prolapso del útero prolapse of the uterus.
prolapso de la válvula mitral mitral valve prolapse.
prolepsis *f.* prolepsis.
proléptico, -ca *adj.* proleptic.
proliferación *f.* proliferation.
  proliferación gingival gingival proliferation.
proliferativo, -va *adj.* proliferative.
prolífero, -ra *adj.* proliferous.
prolífico, -ca *adj.* prolific.
prolígero, -ra *adj.* proligerous.
prolongación *f.* prolongation.
promegaloblasto *m.* promegaloblast.
prometafase *f.* prometaphase.
promielocito *m.* promyelocyte.
prominencia *f.* prominence, prominentia.
prominente *adj.* prominent.
promonocito *m.* promonocyte.
promontorio *m.* promontory.
pronación *f.* pronation.
  pronación del antebrazo pronation of the forearm.
  pronación del pie pronation of the foot.
pronador, -ra *adj.* pronator.
pronato *m.* pronatis.
pronefros *m.* pronephros.
prono *m.* prone.
pronógrado, -da *adj.* pronograde.
pronómetro *m.* pronometer.
pronóstico *m.* prognosis.
pronúcleo *m.* pronucleus.
proótico, -ca *adj.* pro-otic.
propagación *f.* propagation.
propagar *v.* propagate.
properitoneal *adj.* properitoneal.
propiocepción *f.* propioception.
propioceptor, -ra *adj.* proprioceptor.
propioespinal *adj.* propiospinal.
propionacidemia *f.* propionacidemia.
proplasmocito *m.* proplasmacyte.
proporción *f.* ratio.
propósito *m.* propositus.
proptosis *f.* proptosis.
proptómetro *m.* exophthalmometer.
proptosis *f.* proptosis.
propulsión *f.* propulsion.
proqueilia *f.* procheilia, prochilia.
proquilia *f.* procheilia, prochilia.
prorsad prorsad.
prosencéfalo *m.* prosencephalon.
prosodemia *f.* prosodemy.
prosodia *f.* prosody.
prosopagnosia *f.* prosopagnosia.
prosópago *m.* prosopagus.
prosopalgia *f.* prosopalgia.
prosopálgico, -ca *adj.* prosopalgic.
prosopectasia *f.* prosopectasia.
prosoplasia *f.* prosoplasia.
prosopodinia *f.* prosopalgia.
prosopodiplejía *f.* prosodiplegia.
prosopodismorfia *f.* prosopodysmorphia.
prosoponeuralgia *f.* prosoponeuralgia.
prosoplejía *f.* prosopoplegia.
prosopopléjico, -ca *adj.* prosopoplegic.
prosoposquisis *f.* prosoposchisis.
prosopotoracópago *m.* prosopothoracopagus.
próstata *f.* prostate.

prostatalgia *f.* prostatalgia.
prostatectomía *f.* prostatectomy.
prostático, -ca *adj.* prostatic.
prostaticovesical *adj.* prostaticovesical.
prostatismo *m.* prostatism.
prostatitis *f.* prostatitis.
prostatocistitis *f.* prostatocystitis.
prostatocistotomía *f.* prostatocystotomy.
prostatodinia *f.* prostatodynia.
prostatografía *f.* prostatography.
prostatolito *m.* prostatolith.
prostatomegalia *f.* prostatomegaly.
prostatomía *f.* prostatomy.
prostatomiomectomía *f.* prostatomyomectomy.
prostatorrea *f.* prostatorrhea.
prostatotomía *f.* prostatotomy.
prostatovesiculectomía *f.* prostatovesiculectomy.
prostatovesiculitis *f.* prostatovesiculitis.
prosternación *f.* prosternation.
prostético, -ca *adj.* prosthetic.
protamina *f.* protamine.
protanomalía *f.* protanomaly.
protanomalopía *f.* protanomalopia.
protánope *adj.* protanope.
protanopía *f.* protanopia.
proteico, -ca *adj.* protean.
proteido *m.* proteid.
proteína *f.* protein.
proteináceo, -a *adj.* proteinaceous.
proteinemia *f.* proteinemia.
proteinógeno, -na *adj.* proteinogenous.
proteinograma *m.* proteinogram.
proteinosis *f.* proteinosis.
  proteinosis alveolar pulmonar pulmonary alveolar proteinosis.
  proteinosis lipídica lipid proteinosis.
proteinoterapia *f.* proteinotherapy.
proteinuria *f.* proteinuria.
  proteinuria accidental accidental proteinuria.
  proteinuria adventicia adventitious proteinuria.
  proteinuria aislada isolated proteinuria.
  proteinuria atlética athletic proteinuria.
  proteinuria de Bence Jones Bence Jones proteinuria.
  proteinuria colicuativa colliquative proteinuria.
  proteinuria dietética dietetic proteinuria.
  proteinuria digestiva digestive proteinuria.
  proteinuria de emulsión emulsion proteinuria.
  proteinuria enterógena enterogenic proteinuria.
  proteinuria de esfuerzo effort proteinuria.
  proteinuria falsa false proteinuria.
  proteinuria febril febrile proteinuria.
  proteinuria fisiológica physiologic proteinuria.
  proteinuria funcional functional proteinuria.
  proteinuria gestacional gestational proteinuria.
  proteinuria globular globular proteinuria.
  proteinuria gotosa gouty proteinuria.
  proteinuria hematógena hematogenous proteinuria.
  proteinuria hémica hemic proteinuria.
  proteinuria intermitente intermittent proteinuria.
  proteinuria intrínseca intrinsic proteinuria.
  proteinuria lordótica lordotic proteinuria.
  proteinuria mixta mixed proteinuria.

proteinuria nefrógena renal proteinuria.
proteinuria ortostática orthostatic proteinuria.
proteinuria palpatoria palpatory proteinuria.
proteinuria paroxística paroxysmal proteinuria.
proteinuria piógena pyogenic proteinuria.
proteinuria posrenal postrenal proteinuria.
proteinuria postural postural proteinuria.
proteinuria prerrenal prerenal proteinuria.
proteinuria regulatoria regulatory proteinuria.
proteinuria renal renal proteinuria.
proteinuria residual residual proteinuria.
proteinuria serosa serous proteinuria.
proteinuria transitoria transient proteinuria.
proteinuria verdadera true proteinuria.
proteoclástico, -ca *adj.* proteoclastic.
proteohormona *f.* proteohormone.
proteolípido *m.* proteolipid.
proteolisina *f.* proteolysin.
proteólisis *f.* proteolysis.
proteometabólico, -ca *adj.* proteometabolic.
proteometabolismo *m.* proteometabolism.
proteopepsis *f.* proteopepsis.
proteopexis *f.* proteopexy, proteopexis.
proteosoma *m.* proteasome.
proteosuria *f.* proteosuria.
proteoterapia *f.* proteinotherapy.
protésico, -ca *adj.* prosthetic.
prótesis *f.* prosthesis.
prótesis antirreflujo antireflux prosthesis.
prótesis articulada a barras bar joint prosthesis.
prótesis coclear cochlear prosthesis.
prótesis completa complete prosthesis.
prótesis definitiva definitive prosthesis.
prótesis dental, dentaria dental prosthesis.
prótesis de implante implant prosthesis.
prótesis inmediata immediate prosthesis.
prótesis de inserción inmediata immediate insertion prosthesis.
prótesis interina interim prosthesis.
prótesis maxilofacial maxillofacial prosthesis.
prótesis ocular ocular prosthesis.
prótesis parcial partial prosthesis.
prótesis parcial de extensión distal distal extension partial denture.
prótesis parcial fija fixed partial prosthesis.
prótesis parcial removible removable partial prosthesis.
prótesis preparatory preparatory prosthesis.
prótesis provisional provisional prosthesis.
prótesis de prueba trial prosthesis.
prótesis superpuesta overlay prosthesis.
prótesis telescópica telescopic prosthesis.
prótesis temporal temporary prosthesis.
prótesis total full prosthesis.
prótesis transitoria transitional prosthesis.
prótesis de tratamiento treatment prosthesis.
prótesis de válvula cardíaca cardiac valve prosthesis.
proteuria *f.* proteinuria.
Proteus Proteus.
prótido *m.* protide.
protocondrio *m.* protochondrium.
protocolo *m.* protocol.
protocónido *m.* proconid.
protocono *m.* protoconid.
protocoproporfiria *f.* protocoproporphyria.
protodermo *m.* protoderm.
protodiastólico, -ca *adj.* protodiastolic.
protoduodeno *m.* protoduodenum.
protoeritrocito *m.* protoerythrocyte.
protoespasmo *m.* protospasm.

protofilamento *m.* protofilament.
protófito *m.* protophyte.
protoleucocito *m.* protoleukocyte.
protón *m.* proton.
protonefros *m.* protonephron, protonephros.
protoneurona *f.* protoneuron.
protooncogén *m.* proto-oncogene.
protoplasia *f.* protoplasia.
protoplasma *m.* protoplasm.
protoplasmático, -ca *adj.* protoplasmatic, protoplasmic.
protoplasto *m.* protoplast.
protoporfiria *f.* protoporphyria.
protoporfirinuria *f.* protoporphyrinuria.
protosífilis *f.* protosyphilis.
protostoma *m.* protostoma.
prototecosis *f.* protothecosis.
prototipo *m.* prototype.
prototoxina *f.* prototoxin.
protótrofo, -fa *adj.* prototroph.
protovértebra *f.* protovertebra.
protozoacida *m.* protozoacide.
protozoario, -ria *adj.* protozoal.
protozoiasis *f.* protozoosis.
protozoófago, -ga *adj.* protozoophage.
protozoología *f.* protozoology.
protozoo *m.* protozoon.
protozoosis *f.* protozoosis.
protozooterapia *f.* protozootherapy.
protracción *f.* protraction.
protracción mandibular mandibular protraction.
protracción maxilar maxillary protraction.
protractor *m.* protractor.
protripsina *f.* protrypsin.
protrombina *f.* prothrombin.
protrusión *f.* protrusion.
protuberancia *f.* protuberance.
provértebra *f.* provertebra.
provirus *m.* provirus.
provitamina *f.* provitamin.
proxémica *f.* proxemics.
proximal *adj.* proximal.
proximoataxia *f.* proximoataxia.
proximoceptor *m.* proximoceptor.
proximolabial *adj.* proximolabial.
proximolingual *adj.* proximolingual.
proximovestibular *adj.* proximovestibular.
proyección *f.* projection.
proyección errónea erroneous projection.
proyección falsa false projection.
proyección radiológica radiologic projection.
proyección visual visual projection.
prozona *f.* prozone.
prueba *f.* test.
prueba de Denver para el análisis del desarrollo Denver's analytic test for development.
prueba del desarrollo de la integración visuomotora de Beery-Buktenika Beery-Buktenika test of developmental visual motor integration (VMI).
prueba de diagnóstico de la afasia de Boston Boston diagnostic aphasia examination.
prueba del diseño de bloques de Kohs Kohs block design test.
prueba de elección de tarjetas de Wisconsin Wisconsin card sorting test.
prueba de frases incompletas sentence completion test (SCT).
prueba para la impotencia male impotence test (MIT).
prueba inventario clínico multiaxial de Millon Millon clinical multiaxial inventory (MCMI-II).

prueba inventario de personalidad de Eysenk Eysenk personality inventory (EPI).
prueba inventario de personalidad multifásico de Minnesota Minnesota multiphase personality inventory (MMPI-2).
prueba de Kaufman para logros educacionales Kaufman test of educational achievement (K-TEA).
prueba de investigación de laboratorio de enfermedades venéreas venereal disease research laboratory (VDRL) test.
prueba de Machover del dibujo de la figura humana Machover draw-a-person test (MDAP).
prueba de memoria de Wechsler revisada revised Wechsler memory scale test.
prueba de Peabody revisada de vocabulario con imágenes revised Peabody picture vocabulary test (PPVT-R).
prueba de Standford-Binet Standford-Binet test.
prurigeno, -na *adj.* pruriginous.
pruriginoso, -sa *adj.* pruriginous.
prurigo *m.* prurigo.
prurigo agrio prurigo agria.
prurigo de Besnier Besnier's prurigo, prurigo of Besnier.
prurigo crónico multiforme prurigo chronica multiformis.
prurigo estival prurigo aestivalis.
prurigo ferox prurigo ferox.
prurigo gestacional, prurigo gestationis prurigo gestationis.
prurigo de Hebra Hebra's prurigo, prurigo of Hebra.
prurigo infantil prurigo infantilis.
prurigo melanótico melanotic prurigo.
prurigo simple prurigo simplex.
prurigo de verano summer prurigo.
prurítico, -ca *adj.* pruritic.
prurito *m.* itch, pruritus.
prurito de agua water pruritus.
prurito anal, prurito ani pruritus ani.
prurito de avicultor poultryman's itch.
prurito del baño bath itch.
prurito por cereales grain itch.
prurito del coolie coolie itch.
prurito por copra pruritus copra.
prurito cubano Cuban itch.
prurito de los dedos de los pies toe itch.
prurito de escarcha frost itch.
prurito esencial essential pruritus.
prurito generalizado essential pruritus.
prurito idiopático essential pruritus.
prurito de invierno winter itch.
prurito del leñador lumberman's itch.
prurito del nadador swimmer's itch.
prurito de noruega Norway itch.
prurito del panadero baker's itch.
prurito de los pantanos swamp itch.
prurito de san Ignacio Saint Ignatius' itch.
prurito senil senile itch, pruritus senilis.
prurito sintomático symptomatic itch.
prurito del suelo ground itch.
prurito vulvar pruritus vulvae.
psamocarcinoma *m.* psammocarcinoma.
psamoma *m.* psammoma.
psamomatoso, -sa *adj.* psammomatous.
psamoso, -sa *adj.* psammous.
pselafesia *f.* pselaphesia.
pselismo *m.* psellism.
Pseudomonas Pseudomonas.
psicalgia *f.* psychalgia.
psicalia *f.* psychalia.

psicastenia *f.* psychasthenia.
psicoacústica *f.* psychoacoustics.
psicoacústico, -ca *adj.* psychoauditory.
psicoanálisis *m.* psycho-analysis.
psicoanalista *m., f.* psychoanalyst.
psicoauditivo, -va *adj.* psychoauditory.
psicobiología *f.* psychobiology.
psicocatarsis *f.* psychocatharsis.
psicodélico, -ca *adj.* psychedelic.
psicodiagnóstico *m.* psychodiagnosis.
psicodinámica *f.* psychodynamics.
psicodometría *f.* psychodometry.
psicodrama *m.* psychodrama.
psicoendocrinología *f.* psychoendocrinology.
psicoestimulante *m.* psychostimulant.
psicofármaco *m.* psychopharmaceutical.
psicofarmacología *f.* psychopharmacology.
psicofilaxis *f.* psychophylaxis.
psicofísica *f.* psychophysics.
 psicofísica clínica clinical psychophysics.
psicofisiología *f.* psychophysiology.
psicogalvánico, -ca *adj.* psychogalvanic.
psicogénesis *f.* psychogenesis.
psicogenia *f.* psychogenesis.
psicogeriatria *f.* psychogeriatrics.
psicología *f.* psychology.
 psicología clínica clinical psychology.
 psicología cognitiva cognitive psychology.
 psicología comunitaria community psychology.
 psicología conductista behavioral psychology.
 psicología dinámica dynamic psychology.
 psicología de la educación, psicología educacional educational psychology.
 psicología evolutiva developmental psychology.
 psicología existencial existential psychology.
 psicología experimental experimental psychology.
 psicología genética genetic psychology.
 psicología de la Gestalt Gestalt psychology.
 psicología individual individual psychology.
 psicología industrial industrial psychology.
 psicología médica medical psychology.
 psicología de la orientación counseling psychology.
 psicología profunda depth psychology.
 psicología social social psychology.
 psicología del trabajo y de las organizaciones industrial-organizational psychology.
psicólogo, -ga *m., f.* psychologist.
psicoma *m.* sycoma.
psicometría *f.* psychometry.
psicomotor, -ra *adj.* psychomotor.
psiconeurosis *f.* psychoneurosis.
psiconosología *f.* psychonosology.
psicópata *m., f.* psychopath.
psicopatía *f.* psychopathy.
psicopático, -ca *adj.* psychopathic.
psicopatología *f.* psychopathology.
psicosensorial *adj.* psychosensory.
psicosexual *adj.* psychosexual.
psicosis *f.* psychosis.
psicosocial *adj.* psychosocial.
psicosomático, -ca *adj.* psychosomatic.
psicotecnia *f.* psychotechnics.
psicoterapeuta *m., f.* psychotherapist.
psicoterapia *f.* psychotherapy.
 psicoterapia analítica analytic psychotherapy.
 psicoterapia de apoyo supportive psychotherapy.
 psicoterapia breve short-term psychotherapy.
 psicoterapia dinámica dynamic psychotherapy.

 psicoterapia existencial existential psychotherapy.
 psicoterapia de la Gestalt Gestalt psychotherapy.
 psicoterapia grupal, psicoterapia de grupo group psychotherapy.
 psicoterapia psicoanalítica psychoanalytic psychotherapy.
 psicoterapia transaccional trasactional psychotherapy.
psicótico, -ca *adj.* psychotic.
psicotrópico, -ca *adj.* psychotropic.
psicotropo, -pa *adj.* psychotropic.
psilosis *f.* psilosis.
psique *f.* psyche.
psiquiatra *m., f.* psychiatrist.
psiquiatría *f.* psychiatry.
 psiquiatría biológica biological psychiatry.
 psiquiatría comunitaria community psychiatry.
 psiquiatría dinámica dynamic psychiatry.
 psiquiatría existencial existential psychiatry.
 psiquiatría forense forensic psychiatry.
 psiquiatría infantil infantile psychiatry.
 psiquiatría social social psychiatry.
psíquico, -ca *adj.* psychic.
psiquismo *m.* psychism.
psitacosis *f.* psittacosis.
psódimo *m.* psodymus.
psoítis *f.* psoitis.
psomofagia *f.* psomophagia, psophagy.
psorelcosis *f.* psorelcosis.
psorenteritis *f.* psorenteritis.
psoriasiforme *adj.* psoriasiform.
psoriasis *f.* psoriasis.
 psoriasis anular psoriasis annularis, psoriasis annulata.
 psoriasis artropática psoriasis arthropica.
 psoriasis bucal psoriasis buccalis.
 psoriasis circinada psoriasis circinata.
 psoriasis difusa diffused psoriasis, psoriasis diffusa.
 psoriasis discoidea psoriasis discoidea.
 psoriasis espondilítica psoriasis spondylitica.
 psoriasis exfoliativa, psoriasis folicular exfoliative psoriasis.
 psoriasis geográfica psoriasis geographica.
 psoriasis guttata psoriasis guttata.
 psoriasis gyrata psoriasis gyrata.
 psoriasis inveterada psoriasis inveterata.
 psoriasis lingual psoriasis linguae.
 psoriasis liquenoide lichen planus.
 psoriasis numular psoriasis nummularis.
 psoriasis orbicular psoriasis orbicularis.
 psoriasis ostrácea psoriasis ostreacea.
 psoriasis palmar y plantar psoriasis of palms and soles.
 psoriasis punctata, psoriasis punteada psoriasis punctata.
 psoriasis pustulosa generalizada de Zambusch generalized pustular psoriasis of Zambusch.
 psoriasis rupioides psoriasis rupioides.
 psoriasis universal, psoriasis universalis psoriasis universalis.
pterigión *m.* pterygium.
pterigoideo, -a *adj.* pterygoid.
pterigoide *adj.* pterygoid.
pterigoides *m.* pterygoid.
pterigomandibular *adj.* pterygomandibular.
pterigomaxilar *adj.* pterygomaxillare.
pterigopalatino, -na *adj.* pterygopalatine.
pternalgia *f.* pternalgia.
ptilosis *f.* ptilosis.
ptiocrino *m.* ptyocrinous.

ptiriasis *f.* phthiriasis.
 ptiriasis de la cabeza phthiriasis capitis.
 ptiriasis del cuerpo phthiriasis corporis.
 ptiriasis del pubis phthiriasis pubis.
ptosis *f.* ptosis.
 ptosis adiposa ptosis adiposa.
 ptosis falsa false ptosis.
 ptosis de Horner Horner's ptosis.
 ptosis lipomatosa ptosis lipomatosis.
 ptosis simpática ptosis sympathetica.
pubarquia *f.* pubarche.
pubertad *f.* puberty.
 pubertad precoz precocious puberty.
pubes pubes.
pubescencia *f.* pubescence.
pubescente *adj.* pubescent.
pubiofemoral *adj.* pubofemoral.
pubioplastia *f.* pubioplasty.
pubioprostático, -ca *adj.* puboprostatic.
pubiotomía *f.* pubiotomy.
pubis *m.* pubis.
puente¹ *m.* pons.
puente² *m.* bridge.
puericultura *f.* puericulture.
puérpera *f.* puerpera.
puerperal *adj.* puerperal.
puerperio *m.* puerperium.
pulgar *m.* thumb.
 pulgar del tenista tennis thumb.
pulido *m.* polishing.
pulmoaórtico, -ca *adj.* pulmoaortic.
pulmolito *m.* pulmolith.
pulmometría *f.* pulmometry.
pulmómetro *m.* pulmometer.
pulmón *m.* lung.
 pulmón de acero iron lung.
 pulmón por acondicionador de aire air-conditioner lung.
 pulmón ahogado drowned lung.
 pulmón de albañil mason's lung.
 pulmón blanco white lung.
 pulmón cardíaco cardiac lung.
 pulmón de criador de aves bird-breeder's lung, bird-fancier's lung.
 pulmón fibroide fibroid lung.
 pulmón de granjero farmer's lung.
 pulmón húmedo wet lung.
 pulmón de los mineros del carbón coalminer's lung.
 pulmón en panal, pulmón en panal de abeja honeycomb lung.
 pulmón posperfusión postperfusion lung.
 pulmón quieto quiet lung.
 pulmón de soldador welder's lung.
 pulmón de los trabajadores con hongos mushroom-worker's lung.
 pulmón de trabajadores del queso cheese worker's lung.
 pulmón de trillador thresher's lung.
 pulmón urémico uremic lung.
pulmonectomía *f.* pulmonectomy.
pulmonía *f.* pulmonitis.
pulpa *f.* pulp, pulpa.
 pulpa del dedo, pulpa digital pulp of the finger, digital pulp.
 pulpa dental dental pulp.
 pulpa desvitalizada devitalized pulp.
 pulpa esplénica pulpa splenica.
 pulpa expuesta exposed pulp.
 pulpa muerta dead pulp.
 pulpa necrótica necrotic pulp.
 pulpa no vital non-vital pulp.
 pulpa putrefacta putrescent pulp.
 pulpa radicular radicular pulp.
 pulpa vital vital pulp.

pulpación *f.* pulpation.
pulpalgia *f.* pulpalgia.
pulpectomía *f.* pulpectomy.
pulpefacción *f.* pulpifaction.
pulpiforme *adj.* pulpiform.
pulpitis *f.* pulpitis.
  pulpitis hiperplásica hyperplastic pulpitis.
  pulpitis irreversible irreversible pulpitis.
  pulpitis reversible reversible pulpitis.
  pulpitis supurativa suppurative pulpitis.
pulposo, -sa *adj.* pulpy.
pulsación *f.* pulsation.
pulsador *m.* pulsator.
pulsátil *adj.* pulsatile.
pulsión¹ *f.* drive, instinct.
  pulsión agresiva aggressive drive, aggressive instinct.
  pulsión de autoconservación instinct of self-preservation.
  pulsión de dominio instinct to master.
  pulsión destructiva aggressive drive, aggressive instinct.
  pulsión de muerte death instinct.
  pulsión sexual sexual drive, sexual instinct.
  pulsión de vida life instinct.
  pulsión del yo ego instinct.
pulsión² *m.* pulsion.
pulso *m.* pulse, pulsus.
  pulso abdominal abdominal pulse, pulsus abdominalis.
  pulso acelerado pulsus celer.
  pulso acoplado coupled pulse.
  pulso alternante pulsus alternans.
  pulso anacrótico, pulso anacroto anacrotic pulse.
  pulso en bala de cañón cannon ball pulse.
  pulso bigémino bigeminal pulse, pulsus bigeminus.
  pulso bisferiens bisferious pulse, pulsus bisferiens.
  pulso blando soft pulse.
  pulso bulbar bulbar pulse.
  pulso capilar capillary pulse.
  pulso caprizante pulsus caprisans.
  pulso celer celer pulse.
  pulso en cola de ratón mousetail pulse.
  pulso colapsante collapsing pulse.
  pulso cordal cordy pulse.
  pulso cordis pulse cordis.
  pulso de Corrigan Corrigan's pulse.
  pulso cuadrigémino quadrigeminal pulse.
  pulso desigual pulsus inaequalis.
  pulso dicrótico, pulso dicroto dicrotic pulse.
  pulso differens pulsus differens.
  pulso duro hard pulse.
  pulso elástico elastic pulse.
  pulso entóptico entoptic pulse.
  pulso febril febrile pulse.
  pulso filiforme filiform pulse.
  pulso frecuente frequent pulse.
  pulso gaseoso gaseous pulse.
  pulso gutural guttural pulse.
  pulso heterocrónico pulsus heterochronicus.
  pulso igual equal pulse, pulsus aequalis.
  pulso incongruente pulsus incongruens.
  pulso infrecuente pulsus infrequens.
  pulso intermitente intermittent pulse.
  pulso irregular irregular pulse.
  pulso irregular perpetuo pulsus irregularis perpetuus.
  pulso de Kussmaul Kussmaul's pulse.
  pulso largo long pulse.
  pulso lento slow pulse.
  pulso en martillo de agua water-hammer pulse.

  pulso en meseta plateau pulse.
  pulso de Monneret Monneret's pulse.
  pulso monocroto monocrotic pulse.
  pulso móvil movable pulse.
  pulso ondulante undulating pulse.
  pulso de opresión pulsus oppresus.
  pulso paradójico, pulso paradójico de Kussmaul paradoxical pulse, Kussmaul's paradoxical pulse.
  pulso paradójico invertido reversed paradoxical pulse.
  pulso pedio dorsal pedis pulse.
  pulso periférico peripheral pulse.
  pulso a pistón piston pulse.
  pulso policroto polycrotic pulse.
  pulso poplíteo popliteal pulse.
  pulso de Quincke Quincke's pulse.
  pulso radial radial pulse.
  pulso rápido rapid pulse.
  pulso respiratorio respiratory pulse.
  pulso de Riegel Riegel's pulse.
  pulso tardío pulsus tardus.
  pulso tenso tense pulse.
  pulso trémulo pulse tremulus.
  pulso tricrótico, pulso tricroto tricrotic pulse.
  pulso trigeminado, pulso trigémino trigeminal pulse, pulsus trigeminus.
  pulso ungueal, pulso ungular nail pulse.
  pulso vacío, pulso vacuo vacuus pulse, pulsus vacuus.
  pulso del vago pulsus vagus.
  pulso venoso venous pulse, pulsus venosus.
  pulso vermicular vermicular pulse.
  pulso yugular jugular pulse.
pultáceo, -a *adj.* pultaceous.
pululación *f.* pullulation.
pulverización *f.* pulverization.
pulverizar *v.* pulverize.
pulvinado, -da *adj.* pulvinated.
pulvinar pulvinar.
punción *f.* puncture.
  punción de Bernard Bernard's puncture.
  punción cisternal cisternal puncture.
  punción craneal cranial puncture.
  punción diabética diabetic puncture.
  punción digital finger stick.
  punción espinal spinal puncture.
  punción esplénica splenic puncture.
  punción esternal sternal puncture.
  punción exploratoria exploratory puncture.
  punción de Kronecker Kronecker's puncture.
  punción intracraneal intracisternal puncture.
  punción lumbar (PL) lumbar puncture (LP).
  punción de Quincke Quincke's puncture.
  punción raquídea spinal puncture.
  punción suboccipital suboccipital puncture.
  punción del talón heel puncture.
  punción tecal thecal puncture.
  punción ventricular ventricular puncture.
punta *f.* point.
  punta absorbente absorbent point.
  punta de gutapercha gutta-percha point.
  punta de plata silver point.
punteado *m.* stippling.
puntiforme *adj.* punctiform.
punto *m.* point.
  punto de congelación freezing point.
  punto doloroso painful point, point dolorosum.
  punto de ebullición boiling point.
  punto isoeléctrico isoelectric point.
  punto isoiónico isoionic point.
  punto isosbéstico isosbestic point.
  punto J J point.

  punto de máximo impulso point of maximal impulse.
  punto motor motor point.
  punto neutro neutral point.
  punto de osificación point of ossification.
  punto de osificación primario primary point of ossification.
  punto de osificación secundario secondary point of ossification.
  punto de presión pressure point.
  punto de rigor por el calor heat-rigor point.
  punto de rigor por el frío cold-rigor point.
  punto terminal end point.
  punto de Velleix Velleix's point.
punzada *f.* twinge.
pupila *f.* pupil, pupilla.
  pupila de Adie Adie's pupil.
  pupila de Argyll-Robertson Argyll-Robertson pupil.
  pupila artificial artificial pupil.
  pupila de Bumke Bumke's pupil.
  pupila catatónica catatonic pupil.
  pupila fija fixed pupil.
  pupila de Gunn Gunn pupil.
  pupila de Holmes-Adie Holmes-Adie pupil.
  pupila de Horner Horner's pupil.
  pupila de Hutchinson Hutchinson's pupil.
  pupila de Marcus-Gunn Marcus-Gunn pupil.
  pupila en ojo de cerradura keyhole pupil.
  pupila en ojo de gato cat's-eye pupil.
  pupila paradójica paradoxical pupil.
  pupila puntiforme pinhole pupil.
  pupila rígida rigid pupil.
  pupila de Robertson Robertson pupil.
  pupila en rueda dentada cogwheel pupil.
  pupila de Saenger Saenger pupil.
  pupila tónica tonic pupil.
pupilatonía *f.* pupillatonia.
pupilometría *f.* pupilometry.
pupilómetro *m.* pupilometer.
pupilomotor, -ra *adj.* pupillomotor.
pupiloplejía *f.* pupiloplegia.
pupiloscopia *f.* pupilloscopia.
pupilostatómetro *m.* pupillostatometer.
purgante *adj.* purgative.
puriforme *adj.* puriform.
purinemia *f.* purinemia.
puromucoso, -sa *adj.* puromucous.
púrpura¹ purple.
  púrpura visual visual purple.
púrpura² *f.* purpura.
  púrpura abdominal Henoch's purpura.
  púrpura alérgica allergic purpura.
  púrpura anafiláctica anaphylactoid purpura.
  púrpura angioneurótica angioneurotic purpura.
  púrpura atrombocitopénica non-thrombocytopenic purpura.
  púrpura fibrinolítica fibrinolytic purpura.
  púrpura fulminante, púrpura fulminans purpura fulminans.
  púrpura hemorrágica hemorrhagic purpura.
  púrpura de Henoch Henoch's purpura.
  púrpura de Henoch-Schönlein Henoch-Schönlein purpura.
  púrpura maligna malignant purpura.
  púrpura no trombocitopénica non-thrombocytopenic purpura.
  púrpura nerviosa purpura nervosa.
  púrpura psicogénica psychogenic purpura.
  púrpura reumática purpura rheumatica.
  púrpura senil purpura senilis.
  púrpura sintomática purpura symptomatica.
  púrpura trombocitopénica thrombocytopenic purpura.

púrpura trombocitopénica idiopática (PTI) idiopathic thrombocytopenic purpura (ITP).

púrpura trombocitopénica inmune immune thrombocytopenic purpura.

púrpura trombocitopénica trombótica (PTT) thrombotic thrombocytopenic purpura (TTP).

púrpura trombopática, púrpura trombopénica thrombopenic purpura.

púrpura urticans purpura urticans.

púrpura vascular aguda acute vascular purpura.

púrpura de Waldenström Waldenström's purpura.

púrpura yódica iodic purpura, purpura iodica.

purpurífero, -ra *adj.* purpuriferous.

purpurinuria *f.* purpurinuria.

purpurógeno, -na *adj.* purpurogenous.

purulencia *f.* purulence.

purulento, -ta *adj.* purulent.

puruloide *adj.* puruloid.

pus *m.* pus.

pus azul blue pus.

pus caseoso cheesy pus.

pus denso cheesy pus.

pus cuajado curdy pus.

pus licoroso lichorous pus.

pus de salsa de anchoas anchovy sauce pus.

pus sanioso sanious pus.

pus verde green pus.

pústula *f.* pustule.

pústula espongiforme de Kogoj spongiform pustule of Kogoj.

pústula multilocular multilocular pustule.

pústula post mortem pustule postmortem.

pústula simple simple pustule.

pústula unilocular unilocular pustule.

pústula variólica pock pustule.

pustulación *f.* pustulation.

pustular *adj.* pustular.

pustuliforme *adj.* pustuliform.

pustulocrustáceo, -a *adj.* pustulocrustaceous.

pustulosis *f.* pustulosis.

pustulosis palmoplantar pustulosis palmaris et plantaris.

pustulosis vacciniforme aguda pustulosis vacciniformis acuta.

pustuloso, -sa *adj.* pustular.

putrefacción *f.* putrefaction.

putrescencia *f.* putrefaction.

pútrido, -da *adj.* putrid.

quadrat *m.* quadrat.
quale *m.* quale.
quantal *adj.* quantal.
quantum quantum.
queilalgia *f.* cheilalgia.
queilectomía *f.* cheilectomy.
queilectropión *m.* cheilectropion.
queilión *m.* cheilion.
queilitis *f.* cheilitis.
  queilitis actínica actinic cheilitis.
  queilitis angular angular cheilitis.
  queilitis apostematosa apostematous cheilitis.
  queilitis comisural commisural cheilitis.
  queilitis de contacto, queilitis por contacto contact cheilitis.
  queilitis exfoliativa cheilitis exfoliativa.
  queilitis glandular cheilitis glandularis.
  queilitis glandular apostematosa cheilitis glandularis apostematosa.
  queilitis granulomatosa cheilitis granulomatosa.
  queilitis impetiginosa impetiginous cheilitis.
  queilitis migratoria migrating cheilitis.
  queilitis solar solar cheilitis.
  queilitis venenosa, queilitis venenata cheilitis venenata.
  queilitis de Volkmann Volkmann's cheilitis.
queiloalveolosquisis *f.* cheiloalveoloschisis.
queiloangioscopia *f.* cheilangioscopy, cheiloangioscopy.
queilocarcinoma *m.* cheilocarcinoma.
queilofagia *f.* cheilophagia.
queilognatoglososquisis *f.* cheilognathoglossoschisis.
queilognatopalatosquisis *f.* cheilognathopalatoschisis.
queilognatoprosoposquisis *f.* cheilognathoprosoposchisis.
queilognatosquisis *f.* cheilognathoschisis.
queilognatouranosquisis *f.* cheilognathouranoschisis.
queilonco *m.* cheiloncus.
queiloplastia *f.* cheiloplasty.
queilorrafia *f.* cheilorrhaphy.
queiloscopia *f.* cheiloscopy.
queilosis *f.* cheilosis.
  queilosis angular angular cheilosis.
queilosquisis *f.* cheiloschisis.
queilostomatoplastia *f.* cheilostomatoplasty.
queilotomía *f.* cheilotomy.
queiragra *f.* cheiragra.
queiralgia *f.* cheiralgia.
  queiralgia parestésica cheiralgia paresthetica.
queirartritis *f.* cheirarthritis.
queirobraquialgia *f.* cheirobrachialgia.
queirocinestesia *f.* cheirocinesthesia, cheirokinesthesia.
queirocinestésico, -ca *adj.* cheirokinesthesic.
queiroespasmo *m.* cheirospasm.

queirognomía *f.* cheirognomy.
queirognóstico, -ca *adj.* cheirognostic.
queirología *f.* cheirology.
queiromegalia *f.* cheiromegaly.
queiroplastia *f.* cheiroplasty.
queiropodalgia *f.* chiropodalgia.
queiroponfólix *m.* cheiropompholyx.
queiroscopio *m.* cheiroscope.
queirospasmo *m.* cheirospasm.
quejido *m.* grunting.
quelación *f.* chelation.
quelado, -da *adj.* chelate.
quelante *m.* chelating agent.
quelar *v.* chelate.
quelato *m.* chelate.
queloide *m.* cheloid, keloid.
  queloide de acné acne keloid.
  queloide de Addison Addison's keloid.
  queloide de Alibert Alibert's keloid.
  queloide cicatricial cicatricial keloid.
  queloide de las encías keloid of the gums.
  queloide falso false keloid.
  queloide de Hawkins Hawkins' keloid.
queloides *m.* cheloid, keloid.
queloidosis *f.* cheloidosis, keloidosis.
queloma *m.* cheloma.
queloplastia *f.* keloplasty.
quelos *m.* cheloma.
quelotomía *f.* kelotomy.
quemadura *f.* burn.
  quemadura ácida acid burn.
  quemadura por agentes térmicos thermal burn.
  quemadura por álcalis alkali burn.
  quemadura por cemento cement burn, concrete burn.
  quemadura conjuntival conjunctival burn.
  quemadura por contacto contact burn.
  quemadura por cuerda rope burn.
  quemadura eléctrica electric burn, electrical burn.
  quemadura de espesor parcial partial-thickness burn.
  quemadura de espesor total full-thickness burn.
  quemadura por fricción brush burn, friction burn, matt burn.
  quemadura por fulguración flash burn.
  quemadura por napalm napalm burn.
  quemadura de primer grado first degree burn.
  quemadura química chemical burn.
  quemadura por radiación radiation burn.
  quemadura por rayos X X-ray burn.
  quemadura por relámpago flash burn.
  quemadura respiratoria respiratory burn.
  quemadura de segundo grado second degree burn.
  quemadura por soga rope burn.
  quemadura solar solar burn, sun burn, sunburn.
  quemadura superficial superficial burn.

  quemadura de tercer grado third degree burn.
  quemadura térmica thermal burn.
quemazón *f.* burning.
quemisorción *f.* chemisorption.
quemocefalia *f.* chamaecephaly, chemocephalia, chemocephaly.
quemocéfalo, -la *adj.* chamaecephalic, chemocephalic.
quemodectoma *m.* chemodectoma.
quemosis *f.* chemosis.
  quemosis conjuntival conjunctival chemosis.
quemótico, -ca *adj.* chemotic.
quenismógeno, -na *adj.* knismogenic.
quenodesoxicólico, -ca *adj.* chenodeoxycholic (acid).
quenodesoxicolilglicina *f.* chenodeoxycholylglycine.
quenodesoxicoliltaurina *f.* chenodeoxycholyltaurine.
quenoterapia *f.* chenotherapy.
quenotoxina *f.* kenotoxin.
quenutoracoplastia *f.* quenuthoracoplasty.
queratalgia *f.* keratalgia.
queratán-sulfato *m.* keratan sulfate.
queratansulfaturia *f.* keratansulfaturia.
queratectasia *f.* keratectasia.
queratectomía *f.* keratectomy.
  queratectomía fotorrefractiva, queratectomía fotorrefringente photo-refractive keratectomy.
querateína *f.* keratein.
queratiasis *f.* keratiasis.
querático, -ca *adj.* keratic.
queratina *f.* ceratin, keratin.
queratinasa *f.* keratinase.
queratinización *f.* keratinization.
queratinizado, -da *adj.* keratinized.
queratinizar *v.* keratinize.
queratinocito *m.* keratinocyte.
queratinoide *adj.* keratinoid.
queratinoso, -sa *adj.* keratinous.
queratinosoma *m.* keratinosome.
queratitis *f.* keratitis.
  queratitis de acné rosácea acne rosacea keratitis.
  queratitis actínica actinic keratitis.
  queratitis de los aerosoles aerosol keratitis.
  queratitis alfabética, queratitis en alfabeto alphabet keratitis, alphabetical keratitis.
  queratitis ampollosa keratitis bullosa.
  queratitis anafiláctica anaphylactic keratitis.
  queratitis anular annular keratitis.
  queratitis arborescente keratitis arborescens.
  queratitis arrugada furrow keratitis.
  queratitis por aspergillus aspergillus keratitis.
  queratitis en banda band keratitis, band-shaped keratitis, keratitis bandelette, ribbon-like keratitis.

queratitis dendriforme, queratitis dendrítica dendriform keratitis, dendritic keratitis.
queratitis de desecación desiccation keratitis.
queratitis de Dimmer Dimmer's keratitis.
queratitis disciforme, queratitis discoide disciform keratitis, keratitis disciformis.
queratitis entretejida lattice keratitis.
queratitis epitelial difusa epithelial diffuse keratitis.
queratitis esclerosante sclerosing keratitis.
queratitis escrofulosa scrofulous keratitis.
queratitis estriada striate keratitis.
queratitis exfoliativa exfoliative keratitis.
queratitis por exposición exposure keratitis.
queratitis fascicular fascicular keratitis.
queratitis filamentosa filamentary keratitis, keratitis filamentosa.
queratitis flictenular phlyctenular keratitis.
queratitis fugaz periódica keratitis periodica fugax.
queratitis geográfica geographic keratitis.
queratitis herpética herpetic keratitis.
queratitis con hipopión, queratitis de hipopión hypopyon keratitis.
queratitis intersticial interstitial keratitis.
queratitis lagoftálmica lagophthalmic keratitis.
queratitis lineal migratoria keratitis linearis migrans.
queratitis lineal superficial superficial linear keratitis.
queratitis marginal marginal keratitis.
queratitis metaherpética metaherpetic keratitis.
queratitis micótica mycotic keratitis.
queratitis necrogranulomatosa necrogranulomatous keratitis.
queratitis neuroparalítica neuroparalytic keratitis.
queratitis neurotrófica neurotrophic keratitis.
queratitis numular nummular keratitis, keratitis nummularis.
queratitis parenquimatosa parenchymatous keratitis.
queratitis petrificans keratitis petrificans.
queratitis profunda deep keratitis, keratitis profunda.
queratitis punteada, queratitis punctata punctate keratitis, keratitis punctata.
queratitis punteada profunda keratitis punctata profunda.
queratitis punteada superficial superficial punctate keratitis.
queratitis puntiforme superficial de Thygeson Thygeson superficial punctate keratitis.
queratitis purulenta purulent keratitis.
q pustuliforme profunda, queratitis pustulosa profunda keratitis pustuliformis profunda.
queratitis ramificada superficial keratitis ramificata superficialis.
queratitis reticular reticular keratitis.
queratitis rosácea rosacea keratitis.
queratitis seca keratitis sicca.
queratitis secundaria secondary keratitis.
queratitis de la seda artificial artificial silk keratitis.
queratitis de los segadores reaper's keratitis.
queratitis serpiginosa serpiginous keratitis.
queratitis superficial polimorfa polymorphic superficial keratitis.
queratitis supurativa suppurative keratitis.
queratitis tracomatosa trachomatous keratitis.

queratitis trófica trophic keratitis.
queratitis vascular vascular keratitis.
queratitis vasculonebulosa vasculonebulous keratitis.
queratitis vesicular vesicular keratitis.
queratitis xerótica xerotic keratitis.
queratitis zonular zonular keratitis.
queratoacantoma *m.* keratoacanthoma.
queratoangioma *m.* keratoangioma.
queratoatrofodermia *f.* keratoatrophoderma.
queratocele *m.* keratocele.
queratocentesis *f.* keratocentesis.
queratocito *m.* keratocyte.
queratoconjuntivitis *f.* keratoconjunctivitis.
queratoconjuntivitis atópica atopic keratoconjunctivitis.
queratoconjuntivitis de los astilleros shipyard keratoconjunctivitis.
queratoconjuntivitis por destello flash keratoconjunctivitis.
queratoconjuntivitis epidémica epidemic keratoconjunctivitis.
queratoconjuntivitis en flash flash keratoconjunctivitis.
queratoconjuntivitis flictenular phlyctenular keratoconjunctivitis.
queratoconjuntivitis herpética herpetic keratoconjunctivitis.
queratoconjuntivitis limbica superior superior limbic keratoconjunctivitis.
queratoconjuntivitis primaveral vernal keratoconjunctivitis.
queratoconjuntivitis seca keratoconjunctivitis sicca.
queratoconjuntivitis ultravioleta ultraviolet keratoconjunctivitis.
queratoconjuntivitis vernal vernal keratoconjunctivitis.
queratoconjuntivitis viral, queratoconjuntivitis virósica viral keratoconjunctivitis, virus keratoconjunctivitis.
queratocono *m.* keratoconus.
queratodermatitis *f.* keratodermatitis.
queratodermatocele *m.* keratodermatocele.
queratodermia *f.* keratoderma.
queratodermia blenorrágica keratoderma blennorrhagicum.
queratodermia climatérica keratoderma climactericum.
queratodermia endocrina endocrine keratoderma.
queratodermia excéntrica keratoderma eccentrica.
queratodermia linfedematosa lymphedematous keratoderma.
queratodermia mutilante mutilating keratoderma.
queratodermia palmoplantar, queratodermia palmar y plantar palmoplantar keratoderma, keratoderma palmaris et plantaris, keratoderma palmare et plantare.
queratodermia palmoplantar difusa diffuse palmoplantar keratoderma.
queratodermia plantar fisurada keratoderma blennorrhagicum.
queratodermia plantar surcada keratoderma plantare sulcatum.
queratodermia punteada punctate keratoderma.
queratodermia senil senile keratoderma.
queratodermia simétrica symmetric keratoderma, keratoderma symmetrica.
queratodermia de Vohwinkel Vohwinkel's keratoderma.

queratodermia de Vorner Vorner's keratoderma.
queratoectasia *f.* keratoectasia.
queratoescleritis *f.* keratoscleritis.
queratofaquia *f.* keratophakia.
queratogénesis *f.* keratogenesis.
queratogénico, -ca *adj.* keratogenetic.
queratógeno, -na *adj.* keratogenous.
queratoglobo *m.* keratoglobus.
queratohelcosis *f.* keratohelcosis.
queratohemia *f.* keratohemia.
queratohial *adj.* ceratohyal, keratohyal.
queratohialina *f.* keratohyalin.
queratohialino, -na *adj.* kerotohyaline.
queratoide *adj.* keratoid.
queratoideo, -a *adj.* keratoid.
queratoiditis *f.* keratoiditis.
queratoiridociclitis *f.* keratoiridocyclitis.
queratoiridoscopio *m.* keratoiridoscope.
queratoiritis *f.* keratoiritis.
queratoiritis de hipopión hypopyon keratoiritis.
queratoleptinsis *f.* keratoleptynsis.
queratoleucoma *m.* keratoleukoma.
queratólisis *f.* keratolysis.
queratólisis excavada pitted keratolysis.
queratólisis exfoliativa keratolysis exfoliativa.
queratólisis neonatal keratolysis neonatorum.
queratólisis plantar surcada keratolysis plantare sulcatum.
queratólisis del recién nacido keratolysis neonatorum.
queratolítico, -ca *adj.* keratolytic.
queratoma *m.* keratoma.
queratoma hereditario mutilante keratoma hereditarium mutilans.
queratoma palmar y plantar keratoma palmare et plantare.
queratoma senil keratoma senile.
queratomalacia *f.* keratomalacia.
queratometría *f.* keratometry.
queratométrico, -va *adj.* keratometric.
queratómetro *m.* keratometer.
queratomicosis *f.* keratomycosis.
queratomicosis de la lengua, queratomicosis lingual lingual keratomycosis, keratomycosis linguae.
queratomileusis *f.* keratomileusis.
querátomo *m.* keratome.
queratonosis *f.* keratonosus.
queratopatía *f.* keratopathy.
queratopatía ampollar bullous keratopathy.
queratopatía en banda band keratopathy, band-shaped keratopathy.
queratopatia bullosa bullous keratopathy.
queratopatía climática climatic keratopathy.
queratopatía estríada striate keratopathy.
queratopatía filamentosa filamentary keratopathy.
queratopatía del Labrador Labrador keratopathy.
queratopatía lipídica lipid keratopathy.
queratopatía vesicular vesicular keratopathy.
queratoplasia *f.* keratoplasia.
queratoplastia *f.* keratoplasty.
queratoplastia alopática allopathic keratoplasty.
queratoplastia autógena autogenous keratoplasty.
queratoplastia lamelar lamellar keratoplasty.
queratoplastia óptica optic keratoplasty.
queratoplastia no penetrante non-penetrating keratoplasty.

queratoplastia penetrante penetrating keratoplasty.

queratoplastia de refracción refractive keratoplasty.

queratoplastia tectónica tectonic keratoplasty.

queratoproteína *f.* keratoprotein.

queratoprótesis *f.* keratoprosthesis.

queratorrexis *f.* keratorhexis.

queratoscleritis *f.* keratoscleritis.

queratoscopia *f.* keratoscopy.

queratoscopio *m.* keratoscope.

queratósico, -ca *adj.* keratotic.

queratosis *f.* keratosis.

  queratosis actínica actinic keratosis.

  queratosis por alquitrán tar keratosis.

  queratosis arsenical, queratosis por arsénico arsenic keratosis, arsenical keratosis.

  queratosis blenorrágica keratosis blennorrhagica.

  queratosis del estuco stucco keratosis.

  queratosis faríngea keratosis pharyngea.

  queratosis folicular keratosis follicularis.

  queratosis folicular contagiosa keratosis follicularis contagiosa.

  queratosis gonorreica gonorrheal keratosis.

  queratosis lingual keratosis linguae.

  queratosis nigricans keratosis nigricans.

  queratosis obturadora, queratosis obturante, queratosis obturatriz keratosis obturans.

  queratosis palmar y plantar keratosis palmaris et plantaris.

  queratosis pilar, queratosis pilosa, queratosis pilaris keratosis pilaris.

  queratosis punteada keratosis punctata.

  queratosis por radiación radiation keratosis.

  queratosis por rayos roentgen roentgen keratosis.

  queratosis rubra figurata keratosis rubra figurata.

  queratosis seborreica seborrheic keratosis, keratosis seborrheica.

  queratosis senil senile keratosis, keratosis senilis.

  queratosis solar solar keratosis.

queratosulfato *m.* keratosulfate.

queratotomía *f.* keratotomy.

  queratotomía con láser excímer laser excimer keratotomy.

  queratotomía delimitante delimiting keratotomy.

  queratotomía radial radial keratotomy.

  queratotomía refractiva refractive keratotomy.

queratótomo *m.* keratotome.

queratótoro *m.* keratotorus.

querectasia *f.* kerectasis.

querectasis *f.* kerectasis.

querectomía *f.* kerectomy.

querión *m.* kerion.

  querión de Celso kerion of Celso, Celsus kerion, kerion celsi.

querníctero *m.* kernicterus.

querofobia *f.* cherophobia.

queroideo, -a *adj.* keroid.

queromanía *f.* cheromania.

queroterapia *f.* kerotherapy.

querubismo *m.* cherubism.

querulancia *f.* querulousness.

querulante *adj.* querulous.

quiasma *m.* chiasm, chiasma.

  quiasma de Camper Camper's chiasm.

  quiasma de los dedos de la mano, quiasma tendinoso, quiasma tendinoso del músculo flexor superficial de los dedos, quiasma tendinum digitorum manus chiasm of the digits of the hand, tendinous chiasm of the digital tendons, tendinous chiasm of the flexor digitorum sublimis muscle, chiasma tendinum digitorum manus.

  quiasma óptico optic chiasm, chiasma opticum.

quiasmapexia *f.* chiasmapexy.

quiasmático, -ca *adj.* chiasmatic.

quiasmómetro *m.* chiasmometer.

quiastómetro *m.* chiastometer.

quibisítomo *m.* kibisotome.

quiescente *adj.* quiescent.

quijada *f.* jaw.

  quijada de cotorra parrot jaw.

  quijada crujiente crackling jaw.

  quijada de Habsburgo Habsburg jaw.

  quijada hendida cleft jaw.

  quijada en pico de pájaro bird beak jaw.

  quijada de pipa pipe jaw.

quijilla *f.* quigila.

quilacuoso, -sa *adj.* chylaqueous.

quilalgia *f.* chilalgia.

quilangioma *m.* chylangioma.

quilectasia *f.* chylectasia.

quilectomía *f.* chilectomy.

quilectropión *m.* chilectropion.

quilemia *f.* chylemia.

quilhidrosis *f.* chylidrosis.

quilidrosis *f.* chylidrosis.

quilifacción *f.* chylifaction.

quilifaciente *adj.* chylifacient.

quilifactivo, -va *adj.* chylifactive.

quilífero, -ra *adj.* chyliferous.

quilificación *f.* chylification.

quiliforme *adj.* chyliform.

quilitis *f.* chilitis.

quilo *m.* chyle.

quiloacuoso, -sa *adj.* chylaqueous.

quiloalveolosquisis *f.* chiloalveoloschisis.

quilocele *m.* chylocele.

quilodermia *f.* chyloderma.

quilofagia *f.* chilophagia.

quilóforo, -ra *adj.* chylophoric.

quilognatoglososquisis *f.* chilognathoglossoschisis.

quilognatopalatosquisis *f.* chilognathopalatoschisis.

quilognatoprosoposquisis *f.* chilognathoprosoposchisis.

quilognatosquisis *f.* chilognathoschisis.

quilognatouranosquisis *f.* chilognathouranoschisis.

quiloide *adj.* chyloid.

quilología *f.* chylology.

quilomastigiasis *f.* chilomastigiasis, chilomastixiasis.

quilomastixiasis *f.* chilomastigiasis, chilomastixiasis.

quilomastosis *f.* chilomastosis.

quilomediastino *m.* chylomediastinum.

quilomicrografía *f.* chylomicrograph.

quilomicrón *m.* chylomicron.

quilomicronemia *f.* chylomicronemia.

quiloneumotórax *m.* chylopneumothorax.

quilopericardio *m.* chylopericardium.

quilopericarditis *f.* chylopericarditis.

quiloperitoneo *m.* chyloperitoneum.

quiloplastia *f.* chiloplasty.

quilopleura *f.* chylopleura.

quilopodiasis *f.* chilopodiasis.

quilopoyesis *f.* chylopoiesis.

quilopoyético, -ca *adj.* chylopoietic.

quilorrafia *f.* chilorrhaphy.

quilorrea *f.* chylorrhea.

quilosis[1] *f.* chilosis.

quilosis[2] *f.* chylosis.

quilosis[3] *f.* kyllosis.

quiloso, -sa *adj.* chylous.

quilosquisis *f.* chiloschisis.

quilostomatoplastia *f.* chilostomatoplasty.

quilotomía *f.* chilotomy.

quilotórax *m.* chylothorax.

quiluria *f.* chyluria.

quimasa *f.* chymase.

quimera *f.* chimera, chimaera, chiomera.

  quimera de ADN DNA chimera.

  quimera heteróloga heterologous chimera.

  quimera homóloga homologous chimera.

  quimera isóloga isologous chimera.

  quimera por radiación radiation chimera.

quimérico, -ca *adj.* chimeric.

quimerismo *m.* chimerism.

química *f.* chemistry.

  química analítica analytic chemistry, analytical chemistry.

  química aplicada applied chemistry.

  química biológica biological chemistry.

  química clínica clinical chemistry.

  química coloidal, química coloide colloid chemistry.

  química dental dental chemistry.

  química electroanalítica electroanalytic chemistry.

  química estructural structural chemistry.

  química farmacéutica pharmaceutical chemistry.

  química fisiológica physiologic chemistry, physiological chemistry.

  química forense forensic chemistry.

  química industrial industrial chemistry.

  química inorgánica inorganic chemistry.

  química médica medical chemistry.

  química medicinal medicinal chemistry.

  química metabólica metabolic chemistry.

  química mineral mineral chemistry.

  química nuclear nuclear chemistry.

  química orgánica organic chemistry.

  química patológica medical chemistry.

  química de las radiaciones radiation chemistry.

  química de síntesis synthetic chemistry.

  química de superficie surface chemistry.

químico, -ca[1] *m., f.* chemist.

químico, -ca[2] *adj.* chemical.

quimicobiológico, -ca *adj.* chemicobiological.

quimicocauterio *m.* chemicocautery.

quimicofísico, -ca *adj.* chemicophysical.

quimicofisiológico, -ca *adj.* chemicophysiologic.

quimificación *f.* chymification.

quiminosis *f.* cheminosis.

quimioabrasión *f.* chemabrasion.

quimioatractivo, -va *adj.* chemoattractant.

quimioautotrófico, -ca *adj.* chemoautotrophic.

quimioautótrofo, -fa *adj.* chemoautotrophic.

quimioautótrofo *m.* chemoautotroph.

quimiobiodinamia *f.* chemobiodynamics.

quimiocauterio *m.* chemocautery.

quimiocauterizar *v.* chemocauterize.

quimiocauterización *f.* chemocautery.

quimioceptor$$ra *m., f.* chemoceptor.

quimiocinesis *f.* chemokinesis.

quimiocinético, -ca *adj.* chemokinetic.

quimiocirugía *f.* chemosurgery.

quimiocoagulación *f.* chemocoagulation.

quimiodectoma *m.* chemodectoma.

quimiodectomatosis *f.* chemodectomatosis.

quimiodiferenciación *f.* chemodifferentiation.
quimioesterilizante *adj.* chemosterilant.
quimioexfoliación *f.* chemexfoliation.
quimiofarmacodinámico, -ca *adj.* chemopharmacodynamic.
quimiofisiología *f.* chemophysiology.
quimiofisiológico, -ca *adj.* chemicophysiologic.
quimioheterotrófico, -ca *adj.* chemoheterotrophic.
quimioheterótrofo *m.* chemoheterotroph.
quimiohormonal *adj.* chemohormonal.
quimioinmunología *f.* chemoimmunology.
quimiólisis *f.* chemolysis.
quimiolitotrófico, -ca *adj.* chemolithotrophic.
quimiolitótrofo *m.* chemolithotroph.
quimioluminiscencia *f.* chemiluminiscence, chemoluminiscence.
quimiomorfosis *f.* chemomorphosis.
quimionucleólisis *f.* chemonucleolysis.
quimioorganotrófico, -ca *adj.* chemo-organotrophic.
quimioorganotrofo *m.* chemo-organotroph.
quimioósmosis *f.* chemosmosis.
quimiósmosis *f.* chemosmosis.
quimiopalidectomía *f.* chemopallidectomy.
quimiopalidotalamectomía *f.* chemopallidothalamectomy.
quimiopalidotomía *f.* chemopallidotomy.
quimioprevención *f.* chemoprevention.
quimioprofilaxis *f.* chemoprophylaxis.
  quimioprofilaxis primaria primary chemoprophylaxis.
  quimioprofilaxis secundaria secondary chemoprophylaxis.
quimiopsiquiatría *f.* chemopsychiatry.
quimiorrecepción *f.* chemoreception.
quimiorreceptor *m.* chemoreceptor.
  quimiorreceptor bulbar medullary chemoreceptor.
  quimiorreceptor central central chemoreceptor.
  quimiorreceptor periférico peripheral chemoreceptor.
quimiorreflejo *m.* chemoreflex.
quimiorresistencia *f.* chemoresistance.
quimiosensible *adj.* chemosensitive.
quimiosensorial *adj.* chemosensory.
quimioseroterapia *f.* chemoserotherapy.
quimiosíntesis *f.* chemosynthesis.
quimiosintético, -ca *adj.* chemosynthetic.
quimiósmosis *f.* chemosmosis.
quimiosmótico, -ca *adj.* chemosmotic.
quimiosorción *f.* chemosorption.
quimiostato *m.* chemostat.
quimiotáctico, -ca *adj.* chemotactic.
quimiotactismo *m.* chemotaxis.
quimiotaxis *f.* chemotaxis.
  quimiotaxis leucocitaria leukocyte chemotaxis.
  quimiotaxis negativa negative chemotaxis.
  quimiotaxis positiva positive chemotaxis.
quimiotalamectomía *f.* chemothalamectomy.
quimiotalamotomía *f.* chemothalamotomy.
quimiotaxina *f.* chemotaxin.
quimioterapéutico, -ca *adj.* chemotherapeutic.
quimioterapia *f.* chemotherapy.
  quimioterapia adyuvante adjuvant chemotherapy.
  quimioterapia combinada combination chemotherapy.
  quimioterapia de consolidación consolidation chemotherapy.
  quimioterapia intraarterial, quimioterapia

I.A. intraarterial chemotherapy.
  quimioterapia de inducción induction chemotherapy.
  quimioterapia de intensificación intensification chemotherapy.
  quimioterapia radioactiva chemotherapy (unsealed radioactive).
  quimioterapia de salvataje salvage chemotherapy.
quimioterápico, -ca *adj.* chemotherapeutic.
quimiotripsinógeno *m.* chymotrypsinogen.
quimiotrófico, -ca *adj.* chemotrophic.
quimiótrofo *m.* chemotroph.
quimiotrópico, -ca *adj.* chemotropic.
quimiotropismo *m.* chemotropism.
quimismo *m.* chemism.
quimo *m.* chyme.
quimociclógrafo *m.* kymocyclograph.
quimodenina *f.* chymodenin.
quimografía *f.* kymography.
  quimografía roentgen roentgen kymography.
quimógrafo *m.* kymograph.
quimograma *m.* kymogram.
quimopapaína *f.* chymopapain.
quimopoyesis *f.* chymopoiesis.
quimorrea *f.* chymorrhea.
quimosina *f.* chymosin.
quimoso, -sa *adj.* chymous.
quimotripsina *f.* chymotrypsin.
quinasa *f.* kinase.
quinquecúspide *adj.* quinquecuspid.
quinquetubercular *adj.* quinquetubercular.
quintaesencia *f.* quintassence.
quintana *adj.* quintan.
quintillizo, -za *adj.* quintuplet.
quintípara *f.* quintipara.
quintisternal *adj.* quintisternal.
quíntuplo, -pla *adj.* quintuplet.
quiógeno, -na *adj.* kyogenic.
quionablepsia *f.* chionablepsia.
quiotomía *f.* kiotomy.
quiótomo *m.* kiotome.
quiragra *f.* chiragra.
quiral *adj.* chiral.
quiralgia *f.* chiralgia.
quiralidad *f.* chirality.
quirartritis *f.* cheirarthritis.
quirobraquialgia *f.* chirobrachialgia.
quirocinestesia *f.* chirokinesthesia.
quirocinestésico, -ca *adj.* chirokinesthetic.
quiroespasmo *m.* chirospasm.
quirófano *m.* operating room.
quirognomía *f.* cheirognomy.
quirognóstico, -ca *adj.* chirognostic.
quirología *f.* chirology.
quiromegalia *f.* chiromegaly.
quiroplastia *f.* chiroplasty.
quiropodalgia *f.* chiropodalgia.
quiroponfólix *m.* chiropompholyx.
quiropráctica *f.* chiropractics.
quiropraxia *f.* chiropractics.
quiropráctico *m., f.* chiropractor.
quiropractor *m., f.* chiropractor.
quiroscopio *m.* chiroscope.
quirospasmo *m.* chirospasm.
quirtorráquico, -ca *adj.* kyrtorrhachic.
quirurgénico, -ca *adj.* chirurgenic.
quirúrgico, -ca *adj.* chirurgic, surgical.
quiste *m.* cyst.
  quiste abovedado azul blue dome cyst.
  quiste achocolatado chocolate cyst.
  quiste de Acrel Acrel's cyst.
  quiste alantoico allantoic cyst.
  quiste alquitranado tarry cyst.

  quiste alveolar alveolar cyst.
  quiste amniótico amnionic cyst.
  quiste angioblástico angioblastic cyst.
  quiste apical apical cyst.
  quiste apical periodontal apical periodontal cyst.
  quiste aracnoideo arachnoid cyst.
  quiste ateromatoso atheromatous cyst.
  quiste de Baker Baker's cyst.
  quiste de Bartholin, quiste de Bartolino Bartholin's cyst.
  quiste de Blessig Blessig's cyst.
  quiste de la bolsa de Rathke Rathke's pouch cyst.
  quiste de Boyer Boyer's cyst.
  quiste branquial, quiste branquiógeno branchial cyst, branchiogenetic cyst, branchiogenous cyst.
  quiste broncogénico, quiste broncógeno, quiste broncopulmonar, quiste bronquial bronchial cyst, bronchogenic cyst, bronchopulmonary cyst.
  quiste bursal bursal cyst, gallbladder cyst.
  quiste cerebeloso cerebellar cyst.
  quiste cervical cervical cyst.
  quiste de chocolate chocolate cyst.
  quiste del colédoco choledochal cyst, choledochus cyst.
  quiste coloidal, quiste coloide, quiste coloideo colloid cyst, colloidal cyst.
  quiste compuesto compound cyst.
  quiste del conducto craneofaríngeo craniopharyngeal duct cyst.
  quiste del conducto nasopalatino nasopalatine duct cyst.
  quiste del conducto tirogloso thyroglossal duct cyst.
  quiste congénito congenital cyst.
  quiste de Cowper Cowper's cyst.
  quiste craneobucal craniobuccal cyst.
  quiste del cuerpo amarillo corpus luteum cyst, corpora lutea cyst.
  quiste en cúpula azul blue dome cyst.
  quiste cutáneo, quiste cuticular cutaneous cyst, cuticular cyst.
  quiste de Dandy-Walker Dandy-Walker cyst.
  quiste dental dental cyst.
  quiste dentígero dentigerous cyst.
  quiste dentoalveolar dentoalveolar cyst.
  quiste dermoide, quiste dermoideo dermoid cyst.
  quiste dermoide de implantación implantation dermoid cyst.
  quiste dermoide de inclusión inclusion dermoid cyst.
  quiste dermoide del ovario dermoid cyst of the ovary.
  quiste dermoide tiroideo thyroid dermoid cyst.
  quiste dermoide tubárico tubal dermoid cyst.
  quiste por dilatación dilatation cyst.
  quiste por distensión distention cyst.
  quiste por duplicación duplication cyst.
  quiste endometrial endometrial cyst.
  quiste endotelial endothelial cyst.
  quiste entérico, quiste enterógeno enteric cyst, enterogenous cyst.
  quiste ependimario ependymal cyst.
  quiste epidérmico epidermal cyst.
  quiste epidérmico de inclusión epidermal inclusion cyst.
  quiste epidermoide, quiste epidermoideo epidermoid cyst.
  quiste de epidídimo epididymal cyst.

quiste epiploico omental cyst.
quiste epitelial epithelial cyst.
quiste equinocócico, quiste de equinococos echinococcus cyst.
quiste de erupción eruption cyst.
quiste estéril sterile cyst.
quiste por extravasación extravasation cyst.
quiste de exudación, quiste por exudación exudation cyst.
quiste feomicótico phaeomycotic cyst.
quiste fisural fissural cyst.
quiste folicular follicular cyst.
quiste ganglionar ganglionic cyst.
quiste de Gartner, quiste gartneriano Gartner's cyst, Gartner's duct cyst, Gartnerian cyst.
quiste gaseoso gas cyst.
quiste gingival gingival cyst.
quiste globulomaxilar globulomaxillary cyst.
quiste de Gorlin Gorlin cyst.
quiste hemático, quiste hemorrágico blood cyst, hemorrhagic cyst.
quiste de la hendidura branquial branchial cleft cyst.
quiste hepático hepatic cyst, cyst of the liver.
quiste hidatídico hydatid cyst.
quiste hidatídico alveolar alveolar hydatid cyst.
quiste hidatídico multiloculado, quiste hidatídico multilocular multiloculate hydatid cyst, multilocular hydatid cyst.
quiste hidatídico óseo osseous hydatid cyst.
quiste hidatídico unilocular unilocular hydatid cyst.
quiste hijo daughter cyst.
quiste de implantación, quiste por implantación, quiste por inclusión implantation cyst, inclusion cyst.
quiste intraepitelial intraepithelial cyst.
quiste intraluminal intraluminal cyst.
quiste intrapituitario intrapituitary cyst.
quiste de involución, quiste por involución involution cyst.
quiste de Iwanoff Iwanoff's cyst.
quiste de jabón soap cyst.
quiste láctico lacteal cyst.
quiste de la lámina dental dental lamina cyst.
quiste lateral periodontal lateral periodontal cyst.
quiste de leche, quiste de la leche milk cyst.
quiste leptomeníngeo leptomeningeal cyst.
quiste luteínico, quiste lúteo lutein cyst, luteal cyst.
quiste madre mother cyst.
quiste mandibular mediano median mandibular cyst.
quiste en mantequilla butter cyst.
quiste maxilar anterior mediano median anterior maxillary cyst.
quiste meibomiamo, quiste de Meibomio Meibomian cyst.
quiste mesentérico mesenteric cyst.
quiste mesonéfrico, quiste mesonefroide mesonephroid cyst.
quiste mixoide myxoid cyst.
quiste mucoide mucoid cyst.

quiste mucoso mucous cyst.
quiste multilocular multilocular cyst.
quiste nasoalveolar, quiste nasolabial nasoalveolar cyst, nasolabial cyst.
quiste necrótico necrotic cyst.
quiste neural neural cyst.
quiste neurentérico neurenteric cyst.
quiste nevoide nevoid cyst.
quiste nieto granddaughter cyst.
quiste odontogénico, quiste odontógeno odontogenic cyst.
quiste odontogénico calcificante calcifying odontogenic cyst.
quiste odontogénico y queratinizante calcifying and keratinizing odontogenic cyst.
quiste oleoso oil cyst.
quiste ooforético oophoritic cyst.
quiste óseo bone cyst.
quiste óseo aneurismático aneurysmal bone cyst.
quiste óseo hidatídico osseous hydatid cyst.
quiste óseo solitario simple bone cyst, solitary bone cyst, traumatic bone cyst.
quiste óseo de Stafne Stafne bone cyst.
quiste ovárico, quiste del ovario ovarian cyst.
quiste del paladar mediano, quiste palatino mediano median palatal cyst.
quiste pancreático pancreatic cyst.
quiste paranéfrico paranephric cyst.
quiste paraovárico, quiste parovárico paraovarian cyst.
quiste pararrenal paranephric cyst.
quiste parasitario, quiste parásito parasitic cyst.
quiste parovárico paraovarian cyst.
quiste parvilocular parvilocular cyst.
quiste periapical periapical cyst.
quiste pericárdico pericardial cyst.
quiste periodontal periodontal cyst.
quiste periodontal apical apical periodontal cyst.
quiste periodontal lateral lateral periodontal cyst.
quiste en perla, quiste perlado pearl cyst.
quiste pilar, quiste pilífero, quiste piloso pilar cyst, piliferous cyst.
quiste pilonidal pilonidal cyst.
quiste placentario placental cyst.
quiste porencefálico porencephalic cyst.
quiste preauricular congénito congenital preauricular cyst.
quiste primordial primordial cyst.
quiste proliferante, quiste proliferativo proliferation cyst, proliferative cyst.
quiste proliferante del tricolema proliferating tricholemmal cyst.
quiste proligero proligerous cyst.
quiste de protozoarios protozoan cyst.
quiste pseudomucinoso, quiste seudomucinoso pseudomucinous cyst.
quiste queratinizante keratinous cyst.
quiste queratinoso keratinous cyst.
quiste de quilo chyle cyst.
quiste radicular, quiste radiculodental, quiste de la raíz root cyst, radiculodental cyst.
quiste de Rathke Rathke's cyst.

quiste de la red ovárica rete cyst of ovary.
quiste renal renal cyst.
quiste renal multilocular benign multilocular cyst, multilocular cyst, nephroma.
quiste renal simple simple renal cyst.
quiste residual residual cyst.
quiste por retención retention cyst.
quiste de Sampson Sampson's cyst.
quiste sanguíneo blood cyst, sanguineous cyst.
quiste sebáceo sebaceous cyst.
quiste secretorio secretory cyst.
quiste por secuestración sequestration cyst.
quiste secundario secondary cyst.
quiste seminal seminal cyst.
quiste seroso serous cyst.
quiste seudomucinoso pseudomucinous cyst.
quiste simple simple cyst.
quiste sinovial synovial cyst.
quiste subcondral subchondral cyst.
quiste sublingual sublingual cyst.
quiste subsinovial subsynovial cyst.
quiste supraselar suprasellar cyst.
quiste de Tarlov Tarlov's cyst.
quiste tarsal, quiste tarsiano tarsal cyst.
quiste tecal thecal cyst.
quiste tecaluteínico theca-lutein cyst.
quiste teratomatoso teratomatous cyst.
quiste tímico thymic cyst.
quiste tirogloso, quiste tirolingual thyroglossal cyst, thyrolingual cyst.
quiste de Tornwaldt Tornwaldt's cyst.
quiste tricolémico, quiste triquilemal trichilemmal cyst.
quiste tuboovárico tubo-ovarian cyst.
quiste tubular tubular cyst.
quiste umbilical umbilical cyst.
quiste unicameral, quiste unilocular unicameral cyst, unicameral bone cyst, unilocular cyst.
quiste de unión junctional cyst.
quiste uracal, quiste del uraco urachal cyst.
quiste urinario urinary cyst.
quiste vaginal vaginal cyst.
quiste verdadero true cyst.
quiste vitelointestinal vitellointestinal cyst.
quiste vocal intracordal cyst.
quiste de Wolff, quiste wolffiano Wolffian cyst.

quistectomía *f.* cystectomy.
quístico, -ca[1] *adj.* cystic.
quístico, -ca[2] *adj.* cystose, cystous.
quistoduodenostomía *f.* cystduodenostomy.
quistogastrostomía *f.* cystgastrostomy.
quistografía *f.* cystography.
quistoperiquistectomía *f.* cystopericystectomy.
   quistoperiquistectomía subtotal *f.* subtotal cystopericystectomy.
   quistoperiquistectomía total *f.* total cystopericystectomy.
quistoyeyunostomía *f.* cystojejunostomy.
quitina *f.* chitin.
quitinasa *f.* chitinase.
quitinoso, -sa *adj.* chitinous.
quitoneuro *m.* chitoneure.

R r

rabadilla *f.* rump.
rabditiforme *adj.* rhabditiform.
rabditoide *adj.* rhadbitoid.
rabdocito *m.* rhabdocyte.
rabdoesfínter *m.* rhabdosphincter.
rabdofobia *f.* rhabdophobia.
rabdoide *adj.* rhabdoid.
rabdoideo, -a *adj.* rhabdoid.
rabdomioblasto *m.* rhabdomyoblast.
rabdomioblastoma *m.* rhabdomyoblastoma.
rabdomiocondroma *m.* rhabdomyochondroma.
rabdomiólisis *f.* rhabdomyolysis.
 rabdomiólisis por esfuerzo exertional rhabdomyolysis.
 rabdomiólisis paroxística idiopática idiopathic paroxysmal rhabdomyolysis.
rabdomioma *m.* rhabdomyoma.
 rabdomioma granulosa, rabdomioma granulocelular granular cell myoblaste.
rabdomiomixoma *m.* rhabdomyomyxoma.
rabdomiosarcoma *m.* rhabdomyosarcoma.
 rabdomiosarcoma alveolar alveolar rhabdomyosarcoma.
 rabdomiosarcoma alveolar juvenil juvenile alveolar rhabdomyosarcoma.
 rabdomiosarcoma embrionarios embryonal rhabdomyosarcoma.
 rabdomiosarcoma pleomórfico pleomorphic rhabdomyosarcoma.
rabdosarcoma *m.* rhabdosarcoma.
rabdovirus *m.* rhabdovirus.
rabia *f.* rabies.
 rabia falsa false rabies.
 rabia furiosa furious rabies.
 rabia muda dumb rabies.
 rabia paralítica paralytic rabies.
rabicida *adj.* rabicidal.
rábico, -ca *adj.* rabic, rabietic.
rabieta *f.* tantrum.
rabífico, -ca *adj.* rabific.
rabiforme *adj.* rabiform.
rabígeno, -na *adj.* rabigenic.
rabioso, -sa *adj.* rabiate, rabid.
racemato *m.* racemate.
raceme *m.* raceme.
racémico, -ca *adj.* racemic.
racemización *f.* racemization.
racemoso, -sa *adj.* racemose.
racial *adj.* racial.
raciocinio *m.* rationale.
ración *f.* ration.
 ración basal basal ration.
racional *adj.* rational.
racionalidad *f.* rationality.
 racionalidad ética ethical rationality.
 racionalidad técnica technical rationality.
racionalización *f.* rationalization.
racionar *v.* ration.
racismo *m.* racism.

racista *adj.* racist.
racoma *f.* rhacoma.
radarquimografía *f.* radarkymography.
radectomía *f.* radectomy, radiectomy.
radiabilidad *f.* radiability.
radiable *adj.* radiable.
radiación *f.* radiation, radiato.
 radiación acústica acoustic radiation, radiatio acustica.
 radiación adaptativa adaptive radiation.
 radiación alfa alpha radiation.
 radiación ambiental background radiation.
 radiación de aniquilación annihilation radiation.
 radiación atmosférica atmospheric radiation.
 radiación auditiva, radiación auditoria auditory radiation.
 radiación de bajo grado low-level radiation.
 radiación beta beta radiation.
 radiación blanda soft radiation.
 radiación de campo ampliado extended field radiation.
 radiación característica characteristic radiation.
 radiación de convergencia convergent beam therapy.
 radiación corporal total total body radiation.
 radiación corpuscular corpuscular radiation.
 radiación a corta distancia short-distance irradiation.
 radiación cósmica cosmic radiation.
 radiación del cuerpo calloso radiato corporis callosi.
 radiación del cuerpo estriado radiato corporis striati.
 radiación difusa scattered radiation.
 radiación dispersa scattered radiation.
 radiación divergente divergent radiation.
 radiación dura hard radiation.
 radiación electromagnética electromagnetic radiation.
 radiación de fondo background radiation.
 radiación de frenado blemsstrahlung radiation, breaking radiation.
 radiación fotoquímica photochemical radiation.
 radiación fuera de foco off-focus radiation.
 radiación por fugas leakage radiation.
 radiación gamma gamma radiation.
 radiación geniculocalcarina geniculocalcarine radiation.
 radiación de Gratiolet Gratiolet radiation, radiation of Gratiolet.
 radiación heterogénea heterogeneous radiation.
 radiación homogénea homogeneous radiation.
 radiación infrarroja infrared radiation.
 radiación del injerto graft radiation.
 radiación intersticial interstitial radiation.

 radiación intrauterina intrauterine radiation.
 radiación ionizante ionizing radiation.
 radiación no ionizante non-ionizing radiation.
 radiación monocromática monochromatic radiation.
 radiación monoenergética monoenergetic radiation.
 radiación natural natural radiation.
 radiación nuclear nuclear radiation.
 radiación occipitotalámica occipitothalamic radiation.
 radiación óptica optic radiation, radiatio optica.
 radiación piramidal pyramidal radiation, radiatio pyramidalis.
 radiación primaria primary radiation.
 radiación residual remnant radiation.
 radiación de retrodispersión backscatter radiation.
 radiación de Rollier Rollier's radiation.
 radiación secundaria secondary radiation.
 radiación solar solar radiation.
 radiación talámica thalamic radiation, radiation of the thalamus.
 radiación talamotemporal thalamotemporal radiation.
 radiación tegmentaria tegmental radiation.
 radiación térmica thermal radiation.
 radiación ultravioleta ultraviolet radiation.
 radiación útil useful radiation.
 radiación no utilizada stray radiation.
 radiación visible visible radiation.
 radiación de Wernicke Wernicke radiation.
 radiación X X-radiation.
radiactivación *f.* radioactivation.
radiactividad *f.* radioactivity.
radioactividad *f.* radioactivity.
 radiactividad alfa alpha radioactivity.
 radiactividad artificial artificial radioactivity.
 radiactividad beta beta radioactivity.
 radiactividad beta positiva beta positive radioactivity.
 radiactividad específica specific radioactivity.
 radiactividad inducida induced radioactivity.
 radiactividad natural natural radioactivity.
radiactivo, -va *adj.* radioactive.
radioactivo, -va *adj.* radioactive.
radiactor *m.* radioactor.
radiad radiad.
radiado, -da *adj.* radiate.
radial *adj.* radial, radialis.
radián *m.* radian.
radiante *m.* radiant.
radiar *v.* radiate.
radical *m. y adj.* radical.
 ácido radical acid radical.
 radical alcohol alcohol radical.
 radical coloreado, radical de color color radical.

radical cromóforo color radical.
radical hidróxilo hydroxyl radical.
radical libre free radical, oxygen derived free radical.
radical de oxígeno oxygen radical.
radiciforme *adj.* radiciform.
radicoloide *adj.* radiocolloid.
radicotomía *f.* radicotomy.
radicotomía posterior posterior spinal rhizotomy.
radícula *f.* radicle, radicula.
radiculalgia *f.* radiculalgia.
radicular *adj.* radicular.
radiculectomía *f.* radiculectomy.
radiculitis *f.* radiculitis.
radiculitis braquial aguda acute brachial radiculitis.
radiculoganglionitis *f.* radiculoganglionitis.
radiculografía *f.* radiculography.
radiculomedular *adj.* radiculomedullary.
radiculomeningomielitis *f.* radiculomeningomyelitis.
radiculomielopatía *f.* radiculomyelopathy.
radiculoneuritis *f.* radiculoneuritis.
radiculoneuropatía *f.* radiculoneuropathy.
radiculopatía *f.* radiculopathy.
radiectomía *f.* radiectomy.
radielemento *m.* radioelement.
radífero, -ra *adj.* radiferous.
radio¹ *m.* radium.
radio² *m.* radius.
radio del cristalino radius of the lens.
radio curvo radius curvus.
radio fijo radius fixus.
radio de van der Walls van der Walls radius.
radioalergosorbente *adj.* radioallergosorbent.
radioautografía *f.* radioautography.
radioautógrafo *m.* radioautograph.
radioazufre *m.* radiosulfur.
radiobicipital *adj.* radiobicipital.
radiobiología *f.* radiobiology.
radiobiológico, -ca *adj.* radiobiological, radiobiologic.
radiobiólogo, -ga *m., f.* radiobiologist.
radiocalcio *m.* radiocalcium.
radiocáncer *m.* radiocancer.
radiocarbono *m.* radiocarbon.
radiocarcinogénesis *f.* radiocarcinogenesis.
radiocardiografía *f.* radiocardiography.
radiocardiograma *m.* radiocardiogram.
radiocarpal *adj.* radiocarpal.
radiocarpiano, -na *adj.* radiocarpal.
radiocinematografía *f.* radiocinematography, roentgencinematography.
radiocinematógrafo *m.* radiocinematograph.
radiocinematográfico, -ca *adj.* radiocinematographic.
radiocirugía *f.* radiosurgery.
radiocistitis *f.* radiocystitis.
radiocobalto *m.* iradiocobalt.
radiocoloide *m.* radiocolloid.
radiocromatografía *f.* radiochromatograpy.
radiocubital *adj.* radioulnar.
radiocurable *adj.* radiocurable.
radiodensidad *f.* radiodensity.
radiodensimetría *f.* radiodensimetry.
radiodensitometría *f.* radiodensitometry.
radiodenso, -sa *adj.* radiodense.
radiodermatitis *f.* radiodermatitis.
radiodermitis *f.* radiodermitis.
radiodiagnosis *f.* radiodiagnosis.
radiodiagnóstico *m.* radiodiagnosis.
radiodiagnóstico, -ca *m.* radiodiagnostic.
radiodigital *adj.* radiodigital.

radiodoncia *f.* radiodontics.
radiodoncista *m., f.* radiodontist.
radioecología *f.* radioecology.
radioelectrocardiografía *f.* radioelectrocardiography.
radioelectrocardiógrafo *m.* radioelectrocardiograph.
radioelectrocardiograma *m.* radioelectrocardiogram.
radioelemento *m.* radioelement.
radioencefalografía *f.* radioencephalography.
radioencefalograma *m.* radioencephalogram.
radioepidermitis *f.* radioepidermitis.
radioepitelitis *f.* radioepithelitis.
radioesclerómetro *m.* radosclerometer.
radioestereoscopia *f.* radiostereoscopy, radiosteroscopy.
radioestroncio *m.* radiostrontium.
radiofarmacéutico, -ca¹ *adj.* radiopharmaceutic, radiopharmaceutical.
radiofarmacéutico, -ca² *m., f.* radiopharmacist.
radiofarmacia *f.* radiopharmacy.
radiofármaco *m.* radiopharmaceutical preparation.
radiofármaco de investigación research radiopharmaceutical preparation.
radiofármaco diagnóstico diagnostic radiopharmaceutical preparation.
radiofármaco terapéutico therapeutic radiopharmaceutical preparation.
radiofibrinógeno *m.* radiofibrinogen.
radiofísica *f.* radiophysics.
radiofísico, -ca *m., f.* radiophysicist.
radiofósforo *m.* radiophosphorus.
radiofotografía *f.* radiophotography.
radiofrecuencia *f.* radiofrequency.
radiogalio *m.* radiogallium.
radiogénesis *f.* radiogenesis.
radiogenia *f.* radiogenics.
radiogénico, -ca *adj.* radiogenic.
radiógeno *m.* radiogen.
radiógeno, -na *adj.* radiogenic.
radiografía¹ *f.* radiography.
radiografía de aumento magnification radiography.
radiografía por barrido de hendidura slit scan radiography.
radiografía cefalométrica cephalometric radiograph.
radiografía dental dental radiograph.
radiografía digital digital radiography.
radiografía de doble contraste double contrast radiography.
radiografía electrónica electron radiography.
radiografía estereoscópica stereoscopic radiograph.
radiografía magnificada, radiografía de magnificación magnification radiography.
radiografía en masa mass radiography.
radiografía en miniatura en masa mass miniature radiography.
radiografía de mordida bite-wing radiography.
radiografía oclusal, radiografía oclusiva occlusal radiography.
radiografía panorámica panoramic radiography.
radiografía periapical periapical radiography.
radiografía portátil AP AP portable view.
radiografía del relieve de la mucosa mucosal relief radiography.
radiografía de una sección corporal body-

section radiography.
radiografía selectiva selective radiography.
radiografía seriada por planos paralelos body-section radiography.
radiografía seriada, radiografía en serie serial radiography.
radiografía² *f.* radiogram.
radiografía con aleta bite-wing radiogram.
radiografía panorámica panoramic radiogram.
radiográfico, -ca *adj.* radiographic.
radiografista *m., f.* radiographer.
radiograma *m.* radiogram.
radiohierro *m.* radioiron.
radiohumeral *adj.* radiohumeral.
radioinmunidad *f.* radioimmunity.
radioinmunización *f.* radioimmunity.
radioinmunoanálisis (RIA) *m.* radioimmunoassay (RIA).
radioinmunodetección *f.* radioimmunodetection.
radioinmunodifusión *f.* radioimmunodiffusion.
radioinmunoelectroforesis *f.* radioimmunoelectrophoresis.
radioinmunoensayo *m.* radioimmunoassay.
radioinmunología *f.* radioimmunology.
radioinmunológico, -ca *adj.* radioimmunologic.
radioinmunoprecipitación *f.* radioimmunoprecipitation.
radioinmunosorbente *adj.* radioimmunosorbent.
radioinmunoterapia *f.* radioimmunotherapy.
radioiodo *m.* radioactive iodine.
radioisotópico, -ca *adj.* radioisotopic.
radioisótopo *m.* radioisotope.
radiolábil *adj.* radiosensitive.
radiolesión *f.* radiolesion.
radioligando *m.* radioligand.
radiólisis *f.* radiolysis.
radiología *f.* radiology.
radiología bucal oral radiology.
radiología convencional conventional radiology.
radiología dental dental radiology.
radiología diagnóstica diagnostic radiology.
radiología digital digital radiology.
radiología intervencionista interventional radiology.
radiología médica medical radiology.
radiología pediátrica pediatric radiology.
radiológico, -ca *adj.* radiologic, radiological.
radiólogo, -ga *m., f.* radiologist.
radiólogo dental dental radiologist.
radiolucencia *f.* radiolucency.
radiolucente *adj.* radiolucent.
radiolucidez *f.* radiolucency.
radiolúcido, -da *adj.* radiolucent.
radioluminiscencia *f.* radioluminiscence.
radiomarcado *m.* radiolabeling.
radiomarcado, -da *adj.* radiolabeled.
radiomarcaje *m.* radiolabeling.
radiometría *f.* radiometry.
radiómetro *m.* radiometer.
radiómetro fotográfico photographic radiometer.
radiómetro de pastilla pastille radiometer.
radiómetro de película film radiometer.
radiomicrómetro *m.* radiomicrometer.
radiomimético, -ca *adj.* radiomimetic.
radiomuscular *adj.* radiomuscular.
radiomutación *f.* radiomutation.
radionecrosis *f.* radionecrosis.
radioneuritis *f.* radioneuritis.
radionitrógeno *m.* radionitrogen.

radionúcleo *m.* radionucleus.

radonúclido *m.* radionuclide.

radioopacidad *f.* radiopacity.

radioopaco, -ca *adj.* radiopaque.

radiopacidad *f.* radiopacity.

radiopaco, -ca *adj.* radiopaque.

radiopalmar *adj.* radiopalmar.

radiopatología *f.* radiopathology.

radiopelvigrafía *f.* radiopelvigraphy.

radiopelvimetría *f.* radiopelvimetry.

radioplomo *m.* radiolead.

radiopotasio *m.* radiopotassium.

radiopotenciación *f.* radiopotentiation.

radioprotección *f.* radiation protection.

radioprotector *m.* chemical protector.

radioquímica *f.* radiation chemistry, radiochemistry.

radioquímico, -ca *adj.* radiochemical.

radioquimografía *f.* radiokymography, roentgenkymography.

radioquimógrafo *m.* roentgenkymograph.

radioquimograma *m.* roentgenkymogram.

radiorrespondente *adj.* radioresponsive.

radiorreacción *f.* radioreaction.

radiorreaccionante *adj.* radioresponsive.

radiorreceptor *m.* radioreceptor.

radiorresistencia *f.* radioresistance.

   radiorresistencia adquirida acquired radioresistance.

radiorresistente *adj.* radioresistant.

radiosarcoma *m.* X-ray sarcoma.

radiosclerómetro *m.* radiosclerometer.

radioscopia *f.* radioscopy.

radioscópico, -ca *adj.* radioscopic.

radioscopio *m.* radioscope.

radiosensibilidad *f.* radiosensibility, radiosensitiveness, radiosensitivity.

radiosensibilizador *m.* radiosensitizer.

radiosensible *adj.* radiosensitive, radiosensible.

radiosodio *m.* radiosodium.

radiostereoscopia *f.* radiostereoscopy, radiosteroscopy.

radiotanatología *f.* radiothanatology.

radiotelemetría *f.* radiotelemetry.

radioterapeuta *m., f.* radiotherapist.

radioterapéutica *f.* radiotherapeutics.

radioterapéutico, -ca *adj.* radiotherapeutic.

radioterapia *f.* radiation therapy, radiotherapy, X-ray therapy.

   radioterapia de campo ampliado extended field radiotherapy.

   radioterapia corporal total whole-body radiotherapy.

   radioterapia con electrones electron beam radiotherapy.

   radioterapia externa external radiation therapy.

   radioterapia intersticial interstitial radiotherapy.

   radioterapia intracavitaria intracavitary radiotherapy.

   radioterapia con mesones pi negativos (piones) negative pi meson (pion) radiotherapy.

   radioterapia metabólica metabolic radiotherapy.

radiotermia *f.* radiothermy.

radiotiroidectomía *f.* radiothyroidectomy.

radiotiroxina *f.* radiothyroxin.

radiotomografía *f.* radiotomography.

radiotoxemia *f.* radiotoxemia.

radiotoxicidad *f.* radiotoxicity.

radiotoxicología *f.* radiotoxicology.

radiotransparencia *f.* radioparency, radiotransparency.

radiotransparente *adj.* radiotransparent.

radiotrazador *m.* radiotracer.

radioyodado, -da *adj.* radioiodinated.

radioyodo *m.* radioiodine.

radisectomía *f.* radisectomy.

radium radium.

radius radius.

radix radix.

radón *m.* radon.

   radón 219 radon 219 actinon.

   radón 220 radon 220 thoron.

   radón 222 radon 222.

   productos dependientes del radón 222 radon 222 daughter products.

raebocrania *f.* rhaebocrania.

raebosis *f.* rhaebosis.

rafe *m.* raphe.

rafidiospora *f.* raphidiospore.

rágade *f.* rhagade, rhagades.

ragadías *f.* rhagades.

ragadiforme *adj.* rhagadiform.

ragiocrino, -na *adj.* rhagiocrine.

ragocito *m.* ragocyte.

raicilla *f.* rootlet.

   raicilla flagelar flagellar rootlet.

raigón *m.* tooth stump.

Raillietina Raillietina.

raillietiniasis *f.* raillietiniasis.

raíz *f.* root, radix.

rama[1] *f.* branch, ramus.

rama[2] *f.* branch.

ramal *m.* ramal.

ramicotomía *f.* ramicotomy.

ramificación *f.* ramification.

   ramificación falsa false ramification.

ramificado, -da *adj.* branching, ramified.

ramificar *v.* ramify.

ramillete *m.* bouquet, nosegay.

   ramillete de Riolano Riolan's nosegay.

ramisección *f.* ramisection.

ramisectomía *f.* ramisectomy.

ramita *f.* twig, ramulus.

ramitis *f.* ramitis.

ramo *m.* branch, ramus.

ramoso, -sa *adj.* ramose, ramous.

rampa *f.* scala.

rámula *f.* ramulus.

rámulo *m.* ramulus.

ramus ramus.

ramúsculo *m.* ramulus.

ranciar *v.* rancidify.

rancidez *f.* rancidity.

ranciedad *f.* rancidity.

rancio, -cia *adj.* rancid, rank.

rango *m.* range.

   rango de movimiento range of motion.

   rango de acomodación range of accommodation.

   rango dinámico dynamic range.

ranino, -na *adj.* ranine.

ránula *f.* ranula.

   ránula pancreática pancreatic ranula.

ranular *adj.* ranular.

ranura *f.* cleft.

rapto *m.* raptus.

raquial *adj.* rachial.

raquialbuminometría *f.* rachialbuminimetry.

raquialbuminómetro *m.* rachialbuminimeter.

raquialgia *f.* rachialgia.

raquianalgesia *f.* rachianalgesia.

raquianestesia *f.* rachianesthesia, spinal anesthesia.

   raquianestesia hiperbárica hyperbaric rachianesthesia.

   raquianestesia hipobárica hypobaric rachianesthesia.

   raquianestesia isobárica isobaric spinal anesthesia.

raquicentesis *f.* rachicentesis, rachiocentesis.

raquídeo, -a *adj.* rachidial.

raquidiano, -na *adj.* rachidian.

raquiestenosis *f.* rachistenosis.

   raquiestenosis cervical cervical stenosis.

   raquiestenosis lumbar lumbar stenosis.

raquígrafo *m.* rachigraph.

raquilisis *f.* rachilysis.

raquiocampsis *f.* rachiocampsis.

raquiocentesis *f.* rachiocentesis.

raquiocifosis *f.* rachiocyphosis, rachiokyphosis.

raquiodinia *f.* rachiodynia.

raquioescoliosis *m.* rachioscoliosis.

raquiómetro *m.* rachiometer.

raquiomielitis *f.* rachiomyelitis.

raquiópago, -ga *m., f.* rachiopagus, rachipagus.

raquiopatía *f.* rachiopathy, rachipathy.

raquioplejia *f.* rachioplegia.

raquioquisis *f.* rachiochysis, rachychysis.

raquioscoliosis *f.* rachioscoliosis.

raquiotomía *f.* rachiotomy, rachitomy.

raquiótomo *m.* rachiotome, rachitome.

raquípago, -ga *adj.* rachipagus.

raquirresistencia *f.* rachircsistance.

raquirresistente *adj.* rachiresistant.

raquis *m.* rachis.

raquisagra *f.* rachisagra.

raquisensibilidad *f.* rachisensibility.

raquisensible *adj.* rachisensible.

raquisensitivo, -va *adj.* rachisensible.

raquisquisis *f.* rachischisis.

   raquisquisis anterior somatoschisis.

   raquisquisis posterior rachischisis posterior.

   raquisquisis total rachischisis totalis.

raquítico, -ca *adj.* rachitic, rickety.

raquitis *f.* rachitis.

   raquitis fetal rachitis fetalis.

   raquitis fetal anular rachitis fetalis annularis.

   raquitis fetal micromélica rachitis fetalis micromelica.

   raquitis intrauterina rachitis intrauterina.

   raquitis tardía rachitis tarda.

   raquitis uterina rachitis uterina.

raquitismo *m.* rachitis, rickets.

   raquitismo de los adolescentes late rickets, rachitis tarda.

   raquitismo del adulto adult rickets.

   raquitismo agudo acute rickets.

   raquitismo por berilio beryllium rickets.

   raquitismo celiaco celiac rickets.

   raquitismo congénito fetal rickets.

   raquitismo fetal rachitis fetalis.

   raquitismo escorbútico scurvy rickets.

   raquitismo de Glisson Glissonian rickets.

   raquitismo graso fat rickets.

   raquitismo hemorrágico hemorrhagic rachitis.

   raquitismo hepático hepatic rachitis.

   raquitismo hipofosfatémico familiar hypophosphatemic familial rachitis, X-linked hypophosphatemic rachitis.

   raquitismo magro lean rachitis.

   raquitismo refractario refractory rachitis.

   raquitismo refractario a la vitamina D vitamin D-refractory rachitis.

   raquitismo renal renal rachitis.

   raquitismo resistente a la vitamina D vitamin D-resistant rachitis.

   raquitismo por seudodeficiencia pseudodeficiency rachitis.

   raquitismo tardío late rachitis.

raquitismo vitaminorresistente resistant rachitis.

raquitismo vitaminorresistente familiar hipofosfatémico de Fanconi hypophosphataemic familial rachitis, X-linked hypophosphatemic rachitis.

raquitógeno, -na *adj.* rachitogenic.

raquitomía *f.* rachitomy.

raquítomo *m.* rachitome.

rarefacción *f.* rarefaction.

rarificante *adj.* rarefying.

rarificarse *v.* rarefy.

rarificativo, -va *adj.* rarefying.

rascadura *f.* scratch.

rasceta *f.* rasceta.

rasgado, -da *adj.* lacerated.

rasgo *m.* trait.

rasgo adquirido acquired trait.

rasgo de Bombay Bombay trait.

rasgo del carácter, rasgo caracterial character trait.

rasgo categórico categorical trait.

rasgo de células drepanocíticas sickle cell trait.

rasgo codominante codominant trait.

rasgo condicionado por el sexo sex-conditioned trait.

rasgo cromosómico chromosomal trait.

rasgo cualitativo qualitative trait.

rasgo dependiente dependent trait.

rasgo dominante dominant trait.

rasgo hereditario hereditary trait.

rasgo influido por el sexo sex-influenced trait.

rasgo intermedio intermediate trait.

rasgo ligado al sexo sex-linked trait.

rasgo limitado por el sexo sex-limited trait.

rasgo marcador marker trait.

rasgo no penetrante non-penetrant trait.

rasgo de la personalidad personality trait.

rasgo secretor secretor trait.

rash *m.* rash.

rash amoniacal ammonia rash.

rash antitoxina antitoxin rash.

rash astacoide astacoid rash.

rash por calor heat rash, prickly heat rash.

rash cristalino crystal rash.

rash del pañal diaper rash.

rash por drogas drug rash, medicinal rash.

rash de erisipela wildfire rash.

rash errante wandering rash.

rash del Valle del Murray Murray Valley rash.

rash hidatídico hydatid rash.

rash en mariposa butterfly rash.

rash por ortigas nettle rash.

rash por orugas caterpillar rash.

rash en pasa negra black currant rash.

rash roséola rose rash, roseola.

rash sérico serum rash.

rash de verano summer rash.

rasión *f.* rasion.

raspadera *f.* rugine.

raspado *m.* strip, curettage.

raspado apical apical curettage.

raspado por aspiración suction curettage.

raspado radicular root curettage.

raspado subgingival subgingival curettage.

raspado por vacío vacuum curettage.

raspador *m.* raspatory, scaler.

raspador en azada hoe scaler.

raspador sónico sonic scaler.

raspar *v.* rasp.

RAST radio-allergo-(inmuno)sorbent test RAST.

rastreo *m.* scan.

rastreo cromosómico chromosome walking.

rastreo genético genetic screening.

rastreo isotópico isotopic scan.

rastreo isotópico en el carcinoma de tiroides isotopic body scan in thyroid carcinoma.

rastreo lineal linear scan.

rastreo de Meckel Meckel scan.

rastreo de ventilación-perfusión ventilation-perfusion scan.

rastro *m.* track.

rastro germinal germ track.

rata *f.* rat, rattus.

raticida *m.* raticide, mort-aux-rats.

ratón *m.* mouse.

ratón articular joint mouse.

ratón CFW cancer-free white (CFW) mouse.

ratón desnudo nude mouse.

ratón nu/nu nu/nu mouse.

ratón de Nueva Zelanda (ratón NAB) New Zealand Black (NAB) mouse.

Rattus Rattus.

raucedo *f.* raucedo.

rausch rausch.

raya *f.* streak.

raya angioide angioid streak.

raya de Fraunhofer Fraunhofer's line.

raya grasa fatty streak.

raya luminosa de Moore Moore lightning streak.

raya meningítica meningitic streak.

rayo *m.* ray.

rayo actínico actinic ray.

rayo alfa alpha ray.

rayo anódico anode ray.

rayo antirraquítico antirachitic ray.

rayo astral astral ray.

rayo de Becquerel Becquerel ray.

rayo beta beta ray.

rayo blando soft ray.

rayo calórico caloric ray, heat ray.

rayo característico characteristic ray.

rayo catódico cathodic ray.

rayo central central ray.

rayo convergentes convergent ray.

rayo cósmicos cosmic ray.

rayo de Crookes Crookes ray.

rayo delta delta ray.

rayo difuso scattered ray.

rayo digital digital ray.

rayo dinámico dynamic ray.

rayo de dirección direction ray.

rayo directo direct ray.

rayo diseminado scattered ray.

rayo divergente divergent ray.

rayo duro hard ray.

rayo de Finsen Finsen ray.

rayo fluorescente fluorescent ray.

rayo fluorescentes característico characteristic fluorescent ray.

rayo de frenado bremsstrahlung.

rayo gamma gamma ray.

rayo de Grenz Grenz ray.

rayo H H ray.

rayo hertziano Hertzian ray.

rayo incidente incident ray.

rayo indirecto indirect ray.

rayo infraroentgen infraroentgen ray.

rayo infrarrojo infrared ray.

rayo intermedio intermediate ray.

rayo límite, rayo limítrofe border ray.

rayo luminoso luminous ray.

rayo marginal marginal ray.

rayo medular medullary ray.

rayo de Millikan Millikan ray.

rayo monocromático monochromatic ray.

rayo necrobiótico necrobiotic ray.

rayo negativo cathodic ray.

rayo paraaxial paraxial ray.

rayo paracatódico paracathodic ray.

rayo paralelo parallel ray.

rayo positivo positive ray.

rayo primario primary ray.

rayo productores de eritema erythema-producing ray.

rayo químico chemical ray.

rayo reflejado reflected ray.

rayo refractado refracted ray.

rayo roentgen roentgen ray.

rayo de Sagnac Sagnac ray.

rayo secundario secondary ray.

rayo supersónico supersonic ray.

rayo ultrasónico ultrasonic ray.

rayo ultravioleta ultraviolet ray.

rayo ultra X ultra x-ray.

rayo de vidrio glass ray.

rayo vital vital ray.

rayo W W ray.

rayo X x-ray.

raza *f.* race.

razón[1] *f.* rational faculty.

razón[2] *f.* ratio.

razón de bases base ratio.

reabsorber *v.* reabsorb.

reabsorbible *adj.* reabsorbable.

reabsorción *f.* reabsorption.

reabsorción dental externa external tooth reabsorption.

reabsorción dental interna internal tooth reabsorption.

reabsorción gingival gingival reabsorption.

reabsorción interna internal reabsorption.

reabsorción ósea bone reabsorption.

reabsorción de raíces root reabsorption.

reabsorción de rebordes ridge reabsorption.

reabsorción tubular tubular reabsorption.

reabsorción tubular de fosfatos tubular reabsorption of phosphate.

reacción *f.* reaction.

reacción de Abelin Abelin's reaction.

reacción del ácido acético acetic acid reaction.

reacción del ácido nítrico de Bruck Bruck nitric acid reaction.

reacción de ácido periódico de Schiff periodic acid-Schiff reaction.

reacción acoplada coupled reaction.

reacción acelerada accelerated reaction.

reacción ácida acid reaction.

reacción del ácido perfórmico performic acid reaction.

reacción de acortamiento shortening reaction.

reacción acrosómica acrosomal reaction.

reacción de Adamkiewicz Adamkiewicz's reaction.

reacción de adaptación general general-adaptation reaction.

reacción de adrenalina con cloruro férrico ferric chloride reaction of epinephrine.

reacción adversa adverse reaction.

reacción adversa a un fármaco adverse drug reaction.

reacción de aglutinación agglutination test.

reacción de aglutinación de células mixtas mixed cell agglutination reaction.

reacción de aglutinación mixta mixed agglutination reaction.

reacción de agotamiento reaction of exhaustion.

reacción agresiva asocial unsocialized aggressive reaction.

reacción de alargamiento lengthening reaction.
reacción de alarma alarm reaction.
reacción alcalina alkaline reaction.
reacción de aldehído aldehyde reaction.
reacción alérgica allergic reaction.
reacción alérgica cutánea harara.
reacción de alerta arousal reaction.
reacción de Amann Amann's test.
reacción anafiláctica anaphylactic reaction.
reacción anafiláctica cutánea pasiva passive cutaneous anaphylactic reaction.
reacción anafilactoide anaphylactoid reaction.
reacción anamnéstica anamnestic reaction.
reacción anestésica local local anesthetic reaction.
reacción antálgica de anticuerpos heterófilos, reacción antiálgica de anticuerpos heterófilos heterophil antibody reaction.
reacción de antígeno de Debré y Paraf antigen reaction of Debré and Paraf.
reacción antígeno-anticuerpo antigen-antibody reaction.
reacción antígeno-anticuerpo de Forssman Forssman antigen-antibody reaction.
reacción antiglobulínica antiglobulin reaction.
reacción antimónica de Chopra Chopra antimony reaction.
reacción de Arias-Stella Arias-Stella reaction.
reacción del arlequín harlequin reaction.
reacción de Arloing-Courmont Arloing-Courmont test.
reacción de Arnold Arnold's test.
reacción de Arthus Arthus reaction.
reacción asténica psicofisiológica psychophysiologic asthenic reaction.
reacción axónica axon reaction, axonal reaction.
reacción azul de Turnbull Turnbull's blue reaction.
reacción bacteriolítica bacteriolytic test.
reacción de Bareggi Bareggi's reaction.
reacción de Bechterew Bechterew reaction.
reacción de Benedict Benedict's test.
reacción de benzaldehído de Ehrlich Ehrlich's benzaldehyde reaction.
reacción de Besredka Besredka's reaction.
reacción de Bial Bial's test.
reacción bimolecular bimolecular reaction.
reacción de Binz Binz's test.
reacción de Bittorf Bittorf reaction.
reacción de biuret biuret reaction.
reacción de blanqueamiento blanching reaction.
reacción de Bloch Bloch reaction.
reacción de Boedeker Boedeker's test.
reacción de Boltz Boltz's reaction.
reacción de Bordet-Gengou Bordet-Gengou reaction.
reacción de Bourget Bourget's test.
reacción de Braun Baun's test.
reacción de Bremer Bremer's test.
reacción de Brieger Brieger's test.
reacción cadavérica cadaveric reaction.
reacción en cadena chain reaction.
reacción en cadena de polimerasa polymerase chain reaction (PCR).
reacción de Cammidge Cammidge reaction, Cammidge test.
reacción del cáncer cancer reaction.
reacción de Cannizzaro Cannizzaro reaction.
reacción capsular capsular reaction.

reacción caquéctica cachexia reaction.
reacción de caquexia de Brieger Brieger cachexia reaction.
reacción carbamínica carbamino reaction.
reacción de Carr-Price Carr-Price test.
reacción de Castellani Castellani's reaction.
reacción catastrófica catastrophic reaction.
reacción cercana near reaction.
reacción de cierre del párpado lid closure reaction.
reacción circular circular reaction.
reacción citotóxica cytotoxic reaction.
reacción de la conglutinación conglutination reaction.
reacción consensual consensual reaction.
reacción constitucional constitutional reaction.
reacción de conversión conversion reaction.
reacción cortical cortical reaction.
reacción de Crismer Crismer's test.
reacción cromafín, reacción cromafínica chromaffin reaction.
reacción cruzada cross reaction.
reacción ante cuerpos extraños, reacción de cuerpo extraño foreign body reaction.
reacción de cultivo mixto de leucocitos mixed lymphocyte culture reaction.
reacción de Cushing Cushing's reaction.
reacción cutánea cutaneous reaction.
reacción cutánea galvánica galvanic skin reaction.
reacción cutánea de Goetsch Goetsch's skin reaction.
reacción cutánea pasiva de anafilaxia passive cutaneous anaphylaxis reaction.
reacción cutánea psicogalvánica psychogalvanic reaction, psychogalvanic skin reaction.
reacción cutituberculínica cutituberculin reaction.
reacción de chantemesse chantemesse reaction.
reacción de Darányi Darányi's test.
reacción de Day Day's test.
reacción de Debré y Paraf antigen reaction of Debré and Paraf.
reacción decidual decidual reaction.
reacción de Deen Deen's test.
reacción de degeneración (RD) degeneration reaction (DR), reaction of degeneration (RD).
reacción depósito depot reaction.
reacción depresiva depressive reaction.
reacción desencadenante trigger reaction.
reacción de desplazamiento displacement reaction.
reacción de Detre Detre's reaction.
reacción de diazo, reacción diazoica, reacción diazoica de Ehrlich diazo reaction, Ehrlich's diazo reaction, Ehrlich's aldehyde reaction.
reacción de digitonina digitonin reaction.
reacción de Dische Dische reaction.
reacción disergástica dysergastic reaction.
reacción distónica dystonic reaction.
reacción de Dold Dold's test.
reacción dolorosa, reacción de dolor pain reaction.
reacción de dopa dopa reaction.
reacción de Dragendorff Dragendorff's test.
reacción de Dreschsel Dreschsel's test.
reacción de duelo grief reaction.
reacción de Dumont-Pallier Dumont-Pallier's test.
reacción de Dungern Dungern's test.
reacción de eco echo reaction.
reacción de Ehrlich Ehrlich reaction.

reacción endergónica endergonic reaction.
reacción endotérmica endothermal reaction, endothermic reaction.
reacción enzimática enzymatic reaction.
reacción eosinopénica eosinopenic reaction.
reacción eritematosa y edematosa wheal and erythema reaction.
reacción específica specific reaction.
reacción a estrés stress reaction.
reacción exergónica exergonic reaction.
reacción exotérmica exothermal reaction, exothermic reaction.
reacción de fatiga fatigue reaction.
reacción de Fernández Fernández reaction.
reacción de Feulgen Feulgen reaction.
reacción de fijación, reacción de fijación del complemento fixation reaction, complement fixation reaction.
reacción de florence florence reaction.
reacción focal focal reaction.
reacción de Folin Folin's test.
reacción de formación formation reaction.
reacción de Fornet Fornet's reaction.
reacción de Forssman Forssman reaction.
reacción de Foshay Foshay's test.
reacción fotonuclear photonuclear reaction.
reacción fotoquímica photochemical reaction.
reacción de Fouchet Fouchet's test.
reacción de Francis Francis' test.
reacción franklínica de degeneración Franklinic reaction of degeneration.
reacción de Freund, reacción de Freund-Kaminer Freund's reaction, Freund-Kaminer reaction.
reacción fucsinófila fuchsinophil reaction.
reacción de Gangl Gangl's reaction.
reacción de Gell y Coombs Gell and Coombs reaction.
reacción gemistocítica gemistocytic reaction.
reacción de Gerhardt Gerhardt reaction.
reacción de Gmelin Gmelin reaction.
reacción de Gordon Gordon's test.
reacción de Graham Graham's test.
reacción de gran tensión gross stress reaction.
reacción de Gregerson Gregerson and Boas' test.
reacción de grupo group reaction.
reacción de Gubler Gubler's test.
reacción de Günzberg Günzberg's test.
reacción de Gutzeit Gutzeit's test.
reacción de Hammarsten Hammarsten's test.
reacción de Hecht-Weinberg-Gradwohl Hecht-Weinberg-Gradwohl reaction.
reacción de Heller Heller's test.
reacción hemoclástica hemoclastic reaction.
reacción hemolítica posttransfusional hemolytic tranfusion reaction.
reacción de Hench-Aldrich Hench-Aldrich's test.
reacción de Henle Henle reaction.
reacción de Herxheimer Herxheimer reaction.
reacción de Heynsius Heynsius' test.
reacción de Hildebrandt Hildebrandt's test.
reacción hipercinética de la infancia hyperkinetic reaction of childhood.
reacción de hipersensibilidad hypersensivity reaction.
reacción de hipersensibilidad celular cell hypersensitivity reaction.
reacción de hipersensibilidad inmediata immediate hypersensitivity reaction.

reacción de hipersensibilidad retardada delayed hypersensitivity reaction.

reacción de la histamina histamine test.

reacción de Hofmeister Hofmeister's test.

reacción de Hoppe-Seyler Hoppe-Seyler test.

reacción de huida runaway reaction.

reacción de id id reaction.

reacción de identidad reaction of identity.

reacción de identidad parcial reaction of partial identity.

reacción de inhibición de la hemaglutinación hemagglutination inhibition reaction.

reacción de injerto blanco white-graft reaction.

reacción de injerto contra huésped graft vs. host reaction, graft versus-host reaction.

reacción inmediata immediate reaction.

reacción inmune, reacción de inmunidad, reacción inmunitaria immune reaction.

reacción inmunitaria primaria primary immune reaction.

reacción inmunitaria secundaria secondary immune reaction.

reacción intracutánea intracutaneous reaction.

reacción intradérmica intradermal reaction.

reacción inversa reversal reaction.

reacción irreversible irreversible reaction.

reacción de Jacobsthal Jacobsthal's test.

reacción de Jaffé, reacción de Jaffe Jaffé reaction, Jaffe reaction.

reacción de Jaksch von Jaksch's test.

reacción de Jarisch-Herxheimer Jarisch-Herxheimer reaction.

reacción de Johnson Johnson's test.

reacción de Jolles Jolles' test.

reacción de Jolly Jolly reaction.

reacción de Jones y Mote Jones-Mote reaction.

reacción de Kafka Kafka's test.

reacción de Kahn Kahn's test.

reacción de Kerner Kerner's test.

reacción de Klimov Klimow's test.

reacción de Kline Kline's test.

reacción de Kolmer Kolmer's test.

reacción de Kossel Kossel's test.

reacción de Kottmann Kottmann's test.

reacción de Kowarsky Kowarsky's test.

reacción de Krauss Krauss' reaction.

reacción de Kultz Kultz's test.

reacción de Kveim Kveim reaction.

reacción Landau Landau's reaction.

reacción de Landerdorff Ladendorff's test.

reacción de Lange Lange reaction.

reacción de Legal Legal's test.

reacción leprosa, reacción de la lepra lepra reaction.

reacción leucemoide, reacción leucémica leukemic reaction, leukemoid reaction.

reacción leucemoide linfocítica lymphocytic leukemic reaction.

reacción leucemoide mielocítica myelocytic leukemic reaction.

reacción leucemoide monocítica monocytic leukemic reaction.

reacción leucemoide plasmocítica plasmocytic leukemic reaction.

reacción de Lewis Lewis reaction.

reacción de Lieben Lieben's test.

reacción de Liebermann Liebermann's test.

reacción de Liebermann-Burchard Liebermann-Burchard reaction.

reacción de Liebig Liebig's test.

reacción local local reaction.

reacción localizada de Shwartzman localized Shwartzman reaction.

reacción de Lohmann Lohmann reaction.

reacción de Löwenthal Löwenthal reaction.

reacción de Lowy Lowy's test.

reacción de lucha fight reaction.

reacción luminosa light reaction.

reacción en llamarada wheal and flare reaction.

reacción de MacMunn MacMunn's test.

reacción de MacWilliam MacWilliam's test.

reacción de Machado-Guerreiro Machado reaction, Machado-Guerreiro reaction.

reacción de Malerba Malerba's test.

reacción de Maly Maly's test.

reacción de Mandel Mandel's test.

reacción manifiesta de tensión gross stress reaction.

reacción de Mantoux Mantoux's reaction.

reacción de Marchi Marchi reaction.

reacción de Maréchal Maréchal's test.

reacción de Marsh Marsh's test.

reacción de Maschke von Maschke's test.

reacción de Masset Masset's test.

reacción de Mátéfy Mátéfy's test.

reacción de Maumené Maumené's test.

reacción de memoria memory reaction.

reacción de Mendel Mendel's test.

reacción miasténica myasthenic reaction.

reacción de miedo fear reaction, fright reaction.

reacción de Millard Millard's test.

reacción miotónica myotonic reaction.

reacción de Mitsuda Mitsuda reaction.

reacción mixta de leucocitos, reacción mixta de linfocitos mixed leukocyte reaction, mixed lymphocyte reaction.

reacción de Moeller Moeller reaction.

reacción de Mohr Mohr's test.

reacción de Molisch Molisch's reaction.

reacción monomolecular monomolecular reaction.

reacción de Montenegro Montenegro reaction.

reacción de Moretti Moretti's test.

reacción de Moritz Moritz reaction.

reacción de Mörner Mörner's test.

reacción de Moro Moro reaction, percutaneous reaction.

reacción de Mulder Mulder's test.

reacción de Nadi Nadi reaction.

reacción de Nagler Nagler's reaction.

reacción de negativa falsa false negative reaction.

reacción neurotónica neurotonic reaction.

reacción de la ninhidrina ninhydrin reaction.

reacción de no identidad reaction of non-identity.

reacción de Nonne-Apelt Nonne-Apelt reaction.

reacción nuclear nucleal reaction.

reacción de Nylander Nylander's test.

reacción de Obermayer Obermayer's test.

reacción de Oliver Oliver's test.

reacción orbicular orbicularis reaction.

reacción de orden cero zero-order reaction.

reacción de Ott Ott's test.

reacción de oxidación-reducción oxidation-reduction reaction.

reacción de la palmitina palmitin test.

reacción paralérgica parallergic reaction.

reacción parasérica paraserum reaction.

reacción de Pasteur Pasteur's reaction.

reacción de la peroxidasa peroxidase reaction.

reacción de Pettenkofer Pettenkofer's test.

reacción de Petzetakis Petzetakis' reaction.

reacción de la piel skin reaction.

reacción de Pietrowsky Pietrowsky reaction.

reacción de Pirquet, reacción de von Pirquet Pirquet reaction, Pirquet's test.

reacción plasmática plasmal reaction.

reacción de Porter Porter's test.

reacción de Porter-Silber Porter-Silber reaction.

reacción positiva falsa false-positive reaction.

reacción de Posner Posner's reaction.

reacción de Prausnitz-küstner Prausnitz-Küstner reaction.

reacción de Prausnitz-Küstner revertida reversed Prausnitz-Küstner reaction.

reacción de la precipitina precipitin reaction.

reacción primaria primary reaction.

reacción de primer orden first-order reaction.

reacción provocativa de Wassermann provocative wassermann reaction.

reacción próxima near reaction.

reacción de punción puncture reaction.

reacción de punto cercano near-point reaction.

reacción pupilar hemiópica hemiopic pupillary reaction.

reacción pupilar indirecta indirect pupillary reaction.

reacción pupilar vestibular vestibular pupillary reaction.

reacción de Raabe Raabe's test.

reacción de Ralfe Ralfe's test.

reacción de Randolph Randolph's test.

reacción de Rees Rees' test.

reacción refleja del talón heel-tap reaction.

reacción de reflejo booster reaction.

reacción de Reinsch Reinsch's test.

reacción de Remak Remak reaction.

reacción de reticulocitos reticulocyte reaction.

reacción retrasada delayed reaction.

reacción retrasada de blanqueamiento delayed blanch reaction.

reacción de Reuss Reuss' test.

reacción de Riegler Riegler's test.

reacción de Rivalta Rivalta reaction.

reacción de Roberts Roberts' test.

reacción de Romberg Romberg's test.

reacción de roncha y pápula, reacción de roncha y eritema wheal-and-erythema reaction.

reacción de Russo Russo's reaction.

reacción de Sakaguchi Sakaguchi reaction.

reacción de Schardinger Schardinger reaction.

reacción de Schönbein Schönbein's reaction.

reacción de Schultz-Charlton Schultz-Charlton reaction.

reacción de sedimentación, reacción de sedimentación eritrocítica sedimentation reaction, erythrocyte sedimentation reaction.

reacción de segundo juego second-set reaction.

reacción sérica serological reaction, serum reaction.

reacción de seroflocculación de Penn Penn serofloculation reaction.

reacción seudoalérgica pseudoallergic reaction.

reacción de la sífilis syphilis test, serologic test for syphilis.

reacción sintomática symptomatic reaction.

reacción de sobresalto startle reaction, startle reflex.

reacción de sostén supporting reaction.

reacción temprana early reaction.

reacción tendinosa tendon reaction.

reacción de tensión simpática sympathetic stress reaction.

reacción terapéutica negativa negative terapeutic reaction.

reacción termoprecipitina thermoprecipitin reaction.

reacción tifoídica de Deehan Deehan's typhoid reaction.

reacción tipo Arthus Arthus-type test.

reacción del tipo enfermedad del suero serum sickness like reaction.

reacción de tipo reflejo reflex type reaction.

reacción de título de recuerdo recall titer reaction.

reacción de toxina-antitoxina toxin-antitoxin reaction.

reacción transfusional transfusion reaction.

reacción por transfusión sanguínea incompatible incompatible blood transfusion response.

reacción de tricetohidrindeno triketohydrindene reaction.

reacción triple, reacción triple de Lewis triple response of Lewis.

reacción triple azúcar hierro triple sugar iron reaction.

reacción de la tuberculina tuberculin reaction.

reacción unimolecular unimolecular reaction.

reacción vestibular térmica Bárány sign.

reacción viscerosomática viscerosomatic reaction.

reacción vital vital reaction.

reacción de Wernicke Wernicke's reaction.

reacción de Wichbrodt Wichbrodt's reaction.

reacción de Widal Widal's reaction.

reacción de yodato de la adrenalina iodate reaction of epinephrine.

reacción zed zed reaction.

reacción-formación *f.* reaction-formation.

reaccionar *v.* react.

reactancia *f.* reactance.

reactante *m.* reactant.

reactante de fase aguda acute phase reactant.

reactivación *f.* reactivation.

reactivación del suero reactivation of serum.

reactivar *v.* reactivate.

reactividad *f.* reactivity.

reactivo *m.* reagent.

real *adj.* real, true.

realidad *f.* reality.

reamputación *f.* reamputation.

reanimación *f.* resuscitation.

reanimación boca a boca mouth-to-mouth resuscitation.

reanimación cardiopulmonar cardiopulmonary resuscitation.

reaprendizaje *m.* relearning.

rebasar *v.* rebase.

reblandecimiento *m.* softening.

reborde *m.* ridge.

recaída *f.* relapse.

recalcificación *f.* recalcification.

recanalización *f.* recanalization.

recanalizar *v.* recanalize.

recanalizar un vaso recanalize a vessel.

recapar *v.* reline.

recapitulación *f.* recapitulation.

receptáculo *m.* receptaculum.

receptaculum receptaculum.

receptoma *m.* receptoma.

receptor, -ra *m., f. y adj.* receptor.

receptor alfa-adrenérgico alpha-adrenergic receptor.

receptor beta-adrenérgico beta-adrenergic receptor.

receptor colinérgico cholinergic receptor.

receptor de contacto contact receptor.

receptor de dopamina dopamine receptor.

receptor de estiramiento stretch receptor.

receptor de estrógenos estrogen receptor.

receptor Fc Fc receptor.

receptor gustatorio gustatory receptor.

receptor hormonal hormone receptor.

receptor de insulina insulin receptor.

receptor de lipoproteínas de baja densidad (LDL) LDL receptor.

receptor muscarínico muscarinic receptor.

receptor para opiáceo opiate receptor.

receptor de dolor pain receptor.

receptor de presión pressure receptor.

receptor de progesterona progesterone receptor.

receptor químico chemical receptor.

receptor sensitivo sensory receptor.

receptor táctiles touch receptor.

receptor de transfusión receiver of transfusion.

receptor de trasplante receiver of transplant.

receptor universal universal recipient.

receptor de volumen volume receptor.

recesión *f.* recession.

recesión gingival gingival recession.

recesión de síntomas recession of symptoms.

recesión tendinosa tendon recession.

recesividad *f.* recessitivity, recessiveness.

recesivo, -va *adj.* recessive.

receso *m.* recess, recessus.

recessus *m.* recessus.

receta *f.* prescription, recipe.

rechazo *m.* rejection.

rechazo agudo acute rejection.

rechazo celular agudo acute cellular rejection.

rechazo humoral humoral rejection.

rechazo de órgano organ rejection.

rechazo *m.* rebound.

rechinamiento *m.* grancement, gnashing.

recidiva *f.* recidivation, relapse.

recidiva de los tumores tumor relapse.

recidividad *f.* recidivism.

recidivismo *m.* recidivism.

recidivista *m., f.* recidivist.

recién nacido *m.* newborn.

recipiomotor, -ra *adj.* recipiomotor.

reciprocación *f.* reciprocation.

recitado *m.* rehearsal.

reclinación *f.* reclination.

reclusión *f.* reclusion.

reclutamiento *m.* recruitment.

recolección *f.* recollection.

recombinación *f.* recombination.

recombinación bacteriana bacterial recombination.

recombinación genética genetic recombination.

recombinación genética bacteriana bacterial recombination.

recombinante *adj.* recombinant.

recompensa *f.* reward.

recompresión *f.* recompression.

recón *m.* recon.

reconocimiento *m.* recognition.

reconocimiento antigénico en la inmunidad celular antigen recognition in cell-mediated immunity.

reconstitución *f.* reconstitution.

reconstituyente *m.* restorative.

reconstrucción *f.* reconstruction.

reconstrucción holográfica holographic reconstruction.

reconstrucción de la mama breast reconstruction.

recorte de tejidos *m.* tissue trimming.

recremento *m.* recrement.

recrudecimiento *m.* recrudescence.

recrudescencia *f.* recrudescence.

recrudescente *adj.* recrudescent.

rectal *adj.* rectal.

rectalgia *f.* rectalgia.

rectectomía *f.* rectectomy.

rectificación *f.* rectification.

rectificar *v.* rectify.

rectitis *f.* rectitis.

recto *m.* rectum.

recto, -ta *adj.* straight.

rectoabdominal *adj.* rectoabdominal.

rectocele *m.* rectocele.

rectocistotomía *f.* rectocystotomy.

rectoclisis *f.* rectoclysis.

rectococcígeo, -a *adj.* rectococcygeal.

rectococcicopexia *f.* rectococcipexy.

rectococcipexia *f.* rectococcipexy.

rectocolitis *f.* rectocolitis.

rectoperineal *adj.* rectoperineal.

rectoperineorrafia *f.* rectoperineorrhaphy.

rectopexia *f.* rectopexy.

rectoplastia *f.* rectoplasty.

rectorrafia *f.* rectorrhaphy.

rectoscopia *f.* rectoscopy.

rectosigmoide *m.* rectosigmoid.

rectosigmoidectomía *m.* rectosigmoidectomy.

rectosigmoidoscopia *f.* proctosigmoidoscopy.

rectosigmoidoscopio *m.* proctosigmoidoscope.

rectostenosis *f.* rectostenosis.

rectostomía *f.* rectostomy.

rectótomo *m.* rectotome.

rectotomía *f.* rectotomy.

rectouretral *adj.* rectourethral.

rectouterino, -na *adj.* rectouterine.

rectovaginal *adj.* rectovaginal.

rectovesical *adj.* rectovesical.

rectovestibular *adj.* rectovestibular.

rectovulvar *adj.* rectovulvar.

recuento *m.* count.

recuento de Addis Addis count.

recuento de Arneth Arneth count.

recuento de la cresta epidérmica epidermal ridge count.

recuento diferencial differential count.

recuento directo de plaquetas direct platelet count.

recuento de filamentos y no filamentos filament-non-filament count.

recuento indirecto de plaquetas indirect platelet count.

recuento de parásitos parasite count.

recuento de sangre, recuento sanguíneo blood count.

recuento sanguíneo completo complete blood count.

recuento sanguíneo diferencial de glóbulos blancos differential white blood count.

recuento de Schilling Schilling's blood count.

recuerdo *m.* recall.

recumbente *adj.* recumbent.

recuperación[1] *f.* recuperation.
recuperación[2] *f.* recovery.
recuperación de arrastre creep recovery.
recuperación espontánea spontaneous recovery.
recuperación de un óvulo por ultrasonido ultrasonic egg recovery.
recuperación posoperatoria postoperatory recovery.
recuperador *m.* regainer.
recuperarse *v.* recuperate.
recurrencia *f.* recurrence.
recurrente[1] *adj.* recurrent.
recurrente[2] *adj.* relapsing.
recurvación *f.* recurvation.
red *f.* net, rete.
rediferenciación *f.* redifferentiation.
redintegración *f.* redintegration.
redislocación *f.* redislocation, reluxation.
redox *m.* redox.
reducción *f.* reduction.
reducción abierta open reduction.
reducción abierta de fractura open reduction of fracture.
reducción cerrada de fractura closed reduction of fracture.
reducción cerrada closed reduction.
reducción de cromosomas reduction of chromosomes.
reducción de fractura reduction of fracture.
reducción de la mama, reducción mamaria breast reduction, mammaplasty reduction.
reducción en masa reduction en masse.
reduccion-oxidación oxidation reduction.
reducción de peso weight reduction.
reducción de la tuberosidad tuberosity reduction.
reducible *adj.* reducible.
reducir *v.* reduce.
reductor *m.* reductant.
reduplicación *f.* reduplication.
reeducación *f.* reeducation.
reefing *m.* reefing.
reefing del estómago stomach reefing.
reentrada *f.* reentry.
refección *f.* refection.
referencia *f.* reference.
refinación *f.* refining.
refinar *v.* refine.
reflector, -ra *m. y adj.* reflector.
reflejado, -da *adj.* reflected.
reflejar *v.* reflect.
reflejo, -ja *m. y adj.* reflex.
reflejo abdominal abdominal reflex.
reflejo abdominales profundo deep abdominal reflex.
reflejo abdominocardíaco abdominocardiac reflex.
reflejo de Abrams Abrams' heart reflex.
reflejo del abrazo embrace reflex.
reflejo de acomodación accommodation reflex.
reflejo acrominal acromial reflex.
reflejo de actitud attitudinal reflex.
reflejo acusticopalpebral acousticopalpebral reflex.
reflejo adquirido acquired reflex.
reflejo del aductor adductor reflex.
reflejo del aductor cruzado crossed adductor reflex.
reflejo de agarre grasp reflex.
reflejo de alarma threat reflex.
reflejo aliado allied reflex.
reflejo de amenaza threat reflex.
reflejo anal anal reflex.

reflejo antagónico antagonistic reflex.
reflejo aórtico aortic reflex.
reflejo aponeurótico aponeurotic reflex.
reflejo de apoyo supporting reflex.
reflejo aquileo, reflejo aquiliano Achilles reflex.
reflejo del arco costal costal arch reflex.
reflejo articular basal basal joint reflex.
reflejo de atención de la pupila attention reflex of the pupil.
reflejo de Aschner, reflejo de Aschner-Dagnini Aschner's reflex, Aschner-Dagnini reflex.
reflejo auditivo, reflejo aural auditory reflex.
reflejo auditooculógiro audito-oculogyric reflex.
reflejo auriculocervical auriculocervical nerve reflex.
reflejo auriculopalpebral auriculopalpebral reflex.
reflejo auriculopresor auriculopressor reflex.
reflejo auropalpebral auropalpebral reflex.
reflejo axónico axon reflex.
reflejo de Babinski Babinski reflex.
reflejo de Bainbridge Bainbridge reflex.
reflejo de Barkman Barkman's reflex.
reflejo de Bechterew Bechterew's reflex.
reflejo de Bechterew-Mendel Bechterew-Mendel reflex.
reflejo de Benedek Benedek's reflex.
reflejo de Bezold-Jarisch Bezold-Jarisch reflex.
reflejo del biceps, reflejo bicipital biceps reflex.
reflejo del biceps femoral biceps femoris reflex.
reflejo de Bing Bing's reflex.
reflejo de Brain Brain's reflex.
reflejo braquiorradial brachioradial reflex.
reflejo bregmocardíaco bregmocardiac reflex.
reflejo de Brissaud Brissaud's reflex.
reflejo de Brudzinski Brudzinski's reflex.
reflejo bulbocavernoso bulbocavernous reflex, bulbocavernosus reflex.
reflejo bulbonímico bulbonimic reflex.
reflejo en cadena chain reflex.
reflejo de Capp Capp's reflex.
reflejo cardíaco cardiac reflex.
reflejo cardíaco de Abrams Abrams' heart reflex.
reflejo cefálico cephalic reflex.
reflejo cefalopalpebral cephalopalpebral reflex.
reflejo cercano near reflex.
reflejo cerebropupilar cerebropupillary reflex.
reflejo cervical neck reflex.
reflejo de Chaddock Chaddock reflex.
reflejo ciliar ciliary reflex.
reflejo ciliospinal ciliospinal reflex.
reflejo cocleoorbicular cochleo-orbicular reflex.
reflejo cocleopalpebral cochleopalpebral reflex.
reflejo cocleopupilar cochleopupillary reflex.
reflejo compuesto coordinated reflex.
reflejo condicionado conditional reflex, conditioned reflex, trained reflex.
reflejo conjuntival conjunctival reflex.
reflejo consensual luminoso consensual light reflex.
reflejo contralateral contralateral reflex.
reflejo coordinado coordinate reflex, coordinated reflex.

reflejo corneal corneal reflex.
reflejo corneomandibular, reflejo corneomaxilar corneomandibular reflex.
reflejo corneopterigoideo corneopterygoid reflex.
reflejo coronario coronary reflex.
reflejo craneal cranial reflex.
reflejo de la corteza cerebral cerebral cortex reflex.
reflejo cremastérico cremasteric reflex.
reflejo cruzado crossed reflex.
reflejo cuboide digital metatarsal reflex.
reflejo cubitopronador ulnar reflex.
reflejo del cutáneo cutaneous pupillary reflex.
reflejo cutaneoabdominal abominal reflex.
reflejo cutaneoplantar Babinski's sign.
reflejo cutáneo psicogalvánico psychogalvanic skin reflex.
reflejo cutáneo pupilar cutaneous pupillary reflex.
reflejo de Dagnini-Aschner Aschner's reflex.
reflejo del dartos dartos reflex.
reflejo del dedo gordo del pie great-toe reflex.
reflejo de defensa defense reflex.
reflejo digital digital reflex.
reflejo dorsal dorsal reflex.
reflejo epigástrico epigastric reflex.
reflejo de Erben Erben's reflex.
reflejo del esfinter anal anal sphincter reflex.
reflejo escapulohumeral scapulohumeral reflex.
reflejo de Escherich Escherich's reflex.
reflejo escrotal scrotal reflex.
reflejo esofagosalival esophagosalivary reflex.
reflejo espinal spinal reflex.
reflejo estático, reflejo estatocinético static reflex, statokinetic reflex.
reflejo estilorradial styloradial reflex.
reflejo extensor paradójico paradoxical extensor reflex.
reflejo de eyección láctea milk-ejection reflex.
reflejo facial facial reflex.
reflejo faríngeo pharyngeal reflex.
reflejo fásico phasic reflex.
reflejo faucal, reflejo faucial faucial reflex.
reflejo femoral femoral reflex.
reflejo femoroabdominal femoroabdominal reflex.
reflejo flexor flexor reflex.
reflejo flexor paradójico paradoxical flexor reflex.
reflejo del fondo de ojo fundus reflex.
reflejo fotomotor light reflex, direct light reflex.
reflejo gastrocólico gastrocolic reflex.
reflejo gastroileal, reflejo gastroiliaco gastroileal reflex.
reflejo de Gault Gault's cochleopalpebral reflex.
reflejo de Geigel Geigel's reflex.
reflejo de Gifford Gifford's reflex.
reflejo glúteo gluteal reflex.
reflejo de Gordon Gordon reflex.
reflejo de Grünfelder Grünfelder's reflex.
reflejo de Guillain-Barré Guillain-Barré reflex.
reflejo de guiño wink reflex, blink reflex.
reflejo gustatorio-sudorífico gustatory-sudorific reflex.
reflejo gustolagrimal gustolacrimal reflex.
reflejo de Haab Haab's reflex.

reflejo hepatoyugular hepatojugular reflex.

reflejo de Hering-Breuer Hering-Breuer reflex.

reflejo hipogástrico hypogastric reflex.

reflejo de Hirschberg Hirschberg's reflex.

reflejo de hociqueo rooting reflex.

reflejo de Hoffmann Hoffmann's reflex.

reflejo de Hughes Hughes' reflex.

reflejo humoral humoral reflex.

reflejo incondicionado unconditioned reflex, inborn reflex.

reflejo índice-pulgar finger-thumb reflex.

reflejo indirecto indirect reflex.

reflejo infraspinoso infraspinatus reflex.

reflejo inguinal inguinal reflex.

reflejo de inmersión diving reflex.

reflejo interescapular interscapular reflex.

reflejo intrínseco intrinsic reflex.

reflejo invertido inverted reflex.

reflejo investigatorio investigatory reflex.

reflejo ipsilateral ipsilateral reflex.

reflejo de Jacobson Jacobson's reflex.

reflejo de Joffroy Joffroy's reflex.

reflejo de Juster Juster's reflex.

reflejo de Kisch Kisch's reflex.

reflejo de Kocher Kocher's reflex.

reflejo laberíntico labyrinthine reflex.

reflejo laberíntico de enderezamiento labyrinthine righting reflex.

reflejo labial lip reflex.

reflejo lagrimal lacrimal reflex.

reflejo lagrimogustativo lacrimogustatory reflex.

reflejo laríngeo laryngeal reflex.

reflejo laríngeo protector protective laryngeal reflex.

reflejo laringoespástico laryngospastic reflex.

reflejo latente latent reflex.

reflejo de Lidell-Sherrington Lidell-Sherrington reflex.

reflejo de Livierato Abrams' heart reflex.

reflejo del llanto cry reflex.

reflejo de lordosis lordosis reflex.

reflejo de Loven Loven reflex.

reflejo lumbar lumbar reflex.

reflejo luminoso light reflex.

reflejo luminoso directo direct light reflex.

reflejo luminoso tapetal tapetal light reflex.

reflejo de Lust Lust's reflex.

reflejo de Mac Carthy Mac Carthy's reflex.

reflejo de Mc Cormac McCormac's reflex.

reflejo mandibular de guiño jaw-working reflex.

reflejo de la marcha stepping reflex.

reflejo en masa mass reflex.

reflejo del maxilar jaw reflex.

reflejo de Mayer Mayer's reflex.

reflejo mediopubiano mediopubic reflex.

reflejo de Mendel-Bechterew Mendel-Bechterew reflex.

reflejo mentoniano chin reflex.

reflejo metacarpohipotenar metacarpohypothenar reflex.

reflejo metacarpotenar metacarpothenar reflex.

reflejo metatarsiano metatarsal reflex.

reflejo de micción micturition reflex.

reflejo mientérico myenteric reflex.

reflejo miópico myopic reflex.

reflejo miotático myotatic reflex.

reflejo de Mondonesi Mondonesi's reflex.

reflejo de Moro Moro reflex.

reflejo motor muscular muscular reflex.

reflejo muscular muscular reflex.

reflejo muscular plantar plantar muscle reflex.

reflejo de nariz-ojo nose-eye reflex.

reflejo de nariz-puente-párpado nose-bridge-lid reflex.

reflejo nasal nasal reflex.

reflejo nauseoso gag reflex.

reflejo neocardíaco pneocardiac reflex.

reflejo neopneico pneopneic reflex.

reflejo nociceptivo nociceptive reflex.

reflejo nocifensor nocifensor reflex.

reflejo oblicuo externo external oblique reflex.

reflejo ocular eye reflex.

reflejo oculocardíaco oculocardiac reflex.

reflejo oculocefálico oculocephalic reflex.

reflejo oculocefalógiro oculocephalogyric reflex.

reflejo oculofaríngeo oculopharyngeal reflex.

reflejo oculógiro auditivo auditory oculogyric reflex.

reflejo del olécranon olecranon reflex.

reflejo de Oppenheim Oppenheim's reflex.

reflejo opticofacial opticofacial reflex.

reflejo del orbicular de los párpados orbicularis oculi reflex.

reflejo orbicular pupilar orbicularis pupillary reflex.

reflejo de orientación, reflejo orientador orienting reflex.

reflejo óseo bone reflex.

reflejo palatino palatal reflex, palatine reflex.

reflejo palma-mentón palm-chin reflex.

reflejo palmar palmar reflex.

reflejo palmomentoniano palmomental reflex.

reflejo de paracaídas parachute reflex.

reflejo paradójico paradoxical reflex, paradoxical flexor reflex.

reflejo paradójico del tríceps paradoxical triceps reflex.

reflejo patelar knee-jerk reflex.

reflejo patológico pathologic reflex.

reflejo de Pavlov Pavlov's reflex.

reflejo pectoral pectoral reflex.

reflejo de percusión frontal front-tap reflex.

reflejo de percusión plantar sole-tap reflex.

reflejo de Pérez Pérez reflex.

reflejo pericárdico pericardial reflex.

reflejo perióstico periosteal reflex.

reflejo perióstico abdominal superior upper abdominal periosteal reflex.

reflejo de Phillipson Phillipson's reflex.

reflejo pilomotor pilomotor reflex.

reflejo de Piltz Piltz's reflex.

reflejo plantar sole reflex, plantar reflex.

reflejo plantar en hiperflexión Guillain-Barré reflex.

reflejo del plexo celíaco celiac plexus reflex.

reflejo postural postural reflex.

reflejo de prensión, reflejo de prensión forzada grasp reflex, grasping reflex, forced grasping reflex.

reflejo presorreceptor pressoreceptor reflex.

reflejo profundo deep reflex.

reflejo propioceptivo proprioceptive reflex.

reflejo oculocefálico proprioceptive-oculocephalic reflex.

reflejo psicocardíaco psychocardiac reflex.

reflejo psicogalvánico psychogalvanic reflex.

reflejo del pulgar thumb reflex.

reflejo pulmonocoronario pulmonocoronary reflex.

reflejo de la pupila blanca white pupillary reflex.

reflejo pupilar pupillary reflex.

reflejo pupilar-cutáneo pupillary-skin reflex.

reflejo pupilar paradójico paradoxical pupillary reflex.

reflejo pupilar de Westphal Westphal's pupillary reflex.

reflejo radial radial reflex.

reflejo radial invertido inverted radial reflex.

reflejo radiobicipital radiobicipital reflex.

reflejo radioperióstico radioperiosteal reflex.

reflejo rectal rectal reflex.

reflejo rectocardíaco rectocardiac reflex.

reflejo rectolaríngeo rectolaryngeal reflex.

reflejo de Remak Remak's reflex.

reflejo renal renal reflex.

reflejo del retiro withdrawal reflex.

reflejo de Riddoch Riddoch's mass reflex.

reflejo de la risa laughter reflex.

reflejo de la rodilla knee reflex.

reflejo de Roger Roger's reflex.

reflejo rojo red reflex.

reflejo de Rossolimo Rossolimo's reflex.

reflejo rotuliano patellar reflex.

reflejo rotuliano paradójico paradoxical patellar reflex.

reflejo rotuloaductor patello-adductor reflex.

reflejo de Ruggeri Ruggeri's reflex.

reflejo de la sacudida de la rodilla knee-jerk reflex.

reflejo de Schäffer Schäffer's reflex.

reflejo de la seda tornasolada shot-silk reflex.

reflejo semimembranoso, semitendinoso semimembranosus reflex, semitendinosus reflex.

reflejo del seno carotídeo carotid sinus reflex.

reflejo simple simple reflex.

reflejo sincrónico synchronous reflex.

reflejo sinusal sinus reflex.

reflejo de Snellen Snellen's reflex.

reflejo de sobresalto startle reflex.

reflejo de sostén supporting reflex.

reflejo de Starling Starling's reflex.

reflejo de Stookey Stookey's reflex.

reflejo de Strümpell Strümpell's reflex.

reflejo de succión suckling reflex.

reflejo superficial superficial reflex.

reflejo de supinación supination reflex.

reflejo del supinador, reflejo del supinador largo supinator reflex, supinator longus reflex.

reflejo supraorbital, reflejo supraorbitario supraorbital reflex.

reflejo suprarrotuliano suprapatellar reflex.

reflejo supraumbilical supraumbilical reflex.

reflejo tarsofalángico tarsophalangeal reflex.

reflejo tarsofalángico cuboidodigital reflex.

reflejo tendinoso tendon reflex.

reflejo tendinoso de Aquiles, reflejo del tendón de Aquiles Achilles tendon reflex.

reflejo del tendón rotuliano patellar tendon reflex.

reflejo del tobillo ankle reflex.

reflejo tónico tonic reflex.

reflejo de tracción visceral visceral traction reflex.

reflejo del tríceps triceps reflex.

reflejo del tríceps crural triceps surae reflex.

reflejo del trocánter trochanter reflex.

reflejo de Trömner Trömner's reflex.

reflejo tusígeno cough reflex.

reflejo urinario bladder reflex.

reflejo vascular vascular reflex.
reflejo vasovagal vasovagal reflex.
reflejo vasopresor vasopressor reflex.
reflejo venorrespiratorio venorespiratory reflex.
reflejo vesical vesical reflex, bladder reflex.
reflejo vestibuloespinal vestibulospinal reflex.
reflejo viril virile reflex.
reflejo visceral visceral reflex.
reflejo viscerocardíaco viscerocardiac reflex.
reflejo viscerogénico viscerogenic reflex.
reflejo visceromotor visceromotor reflex.
reflejo viscerosensitivo viscerosensory reflex.
reflejo viscerotrófico viscerotrophic reflex.
reflejo de vómito vomiting reflex.
reflejo de Weingrow Weingrow's reflex.
reflejo de Weiss Weiss' reflex.
reflejo de Westphal, reflejo de Westphal-Piltz Westphal pupillary reflex, Westphal-Piltz reflex.
reflexión *f.* reflection.
reflexionar *v.* reflect.
reflexófilo, -la *adj.* reflexophile.
reflexogénico, -ca *adj.* reflexogenic.
reflexógeno, -na *adj.* reflexogenous.
reflexógrafo *m.* reflexograph.
reflexología *f.* reflexology.
reflexómetro *m.* reflexometer.
reflexoterapia *f.* reflexotherapy.
reflujo *m.* reflux.
reflujo abdominoyugular abdominojugular reflux.
reflujo esofágico esophageal reflux.
reflujo gastroesofágico gastroesophageal reflux.
reflujo hepatoyugular hepatojugular reflux.
reflujo uretrorrenal uretrorenal reflux.
reflujo uretrovesiculodeferencial uretrovesiculo-differential reflux.
reflujo vesicoureteral vesicoureteral reflux.
reforzador *m.* reinforcer.
reforzamiento *m.* reinforcement.
reforzamiento de relación variable (RV) variable ratio (VR) reinforcement.
reforzamiento de intervalo fijo fixed-interval reinforcement.
reforzamiento de intervalo variable (IV) variable interval reinforcement (VI).
refracción *f.* refraction.
refracción dinámica dynamic refraction.
refracción doble double refraction.
refracción estática static refraction.
refracción ocular ocular refraction.
refracción oculofaríngea oculopharyngeal refraction.
refraccionista *adj.* refractionist.
refraccionómetro *m.* refractionometer.
refractar *v.* refract.
refractario, -ria *adj.* refractory.
refractividad *f.* refractivity.
refractivo, -va *adj.* refractive.
refractometría *f.* refractometry.
refractómetro *m.* refractometer.
refractura *f.* refracture.
refrangible *adj.* refrangible.
refrescante *adj.* refrigerant.
refrescar *v.* refresh.
refrigeración *f.* refrigeration.
refrigerante *adj.* refrigerant.
refringencia *f.* refringence.
refringente *adj.* refringent.
refuerzo *m.* reinforcement.
refuerzo contingente contingency reinforcement.

refuerzo continuo continuous reinforcement.
refuerzo intermitente intermittent reinforcement.
refuerzo negativo negative reinforcement.
refuerzo parcial partial reinforcement.
refuerzo positivo positive reinforcement.
refuerzo primario primary reinforcement.
refuerzo secundario secondary reinforcement.
refusión *f.* refusion.
regeneración *f.* regeneration.
regeneración aberrante aberrant regeneration.
regenerar *v.* regenerate.
régimen *m.* regimen, diet.
régimen diabético diabetic diet.
régimen de eliminación elimination diet.
región *f.* region.
región abdominal abdominal region.
regional *adj.* regional.
registro *m.* record.
registro de anestesia anesthesia record.
registro de arco facial face-brow record.
registro de cuidados diarios de pacientes daily patient care record.
registro electrocardiografico electrocardiographic record.
registro electroencefalografico electroencefalographic record.
registro funcional de masticación functional chew-in record.
registro hospitalario hospital record.
registro hospitalario de pacientes patient's hospital record.
registro interoclusal interocclusal record.
registro maxilomandibular maxillomandibular record.
registro médico medical record.
registro orientado por problemas problem-oriented record.
registro de perfil profile record.
registro preextracción preextraction record.
registro preoperatorio preoperative record.
registro protrusivo protrusive record.
registro de la relación de oclusión céntrica occluding centric relation record.
registro de la relación intermaxilar terminal terminal jaw relation record.
registro de tejidos tissue record.
registro tridimensional three-dimensional record.
regla¹ *f.* period.
regla² *f.* rule.
regla de Abegg Abegg's rule.
regla de bigeminia rule of bigeminy.
regla del conducto de salida rule of outlet.
regla de Cowling Cowling's rule.
regla de fase phase rule.
regla de Goriaew Goriaew's rule.
regla de Haase Haase's rule.
regla de His His' rule.
regla isométrica isometric ruler.
regla de Jackson Jackson's rule.
regla de Le Bel-van't Hoff Le Bel-van't Hoff rule.
regla de Liebermeister Liebermeister's rule.
regla de Nägele Nägele's rule.
regla de Ogino-Knaus Ogino-Knaus rule.
regla de Prentice Prentice's rule.
regla de Quetelet Quetelet's rule.
regla de Rolleston Rolleston's rule.
regla de Schütz Schütz rule.
regla de Young Young's rule.
regma *f.* rhegma.
regmatógeno, -na *adj.* rhegmetogenous.

regresión *f.* regression.
regresivo, -va *adj.* regressive.
regulación *f.* regulation.
regulador *m.* regulator.
regulador, -ra *adj.* regulatory.
regular *adj.* regular.
regularidad *f.* regularity.
regurgitación *f.* regurgitation.
regurgitación aórtica aortic regurgitation.
regurgitación mitral mitral regurgitation.
regurgitación pulmonar pulmonic regurgitation.
regurgitación tricuspídea tricuspid regurgitation.
regurgitación valvular valvular regurgitation.
regurgitante *adj.* regurgitant.
regurgitar *v.* regurgitate.
rehabilitación *f.* rehabilitation.
rehidratación *f.* rehydratation.
rehidratar *v.* rehydrate.
rehospitalizar *v.* rehospitalize.
reimplantación *f.* reimplantation.
reimplantación intencional intentional replantation.
reimplante *m.* replant.
reinduración *f.* chancre redux.
reinervación *f.* reinnervation.
reinfección *f.* reinfection.
reinhalación *f.* rebreathing.
reinoculación *f.* reinoculation.
reinserción *f.* reattachment.
reintegración *f.* reintegration.
reintubación *f.* reintubation.
reinversión *f.* reinversion.
rejuvenecimiento *m.* rejuvenescence.
relación *f.* relation, relationship.
relación de acomodación-convergencia acomodativa (A/CA) accommodative convergence-accommodation relation.
relación albúmina-globulina (A/G) albumin-globulin (A/G) relation.
relación ALT:AST ALT:AST relation.
relación bucolingual buccolingual relation.
relación cardiotorácica cardiothoracic relation.
relación céntrica adquirida acquired centric relation.
relación cetogénica-anticetogénica (C:A) ketogenic-antiketogenic (K:A) relation.
relación de depuración metabólica de amilasa-creatinina amylase-creatinine clearance relation.
relación de dientes deteriorados y obturados relation of decayed and filled teeth (RDFT).
relación dinámica dynamic relation.
relación excéntrica eccentric relation.
relación excéntrica adquirida acquired eccentric relation.
relación de extracción (E) extraction (E) relation.
relación F/O P/O relation.
relación de flujo flux relation.
relación hipnótica hypnotic relationship.
relación IIR/G IRI/G relation.
relación de inervación terminal absoluta absolute terminal innervation relation.
relación de inervación terminal funcional functional terminal innervation relation.
relación de intercambio respiratorio (R) respiratory exchange (R) relation.
relación intermaxilar intermaxillary relation.
relación intermaxilar céntrica centric jaw relation.

relación intermaxilar protrusiva protrusive jaw relation.
relación intermaxilar de reposo rest jaw relation.
relación intermaxilar sin tensión unstrained jaw relation.
relación lecitina/esfingomielina (L/E) lecithin/sphingomyelin (L/S) relation.
relación M:E M:E relation.
relación de la mano hand relation.
relación maxilomandibular maxillomandibular relation.
relación mediana, relación mediana retruida median retruded relation, median relation.
relación mendeliana Mendelian relation.
relación nuclear-citoplasmática nuclear cytoplasmic relation.
relación nutritiva nutritive relation.
relación de objeto object relationship.
relación oclusal occluding relation.
relación de peso corporal body-weight relation.
relación protrusiva protrusive relation.
relación de los rebordes ridge relation.
relación de reposo rest relation.
relación sadomasoquista sadomasochistic relation.
relación de sangre blood relationship.
relación de sedimentación zeta zeta sedimentation relation (ZSR).
relación de segregación segregation relation.
relación de sexos sex relation.
relación de superficies dentarias deterioradas y obturadas relation of decayed and filled surfaces (RDFS).
relación terapéutica therapeutic relation.
relación ventilación/perfusión (Va/Q) ventilation/perfusion relation (Va/Q).
relajación *f.* relaxation.
relajación cardioesofágica cardioesophageal relaxation.
relajación isométrica isometric relaxation.
relajación isovolumétrica isovolumetric relaxation.
relajación isovolúmica isovolumic relaxation.
relajamiento *m.* relaxation.
relajante *m. y adj.* relaxant.
relajante despolarizante depolarizing relaxant.
relajante muscular muscular relaxant.
relajante del músculo liso smooth muscle relaxant.
relajante neuromuscular neuromuscular relaxant.
relajante no despolarizante non-depolarizing relaxant.
relajar *v.* relax.
relativo, -va *adj.* relative.
remanente *m. y adj.* remanent.
remediable *adj.* remediable.
remedio *m.* remedy.
remedio concordante concordant remedy.
remedio inímico inimic remedy.
remineralización *f.* remineralization.
reminiscencia *f.* reminescence.
remisión *f.* remission.
remisión espontánea spontaneous remission.
remitencia *f.* remittence.
remitente *adj.* remittent.
remitir *v.* remit.
remodelación *f.* remodeling.
renal *adj.* renal.
rénculo *m.* renculus.

renegación *f.* disavowal.
renicápsula *f.* renicapsule.
renicardíaco, -ca *adj.* renicardiac.
renicardio, -dia *adj.* renicardiac.
renículo *m.* reniculus.
reniforme *adj.* reniform.
renipélvico, -ca *adj.* renipelvic.
reniportal *adj.* reniportal.
renipuntura *f.* renipuncture.
renitencia *f.* renitence.
renitis *f.* nephritis.
renocutáneo, -a *adj.* renocutaneous.
renogástrico, -ca *adj.* renogastric.
renogénico, -ca *adj.* renogenic.
renografía *f.* renography.
renograma *m.* renogram.
renointestinal *adj.* renointestinal.
renomegalia *f.* renomegaly.
renopatía *f.* renopathy.
renoprivo, -va *adj.* renoprival.
renopulmonar *adj.* renopulmonary.
renotrófico, -ca *adj.* renotrophic.
renotrofina *f.* renotrophin.
renotrópico, -ca *adj.* renotropic.
renovascular *adj.* renovascular.
rénulo *m.* renunculus.
renúnculo *m.* renunculus.
reobase *f.* rheobase.
reobasis *f.* rheobase.
reobásico, -ca *adj.* rheobasic.
reocardiografía *f.* rheocardiography.
reocordio *m.* rheocord.
reoencefalografía *f.* rheoencephalography.
reoencefalograma *m.* rheoencephalogram.
reograma *f.* rheogram.
reología *f.* rheology.
reólogo, -ga *m., f.* rheologist.
reometría *f.* rheometry.
reómetro *m.* rheometer.
reopexia *f.* rheopexy.
reoscopio *m.* rheoscope.
reóstato *m.* rheostat.
reostosis *f.* rheostosis.
reotaquigrafía *f.* rheotachygraphy.
reotaxis *f.* rheotaxis.
reótomo *m.* rheotome.
reotropismo *m.* rheotropism.
reótropo *m.* rheotrope.
Reoviridae Reoviridae.
Reovirus Reovirus.
reoxidación *f.* reoxidation.
rep roentgen-equivalent-physical.
reparación *f.* reparation, repair.
reparación de ADN dna reparation.
reparación química chemical reparation.
reparación quirúrgica surgical reparation.
reparación tisular tissue reparation.
reparador, -ra *adj.* reparative, restorative.
reparativo, -va *adj.* reparative, restorative.
repelente *adj.* repellent.
repercolación *f.* repercolation.
repetición-compulsión *f.* repetition-compulsion.
replantación *f.* replantation.
repleción *f.* repletion.
réplica *f.* replica.
replicación *f.* replication.
replicador *m.* replicator.
replicar *v.* replicate.
replicasa *f.* replicase.
replicón *m.* replicon.
replisoma *m.* replisome.
repolarización *f.* repolarization.
reposición *f.* repositioning.
reposición gingival gingival repositioning.

reposición mandibular jaw repositioning.
reposición muscular muscle repositioning.
reposicionamiento *m.* set.
repositor *m.* repositor.
reposo *m.* rest.
representación *f.* representation.
represión *f.* repression.
reproducción *f.* reproduction.
reproducción asexual asexual reproduction.
reproducción citogénica cytogenic reproduction.
reproducción sexual sexual reproduction.
reproducción somática somatic reproduction.
reproductivo, -va *adj.* reproductive.
reproductor, -ra *adj.* reproductive.
repudio *m.* repudiation.
repulsión *f.* repulsion.
repululación *f.* repullulation.
resalto *m.* overjet, overjut.
resazurina *f.* resazurin.
resbalamiento *m.* creep.
rescisión *f.* excision.
resecable *adj.* resectable.
resecar *v.* resect.
resección *f.* resection.
resección en cuña wedge resection.
resección de las encías gum resection.
resección escleral scleral resection.
resección estomacal de Reichel-Pólya Reichel-Pólya stomach resection.
resección de Miles Miles resection.
resección muscular muscle resection.
resección radicular, resección de raíces root resection.
resección submucosa (RSM) submucous resection (SMR).
resección transuretral (RTU) transurethral resection (TUR).
resectoscopia *f.* resectocopy.
resectoscopio *m.* resectoscope.
reserva *f.* reserve.
reserva alcalina alkali reserve.
reserva cardíaca cardiac reserve.
reserva respiratoria breathing reserve.
reservorio *m.* reservoir.
reservorio de espermatozoides reservoir of spermatozoa.
reservorio de infección reservoir of infection.
reservorio de Ommaya Ommaya reservoir.
reservorio de virus animal reservoir.
resfriado *m.* cold.
resfriado de la cabeza cold in the head, head cold.
residual *adj.* residual.
residuo *m.* residue.
residuo del día day residue.
resiliencia *f.* resilience.
resistencia *f.* resistance.
resistencia a ácidos y alcohol acid alcohol resistance.
resistencia a los bacteriófagos bateriophage resistance.
resistencia espiratoria expiratory resistance.
resistencia a la fatiga fatigue strength.
resistencia al impacto impact resistance.
resistencia inductiva inductive resistance.
resistencia a la insulina insulin resistance.
resistencia mutua mutual resistance.
resistencia periférica peripheral resistance.
resistencia periférica total (RPT) total peripheral resistance (TPR).
resistencia sináptica synaptic resistance.
resistencia de las vías aéreas airway resistance.
resistor *m.* resistor.

resolución *f.* resolution.
resolutivo, -va *adj.* resolvent.
resolvente *adj.* resolvent.
resolver *v.* resolve.
resonador *m.* resonator.
  resonador de Oudin Oudin resonator.
resonancia *f.* resonance.
  resonancia anfórica amphoric resonance.
  resonancia escódica skodaic resonance.
  resonancia de espín electrónico electron spin resonance.
  resonancia hidatídica hydatic resonance.
  resonancia de madera wooden resonance.
  resonancia magnética magnetic resonance (mr).
  resonancia magnética nuclear nuclear magnetic resonance (Nmr).
  resonancia de olla hendida cracked-pot resonance.
  resonancia timpánica tympanitic resonance.
  resonancia vesicular vesicular resonance.
  resonancia vesiculotimpánica vesiculotympanitic resonance.
  resonancia vocal vocal resonance (Vr).
resonante *adj.* resonant.
resorción *f.* resorption.
resorte *m.* spring.
respirable *adj.* respirable.
respiración *f.* breathing, respiration.
  respiración abdominal abdominal respiration.
  respiración aeróbica aerobic respiration.
  respiración anaeróbica anaerobic respiration.
  respiración anfórica amphoric respiration.
  respiración apnéustica apneustic respiration.
  respiración artificial artificial respiration.
  respiración asistida assisted respiration.
  respiración de Biot Biot's respiration.
  respiración boca a boca mouth-to-mouth respiration.
  respiración de Bouchut Bouchut's respiration.
  respiración broncovesicular broncovesicular respiration.
  respiración bronquial bronchial respiration.
  respiración cerebral cerebral respiration.
  respiración de Cheyne-Stokes Cheyne-Stokes respiration.
  respiración con presión positiva continua continuous positive pressure breathing.
  respiración con presión positiva intermitente intermittent positive pressure breathing.
  respiración con presión positiva negativa positive-negative pressure breathing.
  respiración controlada controlled respiration.
  respiración de Corrigan Corrigan's respiration.
  respiración costal costal respiration.
  respiración cutánea cutaneous respiration.
  respiración diafragmática diaphragmatic respiration.
  respiración por difusión diffusion respiration.
  respiración dividida divided respiration.
  respiración electrofrénica electrophrenic respiration.
  respiración entrecortada interrupted respiration.
  respiración estertorosa stertorous respiration.
  respiración externa external respiration.
  respiración fetal fetal respiration.
  respiración forzada forced respiration.
  respiración glosofaríngea glossopharyngeal breathing.
  respiración hística tissue respiration.
  respiración interna internal respiration.

  respiración interrumpida interrupted respiration.
  respiración de Kussmaul, respiración de Kussmaul-Kien Kussmaul respiration, Kussmaul-Kien's respiration.
  respiración meningítica meningitic respiration.
  respiración de nitrato nitrate respiration.
  respiración oral mouth breathing.
  respiración paradójica paradoxical respiration.
  respiración pueril puerile respiration.
  respiración ruda rude respiration, harsh respiration.
  respiración en rueda dentada cogwheel respiration.
  respiración de sulfato sulfate respiration.
  respiración superficial shallow breathing.
  respiración suplementaria supplementary respiration.
  respiración suspirosa sighing respiration.
  respiración torácica thoracic respiration.
  respiración tubárica, respiración tubular tubular respiration.
  respiración vesicular vesicular respiration.
  respiración vesiculocavernosa vesiculocavernous respiration.
respirador *m.* respirator.
  respirador de circuito abierto open-circuit breathing system.
  respirador controlado por presión pressure-controlled respirator.
  respirador controlado por volumen volume-controlled respirator.
  respirador en coraza cuirass respirator.
  respirador de Drinker Drinker respirator.
  respirador tanque tank respirator.
respirar *v.* respire.
respiratorio, -ria *adj.* respiratory.
respirómetro *m.* respirometer.
  respirómetro de Dräger Dräger respirometer.
  respirómetro de Wright Wright respirometer.
respuesta *f.* response.
  respuesta anamnéstica anamnestic response.
  respuesta bifásica biphasic response.
  respuesta condicionada conditioned response.
  respuesta de curva curve response.
  respuesta de Cushing Cushing response.
  respuesta cutánea galvánica galvanic skin response.
  respuesta de deplección depletion response.
  respuesta de fase tardía late-phase response.
  respuesta de fase temprana early-phase response.
  respuesta de Henry-Gauer Henry-Gauer response.
  respuesta de huida flight response.
  respuesta inmune immune response.
  respuesta isomórfica isomorphic response.
  respuesta de lucha fight response.
  respuesta no condicionada unconditioned response.
  respuesta oculomotora oculomotor response.
  respuesta de orientación orienting response.
  respuesta psicogalvánica psychogalvanic response, psychogalvanic skin response.
  respuesta de reclutamiento recruiting response.
  respuesta de relajación relaxation response.
  respuesta sonomotora sonomotor response.
  respuesta triple triple response.
restablecimiento *m.* recovery.
restauración *f.* restoration.

  restauración colgante overhanging restoration.
  restauración combinada combination restoration.
  restauración compuesta compound restoration.
  restauración de conductos radiculares root canal restoration.
  restauración directa de acrílico direct acrylic restoration.
  restauración directa de resina, restauración directa de resina compuesta direct resin restoration, direct composite resin restoration.
  restauración grabada con ácido acid-etched restoration.
  restauración permanente permanent restoration.
  restauración de silicato silicate restoration.
  restauración temporal temporary restoration.
restaurativo, -va *adj.* restorative.
restibraquio *m.* restibrachium.
restiforme *adj.* restiform.
restis *m.* restis.
restitutio ad integrum restitutio ad integrum.
resto *m.* residue.
  resto adrenal adrenal residue.
  resto celular de Walthard Walthard's cell residue.
  resto de carbono carbon residue.
  resto diurno day residue.
  resto embrionario embryonic residue.
  resto epitelial epithelial residue.
  resto fetal fetal residue.
  resto epiteliales de Malassez Malassez's epithelial residue.
  resto mesonéfrico mesonephric residue.
  resto de precisión precision residue.
  resto suprarrenal adrenal residue.
  resto de Wolff Wolffian residue.
restocitemia *f.* restocythemia.
restricción *f.* restraint.
resublimado, -da *adj.* resublimed.
resucitación *f.* resuscitation.
resucitador *m.* resuscitator.
resultado *m.* result.
resurrección *f.* resuscitation.
retardado *m.* retardate.
retardador *m.* retarder.
rete *f.* rete.
retelioma *m.* rethelioma.
retención *f.* retention.
  retención de orina urine retention, retention of urine.
  retención directa direct retention.
  retención indirecta indirect retention.
  retención placentaria retention of placenta, retention of placental fragments.
  retención protésica denture retention.
  retención de prótesis parciales partial denture retention.
  retención de la respiración breath-holding.
retenedor *m.* retainer.
  retenedor en barra continuo continuous bar retainer.
  retenedor directo direct retainer.
  retenedor de espacio space retainer.
  retenedor extracoronal extracoronal retainer.
  retenedor indirecto indirect retainer.
  retenedor intracoronal intracoronal retainer.
  retenedor de matriz matrix retainer.
retetestis retetestis.
retícula *f.* reticula.

reticulación *f.* reticulation.
reticulado, -da *adj.* reticulated.
reticular *adj.* reticular.
reticulina *f.* reticulin.
retículo *m.* reticulum.
  retículo de Ebner Ebner's reticulum.
  retículo endoplásmico endoplasmic reticulum.
  retículo estrellado stellate reticulum.
  retículo de Kölliker Kölliker's reticulum.
  retículo sarcoplasmático sarcoplasmic reticulum.
  retículo trabecular trabecular reticulum.
reticulocito *m.* reticulocyte.
reticulocitopenia *f.* reticulocytopenia.
reticulocitosis *f.* reticulocytosis.
reticuloendotelial *adj.* reticuloendothelial.
reticuloendotelio *m.* reticuloendothelium.
reticuloendotelioma *m.* reticuloendothelioma.
reticuloendoteliosis *f.* reticuloendotheliosis.
  reticuloendoteliosis leucémica leukemic reticuloendotheliosis.
reticuloespinal *adj.* reticulospinal.
reticulohistiocitoma *m.* reticulohistiocytoma.
reticulohistiocitosis *f.* reticulohistiocytosis.
  reticulohistiocitosis multicéntrica multicentric reticulohistiocytosis.
reticuloide *m.* reticuloid.
  reticuloide actínico actinic reticuloid.
reticuloma *m.* reticuloma.
reticulopenia *f.* reticulopenia.
reticulosarcoma *m.* reticulosarcoma.
reticulosis *f.* reticulosis.
  reticulosis benigna por inoculación benign inoculation reticulosis.
  reticulosis leucémica leukemic reticulosis.
  reticulosis lipomelánica lipomelanic reticulosis.
  reticulosis medular histiocítica histiocytic medullary reticulosis.
  reticulosis mieloide myeloid reticulosis.
  reticulosis pagetoide pagetoid reticulosis.
  reticulosis polimórfica polymorphic reticulosis.
reticulotelio *m.* reticulothelium.
reticulotomía *f.* reticulotomy.
retiforme *adj.* retiform.
retina *f.* retina.
  retina comprimida coarctate retina.
  retina desprendida detached retina.
  retina de kandori fleck retina.
  retina de leopardo leopard retina.
  retina manchada flecked retina.
  retina de seda tornasolada shot-silk retina.
  retina tigroide tigroid retina.
  retina veteada flecked retina.
retináculo *m.* retinaculum.
retinaculum retinaculum.
retinal *adj.* retinal.
retineno *m.* retinene.
retiniano, -na *adj.* retinal.
retinitis *f.* retinitis.
  retinitis actínica actinic retinitis.
  retinitis albuminúrica albuminuric retinitis.
  retinitis angiospástica central central angiospastic retinitis.
  retinitis apoplética apoplectic retinitis.
  retinitis azoémica azotemic retinitis.
  retinitis central recurrente recurrent central retinitis.
  retinitis circinada circinate retinitis.
  retinitis diabética diabetic retinitis.
  retinitis esclopedaria retinitis sclopetaria.

  retinitis esplénica leukemic retinitis.
  retinitis exudativa exudative retinitis.
  retinitis gravídica gravidic retinitis.
  retinitis hemorrágica retinitis hemorrhagica.
  retinitis hipertensiva hypertensive retinitis.
  retinitis de Jacobson Jacobson's retinitis.
  retinitis de Jensen Jensen's retinitis.
  retinitis leucémica leukemic retinitis.
  retinitis metastásica metastatic retinitis.
  retinitis nefrítica retinitis nephritica.
  retinitis pigmentaria, retinitis pigmentosa retinitis pigmentosa.
  retinitis proliferante proliferating retinitis, retinitis proliferans.
  retinitis punteada, retinitis punctata punctate retinitis.
  retinitis purulenta purulent retinitis.
  retinitis renal retinitis nephritica.
  retinitis serosa purulent retinitis.
  retinitis secundaria secondary retinitis.
  retinitis séptica septic retinitis.
  retinitis sifilítica syphilitic retinitis, retinitis syphilitica.
  retinitis simple simple retinitis.
  retinitis solar solar retinitis.
retinoblastoma *m.* retinoblastoma.
retinocitoma *f.* retinocytoma.
retinocoroide *adj.* retinochoroid.
retinocoroiditis *f.* retinochoroiditis.
  retinocoroiditis en perdigón bird shot retinochoroiditis.
  retinocoroiditis yuxtapapilar retinochoroiditis juxtapapillaris.
retinodiálisis *f.* retinodialysis.
retinografía *f.* retinography.
retinoide *adj.* retinoid.
retinomalacia *f.* retinomalacia.
retinopapilitis *f.* retinopapillitis.
  retinopapilitis de los niños prematuros retinopapillitis of premature infants.
retinopatía *f.* retinopathy.
  retinopatía angioespástica central central angiospastic retinopathy.
  retinopatía angiopática angiopathic retinopathy.
  retinopatía arteriosclerótica arteriosclerotic retinopathy.
  retinopatía circinada circinate retinopathy.
  retinopatía por compresión compression retinopathy.
  retinopatía diabética diabetic retinopathy.
  retinopatía disórica dysoric retinopathy.
  retinopatía disproteinémica dysproteinemic retinopathy.
  retinopatía drepanocítica sickle cell retinopathy.
  retinopatía eclámptica eclamptic retinopathy.
  retinopatía eléctrica electric retinopathy.
  retinopatía por estasis venosa venous stasis retinopathy.
  retinopatía estrellada stellate retinopathy.
  retinopatía estrellada idiopática de Leber Leber's idiopathic stellate retinopathy.
  retinopatía exudativa externa external exudative retinopathy.
  retinopatía fótica photo retinopathy.
  retinopatía gravídica gravidic retinopathy.
  retinopatía hipertensiva hypertensive retinopathy.
  retinopatía hipotensiva hypotensive retinopathy.
  retinopatía leucémica leukemic retinopathy.
  retinopatía lipémica lipemic retinopathy.
  retinopatía macular macular retinopathy.

  retinopatía pigmentaria, retinopatía pigmentosa pigmentary retinopathy.
  retinopatía de los prematuros retinopathy of prematurity.
  retinopatía proliferativa proliferative retinopathy.
  retinopatía punctata albescens retinopathy punctata albescens.
  retinopatía renal renal retinopathy.
  retinopatía de la rubéola rubella retinopathy.
  retinopatía serosa central central serous retinopathy.
  retinopatía solar solar retinopathy.
  retinopatía tapetorretiniana tapetoretinal retinopathy.
  retinopatía toxémica del embarazo toxemic retinopathy of preganancy.
  retinopatía tóxica toxic retinopathy.
  retinopatía traumática traumatic retinopathy.
retinopexia *f.* retinopexy.
retinopiesis *f.* retinopiesis.
retinoscopia *f.* retinoscopy.
  retinoscopia borrosa fogging retinoscopy.
  retinoscopia cilíndrica cylinder retinoscopy.
retinoscopio *m.* retinoscope.
  retinoscopio luminoso luminous retinoscope.
  retinoscopio reflector reflecting retinoscope.
retinosis *f.* retinosis.
retinosquisis *f.* retinoschisis.
  retinosquisis juvenil juvenile retinoschisis.
  retinosquisis senil senile retinoschisis.
retintín *m.* tinkle.
retisolución *f.* retisolution.
retoperitelio *m.* retoperithelium.
retorno *m.* return.
  retorno venoso venous return.
retorta *f.* retort.
retortijón *m.* gripe, stomach cramp.
retotelio *m.* retothelium.
retotelioma *m.* retothelioma.
retoteliosis *m.* reticulosis.
retracción *f.* retraction.
  retracción de la aponeurosis palmar Dupuytren's contraction, Dupuytren's contracture.
  retracción gingival gingival retraction.
  retracción mandibular mandibular retraction.
  retracción sistólica de la punta Heim-Kreysig sign.
  retracción del tórax retraction of the chest.
  retracción del útero uterine muscle retraction.
retráctil *adj.* retractile.
retractor *m.* retractor.
  retractor de Moorehead Moorehead's retractor.
retrasado, -da *adj.* retardate.
retraso *m.* retardation.
  retraso de anafase anaphase lag.
  retraso mental mental retardation.
  retraso mental leve mild mental retardation.
  retraso mental moderado moderate mental retardation.
  retraso mental grave severe mental retardation.
  retraso mental profundo profound mental retardation.
  retraso psicomotor psychomotor retardation.
retroacción *f.* feedback.
retroactividad *f.* deferred action.

retroalimentación *f.* feedback.
retroalimentación negativa negative feedback.
retroalimentación positiva positive feedback.
retroauricular *adj.* retroauricular.
retrobronquial *adj.* retrobronchial.
retrobucal *adj.* retrobuccal.
retrobulbar *adj.* retrobulbar.
retrocalcaneobursitis *f.* retrocalcaneobursitis.
retrocardíaco, -ca *adj.* retrocardiac.
retrocateterismo *m.* retrocatheterism.
retrocecal *adj.* retrocecal.
retrocervical *adj.* retrocervical.
retrocesión *f.* retrocession.
retroceso *m.* retrocession.
retroclavicular *adj.* retroclavicular.
retrocólico, -ca *adj.* retrocolic.
retrocolis *m.* retrocollis, retrocollic spasm.
retrodesplazamiento *m.* retrodisplacement.
retrodesviación *f.* retrodeviation.
retroesofágico, -ca *adj.* retroesophageal.
retroespondilolistesis *f.* retrospondylolisthesis.
retroesternal *adj.* retrosternal.
retrofaringe *f.* retropharynx.
retrofaríngeo, -a *adj.* retropharyngeal.
retroflexo, -xa *adj.* retroflexed.
retroflexión *f.* retroflexion.
retroflexionado, -da *adj.* retroflexed.
retrognatia *f.* retrognathia.
retrognático, -ca *adj.* retrognathic.
retrognatismo *m.* retrognathism.
retrógrado, -da *adj.* retrograde.
retrografía *f.* retrography.
retrogresión *f.* retrogression.
retroinsular *adj.* retroinsular.
retroiridiano, -na *adj.* retroiridian.
retrolaberíntico, -ca *adj.* retrolabyrinthine.
retrolental *adj.* retrolental.
retrolenticular *adj.* retrolenticular.
retrolingual *adj.* retrolingual.
retrolistesis *f.* retrolisthesis.
retromamario, -ria *adj.* retromammary.
retromandibular *adj.* retromandibular.
retromastoideo, -a *adj.* retromastoid.
retromaxilar *adj.* retromaxillary.
retromorfosis *f.* retromorphosis.
retronasal *adj.* retronasal.
retroobturación *f.* retrofilling.
retroocular *adj.* retro-ocular.
retroperitoneal *adj.* retroperitoneal.
retroperitonitis *f.* retroperitonitis.
retroperitonitis fibrosa idiopática idiopathic fibrous retroperitonitis.
retroplacentario, -ria *adj.* retroplacental.
retroplasia *f.* retroplasia.
retroposición *f.* retroposition.
retroposón *m.* retroposon.
retropúbico, -ca *adj.* retropubic.
retropuesto, -ta *adj.* retroposed.
retropulsión *f.* retropulsion.
retrorrectal *adj.* retrorectal.
retrosinfisial *adj.* retrosymphysial.
retrospección *f.* retrospection.
retrospectivo, -va *adj.* retrospective.
retrospondilolistesis *f.* retrospondylolisthesis.
retrostalsis *f.* retrostalsis.
retrosternal *adj.* retrosternal.
retrotarsiano, -na *adj.* retrotarsal.
retrouterino, -na *adj.* retrouterine.
retroversioflexión *f.* retroversioflexion.
retroversión *f.* retroversion.

retrovertido, -da *adj.* retroverted.
Retroviridae Retroviridae.
retrovirus *m.* retrovirus.
retroyección *f.* retrojection.
retroyector *m.* retrojector.
retrusión *f.* retrusion.
reuma, reúma *m., f.* rheum, rheuma.
reumatalgia *f.* rheumatalgia.
reumático, -ca *adj.* rheumatic, rheumatismal.
reumaticosis *f.* rheumaticosis.
reumátide *f.* rheumatid.
reumatismo *m.* rheumatism.
reumatismo articular agudo acute articular rheumatism.
reumatismo articular crónico chronic articular rheumatism.
reumatismo capsular de Macleod Macleod's rheumatism.
reumatismo cardíaco rheumatism of the heart.
reumatismo cerebral cerebral rheumatism.
reumatismo crónico chronic rheumatism.
reumatismo deformante chronic articular rheumatism.
reumatismo gonorreico gonorrheal rheumatism.
reumatismo gotoso chronic rheumatism.
reumatismo de Heberden Heberden's rheumatism.
reumatismo inflamatorio inflammatory rheumatism.
reumatismo lumbar lumbar rheumatism.
reumatismo de Macleod Macleod's rheumatism.
reumatismo muscular muscular rheumatism.
reumatismo nudoso nodose rheumatism.
reumatismo óseo osseous rheumatism.
reumatismo palindrómico palindromic rheumatism.
reumatismo de Poncet Poncet's rheumatism.
reumatismo subagudo subacute rheumatism.
reumatismo tuberculoso tuberculous rheumatism.
reumatismo visceral visceral rheumatism.
reumatocelis *f.* rheumatocelis.
reumatología *f.* rheumatology.
reumatólogo, -ga *f.* rheumatologist.
reumatosis *f.* rheumatosis.
reunión *f.* union.
revacunación *f.* revaccination.
revascularización *f.* revascularization.
reversible *adj.* reversible.
reversión *f.* reversion.
revertante *adj.* revertant.
revestimiento *m.* lining.
revivificación *f.* revivification.
reviviscencia *f.* reviviscence.
revulsión *f.* revulsion.
revulsivo, -va *m. y adj.* revulsive.
reyección *f.* rejection.
Rhabditis Rhabditis.
Rhabdoviridae Rhabdoviridae.
Rhinosporidium Rhinosporidium.
Rhinovirus Rhinovirus.
Rhizopus Rhizopus.
Rhodnius prolixus Rhodnius prolixus.
Rhodotorula Rhodotorula.
ribavirina *f.* ribavirin.
riboflavina *f.* riboflavin, riboflavine.
ribonucleoproteína *f.* ribonucleoprotein.
ribonucleósido *m.* ribonucleoside.
ribonucleótido *m.* ribonucleotide.
ribosoma *m.* ribosome.
ribosuria *f.* ribosuria.

Rickettsia Rickettsia.
Rickettsiaceae Rickettsiaceae.
rickettsial *adj.* rickettsial.
rickettsiosis *f.* rickettsiosis.
rickettsiostático, -ca *adj.* rickettsiostatic.
rictus *m.* rictus.
ridectomía *f.* rhytidectomy.
riesgo *m.* risk.
riesgo empírico empiric risk.
riesgo de recurrencia recurrence risk.
rigidez *f.* rigidity.
rigidez anatómica anatomic rigidity.
rigidez cadavérica cadaveric rigidity.
rigidez en caño de plomo lead rigidity, pipe rigidity.
rigidez catatónica catatonic rigidity.
rigidez cerebelosa cerebellar rigidity.
rigidez de decorticación decorticate rigidity.
rigidez de descerebración decerebrate rigidity.
rigidez escleral scleral rigidity.
rigidez extrapiramidal extrapyramidal rigidity.
rigidez hemipléjica hemiplegic rigidity.
rigidez midriática mydriatic rigidity.
rigidez ocular ocular rigidity.
rigidez patológica pathologic rigidity.
rigidez post mortem postmortem rigidity.
rigidez en rueda dentada cogwheel rigidity.
rigor *m.* rigor.
rigor ácido acid rigor.
rigor cálcico calcium rigor.
rigor mortis rigor mortis.
rigor mortis miocárdico myocardial rigor.
rigor nervorum rigor nervorum.
rigor térmico heat rigor.
rigor tremens rigor tremens.
rigótico, -ca *adj.* rhigotic.
rigosis *f.* rhigosis.
rima *f.* rima.
rimoso, -sa *adj.* rimose.
rímula *f.* rimula.
rinal *adj.* rhinal.
rinalergia *f.* rhinallergosis.
rinalergosis *f.* rhinallergosis.
rinalgia *f.* rhinalgia.
rinedema *f.* rhinedema.
rinencefalia *f.* rhinocephalia, rhinocephaly.
rinencefálico, -ca *adj.* rhinencephalic.
rinencéfalo *m.* rhinencephalon.
rinenquisis *f.* rhinenchysis.
rinestesia *f.* rhinesthesia.
rineurínter *m.* rhineurynter.
riniatría *f.* rhinology.
rinión *m.* rhinion.
rinismo *m.* rhinism.
rinitis *f.* rhinitis.
rinitis aguda acute rhinitis.
rinitis alérgica allergic rhinitis.
rinitis analfiláctica anaphylactic rhinitis.
rinitis atrófica atrophic rhinitis.
rinitis caseosa caseous rhinitis, rhinitis caseosa.
rinitis catarral aguda acute catarrhal rhinitis.
rinitis crónica chronic rhinitis.
rinitis cruposa croupous rhinitis.
rinitis eosinofílica no alérgica eosinophilic non-allergic rhinitis.
rinitis escrofulosa scrofulous rhinitis.
rinitis fibrinosa fibrinous rhinitis.
rinitis gangrenosa gangrenous rhinitis.
rinitis hipertrófica hypertrophic rhinitis.
rinitis membranosa membranous rhinitis.
rinitis nerviosa rhinitis nervosa.
rinitis purulenta purulent rhinitis, rhinitis purulenta.

rinitis seca rhinitis sicca.

rinitis seudomembranosa pseudomembranous rhinitis.

rinitis sifilítica syphilitic rhinitis.

rinitis tuberculosa tuberculous rhinitis.

rinitis vasomotora vasomotor rhinitis.

rinoanemómetro *m.* rhinoanemometer.

rinoantritis *f.* rhinoantritis.

rinobión *m.* rhinobyon.

rinocantectomía *f.* rhinocanthectomy.

rinocefalia *f.* rhinocephalia, rhinocephaly.

rinocéfalo *m.* rhinocephalus.

rinocelo *m.* rhinocele.

rinocifectomía *f.* rhinokyphectomy.

rinocifosis *f.* rhinokyphosis.

rinocleisis *f.* rhinocleisis.

rinodacriolito *m.* rhinodacryolith.

rinodimia *f.* rhinodymia.

rinodinia *f.* rhinodynia.

rinoedema *f.* rhinedema.

rinoescleroma *m.* rhinoscleroma.

rinoestenosis *f.* rhinostenosis.

rinofaringe *f.* rhinopharynx.

rinofaríngeo, -a *adj.* rhinopharyngeal.

rinofaringitis *f.* rhinopharyngitis.

rinofaringocele *m.* rhinopharyngocele.

rinofaringolito *m.* rhinopharyngolith.

rinoficomicosis *f.* rhinophycomycosis.

rinofima *m.* rhinophyma.

rinofonía *f.* rhinophonia.

rinógeno, -na *adj.* rhinogenous.

rinolalia *f.* rhinolalia.

rinolalia abierta rhinolalia aperta.

rinolalia cerrada rhinolalia clausa.

rinolaringitis *f.* rhinolaryngitis.

rinolaringología *f.* rhinolaryngology.

rinolitiasis *f.* rhinolithiasis.

rinolito *m.* rhinolith.

rinología *f.* rhinology.

rinológico, -ca *adj.* rhinologic.

rinólogo, -ga *m., f.* rhinologist.

rinomanometria *f.* rhinomanometry.

rinomanómetro *m.* rhynomanometer.

rinomectomía *f.* rhinnommectomy.

rinómetro *m.* rhinometer.

rinomicosis *f.* rhinomycosis.

rinomucormicosis *f.* rhinomucormycosis.

rinonecrosis *f.* rhinonecrosis.

rinoneurosis *f.* rhinoneurosis.

rinopatía *f.* rhinopathy.

rinoplastia *f.* rhinoplasty.

rinoplastia hindú Indian rhinoplasty.

rinoplastia inglesa English rhinoplasty.

rinoplastia italiana Italian rhinoplasty.

rinoplastia de tagliacozzi Tagliacotian operation.

rinopólipo *m.* rhinopolypus.

rinoqueiloplastia *f.* rhinocheiloplasty.

rinoquiloplastia *f.* rhinocheiloplasty.

rinorrafia *f.* rhinorrhaphy.

rinorragia *f.* rhinorrhagia.

rinorrea *f.* rhinorrhea.

rinorrea cerebroespinal cerebrospinal fluid rhinorrhea.

rinorrea gustativa gustatory rhinorrhea.

rinorrea de líquido cefalorraquídeo cerebrospinal fluid rhinorrhea.

rinorreacción *f.* rhinoreaction.

rinosalpingitis *f.* rhinosalpingitis.

rinoscleroma *m.* rhinoscleroma.

rinoscopia *f.* rhinoscopy.

rinoscopia anterior anterior rhinoscopy.

rinoscopia media median rhinoscopy.

rinoscopia posterior posterior rhinoscopy.

rinoscopio *m.* rhinoscope.

rinoseptoplastia *f.* septorhinoplasty.

rinosporidiosis *f.* rhinosporidiosis.

rinostenosis *f.* rhinostenosis.

rinotomía *f.* rhinotomy.

rinotraqueítis *f.* rhinotracheitis.

rinovacunación *f.* rhinovaccination.

rinovirus *m.* rhinovirus.

riñón *m.* kidney.

riñón adiposo amyloid kidney.

riñón amiloide, riñón amiloideo amyloid kidney.

riñón aplastado crush kidney.

riñón de argamasa mortar kidney.

riñón de Armanni-Ebstein Armanni-Ebstein kidney.

riñón arterioloesclerótico arteriolosclerotic kidney.

riñón arterioesclerótico arteriosclerotic kidney.

riñón artificial artificial kidney.

riñón de Askr-Upmark Askr-Upmark kidney.

riñón atrófico atrophic kidney.

riñón cefálico head kidney.

riñón céreo waxy kidney.

riñón cicatricial cicatricial kidney.

riñón contraído contracted kidney.

riñón delantero head kidney.

riñón discoide disk kidney.

riñón doble duplex kidney.

riñón ectópico floating kidney.

riñón errante wandering kidney.

riñón esclerótico sclerotic kidney.

riñón flotante floating kidney.

riñón de Formad Formad's kidney.

riñón fusionado fused kidney.

riñón de Goldblatt Goldblatt kidney.

riñón granular granular kidney.

riñón graso fatty kidney.

riñón en herradura horseshoe kidney.

riñón lardáceo amyloid kidney.

riñón de masilla putty kidney.

riñón meduloesponjoso medullary sponge kidney.

riñón movible movable kidney.

riñón en panqueque pancake kidney.

riñón mural mural kidney.

riñón parietal mural kidney.

riñón pélvico pelvic kidney.

riñón picado por pulgas flea-bitten kidney.

riñón pielonefrítico pyelonephritic kidney.

riñón poliquístico polycystic kidney.

riñón primordial primordial kidney.

riñón quístico cystic kidney.

riñón de Roser-Bradford Roser-Bradford kidney.

riñón supernumerario supernumerary kidney.

riñón trasero hind kidney.

riñón en torta cake kidney.

riñón de vaca cow kidney.

ripa *f.* ripa.

ripofagia *f.* rhypophagy.

risa *f.* laugh, risus.

risa canina risus caninus.

risa y llanto espasmódicos spasmodic crying or laughing.

risa sardónica risus sardonicus.

ritidectomía *f.* rhytidectomy.

ritidoplastia *f.* rhytidoplasty.

ritidosis *f.* rhytidosis.

ritmador *m.* rhythmeur.

rítmico, -ca *adj.* rhythmical.

ritmo *m.* rhythm.

ritmo acoplado coupled rhythm.

ritmo agónico agonal rhythm.

ritmo alfa alpha rhythm.

ritmo auriculoventricular atrioventricular rhythm.

ritmo de Berger Berger rhythm.

ritmo beta beta rhythm.

ritmo bigémico bigeminal rhythm.

ritmo circadiano circadian rhythm.

ritmo circular circus rhythm.

ritmo cuádruple quadruple rhythm.

ritmo delta delta rhythm.

ritmo ectópico ectopic rhythm.

ritmo de escape escape rhythm.

ritmo fetal fetal rhythm.

ritmo de galope cantering rhythm.

ritmo idionodal idionodal rhythm.

ritmo idioventricular idioventricular rhythm.

ritmo nodal nodal rhythm.

ritmo nodal auriculoventricular atrioventricular nodal rhythm.

ritmo nodal coronario coronary nodal rhythm.

ritmo pendular pendulum rhythm.

ritmo rápido fast rhythm.

ritmo reciprocante reciprocating rhythm.

ritmo recíproco reciprocal rhythm.

ritmo recíproco invertido reversed reciprocal rhythm.

ritmo de ruedas de tren trainwheel rhythm.

ritmo sinusal sinus rhythm.

ritmo sinusal coronario coronary sinus rhythm.

ritmo theta theta rhythm.

ritmo de tic-tac tick-tack rhythm.

ritmo trigeminal trigeminal rhythm.

ritmo triple triple rhythm.

ritmo ultradiano ultradian rhythm.

ritmo ventricular ventricular rhythm.

ritmófono *m.* rhythmophone.

ritmoterapia *f.* rhytmotherapy.

ritual *m.* ritual.

rivalidad *f.* rivalry.

rivalidad binocular binocular rivalry.

rivalidad de la retina rivalry of the retina.

rivus lacrimalis *m.* rivus lacrimalis.

rizanestesia *f.* rhizanesthesia.

rizoide *adj.* rhizoid.

rizomelia *f.* rhizomelia.

rizomélico, -ca *adj.* rhizomelic.

rizomeningomielitis *f.* rhizomeningomyelitis.

rizómera *f.* rhizomere.

rizoneura *f.* rhizoneure.

rizoplasto *m.* rhizoplast.

rizópodos *m.* rhizopoda.

rizotomía *f.* rhizotomy.

rizotomía anterior anterior rhizotomy.

rizotomía de facetas facet rhizotomy.

rizotomía posterior posterior rhizotomy.

rizotomía trigeminal trigeminal rhizotomy.

robo *m.* steal.

robo ilíaco iliac steal.

robo renal-esplácnico renal-splanchnic steal.

robo de la sublavia subclavian steal.

roborante *adj.* roborant.

roce *m.* rubbing.

roce de fricción friction rubbing.

roce de fricción pericárdica pericardial friction rubbing.

roce pericárdico pericardial rubbing.

roce pleurítico pleuritic rubbing.

rodamina b *f.* rhodamine b.

rodilla *f.* knee, genu.

rodilla bloqueada locked knee.

rodilla de Brodie Brodie's knee.

rodilla distendida capped knee.

rodilla de mucama housemaid's knee.

rodilla de rugby rugby knee.

rodillera *f.* kneeguard.

rodocito *m.* rhodocyte.
rodofiláctico, -ca *adj.* rhodophylactic.
rodofilaxia *f.* rhodophylaxis.
rodofilaxis *f.* rhodophylaxis.
rodogénesis *f.* rhodogenesis.
rodonalgia *f.* rodonalgia.
roentgen *m.* roentgen.
　roentgen equivalente-físico roentgen equivalent-physical.
　roentgen equivalente-hombre roentgen equivalent-man.
roentgenismo *m.* roentgenism.
roentgenografía *f.* roentgenography.
　roentgenografía en relieve de la mucosa mucosal relief roentgenography.
　roentgenografía seccional sectional roentgenography.
　roentgenografía seriada serial roentgenography.
roentgenograma *m.* roentgenogram.
roentgenología *f.* roentgenology.
roentgenólogo, -ga *m.* roentgenologist.
roentgenometría *f.* roentgenometry.
roentgenómetro *m.* roentgenometer.
roentgenoquimografía *f.* roentgenkymography.
roentgenoquimógrafo *m.* roentgenkymograph.
roentgenoquimograma *m.* roentgenkymogram.
roentgenoscopia *f.* roentgenoscopy.
roentgenoscopio *m.* roentgenoscope.
roentgenoterapia *f.* roentgenotherapy.
rofeocitosis *f.* rhopheocytosis.
rojo *m.* red.
rojo, -ja *adj.* red.
rol *m.* role.
　rol complementario complementary role.
　rol de enfermo sick role.
　rol de género gender role.
　rol no complementario non-complementary role.
　rol sexual sexual role.
rollo *m.* roll.
　rollo escleral scleral roll.
　rollo ilíaco iliac roll.
romadizo *m.* snuffles.
romanopexia *f.* romanopexy.
romanoscopio *m.* romanoscope.
rombencéfalo *m.* rhombencephalon.
rómbico, -ca *adj.* rhombic.
romboatloideo *m.* rhomboatloideus.
romboide *adj.* rhomboid.
rombómero *m.* rhombomere.
rompefuerzas *m.* stress breaker.
roncha *f.* wheal.
ronco, -ca *adj.* hoarse.
rongeur *f.* rongeur.
ronquera *f.* hoarseness.
ronquido *m.* snore.
　ronquido cavernoso cavernous rhoncus.
ropalocitosis *f.* ropalocytosis.
roptria *f.* rhoptry.
rosa *f.* rose.
rosácea *f.* rosacea.
　rosácea hipertrófica hypertrophic rosacea.
rosanilina *f.* rosanilin.
rosario *m.* rosary.
　rosario raquítico rachitic rosary.
roséola *f.* roseola.
　roséola epidémica epidemic roseola.

　roséola idiopática idiopathic roseola.
　roséola infantil roseola infantilis, roseola infantum.
　roséola sifilítica syphilitic roseola.
roseta *f.* rosette.
rostral *adj.* rostral.
rostriforme *adj.* rostriform.
rotación *f.* rotation.
　rotación específica specific rotation.
　rotación intestinal intestinal rotation.
　rotación molecular molecular rotation.
　rotación óptica optical rotation.
rotacismo *m.* rhotacism.
rotador *m. y adj.* rotator.
rotámetro *m.* rotameter.
rotatorio, -ria *adj.* rotator.
Rotavirus Rotavirus.
rotoescoliosis *f.* rotoscoliosis.
rotótomo *m.* rototome.
rótula *f.* rotula, patella.
　rótula deslizable slipping patella.
　rótula flotante floating patella.
rotura *f.* rhexis, rupture.
rozadura *f.* gall.
rubedo *f.* rubedo.
rubefacción *f.* erubescence, rubefaction.
rubefaciente *adj.* rubefacient.
rubella *f.* rubella.
rubéola *f.* rubella, rubeola.
　rubéola escarlatinosa rubeola scarlatinosa, rubeola scarlatiniforma.
rubeosis *f.* rubeosis.
　rubeosis diabética del iris rubeosis iridis diabetica.
　rubeosis iris rubeosis iridis.
rubescente *adj.* rubescent.
rubiginoso, -sa *adj.* rubiginous.
Rubivirus Rubivirus.
rubor *m.* flush, redness, rubor.
　rubor héctico hectic flush.
　rubor malar malar flush.
rubriblasto *m.* rubriblast.
　rubriblasto tipo anemia perniciosa pernicious anemia type rubriblast.
rubricito *m.* rubricyte.
rúbrico, -ca *adj.* rubric.
rubrospinal *adj.* rubrospinal.
ructus ructus.
rudimental *adj.* rudimentary.
rudimentario, -ria *adj.* rudimentary.
rudimento *m.* rudiment.
rueda *f.* wheel.
　rueda de Burlew Burlew wheel.
　rueda dentada cogwheel rigidity.
rufoso, -sa *adj.* rufous.
ruga ruga.
rugitus rugitus.
rugosidad *f.* rugosity.
rugoso, -sa *adj.* rugous, rugose, wrinkled.
ruido *m.* noise, sound, bruit, sonitus.
　ruido ambiental ambient noise.
　ruido aneurismático aneurysmal bruit.
　ruido auricular atrial sound.
　ruido auscultatorio auscultatory sound.
　ruido de bandera bruit de drapeau.
　ruido de bazuqueo succussion sound.
　ruido de Beatty-Bright Beatty-Bright friction sound.
　ruido de campana bell sound.
　ruido de cañón bruit de canon.

　ruido cardíaco cardiac sound.
　ruido de cascabel bruit de grelot.
　ruido de chapoteo bruit de clapotement.
　ruido de chasquido bruit de claquement.
　ruido de coco coconut sound.
　ruido del corazón heart sound.
　ruido del diablo bruit du diable.
　ruido de doble shock double-shock sound.
　ruido de disparo pistol-shot sound.
　ruido de expulsión ejection sound.
　ruido femoral de disparo de revólver pistol-shot femoral sound.
　ruido de fricción friction sound.
　ruido de fricción pericárdica pericardial friction sound.
　ruido de fuelle bruit de soufflet.
　ruido de galope bruit de galop.
　ruido hipocrático hippocratic sound.
　ruido intestinal bowel sound.
　ruido de Korotkoff Korotkoff sound.
　ruido de Leudet bruit de Leudet.
　ruido de lima bruit de lime.
　ruido metálico metallic sound.
　ruido de molino bruit de moulin.
　ruido muscular muscle sound.
　ruido de olla hendida cracked-pot sound.
　ruido de percusión percussion sound.
　ruido de pergamino bruit de parchemin.
　ruido placentario placenta souffle.
　ruido de redoble bruit de rappel.
　ruido respiratorio respiratory sound.
　ruido respiratorio anfórico amphoric breath sound.
　ruido respiratorio bronquial bronchial breath sound.
　ruido respiratorio traqueal tracheal breath sound.
　ruido respiratorio vesicular vesicular breath sound.
　ruido de Roger bruit de Roger.
　ruido de Santini Santini's booming sound.
　ruido de sierra bruit de scie, bruit de rape.
　ruido de silbido de agua water-whistle sound.
　ruido de soplo souffle.
　ruido de succión postussis post-tussis suction sound.
　ruido de sucusión succussion sound.
　ruido de tambor bruit de tambour, bandbox sound.
　ruido de tic-tac tick-tack sound.
　ruido tiroideo thyroid bruit.
　ruido de trío bruit de triolet.
　ruido de vela de barco sail sound.
　ruido de Verstraeten Verstraeten's bruit.
　ruido vocal anfórico amphoric voice sound.
　ruido vocal cavernoso cavernous voice sound.
　ruido de yunque anvil sound.
rumiación *f.* rumination.
Ruminococcus Ruminococcus.
rupia *f.* rupia.
　rupia escarótica rupia escharotica.
rupial *adj.* rupial.
rupiode *adj.* rupioid.
ruptura *f.* break, rupture.
rutidosis *f.* rutidosis.
rutilismo *m.* rutilism.
rutina[1] *f.* habit.
rutina[2] *f.* rutin.
rutósido *m.* rutoside.

S s

S ilíaca del colon *f.* S romanum.
S romana del colon *f.* S romanum.
sabañón *m.* chilblain.
　sabañón necrosado necrotized chilblain.
sabor *m.* flavor.
saburra *f.* saburra.
saburral *adj.* saburral.
sacabocados *m.* punch.
　sacabocados de alfiler pin punch.
　sacabocados de placa plate punch.
sacádico, -ca *adj.* saccadic.
sacarefidrosis *f.* saccharephidrosis.
sacarífero, -ra *adj.* sacchariferous.
sacarificación *f.* saccharification.
sacarímetro *m.* saccharimeter.
sacarina *f.* saccharin.
sacarino, -na *adj.* saccharine.
sacarogalactorrea *f.* saccharogalactorrhea.
sacarolado, -da *m. y adj.* saccharated.
sacarólico, -ca *adj.* saccharated.
sacarolítico, -ca *adj.* saccharolytic.
saracometabólico, -ca *adj.* saccharometabolic.
sacarometabolismo *m.* saccharometabolism.
sacarómetro *m.* saccharometer.
sacaromicético, -ca *adj.* saccharomycetic.
sacaromiceto *m.* Saccharomyces.
sacaromicetólisis *f.* saccharomycetolysis.
sacaromicosis *f.* saccharomycosis.
sacarosa *f.* sucrose.
sacarosemia *f.* sucrosemia.
sacarosuria *f.* sucrosuria.
sacaruria *f.* saccharuria.
Saccharomyces Saccharomyces.
Saccharomycetacea Saccharomycetacea.
Saccharomycopsis Saccharomycopsis.
sacciforme *adj.* sacciform.
saciedad *f.* satiety.
saccus *m.* sac, saccus.
saco *m.* sac, saccus.
sacrad sacrad.
sacral *adj.* sacral.
sacralgia *f.* sacralgia.
sacralización *f.* sacralization.
sacrectomía *f.* sacrectomy.
sacro *m.* sacrum.
　sacro inclinado tilted sacrum.
sacroanterior *adj.* sacroanterior.
sacroartrógeno, -na *adj.* sacroarthogenic.
sacrociático, -ca *adj.* sacrosciatic.
sacrococcígeo, -a *adj.* sacrococcygeal.
sacrocóccix *m.* sacrococcyx.
sacrocoxalgia *f.* sacrocoxalgia.
sacrocoxitis *f.* sacrocoxitis.
sacrodinia *f.* sacrodynia.
sacroespinal *adj.* sacrospinal.
sacroespinoso, -sa *adj.* sacrospinal, sacrospinalis.
sacroileítis *f.* sacroiliitis.
sacroilíaco, -ca *adj.* sacroiliac.

sacroilitis *f.* sacroiliitis.
sacrolistesis *f.* sacrolisthesis.
sacrolumbar *adj.* sacrolumbar.
sacroperineal *adj.* sacroperineal.
sacroposterior *adj.* sacroposterior.
sacrospinoso, -sa *adj.* sacrospinal, sacrospinalis.
sacrotomía *f.* sacrotomy.
sacrotransverso, -sa *adj.* sacrotransverse.
sacrouterino, -na *adj.* sacrouterine.
sacrovertebral *adj.* sacrovertebral.
sactosálpinx *m.* sactosalpinx.
sacudida *f.* jerk, saccade.
　sacudida aductora cruzada crossed adductor jerk.
　sacudida de Aquiles Achilles jerk.
　sacudida del bíceps biceps jerk.
　sacudida del codo elbow jerk.
　sacudida costal rib shaking.
　sacudida cruzada crossed jerk.
　sacudida cruzada de la rodilla crossed knee jerk.
　sacudida del cuádriceps quadriceps jerk.
　sacudida del maxilar jaw jerk.
　sacudida del mentón chin jerk.
　sacudida de la rodilla knee jerk.
　sacudida del supinador supinator jerk.
　sacudida tendinosa tendon jerk.
　sacudida del tobillo ankle jerk.
　sacudida del tríceps crural triceps surae jerk.
sacudidas *f.* shakes.
　sacudidas kwaski kwaski shakes.
　sacudidas del sombrero hatter's shakes.
saculación *f.* sacculation.
　saculación del colon sacculation of the colon.
saculado, -da *adj.* sacculated.
sacular *adj.* saccular.
saculiforme *adj.* sacciform.
sáculo *m.* saccule, sacculus.
saculococlear *adj.* sacculocochlear.
sádico, -ca[1] *m., f.* sadist.
sádico, -ca[2] *adj.* sadistic.
sadismo *m.* sadism.
　sadismo anal anal sadism.
　sadismo oral oral sadism.
　sadismo sexual sexual sadism.
sadomasoquismo *m.* sadomasochism.
sadomasoquista *adj.* sadomasochistic.
safena *f.* saphena.
safenectomía *f.* saphenectomy.
safeno, -na *adj.* saphenous.
safismo *m.* sapphism.
safu *m.* safu.
sagital *adj.* sagittal.
sal *f.* salt, sal.
sala *f.* room, ward.
　sala de aislamiento isolation ward.
　sala de cuidados intensivos intensive therapy room.
　sala de dilatación predelivery room.

　sala de juegos games room.
　sala de operaciones (SO) operating room (OR).
　sala de partos, paritorio delivery room.
　sala posparto postdelivery room.
　sala de reanimación recovery room (RR).
　sala de recuperación recovery room.
　sala de urgencias (SU) emergency room (ER).
salicilemia *f.* salicylemia.
salicilar *v.* salicylate.
salicilatar *v.* salicylate.
salicilismo *m.* salicylism.
salicilterapia *f.* salicyltherapy.
saliciloterapia *f.* salicyltherapy.
salida *f.* outlet.
salidas *f.* output.
saliente *m.* salient.
salificable *adj.* salifiable.
salificar *v.* salify.
salímetro *m.* salimeter.
salino, -na *adj.* saline.
salinómetro *m.* salinometer.
saliva *f.* saliva.
　saliva artificial artificial saliva.
　saliva cordal, saliva de la cuerda chorda saliva.
　saliva filante ropy saliva.
　saliva ganglionar ganglionic saliva.
　saliva lingual lingual saliva.
　saliva parótida, saliva parotídea parotid saliva.
　saliva en reposo resting saliva.
　saliva simpática sympathetic saliva.
　saliva sublingual sublingual saliva.
　saliva submaxilar submaxilar saliva.
salivación *f.* salivation.
salivador, -ra *adj.* salivator.
salival *adj.* salivary.
salivante *adj.* salivant.
salivar *v.* salivate.
salivaria *f.* salivaria.
salivariano, -na *adj.* salivarian.
salivatorio, -ria *adj.* salivatory.
salivolitiasis *f.* salivolithiasis.
salmonela *f.* salmonella.
Salmonella Salmonella.
salmonelosis *f.* salmonellosis.
salpinge *f.* salpinx.
salpingectomía *f.* salpingectomy.
　salpingectomía abdominal abdominal salpingectomy.
salpingenfraxis *f.* salpingemphraxis.
salpíngeo, -a *adj.* salpingian.
salpingiano, -na *adj.* salpingian.
salpingioma *m.* salpingioma.
salpingión *m.* salpingion.
salpingítico, -ca *adj.* salpingitic.
salpingitis *f.* salpingitis.
　salpingitis por cuerpo extraño foreign body salpingitis.

salpingitis de Eustaquio eustachian salpingitis.
salpingitis gonocócica gonococcal salpingitis.
salpingitis gonorreica gonorrheal salpingitis.
salpingitis hemorrágica hemorrhagic salpingitis.
salpingitis hipertrófica hypertrophic salpingitis.
salpingitis intersticial crónica chronic interstitial salpingitis.
salpingitis ístmica nudosa salpingitis isthmica nodosa.
salpingitis mural mural salpingitis.
salpingitis nodular nodular salpingitis.
salpingitis parenquimatosa parenchymatous salpingitis.
salpingitis piógena pyogenic salpingitis.
salpingitis purulenta, salpingitis serosa purulent salpingitis.
salpingitis seudofolicular pseudofollicular salpingitis.
salpingitis tuberculosa tuberculous salpingitis.
salpingitis vegetativa crónica chronic vegetating salpingitis.
salpingocateterismo *m.* salpingocatheterism.
salpingocele *m.* salpingocele.
salpingociesis *f.* salpingocyesis.
salpingoestafilino, -na *adj.* salpingostaphyline.
salpingofaríngeo *m.* salpingopharyngeus.
salpingofaríngeo, -a *adj.* salpingopharyngeal.
salpingografía *f.* salpingography.
salpingólisis *f.* salpingolysis.
salpingolitiasis *f.* salpingolithiasis.
salpingooforectomía *f.* salpingo-oophorectomy.
salpingooforitis *f.* salpingo-oophoritis.
salpingooforocele *m.* salpingo-oophorocele.
salpingoovariectomía *f.* salpingo-ovariectomy.
salpingoperitonitis *f.* salpingoperitonitis.
salpingopexia *f.* salpingopexy.
salpingoplastia *f.* salpingoplasty.
salpingorrafia *f.* salpingorrhaphy.
salpingorragia *f.* salpingorrhagia.
salpingoscopia *f.* salpingoscopy.
salpingoscopio *m.* salpingoscope.
salpingostomía *f.* salpingostomy.
salpingotomía *f.* salpingotomy.
sálpinx, salpinx *f.* salpinx.
saltación *f.* saltation.
saltatorio, ria *adj.* saltatorial, saltatoric, saltatory.
salterial *adj.* psalterial.
saltérico, -ca *adj.* psalterial.
salterio *m.* psalterium.
salubre *adj.* salubrious.
salubridad *f.* salubrity.
salud *f.* health.
  salud familiar family health.
  salud laboral industrial health.
  salud medioambiental environmental health.
  salud mental mental health.
  salud mental comunitaria community mental health.
  salud profesional occupational health.
  salud sexual sexual health.
saludable *adj.* salutary.
saludo alérgico *m.* allergic salute.
saluresis *f.* saluresis.
salurético, -ca *adj.* saluretic.
salutífero, -ra *adj.* salutary.

sanativo, -va *adj.* sanative.
sanatorio *m.* sanatorium.
saneamiento *m.* sanitation.
sanear *v.* sanitize.
sangradera *f.* lancet.
sangrado *m.* bleeding.
  sangrado uterino disfuncional dysfunctional uterine bleeding.
sangrador, -ra *adj.* bleeding.
sangrador *m.* bleeder, bloodletter.
sangradura *f.* bloodletting.
sangramiento *m.* bleeding.
sangrar *v.* bleed.
sangre *f.* blood.
  sangre anticoagulable anticoaguated blood.
  sangre arterial arterial blood.
  sangre central central blood.
  sangre circulante circulating bloodstream.
  sangre del cordón cord blood.
  sangre en crema de fresa strawberry cream blood.
  sangre desfibrinada defibrinated blood.
  sangre entera whole blood.
  sangre esplácnica splanchnic blood.
  sangre estancada sludged blood.
  sangre lacada laked blood, laky blood.
  sangre lodosa sludged blood.
  sangre oculta occult blood.
  sangre periférica peripheral blood.
  sangre total whole blood.
  sangre venosa venous blood.
  sangre venosa mixta mixed venous blood.
sangría *f.* bloodletting.
  sangría general general bloodletting.
  sangría local local bloodletting.
sanguícola *adj.* sanguicolous.
sanguifaciente *adj.* sanguifacient.
sanguífero, -ra *adj.* sanguiferous.
sanguificación *f.* sanguification.
sanguíneo, -a *adj.* sanguine, sanguineous.
sanguinolento, -ta *adj.* sanguinolent.
sanguinopoyético, -ca *adj.* sanguinopoietic.
sanguinopurulento, -ta *adj.* sanguinopurulent.
sanguinoso, -sa *adj.* sanguinous.
sanguisucción *f.* leech.
sanguívoro, -ra *adj.* sanguivorous.
sanguimotor, -ra *adj.* sanguimotor.
sanidad *f.* sanitation, sanity.
sanies *f.* sanies.
saniopurulento, -ta *adj.* saniopurulent.
sanioseroso, -sa *adj.* sanioserous.
sanioso, -sa *adj.* sanious.
sanitario, -ria *adj.* sanitary.
sanitas health.
sano, -na *adj.* healthy.
sápido, -da *adj.* sapid.
sapóforo *m.* sapophore.
saponáceo, -a *adj.* saponaceous.
saponificación *f.* saponification.
sapremia *f.* sapremia.
sapróbico, -ca *adj.* saprobic.
saprodoncia *f.* saprodontia.
saprófilo *m.* saprophyte.
saprófilo, -la *adj.* saprophilous.
saprofítico, -ca *adj.* saprophytic.
saprofitismo *m.* saprophytism.
saprofito, saprófito *m.* saprophyte.
saprogénico, -ca *adj.* saprogenic.
saprógeno, - na *adj.* saprogenous.
sapronosis *f.* sapronosis.
saprozoico, -ca *adj.* saprozoic.
saprozoíto *m.* saprozoite.
saprozoonosis *f.* saprozoonosis.
sarampión *m.* measles.

sarampión alemán German measles.
sarampión atípico atypical measles.
sarampión de los tres días three-day measles.
sarampión hemorrágico hemorrhagic measles.
sarampión negro black measles.
sarampión tropical tropical measles.
sarcina *f.* sarcine.
Sarcina Sarcina.
sarcitis *f.* sarcitis.
sarcoadenoma *m.* sarcoadenoma.
sarcoblasto *m.* sarcoblast.
sarcocarcinoma *m.* sarcocarcinoma.
sarcocele *m.* sarcocele.
sarcocisto *m.* sarcocyst.
sarcocistosis *f.* sarcocystosis.
sarcocito *m.* sarcocyte.
Sarcocystis Sarcocystis.
Sarcodina Sarcodina.
sarcoencondroma *m.* sarcoenchondroma.
sarcogénico, -ca *adj.* sarcogenic.
sarcógeno, -na *adj.* sarcogenic.
sarcohidrocele *m.* sarcohydrocele.
sarcoide *m.* sarcoid.
  sarcoide de Boeck Boeck's sarcoid, sarcoid of Boeck.
  sarcoide de Carier-Roussy Carier-Roussy sarcoid.
  sarcoide de Schaumann Schaumann's sarcoid.
  sarcoide de Spiegler-Fendt Spiegler-Fendt sarcoid.
sarcoidosis *f.* sarcoidosis.
  sarcoidosis cardíaca, sarcoidosis cordis sarcoidosis cordis.
  sarcoidosis hipercalcémica hypercalcemic sarcoidosis.
  sarcoidosis muscular muscular sarcoidosis.
sarcolema *m.* sarcolemma.
sarcolémico, -ca *adj.* sarcolemmic.
sarcolemoso, -sa *adj.* sarcolemmous.
sarcólisis *f.* sarcolysis.
sarcolítico, -ca *adj.* sarcolytic.
sarcólito *m.* sarcolyte.
sarcología *f.* sarcology.
sarcoma *m.* sarcoma.
  sarcoma de Abernethy Abernethy's sarcoma.
  sarcoma adiposo adipose sarcoma.
  sarcoma alveolar de las partes blandas alveolar soft part sarcoma.
  sarcoma ameloblástico ameloblastic sarcoma.
  sarcoma angiolítico angiolithic sarcoma.
  sarcoma botrioide, sarcoma botrioideo, sarcoma botrioides botryoid sarcoma, sarcoma botryoides.
  sarcoma de células fusiformes spindle cell sarcoma.
  sarcoma de células gigantes giant cell sarcoma.
  sarcoma de células de Kupffer Kupffer cell sarcoma.
  sarcoma de células mixtas mixed cell sarcoma.
  sarcoma de células redondas round cell sarcoma.
  sarcoma de células reticulares reticulum cell sarcoma.
  sarcoma cloromatoso chloromatous sarcoma.
  sarcoma condroblástico chondroblastic sarcoma.
  sarcoma embrionario embryonal sarcoma.
  sarcoma del estroma endometrial, sarcoma estrómico endometrial endometrial stromal sarcoma.

sarcoma de Ewing Ewing's sarcoma.
sarcoma fascial fascial sarcoma.
sarcoma fasciculado fascicular sarcoma.
sarcoma fibroblástico fibroblastic sarcoma.
sarcoma fusocelular spindle cell sarcoma.
sarcoma gigantocelular giant cell sarcoma.
sarcoma granulocítico granulocytic sarcoma.
sarcoma hemorrágico idiopático múltiple multiple idiopathic hemorrhagic sarcoma.
sarcoma hemorrágico pigmentado idiopático simple idiopathic multiple pigmented hemorrhagic sarcoma.
sarcoma hidrópico papilar del cuello uterino sarcoma colli uteri hydropicum papillare.
sarcoma de Hodgkin Hodgkin's sarcoma.
sarcoma inmunoblástico immunoblastic sarcoma.
sarcoma inmunoblástico de células B immunoblastic sarcoma of B cells.
sarcoma inmunoblástico de células T immunoblastic sarcoma of T cells.
sarcoma de Kaposi Kaposi's sarcoma.
sarcoma leucocítico leukocytic sarcoma.
sarcoma linfático lymphatic sarcoma.
sarcoma medular medullary sarcoma.
sarcoma melanótico melanotic sarcoma.
sarcoma mielógeno myelogenic sarcoma.
sarcoma osteoblástico osteoblastic sarcoma.
sarcoma osteogénico osteogenic sarcoma.
sarcoma osteogénico telangiectático telangiectatic sarcoma.
sarcoma osteogénico yuxtacortical juxtacortical osteogenic sarcoma.
sarcoma parósteo parosteal sarcoma.
sarcoma perióstico periosteal sarcoma.
sarcoma polimorfo polymorphous sarcoma.
sarcoma reticuloendotelial, sarcoma reticulocítico reticulum cell sarcoma of the brain.
sarcoma seudo-Kaposi pseudo-Kaposi sarcoma.
sarcoma sinovial synovial sarcoma.
sarcoma telangiectásico telangiectatic sarcoma.
sarcomagénesis *f.* sarcomagenesis.
sarcomagénico, -ca *adj.* sarcomagenic.
sarcomágeno, -na *adj.* sarcomagenic.
sarcomatoide *adj.* sarcomatoid.
sarcomatoideo, -a *adj.* sarcomatoid.
sarcomatosis *f.* sarcomastosis.
sarcomatoso, -sa *adj.* sarcomatous.
sarcomelanina *f.* sarcomelanin.
sarcómera *m.* sarcomere.
sarcómero *m.* sarcomere.
sarconema *m.* sarconeme.
sarconfalocele *m.* sarconphalocele.
Sarcophagidae Sarcophagidae.
sarcoplasma *m.* sarcoplasm.
sarcoplásmico, -ca *adj.* sarcoplasmic.
sarcoplasto *m.* sarcoplast.
sarcopoyético, -ca *adj.* sarcopoietic.
Sarcoptes Sarcoptes.
sarcóptico, -ca *adj.* sarcoptic.
sarcóptido *m.* sarcoptid.
sarcoptidosis *f.* sarcoptidosis.
sarcosinemia *f.* sarcosinemia.
sarcosis *f.* sarcosis.
sarcoso, -sa *adj.* sarcous.
Sarcosporidia Sarcosporidia.
sarcosporidiasis *f.* sarcosporidiasis, sarcosporidiosis.
sarcosporidio *m.* sarcosporidium.
sarcosporidiosis *f.* sarcosporidiosis.
sarcosteosis *f.* sarcostosis.
sarcostilo *m.* sarcostyle.
sarcostosis *f.* sarcostosis.

sarcoterapia *f.* sarcotherapeutics, sarcotherapy.
sarcótico, -ca *adj.* sarcotic.
sarcotripsia *f.* sarcotripsy.
sarcotúbulos *m.* sarcotubules.
sarna *f.* scabies.
sarna cubana Cuban itch.
sarna de Noruega Norwegian scabies.
sarnoso, -sa *adj.* scabietic.
sarpullido *m.* tetter.
sarpullido por calor prickly heat tetter.
sarpullido costroso crusted tetter.
sarro *m.* tartar.
satélite *m.* satellite.
satélite cromosoma, satélite cromosómico chromosome satellite.
satélite nucleolar nucleolar satellite.
satélite perineuronal perineuronal satellite.
satelitismo *m.* satellitism.
satelitosis *f.* satellitosis.
satiriasis *f.* satyriasis.
saturación *f.* saturation.
saturación arterial en oxígeno arterial oxygen saturation.
saturación de hemoglobina hemoglobin saturation.
saturación de hierro iron saturation.
saturación de oxígeno oxygen saturation.
saturación de oxígeno en la hemoglobina hemoglobin oxygen saturation.
saturación de oxihemoglobina oxyhemoglobin saturation.
saturación secundaria secondary saturation.
saturación venosa central de oxígeno (SVCO2) central venous oxygen saturation (CVSO2).
saturado, -da *adj.* saturated.
saturnino, -na *adj.* saturnine.
saturnismo *m.* saturnism.
saturnoterapia *f.* saturnotherapy.
saucerización *f.* saucerization.
sauriasis *f.* sauriasis, sauriosis.
sauridermia *f.* sauriderma, sauroderma.
saurodermia *f.* sauroderma.
sauriosis *f.* sauriosis.
sauroide *adj.* sauroid.
scabrities scabrities.
scabrities unguium scabrities unguium.
scan *f.* scan.
scapha scapha.
scapula alata *f.* scapula alata.
Schistosoma Schistosoma.
Schizoblastosporium Schizoblastosporium.
Schizopyrenida Schizopyrenida.
schlusskoagulum *m.* schlusskoagulum.
schwannitis *f.* schwannitis.
schwannoglioma *m.* schwannoglioma.
schwannoma *m.* schwannoma.
schwannoma de células granulosas granular cell schwannoma.
schwannosis *f.* schwannosis.
schwanoma *m.* schwannoma.
Scolopendra Scolopendra.
Scopulariopsis Scopulariopsis.
Scotobacteria Scotobacteria.
screening *m.* screening.
scutulum scutulum.
scutum scutum.
sebáceo, -a *adj.* sebaceous, sebaceus.
sebiagógico, -ca *adj.* sebiagogic.
sebífero, -ra *adj.* sebiferous.
sebíparo, -ra *adj.* sebiparous.
sebo *m.* sebum.
sebolito *m.* sebolith.
seborragia *f.* seborrhea.
seborrea *f.* seborrhea.

seborrea adiposa seborrhea adiposa.
seborrea de la cabeza, seborrea capilar, seborrea capitis seborrhea capitis.
seborrea de la cara seborrhea of the face, seborrhea faciei.
seborrea cérea seborrhea cerea.
seborrea concreta concrete seborrhea.
seborrea corporal seborrhea corporis.
seborrea costrosa concrete seborrhea.
seborrea eccematosa eczematoid seborrhea.
seborrea escamosa neonatal seborrhea squamosa neonatorum.
seborrea facial seborrhea of the face, seborrhea faciei.
seborrea nigra, seborrea nigricans seborrhea nigra.
seborrea oleosa seborrhea oleosa.
seborrea seca seborrhea sicca.
seborreico, -ca *adj.* seborrheic.
seborroide *f.* seborrhoid.
sebotrópico, -ca *adj.* sebotropic.
sebum *m.* sebum.
secante *adj.* dessicant, siccant.
secativo, -va *adj.* siccative.
sección *f.* section, sectio.
sección abdominal abdominal section.
sección alta sectio alta.
sección C C-section.
sección de celoidina celloidin section.
sección cesárea cesarean section.
sección cesárea cervical cervical cesarean section.
sección cesárea cervical baja, sección cesárea cervical inferior low cervical cesarean section.
sección cesárea clásica classical cesarean section.
sección hipogástrica sectio alta.
sección cesárea de Latzko Latzko's cesarean section.
sección cesárea de Munro Kerr Munro Kerr cesarean section.
sección cesárea del segmento inferior lower segment cesarean section.
sección congelada frozen section.
sección coronal coronal section.
sección craneal separada detached cranial section.
sección fina thin section.
sección frontal frontal section.
sección lateral sectio lateralis.
sección mediana sectio mediana.
sección perineal perineal section.
sección de Saemisch Saemisch's section.
sección sagital sagittal section, sagittal sectio.
sección suprapúbica sectio alta.
sección del tallo hipofisario pituitary stalk section.
sección ultrafina ultrathin section.
seclusión *f.* seclusion.
seclusión de la pupila seclusion of the pupil.
seco, -ca *adj.* dry.
secodonto, -ta *adj.* secodont.
secoyosis *f.* sequoiosis.
secreción *f.* secretion.
secreción apocrina apocrine secretion.
secreción autocrina autocrine secretion.
secreción bronquial bronchial secretion.
secreción externa external secretion.
secreción holocrina holocrine secretion.
secreción interna internal secretion.
secreción merocrina merocrine secretion.
secreción paracrina paracrine secretion.
secreción paralítica paralytic secretion.
secreción del pezón nipple discharge.

secreta *f.* secreta.
secretado, -da *adj.* secreted.
secretagogo, -ga *adj.* secretagogue, secreto-gogue.
secretar *v.* secrete.
secretoinhibidor, -ra *m.* secretoinhibitory.
secretoinhibitorio, -ria *adj.* secretoinhibitory.
secretomotor, -ra *adj.* secretomotor.
secreto *m.* secretor.
secretor, -ra *adj.* secretory.
sectario, -ria *adj.* sectarian.
séctil *m. y adj.* sectile.
sector *m.* sector.
sectorial *adj.* sectorial.
secuela *f.* sequela.
secuencia *f.* sequence.
  secuencia ALU ALU sequence.
  secuencia consensuada consensus sequence.
  secuencia de codificación coding sequence.
  secuencia colindante flanking sequence.
  secuencia cruzada cross-sequence.
  secuencia del desarrollo developmental sequence.
  secuencia de inserción insertion sequence.
  secuencia intercalada intervening sequence.
  secuencia de intervención intervening sequence.
  secuencia palindrómica palindromic sequence.
  secuencia reguladora regulatory sequence.
  secuencia de terminación termination sequence.
secuestral *adj.* sequestral.
secuestrante *adj.* sequestrant.
secuestrar *v.* sequester.
secuestrectomía *f.* sequestrectomy.
secuestro *m.* sequestration, sequestrum.
  secuestro farmacológico drug sequestration.
  secuestro primario primary sequestrum.
  secuestro pulmonar pulmonary sequestration, sequestrum pulmonaris.
  secuestro secundario secondary sequestrum.
  secuestro subclavio subclavian sequestration.
  secuestro terciario tertiary sequestrum.
secuestrotomía *f.* sequestrotomy.
secundario, -ria *m. y adj.* secondary.
secundigrávida *f.* secundigravida.
secundina uterina *f.* secundina uteri.
secundinas *f.* afterbirth, secundines.
secundípara *f.* secundipara.
secundiparidad *f.* secundiparity.
sed *f.* thirst.
  sed crepuscular twilight thirst.
  sed falsa false thirst.
  sed insensible insensible thirst.
  sed real true thirst.
  sed subliminal subliminal thirst.
  sed verdadera true thirst.
seda *f.* silk.
  seda dental dental floss.
  seda quirúrgica surgical silk.
  seda virgen virgin silk.
sedación *f.* sedation.
sedal *m.* seton.
sedante *m. y adj.* sedative, sedativus.
  sedante cardíaco cardiac sedative.
  sedante cerebral cerebral sedative.
  sedante gástrico gastric sedative.
  sedante general general sedative.
  sedante intestinal intestinal sedative.
  sedante nervioso nervous sedative.
  sedante raquídeo spinal sedative.
  sedante respiratorio respiratory sedative.
  sedante de tronco nervioso nerve trunk sedative.

  sedante vascular vascular sedative.
sedativo, -va *m. y adj.* sedative, sedativus.
sedentario, -ria *adj.* sedentary.
sedimentable *adj.* sedimentable.
sedimentación *f.* sedimentation, sludging.
  sedimentación eritrocitaria, sedimentación eritrocítica erythrocyte sedimentation.
  sedimentación con formol y éter (Ritchie) formalin ether sedimentation (Ritchie).
sedimentador *m.* sedimentator.
sedimento *m.* sediment.
  sedimento alcalino alkaline ash.
  sedimento urinario urinary sediment.
seducción *f.* seduction.
segmentación *f.* cleavage, segmentation.
  segmentación accesoria accessory cleavage.
  segmentación anormal de las válvulas cardíacas abnormal cleavage of the cardiac valve.
  segmentación casi igual adequal cleavage.
  segmentación completa total cleavage.
  segmentación desigual unequal cleavage.
  segmentación determinada determinate cleavage.
  segmentación discoidal, segmentación discoide discoidal cleavage.
  segmentación ecuatorial equatorial cleavage.
  segmentación del esmalte enamel cleavage.
  segmentación fosforoclásica phosphoroclastic cleavage.
  segmentación haustral haustral segmentation.
  segmentación hidrolítica hydrolytic cleavage.
  segmentación holoblástica holoblastic cleavage.
  segmentación igual equal cleavage.
  segmentación incompleta parcial meroblastic cleavage.
  segmentación indeterminada indeterminate cleavage.
  segmentación meridional meridional cleavage.
  segmentación meroblástica meroblastic cleavage.
  segmentación en mosaico mosaic cleavage.
  segmentación parcial partial cleavage.
  segmentación superficial superficial cleavage.
  segmentación tioclásica, segmentación tioclástica thioclastic cleavage.
  segmentación total total cleavage.
  segmentación de la yema yolk cleavage.
segmentador *m.* segmenter.
Segmentina Segmentina.
segmentario, -ria *adj.* segmental.
segmento *m.* segment, segmentum.
segregación *f.* segregation.
segregador *m.* segregator.
segregar *v.* secrete.
seguimiento horizontal *m.* horizontal pursuit.
seisestesia *f.* seisesthesia.
seismestesia *f.* seismesthesia.
seismocardiografía *f.* seismocardiography.
seismocardiograma *f.* seismocardiogram.
seismoterapia *f.* seismotherapy, sismotherapy.
selección *f.* selection.
  selección aleatoria random selection.
  selección artificial artificial selection.
  selección citológica cytologic selection.
  selección de descendencia progeny selection.
  selección direccional directional selection.
  selección disruptiva disruptive selection.
  selección diversificante diversifying selection.
  selección estabilizante stabilizing selection.

  selección independiente independent assortment.
  selección médica medical selection.
  selección multifásica multiphasic selection.
  selección múltiple multiple selection.
  selección natural natural selection.
  selección neonatal neonatal selection.
  selección prenatal prenatal selection.
  selección de señal gating.
  selección sexual sexual selection.
  selección sesgada truncate selection.
  selección truncada truncate selection.
selectividad *f.* selectivity.
selectivo, -va *adj.* selective.
selene unguium selene unguium.
Selenomonas Selenomonas.
selenosis *f.* selenosis.
sella *f.* sella.
  sella turcica sella turcica.
sellado *m.* seal.
  sellado de bordes border seal.
  sellado palatino, sellado palatino posterior palatal seal, posterior palatal seal.
  sellado periférico peripheral seal.
  sellado pospalatino postpalatal seal.
  sellado velofaríngeo velopharyngeal seal.
sellador *m.* sealant.
  sellador dental dental sealant.
  sellador de fisuras fissure sealant.
  sellador de huecos y fisuras pit and fissure sealant.
sellar *v.* seal.
sello[1] *m.* cachet.
sello[2] *m.* seal.
  sello de bordes border seal.
  sello doble double seal.
  sello palatino posterior posterior palatal seal.
  sello terminal tip seal.
  sello velofaríngeo velopharyngeal seal.
sembrar *v.* seal.
semelincidente *adj.* semelincident.
semelparidad *f.* semelparity.
semélparo, -ra *adj.* semelparous.
semen *m.* semen.
semenología *f.* semenology.
semenólogo, -ga *m., f.* senemologist.
semenuria *f.* semenuria, seminuria.
semiantígeno *m.* semiantigen.
semicanal *m.* semicanal.
semicartilaginoso, -sa *adj.* semicartilaginous.
semicircular *adj.* semicircular.
semicoma *m.* semicoma.
semicomatoso, -sa *adj.* semicomatose.
semiconducto *m.* semicanal, semicanalis.
semiconductor *m.* semiconductor.
semiconsciente *m.* semiconscious.
semicresta *f.* semicrista.
semicuantitativo, -va *adj.* semicuantitative.
semidecusación *f.* semidecussation.
semidesintegración *f.* half-life.
semiespéculo *m.* semispeculum.
semiflexión *f.* semiflexion.
semifluctuante *adj.* semifluctuating.
semilla *f.* seed.
  semilla de oro radiactivo (198 Au) radiogold seed (198 Au).
semiluna *f.* crescent, demilune, semilune, selene.
  semiluna epitelial epithelial crescent.
  semiluna de Giannuzzi Giannuzzi's crescent, crescent of Giannuzzi.
  semiluna glomerular glomerular crescent.
  semiluna miópica myopic crescent.
  semiluna palúdica malarial crescent.
  semiluna roja red half-moon.

semiluna serosas serous demilune.
semiluna sublingual sublingual crescent.
semilunar *adj.* semilunar.
semiluxación *f.* semiluxation.
semimembranoso, -sa *adj.* semimembranous.
semimostruosidad *f.* semimonstrosity.
seminación *f.* semination.
seminal *adj.* seminal.
seminífero, -ra *adj.* seminiferous.
seminología *f.* seminology, semenology.
seminólogo, -ga *m., f.* seminologist.
seminoma *m.* seminoma.
   seminoma espermatocítico spermacytic seminoma.
   seminoma ovárico, seminoma del ovario ovarian seminoma.
seminuria *f.* seminuria, semenuria.
semiografía *f.* semeiography, semiography.
semiología *f.* semeiology, semiology.
semiorbicular *adj.* semiorbicular.
semiótica *f.* semeiotics, semiotics.
semiótico, -ca *adj.* semeiotic, semiotic.
semiparásito *m.* semiparasite.
semipenniforme *adj.* semipenniform.
semipermeable *adj.* semipermeable.
semiplejía *f.* semiplegia.
semipronación *f.* semipronation.
semiprono, -na *adj.* semiprone.
semirrecostado, -da *adj.* semirecumbent.
semirrecumbente *adj.* semirecumbent.
semisideración *f.* semisideration, semisideratio.
semisintético, -ca *adj.* semisynthetic.
semisupinación *f.* semisupination.
semisupino, -na *adj.* semisupine.
semisurco *m.* semisulcus.
semitendinoso, -sa *adj.* semitendinous.
semiterciana *f.* semitertian.
semivida *f.* half-life.
   semivida biológica biologic half-life.
senectud *f.* senium.
senescencia *f.* senescence.
   senescencia dental, senescencia dentaria dental senescence.
senescente *adj.* senescent.
senil *adj.* senile.
senilidad *f.* senility.
senilismo *m.* senilism.
seno *m.* sinus.
senografía *f.* senography.
senógrafo *m.* senograph.
senopía *f.* senopia.
senopsia *f.* senopia.
sensación *f.* sensation.
   sensación de calor sensation of warmth.
   sensación de cinto, sensación en cintura cincture sensation, girdle sensation.
   sensación cutánea skin sensation.
   sensación dérmica dermal sensation.
   sensación diferida delayed sensation.
   sensación epigástrica epigastric sensation.
   sensación de esfuerzo strain sensation.
   sensación especial special sensation.
   sensación general general sensation.
   sensación de impotencia powerlessness.
   sensación luminosa light sensation.
   sensación nueva new sensation.
   sensación objetiva objective sensation.
   sensación primaria primary sensation.
   sensación propioceptiva proprioceptive sensation.
   sensación referida referred sensation.
   sensación refleja reflex sensation.
   sensación retardada, sensación retrasada delayed sensation.

sensación subjetiva subjective sensation.
sensación superficial superficial sensation.
sensación táctil tactile sensation.
sensación de tope end-feel.
sensación transferida transferred sensation.
sensación vascular vascular sensation.
sensibilidad¹ *f.* sensibility.
   sensibilidad articular articular sensibility, joint sensibility.
   sensibilidad cortical cortical sensibility.
   sensibilidad electromuscular electromuscular sensibility.
   sensibilidad epicrítica epicritic sensibility.
   sensibilidad esplacnestésica splanchnesthetic sensibility.
   sensibilidad mesoblástica mesoblastic sensibility.
   sensibilidad ósea bone sensibility.
   sensibilidad palestésica pallesthetic sensibility.
   sensibilidad palmestésica pallesthetic sensibility.
   sensibilidad profunda deep sensibility, deep sensation.
   sensibilidad propioceptiva propioceptive sensibility.
   sensibilidad protopática protopathic sensibility.
   sensibilidad vibratoria vibratory sensibility.
sensibilidad² *f.* sensitivity.
   sensibilidad adquirida acquired sensitivity.
   sensibilidad a los antibióticos antibiotic sensitivity.
   sensibilidad de contraste contrast sensitivity.
   sensibilidad cruzada cross sensitivity.
   sensibilidad cutánea cutaneous sensation.
   sensibilidad diagnóstica diagnostic sensitivity.
   sensibilidad fotoalérgica photoallergic sensitivity.
   sensibilidad fototóxica phototoxic sensitivity.
   sensibilidad idiosincrática idiosyncratic sensitivity.
   sensibilidad magnética magnetic susceptibility.
   sensibilidad marcapaso pacemaker sensitivity.
   sensibilidad motora motor sense.
   sensibilidad a la primaquina primaquine sensitivity.
   sensibilidad proporcional proportional sensitivity.
   sensibilidad de rebote rebound tenderness.
   sensibilidad a la sal salt sensitivity.
   sensibilidad relativa relativa sensitivity.
sensibilígeno, -na *adj.* sensibiligen.
sensibilisina *f.* sensibilisin.
sensibilización *f.* sensitization.
   sensibilización activa active sensitization.
   sensibilización autoeritrocítica autoerythrocyte sensitization.
   sensibilización cruzada cross sensitization.
   sensibilización encubierta covert sensitization.
   sensibilización fotodinámica photodynamic sensitization.
   sensibilización pasiva passive sensitization.
   sensibilización proteica, sensibilización proteínica protein sensitization.
   sensibilización Rh Rh sensitization.
sensibilizado, -da *adj.* sensitized.
sensibilizador, -ra *m. y adj.* sensitizer.
sensibilizante *adj.* sensitizer.

sensible *adj.* sensitive.
sensífero, -ra *adj.* sensiferous.
sensígeno, -na *adj.* sensigenous.
sensímetro *m.* sensimeter.
sensitinógeno *m.* sensitinogen.
sensitivo, -va *adj.* sensory.
sensitivomotor, -ra *adj.* sensorimotor.
sensitivoneural *adj.* sensorineural.
sensitógeno, -na *adj.* sensitogen.
sensitómetro *m.* sensitometer.
sensomotor, -triz *adj.* sensomotor.
sensomóvil *adj.* sensomobile.
sensomovilidad *f.* sensomobility.
sensor, -ra *m. y adj.* sensor.
sensorial *adj.* sensorial.
sensoriglandular *adj.* sensoriglandular.
sensorimuscular *adj.* sensorimuscular.
sensorio *m.* sensorium.
sensorioglandular *adj.* sensoriglandular.
sensoriometabolismo *m.* sensoriometabolism.
sensoriomotor, -triz *adj.* sensorimotor.
sensoriomuscular *adj.* sensorimuscular.
sensoriovascular *adj.* sensorivascular.
sensoriovasomotor, -triz *adj.* sensorivasomotor.
sensual *adj.* sensual.
sensualidad *f.* sensualism.
sensualismo *m.* sensualism.
sentido *m.* sense.
   sentido articular joint sense.
   sentido cinestésico kinesthetic sense.
   sentido del color color sense.
   sentido del dolor pain sense.
   sentido del equilibrio sense of equilibrium.
   sentido espacial, sentido del espacio space sense.
   sentido especial, sentido específico special sense.
   sentido estático static sense.
   sentido estereognóstico stereognostic sense.
   sentido de la forma form sense.
   sentido interno internal sense.
   sentido laberíntico labyrinthine sense.
   sentido luminoso light sense.
   sentido muscular muscle sense, muscular sense.
   sentido de los obstáculos obstacle sense.
   sentido de la posición, sentido de la postura position sense, posture sense.
   sentido de la presión pressure sense.
   sentido propioceptivo propioceptive sense.
   sentido químico chemical sense.
   sentido séptimo seventh sense.
   sentido sexto sixth sense.
   sentido táctil tactile sense.
   sentido de la temperatura temperature sense.
   sentido térmico thermic sense.
   sentido del tiempo time sense.
   sentido del tono tone sense.
   sentido vibratorio vibratory sense.
   sentido visceral visceral sense.
sentimiento *m.* sentiment, feeling.
   sentimiento de culpabilidad feeling of guilt.
   sentimiento de inferioridad feeling of inferiority.
señal *f.* signal, cue.
   señal de angustia *f.* signal of anxiety.
   señal vocal *f.* vocal cue.
señalización pasada *f.* past pointing.
separación *f.* separation.
   separación de dientes separation of teeth.
   separación-individuación separation-individuation.

separación de los maxilares jaw separation.
separación de la retina separation of the retina.
separador[1] *m.* retractor.
separador[2] *m.* separator.
sepedogénesis *f.* sepodonogenesis.
sepedonogénesis *f.* sepodonogenesis.
sepsis *f.* sepsis.
sepsis agranulocítica sepsis agranulocytica.
sepsis del catéter catheter sepsis.
sepsis incarcerada incarcerated sepsis.
sepsis intestinal sepsis intestinalis.
sepsis lenta sepsis lenta.
sepsis murina mouse sepsis, murine sepsis.
sepsis puerperal puerperal sepsis.
septación *f.* septation.
septado, -da *adj.* septate.
septal *adj.* septal.
septana *f.* septan.
septano, -na *adj.* septan.
septátomo *m.* septatome.
septectomía *f.* septectomy.
septemia *f.* septemia.
septicemia *f.* septicemia.
septicemia criptógena cryptogenic septicemia.
septicemia del esputo sputum septicemia.
septicemia flebítica phlebitic septicemia.
septicemia fúngica fungal septicemia.
septicemia meningocócica fulminante aguda acute fulminating meningococcal septicemia.
septicemia de los morfinómanos morphine injector's septicemia.
septicemia de la peste plague septicemia.
septicemia puerperal puerperal septicemia.
septicemia tifoidea, septicemia tifoídica typhoid septicemia.
septicémico, -ca *adj.* septicemic.
séptico, -ca *adj.* septic.
septicocimoide *adj.* septicozymoid.
septicocimoideo, -a *adj.* septicozymoid.
septicoflebitis *f.* septicophlebitis.
septicopiohemia *f.* septicopyemia.
septicopiohemia criptógena cryptogenic septicopyemia.
septicopiohemia espontánea spontaneous septicopyemia.
septicopiohemia metastásica metastatic septicopyemia.
septicopiohémico, -ca *adj.* septicopyemic.
septífero, -ra *adj.* septiferous.
septigrávida *f.* septigravida.
septimetritis *f.* septimetritis.
séptimo par craneal *m.* seventh cranial nerve.
septineuritis *f.* septineuritis.
septineuritis de Nicolau Nicolau's septineuritis.
septípara *f.* septipara.
septo *m.* septum.
septomarginal *adj.* septomarginal.
septonasal *adj.* septonasal.
septoplastia *f.* septoplasty.
septostomía *f.* septostomy.
septostomía auricular por pelota, septostomía con balón balloon atrial septostomy, balloon septostomy.
septotomía *f.* septotomy.
septótomo *m.* septotome.
séptulo *m.* septulum.
séptulo testis septulum testis.
septum *m.* septum.
septúpleto, -ta *adj.* septuplet.
seraféresis *f.* serapheresis, seropheresis.
serangitis *f.* serangitis.

sere *m.* sere.
serempión *m.* serempion.
serendipia *f.* serendipity.
serendipidad *f.* serendipity.
seriado, -da *adj.* serial.
serial *adj.* serial.
serialógrafo *f.* serialograph.
sericita *f.* sericite.
sérico, -ca *adj.* serumal.
serie *f.* series.
serie basófila, serie basofílica basophil series, basophilic series.
serie eosinófila, serie eosinofílica eosinophil series, eosinophilic series.
serie eritrocítica, serie de eritrocitos erythrocytic series, erythrocyte series.
serie granulocítica, serie de granulocitos granulocytic series, granulocyte series.
serie de Hofmeister Hofmeister series.
serie leucocítica leukocytic series.
serie lineal linear array.
serie linfocítica, serie de linfocitos lymphocyte series, lymphocytic series.
serie liotrópica lyotropic series.
serie mielocítica, serie mieloide myeloid series.
serie monocítica monocyte series, monocytic series.
serie neutrofílica, serie de neutrófilos neutrophilic series, neutrophil series.
serie plasmocítica, serie de plasmocitos plasmacytic series, plasmacyte series.
serie trombocítica, serie de trombocitos thrombocytic series, thrombocyte series.
seriescopía *f.* serioscopy.
serioscopía *f.* serioscopy.
seriflujo *m.* seriflux.
serifuga *f.* serifuge.
seriografía *f.* seriography.
seriógrafo *m.* seriograph.
serioscopía *f.* serioscopy.
seriscisión *f.* seriscission.
seroalbúmina *f.* seralbumin.
seroalbuminoso, -sa *adj.* seroalbuminous.
seroalbuminuria *f.* seroalbuminuria.
seroanafilaxis *f.* seroanaphylaxis.
serocima *f.* serozyme.
serocolitis *f.* serocolitis.
seroconversión *f.* seroconversion.
seroconvertir *v.* seroconvert.
serocromo *m.* serochrome.
serocultivo *m.* seroculture.
serodiagnosis *f.* serodiagnosis.
serodiagnóstico *m.* serodiagnosis.
seroencuesta *f.* serosurvey.
seroenteritis *f.* seroenteritis.
seroepidemiología *f.* seroepidemiology.
seroepidemiológico, -ca *adj.* seroepidemiologic, seroepidemiological.
seroféresis *f.* seropheresis.
serofibrinoso, -sa *adj.* serofibrinous.
serofibroso, -sa *adj.* serofibrous.
serofílico, -ca *adj.* serophilic.
serofisiología *f.* serophysiology.
serofloculación *f.* seroflocculation.
serofluido *m.* serofluid.
serogastria *f.* serogastria.
serogenesia *f.* serogenesis.
serogénesis *f.* serogenesis.
seroglobulina *f.* seroglobulin.
seroglucoide *m.* seroglycoid.
serogrupo *m.* serogroup.
serohemorrágico, -ca *adj.* serohemorrhagic.
serohepatitis *f.* serohepatitis.
seroinmunidad *f.* seroimmunity.

seroinversión *f.* seroinversion.
serolactescente *adj.* serolactescent.
serolema *m.* serolemma.
serolipasa *f.* serolipase.
serolisina *f.* serolysin.
serología *f.* serology.
serología diagnóstica diagnostic serology.
serológico, -ca *adj.* serologic, serological.
serólogo, -ga *m.* serologist.
seroma *m.* seroma.
seromembranoso, -sa *adj.* seromembranous.
seromoco *m.* seromocus.
seromucoide *adj.* seromucoid.
seromucoideo, -a *adj.* seromucoid.
seromucoso, -sa *adj.* seromucous.
seromuscular *adj.* seromuscular.
seronegatividad *f.* seronegativity.
seronegativo, -va *adj.* seronegative.
seroneumotórax *m.* seropneumothorax.
seroperitoneo *m.* seroperitoneum.
seroplástico, -ca *adj.* seroplastic.
seropositividad *f.* seropositivity.
seropositivo, -va *adj.* seropositive.
seroprevalecencia *f.* seroprevalence.
seroprevención *f.* seroprevention.
seroprofilaxia *f.* seroprophylaxis.
seroprofilaxis *f.* seroprophylaxis.
seropronóstico *m.* seroprognosis.
seropurulento, -ta *adj.* seropurulent.
seroquístico, -ca *adj.* serocystic.
serorreacción *f.* seroreaction.
serorrecaída *f.* serorelapse.
serorresistente *adj.* serofast, serum-fast, seroresistant.
serosa *f.* serose, serosa.
serosamucina *f.* serosamucin.
serosanguíneo, -a *adj.* serosanguineous, serosanguinous.
seroscopia *f.* seroscopy.
seroseroso, -sa *adj.* seroserous.
serosidad *f.* serosity.
serosinovial *adj.* serosynovial.
serosinovitis *f.* serosynovitis.
serositis *f.* serositis.
serositis múltiple multiple serositis.
seroso, -sa *adj.* serosal, serous.
serotaxis *f.* serotaxis.
seroterapeuta *m., f.* serotherapist.
seroterapia *f.* serotherapy, serum therapy.
serotipificar *v.* serotype.
serotipo *m.* serotype.
serotonina *f.* serotonin.
serotoninérgico, -ca *adj.* serotoninergic.
serotórax *m.* serothorax.
serovacunación *f.* serovaccination.
serovariedad *f.* serovar.
serovigilancia *f.* serosurvey.
serpiente *f.* snake.
serpiginoso, -sa *adj.* serpiginous.
serpigo *m.* serpigo.
serrado, -da *adj.* serrated, serratus.
serratus *adj.* serrated, serratus.
Serratia Serratia.
serrato, -ta *adj.* serratus.
serrefina *f.* serrefine.
serrulado, -da *adj.* serrulate, serrulated.
serum *m.* serum.
serumuria *f.* serumuria.
servicio *m.* department, service.
servicio básico de salud basic health service.
servicio compartido shared service.
servicio diagnóstico diagnostic service.
servicio de hospital de día day health care service.
servicio interno environmental service.

servicio relacionado con la salud health-related service.

servicio de salud maternoinfantil maternal and child (MCH) service.

servicio de toxicología detoxification service.

servicio de urgencias emergency department.

servicio de urgencias de psiquiatría psychiatric emergency service.

sesamoide *adj.* sesamoid.

sesamoideo, -a *adj.* sesamoid.

sesamoiditis *f.* sesamoiditis.

sesgo *m.* bias.

sesgo de detección detection bias.

sésil *adj.* sessile.

sesión *f.* round.

sesión clínico-patológica clinical-pathologic conference.

sesión docente teaching round.

seta *f.* seta.

setáceo, -a *adj.* setaceous.

setífero, -ra *adj.* setiferous, setigerous.

setígero, -ra *adj.* setigerous.

seudactinomicosis *f.* pseudactinomycosis.

seudacusma *f.* pseudacousma.

seudinoma *m.* pseudinoma.

seudoacantosis nigricans *f.* pseudoacanthosis nigricans.

seudoacéfalo *m.* pseudoacephalus.

seudoacondroplasia *f.* pseudoachondroplasia.

seudoacromegalia *f.* pseudacromegaly.

seudoactinomicosis *f.* pseudoactinomycosis.

seudoacusia *f.* pseudacousis.

seudoafia *f.* pseudaphia, pseudoaphia.

seudoagrafía *f.* pseudoagraphia, pseudagraphia.

seudoagramatismo *m.* pseudoagrammatism.

seudoalbuminuria *f.* pseudalbuminuria, pseudoalbuminuira.

seudoalopecia atrófica *f.* pseudoalopecia.

seudoalucinación *f.* pseudohallucination.

seudoalveolar *adj.* pseudoalveolar.

seudoanafiláctico, -ca *adj.* pseudoanaphylactic.

seudoanafilaxia *f.* pseudoanaphylaxis.

seudoanafilaxis *f.* pseudoanaphylaxis.

seudoanemia *f.* pseudoanemia.

seudoaneurisma *m.* pseudoaneurysm.

seudoangina *f.* pseudangina, pseudoangina.

seudoangiosarcoma *m.* pseudoangiosarcoma.

seudoangiosarcoma de Masson Masson's pseudoangiosarcoma.

seudoangostura *f.* pseudonarrowness.

seudoanodoncia *f.* pseudoanodontia.

seudoanorexia *f.* pseudoanorexia.

seudoanquilosis *f.* pseudankylosis, pseudoankylosis.

seudoantagonista *m.* pseudoantagonist.

seudoapendicitis *f.* pseudoappendicitis.

seudoapoplejía *f.* pseudoapoplexy.

seudoapraxia *f.* pseudoapraxia.

seudoarrenia *f.* pseudarrhenia.

seudoartrosis *f.* pseudarthrosis, pseudoarthrosis.

seudoataxia *f.* pseudoataxia.

seudoatetosis *f.* pseudoathetosis.

seudoatrofodermia *m.* pseudoatrophoderma.

seudoatrofodermia del cuello pseudoatrophoderma colli.

seudobacilo *m.* pseudobacillus.

seudobacteria *f.* pseudobacterium.

seudoblenorragia *f.* pseudoblennorrhagia.

seudobronquiectasia *f.* pseudobronchiectasis.

seudobulbar *adj.* pseudobulbar.

seudocardíaco, -ca *adj.* pseudocardiac.

seudocartilaginoso, -sa *adj.* pseudocatilaginous.

seudocartílago *m.* pseudocartilage.

seudocefalocele *m.* pseudocephalocele.

seudocele *m.* pseudocele.

seudoceloma *m.* pseudocelom.

seudocelomado, -da *adj.* pseudocoelomate.

seudochancro *m.* pseudochancre.

seudocianina *f.* pseudocyanin.

seudociesis *f.* pseudocyesis.

seudocilindro *m.* pseudocast.

seudocilindroide *m.* pseudocylindroid.

seudocirrosis *f.* pseudocirrhosis.

seudoclaudicación *f.* pseudoclaudication.

seudoclono *m.* pseudoclonus.

seudoclorosis *f.* pseudochlorosis.

seudocoartación *f.* pseudocoarctation.

seudocolecistitis *f.* pseudocholecystitis.

seudocolesteatoma *m.* pseudocholesteatoma.

seudocoloboma *m.* pseudocoloboma.

seudocoloide *m.* pesudocolloid.

seudocolonia *f.* pseudocolony.

seudocopulación *f.* pseudocopulation.

seudocorea *f.* pseudochorea.

seudocoxalgia *f.* pseudocoxalgia.

seudocriptorquismo *m.* pseudocryptorchism.

seudocrisis *f.* pseudocrisis.

seudocromestesia *f.* pseudochromesthesia.

seudocromhidrosis *f.* pseudochromhidrosis.

seudocromidrosis *f.* pseudochromidrosis, pseudochromhidrosis.

seudocromosoma *m.* pseudochromosome.

seudocrup *m.* pseudocroup.

seudocuerpo lúteo *m.* pseudocorpus luteum.

seudodeciduosis *f.* pseudodeciduosis.

seudodemencia *f.* pseudodementia.

seudodextrocardia *f.* pseudodextrocardia.

seudodiastólico, -ca *adj.* pseudodiastolic.

seudodifteria *f.* pseudodiphtheria.

seudodisentería *f.* pseudodysentery.

seudodispepsia *f.* pseudodyspepsia.

seudodivertículo *m.* pseudodiverticulum.

seudodominante *adj.* pseudodominant.

seudoedema *m.* pseudoedema.

seudoembarazo *m.* pseudopregnancy.

seudoembrionario, -ria *adj.* pseudoembryonic.

seudoencéfalo *m.* pseudoencephalus.

seudoendometritis *f.* pseudoendometritis.

seudoenfisema *m.* pseudoemphysema.

seudoeosinófilo *m.* pseudoeosinophil.

seudoepífisis *f.* pseudoepiphysis.

seudoerisipela *f.* pseudoerysipelas.

seudoerosión *f.* pseudograze.

seudoescarlatina *f.* pseudo-scarlet fever.

seudoesclerema *m.* pseudosclerema.

seudoesclerosis *f.* pseudosclerosis.

seudoesclerosis de Westphal Westphal's pseudosclerosis.

seudoesclerosis de Westphal-Strümpell Westphal-Strümpell pseudosclerosis.

seudoescroto *m.* pseudoscrotum.

seudoestesia *f.* pseudesthesia, pseudoesthesia.

seudoestoma *m.* pseudostoma.

seudoestrabismo *m.* pseudostrabism, pseudostrabismus.

seudoestratificación *f.* pseudostratification.

seudoestratificado, -da *adj.* pseudostratified.

seudoexfoliación *f.* pseudoexfoliation.

seudoexfoliación de la cápsula del cristalino pseudoexfoliation of the lens capsule.

seudoexoforia *f.* pseudoexophoria.

seudoexoftalmia *f.* pseudoexophthalmos.

seudoextrofia *f.* pseudoextrophy.

seudofacodonesis *f.* pseudophakodonesis.

seudofaquia *f.* pseudophakia.

seudoflemón *m.* pseudophlegmon.

seudofluctuación *f.* pseudofluctuation.

seudofotoestesia *f.* pseudophotesthesia.

seudofractura *f.* pseudofracture.

seudofrémito *m.* pseudothrill.

seudoganglión *m.* pseudoganglion.

seudogén *m.* pseudogene.

seudogeusestesia *f.* pseudogeusesthesia.

seudogeusia *f.* pseudogeusia.

seudoginecomastia *f.* pseudogynecomastia.

seudoglioma *m.* pseudoglioma.

seudoglobulina *f.* pseudoglobulin.

seudoglomérulo *m.* pseudoglomerulus.

seudoglótico, -ca *adj.* pseudoglottic.

seudoglotis *f.* pseudoglottis.

seudogonorrea *f.* pseudogonorrhea, pseudogonorrhoea.

seudogota *f.* pseudogout.

seudografía *f.* pseudographia.

seudohaustración *f.* pseudohaustration.

seudohematuria *f.* pseudohematuria.

seudohemofilia *f.* pseudohemophilia.

seudohemoptisis *f.* pseudohemophtysis.

seudohereditario, -ria *adj.* pseudohereditary.

seudohermafrodita *m., f.* pseudohermaphrodite.

seudohermafrodita femenino female pseudohermaphrodite.

seudohermafrodita masculino male pseudohermaphrodite.

seudohermafroditismo *m.* pseudohermafroditism.

seudohermafroditismo femenino female pseudohermafroditism.

seudohermafroditismo masculino male pseudohermafroditism.

seudohernia *f.* pseudohernia.

seudoheterotopia *f.* pseudoheterotopia.

seudohidrartrosis *f.* pseudohydrarthrosis.

seudohidrartrosis de la rodilla pseudohydrarthrosis of the knee.

seudohidrocefalia *f.* pseudohydrocephaly.

seudohidrofobia *f.* pseudohydrophobia.

seudohidronefrosis *f.* pseudohydronephrosis.

seudohifa *f.* pseudohypha.

seudohiperparatiroidismo *m.* pseudohyperparathyroidism.

seudohipertricosis *f.* pseudohypertrichosis.

seudohipertelorismo *m.* pseudohypertelorism.

seudohipertrofia *f.* pseudohypertrophy.

seudohipertrofia muscular muscular pseudohypertrophy.

seudohipertrófico, -ca *adj.* pseudohypertrophic.

seudohipoaldosteronismo *m.* pseudohypoaldosteronism.

seudohipofosfatasia *f.* pseudohypophosphatasia.

seudohiponatremia *f.* pseudohyponatremia.

seudohipoparatiroidismo *m.* pseudohypoparathyroidism.

seudohipotiroidismo *m.* pseudohypothyrodism.

seudoictericia *f.* pseudojaundice.

seudoíctero, -ra *adj.* pseudoicterous.

seudoinfarto *m.* pseudoinfarction.

seudoinfluenza *f.* pseudoinfluenza.

seudointraligamentoso, -sa *adj.* pseudointraligamentous.

seudoión *m.* pseudoion.

seudoisocianina *f.* pseudoisocyanin.
seudoisocromático, -ca *adj.* pseudoisochromatic.
seudolaminar *adj.* pseudolamellar.
seudoleucemia *f.* pseudoleukemia.
seudoleucocitemia *f.* pseudoleukocythemia.
seudoliendre *f.* pseudonit.
seudolinfocito *m.* pseudolymphocyte.
seudolinfoma *m.* pseudolymphoma.
seudolipoma *m.* pseudolipoma.
seudolitiasis *f.* pseudolithiasis.
seudología fantástica *f.* pseudologia phantastica.
seudoluxación *f.* pseudoluxation.
seudomalaria *f.* pseudomalaria.
seudomalignidad *f.* pseudomalignancy.
seudomama *f.* pseudomamma.
seudomegacolon *m.* pseudomegacolon.
seudomelanoma *m.* pseudomelanoma.
seudomelanosis *f.* pseudomelanosis.
seudomembrana *f.* pseudomembrane.
seudomembranoso, -sa *adj.* pseudomembranous.
seudomeningitis *f.* pseudomeningitis.
seudomenstruación *f.* pseudomenstruation.
seudometahemoglobina *f.* pseudomethemoglobin.
seudometaplasia *f.* pseudometaplasia.
seudomiasis *f.* pseudomyasis.
seudomicelio *m.* pseudomycelium.
seudomicosis *f.* pseudomycosis.
seudomicrocefalia *f.* pseudomicrocephaly.
seudomicrocéfalo, -la *adj.* pseudomicrocephalus.
seudomiopía *f.* pseudomyopia.
seudomixoma *m.* pseudomyxoma.
seudomnesia *f.* pseudomnesia.
seudomotor, -ra *adj.* pseudomotor.
seudomucina *f.* pseudomucin.
seudomucinoso, -sa *adj.* pseudomucinous.
seudomutismo *m.* pseudomutism.
seudomutualidad *f.* pseudomutuality.
seudonarcótico, -ca *adj.* pseudonarcotic.
seudonarcotismo *m.* pseudonarcotism.
seudoneoplasia *f.* pseudoneoplasm.
seudoneumonía *f.* pseudoponeumonia.
seudoneuralgia *f.* pseudoneuralgia.
seudoneuritis *f.* pseudoneuritis.
seudoneurofagia *f.* pseudoneuronophagia.
seudoneuroma *m.* pseudoneuroma.
seudonistagmo *m.* pseudonystagmus.
seudoobstrucción *f.* pseudo-obstruction.
seudoocronosis *f.* pseudo-ochronosis.
seudooptograma *m.* pseudo-optogram.
seudoosteomalacia *f.* pseudo-osteomalacia.
seudoóvulo *m.* pseudo-ovum.
seudopaludismo *m.* pseudomalaria.
seudopaño *m.* pseudopannus.
seudopapila *f.* pseudopapilla.
seudopapiledema *m.* pseudopapilledema.
seudoparafrasia *f.* pseudoparaphrasia.
seudoparafrasis *f.* pseudoparaphrasia.
seudoparálisis *f.* pseudoparalysis.
   seudoparálisis atónica congénita congenital atonic pseudoparalysis.
   seudoparálisis espástica spastic pseudoparalysis.
   seudoparálisis general artrítica arthritic general pseudoparalysis.
seudoparaplejía *f.* pseudoparaplegia.
   seudoparaplejía de Basedow Basedow's pseudoparaplegia.
seudoparasitismo *m.* pseudoparasitism.
seudoparásito *m.* pseudoparasite.
seudoparesia *f.* pseudoparesis.

seudopeptona *f.* pseudopeptone.
seudopericárdico, -ca *adj.* pseudopericardial.
seudoperitonitis *f.* pseudoperitonitis.
seudopeste *f.* pseudoplague.
seudoplaqueta *f.* pseudoplatelet.
seudoplasma *m.* pseudoplasm.
seudoplasmodium *m.* pseudoplasmodium.
seudoplejía *f.* pseudoplegia.
seudopleuresía *f.* pseudopleuresy.
seudopleuritis *f.* pseudopleuritis.
seudópodo *m.* pseudopod, pseudopodium.
seudopolicitemia *f.* pseudopolycythemia.
seudopolimelia *f.* pseudopolymelia.
seudopoliomielitis *f.* pseudopoliomyelitis.
seudopólipo *m.* pseudopolyp.
seudopoliposis *f.* pseudopolyposis.
seudoporfiria *f.* pseudoporphyria.
seudoprognatismo *m.* pseudoprognathism.
seudoproteinuria *f.* pseudoproteinuria.
seudopsia *f.* pseudopsia.
seudopterigión *m.* pseudopterygium.
seudoptialismo *m.* pseudoptyalism.
seudoptosis *f.* pseudoptosis.
seudopubertad *f.* pseudopuberty.
   seudopubertad precoz precocious pseudopuberty.
seudoquiloso, -sa *adj.* pseudochylous.
seudoquiste *m.* pseudocyst.
   seudoquiste pancreático pancreatic pseudocyst.
seudorraquitismo *m.* pseudorickets.
seudorreacción *f.* pseudoreaction.
seudorreminiscencia *f.* pseudoreminiscence.
seudorréplica *f.* pseudoreplica.
seudorretinitis pigmentosa *f.* pseudoretinitis pigmentosa.
seudorreumatismo *m.* pseudorheumatism.
seudorroseta *f.* pseudorosette.
seudorrubéola *f.* pseudorubella.
seudosarcoma *m.* pseudosarcoma.
seudosclerema *m.* pseudosclerema.
seudosclerosis *f.* pseudosclerosis.
seudoseudohipoparatiroidismo *m.* pseudopseudohypoparathyroidism.
seudosolución *f.* pseudosolution.
seudosteomalacia *f.* pseudo-osteomalacia.
seudostoma *m.* pseudostoma.
seudotabes *f.* pseudotabes.
   seudotabes de Friedreich Friedreich's pseudotabes.
seudotétanos *m.* pseudotetanus.
seudotialismo *m.* pseudoptyalism.
seudotifoidea *f.* pseudotyphoid.
seudotifus *m.* pseudotyphus.
seudotisis *f.* pseudophthisis.
seudotracoma *m.* pseudotrachoma.
seudotriquinosis *f.* pseudotrichiniasis, pseudotrichinosis.
seudotrismo *m.* pseudotrismus.
seudotronco arterioso *m.* pseudotruncus arteriosus.
seudotubérculo *m.* pseudotubercle.
seudotuberculoma *m.* pseudotuberculoma.
seudotuberculosis *f.* pseudotuberculosis.
   seudotuberculosis estreptotrica humana pseudotuberculosis hominis streptothrica.
seudotumor *m.* pseudotumor.
   seudotumor cerebral pseudotumor cerebri.
   seudotumor inflamatorio inflammatory pseudotumor.
seudouremia *f.* pseudouremia.
seudourticaria *f.* pseudourticaria.
seudovacuna *f.* pseudocowpox.
seudovacuola *f.* pseudovacuole.
seudoválvula *f.* pseudovalve.

seudovaricela *f.* pseudosmallpox.
seudovariola *f.* pseudovariola.
seudoventrículo *m.* pseudoventricle.
seudoviruela *f.* pseudosmallpox.
seudovitamina *f.* pseudovitamin.
seudovómito *m.* pseudovomiting.
seudovoz *f.* pseudovoice.
seudoxantoma *m.* pseudoxanthoma.
   seudoxantoma elástico pseudoxanthoma elasticum.
seudozumbido *m.* pseudobuzzing.
   seudozumbido de oído pseudobuzzing of the ears.
sevicia *f.* ill-treatment.
sexar *v.* sex.
sexdigitado, -da *adj.* sexdigitate.
sexdigitismo *m.* sexdigitism.
sexismo *m.* sexism.
sexo *m.* sex.
   sexo cromosómico chromosomal sex.
   sexo endocrinológico endocrinologic sex.
   sexo genético genetic sex.
   sexo gonadal gonadal sex.
   sexo morfológico morphological sex.
   sexo nuclear nuclear sex.
   sexo psicológico psychological sex.
   sexo seguro safe sex.
   sexo social social sex.
sexología *f.* sexology.
sexopatía *f.* sexopathy.
sextana *f.* sextan.
sextigrávida *f.* sextigravida.
sextillizo, -za *adj.* sextuplet.
sextípara *f.* sextipara.
sexto par craneal *m.* sixth cranial nerve.
sextúpleto, -ta *adj.* sextuplet.
sexual *adj.* sexual.
sexualidad *f.* sexuality.
   sexualidad infantil infantile sexuality.
shashitsu *m.* shashitsu.
Shigella Shigella.
shigella shigella.
shigellosis *f.* shigellosis.
shock *m.* shock.
   shock cultural cultural shock.
   shock de guerra war shock.
shower *f.* shower.
   shower de ácido úrico uric acid shower.
shunt *m.* shunt.
siagantritis *f.* siagantritis.
siagonagra *f.* siagonatra.
siagonantritis *f.* siagonantritis.
sialadenectomía *f.* sialadenectomy.
sialadenitis *f.* sialadenitis.
   sialadenitis inespecífica crónica chronic non-specific sialadenitis.
sialadeno *m.* sialaden.
sialadenografía *f.* sialadenography.
sialadenonco *m.* sialadenoncus.
sialadenosis *f.* sialadenosis.
sialadenotomía *f.* sialadenotomy.
sialagogo, -ga *adj.* sialagogue, sialogogue.
sialogogo, -ga *adj.* sialagogue, sialogogue.
sialaporía *f.* sialaporia.
sialectasia *f.* sialectasia.
sialemesis *f.* sialemesis.
siálico, -ca *adj.* sialic.
sialino, -na *adj.* sialine.
sialismo *m.* sialism, sialismus.
sialoadenectomía *f.* sialoadenectomy.
sialoadenitis *f.* sialoadenitis.
sialoadenotomía *f.* sialoadenotomy, sialadenotomy.
sialoaerofagia *f.* sialoaerophagia, sialoaerophagy.

sialoangiectasla *f.* sialoangiectasis.
sialoangiectasis *f.* sialoangiectasis.
sialoangiogafía *f.* sialoangiography.
sialoangitis *f.* sialoangitis, sialoangiitis.
sialocele *m.* sialocele.
sialodocoplastia *f.* sialodochoplasty.
sialodoquitis *f.* sialodochitis.
sialoductitis *f.* sialoductitis.
sialoestenosis *f.* sialostenosis.
sialofagia *f.* sialophagia, sialophagy.
sialogastrona *f.* sialogastrone.
sialógeno, -na *adj.* sialogenous.
sialogógico, -ca *adj.* sialogogic.
sialografía *f.* sialography.
sialograma *m.* sialogram.
sialojeringa *f.* sialosyrinx.
sialolitiasis *f.* sialolithiasis.
sialolito *m.* sialolith.
sialolitotomía *f.* sialolithotomy.
sialología *f.* sialology.
sialometaplasia *f.* sialometaplasia.
  sialometaplasia necrosante necrotizing sialometaplasia.
sialomucina *f.* sialomucin.
sialorrea *f.* sialorrhea.
sialosemiología *f.* sialosemeiology, sialosemiology.
sialosis *f.* sialosis.
sialosquesis *f.* sialoschesis.
sialostenosis *f.* sialostenosis.
sialótico, -ca *adj.* sialotic.
sibilancia *f.* sibilant rales, wheeze, whistling
rales.
  sibilancia asmatoide asthmatoid sibilant
  rales.
sibilante *adj.* sibilant.
sicasia *f.* sicchasia.
sicativo, -va *adj.* siccative.
sicéfalo, -la *adj.* sycephalous.
sicigia *f.* syzygy.
sicigial *adj.* syzygial.
sicigio *m.* syzygium.
sicnuria *f.* sychnuria.
sicosis *f.* sycosis.
  sicosis de la barba sycosis barbae.
  sicosis cocógena coccogenic sycosis.
  sicosis estafilógena sycosis staphylogenes.
  sicosis lupoide lupoid sycosis.
  sicosis necrotizante de la nuca sycosis nuchae necrotizans.
  sicosis de la nuca sycosis nuchae.
  sicosis parasitaria parasitic sycosis.
  sicosis simple sycosis vulgaris.
  sicosis tarsal sycosis tarsi.
  sicosis vulgar sycosis vulgaris.
sideración *f.* sideration.
sideremia *f.* blood iron.
siderismo *m.* siderism.
sideroblasto *m.* sideroblast.
siderocito *m.* siderocyte.
siderodermia *f.* sideroderma.
siderófago, -ga *m., f.* siderophage.
siderofibrosis *f.* siderofibrosis.
siderófilo *m.* siderophil.
siderófilo, -la *adj.* siderophilous.
sideróforo *m.* siderophore.
siderógeno, -na *adj.* siderogenous.
sideroscopio *m.* sideroscope.
siderosilicosis *f.* siderosilicosis.
siderosis *f.* siderosis.
  siderosis bulbar siderosis bulbi.
  siderosis conjuntival siderosis conjunctivae.
  siderosis hepática hepatic siderosis.
  siderosis nutricional nutritional siderosis.
  siderosis pulmonar pulmonary siderosis.

  siderosis urinaria urinary siderosis.
sideroso, -sa *adj.* siderous.
siderótico, -ca *adj.* siderotic.
siembra *f.* seeding.
sien *f.* temple.
sierra *f.* saw.
  sierra de Adams Adam's saw.
  sierra de alambre de Gigli Gigli's wire saw.
  sierra de amputación amputating saw.
  sierra de bayoneta bayonet saw.
  sierra de Butcher Butcher's saw.
  sierra de cadena chain saw.
  sierra de corona crown saw.
  sierra de escayola cast saw.
  sierra de Farabeuf Farabeuf's saw.
  sierra de Gigli Gigli's saw.
  sierra de Hey Hey's saw.
  sierra de perforación hole saw.
  sierra de separación separating saw.
  sierra de Shrady, sierra subcutánea
  Shrady's saw, subcutaneous saw.
  sierra de Stryker Stryker saw.
sifílide *f.* syphilid.
  sifílide acuminata acuminate syphilid.
  sifílide ampollar bullous syphilid.
  sifílide anular annular syphilid.
  sifílide corimbiforme corymbose syphilid.
  sifílide ectimatosa ecthymatous syphilid.
  sifílide eritematosa erythematous syphilid.
  sifílide folicular follicular syphilid.
  sifílide gomosa gummatous syphilid.
  sifílide impetiginosa impetiginous syphilid.
  sifílide lenticular lenticular syphilid.
  sifílide maculosa pigmentaria macular
  syphilid.
  sifílide miliar miliary syphilid.
  sifílide nodular nodular syphilid.
  sifílide numular nummular syphilid.
  sifílide palmar, sifílide plantar palmar syphilid, plantar syphilid.
  sifílide papulosa papular syphilid.
  sifílide papulosa plana flat papular syphilid.
  sifílide pigmentaria pigmentary syphilid.
  sifílide precoz secondary syphilid.
  sifílide rupial rupial syphilid.
  sifílide secundaria secondary syphilid.
  sifílide tardía tertiary syphilid.
  sifílide terciaria tertiary syphilid.
  sifílide tuberculosa tubercular syphilid.
  sifílide variceliforme, sifílide varioliforme
  varioliform syphilid.
sifilis *f.* syphilis.
  sífilis benigna tardía late benign syphilis.
  sífilis cardiovascular cardiovascular syphilis.
  sífilis congénita congenital syphilis.
  sífilis cuaternaria quaternary syphilis.
  sífilis endémica endemic syphilis.
  sífilis gomosa gummatous syphilis.
  sífilis hereditaria syphilis hereditaria, hereditary syphilis.
  sífilis hereditaria tardía syphilis hereditaria
  tarda.
  sífilis latente latent syphilis.
  sífilis latente precoz early latent syphilis.
  sífilis latente tardía late latent syphilis.
  sífilis meningovascular meningovascular syphilis.
  sífilis parenquimatosa parenchymatous syphilis.
  sífilis primaria primary syphilis.
  sífilis secundaria secondary syphilis.
  sífilis tardía late syphilis.
  sífilis tardía latente late latent syphilis.
  sífilis temprana early syphilis.
  sífilis temprana latente early latent syphilis.

  sífilis terciaria tertiary syphilis.
  sifilis no venérea non-venereal syphilis.
sifilítico, -ca *adj.* syphilitic.
sifilodermia *m.* syphiloderm, syphiloderma.
sifilofima *m.* syphilophyma.
sifilógeno, -na *adj.* siphilogenous.
sifiloide *m.* syphiloid.
sifilología *f.* syphilology.
sifiloma *m.* syphiloma.
sifilopatía *f.* syphilopathy.
sifilosis *f.* syphilosis.
sifiloso, -sa *adj.* syphilous.
sifitoxina *f.* syphitoxin.
sifón *m.* syphon.
sifonaje *m.* syphonage.
slgmatismo *m.* sigmatism, sigmasism.
sigmoide *m. y adj.* sigmoid.
sigmoidectomía *f.* sigmoidectomy.
sigmoideo, -a *adj.* sigmoid.
sigmoides *m.* sigmoid.
sigmoiditis *f.* sigmoiditis.
sigmoidopexia *f.* sigmoidopexy.
sigmoidoproctostomía *f.* sigmoidoproctostomy.
sigmoidorrectostomía *f.* sigmoidorectostomy.
sigmoidoscopia *f.* sigmoidoscopy.
sigmoidoscopio *m.* sigmoidoscope.
sigmoidosigmoidostomía *f.* sigmoidosigmoidostomy.
sigmoidostomía *f.* sigmoidostomy.
sigmoidotomía *f.* sigmoidotomy.
sigmoidovesical *adj.* sigmoidovesical.
sigmoscopio *m.* sigmoscope.
significación *f.* significance.
  significación estadística statistical significance.
signo *m.* sign.
  signo de Aaron Aaron's sign.
  signo de Abadie Abadie's sign.
  signo de Abadie de tabes dorsal Abadie's
  sign of tabes dorsalis.
  signo del abanico fan sign.
  signo accesorio accessory sign.
  signo de Ahlfeld Ahlfeld's sign.
  signo de Allis Allis' sign.
  signo de Amoss Amoss' sign.
  signo de André-Thomas André-Thomas
  sign.
  signo de Angelescu Angelescu's sign.
  signo antecedente antecedent sign.
  signo de Argyll-Robertson Argyll-Robertson's sign.
  signo del arlequín harlequin sign.
  signo de Arroyo Arroyo's sign.
  signo de Auenbrugger Auenbrugger's sign.
  signo de Aufrecht Aufrecht's sign.
  signo de Auspitz Auspitz's sign.
  signo de Babinski Babinski's sign.
  signo de Babinski del dedo gordo Babinski's toe sign.
  signo de Bacelli Bacelli's sign.
  signo de Baillarger Baillarger's sign.
  signo de Ballance Ballance's sign.
  signo de Bard Bard's sign.
  signo de Baruch Baruch's sign.
  signo de Bassler Bassler's sign.
  signo de Bastedo Bastedo's sign.
  signo de Battle Battle's sign.
  signo de Becker Becker's sign.
  *signo de Béclard, signo de madurez de
  Béclard* Béclard's sign.
  signo de Béhier-Hardy Béhier-Hardy sign.
  signo de Bell Bell's sign.
  signo de Bespalov Bespaloff's sign.

signo de Bezold Bezold's sign.
signo de Biederman Biederman's sign.
signo de Bielschowsky Bielschowsky's sign.
signo de Biermer Biermer's sign.
signo de Biernacki Biernacki's sign.
signo de Binda Binda's sign.
signo de Biot Biot's sign.
signo de Bird Bird's sign.
signo de Bjerrum Bjerrum's sign.
signo de Bonnet Bonnet's sign.
signo de Bordier-Frankel Bordier-Frankel sign.
signo de Borsieri Borsieri's sign.
signo de Bouveret Bouveret's sign.
signo de Bragard Bragard's sign.
signo de Branham Branham's sign.
signo de Braun-Fernwald Braun-Fernwald sign.
signo de Braxton-Hicks Braxton-Hicks sign.
signo de Brissaud Brissaud sign.
signo de Brittain Brittain's sign.
signo de Broadbent Broadbent's sign.
signo de Brodie Brodie's sign.
signo del broncograma aéreo bronchogram sign.
signo de Brudzinski Brudzinski's sign.
signo de Bryant Bryant's sign.
signo de Bryson Bryson's sign.
signo de Bychowski Bychowski's sign.
signo del cajón anterior anterior drawer sign.
signo del cajón posterior posterior drawer sign.
signo de Cantelli Cantelli's sign.
signo de Cardarelli Cardarelli's sign.
signo cardinal (de inflamación) cardinal sign (of inflammation).
signo de Carman Carman's sign.
signo de Carvallo Carvallo's sign.
signo de Cejka Cejka's sign.
signo de Chaddock Chaddock's sign.
signo de Chadwick Chadwick's sign.
signo de Charcot Charcot's sign.
signo de Charcot-Marie Charcot-Marie's sign.
signo de Charcot-Vulpian Charcot-Vulpian's sign.
signo de Chase Chase's sign.
signo de Cheyne-Stokes Cheyne-Stokes sign.
signo ciático cruzado de Fajersztajn Fajersztajn crossed sciatic sign.
signo de la cimitarra scimitar sign.
signo clavicular clavicular sign.
signo de Cleeman Cleeman's sign.
signo de Codman Codman's sign.
signo de Cole Cole's sign.
signo de Comolli Comolli's sign.
signo conmemorativo commemorative sign.
signo contralateral contralateral sign.
signo de Coopernail Coopernail sign.
signo de Cope Cope's sign.
signo de Corrigan Corrigan's sign.
signo de Courvoisier Courvoisier's sign.
signo de Crichton-Browne Crichton-Browne's sign.
signo de Crowe Crowe's sign.
signo del cuello neck sign.
signo de la cuerda rope sign.
signo de Cullen Cullen's sign.
signo de Dalrympe Dalrymple's sign.
signo de Damoisseau Damoisseau's sign.
signo de Dance Dance's sign.
signo de Darier Darier's sign.
signo de Davidsohn Davidsohn's sign.
signo del dedo gordo toe sign.

signo de Déjerine Déjerine's sign.
signo de Delbet Delbet's sign.
signo de Demianoff Demianoff's sign.
signo de destello oscilante swinging flashing sign.
signo de Deuel Deuel's sign.
signo del doble conducto duct sign.
signo de Dubois Dubois' sign.
signo de Duchenne Duchenne's sign.
signo de Duncan-Bird Duncan-Bird's sign.
signo de Duroziez Duroziez's sign.
signo de Erichsen Erichsen's sign.
signo de Ewart Ewart's sign.
signo de Faget Faget's sign.
signo físico physical sign.
signo de Forcsheimer Forscheimer's sign.
signo de Fothergill Fothergill's sign.
signo de Friedreich Friedreich's sign.
signo de Froment Froment's sign.
signo de Froment del papel Froment's paper sign.
signo de Gaenslen Gaenslen's sign.
signo de Galeazzi Galeazzi's sign.
signo de Gauss Gauss' sign.
signo de Gerhardt Gerhardt's sign.
signo de Gianelli Gianelli's sign.
signo de Gibson Gibson's sign.
signo de Gifford Gifford's sign.
signo de Glasgow Glasgow's sign.
signo de Gordon Gordon's sign.
signo de Gotron Gotron's sign.
signo de Gowers Gowers' sign.
signo de Graefe, signo de von Graefe Graefe's sign.
signo de Grasset Grasset's sign.
signo de Grey-Turner Grey-Turner's sign.
signo de Griesinger Griesinger's sign.
signo de Guedel Guedel's sign's.
signo de Guillain Guillain's sign.
signo de Gunn Gunn's sign.
signo de Guntz Guntz's sign.
signo de Guttmann Guttmann's sign.
signo de Guye Guye's sign.
signo de Hahn Hahn's sign.
signo de Hamman Hamman's sign.
signo de Heberden Heberden's sign.
signo de Hefke-Turner Hefke-Turner sign.
signo de Hegar Hegar's sign.
signo de Heim-Kreysig Heim-Kreysig sign.
signo de Heimlich Heimlich sign.
signo de Hellat Hellat's sign.
signo de Hennebert Hennebert's sign.
signo de Hertwig-Magendie Hertwig-Magendie sign.
signo de Heryng Heryng's sign.
signo de Hicks Hick's sign.
signo de Higoumenakis Higoumenakis sign.
signo del hilio tapado hilar obliteration sign.
signo de Hoffmann Hoffmann's sign.
signo de Hoffmann-Tinel Hoffmann-Tinel's sign.
signo de Holmes Holmes' sign.
signo de Homans Homans sign.
signo de Hoover Hoover's sign.
signo de Horn Horn's sign.
signo de Hoster Hoster's sign.
signo de Howship-Romberg Howship-Romberg sign.
signo de Hueter Hueter's sign.
signo de Hutchinson Hutchinson's pupillary sign.
signo de Hutter Hutter's sign.
signo indexal indexical sign.
signo interóseo interossei sign.
signo de Jaccoud Jaccoud's sign.

signo de Jacquemier Jacquemier's sign.
signo de Jellinek Jellinek's sign.
signo de Jendrassik Jendrassik's sign.
signo de Joffroy Joffroy's sign.
signo de Keen Keen's sign.
signo de Kehr Kehr's sign.
signo de Kehrer Kehrer's sign.
signo de Kerandel Kerandel's sign.
signo de Kerning Kernig's sign.
signo de Klein Klein's sign.
signo de Kocher Kocher's sign.
signo de Koplik Koplik's sign.
signo de Koranyi Koranyi's sign.
signo de Kreysig Kreysig's sign.
signo de Kussmaul Kussmaul's sign.
signo de Küstner Küstner's sign.
signo de Langoria Langoria's sign.
signo de Lasègue Lasègue's sign.
signo de Laugier Laugier's sign.
signo de Lebhardt Lebhardt's sign.
signo de Leri Leri's sign.
signo de Leser-Trélat Leser-Trélat sign.
signo de Lesieur Lesieur's sign.
signo de Lewinson Lewinson's sign.
signo de Lhermitte Lhermitte's sign.
signo de Lian Lian's sign.
signo de Lichtheim Lichtheim's sign.
signo local local sign.
signo de Ludloff Ludloff's sign.
signo de Lust Lust's sign.
signo de McBurney McBurney's sign.
signo de McEwen McEwen's sign.
signo de Magendie, signo de Magendie-Hertwig Magendie-Hertwig sign.
signo de Magnan Magnan's sign.
signo de Mahler Mahler's sign.
signo de Marañón Marañón's sign.
signo de Marcus Gunn Marcus Gunn's sign.
signo de Marie Marie's sign.
signo de Marie-Foix Marie-Foix sign.
signo meníngeo meningeal sign.
signo del menisco meniscus sign.
signo de Mennell Mennell's sign.
signo de Milian, signo del máximo periférico de Milian Milian's sign.
signo de Minor Minor's sign.
signo de Möbius Moebius' sign, Möbius' sign.
signo de la moneda coin sign.
signo de Müller Müller's sign.
signo de Murphy Murphy's sign.
signo de Musset Musset's sign.
signo de Myerson Myerson's sign.
signo de Naffziger Naffziger sign.
signo de Naunyn Naunyn's sign.
signo de Negro Negro's sign.
signo de Neri Néri's sign.
signo neurológico leve soft neurologic sign.
signo de Nikolsky Nikolsky's sign.
signo objetivo objective sign.
signo del obturador obturator sign.
signo de los ojos de la muñeca doll's eye sign.
signo de Oliver-Cardarelli Oliver's sign.
signo de oposición complementaria complementary opposition sign.
signo de Oppenheim Oppenheim's sign.
signo orbicular sign of the orbicularis.
signo de Osler Osler's sign.
signo de Parkinson Parkinson's sign.
signo de Parrot Parrot's sign.
signo de Pastia Pastia's sign.
signo de Payr Payr's sign.
signo del pico de moco peak mucus sign.
signo de Piskacek Piskacek's sign.
signo de Pitres Pitres' sign.
signo placentario placental sign.

signo de Pool-Schlesinger Pool-Schlesinger sign.
signo de Porter Porter's sign.
signo positivo de embarazo positive sign of pregnancy.
signo de Prehn Prehn's sign.
signo de presunción presumptive sign.
signo probable probable sign.
signo prodrómico prodromic sign.
signo de psoas psoas sign.
signo de la puesta del sol setting-sun sign.
signo del pulgar thumb sign.
signo de la pupila de Marcus Gunn, signo pupilar de Marcus Gunn Marcus Gunn pupil sign, Marcus Gunn's pupillary sign.
signo del puño cerrado de Pitres clenched fist sign.
signo de Queckenstedt Queckenstedt's sign.
signo de Quincke Quincke's sign.
signo de Radovici Radovici's sign.
signo de Raynaud Raynaud's sign.
signo de Remak Remak's sign.
signo de Revilliod Revilliod's sign.
signo de Riesman Riesman's sign.
signo de Roche Roche's sign.
signo de Romaña Romaña's sign.
signo de Romberg-Howship Romberg-Howship sign.
signo de Rosenbach Rosenbach's sign.
signo de Rossolimo Rossolimo's sign.
signo de Rovsing Rovsing's sign.
signo de la rueda dentada cogwheel sign.
signo de Rumpel-Leede Rumpel-Leede sign.
signo de Sanders Sanders' sign.
signo de Saunders Saunders' sign.
signo de Schlesinger Schlesinger's sign.
signo de Schultze Schultze's sign.
signo de Seitz Seitz's sign.
signo de la silueta silhouette sign.
signo de Souques Souques' sign.
signo de Spalding Spalding's sign.
signo de Stellwag Stellwag's sign.
signo de Sternberg Sternberg's sign.
signo de Stewart-Holmes Stewart-Holmes sign.
signo de Stierlin Stierlin's sign.
signo de Stiller Stiller's sign.
signo de Strümpell Strümpell's sign.
signo de Suker Suker's sign.
signo de Sumner Sumner's sign.
signo de Tellais Tellais' sign.
signo de Ten-Horn Ten-Horn's sign.
signo de Thomas Thomas' sign.
signo de Thomayer Thomayer's sign.
signo de Tournay Tournay's sign.
signo de Trendelenburg Trendelenburg's sign.
signo de Troisier Troisier's sign.
signo de Trömner Trömner's sign.
signo de Trousseau Trousseau's sign.
signo de Turner Turner's sign.
signo de Turyn Turyn's sign.
signo de Vanzetti Vanzetti's sign.
signo de la vena vein sign.
signo de Vigouroux Vigouroux's sign.
signo visual visual sign.
signo vital vital sign.
signo de Voltolini Voltolini's sign.
signo de von Graefe von Graefe's sign.
signo de Wahl Wahl's sign.
signo de Walker Walker's sign.
signo de Wartenberg Wartenberg's sign.
signo de Weber Weber's sign.
signo de Weiss Weiss' sign.
signo de Wenckebach Wenckebach's sign.

signo de Wernicke Wernicke's sign.
signo de Westermark Westermark's sign.
signo de Westphal Westphal's sign.
signo de Widowitz Widowitz's sign.
signo de Winterbottom Winterbottom's sign.
signo de Wintrich Wintrich's sign.
signo de Wood Wood's sign.
signo de Zaufal Zaufal's sign.
silbato m. whistle.
silbato de Galton Galton's whistle.
silbido m. whistle.
silencio m. silence.
silencio electrocerebral electrocerebral silence (ECS).
silencioso, -sa adj. silent.
silente adj. silent.
silepsiología f. syllepsiology.
silepsis f. syllepsis.
silicatosis f. silicatosis.
silíceo, -a adj. siliceous, silicious.
silicoantrocosis f. silicoanthrocosis.
silicona f. silicone.
silicona inyectable injectable silicone.
silicosis f. silicosis.
silicoso, -sa adj. silicous.
silicótico, -ca adj. silicotic.
silicotubeculosis f. silicotuberculosis.
silla f. chair, sella.
silla de la base de dentadura denture base sella.
silla de montar saddle.
silla de parto birthing chair.
silla de ruedas wheelchair.
sillar adj. sellar.
silosis f. psilosis.
sllueta f. silhouette.
silueta cardíaca cardiac silhouette.
silviano, -na adj. sylvian.
simbalófono m. symballophone.
simbiología f. symbiology.
simbión m. symbiote.
simbiónico, -ca adj. symbionic.
simbionte m. symbiont.
simbiosis f. symbiosis.
simbiosis antagonista, simbiosis antagónica antagonistic symbiosis, antipathetic symbiosis.
simbiosis conjuntiva conjunctive symbiosis.
simbiosis constructiva constructive symbiosis.
simbiosis diádica dyadic symbiosis.
simbiosis triádica triadic symbiosis.
simbiota m. symbiote.
simbiótico, -ca adj. symbiotic.
simbléfaron m. symblepharon.
simbléfaron anterior anterior symblepharon.
simbléfaron posterior posterior symblepharon.
simbléfaron total total symblepharon.
simblefaropterigión m. symblepharopterygium.
simbolia f. symbolia.
simbolismo m. symbolism.
simbolización f. symbolization.
símbolo m. symbol.
símbolo de radiación radiation symbol.
símbolo validado consensualmente consensual validated symbol.
simbraquidactilia f. symbrachydactyly.
simbraquidactilismo m. symbrachydactylism.
simelia f. symmelia.
simelia apodálica apodial symmelia.
simelia tripódica tripodial symmelia.

simelo m. symmelus.
simestesia f. simesthesia.
simetría f. symmetry.
simetría bilateral bilateral symmetry.
simetría inversa inverse symmetry.
simetría radial radial symmetry.
simétrico, -ca adj. symmetrical, symmetric.
similia similibus curantur similia similibus curantur.
simillimum simillimum, simillimum.
sí mismo m. self.
simpatectomía f. sympathectomy.
simpatectomía periarterial periarterial sympathectomy.
simpatectomizar v. sympathectomize.
simpatia f. sympathy.
simpaticectomía f. sympathicectomy.
simpático m. y adj. sympathetic, sympathic.
simpaticoblasto m. sympathicoblast.
simpaticoblastoma m. sympathicoblastoma.
simpaticogonioma m. sympathicogonioma.
simpaticolítico, -ca adj. sympathicolytic.
simpaticomimético, -ca adj. sympathicomimetic.
simpaticoneuritis f. sympathiconeuritis.
simpaticoparalítico, -ca adj. sympatheticoparalytic.
simpaticopatía f. sympathicopathy.
simpaticoterapia f. sympatheticotherapy.
simpaticotonía f. sympathicotonia, sympatheticotonia.
simpaticotónico, -ca adj. sympatheticotonic, sympathicotonic.
simpaticotripsia f. sympathicotripsy.
simpaticotrópico, -ca adj. sympathicotropic, sympathicotrope.
simpaticótropo, -pa adj. sympathicotrope.
simpatismo m. sympathism.
simpatizador, -ra adj. sympathizer.
simpatizante adj. sympathizer.
simpatoblasto m. sympathoblast.
simpatoblastoma m. sympathoblastoma.
simpatogonioma m. sympathogonioma.
simpatolítico, -ca adj. sympatholytic.
simpatoma m. sympathoma.
simpatomimético, -ca adj. sympathomimetic.
simpatosuprarrenal adj. sympathoadrenal.
simpexión m. sympexion.
simpexis f. sympexis.
simplasma m. symplasm.
simplasmático, -ca adj. symplasmatic.
simple adj. simple.
simpodia f. sympodia.
simporte m. symport.
simptosis f. symptosis.
simulación f. simulation.
simulador m. simulator.
simulador, -ra adj. simulator.
Simulium Simulium.
simultagnosia f. simultanagnosia, simultagnosia.
simultanagnosia f. simultanagnosia, simultagnosia.
simultáneo, -a adj. simultaneous.
sinadelfo m. synadelphus.
sinafimenitis f. synaphymenitis.
sinal adj. sinal.
sinalbúmina f. synalbumin.
sinalgia f. synalgia.
sinálgico, -ca adj. synalgic.
sinanastomosis f. synanastomosis.
sinantema m. synanthem, synanthema.
sinapsis f. synapse, synapsis.
sinapsis en asa loop synapse.

sinapsis axoaxónica, sinapsis axonoaxóni-ca axoaxonic synapse.
sinapsis axodendrítica axodendritic synapse.
sinapsis axodendrosomática axodendrosomatic synapse.
sinapsis axosomática axosomatic synapse.
sinapsis dendrodendrítica dendrodendritic synapse.
sinapsis electrotónica electrotonic synapse.
sinapsis de tránsito en passant synapse.
sináptico, -ca *adj.* synaptic.
sinaptología *f.* synaptology.
sinaptosoma *m.* synaptosome.
sinartrodia *f.* synarthrodia.
sinartrodial *adj.* synarthrodial.
sinartrofisis *f.* synartrophysis.
sinartrosis *f.* synarthrosis.
sinatresis *f.* synathresis.
sinatroisis *f.* synathroisis.
sincainogénesis *f.* synkainogenesis.
sincanto *m.* syncanthus.
sincarion *m.* syncaryon, synkaryon.
sincefalia *f.* syncephaly.
sincéfalo *m.* syncephalus.
sinceloma *m.* syncelom.
sincinesia *f.* syncinesis, synkinesis.
sincinesia de boca y mano mouth and hand syncinesis.
sincinesia homolateral de los miembros homolateral limb syncinesis.
sincinesia imitativa imitative syncinesis.
sincinesis *f.* syncinesis, synkinesis.
sincinético, -ca *adj.* synkinetic.
sincipital *adj.* sincipital.
sincipucio *m.* sinciput, synciput.
sincitial *adj.* syncytial.
sincitio *m.* syncytium.
sincitioide *adj.* syncytoid.
sincitioideo, -a *adj.* syncytoid.
sincitioma *m.* syncytioma.
sincitioma maligno syncytioma malignum.
sincitiotrofoblasto *m.* syncytiotrophoblast.
sincitotoxina *f.* syncytotoxin.
sinclítico, -ca *adj.* synclitic.
sinclitismo *m.* synclitism, sycliticism.
sinclonía *m.* synclonus.
sinclono *m.* synclonus.
sincolia *f.* sycholia.
sincondrectomía *f.* synchondrectomy.
sincondroseotomía *f.* synchondroseotomy.
sincondrosis *f.* synchondrosis.
sincondrotomía *f.* synchondrotomy.
sincopal *adj.* syncopal.
síncope *m.* syncope.
síncope de Adams-Stokes Adams-Stokes syncope.
síncope anginoso syncope anginosa.
síncope cardíaco cardiac syncope.
síncope por deglución, síncope deglutorio swallow syncope, swallowing syncope.
síncope digital digital syncope.
síncope por estiramiento stretching syncope.
síncope laríngeo laryngeal syncope.
síncope local local syncope.
síncope miccional, síncope de micción micturition syncope.
síncope postural postural syncope.
síncope prostático prostatic syncope.
síncope del seno carotídeo carotid sinus syncope.
síncope de la tos, síncope por tos cough syncope.
síncope tusígeno tussive syncope.
síncope vasodepresor vasodepressor syncope.
síncope vasovagal vasovagal syncope.

sincópico, -ca *adj.* syncopic.
sincorial *adj.* synchorial.
sincrónico, -ca *adj.* synchronous.
sincronismo *m.* synchronism.
sincrotón *m.* synchroton.
sindactilia *f.* syndactylia, syndactyly.
sindactilia completa complete syndactyly.
sindactilia complicada complicated syndactyly.
sindactilia doble double syndactyly.
sindactilia parcial partial syndactyly.
sindactilia sencilla single syndactyly.
sindactilia simple simple syndactyly.
sindactilia triple triple syndactyly.
sindactílico, -ca *adj.* syndactylous.
sindactilismo *m.* syndactylism.
sindáctilo, -la *m.* syndactyl, syndactyle.
sindáctilo, -la *adj.* syndactylous.
sindectomía *f.* syndectomy.
sindelfo *m.* syndelphus.
sindesis *f.* syndesis.
sindesmectomía *f.* syndesmectomy.
sindesmitis *f.* syndesmitis.
sindesmitis metatarsiana syndesmitis metatarsea.
sindesmodontoides *adj.* syndesmo-odontoid.
sindesmófito *m.* syndesmophyte.
sindesmografía *f.* syndesmography.
sindesmología *f.* syndesmologia, syndesmology.
sindesmoma *m.* syndesmoma.
sindesmopexia *f.* syndesmopexy.
sindesmoplastia *f.* syndesmoplasty.
sindesmorrafia *f.* syndesmorrhaphy.
sindesmosis *f.* syndesmosis.
sindesmosis radiocubital radioulnar syndesmosis, syndesmosis radio-ulnaris.
sindesmosis tibioperonea tibiofibular syndesmosis, syndesmosis tibiofibularis.
sindesmosis timpanoestapedia syndesmosis tympanostapedia, tympanostapedial syndesmosis.
sindesmotomía *f.* syndesmotomy.
síndrome *m.* syndrome.
síndrome de Aarskog-Scott Aarskog syndrome, Aarskog-Scott syndrome.
síndrome de Aase Aase syndrome.
síndrome de Abercrombie Abercrombie syndrome.
síndrome de abstinencia abstinence syndrome, withdrawal syndrome.
síndrome de abstinencia del alcohol withdrawal syndrome for alcohol.
síndrome de abstinencia de cannabioides withdrawal syndrome for cannabis.
síndrome de abstinencia de hipnóticos withdrawal syndrome for hypnotics.
síndrome de abstinencia de opioides withdrawal syndrome for opioids.
síndrome de abstinencia de sedantes withdrawal syndrome for sedatives.
síndrome de abuso del niño abused-child syndrome.
síndrome de accidente vascular stroke syndrome.
síndrome de Achard Achard syndrome.
síndrome de Achard-Thiers Achard-Thiers syndrome.
síndrome de Achenbach Achenbach syndrome.
síndrome acrofacial acrofacial syndrome.
síndrome de ACTH ectópica ectopic ACTH syndrome.
síndrome del acueducto de Silvio Sylvian aqueduct syndrome.

síndrome de Adair-Dighton Adair-Dighton syndrome.
síndrome de Adams-Stokes Adams-Stokes syndrome.
síndrome de adaptación general (SAG) de Selye Selye general adaptation syndrome (GAS).
síndrome de adaptación local (SAL) local adaptation syndrome (LAS).
síndrome de Addison, síndrome adisoniano Addisonian syndrome.
síndrome de adherencia adherence syndrome.
síndrome de Adie, síndrome de Adie-Reys Adie syndrome, Adie's syndrome.
síndrome adiposogenital adiposogenital syndrome.
síndrome adrenogenital adrenogenital syndrome.
síndrome de aglosia-adactilia aglossia-adactylia syndrome.
síndrome por aglutina de frío cold agglutinin syndrome.
síndrome de agotamiento de sal salt depletion syndrome.
síndrome del agua dura hard water syndrome.
síndrome del agujero rasgado posterior, síndrome del agujero yugular jugular foramen syndrome.
síndrome de Ahumada-del Castillo Ahumada-del Castillo syndrome.
síndrome de Aicardi Aicardi's syndrome.
síndrome de Alajouanine Alajouanine's syndrome.
síndrome de Albright, síndrome de Albright-McCune-Sternberg Albright's syndrome, Albright-McCune-Sternberg syndrome.
síndrome de Albright-Turner Albright-Turner's syndrome.
síndrome alcohólico fetal, síndrome de alcoholismo fetal fetal alcohol syndrome.
síndrome de Aldrich Aldrich syndrome, Aldrich's syndrome.
síndrome alérgico tóxico toxic allergic syndrome.
síndrome de Alezzandrini Alezzandrini's syndrome.
síndrome de Alicia en el país de las maravillas Alice-in-Wonderland syndrome.
síndrome de Allen-Masters Allen-Masters' syndrome.
síndrome de Allemann Allemann's syndrome.
síndrome de Alport Alport's syndrome.
síndrome de Alström Alström syndrome.
síndrome del ama de casa fatigada tired housewife syndrome.
síndrome del amanecer sunrise syndrome.
síndrome de amenorrea-galactorrea amenorrhea-galactorrhea syndrome.
síndrome amiostático amyostatic syndrome.
síndrome amnésico, síndrome amnésico-confabulatorio amnestic syndrome, amnestic-confabulatory syndrome.
síndrome de Andersen Andersen's syndrome.
síndrome de Angelman Angelman's syndrome.
síndrome de Angelucci Angelucci syndrome, Angelucci's syndrome.
síndrome anginoso anginal syndrome, anginose syndrome.
síndrome de angio-osteohipertrofia angio-osteohypertrophy syndrome.
síndrome del ángulo esplénico splenic flexure syndrome.
síndrome del ángulo pontocerebeloso pontocerebellas angle syndrome.

síndrome del anochecer sundowning syndrome.

síndrome de anorexia-caquexia anorexia-cachexia syndrome.

síndrome de ansiedad anxiety syndrome.

síndrome de ansiedad orgánica organic anxiety syndrome.

síndrome anticolinérgico anticholinergic syndrome.

síndrome de Anton Anton's syndrome.

síndrome apálico apallic syndrome.

síndrome de Apert Apert syndrome.

síndrome de Apert-Crouzon Apert-Crouzon's syndrome.

síndrome de Apert-Cushing Apert Cushing's syndrome.

síndrome de aplasia radial-trombocitopenia radial aplasia-thrombocytopenia syndrome.

síndrome de aplastamiento crush syndrome.

síndrome de apnea del sueño sleep apnea syndrome.

síndrome del arco doloroso painful arch syndrome.

síndrome argentafín, síndrome de argentafinoma argentaffinoma syndrome.

síndrome de Argonz-Ahumada del Castillo Argonz-del Castillo syndrome.

síndrome de Arndt-Gottron Arndt-Gottron syndrome.

síndrome de Arnold-Chiari Arnold-Chiari syndrome.

síndrome de la arteria mesentérica superior superior mesenteric artery syndrome.

síndrome de la articulación temporomaxilar temporomandibular joint syndrome.

síndrome del asa aferente afferent loop syndrome.

síndrome del asa ciega blind loops syndrome.

síndrome de Ascher Ascher's syndrome.

síndrome de Asherman Asherman's syndrome.

síndrome de Asherson Asherson's syndrome.

síndrome de aspiración fetal fetal aspiration syndrome.

síndrome de aspiración ácida pulmonar, síndrome de aspiración pulmonar de ácido pulmonary acid aspiration syndrome.

síndrome de asplenia asplenia syndrome.

síndrome del asta anterior anterior cornual syndrome.

síndrome de ataxia y telangiectasia ataxia-telangiectasia syndrome.

síndrome de atrapamiento poplíteo popliteal entrapment syndrome.

síndrome auriculotemporal auriculotemporal syndrome.

síndrome de Avellis Avellis' syndrome.

síndrome de Axenfeld Axenfeld's syndrome.

síndrome de Axenfeld-Schürenberg Axenfeld-Schürenberg syndrome.

síndrome de Ayerza Ayerza's syndrome.

síndrome de Babinski Babinski's syndrome.

síndrome de Babinski-Frölich Babinski-Fröhlich syndrome.

síndrome de Babinski-Nageotte Babinski-Nageotte syndrome, syndrome of Babinski-Nageotte.

síndrome de Babinski-Vazquez Babinski-Vazquez syndrome.

síndrome BADS BADS syndrome.

síndrome de Bäfverstedt Bäfverstedt's syndrome.

síndrome de Balckfan-Diamond Diamond-Balckfan syndrome.

síndrome de Balint Balint's syndrome.

síndrome de Baller-Gerold Baller Gerold syndrome.

síndrome de la banda amniótica amniotic band syndrome.

síndrome de Bannwarth Bannwarth's syndrome.

síndrome de Banti Banti's syndrome.

síndrome de Bardet-Biedl Bardet-Biedl syndrome.

síndrome de Barlow Barlow's syndrome.

síndrome de Barraquer-Simon Barraquer-Simon's syndrome.

síndrome de Barré-Guillain Barré-Guillain syndrome.

síndrome de Barrett Barrett's syndrome.

síndrome de Bart Bart's syndrome.

síndrome de Bartter Bartter's syndrome.

síndrome de Bassen-Kornzweig Bassen-Kornzweig syndrome.

síndrome de Bazex Bazex's syndrome.

síndrome del bazo palúdico hiperreactivo malarial hyperreactive spleen syndrome.

síndrome de Bearn-Kunkel, síndrome de Bearn-Kunkel-Slater Bearn-Kunkel syndrome, Bearn-Kunkel-Slater syndrome.

síndrome de Beckwith, síndrome de Beckwith-Wiedemann Beckwith's syndrome, Beckwith-Wiedemann syndrome.

síndrome de Behçet Behçet's syndrome.

síndrome de Behr Behr's syndrome.

síndrome de Benedikt Benedikt's syndrome, syndrome of Benedikt.

síndrome de Beradinelli Beradinelli's syndrome.

síndrome de Bernard, síndrome de Bernard-Horner Bernard's syndrome, Bernard-Horner syndrome.

síndrome de Bernard-Sergent Bernard-Sergent syndrome.

síndrome de Bernard-Soulier Bernard-Soulier syndrome.

síndrome de Benhardt-Roth Bernhardt-Roth syndrome.

síndrome de Berheim Berheim's syndrome.

síndrome de Bertolotti Bertolotti's syndrome.

síndrome BFD OFD syndrome.

síndrome de Bianchi Bianchi's syndrome.

síndrome de Biedl-Bardet Biedl's syndrome.

síndrome de Biemond Biemond syndrome.

síndrome de Biemond II Biemond syndrome type II.

síndrome de bilis espesada inspissated bile syndrome.

síndrome de Björnstad Björnstad's syndrome.

síndrome de Blatin Blatin's syndrome.

síndrome de Bloch-Sulzberger Bloch-Sulzberger syndrome.

síndrome de Bloom Bloom's syndrome.

síndrome del bloqueo del nistagmo nystagmus blockage syndrome.

síndrome de Blum Blum's syndrome.

síndrome de Boerhaave Boerhaave's syndrome.

síndrome de Bogorad Bogorad's syndrome.

síndrome de la bolsa faríngea pharyngeal pouch syndrome.

síndrome de Bonnevie-Ullrich Bonnevie-Ullrich syndrome.

síndrome de Bonnier Bonnier's syndrome.

síndrome de Böök Böök's syndrome.

síndrome de Börjesson-Forssman-Lehmann Börjesson-Forssman-Lehmann syndrome.

síndrome de Bouillaud Bouillaud's syndrome.

síndrome de bradicardia y taquicardia bradycardia-tachycardia syndrome.

síndrome braquial brachial syndrome.

síndrome de Brennemann Brennemann's syndrome.

síndrome de Briquet Briquet's syndrome.

síndrome de Brissaud-Sicard Brissaud-Sicard syndrome.

síndrome de Bristowe Bristowe's syndrome.

síndrome de Brock Brock syndrome.

síndrome de Brocq-Pautrier Brocq-Pautrier syndrome.

síndrome de Brown Brown's syndrome.

síndrome de Brown-Séquard Brown-Séquard syndrome.

síndrome de Bruns Bruns' syndrome.

síndrome de Brunsting Brunsting's syndrome.

síndrome de Brushfield-Wyatt Brushfield-Wyatt syndrome.

síndrome bucofaciodigital tipo II (BFD) orofaciodigital syndrome, type II (OFD).

síndrome bucofaciodigital tipo III (BFD) orofaciodigital syndrome type III (OFD).

síndrome de Budd-Chiari Budd-Chiari syndrome.

síndrome bulbar bulbar syndrome.

síndrome de Bürger-Grütz Bürger-Grütz syndrome.

síndrome de Burnett Burnett's syndrome.

síndrome de Buschke-Ollendorf Buschke-Ollendorf syndrome.

síndrome de bypass intestinal bowel bypass syndrome.

síndrome de Bywaters Bywaters' syndrome.

síndrome de la cabeza cerrada closed head syndrome.

síndrome de Caffey, síndrome de Caffey-Silverman, síndrome de Caffey-Smith Caffey's syndrome, Caffey-Silverman syndrome, Caffey-Smith syndrome.

síndrome calloso callosal syndrome.

síndrome camptomélico camptomelic syndrome.

síndrome de Canada-Cronkhite Canada-Cronkhite syndrome.

síndrome del canal carpiano carpal tunnel syndrome.

síndrome del canal del tarso tarsal tunnel syndrome.

síndrome de cáncer de Li-Fraumeni Li-Fraumeni cancer syndrome.

síndrome de Capgras Capgras' syndrome.

síndrome de Caplan Caplan's syndrome.

síndrome capsulotalámico capsulo-thalamic syndrome.

síndrome caquéctico-SIDA SIDA-wasting syndrome.

síndrome de cara de diablillo elfin facies syndrome.

síndrome de cara fetal fetal face syndrome.

síndrome de cara silbante, síndrome de cara silbante y mano en capa de molino de viento whistling face syndrome, whistling face-windmill vane hand syndrome.

síndrome carcinoide carcinoid syndrome.

síndrome de carcinoma nevoide de células basales basal cell nevus syndrome.

síndrome cardiofacial cardiofacial syndrome.

síndrome carotídeo de Forssman Forssman's carotid syndrome.

síndrome de Carpenter Carpenter's syndrome.

síndrome de castración funcional prepuberal prepubertal castrate syndrome.

síndrome de cautiverio locked-in syndrome.

síndrome cava superior superior caval syndrome.

síndrome del cayado aórtico aortic arch syndrome.

síndrome de Ceelen, síndrome de Ceelen-Gellestadt Ceelen-Gellestadt syndrome.

síndrome celíaco celiac syndrome.

síndrome de células de Sertoli únicamente Sertoli-cell-only syndrome.

síndrome centroposterior centroposterior syndrome.

síndrome cerebeloso cerebellar syndrome.

síndrome cerebral postraumático posttraumatic brain syndrome.

síndrome del cerebro dividido split-brain syndrome.

síndrome cerebrocardíaco cerebrocardiac syndrome.

síndrome cerebrohepatorrenal cerebrohepatorenal syndrome.

síndrome cervical, síndrome cervicobraquial cervical syndrome, cervicobrachial syndrome.

síndrome cervical postraumático cervical post-traumatic syndrome.

síndrome de Cestan, síndrome de Cestan-Chenais Cestan's syndrome, Cestan-Chenais syndrome.

síndrome de Cestan-Raymond Cestan-Raymond syndrome.

síndrome chancriforme chancriform syndrome.

síndrome de Chandler Chandler's syndrome.

síndrome de Charcot Charcot's syndrome.

síndrome de Charcot-Weiss-Baker Charcot-Weiss-Baker syndrome.

síndrome de Charlin Charlin's syndrome.

síndrome del chasquido clic syndrome.

síndrome de Chauffard, síndrome de Chauffard-Still Chauffard's syndrome, Chauffard-Still syndrome.

síndrome de Chédiak-Higashi Chédiak-Higashi syndrome.

síndrome de Chiari Chiari's syndrome.

síndrome de Chiari-Arnold Chiari-Arnold syndrome.

síndrome de Chiari-Frommel Chiari-Frommel syndrome.

síndrome de Chilaiditi Chilaiditi's syndrome.

síndrome de CHILD CHILD syndrome.

síndrome del choque hemorrágico del dengue (SHFS) dengue hemorrhagic fever shock (DHFS) syndrome.

síndrome de choque de Mengert Mengert's shock syndrome.

síndrome del choque tóxico (SST) toxic shock syndrome (TSS).

síndrome de Chotzen Chotzen's syndrome.

síndrome de Christ-Siemens-Touraine Christ-Siemens-Touraine syndrome.

síndrome de Christian Christian's syndrome.

síndrome de Churg-Strauss Churg-Strauss syndrome.

síndrome de los cilios inmóviles immotile cilia syndrome.

síndrome en ciruela pasa prune-belly syndrome.

síndrome de Citelli Citelli's syndrome.

síndrome de la clara de huevo egg-white syndrome.

síndrome de Clarke-Hadefield Clarke-Hadefield syndrome.

síndrome de la clase turista tourist class syndrome.

síndrome de Claude Claude's syndrome.

síndrome de Claude Bernard-Horner Claude Bernard-Horner syndrome.

síndrome de Clérambault Clerambault syndrome.

síndrome de Clough y Richter Clough and Richter's syndrome.

síndrome de Clouston Clouston's syndrome.

síndrome de Cobb Cobb's syndrome.

síndrome de Cockayne Cockayne's syndrome.

síndrome de Cogan Cogan's syndrome.

síndrome de Cogan-Reese Cogan-Reese's syndrome.

síndrome de Cohen Cohen's syndrome.

síndrome de la cola de caballo cauda equina syndrome.

síndrome de Collet, síndrome de Collet-Sicard Collet's syndrome, Collet-Sicard syndrome.

síndrome del colon irritable irritable colon syndrome.

síndrome compartimental compartmental syndrome.

síndrome del compartimiento tibial anterior anterior tibial compartment syndrome.

síndrome de compresión compression syndrome.

síndrome del conducto de salida torácica thoracic outlet syndrome.

síndrome del conejo rabbit syndrome.

síndrome de congestión pélvica pelvic congestion syndrome.

síndrome de conmoción cerebral concussion syndrome.

síndrome de Conn Conn's syndrome.

síndrome de Conradi-Hünermann Conradi-Hünermann syndrome.

síndrome de conversión de fibrinógeno en fibrina fibrinogen-fibrin conversion syndrome.

síndrome del corazón atlético athletic heart syndrome.

síndrome del corazón del día de fiesta holiday heart syndrome.

síndrome del corazón hipercinético hyperkinetic heart syndrome.

síndrome del corazón izquierdo hipoplásico hypoplastic left heart syndrome.

síndrome de corazón y mano heart-hand syndrome.

síndrome de corazón rígido stiff heart syndrome.

síndrome del cordón anterior anterior cord syndrome.

síndrome del cordón central central cord syndrome.

síndrome del cordón posterior posterior cord syndrome.

síndrome de córnea quebradiza brittle cornea syndrome.

síndrome de Cornelia de Lange Cornelia de Lange's syndrome.

síndrome de coroidopatía vitreorretiniana vitreoretinal choroidopathy syndrome.

síndrome de Costen Costen's syndrome.

síndrome de la costilla cervical cervical rib syndrome.

síndrome costoclavicular costoclavicular syndrome.

síndrome de Cotard Cotard's syndrome.

síndrome de Courvoisier-Terrier Courvoisier-Terrier syndrome.

síndrome de covada couvade syndrome.

síndrome de Cowden Cowden's syndrome.

síndrome de cráneo en hoja de trébol cloverleaf skull syndrome, Kleeblattschadel syndrome.

síndrome craneosinostosis-aplasia radial craniosynostosis-radial aplasia syndrome.

síndrome CREST CREST syndrome.

síndrome de la cresta neural neural crest syndrome.

síndrome de Creutzfeldt-Jakob Creutzfeldt-Jakob syndrome.

síndrome cri du chat cri-du-chat syndrome, cat-cry syndrome.

síndrome de Crigler-Najjar Crigler-Najjar syndrome.

síndrome de criptoftalmia cryptophthalmos syndrome.

síndrome del cromosoma 5p chromosome 5p syndrome.

síndrome del cromosoma X frágil fragile X syndrome.

síndrome cromosómico chromosomal syndrome.

síndrome de Cronkhite, síndrome de Cronkhite-Canada Cronkhite-Canada syndrome.

síndrome de Cross-McKusick-Breen Cross-McKusick-Breen syndrome.

síndrome de Crouzon Crouzon's syndrome.

síndrome CRST CRST syndrome.

síndrome de Cruveilhier-Baumgarten Cruveilhier-Baumgarten syndrome.

síndrome de los cuatro días four-day syndrome.

síndrome del cuerpo estriado syndrome of corpus striatum.

síndrome del cuerpo de Luys body of Luys syndrome.

síndrome de Curtius Curtius syndrome.

síndrome de Cushing Cushing's syndrome.

síndrome de Cyriax Cyriax's syndrome, Cyriax syndrome.

síndrome de Danbolt-Closs Danbolt-Closs syndrome.

síndrome de Dandy-Walker Dandy-Walker syndrome.

síndrome de Danlos Danlos' syndrome.

síndrome de Debré-Sémélaigne Debré-Sémélaigne syndrome.

síndrome de deficiencia de 17-hidroxilasa 17-hydroxylase deficiency syndrome.

síndrome de deficiencia de anticuerpos, síndrome por deficiencia de anticuerpos antibody deficiency syndrome.

síndrome de deficiencia de biotina biotin deficiency syndrome.

síndrome de deficiencia muscular abdominal abdominal muscle deficiency syndrome.

síndrome de deficiencia poliendocrina, síndrome de deficiencia poliglandular polyendocrine deficiency syndrome, polyglandular deficiency syndrome.

síndrome de Degos Degos' syndrome.

síndrome de Déjérine Dejerine's syndrome.

síndrome de Déjerine-Klumpke Déjérine-Klumpke syndrome.

síndrome de Déjerine-Roussy Déjérine-Roussy syndrome.

síndrome de Déjerine-Sottas Déjerine-Sottas syndrome.

síndrome de De Lange De Lange syndrome, De Lange's syndrome.

síndrome de del Castillo del Castillo's syndrome.

síndrome de deleción deletion syndrome.

síndrome de Dennie-Marfan Dennie-Marfan syndrome.

síndrome de dependencia dependency syndrome.

síndrome de depleción salina salt-depletion syndrome.

síndrome depresivo depressive syndrome.

síndrome de deprivación materna maternal deprivation syndrome.

síndrome de De Sanctis-Cacchione De Sanctis-Cachione syndrome.

síndrome de desconexión interhemisférica disconnection syndrome.

síndrome de desequilibrio de diálisis dialysis disequilibrium syndrome.

síndrome de desfibrinación defibrination syndrome.

síndrome de despersonalización depersonalization syndrome.

síndrome diencefálico diencephalic syndrome.

síndrome de dientes y uñas tooth-and-nail syndrome.

síndrome de dificultad respiratoria del adulto (SDRA) adult respiratory distress syndrome (ARDS).

síndrome de dificultad respiratoria aguda acute respiratory distress syndrome.

síndrome de dificultad respiratoria idiopática idiopathic respiratory distress syndrome.

síndrome de dificultad respiratoria del recién nacido respiratory distress syndrome of the newborn.

síndrome de Di George Di George syndrome.

síndrome de Dighton-Adair Dighton-Adair syndrome.

síndrome de Di Guglielmo Di Guglielmo's syndrome.

síndrome discinético dyskinetic syndrome.

síndrome del disco disc syndrome.

síndrome del disco cervical cervical disc syndrome.

síndrome de disforia de género gender dysphoria syndrome.

síndrome de disfunción de la articulación temporomandibular, síndrome de disfunción temporomandibular temporomandibular dysfunction syndrome, temporomandibular joint syndrome.

síndrome de disfunción dolorosa pain dysfunction syndrome.

síndrome de disfunción dolorosa de la articulación temporomandibular temporomandibular joint pain dysfunction syndrome.

síndrome de disfunción placentaria placental dysfunction syndrome.

síndrome disglandular dysglandular syndrome.

síndrome de disociación sensorial con amiotrofia braquial syndrome of sensory dissociation with brachial amyotrophy.

síndrome de disostosis mandibulofacial mandibulofacial dysostosis syndrome.

síndrome de displasia caudal, síndrome de regresión caudal caudal dysplasia syndrome, caudal regresion syndrome.

síndrome de displasia oculodentodigital dysplasia oculodentodigitalia syndrome.

síndrome de disqueratosis intraepitelial hereditaria benigna hereditary benign intraepithelial dyskeratosis syndrome.

síndrome disráfico dysraphic syndrome.

síndrome de distrés respiratorio del recién nacido respiratory distress syndrome of the newborn.

síndrome de distrés respiratorio del adulto (SDRA) adult respiratory distress syndrome (ARDS).

síndrome de dolor-disfunción de la articulación temporomandibular temporomandibular joint pain-function syndrome.

síndrome de dolor y disfunción miofacial myofacial pain-dysfunction syndrome.

síndrome del dolor relámpago flashing pain syndrome.

síndrome de Donath-Landsteiner Donath-Landsteiner syndrome.

síndrome de Donohue Donohue's syndrome.

síndrome del dorso recto straight back syndrome.

síndrome de Down Down's syndrome.

síndrome de Down por traslocación translocation Down syndrome.

síndrome de Dresbach Dresbach's syndrome.

síndrome de Dressler Dressler's syndrome.

síndrome de Duane Duane's syndrome.

síndrome de Dubin-Johnson Dubin-Johnson syndrome.

síndrome de Dubin-Sprinz Dubin-Sprinz syndrome.

síndrome de Dubowitz Dubowitz syndrome.

síndrome de Dubreuil-Chambardel Dubreuil-Chambardel syndrome.

síndrome de Duchenne Duchenne's syndrome.

síndrome de Duchenne-Erb Duchenne-Erb syndrome.

síndrome del dumping dumping syndrome.

síndrome de Duncan Duncan's syndrome.

síndrome de Duplay Duplay's syndrome.

síndrome de Dupré Dupré's syndrome.

síndrome de Dyke-Davidoff Dyke-Davidoff syndrome.

síndrome de Eaton-Lambert Eaton-Lambert syndrome.

síndrome ectrodactilia-displasia ectodérmica-fisuración ectrodactyly-ectodermal dysplasia-clefting syndrome, EEC syndrome.

síndrome de Eddowes Eddowes' syndrome.

síndrome de Edwards Edwards' syndrome.

síndrome de Ehlers-Danlos Ehlers-Danlos.

síndrome de Eisenmenger Eisenmenger's syndrome.

síndrome de Ekbom Ekbom syndrome.

síndrome electrocardiográfico-auscultatorio electrocardiographic-auscultatory syndrome.

síndrome del elevador levator syndrome.

síndrome de Ellis-van Creveld Ellis-van Creveld syndrome.

síndrome de embriaguez punchdrunk syndrome.

síndrome de Emery-Dreifuss Emery-Dreifuss syndrome.

síndrome EMG EMG syndrome.

síndrome de encefalopatía por diálisis dialysis encephalopathy syndrome.

síndrome de encierro locked-in syndrome.

síndrome endotelial iridocorneal endotelio-iridocorneal syndrome.

síndrome de enfermedad eutiroidea euthyroid sick syndrome.

síndrome de enfermedad del suero serum sickness syndrome.

síndrome epifisario epiphyseal syndrome.

síndrome de Epstein Epstein's syndrome.

síndrome de equimosis dolorosa painful-bruising syndrome.

síndrome de Erb Erb's syndrome.

síndrome de eritrodistesia erythrodysthesia syndrome.

síndrome del escaleno scalenus syndrome, scalenus anticus syndrome.

síndrome del escaleno anterior scalenus anterior syndrome.

síndrome escapulocostal scapulocostal syndrome.

síndrome de esferofaquia y braquimorfia spherophakia-brachymorphia syndrome.

síndrome de esfuerzo effort syndrome.

síndrome del espacio retroparotídeo syndrome of retroparotid space.

síndrome de la espalda recta straight back syndrome.

síndrome específico de cultura culture-specific syndrome.

síndrome de esplenomegalia tropical tropical splenomegaly syndrome.

síndrome de estenosis aórtica supravalvular supravalvar aortic stenosis syndrome.

síndrome de estenosis aórtica supravalvular-hipercalcemia infantil supravalvar aortic stenosis-infantile hypercalcemia syndrome.

síndrome de Estocolmo Stockholm syndrome.

síndrome de estrabismo A-V A-V strabismus syndrome.

síndrome de estrecho torácico thoracic outlet syndrome.

síndrome de estrés por cambio de entorno relocation stress syndrome.

síndrome de estrés postraumático posttraumatic stress syndrome.

síndrome de la evacuación gástrica rápida dumping syndrome.

síndrome de la evacuación gástrica en torrente dumping syndrome.

síndrome exoftalmos-macroglosia-gigantismo exophthalmos-macroglossia-gigantism syndrome.

síndrome del eunuco fecundo, síndrome del eunuco fértil fertile eunuch syndrome.

síndrome de Evans Evans' syndrome.

síndrome extrapiramidal extrapyramidal syndrome.

síndrome exónfalo-macroglosia-gigantismo exomphalos-macroglossia-gigantism syndrome.

síndrome de Faber Faber's syndrome.

síndrome de Fabry Fabry's syndrome.

síndrome faciodigitogenital faciodigitogenital syndrome.

síndrome de Fahr Fahr's syndrome.

síndrome de Fallot Fallot's syndrome.

síndrome de Fanconi Fanconi's syndrome.

síndrome de Farber, síndrome de Farber-Uzman Farber syndrome, Farber-Uzman syndrome.

síndrome de fatiga crónica (SFC) chronic fatigue syndrome (CFS).

síndrome de fatiga posvírica postviral fatigue syndrome.

síndrome de Favre-Racouchot Favre-Racouchot syndrome.

síndrome de Fazio-Londe Fazio-Londe's syndrome.

síndrome de Felty Felty's syndrome.

síndrome de feminización testicular testicular feminization syndrome.

síndrome de Fernández-Sotos Sotos syndrome.

síndrome del feto muerto dead fetus syndrome.

síndrome de Fèvre-Languepin Fèvre-Languepin syndrome.

síndrome de fiebre hemorrágica hemorrhagic fever syndrome.

síndrome de Fiessinger Fiessinger's syndrome.

síndrome de Figueira Figueira's syndrome.

síndrome de Fisher Fischer's syndrome.

síndrome de Fitz Fitz's syndrome.

síndrome de Fitz-Hugh-Curtis Fitz-Hugh-Curtis syndrome.

síndrome de Foix-Alajouanine Foix-Alajouanine syndrome.

síndrome de Foix-Cavany-Marie Foix-Cavany-Marie syndrome.

síndrome de Forbes-Albright Forbes-Albright syndrome.

síndrome de Foster-Kennedy Foster-Kennedy's syndrome.

síndrome de Foville Foville's syndrome.

síndrome del fracaso social social breakdown syndrome.

síndrome de Franceschetti Franceschetti's syndrome.

síndrome de Franceschetti-Jadassohn Franceschetti-Jadassohn syndrome.

síndrome de Freeman-Sheldon Freeman-Sheldon syndrome.

síndrome de Frey Frey's syndrome.

síndrome de Friderichsen-Waterhouse Friderichsen-Waterhouse syndrome.

síndrome de Friedmann Friedmann's vasomotor syndrome.

síndrome de Fröhlich Fröhlich's syndrome.

síndrome de Froin Froin's syndrome.

síndrome de Frommel-Chiari Frommel-Chiari syndrome.

síndrome de Fuchs Fuchs' syndrome.

síndrome de fusión cervical cervical fusion syndrome.

síndrome G G syndrome.

síndrome de Gailliard Gailliard's syndrome.

síndrome de galactorrea-amenorrea galactorrhea-amenorrhea syndrome.

síndrome de la gallina enana de Sebright Sebright bantam syndrome.

síndrome ganglionar mucocutáno (SGMC) mucocutaneous lymph node syndrome (MLNS).

síndrome de los ganglios linfáticos mucocutáneos mucocutaneous lymph node syndrome.

síndrome de Ganser Ganser's syndrome, Ganser syndrome.

síndrome de Garcin Garcin's syndrome.

síndrome de Gardner Gardner's syndrome.

síndrome de Gardner-Diamond Gardner-Diamond syndrome.

síndrome de Gasser Gasser's syndrome.

síndrome gastrocardíaco gastrocardiac syndrome.

síndrome de Gee-Herter-Heubner Gee-Herter-Heubner syndrome.

síndrome de Gélineau Gélineau's syndrome.

síndrome del gen contiguo contiguous gene syndrome.

síndrome general de adaptación (SGA) general adaptation syndrome.

síndrome de Gerhardt Gerhardt's syndrome.

síndrome de Gerlier Gerlier's syndrome.

síndrome de Gerstmann Gerstmann's syndrome.

síndrome de Gerstmann-Straussler Gerstmann-Straussler syndrome.

síndrome de Gianotti-Crosti Gianotti-Crosti syndrome.

síndrome de Gilbert Gilbert's syndrome.

síndrome de Gilles de la Tourette Gilles de la Tourette's syndrome.

síndrome de glioma y poliposis glioma-polyposis syndrome.

síndrome del globo pálido pallidal syndrome.

síndrome de glucagonoma glucagonoma syndrome.

síndrome de Goldenhar Goldenhar's syndrome.

síndrome de Goltz Goltz syndrome.

síndrome de Good Good's syndrome.

síndrome de Goodman Goodman syndrome.

síndrome de Goodpasture Goodpasture's syndrome.

síndrome de Gopalan Gopalan's syndrome.

síndrome de Gorham, síndrome de Gorham-Stout Gorham syndrome.

síndrome de Gorlin Gorlin's syndrome.

síndrome de Gorlin-Chaudhry-Moss Gorlin-Chaudhry-Moss syndrome.

síndrome de Gougerot-Carteaud Gougerot-Carteaud syndrome.

síndrome de Gowers Gowers' syndrome.

síndrome de Gradenigo, síndrome de Gradenigo-Lannois Gradenigo's syndrome.

síndrome de Graham Little Graham Little syndrome.

síndrome gris gray syndrome.

síndrome gris espinal gray spinal syndrome.

síndrome de Griscelli Griscelli syndrome.

síndrome de Grönblad-Strandberg Grönblad-Strandberg syndrome.

síndrome de Gruber Gruber's syndrome.

síndrome de Gubler Gubler's syndrome.

síndrome de Guillain-Barré, síndrome de Guillain-Barré-Strohl Guillain-Barré's syndrome.

síndrome del guiño maxilar jaw-winking syndrome.

síndrome del guiño maxilar invertido inversed jaw-winking syndrome.

síndrome de Gunn Gunn's syndrome.

síndrome de Hadefield-Clarke Hadefield-Clarke syndrome.

síndrome de Hallevorden-Spatz Hallervorden-Spatz syndrome.

síndrome del hamartoma múltiple multiple hamartoma syndrome.

síndrome de Hamman Hamman's syndrome.

síndrome de Hamman-Rich Hamman-Rich syndrome.

síndrome de Hand-Schüller-Christian Hand-Schüller-Christian syndrome.

síndrome de Hanhart Hanhart's syndrome.

síndrome de Harada Harada's syndrome.

síndrome de Hare Hare's syndrome.

síndrome de Harris Harris' syndrome.

síndrome de Hartnup Hartnup syndrome.

síndrome de Hayem-Widal Hayem-Widal syndrome.

síndrome de Heerfordt Heerfordt's syndrome.

síndrome de Heidenhain Heidenhain's syndrome.

síndrome de hemangioma-trombocitopenia, síndrome de hemangiomatosis y trombocitopenia hemangioma-thrombocytopenia syndrome.

síndrome hematopoyético hematopoietic syndrome.

síndrome hemolítico-urémico hemolytic-uremic syndrome.

síndrome de la hendidura orbitaria superior superior orbital fissure syndrome.

síndrome de Henoch-Schönlein Henoch-Schönlein syndrome.

síndrome hepatorrenal hepatorenal syndrome.

síndrome de Hermansky-Pudlak Hermansky-Pudlak syndrome.

síndrome de Heyd Heyd syndrome.

síndrome de la hidantonía fetal, síndrome hidantoínico fetal (SHF) fetal hydantoin syndrome (FHS).

síndrome de la hidralacina hydralazine syndrome.

síndrome de hígado y riñón liver-kidney syndrome.

síndrome de Hinman Hinman's syndrome.

síndrome de hiperabducción hyperabduction syndrome.

síndrome de hipercalcemia ectópica ectopic-hypercalcemic syndrome.

síndrome hipercinético hyperkinetic syndrome.

síndrome hiperdinámico hyperdynamic syndrome.

síndrome hipereosinófilo hypereosinophilic syndrome.

síndrome de hiperinmunoglobulina E, síndrome de hiperinmunoglobulinemia E hyperimmunoglobulin E syndrome, hyperimmunoglobulinemia E syndrome.

síndrome de hiperplasia pineal pineal hyperplasia syndrome.

síndrome de hipersensibilidad xifoidea hypersensitive xiphoid syndrome.

síndrome de hipertrofia frenular hypertrophied frenula syndrome.

síndrome de hiperventilación, síndrome de hiperventilación crónica hyperventilation syndrome, chronic hyperventilation syndrome.

síndrome de hiperviscosidad hyperviscosity syndrome.

síndrome hipofisario hypophyseal syndrome, pituitary syndrome.

síndrome de hipoglosia-hipodactilia hypoglossic-hypodactyly syndrome.

síndrome de hipoparatiroidismo hypoparathyroidism syndrome.

síndrome de hipoplasia de cartílago y pelo cartilage-hair hypoplasia syndrome.

síndrome de hipoplasia del corazón izquierdo hypoplastic left heart syndrome.

síndrome de hipoplasia dérmica focal focal dermal hypoplasia syndrome.

síndrome de hipotensión supina supine hypotensive syndrome.

síndrome de histiocitos de color azul marino syndrome of sea-blue histiocyte.

síndrome de Hoffmann-Werdnig Hoffmann-Werdnig syndrome.

síndrome de Holmes-Adie Holmes-Adie syndrome.

síndrome de Holt-Oram Holt-Oram syndrome.

síndrome del hombre rígido stiff-man syndrome.

síndrome de hombro y mano shoulder-hand syndrome.

síndrome de Homén Homén's syndrome.

síndrome de Horner, síndrome de Horner-Bernard Horner's syndrome.

síndrome de Horton Horton's syndrome.

síndrome de hospitalización institutionalism syndrome.

síndrome de Houssay Houssay syndrome.

síndrome de Howel-Evans Howel-Evans' syndrome.

síndrome del hueso quebradizo brittle bone syndrome.

síndrome de Hughlings-Jackson Hughlings-Jackson syndrome.

síndrome de Hunt Hunt's syndrome.

síndrome de Hunter, síndrome de Hunter-Hurler Hunter syndrome, Hunter-Hurler syndrome.

síndrome de Hurler Hurler's syndrome.

síndrome de Hurler-Scheie Hurler-Scheie syndrome.

síndrome de Hutchinson Hutchinson syndrome.

síndrome de Hutchinson-Gilford Hutchinson-Gilford syndrome.

síndrome de Imerslund, síndrome de Imerslund-Graesbeck Imerslund syndrome, Imerslund-Graesbeck syndrome.

síndrome de indiferencia al dolor indifference to pain syndrome.

síndrome de inestabilidad cromosómica chromosomal instability syndrome.

síndrome de infección amniótica de Blane amniotic infection syndrome of Blane.

síndrome inhibitorio inhibitory syndrome.

síndrome de injerto contra huésped runting syndrome.

síndrome de inmadurez pulmonar pulmonary dysmaturity syndrome.

síndrome de inmunodeficiencia immunodeficiency syndrome.

síndrome de inmunodeficiencia adquirida (SIDA) acquired immunodeficiency syndrome (AIDS).

síndrome de inmunodeficiencia celular cellular immunity deficiency syndrome.

síndrome de inmunodeficiencia combinada combined immunodeficiency syndrome.

síndrome de insensibilidad a los andrógenos androgen-insensitivity syndrome.

síndrome de insuficiencia de la arteria basilar basilar artery insufficiency syndrome.

síndrome de insuficiencia del cuerpo lúteo, síndrome de insuficiencia lútea corpus luteum deficiency syndrome.

síndrome de insuficiencia glandular múltiple multiple glandular deficiency syndrome.

síndrome de insuficiencia placentaria placental dysfunction syndrome.

síndrome de insuficiencia respiratoria del adulto adult respiratory distress syndrome (ARDS).

síndrome de insuficiencia respiratoria del recién nacido respiratory distress syndrome of the newborn.

síndrome intestinal funcional functional bowel syndrome.

síndrome intestinal del homosexual gay bowel syndrome.

síndrome de intestino corto short-bowel syndrome.

síndrome del intestino irritable irritable bowel syndrome.

síndrome iris-nevo iris-nevus syndrome.

síndrome de irradiación aguda acute radiation syndrome.

síndrome de Irvine-Gass Irvine-Gass' syndrome.

síndrome de Isaac Isaac's syndrome.

síndrome de Ivemark Ivemark's syndrome.

síndrome de Jackson Jackson's syndrome.

síndrome de Jacod Jacod's syndrome.

síndrome de Jadassohn-Lewandowsky Jadassohn-Lewandowski syndrome.

síndrome de Jahnke Jahnke's syndrome.

síndrome de Jervell y Lange-Nielsen Jervell and Lange-Nielsen syndrome.

síndrome de Jeune Jeune's syndrome.

síndrome de Job Job syndrome.

síndrome de Kanner Kanner's syndrome.

síndrome de Kartagener Kartagener's syndrome.

síndrome de Kasabach-Merrit Kasabach-Merrit syndrome.

síndrome de Kast Kast's syndrome.

síndrome de Katayama Katayama syndrome.

síndrome de Kawasaki Kawasaki syndrome.

síndrome de Kearns-Sayre Kearns-Sayre syndrome.

síndrome de Kellgren Kellgren's syndrome.

síndrome de Kelly-Paterson Kelly-Paterson syndrome.

síndrome de Kennedy Kennedy's syndrome.

síndrome de Kimmelstiel-Wilson Kimmelstiel-Wilson syndrome.

síndrome de Klauder Klauder's syndrome.

síndrome de Klein-Waardenburg Klein-Waardenburg syndrome.

síndrome de Kleine-Levin Kleine-Levin syndrome.

síndrome de Klinefelter Klinefelter's syndrome.

síndrome de Klippel-Feil Klippel-Feil syndrome.

síndrome de Klippel-Trénaunay, síndrome de Klippel-Trénaunay-Weber Klippel-Trénaunay syndrome, Klippel-Trénaunay-Weber syndrome.

síndrome de Klumpke-Déjerine Klumpke-Déjerine syndrome.

síndrome de Kocher-Debré-Sémélaigne Kocher-Debré-Sémélaigne syndrome.

síndrome de Koenig Koenig's syndrome.

síndrome de Koerber-Salus-Elschnig Koerber-Salus-Elschnig syndrome.

síndrome de Korsakov, síndrome de Korsakoff Korsakoff's syndrome.

síndrome de Kostmann Kostmann's syndrome.

síndrome de Krabbe Krabbe's syndrome.

síndrome de Krause Krause's syndrome.

síndrome de Labbé Labbé's neurocirculatory syndrome.

síndrome del lactante blando, síndrome del lactante fláccido floppy infant syndrome.

síndrome del lactante gris gray baby syndrome.

síndrome de lágrimas de cocodrilo syndrome of crocodile tears.

síndrome de Lambert-Eaton Lambert-Eaton syndrome.

síndrome de Landau-Kleffner Landau-Kleffner's syndrome.

síndrome de Landry Landry syndrome.

síndrome de Laron Laron's syndrome.

síndrome de Larsen Larsen's syndrome.

síndrome de Lasègue Lasègue's syndrome.

síndrome de Launois Launois syndrome.

síndrome de Launois-Cléret Launois-Cléret syndrome.

síndrome de Laurence-Biedl, síndrome de Laurence-Moon-Bardet-Biedl, síndrome de Laurence-Moon-Biedl Laurence-Moon-Biedl syndrome.

síndrome de Laurence-Moon Laurence-Moon syndrome.

síndrome de Läwen-Roth Läwen-Roth's syndrome.

síndrome de Lawford Lawford's syndrome.

síndrome de Lawrence-Seip Lawrence-Seip syndrome.

síndrome de leche y álcali, síndrome de leche y alcalinos milk-alkali syndrome.

síndrome de Leigh Leigh syndrome.

síndrome de Lenègre-de Bruix Lenègre's syndrome.

síndrome de Lennox-Gastaut Lennox-Gastaut syndrome.

síndrome de léntigos, síndrome de léntigos múltiples lentigines syndrome, multiple lentigines syndrome.

síndrome del leopardo leopard syndrome.

síndrome de Leri-Weill Leri-Weill syndrome.

síndrome de Leriche Leriche's syndrome.

síndrome de Lermoyez Lermoyez's syndrome.

síndrome de Lesch-Nyham Lesch-Nyham syndrome.

síndrome de Letterer-Siwer Letterer-Siwer syndrome.

síndrome de leucocitos perezosos lazy leucocyte syndrome.

síndrome de Lev Lev's syndrome.

síndrome de Lhermitte y McAlpine Lhermitte and McAlpine syndrome.

síndrome de Libman-Sacks Libman-Sacks syndrome.

síndrome de Liddle Liddle's syndrome.

síndrome de Lightwood Lightwood's syndrome.

síndrome de Lignac, síndrome de Lignac-Fanconi Lignac-Fanconi syndrome.

síndrome de linfoadenopatía lymphadenopathy syndrome.

síndrome de linfoadenopatía generalizada persistente (SLGP) lymphadenopathy syndrome (LAS).

síndrome linfoproliferativo ligado al cromosoma X X-linked lymphoproliferative syndrome.

síndrome de lisis tumoral tumor lysis syndrome.

síndrome de Lobstein Lobstein's syndrome.

síndrome del lóbulo frontal frontal lobe syndrome.

síndrome del lóbulo medio middle lobe syndrome.

síndrome de loculación loculation syndrome.

síndrome de Löffler Löffler's syndrome.

síndrome de Looser-Debray-Milkman Looser-Milkman syndrome.

síndrome de Lorain-Lévi Lorain-Lévi syndrome.

síndrome de Louis-Bar Louis-Bar syndrome.

síndrome de Lowe, síndrome de Lowe-Terry-Mac Lachlan Lowe syndrome, Lowe-Terry-Mac Lachlan syndrome.

síndrome de Lown-Ganong-Levine Lown-Ganong-Levine syndrome.

síndrome lúpico por hidralacina hydralazine lupus syndrome.

síndrome de Lutenbacher Lutenbacher's syndrome.

síndrome de Lyell Lyell's syndrome.

síndrome de Mac Ardle, síndrome de Mac Ardle-Schmid-Pearson McArdle's syndrome.

síndrome de Mackenzie Mackenzie's syndrome.

síndrome de Macleod Macleod's syndrome.

síndrome de Mad Hatter Mad Hatter syndrome.

síndrome de Mafucci Mafucci's syndrome.

síndrome de mala absorción, síndrome de malabsorción malabsortion syndrome.

síndrome de malabsorción de metionina methionine malabsorption syndrome.

síndrome de malformación cerebelobulbar cerebellomedullary malformation syndrome.

síndrome de malformación glomangiomatosa y ósea, síndrome de malformación ósea glomangiomatosa glomangiomatous osseus malformation syndrome.

síndrome de Mallory-Weiss Mallory-Weiss syndrome.

síndrome mandibulooculofacial mandibulo-oculofacial syndrome.

síndrome de mano y hombro hand-shoulder syndrome.

síndrome de mano, pie y útero hand-foot-uterus syndrome.

síndrome de manos y pies hand-and-foot syndrome.

síndrome de Marañón Marañón's syndrome.

síndrome de Marcus Gunn Marcus Gunn syndrome.

síndrome de Marchesani Marchesani's syndrome.

síndrome de Marchiafava-Micheli Marchiafava-Micheli syndrome.

síndrome de Marfan Marfan's syndrome, Marfan syndrome.

síndrome de Margolis Margolis syndrome.

síndrome de Marie Marie's syndrome.

síndrome de Marie-Robinson Marie-Robinson syndrome.

síndrome de Marin Amat Marin Amat syndrome.

síndrome de Marinesco-Sjögren Marinesco-Sjögren syndrome.

síndrome de Markus Markus-Adie syndrome.

síndrome de Maroteaux-Lamy Maroteaux-Lamy syndrome.

síndrome del marteleno mast syndrome.

síndrome de Martorell Martorell's syndrome.

síndrome de Masters-Allen Masters-Allen syndrome.

síndrome de mastocitosis mastocytosis syndrome.

síndrome del maullido, síndrome del maullido de gato cat-cry syndrome, cri-du-chat syndrome.

síndrome de Mauriac Mauriac's syndrome.

síndrome del maxilar inferior y parpadeo jaw-winking syndrome.

síndrome de Mayer-Rokitansky-Küster-Hauser Mayer-Rokitansky-Küster-Hauser syndrome.

síndrome de McArdle McArdle syndrome.

síndrome de McCune-Albright McCune-Albright syndrome.

síndrome de Meadows Meadows' syndrome.

síndrome de Meckel, síndrome de Meckel-Gruber Meckel syndrome, Meckel-Gruber syndrome.

síndrome medicamentoso de Cushing Cushing's medicamentous syndrome.

síndrome de la médula espinal central central cord syndrome.

síndrome de la médula trabada tethered cord syndrome.

síndrome medular anterior anterior medullar syndrome.

síndrome megacístico megacystic syndrome.

síndrome de megacisto y megauréter megacystis-megaureter syndrome.

síndrome de Meige Meige's syndrome.

síndrome de Meigs Meigs' syndrome.

síndrome de Melkersson, síndrome de Melkersson-Rosenthal Melkersson-Rosenthal syndrome.

síndrome de la membrana hialina hyaline membrane syndrome.

síndrome de la membrana pericólica pericolic membrane syndrome.

síndrome de la membrana poplítea popliteal web syndrome.

síndrome de Mendelson Mendelson's syndrome.

síndrome de Ménétrier Ménétrier's syndrome.

síndrome de Ménière Ménière's syndrome.

síndrome de Menkes Menkes' syndrome.

síndrome menopáusico menopausal syndrome.

síndrome de Meyer-Schwickerath y Weyers Meyer-Schwickerath and Weyers syndrome.

síndrome de Meyers-Kowenaar Meyers-Kowenaar syndrome.

síndrome mialgia-eosinofilia inducida por triptófano tryptophan-induced eosinophilia-myalgia syndrome.

síndrome de miastenia grave myasthenia gravis syndrome.

síndrome miasténico myasthenic syndrome (MS).

síndrome microdelecional microdeletion syndrome.

síndrome miedo-tensión-dolor fear-tension-pain syndrome.

síndrome mieloproliferativo myeloproliferative syndrome.

síndrome del miembro fantasma phantom limb syndrome.

síndrome de Mikulicz Mikulicz's syndrome.

síndrome de Milkman, síndrome de Milkman-Looser Milkman's syndrome.

síndrome de Millard-Gubler Millard-Gubler syndrome.

síndrome de Miller-Fisher Miller-Fisher's syndrome.

síndrome de Milles Milles' syndrome.

síndrome de Minkowski-Chauffard Minkowski-Chauffard syndrome.

síndrome de Möbius Möbius' syndrome.

síndrome de Mohr Mohr syndrome.

síndrome de Monakow Monakow's syndrome.

síndrome de Moore Moore's syndrome.

síndrome de Morel Morel's syndrome.

síndrome de Morgagni, síndrome de Morgagni-Stewart-Morel Morgagni's syndrome.

síndrome de Morgagni-Adams-Stokes, síndrome de Morgagni-Stokes-Adams Morgagni-Adams-Stokes syndrome.

síndrome de «morning glory» morning glory syndrome.

síndrome de Morquio, síndrome de Morquio-Ullrich Morquio's syndrome, Morquio-Ullrich syndrome.

síndrome de Morris Morris syndrome.

síndrome de Morsier Morsier's syndrome.

síndrome de Morton Morton syndrome.

síndrome de Morvan Morvan's syndrome.

síndrome de Mournier-Kühn Mounier-Kuhn syndrome.

síndrome de Moynahan Moynahan syndrome.

síndrome de Muckle-Wells Muckle-Wells syndrome.

síndrome de Mucha-Habermann Mucha-Habermann syndrome.

síndrome de muerte hematológica hematologic death syndrome.

síndrome de muerte súbita inexplicada sudden unexplained death syndrome (SUDS).

síndrome de la muerte súbita del lactante (SMSL) sudden infant death syndrome (SIDS).

síndrome de la mujer maltratada (SMM) battered woman syndrome (BWS).

síndrome de Munchausen Munchausen syndrome.

síndrome del muñeco feliz, síndrome del muñeco sonriente happy puppet syndrome.

síndrome muscular papilar papillary muscle syndrome.

síndrome del músculo supraespinoso supraspinatus syndrome.

síndrome de Naegeli Naegeli syndrome.

síndrome de Naffziger Naffziger syndrome.

síndrome de necrosis hipofisaria posparto postpartum pituitary necrosis syndrome.

síndrome nefrítico nephritic syndrome.

síndrome nefrótico nephrotic syndrome.

síndrome nefrótico idiopático idiopathic nephrotic syndrome.

síndrome de Nelson Nelson's syndrome.

síndrome del nervio auriculotemporal auriculotemporal nerve syndrome.

síndrome de Netherton Netherton's syndrome.

síndrome de neurinoma mucoso múltiple multiple mucosal neuroma syndrome.

síndrome neurocirculatorio de Labbé Labbé's neurocirculatory syndrome.

síndrome neurocutáneo neurocutaneous syndrome.

síndrome neuroléptico maligno neuroleptic malignant syndrome.

síndrome del neuroma mucoso mucosal neuroma syndrome.

síndrome del nevo basocelular basal cell nevus syndrome.

síndrome del nevo displásico dysplastic nevus syndrome.

síndrome de nevos de células basales basal cell nevus syndrome.

síndrome de Nezelof Nezelof syndrome.

síndrome del nido vacío empty-nest syndrome.

síndrome del niño apaleado battered child syndrome.

síndrome del niño maltratado battered child syndrome.

síndrome del niño hiperactivo hyperactive child syndrome.

síndrome del niño hipotónico floppy infant syndrome.

síndrome del niño vulnerable vulnerable child syndrome.

síndrome de Noack Noack's syndrome.

síndrome de Nonne Nonne's syndrome.

síndrome de Nonne-Milroy-Meige Nonne-Milroy-Meige syndrome.

síndrome de Noonan Noonan's syndrome.

síndrome de Nothnagel Nothnagel's syndrome.

síndrome OAV OAV syndrome.

síndrome de Obrinsky Obrinsky syndrome.

síndrome de obstrucción del asa gastroyeyunal gastrojejunal loop obstruction syndrome.

síndrome oculobucogenital oculobuccogenital syndrome.

síndrome oculocerebrorrenal oculocerebrorenal syndrome.

síndrome oculocutáneo oculocutaneous syndrome.

síndrome oculofaríngeo oculopharyngeal syndrome.

síndrome oculoglandular de Parinaud Parinaud oculoglandular syndrome.

síndrome oculomandibulofacial oculomandibulofacial syndrome.

síndrome oculovertebral oculovertebral syndrome.

síndrome oculovestibuloauditivo oculovestibulo-auditory syndrome.

síndrome de Ogilvie Ogilvie's syndrome.

síndrome del ojo de gato cat's-eye syndrome, cat-eye syndrome.

síndrome de ojos secos dry eye syndrome.

síndrome de oligodactilia de Weyers Weyer's oligodactyly syndrome.

síndrome de Oppenheim Oppenheim's syndrome.

síndrome orbitario orbital syndrome.

síndrome orofaciodigital orofaciodigital syndrome (OFD).

síndrome de Osler-Rendu-Weber, síndrome de Osler-Weber-Rendu Osler-Rendu-Weber syndrome.

síndrome osteomielofribrótico osteomyelofibrotic syndrome.

síndrome de Ostrum-Furst Ostrum-Furst syndrome.

síndrome otomandibular otomandibular syndrome.

síndrome otopalatodigital otopalatodigital syndrome.

síndrome ovárico residual residual ovary syndrome.

síndrome del ovario poliquístico polycystic ovary syndrome.

síndrome de ovarios resistentes resistant ovary syndrome.

síndrome de Paget-Schrötter Paget-von Schrötter syndrome.

síndrome paleoestriado, síndrome paleoestriatal paleostriatal syndrome.

síndrome de Pancoast Pancoast's syndrome.

síndrome del pañal azul blue diaper syndrome.

síndrome de Papillon-Lefèvre Papillon-Lefèvre syndrome.

síndrome paraneoplásico paraneoplastic syndrome.

síndrome paratrigeminal de Raeder Raeder's paratrigeminal syndrome.

síndrome de la pared abdominal anterior anterior abdominal wall syndrome.

síndrome de Parinaud Parinaud's syndrome.

síndrome de Parkinson Parkinson's syndrome.

síndrome de Parsonage-Turner Parsonage-Turner syndrome.

síndrome de Patau Patau's syndrome.

síndrome de Paterson, síndrome de Paterson-Brown-Kelly, síndrome de Paterson-Kelly Paterson's syndrome, Paterson-Brown-Kelly syndrome, Paterson-Kelly syndrome.

síndrome de Pellizi Pellizi's syndrome.

síndrome de pelo en alambre de acero steel-hair syndrome.

síndrome de pelo ensortijado, síndrome del pelo ensortijado de Menkes kinky-hair syndrome, Menkes' kinky hair syndrome.

síndrome de Pendred Pendred's syndrome.

síndrome de Pepper Pepper syndrome.

síndrome de pequeñez de Seabright Seabright bantam syndrome.

síndrome de pérdida de sal, síndrome por pérdida de sal salt-losing syndrome.

síndrome de persistencia del conducto de Müller persistent Müllerian duct syndrome.

síndrome pertussis pertussis syndrome.

síndrome de Peutz-Jeghers Peutz-Jeghers syndrome.

síndrome de Pfeiffer Pfeiffer's syndrome.

síndrome PHC PHC syndrome.

síndrome de Picchini Picchini's syndrome.

síndrome de Pick Pick's syndrome.

síndrome de Pickwick Pickwickian syndrome.

síndrome del pie urente burning feet syndrome.

síndrome de la piel escaldada, síndrome de la piel escaldada estafilocócica (SPEE) scalded skin syndrome, staphylococcal scalded skin syndrome (SSSS).

síndrome de la piel escaldada no estafilocócica scalded skin non-staphylococcal syndrome.

síndrome de las piernas inquietas, síndrome de las piernas sin reposo restless legs syndrome.

síndrome de Pierre-Robin Pierre-Robin's syndrome.

síndrome de pies quemantes burning feet syndrome.

síndrome de Plummer-Vinson Plummer-Vinson syndrome.

síndrome de Poland Poland's syndrome, Poland syndrome.

síndrome poliglandular endocrino endocrine polyglandular syndrome.

síndrome postadrenalectomía postadrenalectomy syndrome.

síndrome poscardiotomía postcardiotomy syndrome.

síndrome poscolecistectomía, síndrome subsecuente a colecistectomía postcholecystectomy syndrome.

síndrome poscomisurotomía postcommisurotomy syndrome.

síndrome posconmoción, síndrome posconmocional postconcussion syndrome, postconcussional syndrome.

síndrome posflebítico postphlebitic syndrome.

síndrome posgastrectomía postgastrectomy syndrome.

síndrome posinfarto de miocardio postmyocardial infarction syndrome.

síndrome de posmadurez postmaturity syndrome.

síndrome posperfusión postperfusion syndrome.

síndrome pospericardiotomía postpericardiotomy syndrome.

síndrome posprandial idiopático idiopathic postprandial syndrome.

síndrome posradiación postradiation syndrome.

síndrome posrubéola postrubella syndrome.

síndrome posterolateral posterolateral syndrome.

síndrome post-punción lumbar post-lumbar puncture syndrome.

síndrome postransfusional post-transfusion syndrome.

síndrome postraumático post-traumatic syndrome.

síndrome postrombótico post-thrombotic syndrome.

síndrome de Potter Potter's syndrome.

síndrome de Prader-Labhart-Willi, síndrome de Prader-Willi Prader-Willi syndrome.

síndrome de preexcitación preexcitation syndrome.

síndrome preinfarto preinfaction syndrome.

síndrome premotor premotor syndrome.

síndrome del primer arco first arch syndrome.

síndrome de privación materna maternal deprivation syndrome.

síndrome de privación social social breakdown syndrome.

síndrome de Profichet Profichet's syndrome.

síndrome de prolapso de la válvula mitral mitral valve prolapse syndrome.

síndrome del pronador pronator syndrome.

síndrome psicóticos ligados a la cultura culture-bound psychotic syndrome.

síndrome del pterigion pterygium syndrome.

síndrome del pulmón hiperlúcido hyperlucent lung syndrome.

síndrome de Putnam-Dana Putnam-Dana syndrome.

síndrome QT QT syndrome.

síndrome quiasmático chiasma syndrome, chiasmatic syndrome.

síndrome de Rabson-Mendehall Rabson-Mendehall's syndrome.

síndrome por radiación radiation syndrome.

síndrome radicular radicular syndrome.

síndrome de Ramsay-Hunt Ramsay-Hunt syndrome.

síndrome de Raynaud Raynaud's syndrome.

síndrome de Raymond-Cestan Raymond-Cestan syndrome.

síndrome de reacción global global syndrome.

síndrome de Refetoff Refetoff's syndrome.

síndrome de Refsum Refsum's syndrome.

síndrome de regresión testicular embrionaria embryonic testicular regression syndrome.

síndrome de Reifenstein Reifenstein's syndrome.

síndrome de Reiter Reiter's syndrome.

síndrome de Rendu-Osler-Weber Rendu-Osler-Weber syndrome.

síndrome de residuos ováricos ovarian remnant syndrome.

síndrome de respuesta al estrés stress response syndrome.

síndrome del restaurante chino Chinese reaturant syndrome (CRS).

síndrome de retención del sudor sweat retention syndrome.

síndrome de retracción retraction syndrome.

síndrome de retracción vertical de Brown Brown's vertical retraction syndrome.

síndrome de Rett Rett syndrome.

síndrome de Reye Reye's syndrome.

síndrome de Rh nulo Rh null syndrome.

síndrome de Richards-Rundle Richards-Rundle syndrome.

síndrome de Richter Richter's syndrome.

síndrome de Rieger Rieger's syndrome.

síndrome de Riley, síndrome de Riley-Day Riley-Day syndrome.

síndrome de Riley-Smith Riley-Smith syndrome.

síndrome de Roberts Roberts syndrome.

síndrome de Robin Robin's syndrome.

síndrome de Robinow Robinow's syndrome.

síndrome del robo de la subclavia subclavian steal syndrome.

síndrome de Rokitansky-Küster-Hauser Rokitansky-Küster-Hauser syndrome.

síndrome de Romano-Ward Romano-Ward syndrome.

síndrome de Romberg Romberg's syndrome.

síndrome de Romberg-Paessler Romberg-Paessler's syndrome.

síndrome de Rosenthal, síndrome de Ro-

senthal-Dreskin Rosenthal's syndrome.

síndrome de Rosenthal-Kloepfer Rosenthal-Kloepfer syndrome.

síndrome de Roth, síndrome de Roth-Benhardt Roth's syndrome.

síndrome de Rothmund-Thomson Rothmund-Thomson syndrome.

síndrome de Rotor Rotor syndrome.

síndrome de Rotor-Manahan-Florentin Rotor-Manahan-Florentin syndrome.

síndrome de Roussy Roussy-Déjerine syndrome.

síndrome de Roussy-Lévy Roussy-Lévy's syndrome.

síndrome de la rubéola, síndrome de la rubéola congénita rubella syndrome, congenital rubella syndrome.

síndrome de Rubinstein, síndrome de Rubinstein-Taybi Rubinstein-Taybi syndrome.

síndrome rubroespinal del pedúnculo cerebeloso rubrospinal cerebellar peduncle syndrome.

síndrome de Rud Rud's syndrome.

síndrome de ruptura de cromosomas chromosomal breakage syndrome.

síndrome de Russell, síndrome de Russell-Silver Russell's syndrome, Russel-Silver's syndrome.

síndrome de Rust Rust's syndrome.

síndrome de sacudida por latigazo whiplash shake syndrome.

síndrome de Saethre-Chotzen Saethre-Chotzen's syndrome.

síndrome de salida del tórax thoracic outlet syndrome.

síndrome salival premenstrual premenstrual salivary syndrome.

síndrome de Sánchez Salorio Sánchez Salorio syndrome.

síndrome de Sanfilippo Sanfilippo's syndrome.

síndrome de sarampión atípico (SSA) atypical measles syndrome (AMS).

síndrome de Savage Savage syndrome.

síndrome de Schafer Schafer's syndrome.

síndrome de Schanz Schanz syndrome.

síndrome de Schaumann Schaumann's syndrome.

síndrome de Scheie Scheie's syndrome.

síndrome de Schirmer Schirmer's syndrome.

síndrome de Schmidt Schmidt's syndrome.

síndrome de Schmidt (MB) Schmidt's (MB) syndrome.

síndrome de Schönlein-Henoch Schönlein-Henoch syndrome.

síndrome de Schroeder Schroeder's syndrome.

síndrome de Schüller, síndrome de Schüller-Christian Schüller's syndrome.

síndrome de Schultz Schultz syndrome.

síndrome de Schwachman, síndrome de Schwachman-Diamond Schwachman syndrome.

síndrome de Schwartz-Bartter Schwartz-Bartter's syndrome.

síndrome de Schwartz-Jampel Schwartz syndrome.

síndrome de Seabright-Bantam Seabright bantam syndrome.

síndrome de Seckel Seckel's syndrome.

síndrome seco sicca syndrome.

síndrome de secreción inadecuada de hormona antidiurética (SIADH) syndrome of inappropriate antidiuretic hormone secretion (SIADH).

síndrome de secuestro de la sublcavia subclavian steal syndrome.

síndrome de segmentación de la camara anterior anterior chamber cleavage syndrome.

síndrome segmentario segmentary syndrome.

síndrome de Selye Selye's syndrome.

síndrome de Senear-Usher Senear-Usher syndrome.

síndrome del seno carotídeo carotid sinus syndrome.

síndrome del seno cavernoso cavernous sinus syndrome.

síndrome del seno enfermo sick sinus syndrome.

síndrome de sensibilización autoeritrocítica autoerythrocyte sensitization syndrome.

síndrome de separación maternoinfantil maternal-child separation syndrome.

síndrome de seudoclaudicación pseudoclaudication syndrome.

síndrome de Sézary Sézary's syndrome.

síndrome de Sheehan Sheehan's syndrome.

síndrome de Shy-Drager Shy-Drager syndrome.

síndrome de Sicard Sicard's syndrome.

síndrome de Siemens Siemens syndrome.

síndrome de la silla turca vacía, síndrome de la silla vacía empty sella syndrome.

síndrome de Silver, síndrome de Silver-Russel Silver syndrome, Silver-Russel syndrome.

síndrome de Silverskiöld Silverskiöld syndrome.

síndrome de Silvestrini-Corda Silvestrini-Corda syndrome.

síndrome silviano sylvian syndrome.

síndrome sin sentido nonsense syndrome.

síndrome de Sipple Sipple's syndrome.

síndrome siringomiélico syringomelic syndrome.

síndrome del sistema nervioso central, síndrome del SNC central nervous system syndrome, CNS syndrome.

síndrome de Sjögren Sjögren's syndrome.

síndrome de Sjögren-Larsson Sjögren-Larsson syndrome.

síndrome de Sluder Sluder's syndrome.

síndrome de Sly Sly syndrome.

síndrome de Smith-Lemli-Opitz Smith-Lemli-Opitz syndrome.

síndrome de Sneddon Sneddon's syndrome.

síndrome de Sohval-Soffer Sohval-Soffer syndrome.

síndrome de sólo células de Sertoli Sertoli-cell only syndrome.

síndrome del sombrerero loco Mad Hatter syndrome.

síndrome sordocardiaco surdocardiac syndrome.

síndrome de Sorsby Sorsby's syndrome.

síndrome de Spens Spens' syndrome.

síndrome de Sprinz-Dubin, síndrome de Sprinz-Nelson Sprinz-Dubin syndrome, Sprinz-Nelson syndrome.

síndrome de Spurway Spurway's syndrome, Spurway syndrome.

síndrome de Steele-Richardson-Olszewski Steele-Richardson-Olszewski syndrome.

síndrome de Stein-Leventhal Stein-Leventhal syndrome.

síndrome de Stevens-Johnson Stevens-Johnson syndrome.

síndrome de Stewart-Morel Stewart-Morel syndrome.

síndrome de Stewart-Treves Stewart-Treves syndrome.

síndrome de Stickler Stickler's syndrome.

síndrome de Stilling, síndrome de Stilling-Duane, síndrome de Stilling-Turk-Duane Stilling-Turk-Duane syndrome.

síndrome de Stokes-Adams Stokes' syndrome.

síndrome de Strachan Strachan's syndrome.

síndrome de Sturge-Kalischer-Weber, síndrome de Sturge-Weber Sturge-Kalischer-Weber syndrome, Sturge-Weber syndrome.

síndrome subsecuente a cardiotomía postcardiotomy syndrome.

síndrome subsecuente a conmoción postconcussion syndrome, postconcussional syndrome.

síndrome subsecuente a flebitis postphlebitic syndrome.

síndrome subsecuente a gastrectomía postgastrectomy syndrome.

síndrome subsecuente a infarto del miocardio postmyocardial infarction syndrome.

síndrome subsecuente a perfusión postperfusion syndrome.

síndrome subsecuente a pericardiotomía postpericardiotomy syndrome.

síndrome subsecuente a radiación postradiation syndrome.

síndrome subsecuente a transfusión posttransfusion syndrome.

síndrome de sudación gustatoria gustatory sweating syndrome.

síndrome de Sulzberger-Garbe Sulzberger-Garbe syndrome.

síndrome del supraespinoso supraspinatus syndrome.

síndrome de supresión de alcohol alcohol withdrawal syndrome.

síndrome de Sweet Sweet's syndrome.

síndrome de Swyer-James Swyer-James syndrome.

síndrome talámico thalamic syndrome.

síndrome de Tapia Tapia's syndrome.

síndrome del tapón meconial meconium plug syndrome.

síndrome de Taussig-Bing Taussig-Bing syndrome.

síndrome tegmentario tegmental syndrome.

síndrome de telangiectasia nevoide unilateral unilateral nevoid telangiectasia syndrome.

síndrome de Terry Terry's syndrome.

síndrome de los testículos ausentes vanishing testis syndrome.

síndrome de los testículos rudimentarios rudimentary testis syndrome.

síndrome de Thibierge-Weissenbach Thibierge-Weissenbach syndrome.

síndrome de Thiele Thiele's syndrome.

síndrome de Thorn Thorn's syndrome.

síndrome de Tietze Tietze's syndrome.

síndrome de Timme Timme's syndrome.

síndrome tipo enfermedad del suero serum sickness-like syndrome.

síndrome del tipo del lupus lupus like syndrome.

síndrome del tipo pertussis pertussis-like syndrome.

síndrome tirohipofisario thyrohypophyseal syndrome.

síndrome de Tolosa-Hunt Tolosa-Hunt syndrome.

síndrome de Toni-Fanconi Toni-Fanconi syndrome.

síndrome TORCH TORCH syndrome.

síndrome de Tornwaldt Tornwaldt's syndrome.

síndrome de Torre Torre's syndrome.

síndrome de tos nerviosa refleja de Arnold Arnold's nerve reflex cough syndrome.

síndrome de Touraine-Solente-Golé Touraine-Solente-Golé syndrome.

síndrome de Tourette Tourette's syndrome.

síndrome tóxico constitucional anorexia-cachexia syndrome.

síndrome tóxico del polvo orgánico (STPO) organic dust toxic syndrome (ODTS).

síndrome de trabamiento locked-in syndrome.

síndrome de transfusión, síndrome de transfusión placentaria transfusion syndrome, placental transfusion syndrome.

síndrome de trauma por violación rape-trauma syndrome.

síndrome traumático ocular anterior de Frenkel Frenkel's anterior ocular traumatic syndrome.

síndrome de Treacher-Collins, síndrome de Treacher-Collins-Franceschetti Treacher-Collins syndrome, Treacher-Collins-Franceschetti syndrome.

síndrome tricorrinofalángico trichorhinophalangeal syndrome.

síndrome de triple X triple X syndrome.

síndrome de trisomía trisomy syndrome.

síndrome de la trisomía 8 trisomy 8 syndrome.

síndrome de la trisomía 13 trisomy 13 syndrome.

síndrome de la trisomía 18 trisomy 18 syndrome.

síndrome de la trisomía 21 trisomy 21 syndrome.

síndrome de la trisomía 22 trisomy 22 syndrome.

síndrome de trituración crush syndrome.

síndrome de trombocitopenia y ausencia de radio (TAR) thrombocytopenia-absent radius (TAR) syndrome.

síndrome trombólico thrombosis syndrome.

síndrome de trombosis capsular capsular thrombosis syndrome.

síndrome de Trousseau Trousseau's syndrome.

síndrome de tumor del surco superior superior sulcus tumor syndrome.

síndrome del túnel carpiano carpal tunnel syndrome.

síndrome del túnel cubital cubital tunnel syndrome.

síndrome del túnel del tarso tarsal tunnel syndrome.

síndrome de Turcot Turcot syndrome.

síndrome de Turner Turner's syndrome.

síndrome de Turner masculino, síndrome de Turner del varón Turner's male syndrome.

síndrome de Ullrich Ullrich-Bonnevie syndrome.

síndrome de Uehlinger Uehlinger's syndrome.

síndrome de Unna-Thost Unna-Thost syndrome.

síndrome de Unverricht-Lunborg Unverricht-Lundborg syndrome.

síndrome de las uñas amarillas yellow nail syndrome.

síndrome uña-rótula nail-patella syndrome.

síndrome urémico hemolítico hemolytic uremic syndrome.

síndrome uretral urethral syndrome.

síndrome uretral agudo acute urethral syndrome.

síndrome de Usher Usher's syndrome.

síndrome uveocutáneo uveocutaneous syndrome.

síndrome uveoencefalítico uveo-encephalitic syndrome.

síndrome de vaciamiento rápido dumping syndrome.

síndrome de la vaina tendinosa tendon sheath syndrome.

síndrome de la válvula fláccida floppy valve syndrome.

síndrome de van Buchem van Buchem's syndrome.

síndrome de van der Hoeve van der Hoeve's syndrome.

síndrome vascular vascular syndrome.

síndrome vascular encefalotrigeminal, síndrome vascular encefalotrigémino encephalotgeminal vascular syndrome.

síndrome vasomotor de Friedmann Friedmann's vasomotor syndrome.

síndrome vasovagal vasovagal syndrome.

síndrome de la vena cava superior superior vena cava syndrome.

síndrome de la vena rolándica rolandic vein syndrome.

síndrome de Verner-Morrison Verner-Morrison syndrome.

síndrome de Vernet Vernet's syndrome.

síndrome de vérnix amarillo yellow vernix syndrome.

síndrome de Villaret Villaret's syndrome.

síndrome de Vogt Vogt's syndrome.

síndrome de Vogt-Koyanagi Vogt-Koyanagi syndrome.

síndrome de Vohwinkel Vohwinkel's syndrome.

síndrome de Waardenburg Waardenburg's syndrome.

síndrome de Wallenberg, síndrome de Wallemberg-Foix Wallemberg's syndrome.

síndrome de Ward-Romano Ward-Romano syndrome.

síndrome de Waterhouse-Friderichsen Waterhouse-Friderichsen syndrome.

síndrome WDHA WDHA syndrome.

síndrome de Weber Weber's syndrome.

síndrome de Weber-Christian Weber-Christian syndrome.

síndrome de Weber-Cockayne Weber-Cockayne syndrome.

síndrome de Weber-Dubler Weber-Dubler syndrome.

síndrome de Wegener Wegener's syndrome.

síndrome de Weil Weil's syndrome.

síndrome de Weil-Marchesani Weil-Marchesani syndrome.

síndrome de Weingarten Weingarten's syndrome.

síndrome de Werdnig-Hoffman Werdnig-Hoffmann syndrome.

síndrome de Wermer Wermer's syndrome.

síndrome de Werner Werner's syndrome, Werner syndrome.

síndrome de Wernicke Wernicke's syndrome.

síndrome de Wernicke-Korsakoff Wernicke-Korsakoff syndrome.

síndrome de West West's syndrome.

síndrome de Weyers-Thier Weyers-Thier syndrome.

síndrome WHDA WHDA syndrome.

síndrome de Widal Widal's syndrome.

síndrome de Willebrand Willebrand's syndrome.

síndrome de Williams Williams' syndrome.

síndrome de Williams-Campbell Williams-Campell's syndrome.

síndrome de Wilson Wilson's syndrome.

síndrome de Wilson-Mikity Wilson-Mikity syndrome.

síndrome de Winter Winter syndrome.

síndrome de Wiskott-Aldrich Wiskott-Aldrich syndrome.

síndrome de Wittmaack-Ekbon Wittmaack-Ekbon syndrome.

síndrome de Wolff-Parkinson-White Wolff-Parkinson-White syndrome.

síndrome de Wolfram Wolfram syndrome.

síndrome de Woringer-Kolopp Woringer-Kolopp syndrome.

síndrome de Wright Wright's syndrome.

síndrome de Wunderlich Wunderlich's syndrome.

síndrome del X frágil fragile X syndrome.

síndrome XXX XXX syndrome.

síndrome XXY XXY syndrome.

síndrome yeyunal jejunal syndrome.

síndrome de Zellweger Zellweger syndrome.

síndrome de Zieve Zieve's syndrome.

síndrome de Zinser-Cole-Engman Zinser-Cole-Engman syndrome.

síndrome de Zollinger-Ellison Zollinger-Ellison syndrome.

sindrómico, -ca *adj.* syndromic.

sindromología *f.* syndromology.

sinecología *f.* synechology.

sinecotomía *f.* synechotomy.

sinecótomo *m.* synechotome.

sinecrosis *f.* synecrosis.

sinencefalia *f.* synencephaly.

sinencéfalo *m.* synencephalus.

sinencefalocele *m.* synencephalocele.

sinequenterotomía *f.* synechenterotomy.

sinequia *f.* synechia.

sinequia anterior anterior synechia.

sinequia anterior periférica peripheral anterior synechia.

sinequia anterior total total anterior synechia.

sinequia anular annular synechia.

sinequia circular circular synechia.

sinequia pericárdica, sinequia del pericardio synechia pericardii.

sinequia posterior posterior synechia.

sinequia posterior total total posterior synechia.

sinequia total total synechia.

sinequia vulvar synechia vulvae.

sinéresis *f.* syneresis.

sinergético, -ca *adj.* synergetic.

sinergia *f.* synergy, synergia.

sinérgico, -ca *adj.* synergic.

sinergismo *m.* synergism.

sinergista *m.* synergist.

sinergista hipofisario pituitary synergist.

sinergístico, -ca *adj.* synergistic.

sinestesia *f.* synesthesia.

sinestesia álgica synesthesia algica.

sinestesia auditiva auditory synesthesia.

sinestesialgia *f.* synesthesialgia.

sinetión *m.* synaetion.

sineurosis *f.* synneurosis.

sinezesis *f.* synezesis.

sinfalangia *f.* symphalangia, symphalangy.

sinfalangismo *m.* symphalangism.

sinfiocéfalo *m.* symphyocephalus.

sinfiogenético, -ca *adj.* symphyogenetic.

sinfisectomía *f.* symphysiectomy.
sinfisial *adj.* symphyseal.
sinfísico, -ca *adj.* symphysic.
sinfisiectomía *f.* symphysiectomy.
sinfisiólisis *f.* symphysiolysis.
sinfisión *m.* symphysion.
sinfisiorrafia *f.* symphysiorrhaphy.
sinfisiotomía *f.* symphiseotomy, symphysiotomy.
sinfisiótomo *m.* symphiseotome, symphysiotome.
sínfisis *f.* symphysis.
 sinfisis cardíaca cardiac symphysis.
sinfisodactilia *f.* symphisodactylia, symphysodactyly.
singamia *f.* syngamy.
singamo, -ma *adj.* syngamous.
singeneico, -ca *adj.* syngeneic.
singenesioplastia *f.* syngenesioplasty.
singenesioplástico, -ca *adj.* syngenesioplastic.
singenesiotrasplante *m.* syngenesiotrasplantation.
singénesis *f.* syngenesis.
singénico, -ca *adj.* syngenic.
singnatia *f.* syngnathia.
singónico, -ca *adj.* syngonic.
singultación *f.* singultation.
singultoso, -sa *adj.* singultous.
sinicesis *f.* synizesis.
sinidrosis *f.* synidrosis.
sininjerto *m.* syngraft.
sinistral *adj.* sinistral.
sinistralidad *f.* sinistrality.
sinistraural *adj.* sinistraural.
sinistrocardia *f.* sinistrocardia.
sinistrocerebral *adj.* sinistrocerebral.
sinistrocular *adj.* left-eyed, sinistrocular.
sinistrocularidad *f.* sinistrocularity.
sinistrómano, -na *adj.* left-handed, sinistromanual.
sinistropedal *adj.* left-footed, sinistropedal.
sinistrotorsión *f.* sinistrotorsion.
sinneumónico, -ca *adj.* synpneumonic.
sinoatrial *adj.* sinoatrial.
sinoauricular *adj.* sinoauricular.
sinobronquitis *f.* sinobronchitis.
sinoca *f.* synocha.
sinocal *adj.* synochal.
sinocitotoxina *f.* synocytotoxin.
sinoespiral *adj.* sinospiral.
sinofridia *f.* synophridia.
sinofris *f.* synophris.
sinoftalmía *f.* synophthalmia, synophthalmus.
sinónimo, -ma *adj.* synonym.
 sinónimo objetivo objective synonym.
 sinónimo senior senior synonym.
 sinónimo subjetivo subjective synonym.
sinoniquia *f.* synonychia.
sinopsia *f.* synopsis, synopsy.
sinopsis *f.* synopsis, synopsy.
sinoptoscopio *m.* synoptoscope.
sinopulmonar *adj.* sinopulmonary.
sinorquidia *f.* synorchidism.
sinorquismo *m.* synorchism.
sinósqueo *m.* synoscheos.
sinosteología *f.* synosteology.
sinosteotomía *f.* synosteotomy.
sinostosis *f.* synostosis.
 sinostosis tribasilar tribasilar synostosis.
sinostósico, -ca *adj.* synostatic, synosteotic.
sinotia *f.* synotia.
sinoto *m.* synotus.
sinovectomía *f.* synovectomy.
sinovia *f.* synovia.

sinovial *adj.* synovial.
sinovialoma *m.* synovialoma.
sinovina *f.* synovin.
sinovio *m.* synovio.
sinovioblasto *m.* synovioblast.
sinovioma *m.* synovioma.
sinoviortesia *f.* sinoviorthese.
sinoviortesis *f.* synoviorthesis, synoviorthese.
sinoviosarcoma *m.* synoviosarcoma.
sinovíparo, -ra *adj.* synoviparous.
sinovitis *f.* synovitis.
 sinovitis bursal bursal synovitis.
 sinovitis filarial filarial synovitis.
 sinovitis nodular localizada localized nodular synovitis.
 sinovitis purulenta purulent synovitis.
 sinovitis seca dry synovitis, synovitis sicca.
 sinovitis serosa serous synovitis.
 sinovitis simple simple synovitis.
 sinovitis supurada suppurative synovitis.
 sinovitis tendinosa tendinous synovitis.
 sinovitis vaginal vaginal synovitis.
 sinovitis vellonodular pigmentada pigmented villonodular synovitis.
 sinovitis vellosa hemorrágica crónica chronic hemorrhagic villous synovitis.
 sinovitis de vibración, sinovitis por vibración vibration synovitis.
sinquesis *f.* synchesis.
sinquilia *f.* syncheilia, synchilia.
sinquiria *f.* synchiria.
sínquisis *f.* synchysis, synchesis.
 sinquisis centelleante synchysis scintillans.
sintáctico, -ca *adj.* syntactic.
sintaxis *f.* syntaxis.
sintenia *f.* synteny.
sinténico, -ca *adj.* syntenic.
sintenosis *f.* syntenosis.
sínter *m.* sinter.
sintéresis *f.* synteresis.
sinterético, -ca *adj.* synteretic.
sintérmico, -ca *adj.* synthermal.
sintescopio *m.* syntescope.
síntesis *f.* synthesis.
 síntesis de contigüidad synthesis of continuity.
 síntesis de enzima inducible inducible enzyme synthesis.
sintético, -ca *adj.* synthetic.
síntexis *f.* syntexis.
síntoma *m.* symptom.
 síntoma de abstinencia abstinence symptom.
 síntoma accesorio accessory symptom.
 síntoma accidental accidental symptom.
 síntoma de Anton Anton's symptom.
 síntoma aplazado delayed symptom.
 síntoma del arco iris, síntoma en arco iris rainbow symptom.
 síntoma asidente assident symptom.
 síntoma de Bárány Bárány's symptom.
 síntoma de barra cruzada de Fraenkel crossbar symptom of Fraenkel.
 síntoma de Baumès Baumès symptom.
 síntoma de Béhier-Hardy Béhier-Hardy symptom.
 síntoma de Bechterew Bechterew's symptom.
 síntoma de Bezold Bezold's symptom.
 síntoma de Bolognini Bolognini's symptom.
 síntoma de Bonhoeffer Bonhoeffer's symptom.
 síntoma de Brauch-Romberg Brauch-Romberg symptom.
 síntoma de Buerger Buerger's symptom.

 síntoma de Burghart Burghart's symptom.
 síntoma de Capgras Capgras symptom.
 síntoma característico characteristic symptom.
 síntoma de Cardarelli Cardarelli's symptom.
 síntoma cardinal cardinal symptom.
 síntoma de Castellani-Low Castellani-Low symptom.
 síntoma de Colliver Colliver's symptom.
 síntoma concomitante concomitant symptom.
 síntoma consecutivo consecutive symptom.
 síntoma constitucional constitutional symptom.
 síntoma de deficiencia deficiency symptom.
 síntoma de Demarquay Demarquay's symptom.
 síntoma diana target symptom.
 síntoma diferido delayed symptom.
 síntoma directo direct symptom.
 síntoma de disociación dissociation symptom.
 síntoma de Duroziez Duroziez's symptom.
 síntoma de encarcelación incarceration symptom.
 síntoma endotelial endothelial symptom.
 síntoma de Epstein Epstein's symptom.
 síntoma equívoco equivocal symptom.
 síntoma esofagosalival esophagosalivary symptom.
 síntoma estático static symptom.
 síntoma de Fischer Fischer's symptom.
 síntoma focal focal symptom.
 síntoma de Frenkel Frenkel's symptom.
 síntoma de Fröschel Fröschel's symptom.
 síntoma de Ganser Ganser's symptom.
 síntoma general constitutional symptom.
 síntoma de Goldthwait Goldthwait's symptom.
 síntoma de Gordon Gordon's symptom.
 síntoma de Griesinger Griesinger's symptom.
 síntoma de Haenel Haenel's symptom.
 síntoma del halo halo symptom.
 síntoma de Hochenegg Hochenegg's symptom.
 síntoma de Howship Howship's symptom.
 síntoma de incarceración incarceration symptom.
 síntoma indirecto indirect symptom.
 síntoma inducido induced symptom.
 síntoma de Jellinek Jellinek's symptom.
 síntoma de Jonas Jonas symptom.
 síntoma de Kérandel Kérandel's symptom.
 síntoma de Kocher Kocher's symptom.
 síntoma de Kussmaul Kussmaul's symptom.
 síntoma de Lade Lade's symptom.
 síntoma laberíntico labyrinthine symptom.
 síntoma de Liebreich Liebreich's symptom.
 síntoma local local symptom.
 síntoma de localización localizing symptom.
 síntoma de Magendie Magendie's symptom.
 síntoma objetivo objective symptom.
 síntoma de Oehler Oehler's symptom.
 síntoma orientador guiding symptom.
 síntoma pasivo passive symptom.
 síntoma patognomónico pathognomonic symptom.
 síntoma patognomónico negativo negative pathognomonic symptom.
 síntoma de Pel-Ebstein Pel-Ebstein symptom.
 síntoma de Prat Pratt's symptom.
 síntoma precursor, síntoma premonitor precursory symptom, premonitory symptom.

síntoma de presentación presenting symptom.

síntoma prodrómico prodromal symptom.

síntoma racional rational symptom.

síntoma reflejo reflex symptom.

síntoma de Remak Remak's symptom.

síntoma de retiro withdrawal symptom.

síntoma retrasado delayed symptom.

síntoma de Roger Roger's symptom.

síntoma de Romberg-Howship Romberg-Howship symptom.

síntoma señal signal symptom.

síntoma señal de Séguin Séguin's signal symptom.

síntoma de Simon Simon's symptom.

síntoma simpático sympathetic symptom.

síntoma de Sklowsky Sklowsky's symptom.

síntoma de Stellwag Stellwag's symptom.

síntoma de Sterlin Stierlin's symptom.

síntoma subjetivo subjective symptom.

síntoma de supresión withdrawal symptom.

síntoma de Tar Tar's symptom.

síntoma de Trendelenburg Trendelenburg's symptom.

síntoma de Trunecek Trunecek's symptom.

síntoma de vecindad neighborhood symptom.

síntoma de la ventana nasal nostril symptom.

síntoma de Wanner Wanner's symptom.

síntoma de Wartenberg Wartenberg's symptom.

síntoma de Weber Weber's symptom.

síntoma de Wernicke Wernicke's symptom.

síntoma de Westphal Westphal's symptom.

síntoma de Winterbottom Winterbottom's symptom.

sintomático, -ca *adj.* symptomatic.

sintomolítico, -ca *adj.* symptomatolytic, symptomolytic.

sintomatología *f.* symptomatology.

sintonía *f.* syntony.

sintónico, -ca *adj.* syntonic.

sintonina *f.* syntonin.

sintono, -na *adj.* syntone.

sintopia *f.* syntopia.

sintórax *m.* synthorax.

sintripsia *f.* syntripsis.

sintripsis *f.* syntripsis.

sintrofismo *m.* syntrophism.

sintrofoblasto *m.* syntrophoblast.

sintropía *f.* syntropy.

sintropía inversa inverse syntropy.

sintrópico, -ca *adj.* syntropic.

sinuitis *f.* sinuitis.

sinulosis *f.* synulosis.

sinulótico, -ca *adj.* synulotic.

sinuoso, -sa *adj.* sinuate, sinuous.

sinus sinus.

sinusal *adj.* sinusal.

sinusitis *f.* sinusitis.

sinusitis abscendante sinusitis abscendens.

sinusitis crónica chronic sinusitis.

sinusitis frontal frontal sinusitis.

sinusitis etmoidea ethmoid sinusitis.

sinusitis infecciosa del pavo infectious sinusitis of turkeys.

sinusoidal *adj.* sinusoidal.

sinusoidalización *f.* sinusoidalization.

sinusoide *m. y adj.* sinusoid.

sinusotomía *f.* sinusotomy.

sinuspiral *adj.* sinuspiral.

sinuventricular *adj.* sinoventricular, sinuventricular.

Siphunculina Siphunculina.

sirenomelia *f.* sirenomelia.

sirenomelo *m.* sirenomelus.

siriasis *f.* siriasis.

sirigmo *m.* syrigmus.

siringadenoma *m.* syringadenoma.

siringectomía *f.* syringectomy.

siringitis *f.* syringitis.

siringobulbia *f.* syringobulbia.

siringocele *m.* syringocele.

siringocistoadenoma *m.* syringocystadenoma.

siringocistoadenoma papilífero syringocystadenoma papilliferum.

siringocistoma *m.* syringocystoma.

siringoencefalia *f.* syringoencephalia.

siringoide *adj.* syringoid.

siringoma *m.* syringoma.

siringoma condroide chondroid syringoma.

siringomielia *f.* syringomyelia.

siringomielocele *m.* syringomyelocele.

siringotomía *f.* syringotomy.

siringótomo *m.* syringotome.

siruposo, -sa *adj.* syrupy.

sisarcosis *f.* syssarcosis.

sismoterapia *f.* sismotherapy.

sísomo *m.* syssomus.

sistáltico, -ca *adj.* systaltic.

sistema *m.* system.

sistema absorbente absorbent system.

sistema absoluto de unidades absolute system of units.

sistema activador reticular reticular activating system (RAS).

sistema amortiguador buffer system.

sistema APUD APUD system.

sistema de asociación association system.

sistema de aviso de hipoxia hypoxia warning system.

sistema Bertillon Bertillon system.

sistema cardiovascular cardiovascular system.

sistema cefalorraquídeo cerebrospinal system.

sistema cegesimal (CGS) centimeter-gram-second (CGS) system.

sistema centímetro-gramo-segundo (CGS) centimeter-gram-second (CGS) system.

sistema cinético kinetic system.

sistema circulatorio circulatory system.

sistema coloide colloid system.

sistema de conducción del corazón, sistema conductor del corazón conductor system of the heart.

sistema craneosacro craniosacral system.

sistema cromafín chromaffin system.

sistema de la dentina, sistema dentinal dentinal system.

sistema dérmico, sistema dermoide dermal system.

sistema digestivo digestive system.

sistema disperso disperse system.

sistema ecológico ecological system.

sistema endocrino endocrine system.

sistema no específico non-specific system.

sistema esquelético skeletal system.

sistema estático static system.

sistema estesiódico esthesiodic system.

sistema estomatognático stomatognathic system.

sistema extrapiramidal extrapyramidal motor system.

sistema fagocítico mononuclear (SFM) mononuclear phagocyte system (MPS).

sistema genital genital system.

sistema glandular glandular system.

sistema de grupos sanguíneos blood group system.

sistema de Havers, sistema haversiano Haversian system.

sistema hematopoyético, sistema hemopoyético hematopoietic system.

sistema heterogéneo heterogeneous system.

sistema de His-Tawara His-Tawara system.

sistema homogéneo homogeneous system.

sistema indicador indicator system.

sistema inmunitario, sistema inmunológico immune system.

sistema internacional de unidades (SI) international system of units.

sistema interofectivo interofective system.

sistema interrenal interrenal system.

sistema linfático lymphatic system.

sistema locomotor locomotor system.

sistema macrófago system of macrophages.

sistema masticatorio masticatory system.

sistema métrico metric system.

sistema metro-kilogramo-segundo (MKS) meter-kilogram-second (MKS) system.

sistema mononuclear fagocítico mononuclear phagocyte system.

sistema motor extrapiramidal extrapyramidal motor system.

sistema muscular muscular system.

sistema nervioso nervous system.

sistema nervioso autónomo autonomic nervous system.

sistema nervioso central central nervous system.

sistema nervioso involuntario involuntary nervous system.

sistema nervioso metamérico metameric nervous system.

sistema nervioso parasimpático parasympathetic nervous system.

sistema nervioso periférico sistema nervosum periphericum.

sistema nervioso simpático, sistema nervioso del tronco simpático sympathetic nervous system.

sistema nervioso vegetativo vegetative nervous system.

sistema nervioso visceral visceral nervous system.

sistema neuromuscular neuromuscular system.

sistema de nomenclatura de Linneo Linnaean system of nomenclature.

sistema oclusal occlusal system.

sistema oculomotor oculomotor system.

sistema de oxidación-reducción (O-R) oxidation-reduction (O-R) system.

sistema pedal pedal system.

sistema periódico periodic system.

sistema pie-libra-segundo foot-pound-second (FPS) system.

sistema piramidal pyramidal system.

sistema portal portal system.

sistema portal accesorio, sistema portal accesorio de Sappey accessory portal system of Sappey.

sistema presorreceptor pressoreceptor system.

sistema de la properdina properdin system.

sistema de proyección projection system.

sistema de Purkinje Purkinje system.

sistema redox redox system.

sistema renina-angiotensina renin-angiotensin system.

sistema reproductor reproductive system.

sistema respiratorio system respiratorium.

sistema reticular activador ascendente reticular activating system (RAS).
sistema reticuloendotelial reticuloendothelial system.
sistema de retroalimentación feedback system.
sistema sanguíneo vascular blood-vascular system.
sistema de segundas señales second signaling system.
sistema somestésico somesthetic system.
sistema T T system.
sistema tegumentario integumentary system.
sistema toracolumbar thoracolumbar system.
sistema urinario urinary system.
sistema urogenital urogenital system.
sistema vascular, sistema vascular sanguíneo vascular system.
sistema vasomotor vasomotor system.
sistema vegetativo vegetative nervous system.
sistema vertebral-basilar vertebral-basilar system.
sistematizado, -da *adj.* systematized.
sistematología *f.* systematology.
sistémico, -ca *adj.* systemic.
sistemoide *adj.* systemoid.
sístole *f.* systole.
sístole abortada aborted systole.
sístole alternada systole alternans.
sístole arterial arterial systole.
sístole auricular auricular systole.
sístole electromecánica electromechanical systole.
sístole extra extra systole.
sístole prematura premature systole.
sístole tardía late systole.
sístole ventricular ventricular systole.
sistolómetro *m.* systolometer.
sistrema *m.* systremma.
sitio *m.* site, situs.
sitio activo active site.
sitio alostérico allosteric site.
sitio de cambio switching site.
sitio frágil fragile site.
sitio privilegiados privileged site.
sitio receptor receptor site.
sitio de restricción restriction site.
sitio de segmentación cleavage site.
sitiofobia *f.* sitophobia.
sitiología *f.* sitiology.
sitioterapia *f.* sitotherapy.
sitiotropismo *m.* sitotropism.
sitofobia *f.* sitophobia.
sitiofobia *f.* sitophobia.
sitología *f.* sitology.
sitiología *f.* sitology.
sitoterapia *f.* sitotherapy.
sitioterapia *f.* sitotherapy.
sitotoxismo *m.* sitotoxism.
sitotropismo *m.* sitotropism.
sitiotropismo *m.* sitotropism.
situación *f.* situation.
situs situs, site.
situs inversus viscerum situs inversus viscerum.
situs perversus situs perversus.
situs psicoanalítica psychoanalytic site.
situs solitus situs solitus.
situs transversus situs transversus.
snare *m.* snare.
snare caliente, snare galvanocáustico galvanocaustic snare.
snare frío cold snare.

sobreactividad *f.* superactivity.
sobreagudo, -da *adj.* superacute.
sobrealimentación *f.* overfeeding, superalimentation.
sobrecarga *f.* overloading.
sobrecorrección *f.* overcorrection.
sobredeterminación *f.* overdetermination.
sobredosificación *f.* overdosage.
sobredosis *f.* overdose.
sobreexcitación *f.* superexcitation.
sobreextensión *f.* overextension.
sobrefatiga *f.* overstrain.
sobreingesta *f.* hyperingesta.
sobreingestión *f.* hyperingestion.
sobremordida *f.* overbite.
sobresalto *m.* startling.
socia parotidis socia parotidis.
sociología *f.* sociology.
sodemia *f.* sodemia.
sodio *m.* sodium.
sodoku *m.* sodoku.
sodomía *f.* sodomy.
sofisticación *f.* sophistication.
sofoco *m.* flush.
sokosho *m.* sokosho.
sol *m.* sol.
solar *adj.* solar.
solarium *m.* solarium.
solenoide *m.* solenoid.
solenoma *m.* solenoma.
solenoniquia *f.* solenonychia.
solidificación *f.* solidification.
sólido, -da *m. y adj.* solid.
solipsismo *m.* solipsism.
solitario, -ria *adj.* solitary.
solubilidad *f.* solubility.
soluble *adj.* soluble.
solución *f.* solution, solutio.
solum solum.
solutio solution, solutio.
soluto *m.* solute.
solvatación *f.* solvation.
solvato *m.* solvate.
solvólisis *f.* solvolysis.
soma *m.* soma.
somatalgia *f.* somatalgia.
somatestesia *f.* somatesthesia.
somatestésico, -ca *adj.* somatesthesic.
somático, -ca *adj.* somatic.
somatoesplácnico, -ca *adj.* somaticosplanchnic.
somaticovisceral *adj.* somaticovisceral.
somatista *m.* somatist.
somatización *f.* somatization.
somatoagnosia *f.* somatagnosia.
somatoceptor *m.* somatoceptor.
somatoderma *m.* somatoderm.
somatodermo *m.* somatoderm.
somatodídimo, -ma *m.* somatodidymus.
somatodimia *f.* somatodymia.
somatoesplácnico, -ca *adj.* somatosplanchcnic.
somatoesplacnopléurico, -ca *adj.* somatosplanchnopleuric.
somatoforme *adj.* somatoform.
somatogenesia *f.* somatogenesis.
somatogénesis *f.* somatogenesis.
somatogenético, -ca *adj.* somatogenetic.
somatogenia *f.* somatogenesis.
somatogénico, -ca *adj.* somatogenic.
somatograma *m.* somatogram.
somatoliberina *f.* somatoliberin.
somatología *f.* somatology.
somatomamotropina *f.* somatommamotropin.
somatomamotropina coriónica, somatomamotropina coriónica humana (HCS) cho-

rionic somatommamotropin, human chorionic somatommamotropin (HCS).
somatomegalia *f.* somatomegaly.
somatometría *f.* somatometry.
somatómico, -ca *adj.* somatomic.
somátomo *m.* somatome.
somatópago *m.* somatopagus.
somatopatía *f.* somatopathy.
somatopático, -ca *adj.* somatopathic.
somatopleura *f.* somatopleura, somatopleure.
somatopleural *adj.* somatopleural.
somatoprótesis *f.* somatoprosthetics.
somatopsíquico, -ca *adj.* somatopsychic.
somatoscopia *f.* somatoscopy.
somatosensorial *adj.* somatosensory.
somatosexual *adj.* somatosexual.
somatosquisis *f.* somatoschisis.
somatostatina *f.* somatostatin.
somatostatinoma *m.* somatostatinoma.
somatoterapia *f.* somatotherapy.
somatotipia *f.* somatotypy.
somatotipificación *f.* somatotyping.
somatotipo *m.* somatotype.
somatotipología *f.* somatotypology.
somatotonía *f.* somatotonia.
somatotopoagnosia *f.* somatotopagnosia, somatotopagnosis.
somatotopia *f.* somatotopy.
somatotópico, -ca *adj.* somatotopic.
somatotridimo *m.* somatotridymus.
somatotrofo *m.* somatotroph.
somatotrófico, -ca *adj.* somatotrophic.
somatotrópico, -ca *adj.* somatotropic.
sombra *f.* shadow.
sombra acústica acoustic shadow.
sombra mamaria breast shadow.
sombreado *m.* shadow-casting.
somita *m.* somite.
somita occipital occipital somite.
somite *m.* somite.
somito *m.* somite.
somnifaciente *adj.* somnifacient.
somnífero, -ra *adj.* somniferous, somnific.
somnífugo, -ga *adj.* somnifugous.
somnilocuencia *f.* somniloquence.
somnilocuo, -cua *m., f.* somniloquist.
somniloquia *f.* sleeptalking, somniloquy.
somniloquismo *m.* somniloquism.
somnípata *m., f.* somnipathist.
somnipatía *f.* somnipathy.
somnocinematografía *f.* somnocinematography.
somnocinematógrafo *m.* somnocinematograph.
somnolencia *f.* somnolence, somnolency, somnolentia.
somnoliento, -ta *adj.* somnolent.
somnus sleep.
somosfera, somósfera *f.* somosphere.
sonambulismo *m.* sleepwalking, somnambulance, somnambulism.
sonámbulo, -la *m., f.* sleepwalker, somnambulist.
sonda *f.* probe, sound, tube.
sonda de Abbott-Miller Abbott-Miller tube.
sonda de Abbott-Rawson Abbott-Rawson tube.
sonda de ácido nucleico nucleic acid probe.
sonda de alambre wire probe.
sonda de alimentación feeding tube.
sonda de alimentación yeyunal jejunal feeding tube.
sonda de Anel Anel's probe.
sonda articulada de Davis Davis interlocking sound.

sonda de autorretención self-retaining catheter.
sonda de Bellocq Bellocq's sound.
sonda de Béniqué Béniqué's sound.
sonda de Blakemore-Sengstaken Blakemore-Sengstaken tube.
sonda de Bouchut Bouchut's tube.
sonda de Bowman Bowman's sound.
sonda de cálculos stone-searcher.
sonda de Cantor Cantor tube.
sonda de Campbell Campbell sound.
sonda de Carrel Carrel tube.
sonda de Celestin Celestin tube.
sonda de Devine Devine's tube.
sonda de Diamond Diamond's tube.
sonda de drenaje drainage tube.
sonda duodenal duodenal tube.
sonda de Durham Durham tube.
sonda de empiema empyema tube.
sonda endobronquial endobronchial tube.
sonda endotraqueal endotracheal tube.
sonda esofágica esophageal sound, esophageal tube, probang.
sonda esofágica de cerdas bristle probe, horse hair probe.
sonda esofágica de esfera ball probe.
sonda esofágica de torunda sponge probe.
sonda de Ewald Ewald tube.
sonda fibróptica fiberoptic.
sonda de flujo sanguíneo blood flow probe.
sonda de Foley Foley catheter, Foley's catheter.
sonda forrada dressed tube.
sonda gástrica stomach tube.
sonda gástrica de Rehfuss Rehfuss stomach tube.
sonda génica gene probe.
sonda de Guisez Guisez's sound.
sonda de Harris Harris tube.
sonda de intubación intubation tube.
sonda de Jewett Jewett sound.
sonda de Killian Killian's tube.
sonda lagrimal lacrimal probe, lacrimal sound.
sonda de Le Fort Le Fort sound.
sonda de Levin Levin tube.
sonda de luz múltiple multiple-lumen tube.
sonda de magnesita meerschaum probe.
sonda de McCollum McCollum tube.
sonda de McCrea McCrea sound.
sonda de Mercier Mercier's sound.
sonda de Miller-Abbott Miller-Abbott tube.
sonda nasogástrica nasogastric tube.
sonda nasotraqueal nasotracheal tube.
sonda de nefrostomía nephrostomy tube.
sonda de Neuber Neuber's tube.
sonda de O'Dwyer O'Dwyer's tube.
sonda de ojo eyed probe.
sonda de Paul-Mixter Paul-Mixter tube.
sonda periodontal periodontal probe.
sonda prostática prostatic catheter.
sonda de proyectil, sonda para proyectiles bullet probe.
sonda radiactiva radioactive probe.
sonda rectal rectal tube.
sonda de Rehfuss Rehfuss tube.
sonda roma blunt probe.
sonda de Ryle Ryle's tube.
sonda de saco pocket probe.
sonda de Sengstaken-Blakemore Sengstaken-Blakemore tube.
sonda de Shiner Shiner's tube.
sonda de Swan-Ganz Swan-Ganz catheter.
sonda en T T tube.
sonda de tambor drum probe.
sonda de taponamiento tampon tube.

sonda de tijeras scissor probe.
sonda de toracostomía thoracostomy tube.
sonda uretral urethral sound.
sonda uterina uterine sound.
sonda uterina de Simpson Simpson uterine sound.
sonda uterina de Sims Sims uterine sound.
sonda de Van Buren Van Buren sound.
sonda vertebrada vertebrated probe.
sonda viral viral probe.
sonda de Voltolini Voltolini's tube.
sonda de Wangensteen Wangensteen tube.
sonda de Winternitz Winternitz's sound.
sonda yeyunal nasojejunal tube.
sondaje femenino *m.* female catheterization.
sondaje gástrico *m.* gastric intubation.
sondaje masculino *m.* male catheterization.
sondar *v.* probe, sound.
sondeo *m.* probing, sounding.
sonicación *f.* sonication.
sonicado, -da *adj.* sonicate.
sonicar *v.* sonicate.
sónico, -ca *adj.* sonic.
sonido *m.* sound, sonitus.
sonido de aleteo flapping sound.
sonido auscultatorio auscultatory sound.
sonido blanco white sound.
sonido de botella bottle sound.
sonido broncovesicular bronchovesicular sound.
sonido cardíaco heart sound.
sonido de crepitación xifiesternal xiphisternal crunching sound.
sonido entótico entotic sound.
sonido fisiológico physiological sound.
sonido de fricción friction sound.
sonido de fricción de Beatty-Bright Beatty-Bright friction sound.
sonido de fuelle bellows sound.
sonido hipocrático hippocratic sound.
sonido de Korotkoff Korotkoff sound.
sonido metálico metallic sound.
sonido muscular muscle sound.
sonido de pavo real peacock sound.
sonido de percusión percussion sound.
sonido pulmonar pulmonic sound.
sonido respiratorio respiratory sound.
sonido respiratorio anfórico amphoric breath sound.
sonido respiratorio traqueal tracheal breath sound.
sonido respiratorio vesicular vesicular breath sound.
sonífero *m.* sonifer.
sonificación *f.* sonification.
sonificador *m.* sonifier.
sonitus sonitus.
sonografía *f.* sonography.
sonográfico, -ca *adj.* sonographic.
sonógrafo *m.* sonograph.
sonograma *m.* sonogram.
sonolucidez *f.* sonolucency.
sonolúcido, -da *adj.* sonolucent.
sonomotor, -ra *adj.* sonomotor.
sonoquímica *f.* sonochemistry.
sonoro, -ra *adj.* sonorous.
soplete *m.* blowpipe.
soplo *m.* murmur, souffle.
soplo accidental accidental murmur.
soplo anémico anemic murmur.
soplo aórtico aortic murmur.
soplo arterial arterial murmur.
soplo auriculosistólico atriosystolic murmur.
soplo de Austin Flint Austin Flint murmur.
soplo de Cabot-Locke Cabot-Locke murmur.

soplo cardíaco cardiac souffle, heart murmur.
soplo cardiopulmonar, soplo cardiorrespiratorio cardiopulmonary murmur, cardiorespiratory murmur.
soplo de Carey-Coombs Carey-Coombs' murmur.
soplo cerebral brain murmur.
soplo de Cole-Cecil Cole-Cecil murmur.
soplo continuo continuous murmur.
soplo de Coombs Coombs murmur.
soplo creciente, soplo in crescendo crescendo murmur.
soplo de Cruveilhier-Baumgarten Cruveilhier-Baumgarten murmur.
soplo diastólico diastolic murmur.
soplo diastólico apical apical diastolic souffle.
soplo diastólico basal basal diastolic souffle.
soplo diastólico inicial early diastolic murmur.
soplo diastólico tardío late diastolic murmur.
soplo dinámico dynamic murmur.
soplo de Duroziez Duroziez's murmur.
soplo endocárdico endocardial murmur.
soplo esplénico splenic souffle.
soplo de estenosis, soplo estenótico stenosal murmur.
soplo exocardíaco, soplo extracardíaco exocardial murmur, extracardiac murmur.
soplo de eyección ejection murmur, ejection souffle.
soplo fetal fetal souffle.
soplo fisiológico physiological murmur, physiological souffle.
soplo de Flint Flint's murmur.
soplo en forma de rombo diamond-shaped murmur.
soplo de Fräntzel Fräntzel's murmur.
soplo de fuelle bellows murmur.
soplo funcional functional murmur.
soplo funicular funic souffle, funicular souffle.
soplo de gaviota sea gull murmur.
soplo de Gibson Gibson's murmur.
soplo de Graham-Steell Graham-Steell's murmur.
soplo hemático hemic murmur.
soplo de Hodgkin-Key Hodgkin-Key murmur.
soplo holosistólico holosystolic murmur.
soplo inocente innocent murmur.
soplo inorgánico inorganic murmur.
soplo mamario mammary souffle.
soplo de maquinaria machinery murmur.
soplo mesodiastólico mid-diastolic murmur.
soplo mitral mitral murmur, mitral souffle.
soplo de monja nun's murmur.
soplo muscular muscular murmur.
soplo musical musical murmur.
soplo orgánico organic murmur.
soplo pansistólico pansystolic murmur.
soplo pericárdico pericardial murmur.
soplo placentario placental bruit, placental souffle.
soplo pleuropericárdico pleuropericardial murmur.
soplo prediastólico prediastolic murmur.
soplo presistólico presystolic murmur.
soplo pulmonar pulmonary murmur.
soplo de la punta apex murmur.
soplo de regurgitación, soplo regurgitante regurgitant murmur.
soplo de regurgitación aórtica aortic regurgitant murmur.
soplo en reloj de arena hourglass murmur.

soplo respiratorio respiratory murmur.
soplo de Roger Roger's murmur.
soplo en rueda hidráulica water wheel murmur.
soplo en rueda de molino mill wheel murmur.
soplo sistólico systolic murmur.
soplo sistólico apical tardío late apical systolic murmur.
soplo de Steell Steell's murmur.
soplo de Still Still's murmur.
soplo en sube y baja seesaw murmur.
soplo telesistólico late systolic murmur.
soplo tricuspídeo tricuspid murmur, tricuspid souffle.
soplo umbilical umbilical souffle.
soplo uterino uterine souffle.
soplo de vaivén, soplo en vaivén to-and-fro murmur.
soplo vascular vascular murmur.
soplo venoso venous hum, venous murmur.
soplo vesicular vesicular murmur.
sopor *m.* drowsiness, sopor.
soporífero, -ra *adj.* soporiferous.
soporífico, -ca *m. y adj.* soporific.
soporoso, -sa *adj.* soporose, soporous.
soporte *m.* assistant, holder, rest, support, sustentaculum.
soporte auxiliar auxiliary assistant.
soporte intermedio intermediate assistant.
soporte móvil para el brazo mobile arm support.
soporte múltiple multiple assistant.
soporte de oro laminar foil holder, foil assistant.
soporte del peso weight holder.
soporte de precisión precision rest.
soporte primario primary assistant.
soporte secundario secondary assistant.
soporte del tendón rotuliano con ajuste supracondíleo (STR/SC) patellar tendon-bearing supracondular socket (PTB/SC).
soporte del tendón rotuliano con ajuste supracondíleo y suprarrotuliano (STRSC/SR) patellar tendon-bearing supracondular-suprapatellar socket (PTBSC/SPI).
soporte terminal terminal assistant.
soporte vital life support.
soporte vital avanzado pediátrico (SVAP) pediatric advanced life support (PALS).
soporte vital básico basic life support.
soporte vital cardíaco avanzado (SVCA) advanced cardiac life support (ACLS).
sorbefaciente *adj.* sorbefacient.
sorbente *adj.* sorbent.
sorber *v.* sorb.
sordera *f.* deafness.
sordera de Alexander Alexander's deafness.
sordera de alta frecuencia high frequency deafness, high frequency hearing loss.
sordera del calderero boilermaker's deafness.
sordera central central deafness.
sordera cerebral, sordera cortical cerebral deafness, cortical deafness.
sordera de conducción conduction hearing loss, conductive deafness.
sordera funcional functional deafness.
sordera inducida por el ruido noise-induced hearing loss.
sordera industrial industrial deafness.
sordera laberíntica labyrinthine deafness.
sordera mesencefálica midbrain deafness.
sordera de Mondini Mondini deafness.
sordera musical music deafness.
sordera nerviosa, sordera neural nerve deafness, neural deafness.

sordera neurosensorial nerve deafness, neural deafness.
sordera ocupacional occupational deafness.
sordera orgánica organic deafness.
sordera de las palabras word deafness.
sordera palúdica malarial deafness.
sordera perceptiva perceptive deafness.
sordera poslingual postlingual deafness.
sordera prelingual prelingual deafness.
sordera psicogénica psychogenic deafness.
sordera retrococlear retrocochlear deafness.
sordera de Scheibe Scheibe's deafness.
sordera sensorioneural, sordera sensitivo-nerviosa sensorioneural deafness.
sordera de tonos, sordera para los tonos tone deafness.
sordera de tonos bajos low tone deafness.
sordera traumática acústica, sordera por traumatismo acústico acoustic trauma deafness.
sordera unilateral hemianacusia.
sordera verbal word deafness.
sordes *f.* sordes.
sordo, -da *adj.* deaf.
sordomudez *f.* deaf-mutism, surdimutitas.
sordomudez endémica endemic deaf-mutism.
sordomudo, -da *adj.* deaf-mute, surdimute.
sororiación *f.* sororiation.
Spaniopsis Spaniopsis.
Sparganum Sparganum.
spasmus spasmus.
spin *m.* spin.
spin nuclear nuclear spin.
spinnbarkeit *m.* spinnbarkeit.
Spirometra Spirometra.
splay *m.* splay.
splenium *m.* splenium.
splenium del cuerpo calloso splenium corporis callosi.
Sporozoa Sporozoa.
Staphylococcus Staphylococcus.
status *m.* status.
status anginosus status anginosus.
status dysmyelinisatus status dysmyelinisatus.
status dysraphicus status dysraphicus.
status epilepticus status epilepticus.
status lacunaris lacunar state, status lacunaris.
estado marmóreo status marmoratus.
status spongiosus status spongiosus.
status typhosus status typhosus.
Stegomyia Stegomyia.
sternum sternum.
stock *m.* stock.
stoke *m.* stoke.
Stomoxys Stomoxys.
strapping *m.* strapping.
Streptobacillus Streptobacillus.
Streptococcaceae Streptococcaceae.
Streptococcus Streptococcus.
Streptomyces Streptomyces.
Streptomycetaceae Streptomycetaceae.
stria stria.
stromuhr *m.* stromuhr.
Strongyloidea Strongyloidea.
Strongyloides Strongyloides.
Strophantus Strophantus.
subabdominal *adj.* subabdominal.
subabdominoperitoneal *adj.* subabdominoperitoneal.
subacetabular *adj.* subacetabular.
subacromial *adj.* subacromial.
subagudo, -da *adj.* subacute.
subamortiguamiento *m.* underdamping.
subanal *adj.* subanal.

subaórtico, -ca *adj.* subaortic.
subapical *adj.* subapical.
subaponeurótico, -ca *adj.* subaponeurotic.
subaracnoideo, -a *adj.* subarachnoid.
subareolar *adj.* subareolar.
subarqueado, -da *adj.* subarcuate.
subastragalino, -na *adj.* subastragalar.
subastringente *adj.* subastringent.
subatloideo, -a *adj.* subatloidean.
subatómico, -ca *adj.* subatomic.
subaural *adj.* subaural.
subauricular *adj.* subauricular.
subaxial *adj.* subaxial.
subaxil *adj.* subaxial.
subaxilar *adj.* subaxillary.
subbasal *adj.* subbasal.
subbásico, -ca *adj.* subbasal.
subbraquicéfalo, -la *adj.* subbrachycephalic.
subcalcáreo, -a *adj.* subcalcareous.
subcalcarino, -na *adj.* subcalcarine.
subcalloso, -sa *adj.* subcallosal.
subcapsular *adj.* subcapsular.
subcapsuloperióstico, -ca *adj.* subcapsuloperiosteal.
subcardinal *adj.* subcardinal.
subcartilaginoso, -sa *adj.* subcartilaginous.
subcecal *adj.* subcecal.
subcelular *adj.* subcellular.
subcentral *adj.* subcentral.
subcepción *f.* subception.
subcigomático, -ca *adj.* subzygomatic.
subcircunvolución *f.* subgyrus.
subcisura *f.* subfissure.
subclase *f.* subclass.
subclavio, -via *adj.* subclavian.
subclínico, -ca *adj.* subclinical.
subcolateral *adj.* subcollateral.
subcondral *adj.* subchondral.
subconjuntival *adj.* subconjunctival.
subconjuntivitis *f.* subconjunctivitis.
subconsciencia *f.* subconsciousness.
subconsciente *m.* subconscious.
subcontinuo, -nua *adj.* subcontinuous.
subcoracoideo, -a *adj.* subcoracoid.
subcordal *adj.* subchordal.
subcoriónico, -ca *adj.* subchorionic.
subcoroidal *adj.* subchoroidal.
subcoroideo, -a *adj.* subchoroidal.
subcortical *adj.* subcortical.
subcostal *adj.* subcostal.
subcostalgia *f.* subcostalgia.
subcraneal *adj.* subcranial.
subcrepitación *f.* subcrepitation.
subcrepitante *adj.* subcrepitant.
subcrónico, -ca *adj.* subchronic.
subcultivar *v.* subculture.
subcultivo *m.* subculture.
subcultura *f.* subculture.
subcurativo, -va *adj.* subcurative.
subcutáneo, -a *adj.* subcutaneous.
subcuticular *adj.* subcuticular.
subcutis *m.* subcutis.
subdeltoideo, -a *adj.* subdeltoid.
subdental *adj.* subdental.
subdentario, -ria *adj.* subdental.
subdérmico, -ca *adj.* subdermic.
subdiafragmático, -ca *adj.* subdiaphragmatic.
subdorsal *adj.* subdorsal.
subducción *f.* subduction.
subducir *v.* subduct.
subdural *adj.* subdural.
subecuador *m.* infrabulge.
subendimario, -ria *adj.* subendymal.
subendocardíaco, -ca *adj.* subendocardial.

subendocárdico, -ca *adj.* subendocardial.
subendotelial *adj.* subendothelial.
subendotelio *m.* subendothelium.
subependimario, -ria *adj.* subependymal.
subependimoma *m.* subependymoma.
subepidérmico, -ca *adj.* subepidermal, sub-epidermic.
subepiglótico, -ca *adj.* subepiglottic.
subepitelial *adj.* subepithelial.
suberosis *f.* suberosis.
subescafocefalia *f.* subscaphocephaly.
subescapular *adj.* subscapular.
subescleral *adj.* subscleral.
subesclerótico, -ca *adj.* subsclerotic.
subespecialidad *f.* subspeciality.
subespecie *f.* subspecies.
subespinal *m.* subspinale.
subespinoso, -sa *adj.* subspinous.
subesplenio, -nia *adj.* subsplenial.
subestándar *adj.* substandard.
subesternal *adj.* substernal.
subesternomastoideo, -a *adj.* substernomas-toid.
subestimulación con marcapaso *f.* under-drive pacing.
subestructura *f.* substructure.
  subestructura de implante implant sub-structure.
  subestructura de implantes protésicos im-plant denture substructure.
subexcitar *v.* subexcite.
subextensibilidad *f.* subextensibility.
subfamilia *f.* subfamily.
subfaríngeo, -a *adj.* subpharyngeal.
subfascial *adj.* subfascial.
subfecundidad *f.* subfertility.
subfecundo, -da *adj.* subfertile.
subfertilidad *f.* subfertility.
subfilo *m.* subphylum.
subflavo, -va *adj.* subflavous.
subfoliar *adj.* subfoliar.
subfolio *m.* subfolium.
subfolium *m.* subfolium.
subfrénico, -ca *adj.* subphrenic.
subgaleal *adj.* subgaleal.
subgemal *adj.* subgemal.
subgénero *m.* subgenus.
subgerminal *adj.* subgerminal.
subgingival *adj.* subgingival.
subglenoideo, -a *adj.* subglenoid.
subglósico, -ca *adj.* subglossal.
subglositis *f.* subglossitis.
subgloso, -sa *adj.* subglossal.
subglótico, -ca *adj.* subglottic.
subgranular *adj.* subgranular.
subgranuloso, -sa *adj.* subgranular.
subgrundación *f.* subgrundation.
subhepático, -ca *adj.* subhepatic.
subhialoideo, -a *adj.* subhyaloid.
subhioideo, -a *adj.* subhyoid.
subhumeral *adj.* subhumeral.
subictérico, -ca *adj.* subicteric.
subicular *adj.* subicular.
subículo *m.* subiculum.
subiculum *m.* subiculum.
subida de leche *f.* let-down.
subíleon *m.* subilium.
subilíaco, -ca *adj.* subiliac.
subilion *m.* subilium.
subimbibicional *adj.* subimbibitional.
subinfección *f.* subinfection.
subinflamación *f.* subinflammation.
subinflamatorio, -ria *adj.* subinflammatory.
subíntimo, -a *adj.* subintimal.
subintrancia *f.* subintrance.

subintrante *adj.* subintrant.
subinvolución *f.* subinvolution.
  subinvolución uterina, subinvolución del útero uterine subinvolution.
subjetivo, -va *adj.* subjective.
subjetoscopio *m.* subjectoscope.
sublación *f.* sublation, sublatio.
sublatio sublatio.
sublesional *adj.* sublesional.
subletal *adj.* sublethal.
subleucemia *f.* subleukemia.
sublimación *f.* sublimation.
sublimado, -da *m. y adj.* sublimate.
  sublimado corrosivo corrosive sublimate.
sublimar *v.* sublimate.
subliminal *adj.* subliminal.
sublinfemia *f.* sublymphemia.
sublingual *adj.* sublingual.
sublingüitis *f.* sublinguitis.
sublobulillar *adj.* sublobar.
sublóbulo *m.* sublobe.
sublogro *m.* underachievement.
sublumbar *adj.* sublumbar.
subluminal *adj.* subluminal.
subluxación *f.* subluxation.
  subluxación congénita de cadera congeni-tal subluxation of the hip.
  subluxación del hombro shoulder sublux-ation.
  subluxación de Volkmann Volkmann's sub-luxation.
subluxar *v.* subluxate.
submamario, -ria *adj.* submammary.
submandibular *adj.* submandibular.
submarginal *adj.* submarginal.
submaxilar *adj.* submaxillary.
submaxilaritis *f.* submaxillaritis.
submeatal *adj.* submeatal.
submedial *adj.* submedial.
submediano, -na *adj.* submedian.
submembranoso, -sa *adj.* submembranous.
submentoniano, -na *adj.* submental.
submentovértice *m.* submentovertex.
submersión *f.* submersion.
submetacéntrico, -ca *adj.* submetacentric.
submicroscópico, -ca *adj.* submicroscopic, submicroscopal.
submordida *f.* underbite.
submorfo, -fa *adj.* submorphous.
submucosa *f.* submucosa.
submucoso, -sa *adj.* submucosal, submucous.
subnadante *adj.* subnatant.
subnasal *adj.* subnasal.
subnasión *m.* subnasion.
subneural *adj.* subneural.
subnotocordal *adj.* subnotochordal.
subnúcleo *m.* subnucleus.
subnutrición *f.* subnutrition, undernutrition.
suboccipital *adj.* suboccipital.
suboccipitobregmático, -ca *adj.* suboccipi-tobregmatic.
subóptimo, -ma *adj.* suboptimal.
suborbitario, -ria *adj.* suborbital.
suborden *m.* suborder.
suboxidación *f.* suboxidation.
subóxido *m.* suboxide.
subpapilar *adj.* subpapillary.
subpapular *adj.* subpapular.
subparalítico, -ca *adj.* subparalytic.
subparietal *adj.* subparietal.
subpatelar *adj.* subpatellar.
subpectoral *adj.* subpectoral.
subpelviperitoneal *adj.* subpelviperitoneal.
subpericardíaco, -ca *adj.* subpericardial.
subpericárdico, -ca *adj.* subpericardial.

subperióstico, -ca *adj.* subperiosteal.
subperiostiocapsular *adj.* subperiosteocap-sular.
subperitoneal *adj.* subperitoneal.
subperitoneoabdominal *adj.* subperitoneo-abdominal.
subperitoneopélvico, -ca *adj.* subperito-neopelvic.
subpetroso, -sa *adj.* subpetrosal.
subphylum subphylum.
subpial *adj.* subpial.
subpiramidal *adj.* subpyramidal.
subpituitarismo *m.* subpituitarism.
subplatina *f.* substage.
subpleural *adj.* subpleural.
subpléxico, -ca *adj.* subplexal.
subprepucial *adj.* subpreputial.
subproducto *m.* byproduct.
subpúbico, -ca *adj.* subpubic.
subpubiano, -na *adj.* subpubic.
subpulmonar *adj.* subpulmonary.
subpulpal *adj.* subpulpal.
subraquicefálico, -ca *adj.* subbrachycephalic.
subrectal *adj.* subrectal.
subretinal *adj.* subretinal.
subretiniano, -na *adj.* subretinal.
subrotuliano, -na *adj.* subpatellar.
subsartorial *adj.* subsartorial.
subserosa *f.* subserosa.
subseroso, -sa *adj.* subserosal, subserous.
subsibilante *adj.* subsibilant.
subsidencia *f.* subsidence.
subsilviano, -na *adj.* subsylvian.
subsistema *m.* subsystem.
subsistencia *f.* subsistence.
subsónico, -ca *adj.* subsonic.
subsultus tendinum subsultus tendinum.
  subsultus tendinum tendinum clonus sub-sultus tendinum tendinum clonus.
  subsultus tendinum tendinum tendinum subsultus tendinum tendinum tendinum.
subsurco *m.* subsulcus.
subtalámico, -ca *adj.* subthalamic.
subtálamo *m.* subthalamus.
subtalar *adj.* subtalar.
subtarsal *adj.* subtarsal.
subtarsiano, -na *adj.* subtarsal.
subtegumentario, -ria *adj.* subtegumental.
subtemporal *adj.* subtemporal.
subtenial *adj.* subtenial.
subtentorial *adj.* subtentorial.
subterminal *adj.* subterminal.
subtetánico, -ca *adj.* subtetanic.
subtimpánico, -ca *adj.* subtympanic.
subtiroideo *m.* subthyroideus.
subtiroidismo *m.* subthyroidism.
subtotal *adj.* subtotal.
subtrapecial *adj.* subtrapezial.
subtribu *f.* subtribe.
subtrocantéreo, -a *adj.* subtrochanteric.
subtrocanteriano, -na *adj.* subtrochanteric.
subtrocantérico, -ca *adj.* subtrochanteric.
subtroclear *adj.* subtrochlear.
subtuberal *adj.* subtuberal.
subumbilical *adj.* subumbilical.
subungueal *adj.* subungual.
subungular *adj.* subungual.
suburetral *adj.* suburethral.
subvaginal *adj.* subvaginal.
subvalvular *adj.* subvalvular.
subventilación *f.* underventilation.
subvertebral *adj.* subvertebral.
subvitaminosis *f.* subvitaminosis.
subvítreo, -a *adj.* subvitrinal.
subvolución *f.* subvolution.

subyacente *adj.* subjacent.
subyugal *adj.* subjugal.
subzonal *adj.* subzonal.
sucagogo, -ga *m. y adj.* succagogue.
succenturiado, -da *adj.* succenturiate.
succinoso, -sa *adj.* succinous.
succión *f.* suction.
  succión postusiva post-tussive suction.
  succión del pulgar thumbsucking.
  succión de Wangesteen Wangesteen suction.
succionar *v.* suck.
succus succus.
sucedáneo *m.* succedaneum.
sucedáneo, -a *adj.* succedaneous.
sucorrea *f.* succorrhea.
sucrosemia *f.* sucrosemia.
sucrosuria *f.* sucrosuria.
suctorial *adj.* suctorial.
sucus sucus.
sucusión *f.* succussion.
  sucusión hipocrática hippocratic succussion.
sudación *f.* sudation.
sudamen *f.* sudamen.
sudaminal *adj.* sudaminal.
sudán *m.* sudan.
sudanofilia *f.* sudanophilia.
sudanófilo, -la *adj.* sudanophilic, sudanophilous.
sudanófobo, -ba *adj.* sudanophobic.
sudar *v.* sweat.
sudario *m.* sudarium.
sudograma *m.* sudogram.
sudomotor, -ra *adj.* sudomotor.
sudoqueratosis *f.* sudorikeratosis.
sudor *m.* sweat, sudor.
  sudor colicuativo colliquative sweat.
  sudor nocturno night sweat.
  sudor rojo red sweat.
  sudor sanguíneo bloody sweat, sudor cruentus, sudor sanguineus.
  sudor urinoso sudor urinosus.
sudoral *adj.* sudoral.
sudoresis *f.* sudoresis.
sudorífero, -ra *adj.* sudoriferous.
sudorífico, -ca *adj.* sudorific.
sudoríparo, -ra *adj.* sudoriparous.
sudorómetro *m.* sudorometer.
sudorrea *f.* sudorrhea.
suelo *m.* floor, solum.
sueño¹ *m.* dream.
  sueño de ansiedad, sueño ansioso anxiety dream.
  sueño de castigo punishment dream.
  sueño diurno day dream.
sueño² *m.* sleep.
  sueño activo active sleep.
  sueño congelado frozen sleep.
  sueño creciente, sueño en crescendo crescendo sleep.
  sueño crepuscular twilight sleep.
  sueño desincronizado desynchronized sleep.
  sueño eléctrico electric sleep.
  sueño electroterapéutico electrotherapeutic sleep.
  sueño hipnótico hypnotic sleep.
  sueño invernal winter sleep.
  sueño ligero, sueño liviano light sleep.
  sueño de movimientos oculares rápidos (MOR) rapid eye movement sleep, REM sleep.
  sueño NREM NREM sleep.
  sueño de onda rápida fast wave sleep.
  sueño ortodoxo orthodox sleep.
  sueño paradójico paradoxical sleep.
  sueño paroxístico paroxysmal sleep.
  sueño patológico pathologic sleep.

sueño profundo deep sleep.
sueño prolongado prolonged sleep.
sueño que no es de movimientos oculares rápidos non-rapid eye movement sleep.
sueño rápido fast sleep.
sueño REM REM sleep.
sueño sincronizado synchronized sleep.
sueño con sueños dreaming sleep.
sueño S S sleep.
sueño templo temple sleep.
suero *m.* whey, serum.
  suero anticomplementario anticomplementary serum.
  suero antilinfocitario, suero antilinfocítico (SAL) antilymphocyte serum (ALS).
  suero antiplaquetario antiplatelet serum.
  suero combinado, suero sanguíneo combinado pooled serum, pooled blood serum.
  suero de convalecencia, suero de convaleciente convalescent serum.
  suero de convaleciente de sarampión measles convalescent serum.
  suero de Coombs Coombs serum.
  suero de determinación de grupos sanguíneos blood grouping serum.
  suero extraño foreign serum.
  suero hiperinmune hyperimmune serum.
  suero humano human serum.
  suero humano desecado dried human serum.
  suero humano líquido liquid human serum.
  suero humano normal normal human serum.
  suero inmune immune serum.
  suero inmune de escarlatina humana human scarlet-fever immune serum.
  suero inmune de sarampión humano human measles immune serum.
  suero inmune de tos ferina humana human pertussis immune serum.
  suero muscular muscle serum.
  suero normal normal serum.
  suero salado salted serum.
  suero sanguíneo blood serum.
  suero tirolítico, suero tirotóxico thyrotoxic serum.
  suero contra la tos ferina antipertussis serum.
suficiencia *f.* competence.
  suficiencia embrionaria embryonic competence.
  suficiencia inmunológica immunological competence.
sufrimiento *m.* distress, suffering.
  sufrimiento fetal fetal distress.
sufusión *f.* suffusion.
sugestibilidad *f.* suggestibility.
sugestión *f.* suggestion.
  sugestión hipnótica hypnotic suggestion.
  sugestión poshipnótica posthypnotic suggestion.
sugestionabilidad *f.* suggestibility.
sugestionable *adj.* suggestible.
sugestivo, -va *adj.* suggestive.
suicida¹ *m., f.* suicide.
suicida² *adj.* suicidal.
suicidio *m.* suicide.
suicidología *f.* suicidology.
suipestifer *m.* suipestifer.
sujeción *f.* restraint.
  sujeción química chemical restraint.
sujetar *v.* subject.
sujeto *m.* subject.
sukkla pakla *f.* sukkla pakla.
sulciforme *adj.* sulciform.
sulculus sulculus.

sulcus sulcus.
sulfahemoglobina *f.* sulfhemoglobin.
sulfahemoglobinemia *f.* sulfhemoglobinemia.
sulfólisis *f.* sulfolysis.
sulfametahemoglobina *f.* sulfamethemoglobin.
sulfamida *f.* sulfa drug, sulfonamide.
sulfamidemia *f.* sulfonamidemia.
sulfamidocolia *f.* sulfonamidocholia.
sulfamidoterapia *f.* sulfonamidotherapy.
sulfamiduria *f.* sulfonamiduria.
sulfanuria *f.* sulfanuria.
sulfatemia *f.* sulfatemia.
sulfatidosis *f.* sulfatidosis.
sulfohemoglobina *f.* sulfhemoglobin.
sulfohemoglobinemia *f.* sulfhemoglobinemia.
sulfometahemoglobina *f.* sulfmethemoglobin.
sulfomucina *f.* sulfomucin.
sulfoxismo *m.* sulfoxism.
sumación *f.* summation.
  sumación de estímulos summation of stimuli.
  sumación temporal temporal summation.
sumergido *m.* submerged.
sumersión *f.* submersion.
  sumersión de la raíz root submersion.
supedania *f.* suppedania.
superabducción *f.* superabduction.
superacidez *f.* superacidity.
superácido, -da *adj.* superacid.
superacromial *adj.* superacromial.
superactividad *f.* superactivity.
superagudo, -da *adj.* superacute.
superalcalinidad *f.* superalkalinity.
superalimentación *f.* superalimentation.
superanal *adj.* superanal.
superaural *m.* superaurale.
supercentral *adj.* supercentral.
superciliar *adj.* superciliary.
supercilio *m.* supercilium.
supercilium supercilium.
superclase *f.* superclass.
superdicrótico, -ca *adj.* superdicrotic.
superdistensión *f.* superdistention.
superducción *f.* superduction.
superesfenoidal *adj.* supersphenoid.
superestructura *f.* superstructure.
  superestructura de implante, superestructura de prótesis implantada implant superstructure, implant denture superstructure.
superexcitación *f.* superexcitation.
superextendido, -da *adj.* superextended.
superextensión *f.* superextension.
superfamilia *f.* superfamily.
superfecundación *f.* superfecundation.
superfetación *f.* superfetation.
superfibrinación *f.* superfibrination.
superficial *adj.* superficial, superficialis.
superficie *f.* surface.
superflexion *f.* superflexion.
superfunción *f.* superfunction.
superfusión *f.* superfusion.
supergraso, -sa *adj.* superfatted.
superimpregnación *f.* superimpregnation.
superinducir *v.* superinduce.
superinfección *f.* superinfection.
superinvolución *f.* superinvolution.
superior *adj.* superior.
superlactación *f.* superlactation.
superligamen *m.* superligamen.
supermaxilar¹ *adj.* supermaxilla.
supermaxilar² *adj.* supermaxillary.
supermedial *adj.* supermedial.
supermediano, -na *adj.* supermedial.
supermotilidad *f.* supermotility.
supermovilidad *f.* supermotility.

supernadante *adj.* supernatant.
supernumerario, -ria *adj.* supernumerary.
supernutrición *f.* supernutrition.
superoccipital *adj.* superoccipital.
superolateral *adj.* superolateral.
superovulación *f.* superovulation.
superparasitismo *m.* superparasitism.
superparásito *m.* superparasite.
superpetroso, -sa *adj.* superpetrosal.
superpigmentación *f.* superpigmentation.
superposición *f.* overlap, oversampling, superposition.
   superposición horizontal horizontal overlap.
   superposición vertical vertical overlap.
superregeneración *f.* super-regeneration.
superrotuliano, -na *adj.* supergenual.
supersaturar *v.* supersaturate.
supersecreción *f.* supersecretion.
supersensibilidad *f.* supersensitivity.
   supersensibilidad por desuso disuse supersensitivity.
supersesibilización *f.* supersensitization.
supersónica *f.* supersonics.
supersónico, -ca *adj.* supersonic.
supertensión *f.* supertension.
supervascularización *f.* supervascularization.
supervención *f.* supervention.
supervenosidad *f.* supervenosity.
superversión *f.* superversion.
supervirulento, -ta *adj.* supervirulent.
supervisión *f.* supervision.
supervitaminosis *f.* supervitaminosis.
supervivencia *f.* survival.
supervoltaje *m.* supervoltage.
superyacente *adj.* superjacent.
superyó *m.* superego.
supinación *f.* supination.
   supinación del antebrazo supination of the forearm.
   supinación del pie supination of the foot.
supinador *m.* supinator.
supinar *v.* supinate.
supino, -na *adj.* supine.
suplementario, -ria *adj.* supplemental.
suplente *m.* surrogate.
supraacromial *adj.* supra-acromial.
supraamigdalino, -na *adj.* supratonsillar.
supraanal *adj.* supra-anal.
supraauricular *adj.* supra-auricular.
supraaxilar *adj.* supra-axillary.
suprabucal *adj.* suprabuccal.
supracardinal *adj.* supracardinal.
supracerebeloso, -sa *adj.* supracerebellar.
supracerebral *adj.* supracerebral.
supraciliar *adj.* supraciliary.
supraclavicular *adj.* supraclavicular, supraclavicularis.
supraclavicularis major supraclavicularis major.
supraclusión *f.* supraclusion.
supracondíleo, -a *adj.* supracondylar, supracondyloid.
supracoroideo, -a *adj.* suprachoroid.
supracoroides *f.* suprachoroidea.
supracostal *adj.* supracostal.
supracotiloideo, -a *adj.* supracotyloid.
supracraneal *adj.* supracranial.
supracrestal *adj.* supracristal.
supradiafragmático, -ca *adj.* supradiaphragmatic.
supraducción *f.* supraduction.
supraecuatorial *adj.* suprabulge.
supraepicondíleo, -a *adj.* supraepicondylar.
supraepitroclear *adj.* supraepitrochlear.
supraepitrócleo, -a *adj.* supraepitrochlear.

supraescapular *adj.* suprascapular.
supraesclerótico, -ca *adj.* suprascleral.
supraespinal *adj.* supraspinal.
supraespinoso, -sa *adj.* supraspinous.
supraestapedial *adj.* suprastapedial.
supraesternal *adj.* suprasternal.
suprafarmacológico, -ca *adj.* suprapharmacologic.
suprafisiológico, -ca *adj.* supraphysiologic, supraphysiological.
supraglenoideo, -a *adj.* supraglenoid.
supraglótico, -ca *adj.* supraglottic.
suprahepático, -ca *adj.* suprahepatic.
suprahioideo, -a *adj.* suprahyoid.
suprainguinal *adj.* suprainguinal.
supraintestinal *adj.* supraintestinal.
supraliminal *adj.* supraliminal.
supralumbar *adj.* supralumbar.
supramaleolar *adj.* supramalleolar.
supramamario, -ria *adj.* supramammary.
supramandibular *adj.* supramandibular.
supramarginal *adj.* supramarginal.
supramastoideo, -a *adj.* supramastoid.
supramaxilar¹ *m.* supramaxilla.
supramaxilar² *adj.* supramaxillary.
supramáximo, -ma *adj.* supramaximal.
suprameático, -ca *adj.* suprameatal.
supramentale *n.* supramentale.
supramentoniano, -na *adj.* supramental.
supranasal *adj.* supranasal.
supraneural *adj.* supraneural.
supranormal *adj.* supranormal.
supranuclear *adj.* supranuclear.
supraoccipital *adj.* supraoccipital.
supraoclusión *f.* supraocclusion.
supraocular *adj.* supraocular.
supraóptimo, -ma *adj.* supraoptimal.
supraorbitario, -ria *adj.* supraorbital.
suprapatelar *adj.* suprapatellar.
suprapelviano, -na *adj.* suprapelvic.
suprapélvico, -ca *adj.* suprapelvic.
suprapontino, -na *adj.* suprapontine.
suprapúbico, -ca *adj.* suprapubic.
suprarrenal *adj.* adrenal, suprarenal.
suprarrenalectomía *f.* suprarenalectomy.
suprarrenalemia *f.* suprarenalemia.
suprarrenalismo *m.* suprarenalism.
suprarrenalopatía *f.* suprarenalopathy.
suprarrenogénico, -ca *adj.* suprarenogenic.
suprarrenoma *m.* suprarenoma.
suprarrenopatía *f.* suprarenopathy.
suprarrenotrópico, -ca *adj.* suprarenotropic.
suprarrenotropismo *m.* suprarenotropism.
suprarrotuliano, -na *adj.* suprapatellar.
suprascapular *adj.* suprascapular.
supraselar *adj.* suprasellar.
supraseptal *adj.* supraseptal.
suprasilviano, -na *adj.* suprasylvian.
suprasinfisario, -ria *adj.* suprasymphysary.
suprasónica *f.* suprasonics.
supraspinal *adj.* supraspinal.
supraspinoso, -sa *adj.* supraspinous.
suprasternal *adj.* suprasternal.
supratemporal *adj.* supratemporal.
supratentorial *adj.* supratentorial.
supratimpánico, -ca *adj.* supratympanic.
supratonsilar *adj.* supratonsillar.
supratorácico, -ca *adj.* suprathoracic.
supratroclear *adj.* supratrochlear.
supraumbilical *adj.* supraumbilical.
supravaginal *adj.* supravaginal.
supravalvar *adj.* supravalvar.
supravalvular *adj.* supravalvular.
supraventricular *adj.* supraventricular.
supravergencia *f.* supravergence.

supraversión *f.* supraversion.
supravital *adj.* supravital.
supraxifoideo, -a *adj.* supraxiphoid.
supresión *f.* suppression.
   supresión del indicador de referencia referential index deletion.
   supresión de la menstruación suppressed menstruation.
   supresión de la sobreconducción overdrive suppression.
supresor, -ra *m. y adj.* suppressant.
supuración *f.* suppuration.
   supuración alveolodental alveolodental suppuration.
supurante *m. y adj.* suppurant.
supurar *v.* suppurate.
supurativo, -va *adj.* suppurative.
sura *f.* sura.
sural *adj.* sural, suralis.
surcado, -da *adj.* sulcate.
surcamiento *m.* sulcation.
surco *m.* furrow, groove, sulcus.
sursanura *f.* sursanure.
sursunducción *f.* sursumduction.
sursunvergencia *f.* sursumvergence.
sursunversión *f.* sursumversion.
susceptibilidad *f.* susceptibility.
   susceptibilidad genética genetic susceptibility.
susceptible *adj.* susceptible.
suscitar *v.* suscitate.
suspenopsia *f.* suspenopsia.
suspensiómetro *m.* suspensiometer.
suspensión *f.* suspension.
suspensoide *m.* suspensoid.
suspensorio, -ria *m. y adj.* suspensory.
suspiro *m.* sigh.
sustancia *f.* substance, substantia.
sustentacular *adj.* sustentacular.
sustentáculo *m.* sustentaculum.
sustentaculum sustentaculum.
sustitución *f.* replacement, substitution.
   sustitución articular total total joint replacement.
   sustitución de cadera hip replacement.
   sustitución de estímulos stimulus substitution.
   sustitución reptante del hueso creeping substitution of bone.
   sustitución de rodilla knee replacement.
   sustitución de síntomas symptom substitution.
   sustitución total de la cadera total hip replacement.
sustitutivo, -va *m., f. y adj.* substitutive.
sustituto, -ta *m., f.* substitute.
   sustituto materno mother substitute.
   sustituto plasmático plasma substitute.
   sustituto de sangre blood substitute.
   sustituto de volumen volume substitute.
sustituyente *m.* substituent.
susto *m.* fright.
sustracción *f.* substraction.
   sustracción energética energy substraction.
   sustracción híbrida hybrid substraction.
   sustracción temporal temporal substraction.
sustrato *m.* substrate, substratum.
susurro *m.* susurrus.
   susurro auricular susurrus aurium.
sutika *f.* sutika.
sutura¹ *f.* suture, sutura.
   sutura anatómica anatomical suture.
sutura² *f.* suture.
   sutura absorbible absorbable suture, absorbable surgical suture.

sutura acolchada quilted suture.
sutura de afrontamiento, sutura de aproximación approximation suture.
sutura de Albert Albert's suture.
sutura de aposición apposition suture.
sutura de Appolito Appolito's suture.
sutura armónica harmonic suture.
sutura en asa interrupted suture.
sutura atraumática atraumatic suture.
sutura bastarda bastard suture.
sutura de Bell Bell's suture.
sutura de Billroth button suture.
sutura en bolsa de tabaco purse-string suture.
sutura de botón, sutura en botón button suture.
sutura de Bozeman button suture.
sutura en brida bridle suture.
sutura de Bunnell Bunnell's suture.
sutura de cadena, sutura en cadena chain suture.
sutura calada shotted suture.
sutura de catgut catgut suture.
sutura circular circular suture.
sutura de coaptación coaptation suture.
sutura de colchonero mattress suture.
sutura de colchonero en ángulo recto right-angle mattress suture.
sutura compuesta compound suture, quilled suture.
sutura de Connell Connell's suture.
sutura continua continuous suture.
sutura continua corrida continuous running suture.
sutura de cuña y surco wedge-and-groove suture.
sutura de Cushing Cushing's suture.
sutura de Czerny Czerny's suture.
sutura de Czerny-Lembert Czerny-Lembert suture.
sutura demorada delayed suture.
sutura dentada dentate suture, sutura dentata.
sutura diferida delayed suture.
sutura de doble botón double-button suture.
sutura de doble brazo doubly armed suture.
sutura de Doyen lock-stitch suture.

sutura de Dupuytren Dupuytren's suture.
sutura emplumada compound suture, quilled suture.
sutura enterrada buried suture.
sutura ensortijada figure-of-8 suture.
sutura espiral, sutura en espiral spiral suture.
sutura de eversión everting suture.
sutura de Faden Faden's suture.
sutura falsa false suture.
sutura en festón lock-stitch suture.
sutura en forma de 8 figure-of-8 suture.
sutura de Frost Frost's suture.
sutura de Gaillard-Arlt Gaillard-Arlt suture.
sutura de Gély Gély's suture.
sutura de Gould Gould's suture.
sutura de guantero glover's suture.
sutura de Gussenbauer Gussenbauer's suture.
sutura de Halsted Halsted's suture.
sutura hemostática hemostatic suture.
sutura hendida shotted suture.
sutura horizontal de colchonero horizontal mattress suture.
sutura implantada implanted suture.
sutura incluida buried suture.
sutura ininterrumpida uninterrumpted suture.
sutura interrumpida interrupted suture.
sutura intradérmica intradermic suture.
sutura intradérmica de colchonero intradermal matress suture.
sutura de inversión inverting suture.
sutura en jareta purse-string suture.
sutura de Jobert de Lamballe Jobert de Lamballe's suture.
sutura de labio leporino harelip suture.
sutura de Le Dentu Le Dentu's suture.
sutura de Le Fort, sutura de Lejars Le Fort's suture.
sutura de lejos y de cerca far-and-near suture.
sutura de Lembert Lembert suture.
sutura de lengüeta y surco plastic suture.
sutura de manta blanket suture.
sutura metálica wire suture.
sutura de nervio nerve suture.

sutura no absorbible, sutura quirúrgica no absorbible non-absorbable surgical suture.
sutura no interrumpida uninterrupted suture.
sutura notha sutura notha.
sutura en ocho figure-of-8 suture.
sutura de Pancoast Pancoast's suture.
sutura de Paré Pare's suture.
sutura de Parker-Kerr Parker-Kerr suture.
sutura de peletero furrier's suture.
sutura plana suture plana.
sutura por planos plane suture.
sutura plástica plastic suture.
sutura preseccional presection suture.
sutura previa al corte presection suture.
sutura primaria primary suture.
sutura profunda buried suture.
sutura de puntos en asa interrupted suture.
sutura a punto pasado, sutura de punto pasado lock-stitch suture.
sutura de puntos separados interrupted suture.
sutura de puntos en u interrupted suture.
sutura quirúrgica surgical suture.
sutura de relajación relaxation suture.
sutura de retención retention suture.
sutura secundaria secondary suture.
sutura sepultada buried suture.
sutura de Sims Sims' suture.
sutura con soporte bolster suture.
sutura subcuticular subcuticular suture.
sutura superficial superficial suture.
sutura de tensión tension suture.
sutura de transfixión transfixion suture.
sutura de tripa de gusano de seda silkworm gut suture.
sutura vertical de colchonero end-on matress suture.
sutura de zapatero cobbler's suture.
suturación *f.* suturation.
sutural *adj.* sutural.
suturar *v.* stitch.
suturectomía *f.* suturectomy.
Symphoromyia Symphoromyia.
symplex symplex.
sympus sympus.
syncretio syncretio.

T t

tabaco *m.* tobacco.
tabacosis *f.* tabacosis.
tabánidos *m.* tabanid.
tabanka *m.* tabanka.
tábano *m.* gadfly, horsefly, warblefly.
tabaquera anatómica *f.* anatomic snuffbox, anatomical snuffbox, anatomist's snuffbox.
tabaquismo *m.* tabacism, tabagism.
tabardillo *m.* tabardillo.
tabefacción *f.* tabes.
tabes *f.* tabes.
  tabes cerebral cerebral tabes.
  tabes cervical cervical tabes.
  tabes diabética tabes diabetica.
  tabes dorsal tabes dorsalis.
  tabes ergótica tabes ergotica.
  tabes escrofulosa tabes mesenterica.
  tabes espasmódica tabes spasmodica.
  tabes espinal tabes spinalis.
  tabes familiar Friedreich's tabes.
  tabes de Friedreich Friedreich's tabes.
  tabes hereditaria Friedreich's tabes.
  tabes infantil tabes infantum.
  tabes mesaraica tabes mesaraica.
  tabes mesentérica tabes mesenterica.
  tabes periférica peripheral tabes.
  tabes raquídea tabes dorsalis.
  tabes superior cervical tabes.
tabescencia *f.* tabescence.
tabético, -ca *adj.* tabetic.
tabicado, -da *adj.* septate.
tábico, -ca *adj.* tabic.
tabificación *f.* tabification.
tabique *m.* partition, septum.
tabla *f.* table, tabula.
  tabla de Aub-Dubois Aub-Dubois table.
  tabla de colores de Reuss Reuss' color table.
  tabla de colores de Stilling Stilling color table.
  tabla de contingencia contingency table.
  tabla de crecimiento de Tanner Tanner growth table.
  tabla de Mendéleiev Mendeleiev table.
  tabla de mortalidad, tabla de mortalidad demográfica demographic life table.
  tabla periódica periodic table.
  tabla de pies footboard.
  tabla de supervivencia cohort life table, life table.
  tabla de tratamiento rotocinético rotokinetic treatment table.
tablatura *f.* tablature.
tablero de ángulo *m.* angle board.
tableta *f.* tablet.
  tableta de acción prolongada prolonged action tablet.
  tableta de acción repetida repeat action tablet.
  tableta de acción sostenida sustained action tablet.

tableta bucal buccal tablet.
tableta comprimida compressed tablet.
tableta con cubierta entérica enteric coated tablet.
tableta distribuidora dispensing tablet.
tableta hipodérmica hypodermic tablet.
tableta de preparación dispensing tablet.
tableta sublingual sublingual tablet.
tableta triturada triturate tablet.
taboparálisis *f.* taboparalysis.
taboparesis *f.* taboparesis.
tabú *m.* taboo, tabu.
tabula *f.* tabula.
  tabula rasa tabula rasa.
tabulación sistemática *f.* systematic tabulation.
tabular *adj.* tabular.
tacografía *f.* tachography.
tacógrafo *m.* tachograph.
tacograma *m.* tachography.
tacómetro *m.* tachometer.
tacón *m.* heel.
tacticidad *f.* tacticity.
táctico, -ca *adj.* tactic.
táctil *adj.* tactual, tactile.
tactismo *m.* tropism.
tacto *m.* touch, tactus.
  tacto abdominal abdominal touch.
  tacto doble double touch.
  tacto erudito tactus eruditus.
  tacto experimentado tactus expertus.
  tacto mantenido constant touch.
  tacto real royal touch.
  tacto rectal rectal touch.
  tacto vaginal vaginal touch.
  tacto vesical vesical touch.
tactómetro *m.* tactometer.
taedium vitae taedium vitae.
Taenia Taenia.
taenia *f.* taenia.
taeniola *f.* taeniola.
tafofilia *f.* taphophilia.
taheño, -ña *adj.* ginger, red-haired, red-headed.
Taijin kyofusho *m.* Taijin kyofusho.
tajeño, -ña *adj.* ginger, red-haired, red-headed.
talalgia *f.* talalgia.
talamencefálico, -ca *adj.* thalamencephalic.
talamencéfalo *m.* thalamencephalon.
talámico, -ca *adj.* thalamic.
tálamo *m.* thalamus.
talamocortical *adj.* thalamocortical.
talamoencefálico, -ca *adj.* thalamencephalic.
talamoencéfalo *m.* thalamencephalon.
talamolenticular *adj.* thalamolenticular.
talamomamilar *adj.* thalamomillary.
talamotegmental *adj.* thalamotegmental.
talamotomía *f.* thalamotomy.
  talamotomía anterior anterior thalamotomy.
  talamotomía dorsomedial dorsomedial thalamotomy.

talar *adj.* talar.
talasemia *f.* thalassemia.
  talasemia beta beta thalassemia.
  talasemia beta-delta beta-delta thalassemia.
  talasemia de células falciformes sickle cell thalassemia.
  talasemia delta delta thalassemia.
  talasemia drepanocítica sickle cell thalassemia.
  talasemia F F thalassemia.
  talasemia de hemoglobina S hemoglobin S-thalassemia.
  talasemia intermedia thalassemia intermedia.
  talasemia de Lepore Lepore thalassemia.
  talasemia mayor major thalassemia.
  talasemia menor minor thalassemia.
talasofobia *f.* thalassophobia.
talasoposia *f.* thalassoposia.
talasoterapia *f.* thalassotherapy.
talcosis *f.* talcosis.
  talcosis pulmonar pulmonary talcosis.
taliotoxicosis *f.* thallitoxicosis, thallotoxicosis.
talipédico, -ca *adj.* talipedic.
talipedo, -da *adj.* taliped.
talipes talipes.
  talipes arcuato talipes arcuatus.
  talipes calcáneo talipes calcaneus.
  talipes calcaneovalgo talipes calcaneovalgus.
  talipes calcaneovaro talipes calcaneovarus.
  talipes cavo talipes cavus.
  talipes cavovalgo talipes cavovalgus.
  talipes equino talipes equinus.
  talipes equinovalgo talipes equinovalgus.
  talipes equinovaro talipes equinovarus.
  talipes plano talipes planus.
  talipes planovalgo talipes planovalgus.
  talipes plantar talipes plantaris.
  talipes transversoplano talipes transversoplanus.
  talipes valgo talipes valgus.
  talipes varo talipes varus.
talla *f.* height, stature.
  talla baja short stature.
tallador de amalgama *m.* amalgam carver.
talle *m.* waist.
tallo *m.* stalk.
  tallo abdominal abdominal stalk.
  tallo corporal body stalk.
  tallo óptico optic stalk.
  tallo ventral belly stalk.
  tallo vitelino yolk stalk.
talocalcáneo, -a *adj.* talocalcaneal, talocalcanean.
talocrural *adj.* talocrural.
taloescafoideo, -a *adj.* taloscaphoid.
talofibular *adj.* talofibular.
talón *m.* heel, talus.
  talón anterior anterior heel.
  talón doloroso painful heel.

talón de footing jogger's heel.
talón gonocócico gonorrheal heel.
talón de jugador de baloncesto basketball heel.
talón negro black heel.
talón de policía policeman's heel.
talón prominente prominent heel.
talón de Thomas Thomas heel.
talonavicular *adj.* talonavicular.
talónide *m.* talonid.
taloperoneal *adj.* talofibular.
taloperoneo, -a *adj.* talofibular.
talotibial *adj.* talotibial.
talotoxicosis *f.* thallitoxicosis.
talposis *f.* thalposis.
talpótico, -ca *adj.* thalpotic.
talus talus.
tama *f.* tama.
tambalearse *v.* wobble, stagger.
tambor¹ *m.* tambour.
tambor² *m.* eardrum.
tamiz *m.* sieve.
  tamiz molecular molecular sieve.
tamización *f.* sieving.
tamizar *v.* strain.
tampón¹ *m.* buffer.
  tampón de bicarbonato bicarbonate buffer.
  tampón de cacodilato cacodylate buffer.
  tampón de fosfato phosphate buffer.
  tampón de proteínas protein buffer.
  tampón sanguíneo blood buffer.
  tampón TRIS TRIS buffer.
  tampón de veronal veronal buffer.
tampón *m.* sponge, tampon.
  tampón de Corner Corner's tampon.
  tampón menstrual menstrual sponge.
tamuria *f.* thamuria.
tanatobiológico, -ca *adj.* thanatobiologic.
tanatocronología *f.* thanatochronology.
tanatofídico, -ca *adj.* thanatophidial.
tanatofilia *f.* thanatophilia.
tanatofobia *f.* thanatophobia.
tanatofórico, -ca *adj.* thanatophoric.
tanatognomónico, -ca *adj.* thanatognomonic.
tanatoide *adj.* thanatoid.
tanatología *f.* thanatology.
tanatomanía *f.* thanatomania.
tanatómetro *m.* thanatometer.
tanatopsia *f.* thanatopsy.
tanatoquimia *f.* thanatochemistry.
tánatos *m.* thanatos.
tanatosis *f.* thanatosis.
tangencialidad *f.* tangentiality.
tangorreceptor *m.* tangoreceptor.
tanicito *m.* tanycyte.
tanifonía *f.* tanyphonia.
taninación *f.* tannic acid treatment.
tanotopsia *f.* thanotopsia.
taón *m.* taon.
tapeinocefalia *f.* tapeinocephaly, tapinocephaly.
tapeinocefálico, -ca *adj.* tapeinocephalic, tapinocephalic.
tapetal *adj.* tapetal.
tapetocoroideo, -a *adj.* tapetochoroidal.
tapetorretiniano, -na *adj.* tapetoretinal.
tapetorretinopatía *f.* tapetoretinopathy.
tapetum tapetum.
tapinocefalia *f.* tapinocephaly.
tapinocefálico, -ca *adj.* tapinocephalic.
tapiroide *adj.* tapiroid.
tapón¹ *m.* plug.
  tapón de cerumen cerumen plug.
  tapón de Dittrich Dittrich's plug.

tapón de Ecker Ecker's plug.
tapón epitelial epithelial plug.
tapón graso de Imlach Imlach's fat plug.
tapón de Imlach Imlach's fat plug.
tapón mucoso mucous plug.
tapón mucoso cervical mucous plug.
tapón de Traube Traube's plug.
tapón² *m.* pledget, tampon.
  tapón de Corner Corner's tampon.
taponador¹ *m.* plugger.
  taponador de acción retrógada back-action plugger.
  taponador de amalgama amalgam plugger.
  taponador automático automatic plugger.
  taponador de chapa de oro foil plugger.
  taponador de oro gold plugger.
  taponador de pie foot plugger.
  taponador de reversa reverse plugger.
taponador² *m.* packer.
taponamiento *m.* pack, packing, tamponade.
  taponamiento cardíaco cardiac tamponade.
  taponamiento cardíaco crónico chronic tamponade.
  taponamiento del corazón heart tamponade.
  taponamiento crónico chronic tamponade.
  taponamiento esofagogástrico esophagogastric tamponade.
  taponamiento faríngeo throat pack.
  taponamiento con globo balloon tamponade.
  taponamiento de Mikulicz Mikulicz pack.
  taponamiento nasal nasal packing.
  taponamiento pericárdico pericardial tamponade.
  taponamiento periodontal periodontal pack.
  taponamiento de Rose cardiac tamponade.
taponar *v.* tampon.
tapotage *m.* tapotage.
tapotement *m.* tapotement.
taquialimentación *f.* tachyalimentation.
taquiarritmia *f.* tachyarrhythmia.
  taquiarritmia auricular atrial flutter, auricular flutter.
taquiauxesia *f.* tachyauxesis.
taquiauxesis *f.* tachyauxesis.
taquicardia *f.* tachycardia.
  taquicardia auricular atrial tachycardia.
  taquicardia auriculoventricular atrioventricular tachycardia, auriculoventricular tachycardia.
  taquicardia caótica auricular atrial chaotic tachycardia, chaotic atrial tachycardia.
  taquicardia doble double tachycardia.
  taquicardia ectópica ectopic tachycardia.
  taquicardia esencial essential tachycardia.
  taquicardia estrumosa y exoftálmica tachycardia strumosa exophthalmica.
  taquicardia fetal fetal tachycardia.
  taquicardia en franja de puntas tachycardia torsades de pointes.
  taquicardia de Gallavardin Gallavardin's tachycardia.
  taquicardia idiojuncional accelerated idiojunctional rhythm.
  taquicardia intranodal atrioventricular node reentrant tachycardia.
  taquicardia nodal nodal tachycardia.
  taquicardia nodal auriculoventricular atrioventricular nodal tachycardia.
  taquicardia nodal paroxística paroxysmal nodal tachycardia.
  taquicardia ortostática orthostatic tachycardia.

  taquicardia paroxística paroxysmal tachycardia.
  taquicardia paroxística auricular paroxysmal atrial tachycardia.
  taquicardia paroxística ventricular paroxysmal ventricular tachycardia.
  taquicardia refleja reflex tachycardia.
  taquicardia en salvas tachycardia en salves.
  taquicardia sinusal sinus tachycardia.
  taquicardia supraventricular (TSV) supraventricular tachycardia (SVT).
  taquicardia de la unión junctional tachycardia.
  taquicardia ventricular ventricular tachycardia.
  taquicardia ventricular bidireccional bidirectional ventricular tachycardia.
taquicárdico, -ca *adj.* tachycardiac, tachycardic.
taquidisritmia *f.* tachydysrhythmia.
taquifagia *f.* tachyphagia.
taquifilaxia *f.* tachyphylaxia.
taquifilaxis *f.* tachyphylaxis.
taquifrasia *f.* tachyphrasia.
taquifrenia *f.* tachyphrenia.
taquigastria *f.* tachygastria.
taquigénesis *f.* tachygenesis.
taquilalia *f.* tachylalia.
taquimarcapasos *m.* tachypacing.
taquímetro *m.* tachymeter.
taquipnea *f.* tachypnea.
  taquipnea nerviosa nervous tachypnea.
  taquipnea transitoria transient tachypnea.
taquipragia *f.* tachypragia.
taquipsiquia *f.* tachyphrenia.
taquirritmia *f.* tachyrhythmia.
taquisinecia *f.* tachyphylasis.
taquisíntesis *f.* tachysynthesis.
taquisistolia *f.* tachysystole.
  taquisistolia auricular atrial flutter, auricular flutter.
taquistestesia *f.* tachistesthesia.
taquistoscopio *m.* tachistoscope.
taquitropismo *m.* tachytrophism.
taquiurgia *f.* tachypragia.
taquizoíto *m.* tachyzoite.
tara¹ *f.* tare.
tara² *f.* tara.
taraceo *m.* tattoo.
taraxia *f.* taraxy.
taraxígeno *m.* taraxigen.
taraxis *f.* taraxy.
tardanza *f.* lag.
  tardanza del nitrógeno nitrogen lag.
tardío, -a *adj.* late, tardive, tardy.
tarsadenitis *f.* tarsadenitis.
tarsal *adj.* tarsal.
tarsalgia *f.* tarsalgia.
tarsectomía *f.* tarsectomy.
  tarsectomía anterior anterior tarsectomy.
  tarsectomía cuneiforme cuneiform tarsectomy.
  tarsectomía posterior posterior tarsectomy.
tarsectopía *f.* tarsectopia.
tarsiano, -na *adj.* tarsal.
tarsitis *f.* tarsitis.
tarso *m.* tarsus.
tarsoclasia *f.* tarsoclasia.
tarsoclasis *f.* tarsoclasis.
tarsofalángico, -ca *adj.* tarsophalangeal.
tarsofima *m.* tarsophyma.
tarsomalacia *f.* tarsomalacia.
tarsomegalia *f.* tarsomegaly.
tarsometatarsiano, -na *adj.* tarsometatarsal.
tarsoorbitario, -ria *adj.* tarso-orbital.
tarsoplasia *f.* tarsoplasia.

tarsoplastia *f.* tarsoplasty, tarsoplasia.
tarsoptosis *f.* tarsoptosis.
tarsoqueiloplastia *f.* tarsocheiloplasty.
tarsoquiloplastia *f.* tarsocheiloplasty.
tarsorrafia *f.* tarsorrhaphy.
tarsotarsal *adj.* tarsotarsal.
tarsotarsiano, -na *adj.* tarsotarsal.
tarsotibial *adj.* tarsotibial.
tarsotomía *f.* tarsotomy.
tarsus *m.* tarsus.
tartamudez *f.* stuttering.
  tartamudez labiocoreica labiochoreic stuttering.
  tartamudez urinaria urinary stuttering.
  tartamudez vesical urinary stuttering.
tasa *f.* rate.
  tasa bruta de natalidad crude birth rate.
  tasa de embarazos pregnancy rate.
  tasa específica specific rate.
  tasa de falsos negativos false-negative rate.
  tasa de falsos positivos false-positive rate.
  tasa de fertilidad fertility rate.
  tasa de filtración glomerular (TFG) glomerular filtration rate (GFR).
  tasa de formación ósea bone formation rate.
  tasa de morbididad morbidity rate.
  tasa de mortalidad death rate.
  tasa de mortalidad ajustada adjusted death rate.
  tasa de mortalidad estandarizada standardized death rate.
  tasa de mutación mutation rate.
  tasa de nacimientos ajustada refined birth rate.
  tasa real de nacimientos true birth rate.
tatuaje *m.* tattoo, tattooing.
  tatuaje de amalgama amalgam tattoo.
  tatuaje de la córnea tattooing of the cornea.
taurocolaneresis *f.* taurocholaneresis.
taurocolanopoyesis *f.* taurocholanopoiesis.
taurocolemia *f.* taurocholemia.
taurodontismo *m.* taurodontism.
tautomería *f.* tautomerism.
tautomérico, -ca *adj.* tautomeric.
tautomerismo *m.* tautomerism.
tautómero, -ra *adj.* tautomer.
taxis *f.* taxis.
  taxis bipolar bipolar taxis.
  taxis negativa negative taxis.
  taxis positiva positive taxis.
taxón *m.* taxon.
taxonomía *f.* taxonomy.
  taxonomía numérica numerical taxonomy.
taxonómico, -ca *adj.* taxonomic.
taxonomista *m., f.* taxonomist.
taylorismo *m.* taylorism.
taza *f.* cup.
  taza de talón heel cup.
tebaico, -ca *adj.* thebaic.
tebaísmo *m.* thebaism.
teca[1] *f.* theca.
teca[2] *f.* theque.
tecal *adj.* thecal.
techo *m.* roof, tectum.
tecitis *f.* thecitis.
técnica *f.* technique.
  técnica de abrasión con aire airbrasive technique.
  técnica de Alexander Alexander technique.
  técnica de anticuerpos fluorescentes fluorescent antibody technique.
  técnica de Asopa Asopa's technique.
  técnica de aspiración aspiration technique.
  técnica de Barcroft-Warburg Barcroft-Warburg technique.

técnica de Barraquer Barraquer operation.
técnica de Begg Begg technique.
técnica de Berbericht-Hirsch phlebography.
técnica de Camey Camey's neobladder technique.
técnica del campo lavado washed field technique.
técnica coaxial coaxial technique.
técnica cognitiva cognitive technique.
técnica de Cohen cross trigonal technique.
técnica del colgajo pediculado pedicle flap operation.
técnica conductual behavioral technique.
técnica del cono largo long cone technique.
técnica de corrección de incontinencia Marshall-Marchetti-Kranz Marshall-Marchetti-Kranz's technique.
técnica de cuenta de centelleo scintillation counting technique.
técnica de Czepa Czepa's technique.
técnica de DeLorme DeLorme technique.
técnica depilatoria depilatory technique.
técnica de derivación urinaria continente de Benchecround Benchekroun continent vesicostomy.
técnica de Devine-Horton Devine-Horton's technique.
técnica de difusión de tiempo time diffusion technique.
técnica de dilución y filtración dilution-filtration technique.
técnica directa direct technique.
técnica de Dotter Dotter's technique.
técnica de Duckett meatoplasty and granuloplasty repair.
técnica para esterilizar insectos sterile insect technique.
técnica de Ficoll-Hypaque Ficoll-Hypaque technique.
técnica de Frazier Frazier's technique.
técnica de gota colgante hanging drop technique.
técnica de Gregoir Gregoir's technique.
técnica de Hakanson Hakanson's technique.
técnica Hampton Hampton technique.
técnica de Hartel Hartel technique.
técnica de imagen digital digital image technique.
técnica indirecta indirect technique.
técnica de infusión intravenosa intravenous infusion technique.
técnica de inmunoperoxidasa immunoperoxidase technique.
técnica de inyección injection technique.
técnica de Judkins Judkins' technique.
técnica de Kleinschmidt Kleinschmidt technique.
técnica de Kronlein Kronlein's technique.
técnica de Laurell Laurell technique.
técnica de Leboyer Leboyer technique.
técnica de Léger splenoportography.
técnica de Lindt-Wegelins cineangiocardiography.
técnica de machacamiento squash technique.
técnica de manchado de Western Western blot technique.
técnica de las manchas de tinta de Holtzman Holtzman inkblot technique.
técnica de McGoon McGoon technique.
técnica de Merendino Merendino technique.
técnica de Mohs Mohs' technique.
técnica de Mustard Mustard's inflow correction.
técnica de Neviaser Neviaser procedure.

técnica de Nirschl Nirschl procedure.
técnica de Oakley-Fulthorpe Oakley-Fulthorpe technique.
técnica de Ober Ober procedure.
técnica de Ober y Barr Ober and Barr procedure.
técnica de Orr Orr technique.
técnica de Osborne y Cotterill Osborne and Cotterill procedure.
técnica de Oudin Oudin technique.
técnica de pared auricular atrial-wall technique.
técnica de la peroxidasa-antiperoxidasa peroxidase-antiperoxidase technique.
técnica de placa de Jerne Jerne plaque technique.
técnica de quimiocirugía de tejido fresco de Mohs Mohs' fresh tissue chemosurgery.
técnica de relajación relaxation technique.
técnica de relajación condicionada conditioned relaxation technique.
técnica de relajación imaginaria imaginary relaxation technique.
técnica de relajación progresiva de E. Jacobson Jacobson's progressive relaxation technique.
técnica de relajación de Schultz Schultz's relaxation technique.
técnica de relajación de Wolpe Wolpe's relaxation technique.
técnica de re-respiración rebreathing technique.
técnica de reproducción asistida assisted reproduction technique.
técnica de rubor flush technique.
técnica de secado de Southern Southern blot technique.
técnica de secado de Western Western blot technique.
técnica de Seldinger Seldinger's technique.
técnica de Smith-Robinson Smith-Robinson's technique.
técnica de sustracción substraction technique.
técnica de Tennison-Randall Tennison-Randall's technique.
técnica de Trueta Trueta technique.
técnica de ventana cutánea de Rebuck Rebuck skin window technique.
técnica de vibración supersónica supersonic vibration technique.
tecodonto, -ta *adj.* thecodont.
tecoma *m.* thecoma.
tecomatosis *f.* thecomatosis.
tecosoma *m.* schistosome.
tectal *adj.* tectal.
tectiforme *adj.* tectiform.
tectina *f.* tektin.
tectocefalia *f.* tectocephaly.
tectocefálico, -ca *adj.* tectocephalic.
tectoespinal *adj.* tectospinal.
tectología *f.* tectology.
tectónico, -ca *adj.* tectonic.
tectorial *adj.* tectorial.
tectorio *m.* tectorium.
tectorio, -ria *adj.* tectorial.
tectorium tectorium.
tectospinal *adj.* tectospinal.
tectum tectum.
tefromalacia *f.* tephromalacia.
tefromielitis *f.* tephromyelitis.
tefrosis *f.* tephrosis.
tegmen tegmen.
tegmental *adj.* tegmental.
tegmentario, -ria *adj.* tegmental.

tegmento *m.* tegmen, tegmentum.
tegmentotomía *f.* tegmentotomy.
tegmentum tegmentum.
tegumento *m.* integument, tegument, integumentum.
teicopsia *f.* teichopsia.
teinodinia *f.* teinodynia.
tejido *m.* tissue, textus.
 tejido adenoide, tejido adenoideo adenoid tissue.
 tejido adiposo adipose tissue.
 tejido adiposo blanco white adipose tissue.
 tejido adiposo pardo brown adipose tissue.
 tejido adiposo multilocular multilocular adipose tissue.
 tejido adrenógeno adrenogenic tissue.
 tejido areolar areolar tissue.
 tejido blanco target tissue.
 tejido blando del nasión nasion soft tissue.
 tejido cartilaginoso cartilaginous tissue.
 tejido de caucho rubber tissue.
 tejido cavernoso cavernous tissue.
 tejido celular cellular tissue.
 tejido cicatricial cicatricial tissue, scar tissue.
 tejido citógeno adenoid tissue.
 tejido compacto compact tissue.
 tejido condroide chondroid tissue.
 tejido conectivo connective tissue.
 tejido conjuntivo connective tissue.
 tejido conjuntivo laxo loose connective tissue.
 tejido cordal, tejido cordoideo chordal tissue.
 tejido cromafin chromaffin tissue.
 tejido duro hard tissue.
 tejido elástico, tejido elástico amarillo elastic tissue.
 tejido embrionario embryonic tissue.
 tejido endotelial endothelial tissue.
 tejido episcleral, tejido esclerótico episcleral tissue.
 tejido epitelial epithelial tissue.
 tejido eréctil erectile tissue.
 tejido esplénico splenic tissue.
 tejido esponjoso cancellous tissue.
 tejido esquelético skeletal tissue.
 tejido fibroareolar fibroareolar tissue.
 tejido fibroelástico fibroelastic tissue.
 tejido fibrohialino fibrohyaline tissue.
 tejido fibroso fibrous tissue.
 tejido friable friable tissue.
 tejido de Gamgee Gamgee tissue.
 tejido gelatinoso gelatiginous tissue.
 tejido gingival gingival tissue.
 tejido glandular glandular tissue.
 tejido hemopoyético hemopoietic tissue.
 tejido heterólogo heterologous tissue.
 tejido heterotópico heterotopic tissue.
 tejido hílico hylic tissue.
 tejido hiperplástico hyperplastic tissue.
 tejido homólogo homologous tissue.
 tejido intersticial interstitial tissue.
 tejido lardáceo lardaceous tissue.
 tejido lepídico lepidic tissue.
 tejido linfadenoide lymphadenoid tissue.
 tejido linfático lymphatic tissue.
 tejido linfoide, tejido linfoideo lymphoid tissue.
 tejido mesenquimático, tejido mesenquimatoso mesenchymal tissue.
 tejido mesonéfrico mesonephric tissue.
 tejido metanefrogénico metanephrogenic tissue.
 tejido mieloide myeloid tissue.
 tejido mucoso mucous tissue.

 tejido muscular muscular tissue.
 tejido muscular cardíaco cardiac striated tissue.
 tejido muscular estriado esquelético striated skeletal muscular tissue.
 tejido muscular liso smooth muscular tissue.
 tejido nefrogénico nephrogenic tissue.
 tejido nervioso nervous tissue.
 tejido nodular nodal tissue.
 tejido óseo bone tissue, osseous tissue.
 tejido osteógeno osteogenic tissue.
 tejido osteoide osteoid tissue.
 tejido parenquimatoso parenchymatous tissue.
 tejido periapical periapical tissue.
 tejido poroso cancellous tissue.
 tejido primario embryonic tissue.
 tejido primitivo de la pulpa primitive pulp tissue.
 tejido reticulado, tejido reticular, tejido retiforme reticular tissue, retiform tissue.
 tejido de revestimiento investing tissue.
 tejido subcutáneo subcutaneous tissue.
 tejido tuberculoso de granulación tuberculosis granulation tissue.
 tejido de unión junctional tissue.
tela *f.* cloth, tela.
telalgia¹ *f.* telalgia.
telalgia² *f.* thelalgia.
telangiectasia *f.* telangiectasia.
 telangiectasia aracniforme, telangiectasia aracnoide spider telangiectasia.
 telangiectasia capilar capillar telangiectasia.
 telangiectasia cefalooculocutánea cephalo-oculocutaneous telangiectasia.
 telangiectasia esencial essential telangiectasia.
 telangiectasia esencial generalizada generalized essential telangiectasia.
 telangiectasia hemorrágica hereditaria hereditary hemorrhagic telangiectasia.
 telangiectasia linfática telangiectasia lymphatica.
 telangiectasia macular eruptiva persistente telangiectasia macularis eruptiva perstans.
 telangiectasia retiniana retinal telangiectasia.
 telangiectasia verrugosa telangiectasia verrucosa.
 telangiectasia yuxtafoveolar idiopática idiopathic juxtafoveolar telangiectasia.
telangiectásico, -ca *adj.* telangiectatic.
telangiectasis *f.* telangiectasis.
telangiectoide *adj.* telangiectodes.
telangiectoma *m.* telangioma.
telangiitis *f.* telangiitis.
telangioma *m.* telangioma.
telangión *m.* telangion.
telangiosis *f.* telangiosis.
telangitis *f.* telangiitis.
telarca *f.* thelarche.
telarquia, telarquía *f.* thelarche.
telebinocular *m.* telebinocular.
telecanto *m.* telecanthus.
telecardiófono *m.* telecardiophone.
telecardiografia *f.* telecardiography.
telecardiograma *m.* telecardiogram.
teleceptivo, -va *adj.* teleceptive.
teleceptor *m.* teleceptor.
telecinesia *f.* telekinesis.
telecinesis *f.* telekinesis.
telecinético, -ca *adj.* telekinetic.
telecord *m.* telecord.
telectrocardiograma *m.* telectrocardiogram.
telecurieterapia *f.* telecurietherapy.

teledendrita *f.* teledendrite.
teledendron *m.* teledendron.
telediagnóstico *m.* telediagnosis.
telediastólico, -ca *adj.* telediastolic.
teleelectrocardiógrafo *m.* teleelectrocardiograph.
telefluoroscopia *f.* telefluoroscopy.
telelectrocardiograma *m.* telelectrocardiogram.
telemando *m.* telecommand.
telemetría *f.* telemetry.
telémetro *m.* telemeter.
telencefálico, -ca *adj.* telencephalic.
telencefalización *f.* telencephalization.
telencéfalo *m.* telencephalon.
teleneurita *f.* teleneurite.
teleología *f.* teleology.
teleológico, -ca *adj.* teleological.
teleologismo *m.* teleologism.
teleonomía *f.* teleonomy.
teleonómico, -ca *adj.* teleonomic.
teleopsia *f.* teleopsia.
teleorbitismo *m.* teleorbitism.
telépata *m., f.* telepathist.
telepatía *f.* telepathy.
telepatizar *v.* telepathize.
teleplastia *f.* theleplasty.
telequinesia *f.* telekinesis.
teleretismo *m.* thelothism, thelerethism.
telergia *f.* telergy.
telérgico, -ca *adj.* telergic.
telérgico, -ca *m.* teleradium.
telerradiografía *f.* teleradiography.
telerradioterapia *f.* teletherapy.
telerreceptivo, -va *adj.* telereceptive.
telerreceptor *m.* telereceptor.
telerroentgenografía *f.* teleroentgenography.
telerroentgenograma *m.* teleroentgenogram.
telerroentgenoterapia *f.* teleroentgenotherapy.
telesífilis *f.* telesyphilis.
telesis *f.* telesis.
telesistólico, -ca *adj.* telesystolic.
telestesia *f.* telesthesia.
telestetoscopio *m.* telesthetoscope.
teletactor *m.* teletactor.
teleterapia *f.* teletherapy.
teletermómetro *m.* telethermometer.
teligénico, -ca *adj.* thelygenic.
telio *m.* thelium.
telitis *f.* thelitis.
telobiosis *f.* telobiosis.
telocele *f.* telocoele.
telocéntrico, -ca *adj.* telocentric.
telodendrión *m.* telodendron.
telodendron *m.* telodendron.
telofase *f.* telophase.
telofragma *m.* telophragma.
telógeno *m.* telogen.
teloglia *f.* teloglia.
telognosis *f.* telognosis.
telognóstico, -ca *adj.* telognostic.
telolecital *adj.* telolecithal.
telolema *m.* telolemma.
telomerasa *f.* telomerase.
telómero *m.* telomere.
telonco *m.* theloncus.
telopéptido *m.* telopeptide.
teloplastia *f.* theleplasty.
telorismo *m.* telorism.
telorragia *f.* thelorrhagia.
telorreceptor *m.* teloreceptor.
telotismo *m.* telotism.
telurismo *m.* tellurism.
temblor *m.* tremor.

temblor de acción action tremor.

temblor aleteante, temblor de aleteo flapping tremor.

temblor alternante alternating tremor.

temblor arsenical, temblor por arsénico arsenical tremor.

temblor burdo coarse tremor.

temblor de la cabeza head tremor.

temblor cardíaco tremor cordis.

temblor cerebeloso cerebellar tremor.

temblor cerebeloso progresivo progressive cerebellar tremor.

temblor cinético kinetic tremor.

temblor continuo continuous tremor.

temblor esencial, temblor esencial benigno, temblor esencial hereditario benign essential tremor, essential tremor, hereditary essential tremor.

temblor estático static tremor.

temblor familiar familial tremor.

temblor fibrilar fibrillary tremor.

temblor fino fine tremor.

temblor fisiológico physiologic tremor.

temblor grueso coarse tremor.

temblor hepático liver flap.

temblor heredofamiliar heredofamilial tremor.

temblor histérico hysterical tremor.

temblor inducido induced tremor.

temblor de intención, temblor intencional intentional tremor.

temblor intermitente intermittent tremor.

temblor lingual tremor linguae.

temblor mercurial mercurial tremor.

temblor metálico metallic tremor.

temblor muscular muscular tremor.

temblor por opio, temblor opiophagorum tremor opiophagorum.

temblor parkinsoniano Parkinsonian tremor.

temblor pasivo passive tremor.

temblor perioral perioral tremor.

temblor persistente persistent tremor.

temblor postural postural tremor.

temblor de reposo rest tremor, resting tremor.

temblor de ronroneo purring tremor.

temblor saturnino saturnine tremor.

temblor senil senile tremor.

temblor de los tendones, temblor tendinoso tremor tendinum.

temblor tosco coarse tremor.

temblor tóxico toxic tremor.

temblor en trombón de la lengua trombone tremor of the tongue.

temblor volicional, temblor volitivo volitional tremor.

tembloroso, -sa *adj.* tremulous.

temor *m.* fear.

temperamento *m.* temperament.

temperamento atrabiliario, temperamento atrabilioso melancholic temperament.

temperamento bilioso choleric temperament.

temperamento colérico choleric temperament.

temperamento flemático phlegmatic temperament.

temperamento linfático phlegmatic temperament.

temperamento melancólico melancholic temperament.

temperamento sanguíneo sanguine temperament.

temperatura *f.* temperature.

temperatura absoluta absolute temperature.

temperatura ambiental ambient temperature, room temperature.

temperatura axilar axillary temperature.

temperatura basal basal temperature.

temperatura central core temperature.

temperatura corporal body temperature.

temperatura corporal basal basal body temperature.

temperatura crítica critical temperature.

temperatura de desnaturalización del ADN denaturation temperature of DNA.

temperatura del lactante temperature of infant.

temperatura máxima maximum temperature.

temperatura media mean temperature.

temperatura mínima minimum temperature.

temperatura normal normal temperature.

temperatura óptima optimum temperature.

temperatura oral oral temperature.

temperatura rectal rectal temperature.

temperatura sensible sensible temperature.

temperatura subnormal subnormal temperature.

temperatura terapéutica therapeutic temperature.

temperatura timpánica tympanic temperature.

templado *m.* template.

templado quirúrgico surgical template.

templado, -da *adj.* warm.

templar *v.* anneal.

tempoestable *adj.* tempostabile.

tempolábil *adj.* tempolabile.

temporal[1] *adj.* temporal.

temporal[2] *adj.* temporalis.

temporoauricular *adj.* temporoauricular.

temporocigomático, -ca *adj.* temporozygomatic.

temporoesfenoidal *adj.* temporosphenoid.

temporoesfenoideo, -a *adj.* temporosphenoid.

temporofacial *adj.* temporofacial.

temporofrontal *adj.* temporofrontal.

temporohioideo, -a *adj.* temporohyoid.

temporomalar *adj.* temporomalar.

temporomandibular *adj.* temporomandibular.

temporomaxilar *adj.* temporomaxillary.

temporooccipital *adj.* temporooccipital.

temporoparietal *adj.* temporoparietal.

temporopontil *adj.* temporopontile.

temporopontino, -na *adj.* temporopontile.

tempostábil *adj.* tempostabile.

tenacidad *f.* tenacity.

tenacillas *f.* tweezers.

tenal *adj.* thenal.

tenalgia *f.* tenalgia.

tenar *adj.* thenar.

tenaz *adj.* tenacious.

tenaza *f.* tongs.

tenaza de Crutchfield Crutchfield tongs.

tenaza de Gardner-Wells Gardner-Wells tongs.

tendencia *f.* trend.

tendencia curvilínea curvilinear trend.

tendencia de pensamiento trend of thought.

tendencia a la recidiva recidivism.

tendinitis *f.* tendinitis, tendonitis.

tendinitis cálcica, tendinitis calcificada calcific tendinitis.

tendinitis estenosante stenosing tendinitis, tendinitis stenosans.

tendinitis osificante traumática tendinitis ossificans traumatica.

tendinografía *f.* tendinography.

tendinoplastia *f.* tendinoplasty.

tendinoso, -sa *adj.* tendinous.

tendo *m.* tendo.

tendofonía *f.* tendophony.

tendomucina *f.* tendomucin.

tendomucoide *m.* tendomucoid.

tendón *m.* sinew, tendon, tendo.

tendón de Aquiles Achilles' tendon, tendo Achillis.

tendón calcáneo tendo calcaneus.

tendón desgarrado pulled tendon.

tendón de jinete rider's tendon.

tendón del talón heel tendon.

tendosinovitis *f.* tendosynovitis.

tendosinovitis adhesiva adhesive tendosynovitis.

tendosinovitis crepitante tendosynovitis crepitans.

tendosinovitis estenosante tendosynovitis stenosans.

tendosinovitis gonocócica, tendosinovitis gonorreica gonococcic tendosynovitis, gonorrheal tendosynovitis.

tendosinovitis granulosa tendosynovitis granulosa.

tendosinovitis nodular nodular tendosynovitis.

tendosinovitis nodular localizada localized nodular tendosynovitis.

tendosinovitis purulenta, tendosinovitis purulenta aguda tendosynovitis acuta purulenta.

tendosinovitis serosa, tendosinovitis serosa crónica tendosynovitis chronica.

tendosinovitis tuberculosa tuberculous tendosynovitis.

tendosinovitis vellonodular pigmentada villonodular pigmented tendosynovitis.

tendosinovitis vellosa villous tendosynovitis.

tendosinovitis vellosonodular villonodular tendosynovitis.

tendonitis *f.* tendonitis.

tendovaginal *adj.* tendovaginal.

tendovaginitis *f.* tendovaginitis.

tenectomía *f.* tenectomy.

tenésmico, -ca *adj.* tenesmic.

tenesmo *m.* straining, tenesmus.

tenesmo rectal rectal tenesmus.

tenesmo vesical vesical tenesmus.

tenia[1] *f.* tapeworm, taenia.

tenia[2] *f.* tenia, taenia.

tenial *adj.* taenial.

teniamiotomía *f.* teniamyotomy.

teniasis *f.* taeniasis, teniasis.

teniasis somática somatic taeniasis.

tenicida *adj.* teniacide, tenicide.

teniforme *adj.* teniform.

tenífugo, -ga *adj.* taenifugal, taenifuge, teniafugal, teniafuge, tenifugal, tenifuge.

teniola *f.* taeniola, teniola.

teniotoxina *f.* teniotoxin.

tenodesis *f.* tenodesis.

tenodinia *f.* tenodynia.

tenofibrilla *f.* tenofibril.

tenofito *m.* tonophyte.

tenofonía *f.* tenophony.

tenografía *f.* tenography.

tenólisis *f.* tenolysis.

tenomioplastia *f.* tenomyoplasty.

tenomiotomía *f.* tenomyotomy.

tenonectomía *f.* tenonectomy.

tenonitis *f.* tenonitis.

tenonómetro *m.* tenonometer.

tenonostosis *f.* tenonostosis.

tenontagra *f.* tenontagra.

tenontitis *f.* tenontitis.

tenontitis proliferante calcárea, tenontitis prolífica calcárea tenontitis prolifera calcarea.

tenontofima *m.* tenontophyma.

tenontografía *f.* tenontography.
tenontolemitis *f.* tenontolemmitis.
tenontolemnitis *f.* tenontolemmitis.
tenontomioplastia *f.* tenontomyoplasty.
tenontomiotomía *f.* tenontomyotomy.
tenontoplastia *f.* tenontoplasty.
tenontoplástico, -ca *adj.* tenontoplastic.
tenopexia *f.* tenodesis.
tenoplastia *f.* tenoplasty.
tenoplástico, -ca *adj.* tenoplastic.
tenorrafia *f.* tenorrhaphy.
tenorreceptor *m.* tenoreceptor.
tenosinovectomía *f.* tenosinovectomy, tenosynovectomy.
tenosinovitis *f.* tenosynovitis.
tenositis *f.* tenositis.
tenostosis *f.* tenostosis.
tenosuspensión *f.* tenosuspension.
tenosutura *f.* tenosuture.
tenotomía *f.* tenotomy.
  tenotomía de contención curb tenotomy.
  tenotomía graduada graduated tenotomy.
  tenotomía de restricción curb tenotomy.
  tenotomía subcutánea subcutaneous tenotomy.
  tenotomía con sujeción curb tenotomy.
tenotomizar *v.* tenotomize.
tenótomo *m.* tenotome.
tenovaginitis *f.* tenovaginitis.
tensioactivo, -va *adj.* tensioactive.
tensiómetro *m.* tensiometer.
tensión[1] *f.* stress.
tensión[2] *f.* tension.
  tensión arterial arterial tension, arterial pressure.
  tensión arterial media mean arterial pressure.
  tensión de dióxido de carbono carbon-dioxide tension.
  tensión eléctrica electrical tension.
  tensión emocional strain.
  tensión de fatiga fatigue tension.
  tensión final ultimate tension.
  tensión de un gas sanguíneo blood gas tension.
  tensión hística tissue tension.
  tensión intraocular intraocular pressure.
  tensión intravenosa intravenous tension.
  tensión límite ultimate tension.
  tensión muscular muscular tension.
  tensión ocular ocular tension.
  tensión de oxígeno oxygen tension.
  tensión de pared wall tension.
  tensión premenstrual premenstrual tension.
  tensión superficial surface tension.
  tensión superficial interfacial interfacial surface tension.
  tensión tisular tissue tension.
tenso, -sa *adj.* tense.
tensómetro *m.* tensometer.
tensor, -ra *m. y adj.* tensor.
tentativo, -va *adj.* tentative.
tentorial *adj.* tentorial.
tentorium tentorium.
tentum tentum.
teñible *adj.* tinctable.
teñir *v.* stain.
teofilinemia *f.* theophylline determination.
teorema *m.* theorem.
  teorema de Bayes Bayes theorem.
  teorema central del límite central limit theorem.
  teorema de Gibbs Gibbs theorem.
teoría *f.* theory.
  teoría de acción en masa mass action theory.

teoría de la actividad activity theory.
teoría de la adaptación al estrés stress-adaptation theory.
teoría de adsorción de narcosis adsorption theory of narcosis.
teoría del alargamiento del huso spindle elongation theory.
teoría de Altmann Altmann's theory.
teoría del alud avalanche theory.
teoría del anillo contráctil contractile ring theory.
teoría del anticuerpo específico antibody specific theory.
teoría de los antígenos secuestrados sequestered antigen theory.
teoría de aposición apposition theory.
teoría del aprendizaje learning theory.
teoría del aprendizaje social social learning theory.
teoría atómica atomic theory.
teoría de la atribución attribution theory.
teoría de la avalancha avalanche theory.
teoría de ß-oxidación-condensación ß-oxidation-condensation theory.
teoría de Baeyer Baeyer's theory.
teoría bioquímica de Ehrlich Ehrlich's theory.
teoría del blanco target theory.
teoría de Bohr Bohr's theory.
teoría de Bowman Bowman's theory.
teoría de Brønsted Brønsted theory.
teoría de Buergi Buergi's theory.
teoría de Burn y Rand Burn and Rand theory.
teoría de las cadenas laterales, teoría de las cadenas laterales de Ehrlich Ehrlich's side-chain theory, lateral chain theory, side chain theory.
teoría de Cannon Cannon theory.
teoría de Cannon-Bard Cannon-Bard theory.
teoría de la capa germinal germ layer theory.
teoría celular cell theory.
teoría del circuito local local circuit theory.
teoría de la circulación abierta open circulation theory.
teoría de la circulación abierta y cerrada open-closed circulation theory.
teoría de la circulación cerrada closed circulation theory.
teoría de la circulación cerrada y abierta closed-open circulation theory.
teoría de la circulación lenta slow circulation theory.
teoría de la circulación rápida fast circulation theory.
teoría del clon prohibido forbidden clone theory.
teoría cognitiva social social cognitive theory.
teoría de Cohnheim Cohnheim's theory.
teoría coloidal de la narcosis colloid theory of narcosis.
teoría de los colores opuestos opponent colors theory.
teoría de las compuertas del dolor gate theory of pain.
teoría de la comunicación communication theory.
teoría del conductor central core conductor theory.
teoría de control de compuertas gate control theory.
teoría de convergencia y proyección convergence-projection theory.
teoría de la crisis crisis theory.

teoría cuántica quantum theory.
teoría de Darwin, teoría darwiniana Darwinian theory.
teoría de De Bordeau De Bordeau theory.
teoría de De Vries De Vries theory.
teoría de Delecato-Doman Delecato-Doman theory.
teoría del desarrollo de la edad developmental theory of aging.
teoría de la desconexión disengagement theory.
teoría del desgaste wear-and-tear theory.
teoría de Dieulafoy Dieulafoy theory.
teoría del dímero dimer theory.
teoría de los dipolos dipole theory.
teoría de la diseminación linfática de la endometriosis lymphatic dissemination theory of endometriosis.
teoría de la disociación molecular molecular dissociation theory.
teoría de la disonancia cognitiva cognitive dissonance theory.
teoría del doble vínculo double bind theory.
teoría de las dos simpatinas two-sympathin theory.
teoría dualista dualistic theory.
teoría de la duplicidad de la visión duplicity theory of vision.
teoría de Ehrlich Ehrlich's theory.
teoría de los electrones electron theory.
teoría de la emergencia emergency theory.
teoría de la emigración emigration theory.
teoría del encajonamiento incasement theory.
teoría del envejeciemiento de la ateriosclerosis aging theory of atherosclerosis.
teoría del envejecimiento por los radicales libres free-radical theory of aging.
teoría epigenética epigenetic theory.
teoría del equilibrio balance theory, equilibrium theory.
teoría de equilibrio de los sexos balance theory of sex.
teoría evolucionista Darwinian theory.
teoría de expansión de membranas membrane expansion theory.
teoría de los filamentos deslizantes sliding filament theory.
teoría de Flourens Flourens' theory.
teoría del foco ectópico ectopic focus theory.
teoría de la frecuencia frequency theory.
teoría de Frerich Frerich's theory.
teoría de Freud Freud's theory.
teoría gametoide gametoid theory.
teoría de la gastrea, teoría de la gastrea de Haeckel gastrea theory, Haeckel's gastrea theory.
teoría del gate control gate control theory.
teoría germen-plasma germ-plasm theory.
teoría de los gérmenes, teoría germinal germ theory.
teoría de la Gestalt Gestalt theory.
teoría de Golgi Golgi's theory.
teoría de Goltz Goltz's theory.
teoría de Helmholtz de la acomodación Helmholtz theory of accommodation.
teoría de Helmholtz de la audición Helmholtz theory of hearing.
teoría hematógena de la endometriosis hematogenous theory of endometriosis.
teoría de Hering de la visión del color Hering's theory of color vision.
teoría de hidratos microcristalinos de la anestesia hydrate microcrystal theory of anesthesia.

teoría del impacto hit theory.

teoría de la implantación en la producción de endometriosis implantation theory of the production of endometriosis.

teoría de la inactivación del X X-inactivation theory.

teoría de inclusión incasement theory.

teoría de la incrustación encrustation theory.

teoría de la información information theory.

teoría de inhibición enzimática por la narcosis enzyme inhibition theory of narcosis.

teoría de la inmunidad celular, teoría de la inmunidad celular de Metchnikov cellular immunity theory, Metchnikov's cellular immunity theory.

teoría inmunológica del envejecimiento immunologic theory of aging.

teoría de la instrucción instructive theory.

teoría instructiva de los anticuerpos antibody instructive theory.

teoría de instrumento de cuerda stringed instrument theory.

teoría de instrumento de viento reed instrument theory.

teoría de la interacción interactionist theory.

teoría iónica ionic theory.

teoría iónica de la membrana membrane ionic theory.

teoría de James-Lange James-Lange's theory.

teoría de Jung Jung's theory.

teoría de kern kern-plasma relation theory.

teoría de Knoop Knoop theory.

teoría lacaniana Lacan's theory.

teoría de Ladd-Franklin Ladd-Franklin theory.

teoría de Lamarck Lamarckian theory.

teoría de Liebig Liebig theory.

teoría lipoide de la narcosis lipoid theory of narcosis.

teoría mendeliana Mendelian theory.

teoría de metaplasia celómica de la endometriosis celomic metaplasia theory of endometriosis.

teoría de Metchnikov, teoría de Mechnikov, teoría de Metchnikoff Metchnikoff's theory.

teoría de Meyer-Overton de la narcosis Meyer-Overton theory of narcosis.

teoría de la migración migration theory.

teoría mioelástica myoelastic theory.

teoría miógena, teoría miogénica myogenic theory.

teoría monofilética monophyletic theory.

teoría de Monro-Kellie Monro-Kellie's theory.

teoría de las mutaciones De Vries theory.

teoría de mutación somática del cáncer somatic mutation of cancer theory.

teoría de Nernst Nernst's theory.

teoría neurocronáxica neurochronaxic theory.

teoría neurogénica neurogenic theory.

teoría de la neurona, teoría neuronal neuron theory.

teoría de Ollier Ollier's theory.

teoría de omega-oxidación omega-oxidation theory.

teoría de la onda, teoría ondulatoria ondulatory theory.

teoría de Pasteur Pasteur's theory.

teoría del patrón del dolor pattern theory of pain.

teoría de Pauling Pauling theory.

teoría de la permeabilidad en la narcosis permeability theory of narcosis.

teoría de Planck Planck theory.

teoría de la plantilla template theory.

teoría de la polarización de la membrana polarization membrane theory.

teoría polifilética polyphyletic theory.

teoría de la posición place theory.

teoría POU POU theory.

teoría de la preformación, teoría preformacionista preformation theory, preformationism theory.

teoría prescriptiva prescriptive theory.

teoría de privación de oxígeno en la narcosis oxygen deprivation theory of narcosis.

teoría de la puerta gate theory.

teoría del punto de referencia point-de-repère theory.

teoría de los quanta, teoría del quantum quantum theory.

teoría quimicoparasitaria, teoría quimioparasitaria de Miller Miller's chemicoparasitic theory.

teoría de la recapitulación recapitulation theory.

teoría de los receptores en la acción farmacológica receptor theory of drug action.

teoría de recombinación de la línea germinal recombinational germline theory.

teoría de reentrada reentry theory.

teoría de reingreso reentry theory.

teoría de la relación núcleo-plasma kernplasma relation theory.

teoría de la resonancia de la audición, teoría de la resonancia de Traube resonance theory of hearing.

teoría de Ribbert Ribbert's theory.

teoría de Schiefferdecker de la simbiosis Shiefferdecker's symbiosis theory.

teoría de Schön Schön's theory.

teoría de la selección clonal clonal selection theory.

teoría de la selección clonal de la inmunidad clonal-selection theory of immunity.

teoría de la selección natural natural selection theory.

teoría sensorimotora sensorimotor theory.

teoría de la simbiosis de Schiefferdecker Shiefferdecker's symbiosis theory.

teoría del sitio place theory.

teoría de situación situational theory.

teoría de un solo golpe single hit theory.

teoría de Spitzer Spitzer's theory.

teoría de la superficie en ampliación expanding surface theory.

teoría de superproducción overproduction theory.

teoría del teléfono telephone theory.

teoría de la tensión superficial de la narcosis surface tension theory of narcosis.

teoría termodinámica de la narcosis thermodynamic theory of narcosis.

teoría del termostato thermostat theory.

teoría trialista trialistic theory.

teoría unitaria unitarian theory.

teoría de la urgencia emergency theory.

teoría de van't Hoff van't Hoff's theory.

teoría del vínculo bind theory.

teoría visomotora de Getman Getman visuomotor theory.

teoría de Warburg Warburg's theory.

teoría de Weismann Weismann's theory.

teoría de Woods-Fildes Woods-Fildes theory.

teoría del yo self-theory.

teoría de Young-Helmholtz Young-Helmholtz theory of color vision.

teórico, -ca[1] *m., f.* theorist.

teórico, -ca[2] *adj.* theoretical.

terapia *f.* therapeutics, therapy, therapia.

terapia ácida acid therapy.

terapia adyuvante adjuvant therapy.

terapia alcalina alkalitherapy.

terapia ambiental environmental therapy.

terapia de amortiguación buffer therapy.

terapia anticoagulante anticoagulant therapy.

terapia autogénica autogenic therapy.

terapia autosérica autoserum therapy.

terapia de aversión, terapia aversiva aversion therapy.

terapia bacteriana bacterial therapy.

terapia biológica biological therapy.

terapia breve brief therapy.

terapia broncodilatadora en aerosol aerosol bronchodilator therapy.

terapia carbónica carbonic therapy.

terapia centrada en el cliente, terapia centrada en el paciente client-centered therapy.

terapia de Chaoul Chaoul therapy.

terapia de choque shock therapy.

terapia citorreductora cytoreductive therapy.

terapia clínica de humidificación clinical humidity therapy.

terapia cognitiva cognitive therapy.

terapia de colapso collapse therapy.

terapia combinada combined therapy.

terapia de conducta, terapia conductual behavior therapy.

terapia del conducto de la pulpa pulp canal therapy.

terapia del conducto de la raíz root canal therapy.

terapia correctora corrective therapy.

terapia de corriente interferida interference current therapy.

terapia de Curie Curie therapy.

terapia por depósito depot therapy.

terapia diatérmica diathermic therapy.

terapia dirigida directive therapy.

terapia del divorcio divorce therapy.

terapia doble duplex therapy.

terapia electroconvulsiva (TEC) electroconvulsive therapy.

terapia de emanación emanation therapy.

terapia endocrina endocrine therapy.

terapia de esclerosis esclerosing therapy.

terapia específica specific therapy.

terapia esterilizante magna therapia sterilisans magna.

terapia de estimulación stimulation therapy.

terapia existencial existential therapy.

terapia expresiva expressive therapy.

terapia fágica phage therapy.

terapia de la familia, terapia familiar, terapia familiar conjunta family therapy.

terapia familiar extendida extended family therapy.

terapia familiar múltiple multiple family therapy.

terapia física physical therapy.

terapia fotodinámica photodynamic therapy.

terapia con fotorradiación photoradiation therapy.

terapia gaseosa gas therapy.

terapia génica gene therapy.

terapia gestáltica, de la Gestalt Gestalt therapy.

terapia del grito primal primal scream therapy.

terapia de grupo group therapy.
terapia de hambre hunger therapy.
terapia de haz beam therapy.
terapia con heterovacunación heterovaccine therapy.
terapia con hormonas esteroideas steroid hormone therapy.
terapia de humedecimiento humidification therapy.
terapia de Indoklon Indoklon therapy.
terapia de inducción induction therapy.
terapia inespecífica non-specific therapy.
terapia con infrarrojos infrared therapy.
terapia interpersonal interpersonal therapy.
terapia de inhalación inhalation therapy.
terapia de inmunización immunization therapy.
terapia inmunosupresora immunesuppresive therapy.
terapia insulínica de coma, terapia insulínica de subcoma subcoma insulin therapy.
terapia de integración sensorial sensory integrative therapy.
terapia de intercambio plasmático plasma exchange therapy.
terapia interpersonal interpersonal therapy.
terapia intersticial interstitial therapy.
terapia intracavitaria intracavitary therapy.
terapia intralesional intralesional therapy.
terapia intraósea intraosseus therapy.
terapia intravenosa intravenous therapy.
terapia de irritación irritation therapy.
terapia de juego play therapy.
terapia laboral work therapy.
terapia del lenguaje speech therapy.
terapia de liberación release therapy.
terapia lúdica play therapy.
terapia de luz light therapy.
terapia de mantenimiento maintenance drug therapy.
terapia del medio milieu therapy.
terapia de meditación meditation therapy.
terapia megavitamínica megavitamin therapy.
terapia metatrófica metatrophic therapy.
terapia miofuncional myofunctional therapy.
terapia de narcosis narcosis therapy.
terapia no directiva non-directive therapy.
terapia ocupacional occupational therapy.
terapia de oficio art therapy.
terapia de onda corta short wave therapy.
terapia opsónica opsonic therapy.
terapia orgánica organic therapy.
terapia ortodóntica orthodontic therapy.
terapia ortodóntica funcional functional orthodontic therapy.
terapia ortomolecular orthomolecular therapy.
terapia con oxígeno oxygen therapy.
terapia con oxígeno hiperbárico hyperbaric oxygen therapy.
terapia palúdica, terapia de paludización malarial therapy.
terapia paraespecífica paraspecific therapy.
terapia parenteral parenteral therapy.
terapia con plasma plasma therapy.
terapia profunda de rayos X deep roentgen-ray therapy.
terapia proliferación proliferation therapy.
terapia de protección sparing therapy.
terapia con proteínas, terapia con proteínas extrañas, terapia proteínico foreign protein therapy.
terapia psicoanalítica psychoanalytic therapy.

terapia con pulsos pulse therapy.
terapia racional rational therapy.
terapia racional emotiva rational emotive therapy.
terapia con radiación, terapia con radio radiation therapy, radium therapy.
terapia radiológico de alto voltaje high-voltage roentgen therapy.
terapia con rayos ray therapy.
terapia recreativa recreational therapy.
terapia de recurrencia recurrence therapy.
terapia de red social social network therapy.
terapia refleja reflex therapy.
terapia de rejilla grid therapy.
terapia de relación relationship therapy.
terapia de relajación relaxation therapy.
terapia de reposición replacement therapy.
terapia de representación de un rol role playing therapy.
terapia de rotación rotation therapy.
terapia del saturnismo deleading therapy.
terapia sérica serum therapy.
terapia sexual sexual therapy.
terapia de shock shock therapy.
terapia de shock proteico protein shock therapy.
terapia social social therapy.
terapia solar solar therapy.
terapia somática somatic therapy.
terapia sterilisans covergens therapia sterilisans covergens.
terapia sterilisans divergens therapia sterilisans divergens.
terapia sterilisans fractionata therapia sterilisans fractionata.
terapia con sueño electroterapéutico electrotherapeutic sleep therapy.
terapia con suero serum therapy.
terapia de sugestión suggestive therapy.
terapia de sustitución, terapia sustitutiva substitution therapy, substitutive therapy.
terapia con telerradio teleradium therapy.
terapia tiroidea thyroid therapy.
terapia ultrasónica ultrasonic therapy.
terapia ultravioleta ultraviolet therapy.
terapia vacunal heterovaccine therapy.
terapia con vacunas vaccine therapy.
terapeuta *m., f.* therapist.
terapeuta físico physical therapist.
terapeuta del lenguaje speech therapist.
terapeuta ocupacional occupation therapist.
terapeuta sexual sexual therapist.
terapéutico, -ca *adj.* therapeutic.
teras *m.* teras.
teratismo *m.* teratism.
teratismo ceásmico ceasmic teratism.
teratismo ectópico ectopic teratism.
teratismo ectrogénico ectrogenic teratism.
teratismo hipergenético hypergenetic teratism.
teratismo sinfísico symphysic teratism.
teratoblastoma *m.* teratoblastoma.
teratocarcinogénesis *f.* teratocarcinogenesis.
teratocarcinoma *m.* teratocarcinoma.
teratocarcinoma de testículo teratocarcinoma testis.
teratogénesis *f.* teratogenesis.
teratogenético, -ca *adj.* teratogenetic.
teratogenia *f.* teratogenesis.
teratogenicidad *f.* teratogenicity.
teratogénico, -ca *adj.* teratogenic.
teratógeno *m.* teratogen.
teratógeno, -na *adj.* teratogenous.
teratoide[1] *m.* teratoma.
teratoide[2] *adj.* teratoid.

teratología *f.* teratology.
teratológico, -ca *adj.* teratologic.
teratólogo, -ga *m., f.* teratologist.
teratoma *m.* teratoma.
teratoma adulto adult teratoma.
teratoma inmaduro immature teratoma.
teratoma macizo solid teratoma.
teratoma maduro mature teratoma.
teratoma maligno malignant teratoma.
teratoma quístico, teratoma quístico benigno benign cystic teratoma, cystic teratoma.
teratomatoso, -sa *adj.* teratomous.
teratosis *f.* teratosis.
teratospermia *f.* teratospermia.
terciana *f.* tertian fever.
terciano, -na *adj.* tertian.
terciano maligna malignant tertian.
terciario, -ria *adj.* tertiary.
terciarismo *m.* tertiarism.
tercípara *f.* tertipara.
terebintinismo *m.* terebinthinism.
terebración *f.* terebration.
terebrante *adj.* terebrant, terebrating, terebrans.
terencéfalo, -la *adj.* therencephalous.
terigoide *adj.* pterygoid.
terigoideo, -a *adj.* pterygoid.
teriomorfismo *m.* theriomorphism.
terma *f.* therm.
termacogénesis *f.* thermacogenesis.
termaeroterapia *f.* thermaerotherapy.
termaestesia *f.* thermesthesia.
termal *adj.* thermal.
termalgesia *f.* thermalgesia.
termalgia *f.* thermalgia.
termanalgesia *f.* thermanalgesia.
termanestesia *f.* thermanesthesia.
termatología *f.* thermatology.
termelómetro *m.* thermelometer.
termestesia *f.* thermesthesia.
termestesiómetro *m.* thermesthesiometer.
térmico, -ca *adj.* thermal, thermic.
terminación *f.* ending, termination, terminatio.
terminación nerviosa nerve ending.
terminal *m. y adj.* terminal.
terminal C C terminal.
terminal cohesivo cohesive terminal.
terminal inteligente intelligent terminal.
terminal no inteligente dumb terminal.
terminal de visualización de vídeo video display terminal.
término *m.* term, terminus.
terminología *f.* terminology.
terminus *m.* terminus.
termión *m.* thermion.
termistor *m.* thermistor.
termoalgesia *f.* thermoalgesia, thermalgesia.
termoanalgesia *f.* thermoanalgesia, thermanalgesia.
termoanestesia *f.* thermoanesthesia, thermanesthesia.
termocauterectomía *f.* thermocauterectomy.
termocauterio *m.* thermocautery.
termocauterización *f.* thermocautery.
termocoagulación *f.* thermocoagulation.
termocoagulación del trigémino trigeminal thermocoagulation.
termocorriente *f.* thermocurrent.
termocroico, -ca *adj.* thermochroic.
termocroísmo *m.* thermochroism.
termocrosia *f.* thermochrose, thermochrosy.
termocrosis *f.* thermochrosis.
termodifusión *f.* thermodiffusion.
termodilución *f.* thermodilution.

termodinámica *f.* thermodynamics.

termodúrico, -ca *adj.* thermoduric.

termoelectricidad *f.* thermoelectricity.

termoeléctrico, -ca *adj.* thermoelectric.

termoestabilidad *f.* thermostability.

termoestable *adj.* thermostabile, thermostable.

termoestasia *f.* thermostasis.

termoestéresis *f.* thermosteresis.

termoestesia, *f.* thermosthesia, thermesthesia.

termoestesiómetro *m.* thermoesthesiometer, thermesthesiometer.

termoexcitador, -ra *adj.* thermoexcitory.

termofílico, -ca *adj.* thermophilic.

termófilo, -la *adj.* thermophile.

termóforo, -ra *m. y adj.* thermophore.

termogenesia *f.* thermogenesis.

termogénesis *f.* thermogenesis.

   termogénesis sin estremecimiento nonshivering thermogenesis.

termogenético, -ca *adj.* thermogenetic.

termogenia *f.* thermogenics.

termogénico, -ca *adj.* thermogenic, thermogenous.

termogenina *f.* termogenin.

termógeno, -na *adj.* thermogenous.

termografía *f.* thermography.

   termografía con cristal líquido liquid crystal thermography.

   termografía infrarroja infrared thermography.

   termografía por microondas microwave thermography.

termográfico, -ca *adj.* thermographic.

termógrafo *m.* thermograph.

   termógrafo de centelleo continuo continuous scan thermograph.

termograma *m.* thermogram.

termogravímetro *m.* thermogravimeter.

termohiperalgesia *f.* thermohyperalgesia.

termohiperestesia *f.* thermohyperesthesia.

termohipestesia *f.* thermohypesthesia.

termohipoestesia *f.* thermohypesthesia.

termohipostesia *f.* thermohypesthesia.

termoinactivación *f.* thermoinactivation.

termoinhibidor, -ra *adj.* thermoinhibitory.

termoinhibitorio, -ria *adj.* thermoinhibitory.

termointegrador *m.* thermointegrator.

termolábil *adj.* heat labile, thermolabile.

termolámpara *f.* thermolamp.

termolaringoscopio *f.* thermolaryngoscope.

termólisis *f.* thermolysis.

termolítico, -ca *adj.* thermolytic.

termología *f.* thermology.

termomagnetismo *m.* thermoelectricity.

termomasaje *m.* thermomassage.

termometría *f.* thermometry.

   termometría clínica clinical thermometry.

   termometría del oído ear thermometry.

   termometría invasiva invasive thermometry.

termométrico, -ca *adj.* thermometric.

termómetro *m.* thermometer.

   termómetro de aire air thermometer.

   termómetro de alcohol spirit thermometer.

   termómetro con autorregistro self-registering thermometer.

   termómetro axilar axilla thermometer.

   termómetro de Beckmann Beckmann thermometer.

   termómetro bimetálico bimetal thermometer.

   termómetro bucal oral thermometer.

   termómetro cata kata thermometer.

   termómetro de Celsius, termómetro centígrado Celsius thermometer.

termómetro clínico clinical thermometer.

termómetro diferencial differential thermometer.

termómetro electrónico electronic thermometer.

termómetro de Fahrenheit Fahrenheit thermometer.

termómetro para la fiebre fever thermometer.

termómetro de gas gas thermometer.

termómetro Kelvin Kelvin thermometer.

termómetro de líquido en vidrio liquid-in-glass thermometer.

termómetro de máxima maximum thermometer.

termómetro de medio minuto half minute thermometer.

termómetro de la membrana timpánica tympanic membrane thermometer.

termómetro de mercurio mercury thermometer.

termómetro metálico metallic thermometer.

termómetro metastático metastatic thermometer.

termómetro de mínima minimum thermometer.

termómetro óptico optic thermometer.

termómetro de profundidad depth thermometer.

termómetro Rankine Rankine thermometer.

termómetro de Réaumur Réaumur thermometer.

termómetro rectal rectal thermometer.

termómetro de registro recording thermometer.

termómetro de superficie surface thermometer.

termómetro de termopar thermocouple thermometer.

termonuclear *adj.* thermonuclear.

termopalpación *f.* thermopalpation.

termoplacentografía *f.* thermoplacentography.

termoplástico, -ca *adj.* thermoplastic.

termoplejía *f.* thermoplegia.

termopolipnea *f.* thermopolypnea.

termopolipneico, -ca *adj.* thermopolypneic.

termoprecipitación *f.* thermoprecipitation.

termoqueratoplastia *f.* thermokeratoplasty.

termoquímica *f.* thermochemistry.

termorradioterapia *f.* thermoradiotherapy.

termorreceptor, -ra *m., f. y adj.* thermoreceptor.

termorregulación *f.* thermoregulation.

   termorregulación ineficaz ineffective thermoregulation.

   termorregulación neonatal neonatal thermoregulation.

termorregulador, -ra *m. y adj.* thermoregulator.

termorresistencia *f.* thermoresistance.

termorresistente *adj.* thermoresistant.

termoscopio *m.* thermoscope.

termosistáltico, -ca *adj.* thermosystaltic.

termosistaltismo *m.* thermosystaltism.

termostábil *adj.* thermostabile.

termostable *adj.* thermostabile.

termostabilidad *f.* thermostability.

termostasia *f.* thermostasis.

termostato, termóstato *m.* thermostat.

   termostato hipotalámico hypothalamic thermostat.

termostéresis *f.* thermosteresis.

termotáctico, -ca *adj.* thermotactic.

termotaxia *f.* thermotaxis.

termotaxia negativa negative thermotaxis.

termotaxia positiva positive thermotaxis.

termotáxico, -ca *adj.* thermotaxic.

termotaxis *f.* thermotaxis.

termoterapia *f.* thermotherapy.

termótica *f.* thermotics.

termotolerante *adj.* thermotolerant.

termotonómetro *m.* thermotonometer.

termotraqueotomía *f.* thermotracheotomy.

termotrópico, -ca *adj.* thermotropic.

termotropismo *m.* thermotropism.

ternario, -ria *adj.* ternary.

teromorfia *f.* theromorphism.

teromorfismo *m.* theromorphism.

teromorfo, -fa *adj.* theromorph.

terrace terrace.

terreno *m.* ground.

territorialidad *f.* territoriality.

terror *m.* terror.

   terror nocturno night terror.

tesaurismosis *f.* thesaurismosis.

   tesaurismosis amiloide amyloidosis.

tesaurismótico, -ca *adj.* thesaurismotic.

tesaurosis *f.* thesaurosis.

teslaización *f.* teslaization.

test *m.* test.

   test de Allen-Doisy Allen-Doisy test.

   test de Ames Ames' test.

   test de apercepción temática (TAT) thematic apperception test, TAT.

   test de apomorfina apomorphine test.

   test de aptitudes aptitude test.

   test de Bending Bending's test.

   test de eficiencia efficiency test.

   test del edrofonio edrophonium test.

   test epicutáneo epicuteaneous skin test.

   test de Farnsworth Farnsworth's test.

   test gestáltico visomotor gestalt visualmotor test.

   test de infusión infusion test.

   test de inteligencia intelligence test.

   test intracutáneo intradermal skin test.

   test de Langman Langman's test.

   test de Lepromin Lepromin's test.

   test de limulus limulus amebocyte assay.

   test de Mitsuda Mitsuda's test.

   test de Pap Pap's test.

   test de papaverina papaverin test.

   test de perfusión ácida acid-perfusion test.

   test de personalidad personality test.

   test de presión-volumen pressure-volume test.

   test proyectivo projective test.

   test de rendimiento achievement test.

   test de Rorschach Rorschach's test.

   test de Wada Wada's test.

testalgia *f.* testalgia.

testamento vital *m.* living will.

testectomía *f.* testectomy.

testicondo, -da *adj.* testicond.

testicular *adj.* testicular.

testículo *m.* testicle, testis.

   testículo criptorquídico cryptorchid testicle.

   testículo desplazado displaced testicle.

   testículo ectópico ectopic testicle.

   testículo invertido inverted testicle.

   testículo irritable de Cooper Cooper's irritable testicle.

   testículo móvil movable testicle.

   testículo no descendido undescended testicle.

   testículo obstruido obstructed testicle.

   testículo pulposo pulpy testicle.

   testículo de reducción, testículo redux, testis redux relax testicle, testis redux.

testículo retenido retained testicle.
testículo retráctil retractile testicle.
testiculoma *m.* testiculoma.
testiforme *adj.* testoid.
testimonio *m.* testimony.
testitoxicosis *f.* testitoxicosis.
testis testis.
testitis *f.* testitis.
testitoxicosis *f.* testitoxicosis.
testoide *adj.* testoid.
testoideo, -a *adj.* testoid.
testopatía *f.* testopathy.
testosterona *f.* testosterone.
tetanal *adj.* tetanal.
tetania *f.* tetany.
  tetania por alcalosis tetany of alkalosis.
  tetania duradera duration tetany.
  tetania epidémica epidemic tetany.
  tetania por fosfato phosphate tetany.
  tetania gástrica gastric tetany.
  tetania gravídica tetany gravidarum.
  tetania de hiperventilación, tetania por hiperventilación hyperventilation tetany.
  tetania hipocalcémica hypocalcemic tetany.
  tetania infantil infantile tetany.
  tetania latente latent tetany.
  tetania manifiesta manifest tetany.
  tetania neonatal neonatal tetany.
  tetania paratireopriva, tetania paratiropriva parathyroprival tetany, tetany parathyreopriva.
  tetania paratiroidea parathyroid tetany.
  tetania posoperatoria postoperative.
  tetania del recién nacido neonatal tetany.
  tetania reumática rheumatic tetany.
  tetania uterina uterine tetany.
tetánico, -ca *adj.* tetanic.
tetaniforme *adj.* tetaniform.
tetanígeno, -na *adj.* tetanigenous.
tetanismo *m.* tetanism.
tetanización *adj.* tetanization.
tetanizar *v.* tetanize.
tetánodo *m.* tetanode.
tetanoide *adj.* tetanoid.
tetanoideo, -a *adj.* tetanoid.
tetanómetro *m.* tetanometer.
tetanomotor *m.* tetanomotor.
tétanos *m.* tetanus.
  tétanos de abertura anódica anodal opening tetanus.
  tétanos de abertura catódica cathodal opening tetanus.
  tétanos acústico acoustic tetanus.
  tétanos anódico de abertura anodal opening tetanus.
  tétanos anódico de cierre anodal closure tetanus.
  tétanos anticus tetanus anticus.
  tétanos apirético apyretic tetanus.
  tétanos benigno benign tetanus.
  tétanos de Binot splanchnic tetanus.
  tétanos de la cabeza, tétanos cefálico head tetanus.
  tétanos catódico de apertura cathodal opening tetanus.
  tétanos catódico de cierre, tétanos de cierre catódico cathodal closure tetanus.
  tétanos cefálico cephalic tetanus.
  tétanos cefálico de Rose Rose's cephalic tetanus.
  tétanos cerebral cerebral tetanus.
  tétanos de cierre anódico anodal closure tetanus.
  tétanos completo complete tetanus.
  tétanos completus tetanus completus.

tétanos criptogénico, tétanos criptógeno cryptogenic tetanus.
  tétanos crónico chronic tetanus.
  tétanos dorsal tetanus dorsalis.
  tétanos durable anódico anodal duration tetanus.
  tétanos durable catódico cathodal duration tetanus.
  tétanos esplácnico splanchnic tetanus.
  tétanos espontáneo cryptogenic tetanus.
  tétanos extensor extensor tetanus.
  tétanos farmacológico drug tetanus.
  tétanos fisiológico physiological tetanus.
  tétanos flexor flexor tetanus.
  tétanos generalizado generalized tetanus.
  tétanos hidrofóbico, tétanos hidrófobo hydrophobic tetanus.
  tétanos idiopático cryptogenic tetanus.
  tétanos imitativo imitative tetanus.
  tétanos incompleto incomplete tetanus.
  tétanos infantil tetanus infantum.
  tétanos intermitente intermittent tetanus.
  tétanos de Janin cephalic tetanus.
  tétanos de Klemn cephalic tetanus.
  tétanos local local tetanus.
  tétanos medicamentoso drug tetanus.
  tétanos médico cryptogenic tetanus.
  tétanos neonatal, tétanos del neonato, tétanos neonatorum neonatal tetanus, tetanus neonatorum.
  tétanos paralítico cephalic tetanus.
  tétanos parcial partial tetanus.
  tétanos posparto tetanus postpartum.
  tétanos posterior, tétanos póstico, tétanos posticus tetanus posticus.
  tétanos postsérico postserum tetanus.
  tétanos puerperal puerperal tetanus.
  tétanos de los recién nacidos neonatal tetanus, tetanus neonatorum.
  tétanos remitente intermittent tetanus.
  tétanos reumático cryptogenic tetanus.
  tétanos tóxico toxic tetanus.
  tétanos traumático traumatic tetanus.
  tétanos uterino uterine tetanus.
tetanospasmina *f.* tetanospasmin.
tetártanope *m.* tetartanope.
tetartanopía *f.* tetartanopia.
tetartanópico, -ca *adj.* tetartanopic.
tetartanopsia *f.* tetartanopia.
tetartocono *m.* tetartocone.
tetia *f.* tetia.
tetraamelia *f.* tetra-amelia.
tetrablástico, -ca *adj.* tetrablastic.
tetrabraquio *m.* tetrabrachius.
tetrabromofenolftaleína *f.* tetrabromophenolphthalein.
  tetrabromofenolftaleína sódica tetrabromophenolphthalein sodium.
tetracrómico, -ca *adj.* tetrachromic.
tetracrótico, -ca *adj.* tetracrotic.
tetracúspide *adj.* tetracuspid.
tétrada *f.* tetrad.
  tétrada de Fallot tetralogy of Fallot.
tetradactilia *f.* tetradactyly.
tetradáctilo, -la *adj.* tetradactylous.
tetrafocomelia *f.* tetraphocomelia.
tetrágono *m.* tetragonum.
  tetrágono lumbar tetragonum lumbale.
tetragonus tetragonus.
tetrahídrico, -ca *adj.* tetrahydric.
tetralogía *f.* tetralogy.
  tetralogía de Eisenmenger Eisenmenger tetralogy.
  tetralogía de Fallot Fallot's tetralogy, tetralogy of Fallot.

tetramastia *f.* tetramastia.
tetramasto, -ta *adj.* tetramastous.
tetramazia *f.* tetramazia.
tetramelos *m.* tetramelus.
tetramérico, -ca *adj.* tetrameric.
tetrámero, -ra *adj.* tetrameric, tetramerous.
Tetramitus Tetramitus.
tetranoftalmo *m.* tetranophthalmos, tetraophthalmus.
tetranopsia *f.* tetranopsia.
tetraodontoxismo *m.* tetraodontoxism, tetrodotoxism.
tetraoftalmo *m.* tetraophthalmus.
tetraparesia *f.* tetraparesis.
tetraperomelia *f.* tetraperomelia.
tetraplejía *f.* tetraplegia.
tetrapléjico, -ca *adj.* tetraplegic.
tetraploide *adj.* tetraploid.
tetraploidía *f.* tetraploidy.
tetrapódisis *f.* tetrapodisis.
tetrápodo, -da *adj.* tetrapod, tetrapus.
tetrapus tetrapus.
tetráquiro *m.* tetrachirus.
tetrascelo *m.* tetrascelus.
tetrasquelo *m.* tetrascelus.
tetrasomía *f.* tetrasomy.
tetrasómico, -ca *adj.* tetrasomic.
tetráster *m.* tetraster.
tetrastisquiasis *f.* tetrastischiasis.
Tetrastoma Tetrastoma.
tetratómico, -ca *adj.* tetratomic.
tetravacuna *f.* tetravaccine.
tetravalente *adj.* tetravalent.
tetrayodofenolftaleína *f.* tetraiodophenolphthalein.
tetrazolio *m.* tetrazolium.
  nitroazul de tetrazolio tetrazolium nitroblue.
tetrodotoxismo *m.* tetrodotoxism.
tetroftalmo *m.* tetrophthalmus.
tetrosa *f.* tetrose.
texis *f.* texis.
textura *f.* texture.
textural *adj.* textural.
textus textus.
thalamus dorsalis dorsal thalamus.
therapia sterilisans magna therapia sterilisans magna.
thrill *m.* thrill.
  thrill aórtico aortic thrill.
thrombotest *m.* thrombotest.
tiacarana *f.* tiacarana.
tiacida *f.* thiazide.
tiadiacida *f.* thiadiazide, thiadiazine.
tiadiacina *f.* thiadiazide, thiadiazine.
tialagogo, -ga *adj.* ptyalagogue.
tialectasia *f.* ptyalectasis.
tialismo *m.* ptyalism.
  tialismo gravídico gravidic ptyalism.
tialito *m.* ptyalolith.
tialocele *m.* ptyalocele.
tialogénico, -ca *adj.* ptyalogenic.
tialógeno, -na *adj.* ptyalogenic.
tialografía *f.* ptyalography.
tialolitiasis *f.* ptyalolithiasis.
tialolito *m.* ptyalolith.
tialorrea *f.* ptyalorrhea.
tialorreacción *f.* ptyaloreaction.
tialosis *f.* ptyalism.
tiazida *f.* thiazide.
tiazina *f.* thiazin.
tibia *f.* tibia.
  tibia en sable saber tibia, saber-shaped tibia.
  tibia valga tibia valga.
  tibia vara tibia vara.

tibial *adj.* tibial, tibialis.
tibialis *adj.* tibial, tibialis.
tibialgia *f.* tibialgia.
tibio, -bia *adj.* tepid.
tibiocalcáneo, -a *adj.* tibiocalcanean.
tibioescafoideo, -a *adj.* tibioscaphoid.
tibiofemoral *adj.* tibiofemoral.
tibiofibular *adj.* tibiofibular.
tibionavicular *adj.* tibionavicular.
tibioperoneo, -a *adj.* tibioperoneal.
tibiotarsiano, -na *adj.* tibiotarsal.
tic *m.* tic.
  tic convulsivo convulsive tic.
  tic coreico progresivo progressive choreic tic.
  tic crónico chronic tic.
  tic diafragmático diaphragmatic tic.
  tic doloroso, tic doloroso de la cara tic douloureux.
  tic espasmódico spasmodic tic.
  tic facial tic facial.
  tic glosofaríngeo glossopharyngeal tic.
  tic de Guinon jumping tic.
  tic por hábito, tic habitual habit tic.
  tic local local tic.
  tic de mímica, tic mímico mimic tic.
  tic motor complejo complex motor tic.
  tic motor simple simple motor tic.
  tic de pensamiento, tic "de pensée" tic de pensée.
  tic respiratorio diaphragmatic tic.
  tic rotatorio rotatory tic.
  tic saltatorio saltatory tic.
  tic salutatorio bowing tic.
  tic del sueño tic de sommeil.
  tic vocal complejo complex vocal tic.
  tic vocal simple simple vocal tic.
tiemia *f.* thiemia.
tiempo *m.* time.
  tiempo del ápice apex time.
  tiempo de asociación association time.
  tiempo en la circulación circulation time.
  tiempo de circulación normal normal circulation time.
  tiempo de coagulación clotting time.
  tiempo de cromoscopia chromoscopy time.
  tiempo de desaparición fading time.
  tiempo de dextrinización dextrinizing time.
  tiempo de elevación rise time.
  tiempo de espiración forzosa (FET) forced expiratory time (FET).
  tiempo de expulsión del ventrículo izquierdo left ventricular ejection time (LVET).
  tiempo de formación del coágulo clotting time.
  tiempo de generación generation time.
  tiempo de hemorragia bleeding time.
  tiempo de inercia inertia time.
  tiempo de inhibición de tromboplastina tisular tissue thromboplastin inhibition time.
  tiempo de protrombina prothrombin time.
  tiempo de reacción reaction time.
  tiempo de recalcificación recalcification time.
  tiempo de reconocimiento recognition time.
  tiempo de reconstrucción reconstruction time.
  tiempo de recuperación sinoauricular sinoatrial recovery time (SART).
  tiempo de reducción decimal decimal reduction time.
  tiempo de reduplicación doubling time.
  tiempo de relajación relaxation time.
  tiempo de resolución resolving time.
  tiempo de retención retention time.
  tiempo de retracción del coágulo clot retraction time.

tiempo de sangría bleeding time.
tiempo de sangría secundaria secondary bleeding time.
tiempo de sedimentación sedimentation time.
tiempo de sensación sensation time.
tiempo térmico de muerte thermal death time.
tiempo de trombina thrombin.
tiempo de tromboplastina parcial (TTP) partial thromboplastin time (PTT).
tiempo de trombloplastina parcial activada (TTPa) activated partial thromboplastin time (APTT).
tienda *f.* tent, tentorium.
tifemia *f.* typhemia.
tifia *f.* typhia.
tífico, -ca *adj.* typhic.
tiflectasia *f.* typhlectasis.
tiflectomía *f.* typhlectomy.
tiflenteritis *f.* typhlenteritis, typhloenteritis.
tiflitis *f.* typhlitis.
tiflocele *m.* typhlocele.
tiflocolitis *f.* typhlocolitis.
tiflodicliditis *f.* typhlodicliditis.
tifloectasia *f.* typhlectasis.
tifloectomía *f.* typhlectomy.
tifloempiema *m.* typhloempyema.
tifloenteritis *f.* typhloenteritis.
tifloestenosis *f.* typhlostenosis.
tiflolitiasis *f.* typhlolithiasis.
tiflología *f.* typhlology.
tiflomegalia *f.* typhlomegaly.
tiflón *m.* typhlon.
tiflopexia *f.* typhlopexy.
tifloptosis *f.* typhloptosis.
tiflorrafia *f.* typhlorrhaphy.
tiflosis *f.* typhlosis.
tiflostenosis *f.* typhlostenosis.
tiflostomía *f.* typhlostomy.
tifloteritis *f.* typhloteritis.
tiflotomía *f.* typhlotomy.
tifloureterostomía *f.* typhloureterostomy.
tifo *m.* typhus.
tifobacilosis *f.* typhobacillosis.
tifohemia *f.* typhemia.
tifoidal *adj.* typhoidal.
tifoideo, -a *adj.* typhoid.
tifoídico, -ca *adj.* typhous.
tifomalárico, -ca *adj.* typhomalarial.
tifoneumonía *f.* typhopneumonia.
tifopalúdico, -ca *adj.* typhomalarial.
tifopaludismo *m.* typhopaludism.
tifosepsis *f.* typhosepsis.
tifoso, -sa *adj.* typhous.
tifus *m.* typhus.
  tifus abdominal abdominal typhus.
  tifus por ácaros mite-borne typhus.
  tifus amarillo amarillic typhus.
  tifus de Asia septentrional transmitido por garrapatas North Asian tick-borne rickettsiosis.
  tifus australiano por garrapatas Australian tick typhus.
  tifus benigno Brill's disease.
  tifus clásico classic typhus.
  tifus endémico endemic typhus.
  tifus epidémico epidemic typhus.
  tifus europeo European typhus.
  tifus exantemático exanthematous typhus.
  tifus por garrapatas tick typhus.
  tifus hepático Weil's syndrome.
  tifus icterodes yellow fever.
  tifus de las malezas scrob typhus.
  tifus KT KT typhus.

tifus de Manchuria Manchurian typhus.
tifus de los matorrales scrob typhus.
tifus mexicano Mexican typhus.
tifus mitior mitior typhus.
tifus murino murine typhus.
tifus del norte de Asia por garrapata North Asian tick typhus.
tifus de North Queensland por garrapatas North-Queensland tick typhus.
tifus petequial petechial typhus.
tifus por piojos louse-borne typhus.
tifus por pulgas flea-borne typhus.
tifus de Queensland por garrapata Queensland tick typhus.
tifus de la rata rat typhus.
tifus recrudescente recrudescent typhus.
tifus recurrente recurrent fever.
tifus rural rural typhus.
tifus de Sao Paulo Sao Paulo typhus.
tifus de Siberia por garrapata Siberian tick typhus.
tifus de las tiendas shop typhus.
tifus transmitido por garrapatas africanas African tick typhus.
tifus transmitido por piojos louse-borne typhus.
tifus transmitido por pulgas flea-borne typhus.
tifus tropical, tifus de los trópicos tropical typhus.
tifus urbano urban typhus.
tigmotáctico, -ca *adj.* thigmotactic.
tigmotaxia *f.* thigmotaxis.
tigmotaxis *f.* thigmotaxis.
tigmotrópico, -ca *adj.* thigmotropic.
tigmotropismo *m.* thigmotropsm.
tigroide *adj.* tigroid.
tigrólisis *f.* tigrolysis.
tijeras *f.* scissors.
  tijeras canalicular canalicular scissors.
  tijeras de cánula cannula scissors.
  tijeras de craneotomía craniotomy scissors.
  tijeras de Fox Fox scissors.
  tijeras de Liston Liston's scissors.
  tijeras de Smellie Smellie's scissors.
  tijeras de vendaje bandage shears.
  tijeras de Wecker Wecker's scissors.
tilacitis *f.* tylacitis.
tilectomía *f.* tylectomy.
tilión *m.* tylion.
tilmo *m.* tilmus.
tiloma *m.* tyloma.
  tiloma conjuntival tyloma conjunctivae.
tilosis *f.* tylosis.
  tilosis ciliar tylosis ciliaris.
  tilosis lingual tylosis linguae.
  tilosis palmar y plantar tylosis palmaris et plantaris.
tilótico, -ca *adj.* tylotic.
timbre *m.* timbre.
timectomía *f.* thymectomy.
timectomizar *v.* thymectomize.
timelcosis *f.* thymelcosis.
timiasis *f.* thymiasis, thymiosis.
tímico, -ca *adj.* thymic.
timicolinfático, -ca *adj.* thymicolymphatic.
timión, timion *m.* thymion.
timiosis *f.* thymiosis.
timitis *f.* thymitis.
timo *m.* thymus.
  timo accesorio accessory thymus.
timocinético, -ca *adj.* thymokinetic.
timocito *m.* thymocyte.
timógeno, -na *adj.* thymogenic.
timogénico, -ca *adj.* thymogenic.

timolisina *f.* thymolysin.
timólisis *f.* thymolysis.
timolítico, -ca *adj.* thymolytic.
timoma *m.* thymoma.
timopatía *f.* thymopathy.
timopático, -ca *adj.* thymopathic.
timopoyetina *f.* thymopoietin.
timoprivo, -va *adj.* thymoprivous.
timoquesia *f.* thymokesis.
timoquesis *f.* thymokesis.
timosina *f.* thymosin.
timotóxico, -ca *adj.* thymotoxic.
timotrófico, -ca *adj.* thymotrophic.
timpanal *adj.* tympanal.
timpanectomía *f.* tympanectomy.
timpania *f.* tympania, tympany.
  timpania de campana bell tympania.
timpanicidad *f.* tympanicity.
timpánico, -ca *adj.* tympanic.
timpanismo *m.* tympanism.
  timpanismo de Skoda Skoda's tympanism.
  timpanismo uterino uterine tympanism.
timpanítico, -ca *adj.* tympanitic.
timpanitis *f.* bloat, tympanitis.
tímpano *m.* eardrum, tympanum.
timpanoacriloplastia *f.* tympanoacryloplasty.
timpanocentesis *f.* tympanocentesis.
timpanoescamoso, -sa *adj.* tympanosquamosal.
timpanoesclerosis *f.* tympanosclerosis.
timpanoestapédico, -ca *adj.* tympanostapedial.
timpanoeustaquiano, -na *adj.* tympanoeustachian.
timpanógeno, -na *adj.* tympanogenic.
timpanograma *m.* tympanogram.
timpanohial *adj.* tympanohyal.
timpanomáleo, -a *adj.* tympanomalleal.
timpanomalear *adj.* tympanomalleal.
timpanomandibular *adj.* tympanomandibular.
timpanomastoideo, -a *adj.* tympanomastoid.
timpanomastoiditis *f.* tympanomastoiditis.
timpanometría *f.* tympanometry.
timpanométrico, -ca *adj.* tympanometric.
timpanoplastia *f.* tympanoplasty.
timpanoplástico, -ca *adj.* tympanoplastic.
timpanoscamoso, -sa *adj.* tympanosquamosal.
timpanosclerosis *f.* tympanosclerosis.
timpanosimpatectomía *f.* tympanosympathectomy.
timpanoso, -sa *adj.* tympanous.
timpanostapédico, -ca *adj.* tympanostapedial.
timpanotemporal *adj.* tympanotemporal.
timpanotomía *f.* tympanotomy.
timusectomía *f.* thymusectomy.
tinción *f.* tinction.
tindalización *f.* tyndallization.
tinea *f.* ringworm, tinea.
  tinea corporis tinea circinata.
  tinea faciei tinea faciale, tinea faciei.
  tinea favosa tinea favosa.
  tinea imbricata tinea imbricata.
  tinea manus ringworm of the hand, tinea manuum.
  tinea pedis ringworm of the feet.
  tinea vera tinea vera.
tingible *adj.* tingible.
tinnitus *m.* tinnitus.
  tinnitus aurium tinnitus aurium.
  tinnitus cerebral tinnitus cerebri.
  tinnitus en clic clicking tinnitus.
tinoide, -a *adj.* phthinoid.
tinte B *m.* tint B.
tintometría *f.* tintometry.

tintómetro *m.* tintometer.
tintorial *adj.* tinctorial.
tintura *f.* tincture.
tiña *f.* ringworm, tinea.
  tiña amiantácea tinea amiantacea.
  tiña axilar tinea axillaris.
  tiña de la barba tinea barbae.
  tiña de Birmania tinea imbricata.
  tiña de la cabeza tinea capitis.
  tiña de la cara ringworm of the face.
  tiña ciliar tinea ciliorum.
  tiña circinada tinea circinata.
  tiña corporal tinea corporis.
  tiña crural tinea cruris.
  tiña del cuero cabelludo ringworm of the scalp.
  tiña del cuerpo tinea corporis.
  tiña facial tinea faciale, tinea faciei.
  tiña fávica tinea favosa.
  tiña glabra, tiña glabrosa tinea glabrosa.
  tiña imbricada tinea imbricata.
  tiña de la ingle, tiña inguinal ringworm of the groin, tinea inguinalis.
  tiña lupinosa tinea favosa.
  tiña maligna tinea favosa.
  tiña en mancha negra black-dot ringworm.
  tiña de las manos ringworm of the hand, tinea manuum.
  tiña microspórica tinea tonsurans.
  tiña negra tinea nigra.
  tiña nudosa tinea nodosa.
  tiña a parches grises gray-patch ringworm.
  tiña del pie ringworm of the feet.
  tiña podal tinea pedis.
  tiña profunda tinea profunda.
  tiña querion tinea kerion.
  tiña sicosis tinea sycosis.
  tiña tarsal tinea tarsi.
  tiña del tipo del asbesto asbestos-like tinea.
  tiña de Tokelau Tokelau ringworm.
  tiña tonsurante tinea tonsurans.
  tiña tricofítica tinea tonsurans.
  tiña tropical tinea tropicalis.
  tiña ungueal, tiña de las uñas ringworm of the nails, tinea unguium.
  tiña verdadera tinea vera.
  tiña versicolor tinea versicolor.
tiocina *f.* thiozine.
tiodoterapia *f.* thiodotherapy.
tioflavina *f.* thioflavine.
  tioflavina S thioflavine S.
  tioflavina T thioflavine T.
tiogénico, -ca *adj.* thiogenic.
tiógeno, -na *adj.* thiogenic.
tiólisis *f.* thiolysis.
tiónico, -ca *adj.* thionic.
tionina *f.* thionin.
tiopéctico, -ca *adj.* thiopectic, thiopexy.
tiopexia *f.* thiopexy.
tiopéxico, -ca *adj.* thioexic.
tiorredoxina *f.* thioredoxin.
tipificación *f.* typing.
  tipificación por bacteriófagos bacteriophage typing.
  tipificación fágica, tipificación por fagos phage typing.
  tipificación de los grupos sanguíneos blood typing.
  tipificación de los HLA HLA typing.
  tipificación de linfocitos preparados (TLP) primed lymphocyte typing (PLT).
  tipificación de la sangre blood typing.
  tipificación tisular tissue typing.
tipificar *v.* standardize.
tipo *m.* type.

  tipo amiostático y acinético amyostatic-kinetic type.
  tipo asténico asthenic type.
  tipo atlético athletic type.
  tipo azteca Aztec type.
  tipo de búfalo buffalo type.
  tipo de cabeza de pájaro bird's head type.
  tipo constitucional constitutional type.
  tipo escapulohumeral scapulohumeral type.
  tipo esquizoide, tipo esquizotímico schizoid type.
  tipo esténico sthenic type.
  tipo fágico phage type.
  tipo hiperactivo overactive type.
  tipo inestable unstable type.
  tipo de Lorain Lorain type.
  tipo leptosómico asthenic type.
  tipo pícnico pyknic type.
  tipo de prueba de Jaeger Jaeger's test type.
  tipo de prueba de Snellen Snellen's test type.
  tipo salvaje wild type.
  tipo sanguíneo blood type.
  tipo sospechoso suspicious type.
  tipo tinoide phthinoid type.
tipología *f.* typology.
tipioscopio *m.* typoscope.
tiposcopio *m.* typoscope.
tira *f.* strip.
  tira abrasiva abrasive strip.
  tira de lino linen strip.
  tira de Mees Mees' strip.
  tira reactiva dipstrip.
tiranismo *m.* tyrannism.
tiremesis *f.* tyremesis.
tiring *f.* tiring.
tiro *m.* tugging.
  tiro traqueal tracheal tugging.
tiroactivo, -va *adj.* thyroactive.
tiroadenitis *f.* thyroadenitis.
tiroaplasia *f.* thyroaplasia.
tiroaritenoideo, -a *adj.* thyroarytenoid.
tirocardíaco, -ca *adj.* thyrocardiac.
tirocarditis *f.* thyrocarditis.
tirocele *m.* thyrocele.
tirocervical *adj.* thyrocervical.
tirocetonuria *f.* thyroketonuria.
tirocondrotomía *f.* thyrochondrotomy.
tirocricotomía *f.* thyrocricotomy.
tirodésmico, -ca *adj.* thyrodesmic.
tiroepiglótico, -ca *adj.* thyroepiglottic.
tiroesófago *m.* thyroesophageus.
tirofaríngeo, -a *adj.* thyropharyngeal.
tirofima *m.* thyrophyma.
tirofisura *f.* thyrofissure.
tirogénico, -ca *adj.* thyrogenic, thyrogenous.
tirógeno, -na *adj.* thyrogenous.
tiroglobulina *f.* thyroglobulin.
tirogloso, -sa *adj.* thyroglossal.
tirohial *adj.* thyrohyal.
tirohioideo, -a *adj.* thyrohyoid.
tiroidectomía *f.* thyroidectomy.
  tiroidectomía química chemical thyroidectomy.
  tiroidectomía subtotal subtotal thyroidectomy.
  tiroidectomía total total thyroidectomy.
tiroidectomizado, -da *adj.* thyroidectomize.
tiroidectomizar *v.* thyroidectomize.
tiroideo, -a *adj.* thyroid.
tiroides *m.* thyroid.
tiroidismo *m.* thyroidism.
tiroiditis *f.* thyroiditis.
  tiroiditis aguda acute thyroiditis.
  tiroiditis atrófica crónica chronic atrophic thyroiditis.

tiroiditis autoInmune autoimmune thyroiditis.

tiroiditis de células gigantes giant cell thyroiditis.

tiroiditis crónica chronic thyroiditis.

tiroiditis fibrosa fibrous thyroiditis.

tiroiditis fibrosa crónica chronic fibrous thyroiditis.

tiroiditis folicular gigante giant follicular thyroiditis.

tiroiditis granulomatosa, tiroiditis granulomatosa subaguda granulomatous thyroiditis, subacute granulomatous thyroiditis.

tiroiditis de Hashimoto Hashimoto's thyroiditis.

tiroiditis invasora ligneous thyroiditis.

tiroiditis leñosa ligneous thyroiditis.

tiroiditis lígnea ligneous thyroiditis.

tiroiditis linfadenoide crónica, tiroiditis linfocítica crónica chronic lymphadenoid thyroiditis, chronic lymphocytic thyroiditis.

tiroiditis linfocítica focal focal lymphocytic thyroiditis.

tiroiditis linfocítica subaguda subacute lymphocytic thyroiditis.

tiroiditis no supurativa aguda acute nonsuppurative thyroiditis.

tiroiditis parasitaria parasitic thyroiditis.

tiroiditis de Quervain Quervain's thyroiditis.

tiroiditis de Riedel Riedel's thyroiditis.

tiroiditis subaguda subacute thyroiditis.

tiroidización *f.* thyroidization.

tiroidología *f.* thyroidology.

tiroidopatía *f.* thyroidopathy.

tiroidoterapia *f.* thyroidotherapy.

tiroidotomía *f.* thyroidotomy.

tirointoxicación *f.* thyrointoxication.

tirolaríngeo, -a *adj.* thyrolaryngeal.

tiroliberina *f.* thyroliberin.

tirolingual *adj.* thyrolingual.

tiroma *m.* tyroma.

tiromatosis *f.* tyromatosis.

tiromegalia *f.* thyromegaly.

tiromimético, -ca *adj.* thyromimetic.

tirón *m.* pull.

tironco *m.* thyroncus.

tiroparatiroidectomía *f.* thyroparathyroidectomy.

tiroparatiroprivo, -va *adj.* thyroparathyroprivic.

tiropatía *f.* thyropathy.

tiroplastia *f.* thyroplasty.

tiroprivación *f.* thyroprivia.

tiroprivia *f.* thyroprivia.

tiroprivo, -va *adj.* thyroprival.

tiroptosis *f.* thyroptosis.

tirosiluria *f.* tyrosyluria.

tirosinemia *f.* tyrosinemia.

tirosinemia hereditaria hereditary tyrosinemia.

tirosinosis *f.* tyrosinosis.

tirosinurea *f.* tyrosinurea.

tirosinuria *f.* tyrosinuria.

tirosis *f.* tyrosis.

tiroterapia *f.* thyrotherapy.

tirotomía *f.* thyrotomy.

tirótomo *m.* thyrotome.

tirotoxemia *f.* thyrotoxemia.

tirotoxia *f.* thyrotoxia.

tirotóxico, -ca *adj.* thyrotoxic.

tirotoxicón *m.* thyrotoxicon.

tirotoxicosis *f.* thyrotoxicosis, tyrotoxicosis.

tirotoxicosis apática apathetic thyrotoxicosis.

tirotoxicosis medicamentosa thyrotoxicosis medicamentosa.

tirotoxina *f.* thyrotoxin.

tirotoxismo *m.* tyrotoxism.

tirotrofo *m.* thyrotroph.

tirotrópico, -ca *adj.* thyrotropic.

tirotropina *f.* thyrotropin.

tirotropismo *m.* thyrotropism.

tirotropo *m.* thyrotrope.

tiroxina *f.* tyroxine.

tiroxina libre free tyroxine.

tiroxina radiactiva radioactive tyroxine.

tiroxina sódica tyroxine sodium.

tiroxinemia *f.* thyroxinemia.

tiroxínico, -ca *adj.* thyroxinic.

tísico, -ca *adj.* phthisic.

tisiogénesis *f.* phthisiogenesis.

tisiogénico, -ca *adj.* phthisiogenetic.

tisiógeno, -na *adj.* phthisiogenetic.

tisiología *f.* phthisiology.

tisioterapeuta *m., f.* phthisiotherapist.

tisioterapéutico, -ca *adj.* phthisiotherapeutical.

tisioterapia *f.* phthisiotherapy.

tisis *f.* phthisis.

tisis abdominal abdominal phthisis.

tisis aguda granúlica acute miliary phthisis.

tisis antracótica anthracosis.

tisis común tuberculosis of the lungs.

tisis corneal phthisis corneae.

tisis esencial, tisis esencial del globo ocular essential phthisis bulbi.

tisis del globo ocular phthisis bulbi.

tisis laríngea tuberculosis of the larynx.

tisis mesentérica abdominal phthisis.

tisis de los mineros anthracosis.

tisis negra anthracosis.

tisis ocular ocular phthisis.

tisis pulmonar tuberculosis of the lungs.

tisonitis *f.* tysonitis.

tisular *adj.* tissular.

titilación *f.* titillation.

titilomanía *f.* titillomania.

titmus *f.* titmus.

titubeante *adj.* titubant.

titubeo *m.* titubation.

titulación *f.* titration.

titulación colorimétrica colorimetric titration.

titulación complexométrica complexometric titration.

titulación coulométrica coulometric titration.

titulación de Dean y Webb Dean and Webb titration.

titulación potenciométrica potentiometric titration.

titular *v.* titrate.

título *m.* titer.

tixolábil *adj.* thixolabile.

tixotropía *f.* thixotropy.

tixotrópico, -ca *adj.* thixotropic.

tixotropismo *m.* thixotropy.

tobillo *m.* ankle.

tobillo de cubierta deck ankle.

tobillo de sastre tailor's ankle.

tococardiografía *f.* tococardiography.

tocodinagrafía *f.* tocodynagraph.

tocodinágrafo *m.* tocodynagraph.

tocodinamómetro *m.* tocodynamometer.

tocografía *f.* tocography.

tocógrafo *m.* tocograph.

tocólisis *f.* tocolysis.

tocología *f.* tocology.

tocólogo, -ga *m., f.* obstetrician.

tocómetro *m.* tocometer.

tocotransductor *m.* tocotransducer.

todo-trans-retinal all-trans-retinal.

tofáceo, -a *adj.* tophaceus.

tofo *m.* tophus.

tofolipoma *m.* topholipoma.

Togaviridae Togaviridae.

togavirus *m.* togavirus.

toilet *f.* toilet, toilette.

toilette *f.* toilet, toilette.

toilet articular articular toilet.

toilet cadavérica cadaveric toilet.

tolerancia *f.* tolerance.

tolerancia a la actividad activity tolerance.

tolerancia acústica acoustic tolerance.

tolerancia adquirida acquired tolerance.

tolerancia a los álcalis alkali tolerance.

tolerancia baja de zona low-zone tolerance.

tolerancia cruzada crossed tolerance.

tolerancia dividida split tolerance.

tolerancia al dolor tolerance pain.

tolerancia al ejercicio exercise tolerance.

tolerancia elevada de zona high-zone tolerance.

tolerancia farmacológica, tolerancia a los fármacos drug tolerance.

tolerancia a la frustración frustration tolerance.

tolerancia a la glucosa glucose tolerance.

tolerancia individual individual tolerance.

tolerancia inmunológica immunologic tolerance.

tolerancia al oxigeno oxygen tolerance.

tolerancia al trabajo work tolerance.

tolerante *adj.* tolerant.

tolerogénesis *f.* tolerogenesis.

tolerogénico, -ca *adj.* tolerogenic.

tolerógeno *m.* tolerogen.

tolerógeno, -na *adj.* tolerogenic.

toma *f.* collection, sampling.

toma de muestras de las vellosidades coriónicas chorionic villi sampling.

toma programada timed collection.

tomainemia *f.* ptomainemia.

tomainotoxismo *m.* ptomainotoxism.

tomatopía *f.* ptomatopsia, ptomatopsy.

tomatopsia *f.* ptomatopsia, ptomatopsy.

tomento *m.* tomentum.

tomento cerebral tomentum cerebri.

tomoartrografía *f.* tomoarthrography.

tomocámara *f.* tomographic gamma camera.

tomodensitometría *f.* tomodensitometry.

tomografía *f.* tomography.

tomografía axial computadorizada (TAC) computer axial tomography (CAT).

tomografía computadorizada (TC) computed tomography (CT).

tomografía computadorizada por emisión (TCE) emission computed tomography (ECT).

tomografía computadorizada por emisión de fotón único (SPECT) single-photon emission computed tomography (SPECT).

tomografía computadorizada espiral spiral-CT.

tomografía por emisión de positrones (PET) positron emission tomography (PET).

tomografía hipocicloide, tomografía hipocicloidal hypocycloidal tomography.

tomografía lineal linear tomography.

tomografía pulmonar completa full-lung tomography.

tomografía ultrasónica ultrasonic tomography.

tomógrafo *m.* tomograph.

tomograma *m.* tomogram.

tomonivel *m.* tomolevel.

tomosíntesis digital *f.* digital tomosynthesis.
tomotocia *f.* cesarean operation.
tonicidad *f.* tonicity, tonus.
tónico, -ca *m. y adj.* tonic.
tonicoclónico, -ca *adj.* tonicoclonic.
tonificar *v.* tonicize.
tono *m.* tone, tonus.
  tono afectivo affective tone.
  tono broncomotor bronchomotor tone.
  tono cardíaco heart tone.
  tono cardíaco fetal (TCF) fetal heart tone (FHT).
  tono doble de Traube Traube's double tone.
  tono emocional emotional tone.
  tono miógeno myogenic tone.
  tono muscular muscular tone.
  tono neurógeno myogenic tone.
  tono químico chemical tone.
  tono sentimental feeling tone.
  tono vagal vagal tone.
tonoclónico, -ca *adj.* tonoclonic.
tonofante *m.* tonophant.
tonofanto *m.* tonophant.
tonofibrilla *f.* tonofibril.
tonofilamento *m.* tonofilament.
tonografía *f.* tonography.
  tonografía de compresión carotídea carotid compression tonography.
tonógrafo *m.* tonograph.
tonograma *m.* tonogram.
tonometría *f.* tonometry.
  tonometría de aplanación, tonometría de aplanamiento applanation tonometry.
  tonometría de indentación indentation tonometry.
tonómetro *m.* tonometer.
  tonómetro de aplanamiento applanation tonometer.
  tonómetro de aplanamiento de Goldmann Goldmann's applanation tonometer.
  tonómetro electrónico electronic tonometer.
  tonómetro electrónico de MacKay-Marg MacKay-Marg electronic tonometer.
  tonómetro electrónico de Mueller Mueller electronic tonometer.
  tonómetro de Gärtner Gärtner's tonometer.
  tonómetro de impresión impression tonometer.
  tonómetro de indentación indentation tonometer.
  tonómetro de McLean McLean tonometer.
  tonómetro neumático pneumatic tonometer.
  tonómetro de Recklinghausen Recklinghausen tonometer.
  tonómetro de Schiötz Schiötz's tonometer.
tonoplasto *m.* tonoplast.
tonoscilógrafo *m.* tonoscillograph.
tonoscopio *m.* tonoscope.
tonotopicidad *f.* tonotopicity.
tonotópico, -ca *adj.* tonotopic.
tonotrópico, -ca *adj.* tonotropic.
tonsilar *adj.* tonsillar, tonsillary.
tonsilectomía *f.* tonsillectomy.
tonsilitis *f.* tonsillitis.
  tonsilitis caseosoa lacunar tonsillitis.
  tonsilitis lacunar, tonsilitis lagunar lacunar tonsillitis.
  tonsilitis parenquimatosa parenchymatous tonsillitis.
  tonsilitis superficial superficial tonsillitis.
  tonsilitis de Vincent Vincent tonsillitis.
tonsilito *m.* tonsillith.
tonsilolito *m.* tonsillolith.
tonsilomicosis *f.* tonsillomycosis.

tonsilomoniliasis *f.* tonsillomoniliasis.
tonsilopatía *f.* tonsillopathy.
tonsiloscopia *f.* tonsilloscopy.
tonsilotomía *f.* tonsillotomy.
tonsilótomo *m.* tonsillotome.
tonus tonus.
topagnosia *f.* topagnosia, topagnosis.
topagnosis *f.* topagnosis.
topalgia *f.* topalgia.
topar *v.* butt.
topestesia *f.* topesthesia.
Tópica *f.* topography.
tópico *m.* topicum.
tópico, -ca *adj.* topical.
topístico, -ca *adj.* topistic.
topoalgia *f.* topalgia.
topoanestesia *f.* topoanesthesia.
topodisestesia *f.* topodysesthesia.
topofilaxia *f.* topophylaxis.
topofilaxis *f.* topophylaxis.
topognosia *f.* topognosis.
topognosis *f.* topognosis.
topografía *f.* topography.
  topografía anatómica anatomical topography.
topográfico, -ca *adj.* topographic, topographical.
topograma *m.* topogram.
topología *f.* topology.
toponarcosis *f.* toponarcosis.
toponimia *f.* toponymy.
topónimo *m.* toponym.
toporestesia *f.* topoparesthesia.
topopatogenia *f.* topopathogenesis.
topoquímica *f.* topochemistry.
toposcopio *m.* toposcope.
topotermestesiómetro *m.* topothermesthesiometer.
topovacunación *f.* topovaccinotherapy.
topovacunoterapia *f.* topovaccinotherapy.
toque *m.* touching.
toracalgia *f.* thoracalgia.
toracectomía *f.* thoracectomy.
toracentesis *f.* thoracentesis.
torácico, -ca *adj.* thoracic.
toracicoabdominal *adj.* thoracicoabdominal.
toracicoacromial *adj.* thoracicoacromial.
toracicohumeral *adj.* thoracicohumeral.
toracoabdominal *adj.* thoracoabdominal.
toracoacromial *adj.* thoracoacromial.
toracobroncotomía *f.* thoracobronchotomy.
toracocelosquisis *f.* thoracoceloschisis.
toracocentesis *f.* thoracocentesis.
toracocilosis *f.* thoracocyllosis.
toracocirtosis *f.* thoracocyrtosis.
toracodelfo *m.* thoracodelphus.
toracodídimo *m.* thoracodidymus.
toracodinia *f.* thoracodynia.
toracoespinal *adj.* thoracospinal.
toracoestenosis *f.* thoracostenosis.
toracogastrodídimo *m.* thoracogastrodidymus.
toracogastrosquisis *f.* thoracogastroschisis.
toracógrafo *m.* thoracograph.
toracolaparotomía *f.* thoracolaparotomy.
toracólisis *f.* thoracolysis.
toracolumbar *adj.* thoracolumbar.
toracomelo *m.* thoracomelus.
toracometría *f.* thoracometry.
toracómetro *m.* thoracometer.
toracomiodinia *f.* thoracomyodynia.
toraconeumógrafo *m.* thoracopneumograph.
toraconeumoplastia *f.* thoracopneumoplasty.
toracópago *m.* thoracopagus.
toracoparacéfalo *m.* thoracoparacephalus.

toracopatía *f.* thoracopathy.
toracoplastia *f.* thoracoplasty.
  toracoplastia convencional conventional thoracoplasty.
  toracoplastia con costoversión, toracoplastia de costoversión costoversion thoracoplasty.
toracoscopia *f.* thoracoscopy.
toracoscopio *m.* thoracoscope.
toracospinal *adj.* thoracospinal.
toracosquisis *f.* thoracoschisis.
toracostenosis *f.* thoracostenosis.
toracostomía *f.* thoracostomy.
  toracostomía cerrada tube thoracostomy.
toracotomía *f.* thoracotomy.
  toracotomía anteroexterna anterolateral thoracotomy.
  toracotomía posterolateral posterolateral thoracotomy.
toradelfo *m.* thoradelphus.
tórax *m.* chest, thorax.
  tórax alar alar chest.
  tórax asténico keeled chest.
  tórax batiente flail chest.
  tórax enfisematoso emphysematous chest.
  tórax de estallido blast chest.
  tórax ftinoide phthinoid thorax.
  tórax globoso barrel chest.
  tórax inestable flail chest.
  tórax infundibuliforme funne chest, funnel chest.
  tórax óseo bony thorax.
  tórax de paloma pigeon chest.
  tórax paralítico paralytic chest, paralytic thorax.
  tórax de Peyrot Peyrot's thorax.
  tórax de pichón pigeon chest.
  tórax plano flat chest.
  tórax pterigoideo pterygoid chest.
  tórax pulsátil flail thorax.
  tórax en quilla keeled chest.
  tórax raquítico keeled chest.
  tórax tetraédrico tetrahedron chest.
  tórax en tonel barrel chest, barrel-shaped chest.
  tórax de Traube paralytic chest, paralytic thorax.
  tórax de zapatero cobbler's chest.
torcedura *f.* sprain.
tórcula *f.* torcula.
tórico, -ca *adj.* toric.
tormenta *f.* storm.
  tormenta tiroidea, tormenta tirotóxica thyroid storm, thyrotoxic storm.
tormina *f.* tormina.
torminal *adj.* torminal.
tornasol *m.* litmus.
tornillo autorroscante *m.* self-threading pin.
torniquete *m.* tourniquet.
  torniquete de cuero cabelludo scalp tourniquet.
  torniquete de Dupuytren Dupuytren tourniquet.
  torniquete de Esmarch Esmarch tourniquet.
  torniquete neumático pneumatic tourniquet.
  torniquete rotatorio automático automatic rotating tourniquet.
torno dental *m.* dental engine.
toro *m.* torus.
toroso, -sa *adj.* torose, torous.
torpente *adj.* torpent.
torpidez *f.* torpidity.
tórpido, -da *adj.* torpid.
torpor *m.* torpor.

torpor mental clouding of consciousness.
torpor retinal, torpor retinae torpor retinae.
torque *m.* torque.
torsiómetro *m.* torsiometer.
torsión *f.* torsion.
　torsión del cordón espermático torsion of the testis.
　torsión de un diente torsion of a tooth.
　torsión femoral femoral torsion.
　torsión del gancho clasp torsion.
　torsión negativa negative torsion.
　torsión positiva positive torsion.
　torsión testicular, torsión del testículo torsion of the testis.
　torsión tibial tibial torsion.
torsionómetro *m.* torsionometer.
torsiversión *f.* torsiversion.
torso *m.* torso.
torsoclusión *f.* torso-occlusion, torsocclusion.
tortícolis, torticolis *f.* torticollis.
　tortícolis congénita congenital torticollis.
　tortícolis convulsiva spasmodic torticollis.
　tortícolis dermatógena dermatogenic torticollis.
　tortícolis distónica dystonic torticollis.
　tortícolis espasmódica spasmodic torticollis.
　tortícolis espuria spurious torticollis.
　tortícolis falsa spurious torticollis.
　tortícolis fija fixed torticollis.
　tortícolis intermitente intermittent torticollis.
　tortícolis laberíntica labyrinthine torticollis.
　tortícolis miógeno myogenic torticollis.
　tortícolis neurógeno neurogenic torticollis.
　tortícolis ocular ocular torticollis.
　tortícolis refleja reflex torticollis.
　tortícolis reumática, tortícolis reumatoide rheumatoid torticollis.
　tortícolis sintomática symptomatic torticollis.
tortuoso, -sa *adj.* tortuous.
tórulo, torulo *m.* torulus.
toruloma *m.* toruloma.
Torulopsis Torulopsis.
torulopsosis *f.* torulopsosis.
torulosis *f.* torulosis.
torus torus.
tos *f.* cough, tussis.
　tos aneurismática aneurismal tussis.
　tos asmática asthmatic cough.
　tos auditiva, tos auricular ear cough.
　tos de Balme Balme's cough.
　tos bitonal bitonal cough.
　tos blanda wet cough.
　tos de catadores de té tea taster's cough.
　tos por compresión compression cough.
　tos convulsa whooping cough.
　tos coqueluchoide whooping cough.
　tos ferina whooping cough.
　tos dentaria tooth cough.
　tos espasmódica paroxysmal cough.
　tos extrapulmonar extrapulmonary cough.
　tos gástrica stomach cough.
　tos hebética hebetic cough.
　tos húmeda wet cough.
　tos invernal winter cough.
　tos mecánica mechanical cough.
　tos metálica brassy cough.
　tos de Morton Morton's cough.
　tos no productiva non-productive cough.
　tos paroxística paroxysmal cough.
　tos perruna hacking cough.
　tos productiva productive cough.
　tos quintosa whooping cough.
　tos refleja reflex cough.

tos simpática reflex cough.
tos seca dry cough, hacking cough.
tos de Sydenham Sydenham's cough.
tos del tejedor weaver's cough.
tos trigémina, tos trigeminal trigeminal cough.
tosferina *f.* whooping cough.
tósigo *m.* bane.
totemismo *m.* totemism.
totemístico, -ca *adj.* totemistic.
totipotencia *f.* totipotentia.
totipotencial *adj.* totipotential.
totipotencialidad *f.* totipotentiality.
totipotente *adj.* totipotent.
toxalbúmico, -ca *adj.* toxalbumic.
toxanemia *f.* toxanemia.
toxemia *f.* toxemia.
　toxemia alimentaria, toxemia alimenticia alimentary toxemia.
　toxemia eclámptica, toxemia eclamptogénica eclamptic toxemia, eclamptogenic toxemia.
　toxemia del embarazo toxemia of pregnancy.
　toxemia gravídica toxemia of pregnancy.
　toxemia hidatídica hydatid toxemia.
toxémico, -ca *adj.* toxemic.
toxicante *adj.* intoxicant.
toxicemia *f.* toxicemia.
toxicida *adj.* toxicide.
toxicidad *f.* toxicity.
　toxicidad aguda acute toxicity.
　toxicidad coclear cochlear toxicity.
　toxicidad del oxígeno oxygen toxicity.
　toxicidad por oxígeno, toxicidad pulmonar por oxígeno pulmonary oxygen toxicity.
　toxicidad vestibular vestibular toxicity.
tóxico *m.* toxin.
　tóxico irritante irritant poison.
tóxico, -ca *adj.* toxic.
toxicocinética *f.* toxicokinetics.
toxicodermatitis *f.* toxicodermatitis.
toxicodermatosis *f.* toxicodermatosis.
toxicodermia *f.* toxicoderma.
toxicóforo, -ra *adj.* toxipherous.
toxicogénico, -ca *adj.* toxicogenic.
toxicógeno, -na *adj.* toxicogenic.
toxicohemia, toxicemia *f.* toxicohemia, toxicemia.
toxicoide *adj.* toxicoid.
toxicología *f.* toxicolgy.
toxicológico, -ca *adj.* toxicologic.
toxicólogo, -ga *m., f.* toxicologist.
toxicomanía *f.* toxicomania.
toxicómano, -na *m., f.* toxicomaniac.
toxicopéctico, -ca *adj.* toxicopectic.
toxicopexia *f.* toxicopexia, toxicopexy.
toxicosis *f.* toxicosis.
　toxicosis alimenticia, toxicosis alimentaria alimentary toxicosis.
　toxicosis capilar hemorrágica hemorrhagic capillary toxicosis.
　toxicosis endógena endogenic toxicosis.
　toxicosis exógena exogenic toxicosis.
　toxicosis gestacional gestational toxicosis.
　toxicosis de retención retention toxicosis.
　toxicosis tiroidea thyroid toxicosis.
　toxicosis por triyodotironina (T3) triiodothyronine (T3) toxicosis.
toxífero, -ra *adj.* toxiferous.
toxiferoso, -sa *adj.* toxiferous.
toxigenicidad *f.* toxigenicity.
toxigénico, -ca *adj.* toxigenic.
toxígeno, -na *adj.* toxigenic.
toxignomónico, -ca *adj.* toxignomic.
toxiinfección *f.* toxinfection.

toxina *f.* toxin.
toxinemia *f.* toxinemia.
toxínico, -ca *adj.* toxinic.
toxinogenicidad *f.* toxinogenicity.
toxinógeno, -na *adj.* toxinogenic.
toxinogénico, -ca *adj.* toxinogenic.
toxinología *f.* toxinology.
toxinosis *f.* toxinosis.
toxinoterapia *f.* toxinotherapy.
toxipatía *f.* toxipathy.
toxipático, -ca *adj.* toxipathic.
toxiterapia *f.* toxinotherapy.
toxocariásico, -ca *adj.* toxocaral.
toxocariasis *f.* toxocariasis.
toxofílico, -ca *adj.* toxophilic.
toxófilo, -la *adj.* toxophil.
toxofobia *f.* toxophobia.
toxóforo, -ra *adj.* toxophore.
toxogenina *f.* toxogenin.
toxógeno, -na *adj.* toxogen.
toxoglobulina *f.* toxoglobulin.
toxoide *m.* toxoid.
toxoide-antitoxoide *m.* toxoid-antitoxoid.
toxonema *m.* toxoneme.
toxonosis *f.* toxonosis.
toxopéxico, -ca *adj.* toxopexic.
Toxoplasma Toxoplasma.
toxoplasmosis *f.* toxoplasmosis.
　toxoplasmosis adquirida en adultos acquired toxoplasmosis in adults.
　toxoplasmosis congénita congenital toxoplasmosis.
toxoproteína *f.* toxoprotein.
toxuria *f.* toxuria.
trabajo *m.* work.
　trabajo cardíaco dinámico dynamic cardiac work.
　trabajo cardíaco estático static cardiac work.
　trabajo del duelo work of mourning.
　trabajo de parto labor, travail.
　trabajo de parto espontáneo spontaneous labor.
　trabajo respiratorio breathing work.
　trabajo del sueño dream work.
trabamiento *m.* interlocking.
trabécula *f.* trabecula.
trabeculación *f.* trabeculation.
trabeculado, -da *adj.* trabeculate.
trabecular *adj.* trabecular.
trabeculectomía *f.* trabeculectomy.
trabeculoplastia *f.* trabeculoplasty.
　trabeculoplastia láser laser trabeculoplasty.
trabeculotomía *f.* trabeculotomy.
tracción *f.* traction.
　tracción 90-90 90-90 traction.
　tracción ambulatoria ambulatory traction.
　tracción axial axis traction.
　tracción de Bryant Bryant's traction.
　tracción de Buck Buck's traction.
　tracción cefálica head traction.
　tracción cutánea cutaneous traction.
　tracción cutánea adhesiva adhesive skin traction.
　tracción cutánea de Buck Buck's skin traction.
　tracción cutánea de Dunlop Dunlop skin traction.
　tracción cutánea no adhesiva non-adhesive skin traction.
　tracción por el eje axis traction.
　tracción elástica elastic traction.
　tracción equilibrada balanced traction.
　tracción esquelética skeletal traction.
　tracción esquelética de Dunlop Dunlop skeletal traction.

tracción externa external traction.
tracción en halo halo traction.
tracción halopélvica halopelvic traction.
tracción intermaxilar intermaxillary traction.
tracción isométrica isometric traction.
tracción isotónica isotonic traction.
tracción lingual tongue traction.
tracción maxilomandibular, tracción maxilomaxilar maxillomandibular traction.
tracción ortopédica orthopedic traction.
tracción con peso weight traction.
tracción de la piel skin traction.
tracción de Quigley Quigley traction.
tracción rodante de Neufeld Neufeld roller traction.
tracción de Russell Russell traction.
tracción de suspensión de Sayre Sayre's suspension traction.
tracoma *m.* trachoma.
tracoma de Arlt Arlt's trachoma.
tracoma de las cuerdas vocales trachoma of the vocal bands.
tracoma folicular granular trachoma.
tracoma granular granular trachoma.
tracoma de Türck Türck's trachoma.
tracomatoso, -sa *adj.* trachomatous.
tracto *m.* tract, tractus.
tractor *m.* tractor.
tractor de Lowsley Lowsley's tractor.
tractor prostático prostatic tractor.
tractor prostático de Young Young prostatic tractor.
tractor de Syms Syms tractor.
tractor uretral urethral tractor.
tractotomía *f.* tractotomy.
tractotomía anterolateral anterolateral tractotomy.
tractotomía espinal spinal tractotomy.
tractotomía espinotalámica spinothalamic tractotomy.
tractotomía intramedular intramedullary tractotomy.
tractotomía piramidal pyramidal tractotomy.
tractotomía de Schwartz Schwartz tractotomy.
tractotomía de Sjöqvist Sjöqvist tractotomy.
tractotomía trigémina trigeminal tractotomy.
tractotomía de Walker Walker tractotomy.
tractus tractus.
traducción *f.* translation.
traducción de muesca nick translation.
tráfico linfocitario *m.* lymphocytic homing.
tragal *adj.* tragal.
tragion, tragión *m.* tragion.
trago *m.* tragus.
tragofonía *f.* tragophonia, tragophony.
tragomascalia *f.* tragomaschalia.
tragopodia *f.* tragopodia.
tragus tragus.
tramitis *f.* tramitis.
trance *m.* trance.
trance alcohólico alcoholic trance.
trance hipnótico hypnotic trance.
trance inducido induced trance.
trance mortal death trance.
trance de sonambulismo somnambulistic trance.
tranquilizante *m. y adj.* tranquilizer.
tranquilizante mayor major tranquilizer.
tranquilizante menor minor tranquilizer.
transabdominal *adj.* transabdominal.
transacción *f.* transaction.
transacción falsa false transaction.
transacción ulterior ulterior transaction.
transaminasemia *f.* transaminasemia.
transanimación *f.* transanimation.

transaórtico, -ca *adj.* transaortic.
transapendicular *adj.* transappendageal.
transaudiente *adj.* transaudient.
transauricular *adj.* transatrial.
transaxil *adj.* transaxial.
transbasal *adj.* transbasal.
transcalente *adj.* transcalent.
transcapsidación *f.* transcapsidation.
transcalvarial *adj.* transcalvarial.
transcatéter *adj.* transcatheter.
transcervical *adj.* transcervical.
transcitosis *f.* transcytosis.
transcondilar *adj.* transcondylar.
transcondíleo, -a *adj.* transcondyloid.
transcondiloide *adj.* transcondyloid.
transcortical *adj.* transcortical.
transcricotiroideo, -a *adj.* transcricothyroid.
transcripción *f.* transcription.
transcripto, -ta *adj.* transcript.
transcutáneo, -a *adj.* transcutaneous.
transdérmico, -ca *adj.* transdermal.
transducción *f.* transduction.
transducción abortiva abortive transduction.
transducción de alta frecuencia high frequency transduction.
transducción de baja frecuencia low frequency transduction.
transducción completa complete transduction.
transducción especializada specialized transduction.
transducción específica specific transduction.
transducción general general transduction.
transducir *v.* transduce.
transductante *adj.* transductant.
transductor *m.* transducter.
transductor de flujo flow transducter.
transdural *adj.* transdural.
transección *f.* transection.
transeccionar *v.* transect.
transegmental *adj.* transsegmental.
transegmentario, -a *adj.* transsegmental.
transepidérmico, -ca *adj.* transepidermal.
transepitelial *adj.* transepithelial.
transeptal *adj.* transseptal.
transesfenoidal *adj.* transsphenoidal.
transesternal *adj.* transsternal.
transetmoidal *adj.* transethmoidal.
transexual *adj.* transsexual.
transexualismo *m.* transsexualism.
transfaunación *f.* transfaunation.
transfección *f.* transfection.
transfección osmótica osmotic transfection.
transfectoma *f.* transfectoma.
transferencia[1] *f.* transference.
transferencia de carga charge transfer.
transferencia embrionaria embryo transfer.
transferencia génica gene transfer.
transferencia de grupo group transfer.
transferencia intratubárica de gametos (TITG) gamete intrafallopian traction (GIFT).
transferencia lineal de energía (TLE) linear energy traction (LET).
transferencia de tendón tendon transfer.
transferencia[2] *f.* transference.
transferencia negativa negative transference.
transferencia de pensamiento, transferencia por pensamiento extrasensorial thought transference, extrasensory thought transference.
transferencia positiva positive transference.
transfixión *f.* transfixion.
transformación *f.* transformation.

transformación por asbesto asbestos transformation.
transformación bacteriana bacterial transformation.
transformación blástica blastic transformation.
transformación celular cell transformation.
transformación de Fourier (TF) Fourier's transformation (FT).
transformación globular fibrosa transformación G-F) globular-fibrosus transformation, (G-F transformation).
transformación de Lineweaver-Burk Lineweaver-Burk transformation.
transformación linfocitaria, transformación linfocitica, transformación de linfocitos lymphocyte transformation.
transformación de Lobry de Bruyn-van Ekenstein Lobry de Bruyn-van Ekenstein transformation.
transformación logit logit transformation.
transformador *m.* transformer.
transformante *adj.* transformant.
transfosforilación *f.* transphosphorylation.
transfundir *v.* transfuse.
transfusión *f.* transfusion.
transfusión arterial arterial transfusion.
transfusión autóloga autologous transfusion.
transfusión directa direct transfusion.
transfusión por exanguinación, transfusión exanguino exsanguination transfusion.
transfusión fetomaterna fetomaternal transfusion.
transfusión gemelo-gemelar twin-to-twin transfusion.
transfusión por goteo drip transfusion.
transfusión de granulocitos granulocyte transfusion.
transfusión de hemoderivados component therapy.
transfusión indirecta indirect transfusion.
transfusión inmediata immediate transfusion.
transfusión intraperitoneal intraperitoneal transfusion.
transfusión intrauterina intrauterine transfusion.
transfusión de leucocitos buffy coat transfusion.
transfusión mediata mediate transfusion.
transfusión peritoneal peritoneal transfusion.
transfusión placentaria placental transfusion.
transfusión de recambio exchange transfusion.
transfusión recíproca reciprocal transfusion.
transfusión de reemplazo replacement transfusion.
transfusión de sangre blood transfusion.
transfusión subcutánea subcutaneous transfusion.
transfusión de sustitución replacement transfusion.
transfusión de sustitución total total substitution transfusion.
transfusión total total substitution transfusion.
transgenación *f.* transgenation.
transgénico, -ca *adj.* transgenic.
transhiatal *adj.* transhiatal.
transición *f.* transition.
transición cervicotorácica cervicothoracic transition.

transición isomérica isomeric transition.

transición de la vida media midlife transition.

transicional *adj.* transitional.

transilíaco, -ca *adj.* transiliac.

transiliente *adj.* transilient.

transiluminación *f.* transillumination.

transináptico, -ca *adj.* transsynaptic.

transinsular *adj.* transinsular.

transisquiático, -ca *adj.* transischiac.

transístmico, -ca *adj.* transisthmian.

transistmiano, -na *adj.* transisthmian.

tránsito *m.* transit.

tránsito intestinal intestinal transit.

transitorio, -a *adj.* transient.

translateral *adj.* translateral.

translocación *f.* translocation.

translocación balanceada balanced translocation.

translocación equilibrada balanced translocation.

translocación recíproca reciprocal translocation.

translocación robertsoniana Robertsonian translocation.

translúcido, -da *adj.* translucent.

transmembrana *f.* transmembrane.

transmigración *f.* transmigration.

transmigración externa external transmigration.

transmigración interna internal transmigration.

transmisible *adj.* transmissible.

transmisión *f.* transmission.

transmisión doble duplex transmission.

transmisión efáptica ephaptic transmission.

transmisión horizontal horizontal transmission.

transmisión iatrogénica iatrogenic transmission.

transmisión neurohumoral neurohumoral transmission.

transmisión neuromuscular neuromuscular transmission.

transmisión neuroquímica neurochemical transmission.

transmisión de pensamiento thought broadcasting.

transmisión placentaria placental transmission.

transmisión sináptica synaptic transmission.

transmisión transestadial trans-stadial transmission.

transmisión transovárica transovarial transmission.

transmisión vertical vertical transmission.

transmisor, -ra *m.* sender, transmitter.

transmitancia *f.* transmittance.

transmitido, -da por polvo *adj.* dust-borne.

transmural *adj.* transmural.

transocular *adj.* transocular.

transorbitario, -a *adj.* transorbital.

transovárico, -ca *adj.* transovarial.

transpalatino, -na *adj.* tanspalatal.

transparente *adj.* transparent.

transparietal *adj.* transparietal.

transpeptidación *f.* transpeptidation.

transperitoneal *adj.* transperitoneal.

transpirable *adj.* transpirable.

transpiración *f.* transpiration.

transpiración pulmonar pulmonary transpiration.

transpirar *v.* transpire.

transplacentario, -a *adj.* transplacental.

transpleural *adj.* transpleural.

transporte *m.* transport.

transporte activo active transport.

transporte axoplasmático axoplasmic transport.

transporte ciliar del moco ciliary mucus transport.

transporte de hierro iron transport.

transporte de masa bulk transport.

transporte óseo bone transport.

transporte de oxígeno oxygen transport.

transporte pasivo passive transport.

transporte vesicular vesicular transport.

transposición *f.* transposition.

transpúbico, -ca *adj.* transpubic.

transtalámico, -ca *adj.* transthalamic.

transtemporal *adj.* transtemporal.

transtentorial *adj.* transtentorial.

transtermia *f.* transthermia.

transtimpánico, -ca *adj.* transtympanic.

transtorácico, -ca *adj.* transthoracic.

transtoracotomía *f.* transthoracotomy.

transtraqueal *adj.* transtracheal.

transtrocantericosteotomía *f.* transtrochantericosteotomy.

transudación *f.* transudation.

transudado *m.* transudate.

transudar *v.* transudate.

transureteroureterostomía *f.* transureteroureterostomy.

transuretral *adj.* transurethral.

transustanciación *f.* transubstantiation.

transvaginal *adj.* transvaginal.

transvateriano, -na *adj.* transvaterian.

transvector *m.* transvector.

transventricular *adj.* transventricular.

transversal *adj.* transversalis.

transversectomía *f.* transversectomy.

transversión *f.* transversion.

transverso, -sa *adj.* transverse, transversus.

transversocostal *adj.* transversocostal.

tranversotomía *f.* transversotomy.

transvesical *adj.* transvesical.

trapeciforme *adj.* trapeziform.

trapecio *m.* trapezium.

trapeciometacarpiano, -na *adj.* trapeziometacarpal.

trapezoide *adj.* trapezoid.

trapezoideo, -a *adj.* trapezoid.

tráquea *f.* trachea.

traqueal *adj.* tracheal.

traquealgia *f.* trachealgia.

traquectasia *f.* trachectasy.

traqueítis *f.* tracheitis, trachitis.

traquelagra *f.* trachelagra.

traquelalis *m.* trachelalis.

traquelectomía *f.* trachelectomy.

traquelematoma *m.* trachelematoma.

traqueliano, -na *adj.* trachelian.

traquelismo *m.* trachelism, trachelismus.

traquelitis *f.* trachelitis.

traquelocele *m.* trachelocele.

traquelocifosis *f.* trachelokyphosis.

traquelocilosis *f.* trachelocyllosis.

traquelocirtosis *f.* trachelocyrtosis.

traquelocistitis *f.* trachelocystitis.

traquelodinia *f.* trachelodynia.

traquelofima *m.* trachelophyma.

traquelología *f.* trachelology.

traquelólogo, -ga *m., f.* trachelologist.

traquelooccipital *adj.* trachelo-occipitalis.

traquelopano *m.* trachelopanus.

traquelopexia *f.* trachelopexy.

traqueloplastia *f.* tracheloplasty.

traquelorrafia *f.* trachelorrhaphy.

traquelosiringorrafia *f.* trachelosyringorrhaphy.

traquelosquisis *f.* tracheloschisis.

traquelotomía *f.* trachelotomy.

traqueoaerocele *m.* tracheoaerocele.

traqueobiliar *adj.* tracheobiliary.

traqueobroncomalacia *f.* tracheobronchomalacia.

traqueobroncomegalia *f.* tracheobronchomegaly.

traqueobroncoscopia *f.* tracheobronchoscopy.

traqueobronquial *adj.* tracheobronchial.

traqueobronquitis *f.* tracheobronchitis.

traqueocele *m.* tracheocele.

traqueoesofágico, -ca *adj.* tracheoesophageal.

traqueoestenosis *f.* tracheostenosis.

traqueofaríngeo, -a *adj.* tracheopharyngeal.

traqueofistulización *f.* tracheofistulization.

traqueofisura *f.* tracheofissure.

traqueofonesis *f.* tracheophonesis.

traqueofonía *f.* tracheophony.

traqueógeno, -a *adj.* tracheogenic.

traqueolaríngeo, -a *adj.* tracheolaryngeal.

traqueolaringotomía *f.* tracheolaryngotomy.

traqueomalacia *f.* tracheomalacia.

traqueomegalia *f.* tracheomegaly.

traqueopatía *f.* tracheopathia, tracheopathy.

traqueopatía osteoplásica tracheopathia osteoplastica.

traqueopiosis *f.* tracheopyosis.

traqueoplastia *f.* tracheoplasty.

traqueorrafia *f.* tracheorrhaphy.

traqueorragia *f.* tracheirrhagia.

traqueoscopia *f.* tracheoscopy.

traqueoscópico, -ca *adj.* tracheoscopic.

traqueoscopio *m.* tracheoscope.

traqueosquisis *f.* tracheoschisis.

traqueostenosis *f.* tracheostenosis.

traqueostoma *m.* tracheostoma.

traqueostomia *f.* tracheostomy.

traqueostomizar *v.* tracheostomize.

traqueotomía *f.* tracheotomy.

traqueotomía inferior inferior tracheotomy.

traqueotomía superior superior tracheotomy.

traqueotomizar *v.* tracheotomize.

traqueótomo *m.* tracheotome.

traquicromático, -ca *adj.* trachychromatic.

traquifonía *f.* trachyphonia.

traquitis *f.* trachitis.

trascendencia *f.* trascendence.

trascendental *adj.* trascendent.

trascendente *adj.* trascendent.

traslación *f.* traslation.

traslado *m.* transfer.

traslado con pivotación pivot transfer.

traslado por deslizamiento sliding transfer.

traslocación *f.* translocation.

trasonancia *f.* transonance.

trasplantar[1] *v.* transplant.

trasplantar[2] *adj.* trasplantar.

trasplante *m.* transplant, transplantation.

trasplante alogeneico allogeneic transplant.

trasplante autoplástico allogeneic transplant.

trasplante cardíaco, trasplante de corazón heart transplant.

trasplante corneal, trasplante de córnea corneal transplant.

trasplante dental tooth transplant.

trasplante de Gallie Gallie transplant.

trasplante hepático liver transplant.

trasplante heteroplástico heteroplastic transplant.

trasplante heterotópico heterotopic transplant.

trasplante HLA idéntico HLA-identical transplant.

*trasplante **homoplástico*** homoplastic transplant.

*trasplante **homotópico*** homotopic transplant.

*trasplante **isoplástico*** isotransplantation.

*trasplante de **médula ósea*** bone marrow transplant.

*trasplante **ortotópico*** orthotopic transplant.

*trasplante **pancreático*** pancreatic transplant.

*trasplante **pancreaticoduodenal*** pancreaticoduodenal transplant.

*trasplante **postmortem*** postmortem graft.

*trasplante **renal*** renal transplant.

*trasplante **singenesioplástico*** syngenesioplastic transplant.

*trasplante de **tejido fetal*** fetal tissue transplant.

*trasplante **tendinosos**, trasplante del **tendón*** tendon transplant.

trasplantectomía *f.* trasplantectomy.

trasposición *f.* transposition.

*trasposición **corregida de grandes vasos**, trasposición **corregida de grandes arterias*** corrected transposition of great vessels.

*trasposición de **grandes vasos**, trasposición de **grandes arterias**, trasposición de **los troncos arteriales*** transposition of great vessels.

*trasposición **parcial de grandes vasos*** partial transposition of great vessels.

trastorno *m.* disorder.

*trastorno por **abuso de sustancias*** substance abuse disorder.

*trastorno **adaptativo*** adjustment disorder.

*trastorno **afectivo estacional (TAE)*** seasonal affective disorder (SAD).

*trastorno **afectivo*** affective disorder.

*trastorno **amnésicos*** amnestic disorder.

*trastorno de **ansiedad*** anxiety disorder.

*trastorno de **ansiedad generalizada*** generalized anxiety disorder.

*trastorno de **ansiedad inducido por sustancias*** substance-induced anxiety disorder.

*trastorno de **ansiedad por separación*** separative anxiety disorder.

*trastorno **antisocial de la personalidad*** antisocial personality disorder.

*trastorno del **aprendizaje*** learning disorder.

*trastorno de **Asperger*** Asperger's disorder.

*trastorno **autista**, trastorno **autístico*** autistic disorder.

*trastorno **bipolar*** bipolar disorder.

*trastorno **bipolar I*** bipolar I disorder.

*trastorno **bipolar II*** bipolar II disorder.

*trastorno **ciclotímico*** cyclotimic disorder.

*trastorno de la **colágena*** collagen disorder.

*trastorno del **comportamiento*** behavior disorder.

*trastorno del **comportamiento en la niñez y en la adolescencia*** behavior disorder of childhood and adolescence.

*trastorno de la **conducta alimentaria*** eating disorder.

*trastorno del **control de impulsos*** impulse control disorder.

*trastorno de **conversión*** conversion disorder.

*trastorno por **déficit de atención con hiperactividad*** attention-deficit hyperactive disorder.

*trastorno del **desarrollo*** developmental disorder.

*trastorno **delirante*** delusional disorder.

*trastorno del **desarrollo psicológico*** psychological development disorder.

*trastorno de **despersonalización*** despersonalization disorder.

*trastorno **depresivo mayor*** major depressive disorder.

*trastorno **dismórfico corporal*** body dysmorphic disorder.

*trastorno **disociativo*** dissociative disorder.

*trastorno **distímico*** dysthymic disorder.

*trastorno por **dolor*** pain disorder.

*trastorno **específicos del desarrollo del aprendizaje escolar*** academic skill disorder.

*trastorno **espinocerebeloso*** spinocerebellar disorder.

*trastorno **esquizoafectivo*** schizoaffective disorder.

*trastorno **esquizoafectivo*** schizoaffective disorder.

*trastorno **esquizofreniforme*** schizophreniform disorder.

*trastorno **esquizoide de la personalidad*** schizoid personality disorder.

*trastorno **esquizotípico de la personalidad*** schizotypal personality disorder.

*trastorno del **estado del ánimo*** mood disorder.

*trastorno por **estrés agudo*** acute stress disorder.

*trastorno por **estrés postraumático*** posttraumatic stress disorder.

*trastorno **explosivo intermitente*** intermittent explosive disorder.

*trastorno **general del desarrollo**, trastorno **generalizado del desarrollo*** pervasive development disorder.

*trastorno **facticio*** factitious disorder.

*trastorno **funcional*** functional disorder.

*trastorno por **gen simple*** simple-gen disorder.

*trastorno **hereditario*** inherited disorder.

*trastorno **hipocondríaco*** hypochondriac disorder.

*trastorno **histriónico de la personalidad*** histrionic personality disorder.

*trastorno de **identidad disociativo*** dissociative identity disorder.

*trastorno de la **identidad sexual*** sexual identity disorder.

*trastorno por **inmunodeficiencia*** immunodeficiency disorder.

*trastorno **maniacodepresivo*** maniac-depressive disorder.

*trastorno de la **marcha*** gait disorder.

*trastorno **mendeliano*** Mendelian disorder.

*trastorno **mental*** mental disorder.

*trastorno **mental orgánico*** organic mental disorder.

*trastorno **metabólico*** metabolic disorder.

*trastorno **monogénico*** monogenic disorder.

*trastorno **multifactorial*** multifactorial disorder.

*trastorno **narcisista de la personalidad*** narcissistic personality disorder.

*trastorno **neurótico*** neurotic disorder.

*trastorno de **pánico*** panic disorder.

*trastorno de la **personalidad por dependencia*** dependent personality disorder.

*trastorno de **personalidad múltiple*** multiple personality disorder.

*trastorno **obsesivo-compulsivo de la personalidad*** obsessive-compulsive personality disorder.

*trastorno **paranoide de la personalidad*** paranoid personality disorder.

*trastorno de **procesamiento auditivo central*** central auditory processing disorder.

*trastorno **psicótico compartido*** shared psychotic disorder.

*trastorno **psicótico inducido por sustancias*** substance-induced psychotic disorder.

*trastorno de **receptor LDL*** LDL-receptor disorder.

*trastorno **relacionado con sustancias*** disorder related to substances.

*trastorno de **Rett*** Rett disorder.

*trastorno **sexual*** sexual disorder.

*trastorno de **somatización*** somatization disorder.

*trastorno **somatomorfo*** somatoform disorder.

*trastorno del **sueño*** sleep disorder.

*trastorno de **tics*** tic disorder.

trasudación *f.* transudation.

trasudado *m.* transudate.

tratamiento *m.* treatment.

*tratamiento **activo*** active treatment.

*tratamiento **adyuvante*** adjuvant treatment.

*tratamiento de **alta frecuencia*** high-frequency treatment.

*tratamiento **antigénico*** antigen treatment.

*tratamiento **antirrechazo*** anti-rejection treatment.

*tratamiento **autosérico**, tratamiento con **autosueros*** autoserous treatment.

*tratamiento **bajo el agua*** underwater treatment.

*tratamiento de **Bier*** Bier's treatment.

*tratamiento de **Bier combinado*** Bier's combined treatment.

*tratamiento de **Bouchardat*** Bouchardat's treatment.

*tratamiento de **Brehmer*** Brehmer's treatment.

*tratamiento de **Brown-Séquard*** Brown-Séquard's treatment.

*tratamiento **causal*** causal treatment.

*tratamiento de **choque insulínico*** insulin shock treatment.

*tratamiento **coadyuvante*** coadjuvant treatment.

*tratamiento de **coma insulínico**, tratamiento por **coma insulínico*** coma insulinic treatment.

*tratamiento **combinado*** combined modality treatment.

*tratamiento de **conducto radicular*** root canal treatment.

*tratamiento **conservador*** conservative treatment.

*tratamiento **curativo*** curative treatment.

*tratamiento de la **diabetes*** diabetic treatment.

*tratamiento **dietético*** dietetic treatment.

*tratamiento **empírico*** empiric treatment.

*tratamiento **escalonado*** stepped treatment.

*tratamiento **específico*** specific treatment.

*tratamiento **expectante*** expectant treatment.

*tratamiento de **eventración*** eventration treatment.

*tratamiento de **Frenkel*** Frenkel's treatment.

*tratamiento de **Goeckerman*** Goeckerman treatment.

*tratamiento de **Hartel*** Hartel's treatment.

*tratamiento **higiénico*** hygienic treatment.

*tratamiento **inmunosupresor*** immunosuppressive treatment.

*tratamiento de las **intoxicaciones*** poisoning treatment.

*tratamiento **isosérico*** isoserum treatment.

*tratamiento de **Kenny*** Kenny treatment.

tratamiento de Lerich Lerich's treatment.

tratamiento luminoso, tratamiento de luz light treatment.

tratamiento de mascarilla slush treatment.

tratamiento de Matas Matas' treatment.

tratamiento medicinal medicinal treatment.

tratamiento con el método del hilo string method treatment.

tratamiento neoadyuvante neoadjuvant treatment.

tratamiento orgánico organ treatment.

tratamiento de Orr Orr treatment.

tratamiento paliativo palliative treatment.

tratamiento del paludismo malarial treatment.

tratamiento preventivo preventive treatment.

tratamiento profiláctico prophylactic treatment.

tratamiento quirúrgico surgical treatment.

tratamiento radical radical treatment.

tratamiento reptante de Klapp Klapp's creeping treatment.

tratamiento con salicílicos salicyl treatment.

tratamiento de Schlösser Schlösser's treatment.

tratamiento de Semple Semple vaccine.

tratamiento sintomático symptomatic treatment.

tratamiento solar solar treatment.

tratamiento de sostén supporting treatment.

tratamiento de subcoma insulínico subcoma insulin treatment.

tratamiento sustitutivo substitutive treatment.

tratamiento de Tallermann Tallerman treatment.

tratamiento con telerradio teleradium treatment.

tratamiento con timo thymus treatment.

tratamiento con tiroides thyroid treatment.

tratamiento de tres colorantes three dye treatment.

tratamiento de Trueta Trueta treatment.

tratamiento zonal zone treatment.

tratar *v.* treat.

trauma *m.* trauma.

trauma acústico acoustic trauma.

trauma craneoencefálico cranioencephalic trauma.

trauma por herida de bala missile wound trauma.

trauma del nacimiento birth trauma.

trauma obstétrico del plexo braquial birth trauma of the brachial plexus.

trauma oclusal occlusal trauma.

trauma potencial potential trauma.

trauma psíquico psychic trauma.

trauma raquimedular spinal cord trauma.

trauma renal renal trauma.

trauma uretral urethral trauma.

traumastenia *f.* traumasthenia.

traumaterapia *f.* traumatherapy.

traumático, -ca *adj.* traumatic.

traumatismo *m.* traumatism.

traumatismo abdominal abdominal traumatism.

traumatismo abdominal abierto open abdominal traumatism.

traumatismo abdominal cerrado blunt abdominal traumatism.

traumatismo oclusal secundario secondary occlusal traumatism.

traumatizar *v.* traumatize.

traumatofilia *f.* traumatophilia.

traumatógeno, -na *adj.* traumatogenic.

traumatología *f.* traumatology.

traumatólogo, -ga *m.* traumatologist.

traumatonesis *f.* traumatonesis.

traumatopatía *f.* traumatopathy.

traumatópira *f.* traumatopyra.

traumatopnea *f.* traumatopnea.

traumatosepsis *f.* traumatosepsis.

traumatosis *f.* traumatosis.

traumatoterapia *f.* traumatotherapy.

traumatropismo *m.* traumatropism.

travestido, -da *m., f.* transvestite.

travestismo *m.* transvestism.

traviesa *f.* beam.

trayecto *m.* path.

trayector *m.* trajector.

trazado *m.* plot, tracing.

trazador *m.* tracer.

trazador de estilo stylus tracer.

trazador isotópico isotopic tracer.

trazador de punta de aguja needle-point tracer.

trazador de punta de flecha arrow-point tracer.

trazar *v.* plot.

trazo *m.* tracing.

trefina *f.* trephine.

trefinación *f.* trephination.

trefocito *m.* trephocyte.

trema *f.* trema.

Trematoda Trematoda.

trematodiasis *f.* trematodiasis.

trematodos, Trematodes *m.* trematodes, Trematodes.

trematología *f.* thremmatology.

tremoestable *adj.* tremostable.

tremógrafo *m.* tremograph.

tremograma *m.* tremogram.

tremolábil *adj.* tremolabile.

tremor *m.* tremor.

tremorgrama *m.* tremorgram.

trémulo, -la *adj.* tremulous.

tremulor *m.* tremulor.

trendscriber *m.* trendscriber.

trenscription *f.* trendscription.

trepanación *f.* trepanation.

trepanación corneal, trepanación de la córnea corneal trepanation, trepanation of the cornea.

trepanación dental dental trepanation.

trepanación esclerocorneal corneoscleral trepanation.

trepanador, -ra *m., f.* trepanner.

trepanar *v.* trephine.

trépano *m.* drill, trepan.

trépano canulado cannulated drill.

trepidación *f.* trepidation, trepidatio.

trepidación del corazón trepidatio cordis.

trepidante *adj.* trepidant.

Treponema Treponema.

treponemal *adj.* treponemal.

treponematosis *f.* treponematosis.

treponemiasis, treponemosis *f.* treponemiasis.

treponemicida *adj.* treponemicidal.

treponémico, -ca *adj.* treponemal.

treponemosis *f.* treponemiasis.

trepopnea *f.* trepopnea.

treppe *m.* treppe.

trepsia, trepsis *f.* threpsis.

trepsis *f.* threpsis.

tresis *f.* tresis.

tríada *f.* triad.

tríada adrenomedular adrenomedullary triad.

tríada de Andersen Andersen's triad.

tríada de Beck Beck's triad.

tríada de Bezold Bezold's triad.

tríada bucolinguomasticatoria buccolinguomasticatory triad.

tríada de Charcot Charcot's triad.

tríada de compresión aguda acute compression triad.

tríada del cono retiniano triad of the retinal cone.

tríada desgraciada de la rodilla knee triad.

tríada de Dieulafoy Dieulafoy's triad.

tríada de Fallot Fallot's triad.

tríada de Grancher Grancher's triad.

tríada de Hull Hull's triad.

tríada de Hutchinson Hutchinson's triad.

tríada infantil childhood triad.

tríada de Kartagener Kartagener's triad.

tríada de Luciani triad of Luciani.

tríada patológica pathologic triad.

tríada primaria primary triad.

tríada de Saint Saint's triad.

tríada de Schultz triad of Schultz.

tríada de Whipple Whipple's triad.

triaditis *f.* triaditis.

triage triage.

triage neonatal neonatal triage.

triangular *adj.* triangular, triangularis.

triángulo *m.* triangle, triangulum.

triángulo de Burow Burow's triangle.

triángulo escaleno de Burger Burger's scalene triangle.

triángulo de Garland Garland's triangle.

triángulo de Gerhardt Gerhardt's triangle.

triángulo de Grocco Grocco's.

triángulo de Koch Koch's triangle.

triángulo de Minor Minor's triangle.

triángulo quirúrgico surgical triangle.

triángulo de seguridad de Jackson Jackson's safety triangle.

triángulo de Tweed Tweed triangle.

triangulum triangulum.

triantebraquia *f.* triantebrachia.

triárquido, -da *adj.* triorchid.

triatómico, -ca *adj.* triatomic.

Triatominae Triatominae.

tríbada *f.* tribade.

tribadía *f.* tribady.

tribadismo *m.* tribadism.

tribásico, -ca *adj.* tribasic.

tribasilar *adj.* tribasilar.

tribología *f.* tribology.

triboluminiscencia *f.* triboluminiscence.

tribraquia *f.* tribrachia.

tribraquio *m.* tribrachius.

tribu *f.* tribe.

tricálcico, -ca *adj.* tricalcic.

tricalgia *f.* trichalgia.

tricatrofia *f.* trichatrophia.

tricauxis *f.* trichauxis.

tricéfalo *m.* tricephalus.

tricelular *adj.* tricelullar.

triceps *adj.* triceps.

Trichina Trichina.

Trichinella Trichinella.

Trichinella spiralis Trichinella spiralis.

Trichomonadida Trichomonadida.

Trichomonas Trichomonas.

Trichophyton Trichophyton.

Trichoptera Trichoptera.

Trichosporon, Trichosporum Trichosporon, Trichosporum.

Trichosporum Trichosporum.

Trichostomatida Trichostomatida.

Trichostronglyade Trichostronglyade.

Trichostrongylus Trichostrongylus.
trichuriasis *f.* trichuriasis.
Trichuris Trichuris.
Trichuroidea Trichuroidea.
tricíclico, -ca *adj.* tricyclic.
tricípite *adj.* tricipital.
tricipital *adj.* tricipital.
tricoanestesia *f.* trichoanesthesia.
tricobacteria *f.* trichobacteria.
tricobezoar *m.* trichobezoar.
tricocefaliasis *f.* trichocephaliasis.
tricocefalosis *f.* trichocephalosis.
tricocisto *m.* trichocyst.
tricoclasia *f.* trichoclasia, trichoclasis.
tricoclasis *f.* trichoclasis.
tricoclastia *f.* trichoclasis.
tricocriptosis *m.* trichocryptosis.
tricodinia *f.* trichodynia.
tricoepitelioma *m.* trichoepithelioma.
  tricoepitelioma desmoplásico desmoplastic trichoepithelioma.
  tricoepitelioma múltiple hereditario hereditary multiple trichoepithelioma.
  tricoepitelioma papiloso múltiple trichoepithelioma papillosum multiplex.
tricoestesia *f.* trichoesthesia.
tricoestesiómetro *m.* trichoesthesiometer.
tricoestrongilosis *f.* trychostrongylosis.
tricofagia *f.* trichophagy.
tricofibroacantoma *m.* trichofibroacanthoma.
tricofibroepitelioma *m.* trichofibroepithelioma.
tricofítico, -ca *adj.* trichophytic.
tricofítide *f.* trichophytid.
tricofitosis *f.* trichophytosis.
  tricofitosis de la barba trichophytosis barbae.
  tricofitosis de la cabeza trichophytosis capitis.
  tricofitosis crural rural trichophytosis.
  tricofitosis del cuerpo trichophytosis corporis.
  tricofitosis de las uñas trichophytosis unguium.
tricofoliculoma *m.* trichofolliculoma.
tricógeno *m.* trichogen.
tricogenoso, -sa *adj.* trichogenous.
tricoglosia *f.* trichoglossia.
tricografismo *m.* trichographism.
tricohialina *f.* trichohyalin.
tricoide *adj.* trichoid.
tricoideo, -a *adj.* trichoid.
tricoleucocito *m.* tricholeukocyte.
tricolito *m.* tricholith.
tricoma *m.* trichome.
tricomadesis *f.* trichomadesis.
tricomanía *f.* trichomania.
tricomatosis *f.* trichomatosis.
tricomatoso, -sa *adj.* trichomatous.
tricomegalia *f.* trichomegaly.
tricomicetosis *f.* trichomycetosis.
tricomicosis *f.* trichomycosis.
  tricomicosis axilar trichomycosis axillaris.
  tricomicosis cromática trichomycosis chromatica.
  tricomicosis nudosa, tricomicosis nodular trichomycosis nodosa, trichomycosis nodularis.
  tricomicosis palmellina trichomycosis palmellina.
  tricomicosis púbica trichomycosis chromatica.
  tricomicosis pustulosa trichomycosis pustulosa.
tricomona *f.* trichomonad.

tricomonadicida *adj.* trichomonadicidal.
tricomonal *adj.* trichomonal.
tricomoniasis *f.* trichomoniasis.
  tricomoniasis vaginitis trichomoniasis vaginitis.
tricomonicida *adj.* trichomonacidal.
triconocardiasis *f.* trichonocardiosis.
triconodosis *f.* trichonodosis.
triconosis *f.* trichonosis.
  triconosis versicolor versicolor trichonosis.
tricopatía *f.* trichopathy.
tricopático, -ca *adj.* trichopathic.
tricopoliosis *f.* trichopoliosis.
tricoptilosis *f.* trichoptilosis.
tricorne *adj.* tricorn, tricornute.
tricorrea *f.* trichorrhea.
tricorrexia *f.* trichorrhexis.
tricorrexis *f.* trichorrhexis.
  tricorrexis invaginada trichorrhexis invaginata.
  tricorrexis nudosa trichorrhexis nodosa.
tricoscopia *f.* trichoscopy.
tricosis *f.* trichosis.
  tricosis caruncular, tricosis de la carúncula trichosis carunculae.
  tricosis sensitiva trichosis sensitiva.
  tricosis setosa trichosis setosa.
tricosporia *f.* trichosporosis.
tricosporosis *f.* trichosporosis.
tricosquisis *f.* trichoschisis.
tricostasis espinulosa *f.* trichostasis spinulosa.
tricostrongiliasis *f.* trichostrongyliasis.
tricotilomanía *f.* trichotillomania.
tricotiodistrofia *f.* trichothiodystrophy.
tricotomía *f.* trichotomy.
tricotomoso, -sa *adj.* trichotomous.
tricotrofia *f.* trichotrophy.
tricroico, -ca *adj.* trichroic.
tricroísmo *m.* trichroism.
tricromasia *f.* trichromasy.
  tricromasia anómala anomalous trichromasy.
tricromático, -ca *adj.* trichromatic.
tricromatismo *m.* trichromatism.
  tricromatismo anómalo anomalous trichromatism.
tricromatopsia *f.* trichromatopsia.
tricromía *f.* trichromatism.
tricrómico, -ca *adj.* trichromic.
tricrótico, -ca *adj.* trichrotic.
tricrotismo *m.* trichrotism.
tricroto, -ta *adj.* trichrotic.
tricuriasis *f.* trichuriasis.
tricuspidalización *f.* tricuspidalization.
tricúspide *adj.* tricuspid, tricuspidal, tricuspidate.
tridactilia *f.* tridactylism.
tridáctilo, -la *adj.* tridactylous.
tridentado, -da *adj.* tridentate.
tridente *adj.* trident, tridentate.
tridérmico, -ca *adj.* tridermic.
tridermogénesis *f.* tridemogenesis.
tridermona *m.* tridermona.
tridigitado, -da *adj.* tridigitate.
trielcón *m.* trielcon.
triencéfalo, -la *adj.* triencephalous.
triesplácnico, -ca *adj.* trisplanchnic.
trifalangia *f.* triphalangia.
trifalángico, -ca *adj.* triphalangeal.
trifalangismo *m.* triphalangism.
trifásico, -ca *adj.* triphasic.
trífido, -da *adj.* trifid.
trifilocefalia *f.* trifilocephalia.
trifocal *adj.* trifocal.
triftemia *f.* triphthemia.

trifurcación *f.* trifurcation.
trigástrico, -ca *adj.* trigastric.
trigeminal *adj.* trigeminal.
trigeminismo *m.* trigeminy.
trigémino *m.* trigeminus.
trigénico, -ca *adj.* trigenic.
triglicérido *m.* triglyceride.
trigocéfalo, -la *m.* trigocephalus.
trigonal *adj.* trigonal.
trigonitis *f.* trigonitis.
trígono *f.* trigone, trigonum.
trigonocefalia *f.* trigonocephalia, trigonocephaly.
trigonocefálico, -ca *adj.* trigonodephalic.
trigonocéfalo *m.* trigonocephalus.
trigonótomo *m.* trigonotome.
trigonum trigonum.
trihíbrido, -da *adj.* trihybrid.
triiniodimo *m.* triiniodymus.
trilabo *m.* trilabe.
trilaminar *adj.* trilaminar.
trilateral *adj.* trilateral.
trillizo, -za *adj.* triplets.
trilobectomía *f.* trilobectomy.
trilobulado, -da *adj.* trilobate.
trilocular *adj.* trilocular.
trilogía *f.* trilogy.
  trilogía de Fallot Fallot's trilogy.
trilostano *m.* trilostane.
trimensual *adj.* trimensual.
trimérico, -ca *adj.* trimeric.
trímero *m.* trimer.
trimestral *adj.* trimensual.
trimestre *m.* trimester.
trimetilaminuria *f.* trimethylaminuria.
trimorfismo *m.* trimorphism.
trimorfo, -fa *adj.* trimorphous.
trimórfico, -ca *adj.* trimorphous.
trinegativo, -va *adj.* trinegative.
trineural *adj.* trineural.
trinéurico, -ca *adj.* trineural.
trinucleado, -da *adj.* trinucleate.
trinucleótido *m.* trinucleotide.
triocéfalo *m.* triocephalus.
trioftalmo *m.* triophthalmos.
triolismo *m.* triolism.
triónimo *m.* trionym.
triopódimo, -ma *adj.* triopodymus.
triorquidia *f.* triorquidism.
triorquidismo *m.* triorquidism.
triorquio, -a *adj.* triorchid.
trioto, -ta *adj.* triptus.
trióxido *m.* trioxide.
tripánide *f.* trypanid.
tripanocida[1] *m.* trypanocide.
tripanocida[2] *adj.* trypanocidal.
tripanólisis *f.* trypanolysis.
tripanolítico, -ca *adj.* trypanolytic.
tripanosoma *m.* trypanosome.
tripanosomático, -ca *adj.* trypanosomatic.
tripanosomatosis *f.* trypanosomatosis.
tripanosomatotrópico, -ca *adj.* trypanosomatotropic.
tripanosomíaco, -ca *adj.* trypanosomal.
tripanosomiasis *f.* trypanosomiasis.
  tripanosomiasis africana African trypanosomiasis.
  tripanosomiasis del África Occidental West African trypanosomiasis.
  tripanosomiasis del África Oriental East African trypanosomiasis.
  tripanosomiasis aguda acute trypanosomiasis.
  tripanosomiasis americana, tripanosomiasis brasileña Brazilian trypanosomiasis.

tripanosomiasis crónica chronic trypanosomiasis.

tripanosomiasis de Cruz Cruz trypanosomiasis.

tripanosomiasis gambiense Gambian trypanosomiasis.

tripanosomiasis rhodesiense Rhodesian trypanosomiasis.

tripanosomiasis sudamericana South American trypanosomiasis.

tripanosómico, -ca *adj.* trypanosomal, trypanosomic.

tripanosómide *f.* trypanosomid.

trípara *f.* tripara.

tripartito, -ta *adj.* tripartite.

tripesis *f.* trypesis.

triple *adj.* triple.

triplex *m.* triplex.

triplejía *f.* triplegia.

triplete *m.* triplet.

triploblástico, -ca *adj.* triploblastic.

triplocoria *f.* triplokoria.

triploide *adj.* triploid.

triploidia *f.* triploidy.

triplopía *f.* triplopia.

triplopsia *f.* triplopia.

tripnosomiosis *f.* trypanosomiasis.

trípode *m.* tripod.

trípode de la vida, trípode vital tripod of life, vital tripod.

tripodia *f.* tripodia.

tripodismo *m.* tripoding.

tripositivo, -va *adj.* tripositive.

triprósopo *m.* triprosopus.

tripsinizar *v.* trypsinize.

tripsinógeno *m.* trypsinogen.

tripsógeno *m.* trypsogen.

tríptico, -ca *adj.* tryptic.

triptocoria *f.* triptokoria.

triptofanuria *f.* tryptophanuria.

triptofanuria con enanismo tryptophanuria with dwarfism.

triptólisis *f.* tryptolysis.

triptolítico, -ca *adj.* tryptolytic.

triptonemia *f.* tryptonemia.

tripus tripus.

triqulasis *f.* trichiasis.

triquiasis anal anal trichiasis.

triquilémico, -ca *adj.* trichilemmal.

triquilemoma *m.* trichilemmoma.

triquineliasis *f.* trichinelliasis.

triquinelosis *f.* trichinellosis.

triquiniasis *f.* trichiniasis.

triquinífero, -ra *adj.* trichinipherous.

triquinización *f.* trichinization.

triquinoscopio *m.* trichinoscope.

triquinosis *f.* trichinosis.

triquinoso, -sa *adj.* trichinous.

triquión *m.* trichion.

triquitis *f.* trichitis.

trirradiación *f.* triradiation.

trirradiado, -da *adj.* triradiate.

trirradial *adj.* triradial.

trirradio *m.* triradius.

trismico, -ca *adj.* trismic.

trismo *m.* trismus.

trismo capistratus trismus capistratus.

trismo cómico trismus sardonicus.

trismo doloroso trismus dolorificus.

trismo del nacimiento trismus nascentium.

trismo neonatal trismus neonatorum.

trismo del recién nacido trismus neonatorum.

trismo sardónico trismus sardonicus.

trismoide *m.* trismoid.

trismus trismus.

trisomía *f.* trisomy, trisomia.

trisómico, -ca *adj.* trisomic.

trisquiasis *f.* trischiasis.

tristeza *f.* sadness.

tristiquia *f.* tristichia.

trisurcado, -da *adj.* trisulcate.

tritánico, -ca *adj.* tritan.

tritanomalia *f.* tritanomaly.

tritanomalo, -la *adj.* tritanomal.

tritanomalopía *f.* tritanomalopia.

tritánope *adj.* tritanope.

tritanopía *f.* tritanopia.

tritanópico, -ca *adj.* tritanopic.

tritanopsia *f.* tritanopsia.

tritocónide *m.* tritoconid.

tritócono *m.* tritocone.

trituración[1] *f.* grinding.

trituration[2] *f.* trituration.

triturador *m.* triturator.

triturar *v.* triturate.

trivalencia *f.* trivalence.

trivalente *adj.* trivalent.

trivalvo, -va *adj.* trivalve.

trivalvulado, -da *adj.* trivalve.

triyodotironina *f.* triiodothyronine.

trizonal *adj.* trizonal.

trocánter *m.* trochanter.

trócar *m.* trocar.

trócar de Duchenne Duchenne's trocar.

trócar de Durham Durham's trocar.

trócar piloto piloting trocar.

tróclea *f.* trochlea.

troclear *adj.* trochlear.

trocleariforme *adj.* trochleariform.

trococardia *f.* trochocardia.

trococefalia *f.* trochocephalia, trochocephaly.

trocoide *adj.* trochoid.

trocoideo, -a *adj.* trochoid.

trocoides *m.* trochoides.

trocorrizocardia *f.* trocorizocardia.

trofectodermo *m.* trophectoderm.

trofedema *m.* trophedema.

trofesia *f.* trophesy.

trofesial *adj.* trophesial.

trofésico, -ca *adj.* trophesic.

troficidad *f.* trophicity.

trófico, -ca *adj.* trophic.

trofismo *m.* trophism.

trofoblasto *m.* trophoblast.

trofoblastoma *m.* trophoblastoma.

trofocito *m.* trophocyte.

trofocromatina *f.* trophochromatin.

trofocromidia *f.* trophochromidia.

trofodermo *m.* trophoderm.

trofodermatoneurosis *f.* trophodermatoneurosis.

trofodinámica *f.* trophodynamics.

trofoedema *m.* trophedema.

trofolecítico, -ca *adj.* tropholecithal.

trofolecito *m.* tropholecithus.

trofología *f.* trophology.

trofoneurosis *f.* trophoneurosis.

trofoneurosis facial facial trophoneurosis.

trofoneurosis lingual lingual trophoneurosis.

trofoneurosis muscular muscular trophoneurosis.

trofoneurosis de Romberg Romberg's trophoneurosis.

trofoneurótico, -ca *adj.* trophoneurotic.

trofonosis *f.* trophonosis.

trofonúcleo *m.* trophonucleus.

trofopatía *f.* trophopathy.

trofoplasto *m.* trophoplast.

trofospongia *m.* trophospongia.

trofospongio *m.* trophospongia.

trofotaxia *f.* trophotaxis.

trofotaxis *f.* trophotaxis.

trofoterapia *f.* trophotherapy.

trofotropismo *m.* trophotropism.

trombaféresis *f.* thrombapheresis.

trombectomía *f.* thrombectomy.

trombina *f.* thrombin.

trombo *m.* thrombus.

trombo aglutinativo agglutinative thrombus.

trombo agonal agonal thrombus.

trombo agónico agony thrombus.

trombo ante mortem antemortem thrombus.

trombo anular annular thrombus.

trombo autóctono primary thrombus.

trombo biliar bile thrombus.

trombo blanco white thrombus.

trombo calcificado calcified thrombus.

trombo esférico ball thrombus.

trombo estratificado stratified thrombus.

trombo fibrinoso, trombo de fibrina fibrin thrombus.

trombo hialino hyaline thrombus.

trombo infectivo infective thrombus.

trombo de jalea de grosella currant jelly thrombus.

trombo lácteo milk thrombus.

trombo laminado laminated thrombus.

trombo lateral lateral thrombus.

trombo marasmático, trombo marásmico marantic thrombus, marasmatic thrombus.

trombo mixto mixed thrombus.

trombo mural mural thrombus.

trombo obliterante obstructive thrombus.

trombo obstructivo obstructive thrombus.

trombo oclusivo occluding thrombus, occlusive thrombus.

trombo organizado organized thrombus.

trombo pálido pale thrombus.

trombo parásito, trombo parasitario parasitic thrombus.

trombo parietal parietal thrombus.

trombo plaquetario plate thrombus, platelet thrombus.

trombo post mortem post mortem thrombus.

trombo previo a la muerte antemortem thrombus.

trombo primario primary thrombus.

trombo prolongado, trombo propagado propagated thrombus.

trombo rojo red thrombus.

trombo secundario secondary thrombus.

trombo subsecuente a la muerte post mortem thrombus.

trombo traumático traumatic thrombus.

trombo valvular valvular thrombus.

tromboangeítis *f.* thromboangiitis.

tromboangeítis obliterante thromboangiitis obliterans.

tromboangitis *f.* thromboangiitis.

tromboastenia *f.* thrombasthenia.

tromboblasto *m.* thromboblast.

trombocinasa *f.* thrombokinase.

trombocinesia *f.* thrombokinesis.

trombocinesis *f.* thrombokinesis.

trombocinética *f.* thrombokinetics.

trombocisto *m.* thrombocyst.

trombocitaféresis *f.* thrombocytapheresis.

trombocitemia *f.* thrombocythemia.

trombocitemia esencial essential thrombocythemia.

trombocitemia hemorrágica hemorrhagic thrombocythemia.

trombocitemia idiopática idiopathic thrombocythemia.

trombocitemia primaria primary thrombocythemia.

trombocítico, -ca *adj.* thrombocytic.

trombocitócrito *m.* thrombocytocrit.

trombocitólisis *f.* thrombocytolysis.

trombocitopatía *f.* thrombocytopathy.

trombocitopático, -ca *adj.* thrombocytopathic.

trombocitopenia *f.* thrombocytopenia.

trombocitopenia autoinmune autoimmune thrombocytopenia.

trombocitopenia esencial essential thrombocytopenia.

trombocitopenia inmune immune thrombocytopenia.

trombocitopenia isoinmune isoimmune thrombocytopenia.

trombocitopoyesis *f.* thrombocytopoiesis.

trombocitopoyético, -ca *adj.* thrombocytopoietic.

trombocitosis *f.* thrombocytosis.

tromboclasis *f.* thromboclasis.

tromboclástico, -ca *adj.* thromboclastic.

tromboclastografía *f.* thromboclastography.

tromboelastografo *m.* thromboelastograh.

tromboelastograma *m.* thromboelastogram.

tromboembolia *f.* thromboembolism.

tromboembolismo *m.* thromboembolism.

tromboendarterectomía *f.* thromboendarterectomy.

tromboendarteritis *f.* thromboendarteritis.

tromboendocarditis *f.* thromboendocarditis.

tromboestasis *f.* thrombostasis.

trombofilia *f.* thrombophilia.

tromboflebitis *f.* thrombophlebitis.

tromboflebitis iliofemoral posparto postpartum iliofemoral thrombophlebitis.

tromboflebitis migratoria thrombophlebitis migrans.

tromboflebitis purulenta thrombophlebitis purulenta.

tromboflebitis saltarina thrombophlebitis saltans.

trombogénesis *f.* thrombogenesis.

trombógeno, -na *adj.* thrombogenic.

tromboide *adj.* thromboid.

trombolinfangitis *f.* thrombolymphangitis.

trombólisis *f.* thrombolysis.

trombolítico, -ca *adj.* thrombolytic.

trombopatía *f.* thrombopathia, thrombopathy.

trombopenia *f.* thrombopenia, thrombopeny.

tromboplástico, -ca *adj.* thromboplastic.

tromboplástida *f.* thromboplastid.

tromboplastina *f.* thromboplastin.

trombopoyesis *f.* thrombopoiesis.

trombopoyético, -ca *adj.* thrombopoietic.

tromboquinesis *f.* thrombokinesis.

trombosado, -da *adj.* thrombosed.

trombosinusitis *f.* thrombosinusitis.

trombosis *f.* thrombosis.

trombosis agonal agonal thrombosis.

trombosis arterial postraumática post-traumatic arterial thrombosis.

trombosis atrófica atrophic thrombosis.

trombosis cardiaca cardiac thrombosis.

trombosis cerebral cerebral thrombosis.

trombosis por compresión compression thrombosis.

trombosis coronaria coronary thrombosis.

trombosis por dilatación dilatation thrombosis.

trombosis por infección infective thrombosis.

trombosis en lámina plate thrombosis, platelet thrombosis.

trombosis marántica, trombosis marásmica marantic thrombosis, marasmic thrombosis.

trombosis mesentérica, trombosis mesentérica arterial mesenteric thrombosis, mesenteric arterial thrombosis.

trombosis mural mural thrombosis.

trombosis placentaria placental thrombosis.

trombosis plaquetaria plate thrombosis, platelet thrombosis.

trombosis propagante propagating thrombosis.

trombosis puerperal puerperal thrombosis.

trombosis reptante creeping thrombosis.

trombosis de Ribert agonal thrombosis.

trombosis saltarina jumping thrombosis.

trombosis del seno cavernoso cavernous sinus thrombosis.

trombosis sinusal sinus thrombosis.

trombosis traumática traumatic thrombosis.

trombosis venosa venous thrombosis.

trombosis venosa postraumática post-traumatic venous thrombosis.

trombostenina *f.* thrombostenin.

trombótico, -ca *adj.* thrombotic.

tromofonia *f.* thromophonia.

trompa *f.* tube, tuba.

tronco *m.* trunk, truncus.

tropesis *f.* tropesis.

tropía *f.* tropia.

tropicopolita *adj.* tropicopolitan.

tropismo *m.* tropism.

tropocolágena *f.* tropocollagen.

tropocromo, -ma *adj.* tropochrome.

tropómetro *m.* tropometer.

troquelado *m.* imprinting.

troquín *m.* trochin, trochinus.

troquiter *m.* trochiter.

troquiteriano, -na *adj.* trochiterian.

truncado, -da *adj.* truncate, truncatus.

truncal *adj.* truncal.

truncar *v.* truncate.

trusión *f.* trusion.

trusión corporal bodily trusion.

trusión maxilar inferior mandibular trusion.

trusión maxilar superior maxillary trusion.

Trypanosoma Trypanosoma.

Trypanosomatidae Trypanosomatidae.

Trypanosomatina Trypanosomatina.

Tsa *m.* Tsa.

tsetsé *f.* tsetse.

tsutsugamushi tsutsugamushi.

tubárico, -ca *adj.* tubal.

tubario, -ria *adj.* tubal.

tubectomía *f.* tubectomy.

tuber tuber.

tuberculación *f.* tuberculation.

tuberculado, -da *adj.* tuberculate, tuberculated.

tubercular *adj.* tubercular.

tubercúlide *f.* tuberculid.

tuberculígeno, -na *adj.* tuberculigenous.

tuberculina *f.* tuberculin.

tuberculinación *f.* tuberculination.

tuberculinización *f.* tuberculinization.

tuberculinoterapia *f.* tuberculinotherapy.

tuberculitis *f.* tuberculitis.

tubérculo *m.* tubercle, tuberculum.

tuberculocele *m.* tuberculocele.

tuberculocida[1] *m.* tuberculocide.

tuberculocida[2] *adj.* tuberculocidal.

tuberculoderma *m.* tuberculoderma.

tuberculofibroide *m.* tuberculofibroid.

tuberculofibrosis *f.* tuberculofibrosis.

tuberculoide *adj.* tuberculoid.

tuberculoidina *f.* tuberculoidin.

tuberculoma *m.* tuberculoma.

tuberculoma en placa tuberculoma en plaque.

tuberculoopsónico, -ca *adj.* tuberculo-opsonic.

tuberculosilicosis *f.* tuberculosilicosis.

tuberculosis *f.* tuberculosis.

tuberculosis abierta open tuberculosis.

tuberculosis del adulto adult tuberculosis.

tuberculosis aerógena aerogenic tuberculosis.

tuberculosis aguda acute tuberculosis.

tuberculosis antracótica anthracotic tuberculosis.

tuberculosis articular white tumor, chronic tuberculous arthritis.

tuberculosis atenuada attenuated tuberculosis.

tuberculosis atípica atypical tuberculosis.

tuberculosis basal basal tuberculosis.

tuberculosis bucal oral tuberculosis.

tuberculosis cerebral cerebral tuberculosis.

tuberculosis cestódica cestodic tuberculosis.

tuberculosis cutánea cutaneous tuberculosis.

tuberculosis cutánea colicuativa tuberculosis cutis colliquativa.

tuberculosis cutánea liquenoide tuberculosis cutis lichenoides.

tuberculosis cutánea miliar diseminada tuberculosis cutis miliaris disseminata.

tuberculosis cutánea orificial tuberculosis cutis orificialis.

tuberculosis cutis tuberculosis cutis.

tuberculosis cutis folicular diseminada tuberculosis cutis follicularis disseminata.

tuberculosis cutis luposa tuberculosis cutis luposa.

tuberculosis cutis verrugosa tuberculosis cutis verrucosa.

tuberculosis dérmica dermal tuberculosis.

tuberculosis entérica enteric tuberculosis.

tuberculosis espinal spinal tuberculosis, tuberculosis of the spine.

tuberculosis exudativa exudative tuberculosis.

tuberculosis de los ganglios linfáticos tuberculosis of the lymph nodes.

tuberculosis general general tuberculosis.

tuberculosis genital genital tuberculosis.

tuberculosis genitourinaria genitourinary tuberculosis.

tuberculosis hematógena hematogenous tuberculosis.

tuberculosis hilial, tuberculosis hiliar hilus tuberculosis.

tuberculosis de huesos y articulaciones tuberculosis of bones and joints.

tuberculosis de la infancia childhood tuberculosis.

tuberculosis por inhalación inhalation tuberculosis.

tuberculosis intestinal tuberculosis of the intestines.

tuberculosis laríngea tuberculosis of the larynx.

tuberculosis linfoide tuberculosis of the lymph nodes.

tuberculosis liquenoide tuberculosis lichenoides.

tuberculosis miliar, tuberculosis miliar aguda miliary tuberculosis, acute miliary tuberculosis.

tuberculosis miliar diseminada tuberculosis miliaris disseminata.

tuberculosis orificial orificial tuberculosis.

tuberculosis papulonecrótica papulonecrotic tuberculosis.

tuberculosis de la piel tuberculosis of the skin.

tuberculosis posprimaria postprimary tuberculosis.

tuberculosis primaria primary tuberculosis.

tuberculosis primaria de inoculación primary inoculation tuberculosis.

tuberculosis pulmonar pulmonar tuberculosis.

tuberculosis raquidea spinal tuberculosis, tuberculosis of the spine.

tuberculosis de reinfección reinfection tuberculosis.

tuberculosis secundaria secondary tuberculosis.

tuberculosis suprarrenal adrenal tuberculosis.

tuberculosis de tipo infantil childhood type tuberculosis.

tuberculosis traqueobronquial tracheobronchial tuberculosis.

tuberculosis ulcerosa tuberculosis ulcerosa.

tuberculosis verrucosa, tuberculosis verrucosa cutánea warty tuberculosis, tuberculosis verrucosa cutis.

tuberculoso, -sa adj. tuberculous.

tuberculostático, -ca adj. tuberculostatic.

tuberculótico, -ca adj. tuberculotic.

tuberculum tuberculum.

tuberosidad f. tuberosity, tuberositas.

tuberositas tuberositas.

tuberoso, -sa adj. tuberous, tuberosus.

tubo m. tube, tubus.

tubo de Abbott-Rawson Abbott-Rawson tube.

tubo de alimentación feeding tube.

tubo de Bouchut Bouchut's tube.

tubo de Bourdon Bourdon tube.

tubo de Bowman Bowman's tube.

tubo de Cantor Cantor tube.

tubo de Carlen Carlen's tube.

tubo catódico caliente hot-cathode tube.

tubo de Chaoul Chaoul tube.

tubo de Celestin Celestin tube.

tubo de Coolidge Coolidge tube.

tubo de Crookes Crookes' tube.

tubo de descarga discharge tube.

tubo de drenaje drainage tube.

tubo de Durham Durham tube.

tubo de empiema empyema tube.

tubo de ensayo test tube.

tubo de Esmarch Esmarch's tube.

tubo de esputo sputum tube.

tubo de fermentación fermentation tube.

tubo fotomultiplicador photomultiplier tube.

tubo de fusión fusion tube.

tubo de gas gaz tube.

tubo de Geissler, tubo de Geissler-Pluecker Geissler's tube, Geissler-Pluecker tube.

tubo de Hittorf Hittorf tube.

tubo de Leonard Leonard tube.

tubo de Levin Levin tube.

tubo de Martin Martin's tube.

tubo de Mett Mett's tube.

tubo de Miller-Abbott Miller-Abbott tube.

tubo de Moss Moss tube.

tubo de O'Dwyer O'Dwyer's tube.

tubo orotraqueal orotracheal tube.

tubo de Pault-Mixter Paul-Mixter tube.

tubo de rayos catódicos cathode-ray tube.

tubo de rayos X X-ray tube.

tubo de Rehfuss Rehfuss tube.

tubo de Roida Roida's tube.

tubo de rollo roll tube.

tubo de Ryle Ryle's tube.

tubo de Sengstaken-Blakemore Sengstaken-Blakemore tube.

tubo de Souttar Souttar's tube.

tubo de Thunberg Thunberg tube.

tubo de traqueotomía tracheotomy tube.

tubo al vacío, tubo de vacío vacuum tube.

tubo de válvula valve tube.

tubo de Veillon Veillon tube.

tubo vertical vertical tube.

tubo de Wangensteen Wangensteen tube.

tuboabdominal adj. tuboabdominal.

tuboanexopexia f. tuboadnexopexy.

tuboligamentario, -ria adj. tuboligamentous.

tuboligamentoso, -sa adj. tuboligamentous.

tuboovárico, -ca adj. tubo-ovarian.

tuboovariotomía f. tubo-ovariotomy.

tuboovaritis f. tubo-ovaritis.

tuboperitoneal adj. tuboperitoneal.

tuboplastia f. tuboplasty.

tuborrea f. tuborrhea.

tubotimpánico, -ca adj. tubotympanal.

tubotímpano m. tubotympanum.

tubotorsión f. tubotorsion.

tubouterino, -na adj. tubouterine.

tubovaginal adj. tubovaginal.

tubulado, -da adj. tubulous.

tubular adj. tubular.

túbulo m. tubule, tubulus.

tubuloacinar tubuloacinar.

tubulocisto m. tubulocyst.

tubulorracemoso, -sa adj. tuboloracemose.

tubulosacular adj. tubulosaccular.

tubuloso, -sa adj. tubulous.

tubus tubus.

tuerto, -ta adj. one-eyed.

tularemia f. tularemia.

tularemia ganglionar glandular tularemia.

tularemia gastrointestinal gastrointestinal tularemia.

tularemia oculoganglionar oculoglandular tularemia.

tularemia orofaríngea oropharyngeal tularemia.

tularemia pulmonar pulmonary tularemia.

tularemia tifoidica typhoidal tularemia.

tularemia ulceroganglionar ulceroglandular tularemia.

tumefacción f. tumefaction.

tumefaciente adj. tumefacient.

tumescencia f. tumescence.

tumescente adj. tumid, tumidus.

túmido, -da adj. tumid, tumidus.

tumor m. tumor.

tumor de Abrikosov Abrikosov's tumor.

tumor adenoide, tumor adenoideo adenoid tumor.

tumor adenomatoide, tumor adenomatoideo adenomatoid tumor.

tumor adenomatoide ameloblástico ameloblastic adenomatoid tumor.

tumor adiposo adipose tumor.

tumor agudo esplénico acute splenic tumor.

tumor amiloide amiloid tumor.

tumor del ángulo pontocerebeloso cerebellopontine angle tumor.

tumor del ángulo protuberancial pontine angle tumor.

tumor arenoso sand tumor.

tumor de azúcar sugar tumor.

tumor de Bednar Bednar tumor.

tumor benigno benign tumor.

tumor blanco tumor albus, white tumor.

tumor blanco piógeno tumor albus pyogenes.

tumor de la bolsa de Rathke Rathke's pouch tumor.

tumor de Brenner Brenner tumor.

tumor de Brooke Brooke's tumor.

tumor de Burkitt Burkitt's tumor.

tumor en campana dumb-bell tumor.

tumor carcinoide carcinoid tumor.

tumor carcinoide bronquial carcinoid tumor of the bronchus.

tumor cartilaginoso cartilaginous tumor.

tumor cavernoso cavernous tumor.

tumor celular cellular tumor.

tumor de células acinares acinar cell tumor.

tumor de células cromafines chromaffin-cell tumor.

tumor de células gigantes del hueso giant cell tumor of bone.

tumor de células gigantes de la vaina tendinosa giant cell tumor of tendon sheath.

tumor de células granulares, tumor de células granulosas granular cell tumor.

tumor de células de la granulosa granulosa cell tumor.

tumor de células de granulosa y teca granulosa-theca tumor.

tumor de celulas hiliares hilar cell tumor.

tumor de células hiliares del ovario hilar cell tumor of the ovary.

tumor de células de Hortega Hortega cell tumor.

tumor de células de Hürthle Hürthle cell tumor.

tumor de células insulares islet cell tumor.

tumor de células intersticiales de los testículos insterstitial cell tumor of testis.

tumor de células de Leydig Leydig cell tumor.

tumor de células lipoides del ovario lipoid cell tumor of the ovary.

tumor de células luteinizadas de granulosa y teca luteinized granulosa-theca cell tumor.

tumor de células de Merkel Merkel cell tumor.

tumor de células oxífilas oxyphil cell tumor.

tumor de células de Schwann Schwann-cell tumor.

tumor de células de Sertoli Sertoli cell tumor.

tumor de células de Sertoli y Leydig Sertoli-Leydig cell tumor.

tumor de células de teca, tumor de células de la teca theca cell tumor.

tumor cervical tumor colli.

tumor de Codman Codman's tumor.

tumor de colisión collision tumor.

tumor coloide colloid tumor.

tumor de conductos dérmicos dermal duct tumor.

tumor conectivo connective tumor.

tumor cromafín chromaffin tumor.

tumor del cuerpo aórtico aortic body tumor.

tumor del cuerpo carotídeo carotid body tumor.

tumor dermoide dermoid tumor.

tumor desmoide desmoid tumor.

tumor de dureza de marfil ivory-like tumor.

tumor de embarazo, tumor del embarazo pregnancy tumor.

tumor embrionario embryonal tumor, embryonic tumor.

tumor embrioplástico embryoplastic tumor.

tumor endodérmico endodermal sinus tumor.

tumor endometrioide endometrioid tumor.

tumor enquistado encysted tumor.

tumor de Erdhein Erdhein tumor.

tumor eréctil erectile tumor.

tumor esplénico agudo acute splenic tumor.
tumor estercoráceo stercoral tumor.
tumor de Ewing Ewing's tumor.
tumor falso false tumor.
tumor fantasma phantom tumor.
tumor fecal fecal tumor.
tumor fibrocelular fibrocellular tumor.
tumor fibroide fibroid tumor.
tumor fibroplástico fibroplastic tumor.
tumor filoide phyllodes tumor.
tumor gelatinoso gelatinous tumor.
tumor germinal germinal tumor.
tumor del glomo glomus tumor.
tumor del glomo yugular glomus jugulare tumor.
tumor gomoso gummy tumor.
tumor de Godwin Godwin tumor.
tumor de granulosa granulosa tumor.
tumor grasoso fatty tumor.
tumor de Grawitz Grawitz's tumor.
tumor de Gubler Gubler's tumor.
tumor hepatocelular oncocítico oncocytic hepatocelular tumor.
tumor heterólogo heterologous tumor.
tumor heterotípico heterotypic tumor.
tumor hílico hylic tumor.
tumor hinchado de Pott Pott's puffy tumor.
tumor histioide histioid tumor.
tumor homólogo homologous tumor.
tumor homotípico homoiotypic tumor.
tumor infiltrante, tumor infiltrativo infiltrating tumor.
tumor inocente innocent tumor.
tumor de Koenen Koenen's tumor.
tumor de Krompecher ulcus rodens.
tumor de Krukenberg Krukenberg's tumor.
tumor lácteo lacteal tumor.
tumor lienal tumor lienis.
tumor de Lindau Lindau's tumor.
tumor líquido fluid tumor.
tumor maligno malignant tumor.
tumor de marcha march tumor.
tumor de mastocitos mast cell tumor.
tumor melanótico neuroectodérmico melanotic neuroectodermal tumor.
tumor mesonefroide mesonephroid tumor.
tumor micótico fungating tumor.
tumor mixto mixed tumor.
tumor mixto de la glándula salival mixed

tumor of the salivary gland.
tumor mixto de la piel mixed tumor of the skin.
tumor mucoso mucous tumor.
tumor muscular muscular tumor.
tumor de Nélaton Nélaton's tumor.
tumor de Nelson Nelson tumor.
tumor del nervio acústico acoustic nerve tumor.
tumor neuroectodérmico melanótico melanotic neuroectodermic tumor.
tumor neuroepitelial neuroepithelial tumor.
tumor del octavo par eighth nerve tumor.
tumor odontogénico adenomatoide adenomatoid odontogenic tumor.
tumor odontogénico epitelial calcificado calcifying epithelial odontogenic tumor.
tumor odontogénico escamoso squamous odontogenic tumor.
tumor oleoso oil tumor.
tumor organoide organoid tumor.
tumor óseo de células gigantes giant cell tumor of bone.
tumor de Pancoast Pancoast's tumor.
tumor papilar papillary tumor.
tumor parafín paraffin tumor.
tumor pardo brown tumor.
tumor de patata potato tumor.
tumor piloso del cuero cabelludo pilar tumor of the scalp.
tumor de Pindborg Pindborg tumor.
tumor del primordio retiniano retinal anlage tumor.
tumor de quimiorreceptores chemoreceptor tumor.
tumor quístico cystic tumor.
tumor ranino ranine tumor.
tumor de Rathke Rathke's tumor.
tumor de Recklinghausen Recklinghausen's tumor.
tumor en reloj de arena hourglass tumor.
tumor de restos suprarrenales adrenal rest tumor.
tumor del saco vitelino yolk sac tumor.
tumor sacrococcígeo sacrococcygeal tumor.
tumor sanguíneo blood tumor.
tumor de Schmincke Schmincke's tumor.
tumor del surco pulmonar pulmonary sulcus tumor.

tumor del surco pulmonar superior superior pulmonary sulcus tumor.
tumor del surco superior superior sulcus tumor.
tumor del tejido conectivo, tumor del tejido conjuntivo connective-tissue tumor.
tumor teratoide teratoid tumor.
tumor tridérmico tridermic tumor.
tumor en turbante turban tumor.
tumor vascular vascular tumor.
tumor velloso villous tumor.
tumor verdadero true tumor.
tumor verrucoso cicatricial warty cicatricial tumor.
tumor de Warthin Warthin's tumor.
tumor de Wilms Wilms' tumor.
tumor de Zollinger-Ellison Zollinger-Ellison tumor.
tumorafín *adj.* tumoraffin.
tumoricida *f.* tumoricidal.
tumorigénesis *f.* tumorigenesis.
tumorígeno, -na *adj.* tumorigenic.
tumoroso, -sa *adj.* tumorous.
túnel *m.* tunnel.
tungiasis *f.* tungiasis.
túnica *f.* tunic, tunica.
turbidimetría *f.* turbidimetry.
turbidímetro *m.* turbidimeter.
túrbido, -da *adj.* turbid.
turbiedad *f.* turbidity.
turbinado, -da *adj.* turbinate.
turbinal *adj.* turbinal.
turbinectomía *f.* turbinectomy.
turbinotomía *f.* turbinotomy.
turbinótomo *m.* turbinotome.
turbio, -bia *adj.* turbid.
turgencia *f.* turgescence.
turgente *adj.* turgescent.
turgidización *f.* turgidization.
túrgido, -da *adj.* turgid, turgidus.
turricefalia *f.* turricephaly.
tusícula *f.* tussicula.
tusiculación *f.* tussiculation.
tusígeno, -na *adj.* tussigenic.
tusíparo, -ra *adj.* tussigenic.
tusivo, -va *adj.* tussal, tussive.
tussis tussis.
tyndalización *f.* tyndallization.
tzetzé *f.* tzetze.

U u

uartritis *f.* uarthritis.
uberoso, -sa *adj.* uberous.
ubicuitina *f.* ubiquitin.
ubihidroquinona *f.* ubihydroquinone.
ubiquinol *m.* ubiquinol.
ubiquinona *f.* ubiquinone.
ubiquista *adj.* ubiquitous.
ubiquitina *f.* ubiquitin.
ulaganactesis *f.* ulaganactesis.
ulalgia *f.* ulalgia.
ulatrofia *f.* ulatrophy.
   ulatrofia afuncional afunctional ulatrophy.
   ulatrofia atrófica atrophic ulatrophy.
   ulatrofia cálcica calcic ulatrophy.
   ulatrofia isquémica ischemic ulatrophy.
   ulatrofia traumática traumatic ulatrophy.
úlcera *f.* ulcer, sore, ulcus.
   úlcera de Adén Aden ulcer.
   úlcera aftosa aphthous ulcer.
   úlcera aguda por decúbito acute decubitus ulcer.
   úlcera aguda de la vulva ulcus vulvae acutum.
   úlcera de Allingham Allingham's ulcer.
   úlcera ambulante ulcus ambulans.
   úlcera amebiana, úlcera amibiana amebic ulcer.
   úlcera amputante amputating ulcer.
   úlcera anastomótica anastomotic ulcer.
   úlcera en anémona de mar sea anemone ulcer.
   úlcera en anillo, úlcera anular, úlcera anular de la córnea annular ulcer, ring ulcer, ring ulcer of the cornea.
   úlcera anular marginal de la córnea marginal ring ulcer of the cornea.
   úlcera ateromatosa atheromatous ulcer.
   úlcera atónica atonic ulcer.
   úlcera de Barrett Barrett's ulcer.
   úlcera en beso kissing ulcer.
   úlcera blanda, úlcera blanda cutánea soft sore, soft ulcer, ulcus molle, ulcus molle cutis.
   úlcera de Buruli Buruli ulcer.
   úlcera callosa indolent ulcer.
   úlcera cancerosa ulcus cancerosum.
   úlcera del chicle, úlcera de los chicleros bay sore, chicle ulcer, chiclero ulcer.
   úlcera en cinturón girdle ulcer.
   úlcera del conducto pilórico channel ulcer.
   úlcera constitucional constitutional ulcer.
   úlcera corneal catarral catarrhal corneal ulcer.
   úlcera corneal dendrítica dendritic corneal ulcer.
   úlcera corrosiva corrosive ulcer.
   úlcera en cresta de gallo cockscomb ulcer.
   úlcera por cromo chrome sore, chrome ulcer.
   úlcera crónica chronic ulcer.
   úlcera crónica de la pierna, úlcera crural chronic leg ulcer, ulcus cruris.

   úlcera de Cruveilhier Cruveilhier's ulcer.
   úlcera curada healed ulcer.
   úlcera de Curling Curling's ulcer.
   úlcera de los curtidores tanner's ulcer.
   úlcera de Cushing, úlcera de Cushing-Rokitansky Cushing's ulcer.
   úlcera de decúbito, úlcera por decúbito bed sore, decubital ulcer, pressure sore, pressure ulcer.
   úlcera de Delhi Delhi sore, Oriental sore.
   úlcera dendriforme, úlcera dendrítica, úlcera dendrítica corneal dendriform ulcer, dendritic ulcer, dendritic corneal ulcer.
   úlcera dental dental ulcer.
   úlcera del desierto desert sore, desert ulcer, veldt sore.
   úlcera diabética diabetic ulcer.
   úlcera de Dieulafoy Dieulafoy's ulcer.
   úlcera diftérica diphtheritic ulcer.
   úlcera por distensión distention ulcer.
   úlcera duodenal duodenal ulcer.
   úlcera dura hard sore, hard ulcer.
   úlcera elusiva elusive ulcer.
   úlcera escorbútica scorbutic ulcer.
   úlcera esfacelada, úlcera de esfacelo sloughing ulcer.
   úlcera esofágica Barrett's ulcer.
   úlcera de estasis, úlcera por estasis stasis ulcer.
   úlcera estercorácea stercoral ulcer, stercoraceous ulcer.
   úlcera esteroide steroid ulcer.
   úlcera del estómago ulcer of the stomach.
   úlcera de estoma, úlcera estomal, úlcera estómica stoma ulcer, stomal ulcer.
   úlcera de estrés, úlcera por estrés, úlcera de tensión stress ulcer.
   úlcera fagedénica phagedenic ulcer.
   úlcera fagedénica socavante burrowing phagedenic ulcer.
   úlcera fagedénica tropical tropical phagedenic ulcer.
   úlcera fascicular fascicular ulcer.
   úlcera de Fenwick-Hunner Fenwick-Hunner ulcer.
   úlcera fistulosa fistulous ulcer.
   úlcera flemonosa phlegmonous ulcer.
   úlcera folicular follicular ulcer.
   úlcera por frío cold ulcer.
   úlcera fungosa fungating sore.
   úlcera de Gallipolli Gallipolli sore.
   úlcera gangrenosa canker sore.
   úlcera gástrica gastric ulcer.
   úlcera gotosa gouty ulcer.
   úlcera gravitacional gravitational ulcer.
   úlcera gwaliar gwaliar ulcer.
   úlcera herpética herpetic ulcer.
   úlcera de hipopión hypopyon ulcer.
   úlcera de Hunner Hunner's ulcer.
   úlcera indolente indolent ulcer.

   úlcera inflamada inflamed ulcer.
   úlcera inguinal groin ulcer.
   úlcera intergidital ulcus interdigitale.
   úlcera irritable inflamed ulcer.
   úlcera isquémica hipertensiva hypertensive ischemic ulcer.
   úlcera de Jacob Jacob's ulcer.
   úlcera de Kocher, úlcera de Kocher de dilatación Kocher's dilatation ulcer.
   úlcera de Lipschütz Lipschütz ulcer.
   úlcera lupoide, úlcera lupoidea lupoid ulcer.
   úlcera marginal marginal ulcer.
   úlcera de Marjolin Marjolin's ulcer.
   úlcera en matraz flask ulcer.
   úlcera de Meleney, úlcera socavante crónica de Meleney Meleney's chronic undermining ulcer, Meleney's ulcer.
   úlcera micobacteriana mycobacterial ulcer.
   úlcera de Mooren Mooren's ulcer.
   úlcera neumocócica pneumococcus ulcer.
   úlcera neurógena, úlcera neurotrófica neurogenic ulcer, neurotrophic ulcer.
   úlcera oculta concealed ulcer.
   úlcera penetrante penetrating ulcer, ulcus penetrans.
   úlcera péptica peptic ulcer.
   úlcera péptica gigante giant peptic ulcers.
   úlcera perambulante perambulating ulcer.
   úlcera perforante perforating ulcer.
   úlcera pilórica pyloric ulcer.
   úlcera de Plaut Plaut's ulcer.
   úlcera pudenda pudendal ulcer.
   úlcera redonda round ulcer.
   úlcera reptante creeping ulcer.
   úlcera roedora rodent ulcer, ulcus rodens.
   úlcera de Rokitansky-Cushing Rokitansky-Cushing's ulcer.
   úlcera de Saemisch Saemisch's ulcer.
   úlcera de los segadores hypopyon ulcer.
   úlcera serpiginosa serpiginous ulcer.
   úlcera serpenteante de la córnea, úlcera serpiginosa corneal serpent ulcer of the cornea, serpiginous corneal ulcer, ulcus serpens corneae.
   úlcera sifilítica syphilitic ulcer.
   úlcera simple simple ulcer.
   úlcera simple adenógena, úlcera de Nicolas-Favre Nicolas-Favre disease, limphogranuloma venereum.
   úlcera simple vesicante ulcus simplex vesicae.
   úlcera sintomática symptomatic ulcer.
   úlcera siria, úlcera siriaca Syrian ulcer.
   úlcera sublingual sublingual ulcer.
   úlcera submucosa submucous ulcer.
   úlcera de Sutton Sutton's ulcer.
   úlcera de tensión stress ulcer.
   úlcera traumática traumatic ulcer.
   úlcera trófica trophic ulcer.
   úlcera trofoneurótica trophoneurotic ulcer.

úlcera tropical tropical sore, tropical ulcer, ulcus tropicum.

úlcera varicosa varicose ulcer.

úlcera venérea venereal sore, venereal ulcer.

úlcera verrugosa warty ulcer.

úlcera vulvar aguda ulcus vulvae acutum.

úlcera yeyunal, úlcera yeyunal secundaria jejunal ulcer, secondary jejunal ulcer.

úlcera zapadora undermining ulcer.

ulceración *f.* ulceration.

ulceración de labios y pierna lips and leg ulceration.

ulceración traqueal tracheal ulceration.

ulceración de Daguet ulceration of Daguet.

ulcerado, -da *adj.* ulcerated.

ulcerar *v.* ulcerate.

ulcerativo, -va *adj.* ulcerative.

ulcerocáncer *m.* ulcerocancer.

ulcerogangrenoso, -sa *adj.* ulcerogangrenous.

ulcerógeno, -na *adj.* ulcerogenic.

ulceroglandular *adj.* ulceroglandular.

ulcerogranuloma *m.* ulcerogranuloma.

ulceromembranoso, -sa *adj.* ulceromembranous.

ulceroso, -sa *adj.* ulcerous.

ulcus *f.* ulcer, sore, ulcus.

ulcus ambulans ulcus ambulans.

ulcus cruris chronic leg ulcer, leg ulcer, ulcus cruris.

ulcus durum hard ulcer.

ulcus exedens ulcus exedens.

ulcus gástrico gastric ulcer.

ulcus molle ulcus molle.

ulcus rodens rodent ulcer, ulcus rodens.

ulcus serpens serpiginous ulcer.

ulcus tropicum tropical ulcer, ulcus tropicum.

ulcus ventriculi ulcus ventriculi.

ulcus vulvae acutum ulcus vulvae acutum.

ulectomía *f.* ulectomy, oulectomy.

ulegiria *f.* ulegyria.

ulemorragia *f.* ulemorrhagia.

uleritema *m.* ulerythema.

uleritema centrifugo ulerythema centrifugum.

uleritema ofriógeno ulerythema ophryogenes.

uleritema sicosiforme ulerythema sycosiforme.

ulesis *f.* cicatrization.

uliginoso, -sa *adj.* uliginous.

ulitis *f.* ulitis, oulitis.

ulitis micótica fungus ulitis.

ullen *m.* ullen.

ulna ulna.

ulnar *adj.* ulnar.

ulnocarpal *adj.* ulnocarpal.

ulnocarpiano, -na *adj.* ulnocarpal.

ulnorradial *adj.* ulnoradial.

ulocace *f.* ulocace.

ulocarcinoma *m.* ulocarcinoma.

ulodermatitis *f.* ulodermatitis.

uloglositis *f.* uloglossitis.

uloide *adj.* uloid.

uloma *m.* uloncus.

ulonco *m.* uloncus.

ulorragia *f.* ulorrhagia, oulorragia.

ulorrea *f.* ulorrhea.

ulótico, -ca *adj.* ulotic.

ulotomía *f.* ulotomy.

ulotrico, -ca *adj.* ulotrichous.

ulotripsis *f.* ulotripsis.

ultimisternal *adj.* ultimisternal.

ultimobranquial *adj.* ultimobranchial.

ultimoesternal *adj.* ultimisternal.

ultimum moriens ultimum moriens.

ultraacústica *f.* ultrasonics.

ultrabraquicefálico, -ca *adj.* ultrabrachycephalic.

ultrabraquicéfalo, -la *adj.* ultrabrachycephalic.

ultracentrífuga *f.* ultracentrifuge.

ultracentrifugación *f.* ultracentrifugation.

ultradiano, -na *adj.* ultradian.

ultradolicocefálico, -ca *adj.* ultradolichocephalic.

ultradolicocéfalo, -la *adj.* ultradolichocephalic.

ultraestructura *f.* ultrastructure.

ultrafagocitosis *f.* ultraphagocytosis.

ultrafiltración *f.* ultrafiltration.

ultrafiltrado *m.* ultrafiltrate.

ultrafiltro *m.* ultrafilter.

ultraligadura *f.* ultraligation.

ultramicro *m.* ultramicron.

ultramicrón *m.* ultramicron.

ultramicropipeta *f.* ultramicropipet.

ultramicroquímica *f.* ultramicrochemistry.

ultramicroscopía *f.* ultramicroscopy.

ultramicroscópico, -ca *adj.* ultramicroscopic.

ultramicrotomía *f.* ultramicrotomy.

ultramicrotomo, ultramicrótomo *m.* ultramicrotome.

ultromotilidad *f.* ultromotivity.

ultromovilidad *f.* ultromotivity.

ultraprofilaxis *f.* ultraprophylaxis.

ultrarrojo, -ja *adj.* ultra-red.

ultrasónica *f.* ultrasonics.

ultrasónico, -ca *adj.* ultrasonic.

ultrasonido *m.* ultrasound.

ultrasonografía *f.* ultrasonography.

ultrasonografía Doppler Doppler ultrasonography.

ultrasonografía endoscópica endoscopic ultrasonography.

ultrasonografía renal renal ultrasonography.

ultrasonográfico, -ca *adj.* ultrasonographic.

ultrasonograma *m.* ultrasonogram.

ultrasonometría *f.* ultrasonometry.

ultrasonoterapia *f.* ultrasonotherapy.

ultratermo *m.* ultratherm.

ultravioleta *adj.* ultraviolet.

ultravioleta cercana near ultraviolet.

ultravioleta lejana far ultraviolet.

ultravisible *adj.* ultravisible.

ululación *f.* ululation.

umbilectomía *f.* umbilectomy.

umbilicación *f.* umbilication.

umbilicado, -da¹ *adj.* umbilicate.

umbilicado, -da² *adj.* umbilicated.

umbilical *adj.* umbilical.

umbo *m.* umbo.

umbo de la membrana timpánica umbo membranae tympani, umbo of the tympanic membrane.

umbonado, -da *adj.* umbonate.

umbral *m.* threshold.

umbral absoluto absolute threshold.

umbral acromático achromatic threshold.

umbral de audición, umbral auditivo auditory threshold.

umbral del conocimiento, umbral de conciencia, umbral de consciencia threshold of consciousness.

umbral de convulsión, umbral convulsivo convulsant threshold, seizure threshold.

umbral de deglución swallowing threshold.

umbral de desplazamiento displacement threshold.

umbral diferencial differential threshold.

umbral de doble punto double point threshold.

umbral de dolor, umbral doloroso pain threshold.

umbral de dosis dose threshold.

umbral epileptógeno epileptic threshold.

umbral de eritema erythema threshold.

umbral de estímulo stimulus threshold.

umbral galvánico galvanic threshold.

umbral luminoso mínimo minimum light threshold.

umbral neuronal neuron threshold.

umbral de punto doble double point threshold.

umbral de relación relational threshold.

umbral renal renal threshold.

umbral renal de la glucosa renal threshold for glucose.

umbral de resolución threshold of resolution.

umbral de la sensación visual, umbral visual threshold of visual sensation, visual threshold.

umbral de sensibilidad, umbral sensitivo sensitivity threshold, sensory threshold.

umbral titilante de fusión flicker fusion threshold.

umbrascopia *f.* umbrascopy.

uncal *adj.* uncal.

uncartrosis *f.* uncarthrosis.

unciforme *adj.* unciform.

uncinado, -da *adj.* uncinate.

uncinal *adj.* uncinal.

Uncinaria Uncinaria.

Uncinaria americana Uncinaria americana.

Uncinaria duodenalis Uncinaria duodenalis.

uncinaria *f.* hookworm.

uncinaria americana, uncinaria del Nuevo Mundo New World hookworm.

uncinaria europea, uncinaria del Viejo Mundo Old World hookworm.

uncinariasis *f.* uncinariasis.

uncinariático, -ca *adj.* uncinariatic.

uncinariosis *f.* uncinariosis.

unción *f.* unction.

uncipresión *f.* uncipressure.

uncoosificado, -da *adj.* unco-ossified.

uncovertebral *adj.* uncovertebral.

uncus uncus.

uncus del hueso ganchoso uncus of the hamate bone.

ungueal *adj.* ungual.

ungüento *m.* ointment, unguent.

ungüento ocular, ungüento oftálmico eye ointment, ophthalmic ointment.

unguentum *m.* ointment, unguent.

unguícula *f.* unguiculus.

unguiculado, -da *adj.* unguiculate.

unguinal *adj.* unguinal.

unguis¹ lacrimal bone, os lacrimale.

unguis² unguis.

unguis³ unguis.

ungulado, -da *adj.* ungulate.

ungular *adj.* ungular.

uniarticular *adj.* uniarticular.

uniaural *adj.* uniaural.

uniaxial *adj.* uniaxial.

uniaxil *adj.* uniaxial.

unibasal *adj.* unibasal.

unibásico, -ca *adj.* unibasal.

unicameral *adj.* unicameral.

unicelular *adj.* unicellular.

unicentral *adj.* unicentral.

unicéntrico, -ca *adj.* unicentric.

uniceps *adj.* uniceps.

uniceptor *m.* uniceptor.

unicismo *m.* unicism.

unicollis unicollis.

unicornio, -nia *adj.* unicorn, unicornous, unicornis.

unicuspidado, -da *adj.* unicuspidate.

unicúspide *adj.* unicuspid.
unidad *f.* unit.
  unidad absoluta absolute unit.
  unidad amboceptora amboceptor unit.
  unidad de Angström Angström unit.
  unidad de Ansbacher Ansbacher unit.
  unidad antitóxica antitoxin unit.
  unidad Bethesda Bethesda unit.
  unidad Bodansky, unidad de Bodansky Bodansky unit.
  unidad CGS CGS unit.
  unidad clínica clinical unit.
  unidad de Collip Collip unit.
  unidad de Corner-Allen Corner-Allen unit.
  unidad coronaria (UCC), unidad de cuidados coronarios coronary care unit, coronary intensive care unit (CCU).
  unidad de actividad uterina, unidad de Álvarez Caldeiro Montevideo unit.
  unidad de Allen-Doisy Allen-Doisy unit.
  unidad de antígeno antigen unit.
  unidad de calor unit of heat, heat unit.
  unidad de Clauberg Clauberg unit.
  unidad de complemento complement unit.
  unidad de corriente unit of current.
  unidad de cuidados hospitalarios inpatient care unit.
  unidad de cuidados intensivos (UCI) intensive care unit (ICU).
  unidad de cuidados intensivos neonatales (UCIN) neonatal intensive care unit (NICU).
  unidad de Dam Dam unit.
  unidad de exposición exposure unit.
  unidad de Felton Felton's unit.
  unidad de Florey Florey unit.
  unidad de flotación de Svedberg Svedberg flotation unit.
  unidad de formación de colonias colony-forming unit.
  unidad de Hampson Hampson's unit.
  unidad de Hounsfield Hounsfield unit.
  unidad de ingreso psiquiátrico psychiatric inpatient unit.
  unidad de King, unidad de King-Armstrong King unit, King-Armstrong unit.
  unidad de la American Drug Manufacturers Association American Drug Manufacturers' Association unit.
  unidad de Mache Mache's unit.
  unidad de mapeo map unit.
  unidad de masa atómica atomic mass unit.
  unidad de pepsina pepsin unit.
  unidad de peso atómico atomic weight unit.
  unidad de polen de Noon Noon pollen unit.
  unidad de prueba cutánea skin test unit.
  unidad de resistencia resistance unit.
  unidad de resistencia periférica peripheral resistance unit.
  unidad de Somogyi Somogyi unit.
  unidad de Steenbock, unidad Steenbock de vitamina D Steenbock unit, Steenbock unit of vitamin D.
  unidad de tuberculina tuberculin unit.
  unidad dental dental unit.
  unidad eléctrica, unidad electromagnética, unidad electrostática electromagnetic unit, electrostatic unit.
  unidad enzimática enzyme unit.
  unidad específica de olfato specific smell unit.
  unidad hemolítica hemolytic unit.
  unidad inmunizante antitoxic unit.
  unidad internacional international unit.
  unidad internacional de actividad enzimática international unit of enzyme activity.
  unidad internacional de actividad estrógena international unit of estrogenic activity.
  unidad internacional de actividad gonadotrófica international unit of gonadotropic activity.
  unidad internacional de insulina international insulin unit.
  unidad luz light unit.
  unidad MKS meter-kilogram-second (MKS) unit.
  unidad Montevideo Montevideo unit of uterine activity.
  unidad motora, unidad motriz motor unit.
  unidad neonatal neonatal unit.
  unidad Oxford Oxford unit.
  unidad pilosebácea pilosebaceous unit.
  unidad quantum quantum unit.
  unidad rata rat unit.
  unidad ratón mouse unit.
  unidad roentgen roentgen unit.
  unidad SI SI unit.
unidireccional *adj.* unidirectional.
uniflagelado, -da *adj.* uniflagellate.
unifocal *adj.* unifocal.
uniforado, -da *adj.* uniforate.
unigeminal *adj.* unigeminal.
unigémino, -na *adj.* unigeminal.
unigerminal *adj.* unigerminal.
uniglandular *adj.* uniglandular.
unigrávida *adj.* unigravida.
unilaminar *adj.* unilaminar.
unilateral *adj.* unilateral.
unilobar *adj.* unilobar.
unilobular *adj.* unilobar.
unilocular *adj.* unilocular.
unimodal *adj.* unimodal.
unimolecular *adj.* unimolecular.
uninefrectomizado, -da *adj.* uninephrectomized.
uninucleado, -da *adj.* uninucleate.
uninuclear *adj.* uninuclear.
uniocular *adj.* uniocular.
unión[1] *f.* attachment.
  unión aleatoria random mating.
  unión de fricción, unión friccional friction attachment, frictional attachment.
  unión de precisión precision attachment.
  unión en llave, unión llave y paso de llave key attachment, key-and-keyway attachment.
  unión epitelial (de Gottlieb) epithelial attachment (of Gottlieb).
  unión extracoronal extracoronal attachment.
  unión interna internal attachment.
  unión intracoronal intracoronal attachment, slotted attachment.
  unión ortodóntica orthodontic attachment.
  unión paralela parallel attachment.
  unión pericemental pericemental attachment.
  unión por el borde edgewise attachment.
unión[2] *f.* junction.
  unión adherente adherent junction.
  unión amelodentinaria, unión amelodentínica amelodental junction, amelodentinal junction.
  unión amnioembrionaria amnioembryonic junction.
  unión cardioesofágica cardioesophageal junction.
  unión cementodentinaria cementodentinal junction.
  unión cemento-esmalte cementoenamel junction.
  unión coledocoduodenal choledochoduodenal junction.
  unión corticomedular corticomedullary junction.
  unión de brecha gap junction.
  unión de hendidura gap junction.
  unión de intersticio communicating junction.
  unión de los labios junction of the lips.
  unión de nexo, unión nexo gap junction.
  unión dentina-esmalte dentinoenamel junction.
  unión dentinocementaria dentinocemental junction.
  unión dentogingival dentogingival junction.
  unión dermoepidérmica dermoepidermal junction.
  unión electrotónica electrotonic junction.
  unión escamocolumnar squamocolumnar junction.
  unión esofagogástrica esophagogastric junction.
  unión estrecha tight junction.
  unión fibromuscular fibromuscular junction.
  unión gastroesofágica gastroesophageal junction.
  unión ileocecal ileocecal junction.
  unión intercelular intercellular junction.
  unión mioneural myoneural junction.
  unión mucocutánea mucocutaneous junction.
  unión musculotendinosa muscle-tendon junction.
  unión neuroectodérmica neuroectodermal junction.
  unión neuromuscular neuromuscular junction.
  unión neurosomática neurosomatic junction.
  unión ocluyente occluding junction, thight junction.
  unión ósea bony junction, osseous junction.
  unión S.T. S.T. junction.
  unión sináptica synaptic junction.
  unión timpanoestapedia tympanostapedial junction.
  unión ureteropélvica ureteropelvic junction.
  unión ureterovesical ureterovesical junction.
unión[3] *f.* union.
  unión autógena autogenous union.
  unión defectuosa faulty union.
  unión fibrosa fibrous union.
  unión primaria primary union.
  unión secundaria secondary union.
  unión viciosa vicious union.
uniovular *adj.* uniovular.
unipara *adj.* unipara.
uniparental *adj.* uniparental.
uníparo, -ra *adj.* uniparous.
uniperforado, -da *adj.* uniforate.
unipolar *adj.* unipolar.
unipotencia *f.* unipotency.
unipotencial *adj.* unipotential.
unipotente *adj.* unipotent.
unipunción *f.* single-needle dialysis, unipuncture.
unipuntura *f.* single-needle dialysis, unipuncture.
unir *v.* bind.
uniseptado, -da *adj.* uniseptate.
unisexual *adj.* unisexual.
unitabicado, -da *adj.* uniseptate.
unitage unitage.
unitario, -ria *adj.* unitary.
uniterminal *adj.* uniterminal.
univalencia *f.* univalence.
univalente *adj.* univalent.
universal *adj.* universal.

univitelino, -na *adj.* univitelline.
untador *m.* spreader.
uña *f.* fingernail, nail, toenail, unguis.
  uña encarnada, uña incardinada, uñero unguis aduncus.
  uña encarnada, uña incardinada, uñero unguis incarnatus.
  uña acanalada reedy nail.
  uña amarilla yellow nail.
  uña de doble borde double-edge nail.
  uña de Terrry Terry's nail.
  uña en caña reedy nail.
  uña en cáscara de huevo eggshell nail.
  uña en cuchara spoon nail.
  uña en dorso de tortuga turtle-back nail.
  uña en pico de loro parrot beak nail.
  uña en pinza pincer nail.
  uña en raqueta racket nail.
  uña en vaina shell nail.
  uña en vidrio de reloj watch-crystal nail.
  uña encarnada ingrowing toenail, unguis aduncus, unguis incarnatus.
  uña hipocrática hippocratic nail.
  uña incardinada ingrowing toenail, unguis aduncus, unguis incarnatus.
  uña jaspeada leukonychia.
  uña mitad y mitad half and half nail.
  uña con hoyuelos pitted nail.
uñero *m.* ingrown toenail , ingrowing toenail, unguis aduncus, unguis incarnatus.
uperisación *f.* sterilization.
upsiloide *adj.* upsiloide.
uracal *adj.* urachal.
uracilo *m.* uracil.
uraco *m.* urachus.
uracovesical *adj.* urachovesical.
uracrasia *f.* uracrasia.
uracratia *f.* uracratia.
uragogo, -ga *m., f. y adj.* uragogue.
uranálisis *f.* uranalysis.
uranianismo *m.* uranianism.
uranisco *m.* uraniscus.
uraniscocasma *f.* uraniscochasma.
uraniscolalia *f.* uraniscolalia.
uranisconitis *f.* uranisconitis.
uraniscoplastia *f.* uraniscoplasty.
uraniscorrafia *f.* uraniscorrhaphy.
uranismo *m.* uranism.
uranista *adj.* uranist.
uranoestafiloplastia *f.* uranostaphyloplasty.
uranoestafilorrafia *f.* uranostaphylorrhaphy.
uranoestafilosquisis *f.* uranostaphyloschisis.
uranofobia *f.* uranophobia.
uranoplastia *f.* uranoplasty.
uranoplástico, -ca *adj.* uranoplastic.
uranoplejía *f.* uranoplegia.
uranorrafia *f.* uranorrhaphy.
uranosquisis *f.* uranoschisis.
uranosquismo *m.* uranoschism.
uranostafiloplastia *f.* uranostaphyloplasty.
uranostafilorrafia *f.* uranostaphylorrhaphy.
uranostafilosquisis *f.* uranostaphyloschisis.
uranosteoplastia *f.* uranosteoplasty.
uranovelosquisis *f.* uranoveloschisis.
urapostema *f.* urapostema.
uraroma *m.* uraroma.
urartritis *f.* urarthritis.
uratemia *f.* uratemia.
urático, -ca *adj.* uratic.
uratohistequia *f.* uratohistechia.
uratólisis *f.* uratolysis.
uratolítico, -ca *adj.* uratolytic.
uratoma *m.* uratoma.
uratosis *f.* uratosis.
uraturia *f.* uraturia.

urceiforme *adj.* urceiform.
urceolado, -da *adj.* urceolate.
urea *f.* urea.
ureagénesis *f.* ureagenesis.
ureagénico, -ca *adj.* uragenetic.
ureal *adj.* ureal.
ureametría *f.* ureametry.
ureámetro *m.* ureameter.
Ureaplasma Ureaplasma.
  Ureaplasma urealyticum Ureaplasma urealyticum.
ureapoyesis *f.* ureapoiesis.
uredema *m.* uredema.
uredo *f.* uredo.
ureico, -ca *adj.* ureal.
ureina *f.* urein.
urelcosis *f.* urelcosis.
uremia *f.* uremia.
  uremia extrarrenal extrarenal uremia.
  uremia hipercalcémica hypercalcemic uremia.
  uremia prerrenal prerenal uremia.
  uremia de retención retention uremia.
urémico, -ca *adj.* uremic.
urémide *f.* uremide.
uremígeno, -na *adj.* uremigenic.
ureogénesis *f.* ureogenesis.
ureólisis *f.* ureolysis.
ureolítico, -ca *adj.* ureolytic.
ureometría *f.* ureometry.
ureómetro *f.* ureometer.
ureotélico, -ca *adj.* ureotelic.
urequisis *f.* urecchysis.
uresiestesia *f.* uresiesthesia, uresiesthesis.
uresis *f.* uresis.
uréter *f.* ureter.
  uréter circuncaval circumcaval ureter.
  uréter ectópico ectopic ureter.
  uréter enroscado curlicue ureter.
  uréter poscaval postcaval ureter.
  uréter retrocaval retrocaval ureter.
  uréter retroiliaco retroiliac ureter.
ureteral *adj.* ureteral.
ureteralgia *f.* ureteralgia.
uretercistoscopio *m.* uretercystoscope.
ureterectasia *f.* ureterectasia, ureterectasis.
ureterectomía *f.* ureterectomy.
uretérico, -ca *adj.* ureteric.
ureteritis *f.* ureteritis.
  ureteritis glandular ureteritis glandularis.
  ureteritis quistica ureteritis cystica.
ureterocele *m.* ureterocele.
  ureterocele ectópico ectopic ureterocele.
ureterocelectomía *f.* ureterocelectomy.
ureterocelorrafia *f.* ureterocelorrhaphy.
ureterocervical *adj.* ureterocervical.
ureterocistanastomosis *f.* ureterocystanastomosis.
ureterocistoneostomía *f.* ureteroneocystostomy.
ureterocistoscopio *m.* ureterocystoscope.
ureterocistostomía *f.* ureterocystostomy.
ureterocólico, -ca *adj.* ureterocolic.
ureterocolostomía *f.* ureterocolostomy.
ureterocutaneostomía *f.* ureterocutaneostomy.
ureterodiálisis *f.* ureterodyalisis.
ureteroduodenal *adj.* ureteroduodenal.
ureteroectasia *f.* ureteroctasia.
ureteroentérico, -ca *adj.* ureteroenteric.
ureteroenteroanastomosis *f.* ureteroenteroanastomosis.
ureteroenterostomía *f.* ureteroenterostomy.
ureteroestenosis *f.* ureterostenosis.
ureterostegnosis *f.* ureterostegnosis.

ureteroflegma *f.* ureterophlegma.
ureteroflema *f.* ureterophlegma.
ureterografía *f.* ureterography.
ureterograma *m.* ureterogram.
ureteroheminefrectomía *f.* ureteroheminephrectomy.
ureterohidronefrosis *f.* ureterohydronephrosis.
ureteroileostomía *f.* ureteroileostomy.
ureterointestinal *adj.* ureterointestinal.
ureterólisis *f.* ureterolysis.
ureterolitiasis *f.* ureterolithiasis.
ureterolito *m.* ureterolith.
ureterolitotomía *f.* ureterolithotomy.
ureteromeatotomía *f.* ureteromeatotomy.
ureteronefrectomía *f.* ureteronephrectomy.
ureteroneocistostomía *f.* ureteroneocystostomy.
ureteroneopielostomía *f.* ureteroneopyelostomy.
ureteropatía *f.* ureteropathy.
ureteropélvico, -ca *adj.* ureteropelvic.
ureteropelvioneostomía *f.* ureteropelvioneostomy.
ureteropelvioplastia *f.* ureteropelvioplasty.
  ureteropelvioplastia de Culp de Weerd Culp de Weerd ureteropelvioplasty.
  ureteropelvioplastia de Foley en Y-V Foley Y-V ureteropelvioplasty.
  ureteropelvioplastia de Scardino-Prince Scardino-Prince ureteropelvioplasty.
ureteropielitis *f.* ureteropyelitis.
ureteropielografía retrógrada *f.* retrograde ureteropyelography.
ureteropielonefritis *f.* ureteropyelonephritis.
ureteropielonefrostomía *f.* ureteropyelonephrostomy.
ureteropieloneostomía *f.* ureteropyeloneostomy.
ureteropieloplastia *f.* ureteropyeloplasty.
ureteropielostomía *f.* ureteropyelostomy.
ureteropiosis *f.* ureteropyosis.
ureteroplastia *f.* ureteroplasty.
ureteroproctostomía *f.* ureteroproctostomy.
ureterorrafia *f.* ureterorrhaphy.
ureterorragia *f.* ureterorrhagia.
ureterorrectal *adj.* ureterorectal.
ureterorrectoneostomía *f.* ureterorectoneostomy.
ureterorrectostomía *f.* ureterorectostomy.
ureterorrenoscopia *f.* ureterorenoscopy.
ureterorrenoscopio *f.* ureterorenoscope.
ureterosigmoideo, -a *adj.* ureterosigmoid.
ureterosigmoidostomía *f.* ureterosigmoidostomy.
ureterostegnosis *f.* ureterostegnosis.
ureterostenoma *m.* ureterostenoma.
ureterostoma *f.* ureterostoma.
ureterostomía *f.* ureterostomy.
  ureterostomía cutánea cutaneous ureterostomy.
  ureterostomía lumbar subaracnoidea lumbar subarachnoid ureterostomy.
ureterostomosis *f.* ureterostomosis.
ureterostonoma *m.* ureterostonoma.
ureterotomía *f.* ureterotomy.
ureterotrigonoenterostomía *f.* ureterotrigonoenterostomy.
ureterotrigonosigmoidostomía *f.* ureterotrigonosigmoidostomy.
ureteroureteral *adj.* ureteroureteral.
ureteroureterostomía *f.* ureteroureterostomy.
ureterouterino, -na *adj.* ureterouterine.
ureterovaginal *adj.* ureterovaginal.
ureterovesical *adj.* ureterovesical.

ureterovesicoplastia *f.* ureteroesicoplasty.
ureterovesicostomía *f.* ureterovesicostomy.
urético, -ca *adj.* uretic.
uretra *f.* urethra.
　uretra anterior anterior urethra.
　uretra de la mujer, uretra muliebris female urethra.
　uretra del hombre male urethra.
　uretra doble double urethra.
　uretra esponjosa spongy urethra.
　uretra femenina urethra feminina.
　uretra masculina urethra masculina.
　uretra membranosa membranous urethra.
　uretra peneana penile urethra.
　uretra posterior posterior urethra.
　uretra prostática prostatic urethra.
　uretra virilis urethra virilis.
uretral *adj.* urethral.
uretralgia *f.* urethralgia.
uretrámetro *m.* urethrameter.
uretrascopio *m.* urethrascope.
uretratresia *f.* urethratresia.
uretrectomía *f.* urethrectomy.
uretremorragia *f.* urethremorrhagia.
uretrenfraxis *f.* urethremphraxis.
uretreurínter *m.* urethreurynter.
uretrismo *m.* urethrism, urethrismus.
uretritis *f.* urethritis.
　uretritis anterior anterior urethritis.
　uretritis del orificio externo urethritis orificii externi.
　uretritis específica specific urethritis.
　uretritis folicular follicular urethritis.
　uretritis glandular urethritis glandularis.
　uretritis gonocócica, uretritis gonorreica gonococcal urethritis, gonococcic urethritis, gonorrheal urethritis.
　uretritis gotosa gouty urethritis.
　uretritis granular granular urethritis.
　uretritis granulosa urethritis granulosa.
　uretritis inespecífica (UNE) non-specific urethritis (NSU).
　uretritis no gonocócica non-gonococcal urethritis.
　uretritis petrificante urethritis petrificans.
　uretritis posterior posterior urethritis.
　uretritis profiláctica prophylactic urethritis.
　uretritis quística urethritis cystica.
　uretritis simple simple urethritis.
　uretritis venérea urethritis venerea.
uretrobalanoplastia *f.* urethrobalanoplasty.
uretroblenorrea *f.* urethroblennorrhea.
uretrobulbar *adj.* urethrobulbar.
uretrocele *m.* urethrocele.
uretrocistitis *f.* urethrocystitis.
uretrocistografía *f.* urethrocystography.
uretrocistograma *m.* urethrocystogram.
uretrocistometría *f.* urethrocystometry.
uretrocistometrografía *f.* urethrocystometrography.
uretrocistopexia *f.* urethrocystopexy.
uretrodinia *f.* urethrodynia.
uretroescrotal *adj.* urethroscrotal.
uretroespasmo *m.* urethrospasm.
uretroestenosis *f.* urethrostenosis.
uretrofima *m.* urethrophyma.
uretrofraxis *f.* urethrophraxis.
uretrografía *f.* urethrography.
　uretrografía de evacuación voiding urethrography.
uretrometría *f.* urethrometry.
uretrómetro *m.* urethrometer.
uretropeneal *adj.* urethropenile.
uretropeneano, -na *adj.* urethropenile.
uretropeniano, -na *adj.* urethropenile.

uretroperineal *adj.* urethroperineal.
uretroperineoscrotal *adj.* urethroperineoscrotal.
uretropexia *f.* urethropexy.
uretroplastia *f.* urethroplasty.
uretroprostático, -ca *adj.* urethroprostatic.
uretrorrafia *f.* urethrorrhaphy.
uretrorragia *f.* urethrorrhagia.
uretrorrea *f.* urethrorrhea.
uretrorrectal *adj.* urethrorectal.
uretroscopia *f.* urethroscopy.
uretroscópico, -ca *adj.* urethroscopic.
uretroscopio *m.* urethroscope.
uretrospasmo *m.* urethrospasm.
uretrostenosis *f.* urethrostenosis.
uretrostaxis *f.* urethrostaxis.
uretrostomía *f.* urethrostomy.
　uretrostomía perineal perineal urethrostomy.
uretrotomía *f.* urethrotomy.
　uretrotomía externa external urethrotomy.
　uretrotomía interna internal urethrotomy.
　uretrotomía perineal perineal urethrotomy.
uretrótomo *m.* urethrotome.
　uretrótomo de Maisonneuve Maisonneuve's urethrotome.
uretrotrigonitis *f.* urethrotrigonitis.
uretrovaginal *adj.* urethrovaginal.
uretrovesical *adj.* urethrovesical.
uretrovesicopexia *f.* urethrovesicopexy.
urgencia¹ *f.* emergency.
urgencia² *f.* urgency.
　urgencia motora motor urgency.
　urgencia sensorial sensory urgency.
urhidrosis *f.* urhidrosis.
　urhidrosis cristalina urhidrosis crystallina.
urinhidrosis *f.* urhidrosis.
uricacidemia *f.* uricacidemia.
uricaciduria *f.* uricaciduria.
uricemia *f.* uricemia.
úrico, -ca *adj.* uric.
uricocolia *f.* uricocholia.
uricólisis *f.* uricolysis.
uricolítico, -ca *adj.* uricolytic.
uricómetro *m.* uricometer.
　uricómetro de Ruhemann Ruhemann's uricometer.
uricopoyesis *f.* uricopoiesis.
uricosuria *f.* uricosuria.
uricosúrico, -ca *adj.* uricosuric.
uricotélico, -ca *adj.* uricotelic.
uridrosis *f.* uridrosis.
uriestesia *f.* uriesthesis.
urina *f.* urine.
urinable *adj.* urinable.
urinación *f.* urination.
urinálisis *m.* urinalysis.
urinario, -ria *adj.* urinary.
urinemia *f.* urinemia.
urinhidrosis *f.* urinidrosis.
urinífero, -ra *adj.* uriniferous.
urinífico, -ca *adj.* urinific.
uriningismo *m.* uriningism.
uriníparo, -ra *adj.* uriniparous.
urinocrioscopia *f.* urinocryoscopy.
urinófilo, -la *adj.* urinophilous.
urinogenital *adj.* urinogenital.
urinógeno, -na *adj.* urinogenous.
urinoglucosómetro *m.* urinoglucosometer.
urinología *f.* urinology.
urinólogo, -ga *m., f.* urinologist.
urinoma *m.* urinoma.
urinometría *f.* urinometry.
urinómetro *m.* urinometer.
urinoscopia *f.* urinoscopy.
urinosexual *adj.* urinosexual.

urinoso, -sa *adj.* urinous.
uriposia *f.* uriposia.
urisolvente *adj.* urisolvent.
urningismo *m.* urningism.
urnismo *m.* urnism.
uroacidímetro *m.* uroacidimeter.
uroacidómetro *m.* uroacidimeter.
uroamoniacal *adj.* uroammoniac.
uroamónico, -ca *adj.* uroammoniac.
uroantelona *f.* uroanthelone.
uroazómetro *m.* uroazotometer.
uroazotómetro *m.* uroazotometer.
urobilina *f.* urobilin.
urobilinemia *f.* urobilinemia.
urobilinogenemia *f.* urobilinogenemia.
urobilinógeno *m.* urobilinogen.
urobilinogenuria *f.* urobilinogenuria.
urobilinoide *adj.* urobilinoid.
urobilinoideno *m.* urobilinoiden.
urobilinoideo, -a *adj.* urobilinoid.
urobilinuria *f.* urobilinuria.
urocele *m.* urocele.
urocianina *f.* urocyanin.
urocianógeno *m.* urocyanogen.
urocianosis *f.* urocyanosis.
urocinasa *f.* urokinase.
urocinético, -ca *adj.* urokinetic.
urocístico, -ca *adj.* urocystic.
urocistis *f.* urocystis.
urocistitis *f.* urocystitis.
urocisto *m.* urocyst.
uroclepsia *f.* uroclepsia.
urocoproporfiria *f.* urocoproporphyria.
urocrisia *f.* urocrisia, urocrisis.
urocrisis *f.* urocrisis.
urocriterio *m.* urocriterion.
urocromo *m.* urochrome.
urocromógeno *m.* urochromogen.
urodensímetro *m.* urinometer.
urodeo *m.* urodeum.
urodiálisis *f.* urodyalisis.
urodinamia *f.* urodynamics.
urodinámica *f.* urodynamics.
urodinámico, -ca *adj.* urodynamic.
urodinia *f.* urodynia.
urodoquio *m.* urodochium.
uroedema *m.* uroedema.
uroemia *f.* uremia.
uroenterona *f.* uroenterone.
uroeritrina *f.* uroerythrin.
uroespectrina *f.* urospectrin.
urofánico, -ca *adj.* urophanic.
urofeína *f.* urophein.
urofilia *f.* urophilia.
uroflavina *f.* uroflavin.
uroflómetro *m.* uroflometer.
urofluómetro *m.* urofluometer.
urofobia *f.* urophobia.
urofosfómetro *m.* urophosphometer.
urofuscina *f.* urofuscin.
urofuscohematina *f.* urofuscohematin.
urogáster *m.* urogaster.
urogastrona *f.* urogastrone.
urogénesis *f.* urogenesis.
urogenital *adj.* urogenital.
urógeno, -na *adj.* urogenous.
uroglaucina *f.* uroglaucina.
urografía *f.* urography.
　urografía anterógrada anterograde urography.
　urografía ascendente ascending urography.
　urografía cistoscópica cystoscopyc urography.
　urografía descendente descending urography.
　urografía de excreción, urografía excretora, urografía excretoria excretion urography, excretory urography.

urografía intravenosa intravenous urography.

urografía bucal oral urography.

urografía retrógrada retrograde urography.

urograma *m.* urogram.

urogravímetro *m.* urogravimeter.

urohematina *f.* urohematin.

urohematonefrosis *f.* urohematonephrosis.

urohematoporfirina *f.* urohematoporphyrin.

uroheparina *f.* uroheparin.

urohidrosis *f.* urhidrosis.

urohipertensina *f.* urohypertensin.

urolagnia *f.* urolagnia.

urolitiasis *f.* urolithiasis.

urolítico, -ca *adj.* urolithic.

urolito *m.* urolith.

urolitología *f.* urolithology.

urología *f.* urology.

urológico, -ca *adj.* urologic.

urólogo, -ga *m., f.* urologist.

uroluteína *f.* urolutein.

uromancia, uromancía *f.* uromancy.

uromelanina *f.* uromelanin.

uromelo *m.* uromelus.

urometría *f.* urometry.

urométrico, -ca *adj.* urometric.

urómetro *m.* urometer.

uromucoide *m.* uromucoid.

uronco *m.* uroncus.

uronefrosis *f.* uronephrosis.

uronófilo, -la *adj.* uronophile.

uronología *f.* uronology.

urononcometría *f.* urononcometry.

uronoscopia *f.* uronoscopy.

uropatía *f.* uropathy.

uropatía obstructiva obstructive uropathy.

uropatógeno *m.* uropathogen.

uropenia *f.* uropenia.

uropepsina *f.* uropepsin.

uropepsinógeno *m.* uropepsinogen.

uropionefrosis *f.* uropyonephrosis.

uropiouréter *m.* uropyoureter.

uroplania *f.* uroplania.

urópodo *m.* uropod.

uroporfiria *f.* uroporphyria.

uroporfiria eritropoyética erythropoietic uroporphyria.

uroporfirina *f.* uroporphyrin.

uropoyesis *f.* uropoiesis.

uropoyético, -ca *adj.* uropoietic.

uropsamo *m.* uropsammus.

uropterina *f.* uropterin.

uropurpurina *f.* uropurpurin.

uroqueras *m.* urocheras.

uroquesia *f.* urochesia, urochezia.

uroquinasa *f.* urokinase.

uroquinético, -ca *adj.* urokinetic.

urorradiología *f.* uroradiology.

urorragia *f.* urorrhagia.

urorrea *f.* urorrhea.

urorrectal *adj.* urorectal.

urorritmografía *f.* urorhythmography.

urorrodina *f.* urorrhodin.

urorrodinógeno *m.* urorrhodinogen.

urorroseína *f.* uroroseín.

urorroseinógeno *m.* uroroseinogen.

urorrubina *f.* urorubin.

urorrubinógeno *m.* urorubinogen.

urorrubrohematina *f.* urorubrohematin.

urosacarimetría *f.* urosaccharometry.

urosacina *f.* urosacin.

uroscopia *f.* uroscopy.

uroscópico, -ca *adj.* uroscopic.

urosemiología *f.* urosemiology.

urosepsina *f.* urosepsin.

urosepsis *f.* urosepsis.

uroséptico, -ca *adj.* uroseptic.

uroseptina *f.* urosepsin.

urosis *f.* urosis.

urospectrina *f.* urospectrin.

urosqueocele *m.* uroscheocele.

urosquesis *f.* uroschesis.

urostalagmia *f.* urostalagmometry.

urostalagmometría *f.* urostalagmometry.

urostealito *m.* urostealith.

urostomia *f.* urostomy.

urotelial *adj.* urothelial.

urotelio *m.* urothelium.

urotórax *m.* urothorax.

urotoxemia *f.* urosepsis.

urotoxia *f.* urotoxia, urotoxy.

urotoxicidad *f.* urotoxicity.

urotóxico, -ca *adj.* urotoxic.

urotoxina *f.* urotoxin.

urouréter *m.* uroureter.

uroxantina *f.* uroxanthin.

urrodina *f.* urrhodin.

urticación *f.* urtication.

urticante *adj.* urticant.

urticaria *f.* urticaria.

urticaria acuógena aqvuagenic urticaria.

urticaria aguda acute urticaria, urticaria acuta.

urticaria ampollar, urticaria ampollosa, urticaria bullosa bullous urticaria, urticaria bullosa.

urticaria colinérgica cholinergic urticaria.

urticaria confluyente urticaria conferta.

urticaria crónica chronic urticaria, urticaria chronica.

urticaria de contacto contact urticaria.

urticaria endémica, urticaria epidémica urticaria endemica, urticaria epidemica.

urticaria facticia factitious urticaria, urticaria factitia.

urticaria febril febril urticaria, urticaria febrilis.

urticaria fotógena light urticaria.

urticaria fría, urticaria por frío cold urticaria.

urticaria gigante giant urticaria.

urticaria hemorrágica hemorrhagic urticaria, urticaria hemorrhagica.

urticaria macular, urticaria maculosa urticaria maculosa.

urticaria medicamentosa urticaria medicamentosa.

urticaria multiforme endémica urticaria multiformis endemica.

urticaria papular, urticaria papulosa papular urticaria, urticaria papulosa.

urticaria persistente urticaria perstans.

urticaria pigmentosa urticaria pigmentosa.

urticaria pigmentosa juvenil juvenile urticaria pigmentosa.

urticaria por calor heat urticaria.

urticaria por compresión, urticaria por presión pressure urticaria.

urticaria por congelación congelation urticaria.

urticaria solar solar urticaria, urticaria solaris.

urticaria subcutánea urticaria subcutanea.

urticaria tuberosa urticaria tuberosa.

urticaria vesicular urticaria vesiculosa.

urticaria vibratoria vibratory urticaria.

urticarial *adj.* urticarial.

urticariógeno, -na *adj.* urticariogenic.

urticarioso, -sa *adj.* urticarious.

ustilaginismo *m.* ustilaginism.

Ustilago Ustilago.

Ustilago maydis Ustilago maydis.

ustión *m.* ustion.

ustulación *f.* ustulation.

ustus ustus.

uta *f.* uta.

uterino, -na *adj.* uterine.

uterismo *m.* uterismus.

útero *m.* uterus.

útero acervical, útero acólico, uterus acollis uterus acollis.

útero anómalo anomalous uterus.

útero arcuato, útero arqueado, uterus arcuatus arcuate uterus, uterus arcuatus.

útero bicameral sellado, útero bicameral senil, uterus bicameratus vetularum uterus bicameratus vetularum.

útero bicorne bicornate uterus, uterus bicornis.

útero bicorne bicervical uterus bicornis bicollis.

útero bicorne unicervical uterus bicornis unicollis.

útero bífido bifid uterus, uterus bifidus.

útero bilocular uterus bilocularis.

útero biorificial biforate uterus, uterus biforis.

útero bipartido, uterus bipartitus bipartite uterus, uterus bipartitus.

útero cocleado cochleate uterus.

útero cordiforme cordiform uterus, uterus cordiformis.

útero de Couvelaire Couvelaire uterus.

útero de doble boca double-mouthed uterus.

útero didelfo uterus didelphys.

útero doble, uterus duplex separatus double uterus, duplex uterus, uterus duplex.

útero en cinta ribbon uterus.

útero en forma de corazón heart-shaped uterus.

útero en reloj de arena hour glass uterus.

útero en silla de montar saddle-shaped uterus.

útero fetal fetal uterus.

útero grávido gravid uterus.

útero incudiforme incudiform uterus, uterus incudiformis.

útero infantil infantile uterus.

útero masculino masculine uterus, uterus masculinus.

útero parvicólico, uterus parvicollis uterus parvicollis.

útero planifúndico uterus planifundalis.

útero pubescente pubescent uterus.

útero recubierto capped uterus.

útero rudimentario uterus rudimentarius.

útero septado, útero tabicado septate uterus, uterus septus.

útero simple uterus simplex.

útero subseptado, útero subtabicado uterus subseptus.

útero triangular triangular uterus, uterus triangularis.

útero unicorne unicorn uterus, uterus unicornis.

uteroabdominal *adj.* uteroabdominal.

uterocele *m.* uterocele.

uterocervical *adj.* uterocervical.

uterocistostomía *f.* uterocystostomy.

uterodinia *f.* uterodynia.

uterofijación *f.* uterofixation.

uterógeno, -na *adj.* uterogenic.

uterogestación *f.* uterogestation.

uteroglobulina *f.* uteroglobulin.

uterografía *f.* uterography.

uterolito *m.* uterolith.

uterometría *f.* uterometry.

uterómetro *m.* uterometer.

uteroovárico, -ca *adj.* utero-ovarian.
uteroparietal *adj.* uteroparietal.
uteropelviano, -na *adj.* uteropelvic.
uteropélvico, -ca *adj.* uteropelvic.
uteropexia *f.* uteropexy.
uteroplacentario, -ria *adj.* uteroplacental.
uteroplastia *f.* uteroplasty.
uterorragia *f.* metrorrhagia.
uterorrea *f.* leukorrhea.
uterorrectal *adj.* uterorectal.
uterosacro, -cra *adj.* uterosacral.
uterosalpingografía *f.* uterosalpingography.
uterosclerosis *f.* uterosclerosis.
uteroscopia *f.* uteroscopy.
uteroscopio *m.* uteroscope.
uterotermometría *f.* uterothermometry.
uterotomía *f.* uterotomy.
uterotónico, -ca *adj.* uterotonic.
uterotrópico, -ca *adj.* uterotropic.
uterotubárico, -ca *adj.* uterotubal.
uterotubario, -ria *adj.* uterotubal.
uterotubografía *f.* uterotubography.
uterovaginal *adj.* uterovaginal.
uteroventral *adj.* uteroventral.
uterovesical *adj.* uterovesical.
uterus *m.* uterus.
utricular *adj.* utricular.
utriculitis *f.* utriculitis.
utrículo *m.* utricle, utriculus.
  utrículo del oído, utrículo del vestíbulo,
  utrículo vestibular utriculus vestibuli.
  utrículo masculino utriculus masculinus.

utrículo prostático utriculus prostaticus.
utrículo prostático prostatic utricle.
utrículo uretral urethral utricle.
utriculosacular *adj.* utriculosaccular.
utriforme *adj.* utriform.
úvea *f.* uvea, uveal tract.
uveal *adj.* uveal.
uveítico, -ca *adj.* uveitic.
uveítis *f.* uveitis.
  uveítis anterior anterior uveitis.
  uveítis de Förster Förster's uveitis.
  uveítis de Fuchs Fuchs' uveitis.
  uveítis endógena endogenous uveitis.
  uveítis exógena exogenous uveitis.
  uveítis facoanafiláctica phacoanaphylactic
  uveitis.
  uveítis facoantigénica phacoantigenic uveitis.
  uveítis facogénica phacogenic uveitis.
  uveítis facotóxica phacotoxic uveitis.
  uveítis granulomatosa granulomatous uveitis.
  uveítis heterocrómica heterochromic uveitis.
  uveítis inducida por el cristalino lens-induced uveitis.
  uveítis intermedia intermediate uveitis.
  uveítis no granulomatosa non-granulomatous uveitis.
  uveítis posterior posterior uveitis.
  uveítis simpática sympathetic uveitis.
  uveítis total total uveitis.
  uveítis tuberculosa tuberculous uveitis.

uveoencefalitis *f.* uveoencephalitis.
uveoescleritis *f.* uveoscleritis.
uveolaberintitis *f.* uveolabyrinthitis.
uveomeningitis *f.* uveomeningitis.
uveoneuraxitis *f.* uveoneuraxitis.
uveoparotídeo, -a *adj.* uveoparotid.
uveoparotitis *f.* uveoparotitis.
uveoplastia *f.* uveoplasty.
uveoscleritis *f.* uveoscleritis.
uviforme *adj.* uviform.
úvula *f.* uvula.
  úvula bífida bifid uvula.
  úvula bifurcada forked uvula.
  úvula cerebelosa, úvula de cerebelo uvula
  cerebelli, uvula of the cerebellum.
  úvula de Lieutaud Lieutaud's uvula.
  úvula del vermis, úvula vermis uvula vermis.
  úvula fisurada uvula fissa.
  úvula hendida cleft uvula, split uvula.
  úvula palatina palatine uvula, uvula palatina.
  úvula vesical uvula of the bladder.
uvulaptosis *f.* uvulaptosis.
uvular *adj.* uvular.
uvulatomía *f.* uvulatomy.
uvulátomo, -ma *adj.* uvulatome.
uvulectomía *f.* uvulectomy.
uvulitis *f.* uvulitis.
uvulopalatofaringoplastia *f.* uvulopalatopharyngoplasty.
uvuloptosis *f.* uvuloptosis.
uvulotomía *f.* uvulotomy.
uvulótomo *m.* uvulotome.

vaca *f.* cow.
   vaca radiactiva radioactive cow.
vaccígeno, -na *adj.* vaccigenous.
vaccina *f.* vaccina.
vaccinal *adj.* vaccinal.
vaccinia *f.* vaccinia.
   vaccinia fetal fetal vaccinia.
   vaccinia gangrenosa vaccinia gangrenosa.
   vaccinia generalizada generalized vaccinia.
   vaccinia progresiva progressive vaccinia.
vaccinial *adj.* vaccinial.
vacciniculturista *m., f.* vacciniculturist.
vaccinide *f.* vaccinid.
vaccinífero *m.* vaccinifer.
vacciniforme *adj.* vacciniform.
vaccinina *f.* vaccinin.
vacciniola *f.* vacciniola.
vaccinización *f.* vaccinization.
vaccinógeno *m.* vaccinogen.
vaccinógeno, -na *adj.* vaccinogenous.
vaccinoide *adj.* vaccinoid.
vaccinola *f.* vaccinola.
vaccinostilo *m.* vaccinostyle.
vaccinum vaccinum.
vaciado *m.* casting.
   vaciado al vacío vacuum casting.
vacío *m.* vacuum.
   gran vacío high vacuum.
   vacío de Torricelli, vacío torricelliano Torricellian vacuum.
vacuna *f.* vaccine, vaccinum.
   vacuna de aceite oil vaccine.
   vacuna acuosa aqueous vaccine.
   vacuna absorbida de la tos ferina adsorbed pertussis vaccine.
   vacuna absorbida de toxoide diftérico y tetánico y de la tos ferina (DTP) adsorbed diphtheria and tetanus toxoids and pertussis vaccine (DTP).
   vacuna antiamarílica yellow fever vaccine.
   vacuna anticólera, vacuna anticolérica cholera vaccine.
   vacuna anticoqueluchosa pertussis vaccine.
   vacuna antidiftérica diphtheria vaccine.
   vacuna anti-fiebre amarilla yellow fever vaccine.
   vacuna anti-fiebre manchada de las Montañas Rocosas Rocky Mountain spotted fever vaccine.
   vacuna antigripal influenza virus vaccine.
   vacuna antimeningocócica de polisacáridos meningococcal polysaccharide vaccine.
   vacuna antineumocócica pneumococcal vaccine.
   vacuna antiparotiditis, vacuna antiparotidítica mumps virus vaccine.
   vacuna antipertussis pertussis vaccine.
   vacuna antipeste plague vaccine.
   vacuna antipoliomielitis, vacuna antipoliomielítica poliovirus vaccine.

   vacuna antipoliomielítica inactivada (IPV) inactivated poliovirus vaccine (IPV).
   vacuna antipoliomielítica oral (OPV) oral poliovirus vaccine (OPV).
   vacuna antipoliomielítica de Sabin Sabin's oral vaccine.
   vacuna antipoliomielítica de Salk Salk vaccine.
   vacuna antirrábica antirabic vaccine.
   vacuna antirrábica preparada de células diploides humanas, vacuna antirrábica preparada en células diploides humanas (HDRV) human diploid cell rabies vaccine (HDRV).
   vacuna antirrubéola, vacuna antirrubeólica rubella virus vaccine.
   vacuna antirrubeólica de virus vivos live rubella virus vaccine.
   vacuna antisarampión, vacuna antisarampionosa measles vaccine, measles virus vaccine.
   vacuna antitetánica tetanus vaccine.
   vacuna antitífica, vacuna antitifoidea, vacuna antitifus antityphoid vaccine.
   vacuna antitosferinosa pertussis vaccine.
   vacuna antituberculosa tuberculosis vaccine.
   vacuna antivariólica smallpox vaccine.
   vacuna de Aragão yellow fever vaccine.
   vacuna atenuada attenuated vaccine.
   vacuna autógena autogenous vaccine.
   vacuna auxiliar adjuvant vaccine.
   vacuna del bacilo de Calmette-Guérin (BCG) (bacillus) Calmette-Guérin vaccine (BCG).
   vacuna bacteriana, vacuna bactérica bacterial vaccine.
   vacuna bovina bovine vaccine.
   vacuna de Calmette Calmette's vaccine.
   vacuna de Calmette-Guérin Calmette-Guérin vaccine.
   vacuna caprinizada caprinized vaccine.
   vacuna del carbunco anthrax vaccine.
   vacuna coadyuvante adjuvant vaccine.
   vacuna del cólera cholera vaccine.
   vacuna de Cox Cox vaccine.
   vacuna de Dakar Dakar vaccine.
   vacuna de la difteria diphtheria vaccine.
   vacuna duplicativa replicative vaccine.
   vacuna de embrión de pato duck embryo vaccine, duck embryo origin vaccine (DEV).
   vacuna estafilocócica, vacuna de estafilococo staphylococcus vaccine.
   vacuna estreptocócica, vacuna de estreptococos streptococcic vaccine.
   vacuna de la fiebre amarilla yellow fever vaccine.
   vacuna de fracciones virales split virus vaccine.
   vacuna de Haffkine Haffkine's vaccine.

   vacuna de la hepatitis B, vacuna contra la hepatitis B hepatitis B vaccine.
   vacuna heteróloga heterologous vaccine.
   vacuna contra la hidrofobia hydrophobia vaccine.
   vacuna homóloga homologous vaccine.
   vacuna inactivada inactivated vaccine.
   vacuna mixta mixed vaccine.
   vacuna multivalente multivalent vaccine.
   vacuna de organismos muertos killed vaccine.
   vacuna de Pasteur Pasteur vaccine.
   vacuna de la peste plague vaccine.
   vacuna de la poliomielitis poliovirus vaccine.
   vacuna de poliovirus poliovirus vaccine.
   vacuna de polisacáridos neumocócicos pneumococcal polysaccharide vaccine.
   vacuna polivalente combined vaccine, polyvalent vaccine.
   vacuna de la rabia rabies vaccine.
   vacuna recombinante de la hepatitis B recombinant hepatitis B vaccine.
   vacuna de rickettsias atenuadas rickettsia attenuated vaccine.
   vacuna de Sabin Sabin's vaccine.
   vacuna de Sabin bucal Sabin's oral vaccine.
   vacuna de Salk Salk vaccine.
   vacuna del sarampión measles vaccine, measles virus vaccine.
   vacuna contra el sarampión, la parotiditis y la rubéola (MMR) measles, mumps and rubella vaccine (MMR).
   vacuna de Sauer Sauer's vaccine.
   vacuna de Semple Semple's vaccine.
   vacuna sensibilizada, vacuna sensibilizada viva sensitized vaccine.
   vacuna de Spencer-Parker Spencer-Parker vaccine.
   vacuna de stock stock vaccine.
   vacuna de subunidades, vacuna de subunidades virales subunit vaccine.
   vacuna subviral subvirion vaccine.
   vacuna TAB TAB vaccine.
   vacuna del tifo, vacuna de la tifoidea, vacuna del tifus, vacuna contra el tifus typhoid vaccine, typhus vaccine.
   vacuna de la tos ferina, vacuna contra la tos ferina pertussis vaccine, whooping cough vaccine.
   vacuna de toxoide diftérico, tetánico y de la tos ferina (DTP) diphtheria and tetanus toxoids and pertussis vaccine (DTP).
   vacuna de toxoide diftérico, tetánico y antipertussis (DTP) diphtheria, tetanus toxoids and pertussis vaccine (DTP).
   vacuna triple, vacuna triple vírica triple vaccine, trivalent vaccine.
   vacuna de la tuberculosis tuberculosis vaccine.
   vacuna de violeta cristal crystal violet vaccine.

vacuna de la viruela smallpox vaccine.

vacuna de virus inactivados inactivated vaccine.

vacuna de virus inactivado de la parotiditis inactived mumps virus vaccine.

vacuna de virus de influenza, vacuna de virus de la influenza influenza virus vaccine.

vacuna de virus de las paperas mumps virus vaccine.

vacuna de virus de rubéola vivos, vacuna de virus de la rubéola vivos live rubella virus vaccine.

vacuna de virus del sarampión inactivado inactived measles virus vaccine.

vacuna de virus sarampionoso measles virus vaccine.

vacuna de virus vivos atenuados de sarampión live attenuated measles virus vaccine.

vacuna de virus vivos de parotiditis live mumps virus vaccine.

vacuna de virus vivos de rubéola y parotiditis live rubella and mumps virus vaccine.

vacuna de virus vivos de sarampión live measles virus vaccine.

vacuna de virus vivos de sarampión, parotiditis y rubéola live measles, mumps and rubella virus vaccine.

vacuna de virus vivos de sarampión y rubéola live measles and rubella virus vaccine.

vacuna viva live vaccine.

vacunable adj. vaccinable.

vacunación f. vaccination.

vacunación contra la viruela smallpox vaccination.

vacunacionista m., f. vaccinationist.

vacunador, -ra m., f. vaccinator, vaccinist.

vacunador m. vaccinator.

vacunal adj. vaccinal.

vacunar v. vaccinate.

vacunífero, -ra adj. vaccinifer.

vacuniforme adj. vacciniform.

vacunización f. vaccinization.

vacunógeno, -na adj. vaccinogenous.

vacunoide f. vaccinoid.

vacunostilo m. vaccinostyle.

vacunoterapia f. vaccinotherapy.

vacuoextractor m. vacuum extractor.

vacuola f. vacuole.

vacuola acuosa water vacuole.

vacuola alimenticia food vacuole.

vacuola autofágica autophagic vacuole.

vacuola de condensación condensing vacuole.

vacuola contráctil contractile vacuole.

vacuola digestiva digestive vacuole.

vacuola parasitófora parasitophorous vacuole.

vacuola plasmocrina plasmocrine vacuole.

vacuola pulsátil contractile vacuole.

vacuola ragiocrina rhagiocrine vacuole.

vacuolación f. vacuolation.

vacuolado, -da adj. vacuolate, vacuolated.

vacuolar¹ v. vacuolate.

vacuolar² adj. vacuolar.

vacuolización f. vacuolation.

vacuoma m. vacuome.

vacútomo m. vacutome.

vacuum vacuum.

vadum vadum.

vagabundo, -da adj. wandering.

vagal adj. vagal.

vagido m. vagitus.

vagido uterino vagitus uterinus.

vagido vaginal vagitus vaginalis.

vagina f. vagina.

vagina bipartida bipartite vagina.

vagina masculina vagina masculina.

vagina septada septate vagina.

vagina tabicada septate vagina.

vaginado, -da adj. vaginate.

vaginal adj. vaginal.

vaginalectomía f. vaginalectomy.

vaginalitis f. vaginalitis.

vaginalitis plástica plastic vaginalitis.

vaginapexia f. vaginapexy.

vaginar v. vaginate.

vaginectomía f. vaginectomy.

vaginismo m. vaginismus.

vaginismo anterior vulvar vaginismus.

vaginismo mental mental vaginismus.

vaginismo perineal perineal vaginismus.

vaginismo posterior posterior vaginismus.

vaginismo vulvar vulvar vaginismus.

vaginitis f. vaginitis.

vaginitis adhesiva adhesive vaginitis, vaginitis adhaesiva.

vaginitis amebiana, vaginitis amébica amebic vaginitis.

vaginitis atrófica atrophic vaginitis.

vaginitis por Candida Candida vaginitis.

vaginitis diftérica diphtheritic vaginitis.

vaginitis enfisematosa emphysematous vaginitis, vaginitis emphysematosa.

vaginitis por Gardnerella vaginalis Gardnerella vaginalis vaginitis.

vaginitis gaseosa emphysematous vaginitis, vaginitis emphysematosa.

vaginitis granulosa granular vaginitis.

vaginitis inflamatoria descamativa, vaginitis inflamatoria exfoliativa desquamative inflammatory vaginitis.

vaginitis por oxiuros pinworm vaginitis.

vaginitis posmenopáusica postmenopausal vaginitis.

vaginitis quística vaginitis cystica.

vaginitis senil senile vaginitis, vaginitis senilis.

vaginitis testicular, vaginitis testis vaginitis testis.

vaginitis verrugosa granular vaginitis.

vaginitis tricomoniásica trichomonas vaginitis.

vaginoabdominal adj. vaginoabdominal.

vaginocele m. vaginocele.

vaginocutáneo, -a adj. vaginocutaneous.

vaginodinia f. vaginodynia.

vaginofijación f. vaginofixation.

vaginografía f. vaginography.

vaginograma m. vaginogram.

vaginohisterectomía f. vaginohysterectomy.

vaginolabial adj. vaginolabial.

vaginómetro m. vaginometer.

vaginomicosis f. vaginomycosis.

vaginopatía f. vaginopathy.

vaginoperineal adj. vaginoperineal.

vaginoperineoplastia f. vaginoperineoplasty.

vaginoperineorrafia f. vaginoperineorrhaphy.

vaginoperineotomía f. vaginiperineotomy, vaginoperineotomy.

vaginoperitoneal adj. vaginoperitoneal.

vaginopexia f. vaginopexy.

vaginoplastia f. vaginoplasty.

vaginorrectal adj. rectovaginal.

vaginoscopia f. vaginoscopy.

vaginoscopio m. vaginoscope.

vaginosis f. vaginosis.

vaginosis bacteriana bacterial vaginosis.

vaginotomía f. vaginotomy.

vaginouretral adj. urethrovaginal.

vaginouterino, -na adj. uterovaginal.

vaginovesical adj. vaginovesical.

vaginovulvar adj. vaginovulvar.

vagitus vagitus.

vago m. vagus.

vagoaccesorio m. vagoaccessorius.

vagoespinal m. vagoaccessorius.

vagoesplácnico, -ca adj. vagosplanchnic.

vagoglosofaríngeo, -a adj. vagoglossopharyngeal.

vagograma m. vagogram.

vagólisis f. vagolysis.

vagolítico, -ca adj. vagolytic.

vagomimético, -ca adj. vagomimetic.

vagosimpático, -ca adj. vagosympathetic.

vagosplácnico, -ca adj. vagosplanchnic.

vagotomía f. vagotomy.

vagotomía bilateral bilateral vagotomy.

vagotomía de células parietales parietal cell vagotomy.

vagotomía farmacológica pharmacologic vagotomy.

vagotomía médica medical vagotomy.

vagotomía quirúrgica surgical vagotomy.

vagotomía muy selectiva highly selective vagotomy.

vagotomía selectiva selective vagotomy.

vagotomía selectiva proximal (VSP) selective proximal vagotomy.

vagotomía selectiva total (VST) highly selective vagotomy.

vagotomía supraselectiva highly selective vagotomy.

vagotomía troncal (VT) truncal vagotomy.

vagotomía troncular truncal vagotomy.

vagotonía f. vagotonia, vagotony.

vagotónico, -ca adj. vagotonic.

vagotonina f. vagotonin.

vagotrópico, -ca adj. vagotropic.

vagotropismo m. vagotropism.

vagotropo, -pa adj. vagotrope.

vagovagal adj. vagovagal.

vagrante adj. vagrant.

vaguectomía f. vagectomy.

vaharera f. perlèche.

vahído m. giddiness, swoon.

vaina f. sheath, vagina.

vaina caudal caudal sheath.

vaina espiral spiral vagina.

vaina fenestrada fenestrated sheath.

vaina fibrosa fibrous sheath.

vaina medular medullary sheath.

vaina mielínica, vaina de mielina myelin sheath.

vaina mitocondrial mitochondrial sheath.

vaina radicular root sheath.

vaina del resectoscopio resectoscope sheath.

vainillismo m. vanillism.

valado, -da adj. vallate.

valécula f. vallecula.

valecular adj. vallecular.

valencia f. valence, valency.

valencia antigénica antigenic valence.

valencia ecológica ecological valence.

valencia negativa negative valence.

valencia positiva positive valence.

valencia química chemical valence.

valente adj. valent.

valetudinarianismo m. valetudinarianism.

valetudinario, -ria adj. valetudinarian.

valgo, -ga adj. valgus.

valgus adj. valgus.

valgoide adj. valgoid.

validación f. validation.

validación consensuada, validación con-

sensual consensual validation.

validación de datos data validation.

validación de un modelo model validation.

validación de la nomenclatura nomenclatural validation.

validez *f.* validity.

validez concurrente concurrent validity.

validez de construcción constructive validity.

validez de contenido content validity.

validez estructural structural validity.

validez predictiva predictive validity.

validez relacionada con un criterio criterion-related validity.

validez replicativa replicative validity.

válido, -da *adj.* valid.

valinemia *f.* valinemia.

valle *m.* valley.

vallecula vallecula.

vallum vallum.

vallum ungueal, vallum unguis vallum unguis.

valor *m.* value.

valor acetilo acetyl value.

valor de ácido acid value.

valor aditivo additive value.

valor amortiguador buffer value.

valor AT, valor % AT AT value, % AT value.

valor de base homing value.

valor biológico biological value.

valor buffer buffer value.

valor buffer de la sangre buffer value of the blood.

valor C C value.

valor calórico caloric value.

valor calorífico de los alimentos caloric value.

valor clínico medio mean clinical value.

valor de combustible fuel value.

valor convencional de una magnitud conventional value of a magnitude.

valor de criócrito cryocrit value.

valor D D value.

valor energético fisiológico physiological energetic value.

valor extremo de una distribución extreme value of a distribution.

valor fenotípico phenotypic value.

valor GC, valor %GC GC value, %GC value.

valor genotípico genotypic value.

valor globular globular value.

valor de Hehner Hehner value.

valor liminal liminal value.

valor de maduración maturation value.

valor de una magnitud magnitude value.

valor medio mean value.

valor medio cuadrático mean square value.

valor de mejora breeding value.

valor normal normal value.

valor numérico de una magnitud numeric value of a quantity.

valor P P value.

valor de predicción, valor predictivo predictive value.

valor de referencia reference value.

valor de ruptura breakdown value.

valor umbral threshold value.

valor verdadero true value.

valor verdadero de una magnitud true value of a magnitude.

valor yodo iodine value.

valoración¹ *f.* assay.

valoración de células madre stem cell assay.

valoración de cuatro puntos fourpoint assay.

valoración inmunitaria immune assay.

valoración microbiológica microbiological assay.

valoración² *f.* assessment, measurement, testing.

valoración del aparato reproductor femenino female reproductive system assessment.

valoración del aparato urinario urinary system assessment.

valoración de Brazelton Brazelton assessment.

valoración clínica geriátrica de Sandoz Sandoz Clinical Assessment-Geriatric.

valoración del desarrollo de Gesell Gessel developmental assessment.

valoración del dolor pain assessment.

valoración del domicilio home assessment.

valoración de Dubowitz Dubowitz assessment.

valoración física physical assessment.

valoración gestacional gestational assessment.

valoración de la investigación research measurement.

valoración neurológica neurologic assessment.

valoración del paciente anciano assessment of the aging patient.

valoración respiratoria respiratory assessment.

valoración de la sensibilidad general gross sensory testing.

valoración del sistema auditivo auditory system assessment.

valoración del sistema gastrointestinal gastrointestinal system assessment.

valoración del sistema musculoesquelético musculoskeletal system assessment.

valoración del sistema óptico optic system assessment.

valoración del sistema tegumentario integumentary system assessment.

valoración del traslado lift assessment.

valoración³ *f.* analysis, titration.

valoración química titration.

valva¹ *f.* shell, cuspis.

valva² *f.* valve.

valvado, -da *adj.* valvate, valved.

valvar *adj.* valval, valvar.

valviforme *adj.* valviform.

valvoplastia *f.* valvoplasty.

valvotomía *f.* valvotomy.

valvotomía mitral mitral valvotomy.

valvotomía pulmonar pulmonar valvotomy.

valvotomía rectal rectal valvotomy.

valvotomía transventricular cerrada transventricular closed valvotomy.

valvótomo *m.* valvotome.

válvula *f.* valve, valvul, valva.

válvula de Bjork-Shiley Bjork-Shiley valve.

válvula cardíaca artificial artificial cardiac valve, artificial heart valve.

válvula cardíaca protésica prosthetic heart valve.

válvula de Carpentier-Edwards Carpentier-Edwards valve.

válvula de disco cautivo tilting-disc valve.

válvula esférica ball valve.

válvula de Heyer-Pudenz Heyer-Pudenz valve.

válvula reductora reducing valve.

válvula sin respiración doble non-rebreathing valve.

válvula de tipo de esfera ball-type valve.

valvular *adj.* valvular.

valvulitis *f.* valvulitis.

valvulitis reumática rheumatic valvulitis.

valvulopatía cardíaca *f.* valvular heart disease.

valvuloplastia *f.* valvuloplasty.

valvulotomía *f.* valvulotomy.

valvulótomo *m.* valvulotome.

vanadismo *m.* vanadiumism.

vanadiumismo *m.* vanadiumism.

vanilismo *m.* vanillism.

vapocauterización *f.* vapocauterization.

vapor *m.* vapor.

vapor anestésico anesthetic vapor.

vaporario *m.* vaporarium.

vaporización *f.* vaporization.

vaporizador *m.* vaporizer.

vaporizador de cobre copper kettle vaporizer.

vaporizador de flujo flow-over vaporizer.

vaporizador de temperatura compensada temperature-compensated vaporizer.

vaporizar *v.* vaporize.

vaportórax *m.* vaporthorax.

vapoterapia *f.* vapotherapy.

variabilidad *f.* variability.

variabilidad basal de la frecuencia cardíaca fetal baseline variability of fetal heart rate.

variable *f. y adj.* variable.

variable aleatoria random variable.

variable aleatoria continua continuous random variable.

variable aleatoria centrada centered random variable.

variable aleatoria discreta discrete random variable.

variable aleatoria equivalente equivalent random variable.

variable aleatoria tipificada standardized random variable.

variable aleatoria correlacionada correlated random variable.

variable aleatoria idénticamente distribuida identically distributed random variable.

variable aleatoria incorrelacionada uncorrelated random variable.

variable aleatoria no correlacionada uncorrelated random variable.

variable binaria Boolean variable.

variable booleana Boolean variable.

variable compleja complex variable.

variable de control control variable.

variable no controlable non-controllable variable.

variable de decisión control variable.

variable dependiente dependent variable.

variable descriptiva del modelo model descriptive variable.

variable dinámica dynamic variable.

variable de diseño design variable.

variable endógena endogenous variable.

variable de entrada input variable.

variable estadística statistical variable.

variable estadística continua continuous statistical variable.

variable estadística discreta discrete statistical variable.

variable de estado state variable.

variable estocástica random variable.

variable exógena exogenous variable.

variable experimental experimental variable.

variable independiente independent variable.

variable de ingreso input variable.

variable interviniente intervening variable.

variable latente latent variable.

variable lógica Boolean variable.

variable predictiva predictor variable.
variable real real variable.
variable de respuesta output variable.
variable de salida output variable.
variable termodinámica thermodynamic variable.
variable tipificada standardized random variable.
variación *f.* variation.
variación alotípica allotypic variation.
variación antigénica antigenic variation, antigenic shift.
variación bacteriana bacterial variation.
variación casi continua quasi-continuous variation.
variación circadiana circadian variation.
variación continua continuous variation.
variación diaria circadian variation.
variación diurna del estado de ánimo diurnal mood variation.
variación discontinua discotinuous variation.
variación estructural structural change.
variación fenotípica phenotypic variation.
variación idiotípica idiotypic variation.
variación impresa impressed variation.
variación innata inborn variation.
variación isotípica isotypic variation.
variación de Lexis Lexis variation.
variación latido a latido de la frecuencia cardíaca fetal beat-to-beat variation of fetal heart rate.
variación lisa-rugosa (L-R) smooth-rough variation (S-R).
variación merística meristic variation.
variación microbiana microbial variation.
variante *f. y adj.* variant.
variante de fase I I-phase variant.
variante hereditaria de albúmina inherited albumin variant.
varianza *f.* variance.
variato *m.* variate.
varicación *f.* varication.
varice *f.* varix.
variceal *adj.* variceal.
varicectomía *f.* varicotomy.
varicela *f.* chickenpox, varicella.
varicela gangrenosa varicella gangrenosa.
varicela inoculada varicella inoculata.
varicela pustular, varicela pustulosa pustular varicella, varicella pustulosa.
varicela por vacunación vaccination varicella.
varicelación *f.* varicellation.
variceliforme *adj.* varicelliform.
varicelización *f.* varicellization.
variceloide *adj.* varicelloid.
variciforme *adj.* variciform.
varicobléfaron *m.* varicoblepharon.
varicocele *m.* varicocele.
varicocele ovárico ovarian varicocele.
varicocele pélvico pelvic varicocele.
varicocele sintomático symptomatic varicocele.
varicocele tubárico ovarian varicocele.
varicocele tuboovárico tubo-ovarian varicocele.
varicocele uteroovárico utero-ovarian varicocele.
varicocelectomía *f.* varicocelectomy.
varicoflebitis *f.* varicophlebitis.
varicografía *f.* varicography.
varicoide *adj.* varicoid.
varicole *m.* varicole.
variconfalo, varicónfalo *m.* varicomphalus.
varicosclerosación *f.* varicosclerosation.

varicosidad *f.* varicosity.
varicosis *f.* varicosis.
varicoso, -sa *adj.* varicose.
varicotomía *f.* varicotomy.
varícula *f.* varicula.
variedad *f.* variety.
variedad alogénica allogenic variety.
variedad singénica syngenic variety.
variedad xenogénica xenogeneic variety.
varilla *f.* staff.
varilla ranurada grooved staff.
variola *f.* variola.
variola benigna variola benigna.
variola crystallina variola crystallina.
variola sin erupción variola sine eruptione.
variola hemorrágica, variola hemorrhagica variola hemorrhagica.
variola inserta variola inserta.
variola maligna variola maligna.
variola mayor, variola major variola major.
variola menor, variola minor variola minor.
variola miliar, variola miliaris variola miliaris.
variola mitigata variola mitigata.
variola penfigosa, variola pemphigosa variola pemphigosa.
variola silicuosa, variola siliquosa variola siliquosa.
variola vaccinia variola vaccine, variola vaccinia.
variola verdadera, variola vera variola vera.
variola verrugosa, variola verrucosa variola verrucosa.
variolación *f.* variolation.
variolado, -da *adj.* variolate.
variolar *v.* variolate.
variolar *adj.* variolar.
variólico, -ca *adj.* variolic.
varioliforme *adj.* varioliform.
variolización *f.* variolization.
varioloide *adj.* varioloid.
varioloso, -sa *adj.* variolous.
variolovacuna *f.* variolovaccine.
variz *f.* varix.
variz anastomótica anastomotic varix, varix anastomoticus.
variz aneurismática aneurysmal varix.
variz aneurismoide aneurysmoid varix.
variz arterial arterial varix.
variz cirsoide cirsoid varix.
variz conjuntival conjunctival varix.
variz esofágica esophageal varices.
variz gelatinosa gelatinous varix.
variz linfática lymph varix, varix lymphaticus.
variz turbinada turbinal varix.
varo, -ra *adj.* varus.
varoliano, -na *adj.* varolian.
varón *m.* male.
varus varus.
vas vas.
vasal *adj.* vasal.
vasalgia *f.* vasalgia.
vascular *adj.* vascular.
vascularidad *f.* vascularity.
vascularizado, -da *adj.* vascularized.
vascularización *f.* vascularization.
vascularizar *v.* vascularize.
vasculatura *f.* vasculature.
vasculítico, -ca *adj.* vasculitic.
vasculitis *f.* vasculitis.
vasculitis alérgica allergic vasculitis.
vasculitis alérgica cutánea allergic cutaneous vasculitis.
vasculitis cutánea cutaneous vasculitis.
vasculitis hialinizante segmentada, vasculi-

tis hialinizante segmentaria segmented hyalinizing vasculitis.
vasculitis de hipersensibilidad, vasculitis por hipersensibilidad hypersensitivity vasculitis.
vasculitis leucocitoclástica leukocytoclastic vasculitis.
vasculitis livedo livedo vasculitis.
vasculitis necrosante, vasculitis necrotizante necrotizing vasculitis.
vasculitis nodular nodular vasculitis.
vasculitis umbilical umbilical vasculitis.
vasculocardíaco, -ca *adj.* vasculocardiac.
vasculogénesis *f.* vasculogenesis.
vasculógeno, -na *adj.* vasculogenic.
vasculolinfático, -ca *adj.* vasculolymphatic.
vasculomielinopatía *f.* vasculomyelinopathy.
vasculomotor, -ra *adj.* vasculomotor.
vasculomotriz *adj.* vasculomotor.
vasculopatía *f.* vasculopathy.
vasculopatía diabética diabetic vasculopathy.
vasculopatía del injerto graft vasculopathy.
vasculotóxico, -ca *adj.* vasculotoxic.
vasculum vasculum.
vasectomía *f.* vasectomy.
vasectomía cruzada cross over vasectomy.
vasectomizado, -da *adj.* vasectomized.
vaselina *f.* petrolatum.
vaselina blanca white petrolatum.
vaselina hidrófila hydrophilic petrolatum.
vaselina líquida liquid petrolatum, petrolatum liquidum, petroleum jelly.
vaselina líquida ligera, vaselina líquida liviana light liquid petrolatum, petrolatum liquidum leve.
vaselina líquida pesada heavy liquid petrolatum.
vasifacción *f.* vasifaction.
vasifactivo, -va *adj.* vasifactive.
vasiforme *adj.* vasiform.
vasitis *f.* vasitis.
vaso *m.* vessel, vas.
vasoactivo, -va *adj.* vasoactive.
vasocentesis *f.* vasopuncture.
vasoconstricción *f.* vasoconstriction.
vasoconstricción activa active vasoconstriction.
vasoconstricción pasiva passive vasoconstriction.
vasoconstrictivo, -va *adj.* vasoconstrictive.
vasoconstrictor, -ra *adj.* vasoconstrictive, vasoconstrictor.
vasocorona *f.* vasocorona.
vasodepresión *f.* vasodepression.
vasodepresor *m. y adj.* vasodepressor.
vasodilatación *f.* vasodilatation.
vasodilatación activa active vasodilatation.
vasodilatación pasiva passive vasodilatation.
vasodilatación refleja reflex vasodilatation.
vasodilatador, -ra *adj.* vasodilative, vasodilator.
vasodilatativo, -va *adj.* vasodilative.
vasoepididimografía *f.* vasoepididymography.
vasoepididimostomía *f.* vasoepididymostomy.
vasoespasmo *m.* vasospasm.
vasoespasmolítico, -ca *adj.* vasospasmolytic.
vasoespástico, -ca *adj.* vasospastic.
vasoestimulante *adj.* vasostimulant.
vasofactivo, -va *adj.* vasofactive.
vasoformación *f.* vasoformation.
vasoformativo, -va *adj.* vasoformative.
vasografía *f.* vasography.
vasohipertónico, -ca *adj.* vasohypertonic.
vasohipotónico, -ca *adj.* vasohypotonic.

vasoinerte *adj.* vasoinert.
vasoinhibidor *m.* vasoinhibitor.
vasoinhibidor, -ra *adj.* vasoinhibitory.
vasoinhibitorio, -ria *adj.* vasoinhibitory.
vasolábil *adj.* vasolabile.
vasoligadura *f.* vasoligation, vasoligature.
vasomoción *f.* vasomotion.
vasomotor, -ra *adj.* vasomotive.
vasomotorio, -ria *adj.* vasomotorial.
vasomotricidad *f.* vasomotoricity.
vasomovimiento *f.* vasomotion.
vasoneuropatía *f.* vasoneuropathy.
vasoneurosis *f.* vasoneurosis.
vasoorquidostomía *f.* vaso-orchidostomy.
vasoparálisis *f.* vasoparalysis.
vasoparesia *f.* vasoparesis.
vasoparesis *f.* vasoparesis.
vasopermeabilidad *f.* vasopermeability.
vasopresina (VP) *f.* vasopressin (VP).
 vasopresina arginina arginine vasopressin.
vasopresor *m. y adj.* vasopressor.
vasopuntura *f.* vasopuncture.
vasorrafia *f.* vasorrhaphy.
vasorreflejo *m.* vasoreflex.
vasorrelajación *f.* vasorelaxation.
vasorresección *f.* vasoresection.
vasosección *f.* vasosection.
vasosensitivo, -va *adj.* vasosensory.
vasosensorial *adj.* vasosensory.
vasospasmo *m.* vasospasm.
vasospástico, -ca *adj.* vasospastic.
vasostomía *f.* vasostomy.
vasotocina *f.* vasotocin.
 vasotocina arginina arginine vasotocin.
vasotomía *f.* vasotomy.
vasotonía *f.* vasotonia.
vasotónico, -ca *adj.* vasotonic.
vasotribo *m.* vasotribe.
vasotripsia *f.* vasotripsy.
vasotripsina *f.* vasotripsin.
vasotrófico, -ca *adj.* vasotrophic.
vasotrombina *f.* vasothrombin.
vasotrópico, -ca *adj.* vasotropic.
vasovagal *adj.* vasovagal.
vasovasostomía *f.* vasovasostomy.
vasovesiculectomía *f.* vasovesiculectomy.
vasovesiculitis *f.* vasovesiculitis.
vástago de Wrisberg *m.* staff of Wrisberg.
vasto *m.* vastus.
vatímetro *m.* wattmeter.
ve velamentum.
 ve cerebral velamentum cerebri.
vección *f.* vection.
vectocardiografia *f.* vectocardiography.
 vectocardiografia espacial spatial vectocardiography.
vectocardiógrafo *m.* vectocardiograph.
vector *m.* vector.
 vector axial axial vector.
 vector bifuncional bifunctional vector.
 vector biológico biological vector.
 vector de Burger Burger's vector.
 vector de clonación, vector clonal cloning
 vector.
 vector espacial spatial vector.
 vector de expresión expression vector.
 vector instantáneo instantaneous vector.
 vector manifiesto manifest vector.
 vector mecánico pasivo mechanical vector.
 vector medio mean vector.
 vector polar polar vector.
 vector de posición position vector.
 vector recombinante recombinant vector.
 vector transmisor transmitter vector.
 vector transportador shuttle vector.

vectorcardiograma *m.* vectorcardiogram.
vectorial *adj.* vectorial.
vectoriscopio *m.* vectorscope.
vegán *adj.* vegan.
veganismo *m.* veganism.
vegetación *f.* vegetation.
 vegetación adenoide adenoid vegetation.
 vegetación bacteriana bacterial vegetation.
vegetante *adj.* vegetative, vegetans.
vegetarianismo *m.* vegetarianism.
vegetariano, -na *m., f.* vegetarian.
vegetarismo *m.* vegetarianism.
vegetativo, -va *adj.* vegetative.
vehículo *m.* vehicle.
Veillonella Veillonella.
Veillonellaceae Veillonellaceae.
vejez *f.* old age.
vejiga *f.* bladder, vesica.
 vejiga atónica atonic bladder.
 vejiga atónica neurógena atonic neurogenic
 bladder.
 vejiga automática automatic bladder.
 vejiga autónoma, vejiga autonómica autonomic bladder.
 vejiga de baja elasticidad low-compliance
 bladder.
 vejiga biliar vesica biliaris.
 vejiga en cuerda cord bladder.
 vejiga espasmódica hypertonic bladder.
 vejiga espástica spastic bladder.
 vejiga fasciculada fasciculate bladder.
 vesica fellea vesica fellea.
 vejiga fláccida flaccid bladder.
 vejiga de la hiel fasciculate bladder.
 vejiga hipertónica hypertonic bladder.
 vejiga ileal ileal bladder.
 vejiga irritable irritable bladder.
 vejiga medular chard bladder.
 vejiga nerviosa irritable bladder.
 vejiga neurógena, vejiga neurogénica neurogenic bladder.
 vejiga neurogénica autonóma autonomic
 neurogenic bladder.
 vejiga neurogénica desinhibida uninhibited neurogenic bladder.
 vejiga neurogénica refleja reflex neurogenic
 bladder.
 vejiga neuropática neuropathic bladder.
 vejiga no refleja non-reflex bladder.
 vejiga de la orina urinary bladder.
 vejiga prostática, vesica prostatica vesica
 prostatica.
 vejiga refleja reflex bladder.
 vejiga saculada sacculated vesica.
 vejiga seudoneurogénica pseudoneurogenic bladder.
 vejiga de succión sucking blister.
 *vejiga urinaria, vesica urinalis, vesica uri-
 naria* urinary bladder, cystis urinaria, vesica
 urinaria.
veladura *f.* fogging.
velamen *m.* velamen.
velamentum velamentum.
velamentoso, -sa *adj.* velamentous.
velar *adj.* velar.
velicación *f.* vellication.
velicar *v.* vellicate.
velificación *f.* vellication.
veliforme *adj.* veliform.
vello *m.* hair, vellus.
 vello de la oliva vellus olivae.
 vello de la oliva inferior vellus olivae inferioris.
 vello pubiano, vello púbico pubic hair.
vellosidad¹ *f.* villus.
 vellosidad amniotica amniotic villus.

 vellosidad de anclaje anchoring villus.
 vellosidad aracnoideas arachnoid villi.
 vellosidad coriónicas chorionic villi.
 vellosidad de fijación anchoring villus.
 vellosidad flotante floating villus.
 vellosidad intestinales intestinal villi, villi
 intestinale.
 vellosidad del intestino delgado villus of
 the small intestine.
 vellosidad libre free villus.
 vellosidad lingual lingual villus.
 vellosidad pericárdicas pericardial villi, villi
 pericardiaci.
 vellosidad peritoneales peritoneal villi, villi
 peritoneales.
 vellosidad placentaria coriónica chorionic
 villi.
 vellosidad pleurales pleural villi, villi pleurales.
 vellosidad primaria primary villus.
 vellosidad secundaria secondary villus.
 vellosidad sinoviales synovial villi, villi syno-
 viales.
 vellosidad terciaria tertiary villus.
vellosidad² *f.* villosity.
vellositis *f.* villositis.
velloso, -sa *adj.* villose, villous.
velludo, -da *adj.* villose.
velo *m.* veil, velum.
 velo del acueducto aqueduct veil.
 velo de amamantamiento nursing veil.
 velo artificial artificial veil.
 velo de Fick Fick's veil.
 velo de Jackson Jackson's veil.
 velo de Sattler Sattler's veil.
velocidad *f.* rate, speed, velocity.
 velocidad de absorción específica (VAE)
 specific absorption rate (SAR).
 *velocidad circulatoria, velocidad de circu-
 lación* blood flow velocity, circulation rate.
 velocidad de conducción conduction velocity.
 velocidad de conducción nerviosa nerve
 conduction velocity.
 velocidad de crecimiento rate of growth.
 velocidad de enfriamiento cooling rate.
 velocidad de eritrosedimentación erythrocyte sedimentation rate (ESR).
 velocidad de flujo lineal linear flow velocity.
 velocidad de flujo volumétrico volumetric
 flow rate.
 velocidad inherente inherent rate.
 velocidad de intercambio espiratorio expiratory exchange rate.
 velocidad de intercambio respiratorio respiratory exchange rate.
 velocidad máxima maximum velocity.
 velocidad máxima de crecimiento peak
 height velocity.
 *velocidad máxima de flujo espiratorio
 (MEFR)* maximal expiratory flow rate
 (MEFR).
 *velocidad máxima de flujo mesoespirato-
 rio* maximal midexpiratory flow rate.
 velocidad metabólica basal basal metabolic
 rate.
 *velocidad de metabolización cerebral local
 de la glucosa (VMCLG)* local cerebral metabolic rate of glucose utilization (LCMRG).
 velocidad de perfusión perfusion rate.
 velocidad de pulso pulse rate.
 velocidad de sedimentación sedimentation
 rate, sedimentation velocity.
 *velocidad de sedimentación de los glóbulos
 rojos* erythrocyte sedimentation rate (ESR).

velocidad de sedimentación de eritrocitos erythrocyte sedimentation rate (ESR).
velocidad de sedimentación globular (VSG) erythrocyte sedimentation rate (ESR).
velocidad de ultrasonidos velocity of ultrasound.
velocimetría *f.* velocimetry.
velocimetría láser-Doppler laser-Doppler velocimetry.
velofaríngeo, -a *adj.* velopharyngeal.
velogénico, -ca *adj.* velogenic.
velosíntesis *f.* velosynthesis.
velum *m.* veil, velum.
vena *f.* vein, vena.
venacavografía *f.* venacavography.
venacavograma *m.* venacavogram.
venación *f.* venation.
venda *f.* bandage.
venda de Martin Martin's bandage.
venda elástica elastic bandage.
vendaje *m.* bandage, dressing, strapping.
vendaje abdominal abdominal bandage.
vendaje adhesivo adhesive bandage, strap.
vendaje almidonado starch bandage.
vendaje de Barton Barton's bandage.
vendaje de Baynton Baynton's bandage.
vendaje braquial simple en 8 simple figure-of-eight roller arm sling.
vendaje de cabos múltiples many-tailed bandage.
vendaje en capelina, vendaje capelar capeline bandage.
vendaje en chalina scarf bandage.
vendaje circular circular bandage.
vendaje compresivo compression bandage, pressure bandage.
vendaje crucial, vendaje en cruz crucial bandage.
vendaje de cuatro cabos, vendaje de cuatro colas four-tailed bandage.
vendaje de Desault Desault's bandage.
vendaje dextrinado starch bandage.
vendaje elástico elastic bandage.
vendaje enrollado roller bandage.
vendaje enyesado plate bandage.
vendaje de Esmarch Esmarch's bandage.
vendaje con esparadrapo strapping.
vendaje en espiga, vendaje en espica spica bandage.
vendaje espiral spiral bandage.
vendaje espiral inverso spiral reverse bandage.
vendaje en fijación de Gibney Gibney's fixation bandage.
vendaje en figura de ocho figure-of-eight bandage.
vendaje de Galeno Galen's bandage.
vendaje de gasa gauze bandage.
vendaje gelatinado starch bandage.
vendaje de Gibson Gibson's bandage.
vendaje en guante, vendaje en guantelete gauntlet bandage.
vendaje en hamaca hammock bandage.
vendaje de Heliodoro Heliodorus' bandage.
vendaje inamovible immovable bandage.
vendaje inmóvil immovable bandage.
vendaje de inmovilización immobilizing bandage.
vendaje inverso reversed bandage.
vendaje de Martin Martin's bandage.
vendaje de múltiples colas, vendaje de múltiples extremos many-tailed bandage.
vendaje en ocho figure-of-eight bandage.
vendaje protector, vendaje protectivo protective bandage.

vendaje recurrente recurrent bandage.
vendaje en rollo roller bandage.
vendaje de Scultetus Scultetus' bandage.
vendaje en semiguantelete demigauntlet bandage.
vendaje silicatado starch bandage.
vendaje suspensor, vendaje suspensorio suspensory bandage.
vendaje en T T-bandage.
vendaje con tela adhesiva strapping.
vendaje triangular triangular bandage.
vendaje de Velpeau Velpeau's bandage.
vendar *v.* bandage, bind, strap.
venectasia *f.* venectasia.
venectomía *f.* venectomy.
veneer veneer.
venenación *f.* venenation.
venenífero, -ra *adj.* veneniferous.
venenífico, -ca *adj.* venenific.
venenización *f.* venomization.
veneno *m.* poison, venom.
veneno acre, veneno ácrido acrid poison.
veneno de araña spider venom.
veneno de buccino whelk poison.
veneno de fatiga sedative venom.
veneno de flechas arrow poison.
veneno fugu, veneno del fugu fugu poison.
veneno hipostenizante sedative venom.
veneno irritante acrid poison.
veneno kokoi kokoi venom.
veneno narcótico narcotic poison.
veneno de los peces fish poison.
veneno de pez globo puffer poison.
veneno sedante sedative venom.
veneno de las serpientes snake venom.
veneno de víbora viper venom.
veneno de víbora de Russell Russell's viper venom.
venenosalival *adj.* venenosalivary.
venenosidad *f.* venenosity.
venenoso, -sa *adj.* poisonous, venenous, venomous.
venepunción *f.* venipuncture.
venepuntura *f.* venipuncture.
venéreo, -a *adj.* venereal.
venereofobia *f.* venereophobia.
venereología *f.* venereology.
venereólogo, -ga *m., f.* venereologist.
venerrupina *f.* venerupin.
venesección *f.* venesection.
venipuntura *f.* venipuncture.
venisección *f.* venisection.
venisutura *f.* venesuture, venisuture.
venoauricular *adj.* venoauricular, venoatrial.
venoclisis *f.* venoclysis.
venoesclerosis *f.* venosclerosis.
venoestasia *f.* venostasia.
venofibrosis *f.* venofibrosis.
venografía *f.* venography.
venografía esplénica splenic venography.
venografía esplenicoportal splenic portal venography.
venografía transósea transosseous venography.
venografía vertebral vertebral venography.
venograma *f.* venogram.
venoma *m.* venous angioma.
venomosalival *adj.* venomosalivary.
venomotor, -ra *adj.* venomotor.
venooclusivo, -va *adj.* veno-occlusive.
venoperitoneostomía *f.* venoperitoneostomy.
venopresor, -ra *adj.* venopressor.
venopunción *f.* venepuncture.
venosclerosis *f.* venosclerosis.
venosidad *f.* venosity.

venosinusal *adj.* venosinusal.
venoso, -sa *adj.* venous, venose.
venospasmo *m.* venospasm.
venostasis *f.* venostasis.
venóstato *m.* venostat.
venostomía *f.* cutdown, venous cutdown.
venotomía *f.* venotomy.
venosutura *f.* venesuture.
venovenostomía *f.* venovenostomy.
vent vent.
ventana *f.* window, fenestra.
ventana aórtica aortic window.
ventana aortopulmonar aortopulmonary window.
ventana de la cóclea, ventana coclear, fenestra cochleae window of the cochlea, cochlear window, fenestra of the cochlea, fenestra cochleae.
ventana cutánea skin window.
ventana nasal anterior nares, nostril.
ventana novovalis fenestra novovalis.
ventana oval, fenestra ovalis oval window, fenestra ovalis.
ventana redonda round window.
ventana de taquicardia tachycardia window.
ventana vestibular, ventana del vestíbulo, fenestra vestibuli vestibular window, window of the vestibule, fenestra of the vestibule, fenestra vestibuli.
venter venter.
ventilación *f.* ventilation.
ventilación alveolar alveolar ventilation.
ventilación artificial artificial ventilation.
ventilación ascendente upward ventilation.
ventilación asistida assisted ventilation.
ventilación asistida controlada assist-control ventilation.
ventilación asistida intermitente (VAI) intermittent assisted ventilation (IAV).
ventilación asistida de modalidad controlada assist-control mode ventilation.
ventilación colateral collateral ventilation.
ventilación controlada controlled ventilation.
ventilación descendente downward ventilation.
ventilación desperdiciada wasted ventilation.
ventilación de escape exhausting ventilation.
ventilación espontánea spontaneous ventilation.
ventilación mandatoria intermitente intermittent mandatory ventilation (IMV).
ventilación mandatoria intermitente espontánea spontaneous intermittent mandatory ventilation (SIMV).
ventilación mandatoria intermitente sincronizada synchronized intermittent mandatory ventilation (SIMV).
ventilación manual manual ventilation.
ventilación mecánica mechanical ventilation.
ventilación mecánica controlada controlled mechanical ventilation (CMV).
ventilación por minuto, ventilación-minuto minute ventilation.
ventilación de modalidad controlada control mode ventilation.
ventilación obligada intermitente (VOI) intermittent mandatory ventilation (IMV).
ventilación obligada intermitente sincronizada (VOIS) synchronized intermittent mandatory ventilation (SIMV).
ventilación plena plenum ventilation.
ventilación con presión de soporte (VPS) pressure support ventilation (PSV).
ventilación con presión positiva constante constant positive pressure ventilation.

ventilación con presión positiva continua (VPPC) continous positive pressure ventilation (CPPV).

ventilación con presión positiva intermitente intermittent positive pressure ventilation (IPPV).

ventilación pulmonar pulmonary ventilation.

ventilación residual wasted ventilation.

ventilación voluntaria máxima (VVM) maximum voluntary ventilation (MVV).

ventilador *m.* ventilator.

ventilador cíclico combinado combined cycling ventilator.

ventilador en fuelle bellows ventilator.

ventilador fluídico fluidic ventilator.

ventilador a presión pressure ventilator.

ventilador de volumen volume ventilator.

ventilar *v.* ventilate.

ventosa *f.* cup, cupping glass.

ventosa escarificada wet cup.

ventosa fisiológica physiologic cup.

ventosa glaucomatosa glaucomatous cup.

ventosa húmeda wet cup.

ventosa obstétrica obstetric vacuum.

ventosa óptica optic cup.

ventosa seca dry cup.

ventosa de succión suction cup.

ventplante *m.* ventplant.

ventrad ventrad.

ventral *adj.* ventral, ventralis.

ventricornu ventricornu.

ventricornual *adj.* ventricornual.

ventricoso, -sa *adj.* ventricose.

ventricuerno *m.* ventricornu.

ventricular *adj.* ventricular.

ventricularización *f.* ventricularization.

ventriculitis *f.* ventriculitis.

ventrículo *m.* ventricle, ventriculus.

ventriculoauricular (V-A) *adj.* ventriculoatrial (V-A).

ventriculoauriculostomía *f.* ventriculoatriostomy.

ventriculocisternostomía *f.* ventriculocisternostomy.

ventriculocordectomía *f.* ventriculocordectomy.

ventriculofásico, -ca *adj.* ventriculophasic.

ventriculografía *f.* ventriculography.

ventriculografía isotópica isotope ventriculography.

ventriculograma *m.* ventriculogram.

ventriculograma isotópico isotope ventriculogram.

ventriculomastoidostomía *f.* ventriculomastoidostomy.

ventriculometría *f.* ventriculometry.

ventriculomiotomía *f.* ventriculomyotomy.

ventriculoperitoneostomía *f.* ventriculoperitoneostomy.

ventriculoplastia *f.* ventriculoplasty.

ventriculopunción *f.* ventriculopuncture.

ventriculopuntura *f.* ventriculopuncture.

ventriculoscopia *f.* ventriculoscopy.

ventriculoscopio *m.* ventriculoscope.

ventriculostomía *f.* ventriculostomy.

ventriculostomía del tercer ventrículo third ventriculostomy.

ventriculosubaracnoideo, -a *adj.* ventriculosubarachnoid.

ventriculotomía *f.* ventriculotomy.

ventriculovenoso, -sa *adj.* ventriculovenous.

ventriculovenostomía *f.* ventriculovenostomy.

ventriculus *m.* ventricle, ventriculus.

ventricumbente *adj.* ventricumbent.

ventriducción *f.* ventriduction.

ventriducir *v.* ventriduct.

ventrifijación *f.* ventrifixation.

ventriflexión *f.* ventriflexion.

ventrocistorrafia *f.* ventrocystorrhaphy.

ventrodorsad ventrodorsad.

ventrodorsal *adj.* ventrodorsal.

ventrofijación *f.* ventrofixation.

ventrohisteropexia *f.* ventrohisteropexy.

ventroinguinal *adj.* ventroinguinal.

ventrolateral *adj.* ventrolateral.

ventroposterior *adj.* ventroposterior.

ventroptosia *f.* ventroptosia.

ventroptosis *f.* ventroptosis.

ventroscopia *f.* ventroscopy.

ventroso, -sa *adj.* ventrose.

ventrosuspensión *f.* ventrosuspension.

ventrotomía *f.* ventrotomy.

ventrovesicofijación *f.* ventrovesicofixation.

venturímetro *m.* venturimeter.

vénula *f.* venule, venula.

venular *adj.* venula.

venuloso, -sa *adj.* venulous.

verbigeración *f.* verbigeration.

verbomanía *f.* verbomania.

verborrea *f.* verbiage.

verde *adj.* green.

verdina *f.* verdine.

verdoglobina *f.* verdoglobin.

verdohemina *f.* verdohemin.

verdohemocromo *m.* verdohemochrome.

verdohemoglobina *f.* verdohemoglobin.

verdohemocromógeno *m.* verdohemochromogen.

verdoperoxidasa *f.* verdoperoxidase.

verga *f.* penis.

verga palmeada webbed penis, penis palmatus.

vergencia *f.* vergence.

vergencia de una lente vergence of lens.

vermes *m.* vermis.

vermetoide *adj.* vermetoid.

vermiano, -na *adj.* vermian.

vermicida *m.* vermicidal.

vermícula *f.* vermicule.

vermícula viajera traveling vermicule.

vermiculación *f.* vermiculation.

vermicular *adj.* vermicular.

vermículo *m.* vermicule, vermiculus.

vermiculoso, -sa *adj.* vermiculous, vermiculose.

vermifobia *f.* vermiphobia.

vermiforme *adj.* vermiform.

vermífugo, -ga *adj.* vermifugal.

vermilionectomía *f.* vermilionectomy.

vermina *f.* vermin.

verminación *f.* vermination.

verminal *adj.* verminal.

verminosis *f.* verminosis.

verminoso, -sa *adj.* verminous.

verminótico, -ca *adj.* verminotic.

vermis vermis.

vermis cerebeloso, vermis del cerebelo vermis cerebelli.

vermis inferior vermis inferior.

vermis superior vermis superior.

vérmix *m.* vermix.

vermografía *f.* vermography.

vermoide vermiform.

vernier *m.* vernier.

vérnix vernix.

vérnix caseosa vernix caseosa.

verosimilitud biológica *f.* biological plausibility.

verruca *f.* wart, verruga, verruca.

verruciforme *adj.* verruciform.

verrucosis *f.* verrucosis.

verrucosis linfostática lymphostatic verrucosis.

verrucoso, -sa *adj.* verrucous, verrucose.

verruga *f.* wart, verruga, verruca.

verruga acuminada acuminate wart, verruca acuminata.

verruga de alquitrán pitch wart.

verruga de amianto asbestos wart.

verruga común common wart.

verruga del deshollinador soot wart.

verruga digitada digitate wart, verruca digitata.

verruga filiforme filiform wart, verruca filiformis.

verruga fugaz fugitive wart.

verruga genital genital wart.

verruga glabra verruca glabra.

verruga de Hassall-Henle Hassall-Henle wart.

verruga de Henle Henle's wart.

verruga en higo fig wart.

verruga del hollín soot wart.

verruga húmeda moist wart.

verruga infecciosa infectious wart.

verruga juvenil juvenile wart.

verruga madre mother wart.

verruga molusciforme verruca mollusciformis.

verruga en mosaico mosaic wart.

verruga mucocutánea mucocutaneous wart.

verruga periungueal periungual wart.

verruga peruana Peruvian wart, verruga peruana, verruca peruana, verruca peruviana.

verruga plana flat wart, plane wart, verruca plana.

verruga plana juvenil verruca plana juvenilis.

verruga plantar, verruca plantaris plantar wart, verruca plantaris.

verruga de prosector prosector wart.

verruga en punta pointed wart.

verruga de punto printed wart.

verruga seborreica seborrheic verruca, seborrheic wart, verruca seborrheica.

verruga de semilla seed wart.

verruga senil senile wart, verruca senilis.

verruga simple simple wart, verruca simplex.

verruga telangiectásica telangiectatic wart.

verruga tuberculosa tuberculous wart, verruca tuberculosa.

verruga venérea venereal wart.

verruga viral viral wart.

verruga vulgar verruca vulgaris.

verrugoso, -sa *adj.* verrucose, verrucous.

versicolor *adj.* versicolor.

versión *f.* version.

versión abdominal abdominal version.

versión bimanual bimanual version.

versión bipolar bipolar version.

versión de Braxton-Hicks Braxton-Hicks version.

versión cefálica cephalic version.

versión combinada combined version.

versión espontánea spontaneous version.

versión espontánea de Denman Denman's spontaneous version.

versión externa external version.

versión y extracción version and extraction.

versión de Hicks Hicks version.

versión interna internal version.

versión por maniobras externas external version.

versión por maniobras internas internal version.

versión mixta combined version.

versión pelviana pelvic version.

versión podálica podalic version.

versión podálica interna y extracción completa de nalgas internal podalic version and total breech extraction.

versión postural postural version.

versión de Potter Potter's version.

versión de Wright Wright's version.

vértebra *f.* vertebra.

vértebra plana vertebra plana.

vértebra en reloj de arena hourglass vertebra.

vertebrado, -da *adj.* vertebrated.

vertebral *adj.* vertebral.

vertebrarterial *adj.* vertebrarterial.

vertebrectomía *f.* vertebrectomy.

vertebroarterial *adj.* vertebroarterial.

vertebrocondral *adj.* vertebrochondral.

vertebrocostal *adj.* vertebrocostal.

vertebrodidimo, -ma *adj.* vertebrodidymus.

vertebrodimo *m.* vertebrodymus.

vertebroesternal *adj.* vertebrosternal.

vertebrofemoral *adj.* vertebrofemoral.

vertebrógeno, -na *adj.* vertebrogenic.

vertebroilíaco, -ca *adj.* vertebroiliac.

vertebromamario, -ria *adj.* vertebromammary.

vertebrosacro, -cra *adj.* vertebrosacral.

vertebrosternal *adj.* vertebrosternal.

vertedero *m.* spillway, landfill.

vertedero oclusivo *m.* occlusal spillway.

vertedero sanitario *m.* sanitary landfill.

vertex vertex.

vertical[1] *adj.* vertical.

vertical[2] *adj.* vertical, verticalis.

vértice *m.* vertex.

verticomentoniano, -na *adj.* verticomental.

vertiente *f.* slope.

vertiginoso, -sa *adj.* vertiginous.

vértigo *m.* vertigo.

vértigo alternobárico alternobaric vertigo.

vértigo de altura height vertigo.

vértigo angiopático angiopathic vertigo.

vértigo auditivo auditory vertigo.

vértigo aural, vértigo auricular aural vertigo.

vértigo cardíaco, vértigo cardiovascular cardiovascular vertigo.

vértigo central central vertigo.

vértigo cerebral cerebral vertigo.

vértigo de Charcot Charcot's vertigo.

vértigo endémico paralítico endemic paralytic vertigo.

vértigo epidémico epidemic vertigo.

vértigo epiléptico epileptic vertigo.

vértigo esencial essential vertigo.

vértigo estomacal gastric vertigo.

vértigo de falso movimiento, vértigo de movimiento giratorio sham-movement vertigo.

vértigo galvánico galvanic vertigo.

vértigo gástrico gastric vertigo.

vértigo histérico hysterical vertigo.

vértigo horizontal horizontal vertigo.

vértigo de los jinetes rider's vertigo.

vértigo laberíntico labyrinthine vertigo.

vértigo laberíntico paroxístico paroxysmal labyrinthine vertigo.

vértigo laríngeo laryngeal vertigo.

vértigo lateral lateral vertigo.

vértigo litémico lithemic vertigo.

vértigo mecánico mechanical vertigo.

vértigo nocturno nocturnal vertigo.

vértigo objetivo objective vertigo.

vértigo ocular ocular vertigo.

vértigo orgánico organic vertigo.

vértigo paralizante paralyzing vertigo.

vértigo paroxístico posicional benigno, vértigo paroxístico postural benigno benign paroxysmal positional vertigo, benign paroxysmal postural vertigo.

vértigo periférico peripheral vertigo.

vértigo de piloto aéreo pilot's vertigo.

vértigo posicional, vértigo de posición positional vertigo.

vértigo posicional incapacitante disabling positional vertigo.

vértigo postural postural vertigo.

vértigo rotatorio rotary vertigo, rotatory vertigo.

vértigo de los sentidos especiales special sense vertigo.

vértigo sistemático systematic vertigo.

vértigo subjetivo subjective vertigo.

vértigo toxémico, vértigo tóxico toxemic vertigo.

vértigo velloso villous vertigo.

vértigo vertical vertical vertigo.

vértigo voltaico galvanic vertigo.

verum montanum verumontanum.

verumontanum verumontanum.

verumontanitis *f.* verumontanitis.

vesaliano, -na *adj.* vesalian.

vesica *f.* vesica.

vesicación *f.* vesication.

vesical *adj.* vesical.

vesicante *adj.* vesicant.

vesicatorio, -ria *adj.* vesicatory.

vesicoabdominal *adj.* vesicoabdominal.

vesicoampollar *adj.* vesicobullous.

vesicocavernoso, -sa *adj.* vesicocavernous.

vesicocele *m.* vesicocele.

vesicocervical *adj.* vesicocervical.

vesicoclisis *f.* vesicoclysis.

vesicocólico, -ca *adj.* vesicocolic, vesicocolonic.

vesicoentérico, -ca *adj.* vesicoenteric.

vesicoespinal *adj.* vesicospinal.

vesicofijación *f.* vesicofixation.

vesicointestinal *adj.* vesicointestinal.

vesicoperineal *adj.* vesicoperineal.

vesicoprostático, -ca *adj.* vesicoprostatic.

vesicopubiano, -na *adj.* vesicopubic.

vesicopúbico, -ca *adj.* vesicopubic.

vesicopústula *f.* vesicopustule.

vesicorrectal *adj.* vesicorectal.

vesicorrenal *adj.* vesicorenal.

vesicosigmoideo, -a *adj.* vesicosigmoid.

vesicosigmoidostomía *f.* vesicosigmoidostomy.

vesicospinal *adj.* vesicospinal.

vesicostomía *f.* vesicostomy.

vesicotomía *f.* vesicotomy.

vesicoumbilical *adj.* vesicoumbilical.

vesicouracal *adj.* vesicourachal.

vesicoureteral *adj.* vesicoureteral, vesicoureteric.

vesicouretral *adj.* vesicourethral.

vesicouterino, -na *adj.* vesicouterine.

vesicouterovaginal *adj.* vesicouterovaginal.

vesicovaginal *adj.* vesicovaginal.

vesicovaginorrectal *adj.* vesicovaginorectal.

vesícula *f.* blister, vesicle, vesicula.

vesícula acuosa water blister.

vesícula acústica acoustic vesicle.

vesícula alantoica, vesícula alantoidea allantoic vesicle.

vesícula ambulante mobile gallbladder, floating gallbladder, wandering gallbladder.

vesícula amniocardíaca amniocardiac vesicle.

vesícula anterocerebral forebrain vesicle.

vesícula de Ascherson Ascherson's vesicle.

vesícula auditiva auditory vesicle.

vesícula biliar gallbladder, vesicula bilis, vesicula fellea.

vesícula biliar en frambuesa, vesícula biliar en fresa strawberry gallbladder.

vesícula biliar en papel de lija sandpaper gallbladder.

vesícula biliar en reloj de arena hourglass gallbladder.

vesícula blastodérmica blastodermic vesicle.

vesícula cefálica cephalic vesicle.

vesícula cerebral brain vesicle, cerebral vesicle.

vesícula cerebral primaria primary brain vesicle.

vesícula cerebral secundaria secondary brain vesicle.

vesícula compuesta compound vesicle.

vesícula coriónica chorionic vesicle.

vesícula del cristalino lens vesicle.

vesícula encefálica encephalic vesicle.

vesícula encefálica primaria primary brain vesicle.

vesícula espermática falsa false spermatic vesicle.

vesícula de excreción acuosa water expulsion vesicle.

vesícula fagocítica phagocytotic vesicle.

vesícula febril fever blister.

vesícula fellea, vesícula fellis vesicula fellea, vesicula fellis.

vesícula frambesiforme strawberry gallbladder.

vesícula germinal germinal vesicle, vesicula germinalis.

vesícula hemorrágica blood blister.

vesícula intraepidérmica intraepidermal vesicle.

vesícula lenticular lenticular vesicle.

vesícula de Malpighi Malpighian vesicle.

vesícula de la matriz matrix vesicle.

vesícula multilocular compound vesicle.

vesícula ocular ocular vesicle.

vesícula oftálmica ophthalmic vesicle, vesicula ophthalmica.

vesícula óptica optic vesicle.

vesícula olfatoria olfactory vesicle.

vesícula ótica otic vesicle.

vesícula pinocítica pinocytotic vesicle.

vesícula pituitaria pituitary vesicle.

vesícula plasmalémica plasmalemma vesicle.

vesícula prostática prostatic vesicle, vesicula prostatica.

vesícula queriónica kerionic vesicle.

vesícula recubiertas coated vesicle.

vesícula de secreción secretory vesicle.

vesícula seminal seminal vesicle, vesicula seminalis.

vesícula de los sentidos sense vesicle.

vesícula sináptica synaptic vesicle.

vesícula de transferencia transfer vesicle.

vesícula transicional transitional vesicle.

vesícula de transporte transport vesicle.

vesícula umbilical umbilical vesicle, vesicula umbilicalis.

vesiculación *f.* vesiculation.

vesiculado, -da *adj.* vesiculated.

vesicular *adj.* vesicular.

vesiculasa *f.* vesiculase.

vesiculectomía *f.* vesiculectomy.

vesiculiforme *f.* vesiculiform.

vesiculitis *f.* vesiculitis.

vesiculitis seminal seminal vesiculitis.
vesiculobronquial *adj.* vesiculobronchial.
vesiculocavernoso, -sa *adj.* vesiculocavernous.
vesiculografía *f.* vesiculography.
vesiculograma *m.* vesiculogram.
vesiculopapuloso, -sa *adj.* vesiculopapular.
vesiculoprostatitis *f.* vesiculoprostatitis.
vesiculopostular *adj.* vesiculopostular.
vesiculopustuloso, -sa *adj.* vesiculopustular.
vesiculoso, -sa *adj.* vesiculose, vesiculous.
vesiculotimpánico, -ca *adj.* vesiculotympanic.
vesiculotomía *f.* vesiculotomy.
vesiculotubular *adj.* vesiculotubular.
Vesiculovirus Vesiculovirus.
vestibulado, -da *adj.* vestibulate.
vestibular *adj.* vestibular.
vestibuliferia vestibuliferia.
vestíbulo *m.* vestibule, vestibulum.
vestibulocerebelo *m.* vestibulocerebellum.
vestibulococlear *adj.* vestibulochoclear.
vestibuloespinal *adj.* vestibulospinal.
vestibulógeno, -na *adj.* vestibulogenic.
vestibuloocular *adj.* vestibulo-ocular.
vestibuloplastia *f.* vestibuloplasty.
vestibulotomía *f.* vestibulotomy.
vestibulouretral *adj.* vestibulourethral.
vestigial *adj.* vestigial.
vestigio *m.* vestige, vestigium.
  vestigio del proceso vaginal vestige of vaginal process, vestigium processus vaginalis.
veta *f.* veta.
veterinario, -ria[1] *adj.* veterinary.
veterinario, -ria[2] *m., f.* veterinarian.
vía *f.* path, pathway, route, way, via.
  vía accesoria accessory pathway.
  vía de administración route of administration.
  vía aérea artificial artificial airway.
  vía aérea de conducción conducting airway.
  vía aérea inferior lower airway.
  vía aérea oral oral airway.
  vía aérea respiratoria respiratory airway.
  vía aérea superior upper airway.
  vía aferente afferent pathway.
  vía alternativa alternative pathway.
  vía alternativa del complemento alternative complement pathway.
  vía alternativa de la activación del complemento alternative pathway of complement activation.
  vía arterial arterial line.
  vía auditiva auditory pathway.
  vía biliar bile duct, biliary tract.
  vía biosintética biosynthetic pathway.
  vía central central line.
  vía de clivaje axial axial spillway.
  vía de colocación placement path.
  vía condílea condyle path.
  vía de copulación copulation path.
  vía eferente efferent pathway.
  vía de Embden-Meyerhof Embden-Meyerhof pathway.
  vía de Embden-Meyerhof-Parnas Embden-Meyerhof-Parnas pathway.
  vía extrapiramidal extrapyramidal tract.
  vía final común final common pathway.
  vía del fosfato de pentosa, vía del fosfogluconato pentose phosphate pathway.
  vía de fuga spillway.
  vía incisiva incisor path.
  vía internuncial internuncial pathway.
  vía metabólica metabolic pathway.
  vía motora motor pathway.

  vía nasal nasal airway.
  vía natural via naturale.
  vía piramidal pyramidal tract.
  vía de reentrada reentrant pathway.
  vías respiratorias respiratory tract.
  vía respiratoria con obturador esofágico esophageal obturator airway.
  vía sensitiva sensory pathway.
  vías urinarias urinary tract.
  vía visual visual pathway.
viabilidad *f.* viability.
viable *adj.* viable.
vial *m.* vial.
vibesato *m.* vibesate.
víbice *f.* vibex.
vibración *f.* vibration.
  vibración fotoeléctrica photoelectric vibration.
vibrador *m.* vibrator.
vibrante *adj.* vibrative.
vibrátil *adj.* vibratile.
vibrativo, -va *adj.* vibrative.
vibrátodo *m.* vibratode.
vibratorio, -ria *adj.* vibratory.
Vibrio Vibrio.
  vibrio alginolyticus vibrio alginolyticus.
  vibrio cholerae vibrio cholerae.
  Vibrio comma Vibrio comma.
  Vibrio fluvialis Vibrio fluvialis.
  Vibrio furnissii Vibrio furnissii.
  Vibrio mimicus Vibrio mimicus.
  Vibrio parahaemolyticus Vibrio parahaemolyticus.
  Vibrio sputorum Vibrio sputorum.
  Vibrio vulnificus Vibrio vulnificus.
vibrión *m.* vibrio.
vibriosis *f.* vibriosis.
vibrisa *f.* vibrissa.
vibrisal *adj.* vibrisal.
vibriza *f.* vibrissa.
vibrocardiograma *m.* vibrocardiogram.
vibromasajeador *m.* vibromasseur.
vibrómetro *m.* vibrometer.
vibrosensibilidad *f.* pallesthesia.
vibroterapéutica *f.* vibrotherapeutics, vibratory massage.
vibroterapia *f.* vibrotherapeutics.
vicariante *adj.* vicarious.
vicario, -ria *adj.* vicarious.
viciación *f.* vitiation.
viciado, -da *adj.* deformed, distorted.
viciación *f.* vitiation.
viciamiento *f.* vitiation.
vicio *m.* vice, vitium.
  vicio cardíaco vitium cordis.
  vicio de conformación vitium conformationis.
  vicio de primera formación vitium primae formationis.
vicioso, -sa *adj.* vicious.
vida *f.* life.
  vida antenatal prenatal life.
  vida artificial artificial life.
  vida intrauterina prenatal life.
  vida latente latent life.
  vida media average life, mean lifetime.
  vida media biológica biological half life.
  vida media efectiva, vida media eficaz (VME) effective half life (EHL).
  vida media física physical half life.
  vida media plasmática plasma half life.
  vida media de un radionúclido radionuclide half life.
  vida posnatal postnatal life.
  vida potencial potential life.

  vida prenatal prenatal life.
  vida promedio mean lifetime.
  vida sedentaria sedentary living.
  vida sexual sexual life.
  vida uterina prenatal life.
  vida vegetativa vegetative life.
videofluoroscopia *f.* videofluoroscopy.
videognosia *f.* videognosis.
videomicroscopía *f.* videomicroscopy.
videonistagmografía *f.* videonystagmography.
vidriado *m.* glaze.
vidrio *m.* glass.
vientre *m.* belly, venter.
  vientre en alforja venter propendens.
  vientre colgante venter propendens.
  vientre escafoideo scaphoid abdomen.
  vientre de madera wooden belly.
  vientre navicular navicular abdomen.
  vientre propendens venter propendens.
  vientre en tabla wooden belly.
  vientre de tambor drum belly.
vigencia concurrente *f.* concurrent validity.
vigesimonormal *adj.* vigintinormal.
vigilambulismo *m.* vigilambulism.
vigilancia[1] *f.* surveillance, survey.
  vigilancia inmune, vigilancia inmunológica immune surveillance, inmunological surveillance.
  vigilancia metastática metastatic survey.
vigilia *f.* vigilance, wakefulness.
  vigilia de coma coma vigilance.
vigor *m.* vigor.
  vigor híbrido hybrid vigor.
villicinina *f.* villikinin.
villífero, -ra *adj.* villiferous.
villioma *m.* villioma.
villoma *m.* villoma.
villonodular *adj.* villonodular.
villosectomía *f.* villusectomy.
villositis *f.* villositis.
villus villus.
villusectomía *f.* villusectomy.
vinculación *f.* bonding.
  vinculación afectiva *f.* bonding.
  vinculación maternoinfantil *f.* maternal-infant bonding.
vínculo *m.* vinculum.
vinculum vinculum.
violáceo, -a *adj.* violaceous.
violación *f.* rape, violation.
  violación marital marital rape.
  violación de menores statutory rape.
  violación por conocido date rape, acquaintance rape.
violar *v.* rape.
violescente *adj.* violescent.
violeta *adj.* violet.
  violeta de genciana gentian violet.
  violeta de metilo methyl violet.
  violeta de París Paris violet, pentamethyl violet.
vipoma *m.* vipoma.
vipérido, -da *adj.* viperid.
viperino, -na *adj.* viperid.
viraginidad *f.* viraginity.
viral *adj.* viral.
viremia *f.* viremia.
virgen *adj.* virgin.
virginal *adj.* virginal.
virginidad *f.* virginity.
virgofrenia *f.* virgophrenia.
viriasis *f.* viral infection.
viricida *adj.* viricidal.
vírico, -ca *adj.* viral.

viril *adj.* virile.
virilescencia *f.* virilescence.
virilia virilia.
virilidad *f.* virility.
virilígeno, -na *adj.* viriligenic.
viriliscencia *f.* virilescence.
virilismo *m.* virilism.
　virilismo adrenal, virilismo suprarrenal adrenal virilism.
　virilismo prosopopiloso prosopopilary virilism.
virilización *f.* virilization.
virilizador, -ra *adj.* virilizing.
virilizante *adj.* virilizing.
virión *m.* virion.
viripotente *adj.* viripotent.
virocida *m.* virucidal.
virocito *m.* virocyte.
viroide *m.* viroid.
virología *f.* virology.
virólogo, -ga *m., f.* virologist.
viropexis *f.* viropexis.
virósico, -ca *adj.* viral.
virosis *f.* virosis.
　virosis hemorrágica del noroeste bonaerense Argentine hemorrhagic fever.
viroso, -sa *adj.* viral.
virtual *adj.* virtual.
virucida *adj.* viricidal.
viruela *f.* smallpox, variola.
　viruela antillana West Indian smallpox.
　viruela blanca whitepox.
　viruela del camello camelpox.
　viruela coherente coherent smallpox.
　viruela confluente, viruela confluyente confluent smallpox.
　viruela discreta discrete smallpox.
　viruela equina horsepox.
　viruela fulminante fulminating smallpox.
　viruela hemorrágica hemorrhagic smallpox, variola hemorrhagica.
　viruela kaffir kaffir pox.
　viruela maligna malignant smallpox, variola maligna.
　viruela miliar variola miliaris.
　viruela modificada modified smallpox.
　viruela de los monos monkeypox.
　viruela negra black smallpox.
　viruela penfigosa variola pemphigosa.
　viruela rickettsiana rickettsial pox.
　viruela silicuosa variola siliquosa.
　viruela variceloide modified smallpox.
　viruela verrugosa wartpox.
virulencia *f.* virulence.
virulento, -ta *adj.* virulent.
virulicida *adj.* viricidal.
virulífero, -ra *adj.* viruliferous.
viruria *f.* viruria.
virus *m.* virus.
virusemia *f.* virusemia.
virustático, -ca *adj.* virustatic.
vis vis.
viscancia *f.* viscance.
víscera *f.* viscera, viscus.
viscerad viscerad.
visceral *adj.* visceral.
visceralgia *f.* visceralgia.
visceralismo *m.* visceralism.
viscerimotor, -ra *adj.* viscerimotor.
viscerocráneo *m.* viscerocranium.
visceroesquelético, -ca *adj.* visceroskeletal.
visceroesqueleto *m.* visceroskeleton.
viscerogénico, -ca *adj.* viscerogenic.
viscerógrafo *m.* viscerograph.
visceroinhibidor, -ra *adj.* visceroinhibitory.

visceroinhibitorio, -ria *adj.* visceroinhibitory.
visceromegalia *f.* visceromegaly.
visceromotor, -ra *adj.* visceromotor.
visceroparietal *adj.* visceroparietal.
visceroperitoneal *adj.* visceroperitoneal.
visceropleural *adj.* visceropleural.
visceroptosia *f.* visceroptosia, visceroptosis.
visceroptosis *f.* visceroptosis.
viscerosensitivo, -va *adj.* viscerosensory.
viscerosensorial *adj.* viscerosensory.
viscerosomático, -ca *adj.* viscerosomatic.
viscerosquelético, -ca *adj.* visceroskeletal.
viscerotomía *f.* viscerotomy.
viscerótomo *m.* viscerotome.
viscerotonía *f.* viscerotonia.
viscerotrófico, -ca *adj.* viscerotrophic.
viscerotrópico, -ca *adj.* viscerotropic.
viscidez *f.* viscidity.
víscido, -da *adj.* viscid.
viscidosis *f.* viscidosis.
viscoelasticidad *f.* viscoelasticity.
viscogel *m.* viscogel.
viscómetro *m.* viscometer.
viscosa *f.* viscose.
viscosacarosa *f.* viscosaccharose.
viscosidad *f.* viscosity.
　viscosidad absoluta absolute viscosity.
　viscosidad anómala anomalous viscosity.
　viscosidad aparente apparent viscosity.
　viscosidad cinemática kinematic viscosity.
　viscosidad dinámica dynamic viscosity.
　viscosidad de dilatación bulk viscosity.
　viscosidad newtoniana Newtonian viscosity.
　viscosidad relativa relative viscosity.
　viscosidad volumétrica bulk viscosity.
viscosimetría *f.* viscosimetry.
viscosímetro *m.* viscosimeter.
viscoso, -sa *adj.* viscous.
viscus viscus.
visibilidad *f.* visibility.
visible *adj.* visible.
visión *f.* sight, vision.
　visión acromática achromatic vision.
　visión amarilla, visión amarillenta yellow vision.
　visión azul blue vision.
　visión en arco iris rainbow vision.
　visión en aureola halo vision.
　visión baja low vision.
　visión de bastones rod vision.
　visión binocular binocular vision.
　visión central central vision.
　visión de cerca near sight.
　visión de color color vision.
　visión cónica cone vision.
　visión corta short sight.
　visión crepuscular twilight vision.
　visión cromática chromatic vision.
　visión dicromática dichromatic vision.
　visión digital finger vision.
　visión directa direct vision.
　visión diurna day sight.
　visión doble double vision.
　visión escoteritrosa scoterythrous vision.
　visión escotópica scotopic vision.
　visión estereoscópica stereoscopic vision.
　visión facial facial vision.
　visión fotópica photopic vision.
　visión foveal foveal vision.
　visión en halo halo vision.
　visión haploscópica haploscopic vision.
　visión indirecta indirect vision.
　visión iridiscente halo vision.
　visión de lejos long sight, far sight.

　visión monocular monocular vision.
　visión múltiple multiple vision.
　visión nocturna night vision.
　visión oscilante oscillating vision.
　visión de las palabras word vision.
　visión periférica peripheral vision.
　visión de Pick Pick's vision.
　visión pseudoscópica pseudoscopic vision.
　visión roja red vision.
　visión subjetiva subjective vision.
　visión triple triple vision.
　visión tubular tubular vision.
　visión en túnel tunnel vision.
　visión de la vejez old vision.
　visión verde green vision.
visita *f.* visit.
visoauditivo, -va *adj.* visoauditory.
vista *f.* sight, view.
　vista cansada presbyopia.
　vista cercana short sight.
　vista corta short sight.
　vista diurna day sight.
　vista doble double vision.
　vista larga, vista lejana long sight.
　vista nocturna night sight.
　vista oblicua strabismus.
visual *adj.* visual.
visualización *f.* visualization.
　visualización de doble contraste double contrast visualization.
visualizar *v.* visualize.
visuauditivo, -va *adj.* visoauditory.
visuespacial *adj.* visuospatial.
visuoespacial *adj.* visuospatial.
visuognosis *f.* visuognosis.
visuoléxico, -ca *adj.* visuolexic.
visuómetro *m.* visuometer.
visuomoto, -ra *adj.* visuomotor.
visuopsíquico, -ca *adj.* visuopsychic.
visuoscopio *m.* visuoscope.
visuosensitivo, -va *adj.* visuosensory.
visuosensorial *adj.* visuosensory.
vitagonista *adj.* vitagonist.
vital *adj.* vital.
vitalidad *f.* vitality.
vitalismo *m.* vitalism.
vitalístico, -ca *adj.* vitalistic.
vitalizar *v.* vitalize.
vitalómetro *m.* vitalometer.
vitámero *m.* vitamer.
vitámetro *m.* vitameter.
vitamina *f.* vitamin.
vitaminógeno, -na *adj.* vitaminogenic.
vitaminoide *adj.* vitaminoid.
vitaminología *f.* vitaminology.
vitaminoscopio *m.* vitaminoscope.
vitaminoterapia *f.* vitamin therapy.
vitanición *f.* vitanition.
vitazima *f.* vitamin.
vitelar *adj.* vitellary.
viteliforme *adj.* vitelliform.
vitelina *f.* vitelline.
vitelino, -na *adj.* vitelline.
vitellus vitellus.
vitelo *m.* yolk, vitellus.
　vitelo del huevo ovi vitellus.
vitelogénesis *f.* vitellogenesis.
viteloluteína *f.* vitellolutein.
vitelorrubina *f.* vitellorubin.
vitelosa *f.* vitellose.
vitiatina *f.* vitiatin.
vitilígines *f.* vitiligines.
vitiliginoso, -sa *adj.* vitiliginous.
vitíligo *m.* vitiligo.
　vitíligo de la cabeza vitiligo capitis.

vitíligo de **Cazenave** Cazenave's vitiligo.
vitíligo de **Celsus** Celsus' vitiligo.
vitíligo circumnévico circumnevic vitiligo.
vitíligo del iris, vitíligo iridis vitiligo iridis.
vitíligo perinévico, vitíligo perinevoide circumnevic vitiligo.
vitiligoide *adj.* vitiligoidea.
vitium vitium.
vitoquímico, -ca *adj.* vitochemical.
vitrectomía *f.* vitrectomy.
vitrectomía anterior anterior vitrectomy.
vitrectomía posterior posterior vitrectomy.
vitreína *f.* vitrein.
vitreítis *f.* vitreitis.
vítreo *m.* vitreous body, corpus vitreum.
vítreo desprendido detached vitreous body.
vítreo primario primary vitreous body.
vítreo primario hiperplástico persistente primary persistent hyperplastic vitreous body.
vítreo secundario secondary vitreous body.
vítreo terciario tertiary vitreous body.
vítreo, -a *adj.* vitreous.
vitreocapsulitis *f.* vitreocapsulitis.
vitreodentina *f.* vitreodentin.
vitreorragia *f.* vitreous loss.
vitreorretiniano, -na *adj.* vitreoretinal.
vitreorretinopatía *f.* vitreoretinopathy.
vitreorretinopatía familiar exudativa familial exudative vitreoretinopathy.
vitreum vitreum.
vitrificación *f.* vitrification.
vitrina *f.* vitrina.
vitrina ocular vitrina oculi.
vitriolado, -da *adj.* vitriolated.
vitriolaje *m.* vitriolation.
vitriolo *m.* vitriol.
vitriolo azul blue vitriol.
vitriolo blanco white vitriol.
vitriolo cíncico zinc vitriol.
vitriolo verde green vitriol.
vitritis *f.* vitritis.
vitropresión *f.* vitropression.
vitrosina *f.* vitrosin.
vivario *m.* vivarium.
vivencia *f.* internal experience.
vividiálisis *f.* vividialysis.
vividifusión *f.* vividiffusion.
vivificación¹ *f.* quickening.
vivificación² *f.* vivification, vivificatio.
viviparición *f.* viviparition.
viviparidad *f.* viviparity.
vivíparo, -ra *adj.* viviparous.
vivipercepción *f.* viviperception.
vivisección *f.* vivisection.
viviseccionista *m., f.* vivisectionist.
vivisector, -ra *m., f.* vivisector.
vivo, -va *adj.* alive.
vocal *adj.* vocal.
volar *adj.* volar.
volardorsal *adj.* volardorsal.
volátil *adj.* volatile.
volatilización *f.* volatilization.
volatilizador *m.* volatilizer.
volatilizar *v.* volatilize.
volemia *f.* blood volume.
volición *f.* volition.
volitivo, -va *adj.* volitional.
volsella volsella.
voltaico, -ca *adj.* voltaic.
voltaísmo *m.* voltaism.
voltaje *m.* voltage.
voltámetro *m.* voltameter.
voltamperio *m.* voltampere.
voltímetro *m.* voltmeter.
volumen *m.* volume .

volumen atómico atomic volume .
volumen blanco target volume .
volumen celular medio (VCM) mean cell volume (MCV).
volumen de células aglomeradas packed-cell volume (PCV), volume of packed red cells (VPRC).
volumen de cierre closing volume (CV).
volumen de circulación, volumen circulatorio circulation volume , volume of circulation.
volumen por contracción stroke volume .
volumen corpuscular medio (VCM) mean corpuscular volume (MCV).
volumen corriente tidal volume (Vt).
volumen corriente en reposo resting tidal volume .
volumen corriente pulmonar tidal volume (Vt).
volumen crítico critical volume .
volumen diana target volume .
volumen diastólico final end-diastolic volume .
volumen de distribución distribution volume .
volumen eritrocítico red cell volume .
volumen eritrocítico concentrado packed-cell volume (PCV), volume of packed red cells (VPRC).
volumen específico specific volume .
volumen espiratorio forzado (VEF) forced expiratory volume (FEV).
volumen espiratorio de reserva (VER) expiratory reserve volume (ERV).
volumen estándar standard volume .
volumen de fin de diástole end-diastolic volume .
volumen de fin de sístole end-systolic volume.
volumen funcional pulmonar functional residual volume .
volumen inspiratorio de reserva (VIR) inspiratory reserve volume (IRV).
volumen minuto (VM), volumen por minuto (VM) minute volume (MV).
volumen minuto cardíaco minute output volume.
volumen minuto respiratorio respiratory minute volume .
volumen parcial partial volume .
volumen plasmático plasma volume .
volumen de reserva aspiratoria (VRA) inspiratory reserve volume (IRV).
volumen de reserva espiratoria (VRE) expiratory reserve volume (ERV).
volumen de reserva inspiratoria inspiratory reserve volume (IRV).
volumen residual (VR) residual volume (RV).
volumen sanguíneo blood volume .
volumen sistólico systolic volume .
volumen sistólico final end-systolic volume .
volumen telediastólico end-diastolic volume .
volumen tidal (Vt) tidal volume (Vt).
volumen de ventilación pulmonar en reposo resting tidal volume .
volumen de ventilación pulmonar tidal volume (Vt).
volumenómetro *m.* volumenometer.
volumette volumette.
volumetría *f.* volumetry.
volumétrico, -ca *adj.* volumetric.
voluminación *f.* volumination.
volumómetro *m.* volumometer.
voluntad *f.* will.

voluntario, -ria *adj.* voluntary.
voluntomotor, -ra *adj.* voluntomotory.
voluptuosidad *f.* voluptuousness.
voluptuoso, -sa *adj.* voluptuous.
voluta *f.* volute.
volutina *f.* volutin.
volvular *v.* volvulate.
vólvulo *m.* volvulus.
vólvulo gástrico gastric volvulus.
vólvulo neonatal volvulus neonatorum.
volvulosis *f.* volvulosis.
vómer *m.* vomer.
vomeriano, -na *adj.* vomerine.
vomerino, -na *adj.* vomerine.
vomerobasilar *adj.* vomerobasilar.
vomeronasal *adj.* vomeronasal.
vómica *f.* vomica, vomicus.
vomición *f.* vomition, vomiting.
vomicoso, -sa *adj.* vomicose.
vomitar *v.* vomit.
vomitivo *m.* vomitory.
vomitivo, -va *adj.* vomitive.
vómito¹ *m.* vomit.
vómito acetonémico acetonemic vomit.
vómito de Barcoo Barcoo vomit.
vómito bilioso bilious vomit.
vómito de borra de café coffee-ground vomit.
vómito hiperácido gastroxynsis.
vómito negro black vomit, vomitus niger.
vómito en posos de café coffee-ground vomit.
vómito de sangre hematemesis.
vómito² *m.* vomiting.
vómito cerebral cerebral vomiting.
vómito cíclico cyclic vomiting.
vómito electivo hysterical vomiting.
vómito del embarazo vomiting of pregnancy.
vómito epidémico epidemic vomiting.
vómito estercoráceo stercoraceous vomiting.
vómito fecal fecal vomiting.
vómito fecaloideo fecal vomiting.
vómito histérico hysterical vomiting.
vómito incoercible incoercible vomiting.
vómito matinal morning vomiting.
vómito nervioso nervous vomiting.
vómito periódico periodic vomiting.
vómito pernicioso pernicious vomiting.
vómito en escopetazo projectile vomiting.
vómito psicógeno psychogenic vomiting.
vómito recurrente recurrent vomiting.
vómito por retención retention vomiting.
vómito seco dry vomiting.
vómito³ *m.* vomitus.
vómito cruento vomitus cruentus.
vómito marino vomitus marinus.
vómito negro vomitus niger.
vomitorio *m.* vomitory.
vomiturición *f.* vomiturition.
vomitus vomitus.
vomitus cruentus vomitus cruentus.
vomitus gravidarum vomitus gravidarum.
vomitus matutinus potatorum vomitus matutinus potatorum.
vortex vortex.
vórtice *m.* whorl, vortex.
vorticoso, -sa *adj.* vorticose.
voussure *f.* voussure.
vox vox.
voxel *m.* voxel.
voyeur *m.* voyeur.
voyeurismo *m.* voyeurism, scopophilia.
voz *f.* voice, voix, vox.
voz anfórica amphoric voice.
voz bronquial bronchial voice.

voz cavernosa cavernous voice.
voz colérica vox choleraica, vox cholerica.
voz doble double voice.
voz epigástrica epigastric voice.
voz eunucoide eunuchoid voice.
voz de falsete eunuchoid voice.
voz mixedematosa myxedema voice.
voz susurrada whispered voice.
vuelta *f.* tour.
  vuelta de maestro tour de maitre.
vuerómetro *m.* vuerometer.
vulcanizar *v.* vulcanize.
vulgar *adj.* vulgaris.
vulnerabilidad *f.* vulnerability.
vulnerable *adj.* vulnerable.
vulnerante *adj.* vulnerant.
vulnerar *v.* vulnerate.

vulnerario, -ria *m. y adj.* vulnerary.
vulsela *f.* vulsella, vulsellum.
vulsella vulsella.
vulsellum vulsella.
vulva *f.* vulva.
vulvar *adj.* vulval, vulvar.
vulvectomía *f.* vulvectomy.
vulvismo *m.* vulvismus.
vulvitis *f.* vulvitis.
  vulvitis atrófica crónica chronic atrophic vulvitis.
  vulvitis blenorrágica gonorrheal vulvitis.
  vulvitis de células plasmáticas plasma cell vulvitis.
  vulvitis diabética diabetic vulvitis.
  vulvitis diftérica diphtheritic vulvitis.
  vulvitis eccematiforme eczematiform vulvitis.

vulvitis erosiva erosive vulvitis.
vulvitis eccematosa eczematiform vulvitis.
vulvitis flemonosa phlegmonous vulvitis.
vulvitis folicular follicular vulvitis.
vulvitis hipertrófica crónica chronic hypertrophic vulvitis.
vulvitis leucoplásica leukoplakic vulvitis.
vulvitis plasmocelular vulvitis plasmocellularis.
vulvitis pseudoleucoplásica pseudoleukoplakic vulvitis.
vulvocrural *adj.* vulvocrural.
vulvorrectal *adj.* vulvorectal.
vulvouterino, -na *adj.* vulvouterine.
vulvovaginal *adj.* vulvovaginal.
vulvovaginitis *f.* vulvovaginitis.
  vulvovaginitis senil senile vulvovaginitis.

W w

wagaga *f.* wagaga.
wakamba *m.* wakamba.
walleye *m.* wall-eye.
wanganga *f.* wanganga.
wartpox *m.* wartpox.
waterpox *m.* waterpox.
wattage *m.* wattage.
weber *m.* weber.
weismanismo *m.* weismannism.

whartonitis *f.* whartonitis.
wihtigo, windigo, witigo *m.* windigo.
windage *m.* windage.
witzelsucht *m.* witzelsucht.
Wohlfahrtia Wohlfahrtia.
  Wohlfahrtia magnifica Wohlfahrtia magnifica.
  Wohlfahrtia opaca Wohlfahrtia opaca.
  Wohlfahrtia vigil Wohlfahrtia vigil.

wohlfahrtiosis *f.* wohlfahrtiosis.
wolffiano, -na *adj.* Wolffian.
Wolinella Wolinella.
  Wolinella recta Wolinella recta.
W-plastia *f.* W-plasty.
Wuchereria Wuchereria.
  Wuchereria bancrofti Wuchereria bancrofti.
  Wuchereria malayi Wuchereria malayi.
wuchereriasis *f.* wuchereriasis.

xancromático, -ca *adj.* xanchromatic.
xantelasma *m.* xanthelasma.
  xantelasma generalizado generalized xanthelasma.
  xantelasma palpebral, xantelasma palpebrarum xanthelasma palpebrarum.
xantelasmatosis *f.* xanthelasmatosis.
xanthematina *f.* xanthematin.
xantematina *f.* xanthematin.
xantemia *f.* xanthemia.
xanthematina *f.* xanthematin.
xántico, -ca *adj.* xanthic.
xantílico, ca *adj.* xanthylic.
xantina *f.* xanthin, xanthine.
xantinoxidasa *f.* xanthine oxidase.
xantinuria *f.* xanthinuria.
xantinúrico, -ca *adj.* xanthinuric.
xantismo *m.* xanthism.
xantiuria *f.* xanthiuria.
xántixo, -xa *adj.* xanthic.
xantoastrocitoma pleomórfico *m.* pleomorphic xanthoastrocytoma.
xantocianopía *f.* xanthokyanopy.
xantocianopsia *f.* xanthocyanopsia.
xantocistina *f.* xanthocystine.
xantocito *m.* xanthocyte.
xantocroia *f.* xanthochroia.
xancrómico, -ca *adj.* xanthochromatic.
xantocromía *f.* xanthochromia.
  xantocromía estriada palmar xanthochromia striata palmaris.
xantocrómico, -ca *adj.* xanthochromic.
xantocroo, -a *adj.* xanthochroous.
xantoderma *m.* xanthoderma.
xantodermia *f.* xanthodermia.
xantodermo, -ma *adj.* xanthochroous.
xantodonte *adj.* xanthodont.
xantoeritrodermia *f.* xanthoerythrodermia.
xantófano *m.* xanthophane.
xantofibroma tecocelular *m.* xanthofibroma thecocellulare.
xantofosia *f.* xanthophose.
xantofosis *f.* xanthophose.
xantogranuloma *m.* xanthogranuloma.
  xantogranuloma juvenil juvenile xanthogranuloma.
  xantogranuloma necrobiótico necrobiotic xanthogranuloma.
  xantogranuloma de plexos coroideos choroidal plexus xanthogranuloma.
xantogranulomatosis *f.* xanthogranulomatosis.
xantogranulomatoso, -sa *adj.* xanthogranulomatous.
xantoma *m.* xanthoma.
  xantoma craneohipofisario craniohypophyseal xanthoma.
  xantoma diabético, xantoma de los diabéticos diabetic xanthoma, xanthoma diabeticorum.

  xantoma diseminado disseminated xanthoma, xanthoma disseminatum.
  xantoma eruptivo eruptive xanthoma, xanthoma eruptivum.
  xantoma estriado palmar xanthoma striatum palmare.
  xantoma múltiple multiple xanthoma, xanthoma multiplex.
  xantoma de los párpados, xantoma palpebral xanthoma palpebrarum.
  xantoma planar, xantoma plano planar xanthoma, plane xanthoma, xanthoma planum.
  xantoma plano normolipémico normolipemic xanthoma planum.
  xantoma tendinoso tendinous xanthoma, xanthoma tendinosum.
  xantoma tuberoeruptivo tuberoeruptive xanthoma.
  xantoma tuberoso, xantoma tuberoso múltiple tuberous xanthoma, xanthoma tuberosum, xanthoma tuberosum multiplex.
xantomasarcoma *m.* xanthomasarcoma.
xantomatosis *f.* xanthomatosis.
  xantomatosis biliar hipercolesterolémica biliary hypercholesterolemic xanthomatosis.
  xantomatosis bulbar xanthomatosis bulbi.
  xantomatosis cerebrotendinosa cerebrotendinous xanthomatosis.
  xantomatosis colesterémica normal normal cholesteremic xanthomatosis.
  xantomatosis corneal xanthomatosis corneae.
  xantomatosis familiar primaria primary familial xanthomatosis.
  xantomatosis hipercolesterémica familiar familial hypercholesterolemic xanthomatosis.
  xantomatosis idiopática crónica chronic idiopathic xanthomatosis.
  xantomatosis del iris xanthomatosis iridis.
  xantomatosis ósea generalizada xanthomatosis generalisata ossium.
  xantomatosis de Wolman Wolman xanthomatosis.
xantomatoso, -sa *adj.* xanthomatous.
xantopatía *f.* xanthopathy.
xantopía *f.* xanthopia.
xantoproteico, -ca *adj.* xanthoproteic.
xantoproteína *f.* xanthoprotein.
xantopsia *f.* xanthopsia.
xantopsidracia *f.* xanthopsydracia.
xantopsis *f.* xanthopsis.
xantorrubina *f.* xanthorubin.
xantosarcoma *m.* xanthosarcoma.
xantosis *f.* xanthosis.
  xantosis del tabique nasal xanthosis of the septum nasi.
xantoso, -sa *adj.* xanthous.
xantoxito *m.* xanthocyte.
xanturia *f.* xanthuria.
xenembolia *f.* xenembole.

xenentesis *f.* xenenthesis.
xenoantígeno *m.* xenoantigen.
xenobiótico, -ca *adj.* xenobiotic.
xenocitófilo, -la *adj.* xenocythophilic.
xenodiagnosis *f.* xenodiagnosis.
xenodiagnóstico *m.* xenodiagnosis.
xenodiagnóstico, -ca *adj.* xenodiagnostic.
xenofobia *f.* xenophobia.
xenofonía *f.* xenophonia.
xenoftalmía *f.* xenophthalmia.
xenogeneico, -ca *adj.* xenogeneic.
xenogénesis *f.* xenogenesis.
xenogenia *f.* xenogenesis.
xenogénico, -ca[1] *adj.* xenogenic.
xenogénico, -ca[2] *adj.* xenogenous.
xenógeno, -na *adj.* xenogenous.
xenograft *m.* xenograft.
xenoinjerto *m.* xenograft.
xenología *f.* xenology.
xenomenia *f.* xenomenia.
xenoparasitismo *m.* xenoparasitism.
xenoparásito *m.* xenoparasite.
Xenopsylla Xenopsylla.
  Xenopsylla astia Xenopsylla astia.
  Xenopsylla brasiliensis Xenopsylla brasiliensis.
  Xenopsylla cheopis Xenopsylla cheopis.
xenorexia *f.* xenorexia.
xeransia *f.* xeransia, xeransis.
xeransis *f.* xeransis.
xerántico, -ca *adj.* xerantic.
xerasia *f.* xerasia.
xerasial *adj.* xerasial.
xerocolirio *m.* xerocollyrium.
xeroderma *m.* xeroderma.
xerodermia *f.* xeroderma.
  xerodermia pigmentosa xeroderma pigmentosum.
xerodérmico, -ca *adj.* xerodermatic.
xerodermoide *m.* xerodermoid.
  xerodermoide pigmentado pigmented xerodermoid.
xerofagia *f.* xerophagia, xerophagy.
xerofobia *f.* xerophobia.
xeroftalmía *f.* xerophthalmia.
xeroftalmo *m.* xerophthalmus.
xerogel *m.* xerogel.
xerografía *f.* xerography.
xerograma *m.* xerogram.
xeroma *m.* xeroma.
xeromamografía *f.* xeromammography.
xeromenia *f.* xeromenia.
xeromicteria *f.* xeromycteria.
xeroqueilia *f.* xerocheilia, xerochilia.
xeroquilia *f.* xerochilia.
xerorradiografía *f.* xeroradiography.
xerosialografía *f.* xeroxialography.
xerosis *f.* xerosis.
  xerosis conjuntival conjunctival xerosis, xerosis conjuctivae.

xerosis corneal corneal xerosis, xerosis corneae.
xerosis cutánea, xerosis del cutis xerosis cutis.
xerosis parenquimatosa xerosis parenchymatosa.
xerosis superficial xerosis superficialis.
xerostomía *f.* xerostomia.
xerótico, -ca *adj.* xerotic.
xerotipia *f.* xerotripsis.
xerotocia *f.* xerotocia.
xerotomografía *f.* xerotomography.

xerotripsis *f.* xerotripsis.
xifisternal *adj.* xiphisternal.
xifocostal *adj.* xiphocostal.
xifodídimo *m.* xiphodidymus.
xifodimo *m.* xiphodidymus.
xifodinia *f.* xiphodynia.
xifoidalgia *f.* xiphoidalgia.
xifoide *adj.* xiphoid.
xifoides *adj.* xiphoid.
xifoiditis *f.* xiphoiditis.

xifópago *m.* xiphopagus.
xifopagotomía *f.* xiphopagotomy.
xilocetosa *f.* xyloketose.
xilocetosuria *f.* xyloketosuria.
xilosa *f.* xylose.
xilosuria *f.* xylosuria.
xiloterapia *f.* xylotherapy.
xirospasmo *m.* xyrospasm.
xisma *f.* xysma.
xister *f.* xyster.

yantinopsia *f.* ianthinopsia.
yatraléptica *f.* iatraliptics.
yatraléptico, -ca *adj.* iatraliptic.
yatralíptica *f.* iatraliptics.
yatralíptico, -ca *adj.* iatraliptic.
yatreusiología *f.* iatreusiology.
yatreusis *f.* iatreusis.
yátrico, -ca *adj.* iatric.
yatrofísica *f.* iatrophysics.
yatrogénesis *f.* iatrogenesis.
yatrogenia *f.* iatrogeny.
yatrogénico, -ca *adj.* iatrogenic.
yatrógeno, -na *adj.* iatrogenic.
yatrología *f.* iatrology.
yaw *m.* yaw.
yawey *m.* yawey.
yaws *m.* yaws.
yema *f.* bud.
Yersinia Yersinia.
yersiniosis *f.* yersiniosis.
yeso¹ *m.* cast.
yeso² *m.* gypsum, plaster.
yeyunal *adj.* jejunal.
yeyunectomía *f.* jejunectomy.
yeyunitis *f.* jejunitis.
yeyuno *m.* jejunum.
yeyunocecostomía *f.* jejunocecostomy.
yeyunocolostomía *f.* jejunocolostomy.
yeyunografía *f.* jejunography.
yeyunoileal *adj.* jejunoileal.
yeyunoileítis *f.* jejunoileitis.
yeyunoileostomía *f.* jejunoileostomy.
yeyunoplastia *f.* jejunoplasty.

yeyunorrafia *f.* jejunorrhaphy.
yeyunostomía *f.* jejunostomy.
yeyunotomía *f.* jejunotomy.
yeyunoyeyunostomía *f.* jejunojejunostomy.
yin-yang *m.* yin-yang.
yo *m.* ego.
yodación *f.* iodination.
yodado, -da *adj.* iodinated, iodized.
yodar *v.* iodinate, iodize.
yodemia *f.* iodemia.
yódico, -ca *adj.* iodic.
yódide *f.* iododerma.
yodimetría *f.* iodometry.
yodipamida *f.* iodipamide.
yodismo *m.* iodism.
yodizar *v.* iodize.
yodo *m.* iodine.
yodoacetamida *f.* iodoacetamide.
yodobasedow *m.* iodbasedow, jodbasedow.
yodobrásido *m.* yodobrassid.
yodocolesterol *m.* iodocholesterol.
yododermia *m.* iododerma.
yodofilia *f.* iodophilia.
yodófilo *m.* iodinophil, iodinophile, iodophil.
yodófilo, -la *adj.* iodinophil, iodinophile, iodinophilous.
yodoformismo *m.* iodoformism.
yodoftaleína *f.* iodophthalein.
yodogénico, -ca *adj.* iodogenic.
yodoglobulina *f.* iodoglobulin.
yodometría *f.* iodometry.
yodométrico, -ca *adj.* iodometric.
yodopiracet *m.* iodopyracet.

yodoproteínas *f.* iodoproteins.
yodopsina *f.* iodopsin.
yodorresistente *adj.* iodine-fast.
yodoterapia *f.* iodotherapy.
yodotironinas *f.* iodothyronine.
yodotirosinas *f.* iodotyrosine.
yodoventriculografía *f.* iodoventriculography.
yodovolatilización *f.* iodovolatilization.
yoduria *f.* ioduria.
yoduro *m.* iodide.
yonofosia *f.* ionophose.
yotacismo *m.* iotacisme.
yperita *f.* yperite.
yugal *adj.* jugal.
yugo *m.* yoke, jugum.
yugomaxilar *adj.* jugomaxillary.
yugulación *f.* jugulation.
yugular *adj.* jugular.
yuncional *adj.* junctional.
yunque *m.* anvil, incus.
yuxtaangina *f.* juxtangina.
yuxtaarticular *adj.* juxta-articular.
yuxtaepifisario, -ria *adj.* juxtaepiphyseal, juxtaepiphysial.
yuxtaespinal *adj.* juxtaspinal.
yuxtaglomerular *adj.* juxtaglomerular.
yuxtamedular *adj.* juxtamedullary.
yuxtangina *f.* juxtangina.
yuxtapilórico, -ca *adj.* juxtapyloric.
yuxtaposición *f.* juxtaposition.
yuxtaspinal *adj.* juxtaspinal.
yuxtavesical *adj.* juxtavesical.

Zz

zaire *m.* zaire.
zalea *m.* draw-sheet.
zambo, -ba *adj.* knock-kneed.
zapato *m.* shoe.
  zapato para escayola cast shoe.
  zapato de horma normal normal last shoe.
  zapato ortopédico de tacón bajo orthopedic Oxford shoe.
zarantán *m.* zaranthan.
zarigüeya *f.* opossum.
zarzasapogenina *f.* sarsapogenin.
zeiosis *f.* zeiosis.
zeisiano, -na *adj.* Zeissian.
zeísmo *m.* zeism.
zenkerismo *m.* zenkerism.
zenkerizar *v.* zenkerize.
zetácrito *m.* zetacrit.
zetaplastia *f.* Z-plasty.
zigion *m.* zygion.
zigoma *m.* zygoma.
zigzagplastia *f.* zigzagplasty.
zima *f.* zyme.
zimina *f.* zymin.
zimogénesis *f.* zymogenesis.
zimógeno *m.* zymogen.
zimógeno, -na *adj.* zymogenic, zymogenous, zymogic.
zoacantosis *f.* zoacanthosis.
zoantropía *f.* zoanthropy.
zoantrópico, -ca *adj.* zoanthropic.
zoescopio *m.* zoescope.
zoético, -ca *adj.* zoetic.
zoétropo *m.* zoetrope.
zoico, -ca *adj.* zoic.
zoíto *m.* zoite.
zomidina *f.* zomidin.
zomoterapia *f.* zomotherapy.
zona *f.* area, site, zone, zona.
  zona andrógena, zona androgénica androgenic zone.
  zona anelectrónica anelectronic zone.
  zona anelectrotínica anelectrotinic zone.
  zona apical apical zone.
  zona de apoyo rest area.
  zona de bienestar comfort zone.
  zona biocinética biokinetic zone.
  zona de Charcot Charcot's zone.
  zona combinante combining zone.
  zona de comodidad comfort zone.
  zona confortable comfort zone.
  zona cornurradicular cornuradicular zone.
  zona coronal coronal zone, zona corona.
  zona denticulada denticulate zone, zona denticulata.
  zona dentofacial dentofacial zone.
  zona dependiente del timo, zona timodependiente thymus-dependent zone.
  zona dérmica zona dermatica.
  zona de descarga relief area.
  zona desencadenante trigger zone.

zona de deslizamiento gliding zone.
zona de discontinuidad zone of discontinuity.
zona dolorígena, zona dolorógena, zona dolorogénica dolorogenic zone.
zona dorsal de His dorsal zone of His.
zona de entrada entry zone.
zona epileptógena epileptogenic zone, epileptogenous zone.
zona epitelioserosa, zona de epitelio seroso zona epithelioserosa.
zona de equivalencia equivalence zone, zone of equivalence.
zona erógena, zona erotógena erogenous zone, erotogenic zone.
zona de exceso de anticuerpo zone of antibody excess.
zona de exceso de antígeno zone of antigen excess.
zona extravisual extravisual zone.
zona fetal fetal zone.
zona focal focal zone.
zona de Fraunhofer Fraunhofer zone.
zona de Fresnel Fresnel zone.
zona gatillo trigger zone.
zona de Head Head's zone.
zona hiperestésica hyperesthetic zone.
zona hipnógena hypnogenic zone, hypnogenous zone.
zona histerógena hysterogenic zone, hysterogenous zone.
zona ígnea zona ignea.
zona de inhibición inhibition zone.
zona intermedia intermediate zone.
zona isoeléctrica isoelectric zone.
zona latente latent zone.
zona del lenguaje language zone.
zona límite, zona limitrofe border zone.
zona de Looser Looser's zone.
zona marginal marginal zone.
zona nucleolar nucleolar zone.
zona oftálmica zona ophthalmica.
zona placentaria placental zone.
zona polar polar zone.
zona de presión pressure area.
zona primordial de Flechsig Flechsig's primordial zone.
zona proaglutinoide proagglutinoid zone.
zona de proporciones óptimas zone of optimal proportions.
zona pupilar pupillary zone.
zona reflexógena reflexogenic zone.
zona respiratoria respiratory zone.
zona segmentaria segmental zone.
zona visual visual zone.
zonado, -da *adj.* zonate.
zonal *adj.* zonal, zonary.
zonestesia *f.* zonesthesia.
zonificación *f.* zoning.
zonífugo, -ga *adj.* zonifugal.
zonípeto, -ta *adj.* zonipetal.

zónula, zonula *f.* zonule, zonula.
  zónula adherente zonula adherens.
  zónula de oclusión, zónula ocluyente, zonula occludens zonula occludens.
zonular *adj.* zonular.
zonulitis *f.* zonulitis.
zonulólisis *f.* zonulolysis, zonulysis.
zonulotomía *f.* zonulotomy.
zooaglutinina *f.* zoo-agglutinin.
zooanafilactógeno *m.* zooanaphylactogen.
zooantroponosis *f.* zooanthroponosis.
zoobiología *f.* zoobiology.
zoobiotismo *m.* zoobiotism.
zoocinasa *f.* zookinase.
zoodérmico, -ca *adj.* zoodermic.
zoodesecho *m.* zoodetritus.
zoodinámica *f.* zoodynamics.
zoodinámico, -ca *adj.* zoodynamic.
zooerastia *f.* zooerastia.
zooesteroide *m.* zooesteroid.
zooesterol *m.* zoosterol.
zoófago, -ga *m.* zoophagus.
zoofilia *f.* zoophilia.
zoofilismo *m.* zoophilism.
zoófilo, -la *adj.* zoophile.
zoofílico, -ca *adj.* zoophilic.
zoofisiología *f.* zoophysiology.
zoofobia *f.* zoophobia.
zoogénesis *f.* zoogenesis.
zoogenia *f.* zoogeny.
zoógeno, -na *adj.* zoogenous.
zoogeografía *f.* zoogeography.
zoografía *f.* zoography.
zoohormona *f.* zoohormone.
zooinjerto *m.* zoograft, zoografting.
zoolagnia *f.* zoolagnia.
zoología *f.* zoology.
  zoología experimental experimental zoology.
zoom *m.* zoom.
zoomanía *f.* zoomania.
zoomilo *m.* zoomylus.
zoonomía *f.* zoonomy.
zoonosis *f.* zoonosis.
  zoonosis directa direct zoonosis.
zoonótico, -ca *adj.* zoonotic.
zooparasitario, -ria *adj.* zooparasitic.
zooparásito *m.* zooparasite.
zooperal *adj.* zooperal.
zooperia *f.* zoopery.
zooplastia *f.* zooplasty.
zooprecipitinas *f.* zooprecipitins.
zooprofilaxis *f.* zooprophylaxis.
zoopsia *f.* zoopsia.
zooquímica *f.* zoochemistry.
zooquímico, -ca *adj.* zoochemical.
zooquinasa *f.* zookinase.
zoosadismo *m.* zoosadism.
zooscopia *f.* zooscopy.
zoosensitinógeno *m.* zoosensitinogen.
zoosis *f.* zoosis.

zoósmosis *f.* zoosmosis.
zoosperma *m.* zoosperm.
zoospermia *f.* zoospermia.
zoótico, -ca *adj.* zootic.
zootomía *f.* zootomy.
zootomista *m., f.* zootomist.
zootoxina *f.* zootoxin.
zootrófico, -ca *adj.* zootrophic.
zootrofotoxismo *m.* zootrophotixism.
zoster *m.* zoster.
  zoster sine eruptione, zoster sine herpete
  zoster sine eruptione, zoster sine herpete.

zoster geniculado geniculate zoster.
zoster oftálmico ophthalmic zoster, zoster ophthalmicus.
zosteriforme *adj.* zosteriform.
zosteroide *adj.* zosteroid.
Z-plastia *f.* Z-plasty.
zumaque *m.* sumac.
  zumaque de los pantanos, zumaque venenoso poison ivy, poison oak, poison sumac, swamp sumac.
zumbido *m.* hum, bourdonnement, tinnitus.
  zumbido auricular tinnitus, tinnitus aurium.

zumbido de chasquido clicking tinnitus.
zumbido de Leudet Leudet's tinnitus.
zumbido no vibratorio non-vibratory tinnitus.
zumbido objetivo objective tinnitus.
zumbido venoso venous hum, bruit de diable, humming-top murmur.
zumbido vibratorio vibratory tinnitus.
zurdo, -da *m. y adj.* left-handed.
zwiterión *m.* zwitterion.
zwiteriónico, -ca *adj.* zwitterionic.
zwitterion *m.* zwitterion.
zygion *m.* zygion.

Medical Spanish Phrasebook

Greetings and Basics

Hello.	Hola.
My name is. . .	Me llamo…
I am your nurse. (male)	Soy su enfermero.
I am your nurse. (female)	Soy su enfermera.
I am your doctor. (male)	Soy su doctor.
I am your doctor. (female)	Soy su doctora.
Good morning.	Buenos días.
Good afternoon.	Buenas tardes.
Good evening.	Buenas noches.
How are you?	¿Cómo está?
Very well.	Muy bien.
Nice to meet you.	Mucho gusto.
Thank you.	Gracias.
You're welcome.	De nada.
Please.	Por favor.
Do you speak English?	¿Habla inglés?
Do you understand?	¿Entiende?
I don't understand.	No entiendo.
Speak slower, please.	Hable más despacio, por favor.
Repeat, please.	Repita, por favor.
Do you have any questions?	¿Tiene preguntas?

Patient Admission

What is your name?	¿Cómo se llama?
What is your address?	¿Cuál es su dirección?
What is your phone number?	¿Cuál es su número de teléfono?

What is your Social Security number?	¿Cuál es su número de seguro social?
What medical insurance do you have?	¿Cuál seguro médico tiene?
Do you have your medical insurance card?	¿Tiene su tarjeta de seguro médico?
Do you take any medication?	¿Toma medicina?
How old are you?	¿Cuántos años tiene?
What is your date of birth?	¿Cuál es su fecha de nacimiento?
Where are you from?	¿De dónde es?
Are you married? (to a male)	¿Es casado?
Are you married? (to a female)	¿Es casada?
Are you single? (to a male)	¿Es soltero?
Are you single? (to a female)	¿Es soltera?
Are you widowed? (to a male)	¿Es viudo?
Are you widowed? (to a female)	¿Es viuda?
Do you have any children?	¿Tiene hijos?
Do you have a relative with you?	¿Tiene un pariente con usted?
Sign here to give your consent.	Firme aquí para dar su consentimiento.

Medical History

Have you or anyone in your family had . . .	¿Ha tenido o tiene alguien en su familia…
. . . allergies?	… alergias?
. . . asthma?	… asma?
. . . bleeding problems?	… problemas de hemorragia?
. . . breast disease?	… enfermedad de los senos?
. . . bronchitis?	… bronquitis?
. . . cancer? What type?	… cáncer? ¿Qué tipo?
. . . convulsions?	… convulsiones?
. . . diabetes?	… diabetes?
. . . emotional problems or depression?	… problemas emocionales o depresión?
. . . frequent headaches?	… dolores frecuentes de cabeza?
. . . glaucoma?	… glaucoma?
. . . heart attack?	… ataque del corazón?
. . . heart disease?	… enfermedad del corazón?
. . . high blood pressure?	… presión alta?
. . . high cholesterol?	… colesterol alto?
. . . kidney disease?	… enfermedad de los riñones?
. . . liver disease?	… enfermedad del hígado?

. . . obesity?	… obesidad?
. . . osteoporosis?	… osteoporosis?
. . . pneumonia?	… neumonía?
. . . rheumatic fever?	… fiebre reumática?
. . . strokes or blood clots?	… derrames cerebrales o coágulos de sangre?
. . . surgeries? What type?	… operaciones? ¿Qué tipo?
. . . thyroid disease?	… enfermedad de la tiroides?
. . . tuberculosis?	… tuberculosis?
. . . venereal diseases?	… enfermedades venéreas?
Is your mother living or deceased?	¿Está su madre viva o muerta?
Is your father living or deceased?	¿Está su padre vivo o muerto?
Do you smoke?	¿Fuma?
How many cigarettes do you smoke in a day?	¿Cuántos cigarrillos fuma en un día?
Do you drink alcohol?	¿Toma alcohol?
How many beers do you drink in a day?	¿Cuántas cervezas toma en un día?
What drugs do you use for fun?	¿Cuáles drogas usa para divertirse?
How often?	¿Con qué frecuencia?

Would you say that you . . .　　　　**¿Diría que…**

. . . are healthy?	… es saludable?
. . . are sickly?	… es enfermizo?
. . . sometimes get sick?	… a veces se enferma?
. . . never get sick?	… nunca se enferma?

Would you say that your weight . . .　　　　**¿Diría que su peso…**

. . . has gone down?	… ha bajado?
. . . has gone up?	… ha subido?
. . . is the same as always?	… es igual que siempre?
Do you feel less hungry than usual?	¿Siente menos hambre que de costumbre?

Chief Complaint

What's going on?	¿Qué pasa?
What's wrong, sir?	¿Qué tiene, señor?
What's wrong, ma'am?	¿Qué tiene, señora?
Why did you come to the hospital?	¿Por qué vino al hospital?
Do you have pain?	¿Tiene dolor?
When did this problem start?	¿Cuándo comenzó este problema?
Does this stop you from working?	¿Le impide este problema trabajar?

Has this problem affected . . . | ¿Este problema ha afectado . . .

. . . your life at home? | … su casa?

. . . your work? | … su trabajo?

. . . your social activities? | … sus actividades sociales?

Have you had this problem before? | ¿Ha tenido este problema antes?

Did it start suddenly? | ¿Comenzó de repente?

Did it start little by little? | ¿Comenzó poco a poco?

Do you have this problem constantly? | ¿Tiene este problema constantemente?

How many times a day? | ¿Cuántas veces al día?

When do you feel worse . . . | ¿Cuándo se siente peor…

. . . in the morning? | … en la mañana?

. . . in the afternoon? | … en la tarde?

. . . at night? | … en la noche?

Do you have any additional symptoms? | ¿Tiene síntomas adicionales?

Have you seen the doctor lately? | ¿Ha visto al doctor recientemente?

Is there anything that helps relieve this problem? | ¿Hay algo que le ayude a aliviar este problema?

Are you taking medicine you brought from your country? | ¿Toma medicina traída de su país?

What is the worst thing that is happening? | ¿Qué es lo peor que está pasando?

Pain

Do you have pain? | ¿Tiene dolor?

Did it develop slowly? | ¿Le apareció lentamente?

Did it develop suddenly? | ¿Le apareció de repente?

Is there anything that alleviates the pain? | ¿Hay algo que alivie el dolor?

When did the pain begin? | ¿Cuándo comenzó el dolor?

Where does it hurt? | ¿Dónde le duele?

Does it hurt when I apply pressure? | ¿Le duele cuando pongo presión?

Does it hurt when I remove pressure? | ¿Le duele cuando quito presión?

Do you have the pain . . . | ¿Tiene el dolor…

. . . all the time? | … todo el tiempo?

. . . in the morning? | … por la mañana?

. . . at night? | … por la noche?

. . . before eating? | … antes de comer?

. . . after eating? | … después de comer?

What kind of pain is it?	**¿Qué tipo de dolor es?**
A little?	¿Un poco?
A lot?	¿Mucho?
Dull?	¿Sordo?
Severe?	¿Severo?
Mild?	¿Leve?
Sharp?	¿Agudo?
Stabbing?	¿Punzante?
Throbbing?	¿Pulsativo?
Shooting? Like a knife?	¿Fulgurante? ¿Como un cuchillo?
Burning?	¿Quemante?
Constant?	¿Constante?
Intermittent?	¿Intermitente?
Cramping?	¿Como un calambre?

Physical Exam

I am going to examine you. (to a male)	Lo voy a examinar.
I am going to examine you. (to a female)	La voy a examinar.
I am going to tap here.	Voy a dar un golpecito aquí.
I am going to listen to your heart.	Voy a escuchar su corazón.

I am going to take . . .	**Voy a tomar…**
. . . a sample.	… una muestra.
. . . your pulse.	… su pulso.
. . . your blood pressure.	… su presión de sangre.
. . . your temperature.	… su temperatura.

I am going to examine your . . .	**Voy a examinar su…**
. . . abdomen.	… abdomen.
. . . throat.	… garganta.
. . . ear.	… oído.
. . . rectum.	… recto.
. . . vagina.	… vagina.
I am going to palpate your abdomen.	Voy a palpar el abdomen.
Tell me if it hurts.	Dígame si le duele.
Does it hurt when I press down?	¿Le duele cuando presiono?
Does it hurt when I let go?	¿Le duele cuando retiro la mano?
Raise your head.	Levante la cabeza.
Turn on your side.	Dése la vuelta a su lado.

Take a deep breath.	Respire profundo.
Exhale.	Exhale.

Medication Instructions

Take . . .	Tome…
. . . a drop.	… una gota.
. . . a teaspoon.	… una cucharadita.
. . . a tablespoon.	… una cucharada.
. . . a glass.	… un vaso.
. . . two inhalations.	… dos inhalaciones.

Apply it . . .	Aplíquelo…
. . . one time a day.	… una vez al día.
. . . two times a day.	… dos veces al dia.
. . . three. . .	… tres…
. . . four. . .	… cuatro…
. . . five. . .	… cinco…
. . . six . . .	… seis…

This medicine is taken . . .	Esta medicina se toma…
. . . by mouth.	… por la boca.
. . . by rectum.	… por el recto.
. . . intravenously.	… por las venas.
. . . under the tongue.	… por debajo de la lengua.
. . . by patch.	… en parche.
. . . under the skin.	… por debajo de la piel.
. . . orally.	… por la boca.
. . . nasally.	… por la nariz.
Avoid sunlight.	Evite la luz del sol.
Don't drive while taking this medicine.	No maneje cuando tome esta medicina.
Don't take medicine from any healer.	No tome otra medicina de ningún sanador.

Take this medicine . . .	Tome esta medicina…
. . . a half hour before every meal.	… media hora antes de cada comida.
. . . one hour after every meal.	… una hora después de cada comida.
. . . before bedtime.	… antes de acostarse.
. . . with food.	… con la comida.
. . . on an empty stomach.	… con el estómago vacío.

This medicine will . . .

. . . give you diarrhea.

. . . lower your blood sugar.

. . . lower your blood pressure.

. . . relieve fever and inflammation.

. . . relieve your pain.

Esta medicina...

... le dará diarrea.

... le bajará el nivel de su azúcar en la sangre.

... le bajará su presión de sangre.

... le aliviará la fiebre y la inflamación.

... le aliviará el dolor.

Emergencies and Injuries

Did you have . . .

. . . an accident?

. . . an allergic reaction?

. . . an anxiety attack?

. . . bleeding?

. . . a bee sting?

. . . a blow to the head?

. . . a bruise?

. . . a burn?

. . . chest pain?

. . . a cut?

. . . dizziness?

. . . a dog bite?

. . . domestic abuse?

. . . a fall?

. . . a fight?

. . . a fracture?

. . . frostbite?

. . . heat stroke?

. . . an overdose?

. . . pain?

. . . a spasm?

. . . a stabbing?

. . . a stroke?

Can you tell me what happened?

Do you know where you are?

Where does it hurt?

Show me.

¿Tuvo...

... un accidente?

... una reacción alérgica?

... un ataque de ansiedad?

... hemorragia?

... una picadura de abeja?

... un golpe a la cabeza?

... un moretón?

... una quemadura?

... dolor del pecho?

... una cortada?

... mareos?

... una mordida de perro?

... abuso doméstico?

... una caída?

... una pelea?

... una fractura?

... congelamiento?

... insolación?

... una sobredosis?

... dolor?

... un espasmo?

... una puñalada?

... un derrame cerebral?

¿Puede decirme lo que pasó?

¿Sabe dónde está?

¿Dónde le duele?

Enséñeme.

What happened to your . . .

¿Qué le pasa a su...

. . . abdomen?

... abdomen?

. . . ankle?

... tobillo?

. . . arm?

... brazo?

. . . back?

... espalda?

. . . chest?

... pecho?

. . . ear?

... oído?

. . . eye?

... ojo?

. . . face?

... cara?

. . . finger?

... dedo?

. . . foot?

... pie?

. . . hand?

... mano?

. . . head?

... cabeza?

. . . knee?

... rodilla?

. . . leg?

... pierna?

. . . mouth?

... boca?

. . . neck?

... cuello?

. . . nose?

... nariz?

. . . shoulder?

... hombro?

. . . skin?

... piel?

. . . stomach?

... estómago?

. . . teeth?

... dientes?

Was it burned?

¿Fue quemado?

Was it cut?

¿Fue cortado?

Was it fractured?

¿Fue fracturado?

Was it infected?

¿Fue infectado?

Was it swollen?

¿Fue hinchado?

Diagnostic Tests and Treatments

You need to have . . .

Usted necesita tener...

. . . a blood test.

... un examen de sangre.

. . . a neurological exam.

... un examen neurológico.

. . . a pregnancy test.

... una prueba de embarazo.

. . . a scan.

... un escán.

. . . an echocardiogram.

... un ecocardiograma.

. . . an EKG.

... un electrocardiograma.

. . . an ultrasound.

... un examen de ultrasonido.

. . . an x-ray.

... una radiografía.

You need . . .	Usted necesita...
. . . an antibiotic.	… un antibiótico.
. . . a bandage.	… un vendaje.
. . . a blood transfusion.	… una transfusión de sangre.
. . . a cast.	… un yeso.
. . . first aid.	… los primeros auxilios.
. . . an IV.	… un suero.
. . . medicine.	… medicina.
. . . an operation.	… una operación.
. . . oxygen.	… oxígeno.
. . . physical therapy.	… terapia física.
. . . a shot.	… una inyección.
. . . a sling.	… un cabestrillo.
. . . stitches.	… los puntos.
. . . surgery.	… la cirugía.

Specialties

You need to see a specialist in . . .	Necesita ver un especialista en...
. . . ENT.	… los oídos, la nariz y la garganta.
. . . ophthalmology.	… oftalmología.
. . . cardiology.	… cardiología.
. . . gastroenterology.	… gastroenterología.
. . . OB-GYN.	… ginecología.
. . . endocrinology.	… endocrinología.
. . . orthopedics.	… ortopedia.
. . . pediatrics.	… pediatría.
. . . neurology.	… neurología.
. . . dermatology.	… dermatología.
. . . obstetrics.	… obstetricia.
. . . oncology.	… oncología.
. . . psychiatry.	… psiquiatría.
. . . surgery.	… cirugía.

Pregnancy

It is important to take care of yourself during pregnancy.	Es importante cuidar su salud durante su embarazo.
How many times have you been pregnant?	¿Cuántas veces ha estado embarazada?
How many children do you have?	¿Cuántos hijos tiene?
Do you breast-feed them?	¿Les da pecho?
Have you ever been pregnant?	¿Ha estado alguna vez embarazada?

How many . . . **¿Cuántos...**

. . . pregnancies?	… embarazos?
. . . children?	… hijos?
. . . miscarriages?	… abortos espontáneos?
. . . abortions?	… abortos?
What was the date of your last period?	¿Cuándo fue su última regla?

You are . . . weeks pregnant. **Tiene...semanas de embarazo.**

. . . six . . .	… seis…
. . . ten . . .	… diez…
Have you had any bleeding?	¿Ha sangrado?

Birth Control

Are you using birth control now?	¿Usa algún método para evitar el embarazo?

Do you use . . . **¿Usa...**

. . . the pill?	… la píldora anticonceptiva?
. . . the diaphragm?	… el diafragma?
. . . an IUD?	… el dispositivo intrauterino?
. . . condoms?	… preservativos?
. . . the rhythm method?	… el método del ritmo?
. . . abstinence?	… abstinencia?
How long have you used this method?	¿Cuánto tiempo ha usado este método?

Have you experienced any of the following taking the pill? **¿Ha sentido alguna de estas molestias tomando la píldora?**

Headaches?	¿Dolores de cabeza?
Vision changes?	¿Cambios de la visión?
Pain or swelling in the legs?	¿Dolor o hinchazón en las piernas?
Chest pain?	¿Dolor en el pecho?
Shortness of breath?	¿Falta de aire?
Weight loss or gain?	¿Pérdida o aumento de peso?

Diabetic Patients

Are you a diabetic? (to a male)	¿Es diabético?
Are you a diabetic? (to a female)	¿Es diabética?
Do you take insulin?	¿Toma insulina?
What type of insulin?	¿Qué tipo de insulina?
Oral or by injection?	¿Oral o inyectada?
When was the last time you took insulin?	¿Cuándo fue la última vez que tomó insulina?
When did you last eat?	¿Cuándo fue la última vez que comió?
Are you measuring your sugar?	¿Mide su azúcar?
Before and after meals?	¿Antes y después de las comidas?
Are you keeping a record of your sugar levels?	¿Toma notas de los niveles de su azúcar?
Are you taking your insulin?	¿Toma su insulina?
Are you exercising?	¿Hace ejercicio?
Have you had your vision checked?	¿Ha tenido su visión chequeada?
Have you had your feet checked?	¿Ha tenido sus pies chequeados?

You need to have . . .   **Necesita tener...**

. . . blood sugar records.	… notas del nivel del azúcar.
. . . better control of your blood sugar.	… mejor control de los niveles de su azúcar.
. . . a dilated eye exam.	… un examen con los ojos dilatados.
. . . a finger stick test.	… un examen pinchando el dedo.
. . . a foot exam.	… un examen del pie.
. . . a urine protein test.	… un examen de la proteína en la orina.

Pay attention to . . .   **Preste más atención a...**

. . . not smoking.	… evitar fumar.
. . . blood sugar count before and after meals.	… contar el nivel del azúcar antes y después de las comidas.
. . . changes in vision.	… los cambios de la visión.
. . . changes in your skin.	… los cambios de la piel.
. . . decreased sense of touch.	… la disminución del sentido del tacto.
. . . difficulty picking up small objects.	… las dificultades para recoger objetos pequeños.
. . . lack of sensation in any part of the body.	… la falta de sensación en alguna parte del cuerpo.
. . . swelling in your legs or hands.	… la hinchazón en las piernas o las manos.
Eat your meals at the same time each day.	Coma sus comidas a la misma hora cada día.
Take your medicine at the same time each day.	Tomar su medicina a la misma hora cada día.

Monitor your cholesterol level.

Controle el nivel de su colesterol.

Check your blood pressure regularly.

Chequee regularmente su presión de la sangre.

Are you eating measured portions?

¿Come porciones medidas?

You need to have a diet . . .

. . . low in cholesterol.

. . . low in sodium.

. . . low in sugar.

. . . high in fiber.

. . . low in carbohydrates.

Necesita tener una dieta...

… baja en colesterol.

… baja en sodio.

… baja en azúcar.

… alta en fibra.

… baja en carbohidratos.

Cardiovascular System

Do you have . . .

¿Tiene...

Have you had . . .

¿Ha tenido...

. . . cardiovascular disease?

… enfermedad cardiovascular?

. . . chest pain?

… dolor de pecho?

. . . embolism?

… embolismo?

. . . fainting?

… desmayos?

. . . high blood pressure?

… presión alta?

. . . infarction?

… infarto?

. . . irregular heartbeat?

… latidos irregulares del corazón?

. . . low blood pressure?

… presión baja?

. . . mitral valve prolapse?

… prolapso de la válvula mitral?

. . . obesity?

… obesidad?

. . . palpitations?

… palpitaciones?

. . . poor circulation?

… mala circulación de la sangre?

. . . shortness of breath?

… falta de aire?

. . . stroke?

… derrame cerebral?

. . . thrombosis?

… trombosis?

Have you ever had a heart attack?

¿Ha tenido alguna vez un ataque de corazón?

Has this ever happened before?

¿Ha ocurrido esto antes?

Do you have a history of heart problems?

¿Tiene un historial de problemas del corazón?

Have you had . . .

. . . chest pain?

. . . headaches?

¿Ha tenido...

… dolor en el pecho?

… dolores de cabeza?

. . . pressure in your chest?	… presión en el pecho?
. . . shortness of breath?	… falta de aire?
. . . swollen ankles?	… los tobillos hinchados?
. . . dizziness?	… mareos?
. . . irregular heartbeat?	… latidos irregulares del corazón?

Do you have shortness of breath when . . .   **¿Tiene la falta de aire cuando…**

. . . at rest?	… descansa?
. . . walking?	… camina?
. . . climbing stairs?	… sube las escaleras?
. . . exercising?	… hace ejercicio?

Is there anyone in your family who has . . .   **¿Hay alguien en su familia que haya…**

. . . suffered from heart problems?	… sufrido de problemas del corazón?
. . . suffered from high blood pressure?	… sufrido de presión alta?
. . . had a stroke?	… tenido un derrame cerebral?
Where does it hurt?	¿Dónde le duele?
Does the pain radiate to the arms?	¿Corre el dolor a los brazos?
Does it hurt when you breathe?	¿Le duele cuando respira?

You need to have . . .   **Usted necesita tener…**

. . . an angiogram.	… un angiograma.
. . . an angioplasty.	… una angioplastia.
. . . blood tests.	… pruebas de sangre.
. . . a breathing test.	… una prueba de la respiración.
. . . catheterization.	… cateterismo.
. . . a chest x-ray.	… una radiografía del pecho.
. . . an echocardiogram.	… un ecocardiograma.
. . . an EKG.	… un electrocardiograma.
. . . heart surgery.	… cirugía del corazón.
. . . a Holter monitor.	… un monitor de Holter.
. . . an MRI.	… una imagen de resonancia magnética.
. . . a pacemaker.	… un marcapaso.
. . . a stress test.	… un examen del estrés.
. . . a triple bypass.	… un bypass triple.
. . . a quadruple bypass.	… un bypass cuádruple.

Gastrointestinal System

Do you have problems with . . .

. . . abdominal tenderness?

. . . constipation?

. . . diarrhea?

. . . indigestion?

. . . cramps?

. . . vomiting?

. . . dizziness?

Does it hurt when I press here?

Are you moving your bowels normally?

Any blood in the urine or stools?

¿Tiene problemas con...

... dolor tocando el abdomen?

... estreñimiento?

... diarrea?

... indigestión?

... calambres?

... vómitos?

... mareos?

¿Le duele cuando presiono aquí?

¿Es su excremento regular?

¿Hay sangre en la orina o el excremento?

Have you ever had . . .

. . . a stomach ulcer?

. . . inflammatory bowel disease?

. . . history of GI disease or bleeding?

Ha tenido alguna vez...

... una úlcera en el estómago?

... enfermedad inflamatoria del intestino?

... un historial de enfermedad o sangrado gastrointestinal?

Do you have . . .

. . . stomach acid in your throat?

. . . stomach pain?

. . . gas?

. . . a metallic taste in your mouth?

¿Tiene...

... ácido del estómago en la garganta?

... dolor en el estómago?

... gas?

... un sabor metálico en la boca?

Do you eat or drink . . .

. . . more than one cup of coffee a day?

. . . carbonated drinks?

. . . spicy food?

¿Toma...

... más de una taza de café al día?

... bebidas gaseosas?

... la comida picante?

You need to . . .

. . . lower alcohol use.

. . . stop smoking.

. . . stop overeating.

. . . eliminate coffee.

. . . eliminate carbonated drinks.

. . . eliminate spicy food.

. . . sleep with your head elevated.

Necesita...

... bajar el uso del alcohol.

... no fumar.

... dejar de comer demasiado.

... eliminar el café.

... eliminar las bebidas gaseosas.

... eliminar la comida picante.

... dormir con la cabeza elevada.

Neurological Exam

Have you had . . .	¿Ha tenido...
. . . changes or vision problems?	… cambios o problemas con la visión?
. . . fainting?	… desmayos?
. . . dizzy spells?	… mareos?
. . . difficulty moving part of your body?	… dificultad para mover una parte del cuerpo?
. . . problems remembering things?	… problemas recordando cosas?
. . . a recent head injury?	… una herida en la cabeza recientemente?
Are you taking any medications?	¿Toma medicamentos?
What were you doing before you had the seizure?	¿Qué estaba haciendo antes del ataque?
Has it happened before?	¿Ha pasado antes?
Can you describe what happened before the seizure?	¿Puede describir qué pasó justo antes del ataque?
Were you unconscious?	¿Estuvo inconsciente?
For how long?	¿Por cuánto tiempo?
Is there any part of your body that feels . . .	**¿Hay alguna parte de su cuerpo que sienta...**
. . . numb?	… dormida?
. . . like pins and needles?	… como hormigueo?
. . . weak?	… débil sin fuerzas?
. . . painful?	… con dolores?
. . . heavy?	… pesada?
I'm going to check your eyes.	Voy a revisarle los ojos.
Follow my fingers with your eyes without moving your head.	Siga mis dedos con los ojos sin mover la cabeza.
Open your mouth and say "ahhh."	Abra la boca y diga "aaaah".
Shrug your shoulders.	Levante los hombros.
Smile.	Sonría.
Close your eyes.	Cierre los ojos.
Open your eyes.	Abra los ojos.
Touch the tip of your nose with your finger.	Toque la punta de su nariz con el dedo.
I'm going to check your strength.	Voy a chequear su fuerza.
Pull.	Jale.
Push.	Empuje.
Squeeze my fingers.	Apriete mis dedos.
Stand and close your eyes.	Párese y cierre los ojos.
Walk on your toes.	Camine de puntillas.
Walk on your heels.	Camine con los talones.

Mental Health

Do you feel . . .	**¿Siente...**
. . . sadness?	... tristeza?
. . . anxiety?	... ansiedad?
. . . emptiness?	... vacío?
. . . hopelessness?	... desesperanza?
. . . guilt?	... culpabilidad?
. . . worthlessness?	... inutilidad?
. . . irritability?	... irritabilidad?
How long have you felt this way?	¿Hace cuánto tiempo que se ha sentido así?
Do you have interest in activities?	¿Tiene interés en actividades?
Do you have difficulty concentrating?	¿Tiene dificultad para concentrarse?

Do you feel . . .	**¿Siente...**
. . . decreased energy?	... falta de energía?
. . . difficulty concentrating?	... dificultad para concentrarse?
. . . difficulty remembering?	... dificultad para recordar?
. . . insomnia?	... insomnio?
. . . lack of appetite?	... que le falta el apetito?
. . . you eat too much?	... que come demasiado?
. . . you have digestive disorders?	... que tiene trastornos de digestión?
. . . chronic pain?	... dolor crónico?
Do you wake up earlier than normal?	¿Siente que se despierta más temprano que lo normal?
Do you oversleep?	¿Siente que duerme demasiado?
Do you think about dying?	¿Piensa en la muerte?
Do you think about suicide?	¿Piensa en el suicidio?

Do you feel . . .	**¿Siente...**
. . . mania?	... manía?
. . . excessive elation?	... un estado excesivo de elación?
. . . racing thoughts?	... pensamientos acelerados?
. . . irritable?	... irritable?
Do you have more energy than usual?	¿Tiene más energía que lo normal?
Do you have less need for sleep?	¿Necesita dormir menos?
How long have you felt this way?	¿Hace cuánto tiempo que se ha sentido así?